NAVE'S

TOPICAL BIBLE

A DIGEST OF THE HOLY SCRIPTURES

More Than Twenty Thousand Topics and Subtopics
Over One Hundred Thousand References
to the Scriptures

BY ORVILLE J. NAVE, A.M., D.D., LL.D.,

Editor, *Nave's Study Bible*

ROYAL PUBLISHERS, INC.
NASHVILLE, TENNESSEE

ISBN: 0-8407-4993-7

PREFACE

THE OBJECT OF THIS BOOK is to bring together in cyclopedic form and under familiar headings all that the Bible contains on particular subjects. The subjects formulated are of practical value to every profession and to all who desire to consult the Bible.

The method pursued in preparing this Digest has been, first, to analyze topically each verse of the Bible, each series of verses, and each chapter and series of chapters; and, second, to group under suitable headings all the Scriptures related to the subjects found in the analysis. The first verse in the Bible may serve to illustrate: "In the beginning God created the heaven and the earth." "In the beginning." Some authorities interpret this phrase as meaning the beginning of time; therefore the author noted, "Time, Beginning of, Gen. 1:1." Other authorities interpret it as referring to the beginning of the creation; therefore the author noted, "Creation, Beginning of, Gen. 1:1." "In the beginning God created." The author noted, "God, Creator, Gen. 1:1." "In the beginning God created the heaven." Note, "Heaven, Creation of, Gen. 1:1." "In the beginning God created the heaven and the earth." "Earth, Creation of, Gen. 1:1." This process was faithfully adhered to throughout the work.

Three classifications of Scripture verses have been published in America, two of which are erroneously styled "a complete analysis" of the Scriptures. Each author followed, with slight and unimportant modifications in arrangement, Mr. Matthew Talbot's classification of verses made in England over one hundred years ago. Mr. Talbot's mode of treatment was to arrange all verses of the Bible, as best he might, under thirty general headings. When each verse had been assigned under the heading to which it seemed best adapted, the work he undertook was complete. He used no verse more than once, regardless of the many different and distinct subjects it might contain. It was consequently a classification of verses rather than a topical analysis of matter. American publishers have followed this erroneous mode of treatment, and as a result the so-called analyses of the Scriptures hitherto offered to Bible students and Christian teachers have been unsatisfactory. This Digest is an analysis of the matter without regard to verse divisions except for convenience of reference. Verses, parts of verses, series of verses, and chapters are cited or quoted as often as they contain distinct subjects. Numerous verses are repeated from one to thirty

3

times each, according to the number of subjects they contain and their position in extensive citations or extracts. The verse before referred to has been quoted or cited under five different and equally important headings, while other analyses quote it only once. The familiar verse, Rom. 5:1, "Therefore being justified by faith, we have peace with God through our Lord Jesus Christ," is cited under nine headings; namely, Justification, Faith, Peace, Salvation by Faith, Jesus the Saviour, Atonement, Mediation, Propitiation, and Reconciliation, while in other analyses it is used but once, under Justification.

Passages variously interpreted by different religious schools or accepted authorities are cited under the subjects they are claimed to support, without reference to the personal views of the author.

This work is based on the King James Version, but the increasing demand for the readings of the Revised Version constrained me to introduce these readings more liberally than seemed to be required when the work was first published. In the seventh edition, I inserted them where they affect the topical uses of verses. The phrases and sentences affected are set in smaller type than the rest of the text in order to draw attention, and the revised readings and notes of omissions are set in small type at the ends of paragraphs.

To provide against doubt that this Digest would be complete in its classification of matter respecting the principles and practice of law, I secured the assistance of the Honorable John Welch, Judge of the Supreme Court of the State of Ohio, U. S. A., and author of *Welch's Index-Digest of Ohio Decisions.* Judge Welch made a consecutive and analytical study of the Bible for this work, from the standpoint of a learned jurist and successful author, and his notes have been incorporated with the author's. Lawyers, judges, legislators, and statesmen may, therefore, rely on this work as a complete and valuable handbook of the Bible for the purposes of their professions. All subjects relating to the principles and practice of law are classified under headings in common use.

Some subjects abound in the Scriptures to such an extent, and are used so frequently by religious teachers and others, that, were references only given in this work to the books, chapters, and verses containing them, the student would stagger at the thought of developing the topics. In order to make this class of subjects quickly and easily available the verses, or parts of verses, themselves are printed. This method of treatment might have been extended, but the size of a convenient volume had to be taken into consideration. Minor topics are made almost equally available by brief sub-topical divisions followed by references.

One of the most important, and it is believed valuable, features of this book is its elaborate system of cross references to kindred and antithetical subjects. Wide scope is thus given each subject by connecting it with those to which it is related.

Under the sub-topic, INSTANCES OF, are grouped all the illustrative facts that occur in the Scriptures relating to each subject. As a book of illustrations this work should prove valuable. It also contains numerous and elaborate Bible readings, with a wide range of subjects.

It was not the object of the author in preparing this Digest to develop religious subjects only, but to note and classify everything found in the Scriptures. It is believed that it is approximately exhaustive. It is the result of fourteen years of delightful and untiring study of the word of God, aided by my wife, Anna Semans Nave, who has been an indefatigable assistant from the inception of the work. All pioneer works of an analytic character, as well as all noteworthy commentaries, have been consulted, in order to bring into it all useful materials to be found. Its preparation was inspired by the obvious deficiency of such helps in the use of the Scriptures. This deficiency was felt by the author in preparing sermons, lectures, and other forms of religious instruction. The quiet of army garrisons, apart from the rush and distraction of dense communities, has been favorable to its careful preparation. With the belief that it will contribute to make the Scriptures more quickly, easily, and fully available where particular subjects are under consideration, I offer it to the public.

THE AUTHOR

Fort McPherson, Ga.

LIST OF ABBREVIATIONS.

A. V.	for	Authorized Version.	Mic.	for	Micah.
R. V.	"	Revised Version.	Nah.	"	Nahum.
O. T.	"	Old Testament.	Hab.	"	Habakkuk.
N. T.	"	New Testament.	Zeph.	"	Zephaniah.
Gen.	"	Genesis.	Hag.	"	Haggai.
Ex.	"	Exodus.	Zech.	"	Zechariah.
Lev.	"	Leviticus.	Mal.	"	Malachi.
Num.	"	Numbers.	Matt.	"	Matthew.
Deut.	"	Deuteronomy.	Rom.	"	Romans.
Josh.	"	Joshua.	1 Cor.	"	1 Corinthians.
Judg.	"	Judges.	2 Cor.	"	2 Corinthians.
1 Sam.	"	1 Samuel.	Gal.	"	Galatians.
2 Sam.	"	2 Samuel.	Eph.	"	Ephesians.
1 Kin.	"	1 Kings.	Phil.	"	Philippians.
2 Kin.	"	2 Kings.	Col.	"	Colossians.
1 Chr.	"	1 Chronicles.	1 Thess.	"	1 Thessalonians.
2 Chr.	"	2 Chronicles.	2 Thess.	"	2 Thessalonians.
Neh.	"	Nehemiah.	1 Tim.	"	1 Timothy.
Esth.	"	Esther.	2 Tim.	"	2 Timothy.
Psa.	"	Psalms.	Tit.	"	Titus.
Prov.	"	Proverbs.	Philem.	"	Philemon.
Eccl.	"	Ecclesiastes.	Heb.	"	Hebrews.
Song	"	Song of Solomon.	Jas.	"	James.
Isa.	"	Isaiah.	1 Pet.	"	1 Peter.
Jer.	"	Jeremiah.	2 Pet.	"	2 Peter.
Lam.	"	Lamentations.	Rev.	"	Revelation.
Ezek.	"	Ezekiel.	N.	"	North.
Dan.	"	Daniel.	E.	"	East.
Hos.	"	Hosea.	S.	"	South.
Obad.	"	Obadiah.	W.	"	West.

THE TOPICAL BIBLE.

AARON. Lineage of, Ex. 6:16-20; Josh. 21:4,10; 1 Chr. 6:2,3; 23:13. Marriage of, Ex. 6:23. Children of, Ex. 6:23,25; 1 Chr. 6:3; 24:1,2. Descendants of, Ex. 6:23,25; 1 Chr. 6:3-15, 50-53; 24.

Meets Moses in the wilderness and is made spokesman for Moses, Ex. 4:14-16,27-31; 7:1,2. Inspiration of, Ex. 12:1; Lev. 10:8; 11:1; 13:1; 15:1; Num. 2:1; 4:1,17; 18:1; 19:1; 20:12. Commissioned as a deliverer of Israel, Ex. 6:13,26,27; Josh. 24:5; 1 Sam. 12:8; Psa. 77:20; 105:26; Mic. 6:4. Summoned to Sinai with Nadab, Abihu, and seventy elders, Ex. 19:24; 24:1,9,10.

Priesthood of, Ex. 28:1; 29:9; Num. 17;18:1; Psa. 99:6; Heb. 5:4. Consecration of, to the priesthood, Ex. 28; 29; Lev. 8. Enters upon the priestly office, Lev. 9. See PRIEST, HIGH. Descendants of, ordained priests forever, Ex. 28:40-43; 29:9; Num. 3:3; 18:1; 1 Chr. 23:13; 2 Chr. 26:18.

Judges Israel in the absence of Moses, Ex. 24:14. Makes the golden calf, Ex. 32; Acts 7:40; Deut. 9:20,21. Rod of, buds, Num. 17; Heb. 9:4; preserved, Num. 17; Heb. 9:4. Murmured against, by the people, Ex. 5:20,21; 16:2-10; Num. 14:2-5,10; 16:3-11, 41; 20:2; Psa. 106:16. Places pot of manna in the ark, Ex. 16:34. With Hur supports the hands of Moses during battle, Ex. 17:12. His benedictions upon the people, Lev. 9:22; Num. 6:23. Forbidden to mourn the death of his sons, Nadab and Abihu, Lev. 10:6,19. Intercedes for Miriam, Num. 12:11,12. Stays the plague by priestly intercession, Num. 16:46-48. Jealous of Moses, Num. 12:1. His presumption, when the rock is smitten, Num. 20:10-12. Not permitted to enter Canaan, Num. 20:12,23-29. Age of, at death, Ex. 7:7; Num. 33:38,39. Death and burial of, Num. 20:27,28; Deut. 10:6; 32:50.

Character of, Psa. 106:16.

ABADDON, the angel of the bottomless pit, Rev. 9:11.

ABAGTHA, a Persian chamberlain, Esth. 1:10.

ABANA, river of Damascus, 2 Kin. 5:12.

ABARIM. See NEBO.

ABBA, Father, Mark 14:36; Rom. 8:15; Gal. 4:6.

ABDA, father of Adoniram, 1 Kin. 4:6.

ABDEEL, father of Shelemiah, Jer. 36:26.

ABDI, father of Kish, 2 Chr. 29:12.

ABDIEL, a Gadite, 1 Chr. 5:15.

ABDON. 1. A judge of Israel, in the time of the judges, Judg. 12:13-15.

2. A Levitical city, Josh. 21:30; 1 Chr. 6:74.

3. A Benjamite chief, 1 Chr. 8:23.

4. Son of Gibeon, 1 Chr. 8:30; 9:36.

5. Son of Micah, 2 Chr. 34:20. Called also ACHBOR, 2 Kin. 22:12.

ABED-NEGO, called also AZARIAH, a Jewish captive in Babylon, Dan. 1:6-20; 2:17, 49; 3:12-30; Heb. 11:34.

ABEL. 1. Son of Adam. History of, Gen. 4:1-15,25. References to the death of, Matt. 23:35; Luke 11:51; Heb. 11:4; 12:24; 1 John 3:12.

2. A stone, 1 Sam. 6:18.

ABEL-BETH-MAACHAH, called also ABEL-MAIM. A city in the N. of Palestine. Sheba slain in, 2 Sam. 20:14-22. Taken by Benhadad, 1 Kin. 15:20; 2 Chr. 16:4; by Tiglath, 2 Kin. 15:29.

ABEL-MEHOLAH. A city near the Jordan, Judg. 7:22; 1 Kin. 4:12. Elisha's birthplace, 1 Kin. 19:16.

ABEL-MIZRAIM, place where the Israelites mourned for Jacob, Gen. 50:11.

ABEL-SHITTIM. See SHITTIM.

ABETTING. See COMPLICITY.

ABEZ, a city of Issachar, Josh. 19:20.

ABI, mother of Hezekiah, 2 Kin. 18:2. Called ABIJAH, 2 Chr. 29:1.

ABIA. 1. Called also ABIJAH, chief of the twenty-four courses of priests, 1 Chr. 24:10; Neh. 12:4; Luke 1:5.

2. King of Judah. See ABIJAM.

ABIAH. 1. Wife of Hezron, 1 Chr. 2:24

2. Son of Samuel, 1 Sam. 8:1-5; 1 Chr. 6:28

ABI-ALBON, called also ABIEL. One of David's heroes, 2 Sam. 23:31; 1 Chr. 11:32.

ABIASAPH, son of Korah, Ex. 6:24.

7

ABIATHAR. 1. High priest. Called AHIMELECH in 2 Sam. 8:17; 1 Chr. 24:3,6,31, and ABIMELECH, 1 Chr.18:16. Son of Ahimelech, 1 Sam. 22:20. Escapes to David from the vengeance of Saul, who slew the priests in the city of Nob, 1 Sam. 22:20–23, with *vs.* 6–19. Consults the ephod for David, 1 Sam. 22:10; 23:9; 30:7. Associate high priest with Zadok in the reign of David, 2 Sam. 15:35; 20:25; 1 Kin. 4:4; 1 Chr. 15:11, but called AHIMELECH and father of Abiathar, 2 Sam. 8:17; 1 Chr. 18:16. Loyal to David when Absalom rebelled; leaves Jerusalem with the ark of the covenant, but is directed by David to return with the ark, 2 Sam. 15:24–29. Aids David by sending his son from Jerusalem to David with secret information concerning the counsel of Ahithophel, 2 Sam. 15:35,36; 17:15–22; 1 Kin. 2:26. Supports Adonijah's pretensions to the throne, 1 Kin. 1:7. Thrust out of office by Solomon, 1 Kin. 2:26,27, with 1 Sam. 2:31–35.

2. See AHIMELECH.

ABIB, called also NISAN. First month in the Jewish calendar, Ex. 12:2. Passover instituted, and Israelites depart from Egypt in, Ex. 23:15; Deut. 16:1. Tabernacle set up in, Ex. 40:2,17. Israelites arrive at the wilderness of Zin in, Num. 20:1. Enter Canaan in, Josh. 4:19. Jordan's overflow in, 1 Chr. 12:15.

ABIDA, son of Midian, 1 Chr. 1:33.

ABIDAH, a descendant of Abraham, Gen. 25:4.

ABIEL. 1. Saul's grandfather, 1 Sam. 14:51.

2. A Benjamite,1 Sam.9:1. See ABI-ALBON.

ABIEZER. 1. Called also JEEZER, progenitor of the Abiezrites, Num. 26:30; Josh. 17:2; Judg. 6:34; 8:2.

2. One of David's heroes, 2 Sam. 23:27; 1 Chr. 27:12.

ABIGAIL. 1. Nabal's wife. Her wisdom and tact, and marriage to David, 1 Sam. 25; 27:3; 2 Sam. 2:2. Mother of Chileab by David, 2 Sam. 3:3; 1 Chr. 3:1. Taken captive and rescued by David, 1 Sam. 30:1–18.

2. Sister of David, and mother of Amasa, 2 Sam. 17:25; 1 Chr. 2:16,17.

ABIHAIL. 1.Father of Esther, Esth.2:15.

2. The second wife of Rehoboam, 2 Chr. 11:18,19.

3. Father of Zuriel, Num. 3:35.

4. Wife of Abishur, 1 Chr. 2:29.

ABIHU. Son of Aaron, Ex.6:23; Num.3:2. Summoned by God to Sinai, Ex. 24:9. Called to the priesthood, Ex. 28:1. Death of, Lev. 10:1,2; Num. 26:61. Died childless, Num. 3:4.

ABIHUD, called also AHIHUD, son of Bela, 1 Chr. 8:3.

ABIJAH. 1. Son of Jeroboam, 1 Kin. 14:1–18.

2. See ABIA; ABIJAM.

ABIJAM, called also ABIJAH and ABIA. King of Judah, 1 Kin. 14:31; 15:1; 2 Chr. 12:16. History of, 1 Kin. 15:1–8; 2 Chr. 11:22; 13. Succeeded by Asa, 1 Kin. 15:8; 2 Chr. 14:1.

ABILENE, a Roman province in Palestine, Luke 3:1.

ABIMAEL, son of Joktan, Gen. 10:28; 1 Chr. 1:22.

ABIMELECH. 1. King of Gerar, Gen. 20; 21:22–32.

2. King of Gerar, Gen. 26.

3. Son of Gideon, Judg.8:31; 9; 2 Sam.11:21.

4. See ACHISH; AHIMELECH.

ABINADAB. 1. A Levite, in whose house the ark of God rested twenty years, 1 Sam. 7:1,2; 2 Sam. 6:3,4; 1 Chr. 13:7.

2. Son of Jesse, 1 Sam. 16:8; 17:13.

3. Called also ISHUI, son of Saul, 1 Sam. 14:49; 31:2.

4. Father of one of Solomon's purveyors. Called in *R. V.* Ben-Abinadab, 1 Kin. 4:11.

ABINOAM, father of Barak, Judg. 4:6.

ABIRAM. 1. An Israelite who conspired with Dathan against Moses and Aaron, Num. 16; 26:9,10; Deut. 11:6; Psa. 106:17.

2. Son of Hiel, 1 Kin. 16:34.

ABISHAG, wife of David, 1 Kin. 1:1–4; 2:13–25.

ABISHAI. Son of Zeruiah, David's sister, 1 Chr. 2:16. One of David's chief men, 2 Sam. 23:18. Seeks Saul's life, 1 Sam. 26:6-8. Pursues and slays Abner, 2 Sam. 2:24; 3:30. Defeats the Edomites, 1 Chr. 18:12; the Ammonites, 2 Sam. 10:10,14. Seeks the life of Shimei, 2 Sam. 16:9; 19:21. Leads a division of David's army against Absalom, 2 Sam. 18:2,5. Overthrows Sheba, 2 Sam. 20:1-22. Saves David from being slain by a Philistine, 2 Sam. 21:17. Obtains water from the well of Bethlehem for David, 1 Chr. 11:15-20.

ABISHALOM. 1 Kin. 15:2,10. See ABSALOM.

ABISHUA. 1. A high priest, 1 Chr. 6:4, 5,50.

2. A son of Bela, 1 Chr. 8:4.

ABISHUR, son of Shammai, 1 Chr. 2: 28,29.

ABITAL, wife of David, 2 Sam. 3:4; 1 Chr. 3:3.

ABITUB, a Benjamite, 1 Chr. 8:11.

ABIUD, ancestor of Jesus, Matt. 1:13.

ABLUTION, Ex. 19:10,14; Matt. 15:2; Mark 7:2-5,8,9; Luke 11:38; Heb. 9:10. Of priests, Ex. 29:4; 30:18-21; 40:12,31,32; Lev. 8:6; 16:4,24,26,28; Num. 19:7-10,19; 2 Chr. 4:6.

Of burnt offerings, Lev. 1:9,13; 9:14; 2 Chr. 4:6. Of the dead, Acts 9:37. Of infants, Ezek. 16:4. Of the face, Matt. 6:17; feet, Gen. 18:4; 19:2; 24:32; 43:24; Ex. 30:19,21; 40:31; Judg. 19:21; 2 Sam. 11:8; Song 5:3; Luke 7:38,44; John 13:5; 1 Tim. 5:10; hands, Ex. 30:18-21; 40:30-32. Of the hands, as a token of innocency, Deut. 21:6; Psa. 26:6; Matt. 27:24.

For defilement: Of lepers, Lev. 14:8,9; those having bloody issue, Lev. 15:5-13; those having eaten that which died, Lev. 17:15,16.

Traditional forms of, not observed by Jesus, Luke 11:38,39. See PURIFICATION; DEFILEMENT.

FIGURATIVE: Psa. 51:2. Wash me throughly from mine iniquity, and cleanse me from my sin. 7. Purge me with hyssop, and I shall be clean: wash me, and I shall be whiter than snow.

Psa. 65:3. Iniquities prevail against me: *as for* our transgressions, thou shalt purge them away.

Psa. 73:13. Verily I have cleansed my heart *in* vain, and washed my hands in innocency.

Psa. 79:9. Help us, O God of our salvation, for the glory of thy name: and deliver us, and purge away our sins, for thy name's sake.

Prov. 16:6. By mercy and truth iniquity is purged:

Prov. 20:9. Who can say, I have made my heart clean, I am pure from my sin?

Isa. 1:16. Wash you, make you clean; *v.* 18.

Isa. 4:3. And it shall come to pass, *that he that is* left in Zion, and *he that* remaineth in Jerusalem, shall be called holy, *even* every one that is written among the living in Jerusalem: 4. When the Lord shall have washed away the filth of the daughters of Zion, and shall have purged the blood of Jerusalem from the midst thereof by the spirit of judgment, and by the spirit of burning.

Dan. 12:10. Many shall be purified, and made white, and tried. Zech. 13:1; John 13:8.

Acts 22:16. Arise, and be baptized, and wash away thy sins, calling on the name of the Lord.

1 Cor. 5:7. Purge out therefore the old leaven, that ye may be a new lump.

1 Cor. 6:11. But ye are washed, but ye are sanctified, but ye are justified in the name of the Lord Jesus, and by the Spirit of our God. 2 Cor. 7:1; Eph. 5:26.

Tit. 3:5. Not by works of righteousness which we have done, but according to his mercy he saved us, by the washing of regeneration, and renewing of the Holy Ghost; 6. Which he shed on us abundantly through Jesus Christ our Saviour;

Heb. 1:3. Who . . . when he had by himself purged our sins, sat down on the right hand of the Majesty on high.

Heb. 9:14. How much more shall the blood of Christ, who through the eternal Spirit offered himself without spot to God, purge your conscience from dead works to serve the living God? *chap.* 10:22.

Jas. 4:8. Cleanse *your* hands, *ye* sinners; and purify *your* hearts, *ye* doubleminded.

2 Pet. 1:9. But he that lacketh these things is blind, and cannot see afar off, and hath forgotten that he was purged from his old sins.

1 John 1:7. But if we walk in the light, as he is in the light, we have fellowship one with another, and the blood of Jesus Christ his Son cleanseth us from all sin. . . . 9. If we confess our sins, he is faithful and just to forgive us *our* sins, and to cleanse us from all unrighteousness.

Rev. 1:5. Unto him that loved us, and washed us from our sins in his own blood,

Rev. 7:14. These are they which came out of great tribulation, and have washed their robes, and made them white in the blood of the Lamb. Rev. 22:14 [*R. V.*]. See REGENERATION.

ABNER, son of Ner. Cousin of Saul, 1 Sam. 14:50,51, with 1 Sam. 9:1. Captain of the host, 1 Sam. 14:50; 17:55; 26:5,14. Dedicated spoils of war to the tabernacle, 1 Chr. 26:27,28. Loyalty of, to the house of Saul, 2 Sam. 2:8–32. Alienation of, from the house of Saul, 2 Sam. 3:6–21. Murdered by Joab; David's sorrow for, 2 Sam. 3:27–39.

ABOMINATION. Things that are, to God: Idolatry, Deut. 7:25; 27:15; 32:16; unjust weights and measures, Deut. 25:13–16; Prov. 11:1; 20:10,23; uncleanness, Lev. 18: 22; 20:13; Deut. 24:4; incest, Lev. 18:6–18; lying with a woman in her menses, Lev. 18:19; adultery, Lev. 18:20; sodomy, Lev. 18:22,23; offering seed to Molech, Lev. 18:21, or children in sacrifice, Deut. 18:10; sorcery and necromancy, Deut. 18:10,11; the hire of a whore and price of a dog, as a consecrated gift, Deut. 23:18.

UNCLASSIFIED SCRIPTURES RELATING TO: Deut. 22:5. The woman shall not wear that which pertaineth unto a man, neither shall a man put on a woman's garment: for all that do so *are* abomination unto the LORD thy God.

Prov. 3:32. For the froward *is* abomination to the LORD: but his secret *is* with the righteous.

Prov. 6:16. These six *things* doth the LORD hate; yea, seven *are* an abomination unto him: 17. A proud look, a lying tongue, and hands that shed innocent blood, 18. A heart that deviseth wicked imaginations, feet that be swift in running to mischief, 19. A false witness *that* speaketh lies, and he that soweth discord among brethren.

Prov. 8:7. Wickedness *is* an abomination to my lips.

Prov. 11:20. They that are of a froward heart *are* abomination to the LORD.

Prov. 12:22. Lying lips *are* abomination to the LORD: but they that deal truly *are* his delight.

Prov. 15:8. The sacrifice of the wicked *is* an abomination to the LORD: but the prayer of the upright *is* his delight. 9. The way of the wicked *is* an abomination unto the LORD: but he loveth him that followeth after righteousness. 26. The thoughts of the wicked *are* an abomination to the LORD: but *the words* of the pure *are* pleasant words.

Prov. 16:5. Every one *that is* proud in heart *is* an abomination to the LORD: *though* hand *join* in hand, he shall not be unpunished.

Prov. 17:15. He that justifieth the wicked, and he that condemneth the just, even they both *are* abomination to the LORD.

Prov. 20:10. Divers weights, *and* divers measures, both of them *are* alike abomination to the LORD. *v.* 23.

Prov. 21:27. The sacrifice of the wicked *is*

abomination: how much more, *when* he bringeth it with a wicked mind?

Prov. 24:9. The thought of foolishness *is* sin: and the scorner *is* an abomination to men.

Prov. 28:9. He that turneth away his ear from hearing the law, even his prayer *shall be* abomination.

Prov. 29:27. An unjust man *is* an abomination to the just.

ABORTION. Ex. 21:22. If men strive, and hurt a woman with child, so that her fruit depart *from her*, and yet no mischief follow: he shall be surely punished, according as the woman's husband will lay upon him; and he shall pay as the judges *determine.* 23. And if *any* mischief follow, then thou shalt give life for life.

As a judgment, Hos. 9:14. Of animals, caused by thunder, Psa. 29:9.

ABRAHAM, called also ABRAM. Son of Terah, Gen. 11:26,27. Marries Sarah, Gen. 11:29. Dwells in Ur, but removes to Haran, Gen. 11:31; Neh. 9:7; Acts 7:4, and Canaan, Gen. 12:4,5,6; Acts 7:4.

Divine call of, Gen. 12:1–3; Josh. 24:3; Neh. 9:7; Isa. 51:2; Acts 7:2,3; Heb. 11:8. Canaan given to, Gen. 12:1,7; 15:7–21; Ezek. 33:24. Dwells in Beth-el, Gen. 12:8. Sojourns in Egypt, Gen. 12:10–20; 26:1. Deferring to Lot, chooses Hebron, Gen. 13; 14:13; 35:27. Dwells in Gerar, Gen. 20; 21:22–34.

Defeats Chedorlaomer, Gen. 14:5–24; Heb. 7:1. Is blessed by Melchizedek, Gen. 14:18–20; Heb. 7:1–10.

God's covenant with, Gen. 15; 17:1–22; Mic. 7:20; Luke 1:73; Rom. 4:13; 15:8; Heb. 6:13, 14; Gal. 3:6–18,29; 4:22–31. Called ABRAHAM, Gen. 17:5; Neh. 9:7. Circumcision of, Gen. 17:10–14,23–27. Angels appear to, Gen. 18:1–16; 22:11,15; 24:7. His questions about the destruction of the righteous and wicked in Sodom, Gen. 18:23–32. Witnesses the destruction of Sodom, Gen. 19:27,28. Ishmael born to, Gen. 16:3,15. Dwells in Gerar; deceives Abimelech concerning Sarah, his wife, Gen. 20. Isaac born to, Gen. 21:2,3; Gal. 4:22–30. Sends Hagar and Ishmael away, Gen. 21:10–14; Gal. 4:22–30.

Trial of his faith in the offering of Isaac, Gen. 22:1–19; Heb. 11:17; Jas. 2:21. Sarah, his wife, dies, Gen. 23:1,2. He purchases a place for her burial, and buries her in a cave, Gen. 23:3–20. Marries Keturah, Gen. 25:1. Provides a wife for Isaac, Gen. 24.

Children of, Gen. 16:15; 21:2,3; 25:1–4; 1 Chr. 1:32–34. Testament of, Gen. 25:5,6. Wealth of, Gen. 13:2; 24:35; Isa. 51:2. Age of, at different periods, Gen. 12:4; 16:16; 21:5; 25:7. Death, Gen. 15:15; 25:8–10. In Paradise, Matt. 8:11; Luke 13:28; 16:22–31.

Friend of God, Isa. 41:8; 2 Chr. 20:7; Jas. 2:23. Piety of, Gen. 12:7,8; 13:4,18; 18:19; 20:7; 21:33; 22:3–13; 26:5; Neh. 9:7,8; Rom. 4:16–18; 2 Chr. 20:7; Isa. 41:8; Jas. 2:23. A prophet, Gen. 20:7. Faith of, Gen. 15:6; Rom. 4:1–22; Gal. 3:6–9; Heb. 11:8–10, 17–19; Jas. 2:21–24. Unselfishness of, Gen. 13:9;

21:25–30. Independence of, in character, Gen. 14:23; 23:6–16.

Ancestors of, idolatrous, Josh. 24:2. How regarded by his descendants, Matt. 3:9; Luke 13:16,28; 19:9; John 8:33–40,52–59.

ABSALOM, called also ABISHALOM. Son of David by Maacah. 2 Sam. 3:3; 1 Chr. 3:2. Beauty of, 2 Sam. 14:25. Slays Amnon, 2 Sam. 13:22–29. Flees to Geshur, 2 Sam. 13:37, 38. Is permitted by David to return to Jerusalem, 2 Sam. 14:1–24. His demagogism, 2 Sam. 15:2–6,13; conspiracy, 2 Sam. chapters 15–17; death and burial, 2 Sam. 18:9–17. David's mourning for, 2 Sam. 18:33; 19:1–8. Children of, 2 Sam. 14:27; 18:18; 1 Kin. 15:2; 2 Chr. 11:20. Pillar of, 2 Sam. 18:18.

ABSTEMIOUSNESS, Prov. 23:1–3.

INSTANCES OF: Daniel and his Hebrew companions, Dan. 1:8–16. John the Baptist, Matt. 11:18. See ABSTINENCE; TEMPERANCE.

ABSTINENCE, TOTAL. FROM INTOXICATING BEVERAGES: Lev. 10:8. And the LORD spake unto Aaron, saying, 9. Do not drink wine nor strong drink, thou, nor thy sons with thee, when ye go into the tabernacle of the congregation, lest ye die: *it shall be* a statute for ever throughout your generations: 10. And that ye may put difference between holy and unholy, and between unclean and clean.

Num. 6:3. He shall separate *himself* from wine and strong drink, and shall drink no vinegar of wine, or vinegar of strong drink, neither shall he drink any liquor of grapes, nor eat moist grapes, or dried. 4. All the days of his separation shall he eat nothing that is made of the vine tree, from the kernels even to the husk.

Judg. 13:4. Now therefore beware, I pray thee, and drink not wine nor strong drink, and eat not any unclean *thing:* ... 13. And the angel of the LORD said unto Manoah, Of all that I said unto the woman let her beware. 14. She may not eat of any *thing* that cometh of the vine, neither let her drink wine or strong drink.

Esth. 1:8. And the drinking *was* according to the law; none did compel; for so the king had appointed to all the officers of his house, that they should do according to every man's pleasure.

Prov. 23:20. Be not among winebibbers, 31. Look not thou upon the wine when it is red, when it giveth his colour in the cup, *when* it moveth itself aright. 32. At the last it biteth like a serpent, and stingeth like an adder.

Prov. 31:4. *It is* not for kings, O Lemuel, *it is* not for kings to drink wine; nor for princes strong drink:

Jer. 35:6. But they said, We will drink no wine: for Jonadab the son of Rechab our father commanded us, saying, Ye shall drink no wine, *neither* ye, nor your sons forever: 7. Neither shall ye build house, nor sow seed, nor plant vineyard, nor have *any:* but all your days ye shall dwell in tents; that ye may live many days in the land where ye *be* strangers. 8. Thus have we obeyed the voice of Jonadab the son of Rechab our father in all that he hath charged us, to drink no wine all our days, we, our wives, our sons, nor our daughters: 14. The words of Jonadab the son of Rechab, that he commanded his sons not to drink wine, are performed; for unto this day they drink none, but obey their father's commandment: notwithstanding I have spoken unto you, rising early and speaking; but ye hearkened not unto me.

Luke 1:15. For he shall be great in the sight of the Lord, and shall drink neither wine nor strong drink; and he shall be filled with the Holy Ghost, even from his mother's womb.

See TEMPERANCE.

INSTANCES OF: Israelites in the wilderness, Deut. 29:6. Samson, Judg. 16:17, with 13:3-5,13,14; Num. 6:3,4. Daniel, Dan. 1:8,12. Rechabites, Jer. 35:6-14. John the Baptist, Matt. 11:18; Luke 1:15; 7:33.

ACCAD, a city conquered by Nimrod, Gen. 10:10.

ACCESSORY. See COMPLICITY.

ACCHO, called also PTOLEMAIS, a town of Phenicia, Judg. 1:31; Acts 21:7.

ACCOMPLICE. See COMPLICITY.

ACCOUNTABILITY. See RESPONSIBILITY.

ACCURSED, what so called, Deut. 21:23; Josh. 6:17; 7:1; 1 Chr. 2:7; Isa. 65:20; Gal. 1:8.

ACCUSATION, FALSE. Ex. 23:1. Thou shalt not raise a false report: put not thine hand with the wicked to be an unrighteous witness. 7. Keep thee far from a false matter; and the innocent and righteous slay thou not: for I will not justify the wicked.

Lev. 19:16. Thou shalt not go up and down *as* a talebearer among thy people; neither shalt thou stand against the blood of thy neighbour: I *am* the LORD.

Psa. 41:5. Mine enemies speak evil of me. When shall he die, and his name perish? 6. And if he come to see *me*, he speaketh vanity: his heart gathereth iniquity to itself; *when* he goeth abroad, he telleth *it.* 7. All that hate me whisper together against me: against me do they devise my hurt. 8. An evil disease, *say they,* cleaveth fast unto him: and *now* that he lieth he shall rise up no more. 9. Yea, mine own familiar friend, in whom I trusted, which did eat of my bread, hath lifted up *his* heel against me.

Matt. 5:11. Blessed are ye, when *men* shall revile you, and persecute *you,* and shall say all manner of evil against you falsely, for my sake.

Luke 3:14. And the soldiers likewise demanded of him, saying, And what shall we do? And he said unto them, Do violence to no man, neither accuse *any* falsely.

2 Tim. 3:3. Without natural affection, trucebreakers, ¹false accusers.   [¹ R. V. slanderers]

1 Pet. 4:14. If ye be reproached for the name of Christ, happy *are ye;* for the Spirit of glory and of God resteth upon you.

See CONSPIRACY; EVIDENCE; FALSE WITNESS; PERSECUTION; SPEAKING, EVIL; TALEBEARER.

INCIDENTS ILLUSTRATIVE OF: Against Joseph by Potiphar's wife, Gen. 39:7-20; against Joseph's brethren by Joseph, Gen. 42:9-14; against Moses by Korah, Num. 16:3,13; against the prophet Ahimelech by Saul, 1 Sam. 22:11-16; against Abner by Joab, 2 Sam. 3:24-27; against David by the princes of Ammon, 2 Sam. 10:3; against Elijah by Ahab, 1 Kin. 18:17,18; against Naboth by Jezebel, 1 Kin. 21:10,13; against Jews, returned under Ezra, Ezra 4:6-16; Neh. 6:6-8; against Jeremiah, Jer. 26:8,11; 37:13,14; 43:2,3; against Amos, Am. 7:10,11; against Mary, Matt. 1:19; against Jesus, Matt. 9:34; 10:25; 12:2-14; 26:59-61; Mark 3:22; 14:53-65; Luke 23:2; John 18:30; against Stephen, Acts 6:11,13; against Paul, Acts 17:7; 21:28; 24:5, 6,13; 25:2,7; Rom. 3:8; against Paul and Silas, Acts 16:20,21. Satan falsely accuses Job, Job 1:9,10; 2:4,5.

ACELDAMA, the field of blood, Matt. 27:8; Acts 1:19.

ACHAIA, a region of Greece. Paul visits, Acts 18; 19:21; Rom. 16:5; 1 Cor. 16:15; 2 Cor. 1:1. Benevolence of the Christians in, Rom. 15:26; 2 Cor. 9:2; 11:10.

ACHAICUS, a citizen of Corinth, 1 Cor 16:17,18.

ACHAN, sin and punishment of, Josh. 7; 22:20; 1 Chr. 2:7.

ACHAZ. See AHAZ.

ACHBOR. 1. Father of King Baal-hanan, Gen. 36:39; 1 Chr. 1:49.

2. Or ABDON. One of Josiah's courtiers, 2 Kin. 22:14; 2 Chr. 34:20.

3. Father of Elnathan, Jer. 26:22; 36:12,25.

ACHIM, ancestor of Jesus, Matt. 1:14.

ACHISH. King of the Philistines, called also ABIMELECH. David escapes to, 1 Sam. 21:10-15; 27; 28:1,2; 29; 1 Kin. 2:39,40.

ACHMETHA, a Persian city, Ezra 6:2.

ACHOR, a valley near Jericho, Josh. 7:26; 15:7; Isa. 65:10; Hos. 2:15.

ACHSAH, Caleb's daughter, Josh. 15:16-19; Judg. 1:9-13. Called ACHSA, 1 Chr. 2:49.

ACHSHAPH, an ancient city in N. Palestine, Josh. 11:1; 12:20; 19:25.

ACHZIB. 1. A city of Asher, Josh. 19:29; Judg. 1:31.

2. Called also CHEZIB, a city of Judah, Gen. 38:5; Josh. 15:44.

ACRE, the indefinite quantity of land a yoke of oxen could plow in a day, with the kinds of plows, and modes of plowing, used in the times referred to, 1 Sam. 14:14; Isa. 5:10.

ACROSTIC POETRY. See POETRY.

ACTIONS AT LAW, duty of defendant, Matt. 5:40.

See ADJUDICATION; ARBITRATION.

ADADAH, a city of Judah, Josh. 15:22.

ADAH. 1. Wife of Lamech, Gen. 4:19-23

2. Wife of Esau, Gen. 36:10-12.

ADAIAH. 1. Grandfather of Josiah, 2 Kin. 22:1.

2. A musician, 1 Chr. 6:41.

3. A priest, 1 Chr. 9:12; Neh. 11:12.

4. A Benjamite, 1 Chr. 8:21.

5. Father of Maaseiah, 2 Chr. 23:1.

6. Two sons of Bani, Ezra 10:29,39.

7. Son of Joiarib, Neh. 11:5.

ADALIA, son of Haman, Esth. 9:8.

ADAM. 1. The first man. Creation of, Gen. 1:26-28; 2:7; 1 Cor. 15:45; 1 Tim. 2:13. History of, before he sinned, Gen. 1:26-30; 2:16-25. Temptation and sin of, Gen. 3; Job 31:33; Isa. 43:27; Hos. 6:7 [see *R. V.*]; Rom. 5:14-21; 1 Tim. 2:14. Subsequent history of, Gen. 3:20-24; 4:1,2,25; 5:1-5. His death, Gen. 5:5.

Progenitor of the human race, Deut. 32:8; Mal. 2:10. Brought sin into the world,1 Cor. 15:22,45. Type of Christ, Rom. 5:14.

2. A name of Christ, 1 Cor. 15:45,47.

3. A city near the Jordan, Josh. 3:16.

ADAMAH, called also ADAMI, a city of Naphtali,Josh.19:33,36.

ADAMANT, a flint,Ezek. 3:9; Zech. 7:12. See DIAMOND.

ADAMI. See ADAMAH.

ADAR. 1. Twelfth month in Jewish calendar, Ezra 6:15; Esth. 3:7; 8:12; 9:1.

2. Son of Bela, 1 Chr. 8:3.

3. See HAZAR-ADAR.

ADBEEL, son of Ishmael, Gen. 25:13; 1 Chr. 1:29.

ADDAN, called also ADDON, uncertain whether person or town, Ezra 2:59; Neh. 7:61.

ADDER, a venomous serpent,Gen.49:17; Psa. 91:13; 58:4; 140:3; Prov. 23:32.

ADDON. See ADDAN.

ADER, a Benjamite, 1 Chr. 8:15.

ADIEL. 1. A man of the tribe of Simeon, 1 Chr. 4:36.

2. A priest, 1 Chr. 9:12.

3. Father of Azmaveth, 1 Chr. 27:25.

ADIN, a Jewish captive, Ezra 2:15; 8:6; Neh. 7:20.

ADINA,one of David's heroes,1Chr.11:42.

ADINO, one of David's valiant men, 2 Sam. 23:8.

ADITHAIM, a city of Judah,Josh.15:36.

ADJUDICATION AT LAW. TO BE AVOIDED. Prov. 17:14. The beginning of strife *is as* when one letteth out water: therefore leave off contention, before it be meddled with.

Prov. 20:3. *It is* an honour for a man to cease from strife: but every fool will be meddling.

Prov. 25:8. Go not forth hastily to strive, lest *thou know not* what to do in the end thereof, when thy neighbour hath put thee to shame. 9. Debate thy cause with thy neighbour *himself;* and discover not a secret to another: 10. Lest he that heareth *it* put thee to shame, and thine infamy turn not away.

Matt. 5:25. Agree with thine adversary quickly, whiles thou art in the way with him: lest at any time the adversary deliver thee

to the judge, and the judge deliver thee to the officer, and thou be cast into prison.

See ACTIONS AT LAW; ARBITRATION; COMPROMISE; COURTS; JUSTICE.

ADLAI, father of Shaphat, 1 Chr. 27:29.

ADMAH, a city in the vale of Siddim, Gen. 10:19; 14:2; Deut. 29:23; Hos. 11:8.

ADMATHA, a Persian prince,Esth. 1:14.

ADMONITION. SeeWICKED,WARNED.

ADNA. 1. A son of Pahath-Moab, Ezra 10:30.

2. A priest, Neh. 12:15.

ADNAH. 1. One of David's captains, 1 Chr. 12:20.

2. A military chief, 2 Chr. 17:14.

ADONI-BEZEK, king of Bezek, Judg. 1:4-7.

ADONIJAH. 1. Son of David and Haggith, 2 Sam. 3:4; 1 Kin. 1:5,6; 1 Chr. 3:2. Usurpation of, and downfall, 1 Kin. 1. Executed by Solomon, 1 Kin. 2:13 25.

2. A Levite, 2 Chr. 17:8.

3. See ADONIKAM.

ADONIKAM, called also ADONIJAH, a Jew who returned with Ezra from Babylon, Ezra 2:13; Neh. 7:18; 10:16.

ADONIRAM, called also ADORAM,a tax-gatherer, 2 Sam. 20:24; 1 Kin. 4:6; 5:14; 12:18.

ADONI-ZEDEK, a king of Jerusalem, Josh. 10:1-27.

ADOPTION. Gen. 15:3.

OF CHILDREN. INSTANCES OF: Of Joseph's sons, Gen. 48:5,14,16,22. Of Moses, Ex.2:5-10; Acts 7:21; Heb. 11:24. Of Esther, Esth. 2:7.

SPIRITUAL: Ex. 4:22. And thou shalt say unto Pharaoh,Thus saith the LORD, Israel *is* my son, *even* my firstborn: 23. And I say unto thee, Let my son go, that he may serve me: and if thou refuse to let him go, behold, I will slay thy son, *even* thy firstborn.

Num. 6:27. And they shall put my name upon the children of Israel, and I will bless them. Deut. 28:10; 2 Chr. 7:14; Isa. 43:7.

Deut. 14:1. Ye *are* the children of the LORD your God.

Deut. 26:18. The LORD hath avouched thee this day to be his peculiar people, as he hath promised thee, and that *thou* shouldest keep all his commandments.

Deut. 27:9. Moses and the priests the Levites spake unto all Israel, saying, Take heed, and hearken, O Israel; this day thou art become the people of the LORD thy God.

Deut. 32:5. They have corrupted themselves, their spot *is* not *the spot* of his children. 6. Do ye thus requite the LORD, O foolish people and unwise? *is* not he thy father *that* hath bought thee?

2 Sam. 7:14. I will be his father, and he shall be my son.

1 Chr. 22:10. He shall build a house for my name; and he shall be my son, and I *will be* his father; 1 Chr. 28:6.

Prov. 14:26. His children shall have a place of refuge.

Isa. 8:18. Behold, I and the children whom the LORD hath given me

Isa. 43:6. I will say to the north, Give up;

and to the south, Keep not back: bring my sons from far, and my daughters from the ends of the earth;

Isa. 63:16. Doubtless thou *art* our Father, though Abraham be ignorant of us, and Israel acknowledge us not: thou, O LORD, *art* our Father, our Redeemer; thy name *is* from everlasting. *v.* 8.

Jer. 3:19. I said, How shall I put thee among the children, and give thee a pleasant land, a goodly heritage of the hosts of nations? and I said, Thou shalt call me, My father; and shalt not turn away from me.

Jer. 31:9. I am a father to Israel, and Ephraim *is* my firstborn. 20. *Is* Ephraim my dear son? *is he* a pleasant child?

Hos. 1:9. Then said God, Call his name Lo-ammi: for ye *are* not my people, and I will not be your *God.* 10. It shall come to pass, *that* in the place where it was said unto them, Ye *are* not my people, *there* it shall be said unto them, Ye *are* the sons of the living God.

Hos. 11:1. When Israel *was* a child, then I loved him, and called my son out of Egypt.

Matt. 5:9. Blessed *are* the peacemakers: for they shall be called the children of God. 45. That ye may be the children of your Father which is in heaven:

Matt. 13:43. Then shall the righteous shine forth as the sun in the kingdom of their Father.

Luke 6:35. Ye shall be the children of the Highest:

John 1:12. As many as received him, to them gave he [1] power to become [2] the sons of God, even to them that believe on his name: 13. Which were born, not of blood, nor of the will of the flesh, nor of the will of man, but of God. [R. V. [1] the right [2] children]

John 11:52. And not for that nation only, but that also he should gather together in one the children of God that were scattered abroad.

Acts 15:17. That the residue of men might seek after the Lord, and all the Gentiles, upon whom my name is called, saith the Lord, who doeth all these things.

Rom. 8:14. For as many as are led by the Spirit of God, they are the sons of God. 15. For ye have not received the spirit of bondage again to fear; but ye have received the Spirit of adoption, whereby we cry, Abba, Father. 16. The Spirit itself beareth witness with our spirit, that we are the children of God: 17. And if children, then heirs; heirs of God, and joint-heirs with Christ; 19. For the earnest expectation of the creature waiteth for the manifestation of the sons of God. 21. Because the creature itself also shall be delivered from the bondage of corruption into the glorious liberty of the children of God. 29. For whom he did foreknow, he also did predestinate *to be* conformed to the image of the Son, that he might be the firstborn among many brethren.

Rom. 9:8. They which are the children of the flesh, these *are* not the children of God:

but the children of the promise are counted for the seed. *v.* 26; 2 Sam. 7:14; Heb. 1:5.

2 Cor. 6:17. Wherefore come out from among them, and be ye separate, saith the Lord, and touch not the unclean *thing;* and I will receive you, 18. And will be a Father unto you, and ye shall be my sons and daughters, saith the Lord Almighty.

Gal. 3:26. For ye are all the children of God by faith in Christ Jesus. 29. And if ye *be* Christ's, then are ye Abraham's seed, and heirs according to the promise.

Gal. 4:5. To redeem them that were under the law, that we might receive the adoption of sons. 6. And because ye are sons, God hath sent forth the Spirit of his Son into your hearts, crying, Abba, Father. 7. Wherefore thou art no more a servant, but a son; and if a son, then an heir [1] of God through Christ. [[1] R. V. through God]

Eph. 1:5. Having predestinated us unto the adoption of children by Jesus Christ to himself,

Eph. 2:19. Now therefore ye are no more strangers and foreigners, but fellow citizens with the saints, and of the household of God;

Eph. 3:6. That the Gentiles should be fellowheirs, and of the same body, and partakers of his promise in Christ by the gospel: 15. Of whom the whole family in heaven and earth is named,

Phil. 2:15. That ye may be blameless and harmless, the sons of God, without rebuke, in the midst of a crooked and perverse nation, among whom ye shine as lights in the world.

Heb. 2:10. It became him, for whom are all things, and by whom *are* all things, in bringing many sons unto glory, to make the captain of their salvation perfect through sufferings. 11. For both he that sanctifieth and they who are sanctified *are* all of one: for which cause he is not ashamed to call them brethren. 13. Behold I and the children which God hath given me.

Heb. 12:6. Whom the Lord loveth he chasteneth, and scourgeth every son whom he receiveth. 7. If ye endure chastening, God dealeth with you as with sons; for what son is he whom the father chasteneth not? 9... Shall we not much rather be in subjection unto the Father of spirits, and live?

1 John 3:1. Behold what manner of love the Father hath bestowed upon us, that we should be called the sons of God: 2. Beloved, now are we the sons of God, and it doth not yet appear what we shall be: but we know that, when he shall appear, we shall be like him; 10. In this the children of God are manifest, and the children of the devil: whosoever doeth not righteousness is not of God, neither he that loveth not his brother.

1 John 4:4. Ye are of God, little children, and have overcome them; because greater is he that is in you, than he that is in the world.

Rev. 21:7. He that overcometh shall inherit all things; and I will be his God, and he shall be my son.

TYPIFIED, in Israel, Ex. 4:22; Hos. 11:1; Rom. 9:4.

See GOD, FATHERHOOD OF; RIGHTEOUS, UNION OF, WITH CHRIST.

ADORAIM, a city of Judah, 2 Chr. 11:9.

ADORAM. 1. Officer over the tribute, 2 Sam. 20:24.

2. See ADONIRAM.

ADRAMMELECH. 1. An Assyrian idol, 2 Kin. 17:31.

2. Son of Sennacherib, 2 Kin. 19:37; Isa. 37:38.

ADRAMYTTIUM, a city of Mysia, Acts 27:2.

ADRIA, sea of, Acts 27:27.

ADRIEL, Saul's son-in-law, 1 Sam. 18:19; 2 Sam. 21:8,9.

ADULLAM. 1. A cave near the Dead Sea. David takes refuge in, 1 Sam. 22:1; 2 Sam. 23:13; 1 Chr. 11:15. See titles of Psalms 57 and 142.

2. An ancient city of Canaan, Gen. 38:1; Josh. 12:15; 15:35; 2 Chr. 11.7; Neh. 11:30; Mic. 1:15.

ADULTERY. Gen. 20:3. But God came to Abimelech in a dream by night, and said to him, Behold, thou *art but* a dead man, for the woman which thou hast taken; for she *is* a man's wife.

2 Sam. 12:14. Howbeit, because by this deed thou hast given great occasion to the enemies of the LORD to blaspheme, the child also *that is* born unto thee shall surely die.

Job 24:15. The eye also of the adulterer waiteth for the twilight, saying, No eye shall see me: and disguiseth *his* face. 16. In the dark they dig through houses, *which* they had marked for themselves in the daytime: they know not the light. 17. For the morning *is* to them even as the shadow of death: if *one* know *them; they are in* the terrors of the shadow of death. *v.* 18.

Job 31:1. I made a covenant with mine eyes; why then should I think upon a maid? 9. If mine heart have been deceived by a woman, or *if* I have laid wait at my neighbour's door; 10. *Then* let my wife grind unto another, and let others bow down upon her. 11. For this *is* a heinous crime; yet it *is* an iniquity *to be punished by* the judges. 12. For it *is* a fire *that* consumeth to destruction, and would root out all mine increase.

Prov. 2:16. To deliver thee from the strange woman, *even* from the stranger *which* flattereth with her words; 18. Her house inclineth unto death, and her paths unto the dead. 19. None that go unto her return again, neither take they hold of the paths of life. *v.* 17.

Prov 5:3. The lips of a strange woman drop *as* an honeycomb, and her mouth *is* smoother than oil: 4. But her end is bitter as wormwood, sharp as a two-edged sword. *vs.* 5-22.

Prov. 6:24. To keep thee from the evil woman, from the flattery of the tongue of a strange woman. 25. Lust not after her beauty in thine heart; neither let her take thee with her eyelids. 26. For by means of a whorish woman *a man is brought* to a piece of bread: and the adulteress will hunt for the precious life. 27. Can a man take fire in his bosom, and his clothes not be burned? 28. Can one go upon hot coals, and his feet not be burned? 29. So he that goeth in to his neighbour's wife; whosoever toucheth her shall not be innocent. 32. *But* whoso committeth adultery with a woman lacketh understanding: he *that* doeth it destroyeth his own soul. 33. A wound and dishonour shall he get; and his reproach shall not be wiped away.

Prov. 7:5. That they may keep thee from the strange woman, from the stranger *which* flattereth with her words. 6. For at the window of my house I looked through my casement, 7. And beheld among the simple ones, I discerned among the youths, a young man void of understanding, 8. Passing through the street near her corner; and he went the way to her house, 9. In the twilight, in the evening, in the black and dark night: 10. And, behold, there met him a woman *with* the attire of a harlot, and subtle of heart. 11. (She *is* loud and stubborn; her feet abide not in her house: 12. Now *is she* without, now in the streets, and lieth in wait at every corner.) 13. So she caught him, and kissed him, *and* with an impudent face said unto him, 14. *I have* peace offerings with me; this day have I paid my vows. 15. Therefore came I forth to meet thee, diligently to seek thy face, and I have found thee. 16. I have decked my bed with coverings of tapestry, with carved *works*, with fine linen of Egypt. 17. I have perfumed my bed with myrrh, aloes, and cinnamon. 18. Come, let us take our fill of love until the morning: let us solace ourselves with loves. 19. For the goodman *is* not at home, he is gone a long journey: 20. He hath taken a bag of money with him, *and* will come home at the day appointed. 21. With her much fair speech she caused him to yield, with the flattering of her lips she forced him. 22. He goeth after her straightway, as an ox goeth to the slaughter, or as a fool to the correction of the stocks; 23. Till a dart strike through his liver; as a bird hasteth to the snare, and knoweth not that it *is* for his life.

Prov. 9:13. A foolish woman *is* clamorous: *she is* simple, and knoweth nothing. 14. For she sitteth at the door of her house, on a seat in the high places of the city, 15. To call passengers who go right on their ways: 16. Whoso *is* simple, let him turn in hither: and *as for* him that wanteth understanding, she saith to him, 17. Stolen waters are sweet, and bread *eaten* in secret is pleasant. 18. But he knoweth not that the dead *are* there; *and that* her guests *are* in the depths of hell.

Prov. 22:14. The mouth of strange women

is a deep pit: he that is abhorred of the LORD shall fall therein.

Prov. 23:27. For a whore *is* a deep ditch; and a strange woman *is* a narrow pit. 28. She also lieth in wait as *for* a prey, and increaseth the transgressors among men.

Prov. 29:3. He that keepeth company with harlots spendeth *his* substance.

Prov. 30:18. There be three *things which* are too wonderful for me, yea, four which I know not: 19. The way of an eagle in the air; the way of a serpent upon a rock; the way of a ship in the midst of the sea; and the way of a man with a maid. 20. Such *is* the way of an adulterous woman; she eateth, and wipeth her mouth, and saith, I have done no wickedness.

Prov. 31:3. Give not thy strength unto women, nor thy ways to that which destroyeth kings.

Isa. 57:3. But draw near hither, ye sons of the sorceress, the seed of the adulterer and the whore. 4. Against whom do ye sport yourselves? against whom make ye a wide mouth, *and* draw out the tongue? *are* ye not children of transgression, a seed of falsehood,

Jer. 3:1. If a man put away his wife, and she go from him, and become another man's, shall he return unto her again? shall not that land be greatly polluted?

Jer. 5:7. How shall I pardon thee for this? thy children have forsaken me, and sworn by *them that are* no gods: when I had fed them to the full, they then committed adultery, and assembled themselves by troops in the harlots' houses. 8. They were *as* fed horses in the morning: every one neighed after his neighbour's wife.

Jer. 7:9. Will ye steal, murder, and commit adultery, and swear falsely, and burn incense unto Baal, and walk after other gods whom ye know not; 10. And come and stand before me in this house, which is called by my name, and say, We are delivered to do all these abominations?

Jer. 23:10. The land is full of adulterers.

Ezek. 18:5. But if a man be just, and do that which is lawful and right, 6. *And* hath not eaten upon the mountains, neither hath lifted up his eyes to the idols of the house of Israel, neither hath defiled his neighbour's wife, neither hath come near to a menstruous woman, 9. . . . . He *is* just, he shall surely live, saith the Lord GOD.

Hos. 4:1 The LORD hath a controversy with the inhabitants of the land, because *there is* no truth, nor mercy, nor knowledge of God in the land. 2. By swearing, and lying, and killing, and stealing, and committing adultery, they break out, and blood toucheth blood. 11. Whoredom, and wine, and new wine, take away the heart.

Matt. 5:28. Whosoever looketh on a woman to lust after her hath committed adultery with her already in his heart. 32. Whosoever shall put away his wife, saving for the cause of fornication, causeth her to commit adultery: and whosoever shall marry her that

is divorced committeth adultery. **Mark** 10:11,12; Luke 16:18.

Matt. 15:19. Out of the heart proceed evil thoughts, adulteries, fornications, Mark 7:21.

Matt. 19.9. And I say unto you, Whosoever shall put away his wife, except *it be* for fornication, and shall marry another, committeth adultery: and whoso marrieth her which is put away doth commit adultery. Mark 10:11.

Mark 10:19. Thou knowest the commandments, Do not commit adultery, Do not kill, Do not steal, Do not bear false witness, Defraud not, Honour thy father and mother. Jas. 2:11.

Acts 15:20. We write unto them, that they abstain from pollutions of idols, and *from* fornication, *v.* 29.

Rom. 1:28. As they did not like to retain God in *their* knowledge, God gave them over to a reprobate mind, to do those things which are not convenient; 29. Being filled with all unrighteousness, fornication, wickedness, covetousness, . . . 32. Who, knowing the judgment of God, that they which commit such things are worthy of death, not only do the same, but have pleasure in them that do them.

Rom. 7:3. So then if, while *her* husband liveth, she be married to another man, she shall be called an adulteress: but if her husband be dead, she is free from that law; so that she is no adulteress, though she be married to another man.

1 Cor. 5:9. I wrote unto you in an epistle not to company with fornicators: 10. Yet not altogether with the fornicators of this world, or with the covetous, or extortioners, or with idolaters: for then must ye needs go out of the world.

1 Cor. 6:15. Know ye not that your bodies are the members of Christ? shall I then take the members of Christ, and make *them* the members of an harlot? God forbid. 16. What? know ye not that he which is joined to an harlot *is* one body? for two, saith he, shall be one flesh. 18. Flee fornication. Every sin that a man doeth is without the body; but he that committeth fornication sinneth against his own body.

1 Cor. 10:8. Neither let us commit fornication, as some of them committed, and fell in one day three and twenty thousand.

2 Cor. 12:21. *And* lest, when I come again, my God will humble me among you, and *that* I shall bewail many which have sinned already, and have not repented of the uncleanness and fornication and lasciviousness which they have committed.

Gal. 5:19. The works of the flesh are manifest, which are *these;* Adultery, fornication, uncleanness, lasciviousness, 21. Of the which I tell you before, as I have also told *you* in time past, that they which do such things shall not inherit the kingdom of God.

1 Tim. 1:9. Knowing this, that the law is not made for a righteous man, but . . . 10. For whoremongers, for them **that defile**

themselves with mankind, for menstealers, for liars, for perjured persons, and if there be any other thing that is contrary to sound doctrine.

2 Tim. 3:6. For of this sort are they which creep into houses, and lead captive silly women laden with sins, led away with divers lusts,

1 Pet. 4:3. The time past of *our* life may suffice us to have wrought the will of the Gentiles, when we walked in lasciviousness, lusts, . . . 4. Wherein they think it strange that ye run not with *them* to the same excess of riot, speaking evil of *you.*

2 Pet. 2:9. The Lord knoweth how to deliver the godly out of temptations, and to reserve the unjust unto the day of judgment to be punished: 10. But chiefly them that walk after the flesh in the lust of uncleanness. 14. Having eyes full of adultery, and that cannot cease from sin; beguiling unstable souls:

Jude 7. Even as Sodom and Gomorrha, and the cities about them in like manner, giving themselves over to fornication, and going after strange flesh, are set forth for an example, suffering the vengeance of eternal fire.

Rev. 2:20. Notwithstanding I have a few things against thee, because thou sufferest that woman Jezebel . . . to teach and to seduce my servants to commit fornication, . . . 21. And I gave her space to repent of her fornication; and she repented not. 22. Behold, I will cast her into a bed, and them that commit adultery with her into great tribulation, except they repent of their deeds.

Rev. 9:21. Neither repented they of their murders, nor of their sorceries, nor of their fornication,

See LASCIVIOUSNESS; RAPE; SENSUALITY; SODOMY; WHORE; WHOREDOM.

FORBIDDEN: Ex. 20:14. Thou shalt not commit adultery. Deut. 5:18; Matt. 5:27; 19: 18; Luke 18:20; Rom. 13:9; Jas. 2:11.

Lev. 18:20. Moreover thou shalt not lie carnally with thy neighbour's wife, to defile thyself with her.

Lev. 19:29. Do not prostitute thy daughter, to cause her to be a whore; lest the land fall to whoredom, and the land become full of wickedness.

Deut. 23:17. There shall be no whore of the daughters of Israel, nor a sodomite of the sons of Israel.

Acts 15:20. We write unto them, that they abstain from fornication.

Rom. 13:13. Let us walk honestly, as in the day; not in rioting and drunkenness, not in chambering and wantonness.

1 Cor. 5:11. I have written unto you not to keep company, if any man that is called a brother be a fornicator, . . . with such an one no not to eat. *vs.* 9, 10.

1 Cor. 6:13. Now the body *is* not for fornication, but for the Lord; and the Lord for the body. 15. Know ye not that your bodies **are** the members of Christ? shall I then take

the members of Christ, and make *them* the members of an harlot? God forbid. 18. Flee fornication. Every sin that a man doeth is without the body; but he that committeth fornication sinneth against his own body.

1 Cor. 10:8. Neither let us commit fornication, as some of them committed, and fell in one day three and twenty thousand.

Eph. 4:17. This I say therefore, and testify in the Lord, that ye henceforth walk not as other Gentiles walk, in the vanity of their mind; 19. Who, being past feeling, have given themselves over unto lasciviousness, to work all uncleanness with greediness. 20. But ye have not so learned Christ;

Eph. 5:3. But fornication, and all uncleanness, let it not be once named among you, as becometh saints; 11. Have no fellowship with the unfruitful works of darkness, but rather reprove *them.* 12. For it is a shame even to speak of those things which are done of them in secret.

Col. 3:5. Mortify therefore your members which are upon the earth; fornication, uncleanness, inordinate affection, evil concupiscence.

1 Thes. 4:3. This is the will of God, *even* your sanctification, that ye should abstain from fornication: 4. That every one of you should know how to possess his vessel in sanctification and honour; 5. Not in the lust of concupiscence, even as the Gentiles which know not God: 7. For God hath not called us unto uncleanness, but unto holiness.

FORGIVENESS OF: INSTANCES OF. Judg. 19:1-4.

John 8:10. Woman, where are those thine accusers? hath no man condemned thee? 11. She said, No man, Lord. And Jesus said unto her, Neither do I condemn thee: go, and sin no more.

PENALTIES FOR: Gen. 20:7. Now therefore restore the man *his* wife; for he *is* a prophet, and he shall pray for thee, and thou shalt live: and if thou restore *her* not, know thou that thou shalt surely die, thou, and all that *are* thine.

Gen. 26:11. And Abimelech charged all *his* people, saying, He that toucheth this man or his wife shall surely be put to death.

Gen. 38:24. And it came to pass about three months after, that it was told Judah, saying, Tamar thy daughter in law hath played the harlot; and also, behold, she *is* with child by whoredom. And Judah said, Bring her forth, and let her be burnt.

Ex. 22:16. And if a man entice a maid that is not betrothed, and lie with her, he shall surely endow her to be his wife. 17. If her father utterly refuse to give her unto him, he shall pay money according to the dowry of virgins.

Lev. 19:20. And whosoever lieth carnally with a woman, that *is* a bondmaid, betrothed to a husband, and not at all redeemed, nor freedom given her; she shall be scourged: they shall not be put to death, because she was **not** free. 21. And he shall bring his trespass offering unto the LORD, unto the door of the tabernacle of the congregation, *even* a ram for a trespass offering. 22. And the priest shall make an atonement for him with the ram of the trespass offering before the LORD for his sin which he hath done; and the sin which he hath done shall be forgiven him.

Lev. 20:10. And the man that committeth adultery with *another* man's wife, *even he* that committeth adultery with his neighbour's wife, the adulterer and the adulteress shall surely be put to death. 11. And the man that lieth with his father's wife hath uncovered his father's nakedness: both of them shall surely be put to death; their blood *shall be* upon them. 12. And if a man lie with his daughter in law, both of them shall surely be put to death: they have wrought confusion; their blood *shall be* upon them.

Lev. 21:9. And the daughter of any priest, if she profane herself by playing the whore, she profaneth her father: she shall be burnt with fire.

Num. 5:11. And the LORD spake unto Moses, saying. 12. Speak unto the children of Israel, and say unto them, If any man's wife go aside, and commit a trespass against him, 13. And a man lie with her carnally, and it be hid from the eyes of her husband, and be kept close, and she be defiled, and *there be* no witness against her, neither she be taken *with the manner* [in the act, R. V.]; 14. And the spirit of jealousy come upon him, and he be jealous of his wife, and she be defiled: or if the spirit of jealousy come upon him, and he be jealous of his wife, and she be not defiled: 15. Then shall the man bring his wife unto the priest, and he shall bring her offering for her, the tenth *part* of an ephah of barley meal; he shall pour no oil upon it, nor put frankincense thereon; for it *is* an offering of jealousy, an offering of memorial, bringing iniquity to remembrance. 16. And the priest shall bring her near, and set her before the LORD: 17. And the priest shall take holy water in an earthen vessel; and of the dust that is in the floor of the tabernacle the priest shall take, and put *it* into the water: 18. And the priest shall set the woman before the LORD, and uncover the woman's head, and put the offering of memorial in her hands, which *is* the jealousy offering: and the priest shall have in his hand the bitter water that causeth the curse: 19. And the priest shall charge her by an oath, and say unto the woman, If no man have lain with thee, and if thou hast not gone aside to uncleanness *with another* instead of thy husband, be thou free from this bitter water that causeth the curse: 20. But if thou hast gone aside *to another* instead of thy husband, and if thou be defiled, and some man have lain with thee beside thine husband: 21. Then the priest shall charge the woman with an oath of cursing, and the priest shall say unto the woman, The LORD make thee a curse and an oath among thy people,

when the LORD doth make thy thigh to rot, and thy belly to swell: 22. And this water that causeth the curse shall go into thy bowels, to make *thy* belly to swell, and *thy* thigh to rot. And the woman shall say, Amen, Amen. 23. And the priest shall write these curses in a book, and he shall blot *them* out with the bitter water: 24. And he shall cause the woman to drink the bitter water that causeth the curse: and the water that causeth the curse shall enter into her, *and become* bitter. 25. Then the priest shall take the jealousy offering out of the woman's hand, and shall wave the offering before the LORD, and offer it upon the altar: 26. And the priest shall take a handful of the offering, *even* the memorial thereof, and burn *it* upon the altar, and afterward shall cause the woman to drink the water. 27. And when he hath made her to drink the water, then it shall come to pass, *that* if she be defiled, and have done trespass against her husband, that the water that causeth the curse shall enter into her, *and become* bitter, and her belly shall swell, and her thigh shall rot: and the woman shall be a curse among her people. 28. And if the woman be not defiled, but be clean; then she shall be free, and shall conceive seed. 29. This *is* the law of jealousies, when a wife goeth aside *to another* instead of her husband, and is defiled; 30. Or when the spirit of jealousy cometh upon him, and he be jealous over his wife, and shall set the woman before the LORD, and the priest shall execute upon her all this law.

Deut. 22:13. If any man take a wife, and go in unto her, and hate her, 14. And give occasion of speech against her, and bring up an evil name upon her, and say, I took this woman, and when I came to her, I found her not a maid: 15. Then shall the father of the damsel, and her mother, take and bring forth *the tokens of* the damsel's virginity unto the elders of the city in the gate: 16. And the damsel's father shall say unto the elders, I gave my daughter unto this man to wife, and he hateth her: 17. And, lo, he hath given occasions of speech *against her*, saying, I found not thy daughter a maid; and yet these *are the tokens of* my daughter's virginity. And they shall spread the cloth before the elders of the city. 18. And the elders of that city shall take that man and chastise him; 19. And they shall amerce him in a hundred *shekels* of silver, and give *them* unto the father of the damsel, because he hath brought up an evil name upon a virgin of Israel: and she shall be his wife; he may not put her away all his days. 20. But if this thing be true, *and the tokens of* virginity be not found for the damsel: 21. Then they shall bring out the damsel to the door of her father's house, and the men of her city shall stone her with stones that she die; because she hath wrought folly in Israel, to play the whore in her father's house: so shalt thou put evil away from among you. 22. If a man be found lying with a woman married to a husband, then they shall both of them die, *both* the man that lay with the woman, and the woman: so shalt thou put away evil from Israel: 23. If a damsel *that is* a virgin be betrothed unto a husband, and a man find her in the city, and lie with her; 24. Then ye shall bring them both out unto the gate of that city, and ye shall stone them with stones that they die; the damsel, because she cried not, *being* in the city; and the man, because he hath humbled his neighbour's wife: so thou shalt put away evil from among you. 25. But if a man find a betrothed damsel in the field, and the man force her, and lie with her; then the man only that lay with her shall die: 26. But unto the damsel thou shalt do nothing; *there is* in the damsel no sin *worthy* of death: for as when a man riseth against his neighbour, and slayeth him, even so *is* this matter: 27. For he found her in the field, *and* the betrothed damsel cried, and *there was* none to save her. 28. If a man find a damsel *that is* a virgin, which is not betrothed, and lay hold on her, and lie with her, and they be found; 29. Then the man that lay with her shall give unto the damsel's father fifty *shekels* of silver, and she shall be his wife; because he hath humbled her, he may not put her away all his days.

Deut. 27:20. Cursed *be* he that lieth with his father's wife: because he uncovereth his father's skirt: and all the people shall say, Amen. 22. Cursed *be* he that lieth with his sister, the daughter of his father, or the daughter of his mother: and all the people shall say, Amen. 23. Cursed *be* he that lieth with his mother in law: and all the people shall say, Amen.

2 Sam. 12:10. Now therefore the sword shall never depart from thine house; because thou hast despised me, and hast taken the wife of Uriah the Hittite to be thy wife. 11. Thus saith the LORD, Behold, I will raise up evil against thee out of thine own house, and I will take thy wives before thine eyes, and give *them* unto thy neighbour, and he shall lie with thy wives in the sight of this sun. 12. For thou didst *it* secretly: but I will do this thing before all Israel, and before the sun.

Jer. 29:22. The LORD make thee like Zedekiah and like Ahab, whom the king of Babylon roasted in the fire; 23. Because they have committed villany in Israel, and have committed adultery with their neighbours' wives, and have spoken lying words in my name, which I have not commanded them; even I know, and *am* a witness, saith the LORD.

Ezek. 16:38. And I will judge thee, as women that break wedlock and shed blood are judged: 40. They shall also bring up a company against thee, and they shall stone thee with stones, and thrust thee through with their swords. 41. And they shall burn thine houses with fire, and execute judgments upon thee in the sight of many women: and I will

cause thee to cease from playing the harlot, and thou also shalt give no hire any more.

Ezek. 23:45. And the righteous men, they shall judge them after the manner of adulteresses, and after the manner of women that shed blood; because they *are* adulteresses, and blood *is* in their hands. 47. And the company shall stone them with stones, and dispatch them with their swords; they shall slay their sons and their daughters, and burn up their houses with fire. 48. Thus will I cause lewdness to cease out of the land, that all women may be taught not to do after your lewdness.

Mal. 3:5. And I will come near to you to judgment; and I will be a swift witness against the sorcerers, and against the adulterers, and against false swearers, and against those that oppress the hireling in *his* wages, the widow, and the fatherless, and that turn aside the stranger *from his right*, and fear not me, saith the LORD of hosts.

John 8:4. They say unto him, Master, this woman was taken in adultery, in the very act. 5. Now Moses in the law commanded us, that such should be stoned.

1 Cor. 5:1. It is reported commonly *that there is* fornication among you, and such fornication as is not so much as named among the Gentiles, that one should have his father's wife. 2. And ye are puffed up, and have not rather mourned, that he that hath done this deed might be taken away from among you. 3. For I verily, as absent in body, but present in spirit, have judged already, as though I were present, *concerning* him that hath so done this deed, 4. In the name of our Lord Jesus Christ, when ye are gathered together, and my spirit, with the power of our Lord Jesus Christ, 5. To deliver such an one unto Satan for the destruction of the flesh, that the spirit may be saved in the day of the Lord Jesus. 6. Your glorying *is* not good. Know ye not that a little leaven leaveneth the whole lump? 7. Purge out therefore the old leaven, that ye may be a new lump, as ye are unleavened. For even Christ our passover is sacrificed for us: 8. Therefore let us keep the feast, not with old leaven, neither with the leaven of malice and wickedness; but with the unleavened *bread* of sincerity and truth. 9. I wrote unto you in an epistle not to company with fornicators: 10. Yet not altogether with the fornicators of this world, or with the covetous, or extortioners, or with idolaters; for then must ye needs go out of the world. 11. But now I have written unto you not to keep company, if any man that is called a brother be a fornicator, or covetous, or an idolater, or a railer, or a drunkard, or an extortioner; with such an one no not to eat. 12. For what have I to do to judge them also that are without? do not ye judge them that are within? 13. But them that are without God judgeth. Therefore put away from among yourselves that wicked person.

1 Cor. 6:9. Be not deceived: neither forni-

cators nor idolaters, nor adulterers, nor effeminate, nor abusers of themselves with mankind, 10. . . . Shall inherit the kingdom of God.

1 Cor. 10:8. Neither let us commit fornication, as some of them committed, and fell in one day three and twenty thousand.

Gal. 5:19. The works of the flesh are manifest, which are *these;* Adultery, fornication, uncleanness, lasciviousness, 21. Of the which I tell you before, as I have also told *you* in time past, that they which do such things shall not inherit the kingdom of God.

Eph. 5:5. Ye know, that no whoremonger, nor unclean person, hath any inheritance in the kingdom of Christ and of God. 6. Let no man deceive you with vain words: for because of these things cometh the wrath of God upon the children of disobedience.

Heb. 13:4. Whoremongers, and adulterers, God will judge.

Rev. 18:9. And the kings of the earth, who have committed fornication and lived deliciously with her, shall bewail her, and lament for her, when they shall see the smoke of her burning, 10. Standing afar off for the fear of her torment, saying, Alas, alas that great city Babylon, that mighty city! for in one hour is thy judgment come.

Rev. 21:8. But the fearful, and unbelieving, and the abominable, and murderers, and whoremongers, and sorcerers, and idolaters, and all liars, shall have their part in the lake which burneth with fire and brimstone: which is the second death.

Rev. 22:15. For without *are* dogs, and sorcerers, and whoremongers, and murderers, and idolaters, and whosoever loveth and maketh a lie.

FIGURATIVE: Jer. 3:2; Ezek. 16:15,16; Hos. 1. See WHOREDOM; IDOLATRY.

INSTANCES OF: Sodomites, Gen. 19:5-8. Lot, Gen. 19:31-38. Shechem, Gen. 34:2. Reuben, Gen. 35:22. Judah, Gen. 38:1-24. Potiphar's wife, Gen. 39:7-12. The Levite's concubine, Judg. 19:2. The Gibeahites, Judg. 19:22-25. Gilead, Judg. 11:1. Samson, Judg. 16:1. Sons of Eli, 1 Sam. 2:22. David, 2 Sam. 11:1-5. Amnon, 2 Sam. 13:1-20. Absalom, 2 Sam. 16:22. Israelites, Ex. 32:6,25; Jer. 29:23; Ezek. 22:9-11; 33:26; Hos. 7:4. Herod, Matt. 14:3,4; Mark 6:17,18; Luke 3:19. Samaritan woman, John 4:17,18. The woman brought to Jesus in the temple, John 8:4-11. Corinthians, 1 Cor. 5:1-5. Heathen, Eph. 4:17-19; 1 Pet. 4:3.

ADUMMIM, place between the fords of the Jordan and Jerusalem, Josh.15:7; 18:17.

ADVENT. See JESUS, SECOND COMING OF; MILLENNIUM.

ADVERSITY. See AFFLICTIONS, p. 20.

ADVICE. See COUNSEL.

ADVOCATE. Tertullus, Acts 24:1-9. FIGURATIVE 1 John 2:1.

ÆNEAS, healed, Acts 9:33,34.

ÆNON. See ENON.

AFFECTIONS. Should be supremely set upon God, Deut. 6:5; Mark 12:30. Should be set upon the commandments of God, Psa. 19:8-10; 119:20,97,103,167; upon the house and worship of God, 1 Chr. 29:3; Psa. 26:8; 27:4; 84:1,2; upon the people of God, Psa. 16:3; Rom. 12:10; 2 Cor. 7:13-16; 1 Thess. 2:8; upon heavenly things, Col. 3:1,2. Should be zealously engaged for God, Psa. 69:9; 119:139; Gal. 4:18. Christ claims the first place in, Matt. 10:37; Luke 14:26. Enkindled by communion with Christ, Luke 24:32. Blessedness of making God the object of, Psa. 91:14. Should not grow cold, Psa. 106:12,13; Matt. 24:12; Gal. 4:15; Rev. 2:4. Of saints, supremely set on God, Psa. 42:1; 73:25; 119:10. Of the wicked, not sincerely set on God, Isa. 58:1,2; Ezek. 33:31,32; Luke 8:13. Carnal, should be mortified, Rom. 8:13; 13:14; 1 Cor. 9:27; Col. 3:5; 1 Thess. 4:5. Carnal affections crucified in saints, Rom. 6:6; Gal. 5:24. False teachers seek to captivate, Gal. 1:10; 4:17; 2 Tim. 3:6; 2 Pet. 2:3,18; Rev. 2:14,20. Of the wicked, are unnatural and perverted, Rom. 1:31; 2 Tim. 3:3; 2 Pet. 2:10.—*Bible Text-Book.*

AFFLICTED. DUTY TO THE: Job 6:14. To him that is afflicted pity *should be shewed* from his friend.

Job 22:29. When *men* are cast down, then thou shalt say, *There is* lifting up; and he shall save the humble person.

Isa. 58:6. *Is* not this the fast that I have chosen? to loose the bands of wickedness, to undo the heavy burdens, and to let the oppressed go free, and that ye break every yoke? 7. *Is it* not to deal thy bread to the hungry, and that thou bring the poor that are cast out to thy house? when thou seest the naked, that thou cover him; and that thou hide not thyself from thine own flesh? 10. And *if* thou draw out thy soul to the hungry, and satisfy the afflicted soul; then shall thy light rise in obscurity, and thy darkness *be* as the noonday.

Matt. 25:34. The shall the King say unto hem on his right hand, Come, ye blessed of my Father, inherit the kingdom prepared for you from the foundation of the world: 35. For I was an hungered, and ye gave me meat: I was thirsty, and ye gav me drink: I was a stranger, and ye took me in: 36. Naked, and ye clothed me: I was sick, and ye visited me: I was in prison, and ye came unto me. 37. Then shall the righteous answer him, saying, Lord, when saw we thee an hungered, and fed *thee?* or thirsty, and gave *thee* drink? 38. When saw we thee a stranger, and took *thee* in? or naked, and clothed *thee?* 39. Or when saw we thee sick, or in prison, and came unto thee? 40. And the King shall answer and say unto them, Verily I say unto you, Inasmuch as ye have done *it* unto one of the least of these my brethren, ye have done *it* unto me. 41. Then shall he say also unto them on the left hand, Depart from me, ye cursed, into everlasting fire, prepared for the devil and his angels: 42. For I was an hungered, and ye gave me no meat: I was thirsty, and ye gave me no drink: 43. I was a stranger, and ye took me not in: naked, and ye clothed me not: sick, and in prison, and ye visited me not. 44. Then shall they also answer him, saying, Lord, when saw we thee anhungered, or a thirst, or a stranger, or naked, or sick, or in prison, and did not minister unto thee? 45. Then shall he answer them, saying, Verily I say unto you, Inasmuch as ye did *it* not to one of the least of these, ye did *it* not to me.

Luke 10:30. And Jesus answering said, A certain *man* went down from Jerusalem to Jericho, and fell among thieves, which stripped him of his raiment, and wounded *him*, and departed, leaving *him* half dead. 31. And by chance there came down a certain priest that way: and when he saw him, he passed by on the other side. 32. And likewise a Levite, when he was at the place, came and looked *on him*, and passed by on the other side. 33. But a certain Samaritan, as he journeyed, came where he was; and when he saw him, he had compassion *on him*, 34. And went to *him*, and bound up his wounds, pouring in oil and wine, and set him on his own beast, and brought him to an inn, and took care of him. 35. And on the morrow when he departed, he took out two pence, and gave *them* to the host, and said unto him, Take care of him: and whatsoever thou spendest more, when I come again, I will repay thee. 36. Which now of these three, thinkest thou, was neighbour unto him that fell among the thieves? 37. And he said, He that shewed mercy on him. Then said Jesus unto him, Go, and do thou likewise.

Phil. 2:1. If *there be* therefore any consolation in Christ, if any comfort of love, if any fellowship of the Spirit, if any bowels and mercies, 2. Fulfil ye my joy, that ye be likeminded, having the same love, *being* of one accord, of one mind.

1 Tim. 5:10. If she have relieved the afflicted, if she have diligently followed every good work.

Jas. 5:13. Is any among you afflicted? let him pray. Is any merry? let him sing psalms. 14. Is any sick among you? let him call for the elders of the church; and let them pray over him, anointing him with oil in the name of the Lord: 15. And the prayer of faith shall save the sick, and the Lord shall raise him up; and if he have committed sins, they shall be forgiven him.

AFFLICTIONS AND ADVERSITIES. LIST OF SUB-TOPICS: *Miscellany of Minor Sub-Topics, p. 20; Unclassified Scriptures Relating to, p. 20; Benefits of, p. 26; Benefits of, Illustrated, p. 27; Consolation in, p. 28; Deliverance from, p. 34; Design of, p. 34; Despondency in, p. 37; Dispensation of God, p. 37; From Satan, p. 39; Impenitence in, p. 39; As a Judgment, p. 40; Mocking at, p. 39; Murmuring in, p. 39; Obduracy in, p. 39; Penitence in, p. 40; Prayer in, p. 40; Prayer in Answered, p. 46; Prayer for the Afflicted, p. 46; Resignation in, p. 46; Resignation in Exemplified, p. 47; Instances of Resignation in, p. 48.*

MISCELLANY OF MINOR SUB-TOPICS: God regulates the measure of afflictions, Psa. 80:5; Isa. 9:1; Jer. 46:28; determines the continuance of, Gen. 15:13,14; Num. 14:33; Isa. 10:25; Jer. 29:10; does not willingly send, Lam. 3:33. Man is born to, Job 5:6,7; 14:1. Saints appointed to, 1 Thess. 3:3. Consequent upon the fall, Gen. 3:16-19. Sin produces, Job 4:8; Prov. 1:31. Sinners corrected by, 2 Sam. 12:14; Psa. 89:30-32; Isa. 57:17; Acts 13:10, 11. Often severe, Job 16:7-16; Psa. 42:7; 66:12; Jonah 2:3; Rev. 7:14. Always less than deserved, Ezra 9:13; Psa. 103:10. Results of, good, Gen. 50:20; Ex. 1:11,12; Deut. 8:15,16; Jer. 24:5,6; Ezek. 20:37. Tempered with mercy, Psa. 78:38,39; 106:43-46; Isa. 30:18-21; Lam. 3:32; Mic. 7:7-9; Nah. 1:12.

OF SAINTS: To be expected, John 16:33; Acts 14:22. Comparatively light, Acts 20:23, 24; Rom. 8:18; 2 Cor. 4:17. Temporary, Psa. 30:5; 103:9; Isa. 54:7,8; John 16:20; 1 Pet. 1:6; 5:10; joy under, Job 5:17; Jas. 5:11; end in joy and blessedness, Psa. 126:5,6; Isa. 61:2,3; Matt. 5:4; 1 Pet. 4:13,14; often arise from the profession of the gospel, Matt. 24:9; John 15:21; 2 Tim. 3:11,12. Exhibit the love and faithfulness of God, Deut. 8:5; Psa. 119:75; Prov. 3:12; 1 Cor. 11:32; Heb. 12:6,7; Rev. 3:19.

OF THE WICKED: God is glorified in, Ex. 14:4; Ezek. 38:22,23. God holds in derision, Psa. 37:13; Prov. 1:26,27. Are multiplied, Deut. 31:17; Job 20:5; 21:17; Psa. 32:10; continual, Job. 15:20; Eccl. 2:23; Isa. 32:10; often sudden, Psa. 73:19; Prov. 6:15; Isa. 30:13 Rev. 18:10. Are often judicially sent, Job 21:17; Psa. 107:17; Jer. 30:15. Are for examples to others, Psa. 64:7-9; Zeph. 3:6,7; 1 Cor. 10:5,11; 2 Pet. 2:6. Are ineffectual for their conversion, Ex. 9:30; Isa. 9:13; Jer. 2:30; Hag. 2:17. Their persecution of saints, a cause of, Deut. 30:7; Psa. 55:19; Zech. 2:9; 2 Thess. 1:6. Impenitence is a cause of, Prov. 1:30,31; Ezek. 24:13; Amos 4:6-12; Zech. 7:11,12; Rev. 2:21, 22. Sometimes humble them, 1 Kin. 21:27. Frequently harden, Neh. 9:28,29; Jer. 5:3. Produce slavish fear, Job 15:24; Psa. 73:19; Jer. 49:3,5. Saints should not be alarmed at, Prov. 3:25,26.

Exemplified: in Pharaoh and the Egyptians, Ex. 9:14,15; 14:24,25; Ahaziah, 2 Kin. 1:1-4; Gehazi, 2 Kin. 5:27; Jehoram, 2 Chr. 21:12-19; Uzziah, 2 Chr. 26:19-21; Ahaz, etc., 2 Chr. 28:5-8,22.– *Bible Text Book.*

FORSAKEN BY FRIENDS IN. INSTANCES OF: Job 2:9; 19:13-19. David, Psa. 31:11, 12; 41:9; 88:8,18. Jesus, Matt. 26:56. Paul, 2 Tim. 4:16. NATIONAL LESSONS FROM, Joel 1; 2.

UNCLASSIFIED SCRIPTURES RELATING TO: Gen. 3:16. Unto the woman he said, I will greatly multiply thy sorrow and thy conception; in sorrow thou shalt bring forth children; 17. Cursed *is* the ground for thy sake; in sorrow shalt thou eat *of* it all the days of thy life.

Deut. 8:5. Thou shalt also consider in thine heart, that as a man chasteneth his son, *so* the LORD thy God chasteneth thee.

2 Sam. 7:14. I will be his father, and he shall be my son. If he commit iniquity, I will chasten him with the rod of men, and with the stripes of the children of men:

Job 3:1. After this opened Job his mouth, and cursed his day. 2. And Job spake, and said, 3. Let the day perish wherein I was born, and the night *in which* it was said, There is a man child conceived. 4. Let that day be darkness; let not God regard it from above, neither let the light shine upon it. 5. Let darkness and the shadow of death stain it; let a cloud dwell upon it; let the blackness of the day terrify it. 6. *As for* that night, let darkness seize upon it; let it not be joined unto the days of the year; let it not come into the number of the months. 7. Lo, let that night be solitary; let no joyful voice come therein. 8. Let them curse it that curse the day, who are ready to raise up their mourning. 9. Let the stars of the twilight thereof be dark; let it look for light, but *have* none; neither let it see the dawning of the day: 10. Because it shut not up the doors of my *mother's* womb, nor hid sorrow from mine eyes. 11. Why died I not from the womb? *why* did I *not* give up the ghost when I came out of the belly? 12. Why did the knees prevent me? or why the breasts that I should suck? 13. For now should I have lain still and been quiet, I should have slept: then had I been at rest, 14. With kings and counsellors of the earth, which built desolate places for themselves; 15. Or with princes that had gold, who filled their houses with silver: 16. Or as an hidden untimely birth I had not been; as infants *which* never saw light. 17. There the wicked cease *from* troubling; and there the weary be at rest. 18. *There* the prisoners rest together; they hear not the voice of the oppressor. 19. The small and great are there; and the servant *is* free from his master. 20. Wherefore is light given to him that is in misery, and life unto the bitter *in* soul; 21. Which long for death, but it *cometh* not; and dig for it more than for hid treasures; 22. Which rejoice exceedingly, *and* are glad, when they can find the grave? 23. *Why is light given* to a man whose way is hid, and whom God hath hedged in? 24. For my sighing cometh before I eat, and my roarings are poured out like the waters. 25. For the thing which I greatly feared is come upon me, and that which I was afraid of is come unto me. 26. I was not in safety, neither had I rest, neither was I quiet; yet trouble came.

Job 5:6. Although affliction cometh not forth of the dust, neither doth trouble spring out of the ground; 7. Yet man is born unto trouble, as the sparks fly upward. 17. Behold, happy *is* the man whom God correcteth: therefore despise not thou the chastening of the Almighty: 18. For he maketh sore, and bindeth up: he woundeth, and his hands make whole.

Job. 6:1. But Job answered and said, 2. Oh that my grief were thoroughly weighed, and my calamity laid in the balances together! 3. For now it would be heavier than the sand of the sea: therefore my words are swallowed up. 4. For the arrows of the Almighty *are* within me, the poison whereof drinketh up my spirit: the terrors of God do set themselves in array against me. 5. Doth the wild ass bray when he hath grass? or loweth the ox over his fodder? 6. Can that which is unsavoury be eaten without salt? or is there *any* taste in the white of an egg? 7. The things *that* my soul refused to touch *are* as my sorrowful meat. 8. Oh that I might have my request; and that God would grant *me* the thing that I long for! 9. Even that it would please God to destroy me; that he would let loose his hand, and cut me off! 10. Then should I yet have comfort; yea, I would harden myself in sorrow: let him not spare; for I have not concealed the words of the Holy One. 11. What *is* my strength, that I should hope? and what *is* mine end, that I should prolong my life? 12. *Is* my strength the strength of stones? or *is* my flesh of brass? 13. *Is* not my help in me? and is wisdom driven quite from me? 14. To him that is afflicted pity *should be shewed* from his friend; but he forsaketh the fear of the Almighty. 15. My brethren have dealt deceitfully as a brook, *and* as the stream of brooks they pass away; 16. Which are blackish by reason of the ice, *and* wherein the snow is hid: 17. What time they wax warm, they vanish: when it is hot, they are consumed out of their place. 18. The paths of their way are turned aside; they go to nothing, and perish. 19. The troops of Tema looked, the companies of Sheba waited for them. 20. They were confounded because they had hoped; they came thither, and were ashamed. 21. For now ye are nothing; ye see *my* casting down, and are afraid. 22. Did I say, Bring unto me? or, Give a reward for me of your substance? 23. Or, Deliver me from the enemy's hand? or, Redeem me from the hand of the mighty? 24. Teach me, and I will hold my tongue: and cause me to understand wherein I have erred. 25. How forcible are right words! but what doth your arguing reprove? 26. Do ye imagine to reprove words, and the speeches of one that is desperate, *which are* as wind? 27. Yea, ye overwhelm the fatherless, and ye dig *a pit* for your friend. 28. Now therefore be content, look upon me; for *it is* evident unto you if I lie. 29. Return, I pray you, let it not be iniquity; yea, return again, my righteousness *is* in it. 30. Is there iniquity in my tongue? cannot my taste discern perverse things?

Job. 7:2. As a servant earnestly desireth the shadow, and as an hireling looketh for *the reward of* his work: 3. So am I made to possess months of vanity, and wearisome nights are appointed to me. 4. When I lie down, I say, When shall I arise, and the night be gone? and I am full of tossings to and fro unto the dawning of the day. 5. My flesh is clothed with worms and clods of dust; my skin is broken, and become loathsome. 6. My days are swifter than a weaver's shuttle, and are spent without hope.

Job 9:18. He will not suffer me to take my breath, but filleth me with bitterness.

Job 12:5. He that is ready to slip with *his* feet *is as* a lamp despised in the thought of him that is at ease.

Job 14:1. Man *that is* born of a woman *is* of few days, and full of trouble. 22. His flesh upon him shall have pain, and his soul within him shall mourn.

Job 16:6. Though I speak, my grief is not asswaged · and *though* I forbear, what am I eased? 7. But now he hath made me weary: thou hast made desolate all my company. 8. And thou hast filled me with wrinkles, *which* is a witness *against me:* and my leanness rising up in me beareth witness to my face. 9. He teareth *me* in his wrath, who hateth me: he gnasheth upon me with his teeth; mine enemy sharpeneth his eyes upon me. 10. They have gaped upon me with their mouth; they have smitten me upon the cheek reproachfully; they have gathered themselves together against me. 11. God hath delivered me to the ungodly, and turned me over into the hands of the wicked. 12. I was at ease, but he hath broken me asunder: he hath also taken *me* by my neck, and shaken me to pieces, and set me up for his mark. 13. His archers compass me round about, he cleaveth my reins asunder, and doth not spare; he poureth out my gall upon the ground. 14. He breaketh me with breach upon breach: he runneth upon me like a giant.

Job 17:7. Mine eye also is dim by reason of sorrow, and all my members *are* as a shadow. 8. Upright *men* shall be astonied at this, and the innocent shall stir up himself against the hypocrite. 9. The righteous also shall hold on his way, and he that hath clean hands shall be stronger and stronger. 10. But as for you all, do ye return, and come now: for I cannot find *one* wise *man* among you. 11. My days are past, my purposes are broken off, *even* the thoughts of my heart. 12. They change the night into day: the light *is* short because of darkness. 13. If I wait, the grave *is* mine house: I have made my bed in the darkness. 14. I have said to corruption, Thou *art* my father: to the worm, *Thou art* my mother, and my sister. 15. And where *is* now my hope? as for my hope, who shall see it? 16. They shall go down to the bars of the pit, when *our* rest together *is* in the dust.

Job 19:7. Behold, I cry out of wrong, but I am not heard: I cry aloud, but *there is* no judgment. 8. He hath fenced up my way that I cannot pass, and he hath set darkness in my paths. 9. He hath stripped me of my glory, and taken the crown *from* my head. 10. He hath destroyed me on every side, and I am gone: and mine hope hath he removed like a tree. 11. He hath also kindled his wrath against me, and he counteth me unto him as *one of* his enemies. 12. His troops come together, and raise up their way against me, and encamp round about my tabernacle. 13. He hath put my brethren far from me, and mine acquaintance are verily estranged from me. 14. My kinsfolk have failed, and my familiar friends have forgotten me. 15. They that dwell in mine house, and my maids, count me for a stranger: I am an alien in their sight. 16. I called my servant, and he gave *me* no answer: I entreated him with my mouth. 17. My breath is strange to my wife, though I entreated for the children's *sake* of mine own body. 18. Yea, young children despised me: I arose, and they spake against me. 19. All my inward friends abhorred me: and they whom I loved are turned against me. 20. My bone cleaveth to my skin and to my flesh, and I am escaped with the skin of my teeth.

Job 23:10. But he knoweth the way that I take: *when* he hath tried me, I shall come forth as gold.

Job 30:15. Terrors are turned upon me: they pursue my soul as the wind: and my welfare passeth away as a cloud. 16. And now my soul is poured out upon me: the days of affliction have taken hold upon me. 17. My bones are pierced in me in the night season: and my sinews take no rest. 18. By the great force *of my disease* is my garment changed: it bindeth me about as the collar of my coat. 19. He hath cast me into the mire, and I am become like dust and ashes.

Job 33:19. He is chastened also with pain upon his bed, and the multitude of his bones with strong *pain:* 20. So that his life abhorreth bread, and his soul dainty meat. 21. His flesh is consumed away, that it cannot be seen; and his bones *that* were not seen stick out. 22. Yea, his soul draweth near unto the grave, and his life to the destroyers.

Job 36:8. And if *they be* bound in fetters, *and* be holden in cords of affliction; 9. Then he showeth them their work, and their transgressions that they have exceeded. 10. He openeth also their ear to discipline, and commandeth that they return from iniquity. 11. If they obey and serve *him*, they shall spend their days in prosperity, and their years in pleasures. 12. But if they obey not, they shall perish by the sword, and they shall die without knowledge. 15. He delivereth the poor in his affliction, and openeth their ears in oppression.

Psa. 6:6. I am weary with my groaning; all the night make I my bed to swim; I water my couch with my tears. 7. Mine eye is consumed because of grief; it waxeth old because of all mine enemies.

Psa. 18:4. The sorrows of death compassed me, and the floods of ungodly men made me afraid. 5. The sorrows of hell compassed me about: the snares of death prevented me. 6. In my distress I called upon the Lord, and cried unto my God: he heard my voice out of his temple, and my cry came before him, *even* into his ears.

Psa. 31:9. Have mercy upon me, O LORD, for I am in trouble: mine eye is consumed with grief, *yea*, my soul and my belly. 10. For my life is spent with grief, and my years with sighing: my strength faileth because of mine iniquity, and my bones are consumed. 11. I was a reproach among all mine enemies, but especially among my neighbours, and a fear to mine acquaintance: they that did see me without fled from me. 12. I am forgotten as a dead man out of mind: I am like a broken vessel. 13. For I have heard the slander of many: fear *was* on every side: while they took counsel together against me, they devised to take away my life.

Psa. 32:3. When I kept silence, my bones waxed old through my roaring all the day long. 4. For day and night thy hand was heavy upon me: my moisture is turned into the drought of summer.

Psa. 39:1. I said, I will take heed to my ways, that I sin not with my tongue: I will keep my mouth with a bridle, while the wicked is before me. 2. I was dumb with silence, I held my peace, *even* from good; and my sorrow was stirred. 3. My heart was hot within me; while I was musing the fire burned: *then* spake I with my tongue, 4. LORD, make me to know mine end, and the measure of my days, what it *is; that* I may know how frail I *am.*

Psa. 42:6. O my God, my soul is cast down within me: therefore will I remember thee from the land of Jordan, and of the Hermonites, from the hill Mizar. 7. Deep calleth unto deep at the noise of thy waterspouts: all thy waves and thy billows are gone over me.

Psa. 55:4. My heart is sore pained within me: and the terrors of death are fallen upon me. 5. Fearfulness and trembling are come upon me, and horror hath overwhelmed me. 6. And I said, Oh that I had wings like a dove! *for then* would I fly away, and be at rest. 7. Lo, *then* would I wander far off, *and* remain in the wilderness. 8. I would hasten my escape from the windy storm *and* tempest.

Psa. 66:10. For thou, O God, hast proved us: thou hast tried us, as silver is tried. 11. Thou broughtest us into the net; thou laidst affliction upon our loins. 12. Thou hast caused men to ride over our heads; we went through fire and through water: but thou broughtest us out into a wealthy *place.*

Psa. 69:1. Save me, O God, for the waters are come in unto *my* soul. 2. I sink in deep mire, where *there is* no standing: I am come into deep waters, where the floods overflow me. 3. I am weary of my crying: my throat is dried: mine eyes fail while I wait for my God. 20. Reproach hath broken my heart; and I am full of heaviness: and I looked *for some* to take pity, but *there was* none; and for comforters, but I found none.

Psa. 73:10. Therefore his people return hither: and waters of a full *cup* are wrung out to them.

Psa. 77:2. In the day of my trouble I sought the Lord: my sore ran in the night, and ceased not: my soul refused to be comforted. 3. I remembered God, and was troubled: I complained, and my spirit was overwhelmed. 4. Thou holdest mine eyes waking: I am so troubled that I cannot speak.

Psa. 80:5. Thou feedest them with the bread of tears; and givest them tears to drink in great measure. 6. Thou makest us a strife unto our neighbors: and our enemies laugh among themselves.

Psa. 88:3. For my soul is full of troubles: and my life draweth nigh unto the grave. 4. I am counted with them that go down into the pit: I am as a man *that hath* no strength: 5. Free among the dead, like the slain that lie in the grave, whom thou rememberest no more: and they are cut off from thy hand. 6. Thou hast laid me in the lowest pit, in darkness, in the deeps. 7. Thy wrath lieth hard upon me, and thou hast afflicted *me* with all thy waves. 8. Thou hast put away mine acquaintance far from me; thou hast made me an abomination unto them: *I am* shut up, and I cannot come forth. 9. Mine eye mourneth by reason of affliction: LORD, I have called daily upon thee, I have stretched out my hands unto thee. 10. Wilt thou shew wonders to the dead? shall the dead arise *and* praise thee? 11. Shall thy lovingkindness be declared in the grave? *or* thy faithfulness in destruction? 12. Shall thy wonders be known in the dark? and thy righteousness in the land of forgetfulness? 13. But unto thee have I cried, O LORD; and in the morning shall my prayer prevent thee. 14. LORD, why castest thou off my soul? *why* hidest thou thy face from me? 15. I *am* afflicted and ready to die from *my* youth up: *while* I suffer thy terrors I am distracted. 16. Thy fierce wrath goeth over me; thy terrors have cut me off. 17. They came round about me daily like water; they compassed me about together. 18. Lover and friend hast thou put far from me, *and* mine acquaintance into darkness.

Psa. 89:32. Then will I visit their transgression with the rod, and their iniquity with stripes.

Psa. 90:10. The days of our years *are* threescore years and ten; and if by reason of strength *they be* fourscore years, yet *is* their strength labour and sorrow; for it is soon cut off, and we fly away.

Psa. 102:3. For my days are consumed like smoke, and my bones are burned as an hearth. 4. My heart is smitten, and withered like grass; so that I forget to eat my bread. 5. By reason of the voice of my groaning my bones cleave to my skin. 6. I am like a pelican of the wilderness: I am like an owl of the desert. 7. I watch, and am as a sparrow alone upon the house top. 8. Mine enemies reproach me all the day; *and* they that are mad against me are sworn against me. 9. For I have eaten ashes like bread, and mingled my drink with weeping. 10. Because of thine indignation and thy wrath: for thou hast lifted me up, and cast me down. 11. My days *are* like a shadow that declineth; and I am withered like grass.

Psa. 107:4. They wandered in the wilderness in a solitary way; they found no city to dwell in. 5. Hungry and thirsty, their soul fainted in them. 10. Such as sit in darkness and in the shadow of death, *being* bound in affliction and iron; 17. Fools, because of their transgression, and because of their iniquities, are afflicted. 18. Their soul abhorreth all manner of meat; and they draw near unto the gates of death. 19. Then they cry unto the Lord in their trouble, *and* he saveth them out of their distresses.

Psa. 109:22. For I *am* poor and needy, and my heart is wounded within me. 23. I am gone like the shadow when it declineth: I am tossed up and down as the locust. 24. My knees are weak through fasting; and my flesh faileth of fatness.

Psa. 116:3. The sorrows of death compassed me, and the pains of hell gat hold upon me: I found trouble and sorrow.

Psa. 141:7. Our bones are scattered at the grave's mouth, as when one cutteth and cleaveth *wood* upon the earth.

Psa. 143:3. For the enemy hath persecuted my soul; he hath smitten my life down to the ground; he hath made me to dwell in darkness, as those that have been long dead. 4. Therefore is my spirit overwhelmed within me: my heart within me is desolate.

Prov. 3:11. My son, despise not the chastening of the Lord; neither be weary of his correction: 12. For whom the Lord loveth he correcteth; even as a father the son *in whom* he delighteth.

Prov. 12:25. Heaviness in the heart of man maketh it stoop: but a good word maketh it glad.

Prov. 13:12. Hope deferred maketh the heart sick: but *when* the desire cometh, *it is* a tree of life.

Prov. 14:10. The heart knoweth his own bitterness; and a stranger doth not intermeddle with his joy. 13. Even in laughter the heart is sorrowful; and the end of that mirth *is* heaviness.

Prov. 15:13. A merry heart maketh a cheerful countenance: but by sorrow of the heart the spirit is broken. 15. All the days of the afflicted *are* evil: but he that is of a merry heart *hath* a continual feast.

Prov. 17:3. The fining pot *is* for silver, and the furnace for gold: but the Lord trieth the hearts. 22. A merry heart doeth good *like* a medicine: but a broken spirit drieth the bones.

Prov. 18:14. The spirit of a man will sustain his infirmity; but a wounded spirit who can bear?

Eccl. 2:22. For what hath man of all his labour, and of the vexation of his heart, wherein he hath laboured under the sun? 23. For all his days *are* sorrows, and his travail grief; yea, his heart taketh not rest in the night. This is also vanity.

Eccl. 7:2. *It is* better to go to the house of mourning, than to go to the house of feasting: for that *is* the end of all men; and the living will lay *it* to his heart. 3. Sorrow *is* better than laughter: for by the sadness of the countenance the heart is made better. 4. The heart of the wise *is* in the house of mourning; but the heart of fools *is* in the house of mirth.

Isa. 1:6. From the sole of the foot even unto the head *there is* no soundness in it; *but* wounds, and bruises, and putrifying sores: they have not been closed, neither bound up, neither mollified with ointment.

Isa. 24:1. Behold, the Lord maketh the earth empty, and maketh it waste, and turneth it upside down, and scattereth abroad the inhabitants thereof. 2. And it shall be, as with the people, so with the priest; as with the servant, so with his master; as with the maid, so with her mistress; as with the buyer, so with the seller; as with the lender, so with the borrower; as with the taker of usury, so with the giver of usury to him. 3. The land shall be utterly emptied, and utterly spoiled: for the Lord hath spoken this word. 4. The earth mourneth *and* fadeth away, the world languisheth *and* fadeth away, the haughty people of the earth do languish. 5. The earth also is defiled under the inhabitants thereof: because they have transgressed the laws, changed the ordinance, broken the everlasting covenant. 6. Therefore hath the curse devoured the earth, and they that dwell therein are desolate: therefore the inhabitants of the earth are burned, and few men left. 7. The new wine mourneth, the vine languisheth, all the merryhearted do sigh. 8. The mirth of tabrets ceaseth, the noise of them that rejoice endeth, the joy of the harp ceaseth. 9. They shall not drink wine with a song; strong drink shall be bitter to them that drink it. 10. The city of confusion is broken down; every house is shut up, that no man may come in. 11. *There is* a crying for wine in the streets; all joy is darkened, the mirth of the land is gone. 12. In the city is left desolation, and the gate is smitten with destruction. 13. When thus it shall be in the midst of the land among the people, *there shall be* as the shaking of an olive tree, *and* as the gleaning grapes when the vintage is done. 14. They shall lift up their voice, they shall sing for the majesty of the Lord, they shall cry aloud from the sea. 15. Wherefore glorify ye the Lord in the fires, *even* the name of the Lord God of Israel in the isles of the sea. 16. From the uttermost part of the earth have we heard songs, *even* glory to the righteous.

Isa. 26:16. Lord, in trouble have they visited thee; they poured out a prayer *when* thy chastening *was* upon them. 17. Like as a woman with child, *that* draweth near the time of her delivery, is in pain, *and* crieth out in her pangs: so have we been in thy sight, O LORD.

Isa. 48:10. Behold, I have refined thee, but not with silver; I have chosen thee in the furnace of affliction.

Lam. 1:7. Jerusalem remembered in the days of her affliction and of her miseries all her pleasant things that she had in the days of old, when her people fell into the hand of the enemy, and none did help her: . . . 12. *Is it* nothing to you, all ye that pass by ? behold, and see if there be any sorrow like unto my sorrow, which is done unto me, wherewith the LORD hath afflicted *me* in the day of his fierce anger.

Lam. 3:1. I am the man *that* hath seen affliction by the rod of his wrath. 2. He hath led me, and brought *me into* darkness, but not *into* light. 3. Surely against me is he turned; he turneth his hand *against me* all the day. 4. My flesh and my skin hath he made old; he hath broken my bones. 5. He hath builded against me, and compassed *me* with gall and travail. 6. He hath set me in dark places, as *they that be* dead of old. 7. He hath hedged me about, that I cannot get out; he hath made my chain heavy. 8. Also when I cry and shout, he shutteth out my prayer. 9. He hath inclosed my ways with hewn stone; he hath made my paths crooked. 10. He *was* unto me *as* a bear lying in wait, *and as* a lion in secret places. 11. He hath turned aside my ways, and pulled me in pieces; he hath made me desolate. 12. He hath bent his bow, and set me as a mark for the arrow. 13. He hath caused the arrows of his quiver to enter into my reins. 14. I was a derision to all my people; *and* their song all the day. 15. He hath filled me with bitterness, he hath made me drunken with wormwood. 16. He hath also broken my teeth with gravel stones, he hath covered me with ashes. 17. And thou hast removed my soul far off from peace; I forgat prosperity. 18. And I said, My strength and my hope is perished from the LORD: 19. Remembering mine afflictions and my misery, the wormwood and the gall. 20. My soul hath *them* still in remembrance, and is humbled in me. 21. This I recall to my mind, therefore have I hope. 22. *It is of* the LORD'S mercies that we are not consumed, because his compassions fail not. 23. *They are* new every morning: great *is* thy faithfulness. 24. The LORD *is* my portion, saith my soul; therefore will I hope in him. 25. The LORD *is* good unto them that wait for him, to the soul *that* seeketh him. 26. *It is* good that *a man* should both hope and quietly wait for the salvation of the LORD. 27. *It is* good for a man that he bear the yoke in his youth. 28. He sitteth alone and keepeth silence, because he hath borne *it* upon him. 29. He putteth his mouth in the dust; if so be there may be hope. 30. He giveth *his* cheek to him that smiteth him: he is filled full with reproach. 31. For the Lord will not cast off for ever: 32. But though

he cause grief, yet will he have compassion according to the multitude of his mercies. 33. For he doth not afflict willingly **nor** grieve the children of men. 34. To crush under his feet all the prisoners of the earth, 35. To turn aside the right of a man before the face of the Most High, 36. To subvert **a** man in his cause, the Lord approveth not.

Zech. 13:9. And I will bring the third part through the fire, and will refine them as silver is refined, and will try them as gold is tried:

Mark 9:49. For every one shall be salted with fire, [1] and every sacrifice shall be salted with salt. [1 Omitted in R. V.]

John 15:2. Every branch in me that beareth not fruit he taketh away: and every *branch* that beareth fruit, he purgeth **it**, that it may bring forth more fruit.

John 16:33. In the world ye shall have tribulation;

2 Cor. 1:8. For we would not, brethren, have you ignorant of our trouble which came to us in Asia, that we were pressed out of measure, above strength, insomuch that we despaired even of life: 9. But we had the sentence of death in ourselves, that we should not trust in ourselves, but in God which raiseth the dead:

2 Cor. 4:7. But we have this treasure in earthen vessels, that the excellency of the power may be of God, and not of us. 8. *We are* troubled on every side, yet not distressed; *we are* perplexed, but not in despair; 9. Persecuted, but not forsaken; cast down, but not destroyed; 10. Always bearing about in the body the dying of the Lord Jesus, that the life also of Jesus might be made manifest in our body. 11. For we which live are alway delivered unto death for Jesus' sake, that the life also of Jesus might be made manifest in our mortal flesh. 12. So then death worketh in us, but life in you. 16. For which cause we faint not; but though our outward man perish, yet the inward *man* is renewed day by day. 17. For our light affliction, which is but for a moment, worketh for us a far more exceeding *and* eternal weight of glory.

2 Cor. 6:4. But in all *things* approving ourselves as the ministers of God, in much patience, in afflictions, in necessities, in distresses, 5. In stripes, in imprisonments, in tumults, in labours, in watchings, in fastings; 6. By pureness, by knowledge, by longsuffering, by kindness, by the Holy Ghost, by love unfeigned, 7. By the word of truth, by the power of God, by the armour of righteousness on the right hand and on the left, 8. By honour and dishonour, by evil report and good report: as deceivers, and *yet* true; 9. As unknown, and *yet* well known; as dying, and, behold, we live; as chastened, and not killed; 10. As sorrowful, yet alway rejoicing; as poor, yet making many rich; as having nothing, and *yet* possessing all things.

2 Cor. 11:23. In labours more abundant, in stripes above measure, in prisons more frequent, in deaths oft. 24. Of the Jews five

times received I forty *stripes* save one. 25. Thrice was I beaten with rods, once was I stoned, thrice I suffered shipwreck, a night and a day I have been in the deep; 26. *In* journeyings often, *in* perils of waters, *in* perils of robbers, *in* perils by *mine own* countrymen, *in* perils by the heathen, *in* perils in the city, *in* perils in the wilderness, *in* perils in the sea, *in* perils among false brethren; 27. In weariness and painfulness, in watchings often, in hunger and thirst, in fastings often, in cold and nakedness. 28. Beside those things that are without, that which cometh upon me daily, the care of all the churches. 29. Who is weak, and I am not weak? who is offended, and I burn not? 30. If I must needs glory, I will glory of the things which concern my infirmities.

Heb. 12:6. For whom the Lord loveth he chasteneth, and scourgeth every son whom he receiveth. 7. If ye endure chastening, God dealeth with you as with sons; for what son is he whom the father chasteneth not? 9. Furthermore, we have had fathers of our flesh which corrected *us*, and we gave *them* reverence: shall we not much rather be in subjection unto the Father of spirits, and live?

1 Pet. 5:9. Whom resist stedfast in the faith, knowing that the same afflictions are accomplished in your brethren that are in the world.

Rev. 3:19. As many as I love, I rebuke and chasten: be zealous therefore, and repent.

See PENITENTS; PERSECUTION; POOR; SORROW; TEMPTATION.

BENEFITS OF: 1 Kin. 8:33. When thy people Israel be smitten down before the enemy, because they have sinned against thee, and shall turn again to thee, and confess thy name, and pray, and make supplication unto thee in this house: 47. *Yet* if they shall bethink themselves in the land whither they were carried captives, and repent, and make supplication unto thee in the land of them that carried them captives, saying, We have sinned, and have done perversely, we have committed wickedness; 48. And *so* return unto thee with all their heart, and with all their soul, in the land of their enemies, which led them away captive, and pray unto thee toward their land, which thou gavest unto their fathers, the city which thou hast chosen, and the house which I have built for thy name: 49. Then hear thou their prayer and their supplication in heaven thy dwelling place, and maintain their cause. *vs.* 35,49-53; Deut. 4:30,31; 30:1,2; 2 Chr. 6:28-31.

Job 5:6. Although affliction cometh not forth of the dust, neither doth trouble spring out of the ground: 7. Yet man is born unto trouble, as the sparks fly upward. 8. I would seek unto God, and unto God would I commit my cause: 9. Which doeth great things and unsearchable; marvellous things without number: 10. Who giveth rain upon the earth, and sendeth waters upon the fields: 11. To set up on high those that be low: that those which mourn may be exalted to safety.

17. Behold, happy *is* the man whom God correcteth: therefore despise not thou the chastening of the Almighty.

Job 23:10. *When* he hath tried me, I shall come forth as gold.

Psa. 94:12. Blessed *is* the man whom thou chastenest, O LORD, and teachest him out of thy law; 13. That thou mayest give him rest from the days of adversity, until the pit be digged for the wicked.

Prov. 3:11. My son, despise not the chastening of the LORD; neither be weary of his correction: 12. For whom the LORD loveth he correcteth; even as a father the son *in whom* he delighteth. Heb. 12:5.

Eccl. 7:2. It *is* better to go to the house of mourning, than to go to the house of feasting: for that *is* the end of all men: and the living will lay *it* to his heart. 3. Sorrow *is* better than laughter: for by the sadness of the countenance the heart is made better.

Isa. 19:20. And it shall be for a sign and for a witness unto the LORD of hosts in the land of Egypt: for they shall cry unto the LORD because of the oppressors, and he shall send them a saviour, and a great one, and he shall deliver them. 22. And the LORD shall smite Egypt: he shall smite and heal *it:* and they shall return *even* to the LORD, and he shall be entreated of them, and shall heal them.

Isa. 26:9. When thy judgments *are* in the earth, the inhabitants of the world will learn righteousness.

Isa. 27:9. By this therefore shall the iniquity of Jacob be purged; and this *is* all the fruit to take away his sin;

Jer. 2:27. For they have turned *their* back unto me, and not *their* face: but in the time of their trouble they will say, Arise, and save us.

Jer. 22:22. The wind shall eat up all thy pastors, and thy lovers shall go into captivity: surely then shalt thou be ashamed and confounded for all thy wickedness. 23. O inhabitant of Lebanon, that makest thy nest in the cedars, how ¹gracious shalt thou be when pangs come upon thee, the pain as of a woman in travail! [¹ R. V. greatly to be pitied]

Jer. 31:19. Surely after that I was turned, I repented, and after that I was instructed, I smote upon *my* thigh: I was ashamed, yea, even confounded, because I did bear the reproach of my youth.

Lam. 3:27. *It is* good for a man that he bear the yoke in his youth. 28. He sitteth alone and keepeth silence, because he hath borne *it* upon him.

Ezek. 20:37. And I will cause you to pass under the rod, and I will bring you into the bond of the covenant: 43. And there shall ye remember your ways, and all your doings, wherein ye have been defiled; and ye shall lothe yourselves in your own sight for all your evils that ye have committed. Ezek. 6:9.

Hos. 2:6. Therefore, behold, I will hedge up thy way with thorns, and make a wall, that she shall not find her paths. 7. And she shall follow after her lovers, but she shall not overtake them; and she shall seek them, but shall not find *them:* then shall she say, I will go and return to my first husband; for then *was it* better with me than now.

Hos. 5:15. I will go *and* return to my place, till they acknowledge their offence, and seek my face: in their affliction they will seek me ¹early.
[¹ R. V. earnestly]

Rom. 5:3. And not only *so,* but we glory in tribulations also; knowing that tribulation worketh patience: 4. And patience, experience; and experience, hope:

Rom. 8:17. And if children, then heirs; heirs of God, and joint heirs with Christ; if so be that we suffer with *him,* that we may be also glorified together. 28. And we know that all things work together for good to them that love God, to them who are the called according to *his* purpose.

2 Cor. 4:17. For our light affliction, which is but for a moment, worketh for us a far more exceeding *and* eternal weight of glory;

Phil. 1:12. But I would ye should understand, brethren, that the things *which happened* unto me have fallen out rather unto the furtherance of the gospel; 13. So that my bonds in Christ are manifest in all the palace, and in all other *places;* 14. And many of the brethren in the Lord, waxing confident by my bonds, are much more bold to speak the word without fear. 19. For I know that this shall turn to my salvation through your prayer, and the supply of the Spirit of Jesus Christ,

Jas. 1:2. My brethren, count it all joy when ye fall into divers temptations; 3. Knowing *this,* that the trying of your faith worketh patience. 4. But let patience have *her* perfect work, that ye may be perfect and entire, wanting nothing.

12. Blessed *is* the man that endureth temptation: for when he is tried, he shall receive the crown of life, which the Lord hath promised to them that love him.

1 Pet. 1:7. That the trial of your faith, being much more precious than gold that perisheth, though it be tried with fire, might be found unto praise and honour and glory at the appearing of Jesus Christ.

1 Pet. 4:14. If ye be reproached for the name of Christ, happy *are ye;* for the Spirit of glory and of God resteth upon you: ¹on their part he is evil spoken of, but on your part he is glorified.
[¹ Omitted in R. V.]

BENEFITS OF, ILLUSTRATED: Gen. 22:12. And he said, Lay not thine hand upon the lad, neither do thou any thing unto him: for now I know that thou fearest God, seeing thou hast not withheld thy son, thine only *son,* from me. 16. And said, By myself have I sworn, saith the Lord, for because thou hast done this thing, and hast not withheld thy son, thine only *son,* 17. That in blessing I will bless thee, and in multiplying I will multiply thy seed as the stars of the heaven, and as the sand which *is* upon the sea shore; and thy seed shall possess the gate

of his enemies; 18. And in thy seed shall all the nations of the earth be blessed; because thou hast obeyed my voice.

Gen. 32:11. Deliver me, I pray thee, from the hand of my brother, from the hand of Esau: for I fear him, lest he will come and smite me, *and* the mother with the children. with *vs.* 9-31.

Gen. 42:21. And they said one to another, We *are* verily guilty concerning our brother, in that we saw the anguish of his soul, when he besought us, and we would not hear; therefore is this distress come upon us.

Ex. 9:27. And Pharaoh sent, and called for Moses and Aaron, and said unto them, I have sinned this time: the Lord *is* righteous, and I and my people *are* wicked. 28. Entreat the Lord (for *it is* enough) that there be no *more* mighty thunderings and hail; and I will let you go, and ye shall stay no longer.

Ex. 10:7. And Pharaoh's servants said unto him, How long shall this man be a snare unto us? let the men go, that they may serve the Lord their God: knowest thou not yet that Egypt is destroyed? 16. Then Pharaoh called for Moses and Aaron in haste; and he said, I have sinned against the Lord your God, and against you. 17. Now therefore forgive, I pray thee, my sin only this once, and entreat the Lord your God, that he may take away from me this death only. Ex. 12:31-33.

Num. 21:7. Therefore the people came to Moses, and said, We have sinned, for we have spoken against the Lord, and against thee; pray unto the Lord, that he take away the serpents from us.

Judg. 10:6. And the children of Israel did evil again in the sight of the Lord, and served Baalim, and Ashtaroth, and the gods of Syria, and the gods of Zidon, and the gods of Moab, and the gods of the children of Ammon, and the gods of the Philistines, and forsook the Lord, and served not him. 7. And the anger of the Lord was hot against Israel, and he sold them into the hands of the Philistines, and into the hands of the children of Ammon. 8. And that year they vexed and oppressed the children of Israel: eighteen years, all the children of Israel that *were* on the other side Jordan in the land of the Amorites, which *is* in Gilead. 10. And the children of Israel cried unto the Lord, saying, We have sinned against thee, both because we have forsaken our God, and also served Baalim.

1 Sam. 12:9. And when they forgat the Lord their God, he sold them into the hand of Sisera, captain of the host of Hazor, and into the hand of the Philistines, and into the hand of the king of Moab, and they fought against them. 10. And they cried unto the Lord, and said, We have sinned, because we have forsaken the Lord, and have served Baalim and Ashtaroth: but now deliver us out of the hand of our enemies, and we will serve thee.

1 Kin. 13:6. And the king answered and said unto the man of God, Entreat now the

face of the LORD thy God, and pray for me, that my hand may be restored me again. And the man of God besought the LORD, and the king's hand was restored him again, and became as *it was* before. with *vs.* 1-10.

2 Chr. 15:4. But when they in their trouble did turn unto the LORD God of Israel, and sought him, he was found of them.

2 Chr. 33:12. And when he was in affliction, he besought the LORD his God, and humbled himself greatly before the God of his fathers, 13. And prayed unto him: and he was entreated of him, and heard his supplication, and brought him again to Jerusalem into his kingdom. Then Manasseh knew that the LORD he *was* God.

Ezra 9:13. And after all that is come upon us for our evil deeds, and for our great trespass, seeing that thou our God hast punished us less than our iniquities *deserve*, and hast given us *such* deliverance as this; with *vs.* 5-15.

Neh. 9:32. Now therefore, our God, the great, the mighty, and the terrible God, who keepest covenant and mercy, let not all the trouble seem little before thee, that hath come upon us, on our kings, on our princes, and on our priests, and on our prophets, and on our fathers, and on all thy people, since the time of the kings of Assyria unto this day. with *vs.* 4-38.

Job 34:31. Surely it is meet to be said unto God, I have borne *chastisement*, I will not offend *any more:* 32. *That which* I see not teach thou me: if I have done iniquity, I will do no more.

Job 40:1. Moreover the LORD answered Job, and said, 2. Shall he that contendeth with the Almighty instruct *him?* he that reproveth God, let him answer it. 3. Then Job answered the LORD, and said, 4. Behold, I am vile; what shall I answer thee? I will lay mine hand upon my mouth. 5. Once have I spoken; but I will not answer: yea, twice; but I will proceed no further.

Psa. 18:4. The sorrows of death compassed me, and the floods of ungodly men made me afraid. 5. The sorrows of hell compassed me about: the snares of death prevented me. 6. In my distress I called upon the LORD, and cried unto my God: he heard my voice out of his temple, and my cry came before him, *even* into his ears.

Psa. 66:10. For thou, O God, hast proved us: thou hast tried us, as silver is tried. 11. Thou broughtest us into the net; thou laidst affliction upon our loins. 12. Thou hast caused men to ride over our heads; we went through fire and through water: but thou broughtest us out into a wealthy *place*.

Psa. 78:34. When he slew them, then they sought him: and they returned and inquired early after God. 35. And they remembered that God *was* their Rock, and the high God their Redeemer.

Psa. 119:67. Before I was afflicted I went astray: but now have I kept thy word. 71.

It is good for me that I have been afflicted; that I might learn thy statutes.

Isa. 26:16. LORD, in trouble have they visited thee; they poured out a prayer *when* thy chastening *was* upon them.

Jer. 31:18. I have surely heard Ephraim bemoaning himself *thus;* Thou hast chastised me, and I was chastised, as a bullock unaccustomed *to the yoke:* turn thou me, and I shall be turned; for thou *art* the LORD my God. 19. Surely after that I was turned, I repented; and after that I was instructed, I smote upon *my* thigh: I was ashamed, yea, even confounded, because I did bear the reproach of my youth.

Lam. 3:19. Remembering mine affliction and my misery, the wormwood and the gall. 20. My soul hath *them* still in remembrance, and is humbled in me.

Hos. 6:1. Come, and let us return unto the LORD: for he hath torn, and he will heal us; he hath smitten, and he will bind us up.

Jonah 2:1. Then Jonah prayed unto the LORD his God out of the fish's belly, 2. And said, I cried by reason of mine affliction unto the LORD, and he heard me; out of the belly of hell cried I, *and* thou heardest my voice. 3. For thou hadst cast me into the deep, in the midst of the seas; and the floods compassed me about: all thy billows and thy waves passed over me. 4. Then I said, I am cast out of thy sight; yet I will look again toward thy holy temple. 5. The waters compassed me about, *even* to the soul: the depth closed me round about, the weeds were wrapped about my head. 6. I went down to the bottoms of the mountains; the earth with her bars *was* about me for ever: yet hast thou brought up my life from corruption, O LORD my God. 7. When my soul fainted within me I remembered the LORD: and my prayer came in unto thee, into thine holy temple. 8. They that observe lying vanities forsake their own mercy. 9. But I will sacrifice unto thee with the voice of thanksgiving; I will pay *that* that I have vowed. Salvation *is* of the LORD. 10. And the LORD spake unto the fish, and it vomited out Jonah upon the dry *land*.

Luke 15:17. And when he came to himself, he said, How many hired servants of my father's have bread enough and to spare, and I perish with hunger! with *vs.* 11-24.

Acts 8:24. Then answered Simon, and said, Pray ye to the Lord for me, that none of these things which ye have spoken come upon me.

Exemplified: Joseph's brethren, Gen. 42:21. Joseph, Gen. 45:5,7,8. Israel, Deut. 8:3,5. Josiah, 2 Kin. 22:19. Hezekiah, 2 Chr. 32:25, 26. Manasseh, 2 Chr. 33:12. Jonah, Jonah 2:7. Prodigal son, Luke 15:21.

CONSOLATION IN: Gen. 21:17. And God heard the voice of the lad; and the angel of God called to Hagar out of heaven, and said unto her, What aileth thee, Hagar? fear not, for God hath heard the voice of the lad where he *is*. *vs.* 12-21. Gen. 16:7-13.

Gen. 26:24. And the LORD appeared unto him the same night, and said, I *am* the God of Abraham thy father: fear not, for I *am* with thee, and will bless thee, and multiply thy seed for my servant Abraham's sake. with *vs.* 17-33.

Gen. 31:42. Except the God of my father, the God of Abraham, and the fear of Isaac, had been with me, surely thou hadst sent me away now empty. God hath seen mine affliction and the labour of my hands, and rebuked *thee* yesternight.

Ex. 3:7. And the LORD said, I have surely seen the affliction of my people which *are* in Egypt, and have heard their cry by reason of their taskmasters; for I know their sorrows; 8. And I am come down to deliver them out of the hand of the Egyptians, and to bring them up out of that land unto a good land and a large, unto a land flowing with milk and honey. *vs.* 16,17.

Ex. 14:13. And Moses said unto the people, Fear ye not, stand still, and see the salvation of the LORD, which he will shew to you to day: for the Egyptians whom ye have seen to day, ye shall see them again no more for ever. 14. The LORD shall fight for you, and ye shall hold your peace.

Deut. 33:27. The eternal God *is thy* refuge, and underneath *are* the everlasting arms: and he shall thrust out the enemy from before thee; and shall say, Destroy *them.*

2 Sam. 22:28. And the afflicted people thou wilt save: but thine eyes *are* upon the haughty, *that* thou mayest bring *them* down.

Job 5:6. Although affliction cometh not forth of the dust, neither doth trouble spring out of the ground; 7. Yet man is born unto trouble, as the sparks fly upward. 8. I would seek unto God, and unto God would I commit my cause: 9. Which doeth great things and unsearchable; marvellous things without number: 10. Who giveth rain upon the earth, and sendeth waters upon the fields. 11. To set up on high those that be low; that those which mourn may be exalted to safety. 12. He disappointeth the devices of the crafty, so that their hands cannot perform *their* enterprise. 13. He taketh the wise in their own craftiness: and the counsel of the froward is carried headlong. 14. They meet with darkness in the daytime, and grope in the noonday as in the night. 15. But he saveth the poor from the sword, from their mouth, and from the hand of the mighty. 16. So the poor hath hope, and iniquity stoppeth her mouth. 17. Behold, happy *is* the man whom God correcteth: therefore despise not thou the chastening of the Almighty: 18. For he maketh sore, and bindeth up: he woundeth, and his hands make whole. 19. He shall deliver thee in six troubles: yea, in seven there shall no evil touch thee. 20. In famine he shall redeem thee from death: and in war from the power of the sword. 21. Thou shalt be hid from the scourge of the tongue: neither shalt thou be afraid of destruction when it cometh. 22. At destruction and famine

thou shalt laugh: neither shalt thou be afraid of the beasts of the earth. 23. For thou shalt be in league with the stones of the field: and the beasts of the field shall be at peace with thee. 24. And thou shalt know that thy tabernacle *shall be* in peace; and thou shalt visit thy habitation, and shalt not sin. 25. Thou shalt know also that thy seed *shall be* great, and thine offspring as the grass of the earth. 26. Thou shalt come to *thy* grave in a full age, like as a shock of corn cometh in in his season. 27. Lo this, we have searched it, so it *is;* hear it, and know thou *it* for thy good.

Job 11:16. Because thou shalt forget *thy* misery, *and* remember *it* as waters *that* pass away: 17. And *thine* age shall be clearer than the noonday; thou shalt shine forth, thou shalt be as the morning. 18. And thou shalt be secure, because there is hope; yea, thou shalt dig *about thee, and* thou shalt take thy rest in safety. 19. Also thou shalt lie down, and none shall make *thee* afraid; yea, many shall make suit unto thee.

Job 16:5. *But* I would strengthen you with my mouth, and the moving of my lips should assuage *your grief.*

Job 29:25. I chose out their way, and sat chief, and dwelt as a king in the army, as one *that* comforteth the mourners.

Job 31:19. If I have seen any perish for want of clothing, or any poor without covering; 20. If his loins have not b'essed me, and *if* he were *not* warmed with the fleece of my sheep; 21. If I have lifted up my hand against the fatherless, when I saw my help in the gate: 22. *Then* let mine arm fall from my shoulder blade, and mine arm be broken from the bone.

Job 35:10. But none saith, Where *is* God my maker, who giveth songs in the night;

Psa. 9:9. The LORD also will be a refuge for the oppressed, a refuge in times of trouble. 10. And they that know thy name will put their trust in thee: for thou, LORD, hast not forsaken them that seek thee.

Psa. 23:4. Yea, though I walk through the valley of the shadow of death, I will fear no evil: for thou *art* with me; thy rod and thy staff they comfort me.

Psa. 27:5. For in the time of trouble he shall hide me in his pavilion: in the secret of his tabernacle shall he hide me: he shall set me up upon a rock. 6. And now shall mine head be lifted up above mine enemies round about me: therefore will I offer in his tabernacle sacrifices of joy; I will sing, yea, I will sing praises unto the LORD.

Psa. 30:5. For his anger *endureth but* a moment; in his favour *is* life: weeping may endure for a night, but joy cometh in the morning.

Psa. 31:7. I will be glad and rejoice in thy mercy: for thou hast considered my trouble; thou hast known my soul in adversities;

Psa. 34:4. I sought the LORD, and he heard me, and delivered me from all my fears. 19. Many *are* the afflictions of the righteous: but the LORD delivereth him out of them all. 20. He keepeth all his bones: not one of them is broken.

Psa. 37:23. The steps of a *good* man are ordered by the LORD: and he delighteth in his way. 24. Though he fall, he shall not be utterly cast down: for the LORD upholdeth *him with* his hand. 32. The wicked watcheth the righteous, and seeketh to slay him. 33. The LORD will not leave him in his hand, nor condemn him when he is judged.

Psa. 41:3. The LORD will strengthen him upon the bed of languishing: thou wilt make all his bed in his sickness.

Psa. 42:5. Why art thou cast down, O my soul? and *why* art thou disquieted in me? hope thou in God: for I shall yet praise him *for* the help of his countenance.

Psa. 46:1. God *is* our refuge and strength, a very present help in trouble.

Psa. 50:15. Call upon me in the day of trouble: I will deliver thee, and thou shalt glorify me.

Psa. 55:22. Cast thy burden upon the LORD, and he shall sustain thee: he shall never suffer the righteous to be moved.

Psa. 56:8. Thou tellest my wanderings: put thou my tears into thy bottle: *are they* not in thy book? 9. When I cry *unto thee*, then shall mine enemies turn back: this I know; for God *is* for me. 10. In God will I praise *his* word: in the LORD will I praise *his* word.

Psa. 62:1. Truly my soul waiteth upon God: from him *cometh* my salvation. 2. He only *is* my rock and my salvation; *he is* my defence; I shall not be greatly moved. 5. My soul, wait thou only upon God; for my expectation *is* from him. 6. He only *is* my rock and my salvation: *he is* my defence; I shall not be moved. 7. In God *is* my salvation and my glory: the rock of my strength, *and* my refuge, *is* in God. 8. Trust in him at all times; ye people, pour out your heart before him: God *is* a refuge for us. 11. God hath spoken once; twice have I heard this, that power *belongeth* unto God. 12. Also unto thee, O Lord, *belongeth* mercy: for thou renderest to every man according to his work.

Psa. 68:6. God setteth the solitary in families: he bringeth out those which are bound with chains: but the rebellious dwell in a dry *land*.

Psa. 69:20. Reproach hath broken my heart; and I am full of heaviness: and I looked *for some* to take pity, but *there was* none; and for comforters, but I found none. 33. For the LORD heareth the poor, and despiseth not his prisoners.

Psa. 71:20. *Thou*, which hast shewed me great and sore troubles, shalt quicken me again, and shalt bring me up again from the depths of the earth.

Psa. 73:26. My flesh and my heart faileth · *but* God *is* the strength of my heart, and my portion for ever.

Psa. 94:17. Unless the LORD *had been* my help, my soul had almost dwelt in silence. 18. When I said, My foot slippeth; thy mercy, O LORD. held me up. 19. In the multitude of my thoughts within me thy comforts delight my soul.

Psa. 103:13. Like as a father pitieth *his* children, so the LORD pitieth them that fear him. 14. For he knoweth our frame; he remembereth that we *are* dust.

Psa. 112:4. Unto the upright there ariseth light in the darkness: *he is* gracious, and full of compassion, and righteous.

Psa. 119:50. This *is* my comfort in my affliction: for thy word hath quickened me. 52. I remembered thy judgments of old, O LORD; and have comforted myself. 54. Thy statutes have been my songs in the house of my pilgrimage. 92. Unless thy law *had been* my delights, I should then have perished in mine affliction. 143. Trouble and anguish have taken hold on me: *yet* thy commandments *are* my delights.

Psa. 138:3. In the day when I cried thou answeredst me, *and* strengthenedst me *with* strength in my soul. 7. Though I walk in the midst of trouble, thou wilt revive me: thou shalt stretch forth thine hand against the wrath of mine enemies, and thy right hand shall save me. 8. The LORD will perfect *that which* concerneth me: thy mercy, O LORD, *endureth* for ever: forsake not the works of thine own hands.

Psa. 140:12. I know that the LORD will maintain the cause of the afflicted, *and* the right of the poor.

Psa. 145:14. The LORD upholdeth all that fall, and raiseth up all *those that be* bowed down.

Psa. 147:3. He healeth the broken in heart, and bindeth up their wounds.

Prov. 12:13. The wicked is snared by the transgression of *his* lips: but the just shall come out of trouble.

Eccl. 4:1. So I returned, and considered all the oppressions that are done under the sun: and behold the tears of *such as were* oppressed, and they had no comforter; and on the side of their oppressors *there was* power; but they had no comforter.

Isa. 4:6. And there shall be a tabernacle for a shadow in the daytime from the heat, and for a place of refuge, and for a covert from storm and from rain.

Isa. 14:31. Howl, O gate; cry, O city; thou, whole Palestina, *art* dissolved: for there shall come from the north a smoke, and none *shall* be alone in his appointed times. 32. What shall *one* then answer the messengers of the nation? That the LORD hath founded Zion, and the poor of his people shall trust in it.

Isa. 25:4. For thou hast been a strength to the poor, a strength to the needy in his distress, a refuge from the storm, a shadow from the heat. when the blast of the terrible ones *is* as a storm *against* the wall.

Isa. 30:19. For the people shall dwell in Zion at Jerusalem · thou shalt weep no more; he will be very gracious unto thee at the voice of thy cry; when he shall hear it, he will answer thee. 20. And *though* the Lord give you the bread of adversity, and the water of affliction, yet shall not thy teachers be removed into a corner any more, but thine eyes shall see thy teachers:

Isa. 40:1. Comfort ye, comfort ye my people, saith your God. 2. Speak ye comfortably to Jerusalem, and cry unto her, that her warfare is accomplished, that her iniquity is pardoned: for she hath received of the LORD'S hand double for all her sins. 29. He giveth power to the faint; and to *them that have* no might he increaseth strength.

Isa. 41:10. Fear thou not; for I *am* with thee: be not dismayed; for I *am* thy God: I will strengthen thee; yea, I will help thee; yea, I will uphold thee with the right hand of my righteousness. 13. For I the LORD thy God will hold thy right hand, saying unto thee, Fear not; I will help thee. 14. Fear not, thou worm Jacob, *and* ye men of Israel; I will help thee, saith the LORD, and thy Redeemer, the Holy One of Israel. 17. *When* the poor and needy seek water, and *there is* none, *and* their tongue faileth for thirst, I the LORD will hear them, *I* the God of Israel will not forsake them.

Isa. 42:3. A bruised reed shall he not break, and the smoking flax shall he not quench: he shall bring forth judgment unto truth.

Isa. 43:2. When thou passest through the waters, I *will be* with thee; and through the rivers, they shall not overflow thee: when thou walkest through the fire, thou shalt not be burned; neither shall the flame kindle upon thee.

Isa. 49:13. Sing, O heavens; and be joyful, O earth; and break forth into singing, O mountains: for the LORD hath comforted his people, and will have mercy upon his afflicted.

Isa. 50:4. The Lord GOD hath given me the tongue of the learned, that I should know how to speak a word in season to *him that is* weary: he wakeneth morning by morning, he wakeneth mine ear to hear as the learned. 7. For the Lord GOD will help me; therefore shall I not be confounded: therefore have I set my face like a flint, and I know that I shall not be ashamed. 8. *He is* near that justifieth me; who will contend with me? let us stand together: who *is* mine adversary? let him come near to me. 9. Behold, the Lord GOD will help me; who *is* he *that* shall condemn me? lo, they all shall wax old as a garment; the moth shall eat them up. 10. Who *is* among you that feareth the LORD, that obeyeth the voice of his servant, that walketh *in* darkness, and hath no light? let him trust in the name of the LORD, and stay upon his God.

Isa. 51:3. For the LORD shall comfort Zion: he will comfort all her waste places; and he will make her wilderness like Eden, and her desert like the garden of the LORD; joy and gladness shall be found therein, thanksgiving and the voice of melody. 12. I, *even* I, *am* he that comforteth you: who *art* thou, that thou shouldest be afraid of a man *that*

shall die, and of the son of man *which* shall be made *as* grass; with *vs.* 3-13.

Isa. 54:4. Fear not; for thou shalt not be ashamed: neither be thou confounded; for thou shalt not be put to shame: for thou shalt forget the shame of thy youth, and shalt not remember the reproach of thy widowhood any more. 11. O thou afflicted, tossed with tempest, *and* not comforted, behold, I will lay thy stones with fair colours, and lay thy foundations with sapphires.

Isa. 58:10. And *if* thou draw out thy soul to the hungry, and satisfy the afflicted soul; then shall thy light rise in obscurity, and thy darkness *be* as the noonday:

Isa. 61:1. The Spirit of the Lord GOD *is* upon me; because the LORD hath anointed me to preach good tidings unto the meek; he hath sent me to bind up the brokenhearted, to proclaim liberty to the captives, and the opening of the prison to *them that are* bound; 2. To proclaim the acceptable year of the LORD, and the day of vengeance of our God; to comfort all that mourn; 3. To appoint unto them that mourn in Zion, to give unto them beauty for ashes, the oil of joy for mourning, the garment of praise for the spirit of heaviness; that they might be called trees of righteousness, the planting of the LORD, that he might be glorified.

Isa. 63:9. In all their affliction he was afflicted, and the angel of his presence saved them: in his love and in his pity he redeemed them: and he bare them, and carried them all the days of old.

Isa. 66:5. Hear the word of the LORD, ye that tremble at his word; Your brethren that hated you, that cast you out for my name's sake, said, Let the LORD be glorified: but he shall appear to your joy, and they shall be ashamed. 13. As one whom his mother comforteth, so will I comfort you; and ye shall be comforted in Jerusalem. 14. And when ye see *this*, your heart shall rejoice, and your bones shall flourish like an herb and the hand of the LORD shall be known toward his servants, and *his* indignation toward his enemies.

Jer. 31:13. Then shall the virgin rejoice in the dance, both young men and old together: for I will turn their mourning into joy, and will comfort them, and make them rejoice from their sorrow. 25. For I have satiated the weary soul, and I have replenished every sorrowful soul.

Jer. 39:17. But I will deliver thee in that day, saith the LORD; and thou shalt not be given into the hand of the men of whom thou *art* afraid. 18. For I will surely deliver thee, and thou shalt not fall by the sword, but thy life shall be for a prey unto thee; because thou hast put thy trust in me, saith the LORD.

Lam. 3:31. For the Lord will not cast off for ever: 32. But though he cause grief, yet will he have compassion according to the multitude of his mercies. 33. For he doth not afflict willingly, nor grieve the children of men. 57. Thou drewest near in the day *that* I called upon thee: thou saidst, Fear not.

Ezek. 11:16. Therefore say, Thus saith the Lord God; Although I have cast them far off among the heathen, and although I have scattered them among the countries, yet will I be to them as a little sanctuary in the countries where they shall come.

Hos. 2:14. Therefore, behold, I will allure her, and bring her into the wilderness, and speak comfortably unto her. 15. And I will give her her vineyards from thence, and the valley of Achor for a door of hope: and she shall sing there, as in the days of her youth, and as in the day when she came up out of the land of Egypt.

Hos. 6:1. Come, and let us return unto the Lord: for he hath torn, and he will heal us; he hath smitten, and he will bind us up. 2. After two days will he revive us: in the third day he will raise us up, and we shall live in his sight. 3. Then shall we know, *if* we follow on to know the Lord: his going forth is prepared as the morning; and he shall come unto us as the rain, as the latter *and* former rain unto the earth.

Nah. 1:7. The Lord *is* good, a strong hold in the day of trouble; and he knoweth them that trust in him.

Zeph. 3:18. I will gather *them that are* sorrowful for the solemn assembly, *who* are of thee, *to whom* the reproach of it *was* a burden.

Matt. 5:4. Blessed *are* they that mourn: for they shall be comforted. 10. Blessed *are* they which are persecuted for righteousness' sake: for theirs is the kingdom of heaven. 11. Blessed are ye, when *men* shall revile you, and persecute *you*, and shall say all manner of evil against you falsely, for my sake. 12. Rejoice, and be exceeding glad: for great *is* your reward in heaven: for so persecuted they the prophets which were before you.

Matt. 10:29. Are not two sparrows sold for a farthing? and one of them shall not fall on the ground without your father. 30. But the very hairs of your head are all numbered. [Luke 21:18.] 31. Fear ye not therefore, ye are of more value than many sparrows. Luke 12:6,7.

Matt. 11:28. Come unto me, all *ye* that labour and are heavy laden, and I will give you rest.

Matt. 14:27. But straightway Jesus spake unto them, saying, Be of good cheer; it is I; be not afraid. Mark 6:50.

Matt. 25:34. Then shall the King say unto them on his right hand, Come, ye blessed of my Father, inherit the kingdom prepared for you from the foundation of the world: 35. For I was an hungered, and ye gave me meat: I was thirsty, and ye gave me drink: I was a stranger, and ye took me in: 36. Naked, and ye clothed me: I was sick, and ye visited me: I was in prison, and ye came unto me. 40. Inasmuch as ye have done *it* unto one of the least of these my brethren, ye have done *it* unto me.

Matt. 28:5. And the angel answered and said unto the women, Fear not ye: for I know that ye seek Jesus, which was crucified. 9. And as they went to tell his disciples, behold, Jesus met them, saying, All hail. And they came and held him by the feet, and worshipped him. 10. Then said Jesus unto them, Be not afraid: go tell my brethren that they go into Galilee, and there shall they see me.

Luke 6:21. Blessed *are ye* that hunger now: for ye shall be filled. Blessed *are ye* that weep now: for ye shall laugh. 22. Blessed are ye, when men shall hate you, and when they shall separate you *from their company*, and shall reproach *you*, and cast out your name as evil, for the Son of man's sake. 23. Rejoice ye in that day, and leap for joy: for, behold, your reward *is* great in heaven: for in the like manner did their fathers unto the prophets.

Luke 7:13. And when the Lord saw her, he had compassion on her, and said unto her, Weep not.

John 14:1. Let not your heart be troubled: ye believe in God, believe also in me. 16. And I will pray the Father, and he shall give you another Comforter, that he may abide with you for ever; 18. I will not leave you comfortless: I will come to you. 27. Peace I leave with you, my peace I give unto you: not as the world giveth, give I unto you. Let not your heart be troubled, neither let it be afraid.

John 15:18. If the world hate you, ye know that it hated me before *it hated* you. 20. Remember the word that I said unto you, The servant is not greater than his lord. If they have persecuted me, they will also persecute you; if they have kept my saying, they will keep yours also.

John 16:20. Verily, verily, I say unto you, That ye shall weep and lament, but the world shall rejoice: and ye shall be sorrowful, but your sorrow shall be turned into joy. 22. And ye now therefore have sorrow: but I will see you again, and your heart shall rejoice, and your joy no man taketh from you. 33. These things I have spoken unto you, that in me ye might have peace. In the world ye shall have tribulation: but be of good cheer; I have overcome the world.

Acts 12:5. Peter therefore was kept in prison: but prayer was made without ceasing of the church unto God for him.

Acts 23:11. And the night following the Lord stood by him, and said, Be of good cheer, Paul: for as thou hast testified of me in Jerusalem, so must thou bear witness also at Rome.

Rom. 8:28. And we know that all things work together for good to them that love God, to them who are the called according to *his* purpose. 35. Who shall separate us from the love of Christ? *shall* tribulation, or distress, or persecution, or famine, or nakedness, or peril, or sword? 36. As it is written,

For thy sake we are killed all the day long; we are accounted as sheep for the slaughter. 37. Nay, in all these things we are more than conquerors through him that loved us. 38. For I am persuaded, that neither death, nor life, nor angels, nor principalities, nor powers, nor things present, nor things to come, 39. Nor height, nor depth, nor any other creature, shall be able to separate us from the love of God, which is in Christ Jesus our Lord.

Rom. 12:12. Rejoicing in hope; patient in tribulation; continuing instant in prayer; 15. Rejoice with them that do rejoice, and weep with them that weep.

Rom. 15:4. For whatsoever things were written aforetime were written for our learning, that we through patience and comfort of the Scriptures might have hope.

2 Cor. 1:3. Blessed *be* God, even the Father of our Lord Jesus Christ, the Father of mercies, and the God of all comfort; 4. Who comforteth us in all our tribulation, that we may be able to comfort them which are in any trouble, by the comfort wherewith we ourselves are comforted of God. 5. For as the sufferings of Christ abound in us, so our consolation also aboundeth by Christ. 7. And our hope of you *is* stedfast, knowing, that as ye are partakers of the sufferings, so *shall ye be* also of the consolation.

2 Cor. 4:8. *We are* troubled on every side, yet not distressed; *we are* perplexed, but not in despair; 9. Persecuted, but not forsaken; cast down, but not destroyed; 10. Always bearing about in the body the dying of the Lord Jesus, that the life also of Jesus might be made manifest in our body. 16. For which cause we faint not; but though our outward man perish, yet the inward *man* is renewed day by day. 17. For our light affliction, which is but for a moment, worketh for us a far more exceeding *and* eternal weight of glory;

2 Cor. 7:6. Nevertheless God, that comforteth those that are cast down, comforted us by the coming of Titus;

2 Cor. 12:9. And he said unto me, My grace is sufficient for thee: for my strength is made perfect in weakness. Most gladly therefore will I rather glory in my infirmities, that the power of Christ may rest upon me.

Gal. 6:2. Bear ye one another's burdens, and so fulfil the law of Christ.

Phil. 1:19. For I know that this shall turn to my salvation through your prayer, and the supply of the Spirit of Jesus Christ,

1 Thess. 4:13. But I would not have you to be ignorant, brethren, concerning them which are asleep, that ye sorrow not, even as others which have no hope. 16. For the Lord himself shall descend from heaven with a shout, with the voice of the archangel, and with the trump of God: and the dead in Christ shall rise first: 17. Then we which are alive *and* remain shall be caught up together with them in the clouds, to meet the Lord in the air: and so shall we ever be with the Lord. 18. Wherefore comfort one another with these words.

2 Thess. 1:7. And to you who are troubled rest with us, when the Lord Jesus shall be revealed from heaven with his mighty angels.

2 Thess. 2:16. Now, our Lord Jesus Christ himself, and God, even our Father, which hath loved us, and hath given *us* everlasting consolation and good hope through grace, 17. Comfort your hearts, and stablish you in every good word and work.

2 Tim. 2:12. If we suffer, we shall also reign with *him:*

2 Tim. 4:17. Notwithstanding the Lord stood with me, and strengthened me; that by me the preaching might be fully known, and *that* all the Gentiles might hear; and I was delivered out of the mouth of the lion.

Heb. 2:14. Forasmuch then as the children are partakers of flesh and blood, he also himself likewise took part of the same; that through death he might destroy him that had the power of death, that is, the devil; 15. And deliver them, who through fear of death were all their lifetime subject to bondage. 18. For in that he himself hath suffered being tempted, he is able to succour them that are tempted.

Heb. 4:15. For we have not an high priest which cannot be touched with the feeling of our infirmities: but was in all points tempted like as *we are, yet* without sin. 16. Let us therefore come boldly unto the throne of grace, that we may obtain mercy, and find grace to help in time of need.

Heb. 6:18. That by two immutable things, in which *it was* impossible for God to lie, we might have a strong consolation, who have fled for refuge to lay hold upon the hope set before us:

Heb. 12:1. Wherefore, seeing we also are compassed about with so great a cloud of witnesses, let us lay aside every weight, and the sin which doth so easily beset *us*, and let us run with patience the race that is set before us. 2. Looking unto Jesus the author and finisher of *our* faith; who for the joy that was set before him endured the cross, despising the shame, and is set down at the right hand of the throne of God. 3. For consider him that endured such contradiction of sinners against himself, lest ye be wearied and faint in your minds. 4. Ye have not yet resisted unto blood, striving against sin.

Heb. 13:3. Remember them that are in bonds, as bound with them; *and* them which suffer adversity, as being yourselves also in the body. 5. *Let your* conversation *be* without covetousness; *and be* content with such things as ye have: for he hath said, I will never leave thee, nor forsake thee. 6. So that we may boldly say, The Lord *is* my helper, and I will not fear what man shall do unto me.

Jas. 1:12. Blessed *is* the man that endureth temptation; for when he is tried, he shall receive the crown of life, which the Lord hath promised to them that love him. 27. Pure religion and undefiled before God and the Father is this, To visit the fatherless and widows in their affliction, *and* to keep himself unspotted from the world.

Jas. 5:8. Be ye also patient; stablish your hearts: for the coming of the Lord draweth nigh. 10. Take, my brethren, the prophets, who have spoken in the name of the Lord, for an example of suffering affliction, and of patience.

1 Pet. 2:21. For even hereunto were ye called: because Christ also suffered for us, leaving us an example, that ye should follow his steps: 22. Who did no sin, neither was guile found in his mouth: 23. Who, when he was reviled, reviled not again; when he suffered, he threatened not; but committed *himself* to him that judgeth righteously: 24. Who his own self bare our sins in his own body on the tree, that we, being dead to sins, should live unto righteousness: by whose stripes ye were healed.

1 Pet. 4:12. Beloved, think it not strange concerning the fiery trial which is to try you, as though some strange thing happened unto you: 13. But rejoice, inasmuch as ye are partakers of Christ's sufferings, that when his glory shall be revealed, ye may be glad also with exceeding joy. 14. If ye be reproached for the name of Christ, happy *are ye;* for the Spirit of glory and of God resteth upon you.

1 Pet. 5:7. Casting all your care upon him; for he careth for you. 9. Knowing that the same afflictions are accomplished in your brethren that are in the world.

Rev. 2:9. I know thy works, and tribulation, and poverty, (but thou art rich) and *I know* the blasphemy of them which say they are Jews, and are not, but *are* the synagogue of Satan. 10. Fear none of those things which thou shalt suffer: behold, the devil shall cast *some* of you into prison, that ye may be tried; and ye shall have tribulation ten days; be thou faithful unto death, and I will give thee a crown of life.

Rev. 3:2. Be watchful, and strengthen the things which remain, that are ready to die: 10. Because thou hast kept the word of my patience, I also will keep thee from the hour of temptation, which shall come upon all the world, to try them that dwell upon the earth.

Rev. 7:14. These are they which came out of great tribulation, and have washed their robes, and made them white in the blood of the Lamb. 15. Therefore are they before the throne of God, and serve him day and night in his temple: and he that sitteth on the throne shall ¹dwell among them. 16. They shall hunger no more, neither thirst any more; neither shall the sun light on them, nor any heat. 17. For the Lamb which is in the midst of the throne shall feed them, and shall lead them unto living fountains of waters: and God shall wipe away all tears from their eyes.   [¹ R.V. spread his tabernacle over]

DELIVERANCE FROM. See PRAYER ANSWERED.

DESIGN OF; Deut. 8:2. And thou shalt remember all the way which the LORD thy God led thee these forty years in the wilderness, to humble thee, *and* to prove thee, to know what *was* in thine heart, whether thou wouldest keep his commandments, or no. 16. Who fed thee in the wilderness with manna, which thy fathers knew not, that he might humble thee, and that he might prove thee, to do thee good at thy latter end;

Deut. 30:1. And it shall come to pass, when all these things are come upon thee, the blessing and the curse, which I have set before thee, and thou shalt call *them* to mind among all the nations, whither the LORD thy God hath driven thee, 2. And shalt return unto the LORD thy God, and shalt obey his voice according to all that I command thee this day, thou and thy children, with all thine heart, and with all thy soul; 3. That then the LORD thy God will turn thy captivity, and have compassion upon thee, and will return and gather thee from all the nations, whither the LORD thy God hath scattered thee.

Deut. 31:17. Then my anger shall be kindled against them in that day, and I will forsake them, and I will hide my face from them, and they shall be devoured, and many evils and troubles shall befall them: so that they will say in that day, Are not these evils come upon us, because our God *is* not among us?

Judg. 2:21. I also will not henceforth drive out any from before them of the nations which Joshua left when he died: 22. That through them I may prove Israel, whether they will keep the way of the LORD to walk therein, as their fathers did keep *it,* or not.

1 Kin. 8:33. When thy people Israel be smitten down before the enemy, because they have sinned against thee, and shall turn again to thee, and confess thy name, and pray, and make supplication unto thee in this house: 34. Then hear thou in heaven, and forgive the sin of thy people Israel, and bring them again unto the land which thou gavest unto their fathers.   with *vs.* 35-48; 2 Chr. 6:24-31.

2 Chr. 7:13. If I shut up heaven that there be no rain, or if I command the locusts to devour the land, or if I send pestilence among my people; 14. If my people, which are called by my name, shall humble themselves, and pray, and seek my face, and turn from their wicked ways; then will I hear from heaven, and will forgive their sin, and will heal their land.

Job 33:11. He putteth my feet in the stocks, he marketh all my paths. 16. Then he openeth the ears of men, and sealeth their instruction, 17. That he may withdraw man *from his* purpose, and hide pride from man. 18. He keepeth back his soul from the pit, and his life from perishing by the sword. 19. He is chastened also with pain upon his bed, and the multitude of his bones with strong *pain:* 20. So that his life abhorreth bread, and his soul dainty meat. 21. His flesh is consumed away, that it cannot be seen; and his bones *that* were not seen stick out. 22. Yea, his soul draweth near unto the grave, and his life to the destroyers. 23. If there be a messenger with him, an interpreter, one among a thousand, to shew unto man his uprightness; 24. Then he is gracious unto him, and saith, Deliver him from going down to the pit: I have found a ransom. 25. His flesh shall be fresher than a child's: he shall return to the days of his youth: 26. He shall pray unto God, and he will be favourable unto him: and he shall see his face with joy: for he will render unto man his righteousness. 27. He looketh upon men, and *if any* say, I have sinned, and perverted *that which was* right, and it profited me not; 28. He will deliver his soul from going into the pit, and his life shall see the light. 29. Lo, all these *things* worketh God oftentimes with man, 30. To bring back his soul from the pit, to be enlightened with the light of the living.

Job 36:8. And if *they be* bound in fetters, *and* be holden in cords of affliction; 9. Then he sheweth them their work, and their transgressions that they have exceeded. 10. He openeth also their ear to discipline, and commandeth that they return from iniquity.

Psa. 66:10. For thou, O God, hast proved us: thou hast tried us, as silver is tried.

Psa. 106:43. Many times did he deliver them; but they provoked *him* with their counsel, and were brought low for their iniquity. 44. Nevertheless he regarded their affliction, when he heard their cry.

Psa. 107:10. Such as sit in darkness and in the shadow of death, *being* bound in affliction and iron; 11. Because they rebelled against the words of God, and contemned the counsel of the Most High: 12. Therefore he brought down their heart with labour; they fell down, and *there was* none to help. 13. Then they cried unto the LORD in their trouble, *and* he saved them out of their distresses. 14. He brought them out of darkness and the shadow of death, and brake their bands in sunder. 17. Fools, because of their transgression, and because of their iniquities, are afflicted. 18. Their soul abhorreth all manner of meat; and they draw near unto the gates of death. 19. Then they cry unto the LORD in their trouble, *and* he saveth them out of their distresses. 20. He sent his word, and healed them, and delivered *them* from their destructions. 21. Oh that *men* would praise the LORD *for* his goodness, and *for* his wonderful works to the children of men! 23. They that go down to the sea in ships, that do business in great waters; 24. These see the works of the LORD, and his wonders in the deep. 25. For he commandeth, and raiseth the stormy wind, which lifteth up the waves thereof. 26. They mount up to the heaven, they go down again to the depths: their soul is melted because of trouble. 27. They reel to and fro, and stagger like a drunken man, and are at their wit's end. 28. Then they cry unto the LORD in their trouble, and he bringeth them out of their distresses. 29. He mak-

eth the storm a calm, so that the waves thereof are still. 30. Then are they glad because they be quiet; so he bringeth them unto their desired haven. 31. Oh that *men* would praise the LORD *for* his goodness, and *for* his wonderful works to the children of men!

Psa. 119:71. *It is* good for me that I have been afflicted; that I might learn thy statutes.

Eccl. 7:14. In the day of prosperity be joyful, but in the day of adversity consider: God also hath set the one over against the other, to the end that man should find nothing after him.

Isa. 1:25. And I will turn my hand upon thee, and purely purge away thy dross, and take away all thy tin: 26. And I will restore thy judges as at the first, and thy counsellors as at the beginning: afterward thou shalt be called, The city of righteousness, the faithful city. 27. Zion shall be redeemed with judgment and her converts with righteousness.

Isa. 4:3. And it shall come to pass, *that he that is* left in Zion, and *he that* remaineth in Jerusalem, shall be called holy, *even* every one that is written among the living in Jerusalem: 4. When the Lord shall have washed away the filth of the daughters of Zion, and shall have purged the blood of Jerusalem from the midst thereof by the spirit of judgment, and by the spirit of burning.

Isa. 9:13. For the people turneth not unto him that smiteth them, neither do they seek the LORD of hosts. 14. Therefore the LORD will cut off from Israel head and tail, branch and rush, in one day.

Isa. 52:5. Now therefore, what have I here, saith the LORD, that my people is taken away for nought? they that rule over them make them to howl, saith the LORD; and my name continually every day *is* blasphemed. 6. Therefore my people shall know my name: therefore *they shall know* in that day that I *am* he that doth speak: behold, *it is* I.

Jer. 24:5. Thus saith the LORD, the God of Israel; Like these good figs, so will I acknowledge them that are carried away captive of Judah, whom I have sent out of this place into the land of the Chaldeans for *their* good.

Lam. 1:5. Her adversaries are the chief, her enemies prosper; for the LORD hath afflicted her for the multitude of her transgressions:

Ezek. 6:10. And they shall know that I *am* the LORD, *and that* I have not said in vain that I would do this evil unto them.

Ezek. 14:10. And they shall bear ¹ the punishment of their iniquity: 11. That the house of Israel may go no more astray from me, neither be polluted any more with all their transgressions; but that they may be my people, and I may be their God, saith the Lord GOD. [¹ Omitted in R.V.]

Dan. 4:25. That they shall drive thee from men, and thy dwelling shall be with the beasts of the field, and they shall make thee to eat grass as oxen, and they shall wet thee with the dew of heaven, and seven times shall pass over thee, till thou know that the Most High ruleth in the kingdom of men, and giveth it to whomsoever he will. 26. And whereas they commanded to leave the stump of the tree roots; thy kingdom shall be sure unto thee, after that thou shalt have known that the heavens do rule. 27. Wherefore, O king, let my counsel be acceptable unto thee, and break off thy sins by righteousness, and thine iniquities by shewing mercy to the poor; if it may be a lengthening of thy tranquillity. 34. And at the end of the days I Nebuchadnezzar lifted up mine eyes unto heaven, and mine understanding returned unto me, and I blessed the Most High, and I praised and honoured him that liveth for ever, whose dominion *is* an everlasting dominion, and his kingdom *is* from generation to generation:

Hos. 5:15. I will go *and* return to my place, till they acknowledge their offence, and seek my face: in their affliction they will seek me ¹early. [¹ R. V. earnestly]

Amos 4:6. And I also have given you cleanness of teeth in all your cities, and want of bread in all your places: yet have ye not returned unto me, saith the LORD.

Mic. 6:9. The LORD'S voice crieth unto the city, and *the man of* wisdom shall see thy name: hear ye the rod, and who hath appointed it.

Mal. 3:3. And he shall sit *as* a refiner and purifier of silver: and he shall purify the sons of Levi, and purge them as gold and silver, that they may offer unto the LORD an offering in righteousness.

John 9:2. And his disciples asked him, saying, Master, who did sin, this man, or his parents, that he was born blind? 3. Jesus answered, Neither hath this man sinned, nor his parents: but that the works of God should be made manifest in him.

John 11:4. When Jesus heard *that*, he said, This sickness is not unto death, but for the glory of God, that the Son of God might be glorified thereby.

John 15:2. Every *branch* that beareth fruit, he purgeth it, that it may bring forth more fruit.

John 21:19. This spake he, signifying by what death he should glorify God. And when he had spoken this, he saith unto him, Follow me.

1 Cor. 11:32. But when we are judged, we are chastened of the Lord, that we should not be condemned with the world.

2 Cor. 1:4. Who comforteth us in all our tribulation, that we may be able to comfort them which are in any trouble, by the comfort wherewith we ourselves are comforted of God. 5. For as the sufferings of Christ abound in us, so our consolation also aboundeth by Christ. 6. And whether we be afflicted, *it is* for your consolation and salvation, which is effectual in the enduring of the same sufferings which we also suffer: or whether we be comforted, *it is* for your consolation and salvation.

2 Cor. 4:11. For we which live are alway delivered unto death for Jesus' sake, that the life also of Jesus might be made manifest in our mortal flesh. 17. For our light affliction, which is but for a moment, worketh for us a far more exceeding *and* eternal weight of glory:

2 Cor. 12:7. And lest I should be exalted above measure through the abundance of the revelations, there was given to me a thorn in the flesh, the messenger of Satan to buffet me, lest I should be exalted above measure.

Phil. 1:29. For unto you it is given in the behalf of Christ, not only to believe on him, but also to suffer for his sake; 30. Having the same conflict which ye saw in me, and now hear *to be* in me.

2 Thess. 1:4. So that we ourselves glory in you in the churches of God, for your patience and faith in all your persecutions and tribulations that ye endure. 5. *Which is* a manifest token of the righteous judgment of God, that ye may be counted worthy of the kingdom of God, for which ye also suffer:

Heb. 2:10. For it became him, for whom *are* all things, and by whom *are* all things, in bringing many sons unto glory, to make the Captain of their salvation perfect through sufferings. 11. For both he that sanctifieth and they who are sanctified *are* all of one: for which cause he is not ashamed to call them brethren. 12. Saying, I will declare thy name unto my brethren, in the midst of the church will I sing praise unto thee. 13. And again, I will put my trust in him. And again, Behold I and the children which God hath given me. 14. Forasmuch then as the children are partakers of flesh and blood, he also himself likewise took part of the same; that through death he might destroy him that had the power of death, that is, the devil; 15. And deliver them, who through fear of death were all their lifetime subject to bondage. 16. For verily he took not on *him the nature of* angels; but he took on *him* the seed of Abraham. 17. Wherefore in all things it behooved him to be made like unto *his* brethren, that he might be a merciful and faithful high priest in things *pertaining* to God, to make reconciliation for the sins of the people. 18. For in that he himself hath suffered being tempted, he is able to succour them that are tempted.

Heb. 5:8. Though he were a Son, yet learned he obedience by the things which he suffered; 9. And being made perfect, he became the author of eternal salvation unto all them that obey him.

Heb. 12:5. And ye have forgotten the exhortation which speaketh unto you as unto children, My son, despise not thou the chastening of the Lord, nor faint when thou art rebuked of him: 6. For whom the Lord loveth he chasteneth, and scourgeth every son whom he receiveth. 7. If ye endure chastening, God dealeth with you as with sons; for what son is he whom the father chasteneth not? 8. But if ye be without chastisement, whereof all are partakers, then are ye bastards, and not sons. 9. Furthermore, we have had fathers of our flesh which corrected *us*, and we gave *them* reverence: shall we not much rather be in subjection unto the Father of spirits, and live? 10. For they verily for a few days chastened *us* after their own pleasure; but he for *our* profit, that *we* might be partakers of his holiness. 11. Now no chastening for the present seemeth to be joyous, but grievous: nevertheless, afterward it yieldeth the peaceable fruit of righteousness unto them which are exercised thereby.

1 Pet. 1:6. Wherein ye greatly rejoice, though now for a season, if need be, ye are in heaviness through manifold temptations: 7. That the trial of your faith, being much more precious than of gold that perisheth, though it be tried with fire, might be found unto praise and honour and glory at the appearing of Jesus Christ:

1 Pet. 5:10. But the God of all grace, who hath called us unto his eternal glory by Christ Jesus, after that ye have suffered a while, make you perfect, stablish, strengthen, settle *you*.

Rev. 2:10. Fear none of those things which thou shalt suffer: behold, the devil shall cast *some* of you into prison, that ye may be tried; and ye shall have tribulation ten days: be thou faithful unto death, and I will give thee a crown of life.

See BENEFITS OF, above.

DESPONDENCY IN: Job 4:5. But now it is come upon thee, and thou faintest; it toucheth thee, and thou art troubled.

Job 9:16. If I had called, and he had answered me; *yet* would I not believe that he had hearkened unto my voice. 17. For he breaketh me with a tempest, and multiplieth my wounds without cause. 18. He will not suffer me to take my breath, but filleth me with bitterness. 19. If *I speak* of strength, lo, *he is* strong: and if of judgment, who shall set me a time *to plead?* 20. If I justify myself, mine own mouth shall condemn me: *if I say*, I *am* perfect, it shall also prove me perverse. 21. *Though* I *were* perfect, *yet* would I not know my soul: I would despise my life. 22. This *is* one *thing*, therefore I said *it*, He destroyeth the perfect and the wicked. 23. If the scourge slay suddenly, he will laugh at the trial of the innocent. 24. The earth is given into the hand of the wicked: he covereth the faces of the judges thereof; if not, where, *and* who *is* he? 25. Now my days are swifter than a post: they flee away, they see no good. 26. They are passed away as the swift ships: as the eagle *that* hasteth to the prey. 27. If I say, I will forget my complaint, I will leave off my heaviness, and comfort *myself;* 28. I am afraid of all my sorrows, I know that thou wilt not hold me innocent. 29. *If* I be wicked, why then labour I in vain? 30. If I wash myself with snow water, and make my hands never so clean; 31. Yet shalt thou plunge me in the ditch, and mine own

clothes shall abhor me. 32. For *he is* not a man, as I *am, that* I should answer him, *and* we should come together in judgment. 33. Neither is there any daysman betwixt us, *that* might lay his hand upon us both. 34. Let him take his rod away from me, and let not his fear terrify me: 35. *Then* would I speak, and not fear him; but *it is* not so with me.

Psa. 22:1. My God, my God, why hast thou forsaken me? *why art thou so* far from helping me, *and from* the words of my roaring? 2. O my God, I cry in the daytime, but thou hearest not; and in the night season, and am not silent.

Prov. 24:10. *If* thou faint in the day of adversity, thy strength *is* small.

Lam. 3:39. Wherefore doth a living man complain, a man for the punishment of his sins?

Mark 15:34. And at the ninth hour Jesus cried with a loud voice, saying, Eloi, Eloi, lama sabachthani? which is, being interpreted, My God, my God, why hast thou forsaken me? Matt. 27:46.

Luke 18:1. And he spake a parable unto them *to this end*, that men ought always to pray, and not to faint;

DISPENSATION OF GOD: Ex. 4:11. And the LORD said unto him, Who hath made man's mouth? or who maketh the dumb, or deaf, or the seeing, or the blind? have not I the Lord?

Deut. 28:20. The LORD shall send upon thee cursing, vexation, and rebuke, in all that thou settest thine hand unto for to do, until thou be destroyed, and until thou perish quickly; because of the wickedness of thy doings, whereby thou hast forsaken me. With *vs.* 15–68.

Deut. 32:39. See now that I, *even* I, *am* he, and *there is* no god with me: I kill, and I make alive; I wound, and I heal: neither *is there any* that can deliver out of my hand.

Ruth 1:20. And she said unto them, Call me not Naomi, call me Mara: for the Almighty hath dealt very bitterly with me. 21. I went out full, and the LORD hath brought me home again empty: why *then* call ye me Naomi, seeing the Lord hath testified against me; and the Almighty hath afflicted me?

1 Sam. 2:6. The LORD killeth, and maketh alive: he bringeth down to the grave, and bringeth up. 7. The LORD maketh poor, and maketh rich: he bringeth low, and lifteth up.

2 Sam. 16:10. And the king said, What have I to do with you, ye sons of Zeruiah? so let him curse, because the Lord hath said unto him, Curse David. Who shall then say, Wherefore hast thou done so?

2 Kin. 6:33. Behold, this evil *is* of the LORD:

2 Kin. 15:5. The LORD smote the king, so that he was a leper unto the day of his death,

2 Chr. 7:13. If I shut up heaven that there

be no rain, or if I command the locusts to devour the land, or if I send pestilence among my people, with *vs.* 12–22.

Job 1:21. Naked came I out of my mother's womb, and naked shall I return thither: the LORD gave, and the LORD hath taken away: blessed be the name of the LORD.

Job 5:17. Happy *is* the man whom God correcteth: therefore despise not thou the chastening of the Almighty: [*v.* 6.]   18. For he maketh sore, and bindeth up: he woundeth, and his hands make whole.

Job 6:4. The arrows of the Almighty *are* within me, the poison whereof drinketh up my spirit: the terrors of God do set themselves in array against me.

Job 9:12. He taketh away, who can hinder him? who will say unto him, What doest thou?   22. He destroyeth the perfect and the wicked.

Job 10:8. Thine hands have made me and fashioned me together round about; yet thou dost destroy me.

Job 11:10. If he cut off, and shut up, or gather together, then who can hinder him?

Job 12:14. Behold, he breaketh down, and it cannot be built again: he shutteth up a man, and there can be no opening.   15. Behold, he withholdeth the waters, and they dry up: also he sendeth them out, and they overturn the earth.   16. With him *is* strength and wisdom: the deceived and the deceiver *are* his.   17. He leadeth counsellors away spoiled, and maketh the judges fools.   18. He looseth the bond of kings, and girdeth their loins with a girdle.   19. He leadeth princes away spoiled, and overthroweth the mighty.   20. He removeth away the speech of the trusty, and taketh away the understanding of the aged.   21. He poureth contempt upon princes, and weakeneth the strength of the mighty.   22. He discovereth deep things out of darkness, and bringeth out to light the shadow of death.   23. He increaseth the nations, and destroyeth them: he enlargeth the nations, and straiteneth them *again*.   24. He taketh away the heart of the chief of the people of the earth, and causeth them to wander in a wilderness *where there is* no way.   25. They grope in the dark without light, and he maketh them to stagger like a drunken man.

Job 19:6. Know now that God hath overthrown me, and hath compassed me with his net.   21. Have pity upon me, have pity upon me, O ye my friends: for the hand of God hath touched me.

Job 21:17. How oft is the candle of the wicked put out! and *how oft* cometh their destruction upon them! *God* distributeth sorrows in his anger.

Job 23:16. For God maketh my heart soft, and the Almighty troubleth me:

Job 27:2. *As* God liveth, *who* hath taken away my judgment; and the Almighty, *who* hath vexed my soul;

Job 30:11. Because he hath loosed my cord,

and afflicted me, they have also let loose the bridle before me.

Job 34:29. When he giveth quietness, who then can make trouble? and when he hideth *his* face, who then can behold him? whether *it be done* against a nation, or against a man only:

Psa. 38:3. *There is* no soundness in my flesh because of thine anger; neither *is there any* rest in my bones because of my sin.

Psa. 66:11. Thou broughtest us into the net; thou laidst affliction upon our loins.

Psa. 71:20. *Thou*, which hast shewed me great and sore troubles, shalt quicken me again, and shalt bring me up again from the depths of the earth.

Psa. 78:31. The wrath of God came upon them, and slew the fattest of them, and smote down the chosen *men* of Israel.   32. For all this they sinned still, and believed not for his wondrous works.   33. Therefore their days did he consume in vanity, and their years in trouble.   34. When he slew them, then they sought him· and they returned and enquired early after God.

Psa. 88:6. Thou hast laid me in the lowest pit, in darkness, in the deeps.   7. Thy wrath lieth hard upon me, and thou hast afflicted *me* with all thy waves.   16. Thy fierce wrath goeth over me; thy terrors have cut me off.

Psa. 89:38. But thou hast cast off and abhorred, thou hast been wroth with thine anointed.   39. Thou hast made void the covenant of thy servant: thou hast profaned his crown *by casting it* to the ground.   40. Thou hast broken down all his hedges; thou hast brought his strong holds to ruin.   41. All that pass by the way spoil him: he is a reproach to his neighbours.   42. Thou hast set up the right hand of his adversaries; thou hast made all his enemies to rejoice.   43. Thou hast also turned the edge of his sword, and hast not made him to stand in the battle.   44. Thou hast made his glory to cease, and cast his throne down to the ground.   45. The days of his youth hast thou shortened: thou hast covered him with shame.

Psa. 90:7. For we are consumed by thine anger, and by thy wrath are we troubled.   15. Make us glad according to the days *wherein* thou hast afflicted us.

Psa. 102:10. Because of thine indignation and thy wrath: for thou hast lifted me up, and cast me down.   23. He weakened my strength in the way, he shortened my days.

Isa. 30:20. *Though* the Lord give you the bread of adversity, and the water of affliction, yet shall not thy teachers be removed into a corner any more, but thine eyes shall see thy teachers:

Isa. 45:7. I form the light, and create darkness: I make peace, and create evil: I the LORD do all these *things*.

Jer. 45:3. Thou didst say, Woe is me now! for the LORD hath added grief to my sorrow; I fainted in my sighing, and I find no rest.

Lam. 1:5. The LORD hath afflicted her for the multitude of her transgressions:

Lam. 3:1. I *am* the man *that* hath seen affliction by the rod of his wrath.

Dan. 4:24. This *is* the interpretation, O king, and this *is* the decree of the Most High, which is come upon my lord the king: 25. That they shall drive thee from men, and thy dwelling shall be with the beasts of the field, and they shall make thee to eat grass as oxen, and they shall wet thee with the dew of heaven, and seven times shall pass over thee, till thou know that the Most High ruleth in the kingdom of men, and giveth it to whomsoever he will. 26. And whereas they commanded to leave the stump of the tree roots; thy kingdom shall be sure unto thee, after that thou shalt have known that the heavens do rule.

Amos 3:6. Shall there be evil in a city, and the LORD hath not done *it ?*

Jonah 2:3. For thou hadst cast me into the deep, in the midst of the seas; and the floods compassed me about: all thy billows and thy waves passed over me.

Mic. 1:12. For the inhabitant of Maroth waited carefully for good: but evil came down from the LORD unto the gate of Jerusalem.

Rom. 8:20. For the creature was made subject to vanity, not willingly, but by reason of him who hath subjected *the same* in hope,

1 Cor. 11:32. But when we are judged, we are chastened of the Lord, that we should not be condemned with the world.

Heb. 12:10. For they verily for a few days chastened *us* after their own pleasure; but he for *our* profit, that *we* might be partakers of his holiness.

Rev. 3:19. As many as I love, I rebuke and chasten: be zealous therefore, and repent.

FROM SATAN: Job 1; 2; 2 Cor. 12:7. See TEMPTATION.

IMPENITENCE IN. See OBDURACY IN, below.

MOCKING AT: Job 12:5. He that is ready to slip with *his* feet *is as* a lamp despised in the thought of him that is at ease.

Prov. 17:5. Whoso mocketh the poor reproacheth his Maker; *and* he that is glad at calamities shall not be unpunished.

MURMURING IN. See MURMURING.

OBDURACY IN: Lev. 26:23. If ye will not be reformed by me by these things, but will walk contrary unto me; 24. Then will I also walk contrary unto you, and will punish you yet seven times for your sins. *vs.* 27,28.

Job 36:12. But if they obey not, they shall perish by the sword, and they shall die without knowledge. 13. But the hypocrites in heart heap up wrath: they cry not when he bindeth them.

Psa. 78:31. The wrath of God came upon them, and slew the fattest of them, and smote down the chosen *men* of Israel. 32. For all this they sinned still, and believed not for his wondrous works.

Isa. 8:21. And they shall pass through it, hardly bestead and hungry: and it shall come to pass, that when they shall be hungry, they shall fret themselves, and curse their king and their God, and look upward.

Isa. 9:13. The people turneth not unto him that smiteth them, neither do they seek the LORD of hosts.

Isa. 22:12. And in that day did the Lord GOD of hosts call to weeping, and to mourning, and to baldness, and to girding with sackcloth: 13. And behold joy and gladness, slaying oxen, and killing sheep, eating flesh, drinking wine: let us eat and drink; for to morrow we shall die.

Isa. 26:11. LORD, *when* thy hand is lifted up, they will not see: *but* they shall see, and be ashamed for *their* envy at the people; yea, the fire of thine enemies shall devour them.

Isa. 42:25. Therefore he hath poured upon him the fury of his anger, and the strength of battle: and it hath set him on fire round about, yet he knew not; and it burned him, yet he laid *it* not to heart.

Isa. 57:17. For the iniquity of his covetousness was I wroth, and smote him · I hid me, and was wroth, and he went on frowardly in the way of his heart.

Jer. 2:30. In vain have I smitten your children; they received no correction: 35. Thou sayest, Because I am innocent, surely his anger shall turn from me. Behold, I will plead with thee, because thou sayest, I have not sinned.

Jer. 3:3. The showers have been withholden, and there hath been no latter rain; and thou hadst a whore's forehead, thou refusedst to be ashamed.

Jer. 5:3. O LORD, *are* not thine eyes upon the truth? thou hast stricken them, but they have not grieved; thou hast consumed them, *but* they have refused to receive correction: they have made their faces harder than a rock; they have refused to return.

Jer. 7:28. But thou shalt say unto them, This *is* a nation that obeyeth not the voice of the LORD their God, nor receiveth correction: truth is perished, and is cut off from their mouth.

Dan. 9:13. All this evil is come upon us: yet made we not our prayer before the LORD our God, that we might turn from our iniquities.

Hos. 7:9. Strangers have devoured his strength, and he knoweth *it* not; yea, gray hairs are here and there upon him, yet he knoweth not. 10. And the pride of Israel testifieth to his face: and they do not return to the LORD their God, nor seek him for all this. 14. They have not cried unto me with their heart, when they howled upon their beds:

Hos. 9:17. My God will cast them away, because they did not hearken unto him:

Amos 4:6. I also have given you cleanness of teeth in all your cities, and want of bread in all your places; yet have ye not returned unto me, saith the LORD. [*vs.* 7-10.] 11. I have overthrown *some* of you, as God overthrew Sodom and Gomorrah, and ye were as a firebrand plucked out of the burning: yet have ye not returned unto me, saith the LORD.

Zeph. 3:2. She obeyed not the voice; she received not correction: she trusted not in the LORD; she drew not near to her God. 7. I said, Surely thou wilt fear me, thou wilt receive instruction; so their dwelling should not be cut off, howsoever I punished them: but they rose early, *and* corrupted all their doings.

Hag. 2:17. I smote you with blasting and with mildew and with hail in all the labours of your hands; yet ye *turned* not to me, saith the LORD.

Rev. 9:20. And the rest of the men which were not killed by these plagues yet repented not of the works of their hands, that they should not worship devils, and idols of gold, and silver, and brass, and stone, and of wood: which neither can see, nor hear, nor walk: 21. Neither repented they of their murders, nor of their sorceries, nor of their fornication, nor of their thefts.

Rev. 16:9. And men were scorched with great heat, and blasphemed the name of God, which hath power over these plagues: and they repented not to give him glory. 10. And the fifth angel poured out his vial upon the seat of the beast; and his kingdom was full of darkness; and they gnawed their tongues for pain, 11. And blasphemed the God of heaven because of their pains and their sores, and repented not of their deeds. *v.* 21.

As a Judgment. See JUDGMENT.

See IMPENITENCE.

INSTANCES OF: Pharaoh, Ex. 8:19; 9:30-34; 14:5-9. Asa, 2 Chr. 16:12. Ahaz, 2 Chr. 28:22,23.

PENITENCE IN: INSTANCES OF: Pharaoh, Ex. 8:8; 9:27-30; 12:30,31; 14:5-9. David, 2 Sam. 12:15,16,23. Nebuchadnezzar, Dan. 4: 28-37. Levites, Neh. 9:33.

PRAYER IN: Gen. 32:11. Deliver me, I pray thee, from the hand of my brother, from the hand of Esau: for I fear him.

Gen. 43:14. And God Almighty give you mercy before the man, that he may send away your other brother, and Benjamin. If I be bereaved *of my children*, I am bereaved.

Ex. 17:4. And Moses cried unto the LORD, saying, What shall I do unto this people? they be almost ready to stone me.

Num. 20:16. And when we cried unto the LORD, he heard our voice, and sent an angel, and hath brought us forth out of Egypt.

2 Sam. 12:22. While the child was yet alive, I fasted and wept: for I said, Who can tell *whether* God will be gracious to me, that the child may live? 1 Sam. 1:10,11.

2 Sam. 15:31. And David said, O LORD, I pray thee, turn the counsel of Ahithophel into foolishness.

2 Sam. 22:7. In my distress I called upon the LORD, and cried to my God: and he did hear my voice out of his temple, and my cry *did enter* into his ears.

1 Kin. 8:35. When heaven is shut up, and there is no rain, because they have sinned against thee: if they pray toward this place, and confess thy name, and turn from their sin when thou afflictest them: with *vs.* 36-50; 2 Chr. 6:24-39.

2 Kin. 19:16. LORD, bow down thine ear, and hear: open, LORD, thine eyes, and see; and hear the words of Sennacherib, which hath sent him to reproach the living God. 19. Now therefore, O LORD our God, I beseech thee, save thou us out of his hand, that all the kingdoms of the earth may know that thou *art* the LORD God, *even* thou only.

1 Chr. 5:20. They cried to God in the battle, and he was entreated of them; because they put their trust in him.

2 Chr. 14:11. And Asa cried unto the LORD his God, and said, LORD, *it is* nothing with thee to help, whether with many, or with them that have no power: help us, O LORD our God; for we rest on thee, and in thy name we go against this multitude. O LORD, thou *art* our God; let not man prevail against thee.

2 Chr. 20:12. O our God, wilt thou not judge them? for we have no might against this great company that cometh against us; neither know we what to do; but our eyes *are* upon thee. *vs.* 4-13.

2 Chr. 33:12. And when he was in affliction, he besought the LORD his God, and humbled himself greatly before the God of his fathers. 13. And prayed unto him: and he was entreated of him, and heard his supplication, and brought him again to Jerusalem into his kingdom. Then Manasseh knew that the LORD he *was* God.

Neh. 4:4. Hear, O our God; for we are despised: and turn their reproach upon their own head, and give them for a prey in the land of captivity: *vs.* 5,9; Neh. 6:9,14.

Neh. 9:32. Now therefore, our God, the great, the mighty, and the terrible God, who keepest covenant and mercy, let not all the trouble seem little before thee, that hath come upon us, on our kings, on our princes, and on our priests, and on our prophets, and on our fathers, and on all thy people, since the time of the kings of Assyria unto this day.

Job 10:2. I will say unto God, Do not condemn me; shew me wherefore thou contendest with me. 9. Remember, I beseech thee, that thou hast made me as the clay; and wilt thou bring me into dust again? *v.* 15.

Job 13:21. Withdraw thine hand far from me: and let not thy dread make me afraid.

Job 16:20. My friends scorn me: *but* mine eye poureth out *tears* unto God.

Psa. 3:1. LORD, how are they increased that trouble me! many *are* they that rise up against me. 2. Many *there be* which say of my soul, *There is* no help for him in God. 7. Arise, O LORD; save me, O my God:

Psa. 4:1. Hear me when I call, O God of my

righteousness: thou hast enlarged me *when I was* in distress; have mercy upon me, and hear my prayer.

Psa. 5:8. Lead me, O LORD, in thy righteousness because of mine enemies; make thy way straight before my face.

Psa. 6:1. O LORD, rebuke me not in thine anger, neither chasten me in thy hot displeasure. 2. Have mercy upon me, O LORD; for I *am* weak: O LORD, heal me; for my bones are vexed. 3. My soul is also sore vexed: but thou, O LORD, how long? 4. Return, O LORD, deliver my soul: oh save me for thy mercies' sake. *vs.* 5-7.

Psa. 7:1. O LORD my God, in thee do I put my trust: save me from all them that persecute me, and deliver me. 2. Lest he tear my soul like a lion, rending *it* in pieces, while *there is* none to deliver. *vs.* 6,7.

Psa. 9:13. Have mercy upon me, O LORD; consider my trouble *which I suffer* of them that hate me, thou that liftest me up from the gates of death: *v.* 14.

Psa. 10:1. Why standest thou afar off, O LORD? *why* hidest thou *thyself* in times of trouble? 12. Arise, O LORD; O God, lift up thine hand: forget not the humble. *vs.* 13-15.

Psa. 13:1. How long wilt thou forget me, O LORD? for ever? how long wilt thou hide thy face from me? 2. How long shall I take counsel in my soul, *having* sorrow in my heart daily? how long shall mine enemy be exalted over me? 3. Consider *and* hear me, O LORD my God: lighten mine eyes, lest I sleep the *sleep of* death, *v.* 4.

Psa. 16:1. Preserve me, O God for in thee do I put my trust.

Psa. 17:1. Hear the right, O LORD, attend unto my cry, give ear unto my prayer, *that goeth* not out of feigned lips. 6. I have called upon thee, for thou wilt hear me, O God: incline thine ear unto me, *and* hear my speech. 7. Shew thy marvellous lovingkindness, O thou that savest by thy right hand them which put their trust *in thee* from those that rise up *against them.* 8. Keep me as the apple of the eye, hide me under the shadow of thy wings, 9. From the wicked that oppress me, *from* my deadly enemies, *who* compass me about. 13. Arise, O LORD, disappoint him, cast him down, deliver my soul from the wicked, *which is* thy sword: *vs.* 2,14.

Psa. 20:1. The LORD hear thee in the day of trouble; the name of the God of Jacob defend thee, 2. Send thee help from the sanctuary, and strengthen thee out of Zion;

Psa. 22:1. My God, my God, why hast thou forsaken me? *why art thou so* far from helping me, *and from* the words of my roaring? 11. Be not far from me, for trouble *is* near; for *there is* none to help. 19. Be not thou far from me, O LORD: O my strength, haste thee to help me. 20. Deliver my soul from the sword: my darling from the power of the dog. 21. Save me from the lion's mouth: *vs.* 1-21.

Psa. 25:2. O my God, I trust in thee: let me not be ashamed, let not mine enemies triumph over me. 16. Turn thee unto me, and have mercy upon me; for I *am* desolate and afflicted. 17. The troubles of my heart are enlarged: *O* bring thou me out of my distresses. 18. Look upon mine affliction and my pain; and forgive all my sins. 19. Consider mine enemies, for they are many and they hate me with cruel hatred. 22. Redeem Israel, O God, out of all his troubles.

Psa. 27:11. Teach me thy way, O LORD, and lead me in a plain path, because of mine enemies. 12. Deliver me not over unto the will of mine enemies: for false witnesses are risen up against me, and such as breathe out cruelty.

Psa. 28:1. Unto thee will I cry, O LORD my rock: be not silent to me: lest, *if* thou be silent to me, I become like them that go down into the pit.

Psa. 30:9. What profit *is there* in my blood, when I go down to the pit? Shall the dust praise thee? shall it declare thy truth? 10. Hear, O LORD, and have mercy upon me: LORD, be thou my helper.

Psa. 31:1. In thee, O LORD, do I put my trust; let me never be ashamed: deliver me in thy righteousness. 2. Bow down thine ear to me; deliver me speedily: be thou my strong rock, for an house of defence to save me. 3. For thou *art* my rock and my fortress, therefore for thy name's sake lead me, and guide me. 4. Pull me out of the net that they have laid privily for me. for thou *art* my strength. [*vs.* 15-18.] 9. Have mercy upon me, O LORD, for I am in trouble mine eye is consumed with grief, *yea,* my soul and my belly. 14. But I trusted in thee, O LORD: I said, Thou *art* my God. 15. My times *are* in thy hand: deliver me from the hand of mine enemies, and from them that persecute me. 16. Make thy face to shine upon thy servant: save me for thy mercies' sake. 17. Let me not be ashamed, O LORD, for I have called upon thee:

Psa. 35:1. Plead *my cause*, O LORD, with them that strive with me: fight against them that fight against me. 2. Take hold of shield and buckler, and stand up for mine help. 3. Draw out also the spear, and stop *the way* against them that persecute me · say unto my soul, I *am* thy salvation.

17. Lord, how long wilt thou look on? rescue my soul from their destructions, my darling from the lions. 19. Let not them that are mine enemies wrongfully rejoice over me. *neither* let them wink with the eye that hate me without a cause.

22. *This* thou hast seen, O LORD: keep not silence: O Lord, be not far from me. 23. Stir up thyself, and awake to my judgment, *even* unto my cause, my God and my Lord. 25. Let them not say in their hearts, Ah, so would we have it: let them not say, We have swallowed him up.

Psa. 38:1. O Lord, rebuke me not in thy wrath. neither chasten me in thy hot displeasure. 2. For thine arrows stick fast in me, and thy hand presseth me sore. 9. Lord, all my desire *is* before thee; and my groaning is not hid from thee. 10. My heart panteth, my strength faileth me: as for the light of mine eyes, it also is gone from me. 16. *Hear me*, lest *otherwise* they should rejoice over me: when my foot slippeth, they magnify themselves against me.

21. Forsake me not, O LORD: O my God, be not far from me. 22. Make haste to help me. O Lord my salvation. *vs.* 1–22.

Psa. 39:10. Remove thy stroke away from me: I am consumed by the blow of thine hand. 12. Hear my prayer, O LORD, and give ear unto my cry; hold not thy peace at my tears: for I *am* a stranger with thee, *and* a sojourner, as all my fathers *were*. 13. O spare me, that I may recover strength, before I go hence, and be no more.

Psa. 40:13. Be pleased, O LORD, to deliver me: O LORD, make haste to help me. 17. I *am* poor and needy; *yet* the Lord thinketh upon me: thou *art* my help and my deliverer; make no tarrying, O my God. Psa. 70:5.

Psa. 42:9. I will say unto God my rock, Why hast thou forgotten me? why go I mourning because of the oppression of the enemy?

Psa. 43:1. Judge me, O God, and plead my cause against an ungodly nation: O deliver me from the deceitful and unjust man. 2. For thou *art* the God of my strength: why dost thou cast me off? why go I mourning because of the oppression of the enemy? *vs.* 3–5.

Psa. 44:4. Thou art my King, O God: command deliverances for Jacob. 23. Awake, why sleepest thou, O Lord? arise, cast *us* not off for ever.

24. Wherefore hidest thou thy face *and* forgettest our affliction and our oppression? 25. For our soul is bowed down to the dust: our belly cleaveth unto the earth. 26. Arise for our help, and redeem us for thy mercies' sake.

Psa. 50:15. And call upon me in the day of trouble: I will deliver thee, and thou shalt glorify me.

Psa. 54:1. Save me, O God, by thy name, and judge me by thy strength. 2. Hear my prayer, O God; give ear to the words of my mouth. 3. For strangers are risen up against me, and oppressors seek after my soul:

Psa. 55:1. Give ear to my prayer, O God; and hide not thyself from my supplication. 2. Attend unto me, and hear me: I mourn in my complaint, and make a noise; 3. Because of the voice of the enemy, because of the oppression of the wicked; for they cast iniquity upon me, and in wrath they hate me. *vs.* 1–17.

Psa. 56:1. Be merciful unto me, O God: for man would swallow me up; he fighting daily oppresseth me. 2. Mine enemies would daily swallow *me* up: for *they be* many that fight against me, O thou most High. *vs.* 1–13.

Psa. 57:1. Be merciful unto me, O God, be merciful unto me: for my soul trusteth in

thee: yea, in the shadow of thy wings will I make my refuge, until *these* calamities be overpast. 2. I will cry unto God most high; unto God that performeth *all things* for me.

Psa. 59:1. Deliver me from mine enemies, O my God: defend me from them that rise up against me. 2. Deliver me from the workers of iniquity, and save me from bloody men. 4. Awake to help me, and behold. *vs.* 1–17.

Psa. 60:1. O God, thou hast cast us off, thou hast scattered us, thou hast been displeased; O turn thyself to us again. 2. Thou hast made the earth to tremble; thou hast broken it: heal the breaches thereof; for it shaketh. 3. Thou hast shewed thy people hard things: thou hast made us to drink the wine of astonishment. 11. Give us help from trouble: for vain *is* the help of man.

Psa. 61:1. Hear my cry, O God; attend unto my prayer. 2. From the end of the earth will I cry unto thee, when my heart is overwhelmed: lead me to the rock *that* is higher than I.

Psa. 64:1. Hear my voice, O God, in my prayer: preserve my life from fear of the enemy. 2. Hide me from the secret counsel of the wicked; from the insurrection of the workers of iniquity:

Psa. 69:1. Save me, O God; for the waters are come in unto *my* soul.

13. As for me, my prayer *is* unto thee, O Lord, *in* an acceptable time: O God, in the multitude of thy mercy hear me, in the truth of thy salvation. 14. Deliver me out of the mire, and let me not sink: let me be delivered from them that hate me, and out of the deep waters. 15. Let not the waterflood overflow me, neither let the deep swallow me up, and let not the pit shut her mouth upon me.

17. Hide not thy face from thy servant; for I am in trouble: hear me speedily. 18. Draw nigh unto my soul, *and* redeem it: deliver me because of mine enemies. 19. Thou hast known my reproach, and my shame, and my dishonour: mine adversaries *are* all before thee. 29. I *am* poor and sorrowful: let thy salvation, O God, set me up on high. *vs.* 1–36.

Psa. 70:1. *Make haste*, O God, to deliver me: make haste to help me, O LORD. 2. Let them be ashamed and confounded that seek after my soul: *vs.* 3–5.

Psa. 71:1. In thee, O LORD, do I put my trust: let me never be put to confusion. 2. Deliver me in thy righteousness, and cause me to escape: incline thine ear unto me, and save me. 4. Deliver me, O my God, out of the hand of the wicked, out of the hand of the unrighteous and cruel man. *vs.* 1–24.

Psa. 71:9. Cast me not off in the time of old age; forsake me not when my strength faileth. 12. O God, be not far from me: O my God, make haste for my help.

Psa. 74:1. O God, why hast thou cast *us* off for ever? *why* doth thine anger smoke against the sheep of thy pasture? 3. Lift up thy feet unto the perpetual desolations *even* all *that* the enemy hath done wickedly in the sanctuary.

Psa. 74:10. O God, how long shall the adversary reproach? shall the enemy blaspheme thy name for ever? 11. Why withdrawest thou thy hand. even thy right hand? pluck *it* out of thy bosom. 19. O deliver not the soul of thy turtledove unto the multitude *of the wicked:* forget not the congregation of thy poor for ever. 21. O let not the oppressed return ashamed · let the poor and needy praise thy name. 22. Arise, O God, plead thine own cause. remember how the foolish man reproacheth thee daily. 23. Forget not the voice of thine enemies: the tumult of those that rise up against thee increaseth continually. *vs.* 1–23.

Psa. 77:1. I cried unto God with my voice, *even* unto God with my voice; and he gave ear unto me. 2. In the day of my trouble I sought the Lord: 7. Will the Lord cast off for ever? and will he be favourable no more? 8. Is his mercy clean gone for ever? doth *his* promise fail for evermore? 9. Hath God forgotten to be gracious? hath he in anger shut up his tender mercies? *vs.* 1–20.

Psa. 79:1. O God, the heathen are come into thine inheritance; thy holy temple have they defiled; they have laid Jerusalem on heaps. 5. How long, LORD? wilt thou be angry for ever? shall thy jealousy burn like fire?

Psa. 79:8. O remember not against us former iniquities: let thy tender mercies speedily prevent us: for we are brought very low. 9. Help us, O God of our salvation, for the glory of thy name: and deliver us, and purge away our sins, for thy name's sake. *vs.* 1–13.

Psa. 79:11. Let the sighing of the prisoner come before thee; according to the greatness of thy power preserve thou those that are appointed to die; *vs.* 1–11.

Psa. 80:1. Give ear, O Shepherd of Israel, thou that leadest Joseph like a flock; thou that dwellest *between* the cherubims, shine forth.

Psa. 80:3. Turn us again, O God, and cause thy face to shine; and we shall be saved. 4. O LORD God of hosts, how long wilt thou be angry against the prayer of thy people? 5. Thou feedest them with the bread of tears; and givest them tears to drink in great measure. 14. Return, we beseech thee, O God of hosts. look down from heaven, and behold, and visit this vine. *vs.* 1–16.

Psa. 83:1. Keep not thou silence, O God. hold not thy peace, and be not still, O God. 2. For, lo, thine enemies make a tumult: and they that hate thee have lifted up the head. *vs.* 1–18.

Psa. 85:5. Wilt thou be angry with us for ever? wilt thou draw out thine anger to all generations? 6. Wilt thou not revive us again: that thy people may rejoice in thee? 7. Shew us thy mercy, O LORD, and grant us thy salvation.

Psa. 86:1. Bow down thine ear, O LORD, hear me: for I *am* poor and needy. 2. Preserve my soul: for I *am* holy O thou my

God, save thy servant that trusteth in thee. 3. Be merciful unto me, O Lord: for I cry unto thee daily. 4. Rejoice the soul of thy servant. for unto thee, O Lord, do I lift up my soul. *vs.* 1–17.

Psa. 86:16. O turn unto me, and have mercy upon me; give thy strength unto thy servant, and save the son of thine handmaid. 17. Shew me a token for good; that they which hate me may see *it*, and be ashamed . because thou, LORD, hast holpen me, and comforted me.

Psa. 88:9. LORD, I have called daily upon thee, I have stretched out my hands unto thee. 13. Unto thee have I cried, O LORD; and in the morning shall my prayer prevent thee. 14. LORD, why castest thou off my soul? *why* hidest thou thy face from me? *vs.* 10–12.

Psa. 89:46. How long, LORD? wilt thou hide thyself for ever? shall thy wrath burn like fire? 47. Remember how short my time is: wherefore hast thou made all men in vain? 49. Lord, where *are* thy former lovingkindnesses, *which* thou swarest unto David in thy truth?

Psa. 89:50. Remember, Lord, the reproach of thy servants; *how* I do bear in my bosom *the reproach of* all the mighty people; 51. Wherewith thine enemies have reproached, O LORD; wherewith they have reproached the footsteps of thine anointed. *vs.* 39–51.

Psa. 90:15. Make us glad according to the days *wherein* thou hast afflicted us, *and* the years *wherein* we have seen evil.

Psa. 94:1. O God, to whom vengeance belongeth, shew thyself. 2. Lift up thyself, thou judge of the earth: render a reward to the proud. *vs.* 1–23.

Psa. 102:2. Hide not thy face from me in the day *when* I am in trouble; incline thine ear unto me: in the day *when* I call answer me speedily. 24. O my God, take me not away in the midst of my days:

Psa. 106:47. Save us, O LORD our God, and gather us from among the heathen, to give thanks unto thy holy name, and to triumph in thy praise.

Psa. 108:6. That thy beloved may be delivered: save *with* thy right hand, and answer me. 12. Give us help from trouble: for vain *is* the help of man,

Psa. 109 1. Hold not thy peace, O God of my praise; 2. For the mouth of the wicked and the mouth of the deceitful are opened against me: 21 But do thou for me, O GOD the Lord, for thy name's sake: because thy mercy *is* good, deliver thou me. 26. Help me, O LORD my God: O save me according to thy mercy: 27. That they may know that this *is* thy hand; *that* thou, LORD, hast done it. 28. Let them curse, but bless thou: when they arise, let them be ashamed; but let thy servant rejoice. *vs.* 1–31.

Psa. 116:4. Then called I upon the name of the LORD: O LORD, I beseech thee, deliver my soul.

Psa. 119:22. Remove from me reproach and

contempt; for I have kept thy testimonies. 28. My soul melteth for heaviness: strengthen thou me according unto thy word. 39. Turn away my reproach which I fear: for thy judgments *are* good. 41. Let thy mercies come also unto me, O LORD, *even* thy salvation, according to thy word. 42. So shall I have wherewith to answer him that reproacheth me: for I trust in thy word. 76. Let, I pray thee, thy merciful kindness be for my comfort, according to thy word unto thy servant. 77. Let thy tender mercies come unto me, that I may live: for thy law *is* my delight. 82. Mine eyes fail for thy word, saying, When wilt thou comfort me? 84. How many *are* the days of thy servant? when wilt thou execute judgment on them that persecute me? 107. I am afflicted very much: quicken me, O LORD, according unto thy word. 121. Leave me not to mine oppressors. 122. Be surety for thy servant for good: let not the proud oppress me. 123. Mine eyes fail for thy salvation, and for the word of thy righteousness. 134. Deliver me from the oppression of man: so will I keep thy precepts. 145. I cried with *my* whole heart; hear me, O LORD: I will keep thy statutes. 146. I cried unto thee; save me, and I shall keep thy testimonies. 147. I prevented the dawning of the morning, and cried: I hoped in thy word. 148. Mine eyes prevent the *night* watches, that I might meditate in thy word. 149. Hear my voice according unto thy lovingkindness: O LORD, quicken me according to thy judgment. 153. Consider mine affliction, and deliver me: for I do not forget thy law. 154. Plead my cause, and deliver me: quicken me according to thy word. 170. Let my supplication come before thee: deliver me according to thy word. 173. Let thine hand help me; for I have chosen thy precepts.

Psa. 120:2. Deliver my soul, O LORD, from lying lips, *and* from a deceitful tongue.

Psa. 123:3. Have mercy upon us, O LORD, have mercy upon us: for we are exceedingly filled with contempt. 4. Our soul is exceedingly filled with the scorning of those that are at ease, *and* with the contempt of the proud.

Psa. 126:4. Turn again our captivity, O LORD, as the streams in the south.

Psa. 130:1. Out of the depths have I cried unto thee, O LORD. 2. Lord, hear my voice: let thine ears be attentive to the voice of my supplications. *vs.* 1-8.

Psa. 140:4. Keep me, O LORD, from the hands of the wicked; preserve me from the violent man; who have purposed to overthrow my goings. 6. I said unto the LORD, Thou *art* my God: hear the voice of my supplications, O LORD. 7. O GOD the Lord, the strength of my salvation, thou hast covered my head in the day of battle. 8. Grant not, O LORD, the desires of the wicked: further not his wicked device; *lest* they exalt themselves. *vs.* 1-13.

Psa. 141:8. Mine eyes *are* unto thee, O GOD the Lord: in thee is my trust; leave not my

soul destitute. 9. Keep me from the snares *which* they have laid for me, and the gins of the workers of iniquity. *vs.* 1-10.

Psa. 142:1. With my voice unto the LORD did I make my supplication. 2. I poured out my complaint before him; I shewed before him my trouble. 5. I cried unto thee, O LORD: I said, Thou *art* my refuge *and* my portion in the land of the living. 6. Attend unto my cry; for I am brought very low: deliver me from my persecutors; for they are stronger than I. 7. Bring my soul out of prison, that I may praise thy name:

Psa. 143:7. Hear me speedily, O LORD: my spirit faileth: hide not thy face from me, lest I be like unto them that go down into the pit. 8. Cause me to hear thy lovingkindness in the morning; for in thee do I trust: cause me to know the way wherein I should walk; for I lift up my soul unto thee. 9. Deliver me, O LORD, from mine enemies: I flee unto thee to hide me. 11. Quicken me, O Lord, for thy name's sake: for thy righteousness' sake bring my soul out of trouble. *vs.* 1-12.

Isa. 33:2. O LORD, be gracious unto us; we have waited for thee: be thou their arm every morning, our salvation also in the time of trouble.

Isa. 38:2. Then Hezekiah turned his face toward the wall, and prayed unto the LORD, 3. And said, Remember now, O LORD, I beseech thee, how I have walked before thee in truth and with a perfect heart, and have done *that which is* good in thy sight. And Hezekiah wept sore. [2 Kin. 20:3.] 14. Like a crane or a swallow, so did I chatter; I did mourn as a dove: mine eyes fail *with looking* upward: O LORD, I am oppressed; undertake for me. 15. What shall I say? he hath both spoken unto me, and himself hath done *it*: I shall go softly all my years in the bitterness of my soul. 16. O Lord, by these *things men* live, and in all these *things is* the life of my spirit: so wilt thou recover me, and make me to live. 17. Behold, for peace I had great bitterness: but thou hast in love to my soul *delivered it* from the pit of corruption: for thou hast cast all my sins behind thy back. 18. For the grave cannot praise thee, death can *not* celebrate thee: they that go down into the pit cannot hope for thy truth. 19. The living, the living, he shall praise thee, as I *do* this day: the father to the children shall make known thy truth.

Isa. 51:9. Awake, awake, put on strength, O arm of the LORD; awake, as in the ancient days, in the generations of old.

Isa. 63:15. Look down from heaven, and behold from the habitation of thy holiness and of thy glory: where *is* thy zeal and thy strength, the sounding of thy bowels and of thy mercies toward me? are they restrained? 16. Doubtless thou *art* our father, though Abraham be ignorant of us, and Israel acknowledge us not: thou, O LORD, *art* our father, our redeemer; thy name *is* from everlasting. 17. O LORD, why hast thou made us to err from thy ways, *and* hardened our heart from thy fear? Return for thy servants' sake, the tribes of thine inheritance.

Isa. 64:1. Oh that thou wouldest rend the heavens, that thou wouldest come down, that the mountains might flow down at thy presence. 9. Be not wroth very sore, O LORD, neither remember iniquity for ever: behold, see, we beseech thee, we *are* all thy people. 10. Thy holy cities are a wilderness, Zion is a wilderness, Jerusalem a desolation. 11. Our holy and our beautiful house, where our fathers praised thee, is burnt up with fire: and all our pleasant things are laid waste. 12. Wilt thou refrain thyself for these *things*, O LORD? wilt thou hold thy peace, and afflict us very sore?

Jer. 10:24. O LORD, correct me, but with judgment; not in thine anger, lest thou bring me to nothing.

Jer. 14:8. O the hope of Israel, the saviour thereof in time of trouble, why shouldest thou be as a stranger in the land, and as a wayfaring man *that* turneth aside to tarry for a night? 9. Why shouldest thou be as a man astonied, as a mighty man *that* cannot save? yet thou, O LORD, *art* in the midst of us, and we are called by thy name; leave us not. 19. Hast thou utterly rejected Judah? hath thy soul loathed Zion? why hast thou smitten us, and *there is* no healing for us? we looked for peace, and *there is* no good; and for the time of healing, and behold trouble! 20. We acknowledge, O LORD, our wickedness, *and* the iniquity of our fathers: for we have sinned against thee. 21. Do not abhor *us*, for thy name's sake, do not disgrace the throne of thy glory: remember, break not thy covenant with us. Jer. 32:16-25.

Jer. 15:15. O LORD, thou knowest: remember me, and visit me, and revenge me of my persecutors; take me not away in thy long-suffering: know that for thy sake I have suffered rebuke.

Jer. 16:19. O LORD, my strength, and my fortress, and my refuge in the day of affliction, the Gentiles shall come unto thee from the ends of the earth, and shall say, Surely our fathers have inherited lies, vanity, and *things* wherein *there is* no profit.

Jer. 17:17. Be not a terror unto me: thou *art* my ¹hope in the day of evil. 18. Let them be ²confounded that persecute me, but let not me be ²confounded: let them be dismayed, but let not me be dismayed: [R. V. ¹refuge ²ashamed]

Jer. 18:19. Give heed to me, O LORD, and hearken to the voice of them that contend with me. Jer. 20:7,8.

Lam. 1:9. O LORD, behold my affliction: for the enemy hath magnified *himself.* 10. The adversary hath spread out his hand upon all her pleasant things: for she hath seen *that* the heathen entered into her sanctuary, whom thou didst command *that* they should not enter into thy congregation. 11. All her people sigh, they seek bread; they have given their pleasant things for meat to relieve the soul: see, O LORD, and consider: for I am become vile. 20. Behold, O LORD: for I *am* in

distress: my bowels are troubled; mine heart is turned within me; for I have grievously rebelled: abroad the sword bereaveth, at home *there is* as death.

Lam. 2:18. Their heart cried unto the Lord, O wall of the daughter of Zion, let tears run down like a river day and night: give thyself no rest; let not the apple of thine eye cease. 19. Arise, cry out in the night: in the beginning of the watches pour out thine heart like water before the face of the Lord: lift up thy hands toward him for the life of thy young children, that faint for hunger in the top of every street.

Lam. 5:1. Remember, O LORD, what is come upon us: consider, and behold our reproach. 16. The crown is fallen *from* our head: woe unto us, that we have sinned! 17. For this our heart is faint; for these *things* our eyes are dim. 19. Thou, O LORD, remainest for ever; thy throne from generation to generation. 20. Wherefore dost thou forget us for ever, *and* forsake us so long time? 21. Turn thou us unto thee, O LORD, and we shall be turned; renew our days as of old. 22. But thou hast utterly rejected us; thou art very wroth against us. chapters 1-5.

Dan. 6:10. He kneeled upon his knees three times a day, and prayed, and gave thanks before his God, as he did aforetime.

Joel 1:19. O LORD, to thee will I cry: for the fire hath devoured the pastures of the wilderness, and the flame hath burned all the trees of the field.

Jonah 1:14. Wherefore they cried unto the LORD, and said, We beseech thee, O LORD, we beseech thee, let us not perish for this man's life, and lay not upon us innocent blood: for thou, O LORD, hast done as it pleased thee.

Jonah 2:1. Then Jonah prayed unto the LORD his God out of the fish's belly, 2. And said, I cried by reason of mine affliction unto the LORD, and he heard me; out of the belly of hell cried I, *and* thou heardest my voice. 3. For thou hadst cast me into the deep, in the midst of the seas; and the floods compassed me about: all thy billows and thy waves passed over me. 4. Then I said, I am cast out of thy sight; yet I will look again toward thy holy temple. 5. The waters compassed me about, *even* to the soul: the depth closed me round about, the weeds were wrapped about my head. 6. I went down to the bottoms of the mountains; the earth with her bars *was* about me for ever: yet hast thou brought up my life from corruption, O LORD my God. 7. When my soul fainted within me I remembered the LORD: and my prayer came in unto thee, into thine holy temple. 8. They that observe lying vanities forsake their own mercy. 9. But I will sacrifice unto thee with the voice of thanksgiving; I will pay *that* that I have vowed. Salvation *is* of the LORD. 10. And the LORD spake unto the fish, and it vomited out Jonah upon the dry *land.*

Hab. 1:12. *Art* thou not from everlasting,

O LORD my God, mine Holy One? we shall not die. O LORD, thou hast ordained them for judgment; and, O mighty God, thou hast established them for correction. 13. *Thou art* of purer eyes than to behold evil, and canst not look on iniquity: wherefore lookest thou upon them that deal treacherously, *and* holdest thy tongue when the wicked devoureth *the man that is* more righteous than he?

Matt. 8:25. His disciples came to *him* and awoke him, saying, Lord, save us: we perish.

Matt. 14:30. But when he saw the wind boisterous, he was afraid; and beginning to sink, he cried, saying, Lord, save me.

Matt. 15:22. And, behold, a woman of Canaan came out of the same coasts, and cried unto him, saying, Have mercy on me, O Lord, *thou* Son of David; my daughter is grievously vexed with a devil. 23. But he answered her not a word. And his disciples came and besought him, saying, Send her away; for she crieth after us. 24. But he answered and said, I am not sent but unto the lost sheep of the house of Israel. 25. Then came she and worshipped him, saying, Lord, help me. 26. But he answered and said, It is not meet to take the children's bread, and cast *it* to dogs. 27. And she said, Truth, Lord: yet the dogs eat of the crumbs which fall from their master's table. 28. Then Jesus answered and said unto her, O woman, great *is* thy faith: be it unto thee even as thou wilt.

Matt. 26:39. And he went a little farther, and fell on his face, and prayed, saying, O my Father, if it be possible, let this cup pass from me: nevertheless, not as I will, but as thou *wilt*. 42. He went away again the second time, and prayed, saying, O my Father, if this cup may not pass away from me, except I drink it, thy will be done. *v.* 44; Mark 14:36; Luke 22:42.

Matt. 27:46. And about the ninth hour Jesus cried with a loud voice, saying, Eli, Eli, lama sabachthani? that is to say, My God, my God, why hast thou forsaken me? Mark 15:34; Luke 23:46.

Luke 18:1. And he spake a parable unto them *to this end*, that men ought always to pray, and not to faint:

John 11:3. Therefore his sisters sent unto him, saying, Lord, behold, he whom thou lovest is sick.

Acts 4:29. Now, Lord, behold their threatenings: and grant unto thy servants, that with all boldness they may speak thy word, 30. By stretching forth thy hand to heal; and that signs and wonders may be done by the name of thy holy child Jesus.

Acts 7:59. And they stoned Stephen, calling upon *God*, and saying, Lord Jesus, receive my spirit. 60. And he kneeled down, and cried with a loud voice, Lord, lay not this sin to their charge.

2 Cor. 12:8. For this thing I besought the Lord thrice, that it might depart from me.

Jas. 5:13. Is any among you afflicted? let him pray. Is any merry? let him sing psalms. 14. Is any sick among you? let him call for the elders of the church; and let them pray over him, anointing him with oil in the name of the Lord: 15. And the prayer of faith shall save the sick, and the Lord shall raise him up; and if he have committed sins, they shall be forgiven him. 16. Confess *your* faults one to another, and pray one for another, that ye may be healed. The effectual fervent prayer of a righteous man availeth much.

See PRAYER.

PRAYER IN, ANSWERED. See PRAYER, ANSWERED.

PRAYER FOR THE AFFLICTED. See INTERCESSION.

RESIGNATION IN: Job 5:17. Happy *is* the man whom God correcteth: therefore despise not thou the chastening of the Almighty:

Job 13:15. Though he slay me, yet will I trust in him:

Job 34:31. Surely it is meet to be said unto God, I have borne *chastisement*. I will not offend *any more:* 32. *That which* I see not teach thou me: if I have done iniquity, I will do no more. *v.* 34.

Psa. 46:10. Be still, and know that I *am* God: Psa. 4:4; 37:1.

Prov. 3:11. My son, despise not the chastening of the LORD; neither be weary of his correction:

Lam. 3:22. *It is of* the LORD's mercies that we are not consumed, because his compassions fail not. 23. *They are* new every morning: great *is* thy faithfulness. 24. The LORD *is* my portion, saith my soul: therefore will I hope in him. 25. The LORD *is* good unto them that wait for him, to the soul *that* seeketh him. 26. *It is* good that *a man* should both hope and quietly wait for the salvation of the LORD. 27. *It is* good for a man that he bear the yoke in his youth. 28. He sitteth alone and keepeth silence, because he hath borne *it* upon him. 29. He putteth his mouth in the dust; if so be there may be hope. 30. He giveth *his* cheek to him that smiteth him: he is filled full with reproach. 31. For the Lord will not cast off for ever: 32. But though he cause grief, yet will he have compassion according to the multitude of his mercies. 33. For he doth not afflict willingly, nor grieve the children of men. 34. To crush under his feet all the prisoners of the earth, 35. To turn aside the right of a man before the face of the Most High, 36. To subvert a man in his cause, the Lord approveth not. 39. Wherefore doth a living man complain, a man for the punishment of his sins?

Mic. 6:9. The LORD's voice crieth unto the city, and *the man of* wisdom shall see thy name: hear ye the rod, and who hath appointed it.

Matt. 26:39. O my Father, if it be possible, let this cup pass from me: nevertheless, not as I will, but as thou *wilt*. Mark 14:36; Luke 22:42; John 18:11.

Luke 21:19. In your patience possess ye your souls.

Rom. 5:3. And not only *so*, but we glory in tribulations also; knowing that tribulation worketh patience:

Rom. 12:12. Rejoicing in hope; patient in tribulation; continuing instant in prayer;

2 Cor. 12:9. And he said unto me, My grace is sufficient for thee: for my strength is made perfect in weakness. Most gladly therefore will I rather glory in my infirmities, that the power of Christ may rest upon me.

Phil. 2:14. Do all things without murmurings:

Col. 1:11. Strengthened with all might, according to his glorious power, unto all patience and longsuffering with joyfulness;

1 Thess. 3:3. That no man should be moved by these afflictions: for yourselves know that we are appointed thereunto. *v.* 4.

2 Thess. 1:4. So that we ourselves glory in you in the churches of God, for your patience and faith in all your persecutions and tribulations that ye endure;

2 Tim. 2:3. Endure hardness, as a good soldier of Jesus Christ.

2 Tim. 4:5. But watch thou in all things, endure afflictions,

Heb. 10:34. For ye had compassion of me in my bonds, and took joyfully the spoiling of your goods, knowing in yourselves that ye have in heaven a better and an enduring substance.

Heb. 12:3. Consider him that endured such contradiction of sinners against himself, lest ye be wearied and faint in your minds. 4. Ye have not yet resisted unto blood, striving against sin. 5. And ye have forgotten the exhortation which speaketh unto you as unto children, My son, despise not thou the chastening of the Lord, nor faint when thou art rebuked of him: 9. We have had fathers of our flesh which corrected *us*, and we gave *them* reverence: shall we not much rather be in subjection unto the Father of spirits, and live? *vs.* 6-12.

Jas. 1:10. [Let] the rich [rejoice] in that he is made low: because as the flower of the grass he shall pass away.

Jas. 4:7. Submit yourselves therefore to God.

1 Pet. 1:6. Wherein ye greatly rejoice, though now for a season, if need be, ye are in heaviness through manifold temptations:

1 Pet. 2:20. For what glory *is it*, if, when ye be buffeted for your faults, ye shall take it patiently? but if, when ye do well, and suffer *for it*, ye take it patiently, this *is* acceptable with God.

1 Pet. 4:12. Beloved, think it not strange concerning the fiery trial which is to try you, as though some strange thing happened unto you: 13. But rejoice, inasmuch as ye are partakers of Christ's sufferings; that, when his glory shall be revealed, ye may be glad also with exceeding joy. 19. Wherefore, let them that suffer according to the will of God commit the keeping of their souls *to him* in well doing, as unto a faithful Creator.

1 Pet. 5:6. Humble yourselves therefore under the mighty hand of God, that he may exalt you in due time: 7. Casting all your care upon him; for he careth for you.

See RESIGNATION.

RESIGNATION IN, EXEMPLIFIED: Judg. 10:15. And the children of Israel said unto the Lord, We have sinned: do thou unto us whatsoever seemeth good unto thee; deliver us only, we pray thee, this day.

1 Sam. 3:18. And he said, It *is* the Lord: let him do what seemeth him good.

2 Sam. 12:23. Now he is dead, wherefore should I fast? can I bring him back again? I shall go to him, but he shall not return to me.

2 Sam. 15:26. If he thus say, I have no delight in thee; behold, *here am* I, let him do to me as seemeth good unto him.

2 Sam. 16:10. And the king said, What have I to do with you, ye sons of Zeruiah? so let him curse, because the Lord hath said unto him, Curse David. Who shall then say, Wherefore hast thou done so? 12. It may be that the Lord will look on mine affliction, and that the Lord will requite me good for his cursing this day.

2 Sam. 24:14. David said unto Gad, I am in a great strait: let us fall now into the hand of the Lord; for his mercies *are* great: and let me not fall into the hand of man.

2 Kin. 4:26. *Is it* well with the child? And she answered, *It is* well.

2 Kin. 20:19. Then said Hezekiah unto Isaiah, Good *is* the word of the Lord which thou hast spoken. And he said, Is *it* not *good*, if peace and truth be in my days? Isa. 39:8.

Neh. 9:33. Howbeit thou *art* just in all that is brought upon us; for thou hast done right, but we have done wickedly:

Esth. 4:16. And so will I go in unto the king, which *is* not according to the law: and if I perish, I perish.

Job 1:21. Naked came I out of my mother's womb, and naked shall I return thither: the Lord gave, and the Lord hath taken away; blessed be the name of the Lord. 22. In all this Job sinned not, nor charged God foolishly.

Job 2:10. What? shall we receive good at the hand of God, and shall we not receive evil? In all this did not Job sin with his lips.

Job 13:15. Though he slay me, yet will I trust in him: but I will maintain mine own ways before him.

Job 14:14. All the days of my appointed time will I wait, till my change come.

Psa. 39:9. I was dumb, I opened not my mouth; because thou didst *it*.

Psa. 71:20. *Thou*, which hast shewed me great and sore troubles, shalt quicken me again, and shalt bring me up again from the depths of the earth.

Psa. 119:75. I know, O Lord, that thy judgments *are* right, and *that* thou in faithfulness hast afflicted me.

Jer. 10:19. Woe is me for my hurt! my wound is grievous: but I said, Truly this *is* a grief, and I must bear it.

Lam. 1:18. The LORD is righteous; for I have rebelled against his commandment:

Lam. 3:39. Wherefore doth a living man complain, a man for the punishment of his sins?

Dan. 9:14. Therefore hath the LORD watched upon the evil, and brought it upon us: for the LORD our God *is* righteous in all his works which he doeth: for we obeyed not his voice.

Mic. 7:9. I will bear the indignation of the LORD, because I have sinned against him, until he plead my cause, and execute judgment for me: he will bring me forth to the light, *and* I shall behold his righteousness.

Luke 23:40. Dost not thou fear God, seeing thou art in the same condemnation? 41. And we indeed justly; for we receive the due reward of our deeds: but this man hath done nothing amiss.

Acts 21:14. When he would not be persuaded, we ceased, saying, The will of the Lord be done.

Rom. 5:3. And not only *so*, but we glory in tribulations also: knowing that tribulation worketh patience; 4. And patience, experience; and experience, hope:

2 Cor. 6:4. But in all *things* approving ourselves as the ministers of God, in much patience, in afflictions, in necessities, in distresses, 5. In stripes, in imprisonments, in tumults, in labours, in watchings, in fastings; 6. By pureness, by knowledge, by longsuffering, by kindness, by the Holy Ghost, by love unfeigned, 7. By the word of truth, by the power of God, by the armour of righteousness on the right hand and on the left, 8. By honour and dishonour, by evil report and good report: as deceivers, and *yet* true; 9. As unknown, and *yet* well known; as dying, and, behold, we live; as chastened, and not killed; 10. As sorrowful, yet alway rejoicing; as poor, yet making many rich; as having nothing, and *yet* possessing all things.

2 Cor. 7:4. I am filled with comfort, I am exceeding joyful in all our tribulation.

2 Thess. 1:4. We ourselves glory in you in the churches of God, for your patience and faith in all your persecutions and tribulations that ye endure:

Jas. 5:11. Behold, we count them happy which endure. Ye have heard of the patience of Job,and have seen the end of the Lord: that the Lord is very pitiful, and of tender mercy.

See RESIGNATION.

INSTANCES OF RESIGNATION IN: Aaron, at the death of Nadab and Abihu, Lev. 10:1-3. Eli, when judgments against his house were foretold, 1 Sam. 3:15-18. David, at the death of his child, 2 Sam. 12:23. The Shunammite, 2 Kin. 4:18-37. Jesus, in Gethsemane, Matt. 26:39; Mark 14:36; Luke 22:42; John 18:11. Paul and Silas in prison, Acts 16:23-25.

AGABUS, a prophet, Acts 11:28; 21:10.

AGAG. 1. A king of the Amalekites, Num. 24:7.

2. A king of the Amalekites, taken prisoner by Saul, and slain by Samuel, 1 Sam. 15:8,33.

AGAR. See HAGAR.

AGATE, a precious stone, Ex. 28:19; Isa. 54:12; Ezek. 27:16.

AGE, OLD. See OLD AGE.

AGED, gospel invitation to, Matt. 20: 5,6. See OLD AGE.

AGEE, father of Shammah, 2 Sam. 23:11.

AGENCY. IN SALVATION OF MEN: Job 33:14. For God speaketh once, yea twice, *yet man* perceiveth it not. 15. In a dream, in a vision of the night, when deep sleep falleth upon men, in slumberings upon the bed; 16. Then he openeth the ears of men, and sealeth their instruction, 17. That he may withdraw man *from his* purpose, and hide pride from man. 18. He keepeth back his soul from the pit, and his life from perishing by the sword. 19. He is chastened also with pain upon his bed, and the multitude of his bones with strong *pain:* 20. So that his life abhorreth bread, and his soul dainty meat. 21. His flesh is consumed away, that it cannot be seen; and his bones *that* were not seen stick out. 22. Yea, his soul draweth near unto the grave, and his life to the destroyers. 23. If there be a messenger with him, an interpreter, one among a thousand, to shew unto man his uprightness; 24. Then he is gracious unto him, and saith, Deliver him from going down to the pit: I have found a ransom. 25. His flesh shall be fresher than a child's: he shall return to the days of his youth: 26. He shall pray unto God, and he will be favourable unto him: and he shall see his face with joy: for he will render unto man his righteousness. 27. He looketh upon men, and *if any* say, I have sinned, and perverted *that which was* right, and it profited me not; 28. He will deliver his soul from going into the pit, and his life shall see the light. 29. Lo, all these *things* worketh God oftentimes with man, 30. To bring back his soul from the pit, to be enlightened with the light of the living.

Psa. 8:2. Out of the mouth of babes and sucklings hast thou ordained strength because of thine enemies, that thou mightest still the enemy and the avenger.

Matt. 4:19. And he saith unto them, Follow me, and I will make you fishers of men. Luke 5:10.

Matt. 5:13. Ye are the salt of the earth: but if the salt have lost his savour, wherewith shall it be salted? It is thenceforth good for nothing, but to be cast out, and to be trodden under foot of men. 14. Ye are the light of the world. A city that is set on a hill cannot be hid. 15. Neither do men light a candle, and put it under a bushel, but on a candlestick: and it giveth light unto all that are in the house. 16. Let your light so shine before men, that they may see your good works, and glorify your Father which is in heaven.

Luke 1:17. And he shall go before him in the spirit and power of Elias, to turn the hearts of the fathers to the children, and the disobedient to the wisdom of the just; to make ready a people prepared for the Lord.

Luke 10:17. And the seventy returned again with joy, saying, Lord, even the devils are subject unto us through thy name. 21. In that hour Jesus rejoiced in spirit, and said, I thank thee, O Father, Lord of heaven and earth, that thou hast hid these things from the wise and prudent, and hast revealed them unto babes: even so, Father; for so it seemed good in thy sight.

John 15:16. Ye have not chosen me, but I have chosen you, and ordained you, that ye should go and bring forth fruit, and *that* your fruit should remain.

1 Cor. 1:26. For ye see your calling, brethren, how that not many wise men after the flesh, not many mighty, not many noble, *are called:* 27. But God hath chosen the foolish things of the world to confound the wise; and God hath chosen the weak things of the world to confound the things which are mighty; 28. And base things of the world, and things which are despised, hath God chosen, *yea,* and things which are not, to bring to nought things that are: 29. That no flesh should glory in his presence.

1 Thess. 2:4. But as we were allowed of God to be put in trust with the gospel, even so we speak; not as pleasing men, but God, which trieth our hearts.

1 Tim. 1:11. According to the glorious gospel of the blessed God, which was committed to my trust.

1 Tim. 6:20. O Timothy, keep that which is committed to thy trust, avoiding profane *and* vain babblings, and oppositions of science falsely so called:

Jas. 5:20. Let him know, that he which converteth the sinner from the error of his way shall save a soul from death, and shall hide a multitude of sins.

See PREACHING.

IN EXECUTING JUDGMENTS: Gen. 3:15. It shall bruise thy head, and thou shalt bruise his heel.

1 Sam. 15:18. And the LORD sent thee on a journey, and said, Go and utterly destroy the sinners the Amalekites, and fight against them until they be consumed. with *vs.* 1–19.

2 Sam. 7:14. If he commit iniquity, I will chasten him with the rod of men, and with the stripes of the children of men:

2 Kin. 9:6. Thus saith the LORD God of Israel, I have anointed thee king over the people of the LORD, *even* over Israel. 7. And thou shalt smite the house of Ahab thy master, that I may avenge the blood of my servants the prophets, and the blood of all the servants of the LORD, at the hand of Jezebel.

2 Kin. 19:25. Now have I brought it to pass, that thou shouldest be to lay waste fenced cities *into* ruinous heaps. 26. Therefore their inhabitants were of small power, they were dismayed and confounded.

2 Chr. 22:7. He went out with Jehoram against Jehu the son of Nimshi, whom the LORD had anointed to cut off the house of Ahab.

Psa. 17:13. Arise, O LORD, disappoint him, cast him down: deliver my soul from the wicked, *which is* thy sword: 14. From men *which are* thy hand.

Isa. 10:5. O Assyrian, the rod of mine anger, and the staff in their hand is mine indignation. 6. I will send him against a hypocritical nation, and against the people of my wrath will I give him a charge, to take the spoil, and to take the prey, and to tread them down like the mire of the streets.

Isa. 13:5. They come from a far country, from the end of heaven, *even* the LORD, and the weapons of his indignation, to destroy the whole land.

Jer. 27:8. And it shall come to pass, *that* the nation and kingdom which will not serve the same Nebuchadnezzar the king of Babylon, and that will not put their neck under the yoke of the king of Babylon, that nation will I punish, saith the LORD, with the sword, and with the famine, and with the pestilence, until I have consumed them by his hand.

Jer. 51:20. Thou *art* my battle ax *and* weapons of war: for with thee will I break in pieces the nations, and with thee will I destroy kingdoms; 21. And with thee will I break in pieces the horse and his rider; and with thee will I break in pieces the chariot and his rider; 22. With thee also will I break in pieces man and woman; and with thee will I break in pieces old and young; and with thee will I break in pieces the young man and the maid; 23. I will also break in pieces with thee the shepherd and his flock; and with thee will I break in pieces the husbandman and his yoke of oxen; and with thee will I break in pieces captains and rulers. Isa. 41:15.

AGENCY, FREE MORAL. See CONTINGENCIES.

AGRICULTURE. Divine institution of, Gen. 2:15; 3:19,23. Practised by Cain, Gen. 4:2; Noah, Gen. 9:20; Elisha, 1 Kin. 19:19; David, 1 Chr. 27:26–31; Uzziah, 2 Chr. 26:10; Solomon, Eccl. 2:4–6.

God to be acknowledged in, Jer. 5:24; Hos. 2:8. Requires wisdom, Isa. 28:26; diligence, Prov. 27:23,27; Eccl. 11:6; patience, Jas. 5:7; toil, 2 Tim. 2:6. Persons engaged in, called husbandmen, 2 Chr. 26:10; laborers, Matt. 9:37; 20:1; tillers of the ground, Gen. 4:2. Planters of vineyards exempted from military service, Deut. 20:6. Fruits blasted because of sin, Isa. 5:10; 7:23; Jer. 12:13; Joel 1:10,11.

LAWS CONCERNING: Ex. 22:5. If a man shall cause a field or vineyard to be eaten, and shall put in his beast, and shall feed in another man's field; of the best of his own field, and of the best of his own vineyard, shall he make restitution.

6. If fire break out, and catch in thorns, so that the stacks of corn, or the standing corn, or the field, be consumed *therewith;*

he that kindled the fire shall surely make restitution.

Ex. 34:21. Six days shalt thou work, but on the seventh day thou shalt rest: in earing time and in harvest thou shalt rest. Ex. 20:9; 23:12; Deut. 5:13,14.

22. And thou shalt observe the feast of weeks, of the firstfruits of wheat harvest, and the feast of ingathering at the year's end.

Lev. 19:9. And when ye reap the harvest of your land, thou shalt not wholly reap the corners of thy field, neither shalt thou gather the gleanings of thy harvest. 10. And thou shalt not glean thy vineyard, neither shalt thou gather every grape of thy vineyard; thou shalt leave them for the poor and stranger: I am the LORD your God.

19. Ye shall keep my statutes. Thou shalt not let thy cattle gender with a diverse kind: thou shalt not sow thy field with mingled seed: neither shall a garment mingled of linen and woollen come upon thee.

23. And when ye shall come into the land, and shall have planted all manner of trees for food, then ye shall count the fruit thereof as uncircumcised: three years shall it be as uncircumcised unto you: it shall not be eaten of. 24. But in the fourth year all the fruit thereof shall be holy to praise the LORD withal. 25. And in the fifth year shall ye eat of the fruit thereof, that it may yield unto you the increase thereof: I am the LORD your God.

Lev. 25:2. Speak unto the children of Israel, and say unto them, When ye come into the land which I give you, then shall the land keep a sabbath unto the LORD. 3. Six years thou shalt sow thy field, and six years thou shalt prune thy vineyard, and gather in the fruit thereof; 4. But in the seventh year shall be a sabbath of rest unto the land a sabbath for the LORD; thou shalt neither sow thy field, nor prune thy vineyard. [Ex. 23:10,11.] 5. That which groweth of its own accord of thy harvest thou shalt not reap, neither gather the grapes of thy vine undressed: for it is a year of rest unto the land. 6. And the sabbath of the land shall be meat for you; for thee, and for thy servant, and for thy maid, and for thy hired servant, and for thy stranger that sojourneth with thee, 7. And for thy cattle, and for the beast that are in thy land, shall all the increase thereof be meat.

8. And thou shalt number seven sabbaths of years unto thee, seven times seven years: and the space of the seven sabbaths of years shall be unto thee forty and nine years. 9. Then shalt thou cause the trumpet of the jubilee to sound on the tenth day of the seventh month, in the day of atonement shall ye make the trumpet sound throughout all your land. 10. And ye shall hallow the fiftieth year, and proclaim liberty throughout all the land unto all the inhabitants thereof: it shall be a jubilee unto you; and ye shall return every man unto his possession, and ye shall return every man unto his family. 11. A jubilee shall that fiftieth year be unto you: ye shall not sow neither reap that which groweth of itself in it, nor gather the grapes in it of thy vine undressed. 12. For it is the jubilee; it shall be holy unto you: ye shall eat the increase thereof out of the field. 15. According to the number of years after the jubilee thou shalt buy of thy neighbour, and according unto the number of years of the fruits he shall sell unto thee: 16. According to the multitude of years thou shalt increase the price thereof, and according to the fewness of years thou shalt diminish the price of it: for according to the number of the years of the fruits doth he sell unto thee. 19. And the land shall yield her fruit, and ye shall eat your fill, and dwell therein in safety. 20. And if ye shall say, What shall we eat the seventh year? behold, we shall not sow, nor gather in our increase: 21. Then I will command my blessing upon you in the sixth year, and it shall bring forth fruit for three years. 22. And ye shall sow the eighth year, and eat yet of old fruit until the ninth year; until her fruits come in ye shall eat of the old store.

23. The land shall not be sold for ever: for the land is mine; for ye are strangers and sojourners with me. 24. And in all the land of your possession ye shall grant a redemption for the land.

25. If thy brother be waxen poor, and hath sold away some of his possession, and if any of his kin come to redeem it, then shall he redeem that which his brother sold. 26. And if the man have none to redeem it, and himself be able to redeem it; 27. Then let him count the years of the sale thereof, and restore the overplus unto the man to whom he sold it; that he may return unto his possession. 28. But if he be not able to restore it to him, then that which is sold shall remain in the hand of him that hath bought it until the year of jubilee: and in the jubilee it shall go out, and he shall return unto his possession.

Deut. 22:9. Thou shalt not sow thy vineyard with divers seeds: lest the fruit of thy seed which thou hast sown, and the fruit of thy vineyard, be defiled.

10. Thou shalt not plow with an ox and an ass together.

Deut. 23:24. When thou comest into thy neighbour's vineyard, then thou mayest eat grapes thy fill at thine own pleasure; but thou shalt not put any in thy vessel. 25. When thou comest into the standing corn of thy neighbour, then thou mayest pluck the ears with thine hand: but thou shalt not move a sickle unto thy neighbour's standing corn. Matt. 12:1.

Deut. 24:19. When thou cuttest down thine harvest in thy field, and hast forgot a sheaf in the field, thou shalt not go again to fetch it: it shall be for the stranger, for the fatherless, and for the widow: that the

LORD thy God may bless thee in all the work of thine hands. 20. When thou beatest thine olive tree, thou shalt not go over the boughs again : it shall be for the stranger, for the fatherless, and for the widow. 21. When thou gatherest the grapes of thy vineyard, thou shalt not glean *it* afterward: it shall be for the stranger, for the fatherless, and for the widow.

Prov. 3:9. Honor the LORD with thy substance, and with the firstfruits of all thine increase: 10. So shall thy barns be filled with plenty, and thy presses shall burst out with new wine.

Eccl. 5:9. Moreover the profit of the earth is for all : the king *himself* is served by the field.

Prov. 27:23. Be thou diligent to know the state of thy flocks, *and* look well to thy herds: 24. For riches *are* not for ever: and doth the crown *endure* to every generation? 25. The hay appeareth, and the tender grass sheweth itself, and herbs of the mountains are gathered. 26. The lambs *are* for thy clothing, and the goats *are* the price of the field. 27. And *thou shalt have* goats' milk enough for thy food, for the food of thy household, and *for* the maintenance for thy maidens.

FACTS ABOUT: Gen. 8:22. While the earth remaineth, seedtime and harvest, and cold and heat, and summer and winter, and day and night shall not cease.

1 Sam. 13:19. Now there was no smith found throughout all the land of Israel: for the Philistines said, Lest the Hebrews make *them* swords or spears: 20. But all the Israelites went down to the Philistines, to sharpen every man his share, and his coulter, and his ax, and his mattock: 21. Yet they had a file for the mattocks, and for the coulters, and for the forks, and for the axes, and to sharpen the goads.

Isa. 28:24. Doth the plowman plow all day to sow? doth he open and break the clods of his ground? 25. When he hath made plain the face thereof, doth he not cast abroad the fitches, and scatter the cummin, and cast in the principal wheat and the appointed barley and the rie in their place? 26. For his God doth instruct him to discretion, *and* doth teach him. 27. For the fitches are not threshed with a threshing instrument, neither is a cart wheel turned about upon the cummin; but the fitches are beaten out with a staff, and the cummin with a rod. 28. Bread *corn* is bruised; because he will not ever be threshing it, nor break *it with* the wheel of his cart, nor bruise it *with* his horsemen.

Matt. 13:3. And he spake many things unto them in parables, saying, Behold, a sower went forth to sow; 4. And when he sowed, some *seeds* fell by the wayside, and the fowls came and devoured them up: 5. Some fell upon stony places, where they had not much earth: and forthwith they sprung up, because they had no deepness of earth: 6. And

when the sun was up, they were scorched; and because they had no root, they withered away. 7. And some fell among thorns; and the thorns sprung up, and choked them; 8. But other fell into good ground, and brought forth fruit, some an hundredfold, some sixtyfold, some thirtyfold.

2 Cor. 9:6. But this *I say*, He which soweth sparingly shall reap also sparingly; and he which soweth bountifully shall reap also bountifully.

Gal. 6:7. Be not deceived; God is not mocked: for whatsoever a man soweth, that shall he also reap.

See HUSBANDMAN.

FIGURATIVE: Fallow ground, Jer. 4:3. Sowing wheat, but reaping thorns, Jer. 12:13. Parable of the sower, Matt. 13:3–8,19–23; Luke 8:5-15; of the tares, Matt. 13:24–30, 36–43.

OPERATIONS IN. See CHURNING; GLEANING; GRAFTING; IRRIGATION; MANURE; MOWING; PRUNING; REAPING; SOWER; THRESHING.

IMPLEMENTS OF. See AX; CART; FAN; FLAIL; FORK; GOAD; HARROW; MATTOCK; MILL; PLOW; PRUNING-HOOK; SHOVEL; SICKLE; SIEVE.

PRODUCTS OF. See APPLE; BARLEY; BUTTER; CHAFF; CORN; CUCUMBER; DATE; FIG; FITCH; GARLIC; GOURD; GRAPE; HONEY; LEEK; MELON; MILK; OIL; ONION; POMEGRANATE; RYE; STUBBLE; WHEAT; WINE.

ANIMALS OF. See ASS; CAMEL; GOATS; HORSES; KINE; MULES; SHEEP; SWINE.

See also BARN; FENCE; GARNER; VINEYARDS.

AGRIPPA, king, Acts 25:26.

AGUE. Lev. 26:16.

AGUR, son of Jakeh, Prov. 30:1.

AHAB. 1. King of Israel, 1 Kin. 16:29. Marries Jezebel, 1 Kin. 16:31. Idolatry of, 1 Kin. 16:30–33; 18:18,19; 21:25,26; other wickedness of, 2 Kin. 3:2; 2 Chr. 21:6; 22:3,4; Mic. 6:16. Reproved by Elijah; assembles the prophets of Baal, 1 Kin. 18:17–46. Fraudulently confiscates Naboth's vineyard, 1 Kin. 21. Defeats Ben-hadad, 1 Kin. 20. Closing history and death of, 1 Kin. 22; 2 Chr. 18. Succeeded by his son, Ahaziah, 1 Kin. 22:40. Prophecies against, 1 Kin. 20:42; 21:19–24; 22:19–28; 2 Kin. 9:8,25,26. Sons of, murdered, 2 Kin. 10:1-8.

2. A false prophet, Jer. 29:21,22.

AHARAH, called also EHI, and AHIRAM, and AHER, son of Benjamin, Gen. 46:21; Num. 26:38; 1 Chr. 7:12; 8:1.

AHARHEL, son of Harum, 1 Chr. 4:8.

AHASAI, a grandson of Immer, Neh. 11:13.

AHASBAI, father of Eliphelet, 2 Sam. 23:34. See UR, 1 Chr. 11:35.

AHASUERUS. 1. King of Persia, history of. See BOOK OF ESTHER.

2. See ARTAXERXES.

3. Father of Darius, Dan. 9:1.

AHAVA, a river of Babylon, Ezra 8:15, 21,31.

AHAZ. 1. King of Judah, son and successor of Jotham, 2 Kin. 15:38; 16:1; 2 Chr. 27:9; 28:1. Idolatrous abominations of, 2 Kin. 16: 3,4; 2 Chr. 28:2–4,22–25. Kingdom of, invaded by the kings of Syria and Samaria, 2 Kin. 16:5,6; 2 Chr. 28:5–8. Robs the temple to purchase aid from the king of Assyria, 2 Kin. 16:7–9,17,18; 2 Chr. 28:21. Visits Damascus, obtains a novel pattern of an altar, which he substitutes for the altar in the temple in Jerusalem, and otherwise perverts the forms of worship, 2 Kin. 16:10–16. Sundial of, 2 Kin. 20:11; Isa. 38:8. Prophets in the reign of, Isa. 1:1; Hos. 1:1; Mic. 1:1. Prophecies concerning, Isa. 7:13–25. Succeeded by Hezekiah, 2 Kin. 16:20.

2. Son of Micah, 1 Chr. 8:35; 9:41,42.

AHAZIAH. 1. King of Judah. Called AZARIAH and JEHOAHAZ, 2 Chr. 21:17; 25:23. History of, 2 Kin. 8:25–29; 9:16–29. Gifts of, to the temple, 2 Kin. 12:18. Brethren of, slain, 2 Kin. 10:13,14. Succeeded by Athaliah, 2 Chr. 22:10–12.

2. King of Israel. History of, 1 Kin. 22:40, 49,51–53; 2 Chr. 20:35–37; 2 Kin. 1. Succeeded by Jehoram, 2 Kin. 3:1.

AHBAN, son of Abishur, 1 Chr. 2:29.

AHER. See AHARAH.

AHI. 1. Son of Shamer, 1 Chr. 7:34.

2. Son of Abdiel, 1 Chr. 5:15.

AHIA. See AHIMELECH.

AHIAH. 1. Grandson of Phinehas, 1 Sam. 14:3,18.

2. One of Solomon's scribes, 1 Kin. 4:3.

3. A Benjamite, 1 Chr. 8:7.

AHIAM, one of David's heroes, 2 Sam. 23:33. Called also SACAR, 1 Chr. 11:35.

AHIAN, son of Shemidah, 1 Chr. 7:19.

AHIEZER. 1. Captain of the tribe of Dan, Num. 1:12; 2:25,26. Contributes to the tabernacle, Num. 7:66–71.

2. One of David's valiant men, 1 Chr. 12:3.

AHIHUD. 1. A prince of Asher, assists in allotting the land of Canaan among the tribes, Num. 34:27.

2. A son of Bela, 1 Chr. 8:7.

AHIJAH, called also AHIAH. 1. Son of Bela, 1 Chr. 8:7.

2. Son of Jerahmeel, 1 Chr. 2:25.

3. A priest in Shiloh, probably identical with Ahimelech, mentioned in 1 Sam. 22:11. Was priest in Saul's reign, 1 Sam. 14:3,18. Slain, 1 Sam. 22:11–19.

4. One of David's heroes, 1 Chr. 11:36. Called also ELIAM, 2 Sam. 23:34.

5. A Levite who was treasurer in the tabernacle, 1 Chr. 26:20.

6. Son of Shisha, 1 Kin. 4:3.

7. A prophet in Shiloh, 1 Kin. 11:29–39.

8. Father of Baasha, 1 Kin. 15:27,33; 2 Kin. 9:9.

9. An Israelite, who subscribed to the covenant of Nehemiah, Neh. 10:26.

AHIKAM, son of Shaphan, 2 Kin. 22:12–14; 25:22; 2 Chr. 34:20; Jer. 26:24; 39:14; 40:5–16; 41:1–18; 43:6.

AHILUD, father of Baana, 1 Kin. 4:12;

and of Jehoshaphat, 2 Sám.8:16; 20:24; 1 Kin. 4:3; 1 Chr. 18:15.

AHIMAAZ. 1. Father in law of king Saul, 1 Sam. 14:50.

2. Son of Zadok, the high priest. Loyal to David, 2 Sam. 15:36; 17:17–20; 18,19–33; 1 Chr. 6:8,9,53.

3. Solomon's son in law, 1 Kin. 4:15.

AHIMAN. 1. A giant of Hebron, Num. 13:22; Josh. 15:14. 2. A Levite, 1 Chr. 9:17.

AHIMELECH. 1. Called also AHIA. A high priest, during the reign of David. Gives shewbread and the sword of Goliath to David, 1 Sam. 21; Mark 2:26. Slain by command of Saul, 1 Sam. 22:9–22.

2. A Hittite, and friend of David, 1 Sam. 26:6.

AHIMOTH, a Levite, 1 Chr. 6:25.

AHINADAB, son of Iddo, 1 Kin. 4:14.

AHINOAM. 1. Wife of king Saul, 1 Sam. 14:50.

2. Wife of king David, 1 Sam. 25:43; 27:3; 30:5,18; 2 Sam. 3:2.

AHIO. 1. A Levite, who drove the cart bearing the ark, 2 Sam. 6:3,4; 1 Chr. 13:7.

2. A Benjamite, 1 Chr. 8:14.

3. Son of Jehiel, 1 Chr. 8:31; 9:37.

AHIRA, captain of the tribe of Naphtali, Num. 1:15; 2:29; 7:78–83; 10:27.

AHIRAM. See AHARAH.

AHISAMACH, father of Aholiab, Ex. 31:6; 35:34; 38:23.

AHISHAHAR, son of Bilhan,1 Chr. 7:10.

AHISHAR, one of Solomon's household officers, 1 Kin. 4:6.

AHITHOPHEL. One of David's counsellors, 2 Sam. 15:12; 1 Chr. 27:33. Joins Absalom, 2 Sam. 15:31,34; 16:15,20–23; 17:1–23. Probably referred to by David in Psa. 55:12–14. Suicide of, 2 Sam. 17:1–14,23.

AHITUB. 1. High priest, father of Ahiah, 1 Sam. 14:3; 22:9,11,12,20.

2. Father of Zadok, 2 Sam. 8:17; 1 Chr. 18:16.

3. Ruler of the house of God, 1 Chr. 9:11; Neh. 11:11.

4. The Ahitub mentioned in 1 Chr. 6:8,11, 12, is probably identical with the last described above, or else he is confused with Azariah, 2 Chr. 31:10.

AHLAB, a city of Asher, the original inhabitants of which were not expelled, Judg. 1:31.

AHLAI. 1. Daughter of Sheshan, 1 Chr. 2:31,34,35.

2. Father of Zabad, 1 Chr. 11:41.

AHOAH, son of Bela, 1 Chr. 8:4. Called also AHIAH, 1 Chr. 8:7, and IRA, 1 Chr. 7:7.

AHOLAH, name of an imaginary woman, typical of idolatry, Ezek. 23:4,5,36,44.

AHOLIAB, an artificer of the tabernacle, Ex. 31:6; 35:34; 36:1,2; 38:23.

AHOLIBAH, an imaginary character, typical of idolatry, Ezek. 23:4,5,36,44.

AHOLIBAMAH. 1. Wife of Esau, Gen. 36:2,14,25. She is probably identical with Judith, of Gen. 26:34.

2. An Edomitish prince, Gen. 36:41.

AHUMAI, son of Jahath, 1 Chr. 4:2.

AHUZAM, son of Ashur, 1 Chr. 4:6.

AHUZZATH, a friend of Abimelech, Gen. 26:26.

AI. 1. A royal city of the Canaanites. Conquest and destruction of, Josh. 7; 8. Rebuilt, Ezra 2:28. Called also AIJA, Neh. 11: 31; and AIATH, Isa. 10:28. Population of, Josh. 8:25.

2. A city of the Ammonites, Jer. 49:3.

AIAH. See AJAH.

AIATH. See AI.

AIJA. See AI.

AIJALON. See AJALON.

AIJELETH SHAHAR, a musical term which probably indicated the sprightly movement of the music set to Psa. 22. See TITLE.

AIN. 1. A city of Simeon, Josh. 19:7; 15:32; 21:16; 1 Chr. 4:32. Called also ASHAN, 1 Chr. 6:59. Possibly identical with En-Rimmon, Neh. 11:29.

2. A landmark on the northern boundary of Palestine, Num. 34:11.

AJAH, called also AIAH. 1. A Horite, Gen. 36:24; 1 Chr. 1:40.

2. Father of Rizpah, 2 Sam. 3:7; 21:8–11.

AJALON. 1. A city of Dan, Josh. 19:42. Assigned to the Levites, Josh. 21:24; 1 Sam. 14:31; 1 Chr. 6:69. Amorites of, not exterminated, Judg. 1:35.

2. A city of Zebulun, Judg. 12:12.

3. A city of Judah, 2 Chr. 28:18; 11:10.

4. A valley, Josh. 10:12.

AKAN, a Horite, Gen. 36:27. Called also JAAKAN, Deut. 10:6; and JAKAN, 1 Chr. 1:42.

AKKUB. 1. One of the Nethinim, Ezra 2:45.

2. A returned exile, 1 Chr. 9:17; Ezra 2:42; Neh. 7:45; 8:7; 12:25.

3. A son of Elioenai, 1 Chr. 3:24.

AKRABBIM, a chain of hills in the south of Palestine, Num. 34:4; Josh. 15:3; Judg. 1:36.

ALABASTER. A white stone. Vessels made of, Matt. 26:7; Mark 14:3; Luke 7:37.

ALAMETH, son of Becher, 1 Chr. 7:8.

ALAMMELECH, a town of Asher, Josh. 19:26.

ALAMOTH. A musical term, 1 Chr. 15:20. Inscription to Psa. 46. See MUSIC.

ALEMETH. 1. A Levitical city, 1 Chr. 6:60. See ALMON.

2. Son of Jehoadah, 1 Chr. 8:36; or of Jarah, 1 Chr. 9:42.

ALEXANDER. 1. Son of Simon who bore the cross of Jesus, Mark 15:21.

2. A relative of the high priest, present at the defense of Peter and John, Acts 4:6.

3. A Jew of Ephesus, Acts 19:33.

4. A copper-smith, 1 Tim. 1:20; 2 Tim. 4:14.

ALEXANDRIA. A city of Egypt, Acts 6:9. Ships of, Acts 27:6; 28:11. Apollos born in, Acts 18:24.

ALGUM, called also ALMUG, trees of Ophir and Lebanon, 1 Kin. 10:11,12; 2 Chr. 2:8; 9:10,11.

ALIAH. See ALVAH.

ALIAN. See ALVAN.

ALIENS, strangers, heathen. To be treated with justice, Ex. 22:21; 23:9; Lev. 19:33,34; Deut. 1:16; 10:19; 24:14,17; 27:19; Jer. 7:6; 22:3; Ezek. 22:29; Mal. 3:5. Religious privileges of, Ex. 12:48,49; Num. 9:14; 15:14,15. Kindness to Edomites, enjoined, Deut. 23:7. Jews authorized to purchase, as slaves, Lev. 25:44,45; and to take usury from, Deut. 15:3; 23:20; not permitted to make kings of, Deut. 17:15. Forbidden to eat the passover, Ex. 12:45. Partially exempt from Jewish law, Deut. 14:21. Numerous in times of David and Solomon, 2 Sam. 22:45,46; 2. Chr. 2:17; 15:9. Oppressed, Ezek. 22:29. Rights of, Num. 35:15; Josh. 20:9; Ezek. 47:22,23. David's kindness to, 2 Sam. 15:19, 20. Hospitality to, required by Jesus, Matt. 25:35,38,43.

See GLEANING; HEATHEN; HOSPITALITY; INHOSPITABLENESS; PROSELYTE; STRANGERS.

ALLEGORY. Of the trees seeking a king, Judg. 9:8–15. Messiah's kingdom represented under, of the wolf and the lamb dwelling together, Isa. 11:6–8. Wilderness to blossom as the rose, Isa. 35. The two covenants, Gal. 4:24. See PARABLE; SYMBOL.

ALLIANCES. POLITICAL: With idolaters forbidden, Ex. 23:32,33; 34:12–15; Deut. 7:2; Judg. 2:2; 2 Chr. 19:2; 20:37; Isa. 30:2; 31:1; Hos. 4:17; 5:13; 12:1; Ezek. 17:15. Ratification of: By oaths, Gen. 21:23; 26:28–31; Josh. 9:15–20. 1 Sam. 20:16,17; by giving the hand, Lam. 5:6.

See COVENANTS; TREATY.

INSTANCES OF: Between Abraham and Mamre, Eshcol, and Aner, Gen. 14:13. Abraham and Abimelech, Gen. 21:22–32. Isaac and Abimelech, Gen. 26:26–31. Canaanitish nations against Israel, Josh. 9:1,2. Joshua and the Gibeonites, Josh. 9. Moabites, Amalekites, and Ammonites, Judg. 3:12,13. Solomon and Hiram, 1 Kin. 5:12; Amos, 1:9. Asa and Benhadad, 1 Kin. 15:18,19; 2 Chr. 16:3. Jehoshaphat and Ahab, 1 Kin. 22; 2 Chr. 18:1. Jehoshaphat and Ahaziah, 2 Chr. 20:35. Ahaz and Tiglath, 2 Kin. 16:7,8; 2 Chr. 28:16, 21. Rezin and Pekah, 2 Kin. 16:5. Zedekiah and Pharaoh, Jer. 37:1–8; Ezek. 17:15–17.

ALLON. 1. Son of Jedaiah, 1 Chr. 4:37.

2. A city of Naphtali, Josh. 19:33.

ALLON-BACHUTH, place where Rebekah was buried, Gen. 35:8.

ALLOY, OF METALS: Isa. 1:25.

ALMODAD, son of Joktan, Gen. 10:26; 1 Chr. 1:20.

ALMON, Levitical city of Benjamin, Josh. 21:18. Called ALEMETH, 1 Chr. 6:60.

ALMOND, a tree. Fruit of, Gen. 43:11. Aaron's rod of the, Num. 17:8. Bowls of candlestick in the tabernacle fashioned after the nuts of the, Ex. 25:33,34; 37:19,20.

FIGURATIVE USE OF: Eccl. 12:5; Jer. 1:11.

ALMON - DIBLATHAIM. Camping place of Israelites, Num. 33:46,47. Probably identical with Beth-diblathaim, Jer. 48:22. and with Diblath, Ezek. 6:14.

ALMS. Enjoined, Deut. 15:7–11; Matt. 5:42; 19:21; Luke 12:33; 2 Cor. 9:5–7; Gal. 2:10; 1 Tim. 6:18; Heb. 13:16. To be given without ostentation, Matt. 6:1–4; Rom. 12:8; freely, 2 Cor. 9:6,7. Withholding, not of love, 1 John 3:17. Solicited by the unfortunate, John 9:8; Acts 3:2.

See BENEFICENCE; GIFTS; GIVING; LIBERALITY; POOR.

INSTANCES OF GIVING: Zaccheus, Luke 19:8. Dorcas, Acts 9:36. Cornelius, Acts 10:2. The early Christians, Acts 2:44,45; 4:34–37; 6:1–3; 11:29,30; 24:17; Rom. 15:25–28; 1 Cor. 16:1–4; 2 Cor. 8:1–4; 9:1; Heb. 6:10.

ALOES. Used as perfume, Psa. 45:8; Prov. 7:17; Song 4:14; In embalming the dead, John 19:39. Lign-aloes, Num. 24:6.

ALPHA, a title of Christ, Rev. 1:8,11; 21: 6; 22:13. Compare Isa. 41:4; 44:6; 48:12.

ALPHEUS. 1. Father of James, Matt. 10:3; Mark 3:18.

2. Father of Levi, Mark 2:14.

ALTAR. Built by Noah, Gen. 8:20; Abraham, Gen. 12:7,8; 13:18; 22:9; Isaac, Gen. 26:25; Jacob, Gen. 33:20; 35:1–7; Moses, Ex. 17:15; 24:4; Balaam, Num. 23:1,14,29; Joshua, Deut. 27:4–7; Josh. 8:30–32; Reubenites and Gadites, Josh. 22:10,34; Gideon, Judg. 6:26, 27; Samuel, 1 Sam. 7:17; Saul, 1 Sam. 14:35; David, 2 Sam. 24:18,19; Elijah, 1 Kin. 18:31,32.

Mosaic commandments prescribing the construction of, Ex. 20:24–26; Deut. 27:5–7; Josh. 8:30,31. See Ezek. 43:13.

Used in idolatrous worship, Judg. 6:25. 1 Kin. 12:32; 16:32; 18:26; 2 Kin. 16:10; 23:12,15; Isa. 27:9; 65:3; Hos. 8:11; Acts 17:23.

OF BURNT OFFERINGS: called BRAZEN ALTAR, Ex. 39:39; 1 Kin. 8:64; ALTAR OF GOD, Psa. 43:4; ALTAR OF THE LORD, Mal. 2:13.

IN THE TABERNACLE: Pattern of, Ex. 27:1–8. Constructed by Bezaleel, Ex. 38:1–7, with 37:1. Location of, Ex. 40:6,29; Ezek. 8:16; Matt. 23:35. Furniture of, Ex. 27:3–7; 38:3–7; 1 Sam. 2:13,14. Horns of, Ex. 27:2.

How sanctified, Ex. 29:36,37,44; 30:26–28; 40:10; Lev. 8:10,11; Num. 7. See Ezek. 43: 18–27. See BLOOD. Sanctified everything that touched it, Ex. 29:37; 30:29; Matt. 23:18,19. A place of refuge. Ex. 21:14; 1 Kin. 1:50; 2:28.

IN SOLOMON'S TEMPLE: Description of, 2 Chr. 4:1. Renewed by Asa, 2 Chr. 15:8. Removed by Ahaz, and one of idolatrous fashion substituted, 2 Kin. 16:14–17. Cleansed by Hezekiah, 2 Chr. 29:18–24. Repaired by Manasseh, 2 Chr. 33:16. Furniture of, taken to Babylon, 2 Kin. 25:14.

IN SECOND TEMPLE, Ezra 3:1–6.

EZEKIEL'S VISION OF, Ezek. 43:13–27.

See TABERNACLE; TEMPLE.

OF INCENSE: called the GOLDEN ALTAR, Ex. 39:38; Num. 4:11; ALTAR OF SWEET INCENSE, Lev. 4:7; ALTAR BEFORE THE LORD, Lev. 16:18.

Pattern of, Ex. 30:1–5. Constructed, Ex. 37; 25–28. Location of, Ex. 30:6; 40:5,26. A cover made for, of the censers of Korah, Num. 16:36–40. Uses of, Ex. 30:7–10,26,27; 40: 27; Lev. 4:7,18; 8:15; 9:9; 16:12,18. How pre-

pared for carrying, Num. 4:4–15. Carried by the Kohathites, Num. 3:27–31. In Solomon's temple, 1 Kin. 6:19,20; 7:48; 1 Chr. 28:18. Seen in John's vision, Rev. 8:3; 9:13.

AL-TASCHITH. Title of Psa. 57–59; 75. See MUSIC.

ALTRUISM, Disinterested Benevolence. Matt. 20:26. Whosoever will be great among you, let him be your minister; 27. And whosoever will be chief among you, let him be your servant: [Matt. 23:11.] 28. Even as the Son of man came not to be ministered unto, but to minister, and to give his life a ransom for many. Mark 10:43–45; Luke 22:26,27.

Mark 9:35. And he sat down, and called the twelve, and saith unto them, If any man desire to be first, *the same* shall be last of all, and [1] servant of all. 　[1 R. V. minister]

John 13:12. So after he had washed their feet, and had taken his garments, . . . he said unto them, Know ye what I have done to you? 13. Ye call me Master and Lord: and ye say well; for *so* I am. 14. If I then, *your* Lord and Master, have washed your feet; ye also ought to wash one another's feet. 15. For I have given you an example, that ye should do as I have done to you. *vs.* 4–17.

Acts 20:33. I have coveted no man's silver, or gold, or apparel. 34. Yea, ye yourselves know, that these hands have ministered unto my necessities, and to them that were with me. 35. I have shewed you all things, how that so labouring ye ought to support the weak, and to remember the words of the Lord Jesus, how he said, It is more blessed to give than to receive.

Rom. 15:1. We then that are strong ought to bear the infirmities of the weak, and not to please ourselves. 2. Let every one of us please *his* neighbour for *his* good to edification. 3. For even Christ pleased not himself; but, as it is written, The reproaches of them that reproached thee fell on me.

1 Cor. 9:18. What is my reward then? *Verily* that, when I preach the gospel, I may make the gospel of Christ without charge, [1] that I abuse not my power in the gospel. 19. For though I be free from all *men*, yet have I made myself servant unto all, that I might gain the more. 20. And unto the Jews I became as a Jew, that I might gain the Jews; to them that are under the law, as under the law, [not being myself under the law, *is added in R. V.*] that I might gain them that are under the law; 21. To them that are without law, as without law, ([2] being not without law to God, but under [3] the law to Christ,) that I might gain them that are without law. 22. To the weak became I as weak, that I might gain the weak: I am made all things to all *men*, that I might by all means save some.

[R.V. [1] so as not to use to the full my right [2] not being [3] Omitted.]

1 Cor. 10:24. Let no man seek his own, but every man another's [1] *wealth*. 31. Whether therefore ye eat, or drink, or whatsoever ye do, do all to the glory of God. 32. Give

² none offence, neither to the Jews, ³ nor to the ⁴ Gentiles, nor to the church of God : 33. Even as I please all *men* in all *things*, not seeking mine own profit, but the *profit* of many, that they may be saved.

[R. V. ¹ good ² no occasion of stumbling, ɛither ³ or ⁴ Greeks, or]

2 Cor. 4:5. For we preach not ourselves, but Christ Jesus the Lord ; and ourselves your servants for Jesus' sake.

2 Cor. 6:10. As sorrowful, yet alway rejoicing ; as poor, yet making many rich ; as having nothing, and *yet* possessing all things.

2 Cor. 8:9. For ye know the grace of our Lord Jesus Christ, that, though he was rich, yet for your sakes he became poor, that ye through his poverty might be rich.

Gal. 6:10. As we have therefore opportunity, let us ¹ do good unto all *men*, especially unto them who are of the household of faith.   [¹ R. V. work that which is]

Phil. 2:3. *Let* nothing *be done* through strife or vainglory ; but in lowliness of mind let each esteem other better than themselves. 4. Look not every man on his own things, but every man also on the things of others. 5. Let this mind be in you, which was also in Christ Jesus : 6. Who, being in the form of God, thought it not robbery to be equal with God : 7. But ¹ made himself ² of no reputation, and took upon him the form of a servant, ³ and was made in the likeness of men : 8. And being found in fashion as a man, he humbled himself, and became obedient unto death, even the death of the cross.

[R. V. ¹ emptied   ² taking   ³ being]

See ALMS ; BENEFICENCE ; CHARITABLENESS ; DUTY, OF MAN TO MAN : LIBERALITY ; LOVE.

ALUSH, camping place of the Israelites, Num. 33:13.

ALVAH. Duke of Edom, Gen. 36:40. Called ALIAH, 1 Chr. 1:51.

ALVAN. Son of Shobal, Gen. 36:23. Called ALIAN, 1 Chr. 1:40.

AMAD, a town of Asher, Josh. 19:26.

AMAL, son of Helem, 1 Chr. 7:35.

AMALEK. Son of Eliphaz, Gen. 36:12; 1 Chr. 1:36. Probably not the ancestor of the Amalekites mentioned in time of Abraham, Gen. 14:7.

AMALEKITES. A people inhabiting the country S. of Idumea and E. of the Red Sea, Num. 13:29; 14:25; 1 Sam. 15:7; 27:8. Defeated by Chedorlaomer, Gen. 14:7; by Joshua, Ex. 17:8,13; by Gideon, Judg. 7; by Saul, 1 Sam. 14:47,48; 15:1-33; by David, 1 Sam. 27:8,9; 30:1-20; by the Simeonites, 1 Chr. 4:42,43. Defeat the Israelites, Num. 14: 45; Judg. 3:13. Israel commanded to destroy, Deut. 25:17-19; 1 Sam. 28:18. Prophecies against, Ex. 17:14,16; Num. 24:20.

AMAM. A city of Judah, Josh. 15:26. Probably situated within the district assigned afterward to Simeon, Josh. 19:1-9.

AMANA, a mountain mentioned in Song 4:8.

AMANUENSIS, Jer. 36:4; 45:1.

AMARIAH. 1. Two Levites, 1 Chr. 6:7, 52; 23:19 ; 24:23.

2. Chief priest in the reign of Jehoshaphat, 2 Chr. 19:11.

3. A high priest, father of Ahitub, 1 Chr. 6:11; Ezra 7:3.

4. A Levite, who assisted in distributing temple gifts, 2 Chr. 31:15-19.

5. Son of Hizkiah, Zeph. 1:1.

6. Father of Zechariah, Neh. 11:4.

7. A priest, returned from exile, Neh. 10:3; 12:2. Probably identical with one mentioned in Neh. 12:13.

8. A returned exile. Divorces his idolatrous wife, Ezra 10:42.

AMASA. 1. Nephew of David, 2 Sam. 17:25; 1 Chr. 2:17. Joins Absalom, 2 Sam. 17:25. Returns to David, and is made captain of the host, 2 Sam. 19:13. Slain, 2 Sam. 20:8-12; 1 Kin. 2:5,32.

2. Son of Hadlai, 2 Chr. 28:12.

AMASAI. 1. A Levite and ancestor of Samuel, 1 Chr. 6:25,35.

2. Leader of a body of men disaffected toward Saul, who joined David, 1 Chr. 12:18.

3. A priest and trumpeter, 1 Chr. 15:24.

4. A Levite of the Kohathites, 2 Chr. 29:12.

AMASHAI, a chieftain of Judah, Neh. 11:13.

AMASIAH, a chief of the tribe of Judah, 2 Chr. 17:16.

AMAZIAH. 1. A Levite, 1 Chr. 6:45.

2. King of Judah. History of, 2 Kin. 14; 2 Chr. 25.

3. An idolatrous priest at Bethel, Amos 7:10-17.

4. Father of Joshah, 1 Chr. 4:34.

AMBASSADORS. Sent by Moses to Edom, Num. 20:14; to the Amorites, Num. 21:21; by Gibeonites to the Israelites, Josh. 9:4; Israelites to various nations, Judg. 11:12-28; Hiram to David, 2 Sam. 5:11; and Solomon, 1 Kin. 5:1; Benhadad to Ahab, 1 Kin. 20:2-6; Amaziah to Jehoash, 2 Kin. 14: 8; Ahaz to Tiglath, 2 Kin. 16:7; Hoshea to So, 2 Kin. 17:4; Sennacherib through Rabshakeh to Hezekiah, 2 Kin. 19:9; Berodach to Hezekiah, 2 Kin, 20:12; 2 Chr. 32:31; Zedekiah to Egypt, Ezek. 17:15.

Other references to, Prov. 13:17; Isa. 18:2; 30:4 ; 33:7; 36:11; 39:1,2; Luke 14:32.

FIGURATIVE : Job 33:23; Obad. 1; 2 Cor. 5:20; Eph. 6:20.

AMBER, a vegetable fossil, Ezek. 1:4, 27; 8:2.

AMBITION. Falsely charged against Moses, Num. 16:13. Parable of the thistle, illustrating, 2 Kin. 14:9.

UNCLASSIFIED SCRIPTURES RELATING TO: Job 20:6. Though his excellency mount up to the heavens, and his head reach unto the clouds ; 7. *Yet* he shall perish for ever like his own dung : they which have seen him shall say, Where *is* he ?

Psa. 49:11. Their inward thought *is, that* their houses *shall continue* for ever, *and* their dwellingplaces to all generations ; they call *their* lands after their own names. 12. Nevertheless man *being* in honour abideth not ; he is like the beasts *that* perish.

13. This their way *is* their folly: yet their posterity approve their sayings.

Isa. 5:8. Woe unto them that join house to house, *that* lay field to field, till *there be* no place, that they may be placed alone in the midst of the earth!

Hab. 2:5. Yea ¹also, because he transgresseth by wine, *he is* a proud man, neither keepeth at home, who enlargeth his desire as hell, and *is* as death, and cannot be satisfied, but gathereth unto him all nations, and heapeth unto him all people: 6. Shall not all these take up a parable against him, and a taunting proverb against him, and say, Woe to him that increaseth *that which is* not his! how long? and to him that ladeth himself with ²thick clay!

[R. V. ¹ moreover, wine is a treacherous dealer, a haughty ² pledges]

9. Woe to him that ¹coveteth an evil ²covetousness to his house, that he may set his nest on high, that he may be delivered from the power of evil!   [R. V. ¹ getteth   ² gain for]

Matt. 4:8. Again the devil taketh him up into an exceeding high mountain, and sheweth him all the kingdoms of the world, and the glory of them; 9. And saith unto him, All these things will I give thee, if thou wilt fall down and worship me. 10. Then saith Jesus unto him, Get thee hence, Satan: for it is written, Thou shalt worship the Lord thy God, and him only shalt thou serve. Luke 4:5–8.

Matt. 16:26. For what is a man profited, if he shall gain the whole world, and lose his own soul? or what shall a man give in exchange for his soul? Luke 9:25.

Matt. 23:5. But all their works they do for to be seen of men: they make broad their phylacteries, and enlarge the borders of their garments. 6. And love the uppermost rooms at feasts, and the chief seats in the synagogues. [Mark 12:38,39; Luke 11:43.] 7. And greetings in the markets, and to be called of men, Rabbi, Rabbi. 12. And whosoever shall exalt himself shall be abased; and he that shall humble himself shall be exalted.

Mark 9:33. And he came to Capernaum: and being in the house he asked them, What was it that ye disputed among yourselves by the way? [Luke 22:24.] 34. But they held their peace: for by the way they had disputed among themselves, who *should be* the greatest. 35. And he sat down, and called the twelve, and said unto them, If any man desire to be first, *the same* shall be last of all, and servant of all. 36. And he took a child, and set him in the midst of them: and when he had taken him in his arms, he said unto them, 37. Whosoever shall receive one of such children in my name, receiveth me; and whosoever shall receive me, receiveth not me, but him that sent me. Matt. 18:1; Luke 9:46.

Mark 10:35. And James and John, the sons of Zebedee, come unto him, saying, Master, we would that thou shouldest do for us whatsoever we shall desire. [Matt. 20:20.] 36. And he said unto them, What would ye that I should do for you? 37. They said

unto him, Grant unto us that we may sit, one on thy right hand, and the other on thy left hand, in thy glory. 38. But Jesus said unto them, Ye know not what ye ask: can ye drink of the cup that I drink of? and be baptized with the baptism that I am baptized with? 39. And they said unto him, We can. And Jesus said unto them, Ye shall indeed drink of the cup that I drink of; and with the baptism that I am baptized withal shall ye be baptized: 40. But to sit on my right hand and on my left hand is not mine to give; but *it shall be given to them* for whom it is prepared. 41. And when the ten heard *it*, they began to be much displeased with James and John. 42. But Jesus called them *to him*, and saith unto them, Ye know that they which are accounted to rule over the Gentiles exercise lordship over them; and their great ones exercise authority upon them. 43. But so shall it not be among you: but whosoever will be great among you, shall be your minister: 44. And whosoever of you will be chiefest, shall be servant of all. [Luke 22:26.] 45. For even the Son of man came not to be ministered unto, but to minister, and to give his life a ransom for many.

John 5:44. How can ye believe, which receive honour one of another, and seek not the honour that *cometh* from God only?

1 Tim. 3:1. This *is* a true saying, If a man desire the office of a bishop, he desireth a good work.

Jas. 4:1. From whence *come* wars and fightings among you? *come they* not hence, *even* of your lusts that war in your members? 2. Ye lust, and have not: ye kill, and desire to have, and cannot obtain: ye fight and war, yet ye have not, because ye ask not.

1 John 2:16. For all that *is* in the world, the lust of the flesh, and the lust of the eyes, and the pride of life, is not of the Father, but is of the world.

See PRIDE.

INSTANCES OF: Lucifer, Isa. 14:12–15. Eve, Gen. 3:5,6. The builders of Babel, Gen. 11:4. Aaron and Miriam, Num. 12:2–10. Korah and his co-conspirators, Num. 16:3–35. Abimelech, Judg. 9:1–6. Absalom, 2 Sam. 15:1–13; 18:18. Ahithophel, 2 Sam. 17:23. Adonijah, 1 Kin. 1:5. Sennacherib, 2 Kin. 19:23. Haman, Esth. 5:9–13; 6:6–9. Diotrephes, 3 John 9, 10.

AMBUSH. INSTANCES OF: At Ai, Josh. 8:2–22; Shechem, Judg. 9:25,34; Gibeah, Judg. 20:29–41. Near Zemaraim, 2 Chr. 13:13. By Jehoshaphat, 2 Chr. 20:22. See ARMIES.

FIGURATIVE: Jer. 51:12.

AMEN. A word used to reenforce a statement, Num. 5:22; Deut. 27:12–26; Neh. 5:13; 2 Cor. 1:20; Rev. 1:18; 22:20. Used in prayer, 1 Kin. 1:36; 1 Chr. 16:36; Neh. 8:6; Psa. 41:13; 72:19; 89:52; 106:48; Jer. 28:6; Matt. 6:13; 1 Cor. 14:16; Rev. 5:14; 19:4. A title of Christ, Rev. 3:14.

AMETHYST, a precious stone, Ex. 28:19; 39:12; Rev. 21:20.

AMI. See AMON, 3.

AMINADAB. See AMMINADAB.

AMITTAI, father of Jonah, 2 Kin. 14:25; Jonah 1:1.

AMMAH, a mountain, 2 Sam. 2:24.

AMMI, a figurative name given to Israel, Hos. 2:1.

AMMIEL. 1. One of the twelve spies, Num. 13:12.

2. Father of Machir, 2 Sam. 9:4,5; 17:27.

3. Father of Bath-sheba, 1 Chr. 3:5. Called also ELIAM, 2 Sam. 11:3.

4. Son of Obed-edom, 1 Chr. 26:5.

AMMIHUD. 1. Son of Laadan, 1 Chr. 7:26, and father of Elishama, Num. 1:10; 2:18.

2. Father of Shemuel, Num. 34:20.

3. Father of Pedahel, Num. 34:28.

4. Father of the king of Gesher, 2 Sam. 13:37.

5. Son of Omri, 1 Chr. 9:4.

AMMIHUR. See AMMIHUD.

AMMINADAB. 1. Father in law of Aaron, Ex. 6:23. Father of Nashon, Num. 1:7; 2:3. Lineage of, Ruth 4:18-20; 1 Chr. 2:10; Matt. 1:4; Luke 3:33.

2. A son of Kohath, 1 Chr. 6:22.

3. A son of Uzziel, 1 Chr. 15:10,11.

AMMINADIB. See AMMINADAB.

AMMISHADDAI, father of Ahiezer, Num. 1:12.

AMMIZABAD, son of Benaiah, 1 Chr. 27:6.

AMMON. See BEN-AMMI.

AMMONITES. Descendants of Ben-ammi, one of the sons of Lot, Gen. 19:38. Character of, Judg. 10:6; 2 Kin. 23:13; 2 Chr. 20:25; Jer. 27:3,9; Ezek. 25:3,6; Amos 1:13; Zeph. 2:10. Territory of, Num. 21:24; Deut. 2:19; Josh. 12:2; 13:10,25; Judg. 11:13.

Israelites forbidden to disturb, Deut. 2: 19,37. Excluded from the congregation of Israel, Deut. 23:3-6. Confederate with Moabites and Amalekites against Israel, Judg. 3:12,13. Defeated by the Israelites, Judg. 10:7-18; 11:32,33; 12:1-3; 1 Sam. 11; 2 Sam. 8:12; 10; 11:1; 12:26-31; 17:27; 1 Chr. 18:11; 20:1-3; 2 Chr. 20; 26:7,8; 27:5. Conspire against the Jews, Neh. 4:7,8.

Solomon takes wives from, 1 Kin. 11:1; 2 Chr. 12:13; Neh. 13:26. Jews intermarry with, Ezra 9:12; 10:10-44; Neh. 13:23.

Kings of: Baalis, Jer. 40:14; 41:10; Hanun, 2 Sam. 10; 1 Chr. 19; Nahash, 1 Sam. 11; 2 Sam. 10:1,2; 1 Chr. 19:1,2.

Idols of: Milcom, 2 Kin. 23:13; Molech. See MOLECH. Prophecies concerning, Isa. 11:14; Jer. 9:25,26; 25:15-21; 27:1-11; 49:1-6; Ezek. 21:20,28-32; 25:1-11; Dan. 11:41; Amos 1:13-15; Zeph. 2:8-11.

AMNESTY. For political offenses: To Shimei, 2 Sam. 19:16-23; to Amasa, 2 Sam. 19:13, with 17:25.

AMNON. 1. Son of David, 2 Sam. 3:2; Chr. 3:1. Incest of, and death, 2 Sam. 13.

2. Son of Shimon, 1 Chr. 4:20.

AMOK, a priest, Neh. 12:7,20.

AMON. 1. Governor of the city of Samaria, 1 Kin. 22:26; 2 Chr. 18:25.

2. King of Judah, 2 Kin. 21:18-26; 2 Chr. 33:21-25; Zeph. 1:1; Matt. 1:10.

3. Ancestor of one of the families of the Nethinim, Neh. 7:59. Called AMI, Ezra 2:57.

AMORITES. Descendants of Canaan, Gen. 10:15,16; 1 Chr. 1:13,14. Were giants, Amos 2:9. Smitten by Chedorlaomer and rescued by Abraham, Gen. 14.

Territory of, Gen. 14:7; Num. 13:29; 21:13. Deut. 1:4,7,19; 3:8,9; Josh. 5:1; 10:5; 12:2,3; Judg. 1:35,36; 11:22; given to descendants of Abraham, Gen. 15:21; 48:22; Deut. 1:20; 2:26-36; 7:1; Josh. 3:10; Judg. 11:23; Amos 2: 10; allotted to Reuben, Gad, and Manasseh, Num. 32:33-42; Josh. 13:15-21; conquest of, Num. 21:21-30; Josh. 10:11; Judg. 1:34-36.

Chiefs of, Josh. 13:21. Wickedness of, Gen. 15:16; 2 Kin. 21:11; Ezra 9:1. Idolatry of, Judg. 6:10; 1 Kin. 21:26. Judgments denounced against, Ex. 23:24; 33:2; 34:10,11; Deut. 20:17,18. Hornets sent among, Josh. 24:12. Not exterminated, Judg. 1:34-36; 3:1-3,5-8; 1 Sam. 7:14; 2 Sam. 21:2; 1 Kin. 9:20,21; 2 Chr. 8:7. Intermarry with Jews, Ezra 9:1,2; 10:18-44. Kings of, Josh. 10:3-26.

AMOS. A prophet, Amos 1:1. Forbidden to prophesy in Israel, Amos 7:10-17. Vision of, Amos 8:2.

AMOZ, father of Isaiah, 2 Kin. 19:2,20; 20:1; Isa. 1:1; 13:1.

AMPHIPOLIS, a city of Macedonia, Acts 17:1.

AMPLIAS, a disciple, Paul sends greeting to, Rom. 16:8.

AMRAM. 1. Father of Moses, Ex. 6:18, 20; Num. 26:58,59; 1 Chr. 6:3,18; 23:12,13. Head of one of the branches of Levites, Num. 3:19,27; 1 Chr. 26:23. Age of, at death, Ex. 6:20.

2. Son of Bani, Ezra 10:34.

3. Son of Dishon, 1 Chr. 1:41.

AMRAPHEL, king of Shinar, Gen. 14:1,9.

AMUSEMENTS AND WORLDLY PLEASURES. Belong to the works of the flesh, Gal. 5:19,21; are transitory, Job 21: 12,13; Heb. 11:25; vain, Eccl. 2:11; choke the word of God in the heart, Luke 8:14; formed a part of idolatrous worship, Ex. 32:4,6,19, with 1 Cor. 10:7; Judg. 16:23-25.

Lead to rejection of God, Job. 21:12-15; poverty, Prov. 21:17; disregard of the judgments and works of God, Isa. 5:12; Amos 6:1-6; terminate in sorrow, Prov. 14:13; lead to greater evil, Job 1:5; Matt. 14:6-8; the wicked seek for happiness in, Eccl. 2:1.8.

Indulgence in, a proof of folly, Eccl. 7:4; a characteristic of the wicked, Isa. 47:8; Eph. 4:17,19; 2 Tim. 3:4; Tit. 3:3; 1 Pet. 4:3; a proof of spiritual death, 1 Tim. 5:6; an abuse of riches, Jas. 5:1,5; wisdom of abstaining from, Eccl. 7:2,3, shunned by the primitive saints, 1 Pet. 4:3.

Abstinence from, seems strange to the wicked, 1 Pet. 4:4; denounced by God, Isa.

5:11,12; exclude from the kingdom of God, Gal. 5:21; punishment of, Eccl. 11:9; 2 Pet. 2:13; renunciation of, exemplified by Moses, Heb. 11:25.—*Bible Text Book.*

See DANCING; GAMES; PLEASURE, WORLD-LY; WORLDLINESS.

AMZI. 1. A Levite, 1 Chr. 6:46.

2. A priest, Neh. 11:12.

ANAB, a city of Canaan, Josh. 11:21; 15:50.

ANAH. 1. Son of Seir, Gen. 36:20,24, 29; 1 Chr. 1:38.

2. Father in law or mother in law of Esau. An error of copyist, probably, calls him daughter, instead of son, of Zibeon, the Hivite, Gen. 36:2,14,24. Called also BEERI, Gen. 26:34.

ANAHARATH, city on the border of Issachar, Josh. 19:19.

ANAIAH, a priest, probably, who stood by Ezra while reading the law, Neh. 8:4; 10:22.

ANAK, father of three giants, Josh. 15: 13,14; 21:11.

ANAKIM. A race of giants, Num. 13:28-33; Deut. 1:28; 2:10; 9:2. Defeated: By Joshua, Josh. 11:21,22; Caleb, Josh. 14:12,15; 15:13,14; Judg. 1:20. See HEBRON.

ANAMMELECH, an Assyrian idol, 2 Kin. 17:31.

ANAMIM, a tribe descended from Mizraim, Gen. 10:13; 1 Chr. 1:11.

ANAN, a Jew, returned from Babylonian captivity, Neh. 10:26.

ANANI, a descendant of David, 1 Chr. 3:24.

ANANIAH. 1. Son of Maaseiah, Neh. 3:23; 8:4.

2. Town of Benjamin, Neh. 11:32.

ANANIAS. 1. High priest, before whom Paul was tried, Acts 23:2–5; 24:1; 25:2.

2. A covetous member of church at Jerusalem. Falsehood and death of, Acts 5:1-11.

3. A Christian in Damascus, Acts 9:10–18; 22:12–16.

ANARCHY. Isa. 3:5. And the people shall be oppressed, every one by another, and every one by his neighbour: the child shall behave himself proudly against the ancient, and the base against the honourable. 6. When a man shall take hold of his brother of the house of his father, *saying,* Thou hast clothing, be thou our ruler, and *let* this ruin *be* under thy hand: 7. In that day shall he swear, saying, I will not be a healer; for in my house *is* neither bread nor clothing: make me not a ruler of the people. 8. For Jerusalem is ruined, and Judah is fallen: because their tongue and their doings *are* against the LORD, to provoke the eyes of his glory.

Gal. 5:13. For, brethren, ye have been called unto liberty; only *use* not liberty for an occasion to the flesh, but by love serve one another. 14. For all the law is fulfilled in one word, *even* in this; Thou shalt love thy neighbour as thyself.

2 Pet. 2:10. But chiefly them that walk after the flesh in the lust of uncleanness, and despise government. Presumptuous *are* they, selfwilled, they are not afraid to speak evil of dignities. 11. Whereas angels, which are greater in power and might, bring not railing accusation against them before the Lord. 12. But these as natural brute beasts, made to be taken and destroyed, speak evil of the things that they understand not; and shall utterly perish in their own corruption; 13. And shall receive the reward of unrighteousness, *as* they that count it pleasure to riot in the daytime. Spots *they are* and blemishes, sporting themselves with their own deceivings while they feast with you; 14. Having eyes full of adultery, and that cannot cease from sin; beguiling unstable souls: an heart they have exercised with covetous practices; cursed children: 15. Which have forsaken the right way, and are gone astray, following the way of Balaam *the son* of Bosor, who loved the wages of unrighteousness; 16. But was rebuked for his iniquity: the dumb ass speaking with man's voice forbad the madness of the prophet. 17. These are wells without water, clouds that are carried with a tempest; to whom the mist of darkness is reserved for ever. 18. For when they speak great swelling *words* of vanity, they allure through the lusts of the flesh, *through much* wantonness, those that were clean escaped from them who live in error. 19. While they promise them liberty, they themselves are the servants of corruption: for of whom a man is overcome, of the same is he brought in bondage.

Jude 8. Likewise also these *filthy* dreamers defile the flesh, despise dominion, and speak evil of dignities. 9. Yet Michael the archangel, when contending with the devil he disputed about the body of Moses, durst not bring against him a railing accusation, but said, The Lord rebuke thee. 10. But these speak evil of those things which they know not: but what they know naturally, as brute beasts, in those things they corrupt themselves. 11. Woe unto them! for they have gone in the way of Cain, and ran greedily after the error of Balaam for reward, and perished in the gainsaying of Core. 12. These are spots in your feasts of charity, when they feast with you, feeding themselves without fear: clouds *they are* without water, carried about of winds; trees whose fruit withereth, without fruit, twice dead, plucked up by the roots; 13. Raging waves of the sea, foaming out their own shame; wandering stars, to whom is reserved the blackness of darkness for ever.

ANATH, father of Shamgar, Judg. 3:31.

ANATHEMA MARAN-ATHA, 1 Cor. 16:22. See CURSE.

ANATHOTH. 1. A Levitical city in Benjamin, Josh. 21:18; 1 Chr. 6:60. Abiathar confined in, 1 Kin. 2:26. Birthplace of Jeremiah, Jer. 1:1; 32:7-12; of Abiezer, 2 Sam. 23:27; of Jehu, 1 Chr. 12:3. Prophecies against, Jer. 11:21-23. Inhabitants of, after Babylonian captivity, Ezra 2:23; Neh. 7:27.

2. Son of Becher, 1 Chr. 7:8.

3. A Jew, who returned from Babylon, Neh. 10:19.

ANATOMY, human, Job 10:11.

ANCHOR, Acts 27:29,30. FIGURATIVE: Heb. 6:19.

ANCIENT OF DAYS, an appellation of Jehovah, Dan. 7:9,13,22.

ANDREW. An apostle. A fisherman, Matt. 4:18. Of Bethsaida, John 1:44. A disciple of John, John 1:40. Finds Peter, his brother, and brings him to Jesus, John 1:40-42. Call of, Matt. 4:18; Mark 1:16. His name appears in the list of the apostles in Matt. 10:2; Mark 3:18; Luke 6:14. Asks the Master privately about the destruction of the temple, Mark 13:3,4. Tells Jesus of the Greeks who sought to see him, John 12:20-22. Reports the number of loaves at the feeding of the five thousand, John 6:8. Meets with the disciples after the Lord's ascension, Acts 1:13.

ANDRONICUS, kinsman of Paul, Rom. 16:7.

ANEM, a Levitical city, 1 Chr. 6:73.

ANER. 1. A Canaanitish chief, Gen. 14:13,24.

2. A Levitical city of Manasseh, 1 Chr. 6:70.

ANGEL. ONE OF THE HOLY TRINITY: Trinitarian authorities interpret the Scriptures cited under this topic as referring to Christ, who according to this view was the divine presence in the wilderness. Called ANGEL, Acts 7:30,35; MINE ANGEL, Ex. 32:34; ANGEL OF GOD, Ex. 14:19; Judg. 13:6; 2 Sam. 14:17,20; ANGEL OF THE LORD, Ex. 3:2; Judg. 2:1; ANGEL OF HIS PRESENCE, Isa. 63:9.

ANGEL. A CELESTIAL SPIRIT: Called ANGEL OF THE LORD, Matt. 1:20,24; 2:13,19; 28:2; Luke 1:11; Acts 5:19; 8:26; 12:7,23; MORNING STARS, Job 38:7; HOSTS, Gen. 2:1; 32:2; Josh. 5:14; 1 Chr. 12:22; Psa. 33:6; 103:21; Luke 2:13; PRINCIPALITIES, POWERS, Eph. 3:10; Col. 1:16. Created, Gen. 2:1; Neh. 9:6; Col. 1:16. Of different orders, Isa. 6:2; 1 Thes. 4:16; 1 Pet. 3:22; Jude 9; Rev. 12:7. Immortal, Luke 20:36. Worship God, Neh. 9:6; Phil. 2:9-11; Heb. 1:6. Not to be worshipped, Col. 2:18; Rev. 19:10; 22:8,9. Do not marry, Matt. 22:30; Mark 12:25; Luke 20:35. Are obedient, Psa. 103:20; Matt. 6:10; Luke 11:2; 1 Pet. 3:22; 2 Pet. 2:11; Jude 6. Have knowledge of, and interest in, earthly affairs, Matt. 24:36; Luke 15:7,10; 1 Tim. 5:21; 1 Pet. 1:12. To be judged by men, 1 Cor. 6:3. See FUNCTIONS OF, below.

Men called angels, 2 Sam. 19:27. Are examples of meekness, 2 Pet. 2:11; Jude 9. Are wise, 2 Sam. 14:17,20; mighty, Psa. 103:20; 2 Pet. 2:11; holy, Matt. 25:31; Mark 8:38; elect, 1 Tim. 5:21; innumerable, Deut. 33:2; 2 Kin. 6:17; Job 25:3; Psa. 68:17 [R. V. omits angels in v. 17]; Heb. 12:22; Jude 14.

Aspects of, Judg. 13:6; Isa. 6:2; Dan. 10:6; Matt. 28:3. See UNCLASSIFIED SCRIPTURES RELATING TO, below.

FUNCTIONS OF: Guard the way to the tree of life, Gen. 3:24. Law given by, Acts 7:53; Gal. 3:19; Heb. 2:2. Medium of revelation to prophets, 2 Kin. 1:15; Dan. 4:13-17; 8:19; 9:21-27; 10:10-20; Zech. 1:9-11; Acts 8:26; Gal. 3:19; Heb. 2:2; Rev. 1:1; 5:2-14; 7:1-3, 11-17; 8:2-13; chapters 9 to 20; 22:6,16.

Remonstrates with Balaam, Num. 22:22-27. Announces the birth of Samson, Judg. 13; of John the Baptist, Luke 1:11-20; of Jesus, Matt. 1:20,21; Luke 1:28-38; 2:7-15. Warns Joseph to escape to Egypt, Matt. 2:13. Minister to Jesus after the temptation, Matt. 4:11; Mark 1:13; John 1:51; during his passion, Luke 22:43. Present at the tomb of Jesus, Matt. 28:2-6; the ascension, Acts 1:11. Will be with Christ at his second coming, Matt. 25:31; Mark 8:38; 2 Thess. 1:7; Jude 14,15; at the judgment, Matt. 13:39,41,49; 16:27; 24:31; 25:31; Mark 13:27.

MINISTRANT TO THE RIGHTEOUS: Gen. 16:7. And the angel of the LORD found her by a fountain of water in the wilderness, by the fountain in the way to Shur.

Gen. 24:7. He shall send his angel before thee. [Ex. 32:34; 33:2.] 40. The LORD, before whom I walk, will send his angel with thee, and prosper thy way;

Ex. 23:20. Behold, I send an Angel before thee, to keep thee in the way, and to bring thee into the place which I have prepared. 23. For mine Angel shall go before thee, and bring thee in unto the Amorites, and the Hittites, and the Perizzites, and the Canaanites, the Hivites, and the Jebusites; and I will cut them off. Ex. 33:2.

Num. 20:16. And when we cried unto the LORD, he heard our voice, and sent an angel, and hath brought us forth out of Egypt:

1 Kin. 19:5. And as he lay and slept under a juniper tree, behold, then an angel touched him, and said unto him, Arise *and* eat. 6. And he looked, and, behold, *there was* a cake baken on the coals, and a cruse of water at his head. And he did eat and drink, and laid him down again. 7. And the angel of the LORD came again the second time, and touched him, and said, Arise *and* eat; because the journey *is* too great for thee. 8. And he arose, and did eat and drink, and went in the strength of that meat forty days and forty nights unto Horeb the mount of God.

2 Chr. 18:18. Therefore hear the word of the LORD; I saw the LORD sitting upon his throne, and all the host of heaven standing on his right hand and *on* his left.

Psa. 34:7. The angel of the LORD encampeth round about them that fear him, and delivereth them.

Psa. 68:17. The chariots of God *are* twenty thousand, *even* thousands ¹ of angels: 2 Kin. 6:17. [¹ R. V. upon thousands]

Psa. 91:11. For he shall give his angels charge over thee, to keep thee in all thy ways. 12. They shall bear thee up in *their* hands, lest thou dash thy foot against a stone. Matt. 4:6; Luke 4:10,11.

Psa. 104:4. Who maketh [1] his angels spirits; his ministers a flaming fire. [1 R.V. winds his messengers]

Eccl. 5:6. Suffer not thy mouth to cause thy flesh to sin; neither say thou before the angel, that it *was* an error:

Isa. 63:9. In all their affliction he was afflicted, and the angel of his presence saved them:

Dan. 6:22. My God hath sent his angel, and hath shut the lions' mouths, that they have not hurt me: forasmuch as before him innocency was found in me; and also before thee, O king, have I done no hurt.

Dan. 7:10. A fiery stream issued and came forth from before him: thousand thousands ministered unto him, and ten thousand times ten thousand stood before him: the judgment was set, and the books were opened.

Luke 16:22. The beggar died, and was carried by the angels into Abraham's bosom.

John 1:51. Ye shall see heaven open, and the angels of God ascending and descending upon the Son of man.

John 5:4. For an angel went down at a certain season into the pool, and troubled the water. [This passage is omitted in *R. V.*]

Acts 5:19. But the angel of the Lord by night opened the prison doors, and brought them forth, and said, 20. Go, stand and speak in the temple to the people all the words of this life.

Acts 10:3. He saw in a vision evidently about the ninth hour of the day an angel of God coming in to him, and saying unto him, Cornelius. 4. And when he looked on him, he was afraid, and said, What is it, Lord? And he said unto him, Thy prayers and thine alms are come up for a memorial before God. 5. And now send men to Joppa, and call for *one* Simon, whose surname is Peter: 6. He lodgeth with one Simon a tanner, whose house is by the sea side: [1] he shall tell thee what thou oughtest to do.   [1 Omitted in R. V.]

Acts 12:7. And, behold, the angel of the Lord came upon *him*, and a light shined in the prison: and he smote Peter on the side, and raised him up, saying, Arise up quickly. And his chains fell off *his* hands. 8. And the angel said unto him, Gird thyself, and bind on thy sandals. And so he did. And he saith unto him, Cast thy garment about thee and follow me. 9. And he went out, and followed him; and wist not that it was true which was done by the angel; but thought he saw a vision. 10. When they were past the first and the second ward, they came unto the iron gate that leadeth unto the city; which opened to them of his own accord: and they went out, and passed on through one street; and forthwith the angel departed from him.

Heb. 1:7. And of the angels he saith, Who maketh his angels spirits, and his ministers a flame of fire. 14. Are they not all ministering spirits, sent forth to minister for them who shall be heirs of salvation?

Heb. 13:2. Be not forgetful to entertain strangers: for thereby some have entertained angels unawares.

Execute Judgments Upon the Wicked: Gen. 19:1. And there came two angels to Sodom at even; and Lot sat in the gate of Sodom: and Lot seeing *them* rose up to meet them; and he bowed himself with his face toward the ground; 13. We will destroy this place, because the cry of them is waxen great before the face of the Lord; and the Lord hath sent us to destroy it. *vs.* 1-25.

2 Sam. 24:16. And when the angel stretched out his hand upon Jerusalem to destroy it, the Lord repented him of the evil, and said to the angel that destroyed the people, It is enough: stay now thine hand. And the angel of the Lord was by the threshingplace of Araunah the Jebusite. 17. And David spake unto the Lord when he saw the angel that smote the people, and said, Lo, I have sinned, and I have done wickedly: 1 Chr. 21:15, 16.

2 Kin. 19:35. And it came to pass that night, that the angel of the Lord went out, and smote in the camp of the Assyrians an hundred fourscore and five thousand: and when they arose early in the morning, behold, they *were* all dead corpses.

2 Chr. 32:21. And the Lord sent an angel, which cut off all the mighty men of valour, and the leaders and captains in the camp of the king of Assyria. Isa. 37:36.

Psa. 35:5. Let them be as chaff before the wind: and let the angel of the Lord chase *them*. 6. Let their way be dark and slippery: and let the angel of the Lord persecute them.

Psa. 78:49. He cast upon them the fierceness of his anger, wrath, and indignation, and trouble, by sending evil angels *among them*.

Matt. 13:41. The Son of man shall send forth his angels, and they shall gather out of his kingdom all things that offend, and them which do iniquity; 42. And shall cast them into a furnace of fire: there shall be wailing and gnashing of teeth. *vs.* 49, 50.

Acts 12:23. And immediately the angel of the Lord smote him, because he gave not God the glory: and he was eaten of worms, and gave up the ghost.

Acts 27:23. For there stood by me this night the angel of God, whose I am, and whom I serve, 24. Saying, Fear not, Paul; thou must be brought before Cæsar: and, lo, God hath given thee all them that sail with thee.

Jude 14. And Enoch also, the seventh from Adam, prophesied of these, saying, Behold, the Lord cometh with ten thousands of his saints, 15. To execute judgment upon all, and to convince all that are ungodly among them of all their ungodly deeds which they have ungodly committed, and of all their hard *speeches* which ungodly sinners have spoken against him.

Rev. 7:1. And after these things I saw four angels standing on the four corners of the earth, holding the four winds of the earth, that the wind should not blow on the earth, nor on the sea, nor on any tree.   2. And I saw another angel ascending from the east, having the seal of the living God: and he cried with a loud voice to the four angels, to whom it was given to hurt the earth and the sea,

Rev. 9:15. And the four angels were loosed, which were prepared for an hour, and a day, and a month, and a year, for to slay the third part of men.

Rev. 15:1. And I saw another sign in heaven, great and marvellous, seven angels having the seven last plagues; for in them is filled up the wrath of God.

UNCLASSIFIED SCRIPTURES RELATING TO :

Num. 22:35. And the angel of the LORD said unto Balaam, Go with the men: but only the word that I shall speak unto thee, that thou shalt speak.

Deut. 33:2. And he said, The LORD came from Sinai, and rose up from Seir unto them; he shined forth from mount Paran, and he came with ten thousands of saints: from his right hand *went* a fiery law for them.

Job 4:15. Then a spirit passed before my face; the hair of my flesh stood up: 16. It stood still, but I could not discern the form thereof: an image *was* before mine eyes, *there was* silence, and I heard a voice, *saying*, 17. Shall mortal man be more just than God? shall a man be more pure than his maker? 18. Behold, he put no trust in his servants; and his angels he charged with folly: 19. How much less *in* them that dwell in houses of clay, whose foundation *is* in the dust, *which* are crushed before the moth?

Job 38:7. When the morning stars sang together, and all the sons of God shouted for joy?

Psa. 68:17. The chariots of God *are* twenty thousand, *even* thousands ¹ of angels: the Lord *is* among them, *as* in Sinai, in the holy *place*. 2 Kin. 6:17.   [¹ R. V. upon thousands]

Psa. 103:20. Bless the LORD, ye his angels, that excel in strength, that do his commandments, hearkening unto the voice of his word.   21. Bless ye the LORD, all *ye* his hosts; *ye* ministers of his, that do his pleasure.

Psa. 104:4. Who maketh his angels spirits; his ministers a flaming fire: Heb. 1:7.

Psa. 148:2. Praise ye him, all his angels: praise ye him, all his hosts.

Isa. 6:2. Above it stood the seraphims: each one had six wings; with twain he covered his face, and with twain he covered his feet, and with twain he did fly.   5. Then said I, Woe *is* me! for I am undone; because I *am* a man of unclean lips, and I dwell in the midst of a people of unclean lips: for mine eyes have seen the King, the LORD of hosts.   6. Then flew one of the seraphim unto me, having a live coal in his hand, *which* he had taken with the tongs from off

the altar: 7. And he laid *it* upon my mouth, and said, Lo, this hath touched thy lips; and thine iniquity is taken away, and thy sin purged.

Ezek. 1:13. As for the likeness of the living creatures, their appearance *was* like burning coals of fire, *and* like the appearance of lamps: it went up and down among the living creatures; and the fire was bright, and out of the fire went forth lightning.   14. And the living creatures ran and returned as the appearance of a flash of lightning.   24. Like the noise of great waters, as the voice of the Almighty, the voice of speech, as the noise of an host: when they stood, they let down their wings. *vs.* 4–25; Ezek. 10.

Dan. 4:13. I saw in the visions of my head upon my bed, and, behold, a watcher and an holy one came down from heaven; 17. This matter *is* by the decree of the watchers, and the demand by the word of the holy ones:

Dan. 8:13. Then I heard one saint speaking, and another saint said unto that certain *saint* which spake, How long *shall be* the vision *concerning* the daily *sacrifice*, and the transgression of desolation, to give both the sanctuary and the host to be trodden under foot?   14. And he said unto me, Unto two thousand and three hundred days; then shall the sanctuary be cleansed.

Dan. 9:21. Yea, whiles I *was* speaking in prayer, even the man Gabriel, whom I had seen in the vision at the beginning, being caused to fly swiftly, touched me about the time of the evening oblation.   22. And he informed *me*, and talked with me, and said, O Daniel, I am now come forth to give thee skill and understanding.   23. At the beginning of thy supplications the commandment came forth, and I am come to shew *thee;* for thou *art* greatly beloved: therefore understand the matter, and consider the vision.

Zech. 1:12. Then the angel of the LORD answered and said, O LORD of hosts, how long wilt thou not have mercy on Jerusalem and on the cities of Judah, against which thou hast had indignation these threescore and ten years?   13. And the LORD answered the angel that talked with me *with* good words *and* comfortable words.   14. So the angel that communed with me said unto me, Cry thou, saying, Thus saith the LORD of hosts; I am jealous for Jerusalem and for Zion with a great jealousy.

Zech. 6:5. And the angel answered and said unto me, These *are* the four ¹ spirits of the heavens, which go forth from standing before the Lord of all the earth.   [¹ R.V. winds]

Matt. 4:6. If thou be the Son of God, cast thyself down: for it is written, He shall give his angels charge concerning thee; and in *their* hands they shall bear thee up, lest at any time thou dash thy foot against a stone.   11. Then the devil leaveth him, and behold, angels came and ministered unto him.   Mark 1:13.

Matt. 13:41. The Son of man shall send forth his angels, and they shall gather out of his kingdom all things that offend, and them which do iniquity; 42. And shall cast them into a furnace of fire: there shall be wailing and gnashing of teeth.

Matt. 18:10. Take heed that ye despise not one of these little ones; for I say unto you, That in heaven their angels do always behold the face of my Father which is in heaven.

Matt. 24:31. He shall send his angels with a great sound of a trumpet, and they shall gather together his elect from the four winds, from one end of heaven to the other. 36. Of that day and hour knoweth no *man*, no, not the angels of heaven,

Matt. 25:31. The Son of man shall come in his glory, and all the holy angels with him,

Matt. 26:53. Thinkest thou that I cannot now pray to my Father, and he shall presently give me more than twelve legions of angels?

Luke 9:30. And, behold, there talked with him two men, which were Moses and Elias: 31. Who appeared in glory, and spake of his decease which he should accomplish at Jerusalem. Matt. 17:3; Mark 9:4.

Luke 12:8. Whosoever shall confess me before men, him shall the Son of man also confess before the angels of God: 9. But he that denieth me before men shall be denied before the angels of God. Mark 8:38.

Luke 15:10. There is joy in the presence of the angels of God over one sinner that repenteth. *v. 7.*

John 1:51. Hereafter ye shall see heaven open, and the angels of God ascending and descending upon the Son of man.

Acts 7:53. Who have received the law by the disposition of angels,

Acts 8:26. And the angel of the Lord spake unto Philip, saying, Arise, and go toward the south, unto the way that goeth down from Jerusalem unto Gaza, which is desert.

Gal. 3:19. Wherefore then *serveth* the law? It was added because of transgressions, till the seed should come to whom the promise was made; *and it was* ordained by angels in the hand of a mediator.

Eph. 1:20. Which he wrought in Christ when he raised him from the dead, and set *him* at his own right hand in the heavenly *places.* 21. Far above all principality, and power, and might, and dominion, and every name that is named, not only in this world, but also in that which is to come:

Eph. 3:10. That now, unto the principalities and powers in heavenly *places,* might be known by the church the manifold wisdom of God,

Col. 1:16. By him were all things created, that are in heaven, and that are in earth, visible and invisible, whether *they be* thrones, or dominions, or principalities, or powers:

Col. 2:10. And ye are complete in him,

which is the head of all principality and power.

2 Thess. 1:7. When the Lord Jesus shall be revealed from heaven with his mighty angels,

1 Tim. 3:16. ¹God was manifest in the flesh, justified in the Spirit, seen of angels,

[¹ R. V. He who]

1 Tim. 5:21. I charge *thee* before God, and the Lord Jesus Christ, and the elect angels, that thou observe these things without preferring one before another, doing nothing by partiality.

Heb. 1:4. Being made so much better than the angels, as he hath by inheritance obtained a more excellent name than they. 5. For unto which of the angels said he at any time, Thou art my son, this day have I begotten thee? 13. But to which of the angels said he at any time, Sit on my right hand, until I make thine enemies thy footstool?

Heb. 2:2. For if the word spoken by angels was stedfast, and every transgression and disobedience received a just recompence of reward;

7. Thou madest him a little lower than the angels; thou crownedst him with glory and honour, and didst set him over the works of thy hands: with *v.* 5. Psa. 8:5.

16. For verily he took not on *him the nature of* angels; but he took on *him* the seed of Abraham.

Heb. 12:22. But ye are come unto mount Sion, and unto the city of the living God, the heavenly Jerusalem, and to an innumerable company of angels,

Heb. 13:2. Be not forgetful to entertain strangers: for thereby some have entertained angels unawares.

1 Pet. 1:12. Unto whom it was revealed, that not unto themselves, but unto us they did minister the things, which are now reported unto you by them that have preached the gospel unto you with the Holy Ghost sent down from heaven; which things the angels desire to look into.

1 Pet. 3:22. Who is gone into heaven, and is on the right hand of God; angels and authorities and powers being made subject unto him.

2 Pet. 2:11. Angels, which are greater in power and might, bring not railing accusation against them before the Lord.

Rev. 4:8. And the four beasts had each of them six wings about *him;* and *they were* full of eyes within: and they rest not day and night, saying, Holy, holy, holy, Lord God Almighty, which was, and is, and is to come. 9. And when those beasts give glory and honour and thanks to him that sat on the throne, who liveth for ever and ever, 10. The four and twenty elders fall down before him that sat on the throne, and worship him that liveth for ever and ever, and cast their crowns before the throne, saying, 11. Thou art worthy, O Lord, to receive glory and honour and power: for thou hast created all things, and for thy pleasure they are and were created.

Rev. 5:9. And they sung a new song, saying, Thou art worthy to take the book, and to open the seals thereof: for thou wast slain, and hast redeemed us to God by thy blood out of every kindred, and tongue, and people, and nation; 10. And hast made us unto our God kings and priests: and we shall reign on the earth. 11. And I beheld, and I heard the voice of many angels round about the throne and the beasts and the elders: and the number of them was ten thousand times ten thousand, and thousands of thousands;

Rev. 7:9. After this I beheld, and, lo, a great multitude, which no man could number, of all nations, and kindreds, and people, and tongues, stood before the throne, and before the Lamb, clothed with white robes, and palms in their hands; 10. And cried with a loud voice, saying, Salvation to our God which sitteth upon the throne, and unto the Lamb.

Rev. 10:1. And I saw another mighty angel come down from heaven, clothed with a cloud: and a rainbow *was* upon his head, and his face *was* as it were the sun, and his feet as pillars of fire: 2. And he had in his hand a little book open: and he set his right foot upon the sea, and *his* left *foot* on the earth, 3. And cried with a loud voice, as *when* a lion roareth: and when he had cried, seven thunders uttered their voices. 4. And when the seven thunders had uttered their voices, I was about to write: and I heard a voice from heaven saying unto me, Seal up those things which the seven thunders uttered, and write them not. 5. And the angel which I saw stand upon the sea and upon the earth lifted up his hand to heaven, 6. And sware by him that liveth for ever and ever, who created heaven, and the things that therein are, and the earth, and the things that therein are, and the sea, and the things which are therein, that there should be time no longer:

Rev. 14:10. He shall be tormented with fire and brimstone in the presence of the holy angels,

Rev. 18:1. And after these things I saw another angel come down from heaven, having great power; and the earth was lightened with his glory. 2. And he cried mightily with a strong voice, saying, Babylon the great is fallen, is fallen, and is become the habitation of devils, and the hold of every foul spirit, and a cage of every unclean and hateful bird. 3. For all nations have drunk of the wine of the wrath of her fornication, and the kings of the earth have committed fornication with her, and the merchants of the earth are waxed rich through the abundance of her delicacies.

Rev. 19:10. And I fell at his feet to worship him. And he said unto me, See *thou do it* not: I am thy fellowservant, and of thy brethren that have the testimony of Jesus: worship God: for the testimony of Jesus is the spirit of prophecy.

Rev. 22:8. And I John saw these things, and heard *them*. And when I had heard and seen, I fell down to worship before the feet of the angel which shewed me these things. 9. Then saith he unto me, See *thou do it* not: for I am thy fellowservant, and of thy brethren the prophets, and of them which keep the sayings of this book: worship God.

APPEARANCES OF: To Abraham, Gen. 18:2; 22:11-18; Hagar, in the wilderness, Gen. 16:7; Lot, in Sodom, Gen. 19:1-17; Jacob, in his various visions, Gen. 28:12; Moses, Ex. 3:2; Israelites, Ex. 14:19; Judg. 2:1-4; Balaam, Num. 22:31; Joshua, "the captain of the Lord's host," Josh. 5:15; Gideon, Judg. 6:11-22; Manoah, Judg. 13:6,15-20; David, at the threshing floor of Araunah, 2 Sam. 24:16,17; 1 Chr. 21:15,16; Elijah, while he lay under the juniper tree, 1 Kin. 19:5-11; Daniel, in the lions' den, Dan. 6:22; 8:16; 9:21; 10:5-10,16,18; 12:5-7; Shadrach, Meshach, and Abed-nego, in the fiery furnace, Dan. 3:25,28; Zechariah, in a vision, Zech. 2:3; 3:1,2; 4:1; Joseph, in a dream, Matt. 1:20; 2:13,19. At the transfiguration of Jesus, Matt. 17:3; Luke 9:30,31. To Mary, concerning Jesus, Luke 1:26-38; Zacharias, Luke 1:11-20,26-38; the shepherds, Luke 2:9-11,13,14; Jesus, after his temptation, Matt. 4:11; in Gethsemane, Luke 22:43. At the sepulcher, Matt. 28:2-5; Mark 16:5-7; Luke 24:23; John 20:12; the ascension, Acts 1:10,11. To Peter and John, while in prison, Acts 5:19; Philip, Acts 8:26; Cornelius, in a dream, Acts 10:3,30-32; Peter, in prison, Acts 12:7-11; Paul, on the way to Damascus, Acts 27:23; John, in Patmos, Rev. 1:1; 5:2; 7:11; 10:9; 11:1; 17:7; 19:10; 22:8.

FALLEN: Job 4:18; Matt. 25:41; 2 Pet. 2:4; Jude 6; Rev. 12:9.

ANGEL OF THE CHURCHES. Rev. 1:20; 2:1,8,12,18; 3:1,7,14.

ANGER. Gen. 4:6. And the LORD said unto Cain, Why art thou wroth? and why is thy countenance fallen?

Gen. 49:7. Cursed *be* their anger, for *it was* fierce; and their wrath, for it was cruel:

2 Chr. 28:9. Behold, because the LORD God of your fathers was wroth with Judah, he hath delivered them into your hand, and ye have slain them in a rage *that* reacheth up unto heaven.

Job 5:2. For wrath killeth the foolish man, and envy slayeth the silly one.

Job 19:29. For wrath *bringeth* the punishments of the sword, that ye may know *there is* a judgment.

Psa. 37:8. Cease from anger, and forsake wrath: fret not thyself in any wise to do evil.

Psa. 55:3. They cast iniquity upon me, and in wrath they hate me.

Psa. 76:10. Surely the wrath of man shall praise thee: the remainder of wrath shalt thou restrain.

Prov. 6:34. For jealousy *is* the rage of a man: therefore he will not spare in the day of vengeance.

Prov. 12:16. A fool's wrath is presently known: but a prudent *man* covereth shame.

Prov. 14:17. *He that is* soon angry dealeth foolishly: 29. *He that is* slow to wrath *is* of great understanding: but *he that is* hasty of spirit exalteth folly.

Prov. 15:1. A soft answer turneth away wrath: but grievous words stir up anger. 18. A wrathful man stirreth up strife: but *he that is* slow to anger appeaseth strife.

Prov. 16:14. The wrath of a king *is as* messengers of death: but a wise man will pacify it. 29. A violent man enticeth his neighbour, and leadeth him into the way *that is* not good. 32. *He that is* slow to anger *is* better than the mighty; and he that ruleth his spirit than he that taketh a city.

Prov. 17:14. The beginning of strife *is as* when one letteth out water: therefore leave off contention, before it be meddled with.

Prov. 19:11. The discretion of a man deferreth his anger; and *it is* his glory to pass over a transgression. 12. The king's wrath *is* as the roaring of a lion; but his favour *is* as dew upon the grass. 19. A man of great wrath shall suffer punishment: for if thou deliver *him*, yet thou must do it again.

Prov. 21:24. Proud *and* haughty scorner *is* his name, who dealeth in proud wrath.

Prov. 22:24. Make no friendship with an angry man, and with a furious man thou shalt not go: 25. Lest thou learn his ways, and get a snare to thy soul.

Prov. 25:28. He that *hath* no rule over his own spirit *is like* a city *that is* broken down, *and* without walls.

Prov. 27:3. A stone *is* heavy, and the sand weighty; but a fool's wrath *is* heavier than them both. 4. Wrath *is* cruel, and anger *is* outrageous; but who *is* able to stand before envy?

Prov. 29:8. Scornful men bring a city into a snare: but wise *men* turn away wrath. 9. *If* a wise man contendeth with a foolish man, whether he rage or laugh, *there is* no rest. 22. An angry man stirreth up strife, and a furious man aboundeth in transgression.

Prov. 30:33. Surely the churning of milk bringeth forth butter, and the wringing of the nose bringeth forth blood: so the forcing of wrath bringeth forth strife.

Eccl. 7:9. Be not hasty in thy spirit to be angry: for anger resteth in the bosom of fools.

Hos. 7:16. Their princes shall fall by the sword for the rage of their tongue:

Amos 1:11. Thus saith the LORD: For three transgressions of Edom, and for four, I will not turn away *the punishment* thereof; because he did pursue his brother with the sword, and did cast off all pity, and his anger did tear perpetually, and he kept his wrath for ever:

Jonah 4:4. Then said the LORD, Doest thou well to be angry?

Matt. 5:22. But I say unto you, That whosoever is angry with his brother without a cause shall be in danger of the judgment: and whosoever shall say to his brother, Raca, shall be in danger of the council: but whosoever shall say, Thou fool, shall be in danger of hell fire.

2 Cor. 12:20. For I fear, . . . lest *there be* debates, envyings, wraths, strifes, backbitings, whisperings, swellings, tumults:

Gal. 5:19. Now the works of the flesh are manifest, which are *these;* . . . 20. . . . Hatred, variance, emulations, wrath, strife, seditions, heresies, 21. Envyings, [1] murders, drunkenness, revellings, and such like: of the which I [2] tell you before, as I have also told *you* in time past, that they which [3] do such things shall not inherit the kingdom of God.

[R. V. [1] Omitted.   [2] forewarn you, even as I did forewarn you [3] practise]

Eph. 4:26. Be ye angry, and sin not: let not the sun go down upon your wrath: 31. Let all bitterness, and wrath, and anger, and clamour, and evil speaking, be put away from you, with all malice:

Col. 3:8. But now ye also put off all these anger, wrath, malice,

1 Tim. 2:8. I will therefore that men pray every where, lifting up holy hands, without wrath and doubting.

Tit. 1:7. For a bishop must be blameless, as the steward of God; not selfwilled, not soon angry, [1] not given to wine, no striker, not given to filthy lucre;   [[1] R. V. no brawler]

Jas. 1:19. Wherefore, my beloved brethren, let every man be swift to hear, slow to speak, slow to wrath: 20. For the wrath of man worketh not the righteousness of God.

See HATRED; JEALOUSY; MALICE; SPEAKING, EVIL; STRIFE; KINDNESS; MEEKNESS; PATIENCE.

INSTANCES OF: Of Cain slaying Abel, Gen. 4:5-8; Simeon and Levi, on account of the humbling of their sister, Dinah, Gen. 49:5-7; Pharaoh, toward Moses, Ex. 10:11 28; Moses, toward Israel, Ex. 32:19; Num. 20:10, 11; Balaam, toward his ass, Num. 22:27,29; Balak, toward Balaam, Num. 24:10,11; Ephraimites, toward Gideon, for not soliciting their aid against the Midianites, Judg. 8:1; Jonathan, on account of Saul's persecution of David, 1 Sam. 20:34; Saul, toward Jonathan, 1 Sam. 20:30-34; Ahab, because Naboth would not sell his vineyard, 1 Kin. 21:4; Naaman, because Elisha directed him to wash in the Jordan, 2 Kin. 5:12; Asa, because the prophet reproved him, 2 Chr. 16:10; Ephraimites, toward Judah, 2 Chr. 25:10; Uzziah, toward Azariah, the priest, because of his reproof of, 2 Chr. 26:19; Ahasuerus, toward Vashti, Esth. 1:12; Haman, because Mordecai did not salute him, Esth. 3:5; Ahasuerus, toward Haman, Esth. 7:7; Elihu, because Job had beaten his friends in argument, Job 32:3; Moab, Isa. 16:6; Nebuchadnezzar, on account of the insubordination of the three Hebrews, who refused to worship his idol, Dan. 3:13,19; Jonah, because the gourd withered, Jonah 4:1,2,4,9; Herod, toward the wise men who deceived him, Matt. 2:16; people of Nazareth, toward Jesus, Luke 4:28; Paul, toward Ananias,

Acts 23:3; Jews, against Stephen, Acts 7: 54-58.

OF GOD: Ex. 22:24. And my wrath shall wax hot, and I will kill you with the sword; and your wives shall be widows, and your children fatherless.

Ex. 33:5. For the LORD had said unto Moses, Say unto the children of Israel, Ye *are* a stiffnecked people: I will come up into the midst of thee in a moment, and consume thee: therefore now put off thy ornaments from thee, that I may know what to do unto thee.

Num. 11:1. And *when* the people complained, it displeased the LORD : and the LORD heard *it;* and his anger was kindled; and the fire of the LORD burnt among them, and consumed *them that were* in the uttermost parts of the camp. 10. Then Moses heard the people weep throughout their families, every man in the door of his tent: and the anger of the LORD was kindled greatly ; 33. And while the flesh *was* yet between their teeth, ere it was chewed, the wrath of the LORD was kindled against the people, and the LORD smote the people with a very great plague.

Num. 12:9. And the anger of the LORD was kindled against them; and he departed.

Num. 14:11. And the LORD said unto Moses, How long will this people provoke me? and how long will it be ere they believe me, for all the signs which I have shewed among them?

Num. 16:20. And the LORD spake unto Moses and unto Aaron, saying, 21. Separate yourselves from among this congregation, that I may consume them in a moment. *v.* 45.

Num. 25:3. And Israel joined himself unto Baal-peor: and the anger of the LORD was kindled against Israel. 4. And the LORD said unto Moses, Take all the heads of the people, and hang them up before the LORD against the sun, that the fierce anger of the LORD may be turned away from Israel. 11. Phinehas, the son of Eleazar, the son of Aaron the priest, hath turned my wrath away from the children of Israel, while he was zealous for my sake among them, that I consumed not the children of Israel in my jealousy.

Num. 32:10. And the LORD's anger was kindled the same time, and he sware, saying, 11. Surely none of the men that came up out of Egypt, from twenty years old and upward, shall see the land which I sware unto Abraham, unto Isaac, and unto Jacob: because they have not wholly followed me: 13. And the LORD's anger was kindled against Israel, and he made them wander in the wilderness forty years, until all the generation, that had done evil in the sight of the LORD, was consumed.

Deut. 6:14. Ye shall not go after other gods, of the gods of the people which *are* round about you; 15. (For the LORD thy God *is* a jealous God among you) lest the anger of the LORD thy God be kindled against thee, and destroy thee from off the face of the earth.

Deut. 9:13. Furthermore the LORD spake unto me, saying, I have seen this people, and, behold, it *is* a stiffnecked people: 14. Let me alone, that I may destroy them, and blot out their name from under heaven: and I will make of thee a nation mightier and greater than they. [Ex. 32:10.] 18. And I fell down before the LORD, as at the first, forty days and forty nights: I did neither eat bread, nor drink water, because of all your sins which ye sinned, in doing wickedly in the sight of the LORD, to provoke him to anger. 19. For I was afraid of the anger and hot displeasure, wherewith the LORD was wroth against you to destroy you. But the LORD hearkened unto me at that time also, 20. And the LORD was very angry with Aaron to have destroyed him: and I prayed for Aaron also the same time.

Deut. 32:21. They have moved me to jealousy with *that which is* not God ; they have provoked me to anger with their vanities: and I will move them to jealousy with *those which are* not a people; I will provoke them to anger with a foolish nation. 22. For a fire is kindled in mine anger, and shall burn unto the lowest hell, and shall consume the earth with her increase, and set on fire the foundations of the mountains.

Josh. 7:1. But the children of Israel committed a trespass in the accursed thing: for Achan, the son of Carmi, the son of Zabdi, the son of Zerah, of the tribe of Judah, took of the accursed thing: and the anger of the LORD was kindled against the children of Israel. 26. So the LORD turned from the fierceness of his anger.

Josh. 23:16. When ye have transgressed the covenant of the LORD your God, which he commanded you, and have gone and served other gods, and bowed yourself to them; then shall the anger of the LORD be kindled against you, and ye shall perish quickly from off the good land which he hath given unto you.

Judg. 2:12. And they forsook the LORD God of their fathers, which brought them out of the land of Egypt, and followed other gods, of the gods of the people that *were* round about them, and bowed themselves unto them, and provoked the LORD to anger.

Judg. 3:8. Therefore the anger of the LORD was hot against Israel, and he sold them into the hands of Chushan-rishathaim. Judg. 10:7.

1 Sam. 28:18. Because thou obeyedst not the voice of the LORD, nor executedst his fierce wrath upon Amalek, therefore hath the LORD done this thing unto thee this day.

2 Sam. 6:7. And the anger of the LORD was kindled against Uzzah, and God smote him there for *his* error; and there he died by the ark of God.

2 Sam. 22:8. Then the earth shook and trembled; the foundations of heaven moved

and shook, because he was wroth. 9. There went up a smoke out of his nostrils, and fire out of his mouth devoured: coals were kindled by it.

1 Kin. 11:9. And the LORD was angry with Solomon, because his heart was turned from the LORD God of Israel, which had appeared unto him twice.

1 Kin. 16:7. And also by the hand of the prophet Jehu the son of Hanani came the word of the LORD against Baasha, and against his house, even for all the evil that he did in the sight of the LORD, in provoking him to anger with the work of his hands, *vs.* 2-13.

2 Kin. 13:3. And the anger of the LORD was kindled against Israel, and he delivered them into the hand of Hazael king of Syria,

2 Kin. 17:18. Therefore the LORD was very angry with Israel, and removed them out of his sight: there was none left but the tribe of Judah only.

2 Kin. 22:13. Great *is* the wrath of the LORD that is kindled against us, because our fathers have not hearkened unto the words of this book, to do according unto all that which is written concerning us.

2 Kin. 23:26. Notwithstanding the LORD turned not from the fierceness of his great wrath, wherewith his anger was kindled against Judah,

Psa. 7:11. God judgeth the righteous, and God is angry *with the wicked* every day.

Psa. 69:24. Pour out thine indignation upon them, and let thy wrathful anger take hold of them.

Psa. 74:1. O God, why hast thou cast *us* off for ever? *why* doth thine anger smoke against the sheep of thy pasture?

Psa. 76:7. Thou, *even* thou, *art* to be feared: and who may stand in thy sight when once thou art angry?

Psa. 78:21. Therefore the LORD heard *this*, and was wroth: so a fire was kindled against Jacob, and anger also came up against Israel; 38. But he, *being* full of compassion, forgave *their* iniquity, and destroyed *them* not: yea, many a time turned he his anger away, and did not stir up all his wrath. 49. He cast upon them the fierceness of his anger, wrath, and indignation, and trouble, by sending evil angels *among them.* 50. He made a way to his anger; he spared not their soul from death, but gave their life over to the pestilence;

Psa. 85:3. Thou hast taken away all thy wrath: thou hast turned *thyself* from the fierceness of thine anger.

Psa. 90:11. Who knoweth the power of thine anger? even according to thy fear, *so is* thy wrath.

Psa. 103:8. The LORD *is* merciful and gracious, slow to anger, and plenteous in mercy. 9. He will not always chide: neither will he keep *his anger* for ever.

Psa. 106:23. Therefore he said that he would destroy them, had not Moses his chosen stood before him in the breach, to turn away his wrath, lest he should destroy *them.* 29. Thus they provoked *him* to anger with their inventions: and the plague brake in upon them. 32. They angered *him* also at the waters of strife, so that it went ill with Moses for their sakes:

Psa. 110:5. The Lord at thy right hand shall strike through kings in the day of his wrath.

Isa. 5:25. Therefore is the anger of the LORD kindled against his people, and he hath stretched forth his hand against them, and hath smitten them: and the hills did tremble, and their carcases *were* torn in the midst of the streets. For all this his anger is not turned away, but his hand *is* stretched out still. Isa. 9:17,19,21.

Isa. 12:1. And in that day thou shalt say, O LORD, I will praise thee: though thou wast angry with me, thine anger is turned away, and thou comfortedst me.

Isa. 13:9. Behold the day of the LORD cometh, cruel both with wrath and fierce anger, to lay the land desolate: and he shall destroy the sinners thereof out of it. 13. Therefore I will shake the heavens, and the earth shall remove out of her place, in the wrath of the LORD of hosts, and in the day of his fierce anger.

Isa. 30:27. Behold, the name of the LORD cometh from far, burning *with* his anger, and the burden *thereof is* heavy: his lips are full of indignation, and his tongue as a devouring fire:

Isa. 42:25. Therefore he hath poured upon him the fury of his anger, and the strength of battle: and it hath set him on fire round about, yet he knew not; and it burned him, yet he laid *it* not to heart.

Isa. 48:9. For my name's sake will I defer mine anger, and for my praise will I refrain for thee, that I cut thee not off.

Isa. 57:16. For I will not contend for ever, neither will I be always wroth: for the spirit should fail before me, and the souls *which* I have made. 17. For the iniquity of his covetousness was I wroth, and smote him: I hid me, and was wroth, and he went on frowardly in the way of his heart.

Isa. 63:3. I have trodden the winepress alone; and of the people *there was* none with me: for I will tread them in mine anger, and trample them in my fury; and their blood shall be sprinkled upon my garments, and I will stain all my raiment. 4. For the day of vengeance *is* in mine heart, and the year of my redeemed is come. 5. And I looked, and *there was* none to help; and I wondered that *there was* none to uphold: therefore mine own arm brought salvation unto me; and my fury, it upheld me. 6. And I will tread down the people in mine anger, and make them drunk in my fury, and I will bring down their strength to the earth.

Isa. 66:15. For, behold, the LORD will come with fire, and with his chariots like a whirlwind, to render his anger with fury, and his rebuke with flames of fire.

Jer. 3:12. Go and proclaim these words toward the north, and say, Return, thou backsliding Israel, saith the LORD; *and* I will not cause mine anger to fall upon you: for I *am* merciful, saith the LORD, *and* I will not keep *anger* for ever.

Jer. 4:4. Circumcise yourselves to the LORD, and take away the foreskins of your heart, ye men of Judah and inhabitants of Jerusalem: lest my fury come forth like fire, and burn that none can quench *it*, because of the evil of your doings. 8. For this gird you with sackcloth, lament and howl: for the fierce anger of the LORD is not turned back from us.

26. I beheld, and, lo, the fruitful place *was* a wilderness, and all the cities thereof were broken down at the presence of the LORD, *and* by his fierce anger.

Jer. 7:20. Therefore thus saith the Lord GOD; Behold, mine anger and my fury shall be poured out upon this place, upon man, and upon beast, and upon the trees of the field, and upon the fruit of the ground; and it shall burn, and shall not be quenched.

Jer. 10:10. But the LORD *is* the true God, he *is* the living God, and an everlasting king: at his wrath the earth shall tremble, and the nations shall not be able to abide his indignation.

Jer. 17:4. And thou, even thyself, shalt discontinue from thine heritage that I gave thee; and I will cause thee to serve thine enemies in the land which thou knowest not: for ye have kindled a fire in mine anger, *which* shall burn for ever.

Jer. 21:5. And I myself will fight against you with an outstretched hand and with a strong arm, even in anger, and in fury, and in great wrath. 6. And I will smite the inhabitants of this city, both man and beast: they shall die of a great pestilence.

Jer. 23:20. The anger of the LORD shall not return, until he have executed, and till he have performed the thoughts of his heart: in the latter days ye shall consider it perfectly. Jer. 30:24.

Jer. 25:15. For thus saith the LORD God of Israel unto me; Take the wine cup of this fury at my hand, and cause all the nations, to whom I send thee, to drink it. 16. And they shall drink, and be moved, and be mad, because of the sword that I will send among them. 17. Then took I the cup at the LORD's hand, and made all the nations to drink, unto whom the LORD had sent me: 37. And the peaceable habitations are cut down because of the fierce anger of the LORD. 38. He hath forsaken his covert, as the lion: for their land is desolate because of the fierceness of the oppressor, and because of his fierce anger.

Jer. 32:37. Behold, I will gather them out of all countries, whither I have driven them in mine anger, and in my fury, and in great wrath; and I will bring them again unto this place, and I will cause them to dwell safely:

Jer. 33:5. They come to fight with the Chaldeans, but *it is* to fill them with the dead bodies of men, whom I have slain in mine anger and in my fury, and for all whose wickedness I have hid my face from this city.

Jer. 36:7. It may be they will present their supplication before the LORD, and will return every one from his evil way: for great *is* the anger and the fury that the LORD hath pronounced against this people.

Jer. 42:18. For thus saith the LORD of hosts, the God of Israel; As mine anger and my fury hath been poured forth upon the inhabitants of Jerusalem; so shall my fury be poured forth upon you, when ye shall enter into Egypt: and ye shall be an execration, and an astonishment, and a curse, and a reproach; and ye shall see this place no more.

Jer. 44:6. Wherefore my fury and mine anger was poured forth, and was kindled in the cities of Judah and in the streets of Jerusalem; and they are wasted *and* desolate, as at this day.

Jer. 51:45. My people, go ye out of the midst of her, and deliver ye every man his soul from the fierce anger of the LORD.

Lam. 2:1. How hath the Lord covered the daughter of Zion with a cloud in his anger, *and* cast down from heaven unto the earth the beauty of Israel, and remembered not his footstool in the day of his anger! 3. He hath cut off in *his* fierce anger all the horn of Israel: he hath drawn back his right hand from before the enemy, and he burned against Jacob like a flaming fire, *which* devoureth round about. 6. And he hath violently taken away his tabernacle, as *if it were of* a garden: he hath destroyed his places of the assembly: the LORD hath caused the solemn feasts and sabbaths to be forgotten in Zion, and hath despised in the indignation of his anger the king and the priest.

Lam. 4:11. The LORD hath accomplished his fury; he hath poured out his fierce anger, and hath kindled a fire in Zion, and it hath devoured the foundations thereof.

Ezek. 5:13. Thus shall mine anger be accomplished, and I will cause my fury to rest upon them, and I will be comforted: and they shall know that I the LORD have spoken *it* in my zeal, when I have accomplished my fury in them. 15. So it shall be a reproach and a taunt, an instruction and an astonishment unto the nations that *are* round about thee, when I shall execute judgments in thee in anger and in fury and in furious rebukes. I the LORD have spoken *it*.

Ezek. 25:14. And I will lay my vengeance upon Edom by the hand of my people Israel: and they shall do in Edom according to mine anger and according to my fury; and they shall know my vengeance, saith the Lord GOD. 15. Thus saith the Lord GOD; Because the Philistines have dealt by revenge, and have taken vengeance with a despiteful heart, to destroy *it* for the old hatred; 16. Therefore thus saith the Lord GOD; Behold I will stretch out mine hand upon the Philistines, and I will cut off the Cherethims, and destroy the remnant of the sea coast. 17. And I will execute great vengeance upon them with furious rebukes; and they shall know that I *am* the LORD, when I shall lay my vengeance upon them.

Dan. 9:16. O Lord, according to all thy righteousness, I beseech thee, let thine anger and thy fury be turned away from thy city Jerusalem, thy holy mountain: because for our sins, and for the iniquities of our fathers, Jerusalem and thy people *are become* a reproach to all *that are* about us.

Hos. 11:9. I will not execute the fierceness of mine anger, I will not return to destroy Ephraim: for I *am* God, and not man; the Holy One in the midst of thee: and I will not enter into the city.

Hos. 13:11. I gave thee a king in mine anger, and took *him* away in my wrath.

Hos. 14:4. I will heal their backsliding, I will love them freely: for mine anger is turned away from him.

Nah. 1:2. God *is* jealous, and the LORD revengeth; the LORD revengeth, and *is* furious; the LORD will take vengeance on his adversaries, and he reserveth *wrath* for his enemies. 3. The LORD *is* slow to anger, and great in power, and will not at all acquit *the wicked:* the LORD *hath* his way in the whirlwind and in the storm, and the clouds *are* the dust of his feet. 6. Who can stand before his indignation? and who can abide in the fierceness of his anger? his fury is poured out like fire, and the rocks are thrown down by him.

Matt. 22:7. But when the king heard *thereof* he was wroth: and he sent forth his armies, and destroyed those murderers, and burned up their city. 13. Then said the king to the servants, Bind him hand and foot, and take him away, and cast *him* into outer darkness; there shall be weeping and gnashing of teeth.

Rom. 1:18. For the wrath of God is revealed from heaven against all ungodliness and unrighteousness of men, who hold the truth in unrighteousness;

Rom. 2:5. But after thy hardness and impenitent heart treasurest up unto thyself wrath against the day of wrath and revelation of the righteous judgment of God;

Eph. 5:6. Let no man deceive you with vain words: for because of these things cometh the wrath of God upon the children of disobedience.

Col. 3:6. For which things' sake the wrath of God cometh on the children of disobedience:

Heb. 3:11. So I sware in my wrath, They shall not enter into my rest. Heb. 4:3.

Rev. 6:16. And said to the mountains and rocks, Fall on us, and hide us from the face of him that sitteth on the throne, and from the wrath of the Lamb: 17. For the great day of his wrath is come; and who shall be able to stand?

Rev. 14:10. The same shall drink of the wine of the wrath of God, which is poured out without mixture into the cup of his indignation; and he shall be tormented with fire and brimstone in the presence of the holy angels, and in the presence of the Lamb: 11. And the smoke of their torment ascendeth up for ever and ever: and they have no rest day nor night, who worship the beast and his image, and whosoever receiveth the mark of his name.

Rev. 15:1. And I saw another sign in heaven, great and marvellous, seven angels having the seven last plagues; for in them is filled up the wrath of God. 7. And one of the four beasts gave unto the seven angels seven golden vials full of the wrath of God, who liveth for ever and ever.

Rev. 16:19. And the great city was divided into three parts, and the cities of the nations fell: and great Babylon came in remembrance before God, to give unto her the cup of the wine of the fierceness of his wrath.

Rev. 19:15. And out of his mouth goeth a sharp sword, that with it he should smite the nations: and he shall rule them with a rod of iron: and he treadeth the winepress of the fierceness and wrath of Almighty God.

ANIAM, son of Shemidah, 1 Chr. 7:19.

ANIM, a city of Judah, Josh. 15:50.

ANIMALS. Creation of, Gen. 1:24,25; 2:19; Jer. 27:5. Food of, Gen. 1:30. Named, Gen. 2:20. Ordained as food for man, Gen. 9:2,3; Lev. 11:3,9,21,22; Deut. 14:4-6,9,11,20. God's care of, Gen. 9:9,10; Deut. 25:4; Job 38:41; Psa. 36:6; 104:11,21; 147:9; Jonah 4:11; Matt. 6:26; 10:29; Luke 12:6,24; 1 Cor. 9:9. Under the curse, Gen. 3:14; 6:7,17. Suffer under divine judgments, sent upon man, Jer. 7:20; 12:4; 21:6; Ezek. 14:13,17,19-21; Joel 1:18-20. Two of every sort preserved in the ark, Gen. 6:19,20; 7:2,3,5,9,14; 8:19. Suffered the plagues of Egypt, Ex. 8:17; 9:9,10,19; 11:5. Perish at death, Eccl. 3:21; 12:7. Possessed of devils, Matt. 8:31,32; Mark 5:13; Luke 8:33. Clean and unclean, Gen. 8:20; Lev. 7:21; 11; 20:25; Deut. 14:3-20; Acts 10:11-15; 1 Tim. 4:3-5. Offered in sacrifice, Gen. 4:4; 7:2-8; 8:20. See OFFERINGS.

God's control of, Psa. 91:13; Isa. 11:6,8; 35:9; Luke 10:19. Instruments of God's will, Ex. chapters 8, 9 and 10:1-20; Num. 21:6; 22:28; Josh. 24:12; Jer. 8:17; Joel 1:4. Belong to God, Psa. 50:10-12. Sent in judgment, Lev. 26:22; Num. 21:6,7; Deut. 8:15; 28:26; Ezek. 5:17; 14:15; 32:4; Rev. 6:8. Paul contends with, 1 Cor. 15:32. Nature of, Job 39; Psa. 32:9; 49: 12; Eccl. 3:18-21. Habits of, Job 12:7,8; 37:8; 39; 40:20; Psa. 29:9; 104:20-25; Isa. 13:21,22; 34:14; Jas. 3:7. Menstruation of, Jer. 2:24. Facts about breeding, Gen. 30:35-43; 31:8,9. Instincts of, Deut. 32:11; Job 35:11; 39; 40; 41; Psa. 59:6; 104; Prov. 6:6-8; 30:25-28; Jer. 8:7; Matt. 24:28. Abodes of, Job 24:5; 37:8; 39; Psa. 104:20-25; Isa. 34:14; Jer. 2:24; 50:39; Mark 1:13.

See BIRDS; CATTLE; FISH.

BEASTS. SYMBOLICAL: Isa. 30:6; **Dan. 7;**

11,17,19; 8:4; Acts 10:12; Rev. 4:6–9; 5:6–14; 6:1–7; 7:11; 11:7; 13; 14:3,9,11; 15:2; 16:2,10–13; 17; 19:4,19,20; 20:4,10.

CRUELTY TO: INSTANCES OF: Balaam, Num. 22:22–33. Houghing horses, 2 Sam. 8:4; 1 Chr. 18:4.

See HOUGHING.

KINDNESS TO: INSTANCES OF: Jacob, in erecting booths for his cattle, Gen. 33:17. People of Gerar, in providing tents for cattle, 2 Chr. 14:15.

LAWS CONCERNING: Ex. 20:10. But the seventh day *is* the sabbath of the LORD thy God: *in it* thou shalt not do any work, thou, nor thy son, nor thy daughter, thy manservant, nor thy maidservant, nor thy cattle, nor thy stranger that *is* within thy gates: Deut. 5:14.

Ex. 21:28. If an ox gore a man or a woman, that they die: then the ox shall be surely stoned, and his flesh shall not be eaten; but the owner of the ox *shall be* quit. 29. But if the ox were wont to push with his horn in time past, and it hath been testified to his owner, and he hath not kept him in, but that he hath killed a man or a woman; the ox shall be stoned, and his owner also shall be put to death. 30. If there be laid on him a sum of money, then he shall give for the ransom of his life whatsoever is laid upon him. 31. Whether he have gored a son, or have gored a daughter, according to this judgment shall it be done unto him. 32. If the ox shall push a manservant or a maidservant; he shall give unto their master thirty shekels of silver, and the ox shall be stoned. 33. And if a man shall open a pit, or if a man shall dig a pit, and not cover it, and an ox or an ass fall therein; 34. The owner of the pit shall make *it* good, *and* give money unto the owner of them; and the dead *beast* shall be his. 35. And if one man's ox hurt another's, that he die; then they shall sell the live ox, and divide the money of it; and the dead *ox* also they shall divide. 36. Or if it be known that the ox hath used to push in time past, and his owner hath not kept him in; he shall surely pay ox for ox; and the dead shall be his own.

Ex. 22:1. If a man shall steal an ox, or a sheep, and kill it, or sell it; he shall restore five oxen for an ox, and four sheep for a sheep. 2. If a thief be found breaking up, and be smitten that he die, *there shall* no blood *be shed* for him. 3. If the sun be risen upon him, *there shall be* blood *shed* for him; *for* he should make full restitution; if he have nothing, then he shall be sold for his theft. 4. If the theft be certainly found in his hand alive, whether it be ox, or ass, or sheep; he shall restore double.

Ex. 23:5. If thou see the ass of him that hateth thee lying under his burden, and wouldest forbear to help him, thou shalt surely help with him. Deut. 22:4.

12. Six days thou shalt do thy work, and on the seventh day thou shalt rest: that thine ox and thine ass may rest, and the son of thy handmaid, and the stranger, may be refreshed.

Lev. 19:19. Thou shalt not let thy cattle gender with a diverse kind:

Deut. 22:6. If a bird's nest chance to be before thee in the way in any tree, or on the ground, *whether they be* young ones, or eggs, and the dam sitting upon the young, or upon the eggs, thou shalt not take the dam with the young: 7. *But* thou shalt in any wise let the dam go, and take the young to thee; that it may be well with thee, and *that* thou mayest prolong *thy* days.

10. Thou shalt not plow with an ox and an ass together.

Deut. 25:4. Thou shalt not muzzle the ox when he treadeth out *the corn.* 1 Tim. 5:18.

Prov. 12:10. A righteous *man* regardeth the life of his beast; but the tender mercies of the wicked *are* cruel.

Firstlings of. See FIRSTBORN.

Man's dominion over. See MAN, DOMINION OF.

See ADDER; ANT; ANTELOPE; APE; ASP; ASS; BADGER; BAT; BEAR; BEHEMOTH; BIRDS; BOAR; CAMEL; CHAMELEON; CHAMOIS; CHICKENS; COCKATRICE; CONEY; DEER; DOG; DRAGON; DROMEDARY; ELEPHANT; FERRET; FISH; FOX; FROGS; GOAT; GREYHOUND; HARE; HART; HIND; HIPPOPOTAMUS; HORNET; HORSE; KINE; LEOPARD; LEVIATHAN; LION; LIZARD; MOLE; MOUSE; PYGARG; RAM; ROE; SATYR; SCORPION; SERPENT; SHEEP; SWINE; UNICORN; VIPER; WEASEL; WHALE; WOLF; WORM.

See INSECTS.

ANISE, a seed, used as a condiment, Matt. 23:23.

ANNA, a devout widow, Luke 2:36,37.

ANNAS, associate high priest with Caiaphas, Luke 3:2; John 18:13,19,24; Acts 4:6.

ANOINTING. Of the body, Deut. 28: 40; Ruth 3:3; Esth. 2:12; Psa. 92:10; 104:15; 141:5; Prov. 27:9,16; Eccl. 9:8; Song 1:3; 4:10; Isa. 57:9; Amos 6:6; Mic. 6:15. Of guests, 2 Chr. 28:15; Luke 7:46; the sick, Isa. 1:6; Mark 6:13; Luke 10:34; Jas. 5:14; Rev. 3:18; the dead, Matt. 26:12; Mark 14:8; 16:1; Luke 23:56. Of Jesus, as a token of love, Luke 7:37, 38,46; John 11:2; 12:3. Omitted in mourning, 2 Sam. 12:20; 14:2; Isa. 61:3; Dan. 10:3. God preserves those who receive, Psa. 18:50; 20:6; 89:20–23. Saints receive, Isa. 61:3; 1 John 2:20.

IN CONSECRATION. OF HIGH PRIESTS: Ex. 29:7,29; 40:13; Lev. 6:20; 8:12; 16:32; Num. 35:25; Psa. 133:2.

OF PRIESTS: Ex. 28:41; 30:30; 40:15; Lev. 4:3; 8:30; Num. 3:3.

OF KINGS: Judg. 9:8,15; Saul, 1 Sam. 9:16; 10:1; 15:1; David, 1 Sam. 16:3,12,13; 2 Sam. 2:4; 5:3; 12:7; 19:21; 1 Chr. 11:3; Solomon, 1 Kin. 1:39; 1 Chr. 29:22; Jehu, 1 Kin. 19:16; 2 Kin. 9:1–3,6,12; Hazael, 1 Kin. 19:15; Joash, 2 Kin. 11:12; 2 Chr. 23:11; Jehoahaz, 2 Kin. 23:30; Cyrus, Isa. 45:1.

OF PROPHETS: 1 Kin. 19:16.

OF THE TABERNACLE: Ex. 30:26; 40:9; Lev.

8 10; Num. 7.1; altars of, Ex. 30:26-28; 40:10; Lev. 8:11; Num. 7:1; vessels of, Ex. 30:27,28; 40:9,10; Lev. 8:10,11; Num. 7:1.

JACOB'S PILLAR: at Beth-el, Gen. 28:18; 31: 13, 35:14.

See DEDICATION.

FIGURATIVE: Of Christ's kingly and priestly office, Psa. 45:7; 89:20; Isa. 61:1; Dan. 9:24; Luke 4:18; Acts 4:27; 10:38; Heb. 1:9. Of spiritual gifts, 2 Cor. 1:21· 1 John 2:20,27.

TYPIFIED: Ex. 40:13-15; Lev. 8:12; 1 Sam. 16:13; 1 Kin. 19:16.

SYMBOLICAL: of Jesus, Matt. 26: 7-12; John 12:3-7.

ANOINTING OIL. Formula of, given by Moses, Ex. 30:22-25,31-33.

See OIL; OINTMENT.

ANT, Prov.-6:6-8; 30:25.

ANTEDILUVIANS. Worship God, Gen. 4:3,4,26. Occupations of, Gen. 4:2,3, 20-22. Arts of, Gen. 4:2,3,20-22; 6:14-22. Enoch prophesies to, Jude 14,15. Noah preaches to, 2 Pet. 2:5. Wickedness of, Gen. 6:5-7. Destruction of, Gen. 7:1,21-23; Job 22:15-17; Matt. 24:37-39; Luke 17:26,27; 2 Pet. 2:5.

See FLOOD.

Longevity of. See LONGEVITY.

Giants among. See GIANTS.

ANTELOPE. See DEER.

ANTHROPOMORPHISMS, figures of speech, which attribute human forms, acts, and affections to God.

MISCELLANEOUS FIGURES: Gen. 2:2. And on the seventh day God ended his work which he had made; and he rested on the seventh day from all his work which he had made. 3. And God blessed the seventh day, and sanctified it: because that in it he had rested from all his work. [Ex. 31:17.] 19. And out of the ground the LORD God formed every beast of the field, and every fowl of the air; and brought *them* unto Adam to see what he would call them:

Gen. 6:6. And it repented the LORD that he had made man on the earth, and it grieved him at his heart. Ex. 32:14; Judg. 2:18; 1 Sam. 15:35; 2 Sam. 24:16; 1 Chr. 21:15; Psa. 106:45; Jer. 26:19; Amos 7:3.

Gen. 9:16. And the bow shall be in the cloud; and I will look upon it, that I may remember the everlasting covenant between God and every living creature of all flesh that *is* upon the earth.

Gen. 11:5. And the LORD came down to see the city and the tower, which the children of men builded. 7. Go to, let us go down, and there confound their language, that they may not understand one another's speech. Num. 11:25.

Gen. 18:17. And the LORD said, Shall I hide from Abraham that thing which I do; 18. Seeing that Abraham shall surely become a great and mighty nation, and all the nations of the earth shall be blessed in him? 19. For I know him, that he will command his children and his household after him, and they shall keep the way of the LORD, to do jus-

tice and judgment; that the LORD may bring upon Abraham that which he hath spoken of him. 21. I will go down now, and see whether they have done altogether according to the cry of it, which is come unto me; and if not, I will know. 33. And the LORD went his way, as soon as he had left communing with Abraham:

Gen. 19:29. And it came to pass, when God destroyed the cities of the plain, that God remembered Abraham,

Gen. 22:12. And he said, Lay not thine hand upon the lad, neither do thou any thing unto him: for now I know that thou fearest God, seeing thou hast not withheld thy son, thine only *son*, from me.

Gen. 28:13. And, behold, the LORD stood above it,

Gen. 35:13. And God went up from him in the place where he talked with him.

Ex. 2:24. And God heard their groaning, and God remembered his covenant with Abraham, with Isaac, and with Jacob.

Ex. 3:8. And I am come down to deliver them out of the hand of the Egyptians.

Ex. 14:24. And it came to pass, that in the morning watch the LORD looked unto the host of the Egyptians through the pillar of fire and of the cloud,

Ex. 20:5. For I the LORD thy God *am* a jealous God,

Psa. 31:2. Bow down thine ear to me;

Psa. 33:6. By the word of the LORD were the heavens made; and all the host of them by the breath of his mouth.

Psa. 35:1. Plead *my cause*, O LORD, with them that strive with me: fight against them that fight against me. 2. Take hold of shield and buckler, and stand up for mine help. 3. Draw out also the spear, and stop *the way* against them that persecute me: say unto my soul, I *am* thy salvation.

Psa. 36:7. How excellent *is* thy loving-kindness, O God! therefore the children of men put their trust under the shadow of thy wings.

Psa. 57:1. In the shadow of thy wings will I make my refuge, until *these* calamities be overpast.

Psa. 68:17. The chariots of God *are* twenty thousand, *even* thousands of angels:

Psa. 94:9. He that planted the ear, shall he not hear? he that formed the eye, shall he not see?

Psa. 121:4. Behold, he that keepeth Israel shall neither slumber nor sleep.

Isa. 1:15. And when ye spread forth your hands, I will hide mine eyes from you: yea, when ye make many prayers, I will not hear:

Ezek. 1:24. And when they went, I heard the noise of their wings, like the noise of great waters, as the voice of the Almighty, the voice of speech, as the noise of an host: when they stood, they let down their wings. 28. As the appearance of the bow that is in the cloud in the day of rain, so *was* the appearance of the brightness round about. This *was* the appearance of the likeness of the glory of the LORD. And when I saw *it*. I fell upon my face, and I heard a voice of one that spake,

Hab. 1:13. *Thou art* of purer eyes than to behold evil, and canst not look on iniquity : wherefore lookest thou upon them that deal treacherously, *and* holdest thy tongue when the wicked devoureth *the man that is* more righteous than he?

1 Pet. 3:12. For the eyes of the Lord *are* over the righteous, and his ears *are open* unto their prayers: but the face of the Lord *is* against them that do evil.

INTELLECTUAL FACULTIES ATTRIBUTED TO DEITY : Memory, Isa. 43:26; 63:11; assisted by tokens, Gen. 9:16. Reason, Isa. 1:18. Understanding, Psa. 147:5. Will, Rom. 9:19.

MISCELLANEOUS ACTS AND STATES OF MIND ATTRIBUTED TO : Walking, Gen. 3:8; Lev. 26:12; Deut. 23:14; Job 22:14; Hab. 3:15; resting, Gen. 2:2,3; Ex. 20:11; 31:17; Deut. 5:14; Heb. 4:4,10; fainteth not, Isa. 40:28; amazement. Isa. 59:16; 63:5; Mark 6:6; laughing, Psa. 2:4; 37:13; 59:8; Prov. 1:26; sleeping, Psa. 44:23; 78:65; grieved, Gen. 6:6; Judg. 10: 16; Psa. 95:10; Heb. 3:10,17.

Oaths, Isa. 62:8; Heb. 6:16,17; 7:21,28. See OATHS.* See also ANGER OF GOD.

ANTICHRIST. Matt.24:5,23,24,26; Mark 13:6,21,22; Luke 21:8; 2 Thess. 2:3-12; 1 John 2:18,22; 4:3; 2 John 7. To be destroyed, Rev. 19:20; 20:10,15.

ANTIOCH. 1. A city of Syria. Disciples first called Christians in, Acts 11:19-30. Church in, Acts 13:1; 14:26,27. Barnabas and Paul make second visit to, Acts 14:26-28. Dissension in church of, Acts 15:22, with *vs.* 1-35. Paul and Peter's controversy at, Gal. 2:11-15.

2. A city of Pisidia. Persecutes Paul, Acts 13:14-52; 2 Tim. 3:11; Acts 14:19-22; 18:22.

ANTIPAS, a martyr, Rev. 2:13.

ANTIPATRIS, a city in Samaria, Acts 23:31.

ANTOTHIJAH, a Benjamite, 1 Chr. 8:24.

ANUB, son of Coz, 1 Chr. 4:8.

ANVIL, Isa. 41:7.

ANXIETY. See CARE.

APE, in Solomon's zoological collections, 1 Kin. 10:22; 2 Chr. 9:21.

APELLES, a disciple in Rome, Rom. 16:10.

APHARSACHITES, Ezra 5:6; 6:6, with 2 Kin. 17.

APHARSATHCHITES, Ezra 4:9, with 2 Kin. 17.

APHARSITES, Ezra 4:9, with 2 Kin. 17.

APHEK. 1. A city of the tribe of Asher, Josh 19:30. Called APHIK, Judg. 1:31.

* For various additional anthropomorphic expressions and terms, see FIGURATIVE, under the following topics: ARM, EAR, EYE, HAND; see also ANGER OF GOD, ARROW, FOOTSTOOL, HATRED OF GOD, JEALOUSY, SCEPTER, SWORD, THRONE, and such other terms as are used for anthropomorphic purposes.

For a more extended exemplification of anthropomorphic expressions, consult concordances under the terms above cited, and under various grammatical forms of the verbs HATE, HEAR, REPENT, SEE, SMELL, TALK, WALK, etc.

2. A city of the tribe of Issachar. Philistines defeat Israelites at, 1 Sam. 4:1-11. Saul slain at, 1 Sam. 29:1, with chapter 31. Probably the same mentioned in Josh. 12:18 as a royal city of the Canaanites.

3. A city between Damascus and Palestine. Benhadad defeated at, 1 Kin. 20:26-30.

APHEKAH, a city in the mountains of Judah, Josh. 15:53.

APHIAH, a Benjamite, 1 Sam. 9:1.

APHIK. See APHEK, No. 1.

APHRAH, a city, Mic. 1:10. Perhaps identical with OPHRAH, 1 Chr. 4:14.

APHSES, a governor of the temple, 1 Chr. 24:15.

APOLLONIA, a city of Macedonia, Acts 17:1.

APOLLOS. An eloquent Christian convert at Corinth, Acts 18:24-28; 19:1; 1 Cor. 1:12; 3:4-7. Refuses to return to Rome, 1 Cor. 16:12. Paul writes Titus about, Tit. 3:13.

APOLLYON, angel of the bottomless pit, Rev. 9:11.

APOSTASY. Described, Deut. 13:13; Heb. 3:12. Caused by persecution, Matt. 24:9,10; Luke 8:13; by worldliness, 2 Tim. 4:10. Guilt and punishment of, Zeph. 1:4-6; Heb. 10:25-31,39; 2 Pet. 2:17,20-22. Cautions against, Heb. 3:12; 2 Pet. 3:17. Shall abound in the latter days, Matt. 24:12; 2 Thess. 2:3; 1 Tim. 4:1-3.

See ANTICHRIST.

UNCLASSIFIED SCRIPTURES RELATING TO : Deut. 32:15. He forsook God *which* made him, and lightly esteemed the Rock of his salvation.

1 Chr. 28:9. If thou forsake him, he will cast thee off for ever.

Isa. 1:28. The destruction of the transgressors and of the sinners *shall be* together, and they that forsake the LORD shall be consumed.

Isa. 65:11. But ye *are* they that forsake the LORD, that forget my holy mountain, that prepare a table for that troop, and that furnish the drink offering unto that number. 12. Therefore will I number you to the sword, and ye shall all bow down to the slaughter: because when I called, ye did not answer; when I spake, ye did not hear; but did evil before mine eyes, and did choose *that* wherein I delighted not. 13. Therefore thus saith the Lord GOD, Behold, my servants shall eat, but ye shall be hungry: behold, my servants shall drink, but ye shall be thirsty: behold, my servants shall rejoice, but ye shall be ashamed: 14. Behold, my servants shall sing for joy of heart, but ye shall cry for sorrow of heart, and shall howl for vexation of spirit. 15. And ye shall leave your name for a curse unto my chosen: for the Lord GOD shall slay thee, and call his servants by another name: 16. That he who blesseth himself in the earth shall bless himself in the God of truth; and he that sweareth in the earth shall swear by the God of truth; because the former troubles are forgotten, and because they are hid from mine eyes.

Jer. 17:5. Cursed *be* the man whose heart departeth from the LORD. 6. For he shall be like the heath in the desert, and shall not see when good cometh; but shall inhabit the parched places in the wilderness, *in a* salt land and not inhabited.

Ezek. 3:20. When a righteous *man* doth turn from his righteousness, and commit iniquity, and I lay a stumblingblock before him, he shall die: because thou hast not given him warning, he shall die in his sin, and his righteousness which he hath done shall not be remembered; but his blood will I require at thine hand.

Ezek. 18:24. But when the righteous turneth away from his righteousness, and committeth iniquity, *and* doeth according to all the abominations that the wicked *man* doeth, shall he live? All his righteousness that he hath done shall not be mentioned: in his trespass that he hath trespassed, and in his sin that he hath sinned, in them shall he die. 26. When a righteous *man* turneth away from his righteousness, and committeth iniquity, and dieth in them; for his iniquity that he hath done shall he die.

Ezek. 33:12. Therefore, thou son of man, say unto the children of thy people, The righteousness of the righteous shall not deliver him in the day of his transgression: as for the wickedness of the wicked, he shall not fall thereby in the day that he turneth from his wickedness; neither shall the righteous be able to live for his *righteousness* in the day that he sinneth. 13. When I shall say to the righteous, *that* he shall surely live; if he trust to his own righteousness, and commit iniquity, all his righteousnesses shall not be remembered; but for his iniquity that he hath committed, he shall die for it. 18. When the righteous turneth from his righteousness, and committeth iniquity, he shall even die thereby.

Matt. 13:20. But he that received the seed into stony places, the same is he that heareth the word, and anon with joy receiveth it; 21. Yet hath he not root in himself, but dureth for a while: for when tribulation or persecution ariseth because of the word, by and by he is offended. Mark 4:5–17; Luke 8:13.

Matt. 24:10. And then shall many be offended, and shall betray one another, and shall hate one another. *v.* 12.

Luke 11:24. When the unclean spirit is gone out of a man, he walketh through dry places, seeking rest; and finding none, he saith, I will return unto my house whence I came out. 25. And when he cometh, he findeth *it* swept and garnished. 26. Then goeth he, and taketh *to him* seven other spirits more wicked than himself; and they enter in, and dwell there: and the last *state* of that man is worse than the first.

John 15:6. If a man abide not in me, he is cast forth as a branch, and is withered; and men gather them, and cast *them* into the fire, **and they are burned.**

Acts 7:39. Whom our fathers would not obey, but thrust *him* from them, and in their hearts turned back again into Egypt. 40. Saying unto Aaron, Make us gods to go before us: for *as for* this Moses, which brought us out of the land of Egypt, we wot not what is become of him. 41. And they made a calf in those days, and offered sacrifice unto the idol, and rejoiced in the works of their own hands. 42. Then God turned, and gave them up to worship the host of heaven; as it is written in the book of the prophets, O ye house of Israel, have ye offered to me slain beasts and sacrifices *by the space of* forty years in the wilderness? 43. Yea, ye took up the tabernacle of Moloch, and the star of your god Remphan, figures which ye made to worship them : and I will carry you away beyond Babylon.

1 Cor. 9:27. But I keep under my body, and bring *it* into subjection: lest that by any means, when I have preached to others, I myself should be a castaway.

2 Thess. 2:3. Let no man deceive you by any means: for *that day shall not come*, except there come a falling away first, and that man of sin be revealed, the son of perdition; 11. And for this cause God shall send them strong delusion, that they should believe a lie: 12. That they all might be [1] damned who believe not the truth, but had pleasure in unrighteousness. [1 R. V. judged]

1 Tim. 4:1. Now the Spirit speaketh expressly, that in the latter times some shall depart from the faith, giving heed to seducing spirits, and doctrines of devils; 2. Speaking lies in hypocrisy; having their conscience seared with a hot iron;

2 Tim. 3:1. This know also, that in the last days perilous times shall come. 2. For men shall be lovers of their own selves, covetous, boasters, proud, blasphemers, disobedient to parents, unthankful, unholy, 3. Without natural affection, trucebreakers, false accusers, incontinent, fierce, despisers of those that are good, 4. Traitors, heady, highminded, lovers of pleasures more than lovers of God; 5. Having a form of godliness, but denying the power thereof: from such turn away. 6. For of this sort are they which creep into houses, and lead captive silly women laden with sins, led away with divers lusts, 7. Ever learning, and never able to come to the knowledge of the truth. 8. Now as Jannes and Jambres withstood Moses, so do these also resist the truth: men of corrupt minds, reprobate concerning the faith. 9. But they shall proceed no further; for their folly shall be manifest unto all *men*, as theirs also was.

2 Tim. 4:3. For the time will come when they will not endure sound doctrine; but after their own lusts shall they heap to themselves teachers, having itching ears; 4. And they shall turn away *their* ears from the truth, and shall be turned unto fables.

Heb. 6:4. For *it is* impossible for those who were once enlightened, and have **tasted of** the heavenly gift, and were made partakers of the Holy Ghost, 5. And have tasted the good word of God, and the powers of the world to come, 6. If they shall fall away, to renew them again unto repentance; seeing they crucify to themselves the Son of God afresh, and put *him* to an open shame. 7. For the earth which drinketh in the rain that cometh oft upon it, and bringeth forth herbs meet for them by whom it is dressed, receiveth blessing from God: 8. But that which beareth thorns and briers *is* rejected, and *is* nigh unto cursing; whose end *is* to be burned.

Heb. 10:26. For if we sin wilfully after that we have received the knowledge of the truth, there remaineth no more sacrifice for sins, 27. But a certain fearful looking for of judgment and fiery indignation, which shall devour the adversaries. 28. He that despised Moses' law died without mercy under two or three witnesses: 29. Of how much sorer punishment, suppose ye, shall he be thought worthy, who hath trodden under foot the Son of God, and hath counted the blood of the covenant, wherewith he was sanctified, an unholy thing, and hath done despite unto the Spirit of grace?

2 Pet. 2:1. But there were false prophets also among the people, even as there shall be false teachers among you, who privily shall bring in damnable heresies, even denying the Lord that bought them, and bring upon themselves swift destruction. 15. Which have forsaken the right way, and are gone astray, following the way of Balaam *the son* of Bosor, who loved the wages of unrighteousness; 17. These are wells without water, clouds that are carried with a tempest; to whom the mist of darkness is reserved for ever. 20. For if after they have escaped the pollutions of the world through the knowledge of the Lord and Saviour Jesus Christ, they are again entangled therein, and overcome, the latter end is worse with them than the beginning. 21. For it had been better for them not to have known the way of righteousness, than, after they have known *it*, to turn from the holy commandment delivered unto them. 22. But it is happened unto them according to the true proverb, The dog *is* turned to his own vomit again; and the sow that was washed to her wallowing in the mire.

2 Pet. 3:17. Ye therefore, beloved, seeing ye know *these things* before, beware lest ye also, being led away with the error of the wicked, fall from your own stedfastness.

Jude 4. For there are certain men crept in unawares, who were before of old ordained to this condemnation, ungodly men, turning the grace of our God into lasciviousness, and denying the only Lord God, and our Lord Jesus Christ. 5. I will therefore put you in remembrance, though ye once knew this, how that the Lord, having saved the people out of the land of Egypt, afterward destroyed

them that believed not. 6. And the angels which kept not their first estate, but left their own habitation, he hath reserved in everlasting chains under darkness unto the judgment of the great day.

See BACKSLIDING; REPROBACY.

INSTANCES OF: Israelites, Ex. 32; Num. 14. Saul, 1 Sam. 15:26–29; 18:12; 28:15,18. Amaziah, 2 Chr. 25:14,27. Disciples, John 6:66. Judas, Matt. 26:14–16; 27:3–5; Mark 14:10,11; Luke 22:3–6,47,48; Acts 1:16–18. Hymenæus and Alexander, 1 Tim. 1:19,20. Phygellus and Hermogenes, 2 Tim. 1:15.

See ISRAEL, BACKSLIDING OF.

APOSTLE, an appellation of Jesus, Heb. 3:1.

See APOSTLES.

APOSTLES. A title distinguishing the twelve disciples, whom Jesus selected to be intimately associated with himself, Luke 6:13.

Names of, Matt. 10:2. Now the names of the twelve apostles are these; The first, Simon, who is called Peter, and Andrew his brother; James *the son* of Zebedee, and John his brother; 3. Philip, and Bartholomew: Thomas, and Matthew the publican; James *the son* of Alphæus, and Lebbæus, whose surname was Thaddæus; 4. Simon the Canaanite, and Judas Iscariot, who also betrayed him. Mark 3:16–19; Luke 6:13–16; Acts 1:13,26.

Selection of, Matt. 4:18–22; 9:9,10; 10:2–4; Mark 3:13–19; Luke 6:13–16; John 1:43.

Commission of, Matt. 10; 28:19,20; Mark 3:14,15; 6:7–11; 16:15; Luke 9:1–5; 22:28–30; John 20:23; 21:15–19; Acts 1; 2; 10:42. Unlearned, Matt. 11:25; Acts 4:13. Miraculous power given to, Matt. 10:1; Mark 3:15; 6:7; 16:17; Luke 9:1,2; 10:9,17; Acts 2:4,43; 5:12–16; 1 Cor. 14:18; 2 Cor. 12:12. Authority of, see COMMISSION OF, above, and Matt. 16:19; 18:18; 19:28.

Inspiration of, Matt. 10:27; 16:17–19; Luke 24:45; Acts 1:2; 13:9. Duties of, see COMMISSION OF, above, and Luke 24:48; John 15:27; Acts 1:8,21,22; 2:32; 3:15; 4:33; 5:32; 10:39–41; 13:31; 2 Pet. 1:16,18; 1 John 1:1–3. See MINISTERS.

Moral state of, before Pentecost, Matt. 17:17; 18:3; 20:20–22; Luke 9:54,55. Slow to receive Jesus, as Messiah, Matt. 14:33. Forsake Jesus, Mark 14:50.

Fail to comprehend the nature and mission of Jesus, and the nature of the kingdom he came to establish, Matt. 8:25–27; 15:23; 16: 8–12,21,22; 19:25; Mark 4:13; 6:51,52; 8:17,18, 9:9,10,31,32; 10:13,14; Luke 9:44,45; 18:34; 24:19,21; John 4:32,33; 10:6; 11:12,13; 12:16; 13:6–8; 14:5–9,22; 16:6,17,18,32; 20:9; 21:12; Acts 1:6.

See BARNABAS; MATTHIAS; MINISTERS; PAUL.

FALSE: 2 Cor. 11:13; Rev. 2:2.

See TEACHERS, FALSE.

APOSTROPHE, to death and the grave, Hos. 13:14; 1 Cor. 15:55.

APOTHECARY, a compounder of

drugs, Ex. 30:25,35: 37:29; 2 Chr. 16:14; Neh. 3:8. Ointment of, Eccl. 10:1.

APPAIM, son of Nadab, 1 Chr. 2:30,31.

APPEAL. Paul makes, to Cæsar, Acts 25:10,11,21–27; 26:32; 28:19.

See CHANGE OF VENUE; COURTS, SUPERIOR AND INFERIOR.

APPETITE. Kept in subjection, Dan. 1:8–16; 1 Cor. 9:27.

See TEMPERANCE.

APPHIA, a Christian at Colosse, Philem. 2.

APPII-FORUM, a market town in Italy, Acts 28:15.

APPLE, a fruit, Prov. 25:11; Song 2:3, 5; 7:8; 8:5; Joel 1:12.

AQUILA AND PRISCILLA. Christians at Corinth. Acts 18:1–3,18,19,26. Friendship of, for Paul, Rom. 16:3,4. Paul sends salutations to, 2 Tim. 4:19.

AR, a city of Moab, Num. 21:15; Deut. 2: 9,18,24,29. Destruction of, Num. 21:26–30; Isa. 15:1.

ARA, son of Jether, 1 Chr. 7:38.

ARAB, a city of Judah, Josh. 15:52.

ARABAH. See BETH-ARABAH.

ARABIA. Tributary to Solomon, 2 Chr. 9:14, and Jehoshaphat, 2 Chr. 17:11. Exports of, Ezek. 27:21. Prophecies against, Isa. 21:13; Jer. 25:24. Paul visits, Gal. 1:17.

ARABIANS. Pay tribute to Solomon, 2 Chr. 9:14; to Jehoshaphat, 2 Chr. 17:11. Invade and defeat Judah, 2 Chr. 21:16,17; 22:1. Defeated by Uzziah, 2 Chr. 26:7. Oppose Nehemiah's rebuilding the walls of Jerusalem, Neh. 2:19; 4:7. Commerce of, Ezek. 27: 21. Gospel preached to, Acts 2:11; Gal. 1:17. Prophecies concerning, Isa. 21:13–17; 42:11; 60:7; Jer. 25:24.

ARAD. 1. A city on the S. of Canaan, Num. 21:1; 33:40. Subdued by Joshua, Josh. 12:14.

2. Son of Beriah, 1 Chr. 8:15.

ARAH. 1. Son of Ulla, 1 Chr. 7:39.

2. An Israelite, whose descendants returned from Babylon, Ezra 2:5; Neh. 7:10. Probably identical with ARAH in Neh. 6:18.

ARAM, the name of various regions, and of several men. The word signifies highlands, and is applied in its compounds to various highland districts of Syria.

1. The region whence Balaam came at Balak's command, Num. 23:7.

2. A region N. of Canaan, 1 Chr. 2:23.

3. Son of Shem, Gen. 10:22,23; 1 Chr. 1:17.

4. Son of Kemuel, Gen. 22:21.

5. Son of Shamer, 1 Chr. 7:34.

ARAN, son of Dishan, Gen. 36:28; 1 Chr. 1:42.

ARARAT. A district of Armenia, Jer. 51:27. Ark rested in mountains of, Gen. 8:4. Assassins of Sennacherib take refuge in, Isa. 37:38.

ARAUNAH. A Jebusite from whom David bought a site for an altar, 2 Sam. 24: 16–24. Called also ORNAN, 1 Chr. 21:15–25.

ARBA. 1. Father of Anak, Josh. 15:13.

2. See HEBRON.

ARBITRATION. INSTANCES OF: The two harlots before Solomon, 1 Kin. 3:16–28. Urged by Paul, as a mode of action for Christians, 1 Cor. 6:1–8.

See COURT.

ARCHANGEL. 1 Thess. 4:16; Jude 9. See ANGEL.

ARCHELAUS, a ruler of Judæa, Matt. 2:22.

ARCHERY. Practised by Ishmael, Gen. 21:20; Esau, Gen. 27:3; Jonathan, 1 Sam. 20: 20,36,37; sons of Ulam, 1 Chr. 8:40; Philistines, 1 Sam. 31:1–3; 1 Chr. 10:3; Persians, Isa. 13:17,18; people of Kedar, Isa. 21:17; Syrians, 1 Kin. 22:31–34; Israelites, 2 Sam. 1:18; 1 Chr. 5:18; 12:2; 2 Chr. 14:8; 26:14; Neh. 4:13; Zech. 9:13; Lydians, Jer. 46:9.

In war, Gen. 49:23; Judg. 5:11; 1 Sam. 31; 3; Isa. 22:3; Jer. 4:29; 51:3; Zech. 10:4.

See ARROW; ARMIES; BOW; WAR.

ARCHEVITES, inhabitants of Samaria, Ezra 4:9.

ARCHI, a city of Ephraim, Josh. 16:2.

ARCHIPPUS, a disciple at Colosse, Col. 4:17; Philem. 2.

ARCHITECTURE, Heb. 3:3,4.

FIGURATIVE: Eph. 2:21,22.

See ART; HOUSE; TABERNACLE; TEMPLE.

ARCTURUS, constellation of, Job 9:9; 38:32.

ARD. 1. Son of Benjamin, Gen. 46:21.

2. Son of Bela, Num. 26:40.

ARDON, son of Caleb, 1 Chr. 2:18.

ARELI, son of Gad, Gen. 46:16.

AREOPAGUS, Mars' Hill, Acts 17:19.

ARETAS, a ruler of Syria, 2 Cor. 11:32.

ARGOB. 1. A region E. of the Jordan, Deut. 3:4,13,14; 1 Kin. 4:13.

2. A courtier of Pekah, 2 Kin. 15:25.

ARIDAI, son of Haman, Esth. 9:9.

ARIDATHA, son of Haman, Esth. 9:8.

ARIEH, a conspirator with Pekah, 2 Kin. 15:25.

ARIEL. 1. A messenger from Ezra to Iddo, Ezra 8:16.

2. A symbolical name for Jerusalem, Isa. 29:1,2,7.

ARIMATHEA, called also RAMAH. A town five miles N. of Jerusalem, Matt. 27:57; Mark 15:43; Luke 23:51; John 19:38.

ARIOCH. 1. King of Ellasar, Gen. 14:1,9.

2. Captain of Nebuchadnezzar's guard, Dan. 2:14,15,24,25.

ARISAI, son of Haman, Esth. 9:9.

ARISTARCHUS, a companion of Paul, Acts 19:29; 20:4; 27:2; Col. 4:10; Philem. 24.

ARISTOBULUS, a Christian at Rome, Rom. 16:10.

ARK. 1. NOAH'S. Directions for building of, Gen. 6:14–16. Noah and family preserved in, Gen. 6:18; 7;8; Matt. 24:38; Heb. 11:7; 1 Pet. 3:20. Animals saved in, Gen. 6:19, 20; 7:1–16.

2. OF BULRUSHES, Ex. 2:3.

3. IN THE TABERNACLE. Called ARK OF THE COVENANT, Num. 10:33; Deut. 31:26; Josh. 4:7; 1 Sam. 4:3; 2 Sam. 15:24; 1 Chr. 15:25; 17:1; Jer. 3:16; Heb. 9:4; OF THE TESTIMONY, Ex. 30:6; OF

THE LORD, Josh. 4:11; 1 Sam. 4:6; 6:1; 2 Sam. 6:9; 1 Kin. 8:4; OF GOD, 1 Sam. 3:3; 4:11,17,22; 6:3; 14:18; 2 Sam. 6:7; 7:2; 15:25; 1 Chr. 13:12; 15:1,2,15,24; 16:1; OF GOD'S STRENGTH, 2 Chr. 6:41.

Sanctification of, Ex. 30:26. Ceremonies connected with, on the day of atonement, Lev. 16:13-15. Holy, 2 Chr. 8:11; 35:3.

An oracle of God, Num. 10:33; 14:44; Josh. 7:6-15; Judg. 20:27,28; 1 Sam. 4:3,4,7; 1 Chr. 13:3; 1 Chr. 16:4,37; 2 Chr. 6:41; Psa. 132:8. See MERCY SEAT.

Directions for making, Ex. 25:10-15; 35:12. Construction of, Ex. 37:1-5; Deut. 10:3.

Contents of: The law, Ex. 25:16,21; 40:20; Deut. 10:5; 31:26; 1 Kin. 8:9; 2 Chr. 5:10. Aaron's rod, Num. 17:10; Heb. 9:4. Pot of manna, Ex. 16:33,34; Heb. 9:4.

Place of, Ex. 26:33; 40:21; 1 Sam. 3:3; 2 Sam. 7:2; Heb. 9:2-4.

How prepared for conveyance, Num. 4:5,6. Carried by Kohathites, Num. 3:30,31; 4:4,15; Deut. 10:8; 1 Chr. 15:2,15. On special occasions carried by priests: Crossing Jordan, Josh. 3:6,14; siege of Jericho, Josh. 6:6.

Taken to battle, Josh. 6:6-20; 1 Sam. 4:3-22. Captured by the Philistines, 1 Sam. 4:10,11; Psa. 78:61. Returned by the Philistines, 1 Sam. 6. Remains at the house of Abinadab, 1 Sam. 7:1,2; 2 Sam. 6:4; in the house of Obed-edom, 2 Sam. 6:9-11.

Set up in Shiloh, Josh. 18:1; Judg. 20:27,28; 1 Sam. 4:3,4; in Jerusalem, 2 Sam. 6:12-17; 1 Chr. 6:31; 15; 16:1. Removed from Jerusalem by Zadok at the time of Absalom's revolt, but returned by command of David, 2 Sam. 15:24-29. Transferred to Solomon's temple, 1 Kin. 8:6-9; 2 Chr. 5:2-9; 35:3.

Prophecy concerning, Jer. 3:16. In John's vision, Rev. 11:19.

ARKITES, descendants of Canaan, Gen. 10:17; 1 Chr. 1:15.

ARM. FIGURATIVE USE OF: Ex. 6:6. I will redeem you with a stretched out arm, and with great judgments:

Ex. 15:16. Fear and dread shall fall upon them; by the greatness of thine arm they shall be as still as a stone; till thy people pass over, O LORD, till the people pass over, *which* thou hast purchased.

Deut. 4:34. Or hath God assayed to go *and* take him a nation from the midst of *another* nation, by temptations, by signs, and by wonders, and by war, and by a mighty hand, and by a stretched out arm, and by great terrors, according to all that the LORD your God did for you in Egypt before your eyes? Deut. 7:19; 9:29; 26:8; Acts 13:17.

Deut. 5:15. The LORD thy God brought thee out thence through a mighty hand and by a stretched out arm : Psa. 136:12.

Deut. 11:2. And know ye this day: for I *speak* not with your children which have not known, and which have not seen the chastisement of the LORD your God, his greatness, his mighty hand, and his stretched out arm,

Deut. 33:27. The eternal God *is thy* refuge, and underneath *are* the everlasting arms:

1 Kin. 8:42. (For they shall hear of thy great name, and of thy strong hand, and of thy stretched out arm :) when he shall come and pray toward this house; 2 Chr. 6:32.

2 Kin. 17:36. But the LORD, who brought you up out of the land of Egypt with great power and a stretched out arm, him shall ye fear, and him shall ye worship, and to him shall ye do sacrifice.

Psa. 77:15. Thou hast with *thine* arm redeemed thy people, the sons of Jacob and Joseph.

Psa. 89:10. Thou hast scattered thine enemies with thy strong arm. 13. Thou hast a mighty arm : strong is thy hand, *and* high is thy right hand. 21. With whom my hand shall be established : mine arm also shall strengthen him.

Psa. 98:1. O sing unto the LORD a new song; for he hath done marvellous things : his right hand, and his holy arm, hath gotten him the victory.

Song 2:6. His left hand *is* under my head, and his right hand doth embrace me.

Isa. 33:2. Be thou their arm every morning, our salvation also in the time of trouble.

Isa. 40:10. Behold, the Lord GOD will come with strong *hand*, and his arm shall rule for him : 11. He shall feed his flock like a shepherd : he shall gather the lambs with his arm, and carry *them* in his bosom, *and* shall gently lead those that are with young.

Isa. 51:5. My righteousness *is* near ; my salvation is gone forth, and mine arms shall judge the people ; the isles shall wait upon me, and on mine arm shall they trust. 9. Awake, awake, put on strength, O arm of the LORD ; awake, as in the ancient days, in the generations of old.

Isa. 52:10. The LORD hath made bare his holy arm in the eyes of all the nations ; and all the ends of the earth shall see the salvation of our God.

Isa. 53:1. Who hath believed our report ? and to whom is the arm of the LORD revealed ?

Isa. 59:16. His arm brought salvation unto him ; and his righteousness, it sustained him.

Isa. 62:8. The LORD hath sworn by his right hand, and by the arm of his strength,

Isa. 63:5. And I looked, and *there was* none to help ; and I wondered that *there was* none to uphold : therefore mine own arm brought salvation unto me ; and my fury, it upheld me. 12. That led *them* by the right hand of Moses with his glorious arm, dividing the water before them, to make himself an everlasting name ?

Jer. 21:5. And I myself will fight against you with an outstretched hand and with a strong arm, even in anger, and in fury, and in great wrath. Ezek. 20:33.

Jer. 27:5. I have made the earth, the man and the beast that *are* upon the ground, by my great power and by my outstretched arm, Jer. 32:17.

Luke 1:51. He hath shewed strength with his arm;

See ANTHROPOMORPHISMS.

ARMAGEDDON, a symbolical name, Rev. 16:16.

ARMENIA, a region in Western Asia, 2 Kin. 19:37; Jer. 51:27. Assassins of Sennacherib take refuge in, Isa. 37:38.

ARMIES. Who of the Israelites were subject to service in, Num. 1:2,3; 26:2; 2 Chr. 25:5; who were exempt from service in, Num. 1:47-50; 2:33; Deut, 20:5-9; Judg. 7:3. Enumeration of Israel's military forces, Num. 1:2,3; 26:2; 1 Sam. 11:8; 2 Sam. 18:1,2; 24:1-9; 1 Kin. 20:15; 2 Chr. 25:5. Levies for, Num. 31:4; Judg. 20:10. Compulsory service in, 1 Sam. 14:52. See COWARDICE.

How officered: Commander-in-chief, 1 Sam. 14:50; 2 Sam. 2:8; 8:16; 17:25; 19:13; 20:23; generals of corps and divisions, Num. 2:3-31; 1 Chr. 27:1-22; 2 Chr, 17:12-19; captains of thousands, Num. 31:14,48; 1 Sam. 17:18; 1 Chr. 28:1; 2 Chr. 25:5; of hundreds, Num. 31: 14,48; 2 Kin. 11:15; 1 Chr. 28:1; 2 Chr. 25:5; of fifties, 2 Kin. 1:9; Isa. 3:3. See CAVALRY; CHARIOTS.

Rendezvous of. Methods employed in effecting: Sounding a trumpet, Num. 10:9; Judg. 3:27; 6:34; 1 Sam. 13:3,4; cutting oxen in pieces, and sending the pieces throughout Israel, 1 Sam. 11:7. Refusal to obey the summons, instance of, Judg. 21:5-11, with Judg. 20.

Tactics: Camp and march, Num. 2. March in ranks, Ex. 13:18 [marg.]; 1 Chr. 12:33; Joel 2:7. Move, in attack, in three divisions, Judg. 7:16; 9:43; 1 Sam. 11:11; 13:17,18; 2 Sam. 18:2; Job 1:17. Flanks called wings, Isa. 8:8. See STRATEGY.

Orders delivered with trumpets, 2 Sam. 2: 28; 18:16; 20:1,22; Neh. 4:18,20.

Stratagems: Ambushes, at Ai, Josh. 8:2-22; Shechem, Judg. 9:25,34; Gibeah, Judg. 20:29-43; Zemaraim, 2 Chr. 13:13. By Jehoshaphat, 2 Chr. 20:22. Reconnoissances: Of Jericho, Josh. 2:1-24; Ai, Josh. 7:2,3; Beth-el, Judg. 1:23,24; Laish, Judg. 18:2-10. Night attacks, Gen. 14:15; Judg. 7:16-22. Decoy, Josh. 8:4-22; Judg. 20:29-43; Neh. 6. Delay, 2 Sam. 17:7-14. Celerity of action: Abraham, in pursuit of Chedorlaomer, Gen. 14:14,15. Joshua, against the Amorites, Josh. 10:6,9; the confederated kings, Josh. 11:7. David's attack upon the Philistines, 2 Sam. 5:23-25. Forced marches, Isa. 5:26,27. Sieges: Jer. 39:1; of Jericho, Josh. 6; Samaria, 2 Kin. 6:24-33; 7; Jerusalem, 2 Kin. 25: 1-3.

"Engines" used, 2 Chr. 26:15; Jer. 6:6 [marg.]; Ezek. 26:9. Fortifications, Judg. 9:31; 2 Sam. 5:9; 2 Kin. 25:1; 2 Chr. 11:11; 26: 9; Neh. 3:8; 4:2; Isa. 22:10; 25:12; 29:3; 32:14; Jer. 6:6; 32:24; 33:4; 51:53; Ezek. 4:2; 17:17; 21:22; 26:8; 33:27; Dan. 11:15, 19; Nah. 2:1; 3:14.

Standards, Num. 2:2,3,10,17,18,25,31,34; 10: 14,18,22,25. Uniforms of, Ezek. 23:6,12; Nah.

2:3. Standing armies, 1 Sam. 13:2; 1 Chr. 27; 2 Chr. 1:14; 17:12-19; 26:11-15.

Religious ceremonies attending: Seeking counsel from God before battle, Num. 27:21; Judg. 1:1; 1 Sam. 14:19,37-41; 23:2-12; 30:8; 2 Sam. 2:1; 5:19,23; 1 Kin. 22:7-28; 2 Kin. 3:11-19; 1 Chr. 14:10,14; Jer. 37:7-10; sacrifices, 1 Sam. 13:11,12; purifications, Num. 31:19-24. prophets prophesy before, 2 Chr. 20:14-17; holiness enjoined, Deut. 23:9; officers consecrate themselves to God, 2 Chr. 17:16. Army choir and songs, 2 Chr. 20:21,22. Ark taken to battle, Josh. 6:6,7,13; 1 Sam. 4:4-11.

Divine assistance to: When Aaron and Hur held up Moses' hands, Ex. 17:11,12; in siege of Jericho, Josh. 6; sun stands still, Josh. 10:11-14; Gideon's victory. Judg. 7; Samaria's deliverances, 1 Kin. 20; 2 Kin. 7; Jehoshaphat's victories, 2 Kin. 3; 2 Chr. 20; angel of the Lord smites the Assyrians, 2 Kin. 19:35.

Determine royal succession, 2 Sam. 2:8-10; 1 Kin. 16:16; 2 Kin. 11:4-12.

Composed of insurgents, 1 Sam. 22:1,2. Mercenaries, 2 Sam. 10:6; 1 Chr. 19:6,7; 2 Chr. 25:5,6. Confederated, Josh. 10:1-5; 11: 1-5; Judg. 1:3; 2 Sam. 10:6,15,16,19; 1 Kin. 15:20; 22:1-4; 2 Kin. 16:9; 18:19-21; 1 Chr. 19: 6,7; 2 Chr. 16:2-9; 18:1,3; 20:1; 22:5; 28:16,20; Psa. 83:1-12; Isa. 7:1-9; 8:9-12; 54:15. Exhorted before battle, Deut. 20:1-9. Battle shouts, Judg. 7:18; 1 Sam. 17:20,52. Triumphs of, celebrated: With songs, Judg. 5; 1 Sam. 18:6,7; music, 2 Chr. 20:28; dancing, 1 Sam. 18:6,7.

Rewards for meritorious conduct: The general offers his daughter in marriage, Josh. 15: 16,17; king offers his daughter, 1 Sam. 17:25; 18:17-28; promotion, 2 Sam. 23:8-39; 1 Chr. 11:6,10-47; share the spoils, Num. 31:25-47.

Children instructed in military arts, 2 Sam. 1:18.

Insubordination in, punished, Achan, Josh. 7. Check roll-call, 1 Sam. 14:17; Num. 31:48,49.

Panics: Isa. 30:17; among the Midianites, Judg. 7:21; Philistines, 1 Sam. 14:15-19; Syrians, 2 Kin. 7:7-15. Soldiers destroy each other to escape captivity, 1 Sam. 14:20; 31:4-6.

Champions fight instead of, 1 Sam. 17: 8-53; 2 Sam. 2:14-17; 21:15-22. Confidence in, vain, Psa. 33:16; 44:6. Escort duty performed by, 2 Kin. 1:9; Acts 23:23,24,31-33.

Roman army: Captains [R. V. marg., military tribunes] of, Acts 22:24-29; centurions, Matt. 8:5,8; 27:54; Luke, 7:2; 23:47; Acts 10:1, 7,22; 21:32; 22:26; 23:17,23; 24:23; 27:1,11,43; 28: 16. Divided into "bands" [R. V. marg., cohorts], Acts 10:1; 27:1.

For other than armies of the Israelites and Romans, see AMALEKITES; ASSYRIA; BABYLON; EGYPTIANS; MIDIANITES; PERSIA; SYRIA.

For commissaries of, see COMMISSARY.

For weapons used, see ARMOR.

See AMBUSH; CAVALRY; FORT; GARRISON; HERALD; HOSTAGE; NAVY; RECONNOISSANCE; SIEGE; SOLDIERS; SPIES; STANDARD; STRATEGY; TRUCE; WAR.

FIGURATIVE: Deut. 33:2; 2 Kin. 6:17; Psa. 34:7; 68:17; Rev. 9:16.

ARMONI, son of Saul, 2 Sam. 21:8.

ARMOR, the equipment of a soldier, Jer. 46:3,4; Eph. 6:14–17.

See BREASTPLATE; BRIGANDINE; COAT OF MAIL; GREAVE; HABERGEON; HELMET; SHIELD.

FIGURATIVE: Rom. 13:12; 2 Cor. 6:7; 10: 4; Eph. 6:11-17; 1 Thess. 5:8.

ARMOR-BEARER, an attendant who carried a soldier's equipment. Of Abimelech, Judg. 9:54; Jonathan, 1 Sam. 14:6,7,12, 14,17; Saul, 1 Sam. 16:21; 31:6; Goliath, 1 Sam. 17:7; Joab, 2 Sam. 18:15.

ARMORY. A place for the storage of armor, Neh. 3:19; Song 4;4; Isa. 22:8; 39:2. In different parts of the kingdom, 1 Kin. 10:17; 2 Chr. 11:12.

See JERUSALEM.

FIGURATIVE: Jer. 50:25.

ARMS. See ARMOR; ARROW; ARTILLERY; BATTLE-AX; BATTERING-RAM; BOW; CHARIOT; DAGGER; DART; ENGINE; JAVELIN; SHIELD; SLING; SPEAR; SWORD.

ARNAN, patronymic of a family descended from David, 1 Chr. 3:21.

ARNON. A river emptying into the Dead Sea from the east. Boundary between Moabites and Amorites, Num. 21:13,14,26; 22:36; Deut. 2:24,36; 3:8,16; Josh. 12:1. Fords of, Isa. 16:2. Miracles at, Num. 21:14.

AROD, son of Gad. Num. 26:17.

ARODI, descendants of Arod, Gen. 46:16.

AROER. 1. A city of the Amorites in the valley of the river Arnon, Deut. 4:48. Conquered by Israelites, Deut. 2:36; 3:12; Judg. 11:26. Taken by Hazael, 2 Kin. 10:33.

2. A city built, or, probably more correctly, rebuilt, by the Gadites, Num. 32:34; Josh. 13:25. Jephthah smites the Ammonites at, Judg. 11:33.

3. A city in Judah, 1 Sam. 30:28. Birthplace of two of David's heroes, 1 Chr. 11:44.

ARPAD, called also ARPHAD. A fortified city of Syria, perhaps identical with Arvad, 2 Kin. 18:34; 19:13. Idols of, Isa. 36:19.

ARPHAD. See ARPAD.

ARPHAXAD, son of Shem, Gen. 10:22; 11:10-13; 1 Chr. 1:17,18,24; Luke 3:36.

ARREST. Of Jesus, Matt. 26:57; Mark 14:46; Luke 22:54; John 18:12; apostles, Acts 5:17,18; 6:12; Paul and Silas, Acts 16:19; Paul, Acts 21:30. Paul authorized to arrest Christians, Acts 9:2.

See EXTRADITION; PRISON; PRISONERS.

ARROGANCE. 1 Sam. 2:3. Talk no more so exceeding proudly; let *not* arrogancy come out of your mouth: for the LORD *is* a God of knowledge, and by him actions are weighed.

Prov. 8:13. Pride, and arrogancy, and the evil way, and the froward mouth, do I hate.

Isa. 13:11. I will cause the arrogancy of the proud to cease, and will lay low the haughtiness of the terrible.

See PRIDE.

ARROW, a weapon. Used in hunting, Gen. 21:20; 27:3; in war, 1 Sam. 31:3; 2 Sam.

22:15; 1 Kin. 22:34; 2 Kin. 19:32; Psa. 7:13; Isa. 22:3; Jer. 51:3. Divination by, Ezek. 21: 21. Shot by Jonathan as a sign to David, 1 Sam. 20:20–42. Shot by Joash as a sign against the Syrians, 2 Kin. 13:14-19.

FIGURATIVE: Num. 24:8; Deut. 32:23,42; Job 6:4; Psa. 11:2; 21:12; 38:2; 45:5; 57:4; 58:7; 91:5; 120:4; 144:6; Prov. 25:18; Lam. 3:12,13; Ezek. 5:16; Hab. 3:11.

ARSON. Psa. 74:7,8. Law concerning, Ex. 22:6.

INSTANCES OF: By Samson, Judg. 15:4, 5; Absalom, 2 Sam. 14:30; Zimri, 1 Kin. 16:18.

ART. PRIMITIVE: Invention of musical instruments and instruments of iron and copper [*A. V.*, brass], Gen. 4:21,22. Carpentry, Gen. 6:14–16; Ex. 31:2–9. Of the apothecary or perfumer, Ex. 30:25,35; armorer, 1 Sam. 8:12; baker, Gen. 40:1; 1 Sam. 8:13; barber, Isa. 7:20; Ezek. 5:1; brickmaker, Gen. 11:3; Ex. 5:7,8,18; calker, Ezek. 27:9,27; compounding confections, 1 Sam. 8:13; gardener, Jer. 29:5; John 20:15; goldsmith, Isa. 40:19; mariner, Ezek. 27:8,9; mason, 2 Sam. 5:11; 2 Chr. 24:12; musician, 1 Sam. 18:6; 1 Chr. 15: 16; potter, Isa. 64:8; Jer. 18:3; Lam. 4:2; Zech. 11:13; refiner of metals, 1 Chr. 28:18; Mal. 3: 2,3; ropemaker, Judg. 16:11; stonecutter, Ex. 20:25; 1 Chr. 22:15; shipbuilder, 1 Kin. 9:26; smelter of metals, Job 28:2; spinner, Ex. 35: 25; Prov. 31:19; tailor, Ex. 28:3; tanner, Acts 9:43: 10:6; tentmaker, Gen. 4:20; Acts 18:3; weaver, Ex. 35:35; John 19:23; wine maker, Neh. 13:15; Isa. 63:3.

ARTISANS, SKILLFUL: Jubal, Gen. 4:21; Tubal-cain, Gen. 4:22; Bezaleel and Aholiab, Ex. 31:2–14; 35:30–35; Hiram, 1 Kin. 7:13–51; 2 Chr. 2:13,14.

For the various arts practised, and products manufactured, in ancient times, see APOTHECARY; BEATEN WORK; BRASS; BREAD; BRICK; CARPENTRY; CARVING; CONFECTIONER; COPPER; DRAWING; DYEING; EMBROIDERY; ENGRAVING; FULLER; GOLDSMITH; LAPIDARY; LEATHER; LIME; MASON; MASTER WORKMAN; MOLDING; MUSIC; PAINTING; PAPER; PARCHMENT; PICTURES; POTTERY; ROPES; SHIPS; SILK; SILVERSMITH; SMITH; SOAP; SPINNING; SUN-DIAL; TAPESTRY; TAILORING; TENTS; WEAVING; WINE.

ARTAXERXES. 1. A Persian king, probably identical with AHASUERUS. Prohibits the rebuilding of Jerusalem, Ezra 4:7-24.

2. King of Persia. Decrees of, in behalf of the Jews, Ezra 7; Neh. 2: 5:14.

ARTEMAS, a companion of Paul, Tit. 3:12.

ARTILLERY. 1 Sam. 20:40. See ARMS.

ARTISAN. See ART; MASTER WORKMAN.

ARUBOTH, a district laid under tribute to Solomon's commissariat, 1 Kin. 4:10.

ARUMAH, a place near Shechem, Judg. 9:41.

ARVAD, an island near Zidon, Ezek. 27:8,11.

ARVADITES, descendants of Canaan, Gen. 10:18; 1 Chr. 1:16; Ezek. 27:8,11.

ARZA, a steward of Elah, 1 Kin. 16:9.

ASA. 1. King of Judah, 1 Kin. 15:8–24; 1 Chr. 3:10; 2 Chr. 14; 15; 16; Matt. 1:7.

2. A Levite, 1 Chr. 9:16.

ASAHEL. 1. Nephew of David, and one of his captains, 2 Sam. 2:18–24,32; 3:27; 23:24; 1 Chr. 2:16; 11:26; 27:7.

2. A Levite, commissioned by Jehoshaphat to teach the law to Judah, 2 Chr. 17:8.

3. A Levite, who had charge of tithes, 2 Chr. 31:13.

4. Father of Jonathan, Ezra 10:15.

ASAHIAH, an officer of King Josiah, 2 Kin. 22:12–20; 2 Chr. 34:20–28.

ASAIAH. 1. A descendant of Simeon, 1 Chr. 4:36.

2. A Levite, 1 Chr. 6:30. Probably identical with a man of same name mentioned in 1 Chr. 15:6,11.

3. A Shilonite, 1 Chr. 9:5.

ASAPH. 1. Father of Joah, 2 Kin. 18:18; Isa. 36:3,22.

2. Son of Berachiah. One of the three leaders of music in David's organization of the tabernacle service, 1 Chr. 15:16–19; 16:5–7; 25:1–9; 2 Chr. 5:12; 35:15; Neh. 12:46. Appointed to sound the cymbals in the temple choir, 1 Chr. 15:17,19; 16:5,7. A composer of sacred lyrics, 2 Chr. 29:13–30. See titles of Psa. 50 and 73–83, inclusive. Descendants of, in the temple choir, 1 Chr. 25:1–9; 2 Chr. 20:14; 29:13; Ezra 2:41; 3:10; Neh. 7:44; 11:22.

3. A Levite, whose descendants dwelt in Jerusalem after the exile, 1 Chr. 9:15.

4. A Kohath Levite, 1 Chr. 26:1.

5. Keeper of forests, Neh. 2:8.

ASAREEL, son of Jehaleleel, 1 Chr. 4:16.

ASARELAH. One of the temple choir, 1 Chr. 25:2,14; probably identical with AZA-REEL. *v.* 18.

ASCENSION. Of Elijah, 2 Kin. 2:1–18. Of Jesus, Mark 16:19,20; Luke 24:50–53; Acts 1:9–12. Of two witnesses, Rev. 11:12.

ASCETICISM, a philosophy that leads to severe austerities in subordinating the body to the control of the moral attributes of the mind. Extreme application of, rebuked by Jesus, Matt. 11:19; Luke 7:34; by Paul, Col. 2:20–23; 1 Tim. 4:1–4,8. See STOICISM.

INSTANCES OF THE PRACTICE OF: John the Baptist, Matt. 11:18; Luke 7:33. Those who practised celibacy "for the kingdom of heaven's sake," Matt. 19:12.

ASENATH, wife of Joseph, Gen. 41:45, 50; 46:20.

ASER. See ASHER.

ASH, a tree, Isa. 44:14.

ASHAN, a Levitical city of Judah, later of Simeon, Josh. 15:42; 19:7; 1 Chr. 4:32; 6:59. See AIN.

ASHBEA, a descendant of Shelah, 1 Chr. 4:21.

ASHBEL, son of Benjamin, Gen. 46:21; Num. 26:38, 1 Chr. 8:1.

ASHCHENAZ. See ASHKENAZ.

ASHDOD. A city of the Philistines,

Josh. 13:3; 1 Sam. 6:17; Amos 3:9. Ana kim inhabit, Josh. 11:22. Assigned to Judah, Josh. 15:47. Dagon's temple in, in which was deposited the ark, 1 Sam. 5. Conquest of, by Uzziah, 2 Chr. 26:6; by Tartan, Isa. 20:1. People of, conspire against the Jews, Neh. 4:7,8. Jews intermarry with, Neh. 13:23,24. Prophecies concerning, Jer. 25:20; Amos 1:8; 3; Zeph. 2:4; Zech. 9:6. Called AZOTUS, Acts 8:40.

ASHDOTH-PISGAH, the water courses flowing from Mount Pisgah, Deut. 3:17; 4:49; Josh. 12:3; 13:20.

ASHER. 1. Son of Jacob, by Zilpah, Gen. 30:13; 35:26; 49:20; Ex. 1:4; 1 Chr. 2:2. Descendants of, Gen. 46:17; Num. 26; 44–47.

2. Tribe of: Census of, by families, Num. 1:40,41; 26:44–47; 1 Chr. 7:40; 12:36. Station of, in camp, Num. 2:25,27. Prophecies concerning, by Moses, Deut. 33:24,25; by John, Rev. 7:6. Allotment to, of land in Canaan, Josh. 19:24–31; Ezek. 48:2. Upbraided by Deborah, Judg. 5:17. Summoned by Gideon, Judg. 6:35; 7:23. Join Hezekiah, 2 Chr. 30:11.

3. A city of Shechem, Josh. 17:7; 1 Kin. 4:16.

ASHES. Uses of, in purification, Num. 19:9,10,17; Heb. 9:13. A symbol of mourning, 2 Sam. 13:19; Esth. 4:1,3. Sitting in, Job 2:8; Isa. 58:5; Jer. 6:26; Ezek. 27:30; Jonah 3:6; Luke 10:13. Repenting in, Job 42:6; Dan. 9:3; Jonah 3:6; Matt. 11:21; Luke 10:13. Disguises in, 1 Kin. 20:38,41.

ASHIMA, an idol, 2 Kin. 17:30.

ASHKELON, called also ASKELON. One of the five chief cities of the Philistines, Josh. 13:3. Captured by the people of Judah, Judg. 1:18. Samson slays thirty men of, Judg. 14:19. Emerods (tumors, *R. V.*) of, 1 Sam. 6:17. Prophecies concerning, Jer. 25:20; 47:5,7; Amos 1:8; Zeph. 2:4,7; Zech. 9:5.

ASHKENAZ, called also ASHCHENAZ. Son of Gomer, Gen. 10:3; 1 Chr. 1:6. Descendants of, Jer. 51:27.

ASHNAH, name of two towns in Judah, Josh. 15:33,43.

ASHPENAZ, a prince in Nebuchadnezzar's court, Dan. 1:3.

ASHRIEL. See ASRIEL.

ASHTAROTH. 1. Plural form of ASHTORETH, which see.

2. The capital city of Bashan, Deut. 1:4; Josh. 9:10. Giants dwell at, Josh. 12:4. Allotted to Manasseh, Josh. 13:31; 1 Chr. 6:71. Possibly identical with ASHTEROTH KARNAIM, mentioned in Gen. 14:5.

ASHTEROTH KARNAIM, an ancient city of Palestine taken by Chedorlaomer. Gen. 14:5.

ASHTORETH. An idol of the Philistines, Zidonians, and Phenicians. Probably identical with queen of heaven, Jer. 7:18. Worshiped by Israelites, Judg. 2:13; 10:6; 1 Sam. 7:3,4; 12:10; 1 Kin. 11:5,33; 2 Kin. 23:13. Temple of, 1 Sam. 31:10. High places of, at Jerusalem, destroyed, 2 Kin. 23:13.

ASHUR, son of Hezron, 1 Chr. 2:24; 4:5.

ASHURITES (possibly GESHURITES), 2 Sam. 2:9; Ezek. 27:6.

ASHVATH, son of Japhlet, 1 Chr. 7:33.

ASIA. Inhabitants of, in Jerusalem, at Pentecost, Acts 2:9; 21:27; 24:18. Paul and Silas forbidden by the Holy Ghost to preach in, Acts 16:6. Gospel preached in, by Paul, Acts 19; 20:4. Paul leaves, Acts 20:16. Churches of, 1 Cor. 16:19; Rev. 1:4,11.

ASIEL, grandfather of Jehu, 1 Chr. 4:35.

ASKELON. See ASHKELON.

ASNAH, descendants of, return to Jerusalem, Ezra 2:50.

ASNAPPER, a noble Assyrian prince, who colonized the cities of Samaria after the Israelites were taken captive to Assyria, Ezra 4:10.

See SAMARIA.

ASP. A venomous serpent, Deut. 32:33; Job 20:14,16; Isa. 11:8; Rom. 3:13. Venom of, illustrates the speech of the wicked, Psa. 140:3; Rom. 3:13; injurious effects of wine, Deut. 32:33; Prov. 23:32. Deprived of venom, illustrates conversion, Isa. 11:8,9.

ASPATHA, son of Haman, Esth. 9:7.

ASPHALTUM. See SLIME.

ASRIEL, called also ASHRIEL, son of Manasseh, Josh. 17:2; 1 Chr. 7:14.

ASS. DOMESTICATED: Herds of, Gen. 12:16; 24:35; 32:5; 34:28; Num. 31:34,45; 1 Chr. 5:21; Ezra 2:67; Neh. 7:69.

USED for riding, Gen. 22:3; Num. 22: 21–33; Josh. 15:18; Judg. 1:14; 5:10; 1 Sam. 25: 23; 2 Chr. 28:15; Zech. 9:9; by Jesus, Matt. 21: 2,5; Luke 13:15; John 12:14,15; Zech. 9:9; carrying burdens, Gen. 42:26; 2 Sam. 16:1; Isa. 30:6; drawing chariots, Isa. 21:7; for food, 2 Kin. 6:25. Not to be yoked with an ox, Deut. 22:10. Rest on Sabbath, Ex. 23:12. Bridles for, Prov. 26:3. Jawbone of, used by Samson with which to slay Philistines, Judg. 15:15–17.

FIRSTLINGS OF, redeemed, Ex. 13:13; 34:20.

WILD: Job. 6:5; 24:5; 39:5; Psa. 104:11; Isa. 32:14; Jer. 2:24; 14:6; Hos. 8:9.

ASSASSINATION. David's abhorrence of, 2 Sam. 4:9–12. Laws prohibiting, Deut. 27:24.

INSTANCES OF: Of Eglon, by Ehud, Judg. 3:15–22; Abner, by Joab, 2 Sam. 3:27; Ish-bosheth, by the sons of Rimmon, 2 Sam. 4:5–7; Amnon, by Absalom, 2 Sam. 13:28,29; Amasa, by Joab, 2 Sam. 20:9,10; Joash, by his servants, 2 Kin. 12:20; Sennacherib, by his sons, 2 Kin. 19:37; Isa. 37:38.

ASSAULT AND BATTERY. LAWS CONCERNING: Ex. 21:15. And he that smiteth his father, or his mother, shall be surely put to death.

18. And if men strive together, and one smite another with a stone, or with *his* fist, and he die not, but keepeth *his* bed : 19. If he rise again, and walk abroad upon his staff, then shall he that smote *him* be quit: only he shall pay *for* the loss of his time, and shall cause *him* to be thoroughly healed.

22. If men strive, and hurt a woman with **child,** so that her fruit depart *from her,* and

yet no mischief follow: he shall be surely punished, according as the woman's husband will lay upon him; and he shall pay as the judges *determine.* 23. And if *any* mischief follow, then thou shalt give life for life, 24. Eye for eye, tooth for tooth, hand for hand, foot for foot, 25. Burning for burning, wound for wound, stripe for stripe.

26. And if a man smite the eye of his servant, or the eye of his maid, that it perish; he shall let him go free for his eye's sake. 27. And if he smite out his manservant's tooth, or his maidservant's tooth; he shall let him go free for his tooth's sake.

Deut. 17:8. If there arise a matter too hard for thee in judgment, between blood and blood, between plea and plea, and between stroke and stroke, *being* matters of controversy within thy gates: then shalt thou arise, and get thee up into the place which the LORD thy God shall choose; 9. And thou shalt come unto the priests the Levites, and unto the judge that shall be in those days, and enquire; and they shall shew thee the sentence of judgment: 10. And thou shalt do according to the sentence, which they of that place which the LORD shall choose shall shew thee; and thou shalt observe to do according to all that they inform thee: 11. According to the sentence of the law which they shall teach thee, and according to the judgment which they shall tell thee, thou shalt do: thou shalt not decline from the sentence which they shall shew thee, to the right hand, nor *to* the left. 12. And the man that will do presumptuously, and will not hearken unto the priest that standeth to minister there before the LORD thy God, or unto the judge, even that man shall die: and thou shalt put away the evil from Israel.

Matt. 5:38, Ye have heard that it hath been said, An eye for an eye, and a tooth for a tooth: 39. But I say unto you, That ye resist not evil: but whosoever shall smite thee on thy right cheek, turn to him the other also.

THE SMITING OF JESUS: Prophecies of, Isa. 50:6; Lam. 3:30. The attacks upon, Matt. 26:67; 27:30; Mark 14:65; Luke 22:63; John 19:3.

See STRIPES; STONING.

ASSHUR, son of Shem, and ancestor of the Assyrians, Gen. 10:11,22; 1 Chr. 1:17; Ezek. 32:22.

See ASSYRIA.

ASSHURIM, descendants of Dedan, Gen. 25:3.

ASSIR. 1. Son of Korah, Ex. 6:24; 1 Chr. 6:22.

2. Son of Ebiasaph, 1 Chr. 6:23,37.

3. Son of Jeconiah, 1 Chr. 3:17.

ASSOS, a seaport in Mysia, Acts 20:13,14.

ASSURANCE. Produced by faith, Eph. 3:12; 2 Tim. 1:12; Heb. 10:22. Made full by hope, Heb. 6:11,19. Confirmed by love, 1 John 3:14,19; 4:18. Is the effect of righteousness, Isa. 32:17. Is abundant in the understanding of the gospel, Col. 2:2; 1 Thess. 1:5.

SAINTS PRIVILEGED TO HAVE, of their election, Psa. 4:3; 1 Thess. 1:4; their redemption, Job 19:25; their adoption, Rom. 8:16; 1 John 3:2; their salvation, Isa. 12:2; eternal life, 1 John 5:13; the unalienable love of God, Rom. 8:38,39; union with God and Christ, 1 Cor. 6:15; 2 Cor. 13:5; Eph. 5:30; 1 John 2:5; 4:13; peace with God by Christ, Rom. 5:1: preservation, Psa. 3:6; 8; 27:3-5; 46:1-3; answers to prayer, 1 John 3:22; 5:14,15; comfort in affliction, Psa. 73:26; Luke 4:18; 2 Cor. 4:8-10,16-18; continuance in grace, Phil. 1:6; a support in death, Psa. 23:4; a glorious resurrection, Job 19:26; Psa. 17:15; Phil. 3:21; 1 John 3:2; a kingdom, Heb. 12:28; Rev. 5:10; a crown, 2 Tim. 4:7,8; Jas. 1:12. Saints give diligence to attain, 2 Pet. 1:10,11; strive to maintain, Heb. 3:14,18. Confident hope in God restores, Psa. 42:11.

Exemplified: David, Psa. 23:4; 73:24-26; Paul, 2 Tim. 1:12; 4:18.—*Bible Text Book.*

See FAITH.

ASSYRIA. An empire founded by Nimrod, Gen. 10:8-12; Mic. 5:6. It extended from east of the Tigris, Gen. 2:14; 10:11; possibly to Egypt, Gen. 25:18. Its armies invade the land of Israel under Pul, 2 Kin. 15:19; 1 Chr. 5:26; Tiglath, 2 Kin. 15:29; 1 Chr. 5:6,26; Shalmaneser, 2 Kin. 17:3-6,24-27; 18:9-12; Jer. 50:17; Sennacherib, 2 Kin. 18:13-37; 19; 2 Chr. 32; Isa. chapters 36; 37.

Army of, destroyed by the angel of the Lord, Isa. 37:36. Alliances with, sought by Judah and Israel, Hos. 5:13. Israelites subject to, Lam. 5:6. Israelites carried captive into, 2 Kin. 17:3-23. Jews carried captive to, 2 Kin. chapters 24; 25; 2 Chr. 36:5-21. Invaded by Pharaoh-nechoh, 2 Kin. 23:29.

Commerce of, Ezek. 27:23. Productiveness of, Isa. 36:17.

Prophecies concerning, Isa. 7:17-25; 8:4-10; 10:5-34; 14:24-28; 19:23-25; 20; 30:27-33; 31:8,9; 37:21-35; Jer. 1:15; Ezek. 31; Jonah 3:1-4; Nah. chapters 1-3; Zeph. 2:13-15; Zech. 10:11.

Prophecies of captivity of Israelites in, Hos. 9:3; 11:5,11.

Idols of. See ADRAMMELECH, ANAMMELECH, NISROCH, TARTAK.

ASTROLOGY, Isa. 47:13; Jer. 10:1,2; Dan. 1:20; 2:27; 4:7; 5:7.

See ASTRONOMY; SORCERY.

ASTRONOMY. Job 26:7. He stretcheth out the north over the empty place, *and* hangeth the earth upon nothing. 13. By his spirit he hath garnished the heavens; his hand hath formed the crooked serpent.

Job 37:18. Hast thou with him spread out the sky, *which is* strong, *and* is a molten looking glass?

Job 38:31. Canst thou bind the sweet influences of Pleiades, or loose the bands of Orion? 32. Canst thou bring forth Mazzaroth in his season? or canst thou guide Arcturus with his sons? 33. Knowest thou the ordinances of heaven? canst thou set the dominion thereof in the earth?

Psa. 8:3. When I consider thy heavens, the work of thy fingers, the moon and the stars, which thou hast ordained;

Psa. 19:1. The heavens declare the glory of God; and the firmament sheweth his handywork. 2. Day unto day uttereth speech, and night unto night sheweth knowledge. 3. *There is* no speech nor language, *where* their voice is not heard. 4. Their line is gone out through all the earth, and their words to the end of the world. In them hath he set a tabernacle for the sun, 5. Which *is* as a bridegroom coming out of his chamber, *and* rejoiceth as a strong man to run a race. 6. His going forth *is* from the end of the heaven, and his circuit unto the ends of it: and there is nothing hid from the heat thereof.

Psa. 68:33. To him that rideth upon the heavens of heavens, *which were* of old;

Psa. 136:5. To him that by wisdom made the heavens: for his mercy *endureth* for ever. 6. To him that stretched out the earth above the waters: for his mercy *endureth* for ever. 7. To him that made great lights: for his mercy *endureth* for ever: 8. The sun to rule by day: for his mercy *endureth* for ever: 9. The moon and stars to rule by night: for his mercy *endureth* for ever.

Isa. 13:10. For the stars of heaven and the constellations thereof shall not give their light: the sun shall be darkened in his going forth, and the moon shall not cause her light to shine.

Isa. 40:22. *It is* he that sitteth upon the circle of the earth, and the inhabitants thereof *are* as grasshoppers; that stretcheth out the heavens as a curtain, and spreadeth them out as a tent to dwell in: 26. Lift up your eyes on high, and behold who hath created these *things*, that bringeth out their host by number: he calleth them all by names by the greatness of his might, for that *he is* strong in power; not one faileth.

Isa. 47:13. Let now the astrologers, the stargazers, the monthly prognosticators, stand up, and save thee from *these things* that shall come upon thee.

Jer. 31:35. Thus saith the LORD, which giveth the sun for a light by day, *and* the ordinances of the moon and of the stars for a light by night, which divideth the sea when the waves thereof roar; The LORD of hosts *is* his name: 36. If those ordinances depart from before me, saith the LORD, *then* the seed of Israel also shall cease from being a nation before me for ever. 37. Thus saith the LORD; If heaven above can be measured, and the foundations of the earth searched out beneath, I will also cast off all the seed of Israel for all that they have done, saith the LORD.

Jer. 33:22. As the host of heaven cannot be numbered, neither the sand of the sea measured: so will I multiply the seed of David my servant, and the Levites that minister unto me.

Amos 5:8. *Seek him* that maketh the [1 seven] stars and Orion, and turneth the shadow of death into the morning, and maketh the day dark with night: that calleth for the waters of the sea, and poureth them out upon the face of the earth: The LORD *is* his name: [1 R. V. Pleiades]

1 Cor. 15:41. *There is* one glory of the sun, and another glory of the moon, and another glory of the stars: for *one* star differeth from *another* star in glory.

Jude 13. Raging waves of the sea, foaming out their own shame; wandering stars, to whom is reserved the blackness of darkness for ever.

SIDEREAL PHENOMENA: Josh. 10:12. Then spake Joshua to the LORD in the day when the LORD delivered up the Amorites before the children of Israel, and he said in the sight of Israel, Sun, stand thou still upon Gibeon; and thou, Moon, in the valley of Ajalon. 13. And the sun stood still, and the moon stayed, until the people had avenged themselves upon their enemies. *Is* not this written in the book of Jasher? So the sun stood still in the midst of heaven, and hastened not to go down about a whole day. 14. And there was no day like that before it or after it, that the LORD hearkened unto the voice of a man: for the LORD fought for Israel.

Job 9:6. Which shaketh the earth out of her place, and the pillars thereof tremble. 7. Which commandeth the sun, and it riseth not; and sealeth up the stars. 8. Which alone spreadeth out the heavens, and treadeth upon the waves of the sea. 9. Which maketh Arcturus, Orion, and Pleiades, and the chambers of the south.

Eccl. 1:5. The sun also ariseth, and the sun goeth down, and hasteth to his place where he arose.

Isa. 13:13. Therefore I will shake the heavens, and the earth shall remove out of her place, in the wrath of the LORD of hosts, and in the day of his fierce anger.

Isa. 34:4. And all the host of heaven shall be dissolved, and the heavens shall be rolled together as a scroll: and all their host shall fall down, as the leaf falleth off from the vine, and as a falling *fig* from the fig tree.

Ezek. 32:7. And when I shall put thee out, I will cover the heaven, and make the stars thereof dark; I will cover the sun with a cloud, and the moon shall not give her light. 8. All the bright lights of heaven will I make dark over thee, and set darkness upon thy land, saith the Lord GOD.

Matt. 24:29. Immediately after the tribulation of those days shall the sun be darkened, and the moon shall not give her light, and the stars shall fall from heaven, and the powers of the heavens shall be shaken: [Mark 13:24,25.] 35. Heaven and earth shall pass away, but my words shall not pass away.

Matt. 27:45. Now from the sixth hour there was darkness over all the land unto the ninth hour.

Luke 21:25. And there shall be signs in the sun, and in the moon, and in the stars;

Luke 23:44. And it was about the sixth hour, and there was a darkness over all the earth until the ninth hour. 45. And the sun was darkened, and the veil of the temple was rent in the midst.

Acts 2:19. And I will shew wonders in heaven above, and signs in the earth beneath; blood, and fire, and vapour of smoke: 20. The sun shall be turned into darkness, and the moon into blood, before that great and notable day of the Lord come:

2 Pet. 3:10. But the day of the Lord will come as a thief in the night; in the which the heavens shall pass away with a great noise, and the elements shall melt with fervent heat, the earth also and the works that are therein shall be burned up.

Rev. 6:12. And I beheld when he had opened the sixth seal, and, lo, there was a great earthquake; and the sun became black as sackcloth of hair, and the moon became as blood; 13. And the stars of heaven fell unto the earth, even as a fig tree casteth her untimely figs, when she is shaken of a mighty wind. 14. And the heaven departed as a scroll when it is rolled together;

Rev. 8:10. And the third angel sounded, and there fell a great star from heaven, burning as it were a lamp, and it fell upon the third part of the rivers, and upon the fountains of waters; 11. And the name of the star is called Wormwood: and the third part of the waters became wormwood; and many men died of the waters, because they were made bitter. 12. And the fourth angel sounded, and the third part of the sun was smitten, and the third part of the moon, and the third part of the stars; so as the third part of them was darkened, and the day shone not for a third part of it, and the night likewise.

Rev. 9:1. And the fifth angel sounded, and I saw a star fall from heaven unto the earth: and to him was given the key of the bottomless pit. 2. And he opened the bottomless pit; and there arose a smoke out of the pit, as the smoke of a great furnace; and the sun and the air were darkened by reason of the smoke of the pit.

Rev. 10:1. And I saw another mighty angel come down from heaven, clothed with a cloud: and a rainbow *was* upon his head, and his face *was* as it were the sun, and his feet as pillars of fire: 2. And he had in his hand a little book open: and he set his right foot upon the sea, and *his* left *foot* on the earth,

Rev. 12:3. And there appeared another wonder in heaven; and behold a great red dragon, having seven heads and ten horns, and seven crowns upon his heads. 4. And his tail drew the third part of the stars of heaven, and did cast them to the earth:

Rev. 13:13. And he doeth great wonders, so that he maketh fire come down from heaven on the earth in the sight of men,

Rev. 16:8. And the fourth angel poured out his vial upon the sun; and power was given unto him to scorch men with fire. 9. And men were scorched with great heat

Rev. 19:11. And I saw heaven opened, and behold a white horse; and he that sat upon him was called Faithful and True, and in righteousness he doth judge and make war. 12. His eyes were as a flame of fire, and on his head were many crowns; and he had a name written, that no man knew, but he himself. 13. And he was clothed with a vesture dipped in blood: and his name is called The Word of God. 14. And the armies which were in heaven followed him upon white horses, clothed in fine linen, white and clean.

Rev. 21:1. And I saw a new heaven and a new earth: for the first heaven and the first earth were passed away;

See CONSTELLATIONS; ECLIPSE; HEAVEN; METEOROLOGY; MOON; STARS; SUN.

ASUPPIM, a temple gate, 1 Chr. 26:15,17.

ASYNCRITUS, a disciple at Rome, Rom. 16:14.

ATAD, the place where the sons of Jacob mourned for their father, Gen. 50:10,11.

ATARAH, wife of Jerahmeel, 1 Chr. 2:26.

ATAROTH, called also ATROTH. 1. A city E. of Jordan, Num. 32:3,34.

2. A city, or possibly two different cities, of Ephraim, Josh. 16:2,5,7; 18:13.

3. A city of Judah, 1 Chr. 2:54. Called ATROTH-BETH-JOAB [R. V.].

4. A city of Gad, Num. 32:35.

ATAROTH-ADAR, called also ATA-ROTH-ADDAR. See ATAROTH, 2.

ATER. 1. A descendant of Hezekiah, who returned from Babylon, Ezra 2:16; Neh. 7:21.

2. A porter, Ezra 2:42; Neh. 7:45.

3. An Israelite, who subscribed to Nehemiah's covenant, Neh. 10:17.

ATHACH, a city of Judah, 1 Sam. 30:30.

ATHAIAH, perhaps identical with ASA-IAH, Neh. 11:4.

ATHALIAH. 1. Wife of Jehoram, king of Judah, 2 Kin. 8:18,26; 11:1–3,12–16,20; 2 Chr. 22:10–12; 23:12–15,21.

2. Son of Jehoram, 1 Chr. 8:26.

3. Father of Jeshaiah, Ezra 8:7.

ATHEISM. Psa. 10:4. The wicked in the pride of his countenance, saith, He will not require it. All his thoughts are, There is no God. Psa. 14:1. The fool hath said in his heart, There is no God. Psa. 53:1.

ARGUMENTS AGAINST: Job 12:7. But ask now the beasts, and they shall teach thee: and the fowls of the air, and they shall tell thee: 8. Or speak to the earth, and it shall teach thee: and the fishes of the sea shall declare unto thee. 9. Who knoweth not in all these that the hand of the LORD hath wrought this? 10. In whose hand is the soul of every living thing, and the breath of all mankind. 11. Doth not the ear try words? and the mouth taste his meat? 12. With the ancient is wisdom; and in length of days understanding. 13. With him is wisdom and strength, he hath counsel and understanding. 14. Behold, he breaketh down, and it cannot be built again: he shut-

teth up a man, and there can be no opening. 15. Behold, he withholdeth the waters, and they dry up: also he sendeth them out, and they overturn the earth. 16. With him is strength and wisdom: the deceived and the deceiver are his. 17. He leadeth counsellors away spoiled, and maketh the judges fools. 18. He looseth the bond of kings, and girdeth their loins with a girdle. 19. He leadeth princes away spoiled, and overthroweth the mighty. 20. He removeth away the speech of the trusty, and taketh away the understanding of the aged. 21. He poureth contempt upon princes, and weakeneth the strength of the mighty. 22. He discovereth deep things out of darkness, and bringeth out to light the shadow of death. 23. He increaseth the nations, and destroyeth them: he enlargeth the nations, and straiteneth them again. 24. He taketh away the heart of the chief of the people of the earth, and causeth them to wander in a wilderness where there is no way. 25. They grope in the dark without light, and he maketh them to stagger like a drunken man.

Rom. 1:19. Because that which may be known of God is manifest in them: for God hath shewed it unto them. 20. For the invisible things of him from the creation of the world are clearly seen, being understood by the things that are made, even his eternal power and Godhead; so that they are without excuse:

See GOD; FAITH; UNBELIEF.

ATHENS, a city of Greece, Acts 17:15–34; 1 Thess. 3:1.

ATHLAI, a son of Bebai, Ezra 10:28.

ATOMS OF MATTER, Prov. 8:26.

ATONEMENT. For tabernacle and furniture, Lev. 16:15–20,33. In consecration of the Levites, Num. 8:21. For those defiled by the dead, Num. 6:11. Made for houses, Lev. 14:53.

For sin, see below.

By meat offerings, Lev. 5:11–13; by jewels, Num. 31:50; by money, Ex. 30:12–16; Lev. 5: 15,16; 2 Kin. 12:16; by incense, Num. 16:46–50; by animals, see below; by Jesus, see below.

DAY OF: Time of, Ex. 30:10; Lev. 23:27; 25:9; Num. 29:7. How observed, Ex. 30:10: Lev. 16:2–34; 23:27–32; Num. 29:7–11; Heb. 5:3; 9:7.

MADE BY ANIMAL SACRIFICES: Ex. 29: 36. And thou shalt offer every day a bullock for a sin offering for atonement: and thou shalt cleanse the altar, when thou hast made an atonement for it, and thou shalt anoint it, to sanctify it.

Lev. 1:4. And he shall put his hand upon the head of the burnt offering; and it shall be accepted for him to make atonement for him.

Lev. 4:13. And if the whole congregation of Israel sin through ignorance, and the thing be hid from the eyes of the assembly, and they have done somewhat against any of the commandments of the LORD concern-

ing things which should not be done, and are guilty; 14. When the sin, which they have sinned against it, is known, then the congregation shall offer a young bullock for the sin, and bring him before the tabernacle of the congregation. 15. And the elders of the congregation shall lay their hands upon the head of the bullock before the LORD: and the bullock shall be killed before the LORD. 17. And the priest shall dip his finger *in some* of the blood, and sprinkle *it* seven times before the LORD, *even* before the vail. 18. And he shall put *some* of the blood upon the horns of the altar which *is* before the LORD, that *is* in the tabernacle of the congregation, and shall pour out all the blood at the bottom of the altar of the burnt offering, which *is at* the door of the tabernacle of the congregation.

Lev. 4:20. And he shall do with the bullock as he did with the bullock for a sin offering, so shall he do with this: and the priest shall make an atonement for them, and it shall be forgiven them.

22. When a ruler hath sinned, and done *somewhat* through ignorance *against* any of the commandments of the LORD his God *concerning things* which should not be done, and is guilty; 23. Or if his sin, wherein he hath sinned, come to his knowledge; he shall bring his offering, a kid of the goats, a male without blemish: 24. And he shall lay his hand upon the head of the goat, and kill it in the place where they kill the burnt offering before the LORD: it *is* a sin offering. 25. And the priest shall take of the blood of the sin offering with his finger, and put *it* upon the horns of the altar of burnt offering, and shall pour out his blood at the bottom of the altar of burnt offering. 26. And he shall burn all his fat upon the altar, as the fat of the sacrifice of peace offerings: and the priest shall make an atonement for him as concerning his sin, and it shall be forgiven him. 27. And if any one of the common people sin through ignorance, while he doeth *somewhat against* any of the commandments of the LORD *concerning things* which ought not to be done, and be guilty; 28. Or if his sin, which he hath sinned, come to his knowledge; then he shall bring his offering, a kid of the goats, a female without blemish, for his sin which he hath sinned. 29. And he shall lay his hand upon the head of the sin offering, and slay the sin offering in the place of the burnt offering. 30. And the priest shall take of the blood thereof with his finger, and put *it* upon the horns of the altar of burnt offering, and shall pour out all the blood thereof at the bottom of the altar. 31. And he shall take away all the fat thereof, as the fat is taken away from off the sacrifice of peace offerings; and the priest shall burn *it* upon the altar for a sweet savour unto the LORD; and the priest shall make an atonement for him, and it shall be forgiven him. 32. And if he bring a lamb for a sin offering, he shall bring it a female without blemish. 33. And he shall lay his hand upon the head of the sin offering, and slay it for a sin offering in the place where they kill the burnt offering. 34. And the priest shall take of the blood of the sin offering with his finger, and put *it* upon the horns of the altar of burnt offering, and shall pour out all the blood thereof at the bottom of the altar: 35. And he shall take away all the fat thereof, as the fat of the lamb is taken away from the sacrifice of the peace offerings; and the priest shall burn them upon the altar, according to the offerings made by fire unto the LORD: and the priest shall make an atonement for his sin that he hath committed, and it shall be forgiven him.

Lev. 5:6. And he shall bring his trespass offering unto the LORD for his sin which he hath sinned, a female from the flock, a lamb or a kid of the goats, for a sin offering; and the priest shall make an atonement for him concerning his sin. 7. And if he be not able to bring a lamb, then he shall bring for his trespass, which he hath committed, two turtledoves, or two young pigeons, unto the LORD; one for a sin offering, and the other for a burnt offering. 8. And he shall bring them unto the priest, who shall offer *that* which *is* for the sin offering first, and wring off his head from his neck, but shall not divide *it* asunder: 9. And he shall sprinkle of the blood of the sin offering upon the side of the altar; and the rest of the blood shall be wrung out at the bottom of the altar: it *is* a sin offering. 10. And he shall offer the second *for* a burnt offering, according to the manner: and the priest shall make an atonement for him for his sin which he hath sinned, and it shall be forgiven him.

Lev. 6:7. And the priest shall make an atonement for him before the LORD: and it shall be forgiven him for any thing of all that he hath done in trespassing therein.

Lev. 9:7. And Moses said unto Aaron, Go unto the altar, and offer thy sin offering, and thy burnt offering, and make an atonement for thyself, and for the people: and offer the offering of the people, and make an atonement for them; as the LORD commanded.

Lev. 10:17. Wherefore have ye not eaten the sin offering in the holy place, seeing it *is* most holy, and *God* hath given it you to bear the iniquity of the congregation, to make atonement for them before the LORD?

Lev. 12:6. And when the days of her purifying are fulfilled, for a son, or for a daughter, she shall bring a lamb of the first year for a burnt offering, and a young pigeon, or a turtledove, for a sin offering, unto the door of the tabernacle of the congregation, unto the priest: 7. Who shall offer it before the LORD, and make an atonement for her; and she shall be cleansed from the issue of her blood. This *is* the law for her that hath borne a male or a female. 8. And if she be not able to bring a lamb, then she shall bring two turtles, or two young pigeons; the one for the burnt offering, and the other for a sin offering: and the priest shall make an atonement for her, and she shall be clean. Lev. 14:12. And the priest shall take one he lamb, and offer him for a trespass offering, and the log of oil, and wave them *for* a wave offering before the LORD: 13. And he shall slay the lamb in the place where he shall kill the sin offering and the burnt offering, in the holy place: for as the sin offering *is* the priest's, *so is* the trespass offering: it *is* most holy: 14. And the priest shall take *some* of the blood of the trespass offering, and the priest shall put *it* upon the tip of the right ear of him that is to be cleansed, and upon the thumb of his right hand, and upon the great toe of his right foot: 15. And the priest shall take *some* of the log of oil, and pour *it* into the palm of his own left hand: 16. And the priest shall dip his right finger in the oil that *is* in his left hand, and shall sprinkle of the oil with his finger seven times before the LORD: 17. And of the rest of the oil that *is* in his hand shall the priest put upon the tip of the right ear of him that is to be cleansed, and upon the thumb of his right hand, and upon the great toe of his right foot, upon the blood of the trespass offering: 18. And the remnant of the oil that *is* in the priest's hand he shall pour upon the head of him that is to be cleansed: and the priest shall make an atonement for him before the LORD. 19. And the priest shall offer the sin offering, and make an atonement for him that is to be cleansed from his uncleanness; and afterward he shall kill the burnt offering: 20. And the priest shall offer the burnt offering and the meat offering upon the altar: and the priest shall make an atonement for him, and he shall be clean. 21. And if he *be* poor, and cannot get so much; then he shall take one lamb *for* a trespass offering to be waved, to make an atonement for him, and one tenth deal of fine flour mingled with oil for a meat offering, and a log of oil; 22. And two turtledoves, or two young pigeons, such as he is able to get; and the one shall be a sin offering, and the other a burnt offering. 23. And he shall bring them on the eighth day for his cleansing unto the priest, unto the door of the tabernacle of the congregation, before the LORD. 24. And the priest shall take the lamb of the trespass offering, and the log of oil, and the priest shall wave them *for* a wave offering before the LORD: 25. And he shall kill the lamb of the trespass offering, and the priest shall take *some* of the blood of the trespass offering, and put *it* upon the tip of the right ear of him that is to be cleansed, and upon the thumb of his right hand, and upon the great toe of his right foot. 26. And the priest shall pour of the oil into the palm of his own left hand: 27. And the priest shall sprinkle with his right finger *some* of the oil that *is* in his left hand seven times before the

LORD: 28. And the priest shall put of the oil that *is* in his hand upon the tip of the right ear of him that is to be cleansed, and upon the thumb of his right hand, and upon the great toe of his right foot, upon the place of the blood of the trespass offering: 29. And the rest of the oil that *is* in the priest's hand he shall put upon the head of him that is to be cleansed, to make an atonement for him before the LORD. 30. And he shall offer the one of the turtledoves, or of the young pigeons, such as he can get; 31. *Even* such as he is able to get, the one *for* a sin offering, and the other *for* a burnt offering, with the meat offering: and the priest shall make an atonement for him that is to be cleansed before the LORD. 32. This *is* the law *of him* in whom *is* the plague of leprosy, whose hand is not able to get *that which pertaineth* to his cleansing.

Lev. 16:6. And Aaron shall offer his bullock of the sin offering, which *is* for himself, and make an atonement for himself, and for his house. 10. But the goat, on which the lot fell to be the scapegoat, shall be presented alive before the LORD, to make an atonement with him, *and* to let him go for a scapegoat into the wilderness. 11. And Aaron shall bring the bullock of the sin offering, which *is* for himself, and shall make an atonement for himself, and for his house, and shall kill the bullock of the sin offering which *is* for himself: 15. Then shall he kill the goat of the sin offering, that *is* for the people, and bring his blood within the vail, and do with that blood as he did with the blood of the bullock, and sprinkle it upon the mercy seat, and before the mercy seat: 16. And he shall make an atonement for the holy *place*, because of the uncleanness of the children of Israel, and because of their transgressions in all their sins: and so shall he do for the tabernacle of the congregation, that remaineth among them in the midst of their uncleanness. 17. And there shall be no man in the tabernacle of the congregation when he goeth in to make an atonement in the holy *place*, until he come out, and have made an atonement for himself, and for his household, and for all the congregation of Israel. 18. And he shall go out unto the altar that *is* before the LORD, and make an atonement for it: and shall take of the blood of the bullock, and of the blood of the goat, and put *it* upon the horns of the altar round about. 19. And he shall sprinkle of the blood upon it with his finger seven times, and cleanse it, and hallow it from the uncleanness of the children of Israel. 24. And he shall wash his flesh with water in the holy place, and put on his garments, and come forth, and offer his burnt offering, and the burnt offering of the people, and make an atonement for himself, and for the people. 25. And the fat of the sin offering shall he burn upon the altar. 26. And he that let go the goat for the scapegoat shall wash his clothes, and bathe his flesh in water, and afterward come into the camp. 27. And the bullock *for* the sin offering, and the goat *for* the sin offering, whose blood was brought in to make atonement in the holy *place*, shall one carry forth without the camp; and they shall burn in the fire their skins, and their flesh, and their dung. 28. And he that burneth them shall wash his clothes, and bathe his flesh in water, and afterward he shall come into the camp. 29. And *this* shall be a statute for ever unto you: *that* in the seventh month, on the tenth *day* of the month, ye shall afflict your souls, and do no work at all, *whether it be* one of your own country, or a stranger that sojourneth among you: 30. For on that day shall *the priest* make an atonement for you, to cleanse you, *that* ye may be clean from all your sins before the LORD. 31. It *shall be* a sabbath of rest unto you, and ye shall afflict your souls, by a statute for ever. 32. And the priest, whom he shall anoint, and whom he shall consecrate to minister in the priest's office in his father's stead, shall make the atonement, and shall put on the linen clothes, *even* the holy garments: 33. And he shall make an atonement for the holy sanctuary, and he shall make an atonement for the tabernacle of the congregation, and for the altar, and he shall make an atonement for the priests, and for all the people of the congregation. 34. And this shall be an everlasting statute unto you, to make an atonement for the children of Israel for all their sins once a year. And he did as the LORD commanded Moses.

Lev. 17:11. For the life of the flesh *is* in the blood: and I have given it to you upon the altar to make an atonement for your souls: for it *is* the blood *that* maketh an atonement for the soul.

Lev. 19:22. And the priest shall make an atonement for him with the ram of the trespass offering before the LORD for his sin which he hath done: and the sin which he hath done shall be forgiven him.

Num. 15:22. And if ye have erred, and not observed all these commandments, which the LORD hath spoken unto Moses, 23. *Even* all that the LORD hath commanded you by the hand of Moses, from the day that the LORD commanded *Moses*, and henceforward among your generations: 24. Then it shall be, if *aught* be committed by ignorance without the knowledge of the congregation, that all the congregation shall offer one young bullock for a burnt offering, for a sweet savour unto the LORD, with his meat offering, and his drink offering, according to the manner, and one kid of the goats for a sin offering. 25. And the priest shall make an atonement for all the congregation of the children of Israel, and it shall be forgiven them; for it *is* ignorance: and they shall bring their offering, a sacrifice made by fire unto the LORD, and their sin offering before the LORD, for their ignorance: 26. And it shall be forgiven all the congregation of the children of Israel, and the stranger that sojourneth

among them; seeing all the people *were* in ignorance. 27. And if any soul sin through ignorance, then he shall bring a she goat of the first year for a sin offering. 28. And the priest shall make an atonement for the soul that sinneth ignorantly when he sinneth by ignorance before the LORD, to make an atonement for him; and it shall be forgiven him.

Num. 28:30. One kid of the goats, to make an atonement for you. *v.* 22; Num.29:5,10,11.

Heb. 9:22. And almost all things are by the law purged with blood; and without shedding of blood is no remission.

MADE BY JESUS: Divinely ordained: Luke 2:30,31; Gal. 4:4,5; Eph. 1:3–12,17–22; 2:4–10; Col. 1:19,20; 1 Pet. 1:20; Rev. 13:8. A mystery, 1 Cor. 2:7, with context; 1 Pet. 1:8–12. Made but once, Heb.7:27; 9:24–28; 10:10,12, 14; 1 Pet. 3:18. Redemption by, Matt. 20:28; Acts 20:28; Gal.3:13; 1 Tim. 2:6; Heb.9:12; Rev. 5:9. Typified, Gen. 4:4,with Heb. 11:4; Gen. 22:2,with Heb. 11:17,19; Ex. 12:5,11,14, with 1 Cor. 5:7; Ex. 24:8, with Heb. 9:20; Lev. 16: 30,34, with Heb. 9:7,12,28; Lev. 17:11, with Heb. 9:22.

See SALVATION, PLAN OF.

UNCLASSIFIED SCRIPTURES RELAT-ING TO: Psa. 40:6. Sacrifice and offering thou didst not desire; mine ears hast thou opened: burnt offering and sin offering hast thou not required. 7. Then said I, Lo, I come: in the volume of the book *it is* written of me, 8. I delight to do thy will, O my God: yea, thy law *is* within my heart. Heb. 10:5–9.

Isa. 53:4. Surely he hath borne our griefs, and carried our sorrows: yet we did esteem him stricken, smitten of God, and afflicted. 5. But he *was* wounded for our transgressions, *he was* bruised for our iniquities: the chastisement of our peace *was* upon him; and with his stripes we are healed. 6. All we like sheep have gone astray; we have turned every one to his own way; and the LORD hath laid on him the iniquity of us all. 7. He was oppressed, and he was afflicted, yet he opened not his mouth: he is brought as a lamb to the slaughter, and as a sheep before her shearers is dumb, so he openeth not his mouth. 8. He was taken from prison and from judgment: and who shall declare his generation? for he was cut off out of the land of the living: for the transgression of my people was he stricken. 10. Yet it pleased the LORD to bruise him; he hath put *him* to grief: when thou shalt make his soul an offering for sin, he shall see *his* seed, he shall prolong *his* days, and the pleasure of the LORD shall prosper in his hand. 11. He shall see of the travail of his soul, *and* shall be satisfied: by his knowledge shall my righteous servant justify many; for he shall bear their iniquities. 12. Therefore will I divide him *a portion* with the great, and he shall divide the spoil with the strong; because he hath poured out his soul unto death: and he was numbered with the transgressors; and he bare the sin of many, and made intercession for the transgressors.

Dan. 9:24. Seventy weeks are determined upon thy people and upon thy holy city, to finish the transgression, and to make an end of sins, and to make reconciliation for iniquity, and to bring in everlasting righteousness, and to seal up the vision and prophecy, and to anoint the most Holy. 25. Know therefore and understand, *that* from the going forth of the commandment to restore and to build Jerusalem unto the Messiah the Prince, *shall be* seven weeks, and threescore and two weeks: the street shall be built again, and the wall, even in troublous times. 26. And after threescore and two weeks shall Messiah be cut off, but not for himself: and the people of the prince that shall come shall destroy the city and the sanctuary; and the end thereof *shall be* with a flood, and unto the end of the war desolations are determined. 27. And he shall confirm the covenant with many for one week: and in the midst of the week he shall cause the sacrifice and the oblation to cease, and for the overspreading of abominations he shall make *it* desolate, even until the consummation, and that determined shall be poured upon the desolate.

Zech. 13:1. In that day there shall be a fountain opened to the house of David and to the inhabitants of Jerusalem for sin and for uncleanness.

Matt. 26:28. For this is my blood of the new testament, which is shed for many for the remission of sins. Luke 22:20.

Luke 24:46. And said unto them, Thus it is written, and thus it behoved Christ to suffer, and to rise from the dead the third day: 47. And that repentance and remission of sins should be preached in his name among all nations, beginning at Jerusalem.

John 1:29. The next day John seeth Jesus coming unto him, and saith, Behold the Lamb of God, which taketh away the sin of the world. *v.* 36.

John 6:51. The bread that I will give is my flesh, which I will give for the life of the world.

John 11:49. And one of them, *named* Caiaphas, being the high priest that same year, said unto them, Ye know nothing at all, 50. Nor consider that it is expedient for us, that one man should die for the people, and that the whole nation perish not. 51. And this spake he not of himself: but being high priest that year, he prophesied that Jesus should die for that nation;

Acts 17:2. And Paul, as his manner was, went in unto them, and three sabbath days reasoned with them out of the scriptures. 3. Opening and alleging, that Christ must needs have suffered, and risen again from the dead; and that this Jesus, whom I preach unto you, is Christ.

Acts 20:28. Take heed therefore unto yourselves, and to all the flock, over the which the Holy Ghost hath made you overseers, to feed the church of God, which he hath purchased with his own blood.

Rom. 3:24. Being justified freely by his grace through the redemption that is in Christ Jesus: 25. Whom God hath set forth *to be* a propitiation through faith in his blood, to declare his righteousness for the remission of sins that are past, through the forbearance of God; 26. To declare, *I say*, at this time his righteousness: that he might be just, and the justifier of him which believeth in Jesus.

Rom. 4:25. Who was delivered for our offences, and was raised again for our justification.

Rom. 5:1. Therefore being justified by faith, we have peace with God through our Lord Jesus Christ: 2. By whom also we have access by faith into this grace wherein we stand, and rejoice in hope of the glory of God. 6. For when we were yet without strength, in due time Christ died for the ungodly. 7. For scarcely for a righteous man will one die: yet peradventure for a good man some would even dare to die. 8. But God commendeth his love toward us, in that, while we were yet sinners, Christ died for us. 9. Much more then, being now justified by his blood, we shall be saved from wrath through him. 10. For if, when we were enemies, we were reconciled to God by the death of his Son, much more, being reconciled, we shall be saved by his life. 11. And not only *so*, but we also joy in God through our Lord Jesus Christ, by whom we have now received the [1] atonement. 15. But not as the offence, so also *is* the free gift. For if through the offence of one many be dead, much more the grace of God, and the gift by grace, *which is* by one man, Jesus Christ, hath abounded unto many. 16. And not as *it was* by one that sinned, *so is* the gift: for the judgment *was* by one to condemnation, but the free gift *is* of many offences unto justification. 17. For if by one man's offence death reigned by one; much more they which receive abundance of grace and of the gift of righteousness shall reign in life by one, Jesus Christ. 18. Therefore as by the offence of one *judgment came* upon all men to condemnation; even so by the righteousness of one *the free gift came* upon all men unto justification of life. 19. For as by one man's disobedience many were made sinners, so by the obedience of one shall many be made righteous. 20. Moreover the law entered, that the offence might abound. But where sin abounded, grace did much more abound: 21. That as sin hath reigned unto death, even so might grace reign through righteousness unto eternal life by Jesus Christ our Lord.   [1 R. V. reconciliation]

1 Cor. 1:17. For Christ sent me not to baptize, but to preach the gospel: not with wisdom of words, lest the cross of Christ should be made of none effect. 18. For the preaching of the cross is to them that perish foolishness; but unto us which are saved it is the power of God. 23. But we preach Christ crucified, unto the Jews a stumblingblock,

and unto the Greeks foolishness; 24. But unto them which are called, both Jews and Greeks, Christ the power of God, and the wisdom of God.

1 Cor. 15:3. For I delivered unto you first of all that which I also received, how that Christ died for our sins according to the scriptures;

2 Cor. 5:18. And all things *are* of God, who hath reconciled us to himself by Jesus Christ, and hath given to us the ministry of reconciliation; 19. To wit, that God was in Christ, reconciling the world unto himself, not imputing their trespasses unto them; and hath committed unto us the word of reconciliation.

Gal. 1:3. Grace *be* to you, and peace, from God the Father, and *from* our Lord Jesus Christ, 4. Who gave himself for our sins, that he might deliver us from this present evil world, according to the will of God and our Father:

Gal. 4:4. But when the fulness of the time was come, God sent forth his Son, made of a woman, made under the law, 5. To redeem them that were under the law, that we might receive the adoption of sons.

Eph. 1:7. In whom we have redemption through his blood, the forgiveness of sins, according to the riches of his grace;

Eph. 2:13. But now in Christ Jesus ye who sometimes were far off are made nigh by the blood of Christ. 14. For he is our peace, who hath made both one, and hath broken down the middle wall of partition *between us;* 15. Having abolished in his flesh the enmity, *even* the law of commandments *contained* in ordinances; for to make in himself of twain one new man, *so* making peace; 16. And that he might reconcile both unto God in one body by the cross, having slain the enmity thereby: 17. And came and preached peace to you which were afar off, and to them that were nigh. 18. For through him we both have access by one Spirit unto the Father

Eph. 5:2. Walk in love, as Christ also hath loved us, and hath given himself for us an offering and a sacrifice to God for a sweet-smelling savour. *v.* 25.

Col. 1:14. In whom we have redemption ¹through his blood, *even* the forgiveness of sins; 19. For it pleased *the Father* that in him should all fulness dwell; 20. And, having made peace through the blood of his cross, by him to reconcile all things unto himself; by him, *I say,* whether *they be* things in earth, or things in heaven. 21. And you, that were sometime alienated and enemies in *your* mind by wicked works, yet now hath he reconciled 22. In the body of his flesh through death, to present you holy and unblameable and unreproveable in his sight: [¹ Omitted in R. V.]

1 Thess. 5:9. For God hath not appointed us to wrath, but to obtain salvation by our Lord Jesus Christ, 10. Who died for us, that, whether we wake or sleep, we should live together with him.

1 Tim. 2:5. For *there is* one God, and one mediator between God and men, the man Christ Jesus; 6. Who gave himself a ransom for all, to be testified in due time.

Tit. 2:14. Who gave himself for us, that he might redeem us from all iniquity, and purify unto himself a peculiar people, zealous of good works.

Heb. 1:3. Who being the brightness of *his* glory, and the express image of his person, and upholding all things by the word of his power, when he had by himself purged our sins, sat down on the right hand of the Majesty on high;

Heb. 2:9. That he by the grace of God should taste death for every man. 17. Wherefore in all things it behoved him to be made like unto *his* brethren, that he might be a merciful and faithful high priest in things *pertaining* to God, to make reconciliation for the sins of the people.

Heb. 9:12. Neither by the blood of goats and calves, but by his own blood he entered in once into the holy place, having obtained eternal redemption *for us.* 13. For if the blood of bulls and of goats, and the ashes of an heifer sprinkling the unclean, sanctifieth to the purifying of the flesh: 14. How much more shall the blood of Christ, who through the eternal Spirit offered himself without spot to God, purge your conscience from dead works to serve the living God? 15. And for this cause he is the mediator of the new testament, that by means of death, for the redemption of the transgressions *that were* under the first testament, they which are called might receive the promise of eternal inheritance. 25. Nor yet that he should offer himself often, as the high priest entereth into the holy place every year with blood of others; 26. For then must he often have suffered since the foundation of the world: but now once in the end of the world hath he appeared to put away sin by the sacrifice of himself.

Heb. 10:1. For the law having a shadow of good things to come, *and* not the very image of the things, can never with those sacrifices which they offered year by year continually make the comers thereunto perfect. 2. For then would they not have ceased to be offered? because that the worshippers once purged should have had no more conscience of sins. 3. But in those *sacrifices there is* a remembrance again *made* of sins every year. 4. For *it is* not possible that the blood of bulls and of goats should take away sins. 5. Wherefore when he cometh into the world, he saith, Sacrifice and offering thou wouldest not, but a body hast thou prepared me: 6. In burnt offerings and *sacrifices* for sin thou hast had no pleasure. 7. Then said I, Lo, I come (in the volume of the book it is written of me,) to do thy will, O God. 8. Above when he said, Sacrifice and offering and burnt offerings and *offering* for sin thou wouldest not, neither hadst pleasure *therein;* which are offered by the law; 9.

Then said he, Lo, I come to do thy will, O God. He taketh away the first, that he may establish the second. 10. By the which will we are sanctified through the offering of the body of Jesus Christ once *for all.* 11. And every priest standeth daily ministering and offering oftentimes the same sacrifices, which can never take away sins: 12. But this man, after he had offered one sacrifice for sins for ever, sat down on the right hand of God; 18. Now where remission of these *is, there is* no more offering for sin. 19. Having therefore, brethren, boldness to enter into the holiest by the blood of Jesus, 20. By a new and living way, which he hath consecrated for us, through the veil, that is to say, his flesh;

Heb. 12:24. And to Jesus the mediator of the new covenant, and to the blood of sprinkling, that speaketh better things than *that of* Abel.

Heb. 13:12. Wherefore Jesus also, that he might sanctify the people with his own blood, suffered without the gate. 20. Now the God of peace, that brought again from the dead our Lord Jesus, that great shepherd of the sheep, through the blood of the everlasting covenant, 21. Make you perfect in every good work to do his will,

1 Pet. 1:18. Forasmuch that ye know that ye were not redeemed with corruptible things, *as* silver and gold, from your vain conversation *received* by tradition from your fathers; 19. But with the precious blood of Christ, as of a lamb without blemish and without spot: 20. Who verily was foreordained before the foundation of the world, but was manifest in these last times for you,

1 Pet. 2:24. Who his own self bare our sins in his own body on the tree, that we, being dead to sins, should live unto righteousness: by whose stripes ye were healed.

1 Pet. 3:18. For Christ also hath once suffered for sins, the just for the unjust, that he might bring us to God, being put to death in the flesh, but quickened by the Spirit:

1 John 1:7. The blood of Jesus Christ his Son cleanseth us from all sin.

1 John 2:2. He is the propitiation for our sins: and not for ours only, but also for *the sins of* the whole world.

1 John 3:5. Ye know that he was manifested to take away our sins; and in him is no sin.

1 John 4:10. Herein is love, not that we loved God, but that he loved us, and sent his Son *to be* a propitiation for our sins.

1 John 5:6. This is he that came by water and blood, *even* Jesus Christ; not by water only, but by water and blood.

Rev. 1:5. Unto him that loved us, and washed us from our sins in his own blood,

Rev. 5:9. And they sung a new song, saying, Thou art worthy to take the book, and to open the seals thereof: for thou wast slain, and hast redeemed us to God by thy blood out of every kindred, and tongue, and people, and nation;

Rev. 7:14. And he said to me, These are they which came out of great tribulation, and have washed their robes, and made them white in the blood of the Lamb.

Rev. 12:11. And they overcame him by the blood of the Lamb, and by the word of their testimony; and they loved not their lives unto the death.

See BLOOD; JESUS, DEATH OF, MISSION OF, SUFFERINGS OF; REDEMPTION; SALVATION.

ATTAI. 1. A Gadite warrior, 1 Chr. 12:11.

2. Son of Rehoboam, 2 Chr. 11:20.

3. Grandson of Sheshan, 1 Chr. 2:35,36.

ATTALIA, a seaport of Pamphylia, Acts 14:25.

ATTORNEY, employed, Acts 24:1,2. See LAWYER.

AUGUSTUS, a title of Roman emperors, Luke 2:1; Acts 25:21,25; 27:1.

ATROPHY, of the hand, Matt. 12:10–13.

ATTRIBUTES OF GOD. See GOD.

AVA, called also IVAH. A district near Babylon, 2 Kin. 17:24; 18:34; 19:13. See Ezra 4:9.

AVARICE. Eccl. 4:7. Then I returned, and I saw vanity under the sun. 8. There is one *alone,* and *there is* not a second; yea, he hath neither child nor brother: yet *is there* no end of all his labour; neither is his eye satisfied with riches; neither *saith he,* For whom do I labour, and bereave my soul of good? This *is* also vanity, yea, it *is* a sore travail.

Eccl. 5:10. He that loveth silver shall not be satisfied with silver; nor he that loveth abundance with increase: this *is* also vanity. 11. When goods increase, they are increased that eat them: and what good *is there* to the owners thereof, saving the beholding *of them* with their eyes?

1 Tim. 3:2. A bishop then must be blameless, the husband of one wife, vigilant, sober, of good behaviour, given to hospitality, apt to teach; 3. Not given to wine, no striker, not greedy of filthy lucre; but patient, not a brawler, not covetous. Tit. 1:7.

1 Tim. 6:5. Perverse disputings of men of corrupt minds, and destitute of the truth, supposing that [1] gain is godliness: from such withdraw thyself. 10. For the love of money is the root of all evil: which while some coveted after, they have erred from the faith, and pierced themselves through with many sorrows. [1 R. V. godliness is a way of gain]

See COVETOUSNESS; RICH; RICHES.

INSTANCES OF: The descendants of Joseph, Josh. 17:14–18.

AVEN. 1. "The plain of the Sun," Amos 1:5.

2. Another name for ON, Ezek. 30:17.

3. BETH-AVEN, Hos. 10:8.

AVENGER OF BLOOD. Premosaic, Gen. 9:5,6. Cain fears, Gen. 4:14,15. Lamech fears, Gen. 4:24. Law concerning, set aside by David, 2 Sam. 14:4–11.

See HOMICIDE.

FIGURATIVE: Psa. 8:2; 44:16; Rom. 13:4; 1 Thess. 4:6.

SCRIPTURES RELATING TO: Gen. 9:5. And surely your blood of your lives will I require; at the hand of every beast will I require it, and at the hand of man; at the hand of every man's brother will I require the life of man. 6. Whoso sheddeth man's blood, by man shall his blood be shed: for in the image of God made he man.

Num. 35:19. The revenger of blood himself shall slay the murderer: when he meeteth him, he shall slay him. 20. But if he thrust him of hatred, or hurl at him by laying of wait, that he die; 21. Or in enmity smite him with his hand, that he die: he that smote *him* shall surely be put to death: *for* he *is* a murderer: the revenger of blood shall slay the murderer, when he meeteth him. 22. But if he thrust him suddenly without enmity, or have cast upon him any thing without laying of wait, 23. Or with any stone, wherewith a man may die, seeing *him* not, and cast *it* upon him, that he die, and *was* not his enemy, neither sought his harm: 24. Then the congregation shall judge between the slayer and the revenger of blood according to these judgments: 25. And the congregation shall deliver the slayer out of the hand of the revenger of blood, and the congregation shall restore him to the city of his refuge, whither he was fled: and he shall abide in it unto the death of the high priest, which was anointed with the holy oil. 26. But if the slayer shall at any time come without the border of the city of his refuge, whither he was fled; 27. And the revenger of blood find him without the borders of the city of his refuge, and the revenger of blood kill the slayer; he shall not be guilty of blood: 28. Because he should have remained in the city of his refuge until the death of the high priest: but after the death of the high priest the slayer shall return into the land of his possession. 29. So these *things* shall be for a statute of judgment unto you throughout your generations in all your dwellings.

Deut. 19:4. And this *is* the case of the slayer, which shall flee thither, that he may live: Whoso killeth his neighbour ignorantly, whom he hated not in time past; 5. As when a man goeth into the wood with his neighbour to hew wood, and his hand fetcheth a stroke with the ax to cut down the tree, and the head slippeth from the helve, and lighteth upon his neighbour, that he die; he shall flee unto one of those cities, and live: 6. Lest the avenger of the blood pursue the slayer, while his heart is hot, and overtake him, because the way is long, and slay him; whereas he *was* not worthy of death, inasmuch as he hated him not in time past. 7. Wherefore I command thee, saying, Thou shalt separate three cities for thee. 8. And if the LORD thy God enlarge thy coast, as he hath sworn unto thy fathers, and give thee all the land which he promised to give unto thy fathers; 9. If thou shalt keep all these commandments to do them, which I command thee this day, to love the LORD

thy God, and to walk ever in his ways; then shalt thou add three cities more for thee, besides these three: 10. That innocent blood be not shed in thy land, which the LORD thy God giveth thee *for* an inheritance, and *so* blood be upon thee. 11. But if any man hate his neighbour, and lie in wait for him, and rise up against him, and smite him mortally that he die, and fleeth into one of these cities: 12. Then the elders of his city shall send and fetch him thence, and deliver him unto the hand of the avenger of blood, that he may die. 13. Thine eye shall not pity him, but thou shalt put away *the guilt* of innocent blood from Israel, that it may go well with thee.

Josh 20:1. The LORD also spake unto Joshua, saying, 2. Speak to the children of Israel, saying, Appoint out for you cities of refuge, whereof I spake unto you by the hand of Moses: 3. That the slayer that killeth *any* person unawares *and* unwittingly may flee thither: and they shall be your refuge from the avenger of blood. 4. And when he that doth flee unto one of those cities shall stand at the entering of the gate of the city, and shall declare his cause in the ears of the elders of that city, they shall take him into the city unto them, and give him a place, that he may dwell among them. 5. And if the avenger of blood pursue after him, then they shall not deliver the slayer up into his hand; because he smote his neighbour unwittingly, and hated him not beforetime. 6. And he shall dwell in that city, until he stand before the congregation for judgment, *and* until the death of the high priest that shall be in those days: then shall the slayer return, and come unto his own city, and unto his own house, unto the city from whence he fled. 7. And they appointed Kedesh in Galilee in mount Naphtali, and Shechem in mount Ephraim, and Kirjath-arba, which *is* Hebron, in the mountain of Judah. 8. And on the other side Jordan by Jericho eastward, they assigned Bezer in the wilderness upon the plain out of the tribe of Reuben, and Ramoth in Gilead out of the tribe of Gad, and Golan in Bashan out of the tribe of Manasseh. 9. These were the cities appointed for all the children of Israel, and for the stranger that sojourneth among them, that whosoever killeth *any* person at unawares might flee thither, and not die by the hand of the avenger of blood, until he stood before the congregation.

AVIM. 1. A city of Benjamin, Josh. 18:23. 2. A tribe in southern Palestine. See AVITES.

AVITES. 1. A nation in southern part of Canaan, Deut. 2:23; Josh. 13:3. 2. Colonists of Samaria, 2 Kin. 17:31.

AVITH, capital city of the Edomites, Gen. 36:35; 1 Chr. 1:46.

AWL, a tool, Ex. 21:6; Deut. 15:17.

AX. An implement, Deut. 19:5; 1 Sam. 13: 20,21; 2 Sam. 12:31; Psa. 74:5,6. Elisha causes to swim, 2 Kin. 6:5,6. Battle-ax, Ezek. 26:9.

FIGURATIVE: Jer. 46:22; 51:20; Matt. 3:10.

AXLETREE, part of a wheeled vehicle, 1 Kin. 7:32,33.

AZAL, a place near Jerusalem, Zech. 14:5.

AZALIAH, father of Shaphan, 2 Kin. 22:3; 2 Chr. 34:8.

AZANIAH, father of Jeshua, Neh. 10:9.

AZARAEL. See AZAREEL.

AZAREEL. 1. An Aaronite of the family of Korah, 1 Chr. 12:6.

2. A musician in the temple, 1 Chr. 25:18; Called UZZIEL, v. 4.

3. A Danite prince, 1 Chr. 27:22.

4. A son of Bani, Ezra 10:41.

5. A priest, Neh. 11:13; 12:36.

AZARIAH. 1. Son of Ethan, 1 Chr. 2:8.

2. Son of Jehu, 1 Chr. 2:38,39.

3. Son of Zadok, 1 Kin. 4:2; perhaps identical with No. 6, below.

4. Captain of Solomon's guards, 1 Kin. 4:5.

5. A prophet, called ODED, 2 Chr. 15:1; v. 8.

6. A high priest, 1 Chr. 6:9. Called also AMARIAH, 2 Chr. 19:11.

7. Son of Jehoshaphat, 2 Chr. 21:2.

8. King of Judah, called AHAZIAH, 2 Chr. 22:6. See AHAZIAH.

9. Son of Jeroham, 2 Chr. 23:1.

10. Son of Obed, 2 Chr. 23:1.

11. Son of Johanan, possibly identical with ZECHARIAH, son of Jehoiada, 1 Chr. 6: 10,11; 2 Chr. 24:20-22.

12. See UZZIAH, king of Judah.

13. Chief of the tribe of Ephraim, 2 Chr. 28:12.

14. A Levite, 1 Chr. 6:36. In v. 24 called UZZIAH.

15. High priest in Hezekiah's reign, 2 Chr. 31:10,13. Probably identical with AHITUB mentioned in 1 Chr. 6:11,12.

16. Son of Hilkiah, 1 Chr. 6:13,14; 9:11; Ezra 7:1,3.

17. Son of Hoshaiah, Jer. 43:2-7.

18. Hebrew name of ABED-NEGO, Dan. 1: 7,19.

19. A captive returned from Babylon, Neh. 7:7; 10:2. Called also SERAIAH, Ezra 2:2.

AZAZ, father of Bela, 1 Chr. 5:8.

AZAZEL, the scapegoat, Lev. 16:8,10,26.

AZAZIAH. 1. A harper in the temple, 1 Chr. 15:21.

2. Father of Hoshea, 1 Chr. 27:20.

3. Overseer in temple, 2 Chr. 31:13.

AZBUK, father of Nehemiah, Neh. 3:16.

AZEKAH, a town of Judah, Josh. 10:10, 11; 15:35; 1 Sam. 17:1; 2 Chr. 11:9; Neh. 11: 30; Jer. 34:7.

AZEL, a Benjamite, 1 Chr. 8:37,38; 9:43, 44.

AZEM, a city in the S. of Judah. Called also EZEM, Josh. 15:29; 19:3; 1 Chr. 4:29.

AZGAD. 1. Ancestor of certain captives who returned from Babylon, Ezra 2: 12; Neh. 7:17.

2. A returned exile, Ezra 8:12.

3. A chief who signed Nehemiah's covenant, Neh. 10:15.

AZIEL, a temple musician, 1 Chr. 15:20.

AZIZA, son of Zattu, Ezra 10:27.

AZMAVETH. 1. One of David's heroes 2 Sam. 23:31; 1 Chr. 11:33.

2. A descendant of Jonathan, 1 Chr. 8:36, 9:42.

3. Son of Adiel, 1 Chr. 27:25.

4. A village of Judah or Benjamin, Ezra 2:24; Neh. 12:29. Called BETH-AZMAVETH, Neh. 7:28.

AZMON, a place on the S. of Canaan, Num. 34:4,5; Josh. 15:4.

AZNOTH-TABOR, a town in Naphtali, Josh. 19:34.

AZOR, ancestor of Jesus, Matt. 1:13,14. Perhaps identical with AZRIKAM, 1 Chr. 3:23.

AZOTUS. See ASHDOD.

AZRIEL. 1. A chief of Manasseh, 1 Chr. 5:24.

2. Father of Jerimoth, 1 Chr. 27:19.

3. Father of Seriah, Jer. 36:26.

AZRIKAM. 1. Son of Neraiah, 1 Chr. 3:23.

2. Son of Azel, 1 Chr. 8:38; 9:44.

3. A Levite, 1 Chr. 9:14; Neh. 11:15.

4. Governor of the house of Ahaz, 2 Chr. 28:7.

AZUBAH. 1. Mother of Jehoshaphat, 1 Kin. 22:42; 2 Chr. 20:31.

2. Wife of Caleb, 1 Chr. 2:18,19.

AZUR, father of Jaazaniah, Ezek. 11:1.

AZZAH, a city of the Philistines. See GAZA.

AZZAN, father of Paltiel, Num. 34:26.

AZZUR. 1. An Israelite, who sealed Nehemiah's covenant, Neh. 10:17.

2. A Gibeonite, Jer. 28:1.

B

BAAL. 1. An idol of the Phenicians, god of the sun. Wickedly worshiped by the Israelites in the time of the judges, Judg. 2: 10-23; 1 Sam. 7:3,4; by the kingdom of Israel, 2 Kin. 17:16; Jer. 23:13; Hos. 1; 2; 13:1; under Ahab, 1 Kin. 16:31-33; 18:18; 19:18; Jehoram. 2 Kin. 3:2; by the Jews, 2 Kin. 21:3; 2 Chr. 22:2-4; 24:7; 28:2; 33:3. Jeremiah expostulates against the worship of, Jer. 2:8,23; 7:9.

Altars, destroyed by Gideon, Judg. 6: 25-32; by Jehoiada, 2 Kin. 11:18; by Josiah, 2 Kin. 23:4,5.

Prophets of, slain by Elijah, 1 Kin. 18:40. All worshipers of, destroyed by Jehu, 2 Kin. 10:18-25.

2. A Benjamite, 1 Chr. 8:30; 9:36.

3. A Reubenite, 1 Chr. 5:5.

4. A city in the tribe of Simeon, 1 Chr. 4: 33. Called BAALATH-BEER, Josh. 19:8.

BAALAH. 1. A city in the S. of Judah, Josh. 15:29. Apparently identical with BALAH, Josh. 19:3; and BILHAH, 1 Chr. 4:29.

2. A city in the N. of Judah called also KIRJATH-JEARIM, which see.

3. A mountain in Judah, Josh. 15:11. Probably identical with MOUNT JEARIM. v. 10.

BAALATH, a city of Dan, Josh. 19:44; 1 Kin. 9:18; 2 Chr. 8:6.

BAALATH-BEER. See BAAL, No. 4.

BAAL-BERITH. A god of the Shechemites, Judg. 9:4. Worshiped by Israelites, Judg. 8:33. Called BERITH, Judg. 9:46.

BAALE, a city of Judah, 2 Sam. 6:2. See KIRJATH-JEARIM.

BAAL-GAD. A city of the Canaanites, Josh. 11:17; 12:7; 13:5. Probably identical with BAAL-HERMON, Judg. 3:3; 1 Chr. 5:23.

BAAL-GUR. See GUR-BAAL.

BAAL-HAMON. A place in Mount Ephraim, Song 8:11. Called HAMMON, Josh. 19:28.

BAAL-HANAN. 1. A king of Edom, Gen. 36:38,39; 1 Chr. 1:49,50.

2. One of David's overseers, 1 Chr. 27:28.

BAAL-HAZOR, the place where Amnon was slain, 2 Sam. 13:23.

BAAL-HERMON. 1. A city near Mount Hermon, 1 Chr. 5:23. Identical with BAAL-GAD, which see.

2. A mountain of Lebanon, Judg. 3:3.

BAALIM, plural form of BAAL, Judg. 2:11; 1 Sam. 7:4; Hos. 2:13,17; 11:2. See BAAL.

BAALI, an appellation of JEHOVAH, Hos. 2:16.

BAALIS, king of the Ammonites, Jer. 40:14.

BAAL-MEON. A city of the Reubenites, Num. 32:38; 1 Chr. 5:8; Ezek. 25:9. Called BETH-MEON, Jer. 48:23; BETH-BAAL-MEON, Josh. 13:17; BEON, Num. 32:3.

BAAL-PEOR, an idol of Moab, Num. 25:3,5; Deut. 4:3; Psa. 106:28; Hos. 9:10.

BAAL-PERAZIM. A place in the valley of Rephaim, 2 Sam. 5:20; 1 Chr. 14:11. Called PERAZIM, Isa. 28:21.

BAAL-SHALISHA, a place near Gilgal, 1 Sam. 9:4; 2 Kin. 4:42.

BAAL-TAMAR, a place near Gibeah, Judg. 20:33.

BAAL-ZEBUB, a god of the Philistines, 2 Kin. 1:2,3,6,16.

BAAL-ZEPHON, an Egyptian city on the Red Sea, Ex. 14:2,9; Num. 33:7.

BAANA. 1. Son of Ahilud, 1 Kin. 4:12.

2. Father of Zadok, Neh. 3:4.

BAANAH. 1. A captain of Ish-bosheth's army, 2 Sam. 4:2,5,6,9.

2. Father of Heleb, 2 Sam. 23:29; 1 Chr. 11:30.

3. A chief Jew of the exile, Ezra. 2:2; Neh. 7:7; 10:27.

4. The name is spelled BAANA [R. V.]. Son of Hushai, 1 Kin. 4:16.

BAARA, wife of Shaharaim, 1 Chr. 8:8. Called HODESH, v. 9.

BAASEIAH, a Levite, 1 Chr. 6:40.

BAASHA, king of Israel, 1 Kin. 15:16-22,27-34; 16:1-7; 21:22; 2 Kin. 9:9; 2 Chr. 16:1-6; Jer. 41:9.

BABBLER, a sarcastic epithet applied to St. Paul, Acts 17:18.

BABEL, a city in the plain of Shinar.

Tower built, and tongues confused at, Gen. 11:1-9.

See BABYLON.

BABES. In the mouths of, is praise perfected, Matt. 21:16. A symbol of the guileless, Psa. 8:2; Matt. 11:25; Luke 10:21; of the children of the kingdom of heaven, Matt. 18:2-6; Mark 10:15; Luke 18:17.

FIGURATIVE: Of weak Christians, Rom. 2:20; 1 Cor. 3:1; Heb. 5:13; 1 Pet. 2:2.

See CHILDREN; PARENTS.

BABYLON. 1. CITY OF: Built by Nimrod, Gen. 10:10. In the land of Shinar, Gen. 10:10; 11:2. Tower of, Gen. 11:1-9. Capital of the kingdom of Babylon, Dan. 4:30; 2 Kin. 25: 13; 2 Chr. 36:6,7,10,18,20. Gates of, Isa. 45:1, 2; Jer. 51:58. Walled, Jer. 51:44,58. Splendor of, Isa. 14:4.

Peter writes from, 1 Pet. 5:13.

Prophecies concerning, Psa. 87:4; 137:8,9; Isa. 13; 14:4-26; 21:1-10; 46:1,2; 47; 48:14,20; Jer. 21:4-10; 25:12-14; 27:1-11; 28:14; 32:28; 34: 2,3; 42:11,12:43; 46:13-26; 49:28-30; 50; 51; Ezek. 21:19; 26; 29:17-20; 30:10; 32:11; Dan. 2:21-38; 4:10-26; 5:25-29; 7; Hab. 1:5-11; Zech. 2:7-9.

FIGURATIVE: Rev. 14:8; 16:19; 17; 18.

2. EMPIRE OF.* Founded by Nimrod, Gen. 10:10. Called LAND OF SHINAR, Gen. 10: 10; 11:2; 14:1,9; Isa. 11:11; Dan 1:2; Zech. 5:11; SHESHACH, Jer. 25:26; 51; 41; MERATHAIM, Jer. 50:21. Called also CHALDEA, which see.

Divisions of, 2 Kin. 17:24; 24:7; Isa. 23:12, 13; Dan. 3:1; Acts 7:4. Extent of, at the time of Nebuchadnezzar, Dan. 2:37,38; 4:1; 6:1; of Ahasuerus, Esth. 1:1; 8:9; 9:30.

Armies of, invade ancient Canaan, Gen. 14; Samaria, 2 Kin. 17:5-24; Judah, 2 Kin. 24: 1-16. Jews carried to, 2 Kin. 25; 1 Chr. 9:1; 2 Chr.33:11; 36:17-21; Jer.32:2; 39; 52. Colonists from, sent to Samaria, Ezra 4:9,10,with 2 Kin. 17:29-32. Conquest of Egypt, by 2 Kin. 24:7.

Prophecies of conquests by, 2 Kin. 20:16-19; Jer. 20:4-7; 21; 22; 25:1-11; 27; 28; 29; 32:28, 29; 34; 36:29; 38:17,18; 43:8-13; 46:13-26; Ezek. 12; 17; 19; 21; 24; 26; 29:18-20; 30; 32.

Prophetic denunciations against, Psa. 137: 8,9; Isa. 13; 14:21; 43:14-17; 47; Jer. 50; 51.

GOVERNMENT OF: A limited monarchy, Esth. 1:13-19; 8:8; Dan. 6:8,14,17. Tyrannical, Esth. 3:7-15; Dan. 3.

Sovereigns of. See BELSHAZZAR; CYRUS; DARIUS; EVIL-MERODACH; NEBUCHADNEZZAR.

BACA, valley of, Psa. 84:6.

BACKBITING. Psa. 15:1. LORD, who shall abide in thy tabernacle? who shall dwell in thy holy hill? 2. He that walketh uprightly, and worketh righteousness, and speaketh the truth in his heart. 3. *He that* backbiteth not with his tongue, nor doeth evil to his neighbour, nor taketh up a reproach against his neighbour.

Prov. 25:23. The north wind ¹ driveth away rain: so *doth* ²an angry countenance a backbiting tongue. [R. V. ¹ bringeth forth ²a backbiting tongue an angry countenance.]

---

* For Biblical history of the people and regions ruled at different times under the empire, see ASSYRIA; CHALDEA; PERSIA.

Rom. 1:28. And even as they did not like to retain God in *their* knowledge, God gave them over to a reprobate mind, to do those things which are not convenient; 30. Backbiters, haters of God, despiteful,

2 Cor. 12:20. For I fear, lest, when I come, I shall not find you such as I would, and *that* I shall be found unto you such as ye would not: lest *there* be debates, envyings, wraths, strifes, backbitings, whisperings, swellings, tumults:

See Accusation, False; Slander; Speaking, Evil.

BACKSLIDERS. Lev. 26:14. But if ye will not hearken unto me, and will not do all these commandments; 15. And if ye shall despise my statutes, or if your soul abhor my judgments, so that ye will not do all my commandments, *but* that ye break my covenant: 16. I also will do this unto you; I will even appoint over you terror, consumption, and the burning ague, that shall consume the eyes, and cause sorrow of heart: and ye shall sow your seed in vain, for your enemies shall eat it. 17. And I will set my face against you, and ye shall be slain before your enemies: they that hate you shall reign over you; and ye shall flee when none pursueth you. 18. And if ye will not yet for all this hearken unto me, then I will punish you seven times more for your sins. 19. And I will break the pride of your power; and I will make your heaven as iron, and your earth as brass: 20. And your strength shall be spent in vain: for your land shall not yield her increase, neither shall the trees of the land yield their fruits. 21. And if ye walk contrary unto me, and will not hearken unto me; I will bring seven times more plagues upon you according to your sins. 22. I will also send wild beasts among you, which shall rob you of your children, and destroy your cattle, and make you few in number; and your *high* ways shall be desolate. 23. And if ye will not be reformed by me by these things, but will walk contrary unto me; 24. Then will I also walk contrary unto you, and will punish you yet seven times for your sins. 25. And I will bring a sword upon you, that shall avenge the quarrel of *my* covenant: and when ye are gathered together within your cities, I will send the pestilence among you; and ye shall be delivered into the hand of the enemy. 26. *And* when I have broken the staff of your bread, ten women shall bake your bread in one oven, and they shall deliver *you* your bread again by weight: and ye shall eat, and not be satisfied. 27. And if ye will not for all this hearken unto me, but walk contrary unto me; 28. Then I will walk contrary unto you also in fury; and I, even I, will chastise you seven times for your sins. 29. And ye shall eat the flesh of your sons, and the flesh of your daughters shall ye eat. 30. And I will destroy your high places, and cut down your images, and cast your carcases upon the carcases of your idols, and my soul shall

abhor you. 31. And I will make your cities waste, and bring your sanctuaries unto desolation, and I will not smell the savour of your sweet odours. 32. And I will bring the land into desolation: and your enemies which dwell therein shall be astonished at it. 33. And I will scatter you among the heathen, and will draw out a sword after you: and your land shall be desolate, and your cities waste. 34. Then shall the land enjoy her sabbaths, as long as it lieth desolate, and ye *be* in your enemies' land; *even* then shall the land rest, and enjoy her sabbaths. 35. As long as it lieth desolate it shall rest; because it did not rest in your sabbaths, when ye dwelt upon it. 36. And upon them that are left *alive* of you I will send a faintness into their hearts in the lands of their enemies; and the sound of a shaken leaf shall chase them; and they shall flee, as fleeing from a sword; and they shall fall when none pursueth. 37. And they shall fall one upon another, as it were before a sword, when none pursueth: and ye shall have no power to stand before your enemies. 38. And ye shall perish among the heathen, and the land of your enemies shall eat you up. 39. And they that are left of you shall pine away in their iniquity in your enemies' lands; and also in the iniquities of their fathers shall they pine away with them. 40. If they shall confess their iniquity, and the iniquity of their fathers, with their trespass which they trespassed against me, and that also they have walked contrary unto me; 41. And *that* I also have walked contrary unto them, and have brought them into the land of their enemies; if then their uncircumcised hearts be humbled, and they then accept of the punishment of their iniquity: 42. Then will I remember my covenant with Jacob, and also my covenant with Isaac, and also my covenant with Abraham will I remember; and I will remember the land.

Deut. 4:9. Only take heed to thyself, and keep thy soul diligently, lest thou forget the things which thine eyes have seen, and lest they depart from thy heart all the days of thy life:

Deut. 8:11. Beware that thou forget not the Lord thy God, in not keeping his commandments, and his judgments, and his statutes, which I command thee this day: 12. Lest *when* thou hast eaten and art full, and hast built goodly houses, and dwelt *therein;* 13. And *when* thy herds and thy flocks multiply, and thy silver and thy gold is multiplied, 14. Then thine heart be lifted up, and thou forget the Lord thy God, which brought thee forth out of the land of Egypt, from the house of bondage;

Deut. 28:58. If thou wilt not observe to do all the words of this law that are written in this book, that thou mayest fear this glorious and fearful name, THE LORD THY GOD; 59. Then the Lord will make thy plagues wonderful, and the plagues of thy seed, *even* great plagues, and of long continuance, **and** sore sicknesses, and of long continuance.

63. And it shall come to pass, *that* as the LORD rejoiced over you to do you good, and to multiply you; so the LORD will rejoice over you to destroy you, and to bring you to nought; *vs.* 15–68; 1 Kin. 9:6–9.

Deut. 29:18. Lest there should be among you man, or woman, or family, or tribe, whose heart turneth away this day from the LORD our God, ... lest there should be among you a root that beareth gall and wormwood; *vs.* 18–28.

Deut. 32:15. But Jeshurun waxed fat, and kicked : thou art waxen fat, thou art grown thick, thou art covered *with fatness;* then he forsook God *which* made him, and lightly esteemed the Rock of his salvation. 16. They provoked him to jealousy with strange *gods*, with abominations provoked they him to anger. 17. They sacrificed unto devils, not to God; to gods whom they knew not, to new *gods that* came newly up, whom your fathers feared not. 18. Of the Rock *that* begat thee thou art unmindful, and hast forgotten God that formed thee. 19. And when the LORD saw *it*, he abhorred *them*, because of the provoking of his sons, and of his daughters. 20. And he said, I will hide my face from them, I will see what their end *shall be:* for they *are* a very froward generation, children in whom *is* no faith. 21. They have moved me to jealousy with *that which is* not God; they have provoked me to anger with their vanities: and I will move them to jealousy with *those which are* not a people; I will provoke them to anger with a foolish nation. 22. For a fire is kindled in mine anger, and shall burn unto the lowest hell, and shall consume the earth with her increase, and set on fire the foundations of the mountains. 23. I will heap mischiefs upon them; I will spend mine arrows upon them. 24. *They shall be* burnt with hunger, and devoured with burning heat, and with bitter destruction: I will also send the teeth of beasts upon them, with the poison of serpents of the dust. 25. The sword without, and terror within, shall destroy both the young man and the virgin, the suckling *also* with the man of gray hairs. 26. I said, I would scatter them into corners, I would make the remembrance of them to cease from among men: 27. Were it not that I feared the wrath of the enemy, lest their adversaries should behave themselves strangely, *and* lest they should say, Our hand *is* high, and the LORD hath not done all this. 28. For they *are* a nation void of counsel, neither *is there any* understanding in them. 29. O that they were wise, *that* they understood this, *that* they would consider their latter end! 30. How should one chase a thousand, and two put ten thousand to flight, except their Rock had sold them, and the LORD had shut them up?

Josh. 24:27. And Joshua said . . . Behold, this stone shall be a witness unto us; for it hath heard all the words of the LORD which he spake unto us; it shall be therefore a witness unto you, lest ye deny your God. *vs.* 20–27.

2 Chr. 15:2. And he went out to meet Asa, and said unto him, Hear ye me, Asa, and all Judah and Benjamin; The LORD *is* with you, while ye be with him; and if ye seek him, he will be found of you; but if ye forsake him, he will forsake you. 3. Now for a long season Israel *hath been* without the true God, and without a teaching priest, and without law. 4. But when they in their trouble did turn unto the LORD God of Israel, and sought him, he was found of them.

Ezra 8:22. The hand of our God *is* upon all them for good that seek him; but his power and his wrath *is* against all them that forsake him.

Job 34:26. He striketh them as wicked men in the open sight of others; 27. Because they turned back from him, and would not consider any of his ways:

Psa. 44:20. If we have forgotten the name of our God, or stretched out our hands to a strange god; 21. Shall not God search this out? for he knoweth the secrets of the heart.

Psa. 73:27. For, lo, they that are far from thee shall perish: thou hast destroyed all them that go a whoring from thee.

Psa. 85:8. I will hear what God the LORD will speak: for he will speak peace unto his people, and to his saints: but let them not turn again to folly.

Psa. 125:5. As for such as turn aside unto their crooked ways, the LORD shall lead them forth with the workers of iniquity:

Prov. 2:17. Which forsaketh the guide of her youth, and forgetteth the covenant of her God.

Prov. 14:14. The backslider in heart shall be filled with his own ways:

Prov. 24:16. For a just *man* falleth seven times and riseth up again: but the wicked shall fall into mischief.

Prov. 26:11. As a dog ¹ returneth to his vomit, so a fool returneth to his folly.

[¹ R. V. that returneth to his vomit, *so is* a fool that repeateth]

Jer. 17:13. O LORD, the hope of Israel, all that forsake thee shall be ashamed, *and* they that depart from me shall be written in the earth, because they have forsaken the LORD,

Ezek. 3:20. Again, When a righteous *man* doth turn from his righteousness, and commit iniquity, and I lay a stumblingblock before him, he shall die: because thou hast not given him warning, he shall die in his sin, and his righteousness which he hath done shall not be remembered; but his blood will I require at thine hand.

Ezek. 18:26. When a righteous *man* turneth away from his righteousness, and committeth iniquity, and dieth in them; for his iniquity that he hath done shall he die. *v.* 24.

Ezek. 23:35. Therefore thus saith the Lord GOD; Because thou hast forgotten me, and cast me behind thy back, therefore bear thou also thy lewdness and thy whoredoms.

Ezek. 33:12. Therefore, thou son of man, say unto the children of thy people, The righteousness of the righteous shall not deliver him in the day of his transgression: as for the wickedness of the wicked, he shall not fall thereby in the day that he turneth from his wickedness; neither shall the righteous be able to live for his *righteousness* in the day that he sinneth. 13. When I shall say to the righteous, *that* he shall surely live; if he trust to his own righteousness, and commit iniquity, all his righteousness shall not be remembered; but for his iniquity that he hath committed, he shall die for it. 18. When the righteous turneth from his righteousness, and committeth iniquity, he shall even die thereby.

Hos. 11:7. And my people are bent to backsliding from me: though they called them to the most High, none at all would exalt *him.* 8. How shall I give thee up, Ephraim? *how* shall I deliver thee, Israel? how shall I make thee as Admah? *how* shall I set thee as Zeboim? mine heart is turned within me, my repentings are kindled together.

Jonah 2:4. Then I said, I am cast out of thy sight; yet I will look again toward thy holy temple.

Matt. 5:13. If the salt have lost his savour, wherewith shall it be salted? it is thenceforth good for nothing, but to be cast out, and to be trodden under foot of men. Mark 9:50.

Matt. 24:12. Because iniquity shall abound, the love of many shall wax cold.

Matt. 26:31. All ye shall be offended because of me this night: for it is written, I will smite the shepherd, and the sheep of the flock shall be scattered abroad.

Mark 4:7. And some fell among thorns, and the thorns grew up, and choked it, and it yielded no fruit. 15. And these are they by the way side, where the word is sown; but when they have heard, Satan cometh immediately, and taketh away the word that was sown in their hearts. 16. And these are they likewise which are sown on stony ground; who, when they have heard the word, immediately receive it with gladness; 17. And have no root in themselves, and so endure but for a time: afterward, when affliction or persecution ariseth for the word's sake, immediately they are offended. 18. And these are they which are sown among thorns; such as hear the word, 19. And the cares of this world, and the deceitfulness of riches, and the lusts of other things entering in, choke the word, and it becometh unfruitful.

Mark 8:38. Whosoever therefore shall be ashamed of me and of my words in this adulterous and sinful generation; of him also shall the Son of man be ashamed, when he cometh in the glory of his Father with the holy angels.

Luke 9:62. No man, having put his hand to the plough, and looking back, is fit for the kingdom of God.

Luke 11:21. When a strong man armed keepeth his palace, his goods are in peace: 22. But when a stronger than he shall come upon him, and overcome him, he taketh from him all his armour wherein he trusted,

and divideth his spoils. 23. He that is not with me is against me: and he that gathereth not with me scattereth. 24. When the unclean spirit is gone out of a man, he walketh through dry places, seeking rest; and finding none, he saith, I will return unto my house whence I came out. 25. And when he cometh, he findeth *it* swept and garnished. 26. Then goeth he, and taketh *to him* seven other spirits more wicked than himself; and they enter in, and dwell there: and the last *state* of that man is worse than the first. Matt. 12:45.

Luke 17:32. Remember Lot's wife.

John 6:67. Then said Jesus unto the twelve, Will ye also go away?

John 15:6. If a man abide not in me, he is cast forth as a branch, and is withered; and men gather them, and cast *them* into the fire, and they are burned.

1 Cor. 10:1. Moreover, brethren, I would not that ye should be ignorant, how that all our fathers were under the cloud, and all passed through the sea; 2. And were all baptized unto Moses in the cloud and in the sea; 3. And did all eat the same spiritual meat; 4. And did all drink the same spiritual drink: for they drank of that spiritual Rock that followed them: and that Rock was Christ. 5. But with many of them God was not well pleased: for they were overthrown in the wilderness. 6. Now these things were our examples, to the intent we should not lust after evil things, as they also lusted. 7. Neither be ye idolaters, as *were* some of them; as it is written, The people sat down to eat and drink, and rose up to play. 8. Neither let us commit fornication, as some of them committed, and fell in one day three and twenty thousand. 9. Neither let us tempt Christ, as some of them also tempted, and were destroyed of serpents. 10. Neither murmur ye, as some of them also murmured, and were destroyed of the destroyer. 11. Now all these things happened unto them for ensamples: and they are written for our admonition, upon whom the ends of the world are come. 12. Wherefore let him that thinketh he standeth take heed lest he fall. 13. There hath no temptation taken you but such as is common to man: but God *is* faithful, who will not suffer you to be tempted above that ye are able; but will with the temptation also make a way to escape, that ye may be able to bear *it.*

2 Cor. 12:20. For I fear, lest, when I come, I shall not find you such as I would, and *that* I shall be found unto you such as ye would not: lest *there be* debates, envyings, wraths, strifes, backbitings, whisperings, swellings, tumults: 21. *And* lest, when I come again, my God will humble me among you, and *that* I shall bewail many which have sinned already, and have not repented of the uncleanness and fornication and lasciviousness which they have committed.

Gal. 1:6. I marvel that ye are so soon removed from him that called you into the grace of Christ unto another gospel: *v. 7.*

Gal. 3:1. O foolish Galatians, who hath bewitched you, ¹ that ye should not obey the truth, before whose eyes Jesus Christ hath been evidently set forth, crucified among you? [¹ Omitted in R. V.]

Gal. 4:9. But now, after that ye have known God, or rather are known of God, how turn ye again to the weak and beggarly elements, whereunto ye desire again to be in bondage? 10. Ye observe days, and months, and times, and years. 11. I am afraid of you, lest I have bestowed upon you labour in vain.

Gal. 5:7. Ye did run well; who did hinder you that ye should not obey the truth?

1 Tim. 1:19. Holding faith, and a good conscience; which some having put away concerning faith have made shipwreck:

1 Tim. 5:15. Some are already turned aside after Satan.

1 Tim. 6:10. The love of money is the root of all evil: which while some coveted after, they have erred from the faith, and pierced themselves through with many sorrows. 20. O Timothy, keep that which is committed to thy trust, avoiding profane *and* vain babblings, and oppositions of science falsely so called: 21. Which some professing have erred concerning the faith.

2 Tim. 1:8. Be not thou therefore ashamed of the testimony of our Lord, nor of me his prisoner:

2 Tim. 2:12. If we deny *him*, he also will deny us:

2 Tim. 4:10. For Demas hath forsaken me, having loved this present world,

Heb. 3:12. Take heed, brethren, lest there be in any of you an evil heart of unbelief, in departing from the living God. 13. But exhort one another daily, while it is called To day; lest any of you be hardened through the deceitfulness of sin.

Heb. 4:1. Let us therefore fear, lest, a promise being left *us* of entering into his rest, any of you should seem to come short of it. 11. Let us labour therefore to enter into that rest, lest any man fall after the same example of unbelief.

Heb. 5:11. Of whom we have many things to say, and hard to be uttered, seeing ye are dull of hearing. 12. For when for the time ye ought to be teachers, ye have need that one teach you again which *be* the first principles of the oracles of God; and are become such as have need of milk, and not of strong meat.

Heb. 6:4. *It is* impossible for those who were once enlightened, and have tasted of the heavenly gift, and were made partakers of the Holy Ghost, 5. And have tasted the good word of God, and the powers of the world to come, 6. If they shall fall away, to renew them again unto repentance; seeing they crucify to themselves the Son of God afresh, and put *him* to an open shame. 7 For the earth which drinketh in the rain

that cometh oft upon it, and bringeth forth herbs meet for them by whom it is dressed, receiveth blessing from God: 8. But that which beareth thorns and briers *is* rejected, and *is* nigh unto cursing; whose end *is to* be burned.

Heb. 10:26. If we sin wilfully after that we have received the knowledge of the truth, there remaineth no more sacrifice for sins, 27. But a certain fearful looking for of judgment and fiery indignation, which shall devour the adversaries. 28. He that despised Moses' law died without mercy under two or three witnesses: 29. Of how much sorer punishment, suppose ye, shall he be thought worthy, who hath trodden under foot the Son of God, and hath counted the blood of the covenant, wherewith he was sanctified, an unholy thing, and hath done despite unto the Spirit of grace? 38. If *any man* draw back, my soul shall have no pleasure in him. 39. But we are not of them who draw back unto perdition;

Heb. 11:14. For they that say such things declare plainly that they seek a country. 15. And truly, if they had been mindful of that *country* from whence they came out, they might have had opportunity to have returned.

Heb. 12:15. Looking diligently lest any man fail of the grace of God; lest any root of bitterness springing up trouble *you*, and thereby many be defiled;

2 Pet. 1:9. He that lacketh these things is blind, and cannot see afar off, and hath forgotten that he was purged from his old sins.

2 Pet. 2:20. For if after they have escaped the pollutions of the world through the knowledge of the Lord and Saviour Jesus Christ, they are again entangled therein, and overcome, the latter end is worse with them than the beginning. 21. For it had been better for them not to have known the way of righteousness, than, after they have known *it*, to turn from the holy commandment delivered unto them.

2 John 9. Whosoever transgresseth, and abideth not in the doctrine of Christ, hath not God.

Rev. 2:4. I have *somewhat* against thee, because thou hast left thy first love. 5. Remember therefore from whence thou art fallen, and repent, and do the first works; or else I will come unto thee quickly, and will remove thy candlestick out of his place, except thou repent. 21. I gave her space to repent of her fornication; and she repented not. 22. Behold, I will cast her into a bed, and them that commit adultery with her into great tribulation, except they repent of their deeds. 23. And I will kill her children with death;

Rev. 3:2. Be watchful, and strengthen the things which remain, that are ready to die: for I have not found thy works perfect before God. 3. Remember therefore how thou hast received and heard, and hold fast, and repent. If therefore thou shalt not watch

I will come on thee as a thief, and thou shalt not know what hour I will come upon thee.

Rev. 21:8. The fearful, and unbelieving, . . . shall have their part in the lake which burneth with fire and brimstone: which is the second death.

See APOSTASY; BACKSLIDING OF ISRAEL, below; CHURCH, BACKSLIDDEN; REPROBACY.

INSTANCES OF: Saul, 1 Sam. 15:11,26–28. Solomon, 1 Kin. 11:4–40; Neh. 13:26. Amon, 2 Kin. 21:22,23. Rehoboam, 2 Chr.12:1,2. Asa, 2 Chr. 16:7–9. Joash, 2 Chr. 24:24. Amaziah, 2 Chr. 25:27. Syrians, Isa. 17:10,11. Jonah, Jonah 1:3. The disciples, Matt. 26:56; John 6: 66. Peter, Matt. 26:69–75. Corinthian Christians, 1 Cor. 5:1–8; 2 Cor. 12:20,21. Galatians, Gal. 1.6; 3:1; 4:9–11; 5:6,7. Hymenæus and Alexander, 1 Tim. 1:19,20. Phygellus and Hermogenes, 2 Tim. 1:15. Demas, 2 Tim. 4: 10. Churches of Asia, 1 Tim. 5:15; Rev. 2:4, 14,15,20; 3:2,3,15–18.

PROMISES TO: Lev. 26:40. If they shall confess their iniquity, and the iniquity of their fathers, with their trespass which they trespassed against me, and that also they have walked contrary unto me; 41. And *that* I also have walked contrary unto them, and have brought them into the land of their enemies; if then their uncircumcised hearts be humbled, and they then accept of the punishment of their iniquity: 42. Then will I remember my covenant with Jacob, and also my covenant with Isaac, and also my covenant with Abraham will I remember; and I will remember the land.

Deut. 4:29. But if from thence thou shalt seek the LORD thy God, thou shalt find *him*, if thou seek him with all thy heart and with all thy soul. 30. When thou art in tribulation, and all these things are come upon thee, *even* in the latter days, if thou turn to the LORD thy God, and shalt be obedient unto his voice; *v.* 31.

Deut. 30:1. And it shall come to pass, when all these things are come upon thee, the blessing and the curse, which I have set before thee, and thou shalt call *them* to mind among all the nations, whither the LORD thy God hath driven thee, 2. And shalt return unto the LORD thy God, and shalt obey his voice according to all that I command thee this day, thou and thy children, with all thine heart, and with all thy soul; 3. That then the LORD thy God will turn thy captivity, and have compassion upon thee, and will return and gather thee from all the nations, whither the LORD thy God hath scattered thee. 4. If *any* of thine be driven out unto the utmost *parts* of heaven, from thence will the LORD thy God gather thee, and from thence will he fetch thee: 5. And the LORD thy God will bring thee into the land which thy fathers possessed, and thou shalt possess it; and he will do thee good, and multiply thee above thy fathers. 6. And the LORD thy God will circumcise thine heart, and the heart of thy seed, to love the LORD thy God with all thine heart, and with

all thy soul, that thou mayest live. 7. And the LORD thy God will put all these curses upon thine enemies, and on them that hate thee, which persecuted thee. 8. And thou shalt return and obey the voice of the LORD, and do all his commandments which I command thee this day. 9. And the LORD thy God will make thee plenteous in every work of thine hand, in the fruit of thy body, and in the fruit of thy cattle, and in the fruit of thy land, for good: for the LORD will again rejoice over thee for good, as he rejoiced over thy fathers: 10. If thou shalt hearken unto the voice of the LORD thy God, to keep his commandments and his statutes which are written in this book of the law, *and* if thou turn unto the LORD thy God with all thine heart, and with all thy soul.

Deut. 32:26. I said, I would scatter them into corners, I would make the remembrance of them to cease from among men: 28. For they *are* a nation void of counsel, 29. O that they were wise, *that* they understood this, *that* they would consider their latter end!

1 Kin. 8:33. When thy people Israel be smitten down before the enemy, because they have sinned against thee, and shall turn again to thee, and confess thy name, and pray, and make supplication unto thee in this house: 34. Then hear thou in heaven, and forgive the sin of thy people Israel, and bring them again unto the land which thou gavest unto their fathers. *vs.* 35–53.

2 Chr. 30:9. For if ye turn again unto the LORD, your brethren and your children *shall find* compassion before them that lead them captive, so that they shall come again into this land: for the LORD your God *is* gracious and merciful, and will not turn away *his* face from you, if ye return unto him.

Job 22:23. If thou return to the Almighty, thou shalt be built up, thou shalt put away iniquity far from thy tabernacles. 24. Then shalt thou lay up gold as dust, and the *gold* of Ophir as the stones of the brooks. 25. Yea, the Almighty shall be thy defence, and thou shalt have plenty of silver. 26. For then shalt thou have thy delight in the Almighty, and shalt lift up thy face unto God. 27. Thou shalt make thy prayer unto him, and he shall hear thee, and thou shalt pay thy vows. 28. Thou shalt also decree a thing, and it shall be established unto thee: and the light shall shine upon thy ways. 29. When *men* are cast down, then thou shalt say, *There is* lifting up: and he shall save the humble person. 30. He shall deliver the island of the innocent: and it is delivered by the pureness of thine hands.

Psa. 17.5. Hold up my goings in thy paths, *that* my footsteps slip not.

Psa. 56:13. For thou hast delivered my soul from death: *wilt* not *thou deliver* my feet from falling, that I may walk before God in the light of the living?

Psa. 81:13. Oh that my people had hearkened unto me, *and* Israel had walked in my ways! 14. I should soon have subdued their enemies, and turned my hand against their adversaries.

Isa. 42:3. A bruised reed shall he not break, and the smoking flax shall he not quench: he shall bring forth judgment unto truth.

Isa. 57:18. I have seen his ways, and will heal him: I will lead him also, and restore comforts unto him and to his mourners. 19. I create the fruit of the lips; Peace, peace to *him that is* far off, and to *him that is* near, saith the LORD; and I will heal him.

Jer. 3:4. Wilt thou not from this time cry unto me, My father, thou *art* the guide of my youth? 5. Will he reserve *his anger* for ever? will he keep *it* to the end? 6. The LORD said also unto me in the days of Josiah the king, Hast thou seen *that* which backsliding Israel hath done? she is gone up upon every high mountain and under every green tree, and there hath played the harlot. 7. And I said after she had done all these *things*, Turn thou unto me. But she returned not. 12. Go and proclaim these words toward the north, and say, Return, thou backsliding Israel, saith the LORD; *and* I will not cause mine anger to fall upon you: for I *am* merciful, saith the LORD, *and* I will not keep *anger* for ever. 13. Only acknowledge thine iniquity, that thou hast transgressed against the LORD thy God, and hast scattered thy ways to the strangers under every green tree, and ye have not obeyed my voice, saith the LORD. 14. Turn, O backsliding children, saith the LORD; for I am married unto you: and I will take you one of a city, and two of a family, and I will bring you to Zion: 15. And I will give you pastors according to mine heart, which shall feed you with knowledge and understanding. 16. And it shall come to pass, when ye be multiplied and increased in the land, in those days, saith the LORD, they shall say no more, The ark of the covenant of the LORD: neither shall it come to mind: neither shall they remember it; neither shall they visit *it;* neither shall *that* be done any more. 17. At that time they shall call Jerusalem the throne of the LORD; and all the nations shall be gathered unto it, to the name of the LORD, to Jerusalem: neither shall they walk any more after the imagination of their evil heart. 18. In those days the house of Judah shall walk with the house of Israel, and they shall come together out of the land of the north to the land that I have given for an inheritance unto your fathers. 19. But I said, How shall I put thee among the children, and give thee a pleasant land, a goodly heritage of the hosts of nations? and I said, Thou shalt call me, My father; and shalt not turn away from me. 20. Surely *as* a wife treacherously departeth from her husband, so have ye dealt treacherously with me, O house of Israel, saith the LORD. 21. A voice was heard upon the high places, weeping *and* supplications of the children of Israel: for they have perverted their way, *and* they have forgotten the LORD their God. 22. Return, ye backsliding children, *and* I will heal your backslidings. Behold, we come unto thee; for thou *art* the LORD our God.

Jer. 4:1. If thou wilt return, O Israel, saith the LORD, return unto me: and if thou wilt put away thine abominations out of my sight, then shalt thou not remove. 2. And thou shalt swear, The LORD liveth, in truth, in judgment, and in righteousness; and the nations shall bless themselves in him, and in him shall they glory. 14. O Jerusalem, wash thine heart from wickedness, that thou mayest be saved. How long shall thy vain thoughts lodge within thee?

Jer. 6:16. Thus saith the LORD, Stand ye in the ways, and see, and ask for the old paths, where *is* the good way, and walk therein, and ye shall find rest for your souls.

Hos. 14:4. I will heal their backsliding, I will love them freely: for mine anger has turned away from him.

Zech. 10:6. And I will strengthen the house of Judah, and I will save the house of Joseph, and I will bring them again to place them; for I have mercy upon them: and they shall be as though I had not cast them off: for I *am* the LORD their God, and will hear them.

Mal. 3:7. Even from the days of your fathers ye are gone away from mine ordinances, and have not kept *them.* Return unto me, and I will return unto you, saith the LORD of hosts. But ye said, Wherein shall we return?

Matt. 23:37. O Jerusalem, Jerusalem, *thou* that killest the prophets, and stonest them which are sent unto thee, how often would I have gathered thy children together, even as a hen gathereth her chickens under *her* wings, and ye would not!

Rev. 3:8. I know thy works: behold, I have set before thee an open door, and no man can shut it: for thou hast a little strength, and hast kept my word, and hast not denied my name. 15. I know thy works, that thou art neither cold nor hot: I would thou wert cold or hot. 16. So then because thou art lukewarm, and neither cold nor hot, I will spue thee out of my mouth. 17. Because thou sayest, I am rich, and increased with goods, and have need of nothing; and knowest not that thou art wretched, and miserable, and poor, and blind, and naked: 18. I counsel thee to buy of me gold tried in the fire, that thou mayest be rich; and white raiment, that thou mayest be clothed, and *that* the shame of thy nakedness do not appear; and anoint thine eyes with eyesalve, that thou mayest see. 19. As many as I love, I rebuke and chasten: be zealous therefore, and repent. 20. Behold, I stand at the door, and knock: if any man hear my voice, and open the door, I will come in to him, and will sup with him, and he with me. 21. To him that overcometh will I grant to sit with me in my throne, even as I also overcame, and am set down with my Father in his throne.

See PENITENCE; PENITENT; SEEKERS.

RETURN OF: Psa. 80:3. Turn us again, O God, and cause thy face to shine; and we shall be saved. 4. O LORD God of hosts, how long wilt thou be angry against the prayer of thy people? 5. Thou feedest them with the bread of tears; and givest them tears to drink in great measure. 6. Thou makest us a strife unto our neighbours: and our enemies laugh among themselves. 7. Turn us again, O God of hosts, and cause thy face to shine; and we shall be saved. 14. Return, we beseech thee, O God of hosts: look down from heaven, and behold, and visit this vine; 15. And the vineyard which thy right hand hath planted, and the branch *that* thou madest strong for thyself. 16. *It is* burned with fire, *it is* cut down: they perish at the rebuke of thy countenance. 17. Let thy hand be upon the man of thy right hand, upon the son of man *whom* thou madest strong for thyself. 18. So will not we go back from thee: quicken us, and we will call upon thy name. 19. Turn us again, O LORD God of hosts, cause thy face to shine; and we shall be saved.

Isa. 17:7. At that day shall a man look to his Maker, and his eyes shall have respect to the Holy One of Israel.

Isa. 29:24. They also that erred in spirit shall come to understanding, and they that murmured shall learn doctrine.

Isa. 31:6. Turn ye unto *him from* whom the children of Israel have deeply revolted. 7. For in that day every man shall cast away his idols of silver, and his idols of gold, which your own hands have made unto you *for* a sin.

Jer. 50:4. In those days, and in that time, saith the LORD, the children of Israel shall come, they and the children of Judah together, going and weeping: they shall go, and seek the LORD their God. 5. They shall ask the way to Zion with their faces thitherward, *saying*, Come, and let us join ourselves to the LORD in a perpetual covenant *that* shall not be forgotten. 6. My people hath been lost sheep: their shepherds have caused them to go astray, they have turned them away *on* the mountains: they have gone from mountain to hill, they have forgotten their restingplace.

Hos. 3:5. Afterward shall the children of Israel return, and seek the LORD their God, and David their king; and shall fear the LORD and his goodness in the latter days.

Hos. 6:1. Come, and let us return unto the LORD: for he hath torn, and he will heal us; he hath smitten, and he will bind us up. 2. After two days will he revive us: in the third day he will raise us up, and we shall live in his sight. 3. Then shall we know, *if* we follow on to know the LORD: his going forth is prepared as the morning: and he shall come unto us as the rain, as the latter *and* former rain unto the earth.

INSTANCES OF: Jews, Ezra 6:16–21; 10. David, Psa. 51. Jonah, Jonah 2; 3. Peter, Matt.

26:75; Mark 14:72; Luke 22:62. Thomas, John 20:27–29.

BACKSLIDING OF ISRAEL: Ex. 17:7. And he called the name of the place Massah, and Meribah, because of the chiding of the children of Israel, and because they tempted the LORD, saying, Is the LORD among us, or not?

Deut. 4:25. When thou shalt beget children, and children's children, and ye shall have remained long in the land, and shall corrupt *yourselves*, and make a graven image, *or* the likeness of any *thing*, and shall do evil in the sight of the LORD thy God, to provoke him to anger: 26. I call heaven and earth to witness against you this day, that ye shall soon utterly perish from off the land whereunto ye go over Jordan to possess it; ye shall not prolong *your* days upon it, but shall utterly be destroyed. 27. And the LORD shall scatter you among the nations, and ye shall be left few in number among the heathen, whither the LORD shall lead you. 28. And there ye shall serve gods, the work of men's hands, wood and stone, which neither see, nor hear, nor eat, nor smell. 29. But if from thence thou shalt seek the LORD thy God, thou shalt find *him*, if thou seek him with all thy heart and with all thy soul. 30. When thou art in tribulation, and all these things are come upon thee, *even* in the latter days, if thou turn to the LORD thy God, and shalt be obedient unto his voice; 31. (For the LORD thy God *is* a merciful God;) he will not forsake thee, neither destroy thee, nor forget the covenant of thy fathers which he sware unto them.

Deut. 31:16. And the LORD said unto Moses, Behold, thou shalt sleep with thy fathers; and this people will rise up, and go a whoring after the gods of the strangers of the land, whither they go *to be* among them, and will forsake me, and break my covenant which I have made with them. 17. Then my anger shall be kindled against them in that day, and I will forsake them, and I will hide my face from them, and they shall be devoured, and many evils and troubles shall befall them; so that they will say in that day, Are not these evils come upon us, because our God *is* not among us? 18. And I will surely hide my face in that day for all the evils which they shall have wrought, in that they are turned unto other gods. 19. Now therefore write ye this song for you, and teach it the children of Israel: put it in their mouths, that this song may be a witness for me against the children of Israel. 20. For when I shall have brought them into the land which I sware unto their fathers, that floweth with milk and honey; and they shall have eaten and filled themselves, and waxen fat; then will they turn unto other gods, and serve them, and provoke me, and break my covenant. 21. And it shall come to pass, when many evils and troubles are befallen them, that this song shall testify against them as a witness; for it shall not be forgotten out of the mouths of their seed: for I know their imagination which they go about, even now, before I have brought them into the land which I sware. 22. Moses therefore wrote this song the same day, and taught it the children of Israel. 23. And he gave Joshua the son of Nun a charge, and said, Be strong and of a good courage: for thou shalt bring the children of Israel into the land which I sware unto them: and I will be with thee. 24. And it came to pass, when Moses had made an end of writing the words of this law in a book, until they were finished, 25. That Moses commanded the Levites, which bare the ark of the covenant of the LORD, saying, 26. Take this book of the law, and put it in the side of the ark of the covenant of the LORD your God, that it may be there for a witness against thee. 27. For I know thy rebellion, and thy stiff neck: behold, while I am yet alive with you this day, ye have been rebellious against the LORD; and how much more after my death? 28. Gather unto me all the elders of your tribes, and your officers, that I may speak these words in their ears, and call heaven and earth to record against them. 29. For I know that after my death ye will utterly corrupt *yourselves*, and turn aside from the way which I have commanded you; and evil will befall you in the latter days; because ye will do evil in the sight of the LORD, to provoke him to anger through the work of your hands. 30. And Moses spake in the ears of all the congregation of Israel the words of this song, until they were ended.

Deut. 32:5. They have corrupted themselves, their spot *is* not *the spot* of his children: *they are* a perverse and crooked generation. 6. Do ye thus requite the LORD, O foolish people and unwise? *is* not he thy father *that* hath bought thee? hath he not made thee and established thee? 15. But Jeshurun waxed fat, and kicked: thou art waxen fat, thou art grown thick, thou art covered *with fatness;* then he forsook God *which* made him, and lightly esteemed the Rock of his salvation. *v.* 18; Num. 14:43; Judg. 2:12; 10:12–14.

2 Chr. 24:20. Thus saith God, Why transgress ye the commandments of the LORD, that ye cannot prosper? because ye have forsaken the LORD he hath also forsaken you. 2 Kin. 18:1,12; 2 Chr. 13:11; 27:2; 29:6,8.

Ezra 9:10. Now, O our God, what shall we say after this? for we have forsaken thy commandments, 13. And after all that is come upon us for our evil deeds, and for our great trespass, seeing that thou our God hast punished us less than our iniquities *deserve*, and hast given us *such* deliverance as this; 14. Should we again break thy commandments, and join in affinity with the people of these abominations? wouldest not thou be angry with us till thou hadst consumed *us*, so that *there should be* no remnant nor escaping?

Neh. 9:26. Nevertheless they were disobedient, and rebelled against thee, and cast thy law behind their backs, and slew thy prophets which testified against them to turn them to thee, and they wrought great provocations.

Psa. 78:10. They kept not the covenant of God, and refused to walk in his law; 11. And forgat his works, and his wonders that he had shewed them. 40. How oft did they provoke him in the wilderness, *and* grieve him in the desert! 41. Yea, they turned back and tempted God, and limited the Holy One of Israel. 42. They remembered not his hand, *nor* the day when he delivered them from the enemy. 43. How he had wrought his signs in Egypt, and his wonders in the field of Zoan: 56. Yet they tempted and provoked the most high God, and kept not his testimonies: 57. But turned back, and dealt unfaithfully like their fathers: they were turned aside like a deceitful bow. 58. For they provoked him to anger with their high places, and moved him to jealousy with their graven images. 59. When God heard *this* he was wroth, and greatly abhorred Israel: 60. So that he forsook the tabernacle of Shiloh, the tent *which* he placed among men; 61. And delivered his strength into captivity, and his glory into the enemy's hand. 62. He gave his people over also unto the sword; and was wroth with his inheritance. 63. The fire consumed their young men; and their maidens were not given to marriage. 64. Their priests fell by the sword; and their widows made no lamentation.

Psa. 106:13. They soon forgat his works; they waited not for his counsel: 14. But lusted exceedingly in the wilderness, and tempted God in the desert.

Isa. 1:4. Ah sinful nation, a people laden with iniquity, a seed of evildoers, children that are corrupters: they have forsaken the LORD, they have provoked the Holy One of Israel unto anger, they are gone away backward. 5. Why should ye be stricken any more? ye will revolt more and more: the whole head is sick, and the whole heart faint. 6. From the sole of the foot even unto the head *there is* no soundness in it; *but* wounds, and bruises, and putrifying sores: they have not been closed, neither bound up, neither mollified with ointment. 7. Your country *is* desolate, your cities *are* burned with fire: your land, strangers devour it in your presence, and *it is* desolate, as overthrown by strangers. 21. How is the faithful city become an harlot! it was full of judgment; righteousness lodged in it; but now murderers. 22. Thy silver is become dross, thy wine mixed with water: Isa. 50:1.

Isa. 2:6. Thou hast forsaken thy people the house of Jacob, because they be replenished from the east, and *are* soothsayers like the Philistines, and they please themselves in the children of strangers.

Isa. 5:24. As the fire devoureth the stubble and the flame consumeth the chaff, *so* their root shall be as rottenness, and their blossom shall go up as dust: because they have cast away the law of the LORD of hosts, and despised the word of the Holy One of Israel. *vs.* 12–30.

Isa. 9:16. For the leaders of this people cause *them* to err; and *they that are* led of them *are* destroyed. *vs.* 13–21.

Isa. 17:10. Because thou hast forgotten the God of thy salvation, and hast not been mindful of the rock of thy strength, therefore shalt thou plant pleasant plants, and shalt set it with strange slips: 11. In the day shalt thou make thy plant to grow, and in the morning shalt thou make thy seed to flourish: *but* the harvest *shall be* a heap in the day of grief and of desperate sorrow.

Isa. 24:5. The earth also is defiled under the inhabitants thereof; because they have transgressed the laws, changed the ordinance, broken the everlasting covenant. 6. Therefore hath the curse devoured the earth, and they that dwell therein are desolate: therefore the inhabitants of the earth are burned, and few men left.

Isa. 30:9. That this *is* a rebellious people, lying children, children *that* will not hear the law of the LORD: 15. For thus saith the Lord GOD, the Holy One of Israel; In returning and rest shall ye be saved; in quietness and in confidence shall be your strength: and ye would not.

Isa. 31:6. Turn ye unto *him from* whom the children of Israel have deeply revolted.

Isa. 43:22. But thou hast not called upon me, O Jacob; but thou hast been weary of me, O Israel. 24. Thou hast bought me no sweet cane with money, neither hast thou filled me with the fat of thy sacrifices: but thou hast made me to serve with thy sins, thou hast wearied me with thine iniquities.

Isa. 51:17. Awake, awake, stand up, O Jerusalem, which hast drunk at the hand of the LORD the cup of his fury; thou hast drunken the dregs of the cup of trembling, *and* wrung *them* out. *vs.* 18–20.

Isa. 63:17. O LORD, why hast thou made us to err from thy ways, *and* hardened our heart from thy fear?

Isa. 65:2. I have spread out my hands all the day unto a rebellious people, which walketh in a way *that was* not good, after their own thoughts; 3. A people that provoketh me to anger continually to my face;

Jer. 2:5. Thus saith the LORD, What iniquity have your fathers found in me, that they are gone far from me, and have walked after vanity, and are become vain?

11. Hath a nation changed *their* gods, which *are* yet no gods? but my people have changed their glory for *that which* doth not profit. 12. Be astonished, O ye heavens, at this, and be horribly afraid, be ye very desolate, saith the LORD. 13. For my people have committed two evils; they have forsaken me the fountain of living waters, *and* hewed them out cisterns, broken cisterns, that can hold no water.

17. Hast thou not procured this unto thyself, in that thou hast forsaken the LORD thy God, when he led thee by the way? 19.

Thine own wickedness shall correct thee, and thy backslidings shall reprove thee: know therefore and see that *it is* an evil *thing* and bitter, that thou hast forsaken the LORD thy God, and that my fear *is* not in thee, saith the Lord GOD of hosts.

21. Yet I had planted thee a noble vine, wholly a right seed: how then art thou turned into the degenerate plant of a strange vine unto me? 27. They have turned *their* back unto me, and not *their* face: but in the time of their trouble they will say, Arise, and save us.

31. Have I been a wilderness unto Israel? a land of darkness? wherefore say my people, We are lords; we will come no more unto thee? 32. Can a maid forget her ornaments, *or* a bride her attire? yet my people have forgotten me days without number.

Jer. 3:21. A voice was heard upon the high places, weeping *and* supplications of the children of Israel: for they have perverted their way, *and* they have forgotten the LORD their God. *vs.* 1–25.

Jer. 5:19. When ye shall say, Wherefore doeth the LORD our God all these *things* unto us? then shalt thou answer them, Like as ye have forsaken me, and served strange gods in your land, so shall ye serve strangers in a land *that is* not yours. 23. But this people hath a revolting and a rebellious heart; they are revolted and gone. *vs.* 1–31; Jer. 11:9–17.

Jer. 6:30. Reprobate silver shall *men* call them, because the LORD hath rejected them. Ezek. 22:18.

Jer. 7:12. Go ye now unto my place which *was* in Shiloh, where I set my name at the first, and see what I did to it for the wickedness of my people Israel. *vs.* 13–34.

Jer. 8:5. Why *then* is this people of Jerusalem slidden back by a perpetual backsliding? they hold fast deceit, they refuse to return. 14. Why do we sit still? assemble yourselves, and let us enter into the defenced cities, and let us be silent there: for the LORD our God hath put us to silence, and given us water of gall to drink, because we have sinned against the LORD. 15. We looked for peace, but no good *came; and* for a time of health, and behold trouble! *vs.* 1–22.

Jer. 10:20. My tabernacle is spoiled, and all my cords are broken: my children are gone forth of me, and they *are* not: *there is* none to stretch forth my tent any more, and to set up my curtains. 21. For the pastors are become brutish, and have not sought the LORD: therefore they shall not prosper, and all their flocks shall be scattered. *vs.* 17–22.

Jer. 12:7. I have forsaken mine house, I have left mine heritage; I have given the dearly beloved of my soul into the hand of her enemies.

Jer. 13:24. Therefore will I scatter them as the stubble that passeth away by the wind of the wilderness. 25. This *is* thy lot, the portion of thy measures from me, saith the LORD; because thou hast forgotten me, and trusted in falsehood.

Jer. 14:7. O LORD, though our iniquities testify against us, do thou *it* for thy name's sake: for our backslidings are many; we have sinned against thee. 10. Thus saith the LORD unto this people, Thus have they loved to wander, they have not refrained their feet, therefore the LORD doth not accept them; he will now remember their iniquity, and visit their sins.

Jer. 15:1. Thus saith the LORD unto me, Though Moses and Samuel stood before me, *yet* my mind *could* not *be* toward this people: cast *them* out of my sight, and let them go forth. *vs.* 2–14.

Jer. 18:13. Therefore thus saith the LORD; Ask ye now among the heathen, who hath heard such things: the virgin of Israel hath done a very horrible thing. 14. Will *a man* leave the snow of Lebanon *which cometh* from the rock of the field? *or* shall the cold flowing waters that come from another place be forsaken? 15. Because my people hath forgotten me, they have burned incense to vanity, and they have caused them to stumble in their ways *from* the ancient paths, to walk in paths, *in* a way not cast up; Jer. 19.

Jer. 32:31. This city hath been to me *as* a provocation of mine anger and of my fury from the day that they built it even unto this day; that I should remove it from before my face, *v.* 30.

Jer. 50:6. My people hath been lost sheep: their shepherds have caused them to go astray, they have turned them away *on* the mountains: they have gone from mountain to hill, they have forgotten their restingplace.

Ezek. 2:3. And he said unto me, Son of man, I send thee to the children of Israel, to a rebellious nation that hath rebelled against me: they and their fathers have transgressed against me, *even* unto this very day. 4. For *they are* impudent children and stiffhearted. I do send thee unto them; and thou shalt say unto them, Thus saith the Lord GOD. 5. And they, whether they will hear, or whether they will forbear, (for they *are* a rebellious house,) yet shall know that there hath been a prophet among them. 6. And thou, son of man, be not afraid of them, neither be afraid of their words, though briers and thorns *be* with thee, and thou dost dwell among scorpions: be not afraid of their words, nor be dismayed at their looks, though they *be* a rebellious house. 7. And thou shalt speak my words unto them, whether they will hear, or whether they will forbear: for they *are* most rebellious. 8. But thou, son of man, hear what I say unto thee; Be not thou rebellious like that rebellious house: open thy mouth, and eat that I give thee.

Ezek. 5:6. She hath changed my judgments into wickedness more than the nations, and my statutes more than the countries that *are* round about her: for they have refused my judgments and my statutes, they have not walked in them. *vs.* 1–17.

Ezek. 11:21. *As for them* whose heart walketh after the heart of their detestable things and their abominations, I will recompense their way upon their own heads, saith the Lord GOD. *vs.* 1–21. [See Parable of the Vine, Ezek. 15.]

Ezek. 16:43. Because thou hast not remembered the days of thy youth, but hast fretted me in all these *things;* behold, therefore I also will recompense thy way upon *thine* head, saith the Lord GOD: [See Parables of an Unfaithful Wife, Ezek. 16; 23; Hos. 2; 3.]

Hos. 1:6. And *God* said unto him, Call her name Lo-ruhamah: for I will no more have mercy upon the house of Israel; but I will utterly take them away. 9. Then said *God*, Call his name Lo-ammi: for ye *are* not my people, and I will not be your *God.* *vs.* 1–9.

Hos. 4:6. My people are destroyed for lack of knowledge: because thou hast rejected knowledge, I will also reject thee, that thou shalt be no priest to me: seeing thou hast forgotten the law of thy God, I will also forget thy children. 10. They shall eat, and not have enough: they shall commit whoredom, and shall not increase: because they have left off to take heed to the LORD. *v.* 16.

Hos. 5:11. Ephraim *is* oppressed *and* broken in judgment, because he willingly walked after the commandment. 12. Therefore *will* I *be* unto Ephraim as a moth, and to the house of Judah as rottenness. *vs.* 1–15.

Hos. 6:4. O Ephraim, what shall I do unto thee? O Judah, what shall I do unto thee? for your goodness *is* as a morning cloud, and as the early dew it goeth away. 7. They like ¹men have transgressed the covenant: there have they dealt treacherously against me. *vs.* 4–11; Hos. 8:14; 9:1–17; 13:16.   [¹ R. V. Adam]

Hos. 11:2. *As* they called them, so they went from them: 7. And my people are bent to backsliding from me: though they called them to the most High, none at all would exalt *him.*

Hos. 14:1. O Israel, return unto the LORD thy God; for thou hast fallen by thine iniquity.

Amos. 2:4. Thus saith the LORD; for three transgressions of Judah, and for four, I will not turn away *the punishment* thereof; because they have despised the law of the LORD, and have not kept his commandments, and their lies caused them to err, after the which their fathers have walked:

Zeph. 1:6. Them that are turned back from the LORD; and *those* that have not sought the LORD, nor enquired for him.

Mal. 1:6. A son honoureth *his* father, and a servant his master: if then I *be* a father, where *is* mine honour? and if I *be* a master, where *is* my fear? saith the LORD of hosts unto you, O priests, that despise my name. And ye say, Wherein have we despised thy name?

Mal. 3:7. Even from the days of your fathers ye are gone away from mine ordinances, and have not kept *them.* Return unto me, and I will return unto you, saith the LORD of hosts. But ye said, Wherein shall we return?

Heb. 3:16. For some, when they had heard, did provoke: howbeit not all that came out of Egypt by Moses. 17. But with whom was he grieved forty years? *was it* not with them that had sinned, whose carcases fell in the wilderness? 18. And to whom sware he that they should not enter into his rest, but to them that 1 believed not?   [1 R. V. were disobedient]

INSTANCES OF ISRAEL'S BACKSLIDING: At Meribah, Ex. 17:1-7; when Aaron made the golden calf, Ex. 32; after Joshua's death, Judg. 2; during Asa's reign, 2 Chr. 15; Hezekiah's reign, 2 Chr. 30:2-12.

BAD COMPANY. See COMPANY, EVIL.

BADGER. [*R. V.*, SEAL or PORPOISE.] Skins of, used for covering of tabernacle, Ex. 25:5; 26:14; 35:7,23; 36:19; 39:34; Num. 4:6,8, 10,11,12,14,25. For shoes, Ezek. 16:10. [*R. V.*, SEALSKIN.]

BAGPIPE. [*R. V.*,] a musical instrument, Dan. 3:5.

BAHURIM, a village between the fords of the Jordan and Jerusalem, 2 Sam. 3:16; 16:5; 17:18; 19:16; 1 Kin. 2:8.

BAIL. See SURETY; CREDITOR; DEBT; DEBTOR.

BAJITH, a place of idolatrous worship in Moab, Isa. 15:2.

BAKBAKKAR, a Levite, 1 Chr. 9:15.

BAKBUK, an ancestor of the Nethinim, Ezra 2:51; Neh. 7:53.

BAKBUKIAH, a Levite, Neh. 11:17; 12:9,25.

BAKER, 1 Sam. 8:13; Jer. 37:21; Hos. 7:4,6. Pharaoh's chief baker, Gen. 40.

See BREAD.

BALAAM, son of Beor. From Mesopotamia, Deut. 23:4. A soothsayer, Josh. 13:22. A prophet, Num. 24:2-9; 2 Pet. 2:15,16. Balak sends for, to curse Israel, Num. 22:5-7; Josh. 24:9; Neh. 13:2; Mic. 6:5. Anger of, rebuked by his ass, Num. 22:22-35; 2 Pet.2:16. Counsel of, an occasion of Israel's corruption with the Midianites, Num. 31:16; Rev. 2:14, 15. Covetousness of, 2 Pet. 2:15; Jude 11. Death of, Num. 31:8; Josh. 13:22.

BALAC. See BALAK.

BALAH, a city of Simeon, Josh. 19:3. Called BILHAH, 1 Chr. 4:29.

BALAK, king of Moab, Num. 22:4; Josh. 24:9; Judg. 11:25; Mic. 6:5. Tries to bribe Balaam to curse Israel, Num. 22:5-7,15-17. See BALAAM.

BALANCES. Used for weighing, Job 31:6; Isa. 40:12,15; Ezek.5:1. Money weighed with, Isa. 46:6; Jer. 32:10. Must be just, Lev. 19:36; Prov. 16:11; Ezek. 45:10. False balance used, Hos. 12:7; Amos 8:5; Mic. 6:11; an abomination, Prov. 11:1; 20:23.

FIGURATIVE: Job 6:2; 31:6; Psa. 62:9; Isa. 40:12; Dan. 5:27; Rev. 6:5.

BALDNESS, Lev. 13:40,41. A judgment. Isa. 3:24; Jer. 47:5; 48:37; Ezek. 7:18. Artificial, a sign of mourning, Isa. 22:12; Jer. 16:6; Ezek. 27:31; 29:18; Amos. 8:10; Mic. 1:16.

Artificial, as an idolatrous practice, forbidden, Lev. 21:5; Deut. 14:1.

INSTANCES OF: Elisha, 2 Kin. 2:23.

BALL, playing at, Isa. 22:18.

BALM, a medicinal balsam, Gen. 37:25; 43:11; Jer. 8:22; 46:11; 51:8; Ezek. 27:17.

BAMAH, a high place, Ezek. 20:29.

BAMOTH. A camping place of the Israelites, Num. 21:19,20. Called BAMOTH-BAAL, a city of Reuben, Josh. 13:17.

BANI. 1. A Gadite, 2 Sam. 23:36.

2. A Levite, 1 Chr. 6:46.

3. A descendant of Pharez, 1 Chr. 9:4.

4. Father of returned exiles, Ezra 2:10; 10:29. Called BINNUI, Neh. 7:15.

5. A Levite of the returned exiles, Neh. 3: 17; 8:7; 9:4,5; 10:13; 11:22.

BANISHMENT, Ezra 7:26. Of Adam and Eve, from Eden, Gen. 3:22-24. Of Cain, to be "a fugitive and vagabond," Gen. 4:14. Of Jews, from Rome, Acts 18:2. Of John, to Patmos, Rev. 1:9.

See EXILE.

BANNER. FIGURATIVE: Psa. 20:5; 60:4; Song 2:4; 6:4; Isa. 13:2.

See ENSIGN; STANDARD.

BANQUET. See FEASTS.

BAPTISM. JOHN'S: Matt. 3:5. Then went out to him Jerusalem, and all Judæa, and all the region round about Jordan, 6. And were baptized of him in Jordan, confessing their sins. 7. But when he saw many of the Pharisees and Sadducees come to his baptism, he said unto them, O generation of vipers, who hath warned you to flee from the wrath to come? 8. Bring forth therefore fruits meet for repentance: 11. I indeed baptize you with water unto repentance: but he that cometh after me is mightier than I, whose shoes I am not worthy to bear: he shall baptize you with the Holy Ghost, and *with* fire: 13. Then cometh Jesus from Galilee to Jordan unto John, to be baptized of him. 14. But John forbad him, saying, I have need to be baptized of thee, and comest thou to me? 15. And Jesus answering said unto him, Suffer *it to be so* now: for thus it becometh us to fulfil all righteousness. Then he suffered him. 16. And Jesus, when he was baptized, went up straightway out of the water: and, lo, the heavens were opened unto him, and he saw the Spirit of God descending like a dove, and lighting upon him: Mark 1:8-10; Luke 3:7,8; John 10:40.

Matt. 21:25. The baptism of John, whence was it? from heaven, or of men? Mark 11:30; Luke 20:4.

Mark 1:4. John did baptize in the wilderness, and preach the baptism of repentance for the remission of sins. 5. And there went out unto him all the land of Judæa, and they of Jerusalem, and were all baptized of him in the river of Jordan, confessing their sins.

Luke 3:12. Then came also publicans to be baptized, and said unto him, Master, what shall we do? 21. When all the people were baptized, it came to pass, that Jesus also being baptized, and praying, the heaven was opened.

Luke 7:29. All the people that heard *him*, and the publicans, justified God, being baptized with the baptism of John. 30. But the Pharisees and lawyers rejected the counsel of God against themselves, being not baptized of him.

John 1:25. And they asked him, and said unto him, Why baptizest thou then, if thou be not that Christ, nor Elias, neither that prophet? 26. John answered them, saying, I baptize with water: but there standeth one among you, whom ye know not; 28. These things were done in Bethabara beyond Jordan, where John was baptizing. 31. I knew him not: but that he should be made manifest to Israel, therefore am I come baptizing with water. 33. He that sent me to baptize with water, the same said unto me, Upon whom thou shalt see the Spirit descending, and remaining on him, the same is he which baptizeth with the Holy Ghost.

John 3:23. And John also was baptizing in Ænon, near to Salim, because there was much water there: and they came, and were baptized.

Acts 1:5. John truly baptized with water; but ye shall be baptized with the Holy Ghost not many days hence. 22. Beginning from the baptism of John, unto that same day that he was taken up from us, must one be ordained to be a witness with us of his resurrection.

Acts 10:37. That word, *I say*, ye know, which was published throughout all Judæa, and began from Galilee, after the baptism which John preached;

Acts 11:16. Then remembered I the word of the Lord, how that he said, John indeed baptized with water; but ye shall be baptized with the Holy Ghost. Acts 18:25.

Acts 19:3. And he said unto them, Unto what then were ye baptized? And they said, Unto John's baptism. 4. Then said Paul, John verily baptized with the baptism of repentance, saying unto the people, that they should believe on him which should come after him, that is, on Christ Jesus.

CHRISTIAN: Matt. 28:19. Go ye therefore, and teach all nations, baptizing them in the name of the Father, and of the Son, and of the Holy Ghost:

Mark 16:16. He that believeth and is baptized shall be saved;

John 3:5. Jesus answered, Verily, verily, I say unto thee, Except a man be born of water and *of* the Spirit, he cannot enter into the kingdom of God. 22. After these things came Jesus and his disciples into the land of Judæa; and there he tarried with them, and baptized.

John 4:1. The Lord knew how the Pharisees had heard that Jesus made and baptized more disciples than John, 2. (Though Jesus himself baptized not, but his disciples,)

Acts 1:5. John truly baptized with water; but ye shall be baptized with the Holy Ghost not many days hence. 22. Beginning from the baptism of John, unto that same day that he was taken up from us, must one be

ordained to be a witness with us of his resurrection.

Acts 2:38. Peter said unto them, Repent, and be baptized every one of you in the name of Jesus Christ for the remission of sins, and ye shall receive the gift of the Holy Ghost. 41. Then they that gladly received his word were baptized: and the same day there were added *unto them* about three thousand souls.

Acts 8:12. When they believed Philip preaching the things concerning the kingdom of God, and the name of Jesus Christ, they were baptized, both men and women. 13. Then Simon himself believed also: and when he was baptized, he continued with Philip, *v.* 16.

36. And as they went on *their* way, they came unto a certain water: and the eunuch said, See, *here is* water; what doth hinder me to be baptized? [1] 37. Philip said, If thou believest with all thine heart, thou mayest. And he answered and said, I believe that Jesus Christ is the Son of God. 38. And he commanded the chariot to stand still: and they went down both into the water, both Philip and the eunuch; and he baptized him. [1 Omitted in R. V.]

Acts 9:18. And immediately there fell from his eyes as it had been scales: and he received sight forthwith, and arose, and was baptized.

Acts 10:46. Then answered Peter, 47. Can any man forbid water, that these should not be baptized, which have received the Holy Ghost as well as we? 48. And he commanded them to be baptized in the name of the Lord.

Acts 16:14. And a certain woman named Lydia, a seller of purple, of the city of Thyatira, which worshipped God, heard *us:* whose heart the Lord opened, that she attended unto the things which were spoken of Paul. 15. And when she was baptized, and her household, she besought *us*, saying, If ye have judged me to be faithful to the Lord, come into my house, and abide *there*. 33. He took them the same hour of the night, and washed *their* stripes; and was baptized, he and all his, straightway.

Acts 18:8. Many of the Corinthians hearing believed, and were baptized. 25. This man was instructed in the way of the Lord; and being fervent in the spirit, he spake and taught diligently the things of the Lord, knowing only the baptism of John.

Acts 19:4. Then said Paul, John verily baptized with the baptism of repentance, saying unto the people, that they should believe on him which should come after him, that is, on Christ Jesus. 5. When they heard *this*, they were baptized in the name of the Lord Jesus.

Acts 22:16. And now why tarriest thou? arise, and be baptized, and wash away thy sins, calling on the name of the Lord.

Rom. 6:3. Know ye not, that so many of us as were baptized into Jesus Christ were baptized into his death? 4. Therefore we are buried with him by baptism into death: that like as Christ was raised up from the dead by the glory of the Father, even so we also should walk in newness of life.

1 Cor. 1:13. Were ye baptized in the name of Paul? 14. I thank God that I baptized none of you, but Crispus and Gaius; 15. Lest any should say that I had baptized in mine own name. 16. And I baptized also the household of Stephanas: besides, I know not whether I baptized any other. 17. For Christ sent me not to baptize, but to preach the gospel:

1 Cor. 10:1. Moreover, brethren, I would not that ye should be ignorant, how that all our fathers were under the cloud, and all passed through the sea; 2. And were all baptized unto Moses in the cloud and in the sea;

1 Cor. 12:13. By one Spirit are we all baptized into one body, whether *we be* Jews or Gentiles, whether *we be* bond or free; and have been all made to drink into one Spirit.

1 Cor. 15:29. What shall they do which are baptized for the dead, if the dead rise not at all? why are they then baptized for the dead?

Gal. 3:27. As many of you as have been baptized into Christ have put on Christ.

Eph. 4:5. One Lord, one faith, one baptism,

Eph. 5:26. That he might sanctify and cleanse it with the washing of water by the word,

Col. 2:12. Buried with him in baptism, wherein also ye are risen with *him* through the faith of the operation of God, who hath raised him from the dead.

Heb. 6:2. Of the doctrine of baptisms, and of laying on of hands, and of resurrection of the dead, and of eternal judgment.

1 Pet. 3:18. Christ also hath once suffered for sins, the just for the unjust, that he might bring us to God, being put to death in the flesh, but quickened by the Spirit: 21. The like figure whereunto *even* baptism doth also now save us (not the putting away of the filth of the flesh, but the answer of a good conscience toward God,) by the resurrection of Jesus Christ:

OF THE HOLY GHOST: Isa. 44:3. I will pour my spirit upon thy seed, and my blessing upon thine offspring:

Joel 2:28. And it shall come to pass afterward, *that* I will pour out my spirit upon all flesh; and your sons and your daughters shall prophesy, your old men shall dream dreams, your young men shall see visions: 29. And also upon the servants and upon the handmaids in those days will I pour out my spirit.

Zech. 12:10. And I will pour upon the house of David, and upon the inhabitants of Jerusalem, the spirit of grace and of supplications: and they shall look upon me whom they have pierced, and they shall mourn for him, as one mourneth for *his* only *son*, and shall be in bitterness for him, as one that is in bitterness for *his* firstborn.

Matt. 3:11. I indeed baptize you with water unto repentance: but he that cometh after me is mightier than I, whose shoes I am not worthy to bear: he shall baptize you with the Holy Ghost, and *with* fire: [Mark 1:8; Luke

3:16.] 16. And Jesus, when he was baptized, went up straightway out of the water: and, lo, the heavens were opened unto him, and he saw the Spirit of God descending like a dove, and lighting upon him: Luke 3:22; John 1:32,33.

Luke 24:49. And, behold, I send the promise of my Father upon you: but tarry ye in the city of Jerusalem, until ye be endued with power from on high.

John 3:5. Jesus answered, Verily, verily, I say unto thee, Except a man be born of water and *of* the Spirit, he cannot enter into the kingdom of God.

Acts 1:5. John truly baptized with water; but ye shall be baptized with the Holy Ghost not many days hence.

Acts 2:1. And when the day of Pentecost was fully come, they were all with one accord in one place. 2. And suddenly there came a sound from heaven as of a rushing mighty wind, and it filled all the house where they were sitting. 3. And there appeared unto them cloven tongues like as of fire, and it sat upon each of them. 4. And they were all filled with the Holy Ghost, and began to speak with other tongues, as the Spirit gave them utterance. 38. Peter said unto them, Repent, and be baptized every one of you in the name of Jesus Christ for the remission of sins, and ye shall receive the gift of the Holy Ghost. 41. Then they that gladly received his word were baptized: and the same day there were added *unto them* about three thousand souls.

Acts 8:15. Who [Peter and John], when they were come down, prayed for them, that they might receive the Holy Ghost: 16. (For as yet he was fallen upon none of them: only they were baptized in the name of the Lord Jesus.) 17. Then laid they *their* hands on them, and they received the Holy Ghost.

Acts 10:38. How God anointed Jesus of Nazareth with the Holy Ghost and with power: 44. While Peter yet spake these words, the Holy Ghost fell on all them which heard the word. 45. And they of the circumcision which believed were astonished, as many as came with Peter, because that on the Gentiles also was poured out the gift of the Holy Ghost. 47. Can any man forbid water, that these should not be baptized, which have received the Holy Ghost as well as we?

Acts 11:15. And as I began to speak, the Holy Ghost fell on them, as on us at the beginning. 16. Then remembered I the word of the Lord, how that he said, John indeed baptized with water; but ye shall be baptized with the Holy Ghost.

Acts 19:2. He said unto them, Have ye received the Holy Ghost since ye believed? And they said unto him, We have not so much as heard whether there be any Holy Ghost. 6. And when Paul had laid *his* hands upon them, the Holy Ghost came on them; 1 Cor. 12:13. By one Spirit are we all baptized into one body, whether *we be* Jews or Gentiles, whether *we be* bond or free: and have been all made to drink into one Spirit.

Tit. 3:5. Not by works of righteousness which we have done, but according to his mercy he saved us, by the washing of regeneration, and renewing of the Holy Ghost; 6. Which he shed on us abundantly through Jesus Christ our Saviour;

1 Pet. 3:20. Which sometime were disobedient, when once the longsuffering of God waited in the days of Noah, while the ark was a preparing, wherein few, that is, eight souls were saved by water. 21. The like figure whereunto *even* baptism doth also now save us (not the putting away of the filth of the flesh, but the answer of a good conscience toward God,) by the resurrection of Jesus Christ:

See HOLY SPIRIT.

BARABBAS, a prisoner released by Pilate, Matt. 27:16-26; Mark 15:7-15; Luke 23:18-25; John 18:40; Acts 3:14.

BARACHEL, father of Elihu, Job 32:2, 6.

BARACHIAH. Called also BERECHIAH, father of Zechariah, Zech. 1:1,7. Called BARACHIAS in Matt. 23:35.

BARAK, a judge in Israel, Judg. 4; 5; Heb. 11:32.

BARBARIAN, a foreigner, Acts 28:2-4; Rom. 1:14; 1 Cor. 14:11; Col. 3:11.

See STRANGER.

BARBER, Ezek. 5:1.

BARIAH, son of Shechaniah, 1 Chr. 3:22.

BAR-JESUS, a false prophet, Acts 13:6.

BAR-JONA, surname of Peter, Matt. 16:17.

BARKOS, a Jew whose descendants returned from exile, Ezra 2:53; Neh. 7:55.

BARLEY. A product of Egypt, Ex. 9:31; Palestine, Deut. 8:8; 1 Chr. 11:13; Jer. 41:8. Fed to horses, 1 Kin. 4:28. Used in offerings, Num. 5:15; Ezek. 45:15. Traffic in, 2 Chr. 2:10; Hos. 3:2. Tribute in, 2 Chr. 27:5. Priests estimated value of, Lev. 27:16; 2 Kin. 7:1; Rev. 6:6. Absalom burns Joab's field of, 2 Sam. 14:30.

Loaves of, John 6:9,13.

BARN, 2 Kin. 6:27; Job 39:12; Prov. 3:10; Joel 1:17; Hag. 2:19; Matt. 6:26; 13:30; Luke 12:18,24.

See GARNER.

BARNABAS, called also JOSES. A prophet, Acts 13:1. An apostle, Acts 14:14. A Levite who gave his possessions to be owned in common with other disciples, Acts 4:36,37. Goes to Tarsus to find Paul, brings him to Antioch, Acts 11:25,26. Accompanies Paul to Jerusalem, Acts 11:30. Returns with Paul to Antioch, Acts 12:25. Goes with Paul to Seleucia, Acts 13; to Iconium, Acts 14:1-7. Called Jupiter, Acts 14:12-18. Goes to Derbe, Acts 14:20. Is sent as a commissioner to Jerusalem, Acts 15; Gal. 2:1-9. Disaffected towards Paul, Acts 15:36-39. Is reconciled to Paul, 1 Cor. 9:6. Piety of, Acts 11:24. Devotion of, to Jesus, Acts 15:26.

BARREL, an earthen jar, 1 Kin. 17:12, 14,16; 18:33.

BARRENNESS, sterility of women. A reproach, Gen. 30:22,23; 1 Sam. 1:6,7;

2:1-11; Isa. 4:1; Luke 1:25. Miraculously removed, Instances of: Sarai, Gen. 17:15-21; Rebecca, Gen. 25:21; Manoah's wife, Judg. 13; Hannah, 1 Sam. 1:6-20; Elisabeth, Luke 1:5-25. Sent as a judgment, Gen. 20:17,18.

See CHILDLESSNESS.

BARSABAS. 1. Surname of Joseph, Acts 1:23.

2. Judas, Acts 15:22.

BARTER. See COMMERCE.

BARTHOLOMEW, one of the apostles, Matt. 10:3; Mark 3:18; Luke 6:14; Acts 1:13.

BARTIMEUS, a blind man, Mark 10:46-52; Matt. 20:29-34; Luke 18:35-43.

BARUCH. 1. An amanuensis of Jeremiah, Jer. 32:12-16; 36:4-32; 43:3-6; 45:1,2.

2. Son of Labai, Neh. 3:20; 10:6.

3. A descendant of Pharez, Neh. 11:5.

BARZILLAI. 1. A friend of David, 2 Sam. 17:27-29; 19:31-39; 1 Kin. 2:7; Ezra 2:61; Neh. 7:63.

2. Father of Adriel, 2 Sam. 21:8.

3. A priest, Ezra 2:61; Neh. 7:63.

BASHAN. A region E. of the Jordan and N. of Arnon, Gen. 14:5. Og, king of, Josh. 13:12. Allotted to the two and one half tribes, which had their possession E. of the Jordan, Num. 32:33; Deut. 3:10-14; Josh. 12:4-6; 13:29-31; 17:1. Invaded and taken by Hazael, king of Syria, 2 Kin. 10: 32,33. Retaken by Jehoash, 2 Kin. 13:25. Fertility and productiveness of, Isa. 33:9; Jer. 50:19; Nah. 1:4. Forests of, famous, Isa. 2:13; Ezek. 27:6; Zech. 11.2. Distinguished for its fine cattle, Deut. 32:14; Psa. 22:12; Ezek. 39:18; Amos 4:1; Mic. 7:14.

See ARGOB; ASHTAROTH; EDREI; JAIR.

BASHAN-HAVOTH-JAIR, a name given to Argob, Deut. 3:14.

BASHEMATH, wife of Esau, Gen. 26: 34; 36:3,4,10,13,17.

BASIN. Made of gold, 1 Kin. 7:50; 1 Chr. 28:17; 2 Chr. 4:8,22; Ezra 1:10; 8:27; of brass, Ex. 27:3; 38:3; 1 Kin. 7:45.

See TABERNACLE, FURNITURE OF.

BASKET, Gen. 40:16,17; Ex. 29:3,23,32; Lev. 8:2; Num. 6:15; Deut. 26:2; 28:5,17; 2 Kin. 10:7. Received the fragments after the miracles of the loaves, Matt. 14:20; 15:37; 16: 9,10. Paul let down from the wall in, Acts 9:25; 2 Cor. 11:33.

BASMATH, daughter of Solomon, 1 Kin. 4:15.

BASON. See BASIN.

BASTARD, excluded from the congregation, Deut. 23:2.

INSTANCES OF: Ishmael, Gen. 16:3,15; Gal. 4:22; Moab and Ammon, Gen. 19:36,37; Jephthah, Judg. 11:1; David's child by Bathsheba, 2 Sam. 11:2-5.

FIGURATIVE: Zech. 9:6; Heb. 12:8.

BAT, Lev. 11:19; Deut. 14:18; Isa. 2:20.

BATH, a Hebrew measure for liquids, containing about eight gallons, three quarts, 1 Kin. 7:26,38; Ezra 7:22; Isa. 5:10; Ezek. 45: 10,11,14.

BATHING. See ABLUTION; PURIFICATION.

BATH-RABBIM, a gate in the city of Heshbon, Song 7:4.

BATH-SHEBA, wife of Uriah and later wife of David. Called BATH-SHUA, 1 Chr. 3:5. Adultery of, 2 Sam. 11:2–5. Solomon's mother, 1 Kin. 1:11–31; 2:13–21; 1 Chr. 3:5.

BATTERING-RAM, 2 Sam. 20:15; Ezek. 4:2; 21:22.

BATTERY. See ASSAULT AND BATTERY.

BATTLE. Shouting in, Judg. 7:20; 1 Sam. 17:20. Priests in, 2 Chr. 13:12. Prayer before: By Asa, 2 Chr. 14:11; by Jehoshaphat, 2 Chr. 20:3–12.

See ARMIES ; WAR.

BATTLE-AX, Jer. 51:20.

BATTLEMENTS, on roofs of houses, Deut. 22:8; on walls, Jer. 5:10.

BAVAI, builds the wall of Jerusalem, Neh. 3:18.

BAY TREE, Psa. 37:35.

BAZLITH, called also BAZLUTH, one of the Nethinim, Ezra 2:52; Neh. 7:54.

BDELLIUM, Gen. 2:12; Num. 11:7.

BEACON, Isa. 30:17; Jer. 6:1.

See ENSIGN ; STANDARD.

BEALIAH, an Israelite, who joined David at Ziklag, 1 Chr. 12:5.

BEAM, weaver's, 1 Sam. 17:7; 2 Sam. 21:19.

FIGURATIVE: Matt. 7:3; Luke 6:41.

BEAN, 2 Sam. 17:28; Ezek. 4:9.

BEAR. Ferocity of, 2 Sam. 17:8; Prov. 17:12; 28:15; Isa. 11:7; 59:11; Lam. 3:10; Hos. 13:8; Amos. 5:19. Killed by David, 1 Sam. 17:34–37. Two destroy the children of Beth-el, who mocked Elisha, 2 Kin. 2:24.

FIGURATIVE: Dan. 7:5; Rev. 13:2.

BEARD. Worn long by Aaron, Psa. 133:2; Samson, Judg. 16:17; David, 1 Sam. 21:13; Ezek. 5:1. Shaven by Egyptians, Gen. 41:14. Untrimmed in mourning, 2 Sam. 19:24. Plucked, Ezra 9:3. Cut, Isa. 7:20; 15:2; Jer. 41:5; 48:37. Lepers required to shave, Lev. 13:29–33; 14:9. Idolatrous practice of marring, forbidden, Lev. 19:27; 21:5. Beards of David's ambassadors half shaven by the king of the Amorites, 2 Sam. 10:4.

BEASTS. See ANIMALS.

BEATEN WORK, of metals, Ex. 25:18; 37:17,22; Num. 8:4.

BEATING, as a punishment, Ex. 5:14; Deut. 25:3; Mark 13:9; Acts 5:40; 16:22,37; 18:17; 21:32; 22:19.

See ASSAULT ; PUNISHMENT.

BEAUTY. Vanity of, Psa. 39:11. Prov. 6:25; 31:30; Isa. 3:24; Ezek. 16:14; 28:17. Consumeth away, Psa. 39:11; 49:14.

INSTANCES OF: Sarah, Gen. 12:11. Rebekah, Gen. 24:16. Rachel, Gen. 29:17. Joseph, Gen. 39:6. Moses, Ex. 2:2; Heb. 11:23. David, 1 Sam. 16:12,18. Bath-sheba, 2 Sam. 11:2. Tamar, 2 Sam. 13:1. Absalom, 2 Sam. 14:25. Abishag, 1 Kin. 1:4. Vashti, Esth. 1:11. Esther, Esth. 2:7.

SPIRITUAL: 1 Chr. 16:29; Psa. 27:4; 29:2; 45:11; 90:17; 110:3; Isa. 52:7; Ezek. 16:14; Zech. 9:17.

BEAUTY AND BANDS, the staves, broken, Zech. 11:7.

BEBAI, the name of three Jews whose descendants came from exile, Ezra 2:11; 8:11; 10:28; Neh. 7:16; 10:15.

BECHER. 1. Son of Benjamin, Gen. 46:21, 1 Chr. 7:6,8.

2. Son of Ephraim, Num. 26:35. Called BERED, 1 Chr. 7:20.

BECHORATH, son of Aphiah, 1 Sam. 9:1.

BED. Made of wood, Song 3:7–9; of iron, Deut 3:11; of ivory, Amos 6:4; of gold and silver, Esth. 1:6. Used at meals, Amos 6:4. Exempt from execution for debt, Prov. 22:27. Perfumed, Prov. 7:17.

FIGURATIVE: Psa. 139:8.

BEDAN. 1. One of the deliverers of Israel, 1 Sam. 12:11, possibly identical with Abdon.

2. Son of Ullam, 1 Chr. 7:17.

BEE. In Palestine, Deut. 1:44; Judg. 14: 8; Psa. 118:12; Isa. 7:18. Called by hissing, Isa. 7:18.

See HONEY.

BEELIADA, son of David, 1 Chr. 14:7. Called ELIADA, 2 Sam. 5:16; 1 Chr. 3:8.

BEELZEBUB. The prince of devils, Matt. 10:25; 12:24,27; Mark 3:22; Luke 11:15, 18,19. Messengers sent to inquire of, by Ahaziah, 2 Kin. 1:2.

See BAAL-ZEBUB.

BEER. 1. A station of the Israelites, Num. 21:16–18.

2. A town in the tribe of Judah, Judg. 9:21.

BEERA, son of Zophah, 1 Chr. 7:37.

BEERAH, a Reubenite, 1 Chr. 5:6.

BEER-ELIM, a city of Moab, Isa. 15:8.

BEERI. 1. A Hittite, Gen. 26:34. See ANAH.

2. Father of Hosea, Hos. 1:1.

BEER-LAHAI-ROI, called also LAHAI-ROI, a well, Gen. 16:14; 24:62; 25:11.

BEEROTH. 1. A station of the Israelites. Aaron died at, Deut. 10:6. See BENE-JAAKAN.

2. A city of the Hivites, Josh. 9:17; 18:25; 2 Sam 4:2; Ezra 2:25; Neh. 7:29.

BEER-SHEBA. 1. The most southern city of Palestine, Judg. 20:1. Named by Abraham, who dwelt there, Gen. 21:31–33; 22:19. The dwelling place of Isaac, Gen. 26:23. Jacob went out from, toward Haran, Gen. 28:10. Sacrifices offered at, by Jacob when journeying to Egypt, Gen. 46:1. In the inheritance of Judah, Josh. 15:20,28; 2 Sam. 24:7. Afterward assigned to Simeon, Josh. 19:2,9; 1 Chr. 4:28. Two sons of Samuel were judges at, 1 Sam. 8:2. Became a seat of idolatrous worship, Amos. 5:5; 8:14.

2. Well of, belonged to Abraham and Isaac, Gen. 21:25,26.

3. Wilderness of. Hagar miraculously sees a well in, Gen. 21:14–19. An angel fed Elijah in, 1 Kin. 19:5,7.

BEESH-TERAH, a Levitical city, Josh. 21:27. Called ASHTAROTH, 1 Chr. 6:71.

BEETLE, authorized as food, Lev. 11:22.

BEGGARS. Set among princes, 1 Sam. 2:8. Not the seed of the righteous, Psa. 37:

25. The children of the wicked, Psa. 109:10; Prov. 20:4; Luke 16:3.

INSTANCES OF: Bartimeus, Mark 10:46. Lazarus, Luke 16:20–22; the blind man, John 9:8. The lame man, Acts 3:2–5.

See POOR.

BEHEADING. Execution by: Of John, Matt. 14:10; Mark 6:27: of James, Acts. 12:2; of the martyrs, Rev. 20:4.

See PUNISHMENT.

BEHEMOTH, an amphibious animal, Job. 40:15.

BEKAH, a half shekel, about 31 cents, Ex. 38:26.

BEL, a Babylonian god, Isa. 46:1; Jer. 50: 2; 51:44.

BELA. 1. A city called also Zoar, Gen. 14:2,8.

2. King of Edom, Gen. 36:32,33; 1 Chr. 1: 43,44.

3. Son of Benjamin, Num. 26:38,40; 1 Chr. 7:6,7; 8:1,3. Called BELAH, Gen. 46:21.

4. Son of Azaz, 1 Chr. 5:8.

BELIAL, lawlessness, Deut. 13:13; 2 Cor. 6:15.

BELIEVER. See RIGHTEOUS.

BELIEVING. See FAITH.

BELL. Attached to the hem of the priest's robe, Ex. 28:33,34; 39:25,26. On horses, Zech. 14:20.

BELLOWS, used with the furnace of the founder, Jer. 6:29.

BELLY, used figuratively for the seat of the affections, Job. 15:2,35; 20:20; Psa. 44:25; Prov. 18:20; 20:27,30; Hab. 3:16; John 7:38; Tit. 1:12.

BELSHAZZAR, king of Babylon, Dan. 5:1–30.

BELTESHAZZAR, name given Daniel, Dan. 1:7.

See DANIEL.

BEN, a Levite, 1 Chr. 15:18.

BEN-ABINADAB. See ABINADAB.

BENAIAH. 1. Son of Jehoiada, commander of the Cherethites and Pelethites, 2 Sam. 8:18; 1 Kin. 1:38. A distinguished warrior, 2 Sam. 23:20–23: 1 Chr. 11:22–25; 27:5,6. Loyal to Solomon, 1 Kin. 1:2; 4:4.

2. An Ephraimite, and distinguished warrior, 2 Sam. 23:30; 1 Chr. 11:31; 27:14.

3. A Levitical musician, 1 Chr. 15:18,20; 16:5.

4. A priest, 1 Chr. 15:24; 16:6.

5. Son of Jeiel, 2 Chr. 20:14.

6. A Levite in time of Hezekiah, 2 Chr. 31:13.

7. A chief of the Simeonites, 1 Chr. 4:36.

8. Father of Pelatiah, Ezek. 11:1,13.

9. Son of Parosh, Ezra 10:25.

10. Son of Pahath-moab, Ezra 10:30.

11. Son of Bani, Ezra 10:35.

12. Son of Nebo, Ezra 10:43.

BEN-AMMI, son of Lot, Gen. 19:38.

BENCH, of ivory, Ezek. 27:6.

BEN-DEKAR [R. V.]. See DEKAH.

BENE-BERAK, a city of Dan, Josh. 19:45.

BENEDICTIONS. Divinely appointed, Deut. 10:8; 21:5; Num. 6:23–26. By God, upon creatures he had made, Gen. 1:22; upon man, Gen. 1:28; upon Noah, Gen. 9:1,2.

INSTANCES OF: By Melchizedek, upon Abraham, Gen. 14:19,20; Heb. 7:7. By Bethuel's household, upon Rebekah, Gen. 24:60. By Isaac, upon Jacob, Gen. 27:23–29,37; 28: 1–4; upon Esau, Gen. 27:39,40. By Jacob, upon Pharaoh, Gen. 47:7–10; upon Joseph's sons, Gen. 48; upon his own sons, Gen. 49. By Moses, upon the tribes of Israel, Deut. 33. By Aaron, Lev. 9:22,23; by half the tribes, who stood on mount Gerizim, Deut. 11:29,30; 27:11–13; Josh. 8:33. By Joshua, upon Caleb, Josh. 14:13; upon the Reubenites and Gadites, and half tribe of Manasseh, Josh. 22:6,7. By Naomi, upon Ruth and Orpah, Ruth 1:8,9. By the people, upon Ruth, Ruth 4:11,12. By Eli, upon Elkanah, 1 Sam. 2:20. By David, upon the people, 2 Sam. 6:18; upon Barzillai, 2 Sam. 19:39. By Araunah, upon David, 2 Sam. 24:23. By Solomon, upon the people, 1 Kin. 8:14,55–58; 2 Chr. 6:3. By Simeon, upon Jesus, Luke 2:34. By Jesus, Luke 24:50.

LEVITICAL, FORMS OF: Num. 6:23. On this wise ye shall bless the children of Israel, saying unto them, 24. The LORD bless thee, and keep thee: 25. The LORD make his face shine upon thee, and be gracious unto thee: 26. The LORD lift up his countenance upon thee, and give thee peace.

APOSTOLIC, FORMS OF: Rom. 1:7. To all that be in Rome, beloved of God, called *to be* saints: Grace to you and peace from God our Father, and the Lord Jesus Christ. 1 Cor. 1:3; 2 Cor. 1:2; Gal. 1:3; Eph. 1:2; Phil. 1:2; Col. 1:2; 1 Thess. 1:1; 2 Thess. 1:2; 2 Tim. 1:2; Philem. 3.

Rom. 15:5. Now the God of patience and consolation grant you to be likeminded one toward another according to Christ Jesus: 6. That ye may with one mind *and* one mouth glorify God, even the Father of our Lord Jesus Christ.

13. Now the God of hope fill you with all joy and peace in believing, that ye may abound in hope, through the power of the Holy Ghost.

33. Now the God of peace *be* with you all. Amen.

Rom. 16:20. The grace of our Lord Jesus Christ *be* with you. Amen. [1] *v.* 24; 1 Cor. 16:23; Phil. 4:23; 1 Thess. 5:28; 2 Thess. 3:18; Rev. 22:21.   [1 Omitted in R. V.]

2 Cor. 13:14. The grace of the Lord Jesus Christ, and the love of God, and the communion of the Holy Ghost, *be* with you all. Amen.

Gal. 6:16. And as many as walk according to this rule, peace *be* on them, and mercy, and upon the Israel of God.

18. Brethren, the grace of our Lord Jesus Christ *be* with your spirit. Amen. Philem. 25.

Eph. 6:23. Peace *be* to the brethren, and love with faith, from God the Father and the Lord Jesus Christ. 24. Grace *be* with all them that love our Lord Jesus Christ in sincerity. Amen.

2 Thess. 3:16. Now the Lord of peace himself give you peace always by all means. The Lord *be* with you all.

18. The grace of our Lord Jesus Christ *be* with you all. Amen.

1 Tim. 1:2. Grace, mercy, *and* peace, from God our Father and Jesus Christ our Lord.

1 Tim. 6:21. Grace *be* with thee.

2 Tim. 4:22. The Lord Jesus Christ *be* with thy spirit. Grace *be* with you. Amen.

Tit. 3:15. Grace *be* with you all. Amen.

Heb. 13:20. Now the God of peace, that brought again from the dead our Lord Jesus, that great shepherd of the sheep, through the blood of the everlasting covenant, 21. Make you perfect in every good work to do his will, working in you that which is wellpleasing in his sight, through Jesus Christ; to whom *be* glory for ever and ever. Amen.

25. Grace *be* with you all. Amen.

1 Pet. 1:2. Grace unto you, and peace, be multiplied.

1 Pet. 5:10. But the God of all grace, who hath called us unto his eternal glory by Christ Jesus, after that ye have suffered a while, make you perfect, stablish, strengthen, settle *you*. 11. To him *be* glory and dominion for ever and ever. Amen.

14. Peace *be* with you all that are in Christ Jesus. Amen.

2 Pet. 1:2. Grace and peace be multiplied unto you through the knowledge of God, and of Jesus our Lord, 3. According as his divine power hath given unto us all things that *pertain* unto life and godliness, through the knowledge of him that hath called us to glory and virtue: 4. Whereby are given unto us exceeding great and precious promises: that by these ye might be partakers of the divine nature, having escaped the corruption that is in the world through lust.

2 John 3. Grace be with you, mercy, *and* peace, from God the Father, and from the Lord Jesus Christ, the Son of the Father, in truth and love.

Jude 2. Mercy unto you, and peace, and love, be multiplied.

BENEFACTOR, Luke 22:25.

BENEFICENCE. Deut. 15:7. If there be among you a poor man of one of thy brethren within any of thy gates in thy land which the LORD thy God giveth thee, thou shalt not harden thine heart, nor shut thine hand from thy poor brother: 8. But thou shalt open thine hand wide unto him, and shalt surely lend him sufficient for his need, *in that* which he wanteth. 9. Beware that there be not a thought in thy wicked heart, saying, The seventh year, the year of release, is at hand; and thine eye be evil against thy poor brother, and thou givest him nought; and he cry unto the LORD against thee, and it be sin unto thee. 10. Thou shalt surely give him, and thine heart shall not be grieved when thou givest unto him: because

that for this thing the LORD thy God shall bless thee in all thy works, and in all that thou puttest thine hand unto. 11. For the poor shall never cease out of the land: therefore I command thee, saying, Thou shalt open thine hand wide unto thy brother, to thy poor, and to thy needy, in thy land. 12. *And* if thy brother, an Hebrew man, or a Hebrew woman, be sold unto thee, and serve thee six years; then in the seventh year thou shalt let him go free from thee. 13. And when thou sendest him out free from thee, thou shalt not let him go away empty: 14. Thou shalt furnish him liberally out of thy flock, and out of thy floor, and out of thy winepress: *of that* wherewith the LORD thy God hath blessed thee thou shalt give unto him. 15. And thou shalt remember that thou wast a bondman in the land of Egypt, and the LORD thy God redeemed thee: therefore I command thee this thing to day. 18. It shall not seem hard unto thee, when thou sendest him away free from thee; for he hath been worth a double hired servant *to thee*, in serving thee six years: and the LORD thy God shall bless thee in all that thou doest. Lev. 25:35-43.

Psa. 41:1. Blessed *is* he that considereth the poor: the LORD will deliver him in time of trouble.

Psa. 112:9. He hath dispersed, he hath given to the poor; his righteousness endureth for ever; his horn shall be exalted with honour.

Prov. 3:27. Withhold not good from them to whom it is due, when it is in the power of thine hand to do *it*. 28. Say not unto thy neighbour, Go, and come again, and to morrow I will give; when thou hast it by thee.

Prov. 11:25. The liberal soul shall be made fat: and he that watereth shall be watered also himself.

Prov. 22:9. He that hath a bountiful eye shall be blessed; for he giveth of his bread to the poor.

Prov. 25:21. If thine enemy be hungry, give him bread to eat; and if he be thirsty, give him water to drink: 22. For thou shalt heap coals of fire upon his head, and the LORD shall reward thee.

Prov. 28:27. He that giveth unto the poor shall not lack: but he that hideth his eyes shall have many a curse.

Isa. 58:6. *Is* not this the fast that I have chosen? to loose the bands of wickedness, to undo the heavy burdens, and to let the oppressed go free, and that ye break every yoke? 7. *Is it* not to deal thy bread to the hungry, and that thou bring the poor that are cast out to thy house? when thou seest the naked, that thou cover him; and that thou hide not thyself from thine own flesh? 10. And *if* thou draw out thy soul to the hungry, and satisfy the afflicted soul; then shall thy light rise in obscurity, and thy darkness *be* as the noon day: 11. And the LORD shall guide thee continually, and satisfy thy soul in drought, and make fat thy bones: and thou shalt be like a watered garden, and like a spring of water, whose waters fail not.

Ezek. 18:5. But if a man be just, and do that which is lawful and right, . . . 7. And hath not oppressed any, *but* hath restored to the debtor his pledge, hath spoiled none by violence, hath given his bread to the hungry, and hath covered the naked with a garment; 8. He *that* hath not given forth upon usury, neither hath taken any increase, *that* hath withdrawn his hand from iniquity, hath executed true judgment between man and man, 9. Hath walked in my statutes, and hath kept my judgments, to deal truly ; he *is* just, he shall surely live, saith the Lord GOD.

Matt. 5:42. Give to him that asketh thee, and from him that would borrow of thee turn not thou away.

Matt. 19:21. Jesus said unto him, If thou wilt be perfect, go *and* sell that thou hast, and give to the poor, and thou shalt have treasure in heaven : Mark 10:21.

Matt. 25:35. For I was an hungred, and ye gave me meat: I was thirsty, and ye gave me drink : I was a stranger, and ye took me in : 36. Naked, and ye clothed me : I was sick, and ye visited me : I was in prison, and ye came unto me. 37. Then shall the righteous answer him, saying, Lord, when saw we thee an hungred, and fed *thee ?* or thirsty, and gave *thee* drink ? 38. When saw we thee a stranger, and took *thee* in ? or naked, and clothed *thee ?* 39. Or when saw we thee sick, or in prison, and came unto thee ? 40. And the King shall answer and say unto them, Verily I say unto you, Inasmuch as ye have done *it* unto one of the least of these my brethren, ye have done *it* unto me. 41. Then shall he say also unto them on the left hand, Depart from me, ye cursed, into everlasting fire, prepared for the devil and his angels: 42. For I was an hungred, and ye gave me no meat: I was thirsty, and ye gave me no drink : 43. I was a stranger, and ye took me not in : naked, and ye clothed me not : sick, and in prison, and ye visited me not. 44. Then shall they also answer him, saying, Lord, when saw we thee an hungred, or athirst, or a stranger, or naked, or sick, or in prison, and did not minister unto thee ? 45. Then shall he answer them, saying, Verily I say unto you, Inasmuch as ye did *it* not to one of the least of these, ye did *it* not to me.

Mark 9:41. For whosoever shall give you a cup of water to drink in my name, because ye belong to Christ, verily I say unto you, he shall not lose his reward.

Luke 3:11. He that hath two coats, let him impart to him that hath none; and he that hath meat, let him do likewise.

Luke 11:41. But rather give alms of such things as ye have; and, behold, all things are clean unto you.

Acts 6:1. And in those days, when the **number** of the disciples was multiplied, there arose a murmuring of the Grecians against the Hebrews, because their widows were neglected in the daily ministration. 2. Then the twelve called the multitude of the disciples *unto them*, and said, It is not reason that we should leave the word of God, and serve tables. 3. Wherefore, brethren, look ye out among you seven men of honest report, full of the Holy Ghost and wisdom, whom we may appoint over this business. 4. But we will give ourselves continually to prayer, and to the ministry of the word.

Acts 11:29. Then the disciples, every man according to his ability, determined to send relief unto the brethren which dwelt in Judæa : 30. Which also they did, and sent it to the elders by the hands of Barnabas and Saul.

Rom. 15:25. But now I go unto Jerusalem to minister unto the saints. 26. For it hath pleased them of Macedonia and Achaia to make a certain contribution for the poor saints which are at Jerusalem. 27. It hath pleased them verily ; and their debtors they are. For if the Gentiles have been made partakers of their spiritual things, their duty is also to minister unto them in carnal things.

1 Cor. 13:3. And though I bestow all my goods to feed *the poor*, and though I give my body to be burned, and have not charity, it profiteth me nothing.

1 Cor. 16:1. Now concerning the collection for the saints, as I have given order to the churches of Galatia, even so do ye. 2. Upon the first *day* of the week let every one of you lay by him in store, as [1] *God* hath prospered him, that there be no gatherings when I come. 3. And when I come, whomsoever ye shall approve by *your* letters, them will I send to bring your liberality unto Jerusalem. [1 R. V. he may prosper]

2 Cor. 8:1. Moreover, brethren, we do you to wit of the grace of God bestowed on the churches of Macedonia ; 2. How that in a great trial of affliction the abundance of their joy and their deep poverty abounded unto the riches of their liberality. 3. For to *their* power, I bear record, yea, and beyond *their* power *they were* willing of themselves; 4. Praying us with much entreaty that we would receive the gift, and *take upon us* the fellowship of the ministering to the saints. 5. And *this they did*, not as we hoped, but first gave their own selves to the Lord, and unto us by the will of God. 6. Insomuch that we desired Titus, that as he had begun, so he would also finish in you the same grace also. 7. Therefore, as ye abound in every *thing, in* faith, and utterance, and knowledge, and *in* all diligence, and *in* your love to us, *see* that ye abound in this grace also. 8. I speak not by commandment, but by occasion of the forwardness of others, and to prove the sincerity of your love. 9. For ye know the grace of our Lord Jesus Christ, that, though he was rich, yet for your sakes

he became poor, that ye through his poverty might be rich. 10. And herein I give *my* advice: for this is expedient for you, who have begun before, not only to do, but also to be forward a year ago. 11. Now therefore perform the doing *of it;* that as *there was* a readiness to will, so *there may be* a performance also out of that which ye have. 12. For if there be first a willing mind, *it is* accepted according to that a man hath, *and* not according to that he hath not. 13. For *I mean* not that other men be eased, and ye burdened: 14. But by an equality, *that* now at this time your abundance *may be a supply* for their want, that their abundance also may be *a supply* for your want: that there may be equality: 15. As it is written, He that *had gathered* much had nothing over; and he that *had gathered* little had no lack. 24. Wherefore shew ye to them, and before the churches, the proof of your love, and of our boasting on your behalf.

2 Cor. 9:1. For as touching the ministering to the saints, it is superfluous for me to write to you: 2. For I know the forwardness of your mind, for which I boast of you to them of Macedonia, that Achaia was ready a year ago; and your zeal hath provoked very many. 3. Yet have I sent the brethren, lest our boasting of you should be in vain in this behalf; that, as I said, ye may be ready: 4. Lest haply if they of Macedonia come with me, and find you unprepared, we (that we say not, ye) should be ashamed in this same confident boasting. 5. Therefore I thought it necessary to exhort the brethren, that they would go before unto you and make up beforehand your bounty, whereof ye had notice before, that the same might be ready, as *a matter of* bounty, and not as *of* covetousness. 6. But this *I say*, He which soweth sparingly shall reap also sparingly; and he which soweth bountifully shall reap also bountifully. 7. Every man according as he purposeth in his heart, *so let him give;* not grudgingly, or of necessity: for God loveth a cheerful giver. 8. And God *is* able to make all grace abound toward you: that ye, always having all sufficiency in all *things*, may abound to every good work: 9. (As it is written, He hath dispersed abroad; he hath given to the poor: his righteousness remaineth for ever. 10. Now he that ministereth seed to the sower both minister bread for *your* food, and multiply your seed sown, and increase the fruits of your righteousness;) 11. Being enriched in every thing to all bountifulness, which causeth through us thanksgiving to God. 12. For the administration of this service not only supplieth the want of the saints, but is abundant also by many thanksgivings unto God; 13. Whiles by the experiment of this ministration they glorify God for your professed subjection unto the gospel of Christ, and for *your* liberal distribution unto them, and unto all *men;* 14. And by their prayer for you, which long after you for the exceeding grace of God in you. 15. Thanks *be* unto God for his unspeakable gift.

Gal. 2:10. Only *they would* that we should remember the poor; the same which I also was forward to do.

Phil. 4:10. But I rejoiced in the Lord greatly, that now at the last your care of me hath flourished again; wherein ye were also careful, but ye lacked opportunity. 11. Not that I speak in respect of want: for I have learned, in whatsoever state I am, *therewith* to be content. 12. I know both how to be abased, and I know how to abound: every where and in all things I am instructed both to be full and to be hungry, both to abound and to suffer need. 13. I can do all things through Christ which strengtheneth me. 14. Notwithstanding ye have well done, that ye did communicate with my affliction. 15. Now ye Philippians know also, that in the beginning of the gospel, when I departed from Macedonia, no church communicated with me as concerning giving and receiving, but ye only. 16. For even in Thessalonica ye sent once and again unto my necessity. 17. Not because I desire a gift: but I desire fruit that may abound to your account. 18. But I have all, and abound: I am full, having received of Epaphroditus the things *which were sent* from you, an odour of a sweet smell, a sacrifice acceptable, well-pleasing to God.

1 Tim. 5:8. But if any provide not for his own, and specially for those of his own house, he hath denied the faith, and is worse than an infidel. 16. If any man or woman that believeth have widows, let them relieve them, and let not the church be charged; that it may relieve them that are widows indeed.

1 Tim. 6:18. That they do good, that they be rich in good works, ready to distribute, willing to communicate;

Heb. 6:10. For God *is* not unrighteous to forget your work and labour of love, which ye have shewed toward his name, in that ye have ministered to the saints, and do minister.

Heb. 13:16. But to do good and to communicate forget not: for with such sacrifices God is well pleased.

Jas. 2:15. If a brother or sister be naked, and destitute of daily food, 16. And one of you say unto them, Depart in peace, be *ye* warmed and filled; notwithstanding ye give them not those things which are needful to the body; what *doth it* profit?

1 John 3:17. But whoso hath this world's good, and seeth his brother have need, and shutteth up his bowels *of compassion* from him, how dwelleth the love of God in him?

See ALMS; LIBERALITY; POOR, DUTIES TO; RICH; RICHES.

INSTANCES OF: The old man of Gibeah, Judg. 19:16–21. Boaz, Ruth 2. The returned exile Jews, Neh. 5:8–12; 8:10,11. Job, Job 29: 11–17; 31:16–23. The Temanites, Isa. 21:14. The good Samaritan, Luke 10:33–35. Zacchæus, Luke 19:8. The first Christians, Acts 2:44–46; 4:32–37. Cornelius, Acts 10:2,4. Onesiphorus, 2 Tim. 1:16–18.

See ALMS; POOR, DUTY TO.

BEN-GEBER [*R. V.*, 1 Kin. 4:13]. See GEBER.

BENE-JAAKAN. A tribe that gave its name to certain wells in the wilderness, Num. 33:31,32. Called BEEROTH, Deut. 10:6.

BENEVOLENCE. See ALMS; BENEFI-CENCE; CHARITABLENESS; LIBERALITY; LOVE.

BEN-HADAD. 1. King of Syria, 1 Kin. 15:18–20; 2 Chr. 16:2–4.

2. A king of Syria, who reigned in the time of Ahab, son of Ben-hadad I., 1 Kin. 20; 2 Kin. 5; 6; 7; 8:7–15.

3. Son of Hazael and king of Syria, 2 Kin. 13:3,24,25; Amos 1:4.

BEN-HAIL, a prince of Judah, 2 Chr. 17:7.

BEN-HANAN, a son of Shimon, 1 Chr. 4:20.

BEN-HUR [*R. V.*]. See HUR.

BENINU, a Levite, Neh. 10:13.

BENJAMIN. 1. Son of Jacob by Rachel, Gen. 35:18,24; 46:19. Taken into Egypt, Gen. chapters 42–45. Prophecy concerning, Gen. 49:27. Descendants of, Gen. 46:21; Num. 26:38–41.

2. TRIBE OF: Census of, at Sinai, Num. 1: 37; in the plain of Moab, Num. 26:41. Clans of, Num. 26:38–40; 1 Chr. 7:6–12; 8. Position of, in camp and march, Num. 2:18,22. Moses' benediction upon, Deut. 32:12. Allotment in the land of Canaan, Josh. 18:11–28. Reallot-ment, Ezek. 48:23. Did not exterminate the Jebusites, Judg. 1:21. Join Deborah in the war against Sisera, Judg. 5:14. Territory of, invaded by the Ammonites, Judg. 10:9. Did not avenge the crime of the Gibeonites against the Levite's concubine, the war that followed, Judg. 19; 20. Saul, the first king of Israel, from, 1 Sam. 9:1,17; 10:20,21. Its rank in the time of Samuel, 1 Sam. 9:21. Jerusalem within the territory of, Jer. 6:1. A company of, joins David at Ziklag, 1 Chr. 12:1,2,16. Not enrolled by Joab when he took a census of the military forces of Is-rael, 1 Chr. 21:6. Loyal to Ish-bosheth, the son of Saul, 2 Sam. 2:9,15,31; 1 Chr. 12:29. Subsequently joins David, 2 Sam. 3:19; 19: 16,17. Loyal to Rehoboam, 1 Kin. 12:21; 2 Chr. 11:1. Military forces of, in the reign of Asa, 2 Chr. 14:8; of Jehoshaphat, 2 Chr. 17: 17. Skill in archery and as slingers of stones, Judg. 3:15; 20:16; 1 Chr. 8:40; 12:2. Return to Palestine from the exile in Babylon, Ezra 1:5. Saints of, seen in John's vision, Rev. 7:8. Paul, of the tribe of, Rom. 11:1; Phil. 3:5.

See ISRAEL.

3. Grandson of Benjamin, 1 Chr. 7:10.

4. A son of Harim, Ezra 10:32; probably identical with the man mentioned in Neh. 3:23.

5. A Jew who assisted in purifying the wall of Jerusalem, Neh. 12:34.

6. A gate of Jerusalem, Jer. 20:2; 37:13; 38: 7; Zech. 14:10.

BENO, a descendant of Merari, 1 Chr. 24: 26,27.

BEN-ONI, name given Benjamin by Rachel, Gen. 35:18.

BEN-ZOHETH, son of Ishi,1 Chr. 4:20.

BEON, a place E. of Jordan, probably same as BAAL-MEON, Num. 32:3,38, which see.

BEOR. 1. Father of Bela, Gen. 36:32; 1 Chr. 1:43.

2. Father of Balaam, Num. 22:5. Called BOSOR, 2 Pet. 2:15.

BEQUESTS. See WILLS.

BERA, king of Sodom, Gen. 14:2.

BERACHAH. 1. An Israelite, who joined David at Ziklag, 1 Chr. 12:3. 2. A valley in the S. of Judah, where the Is-raelites blessed the Lord for a victory, 2 Chr. 20:26.

BERACHIAH. See BERECHIAH.

BERAIAH, son of Shimhi, 1 Chr. 8:21.

BEREA, a city in the S. of Macedonia, Acts 17:10,13; 20:4.

BEREAVEMENT. From God, Ex. 12: 29; Hos. 9:12. Mourning in, forbidden to Aaron, on account of his son's wickedness, Lev. 10:6; and to Ezekiel, for his wife, Ezek. 24:16–18.

INSTANCES OF: Abraham,of Sarah,Gen. 23:2. Jacob, of Joseph, Gen. 37:34,35. Joseph, of his father, Gen. 50:1,4. The Egyptians, of their firstborn, Ex. 12:29–33. Naomi, of her husband, Ruth 1:3,5,20,21. David, of his child by Bath-sheba, 2 Sam. 12:15–23; of Ab-salom, 2 Sam. 18:33; 19:4.

RESIGNATION IN: 2 Sam. 12:22. And he said, While the child was yet alive, I fasted and wept: for I said, Who can tell *whether* GOD will be gracious to me, that the child may live? 23. But now he is dead, where-fore should I fast? can I bring him back again? I shall go to him, but he shall not return to me.

Job 1:18. While he *was* yet speaking, there came also another, and said, Thy sons and thy daughters *were* eating and drinking wine in their eldest brother's house: 19. And, behold, there came a great wind from the wilderness, and smote the four corners of the house, and it fell upon the young men, and they are dead; and I only am escaped alone to tell thee. 20. Then Job arose, and rent his mantle, and shaved his head, and fell down upon the ground, and worshipped, 21. And said, Naked came I out of my mother's womb, and naked shall I return thither: the LORD gave, and the LORD hath taken away; blessed be the name of the LORD.

Eccl. 7:2. *It is* better to go to the house of mourning, than to go to the house of feast-ing: for that *is* the end of all men; and the living will lay *it* to his heart. 3. Sorrow *is* better than laughter: for by the sadness of the countenance the heart is made better. 4. The heart of the wise *is* in the house of mourning; but the heart of fools *is* in the house of mirth.

1 Thess. 4:13. But I would not have you to be ignorant, brethren, concerning them which are asleep, that ye sorrow not, even as others which have no hope. 14. For if we believe that Jesus died and rose again, even so them also which sleep in Jesus will God bring with him. 15. For this we say unto you by the word of the Lord, that we which are alive *and* remain unto the coming of the Lord shall not prevent them which are asleep. 16. For the Lord himself shall descend from heaven with a shout, with the voice of the archangel, and with the trump of God: and the dead in Christ shall rise first: 17. Then we which are alive *and* remain shall be caught up together with them in the clouds, to meet the Lord in the air: and so shall we ever be with the Lord. 18. Wherefore comfort one another with these words.

See AFFLICTION, COMFORT IN; RESIGNATION IN. See also RESIGNATION.

BERECHIAH. 1. Father of Asaph, 1 Chr. 15:17,23. Called BERACHIAH, 1 Chr. 6:39.

2. A warrior of Ephraim, 2 Chr. 28:12.

3. A brother of Zerubbabel, 1 Chr. 3:20.

4. Son of Asa, 1 Chr. 9:16.

5. Son of Iddo, Zech. 1:1,7.

6. Son of Meshezabeel, Neh. 3:4,30; 6:18.

BERED. 1. A town in the S. of Palestine, Gen. 16:14.

2. A son of Shuthelah, 1 Chr. 7:20; probably same as BECHER, Num. 26:35.

BERI, son of Zophah, 1 Chr. 7:36.

BERIAH. 1. Son of Asher, Gen. 46:17; Num. 26:44,45; 1 Chr. 7:30.

2. Son of Ephraim, 1 Chr. 7:20–23.

3. A Benjamite, 1 Chr. 8:13.

4. Son of Shimei, 1 Chr. 23:10,11.

BERITH. See BAAL-BERITH.

BERNICE, daughter of Agrippa, Acts 25:13,23; 26.30.

BERODACH-BALADAN. See MERODACH-BALADAN.

BEROTHAH, part of the northern boundary of Canaan, Ezek. 47:16.

BEROTHAI, a city of Zobah, 2 Sam. 8:8.

BERYL. A precious stone, Song 5:14; Ezek. 1:16; 10:9. Set in the breastplate, Ex. 28:20; 39:13. John saw, in the foundation of the new Jerusalem, Rev. 21:20.

BESAI, one of the Nethinim, Ezra 2:49; Neh. 7:52.

BESODEIAH, father of Meshullam, Neh. 3:6.

BESOR, a brook near Gaza, 1 Sam. 30:9, 10,21.

BESTIALITY. Ex. 22:19. Whosoever lieth with a beast shall surely be put to death.

Lev. 18:23. Neither shalt thou lie with any beast to defile thyself therewith: neither shall any woman stand before a beast to lie down thereto: it *is* confusion.

Lev. 20:16. And if a woman approach unto any beast, and lie down thereto, thou shalt kill the woman, and the beast: they shall surely be put to death; their blood *shall be* upon them.

See SODOMY.

BETAH, a city belonging to Hadadezer, 2 Sam. 8:8.

BETEN, a city of Asher, Josh. 19:25.

BETHABARA. A city E. of the Jordan, Judg. 7:24. John testifies to Christ's messiahship, and baptizes at, John 1:28; Jesus at, John 10:39–42.

BETH-ANATH, a fortified city of Naphtali, Josh. 19:38; Judg. 1:33.

BETH-ANOTH, a city in Judah, Josh. 15:59.

BETHANY. A village on the eastern slope of the Mount of Olives, John 11:18. Mary, Martha, and Lazarus dwell at, Luke 10:38–41. Lazarus dies and is raised to life at, John 11. Jesus attends a feast in, Matt. 26:6–13; John 12:1–9. The colt on which Jesus made his triumphal entry into Jerusalem obtained at, Mark 11:1–11. Jesus sojourns at, Matt. 21:17; Mark 11:11,12,19.

BETH-ARABAH. A city in the valley of the Dead Sea, Josh. 15:6,61; 18:22. Called ARABAH, Josh. 18:18.

BETH-ARAM. A fortified city of Gad, Josh. 13:27. Probably identical with BETH-HARAN, Num. 32:36.

BETH-ARBEL, a city spoiled by Shalman, Hos. 10:14.

BETH-AVEN, a place on the mountains of Benjamin, Josh. 7:2; 18:12; 1 Sam. 13:5; 14: 23; Hos. 4:15; 5:8; 10:5.

BETH-AZMAVETH. A town of Benjamin, Neh. 7:28. Called AZMAVETH, Neh. 12:29; Ezra 2:24.

BETH-BAAL-MEON. A place in the tribe of Reuben, Josh. 13:17. Called BAAL-MEON, Num. 32:38; Ezek. 25:9; and BEON, Num. 32:3; and BETH-MEON, Jer. 48:23. Subdued by the Israelites, Num. 32:3,4. Assigned to the Reubenites. Josh. 13:17.

BETH-BARAH, a place E. of Jordan, Judg. 7:24.

BETH-BIREI, a town of Simeon, 1 Chr. 4:31.

See BETH-LEBAOTH.

BETH-CAR, a place W. of Mizpeh, 1 Sam. 7:11.

BETH-DAGON. 1. A city of Judah, Josh. 15:41.

2. A city of Asher, Josh. 19:27.

BETH-DIBLATHAIM. A city of Moab, Jer. 48:22. Called ALMON-DIBLATHAIM, Num. 33:46.

BETH-EL. 1. A city N. of Jerusalem. The ancient city adjacent to, and finally embraced in, was called LUZ. Josh. 18:13; Judg. 1:23–26. Abraham establishes an altar at, Gen. 12:8; 13:3,4. The place where Jacob saw the vision of the ladder, Gen. 28:10–22; 31:13; Hos. 12:4; and builds an altar at, Gen. 35:1–15. Deborah dies at, Gen. 35:8. Conquered by Joshua, Josh. 8:17, with chapter 12:16; by the house of Joseph, Judg. 1:22–26. Allotted to Benjamin, Josh. 18:13,22. Court of justice held at, by Deborah, Judg. 4:5; by Samuel, 1 Sam. 7:16.

Tabernacle at, and called HOUSE OF GOD, Judg. 20:18,31; 21:2. Jeroboam institutes idolatrous worship at, 1 Kin. 12:25-33; 2 Kin. 10:29. Idolatry at, Jer. 48:13; Amos 4:4. Shalmanezer sends a priest to, 2 Kin. 17:27,28. Prophecies against the idolatrous altars at, 1 Kin. 13:1-6,32; 2 Kin. 23:4,15-20; Amos 3:14. The school of prophets at, 2 Kin. 2:3. Children of, mock Elisha, 2 Kin. 2:23,24. People of, return from Babylon, Ezra 2:28; Neh. 7:32. Prophecies against, Amos 5:5.

2. A city in the S. of Judah, 1 Sam. 30:27.

3. A mountain, 1 Sam. 13:2.

BETH-EL-APHRAH [R. V.], APHRAH [A. V.], a place in Philistia, Mic. 1:10.

BETH-EMEK, a city of Asher, Josh. 19:27.

BETHER, mountains of, Song 2:17.

BETHESDA, pool of, John 5:2-4.

BETH-EZEL, a town of Judah, Mic. 1:11.

BETH-GADER. A place in Judah, 1 Chr. 2:51. Probably identical with GEDER, Josh. 12:13; and with GEDOR in Josh. 15:58.

BETH-GAMUL, a city of Moab, Jer. 48:23.

BETH-HACCEREM, a mountain in Judah, Neh. 3:14; Jer. 6:1.

BETH-HAGGAN. A garden house, 2 Kin. 9:27. Probably identical with EN-GANNIM, Josh. 19:21.

BETH-HANAN. See ELON-BETH-HANAN.

BETH-HARAN. A fortified city E. of Jordan, Num. 32:36. Probably identical with BETH-ARAM, Josh. 13:27.

BETH-HOGLA, a place on the border of Judah, Josh. 15:6; 18:19,21.

BETH-HORON. Two ancient cities of Canaan, near which Joshua defeated the Amorites, Josh. 10:10,11; 16:3,5; 18:13; 1 Sam. 13:18; 1 Chr. 7:24. Solomon builds, 1 Kin. 9:17; 2 Chr. 8:5. Taken from Judah by the ten tribes, 2 Chr. 25:13.

BETH-JESHIMOTH. A place in Moab, Josh. 12:3; 13:20; Ezek. 25:9. Called BETH-JESIMOTH, Num. 33:49.

BETH-JOAB. See ATAROTH.

BETH-LEBAOTH. A town of Simeon, Josh. 19:6. Called LEBAOTH, Josh. 15:32, and BETH-BIREI, 1 Chr. 4:31.

BETHLEHEM. A city S. W. of Jerusalem, Judg. 17:7; 19:18. Called EPHRATAH and EPHRATH, Gen. 48:7; Psa. 132:6; Mic. 5:2; and BETH-LEHEM-JUDAH, Judg. 17:7-9; 19:1, 18; Ruth 1:1; 1 Sam. 17:12. Rachel dies and is buried at, Gen. 35:16,19; 48:7. The city of Boaz, Ruth 1:1,19; 2:4; 4. Taken and held by the Philistines, 2 Sam. 23:14-16. Jeroboam converts it into a military stronghold, 2 Chr. 11:6. The city of Joseph, Matt. 2:5,6; Luke 2:4. Birthplace of Jesus, Mic. 5:2; Matt. 2; Luke 2:4,15. Herod slays the children of, Matt. 2:16-18.

2. A town of Zebulun, six miles W. of Nazareth, Josh. 19:15. Israel judged at, Judg. 12:10.

BETH-MAACHAH, a city of Manasseh, 2 Sam. 20:14,15,18; 2 Kin. 15:29.

BETH-MARCABOTH. A town of Simeon, Josh. 19:5; 1 Chron. 4:31. Probably identical with MADMANNAH, Josh. 15:31.

BETH-MEON. See BAAL-MEON.

BETH-NIMRAH. A fenced city E. of Jordan, Josh. 13:27. Called NIMRAH, Num. 32:3.

BETH-PALET. A city in Judah, Josh. 15:27. Called BETH-PHELET, Neh. 11:26.

BETH-PAZZEZ, a town of Issachar, Josh. 19:21.

BETH-PEOR. A place in the tribe of Reuben, Deut. 3:29; 4:46; 34:6. Near the burial place of Moses, Josh. 13:20.

BETHPHAGE, a village on the Mount of Olives, Matt. 21:1; Mark 11:1; Luke 19:29.

BETH-PHELET. See BETH-PALET.

BETH-RAPHA, son of Eshton, 1 Chr. 4:12.

BETH-REHOB. A place in Dan, Judg. 18:28; 2 Sam. 10:6. Called REHOB, v. 8.

BETHSAIDA. 1. A city of Galilee. The city of Philip, Andrew, and Peter, John 1:44; 12:21. Jesus visits, Mark 6:45; cures a blind man in, Mark 8:22; prophecies against, Matt. 11:21; Luke 10:13.

2. Desert of, E. of the sea of Galilee, Jesus feeds five thousand people in, Luke 9:10; Matt. 14:13; Mark 6:32.

BETH-SHAN. See BETH-SHEAN.

BETH-SHEAN. A city of Manasseh, 1 Chr. 7:29; Josh. 17:11. Not subdued, Judg. 1:27. Bodies of Saul and his sons exposed in, 1 Sam. 31:10,12. Called BETH-SHAN, 1 Sam. 31:10,12; 2 Sam. 21:12. District of, under tribute to Solomon's commissariat, 1 Kin. 4:12.

BETH-SHEMESH. 1. A sacerdotal city of Dan, Josh. 21:16; 1 Sam. 6:15; 1 Chr. 6:59. On the northern border of Judah, Josh. 15:10; 1 Sam. 6:9,12. In later times transferred to Judah, 2 Kin. 14:11. Mentioned in Solomon's commissary districts, 1 Kin. 4:9. Amaziah taken prisoner at, 2 Kin. 14:11-13; 2 Chr. 25:21-23. Retaken by the Philistines, 2 Chr. 28:18. Called IR-SHEMESH, Josh 19:41.

2. A city near Jerusalem, Josh. 19:22.

3. A fortified city of Naphtali, Josh. 19:38; Judg. 1:33.

4. An idolatrous temple, Jer. 43:13.

BETH-SHITTAH, a place near the Jordan, Judg. 7:22.

BETH-TAPPUAH, a town of Judah, Josh. 15:53.

BETHUEL, son of Nahor, father of Rebekah, Gen. 22:22,23; 24:15,24; 25:20; 28:2,5.

BETHUL. A city of Simeon, Josh. 19:4. Called CHESIL, Josh. 15:30, and BETHUEL, 1 Chr. 4:30.

BETH-ZUR, a town in Judah, Josh. 15:58; 1 Chr. 2:45; 2 Chr. 11:7; Neh. 3:16.

BETONIM, a town of Gad, Josh. 13:26.

BETRAYAL. Of Jesus, Matt. 26:14-16, 45-50; Mark 14:10,11; Luke 22:3-6; 22:47,48; John 13:21. Of others, foretold, Matt. 20:18;

24:10. Of David, by Doeg, 1 Sam. 22:9,10, with chapter 21:1–10. Of cities, Judg. 1:24,25.

See CONFIDENCE BETRAYED.

BETROTHAL. Of Jacob, Gen. 29:18–30. Exempts from military duty, Deut. 20:7. A quasi marriage, Matt. 1:18; Luke 1:27.

FIGURATIVE: Isa. 62:4; Hos. 2:19,20; 2 Cor. 11:2.

See MARRIAGE.

BETTING, by Samson, Judg. 14:12–19.

BEULAH, Isa. 62:4.

BEZAI. 1. Head of a Jewish family, which returned from Babylon, Ezra 2:17; Neh. 7:23.

2. A family that sealed the covenant with Nehemiah, Neh. 10:18.

BEZALEEL. 1. A divinely inspired mechanic and master workman, who built the tabernacle, Ex. 31:2; 35:30–35; 36:1; 37:1; 38:1–7,22.

2. Son of Pahath-moab. Ezra 10:30.

BEZEK. 1. Residence of Adoni-bezek, Judg. 1:5.

2. A rendezvous of Israel under Saul, 1 Sam. 11:8.

BEZER. 1. A city of refuge, E. of the Jordan, Deut. 4:43; Josh. 20:8; 21:36; 1 Chr. 6:78.

2. Son of Zophah, 1 Chr. 7:37.

BIBLE. See LAW OF MOSES; WORD OF GOD.

BICHRI, a Benjamite, 2 Sam. 20.

BIDKAR, Jehu's captain, 2 Kin. 9:25.

BIER, 2 Sam. 3:31; Luke 7:14.

BIGAMY. See POLYGAMY.

BIGOTRY. Isa. 65:5. Which say, Stand by thyself, come not near to me; for I am holier than thou. These *are* a smoke in my nose, a fire that burneth all the day.

Mark 2:16. And when the scribes and Pharisees saw him eat with publicans and sinners, they said unto his disciples, How is it that he eateth and drinketh with publicans and sinners? Luke 15:2.

Luke 9:49. And John answered and said, Master, we saw one casting out devils in thy name; and we forbad him, because he followeth not with us. 50. And Jesus said to him, Forbid *him* not: for he that is not against us is for us.

Luke 18:9. And he spake this parable unto certain which trusted in themselves that they were righteous, and despised others: 10. Two men went up into the temple to pray; the one a Pharisee and the other a publican. 11. The Pharisee stood and prayed thus with himself, God, I thank thee that I am not as other men *are*, extortioners, unjust, adulterers, or even as this publican. 12. I fast twice in the week, I give tithes of all that I possess. 13. And the publican, standing afar off, would not lift up so much as *his* eyes unto heaven, but smote upon his breast, saying, God be merciful to me a sinner. 14. I tell you, this man went down to his house justified *rather* than the other: for every one that exalteth himself shall be abased:

and he that humbleth himself shall be exalted.

Acts 10:28. And he said unto them, Ye know how that it is an unlawful thing for a man that is a Jew to keep company, or come unto one of another nation; but God hath shewed me that I should not call any man common or unclean. 45. And they of the circumcision which believed were astonished, as many as came with Peter, because that on the Gentiles also was poured out the gift of the Holy Ghost.

Acts 18:12. And when Gallio was the deputy of Achaia, the Jews made insurrection with one accord against Paul, and brought him to the judgment seat, 13. Saying, This *fellow* persuadeth men to worship God contrary to the law.

PAUL'S ARGUMENT AGAINST: Rom. 3:1. What advantage then hath the Jew? or what profit *is there* of circumcision? 2. Much every way: chiefly, because that unto them were committed the oracles of God. 3. For what if some did not believe? shall their unbelief make the faith of God without effect? 4. God forbid: yea, let God be true, but every man a liar; as it is written, That thou mightest be justified in thy sayings, and mightest overcome when thou art judged. 5. But if our unrighteousness commend the righteousness of God, what shall we say? *Is* God unrighteous who taketh vengeance? (I speak as a man) 6. God forbid: for then how shall God judge the world? 7. For if the truth of God hath more abounded through my lie unto his glory; why yet am I also judged as a sinner? 8. And not *rather*, (as we be slanderously reported, and as some affirm that we say,) Let us do evil, that good may come? whose damnation is just. 9. What then? are we better *than they?* No, in no wise: for we have before proved both Jews and Gentiles, that they are all under sin; 10. As it is written, There is none righteous, no, not one: 11. There is none that understandeth, there is none that seeketh after God. 12. They are all gone out of the way, they are together become unprofitable; there is none that doeth good, no, not one. 13. Their throat *is* an open sepulchre; with their tongues they have used deceit: the poison of asps *is* under their lips: 14. Whose mouth *is* full of cursing and bitterness: 15. Their feet *are* swift to shed blood: 16. Destruction and misery *are* in their ways: 17. And the way of peace have they not known: 18. There is no fear of God before their eyes. 19. Now we know that what things soever the law saith, it saith to them who are under the law: that every mouth may be stopped, and all the world may become guilty before God. 20. Therefore by the deeds of the law there shall no flesh be justified in his sight: for by the law *is* the knowledge of sin. 21. But now the righteousness of God without the law is manifested, being witnessed by the law and the prophets; 22. Even the righteousness of

God *which is* by faith of Jesus Christ unto all and upon all them that believe : for there is no difference : 23. For all have sinned, and come short of the glory of God ;

Rom. 4:1. What shall we say then that Abraham our father, as pertaining to the flesh, hath found ? 2. For if Abraham were justified by works, he hath *whereof* to glory ; but not before God. 3. For what saith the scripture ? Abraham believed God, and it was counted unto him for righteousness. 4. Now to him that worketh is the reward not reckoned of grace, but of debt. 5. But to him that worketh not, but believeth on him that justifieth the ungodly, his faith is counted for righteousness. 6. Even as David also describeth the blessedness of the man, unto whom God imputeth righteousness without works. 7. *Saying*, Blessed *are* they whose iniquities are forgiven, and whose sins are covered. 8. Blessed *is* the man to whom the Lord will not impute sin. 9. *Cometh* this blessedness then upon the circumcision *only*, or upon the uncircumcision also ? for we say that faith was reckoned to Abraham for righteousness. 10. How was it then reckoned ? when he was in circumcision, or in uncircumcision ? Not in circumcision, but in uncircumcision. 11. And he received the sign of circumcision, a seal of the righteousness of the faith which *he had yet* being uncircumcised : that he might be the father of all them that believe, though they be not circumcised ; that righteousness might be imputed unto them also : 12. And the father of circumcision to them who are not of the circumcision only, but who also walk in the steps of that faith of our father Abraham, which *he had* being *yet* uncircumcised. 13. For the promise, that he should be the heir of the world, *was* not to Abraham, or to his seed, through the law, but through the righteousness of faith. 14. For if they which are of the law *be* heirs, faith is made void, and the promise made of none effect : 15. Because the law worketh wrath : for where no law is, *there is* no transgression. 16. Therefore *it is* of faith, that *it might be* by grace ; to the end the promise might be sure to all the seed ; not to that only which is of the law, but to that also which is of the faith of Abraham ; who is the father of us all, 23. Now it was not written for his sake alone, that it was imputed to him ; 24. But for us also, to whom it shall be imputed, if we believe on him that raised up Jesus our Lord from the dead ; 25 Who was delivered for our offences, and was raised again for our justification.

INSTANCES OF : Joshua. through envy seeking to suppress Eldad and Medad, who were prophesying, Num. 11:27-29. Jews with regard to the Samaritans. John 4:9,27; in rejecting the teachings of Jesus at Nazareth, Luke 4:28; falsely accusing Jesus of blasphemy, John 5:18; of being a gluttonous man and winebibber, Matt. 11:18,19; of keeping company with sinners, Luke 7:39; 15:2; 19:5-7; of not conforming to the tradi-

tions, Luke 11:38,39; in their treatment of the young man who was born blind, whom Jesus restored to sight, John 9:28,29,34; with regard to Paul's preaching, Acts 21:28,29; 22:22. Of the Samaritans in refusing to receive Jesus, Luke 9:52,53. Of the disciples in forbidding children to be brought to Jesus, Matt. 19:13; Mark 10:13; Luke 18:15. Of the early Christians : In opposing the preaching of the gospel to the Gentiles, Acts 10:45; 11:2,3; 21:20-25; in regard to circumcision, Acts 15:1-10,24; Gal. 2:3-5.

The Jews, Rom. 10:2,3; in persecutions, 1 Thess. 2:15,16. Of John in forbidding the casting out of devils by one who followed not Jesus, Mark 9:38-40; Luke 9:49,50; James and John in desiring to call down fire upon the Samaritans who would not receive Jesus, Luke 9:51-56. Of Saul, in persecuting the Christians, Acts 22:3,4, with 9:1-5; Acts 26:9; Gal. 1:13,14; Phil. 3:6.

See INTOLERANCE, RELIGIOUS ; PERSECUTION ; UNCHARITABLENESS.

BIGTHAN, a conspiring Persian courtier, Esth. 2:21-23; 6:2.

BIGVAI, head of Jewish family, Ezra 2:2; 8:14; Neh. 7:7,19; 10:16.

BILDAD, one of Job's friends, Job 2:11; 8:1; 18:1; 25:1.

BILEAM. A town of Manasseh, 1 Chr. 6:70. Called IBLEAM, Josh. 17:11; GATH-RIMMON, Josh. 21:25.

BILGAH. 1. One of the chiefs of the sacerdotal courses in the temple, 1 Chr. 24:14. 2. A priest, Neh. 12:5,18, perhaps identical with BILGAI, Neh. 10:8.

BILGAI, a priest, Neh. 10:8.

BILHAH. 1. Rachael's servant, bears children by Jacob, Gen. 29:29; 30:3,4; 37:2. Mother of Dan and Naphtali, Gen. 30:1-8; 35:25; 46:23,25. Reuben's incest with, Gen. 35:22; 49:4.

2. A place in the land of Simeon, 1 Chr. 4:29. Called BALAH, Josh. 19:3; and BAALAH, Josh. 15:29.

BILHAN. 1. A Horite chief, Gen. 36:27; 1 Chr. 1:42.

2. A Benjamite, 1 Chr. 7:10.

BILL OF DIVORCE. See DIVORCE.

BILSHAN, a Jew of the captivity, Ezra 2:2; Neh. 7:7.

BIMHAL, son of Japhlet, 1 Chr. 7:33.

BINEA, a descendant of King Saul, 1 Chr. 8:37; 9:43.

BINNUI. 1. A Jew of the captivity, Neh. 7:15. Called BANI, Ezra 2:10.

2. A Levite of the captivity, Neh. 12:8; 3:24; 10:9.

3. Father of Noadiah, Ezra 8:33.

4. Son of Pahath-moab, Ezra 10:30.

5. Son of Bani, Ezra 10:38.

BIRDS. Creation of, on the fifth creative day, Gen. 1:20-30. Man's dominion over, Gen. 1:26,28; 9:2,3; Psa. 8:5-8; Jer. 27:6; Dan. 2:38; Jas. 3:7. Appointed for food, Gen. 9:2,3; Deut. 14:11-20. What species were unclean, Lev. 11:13-20; Deut. 14:12-19.

Used for sacrifice, see DOVE ; PIGEON. Divine care of, Job 38:41; Psa. 147:9; Matt.10:29; Luke 12:6,24. Songs of, at the break of day, Psa. 104:12; Eccl. 12:4; Song 2:12. Domesticated, Job 41:5; Jas. 3:7. Solomon's proverbs of, 1 Kin. 4:33. Nests of, Psa. 104:17; Matt. 8:20; 13:32. Instincts of, Prov. 1:17. Habits of, Job 39:13–18,26–30. Migrate, Jer. 8:7.

Mosaic law protected the mother from being taken with the young,Deut. 22:6,7. Cages of, Jer. 5:27; Rev. 18:2.

See SNARES.

FIGURATIVE: Isa. 16:2; 46:11; Jer. 12:9; Ezek. 39:4. Symbolical, Dan. 7:6.

See BITTERN; CHICKEN; CORMORANT; CRANE; CUCKOO; DOVE; EAGLE; FALCON; GLEDE; HAWK; HEN; HERON; KITE; LAPWING; NIGHT HAWK; OSPREY; OSSIFRAGE; OSTRICH; OWL; PARTRIDGE; PEACOCK; PELICAN; PIGEON; QUAIL; RAVEN; SPARROW; STORK; SWALLOW; SWAN; VULTURE.

BIRSHA, a king of Gomorrah, Gen. 14: 2-10.

BIRTH. Pangs in giving, Psa. 48:6; Isa. 13:8; 21:3; Jer. 4:31; 6:24; 30:6; 31:8. Giving, ordained to be in sorrow, Gen. 3:16.

See ABORTION; CHILDREN.

BIRTHDAY. Celebrated by feasts,Gen. 40:20; Matt.14:6. Cursed, Job 3; Jer. 20:14,18.

BIRTHRIGHT. Belonged to the firstborn, Deut. 21:15,16. Entitled the firstborn to a double portion of inheritance, Deut.21: 15–17; royal succession,2 Chr. 21:3. An honorable title, Ex. 4:22; Psa. 89:27; Jer. 31:9; Rom. 8:29; Col. 1:15; Heb. 1:6; 12:23; Rev.1:5.

Sold by Esau, Gen. 25:29–34; 27:36,with 25: 33; Heb. 12:16; Rom. 9:12,13. Forfeited by Reuben, 1 Chr. 5:1,2. Set aside: That of Manasseh, Gen. 48:15–20; Adonijah, 1 Kin. 2:15; Hosah's son, 1 Chr. 26:10.

See FIRSTBORN.

BIRZAVITH, a descendant of Asher, 1 Chr. 7:31.

BISHLAM, a Samaritan who obstructed the rebuilding of the temple at Jerusalem, Ezra 4:7-24.

BISHOP. Phil. 1:1. Paul and Timotheus, the servants of Jesus Christ, to all the saints in Christ Jesus which are at Philippi, with the bishops [marg. R. V., overseers] and deacons:

Acts 20:28. Take heed therefore unto yourselves, and to all the flock, over the which the Holy Ghost hath made you overseers [R. V., bishops], to feed the church of God, which he hath purchased with his own blood.

1 Tim. 3:2. A bishop [marg. R. V., overseer] then must be blameless, the husband of one wife, vigilant, sober, of good behaviour, given to hospitality, apt to teach; 3. Not given to wine, no striker, not greedy of filthy lucre; but patient, not a brawler, not covetous; 4. One that ruleth well his own house, having his children in subjection with all gravity; 5. (For if a man know not how to rule his own house, how shall he take care of the church of God ?) 6.Not a novice, lest being lifted up with pride he fall

into the condemnation of the devil. 7. Moreover he must have a good report of them which are without; lest he fall into reproach and the snare of the devil.

Tit. 1:5. For this cause left I thee in Crete, that thou shouldest set in order the things that are wanting, and ordain elders in every city, as I had appointed thee: 6. If any be blameless, the husband of one wife, having faithful children not accused of riot or unruly. 7. For a bishop [marg. R. V., overseer] must be blameless, as the steward of God; not selfwilled, not soon angry, 1 not given to wine, no striker, not given to filthy lucre; 8. But a lover of hospitality, a lover of good men, sober, just, holy, temperate; 9. Holding fast the faithful word as he hath been taught, that he may be able by sound doctrine both to exhort and to convince the gainsayers. 10. For there are many unruly and vain talkers and deceivers, specially they of the circumcision: 11. Whose mouths must be stopped, who subvert whole houses, teaching things which they ought not, for filthy lucre's sake.   [1 R. V. no brawler]

A TITLE OF JESUS: 1 Pet. 2:25.

See ELDER.

BIT, part of a bridle, Psa. 32:9; Jas. 3:3.

BITHIAH, daughter of Pharaoh, 1 Chr. 4:18.

BITHRON, a district bordering on the Jordan, 2 Sam. 2:29.

BITHYNIA, a Roman province in Asia Minor, Acts 16:7; 1 Pet. 1:1.

BITTER HERBS, eaten symbolically with the passover, Ex. 12:8; Num. 9:11.

BITTER WATER. At Marah, Ex. 15: 23. A ceremonial water used by the priest, Num. 5:18–27.

BITTERN [R. V., porcupine], Isa. 14: 23; 34:11; Zeph. 2:14.

BITUMEN [marg. R. V., slime], an inflammable mineral, Gen. 11:3; 14:10; Ex. 2:3.

See PETROLEUM.

BIZJOTHJAH, a town in Judah, Josh. 15:28. Called BIZJOTHJAH-BAALAH, v. 32; BAALATH-BEER, Josh. 19:8; and BALAH, Josh. 19:3.

BIZTHA, a Persian chamberlain, Esth. 1:10.

BLACKNESS. FIGURATIVE: Job 30: 30; Joel 2:6. Blackness of darkness, Jude 13. See COLOR, SYMBOLICAL.

BLACKSMITH. See SMITH.

BLAIN, an inflammatory abscess, Ex. 9:9,10.

BLASPHEMY. Ex. 20:7. Thou shalt not take the name of the LORD thy God in vain; for the LORD will not hold him guiltless that taketh his name in vain. Deut. 5:11.

Lev. 19:12. Ye shall not swear by my name falsely, neither shalt thou profane the name of thy God: Lev. 22:32.

Lev. 24:10. And the son of an Israelitish woman, whose father was an Egyptian, went out among the children of Israel: and this son of the Israelitish woman and a man of

Israel strove together in the camp; 11. And the Israelitish woman's son blasphemed the name *of the* LORD, and cursed. And they brought him unto Moses: (and his mother's name *was* Shelomith, the daughter of Dibri, of the tribe of Dan:) 12. And they put him in ward, that the mind of the LORD might be shewed them. 13. And the LORD spake unto Moses, saying, 14. Bring forth him that hath cursed without the camp; and let all that heard *him* lay their hands upon his head, and let all the congregation stone him. 15. And thou shalt speak unto the children of Israel, saying, Whosoever curseth his God shall bear his sin. 16. And he that blasphemeth the name of the LORD, he shall surely be put to death, *and* all the congregation shall certainly stone him: as well the stranger, as he that is born in the land, when he blasphemeth the name *of the* LORD, shall be put to death.

2 Kin. 19:22. Whom hast thou reproached and blasphemed? and against whom hast thou exalted *thy* voice, and lifted up thine eyes on high? *even* against the Holy *One* of Israel. Isa. 37:23.

2 Chr. 32:19. They spake against the God of Jerusalem, as against the gods of the people of the earth, *which were* the work of the hands of man.

*Job 9:16. If I had called, and he had answered me; *yet* would I not believe that he had hearkened unto my voice. 17. For he breaketh me with a tempest, and multiplieth my wounds without cause. 18. He will not suffer me to take my breath, but filleth me with bitterness. 34. Let him take his rod away from me, and let not his fear terrify me: 35. *Then* would I speak, and not fear him; but *it is* not so with me.

*Job 10:2. I will say unto God, Do not condemn me; shew me wherefore thou contendest with me. 3. *Is it* good unto thee that thou shouldest oppress, that thou shouldest despise the work of thine hands, and shine upon the counsel of the wicked? 4. Hast thou eyes of flesh, or seest thou as man seeth? 5. *Are* thy days as the days of man? *are* thy years as man's days, 6. That thou enquirest after mine iniquity, and searchest after my sin? 7. Thou knowest that I am not wicked; and *there is* none that can deliver out of thine hand.

*Job 13:7. Will ye speak wickedly for God? and talk deceitfully for him? 8. Will ye accept his person? will ye contend for God? 9. Is it good that he should search you out? or as one man mocketh another, do ye *so* mock him?

*25. Wilt thou break a leaf driven to and fro? and wilt thou pursue the dry stubble? 26. For thou writest bitter things against me, and makest me to possess the iniquities of my youth. 27. Thou puttest my feet also in the stocks, and lookest narrowly unto all my paths; thou settest a print upon the heels of my feet.

*Job 15:13. Thou turnest thy spirit against

God, and lettest *such* words go out of thy mouth? 25. For he stretcheth out his hand against God, and strengtheneth himself against the Almighty. 26. He runneth upon him, *even* on *his* neck, upon the thick bosses of his bucklers.

*Job 16:9. He teareth *me* in his wrath, who hateth me: he gnasheth upon me with his teeth; mine enemy sharpeneth his eyes upon me. 11. God hath delivered me to the ungodly, and turned me over into the hands of the wicked. 12. I was at ease, but he hath broken me asunder: he hath also taken *me* by my neck, and shaken me to pieces, and set me up for his mark. 13. His archers compass me round about, he cleaveth my reins asunder, and doth not spare; he poureth out my gall upon the ground. 14. He breaketh me with breach upon breach. he runneth upon me like a giant.

*Job 19:6. Know now that God hath overthrown me, and hath compassed me with his net. 7. Behold, I cry out of wrong, but I am not heard: I cry aloud, but *there is* no judgment. 21. Have pity upon me, have pity upon me, O ye my friends; for the hand of God hath touched me. 22. Why do ye persecute me as God, and are not satisfied with my flesh?

Job 21:13. They spend their days in wealth, and in a moment go down to the grave. 14. Therefore they say unto God, Depart from us; for we desire not the knowledge of thy ways.

*Job 22:12. *Is* not God in the height of heaven? and behold the height of the stars, how high they are! 13. And thou sayest, How doth God know? can he judge through the dark cloud? 14. Thick clouds *are* a covering to him, that he seeth not; and he walketh in the circuit of heaven. 17. Which said unto God, Depart from us: and what can the Almighty do for them?

Job 30:21. Thou art become cruel to me: with thy strong hand thou opposest thyself against me.

*Job 33:10. Behold, he findeth occasions against me, he counteth me for his enemy, 11. He putteth my feet in the stocks, he marketh all my paths.

*Job 34:5. For Job hath said, I am righteous: and God hath taken away my judgment. 6. Should I lie against my right? my wound *is* incurable without transgression.

*9. For he hath said, It profiteth a man nothing that he should delight himself with God. 16. If now *thou hast* understanding, hear this: hearken to the voice of my words. 17. Shall even he that hateth right govern? and wilt thou condemn him that is most just? 18. *Is it fit* to say to a king, *Thou art* wicked? *and* to princes, *Ye are* ungodly? 19. *How much less to him* that accepteth not the persons of princes, nor

---

* Interpreted by some authorities as blasphemy.

regardeth the rich more than the poor? for they all *are* the work of his hands. 37. For he addeth rebellion unto his sin, he clappeth *his hands* among us, and multiplieth his words against God.

*Job 37:20. Shall it be told him that I speak? if a man speak, surely he shall be swallowed up.

*Job 40:2. Shall he that contendeth with the Almighty instruct *him?* he that reproveth God, let him answer it.

Psa. 10:11. He hath said in his heart, God hath forgotten: he hideth his face; he will never see *it.* 13. Wherefore doth the wicked contemn God? he hath said in his heart, Thou wilt not require *it.*

Psa. 50:21. These *things* hast thou done, and I kept silence; thou thoughtest that I was altogether *such an one* as thyself: *but* I will reprove thée, and set *them* in order before thine eyes.

Psa. 73:9. They set their mouth against the heavens, and their tongue walketh through the earth. 11. And they say, How doth God know? and is there knowledge in the most High?

Psa. 74:18. Remember this, *that* the enemy hath reproached, O LORD, and *that* the foolish people have blasphemed thy name.

Psa. 78:19. Yea, they spake against God; they said, Can God furnish a table in the wilderness? 20. Behold, he smote the rock, that the waters gushed out, and the streams overflowed; can he give bread also? can he provide flesh for his people?

Psa. 94:7. Yet they say, The LORD shall not see, neither shall the God of Jacob regard it.

Psa. 139:20. For they speak against thee wickedly, *and* thine enemies take *thy name* in vain.

Prov. 30:8. Remove far from me vanity and lies: give me neither poverty nor riches; feed me with food convenient for me: 9. Lest I be full, and deny *thee,* and say, Who *is* the LORD? or lest I be poor, and steal, and take the name of my God *in vain. v.* 7.

Isa. 8:21. When they shall be hungry, they shall fret themselves, and curse their king and their God, and look upward. 22. And *they shall be* driven to darkness.

Isa. 29:15. Woe unto them that seek deep to hide their counsel from the LORD, and their works are in the dark, and they say, Who seeth us? and who knoweth us? 16. Surely your turning of things upside down shall be esteemed as the potter's clay: for shall the work say of him that made it, He made me not? or shall the thing framed say of him that framed it, He had no understanding?

Isa. 36:15. Neither let Hezekiah make you trust in the LORD, saying, The LORD will surely deliver us: this city shall not be delivered into the hand of the king of Assyria. 18. *Beware* lest Hezekiah persuade

you, saying, The LORD will deliver us. Hath any of the gods of the nations delivered his land out of the hand of the king of Assyria? 20. Who *are they* among all the gods of these lands, that have delivered their land out of my hand, that the LORD should deliver Jerusalem out of my hand? 21. But they held their peace, and answered him not a word: for the king's commandment was, saying, Answer him not.

Isa. 37:10. Thus shall ye speak to Hezekiah king of Judah, saying, Let not thy God, in whom thou trustest, deceive thee, saying, Jerusalem shall not be given into the hand of the king of Assyria.

Isa. 40:27. Why sayest thou, O Jacob, and speakest, O Israel, My way is hid from the LORD, and my judgment is passed over from my God?

Isa. 45:9. Woe unto him that striveth with his Maker! *Let* the potsherd *strive* with the potsherds of the earth. Shall the clay say to him that fashioneth it, What makest thou? or thy work, He hath no hands?

Isa. 52:5. Now therefore, what have I here, saith the LORD, that my people is taken away for nought? they that rule over them make them to howl, saith the LORD; and my name continually every day *is* blasphemed.

Isa. 65:7. Your iniquities and the iniquities of your fathers together, saith the LORD, which have burned incense upon the mountains, and blasphemed me upon the hills: therefore will I measure their former work into their bosom.

Jer. 4:10. Then said I, Ah, Lord GOD! surely thou hast greatly deceived this people and Jerusalem, saying, Ye shall have peace; whereas the sword reacheth unto the soul.

Jer. 17:15. Behold, they say unto me, Where *is* the word of the LORD? let it come now.

Jer. 20:7. O LORD, thou hast deceived me, and I was deceived: thou art stronger than I and hast prevailed: I am in derision daily, every one mocketh me.

Jer. 23:10. For the land is full of adulterers; for because of swearing the land mourneth;

Ezek. 8:12. Then said he unto me, Son of man, hast thou seen what the ancients of the house of Israel do in the dark, every man in the chambers of his imagery? for they say, the LORD seeth us not; the LORD hath forsaken the earth.

Ezek. 9:9. Then said he unto me, The iniquity of the house of Israel and Judah *is* exceeding great, and the land is full of blood, and the city full of perverseness: for they say, The LORD hath forsaken the earth, and the LORD seeth not.

Ezek. 18:25. Yet ye say, The way of the Lord is not equal. Hear now, O house of Israel, Is not my way equal? are not your ways unequal?

Ezek. 20:27. Your fathers have blas-

* Interpreted by some authorities as blasphemy.

phemed me, in that they have committed a trespass against me.

Ezek. 33:17. Yet the children of thy people say, The way of the Lord is not equal: but as for them, their way is not equal. 18. When the righteous turneth from his righteousness, and committeth iniquity, he shall even die thereby. 19. But if the wicked turn from his wickedness, and do that which is lawful and right, he shall live thereby. 20. Yet ye say, The way of the Lord is not equal. O ye house of Israel, I will judge you every one after his ways.

Ezek. 35:12. I have heard all thy blasphemies which thou hast spoken. 13. Ye have boasted against me, and have multiplied your words against me: I have heard *them*.

Dan. 7:25. He shall speak *great* words against the most High.

Dan. 11:36. And the king shall do according to his will; and he shall exalt himself, and magnify himself above every god, and shall speak marvellous things against the God of gods, and shall prosper till the indignation be accomplished: 37. Neither shall he regard the ¹God of his fathers, . . . for he shall magnify himself above all. [¹ R. V. gods]

Hos. 7:13. Woe unto them! for they have fled from me: destruction unto them! because they have transgressed against me: though I have redeemed them, yet they have spoken lies against me.

Zeph. 1:12. And it shall come to pass at that time *that* I will search Jerusalem with candles, and punish the men that are settled on their lees: that say in their heart, The LORD will not do good, neither will he do evil.

Zech. 5:3. This *is* the curse that goeth forth over the face of the whole earth: for every one that stealeth shall be cut off *as* on this side according to it; and every one that sweareth shall be cut off *as* on that side according to it. 4. I will bring it forth, saith the LORD of hosts, and it shall enter into the house of the thief, and into the house of him that sweareth falsely by my name: and it shall remain in the midst of his house, and shall consume it with the timber thereof and the stones thereof.

Mal. 3:13. Your words have been stout against me, saith the LORD. Yet ye say, What have we spoken *so much* against thee? 14. Ye have said, It *is* vain to serve God: and what profit *is it* that we have kept his ordinance, and that we have walked mournfully before the LORD of hosts?

Matt. 10:25. They have called the master of the house Beelzebub, how much more *shall they call* them of his household?

Matt. 12:31. Wherefore I say unto you, All manner of sin and blasphemy shall be forgiven unto men: but the blasphemy *against* the *Holy* Ghost shall not be forgiven unto men: 32. And whosoever speaketh a word against the Son of man, it shall be forgiven him: but whosoever speaketh against the Holy Ghost, it shall not be for-

given him, neither in this world, neither in the *world* to come. Mark 3:29,30; Luke 12:10.

Matt. 15:19. Out of the heart proceed . . . ¹ blasphemies: [¹ R. V. railings]

Mark 7:21. For from within, out of the heart of men, proceed evil thoughts, adulteries, fornications, murders, 22. Thefts, covetousness, wickedness, deceit, lasciviousness, an evil eye, blasphemy, pride, foolishness: 23. All these evil things come from within, and defile the man.

John 19:7. The Jews answered him, We have a law, and by our law he ought to die, because he made himself the Son of God.

Rom. 2:24. The name of God is blasphemed among the Gentiles through you, as it is written, 2 Sam. 12:14.

1 Cor. 12:3. Wherefore I give you to understand, that no man speaking by the Spirit of God calleth Jesus accursed: and *that* no man can say that Jesus is the Lord, but by the Holy Ghost.

Col. 3:8. Put off all these; . . . blasphemy, filthy communication out of your mouth.

2 Thess. 2:4. Who opposeth and exalteth himself above all that is called God, or that is worshipped; so that he as God sitteth in the temple of God, shewing himself that he is God.

2 Tim. 3:2. For men shall be lovers of their own selves, covetous, boasters, proud, blasphemers. Rev. 16:11. [¹ R. V. railers]

Heb. 10:29. Of how much sorer punishment, suppose ye, shall he be thought worthy, who hath trodden under foot the Son of God, and hath counted the blood of the covenant, wherewith he was sanctified, an unholy thing, and hath done despite unto the Spirit of grace?

Jas. 2:7. Do not they blaspheme that worthy name by the which ye are called?

Jas. 3:10. Out of the same mouth proceedeth blessing and cursing. My brethren, these things ought not so to be.

Jas. 5:12. Above all things, my brethren, swear not, neither by heaven, neither by the earth, neither by any other oath: but let your yea be yea; and *your* nay, nay; lest ye fall into condemnation.

2 Pet. 3:3. Knowing this first, that there shall come in the last days scoffers, walking after their own lusts, 4. And saying, Where is the promise of his coming? for since the fathers fell asleep, all things continue as *they were* from the beginning of the creation.

Rev. 13:1. And I stood upon the sand of the sea, and saw a beast rise up out of the sea, . . . and upon his heads the name of blasphemy. 6. He opened his mouth in blasphemy against God, to blaspheme his name, and his tabernacle, and them that dwell in heaven.

Rev. 16:9. Men were scorched with great heat, and blasphemed the name of God, which hath power over these plagues: 21. Men blasphemed God because of the plague of the hail;

Rev. 17:3. I saw a woman sit upon a scarlet coloured beast, full of names of blasphemy.

Prophecy of, Rev. 13:1,5,6; 16:9,11,21; 17:3.

INSTANCES OF: The depraved son of Shelomith, who, in an altercation with an Israelite, cursed God, Lev. 24:10-16. Of the Israelites, in murmuring against God, Num. 21:5,6. Infidels, who used the adultery of David as an occasion to blaspheme, 2 Sam. 12:14. Shimei, in his malice toward David, 2 Sam. 16:5. Rabshakeh, in the siege of Jerusalem, 2 Kin. 18:22; 19; Isa. 36:15-20; 37: 10-33. Job's wife, when she exhorted Job to curse God and die, Job 2:9. Peter, when accused of being a disciple of Jesus, Matt. 26:74; Mark 14:71. The revilers of Jesus, when he was crucified, Matt. 27:40-44,63. The early Christians, persecuted by Saul of Tarsus, compelled to blaspheme the name of Jesus, Acts 26:11; 1 Tim. 1:13. Two disciples, Hymenæus and Alexander, who were delivered unto Satan that they might learn not to blaspheme, 1 Tim. 1:20. Man of sin, 2 Thess. 2:3,4. Backslidden Ephesians, Rev. 2:9.

FALSE INDICTMENTS FOR: Of Naboth, 1 Kin. 21:13; Jesus, Matt. 26:65; Mark 14:58; Luke 22:70,71; John 19:7; Stephen, Acts 6:11, 13. Jesus falsely accused of, previously to his trial, Mark 2:7; Luke 5:21.

BLASTING. Blight, 1 Kin. 8:37. Sent as a judgment, Deut. 28:22; 2 Kin. 19:7; Isa. 37:7; Amos 4:9; Hag. 2:17.

FIGURATIVE: Ex. 15:8; 2 Sam. 22:16; Job 4:9; Psa. 18:15.

BLASTUS, one of Herod's officers, Acts 12:20.

BLEMISH, a physical deformity. Debarred sons of Aaron from exercise of priestly offices, Lev. 21:17-23. Animals with, forbidden to be used for sacrifice, Lev. 22: 19-25.

FIGURATIVE: Eph. 5:27; 1 Pet. 1:19.

BLESSING. For blessing before eating, see PRAYER; THANKSGIVING AND PRAYER BEFORE TAKING FOOD. See also BENEDICTIONS.

RESPONSIVE BLESSINGS OF THE LAW: Deut. 28:1. And it shall come to pass, if thou shalt hearken diligently unto the voice of the LORD thy God, to observe *and* to do all his commandments which I command thee this day, that the LORD thy God will set thee on high above all nations of the earth: 2. And all these blessings shall come on thee, and overtake thee, if thou shalt hearken unto the voice of the LORD thy God. 3. Blessed *shalt* thou *be* in the city, and blessed *shalt* thou *be* in the field. 4. Blessed *shall be* the fruit of thy body, and the fruit of thy ground, and the fruit of thy cattle, the increase of thy kine, and the flocks of thy sheep. 5. Blessed *shall be* thy basket and thy store. 6. Blessed *shalt* thou *be* when thou comest in, and blessed *shalt* thou *be* when thou goest out. 7. The LORD shall cause thine enemies that rise up against thee to be smitten before thy face: they shall come out

against thee one way, and flee before thee seven ways. 8. The LORD shall command the blessing upon thee in thy storehouses, and in all that thou settest thine hand unto; and he shall bless thee in the land which the LORD thy God giveth thee. 9. The LORD shall establish thee an holy people unto himself, as he hath sworn unto thee, if thou shalt keep the commandments of the LORD thy God, and walk in his ways. 10. And all the people of the earth shall see that thou art called by the name of the LORD; and they shall be afraid of thee. 11. And the LORD shall make thee plenteous in goods, in the fruit of thy body, and in the fruit of thy cattle, and in the fruit of thy ground, in the land which the LORD sware unto thy fathers to give thee. 12. The LORD shall open unto thee his good treasure, the heaven to give the rain unto thy land in his season, and to bless all the work of thine hand: and thou shalt lend unto many nations, and thou shalt not borrow. 13. And the LORD shall make thee the head, and not the tail; and thou shalt be above only, and thou shalt not be beneath; if that thou hearken unto the commandments of the LORD thy God, which I command thee this day, to observe and to do *them:* 14. And thou shalt not go aside from any of the words which I command thee this day, *to* the right hand, or *to* the left, to go after other gods to serve them.

For the responsive CURSES of the law, see CURSE.

DIVINE, CONTINGENT UPON OBEDIENCE: Ex. 15:26. If thou wilt diligently hearken to the voice of the LORD thy God, and wilt do that which is right in his sight, and wilt give ear to his commandments, and keep all his statutes, I will put none of these diseases upon thee, which I have brought upon the Egyptians: for I *am* the LORD that healeth thee.

Ex. 19:5. Now therefore, if ye will obey my voice indeed, and keep my covenant, then ye shall be a peculiar treasure unto me above all people: for all the earth *is* mine:

Ex. 20:6. And shewing mercy unto thousands of them that love me, and keep my commandments.

Ex. 23:22. If thou shalt indeed obey his voice, and do all that I speak; then I will be an enemy unto thine enemies, and an adversary unto thine adversaries.

Lev. 26:3. If ye walk in my statutes, and keep my commandments, and do them 4. Then I will give you rain in due season, and the land shall yield her increase, and the trees of the field shall yield their fruit. 5. And your threshing shall reach unto the vintage, and the vintage shall reach unto the sowing time: and ye shall eat your bread to the full, and dwell in your land safely. 6. And I will give peace in the land, and ye shall lie down, and none shall make *you* afraid: and I will rid evil beasts out of the land, neither shall the sword go through your land. 7. And ye shall chase your enemies, and they shall fall before you by the sword. 8. And five of you shall chase an hundred, and an hundred of you shall put ten thousand to flight: and your enemies shall fall before you by the sword. 9. For I will have respect unto you, and make you fruitful, and multiply you, and establish my covenant with you. 10. And ye shall eat old store, and bring forth the old because of the new. 11. And I will set my tabernacle among you: and my soul shall not abhor you. 12. And I will walk among you, and will be your God, and ye shall be my people. 13. I *am* the LORD your God, which brought you forth out of the land of Egypt, that ye should not be their bondmen; and I have broken the bands of your yoke, and made you go upright. 14. But if ye will not hearken unto me, and will not do all these commandments: 15. And if ye shall despise my statutes, or if your soul abhor my judgments, so that ye will not do all my commandments, *but* that ye break my covenant: 16. I also will do this unto you; I will even appoint over you terror, consumption, and the burning ague, that shall consume the eyes, and cause sorrow of heart: and ye shall sow your seed in vain, for your enemies shall eat it. 17. And I will set my face against you, and ye shall be slain before your enemies: they that hate you shall reign over you; and ye shall flee when none pursueth you. 18. And if ye will not yet for all this hearken unto me, then I will punish you seven times more for your sins. 19. And I will break the pride of your power; and I will make your heaven as iron, and your earth as brass: 20. And your strength shall be spent in vain: for your land shall not yield her increase, neither shall the trees of the land yield their fruits. 21 And if ye walk contrary unto me, and will not hearken unto me; I will bring seven times more plagues upon you according to your sins. 22. I will also send wild beasts among you, which shall rob you of your children, and destroy your cattle, and make you few in number; and your *high* ways shall be desolate. 23. And if ye will not be reformed by me by these things, but will walk contrary unto me; 24. Then will I also walk contrary unto you, and will punish you yet seven times for your sins. 25. And I will bring a sword upon you, that shall avenge the quarrel of *my* covenant: and when ye are gathered together within your cities, I will send the pestilence among you; and ye shall be delivered into the hand of the enemy. 26. *And* when I have broken the staff of your bread, ten women shall bake your bread in one oven, and they shall deliver *you* your bread again by weight: and ye shall eat, and not be satisfied. 27. And if ye will not for all this hearken unto me, but walk contrary unto me; 28. Then I will walk contrary unto you also in fury; and I, even I, will chastise you seven times for your sins. 29. And ye shall eat the flesh of your

sons, and the flesh of your daughters shall ye eat. 30. And I will destroy your high places, and cut down your images, and cast your carcases upon the carcases of your idols, and my soul shall abhor you. 31. And I will make your cities waste, and bring your sanctuaries unto desolation, and I will not smell the savour of your sweet odours. 32. And I will bring the land into desolation: and your enemies which dwell therein shall be astonished at it. 33. And I will scatter you among the heathen, and will draw out a sword after you: and your land shall be desolate, and your cities waste. 34. Then shall the land enjoy her sabbaths, as long as it lieth desolate, and ye *be* in your enemies' land; *even* then shall the land rest, and enjoy her sabbaths. 35. As long as it lieth desolate it shall rest; because it did not rest in your sabbaths, when ye dwelt upon it. 36. And upon them that are left *alive* of you I will send a faintness into their hearts in the lands of their enemies; and the sound of a shaken leaf shall chase them; and they shall flee as fleeing from a sword; and they shall fall when none pursueth. 37. And they shall fall one upon another, as it were before a sword, when none pursueth: and ye shall have no power to stand before your enemies. 38. And ye shall perish among the heathen, and the land of your enemies shall eat you up. 39. And they that are left of you shall pine away in their iniquity in your enemies' lands; and also in the iniquities of their fathers shall they pine away with them. 40. If they shall confess their iniquity, and the iniquity of their fathers, with their trespass which they trespassed against me, and that also they have walked contrary unto me; 41. And *that* I also have walked contrary unto them, and have brought them into the land of their enemies; if then their uncircumcised hearts be humbled, and they then accept of the punishment of their iniquity: 42. Then will I remember my covenant with Jacob, and also my covenant with Isaac, and also my covenant with Abraham will I remember; and I will remember the land. 43. The land also shall be left of them, and shall enjoy her sabbaths, while she lieth desolate without them: and they shall accept of the punishment of their iniquity; because, even because they despised my judgments, and because their soul abhorred my statutes.

Deut. 4:1. Now therefore hearken, O Israel, unto the statutes and unto the judgments, which I teach you, for to do *them*, that ye may live, and go in and possess the land which the LORD God of your fathers giveth you. 40. Thou shalt keep therefore his statutes, and his commandments, which I command thee this day, that it may go well with thee, and with thy children after thee, and that thou mayest prolong *thy* days upon the earth, which the LORD thy God giveth thee, for ever.

Deut. 5:10. Shewing mercy unto thousands

of them that love me and keep my commandments. 29. O that there were such an heart in them, that they would fear me, and keep all my commandments always, that it might be well with them, and with their children for ever! Deut. 29:9.

Deut. 7:9. Know therefore that the Lord thy God, he *is* God, the faithful God, which keepeth covenant and mercy with them that love him and keep his commandments to a thousand generations; 12. Wherefore it shall come to pass, if ye hearken to these judgments, and keep, and do them, that the Lord thy God shall keep unto thee the covenant and the mercy which he sware unto thy fathers: 13. And he will love thee, and bless thee, and multiply thee: he will also bless the fruit of thy womb, and the fruit of thy land, thy corn, and thy wine, and thine oil, the increase of thy kine, and the flocks of thy sheep, in the land which he sware unto thy fathers to give thee. 14. Thou shalt be blessed above all people: there shall not be male or female barren among you, or among your cattle. 15. And the Lord will take away from thee all sickness, and will put none of the evil diseases of Egypt, which thou knowest, upon thee; but will lay them upon all *them* that hate thee.

Deut. 11:26. Behold, I set before you this day a blessing and a curse; 27. A blessing, if ye obey the commandments of the Lord your God, which I command you this day: *v.* 28.

Deut. 12:28. Observe and hear all these words which I command thee, that it may go well with thee, and with thy children after thee for ever, when thou doest *that which is* good and right in the sight of the Lord thy God.

Deut. 15:4. For the Lord shall greatly bless thee in the land which the Lord thy God giveth thee *for* an inheritance to possess it: 5. Only if thou carefully hearken unto the voice of the Lord thy God, to observe to do all these commandments which I command thee this day.

Deut. 28:1. And it shall come to pass, if thou shalt hearken diligently unto the voice of the Lord thy God, to observe *and* to do all his commandments which I command thee this day, that the Lord thy God will set thee on high above all nations of the earth: 2. And all these blessings shall come on thee, and overtake thee, if thou shalt hearken unto the voice of the Lord thy God. 3. Blessed *shalt* thou *be* in the city, and blessed *shalt* thou *be* in the field. 4. Blessed *shall be* the fruit of thy body, and the fruit of thy ground, and the fruit of thy cattle, the increase of thy kine, and the flocks of thy sheep. 5. Blessed *shall be* thy basket and thy store. 6. Blessed *shalt* thou *be* when thou comest in, and blessed *shalt* thou *be* when thou goest out. 7. The Lord shall cause thine enemies that rise up against thee to be smitten before thy face: they shall come out against thee one way, and flee before thee seven ways. 8. The Lord shall command the blessing upon thee in thy storehouses, and in all that thou settest thine hand unto; and he shall bless thee in the land which the Lord thy God giveth thee. 9. The Lord shall establish thee an holy people unto himself, as he hath sworn unto thee, if thou shalt keep the commandments of the Lord thy God, and walk in his ways. 10. And all people of the earth shall see that thou art called by the name of the Lord; and they shall be afraid of thee. 11. And the Lord shall make thee plenteous in goods, in the fruit of thy body, and in the fruit of thy cattle, and in the fruit of thy ground, in the land which the Lord sware unto thy fathers to give thee. 12. The Lord shall open unto thee his good treasure, the heaven to give thee rain unto thy land in his season, and to bless all the work of thine hand: and thou shalt lend unto many nations, and thou shalt not borrow. 13. And the Lord shall make thee the head, and not the tail; and thou shalt be above only, and thou shalt not be beneath; if that thou hearken unto the commandments of the Lord thy God, which I command thee this day, to observe and to do *them*. 14. And thou shalt not go aside from any of the words which I command thee this day, *to* the right hand, or *to* the left, to go after other gods to serve them.

Deut. 30:1. And it shall come to pass, when all these things are come upon thee, the blessing and the curse, which I have set before thee, and thou shalt call *them* to mind among all the nations, whither the Lord thy God hath driven thee, 2. And shalt return unto the Lord thy God, and shalt obey his voice according to all that I command thee this day, thou and thy children, with all thine heart, and with all thy soul; 3. That then the Lord thy God will turn thy captivity, and have compassion upon thee, and will return and gather thee from all the nations, whither the Lord thy God hath scattered thee. 4. If *any* of thine be driven out unto the outmost *parts* of heaven, from thence will the Lord thy God gather thee, and from thence will he fetch thee: 5. And the Lord thy God will bring thee into the land which thy fathers possessed, and thou shalt possess it; and he will do thee good, and multiply thee above thy fathers. 6. And the Lord thy God will circumcise thine heart, and the heart of thy seed, to love the Lord thy God with all thine heart, and with all thy soul, that thou mayest live. 7. And the Lord thy God will put all these curses upon thine enemies, and on them that hate thee, which persecuted thee. 8. And thou shalt return and obey the voice of the Lord, and do all his commandments which I command thee this day. 9. And the Lord thy God will make thee plenteous in every work of thine hand, in the fruit of thy body, and in the fruit of thy cattle, and in the fruit of thy land, for good: for the Lord will again rejoice over thee for good, as he rejoiced over thy fathers: 10. If thou shalt hearken unto the voice of the LORD thy God, to keep his commandments and his statutes which are written in this book of the law, *and* if thou turn unto the LORD thy God with all thine heart, and with all thy soul. 15. See, I have set before thee this day life and good, and death and evil; 16. In that I command thee this day to love the LORD thy God, to walk in his ways, and to keep his commandments and his statutes and his judgments, that thou mayest live and multiply: and the LORD thy God shall bless thee in the land whither thou goest to possess it. 17. But if thine heart turn away, so that thou wilt not hear, but shalt be drawn away, and worship other gods, and serve them; 18. I denounce unto you this day, that ye shall surely perish, *and that* ye shall not prolong *your* days upon the land, whither thou passest over Jordan to go to possess it. 19. I call heaven and earth to record this day against you, *that* I have set before you life and death, blessing and cursing: therefore choose life, that both thou and thy seed may live: 20. That thou mayest love the LORD thy God, *and* that thou mayest obey his voice, and that thou mayest cleave unto him: for he *is* thy life, and the length of thy days: that thou mayest dwell in the land which the LORD sware unto thy fathers, to Abraham, to Isaac, and to Jacob, to give them.

Josh. 1:8. This book of the law shall not depart out of thy mouth; . . . for then thou shalt make thy way prosperous, and then thou shalt have good success.

1 Kin. 2:3. Keep the charge of the LORD thy God to walk in his ways, to keep his statutes, and his commandments, and his judgments, and his testimonies, as it is written in the law of Moses, that thou mayest prosper in all that thou doest, and whithersoever thou turnest thyself: 4. That the LORD may continue his word which he spake concerning me, saying, If thy children take heed to their way, to walk before me in truth with all their heart and with all their soul, there shall not fail thee (said he) a man on the throne of Israel.

1 Kin. 3:14. If thou wilt walk in my ways, to keep my statutes and my commandments, as thy father David did walk, then I will lengthen thy days.

1 Kin. 8:23. And he said, LORD God of Israel, *there is* no God like thee, in heaven above, or on earth beneath, who keepest covenant and mercy with thy servants that walk before thee with all their heart:

1 Kin. 9:3. And the LORD said unto him, I have heard thy prayer and thy supplication, that thou hast made before me: I have hallowed this house, which thou hast built, to put my name there for ever; and mine eyes and mine heart shall be there perpetually. 4. And if thou wilt walk before me, as David thy father walked, in integrity of heart, and in uprightness, to do according to all that I have commanded thee, *and* wilt keep my statutes and my judgments: 5. Then I will

establish the throne of thy kingdom upon Israel for ever, as I promised to David thy father, saying, There shall not fail thee a man upon the throne of Israel. 6. *But* if ye shall at all turn from following me, ye or your children, and will not keep my commandments *and* my statutes which I have set before you, but go and serve other gods, and worship them: 7. Then will I cut off Israel out of the land which I have given them; and this house, which I have hallowed for my name, will I cast out of my sight; and Israel shall be a proverb and a byword among all people: 8. And at this house, *which* is high, every one that passeth by it shall be astonished, and shall hiss; and they shall say, Why hath the LORD done thus unto this land, and to this house? 9. And they shall answer, Because they forsook the LORD their God, who brought forth their fathers out of the land of Egypt, and have taken hold upon other gods, and have worshipped them, and served them: therefore hath the LORD brought upon them all this evil. 2 Chr. 7:17–22.

1 Chr. 22:13. Then shalt thou prosper, if thou takest heed to fulfil the statutes and judgments which the LORD charged Moses with concerning Israel: be strong, and of good courage; dread not, nor be dismayed.

1 Chr. 28:7. Moreover I will establish his kingdom for ever, if he be constant to do my commandments and my judgments, as at this day. 8. Keep and seek for all the commandments of the LORD your God: that ye may possess this good land, and leave *it* for an inheritance for your children after you for ever.

2 Chr. 26:5. And he sought God in the days of Zechariah, who had understanding in the visions of God: and as long as he sought the LORD, God made him to prosper.

2 Chr. 27:6. So Jotham became mighty, because he prepared his ways before the LORD his God.

2 Chr. 30:9. For if ye turn again unto the LORD, your brethren and your children *shall find* compassion before them that lead them captive, so that they shall come again into this land: for the LORD your God *is* gracious and merciful, and will not turn away *his* face from you, if ye return unto him.

2 Chr. 31:10. Since *the people* began to bring the offerings into the house of the LORD, we have had enough to eat, and have left plenty: for the LORD hath blessed his people; and that which is left *is* this great store.

Job. 36:11. If they obey and serve *him*, they shall spend their days in prosperity, and their years in pleasures.

Prov. 3:1. My son, forget not my law; but let thine heart keep my commandments: 2. For length of days, and long life, and peace, shall they add to thee.

Prov. 16:7. When a man's ways please the LORD, he maketh even his enemies to be at peace with him.

Isa. 1:19. If ye be willing and obedient, ye shall eat the good of the land.

Jer. 7:3. Thus saith the Lord of hosts, the God of Israel, Amend your ways and your doings, and I will cause you to dwell in this place. 4. Trust ye not in lying words, saying, The temple of the Lord, The temple of the Lord, The temple of the Lord, *are* these. 5. For if ye thoroughly amend your ways and your doings; if ye thoroughly execute judgment between a man and his neighbour; 6. *If* ye oppress not the stranger, the fatherless, and the widow, and shed not innocent blood in this place, neither walk after other gods to your hurt: 7. Then will I cause you to dwell in this place, in the land that I gave to your fathers, for ever and ever. 23. But this thing commanded I them, saying, Obey my voice, and I will be your God, and ye shall be my people: and walk ye in all the ways that I have commanded you, that it may be well unto you.

Jer. 11:1. The word that came to Jeremiah from the Lord, saying, 2. Hear ye the words of this covenant, and speak unto the men of Judah, and to the inhabitants of Jerusalem; 3. And say thou unto them, Thus saith the Lord God of Israel; Cursed *be* the man that obeyeth not the words of this covenant, 4. Which I commanded your fathers in the day *that* I brought them forth out of the land of Egypt, from the iron furnace, saying, Obey my voice, and do them, according to all which I command you: so shall ye be my people, and I will be your God: 5. That I may perform the oath which I have sworn unto your fathers, to give them a land flowing with milk and honey, as *it is* this day. Then answered I, and said, So be it, O Lord.

Jer. 12:16. And it shall come to pass, if they will diligently learn the ways of my people, to swear by my name, The Lord liveth; as they taught my people to swear by Baal; then shall they be built in the midst of my people.

Jer. 15:19. Therefore thus saith the Lord, If thou return, then will I bring thee again, *and* thou shalt stand before me: and if thou take forth the precious from the vile, thou shalt be as my mouth: let them return unto thee; but return not thou unto them. 20. And I will make thee unto this people a fenced brasen wall: and they shall fight against thee, but they shall not prevail against thee: for I *am* with thee to save thee and to deliver thee, saith the Lord. 21. And I will deliver thee out of the hand of the wicked, and I will redeem thee out of the hand of the terrible.

Jer. 17:24. And it shall come to pass, if ye diligently hearken unto me, saith the Lord, to bring in no burden through the gates of this city on the sabbath day, but hallow the sabbath day, to do no work therein; 25. Then shall there enter into the gates of this city kings and princes sitting upon the throne of David, riding in chariots and on horses, they, and their princes, the men of Judah, and the inhabitants of Jerusalem: and this city shall remain for ever. 26. And they shall come from the cities of Judah, and from the places about Jerusalem, and from the land of Benjamin, and from the plain, and from the mountains, and from the south, bringing burnt offerings, and sacrifices, and meat offerings, and incense, and bringing sacrifices of praise, unto the house of the Lord. 27. But if ye will not hearken unto me to hallow the sabbath day, and not to bear a burden, even entering in at the gates of Jerusalem on the sabbath day; then will I kindle a fire in the gates thereof, and it shall devour the palaces of Jerusalem, and it shall not be quenched.

Jer. 22:4. For if ye do this thing indeed, then shall there enter in by the gates of this house kings sitting upon the throne of David, riding in chariots and on horses, he, and his servants, and his people. 5. But if ye will not hear these words, I swear by myself, saith the Lord, that this house shall become a desolation.

15. Shalt thou reign, because thou closest *thyself* in cedar? did not thy father eat and drink, and do judgment and justice, *and* then *it was* well with him? 16. He judged the cause of the poor and needy; then *it was* well *with him: was* not this to know me? saith the Lord.

Zech. 3:7. Thus said the Lord of hosts; If thou wilt walk in my ways, and if thou wilt keep my charge, then thou shalt also judge my house, and shalt also keep my courts, and I will give thee places to walk among these that stand by.

Mal. 3:10. Bring ye all the tithes into the storehouse, that there may be meat in mine house, and prove me now herewith, saith the Lord of hosts, if I will not open you the windows of heaven, and pour you out a blessing, that *there shall* not *be room* enough *to receive it.* 11. And I will rebuke the devourer for your sakes, and he shall not destroy the fruits of your ground; neither shall your vine cast her fruit before the time in the field, saith the Lord of hosts. 12. And all nations shall call you blessed: for ye shall be a delightsome land, saith the Lord of hosts.

Matt. 10:22. He that endureth to the end shall be saved. Matt. 24:13; Mark 13:13.

Col. 1:22. To present you holy and unblameable and unreproveable in his sight: 23. If ye continue in the faith grounded and settled, and *be* not moved away from the hope of the gospel, which ye have heard, *and* which was preached to every creature which is under heaven;

Heb. 3:6. But Christ as a son over his own house; whose house are we, if we hold fast the confidence and the rejoicing of the hope firm unto the end. 14. For we are made partakers of Christ, if we hold the beginning of our confidence stedfast unto the end;

Heb. 6:11. And we desire that every one

of you do shew the same diligence to the full assurance of hope unto the end: 12. That ye be not slothful, but followers of them who through faith and patience inherit the promises.

Heb. 10:36. For ye have need of patience, that, after ye have done the will of God, ye might receive the promise.

Rev. 2:10. Be thou faithful unto death, and I will give thee a crown of life.

See FAITHFULNESS; CONTINGENCIES.

SPIRITUAL, FROM GOD: Gen. 49:24. His bow abode in strength, and the arms of his hands were made strong by the hands of the mighty *God* of Jacob;

Ex. 15:2. The LORD *is* my strength and song, and he is become my salvation:

Ex. 33:16. Wherein shall it be known here that I and thy people have found grace in thy sight? *is it* not in that thou goest with us? so shall we be separated, I and thy people, from all the people that *are* upon the face of the earth.

Lev. 21:8. I the LORD, which sanctify you, *am* holy. Ex. 31:13.

Deut. 33:25. Thy shoes *shall be* iron and brass; and as thy days, *so shall* thy strength *be.* 27. The eternal God *is thy* refuge, and underneath *are* the everlasting arms: and he shall thrust out the enemy from before thee; and shall say, Destroy *them.*

1 Sam. 2:4. The bows of the mighty men *are* broken, and they that stumbled are girded with strength.

Neh. 8:10. *This* day *is* holy unto our Lord: neither be ye sorry; for the joy of the LORD is your strength.

Job. 23:6. Will he plead against me with *his* great power? No; but he would put *strength* in me.

Psa. 18:1. I will love thee, O LORD, my strength. 2. The LORD *is* my rock, and my fortress, and my deliverer; my God, my strength, in whom I will trust; my buckler, and the horn of my salvation, *and* my high tower. 28. Thou wilt light my candle: the LORD my God will enlighten my darkness. 32. *It is* God that girdeth me with strength, and maketh my way perfect. 35. Thou hast also given me the shield of thy salvation: and thy right hand hath holden me up, and thy gentleness hath made me great. 36. Thou hast enlarged my steps under me, that my feet did not slip. Psa. 144:1, 2.

Psa. 23:2. He maketh me to lie down in green pastures: he leadeth me beside the still waters. 3. He restoreth my soul: he leadeth me in the paths of righteousness for his name's sake.

Psa. 27:14. Wait on the LORD: be of good courage, and he shall strengthen thine heart: wait, I say, on the LORD.

Psa. 28:8. The LORD *is* their strength, and he *is* the saving strength of his anointed.

Psa. 29:11. The LORD will give strength unto his people;

Psa. 30:7. LORD, by thy favour thou hast made my mountain to stand strong: thou didst hide thy face, *and* I was troubled.

Psa. 31:24. Be of good courage, and he shall strengthen your heart, all ye that hope in the LORD.

Psa. 37:6. He shall bring forth thy righteousness as the light, and thy judgment as the noonday. 17. The LORD upholdeth the righteous. 24. Though he fall, he shall not be utterly cast down: for the LORD upholdeth *him with* his hand. 39. The salvation of the righteous *is* of the LORD: *he is* their strength in the time of trouble.

Psa. 52:8. I *am* like a green olive tree in the house of God: I trust in the mercy of God for ever and ever.

Psa. 55:22. Cast thy burden upon the LORD, and he shall sustain thee: he shall never suffer the righteous to be moved.

Psa. 61:5. Thou, O God, hast heard my vows: thou hast given *me* the heritage of those that fear thy name.

Psa. 63:8. My soul followeth hard after thee: thy right hand upholdeth me.

Psa. 66:9. Which holdeth our soul in life, and suffereth not our feet to be moved.

Psa. 68:18. Thou hast received gifts for men; yea, *for* the rebellious also, that the LORD God might dwell *among them.* 28. Thy God hath commanded thy strength: strengthen, O God, that which thou hast wrought for us. 35. The God of Israel *is* he that giveth strength and power unto *his* people.

Psa. 71:16. I will go in the strength of the Lord GOD; I will make mention of thy righteousness, *even* of thine only.

Psa. 72:6. He shall come down like rain upon the mown grass: as showers *that* water the earth. 17. *Men* shall be blessed in him: all nations shall call him blessed.

Psa. 73:23. I *am* continually with thee: thou hast holden *me* by my right hand. 26. My flesh and my heart faileth: *but* God *is* the strength of my heart, and my portion for ever.

Psa. 81:10. Open thy mouth wide, and I will fill it.

Psa. 84:5. Blessed *is* the man whose strength *is* in thee; in whose heart *are* the ways *of them.* 11. The LORD God *is* a sun and shield: the LORD will give grace and glory: no good *thing* will he withhold from them that walk uprightly.

Psa. 89:17. Thou *art* the glory of their strength: and in thy favour our horn shall be exalted.

Psa. 92:12. The righteous shall flourish like the palm tree: he shall grow like a cedar in Lebanon. 13. Those that be planted in the house of the LORD shall flourish in the courts of our God. 14. They shall still bring forth fruit in old age; they shall be fat and flourishing; Psa. 1:3.

Psa. 94:17. Unless the LORD *had been* my help, my soul had almost dwelt in silence. 18. When I said, My foot slippeth; thy mercy, O LORD, held me up.

Psa. 105:4. Seek the LORD, and his strength:

Psa. 119:32. I will run the way of thy commandments, when thou shalt enlarge my heart. 102. I have not departed from thy judgments: for thou hast taught me.

Psa. 132:15. I will abundantly bless her provision: I will satisfy her poor with bread. 16. I will also clothe her priests with salvation; and her saints shall shout aloud for joy.

Psa. 138:3. In the day when I cried thou answeredst me, *and* strengthenedst me *with* strength in my soul. 8. The LORD will perfect *that which* concerneth me: thy mercy, O LORD, *endureth* for ever: forsake not the works of thine own hands.

Psa. 146:5. Happy *is he* that *hath* the God of Jacob for his help, whose hope *is* in the LORD his God:

Prov. 10:29. The way of the LORD *is* strength to the upright:

Prov. 16:6. By the fear of the LORD *men* depart from evil.

Isa. 1:25. I will turn my hand upon thee, and purely purge away thy dross, and take away all thy tin:

Isa. 4:3. And it shall come to pass, *that he that is* left in Zion, and *he that* remaineth in Jerusalem, shall be called holy, *even* every one that is written among the living in Jerusalem: 4. When the Lord shall have washed away the filth of the daughters of Zion, and shall have purged the blood of Jerusalem from the midst thereof by the spirit of judgment, and by the spirit of burning.

Isa. 6:6. Then flew one of the seraphims unto me, having a live coal in his hand, *which* he had taken with the tongs from off the altar: 7. And he laid *it* upon my mouth, and said, Lo, this hath touched thy lips; and thine iniquity is taken away, and thy sin purged.

Isa. 26:12. LORD, thou wilt ordain peace for us: for thou also hast wrought all our works in us.

Isa. 28:6. For a spirit of judgment to him that sitteth in judgment, and for strength to them that turn the battle to the gate.

Isa. 33:5. The LORD is exalted; for he dwelleth on high: he hath filled Zion with judgment and righteousness. 6. Wisdom and knowledge shall be the stability of thy times, *and* strength of salvation: the fear of the LORD *is* his treasure.

Isa. 40:11. He shall feed his flock like a shepherd: he shall gather the lambs with his arm, and carry *them* in his bosom, *and* shall gently lead those that are with young. 29. He giveth power to the faint; and to *them that have* no might he increaseth strength. 31. They that wait upon the LORD shall renew *their* strength; they shall mount up with wings as eagles; they shall run, and not be weary; *and* they shall walk, and not faint.

Isa. 41:10. Fear thou not; for I *am* with thee: be not dismayed; for I *am* thy God:

I will strengthen thee; yea, I will help thee yea, I will uphold thee with the right hand of my righteousness. 13. For I the LORD thy God will hold thy right hand, saying unto thee, Fear not: I will help thee. 14. Fear not, thou worm Jacob, *and* ye men of Israel; I will help thee, saith the LORD, and thy redeemer, the Holy One of Israel. 17. *When* the poor and needy seek water, and *there is* none, *and* their tongue faileth for thirst, I the LORD will hear them, *I* the God of Israel will not forsake them. 18. I will open rivers in high places, and fountains in the midst of the valleys: I will make the wilderness a pool of water, and the dry land springs of water.

Isa. 44:3. I will pour water upon him that is thirsty, and floods upon the dry ground: I will pour my spirit upon thy seed, and my blessing upon thine offspring:

Isa. 45:8. Drop down, ye heavens, from above, and let the skies pour down righteousness: let the earth open, and let them bring forth salvation, and let righteousness spring up together; I the LORD have created it. 24. Surely, shall *one* say, in the LORD have I righteousness and strength: *even* to him shall *men* come;

Isa. 54:17. No weapon that is formed against thee shall prosper; and every tongue *that* shall rise against thee in judgment thou shalt condemn. This *is* the heritage of the servants of the LORD, and their righteousness *is* of me, saith the LORD.

Isa. 57:19. I create the fruit of the lips; Peace, peace to *him that is* far off, and to *him that is* near, saith the LORD; and I will heal him.

Isa. 58:8. Then shall thy light break forth as the morning, and thine health shall spring forth speedily; and thy righteousness shall go before thee; the glory of the LORD shall be thy rereward. 10. Then shall thy light rise in obscurity, and thy darkness *be* as the noon day: 11. And the LORD shall guide thee continually, and satisfy thy soul in drought, and make fat thy bones: and thou shalt be like a watered garden, and like a spring of water, whose waters fail not.

Jer. 31:12. They shall come and sing in the height of Zion, and shall flow together to the goodness of the LORD, . . . and their soul shall be as a watered garden; and they shall not sorrow any more at all. 14. I will satiate the soul of the priests with fatness, and my people shall be satisfied with my goodness, saith the LORD. 33. I will put my law in their inward parts, and write it in their hearts; and will be their God, and they shall be my people.

Ezek. 16:14. Thy renown went forth among the heathen for thy beauty: for it *was* perfect through my comeliness, which I had put upon thee. saith the Lord GOD.

Dan. 11:32. The people that do know their God shall be strong, and do *exploits*.

Hos. 6:3. Then shall we know *if* we follow on to know the LORD: his going forth is prepared as the morning; and he shall come unto us as the rain, as the latter ¹*and former* rain unto the earth.   [¹ R. V. rain that watereth]

Hos. 14:5. I will be as the dew unto Israel: he shall grow as the lily, and cast forth his roots as Lebanon. 8. Ephraim *shall say,* What have I to do any more with idols? I have heard *him,* and observed him: . . . From me is thy fruit found. *vs.* 6,7.

Hab. 3:19. The LORD God *is* my strength, and he will make my feet like hinds' *feet,* and he will make me to walk upon mine high places.

Zech. 10:12. I will strengthen them in the LORD; and they shall walk up and down in his name, saith the LORD.

Zech. 12:8. In that day shall the LORD defend the inhabitants of Jerusalem; and he that is feeble among them at that day shall be as David; and the house of David *shall be* as God, as the angel of the LORD before them.

Mal. 3:2. He *is* like a refiner's fire, and like fullers' sope: 3. He shall sit *as* a refiner and purifier of silver: and he shall purify the sons of Levi, and purge them as gold and silver, that they may offer unto the LORD an offering in righteousness.

Mal. 4:2. Unto you that fear my name shall the Sun of righteousness arise with healing in his wings;

John 1:16. Of his fulness have all we received, and grace for grace.

John 17:11. Holy Father, keep through thine own name those whom thou hast given me, that they may be one, as we *are.*

Acts 20:32. And now, brethren, I commend you to God, and to the word of his grace, which is able to build you up, and to give you an inheritance among all them which are sanctified.

Rom. 9:23. That he might make known the riches of his glory on the vessels of mercy, which he had afore prepared unto glory,

Rom. 14:4. Yea, he shall be holden up: for God is able to make him stand.

1 Cor. 12:6. There are diversities of operations, but it is the same God which worketh all in all.

1 Cor. 13:10. But when that which is perfect is come, then that which is in part shall be done away. 12. For now we see through a glass, darkly; but then face to face: now I know in part; but then shall I know even as also I am known.

1 Cor. 15:10. By the grace of God I am what I am: and his grace which *was bestowed* upon me was not in vain; but I laboured more abundantly than they all: yet not I, but the grace of God which was with me.

2 Cor. 1:21. Now he which stablisheth us with you in Christ, and hath anointed us, *is* God; 22. Who hath also sealed us, and given the earnest of the Spirit in our hearts.

2 Cor. 3:5. Not that we are sufficient of ourselves to think any thing as of ourselves; but our sufficiency *is* of God;

2 Cor. 5:5. He that hath wrought us for the selfsame thing *is* God, who also hath given unto us the earnest of the Spirit.

2 Cor. 9:8. God *is* able to make all grace abound toward you; that ye, always having all sufficiency in all *things,* may abound to every good work:

2 Cor. 10:4. The weapons of our warfare *are* not carnal, but mighty through God to the pulling down of strong holds;

Eph. 3:20. Now unto him that is able to do exceeding abundantly above all that we ask or think, according to the power that worketh in us,

Phil. 1:6. Being confident of this very thing, that he which hath begun a good work in you will perform *it* until the day of Jesus Christ:

Phil. 2:13. It is God which worketh in you both to will and to do of *his* good pleasure.

Phil. 4:7. The peace of God, which passeth all understanding, shall keep your hearts and minds through Christ Jesus. 19. My God shall supply all your need according to his riches in glory by Christ Jesus.

Col. 1:11. Strengthened with all might, according to his glorious power, unto all patience and longsuffering with joyfulness; 12. Giving thanks unto the Father, which hath made us meet to be partakers of the inheritance of the saints in light:

1 Thess. 5:24. Faithful *is* he that calleth you, who also will do *it.*

Heb. 12:10. For they verily for a few days chastened *us* after their own pleasure; but he for *our* profit, that *we* might be partakers of his holiness. 11. Now no chastening for the present seemeth to be joyous, but grievous: nevertheless afterward it yieldeth the peaceable fruit of righteousness unto them which are exercised thereby.

Jas. 1:17. Every good gift and every perfect gift is from above, and cometh down from the Father of lights, with whom is no variableness, neither shadow of turning. *v.* 18.

1 Pet. 1:5. Who are kept by the power of God through faith unto salvation ready to be revealed in the last time.

2 Pet. 1:2. Grace and peace be multiplied unto you through the knowledge of God, and of Jesus our Lord, 3. . . . His divine power hath given unto us all things that *pertain* unto life and godliness, through the knowledge of him that hath called us to glory and virtue: 4. Whereby are given unto us exceeding great and precious promises: that by these ye might be partakers of the divine nature, having escaped the corruption that is in the world through lust.

1 John 1:9. If we confess our sins, he is faithful and just to forgive us *our* sins, and to cleanse us from all unrighteousness.

1 John 4:4. Ye are of God, little children, and have overcome them: because greater is he that is in you, than he that is in the world.

Jude 1. To them that are sanctified by God the Father, and preserved in Jesus Christ, *and* called: 24. Now unto him that is able to keep you from falling, and to present *you* faultless before the presence of his glory with exceeding joy,

See REGENERATION; SANCTIFICATION.

TEMPORAL, FROM GOD: Gen. 1:30. And to every beast of the earth, and to every fowl of the air, and to every thing that creepeth upon the earth, wherein *there is* life, *I have given* every green herb for meat: and it was so.

Gen. 8:22. While the earth remaineth, seedtime and harvest, and cold and heat, and summer and winter, and day and night shall not cease.

Gen. 9:1. God blessed Noah and his sons, and said unto them, Be fruitful, and multiply, and replenish the earth. 3. Every moving thing that liveth shall be meat for you; even as the green herb have I given you all things. *v.* 2.

Gen. 22:17. In blessing I will bless thee, and in multiplying I will multiply thy seed as the stars of the heaven, and as the sand which *is* upon the sea shore; and thy seed shall possess the gate of his enemies; Gen. 26:4,5.

Gen. 28:20. And Jacob vowed a vow, saying, If God will be with me, and will keep me in this way that I go, and will give me bread to eat, and raiment to put on, 21. So that I come again to my father's house in peace; then shall the LORD be my God:

Gen. 49:24. His bow abode in strength, and the arms of his hands were made strong by the hands of the mighty *God* of Jacob; 25. *Even* by the God of thy father, who shall help thee; and by the Almighty, who shall bless thee with blessings of heaven above, blessings of the deep that lieth under, blessings of the breasts, and of the womb: *vs.* 11,12,20.

Ex. 23:22. If thou shalt indeed obey his voice, and do all that I speak; then I will be an enemy unto thine enemies, and an adversary unto thine adversaries.

Ex. 34:24. Neither shall any man desire thy land, when thou shalt go up to appear before the LORD thy God thrice in the year.

Lev. 25:20. And if ye shall say, What shall we eat the seventh year? behold, we shall not sow, nor gather in our increase: 21. Then I will command my blessing upon you in the sixth year, and it shall bring forth fruit for three years. 22. And ye shall sow the eighth year, and eat *yet* of old fruit until the ninth year; until her fruits come in ye shall eat *of* the old *store.*

Lev. 26:4. I will give you rain in due season, and the land shall yield her increase, and the trees of the field shall yield their fruit. 5. And your threshing shall reach unto the vintage, and the vintage shall reach unto the sowing time: and ye shall eat your bread to the full, and dwell in your land safely. 6. I will give peace in the land, and ye shall lie down, and none shall make *you* afraid: and I will rid evil beasts out of the land, neither shall the sword go through your land. 7. And ye shall chase your enemies, and they shall fall before you by the sword. 8. And five of you shall chase an hundred, and an hundred of you shall put ten thousand to flight: and your enemies shall fall before you by the sword. 9. For I will have respect unto you, and make you fruitful, and multiply you, and establish my covenant with you. 10. And ye shall eat old store, and bring forth the old because of the new.

Deut. 1:10. The LORD your God hath multiplied you, and, behold, ye *are* this day as the stars of heaven for multitude.

Deut. 2:7. The LORD thy God hath blessed thee in all the works of thy hand: he knoweth thy walking through this great wilderness: these forty years the LORD thy God *hath been* with thee; thou hast lacked nothing.

Deut. 4:4. Ye that did cleave unto the LORD your God *are* alive every one of you this day. *v.* 40; Num. 10:29; Deut. 5:33; 6:2–25; 12:28.

Deut. 7:13. He will love thee, and bless thee, and multiply thee: he will also bless the fruit of thy womb, and the fruit of thy land, thy corn, and thy wine, and thine oil, the increase of thy kine, and the flocks of thy sheep, in the land which he sware unto thy fathers to give thee. 14. Thou shalt be blessed above all people: there shall not be male or female barren among you, or among your cattle. 15. And the LORD will take away from thee all sickness, and will put none of the evil diseases of Egypt, which thou knowest, upon thee; *vs.* 16–24; Ex. 15: 26; 23:25,26.

Deut. 8:3. And he humbled thee, and suffered thee to hunger, and fed thee with manna, which thou knewest not, neither did thy fathers know; that he might make thee know that man doth not live by bread only, but by every *word* that proceedeth out of the mouth of the LORD doth man live. 4. Thy raiment waxed not old upon thee, neither did thy foot swell, these forty years. 5. Thou shalt also consider in thine heart, that, as a man chasteneth his son, *so* the LORD thy God chasteneth thee. 6. Therefore thou shalt keep the commandments of the LORD thy God, to walk in his ways, and to fear him. 7. For the LORD thy God bringeth thee into a good land, a land of brooks of water, of fountains and depths that spring out of valleys and hills; 8. A land of wheat, and barley, and vines, and fig trees, and pomegranates; a land of oil olive, and honey; 9. A land wherein thou shalt eat bread without scarceness, thou shalt not lack any *thing* in it; a land whose stones *are* iron, and out of whose hills thou mayest dig brass. 10. When thou hast eaten and art full, then thou shalt bless the LORD thy God for the good land which he hath given thee. 15. Who led thee through that great and terrible wilderness, *wherein were* fiery serpents, and scorpions, and drought, where *there was* no water; who brought thee forth water out of the rock of flint; 16. Who fed thee in the wilderness with manna, which thy fathers knew not, that he might humble thee, and that he might prove thee, to do thee good at thy latter end; 17. And thou say in thine heart, My power and the might of *mine* hand hath gotten me this wealth. 18. But thou shalt remember the LORD thy God: for *it is* he that giveth thee power to get wealth, that he may establish his covenant which he sware unto thy fathers, as *it is* this day. *vs.* 1,2.

Deut. 10:18. He doth execute the judgment of the fatherless and widow, and loveth the stranger, in giving him food and raiment.

Deut. 11:12. A land which the LORD thy God careth for: the eyes of the LORD thy God *are* always upon it, from the beginning of the year even unto the end of the year. *vs.* 13-15.

Deut. 12:7. Ye shall eat before the LORD your God, and ye shall rejoice in all that ye put your hand unto, ye and your households, wherein the LORD thy God hath blessed thee.

Deut. 15:4. For the LORD shall greatly bless thee in the land which the LORD thy God giveth thee *for* an inheritance to possess it: 6. For the LORD thy God blesseth thee, as he promised thee: and thou shalt lend unto many nations, but thou shalt not borrow; and thou shalt reign over many nations, but they shall not reign over thee. Deut. 26:18,19.

Deut. 28:7. The LORD shall cause thine enemies that rise up against thee to be smitten before thy face: they shall come out against thee one way, and flee before thee seven ways. 8. The LORD shall command the blessing upon thee in thy storehouses, and in all that thou settest thine hand unto; and he shall bless thee in the land which the LORD thy God giveth thee.

Deut. 29:5. I have led you forty years in the wilderness: your clothes are not waxen old upon you, and thy shoe is not waxen old upon thy foot. Deut. 8:4.

Deut. 32:13. He made him ride on the high places of the earth, that he might eat the increase of the fields; and he made him to suck honey out of the rock, and oil out of the flinty rock; 14. Butter of kine, and milk of sheep, with fat of lambs, and rams of the breed of Bashan, and goats, with the fat of kidneys of wheat; and thou didst drink the pure blood of the grape.

Josh. 1:8. This book of the law shall not depart out of thy mouth: but thou shalt meditate therein day and night, that thou mayest observe to do according to all that is written therein: for then thou shalt make thy way prosperous, and then thou shalt have good success.

Ruth 1:6. She had heard in the country of Moab how that the LORD had visited his people in giving them bread.

1 Sam. 2:7. The LORD maketh poor, and maketh rich: he bringeth low, and lifteth up. 8. He raiseth up the poor out of the dust, *and* lifteth up the beggar from the dunghill, to set *them* among princes, and to make them inherit the throne of glory:

2 Sam. 7:8. Now therefore so shalt thou say unto my servant David. Thus saith the LORD of hosts, I took thee from the sheepcote, from following the sheep, to be ruler over my people, over Israel: 9. And I was with thee withersoever thou wentest, and have cut off all thine enemies out of thy sight, and have made thee a great name, like unto the name of the great *men* that *are* in the earth. 1 Chr. 17:7,8.

1 Chr. 29:12. Both riches and honour *come* of thee, and thou reignest over all; and in thine hand *is* power and might; and in thine hand *it is* to make great, and to give strength unto all. 14. All things *come* of thee, and of thine own have we given thee. 16. O LORD our God, all this store that we have prepared to build thee an house for thine holy name *cometh* of thine hand, and *is* all thine own.

2 Chr. 1:12. Wisdom and knowledge *is* granted unto thee; and I will give thee riches, and wealth, and honour, such as none of the kings have had that *have been* before thee, neither shall there any after thee have the like.

2 Chr. 31:10. Since *the people* began to bring the offerings into the house of the LORD, we have had enough to eat, and have left plenty: for the LORD hath blessed his people; and that which is left *is* this great store.

Ezra 8:22. The hand of our God *is* upon all them for good that seek him; but his power and his wrath *is* against all them that forsake him.

Neh. 8:10. Then he said unto them, Go your way, eat the fat, and drink the sweet, and send portions unto them for whom nothing is prepared: for *this* day *is* holy unto our Lord: neither be ye sorry; for the joy of the LORD is your strength.

Job 5:10. Who giveth rain upon the earth, and sendeth waters upon the fields:

Job 12:23. He increaseth the nations, and destroyeth them: he enlargeth the nations, and straiteneth them *again.*

Job 22:18. He filled their houses with good *things:*

Job 37:6. He saith to the snow, Be thou *on* the earth; likewise to the small rain, and to the great rain of his strength. 10. By the breath of God frost is given: and the breadth of the waters is straitened. 13. He causeth it to come, whether for correction, or for his land, or for mercy. 16. Dost thou know ... 17. How thy garments *are* warm, when he quieteth the earth by the south *wind?*

Job 38:25. Who hath divided a watercourse for the overflowing of waters, or a way for the lightning of thunder; 26. To cause it to rain on the earth, *where* no man *is; on* the wilderness, wherein *there is* no man; 27. To satisfy the desolate and waste *ground;* and to cause the bud of the tender herb to spring forth? 41. Who provideth for the raven his food? when his young ones cry unto God, they wander for lack of meat. *vs.* 1–41.

Psa. 21:3. Thou preventest him with the blessings of goodness: thou settest a crown of pure gold on his head. 4. He asked life of thee, *and* thou gavest *it* him, *even* length of days for ever and ever. 5. His glory *is* great in thy salvation: honour and majesty hast thou laid upon him.

Psa. 23:1. The LORD *is* my shepherd: I shall not want. 5. Thou preparest a table before me in the presence of mine enemies: thou anointest my head with oil; my cup runneth over.

Psa. 34:10. The young lions do lack, and suffer hunger: but they that seek the LORD shall not want any good *thing.*

Psa. 36:6. O LORD, thou preservest man and beast.

Psa. 44:3. For they got not the land in possession by their own sword, neither did their own arm save them: but thy right hand, and thine arm, and the light of thy countenance, because thou hadst a favour unto them.

Psa. 65:8. Thou makest the outgoings of the morning and evening to rejoice. 9. Thou visitest the earth, and waterest it: thou greatly enrichest it with the river of God, *which* is full of water: thou preparest them corn, when thou hast so provided for it. 10. Thou waterest the ridges thereof abundantly: thou settlest the furrows thereof: thou makest it soft with showers: thou blessest the springing thereof. 11. Thou crownest the year with thy goodness; and thy paths drop fatness. *vs.* 12,13.

Psa. 68:6. God setteth the solitary in families: he bringeth out those which are bound with chains: 9. Thou, O God, didst send a plentiful rain, whereby thou didst confirm thine inheritance, when it was weary. 10. Thy congregation hath dwelt therein: thou, O God, hast prepared of thy goodness for the poor.

19. Blessed *be* the Lord, *who* daily loadeth us *with benefits, even* the God of our salvation.

Psa. 69:35. God will save Zion, and will build the cities of Judah: that they may dwell there, and have it in possession. 36. The seed also of his servants shall inherit it: and they that love his name shall dwell therein.

Psa. 81:16. He should have fed them also with the finest of the wheat: and with honey out of the rock should I have satisfied thee. *vs.* 13–15.

Psa. 85:12. Yea, the LORD shall give *that which is* good; and our land shall yield her increase.

Psa. 91:1. He that dwelleth in the secret place of the most High shall abide under the shadow of the Almighty. 2. I will say of the LORD, *He is* my refuge and my fortress: my God; in him will I trust. 3. Surely he shall deliver thee from the snare of the fowler, *and* from the noisome pestilence. 4. He shall cover thee with his feathers, and under his wings shalt thou trust: his truth *shall be thy* shield and buckler. 5. Thou shalt not be afraid for the terror by night; *nor* for the arrow *that* flieth by day: 6. *Nor* for the pestilence *that* walketh in darkness; *nor* for the destruction *that* wasteth at noonday. 7. A thousand shall fall at thy side, and ten thousand at thy right hand; *but* it shall not come nigh thee. 8. Only with thine eyes shalt thou behold and see the reward of the wicked. 9. Because thou hast made the LORD, *which is* my refuge, *even* the most High, thy habitation; 10. There shall no evil befall thee, neither shall any plague come nigh thy dwelling. 11. For he shall give his angels charge over thee, to keep thee in all thy ways. 12. They shall bear thee up in *their* hands, lest thou dash thy foot against a stone. 13. Thou shalt tread upon the lion and adder: the young lion and the dragon shalt thou trample under feet. 14. Because he hath set his love upon me, therefore will I deliver him: I will set him on high, because he hath known my name. 15. He shall call upon me, and I will answer him: I *will be* with him in trouble; I will deliver him, and honour him. 16. With long life will I satisfy him, and shew him my salvation.

Psa. 103:2. Bless the LORD, O my soul, and forget not all his benefits: 3. Who forgiveth all thine iniquities; who healeth all thy diseases; 4. Who redeemeth thy life from destruction; who crowneth thee with lovingkindness and tender mercies; 5. Who satisfieth thy mouth with good *things; so that* thy youth is renewed like the eagle's.

Psa. 104:14. He causeth the grass to grow for the cattle, and herb for the service of man: that he may bring forth food out of the earth; 15. And wine *that* maketh glad the heart of man, *and* oil to make *his* face to shine, and bread *which* strengtheneth man's heart. 27. These wait all upon thee; that thou mayest give *them* their meat in due season. 28. *That* thou givest them they gather: thou openest thine hand, they are filled with good. *vs.* 1–35.

Psa. 105:24. He increased his people greatly; and made them stronger than their enemies.

Psa. 107:35. He turneth the wilderness into a standing water, and dry ground into water-springs. 36. And there he maketh the hungry to dwell, that they may prepare a city for habitation; 37. And sow the fields, and plant vineyards, which may yield fruits of increase. 38. He blesseth them also, so that they are multiplied greatly; and suffereth not their cattle to decrease.

Psa. 111:5. He hath given meat unto them that fear him: he will ever be mindful of his covenant.

Psa. 113:9. He maketh the barren woman to keep house, *and to be* a joyful mother of children.

Psa. 115:16. The heaven, *even* the heavens, *are* the LORD'S: but the earth hath he given to the children of men.

Psa. 127:1. Except the LORD build the house, they labour in vain that build it: except the LORD keep the city, the watchman waketh *but* in vain. 2. *It is* vain for you to rise up early, to sit up late, to eat the bread of sorrows: *for* so he giveth his beloved sleep. 3. Lo, children *are* an heritage of the LORD: *and* the fruit of the womb *is his* reward. 4. As arrows *are* in the hand of a mighty man; so *are* children of the youth. 5. Happy *is* the man that hath his quiver full of them: they shall not be ashamed, but they shall speak with the enemies in the gate.

Psa. 135:7. He causeth the vapours to ascend from the ends of the earth; he maketh lightnings for the rain; he bringeth the wind out of his treasuries,

Psa. 136:25. Who giveth food to all flesh: for his mercy *endureth* for ever. *vs.* 1–26.

Psa. 144:12. That our sons *may be* as plants grown up in their youth; *that* our daughters *may be* as corner stones, polished *after* the similitude of a palace: 13. *That* our garners *may be* full, affording all manner of store: *that* our sheep may bring forth thousands and ten thousands in our streets: 14. *That* our oxen *may be* strong to labour; *that there be* no breaking in, nor going out; that *there be* no complaining in our streets. 15. Happy *is that* people, that is in such a case: *yea*, happy *is that* people, whose God *is* the LORD.

Psa. 145:15. The eyes of all wait upon thee; and thou givest them their meat in due season. 16. Thou openest thine hand, and satisfiest the desire of every living thing.

Psa. 146:5. Happy *is he* that *hath* the God of Jacob for his help, whose hope *is* in the LORD his God: 6. Which made heaven, and earth, the sea, and all that therein *is:* which keepeth truth for ever: 7. Which executeth judgment for the oppressed: which giveth food to the hungry. The LORD looseth the prisoners: 8. The LORD openeth *the eyes of* the blind: the LORD raiseth them that are bowed down: the LORD loveth the righteous: 9. The LORD preserveth the strangers; he relieveth the fatherless and widow: but the way of the wicked he turneth upside down.

Psa. 147:8. Who covereth the heaven with clouds, who prepareth rain for the earth, who maketh grass to grow upon the mountains. 9. He giveth to the beast his food, *and* to the young ravens which cry. 13. He hath strengthened the bars of thy gates; he hath blessed thy children within thee. 14. He maketh peace *in* thy borders, *and* filleth thee with the finest of the wheat.

Eccl. 2:24. *There is* nothing better for a man, *than* that he should eat and drink, and that he should make his soul enjoy good in his labour. This also I saw, that it *was* from the hand of God.

Eccl. 3:13. And also that every man should eat and drink, and enjoy the good of all his labour, it *is* the gift of God.

Eccl. 5:19. Every man also to whom God hath given riches and wealth, and hath given him power to eat thereof, and to take his portion, and to rejoice in his labour; this *is* the gift of God.

Isa. 25:4. For thou hast been a strength to the poor, a strength to the needy in his distress, a refuge from the storm, a shadow from the heat, when the blast of the terrible ones *is* as a storm *against* the wall.

Isa. 30:23. Then shall he give the rain of thy seed, that thou shalt sow the ground withal; and bread of the increase of the earth, and it shall be fat and plenteous: in that day shall thy cattle feed in large pastures. 26. Moreover the light of the moon shall be as the light of the sun, and the light of the sun shall be sevenfold, as the light of seven days, in the day that the LORD bindeth up the breach of his people, and healeth the stroke of their wound. *vs.* 24, 25.

Isa. 31:1. Woe to them that go down to Egypt for help; and stay on horses, and trust in chariots, because *they are* many; and in horsemen, because they are very strong; but they look not unto the Holy One of Israel, neither seek the LORD! 2. Yet he also *is* wise, and will bring evil, and will not call back his words: but will arise against the house of the evildoers, and against the help of them that work iniquity.

Isa. 33:15. He that walketh righteously, and speaketh uprightly; he that despiseth the gain of oppressions, that shaketh his hands from holding of bribes, that stoppeth his ears from hearing of blood, and shutteth his eyes from seeing evil; 16. He shall dwell on high: his place of defence *shall be* the munitions of rocks: bread shall be given him; his waters *shall be* sure.

Isa. 43:20. The beast of the field shall honour me, the dragons and the owls: because I give waters in the wilderness, *and* rivers in the desert, to give drink to my people, my chosen.

Isa. 48:21. They thirsted not *when* he led them through the deserts: he caused the waters to flow out of the rock for them: he clave the rock also, and the waters gushed out.

Isa. 51:2. Look unto Abraham your father, and unto Sarah *that* bare you: for I called him alone, and blessed him, and increased him.

Isa. 55:10. For as the rain cometh down, and the snow from heaven, and returneth not thither, but watereth the earth, and maketh it bring forth and bud, that it may give seed to the sower, and bread to the eater:

Jer. 5:24. Neither say they in their heart, Let us now fear the LORD our God, that giveth rain, both the former and the latter, in his season: he reserveth unto us the appointed weeks of the harvest.

Jer. 10:13. When he uttereth his voice, *there is* a multitude of waters in the heavens, and he causeth the vapours to ascend from the ends of the earth; he maketh lightnings with rain and bringeth forth the wind out of his treasures. Jer. 51:16.

Jer. 14:22. Are there *any* among the vanities of the Gentiles that can cause rain? or can the heavens give showers? *art* not thou he, O LORD our God? therefore we will wait upon thee: for thou hast made all these *things*.

Jer. 27:4. Thus saith the LORD of hosts, the God of Israel; Thus shall ye say unto your masters; 5. I have made the earth, the man and the beast that *are* upon the ground, by my great power and by my outstretched arm, and have given it unto whom it seemed meet unto me. 6. And now have I given all these lands into the hand of Nebuchadnezzar the king of Babylon, my servant; and the beasts of the field have I given him also to serve him.

Jer. 30:19. Out of them shall proceed thanksgiving and the voice of them that make merry: and I will multiply them, and they shall not be few; I will also glorify them, and they shall not be small.

Jer. 31:35. Thus saith the LORD, which giveth the sun for a light by day, *and* the ordinances of the moon and of the stars for a light by night, which divideth the sea when the waves thereof roar; The LORD of hosts *is* his name:

Ezek. 36:30. I will multiply the fruit of the tree, and the increase of the field, that ye shall receive no more reproach of famine among the heathen. 36. Then the heathen that are left round about you shall know that I the LORD build the ruined *places, and* plant that that was desolate: I the LORD have spoken *it*, and I will do *it*. 38. As the holy flock, as the flock of Jerusalem in her solemn feasts; so shall the waste cities be filled with flocks of men: and they shall know that I *am* the LORD. *vs.* 28–38.

Dan. 5:18. The most high God gave Nebuchadnezzar thy father a kingdom, and majesty, and glory, and honour:

Dan. 6:20. And when he came to the den, he cried with a lamentable voice unto Daniel: *and* the king spake and said to Daniel, O Daniel, servant of the living God, is thy God, whom thou servest continually, able to deliver thee from the lions? 22. My God hath sent his angel, and hath shut the lions' mouths, that they have not hurt me: forasmuch as before him innocency was found in me; and also before thee, O king, have I done no hurt.

Hos. 2:8. She did not know that I gave her corn, and wine, and oil, and multiplied her silver and gold, *which* they prepared for Baal.

Hos. 11:3. I taught Ephraim also to go, taking them [1] by their arms; but they knew not that I healed them. [¹ R. V. on my]

Joel 2:21. Fear not, O land; be glad and rejoice: for the LORD will do great things. 23. Be glad then, ye children of Zion, and rejoice in the LORD your God: for he hath given you the former rain moderately, and

he will cause to come down for you the rain, the former rain, and the latter rain in the first *month*. 26. Ye shall eat in plenty, and be satisfied, and praise the name of the LORD your God, that hath dealt wondrously with you: and my people shall never be ashamed.

Amos 4:7. I have withholden the rain from you, when *there were* yet three months to the harvest: and I caused it to rain upon one city, and caused it not to rain upon another city: one piece was rained upon, and the piece whereupon it rained not withered.

Jonah 4:6. And the LORD God prepared a gourd, and made *it* to come up over Jonah, that it might be a shadow over his head, to deliver him from his grief. So Jonah was exceeding glad of the gourd.

Zech. 10:1. Ask ye of the LORD rain in the time of the latter rain; *so* the LORD shall make bright clouds, and give them showers of rain, to every one grass in the field.

Mal. 3:10. Bring ye all the tithes into the storehouse, that there may be meat in mine house, and prove me now herewith, saith the LORD of hosts, if I will not open you the windows of heaven, and pour you out a blessing, that *there shall* not *be room* enough *to receive it.* 12. All nations shall call you blessed: for ye shall be a delightsome land, saith the LORD of hosts. *v.* 11.

Matt. 5:45. That ye may be the children of your Father which is in heaven: for he maketh his sun to rise on the evil and on the good, and sendeth rain on the just and on the unjust.

Matt. 6:26. Behold the fowls of the air: for they sow not, neither do they reap, nor gather into barns; yet your heavenly Father feedeth them. Are ye not much better than they? 30. Wherefore, if God so clothe the grass of the field, which to day is, and to morrow is cast into the oven, *shall he* not much more *clothe* you, O ye of little faith? 31. Therefore take no thought, saying, What shall we eat? or, What shall we drink? or, Wherewithal shall we be clothed? 32. (For after all these things do the Gentiles seek:) for your heavenly Father knoweth that ye have need of all these things. 33. But seek ye first the kingdom of God, and his righteousness; and all these things shall be added unto you.

Matt. 10:29. Are not two sparrows sold for a farthing? and one of them shall not fall on the ground without your Father.

Luke 12:22. And he said unto his disciples, Therefore I say unto you, Take no thought for your life, what ye shall eat; neither for the body, what ye shall put on. 23. The life is more than meat, and the body *is more* than raiment. 24. Consider the ravens: for they neither sow nor reap; which neither have storehouse nor barn: and God feedeth them: how much more are ye better than the fowls? 25. And which of you with taking thought can add to his stature one cubit? 26. If ye then be not able to do that thing which is least, why take ye thought for the rest? 27. Consider the lilies how they grow: they toil not, they spin not; and yet I say unto you, that Solomon in all his glory was not arrayed like one of these. 28. If then God so clothe the grass, which is to day in the field, and to morrow is cast into the oven; how much more *will he clothe* you, O ye of little faith? 29. And seek not ye what ye shall eat, or what ye shall drink, neither be ye of doubtful mind. 30. For all these things do the nations of the world seek after: and your Father knoweth that ye have need of these things. 31. But rather seek ye the kingdom of God; and all these things shall be added unto you.

John 6:31. Our fathers did eat manna in the desert; as it is written, He gave them bread from heaven to eat.

Acts 14:17. He left not himself without witness, in that he did good, and gave us rain from heaven, and fruitful seasons, filling our hearts with food and gladness.

1 Cor. 2:9. Eye hath not seen, nor ear heard, neither have entered into the heart of man, the things which God hath prepared for them that love him.

1 Cor. 16:2. Upon the first *day* of the week let every one of you lay by him in store, as [1]*God* hath prospered him. [1 R. V. he may prosper]

2 Cor. 7:6. Nevertheless God, that comforteth those that are cast down, comforted us by the coming of Titus;

2 Cor. 9:8. And God *is* able to make all grace abound toward you; that ye, always having all sufficiency in all *things*, may abound to every good work: 9. (As it is written, He hath dispersed abroad; he hath given to the poor: his righteousness remaineth for ever. 10. Now he that ministereth seed to the sower both minister bread for *your* food, and multiply your seed sown, and increase the fruits of your righteousness:)

Phil. 4:19. But my God shall supply all your need according to his riches in glory by Christ Jesus.

2 Pet. 2:7. And delivered just Lot, vexed with the filthy conversation of the wicked: 8. (For that righteous man dwelling among them, in seeing and hearing, vexed *his* righteous soul from day to day with *their* unlawful deeds:) 9. The Lord knoweth how to deliver the godly out of temptations, See GOD, GOODNESS OF, PROVIDENCE OF.

TEMPORAL, FROM GOD, EXEMPLIFIED: To Noah, at the time of the flood, Gen. 7:1; Abraham, Gen. 24:1; Isaac, Gen. 26: 12–24,28; Jacob, Gen. 35:9–15; Israelites, in Egypt, Ex. 11:3; in the wilderness, supplying water, Ex. 17:1-7; Num 20:10,11; Psa. 78:15–20; 105:41; manna, Ex. 16:14,31; Num. 11:7–9; Neh. 9:15; Psa. 78:23,24; quails, Num. 11: 31–33; Psa. 78:23–30; 105:40. To David, 2 Sam. 5:10; 1 Chr. 14:17; Obed-edom, 2 Sam. 6:11; Solomon, 1 Kin. 3:13; 1 Chr. 29:25; 2 Chr. 1:1; Elijah, fed by ravens, 1 Kin. 17: 2–7; by an angel, 1 Kin. 19:5–8. To the

widow of Zerephath, 1 Kin. 17:12–16. Hezekiah prospered, 2 Kin. 18:6,7; 2 Chr. 32:29; restored to health, 2 Kin. 20:1-7; Asa, 2 Chr. 14:6,7; Jehoshaphat, 2 Chr. 17:3–5; 20:30; Uzziah, 2 Chr. 26:5–15; Jotham, 2 Chr. 27:6; Job, Job 1:10; 42:10,12; Daniel, Dan. 1:9.

TEMPORAL, PRAYER FOR: Gen. 27:28. God give thee of the dew of heaven, and the fatness of the earth, and plenty of corn and wine: 29. Let people serve thee, and nations bow down to thee:

Gen. 28:20. And Jacob vowed a vow, saying, If God will be with me, and will keep me in this way that I go, and will give me bread to eat, and raiment to put on, 21. So that I come again to my father's house in peace; then shall the LORD be my God: *vs.*3,4.

Gen. 48:16. The Angel which redeemed me from all evil, bless the lads; and let my name be named on them, and the name of my fathers Abraham and Isaac; and let them grow into a multitude in the midst of the earth.

Deut. 1:11. (The LORD God of your fathers make you a thousand times so many more as ye *are*, and bless you, as he hath promised you!)

Deut. 26:15. Look down from thy holy habitation, from heaven, and bless thy people Israel, and the land which thou hast given us, as thou swarest unto our fathers, a land that floweth with milk and honey.

Deut. 33:11. Bless, LORD, his substance, and accept the work of his hands: smite through the loins of them that rise against him, and of them that hate him, that they rise not again. 13. Blessed of the LORD *be* his land, for the precious things of heaven, for the dew, and for the deep that coucheth beneath, 16. And for the precious things of the earth, and fulness thereof, and *for* the good will of him that dwelt in the bush: let *the blessing* come upon the head of Joseph, 24. *Let* Asher *be* blessed with children; let him be acceptable to his brethren, and let him dip his foot in oil. *vs.* 14,15.

1 Kin. 8:36. Then hear thou in heaven, and forgive the sin of thy servants, and of thy people Israel, that thou teach them the good way wherein they should walk, and give rain upon thy land, which thou hast given to thy people for an inheritance. *vs.* 35–50.

1 Chr. 4:10. Oh that thou wouldest bless me indeed, and enlarge my coast, and that thine hand might be with me, and that thou wouldest keep *me* from evil, that it may not grieve me!

1 Chr. 17:27. Let it please thee to bless the house of thy servant, that it may be before thee for ever: for thou blessest, O LORD, and *it shall be* blessed for ever.

Psa. 28:9. Save thy people, and bless thine inheritance: feed them also, and lift them up for ever.

Psa. 36:11. Let not the foot of pride come against me, and let not the hand of the wicked remove me.

Prov. 30:8. Give me neither poverty nor riches; feed me with food convenient for me:

Matt. 6:11. Give us this day our daily bread.

Rom. 1:10. Making request, if by any means now at length I might have a prosperous journey by the will of God to come unto you.

1 Thess. 3:11. Now God himself and our Father, and our Lord Jesus Christ, direct our way unto you.

3 John 2. Beloved, I wish above all things that thou mayest prosper and be in health, even as thy soul prospereth.

See AFFLICTION, PRAYER IN; PRAYER; PROSPERITY.

TEMPORAL BLESSINGS, PRAYER FOR. INSTANCES OF: Abraham, Gen. 15:2-4. Abraham's servant, Gen. 24:12. Laban, Gen. 24:60. Isaac, Gen. 25:21. Hannah, 1 Sam. 1:11. Elijah, 1 Kin. 17:20,21; 18:42,44; Jas. 5:17,18. Ezra, Ezra 8:21-23. Nehemiah, Neh. 1:11; 2:4; 6:9.

BLIND. Cruelty to, forbidden, Lev. 19:14; Deut. 27:18. Hated by David, 2 Sam. 5:8.

See BLINDNESS.

BLINDNESS. Disqualified for priestly office, Lev. 21:18. Of animals, disqualified for a sacrifice, Lev. 22.22; Deut. 15:21; Mal. 1:8. Miraculously inflicted upon the Sodomites, Gen. 19:11; Syrians, 2 Kin. 6:18-23; Saul of Tarsus, Acts 9:8,9; Elymas, Acts 13:11. Sent as a judgment, Deut. 28:28.

Miraculous healing of, Matt. 9:27-30; 11:5; 12:22; 21:14; of Bartimæus, Matt. 20:30-34; Mark 10:46-52; a man of Bethsaida, Mark 8:22-25; man born blind, John 9:1-7.

INSTANCES OF: Isaac, Gen. 27:1. Jacob, Gen. 48:10. Eli, 1 Sam. 4:15. Ahijah, 1 Kin. 14:4.

SPIRITUAL: Ex. 5:2. And Pharaoh said, Who is the LORD, that I should obey his voice to let Israel go? I know not the LORD, neither will I let Israel go.

Deut. 29:4. Yet the LORD hath not given you an heart to perceive, and eyes to see, and ears to hear, unto this day.

Deut. 32:28. For they are a nation void of counsel, neither is there any understanding in them. 29. O that they were wise, that they understood this, that they would consider their latter end!

Judg. 16:20. And he wist not that the LORD was departed from him.

Job 21:14. Therefore they say unto God, Depart from us; for we desire not the knowledge of thy ways.

Job 22:13. How doth God know? can he judge through the dark cloud? 14. Thick clouds are a covering to him, that he seeth not; and he walketh in the circuit of heaven.

Psa. 10:5. Thy judgments are far above out of his sight: 6. He hath said in his heart, I shall not be moved: for I shall never be in adversity.

Psa. 14:1. The fool hath said in his heart, There is no God. 4. Have all the workers of iniquity no knowledge?

Psa. 73:22. So foolish was I, and ignorant: I was as a beast before thee. with vs. 2-28.

Psa. 79:6. Pour out thy wrath upon the heathen that have not known thee, and upon the kingdoms that have not called upon thy name.

Psa. 82:5. They know not, neither will they understand; they walk on in darkness:

Psa. 92:6. A brutish man knoweth not; neither doth a fool understand this.

Psa. 94:7. They say, The LORD shall not see, neither shall the God of Jacob regard it. 8. Understand, ye brutish among the people: and ye fools, when will ye be wise?

Psa. 95:10. It is a people that do err in their heart, and they have not known my ways:

Psa. 119:18. Open thou mine eyes, that I may behold wondrous things out of thy law.

Prov. 1:7. Fools despise wisdom and instruction. 22. How long, ye simple ones, will ye love simplicity? and the scorners delight in their scorning, and fools hate knowledge? 29. They hated knowledge, and did not choose the fear of the LORD: 30. They would none of my counsel: they despised all my reproof.

Prov. 4:19. The way of the wicked is as darkness: they know not at what they stumble. Prov. 7:7-23.

Prov. 10:21. Fools die for want of wisdom.

Prov. 13:18. Poverty and shame shall be to him that refuseth instruction:

Prov. 14:12. There is a way which seemeth right unto a man, but the end thereof are the ways of death.

Prov. 17:16. Wherefore is there a price in the hand of a fool to get wisdom, seeing he hath no heart to it?

Prov. 19:2. That the soul be without knowledge, it is not good; 3. The foolishness of man perverteth his way: and his heart fretteth against the LORD.

Prov. 28:5. Evil men understand not judgment: but they that seek the LORD understand all things.

Eccl. 7:25. I applied mine heart to know, and to search, and to seek out wisdom, and the reason of things, and to know the wickedness of folly, even of foolishness and madness:

Isa. 1:3. The ox knoweth his owner, and the ass his master's crib: but Israel doth not know, my people doth not consider.

Isa. 5:13. Therefore my people are gone into captivity, because they have no knowledge: 20. Woe unto them that call evil good, and good evil; that put darkness for light, and light for darkness; that put bitter for sweet, and sweet for bitter!

Isa. 6:9. Hear ye indeed, but understand not; and see ye indeed, but perceive not. 10. Make the heart of this people fat, and make their ears heavy, and shut their eyes; lest they see with their eyes, and hear with their ears, and understand with their heart, and convert, and be healed. Matt. 13:14; John 12:38–41.

Isa. 9:2. The people that walked in darkness have seen a great light: they that dwell in the land of the shadow of death, upon them hath the light shined.

Isa. 26:10. Let favour be shewed to the wicked, *yet* will he not learn righteousness; in the land of uprightness will he deal unjustly, and will not behold the majesty of the Lord. 11. Lord, *when* thy hand is lifted up, they will not see:

Isa. 27:11. It *is* a people of no understanding: therefore he that made them will not have mercy on them, and he that formed them will shew them no favour.

Isa. 28:13. But the word of the Lord was unto them precept upon precept, precept upon precept; line upon line, line upon line; here a little, *and* there a little; that they might go, and fall backward, and be broken, and snared, and taken. 15. Because ye have said, We have made a covenant with death, and with hell are we at agreement; when the overflowing scourge shall pass through, it shall not come unto us: for we have made lies our refuge, and under falsehood have we hid ourselves:

Isa. 29:10. The Lord hath poured out upon you the spirit of deep sleep, and hath closed your eyes: the prophets and your rulers, the seers hath he covered. 11. And the vision of all is become unto you as the words of a book that is sealed, which *men* deliver to one that is learned, saying, Read this, I pray thee: and he saith, I cannot; for it *is* sealed: 12. And the book is delivered to him that is not learned, saying, Read this, I pray thee: and he saith, I am not learned.

Isa. 40.21. Have ye not known? have ye not heard? hath it not been told you from the beginning? have ye not understood from the foundations of the earth? 27. Why sayest thou, O Jacob, and speakest, O Israel, My way is hid from the Lord, and my judgment is passed over from my God? 28. Hast thou not known? hast thou not heard, *that* the everlasting God, the Lord, the Creator of the ends of the earth, fainteth not, neither is weary? *there is* no searching of his understanding.

Isa. 42:6. I the Lord have called thee in righteousness, and will hold thine hand, and will keep thee, and give thee for a covenant of the people, for a light of the Gentiles; 7. To open the blind eyes, to bring out the prisoners from the prison, *and* them that sit in darkness out of the prison house. 18. Hear, ye deaf; and look, ye blind, that ye may see. 19. Who *is* blind, but my servant? or deaf, as my messenger *that* I sent? who *is* blind as *he that is* perfect, and blind as the Lord's servant? 20. Seeing many things, but thou observest not; opening the ears, but he heareth not.

Isa. 44:18. They have not known nor understood: for he hath shut their eyes, that

they cannot see; *and* their hearts that they cannot understand. 19. And none considereth in his heart, neither *is there* knowledge nor understanding to say, I have burned part of it in the fire; yea, also I have baked bread upon the coals thereof; I have roasted flesh, and eaten *it:* and shall I make the residue thereof an abomination? shall I fall down to the stock of a tree? 20. He feedeth on ashes: a deceived heart hath turned him aside, that he cannot deliver his soul, nor say, Is there not a lie in my right hand?

Isa. 48:8. Yea, thou heardest not; yea, thou knewest not; yea, from that time *that* thine ear was not opened: for I knew that thou wouldest deal very treacherously, and wast called a transgressor from the womb.

Isa. 56:10. His watchmen *are* blind; they are all ignorant, they *are* all dumb dogs, they cannot bark; sleeping, lying down, loving to slumber.

Isa. 60:2. Darkness shall cover the earth, and gross darkness the people:

Jer. 2:8. The priest said not, Where *is* the Lord? and they that handle the law knew me not:

Jer. 4:22. My people *is* foolish, they have not known me; they *are* sottish children, and they have none understanding: they *are* wise to do evil, but to do good they have no knowledge.

Jer. 5:4. I said, Surely these *are* poor; they are foolish: for they know not the way of the Lord, *nor* the judgment of their God. 5. I will get me unto the great men, and will speak unto them; for they have known the way of the Lord, *and* the judgment of their God: but these have altogether broken the yoke, *and* burst the bonds. 21. Hear now this, O foolish people, and without understanding; which have eyes, and see not; which have ears, and hear not:

Jer. 8:7. Yea, the stork in the heaven knoweth her appointed times; and the turtle and the crane and the swallow observe the time of their coming; but my people know not the judgment of the Lord. 8. How do ye say, We *are* wise, and the law of the Lord *is* with us? Lo, certainly in vain made he *it;* the pen of the scribes *is* in vain. 9. The wise *men* are ashamed, they are dismayed and taken: lo, they have rejected the word of the Lord; and what wisdom *is* in them?

Jer. 9:3. They proceed from evil to evil, and they know not me, saith the Lord. 6. Through deceit they refuse to know me, saith the Lord.

Jer. 16:10. And it shall come to pass, when thou shalt shew these people all these words, and they shall say unto thee, Wherefore hath the Lord pronounced all this great evil against us? or what *is* our iniquity? or what *is* our sin that we have committed against the Lord our God?

Jer. 17:9. The heart *is* deceitful above all *things,* and desperately ˈ wicked: who can know it? [¹ R. V. sick]

Ezek. 12:2. Son of man, thou dwellest in the midst of a rebellious house, which have eyes to see, and see not; they have ears to hear, and hear not: for they *are* a rebellious house.

Dan. 12:10. None of the wicked shall understand; but the wise shall understand.

Hos. 4:1. The LORD hath a controversy with the inhabitants of the land, because *there is* no truth, no mercy, nor knowledge of God in the land. 6. My people are destroyed for lack of knowledge: because thou hast rejected knowledge, I will also reject thee, that thou shalt be no priest to me: 14. The people *that* doth not understand shall fall.

Hos. 5:4. They will not frame their doings to turn unto their God: . . . and they have not known the LORD.

Hos. 7:11. Ephraim also is like a silly dove without heart:

Amos 9:10. All the sinners of my people shall die by the sword, which say, The evil shall not overtake nor prevent us.

Mic. 4:12. They know not the thoughts of the LORD, neither understand they his counsel.

Matt. 5:15. Neither do men light a candle, and put it under a bushel, but on a candlestick; and it giveth light unto all that are in the house. 16. Let your light so shine before men, that they may see your good works, and glorify your Father which is in heaven.

Matt. 6:23. If thine eye be evil, thy whole body shall be full of darkness. If therefore the light that is in thee be darkness, how great *is* that darkness! Isa. 6:9,10.

Matt. 13:13. Therefore speak I to them in parables: because they seeing see not; and hearing they hear not, neither do they understand. 14. And in them is fulfilled the prophecy of Esaias, which saith, By hearing ye shall hear, and shall not understand; and seeing ye shall see, and shall not perceive: 15. For this people's heart is waxed gross, and *their* ears are dull of hearing, and their eyes they have closed; lest at any time they should see with *their* eyes, and hear with *their* ears, and should understand with *their* heart, and should be converted, and I should heal them. 16. But blessed *are* your eyes, for they see: and your ears, for they hear. 19. When any one heareth the word of the kingdom, and understandeth *it* not, then cometh the wicked *one*, and catcheth away that which was sown in his heart. Mark 4: 15; Luke 8:12.

Matt. 15:14. They be blind leaders of the blind. And if the blind lead the blind, both shall fall into the ditch.

Matt. 16:3. O *ye* hypocrites, ye can discern the face of the sky; but can ye not *discern* the signs of the times?

Matt. 22:29. Jesus answered and said unto them, Ye do err, not knowing the scriptures, nor the power of God. Mark 12:24.

Matt. 23:19. *Ye* fools and blind: for whether *is* greater, the gift, or the altar that sanctifieth the gift? 24. *Ye* blind guides, which strain at [out, *R. V.*] a gnat, and swallow a camel. 26. *Thou* blind Pharisee, cleanse first that *which is* within the cup and platter, that the outside of them may be clean also. *vs.* 16-24.

Mark 4:11. And he said unto them, Unto you it is given to know the mystery of the kingdom of God: but unto them that are without, all *these* things are done in parables: 12. That seeing they may see, and not perceive; and hearing they may hear, and not understand; lest at any time they should be converted, and *their* sins should be forgiven them. Luke 8:10.

Mark 6:52. They considered not *the miracle* of the loaves: for their heart was hardened.

Mark 7:18. And he saith unto them, Are ye so without understanding also? Do ye not perceive, that whatsoever thing from without entereth into the man *it* cannot defile him;

Luke 4:18. The Spirit of the Lord *is* upon me, because he hath anointed me to preach the gospel to the poor; he hath sent me to heal the brokenhearted, to preach deliverance to the captives, and recovering of sight to the blind, to set at liberty them that are bruised,

Luke 11:52. Woe unto you, lawyers! for ye have taken away the key of knowledge: ye enter not in yourselves, and them that were entering in ye hindered.

Luke 12:48. He that knew not, and did commit things worthy of stripes, shall be beaten with few *stripes*. 57. Yea, and why even of yourselves judge ye not what is right?

Luke 19:42. If thou hadst known, even thou, at least in this thy day, the things *which belong* unto thy peace! but now they are hid from thine eyes.

Luke 23:34. Then said Jesus, Father, forgive them; for they know not what they do.

John 1:5. The light shineth in darkness; and the darkness comprehended it not. 10. He was in the world, and the world was made by him, and the world knew him not.

John 3:4. Nicodemus saith unto him, How can a man be born when he is old? can he enter the second time into his mother's womb, and be born? 7. Marvel not that I said unto thee, Ye must be born again. 19. This is the condemnation, that light is come into the world, and men loved darkness rather than light, because their deeds were evil. 20. Every one that doeth evil hateth the light, neither cometh to the light, lest his deeds should be reproved. 31. He that is of the earth is earthly, and speaketh of the earth: *vs.* 9-12.

John 4:10. Jesus answered and said unto her, If thou knewest the gift of God, and who it is that saith to thee, Give me to drink; thou wouldest have asked of him, and he would have given thee living water. 22. Ye worship ye know not what: *vs.* 11,15.

John 6:52. The Jews therefore strove among themselves, saying, How can this man give us *his* flesh to eat? 60. Many therefore of his disciples, when they had heard *this*, said, This is an hard saying; who can hear it?

John 7:28. Then cried Jesus in the temple as he taught, saying, Ye both know me, and ye know whence I am: and I am not come of myself, but he that sent me is true, whom ye know not.

John 8:12: Then spake Jesus again unto them, saying, I am the light of the world: he that followeth me shall not walk in darkness, but shall have the light of life. 15. Ye judge after the flesh; 19. Ye neither know me, nor my Father: if ye had known me, ye should have known my Father also. 27. They understood not that he spake to them of the Father. 33. They answered him, We be Abraham's seed, and were never in bondage to any man: how sayest thou, Ye shall be made free? 42. Jesus said unto them, If God were your Father, ye would love me: for I proceeded forth and came from God; neither came I of myself, but he sent me. 43. Why do ye not understand my speech? *even* because ye cannot hear my word. 52. Then said the Jews unto him, Now we know that thou hast a devil. Abraham is dead, and the prophets; and thou sayest, If a man keep my saying, he shall never taste of death. 54. Jesus answered, . . . 55. Yet ye have not known him; but I know him: and if I should say, I know him not, I shall be a liar like unto you: 57. Then said the Jews unto him, Hast thou seen Abraham?

John 9:29. We know that God spake unto Moses; *as for* this *fellow*, we know not from whence he is. 30. The man answered and said unto them, Why, herein is a marvellous thing, that ye know not from whence he is, and *yet* he hath opened mine eyes. 39. Jesus said, For judgment I am come into this world, that they which see not might see; and that they which see might be made blind. *vs.* 30–38.

John 12:38. That the saying of Esaias the prophet might be fulfilled, which he spake, Lord, who hath believed our report? and to whom hath the arm of the Lord been revealed? Isa. 53:1.

John 14:17. The Spirit of truth; whom the world cannot receive, because it seeth him not, neither knoweth him:

John 15:21. But all these things will they do unto you for my name's sake, because they know not him that sent me.

John 16:2. They shall put you out of the synagogues: yea, the time cometh, that whosoever killeth you will think that he doeth God service. 3. These things will they do unto you, because they have not known the Father, nor me.

John 17:25. O righteous Father, the world hath not known thee:

Acts 3:17. Now, brethren, I wot that through ignorance ye did *it*, as *did* also your rulers.

Acts 13:27. They that dwell at Jerusalem, and their rulers, because they knew him not, nor yet the voices of the prophets which are read every sabbath day, they have fulfilled *them* in condemning *him*.

Acts 17:23. For as I passed by, and beheld your devotions, I found an altar with this inscription, TO THE UNKNOWN GOD. Whom therefore ye ignorantly worship, him declare I unto you.

Acts 19:2. We have not so much as heard whether there be any Holy Ghost.

Acts 26:18. To open their eyes, *and* to turn *them* from darkness to light, and *from* the power of Satan unto God, that they may receive forgiveness of sins, and inheritance among them which are sanctified by faith that is in me.

Rom. 1:19. That which may be known of God is manifest in them; for God hath shewed *it* unto them. 20. For the invisible things of him from the creation of the world are clearly seen, being understood by the things that are made, *even* his eternal power and Godhead; so that they are without excuse: 21. When they knew God, they glorified *him* not as God, neither were thankful; but became vain in their imaginations, and their foolish heart was darkened. 22. Professing themselves to be wise, they became fools, 28. And even as they did not like to retain God in *their* knowledge, God gave them over to a reprobate mind, to do those things which are not convenient; 29. Being filled with all unrighteousness, fornication, wickedness, covetousness, maliciousness; full of envy, murder, debate, deceit, malignity; whisperers, 30. Backbiters, haters of God, despiteful, proud, boasters, inventors of evil things, disobedient to parents, 31. Without understanding, covenantbreakers, without natural affection, implacable, unmerciful: 32. Who knowing the judgment of God, that they which commit such things are worthy of death, not only do the same, but have pleasure in them that do them.

Rom. 2:4. Despisest thou the riches of his goodness and forbearance and longsuffering; not knowing that the goodness of God leadeth thee to repentance?

Rom. 11:25. Blindness in part is happened to Israel, until the fulness of the Gentiles be come in.

1 Cor. 1:18. The preaching of the cross is to them that perish foolishness; 20. Where *is* the wise? where *is* the scribe? where *is* the disputer of this world? hath not God made foolish the wisdom of this world? 21. The world by wisdom knew not God,

1 Cor. 2:8. Which none of the princes of this world knew: for had they known *it*, they would not have crucified the Lord of glory. 14. The natural man receiveth not the things of the Spirit of God: for they are foolishness unto him: neither can he know *them*, because they are spiritually discerned. 15. He that is spiritual judgeth all things, yet he himself is judged of no man.

1 Cor. 15:34. Some have not the knowledge of God: I speak *this* to your shame.

2 Cor. 3:14. Their minds were blinded: for until this day remaineth the same vail untaken away in the reading of the old testament: 15. Even unto this day, when Moses is read, the vail is upon their heart.

2 Cor. 4:3. If our gospel be hid, it is hid to them that are lost: 4. In whom the god of this world hath blinded the minds of them which believe not, lest the light of the glorious gospel of Christ, who is the image of God, should shine unto them. 6. For God, who commanded the light to shine out of darkness, hath shined in our hearts, to *give* the light of the knowledge of the glory of God in the face of Jesus Christ.

Gal. 4:8. Howbeit then, when ye knew not God, ye did service unto them which by nature are no gods.

Eph. 4:18. Having the understanding darkened, being alienated from the life of God through the ignorance that is in them, because of the blindness of their heart:

Eph. 5:8. Ye were sometimes [once, *R. V.*] darkness, but now *are ye* light in the Lord:

Col. 1:13. Who hath delivered us from the power of darkness, and hath translated *us* into the kingdom of his dear Son:

1 Thess. 4:4. That every one of you should know how to possess his vessel in sanctification and honour; 5. Not in the lust of concupiscence. even as the Gentiles which know not God.

1 Thess. 5:4. But ye, brethren, are not in darkness. that that day should overtake you as a thief. 5. Ye are all the children of light and the children of the day: we are not of the night, nor of darkness. 6. Therefore let us not sleep, as *do* others; but let us watch and be sober. 7. For they that sleep sleep in the night; and they that be drunken are drunken in the night.

2 Thess. 1:8. In flaming fire taking vengeance on them that know not God, and that obey not the gospel of our Lord Jesus Christ:

2 Thess. 2:11. And for this cause God shall send them [1]strong delusion, that they should believe a lie: 12. That they all might be [2]damned who believed not the truth, but had pleasure in unrighteousness.

[R.V. [1]a working of error   [2]judged]

2 Tim. 3:7. Ever learning, and never able to come to the knowledge of the truth. 13. Evil men and seducers shall wax worse and worse, deceiving, and being deceived.

Tit. 1:16. They profess that they know God; but in works they deny *him*,

Heb. 5:11. Ye are dull of hearing. 12. For when for the time ye ought to be teachers, ye have need that one teach you again which *be* the first principles of the oracles of God; and are become such as have need of milk, and not of strong meat.

1 Pet. 1:14. As obedient children, not fashioning yourselves according to the former lusts in your ignorance:

1 Pet. 2:9. But ye *are* a chosen generation,

a royal priesthood. an holy nation, a peculiar people; that ye should shew forth the praises of him who hath called you out of darkness into his marvellous light:

2 Pet. 1:9. He that lacketh these things is blind, and cannot see afar off, and hath forgotten that he was purged from his old sins.

2 Pet. 3:16. As also in all *his* epistles, speaking in them of these things; in which are some things hard to be understood, which they that are unlearned and unstable wrest, as *they do* also the other scriptures, unto their own destruction.

1 John 1:6. If we say that we have fellowship with him, and walk in darkness, we lie, and do not the truth: 8. If we say that we have no sin, we deceive ourselves, and the truth is not in us.

1 John 2:4. He that saith, I know him, and keepeth not his commandments, is a liar. and the truth is not in him. 9. He that saith he is in the light, and hateth his brother, is in darkness even until now. 11. But he that hateth his brother is in darkness, and walketh in darkness, and knoweth not whither he goeth, because that darkness hath blinded his eyes.

1 John 3:1. The world knoweth us not, because it knew him not. 6. Whosoever sinneth hath not seen him, neither known him.

1 John 4:8. He that loveth not knoweth not God; for God is love.

3 John 11. He that doeth evil hath not seen God.

Jude 10. But these speak evil of those things which they know not: but what they know naturally, as brute beasts, in those things they corrupt themselves.

Rev. 3:17. Thou sayest, I am rich, and increased with goods, and have need of nothing; and knowest not that thou art wretched, and miserable, and poor, and blind, and naked:

See AFFLICTION, OBDURACY IN; MAN, IGNORANCE OF; GOD, PROVIDENCE OF, MISUNDERSTOOD.

INSTANCES OF: Israelites, Num. chapters 16; 17. Moab, 2 Kin. 3:27. Scribes, Matt. 9:3. See in the printed text above for other instances.

BLOOD. Is the life, Gen. 9:4; Lev. 17:11,14; 19:16; Deut. 12:23; Matt. 27:4,24. Forbidden to be used as food, Gen. 9:4; Lev. 3:17; 7:26,27; 17:10-14; 19:26; Deut. 12:16,23; 15:23; Ezek. 33:25; Acts 15:20,29; 21:25. Plague of, Ex. 7:17-25; Psa. 78:44; 105:29.

SACRIFICIAL: Without shedding of, no remission, Heb. 9:22. Sprinkled on altar and people, Ex. 24:6-8; Ezek. 43:18,20. Sprinkled on door posts, Ex. 12:7-23; Heb. 11:28.

OF SIN OFFERING: Sprinkled seven times before the vail. Lev. 4:5,6,17; on horns of the altar of sweet incense, and at the bottom of the altar of burnt offering. Ex. 30:10; Lev. 4:7,18,25,30; 5:9; 9:9,12. Of bullock of sin offering, put on the horns of the altar. Ex. 29:12; Lev. 8:15; poured at the bottom of the altar, Ex. 29:12; Lev. 8:15. See OFFERINGS.

OF TRESPASS OFFERING: Sprinkled on the altar, Lev. 7:2. See OFFERINGS.

OF BURNT OFFERING: Sprinkled round about, and upon the altar, Ex. 29:16; Lev. 1: 5:11,15; 8:19; Deut. 12:27. See OFFERINGS. Used for cleansing of leprosy, Lev. 14:6,7, 17,28,51,52. See OFFERINGS.

OF PEACE OFFERING: Sprinkled about the altar, Lev. 3:2,8,13; 9:19. Blood of the ram of consecration put on tip of right ear, thumb, and great toe of, and sprinkled upon, Aaron and his sons, Ex. 29:20,21; Lev. 8:23,24,30. See OFFERINGS.

OF ATONEMENT: Sprinkled on mercy seat, Lev. 16:14,15,18,19,27; 17:11. See OFFERINGS.

BLOOD OF THE COVENANT: Ex. 24:5–8; Zech. 9:11; Matt. 26:28; Heb. 9:18,19,22; 10:29; 13:20. See OFFERINGS.

FIGURATIVE: Of victories, Psa. 58:10; of oppression and cruelty, Hab. 2:12; of destruction, Ezek. 35:6; of guilt, Lev. 20:9; 2 Sam. 1:16; Ezek. 18:13; of judgments, Ezek. 16:38; Rev. 16:6.

OF SACRIFICES, TYPICAL OF THE ATONING BLOOD OF CHRIST: Heb. 9:6. Now when these things were thus ordained, the priests went always into the first tabernacle, accomplishing the service of God. 7. But into the second *went* the high priest alone once every year, not without blood, which he offered for himself, and *for* the errors of the people: 8. The Holy Ghost this signifying, that the way into the holiest of all was not yet made manifest, while as the first tabernacle was yet standing: 9. Which *was* a figure for the time then present, in which were offered both gifts and sacrifices, that could not make him that did the service perfect, as pertaining to the conscience; 10. *Which stood* only in meats and drinks, and divers washings, and carnal ordinances, imposed *on them* until the time of reformation. 11. But Christ being come an high priest of good things to come, by a greater and more perfect tabernacle, not made with hands, that is to say, not of this building; 12. Neither by the blood of goats and calves, but by his own blood he entered in once into the holy place, having obtained eternal redemption *for us*. 13. For if the blood of bulls and of goats, and the ashes of an heifer sprinkling the unclean, sanctifieth to the purifying of the flesh: 14. How much more shall the blood of Christ, who through the eternal Spirit offered himself without spot to God, purge your conscience from dead works to serve the living God? 15. And for this cause he is the mediator of the new testament, that by means of death, for the redemption of transgressions *that were* under the first testament, they which are called might receive the promise of eternal inheritance. 16. For where a testament *is*, there must also of necessity be the death of the testator. 17. For a testament *is* of force after men are dead: otherwise it is of no strength at all while the testator liveth. 18. Whereupon neither the first *testament* was dedicated without blood: 19. For when Moses had spoken every precept to all the people according to the law, he took the blood of calves and of goats, with water, and scarlet wool, and hyssop, and sprinkled both the book, and all the people, 20. Saying, This *is* the blood of the testament which God hath enjoined unto you. 21. Moreover he sprinkled with blood both the tabernacle, and all the vessels of the ministry. 22. And almost all things are by the law purged with blood; and without shedding of blood is no remission. 23. *It was* therefore necessary that the patterns of things in the heavens should be purified with these; but the heavenly things themselves with better sacrifices than these. 24. For Christ is not entered into the holy places made with hands, *which are* the figures of the true; but into heaven itself, now to appear in the presence of God for us: 25. Nor yet that he should offer himself often, as the high priest entereth into the holy place every year with blood of others; 26. For then must he often have suffered since the foundation of the world: but now once in the end of the world hath he appeared to put away sin by the sacrifice of himself. 27. And as it is appointed unto men once to die, but after this the judgment: 28. So Christ was once offered to bear the sins of many; and unto them that look for him shall he appear the second time without sin unto salvation.

OF CHRIST: Matt. 26:28. For this is my blood of the new testament, which is shed for many for the remission of sins. Mark 14:24; Luke 22:20.

John 6:53. Then Jesus said unto them, Verily, verily, I say unto you, Except ye eat the flesh of the Son of man, and drink his blood, ye have no life in you. 54. Whoso eateth my flesh, and drinketh my blood, hath eternal life; and I will raise him up at the last day. 55. For my flesh is meat indeed, and my blood is drink indeed. 56. He that eateth my flesh, and drinketh my blood, dwelleth in me, and I in him.

John 19:34. But one of the soldiers with a spear pierced his side, and forthwith came there out blood and water.

Acts 20:28. Take heed therefore unto yourselves, and to all the flock, over the which the Holy Ghost hath made you overseers, to feed the church of God, which he hath purchased with his own blood.

Rom. 3:24. Being justified freely by his grace through the redemption that is in Christ Jesus: 25. Whom God hath set forth *to be* a propitiation through faith in his blood, to declare his righteousness for the remission of sins that are past, through the forbearance of God;

Rom. 5:9. Much more then, being now justified by his blood, we shall be saved from wrath through him.

1 Cor. 10:16. The cup of blessing which we bless, is it not the communion of the blood of Christ? The bread which we break,

is it not the communion of the body of Christ?

1 Cor. 11:25. After the same manner also *he took* the cup, when he had supped, saying, This cup is the new testament in my blood: this do ye, as oft as ye drink *it*, in remembrance of me.

Eph. 1:7. In whom we have redemption through his blood, the forgiveness of sins, according to the riches of his grace;

Eph. 2:13. But now in Christ Jesus ye who sometimes were far off are made nigh by the blood of Christ. 16. And that he might reconcile both unto God in one body by the cross, having slain the enmity thereby:

Col. 1:14. In whom we have redemption [1] through his blood, *even* the forgiveness of sins: 20. And, having made peace through the blood of his cross, by him to reconcile all things unto himself; by him, *I say*, whether *they be* things in earth, or things in heaven.   [1 Omitted in R. V.]

Heb. 9:12. Neither by the blood of goats and calves, but by his own blood he entered in once into the holy place, having obtained eternal redemption *for us*. 13. For if the blood of bulls and of goats, and the ashes of an heifer sprinkling the unclean, sanctifieth to the purifying of the flesh: 14. How much more shall the blood of Christ, who through the eternal Spirit offered himself without spot to God, purge your conscience from dead works to serve the living God?

Heb. 10:19. Having therefore, brethren, boldness to enter into the holiest by the blood of Jesus, 20. By a new and living way, which he hath consecrated for us, though the veil, that is to say, his flesh; 29. Of how much sorer punishment, suppose ye, shall he be thought worthy, who hath trodden under foot the Son of God, and hath counted the blood of the covenant, wherewith he was sanctified, an unholy thing, and hath done despite unto the Spirit of grace?

Heb. 12:24. And to Jesus the mediator of the new covenant, and to the blood of sprinkling, that speaketh better things than *that* of Abel.

Heb. 13:12. Wherefore Jesus also, that he might sanctify the people with his own blood, suffered without the gate. 20. Now the God of peace, that brought again from the dead our Lord Jesus, that great shepherd of the sheep, through the blood of the everlasting covenant,

1 Pet. 1:2. Elect according to the foreknowledge of God the Father, through sanctification of the Spirit, unto obedience and sprinkling of the blood of Jesus Christ: 18. Forasmuch as ye know that ye were not redeemed with corruptible things, *as* silver and gold, from your vain conversation *received* by tradition from your fathers; 19. But with the precious blood of Christ, as of a lamb without blemish and without spot:

1 John 1:7. But if we walk in the light, as he is in the light, we have fellowship one with another, and the blood of Jesus Christ his Son cleanseth us from all sin.

1 John 5:6. This is he that came by water and blood, *even* Jesus Christ; not by water only, but by water and blood. 8. There are three that bear witness in earth, the spirit, and the water, and the blood: and these three agree in one.

Rev. 1:5. Unto him that loved us, and washed us from our sins in his own blood, 6. And hath made us kings and priests unto God and his Father; to him *be* glory and dominion for ever and ever.

Rev. 5:9. And they sung a new song, saying, Thou art worthy to take the book, and to open the seals thereof: for thou wast slain, and hast redeemed us to God by thy blood out of every kindred, and tongue, and people, and nation;

Rev. 7:14. And he said to me, These are they which came out of great tribulation, and have washed their robes, and made them white in the blood of the Lamb.

Rev. 12:11. And they overcame him by the blood of the Lamb, and by the word of their testimony;

See ATONEMENT; JESUS, MISSION OF, SUFFERINGS OF.

BLUE. See COLOR.

BLUSHING, with shame, Ezra 9:6; Jer. 6:15; 8:12.

BOANERGES, surname of the sons of Zebedee, Mark 3:17.

BOAR, WILD, Psa. 80:13. See SWINE.

BOASTING. Prov. 20:14; 25:14; 27:1; Isa. 10:15; Jer. 9:23; Rom. 1: 30; Jas. 3:5; 4:16. Of evil, Psa. 52:1.

INSTANCES OF: Goliath, 1 Sam. 17. Benhadad, 1 Kin. 20:10. Sennacherib, 2 Kin. 18:19; Isa. 10:8–15. The disciples, Luke 10:17, with *v*. 20.

SPIRITUAL: Psa. 49:6. They that trust in their wealth, and boast themselves in the multitude of their riches; 7. None *of them* can by any means redeem his brother, nor give to God a ransom for him: 8. (For the redemption of their soul *is* precious, and it ceaseth for ever:) 9. That he should still live for ever, *and* not see corruption.

Psa. 52:1. Why boastest thou thyself in mischief, O mighty man? the goodness of God *endureth* continually.

Psa. 94:4. *How long* shall they utter *and* speak hard things? *and* all the workers of iniquity boast themselves?

Rom. 3:27. Where *is* boasting then? It is excluded. By what law? of works? Nay: but by the law of faith. *vs*. 1–31.

Rom. 11:17. And if some of the branches be broken off, and thou, being a wild olive tree, wert graffed in among them, and with them partakest of the root and fatness of the olive tree; 18. Boast not against the branches. But if thou boast, thou bearest not the root, but the root thee. 19. Thou wilt say then, The branches were broken off, that I might be graffed in. 20. Well; because of unbelief they were broken off, and thou standest by faith. Be not high-minded, but fear: 21. For if God spared not the natural branches, *take heed* lest he also spare not thee.

1 Cor. 1:29. That no flesh should glory in his presence. *vs.* 17-31.

1 Cor. 4:6. And these things, brethren, I have in a figure transferred to myself and *to* Apollos for your sakes; that ye might learn in us not to think *of men* above that which is written, that no one of you be puffed up for one against another. 7. For who maketh thee to differ *from another?* and what hast thou that thou didst not receive? now if thou didst receive *it,* why dost thou glory, as if thou hadst not received *it?*

2 Cor. 10:12. For we dare not make ourselves of the number, or compare ourselves with some that commend themselves: but they measuring themselves by themselves, and comparing themselves among themselves, are not wise. 13. But we will not boast of things without *our* measure, but according to the measure of the rule which God hath distributed to us, a measure to reach even unto you. 14. For we stretch not ourselves beyond *our measure,* as though we reached not unto you: for we are come as far as to you also in *preaching* the gospel of Christ: 15. Not boasting of things without *our* measure, *that is,* of other men's labours; but having hope, when your faith is increased, that we shall be enlarged by you according to our rule abundantly, 16. To preach the gospel in the *regions* beyond you, *and* not to boast in another man's line of things made ready to our hand. 17. But he that glorieth, let him glory in the Lord. 18. For not he that commendeth himself is approved, but whom the Lord commendeth.

Eph. 2:8. For by grace are ye saved through faith; and that not of yourselves: *it is* the gift of God: 9. Not of works, lest any man should boast. 10. For we are his workmanship, created in Christ Jesus unto good works, which God hath before ordained that we should walk in them.

BOAT. See SHIP.

BOAZ. 1. An ancestor of Jesus, Matt. 1:5; Luke 3:32. History of, Ruth, chapters 2-4.

2. One of the brazen pillars of the temple, 1 Kin. 7:21; 2 Chr. 3:17.

BOCHERU, son of Azel, 1 Chr. 8:38; 9:44.

BOCHIM, a place W. of Jordan, near Gilgal, Judg. 2:1,5.

BODY, called HOUSE, 2 Cor. 5:1; HOUSE OF CLAY, Job 4:19; THE TEMPLE OF GOD, 1 Cor. 3:16; 6:15,19.

Corruptible, Job 17:14; 1 Cor. 15:53,54. Resurrection of, 1 Cor. 15:19-54. See RESURRECTION.

BOHAN, a Reubenite, Josh. 15:6; 18:17.

BOIL, a tumor. Plague of Egyptians, Ex. 9:9,10; Deut. 28:27,35; of the Philistines [*R. V.,* tumors], 1 Sam. 5:6,9; 1 Sam. 6:5. Of Hezekiah, healed, 2 Kin. 20:7; Isa. 38:21. Of Job, Job 2:7,8. Levitical ceremonies prescribed for, Lev. 13:18-23.

BOILING POT, parable of, Ezek. 24:3-5.

BOLDNESS. OF THE RIGHTEOUS: Prov. 14:26. In the fear of the LORD *is* strong confidence: and his children shall have a place of refuge.

Prov. 28:1. The wicked flee when no man pursueth: but the righteous are bold as a lion.

Eph. 3:12. In whom we have boldness and access with confidence by the faith of him.

Heb. 4:16. Let us therefore come boldly unto the throne of grace, that we may obtain mercy, and find grace to help in time of need.

Heb. 10:19. Having therefore, brethren, boldness to enter into the holiest by the blood of Jesus,

Heb. 13:6. So that we may boldly say, The Lord *is* my helper, and I will not fear what man shall do unto me.

1 John 2:28. And now, little children, abide in him; that, when he shall appear, we may have confidence, and not be ashamed before him at his coming.

1 John 4:17. Herein is our love made perfect, that we may have boldness in the day of judgment: because as he is, so are we in this world.

INSTANCES OF, IN PRAYER: Abraham, Gen. 18:23-32; Moses, Ex. 33:12-18.

See COURAGE.

BOLT, FIERY, Hab. 3:5.

BOND, to keep the peace, Acts 17:9.

BONDAGE, of Israelites in Egypt, Ex. 1:14; 2:23; 6:6; in PERSIA, Ezra 9:9.

See EMANCIPATION; SERVANT.

BONDMAN. See SERVANT.

BONES. Vision of the dry, Ezek. 37:1-14. None of Christ's broken, Psa. 34:20; John 19:36.

BONNET, a turban. Worn by priests, Ex. 28:40; 29:9; 39:28; Lev. 8:13; Ezek. 44:18; by women, Isa. 3:20.

See DRESS.

BOOK. Genealogies kept in, Gen. 5:1. Law of Moses written in, Num. 5:23; Deut. 17:18; 31:9,24,26 ; 2 Kin. 22:8. Topography of Palestine, recorded in, Josh. 18:9.

Chronicles of the times kept in: By Jasher, Josh. 10:13; 2 Sam. 1:18; Samuel, Nathan, and Gad, 1 Sam. 10:25; 1 Chr. 29:29; Iddo, 2 Chr. 12:15; 13:22; Isaiah, 2 Chr. 26:22; 32:32; Isa. 8:1. Of the kings of Judah and Israel: Of David, 1 Chr. 27:24; Solomon, 1 Kin. 11:41; Jehu, 2 Chr. 20:34; of other kings, 2 Chr. 24: 27; 16:11; 25:26; 27:7; 28:26; 35:27; 36:8; of the kings of Israel, 1 Kin. 14:19; 2 Chr. 20:34; 33: 18. Other records kept in, Ezra 4:15; 6:1,2: Esth. 6:1; 9:32; Jer. 32:12; Acts 19:19.

Prophecies written in, by Jeremiah, Jer. 25:13; 30:2; 45:1; 51:60,63; Dan. 9:2. Other prophecies written in, 2 Chr. 33:18,19. Lamentations written in, 2 Chr. 35:25. Numerous, Eccl. 12:12. Eating of, Jer. 15:16; Ezek. 2:8-10; 3:1-3; Rev. 10:2-10. Of magic, Acts 19:19.

Paul's left at Troas, 2 Tim. 4:13.

Made in a roll, Jer. 36:4; Zech. 5:1. Sealed, Isa. 29:11; Dan. 12:4; Rev. 5:1-5.

Kirjath-jearim was called Kirjath-sepher, which signifies a city of books, Josh. 15:15, 16; Judg. 1:11,12.

OF LIFE: Ex. 32:32. Yet now, if thou wilt forgive their sin—; and if not, blot me, I pray thee, out of thy book which thou hast written. 33. And the LORD said unto Moses, Whosoever hath sinned against me, him will I blot out of my book.

Psa. 69:28. Let them be blotted out of the book of the living, and not be written with the righteous.

Psa. 87:6. The LORD shall count, when he writeth up the people, *that* this *man* was born there.

Dan. 12:1. And at that time shall Michael stand up, the great prince which standeth for the children of thy people: and there shall be a time of trouble, such as never was since there was a nation *even* to that same time: and at that time thy people shall be delivered, every one that shall be found written in the book.

Luke 10:20. Notwithstanding in this rejoice not, that the spirits are subject unto you; but rather rejoice, because your names are written in heaven.

Phil. 4:3. I entreat thee also, true yokefellow, help those women which laboured with me in the gospel, with Clement also, and *with* other my fellowlabourers, whose names *are* in the book of life.

Rev. 3:5. He that overcometh, the same shall be clothed in white raiment; and I will not blot out his name out of the book of life, but I will confess his name before my Father, and before his angels.

Rev. 13:8. And all that dwell upon the earth shall worship him, whose names are not written in the book of life of the Lamb slain from the foundation of the world.

Rev. 17:8. And they that dwell on the earth shall wonder, whose names were not written in the book of life from the foundation of the world, when they behold the beast that was, and is not, and yet is.

Rev. 20:12. And I saw the dead, small and great, stand before God; and the books were opened: and another book was opened, which is *the book* of life: and the dead were judged out of those things which were written in the books, according to their works. 15. And whosoever was not found written in the book of life was cast into the lake of fire.

Rev. 21:27. And there shall in no wise enter into it any thing that defileth, neither *whatsoever* worketh abomination, or *maketh* a lie: but they which are written in the Lamb's book of life.

Rev. 22:19. And if any man shall take away from the words of the book of this prophecy, God shall take away his part out of the *book* of life, and out of the holy city, and *from* the things which are written in this book.   [* R. V. tree]

OF REMEMBRANCE: Psa. 56:8. Thou tellest my wanderings: put thou my tears into thy bottle: *are they* not in thy book?

Psa. 139:16. Thine eyes did see my substance, yet being unperfect; and in thy book all *my members* were written, *which* in continuance were fashioned, when *as yet there was* none of them.

Mal. 3:16. Then they that feared the LORD spake often one to another: and the LORD hearkened, and heard *it*, and a book of remembrance was written before him for them that feared the LORD, and that thought upon his name.

BOOTH. Made of boughs, Jonah 4:5; made for cattle, Gen. 33:17; watchmen, Job 27:18; Isa. 1:8; 24:20. Prescribed for the Israelites to dwell in, during the Feast of Tabernacles, to celebrate their wanderings in the wilderness, Lev. 23:40–43; Neh. 8:15,16.

BOOZ. See BOAZ.

BORING THE EAR, a token of servitude for life, Ex. 21:6.

BORROWING. Ex. 22:14. And if a man borrow *ought* of his neighbour, and it be hurt, or die, the owner thereof *being* not with it, he shall surely make *it* good. 15. *But* if the owner thereof *be* with it, he shall not make *it* good: if it *be* an hired *thing*, it came for his hire.

Neh. 5:1. And there was a great cry of the people and of their wives against their brethren the Jews. 2. For there were that said, We, our sons, and our daughters, *are* many: therefore we take up corn *for them*, that we may eat, and live. 3. *Some* also there were that said, We have mortgaged our lands, vineyards, and houses, that we might buy corn, because of the dearth. 4. There were also that said, We have borrowed money for the king's tribute, *and that upon* our lands and vineyards. 5. Yet now our flesh *is* as the flesh of our brethren, our children as their children: and, lo, we bring into bondage our sons and our daughters to be servants, and *some* of our daughters are brought unto bondage *already:* neither *is it* in our power to redeem them; for other men have our lands and vineyards. 6. And I was very angry when I heard their cry and these words. 7. Then I consulted with myself, and I rebuked the nobles, and the rulers, and said unto them, Ye exact usury, every one of his brother. And I set a great assembly against them. 8. And I said unto them, We after our ability have redeemed our brethren the Jews, which were sold unto the heathen; and will ye even sell your brethren? or shall they be sold unto us? Then held they their peace, and found nothing *to answer.* 9. Also I said, It *is* not good that ye do: ought ye not to walk in the fear of our God because of the reproach of the heathen our enemies? 10. I likewise, *and* my brethren, and my servants, might exact of them money and corn: I pray you, let us leave off this usury. 11. Restore, I pray you, to them, even this day, their lands, their vineyards, their oliveyards, and their houses, also the hundredth *part* of the money, and of the corn, the wine, and the oil, that ye exact of them. 12. Then said they, We will restore *them*, and will require nothing of them; so will we do as thou sayest. Then I called the priests, and took an oath of them, that they should do according to this promise. 13. Also I shook my lap, and said, So God shake out every man from his house, and from his labour, that performeth not this promise, even thus be he shaken out, and emptied. And all the congregation said, Amen, and praised the LORD. And the people did according to this promise.

Psa. 37:21. The wicked borroweth, and payeth not again:

Prov. 22:7. The rich ruleth over the poor, and the borrower *is* servant to the lender.

Matt. 5:42. Give to him that asketh thee, and from him that would borrow of thee turn not thou away.

See LENDING; INTEREST.

INSTANCES OF: Israelites from the Egyptians, Ex. 3:22; 11:2; 12:35.

Borrowing trouble, see TROUBLE, BORROWING.

BOSCATH. See BOZKATH.

BOSOR. See BEOR; BOZRAH.

BOSS, of a shield, Job 15:26.

BOTANY. Laws of nature in the vegetable kingdom uniform in action, Matt. 7:16-18,20; Luke 6:43,44; 1 Cor. 15:36-38; Gal. 6:7. Lily, beauty of, Matt. 6:28,29. He that soweth sparingly shall reap also sparingly, 2 Cor. 9:6.

See ALGUM; ALMOND; ALOE; ANISE; APPLE; ASH; BALM; BARLEY; BAY; BEAN; BOX; BRAMBLE; BULRUSH; CAMPHIRE; CANE; CASSIA; CEDAR; CHESTNUT; CINNAMON; COCKLE; CORIANDER; CORN; CUCUMBER; CUMMIN; CYPRESS; DATE; EBONY; ELM; FIG TREE; FIR TREE; FITCH; FLAG; FLAX; FRANKINCENSE; GALBANUM; GALL; GARLIC; GOPHERWOOD; GOURD; GRASS; HAZEL; HEATH; HEMLOCK; HUSK; HYSSOP; JUNIPER; LEEKS; LENTILE; LILY; MALLOW; MANDRAKE; MELON; MILLET; MINT; MULBERRY; MUSTARD; MYRRH; MYRTLE; NETTLE; NUT; OAK; OLIVE; ONION; PALM; PINE; POMEGRANATE; POPLAR; REED; ROSE; RUE; RYE; SAFFRON; SHITTIM; SPIKENARD; STACTE; SYCAMINE; SYCAMORE; TARE; TEIL; THISTLE; THORN; THYINE; VINE; WHEAT; WILLOW; WORMWOOD.

BOTANICAL GARDENS [park, probably], Eccl. 2:5,6, with 1 Kin. 4:33; 10:22.

BOTCH. See BOIL.

BOTTLE, Gen. 21:14. Made of skins, Josh. 9:4,13; Job 32:19; Psa. 119:83; Matt. 9:17; Mark 2:22; Luke 5:37,38; of clay, Isa. 30:14; Jer. 19:1,10; 48:12. Used as a lachrymatory, Psa. 56:8.

See PITCHER.

BOW. 1. A WEAPON: Gen. 21:16,20. Made of brass [*R. V.*], 2 Sam. 22:35; Job 20:24; Psa. 18:34; of wood, Ezek. 39:9. Used in war, Isa. 13:18; Lam. 2:4; Ezek. 39:3. Used by the Elamites, Jer. 49:35. David instructed the Israelites in the use of, by writing war song to, 2 Sam. 1:18. Used in hunting.

See ARCHERY; ARROW.

FIGURATIVE: Gen. 49:24; Job 16:13; 29:

20; Psa. 78:57; Lam. 3:12; Hos. 1:5; Hab. 3:9; Rev. 6:2.

2. **A TOKEN IN THE CLOUDS:** Gen. 9:8. And God spake unto Noah, and to his sons with him, saying, 9. And I, behold, I establish my covenant with you, and with your seed after you; 10. And with every living creature that *is* with you, of the fowl, of the cattle, and of every beast of the earth with you; from all that go out of the ark, to every beast of the earth. 11. And I will establish my covenant with you; neither shall all flesh be cut off any more by the waters of a flood; neither shall there any more be a flood to destroy the earth. 12. And God said, This *is* the token of the covenant which I make between me and you and every living creature that *is* with you, for perpetual generations: 13. I do set my bow in the cloud, and it shall be for a token of a covenant between me and the earth. 14. And it shall come to pass, when I bring a cloud over the earth, that the bow shall be seen in the cloud: 15. And I will remember my covenant, which *is* between me and you and every living creature of all flesh; and the waters shall no more become a flood to destroy all flesh. 16. And the bow shall be in the cloud; and I will look upon it, that I may remember the everlasting covenant between God and every living creature of all flesh that *is* upon the earth. 17. And God said unto Noah, This *is* the token of the covenant, which I have established between me and all flesh that *is* upon the earth.

Ezek. 1:28. As the appearance of the bow that is in the cloud in the day of rain, so *was* the appearance of the brightness round about. This *was* the appearance of the likeness of the glory of the LORD. And when I saw *it*, I fell upon my face, and I heard a voice of one that spake.

Rev. 4:3. And he that sat was to look upon like a jasper and a sardine stone: and *there was* a rainbow round about the throne, in sight like unto an emerald.

Rev. 10:1. And I saw another mighty angel come down from heaven, clothed with a cloud: and a rainbow *was* upon his head, and his face *was* as it were the sun, and his feet as pillars of fire:

BOWELS. Diseased, 2 Chr. 21:15-20. Judas', gushed out, Acts 1:18.

FIGURATIVE: Of the sensibilities, Gen. 43:30; 1 Kin. 3:26; Job 30:27; Psa. 22:14; Song 5:4; Jer. 4:19; 31:20; Lam. 1:20; Phil. 1:8; 2:1; Col. 3:12; 1 John 3:17.

See HEART.

BOWING, in worship, 2 Chr. 7:3. See WORSHIP, ATTITUDES IN.

BOWL. Made of gold: For the tabernacle, Ex. 25:29; 37:16; temple, 1 Kin. 7:50; 1 Chr. 28:17; 2 Chr. 4:8; of silver, Num. 4:7; 7:13, 19,25,31,37,43,49,55,61,67,73,79,84. Stamped "Holiness to the Lord," Zech. 14:20,21.

See BASIN.

FIGURATIVE: Eccl. 12:6.

BOX. For oil, 2 Kin. 9:1-3. Made of

alabaster, Matt. 26:7; Mark 14:3; Luke 7:37.

BOXING. Figurative, 1 Cor. 9:26 [R. V.].

BOX TREE, Isa. 41:19; 60:13.

BOZEZ, a rock near Gibeah, 1 Sam. 14:4.

BOZKATH, a city of Judah, Josh. 15: 39; 2 Kin. 22:1.

BOZRAH. 1. A city of Edom, Gen. 36: 33. Sheep of, Mic. 2:12. Prophecies concerning, Isa. 34:6; 63:1; Jer. 49:13,22; Amos 1:12.
2. A town of Moab, Jer. 48:24.

BRACELET. Present of, Gen. 24:22. Worn by women, Gen. 24:30; Isa. 3:19; by men, Gen. 38:18,25. Dedicated to the tabernacle, Ex. 35:22; Num. 31:50. Taken as spoils, Num. 31:50; 2 Sam. 1:10.

FIGURATIVE: Ezek. 16:11.

BRAMBLE, Isa. 34:13; Luke 6:44. Allegory of, Judg. 9:14,15.

BRANCH, FIGURATIVE: Prov. 11:28; Hos. 14:6; Isa. 60:21; John 15:2–5. Pruning of, Isa. 18:5; Dan. 4:14; John 15:6; Rom. 11: 17,21. Fruitless, cut off, John 15:2,6. A title of Christ, Psa. 80:15; Isa. 4:2; 11:1; Jer. 23:5; 33:15; Zech. 3:8; 6:12. Symbolic name of Joshua, Zech. 6:12.

See Grafting.

BRASS, or more probably Copper. Smelted, Ezek. 22:20; Job 28:2. A mineral of Canaan, Deut. 8:9; Josh. 22:8; of Syria, 2 Sam. 8:8. Tyrians traded in, Ezek. 27:13. Abundance of, for the temple, 1 Kin. 7:47; 1 Chr. 22:14. Articles made of: altar, vessels, and other articles of the tabernacle and temple, Ex. 38:28–31; 1 Kin. 7:14–47; Ezra 8: 27; cymbals, 1 Chr. 15:19; trumpets, 1 Cor. 13:1; armor, 1 Sam. 17:5,6; 2 Chr. 12:10; bows, see Bows; fetters, Judg. 16:21; 2 Kin. 25:7; gates, Psa. 107:16; Isa. 45:2; bars, 1 Kin. 4:13; idols, Dan. 5:4; Rev. 9:20; mirrors, Ex. 38:8; household vessels, Mark 7:4; money, Matt. 10:9; Mark 12:41 [marg.].

Workers in: Tubal-cain, Gen. 4:22; Hiram, 1 Kin. 7:14; Alexander, 2 Tim. 4:14.

See Brazier; Copper; Molding.

FIGURATIVE: Lev. 26:19; Deut. 33:25; Isa. 48:4; Jer. 1:18; Ezek. 1:7; Dan. 2:32,39; 7:19; 10:6; Zech. 6:1; Rev. 1:15.

BRAVERY. See Boldness; Courage.

BRAY, to pound, Prov. 27:22.

BRAZEN SEA. See Laver.

BRAZEN SERPENT. Made by Moses for the healing of the Israelites, Num. 21:9. Worshiped by Israelites, 2 Kin. 18:4. A symbol of Christ, John 3:14,15.

BRAZIER. 1. An artificer in brass and copper, Gen. 4:22; 2 Tim. 4:14.
2. A utensil used for warming houses, Jer. 36:22–24.

BREAD. Called the Staff of Life, Ezek. 4:16; 5:16; 14:13.

Kinds of: Bread of affliction, 1 Kin. 22:27; Psa. 127:2; Hos. 9:4; Isa. 30:20; leavened, Lev. 7:13; 23:17; Hos. 7:4; Amos 4:5; Matt. 13:33; unleavened, Gen. 19:3; Ex. 29:2; Judg. 6:19; 1 Sam. 28:24.

Made of wheat flour, Ex. 29:2; 1 Kin. 4:22;

5:11; Psa. 81:16; manna, Num. 11:8; **meal, 1** Kin. 17:12; barley, Judg. 7:13.

How Prepared: Mixed with oil, Ex. 29:2, 23; honey, Ex. 16:31; with leaven, or ferment, see leavened, in paragraph above. also see Leaven, Kneaded, Gen. 18:6; Ex. 8:3; 12:34; 1 Sam. 28:24; 2 Sam. 13:8; Jer. 7: 18; Hos. 7:4. Made into loaves, 1 Sam. 10:3; 17:17; 25:18; 1 Kin. 14:3; Mark 8:14; cakes, 2 Sam. 6:19; 1 Kin. 17:12; wafers, Ex. 16:21; 29:23; cracknels, 1 Kin. 14:3. Baked in ovens, Ex. 8:3; Lev. 2:4; 7:9; 11:35; 26:26; Hos. 7:4; in pans, Lev. 2:5,7; 2 Sam. 13:6–9; on hearths, Gen. 18:6; on coals, 1 Kin. 19:6; Isa. 44:19; John 21:9.

Made by men, Gen. 40:2; women, Lev. 26:26; 1 Sam. 8:13, Jer. 7:18. Traffic in, Jer. 37:21; Mark 6:37.

Sacrificed, Lev. 21:6,8,17,21,22; 22:25; 1 Sam. 2:36; 2 Kin. 23:9. By idolaters, Jer. 7:18; 44:19.

See Shewbread; Offerings.

FIGURATIVE: Isa. 55:2; 1 Cor. 10:17; 2 Cor. 9:10. Christ, John 6:32–35.

SYMBOLICAL: Of the body of Christ, Matt. 26:26; Acts 20:7; 1 Cor. 11:23,24.

BREASTPLATE. 1. For high priest, Ex. 25:7. Directions for the making of, Ex. 28:15–30. Made by Bezaleel, Ex. 39:8,21. Freewill offering of materials for, Ex. 35:9, 27. Worn by Aaron, Ex. 29:5; Lev. 8:8.
2. Armor for soldiers, Rev. 9:9,17.

FIGURATIVE: Isa. 59:17. For he put on righteousness as a breastplate, and an helmet of salvation upon his head;

Eph. 6:14. Stand therefore, having your loins girt about with truth, and having on the breastplate of righteousness;

1 Thess. 5:8. But let us, who are of the day, be sober, putting on the breastplate of faith and love; and for an helmet the hope of salvation.

BREATH. Of life, Gen. 2:7; 7:22; Acts 17:25. Of God, 2 Sam. 22:16; Job 4:9; 15:30; 33:4; 37:10; Psa. 18:15; 33:6; Isa. 30:33.

FIGURATIVE: Ezek. 37:9.

BREECHES, for the priests, Ex. 28:42; 39:28; Lev. 6:10; 16:4; Ezek. 44:18.

BRIBERY. Ex. 23:8. And thou shalt take no gift: for the gift blindeth the wise, and perverteth the words of the righteous.

Deut. 16:18. Judges and officers shalt thou make thee in all thy gates, which the Lord thy God giveth thee, throughout thy tribes: and they shall judge the people with just judgment. 19. Thou shalt not wrest judgment; thou shalt not respect persons, neither take a gift: for a gift doth blind the eyes of the wise, and pervert the words of the righteous.

Deut. 27:25. Cursed *be* he that taketh reward to slay an innocent person.

1 Sam. 8:1. And it came to pass, when Samuel was old, that he made his sons judges over Israel. 3. And his sons walked not in his ways, but turned aside after lucre, and took bribes, and perverted judgment.

Job 15:34. Fire shall consume the tabernacles of bribery.

Psa. 26:9. Gather not my soul with sinners, nor my life with bloody men: 10. In whose hands is mischief, and their right hand is full of bribes.

Prov. 15:27. He that is greedy of gain troubleth his own house; but he that hateth gifts shall live.

Prov. 17:8. A gift is as a precious stone in the eyes of him that hath it: whithersoever it turneth, it prospereth. 23. A wicked man taketh a gift out of the bosom to pervert the ways of judgment.

Prov. 18:16. A man's gift maketh room for him, and bringeth him before great men.

Prov. 21:14. A gift in secret pacifieth anger: and a reward in the bosom strong wrath.

Prov. 25:14. Whoso boasteth himself of a false gift is like clouds and wind without rain.

Prov. 28:21. To have respect of persons is not good: for for a piece of bread that man will transgress.

Prov. 29:4. The king by judgment establisheth the land: but he that receiveth gifts overthroweth it.

Eccl. 7:7. A gift destroyeth the heart.

Isa. 1:23. Thy princes are rebellious, and companions of thieves: every one loveth gifts, and followeth after rewards: they judge not the fatherless, neither doth the cause of the widow come unto them.

Isa. 5:22. Woe unto them that are mighty to drink wine, and men of strength to mingle strong drink: 23. Which justify the wicked for reward, and take away the righteousness of the righteous from him!

Isa. 33:15. He that walketh righteously, and speaketh uprightly; he that despiseth the gain of oppressions, that shaketh his hands from holding of bribes, that stoppeth his ears from hearing of blood, and shutteth his eyes from seeing evil; 16. He shall dwell on high: his place of defence shall be the munitions of rocks: bread shall be given him; his waters shall be sure.

Ezek. 13:19. And will ye pollute me among my people for handfuls of barley and for pieces of bread, to slay the souls that should not die, and to save the souls alive that should not live, by your lying to my people that hear your lies?

Ezek. 22:12. In thee have they taken gifts to shed blood; thou hast taken usury and increase, and thou hast greedily gained of thy neighbours by extortion, and hast forgotten me, saith the Lord God. 13. Behold, therefore I have smitten mine hand at thy dishonest gain which thou hast made, and at thy blood which hath been in the midst of thee.

Amos 2:6. Thus saith the Lord; For three transgressions of Israel, and for four, I will not turn away the punishment thereof; because they sold the righteous for silver, and the poor for a pair of shoes;

Amos 5:12. For I know your manifold transgressions and your mighty sins: they afflict the just, they take a bribe, and they turn aside the poor in the gate from their right.

Mic. 7:3. That they may do evil with both hands earnestly, the prince asketh, and the judge asketh for a reward;

INSTANCES OF: Delilah, Judg. 16:5. Samuel's sons. See above. The false prophet, Shemaiah, Neh. 6:10-13. Ben-hadad, 1 Kin. 15:19. Haman bribes Ahasuerus to destroy the Jews, Esth. 3:9. Chief priests bribe Judas, Matt. 26:15; 27:3-9; Mark 14:11; Luke 22:5. Soldiers bribed to declare that the disciples stole the body of Jesus, Matt. 28:12-15. Felix seeks a bribe from Paul, Acts 24:26.

BRICK. Used in building: Babel, Gen. 11:3; cities in Egypt, Ex. 1:11,14; houses, Isa. 9:10; altars, Isa. 65:3. Made by Israelites, Ex. 5:7-19; 2 Sam. 12:31; Jer. 43:9; Nah. 3:14.

BRICK-KILN, Jer. 43:9; Nah. 3:14. Captives tortured in, 2 Sam. 12:31.

BRIDE. Ornaments of, Isa. 49:18; 61:10; Jer. 2:32; Rev. 21:2. Presents to, Gen. 24:53. Maids of, Gen. 24:59,61; 29:24,29.

FIGURATIVE: Psa. 45:10-17; Ezek. 16:8-14; Rev. 19:7,8; 21:2,9; 22:17.

BRIDEGROOM. Ornaments of, Isa. 61:10. Exempt from military duty, Deut. 24:5. Companions of, Judg. 14:11. Joy with, Matt. 9:15; Mark 2:19,20; Luke 5:34,35. Parable of, Matt. 25:1-13. Song of, Song 4:7-16.

FIGURATIVE: Ezek. 16:8-14.

BRIDLE, Psa. 32:9; Prov. 26:3; Rev. 14:20.

FIGURATIVE: 2 Kin. 19:28; Psa. 39:1; Jas. 1:26.

See BIT.

BRIER. FIGURATIVE: Isa. 5:6; 55:13; Ezek. 2:6; 28:24.

BRIGANDINE, a coat of mail, Jer. 46:4; 51:3.

BRIMSTONE, Fire and, rained upon Sodom, Gen. 19:24; Luke 17:29. In Palestine, Deut. 29:23.

FIGURATIVE: Job. 18:15; Psa. 11:6; Isa. 30:33; Ezek. 38:22; Rev. 9:17,18; 14:10; 19:20; 21:8.

BROOK. See RIVER.

BROTH, Judg. 6:19,20; 2 Kin. 4:38; Isa. 65:4. Symbolical, Ezek. 24:5.

BROTHEL. See HIGH PLACE.

BROTHER. Signifies a relative, Gen. 14:16; 29:12; neighbor, Deut. 23:7; Judg. 21:6; Neh. 5:7; any Israelite, Jer. 34:9; Obad. 10; mankind, Gen. 9:5; Matt. 18:35; 1 John 3:15; companion, 2 Sam. 1:26; 1 Kin. 13:30; 20:33. Love of, Prov. 17:17; 18:24; Song 8:1. Unfaithful, Prov. 27:10. Reuben's love for Joseph, Gen. 37:21,22. Joseph's, for his brethren, Gen. 43:30-34; 45:1-5; 50:19-25.

A fraternal epithet, especially among Christians. Instituted by Christ, Matt. 12:50; 25:40; Heb. 2:11,12. Used by disciples, Acts 9:17; 21:20; Rom. 16:23; 1 Cor. 7:12; 2 Cor. 2:13; Peter, 1 Pet. 1:22. Used among the Israelites, Lev. 19:17; Deut. 22:1-4.

Brother's widow, law concerning Levirate marriage of, Deut. 25:5-10; Matt. 22:24; Mark 12:19; Luke 20:28.

BROTHERLY KINDNESS. See BROTHER; CHARITABLENESS; FELLOWSHIP; FRATERNITY; FRIENDSHIP; LOVE.

BUCKET, Num. 24:7; Isa. 40:15.

BUCKLER. See SHIELD.

BUILDER, of the tabernacle. See BEZALEEL; MASTER WORKMAN.

FIGURATIVE: Psa. 118:22; Matt. 21:42; Acts 4:11; 1 Pet. 2:7; Heb. 11:10.

See CARPENTER.

BUILDING. FIGURATIVE: 2 Cor. 5:1.

BUKKI. 1. Son of Abishua, 1 Chr. 6:5, 51; Ezra 7:4.

2. A prince of Dan, Num. 34:22.

BUKKIAH, a Levite, 1 Chr. 25:4,13.

BUL, the eighth month [November]. The temple completed in, 1 Kin. 6:38. Jeroboam institutes an idolatrous feast in, to correspond with the Feast of Tabernacles, 1 Kin. 12:32,33; 1 Chr. 27:11.

BULL, wild, caught in nets, Isa. 51:20. Blood of, in sacrifice, Heb. 9:13; 10:4.

See BULLOCK; OFFERINGS.

BULLOCK, OR OX [Synonymous terms in *A. V.*]. Uses of: For sacrifice, Ex. 29:3, 10-14,36; Lev. 4:8,16; Num. 7:87,88; 28:11-31; 29; plowing, 1 Sam. 14:14; 1 Kin. 19:19; Prov. 14:4; Isa. 32:20; Jer. 31:18; treading out corn, Deut. 25:4; with wagons, Num. 7:3-8; 2 Sam. 6:3-6.

Laws concerning: Trespass by, Ex. 21:28-36; theft of, Ex. 22:1-10; rest for, Ex. 23:12; not to be muzzled, when treading grain, Deut. 25:4; 1 Cor. 9:9; 1 Tim. 5:18; not to be yoked with an ass, Deut. 22:10.

Twelve brazen, under the molten sea in Solomon's temple, 1 Kin. 7:25; 2 Chr. 4:4; Jer. 52:20.

See BULL; CATTLE.

SYMBOLICAL: Ezek. 1:10; Rev. 4:7.

BULRUSH [papyrus, *R. V.*], Moses' ark of, Ex. 2:3. Boats made of, Isa.18:2.

FIGURATIVE: Isa. 58:5.

BULWARK, Deut. 20:20; 2 Chr. 26:15; Eccl. 9:14.

FIGURATIVE: Psa. 48:13; Isa. 26:1.

BUNAH, son of Jerahmeel, 1 Chr. 2:25.

BUNNI. 1. A Levite, a teacher with Ezra, Neh. 9:4.

2. Ancestor of Shemaiah, Neh. 11:15.

3. A family of Jews, Neh. 10:15.

BURDEN. FIGURATIVE: Of oppressions, Isa. 58:6; Matt. 23:4; Luke 11:46; Gal. 6:2. Of the prophetic message, Isa. 13:1; 15:1; 17:1; 19:1.

BURGLARY. See THEFT.

BURIAL. Rites of, Jer. 34:5. Soon after death, Deut. 21:23; Josh. 8:29; John 19:38-42; Acts 5:9,10. With spices, 2 Chr. 16:14; Mark 16:1; Luke 23:56. Bier used at, 2 Sam. 3:31; Luke 7:14. Attended by relatives and friends: Of Jacob, Gen. 50:5-9; Abner, 2 Sam. 3:31; child of Jeroboam, 1 Kin. 14:13; the son of the widow of Nain, Luke 7:12,13; Stephen, Acts 8:2.

Lack of, a disgrace, 2 Kin. 9:10; Prov. 30: 17; Jer. 16:4; 22:19; Ezek. 39:15. Directions given about, before death, by Jacob, Gen. 49:29,30; Joseph, Gen. 50:25. Burial of Gog, [multitude] requiring 7 months, Ezek. 39: 12,13.

BURYING PLACES: Bought by Abraham, Gen. 23; 25:9. Prepared by Jacob, Gen. 50:5; Asa, 2 Chr. 16:14; Joseph, Matt. 27:60. On hills, 2 Kin. 23:16; Josh. 24:33. In valleys, Jer. 7:32.

Family, Gen. 47:30; 49:29; Acts 7:16. Of kings, 1 Kin. 2:10; 2 Chr. 32:33; a place of honor, 2 Chr. 24:16,25; 21:20. For poor and strangers, Jer. 26:23; Matt. 27:7.

Tombs: In houses, 1 Sam. 25:1; 1 Kin. 2:34; in gardens, 2 Kin. 21:18,26; John 19:41; in caves, Gen. 23:9; under trees, Deborah's, Gen. 35:8; King Saul's, 1 Sam. 31:13.

Closed with stones, Matt. 27:60,66; John 11:38; 20:1. Sealed, Matt. 27:66. Marked with pillars, Rachel's, Gen. 35:20, and inscriptions, 2 Kin. 23:17. Painted and garnished, Matt. 23:27,29. With shelves, Isa. 14:15. Demoniacs dwelt in, Matt. 8:28. Any who touched, were unclean, Num. 19:16,18; Isa. 65:4. Refused to the dead, Rev. 11:9. Robbed, Jer. 8:1.

See CREMATION; DEAD, THE; DEATH; ELEGY; GRAVE; MOURNING.

FIGURATIVE: Isa. 22:16; Rom. 6:4; Col. 2:12.

BURNING, as a punishment. See PUNISHMENT.

BURNING BUSH, Ex. 3:2-5; Acts 7:30.

BURNT OFFERING. See OFFERINGS, BURNT.

BUSH, BURNING. See BURNING BUSH.

BUSHEL, about one peck, Matt. 5:15; Mark, 4:21; Luke 11:33.

BUSYBODY. Lev. 19:16. Thou shalt not go up and down *as* a talebearer among thy people : neither shalt thou stand against the blood of thy neighbour : I *am* the LORD.

Prov. 20:3. *It is* an honour for a man to cease from strife : but every fool will be meddling.

2 Thess. 3:11. For we hear that there are some which walk among you disorderly, working not at all, but are busybodies. 12. Now them that are such we command and exhort by our Lord Jesus Christ that with quietness they work, and eat their own bread.

1 Tim. 5:13. And withal they learn *to be* idle, wandering about from house to house : and not only idle, but tattlers also and busybodies, speaking things which they ought not.

1 Pet. 4:15. But let none of you suffer as a murderer, or *as* a thief, or *as* an evil doer, or as a busybody in other men's matters.

See TALEBEARER; SPEAKING, EVIL.

BUTLER. Pharaoh's, imprisoned and released, Gen. 40; 1 Kin. 10:5; 2 Chr. 9:4; Neh. 1:11; 2:1.

BUTTER, Gen. 18:8; Deut. 32:14; Judg.

5:25; 2 Sam. 17:29; Job. 20:17; Isa. 7:15,22.
Made by churning, Prov. 30:33.

BUZ. 1. Son of Nahor, Gen. 22:21.

2. Father of Jahdo, 1 Chr. 5:14.

BUZZI, father of Ezekiel, Ezek. 1:3.

C

CAB, a dry measure containing about two quarts, 2 Kin. 6:25.
See MEASURE.

CABBON, a place in Judah, Josh. 15:40.

CABINET, heads of departments in government. David's, 2 Sam. 8:15–18; 15:12; 20:23–26; 1 Chr. 27:32–34; Solomon's, 1 Kin. 4:1–7; Hezekiah's, Isa. 36:3: Artaxerxes', Ezra 7:14.
See COUNSELLOR; MINISTER, PRIME.

CABUL. 1. A city in the N. of Palestine, Josh. 19:27.

2. Name given by Hiram to certain cities in Galilee, 1 Kin. 9:13.

CÆSAR. 1. AUGUSTUS, Luke 2:1.

2. TIBERIUS, Luke 3:1; 20:22.

3. CLAUDIUS, Acts 11:28.

4. NERO, Phil. 4:22.

CÆSAREA. A seaport in Palestine. Home of Philip, Acts 8:40; 21:8; Cornelius, the centurion, Acts 10:1,24; Herod, Acts 12: 19–23; Felix, Acts 23:23,24. Paul conveyed to, by the disciples to save him from his enemies, Acts 9:30; by Roman soldiers to be tried by Felix, Acts 23:23–35.

CÆSAREA PHILIPPI, a city in the N. of Palestine; visited by Jesus, Matt. 16: 13; Mark 8:27; Luke 9:18.

CAGE, for birds, unclean, Jer. 5:27; Rev. 18:2.

CAIAPHAS. High priest, Luke 3:2; son-in-law of Annas, John 18:13. Prophesies concerning Jesus, John 11:49–51; 18:14. Jesus tried before, Matt. 26:2,3,57,63–65; John 18: 24,28. Peter and other disciples accused before, Acts 4:1–22.

CAIN. 1. Son of Adam, Gen. 4:1. Jealousy and crime of, Gen. 4:3–15; Heb. 11:4; 1 John 3:12; Jude 11. Sojourns in the land of Nod, Gen. 4:16. Children and descendants of, Gen. 4:17,18.

2. A city of Judah, Josh. 15:57.

CAINAN. 1. Called also KENAN. Son of Enos, Gen. 5:9–15; 1 Chr. 1:2; Luke 3:37.

2. Son of Arphaxad, Luke 3:36.

CALAH, an ancient city of Assyria, Gen. 10:11,12.

CALAMUS. A sweet cane of Palestine, Song 4:14; Ezek. 27:19. An ingredient of the holy ointment, Ex. 30:23; Isa. 43:24. Commerce in, Jer. 6:20, Ezek. 27:19.

CALCOL, son of Zerah, 1 Chr. 2:6.

CALDRON, in the tabernacle, 1 Sam. 2:14; temple, 2 Chr. 35:13; Jer. 52:18,19.

FIGURATIVE: Ezek. 11:3–11.

CALEB. One of the two survivors of the Israelites permitted to enter the land of promise, Num. 14:30,38; 26:63–65; 32:11–13; Deut. 1:34–36; Josh. 14:6–15. Sent to Canaan as a spy, Num. 13:6. Brings favorable re-

port, Num. 13:26–30; 14:6–9. Assists in dividing Canaan, Num. 34:19. Life of, miraculously saved, Num. 14:10–12. Leader of the Israelites after Joshua's death, Judg. 1:11,12. Age of, Josh. 14:7–10. Inheritance of, Josh. 14:6–15; 15:13–16. Descendants of, 1 Chr. 4:15.

CALEB-EPHRATAH, a place near Beth-lehem, 1 Chr. 2:24.

CALF. Offered in sacrifice, Mic. 6:6. Golden, made by Aaron, Ex. 32; Deut. 9:16; Neh. 9:18; Psa. 106:19; Acts 7:41.

Images of, set up in Beth-el and Dan by Jeroboam, 1 Kin. 12:28–33; 2 Kin. 10:29. Worshiped by Jehu, 2 Kin. 10:29. Prophecies against the golden calves at Beth-el, 1 Kin. 13:1–5,32; Jer. 48:13; Hos. 8:5,6; 10:5,6, 15; 13:2; Amos 3:14; 4:4; 8:14. Altars of, destroyed, 2 Kin. 23:4,15–20.

"Calves of the lips," a metaphor signifying worship, Hos.14:2.

CALKERS, Ezek. 27:9,27.

CALL, PERSONAL: By Christ, Isa. 55:5; Rom. 1:6; by his Spirit, Rev. 22:17; by his works, Psa. 19:2,3; Rom. 1:20; by his ministers, Jer. 35:15; 2 Cor. 5:20; by his gospel, 2 Thess. 2:14. Is from darkness to light, 1 Pet. 2:9. Addressed to all, Isa. 45:22; Matt. 20:16. Most reject, Prov. 1:24: Matt 20:16. Effectual to saints, Psa. 110:3; Acts 13:48; 1 Cor. 1:24. Not to many wise, 1 Cor. 1:26.

To saints, is of grace, Gal. 1:6; 2 Tim. 1:9; according to the purpose of God, Rom. 8:28; 9:11,23,24, without repentance, Rom. 11:29; high, Phil. 3:14; holy, 2 Tim. 1:9; heavenly, Heb. 3:1; to fellowship with Christ, 1 Cor. 1:9; to holiness, 1 Thess. 4:7; to a prize, Phil. 3:14; to liberty, Gal. 5:13; to peace, 1 Cor. 7:15; Col. 3:15; to glory and virtue, 2 Pet. 1:3; to the eternal glory of Christ, 2 Thess. 2:14; 1 Pet. 5:10; to eternal life, 1 Tim. 6:12.

Partakers of, justified, Rom. 8:30; walk worthy of, Eph. 4:1; 2 Thess. 1:11; blessedness of receiving, Rev. 19:9; is to be made sure, 2 Pet. 1:10; praise God for, 1 Pet. 2:9; illustrated, Prov. 8:3,4; Matt. 3:3–9.

Rejection of, leads to judicial blindness, Isa. 6:9, with Acts 28:24–27; Rom. 11:8–10; delusion, Isa. 66:4; 2 Thess. 2:10,11; withdrawal of the means of grace, Jer. 26:4–6; Acts 13:46; 18:6; Rev. 2:5; temporal judgments, Isa. 28:12; Jer. 6:16,19; 35:17; Zech. 7: 12–14; rejection by God, Prov. 1:24–32; Jer. 6:19,30; condemnation, John 12:48; Heb. 2: 1–3; 12:25; destruction, Prov. 29:1; Matt. 22: 3–7.—*Bible Text-Book.*

TO SPECIAL RELIGIOUS DUTY: OF ABRAHAM, Gen. 12:1. Now the LORD had said unto Abram, Get thee out of thy country, and from thy kindred, and from thy father's house, unto a land that I will shew thee: 2. And I will make of thee a great nation, and I will bless thee, and make thy name great; and thou shalt be a blessing: 3. And I will bless them that bless thee, and curse him that curseth thee: and in thee shall all families of the earth be blessed.

Isa. 51:2. Look unto Abraham your father, and unto Sarah *that* bare you: for I called him alone, and blessed him, and increased him.

Heb. 11:8. By faith Abraham, when he was called to go out into a place which he should after receive for an inheritance, obeyed;

Moses: Ex. 3:2. And the angel of the Lord appeared unto him in a flame of fire out of the midst of a bush: and he looked, and, behold, the bush burned with fire, and the bush *was* not consumed. 4. And when the Lord saw that he turned aside to see, God called unto him out of the midst of the bush, and said, Moses, Moses. And he said, Here *am* I. 10. Come now therefore, and I will send thee unto Pharaoh, that thou mayest bring forth my people the children of Israel out of Egypt.

Ex. 4:1. And Moses answered and said, But, behold, they will not believe me, nor hearken unto my voice: for they will say, The Lord hath not appeared unto thee. 2. And the Lord said unto him, What *is* that in thine hand? And he said, A rod. 3. And he said, Cast it on the ground. And he cast it on the ground, and it became a serpent; and Moses fled from before it. 4. And the Lord said unto Moses, Put forth thine hand, and take it by the tail. And he put forth his hand, and caught it, and it became a rod in his hand: 5. That they may believe that the Lord God of their fathers, the God of Abraham, the God of Isaac, and the God of Jacob, hath appeared unto thee. 6. And the Lord said furthermore unto him, Put now thine hand into thy bosom. And he put his hand into his bosom: and when he took it out, behold, his hand *was* leprous as snow. 7. And he said, Put thine hand into thy bosom again. And he put his hand into his bosom again; and plucked it out of his bosom, and, behold, it was turned again as his *other* flesh. 8. And it shall come to pass, if they will not believe thee, neither hearken to the voice of the first sign, that they will believe the voice of the latter sign. 9. And it shall come to pass, if they will not believe also these two signs, neither hearken unto thy voice, that thou shalt take of the water of the river, and pour *it* upon the dry *land:* and the water which thou takest out of the river shall become blood upon the dry *land.* 10. And Moses said unto the Lord, O my Lord, I *am* not eloquent, neither heretofore, nor since thou hast spoken unto thy servant: but I *am* slow of speech and of a slow tongue. 11. And the Lord said unto him, Who hath made man's mouth? or who maketh the dumb, or deaf, or the seeing, or the blind? have not I the Lord? 12. Now therefore go, and I will be with thy mouth, and teach thee what thou shalt say. 13. And he said, O my Lord, send, I pray thee, by the hand *of him whom* thou wilt send. 14. And the anger of the Lord was kindled against Moses, and he said, *Is* not

Aaron the Levite thy brother? I know that he can speak well. And also, behold, he cometh forth to meet thee: and when he seeth thee, he will be glad in his heart. 15. And thou shalt speak unto him, and put words in his mouth: and I will be with thy mouth, and with his mouth, and will teach you what ye shall do. 16. And he shall be thy spokesman unto the people: and he shall be, *even* he shall be to thee instead of a mouth, and thou shalt be to him instead of God.

Psa. 105:26. He sent Moses his servant; *and* Aaron whom he had chosen.

Acts 7:34. I have seen, I have seen the affliction of my people which is in Egypt, and I have heard their groaning, and am come down to deliver them. And now come, I will send thee into Egypt. 35. This Moses whom they refused, saying, Who made thee a ruler and a judge? the same did God send *to be* a ruler and a deliverer by the hand of the angel which appeared to him in the bush.

Aaron and His Sons: Ex. 4:14-16, see above, and Psa. 105:26.

Ex. 28:1. And take thou unto thee Aaron thy brother, and his sons with him, from among the children of Israel, that he may minister unto me in the priest's office, *even* Aaron, Nadab and Abihu, Eleazar and Ithamar, Aaron's sons.

Heb. 5:4. And no man taketh this honour unto himself, but he that is called of God as *was* Aaron.

Joshua: Num. 27:18. And the Lord said unto Moses, Take thee Joshua the son of Nun, a man in whom *is* the spirit, and lay thine hand upon him; 19. And set him before Eleazar the priest, and before all the congregation; and give him a charge in their sight. 22. And Moses did as the Lord commanded him: and he took Joshua, and set him before Eleazar the priest, and before all the congregation: 23. And he laid his hands upon him, and gave him a charge, as the Lord commanded by the hand of Moses.

Deut. 31:14. And the Lord said unto Moses, Behold, thy days approach that thou must die: call Joshua, and present yourselves in the tabernacle of the congregation, that I may give him a charge. And Moses and Joshua went, and presented themselves in the tabernacle of the congregation.

23. And he gave Joshua the son of Nun a charge, and said, Be strong and of a good courage: for thou shalt bring the children of Israel into the land which I sware unto them: and I will be with thee.

Josh. 1:1. Now after the death of Moses the servant of the Lord, it came to pass, that the Lord spake unto Joshua the son of Nun, Moses' minister, saying, 2. Moses my servant is dead; now therefore arise, go over this Jordan, thou, and all this people, unto the land which I do give to them, *even* to the children of Israel. 3. Every place that the sole of your foot shall tread upon, that have I given unto you, as I said unto Moses. 4. From the wilderness and this Lebanon even unto the great river, the river Euphrates, all the land of the Hittites, and unto the great sea toward the going down of the sun, shall be your coast. 5. There shall not any man be able to stand before thee all the days of thy life: as I was with Moses, *so* I will be with thee: I will not fail thee, nor forsake thee. 6. Be strong and of a good courage: for unto this people shalt thou divide for an inheritance the land, which I sware unto their fathers to give them. 7. Only be thou strong and very courageous, that thou mayest observe to do according to all the law, which Moses my servant commanded thee: turn not from it *to* the right hand or *to* the left, that thou mayest prosper whithersoever thou goest. 8. This book of the law shall not depart out of thy mouth; but thou shalt meditate therein day and night, that thou mayest observe to do according to all that is written therein: for then thou shalt make thy way prosperous, and then thou shalt have good success. 9. Have not I commanded thee? Be strong and of a good courage; be not afraid, neither be thou dismayed: for the LORD thy God *is* with thee whithersoever thou goest.

GIDEON: Judg. 6:11. And there came an angel of the LORD, and sat under an oak which *was* in Ophrah, that *pertained* unto Joash the Abi-ezrite: and his son Gideon threshed wheat by the winepress, to hide *it* from the Midianites. 12. And the angel of the LORD appeared unto him, and said unto him, The LORD *is* with thee, thou mighty man of valour. 13. And Gideon said unto him, O my Lord, if the LORD be with us, why then is all this befallen us? and where *be* all his miracles which our fathers told us of, saying, Did not the LORD bring us up from Egypt? but now the LORD hath forsaken us, and delivered us into the hands of the Midianites. 14. And the LORD looked upon him, and said, Go in this thy might, and thou shalt save Israel from the hand of the Midianites: have not I sent thee? 15. And he said unto him, O my Lord, wherewith shall I save Israel? behold, my family *is* poor in Manasseh, and I *am* the least in my father's house. 16. And the LORD said unto him, Surely I will be with thee, and thou shalt smite the Midianites as one man.

SAMUEL: 1 Sam. 3:4. That the LORD called Samuel: and he answered, Here *am* I. 5. And he ran unto Eli, and said, Here *am* I; for thou calledst me. And he said, I called not; lie down again. And he went and lay down. 6. And the LORD called yet again, Samuel. And Samuel arose and went to Eli, and said, Here *am* I; for thou didst call me. And he answered, I called not, my son; lie down again. 7. Now Samuel did not yet know the LORD, neither was the word of the LORD yet revealed unto him.

8. And the LORD called Samuel again the third time. And he arose and went to Eli, and said, Here *am* I; for thou didst call me. And Eli perceived that the LORD had called the child. 9. Therefore Eli said unto Samuel, Go, lie down: and it shall be, if he call thee, that thou shalt say, Speak, LORD; for thy servant heareth. So Samuel went and lay down in his place. 10. And the LORD came, and stood, and called as at other times, Samuel, Samuel. Then Samuel answered, Speak; for thy servant heareth.

SOLOMON: 1 Chr. 28:6. And he said unto me, Solomon thy son, he shall build my house and my courts: for I have chosen him *to be* my son, and I will be his father. 10. Take heed now; for the LORD hath chosen thee to build an house for the sanctuary: be strong, and do *it*.

JEHU: 2 Kin. 9:6. And he arose, and went into the house; and he poured the oil on his head, and said unto him, Thus saith the LORD God of Israel, I have anointed thee king over the people of the LORD, *even* over Israel. 7. And thou shalt smite the house of Ahab thy master, that I may avenge the blood of my servants the prophets, and the blood of all the servants of the LORD, at the hand of Jezebel.

2 Chr. 22:7. And the destruction of Ahaziah was of God by coming to Joram: for when he was come, he went out with Jehoram against Jehu the son of Nimshi, whom the LORD had anointed to cut off the house of Ahab.

CYRUS: Isa. 45:1. Thus saith the LORD to his anointed, to Cyrus, whose right hand I have holden, to subdue nations before him; and I will loose the loins of kings, to open before him the two leaved gates; and the gates shall not be shut; 2. I will go before thee, and make the crooked places straight: I will break in pieces the gates of brass, and cut in sunder the bars of iron: 3. And I will give thee the treasures of darkness, and the hidden riches of secret places, that thou mayest know that I, the LORD, whch call *thee* by thy name, *am* the God of Israel. 4. For Jacob my servant's sake, and Israel mine elect, I have even called thee by thy name: I have surnamed thee, though thou hast not known me.

AMOS: Amos 7:14. Then answered Amos, and said to Amaziah, I *was* no prophet, neither *was* I a prophet's son; but I *was* an herdman, and a gatherer of sycomore fruit: 15. And the LORD took me as I followed the flock, and the LORD said unto me, Go, prophesy unto my people Israel.

APOSTLES: Matt. 4:18. And Jesus, walking by the sea of Galilee, saw two brethren, Simon called Peter, and Andrew his brother, casting a net into the sea: for they were fishers. 19. And he saith unto them, Follow me, and I will make you fishers of men. 20. And they straightway left *their* nets, and followed him. [Mark 1:16,17.] 21. And going on from thence, he saw other two brethren, James *the son* of Zebedee, and John his brother, in a ship with Zebedee their father, mending their nets; and he called them. 22. And they immediately left the ship and their father, and followed him. Mark 3:13-19; Luke 6:13-15.

Mark 2:14. And as he passed by, he saw Levi the *son* of Alphæus sitting at the receipt of custom, and said unto him, Follow me. And he arose and followed him. Matt. 9:9; Luke 5:27.

John 15:16. Ye have not chosen me, but I have chosen you, and ordained you, that ye should go and bring forth fruit, and *that* your fruit should remain:

THE RICH YOUNG MAN: Mark 10:21. Then Jesus beholding him loved him, and said unto him, One thing thou lackest: go thy way, sell whatsoever thou hast, and give to the poor, and thou shalt have treasure in heaven: and come, take up the cross, and follow me. 22. And he was sad at that saying, and went away grieved: for he had great possessions.

PAUL: Acts 9:4. And he fell to the earth, and heard a voice saying unto him, Saul, Saul, why persecutest thou me? 5. And he said, Who art thou, Lord? And the Lord said, I am Jesus whom thou persecutest: ¹ *it is* hard for thee to kick against the pricks. 6. And he trembling and astonished said, Lord, what wilt thou have me to do? And the Lord *said* unto him, Arise, and go into the city, and it shall be told thee what thou must do.   [¹ Omitted in R. V.]

15. But the Lord said unto him, Go thy way: for he is a chosen vessel unto me, to bear my name before the Gentiles, and kings, and the children of Israel: 16. For I will shew him how great things he must suffer for my name's sake.

Acts 13:2. As they ministered to the Lord, and fasted, the Holy Ghost said, Separate me Barnabas and Saul for the work whereunto I have called them. 3. And when they had fasted and prayed, and laid *their* hands on them, they sent *them* away.

Rom. 1:1. Paul, a servant of Jesus Christ, called *to be* an apostle, separated unto the gospel of God. 1 Cor. 1:1; 2 Cor. 1:1; Gal. 1:1; Eph. 1:1; Col. 1:1; 1 Tim. 1:1; 2 Tim. 1:1.

ALL WHO ARE CALLED OF GOD: Rom. 8:30. Moreover, whom he did predestinate, them he also called: and whom he called, them he also justified: and whom he justified, them he also glorified.

1 Cor. 1:2. Unto the church of God which is at Corinth, to them that are sanctified in Christ Jesus, called *to be* saints, with all that in every place call upon the name of Jesus Christ our Lord, both their's and our's:

9. God *is* faithful, by whom ye were called unto the fellowship of his Son Jesus Christ our Lord.

24. But unto them which are called, both Jews and Greeks, Christ the power of God, and the wisdom of God.

1 Thess. 2:11. As ye know how we ex-

horted and comforted and charged every one of you, as a father *doth* his children, 12. That ye would walk worthy of God, who hath called you unto his kingdom and glory.

2 Thess. 2:13. But we are bound to give thanks always to God for you, brethren beloved of the Lord, because God hath from the beginning chosen you to salvation through sanctification of the Spirit and belief of the truth: 14. Whereunto he called you by our gospel, to the obtaining of the glory of our Lord Jesus Christ.

2 Tim. 1:9. Who hath saved us, and called *us* with an holy calling, not according to our works, but according to his own purpose and grace, which was given us in Christ Jesus before the world began,

Heb. 3:1. Wherefore, holy brethren, partakers of the heavenly calling, consider the Apostle and High Priest of our profession, Christ Jesus; 2. Who was faithful to him that appointed him, as also Moses *was faithful* in all his house.

7. Wherefore as the Holy Ghost saith, To day if ye will hear his voice, 8. Harden not your hearts, as in the provocation, in the day of temptation in the wilderness:

1 Pet. 5:10. But the God of all grace, who hath called us unto his eternal glory by Christ Jesus, after that ye have suffered a while, make you perfect, stablish, strengthen, settle *you.*

2 Pet. 1:3. According as his divine power hath given unto us all things that *pertain* unto life and godliness, through the knowledge of him that hath called us to glory and virtue: 10. Wherefore the rather, brethren, give diligence to make your calling and election sure: for if ye do these things, ye shall never fall:

Jude 1. Jude, the servant of Jesus Christ, and brother of James, to them that are sanctified by God the Father, and preserved in Jesus Christ, *and* called:

Rev. 17:14. These shall make war with the Lamb, and the Lamb shall overcome them: for he is Lord of lords, and King of kings: and they that are with him *are* called, and chosen, and faithful.

See MINISTERS, CALL OF; BACKSLIDERS; SEEKERS.

CALNEH, called also CANNEH and CALNO, a city of Assyria, Gen. 10:10; Isa. 10:9; Ezek. 27:23; Amos 6:2.

CALVARY, called also GOLGOTHA, place where Jesus was crucified, Matt. 27:33; Mark 15:22; Luke 23:33; John 19:17.

CAMEL, herds of, Gen. 12:16; 24:35; Gen. 30:43; 1 Sam. 30:17; 1 Chr. 27:30; Job. 1:3,17; Isa. 60:6.

Docility of, Gen. 24:11. Uses of: For riding, Gen. 24:10,61,64; 31:17; posts, Esth. 8:10, 14; Jer. 2:23; drawing chariots, Isa. 21:7; for carrying burdens, Gen. 24:10; 37:25; 1 Kin. 10:2; 2 Kin. 8:9; 1 Chr. 12:40; Isa. 30:6; for cavalry, 1 Sam. 30:17; for milk, Gen. 32:15. Forbidden as food, Lev. 11:4. Hair of, made into cloth, Matt. 3:4; Mark 1:6

Ornaments of, Judg. 8:21,26. Stables for, Ezek. 25:5.

CAMON, place where Jair was buried, Judg. 10:5.

CAMP, of the Israelites about the tabernacle, Num. 2; 3.

See ITINERARY.

CAMPHIRE [Henna, *R. V.*], a shrub bearing fragrant flowers, not related to camphor, Song 1:14; 4:13.

CANA. Marriage at, John 2:1-11. Nobleman's son healed at, John 4:46,47. Nathanael's home at, John 21:2.

CANAAN. 1. Son of Ham, Gen. 9:18, 22,25-27. Descendants of, Gen. 10:6,15; 1 Chr. 1:8,13.

2. Land of,* Gen. 11:31; 17:8; 23:2. Called THE SANCTUARY, Ex. 15:17; PALESTINE, Ex. 15:14; LAND OF ISRAEL, 1 Sam. 13:19; OF THE HEBREWS, Gen. 40:15; OF THE JEWS, Acts 10:39; OF PROMISE, Heb. 11:9; HOLY LAND, Zech. 2:12; LORD'S LAND, Hos. 9:3; IMMANUEL'S LAND, Isa. 8:8; BEULAH, Isa. 62:4.

Promised to Abraham and his seed, Gen. 12:1-7; 13:14-17; 15:18-21; 17:8; Deut. 12:9,10; Psa. 105:11; renewed to Isaac, Gen. 26:3. Extent of: According to the promise, Gen. 15:18: Ex. 23:31; Deut. 11:24; Josh. 1:4; 15:1; after the conquest by Joshua, Josh. 12:1-8; in Solomon's time, 1 Kin 4:21,24; 2 Chr. 7:8; 9:26. Prophecy concerning, after the restoration of Israel, Ezek. 47:13-20.

Fertility of, Deut. 8:7-9; 11:10-13. Fruitfulness of, Num. 13:27; 14:7,8; Jer. 2:7; 32:22. Products of: Fruits, Deut. 8:8; Jer. 40:10,12; mineral, Deut. 8:9. Exports of, Ezek. 27:17.

Famines in, Gen. 12:10; 26:1; 47:13; Ruth 1:1; 2 Sam. 21:1; 1 Kin. 17. See FAMINE.

Spies sent into, by Moses, Num. 13:17-29. Conquest of, by the Israelites, Num. 21:21-35; Deut. 3:3-6; Josh. chapters 6-12; Psa. 44:1-3. Divided by lot among the twelve tribes, and families, Num. 26:55,56; 33:54; 34:13; by Joshua, Eleazar and a prince from each tribe, Num. 34:16-29; 35:1-8; Josh. chapters 14-19. Divided into twelve provinces by Solomon, 1 Kin. 4:7-19. Into two kingdoms, Judah and Israel, 1 Kin. 11:29-36; 12:16-21. Roman provinces of, Luke 3:1; John 4:3,4.

CANAANITES. Eleven nations, descended from Canaan, Gen. 10:15-19; Deut. 7:1; 1 Chr. 1:13-16. Territory of, Gen. 10:19; 12:6; 15:18; Ex. 23:31; Num. 13:29; 34:1-12; Josh. 1:4; 5:1; given to the Israelites, Gen. 12:6,7; 15:18; 17:8; Ex. 23:23; Deut. 7:1-3; 32:49; Psa. 135:11,12.

Wickedness of, Gen. 13:13; Lev. 18:25,27, 28; 20:23. To be expelled from the land, Ex. 33:2; 34:11. To be destroyed, Ex. 23:23,24; Deut. 19:1; 31:3-5. Not expelled, Josh. 17:12-18; Judg. 1:1-33; 3:1-3. Defeat the Israelites, Num. 14:45; Judg. 4:1-3. Defeated by the Israelites, Num. 21:1-3; Josh. 11:1-16; Judg. 4:4-24; by the Egyptians, 1 Kin. 9:16. Chariots of, Josh. 17:18.

* The history of this region is involved in that of the Israelites. The student is therefore referred to Israel, History of. See also CANAANITES.

Isaac forbidden by Abraham to take a wife from, Gen. 28:1. Judah marries a woman of, Gen. 38:2; 1 Chr. 2:3. The exile Jews take wives from, Ezra 9:2.

Prophecy concerning, Gen. 9:25-27.

CANDACE, queen of Ethiopia, Acts 8:27.

CANDIDATE. Refuses to make promises, 2 Chr. 10:3-16. Electioneering by, instance of, Absalom, 2 Sam. 15:1-6.

CANDLE. Revised version and commentators substitute lamp for candle throughout the Scriptures.

See LAMP.

CANDLESTICK. OF THE TABERNACLE: Made after divine pattern, Ex. 25:31-40; 37:17-24; Num. 8:4. Place of, Ex. 26:35; 40:24,25; Heb. 9:2. Furniture of, Ex. 25:38; 37:23; Num. 4:9,10. Burned every night, Ex. 27:20,21. Trimmed every morning, Ex. 30:7. Carried by Kohathites, Num. 4:4,15. Called THE LAMP OF GOD, 1 Sam. 3:3.

OF THE TEMPLE: Ten branches of, 1 Kin. 7:49,50. Of gold, 1 Chr. 28:15; 2 Chr. 4:20. Taken with other spoils to Babylon, Jer. 52:19.

SYMBOLICAL: Zech. 4:2,11; Rev. 1:12,13,20; 2:5; 11:4.

CANE. See CALAMUS.

CANKER, FIGURATIVE: 2 Tim. 2:17.

CANKERWORM, sent as a judgment, Joel 1:4; 2:25: Nah. 3:15,16.

CANNEH. See CALNEH.

CANNIBALISM, Lev. 26:29; Deut. 28:53-57; 2 Kin. 6:28,29; Jer. 19:9; Lam. 2:20; 4:10; Ezek. 5:10.

CAPERNAUM. A city on the shore of the Sea of Galilee. Jesus chose as the place of his abode, Matt. 4:13; Luke 4:31. Miracles of Jesus performed at, Matt. 9:1 26; 17:24-27; Mark 1:21-45; 2; 3:1-6; Luke 7:1-10; John 4:46-53; 6:17-25,59.

His prophecy against, Matt. 11:23; Luke 10:15.

CAPHTOR, a country now unknown, Deut. 2:23.

CAPHTORIM, people of Caphtor, Gen. 10:14; 1 Chr. 1:12; Deut. 2:23; Jer. 47:4; Amos 9:7.

CAPITAL PUNISHMENT. See PUNISHMENT.

CAPITAL AND LABOR. Strife between, Matt. 21:33-41; Mark 12:1-9; Luke 20:9-16.

See EMPLOYEE; EMPLOYER; MASTER; RICH, THE; SERVANT.

CAPPADOCIA, easternmost province of Asia Minor, Acts 2:9; 1 Pet. 1:1.

CAPTAIN. Commander-in-chief of an army, Deut. 20:9; Judg. 4:2; 1 Sam. 14:50; 1 Kin. 2:35; 16:16; 1 Chr. 27:34. Of the tribes, Num. 2. Of thousands, Num. 31:48; 1 Sam. 17:18; 1 Chr. 28:1. Of hundreds, 2 Kin. 11:15. See CENTURION. Of fifties. 2 Kin. 1:9; Isa. 3:3. Of the guard, Gen. 37:36; 2 Kin. 25:8. Of the ward, Jer. 37:13.

Signifying any commander, as 1 Sam. 9:16; 22:2; 2 Kin. 20:5; leader, 1 Chr. 11:21; 12:34; 2 Chr. 17:14-19; John 18:12.

David's captains, or chief heroes, 2 Sam. 23; 1 Chr. chapters 11,12.   King appoints, 1 Sam. 18:13; 2 Sam. 17:25; 18:1.

Angel of the Lord, called, Josh. 5:14; 2 Chr. 13:12.   Christ called, Heb. 2:10.

See ARMIES.

CAPTIVE. Prisoner of war, Gen. 14:12; 1 Sam. 30:1,2. Cruelty to: Putting to death, Num. 31:9-20; Deut. 20:13; 21:10; Josh. 8:29; 10:15-40; 11:11; Judg. 7:25; 8:21; 21:11; 1 Sam. 15:32,33; 2 Sam. 8:2; 2 Kin. 8:12; Jer. 39:6; twenty thousand, by Amaziah, 2 Chr. 25:11, 12; ripping women with child, 2 Kin. 8:12; 15:16; Amos 1:13; tortured under saws and harrows, 2 Sam. 12:31; 1 Chr. 20:3; blinded, Judg. 16:21; Jer. 39:7; maimed, Judg. 1:6,7; ravished, Lam. 5:11-13; Zech. 14:2; enslaved, Deut. 20:14; 2 Kin. 5:2; Psa. 44:12; Joel 3:6; robbed, Ezek. 23:25,26; confined in pits, Isa. 51:14. Other indignities to, Isa. 20:4.

Kindness to, 2 Kin. 25:27-30; Psa. 106:46. Advanced to positions in state, Gen. 41:39-45; Esth. 2:8; Dan. 1.

CAPTIVITY. Of the Israelites foretold, Lev. 26:33; Deut. 28:36; of the ten tribes, 2 Kin. 17:6,23,24; 18:9-12.

Of Judah in Babylon, prophecy of, Isa. 39: 6; Jer. 13:19; 20:4; 25:2-11; 32:28, etc.; fulfilled, 2 Kin. 24:11-16; 25; 2 Chr. 36; Jer. 52: 28-30. Jews return from, Ezra, chapters 2; 3; 8. Israelites in, promises to, Neh. 1:9.

As a judgment, Ezra 5:12; 9:7; Isa. 5:13; Jer. 29:17-19; Lam. 1:3-5; Ezek. 39:23,24.

FIGURATIVE: Isa. 61:1; Rom. 7:23; 1 Cor. 9:27; 2 Cor. 10:5; 2 Tim. 2:26; 3:6. "Captivity led captive," Judg. 5:12; Psa. 68:18; Eph. 4:8.

CARBUNCLE. A precious stone, Isa. 54: 12; Ezek. 28:13. One of the precious stones set in breastplate, Ex. 28:17; 39:10.

CARCAS, a Persian chamberlain, Esth. 1:10.

CARCHEMISH, a Babylonian city on the Euphrates, against which the king of Egypt made war, 2 Chr. 35:20; Isa. 10:9; Jer. 46:2.

CARE, WORLDLY: Psa. 39:6. Surely every man walketh in a vain shew: surely they are disquieted in vain: he heapeth up *riches*, and knoweth not who shall gather them.

Psa. 127:2. *It is* vain for you to rise up early, to sit up late, to eat the bread of sorrows: *for* so he giveth his beloved sleep.

Eccl. 4:8. There is one *alone*, and *there is* not a second; yea, he hath neither child nor brother: yet *is there* no end of all his labour: neither is his eye satisfied with riches; neither *saith he*, For whom do I labour, and bereave my soul of good? This *is* also vanity, yea, it *is* a sore travail.

Matt. 6:25. Therefore I say unto you, Take no thought [be not anxious, *R. V.*] for your life, what ye shall eat, or what ye shall drink; nor yet for your body, what ye shall put on. Is not the life more than meat, and the body than raiment? 26. Behold the fowls of the air: for they sow not, neither do they reap, nor gather into barns; yet your heavenly Father feedeth them. Are ye not much better than they? 27. Which of you by taking thought [by being anxious, *R. V.*] can add one cubit unto his stature? 28. And why take ye thought for raiment? Consider the lilies of the field, how they grow; they toil not, neither do they spin. [Luke 12:27]. 29. And yet I say unto you, That even Solomon in all his glory was not arrayed like one of these. 30. Wherefore, if God so clothe the grass of the field, which to-day is, and to-morrow is cast into the oven, *shall he* not much more *clothe* you, O ye of little faith? 31. Therefore take no thought [be not therefore anxious, *R. V.*], saying, What shall we eat? or, What shall we drink? or, Wherewithal shall we be clothed? 32. (For after all these things do the Gentiles seek:) for your heavenly Father knoweth that ye have need of all these things. 33. But seek ye first the kingdom of God, and his righteousness; and all these things shall be added unto you. 34. Take therefore no thought [be not therefore anxious, *R. V.*] for the morrow: for the morrow shall take thought for the things of itself. Sufficient unto the day *is* the evil thereof.

Matt. 13:22. He also that received seed among the thorns is he that heareth the word; and the care of this world, and the deceitfulness of riches, choke the word, and he becometh unfruitful. Mark 4:19; Luke 8:14.

Luke 14:18. And they all with one *consent* began to make excuse. The first said unto him, I have bought a piece of ground, and I must needs go and see it: I pray thee have me excused. 19. And another said, I have bought five yoke of oxen, and I go to prove them: I pray thee have me excused. 20. And another said, I have married a wife, and therefore I cannot come.

Luke 21:34. Take heed to yourselves, lest at any time your hearts be overcharged with surfeiting, and drunkenness, and cares of this life, and *so* that day come upon you unawares.

1 Cor. 7:32. But I would have you without carefulness. He that is unmarried careth for the things that belong to the Lord, how he may please the Lord: 33. But he that is married careth for the things that are of the world, how he may please *his* wife.

Phil. 4:6. Be careful for nothing; but in every thing by prayer and supplication with thanksgiving let your requests be made known unto God.

2 Tim. 2:4. No man that warreth entangleth himself with the affairs of *this* life; that he may please him who hath chosen him to be a soldier.

See CARNAL MINDEDNESS; RICHES; WORLDLINESS.

REMEDY FOR: Psa. 37:5. Commit thy way unto the LORD; trust also in him; and he shall bring *it* to pass.

Psa. 55:22. Cast thy burden upon the LORD, and he shall sustain thee: he shall never suffer the righteous to be moved.

Prov. 16:3. Commit thy works unto the LORD, and thy thoughts shall be established.

Jer. 17:7. Blessed *is* the man that trusteth in the LORD, and whose hope the LORD is. 8. For he shall be as a tree planted by the waters, and *that* spreadeth out her roots by the river, and shall not see when heat cometh, but her leaf shall be green; and shall not be careful in the year of drought, neither shall cease from yielding fruit.

Matt. 6:26. Behold the fowls of the air: for they sow not, neither do they reap, nor gather into barns; yet your heavenly Father feedeth them. Are ye not much better than they? 27. Which of you by taking thought can add one cubit unto his stature? 28. And why take ye thought for raiment? Consider the lilies of the field, how they grow; they toil not, neither do they spin: 29. And yet I say unto you, That even Solomon in all his glory was not arrayed like one of these. 30. Wherefore, if God so clothe the grass of the field, which to day is, and to morrow is cast into the oven, *shall he* not much more *clothe* you, O ye of little faith? 31. Therefore take no thought, saying, What shall we eat? or, What shall we drink? or, Wherewithal shall we be clothed? 32. (For after all these things do the Gentiles seek:) for your heavenly Father knoweth that ye have need of all these things. 33. But seek ye first the kingdom of God, and his righteousness; and all these things shall be added unto you. 34. Take therefore no thought for the morrow: for the morrow shall take thought for the things of itself. Sufficient unto the day *is* the evil thereof. Luke 12:22–32.

Phil. 4:6. Be careful for nothing; but in every thing by prayer and supplication with thanksgiving let your requests be made known unto God. 7. And the peace of God, which passeth all understanding, shall keep your hearts and minds through Christ Jesus.

Heb. 13:5. Let *your* conversation *be* without covetousness; *and be* content with such things as ye have: for he hath said, I will never leave thee, nor forsake thee.

1 Pet. 5:6. Humble yourselves therefore under the mighty hand of God, that he may exalt you in due time: 7. Casting all your care upon him; for he careth for you.

INSTANCES OF: Martha, Luke 10:40,41. Certain persons who desired to follow Jesus, Matt. 8:19–22; Luke 9:57–62.

See RICH, THE.

CAREAH. See KAREAH.

CARMEL. 1. A fertile and picturesque mountain in Palestine, Song 7:5; Isa. 33:9; 35:2; Jer. 46:18; 50:19; Amos. 1:2. Forests of, 2 Kin. 19:23. Caves of, Amos 9:3; Mic. 7:14. An idolatrous high place upon; Elijah builds an altar upon, and confounds the worshipers of Baal, putting to death four hundred and fifty of its prophets, 1 Kin. 18:17–46. Elisha's abode in, 2 Kin. 2:25; 4:25.

2. A city of Judah, Josh. 15:55. Saul erects a memorial at, 1 Sam. 15:12. Nabal's

possessions at, 1 Sam. 25:2. King Uzziah, who delighted in agriculture, had vineyards at, 2 Chr. 26:10.

CARMI. 1. Son of Reuben, Gen. 46:9; Ex. 6:14.

2. Son of Hezron, 1 Chr. 4:1. Called CHELUBAI, 1 Chr. 2:9, and CALEB, *v.* 18.

3. Father of Achan, Josh. 7:1,18; 1 Chr. 2:7.

CARNAL MINDEDNESS. Rom. 8:6. For to be carnally minded *is* death; but to be spiritually minded *is* life and peace. 7. Because the carnal mind *is* enmity against God: for it is not subject to the law of God, neither indeed can be. 8. So then they that are in the flesh cannot please God.

Gal. 6:8. For he that soweth to his flesh shall of the flesh reap corruption; but he that soweth to the Spirit shall of the Spirit reap life everlasting.

Jas. 4:4. Ye adulterers and adulteresses, know ye not that the friendship of the world is enmity with God? whosoever therefore will be a friend of the world is the enemy of God.

See CARE, WORLDLY; RICHES; SIN, FRUITS OF; WORLDLINESS.

CARPENTRY. Building the ark, Gen. 6:14–16. Tabernacle, and furniture of, Ex. 31:2–9. See TABERNACLE. David's palace, 2 Sam. 5:11. Temple, 2 Kin. 12:11; 22:6. See TEMPLE. Making idols, Isa. 41:7; 44:13. Carpenters, Jer. 24:1; Zech. 1:20; Joseph, Matt. 13:55; Jesus, Mark 6:3.

See CARVING; MASTER WORKMAN.

CARPET, Prov. 31:22. [*R. V.*]

CARPUS, a Christian at Troas, 2 Tim. 4:13.

CARSHENA, a Persian prince, Esth. 1:14.

CART, 1 Sam. 6:7–14; 2 Sam. 6:3; Isa. 28:27,28.

See WAGON.

CARVING. Woodwork of the temple was decorated with carvings of flowers, cherubim, and palm trees, 1 Kin. 6:18,29,32,35; Psa. 74:6. Beds decorated with, Prov. 7:16. Idols manufactured by, Deut. 7:5; Isa. 44: 9–17; 45:20; Hab. 2:18,19. Persons skilled in: Bezaleel, Ex. 31:5; Hiram, 1 Kin. 7:13–51; 2 Chr. 2:13,14.

CASIPHIA, a place in the Persian empire, Ezra 8:17.

CASLUHIM, a people whose progenitor was a son of Mizraim, Gen. 10:14; 1 Chr. 1:12.

CASSIA. An aromatic plant, probably cinnamon, Psa. 45:8; Ezek. 27:19. An ingredient of the sacred oil, Ex. 30:24.

CASTING. See MOLDING.

CASTLE. A tower, Gen. 25:16; Num. 31:10; 1 Chr. 11:5,7; 2 Chr. 17:12; 27:4; Acts 21:34,37; 23:10,16,32. Bars of, Prov. 18:19. For the doctrine, "The house is my castle," see Deut. 24:10,11.

See FORT; TOWER.

CASTOR AND POLLUX, name of a ship, Acts 28:11.

CATERPILLAR. Sent as a judgment.

1 Kin. 8:37; Psa. 78:46; Psa. 105:34; Jer. 51:27. Joel 1:4; 2:25.

CATHOLICITY. Liberality of religious sentiment.

INCULCATED: Mark 9:38. And John answered him, saying, Master, we saw one casting out devils in thy name, and he followeth not us: and we forbad him, because he followeth not us. 39. But Jesus said, Forbid him not: for there is no man which shall do a miracle in my name, that can lightly speak evil of me. 40. For he that is not against us is on our part. 41. For whosoever shall give you a cup of water to drink in my name, because ye belong to Christ, verily I say unto you, he shall not lose his reward. Luke 9:49,50.

Acts 10:1. There was a certain man in Cæsarea called Cornelius, a centurion of the band called the Italian *band*, 2. A devout *man*, and one that feared God with all his house, which gave much alms to the people, and prayed to God alway. 3. He saw in a vision evidently about the ninth hour of the day an angel of God coming in to him, and saying unto him, Cornelius. 4. And when he looked on him, he was afraid, and said, What is it, Lord? And he said unto him, Thy prayers and thine alms are come up for a memorial before God. 5. And now send men to Joppa, and call for *one* Simon, whose surname is Peter: 6. He lodgeth with one Simon a tanner, whose house is by the sea side: he shall tell thee what thou oughtest to do. 7. And when the angel which spake unto Cornelius was departed, he called two of his household servants, and a devout soldier of them that waited on him continually; 8. And when he had declared all *these* things unto them, he sent them to Joppa. 9. On the morrow, as they went on their journey, and drew nigh unto the city, Peter went up upon the housetop to pray about the sixth hour: 10. And he became very hungry, and would have eaten: but while they made ready, he fell into a trance, 11. And saw heaven opened, and a certain vessel descending unto him, as it had been a great sheet knit at the four corners, and let down to the earth: 12. Wherein were all manner of fourfooted beasts of the earth, and wild beasts, and creeping things, and fowls of the air. 13. And there came a voice to him, Rise, Peter; kill, and eat. 14. But Peter said, Not so, Lord; for I have never eaten any thing that is common or unclean. 15. And the voice *spake* unto him again the second time, What God hath cleansed, *that* call not thou common. 16. This was done thrice: and the vessel was received up again into heaven. 17. Now while Peter doubted in himself what this vision which he had seen should mean, behold, the men which were sent from Cornelius had made inquiry for Simon's house, and stood before the gate, 18. And called, and asked whether Simon, which was surnamed Peter, were lodged there. 19. While Peter thought on the vision,

the Spirit said unto him, Behold, three men seek thee. 20. Arise therefore, and get thee down, and go with them, doubting nothing: for I have sent them. 21. Then Peter went down to the men which were sent unto him from Cornelius; and said, Behold, I am he whom ye seek: what *is* the cause wherefore ye are come? 22. And they said, Cornelius the centurion, a just man, and one that feareth God, and of good report among all the nation of the Jews, was warned from God by an holy angel to send for thee into his house, and to hear words of thee. 23. Then called he them in, and lodged *them*. And on the morrow Peter went away with them, and certain brethren from Joppa accompanied him. 24. And the morrow after they entered into Cæsarea. And Cornelius waited for them, and had called together his kinsmen and near friends. 25. And as Peter was coming in, Cornelius met him, and fell down at his feet, and worshipped *him*. 26. But Peter took him up, saying, Stand up; I myself also am a man. 27. And as he talked with him, he went in, and found many that were come together. 28. And he said unto them, Ye know how that it is an unlawful thing for a man that is a Jew to keep company, or come unto one of another nation; but God hath shewed me that I should not call any man common or unclean. 29. Therefore came I *unto you* without gainsaying, as soon as I was sent for: I ask therefore for what intent ye have sent for me? 30. And Cornelius said, Four days ago I was fasting until this hour; and at the ninth hour I prayed in my house, and, behold, a man stood before me in bright clothing, 31. And said, Cornelius, thy prayer is heard, and thine alms are had in remembrance in the sight of God. 32. Send therefore to Joppa, and call hither Simon, whose surname is Peter; he is lodged in the house of *one* Simon a tanner by the sea side: who, when he cometh, shall speak unto thee. 33. Immediately therefore I sent to thee; and thou hast well done that thou art come. Now therefore are we all here present before God, to hear all things that are commanded thee of God. 34. Then Peter opened *his* mouth, and said, Of a truth I perceive that God is no respecter of persons. 35. But in every nation he that feareth him, and worketh righteousness, is accepted with him. 36. The word which *God* sent unto the children of Israel, preaching peace by Jesus Christ: (he is Lord of all:) 37. That word, *I say*, ye know, which was published throughout all Judæa, and began from Galilee, after the baptism which John preached: 38. How God anointed Jesus of Nazareth with the Holy Ghost and with power: who went about doing good, and healing all that were oppressed of the devil; for God was with him. 39. And we are witnesses of all things which he did both in the land of the Jews, and in Jerusalem; whom they slew and hanged on a tree: 40. Him God raised up the third day, and shewed him openly; 41. Not to all the people, but unto witnesses chosen before of God, *even* to us, who did eat and drink with him after he rose from the dead. 42. And he commanded us to preach unto the people, and to testify that it is he which was ordained of God *to be* the Judge of quick and dead. 43. To him give all the prophets witness, that through his name whosoever believeth in him shall receive remission of sins. 44. While Peter yet spake these words, the Holy Ghost fell on all them which heard the word. 45. And they of the circumcision which believed were astonished, as many as came with Peter, because that on the Gentiles also was poured out the gift of the Holy Ghost. 46. For they heard them speak with tongues, and magnify God. Then answered Peter, 47. Can any man forbid water, that these should not be baptized, which have received the Holy Ghost as well as we? 48. And he commanded them to be baptized in the name of the LORD. Then prayed they him to tarry certain days.

Acts 11:17. Forasmuch then as God gave them the like gift as *he did* unto us, who believed on the Lord Jesus Christ, what was I, that I could withstand God? 18. When they heard these things, they held their peace, and glorified God, saying, Then hath God also to the Gentiles granted repentance unto life.

Acts 15:1. And certain men which came down from Judæa taught the brethren, *and said*, Except ye be circumcised after the manner of Moses, ye cannot be saved. 2. When therefore Paul and Barnabas had no small dissension and disputation with them, they determined that Paul and Barnabas, and certain other of them, should go up to Jerusalem unto the apostles and elders about this question. 3. And being brought on their way by the church, they passed through Phenice and Samaria, declaring the conversion of the Gentiles: and they caused great joy unto all the brethren. 4. And when they were come to Jerusalem, they were received of the church, and *of* the apostles and elders, and they declared all things that God had done with them. 5. But there rose up certain of the sect of the Pharisees which believed, saying, That it was needful to circumcise them, and to command *them* to keep the law of Moses.

6. And the apostles and elders came together for to consider of this matter. 7. And when there had been much disputing, Peter rose up, and said unto them, Men *and* brethren, ye know how that a good while ago God made choice among us, that the Gentiles by my mouth should hear the word of the gospel, and believe. 8. And God, which knoweth the hearts, bare them witness, giving them the Holy Ghost, even as *he did* unto us: 9. And put no difference between us and them, purifying their hearts by faith. 10. Now therefore why tempt ye God, to put a yoke upon the neck of the disciples, which neither our fathers nor we were able to bear? 11. But we believe that through the grace of the Lord Jesus Christ we shall be saved, even as they.

12. Then all the multitude kept silence, and gave audience to Barnabas and Paul, declaring what miracles and wonders God had wrought among the Gentiles by them. 13. And after they had held their peace, James answered, saying, Men *and* brethren, hearken unto me: 14. Simeon hath declared how God at the first did visit the Gentiles, to take out of them a people for his name. 15. And to this agree the words of the prophets: as it is written, 16. After this I will return, and will build again the tabernacle of David, which is fallen down; and I will build again the ruins thereof, and I will set it up: 17. That the residue of men might seek after the Lord, and all the Gentiles, upon whom my name is called, saith the Lord, who doeth all these things. 18. Known unto God are all his works from the beginning of the world. 19. Wherefore my sentence is, that we trouble not them, which from among the Gentiles are turned to God: 20. But that we write unto them, that they abstain from pollutions of idols, and *from* fornication, and *from* things strangled, and *from* blood. 21. For Moses of old time hath in every city them that preach him, being read in the synagogues every sabbath day. 22. Then pleased it the apostles and elders, with the whole church, to send chosen men of their own company to Antioch with Paul and Barnabas; *namely*, Judas surnamed Barsabas, and Silas, chief men among the brethren: 23. And they wrote *letters* by them after this manner; The apostles and elders and brethren *send* greeting unto the brethren which are of the Gentiles in Antioch and Syria and Cilicia: 24. Forasmuch as we have heard, that certain which went out from us have troubled you with words, subverting your souls, saying, Ye *must* be circumcised, and keep the law; to whom we gave no *such* commandment: 25. It seemed good unto us, being assembled with one accord, to send chosen men unto you with our beloved Barnabas and Paul, 26. Men that have hazarded their lives for the name of our Lord Jesus Christ. 27. We have sent therefore Judas and Silas, who shall also tell *you* the same things by mouth. 28. For it seemed good to the Holy Ghost, and to us, to lay upon you no greater burden than these necessary things; 29. That ye abstain from meats offered to idols, and from blood, and from things strangled, and from fornication: from which if ye keep yourselves, ye shall do well. Fare ye well. 30. So when they were dismissed, they came to Antioch: and when they had gathered the multitude together, they delivered the epistle: 31. *Which* when they had read, they rejoiced for the consolation.

Rom. 1:1. Paul, a servant of Jesus Christ, called *to be* an apostle, separated unto the gospel of God. 2. (Which he had promised afore by his prophets in the holy scriptures.) 3. Concerning his Son Jesus Christ our Lord, which was made of the seed of David according to the flesh; 4. And declared *to be* the Son of God with power, according to the Spirit of holiness, by the resurrection from the dead: 5. By whom we have received grace and apostleship, for obedience to the faith among all nations, for his name: 6. Among whom are ye also the called of Jesus Christ: 7. To all that be in Rome, beloved of God, called *to be* saints: Grace to you and peace from God our Father, and the Lord Jesus Christ.

14. I am debtor both to the Greeks, and to the Barbarians; both to the wise, and to the unwise. 15. So, as much as in me is, I am ready to preach the gospel to you that are at Rome also. 16. For I am not ashamed of the gospel of Christ: for it is the power of God unto salvation to every one that believeth; to the Jew first, and also to the Greek.

Rom. 3:20. Therefore by the deeds of the law there shall no flesh be justified in his sight: for by the law *is* the knowledge of sin. 21. But now the righteousness of God without the law is manifested, being witnessed by the law and the prophets; 22. Even the righteousness of God *which is* by faith of Jesus Christ unto all and upon all them that believe: for there is no difference: 23. For all have sinned, and come short of the glory of God; 24. Being justified freely by his grace through the redemption that is in Christ Jesus: 25. Whom God hath set forth *to be* a propitiation through faith in his blood, to declare his righteousness for the remission of sins that are past, through the forbearance of God; 26. To declare, *I say*, at this time his righteousness: that he might be just, and the justifier of him which believeth in Jesus. 27. Where *is* boasting then? It is excluded. By what law? of works? Nay: but by the law of faith. 28. Therefore we conclude that a man is justified by faith without the deeds of the law. 29. *Is he* the God of the Jews only? *is he* not also of the Gentiles? Yes, of the Gentiles also: 30. Seeing *it is* one God, which shall justify the circumcision by faith, and uncircumcision through faith. 31. Do we then make void the law through faith? God forbid: yea, we establish the law.

Rom. 4:1. What shall we say then that Abraham our father, as pertaining to the flesh, hath found? 2. For if Abraham were justified by works, he hath *whereof* to glory; but not before God. 3. For what saith the scripture? Abraham believed God, and it was counted unto him for righteousness. 4. Now to him that worketh is the reward not reckoned of grace, but of debt. 5. But to him that worketh not, but believeth on him that justifieth the ungodly, his faith is counted for righteousness. 6. Even as David also describeth the blessedness of the man, unto whom God imputeth

righteousness without works. 7. *Saying*, Blessed *are* they whose iniquities are forgiven, and whose sins are covered. 8. Blessed *is* the man to whom the Lord will not impute sin. 9. *Cometh* this blessedness then upon the circumcision *only*, or upon the uncircumcision also? for we say that faith was reckoned to Abraham for righteousness. 10. How was it then reckoned? when he was in circumcision, or in uncircumcision? Not in circumcision, but in uncircumcision. 11. And he received the sign of circumcision, a seal of the righteousness of the faith which *he had yet* being uncircumcised; that he might be the father of all them that believe, though they be not circumcised; that righteousness might be imputed unto them also: 12. And the father of circumcision to them who are not of the circumcision only, but who also walk in the steps of that faith of our father Abraham, which *he had* being *yet* uncircumcised. 13. For the promise, that he should be the heir of the world, *was* not to Abraham, or to his seed, through the law, but through the righteousness of faith. 14. For if they which are of the law *be* heirs, faith is made void, and the promise made of none effect: 15. Because the law worketh wrath: for where no law is, *there* is no transgression. 16. Therefore *it is* of faith that *it might be* by grace; to the end the promise might be sure to all the seed; not to that only which is of the law, but to that also which is of the faith of Abraham; who is the father of us all, 17. (As it is written, I have made thee a father of many nations,) before him whom he believed, *even* God, who quickeneth the dead, and calleth those things which be not as though they were: 18. Who against hope believed in hope, that he might become the father of many nations, according to that which was spoken, So shall thy seed be. 19. And being not weak in faith, he considered not his own body now dead, when he was about an hundred years old, neither yet the deadness of Sarah's womb: 20. He staggered not at the promise of God through unbelief; but was strong in faith, giving glory to God; 21. And being fully persuaded that, what he had promised, he was able also to perform. 22. And therefore it was imputed to him for righteousness. 23. Now it was not written for his sake alone, that it was imputed to him; 24. But for us also, to whom it shall be imputed, if we believe on him that raised up Jesus our LORD from the dead; 25. Who was delivered for our offences, and was raised again for our justification.

Rom. 5:1. Therefore being justified by faith, ¹ we have peace with God through our Lord Jesus Christ: 2. By whom also we have access by faith into this grace wherein we stand, and rejoice in hope of the glory of God. [¹ R. V. let us]

Gal. 3:27. For as many of you as have been baptized into Christ have put on

Christ. 28. There is neither Jew nor Greek, there is neither bond nor free, there is neither male nor female: for ye are all one in Christ Jesus.

Eph. 2:14. For he is our peace, who hath made both one, and hath broken down the middle wall of partition *between us;* 15. Having abolished in his flesh the enmity, *even* the law of commandments *contained* in ordinances; for to make in himself of twain one new man, *so* making peace; 16. And that he might reconcile both unto God in one body by the cross, having slain the enmity thereby: 17. And came and preached peace to you which were afar off, and to them that were nigh.

Col. 3:11. Where there is neither Greek nor Jew, circumcision nor uncircumcision, Barbarian, Scythian, bond *nor* free: but Christ *is* all, and in all. 12. Put on therefore, as the elect of God, holy and beloved, bowels of mercies, kindness, humbleness of mind, meekness, longsuffering; 13. Forbearing one another, and forgiving one another, if any man have a quarrel against any: even as Christ forgave you, so also *do* ye. 14. And above all these things *put on* charity, which is the bond of perfectness. 15. And let the peace of God rule in your hearts, to the which also ye are called in one body; and be ye thankful.

See HEATHEN; STRANGERS.

INSTANCES OF: Solomon, in his prayer, 1 Kin. 8:41-43. Paul, in recognizing devout heathen, Acts 13:16,26,42,43. Peter, Acts 10: 34,35. Rulers of the synagogue at Salamis, permitting the Apostles to preach, Acts 13:5.

CATTLE, of the bovine species. Used for sacrifice, 1 Kin. 8:63. See HEIFER; OFFERINGS. Sheltered, Gen. 33:17. Stall-fed, Prov. 15:17.

Gilead adapted to the raising of, Num. 32: 1-4, and Bashan, Psa. 22:12; Ezek. 39:18; Amos 4:1.

See ANIMALS; BULL; BULLOCK; COW; HEIFER; KINE; OFFERING.

CAUL. 1. Probably the upper lobe of the liver. Burnt with sacrifice, Ex. 29:13, 22; Lev. 3:4,10,15; 4:9; 7:4; 8:16,25; 9:10,19. 2. Netted caps, Isa. 3:18.

CAUTION. See EXPEDIENCY; PRUDENCE.

CAVALRY. Mounted on horses, Ex. 14:23; 1 Sam. 13:5; 2 Sam. 8:4; 1 Kin. 4:26; 2 Chr. 8:6; 9:25; 12:3; Isa. 30:16; 31:1; Jer. 4:29; Zech. 10:5; Rev. 9:16-18; on camels, 1 Sam. 30:17.

See ARMIES.

CAUSE. See ACTIONS AT LAW.

CAVE. Used as a dwelling: By Lot, Gen. 19:30; Elijah, 1 Kin. 19:9; Israelites, Ezek. 33:27; saints, Heb. 11:38. Place of refuge, Josh. 10:16-27; Judg. 6.2; 1 Sam. 13:6; 1 Kin. 18:4,13; 19:9,13. Burial place, Gen. 23:9-20; 25:9; 49:29-32; 50:13; John 11:38.

Of Adullam, 1 Sam. 22:1; 2 Sam. 23:13; 1 Chr. 11:15. En-gedi, 1 Sam. 24:3-8.

CEDAR. Valuable for building pur-

poses, Isa. 9:10. David's ample provision of, in Jerusalem, for the temple, 2 Chr. 1:15; 22:4. Furnished by Hiram, king of Tyre, for Solomon's temple, 1 Kin. 5:6-10; 9:11; 2 Chr. 2:16. Used in rebuilding the temple, Ezra 3:7; in David's palace, 2 Sam. 5:11; 1 Chr. 17:1; in Solomon's palace, 1 Kin. 7:2; for masts of ships, Ezek. 27:5; in purifications, Lev. 14:4,6,49-52; Num. 19:6.

FIGURATIVE: Psa. 72:16; 92:12; Isa. 2:13; 14:8; Jer. 22:7; Ezek. 31:3; Zech. 11:2.

CEDRON. Called also KIDRON. Brook of, running S. under the eastern wall of Jerusalem, 1 Kin. 2:37; Neh. 2:15; Jer. 31:40. Idols destroyed on the banks of: By Asa, 1 Kin. 15:13; Josiah, 2 Kin. 23:6,12; Hezekiah, 2 Chr. 29:16.

Its channel changed by Hezekiah, 2 Chr. 32:4.

CELIBACY. Matt. 19:10. His disciples say unto him, If the case of the man be so with *his* wife, it is not good to marry. 11. But he said unto them, All *men* cannot receive this saying, save *they* to whom it is given. 12. For there are some eunuchs, which were so born from *their* mother's womb: and there are some eunuchs which were made eunuchs of men: and there be eunuchs, which have made themselves eunuchs for the kingdom of heaven's sake. He that is able to receive *it*, let him receive *it.*

1 Cor. 7:1. Now concerning the things whereof ye wrote unto me: *It is* good for a man not to touch a woman. 2. Nevertheless, *to avoid* fornication, let every man have his own wife, and let every woman have her own husband. 7. For I would that all men were even as I myself. But every man hath his proper gift of God, one after this manner, and another after that. 8. I say therefore to the unmarried and widows, It is good for them if they abide even as I. 9. But if they cannot contain, let them marry: for it is better to marry than to burn.

25. Now concerning virgins I have no commandment of the Lord: yet I give my judgment, as one that hath obtained mercy of the Lord to be faithful. 26. I suppose therefore that this is good for the present distress, *I say,* that *it is* good for a man so to be.

32. But I would have you without carefulness. He that is unmarried careth for the things that belong to the Lord, how he may please the Lord: 33. But he that is married careth for the things that are of the world, how he may please *his* wife. 34. There is difference *also* between a wife and a virgin. The unmarried woman careth for the things of the Lord, that she may be holy both in body and in spirit: but she that is married careth for the things of the world, how she may please *her* husband. 35. And this I speak for your own profit; not that I may cast a snare upon you, but for that which is comely, and that ye may attend upon the Lord without distraction. 36. But if any man think that he behaveth himself

uncomely toward his virgin, if she pass the flower of *her* age, and need so require, let him do what he will, he sinneth not: let them marry. 37. Nevertheless he that standeth stedfast in his heart, having no necessity, but hath power over his own will, and hath so decreed in his heart that he will keep his virgin, doeth well. 38. So then he that giveth *her* in marriage doeth well; but he that giveth *her* not in marriage doeth better. 39. The wife is bound by the law as long as her husband liveth; but if her husband be dead, she is at liberty to be married to whom she will; only in the Lord. 40. But she is happier if she so abide, after my judgment: and I think also that I have the Spirit of God.

1 Cor. 9:5. Have we not power to lead about a sister, a wife, as well as other apostles, and *as* the brethren of the Lord, and Cephas?

1 Tim. 4:1. Now the Spirit speaketh expressly, that in the latter times some shall depart from the faith, giving heed to seducing spirits, and doctrines of devils; 2. Speaking lies in hypocrisy; having their conscience seared with a hot iron; 3. Forbidding to marry, *and commanding* to abstain from meats, which God hath created to be received with thanksgiving of them which believe and know the truth.

Rev. 14:1. And I looked, and, lo, a Lamb stood on the mount Sion, and with him an hundred forty *and* four thousand, having his Father's name written in their foreheads. 4. These are they which were not defiled with women; for they are virgins. These are they which follow the Lamb whithersoever he goeth. These were redeemed from among men, *being* the firstfruits unto God and to the Lamb. with *vs.* 2-5.

CELLAR, for wine, 1 Chr. 27:27. Oil, 1 Chr. 27:28.

CENCHREA, a city of Corinth, Acts 18:18; Rom. 16:1.

CENSER. Used for offering incense, Lev. 16:12; Num. 4:14; 16:6,7,16–18,46; Rev. 8:3. For the temple, made of gold, 1 Kin. 7:50; 2 Chr. 4:22; Heb. 9:4. Those which Korah used were converted into plates, Num. 16:37–39. Used in idolatrous rites, Ezek. 8:11.

SYMBOLICAL: Rev. 8:3,5.

CENSORIOUSNESS. See UNCHARITABLENESS; SPEAKING, EVIL; CHARITABLENESS.

CENSUS. Numbering of Israel by Moses, Ex. 38:26; Num. 1; 3:14–43; 26; by David, 2 Sam. 24:1-9; 1 Chr. 21:1–8; 27:24.

A poll tax to be levied at each, Ex. 30:12-16; 38:26.

Of the Roman Empire, by Cæsar, Luke 2:1-3 [R. V.].

CENTURION. A commander of one hundred soldiers in the Roman army, Mark 15:44,45; Acts 21:32; 22:25,26; 23:17,23; 24:23. Of Capernaum, comes to Jesus in behalf of his servant, Matt. 8:5-13; Luke 7:1-10. In

charge of the soldiers who crucified Jesus, testifies, "Truly this was the Son of God," Matt. 27:54; Mark 15:39; Luke 23:47.

See CORNELIUS, JULIUS.

CEPHAS. See PETER.

CESAR. See CÆSAR.

CESAREA. See CÆSAREA.

CESAREA PHILIPPI. See CÆSAREA PHILIPPI.

CHAFF, FIGURATIVE: Job 21:18; Psa. 1:4; 35:5; Isa. 17:13; Dan. 2:35; Hos. 13:3; Matt. 3:12; Luke 3:17.

CHAINS. Used as ornaments. Worn by princes, Gen. 41:42; Dan. 5:7,29. Worn on ankles, Num. 31:50; Isa. 3:19; on the breastplate of high priest, Ex. 28:14; 39:15. As ornaments on camels, Judg. 8:26. A partition of, in the temple, 1 Kin. 6:21; 7:17.

Used to confine prisoners, Psa. 68:6; 149:8; Jer. 40:4; Acts 12:6,7; 21:33; 28:20; 2 Tim. 1:16.

See FETTERS.

FIGURATIVE: Psa. 73:6; Prov. 1:9; Lam. 3:7; Ezek. 7:23–27; Jude 6; 2 Pet. 2:4; Rev. 20:1.

CHALCEDONY, a precious stone, Rev. 21:19.

CHALCOL, called also CALCOL. Son of Nahor, 1 Kin. 4:31; 1 Chr. 2:6.

CHALDEA, the southern portion of Babylonia. Often used interchangeably with Babylon, as the name of the empire founded in the valley of the Euphrates. Abraham a native of, Gen. 11:28,31; 15:7. Founded [R. V., destroyed] by the Assyrians, Isa. 23:13. Character of its people, Hab. 1:6.

See BABYLON; CHALDEANS.

CHALDEANS, learned and wise men of the east, Dan. 1:4; 2:2; 4:7; 5:7; Jer. 50:35.

CHALK, Isa. 27:9.

CHAMBERLAIN, an officer of a king, 2 Kin. 23:11; Esth. 1:10–15; 2:3–21; 4:4,5; Acts 12:20; Rom. 16:23.

CHAMELEON, forbidden as food, Lev. 11:30.

CHAMOIS, a species of antelope, Deut. 14:5.

CHAMPAIGN, a flat, open country, Deut. 11:30.

CHAMPIONSHIP. Battles were decided by. INSTANCES OF: Goliath and David, 1 Sam. 17:8-53. Young men of David's and Abner's armies, 2 Sam. 2:14-17. Representatives of the Philistines' and David's armies, 2 Sam. 21:15-22.

CHANAAN. See CANAAN.

CHANCELLOR, a state officer, Ezra 4: 8,9,17.

See CABINET.

CHANGE OF VENUE. Granted Paul, Acts 23:17-35. Declined by Paul, Acts. 25: 9,11.

CHAPITER, head of a pillar, Ex. 36: 38; 1 Kin. 7:16–42; 2 Kin. 25:17; 2 Chr. 4:12, 13; Jer. 52:22.

CHARACTER. OF SAINTS: Attentive to Christ's voice, John 10:3,4; blameless and harmless, Phil. 2:15; bold, Prov. 28:1; contrite, Isa. 57:15; 66:2; devout, Acts 8:2; 22:12;

faithful, Rev. 17:14; fearing God, Mal. 3:16; Acts 10:2; following Christ, John 10:4,27; godly, Psa. 4:3; 2 Pet. 2:9; guileless, John 1: 47; holy, Deut. 7:6; 14:2; Col. 3:12; humble, Psa. 34:2; 1 Pet. 5:5; hungering for righteousness, Matt. 5:6; just, Gen. 6:9; Hab. 2:4; Luke 2:25; led by the Spirit, Rom. 8:14; liberal, Isa. 32:8; 2 Cor. 9:13; loathing themselves, Ezek. 20:43; loving, Col. 1:4; 1 Thess. 4:9; lowly, Prov. 16:19; meek, Isa. 29:19; Matt. 5:5; merciful, Psa. 37:26; Matt. 5:7; new creatures, 2 Cor. 5:17; Eph. 2:10; obedient, Rom. 16:19; 1 Pet. 1:14; poor in spirit, Matt. 5:3; prudent, Prov. 16:21; pure in heart, Matt. 5:8; 1 John 3:3; righteous, Isa. 60:21; Luke 1:6; sincere, 2 Cor. 1:12; 2:17; steadfast, Acts 2:42; Col. 2:5; taught of God, Isa. 54:13; 1 John 2:27; true, 2 Cor. 6:8; undefiled, Psa. 119:1; upright. 1 Kin. 3:6; Psa. 15:2; watchful, Luke 12:37; zealous of good works, Tit. 2:14.

See RIGHTEOUS, DESCRIBED.

OF THE WICKED: Abominable, Rev. 21:8; alienated from God, Eph. 4:18; Col. 1:21; blasphemous, Luke 22:65; Rev. 16:9; blinded, 2 Cor. 4:4; Eph. 4:18; boastful, Psa. 10:3; 49:6; conspiring against saints, Neh. 4:8; 6:2; Psa. 38:12; corrupt, Matt. 7:17; Eph. 4:22; covetous, Mic. 2:2; Rom. 1:29; deceitful, Psa. 5:6; Rom. 3:13; delighting in the iniquity of others, Prov. 2:14; Rom. 1:32; despising saints, Neh. 2:19; 4:2; 2 Tim. 3:3,4; destructive, Isa. 59:7; disobedient, Neh. 9:26; Tit. 3:3; 1 Pet. 2:7; enticing to evil, Prov. 1:10–14; 2 Tim. 3:6; envious, Neh. 2:10; Tit. 3:3; evildoers, Jer. 13:23; Mic. 7:3; fearful, Prov. 28: 1; Rev. 21:8; fierce, Prov. 16:29; 2 Tim. 3:3; foolish, Deut. 32:6; Psa. 5:5; forgetting God, Job 8:13; fraudulent, Psa. 37:21; Mic. 6:11; froward, Prov. 21:8; Isa. 57:17; glorying in their shame, Phil. 3:19; hard-hearted, Ezek. 3:7; hating the light, Job 24:13; John 3:20; heady and high-minded, 2 Tim. 3:4; hostile to God, Rom. 8:7; Col. 1:21; hypocritical, Isa. 29:13; 2 Tim. 3:5; ignorant of God, Hos. 4:1; 2 Thess. 1:8; impudent, Ezek. 2:4; incontinent, 2 Tim. 3:3; infidel, Psa. 10:4; 14:1; loathsome, Prov. 13:5; lovers of pleasure, not of God, 2 Tim. 3:4; lying, Psa. 58:3; 62:4; Isa. 59:4; mischievous, Prov. 24:8; Mic. 7:3; murderous, Psa. 10:8; 94:6; Rom. 1:29; prayerless, Job 21:15; Psa. 53:4; persecuting, Psa. 69:26; 109: 16; perverse, Deut. 32:5; proud, Psa. 59:12; Obad. 3; 2 Tim. 3:2; rebellious, Isa. 1:2; 30:9; rejoicing in the affliction of saints, Psa. 35: 15; reprobate, 2 Cor. 13:5; 2 Tim. 3:8; Tit. 1: 16; selfish, 2 Tim. 3:2; sensual, Phil. 3:19; Jude, 19; sold under sin, 1 Kin. 21:20; 2 Kin. 17:17; stiff-hearted, Ezek. 2:4; stiff-necked, Ex. 33:5; Acts 7:51; uncircumcised in heart, Jer. 9:26; unclean, Isa. 64:6; Eph. 4:19; unjust, Prov. 11:7; Isa. 26:18; unmerciful, Rom. 1:31; ungodly, Prov. 16:27; unholy, 2 Tim. 3:2; unprofitable, Matt. 25:30; Rom. 3:12; unruly, Tit. 1:10; unthankful, Luke 6:35; 2 Tim. 3:2; untoward, Acts 2:40; unwise, Deut. 32:6. —*Bible Text Book.*

See WICKED, DESCRIBED.

GOOD: Prov. 22:1. A *good* name *is* rather to be chosen than great riches, *and* loving favour rather than silver and gold. Eccl. 7:1.

DEFAMATION OF, PUNISHED: Deut. 22:13. If any man take a wife, and go in unto her, and hate her, 14. And give occasions of speech against her, and bring up an evil name upon her, and say, I took this woman, and when I came to her, I found her not a maid: 15. Then shall the father of the damsel, and her mother, take and bring forth *the tokens of* the damsel's virginity unto the elders of the city in the gate. 16. And the damsel's father shall say unto the elders, I gave my daughter unto this man to wife, and he hateth her; 17. And, lo, he hath given occasions of speech *against her*, saying, I found not thy daughter a maid; and yet these *are the tokens of* my daughter's virginity. And they shall spread the cloth before the elders of the city. 18. And the elders of that city shall take that man and chastise him; 19. And they shall amerce him in an hundred *shekels* of silver, and give *them* unto the father of the damsel, because he hath brought up an evil name upon a virgin of Israel: and she shall be his wife; he may not put her away all his days.

REVEALED IN COUNTENANCE: Isa. 3:9. The shew of their countenance doth witness against them; and they declare their sin as Sodom, they hide *it* not. Woe unto their soul! for they have rewarded evil unto themselves. See COUNTENANCE; FACE.

FIRMNESS OF: Psa. 57:7. My heart is fixed, O God, my heart is fixed: I will sing and give praise. Psa. 108:1; 112:7.

Matt. 10:22. And ye shall be hated of all *men* for my name's sake: but he that endureth to the end shall be saved.

Mark 4:20. And these are they which are sown on good ground; such as hear the word, and receive *it*, and bring forth fruit, some thirtyfold, some sixty, and some an hundred.

1 Cor. 7:20. Let every man abide in the same calling wherein he was called.

2 Thess. 2:15. Therefore, brethren, stand fast, and hold the traditions which ye have been taught, whether by word or our epistle.

2 Thess. 3:3. But the Lord is faithful, who shall stablish you, and keep *you* from evil.

Heb. 10:23. Let us hold fast the profession of *our* faith without wavering; (for he *is* faithful that promised;)

Heb. 13:9. Be not carried about with divers and strange doctrines. For *it is* a good thing that the heart be established with grace: not with meats, which have not profited them that have been occupied therein.

Jas. 1:25. But whoso looketh into the perfect law of liberty, and continueth *therein*, he being not a forgetful hearer, but a doer of the work, this man shall be blessed in his deed.

INSTANCES OF FIRMNESS: Joseph in resisting Potiphar's wife, Gen. 39:7–12; Pilate, John 19:22; Paul, Acts 20:22–24; 21:13,14.

See DECISION; STABILITY.

INSTABILITY OF: Prov. 24:21. My son, fear thou the LORD and the king: *and* meddle not with them that are given to change: 22. For their calamity shall rise suddenly; and who knoweth the ruin of them both?

Prov. 27:8. As a bird that wandereth from her nest, so *is* a man that wandereth from his place.

Jer. 2:36. Why gaddest thou about so much to change thy way? thou also shalt be ashamed of Egypt, as thou wast ashamed of Assyria.

Hos. 6:4. O Ephraim, what shall I do unto thee? O Judah, what shall I do unto thee? for your goodness *is* as a morning cloud, and as the early dew it goeth away.

Hos. 7:8. Ephraim, he hath mixed himself among the people: Ephraim is a cake not turned.

Hos. 10:2. Their heart is divided; now shall they be found faulty: he shall break down their altars, he shall spoil their images.

Matt. 13:19. When any one heareth the word of the kingdom, and understandeth *it* not, then cometh the wicked *one*, and catcheth away that which was sown in his heart. This is he which received seed by the way side. 20. But he that received the seed into stony places, the same is he that heareth the word, and anon with joy receiveth it; 21. Yet hath he not root in himself, but dureth for a while: for when tribulation or persecution ariseth because of the word, by and by he is offended. 22. He also that received seed among the thorns is he that heareth the word; and the care of this world, and the deceitfulness of riches, choke the word, and he becometh unfruitful. Mark 4:15–19; Luke 8:5–15.

Luke 9:59. And he said unto another, Follow me. But he said, Lord, suffer me first to go and bury my father. 60. Jesus said unto him, Let the dead bury their dead: but go thou and preach the kingdom of God. 61. And another also said, Lord, I will follow thee; but let me first go bid them farewell, which are at home at my house. 62. And Jesus said unto him, No man, having put his hand to the plough, and looking back, is fit for the kingdom of God. Matt. 8:19–22.

Eph. 4:14. That we *henceforth* be no more children, tossed to and fro, and carried about with every wind of doctrine, by the sleight of men, *and* cunning craftiness, whereby they lie in wait to deceive;

Jas. 1:6. But let him ask in faith, nothing ¹wavering. For he that ²wavereth is like a wave of the sea driven with the wind and tossed. 7. For let not that man think that he shall receive any thing of the Lord. 8. A double minded man *is* unstable in all his ways.   [R. V. ¹doubting ²doubteth]

Jas. 4:8. Draw nigh to God, and he will draw nigh to you. Cleanse *your* hands, *ye* sinners; and purify *your* hearts, *ye* double minded.

2 Pet. 2:14. Having eyes full of adultery, and that cannot cease from sin; beguiling unstable souls:

See INDECISION; INSTABILITY, DECISION; PERSEVERANCE; STABILITY.

INSTANCES OF INSTABILITY. REUBEN: Gen. 49:3. Reuben, thou *art* my firstborn, my might, and the beginning of my strength, the excellency of dignity, and the excellency of power: 4. Unstable as water, thou shalt not excel; because thou wentest up to thy father's bed; then defiledst thou *it*: he went up to my couch.

PHARAOH: Ex. 8:15. But when Pharaoh saw that there was respite, he hardened his heart, and hearkened not unto them; as the LORD had said. 32. And Pharaoh hardened his heart at this time also, neither would he let the people go.

Ex. 9:34. And when Pharaoh saw that the rain and the hail and the thunders were ceased, he sinned yet more, and hardened his heart, he and his servants.

Ex. 14:5. And it was told the king of Egypt that the people fled: and the heart of Pharaoh and of his servants was turned against the people, and they said, Why have we done this, that we have let Israel go from serving us?

SOLOMON: 1 Kin. 11:4. For it came to pass, when Solomon was old, *that* his wives turned away his heart after other gods: and his heart was not perfect with the LORD his God, as *was* the heart of David his father. 5. For Solomon went after Ashtoreth the goddess of the Zidonians, and after Milcom the abomination of the Ammonites. 6. And Solomon did evil in the sight of the LORD, and went not fully after the LORD, as *did* David his father. 7. Then did Solomon build an high place for Chemosh, the abomination of Moab, in the hill that *is* before Jerusalem, and for Molech, the abomination of the children of Ammon. 8. And likewise did he for all his strange wives, which burnt incense and sacrificed unto their gods.

ISRAELITES: Ex. 32:8. They have turned aside quickly out of the way which I commanded them: they have made them a molten calf, and have worshipped it, and have sacrificed thereunto, and said, These *be* thy gods, O Israel, which have brought thee up out of the land of Egypt.

Judg. 2:17. And yet they would not hearken unto their judges, but they went a whoring after other gods, and bowed themselves unto them: they turned quickly out of the way which their fathers walked in, obeying the commandments of the LORD; *but* they did not so. 19. And it came to pass, when the judge was dead, *that* they returned, and corrupted *themselves* more than their fathers, in following other gods to serve them, and to bow down unto them; they ceased not from their own doings, nor from their stubborn way.

2 Chr. 11:17. So they strengthened the kingdom of Judah, and made Rehoboam the son of Solomon strong, three years: for three years they walked in the way of David and Solomon.

2 Chr. 12:1. And it came to pass when Rehoboam had established the kingdom, and had strengthened himself, he forsook the law of the LORD, and all Israel with him.

King Saul in his treatment of David, 1 Sam. chapters 18; 19.

CHARASHIM, valley of, 1 Chr. 4:14; Neh. 11:35.

CHARGE, delivered to ministers. See MINISTERS.

CHARGER, a dish. Dedicated to the tabernacle, Num. 7:13,19,25,31,37,43,49,55,61, 67,73,79,84,85. John Baptist's head carried on, Matt. 14:8,11.

CHARIOT. For war, Ex. 14:7,9,25; Josh. 11:4; 1 Sam. 13:5; 1 Kin. 20:1,25; 2 Kin. 6:14; 2 Chr. 12:2,3; Psa. 20:7; 46:9; Jer. 46:9; 47:3; 51:21; Joel 2:5; Nah. 2:3,4; 3:2. Wheels of Pharaoh's, providentially taken off, Ex. 14:25.

Commanded by captains, Ex. 14:7; 1 Kin. 9:22; 22:31-33; 2 Kin. 8:21. Made of iron, Josh. 17:18; Judg. 1:19. Introduced among Israelites by David, 2 Sam. 8:4. Imported from Egypt by Solomon, 1 Kin. 10:26-29. Cities for, 1 Kin. 9:19; 2 Chr. 1:14; 8:6; 9:25. Royal, Gen. 41:43; 46:29; 2 Kin. 5:9; 2 Chr. 35: 24; Jer. 17:25; Acts 8:29. Drawn by camels, Isa. 21:7; Mic. 1:13.

Traffic in, Rev. 18:13. Kings ride in, 2 Chr. 35:24; Jer. 17:25; 22:4. Cherubim in Solomon's temple mounted on, 1 Chr. 28:18.

FIGURATIVE: Chariots of God, Psa. 68:17; 104:3; 2 Kin. 6:17; Isa. 66:15; Hab. 3:8; Rev. 9:9.

SYMBOLICAL: Zech. 6:1-8; 2 Kin. 2:11,12.

CHARISM. An inspired gift, bestowed on the apostles and early Christians, Matt. 10:1,8; Mark 16:17,18; Luke 10:1,9,17,19; Acts 2:4; 10:44-46; 19:6; 1 Cor. 12.

See MIRACLES; TONGUES.

CHARITABLENESS. Prov. 10:12. Hatred stirreth up strifes: but love covereth all sins.

Prov. 17:9. He that covereth a transgression seeketh love; but he that repeateth a matter separateth *very* friends.

Matt. 5:23. Therefore if thou bring thy gift to the altar, and there rememberest that thy brother hath ought against thee; 24. Leave there thy gift before the altar, and go thy way; first be reconciled to thy brother, and then come and offer thy gift.

Matt. 6:14. For if ye forgive men their trespasses, your heavenly Father will also forgive you: 15. But if ye forgive not men their trespasses, neither will your Father forgive your trespasses.

Matt. 7:1. Judge not, that ye be not judged. 2. For with what judgment ye judge, ye shall be judged: and with what measure ye mete, it shall be measured to you again. 3. And why beholdest thou the mote that is in thy brother's eye, but considerest not the beam that is in thine own eye? 4. Or how wilt thou say to thy brother, Let me pull out the mote out of thine eye; and, behold, a beam *is* in thine own eye? 5. Thou hypocrite, first cast out the beam out of thine own eye; and then shalt thou see clearly to cast out the mote out of thy brother's eye. Luke 6:37-42.

Matt. 18:21. Then came Peter to him, and said, Lord, how oft shall my brother sin against me, and I forgive him? till seven times? 22. Jesus saith unto him, I say not unto thee, Until seven times: but, Until seventy times seven.

23. Therefore is the kingdom of heaven likened unto a certain king, which would take account of his servants. 24. And when he had begun to reckon, one was brought unto him, which owed him ten thousand talents. 25. But forasmuch as he had not to pay, his lord commanded him to be sold, and his wife, and children, and all that he had, and payment to be made. 26. The servant therefore fell down, and worshipped him, saying, Lord, have patience with me, and I will pay thee all. 27. Then the lord of that servant was moved with compassion, and loosed him, and forgave him the debt. 28. But the same servant went out, and found one of his fellowservants, which owed him an hundred pence: and he laid hands on him, and took *him* by the throat, saying, Pay me that thou owest. 29. And his fellowservant fell down at his feet, and besought him, saying, Have patience with me, and I will pay thee all. 30. And he would not: but went and cast him into prison, till he should pay the debt. 31. So when his fellowservants saw what was done, they were very sorry, and came and told unto their lord all that was done. 32. Then his lord, after that he had called him, said unto him, O thou wicked servant, I forgave thee all that debt, because thou desiredst me: 33. Shouldest not thou also have had compassion on thy fellowservant, even as I had pity on thee? 34. And his lord was wroth, and delivered him to the tormentors, till he should pay all that was due unto him. 35. So likewise shall my heavenly Father do also unto you, if ye from your hearts forgive not every one his brother their trespasses.

Luke 6:36. Be ye therefore merciful, as your Father also is merciful. 37. Judge not, and ye shall not be judged: condemn not and ye shall not be condemned: forgive, and ye shall be forgiven:

Luke 17:3. Take heed to yourselves: If thy brother trespass against thee, rebuke him; and if he repent, forgive him. 4. And if he trespass against thee seven times in a day, and seven times in a day turn again to thee, saying, I repent; thou shalt forgive him.

John 7:24. Judge not according to the appearance, but judge righteous judgment.

Rom. 14:1. Him that is weak in the faith receive ye, *but* not to doubtful disputations.

2. For one believeth that he may eat all things: another, who is weak, eateth herbs. 3. Let not him that eateth despise him that eateth not; and let not him which eateth not judge him that eateth: for God hath received him. 4. Who art thou that judgest another man's servant? to his own master he standeth or falleth. Yea, he shall be holden up: for God is able to make him stand. 5. One man esteemeth one day above another: another esteemeth every day *alike*. Let every man be fully persuaded in his own mind. 6. He that regardeth the day, regardeth *it* unto the Lord; and he that regardeth not the day, to the Lord he doth not regard *it*. He that eateth, eateth to the Lord, for he giveth God thanks; and he that eateth not, to the Lord he eateth not, and giveth God thanks. 7. For none of us liveth to himself, and no man dieth to himself. 8. For whether we live, we live unto the Lord; and whether we die, we die unto the Lord: whether we live therefore, or die, we are the Lord's. 9. For to this end Christ both died, and rose, and revived, that he might be Lord both of the dead and living. 10. But why dost thou judge thy brother? or why dost thou set at nought thy brother? for we shall all stand before the judgment seat of Christ. 11. For it is written, *As* I live, saith the Lord, every knee shall bow to me, and every tongue shall confess to God. 12. So then every one of us shall give account of himself to God. 13. Let us not therefore judge one another any more: but judge this rather, that no man put a stumblingblock or an occasion to fall in *his* brother's way. 14. I know, and am persuaded by the Lord Jesus, that *there is* nothing unclean of itself: but to him that esteemeth any thing to be unclean, to him *it is* unclean. 15. But if thy brother be grieved with *thy* meat, now walkest thou not charitably. Destroy not him with thy meat, for whom Christ died. 16. Let not then your good be evil spoken of: 17. For the kingdom of God is not meat and drink; but righteousness, and peace, and joy in the Holy Ghost. 18. For he that in these things serveth Christ *is* acceptable to God, and approved of men. 19. Let us therefore follow after the things which make for peace, and things wherewith one may edify another. 20. For meat destroy not the work of God. All things indeed *are* pure; but *it is* evil for that man who eateth with offence. 21. *It is* good neither to eat flesh, nor to drink wine, nor *any thing* whereby thy brother stumbleth, or is offended, or is made weak. 22. Hast thou faith? have *it* to thyself before God. Happy *is* he that condemneth not himself in that thing which he alloweth. 23. And he that doubteth is damned if he eat, because *he eateth* not of faith: for whatsoever *is* not of faith is sin.

1 Cor. 4:5. Therefore judge nothing before the time, until the Lord come, who both will bring to light the hidden things of darkness, and will make manifest the counsels of the hearts: and then shall every man have praise of God.

1 Cor. 10:28. But if any man say unto you, This is offered in sacrifice ¹ unto idols, eat not for his sake that shewed it, and for conscience sake: ¹ for the earth *is* the Lord's, and the fulness thereof: 29. Conscience, I say, not thine own, but of the other: for why is my liberty judged of another *man's* conscience? 30. For if I by grace be a partaker, why am I evil spoken of for that for which I give thanks? 31. Whether therefore ye eat, or drink, or whatsoever ye do, do all to the glory of God. 32. Give none offence, neither to the Jews, nor to the Gentiles, nor to the church of God: 33. Even as I please all *men* in all *things*, not seeking mine own profit, but the *profit* of many, that they may be saved. [¹ Omitted in R. V.]

1 Cor. 13:1. Though I speak with the tongues of men and of angels, and have not charity [*R. V.*, love], I am become *as* sounding brass, or a tinkling cymbal. 2. And though I have *the gift of* prophecy, and understand all mysteries, and all knowledge; and though I have all faith, so that I could remove mountains, and have not charity, I am nothing. 3. And though I bestow all my goods to feed *the poor*, and though I give my body to be burned, and have not charity, it profiteth me nothing.

4. Charity suffereth long, *and* is kind; charity envieth not; charity vaunteth not itself, is not puffed up, 5. Doth not behave itself unseemly, seeketh not her own, is not easily provoked, thinketh no evil; 6. Rejoiceth not in iniquity, but rejoiceth in the truth; 7. Beareth all things, believeth all things, hopeth all things, endureth all things. 8. Charity never faileth: but whether *there be* prophecies, they shall fail; whether *there be* tongues, they shall cease; whether *there be* knowledge, it shall vanish away. 9. For we know in part, and we prophesy in part. 10. But when that which is perfect is come, then that which is in part shall be done away. 11. When I was a child, I spake as a child, I understood as a child, I thought as a child: but when I became a man, I put away childish things. 12. For now we see through a glass, darkly; but then face to face: now I know in part; but then shall I know even as also I am known. 13. And now abideth faith, hope, charity, these three; but the greatest of these *is* charity.

1 Cor. 16:14. Let all your things be done with charity.

Gal. 6:1. Brethren, if a man be overtaken in a fault, ye which are spiritual, restore such an one in the spirit of meekness; considering thyself, lest thou also be tempted.

Eph. 4:32. And be ye kind one to another, tenderhearted, forgiving one another, even as God for Christ's sake hath forgiven you.

Col. 3:13. Forbearing one another, and forgiving one another, if any man have a quarrel against any: even as Christ forgave you, so also *do* ye.   14. And above all these things *put on* charity, which is the bond of perfectness.

1 Tim. 1:5. Now the end of the commandment is charity out of a pure heart, and *of* a good conscience, and *of* faith unfeigned:

1 Tim. 4:12. Let no man despise thy youth; but be thou an example of the believers, in word, in conversation, in charity, in spirit, in faith, in purity.

2 Tim. 2:22. Flee also youthful lusts: but follow righteousness, faith, charity, peace, with them that call on the Lord out of a pure heart.

Jas. 2:13. For he shall have judgment without mercy, that hath shewed no mercy; and mercy rejoiceth against judgment.

Jas. 4:11. Speak not evil one of another, brethren. He that speaketh evil of *his* brother, and judgeth his brother, speaketh evil of the law, and judgeth the law: but if thou judge the law, thou art not a doer of the law, but a judge.   12. There is one lawgiver, who is able to save and to destroy: who art thou that judgest another?

1 Pet. 3:9. Not rendering evil for evil, or railing for railing: but contrariwise blessing; knowing that ye are thereunto called, that ye should inherit a blessing.

1 Pet. 4:8. And above all things have fervent charity among yourselves: for charity shall cover a multitude of sins.

See LOVE; UNCHARITABLENESS.

CHARITY. See ALMS; BENEFICENCE; LIBERALITY; LOVE.

CHARMERS AND CHARMING. Isa. 19:3; Jer. 8:17. Prohibited, Deut. 18:11. Of serpents, Psa. 58:4,5; Jer. 8:17.

See SORCERY.

CHARRAN. See HARAN.

CHASTISEMENT. FROM GOD: Lev. 26:28. Then I will walk contrary unto you also in fury; and I, even I, will chastise you seven times for your sins.

Deut. 11:2. And know ye this day: for *I speak* not with your children which have not known, and which have not seen the chastisement of the LORD your God, his greatness, his mighty hand, and his stretched out arm,   3. And his miracles, and his acts, which he did in the midst of Egypt unto Pharaoh the king of Egypt, and unto all his land;   4. And what he did unto the army of Egypt, unto their horses, and to their chariots; how he made the water of the Red sea to overflow them as they pursued after you, and *how* the LORD hath destroyed them unto this day;   5. And what he did unto you in the wilderness, until ye came into this place;   6. And what he did unto Dathan and Abiram, the sons of Eliab, the son of Reuben: how the earth opened her mouth, and swallowed them up, and their households, and their tents, and all the substance that *was* in their possession, in the midst of all Israel: 7. But your eyes have seen all the great acts of the LORD which he did.   8. Therefore shall ye keep all the

commandments which I command you this day, that ye may be strong, and go in and possess the land whither ye go to possess it;   9. And that ye may prolong *your* days in the land, which the LORD sware unto your fathers to give unto them and to their seed, a land that floweth with milk and honey.

2 Sam. 7:14. I will be his father, and he shall be my son. If he commit iniquity, I will chasten him with the rod of men, and with the stripes of the children of men: 15. But my mercy shall not depart away from him, as I took *it* from Saul, whom I put away before thee.

2 Chr. 6:24. And if thy people Israel be put to the worse before the enemy, because they have sinned against thee; and shall return and confess thy name, and pray and make supplication before thee in this house; 25. Then hear thou from the heavens, and forgive the sin of thy people Israel, and bring them again unto the land which thou gavest to them and to their fathers.   26. When the heaven is shut up, and there is no rain, because they have sinned against thee: *yet* if they pray toward this place, and confess thy name, and turn from their sin, when thou dost afflict them;   27. Then hear thou from heaven, and forgive the sin of thy servants, and of thy people Israel, when thou hast taught them the good way, wherein they should walk; and send rain upon thy land, which thou hast given unto thy people for an inheritance.   28. If there be dearth in the land, if there be pestilence, if there be blasting or mildew, locusts, or caterpillers; if their enemies besiege them in the cities of their land; whatsoever sore, or whatsoever sickness *there be:*   29. *Then* what prayer *or* what supplication soever shall be made of any man, or of all thy people Israel, when every one shall know his own sore and his own grief, and shall spread forth his hands in this house: 30. Then hear thou from heaven thy dwelling place, and forgive, and render unto every man according unto all his ways, whose heart thou knowest; (for thou only knowest the hearts of the children of men:)   31. That they may fear thee, to walk in thy ways, so long as they live in the land which thou gavest unto our fathers.

2 Chr. 7:13. If I shut up heaven that there be no rain, or if I command the locusts to devour the land, or if I send pestilence among my people;   14. If my people, which are called by my name, shall humble themselves, and pray, and seek my face, and turn from their wicked ways; then will I hear from heaven, and will forgive their sin, and will heal their land.

Job 5:17. Behold, happy *is* the man whom God correcteth: therefore despise not thou the chastening of the Almighty:

Job 33:19. He is chastened also with pain upon his bed, and the multitude of his bones with strong *pain:*

Psa. 6:1. O LORD, rebuke me not in thine

anger, neither chasten me in thy hot displeasure. Psa. 38:1.

Psa. 73:14. For all the day long have I been plagued, and chastened every morning.

Psa. 89:32. Then will I visit their transgression with the rod, and their iniquity with stripes.

Psa. 94:12. Blessed *is* the man whom thou chastenest, O Lord, and teachest him out of thy law; 13. That thou mayest give him rest from the days of adversity, until the pit be digged for the wicked.

Psa. 106:41. And he gave them into the hand of the heathen; and they that hated them ruled over them. 42. Their enemies also oppressed them, and they were brought into subjection under their hand. 43. Many times did he deliver them; but they provoked *him* with their counsel, and were brought low for their iniquity. 44. Nevertheless he regarded their affliction, when he heard their cry:

Psa. 107:17. Fools because of their transgression, and because of their iniquities, are afflicted. 18. Their soul abhorreth all manner of meat; and they draw near unto the gates of death. 19. Then they cry unto the Lord in their trouble, *and* he saveth them out of their distresses. 20. He sent his word, and healed them, and delivered *them* from their destructions. 21. Oh that *men* would praise the Lord *for* his goodness, and *for* his wonderful works to the children of men! 23. They that go down to the sea in ships, that do business in great waters; 24. These see the works of the Lord, and his wonders in the deep. 25. For he commandeth, and raiseth the stormy wind, which lifteth up the waves thereof. 26. They mount up to the heaven, they go down again to the depths: their soul is melted because of trouble. 27. They reel to and fro, and stagger like a drunken man, and are at their wit's end. 28. Then they cry unto the Lord in their trouble, and he bringeth them out of their distresses. 29. He maketh the storm a calm, so that the waves thereof are still. 30. Then are they glad because they be quiet; so he bringeth them unto their desired haven. 31. Oh that *men* would praise the Lord *for* his goodness, and *for* his wonderful works to the children of men!

Psa. 118:18. The Lord hath chastened me sore: but he hath not given me over unto death.

Psa. 119:67. Before I was afflicted I went astray: but now have I kept thy word. 75. I know, O Lord, that thy judgments *are* right, and *that* thou in faithfulness hast afflicted me.

Prov. 3:11. My son, despise not the chastening of the Lord; neither be weary of his correction: 12. For whom the Lord loveth he correcteth; even as a father the son *in whom* he delighteth.

Isa. 26:16. Lord, in trouble have they visited thee, they poured out a prayer *when* thy chastening *was* upon them.

Isa. 42:25. Therefore he hath poured upon him the fury of his anger, and the strength of battle: and it hath set him on fire round about, yet he knew not; and it burned him, yet he laid *it* not to heart.

Isa. 53:4. Surely he hath borne our griefs, and carried our sorrows: yet we did esteem him stricken, smitten of God, and afflicted. 5. But he *was* wounded for our transgressions, *he was* bruised for our iniquities: the chastisement of our peace *was* upon him; and with his stripes we are healed.

Isa. 57:16. For I will not contend for ever, neither will I be always wroth: for the spirit should fail before me, and the souls *which* I have made. 17. For the iniquity of his covetousness was I wroth, and smote him: I hid me, and was wroth, and he went on frowardly in the way of his heart. 18. I have seen his ways, and will heal him: I will lead him also, and restore comforts unto him and to his mourners.

Jer. 2:30. In vain have I smitten your children; they received no correction: your own sword hath devoured your prophets, like a destroying lion.

Jer. 30:14. All thy lovers have forgotten thee; they seek thee not; for I have wounded thee with the wound of an enemy, with the chastisement of a cruel one, for the multitude of thine iniquity; *because* thy sins were increased.

Jer. 31:18. I have surely heard Ephraim bemoaning himself *thus;* Thou hast chastised me, and I was chastised, as a bullock unaccustomed *to the yoke:* turn thou me, and I shall be turned; for thou *art* the Lord my God. 19. Surely after that I was turned, I repented; and after that I was instructed, I smote upon *my* thigh: I was ashamed, yea, even confounded, because I did bear the reproach of my youth. 20. *Is* Ephraim my dear son? *is he* a pleasant child? for since I spake against him, I do earnestly remember him still: therefore my bowels are troubled for him; I will surely have mercy upon him, saith the Lord.

Jer. 46:28. Fear thou not, O Jacob my servant, saith the Lord: for I *am* with thee; for I will make a full end of all the nations whither I have driven thee: but I will not make a full end of thee, but correct thee in measure; yet will I not leave thee wholly unpunished.

Lam. 1:5. Her adversaries are the chief, her enemies prosper; for the Lord hath afflicted her for the multitude of her transgressions: her children are gone into captivity before the enemy.

Hos. 7:12. When they shall go, I will spread my net upon them; I will bring them down as the fowls of the heaven; I will chastise them, as their congregation hath heard.

Hos. 10:10. *It is* in my desire that I should chastise them; and the people shall be gathered against them, when they shall bind themselves in their two furrows.

Hag. 2:17. I smote you with blasting and

with mildew and with hail in all the labours of your hands; yet ye *turned* not to me, saith the LORD.

Heb. 12:5. And ye have forgotten the exhortation which speaketh unto you as unto children, My son, despise not thou the chastening of the LORD, nor faint when thou art rebuked of him: 6. For whom the LORD loveth he chasteneth, and scourgeth every son whom he receiveth. 7. If ye endure chastening, God dealeth with you as with sons; for what son is he whom the father chasteneth not? 8. But if ye be without chastisement, whereof all are partakers, then are ye bastards, and not sons. 9. Furthermore, we have had fathers of our flesh which corrected *us*, and we gave *them* reverence: shall we not much rather be in subjection unto the Father of spirits, and live? 10. For they verily for a few days chastened *us* after their own pleasure; but he for *our* profit, that *we* might be partakers of his holiness. 11. Now no chastening for the present seemeth to be joyous, but grievous: nevertheless afterward it yieldeth the peaceable fruit of righteousness unto them which are exercised thereby.

Rev. 3:19. As many as I love, I rebuke and chasten: be zealous therefore, and repent.

See AFFLICTION, DESIGN OF; JUDGMENTS; PUNISHMENT; WICKED, PUNISHMENT OF.

CHASTITY. Ex. 20:14. Thou shalt not commit adultery.

Job. 31:1. I made a covenant with mine eyes; why then should I think upon a maid?

Prov. 2:10. When wisdom entereth into thine heart, and knowledge is pleasant unto thy soul: 11. Discretion shall preserve thee, understanding shall keep thee: 16. To deliver thee from the strange woman, *even* from the stranger *which* flattereth with her words; 17. Which forsaketh the guide of her youth, and forgetteth the covenant of her God. 18. For her house inclineth unto death, and her paths unto the dead. 19. None that go unto her return again, neither take they hold of the paths of life. 20. That thou mayest walk in the way of good *men*, and keep the paths of the righteous. 21. For the upright shall dwell in the land, and the perfect shall remain in it. 22. But the wicked shall be cut off from the earth, and the transgressors shall be rooted out of it.

Prov. 5:15. Drink waters out of thine own cistern, and running waters out of thine own well. 16. Let thy fountains be dispersed abroad, *and* rivers of waters in the streets. 17. Let them be only thine own, and not strangers' with thee. 18. Let thy fountain be blessed: and rejoice with the wife of thy youth. 19. *Let her be as* the loving hind and pleasant roe; let her breasts satisfy thee at all times; and be thou ravished always with her love. 20. And why wilt thou, my son, be ravished with a strange woman, and embrace the bosom of a stranger? 21. For the ways of man *are* before the eyes of the LORD, and he pondereth all his goings.

Prov. 6:24. To keep thee from the evil woman, from the flattery of the tongue of a strange woman. 25. Lust not after her beauty in thine heart; neither let her take thee with her eyelids.

Prov. 7:1. My son, keep my words, and lay up my commandments with thee. 2. Keep my commandments, and live; and my law as the apple of thine eye. 3. Bind them upon thy fingers, write them upon the table of thine heart. 4. Say unto wisdom, Thou *art* my sister; and call understanding *thy* kinswoman: 5. That they may keep thee from the strange woman, from the stranger *which* flattereth with her words.

Prov. 31:3. Give not thy strength unto women, nor thy ways to that which destroyeth kings.

Matt. 5:28. But I say unto you, That whosoever looketh on a woman to lust after her hath committed adultery with her already in his heart.

Acts 15:20. But that we write unto them, that they abstain from pollutions of *idols*, and *from* fornication,

Rom. 13:13. Let us walk honestly, as in the day; not in rioting and drunkenness, not in chambering and wantonness,

1 Cor. 6:13. Meats for the belly, and the belly for meats: but God shall destroy both it and them. Now the body *is* not for fornication, but for the Lord; and the Lord for the body. 14. And God hath both raised up the Lord, and will also raise up us by his own power. 15. Know ye not that your bodies are the members of Christ? shall I then take the members of Christ, and make *them* the members of an harlot? God forbid. 16. What? know ye not that he which is joined to an harlot is one body? for two, saith he, shall be one flesh. 17. But he that is joined unto the Lord is one spirit. 18. Flee fornication. Every sin that a man doeth is without the body; but he that committeth fornication sinneth against his own body. 19. What? know ye not that your body is the temple of the Holy Ghost *which is* in you, which ye have of God, and ye are not your own?

1 Cor. 7:1. Now concerning the things whereof ye wrote unto me: *It is* good for man not to touch a woman. 2. Nevertheless, *to avoid* fornication, let every man have his own wife, and let every woman have her own husband.

7. For I would that all men were even as I myself. But every man hath his proper gift of God, one after this manner, and another after that. 8. I say therefore to the unmarried and widows, It is good for them if they abide even as I. 9. But if they cannot contain, let them marry: for it is better to marry than to burn.

25. Now concerning virgins I have no commandment of the Lord: yet I give my judgment, as one that hath obtained mercy of the Lord to be faithful. 26. I suppose therefore that this is good for the present distress,

I say, that *it is* good for a man so to be. 36. But if any man think that he behaveth himself uncomely toward his virgin, if she pass the flower of her *age*, and need so require, let him do what he will, he sinneth not: let them marry. 37. Nevertheless he that standeth stedfast in his heart, having no necessity, but hath power over his own will, and hath so decreed in his heart that he will keep his virgin, doeth well.

Eph. 5:3. But fornication, and all uncleanness, or covetousness, let it not be once named among you, as becometh saints;

Col. 3:5. Mortify therefore your members which are upon the earth; fornication, uncleanness, inordinate affection, evil concupiscence, and covetousness, which is idolatry:

1 Thess. 4:3. For this is the will of God, *even* your sanctification, that ye should abstain from fornication: 7. For God hath not called us unto uncleanness, but unto holiness.

Rev. 14:1. And I looked, and, lo, a Lamb stood on the mount Sion, and with him an hundred forty *and* four thousand, having his Father's name written in their foreheads. 2. And I heard a voice from heaven, as the voice of many waters, and as the voice of a great thunder: and I heard the voice of harpers harping with their harps: 3. And they sung as it were a new song before the throne, and before the four beasts, and the elders: and no man could learn that song but the hundred *and* forty *and* four thousand, which were redeemed from the earth. 4. These are they which were not defiled with women; for they are virgins. These are they which follow the Lamb whithersoever he goeth. These were redeemed from among men, *being* the firstfruits unto God and to the Lamb. 5. And in their mouth was found no guile: for they are without fault before the throne of God.

See CONTINENCE.

INSTANCES OF: Joseph, Gen. 39:7-20; Boaz, Ruth 3:6-13; Paul, 1 Cor. 7.

CHEATING. See DISHONESTY.

CHEBAR, a river of Mesopotamia, Ezek. 1:1,3; 3:15,23; 10:15,22; 43:3.

CHEDORLAOMER, king of Elam, Gen. 14:1-16.

CHEERFULNESS. See CONTENTMENT.

CHEESE, 1 Sam. 17:18; 2 Sam. 17:29; Job 10:10.

CHELAL, son of Pahath-moab, Ezra, 10:30.

CHELLUH, son of Bani, Ezra 10:35.

CHELUB. 1. A descendant of Caleb, 1 Chr. 4:11.

2. Father of Ezri, 1 Chr. 27:26.

CHELUBI. Son of Hezron, 1 Chr. 2:9. Called CALEB, *vs.* 18,42.

CHEMARIM, a term descriptive of idolatrous priests, Zeph. 1:4; Hos. 10:5; 2 Kin. 23:15.

CHEMOSH, an idol of the Moabites and Ammonites, 1 Kin. 11:7,33; 2 Kin. 23:13; Jer. 48:7,13,46; and Amorites, Judg. 11:24.

CHENAANAH. 1. Father of the false prophet Zedekiah, 1 Kin. 22:11,24; 2 Chr. 18: 10,23.

2. Brother of Ehud, 1 Chr. 7:10.

CHENANI, a Levite, Neh. 9:4.

CHENANIAH. 1. A Levite, 1 Chr. 15. 22,27.

2. An Izharite, 1 Chr. 26:29.

CHEPHAR-HAAMMONAI, a town of Benjamin, Josh. 18:24.

CHEPHIRAH, a city of the Hivites, Josh. 9:17; 18:26; Ezra 2:25; Neh. 7:29.

CHERAN, a Horite, Gen. 36:26; 1 Chr. 1:41.

CHERETHITES. A Philistine tribe, which adhered to David, and with the Pelethites formed his bodyguard, 1 Sam. 30:14, 16; 2 Sam. 8:18; 15:18; 20:7,23; 1 Kin. 1:38,44; 1 Chr. 18:17; Ezek. 25:16; Zeph. 2:5. Solomon's escort at his coronation, 1 Kin. 1:38.

CHERITH, a brook near Jericho, 1 Kin. 17:3-7.

CHERUB, name of a place or person, Ezra 2:59; Neh. 7:61.

CHERUBIM. Eastward of the garden of Eden, Gen. 3:24.

In the tabernacle, Ex. 25:18-20; 37:7-9. Ark rested beneath the wings of, 1 Kin. 8:6,7; 2 Chr. 5:7,8; Heb. 9:5. Figures of, embroidered on walls of tabernacle, Ex. 26:1; 36:8; and on the vail, Ex. 26:31; 36:35.

In the temple, 1 Kin. 6:23-29; 2 Chr. 3:10-13. Figures of, on the vail, 2 Chr. 3:14; walls, 1 Kin. 6:29-35; 2 Chr. 3:7; lavers, 1 Kin. 7:29,36. In Ezekiel's vision of the temple, Ezek. 41:18-20,25.

FIGURATIVE: Ezek. 28:14,16.

SYMBOLICAL: Ezek. 1; 10.

CHESALON, a landmark in the N. boundary of Judah, Josh. 15:10.

CHESED, son of Nahor, Gen. 22:22.

CHESIL. A town in the S. of Palestine, Josh. 15:30. Probably identical with BETHUL, Josh. 19:4, and BETHUEL, 1 Chr. 4:30.

CHEST, for money, 2 Kin. 12:9; 2 Chr. 24:8-11.

CHESTNUT TREE, Gen. 30:37; Ezek. 31:8.

CHESULLOTH. A city of Issachar, Josh. 19:18. Probably identical with CHISLOTH-TABOR, of *v.* 12, and TABOR, 1 Chr. 6:77.

CHEZIB. Birthplace of Shelah, Gen. 38: 5, probably identical with CHOZEBA, 1 Chr. 4:22, and ACHZIB, Josh. 15:44.

CHICKENS, Matt. 23:37; broods her young, Luke 13:34.

CHIDON. Place where Uzza was stricken to death, 1 Chr. 13:9. Called NACHON's threshingfloor, 2 Sam. 6:6.

CHIDING. Cain chides God, Gen. 4:13, 14. Pharaoh chides Abraham, for calling his wife his sister, Gen. 12:18,19. Abimelech chides Abraham for a like offense, Gen. 20: 9,10. Abimelech chides Isaac for similar conduct, Gen. 26:9,10. Isaac and Laban chide each other, Gen. 31:26-42. Jacob chides Simeon and Levi for slaying Hamor and Shechem, Gen. 34:30. Reuben chides his brethren for their treatment of Joseph, Gen.

42:22. Israelites chide Moses and tempt God, Ex. 17:7. Deborah chides Israel in her epic, Judg. 5:16–23. David chides Joab for slaying Abner, 2 Sam. 3:28–31. Joab chides David for lamenting the death of Absalom, 2 Sam. 19:5–7.

Jesus chides his disciples on account of their unbelief, Matt. 8:26; 14:31; 16:8–11; 17:17; Mark 4:40; Luke 8:25; for slowness of heart, Matt. 15:16; 16:8,9,11; Mark 7:18; Luke 24:25; John 14:9; for sleeping in Gethsemane, Matt. 26:40; Mark 14:27; for forbidding children to be brought to him, Matt. 19:14; Mark 10:14; Luke 18:16.

CHILDLESSNESS. A reproach, Gen. 16:2; 29:32; 30:1–3,13; 1 Sam 1:6; Isa. 4:1; Luke 1:25.

See BARRENNESS. .

CHILDREN. INDEX OF SUB-TOPICS: *Miscellany; The Gift of God,* p. 167; *God's Care of,* p. 168; *A Blessing,* p. 168; *Commandments to,* p. 168; *Counsel of Parents to,* p. 169; *Instruction of,* p. 169; *False Instruction of,* p. 170; *Prayer in Behalf of,* p. 170; *Promises and Assurances to,* p. 171; *Of the Righteous, Blessed of God,* p. 171; *Correction of,* p. 172; *Punishment of,* p. 172; *Good,* p. 173; *Wicked,* p. 173; *Worship, Attend Divine,* p. 174; *Symbolical of the Regenerated,* p. 174.

In answer to prayer: To Abraham, Gen. 15:2–5, with Gen. 21:1,2; Isaac, Gen. 25:21; Leah, Gen. 30:17–22; Rachel, Gen. 30:22–24; Hannah, 1 Sam. 1:9–20; Zacharias, Luke 1:13.

Treatment of, at birth, Ezek. 16:4–6; Luke 2:7,12. Circumcision of. See CIRCUMCISION.

Dedicated to God in infancy: Samson, Judg. 13:5,7; Samuel, 1 Sam. 1:24–28. Promised to the righteous, Deut. 7:12,14; Job 5: 25; Psa. 128:2,3,4,6. Weaning of, Gen. 21:8; 1 Sam. 1:22; 1 Kin. 11:20; Psa. 131:2; Isa. 28:9. Nurses for, Ex. 2:7–9; Acts 7:20; Ruth 4:16; 2 Sam. 4:4; 2 Kin. 11:2. Taught to walk, Hos. 11:3. Tutors and governors for, 2 Kin. 10:1; Acts 22:3; Gal. 3:24; 4:1,2. Bastard, excluded from the privileges of the congregation, Deut. 23:2; Heb. 12:8.

Early piety of: Samuel, 1 Sam. 2:18; 3; Jeremiah, Jer. 1:5–7; John the Baptist, Luke 1:15,80. Jesus, Luke 2:40,46,47,52.

Difference made between male and female, in Mosaic law, Lev. 12. Partiality of parents among: Rebekah for Jacob, Gen. 27:6–17; Jacob for Joseph, Gen. 37:3,4. Partiality among, forbidden, Deut. 21:15–17;

Love of, for parents: Of Ruth, Ruth 1:16–18; Jesus, John 19:26,27.

Sacrificed, 2 Kin. 17:31; Ezek. 16:20,21. Caused to pass through fire, 2 Kin. 16:3; Jer. 32:35; Ezek. 16:21.

Sold for debt, 2 Kin. 4:1; Neh. 5:5; Job 24: 9; Matt. 18:25. Sold in marriage, law concerning, Ex. 21:7–11; instance of, Leah and Rachel, Gen. 29:15–30.

Edict to murder: Of Pharaoh, Ex. 1:22; of Jehu, 2 Kin. 10:1–8; of Herod, Matt. 2:16–18. Eaten, see CANNIBALISM.

Share benefits of covenant privileges guaranteed to parents, Gen. 6:18; 12:7; 13:15; 17: 7,8; 19:12; 21:13; 26:3–5,24; Lev. 26:44,45; Isa. 65:23; 1 Cor. 7:14. Bound by covenants of parents, Gen. 17:9–14. Involved in guilt of parents, Ex. 20:5; 34:7; Lev. 20:5; 26:39–42; Num. 14:18,33; 1 Kin. 21:29; Job 21:19; Psa. 37:28; Isa. 14:20,21; 65:6,7; Jer. 32:18; Dan. 6: 24. Not punished for parents' sake, Jer. 31: 29,30; Ezek. 18:1–30.

Death of, as a judgment upon parents: Firstborn of Egypt, Ex. 12:29; sons of Eli, 1 Sam. 3:13,14; sons of Saul, 1 Sam. 28:18,19; David's child by Uriah's wife, 2 Sam.12:14–19.

Miracles in behalf of: Raised from the dead by Elijah, 1 Kin. 17:17–23; by Elisha, 2 Kin. 4:17–36; by Jesus, Matt. 9:18,24–26; Mark 5:35–42; Luke 7:13–15; 8:49–56; healing of, Matt. 15:28; 17:18; Mark 7:29,30; 9:23–27; Luke 8:42–56; 9:38–42; John 4:46–54.

Character of, known by conduct, Prov. 20:11. Blessed by Jesus, Matt. 19:13–15; Mark 10:13–16; Luke, 18:15,16. Future state of, Matt. 18:10; 19:14. Minors, Gal. 4:1,2. Of ministers, 1 Tim. 3:4; Tit. 1:6. Alienated, Ishmael, to gratify Sarah, Gen. 21:9–15.

Amusements of, Job 21:11; Zech. 8:5; Matt. 11:16,17; Luke 7:31,32.

Adopted. See ADOPTION.

THE GIFT OF GOD: Gen. 4:1. And Adam knew Eve his wife; and she conceived, and bare Cain, and said, I have gotten a man from the LORD. 25. And Adam knew his wife again; and she bare a son, and called his name Seth: For God, *said she,* hath appointed me another seed instead of Abel, whom Cain slew.

Gen. 17:16. And I will bless her, and give thee a son also of her: yea, I will bless her, and she shall be *a mother* of nations; kings of people shall be of her. 20. And as for Ishmael, I have heard thee: Behold, I have blessed him, and will make him fruitful, and will multiply him exceedingly; twelve princes shall he beget, and I will make him a great nation.

Gen. 28:3. And God Almighty bless thee, and make thee fruitful, and multiply thee, that thou mayest be a multitude of people;

Gen. 29:32. And Leah conceived, and bare a son, and she called his name Reuben: for she said, Surely the LORD hath looked upon my affliction; now therefore my husband will love me. 33. And she conceived again, and bare a son; and said, Because the LORD hath heard that I *was* hated, he hath therefore given me this *son* also: and she called his name Simeon. 34. And she conceived again, and bare a son; and said, Now this time will my husband be joined unto me, because I have born him three sons: therefore was his name called Levi. 35. And she conceived again, and bare a son: and she said, Now will I praise the LORD: therefore she called his name Judah: and left bearing.

Gen. 30:2. And Jacob's anger was kindled against Rachel: and he said, *Am* I in God's stead, who hath withheld from thee the fruit of the womb? 6. And Rachel said, God hath judged me, and hath also heard my voice, and hath given me a son: therefore called she his name Dan.   17. And God hearkened unto Leah, and she conceived, and bare Jacob the fifth son.   18. And Leah said, God hath given me my hire, because I have given my maiden to my husband: and she called his name Issachar.   19. And Leah conceived again, and bare Jacob the sixth son.   20. And Leah said, God hath endued me with a good dowry; now will my husband dwell with me, because I have born him six sons: and she called his name Zebulun.   22. And God remembered Rachel, and God hearkened to her and opened her womb.   23. And she conceived, and bare a son; and said, God hath taken away my reproach: 24. And she called his name Joseph; and said, The Lord shall add to me another son.

Gen. 33:5. And he lifted up his eyes, and saw the women and the children, and said, Who *are* those with thee? And he said, The children which God hath graciously given thy servant.

Ruth 4:13. So Boaz took Ruth, and she was his wife: and when he went in unto her, the Lord gave her conception, and she bare a son.

Job 1:21. The Lord gave, and the Lord hath taken away; blessed be the name of the Lord.

I'sa. 107:38. He blesseth them also, so that they are multiplied greatly; and suffereth not their cattle to decrease.   41. Yet setteth he the poor on high from affliction, and maketh *him* families like a flock.

Psa. 113:9. He maketh the barren woman to keep house, *and to be* a joyful mother of children.   Praise ye the Lord.

Psa. 127:3. Lo, children *are* an heritage of the Lord: *and* the fruit of the womb *is his* reward.

GOD'S CARE OF: Ex. 22:22. Ye shall not afflict any widow, or fatherless child.   23. If thou afflict them in any wise, and they cry at all unto me, I will surely hear their cry: 24. And my wrath shall wax hot, and I will kill you with the sword; and your wives shall be widows, and your children fatherless.

Deut. 10:18. He doth execute the judgment of the fatherless and widow, and loveth the stranger, in giving him food and raiment.

Deut. 14:29. The stranger, and the fatherless, and the widow, which *are* within thy gates, shall come, and shall eat and be satisfied; that the Lord thy God may bless thee in all the work of thine hand which thou doest.

Job 29:12. I delivered the poor that cried, and the fatherless, and *him that had* none to help him.

Psa. 10:14. Thou art the helper of the fatherless.   17. Thou wilt cause thine ear to hear: 18. To judge the fatherless and the oppressed, that the man of the earth may no more oppress.

Psa. 27:10. When my father and my

mother forsake me, then the Lord will take me up.

Psa. 68:5. A father of the fatherless, and a judge of the widows, *is* God in his holy habitation.

Psa. 146:9. The Lord . . . relieveth the fatherless and widow:

Jer. 49:11. Leave thy fatherless children, I will preserve *them* alive; and let thy widows trust in me.

Hos. 14:3. In thee the fatherless findeth mercy.

Mal. 3:5. I will be a swift witness against . . . those that oppress . . . the widow, and the fatherless.

A BLESSING: Gen. 5:29. And he called his name Noah, saying, This *same* shall comfort us concerning our work and toil of our hands, because of the ground which the Lord hath cursed.

Gen. 30:1. And when Rachel saw that she bare Jacob no children, Rachel envied her sister; and said unto Jacob, Give me children, or else I die.

Psa. 127:3. Lo, children *are* an heritage of the Lord: *and* the fruit of the womb *is his* reward.   4. As arrows *are* in the hand of a mighty man; so *are* children of the youth.   5. Happy *is* the man that hath his quiver full of them: they shall not be ashamed, but they shall speak with the enemies in the gate.

Prov. 17:6. Children's children *are* the crown of old men; and the glory of children *are* their fathers.

Isa. 54:1. Sing, O barren, thou *that* didst not bear; break forth into singing, and cry aloud, thou *that* didst not travail with child: for more *are* the children of the desolate than the children of the married wife, saith the Lord.

Jer. 20:15. Cursed *be* the man who brought tidings to my father, saying, A man child is born unto thee; making him very glad.

COMMANDMENTS TO: Ex. 20:12. Honour thy father and thy mother: that thy days may be long upon the land which the Lord thy God giveth thee.   Deut. 5:16; Matt. 15:4; 19:19; Mark 10:19; Luke 18:20; Eph. 6:2,3.

Lev. 19:3. Fear every man his mother, and his father.

32. Thou shalt rise up before the hoary head, and honour the face of the old man.

Psa. 119:9. Wherewithal shall a young man cleanse his way? by taking heed *thereto* according to thy word.

Psa. 148:12. Young men, and maidens; old men, and children: 13. Let them praise the name of the Lord:

Prov. 1:8. My son, hear the instruction of thy father, and forsake not the law of thy mother: 9. For they *shall be* an ornament of grace unto thy head, and chains about thy neck.

Prov. 3:1. My son, forget not my law; but let thine heart keep my commandments: 2. For length of days, and long life, and peace, shall they add to thee.   3. Let not mercy and truth forsake thee: bind them about thy neck; write them upon the table of thine heart:

Prov. 4:1. Hear, ye children, the instruction of a father, and attend to know understanding. 2. For I give you good doctrine, forsake ye not my law. 3. For I was my father's son, tender and only *beloved* in the sight of my mother. 4. He taught me also, and said unto me, Let thine heart retain my words: keep my commandments, and live. 10. Hear, O my son, and receive my sayings; and the years of thy life shall be many. 11. I have taught thee in the way of wisdom; I have led thee in right paths. 20. My son, attend to my words; incline thine ear unto my sayings. 21. Let them not depart from thine eyes, keep them in the midst of thine heart. 22. For they *are* life unto those that find them, and health to all their flesh.

Prov. 5:1. My son, attend unto my wisdom, *and* bow thine ear to my understanding: 2. That thou mayest regard discretion, and *that* thy lips may keep knowledge.

Prov. 6:20. My son, keep thy father's commandment, and forsake not the law of thy mother: 21. Bind them continually upon thine heart, *and* tie them about thy neck. 22. When thou goest, it shall lead thee; when thou sleepest, it shall keep thee; and *when* thou awakest, it shall talk with thee. 23. For the commandment *is* a lamp; and the law *is* light; and reproofs of instruction *are* the way of life: 24. To keep thee from the evil woman, from the flattery of the tongue of a strange woman. 25. Lust not after her beauty in thine heart: neither let her take thee with her eyelids.

Prov. 8:32. Hearken unto me, O ye children: for blessed *are they that* keep my ways. 33. Hear instruction, and be wise, and refuse it not.

Prov. 23:22. Hearken unto thy father that begat thee, and despise not thy mother when she is old. 26. My son, give me thine heart, and let thine eyes observe my ways.

Prov. 27:11. My son, be wise, and make my heart glad, that I may answer him that reproacheth me.

Eccl. 12:1. Remember now thy Creator in the days of thy youth, while the evil days come not, nor the years draw nigh, when thou shalt say, I have no pleasure in them.

Lam. 3:27. *It is* good for a man that he bear the yoke in his youth.

Eph. 6:1. Children, obey your parents in the Lord: for this is right.

Col. 3:20. Children, obey *your* parents in all things: for this is well pleasing unto the Lord.

1 Tim. 4:12. Let no man despise thy youth; but be thou an example of the believers, in word, in conversation, in charity, in spirit, in faith, in purity.

2 Tim. 2:22. Flee also youthful lusts: but follow righteousness, faith, charity, peace, with them that call on the Lord out of a pure heart.

Tit. 2:6. Young men likewise exhort to be sober minded.

See YOUNG MEN.

COUNSEL OF PARENTS TO: 1 Kin. 2:1. Now the days of David drew nigh that he should die; and he charged Solomon his son, saying, 2. I go the way of all the earth: be thou strong therefore, and shew thyself a man; 3. And keep the charge of the LORD thy God, to walk in his ways, to keep his statutes, and his commandments, and his judgments, and his testimonies, as it is written in the law of Moses, that thou mayest prosper in all that thou doest, and whithersoever thou turnest thyself: 4. That the LORD may continue his word which he spake concerning me, saying, If thy children take heed to their way, to walk before me in truth with all their heart and with all their soul, there shall not fail thee (said he) a man on the throne of Israel.

1 Chr. 22:6. Then he called for Solomon his son, and charged him to build an house for the LORD God of Israel. 7. And David said to Solomon, My son, as for me, it was in my mind to build an house unto the name of the LORD my God: 8. But the word of the LORD came to me, saying, Thou hast shed blood abundantly, and hast made great wars: thou shalt not build an house unto my name, because thou hast shed much blood upon the earth in my sight. 9. Behold, a son shall be born to thee, who shall be a man of rest; and I will give him rest from all his enemies round about: for his name shall be Solomon, and I will give peace and quietness unto Israel in his days. 10. He shall build an house for my name; and he shall be my son, and I *will be* his father; and I will establish the throne of his kingdom over Israel for ever. 11. Now, my son, the LORD be with thee; and prosper thou, and build the house of the LORD thy God, as he hath said of thee. [1 Chr. 28:9,10,20.] 12. Only the LORD give thee wisdom and understanding, and give thee charge concerning Israel, that thou mayest keep the law of the LORD thy God. 13. Then shalt thou prosper, if thou takest heed to fulfil the statutes and judgments which the LORD charged Moses with concerning Israel: be strong, and of good courage; dread not, nor be dismayed.

See PARENTS.

INSTRUCTION OF: Ex. 13:8. And thou shalt shew thy son in that day, saying, *This is done* because of that *which* the LORD did unto me when I came forth out of Egypt. 9. And it shall be for a sign unto thee upon thine hand, and for a memorial between thine eyes, that the LORD's law may be in thy mouth: for with a strong hand hath the LORD brought thee out of Egypt. 10. Thou shalt therefore keep this ordinance in his season from year to year. 14. And it shall be when thy son asketh thee in time to come, saying, What *is* this? that thou shalt say unto him, By strength of hand the LORD brought us out from Egypt, from the house of bondage: 15. And it came to pass, when Pharaoh would hardly let us go, that the LORD slew all the firstborn in the land of Egypt, both the firstborn of man, and the firstborn of beast: therefore I sacrifice to the LORD all that openeth the matrix, being males; but all the firstborn of my children I redeem; 16. And it shall be for a token upon thine hand, and for frontlets between thine eyes: for by strength of hand the LORD brought us forth out of Egypt.

Deut. 4:9. Only take heed to thyself, and keep thy soul diligently, lest thou forget the things which thine eyes have seen, and lest they depart from thy heart all the days of thy life: but teach them thy sons, and thy sons' sons; 10. *Specially* the day that thou stoodest before the LORD thy God in Horeb, when the LORD said unto me, Gather me the people together, and I will make them hear my words, that they may learn to fear me all the days that they shall live upon the earth, and *that* they may teach their children.

Deut. 6:6. And these words, which I command thee this day, shall be in thine heart: 7. And thou shalt teach them diligently unto thy children, and shalt talk of them when thou sittest in thine house, and when thou walkest by the way, and when thou liest down, and when thou risest up. 8. And thou shalt bind them for a sign upon thine hand, and they shall be as frontlets between thine eyes. 9. And thou shalt write them upon the posts of thy house, and on thy gates.

Deut. 11:19. And ye shall teach them your children, speaking of them when thou sittest in thine house, and when thou walkest by the way, when thou liest down, and when thou risest up. 20. And thou shalt write them upon the door posts of thine house, and upon thy gates.

Deut. 31:12. Gather the people together, men, and women, and children, and thy stranger that *is* within thy gates, that they may hear, and that they may learn, and fear the LORD your God, and observe to do all the words of this law: 13. And *that* their children, which have not known *any thing*, may hear, and learn to fear the LORD your God, as long as ye live in the land whither ye go over Jordan to possess it.

Josh. 8:35. There was not a word of all that Moses commanded, which Joshua read not before all the congregation of Israel, with the women, and the little ones, and the strangers that were conversant among them.

Psa. 34:11. Come, ye children, hearken unto me: I will teach you the fear of the LORD.

Psa. 78:1. Give ear, O my people, *to* my law: incline your ears to the words of my mouth. 2. I will open my mouth in a parable: I will utter dark sayings of old: 3. Which we have heard and known, and our

fathers have told us. 4. We will not hide *them* from their children, shewing to the generation to come the praises of the LORD, and his strength, and his wonderful works that he hath done. 5. For he established a testimony in Jacob, and appointed a law in Israel, which he commanded our fathers, that they should make them known to their children: 6. That the generation to come might know *them, even* the children *which* should be born; *who* should arise and declare *them* to their children: 7. That they might set their hope in God, and not forget the works of God, but keep his commandments: 8. And might not be as their fathers, a stubborn and rebellious generation; a generation *that* set not their heart aright, and whose spirit was not stedfast with God.

Prov. 1:1. The Proverbs of Solomon the son of David, king of Israel; 4. To give subtilty to the simple, to the young man knowledge and discretion.

Prov. 22:6. Train up a child in the way he should go: and when he is old, he will not depart from it.

Isa. 28:9. Whom shall he teach knowledge? and whom shall he make to understand doctrine? *them that are* weaned from the milk, *and* drawn from the breasts. 10. For precept *must be* upon precept, precept upon precept; line upon line, line upon line; here a little, *and* there a little:

Joel 1:3. Tell ye your children of it, and *let* your children *tell* their children, and their children another generation.

John 21:15. Feed my lambs.

Acts 22:3. I am verily a man *which am* a Jew, born in Tarsus, *a city* in Cilicia, yet brought up in this city at the feet of Gamaliel, *and* taught according to the perfect manner of the law of the fathers, and was zealous toward God, as ye all are this day.

See INSTRUCTION. For SOLOMON'S INSTRUCTION OF YOUNG MEN AND CHILDREN, see YOUNG MEN.

BY TUTORS. See TUTOR.

FALSE INSTRUCTION OF: Mark 7:9. And he said unto them, Full well ye reject the commandment of God, that ye may keep your own tradition. 10. For Moses said, Honour thy father and thy mother; and, Whoso curseth father or mother, let him die the death: 11. But ye say, If a man shall say to his father or mother, It *is* Corban, that is to say, a gift, by whatsoever thou mightest be profited by me; *he shall be free.* 12. And ye suffer him no more to do ought for his father or his mother; 13. Making the word of God of none effect through your tradition, which ye have delivered: and many such like things do ye.

PRAYER IN BEHALF OF: Gen. 17:18. Abraham said unto God, O that Ishmael might live before thee!

2 Sam. 12:16. David therefore besought God for the child; and David fasted, and went in, and lay all night upon the earth

1 Chr. 22:12. Only the LORD give **thee**

wisdom and understanding, and give thee charge concerning Israel, that thou mayest keep the law of the LORD thy God.

1 Chr. 29:19. And give unto Solomon my son a perfect heart, to keep thy commandments, thy testimonies, and thy statutes, and to do all *these things*, and to build the palace, *for* the which I have made provision.

Job 1:5. And it was so, when the days of *their* feasting were gone about, that Job sent and sanctified them [his children], and rose up early in the morning, and offered burnt offerings *according* to the number of them all: for Job said, It may be that my sons have sinned, and cursed God in their hearts. Thus did Job continually.

PROMISES AND ASSURANCES TO: Prov. 3:1. My son, forget not my law; but let thine heart keep my commandments: 2. For length of days, and long life, and peace, shall they add to thee. 3. Let not mercy and truth forsake thee: bind them about thy neck; write them upon the table of thine heart: 4. So shalt thou find favour and good understanding in the sight of God and man. 5. Trust in the LORD with all thine heart; and lean not unto thine own understanding. 6. In all thy ways acknowledge him, and he shall direct thy paths. 7. Be not wise in thine own eyes: fear the LORD, and depart from evil. 8. It shall be health to thy navel, and marrow to thy bones. 9. Honour the LORD with thy substance, and with the firstfruits of all thine increase: 10. So shall thy barns be filled with plenty, and thy presses shall burst out with new wine.

Prov. 8:17. I love them that love me; and those that seek me early shall find me. 32. Hearken unto me, O ye children: for blessed *are they that* keep my ways.

Prov. 23:15. My son, if thine heart be wise, my heart shall rejoice, even mine. 16. Yea, my reins shall rejoice, when thy lips speak right things. 24. The father of the righteous shall greatly rejoice: and he that begetteth a wise *child* shall have joy of him. 25. Thy father and thy mother shall be glad, and she that bare thee shall rejoice.

Prov. 29:3. Whoso loveth wisdom rejoiceth his father:

Isa. 40:11. He shall gather the lambs with his arm, and carry *them* in his bosom,

Isa. 54:13. All thy children *shall be* taught of the LORD; and great *shall be* the peace of thy children.

Matt. 18:4. Whosoever therefore shall humble himself as this little child, the same is greatest in the kingdom of heaven. 5. And whoso shall receive one such little child in my name receiveth me. 10. Despise not one of these little ones: for I say unto you, That in heaven their angels do always behold the face of my Father which is in heaven. Mark 9:37; Luke 9:48.

Matt. 19:14. Jesus said, Suffer little children, and forbid them not, to come unto me:

for of such is the kingdom of heaven. 15. And he laid *his* hands on them. Luke 18: 15,16.

Mark 10:16. He took them up in his arms, put *his* hands upon them, and blessed them. *vs.* 13–15

Acts 2:39. The promise is unto you, and to your children,

1 John 2:12. Little children, ... your sins are forgiven you for his name's sake. 13. Young men, ... ye have overcome the wicked one. Little children, ... ye have known the Father.

See YOUNG MEN.

OF THE RIGHTEOUS, BLESSED OF GOD: Gen. 6:18. But with thee will I establish my covenant; and thou shalt come into the ark, thou, and thy sons, and thy wife, and thy sons' wives with thee.

Gen. 7:1. Come thou and all thy house into the ark; for thee have I seen righteous before me in this generation.

Gen. 12:7. And the LORD appeared unto Abram, and said, Unto thy seed will I give this land: and there builded he an altar unto the LORD, who appeared unto him.

Gen. 13:15. For all the land which thou seest, to thee will I give it, and to thy seed for ever.

Gen. 17:7. And I will establish my covenant between me and thee and thy seed after thee in their generations for an everlasting covenant, to be a God unto thee, and to thy seed after thee. 8. And I will give unto thee, and to thy seed after thee, the land wherein thou art a stranger, all the land of Canaan, for an everlasting possession; and I will be their God.

Gen. 19:12. And the men said unto Lot, Hast thou here any besides? son in law, and thy sons, and thy daughters, and whatsoever thou hast in the city, bring *them* out of this place:

15. And when the morning arose, then the angels hastened Lot, saying, Arise, take thy wife, and thy two daughters, which are here; lest thou be consumed in the iniquity of the city. 16. And while he lingered, the men laid hold upon his hand, and upon the hand of his wife, and upon the hand of his two daughters; the LORD being merciful unto him: and they brought him forth, and set him without the city.

Gen. 21:13. And also of the son of the bondwoman will I make a nation, because he *is* thy seed.

Gen. 26:3. Sojourn in this land, and I will be with thee, and will bless thee; for unto thee, and unto thy seed, I will give all these countries, and I will perform the oath which I sware unto Abraham thy father; 4. And I will make thy seed to multiply as the stars of heaven, and will give unto thy seed all these countries; and in thy seed shall all the nations of the earth be blessed; 24. And the LORD appeared unto him the same night, and said, I *am* the God of Abraham thy father: fear not, for I *am* with thee, and will bless thee, and multiply thy seed for my servant Abraham's sake.

Lev. 26:44. And yet for all that, when they be in the land of their enemies, I will not cast them away, neither will I abhor them, to destroy them utterly, and to break my covenant with them: for I *am* the Lord their God. 45. But I will for their sakes remember the covenant of their ancestors, whom I brought forth out of the land of Egypt in the sight of the heathen, that I might be their God: I *am* the Lord.

Deut. 4:37. And because he loved thy fathers, therefore he chose their seed after them, and brought thee out in his sight with his mighty power out of Egypt;

Deut. 10:15. Only the Lord had a delight in thy fathers to love them, and he chose their seed after them, *even* you above all people, as *it is* this day.

Deut. 12:28. Observe and hear all these words which I command thee, that it may go well with thee, and with thy children after thee for ever, when thou doest *that which is* good and right in the sight of the Lord thy God.

1 Kin. 11:13. I will not rend away all the kingdom; *but* will give one tribe to thy son for David my servant's sake,

1 Kin. 15:4. For David's sake did the Lord his God give him a lamp in Jerusalem, to set up his son after him,

2 Kin. 8:19. The Lord would not destroy Judah for David his servant's sake, as he promised him to give him alway a light, *and* to his children.

Psa. 37:26. *He is* ever merciful, and lendeth; and his seed *is* blessed.

Psa. 102:28. The children of thy servants shall continue, and their seed shall be established before thee.

Psa. 103:17. But the mercy of the Lord *is* from everlasting to everlasting upon them that fear him, and his righteousness unto children's children; 18. To such as keep his covenant, and to those that remember his commandments to do them.

Psa. 112:2. His seed shall be mighty upon earth: the generation of the upright shall be blessed. 3. Wealth and riches *shall be* in his house:

Prov. 3:33. The curse of the Lord *is* in the house of the wicked: but he blesseth the habitation of the just.

Prov. 11:21. *Though* hand *join* in hand, the wicked shall not be unpunished: but the seed of the righteous shall be delivered.

Prov. 12:7. The wicked are overthrown, and *are* not: but the house of the righteous shall stand.

Prov. 13:22. A good *man* leaveth an inheritance to his children's children: and the wealth of the sinner *is* laid up for the just.

Prov. 20:7. The just *man* walketh in his integrity: his children *are* blessed after him.

Isa. 44:3. I will pour my spirit upon thy seed, and my blessing upon thine offspring:

4. And they shall spring up *as* among the grass, as willows by the water courses. 5. One shall say, I *am* the Lord's; and another shall call *himself* by the name of Jacob; and another shall subscribe *with* his hand unto the Lord, and surname *himself* by the name of Israel.

Isa. 65:23. They shall not labour in vain, nor bring forth for trouble; for they *are* the seed of the blessed of the Lord, and their offspring with them.

Jer. 32:39. And I will give them one heart, and one way, that they may fear me for ever, for the good of them, and of their children after them:

Acts 2:39. The promise is unto you, and to your children,

1 Cor. 7:14. The unbelieving husband is sanctified by the wife, and the unbelieving wife is sanctified by the husband: else were your children unclean; but now are they holy.

CORRECTION OF: Prov. 13:24. He that spareth his rod hateth his son: but he that loveth him chasteneth him betimes.

Prov. 19:18. Chasten thy son while there is hope, and let not thy soul spare for his crying.

Prov. 22:15. Foolishness *is* bound in the heart of a child; *but* the rod of correction shall drive it far from him.

Prov. 23:13. Withhold not correction from the child: for *if* thou beatest him with the rod, he shall not die. 14. Thou shalt beat him with the rod, and shalt deliver his soul from hell.

Prov. 29:15. The rod and reproof give wisdom: but a child left *to himself* bringeth his mother to shame. 17. Correct thy son, and he shall give thee rest; yea, he shall give delight unto thy soul.

Eph. 6:4. And, ye fathers, provoke not your children to wrath: but bring them up in the nurture and admonition of the Lord.

Col. 3:21. Fathers, provoke not your children *to anger*, lest they be discouraged.

PUNISHMENT OF: Ex. 21:15. And he that smiteth his father, or his mother, shall be surely put to death. 17. And he that curseth his father, or his mother, shall surely be put to death.

Lev. 20:9. For every one that curseth his father or his mother shall be surely put to death: he hath cursed his father or his mother; his blood *shall be* upon him.

Deut. 21:18. If a man have a stubborn and rebellious son, which will not obey the voice of his father, or the voice of his mother, and *that*, when they have chastened him, will not hearken unto them: 19. Then shall his father and his mother lay hold on him, and bring him out unto the elders of his city, and unto the gate of his place; 20. And they shall say unto the elders of his city, This our son *is* stubborn and rebellious, he will not obey our voice; *he is* a glutton, and a drunkard. 21. And all the men of his city shall stone him with stones, that he die: so shalt thou put evil away from among you; and all Israel shall hear, and fear.

Deut. 27:16. Cursed *be* he that setteth light by his father or his mother: and all the people shall say, Amen.

Matt. 15:4. For God commanded, saying, Honour thy father and mother. And, He that curseth father or mother, let him die the death. Mark 7:10.

GOOD: The Lord is with, 1 Sam. 3:19. Know the Scriptures, 2 Tim. 3:15. Their obedience to parents is well pleasing to God, Col. 3:20. Partake of the promises of God, Acts 2:39. Shall be blessed, Prov. 3:1–4; Eph. 6:2,3. Show love to parents, Gen. 46:29. Obey parents, Gen. 28:7; 47:30. Attend to parental teaching, Prov. 13:1. Take care of parents, Gen. 45:9–11; 47:12; Matt. 15:5. Make their parents' hearts glad, Prov. 10:1; 23:24; 29:17. Honor the aged, Job 32:6,7. Character of, illustrates conversion, Matt. 18:3. Illustrative of a teachable spirit, Matt. 18:4.

UNCLASSIFIED SCRIPTURES RELATING TO: Neh. 12:43. Also that day they offered great sacrifices, and rejoiced: for God had made them rejoice with great joy: the wives also and the children rejoiced: so that the joy of Jerusalem was heard even afar off.

Prov. 10:1. A wise son maketh a glad father:

Prov. 13:1. A wise son *heareth* his father's instruction:

Prov. 15:5. He that regardeth reproof is prudent. 20. A wise son maketh a glad father:

Prov. 28:7. Whoso keepeth the law *is* a wise son:

Eccl. 4:13. Better *is* a poor and a wise child than an old and foolish king, who will no more be admonished.

Mal. 1:6. A son honoureth *his* father,

Matt. 21:15. The chief priests . . . saw . . . the children crying in the temple, and saying, Hosanna to the son of David; 16. Out of the mouth of babes and sucklings thou hast perfected praise. Psa. 8:2.

INSTANCES OF: Shem and Japheth, Gen. 9:23. Isaac, Gen. 22:6–12. Esau, Gen. 28:6–9. Judah, Gen. 44:18–34. Joseph, Gen. 45:9–13; 46:29; 47:11,12; 48:12; 50:1–13. Moses, Ex. 15:2; 18:7. Jephthah's daughter, Judg. 11:36. Samson, Judg. 13:24. Ruth, Ruth 1:15–17. Samuel, 1 Sam. 2:26; 3:10. Saul, 1 Sam. 9:5. David, 1 Sam. 22:3,4; Psa. 71:5,17. Solomon, 1 Kin. 2:19,20; 3:3–13. Abijah, 1 Kin. 14:13. Obadiah, 1 Kin. 18:12. Jehoshaphat, 1 Kin. 22:43; 2 Chr. 17:3. The Israelitish maid, captive in Syria, 2 Kin. 5:2–4. Jewish children, 2 Chr. 20:13; Neh. 8:3. Josiah, 2 Chr. 34:1–3. Job, Job 29:4. Elihu, Job 32:4–7. Jeremiah, Jer. 1:5–7. Children in the temple, Matt. 21:15. John, Luke 1:80. Jesus, Luke 2:52. Timothy, 2 Tim. 3:15.

WICKED: Gen. 8:21. The imagination of man's heart *is* evil from his youth;

Ex. 21:15. And he that smiteth his father, or his mother, shall be surely put to death. 17. And he that curseth his father, or his mother, shall surely be put to death. Mark 7:10.

Num. 32:14. Ye are risen up in your father's stead, an increase of sinful men, to augment yet the fierce anger of the LORD toward Israel.

Deut. 21:18. If a man have a stubborn and rebellious son, which will not obey the voice of his father, or the voice of his mother, and *that*, when they have chastened him, will not hearken unto them: 19. Then shall his father and his mother lay hold on him, and bring him out unto the elders of his city, and unto the gate of his place; 20. And they shall say unto the elders of his city, This our son *is* stubborn and rebellious, he will not obey our voice; *he is* a glutton, and a drunkard. 21. And all the men of his city shall stone him with stones, that he die: so shalt thou put evil away from among you; and all Israel shall hear, and fear.

Deut. 27:16. Cursed *be* he that setteth light by his father or his mother. And all the people shall say, Amen.

Job 13:26. For thou writest bitter things against me, and makest me to possess the iniquities of my youth.

Job 19:18. Yea, young children despised me; I arose, and they spake against me.

Job 20:11. His bones are full [1] *of the sin* of his youth, which shall lie down with him in the dust. [1 Omitted in R. V.]

Job 30:1. *They that are* younger than I have me in derision, 12. The youth; they push away my feet, and they raise up against me the ways of their destruction.

Psa. 144:7. Send thine hand from above; [1] rid me, and deliver me out of great waters, from the hand of [2] strange children; 8. Whose mouth speaketh vanity, and their right hand *is* a right hand of falsehood. 11. [1] Rid me, and deliver me from the hand of [2] strange children, whose mouth speaketh vanity, and their right hand *is* a right hand of falsehood: [R. V. 1 rescue   2 strangers]

Prov. 7:7. Among the simple ones, I discerned among the youths, a young man void of understanding,

Prov. 10:1. The proverbs of Solomon. A wise son maketh a glad father: but a foolish son *is* the heaviness of his mother.

Prov. 13:1. A wise son *heareth* his father's instruction: but a scorner heareth not rebuke.

Prov. 15:5. A fool despiseth his father's instruction: but he that regardeth reproof is prudent. 20. A wise son maketh a glad father: but a foolish man despiseth his mother.

Prov. 17:2. A wise servant shall have rule over a son that causeth shame, 21. He that begetteth a fool *doeth it* to his sorrow: and the father of a fool hath no joy. 25. A foolish son *is* a grief to his father, and bitterness to her that bare him. Prov. 19:13.

Prov. 19:26. He that wasteth *his* father, *and* chaseth away *his* mother, *is* a son that causeth shame, and bringeth reproach.

Prov. 20:20. Whoso curseth his father or his mother, his lamp shall be put out in obscure darkness.

Prov. 22:15. Foolishness *is* bound in the heart of a child; *but* the rod of correction shall drive it far from him.

Prov. 23:22. Hearken unto thy father that begat thee, and despise not thy mother when she is old.

Prov. 28:7. Whoso keepeth the law *is* a wise son: but he that is a companion of riotous *men* shameth his father. 24. Whoso robbeth his father or his mother,, and saith, It *is* no transgression; the same *is* the companion of a destroyer.

Prov. 30:11. *There is* a generation *that* curseth their father, and doth not bless their mother. 17. The eye *that* mocketh at *his* father, and despiseth to obey *his* mother, the ravens of the valley shall pick it out, and the young eagles shall eat it.

Eccl. 11:9. Rejoice, O young man, in thy youth; and let thy heart cheer thee in the days of thy youth, and walk in the ways of thine heart, and in the sight of thine eyes: but know thou, that for all these *things* God will bring thee into judgment. 10. Therefore remove sorrow from thy heart, and put away evil from thy flesh: for childhood and youth *are* vanity.

Isa. 3:5. And the people shall be oppressed, every one by another, and every one by his neighbour: the child shall behave himself proudly against the ancient, and the base against the honourable.

Jer. 3:25. We have sinned against the LORD our God, we and our fathers, from our youth even unto this day, and have not obeyed the voice of the LORD our God.

Jer. 7:17. Seest thou not what they do in the cities of Judah and in the streets of Jerusalem? 18. The children gather wood, and the fathers kindle the fire, and the women knead *their* dough, to make cakes to the queen of heaven, and to pour out drink offerings unto other gods, that they may provoke me to anger.

Jer. 32:30. The children of Israel and the children of Judah have only done evil before me from their youth:

Ezek. 22:7. In thee have they set light by father and mother:

Mic. 7:6. For the son dishonoureth the father, the daughter riseth up against her mother, the daughter in law against her mother in law; a man's enemies *are* the men of his own house.

Mark 13:12. Now the brother shall betray the brother to death, and the father the son; and children shall rise up against *their* parents, and shall cause them to be put to death.

Rom. 1:30. [Reprobates are] Backbiters, haters of God, despiteful, proud, boasters,

inventors of evil things, disobedient **to** parents,

2 Tim. 3:2. For men shall be lovers of their own selves, covetous, boasters, proud, blasphemers, disobedient to parents, unthankful, unholy,

WICKED, INSTANCES OF: Canaan, Gen. 9: 25. Lot's daughters, Gen. 19:14,30–38. Ishmael, Gen. 21:9. Eli's sons, 1 Sam. 2:12,22–25. Samuel's sons, 1 Sam. 8:3. Absalom, 2 Sam. 15. Adonijah, 1 Kin. 1:5. Abijam, 1 Kin. 15:3. Ahaziah, 1 Kin. 22:52. Children at Beth-el, 2 Kin. 2:23,24. Samaritans' descendants, 2 Kin. 17:41. Adrammelech and Sharezer, 2 Kin. 19:37; 2 Chr. 32:21. Amon, 2 Kin. 21:21.

WORSHIP, ATTEND DIVINE: Josh. 8:35. There was not a word of all that Moses commanded, which Joshua read not before all the congregation of Israel, with the women, and the little ones, and the strangers that were conversant among them.

2 Chr. 20:13. And all Judah stood before the LORD, with their little ones, their wives, and their children.

2 Chr. 31:16. Beside their genealogy of males, from three years old and upward, *even* unto every one that entereth into the house of the LORD, his daily portion for their service in their charges according to their courses;

Ezra. 8:21. Then I proclaimed a fast there, at the river of Ahava, that we might afflict ourselves before our God, to seek of him a right way for us, and for our little ones, and for all our substance.

Neh. 8:2. And Ezra the priest brought the law before the congregation both of men and women, and all that could hear with understanding, upon the first day of the seventh month. 3. And he read therein before the street that *was* before the water gate from the morning until midday, before the men and the women, and those that could understand; and the ears of all the people *were* *attentive* unto the book of the law.

Neh. 12:43. Also that day they offered great sacrifices, and rejoiced: for God had made them rejoice with great joy: the wives also and the children rejoiced: so that the joy of Jerusalem was heard even afar off.

Matt. 21:15. And when the chief priests and scribes saw the wonderful things that he did, and the children crying in the temple, and saying, Hosanna to the Son of David; they were sore displeased,

Luke 2:46. And it came to pass, that after three days they found him in the temple, sitting in the midst of the doctors, both hearing them, and asking them questions.

SYMBOLICAL OF THE REGENERATED: Matt. 18:2. And Jesus called a little child unto him, and set him in the midst of them, 3. And said, Verily I say unto you, Except ye be converted, and become as little children, ye shall not enter into the kingdom of heaven. 4. Whosoever therefore shall humble himself as this little child, the same **is**

greatest in the kingdom of heaven. 5. And whoso shall receive one such little child in my name receiveth me. 6. But whoso shall offend one of these little ones which believe in me, it were better for him that a millstone were hanged about his neck, and *that* he were drowned in the depth of the sea.

Mark 9:36. And he took a child, and set him in the midst of them: and when he had taken him in his arms, he said unto them, 37. Whosoever shall receive one of such children in my name, receiveth me: and whosoever shall receive me, receiveth not me, but him that sent me.

Mark 10:15. Verily I say unto you, whosoever shall not receive the kingdom of God as a little child, he shall not enter therein.

Luke 9:46. Then there arose a reasoning among them, which of them should be greatest. 47. And Jesus, perceiving the thought of their heart, took a child, and set him by him, 48. And said unto them, Whosoever shall receive this child in my name receiveth me: and whosoever shall receive me, receiveth him that sent me: for he that is least among you all, the same shall be great.

FIGURATIVE: 1 Cor. 13:11. When I was a child, I spake as a child, I understood as a child, I thought as a child: but when I became a man, I put away childish things.

1 Cor. 14:20. Brethren, be not children in understanding: howbeit in malice be ye children, but in understanding be men.

1 Pet. 2:2. As newborn babes, desire the sincere milk of the word, that ye may grow thereby:

See BABES; YOUNG MEN.

CHILDREN OF GOD. See RIGHTEOUS.

CHILEAB. A son of David, 2 Sam. 3:3. Called DANIEL, 1 Chr. 3:1.

CHILION, a son of Naomi, Ruth 1:2,4,5; 4:9.

CHILMAD, merchants of, Ezek. 27:23.

CHIMHAM, a Gileadite, 2 Sam. 19:37,38, 40; Jer. 41:17.

CHIMNEY, Hos. 13:3.

CHINESE. Sinim in Isa. 49:12 is believed by many authorities to be a reference to the Chinese.

CHINNERETH. Called also CHINNEROTH, CINNERETH and CINNEROTH. 1. A district in the N. of Palestine, Josh. 11:2; 1 Kin. 15:20.

2. A city in Naphtali, Josh. 19:35.

3. The sea of, Num. 34:11; Josh. 12:3; 13:27. See GALILEE, SEA OF.

CHINNEROTH. See CHINNERETH.

CHIOS, an island W. of Smyrna, Acts 20:15.

CHISLEU, ninth month in the Israelitish calendar, Ezra 10:9; Neh. 1:1; Jer. 36:22.

CHISLON, father of Eldad, Num. 34:21.

CHISLOTH-TABOR. A place on the border of Zebulun, Josh. 19:12. Called TABOR, 1 Chr. 6:77. Probably same as CHESULLOTH, Josh. 19:18.

CHITTIM. Descendants of Javan, Gen. 10:4. Probably inhabited islands of the Mediterranean, Isa. 23:1,12; Jer. 2:10. Their commerce, Ezek. 27:6. Prophecies concerning, Num. 24:24; Dan. 11:30.

CHIUN, called also Remphan, a god of the Phenicians, Amos 5:26; Acts 7:43.

CHLOE, a Christian of Corinth, 1 Cor. 1:11.

CHOICE. Between judgments, by David, 2 Sam. 24:12; 1 Chr. 21:11-13.

THE SINNER'S: Deut. 30:19. I call heaven and earth to record this day against you, *that* I have set before you life and death, blessing and cursing: therefore choose life, that both thou and thy seed may live: 20. That thou mayest love the LORD thy God, *and* that thou mayest obey his voice, and that thou mayest cleave unto him: for he *is* thy life, and the length of thy days: that thou mayest dwell in the land which the LORD sware unto thy fathers, to Abraham, to Isaac, and to Jacob, to give them.

Josh. 24:15. And if it seem evil unto you to serve the LORD, choose you this day whom ye will serve; whether the gods which your fathers served that *were* on the other side of the flood, or the gods of the Amorites, in whose land ye dwell: but as for me and my house, we will serve the LORD. 16. And the people answered and said, God forbid that we should forsake the LORD, to serve other gods; 17. For the LORD our God, he *it is* that brought us up and our fathers out of the land of Egypt, from the house of bondage, and which did those great signs in our sight, and preserved us in all the way wherein we went, and among all the people through whom we passed: 18. And the LORD drave out from before us all the people, even the Amorites which dwelt in the land: *therefore* will we also serve the LORD; for he *is* our God.

1 Kin. 18:21. And Elijah came unto all the people, and said, How long halt ye between two opinions? if the LORD *be* God, follow him: but if Baal, *then* follow him. And the people answered him not a word.

See CONTINGENCIES; BLESSINGS, CONTINGENT ON OBEDIENCE.

CHOOSING. See CHOICE.

CHOR-ASHAN. A town in Judah, 1 Sam. 30:30. Perhaps identical with ASHAN, Josh. 15:42.

CHORAZIN, denunciation against, Matt. 11:21; Luke 10:13.

CHORUSES. See MUSIC.

CHOSEN, OR ELECTED: Matt. 20:16. [1] For many be called, but few chosen. Matt. 22:14.

1 Pet. 2:9. But ye *are* a chosen generation, a royal priesthood, an holy nation, a peculiar people; that ye should shew forth the praises of him who hath called you out of darkness into his marvellous light: [[1] Omitted in R. V.]

Rev. 17:14. These shall make war with the Lamb, and the Lamb shall overcome them: for he is Lord of lords, and King of kings: and they that are with him *are* called, and chosen, and faithful.

See FOREKNOWLEDGE; PREDESTINATION.

CHOZEBA, a city of Judah, 1 Chr. 4:22. See CHEZIB; ACHZIB.

CHRIST. See JESUS, THE CHRIST.

CHRISTIAN. Believers called, Acts 11:26; 26:28; 1 Pet. 4:16. See RIGHTEOUS.

CHRONOLOGY. Jewish year instituted, Ex. 12:2. See TIME.

CHRYSOLYTE, a precious stone, Rev. 21:20.

CHRYSOPRASUS, a precious stone, Rev. 21:20.

CHUB, a people who were an ally tribe to Egypt, and probably inhabited Africa, Ezek. 30:5.

CHUN, a Syrian city, 1 Chr. 18:8. See BETAH; BEROTHAI.

CHURCH, place of worship.
Called COURTS, Psa. 65:4; 84:2,10; 92:13; 96:8; 100:4; 116:19; Isa. 1:12; 62:9; Zech. 3:7; HOUSE OF GOD, Gen. 28:17,22; Josh. 9:23; Judg. 18:31; 20:18,26; 21:2; 1 Chr. 9:11; 24:5; 2 Chr. 5:14; 22:12; 24:13; 33:7; 36:19; Ezra 5:8,15; 7:20,23; Neh. 6:10; 11:11; 13:11; Psa. 42:4; 52:8; 55:14; 84:10; Eccl. 5:1; Isa. 2:3; Hos. 9:8; Joel 1:16; Mic. 4:2; Zech. 7:2; Matt. 12:4; 1 Tim. 3:15; Heb. 10:21; 1 Pet. 4:17; HOUSE OF THE LORD, Ex. 23:19; 34:26; Deut. 23:18; Josh. 6:24; Judg. 19:18; 1 Sam. 1:7,24; 2 Sam. 12:20; 1 Kin. 3:1; 6:37; 7:40; 8:10,63; 10:5; 2 Kin. 11:3,4,15,18,19; 12:4,9, 10,13,16; 16:18; 20:8; 23:2,7,11; 25:9; 1 Chr. 6:31; 22:1,11,14; 23:4; 26:12; 2 Chr. 8:16; 26:21; 29:5,15; 33.15; 34:15; 36:14; Ezra 7:27; Psa. 23:6; 27:4; 92:13; 116:19; 118:26; 122:1,9; 134:1; Isa. 2:2; 37:14; Jer. 17:26; 20:1,2; 26:2,7; 28:1, 5; 29:26; 35:2; 36:5,6; 38:14; 41:5; 51:51; Lam. 2:7; Ezek. 44:4; Hag. 1:2; Zech. 8:9; SANCTUARY, Ex. 25:8; Lev. 19:30; 21:12; Num. 3:28; 4:12; 7:9; 8:19; 10:21; 18:1,5; 19:20; 1 Chr. 9:29; 22:19; 24:5; 28:10; 2 Chr. 20:8; 26:18; 29:21; 30:8,19; Neh. 10:39; Psa. 20:2; 28:2 (*marg.*); 63:2; 68:24; 73:17; 74:3,7; 77:13; 78:69; 150:1; Isa. 16:12; 63:18; Lam. 2:7,20; 4:1; Ezek. 5:11; 42:20; 44:5,27; 45:3; 48:8,21; Dan. 8:11,13,14; 9:17,26; 11:31; Heb. 8:2; 9:1,2; HOUSE OF PRAYER, Isa. 56:7; Matt. 21:13; TABERNACLE, Ex. 26:1; Lev. 26:11; Josh. 22:19; Psa. 15:1; 61:4; 76:2; Heb. 8:2,5; 9:2,11; Rev. 13:6; 21:3; TEMPLE, 1 Sam. 1:9; 3:3; 2 Kin. 11:10,13; Ezra 4:1; Psa. 5:7; 11:4; 27:4; 29:9; 48:9; 68:29; Isa. 6:1; Mal. 3:1; Matt. 4:5; 23:16; Luke 18:10; 24:53; ZION, Psa. 9:11; 48:11; 74:2; 132:13; 137:1; Isa. 35:10; Jer. 31:6; 50:5; Joel 2:1,15; HOLY PLACE, Ex. 28:29; 38:24; Lev. 6:16; 10:17; 14:13; 16:2-24; Josh. 5:15; 1 Kin. 8:8; 1 Chr. 23:32; 2 Chr. 29:5; 30:27; 35:5; Ezra 9:8. Psa. 24:3; 46:4; 68:17; Eccl. 8:10; Isa. 57:15; Ezek. 41:4; 42:13; 45:4; Matt. 24:15; Acts 6:13; 21:28; Heb. 9:12,25; HOLY TEMPLE, Psa. 5:7; 11:4; 65:4; 79:1; 138:2; Jonah 2:4,7; Mic. 1:2; Hab. 2:20; Eph. 2:21; 3:17; MY FATHER'S HOUSE, John 2:16; 14:2.

HOLY; Ex. 30:26. And thou shalt anoint the tabernacle of the congregation therewith, and the ark of the testimony, 27. And the table and all his vessels, and the candle-stick and his vessels, and the altar of incense, 28. And the altar of burnt offering with all his vessels, and the laver and his foot. 29. And thou shalt sanctify them, that they may be most holy: whatsoever toucheth them shall be holy.

Ex. 40:9. And thou shalt take the anointing oil, and anoint the tabernacle, and all that *is* therein, and shalt hallow it, and all the vessels thereof: and it shall be holy.

Lev. 8:10. And Moses took the anointing oil, and anointed the tabernacle and all that *was* therein, and sanctified them. 11. And he sprinkled thereof upon the altar seven times, and anointed the altar and all his vessels, both the laver and his foot, to sanctify them.

Lev. 16:33. And he shall make an atonement for the holy sanctuary,

Lev. 19:30. Ye shall keep my sabbaths, and reverence my sanctuary: I *am* the LORD.

Lev. 21:12. Neither shall he go out of the sanctuary, nor profane the sanctuary of his God; for the crown of the anointing oil of his God *is* upon him: I *am* the LORD.

Num. 7:1. And it came to pass on the day that Moses had fully set up the tabernacle, and had anointed it, and sanctified it, and all the instruments thereof, both the altar and all the vessels thereof, and had anointed them, and sanctified them;

1 Kin. 9:3. And the LORD said unto him, I have heard thy prayer and thy supplication, that thou hast made before me: I have hallowed this house, which thou hast built, to put my name there for ever; and mine eyes and mine heart shall be there perpetually.

1 Chr. 29:3. Moreover, because I have set my affection to the house of my God, I have of mine own proper good, of gold and silver, *which* I have given to the house of my God, over and above all that I have prepared for the holy house,

2 Chr. 3:8. And he made the most holy house,

Isa. 64:11. Our holy and our beautiful house, where our fathers praised thee, is burned up with fire.

Ezek. 23:39. For when they had slain their children to their idols, then they came the same day into my sanctuary to profane it; and, lo, thus have they done in the midst of mine house.

1 Cor. 3:17. If any man defile the temple of God, him shall God destroy: for the temple of God is holy, which *temple* ye are.

EDIFICES. See SYNAGOGUE; TABERNACLE; TEMPLE.

CHURCH, the collective body of believers.

INDEX OF SUB-TOPICS: *Miscellany of Minor Sub-topics, p. 177; Unclassified Scriptures Relating to, p. 177; Backslidden, p. 182; Beneficence of, p. 183; Christ, Head of, p. 183; Christian. Divinely Established, p. 184; Corruption in, p. 185; Decrees of, p. 186; Design of, p. 186; Discipline in, p. 189;*

Dissensions in, p. 186; *Duty of, to Ministers*, p. 186; *Government of*, p. 186; *Love for*, p. 193; *Membership in*, p. 193; *Prophecies Concerning*, p. 194; *List of Christian*, p. 203; *Unity of*, p. 203; *Triumphant*, p. 203; *Church and State*, p. 204.

MISCELLANY OF MINOR SUB-TOPICS: Called in the O. T., THE CONGREGATION, Ex. 12:3,6,19,47; 16:1,2,9,10,22; Lev. 4:13,15; 10:17; 24:14.

Called in the N. T., CHURCH. Matt. 16:18; 18:17; Acts 2:47; 1 Cor. 11·18; 14:19,23,28,33, 34; 15:9; Gal. 1:13.

Called also ASSEMBLY OF THE SAINTS, Psa. 89:7; ASSEMBLY OF THE UPRIGHT, Psa. 111:1; BODY OF CHRIST, Eph. 1:22,23; Col. 1:24; BRANCH OF GOD'S PLANTING, Isa. 60:21; BRIDE OF CHRIST, Rev. 21:9; CHURCH OF GOD, Acts 20:28; CHURCH OF THE LIVING GOD, 1 Tim. 3:15; CHURCH OF THE FIRSTBORN, Heb. 12:23; CITY OF THE LIVING GOD, Heb. 12:22; CONGREGATION OF SAINTS, Psa. 149:1; CONGREGATION OF THE LORD'S POOR, Psa. 74:19; DOVE, Song 2:14; 5:2; FAMILY IN HEAVEN AND EARTH, Eph. 3:15; FLOCK OF GOD, Ezek. 34:15; 1 Pet. 5:2; FOLD OF CHRIST, John 10:16; GENERAL ASSEMBLY OF THE FIRSTBORN, Heb. 12:23; GOLDEN CANDLESTICK, Rev. 1:20; GOD'S BUILDING, 1 Cor. 3:9; GOD'S HUSBANDRY, 1 Cor. 3:9; GOD'S HERITAGE, Joel 3:2; 1 Pet. 5:3; HABITATION OF GOD, Eph. 2:22; HEAVENLY JERUSALEM, Gal 4:26; Heb. 12:22; HOLY CITY, Rev. 21:2; HOLY MOUNTAIN, Zech. 8:3; HOLY HILL, Psa. 2:6; 15:1; HOUSE OF GOD, 1 Tim. 3:15; Heb. 10:21; THE GOD OF JACOB, Isa. 2:3; HOUSE OF CHRIST, Heb. 3:6; HOUSEHOLD OF GOD, Eph. 2:19; INHERITANCE, Psa. 28:9; Isa. 19:25; ISRAEL OF GOD, Gal. 6:16; KING'S DAUGHTER, Psa. 45:13; KINGDOM OF GOD, Matt. 6:33; 12:28; 19:24; 21:31; KINGDOM OF HEAVEN, Matt. 3:2; 4:17; 10:7; 5:3,10,19,20; HIS KINGDOM, Psa. 103:19; 145:12; Matt. 16:28; Luke, 1:33; MY KINGDOM, John 18:36; THY KINGDOM, Psa. 45:6; 145:11,13; Matt.6:10; Luke 23:42; LAMB'S BRIDE, Eph. 5:22–32; Rev. 22:17; LAMB'S WIFE, Rev. 19:7-9; 21:9; LOT OF GOD'S INHERITANCE, Deut. 32:9; MOUNT ZION, Heb. 12:22; MOUNTAIN OF THE LORD'S HOUSE, Isa. 2:2; NEW JERUSALEM, Rev. 21:2; PILLAR AND GROUND OF THE TRUTH, 1 Tim. 3:15; PLACE OF GOD'S THRONE, Ezek. 43:7; PLEASANT PORTION, Jer. 12:10; SANCTUARY OF GOD, Psa. 114:2; SISTER OF CHRIST, Song 4:12; 5:2; SPIRITUAL HOUSE, 1 Pet. 2:5; SPOUSE OF CHRIST, Song 4:12; 5:1; STRENGTH AND GLORY OF GOD, Psa. 78:61; SOUGHT OUT, A CITY NOT FORSAKEN, Isa. 62:12; THE LORD'S PORTION, Deut. 32:9; TEMPLE OF GOD, 1 Cor. 3:16,17; TEMPLE OF THE LIVING GOD, 2 Cor. 6:16; VINEYARD, Jer. 12:10; Matt. 21:41.

Christ's love for, John 10:8,11,12; Eph. 5: 25–32; Rev. 3:9.

Loved by believers, Psa. 87:7; 137:5; 1 Cor. 12:25; 1 Thess. 4:9; is prayed for, Psa. 122:6; Isa. 62:6; dear to God, Psa. 43·4; safe under his care. Psa. 46:1,2,5; salt and light of the world, Matt. 5:13.

Militant, Song 6:10; Phil. 2:25; 2 Tim. 2:3;

4:7; Philem. 2. God defends, Psa. 89:18; Isa. 4:5; 49:25; Matt. 16:18. God provides ministers for, Jer. 3:15; Eph. 4:11,12. Is glorious, Psa. 45:13; Eph. 5:27. Is clothed in righteousness, Rev. 19:8. Believers continually added to, by the Lord, Acts. 2:47; 5:14; 11:24. Unity of, Rom. 12:5; 1 Cor. 10:17; 12:12; Gal. 3:28; Eph. 4:4. Privileges of, Psa. 36:8; 87:5. Worship of, to be attended, Heb. 10:25. Harmonious fellowship of, Psa. 133; John 13:34; Acts 4:32; Phil. 1:4; 2:1; 1 John 3; 4. Divisions in, to be shunned, Rom. 16:17; 1 Cor. 1:10; 3:3. Baptized into by one Spirit, 1 Cor. 12:13. Ministers commanded to feed, Acts. 20:28. Is edified by the word, Rom. 12:6; 1 Cor. 14:4,13; Eph. 4:15,16; Col. 3:16. The wicked persecute, Acts 8:1-3; 1 Thess. 2:14,15. Not to be despised, 1 Cor. 11:22. Defiling of will be punished, 1 Cor. 3:17. Extent of, predicted, Isa. 2:2; Ezek. 17:22–24; Dan. 2:34,35.

See ECCLESIASTICISM; JESUS, KINGDOM OF; MINISTERS; USURPATION, IN ECCLESIASTICAL AFFAIRS.

UNCLASSIFIED SCRIPTURES RELATING TO: Deut. 32:9. The Lord's portion *is* his people; Jacob *is* the lot of his inheritance.

Psa. 2:6. Yet have I set my King upon my holy hill of Zion.

Psa. 9:11. Sing praises to the LORD, which dwelleth in Zion:

14. That I may shew forth all thy praise in the gates of the daughter of Zion: I will rejoice in thy salvation.

Psa. 14:7. Oh that the salvation of Israel *were come* out of Zion! when the LORD bringeth back the captivity of his people, Jacob shall rejoice, *and* Israel shall be glad. Psa. 53:6.

Psa. 20:2. Send thee help from the sanctuary, and strengthen thee out of Zion;

Psa. 46:4. *There is* a river, the streams whereof shall make glad the city of God, the holy *place* of the tabernacles of the Most High. 5. God *is* in the midst of her; she shall not be moved: God shall help her, *and that* right early.

Psa. 48:1. Great *is* the LORD, and greatly to be praised in the city of our God, *in* the mountain of his holiness. 2. Beautiful for situation, the joy of the whole earth, *is* mount Zion, *on* the sides of the north, the city of the great King. 11. Let mount Zion rejoice, let the daughters of Judah be glad, because of thy judgments. 12. Walk about Zion, and go round about her: tell the towers thereof. 13. Mark ye well her bulwarks, consider her palaces; that ye may tell *it* to the generation following.

Psa. 50:2. Out of Zion, the perfection of beauty, God hath shined.

Psa. 51:18. Do good in thy good pleasure unto Zion: build thou the walls of Jerusalem.

Psa. 65:1. Praise waiteth for thee, O God, in Sion:

Psa. 69:35. God will save Zion, and will build the cities of Judah: that they may dwell there, and have it in possession. 36. The seed also of his servants shall inherit it:

and they that love his name shall dwell therein.

Psa. 74:2. Remember thy congregation, *which* thou hast purchased of old; the rod of thine inheritance, *which* thou hast redeemed; this mount Zion, wherein thou hast dwelt.

Psa. 84:1. How amiable *are* thy tabernacles, O LORD of hosts! 2. My soul longeth, yea, even fainteth for the courts of the LORD: my heart and my flesh crieth out for the living God. 3. Yea, the sparrow hath found an house, and the swallow a nest for herself, where she may lay her young, *even* thine altars, O LORD of hosts, my King, and my God. 4. Blessed *are* they that dwell in thy house: they will be still praising thee. 5. Blessed *is* the man whose strength *is* in thee; in whose heart *are* the ways *of them*. 6. *Who* passing through the valley of Baca make it a well; the rain also filleth the pools. 7. They go from strength to strength, *every one of them* in Zion appeareth before God. 8. O LORD God of hosts, hear my prayer: give ear, O God of Jacob. 9. Behold, O God our shield, and look upon the face of thine anointed. 10. For a day in thy courts *is* better than a thousand. I had rather be a doorkeeper in the house of my God, than to dwell in the tents of wickedness.

Psa. 87:1. His foundation *is* in the holy mountains. 2. The LORD loveth the gates of Zion more than all the dwellings of Jacob. 3. Glorious things are spoken of thee, O city of God. 4. I will make mention of Rahab and Babylon to them that know me: behold Philistia, and Tyre, with Ethiopia; this *man* was born there. 5. And of Zion it shall be said, This and that man was born in her: and the highest himself shall establish her. 6. The LORD shall count, when he writeth up the people, *that* this *man* was born there.

Psa. 99:2. The LORD *is* great in Zion; and he *is* high above all the people.

Psa. 102:13. Thou shalt arise, *and* have mercy upon Zion: for the time to favour her, yea, the set time, is come. 14. For thy servants take pleasure in her stones, and favour the dust thereof. 16. When the LORD shall build up Zion, he shall appear in his glory. 19. For he hath looked down from the height of his sanctuary; from heaven did the LORD behold the earth: 20. To hear the groaning of the prisoner; to loose those that are appointed to death; 21. To declare the name of the LORD in Zion, and his praise in Jerusalem;

Psa. 110:2. The LORD shall send the rod of thy strength out of Zion: rule thou in the midst of thine enemies.

Psa. 111:1. I will praise the LORD with *my* whole heart, in the assembly of the upright, and *in* the congregation.

Psa. 114:2. Judah was his sanctuary, *and* Israel his dominion.

Psa. 125:1. They that trust in the LORD *shall be* as mount Zion, *which* cannot be removed, *but* abideth for ever.

Psa. 126:1. When the LORD turned again the captivity of Zion, we were like them that dream. 2. Then was our mouth filled with laughter, and our tongue with singing: then said they among the heathen, the LORD hath done great things for them.

Psa. 129:5. Let them all be confounded and turned back that hate Zion.

Psa. 132:13. For the LORD hath chosen Zion; he hath desired *it* for his habitation. 14. This *is* my rest for ever: here will I dwell; for I have desired it. 15. I will abundantly bless her provision: I will satisfy her poor with bread. 16. I will also clothe her priests with salvation: and her saints shall shout aloud for joy.

Psa. 133:1. Behold, how good and how pleasant *it is* for brethren to dwell together in unity! 2. *It is* like the precious ointment upon the head, that ran down upon the beard, *even* Aaron's beard: that went down to the skirts of his garments; 3. As the dew of Hermon, *and as the dew* that descended upon the mountains of Zion: for there the LORD commanded the blessing, *even* life for evermore.

Psa. 134:1. Behold, bless ye the LORD, all *ye* servants of the LORD, which by night stand in the house of the LORD. 2. Lift up your hands *in* the sanctuary, and bless the LORD. 3. The LORD that made heaven and earth bless thee out of Zion.

Psa. 137:1. By the rivers of Babylon, there we sat down, yea, we wept, when we remembered Zion. 2. We hanged our harps upon the willows in the midst thereof. 3. For there they that carried us away captive required of us a song; and they that wasted us *required of us* mirth, *saying*, Sing us *one* of the songs of Zion. 4. How shall we sing the LORD'S song in a strange land? 5. If I forget thee, O Jerusalem, let my right hand forget *her cunning*. 6. If I do not remember thee, let my tongue cleave to the roof of my mouth; if I prefer not Jerusalem above my chief joy.

Psa. 149:2. Let Israel rejoice in him that made him: let the children of Zion be joyful in their King.

Isa. 1:8. The daughter of Zion is left as a cottage in a vineyard, as a lodge in a garden of cucumbers, as a besieged city. 27. Zion shall be redeemed with judgment, and her converts with righteousness.

Isa. 2:3. And many people shall go and say, Come ye, and let us go up to the mountain of the LORD, to the house of the God of Jacob; and he will teach us of his ways, and we will walk in his paths: for out of Zion shall go forth the law, and the word of the LORD from Jerusalem.

Isa. 4:2. In that day shall the branch of the LORD be beautiful and glorious, and the fruit of the earth *shall be* excellent and comely for them that are escaped of Israel. 3. And it shall come to pass, *that he that is* left in Zion, and *he that* remaineth in Jerusalem, shall be called holy, *even* every one that is written among the living in Jerusalem: 4. When the

Lord shall have washed away the filth of the daughters of Zion, and shall have purged the blood of Jerusalem from the midst thereof by the spirit of judgment, and by the spirit of burning. 5. And the LORD will create upon every dwelling place of mount Zion, and upon her assemblies, a cloud and smoke by day, and the shining of a flaming fire by night: for upon all the glory *shall be* a defence. 6. And there shall be a tabernacle for a shadow in the daytime from the heat, and for a place of refuge, and for a covert from storm and from rain.

Isa. 12:6. Cry out and shout, thou inhabitant of Zion: for great *is* the Holy One of Israel in the midst of thee.

Isa. 14:32. What shall *one* then answer the messengers of the nation? That the LORD hath founded Zion, and the poor of his people shall trust in it.

Isa. 24:23. Then the moon shall be confounded, and the sun ashamed, when the LORD of hosts shall reign in mount Zion, and in Jerusalem, and before his ancients gloriously.

Isa. 27:2. In that day sing ye unto her, A vineyard of red wine. 3. I the LORD do keep it; I will water it every moment: lest *any* hurt it, I will keep it night and day.

Isa. 28:5. In that day shall the LORD of hosts be for a crown of glory, and for a diadem of beauty, unto the residue of his people, 16. Therefore thus saith the Lord GOD, Behold, I lay in Zion for a foundation a stone, a tried stone, a precious corner *stone*, a sure foundation: he that believeth shall not make haste.

Isa. 31:4. For thus hath the LORD spoken unto me, Like as the lion and the young lion roaring on his prey, when a multitude of shepherds is called forth against him, *he* will not be afraid of their voice, nor abase himself for the noise of them: so shall the LORD of hosts come down to fight for mount Zion, and for the hill thereof. 5. As birds flying, so will the LORD of hosts defend Jerusalem; defending also he will deliver it; *and* passing over he will preserve *it.*

Isa. 33:5. The LORD is exalted; . . . he hath filled Zion with judgment and righteousness. 14. The sinners in Zion are afraid; fearfulness hath surprised the hypocrites. 20. Look upon Zion, the city of our solemnities: thine eyes shall see Jerusalem a quiet habitation, a tabernacle *that* shall not be taken down; not one of the stakes thereof shall ever be removed, neither shall any of the cords thereof be broken. 21. But there the glorious LORD *will be* unto us a place of broad rivers *and* streams; wherein shall go no galley with oars, neither shall gallant ship pass thereby. 22. For the LORD *is* our judge, the LORD *is* our lawgiver, the LORD *is* our King; he will save us. 23. Thy tacklings are loosed; they could not well strengthen their mast, they could not spread the sail: then is the prey of a great spoil divided; the lame take the prey. 24. And the inhabitant shall not say, I am

sick; the people that dwell therein *shall be* forgiven *their* iniquity.

Isa. 35:1. The wilderness and the solitary place shall be glad for them; and the desert shall rejoice, and blossom as the rose. 2. It shall blossom abundantly, and rejoice even with joy and singing: the glory of Lebanon shall be given unto it, the excellency of Carmel and Sharon, they shall see the glory of the LORD, *and* the excellency of our God. 3. Strengthen ye the weak hands, and confirm the feeble knees. 4. Say to them *that are* of a fearful heart, Be strong, fear not: behold, your God will come *with* vengeance, *even* God *with* a recompence; he will come and save you. 5. Then the eyes of the blind shall be opened, and the ears of the deaf shall be unstopped. 6. Then shall the lame *man* leap as an hart, and the tongue of the dumb sing: for in the wilderness shall waters break out, and streams in the desert. 7. And the parched ground shall become a pool, and the thirsty land springs of water: in the habitation of dragons, where each lay, *shall be* grass with reeds and rushes. 8. And an highway shall be there, and a way, and it shall be called The way of holiness; the unclean shall not pass over it; but it *shall be* for those: the wayfaring men, though fools, shall not err *therein.* 9. No lion shall be there, nor *any* ravenous beast shall go up thereon, it shall not be found there: but the redeemed shall walk *there:* 10. And the ransomed of the LORD shall return, and come to Zion with songs and everlasting joy upon their heads: they shall obtain joy and gladness, and sorrow and sighing shall flee away.

Isa. 40:9. O Zion, that bringest good tidings, get thee up into the high mountain; O Jerusalem, that bringest good tidings, lift up thy voice with strength; lift *it* up, be not afraid; say unto the cities of Judah, Behold your God! 10. Behold, the Lord GOD will come with strong *hand,* and his arm shall rule for him: behold, his reward *is* with him, and his work before him. 11. He shall feed his flock like a shepherd: he shall gather the lambs with his arm, and carry *them* in his bosom, *and* shall gently lead those that are with young.

Isa. 43:1. But now thus saith the LORD that created thee, O Jacob, and he that formed thee, O Israel, Fear not: for I have redeemed thee, I have called *thee* by thy name; thou *art* mine. 2. When thou passest through the waters, I *will be* with thee; and through the rivers, they shall not overflow thee: when thou walkest through the fire, thou shalt not be burned; neither shall the flame kindle upon thee. 3. For I *am* the LORD thy God, the Holy One of Israel, thy Saviour: I gave Egypt *for* thy ransom, Ethiopia and Seba for thee. 4. Since thou wast precious in my sight, thou hast been honourable, and I have loved thee: therefore will I give men for thee, and people for thy life. 5. Fear not: for I *am* with thee· I will bring thy seed from the east, and gather thee from the west; 6. I will say to the north, Give up; and to the south, Keep not back: bring my sons from far, and my daughters from the ends of the earth; 7. Every one that is called by my name: for I have created him for my glory, I have formed him; yea, I have made him. 21. This people have I formed for myself; they shall shew forth my praise. 25. I, *even* I, *am* he that blotteth out thy transgressions for mine own sake, and will not remember thy sins.

Isa. 44:23. Sing, O ye heavens; for the Lord hath done *it:* shout, ye lower parts of the earth: break forth into singing, ye mountains, O forest, and every tree therein: for the Lord hath redeemed Jacob, and glorified himself in Israel.

Isa. 49:14. But Zion said, The Lord hath forsaken me, and my Lord hath forgotten me. 15. Can a woman forget her sucking child, that she should not have compassion on the son of her womb? yea, they may forget, yet will I not forget thee. 16. Behold, I have graven thee upon the palms of *my* hands; thy walls *are* continually before me. 17. Thy children shall make haste; thy destroyers and they that made thee waste shall go forth of thee.

Isa. 52:1. Awake, awake; put on thy strength, O Zion; put on thy beautiful garments, O Jerusalem, the holy city: for henceforth there shall no more come into thee the uncircumcised and the unclean. 2. Shake thyself from the dust; arise, *and* sit down, O Jerusalem: loose thyself from the bands of thy neck, O captive daughter of Zion. 7. How beautiful upon the mountains are the feet of him that bringeth good tidings, that publisheth peace; that bringeth good tidings of good, that publisheth salvation: that saith unto Zion, Thy God reigneth! 8. Thy watchmen shall lift up the voice; with the voice together shall they sing: for they shall see eye to eye, when the Lord shall bring again Zion. 9. Break forth into joy, sing together, ye waste places of Jerusalem: for the Lord hath comforted his people, he hath redeemed Jerusalem. 10. The Lord hath made bare his holy arm in the eyes of all the nations; and all the ends of the earth shall see the salvation of our God. 11. Depart ye, depart ye, go ye out from thence, touch no unclean *thing;* go ye out of the midst of her; be ye clean, that bear the vessels of the Lord. 12. For ye shall not go out with haste, nor go by flight: for the Lord will go before you; and the God of Israel *will be* your rereward.

Isa. 59:20. And the Redeemer shall come to Zion, and unto them that turn from transgression in Jacob, saith the Lord.

Isa. 60:1. Arise, shine; for thy light is come, and the glory of the Lord is risen upon thee. 2. For, behold, the darkness shall cover the earth, and gross darkness the people: but the Lord shall rise upon thee, and his glory shall be seen upon thee. 3. And the Gentiles shall come to thy light, and kings to the brightness of thy rising. 4. Lift up thine eyes round about, and see: all they gather themselves together, they come to thee: thy sons shall

come from far, and thy daughters shall be nursed at *thy* side. 5. Then thou shalt see, and flow together, and thine heart shall fear, and be enlarged; because the abundance of the sea shall be converted unto thee, the forces of the Gentiles shall come unto thee. 6. The multitude of camels shall cover thee, the dromedaries of Midian and Ephah; all they from Sheba shall come: they shall bring gold and incense; and they shall shew forth the praises of the Lord. 19. But the Lord shall be unto thee an everlasting light, and thy God thy glory. 20. Thy sun shall no more go down; neither shall thy moon withdraw itself: for the Lord shall be thine everlasting light, and the days of thy mourning shall be ended. 21. Thy people also *shall be* all righteous: they shall inherit the land for ever, the branch of my planting, the work of my hands, that I may be glorified.

Isa. 61:1. The Spirit of the Lord God *is* upon me; because the Lord hath anointed me to preach good tidings unto the meek; he hath sent me to bind up the brokenhearted, to proclaim liberty to the captives, and the opening of the prison to *them that are* bound; 2. To proclaim the acceptable year of the Lord, and the day of vengeance of our God; to comfort all that mourn; 3. To appoint unto them that mourn in Zion, to give unto them beauty for ashes, the oil of joy for mourning, the garment of praise for the spirit of heaviness; that they might be called trees of righteousness, the planting of the Lord, that he might be glorified.

Isa. 62:1. For Zion's sake will I not hold my peace, and for Jerusalem's sake I will not rest, until the righteousness thereof go forth as brightness, and the salvation thereof as a lamp *that* burneth. 3. Thou shalt also be a crown of glory in the hand of the Lord, and a royal diadem in the hand of thy God. 11. Behold, the Lord hath proclaimed unto the end of the world, Say ye to the daughter of Zion, Behold, thy salvation cometh; behold, his reward *is* with him, and his work before him. 12. And they shall call them, The holy people, The redeemed of the Lord: and thou shalt be called, Sought out, A city not forsaken.

Isa. 66:8. Who hath heard such a thing? who hath seen such things? Shall the earth be made to bring forth in one day? *or* shall a nation be born at once? for as soon as Zion travailed, she brought forth her children. 18. For I *know* their works and their thoughts: it shall come, that I will gather all nations and tongues; and they shall come, and see my glory.

Jer. 3:14. Turn, O backsliding children, saith the Lord; for I am married unto you: and I will take you one of a city, and two of a family, and I will bring you to Zion: 15. And I will give you pastors according to mine heart, which shall feed you with knowledge and understanding.

Jer. 12:10. Many pastors have destroyed my vineyard, they have trodden my portion under foot, they have made my pleasant portion a desolate wilderness.

Jer. 13:11. For as the girdle cleaveth to the loins of a man, so have I caused to cleave unto me the whole house of Israel and the whole house of Judah, saith the LORD; that they might be unto me for a people, and for a name, and for a praise, and for a glory: but they would not hear.

Jer. 31:6. For there shall be a day, *that* the watchman upon the mount Ephraim shall cry, Arise ye, and let us go up to Zion unto the LORD our God. 7. For thus saith the LORD; Sing with gladness for Jacob, and shout among the chief of the nations: publish ye, praise ye, and say, O LORD, save thy people, the remnant of Israel. 12. Therefore they shall come and sing in the height of Zion, and shall flow together to the goodness of the LORD, for wheat, and for wine, and for oil, and for the young of the flock and of the herd: and their soul shall be as a watered garden; and they shall not sorrow any more at all. 23. The LORD bless thee, O habitation of justice, *and* mountain of holiness.

Jer 33:9. It shall be to me a name of joy, a praise and an honour before all the nations of the earth, which shall hear all the good that I do unto them:

Ezek. 43:7. And he said unto me, Son of man, the place of my throne, and the place of the soles of my feet, where I will dwell in the midst of the children of Israel for ever, and my holy name, shall the house of Israel no more defile, *neither* they, nor their kings, by their whoredom, nor by the carcases of their kings in their high places.

Joel 2:1. Blow ye the trumpet in Zion, and sound an alarm in my holy mountain: let all the inhabitants of the land tremble: for the day of the LORD cometh, for *it is* nigh at hand; 15. Blow the trumpet in Zion, sanctify a fast, call a solemn assembly: 16. Gather the people, sanctify the congregation, assemble the elders, gather the children, and those that suck the breasts: let the bridegroom go forth of his chamber, and the bride out of her closet. 17. Let the priests, the ministers of the LORD, weep between the porch and the altar, and let them say, Spare thy people. O LORD, and give not thine heritage to reproach, that the heathen should rule over them; wherefore should they say among the people, Where *is* their God?

Zech. 8:3. Jerusalem shall be called a city of truth; and the mountain of the LORD of hosts the holy mountain.

Matt. 13:24. The kingdom of heaven is likened unto a man which sowed good seed in his field:

Matt. 16:18. That thou art Peter, and upon this rock I will build my church; and the gates of hell shall not prevail against it.

Acts 7:38. This is he, that was in the church in the wilderness with the angel which spake to him in the mount Sina,

Acts 20:28. Take heed therefore unto yourselves, and to all the flock, over the which the Holy Ghost hath made you overseers, to feed the church of God, which he hath purchased with his own blood.

1 Cor. 3:9. Ye are God's husbandry, *ye are* God's building.

1 Cor. 12:28. And God hath set some in the church, first apostles, secondarily prophets, thirdly teachers, after that miracles, then gifts of healings, helps, governments, diversities of tongues.

1 Cor. 15:9. I persecuted the church of God.

2 Cor. 8:1. The grace of God bestowed on the churches of Macedonia;

Eph. 1:22. And hath put all *things* under his feet, and gave him *to be* the head over all *things* to the church, 23. Which is his body, the fulness of him that filleth all in all.

Eph. 2:21. In whom all the building fitly framed together groweth unto an holy temple in the Lord: 22. In whom ye also are builded together for an habitation of God through the Spirit.

Eph. 3:15. The whole family in heaven and earth . . . 21. Unto him *be* glory in the church by Christ Jesus throughout all ages, world without end.

Eph. 5:23. For the husband is the head of the wife, even as Christ is the head of the church: and he is the saviour of the body. 24. Therefore as the church is subject unto Christ, so *let* the wives *be* to their own husbands in every thing. 25. Husbands, love your wives, even as Christ also loved the church, and gave himself for it; 26. That he might sanctify and cleanse it with the washing of water by the word, 27. That he might present it to himself a glorious church, not having spot, or wrinkle, or any such thing; but that it should be holy and without blemish. 29. For no man ever yet hated his own flesh; but nourisheth and cherisheth it, even as the Lord the church:

Col. 1:24. The afflictions of Christ in my flesh for his body's sake, which is the church.

1 Tim. 3:14. These things write I unto thee, . . . 15. . . . That thou mayest know how thou oughtest to behave thyself in the house of God, which is the church of the living God, the pillar and ground of the truth.

Heb. 3:6. Christ as a son over his own house; whose house are we,

Heb. 12:22. Ye are come unto mount Sion, and unto the city of the living God, the heavenly Jerusalem, and to an innumerable company of angels, 23. To the general assembly and church of the firstborn, which are written in heaven, and to God the Judge of all, and to the spirits of just men made perfect,

1 Pet. 2:5. Ye also, as lively stones, are built up a spiritual house, an holy priesthood, to offer up spiritual sacrifices,

Rev. 1:20. The seven candlesticks which thou sawest are the seven churches.

Rev. 21:2. I John saw the holy city, new

Jerusalem, coming down from God out of heaven, prepared as a bride adorned for her husband. 10. The holy Jerusalem, descending out of heaven from God, 11. Having the glory of God: 23. The city had no need of the sun, neither of the moon, to shine in it: for the glory of God did lighten it, and the Lamb *is* the light thereof.

BACKSLIDDEN: Psa. 12:1. Help, LORD; for the godly man ceaseth; for the faithful fail from among the children of men.

Psa. 80:1. Give ear, O Shepherd of Israel, thou that leadest Joseph like a flock; thou that dwellest *between* the cherubim, shine forth. 2. Before Ephraim and Benjamin and Manasseh stir up thy strength, and come *and* save us. 3. Turn us again, O God, and cause thy face to shine; and we shall be saved. 4. O LORD God of hosts, how long wilt thou be angry against the prayer of thy people? 5. Thou feedest them with the bread of tears; and givest them tears to drink in great measure. 6. Thou makest us a strife unto our neighbours: and our enemies laugh among themselves. 7. Turn us again, O God of hosts, and cause thy face to shine; and we shall be saved. 8. Thou hast brought a vine out of Egypt: thou hast cast out the heathen, and planted it. 9. Thou preparedst *room* before it, and didst cause it to take deep root, and it filled the land. 10. The hills were covered with the shadow of it, and the boughs thereof *were like* the goodly cedars. 11. She sent out her boughs unto the sea, and her branches unto the river. 12. Why hast thou *then* broken down her hedges, so that all they which pass by the way do pluck her? 13. The boar out of the wood doth waste it, and the wild beast of the field doth devour it. 14. Return, we beseech thee, O God of hosts: look down from heaven, and behold, and visit this vine; 15. And the vineyard which thy right hand hath planted, and the branch *that* thou madest strong for thyself. 16. *It is* burned with fire, *it is* cut down: they perish at the rebuke of thy countenance. 17. Let thy hand be upon the man of thy right hand, upon the son of man *whom* thou madest strong for thyself. 18. So will not we go back from thee: quicken us, and we will call upon thy name. 19. Turn us again, O LORD God of hosts, cause thy face to shine; and we shall be saved.

Isa. 1:2. Hear, O heavens, and give ear, O earth: for the LORD hath spoken, I have nourished and brought up children, and they have rebelled against me. 3. The ox knoweth his owner, and the ass his master's crib: *but* Israel doth not know, my people doth not consider. 4. Ah sinful nation, a people laden with iniquity, a seed of evildoers, children that are corrupters: they have forsaken the LORD, they have provoked the Holy One of Israel unto anger, they are gone away backward. *vs.* 5-27; 17:9-11; 43:22-28; Jer. 2:5-34; 3:1-25; 8:5-22.

Jer. 9:1. Oh that my head were waters,

and mine eyes a fountain of tears, that I might weep day and night for the slain of the daughter of my people! 2. Oh that I had in the wilderness a lodging place of wayfaring men: that I might leave my people, and go from them! for they *be* all adulterers, an assembly of treacherous men. 3. And they bend their tongues *like* their bow *for* lies: but they are not valiant for the truth upon the earth; for they proceed from evil to evil, and they know not me, saith the LORD.

Jer. 10:19. Woe is me for my hurt! my wound is grievous: but I said, Truly this *is* a grief, and I must bear it. 20. My tabernacle is spoiled, and all my cords are broken: my children are gone forth of me, and they *are* not: *there is* none to stretch forth my tent any more, and to set up my curtains. 21. For the pastors are become brutish, and have not sought the LORD: therefore they shall not prosper, and all their flocks shall be scattered. 22. Behold, the noise of the bruit is come, and a great commotion out of the north country, to make the cities of Judah desolate, *and* a den of dragons. Jer. 18:11-17; 50:4-7; Ezek. 2:3-5; 5:5 17; 16:23; Hos. 2; 4; 6; Joel 2; Amos 6; Matt. 21:33-46; Mark 12:1-12.

Luke 13:6. He spake also this parable: A certain *man* had a fig tree planted in his vineyard: and he came and sought fruit thereon, and found none. 7. Then said he unto the dresser of his vineyard, Behold, these three years I come seeking fruit on this fig tree, and find none: cut it down; why cumbereth it the ground? 8. And he answering said unto him, Lord, let it alone this year also, till I shall dig about it, and dung *it:* 9. And if it bear fruit, *well:* and if not, *then* after that thou shalt cut it down.

Rev. 2:1. Unto the angel of the church of Ephesus write; These things saith he that holdeth the seven stars in his right hand, who walketh in the midst of the seven golden candlesticks; 2. I know thy works, and thy labour, and thy patience, and how thou canst not bear them which are evil: and thou hast tried them which say they are apostles, and are not, and hast found them liars: 3. And hast borne, and hast patience, and for my name's sake hast laboured, and hast not fainted. 4. Nevertheless I have *somewhat* against thee, because thou hast left thy first love. 5. Remember therefore from whence thou art fallen, and repent, and do the first works; or else I will come unto thee quickly, and will remove thy candlestick out of his place, except thou repent. 6. But this thou hast, that thou hatest the deeds of the Nicolaitanes, which I also hate.

12. And to the angel of the church in Pergamos write; These things saith he which hath the sharp sword with two edges; 13. I know thy works, and where thou dwellest, *even* where Satan's seat *is:* and thou holdest fast my name, and hast not denied my faith, even in those days wherein Antipas *was* my

faithful martyr, who was slain among you, where Satan dwelleth. 14. But I have a few things against thee, because thou hast there them that hold the doctrine of Balaam, who taught Balak to cast a stumblingblock before the children of Israel, to eat things sacrificed unto idols, and to commit fornication. 15. So hast thou also them that hold the doctrine of the Nicolaitanes, which thing I hate. 16. Repent; or else I will come unto thee quickly, and will fight against them with the sword of my mouth. 18. And unto the angel of the church in Thyatira write; These things saith the Son of God, who hath his eyes like unto a flame of fire, and his feet *are* like fine brass; 19. I know thy works, and charity, and service, and faith, and thy patience, and thy works; and the last *to be* more than the first. 20. Notwithstanding I have a few things against thee, because thou sufferest that woman Jezebel, which calleth herself a prophetess, to teach and to seduce my servants to commit fornication, and to eat things sacrificed unto idols. 21. And I gave her space to repent of her fornication; and she repented not. 22. Behold, I will cast her into a bed, and them that commit adultery with her into great tribulation, except they repent of their deeds. 23. And I will kill her children with death; and all the churches shall know that I am he which searcheth the reins and hearts: and I will give unto every one of you according to your works. 24. But unto you I say, and unto the rest in Thyatira, as many as have not this doctrine, and which have not known the depths of Satan, as they speak; I will put upon you none other burden. 25. But that which ye have *already* hold fast till I come.

Rev. 3:1. And unto the angel of the church in Sardis write; These things saith he that hath the seven Spirits of God, and the seven stars; I know thy works, that thou hast a name that thou livest, and art dead. 2. Be watchful, and strengthen the things which remain, that are ready to die: for I have not found thy works perfect before God. 3. Remember therefore how thou hast received and heard, and hold fast, and repent. If therefore thou shalt not watch, I will come on thee as a thief, and thou shalt not know what hour I will come upon thee. 4. Thou hast a few names even in Sardis which have not defiled their garments; and they shall walk with me in white: for they are worthy.

14. And unto the angel of the church of the Laodiceans write; These things saith the Amen, the faithful and true witness, the beginning of the creation of God; 15. I know thy works, that thou art neither cold nor hot: I would thou wert cold or hot. 16. So then because thou art lukewarm, and neither cold nor hot, I will spue thee out of my mouth. 17. Because thou sayest, I am rich, and increased with goods, and have need of nothing; and knowest not that thou

art wretched, and miserable, and poor, and blind, and naked: 18. I counsel thee to buy of me gold tried in the fire, that thou mayest be rich; and white raiment, that thou mayest be clothed, and *that* the shame of thy nakedness do not appear; and anoint thine eyes with eyesalve, that thou mayest see. 19. As many as I love, I rebuke and chasten: be zealous therefore, and repent. 20. Behold, I stand at the door, and knock: if any man hear my voice, and open the door, I will come in to him, and will sup with him, and he with me.

Backslidings of Israel. See sub-topic BACKSLIDING OF ISRAEL, under BACKSLIDERS. See CORRUPTION IN, below; BACKSLIDERS.

BENEFICENCE OF. See BENEFICENCE; GIVING; LIBERALITY.

CHRIST, HEAD OF: Psa. 118:22. The stone *which* the builders refused is become the head *stone* of the corner. 23. This is the LORD'S doing; it *is* marvellous in our eyes. Matt. 21:42,43; Mark 12:10; Luke 20:17,18; 1 Pet. 2:7.

Isa. 33:22. The Lord *is* our judge, the Lord *is* our lawgiver, the Lord *is* our king; he will save us.

Isa. 55:4. I have given him *for* a witness to the people, a leader and commander to the people.

Matt. 12:6. But I say unto you, That in this place is *one* greater than the temple. 8. The Son of man is Lord even of the sabbath day. Mark 2:28; Luke 6:5.

Matt. 23:8. Be not ye called Rabbi: for one is your Master, *even* Christ; and all ye are brethren. 10. Neither be ye called masters: for one is your Master, *even* Christ.

John 13:13. Ye call me Master and Lord: and ye say well; for *so* I am.

John 15:1. I am the true vine, and my Father is the husbandman. 2. Every branch in me that beareth not fruit he taketh away: and every *branch* that beareth fruit, he purgeth it, that it may bring forth more fruit. 3. Now ye are clean through the word which I have spoken unto you. 4. Abide in me, and I in you. As the branch cannot bear fruit of itself, except it abide in the vine; no more can ye, except ye abide in me. 5. I am the vine, ye *are* the branches: He that abideth in me, and I in him, the same bringeth forth much fruit: for without me ye can do nothing. 6. If a man abide not in me, he is cast forth as a branch, and is withered: and men gather them, and cast *them* into the fire, and they are burned. 7. If ye abide in me, and my words abide in you, ye shall ask what ye will, and it shall be done unto you. 8. Herein is my Father glorified, that ye bear much fruit; so shall ye be my disciples.

Acts 2:36. Let all the house of Israel know assuredly, that God hath made that same Jesus, whom ye have crucified, both Lord and Christ.

Rom. 8.29. For whom he did foreknow, he also did predestinate *to be* conformed to the image of his Son, that he might be the firstborn among many brethren.

Rom. 9:5. Christ, who is over all, God blessed for ever.

1 Cor. 3:11. For other foundation can no man lay than that is laid, which is Jesus Christ.

1 Cor. 11:3. I would have you know, that the head of every man is Christ;

1 Cor. 12:5. There are differences of administrations, but the same Lord.

Eph. 1:10. That in the dispensation of the fulness of times he might gather together in one all things in Christ, both which are in heaven, and which are on earth; *even* in him: 22. Hath put all *things* under his feet, and gave him *to be* the head over all *things* to the church, 23. Which is his body, the fulness of him that filleth all in all.

Eph. 2:20. Are built upon the foundation of the apostles and prophets, Jesus Christ himself being the chief corner *stone;* 21. In whom all the building fitly framed together groweth unto an holy temple in the Lord: 22. In whom ye also are builded together for an habitation of God through the Spirit.

Eph. 4:15. Speaking the truth in love, may grow up into him in all things, which is the head, *even* Christ:

Eph. 5:23. For the husband is the head of the wife, even as Christ is the head of the church: and he is the saviour of the body. 24. Therefore as the church is subject unto Christ, so *let* the wives *be* to their own husbands in every thing. 25. Husbands, love your wives, even as Christ also loved the church, and gave himself for it; 26. That he might sanctify and cleanse it with the washing of water by the word, 27. That he might present it to himself a glorious church, not having spot, or wrinkle, or any such thing; but that it should be holy and without blemish. 28. So ought men to love their wives as their own bodies. He that loveth his wife loveth himself. 29. For no man ever yet hated his own flesh, but nourisheth and cherisheth it, even as the Lord the church: 30. For we are members of his body, of his flesh, and of his bones. 31. For this cause shall a man leave his father and mother, and shall be joined unto his wife, and they two shall be one flesh. 32. This is a great mystery: but I speak concerning Christ and the church.

Col. 1:13. Hath translated *us* into the kingdom of his dear Son: 18. He is the head of the body, the church: who is the beginning, the firstborn from the dead; that in all *things* he might have the preeminence.

Col. 2:10. And ye are complete in him, which is the head of all principality and power: 19. The Head, from which all the body by joints and bands having nourishment ministered, and knit together, increaseth with the increase of God.

Col. 3:11. Christ *is* all, and in all.

Heb. 3:3. This *man* was counted worthy of more glory than Moses, inasmuch as he who hath builded the house hath more honour than the house. 6. Christ as a son over his own house; whose house are we,

Rev. 1:13. And in the midst of the seven candlesticks *one* like unto the Son of man,

Rev. 2:1. These things saith he that holdeth the seven stars in his right hand, who walketh in the midst of the seven golden candlesticks; 9. I know thy works, and tribulation, and poverty, (but thou art rich) and *I know* the blasphemy of them which say they are Jews, and are not, but *are* the synagogue of Satan. 12. These things saith he which hath the sharp sword with two edges; 13. I know thy works, and where thou dwellest, *even* where Satan's seat *is:* and thou holdest fast my name, and hast not denied my faith, even in those days wherein Antipas *was* my faithful martyr, who was slain among you, where Satan dwelleth. 18. These things saith the Son of God, who hath his eyes like unto a flame of fire, and his feet *are* like fine brass; 19. I know thy works, and charity, and service, and faith, and thy patience, and thy works; and the last *to be* more than the first.

Rev. 3:1. These things saith he that hath the seven Spirits of God, and the seven stars; 7. These things saith he that is holy, he that is true, he that hath the key of David, he that openeth, and no man shutteth; and shutteth, and no man openeth;

Rev. 5:6. Lo, in the midst of the throne and of the four beasts, and in the midst of the elders, stood a Lamb as it had been slain, having seven horns and seven eyes, which are the seven Spirits of God sent forth into all the earth.

Rev. 21:22. I saw no temple therein: for the Lord God Almighty and the Lamb are the temple of it. 23. And the city had no need of the sun, neither of the moon, to shine in it: for the glory of God did lighten it, and the Lamb *is* the light thereof.

Rev. 22:16. I Jesus have sent mine angel to testify unto you these things in the churches. I am the root and the offspring of David, *and* the bright and morning star.

See JESUS, KINGDOM OF.

CHRISTIAN, DIVINELY ESTABLISHED:
Matt. 16:15. He saith unto them, But whom say ye that I am? 16. And Simon Peter answered and said, Thou art the Christ, the Son of the living God. 17. And Jesus answered and said unto him, Blessed art thou, Simon Bar-jona: for flesh and blood hath not revealed *it* unto thee, but my Father which is in heaven. 18. And I say also unto thee, That thou art Peter, and upon this rock I will build my church; and the gates of hell shall not prevail against it.

Eph. 2:20. And are built upon the foundation of the apostles and prophets, Jesus Christ himself being the chief corner *stone;* 21. In whom all the building fitly framed together groweth unto an holy temple in the Lord: 22. In whom ye also are builded together for an habitation of God through the Spirit.

1 Thess. 1:1. Paul, and Silvanus, and Timotheus, unto the church of the Thessalonians *which is* in God the Father and *in* the Lord Jesus Christ:

2 Thess. 1:1. Paul, and Silvanus, and Timotheus, unto the church of the Thessalonians in God our Father and the Lord Jesus Christ:

1 Tim. 3:15. But if I tarry long, that thou mayest know how thou oughtest to behave thyself in the house of God, which is the church of the living God, the pillar and ground of the truth.

CORRUPTION IN: Hos. 4:9. And there shall be, like people, like priest: and I will punish them for their ways, and reward them their doings.

Mic. 3:1. And I said, Hear, I pray you, O heads of Jacob, and ye princes of the house of Israel; *Is it* not for you to know judgment? 2. Who hate the good, and love the evil; who pluck off their skin from off them, and their flesh from off their bones; 3. Who also eat the flesh of my people, and flay their skin from off them; and they break their bones, and chop them in pieces, as for the pot, and as flesh within the caldron. 4. Then shall they cry unto the LORD, but he will not hear them: he will even hide his face from them at that time, as they have behaved themselves ill in their doings. 9. Hear this, I pray you, ye heads of the house of Jacob, and princes of the house of Israel, that abhor judgment, and pervert all equity. 11. The heads thereof judge for reward, and the priests thereof teach for hire, and the prophets thereof divine for money: yet will they lean upon the LORD, and say, *Is* not the LORD among us? none evil can come upon us.

Matt. 21:33. Hear another parable: There was a certain householder, which planted a vineyard, and hedged it round about, and digged a winepress in it, and built a tower, and let it out to husbandmen, and went into a far country: 34. And when the time of the fruit drew near, he sent his servants to the husbandmen, that they might receive the fruits of it. 35. And the husbandmen took his servants, and beat one, and killed another, and stoned another. 36. Again, he sent other servants more than the first: and they did unto them likewise. 37. But last of all he sent unto them his son, saying, They will reverence my son. 38. But when the husbandmen saw the son, they said among themselves, This is the heir; come, let us kill him, and let us seize on his inheritance. 39. And they caught him, and cast *him* out of the vineyard, and slew *him*. 40. When the lord therefore of the vineyard cometh, what will he do unto those husbandmen? 41. They say unto him, He will miserably destroy those wicked men, and will let out *his* vineyard unto other husbandmen, which shall render him the fruits in their seasons. 45. And when the chief priests and Pharisees had heard his parables, they perceived that he spake of them. Mark 12:1-12.

Matt. 23:2. The scribes and the Pharisees sit in Moses' seat: 3. All therefore whatsoever they bid you observe, *that* observe and do; but do not ye after their works: for they say, and do not. 4. For they bind heavy burdens and grievous to be borne, and lay *them* on men's shoulders; but they *themselves* will not move them with one of their fingers. 5. But all their works they do for to be seen of men: they make broad their phylacteries, and enlarge the borders of their garments, 6. And love the uppermost rooms at feasts, and the chief seats in the synagogues, 7. And greetings in the markets, and to be called of men, Rabbi, Rabbi. 13. But woe unto you, scribes and Pharisees, hypocrites! for ye shut up the kingdom of heaven against men: for ye neither go in *yourselves*, neither suffer ye them that are entering to go in. 14. Woe unto you, scribes and Pharisees, hypocrites! for ye devour widows' houses, and for a pretence make long prayer: therefore ye shall receive the greater damnation. [Omitted in R. V.] 15. Woe unto you, scribes and Pharisees, hypocrites! for ye compass sea and land to make one proselyte; and when he is made, ye make him twofold more the child of hell than yourselves. 16. Woe unto you, *ye* blind guides, which say, Whosoever shall swear by the temple, it is nothing; but whosoever shall swear by the gold of the temple, he is a debtor! 17. *Ye* fools and blind: for whether is greater, the gold, or the temple that sanctifieth the gold? 18. And, Whosoever shall swear by the altar, it is nothing; but whosoever sweareth by the gift that is upon it, he is guilty. 19. *Ye* fools and blind: for whether *is* greater, the gift, or the altar that sanctifieth the gift? 20. Whoso therefore shall swear by the altar, sweareth by it, and by all things thereon. 21. And whoso shall swear by the temple, sweareth by it, and by him that dwelleth therein. 22. And he that shall swear by heaven, sweareth by the throne of God, and by him that sitteth thereon. 23. Woe unto you, scribes and Pharisees, hypocrites! for ye pay tithes of mint and anise and cummin, and have omitted the weightier *matters* of the law, judgment, mercy, and faith: these ought ye to have done, and not to leave the other undone. 24. *Ye* blind guides, which strain at a [R.V. out the] gnat, and swallow a [R.V. the] camel. 25. Woe unto you, scribes and Pharisees, hypocrites! for ye make clean the outside of the cup and of the platter, but within they are full of extortion and excess. 26. *Thou* blind Pharisee, cleanse first that *which is* within the cup and platter, that the outside of them may be clean also. 27. Woe unto you, scribes and Pharisees, hypocrites! for ye are like unto whited sepulchres, which indeed appear beautiful outward, but are within full of dead *men's* bones, and of all uncleanness. 28. Even so ye also outwardly appear righteous unto men, but within ye are full of hypocrisy and iniquity. 29. Woe unto you, scribes and Pharisees, hypocrites! because ye build the tombs of the prophets, and garnish the sepulchres of the righteous, 30. And say, If we had been in the days of our fathers, we would not have been partakers with them in the blood of the prophets. 31. Wherefore ye be witnesses unto yourselves, that ye are the children of them which killed the prophets. 32. Fill ye up then the measure of your fathers. 33. *Ye* serpents, *ye* generation of vipers, how can ye escape the damnation of hell?

Matt. 26:59. Now the chief priests, and elders, and all the council, sought false witness against Jesus, to put him to death; 60. But found none: yea, though many false witnesses came, *yet* found they none. At the last came two false witnesses, 61. And said, This *fellow* said, I am able to destroy the temple of God, and to build it in three days. 62. And the high priest arose, and said unto him, Answerest thou nothing? what *is it which* these witness against thee? 63. But Jesus held his peace. And the high priest answered and said unto him, I adjure thee by the living God, that thou tell us whether thou be the Christ, the Son of God. 64. Jesus saith unto him, Thou hast said: nevertheless I say unto you, Hereafter shall ye see the Son of man sitting on the right hand of power, and coming in the clouds of heaven. 65. Then the high priest rent his clothes, saying, He hath spoken blasphemy; what further need have we of witnesses? behold, now ye have heard his blasphemy. 66. What think ye? They answered and said, He is guilty of death. 67. Then did they spit in his face, and buffeted him; and others smote *him* with the palms of their hands, 68. Saying, Prophesy unto us, thou Christ, Who is he that smote thee?

Mark 14:10. And Judas Iscariot, one of the twelve, went unto the chief priests, to betray him unto them. 11. And when they heard *it*, they were glad, and promised to give him money. And he sought how he might conveniently betray him. Matt. 26:14-16; Luke 22:3-6.

See BACKSLIDERS, BACKSLIDING OF ISRAEL.

DECREES OF: Acts 15:28. For it seemed good to the Holy Ghost, and to us, to lay upon you no greater burden than these necessary things; 29. That ye abstain from meats offered to idols, and from blood, and from things strangled, and from fornication: from which if ye keep yourselves, ye shall do well. Fare ye well.

Acts 16:4. And as they went through the cities, they delivered them the decrees for to keep, that were ordained of the apostles and elders which were at Jerusalem.

DESIGN OF: Rom. 3:2. Unto them were committed the oracles of God.

Rom. 9:4. Who are Israelites; to whom *pertaineth* the adoption, and the glory, and the covenants, and the giving of the law, and the service *of God*, and the promises;

Eph. 2:20. And are built upon the foundation of the apostles and prophets, Jesus Christ himself being the chief corner *stone;* 21. In whom all the building fitly framed together groweth unto an holy temple in the Lord: 22. In whom ye also are builded together for an habitation of God through the Spirit.

1 Tim. 3:15. But if I tarry long, that thou mayest know how thou oughtest to behave thyself in the house of God, which is the church of the living God, the pillar and ground of the truth.

DISSENSIONS IN: 1 Cor. 1:11-13; 3:3,4; 11:18,19; 2 Cor. 12:20,21.

DUTY OF, TO MINISTERS: Deut. 12:19. Take heed to thyself that thou forsake not the Levite as long as thou livest upon the earth.

1 Cor. 16:10. Now if Timotheus come, see that he may be with you without fear: for he worketh the work of the Lord, as I also *do*. 11. Let no man therefore despise him: but conduct him forth in peace, that he may come unto me: for I look for him with the brethren.

Phil. 2:29. Receive him therefore in the Lord with all gladness; and hold such in reputation:

Phil. 4:10. But I rejoiced in the Lord greatly, that now at the last your care of me hath flourished again; wherein ye were also careful, but ye lacked opportunity. 11. Not that I speak in respect of want: for I have learned, in whatsoever state I am, *therewith* to be content. 12. Every where and in all things I am instructed both to be full and to be hungry, both to abound and to suffer need. 14. Notwithstanding ye have well done, that ye did communicate with my affliction. 15. Now ye Philippians know also, that in the beginning of the gospel, when I departed from Macedonia, no church communicated with me as concerning giving and receiving, but ye only. 16. For even in Thessalonica ye sent once and again unto my necessity. 17. Not because I desire a gift: but I desire fruit that may abound to your account. 18. But I have all, and abound: I am full, having received of Epaphroditus the things *which were sent* from you, an odour of a sweet smell, a sacrifice acceptable, wellpleasing to God.

1 Thess. 5:12. And we beseech you, brethren, to know them which labour among you, and are over you in the Lord, and admonish you: 13. And to esteem them very highly in love for their work's sake.

1 Tim. 5:17. Let the elders that rule well be counted worthy of double honour, especially they who labour in the word and doctrine.

Heb. 13:7. Remember them which have the rule over you, who have spoken unto you the word of God: whose faith follow, considering the end of *their* conversation. 17. Obey them that have the rule over you, and submit yourselves: for they watch for your souls, as they that must give account, that they may do it with joy, and not with grief: for that *is* unprofitable for you.

See MINISTERS, DUTY OF CHURCH TO. p. 860.

GOVERNMENT OF, MOSAIC AND CHRISTIAN: Deut. 17:8. If there arise a matter too hard for thee in judgment, between blood and blood, between plea and plea, and between stroke and stroke, *being* matters of controversy within thy gates: then shalt thou arise, and get thee up into the place which the LORD thy God shall choose; 9. And thou shalt come unto the priests the Levites, and unto the judge that shall be in those days, and enquire; and they shall shew thee the sentence of judgment: 10. And thou shalt do according to the sentence, which they of that place which the LORD shall choose shall shew thee; and thou shalt observe to do according to all that they inform thee: 11. According to the sentence of the law which they shall teach thee, and according to the judgment which they shall tell thee, thou shalt do: thou shalt not decline from the sentence which they shall shew thee, *to* the right hand, nor *to* the left. 12. And the man that will do presumptuously, and will not hearken unto the priest that standeth to minister there before the LORD thy God, or unto the judge, even that man shall die: and thou shalt put away the evil from Israel. 13. And all the people shall hear, and fear, and do no more presumptuously.

Matt. 16:19. And I will give unto thee the keys of the kingdom of heaven: and whatsoever thou shalt bind on earth shall be bound in heaven: and whatsoever thou shalt loose on earth shall be loosed in heaven.

Luke 9:46. Then there arose a reasoning among them, which of them should be greatest. 47. And Jesus, perceiving the thought of their heart, took a child, and set him by him. 48. And said unto them, Whosoever shall receive this child in my name receiveth me: and whosoever shall receive me receiveth him that sent me: for he that is least among you all, the same shall be great.

Luke 22:24. And there was also a strife among them, which of them should be accounted the greatest. 25. And he said unto them, The Kings of the Gentiles exercise lordship over them; and they that exercise authority upon them are called benefactors. 26. But ye *shall* not *be* so: but he that is greatest among you, let him be as the younger; and he that is chief, as he that doth serve. 27. For whether *is* greater, he that sitteth at meat, or he that serveth? *is* not he that sitteth at meat? but I am among you as he that serveth. 28. Ye are they which have continued with me in my temptations. 29. And I appoint unto you a kingdom, as my Father hath appointed unto me: 30. That ye may eat and drink at my table in my kingdom, and sit on thrones judging the twelve tribes of Israel.

John 20:23. Whose soever sins ye remit, they are remitted unto them; *and* whose soever *sins* ye retain, they are retained.

Acts 1:15. Peter stood up in the midst of the disciples, and said, (the number of names together were about an hundred and twenty). 23. They appointed two, Joseph called Barsabas, who was surnamed Justus, and Matthias. 24. And they prayed, and said, Thou, Lord, which knowest the hearts of all *men*, shew whether of these two thou hast chosen, 25. That he may take part of this ministry and apostleship, from which Judas by transgression fell, that he might go to his own place. 26. And they gave forth their lots; and the lot fell upon Matthias; and he was numbered with the eleven apostles.

Acts 6:2. The twelve called the multitude of the disciples *unto them*, and said, It is not reason that we should leave the word of God, and serve tables. 3. Brethren, look ye out among you seven men of honest report, full of the Holy Ghost and wisdom, whom we may appoint over this business. 5. The saying pleased the whole multitude: and they chose Stephen, a man full of faith and of the Holy Ghost, and Philip, . . . 6. Whom they set before the apostles: and when they had prayed, they laid *their* hands on them.

Acts 11:22. Tidings of these things came unto the ears of the church which was in Jerusalem: and they sent forth Barnabas, that he should go as far as Antioch. 29. The disciples, every man according to his ability, determined to send relief unto the brethren which dwelt in Judæa: 30. Which also they did, and sent it to the elders by the hands of Barnabas and Saul.

Acts 13:1. There were in the church that was at Antioch certain prophets and teachers; as Barnabas, and Simeon, . . . 3. When they had fasted and prayed, and laid *their* hands on them, they sent *them* away. 5. They had also John to *their* minister.

Acts 14:23. When they had ordained them elders in every church, and had prayed with fasting, they commended them to the Lord,

Acts 15:1. And certain men which came down from Judæa taught the brethren, *and said*, Except ye be circumcised after the manner of Moses, ye cannot be saved. 2. When therefore Paul and Barnabas had no small dissension and disputation with them, they determined that Paul and Barnabas, and certain other of them, should go up to Jerusalem unto the apostles and elders about this question. 3. And being brought on their way by the church, they passed through Phenice and Samaria, declaring the conversion of the Gentiles: and they caused great joy unto all the brethren. 4. And when they were come to Jerusalem, they were received of the church, and *of* the apostles and elders, and they declared all things that God had done with them. 5. But there rose up certain of the sect of the Pharisees which believed, saying, That it was needful to circumcise them, and to command *them* to keep the law of Moses. 6. And the apostles and elders came together for to consider of this matter. 7. And when there had been much disputing, Peter rose up, and said unto them, Men *and* brethren, ye know how that a good while ago God made choice among us, that the Gentiles by my mouth should hear the word of the gospel, and believe. 8. And God, which knoweth the hearts, bare them witness, giving them the Holy Ghost, even as *he did* unto us; 9. And put no difference between us and them, purifying their hearts by faith. 10. Now therefore why tempt ye God, to put a yoke upon the neck of the disciples, which neither our fathers nor we were able to bear? 11. But we believe that through the grace of the Lord Jesus Christ we shall be saved, even as they. 12. Then all the multitude kept silence, and gave audience to Barnabas and Paul, declaring what miracles and wonders God had wrought among the Gentiles by them. 13. And after they had held their peace, James answered, saying, Men *and* brethren, hearken unto me: 14. Simeon hath declared how God at the first did visit the Gentiles, to take out of them a people for his name. 15. And to this agree the words of the prophets; as it is written, 16. After this I will return, and will build again the tabernacle of David, which is fallen down; and I will build again the ruins thereof, and I will set it up: 17. That the residue of men might seek after the Lord, and all the Gentiles, upon whom my name is called, saith the Lord, who doeth all these things. 18. Known unto God are all his works from the beginning of the world. 19. Wherefore my sentence is, that we trouble not them, which from among the Gentiles are turned to God: 20. But that we write unto them, that they abstain from pollutions of idols, and *from* fornication, and *from* things strangled, and *from* blood. 21. For Moses of old time hath in every city them that preach him, being read in the synagogues every sabbath day. 22. Then pleased it the apostles and elders, with the whole church, to send chosen men of their own company to Antioch with Paul and Barnabas; *namely,* Judas surnamed Barsabas, and Silas, chief men among the brethren: 23. And they wrote *letters* by them after this manner; The apostles and elders and brethren *send* greeting unto the brethren which are of the Gentiles in Antioch and Syria and Cilicia: 24. Forasmuch as we have heard, that certain which went out from us have troubled you with words, subverting your souls, saying, *Ye must* be circumcised, and keep the law: to whom we gave no *such* commandment: 25. It seemed good unto us, being assembled with one accord, to send chosen men unto you with our beloved Barnabas and Paul. 26. Men that have hazarded their lives for the name of our Lord Jesus Christ. 27. We have sent therefore Judas and Silas, who shall also tell *you* the same things by mouth. 28. For it seemed good to the Holy Ghost, and to us, to lay upon you no greater burden than these necessary things; 29. That ye abstain from meats offered to idols, and from blood, and from things strangled, and from fornication: from which if ye keep yourselves, ye shall do well. Fare

ye well. 30. So when they were dismissed, they came to Antioch: and when they had gathered the multitude together, they delivered the epistle: 31. *Which* when they had read, they rejoiced for the consolation.

Acts 16:4. And as they went through the cities, they delivered them the decrees for to keep, that were ordained of the apostles and elders which were at Jerusalem. 5. And so were the churches established in the faith, and increased in number daily.

Acts 20:17. From Miletus he sent to Ephesus, and called the elders of the church. 28. Take heed therefore unto yourselves, and to all the flock, over the which the Holy Ghost hath made you overseers, to feed the church of God, which he hath purchased with his own blood.

1 Cor. 7:17. As God hath distributed to every man, as the Lord hath called every one, so let him walk. And so ordain I in all churches.

1 Cor. 11:2. I praise you, brethren, that ye remember me in all things, and keep the ordinances, as I delivered *them* to you. 33. When ye come together to eat, tarry one for another. 34. And if any man hunger, let him eat at home; that ye come not together unto condemnation. And the rest will I set in order when I come.

1 Cor. 12:5. There are differences of administrations, but the same Lord. 28. God hath set some in the church, first apostles, secondarily prophets, thirdly teachers, after that miracles, then gifts of healings, helps, governments, diversities of tongues.

1 Cor. 14:26. How is it then, brethren? when ye come together, every one of you hath a psalm, hath a doctrine, hath a tongue, hath a revelation, hath an interpretation. Let all things be done unto edifying. 33. God is not *the author* of confusion, but of peace, as in all churches of the saints. 40. Let all things be done decently and in order.

1 Cor. 16:3. When I come, whomsoever ye shall approve by *your* letters, them will I send to bring your liberality unto Jerusalem. 16. Submit yourselves unto such, and to every one that helpeth with *us,* and laboureth.

2 Cor. 2:6. Sufficient to such a man *is* this punishment, which *was inflicted* of many. 7. So that contrariwise ye *ought* rather to forgive *him,* and comfort *him,* lest perhaps such a one should be swallowed up with overmuch sorrow. *vs.* 2–11.

Gal. 2:9. When James, Cephas, and John. who seemed to be pillars, perceived the grace that was given unto me, they gave to me and Barnabas the right hands of fellowship; that we *should go* unto the heathen, and they unto the circumcision. 10. Only *they would* that we should remember the poor:

Eph. 4:11. He gave some, apostles; and some, prophets; and some, evangelists; and some, pastors and teachers: 12. For the perfecting of the saints, for the work of the ministry, for the edifying of the body of Christ:

Phil. 1:1. Paul and Timotheus, . . . to all the saints in Christ Jesus which are at Philippi, with the bishops and deacons:

1 Tim. 3:1. If a man desire the office of a bishop, he desireth a good work. 2. A bishop then must be blameless, . . . 5. (For if a man know not how to rule his own house, how shall he take care of the church of God?) 8. Likewise *must* the deacons *be* grave, not doubletongued, not given to much wine, not greedy of filthy lucre; 9. Holding the mystery of the faith in a pure conscience. 10. And let these also first be proved; then let them use the office of a deacon, being *found* blameless. 11. Even so *must their* wives *be* grave, not slanderers, sober, faithful in all things. 12. Let the deacons be the husbands of one wife, ruling their children and their own houses well. 13. For they that have used the office of a deacon will purchase to themselves a good degree, and great boldness in the faith which is in Christ Jesus. *vs.* 1–13.

1 Tim. 4:14. Neglect not the gift that is in thee, which was given thee by prophecy, with the laying on of the hands of the presbytery.

1 Tim. 5:1. Rebuke not an elder, but intreat *him* as a father; *and* the younger men as brethren; 17. Let the elders that rule well be counted worthy of double honour, especially they who labour in the word and doctrine. 22. Lay hands suddenly on no man, neither be partaker of other men's sins:

2 Tim. 1:6. I put thee in remembrance that thou stir up the gift of God, which is in thee by the putting on of my hands.

Tit. 1:5. For this cause left I thee in Crete, that thou shouldest set in order the things that are wanting, and ordain elders in every city, as I had appointed thee:

Heb. 13:17. Obey them that have the rule over you, and submit yourselves: 24. Salute all them that have the rule over you, and all the saints.

Jas. 5:14. Is any sick among you? let him call for the elders of the church; and let them pray over him, anointing him with oil in the name of the Lord: 15. And the prayer of faith shall save the sick,

1 Pet. 5:1. The elders which are among you I exhort, who am also an elder, . . . 2. Feed the flock of God which is among you, taking the oversight *thereof*, not by constraint, but willingly; not for filthy lucre, but of a ready mind; 3. Neither as being lords over *God's* heritage, but being ensamples to the flock.

3 John 9. I wrote unto the church: but Diotrephes, who loveth to have the preeminence among them, receiveth us not. 10. Wherefore, if I come, I will remember his deeds which he doeth, prating against us with malicious words: and not content therewith, neither doth he himself receive the brethren, and forbiddeth them that would, and casteth *them* out of the church.

Jude 22. And of some have compassion,

making a difference: 23. And others save with fear, pulling *them* out of the fire; hating even the garment spotted by the flesh.

See MINISTERS, DUTIES OF.

RULES OF DISCIPLINE IN, MOSAIC AND CHRISTIAN: Gen. 17:14. And the uncircumcised man child whose flesh of his foreskin is not circumcised, that soul shall be cut off from his people; he hath broken my covenant.

Ex. 12:15. Seven days shall ye eat unleavened bread; even the first day ye shall put away leaven out of your houses: for whosoever eateth leavened bread from the first day until the seventh day, that soul shall be cut off from Israel.

Ex. 30:33. Whosoever compoundeth *any* like it, or whosoever putteth *any* of it upon a stranger, shall even be cut off from his people. 37. And *as for* the perfume which thou shalt make, ye shall not make to yourselves according to the composition thereof: it shall be unto thee holy for the LORD. 38. Whosoever shall make like unto that, to smell thereto, shall even be cut off from his people.

Lev. 7:27. Whatsoever soul *it be* that eateth any manner of blood, even that soul shall be cut off from his people.

Lev. 17:8. And thou shalt say unto them, Whatsoever man *there be* of the house of Israel, or of the strangers which sojourn among you, that offereth a burnt offering or sacrifice, 9. And bringeth it not unto the door of the tabernacle of the congregation, to offer it unto the LORD; even that man shall be cut off from among his people.

Lev. 19:5. And if ye offer a sacrifice of peace offerings unto the LORD, ye shall offer it at your own will. 6. It shall be eaten the same day ye offer it, and on the morrow: and if ought remain until the third day, it shall be burnt in the fire. 7. And if it be eaten at all on the third day, it *is* abominable; it shall not be accepted. 8. Therefore *every one* that eateth it shall bear his iniquity, because he hath profaned the hallowed thing of the LORD: and that soul shall be cut off from among his people.

Lev. 20:18. And if a man shall lie with a woman having her sickness, and shall uncover her nakedness; he hath discovered her fountain, and she hath uncovered the fountain of her blood: and both of them shall be cut off from among their people.

Lev. 22:3. Say unto them, Whosoever *he be* of all your seed among your generations, that goeth unto the holy things, which the children of Israel hallow unto the LORD, having his uncleanness upon him, that soul shall be cut off from my presence: I *am* the LORD.

Num. 9:13. But the man that *is* clean, and is not in a journey, and forbeareth to keep the passover, even the same soul shall be cut off from among his people: because he brought not the offering of the LORD in his appointed season, that man shall bear his sin.

Num. 15:31. Because he hath despised the word of the LORD, and hath broken his commandment, that soul shall utterly be cut off, his iniquity *shall be* upon him.

Num. 19:13. Whosoever toucheth the dead body of any man that is dead, and purifieth not himself, defileth the tabernacle of the LORD; and that soul shall be cut off from Israel: because the water of separation was not sprinkled upon him, he shall be unclean; his uncleanness *is* yet upon him.

20. But the man that shall be unclean, and shall not purify himself, that soul shall be cut off from among the congregation, because he hath defiled the sanctuary of the LORD: the water of separation hath not been sprinkled upon him; he *is* unclean.

Deut. 13:12. If thou shalt hear *say* in one of thy cities, which the LORD thy God hath given thee to dwell there, saying, 13. *Certain* men, the children of Belial, are gone out from among you, and have withdrawn the inhabitants of their city, saying, Let us go and serve other gods, which ye have not known; 14. Then shalt thou enquire, and make search, and ask diligently; and, behold, *if it be* truth, *and* the thing certain, *that* such abomination is wrought among you; 15. Thou shalt surely smite the inhabitants of that city with the edge of the sword, destroying it utterly, and all that *is* therein, and the cattle thereof, with the edge of the sword. 16. And thou shalt gather all the spoil of it into the midst of the street thereof, and shalt burn with fire the city, and all the spoil thereof every whit, for the LORD thy God: and it shall be an heap for ever; it shall not be built again. 17. And there shall cleave nought of the cursed thing to thine hand: that the LORD may turn from the fierceness of his anger, and shew thee mercy, and have compassion upon thee, and multiply thee, as he hath sworn unto thy fathers; 18. When thou shalt hearken to the voice of the LORD thy God, to keep all his commandments which I command thee this day, to do *that which is* right in the eyes of the LORD thy God.

Deut. 17:2. If there be found among you, within any of thy gates which the LORD thy God giveth thee, man or woman, that hath wrought wickedness in the sight of the LORD thy God, in transgressing his covenant, 3. And hath gone and served other gods, and worshipped them, either the sun, or moon, or any of the host of heaven, which I have not commanded; 4. And it be told thee, and thou hast heard *of it*, and enquired diligently, and, behold, *it be* true, *and* the thing certain, *that* such abomination is wrought in Israel: 5. Then shalt thou bring forth that man or that woman, which have committed that wicked thing, unto thy gates, *even* that man or that woman, and shalt stone them with stones, till they die. 6. At the mouth of two witnesses, or three witnesses, shall he that is worthy of death be put to death; *but* at the mouth of one wit-

ness he shall not be put to death. 7. The hands of the witnesses shall be first upon him to put him to death, and afterward the hands of all the people. So thou shalt put the evil away from among you. 8. If there arise a matter too hard for thee in judgment, between blood and blood, between plea and plea, and between stroke and stroke, *being* matters of controversy within thy gates: then shalt thou arise, and get thee up into the place which the LORD thy God shall choose; 9. And thou shalt come unto the priests the Levites, and unto the judge that shall be in those days, and enquire; and they shall shew thee the sentence of judgment: 10. And thou shalt do according to the sentence, which they of that place which the LORD shall choose shall shew thee; and thou shalt observe to do according to all that they inform thee: 11. According to the sentence of the law which they shall teach thee, and according to the judgment which they shall tell thee, thou shalt do; thou shalt not decline from the sentence which they shall shew thee, *to* the right hand, nor *to* the left. 12. And the man that will do presumptuously, and will not hearken unto the priest that standeth to minister there before the LORD thy God, or unto the judge, even that man shall die: and thou shalt put away the evil from Israel. 13. And all the people shall hear, and fear, and do no more presumptuously.

Deut. 19:16. If a false witness rise up against any man to testify against him *that which is* wrong; 17. Then both the men, between whom the controversy *is*, shall stand before the LORD, before the priests and the judges, which shall be in those days; 18. And the judges shall make diligent inquisition: and, behold, *if* the witness *be* a false witness, *and* hath testified falsely against his brother; 19. Then shall ye do unto him, as he had thought to have done unto his brother: so shalt thou put the evil away from among you. 20. And those which remain shall hear, and fear, and shall henceforth commit no more any such evil among you. 21. And thine eye shall not pity: *but* life *shall* go for life, eye for eye, tooth for tooth, hand for hand, foot for foot.

Deut. 21:1. If *one* be found slain in the land which the LORD thy God giveth thee to possess it, lying in the field, *and* it be not known who hath slain him: 2. Then thy elders and thy judges shall come forth, and they shall measure unto the cities which *are* round about him that is slain: 3. And it shall be, *that* the city *which is* next unto the slain man, even the elders of that city shall take an heifer, which hath not been wrought with, *and* which hath not drawn in the yoke; 4. And the elders of that city shall bring down the heifer unto a rough valley, which is neither eared nor sown, and shall strike off the heifer's neck there in the valley: 5. And the priests the sons of Levi shall come near; for them the LORD thy

God hath chosen to minister unto him, and to bless in the name of the LORD; and by their word shall every controversy and every stroke be *tried:* 6. And all the elders of that city, *that are* next unto the slain *man,* shall wash their hands over the heifer that is beheaded in the valley: 7. And they shall answer and say, Our hands have not shed this blood, neither have our eyes seen *it.* 8. Be merciful, O LORD, unto thy people Israel, whom thou hast redeemed, and lay not innocent blood unto thy people of Israel's charge. And the blood shall be forgiven them. 9. So shalt thou put away the *guilt of* innocent blood from among you, when thou shalt do *that which is* right in the sight of the LORD.

18. If a man have a stubborn and rebellious son, which will not obey the voice of his father, or the voice of his mother, and *that,* when they have chastened him, will not hearken unto them: 19. Then shall his father and his mother lay hold on him, and bring him out unto the elders of his city, and unto the gate of his place; 20. And they shall say unto the elders of his city, This our son *is* stubborn and rebellious, he will not obey our voice; *he is* a glutton, and a drunkard. 21. And all the men of his city shall stone him with stones, that he die: so shalt thou put evil away from among you; and all Israel shall hear, and fear.

Deut. 22:13. If any man take a wife, and go in unto her, and hate her, 14. And give occasions of speech against her, and bring up an evil name upon her, and say, I took this woman, and when I came to her, I found her not a maid: 15. Then shall the father of the damsel, and her mother, take and bring forth *the tokens of* the damsel's virginity unto the elders of the city in the gate: 16. And the damsel's father shall say unto the elders, I gave my daughter unto this man to wife, and he hateth her; 17. And, lo, he hath given occasions of speech *against her,* saying, I found not thy daughter a maid; and yet these *are the tokens of* my daughter's virginity. And they shall spread the cloth before the elders of the city. 18. And the elders of that city shall take that man and chastise him; 19. And they shall amerce him in an hundred *shekels* of silver, and give *them* unto the father of the damsel, because he hath brought up an evil name upon a virgin of Israel: and she shall be his wife; he may not put her away all his days. 20. But if this thing be true, *and the tokens of* virginity be not found for the damsel: 21. Then they shall bring out the damsel to the door of her father's house, and the men of her city shall stone her with stones that she die: because she hath wrought folly in Israel, to play the whore in her father's house: so shalt thou put evil away from among you.

22. If a man be found lying with a woman married to an husband, then they shall both of them die, *both* the man that lay with the woman, and the woman: so shalt thou put away evil from Israel.

23. If a damsel *that is* a virgin be betrothed unto an husband, and a man find her in the city, and lie with her; 24. Then ye shall bring them both out unto the gate of that city, and ye shall stone them with stones that they die; the damsel, because she cried not, *being* in the city; and the man, because he hath humbled his neighbour's wife: so thou shalt put away evil from among you. 25. But if a man find a betrothed damsel in the field, and the man force her, and lie with her; then the man only that lay with her shall die: 26. But unto the damsel thou shalt do nothing; *there is* in the damsel no sin *worthy* of death: for as when a man riseth against his neighbour, and slayeth him, even so *is* this matter: 27. For he found her in the field, *and* the betrothed damsel cried, and *there was* none to save her. 28. If a man find a damsel *that is* a virgin, which is not betrothed, and lay hold on her, and lie with her, and they be found; 29. Then the man that lay with her shall give unto the damsel's father fifty *shekels* of silver, and she shall be his wife; because he hath humbled her, he may not put her away all his days.

Ezra 10:7. And they made proclamation throughout Judah and Jerusalem unto all the children of the captivity, that they should gather themselves together unto Jerusalem; 8. And that whosoever would not come within three days, according to the counsel of the princes and the elders, all his substance should be forfeited, and himself separated from the congregation of those that had been carried away. *vs.* 1-44.

Matt. 16:19. And I will give unto thee the keys of the kindom of heaven: and whatsoever thou shalt bind on earth shall be bound in heaven: and whatsoever thou shalt loose on earth shall be loosed in heaven. John 20:23.

Matt. 18:15. Moreover if thy brother shall trespass against thee, go and tell him his fault between thee and him alone: if he shall hear thee, thou hast gained thy brother. 16. But if he will not hear *thee, then* take with thee one or two more, that in the mouth of two or three witnesses every word may be established. 17. And if he shall neglect to hear them, tell *it* unto the church: but if he neglect to hear the church, let him be unto thee as an heathen man and a publican. 18. Verily I say unto you, Whatsoever ye shall bind on earth shall be bound in heaven: and whatsoever ye shall loose on earth shall be loosed in heaven.

John 9:22. These *words* spake his parents, because they feared the Jews: for the Jews had agreed already, that if any man did confess that he was Christ, he should be put out of the synagogue. 34. They answered and said unto him, Thou wast altogether born in sins, and dost thou teach us? And they cast him out. 35. Jesus heard that they had cast him out; and when he had found him, he said unto him, Dost thou believe on the Son of God?

John 16:2. They shall put you out of the synagogues: yea, the time cometh, that whosoever killeth you will think that he doeth God service.

Rom. 14:1. Him that is weak in the faith receive ye, *but* not to doubtful disputations.

Rom. 15:1. We then that are strong ought to bear the infirmities of the weak, *vs.* 1–3.

Rom. 16:17. Mark them which cause divisions and offences contrary to the doctrine which ye have learned; and avoid them.

1 Cor. 4:19. I will come to you shortly, if the Lord will, and will know, not the speech of them which are puffed up, but the power. 21. What will ye? shall I come unto you with a rod, or in love, and *in* the spirit of meekness?

1 Cor. 5:1. It is reported commonly *that there is* fornication among you, and such fornication as is not so much as named among the Gentiles, that one should have his father's wife. 2. Ye are puffed up, and have not rather mourned, that he that hath done this deed might be taken away from among you. 4. In the name of our Lord Jesus Christ, when ye are gathered together, and my spirit, with the power of our Lord Jesus Christ. 5. To deliver such an one unto Satan for the destruction of the flesh, that the spirit may be saved in the day of the Lord Jesus. 6. Your glorying *is* not good. Know ye not that a little leaven leaveneth the whole lump? 7. Purge out therefore the old leaven, that ye may be a new lump, as ye are unleavened. 11. I have written unto you not to keep company, if any man that is called a brother be a fornicator, or covetous, or an idolater, or a railer, or a drunkard, or an extortioner; with such an one no not to eat. 12. What have I to do to judge them also that are without? do not ye judge them that are within? 13. Therefore put away from among yourselves that wicked person.

1 Cor. 16:22. If any man love not the Lord Jesus Christ, let him be Anathema Maranatha.

2 Cor. 2:6. Sufficient to such a man *is* this punishment, which *was inflicted* of many. 7. Ye *ought* rather to forgive *him*, and comfort *him*, lest perhaps such a one should be swallowed up with overmuch sorrow. 8. Wherefore I beseech you that ye would confirm *your* love toward him. 10. To whom ye forgive any thing, I *forgive* also: for if I forgave any thing, to whom I forgave *it*, for your sakes *forgave I it* in the person of Christ; 11. Lest Satan should get an advantage of us: for we are not ignorant of his devices.

2 Cor. 6:14. Be ye not unequally yoked together with unbelievers: for what fellowship hath righteousness with unrighteousness? and what communion hath light with darkness? 15. And what concord hath Christ

with Belial? or what part hath he that believeth with an infidel?

2 Cor. 7:8. For though I made you sorry with a letter, I do not repent, though I did repent: for I perceive that the same epistle hath made you sorry, though *it were* but for a season. 2 Cor. 10:1–11.

2 Cor. 13:1. In the mouth of two or three witnesses shall every word be established. 2. I told you before, and foretell you, as if I were present, the second time; and being absent now I write to them which heretofore have sinned, and to all other, that, if I come again, I will not spare: 10. I write these things being absent, lest being present I should use sharpness, according to the power which the Lord hath given me to edification, and not to destruction.

Gal. 5:10. He that troubleth you shall bear his judgment, whosoever he be. 12. I would they were even cut off which trouble you.

Gal. 6:1. Brethren, if a man be overtaken in a fault, ye which are spiritual, restore such an one in the spirit of meekness; considering thyself, lest thou also be tempted.

1 Thess. 5:14. Now we exhort you, brethren, warn them that are unruly, comfort the feebleminded, support the weak, be patient toward all *men*.

2 Thess. 3:6. We command you, brethren, in the name of our Lord Jesus Christ, that ye withdraw yourselves from every brother that walketh disorderly, and not after the tradition which he received of us. 14. If any man obey not our word by this epistle, note that man, and have no company with him, that he may be ashamed. 15. Yet count *him* not as an enemy, but admonish *him* as a brother.

1 Tim. 1:19. Holding faith, and a good conscience; which some having put away concerning faith have made shipwreck: 20. Of whom is Hymenæus and Alexander; whom I have delivered unto Satan, that they may learn not to blaspheme.

1 Tim. 5:1. Rebuke not an elder, but entreat *him* as a father; *and* the younger men as brethren; 2. The elder women as mothers; the younger as sisters, with all purity.

19. Against an elder receive not an accusation, but before two or three witnesses.

20. Them that sin rebuke before all, that others also may fear.

1 Tim. 6:3. If any man teach otherwise, and consent not to wholesome words, *even* the words of our Lord Jesus Christ, and to the doctrine which is according to godliness; 4. He is proud, knowing nothing, but doting about questions and strifes of words, whereof cometh envy, strife, railings, evil surmisings, 5. Perverse disputings of men of corrupt minds, and destitute of the truth, supposing that [1] gain is godliness: from such withdraw thyself.

[R. V. godliness is a way of gain;

2 Tim. 4:2. Reprove, rebuke, exhort with all longsuffering and doctrine.

Tit. 1:13. Rebuke them sharply, that they may be sound in the faith;

Tit. 2:15. These things speak, and exhort, and rebuke with all authority. Let no man despise thee.

Tit. 3:10. A man that is an heretick after the first and second admonition reject; 11. Knowing that he that is such is subverted, and sinneth, being condemned of himself.

2 John 10. If there come any unto you, and bring not this doctrine, receive him not into *your* house, neither bid him God speed: 11. For he that biddeth him God speed is partaker of his evil deeds.

Jude 22. And of some have compassion, making a difference: 23. And others save with fear, pulling *them* out of the fire; hating even the garment spotted by the flesh.

Rev. 22:19. And if any man shall take away from the words of the book of this prophecy, God shall take away his part out of the book of life, and out of the holy city, and *from* the things which are written in this book.

See Excommunication; Ministers, Duties of.

LOVE FOR: Psa. 102:14. Thy servants take pleasure in her stones, and favour the dust thereof.

Psa. 122:6. Pray for the peace of Jerusalem: they shall prosper that love thee. 9. Because of the house of the Lord our God I will seek thy good.

Psa. 128:5. The Lord shall bless thee out of Zion: and thou shalt see the good of Jerusalem all the days of thy life. 6. Yea, thou shalt see thy children's children, *and* peace upon Israel.

Psa. 137:1. By the rivers of Babylon, there we sat down, yea, we wept, when we remembered Zion. 2. We hanged our harps upon the willows in the midst thereof. 3. For there they that carried us away captive required of us a song; and they that wasted us *required of us* mirth, *saying,* Sing us *one* of the songs of Zion. 4. How shall we sing the Lord's song in a strange land? 5. If I forget thee, O Jerusalem, let my right hand forget her *cunning.* 6. If I do not remember thee, let my tongue cleave to the roof of my mouth; if I prefer not Jerusalem above my chief joy.

Isa. 22:4. Look away from me; I will weep bitterly, labour not to comfort me, because of the spoiling of the daughter of my people.

Isa. 58:12. *They that shall be* of thee shall build the old waste places: thou shalt raise up the foundations of many generations; and thou shalt be called, The repairer of the breach, The restorer of paths to dwell in.

Isa. 62:1. For Zion's sake will I not hold my peace, and for Jerusalem's sake I will not rest, until the righteousness thereof go forth as brightness, and the salvation thereof as a lamp *that* burneth. 6. I have set watchmen upon thy walls, O Jerusalem, *which* shall never hold their peace day nor night: ye that make mention of the Lord, keep not silence, 7. And give him no rest, till he establish, and till he make Jerusalem a praise in the earth.

Isa. 66:10. Rejoice ye with Jerusalem, and be glad with her, all ye that love her: rejoice for joy with her, all ye that mourn for her: 13. Ye shall be comforted in Jerusalem. 14. And when ye see *this,* your heart shall rejoice, and your bones shall flourish like an herb:

Jer. 9:1. Oh that my head were waters, and mine eyes a fountain of tears, that I might weep day and night for the slain of the daughter of my people!

Jer. 14:17. Let mine eyes run down with tears night and day, and let them not cease: for the virgin daughter of my people is broken with a great breach, with a very grievous blow.

Jer. 51:50. Ye that have escaped the sword, ... remember the Lord afar off, and let Jerusalem come into your mind. 51. We are confounded, because we have heard reproach: shame hath covered our faces: for strangers are come into the sanctuaries of the Lord's house.

Lam. 2:11. Mine eyes do fail with tears, my bowels are troubled, my liver is poured upon the earth, for the destruction of the daughter of my people; because the children and the sucklings swoon in the streets of the city.

Lam. 3:48. Mine eye runneth down with rivers of water for the destruction of the daughter of my people. 49. Mine eye trickleth down, and ceaseth not, without any intermission, 50. Till the Lord look down, and behold from heaven. 51. Mine eye affecteth mine heart because of all the daughters of my city. chapters 1-5.

MEMBERSHIP IN: Isa. 44:5. One shall say, I *am* the Lord's; and another shall call *himself* by the name of Jacob; and another shall subscribe *with* his hand unto the Lord, and surname *himself* by the name of Israel.

Ezek. 44:6. And thou shalt say to the rebellious, *even* to the house of Israel, Thus saith the Lord God; O ye house of Israel, let it suffice you of all your abominations, 7. In that ye have brought *into my sanctuary* strangers, uncircumcised in heart, and uncircumcised in flesh, to be in my sanctuary, to pollute it, *even* my house, when ye offer my bread, the fat and the blood, and they have broken my covenant because of all your abominations. 9. Thus saith the Lord God; No stranger, uncircumcised in heart, nor uncircumcised in flesh, shall enter into my sanctuary, of any stranger that *is* among the children of Israel.

Matt. 12:50. For whosoever shall do the will of my Father which is in heaven. the same is my brother, and sister, and mother.

Luke 18:16. Suffer little children to come unto me, and forbid them not: for of such is the kingdom of God. Matt. 19:14; Mark 10:14.

John 15:5. I am the vine, ye *are* the branches: He that abideth in me, and I in him, the same bringeth forth much fruit; for without me ye can do nothing. 6. If a man abide not in me, he is cast forth as a branch, and is withered; and men gather them, and cast *them* into the fire, and they are burned.

Acts 2:41. Then they that gladly received his word were baptized: and the same day there were added *unto them* about three thousand souls. 47. Praising God, and having favour with all the people. And the Lord added to the church daily such as should be saved.

Acts 4:4. Howbeit many of them which heard the word believed; and the number of the men was about five thousand.

Acts 5:14. And believers were the more added to the Lord, multitudes both of men and women;

Acts 9:35. And all that dwelt at Lydda and Saron saw him, and turned to the Lord. 42. And it was known throughout all Joppa; and many believed in the Lord.

Acts 11:21. And the hand of the Lord was with them: and a great number believed, and turned unto the Lord.

Rom. 12:4. For as we have many members in one body, and all members have not the same office: 5. So we, *being* many, are one body in Christ, and every one members one of another.

1 Cor. 3:11. For other foundation can no man lay than that is laid, which is Jesus Christ. 12. Now if any man build upon this foundation gold, silver, precious stones, wood, hay, stubble; 13. Every man's work shall be made manifest: for the day shall declare it, because it shall be revealed by fire; and the fire shall try every man's work of what sort it is. 14. If any man's work abide which he hath built thereupon, he shall receive a reward. 15. If any man's work shall be burned, he shall suffer loss: but he himself shall be saved; yet so as by fire.

1 Cor. 12:12. For as the body is one, and hath many members, and all the members of that one body, being many, are one body: so also *is* Christ. 13. For by one Spirit are we all baptized into one body, whether *we be* Jews or Gentiles, whether *we be* bond or free; and have been all made to drink into one Spirit. 14. For the body is not one member, but many. 15. If the foot shall say, Because I am not the hand, I am not of the body; is it therefore not of the body? 16. And if the ear shall say, Because I am not the eye, I am not of the body; is it therefore not of the body? 17. If the whole body *were* an eye, where *were* the hearing? If the whole *were* hearing, where *were* the smelling? 18. But now hath God set the members every one of them in the body, as it hath pleased him. 19. And if they were all one member, where *were* the body? 20. But now *are they* many members, yet but one body. 21. And the eye cannot say unto the hand, I have no need of thee: nor again the head to the feet, I have no need of you. 22. Nay, much more those members of the body, which seem to be more feeble, are

necessary: 23. And those *members* of the body, which we think to be less honourable, upon these we bestow more abundant honour; and our uncomely *parts* have more abundant comeliness. 24. For our comely *parts* have no need; but God hath tempered the body together, having given more abundant honour to that *part* which lacked: 25. That there should be no schism in the body; but *that* the members should have the same care one for another. 26. And whether one member suffer, all the members suffer with it; or one member be honoured, all the members rejoice with it. 27. Now ye are the body of Christ, and members in particular. 28. And God hath set some in the church, first apostles, secondarily prophets, thirdly teachers, after that miracles, then gifts of healings, helps, governments, diversities of tongues.

Eph. 4:25. We are members one of another.

Eph. 5:30. We are members of his body, of his flesh, and of his bones.

Phil. 4:3. Help those women which laboured with me in the gospel, with Clement also, and *with* other my fellowlabourers, whose names *are* in the book of life.

Rev. 21:27. And there shall in no wise enter into it any thing that defileth, neither *whatsoever* worketh abomination, or *maketh* a lie: but they which are written in the Lamb's book of life.

See RIGHTEOUS, DESCRIBED.

PROPHECIES CONCERNING PROSPERITY OF: Gen. 12:3. In thee shall all families of the earth be blessed.

Gen. 49:10. Unto him *shall* the gathering of the people *be.*

Deut. 32:21. I will move them to jealousy with *those which are* not a people; I will provoke them to anger with a foolish nation.

Psa. 2:8. Ask of me, and I shall give *thee* the heathen *for* thine inheritance, and the uttermost parts of the earth *for* thy possession.

Psa. 22:27. All the ends of the world shall remember and turn unto the LORD: and all the kindreds of the nations shall worship before thee. 28. For the kingdom *is* the LORD'S: and he *is* the governor among the nations. 29. All *they that be* fat upon earth shall eat and worship: all they that go down to the dust shall bow before him: and none can keep alive his own soul. 30. A seed shall serve him: it shall be accounted to the Lord for a generation. 31. They shall come, and shall declare his righteousness unto a people that shall be born, that he hath done *this.*

Psa. 46:4. *There is* a river, the streams whereof shall make glad the city of God, the holy *place* of the tabernacles of the most High. 10. Be still, and know that I *am* God: I will be exalted among the heathen, I will be exalted in the earth.

Psa. 65:2. O thou that hearest prayer, unto thee shall all flesh come.

Psa. 66:4. All the earth shall worship thee, and shall sing unto thee; they shall sing *to* thy name.

Psa. 68:31. Princes shall come out of Egypt; Ethiopia shall soon stretch out her hands unto God. 32. Sing unto God, ye kingdoms of the earth; O sing praises unto the Lord :

Psa. 69:35. God will save Zion, and will build the cities of Judah: that they may dwell there, and have it in possession. 36. The seed also of his servants shall inherit it: and they that love his name shall dwell therein.

Psa. 72:2. He shall judge thy people with righteousness, and thy poor with judgment. 3. The mountains shall bring peace to the people, and the little hills, by righteousness. 4. He shall judge the poor of the people, he shall save the children of the needy, and shall break in pieces the oppressor. 7. In his days shall the righteous flourish; and abundance of peace so long as the moon endureth. 8. He shall have dominion also from sea to sea, and from the river unto the ends of the earth. 9. They that dwell in the wilderness shall bow before him; and his enemies shall lick the dust. 10. The kings of Tarshish and of the isles shall bring presents : the kings of Sheba and Seba shall offer gifts. 11. Yea, all kings shall fall down before him : all nations shall serve him. 16. There shall be an handful of corn in the earth upon the top of the mountains; the fruit thereof shall shake like Lebanon : and *they* of the city shall flourish like grass of the earth. 19. Blessed *be* his glorious name for ever: and let the whole earth be filled *with* his glory; *vs.* 1–20.

Psa. 85:10. Mercy and truth are met together; righteousness and peace have kissed *each other.* 11. Truth shall spring out of the earth; and righteousness shall look down from heaven. 12. Yea, the Lord shall give *that which is* good; and our land shall yield her increase.

Psa. 86:9. All nations whom thou hast made shall come and worship before thee, O Lord; and shall glorify thy name.

Psa. 87:4. I will make mention of Rahab and Babylon to them that know me :

Psa. 89:25. I will set his hand also in the sea, and his right hand in the rivers. 29. His seed also will I make *to endure* for ever, and his throne as the days of heaven. 36. His seed shall endure for ever, and his throne as the sun before me. 37. It shall be established for ever as the moon, and *as* a faithful witness in heaven. *vs.* 1–37.

Psa. 96:11. Let the heavens rejoice, and let the earth be glad; let the sea roar, and the fulness thereof. 12. Let the field be joyful, and all that *is* therein : then shall all the trees of the wood rejoice 13. Before the Lord : for he cometh, for he cometh to judge the earth : he shall judge the world with righteousness, and the people with his truth. *vs.* 1–13.

Psa. 102:13. Thou shalt arise, *and* have mercy upon Zion : for the time to favour her, yea, the set time, is come. 14. For thy servants take pleasure in her stones, and favour the dust thereof. 15. So the heathen shall fear the name of the Lord, and all the kings of the earth thy glory. 16. When the Lord shall build up Zion, he shall appear in his glory. 18. This shall be written for the generation to come : and the people which shall be created shall praise the Lord. 19. For he hath looked down from the height of his sanctuary ; from heaven did the Lord behold the earth ; 20. To hear the groaning of the prisoner ; to loose those that are appointed to death ; 21. To declare the name of the Lord in Zion, and his praise in Jerusalem ; 22. When the people are gathered together, and the kingdoms, to serve the Lord.

Psa. 110:3. Thy people *shall be* willing in the day of thy power, in the beauties of holiness from the womb of the morning : thou hast the dew of thy youth. *vs.* 1–7.

Psa. 113:3. From the rising of the sun unto the going down of the same the Lord's name *is* to be praised.

Psa. 118:24. This *is* the day *which* the Lord hath made ; we will rejoice and be glad in it.

Psa. 126:5. They that sow in tears shall reap in joy. 6. He that goeth forth and weepeth, bearing precious seed, shall doubtless come again with rejoicing, bringing his sheaves *with him.*

Psa. 132:15. I will abundantly bless her provision : I will satisfy her poor with bread. 16. I will also clothe her priests with salvation : and her saints shall shout aloud for joy. 17. There will I make the horn of David to bud : I have ordained a lamp for mine anointed. 18. His enemies will I clothe with shame : but upon himself shall his crown flourish.

Psa. 138:4. All the kings of the earth shall praise thee, O Lord, when they hear the words of thy mouth. 5. Yea, they shall sing in the ways of the Lord : for great *is* the glory of the Lord.

Psa. 145:10. All thy works shall praise thee, O Lord; and thy saints shall bless thee. 11. They shall speak of the glory of thy kingdom, and talk of thy power;

Isa. 2:2. It shall come to pass in the last days, *that* the mountain of the Lord's house shall be established in the top of the mountains, and shall be exalted above the hills; and all nations shall flow unto it. 3. Many people shall go and say, Come ye, and let us go up to the mountain of the Lord, to the house of the God of Jacob; and he will teach us of his ways, and we will walk in his paths : for out of Zion shall go forth the law, and the word of the Lord from Jerusalem. 4. He shall judge among the nations, and shall rebuke many people; and they shall beat their swords into plowshares, and their spears into pruninghooks : nation shall not lift up sword against nation, neither shall they learn war any more. *v.* 5.

Isa. 4:2. In that day shall the branch of the LORD be beautiful and glorious, and the fruit of the earth *shall be* excellent and comely for them that are escaped of Israel. 3. And it shall come to pass, *that he that is* left in Zion, and *he that* remaineth in Jerusalem, shall be called holy, *even* every one that is written among the living in Jerusalem: 5. And the LORD will create upon every dwelling place of mount Zion, and upon her assemblies, a cloud and smoke by day, and the shining of a flaming fire by night: for upon all the glory *shall be* a defence. 6. And there shall be a tabernacle for a shadow in the daytime from the heat, and for a place of refuge, and for a covert from storm and from rain.

Isa. 9:2. The people that walked in darkness have seen a great light: they that dwell in the land of the shadow of death, upon them hath the light shined. 6. The government shall be upon his shoulder: and his name shall be called Wonderful, Counsellor, The mighty God, The everlasting Father, The Prince of Peace. 7. Of the increase of *his* government and peace *there shall be* no end, upon the throne of David, and upon his kingdom, to order it, and to establish it with judgment and with justice from henceforth even for ever. *vs.* 1–7.

Isa. 11:6. The wolf also shall dwell with the lamb, and the leopard shall lie down with the kid; and the calf and the young lion and the fatling together; and a little child shall lead them. 7. And the cow and the bear shall feed; their young ones shall lie down together: and the lion shall eat straw like the ox. 8. And the sucking child shall play on the hole of the asp, and the weaned child shall put his hand on the cockatrice' den. 9. They shall not hurt nor destroy in all my holy mountain: for the earth shall be full of the knowledge of the LORD, as the waters cover the sea. 10. And in that day there shall be a root of Jesse, which shall stand for an ensign of the people; to it shall the Gentiles seek: and his rest shall be glorious. *vs.* 1–10.

Isa. 18:7. In that time shall the present be brought unto the LORD of hosts of a people scattered and peeled, and from a people terrible from their beginning hitherto; a nation meted out and trodden under foot, whose land the rivers have spoiled, to the place of the name of the LORD of hosts, the mount Zion.

Isa. 19:24. In that day shall Israel be the third with Egypt and with Assyria, *even* a blessing in the midst of the land: 25. Whom the LORD of hosts shall bless, saying, Blessed *be* Egypt my people, and Assyria the work of my hands, and Israel mine inheritance.

Isa. 23:17. And it shall come to pass after the end of seventy years, that the LORD will visit Tyre, and she shall turn to her hire, and shall commit fornication with all the kingdoms of the world upon the face of the earth. 18. And her merchandise and her hire shall be holiness to the LORD: it shall not be treasured nor laid up; for her merchandise shall be for them that dwell before the LORD, to eat sufficiently, and for durable clothing.

Isa. 24:16. From the uttermost part of the earth have we heard songs,

Isa. 25:6. In this mountain shall the LORD of hosts make unto all people a feast of fat things, a feast of wines on the lees, of fat things full of marrow, of wines on the lees well refined. 7. And he will destroy in this mountain the face of the covering cast over all people, and the vail that is spread over all nations. 8. He will swallow up death in victory; and the Lord GOD will wipe away tears from off all faces; and the rebuke of his people shall he take away from off all the earth: for the LORD hath spoken *it*.

Isa. 29:18. In that day shall the deaf hear the words of the book, and the eyes of the blind shall see out of obscurity, and out of darkness. 19. The meek also shall increase *their* joy in the LORD, and the poor among men shall rejoice in the Holy One of Israel. *vs.* 18–24.

Isa. 30:20. And *though* the Lord give you the bread of adversity, and the water of affliction, yet shall not thy teachers be removed into a corner any more, but thine eyes shall see thy teachers:

Isa. 32:3. The eyes of them that see shall not be dim, and the ears of them that hear shall hearken. 4. The heart also of the rash shall understand knowledge, and the tongue of the stammerers shall be ready to speak plainly. 15. Until the spirit be poured upon us from on high, and the wilderness be a fruitful field, and the fruitful field be counted for a forest. 16. Then judgment shall dwell in the wilderness, and righteousness remain in the fruitful field. 17. And the work of righteousness shall be peace; and the effect of righteousness quietness and assurance for ever. *vs.* 1–20.

Isa. 33:20. Look upon Zion, the city of our solemnities: thine eyes shall see Jerusalem a quiet habitation, a tabernacle *that* shall not be taken down; not one of the stakes thereof shall ever be removed, neither shall any of the cords thereof be broken. 21. But there the glorious LORD *will be* unto us a place of broad rivers *and* streams: wherein shall go no galley with oars, neither shall gallant ship pass thereby. *vs.* 5,13–24.

Isa. 35:1. The wilderness and the solitary place shall be glad for them; and the desert shall rejoice, and blossom as the rose. 2. It shall blossom abundantly, and rejoice even with joy and singing: the glory of Lebanon shall be given unto it, the excellency of Carmel and Sharon, they shall see the glory of the LORD, *and* the excellency of our God. 5. The eyes of the blind shall be opened, and the ears of the deaf shall be unstopped. 6. Then shall the lame *man* leap as an hart, and the tongue of the dumb sing: for in the wilderness shall waters break out, and streams in the desert. 7. And the parched ground shall become a pool, and the thirsty land springs of water: in the habitation of dragons, where each lay, *shall be* grass with reeds and rushes. *vs.* 1-10; 41:17-20.

Isa. 40:5. The glory of the LORD shall be revealed, and all flesh shall see *it* together: for the mouth of the LORD hath spoken *it*. *vs.* 4-11.

Isa. 42:3. He shall bring forth judgment unto truth. 4. He shall not fail nor be discouraged, till he have set judgment in the earth: and the isles shall wait for his law. *vs.* 1-12.

Isa. 44:3. I will pour water upon him that is thirsty, and floods upon the dry ground: I will pour my spirit upon thy seed, and my blessing upon thine offspring: 4. And they shall spring up *as* among the grass, as willows by the water courses. 5. One shall say, I *am* the LORD's; and another shall call *himself* by the name of Jacob; and another shall subscribe *with* his hand unto the LORD, and surname *himself* by the name of Israel.

Isa. 45:8. Drop down, ye heavens, from above, and let the skies pour down righteousness: let the earth open, and let them bring forth salvation, and let righteousness spring up together; I the LORD have created it. 14. Thus saith the LORD, The labour of Egypt, and merchandise of Ethiopia and of the Sabeans, men of stature, shall come over unto thee, and they shall be thine: they shall come after thee; in chains they shall come over, and they shall fall down unto thee, they shall make supplication unto thee, *saying*, Surely God *is* in thee; and *there is* none else, *there is* no God. 23. I have sworn by myself, the word has gone out of my mouth *in* righteousness, and shall not return, That unto me every knee shall bow, every tongue shall swear. 24. Surely, shall *one* say, in the LORD have I righteousness and strength: *even* to him shall *men* come; *v.* 6.

Isa. 46:12. Hearken unto me, ye stouthearted, that *are* far from righteousness: 13. I bring near my righteousness; it shall not be far off, and my salvation shall not tarry: and I will place salvation in Zion for Israel my glory.

Isa. 49:6. It is a light thing that thou shouldest be my servant to raise up the tribes of Jacob, and to restore the preserved of Israel: I will also give thee for a light to the Gentiles, that thou mayest be my salvation unto the end of the earth. 7. Thus saith the LORD, the Redeemer of Israel, *and* his Holy One, to him whom man despiseth, to him whom the nation abhorreth, to a servant of rulers, Kings shall see and arise, princes also shall worship, because of the LORD that is faithful, *and* the Holy One of Israel, and he shall choose thee. 8. Thus saith the LORD, In an acceptable time have I heard thee, and in a day of salvation have I helped thee: and I will preserve thee, and give thee for a covenant of the people, to establish the earth, to cause to inherit the desolate heritages; 9. That thou mayest say to the prisoners, Go forth; to them that *are*

in darkness, Shew yourselves. They shall feed in the ways, and their pastures *shall be* in all high places. 10. They shall not hunger nor thirst; neither shall the heat nor sun smite them : for he that hath mercy on them shall lead them, even by the springs of water shall he guide them. 11. And I will make all my mountains a way, and my highways shall be exalted. 12. Behold, these shall come from far: and, lo, these from the north and from the west; and these from the land of Sinim. 18. Lift up thine eyes round about, and behold: all these gather themselves together, *and* come to thee. *As* I live, saith the LORD, thou shalt surely clothe thee with them all, as with an ornament, and bind them *on thee*, as a bride *doeth*. *vs.* 18-23.

Isa. 51:3. The LORD shall comfort Zion: he will comfort all her waste places; and he will make her wilderness like Eden, and her desert like the garden of the LORD; joy and gladness shall be found therein, thanksgiving, and the voice of melody. 5. My righteousness *is* near; my salvation is gone forth, and mine arms shall judge the people; the isles shall wait upon me, and on mine arm shall they trust. 6. Lift up your eyes to the heavens, and look upon the earth beneath: for the heavens shall vanish away like smoke, and the earth shall wax old like a garment, and they that dwell therein shall die in like manner: but my salvation shall be for ever, and my righteousness shall not be abolished. 8. For the moth shall eat them up like a garment, and the worm shall eat them like wool: but my righteousness shall be for ever, and my salvation from generation to generation. *vs.* 3-16.

Isa. 52:1. Awake, awake; put on thy strength, O Zion; put on thy beautiful garments, O Jerusalem, the holy city: for henceforth there shall no more come into thee the uncircumcised and the unclean. 2. Shake thyself from the dust; arise, *and* sit down, O Jerusalem: loose thyself from the bands of thy neck, O captive daughter of Zion. 7. How beautiful upon the mountains are the feet of him that bringeth good tidings, that publisheth peace; that bringeth good tidings of good, that publisheth salvation; that saith unto Zion, Thy God reigneth! 8. Thy watchmen shall lift up the voice; with the voice together shall they sing: for they shall see eye to eye, when the LORD shall bring again Zion. 10. The LORD hath made bare his holy arm in the eyes of all the nations; and all the ends of the earth shall see the salvation of our God. 15. So shall he sprinkle many nations; the kings shall shut their mouths at him: for *that* which has not been told them shall they see; and *that* which they had not heard shall they consider. *vs.* 1-15.

Isa. 53:10. When thou shalt make his soul an offering for sin, he shall see *his* seed, he shall prolong *his* days, and the pleasure of the LORD shall prosper in his hand. 11. He shall see of the travail of his soul, *and* shall be satisfied: by his knowledge shall my righteous servant justify many; for he shall bear their iniquities. 12. Therefore will I divide him *a portion* with the great, and he shall divide the spoil with the strong;

Isa. 54:1. Sing, O barren, thou *that* didst not bear; break forth into singing, and cry aloud, thou *that* didst not travail with child: for more *are* the children of the desolate than the children of the married wife, saith the LORD. 2. Enlarge the place of thy tent, and let them stretch forth the curtains of thine habitations: spare not, lengthen thy cords, and strengthen thy stakes; 3. For thou shalt break forth on the right hand and on the left; and· thy seed shall inherit the Gentiles, and make the desolate cities to be inhabited.· 4. Thou shalt forget the shame of thy youth,and shalt not remember the reproach of thy widowhood any more. 5. The LORD of hosts *is* his name; and thy Redeemer the Holy One of Israel; The God of the whole earth shall he be called. 11. O thou afflicted, tossed with tempest, *and* not comforted, behold, I will lay thy stones with fair colours, and lay thy foundation with sapphires. 12. And I will make thy windows of agates, and thy gates of carbuncles, and all thy borders of ·pleasant stones. 13. And all thy children *shall be* taught of the LORD; and great *shall be* the peace of thy children. 14. In righteousness shalt thou be established: thou shalt be far from oppression ; for thou shalt not fear: and from terror; for it shall not come near thee. *vs.* 1-17.

Isa. 55:5. Behold, thou shalt call a nation *that* thou knowest not, and nations *that* knew not thee shall run unto thee because of the LORD thy God, and for the Holy One of Israel; for he hath glorified thee. 10. For as the rain cometh down, and the snow from heaven, and returneth not thither, but watereth the earth, and maketh it bring forth and bud, that it may give seed to the sower, and bread to the eater: 11. So shall my word be that goeth forth out of my mouth: it shall not return unto me void, but it shall accomplish that which I please, and it shall prosper *in the thing* whereto I sent it. 12. Ye shall go out with joy, and be led forth with peace: the mountains and the hills shall break forth before you into singing, and all the trees of the field shall clap *their* hands. 13. Instead of the thorn shall come up the fir tree, and instead of the brier shall come up the myrtle tree: and it shall be to the LORD for a name, for an everlasting sign *that* shall not be cut off. *vs.* 1-13.

Isa. 56:7. Mine house shall be called an house of prayer for all people. 8. The Lord GOD which gathereth the outcasts of Israel saith, Yet will I gather *others* to him, beside those that are gathered unto him. *vs.* 3-8.

Isa. 59:19. So shall they fear the name of the LORD from the west, and his glory from the rising of the sun. When the enemy shall come in like a flood, the Spirit of the

LORD shall lift up a standard against him. *vs.* 19-21.

Isa. 60:1. Arise, shine; for thy light is come, and the glory of the LORD is risen upon thee. 3. The Gentiles shall come to thy light, and kings to the brightness of thy rising. 4. Lift up thine eyes round about, and see: all they gather themselves together, they come to thee: thy sons shall come from far, and thy daughters shall be nursed at *thy* side. 5. Then thou shalt see, and flow together, and thine heart shall fear, and be enlarged; because the abundance of the sea shall be converted unto thee, the forces of the Gentiles shall come unto thee. 7. All the flocks of Kedar shall be gathered together unto thee, the rams of Nebaioth shall minister unto thee: they shall come up with acceptance on mine altar, and I will glorify the house of my glory. 8. Who *are* these *that* fly as a cloud, and as the doves to their windows? 9. Surely the isles shall wait for me, and the ships of Tarshish first, to bring thy sons from far, their silver and their gold with them, unto the name of the LORD thy God, and to the Holy One of Israel, because he hath glorified thee. 19. The sun shall be no more thy light by day; neither for brightness shall the moon give light unto thee: but the LORD shall be unto thee an everlasting light, and thy God thy glory. 20. Thy sun shall no more go down; neither shall thy moon withdraw itself: for the LORD shall be thine everlasting light, and the days of thy mourning shall be ended. *vs.* 1-22.

Isa. 61:1. The Spirit of the Lord GOD *is* upon me; because the LORD hath anointed me to preach good tidings unto the meek; he hath sent me to bind up the brokenhearted, to proclaim liberty to the captive, and the opening of the prison to *them that are* bound; 2. To proclaim the acceptable year of the LORD, and the day of vengeance of our God; to comfort all that mourn; 3. To appoint unto them that mourn in Zion, to give unto them beauty for ashes, the oil of joy for mourning, 6. But ye shall be named the Priests of the LORD: *men* shall call you the Ministers of our God: ye shall eat the riches of the Gentiles, and in their glory shall ye boast yourselves. 9. Their seed shall be known among the Gentiles, and their offspring among the people: all that see them shall acknowledge them, that they *are* the seed *which* the LORD hath blessed. 11. As the earth bringeth forth her bud, and as the garden causeth the things that are sown in it to spring forth; so the Lord GOD will cause righteousness and praise to spring forth before all the nations. *vs.* 1-11.

Isa. 62:2. The Gentiles shall see thy righteousness, and all kings thy glory: and thou shalt be called by a new name, which the mouth of the LORD shall name. 3. Thou shalt also be a crown of glory in the hand of the LORD, and a royal diadem in the hand of thy God. 12. They shall call them, The holy people, The redeemed of the LORD: and thou shalt be called, Sought out, A city not forsaken. *vs.* 1-12.

Isa. 65:1. I am sought of *them that* asked not *for me;* I am found of *them that* sought me not: I said, Behold me, behold me, unto a nation *that* was not called by my name. 17. For, behold, I create new heavens and a new earth: and the former shall not be remembered, nor come into mind. 18. But be ye glad and rejoice for ever *in that* which I create: for, behold, I create Jerusalem a rejoicing, and her people a joy. 19. And I will rejoice in Jerusalem, and joy in my people: and the voice of weeping shall be no more heard in her, nor the voice of crying. 23. They shall not labour in vain, nor bring forth for trouble; for they *are* the seed of the blessed of the LORD, and their offspring with them. 24. And it shall come to pass, that before they call, I will answer; and while they are yet speaking, I will hear. 25. The wolf and the lamb shall feed together, and the lion shall eat straw like the bullock: and dust *shall be* the serpent's meat. They shall not hurt nor destroy in all my holy mountain, saith the LORD. *vs.* 1-25.

Isa. 66:12. Behold, I will extend peace to her like a river, and the glory of the Gentiles like a flowing stream: then shall ye suck, ye shall be borne upon *her* sides, and be dandled upon *her* knees. 19. I will set a sign among them, and I will send those that escape of them unto the nations, *to* Tarshish, Pul, and Lud, that draw the bow, *to* Tubal, and Javan, *to* the isles afar off, that have not heard my fame, neither have seen my glory; and they shall declare my glory among the Gentiles. 23. It shall come to pass, *that* from one new moon to another, and from one sabbath to another, shall all flesh come to worship before me, saith the LORD. *vs.* 7-23.

Jer. 3:17. They shall call Jerusalem the throne of the LORD; and all the nations shall be gathered unto it, to the name of the LORD, to Jerusalem: neither shall they walk any more after the imagination of their evil heart.

Jer. 4:2. The nations shall bless themselves in him, and in him shall they glory.

Jer. 16:19. The Gentiles shall come unto thee from the ends of the earth, and shall say, Surely our fathers have inherited lies, vanity, and *things* wherein *there is* no profit. 20. Shall a man make gods unto himself, and they *are* no gods? 21. Therefore, behold, I will this once cause them to know, I will cause them to know mine hand and my might; and they shall know that my name *is* The LORD.

Jer. 31:7. For thus saith the LORD; Sing with gladness for Jacob, and shout among the chief of the nations: publish ye, praise ye, and say, O LORD, save thy people, the remnant of Israel. 8. Behold, I will bring them from the north country, and gather them from the coasts of the earth, *and* with them the blind and the lame, the woman with child and her that travaileth with child together: a great company shall return thither. 9. They shall come with weeping, and with supplications will I lead them: I will cause them to walk by the rivers of waters in a straight way, wherein they shall not stumble: for I am a father to Israel, and Ephraim *is* my firstborn. 34. They shall teach no more every man his neighbour, and every man his brother, saying, Know the LORD: for they shall all know me, from the least of them unto the greatest of them, saith the LORD: for I will forgive their iniquity, and I will remember their sin no more.

Jer. 33:22. As the host of heaven cannot be numbered, neither the sand of the sea measured; so will I multiply the seed of David my servant, and the Levites that minister unto me.

Ezek. 17:22. Thus saith the Lord GOD; I will also take of the highest branch of the high cedar, and will set *it;* I will crop off from the top of his young twigs a tender one, and will plant *it* upon an high mountain and eminent: 23. In the mountain of the height of Israel will I plant it: and it shall bring forth boughs, and bear fruit, and be a goodly cedar: and under it shall dwell all fowl of every wing; in the shadow of the branches thereof shall they dwell. 24. And all the trees of the field shall know that I the LORD have brought down the high tree, have exalted the low tree, have dried up the green tree, and have made the dry tree to flourish: I the LORD have spoken and have done *it*.

Ezek. 34:26. I will make them and the places round about my hill a blessing; and I will cause the shower to come down in his season; there shall be showers of blessing. 29. And I will raise up for them a plant of renown, and they shall be no more consumed with hunger in the land, neither bear the shame of the heathen any more. 30. Thus shall they know that I the LORD their God *am* with them, and *that* they, *even* the house of Israel, *are* my people, saith the Lord GOD. 31. And ye my flock, the flock of my pasture, *are* men, *and* I *am* your God, saith the Lord GOD. *vs.* 23-31.

Ezek. 47:3. When the man that had the line in his hand went forth eastward, he measured a thousand cubits, and he brought me through the waters; the waters *were* to the ancles. 4. Again he measured a thousand, and brought me through the waters; the waters *were* to the knees. Again he measured a thousand, and brought me through; the waters *were* to the loins. 5. Afterward he measured a thousand; *and it was* a river that I could not pass over: for the waters were risen, waters to swim in, a river that could not be passed over. 7. Now when I had returned, behold, at the bank of the river *were* very many trees on the one side and on the other. 8. Then said he unto me, These waters issue out toward the east country, and go down into the desert, and go into the sea: *which being* brought forth into the sea, the waters shall be healed. 9. And it shall come to pass, *that* every thing that liveth, which moveth, whithersoever the rivers shall come, shall live: and there shall be a very great multitude of fish, because these waters shall come thither: for they shall be healed; and every thing shall live whither the river cometh. 12. And by the river upon the bank thereof, on this side and on that side, shall grow all trees for meat, whose leaf shall not fade, neither shall the fruit thereof be consumed: it shall bring forth new fruit according to his months, because their waters they issued out of the sanctuary: and the fruit thereof shall be for meat, and the leaf thereof for medicine. *vs.* 1-12.

Dan. 2:35. And the stone that smote the image became a great mountain, and filled the whole earth. 44. In the days of these kings shall the God of heaven set up a kingdom, which shall never be destroyed: and the kingdom shall not be left to other people, *but* it shall break in pieces and consume all these kingdoms, and it shall stand for ever. *v.* 45.

Dan. 7:13. I saw in the night visions, and, behold, *one* like the Son of man came with the clouds of heaven, and came to the Ancient of days, and they brought him near before him. 14. And there was given him dominion, and glory, and a kingdom, that all people, nations, and languages, should serve him: his dominion *is* an everlasting dominion, which shall not pass away, and his kingdom *that* which shall not be destroyed. 18. But the saints of the most High shall take the kingdom, and possess the kingdom for ever, even for ever and ever. 22. Until the Ancient of days came, and judgment was given to the saints of the most High; and the time came that the saints possessed the kingdom. 27. The kingdom and dominion, and the greatness of the kingdom under the whole heaven, shall be given to the people of the saints of the most High, whose kingdom *is* an everlasting kingdom, and all dominions shall serve and obey him.

Dan. 12:4. Seal the book, *even* to the time of the end: many shall run to and fro, and knowledge shall be increased. *vs.* 1-13.

Joel 2:26. Ye shall eat in plenty, and be satisfied, and praise the name of the LORD your God, that hath dealt wondrously with you: and my people shall never be ashamed. 27. And ye shall know that I *am* in the midst of Israel, and that I *am* the LORD your God, and none else: and my people shall never be ashamed. 28. And it shall come to pass afterward, *that* I will pour out my Spirit upon all flesh; and your sons and your daughters shall prophesy, your old men shall dream dreams, your young men shall see visions: 29. And also upon the servants and upon the handmaids in those days will I pour out my Spirit. 30. And I will shew wonders in the heavens and in the earth, blood, and fire, and pillars

of smoke. 31. The sun shall be turned into darkness, and the moon into blood, before the great and the terrible day of the LORD come. 32. And it shall come to pass, *that* whosoever shall call on the name of the LORD shall be delivered: for in mount Zion and in Jerusalem shall be deliverance, as the LORD hath said, and in the remnant whom the LORD shall call. Acts. 2:16-21.

Joel 3:18. It shall come to pass in that day, *that* the mountains shall drop down new wine, and the hills shall flow with milk, and all the rivers of Judah shall flow with waters, and a fountain shall come forth of the house of the LORD, and shall water the valley of Shittim.

Amos 9:11. In that day will I raise up the tabernacle of David that is fallen, and close up the breaches thereof; and I will raise up his ruins, and I will build it as in the days of old: 12. That they may possess the remnant of Edom, and of all the heathen, which are called by my name, saith the LORD that doeth this.

Mic. 4:3. He shall judge among many people, and rebuke strong nations afar off; and they shall beat their swords into plowshares, and their spears into pruninghooks: nation shall not lift up a sword against nation, neither shall they learn war any more. 4. But they shall sit every man under his vine and under his fig tree; and none shall make *them* afraid: for the mouth of the LORD of hosts hath spoken *it*. *vs.* 1-7.

Mic. 5:2. But thou, Bethlehem Ephratah, *though* thou be little among the thousands of Judah, *yet* out of thee shall he come forth unto me *that is* to be ruler in Israel; whose goings forth *have been* from of old, from everlasting. 4. And he shall stand and feed in the strength of the LORD, in the majesty of the name of the LORD his God; and they shall abide: for now shall he be great unto the ends of the earth. 7. And the remnant of Jacob shall be in the midst of many people as a dew from the LORD, as the showers upon the grass, that tarrieth not for man, nor waiteth for the sons of men. *vs.* 2-15.

Hab. 2:14. The earth shall be filled with the knowledge of the glory of the LORD, as the waters cover the sea.

Zeph. 2:11. The LORD *will be* terrible unto them: for he will famish all the gods of the earth; and *men* shall worship him, every one from his place, *even* all the isles of the heathen.

Zeph. 3:9. Then will I turn to the people a pure language, that they may all call upon the name of the LORD, to serve him with one consent. *vs.* 9-20.

Hag. 2:7. And I will shake all nations, and the desire of all nations shall come: and I will fill this house with glory, saith the LORD of hosts. 8. The silver *is* mine, and the gold *is* mine, saith the LORD of hosts. 9. The glory of this latter house shall be greater than of the former, saith the LORD of hosts: and in this place will I give peace, saith the LORD of hosts.

Zech. 2:10. Sing and rejoice, O daughter of Zion: for, lo, I come, and I will dwell in the midst of thee, saith the LORD. 11. And many nations shall be joined to the LORD in that day, and shall be my people: and I will dwell in the midst of thee, and thou shalt know that the LORD of hosts hath sent me unto thee.

Zech. 6:15. They *that are* far off shall come and build in the temple of the LORD,

Zech. 8:20. *It shall* yet *come to pass,* that there shall come people, and the inhabitants of many cities: 21. And the inhabitants of one *city* shall go to another, saying, Let us go speedily to pray before the LORD, and to seek the LORD of hosts: I will go also. 22. Yea, many people and strong nations shall come to seek the LORD of hosts in Jerusalem, and to pray before the LORD. 23. Thus saith the LORD of hosts; In those days *it shall come to pass,* that ten men shall take hold out of all languages of the nations, even shall take hold of the skirt of him that is a Jew, saying, We will go with you: for we have heard *that* God *is* with you.

Zech. 9:1. The eyes of man, as of all the tribes of Israel, *shall be* toward the LORD. 10. I will cut off the chariot from Ephraim, and the horse from Jerusalem, and the battle bow shall be cut off: and he shall speak peace unto the heathen: and his dominion *shall be* from sea *even* to sea, and from the river *even* to the ends of the earth. *vs.* 9–17.

Zech. 14:8. It shall be in that day, *that* living waters shall go out from Jerusalem; half of them toward the former sea, and half of them toward the hinder sea: in summer and in winter shall it be. 9. And the LORD shall be king over all the earth: in that day shall there be one LORD, and his name one. 16. And it shall come to pass, *that* every one that is left of all the nations which came against Jerusalem shall even go up from year to year to worship the King, the LORD of hosts, and to keep the feast of tabernacles. *vs.* 8–21.

Mal. 1:11. From the rising of the sun even unto the going down of the same my name *shall be* great among the Gentiles; and in every place incense *shall be* offered unto my name, and a pure offering: for my name *shall be* great among the heathen, saith the LORD of hosts.

Matt. 8:11. Many shall come from the east and west, and shall sit down with Abraham, and Isaac, and Jacob, in the kingdom of heaven.

Matt. 11:11. There hath not risen a greater than John the Baptist: notwithstanding he that is least in the kingdom of heaven is greater than he.

Matt. 13:16. But blessed *are* your eyes, for they see: and your ears, for they hear. 17. For verily I say unto you, That many prophets and righteous *men* have desired to see *those things* which ye see, and have not seen

them; and to hear *those things* which ye hear, and have not heard *them.* 31. The kingdom of heaven is like to a grain of mustard seed, which a man took, and sowed in his field: 32. Which indeed is the least of all seeds: but when it is grown, it is the greatest among herbs, and becometh a tree, so that the birds of the air come and lodge in the branches thereof. 33. The kingdom of heaven is like unto leaven, which a woman took, and hid in three measures of meal, till the whole was leavened.

Matt. 16:18. Upon this rock I will build my church; and the gates of hell shall not prevail against it.

Mark 4:26. So is the kingdom of God, as if a man should cast seed into the ground; 27. And should sleep, and rise night and day, and the seed should spring and grow up, he knoweth not how. 28. For the earth bringeth forth fruit of herself: first the blade, then the ear, after that the full corn in the ear. 29. But when the fruit is brought forth, immediately he putteth in the sickle, because the harvest is come. *vs.* 30–32.

Luke 7:22. Then Jesus answering said unto them, Go your way, and tell John what things ye have seen and heard; how that the blind see, the lame walk, the lepers are cleansed, the deaf hear, the dead are raised, to the poor the gospel is preached. Matt. 11:5.

John 8:35. The servant abideth not in the house for ever: *but* the Son abideth ever.

John 10:16. Other sheep I have, which are not of this fold: them also I must bring, and they shall hear my voice; and there shall be one fold, *and* one shepherd.

Rom. 1:5. By whom we have received grace and apostleship, for obedience to the faith among all nations, for his name: 6. Among whom are ye also the called of Jesus Christ: 7. To all that be in Rome, beloved of God, called *to be* saints: Grace to you and peace from God our Father, and the Lord Jesus Christ.

1 Cor. 15:24. Then *cometh* the end, when he shall have delivered up the kingdom to God, even the Father; when he shall have put down all rule and all authority and power. 25. For he must reign, till he hath put all enemies under his feet. 26. The last enemy *that* shall be destroyed *is* death. 27. For he hath put all things under his feet. But when he saith all things are put under *him, it is* manifest that he is excepted, which did put all things under him. 28. And when all things shall be subdued unto him, then shall the Son also himself be subject unto him that put all things under him, that God may be all in all.

Eph. 1:10. That in the dispensation of the fulness of times he might gather together in one all things in Christ, both which are in heaven, and which are on earth; *even* in him:

Heb. 12:23. To the general assembly and church of the firstborn, which are written in heaven, and to God the Judge of all, and to the spirits of just men made perfect, 24. And to Jesus the mediator of the new covenant, and to the blood of sprinkling, that speaketh better things than *that of* Abel. 27. This *word,* Yet once more, signifieth the removing of those things that are shaken, as of things that are made, that those things which cannot be shaken may remain. 28. Wherefore we receiving a kingdom which cannot be moved, let us have grace, whereby we may serve God acceptably with reverence and godly fear:

Rev. 5:10. And hast made us unto our God kings and priests: and we shall reign on the earth. 13. And every creature which is in heaven, and on the earth, and under the earth, and such as are in the sea, and all that are in them, heard I saying, Blessing, and honour, and glory, and power, *be* unto him that sitteth upon the throne, and unto the Lamb for ever and ever. 14. And the four beasts said, Amen. And the four *and* twenty elders fell down and worshipped him that liveth for ever and ever.

Rev. 11:15. The seventh angel sounded; and there were great voices in heaven, saying, The kingdoms of this world are become *the kingdoms* of our Lord, and of his Christ; and he shall reign for ever and ever.

Rev. 12:10. I heard a loud voice saying in heaven, Now is come salvation, and strength, and the kingdom of our God, and the power of his Christ: for the accuser of our brethren is cast down, which accused them before our God day and night.

Rev. 15:4. Who shall not fear thee, O Lord, and glorify thy name? for *thou* only *art* holy: for all nations shall come and worship before thee; for thy judgments are made manifest.

Rev. 20:4. And I saw thrones, and they sat upon them, and judgment was given unto them: and *I saw* the souls of them that were beheaded for the witness of Jesus, and for the word of God, and which had not worshipped the beast, neither his image, neither had received *his* mark upon their foreheads, or in their hands; and they lived and reigned with Christ a thousand years. 5. But the rest of the dead lived not again until the thousand years were finished. This *is* the first resurrection. 6. Blessed and holy *is* he that hath part in the first resurrection: on such the second death hath no power, but they shall be priests of God and of Christ, and shall reign with him a thousand years.

Rev. 21:9. And there came unto me one of the seven angels which had the seven vials full of the seven last plagues, and talked with me, saying, Come hither, I will shew thee the bride, the Lamb's wife. 10. And he carried me away in the spirit to a great and high mountain, and shewed me that great city, the holy Jerusalem, descending out of heaven from God, 11. Having the glory of God: and her light *was* like unto a stone most precious, even like a jasper stone, clear as crystal; 12. And had a wall great and high, *and* had twelve gates, and at the gates twelve angels, and names written thereon, which are *the names* of the twelve tribes of the children of Israel: 13. On the east three gates; on the north three gates; on the south three gates; and on the west three gates. 14. And the wall of the city had twelve foundations, and in them the names of the twelve apostles of the Lamb. 15. And he that talked with me had a golden reed to measure the city, and the gates thereof, and the wall thereof. 16. And the city lieth foursquare, and the length is as large as the breadth: and he measured the city with the reed, twelve thousand furlongs. The length and the breadth and the height of it are equal. 17. And he measured the wall thereof, an hundred *and* forty *and* four cubits, *according to* the measure of a man, that is, of the angel. 18. And the building of the wall of it was *of* jasper, and the city *was* pure gold, like unto clear glass. 19. And the foundations of the wall of the city *were* garnished with all manner of precious stones. The first foundation *was* jasper; the second sapphire; the third, a chalcedony; the fourth, an emerald; 20. The fifth, sardonyx; the sixth, sardius; the seventh, chrysolyte; the eighth, beryl; the ninth, a topaz; the tenth, a chrysoprasus; the eleventh, a jacinth; the twelfth, an amethyst. 21. And the twelve gates *were* twelve pearls; every several gate was of one pearl: and the street of the city *was* pure gold, as it were transparent glass. 22. And I saw no temple therein: for the Lord God Almighty and the Lamb are the temple of it. 23. And the city had no need of the sun, neither of the moon, to shine in it: for the glory of God did lighten it, and the Lamb *is* the light thereof. 24. And the nations of them which are saved shall walk in the light of it: and the kings of the earth do bring their glory and honour into it. 25. And the gates of it shall not be shut at all by day: for there shall be no night there. 26. And they shall bring the glory and honour of the nations into it. 27. And there shall in no wise enter into it any thing that defileth, neither *whatsoever* worketh abomination, or *maketh* a lie: but they which are written in the Lamb's book of life.

Rev. 22:1. And he shewed me a pure river of water of life, clear as crystal, proceeding out of the throne of God and of the Lamb. 2. In the midst of the street of it, and on either side of the river, *was there* the tree of life, which bare twelve *manner of* fruits, *and* yielded her fruit every month: and the leaves of the tree *were* for the healing of the nations. 3. And there shall be no more curse: but the throne of God and of the Lamb shall be in it; and his servants shall serve him: 4. And they shall see his face; and his name *shall be* in their foreheads. 5. And there shall be no night there; and they need no candle, neither light of the sun; for the Lord God giveth them light: and they shall reign for ever and ever.

See JESUS, KINGDOM OF.

LIST OF CHRISTIAN CHURCHES: Antioch, Acts 13:1. Asia, 1 Cor. 16:19; Rev. 1: 4. Babylon, 1 Pet. 5:13. Cenchrea, Rom. 16:1. Cæsarea, Acts 18:22. Cilicia, Acts 15: 41. Corinth, 1 Cor. 1:2. Ephesus, Eph. 1: 22; Rev. 2:1. Galatia, Gal. 1:2. Galilee, Acts 9:31. Jerusalem, Acts 15:4. Joppa, Acts 9:42. Judæa, Acts 9:31. Laodicea, Rev. 3:14. Pergamos, Rev. 2:12. Philadelphia, Rev. 3:7. Samaria, Acts 9:31. Sardis, Rev. 3:1. Smyrna, Rev. 2:8. Syria, Acts 15:41. Thessalonica, 1 Thess. 1:1. Thyatira, Rev. 2:18.

UNITY OF: Psa. 133:1. Behold, how good and how pleasant *it is* for brethren to dwell together in unity !

John 10:16. Other sheep I have, which are not of this fold : them also I must bring, and they shall hear my voice; and there shall be one fold, *and* one shepherd.

John 17:11. Holy Father, keep through thine own name those whom thou hast given me, that they may be one, as we *are*. 21. That they all may be one; as thou, Father, *art* in me, and I in thee, that they also may be one in us: that the world may believe that thou hast sent me. 22. And the glory which thou gavest me I have given them : that they may be one, even as we are one : 23. I in them, and thou in me, that they may be made perfect in one; and that the world may know that thou hast sent me, and hast loved them, as thou hast loved me.

Rom. 12:4. As we have many members in one body, and all members have not the same office : 5. So we, *being* many, are one body in Christ, and every one members one of another.

1 Cor. 10:17. We *being* many are one bread, *and* one body : for we are all partakers of that one bread.

1 Cor. 12:5. There are differences of administrations, but the same Lord. 12. As the body is one, and hath many members, and all the members of that one body, being many, are one body : so also *is* Christ. 13. For by one Spirit are we all baptized into one body, whether *we be* Jews or Gentiles, whether *we be* bond or free; and have been all made to drink into one Spirit. 26. And whether one member suffer, all the members suffer with it; or one member be honoured, all the members rejoice with it. 27. Now ye are the body of Christ, and members in particular. *vs.* 12–27.

Gal. 3:26. Ye are all the children of God by faith in Christ Jesus. 27. For as many of you as have been baptized into Christ have put on Christ. 28. There is neither Jew nor Greek, there is neither bond nor free, there is neither male nor female : for ye are all one in Christ Jesus.

Eph. 1:10. That in the dispensation of the fulness of times he might gather together in one all things in Christ, both which are in heaven, and which are on earth ; *even* in him:

Eph. 2:14. For he is our peace, who hath made both one, and hath broken down the middle wall of partition *between us ;* 15. Having abolished in his flesh the enmity, *even* the law of commandments *contained* in ordinances ; for to make in himself of twain one new man, *so* making peace ; 16. And that he might reconcile both unto God in one body by the cross, having slain the enmity thereby: 17. And came and preached peace to you which were afar off, and to them that were nigh. 18. For through him we both have access by one Spirit unto the Father. 19. Ye are no more strangers and foreigners, but fellowcitizens with the saints, and of the household of God ; 21. In whom all the building fitly framed together groweth unto an holy temple in the Lord :

Eph. 3:6. The Gentiles should be fellowheirs, and of the same body, and partakers of his promise in Christ by the gospel : 15. Of whom the whole family in heaven and earth is named,

Eph. 4:4. *There is* one body, and one Spirit, even as ye are called in one hope of your calling ; 5. One Lord, one faith, one baptism, 6. One God and Father of all, who *is* above all, and through all, and in you all. 12. For the perfecting of the saints, for the work of the ministry, for the edifying of the body of Christ : 13. Till we all come in the unity of the faith, and of the knowledge of the Son of God, unto a perfect man, unto the measure of the stature of the fulness of Christ : 16. From whom the whole body fitly joined together and compacted by that which every joint supplieth, according to the effectual working in the measure of every part, maketh increase of the body unto the edifying of itself in love. 25. We are members one of another.

Col. 3:11. There is neither Greek nor Jew, circumcision nor uncircumcision, Barbarian, Scythian, bond *nor* free: but Christ *is* all, and in all. 15. Let the peace of God rule in your hearts, to the which also ye are called in one body ;

See ECCLESIASTICISM.

TRIUMPHANT: Gal. 4:26. Jerusalem which is above is free, which is the mother of us all.

Heb. 12:22. But ye are come unto mount Sion, and unto the city of the living God, the heavenly Jerusalem, and to an innumerable company of angels. 23. To the general assembly and church of the firstborn, which are written in heaven, and to God the Judge of all, and to the spirits of just men made perfect.

Rev. 3:12. Him that overcometh will I make a pillar in the temple of my God, and he shall go no more out : and I will write upon him the name of my God, and the name of the city of my God, *which is* new Jerusalem, which cometh down out of heaven from my God : and *I will write upon him* my new name.

Rev. 21:3. And I heard a great voice out

of heaven saying, Behold, the tabernacle of God *is* with men, and he will dwell with them, and they shall be his people, and God himself shall be with them, *and be* their God. 10. And he carried me away in the spirit to a great and high mountain, and shewed me that great city, the holy Jerusalem, descending out of heaven from God.

CHURCH AND STATE.* ECCLESIASTICAL POWER SUPERIOR TO CIVIL: Appoints kings, 1 Sam. 10:1. Directs administration, 1 Sam. 15:1-4. Reproves rulers, 1 Sam. 15:14-35. Withdraws support and anoints a successor, 1 Sam. 16:1-13; 2 Kin. 9:1-26; 11:4-12. Attempted usurpation of ecclesiastical functions by civil authorities, reproved, 1 Sam. 13:8-14; 2 Chr. 26:16-21.

STATE SUPERIOR TO THE CHURCH: David, in organizing the priests and Levites in courses, and appointing musicians, instruments, and other details of religious services, 1 Chr. 23; 24; 25; 2 Chr. 35:4. Solomon, in thrusting Abiathar out of the high priest's office, 1 Kin. 2:26,27; in overshadowing the ecclesiastical in building the temple, and officiating primarily in the dedication, intercessory or priestly prayer, pronouncing the benediction, etc., 1 Kin. chapters 5-8. Hezekiah, in reorganizing temple service, 2 Chr. 31:2-19. Jeroboam, in subverting the Jewish religion, 1 Kin. 12:26-33. Manasseh, in subverting, and afterward restoring, the true religion, 2 Chr. 33:2-9,15-17. Jehoash, in supervising the repairs of the temple, 2 Kin. 12:4-18. Ahaz, in transforming the altars, 2 Kin. 16:10-16. Josiah, in exercising the function of the priests in the temple, 2 Chr. 34:29-33.

STATE FAVORABLE TO THE CHURCH: Cyrus, in his proclamation to restore the temple at Jerusalem, 2 Chr. 36:22,23; Ezra 1:1-11. Darius, in his edict furthering the restoration of the temple, Ezra 6:1-14. Artaxerxes, in exempting priests, Levites, and other temple functionaries from taxes, Ezra 7:24.

See GOVERNMENT; TAX.

CHURNING, Prov. 30:33. See BUTTER.

CHUSHAN-RISHATHAIM, king of Mesopotamia, Judg. 3:8-10.

CHUZA, Herod's steward, Luke 8:3.

CILICIA. Maritime province of Asia Minor. Jews dwell in, Acts 6:9. Churches of, Acts 15:23,41; Gal. 1:21.

SEA OF, Acts 27:5.

CINNAMON. A spice, Prov. 7:17; Song 4:14; Rev. 18:13. An ingredient of the sacred oil, Ex. 30:23.

CINNERETH. See CHINNERETH; GALLEE, SEA OF.

* Identical in the theocratic period. No particular Scriptures can be cited, but the student is directed to the legislative, judicial, and administrative functions of Moses, Joshua, the Judges, and Samuel as shown in the books of Exodus, Leviticus, Numbers, Deuteronomy, Joshua, Judges, and Samuel, and to the sub-topics Government, p.186, and Rules of Discipline, p. 189, where it is evident that civil and ecclesiastical functions are united.

CIRCUMCISION. Institution of, Gen. 17:10-14; Lev. 12:3; John 7:22; Acts 7:8; Rom. 4:11. A seal of righteousness, Rom. 2:25-29; 4:11. Performed on all males on the eighth day, Gen. 17:12,13; Lev. 12:3; Phil. 3:5. Rite of, observed on the Sabbath, John 7:23. A prerequisite of the privileges of the passover, Ex. 12:48. Child named at the time of, Gen. 21:3,4; Luke 1:59; 2:21. Neglect of, punished, Gen. 17:14; Ex. 4:24. Neglected, Josh. 5:7. Covenant promises of, Gen. 17:4-14; Acts 7:8; Rom. 3:1; 4:11; 9:7-13; Gal. 5:3. Necessity of, falsely taught by Judaizing Christians, Acts 15:1. Paul's argument against the continuance of, Rom. 2:25,28; Gal. 6:13. Characterized by Paul as a yoke, Acts 15:10. Abrogated, Acts 15:5-29; Rom. 3:30; 4:9-11; 1 Cor. 7:18,19; Gal. 2:3,4; 5:2-11; 6:12; Eph. 2:11,15; Col. 2:11; 3:11.

INSTANCES OF: Abraham, Gen. 17:23-27; 21:3,4. Shechemites, Gen. 34:24. Moses, Ex. 4:25. Israelites at Gilgal, Josh. 5:2-9. John the Baptist, Luke 1:59. Jesus, Luke 2:21. Paul, Phil. 3:5. Timothy, Acts 16:3.

FIGURATIVE: Ex. 6:12; Deut. 10:16; 30:6; Jer. 4:4; 6:10; 9:26; Rom. 2:28,29; 15:8; Phil. 3:3; Col. 2:11; 3:11.

A designation of the Jews, Acts 10:45; 11:2; Gal. 2:9; Eph. 2:11; Col. 4:11; Tit. 1:10; of Christians, Phil. 3:3.

CIS. See KISH.

CISTERN. Isa. 36:16. Broken, Jer. 2:13. **FIGURATIVE:** 2 Kin. 18:31; Prov. 5:15; Eccl. 12:6. See WELLS.

CITIES. Ancient, Gen. 4:17; 10:10-12. Fortified, Num. 32:36; Deut. 9:1; Josh. 10:20; 14:12; 2 Chr. 8:5; 11:10-12; 17:2,19; 21:3; Isa. 23:11. Gates of, see GATES. Designated as: Royal, Josh. 10:2; 1 Sam. 27:5; 2 Sam. 12:26; 1 Chr. 11:7; treasure, Gen. 41:48; Ex. 1:11; 1 Kin. 9:19; 2 Chr. 8:4; 16:4; 17:12; chariot, 2 Chr. 1:14; 8:6; 9:25; merchant, Isa. 23:11; Ezek. 17:4; 27:3.

Town clerk of, Acts 19:35. Government of, by rulers, Neh. 3:9,12,17,18; 7:2. See GOVERNMENT.

Suburbs of, Num. 35:3-5; Josh. 14:4.

Watchmen of, see WATCHMAN.

FIGURATIVE: Heb. 11:10,16; 12:22; 13:14.

CITIES OF REFUGE. See REFUGE, CITIES OF.

CITIZENS. DUTIES OF: Ex. 22:28. Thou shalt not revile the gods, nor curse the ruler of thy people. Acts 23:5.

Num. 27:20. Thou shalt put *some* of thine honour upon him, that all the congregation of the children of Israel may be obedient.

Ezra 6:10. That they may offer sacrifices of sweet savours unto the God of heaven, and pray for the life of the king, and of his sons.

Ezra 7:26. Whosoever will not do the law of thy God, and the law of the king, let judgment be executed speedily upon him, whether *it be* unto death, or to banishment, or to confiscation of goods, or to imprisonment.

Ezra 10:8. Whosoever would not come

within three days, according to the counsel of the princes and the elders, all his substance should be forfeited, and himself separated from the congregation of those that had been carried away.

Prov. 16:14. The wrath of a king *is as* messengers of death: but a wise man will pacify it. 15. In the light of the king's countenance *is* life; and his favour *is* as a cloud of the latter rain.

Prov. 24:21. My son, fear thou the LORD and the king: *and* meddle not with them that are given to change:

Prov. 25:6. Put not forth thyself in the presence of the king, and stand not in the place of great *men:* 7. For better *it is* that it be said unto thee, Come up hither; than that thou shouldest be put lower in the presence of the prince whom thine eyes have seen. 15. By long forbearing is a prince persuaded, and a soft tongue breaketh the bone.

Eccl. 8:2. I *counsel thee* to keep the king's commandment, and *that* in regard of the oath of God. 3. Be not hasty to go out of his sight: stand not in an evil thing; for he doeth whatsoever pleaseth him. 4. Where the word of a king *is, there is* power, and who may say unto him, What doest thou?

Eccl. 10:4. If the spirit of the ruler rise up against thee, leave not thy place; for yielding pacifieth great offences. 20. Curse not the king, no, not in thy thought; and curse not the rich in thy bedchamber: for a bird of the air shall carry the voice, and that which hath wings shall tell the matter.

Jer. 29:7. Seek the peace of the city whither I have caused you to be carried away captives, and pray unto the LORD for it: for in the peace thereof shall ye have peace.

Matt. 17:24. They that received tribute *money* came to Peter, and said, Doth not your master pay tribute? 25. He saith, Yes. And when he was come into the house, Jesus prevented him, saying, What thinkest thou, Simon? of whom do the kings of the earth take custom or tribute? of their own children, or of strangers? 26. Peter saith unto him, Of strangers. Jesus saith unto him, Then are the children free. 27. Notwithstanding, lest we should offend them, go thou to the sea, and cast an hook, and take up the fish that first cometh up; and when thou hast opened his mouth, thou shalt find a piece of money: that take, and give unto them for me and thee.

Matt. 22:17. Tell us therefore, What thinkest thou? Is it lawful to give tribute unto Cæsar, or not? 18. But Jesus perceived their wickedness, and said, Why tempt ye me, ye hypocrites? 19. Shew me the tribute money. And they brought unto him a penny. 20. And he saith unto them, Whose *is* this image and superscription? 21. They say unto him, Cæsar's. Then saith he unto them, Render therefore unto Cæsar the things that are Cæsar's; and unto God the

things that are God's. Mark 12:14–17; Luke 20:22–25.

Acts 19:36. Ye ought to be quiet, and to do nothing rashly. *vs.* 35–41.

Rom. 13:1. Let every soul be subject unto the higher powers. For there is no power but of God: the powers that be are ordained of God. 2. Whosoever therefore resisteth the power, resisteth the ordinance of God: and they that resist shall receive to themselves damnation. 3. For rulers are not a terror to good works, but to the evil. Wilt thou then not be afraid of the power? do that which is good, and thou shalt have praise of the same: 5. Ye must needs be subject, not only for wrath, but also for conscience sake. 6. For this cause pay ye tribute also: for they are God's ministers, attending continually upon this very thing. 7. Render therefore to all their dues: tribute to whom tribute *is due;* custom to whom custom; fear to whom fear; honour to whom honour.

1 Tim. 2:1. I exhort therefore, that, first of all, supplications, prayers, intercessions, *and* giving of thanks, be made for all men; 2. For kings, and *for* all that are in authority; that we may lead a quiet and peaceable life in all godliness and honesty.

Tit. 3:1. Put them in mind to be subject to principalities and powers, to obey magistrates,

1 Pet. 2:13. Submit yourselves to every ordinance of man for the Lord's sake: whether it be to the king, as supreme; 14. Or unto governors, as unto them that are sent by him for the punishment of evildoers, and for the praise of them that do well. 15. For so is the will of God, that with well doing ye may put to silence the ignorance of foolish men: 16. As free, and not using *your* liberty for a cloke of maliciousness, but as the servants of God. 17. Honour all *men.* Love the brotherhood. Fear God. Honour the king.

RIGHTS OF: Job 34:18. *Is it fit* to say to a king, *Thou art* wicked? *and* to princes, *Ye are* ungodly?

Prov. 14:28. In the multitude of people *is* the king's honour: but in the want of people *is* the destruction of the prince. 35. The king's favour *is* toward a wise servant: but his wrath is *against* him that causeth shame.

Prov. 22:11. He that loveth pureness of heart, *for* the grace of his lips the king *shall be* his friend.

Prov. 23:1. When thou sittest to eat with a ruler, consider diligently what *is* before thee: 2. And put a knife to thy throat, if thou *be* a man given to appetite. 3. Be not desirous of his dainties: for they *are* deceitful meat.

Acts 16:37. They have beaten us openly uncondemned, being Romans, and have cast *us* into prison; and now do they thrust us out privily? nay verily; but let them come themselves and fetch us out.

Acts 19:36. Seeing then that these **things**

cannot be spoken against, ye ought to be quiet, and to do nothing rashly. 37. For ye have brought hither these men, which are neither robbers of caurches, nor yet blasphemers of your goddess. 38. Wherefore if Demetrius, and the craftsmen which are with him, have a matter against any man, the law is open, and there are deputies: let them implead one another. 39. But if ye enquire any thing concerning other matters, it shall be determined in a lawful assembly.

Acts 22:25. And as they bound him with thongs, Paul said unto the centurion that stood by, Is it lawful for you to scourge a man that is a Roman, and uncondemned? 26. When the centurion heard *that*, he went and told the chief captain, saying, Take heed what thou doest: for this man is a Roman. 27. Then the chief captain came, and said unto him, Tell me, art thou a Roman? He said, Yea. 28. And the chief captain answered, With a great sum obtained I this freedom. And Paul said, But I was *free* born. 29. Then straightway they departed from him which should have examined him: and the chief captain also was afraid, after he knew that he was a Roman, and because he had bound him.

Acts 25:16. It is not the manner of the Romans to deliver any man to die, before that he which is accused have the accusers face to face, and have licence to answer for himself concerning the crime laid against him. *vs.* 5,10; Acts 24:18,19.

See CHANGE OF VENUE; COURTS; GOVERNMENT; JUSTICE.

LOYAL, INSTANCES OF: Israelites, Josh. 1:16-18; 2 Sam. 3:36,37; 15:23,30; 18:3; 21:17; 1 Chr. 12:38. David, 1 Sam. 24:6-10; 26:6-16; 2 Sam. 1:14. Hushai, 2 Sam. 17:15,16. David's soldiers, 2 Sam. 18:12,13; 23:15,16. Joab, 2 Sam. 19:5,6. Barzillai, 2 Sam. 19:32. Jehoiada, 2 Kin. 11:4-12; Mordecai, Esth. 2:21-23.

WICKED AND TREASONABLE: Prov. 17: 11. An evil *man* seeketh only rebellion: therefore a cruel messenger shall be sent against him.

Prov. 19:10. Delight is not seemly for a fool: much less for a servant to have rule over princes. 12. The king's wrath *is* as the roaring of a lion; but his favour *is* as dew upon the grass. Prov. 20:2.

2 Pet. 2:10. Them that walk after the flesh in the lust of uncleanness, and despise government. Presumptuous *are they*, selfwilled, they are not afraid to speak evil of dignities. 2 Tim. 3:1-4.

Jude 8. These *filthy* dreamers despise dominion, and speak evil of dignities.

See ANARCHY.

INSTANCES OF WICKED: Miriam and Aaron, Num. 12:1-11. Korah, Dathan and Abiram, Num. 16; 26:9. Shechemites, Judg. 9:22. Ephraimites, Judg. 12:1-4. Israelites, 1 Sam. 10:27; 1 Kin. 12:16-19. Absalom, 2 Sam. 15:10-13. Ahithophel, 2 Sam. 17:1-4. Sheba, 2 Sam. 20:1,2. Adonijah, 1 Kin. 1:5-7. Hadad and Jeroboam, 1 Kin. 11:14-26.

Baasha, 1 Kin. 15:27. Zimri, 1 Kin. 16:9. Jozachar and Jozabad, 2 Kin. 12:19-21; 14:5; of Amaziah, 2 Kin. 14:19; of Amon, 2 Kin. 21:23. Shallum, 2 Kin. 15:10. Menahem, 2 Kin. 15:14. Pekah, 2 Kin. 15:25. Hoshea, 2 Kin. 15:30. Sons, Sennacherib, 2 Kin. 19:37. Ishmael, Jer. 40:14-16; 41. Bigthan and Teresh, Esth. 2:21. Jews, Ezek. 17:12-20. Barabbas, Mark 15:7. Theudas and four hundred seditious persons, Acts 5:36,37. An Egyptian, Acts 21:38.

See COUNTRY, LOVE OF; GOVERNMENT; RULERS; PATRIOTISM.

FIGURATIVE: Phil. 3:20 [*R. V.*]; Eph. 2:19.
CIVIL DAMAGES. See DAMAGES.
CIVIL ENGINEERING, Josh. 18:9; Job 28:9-11.

CIVIL SERVICE. SCHOOL FOR: Dan. 1:3. And the king spake unto Ashpenaz the master of his eunuchs, that he should bring *certain* of the children of Israel, and of the king's seed, and of the princes; 4. Children in whom *was* no blemish, but well favoured, and skilful in all wisdom, and cunning in knowledge, and understanding science, and such as *had* ability in them to stand in the king's palace, and whom they might teach the learning and the tongue of the Chaldeans. 5. And the king appointed them a daily provision of the king's meat, and of the wine which he drank: so nourishing them three years, that at the end thereof they might stand before the king. 17. As for these four children, God gave them knowledge and skill in all learning and wisdom: and Daniel had understanding in all visions and dreams. 18. Now at the end of the days that the king had said he should bring them in, then the prince of the eunuchs brought them in before Nebuchadnezzar. 19. And the king communed with them: and among them all was found none like Daniel, Hananiah, Mishael, and Azariah: therefore stood they before the king. 20. And in all matters of wisdom *and* understanding, that the king enquired of them, he found them ten times better than all the magicians *and* astrologers that *were* in all his realm. 21. And Daniel continued *even* unto the first year of king Cyrus.

COMPETITIVE EXAMINATIONS FOR APPOINTMENT IN. See above, SCHOOL FOR.

APPOINTMENT IN, ON ACCOUNT OF MERIT: Gen. 39:1. And Joseph was brought down to Egypt; and Potiphar, an officer of Pharaoh, captain of the guard, an Egyptian, bought him of the hands of the Ishmaelites, which had brought him down thither. 2. And the LORD was with Joseph, and he was a prosperous man; and he was in the house of his master the Egyptian 3. And his master saw that the LORD *was* with him, and that the LORD made all that he did to prosper in his hand. 4. And Joseph found grace in his sight, and he served him: and he made him overseer over his house, and all *that* he had he put into his hand. 5. And it came to pass from the time *that* he had made him overseer in his house, and over all that he had, that the LORD blessed the Egyptian's house for Joseph's sake; and the blessing of the LORD was upon all that he had in the house, and in the field. 6. And he left all that he had in Joseph's hand; and he knew not ought he had, save the bread which he did eat. And Joseph was a goodly person, and well favoured.

Gen. 41:38. And Pharaoh said unto his servants, Can we find *such a one* as this *is*, a man in whom the Spirit of God *is?* 39. And Pharaoh said unto Joseph, Forasmuch as God hath shewed thee all this, *there is* none so discreet and wise as thou *art:* 40. Thou shalt be over my house, and according unto thy word shall all my people be ruled: only in the throne will I be greater than thou. 41. And Pharaoh said unto Joseph, See, I have set thee over all the land of Egypt. 42. And Pharaoh took off his ring from his hand, and put it upon Joseph's hand, and arrayed him in vestures of fine linen, and put a gold chain about his neck; 43. And he made him to ride in the second chariot which he had; and they cried before him, Bow the knee: and he made him *ruler* over all the land of Egypt. 44. And Pharaoh said unto Joseph, I *am* Pharaoh, and without thee shall no man lift up his hand or foot in all the land of Egypt.

1 Kin. 11:28. And the man Jeroboam *was* a mighty man of valour: and Solomon seeing the young man that he was industrious, he made him ruler over all the charge of the house of Joseph.

Esth. 6:1. On that night could not the king sleep, and he commanded to bring the book of records of the chronicles; and they were read before the king. 2. And it was found written, that Mordecai had told of Bigthana and Teresh, two of the king's chamberlains, the keepers of the door, who sought to lay hands on the king Ahasuerus. 3. And the king said, What honour and dignity hath been done to Mordecai for this? Then said the king's servants that ministered unto him, There is nothing done for him. 4. And the king said, Who *is* in the court? Now Haman was come into the outward court of the king's house, to speak unto the king to hang Mordecai on the gallows that he had prepared for him. 5. And the king's servants said unto him, Behold, Haman standeth in the court. And the king said, Let him come in. 6. So Haman came in. And the king said unto him, What shall be done unto the man whom the king delighteth to honour? Now Haman thought in his heart, To whom would the king delight to do honour more than to myself? 7. And Haman answered the king, For the man whom the king delighteth to honour, 8. Let the royal apparel be brought which the king *useth* to wear, and the horse that the king rideth upon, and the crown royal which is set upon his head: 9. And let this apparel and horse be delivered to the hand

of one of the king's most noble 'princes, that they may array the man *withal* whom the king delighteth to honour, and bring him on horseback through the street of the city, and proclaim before him, Thus shall it be done to the man whom the king delighteth to honour. 10. Then the king said to Haman, Make haste, *and* take the apparel and the horse, as thou hast said, and do even so to Mordecai the Jew, that sitteth at the king's gate: let nothing fail of all that thou hast spoken. 11. Then took Haman the apparel and the horse, and arrayed Mordecai, and brought him on horseback through the street of the city, and proclaimed before him, Thus shall it be done unto the man whom the king delighteth to honour.

Dan. 1:17. As for these four children, God gave them knowledge and skill in all learning and wisdom: and Daniel had understanding in all visions and dreams. 18. Now at the end of the days that the king had said he should bring them in, then the prince of the eunuchs brought them in before Nebuchadnezzar. 19. And the king communed with them; and among them all was found none like Daniel, Hananiah, Mishael, and Azariah: therefore stood they before the king. 20. And in all matters of wisdom *and* understanding, that the king enquired of them, he found them ten times better than all the magicians *and* astrologers that *were* in all his realm. 21. And Daniel continued *even* unto the first year of king Cyrus.

Matt. 25:14. For *the kingdom of heaven is* as a man travelling into a far country, *who* called his own servants, and delivered unto them his goods. 15. And unto one he gave five talents, to another two, and to another one; to every man according to his several ability; and straightway took his journey. 23. His lord said unto him, Well done, good and faithful servant; thou hast been faithful over a few things, I will make thee ruler over many things: enter thou into the joy of thy lord. 24. Then he which had received the one talent came and said, Lord, I knew thee that thou art an hard man, reaping where thou hast not sown, and gathering where thou hast not strawed: 25. And I was afraid, and went and hid thy talent in the earth: lo, *there* thou hast *that is* thine. 26. His lord answered and said unto him, *Thou* wicked and slothful servant, thou knewest that I reap where I sowed not, and gather where I have not strawed: 27. Thou oughtest therefore to have put my money to the exchangers, and *then* at my coming I should have received mine own with usury. 28. Take therefore the talent from him, and give *it* unto him which hath ten talents. 29. For unto every one that hath shall be given, and he shall have abundance: but from him that hath not shall be taken away even that which he hath. 30. And cast ye the unprofitable servant into outer darkness: there shall be weeping and gnashing of teeth. Luke 19: 12-27.

CORRUPTION IN: Neh. 5:15. But the former governors that *had been* before me were chargeable unto the people, and had taken of them bread and wine, beside forty shekels of silver; yea, even their servants bare rule over the people: but so did not I, because of the fear of God.

Dan. 6:4. Then the presidents and princes sought to find occasion against Daniel concerning the kingdom; but they could find none occasion nor fault; forasmuch as he *was* faithful, neither was there any error or fault found in him. 5. Then said these men, We shall not find any occasion against this Daniel, except we find *it* against him concerning the law of his God. 6. Then these presidents and princes assembled together to the king, and said thus unto him, King Darius, live for ever. 7. All the presidents of the kingdom, the governors, and the princes, the counsellors, and the captains, have consulted together to establish a royal statute, and to make a firm decree, that whosoever shall ask a petition of any God or man for thirty days, save of thee, O king, he shall be cast into the den of lions. 8. Now, O king, establish the decree, and sign the writing, that it be not changed, according to the law of the Medes and Persians, which altereth not. 9. Wherefore king Darius signed the writing and the decree. 10. Now when Daniel knew that the writing was signed, he went into his house; and, his windows being open in his chamber toward Jerusalem, he kneeled upon his knees three times a day, and prayed, and gave thanks before his God, as he did aforetime. 11. Then these men assembled, and found Daniel praying and making supplication before his God. 12. Then they came near, and spake before the king concerning the king's decree; Hast thou not signed a decree, that every man that shall ask *a petition* of any God or man within thirty days, save of thee, O king, shall be cast into the den of lions? The king answered and said, The thing *is* true, according to the law of the Medes and Persians, which altereth not. 13. Then answered they and said before the king, That Daniel, which *is* of the children of the captivity of Judah, regardeth not thee, O king, nor the decree that thou hast signed, but maketh his petition three times a day. 14. Then the king, when he heard *these* words, was sore displeased with himself, and set *his* heart on Daniel to deliver him: and he laboured till the going down of the sun to deliver him. 15. Then these men assembled unto the king, and said unto the king, Know, O king, that the law of the Medes and Persians *is*, That no decree nor statute which the king establisheth may be changed. 16. Then the king commanded, and they brought Daniel, and cast *him* into the den of lions. *Now* the king spake and said unto Daniel,

Thy God whom thou servest continually, he will deliver thee. 17. And a stone was brought, and laid upon the mouth of the den; and the king sealed it with his own signet, and with the signet of his lords; that the purpose might not be changed concerning Daniel.

Mark 15:15. And *so* Pilate, willing to content the people, released Barabbas unto them, and delivered Jesus, when he had scourged *him*, to be crucified.

Acts 24:26. He hoped also that money should have been given him of Paul, that he might loose him: wherefore he sent for him the oftener, and communed with him. See BRIBERY.

REFORM IN: Neh. 5:14. Moreover from the time that I was appointed to be their governor in the land of Judah, from the twentieth year even unto the two and thirtieth year of Artaxerxes the king, *that is,* twelve years, I and my brethren have not eaten the bread of the governor. 15. But the former governors that *had been* before me were chargeable unto the people, and had taken of them bread and wine, besides forty shekels of silver; yea, even their servants bare rule over the people: but so did not I, because of the fear of God.

INFLUENCE IN: 1 Kin. 1:11. Wherefore Nathan spake unto Bath-sheba the mother of Solomon, saying, Hast thou not heard that Adonijah the son of Haggith doth reign, and David our lord knoweth *it* not? 12. Now therefore come, let me, I pray thee, give thee counsel, that thou mayest save thine own life, and the life of thy son Solomon. 13. Go and get thee in unto king David, and say unto him, Didst not thou, my lord, O king, swear unto thine handmaid, saying, Assuredly Solomon thy son shall reign after me, and he shall sit upon my throne? why then doth Adonijah reign? 14. Behold, while thou yet talkest there with the king, I also will come in after thee, and confirm thy words. 15. And Bath-sheba went in unto the king into the chamber: and the king was very old; and Abishag the Shunammite ministered unto the king. 16. And Bath-sheba bowed, and did obeisance unto the king. And the king said, What wouldest thou? 17. And she said unto him, My lord, thou swarest by the LORD thy God unto thine handmaid, *saying,* Assuredly Solomon thy son shall reign after me, and he shall sit upon my throne. 18. And now, behold, Adonijah reigneth; and now, my lord the king, thou knowest *it* not: 20. And thou, my lord, O king, the eyes of all Israel *are* upon thee, that thou shouldest tell them who shall sit on the throne of my lord the king after him. 21. Otherwise it shall come to pass, when my lord the king shall sleep with his fathers, that I and my son Solomon shall be counted offenders. 29. And the king sware, and said, *As* the LORD liveth, that hath redeemed my soul out of all distress, 30. Even as I sware unto thee by the LORD God of Israel, saying,

Assuredly Solomon thy son shall reign after me, and he shall sit upon my throne in my stead; even so will I certainly do this day. 31. Then Bath-sheba bowed with *her* face to the earth, and did reverence to the king, and said, Let my lord king David live for ever. *vs.* 5-40.

2 Kin. 4:13. And he said unto him, Say now unto her, Behold, thou hast been careful for us with all this care; what *is* to be done for thee? wouldest thou be spoken for to the king, or to the captain of the host? And she answered, I dwell among mine own people.

Matt. 20:20. Then came to him the mother of Zebedee's children with her sons, worshipping *him*, and desiring a certain thing of him. 21. And he said unto her, What wilt thou? She said unto him, Grant that these my two sons may sit, the one on thy right hand, and the other on the left, in thy kingdom. 22. But Jesus answered and said, Ye know not what ye ask. Are ye able to drink of the cup that I shall drink of, and to be baptized with the baptism that I am baptized with? They say unto him, We are able. 23. And he saith unto them, Ye shall drink indeed of my cup, and be baptized with the baptism that I am baptized with: but to sit on my right hand, and on my left, is not mine to give, but *it shall be given to them* for whom it is prepared of my Father. Mark 10:35.

CLAIRVOYANCE, 1 Sam. 28:13,14; 2 Kin. 6:15-17.

See SORCERY.

CLAUDA, an island near Crete, Acts 27:16.

CLAUDIA, a female disciple, 2 Tim. 4:21.

CLAUDIUS, emperor of Rome, Acts 11: 28; 18:2.

CLAUDIUS LYSIUS, a Roman military officer, Acts 21:31-40; 22:23-30. Sends Paul to Felix, 23:10-35.

CLAY. Man formed from, Job 33:6. Seals made of, Job 38:14. Used by potter, Isa. 29: 16; 41:25; 45:9. Blind man's eyes anointed with, John 9:6.

FIGURATIVE: Job 4:19; Psa. 40:2; Isa. 45: 9; 64:8; Jer. 18:6; Rom. 9:21.

SYMBOLICAL: Dan. 2:33-41.

CLEAN AND UNCLEAN ANIMALS. See ANIMALS. Of BIRDS, see BIRDS. Of FISH, see FISH. Of INSECTS, see INSECTS.

CLEANLINESS. Taught by frequent ablutions.

See ABLUTION; PURIFICATION.

Regulation relating to, in camp, Deut. 23: 12-14.

FIGURATIVE: Psa. 51:7,10; 73:1; Prov. 20: 9; Isa. 1:16; Ezek. 36:25; 1 John 1:7,9; Rev. 1:5.

CLEANSING. See ABLUTION.

CLEMENCY. Of David toward disloyal subjects: Shimei, 2 Sam. 16:5-13; 19:16-23; Amasa, 2 Sam. 19:13, with 2 Sam. 17:25.

DIVINE, see GOD, LONGSUFFERING OF, and MERCY OF.

CLEMENT, a disciple at Philippi, Phil. 4:3.

CLEOPAS, a disciple to whom Jesus appeared after his resurrection, Luke 24:18.

CLEOPHAS, husband of one of the Marys, John 19:25.

CLERGYMAN. See MINISTER.

CLERK, town, Acts 19:35.

CLOAK, Paul's, left at Troas, 2 Tim. 4:13.

FIGURATIVE: John 15:22; 1 Pet. 2:16.

CLOSET. Used as a place for prayer, Matt. 6:6.

CLOTHING, of the Israelites, waxed not old, Deut. 8:4; 29:5; Neh. 9:21.

See DRESS.

CLOUD. FIGURATIVE: Jer. 4:13; Hos. 6:4; 13:3.

SYMBOLICAL: Rev. 14:14.

PILLAR OF: Ex. 13:21. And the LORD went before them by day in a pillar of a cloud, to lead them the way; and by night in a pillar of fire, to give them light; to go by day and night. 22. He took not away the pillar of the cloud by day, nor the pillar of fire by night, *from* before the people.

Ex. 14:19. And the angel of God, which went before the camp of Israel, removed and went behind them; and the pillar of the cloud went from before their face, and stood behind them: 24. And it came to pass, that in the morning watch the LORD looked unto the host of the Egyptians through the pillar of fire and of the cloud, and troubled the host of the Egyptians,

Ex. 16:10. And it came to pass, as Aaron spake unto the whole congregation of the children of Israel, that they looked toward the wilderness, and, behold, the glory of the LORD appeared in the cloud.

Ex. 19:9. And the LORD said unto Moses, Lo, I come unto thee in a thick cloud, that the people may hear when I speak with thee, and believe thee for ever. And Moses told the words of the people unto the LORD. 16. And it came to pass on the third day in the morning, that there were thunders and lightnings, and a thick cloud upon the mount, and the voice of the trumpet exceedingly loud; so that all the people that *was* in the camp trembled.

Ex. 24:16. And the glory of the LORD abode upon mount Sinai, and the cloud covered it six days: and the seventh day he called unto Moses out of the midst of the cloud. 17. And the sight of the glory of the LORD *was* like devouring fire on the top of the mount in the eyes of the children of Israel. 18. And Moses went into the midst of the cloud, and gat him up into the mount: and Moses was in the mount forty days and forty nights.

Ex. 33:9. And it came to pass, as Moses entered into the tabernacle, the cloudy pillar descended, and stood *at* the door of the tabernacle, and *the* LORD talked with Moses. 10. And all the people saw the cloudy pillar stand *at* the tabernacle door: and all the people rose up and worshipped, every man in *his* tent door.

Ex. 34:5. And the LORD descended in the

cloud, and stood with him there, and proclaimed the name of the LORD.

Ex. 40:36. And when the cloud was taken up from over the tabernacle, the children of Israel went onward in all their journeys: 37. But if the cloud were not taken up, then they journeyed not till the day that it was taken up. 38. For the cloud of the LORD *was* upon the tabernacle by day, and fire was on it by night, in the sight of all the house of Israel, throughout all their journeys.

Lev. 16:2. And the LORD said unto Moses, Speak unto Aaron thy brother, that he come not at all times into the holy *place* within the vail before the mercy seat, which *is* upon the ark; that he die not: for I will appear in the cloud upon the mercy seat.

Num. 9:15. And on the day that the tabernacle was reared up the cloud covered the tabernacle, *namely*, the tent of the testimony: and at even there was upon the tabernacle as it were the appearance of fire, until the morning. 16. So it was alway: the cloud covered it *by day*, and the appearance of fire by night. 17. And when the cloud was taken up from the tabernacle, then after that the children of Israel journeyed: and in the place where the cloud abode, there the children of Israel pitched their tents. 18. At the commandment of the LORD the children of Israel journeyed, and at the commandment of the LORD they pitched: as long as the cloud abode upon the tabernacle they rested in their tents. 19. And when the cloud tarried long upon the tabernacle many days, then the children of Israel kept the charge of the LORD, and journeyed not. 20. And *so* it was, when the cloud was a few days upon the tabernacle; according to the commandment of the LORD they abode in their tents, and according to the commandment of the LORD they journeyed. 21. And *so* it was, when the cloud abode from even unto the morning, and *that* the cloud was taken up in the morning, then they journeyed: whether *it was* by day or by night that the cloud was taken up, they journeyed. 22. Or *whether it were* two days, or a month, or a year, that the cloud tarried upon the tabernacle, remaining thereon, the children of Israel abode in their tents, and journeyed not: but when it was taken up, they journeyed. 23. At the commandment of the LORD they rested in the tents, and at the commandment of the LORD they journeyed: they kept the charge of the LORD, at the commandment of the LORD by the hand of Moses.

Num. 10:11. And it came to pass on the twentieth *day* of the second month, in the second year, that the cloud was taken up from off the tabernacle of the testimony. 12. And the children of Israel took their journeys out of the wilderness of Sinai; and the cloud rested in the wilderness of Paran.

33. And they departed from the mount of the LORD three days' journey: and the ark of the covenant of the LORD went before

them in the three days' journey, to search out a resting place for them. 34. And the cloud of the LORD *was* upon them by day, when they went out of the camp. 35. And it came to pass, when the ark set forward, that Moses said, Rise up, LORD, and let thine enemies be scattered; and let them that hate thee flee before thee. 36. And when it rested, he said, Return, O LORD, unto the many thousands of Israel.

Num. 11:25. And the LORD came down in a cloud, and spake unto him, and took of the spirit that *was* upon him, and gave *it* unto the seventy elders: and it came to pass, *that*, when the spirit rested upon them, they prophesied, and did not cease.

Num. 12:5. And the LORD came down in the pillar of the cloud, and stood *in* the door of the tabernacle, and called Aaron and Miriam: and they both came forth. 10. And the cloud departed from off the tabernacle; and, behold, Miriam *became* leprous, *white* as snow: and Aaron looked upon Miriam, and, behold, *she was* leprous.

Num. 14:10. And the glory of the LORD appeared in the tabernacle of the congregation before all the children of Israel.

Num. 16:19. And Korah gathered all the congregation against them unto the door of the tabernacle of the congregation: and the glory of the LORD appeared unto all the congregation. 42. And it came to pass, when the congregation was gathered against Moses and against Aaron, that they looked toward the tabernacle of the congregation: and, behold, the cloud covered it, and the glory of the LORD appeared.

Deut. 1:33. Who went in the way before you, to search you out a place to pitch your tents *in*, in fire by night, to shew you by what way ye should go, and in a cloud by day.

Deut. 31:15. And the LORD appeared in the tabernacle in a pillar of a cloud: and the pillar of a cloud stood over the door of the tabernacle.

1 Kin. 8:10. And it came to pass, when the priests were come out of the holy *place*, that the cloud filled the house of the LORD. 11. So that the priests could not stand to minister because of the cloud: for the glory of the LORD had filled the house of the LORD.

2 Chr. 7:1. Now when Solomon had made an end of praying, the fire came down from heaven, and consumed the burnt offering and the sacrifices; and the glory of the LORD filled the house. 2. And the priests could not enter into the house of the LORD, because the glory of the LORD had filled the LORD's house. 3. And when all the children of Israel saw how the fire came down, and the glory of the LORD upon the house, they bowed themselves with their faces to the ground upon the pavement, and worshipped, and praised the LORD, *saying*, For *he is* good; for his mercy *endureth* for ever.

Neh. 9:12. Moreover thou leddest them in the day by a cloudy pillar; and in the night by a pillar of fire, to give them light in the way wherein they should go.

19. Yet thou in thy manifold mercies forsookest them not in the wilderness: the pillar of the cloud departed not from them by day, to lead them in the way; neither the pillar of fire by night, to shew them light, and the way wherein they should go.

Psa. 78:14. In the daytime also he led them with a cloud, and all the night with a light of fire.

Psa. 105:39. He spread a cloud for a covering; and fire to give light in the night.

Isa. 4:5. And the LORD will create upon every dwelling place of mount Zion, and upon her assemblies, a cloud and smoke by day, and the shining of a flaming fire by night: for upon all the glory *shall be* a defence.

Isa. 6:1. In the year that king Uzziah died I saw also the Lord sitting upon a throne, high and lifted up, and his train filled the temple. 4. And the posts of the door moved at the voice of him that cried, and the house was filled with smoke.

Ezek. 10:18. Then the glory of the LORD departed from off the threshold of the house, and stood over the cherubims. 19. And the cherubims lifted up their wings, and mounted up from the earth in my sight: when they went out, the wheels also *were* beside them, and *every one* stood at the door of the east gate of the LORD's house; and the glory of the God of Israel *was* over them above.

Ezek. 11:22. Then did the cherubims lift up their wings, and the wheels beside them; and the glory of the God of Israel *was* over them above. 23. And the glory of the LORD went up from the midst of the city, and stood upon the mountain which *is* on the east side of the city.

Matt. 17:5. While he yet spake, behold, a bright cloud overshadowed them: and behold a voice out of the cloud, which said, This is my beloved Son, in whom I am well pleased; hear ye him. Luke 9:34,35.

Luke 2:8. And there were in the same country shepherds abiding in the field, keeping watch over their flock by night. 9. And, lo, the angel of the Lord came upon them, and the glory of the Lord shone round about them: and they were sore afraid.

APPEARANCES OF: IN EZEKIEL'S VISION, Ezek. 10:3,4,18; 11:22,23.

CNIDUS, a city in Asia Minor, Acts 27:7.

COAL. FIGURATIVE: Prov. 25:22.

SYMBOLICAL: Isa. 6:6,7; 2 Sam. 14:7.

COAL OIL. See OIL.

COAT OF MAIL, 1 Sam. 17:5,38; 1 Kin. 22:34; 2 Chr. 18:33.

COCKATRICE, a fabulous serpent.

FIGURATIVE: Isa. 11:8; 14:29; 59:5; Jer. 8:17.

COCK CROWING, Matt. 26:34,74,75; Mark 13:35; 14:30,68,72.

COCKLE, a general term for obnoxious plants, Job 31:40.

COERCION. RELIGIOUS: Ex. 22:20. He that sacrificeth unto *any* god, save unto the LORD only, he shall be utterly destroyed.

2 Chr. 15:12. And they entered into a covenant to seek the LORD God of their fathers with all their heart and with all their soul; 13. That whosoever would not seek the LORD God of Israel should be put to death, whether small or great, whether man or woman. 14. And they sware unto the LORD with a loud voice, and with shouting, and with trumpets, and with cornets. 15. And all Judah rejoiced at the oath: for they had sworn with all their heart, and sought him with their whole desire; and he was found of them: and the LORD gave them rest round about.

Dan. 3:2. Then Nebuchadnezzar the king sent to gather together the princes, the governors, and the captains, the judges, the treasurers, the counsellors, the sheriffs, and all the rulers of the provinces, to come to the dedication of the image which Nebuchadnezzar the king had set up. 3. Then the princes, the governors, and captains, the judges, the treasurers, the counsellors, the sheriffs, and all the rulers of the provinces, were gathered together unto the dedication of the image that Nebuchadnezzar the king had set up; and they stood before the image that Nebuchadnezzar had set up. 4. Then an herald cried aloud, To you it is commanded, O people, nations, and languages, 5. *That* at what time ye hear the sound of the cornet, flute, harp, sackbut, psaltery, dulcimer, and all kinds of musick, ye fall down and worship the golden image that Nebuchadnezzar the king hath set up: 6. And whoso falleth not down and worshippeth shall the same hour be cast into the midst of a burning fiery furnace. *vs.* 1-30.

29. Therefore I make a decree, That every people, nation, and language, which speak any thing amiss against the God of Shadrach, Meshach, and Abed-nego, shall be cut in pieces, and their houses shall be made a dunghill: because there is no other God that can deliver after this sort.

Dan. 6:26. I make a decree, That in every dominion of my kingdom men tremble and fear before the God of Daniel: for he *is* the living God, and stedfast for ever, and his kingdom *that* which shall not be destroyed, and his dominion *shall be even* unto the end. 27. He delivereth and rescueth, and he worketh signs and wonders in heaven and in earth, who hath delivered Daniel from the power of the lions.

See INTOLERANCE.

COFFER, a chest, 1 Sam. 6:8,11,15; Ezek. 27:24.

See TREASURY.

COFFIN, Gen. 50:26.

See BURIAL.

COL-HOZEH, father of Baruch, Neh. 11:5.

COIN. See MONEY.

COLLEGE, second quarter of the city of Jerusalem, 2 Kin. 22:14; 2 Chr. 34:22.

See SCHOOL.

COLLECTION, of money, for the poor.

See ALMS; BENEFICENCE; GIVING; LIBER-
ALITY.

COLLUSION. IN SIN: Lev. 20:4. And
if the people of the land do any ways hide
their eyes from the man, when he giveth of
his seed unto Molech, and kill him not: 5.
Then I will set my face against that man,
and against his family, and will cut him off,
and all that go a whoring after him, to commit whoredom with Molech, from among
their people.

See COMPLICITY; CONNIVANCE.

COLONIZATION. Of conquered countries and people, 2 Kin. 17:6,24; Ezra 4:9,10.

COLORS. Symbolical uses of.

BLACK: A SYMBOL OF AFFLICTION AND
CALAMITY. Job 3:5. Let darkness and the
shadow of death stain it; let a cloud dwell
upon it; let the blackness of the day terrify it.

Job 10:20. *Are* not my days few? cease
then, and let me alone, that I may take
comfort a little, 21. Before I go *whence* I
shall not return, *even* to the land of darkness and the shadow of death; 22. A land
of darkness, as darkness *itself; and* of the
shadow of death, without any order, and
where the light *is* as darkness.

Job 30:26. When I looked for good, then
evil came *unto me:* and when I waited for
light, there came darkness.

Psa. 107:10. Such as sit in darkness and in
the shadow of death, *being* bound in affliction and iron; 11. Because they rebelled
against the words of God, and contemned
the counsel of the Most High:

Psa. 143:3. For the enemy hath persecuted my soul; he hath smitten my life down
to the ground; he hath made me to dwell
in darkness, as those that have been long
dead.

Isa. 5:30. And in that day they shall roar
against them like the roaring of the sea:
and if *one* look unto the land, behold darkness *and* sorrow, and the light is darkened
in the heavens thereof.

Isa. 8:22. And they shall look unto the
earth; and behold trouble and darkness,
dimness of anguish; and *they shall be* driven
to darkness.

Isa. 9:19. Through the wrath of the LORD
of hosts is the land darkened, and the people
shall be as the fuel of the fire: no man shall
spare his brother.

Isa. 24:11. *There is* a crying for wine in
the streets; all joy is darkened, the mirth
of the land is gone.

Isa. 50:3. I clothe the heavens with blackness, and I make sackcloth their covering.

Joel 2:6. Before their face the people shall
be much pained: all faces shall gather blackness. 10. The earth shall quake before
them; the heavens shall tremble: the sun
and the moon shall be dark, and the stars
shall withdraw their shining:

Joel 3:14. Multitudes, multitudes in the
valley of decision: for the day of the LORD
is near in the valley of decision. 15. The

sun and the moon shall be darkened, and
the stars shall withdraw their shining.

Amos 5:8. *Seek him* that maketh the
seven stars and Orion, and turneth the
shadow of death into the morning, and
maketh the day dark with night: that calleth for the waters of the sea, and poureth
them out upon the face of the earth: The
LORD *is* his name:

Nah. 2:10. She is empty, and void, and
waste: and the heart melteth, and the
knees smite together, and much pain *is* in
all loins, and the faces of them all gather
blackness.

Zeph. 1:14. The great day of the LORD *is*
near, *it is* near, and hasteth greatly, *even*
the voice of the day of the LORD: the mighty
man shall cry there bitterly. 15. That day
is a day of wrath, a day of trouble and distress, a day of wasteness and desolation, a
day of darkness and gloominess, a day of
clouds and thick darkness,

Matt. 8:12. But the children of the kingdom shall be cast out into outer darkness:
there shall be weeping and gnashing of
teeth.

Matt. 22:13. Then said the king to the
servants, Bind him hand and foot, and take
him away, and cast *him* into outer darkness; there shall be weeping and gnashing
of teeth.

Matt. 25:30. And cast ye the unprofitable
servant into outer darkness: there shall be
weeping and gnashing of teeth.

2 Pet. 2:4. For if God spared not the angels that sinned, but cast *them* down to hell,
and delivered *them* into chains of darkness,
to be reserved unto judgment:

Jude 13. Wandering stars, to whom is reserved the blackness of darkness for ever.

Rev. 16:10. And the fifth angel poured out
his vial upon the seat of the beast; and his
kingdom was full of darkness· and they
gnawed their tongues for pain,

BLUE: SYMBOL OF DEITY. Ex. 24:10; Jer.
10:9; Ezek. 1:26; 10:1. One of the predom-
inating symbolical colors in the drapery and
furnishings of the tabernacle and temple,
and vestments of priests.

Ex. 25:3. And this *is* the offering which
ye shall take of them; gold, and silver, and
brass, 4. And blue, and purple, and scarlet, and fine linen, and goats' *hair,*

Ex. 26:1. Moreover thou shalt make the
tabernacle *with* ten curtains *of* fine twined
linen, and blue, and purple, and scarlet:
with cherubims of cunning work shalt thou
make them.

Ex. 28:28. And they shall bind the breastplate by the rings thereof unto the rings of
the ephod with a lace of blue, that *it* may
be above the curious girdle of the ephod,
and that the breastplate be not loosed from
the ephod. *v.* 37.

Ex. 38:18. And the hanging for the gate of
the court *was* needlework, *of* blue, and purple, and scarlet, and fine twined linen: and
twenty cubits *was* the length, and the height

in the breadth *was* five cubits, answerable to the hangings of the court.

Ex. 39:1. And of the blue, and purple, and scarlet, they made cloths of service, to do service in the holy *place*, and made holy garments for Aaron; as the LORD commanded Moses. 2. And he made the ephod *of* gold, blue, and purple, and scarlet, and fine twined linen. 3. And they did beat the gold into thin plates, and cut *it into* wires, to work *it* in the blue, and in the purple, and in the scarlet, and in the fine linen, *with* cunning work. 4. They made shoulderpieces for it, to couple *it* together: by the two edges was it coupled together. 5. And the curious girdle of his ephod, that *was* upon it, *was* of the same, according to the work thereof; *of* gold, blue, and purple, and scarlet, and fine twined linen; as the LORD commanded Moses. 21. And they did bind the breastplate by his rings unto the rings of the ephod with a lace of blue, that it might be above the curious girdle of the ephod. 24. And they made upon the hems of the robe pomegranates *of* blue, and purple, and scarlet, *and* twined *linen*. 29. And a girdle *of* fine twined linen, and blue, and purple, and scarlet, *of* needlework; as the LORD commanded Moses. 31. And they tied unto it a lace of blue, to fasten *it* on high upon the mitre; as the LORD commanded Moses.

Num. 4:5. And when the camp setteth forward, Aaron shall come, and his sons, and they shall take down the covering vail, and cover the ark of testimony with it: 6. And shall put theron the covering of badgers' skins, and shall spread over *it* a cloth wholly of blue, and shall put in the staves thereof. 7. And upon the table of shewbread they shall spread a cloth of blue, and put thereon the dishes, and the spoons, and the bowls, and covers to cover withal: and the continual bread shall be thereon: 8. And they shall spread upon them a cloth of scarlet, and cover the same with a covering of badgers' skins, and shall put in the staves thereof. 9. And they shall take a cloth of blue, and cover the candlestick of the light, and his lamps, and his tongs, and his snuffdishes, and all the oil vessels thereof, wherewith they minister unto it: 10. And they shall put it and all the vessels thereof within a covering of badgers' skins, and shall put *it* upon a bar. 11. And upon the golden altar they shall spread a cloth of blue, and cover it with a covering of badgers' skins, and shall put to the staves thereof: 12. And they shall take all the instruments of ministry, wherewith they minister in the sanctuary, and put *them* in a cloth of blue, and cover them with a covering of badgers' skins, and shall put *them* on a bar:

Num. 15:38. Speak unto the children of Israel, and bid them that they make them fringes in the borders of their garments throughout their generations, and that they put upon the fringe of the borders a rib-

band of blue: 39. And it shall be unto you for a fringe, that ye may look upon it, and remember all the commandments of the LORD, and do them; and that ye seek not after your own heart and your own eyes, after which ye use to go a whoring: 40. That ye may remember, and do all my commandments, and be holy unto your God.

2 Chr. 2:7. Send me now therefore a man cunning to work in gold, and in silver, and in brass, and in iron, and in purple, and crimson, and blue, and that can skill to grave with the cunning men that *are* with me in Judah and in Jerusalem, whom David my father did provide.   *v.* 14; 3:14.

For additional reference, see passages below under CRIMSON.

SYMBOL OF ROYALTY, Esth. 8:15; Ezek. 23: 6. See CRIMSON, below.

CRIMSON, RED, PURPLE, AND SCARLET, SYMBOLS OF VARIOUS IDEAS: Of *iniquity*, Isa. 1:18; Rev. 17:3,4; 18:12,16; of *royalty*, Judg. 8:26; Dan. 5:7,16,29; Matt. 27:28; *prosperity*, 2 Sam. 1:24; Prov. 31:21; Lam. 4:5; *conquest*, Nah. 2:3; Rev. 12:3.

These colors figured largely in the symbolisms of the tabernacle furnishings, and priestly vestments and functions, *as types and shadows of the atonement.*

Ex. 25:3. And this *is* the offering which ye shall take of them; gold, and silver, and brass, 4. And blue, and purple, and scarlet, and fine linen, and goats' *hair*, 5. And rams' skins dyed red, and badgers' skins, and shittim wood.

Ex. 26:1. Moreover thou shalt make the tabernacle *with* ten curtains *of* fine twined linen, and blue, and purple, and scarlet: 14. And thou shalt make a covering for the tent *of* rams' skins dyed red, and a covering above *of* badgers' skins.   chapter 25:5. 31. And thou shalt make a vail *of* blue, and purple, and scarlet, and fine twined linen of cunning work: with cherubims shall it be made.   chapter 36:35,37. 36. And thou shalt make an hanging for the door of the tent, *of* blue, and purple, and scarlet, and fine twined linen, wrought with needlework.

Ex. 27:16. And for the gate of the court *shall be* an hanging of twenty cubits, *of* blue, and purple, and scarlet, and fine twined linen, wrought with needlework: chapter 38:18,23.

Ex. 28:4. And these *are* the garments which they shall make; a breastplate, and an ephod, and a robe, and a broidered coat, a mitre, and a girdle: and they shall make holy garments for Aaron thy brother, and his sons, that he may minister unto me in the priest's office.   chapter 39:1. 5. And they shall take gold, and blue, and purple, and scarlet, and fine linen. 6. And they shall make the ephod *of* gold, *of* blue, and *of* purple, *of* scarlet, and fine twined linen, with cunning work.   chapter 39:2,3,5. 8. And the curious girdle of the ephod, which *is* upon it, shall be of the same, according to the work thereof; *even of* gold, *of* blue, and purple, and scarlet, and fine twined linen. Ex. 39:29.

15. And thou shalt make the breastplate of judgment with cunning work; after the work of the ephod thou shalt make it; *of* gold, *of* blue, and *of* purple, and *of* scarlet, and *of* fine twined linen, shalt thou make it. Ex. 39:8.

31. And thou shalt make the robe of the ephod all *of* blue.

33. And *beneath* upon the hem of it thou shalt make pomegranates *of* blue, and *of* purple, and *of* scarlet,

Ex. 35:5. Take ye from among you an offering unto the LORD: whosoever *is* of a willing heart, let him bring it, an offering of the LORD; gold, and silver, and brass, 6. And blue, and purple, and scarlet, and fine linen, and goats' *hair*, 7. And rams' skins dyed red, and badgers' skins, Ex. 25:4; 35:23, 25,35; 36:8,19; 39.

Lev. 14:4. Then shall the priest command to take for him that is to be cleansed two birds alive *and* clean, and cedar wood, and scarlet, and hyssop: *vs.* 6,49,51,52.

Num. 4:7. And upon the table of shewbread they shall spread a cloth of blue, and put thereon the dishes, and the spoons, and the bowls, and covers to cover withal: and the continual bread shall be thereon: 8. And they shall spread upon them a cloth of scarlet, and cover the same with a covering of badgers' skins, and shall put in the staves thereof.

13. And they shall take away the ashes from the altar, and spread a purple cloth thereon:

Num. 19:2. This *is* the ordinance of the law which the LORD hath commanded, saying, Speak unto the children of Israel, that they bring thee a red heifer without spot, wherein *is* no blemish, *and* upon which never came yoke: 5. And *one* shall burn the heifer in his sight; her skin, and her flesh, and her blood, with her dung, shall he burn: 6. And the priest shall take cedar wood, and hyssop, and scarlet, and cast *it* into the midst of the burning of the heifer.

Isa. 63:1. Who *is* this that cometh from Edom, with dyed garments from Bozrah? this *that is* glorious in his apparel, travelling in the greatness of his strength? I that speak in righteousness, mighty to save. 2. Wherefore *art thou* red in thine apparel, and thy garments like him that treadeth in the winefat? 3. I have trodden the winepress alone; and of the people *there was* none with me: for I will tread them in mine anger, and trample them in my fury; and their blood shall be sprinkled upon my garments, and I will stain all my raiment.

Heb. 9:19. For when Moses had spoken every precept to all the people according to the law, he took the blood of calves and of goats, with water, and scarlet wool, and hyssop, and sprinkled both the book, and all the

people. 20. Saying, This *is* the blood of the testament which God hath enjoined unto you. 21. Moreover he sprinkled with blood both the tabernacle, and all the vessels of the ministry. 22. And almost all things are by the law purged with blood; and without shedding of blood is no remission. 23. *It was* therefore necessary that the patterns of things in the heavens should be purified with these; but the heavenly things themselves with better sacrifices than these.

WHITE: SYMBOL OF HOLINESS. The highpriest's holy garments were of white linen, Lev. 16:4,32. Choir singers arrayed in white, 2 Chr. 5:12.

SCRIPTURES EMPLOYING THE SYMBOL:

Psa. 51:7. Purge me with hyssop, and I shall be clean: wash me, and I shall be whiter than snow.

Eccl. 9:8. Let thy garments be always white;

Isa. 1:18. Come now, and let us reason together, saith the LORD: though your sins be as scarlet, they shall be as white as snow; though they be red like crimson, they shall be as wool.

Dan. 7:9. I beheld till the thrones were cast down, and the Ancient of days did sit, whose garment *was* white as snow, and the hair of his head like the pure wool: his throne *was like* the fiery flame, *and* his wheels *as* burning fire.

Dan. 11:35. And *some* of them of understanding shall fall, to try them, and to purge, and to make *them* white, *even* to the time of the end:

Dan. 12.10. Many shall be purified, and made white, and tried;

Matt. 17:1. After six days Jesus taketh Peter, James, and John his brother, and bringeth them up into an high mountain apart, 2. And was transfigured before them: and his face did shine as the sun, and his raiment was white as the light. Mark 9:3.

Matt. 28:2. And, behold, there was a great earthquake: for the angel of the Lord descended from heaven; and came and rolled back the stone from the door, and sat upon it. 3. His countenance was like lightning, and his raiment white as snow:

Rev. 1:13. And in the midst of the seven candlesticks *one* like unto the Son of man, clothed with a garment down to the foot, and girt about the paps with a golden girdle. 14. His head and *his* hairs *were* white like wool, as white as snow; and his eyes *were* as a flame of fire;

Rev. 2:17. And will give him a white stone, and in the stone a new name written, which no man knoweth saving he that receiveth *it*.

Rev. 3:4. Thou hast a few names even in Sardis which have not defiled their garments; and they shall walk with me in white: for they are worthy. 5. He that overcometh, the same shall be clothed in white raiment; and I will not blot out his name out of the book of life, but I will confess his name before my Father, and before his angels. 18. I counsel thee to buy of me gold tried in the fire, that thou mayest be rich ; and white raiment, that thou mayest be clothed,

Rev. 4:4. And round about the throne *were* four and twenty seats : and upon the seats I saw four and twenty elders sitting, clothed in white raiment ;

Rev. 6:2. And I saw, and behold a white horse : and he that sat on him had a bow ; and a crown was given unto him : and he went forth conquering, and to conquer. 11. And white robes were given unto every one of them ;

Rev. 7:9. After this I beheld, and, lo, a great multitude, which no man could number, of all nations, and kindreds, and people, and tongues, stood before the throne, and before the Lamb, clothed with white robes, and palms in their hands ;

13. And one of the elders answered, saying unto me, What are these which are arrayed in white robes? and whence came they? 14. And I said unto him, Sir, thou knowest. And he said to me, These are they which came out of great tribulation, and have washed their robes, and made them white in the blood of the Lamb.

Rev. 15:6. And the seven angels came out of the temple, having the seven plagues, clothed in pure and white linen, and having their breasts girded with golden girdles.

Rev. 19:8. And to her was granted that she should be arrayed in fine linen, clean and white : for the fine linen is the righteousness of saints. 11. And I saw heaven opened, and behold a white horse ; and he that sat upon him *was* called Faithful and True, and in righteousness he doth judge and make war. 14. And the armies *which were* in heaven followed him upon white horses, clothed in fine linen, white and clean.

Rev. 20:11. And I saw a great white throne, and him that sat on it, from whose face the earth and the heaven fled away ; and there was found no place for them.

COLOSSE, a city of Phrygia, Col. 1:2,7,8.

COLT, ridden by Jesus, Matt. 21:2,5,7; Mark 11:2; John 12:15.

COMFORT. See Affliction, Consolation in; Righteous, Promises to.

COMFORTER. See God, Grace of; Holy Spirit.

COMMANDMENTS. Ex. 13:8. And thou shalt shew thy son in that day, saying, *This is done* because of that *which* the Lord did unto me when I came forth out of Egypt. 9. And it shall be for a sign unto thee upon thine hand, and for a memorial between thine eyes, that the Lord's law may be in thy mouth : for with a strong hand hath the Lord brought thee out of Egypt. 10. Thou shalt therefore keep this ordinance in his season from year to year.

Ex. 20:3. Thou shalt have no other gods before me.

4. Thou shalt not make unto thee any graven image, or any likeness *of any thing* that *is* in heaven above, or that *is* in the earth beneath, or that *is* in the water under the earth : 5. Thou shalt not bow down thyself to them, nor serve them : for I the Lord thy God *am* a jealous God, visiting the iniquity of the fathers upon the children unto the third and fourth *generation* of them that hate me ; 6. And shewing mercy unto thousands of them that love me, and keep my commandments.

7. Thou shalt not take the name of the Lord thy God in vain : for the Lord will not hold him guiltless that taketh his name in vain.

8. Remember the sabbath day to keep it holy. 9. Six days shalt thou labour, and do all thy work : 10. But the seventh day *is* the sabbath of the Lord thy God : *in it* thou shalt not do any work, thou, nor thy son, nor thy daughter, thy manservant, nor thy maidservant, nor thy cattle, nor thy stranger that *is* within thy gates : 11. For *in* six days the Lord made heaven and earth, the sea, and all that in them *is*, and rested the seventh day : wherefore the Lord blessed the sabbath day and hallowed it.

12. Honour thy father and thy mother : that thy days may be long upon the land which the Lord thy God giveth thee.

13. Thou shalt 1 not kill.   [1 R. V. do no murder)

14. Thou shalt not commit adultery.

15. Thou shalt not steal.

16. Thou shalt not bear false witness against thy neighbour.

17. Thou shalt not covet thy neighbour's house, thou shalt not covet thy neighbour's wife, nor his manservant, nor his maidservant, nor his ox, nor his ass, nor any thing that *is* thy neighbour's. Deut. 5:6-21.

Deut. 4:5. Behold, I have taught you statutes and judgments, even as the Lord my God commanded me, that ye should do so in the land whither ye go to possess it. 9. Only take heed to thyself, and keep thy soul diligently, lest thou forget the things which thine eyes have seen, and lest they depart from thy heart all the days of thy life : but teach them thy sons, and thy sons' sons ; 10. *Specially* the day that thou stoodest before the Lord thy God in Horeb, when the Lord said unto me, Gather me the people together, and I will make them hear my words, that they may learn to fear me all the days that they shall live upon the earth, and *that* they may teach their children.

Deut. 6:4. Hear, O Israel : The Lord our God *is* one Lord : 5. And thou shalt love the Lord thy God with all thine heart, and with all thy soul, and with all thy might. 6. And these words, which I command thee this day, shall be in thine heart : 7. And thou shalt teach them diligently unto thy children, and shalt talk of them when thou sittest in thine house, and when thou walkest by the way, and when thou liest down, and when thou risest up. 8. And thou shalt bind them for a sign upon thine hand,

and they shall be as frontlets between thine eyes. 9. And thou shalt write them upon the posts of thy house, and on thy gates.

Deut. 11:18. Therefore shall ye lay up these my words in your heart and in your soul, and bind them for a sign upon your hand, that they may be as frontlets between your eyes. 19. And ye shall teach them your children, speaking of them when thou sittest in thine house, and when thou walkest by the way, when thou liest down, and when thou risest up. 20. And thou shalt write them upon the door posts of thine house, and upon thy gates: 21. That your days may be multiplied, and the days of your children, in the land which the LORD sware unto your fathers to give them, as the days of heaven upon the earth.

Deut. 32:46. And he said unto them, Set your hearts unto all the words which I testify among you this day, which ye shall command your children to observe to do, all the words of this law. 47. For it *is* not a vain thing for you; because it *is* your life: and through this thing ye shall prolong *your* days in the land, whither ye go over Jordan to possess it.

Josh. 8:30. Then Joshua built an altar unto the LORD God of Israel in mount Ebal, 31. As Moses the servant of the LORD commanded the children of Israel, as it is written in the book of the law of Moses, an altar of whole stones, over which no man hath lift up *any* iron: and they offered thereon burnt offerings unto the LORD, and sacrificed peace offerings. 32. And he wrote there upon the stones a copy of the law of Moses, which he wrote in the presence of the children of Israel. 33. And all Israel, and their elders, and officers, and their judges, stood on this side the ark and on that side before the priests the Levites, which bare the ark of the covenant of the LORD, as well the stranger, as he that was born among them; half of them over against mount Gerizim, and half of them over against mount Ebal; as Moses the servant of the LORD had commanded before, that they should bless the people of Israel. 34. And afterward he read all the words of the law, the blessings and cursings, according to all that is written in the book of the law. 35. There was not a word of all that Moses commanded, which Joshua read not before all the congregation of Israel, with the women, and the little ones, and the strangers that were conversant among them.

2 Chr. 17:7. Also in the third year of his reign he sent to his princes, . . . to teach in the cities of Judah. 8. And with them *he sent* Levites, . . . and with them Elishama and Jehoram, priests. 9. And they taught in Judah and *had* the book of the law of the LORD with them, and went about throughout all the cities of Judah, and taught the people.

Neh. 8:2. And Ezra the priest brought the law before the congregation both of men and women, and all that could hear with understanding, upon the first day of the seventh month. 3. And he read therein before the street that *was* before the water gate from the morning until midday, before the men and the women, and those that could understand; and the ears of all the people *were attentive* unto the book of the law. 4. And Ezra the scribe stood upon a pulpit of wood, which they had made for the purpose; 5. And Ezra opened the book in the sight of all the people, (for he was above all the people;) and when he opened it, all the people stood up: 6. And Ezra blessed the LORD, the great God. And all the people answered, Amen, Amen, with lifting up their hands: and they bowed their heads, and worshipped the LORD with *their* faces to the ground. 7. Also Jeshua, and Bani, and Sherebiah, Jamin, Akkub, Shabbethai, Hodijah, Maaseiah, Kelita, Azariah, Jozabad, Hanan, Pelaiah, and the Levites, caused the people to understand the law: and the people *stood* in their place. 8. So they read in the book in the law of God distinctly, and gave the sense, and caused *them* to understand the reading.

Psa. 78:1. Give ear, O my people, *to* my law: incline your ears to the words of my mouth. 2. I will open my mouth in a parable: I will utter dark sayings of old: 3. Which we have heard and known, and our fathers have told us. 4. We will not hide *them* from their children, shewing to the generation to come the praises of the LORD, and his strength, and his wonderful works that he hath done. 5. For he established a testimony in Jacob, and appointed a law in Israel, which he commanded our fathers, that they should make them known to their children: 6. That the generation to come might know *them, even* the children *which* should be born; *who* should arise and declare *them* to their children: 7. That they might set their hope in God, and not forget the works of God, but keep his commandments:

Prov. 3:3. Let not mercy and truth forsake thee: bind them about thy neck; write them upon the table of thine heart: 4. So shalt thou find favour and good understanding in the sight of God and man.

Prov. 6:20. My son, keep thy father's commandment, and forsake not the law of thy mother: 21. Bind them continually upon thine heart, *and* tie them about thy neck.

Prov. 7:1. My son, keep my words, and lay up my commandments with thee. 2. Keep my commandments, and live; and my laws as the apple of thine eye. 3. Bind them upon thy fingers, write them upon the table of thine heart. 4. Say unto wisdom, Thou *art* my sister; and call understanding *thy* kinswoman:

Isa. 57:8. Behind the doors also and the posts hast thou set up thy remembrance:

Jer. 11:4. I commanded your fathers in the day *that* I brought them forth out of the land of Egypt, from the iron furnace, saying, Obey my voice, and do them, according to all which I command you: so shall ye be my people, and I will be your God:

Zech. 7:9. Thus speaketh the LORD of hosts, saying, Execute true judgment, and shew mercy and compassions every man to his brother: 10. And oppress not the widow, nor the fatherless, the stranger, nor the poor; and let none of you imagine evil against his brother in your heart.

Zech. 8:16. These *are* the things that ye shall do; Speak ye every man the truth to his neighbour; execute the judgment of truth and peace in your gates: 17. And let none of you imagine evil in your hearts against his neighbour; and love no false oath: for all these *are things* that I hate, saith the LORD.

PRECEPTS OF JESUS. EXPLICITLY STATED, OR IMPLIED IN DIDACTIC DISCOURSE: Matt. 5:16, Let your light so shine before men, that they may see your good works, and glorify your Father which is in heaven. 22. But I say unto you, That whosoever is angry with his brother without a cause shall be in danger of the judgment: and whosoever shall say to his brother, Raca, shall be in danger of the council: but whosoever shall say, Thou fool, shall be in danger of hell fire. 23. Therefore if thou bring thy gift to the altar, and there rememberest that thy brother hath aught against thee; 24. Leave there thy gift before the altar, and go thy way; first be reconciled to thy brother, and then come and offer thy gift.

27. Ye have heard that it was said by them of old time, Thou shalt not commit adultery: 28. But I say unto you, That whosoever looketh on a woman to lust after her hath committed adultery with her already in his heart. 29. And if thy right eye offend thee, pluck it out, and cast *it* from thee: for it is profitable for thee that one of thy members should perish, and not *that* thy whole body should be cast into hell. 30. And if thy right hand offend thee, cut it off, and cast *it* from thee: for it is profitable for thee that one of thy members should perish, and not *that* thy whole body should be cast into hell. 31. It hath been said, Whosoever shall put away his wife, let him give her a writing of divorcement: 32. But I say unto you, That whosoever shall put away his wife, saving for the cause of fornication, causeth her to commit adultery: and whosoever shall marry her that is divorced committeth adultery.

33. Again, ye have heard that it hath been said by them of old time, Thou shalt not forswear thyself, but shalt perform unto the Lord thine oaths: 34. But I say unto you, Swear not at all; neither by heaven; for it is God's throne: 35. Nor by the earth; for it is his footstool: neither by Jerusalem; for it is the city of the great King. 36.

Neither shalt thou swear by thy head, because thou canst not make one hair white or black. 37. But let your communication be, Yea, yea; Nay, nay: for whatsoever is more than these cometh of evil.

38. Ye have heard that it hath been said, An eye for an eye, and a tooth for a tooth: 39. But I say unto you, That ye resist not evil: but whosoever shall smite thee on thy right cheek, turn to him the other also. 40. And if any man will sue thee at the law, and take away thy coat, let him have *thy* cloke also. 41. And whosoever shall compel thee to go a mile, go with him twain. 42. Give to him that asketh thee, and from him that would borrow of thee turn not thou away.

43. Ye have heard that it hath been said, Thou shalt love thy neighbour, and hate thine enemy. 44. But I say unto you, Love your enemies, bless them that curse you, do good to them that hate you, and pray for them which despitefully use you, and persecute you; 45. That ye may be the children of your Father which is in heaven: for he maketh his sun to rise on the evil and on the good, and sendeth rain on the just and on the unjust. 46. For if ye love them which love you, what reward have ye? do not even the publicans the same? 47. And if ye salute your brethren only, what do ye more *than others?* do not even the publicans so? 48. Be ye therefore perfect, even as your Father which is in heaven is perfect. Luke 6:27–36.

Matt. 6:1. Take heed that ye do not your alms before men, to be seen of them: otherwise ye have no reward of your Father which is in heaven. 2. Therefore when thou doest *thine* alms, do not sound a trumpet before thee, as the hypocrites do in the synagogues and in the streets, that they may have glory of men. Verily I say unto you, They have their reward. 3. But when thou doest alms, let not thy left hand know what thy right hand doeth: 4. That thine alms may be in secret: and thy Father which seeth in secret himself shall reward thee openly.

6. But thou, when thou prayest, enter into thy closet, and when thou hast shut thy door, pray to thy Father which is in secret; and thy Father which seeth in secret shall reward thee openly. 7. But when ye pray, use not vain repetitions as the heathen *do:* for they think that they shall be heard for their much speaking. 8. Be not ye therefore like unto them: for your Father knoweth what things ye have need of, before ye ask him.

16. Moreover when ye fast, be not, as the hypocrites, of a sad countenance: for they disfigure their faces, that they may appear unto men to fast. Verily I say unto you, They have their reward. 17. But thou, when thou fastest, anoint thine head, and wash thy face; 18. That thou appear not unto men to fast, but unto thy Father which is

in secret: and thy Father, which seeth in secret, shall reward thee openly.

19. Lay not up for yourselves treasures upon earth, where moth and rust doth corrupt, and where thieves break through and steal: 20. But lay up for yourselves treasures in heaven, where neither moth nor rust doth corrupt, and where thieves do not break through nor steal: 21. For where your treasure is, there will your heart be also.

22. The light of the body is the eye: if therefore thine eye be single, thy whole body shall be full of light. 23. But if thine eye be evil, thy whole body shall be full of darkness. If therefore the light that is in thee be darkness, how great is that darkness! 24. No man can serve two masters: for either he will hate the one, and love the other; or else he will hold to the one, and despise the other. Ye cannot serve God and mammon. 25. Therefore I say unto you, Take no thought for your life, what ye shall eat, or what ye shall drink; nor yet for your body, what ye shall put on. Is not the life more than meat, and the body than raiment? 31. Therefore take no thought, saying, What shall we eat? or, What shall we drink? or, Wherewithal shall we be clothed? 32. (For after all these things do the Gentiles seek:) for your heavenly Father knoweth that ye have need of all these things. 33. But seek ye first the kingdom of God, and his righteousness; and all these things shall be added unto you. 34. Take therefore no thought for the morrow: for the morrow shall take thought for the things of itself. Sufficient unto the day is the evil thereof. Luke 12:12-31.

Matt. 7:1. Judge not, that ye be not judged. 2. For with what judgment ye judge, ye shall be judged: and with what measure ye mete, it shall be measured to you again. 3. And why beholdest thou the mote that is in thy brother's eye, but considerest not the beam that is in thine own eye? 4. Or why wilt thou say to thy brother, Let me pull out the mote out of thine eye; and, behold, a beam is in thine own eye? 5. Thou hypocrite, first cast out the beam out of thine own eye; and then shalt thou see clearly to cast out the mote out of thy brother's eye. Luke 6:37-42.

6. Give not that which is holy unto the dogs, neither cast ye your pearls before swine, lest they trample them under their feet, and turn again and rend you. 7. Ask, and it shall be given you; seek, and ye shall find; knock, and it shall be opened unto you: 8. For every one that asketh receiveth; and he that seeketh findeth; and to him that knocketh it shall be opened. 9. Or what man is there of you, whom if his son ask bread, will he give him a stone? 10. Or if he ask a fish, will he give him a serpent? 11. If ye then, being evil, know how to give good gifts unto your children, how much more shall your Father which is in heaven give good things to them that

ask him? 12. Therefore all things whatsoever ye would that men should do to you, do ye even so to them: for this is the law and the prophets. 13. Enter ye in at the strait gate: for wide is the gate, and broad is the way, that leadeth to destruction, and many there be which go in thereat: 14. Because strait is the gate, and narrow is the way, which leadeth unto life, and few there be that find it. Luke 13:24.

15. Beware of false prophets, which come to you in sheep's clothing, but inwardly they are ravening wolves. 16. Ye shall know them by their fruits. Do men gather grapes of thorns, or figs of thistles? 17. Even so every good tree bringeth forth good fruit; but a corrupt tree bringeth forth evil fruit. 18. A good tree cannot bring forth evil fruit, neither can a corrupt tree bring forth good fruit. 19. Every tree that bringeth not forth good fruit is hewn down, and cast into the fire. 20. Wherefore by their fruits ye shall know them.

21. Not every one that saith unto me, Lord, Lord, shall enter into the kingdom of heaven; but he that doeth the will of my Father which is in heaven. 22. Many will say to me in that day, Lord, Lord, have we not prophesied in thy name? and in thy name have cast out devils? and in thy name done many wonderful works? 23. And then will I profess unto them, I never knew you: depart from me, ye that work iniquity. 24. Therefore whosoever heareth these sayings of mine, and doeth them, I will liken him unto a wise man, which built his house upon a rock: 25. And the rain descended, and the floods came, and the winds blew, and beat upon that house; and it fell not: for it was founded upon a rock. 26. And every one that heareth these sayings of mine, and doeth them not, shall be likened unto a foolish man, which built his house upon the sand: 27. And the rain descended, and the floods came, and the winds blew, and beat upon that house; and it fell: and great was the fall of it. 28. And it came to pass, when Jesus had ended these sayings, the people were astonished at his doctrine: 29. For he taught them as one having authority, and not as the scribes.

Matt. 16:24. Then said Jesus unto his disciples, If any man will come after me, let him deny himself, and take up his cross, and follow me. Mark 8:34.

Matt. 18:8. Wherefore if thy hand or thy foot offend thee, cut them off, and cast them from thee; it is better for thee to enter into life halt or maimed, rather than having two hands or two feet to be cast into everlasting fire. 9. And if thine eye offend thee, pluck it out, and cast it from thee: it is better for thee to enter into life with one eye, rather than having two eyes to be cast into hell fire. 10. Take heed that ye despise not one of these little ones; for I say unto you, That in heaven their angels do always behold the face of my Father which is in heaven.

15. Moreover if thy brother shall trespass against thee, go and tell him his fault between thee and him alone : if he shall hear thee, thou hast gained thy brother. 16. But if he will not hear *thee, then* take with thee one or two more, that in the mouth of two or three witnesses every word may be established. 17. And if he shall neglect to hear them, tell *it* unto the church : but if he neglect to hear the church, let him be unto thee as an heathen man and a publican.

21. Then came Peter to him, and said, Lord, how oft shall my brother sin against me, and I forgive him ? till seven times ? 22. Jesus saith unto him, I say not unto thee, Until seven times : but, Until seventy times seven.

Matt. 19:16. And, behold, one came and said unto him, Good Master, what good thing shall I do, that I may have eternal life ? 17. And he said unto him, Why callest thou me good ? *there is* none good but one, *that is,* God : but if thou wilt enter into life, keep the commandments. 18. He saith unto him, Which ? Jesus said, Thou shalt do no murder, Thou shalt not commit adultery, Thou shalt not steal, Thou shalt not bear false witness, 19. Honour thy father and *thy* mother : and, Thou shalt love thy neighbour as thyself. Mark 10:17-22.

Matt. 20:25. But Jesus called them *unto him*, and said, Ye know that the princes of the Gentiles exercise dominion over them, and they that are great exercise authority upon them. 26. But it shall not be so among you : but whosoever will be great among you, let him be your minister ; 27. And whosoever will be chief among you, let him be your servant : 28. Even as the Son of man came not to be ministered unto, but to minister, and to give his life a ransom for many.

Matt. 22:34. But when the Pharisees had heard that he had put the Sadducees to silence, they were gathered together. 35. Then one of them, *which was* a lawyer, asked *him a question*, tempting him, and saying, 36. Master, which *is* the great commandment in the law ? 37. Jesus said unto him, Thou shalt love the Lord thy God with all thy heart, and with all thy soul, and with all thy mind. 38. This is the first and great commandment. 39. And the second *is* like unto it, Thou shalt love thy neighbour as thyself. 40. On these two commandments hang all the law and the prophets. Luke 10:28-37.

Matt. 24:42. Watch therefore : for ye know not what hour your Lord doth come. 43. But know this, that if the goodman of the house had known in what watch the thief would come, he would have watched, and would not have suffered his house to be broken up. 44. Therefore be ye also ready : for in such an hour as ye think not the Son of man cometh. 45. Who then is a faithful and wise servant, whom his lord hath made ruler over his household, to give them meat in due season ? 46. Blessed *is* that servant, whom his lord when he cometh shall find so

doing. 47. Verily I say unto you, That he shall make him ruler over all his goods. 48. But and if that evil servant shall say in his heart, My lord delayeth his coming ; 49. And shall begin to smite *his* fellowservants, and to eat and drink with the drunken ; 50. The lord of that servant shall come in a day when he looketh not for *him*, and in an hour that he is not aware of, 51. And shall cut him asunder, and appoint *him* his portion with the hypocrites : there shall be weeping and gnashing of teeth.

Matt. 25:34. Then shall the King say unto them on his right hand, Come, ye blessed of my Father, inherit the kingdom prepared for you from the foundation of the world : 35. For I was an hungred, and ye gave me meat : I was thirsty, and ye gave me drink : I was a stranger, and ye took me in : 36. Naked, and ye clothed me : I was sick, and ye visited me : I was in prison, and ye came unto me. 37. Then shall the righteous answer him, saying, Lord, when saw we thee an hungred, and fed *thee ?* or thirsty, and gave *thee* drink ? 38. When saw we thee a stranger, and took *thee* in ? or naked, and clothed *thee ?* 39. Or when saw we thee sick, or in prison, and came unto thee ? 40. And the King shall answer and say unto them, Verily I say unto you, Inasmuch as ye have done *it* unto one of the least of these my brethren, ye have done *it* unto me. 41. Then shall he say also unto them on the left hand, Depart from me, ye cursed, into everlasting fire, prepared for the devil and his angels : 42. For I was an hungred, and ye gave me no meat : I was thirsty, and ye gave me no drink : 43. I was a stranger, and ye took me not in : naked, and ye clothed me not : sick, and in prison, and ye visited me not. 44. Then shall they also answer him, saying, Lord, when saw we thee an hungred, or athirst, or a stranger, or naked, or sick, or in prison, and did not minister unto thee ? 45. Then shall he answer them, saying, Verily I say unto you, Inasmuch as ye did *it* not to one of the least of these, ye did *it* not to me. 46. And these shall go away into everlasting punishment : but the righteous into life eternal.

Mark 6:7. And he called *unto him* the twelve, and began to send them forth by two and two ; and gave them power over unclean spirits ; [Matt. 10:5-42.] 8. And commanded them that they should take nothing for *their* journey, save a staff only ; no scrip, no bread, no money in *their* purse : 9. But *be* shod with sandals ; and not put on two coats. 10. And he said unto them, In what place soever ye enter into an house, there abide till ye depart from that place. 11. And whosoever shall not receive you, nor hear you, when ye depart thence, shake off the dust under your feet for a testimony against them. [1] Verily I say unto you, It shall be more tolerable for Sodom and Gomorrha in the day of judgment, than for that city. [1 Omitted in R. V.]

Mark 9:35. **And he sat down, and called**

the twelve, and saith unto them, If any man desire to be first, *the same* shall be last of all, and servant of all.

38. And John answered him, saying, Master, we saw one casting out devils in thy name, and he followeth not us: and we forbad him, because he followeth not us. 39. But Jesus said, Forbid him not: for there is no man which shall do a miracle in my name, that can lightly speak evil of me.

42. Whosoever shall offend one of *these* little ones that believe in me, it is better for him that a millstone were hanged about his neck, and he were cast into the sea. 43. And if thy hand offend thee, cut it off: it is better for thee to enter into life maimed, than having two hands to go into hell, into the fire that never shall be quenched: 44. Where their worm dieth not, and the fire is not quenched. 45. And if thy foot offend thee, cut it off: it is better for thee to enter halt into life, than having two feet to be cast into hell, 1 into the fire that never shall be quenched: 46. Where their worm dieth not, and the fire is not quenched. 47. And if thine eye offend thee, pluck it out: it is better for thee to enter into the kingdom of God with one eye, than having two eyes to be cast into hell fire: 48. Where their worm dieth not, and the fire is not quenched. 49. For every one shall be salted with fire, 1 and every sacrifice shall be salted with salt. 50. Salt *is* good: but if the salt have lost his saltness, wherewith will ye season it? Have salt in yourselves, and have peace one with another.   [1 Omitted in R. V.]

Mark 10:9. What therefore God hath joined together, let not man put asunder. 11. And he saith unto them, Whosoever shall put away his wife, and marry another, committeth adultery against her. 12. And if a woman shall put away her husband, and be married to another, she committeth adultery.

Mark 11:22. And Jesus answering saith unto them, Have faith in God.

Mark 12:17. And Jesus answering said unto them, Render unto Cæsar the things that are Cæsar's, and to God the things that are God's. Matt. 22:21.

Mark 13:33. Take ye heed, watch and pray: for ye know not when the time is. 34. *For the Son of man is* as a man taking a far journey, who left his house, and gave authority to his servants, and to every man his work, and commanded the porter to watch. 35. Watch ye therefore: for ye know not when the master of the house cometh, at even, or at midnight, or at the cockcrowing, or in the morning: 36. Lest coming suddenly he find you sleeping. 37. And what I say unto you I say unto all, Watch.

Luke 12:15. And he said unto them, Take heed, and beware of covetousness: for a man's life consisteth not in the abundance of the things which he possesseth.

John 7:24. Judge not according to the appearance, but judge righteous judgment.

John 13:34. A new commandment I give unto you, That ye love one another; as I have loved you, that ye also love one another. 35. By this shall all *men* know that ye are my disciples, if ye have love one to another.

John 14:11. Believe me that I *am* in the Father, and the Father in me: or else believe me for the very works' sake.

15. If ye love me, keep my commandments.

23. Jesus answered and said unto him, If a man love me, he will keep my words: and my Father will love him, and we will come unto him, and make our abode with him. 24. He that loveth me not keepeth not my sayings: and the word which ye hear is not mine, but the Father's which sent me.

John 15:2. Every branch in me that beareth not fruit, he taketh away: and every *branch* that beareth fruit, he purgeth it, that it may bring forth more fruit. 4. Abide in me, and I in you. As the branch cannot bear fruit of itself, except it abide in the vine; no more can ye, except ye abide in me. 5. He that abideth in me, and I in him, the same bringeth forth much fruit: for without me ye can do nothing. 7. If ye abide in me, and my words abide in you, ye shall ask what ye will, and it shall be done unto you. 8. Herein is my Father glorified, that ye bear much fruit; so shall ye be my disciples. 9. As the Father hath loved me, so have I loved you: continue ye in my love. 10. If ye keep my commandments, ye shall abide in my love; even as I have kept my Father's commandments, and abide in his love. 11. These things have I spoken unto you, that my joy might remain in you, and *that* your joy might be full. 12. This is my commandment, That ye love one another, as I have loved you. 14. Ye are my friends, if ye do whatsoever I command you. 17. These things I command you, that ye love one another. 20. Remember the word that I said unto you, The servant is not greater than his lord. If they have persecuted me, they will also persecute you; if they have kept my saying, they will keep your's also. 21. But all these things will they do unto you for my name's sake, because they know not him that sent me. 22. If I had not come and spoken unto them, they had not had sin: but now they have no cloke for their sin.

See DECALOGUE; TABLES.

PRECEPTS OF ST. PAUL. EXPLICITLY STATED OR IMPLIED IN DIDACTIC EPISTLES: Rom. 12.1. I beseech you therefore, brethren, by the mercies of God, that ye present your bodies a living sacrifice, holy, acceptable unto God, *which is* your reasonable service. 2. And be not conformed to this world: but be ye transformed by the renewing of your mind, that ye may prove what *is* that good, and acceptable, and perfect, will of God. 3. For I say, through the grace given unto me, to every man that is among you, not to think *of himself* more highly than he ought to think; but to think soberly, according as God hath dealt to every man the measure of faith.

6. Having then gifts differing according to the grace that is given to us, whether prophecy, *let us prophesy* according to the proportion of faith; 7. Or ministry, *let us wait* on *our* ministering: or he that teacheth, on teaching; 8. Or he that exhorteth, on exhortation: he that giveth, *let him do it* with simplicity; he that ruleth, with diligence; he that sheweth mercy, with cheerfulness. 9. *Let* love be without dissimulation. Abhor that which is evil; cleave to that which is good.

10. *Be* kindly affectioned one to another with brotherly love; in honour preferring one another; 11. Not slothful in business; fervent in spirit; serving the Lord; 12. Rejoicing in hope; patient in tribulation; continuing instant in prayer; 13. Distributing to the necessity of saints; given to hospitality. 14. Bless them which persecute you: bless, and curse not. 15. Rejoice with them that do rejoice, and weep with them that weep.

16. *Be* of the same mind one toward another. Mind not high things, but condescend to men of low estate. Be not wise in your own conceits. 17. Recompense to no man evil for evil. Provide things honest in the sight of all men. 18. If it be possible, as much as lieth in you, live peaceably with all men. 19. Dearly beloved, avenge not yourselves, but *rather* give place unto wrath: for it is written, Vengeance *is* mine; I will repay, saith the Lord. 20. Therefore if thine enemy hunger, feed him; if he thirst, give him drink: for in so doing thou shalt heap coals of fire on his head. 21. Be not overcome of evil, but overcome evil with good.

Rom. 13:8. Owe no man any thing, but to love one another: for he that loveth another hath fulfilled the law. 9. For this, Thou shalt not commit adultery, Thou shalt not kill, Thou shalt not steal, Thou shalt not bear false witness, Thou shalt not covet; and if *there be* any other commandment, it is briefly comprehended in this saying, namely, Thou shalt love thy neighbour as thyself. 10. Love worketh no ill to his neighbour: therefore love *is* the fulfilling of the law. 11. And that, knowing the time, that now *it is* high time to awake out of sleep: for now *is* our salvation nearer than when we believed. 12. The night is far spent, the day is at hand: let us therefore cast off the works of darkness, and let us put on the armour of light. 13. Let us walk honestly, as in the day; not in rioting and drunkenness, not in chambering and wantonness, not in strife and envying. 14. But put ye on the Lord Jesus Christ, and make not provision for the flesh, to *fulfil* the lusts *thereof.*

Rom. 14:19. Let us therefore follow after the things which make for peace, and things wherewith one may edify another. 20. For meat destroy not the work of God. All things indeed *are* pure; but *it is* evil for that man who eateth with offence. 21. *It is* good neither to eat flesh, nor to drink wine, nor *any thing* whereby thy brother stumbleth, or is offended, or is made weak.

Rom. 15:1. We then that are strong ought to bear the infirmities of the weak, and not to please ourselves. 2. Let every one of us please *his* neighbour for *his* good to edification.

1 Cor. 8:1. Now as touching things offered unto idols, we know that we all have knowledge. Knowledge puffeth up, but charity edifieth. 7. Howbeit *there is* not in every man that knowledge: for some with conscience of the idol unto this hour eat *it* as a thing offered unto an idol; and their conscience being weak is defiled. 8. But meat commendeth us not to God: for neither, if we eat, are we the better; neither, if we eat not, are we the worse. 9. But take heed lest by any means this liberty of yours become a stumblingblock to them that are weak. 10. For if any man see thee which hast knowledge sit at meat in the idol's temple, shall not the conscience of him which is weak be emboldened to eat those things which are offered to idols; 11. And through thy knowledge shall the weak brother perish, for whom Christ died? 12. But when ye sin so against the brethren, and wound their weak conscience, ye sin against Christ. 13. Wherefore, if meat make my brother to offend, I will eat no flesh while the world standeth, lest I make my brother to offend.

1 Cor. 10:7. Neither be ye idolaters, as *were* some of them; as it is written, The people sat down to eat and drink, and rose up to play. 8. Neither let us commit fornication, as some of them committed, and fell in one day three and twenty thousand.

9. Neither let us tempt Christ, as some of them also tempted, and were destroyed of serpents. 10. Neither murmur ye, as some of them also murmured, and were destroyed of the destroyer.

24. Let no man seek his own, but every man another's *wealth.* 28. But if any man say unto you, This is offered in sacrifice unto idols, eat not for his sake that shewed it, and for conscience sake: for the earth *is* the Lord's, and the fulness thereof: 29. Conscience, I say, not thine own, but of the other: for why is my liberty judged of another *man's* conscience? 31. Whether therefore ye eat, or drink, or whatsoever ye do, do all to the glory of God. 32. Give none offence, neither to the Jews, nor to the Gentiles, nor to the church of God ·

1 Cor. 14:20. Brethren, be not children in understanding: howbeit in malice be ye children, but in understanding be men.

1 Cor. 16:13. Watch ye, stand fast in the faith, quit you like men, be strong. 14. Let all your things be done with charity.

2 Cor. 13:7. Now I pray to God that ye do no evil; not that we should appear approved,

but that ye should do that which is honest, though we be as reprobates.

Gal. 5:1. Stand fast therefore in the liberty wherewith Christ hath made us free, and be not entangled again with the yoke of bondage. 16. *This* I say then, Walk in the Spirit, and ye shall not fulfil the lust of the flesh.

Gal. 6:1. Brethren, if a man be overtaken in a fault, ye which are spiritual, restore such an one in the spirit of meekness; considering thyself, lest thou also be tempted. 2. Bear ye one another's burdens, and so fulfil the law of Christ.

Eph. 4:1. I therefore, the prisoner of the Lord, beseech you that ye walk worthy of the vocation wherewith ye are called. 2. With all lowliness and meekness, with longsuffering, forbearing one another in love; 3. Endeavouring to keep the unity of the Spirit in the bond of peace.

26. Be ye angry, and sin not: let not the sun go down upon your wrath: 27. Neither give place to the devil.

28. Let him that stole steal no more: but rather let him labour, working with *his* hands the thing which is good, that he may have to give to him that needeth.

29. Let no corrupt communication proceed out of your mouth, but that which is good to the use of edifying, that it may minister grace unto the hearers.

30. And grieve not the Holy Spirit of God, whereby ye are sealed unto the day of redemption.

31. Let all bitterness, and wrath, and anger, and clamour, and evil speaking, be put away from you, with all malice: 32. And be ye kind one to another, tenderhearted, forgiving one another, even as God for Christ's sake hath forgiven you.

Eph. 5:1. Be ye therefore followers of God, as dear children; 2. And walk in love, as Christ also hath loved us, and hath given himself for us an offering and a sacrifice to God for a sweetsmelling savour.

3. But fornication, and all uncleanness, or covetousness, let it not be once named among you, as becometh saints; 4. Neither filthiness, nor foolish talking, nor jesting, which are not convenient: but rather giving of thanks. 5. For this ye know, that no whoremonger, nor unclean person, nor covetous man, who is an idolater, hath any inheritance in the kingdom of Christ and of God. 6. Let no man deceive you with vain words: for because of these things cometh the wrath of God upon the children of disobedience.

11. Have no fellowship with the unfruitful works of darkness, but rather reprove *them.*

15. See then that ye walk circumspectly, not as fools, but as wise, 16. Redeeming the time, because the days are evil

17. Wherefore be ye not unwise, but understanding what the will of the Lord *is.*

18. And be not drunk with wine, wherein is excess; but be filled with the Spirit; 19. Speaking to yourselves in psalms and hymns and spiritual songs, singing and making melody in your heart to the Lord; 20. Giving thanks always for all things unto God and the Father in the name of our Lord Jesus Christ; 21. Submitting yourselves one to another in the fear of [1] God. [1 R. V. Christ]

Eph. 6:10. Finally, my brethren, be strong in the Lord, and in the power of his might.

11. Put on the whole armour of God, that ye may be able to stand against the wiles of the devil. 13. Wherefore, take unto you the whole armour of God, that ye may be able to withstand in the evil day, and having done all, to stand. 14. Stand therefore, having your loins girt about with truth, and having on the breastplate of righteousness; 15. And your feet shod with the preparation of the gospel of peace; 16. Above all, taking the shield of faith, wherewith ye shall be able to quench all the fiery darts of the wicked. 17. And take the helmet of salvation, and the sword of the Spirit, which is the word of God: 18. Praying always with all prayer and supplication in the Spirit, and watching thereunto with all perseverance and supplication for all saints;

Phil. 1:27. Let your conversation be as it becometh the gospel of Christ: that whether I come and see you, or else be absent, I may hear of your affairs, that ye stand fast in one spirit, with one mind striving together for the faith of the gospel; 28. And in nothing terrified by your adversaries: which is to them an evident token of perdition, but to you of salvation, and that of God.

Phil. 2:2. Fulfil ye my joy, that ye be likeminded, having the same love, *being* of one accord, of one mind.

3. *Let* nothing *be done* through strife or vainglory; but in lowliness of mind let each esteem other better than themselves.

4. Look not every man on his own things, but every man also on the things of others.

5. Let this mind be in you, which was also in Christ Jesus: 6. Who, being in the form of God, thought it not [1] robbery to be equal with God: 7. But [2] made himself of no reputation, and took upon him the form of a servant, and was made in the likeness of men: 8. And being found in fashion as a man, he humbled himself, and became obedient unto death, even the death of the cross.

[R. V. 1 a prize   2 emptied himself, taking]

12. Wherefore, my beloved, as ye have always obeyed, not as in my presence only, but how much more in my absence, work out your own salvation with fear and trembling: 13. For it is God which worketh in you both to will and to do of *his* good pleasure.

14. Do all things without murmurings and disputings: 15. That ye may be blameless and harmless, the sons of God, without rebuke, in the midst of a crooked and per-

verse nation, among whom ye shine as lights in the world; 16. Holding forth the word of life;

Phil. 4:4. Rejoice in the Lord alway: *and* again I say, Rejoice.

5. Let your moderation be known unto all men.

6. Be careful for nothing; but in every thing by prayer and supplication with thanksgiving let your requests be made known unto God.

8. Finally, brethren, whatsoever things are true, whatsoever things *are* honest, whatsoever things *are* just, whatsoever things *are* pure, whatsoever things *are* lovely, whatsoever things *are* of good report; if *there be* any virtue, and if *there be* any praise, think on these things.

9. Those things, which ye have both learned, and received, and heard, and seen in me, do: and the God of peace shall be with you.

Col. 2:6. As ye have therefore received Christ Jesus the Lord, *so* walk ye in him:

16. Let no man therefore judge you in meat, or in drink, or in respect of an holy day, or of the new moon, or of the sabbath *days:* 20. Wherefore if ye be dead with Christ from the rudiments of the world, why, as though living in the world, are ye subject to ordinances, 21. (Touch not; taste not; handle not: 22. Which all are to perish with the using;) after the commandments and doctrines of men? 23. Which things have indeed a shew of wisdom in will worship, and humility, and neglecting of the body; not in any honour to the satisfying of the flesh.

Col. 3:1. If ye then be risen with Christ, seek those things which are above, where Christ sitteth on the right hand of God.

2. Set your affection on things above, not on things on the earth.

5. Mortify therefore your members which are upon the earth; fornication, uncleanness, inordinate affection, evil concupiscence, and covetousness, which is idolatry:

8. But now ye also put off all these; anger, wrath, malice, blasphemy, filthy communication out of your mouth.

9. Lie not one to another, seeing that ye have put off the old man with his deeds; 12. Put on therefore, as the elect of God, holy and beloved, bowels of mercies, kindness, humbleness of mind, meekness, longsuffering; 13. Forbearing one another, and forgiving one another, if any man have a quarrel against any: even as Christ forgave you, so also *do* ye. 14. And above all these things *put on* charity, which is the bond of perfectness. 15. And let the peace of God rule in your hearts, to the which also ye are called in one body; and be ye thankful. 16. Let the word of Christ dwell in you richly in all wisdom; teaching and admonishing one another in psalms and hymns and spiritual songs, singing with grace in your hearts to the Lord. 17. And whatsoever ye do in word

or deed, *do* all in the name of the Lord Jesus, giving thanks to God and the Father by him. 23. And whatsoever ye do, do *it* heartily, as to the Lord, and not unto men;

1 Thess. 3:12. And the Lord make you to increase and abound in love one toward another, and toward all *men*, even as we *do* toward you.

1 Thess. 4:1. Furthermore then we beseech you, brethren, and exhort *you* by the Lord Jesus, that as ye have received of us how ye ought to walk and to please God, *so* ye would abound more and more.

3. For this is the will of God, *even* your sanctification, that ye should abstain from fornication: 5. Not in the lust of concupiscence, even as the Gentiles which know not God: 6. That no *man* go beyond and defraud his brother in *any* matter: because that the Lord *is* the avenger of all such, as we also have forewarned you and testified.

9. But as touching brotherly love ye need not that I write unto you: for ye yourselves are taught of God to love one another. 10. And indeed ye do it toward all the brethren which are in all Macedonia: but we beseech you, brethren, that ye increase more and more; 11. And that ye study to be quiet, and to do your own business, and to work with your own hands, as we commanded you; 12. That ye may walk honestly toward them that are without, and *that* ye may have lack of nothing.

1 Thess. 5:6. Therefore let us not sleep as *do* others; but let us watch and be sober. 8. But let us, who are of the day, be sober, putting on the breastplate of faith and love; and for an helmet, the hope of salvation.

12. And we beseech you, brethren, to know them which labour among you, and are over you in the Lord, and admonish you; 13. And to esteem them very highly in love for their work's sake. *And* be at peace among yourselves.

14. Now we exhort you, brethren, warn them that are unruly, comfort the feebleminded, support the weak, be patient toward all *men*.

15. See that none render evil for evil unto any *man;* but ever follow that which is good, both among yourselves, and to all *men*.

16. Rejoice evermore.

17. Pray without ceasing.

18. In every thing give thanks: for this is the will of God in Christ Jesus concerning you.

19. Quench not the Spirit.

20. Despise not prophesyings.

21. Prove all things; hold fast that which is good.

22. Abstain from all appearance of evil.

2 Thess. 2:15. Therefore, brethren, stand fast, and hold the traditions which ye have been taught, whether by word, or our epistle.

2 Thess. 3:6. Now we command you, brethren, in the name of our Lord Jesus Christ, that ye withdraw yourselves from every

brother that walketh disorderly, and not after the tradition which he received of us. 7. For yourselves know how ye ought to follow us: for we behaved not ourselves disorderly among you; 8. Neither did we eat any man's bread for nought; but wrought with labour and travail night and day, that we might not be chargeable to any of you: 9. Not because we have not power, but to make ourselves an ensample unto you to follow us. 10. For even when we were with you, this we commanded you, that if any would not work, neither should he eat. 11. For we hear that there are some which walk among you disorderly, working not at all, but are busybodies. 12. Now them that are such we command and exhort by our Lord Jesus Christ, that with quietness they work, and eat their own bread.

13. But ye, brethren, be not weary in well doing.

14. And if any man obey not our word by this epistle, note that man, and have no company with him, that he may be ashamed. 15. Yet count *him* not as an enemy, but admonish *him* as a brother.

1 Tim. 1:4. Neither give heed to fables and endless genealogies, which minister questions, rather than godly edifying which is in faith: *so do.*

1 Tim. 2:1. I exhort therefore, that, first of all, supplications, prayers, intercessions, *and* giving of thanks, be made for all men; 2. For kings, and *for* all that are in authority; that we may lead a quiet and peaceable life in all godliness and honesty. 8. I will therefore that men pray every where, lifting up holy hands, without wrath and doubting.

9. In like manner also, that women adorn themselves in modest apparel, with shamefacedness and sobriety; not with broided hair, or gold, or pearls, or costly array; 10. But (which becometh women professing godliness) with good works. 11. Let the woman learn in silence with all subjection. 12. But I suffer not a woman to teach, nor to usurp authority over the man, but to be in silence.

1 Tim. 3:2. A bishop then must be blameless, the husband of one wife, vigilant, sober, of good behaviour, given to hospitality, apt to teach; 3. Not given to wine, no striker, not greedy of filthy lucre; but patient, not a brawler, not covetous; 4. One that ruleth well his own house, having his children in subjection with all gravity; 5. (For if a man know not how to rule his own house, how shall he take care of the church of God?) 6. Not a novice, lest being lifted up with pride he fall into the condemnation of the devil. 7. Moreover he must have a good report of them which are without; lest he fall into reproach and the snare of the devil.

8. Likewise *must* the deacons *be* grave, not doubletongued, not given to much wine, not greedy of filthy lucre; 9. Holding the mystery of the faith in a pure conscience. 10. And let these also first be proved; then let them use the office of a deacon, being *found* blameless.

11. Even so *must their* wives *be* grave, not slanderous, sober, faithful in all things.

12. Let the deacons be the husbands of one wife, ruling their children and their own houses well. 13. For they that have used the office of a deacon well purchase to themselves a good degree, and great boldness in the faith which is in Christ Jesus.

1 Tim. 4:1. Now the Spirit speaketh expressly, that in the latter times some shall depart from the faith, giving heed to seducing spirits, and doctrines of devils; 2. Speaking lies in hypocrisy; having their conscience seared with a hot iron; 3. Forbidding to marry, *and commanding* to abstain from meats, which God hath created to be received with thanksgiving of them which believe and know the truth. 4. For every creature of God *is* good, and nothing to be refused, if it be received with thanksgiving: 5. For it is sanctified by the word of God and prayer.

6. If thou put the brethren in remembrance of these things, thou shalt be a good minister of Jesus Christ, nourished up in the words of faith and of good doctrine, whereunto thou hast attained.

7. But refuse profane and old wives' fables, and exercise thyself *rather* unto godliness.

12. Be thou an example of the believers, in word, in conversation, in charity, in spirit, in faith, in purity.

13. Till I come, give attendance to reading, to exhortation, to doctrine.

14. Neglect not the gift that is in thee, which was given thee by prophecy, with the laying on of the hands of the presbytery.

15. Meditate upon these things; give thyself wholly to them; that thy profiting may appear to all.

16. Take heed unto thyself, and unto the doctrine; continue in them: for in doing this thou shalt both save thyself, and them that hear thee.

1 Tim. 5:1. Rebuke not an elder, but intreat *him* as a father; *and* the younger men as brethren; 2. The elder women as mothers; the younger as sisters, with all purity.

3. Honour widows that are widows indeed. 4. But if any widow have children or nephews, let them learn first to shew piety at home, and to requite their parents: for that is good and acceptable before God. 5. Now she that is a widow indeed, and desolate, trusteth in God, and continueth in supplications and prayers night and day. 6. But she that liveth in pleasure is dead while she liveth. 7. And these things give in charge, that they may be blameless.

8. But if any provide not for his own, and specially for those of his own house, he hath denied the faith, and is worse than an infidel.

9. Let not a widow be taken into the num-

ber under threescore years old, having been the wife of one man. 10. Well reported of for good works; if she have brought up children, if she have lodged strangers, if she have washed the saints' feet, if she have relieved the afflicted, if she have diligently followed every good work.

11. But the younger widows refuse: for when they have begun to wax wanton against Christ, they will marry; 12. Having damnation, because they have cast off their first faith. 13. And withal they learn *to be* idle, wandering about from house to house; and not only idle, but tattlers also and busybodies, speaking things which they ought not.

14. I will therefore that the younger women marry, bear children, guide the house, give none occasion to the adversary to speak reproachfully. 16. If any man or woman that believeth have widows, let them relieve them, and let not the church be charged; that it may relieve them that are widows indeed.

17. Let the elders that rule well be counted worthy of double honour, especially they who labour in the word and doctrine. 18. For the scripture saith, Thou shalt not muzzle the ox that treadeth out the corn. And, The labourer *is* worthy of his reward.

19. Against an elder receive not an accusation, but before two or three witnesses.

20. Them that sin rebuke before all, that others also may fear.

21. I charge *thee* before God, and the Lord Jesus Christ, and the elect angels, that thou observe these things without preferring one before another, doing nothing by partiality.

1 Tim. 6:11. But thou, O man of God, flee these things; and follow after righteousness, godliness, faith, love, patience, meekness. 12. Fight the good fight of faith, lay hold on eternal life, whereunto thou art also called, and hast professed a good profession before many witnesses. 13. I give thee charge in the sight of God, 14. That thou keep *this* commandment without spot, unrebukeable, until the appearing of our Lord Jesus Christ:

17. Charge them that are rich in this world, that they be not highminded, nor trust in uncertain riches, but in the living God, who giveth us richly all things to enjoy; 18. That they do good, that they be rich in good works, ready to distribute, willing to communicate; 19. Laying up in store for themselves a good foundation against the time to come, that they may lay hold on ¹ eternal life.

[¹ R. V. the life which is life indeed]

20. Keep that which is committed to thy trust, avoiding profane *and* vain babblings, and oppositions of science falsely so called:

2 Tim. 1:13. Hold fast the form of sound words, which thou hast heard of me, in faith and love which is in Christ Jesus. 14. That good thing which was committed unto thee keep by the Holy Ghost which dwelleth in us.

2 Tim. 2:19. Let every one that nameth the name of Christ depart from iniquity.

22. Flee also youthful lusts: but follow righteousness, faith, charity, peace, with them that call on the Lord out of a pure heart.

23. But foolish and unlearned questions avoid, knowing that they do gender strifes.

24. And the servant of the Lord must not strive; but be gentle unto all *men*, apt to teach, patient, 25. In meekness instructing those that oppose themselves; if God peradventure will give them repentance to the acknowledging of the truth;

2 Tim. 3:2. For men shall be lovers of their own selves, covetous, boasters, proud, blasphemers, disobedient to parents, unthankful, unholy, 3. Without natural affection, trucebreakers, false accusers, incontinent, fierce, despisers of those that are good, 4. Traitors, heady, highminded, lovers of pleasures more than lovers of God; 5. Having a form of godliness, but denying the power thereof: from such turn away.

Tit. 1:5. For this cause left I thee in Crete, that thou shouldest set in order the things that are wanting, and ordain elders in every city, as I had appointed thee: 6. If any be blameless, the husband of one wife, having faithful children not accused of riot or unruly. 7. For a bishop must be blameless, as the steward of God; not selfwilled, not soon angry, not given to wine, no striker, not given to filthy lucre; 8. But a lover of hospitality, a lover of good men, sober, just, holy, temperate; 9. Holding fast the faithful word as he hath been taught, that he may be able by sound doctrine both to exhort and to convince the gainsayers. 10. For there are many unruly and vain talkers and deceivers, specially they of the circumcision: 11. Whose mouths must be stopped, who subvert whole houses, teaching things which they ought not, for filthy lucre's sake. 12. One of themselves, *even* a prophet of their own, said, The Cretians *are* alway liars, evil beasts, slow bellies. 13. This witness is true. Wherefore rebuke them sharply, that they may be sound in the faith; 14. Not giving heed to Jewish fables, and commandments of men, that turn from the truth.

Tit. 2:2. That the aged men be sober, grave, temperate, sound in faith, in charity, in patience. 3. The aged women likewise, that *they be* in behaviour as becometh holiness, not false accusers, not given to much wine, teachers of good things; 4. That they may teach the young women to be sober, to love their husbands, to love their children, 5. *To be* discreet, chaste, keepers at home, good, obedient to their own husbands, that the word of God be not blasphemed.

9. *Exhort* servants to be obedient unto their own masters, *and* to please *them* well in all *things;* not answering again; 10. Not purloining, but shewing all good fidelity; that they may adorn the doctrine of God our Saviour in all things.

11. For the grace of God that bringeth salvation hath appeared to all men. 12. Teach-

ing us that, denying ungodliness and worldly lusts, we should live soberly, righteously, and godly, in this present world;

Tit. 3:1. Put them in mind to be subject to principalities and powers, to obey magistrates, to be ready to every good work. 2. To speak evil of no man, to be no brawlers, *but* gentle, shewing all meekness unto all men.

8. *This is* a faithful saying, and these things I will that thou affirm constantly, that they which have believed in God might be careful to maintain good works. These things are good and profitable unto men.

Heb. 6:1. Therefore leaving the principles of the doctrine of Christ, let us go on unto perfection; not laying again the foundation of repentance from dead works, and of faith toward God, 11. And we desire that every one of you do shew the same diligence to the full assurance of hope unto the end: 12. That ye be not slothful, but followers of them who through faith and patience inherit the promises.

Heb. 10:22. Let us draw near with a true heart in full assurance of faith, having our hearts sprinkled from an evil conscience, and our bodies washed with pure water.

23. Let us hold fast the profession of *our* faith without wavering; (for he *is* faithful that promised;) 24. And let us consider one another to provoke unto love and to good works: 25. Not forsaking the assembling of ourselves together, as the manner of some *is;* but exhorting *one another:* and so much the more, as ye see the day approaching.

Heb. 12:1. Wherefore seeing we also are compassed about with so great a cloud of witnesses, let us lay aside every weight, and the sin which doth so easily beset *us,* and let us run with patience the race that is set before us, 2. Looking unto Jesus the author and finisher of *our* faith; who for the joy that was set before him endured the cross, despising the shame, and is set down at the right hand of the throne of God. 3. For consider him that endured such contradiction of sinners against himself, lest ye be wearied and faint in your minds. 4. Ye have not yet resisted unto blood, striving against sin. 5. And ye have forgotten the exhortation which speaketh unto you as unto children, My son, despise not thou the chastening of the Lord, nor faint when thou art rebuked of him:

12. Wherefore lift up the hands which hang down, and the feeble knees; 13. And make straight paths for your feet, lest that which is lame be turned out of the way; but let it rather be healed. 14. Follow peace with all *men,* and holiness, without which no man shall see the Lord: 15. Looking diligently lest any man fail of the grace of God; lest any root of bitterness springing up trouble *you,* and thereby many be defiled; 16. Lest there *be* any fornicator, or profane person, as Esau, who for one morsel of meat sold his birthright.

Heb. 13:1. Let brotherly love continue.

2. Be not forgetful to entertain strangers: for thereby some have entertained angels unawares.

3. Remember them that are in bonds, as bound with them; *and* them which suffer adversity, as being yourselves also in the body.

5. *Let your* conversation *be* without covetousness; *and be* content with such things as ye have: for he hath said, I will never leave thee, nor forsake thee.

7. Remember them which have the rule over you, who have spoken unto you the word of God: whose faith follow, considering the end of *their* conversation.

9. Be not carried about with divers and strange doctrines. For *it is* a good thing that the heart be established with grace; not with meats, which have not profited them that have been occupied therein.

15. By him therefore let us offer the sacrifice of praise to God continually, that is, the fruit of *our* lips giving thanks to his name.

16. But to do good and to communicate forget not: for with such sacrifices God is well pleased.

17. Obey them that have the rule over you, and submit yourselves: for they watch for your souls, as they that must give account, that they may do it with joy, and not with grief: for that *is* unprofitable for you.

OTHER APOSTLES: Precepts of, Explicitly Stated or Implied in Didactic Epistles. Jas. 1:16. Do not err, my beloved brethren. 19. Wherefore, my beloved brethren, let every man be swift to hear, slow to speak, slow to wrath:

21. Wherefore lay apart all filthiness and superfluity of naughtiness, and receive with meekness the engrafted word, which is able to save your souls.

22. But be ye doers of the word, and not hearers only, deceiving your own selves.

Jas. 2:1. My brethren, have not the faith of our Lord Jesus Christ, *the Lord* of glory, with respect of persons. 2. For if there come unto your assembly a man with a gold ring, in goodly apparel, and there come in also a poor man in vile raiment; 3. And ye have respect to him that weareth the gay clothing, and say unto him, Sit thou here in a good place; and say to the poor, Stand thou there, or sit here under my footstool: 4. Are ye not then partial in yourselves, and are become judges of evil thoughts?

8. If ye fulfil the royal law according to the scripture, Thou shalt love thy neighbour as thyself, ye do well: 9. But if ye have respect to persons, ye commit sin, and are convinced of the law as transgressors. 10. For whosoever shall keep the whole law, and yet offend in one *point,* he is guilty of all. 11. For he that said, Do not commit adultery, said also, Do not kill. Now if thou commit no adultery, yet if thou kill, thou art become a transgressor of the law. 12. So speak ye, and so do, as they that shall be judged by the law of liberty.

Jas. 3:1. My brethren, be not many masters, knowing that we shall receive the greater condemnation.

Jas. 4:7. Submit yourselves therefore to God. Resist the devil and he will flee from you.

8. Draw nigh to God, and he will draw nigh to you. Cleanse *your* hands, *ye* sinners; and purify *your* hearts, *ye* double minded.

9. Be afflicted, and mourn, and weep: let your laughter be turned to mourning, and *your* joy to heaviness.

10. Humble yourselves in the sight of the Lord, and he shall lift you up.

11. Speak not evil one of another, brethren. He that speaketh evil of *his* brother, and judgeth his brother, speaketh evil of the law, and judgeth the law: but if thou judge the law, thou art not a doer of the law, but a judge.

13. Go to now, ye that say, To day or to morrow we will go into such a city, and continue there a year, and buy and sell, and get gain: 14. Whereas ye know not what *shall be* on the morrow. For what *is* your life? It is even a vapour, that appeareth for a little time, and then vanisheth away. 15. For that ye *ought* to say, If the Lord will, we shall live, and do this, or that.

Jas. 5:7. Be patient therefore, brethren, unto the coming of the Lord. Behold, the husbandman waiteth for the precious fruit of the earth, and hath long patience for it, until he receive the early and latter rain. 8. Be ye also patient; stablish your hearts: for the coming of the Lord draweth nigh.

9. Grudge not one against another, brethren, lest ye be condemned: behold, the judge standeth before the door. 10. Take, my brethren, the prophets, who have spoken in the name of the Lord, for an example of suffering affliction, and of patience. 11. Behold, we count them happy which endure. Ye have heard of the patience of Job, and have seen the end of the Lord; that the Lord is very pitiful, and of tender mercy.

12. But above all things, my brethren, swear not, neither by heaven, neither by the earth, neither by any other oath: but let your yea be yea; and *your* nay, nay; lest ye fall into condemnation.

16. Confess *your* faults one to another, and pray one for another, that ye may be healed.

1 Pet. 1:13. Wherefore gird up the loins of your mind, be sober, and hope to the end for the grace that is to be brought unto you at the revelation of Jesus Christ; 14. As obedient children, not fashioning yourselves according to the former lusts in your ignorance: 15. But as he which hath called you is holy, so be ye holy in all manner of conversation; 16. Because it is written, Be ye holy; for I am holy. 17. And if ye call on the Father, who without respect of persons judgeth according to every man's work, pass the time of your sojourning *here* in fear:

1 Pet. 2:11. Dearly beloved, I beseech *you* as strangers and pilgrims, abstain from fleshly lusts, which war against the soul: 12. Having your conversation honest among the Gentiles: that, whereas they speak against you as evildoers, they may by *your* good works, which they shall behold, glorify God in the day of visitation.

13. Submit yourselves to every ordinance of man for the Lord's sake · whether it be to the king, as supreme; 14. Or unto governors, as unto them that are sent by him for the punishment of evildoers, and for the praise of them that do well. 15. For so is the will of God, that with well doing ye may put to silence the ignorance of foolish men: 16. As free, and not using *your* liberty for a cloke of maliciousness, but as the servants of God.

17. Honour all *men.*
Love the brotherhood.
Fear God.
Honour the king.

18. Servants, *be* subject to *your* masters with all fear; not only to the good and gentle, but also to the froward. 19. For this *is* thankworthy, if a man for conscience toward God endure grief, suffering wrongfully. 20. For what glory *is it,* if, when ye be buffeted for your faults, ye shall take it patiently? but if, when ye do well, and suffer *for it,* ye take it patiently, this *is* acceptable with God. 21. For even hereunto were ye called: because Christ also suffered for us, leaving us an example, that ye should follow his steps: 22. Who did no sin, neither was guile found in his mouth: 23. Who, when he was reviled, reviled not again; when he suffered, he threatened not; but committed *himself* to him that judgeth righteously: 24. Who his own self bare our sins in his own body on the tree, that we, being dead to sins, should live unto righteousness: by whose stripes ye were healed. 25. For ye were as sheep going astray; but are now returned unto the Shepherd and Bishop of your souls.

1 Pet. 3:8. Finally, *be ye* all of one mind, having compassion one of another, love as brethren, *be* pitiful, *be* courteous: 9. Not rendering evil for evil, or railing for railing: but contrariwise blessing; knowing that ye are thereunto called, that ye should inherit a blessing.

10. For he that will love life, and see good days, let him refrain his tongue from evil, and his lips that they speak no guile: 11. Let him eschew evil, and do good; let him seek peace, and ensue it. 12. For the eyes of the Lord *are* over the righteous, and his ears *are open* unto their prayers: but the face of the Lord *is* against them that do evil.

15. But sanctify the Lord God in your hearts: and *be* ready always to *give* an answer to every man that asketh you a reason of the hope that is in you with meekness and fear: 16. Having a good conscience;

that, whereas they speak evil of you, as of evildoers, they may be ashamed that falsely accuse your good conversation in Christ. 17. For *it is* better, if the will of God be so, that ye suffer for well doing, than for evil doing.

1 Pet. 4:1. Forasmuch then as Christ hath suffered for us in the flesh, arm yourselves likewise with the same mind: for he that hath suffered in the flesh hath ceased from sin; 2. That he no longer should live the rest of *his* time in the flesh to the lusts of men, but to the will of God.

3. For the time past of *our* life may suffice us to have wrought the will of the Gentiles, when we walked in lasciviousness, lusts, excess of wine, revellings, banquetings, and abominable idolatries: 4. Wherein they think it strange that ye run not with *them* to the same excess of riot, speaking evil of *you:* 5. Who shall give account to him that is ready to judge the quick and the dead. 6. For for this cause was the gospel preached also to them that are dead, that they might be judged according to men in the flesh, but live according to God in the spirit.

7. But the end of all things is at hand: be ye therefore sober, and watch unto prayer. 8. And above all things have fervent charity among yourselves: for charity shall cover the multitude of sins.

9. Use hospitality one to another without grudging. 10. As every man hath received the gift, *even so* minister the same one to another, as good stewards of the manifold grace of God.

11. If any man speak, *let him speak* as the oracles of God; if any man minister, *let him do it* as of the ability which God giveth: that God in all things may be glorified through Jesus Christ, to whom be praise and dominion for ever and ever. Amen.

12. Beloved, think it not strange concerning the fiery trial which is to try you, as though some strange thing happened unto you: 13. But rejoice, inasmuch as ye are partakers of Christ's sufferings; that, when his glory shall be revealed, ye may be glad also with exceeding joy.

14. If ye be reproached for the name of Christ, happy *are ye;* for the spirit of glory and of God resteth upon you: ¹ on their part he is evil spoken of, but on your part he is glorified.   [¹ Omitted in R. V.]

15. But let none of you suffer as a murderer, or *as* a thief, or *as* an evildoer, or as a busybody in other men's matters. 16. Yet if *any man suffer* as a Christian, let him not be ashamed; but let him glorify God on this behalf.

1 Pet. 5:1. The elders which are among you I exhort, who am also an elder, and a witness of the sufferings of Christ, and also a partaker of the glory that shall be revealed: 2. Feed the flock of God which is among you, taking the oversight *thereof,* not by constraint, but willingly; not for

filthy lucre, but of a ready mind. 3. Neither as being lords over *God's* heritage, but being ensamples to the flock.

5. Likewise, ye younger, submit yourselves unto the elder. Yea, all *of you* be subject one to another, and be clothed with humility: for God resisteth the proud, and giveth grace to the humble.

6. Humble yourselves therefore under the mighty hand of God, that he may exalt you in due time: 7. Casting all your care upon him; for he careth for you.

8. Be sober, be vigilant; because your adversary the devil, as a roaring lion, walketh about, seeking whom he may devour: 9. Whom resist stedfast in the faith, knowing that the same afflictions are accomplished in your brethren that are in the world.

2 Pet. 1:5. And beside this, giving all diligence, add to your faith virtue; and to virtue knowledge; 6. And to knowledge temperance; and to temperance patience; and to patience godliness; 7. And to godliness brotherly kindness; and to brotherly kindness charity.

10. Wherefore the rather, brethren, give diligence to make your calling and election sure: for if ye do these things, ye shall never fall:

2 Pet. 3:14. Wherefore, beloved, seeing that ye look for such things, be diligent that ye may be found of him in peace, without spot, and blameless.

18. But grow in grace, and *in* the knowledge of our Lord and Saviour Jesus Christ.

1 John 2:15. Love not the world, neither the things *that are* in the world. If any man love the world, the love of the Father is not in him.

28. And now, little children, abide in him; that, when he shall appear, we may have confidence, and not be ashamed before him at his coming.

1 John 3:10. In this the children of God are manifest, and the children of the devil: whosoever doeth not righteousness is not of God, neither he that loveth not his brother. 11. For this is the message that ye heard from the beginning, that we should love one another. 12. Not as Cain, *who* was of that wicked one, and slew his brother. And wherefore slew he him? Because his own works were evil, and his brother's righteous.

13. Marvel not, my brethren, if the world hate you.

14. We know that we have passed from death unto life, because we love the brethren. He that loveth not *his* brother abideth in death. 15. Whosoever hateth his brother is a murderer: and ye know that no murderer hath eternal life abiding in him. 16. Hereby perceive we ¹ the love ¹ *of God,* because he laid down his life for us: and we ought to lay down *our* lives for the brethren.   [¹ Omitted in R. V.]

17. But whoso hath this world's good, and

seeth his brother have need, and shutteth up his bowels *of compassion* from him, how dwelleth the love of God in him? 18. My little children, let us not love in word, neither in tongue; but in deed and in truth. 19. And hereby we know that we are of the truth, and shall assure our hearts before him. 20. For if our heart condemn us, God is greater than our heart, and knoweth all things. 21. Beloved, if our heart condemn us not, *then* have we confidence toward God.

22. And whatsoever we ask, we receive of him, because we keep his commandments, and do those things that are pleasing in his sight.

23. And this is his commandment, That we should believe on the name of his Son Jesus Christ, and love one another, as he gave us commandment.

1 John 4:1. Beloved, believe not every spirit, but try the spirits whether they are of God: because many false prophets are gone out into the world.

7. Beloved, let us love one another: for love is of God; and every one that loveth is born of God, and knoweth God. 8. He that loveth not knoweth not God; for God is love.

11. Beloved, if God so loved us, we ought also to love one another.

12. If we love one another, God dwelleth in us, and his love is perfected in us.

15. Whosoever shall confess that Jesus is the Son of God, God dwelleth in him, and he in God.

16. And we have known and believed the love that God hath to us. God is love; and he that dwelleth in love dwelleth in God, and God in him.

21. And this commandment have we from him, That he who loveth God love his brother also.

1 John 5:21. Little children, keep yourselves from idols.

2 John 5. And now I beseech thee, lady, not as though I wrote a new commandment unto thee, but that which we had from the beginning, that we love one another.

6. And this is love, that we walk after his commandments. This is the commandment, That, as ye have heard from the beginning, ye should walk in it.

3 John 11. Beloved, follow not that which is evil, but that which is good. He that doeth good is of God: but he that doeth evil hath not seen God.

Jude 3. Beloved, when I gave all diligence to write unto you of the common salvation, it was needful for me to write unto you, and exhort *you* that ye should earnestly contend for the faith which was once delivered unto the saints. 4. For there are certain men crept in unawares, who were before of old ordained to this condemnation, ungodly men, turning the grace of our God into lasciviousness, and denying the only Lord God, and our Lord Jesus Christ.

20. But ye, beloved, building up yourselves on your most holy faith, praying in the Holy Ghost, 21. Keep yourselves in the love of God, looking for the mercy of our Lord Jesus Christ unto eternal life.

22. And of some have compassion, making a difference: 23. And others save with fear, pulling *them* out of the fire; hating even the garment spotted by the flesh.

Rev. 3:11. Behold, I come quickly: hold that fast which thou hast, that no man take thy crown. 18. I counsel thee to buy of me gold tried in the fire, that thou mayest be rich; and white raiment, that thou mayest be clothed, and *that* the shame of thy nakedness do not appear; and anoint thine eyes with eyesalve, that thou mayest see. 19. As many as I love, I rebuke and chasten: be zealous therefore, and repent.

Rev. 22:17. And the Spirit and the bride say, Come. And let him that heareth say, Come. And let him that is athirst come. And whosoever will, let him take the water of life freely.

See ADULTERY; CHILDREN; CITIZEN; HOMICIDE; INSTRUCTION; MINISTERS; OBEDIENCE, ENJOINED; SERVANTS; THEFT; WIFE; WOMAN and other topics.

OF MEN: Isa. 29:13. Wherefore the Lord said, Forasmuch as this people draw near *me* with their mouth, and with their lips do honour me, but have removed their heart far from me, and their fear toward me is taught by the precept of men:

Matt. 15:2. Why do thy disciples transgress the tradition of the elders? for they wash not their hands when they eat bread. 3. But he answered and said unto them, Why do ye also transgress the commandment of God by your tradition? 4. For God commanded, saying, Honour thy father and mother: and, He that curseth father or mother, let him die the death. 5. But ye say, Whosoever shall say to *his* father or *his* mother, *It is* a gift, by whatsoever thou mightest be profited by me; 6. And honour not his father or his mother, *he shall be free.* Thus have ye made the commandment of God of none effect by your tradition. 7. *Ye* hypocrites, well did Esaias prophesy of you, saying, 8. This people draweth nigh unto me with their mouth, and honoureth me with *their* lips; but their heart is far from me. 9. But in vain they do worship me, teaching *for* doctrines the commandments of men. 10. And he called the multitude, and said unto them, Hear, and understand: 11. Not that which goeth into the mouth defileth a man; but that which cometh out of the mouth, this defileth a man. 12. Then came his disciples, and said unto him, Knowest thou that the Pharisees were offended, after they heard this saying? 13. But he answered and said, Every plant, which my heavenly Father hath not planted, shall be rooted up. 14. Let them alone: they be blind leaders of the blind. And if the blind lead the blind, both shall fall into the ditch. 15. Then answered Peter and said unto him, Declare unto us this parable. 16. And Jesus said, Are ye also yet without understanding? 17. Do not ye yet understand, that whatsoever entereth in at the mouth goeth into the belly, and is cast out into the draught? 18. But those things which proceed out of the mouth come forth from the heart; and they defile the man. 19. For out of the heart proceed evil thoughts, murders, adulteries, fornications, thefts, false witness, blasphemies: 20. These are *the things* which defile a man: but to eat with unwashen hands defileth not a man. Mark 7:2-23.

Rom. 14:1. Him that is weak in the faith receive ye, *but* not to doubtful disputations. 2. For one believeth that he may eat all things: another, who is weak, eateth herbs. 3. Let not him that eateth despise him that eateth not; and let not him which eateth not judge him that eateth: for God hath received him. 4. Who art thou that judgest another man's servant? to his own master he standeth or falleth. Yea, he shall be holden up: for God is able to make him stand. 5. One man esteemeth one day above another: another esteemeth every day *alike.* Let every man be fully persuaded in his own mind. 6. He that regardeth the day, regardeth *it* unto the Lord: and he that regardeth not the day, to the Lord he doth not regard *it.* He that eateth, eateth to the Lord, for he giveth God thanks; and he that eateth not, to the Lord he eateth not, and giveth God thanks. 10. But why dost thou judge thy brother? or why dost thou set at nought thy brother? for we shall all stand before the judgment seat of Christ. 11. For it is written, *As* I live, saith the Lord, every knee shall bow to me, and every tongue shall confess to God. 12. So then every one of us shall give account of himself to God. 13. Let us not therefore judge one another any more: but judge this rather, that no man put a stumblingblock or an occasion to fall in *his* brother's way. 14. I know, and am persuaded by the Lord Jesus, that *there is* nothing unclean of itself: but to him that esteemeth any thing to be unclean, to him *it is* unclean. 15. But if thy brother be grieved with *thy* meat, now walkest thou not charitably. Destroy not him with thy meat, for whom Christ died. 16. Let not then your good be evil spoken of: 17. For the kingdom of God is not meat and drink; but righteousness, and peace, and joy in the Holy Ghost. 18. For he that in these things serveth Christ *is* acceptable to God, and approved of men. 19. Let us therefore follow after the things which make for peace, and things wherewith one may edify another. 20. For meat destroy not the work of God. All things indeed *are* pure: but *it is* evil for that man who eateth with offence. 21. *It is* good neither to eat flesh, nor to drink wine, nor *any thing*

whereby thy brother stumbleth, or is offended, or is made weak. 22. Hast thou faith? have *it* to thyself before God. Happy *is* he that condemneth not himself in that thing which he alloweth. 23. And he that doubteth is damned if he eat, because *he eateth* not of faith: for whatsoever *is* not of faith is sin.

1 Tim. 4:1. Now the Spirit speaketh expressly, that in the latter times some shall depart from the faith, giving heed to seducing spirits, and doctrines of devils; 2. Speaking lies in hypocrisy; having their conscience seared with a hot iron; 3. Forbidding to marry, *and commanding* to abstain from meats, which God hath created to be received with thanksgiving of them which believe and know the truth.

COMMERCE. Laws concerning, Lev. 19:36,37; 25:14,17. Carried on by means of caravans, Gen. 37:25,27; Isa. 60:6; ships, 1 Kin. 9:27,28; 10:11; 22:48; Psa. 107:23-30; Prov. 31:14; Rev. 18:19. Conducted in fairs, Ezek. 27:12,19; Matt. 11:16. Of the Arabians, Isa. 60:6; Jer. 6:20; Ezek. 27:21-24; Egyptians, Gen. 42:2-34; Ethiopians, Isa. 45:14; Ishmaelites, Gen. 37:27,28; Israelites, 1 Kin. 9: 26-28; Neh. 3:31-32; Ezek. 27:17; Ninevites, Nah. 3:16; Syrians, Ezek. 27:16,18; Tyrians, 2 Sam. 5:11; 1 Kin. 5:6; Isa. 23:8; Ezek. 27: 28:5; Zidonians, Isa. 23:2; Ezek. 27:8; Babylonians, Rev. 18:3,11-13; Jews, Ezek. 27:17 From Tarshish, Jer. 10:9; Ezek. 27:25.

Evil practices connected with, Prov. 29:14; Ezek. 22:13; Hos. 12:7.

Articles of: Apes, 1 Kin. 10:22; balm, Gen. 37:25; blue cloth, Ezek. 27:24; brass, Ezek. 27:13; Rev. 18:12; cinnamon, Rev. 18:13; corn, 1 Kin. 5:11; Ezek. 27:17; cattle, Ezek. 27:21; chest of rich apparel, Ezek. 27:24; chariots, 1 Kin. 10:29; Rev. 18:13; clothes for chariots, Ezek. 27:20; embroidery, Ezek. 27:16,24; frankincense, Jer. 6:20; Rev. 18:13; gold, 1 Kin. 9:28; 10:22; 2 Chr. 8:18; Isa. 60:6; Rev. 18:12; honey, Ezek. 27:17; horses, 1 Kin. 10: 29; Ezek. 27:14; Rev. 18:13; ivory, 1 Kin. 10: 22; 2 Chr. 9:21; Ezek. 27:15; Rev. 18:12; iron and steel, Ezek. 27:12,19; land, Gen. 23:13-16; Ruth, 4:3; lead, Ezek. 27:12; linen, 1 Kin. 10: 28; Rev. 18:12; oil, 1 Kin. 5:11; Ezek. 27:17; pearls, Rev. 18:12; peacocks, 1 Kin. 10:22; perfumes, Song 3:6; precious stones, Ezek. 27:16,22; 28:13,16; Rev. 18:12; purple, Ezek. 27:16; Rev. 18:12; sheep, Rev. 18:13; slaves, Gen. 37:28,36; Deut. 24:7; silk, Rev. 18:12; silver, 1 Kin. 10:22; 2 Chr. 9:21; Rev. 18:12; sweet cane, Jer. 6:20; thyine wood, Rev. 18: 12; timber, 1 Kin. 5:6,8; tin, Ezek. 27:12; wheat, Rev. 18:13; white wool, Ezek. 27:18; wine, 2 Chr. 2:15; Ezek. 27:18; Rev. 18:13; bodies and souls of men, Rev. 18:13.

Transportation of passengers, Jonah 1:3; Acts 21:2; 27:2,6,37.

See MERCHANT; TARSHISH; TRADE; TRAFFIC.

COMMISSARY. For armies, cattle driven with, 2 Kin. 3:9. See ARMIES. For royal households, 1 Kin. 4:7-19,27,28.

COMMONWEALTH. FIGURATIVE:
Phil. 3:20 [*R. V.* marg.].

COMMUNION. WITH GOD: Psa. 16:7.
I will bless the LORD, who hath given me
counsel: my reins also instruct me in the
night seasons.

John 14:16. And I will pray the Father,
and he shall give you another Comforter,
that he may abide with you for ever; 17.
Even the Spirit of truth; whom the world
cannot receive, because it seeth him not,
neither knoweth him: but ye know him; for
he dwelleth with you, and shall be in you.
18. I will not leave you comfortless: I will
come to you. 23. Jesus answered and said
unto him, If a man love me, he will keep my
words: and my Father will love him, and
we will come unto him, and make our abode
with him.

1 Cor. 10:16. The cup of blessing which we
bless, is it not the communion of the blood of
Christ? The bread which we break, is it not
the communion of the body of Christ?

2 Cor. 6:16. And what agreement hath the
temple of God with idols? for ye are the
temple of the living God; as God hath said,
I will dwell in them, and walk in *them;* and
I will be their God, and they shall be my
people.

2 Cor. 13:14. The grace of the Lord Jesus
Christ, and the love of God, and the com-
munion of the Holy Ghost, *be* with you all.
Amen.

Gal. 4:6. And because ye are sons, God
hath sent forth the Spirit of his Son into
your hearts, crying, Abba, Father.

Phil. 2:1. If *there be* therefore any consolation in Christ, if any comfort of love, if
any fellowship of the Spirit, if any bowels
and mercies, 2. Fulfil ye my joy, that ye be
likeminded, having the same love, *being* of
one accord, of one mind.

1 John 1:3. Truly our fellowship *is* with
the Father, and with his Son Jesus Christ.

Rev. 3:20. Behold, I stand at the door, and
knock: if any man hear my voice, and open
the door, I will come in to him, and will sup
with him, and he with me.

See FELLOWSHIP.

INSTANCES OF: Enoch, Gen. 5:22,24.
Noah, Gen. 6:9,13–22; 8:15–17. Abraham,
Gen. 12:1–3,7; 17:1,2; 18:1–33; 22:1,2,11,12,16–
18. Hagar, Gen.16:8–12. Isaac,Gen.26:2,24.
Isaac, in dreams, Gen. 28:13,15; 31:3; 35:1,7;
46:2–4. Moses, Ex. 3; 4:1–17; 33:9,11; 34:28;
Num. 12:8. Joshua, Josh.1:1–9; 6:2–5; 7:10–15;
8:1,2; 20:1–6. Gideon, Judg. 6:11–24. Solomon,
1 Kin. 3:5–14; 2 Chr. 1:7–12.

OF SAINTS: 1 Sam. 23:16. And Jonathan
Saul's son arose, and went to David into the
wood, and strengthened his hand in God.

Psa. 55:14. We took sweet counsel together,
and walked unto the house of God in company.

Psa. 119:63. I *am* a companion of all *them*
that fear thee, and of them that keep thy
precepts.

Psa. 133:1. Behold, how good and how
pleasant *it is* for brethren to dwell together
in unity! 2. *It is* like the precious ointment
upon the head, that ran down upon the
beard, *even* Aaron's beard: that went down
to the skirts of his garments; 3. As the dew
of Hermon, *and as the dew* that descended
upon the mountains of Zion: for there the
LORD commanded the blessing, *even* life for
evermore.

Amos 3:3. Can two walk together, except
they be agreed?

Mal. 3:16. They that feared the LORD spake
often one to another: and the LORD hearkened, and heard *it,* and a book of remembrance was written before him for them that
feared the LORD, and that thought upon his
name.

Luke 22:32. When thou art converted,
strengthen thy brethren.

Luke 24:32. They said one to another, Did
not our heart burn within us, while he talked
with us by the way, and while he opened to
us the scriptures? *v.* 17.

John 17:20. Neither pray I for these alone,
but for them also which shall believe on me
through their word; 21. That they all may
be one; as thou, Father, *art* in me, and I
in thee, that they also may be one in us:
that the world may believe that thou hast
sent me.

Acts 2:42. They continued stedfastly in
the apostles' doctrine and fellowship, and in
breaking of bread, and in prayers.

Rom. 12:15. Rejoice with them that do rejoice, and weep with them that weep.

1 Cor. 10:16. The cup of blessing which we
bless, is it not the communion of the blood of
Christ? The bread which we break, is it not
the communion of the body of Christ? 17.
For we *being* many are one bread, *and* one
body: for we are all partakers of that one
bread.

1 Cor. 12:12. For as the body is one, and
hath many members, and all the members
of that one body, being many, are one body:
so also *is* Christ. 13. For by one Spirit are
we all baptized into one body, whether *we be*
Jews or Gentiles, whether *we be* bond or
free; and have been all made to drink into
one Spirit.

2 Cor. 6:14. Be ye not unequally yoked together with unbelievers: for what fellowship
hath righteousness with unrighteousness?
and what communion hath light with darkness? 15. And what concord hath Christ
with Belial? or what part hath he that believeth with an infidel? 16. And what agreement hath the temple of God with idols? for
ye are the temple of the living God; as God
hath said, I will dwell in them, and walk in
them; and I will be their God, and they
shall be my people. 17. Wherefore come
out from among them, and be ye separate,
saith the Lord, and touch not the unclean
thing; and I will receive you, 18. And will
be a Father unto you, and ye shall be my
sons and daughters, saith the Lord Almighty.

Eph. 4:1. I therefore, the prisoner of the Lord, beseech you that ye walk worthy of the vocation wherewith ye are called, 2. With all lowliness and meekness, with longsuffering, forbearing one another in love; 3. Endeavouring to keep the unity of the Spirit in the bond of peace.

Eph. 5:11. And have no fellowship with the unfruitful works of darkness, but rather reprove *them*.

Col. 3:16. Teaching and admonishing one another in psalms and hymns and spiritual songs,

1 Thess. 4:18. Comfort one another with these words.

1 Thess. 5:11. Comfort yourselves together, and edify one another, even as also ye do. 14. We exhort you, brethren, warn them that are unruly, comfort the feebleminded, support the weak, be patient toward all *men*.

Heb. 3:13. Exhort one another daily, while it is called To day; lest any of you be hardened through the deceitfulness of sin.

Heb. 10:24. Let us consider one another to provoke unto love and to good works: 25. Not forsaking the assembling of ourselves together, as the manner of some *is;* but exhorting *one another:*

Jas. 5:16. Confess *your* faults one to another, and pray one for another, that ye may be healed.

1 John 1:3. That which we have seen and heard declare we unto you, that ye also may have fellowship with us: 7. If we walk in the light, as he is in the light, we have fellowship one with another, and the blood of Jesus Christ his Son cleanseth us from all sin.

See FELLOWSHIP.

COMMUNISM. Acts 2:44. And all that believed were together, and had all things common; 45. And sold their possessions and goods, and parted them to all *men*, as every man had need.

Acts 4:32. And the multitude of them that believed were of one heart and of one soul: neither said any *of them* that ought of the things which he possessed was his own; but they had all things common. 34. Neither was there any among them that lacked: for as many as were possessors of lands or houses sold them, and brought the prices of the things that were sold. 35. And laid *them* down at the apostles' feet: and distribution was made unto every man according as he had need. 36. And Joses, who by the apostles was surnamed Barnabas, (which is, being interpreted, The son of consolation,) a Levite, *and* of the country of Cyprus, 37. Having land, sold *it*, and brought the money, and laid *it* at the apostles' feet.

Acts 5:1. But a certain man named Ananias, with Sapphira his wife, sold a possession, 2. And kept back *part* of the price, his wife also being privy *to it*, and brought a certain part, and laid *it* at the apostles' feet. 3. But Peter said, Ananias, why hath Satan filled thine heart to lie to the Holy

Ghost, and to keep back *part* of the price of the land? 4. Whiles it remained, was it not thine own? and after it was sold, was it not in thine own power? why hast thou conceived this thing in thine heart? thou hast not lied unto men, but unto God. 5. And Ananias hearing these words fell down, and gave up the ghost: and great fear came on all them that heard these things. 6. And the young men arose, wound him up, and carried *him* out, and buried *him*. 7. And it was about the space of three hours after, when his wife, not knowing what was done, came in. 8. And Peter answered unto her, Tell me whether ye sold the land for so much? And she said, Yea, for so much. 9. Then Peter said unto her, How is it that ye have agreed together to tempt the Spirit of the Lord? behold, the feet of them which have buried thy husband *are* at the door, and shall carry thee out. 10. Then fell she down straightway at his feet, and yielded up the ghost: and the young men came in, and found her dead, and, carrying *her* forth, buried *her* by her husband.

COMPANY, EVIL: Gen. 19:15. And when the morning arose, then the angels hastened Lot, saying, Arise, take thy wife, and thy two daughters, which are here; lest thou be consumed in the iniquity of the city.

Gen. 49:6. Come not thou into their secret; unto their assembly, mine honour, be not thou united: for in their anger they slew a man, and in their selfwill they digged down a wall.

Ex. 23:2. Thou shalt not follow a multitude to *do* evil; 32. Make no covenant with them, nor with their gods. 33. They shall not dwell in thy land, lest they make thee sin against me: for if thou serve their gods, it will surely be a snare unto thee. Ex. 34: 12–15; Deut. 7:2–4; Josh. 23:6–13.

Lev. 18:3. After the doings of the land of Egypt, wherein ye dwelt, shall ye not do: and after the doings of the land of Canaan, whither I bring you, shall ye not do: neither shall ye walk in their ordinances. Lev. 20:23.

Num. 16:26. And he spake unto the congregation, saying, Depart, I pray you, from the tents of these wicked men, and touch nothing of their's, lest ye be consumed in all their sins. *vs.* 21–26.

Num. 33:55. If ye will not drive out the inhabitants of the land from before you; then it shall come to pass, that those which ye let remain of them *shall be* pricks in your eyes, and thorns in your sides, and shall vex you in the land wherein ye dwell. Judg. 2: 1–3.

Deut. 12:30. Take heed to thyself that thou be not snared by following them, after that they be destroyed from before thee; and that thou enquire not after their gods, saying, How did these nations serve their gods? even so will I do likewise.

2 Sam. 23:6. *The sons* of Belial *shall be* all of them as thorns thrust away, because they cannot be taken with hands: 7. But the

man *that* shall touch them must be fenced with iron and the staff of a spear;

2 Chr. 19:2. And Jehu the son of Hanani the seer went out to meet him, and said to king Jehoshaphat, Shouldest thou help the ungodly, and love them that hate the LORD? therefore *is* wrath upon thee from before the LORD.

Ezra 9:14. Should we again break thy commandments, and join in affinity with the people of these abominations? wouldest not thou be angry with us till thou hadst consumed *us*, so that *there should be* no remnant nor escaping?

Psa. 1:1. Blessed *is* the man that walketh not in the counsel of the ungodly, nor standeth in the way of sinners, nor sitteth in the seat of the scornful.

Psa. 6:8. Depart from me, all ye workers of iniquity;

Psa. 15:4. In whose eyes a vile person is contemned;

Psa. 26:4. I have not sat with vain persons, neither will I go in with dissemblers. 5. I have hated the congregation of evildoers; and will not sit with the wicked. 9. Gather not my soul with sinners, nor my life with bloody men:

Psa. 28:3. Draw me not away with the wicked, and with the workers of iniquity, which speak peace to their neighbours, but mischief *is* in their hearts.

Psa. 31:6. I have hated them that regard lying vanities:

Psa. 50:18. When thou sawest a thief, then thou consentedst with him, and hast been partaker with adulterers.

Psa. 84:10. For a day in thy courts *is* better than a thousand. I had rather be a doorkeeper in the house of my God, than to dwell in the tents of wickedness.

Psa. 101:4. A froward heart shall depart from me: I will ¹ not know a wicked *person.* 7. He that worketh deceit shall not dwell within my house: he that telleth lies shall not tarry in my sight.   [¹ R. V. know no evil thing]

Psa. 106:34. They did not destroy the nations, concerning whom the LORD commanded them: 35. But were mingled among the heathen, and learned their works.

Psa. 119:115. Depart from me, ye evildoers: for I will keep the commandments of my God.

Psa. 120:5. Woe is me, that I sojourn in Mesech, *that* I dwell in the tents of Kedar! 6. My soul hath long dwelt with him that hateth peace. 7. I *am for* peace: but when I speak, they *are* for war.

Psa. 139:19. Surely thou wilt slay the wicked, O God: depart from me therefore, ye bloody men. 21. Do not I hate them, O LORD, that hate thee? and am not I grieved with those that rise up against thee? 22. I hate them with perfect hatred: I count them mine enemies.

Psa. 141:4. Incline not my heart to *any* evil thing, to practise wicked works with men that work iniquity: and let me not eat of their dainties.

Prov. 1:10. My son, if sinners entice thee, consent thou not. 11. If they say, Come with us, . . . 14. Cast in thy lot among us; let us all have one purse: 15. My son, walk not thou in the way with them; refrain thy foot from their path:

Prov. 2:11. Discretion shall preserve thee, understanding shall keep thee: 12. To deliver thee from the way of the evil *man*, from the man that speaketh froward things; 16. To deliver thee from the strange woman, *even* from the stranger *which* flattereth with her words; 19. None that go unto her return again, neither take they hold of the paths of life.

Prov. 4:14. Enter not into the path of the wicked, and go not in the way of evil *men*. 15. Avoid it, pass not by it, turn from it, and pass away.

Prov. 5:8. Remove thy way far from her, and come not nigh the door of her house:

Prov. 9:6. Forsake the foolish, and live;

Prov. 12:11. He that followeth vain *persons is* void of understanding. 26. The righteous *is* more excellent than his neighbour: but the way of the wicked seduceth them.

Prov. 13:20. A companion of fools shall be destroyed.

Prov. 14:7. Go from the presence of a foolish man, when thou perceivest not *in him* the lips of knowledge.

Prov. 16:29. A violent man enticeth his neighbour, and leadeth him into the way *that is* not good.

Prov. 17:12. Let a bear robbed of her whelps meet a man, rather than a fool in his folly.

Prov. 20:19. Meddle not with him that flattereth with his lips.

Prov. 22:5. Thorns *and* snares *are* in the way of the froward: he that doth keep his soul shall be far from them. 10. Cast out the scorner, and contention shall go out; 24. Make no friendship with an angry man; and with a furious man thou shalt not go: 25. Lest thou learn his ways, and get a snare to thy soul.

Prov. 23:6. Eat thou not the bread of *him that hath* an evil eye, neither desire thou his dainty meats: 20. Be not among winebibbers; among riotous eaters of flesh:

Prov. 24:1. Be not thou envious against evil men, neither desire to be with them.

Prov. 28:7. He that is a companion of riotous *men* shameth his father. 19. He that followeth after vain *persons* shall have poverty enough.

Prov. 29:16. When the wicked are multiplied, transgression increaseth: 24. Whoso is partner with a thief hateth his own soul: he heareth cursing, and bewrayeth *it* not.

Eccl. 9:18. One sinner destroyeth much good.

Isa. 1:23. Thy princes *are* rebellious, and companions of thieves:

Isa. 6:5. Then said I, Woe *is* me! for I am undone; because I *am* a man of unclean lips, and I dwell in the midst of a people of unclean lips: for mine eyes have seen the King, the LORD of hosts.

Isa. 8:11. For the LORD spake thus to me with a strong hand, and instructed me that I should not walk in the way of this people, saying, 12. Say ye not, A confederacy, to all *them to* whom this people shall say, A confederacy;

Jer. 2:25. Withhold thy foot from being unshod, and thy throat from thirst: but thou saidst, There is no hope: no; for I have loved strangers, and after them will I go.

Jer. 9:2. Oh that I had in the wilderness a lodging place of wayfaring men; that I might leave my people, and go from them! for they *be* all·adulterers, an assembly of treacherous men.

Jer. 15:17. I sat not in the assembly of the mockers, nor rejoiced; I sat alone because of thy hand:

Jer. 51:6. Flee out of the midst of Babylon, and deliver every man his soul: be not cut off in her iniquity; 45. My people, go ye out of the midst of her, and deliver ye every man his soul from the fierce anger of the LORD.

Hos. 4:17. Ephraim *is* joined to idols: let him alone.

Hos. 7:5. In the day of our king the princes have made *him* sick with bottles of wine; he stretched out his hand with scorners. 8. Ephraim, he hath mixed himself among the people; Ephraim is a cake not turned. 9. Strangers have devoured his strength, and he knoweth *it* not:

Mic. 6:16. For the statutes of Omri are kept, and all the works of the house of Ahab, and ye walk in their counsels; that I should make thee a desolation, and the inhabitants thereof an hissing: therefore ye shall bear the reproach of my people.

Matt. 24:12. Because iniquity shall abound, the love of many shall wax cold.

Rom. 16:17. Now I beseech you, brethren, mark them which cause divisions and offences contrary to the doctrine which ye have learned; and avoid them. 18. For they that are such serve not our Lord Jesus Christ, but their own belly; and by good words and fair speeches deceive the hearts of the simple.

1 Cor. 5:6. Know ye not that a little leaven leaveneth the whole lump? 9. I wrote unto you in an epistle not to company with fornicators: 10. Yet not altogether with the fornicators of this world, or with the covetous, or extortioners, or with idolaters; for then must ye needs go out of the world. 11. But now I have written unto you not to keep company, if any man that is called a brother be a fornicator, or covetous, or an idolater or a railer, or a drunkard, or an extortioner; with such an one no not to eat. Gal. 5:9.

1 Cor. 15:33. Be not deceived: evil communications corrupt good manners.

2 Cor. 6:14. Be ye not unequally yoked together with unbelievers: for what fellowship hath righteousness with unrighteousness? and what communion hath light with dark-

ness? 15. And what concord hath Christ with Belial? or what part hath he that believeth with an infidel? 17. Wherefore come out from among them, and be ye separate, saith the Lord, and touch not the unclean *thing;*

Eph. 5:6. Let no man deceive you with vain words: for because of these things cometh the wrath of God upon the children of disobedience. 7. Be not ye therefore partakers with them. 11. Have no fellowship with the unfruitful works of darkness, but rather reprove *them.*

2 Thess. 3:6. Now we command you, brethren, in the name of our Lord Jesus Christ, that ye withdraw yourselves from every brother that walketh disorderly, and not after the tradition which he received of us.

1 Tim 5:22. Lay hands suddenly on no man, neither be partaker of other men's sins: keep thyself pure.

1 Tim. 6:5. Perverse disputings of men of corrupt minds, and destitute of the truth, supposing that [1] gain is godliness: from such withdraw thyself.   [1 R. V. godliness is a way of gain]

2 Tim. 3:4. Traitors, heady, highminded, lovers of pleasures more than lovers of God; 5. Having a form of godliness, but denying the power thereof: from such turn away.

2 Pet. 2:7. And delivered just Lot, vexed with the filthy conversation of the wicked: 8. (For that righteous man dwelling among them, in seeing and hearing, vexed *his* righteous soul from day to day with *their* unlawful deeds;) 18. For when they speak great swelling *words* of vanity, they allure through the lusts of the flesh, *through much* wantonness, those that were clean escaped from them who live in error.

2 John 10. If there come any unto you, and bring not this doctrine, receive him not into *your* house, neither bid him God speed: 11. For he that biddeth him God speed is partaker of his evil deeds.

Rev. 2:2. I know thy works, and thy labour, and thy patience, and how thou canst not bear them which are evil: and thou hast tried them which say they are apostles, and are not, and hast found them liars:

Rev. 18:4. And I heard another voice from heaven, saying, Come out of her, my people, that ye be not partakers of her sins, and that ye receive not of her plagues.

GOOD: Prov. 13:20. He that walketh with wise *men* shall be wise: but a companion of fools shall be destroyed.

See COMMUNION OF SAINTS; EXAMPLE; FELLOWSHIP; INFLUENCE.

COMPASSES, CARPENTER'S: Isa. 44:13.

COMPASSION. OF GOD: See GOD, MERCY OF.

OF CHRIST: See JESUS, COMPASSION OF.

COMPLAINT. See MURMURING.

COMPLICITY. Psa. 50:18. When thou sawest a thief, then thou consentedst with him, and hast been partaker with adulterers.

Prov. 29:24. Whoso is partner with a thief

hateth his own soul: he heareth cursing, and bewrayeth *it* not.

Rom. 1:32. Who knowing the judgment of God, that they which commit such things are worthy of death, not only do the same, but have pleasure in them that do them.

2 John 10. If there come any unto you, and bring not this doctrine, receive him not into *your* house, neither bid him God speed: 11. For he that biddeth him God speed is partaker of his evil deeds.

INSTANCES OF: The daughter of Herodias, in asking for the head of John the Baptist, Matt. 14:8; Mark 6:25. Pilate, in the death of Jesus, Matt. 27:17-26; Mark 15:9-15; Luke 23:13-25; John 19:13-16. Paul, in the stoning of Stephen, Acts 7:58.

See COLLUSION; CONNIVANCE; CONSPIRACY.

COMPROMISE. BEFORE LITIGATION, ENJOINED: Prov. 25:8. Go not forth hastily to strive, lest *thou know not* what to do in the end thereof, when thy neighbour hath put thee to shame. 9. Debate thy cause with thy neighbour *himself;* and discover not a secret to another: 10. Lest he that heareth *it* put thee to shame, and thine infamy turn not away.

Luke 12:58. When thou goest with thine adversary to the magistrate, *as thou art* in the way, give diligence that thou mayest be delivered from him; lest he hale thee to the judge, and the judge deliver thee to the officer, and the officer cast thee into prison. 59. I tell thee, thou shalt not depart thence, till thou hast paid the very last mite. Matt. 5:25,26.

See ADJUDICATION; ARBITRATION; JUSTICE; COURT.

CONCEIT. Prov. 3:5. Trust in the LORD with all thine heart; and lean not unto thine own understanding. 7. Be not wise in thine own eyes:

Prov. 12:15. The way of a fool *is* right in his own eyes: but he that hearkeneth unto counsel *is* wise.

Prov. 23:4. Cease from thine own wisdom.

Prov. 26:5. Answer a fool according to his folly, lest he be wise in his own conceit. 12. Seest thou a man wise in his own conceit? *there is* more hope of a fool than of him. 16. The sluggard *is* wiser in his own conceit than seven men that can render a reason.

Prov. 28:11. The rich man *is* wise in his own conceit; but the poor that hath understanding searcheth him out. 26. He that trusteth in his own heart is a fool:

Isa. 5:21. Woe unto *them that are* wise in their own eyes, and prudent in their own sight!

Jer. 9:23. Thus saith the LORD, Let not the wise *man* glory in his wisdom, neither let the mighty *man* glory in his might, let not the rich *man* glory in his riches:

Luke 18:11. The Pharisee stood and prayed thus with himself, God, I thank thee, that I am not as other men *are*, extortioners, unjust, adulterers, or even as this publican.

12. I fast twice in the week, I give tithes of all that I possess.

Rom. 1:22. Professing themselves to be wise, they became fools,

Rom. 11:25. For I would not, brethren, that ye should be ignorant of this mystery, lest ye should be wise in your own conceits; that blindness in part is happened to Israel, until the fulness of the Gentiles be come in.

Rom. 12:16. Be not wise in your own conceits.

See HYPOCRISY; PRIDE.

CONCEPTION. MIRACULOUS: By Sarah, Gen. 21:1,2; Rebekah, Gen. 25:21; Rachel, Gen. 30:22; Manoah's wife, Judg. 13:3-24; Hannah, 1 Sam. 1:19,20; Elisabeth, Luke 1:24,25,36,37,58; Mary, Matt. 1:18,20; Luke 1:31-35.

CONCISION, a term for circumcision, Phil. 3:2.

CONCUBINAGE. LAWS CONCERNING: Ex. 21:7-11; Lev. 19:20-22; Deut. 21:10-14. Concubines might be dismissed, Gen. 21:9-14. Called WIVES, Gen. 37:2; Judg. 19:3-5. Children of, not heirs, Gen. 15:4; 21:10.

Practiced by Abraham, Gen. 16:3; 25:6; 1 Chr. 1:32; Nahor, Gen. 22:23,24; Jacob, Gen. 30:4; Eliphaz, Gen. 36:12; Gideon, Judg. 8:31; a Levite, Judg. 19:1; Caleb, 1 Chr. 2:46-48; Manasseh, 1 Chr. 7:14; Saul, 2 Sam. 3:7; David, 2 Sam. 5:13; 15:16; Solomon, 1 Kin. 11:3; Rehoboam, 2 Chr. 11:21; Abijah, 2 Chr. 13:21; Belshazzar, Dan. 5:2.

See MARRIAGE; POLYGAMY.

CONCUPISCENCE. See LASCIVIOUSNESS.

CONDEMNATION, SELF. See SELF-CONDEMNATION.

CONDESCENSION OF GOD. In reasoning with his creatures: Sets forth his reasons for sending the flood, Gen. 6:11-13. Enters into covenant with Abraham, Gen. 15:1-21; 18:1-22. Indulges Abraham's intercession for Sodom, Gen. 18:23-33. Warns Abimelech in a dream, Gen. 20:3-7. Reasons with Moses, Ex. 4:2-17. Sends flesh to the Israelites in consequence of their murmuring, Ex. 16:12. Indulges Moses' prayer to behold his glory, Ex. 33:18-23. Indulges Gideon's tests, Judg. 6:36-40. Reasons with Job, Job 38; 39; 40; 41. Invites sinners, saying, "Come now, and let us reason together," Isa. 1:18-20. Expostulates with backsliding Israel, Isa. 41:21-24; 43:1-19; 65:1-16; Jer. 3:1-15; 4:1-31; 7:1-34; Ezek. 18:25-32; 33: 10-20; Hos. 2; Mic. 6:1-9; Mal. 3:7-15.

SCRIPTURES RELATING TO: Psa. 8:4. What is man, that thou art mindful of him? and the son of man, that thou visitest him? 5. For thou hast made him a little lower than [the angels, and hast crowned him with glory and honour. 6. Thou madest him to have dominion over the works of thy hands; thou hast put all *things* under his feet: [1 R. V. God]

Psa. 113:5. Who *is* like unto the LORD our God, who dwelleth on high, 6. Who humbleth *himself* to behold *the things that are* in heaven, and in the earth!

Psa. 144:3. LORD, what *is* man, that thou takest knowledge of him! *or* the son of man, that thou makest account of him!

Isa. 45:11. Thus saith the LORD, the Holy One of Israel, and his Maker, Ask me of things to come concerning my sons, and concerning the work of my hands command ye me.

John 3:16. For God so loved the world, that he gave his only begotten Son, that whosoever believeth in him should not perish, but have everlasting life.

Rom. 5:8. But God commendeth his love toward us, in that, while we were yet sinners, Christ died for us.

Heb. 2:11. For both he that sanctifieth and they who are sanctified *are* all of one: for which cause he is not ashamed to call them brethren,

Heb. 6:17. Wherein God, willing more abundantly to shew unto the heirs of promise the immutability of his counsel, confirmed *it* by an oath: 18. That by two immutable things, in which *it was* impossible for God to lie, we might have a strong consolation, who have fled for refuge to lay hold upon the hope set before us:

1 John 4:10. Herein is love, not that we loved God, but that he loved us, and sent his Son *to be* the propitiation for our sins. 19. We love him, because he first loved us.

CONDOLENCE. INSTANCES OF: David, to Hanun, 2 Sam. 10:2. King of Babylon, to Hezekiah, 2 Kin. 20:12,13. The three friends of, to Job, Job 2:11. Jesus, to Mary and Martha, John 11:23-35.

See AFFLICTION, COMFORT IN; SYMPATHY.

CONEY, Lev. 11:5; Deut. 14:7; Psa. 104: 18; Prov. 30:26.

CONFECTIONER, 1 Sam. 8:13.

CONFEDERACIES. INSTANCES OF: Of kings, Gen. 14:1,2; Josh. 10:1-5; 11:1-5; 1 Kin. 20:1.

See ALLIANCES.

CONFESSION. OF CHRIST: Matt. 7: 21. Not every one that saith unto me, Lord, Lord, shall enter into the kingdom of heaven; but he that doeth the will of my Father which is in heaven. 22. Many will say to me in that day, Lord, Lord, have we not prophesied in thy name? and in thy name have cast out devils? and in thy name done many wonderful works? 23. And then will I profess unto them, I never knew you: depart from me, ye that work iniquity.

Matt. 10:32. Whosoever therefore shall confess me before men, him will I confess also before my Father which is in heaven. 33. But whosoever shall deny me before men, him will I also deny before my Father which is in heaven. Luke 12:8.

John 1:15. John bare witness of him, and cried, saying, This was he of whom I spake, He that cometh after me is preferred before

me: for he was before me. 16. And of his fulness have all we received, and grace for grace. 17. For the law was given by Moses, *but* grace and truth came by Jesus Christ. 18. No man hath seen God at any time; the only begotten Son, which is in the bosom of the Father, he hath declared *him*. Matt. 3:11.

John 9:22. These *words* spake his parents, because they feared the Jews: for the Jews had agreed already, that if any man did confess that he was Christ, he should be put out of the synagogue. 23. Therefore said his parents, He is of age; ask him. 24. Then again called they the man that was blind, and said unto him, Give God the praise: we know that this man is a sinner. 25. He answered and said, Whether he be a sinner *or no*, I know not: one thing I know, that, whereas I was blind, now I see. 26. Then said they to him again, What did he to thee? how opened he thine eyes? 27. He answered them, I have told you already, and ye did not hear: wherefore would ye hear *it* again? will ye also be his disciples? 28. Then they reviled him, and said, Thou art his disciple; but we are Moses' disciples. 29. We know that God spake unto Moses: *as for* this *fellow*, we know not from whence he is. 30. The man answered and said unto them, Why herein is a marvellous thing, that ye know not from whence he is, and *yet* he hath opened mine eyes. 31. Now we know that God heareth not sinners: but if any man be a worshipper of God, and doeth his will, him he heareth. 32. Since the world began was it not heard that any man opened the eyes of one that was born blind. 33. If this man were not of God, he could do nothing. 34. They answered and said unto him, Thou wast altogether born in sins, and dost thou teach us? And they cast him out. 35. Jesus heard that they had cast him out; and when he had found him, he said unto him, Dost thou believe on the Son of God? 36. He answered and said, Who is he, Lord, that I might believe on him? 37. And Jesus said unto him, Thou hast both seen him, and it is he that talketh with thee. 38. And he said, Lord, I believe. And he worshipped him.

John 12:42. Nevertheless among the chief rulers also many believed on him; but because of the Pharisees they did not confess *him*, lest they should be put out of the synagogue: 43. For they loved the praise of men more than the praise of God.

Acts 8:35. Then Philip opened his mouth, and began at the same scripture, and preached unto him Jesus. 36. And as they went on *their* way, they came unto a certain water: and the eunuch said, See, *here is* water; what doth hinder me to be baptized? [1] 37. And Philip said, If thou believest with all thine heart, thou mayest. And he answered and said, I believe that Jesus Christ is the Son of God.

[1] Omitted in R. V.

Acts 18:5. And when Silas and Timotheus

were come from Macedonia, Paul was pressed in the spirit, and testified to the Jews that Jesus was Christ.

Acts 19:4. Then said Paul, John verily baptized with the baptism of repentance, saying unto the people, that they should believe on him which should come after him, that is, on Christ Jesus. 5. When they heard this, they were baptized in the name of the Lord Jesus.

Rom. 10:9. That if thou shalt confess with thy mouth the Lord Jesus, and shalt believe in thine heart that God hath raised him from the dead, thou shalt be saved. 10. For with the heart man believeth unto righteousness; and with the mouth confession is made unto salvation. 11. For the scripture saith, Whosoever believeth on him shall not be ashamed.

1 Cor. 12:3. Wherefore I give you to understand, that no man speaking by the Spirit of God calleth Jesus accursed: and that no man can say that Jesus is the Lord, but by the Holy Ghost.

1 John 1:6. If we say that we have fellowship with him, and walk in darkness, we lie, and do not the truth:

1 John 2:4. He that saith, I know him, and keepeth not his commandments, is a liar, and the truth is not in him.

1 John 4:2. Hereby know ye the Spirit of God: Every spirit that confesseth that Jesus Christ is come in the flesh is of God: 3. And every spirit that confesseth not ¹ that Jesus ¹ Christ is come in the flesh is not of God: and this is that spirit of antichrist whereof ye have heard that it should come; and even now already is it in the world.   [¹ Omitted in R. V.]

15. Whosoever shall confess that Jesus is the Son of God, God dwelleth in him, and he in God.

See TESTIMONY, RELIGIOUS.

OF SIN: See SIN, CONFESSION OF.

CONFIDENCE. BETRAYED: INSTANCES OF: Joshua, by the Gibeonites, Josh. 9:3-15. Eglon, by Ehud, Judg. 3:15-23. A himelech, by David, 1 Sam. 21:1-9. Abner, by Joab, 2 Sam. 3:27. Amasa, by Joab, 2 Sam. 20:9,10. The worshipers of Baal, by Jehu, 2 Kin. 10:18-28.

See BETRAYAL.

FALSE: Deut. 29:18. Lest there should be among you man, or woman, or family, or tribe, whose heart turneth away this day from the LORD our God, to go and serve the gods of these nations: lest there should be among you a root that beareth gall and wormwood; 19. And it come to pass, when he heareth the words of this curse, that he bless himself in his heart, saying, I shall have peace, though I walk in the imagination of mine heart, to add drunkenness to thirst:

1 Kin. 20:11. Let not him that girdeth on his harness boast himself as he that putteth it off.

2 Kin. 18:21. Thou trustest upon the staff of this bruised reed, even upon Egypt, on which if a man lean, it will go into his hand, and pierce it: Isa. 36:6.

Job 11:20. Their hope shall be as the giving up of the ghost.

Job 15:31. Let not him that is deceived trust in vanity: for vanity shall be his recompence.

Job 29:18. I said, I shall die in my nest, and I shall multiply my days as the sand.

Psa. 10:6. He hath said in his heart, I shall not be moved: for I shall never be in adversity.

Psa. 20:7. Some trust in chariots, and some in horses: but we will remember the name of the LORD our God. 8. They are brought down and fallen: but we are risen, and stand upright.

Psa. 30:6. In my prosperity I said, I shall never be moved.

Psa. 33:16. There is no king saved by the multitude of an host: a mighty man is not delivered by much strength. 17. An horse is a vain thing for safety: neither shall he deliver any by his great strength.

Psa. 36:2. He flattereth himself in his own eyes, until his iniquity be found to be hateful.

Psa. 44:6. I will not trust in my bow, neither shall my sword save me.

Psa. 49:6. They that trust in their wealth, and boast themselves in the multitude of their riches; 7. None of them can by any means redeem his brother, nor give to God a ransom for him:

Psa. 52:7. Lo, this is the man that made not God his strength; but trusted in the abundance of his riches, and strengthened himself in his wickedness.

Psa. 60:11. Give us help from trouble: for vain is the help of man. Psa. 108:12.

Prov. 14:16. A wise man feareth, and departeth from evil: but the fool rageth, and is confident.

Prov. 16:25. There is a way that seemeth right unto a man, but the end thereof are the ways of death.

Prov. 18:11. The rich man's wealth is his strong city, and as an high wall in his own conceit.

Prov. 23:4. Cease from thine own wisdom.

Prov. 26:12. Seest thou a man wise in his own conceit? there is more hope of a fool than of him.

Prov. 28:26. He that trusteth in his own heart is a fool:

Prov. 29:26. Many seek the ruler's favour: but every man's judgment cometh from the LORD.

Isa. 2:22. Cease ye from man, whose breath is in his nostrils: for wherein is he to be accounted of?

Isa. 5:21. Woe unto them that are wise in their own eyes, and prudent in their own sight!

Isa. 8:12. Say ye not, A confederacy, to all them to whom this people shall say, A confederacy;

Isa. 9:9. And all the people shall know, even Ephraim and the inhabitant of Samaria, that say in the pride and stoutness of heart, 10. The bricks are fallen down, but we will build with hewn stones: the sycomores are cut down, but we will change *them into* cedars.

Isa. 22:11. Ye made also a ditch between the two walls for the water of the old pool: but ye have not looked unto the maker thereof, neither had respect unto him that fashioned it long ago.

Isa. 28:15. We have made a covenant with death, and with hell are we at agreement; when the overflowing scourge shall pass through, it shall not come unto us: for we have made lies our refuge, and under falsehood have we hid ourselves:

18. Your covenant with death shall be disannulled, and your agreement with hell shall not stand; when the overflowing scourge shall pass through, then ye shall be trodden down by it.

Isa. 30:1. Woe to the rebellious children, saith the LORD, that take counsel, but not of me; and that cover with a covering, but not of my spirit, that they may add sin to sin: 2. That walk to go down into Egypt, and have not asked at my mouth;

5. They were all ashamed of a people *that* could not profit them, nor be an help nor profit, but a shame, and also a reproach. 7. For the Egyptians shall help in vain, and to no purpose: therefore have I cried concerning this. Their strength *is* to sit still. Isa. 20:5.

10. Which say to the seers, See not; and to the prophets, Prophesy not unto us right things, speak unto us smooth things, prophesy deceits: 15. For thus saith the Lord GOD, the Holy One of Israel: In returning and rest shall ye be saved; in quietness and in confidence shall be your strength: and ye would not. 16. But ye said, No; for we will flee upon horses; therefore shall ye flee: and, We will ride upon the swift; therefore shall they that pursue you be swift.

Isa. 31:1. Woe to them that go down to Egypt for help; and stay on horses, and trust in chariots, because *they are* many; and in horsemen, because they are very strong; but they look not unto the Holy One of Israel, neither seek the LORD! 3. Now the Egyptians *are* men, and not God; and their horses flesh, and not spirit. When the LORD shall stretch out his hand, both he that helpeth shall fall, and he that is holpen shall fall down, and they all shall fail together.

Isa. 47:7. And thou saidst, I shall be a lady for ever: *so* that thou didst not lay these *things* to thy heart, neither didst remember the latter end of it.

8. Therefore hear now this, *thou that art* given to pleasures, that dwellest carelessly, that sayest in thine heart, I *am*, and none else beside me; I shall not sit *as* a widow, neither shall I know the loss of children: 10. Thou hast trusted in thy wickedness: thou hast said, None seeth me. Thy wisdom and thy knowledge, it hath perverted thee;

Isa. 56:12. Come ye, *say they,* I will fetch wine, and we will fill ourselves with strong drink; and to morrow shall be as this day, *and* much more abundant.

Isa. 57:13. When thou criest, let thy companies deliver thee; but the wind shall carry them all away; vanity shall take *them:* but he that putteth his trust in me shall possess the land, and shall inherit my holy mountain;

Jer. 2:13. For my people have committed two evils; they have forsaken me the fountain of living waters, *and* hewed them out cisterns, broken cisterns, that can hold no water.

18. What hast thou to do in the way of Egypt, to drink the waters of Sihor? or what hast thou to do in the way of Assyria, to drink the waters of the river? 22. For though thou wash thee with nitre [lye, *R. V.*], and take thee much sope, *yet* thine iniquity is marked before me, saith the Lord GOD. 23. How canst thou say, I am not polluted, I have not gone after Baalim? see thy way in the valley, know what thou hast done: *thou art* a swift dromedary traversing her ways; 37. The Lord hath rejected thy confidences, and thou shalt not prosper in them.

Jer. 3:23. In vain *is salvation hoped for* from the hills, *and from* the multitude of mountains:

Jer. 5:17. They shall impoverish thy fenced cities, wherein thou trustedst, with the sword.

Jer. 6:14. They have healed also the hurt *of the daughter* of my people slightly, saying, Peace, peace; when *there is* no peace. Jer. 8:11.

Jer. 7:8. Behold, ye trust in lying words, that cannot profit.

Jer. 12:5. *If* in the land of peace, *wherein* thou trustedst, *they wearied thee,* then how wilt thou do in the swelling of Jordan?

Jer. 14:13. Then said I, Ah, Lord GOD! behold, the prophets say unto them, Ye shall not see the sword, neither shall ye have famine; but I will give you assured peace

Jer. 17:5. Thus saith the LORD: Cursed *be* the man that trusteth in man, and maketh flesh his arm, and whose heart departeth from the LORD.

Jer. 21:13. Behold, I *am* against thee, O inhabitant of the valley, *and* rock of the plain, saith the LORD; which say, Who shall come down against us? or who shall enter into our habitations?

Jer. 23:17. They say unto every one that walketh after the imagination of his own heart, No evil shall come upon you.

Jer. 48:7. Because thou hast trusted in thy works and in thy treasures, thou shalt also be taken: 11. Moab hath been at ease from his youth, and he hath settled on his lees.

Jer. 49:4. Wherefore gloriest thou in the valleys, thy flowing valley, O backsliding daughter? that trusted in her treasures, *saying,* Who shall come unto me? 5. Behold, I will bring a fear upon thee, saith the Lord GOD of hosts, from all those that be about thee; and ye shall be driven out every man right forth; and none shall gather up him that wandereth.

Lam. 4:17. As for us, our eyes as yet failed for our vain help: in our watching we have watched for a nation *that* could not save *us*.

Ezek. 8:12. Then said he unto me, Son of man, hast thou seen what the ancients of the house of Israel do in the dark, every man in the chambers of his imagery? for they say, The LORD seeth us not; the LORD hath forsaken the earth.

Ezek. 13:10. They have seduced my people, saying, Peace; and *there was* no peace; and one built up a wall, and, lo, others daubed it with untempered *morter :* 11. There shall be an overflowing shower; and ye, O great hailstones, shall fall; and a stormy wind shall rend *it*.

Ezek. 29:6. And all the inhabitants of Egypt shall know that I *am* the LORD, because they have been a staff of reed to the house of Israel. 7. When they took hold of thee by thy hand, thou didst break, and rend all their shoulder: and when they leaned upon thee, thou breakest, and madest all their loins to be at a stand.

Ezek. 30:8. And they shall know that I *am* the LORD, when I have set a fire in Egypt, and *when* all her helpers shall be destroyed.

Hos. 5:13. Then went Ephraim to the Assyrian, and sent to king Jareb: yet could he not heal you, nor cure you of your wound.

Hos. 7:9. Strangers have devoured his strength, and he knoweth *it* not: yea, gray hairs are here and there upon him, yet he knoweth not. 11. Ephraim also is like a silly dove without heart: they call to Egypt, they go to Assyria. *vs.* 11–16.

Hos. 10:13. Ye have eaten the fruit of lies: because thou didst trust in thy way, in the multitude of thy mighty men.

Hos. 12:1. Ephraim feedeth on wind, and followeth after the east wind: he daily increaseth lies and desolation;

Hos. 14:3. Asshur shall not save us; we will not ride upon horses: neither will we say any more to the work of our hands, Ye *are* our gods:

Amos 6:1. Woe to them *that are* at ease in Zion, and trust in the mountain of Samaria. 3. Ye that put far away the evil day, and cause the seat of violence to come near; [*vs.* 1–7.] 13. Ye which rejoice in a thing of nought, which say, Have we not taken to us horns by our own strength?

Amos 9:10. All the sinners of my people shall die by the sword, which say, The evil shall not overtake nor prevent us.

Obad. 3. The pride of thine heart hath deceived thee, thou that dwellest in the clefts of the rock, whose habitation *is* high; that saith in his heart, Who shall bring me down to the ground?

Mic. 3:11. The heads thereof judge for reward, and the priests thereof teach for hire, and the prophets thereof divine for money: yet will they lean upon the LORD, and say,

Is not the LORD among us? none evil can come upon us.

Zeph. 1:12. And it shall come to pass at that time, *that* I will search Jerusalem with candles, and punish the men that are settled on their lees: that say in their heart, The LORD will not do good, neither will he do evil.

Zeph. 2:15. This *is* the rejoicing city that dwelt carelessly, that said in her heart, I *am*, and *there is* none beside me: how is she become a desolation, a place for beasts to lie down in! every one that passeth by her shall hiss, *and* wag his hand.

Zech. 4:6. Then he answered and spake unto me, saying, This *is* the word of the LORD unto Zerubbabel, saying, Not by might, nor by power, but by my spirit, saith the LORD of hosts.

Matt. 25:5. While the bridegroom tarried, they all slumbered and slept.

Mark 10:24. But Jesus answereth again, and saith unto them, Children, how hard is it for them that trust in riches to enter into the kingdom of God!

Mark 14:29. But Peter said unto him, Although all shall be offended, yet *will* not I. 30. And Jesus saith unto him, Verily I say unto thee, That this day, *even* in this night, before the cock crow twice, thou shalt deny me thrice. 31. But he spake the more vehemently, If I should die with thee, I will not deny thee in any wise. Likewise also said they all. Matt. 26:33–35; Luke 22:33, 34; John 13:37, 38.

Luke 11:35. Take heed therefore that the light which is in thee be not darkness.

Luke 12:19. I will say to my soul, Soul, thou hast much goods laid up for many years; take thine ease, eat, drink, *and* be merry. 20. But God said unto him, Thou fool, this night thy soul shall be required of thee:

Luke 17:26. And as it was in the days of Noe, so shall it be also in the days of the Son of man. 27. They did eat, they drank, they married wives, they were given in marriage, until the day that Noe entered into the ark, and the flood came, and destroyed them all. 28. Likewise also as it was in the days of Lot; they did eat, they drank, they bought, they sold, they planted, they builded; 29. But the same day that Lot went out of Sodom it rained fire and brimstone from heaven, and destroyed *them* all. 30. Even thus shall it be in the day when the Son of man is revealed.

Luke 18:9. And he spake this parable unto certain which trusted in themselves that they were righteous, and despised others: 10. Two men went up into the temple to pray; the one a Pharisee, and the other a publican. 11. The Pharisee stood and prayed thus with himself, God, I thank thee, that I am not as other men *are*, extortioners, unjust, adulterers, or even as this publican. 12. I fast twice in the week, I give tithes of all that I possess. 13. And the publican, standing afar off, would not lift up so much as *his* eyes unto heaven, but smote upon his breast, saying, God be merciful to me a sinner. 14. I tell you, this man went down to his house justified *rather* than the other: for every one that exalteth himself shall be abased; and he that humbleth himself shall be exalted.

John 5:45. Do not think that I will accuse you to the Father: there is *one* that accuseth you, *even* Moses, in whom ye trust.

Rom. 2:3. Thinkest thou this, O man, that judgest them which do such things, and doest the same, that thou shalt escape the judgment of God?

Rom. 12:16. Be not wise in your own conceits.

1 Cor. 3:21. Let no man glory in men.

2 Cor. 1:9. But we had the sentence of death in ourselves, that we should not trust in ourselves, but in God.

Gal. 6:7. Be not deceived; God is not mocked: for whatsoever a man soweth, that shall he also reap. 8. For he that soweth to his flesh shall of the flesh reap corruption:

1 Thess. 5:3. When they shall say, Peace and safety; then sudden destruction cometh upon them, as travail upon a woman with child; and they shall not escape.

1 Tim. 6:17. Charge them that are rich in this world, that they be not highminded, nor trust in uncertain riches, but in the living God, who giveth us richly all things to enjoy;

Jas. 4:13. Go to now, ye that say, To day or to morrow we will go into such a city, and continue there a year, and buy and sell, and get gain: 14. Whereas ye know not what *shall be* on the morrow. 15. For that ye *ought* to say, If the Lord will, we shall live, and do this, or that.

Rev. 18:7. How much she hath glorified herself, and lived deliciously, so much torment and sorrow give her: for she saith in her heart, I sit a queen, and am no widow, and shall see no sorrow. 8. Therefore shall her plagues come in one day, death, and mourning, and famine; and she shall be utterly burned with fire: for strong *is* the Lord God who judgeth her.

See BLINDNESS, SPIRITUAL; CONCEIT.

INSTANCES OF: Builders of Babel, Gen. 11:4. Saul, 1 Sam. 13:8–14. Sennacherib, 2 Kin. 19:23. Asa, 2 Chr. 16:7–9. Hezekiah, Isa. 22: 11. Jonah, Jonah 1:3–5. Peter, Matt. 26: 33–35; Luke 22:33,34. Paul, Phil. 1:25; 2: 23,24.

CONFISCATION. Of property: By David, that of Mephibosheth, 2 Sam. 16:4. By Ahab, of Naboth's vineyard, 1 Kin. 21:7–16. By Ahasuerus, of Haman's house, Esth. 8:1. As a penalty, Ezra 10:8.

CONFUSION, of tongues, Gen. 11:1–9.

CONGESTION, Lev. 13:28; Deut. 28:22.

CONGREGATION, those who were excluded from, Deut. 23:1–3.

See CHURCH; EXCOMMUNICATION.

CONIAH. See JEHOIACHIN.

CONNIVANCE. Prov. 10:10. He that winketh with the eye causeth sorrow: but a prating fool shall fall.

1 Sam. 3:11. And the LORD said to Samuel, Behold, I will do a thing in Israel, at which both the ears of every one that heareth it shall tingle. 12. In that day I will perform against Eli all *things* which I have spoken concerning his house: when I begin, I will also make an end. 13. For I have told him that I will judge his house for ever for the iniquity which he knoweth; because his sons made themselves vile, and he restrained them not.

See COLLUSION; COMPLICITY; CONSPIRACY.

CONONIAH, name of two Israelites, 2 Chr. 31:12,13; 35:9.

CONSCIENCE. Job 15:21. A dreadful sound is in his ears: in prosperity the destroyer shall come upon him. 24. Trouble and anguish shall make him afraid; they shall prevail against him, as a king ready to the battle.

Job 27:6. My righteousness I hold fast, and will not let it go: my heart shall not reproach *me* so long as I live.

Prov. 20:12. The hearing ear, and the seeing eye, the LORD hath made even both of them.

Matt. 6:22. The light of the body is the eye: if therefore thine eye be single, thy whole body shall be full of light. 23. But if thine eye be evil, thy whole body shall be full of darkness. If therefore the light that is in thee be darkness, how great is that darkness!

Luke 11:33. No man, when he hath lighted a candle, putteth *it* in a secret place, neither under a bushel, but on a candlestick, that they which come in may see the light. [Matt. 5:15,16.] 34. The light of the body is the eye: therefore when thine eye is single, thy whole body also is full of light; but when *thine eye* is evil, thy body also *is* full of darkness. [Matt. 6:22.] 35. Take heed therefore that the light which is in thee be not darkness. 36. If thy whole body therefore *be* full of light, having no part dark, the whole shall be full of light, as when the bright shining of a candle doth give thee light.

Acts 23:1. And Paul, earnestly beholding the council, said, Men *and* brethren, I have lived in all good conscience before God until this day.

Acts 24:16. And herein do I exercise myself, to have always a conscience void of offence toward God, and *toward* men.

Rom. 2:14. When the Gentiles, which have not the law, do by nature the things contained in the law, these, having not the law, are a law unto themselves: 15. Which shew the work of the law written in their hearts, their conscience also bearing witness, and *their* thoughts the mean while accusing or else excusing one another;

Rom. 7:15. For that which I do I allow not: for what I would, that do I not; but what I hate, that do I. 16. If then I do that which I would not, I consent unto the law that *it is* good. 17. Now then it is no more I that do it, but sin that dwelleth in me. 18. For I know that in me (that is, in my flesh,) dwelleth no good thing: for to will is present with me; but *how* to perform that which is good I find not. 19. For the good that I would I do not: but the evil which I would not, that I do. 20. Now if I do that I would not, it is no more I that do it, but sin that dwelleth in me. 21. I find then a law, that, when I would do good, evil is present with me. 22. For I delight in the law of God after the inward man: 23. But I see another law in my members, warring against the law of my mind, and bringing me into captivity to the law of sin which is in my members.

Rom. 9:1. I say the truth in Christ, I lie not, my conscience also bearing me witness in the Holy Ghost,

Rom. 14:1. Him that is weak in the faith receive ye, *but* not to doubtful disputations. 2. For one believeth that he may eat all things: another, who is weak, eateth herbs. 3. Let not him that eateth despise him that eateth not; and let not him which eateth not judge him that eateth: for God hath received him. 4. Who art thou that judgest another man's servant? to his own master he standeth or falleth. Yea, he shall be holden up: for God is able to make him stand. 5. One man esteemeth one day above another: another esteemeth every day *alike.* Let every man be fully persuaded in his own mind. 6. He that regardeth the day, regardeth *it* unto the Lord; and he that regardeth not the day, to the Lord he doth not regard *it.* He that eateth, eateth to the Lord, for he giveth God thanks; and he that eateth not, to the Lord he eateth not, and giveth God thanks. 7. For none of us liveth to himself, and no man dieth to himself. 8. For whether we live, we live unto the Lord; and whether we die, we die unto the Lord: whether we live therefore, or die, we are the Lord's. 9. For to this end Christ both died, and rose, and revived, that he might be Lord both of the dead and living. 10. But why dost thou judge thy brother? or why dost thou set at nought thy brother? for we shall all stand before the judgment seat of Christ. 11. For it is written, *As* I live, saith the Lord, every knee shall bow to me, and every tongue shall confess to God. 12. So then every one of us shall give account of himself to God. 13. Let us not therefore judge one another any more: but judge this rather, that no man put a stumblingblock or an occasion to fall in *his* brother's way. 14. I know, and am persuaded by the Lord Jesus, that *there is* nothing unclean of itself: but to him that esteemeth any thing to be unclean, to him *it is* unclean. 15. But if thy brother be grieved with *thy* meat, now walkest thou not charitably. Destroy not him with thy meat, for whom Christ died. 16. Let not then your good be evil spoken of: 17. For the kingdom of God is not meat and drink; but righteousness, and peace, and joy in the Holy Ghost. 18. For he that in these things serveth Christ *is* acceptable to God, and approved of men. 19. Let us therefore follow after the things which make for peace, and things wherewith one may edify another. 20. For meat destroy not the work of God. All things indeed *are* pure; but *it is* evil for that man who eateth with offence. 21. *It is* good neither to eat flesh, nor to drink wine, nor *any thing* whereby thy brother stumbleth, or is offended, or is made weak. 22. Hast thou faith? have *it* to thyself before God. Happy is he that condemneth not himself in that thing which he alloweth. 23. And he that doubteth is damned if he eat, because *he eateth* not of faith: for whatsoever *is* not of faith is sin.

1 Cor. 8:7. Howbeit *there is* not in every man that knowledge: for some with conscience of the idol unto this hour eat *it* as a thing offered unto an idol; and their conscience being weak is defiled. 9. But take heed lest by any means this liberty of yours become a stumblingblock to them that are weak. 10. For if any man see thee which hast knowledge sit at meat in the idol's temple, shall not the conscience of him which is weak be emboldened to eat those things which are offered to idols; 11. And through thy knowledge shall the weak brother perish, for whom Christ died? 12. But when ye sin so against the brethren, and wound their weak conscience, ye sin against Christ. 13. Wherefore, if meat make my brother to offend, I will eat no flesh while the world standeth, lest I make my brother to offend.

1 Cor. 10:27. If any of them that believe not bid you *to a feast,* and ye be disposed to go; whatsoever is set before you, eat, asking no question for conscience sake. 28. But if any man say unto you, This is offered in sacrifice unto idols, eat not for his sake that shewed it, and for conscience sake: for the earth *is* the Lord's, and the fulness thereof: 29. Conscience, I say, not thine own, but of the other: for why is my liberty judged of another *man's* conscience? 30. For if I by grace be a partaker, why am I evil spoken of for that for which I give thanks? 31. Whether therefore ye eat, or drink, or whatsoever ye do, do all to the glory of God. 32. Give none offence, neither to the Jews, nor to the Gentiles, nor to the church of God:

2 Cor. 1:12. For our rejoicing is this, the testimony of our conscience, that in simplicity and godly sincerity, not with fleshly wisdom, but by the grace of God, we have

had our conversation in the world, and more abundantly to you-ward.

2 Cor. 4:2. But have renounced the hidden things of dishonesty, not walking in craftiness, nor handling the word of God deceitfully; but by manifestation of the truth commending ourselves to every man's conscience in the sight of God.

2 Cor. 5:11. Knowing therefore the terror of the Lord, we persuade men; but we are made manifest unto God; and I trust also are made manifest in your consciences.

1 Tim. 1:5. Now the end of the commandment is charity out of a pure heart, and of a good conscience, and of faith unfeigned: 19. Holding faith, and a good conscience; which some having put away concerning faith have made shipwreck:

1 Tim. 3:9. Holding the mystery of the faith in a pure conscience.

Heb. 9:14. How much more shall the blood of Christ, who through the eternal Spirit offered himself without spot to God, purge your conscience from dead works to serve the living God?

Heb. 10:22. Let us draw near with a true heart in full assurance of faith, having our hearts sprinkled from an evil conscience, and our bodies washed with pure water.

Heb. 13:18. Pray for us: for we trust we have a good conscience, in all things willing to live honestly.

1 Pet. 2:19. For this is thankworthy, if a man for conscience toward God endure grief, suffering wrongfully.

1 Pet. 3:16. Having a good conscience; that, whereas they speak evil of you, as of evildoers, they may be ashamed that falsely accuse your good conversation in Christ. 21. The like figure whereunto even baptism doth also now save us (not the putting away of the filth of the flesh, but the answer of a good conscience toward God,) by the resurrection of Jesus Christ:

1 John 3:20. If our heart condemn us, God is greater than our heart, and knoweth all things. 21. Beloved, if our heart condemn us not, then have we confidence toward God.

FAITHFUL: Instances of: Of Pharaoh, when he took Abraham's wife for a concubine, Gen. 12:18,19. Of Abimelech, when he took Isaac's wife for a concubine, Gen. 26: 9-11. Of Jacob, in his care of Laban's property, Gen. 31:39. Of Joseph, when Potiphar's wife tried to seduce him, Gen. 39:7-12. Of Nehemiah, in the matter of taxes, Neh. 5:15. Of Daniel, in refusing to eat of the king's meat and wine, Dan.1:8. Of Peter, in declaring the whole counsel of God, Acts 4:19,20; 5:29.

See Honesty; Integrity.

GUILTY: Job 15:21. A dreadful sound is in his ears: in prosperity the destroyer shall come upon him. 24. Trouble and anguish shall make him afraid; they shall prevail against him, as a king ready to the battle.

Psa. 51:1. Have mercy upon me, O God, according to thy lovingkindness: accord-

ing unto the multitude of thy tender mercies blot out my transgressions. 2. Wash me thoroughly from mine iniquity, and cleanse me from my sin. 3. For I acknowledge my transgressions: and my sin is ever before me. 4. Against thee, thee only, have I sinned, and done this evil in thy sight: that thou mightest be justified when thou speakest, and be clear when thou judgest. 7. Purge me with hyssop, and I shall be clean: wash me, and I shall be whiter than snow. 8. Make me to hear joy and gladness; that the bones which thou hast broken may rejoice. 9. Hide thy face from my sins, and blot out all mine iniquities. 10. Create in me a clean heart, O God: and renew a right spirit within me. 11. Cast me not away from thy presence; and take not thy holy spirit from me. 12. Restore unto me the joy of thy salvation; and uphold me with thy free spirit. 13. Then will I teach transgressors thy ways; and sinners shall be converted unto thee. 14. Deliver me from bloodguiltiness, O God, thou God of my salvation: and my tongue shall sing aloud of thy righteousness.

Psa. 73:21. Thus my heart was grieved, and I was pricked in my reins.

Prov. 28:1. The wicked flee when no man pursueth: but the righteous are bold as a lion.

Isa. 59:9. Therefore is judgment far from us, neither doth justice overtake us: we wait for light, but behold obscurity; for brightness, but we walk in darkness. 10. We grope for the wall like the blind, and we grope as if we had no eyes: we stumble at noon day as in the night; we are in desolate places as dead men. 11. We roar all like bears, and mourn sore like doves: we look for judgment, but there is none; for salvation, but it is far off from us. 12. For our transgressions are multiplied before thee, and our sins testify against us: for our transgressions are with us; and as for our iniquities, we know them; 13. In transgressing and lying against the Lord, and departing away from our God, speaking oppression and revolt, conceiving and uttering from the heart words of falsehood. 14. And judgment is turned away backward, and justice standeth afar off: for truth is fallen in the street, and equity cannot enter.

Matt. 27:3. Then Judas, which had betrayed him, when he saw that he was condemned, repented himself, and brought again the thirty pieces of silver to the chief priests and elders, 4. Saying, I have sinned in that I have betrayed the innocent blood. And they said, What is that to us? see thou to that. 5. And he cast down the pieces of silver in the temple, and departed, and went and hanged himself.

Mark 6:14. And king Herod heard of him; (for his name was spread abroad:) and he said, That John the Baptist was risen from the dead, and therefore mighty works do shew forth themselves in him. 16. But when Herod heard *thereof*, he said, It is John, whom I beheaded : he is risen from the dead. Matt. 14:1,2.

John 8:9. And they which heard *it*, being convicted by *their own* conscience, went out one by one. beginning at the eldest, *even* unto the last : and Jesus was left alone, and the woman standing in the midst.

Acts 2:37. Now when they heard *this*, they were pricked in their heart, and said unto Peter and to the rest of the apostles, Men *and* brethren, what shall we do?

1 Tim. 4:2. Speaking lies in hypocrisy : having their conscience seared with a hot iron ;

Tit. 1:15. Unto the pure all things *are* pure : but unto them that are defiled and unbelieving *is* nothing pure; but even their mind and conscience is defiled.

Heb. 9:14. How much more shall the blood of Christ, who through the eternal Spirit offered himself without spot to God, purge your conscience from dead works to serve the living God ?

Heb. 10:26. For if we sin wilfully after that we have received the knowledge of the truth, there remaineth no more sacrifice for sins, 27. But a certain fearful looking for of judgment and fiery indignation, which shall devour the adversaries.

INSTANCES OF : Of Adam and Eve, after they sinned, Gen. 3:7,8. Of Jacob, after he defrauded Esau, Gen. 33:1–12. Of Joseph's brethren, Gen. 42:21; 44:16. Of Pharaoh, after the plagues, Ex. 9:27. Of Micah, after stealing, Judg. 17:2. Of David, for having cut off Saul's skirt, 1 Sam. 24:5; for having numbered the children of Israel, 2 Sam. 24:10; for his adultery, and murder of Uriah, Psa. 32; 38; 40: 11,12; 51; for numbering Israel, 1 Chr. 21:1–7. Of the lepers of Samaria, 2 Kin. 7:8–10. Of the old prophet of Beth-el, 1 Kin. 13:29–32. Of Herod, for beheading John the Baptist, Matt. 14:2; Luke 9:7. Of Peter, after denying the Lord, Matt. 26:75; Mark 14:72; Luke 22:62. Of Judas, after betraying the Lord, Matt. 27:3–5. The accusers of the woman taken in adultery. John 8:9.

DEAD : Prov. 16:25. There is a way that seemeth right unto a man, but the end thereof *are* the ways of death.

Prov. 30:20. Such is the way of an adulterous woman ; she eateth, and wipeth her mouth, and said, I have done no wickedness.

Jer. 6:15. Were they ashamed when they had committed abomination? nay, they were not at all ashamed, neither could they blush : therefore they shall fall among them that fall : at the time *that* I visit them they shall be cast down, saith the LORD.

Amos 6:1. Woe to them *that are* at ease in Zion, and trust in the mountain of Samaria, *which are* named chief of the nations, to whom the house of Israel came ! 3. Ye that put far away the evil day, and cause the seat of violence to come near ;

4. That lie upon beds of ivory, and stretch themselves upon their couches, and eat the lambs out of the flock, and the calves out of the midst of the stall; 5. That chant to the sound of the viol, *and* invent to themselves instruments of musick, like David ; 6. That drink wine in bowls, and anoint themselves with the chief ointments : but they are not grieved for the affliction of Joseph.

John 16:2. They shall put you out of the synagogues : yea, the time cometh, that whosoever killeth you will think that he doeth God service. 3. And these things will they do unto you, because they have not known the Father, nor me.

Rom. 1:21. Because that, when they knew God, they glorified him not as God, neither were thankful ; but became vain in their imaginations, and their foolish heart was darkened. 22. Professing themselves to be wise, they became fools, 23. And changed the glory of the uncorruptible God into an image made like to corruptible man, and to birds, and fourfooted beasts, and creeping things. 24. Wherefore God also gave them up to uncleanness through the lusts of their own hearts, to dishonour their own bodies between themselves : 25. Who changed the truth of God into a lie, and worshipped and served the creature more than the Creator, who is blessed for ever.

Eph. 4:17. This I say therefore, and testify in the Lord, that ye henceforth walk not as other Gentiles walk, in the vanity of their mind. 18. Having the understanding darkened, being alienated from the life of God through the ignorance that is in them, because of the blindness of their heart : 19. Who being past feeling have given themselves over unto lasciviousness, to work all uncleanness with greediness.

1 Tim. 4:2. Speaking lies in hypocrisy ; having their conscience seared with a hot iron ;

Tit. 1:15. Unto the pure all things *are* pure : but unto them that are defiled and unbelieving *is* nothing pure ; but even their mind and conscience is defiled.

See BLINDNESS, SPIRITUAL.

CONSCIENCE MONEY, Judg. 17:2; 2 Kin. 12:16; Matt. 27:3–5.

See MONEY, SIN MONEY.

CONSCIENTIOUSNESS. See INTEGRITY.

CONSCRIPTION, of soldiers, 1 Sam. 14:52.

See ARMIES.

CONSECRATED THINGS, laws regarding. Lev. 27; Num. 18:8–32.

See FIRSTBORN ; FIRSTFRUITS.

CONSECRATION. Of Aaron, see AARON. Of priests, see PRIESTS. Of the altar, see ALTAR. Of the temple, see TEMPLE, DEDICATION OF. See also OFFERINGS.

PERSONAL : Psa. 51:17. The sacrifices of God *are* a broken spirit : a broken and a contrite heart, O God, thou wilt not despise.

Matt. 13:44. Again, the kingdom of heaven is like unto treasure hid in a field : the which when a man hath found, he hideth, and for joy thereof goeth and selleth all that he hath, and buyeth that field.

45. Again, the kingdom of heaven is like unto a merchantman, seeking goodly pearls : 46. Who, when he had found one pearl of great price, went and sold all that he had, and bought it.

Rom. 6:13. Neither yield ye your members *as* instruments of unrighteousness unto sin : but yield yourselves unto God, as those that are alive from the dead, and your members *as* instruments of righteousness unto God.

16. Know ye not, that to whom ye yield yourselves servants to obey, his servants ye are to whom ye obey ; whether of sin unto death, or of obedience unto righteousness ?

19. I speak after the manner of men because of the infirmity of your flesh : for as ye have yielded your members servants to uncleanness and to iniquity unto iniquity ; even so now yield your members servants to righteousness unto holiness.

Rom. 12:1. I beseech you therefore, brethren, by the mercies of God, that ye present your bodies a living sacrifice, holy, acceptable unto God, *which is* your reasonable service.

2 Cor. 8:5. And *this they did*, not as we hoped, but first gave their own selves to the Lord,

CONDITIONAL: Gen. 28:20. And Jacob vowed a vow, saying, If God will be with me, and will keep me in this way that I go, and will give me bread to eat, and raiment to put on, 21. So that I come again to my father's house in peace ; then shall the LORD be my God : 22. And this stone, which I have set *for* a pillar, shall be God's house ; and of all that thou shalt give me I will surely give the tenth unto thee.

2 Sam. 15:7. And it came to pass after forty years, that Absalom said unto the king, I pray thee, let me go and pay my vow, which I have vowed unto the LORD, in Hebron. 8. For thy servant vowed a vow while I abode at Geshur in Syria, saying, If the LORD shall bring me again indeed to Jerusalem, then I will serve the LORD.

See DEDICATION ; OFFERINGS.

INSTANCES OF: Cain and Abel. Gen. 4: 4-7.

Abraham, of Isaac, Gen. 22:9-12. Jephthah, of his daughter, Judg. 11:30,31,34-40. Hannah, of Samuel, 1 Sam. 1:11,24-28. David consecrates the water obtained by his valiant warriors, 2 Sam. 23:16. Zichri, of himself, 2 Chr. 17:16.

CONSISTENCY. Neh. 5:9. Also I said, It *is* not good that ye do : ought ye not to walk in the fear of our God because of the reproach of the heathen our enemies ?

Matt. 6:24. No man can serve two masters : for either he will hate the one, and love the other ; or else he will hold to the one, and despise the other. Ye cannot serve God and mammon. Luke 16:13.

Rom. 14:22. Hast thou faith? have *it* to thyself before God. Happy *is* he that condemneth not himself in that thing which he alloweth.

1 Cor. 10:21. Ye cannot drink the cup of the Lord, and the cup of devils : ye cannot be partakers of the Lord's table, and of the table of devils.

See DECEIT ; EXPEDIENCY ; HYPOCRISY ; INCONSISTENCY ; OBDURACY ; PRUDENCE.

CONSOLATION. See AFFLICTION, CONSOLATION IN ; HOLY SPIRIT.

CONSPIRACY. LAW AGAINST : Ex. 23:1. Thou shalt not raise a false report : put not thine hand with the wicked to be an unrighteous witness.

2. Thou shalt not follow a multitude to *do* evil ; neither shalt thou speak in a cause to decline after many to wrest *judgment :*

INSTANCES OF: Joseph's brethren, against Joseph, Gen. 37:18-20. Miriam and Aaron, against Moses, Num. 12; 14:4; 16:1-35. Abimelech, against Gideon's sons, Judg. 9:1-6. Gaal, against Abimelech, Judg. 9:23-41. Delilah, against Samson, Judg. 16:4-21. Abner, against Ish-bosheth, 2 Sam. 3:7-21. Of Absalom, 2 Sam. 15:10-13. Of Jeroboam, 1 Kin. 14:2. Of Baasha, 1 Kin. 15:27. Of Zimri, 1 Kin. 16:9. Of Jezebel, against Naboth, 1 Kin. 21:8-13. Of Jehu, 2 Kin. 9:14-26. Of Jehoiada, 2 Kin. 11: 4-16. Of servants, against Joash, 2 Kin. 12:20.

People in Jerusalem, against Amaziah, 2 Kin. 14:19. Shallum, against Zachariah, 2 Kin. 15:10. Pekahiah, 2 Kin. 15:23-25. Pekah, 2 Kin. 15:30. Amon, 2 Kin. 21:23. Sennacherib, 2 Kin. 19:37. Amaziah, 2 Chr. 25:27. Ahasuerus, Esth. 2:21-23. Jeremiah, Jer. 18:18. Daniel, Dan. 6:4-17. Shadrach, Meshach, and Abed-nego, Dan. 3:8-18.

Against Jesus, Jer. 11:9,19; Matt. 12:14; 21: 38-41; 26:3,4; 27:1,2; Mark 3:6. Paul, Acts 18: 12; 23:12-15.

Falsely accused of : Jonathan, 1 Sam. 22:8.

CONSTANCY. In obedience, Psa. 119: 31,33. In friendship, Prov. 27:10. Under suffering, Matt. 5:12; Heb. 12:5; 1 Pet. 4:12-16. In prayer, Luke 18:1; Rom. 12:12; Eph. 6:18; Col. 4:2; 1 Thess. 5:17. In beneficence, Gal. 6:9. In profession, Heb. 10:23.

INSTANCES OF: Ruth 1:14; Jonathan, 1 Sam. 18:1; 20:16; Priscilla and Aquila, Rom. 16:3,4.—*Bible Text Book.*

See CHARACTER ; STABILITY.

CONSTELLATIONS. Isa. 13:10. The serpent, Job 26:13. Orion, Job 9:9; Amos 5:8.

See ASTRONOMY.

CONSTITUTION. AGREEMENT BETWEEN THE RULER AND PEOPLE: Deut. 17:18. And it shall be, when he sitteth upon the throne of his kingdom, that he shall write him a copy of this law in a book out of *that which is* before the priests the Levites : 19. And it shall be with him, and he shall read therein all the days of his life : that he may learn to fear the LORD his God, to keep all the words of this law and these statutes, to do them: 20. That his heart be not lifted up above his brethren, and that he turn not aside from the commandment, to the right hand, or to the left: to the end that he may prolong *his* days in his kingdom, he, and his children, in the midst of Israel.

2 Sam. 5:3. So all the elders of Israel came to the king of Hebron; and king David made a league with them in Hebron before the LORD: and they anointed David king over Israel.

2 Chr. 23:2. And they went about in Judah, and gathered the Levites out of all the cities of Judah, and the chief of the fathers of Israel, and they came to Jerusalem. 3. And all the congregation made a covenant with the king in the house of God. And he said unto them, Behold, the king's son shall reign, as the LORD hath said of the sons of David.

Jer. 34:8. *This is* the word that came unto Jeremiah from the LORD, after that the king Zedekiah had made a covenant with all the people which *were* at Jerusalem, to proclaim liberty unto them; 9. That every man should let his manservant, and every man his maidservant, *being* an Hebrew or an Hebrewess, go free; that none should serve himself of them, to wit, of a Jew his brother. 10. Now when all the princes, and all the people, which had entered into the covenant, heard that every one should let his manservant, and every one his maidservant, go free, that none should serve themselves of them any more; then they obeyed, and let *them* go. 11. But afterward they turned, and caused the servants and the handmaids, whom they had let go free, to return, and brought them into subjection for servants and for handmaids.

Dan. 6:12. Then they came near, and spake before the king concerning the king's decree; Hast thou not signed a decree, that every man that shall ask *a petition* of any God or man within thirty days, save of thee, O king, shall be cast into the den of lions? The king answered and said, The thing *is* true, according to the law of the Medes and Persians, which altereth not. 13. Then answered they and said before the king, That Daniel, which *is* of the children of the captivity of Judah, regardeth not thee, O king, nor the decree that thou hast signed, but maketh his petition three times a day. 14. Then the king, when he heard *these* words, was sore displeased with himself, and set *his* heart on Daniel to deliver him: and he laboured till the going down of the sun to deliver him. 15. Then these men assembled unto the king, and said unto the king, Know, O king, that the law of the Medes and Persians *is*, That no decree nor statute which the king establisheth may be changed.

CONSUMPTION, Lev. 26:16; Deut. 28:22.

CONTEMPT OF COURT. See COURT.

CONTENTION. See STRIFE.

CONTENTMENT. Psa. 16:6. The lines are fallen unto me in pleasant *places;* yea, I have a goodly heritage.

Psa. 37:7. Rest in the LORD, and wait patiently for him: fret not thyself because of him who prospereth in his way, 16. A little that a righteous man hath *is* better than the riches of many wicked.

Prov. 14:14. A good man *shall be satisfied* from himself. *v.* 10.

Prov. 15:13. A merry heart maketh a cheerful countenance: 15. He that is of a merry heart *hath* a continual feast. 30. The light of the eyes rejoiceth the heart: *and* a good report maketh the bones fat.

Prov. 16:8. Better *is* a little with righteousness than great revenues without right.

Prov. 17:1. Better is a dry morsel, and quietness therewith, than an house full of sacrifices *with* strife. 22. A merry heart doeth good *like* a medicine:

Prov. 30:8. Give me neither poverty nor riches; feed me with food convenient for me:

Eccl. 2:24. *There is* nothing better for a man, *than* that he should eat and drink, and *that* he should make his soul enjoy good in his labour. Eccl. 3:12,13; 8:15.

Eccl. 4:6. Better *is* an handful *with* quietness, than both the hands full *with* travail and vexation of spirit.

Eccl. 5:12. The sleep of a labouring man *is* sweet, whether he eat little or much:

Eccl. 6:9. Better *is* the sight of the eyes than the wandering of the desire: *vs.* 7,8.

Eccl. 9:7. Go thy way, eat thy bread with joy, and drink thy wine with a merry heart: for God now accepteth thy works. 8. Let thy garments be always white; and let thy head lack no ointment. 9. Live joyfully with the wife whom thou lovest all the days of the life of thy vanity, which he hath given thee under the sun,

Luke 3:14. And the soldiers likewise demanded of him, saying, And what shall we do? And he said unto them, Do violence to no man, neither accuse *any* falsely; and be content with your wages.

1 Cor. 7:17. As God hath distributed to every man, as the Lord hath called every one, so let him walk. 20. Let every man abide in the same calling wherein he was called. 21. Art thou called *being* a servant? care not for it: but if thou mayest be made free, use *it* rather. 24. Brethren, let every man, wherein he is called, therein abide with God.

Gal. 5:26. Let us not be desirous of vain glory, provoking one another, envying one another.

Phil. 4:11. Not that I speak in respect of want: for I have learned, in whatsoever state I am, *therewith* to be content. 12. I know both how to be abased, and I know how to abound: every where and in all things I am instructed both to be full and to be hungry, both to abound and to suffer need.

1 Tim. 6:6. Godliness with contentment is great gain. 7. For we brought nothing into

this world, *and it is* certain we can carry nothing out. 8. And having food and raiment let us be therewith content.

Heb. 13:5. *Be* content with such things as ye have: for he hath said, I will never leave thee, nor forsake thee.

See AFFLICTION, RESIGNATION IN; RESIGNATION.

INSTANCES OF: Esau, in refusing Jacob's present, Gen. 33:9. Barzillai, in refusing to go with David to Jerusalem, 2 Sam. 19:33–37. The Shunammite, in refusing to make a request of Elisha, 2 Kin. 4:13.

CONTINENCE. Job. 31:1. I made a covenant with mine eyes; why then should I think upon a maid?

Matt. 5:27. Ye have heard that it was said by them of old time, Thou shalt not commit adultery: 28. But I say unto you, That whosoever looketh on a woman to lust after her hath committed adultery with her already in his heart.

Matt. 19:12. There be eunuchs, which have made themselves eunuchs for the kingdom of heaven's sake.

Rom. 13:13. Let us walk honestly, as in the day; not in rioting and drunkenness, not in chambering and wantonness, not in strife and envying.

1 Cor. 7:1. Now concerning the things whereof ye wrote unto me: *It is* good for a man not to touch a woman. 2. Nevertheless, *to avoid* fornication, let every man have his own wife, and let every woman have her own husband. 3. Let the husband render unto the wife due benevolence: and likewise also the wife unto the husband. 4. The wife hath not power of her own body, but the husband: and likewise also the husband hath not power of his own body, but the wife. 5. Defraud ye not one the other, except *it be* with consent for a time, that ye may give yourselves to fasting and prayer; and come together again, that Satan tempt you not for your incontinency. 6. But I speak this by permission, *and* not of commandment. 7. For I would that all men were even as I myself. But every man hath his proper gift of God, one after this manner, and another after that. 8. I say therefore to the unmarried and widows, It is good for them if they abide even as I. 9. But if they cannot contain, let them marry: for it is better to marry than to burn.

25. Now concerning virgins I have no commandment of the Lord: yet I give my judgment, as one that hath obtained mercy of the Lord to be faithful. 26. I suppose therefore that this is good for the present distress, *I say*, that *it is* good for a man so to be. 27. Art thou bound unto a wife? seek not to be loosed. Art thou loosed from a wife? seek not a wife. 28. But and if thou marry, thou hast not sinned; and if a virgin marry, she hath not sinned. Nevertheless such shall have trouble in the flesh: but I spare you. 29. But this I say, brethren, the the time *is* short: it remaineth, that both

they that have wives be as though they had none; 36. But if any man think that he behaveth himself uncomely toward his virgin, if she pass the flower of *her* age, and need so require, let him do what he will, he sinneth not: let them marry. 37. Nevertheless he that standeth stedfast in his heart, having no necessity, but hath power over his own will, and hath so decreed in his heart that he will keep his virgin, doeth well. 38. So then he that giveth *her* in marriage doeth well; but he that giveth *her* not in marriage doeth better.

1 Cor. 9:27. But I keep under my body, and bring *it* into subjection: lest that by any means, when I have preached to others, I myself should be a castaway.

Col. 3:5. Mortify therefore your members which are upon the earth; fornication, uncleanness, inordinate affection, evil concupiscence.

1 Tim. 4:12. Let no man despise thy youth; but be thou an example of the believers, in word, in conversation, in charity, in spirit, in faith, in purity.

1 Tim. 5:1. Rebuke not an elder, but intreat *him* as a father; *and* the younger men as brethren; 2. The elder women as mothers; the younger as sisters, with all purity.

Rev. 14:1. And I looked, and, lo, a Lamb stood on the mount Sion, and with him an hundred forty *and* four thousand, having his Father's name written in their foreheads. 4. These are they which were not defiled with women; for they are virgins. These are they which follow the Lamb whithersoever he goeth. These were redeemed from among men, *being* the firstfruits unto God and to the Lamb. 5. And in their mouth was found no guile: for they are without fault before the throne of God.

See CHASTITY.

INSTANCES OF: Joseph, Gen. 39:7–12. Uriah, 2 Sam. 11:8–13. Boaz, Ruth 3:6–13. Joseph, husband of Mary, Matt. 1:24,25. Paul, 1 Cor. 7:8.

CONTINENTS, Gen. 1:9,10; Job 26:7,10; 28:8–11; 38:4–18; Psa. 95:5; 104:5–9; 136:6; Prov. 8:29; 30:4.

See GEOLOGY.

CONTINGENCIES. IN DIVINE GOVERNMENT OF MAN: Gen. 2:16. And the LORD God commanded the man, saying, Of every tree of the garden thou mayest freely eat: 17. But of the tree of the knowledge of good and evil, thou shalt not eat of it: for in the day that thou eatest thereof thou shalt surely die.

Gen. 3:3. But of the fruit of the tree which *is* in the midst of the garden, God hath said, Ye shall not eat of it, neither shall ye touch it, lest ye die.

Gen. 4:7. If thou doest well shalt thou not be accepted? and if thou doest not well, sin lieth at the door.

Gen. 18:19. For I know him, that he will command his children and his household after him, and they shall keep the way of the

LORD, to do justice and judgment; that the LORD may bring upon Abraham that which he hath spoken of him.

Ex. 19:5. Now therefore, if ye will obey my voice indeed, and keep my covenant, then ye shall be a peculiar treasure unto me above all people: for all the earth is mine:

Lev. 26:3. If ye walk in my statutes, and keep my commandments, and do them; 4. Then I will give you rain in due season, and the land shall yield her increase, and the trees of the field shall yield their fruit. vs. 3–13.

14. But if ye will not hearken unto me, and will not do all these commandments; 15. And if ye shall despise my statutes, or if your soul abhor my judgments, so that ye will not do all my commandments, but that ye break my covenant: 16. I also will do this unto you; I will even appoint over you terror, consumption, and the burning ague, that shall consume the eyes, and cause sorrow of heart: and ye shall sow your seed in vain, for your enemies shall eat it. vs. 14–28.

Deut. 7:12. Wherefore it shall come to pass, if ye hearken to these judgments, and keep, and do them, that the LORD thy God shall keep unto thee the covenant and the mercy which he sware unto thy fathers: vs. 13–26.

Deut. 11:26. Behold, I set before you this day a blessing and a curse; 27. A blessing, if ye obey the commandments of the LORD your God, which I command you this day: 28. And a curse, if ye will not obey the commandments of the LORD your God, but turn aside out of the way which I command you this day, to go after other gods, which ye have not known.

Deut. 30:15. See, I have set before thee this day life and good, and death and evil; 16. In that I command thee this day to love the LORD thy God, to walk in his ways, and to keep his commandments and his statutes and his judgments, that thou mayest live and multiply: and the LORD thy God shall bless thee in the land whither thou goest to possess it. 19. I call heaven and earth to record this day against you, that I have set before you life and death, blessing and cursing: therefore choose life, that both thou and thy seed may live:

Josh. 24:15. And if it seem evil unto you to serve the LORD, choose you this day whom ye will serve; whether the gods which your fathers served that were on the other side of the flood, or the gods of the Amorites, in whose land ye dwell: but as for me and my house, we will serve the LORD.

2 Sam. 24:12. Go and say unto David, Thus saith the LORD, I offer thee three things; choose thee one of them, that I may do it unto thee. 13. So Gad came to David, and told him, and said unto him, Shall seven years of famine come unto thee in thy land? or wilt thou flee three months before thine enemies, while they pursue thee? or

that there be three days' pestilence in thy land? now advise, and see what answer I shall return to him that sent me. 14. And David said unto Gad, I am in a great strait: let us fall now into the hand of the LORD; for his mercies are great: and let me not fall into the hand of man.

1 Kin. 3:14. And if thou wilt walk in my ways, to keep my statutes and my commandments, as thy father David did walk, then I will lengthen thy days.

1 Kin. 20:42. And he said unto him, Thus saith the LORD, Because thou hast let go out of thy hand a man whom I appointed to utter destruction, therefore thy life shall go for his life, and thy people for his people.

1 Chr. 28:7. Moreover I will establish his kingdom for ever, if he be constant to do my commandments and my judgments, as at this day.

2 Chr. 26:5. And he sought God in the days of Zechariah, who had understanding in the visions of God: and as long as he sought the LORD, God made him to prosper.

Job 36:11. If they obey and serve him, they shall spend their days in prosperity, and their years in pleasures. 12. But if they obey not, they shall perish by the sword, and they shall die without knowledge.

Jer. 11:4. Which I commanded your fathers in the day that I brought them forth out of the land of Egypt, from the iron furnace, saying, Obey my voice, and do them, according to all which I command you: so shall ye be my people, and I will be your God:

Jer. 12:17. But if they will not obey, I will utterly pluck up and destroy that nation, saith the LORD.

Jer. 18:8. If that nation, against whom I have pronounced, turn from their evil, I will repent of the evil that I thought to do unto them. 9. And at what instant I shall speak concerning a nation, and concerning a kingdom, to build and to plant it; 10. If it do evil in my sight, that it obey not my voice, then I will repent of the good, wherewith I said I would benefit them.

Jer. 22:4. For if ye do this thing indeed, then shall there enter in by the gates of this house kings sitting upon the throne of David, riding in chariots and on horses, he, and his servants, and his people. 5. But if ye will not hear these words, I swear by myself, saith the LORD, that this house shall become a desolation.

Ezek. 33:14. Again, when I say unto the wicked, Thou shalt surely die; if he turn from his sin, and do that which is lawful and right; 15. If the wicked restore the pledge, give again that he had robbed, walk in the statutes of life, without committing iniquity; he shall surely live, he shall not die. 16. None of his sins that he hath committed shall be mentioned unto him: he hath done that which is lawful and right; he shall surely live.

Jonah 3:10. And God saw their works, that they turned from their evil way; and God repented of the evil, that he had said that he would do unto them; and he did *it* not.

Matt. 19:17. If thou wilt enter into life, keep the commandments.

Matt. 23:37. O Jerusalem, Jerusalem, *thou* that killest the prophets, and stonest them which are sent unto thee, how often would I have gathered thy children together, even as a hen gathereth her chickens under *her* wings, and ye would not!

Matt. 26:39. O my Father, if it be possible, let this cup pass from me: nevertheless not as I will, but as thou *wilt. v.* 42.

Mark 11:26. ¹ But if ye do not forgive, neither will your Father which is in heaven forgive your trespasses.   (¹ Omitted in R. V.)

John 9:41. Jesus said unto them, If ye were blind, ye should have no sin: but now ye say, We see; therefore your sin remaineth.

John 14:23. Jesus answered and said unto him, If a man love me, he will keep my words: and my Father will love him, and we will come unto him, and make our abode with him.

John 15:6. If a man abide not in me, he is cast forth as a branch, and is withered; and men gather them, and cast *them* into the fire, and they are burned. 7. If ye abide in me, and my words abide in you, ye shall ask what ye will, and it shall be done unto you.

Col. 1:22. To present you holy and unblameable and unreproveable in his sight: 23. If ye continue in the faith grounded and settled, and *be* not moved away from the hope of the gospel, which ye have heard, *and* which was preached to every creature which is under heaven; whereof I Paul am made a minister;

2 Thess. 2:8. And then shall that Wicked be revealed, whom the Lord shall consume with the spirit of his mouth, and shall destroy with the brightness of his coming: 9. *Even him,* whose coming is after the working of Satan with all power and signs and lying wonders, 10. And with all deceivableness of unrighteousness in them that perish; because they received not the love of the truth, that they might be saved.

Heb. 3:14. For we are made partakers of Christ, if we hold the beginning of our confidence stedfast unto the end;

Rev. 2:22. Behold, I will cast her into a bed, and them that commit adultery with her into great tribulation, except they repent of their deeds.

Rev. 3:3. Remember therefore how thou hast received and heard, and hold fast, and repent. If therefore thou shalt not watch, I will come on thee as a thief, and thou shalt not know what hour I will come upon thee.

Rev. 22:17. And whosoever will, let him take the water of life freely.

See BLESSINGS, CONTINGENT ON OBEDIENCE; PREDESTINATION; WILL.

CONTRACTS. Between Abraham and Abimelech, concerning wells of water, Gen. 21:25-32; violated, Gen. 26:15. First contract between Laban and Jacob for Laban's daughter, Gen. 29:15-20,27-30; violated, Gen. 29:23-27; second contract, Gen. 30:28-34; violated, Gen. 30:37-43; 31:7; for cattle, Gen. 30:27-29,31-34. See FRAUD.

Between Solomon and Hiram, 1 Kin. 5:9-11; 9:11.

Dissolved: By mutual consent, Ex. 4:18; by blotting out, Col. 2:14. Modes of ratifying: By giving presents, Gen. 21:25-30; 1 Sam. 18:4; by consummating in the presence of the public at the gate of the city, Gen. 23:18; Ruth, 4:1,2; by erecting a heap of stones, Gen. 31:44-54; by oaths, Gen. 26:3,31; Josh. 9:15,20; 1 Chr. 16:16; Heb. 6: 16,17; by joining hands, Prov. 6:1; 11:21; 17: 18; 22:26; Ezek. 17:18; with salt, Num. 18: 19; by taking off the shoe, Ruth 4:6-8; written instrument, Jer. 32:10-15.

See COVENANTS; VOWS.

SCRIPTURES ILLUSTRATIVE OF THE BINDING FORCE OF: Ex. 21:2. If thou buy an Hebrew servant, six years he shall serve: and in the seventh he shall go out free for nothing. 3. If he came in by himself, he shall go out by himself: if he were married, then his wife shall go out with him. 4. If his master have given him a wife, and she have born him sons or daughters; the wife and her children shall be her master's, and he shall go out by himself. 5. And if the servant shall plainly say, I love my master, my wife, and my children; I will not go out free: 6. Then his master shall bring him unto the judges; he shall also bring him to the door, or unto the door post; and his master shall bore his ear through with an aul; and he shall serve him for ever.

Lev. 6:1. And the LORD spake unto Moses, saying, 2. If a soul sin, and commit a trespass against the LORD, and lie unto his neighbour in that which was delivered him to keep, 4. Then it shall be, because he hath sinned, and is guilty, that he shall restore that which he took violently away, or the thing which he hath deceitfully gotten, or that which was delivered him to keep, or the lost thing which he found, 5. Or all that about which he hath sworn falsely; he shall even restore it in the principal, and shall add the fifth part more thereto, *and* give it unto him to whom it appertaineth, in the day of his trespass offering. 6. And he shall bring his trespass offering unto the LORD, a ram without blemish out of the flock, with thy estimation, for a trespass offering, unto the priest: 7. And the priest shall make an atonement for him before the LORD: and it shall be forgiven him for any thing of all that he hath done in trespassing therein.

Josh. 9:3. And when the inhabitants of Gibeon heard what Joshua had done unto Jericho and to Ai, 4. They did work wilily, and went and made as if they had been ambassadors, and took old sacks upon their asses, and wine bottles, old, and rent, and bound up; 5. And old shoes and clouted upon their feet, and old garments upon them; and all the bread of their provision was dry *and* mouldy. 6. And they went to Joshua unto the camp at Gilgal, and said unto him, and to the men of Israel, We be come from a far country: now therefore make ye a league with us. 7. And the men of Israel said unto the Hivites, Peradventure ye dwell among us; and how shall we make a league with you? 8. And they said unto Joshua, We *are* thy servants. And Joshua said unto them, Who *are* ye? and from whence come ye? 9. And they said unto him, From a very far country thy servants are come because of the name of the Lord thy God: . . . . 15. And Joshua made peace with them, and made a league with them, to let them live: and the princes of the congregation sware unto them.

16. And it came to pass at the end of three days after they had made a league with them, that they heard that they *were* their neighbours, and *that* they dwelt among them. 18. And the children of Israel smote them not, because the princes of the congregation had sworn unto them by the Lord God of Israel. And all the congregation murmured against the princes. 19. But all the princes said unto all the congregation, We have sworn unto them by the Lord God of Israel: now therefore we may not touch them. With *vs.* 20-27.

Matt. 20:1. For the kingdom of heaven is like unto a man *that is* an householder, which went out early in the morning to hire labourers into his vineyard. 2. And when he had agreed with the labourers for a penny a day, he sent them into his vineyard. 3. And he went out about the third hour, and saw others standing idle in the marketplace, 4. And said unto them: Go ye also into the vineyard, and whatsoever is right I will give you. And they went their way. 5. Again he went out about the sixth and ninth hour, and did likewise. 6. And about the eleventh hour he went out, and found others standing idle, and saith unto them, Why stand ye here all the day idle? 7. They say unto him, Because no man hath hired us. He saith unto them, Go ye also into the vineyard; ¹ and whatsoever is right, *that* shall ye receive. 8. So when even was come, the lord of the vineyard saith unto his steward, Call the labourers, and give them *their* hire, beginning from the last unto the first. 9. And when they came that *were hired* about the eleventh hour, they received every man a penny. 10. But when the first came, they supposed that they should have received more; and they likewise received every man a penny. 11. And when they had received *it*, they murmured against the goodman of the house, 12. Saying, These last have wrought *but* one hour, and

thou hast made them equal unto us, which have borne the burden and heat of the day. 13. But he answered one of them, and said, Friend, I do thee no wrong: didst not thou agree with me for a penny? 14. Take *that* thine *is*, and go thy way: I will give unto this last, even as unto thee. 15. Is it not lawful for me to do what I will with mine own? Is thine eye evil, because I am good? 16. So the last shall be first, and the first last: ¹ for many be called, but few chosen. [¹ Omitted in R. V.]

Gal. 3:15. Brethren, I speak after the manner of men; Though *it be* but a man's covenant, yet *if it be* confirmed, no man disannulleth, or addeth thereto.

See Covenant; Land.

CONTRITION. See Repentance; Sin, Confession of.

CONVENTION, for counsel, Prov. 15:22.

CONVERSATION. Matt. 5:37. But let your communication be, Yea, yea; Nay, nay: for whatsoever is more than these cometh of evil.

Matt. 12:35. A good man out of the good treasure of the heart bringeth forth good things: and an evil man out of the evil treasure bringeth forth evil things. 36. But I say unto you, That every idle word that men shall speak, they shall give account thereof in the day of judgment. 37. For by thy words thou shalt be justified, and by thy words thou shalt be condemned.

Eph. 4:29. Let no corrupt communication proceed out of your mouth, but that which is good to the use of edifying, that it may minister grace unto the hearers.

Col. 3:8. But now ye also put off all these; anger, wrath, malice, blasphemy, filthy communication out of your mouth.

Col. 4:6. Let your speech *be* alway with grace, seasoned with salt, that ye may know how ye ought to answer every man.

Jas. 5:12. But above all things, my brethren, swear not, neither by heaven, neither by the earth, neither by any other oath: but let your yea be yea; and *your* nay, nay; lest ye fall into condemnation.

See Tongue.

CONVERSION. See Regeneration. **INSTANCES OF:** See Converts, below.

CONVERTS. "Wayside," Matt. 13:4, 19. "Stony ground," Matt. 13:5,20,21. "Choked," Matt. 13:7,22. "Good ground," Matt. 13:8,23; Luke 8:4-15.

See Backsliders; Proselytes; Revivals.

INSTANCES OF: Ruth, Ruth 1:16. Nebuchadnezzar, Dan. 4. The mariners with Jonah, Jonah 1:5,6,9,14,16. Ninevites, Jonah 3. Gadarenes, Luke 8:35-39. The Samaritans, John 4:28-42. The thief on the cross, Luke 23:39-43. At Pentecost, three thousand, Acts 2:41. Post-pentecostal, Acts 4:4. The eunuch, Acts 8:35-38. Saul of Tarsus, Acts 9:3-18. Sergius Paulus, Acts 13: 7,12; 26:12-23. Cornelius, Acts 10. Jews and Greeks at Antioch, Acts 13:43. Lydia, Acts 16:14,15. Jailer, Acts 16:27-34. Greeks, Acts 17:4,12.

ZEALOUS: INSTANCES OF: Nebuchadnezzar, Dan. 3:29; 4:1–37. Andrew, John 1: 40,41. Philip, John 1:43–45. The woman of Samaria, John 4:28,29. The man possessed of demons, Luke 8:39. The blind men, Matt. 9:31; John 9:8–38. The dumb man, Mark 7:36.

CONVEYANCE. OF LAND: See LAND.

CONVICTION. OF SIN: Gen. 4:13. Cain said unto the LORD, My punishment *is* greater than I can bear.

Deut. 28:65. And among these nations shalt thou find no ease, neither shall the sole of thy foot have rest: but the LORD shall give thee there a trembling heart, and failing of eyes, and sorrow of mind: 66. And thy life shall hang in doubt before thee; and thou shalt fear day and night, and shalt have none assurance of thy life: 67. In the morning thou shalt say, Would God it were even! and at even thou shalt say, Would God it were morning! for the fear of thine heart wherewith thou shalt fear, and for the sight of thine eyes which thou shalt see.

Job 40:4. Behold, I am vile; what shall I answer thee? I will lay mine hand upon my mouth. 5. Once have I spoken; but I will not answer: yea, twice; but I will proceed no further.

Psa. 31:10. My life is spent with grief, and my years with sighing: my strength faileth because of mine iniquity, and my bones are consumed.

Psa. 38:1. O LORD, rebuke me not in thy wrath: neither chasten me in thy hot displeasure. 2. For thine arrows stick fast in me, and thy hand presseth me sore. 3. *There* is no soundness in my flesh because of thine anger; neither *is there any* rest in my bones because of my sin. 4. For mine iniquities are gone over mine head: as an heavy burden they are too heavy for me. 5. My wounds stink *and* are corrupt because of my foolishness. 6. I am troubled; I am bowed down greatly; I go mourning all the day long. 7. For my loins are filled with a loathsome *disease:* and *there is* no soundness in my flesh. 8. I am feeble and sore broken: I have roared by reason of the disquietness of my heart. 9. Lord, all my desire *is* before thee; and my groaning is not hid from thee. 10. My heart panteth, my strength faileth me: as for the light of mine eyes, it also is gone from me. 11. My lovers and my friends stand aloof from my sore; and my kinsmen stand afar off. 12. They also that seek after my life lay snares *for me:* and they that seek my hurt speak mischievous things, and imagine deceits all the day long. 13. But I, as a deaf *man,* heard not; and *I was* as a dumb man *that* openeth not his mouth. 14. Thus I was as **a** man that heareth not, and in whose mouth *are* no reproofs. 15. For in thee, O LORD, do I hope: thou wilt hear, O Lord my God. 16. For I said, *Hear me,* lest *otherwise* they

should rejoice over me: when my foot slippeth, they magnify *themselves* against me. 17. For I *am* ready to halt, and my sorrow *is* continually before me. 18. For I will declare mine iniquity; I will be sorry for my sin. 19. But mine enemies *are* lively, *and* they are strong: and they that hate me wrongfully are multiplied. 20. They also that render evil for good are mine adversaries; because I follow *the thing that* good *is.* 21. Forsake me not, O LORD: O my God, be not far from me. 22. Make haste to help me, O Lord my salvation.

Psa. 51:1. Have mercy upon me, O God, according to thy lovingkindness: according unto the multitude of thy tender mercies blot out my transgressions. 2. Wash me throughly from mine iniquity, and cleanse me from my sin. 3. For I acknowledge my transgressions: and my sin *is* ever before me. 4. Against thee, thee only, have I sinned, and done *this* evil in thy sight: that thou mightest be justified when thou speakest, *and* be clear when thou judgest. 7. Purge me with hyssop, and I shall be clean: wash me, and I shall be whiter than snow. 8. Make me to hear joy and gladness; *that* the bones *which* thou hast broken may rejoice. 9. Hide thy face from my sins, and blot out all mine iniquities. 10. Create in me a clean heart, O God; and renew a right spirit within me. 11. Cast me not away from thy presence; and take not thy holy spirit from me. 12. Restore unto me the joy of thy salvation; and uphold me *with thy* free spirit. 13. *Then* will I teach transgressors thy ways; and sinners shall be converted unto thee. 14. Deliver me from bloodguiltiness, O God, thou God of my salvation: *and* my tongue shall sing aloud of thy righteousness. 15. O Lord, open thou my lips; and my mouth shall shew forth thy praise. 16. For thou desirest not sacrifice; else would I give *it:* thou delightest not in burnt offering. 17. The sacrifices of God *are* a broken spirit: a broken and a contrite heart, O God, thou wilt not despise.

Isa. 6:5. Woe *is* me! for I am undone; because I *am* a man of unclean lips, and I dwell in the midst of a people of unclean lips: for mine eyes have seen the King, the LORD of hosts.

Lam. 1:20. Behold, O LORD; for I *am* in distress: my bowels are troubled; mine heart is turned within me; for I have grievously rebelled:

Ezek. 7:16. But they that escape of them shall escape, and shall be on the mountains like doves of the valleys, all of them mourning, every one for his iniquity. 17. All hands shall be feeble, and all knees shall be weak *as* water. 18. They shall also gird *themselves* with sackcloth, and horror shall cover them; and shame *shall be* upon all faces, and baldness upon all their heads. 25. They shall seek peace, and *there shall be* none. 26. Mischief shall come upon mischief, and rumour shall be upon rumour;

then shall they seek a vision of the prophet; but the law shall perish from the priest, and counsel from the ancients.

Ezek. 33:10. Therefore, O thou son of man, speak unto the house of Israel; thus ye speak, saying, If our transgressions and our sins *be* upon us, and we pine away in them, how should we then live?

Mic. 7:17. They shall lick the dust like a serpent, they shall move out of their holes like worms of the earth: they shall be afraid of the LORD our God, and shall fear because of thee.

Luke 5:8. When Simon Peter saw *it*, he fell down at Jesus' knees, saying, Depart from me; for I am a sinful man, O Lord.

Acts 2:37. Now when they heard *this*, they were pricked in their heart, and said unto Peter and to the rest of the apostles, Men *and* brethren, what shall we do?

Acts 9:6. ¹ He trembling and astonished said, Lord, what wilt thou have me to do?　　[¹ Omitted in R. V.]

Acts 16:29. He called for a light, and sprang in, and came trembling, and fell down before Paul and Silas, 30. And brought them out, and said, Sirs, what must I do to be saved?

Rom. 2:15. Which shew the work of the law written in their hearts, their conscience also bearing witness, and *their* thoughts the mean while accusing or else excusing one another;

1 Cor. 14:24. If all prophesy, and there come in one that believeth not, or *one* unlearned, he is convinced of all, he is judged of all: 25. And thus are the secrets of his heart made manifest; and so falling down on *his* face he will worship God, and report that God is in you of a truth.

See SIN, CONFESSION OF.

INSTANCES OF: Adam and Eve, after their disobedience, Gen. 3:8-10. Joseph's brethren, on account of their cruelty to Joseph, Gen. 42:21,22; 44:16; 45:3; 50:15-21. Pharaoh: After the plague of hail, Ex. 9:27, 28; the plague of locusts, Ex. 10:16,17; the death of the firstborn, Ex. 12:31. The Israelites: After being rebuked and punished for worshiping the golden calf, Ex. 33:4; the death of the ten spies, and their being sentenced to wander forty years, Num. 14:39,40; their murmuring against God and being bitten by fiery serpents, Num. 21:7. Saul, after sparing Agag and the best of the spoils, 1 Sam. 15:24. David, after the pestilence sent on account of his numbering the people, 1 Chr. 21:30. See PSALMS, PENITENTIAL. Widow of Zarephath, when her son died, 1 Kin. 17:18. Belshazzar, when he "saw the part of the hand that wrote," Dan. 5:6. Darius, when Daniel was in the lions' den. Dan. 6:18. Mariners: After casting Jonah into the sea, Jonah 1:16; at the preaching of Jonah, Jonah 3; Matt. 12:41; Luke 11:32. Jonah, in the whale's belly, Jonah 2. Herod, when he heard of the fame of Jesus, Matt. 14:2; Mark 6:14; Luke 9:7. Jews, when Jesus commanded the guiltless man to cast the first stone at the woman

taken in adultery, John 8:9. Judas, after his betrayal of Jesus, Matt. 27:3-5. Saul of Tarsus, when he saw Jesus on the way to Damascus, Acts 9:4-18. Felix, under the preaching of Paul, Acts 24:25. Philippian jailer, after the earthquake, Acts 16:30.

See WICKED.

FROM GOD: Job 33:14. For God speaketh once, yea twice, *yet man* perceiveth it not. 15. In a dream, in a vision of the night, when deep sleep falleth upon men, in slumberings upon the bed; 16. Then he openeth the ears of men, and sealeth their instruction, 17. That he may withdraw man *from his* purpose, and hide pride from man. 18. He keepeth back his soul from the pit, and his life from perishing by the sword. 19. He is chastened also with pain upon his bed, and the multitude of his bones with strong *pain:* 20. So that his life abhorreth bread, and his soul dainty meat. 21. His flesh is consumed away, that it cannot be seen; and his bones *that* were not seen stick out. 22. Yea, his soul draweth near unto the grave, and his life to the destroyers. 23. If there be a messenger with him, an interpreter, one among a thousand, to shew unto man his uprightness: 24. Then he is gracious unto him, and saith, Deliver him from going down to the pit: I have found a ransom. 25. His flesh shall be fresher than a child's: he shall return to the days of his youth: 26. He shall pray unto God, and he will be favourable unto him: and he shall see his face with joy: for he will render unto man his righteousness. 27. He looketh upon men, and *if any* say, I have sinned, and perverted *that which was* right, and it profited me not; 28. He will deliver his soul from going into the pit, and his life shall see the light. 29. Lo, all these *things* worketh God oftentimes with man, 30. To bring back his soul from the pit, to be enlightened with the light of the living.

John 6:44. No man can come to me, except the Father which hath sent me draw him: and I will raise him up at the last day. 45. It is written in the prophets, And they shall be all taught of God. Every man therefore that hath heard, and hath learned of the Father, cometh unto me.

John 16:7. Nevertheless I tell you the truth; It is expedient for you that I go away: for if I go not away, the Comforter will not come unto you; but if I depart, I will send him unto you. 8. And when he is come, he will reprove the world of sin, and of righteousness, and of judgment: 9. Of sin, because they believe not on me; 10. Of righteousness, because I go to my Father, and ye see me no more; 11. Of judgment, because the prince of this world is judged.

Acts 16:14. And a certain woman named Lydia, a seller of purple, of the city of Thyatira, which worshipped God, heard *us:* whose heart the Lord opened, that she attended unto the things which were spoken of Paul.

See PENITENTS; REMORSE; REPENTANCE; SIN, CONFESSION OF.

UNJUST, OF INNOCENT PERSONS: See ACCUSATION, FALSE; INDICTMENTS.

CONVOCATION, HOLY: Three held annually by the Israelites, Lev. 23.
See FEASTS.

COOKING. A kid might not be seethed in the mother's milk, Deut. 14:21. Spice used in, Ezek. 24:10. Ephraim, a cake unturned, Hos. 7:8. In the temple, Ezek. 46:19-24.
See BREAD; OVEN.

COOS, an island, Paul visits, in the Mediterranean, Acts 21:1.

COPPER, incorrectly translated brass, Deut. 8:9.
See BRASS.

COPULATION. Forbidden between persons near of kin, Lev. 18:6-16. During menses, Lev. 15:19; 18:19; with animals.
See ADULTERY; LASCIVIOUSNESS; SODOMY.

COR. A measure for liquids and solids, containing ten ephahs, or baths, and equal to the homer, Ezek. 45:14. Rendered measure in 1 Kin. 4:22; 5:11; 2 Chr. 2:10; 27:5; Ezra 7:22; Luke 16:7.
See MEASURES.

CORAL, Job 28:18; Ezek. 27:16.

CORBAN, an oblation, Mark 7:11.

CORD. Ancient uses of: In casting lots, Mic. 2:5; fastening tents, Ex. 35:18; 39:40; Isa. 54:2; leading or binding animals, Psa. 118:27; Hos. 11:4; hitching to cart or plough, Job 39:10; binding prisoners, Judg. 15:13; measuring ground, 2 Sam. 8:2; Josh. 17:14; Psa. 78:55; Amos 7:17; Zech. 2:1; worn on the head as a sign of submission, 1 Kin. 20:31.
FIGURATIVE: Of spiritual blessings, Psa. 16:6. Of sin, Prov. 5:22. Of life, Eccl. 12:6. Of friendship, Eccl. 4:12; Hos. 11:4.
SYMBOLICAL USES OF: Token in mourning, 1 Kin. 20:31-33; Job 36:8. Signifying an inheritance, Josh. 17:14.

CORIANDER, a spice, Ex. 16:31; Num. 11:7.

CORINTH, a city of Achaia. Visited: By Paul, Acts 18; 2 Cor. 12:14; 13:1; with 1 Cor. 16:5-7; and 2 Cor. 1:16; Apollos, Acts 19:1; Titus, 2 Cor. 8:16,17; 12:18. Erastus, a Christian of, Rom. 16:23; 2 Tim. 4:20.
CHURCH OF: Schism in, 1 Cor. 1:12; 3:4. Immortalities in, 1 Cor. 5; 11. Writes to Paul, 1 Cor. 7:1. Alienation of, from Paul, 2 Cor. 10. Abuse of ordinances in, 1 Cor. 11:22; 14. Heresies in, 1 Cor. 15:12; 2 Cor. 11. Lawsuits in, 1 Cor. 6. Liberality of, 2 Cor. 9. Paul's letters to, 1 Cor. 1:2; 16:21-24; 2 Cor. 1:1,13.

CORMORANT, a bird forbidden as food, Lev. 11:17; Deut. 14:17; Isa. 34:11; Zeph. 2:14.

CORN. A general term applied to all grains. In valleys, Psa. 65:13; Mark 4:28. A product of Egypt, Gen. 41:47-49; Palestine, Deut. 33:28; Ezek. 27:17. Parched, Ruth 2:14; 1 Sam. 17:17; 25:18; 2 Sam. 17:28. Ground, 2 Sam. 17:19. Eaten by the Israelites, Josh. 5:11,12. Shocks of, burnt, Judg.

15:5. Heads of, plucked by Christ's disciples, Matt. 12:1. Mosaic laws concerning, Ex. 22:6; Deut. 23:25.
FIGURATIVE: Psa. 72:16; Hos. 14:7; John 12:24. Symbolical, Gen. 41:5.
See BARLEY; BARN; BREAD; FIRSTFRUITS; GLEANING; HARVEST; REAPING; RYE; THRESHING; TITHES; WHEAT.

CORNELIUS, a Roman centurion, Acts 10.

CORNERSTONE, Job 38:6. See STONE.
FIGURATIVE: Psa. 144:12. Of Christ, Psa. 118:22; Isa. 28:16; Matt. 21:42; Mark 12:10; Luke 20:17; Acts 4:11; 1 Cor. 3:11; Eph. 2:20; 1 Pet. 2:6.

CORNET. See TRUMPET.

CORPORAL PUNISHMENT. See PUNISHMENT.

CORPULENCY. INSTANCES OF: Eglon, Judg. 3:17; Eli, 1 Sam. 4:18.

CORRECTION. See AFFLICTION, DESIGN OF; CHASTISEMENT; CHILDREN, CORRECTION OF; PARENTS; PUNISHMENT; SCOURGING.

CORRUPTION. PHYSICAL DECOMPOSITION: Lev. 22:25. After death, Gen. 3:19; Job 17:14; 21:26; 34:15; Psa. 16:10; 49:9; 104:29; Eccl. 3:20; 12:7; Jonah, 2:6; Acts 2:27, 31; 13:34-37; 1 Cor. 15:42,50.
FIGURATIVE: Of sin, Isa. 38:17; Rom. 8: 21; Gal. 6:8; 2 Pet. 1:4; 2:12,19. Mount of, 2 Kin. 23:13.
JUDICIAL: See COURT; GOVERNMENT; JUDGE.
ECCLESIASTICAL: See CHURCH, CORRUPT; MINISTERS.
POLITICAL: See BRIBERY; CIVIL SERVICE; GOVERNMENT; POLITICS.

COSMETICS, 2 Kin. 9:30; Jer. 4:30; Ezek. 23:40.

COTTON, Ex. 25:4 [R. V. marg.].

COUNCIL, Apostolic, Acts 15:1-29. Of War, 2 Sam. 16:20; 17:1-4; 2 Sam. 17:5-15.

COUNSEL. Prov. 1:5. A wise *man* will hear, and will increase learning; and a man of understanding shall attain unto wise counsels:

Prov. 9:9. Give *instruction* to a wise *man*, and he will be yet wiser; teach a just *man*, and he will increase in learning.

Prov. 11:14. Where no counsel *is*, the people fall: but in the multitude of counsellors *there is* safety.

Prov. 12:15. The way of a fool *is* right in his own eyes: but he that hearkeneth unto counsel *is* wise.

Prov. 15:22. Without counsel purposes are disappointed: but in the multitude of counsellors they are established.

Prov. 19:20. Hear counsel, and receive instruction, that thou mayest be wise in thy latter end.

Prov. 20:18. *Every* purpose is established by counsel: and with good advice make war.

Prov. 24:6. For by wise counsel thou shalt make thy war: and in multitude of counsellors *there is* safety.

Prov. 27:9. Ointment and perfume rejoice

the heart : so *doth* the sweetness of a man's friend by hearty counsel.

See PRUDENCE.

REJECTED: Prov. 1:24. Because I have called, and ye refused ; I have stretched out my hand, and no man regarded ; 25. But ye have set at nought all my counsel, and would none of my reproof : 26. I will also laugh at your calamities ; I will mock when your fear cometh ; 27. When your fear cometh as desolation, and your destruction cometh as a whirlwind ; when distress and anguish cometh upon you. 28. Then shall they call upon me, but I will not answer ; they shall seek me early, but they shall not find me : 29. For that they hated knowledge, and did not choose the fear of the LORD : 30. They would none of my counsel : they despised all my reproof. 31. Therefore shall they eat of the fruit of their own way, and be filled with their own devices. 32. For the turning away of the simple shall slay them, and the prosperity of fools shall destroy them. 33. But whoso hearkeneth unto me shall dwell safely, and shall be quiet from fear of evil.

INSTANCES OF : By Rehoboam, 1 Kin. 12: 8-16. By the rich young ruler, Matt. 19:22.

COUNSELLOR. A wise man, versed in law and diplomacy, 1 Chr. 27:32,33. Ahithophel was, to David, 1 Chr.27:33; 2 Sam.16:23; to Absalom, 2 Sam. 16:23. Was member of the Sanhedrin at Jerusalem, Mark 15:43; Luke 23:50,51. A title of Christ, Isa. 9:6.

COUNTENANCE. Angry, Prov. 25:23. Cheerful, Job 29:24; Psa. 4:6; 21:6; 44:3; Prov. 15:13; 27:17. Fierce, Deut. 28:50; Dan. 8:23. Guilty, Gen. 4:5; Isa. 3:9. Health indicated in, Psa. 42:11; 43:5. Pride in, 2 Kin. 5:1; Psa. 10:4. Reading of, Gen. 31:2,5. Sad, 1 Sam. 1:18; Neh. 2:2,3; Eccl. 7:3; Ezek. 27:35; Dan. 1:15; 5:6. Transfigured, Ex. 34:29-35; 2 Cor. 3:7,13; Luke 9:29.

See FACE.

COUNTRY. LOVE OF : Judg. 5:1. Then sang Deborah and Barak the son of Abinoam on that day, saying. 2. Praise ye the LORD for the avenging of Israel, when the people willingly offered themselves. 3. Hear, O ye kings ; give ear, O ye princes ; I, *even* I, will sing unto the LORD ; I will sing *praise* to the LORD God of Israel. 4. LORD, when thou wentest out of Seir, when thou marchedst out of the field of Edom, the earth trembled, and the heavens dropped, the clouds also dropped water. 5. The mountains melted from before the LORD, *even* that Sinai from before the LORD God of Israel. 6. In the days of Shamgar the son of Anath, in the days of Jael, the highways were unoccupied, and the travellers walked through byways. 7. *The inhabitants of* the villages ceased, they ceased in Israel, until that I Deborah arose, that I arose a mother in Israel. 8. They chose new gods ; then *was* war in the gates : was there a shield or spear seen among forty thousand in Israel ? 9. My heart *is* toward the governors of Israel, that

offered themselves willingly among the people. Bless ye the LORD. 10. Speak, ye that ride on white asses, ye that sit in judgment, and walk by the way. 11. *They that are delivered* from the noise of archers in the places of drawing water, there shall they rehearse the righteous acts of the LORD, *even* the righteous acts *toward the inhabitants* of his villages in Israel : then shall the people of the LORD go down to the gates. 12. Awake, awake, Deborah : awake, awake, utter a song : arise, Barak, and lead thy captivity captive, thou son of Abinoam. 13. Then he made him that remaineth have dominion over the nobles among the people : the LORD made me have dominion over the mighty. 14. Out of Ephraim *was there* a root of them against Amalek ; after thee, Benjamin, among thy people ; out of Machir came down governors, and out of Zebulun they that handle the pen of the writer. 15. And the princes of Issachar *were* with Deborah ; even Issachar, and also Barak : he was sent on foot into the valley. For the divisions of Reuben *there were* great thoughts of heart. 16. Why abodest thou among the sheepfolds, to hear the bleatings of the flocks ? For the divisions of Reuben *there were* great searchings of heart. 17. Gilead abode beyond Jordan : and why did Dan remain in ships ? Asher continued on the sea shore, and abode in his breaches. 18. Zebulun and Naphtali *were* a people *that* jeoparded their lives unto the death in the high places of the field. 19. The kings came *and* fought, then fought the kings of Canaan in Taanach by the waters of Megiddo ; they took no gain of money. 20. They fought from heaven ; the stars in their courses fought against Sisera. 21. The river of Kishon swept them away, that ancient river, the river Kishon. O my soul, thou hast trodden down strength. 22. Then were the horsehoofs broken by the means of the pransings, the pransings of their mighty ones. 23. Curse ye Meroz, said the angel of the LORD, curse ye bitterly the inhabitants thereof ; because they came not to the help of the LORD, to the help of the LORD against the mighty. 24. Blessed above women shall Jael the wife of Heber the Kenite be ; blessed shall she be above women in the tent. 25. He asked water, *and* she gave *him* milk ; she brought forth butter in a lordly dish. 26. She put her hand to the nail, and her right hand to the workman's hammer ; and with the hammer she smote Sisera, she smote off his head, when she had pierced and stricken through his temples. 27. At her feet he bowed, he fell, he lay down : at her feet he bowed, he fell : where he bowed, there he fell down dead. 28. The mother of Sisera looked out at a window, and cried through the lattice, Why is his chariot *so* long in coming ? why tarry the wheels of his chariots ? 29. Her wise ladies answered her, yea, she returned answer to herself. 30. Have they not sped ? have they *not* divided the prey ; to every man a damsel *or* two ; to Sisera a prey of divers colours, a prey of divers colours of needlework, of divers colours of needlework on both sides, *meet* for the necks of *them that take* the spoil? 31. So let all thine enemies perish, O LORD: but *let* them that love him *be* as the sun when he goeth forth in his might. And the land had rest forty years.

2 Sam. 10:12. Be of good courage, and let us play the men for our people, and for the cities of our God: and the LORD do that which seemeth him good.

Neh. 1:1. The words of Nehemiah the son of Hachaliah. And it came to pass in the month Chisleu, in the twentieth year, as I was in Shushan the palace, 2. That Hanani, one of my brethren, came, he and *certain* men of Judah; and I asked them concerning the Jews that had escaped, which were left of the captivity, and concerning Jerusalem. 3. And they said unto me, The remnant that are left of the captivity there in the province *are* a great affliction and reproach : the wall of Jerusalem also *is* broken down, and the gates thereof are burned with fire.

4. And it came to pass, when I heard these words, that I sat down and wept, and mourned *certain* days, and fasted, and prayed before the God of heaven, 5. And said, I beseech thee, O LORD God of heaven, the great and terrible God, that keepeth covenant and mercy for them that love him and observe his commandments: 6. Let thine ear now be attentive, and thine eyes open, that thou mayest hear the prayer of thy servant, which I pray before thee now, day and night, for the children of Israel thy servants, and confess the sins of the children of Israel, which we have sinned against thee : both I and my father's house have sinned. 7. We have dealt very corruptly against thee, and have not kept the commandments, nor the statutes, nor the judgments, which thou commandedst thy servant Moses. 8. Remember, I beseech thee, the word that thou commandedst thy servant Moses, saying, *If* ye transgress, I will scatter you abroad among the nations : 9. But *if* ye turn unto me, and keep my commandments, and do them ; though there were of you cast out unto the uttermost part of the heaven, *yet* will I gather them from thence, and will bring them unto the place that I have chosen to set my name there. 10. Now these *are* thy servants and thy people, whom thou hast redeemed by thy great power, and by thy strong hand. 11. O Lord, I beseech thee, let now thine ear be attentive to the prayer of thy servant, and to the prayer of thy servants, who desire to fear thy name : and prosper, I pray thee, thy servant this day, and grant him mercy in the sight of this man. For I was the king's cupbearer.

Neh. 2:1. And it came to pass in the month Nisan, in the twentieth year of Artaxerxes the king, *that* wine *was* before him : and I

took up the wine, and gave *it* unto the king. Now I had not been *beforetime* sad in his presence. 2. Wherefore the king said unto me, Why *is* thy countenance sad, seeing thou *art* not sick? this *is* nothing *else* but sorrow of heart. Then I was very sore afraid, 3. And said unto the king, Let the king live for ever : why should not my countenance be sad, when the city, the place of my fathers' sepulchres, *lieth* waste, and the gates thereof are consumed with fire? 4. Then the king said unto me, For what dost thou make request? So I prayed to the God of heaven. 5. And I said unto the king, If it please the king, and if thy servant have found favour in thy sight, that thou wouldest send me unto Judah, unto the city of my fathers' sepulchres, that I may build it. 6. And the king said unto me, (the queen also sitting by him,) For how long shall thy journey be? and when wilt thou return? So it pleased the king to send me ; and I set him a time. 7. Moreover I said unto the king, If it please the king, let letters be given me to the governors beyond the river, that they may convey me over till I come into Judah; 8. And a letter unto Asaph the keeper of the king's forest, that he may give me timber to make beams for the gates of the palace which *appertained* to the house, and for the wall of the city, and for the house that I shall enter into. And the king granted me, according to the good hand of my God upon me. 9. Then I came to the governors beyond the river, and gave them the king's letters. Now the king had sent captains of the army and horsemen with me. 10. When Sanballat the Horonite, and Tobiah the servant, the Ammonite, heard *of it*, it grieved them exceedingly that there was come a man to seek the welfare of the children of Israel. 11. So I came to Jerusalem, and was there three days. 12. And I arose in the night, I and some few men with me ; neither told I *any* man what my God had put in my heart to do at Jerusalem : neither *was there any* beast with me, save the beast that I rode upon. 13. And I went out by night by the gate of the valley, even before the dragon well, and to the dung port, and viewed the walls of Jerusalem, which were broken down, and the gates thereof were consumed with fire. 14. Then I went on to the gate of the fountain, and to the king's pool : but *there was* no place for the beast *that was* under me to pass. 15. Then went I up in the night by the brook, and viewed the wall, and turned back, and entered by the gate of the valley, and *so* returned. 16. And the rulers knew not whither I went, or what I did ; neither had I as yet told *it* to the Jews, nor to the priests, nor to the nobles, nor to the rulers, nor to the rest that did the work. 17. Then said I unto them, Ye see the distress that we *are* in, how Jerusalem *lieth* waste, and the gates thereof are burned with fire : come, and let us build up the wall of Jerusalem, that we be no more a reproach. 18. Then I told them of the hand of my God which was good upon me; as also the king's words that he had spoken unto me. And they said, Let us rise up and build. So they strengthened their hands for *this* good *work*. 19. But when Sanballat the Horonite, and Tobiah the servant, the Ammonite, and Geshem the Arabian, heard *it*, they laughed us to scorn, and despised us, and said, What *is* this thing that ye do? will ye rebel against the king? 20. Then answered I them, and said unto them, The God of heaven, he will prosper us; therefore we his servants will arise and build: but ye have no portion, nor right, nor memorial, in Jerusalem. chapters 3-6.

Neh. 5:1. And there was a great cry of the people and of their wives against their brethren the Jews. 2. For there were that said, We, our sons, and our daughters, *are* many: therefore we take up corn *for them*, that we may eat, and live. 3. *Some* also there were that said, We have mortgaged our lands, vineyards, and houses, that we might buy corn, because of the dearth. 4. There were also that said, We have borrowed money for the king's tribute, *and that upon* our lands and vineyards. 5. Yet now our flesh *is* as the flesh of our brethren, our children as their children: and, lo, we bring into bondage our sons and our daughters to be servants, and *some* of our daughters are brought unto bondage *already:* neither *is it* in our power *to redeem them;* for other men have our lands and vineyards. 6. And I was very angry when I heard their cry and these words. 7. Then I consulted with myself, and I rebuked the nobles, and the rulers, and said unto them, Ye exact usury, every one of his brother. And I set a great assembly against them. 8. And I said unto them, We after our ability have redeemed our brethren the Jews, which were sold unto the heathen; and will ye even sell your brethren? or shall they be sold unto us? Then held they their peace, and found nothing *to answer*. 9. Also I said, It *is* not good that ye do: ought ye not to walk in the fear of our God because of the reproach of the heathen our enemies? 10. I likewise, *and* my brethren, and my servants, might exact of them money and corn: I pray you, let us leave off this usury. 11. Restore, I pray you, to them, even this day, their lands, their vineyards, their oliveyards, and their houses, also the hundredth *part* of the money, and of the corn, the wine, and the oil, that ye exact of them. 12. Then said they, We will restore *them*, and will require nothing of them; so will we do as thou sayest. Then I called the priests, and took an oath of them, that they should do according to this promise. 13. Also I shook my lap, and said, So God shake out every man from his house, and from his labour, that performeth not this promise, even thus be he shaken out, and emptied. And all the con-

gregation said, Amen, and praised the LORD. And the people did according to this promise. 14. Moreover from the time that I was appointed to be their governor in the land of Judah, from the twentieth year even unto the two and thirtieth year of Artaxerxes the king, *that is*, twelve years, I and my brethren have not eaten the bread of the governor. 15. But the former governors that *had been* before me were chargeable unto the people, and had taken of them bread and wine, beside forty shekels of silver; yea, even their servants bare rule over the people: but so did not I, because of the fear of God. 16. Yea, also I continued in the work of this wall, neither bought we any land: and all my servants *were* gathered thither unto the work. 17. Moreover *there were* at my table an hundred and fifty of the Jews and rulers, beside those that came unto us from among the heathen that *are* about us. 18. Now *that* which was prepared *for me* daily *was* one ox *and* six choice sheep; also fowls were prepared for me, and once in ten days store of all sorts of wine: yet for all this required not I the bread of the governor, because the bondage was heavy upon this people.

Psa. 137:1. By the rivers of Babylon, there we sat down, yea, we wept, when we remembered Zion. 2. We hanged our harps upon the willows in the midst thereof. 3. For there they that carried us away captive required of us a song; and they that wasted us *required of us* mirth, *saying*, Sing us *one* of the songs of Zion. 4. How shall we sing the LORD's song in a strange land? 5. If I forget thee, O Jerusalem, let my right hand forget *her cunning*. 6. If I do not remember thee, let my tongue cleave to the roof of my mouth; if I prefer not Jerusalem above my chief joy.

The Jews held church and country as one, therefore see CHURCH, LOVE OF. See also PATRIOTISM.

COURAGE. Enjoined upon Joshua, Deut. 31:7,8,22,23; Josh. 1:1-9; the Israelites, Lev. 26:6-8; 2 Chr. 32:7,8; Solomon, 1 Chr. 22:13; 28:20; Asa, 2 Chr. 15:1-7. Enjoined by Jehoshaphat upon the judicial and executive officers he appointed, 2 Chr. 19:11.

SCRIPTURES RELATING TO: Prov. 28:1. The wicked flee when no man pursueth: but the righteous are bold as a lion.

Ezek. 2:6. And thou, son of man, be not afraid of them, neither be afraid of their words, though briers and thorns *be* with thee, and thou dost dwell among scorpions: be not afraid of their words, nor be dismayed at their looks, though they *be* a rebellious house.

Ezek. 3:9. As an adamant harder than flint have I made thy forehead: fear them not, neither be dismayed at their looks, though they *be* a rebellious house.

1 Cor. 16:13. Watch ye, stand fast in the faith, quit you like men, be strong.

Phil. 1:27. That ye stand fast in one spirit, with one mind striving together for the faith of the gospel; 28. And in nothing terrified by your adversaries : which is to them an evident token of perdition, but to you of salvation, and that of God.

2 Tim. 1:7. For God hath not given us the spirit of fear; but of power, and of love, and of a sound mind.

INSTANCES OF THE COURAGE OF CONVICTION: Abraham, in leaving his fatherland, Gen. 12:1-9; in offering Isaac, Gen. 22:1-14. Gideon, in destroying the altar of Baal, Judg. 6:25-31. Ezra, in undertaking the perilous journey from Babylon to Palestine without a guard, Ezra 8:22,23.

The Jews, in returning answer to Tatnai, Ezra 5·11. The three Hebrews, who refused to bow down to the image of Nebuchadnezzar, Dan. 3:16-18. Daniel, in persisting in prayer, regardless of the edict against praying, Dan. 6:10. Peter and John, in refusing to obey men, rather than God, Acts 4:19; 5:29.

See MINISTERS, COURAGE OF ; REPROOF.

INSTANCES OF PERSONAL BRAVERY: Joshua and Caleb, in advising that Israel go at once and possess the land, Num. 13:30; 14:6-12. Othniel, in smiting Kirjath-sepher, Josh. 15:16,17. Gideon, in attacking the confederate armies of the Midianites and Amalekites with three hundred men, Judg. 7:7-23. Deborah, in leading Israel's armies, Judg. 4. Jael, in slaying Sisera, Judg. 4:18-22. Agag, in the indifference with which he faced death, 1 Sam. 15:32,33. David, in slaying Goliath, 1 Sam. 17:32-50; in entering into the tent of Saul, and carrying away Saul's spear, 1 Sam. 26:7-12. David's captains, 2 Sam. 23. Joab, in reproving King David, 2 Sam. 19:5-7. Nehemiah, in refusing to take refuge in the temple, Neh. 6:10-13. Esther, in going to the king to save her people, Esth. 4:8,16; chapters 5-7.

Joseph of Arimathæa, in caring for the body of Jesus, Mark 15:43. Thomas, in being willing to die with Jesus, John 11:16. Peter and other disciples, Acts 3:12-26; 4:9-13,19, 20,31. The apostles, under persecution, Acts 5:21,29-32. Paul, in going to Jerusalem, despite his impressions that bonds and imprisonments awaited him, Acts 20:22-24; 24: 14,25.

See BOLDNESS OF THE RIGHTEOUS ; MINISTERS ; REPROOF, FAITHFULNESS IN. COWARDICE.

COURT, ECCLESIASTICAL: 1 Chr. 26: 29. Of the Izharites, Chenaniah and his sons *were* for the outward business over Israel, for officers and judges. 30. *And* of the Hebronites, Hashabiah and his brethren, . . . *were* officers among them of Israel on this side Jordan westward in all the business of the LORD, and in the service of the king. 31. Among the Hebronites *was* Jerijah the chief, *even* among the Hebronites, according to the generations of his fathers. 32. And his brethren, men of valour,

were . . . for every matter pertaining to God, and affairs of the king.

2 Chr. 19:8. Moreover in Jerusalem did Jehoshaphat set of the Levites, and *of* the priests, and of the chief of the fathers of Israel, for the judgment of the LORD, and for controversies, when they returned to Jerusalem. 9. And he charged them, saying, Thus shall ye do in the fear of the LORD, faithfully, and with a perfect heart. 10. And what cause soever shall come to you of your brethren that dwell in their cities, between blood and blood, between law and commandment, statutes and judgments, ye shall even warn them that they trespass not against the LORD, and *so* wrath come upon you, and upon your brethren : this do, and ye shall not trespass. 11. And, behold, Amariah the chief priest *is* over you in all matters of the LORD;

Matt. 18:15. Moreover if thy brother shall trespass against thee, go and tell him his fault between thee and him alone : if he shall hear thee, thou hast gained thy brother. 16. But if he will not hear *thee*, *then* take with thee one or two more, that in the mouth of two or three witnesses every word may be established. 17. And if he shall neglect to hear them, tell *it* unto the church : but if he neglect to hear the church, let him be unto thee as an heathen man and a publican. 18. Verily I say unto you, Whatsoever ye shall bind on earth shall be bound in heaven : and whatsoever ye shall loose on earth shall be loosed in heaven.

John 20:23. Whose soever sins ye remit, they are remitted unto them ; *and* whose soever *sins* ye retain, they are retained.

See CHURCH, DISCIPLINE IN.

CIVIL: Held at the tabernacle, Num. 27:2; the gates of cities, Deut. 21:19; 22:15; 25:7; Josh. 20:4; Ruth 4:1; Zech. 8:16; under a palmtree, Judg. 4:5.

COMPOSITION OF, AND MODE OF PROCEDURE : Ex. 18:25. And Moses chose able men out of all Israel, and made them heads over the people, rulers of thousands, rulers of hundreds, rulers of fifties, and rulers of tens. 26. And they judged the people at all seasons : the hard causes they brought unto Moses, but every small matter they judged themselves.

Deut. 1:15. So I took the chief of your tribes, wise men, and known, and made them heads over you, captains over thousands, and captains over hundreds, and captains over fifties, and captains over tens, and officers among your tribes. 16. And I charged your judges at that time, saying, Hear *the causes* between your brethren, and judge righteously between *every* man and his brother, and the stranger *that is* with him. 17. Ye shall not respect persons in judgment ; *but* ye shall hear the small as well as the great ; ye shall not be afraid of the face of man ; for the judgment *is* God's : and the cause that is too hard for you, bring *it* unto me, and I will hear it.

Deut. 17:9. And thou shalt come unto the priests the Levites, and unto the judge that shall be in those days, and enquire; and they shall shew thee the sentence of judgment:

Ruth 4:2. And he took ten men of the elders of the city, and said, Sit ye down here. And they sat down. 3. And he said unto the kinsman, Naomi, that is come again out of the country of Moab, selleth a parcel of land, which *was* our brother Elimelech's: 4. And I thought to advertise thee, saying, Buy *it* before the inhabitants, and before the elders of my people. If thou wilt redeem *it*, redeem *it:* but if thou wilt not redeem *it*, *then* tell me, that I may know: for *there is* none to redeem *it* beside thee; and I *am* after thee. And he said, I will redeem *it*. 5. Then said Boaz, What day thou buyest the field of the hand of Naomi, thou must buy *it* also of Ruth the Moabitess, the wife of the dead, to raise up the name of the dead upon his inheritance.

1 Chr. 26:29. Of the Izharites, Chenaniah and his sons *were* for the outward business over Israel, for officers and judges. *vs.* 30–32.

2 Chr. 19:8. Moreover in Jerusalem did Jehoshaphat set of the Levites, and *of* the priests, and of the chief of the fathers of Israel, for the judgment of the LORD, and for controversies, when they returned to Jerusalem. 9. And he charged them, saying, Thus shall ye do in the fear of the LORD, faithfully, and with a perfect heart. 10. And what cause soever shall come to you of your brethren that dwell in their cities, between blood and blood, between law and commandment, statutes and judgments, ye shall even warn them that they trespass not against the LORD, and *so* wrath come upon you, and upon your brethren: this do, and ye shall not trespass. 11. And, behold, Amariah the chief priest *is* over you in all matters of the LORD; and Zebadiah the son of Ishmael, . . . of the house of Judah, for all the king's matters:

Mark 14:53. And they led Jesus away to the high priest: and with him were assembled all the chief priests and the elders and the scribes. 55. And the chief priests and all the council sought for witness against Jesus to put him to death; and found none. 56. For many bare false witness against him, but their witness agreed not together. 57. And there arose certain, and bare false witness against him, saying, 58. We heard him say, I will destroy this temple that is made with hands, and within three days I will build another made without hands. 59. But neither so did their witness agree together. 60. And the high priest stood up in the midst, and asked Jesus, saying, Answerest thou nothing? what *is it which* these witness against thee? 61. But he held his peace, and answered nothing. Again the high priest asked him, and said unto him, Art thou the Christ, the Son of the Blessed? 62. And Jesus said, I am: and ye shall see the Son of man sitting on the right

hand of power, and coming in the clouds of heaven. 63. Then the high priest rent his clothes, and saith, What need we any further witnesses? 64. Ye have heard the blasphemy: what think ye? And they all condemned him to be guilty of death. 65. And some began to spit on him, and to cover his face, and to buffet him, and to say unto him, Prophesy: and the servants did strike him with the palms of their hands.

Mark 15:1. And straightway in the morning the chief priests held a consultation with the elders and scribes and the whole council, and bound Jesus, and carried *him* away, and delivered *him* to Pilate. Matt. 26:54–71; Luke 22:50–71; John 18:13–28.

Acts 5:17. Then the high priest rose up, and all they that were with him, (which is the sect of the Sadducees,) and were filled with indignation, 18. And laid their hands on the apostles, and put them in the common prison. 19. But the angel of the Lord by night opened the prison doors, and brought them forth, and said, 20. Go, stand and speak in the temple to the people all the words of this life. 21. And when they heard *that*, they entered into the temple early in the morning, and taught. But the high priest came, and they that were with him, and called the council together, and all the senate of the children of Israel, and sent to the prison to have them brought. 25. Then came one and told them, saying, Behold, the men whom ye put in prison are standing in the temple, and teaching the people. 26. Then went the captain with the officers, and brought them without violence: for they feared the people, lest they should have been stoned. 27. And when they had brought them, they set *them* before the council: and the high priest asked them, 28. Saying, Did not we straitly command you that ye should not teach in this name? and, behold, ye have filled Jerusalem with your doctrine, and intend to bring this man's blood upon us. 34. Then stood there up one in the council, a Pharisee, named Gamaliel, a doctor of the law, had in reputation among all the people, and commanded to put the apostles forth a little space; 38. And now I say unto you, Refrain from these men, and let them alone: for if this counsel or this work be of men, it will come to nought: 39. But if it be of God, ye cannot overthrow it; lest haply ye be found even to fight against God. 40. And to him they agreed: and when they had called the apostles, and beaten *them*, they commanded that they should not speak in the name of Jesus, and let them go. 41. And they departed from the presence of the council, rejoicing that they were counted worthy to suffer shame for his name.

See JUDGE; JUSTICE; PRIEST, JUDICIAL FUNCTIONS OF.

CIRCUIT: 1 Sam. 7:15. And Samuel judged Israel all the days of his life. 16. And he went from year to year in circuit to Beth-el, and Gilgal, and Mizpeh, and judged Israel in all those places. 17. And his return *was* to Ramah;

for there *was* his house; and there he judged Israel; and there he built an altar unto the Lord.

SUPERIOR, AND INFERIOR: Ex. 18:21. Moreover thou shalt provide out of all the people able men, such as fear God, men of truth, hating ¹ covetousness; and place *such* over them *to be* rulers of thousands, *and* rulers of hundreds, rulers of fifties, and rulers of tens. 22. And let them judge the people at all seasons: and it shall be, *that* every great matter they shall bring unto thee, but every small matter they shall judge: so shall it be easier for thyself, and they shall bear *the burden* with thee. 23. If thou shalt do this thing, and God command thee *so*, then thou shalt be able to endure, and all this people shall also go to their place in peace. 24. So Moses hearkened to the voice of his father in law, and did all that he had said. 25. And Moses chose able men out of all Israel, and made them heads over the people, rulers of thousands, rulers of hundreds, rulers of fifties, and rulers of tens. 26. And they judged the people at all seasons: the hard causes they brought unto Moses, but every small matter they judged themselves.   [¹ R. V. unjust gain]

Deut. 1:15. So I took the chief of your tribes, wise men, and known, and made them heads over you, captains over thousands, and captains over hundreds, and captains over fifties, and captains over tens, and officers among your tribes. 16. And I charged your judges at that time, saying, Hear *the causes* between your brethren, and judge righteously between *every* man and his brother, and the stranger *that is* with him. 17. Ye shall not respect persons in judgment; *but* ye shall hear the small as well as the great; ye shall not be afraid of the face of man; for the judgment *is* God's: and the cause that is too hard for you, bring *it* unto me, and I will hear it.

Deut. 17:8. If there arise a matter too hard for thee in judgment, between blood and blood, between plea and plea, and between stroke and stroke, *being* matters of controversy within thy gates: then shalt thou arise, and get thee up into the place which the Lord thy God shall choose; 9. And thou shalt come unto the priests the Levites, and unto the judge that shall be in those days, and enquire; and they shall shew thee the sentence of judgment: 10. And thou shalt do according to the sentence, which they of that place which the Lord shall choose shall shew thee; and thou shalt observe to do according to all that they inform thee: 11. According to the sentence of the law which they shall teach thee, and according to the judgment which they shall tell thee, thou shalt do: thou shalt not decline from the sentence which they shall shew thee, *to* the right hand, nor *to* the left. 12. And the man that will do presumptuously, and will not hearken unto the priest that standeth to minister there before the Lord thy God, or unto the judge, even that man shall die: and thou shalt put away the

evil from Israel. 13. And all the people shall hear, and fear, and do no more presumptuously.

2 Chr. 19:5. And he set judges in the land throughout all the fenced cities of Judah, city by city, 6. And said to the judges, Take heed what ye do: for ye judge not for man, but for the Lord, who *is* with you in the judgment. 7. Wherefore now let the fear of the Lord be upon you; take heed and do *it:* for *there is* no iniquity with the Lord our God, nor respect of persons, nor taking of gifts. 8. Moreover in Jerusalem did Jehoshaphat set of the Levites, and *of* the priests, and of the chief of the fathers of Israel, for the judgment of the Lord, and for controversies, when they returned to Jerusalem. 9. And he charged them, saying, Thus shall ye do in the fear of the Lord, faithfully, and with a perfect heart. 10. And what cause soever shall come to you of your brethren that dwell in their cities, between blood and blood, between law and commandment, statutes and judgments, ye shall even warn them that they trespass not against the Lord, and *so* wrath come upon you, and upon your brethren: this do, and ye shall not trespass.

JUSTICE REQUIRED OF: Ex. 23:2. Thou shalt not follow a multitude to *do* evil; neither shalt thou speak in a cause to decline after many to wrest *judgment:* 3. Neither shalt thou countenance a poor man in his cause. 6. Thou shalt not wrest the judgment of thy poor in his cause. 7. Keep thee far from a false matter; and the innocent and righteous slay thou not: for I will not justify the wicked. 8. And thou shalt take no gift: for the gift blindeth the wise, and perverteth the words of the righteous.

Deut. 1:16. And I charged your judges at that time, saying, Hear *the causes* between your brethren, and judge righteously between *every* man and his brother, and the stranger *that is* with him. 17. Ye shall not respect persons in judgment; *but* ye shall hear the small as well as the great; ye shall not be afraid of the face of man; for the judgment *is* God's: and the cause that is too hard for you, bring *it* unto me, and I will hear it.

Deut. 25:1. If there be a controversy between men, and they come unto judgment, that *the judges* may judge them; then they shall justify the righteous, and condemn the wicked.

2 Chr. 19:5. And he set judges in the land throughout all the fenced cities of Judah, city by city, 6. And said to the judges, Take heed what ye do: for ye judge not for man, but for the Lord, who *is* with you in the judgment. 7. Wherefore now let the fear of the Lord be upon you; take heed and do *it:* for *there is* no iniquity with the Lord our God, nor respect of persons, nor taking of gifts. 8. Moreover in Jerusalem did Jehoshaphat set of the Levites, and *of* the

priests, and of the chief of the fathers of Israel, for the judgment of the LORD, and for controversies, when they returned to Jerusalem. 9. And he charged them, saying. Thus shall ye do in the fear of the LORD, faithfully, and with a perfect heart. 10. And what cause soever shall come to you of your brethren that dwell in their cities, between blood and blood, between law and commandment, statutes and judgments, ye shall even warn them that they trespass not against the LORD, and *so* wrath come upon you, and upon your brethren: this do, and ye shall not trespass.

See JUDGE; JUSTICE.

SENTENCE OF, FINAL AND OBLIGATORY: Deut. 17:8. If there arise a matter too hard for thee in judgment, between blood and blood, between plea and plea, and between stroke and stroke, *being* matters of controversy within thy gates: then shalt thou arise, and get thee up into the place which the LORD thy God shall choose; 9. And thou shalt come unto the priests the Levites, and unto the judge that shall be in those days, and enquire; and they shall shew thee the sentence of judgment: 10. And thou shalt do according to the sentence, which they of that place which the LORD shall choose shall shew thee; and thou shalt observe to do according to all that they inform thee: 11. According to the sentence of the law which they shall teach thee, and according to the jugdment which they shall tell thee, thou shalt do: thou shalt not decline from the sentence which they shall shew thee, *to* the right hand, nor *to* the left. 12. And the man that will do presumptuously, and will not hearken unto the priest that standeth to minister there before the LORD thy God, or unto the judge, even that man shall die: and thou shalt put away the evil from Israel.

CONTEMPT OF: Deut. 17:8. If there arise a matter too hard for thee in judgment, between blood and blood, between plea and plea, and between stroke and stroke, *being* matters of controversy within thy gates: then shalt thou arise, and get thee up into the place which the LORD thy God shall choose; 9. And thou shalt come unto the priests the Levites, and unto the judge that shall be in those days, and enquire; and they shall shew thee the sentence of judgment: 10. And thou shalt do according to the sentence, which they of that place which the LORD shall choose shall shew thee; and thou shalt observe to do according to all that they inform thee: 11. According to the sentence of the law which they shall teach thee, and according to the judgment which they shall tell thee, thou shalt do: thou shalt not decline from the sentence which they shall shew thee, *to* the right hand, nor *to* the left. 12. And the man that will do presumptuously, and will not hearken unto the priest that standeth to minister there before the LORD thy God, or unto the judge, even that

man shall die: and thou shalt put away the evil from Israel. 13. And all the people shall hear, and fear, and do no more presumptuously.

Mic. 5:1. They shall smite the judge of Israel with a rod upon the cheek.

Acts 23:1. And Paul, earnestly beholding the council, said, Men *and* brethren, I have lived in all good conscience before God until this day. 2. And the high priest Ananias commanded them that stood by him to smite him on the mouth. 3. Then said Paul unto him, God shall smite thee, *thou* whited wall: for sittest thou to judge me after the law, and commandest me to be smitten contrary to the law? 4. And they that stood by said, Revilest thou God's high priest? 5. Then said Paul, I wist not, brethren, that he was the high priest: for it is written, Thou shalt not speak evil of the ruler of thy people.

CORRUPT: Prov. 17:15. He that justifieth the wicked, and he that condemneth the just, even they both *are* abomination to the LORD.

Prov. 29:26. Many seek the ruler's favour; but *every* man's judgment *cometh* from the LORD.

Isa. 1:23. Thy princes *are* rebellious, and companions of thieves: every one loveth gifts, and followeth after rewards: they judge not the fatherless, neither doth the cause of the widow come unto them.

Isa. 5:23. Which justify the wicked for reward, and take away the righteousness of the righteous from him!

Isa. 10:1. Woe unto them that decree unrighteous decrees, and that write grievousness *which* they have prescribed; 2. To turn aside the needy from judgment, and to take away the right from the poor of my people, that widows may be their prey, and *that* they may rob the fatherless!

Mic. 3:11. The heads thereof judge for reward, and the priests thereof teach for hire, and the prophets thereof divine for money.

Mic. 7:3. That they may do evil with both hands earnestly, the prince asketh, and the judge *asketh* for a reward; and the great *man*, he uttereth his mischievous desire: so they wrap it up.

Zeph. 3:3. Her princes within her *are* roaring lions; her judges *are* evening wolves; they gnaw not the bones till the morrow.

Matt. 26:59. Now the chief priests, and elders, and all the council, sought false witness against Jesus, to put him to death; 60. But found none: yea, though many false witnesses came, *yet* found they none. At the last came two false witnesses, 61. And said, This *fellow* said, I am able to destroy the temple of God, and to build it in three days. 62. And the high priest arose, and said unto him, Answerest thou nothing? what *is it which* these witness against thee?

Matt. 27:18. For he knew that for envy they had delivered him. [Mark 15:10.] 19. When he was set down on the judgment seat, his wife sent unto him, saying, Have thou nothing to do with that just man: for I have suffered many things this day in a dream because of him. 20. But the chief priests and elders persuaded the multitude that they should ask Barabbas, and destroy Jesus. 21. The governor answered and said unto them, Whether of the twain will ye that I release unto you? They said, Barabbas. 22. Pilate saith unto them, What shall I do then with Jesus which is called Christ? *They* all say unto him, Let him be crucified. 23. And the governor said, Why, what evil hath he done? But they cried out the more, saying, Let him be crucified. 24. When Pilate saw that he could prevail nothing, but *that* rather a tumult was made, he took water, and washed *his* hands before the multitude, saying, I am innocent of the blood of this just person: see ye *to it.* 25. Then answered all the people, and said, His blood *be* on us and on our children. 26. Then released he Barabbas unto them: and when he had scourged Jesus, he delivered *him* to be crucified.

Mark 14:53. And they led Jesus away to the high priest: and with him were assembled all the chief priests and the elders and the scribes. 55. And the chief priests and all the council sought for witness against Jesus to put him to death; and found none. 56. For many bare false witness against him, but their witness agreed not together. 57. And there arose certain, and bare false witness against him, saying, 58. We heard him say, I will destroy this temple that is made with hands, and within three days I will build another made without hands. 59. But neither so did their witness agree together. 60. And the high priest stood up in the midst, and asked Jesus, saying, Answerest thou nothing? what *is it which* these witness against thee? 61. But he held his peace, and answered nothing. Again the high priest asked him, and said unto him, Art thou the Christ, the Son of the Blessed? 62. And Jesus said, I am: and ye shall see the Son of man sitting on the right hand of power, and coming in the clouds of heaven. 63. Then the high priest rent his clothes, and said, What need we any further witnesses? 64. Ye have heard the blasphemy: what think ye? And they all condemned him to be guilty of death. 65. And some began to spit on him, and to cover his face, and to buffet him, and to say unto him, Prophesy: and the servants did strike him with the palms of their hands.

Acts 4:15. But when they had commanded them to go aside out of the council, they conferred among themselves, 16. Saying, What shall we do to these men? for that indeed a notable miracle hath been done by them *is* manifest to all them that dwell in Jerusalem; and we cannot deny *it.* 17. But that it spread no further among the people, let us straitly threaten them, that they speak henceforth to no man in this name. 18. And they called them, and commanded them not to speak at all nor teach in the name of Jesus.

Acts 6:11. Then they suborned men, which

said, We have heard him speak blasphemous words against Moses, and *against* God. 12. And they stirred up the people, and the elders, and the scribes, and came upon *him*, and caught him, and brought *him* to the council, 13. And set up false witnesses, which said, This man ceaseth not to speak blasphemous words against this holy place, and the law: 14. For we have heard him say, that this Jesus of Nazareth shall destroy this place, and shall change the customs which Moses delivered us.

Acts 24:26. He hoped also that money should have been given him of Paul, that he might loose him: wherefore he sent for him the oftener, and communed with him. 27. But after two years Porcius Festus came into Felix' room: and Felix, willing to shew the Jews a pleasure, left Paul bound.

See BRIBERY; JUDGE; JUSTICE.

ACCUSED SPOKE IN HIS OWN DEFENSE: Jer. 26:11. Then spake the priests and the prophets unto the princes and to all the people, saying, This man *is* worthy to die; for he hath prophesied against this city, as ye have heard with your ears. 12. Then spake Jeremiah unto all the princes and to all the people, saying, The LORD sent me to prophesy against this house and against this city all the words that ye have heard. 13. Therefore now amend your ways and your doings, and obey the voice of the LORD your God; and the LORD will repent him of the evil that he hath pronounced against you. 14. As for me, behold, I *am* in your hand: do with me as seemeth good and meet unto you. 15. But know ye for certain, that if ye put me to death, ye shall surely bring innocent blood upon yourselves, and upon this city, and upon the inhabitants thereof: for of a truth the LORD hath sent me unto you to speak all these words in your ears. 16. Then said the princes and all the people unto the priests and to the prophets; This man *is* not worthy to die: for he hath spoken to us in the name of the LORD our God.

Mark 15:3. And the chief priests accused him of many things: but he answered nothing. 4. And Pilate asked him again, saying, Answerest thou nothing? behold how many things they witness against thee. 5. But Jesus yet answered nothing; so that Pilate marvelled.

Acts 4:8. Then Peter, filled with the Holy Ghost, said unto them, Ye rulers of the people, and elders of Israel, 9. If we this day be examined of the good deed done to the impotent man, by what means he is made whole; 10. Be it known unto you all, and to all the people of Israel, that by the name of Jesus Christ of Nazareth, whom ye crucified, whom God raised from the dead, *even* by him doth this man stand here before you whole. 11. This is the stone which was set at nought of you builders, which is become the head of the corner. 12. Neither is there salvation in any other: for there is none other name under heaven given among men, whereby we must be saved. 18. And they called them, and commanded them not to speak at all nor teach in the name of Jesus. 19. But Peter and John answered and said unto them, Whether it be right in the sight of God to hearken unto you more than unto God, judge ye. 20. For we cannot but speak the things which we have seen and heard.

Acts 5:29. Then Peter and the *other* apostles answered and said, We ought to obey God rather than men. 30. The God of our fathers raised up Jesus, whom ye slew and hanged on a tree. 31. Him hath God exalted with his right hand *to be* a Prince and a Saviour, for to give repentance to Israel, and forgiveness of sins. 32. And we are his witnesses of these things; and *so is* also the Holy Ghost, whom God hath given to them that obey him.

Acts 7:1. Then said the high priest, Are these things so? 2. And he [Stephen] said, Men, brethren, and fathers, hearken; The God of glory appeared unto our father Abraham, when he was in Mesopotamia, before he dwelt in Charran, 3. And said unto him, Get thee out of thy country, and from thy kindred, and come into the land which I shall shew thee. 4. Then came he out of the land of the Chaldæans, and dwelt in Charran: and from thence, when his father was dead, he removed him into this land, wherein ye now dwell. 5. And he gave him none inheritance in it, no, not *so much as* to set his foot on: yet he promised that he would give it to him for a possession, and to his seed after him, when *as yet* he had no child. 6. And God spake on this wise, That his seed should sojourn in a strange land; and that they should bring them into bondage, and entreat *them* evil four hundred years. 7. And the nation to whom they shall be in bondage will I judge, said God: and after that shall they come forth, and serve me in this place. 8. And he gave him the covenant of circumcision: and so *Abraham* begat Isaac, and circumcised him the eighth day; and Isaac *begat* Jacob; and Jacob *begat* the twelve patriarchs. 9. And the patriarchs, moved with envy, sold Joseph into Egypt: but God was with him, 10. And delivered him out of all his afflictions, and gave him favour and wisdom in the sight of Pharaoh king of Egypt; and he made him governor over Egypt and all his house. 11. Now there came a dearth over all the land of Egypt and Chanaan, and great affliction: and our fathers found no sustenance. 12. But when Jacob heard that there was corn in Egypt, he sent out our fathers first. 13. And at the second *time* Joseph was made known to his brethren; and Joseph's kindred was made known unto Pharaoh. 14. Then sent Joseph, and called his father Jacob to *him*, and all his kindred, threescore and fifteen souls. 15. So Jacob went down into Egypt, and died, he, and our fathers, 16. And were carried over into Sychem, and laid in the sepulchre that Abraham bought for a sum of money of the sons of Emmor, *the father* of Sychem. 17. But when the time of the promise drew nigh, which God had sworn to Abraham, the people grew and multiplied in Egypt, 18. Till another king arose, which knew not Joseph. 19. The same dealt subtilly with our kindred, and evil entreated our fathers, so that they cast out their young children, to the end they might not live. 20. In which time Moses was born, and was exceeding fair, and nourished up in his father's house three months: 21. And when he was cast out, Pharaoh's daughter took him up, and nourished him for her own son. 22. And Moses was learned in all the wisdom of the Egyptians, and was mighty in words and in deeds. 23. And when he was full forty years old, it came into his heart to visit his brethren the children of Israel. 24. And seeing one *of them* suffer wrong, he defended *him*, and avenged him that was oppressed, and smote the Egyptian: 25. For he supposed his brethren would have understood how that God by his hand would deliver them: but they understood not. 26. And the next day he shewed himself unto them as they strove, and would have set them at one again, saying, Sirs, ye are brethren; why do ye wr ng one to another? 27. But he that did his neighbour wrong thrust him away saying, Who made thee a ruler and a judge over us? 28. Wilt thou kill me, as thou diddest the Egyptian yesterday? 29. Then fled Moses at this saying, and was a stranger in the land of Madian, where he begat two sons. 30. And when forty years were expired, there appeared to him in the wilderness of mount Sina an angel of the Lord in a flame of fire in a bush. 31. When Moses saw *it*, he wondered at the sight: and as he drew near to behold *it*, the voice of the Lord came unto him, 32. *Saying,* I *am* the God of thy fathers, the God of Abraham, and the God of Isaac, and the God of Jacob. Then Moses trembled, and durst not behold. 33. Then said the Lord to him, Put off thy shoes from thy feet: for the place where thou standest is holy ground. 34. I have seen, I have seen the affliction of my people which is in Egypt, and I have heard their groaning, and am come down to deliver them. And now come, I will send thee into Egypt. 35. This Moses whom they refused, saying, Who made thee a ruler and a judge? the same did God send *to be* a ruler and a deliverer by the hand of the angel which appeared to him in the bush. 36. He brought them out, after that he had shewed wonders and signs in the land of Egypt, and in the Red sea, and in the wilderness forty years. 37. This is that Moses, which said unto the children of Israel, A prophet shall the Lord your God raise up unto you of your brethren, like unto me; him shall ye hear. 38. This is he, that was in the church in the wilderness with the angel which spake to him in the mount Sina, and *with* our fathers: who received the lively oracles to give unto us: 39. To whom our fathers would not obey, but thrust *him* from them, and in their hearts turned back again into Egypt, 40. Saying unto Aaron, Make us gods to go before us: for *as for* this Moses, which brought us out of the land of Egypt, we wot not what is become of him. 41. And they made a calf in those days, and offered sacrifice unto the idol, and rejoiced in the works of their own hands. 42. Then God turned, and gave them up to worship the host of heaven; as it is written in the book of the prophets, O ye house of Israel, have ye offered to me slain beasts and sacrifices *by the space of* forty years in the wilderness? 43. Yea, ye took up the tabernacle of Moloch, and the star of your god Remphan, figures which ye made to worship them: and I will carry you away beyond Babylon. 44. Our fathers had the tabernacle of witness in the wilderness, as he had appointed, speaking unto Moses, that he should make it according to the fashion that he had seen. 45. Which also our fathers that came after brought in with Jesus into the possession of the Gentiles, whom God drave out before the face of our fathers, unto the days of David; 46. Who found favour before God, and desired to find a tabernacle for the God of Jacob. 47. But Solomon built him an house. 48. Howbeit the most High dwelleth not in temples made with hands; as saith the prophet, 49. Heaven *is* my throne, and earth *is* my footstool: what house will ye build me? saith the Lord: or what *is* the place of my rest? 50. Hath not my hand made all these things? 51. Ye stiffnecked and uncircumcised in heart and ears, ye do always resist the Holy Ghost: as your fathers *did*, so *do* ye. 52. Which of the prophets have not your fathers persecuted? and they have slain them which shewed before of the coming of the Just One; of whom ye have been now the betrayers and murderers: 53. Who have received the law by the disposition of angels, and have not kept *it*. 54. When they heard these things, they were cut to the heart, and they gnashed on him with *their* teeth. 55. But he, being full of the Holy Ghost, looked up stedfastly into heaven, and saw the glory of God, and Jesus standing on the right hand of God, 56. And said, Behold, I see the heavens opened, and the Son of man standing on the right hand of God.

Acts 23:1. And Paul, earnestly beholding the council, said, Men *and* brethren, I have lived in all good conscience before God until this day. 2. And the high priest Ananias commanded them that stood by him to smite him on the mouth. 3. Then said Paul unto him, God shall smite thee, *thou* whited wall: for sittest thou to judge me after the law, and commandest me to be smitten contrary to the law? 4. And they that stood by said, Revilest thou God's high priest? 5. Then said Paul, I wist not, brethren, that he was

the high priest: for it is written, Thou shalt not speak evil of the ruler of thy people. 6. But when Paul perceived that the one part were Sadducees, and the other Pharisees, he cried out in the council, Men *and* brethren, I am a Pharisee, the son of a Pharisee: of the hope-and resurrection of the dead I am called in question. 7. And when he had so said, there arose a dissension between the Pharisees and the Sadducees: and the multitude was divided.

Acts 26:1. Then Agrippa said unto Paul, Thou art permitted to speak for thyself. Then Paul stretched forth the hand, and answered for himself: 2. I think myself happy, king Agrippa, because I shall answer for myself this day before thee touching all the things whereof I am accused of the Jews: 3. Especially *because I know* thee to be expert in all customs and questions which are among the Jews: wherefore I beseech thee to hear me patiently. 4. My manner of life from my youth, which was at the first among mine own nation at Jerusalem, know all the Jews; 5. Which knew me from the beginning, if they would testify, that after the most straitest sect of our religion I lived a Pharisee. 6. And now I stand and am judged for the hope of the promise made of God unto our fathers: 7. Unto which *promise* our twelve tribes, instantly serving *God* day and night, hope to come. For which hope's sake, king Agrippa, I am accused of the Jews. 8. Why should it be thought a thing incredible with you, that God should raise the dead? 9. I verily thought with myself, that I ought to do many things contrary to the name of Jesus of Nazareth. 10. Which thing I also did in Jerusalem: and many of the saints did I shut up in prison, having received authority from the chief priests; and when they were put to death, I gave my voice against *them*. 11. And I punished them oft in every synagogue, and compelled *them* to blaspheme; and being exceedingly mad against them, I persecuted *them* even unto strange cities. 12. Whereupon as I went to Damascus with authority and commission from the chief priests, 13. At midday, O king, I saw in the way a light from heaven, above the brightness of the sun, shining round about me and them which journeyed with me. 14. And when we were all fallen to the earth, I heard a voice speaking unto me, and saying in the Hebrew tongue, Saul, Saul, why persecutest thou me? *it is* hard for thee to kick against the pricks. 15. And I said, Who art thou, Lord? And he said, I am Jesus whom thou persecutest. 16. But rise, and stand upon thy feet: for I have appeared unto thee for this purpose, to make thee a minister and a witness both of these things which thou hast seen, and of those things in the which I will appear unto thee; 17. Delivering thee from the people, and *from* the Gentiles, unto whom now I send thee, 18. To open their eyes, *and* to turn *them* from darkness to light, and *from* the power of

Satan unto God, that they may receive forgiveness of sins, and inheritance among them which are sanctified by faith that is in me. 19. Whereupon, O king Agrippa, I was not disobedient unto the heavenly vision; 20. But shewed first unto them of Damascus, and at Jerusalem, and throughout all the coasts of Judæa, and *then* to the Gentiles, that they should repent and turn to God, and do works meet for repentance. 21. For these causes the Jews caught me in the temple, and went about to kill *me.* 22. Having therefore obtained help of God, I continue unto this day, witnessing both to small and great, saying none other things than those which the prophets and Moses did say should come: 23. That Christ should suffer, *and* that he should be the first that should rise from the dead, and should shew light unto the people, and to the Gentiles. 24. And as he thus spake for himself, Festus said with a loud voice, Paul, thou art beside thyself; much learning doth make thee mad. 25. But he said, I am not mad, most noble Festus; but speak forth the words of truth and soberness. 26. For the king knoweth of these things, before whom also I speak freely; for I am persuaded that none of these things are hidden from him; for this thing was not done in a corner. 27. King Agrippa, believest thou the prophets? I know that thou believest. 28. Then Agrippa said unto Paul, Almost thou persuadest me to be a Christian. 29. And Paul said, I would to God, that not only thou, but also all that hear me this day, were both almost, and altogether such as I am, except these bonds. 30. And when he had thus spoken, the king rose up, and the governor, and Bernice, and they that sat with them: 31. And when they were gone aside, they talked between themselves, saying, This man doeth nothing worthy of death or of bonds. 32. Then said Agrippa unto Festus, This man might have been set at liberty, if he had not appealed unto Cæsar.

See APPEAL; PUNISHMENT; WITNESS.

COURTESY. See MANNERS.

COURTSHIP. Ancient customs of: Suitor visited the maid, Judg. 14:7; women proposed marriage, Ruth 3:9-13.

See MARRIAGE.

COVENANT. Sacred, Josh. 9:18-21; Gal. 3:15. Binding, Josh. 9:18-20; Jer. 34:8-21; Ezek. 17:14-18; Gal. 3:15. Binding, not only on those who make them, but on those who are represented, Deut. 29:14,15.

Blood of, Ex. 24:8. Book of, Ex. 24:7. The Mosaic law called a covenant, Ex. 34:28.

See CONTRACTS; VOWS.

OF MEN WITH MEN: Breach of, punished, 2 Sam. 21:1-6; Jer. 34:8-22; Ezek. 17: 13-19. National, see ALLIANCES.

Ratified: By giving the hand, Ezra 10:19; Lam. 5:6; Ezek. 17:18; loosing the shoe, Ruth 4:7-11; written and sealed, Neh. 9:38; Jer. 32:10-12; by giving presents, Gen. 21:27-30; 1 Sam. 18:3,4; by making a feast, Gen. 26:30; by a monument, Gen. 31:45, 46, 49-53; by salt-

ing, Lev. 2:13; Num. 18:19; 2 Chr. 13:5; by offering a sacrifice, Gen. 15:9-17; Jer. 34:18,19; by oath, see OATH.

See CONTRACTS.

INSTANCES OF: Abraham and Abimelech, Gen. 21:22-32. Abimelech and Isaac, Gen. 26:26-31. Jacob and Laban, Gen. 31:44-54. Jonathan and David, 1 Sam. 18:3,4; 20:16,42; 2 Sam. 21:7. Jews with each other, to serve God, 2 Chr. 15:12-15; Neh. 10:28-32. King Zedekiah and his subjects, Jer. 34:8. Ahab with Benhadad, 1 Kin. 20:34. Subjects with sovereign, 2 Chr. 23:1-3,16.

OF GOD WITH MEN: Confirmed with an oath, Gen. 22:16; 26:3; 50:24; Psa. 89:35; 105:9; Luke 1:73; Heb. 6:13,17,18. Binding, Lev. 26: Jer. 11:2,3; Gal. 3:15. Everlasting, Gen. 8:20-22; 9:1-17; Psa. 105:8,10; Isa. 54:10; 61:8. God faithful to, Lev. 26:44,45; Deut. 4:31; 7:8,9; Judg. 2:1; 1 Kin. 8:23; Psa. 105:8-11; 106:45; 111:5; Mic. 7:20. Repudiated by God on account of Jews' idolatry, Jer. 44:26,27; Heb. 8:9. Broken by the Jews, Jer. 22:9; Ezek. 16:59; Heb. 8:9. Punishments for breaking of, Lev. 26:25-46.

INSTANCES OF: Of the sabbath, Ex. 31: 16. Of the Ten Commandments, Ex. 34: 28; Deut. 5:2,3; 9:9. With Adam, Gen. 2:16, 17; Noah, Gen. 8:16; 9:8-17; Abraham, Gen. 12:1-3; 15; 17:1-22; Ex. 6:4-8; Psa. 105: 8-11; Rom. 9:7-13; Gal. 3. See CIRCUMCISION. With Isaac, Gen. 17:19; Jacob, Gen. 28:13-15. With the Israelites to deliver them from Egypt, Ex. 6:4-8. With Phinehas, Num. 25:12,13. With Israel, at Horeb, Deut. 5:2,3; in Moab, Deut. 29:1-15. Of the Levites, Neh. 13:29; Mal. 2:4,5. With David, 2 Sam. 7:12-16; 1 Chr. 17:11-14; 2 Chr. 6:16. With David and his house, 2 Sam. 23:5; Psa. 89:20-37; Jer. 33:21. With his people, Isa. 55:3; 59:21. To be confirmed, Dan. 9:27.

THE SECOND COVENANT: Jer. 31:31. Behold, the days come, saith the LORD, that I will make a new covenant with the house of Israel, and with the house of Judah: 32. Not according to the covenant that I made with their fathers in the day *that* I took them by the hand to bring them out of the land of Egypt; which my covenant they brake, although I was an husband unto them, saith the LORD: 33. But this *shall be* the covenant that I will make with the house of Israel; After those days, saith the LORD, I will put my law in their inward parts, and write it in their hearts; and will be their God, and they shall be my people. 34. And they shall teach no more every man his neighbour, and every man his brother, saying, Know the LORD: for they shall all know me, from the least of them unto the greatest of them, saith the LORD: for I will forgive their iniquity, and I will remember their sin no more.

Heb. 8:4. For if he were on earth, he should not be a priest, seeing that there are priests that offer gifts according to the law: 5. Who serve unto the example and shadow of heavenly things, as Moses was admonished of God when he was about to make the tabernacle: for, See, saith he, *that* thou make all things according to the pattern shewed to thee in the mount. 6. But now hath he obtained a more excellent ministry, by how much also he is the mediator of a better covenant, which was established upon better promises. 7. For if that first *covenant* had been faultless, then should no place have been sought for the second. 8. For finding fault with them, he saith, Behold, the days come, saith the Lord, when I will make a new covenant with the house of Israel and with the house of Judah: 9. Not according to the covenant that I made with their fathers, in the day when I took them by the hand to lead them out of the land of Egypt; because they continued not in my covenant, and I regarded them not, saith the Lord. 10. For this *is* the covenant that I will make with the house of Israel after those days, saith the Lord; I will put my laws into their mind, and write them in their hearts: and I will be to them a God, and they shall be to me a people: 11. And they shall not teach every man his neighbour, and every man his brother, saying, Know the Lord: for all shall know me, from the least to the greatest. 12. For I will be merciful to their unrighteousness, and their sins and their iniquities will I remember no more. 13. In that he saith, A new *covenant*, he hath made the first old. Now that which decayeth and waxeth old *is* ready to vanish away.

Heb. 12:18. For ye are not come unto the mount that might be touched, and that burned with fire, nor unto blackness, and darkness, and tempest, 19. And the sound of a trumpet, and the voice of words; which *voice* they that heard intreated that the word should not be spoken to them any more: 20. (For they could not endure that which was commanded, And if so much as a beast touch the mountain, it shall be stoned, or thrust through with a dart: 21. And so terrible was the sight, *that* Moses said, I exceedingly fear and quake:) 22. But ye are come unto mount Sion, and unto the city of the living God, the heavenly Jerusalem, and to an innumerable company of angels, 23. To the general assembly and church of the firstborn, which are written in heaven, and to God the Judge of all, and to the spirits of just men made perfect, 24. And to Jesus the mediator of the new covenant, and to the blood of sprinkling, that speaketh better things than *that of* Abel.

Heb. 13:20. Now the God of peace, that brought again from the dead our Lord Jesus, that great shepherd of the sheep, through the blood of the everlasting covenant.

OF MAN WITH GOD: Jacob, Gen. 28:20-22. Joshua, Josh. 24:25, with *vs.* 19-28. Absalom, 2 Sam. 15:7,8. Jehoiada and Joash, 2 Kin. 11:17. Josiah, 2 Kin. 23:3. Asa, 2 Chr. 15:12-15. Nehemiah, Neh. 9:38; 10. Israelites, Jer. 50:5. See Vows.

COVETOUSNESS. Ex. 18:21. Moreover thou shalt provide out of all the people able men, such as fear God, men of truth, hating ¹ covetousness; 　　[¹ R. V. unjust gain]

Ex. 20:17. Thou shalt not covet thy neighbour's house, thou shalt not covet thy neighbour's wife, nor his manservant, nor his maidservant, nor his ox, nor his ass, nor any thing that *is* thy neighbour's. Deut. 5:21.

Neh. 5:7. Then I consulted with myself, and I rebuked the nobles, and the rulers and said unto them, Ye exact usury, every one of his brother.

Job 20:15. He hath swallowed down riches, and he shall vomit them up again: God shall cast them out of his belly.

Job 31:24. If I have made gold my hope, or have said to the fine gold, *Thou art* my confidence; 25. If I rejoiced because my wealth *was* great, and because mine hand had gotten much; 28. This also *were* an iniquity *to be punished by* the judge: for I should have denied the God *that is* above.

Psa. 10:3. For the wicked boasteth of his heart's desire, and blesseth the covetous, *whom* the LORD abhorreth.

Psa. 119:36. Incline my heart unto thy testimonies, and not to covetousness.

Prov. 1:19. So *are* the ways of every one that is greedy of gain; *which* taketh away the life of the owners thereof.

Prov. 11:24. *There is* that withholdeth more than is meet, but *it tendeth* to poverty. 26. He that withholdeth corn, the people shall curse him:

Prov. 15:27. He that is greedy of gain troubleth his own house;

Prov. 21:25. The desire of the slothful killeth him; for his hands refuse to labour. 26. He coveteth greedily all the day long: but the righteous giveth and spareth not.

Prov. 22:16. He that oppresseth the poor to increase his *riches, and* he that giveth to the rich, *shall* surely *come* to want.

Prov. 23:4. Labour not to be rich; 5. Wilt thou set thine eyes upon that which is not? for *riches* certainly make themselves wings; they fly away as an eagle toward heaven.

Prov. 30:8. Give me neither poverty nor riches; feed me with food convenient for me: 9. Lest I be full, and deny *thee*, and say, Who *is* the LORD?

Eccl. 1:8. All things *are* full of labour: man cannot utter *it:* the eye is not satisfied with seeing, nor the ear filled with hearing. *vs.* 2-8.

Eccl. 4:8. There is one *alone*, and *there is* not a second; yea, he hath neither child nor brother: yet *is there* no end of all his labour; neither is his eye satisfied with riches; neither *saith he*, For whom do I labour, and bereave my soul of good?

Eccl. 5:10. He that loveth silver shall not be satisfied with silver; nor he that loveth abundance with increase: this *is* also vanity. 11. When goods increase, they are increased that eat them: and what good *is there* to the owners thereof, saving the beholding *of them* with their eyes?

Isa. 1:23. Thy princes *are* rebellious, and companions of thieves: every one loveth gifts, and followeth after rewards: they judge not the fatherless, neither doth the cause of the widow come unto them.

Isa. 5:8. Woe unto them that join house to house, *that* lay field to field, till *there be* no place, that they may be placed alone in the midst of the earth!

Isa. 56:11. Yea, *they are* greedy dogs *which* can never have enough, and they *are* shepherds *that* cannot understand: they all look to their own way, every one for his gain, from his quarter.

Isa. 57:17. For the iniquity of his covetousness was I wroth, and smote him: I hid me, and was wroth, and he went on frowardly in the way of his heart.

Jer. 6:13. From the least of them even unto the greatest of them every one *is* given to covetousness;

Jer. 8:10. Therefore will I give their wives unto others, *and* their fields to them that shall inherit *them:* for every one from the least even unto the greatest is given to covetousness, from the prophet even unto the priest every one dealeth falsely.

Jer. 17:11. *As* the partridge sitteth *on eggs,* and hatcheth *them* not; *so* he that getteth riches, and not by right, shall leave them in the midst of his days, and at his end shall be a fool.

Jer. 22:17. But thine eyes and thine heart *are* not but for thy covetousness, and for to shed innocent blood, and for oppression, and for violence, to do *it.*

Jer. 51:13. O thou that dwellest upon many waters, abundant in treasures, thine end is come, *and* the measure of thy covetousness.

Ezek. 22:12. In thee have they taken gifts to shed blood; thou hast taken usury and increase, and thou hast greatly gained of thy neighbours by extortion, and hast forgotten me, saith the Lord God. 13. Behold, therefore I have smitten mine hand at thy dishonest gain which thou hast made, and at thy blood which hath been in the midst of thee.

Ezek. 33:31. And they come unto thee as the people cometh, and they sit before thee *as* my people, and they hear thy words, but they will not do them: for with their mouth they shew much love, *but* their heart goeth after their covetousness.

Hos. 4:18. Her rulers *with* shame do love, Give ye.

Hos. 10:1. Israel *is* an empty vine, he bringeth forth fruit unto himself:

Mic. 2:2. They covet fields, and take *them* by violence; and houses, and take *them* away: so they oppress a man and his house, even a man and his heritage.

Mic. 3:11. The heads thereof judge for re-

ward, and the priests thereof teach for hire, and the prophets thereof divine for money:

Mic. 7:3. That they may do evil with both hands earnestly, the prince asketh, and the judge *asketh* for a reward; and the great *man,* he uttereth his mischievous desire: so they wrap it up.

Hab. 1:15. They take up all of them with the angle, they catch them in their net, and gather them in their drag: therefore they rejoice and are glad. 16. Therefore they sacrifice unto their net, and burn incense unto their drag; because by them their portion *is* fat, and their meat plenteous.

Hab. 2:5. Yea [1] also, because he transgresseth by wine, *he is* a proud man, neither keepeth at home, who enlargeth his desire as hell, and *is* as death, and cannot be satisfied, but gathereth unto him all nations, and heapeth unto him all people: 6. Shall not all these take up a parable against him, and a taunting proverb against him, and say, Woe to him that increaseth *that which is* not his! how long? and to him that ladeth himself with [2] thick clay! 7. Shall they not rise up suddenly that shall bite thee, . . . and thou shalt be for booties unto them? 8. Because thou hast spoiled many nations, all the remnant of the people shall spoil thee: because of men's blood, and *for* the violence of the land, of the city, and of all that dwell therein. 9. Woe to him that [3] coveteth an evil [4] covetousness to his house, that he may set his nest on high, that he may be delivered from the power of evil!

[R. V. [1] moreover, wine is a treacherous dealer, a haughty [2] pledges [3] getteth [4] gain for]

Hag. 1:6. Ye have sown much, and bring in little; ye eat, but ye have not enough; ye drink, but ye are not filled with drink; ye clothe you, but there is none warm; and he that earneth wages, earneth wages *to put it* into a bag with holes.

Mal. 1:10. Who *is there* even among you that would shut the doors *for nought?* neither do ye kindle *fire* on mine altar for nought.

Matt. 6:19. Lay not up for yourselves treasures upon earth, where moth and rust doth corrupt, and where thieves break through and steal: 20. But lay up for yourselves treasures in heaven, where neither moth nor rust doth corrupt, and where thieves do not break through nor steal: 21. For where your treasure is, there will your heart be also.

24. No man can serve two masters: for either he will hate the one, and love the other: or else he will hold to the one, and despise the other. Ye cannot serve God and mammon. 25. Therefore I say unto you, Take no thought for your life, what ye shall eat, or what ye shall drink; nor yet for your body, what ye shall put on. Is not the life more than meat, and the body than raiment?

31. Therefore take no thought, saying, What shall we eat? or, What shall we drink? or, Wherewithal shall we be clothed?

32. (For after all these things do the Gentiles seek:) for your heavenly Father knoweth that ye have need of all these things. 33. But seek ye first the kingdom of God, and his righteousness; and all these things shall be added unto you.

Matt. 13:22. He also that received seed among the thorns is he that heareth the word; and the care of this world, and the deceitfulness of riches, choke the word, and he becometh unfruitful. Mark 4:19; Luke 7:14.

Matt. 16:26. What is a man profited, if he shall gain the whole world, and lose his own soul?

Matt. 19:24. It is easier for a camel to go through the eye of a needle, than for a rich man to enter into the kingdom of God. v. 23; Luke 18:24,25.

Matt. 22:5. They made light of *it*, and went their ways, one to his farm, another to his merchandise: *vs.* 1-14.

Mark 7:21. Out of the heart proceed . . . 22. Covetousness, . . . 23. These evil things come from within, and defile the man.

Luke 12:15. And he said unto them, Take heed, and beware of covetousness: for a man's life consisteth not in the abundance of the things which he possesseth. [See parable of rich man, *vs.* 16-21.] 33. Sell that ye have, and give alms; provide yourselves bags which wax not old, a treasure in the heavens that faileth not, where no thief approacheth, neither moth corrupteth. 34. For where your treasure is, there will your heart be also. Matt. 6:21.

Luke 14:18. They all with one *consent* began to make excuse. The first said unto him, I have bought a piece of ground, and I must needs go and see it: I pray thee have me excused. *vs.* 16-24.

John 6:26. Jesus answered them and said, Verily, verily, I say unto you, Ye seek me, not because ye saw the miracles, but because ye did eat of the loaves, and were filled. 27. Labour not for the meat which perisheth, but for that meat which endureth unto everlasting life, which the Son of man shall give unto you: for him hath God the Father sealed.

Rom. 1:29. Being filled with all unrighteousness, fornication, wickedness, covetousness, maliciousness;

Rom. 13:9. For this, Thou shalt not commit adultery, Thou shalt not kill, Thou shalt not steal, Thou shalt not bear false witness, Thou shalt not covet;

1 Cor. 5:11. But now I have written unto you not to keep company, if any man that is called a brother be a fornicator, or covetous, or an idolater, or a railer, or a drunkard, or an extortioner; with such an one no not to eat.

Eph. 5:3. But fornication, and all uncleanness or covetousness, let it not be once named among you, as becometh saints; 5. For this ye know, that no whoremonger, nor unclean person, nor covetous man, who

is an idolater, hath any inheritance in the kingdom of Christ and of God. 1 Cor. 6:10.

Col. 3:2. Set your affection on things above, not on things on the earth. 5. Mortify therefore your members which are upon the earth; . . . and covetousness, which is idolatry: 6. For which things' sake the wrath of God cometh on the children of disobedience.

Phil. 3:18. (For many walk, of whom I have told you often, and now tell you even weeping, *that they are* the enemies of the cross of Christ: 19. Whose end *is* destruction, whose God *is their* belly, and *whose* glory *is* in their shame, who mind earthly things.)

1 Thess. 2:5. For neither at any time used we flattering words, as ye know, nor a cloke of covetousness; God *is* witness:

1 Tim. 3:3. Not given to wine, no striker, not greedy of filthy lucre; but patient, not a brawler, not covetous; Tit. 1:11.

1 Tim. 6:5. Perverse disputings of men of corrupt minds, and destitute of the truth, supposing that [1] gain is godliness: from such withdraw thyself. 6. But godliness with contentment is great gain. 7. For we brought nothing into *this* world, *and it is* certain we can carry nothing out. 8. And having food and raiment let us be therewith content. [R. V. godliness is a way of gain]

9. But they that will be rich fall into temptation and a snare, and *into* many foolish and hurtful lusts, which drown men in destruction and perdition. 10. For the love of money is the root of all evil: which while some coveted after, they have erred from the faith, and pierced themselves through with many sorrows. 11. But thou, O man of God, flee these things, and follow after righteousness, godliness, faith, love, patience, meekness.

17. Charge them that are rich in this world, that they be not highminded, nor trust in uncertain riches, but in the living God, who giveth us richly all things to enjoy:

2 Tim. 3:2. Men shall be lovers of their own selves, covetous.

Tit. 1:7. For a bishop must be blameless, as the steward of God; not selfwilled, not soon angry, not given to wine, no striker, not given to filthy lucre:

Heb. 13:5. *Let your* conversation *be* without covetousness; *and be* content with such things as ye have:

Jas. 4:2. Ye lust, and have not; ye kill, and desire to have, and cannot obtain: 13. Go to now, ye that say, To day or to morrow we will go into such a city, and continue there a year, and buy and sell, and get gain: 14. Whereas ye know not what *shall be* on the morrow. *vs.* 13-17.

1 Pet. 5:2. Feed the flock of God which is among you, taking the oversight *thereof*, not by constraint, but willingly; not for filthy lucre, but of a ready mind:

2 Pet. 2:3. And through covetousness shall

they with feigned words make merchandise of you: whose judgment now of a long time lingereth not, and their damnation slumbereth not. 14. Having eyes full of adultery, and that cannot cease from sin; beguiling unstable souls: an heart they have exercised with covetous practices; cursed children: *vs.* 15,16.

1 John 2:15. Love not the world, neither the things *that are* in the world. If any man love the world, the love of the Father is not in him. *vs.* 16,17.

Jude 11. Woe unto them! for they have gone in the way of Cain, and ran greedily after the error of Balaam for reward, and perished in the gainsaying of Core.

See AVARICE; RICH; RICHES; WORLDLINESS.

INSTANCES OF: Eve, in desiring the forbidden fruit, Gen: 3:6. Lot, in choosing the plain of the Jordan, Gen. 13:10–13. Laban, in giving Rebekah to be Isaac's wife, Gen. 24: 29–51; in deceiving Jacob when he served him seven years for Rachel, Gen. 29:15–30; in deceiving Jacob in wages, Gen. 31:7,15, 41,42. Jacob, in defrauding Esau of his father's blessing, Gen. 27:6–29; in defrauding Laban of his flocks and herds, Gen. 30:35–43; in buying Esau's birthright, Gen. 25:31. Balaam, in loving the wages of unrighteousness, 2 Pet. 2:15, with Num. 22. Achan, in hiding the treasure, Josh. 7:21. Eli's sons, in taking the flesh of the sacrifice, 1 Sam. 2:13–17. Samuel's sons, in taking bribes, 1 Sam. 8:3. Saul, in sparing Agag and the booty, 1 Sam. 15:8,9. David, of Bath-sheba, 2 Sam. 11:2–5. Ahab, in desiring Naboth's vineyard, 1 Kin. 21:2–16. Gehazi, in taking a gift from Naaman, 2 Kin. 5:20–27. Jews, in exacting usury of their brethren, Neh. 5:1–11; in keeping back the portion of the Levites, Neh. 13:10; in building fine houses while the house of the Lord lay waste, Hag. 1:4–9; in following Jesus for the loaves and fishes, John 6:26. Money changers in the temple, Matt. 21:12,13; Luke 19:45,46; John 2:14–16. The rich young ruler, Matt. 19:16–22. The rich fool, Luke 12:15–21. Judas, in betraying Jesus for twenty pieces of silver, Matt. 26:15,16; Mark 14:10,11; Luke 22:3–6; John 12·6. The unjust steward, Luke 16:1–8. The Pharisees. Luke 16:14. Simon Magus, in trying to buy the gift of the Holy Ghost, Acts 8:18–23. The sorcerers, in filing complaint against Paul and Silas, Acts 16:19. Demetrius, in raising a riot against Paul and Silas, Acts 19: 24,27. Felix, in hoping for a bribe from Paul, Acts 24:26. Demas, in forsaking Paul for love of the world, 2 Tim. 4:10.

See AVARICE; BRIBERY; RICH; RICHES.

COW. Used for draught, 1 Sam. 6:7–12; Hos. 10:11. Milk of, used for food. See MILK. See CATTLE; KINE.

FIGURATIVE: Amos 4:1.

COWARDICE. Lev. 26:36. And upon them that are left *alive* of you I will send a faintness into their hearts in the lands of their enemies; and the sound of a shaking leaf shall chase them; and they shall flee, as fleeing from a sword: and they shall fall when none pursueth. 37. And they shall fall one upon another, as it were before a sword, when none pursueth: and ye shall have no power to stand before your enemies.

Deut. 20:8. And the officers shall speak further unto the people, and they shall say, What man *is there that is* fearful and fainthearted? let him go and return unto his house, lest his brethren's heart faint as well as his heart.

Deut. 32:30. How should one chase a thousand, and two put ten thousand to flight, except their Rock had sold them, and the LORD had shut them up?

Josh. 7:5. The hearts of the people melted, and became as water.

Josh. 23:10. One man of you shall chase a thousand:

Judg. 7:3. Now therefore go to, proclaim in the ears of the people, saying, Whosoever *is* fearful and afraid, let him return and depart early from mount Gilead. And there returned of the people twenty and two thousand: and there remained ten thousand.

Job 15:24. Trouble and anguish shall make him afraid; they shall prevail against him, as a king ready to the battle.

Job 18:11. Terrors shall make him afraid on every side, and shall drive him to his feet.

Prov. 28:1. The wicked flee when no man pursueth: but the righteous are bold as a lion.

Prov. 29:25. The fear of man bringeth a snare:

Isa. 51:12. I, *even I, am* he that comforteth you: who *art* thou, that thou shouldest be afraid of man *that* shall die, and of the son of man *which* shall be made *as* grass; 13. And forgettest the LORD thy maker, that hath stretched forth the heavens, and laid the foundations of the earth; and hast feared continually every day because of the fury of the oppressor, as if he were ready to destroy? and where *is* the fury of the oppressor?

Gal. 6:12. As many as desire to make a fair shew in the flesh, they constrain you to be circumcised; only lest they should suffer persecution for the cross of Christ.

2 Tim. 4:16. At my first answer no man stood with me, but all *men* forsook me:

See COURAGE.

INSTANCES OF: Adam, in attempting to shift responsibility for his sin upon Eve, Gen. 3:12. Abraham, in calling his wife his sister, Gen. 12:11–19; 20:2–12. Isaac, in calling his wife his sister, Gen. 26:7–9. Jacob, in flying from Laban, Gen. 31:31. Aaron, in yielding to the Israelites, when they demanded an idol, Ex. 32:22–24. The ten spies, Num. 13:28, 31–33. Israelites, in fearing to attempt the conquest of Canaan, Num. 14:1–5; Deut. 1:26–28; in the battle with the people of Ai, Josh. 7:5; to meet Goliath, 1 Sam. 17:24; to fight with the Philistines, 1 Sam. 13:6,7. Twenty

thousand of Gideon's army, Judg. 7:3. Ephraimites, Psa. 78:9. Ephraimites and Ma-
nassehites, Josh. 17:14-18. Amoritish kings,
Josh. 10:16. Canaanites, Josh. 2:11; 5:1.
Samuel, fearing to obey God's command to
anoint a king in Saul's stead, 1 Sam. 16:2.
David, in fleeing from Absalom, 2 Sam. 15:
13-17. Nicodemus, in coming to Jesus by
night, John 3:1,2. Joseph of Arimathæa,
secretly a disciple, John 19:38. Parents of
the blind man, who was restored to sight,
John 9:22. Early converts among the rulers,
John 12:42,43. Disciples, in the storm at sea,
Matt. 8:26; Mark 4:38; Luke 8:25; when they
saw Jesus walking on the sea, Matt. 14:25;
Mark 6:50; John 6:19; when Jesus was ap-
prehended, Matt. 26:56. Peter, in denying the
Lord, Matt. 26:69-74; Mark 14:66-72; Luke 22:
54-60; John 18:16,17,25,27. Pilate, in con-
demning Jesus, through fear of the people,
John 19:12-16. Guards of the sepulcher of
Jesus, Matt. 28:4. The Philippian jailer,
Acts 16:27. Peter and other Christians, at
Antioch, Gal. 2:11-14.

COZ, father of Anub, 1 Chr. 4:8.

COZBI, daughter of Zur, Num. 25:15,18.

CRACKNEL, a biscuit or cake, hard
baked, 1 Kin. 14:3.

CRAFTINESS. INSTANCES OF: Satan, in the temptation of Eve, Gen. 3:1-5.
Jacob, in purchase of Esau's birthright, Gen.
25:31-33; obtaining Isaac's blessing, Gen.
27:6-29; in management of Laban's flocks
and herds, Gen. 30:31-43. Gibeonites, in deceiving Joshua and the Israelites into a
treaty, Josh. 9:3-15. Sanballat, in trying
to deceive Nehemiah into a conference,
Neh. 6. Jews, in seeking to entangle the
Master, Matt. 22:15-17,24-28; Mark 12:13,
14,18-23; Luke 20:19-26; in seeking to slay
Jesus, Matt. 26:4; Mark 14:1.

CRAFTSMAN. See ART; MASTER
WORKMAN.

CRANE, an amphibious bird, Isa. 38:14;
Jer. 8:7.

CREATION. Beginning of, Gen. 1:1.
History of, Gen. 1; 2.

See ANIMALS; BIRDS; EARTH; FISH; GRASS;
HEAVENS; MAN; MOON; SEAS; STARS; SUN;
WATER; WOMAN.

See GOD, CREATOR: JESUS, CREATOR.

CREATURE. See CREATION; GOD,
CREATOR; MAN, CREATED.

NEW CREATURE: 2 Cor. 5:17. Therefore
if any man be in Christ, he is a new creature: old things are passed away; behold,
all things are become new.

Gal. 6:15. For in Christ Jesus neither
circumcision availeth any thing, nor uncircumcision, but a new creature.

See REGENERATION.

CREDITOR. LAWS CONCERNING:
Ex. 21:2. If thou buy an Hebrew servant,
six years he shall serve: and in the seventh
he shall go out free for nothing. 3. If he
came in by himself, he shall go out by himself: if he were married, then his wife shall
go out with him. 4. If his master have

given him a wife, and she have born him
sons or daughters; the wife and her children shall be her master's, and he shall go
out by himself. 5. And if the servant shall
plainly say, I love my master, my wife, and
my children; I will not go out free: 6. Then
his master shall bring him unto the judges;
he shall also bring him to the door, or unto
the door post; and his master shall bore his
ear through with an awl; and he shall serve
him for ever.

Ex. 22:25. If thou lend money to any of
my people that is poor by thee, thou shalt
not be to him as a usurer, neither shalt thou
lay upon him usury. 26. If thou at all take
thy neighbour's raiment to pledge, thou
shalt deliver it unto him by that the sun
goeth down: 27. For that is his covering
only, it is his raiment for his skin: wherein
shall he sleep? and it shall come to pass,
when he crieth unto me, that I will hear;
for I am gracious.

Lev. 25:14. And if thou sell ought unto
thy neighbour, or buyest ought of thy neighbour's hand, ye shall not oppress one another: 15. According to the number of years
after the jubile thou shalt buy of thy neighbour, and according unto the number of
years of the fruits he shall sell unto thee:
16. According to the multitude of years
thou shalt increase the price thereof, and
according to the fewness of years thou shalt
diminish the price of it: for according to
the number of the years of the fruits doth
he sell unto thee. 17. Ye shall not therefore oppress one another; but thou shalt fear
thy God: for I am the LORD your God.

35. And if thy brother be waxen poor,
and fallen in decay with thee; then thou
shalt relieve him: yea, though he be a
stranger, or a sojourner; that he may live
with thee. 36. Take thou no usury of him,
or increase: but fear thy God; that thy
brother may live with thee. 37. Thou shalt
not give him thy money upon usury, nor
lend him thy victuals for increase.

Deut. 15:2. And this is the manner of the
release: Every creditor that lendeth ought
unto his neighbour shall release it; he shall
not exact it of his neighbour, or of his
brother; because it is called the LORD's release. 3. Of a foreigner thou mayest exact
it again: but that which is thine with thy
brother thine hand shall release;

Deut. 23:19. Thou shalt not lend upon
usury to thy brother; usury of money,
usury of victuals, usury of any thing that
is lent upon usury: 20. Unto a stranger
thou mayest lend upon usury; but unto thy
brother thou shalt not lend upon usury:
that the LORD thy God may bless thee in all
that thou settest thine hand to in the land
whither thou goest to possess it.

Deut. 24:6. No man shall take the nether
or the upper millstone to pledge: for he
taketh a man's life to pledge. 10. When
thou dost lend thy brother any thing, thou
shalt not go into his house to fetch his

pledge. 11. Thou shalt stand abroad, and the man to whom thou dost lend shall bring out the pledge abroad unto thee. 12. And if the man be poor, thou shalt not sleep with his pledge: 13. In any case thou shalt deliver him the pledge again when the sun goeth down, that he may sleep in his own raiment, and bless thee: and it shall be righteousness unto thee before the LORD thy God.

17. Thou shalt not pervert the judgment of the stranger, nor of the fatherless; nor take a widow's raiment to pledge:

Matt. 5:42. Give to him that asketh thee, and from him that would borrow of thee turn not thou away.

Luke 6:34. And if ye lend to them of whom ye hope to receive, what thank have ye? for sinners also lend to sinners, to receive as much again.

OPPRESSIONS OF: 2 Kin. 4:1. Now there cried a certain woman of the wives of the sons of the prophets unto Elisha, saying, Thy servant my husband is dead; and thou knowest that thy servant did fear the LORD: and the creditor is come to take unto him my two sons to be bondmen.

Neh. 5:1. And there was a great cry of the people and of their wives against their brethren the Jews. 2. For there were that said, We, our sons, and our daughters, are many: therefore we take up corn for them, that we may eat, and live. 3. Some also there were that said, We have mortgaged our lands, vineyards, and houses, that we might buy corn, because of the dearth. 4. There were also that said, We have borrowed money for the king's tribute, and that upon our lands and vineyards. 5. Yet now our flesh is as the flesh of our brethren, our children as their children: and, lo, we bring into bondage our sons and our daughters to be servants, and some of our daughters are brought unto bondage already: neither is it in our power to redeem them; for other men have our lands and vineyards. 6. And I was very angry when I heard their cry and these words. 7. Then I consulted with myself, and I rebuked the nobles, and the rulers, and said unto them, Ye exact usury, every one of his brother. And I set a great assembly against them. 8. And I said unto them, We after our ability have redeemed our brethren the Jews, which were sold unto the heathen; and will ye even sell your brethren? or shall they be sold unto us? Then held they their peace, and found nothing to answer. 9. Also I said, It is not good that ye do: ought ye not to walk in the fear of our God because of the reproach of the heathen our enemies? 10. I likewise, and my brethren, and my servants, might exact of them money and corn: I pray you, let us leave off this usury. 11. Restore, I pray you, to them, even this day, their lands, their vineyards, their olive-yards, and their houses, also the hundredth part of the money, and of the corn, the wine, and the oil, that ye exac' of them. 12. Then

said they, We will restore them, and will require nothing of them; so will we do as thou sayest. Then I called the priests, and took an oath of them, that they should do according to this promise. 13. Also I shook my lap, and said, So God shake out every man from his house, and from his labour, that performeth not this promise, even thus be he shaken out, and emptied. And all the congregation said, Amen, and praised the LORD. And the people did according to this promise.

Job 20:18. That which he laboured for shall he restore, and shall not swallow it down: according to his substance shall the restitution be, and he shall not rejoice therein. 19. Because he hath oppressed and hath forsaken the poor; because he hath violently taken away an house which he builded not; 20. Surely he shall not feel quietness in his belly, he shall not save of that which he desired.

Job 22:6. For thou hast taken a pledge from thy brother for nought, and stripped the naked of their clothing.

Job 24:3. They drive away the ass of the fatherless, they take the widow's ox for a pledge. 9. They pluck the fatherless from the breast, and take a pledge of the poor. 10. They cause him to go naked without clothing, and they take away the sheaf from the hungry:

Prov. 22:26. Be not thou one of them that strike hands, or of them that are sureties for debts. 27. If thou hast nothing to pay, why should he take away thy bed from under thee?

Matt. 5:25. Agree with thine adversary quickly, whiles thou art in the way with him; lest at any time the adversary deliver thee to the judge, and the judge deliver thee to the officer, and thou be cast into prison. 26. Verily I say unto thee, Thou shalt by no means come out thence, till thou hast paid the uttermost farthing. Luke 12:58,59.

Matt. 18:28. But the same servant went out, and found one of his fellowservants, which owed him an hundred pence: and he laid hands on him, and took him by the throat, saying, Pay me that thou owest. 29. And his fellowservant fell down at his feet, and besought him, saying, Have patience with me, and I will pay thee all. 30. And he would not: but went and cast him into prison, till he should pay the debt. 31. So when his fellowservants saw what was done, they were very sorry, and came and told unto their lord all that was done. 32. Then his lord, after that he had called him, said unto him, O thou wicked servant, I forgave thee all that debt, because thou desiredst me: 33. Shouldest not thou also have had compassion on thy fellowservant, even as I had pity on thee? 34. And his lord was wroth, and delivered him to the tormentors, till he should pay all that was due unto him. 35. So likewise shall my heavenly Father do also unto you, if ye from your hearts forgive not every one his brother their trespasses.

MERCIFUL: Psa. 112:5. A good man sheweth favour, and lendeth: he will guide his affairs with discretion.

Matt. 18:23. Therefore is the kingdom of heaven likened unto a certain king, which would take account of his servants. 24. And when he had begun to reckon, one was brought unto him, which owed him ten thousand talents. 25. But forasmuch as he had not to pay, his lord commanded him to be sold, and his wife, and children, and all that he had, and payment to be made. 26. The servant therefore fell down, and worshipped him, saying, Lord, have patience with me, and I will pay thee all. 27. Then the lord of that servant was moved with compassion, and loosed him, and forgave him the debt.

Luke 7:41. There was a certain creditor which had two debtors: the one owed five hundred pence, and the other fifty. 42. And when they had nothing to pay, he frankly forgave them both. Tell me therefore, which of them will love him most? 43. Simon answered and said, I suppose that *he*, to whom he forgave most. And he said unto him, Thou hast rightly judged.

See DEBT; DEBTOR; JUBILEE; SURETY.

CREED. See DECREES; LAW OF MOSES; ECCLESIASTICISM; TRADITION.

CREEPING THINGS. A general term for animals, Gen. 1:26; Lev. 11:20-23,29-31,42; Psa. 104:20,25; Rom. 1:23. Unclean, Lev. 5:2; 11:20,29-44; Deut. 14:19. Clean, Lev. 11:21,22. Uses of, in idolatrous worship, Ezek. 8:10.

CREMATION, Josh. 7:25; 1 Sam. 31:12; 2 Kin. 23:20; Amos 2:1; 6:10. See BURIAL.

CRESCENS, a disciple with Paul at Rome, 2 Tim. 4:10.

CRETE. An island in the Mediterranean Sea. Visited by Paul, Acts 27:7,12,13,21; Titus, Tit. 1:5. Character of the inhabitants of, Acts 2:11; Tit. 1:12.

CRIB, used for grain, Job 39:9; Prov. 14:4; Isa. 1:3.

CRIME. PARTIAL LISTS OF: Ezek. 22:8. Thou hast despised mine holy things, and hast profaned my sabbaths. 9. In thee are men that carry tales to shed blood: and in thee they eat upon the mountains: in the midst of thee they commit lewdness. 10. In thee have they discovered their fathers' nakedness: in thee have they humbled her that was set apart for pollution. 11. And one hath committed abomination with his neighbour's wife; and another hath lewdly defiled his daughter in law; and another in thee hath humbled his sister, his father's daughter. 12. In thee have they taken gifts to shed blood; thou hast taken usury and increase, thou hast greedily gained of thy neighbours by extortion, and hast forgotten me, saith the Lord GOD. 27. Her princes in the midst thereof *are* like wolves ravening the prey, to shed blood, *and* to destroy souls, to get dishonest gain. 28. And her prophets have daubed them with untempered *morter*, seeing vanity, and divining lies unto them, saying, Thus saith the

Lord GOD, when the LORD hath not spoken. 29. The people of the land have used oppression, and exercised robbery, and have vexed the poor and needy: yea, they have oppressed the stranger wrongfully. 30. And I sought for a man among them, that should make up the hedge, and stand in the gap before me for the land, that I should not destroy it: but I found none.

Hos. 4:1. Hear the word of the LORD, ye children of Israel: for the LORD hath a controversy with the inhabitants of the land, because *there is* no truth, nor mercy, nor knowledge of God in the land. 2. By swearing, and lying, and killing, and stealing, and committing adultery, they break out, and blood toucheth blood.

Matt. 15:19. For out of the heart proceed evil thoughts, murders, adulteries, fornications, thefts, false witness, blasphemies: Mark 7:21,22.

Rom. 1:24. Wherefore God also gave them up to uncleanness through the lusts of their own hearts, to dishonour their own bodies between themselves: 29. Being filled with all unrighteousness, fornication, wickedness, covetousness, maliciousness; full of envy, murder, debate, deceit, malignity; whisperers, 30. Backbiters, haters of God, despiteful, proud, boasters, inventors of evil things, disobedient to parents, 31. Without understanding, covenantbreakers, without natural affection, implacable, unmerciful: 32. Who knowing the judgment of God, that they which commit such things are worthy of death, not only do the same, but have pleasure in them that do them.

Rom. 3:14. Whose mouth *is* full of cursing and bitterness: 15. Their feet *are* swift to shed blood: 16. Destruction and misery *are* in their ways: 17. And the way of peace have they not known: 18. There is no fear of God before their eyes.

Rom. 13:9. For this, Thou shalt not commit adultery, Thou shalt not kill, Thou shalt not steal, Thou shalt not bear false witness, Thou shalt not covet;

1 Cor. 5:11. But now I have written unto you not to keep company, if any man that is called a brother be a fornicator, or covetous, or an idolater, or a railer, or a drunkard, or an extortioner; with such an one no not to eat.

Gal. 5:19. Now the works of the flesh are manifest, which are *these:* Adultery, fornication, uncleanness, lasciviousness, 20. Idolatry, witchcraft, hatred, variance, emulations, wrath, strife, seditions, heresies, 21. Envyings, murders, drunkenness, revellings, and such like: of the which I tell you before, as I have also told *you* in time past, that they which do such things shall not inherit the kingdom of God.

See under terms by which various crimes are known, ADULTERY, ARSON, HOMICIDE, THEFT, and the like.

See PUNISHMENT.

CRIMINALS. Released at feasts, Matt.

27:15,21; Mark 15:6; Luke 23:17. Confined in prisons, Gen. 39:20–23; Ezra 7:26; Acts 4:3; 12: 4,5; 16:19–40; in dungeons, Gen. 40:15; 41:14; Ex. 12:29; Isa. 24:22; Jer. 37:16; 38:10; Lam. 3:53,55.

Cruelty to. See SCOURGING; STONING; MOCKING.

Punishment of. See various crimes, such as ADULTERY, ARSON, HOMICIDE, etc. See also PUNISHMENTS.

CRIMINATION. See SELF-CRIMINA-TION.

CRIMSON. See COLOR.

CRISPING PINS, Isa. 3:22.

CRISPUS, a ruler at Corinth, Acts 18:8; 1 Cor. 1:14.

CRITICISM, UNJUST. See UNCHARI-TABLENESS.

CROCODILE. See DRAGON.

CROSS. Jesus crucified on, Matt. 27:32; Mark 15:21; Luke 23:26; Acts 2:23,36; 4:10; 1 Cor. 1:23; 2:2,8; Eph. 2:16; Phil. 2:8; Col. 1:20; 2:14; Heb.12:2. Borne by Simon, Matt. 27:32; Mark 15:21; Luke 23:26; by Jesus,John 19:17.

FIGURATIVE: Matt. 10:38. And he that taketh not his cross, and followeth after me, is not worthy of me. Luke 14:27.

Matt. 16:24. Then said Jesus unto his disciples, If any *man* will come after me, let him deny himself, and take up his cross, and follow me. Mark 8:34; Luke 9:23.

Mark 10:21. Then Jesus beholding him loved him, and said unto him, One thing thou lackest: go thy way, sell whatsoever thou hast, and give to the poor, and thou shalt have treasure in heaven: and come, take up the cross, and follow me.

1 Cor. 1:17. For Christ sent me not to baptize, but to preach the gospel: not with wisdom of words, lest the cross of Christ should be made of none effect. 18. For the preaching of the cross is to them that perish foolishness; but unto us which are saved it is the power of God.

Gal. 5:11. And I, brethren, if I yet preach circumcision, why do I yet suffer persecution? then is the offence of the cross ceased.

Gal. 6:14. But God forbid that I should glory, save in the cross of our Lord Jesus Christ, by whom the world is crucified unto me, and I unto the world.

Phil. 3:18. For many walk, of whom I have told you often, and now tell you even weeping, *that they are* the enemies of the cross of Christ:

See CRUCIFIXION; SELF-DENIAL.

CROSS-QUESTIONING, Prov. 20:5. See WITNESS.

CROWN. Prescribed for priests, Ex. 29:6; 39:30; Lev. 8:9. Worn by kings, 2 Sam. 1:10; 12:30; 2 Kin. 11:12; Esth. 6:8; Song 3:11; Rev. 6:2; by queens, Esth. 1:11; 2:17; 8:15. Made of gold, Psa. 21:3; Zech. 6:11. Of victory, 2 Tim. 2:5. An ornament, Ezek. 23:42; 16:12. Set with gems, 2 Sam. 12:30; 1 Chr. 20:2; Zech. 9:16; Isa. 62:3.

Of thorns, Matt.27:29; Mark 15:17; John 19:5.

FIGURATIVE: Isa. 28:5. In that day shall the LORD of hosts be for a crown of glory, and for a diadem of beauty, unto the residue of his people.

1 Cor. 9:25. And every man that striveth for the mastery is temperate in all things. Now they *do it* to obtain a corruptible crown; but we an incorruptible.

2 Tim. 4:8. Henceforth there is laid up for me a crown of righteousness, which the Lord, the righteous judge, shall give me at that day: and not to me only, but unto all them also that love his appearing.

Jas. 1:12. Blessed *is* the man that endureth temptation: for when he is tried, he shall receive the crown of life, which the Lord hath promised to them that love him.

1 Pet. 5:4. And when the chief Shepherd shall appear, ye shall receive a crown of glory that fadeth not away.

Rev. 2:10. Fear none of those things which thou shalt suffer: behold, the devil shall cast *some* of you into prison, that ye may be tried; and ye shall have tribulation ten days: be thou faithful unto death, and I will give thee a crown of life.

Rev. 3:11. Behold, I come quickly: hold that fast which thou hast, that no man take thy crown.

SYMBOLICAL: Rev. 4:4,10; 6:2; 9:7; 12:1,3; 13:1; 14:14; 19:12.

CRUCIFIXION. The reproach of, Gal. 3:13; 5:11. Of Jesus, see JESUS, HISTORY OF. Of two malefactors, Matt. 27:38. Of disciples, foretold, Matt. 23:34.

See CROSS.

FIGURATIVE: Rom. 6:6. Knowing this, that our old man is crucified with *him*, that the body of sin might be destroyed, that henceforth we should not serve sin.

Gal. 2:20. I am crucified with Christ:

Gal. 5:24. And they that are Christ's have crucified the flesh with the affections and lusts.

Gal. 6:14. But God forbid that I should glory, save in the cross of our Lord Jesus Christ, by whom the world is crucified unto me, and I unto the world.

See CROSS, FIGURATIVE.

CRUELTY. INSTANCES OF: Of Sarah to Hagar, Gen. 16:6; 21:9–14. Egyptians to the Israelites, Ex. 5:6–18. Peninnah to Hannah, 1 Sam. 1:4–7; 2:3. Of Jews to Jesus, Matt. 26:67; 27:28–31; soldiers to Jesus, Luke 22:64; John 19:3. In war, Isa. 13:16,18.

See ANIMALS, CRUELTY TO; KINDNESS; LOVE; MALICE; PRISONERS OF WAR.

CRUSE, a vessel for liquids, 1 Sam. 26:11; 1 Kin. 14:3; 2 Kin. 2:20.

CRYSTAL, a precious stone, Job 28:17; Ezek. 1:22; Rev. 4:6; 21:11; 22:1.

CUBIT.* A measure of distance, Gen. 6:16; Deut. 3:11; Ezek. 40:5; 43:13; Rev. 21:17. Who can add to his height, Matt. 6:27; Luke 12:25.

*According to latest and best authorities the Israelites probably employed the Egyptian cubit. The ordinary Egyptian cubit was 20.24 inches. The sacred was 31.888 inches, and these are the probable biblical measurements.

CUCKOO, a bird. Forbidden as food, Lev. 11:16; Deut. 14:15.

CUCUMBER, Num. 11:5; Isa. 1:8.

CUD, chewing of, was one of the facts by which clean and unclean animals were distinguished, Lev. 11:3-8; Deut. 14:3-8.

CUMMIN, a plant bearing a small aromatic seed, Isa. 28:25,27; Matt. 23:23.

CUP. Gen. 40:11; 2 Sam. 12:3; 1 Kin. 7:26; Matt. 23:25. Made of silver, Gen. 44:2; gold, 1 Chr. 28:17; Jer. 52:19. Used in the institution of the Lord's Supper, Matt. 26:27; Mark 14:23; Luke 22:20; 1 Cor. 10:21. Of the table of devils, 1 Cor. 10:21.

FIGURATIVE: Of sorrow, Psa. 11:6; 73:10; 75:8; Isa. 51:17,22; Jer. 25:15-28; Ezek. 23:31-34; Matt. 20:22,23; 26:39; Mark 14:36; Luke 22:42; John 18:11; Rev. 14:10. Of consolation, Jer. 16:7. Of joy, Psa. 23:5. Of salvation, Psa. 116:13.

CUPBEARER, Gen. 40:1,11; 1 Kin. 10:5; 2 Chr. 9:4; Neh. 1:11.

CUPIDITY. See AVARICE; COVETOUSNESS; LUST.

CURES, miraculous. See MIRACLES.

See DISEASES; PHYSICIAN.

CURIOSITY. Prov. 27:20. Hell and destruction are never full; so the eyes of man are never satisfied.

Eccl. 7:21. Also take no heed unto all words that are spoken; lest thou hear thy servant curse thee:

INSTANCES OF: Of Eve, Gen. 3:6. Of Abraham, to know whether God would destroy the righteous in Sodom, Gen. 18:23-32. Of Jacob, to know the name of the angel, Gen. 32:29. Of the Israelites, to see God, Ex. 19:21,24; to witness the offering in the holy of holies, Num. 4:19,20. Of Manoah, to know the name of an angel, Judg. 13:17,18. Of the people of Beth-shemish, to see inside the ark, 1 Sam. 6:19. Of the Babylonians, to see Hezekiah's treasures, 2 Kin. 20:13. Of Daniel, to know a vision, Dan. 12:8,9. Of Peter, to know what was being done with Jesus, Matt. 26:58; to know what John would be appointed to do, John 21:21,22. A disciple, to know if there be few that be saved, Luke 13:23. Of Herod, to see Jesus, Luke 9:9; 23:8. Of the Jews, to see Lazarus, after he was raised from the dead, John, 12:9; and to see Jesus, John 12:20,21. Of the disciples, to know whether Jesus would restore the kingdom of the Jews, Acts 1:6,7. Of the Athenians, to hear some new thing, Acts 17:19-21. Of angels, to look into the mysteries of salvation, 1 Pet. 1:12.

CURSE. Denounced against the serpent, Gen. 3:14,15; against Adam and Eve, Gen. 3:15-19; against the ground, Gen. 3:17,18; against Cain, Gen. 4:11-16; against Canaan, Noah's son, Gen. 9:24-27; against Meroz, Judg. 5:23; against Gehazi, 2 Kin. 5:27. Barak commands Balaam to curse Israel, Num. 22:6; 23:11.

See BENEDICTIONS.

CURSES OF THE MOSAIC LAW: Deut. 27:1. And Moses with the elders of Israel commanded the people, saying, Keep all the commandments which I command you this day. 2. And it shall be on the day when ye shall pass over Jordan unto the land which the LORD thy God giveth thee, that thou shalt set thee up great stones, and plaister them with plaister: 3. And thou shalt write upon them all the words of this law, when thou art passed over, that thou mayest go in unto the land which the LORD thy God giveth thee, a land that floweth with milk and honey; as the LORD God of thy fathers hath promised thee. 4. Therefore it shall be when ye be gone over Jordan, that ye shall set up these stones, which I command you this day, in mount Ebal, and thou shalt plaister them with plaister. 5. And there shalt thou build an altar unto the LORD thy God, an altar of stones: thou shalt not lift up any iron tool upon them. 6. Thou shalt build the altar of the LORD thy God of whole stones: and thou shalt offer burnt offerings thereon unto the LORD thy God: 7. And thou shalt offer peace offerings, and shalt eat there, and rejoice before the LORD thy God. 8. And thou shalt write upon the stones all the words of this law very plainly. 9. And Moses and the priests the Levites spake unto all Israel, saying, Take heed, and hearken, O Israel; this day thou art become the people of the LORD thy God. 10. Thou shalt therefore obey the voice of the LORD thy God, and do his commandments and his statutes, which I command thee this day. 11. And Moses charged the people the same day, saying, 12. These shall stand upon mount Gerizim to bless the people, when ye are come over Jordan; Simeon, and Levi, and Judah, and Issachar, and Joseph, and Benjamin: 13. And these shall stand upon mount Ebal to curse; Reuben, Gad, and Asher, and Zebulun, Dan, and Naphtali. 14. And the Levites shall speak, and say unto all the men of Israel with a loud voice, 15. Cursed be the man that maketh any graven or molten image, an abomination unto the LORD, the work of the hands of the craftsman, and putteth it in a secret place: and all the people shall answer and say, Amen. 16. Cursed be he that setteth light by his father or his mother. And all the people shall say, Amen. 17. Cursed be he that removeth his neighbour's landmark. And all the people shall say, Amen. 18. Cursed be he that maketh the blind to wander out of the way. And all the people shall say, Amen. 19. Cursed be he that perverteth the judgment of the stranger, fatherless, and widow. And all the people shall say, Amen. 20. Cursed be he that lieth with his father's wife; because he uncovereth his father's skirt. And all the people shall say, Amen. 21. Cursed be he that lieth with any manner of beast. And all the people shall say, Amen. 22. Cursed be he that lieth with his sister, the daughter of his father, or the daughter of his mother. And all the people shall say, Amen. 23.

Cursed *be* he that lieth with his mother in law. And all the people shall say, Amen. 24. Cursed *be* he that smiteth his neighbour secretly. And all the people shall say, Amen. 25. Cursed *be* he that taketh reward to slay an innocent person. And all the people shall say, Amen. 26. Cursed *be* he that confirmeth not *all* the words of this law to do them. And all the people shall say, Amen.

Josh. 8:30. Then Joshua built an altar unto the LORD God of Israel in mount Ebal, 31. As Moses the servant of the LORD commanded the children of Israel, as it is written in the book of the law of Moses, an altar of whole stones, over which no man hath lift up *any* iron : and they offered thereon burnt offerings unto the LORD, and sacrificed peace offerings. 32. And he wrote there upon the stones a copy of the law of Moses, which he wrote in the presence of the children of Israel. 33. And all Israel, and their elders, and officers, and their judges, stood on this side the ark and on that side before the priests the Levites, which bare the ark of the covenant of the LORD, as well the stranger, as he that was born among them; half of them over against mount Gerizim, and half of them over against mount Ebal ; as Moses the servant of the LORD had commanded before, that they should bless the people of Israel. 34. And afterward he read all the words of the law, the blessings and cursings, according to all that is written in the book of the law.

See BLESSINGS.

CURSING. Of parents : Ex. 21:17; Matt. 15:4; Mark 7:10. Shimei curses David, 2 Sam. 16:5–8. The precepts of Jesus concerning, Matt. 5:44; Luke 6:28. Apostolic, Rom. 12:14.

See ANATHEMA MARAN-ATHA ; BLASPHEMY ; GOD, NAME OF, NOT TO BE PROFANED ; OATH.

CURTAINS. For tabernacle, Ex. 26; 27: 9–18; 36:8–18. In the palace of Ahasuerus, Esth. 1:6.

See TABERNACLE ; TAPESTRY.

FIGURATIVE : Isa. 40:22; 54:2; Jer. 4:20; 10:20; 49:29.

CUSH. 1. Son of Ham, Gen. 10:6–8; 1 Chr. 1:8–10.

2. A Benjamite, title of, Psa. 7.

3. Land of, Gen. 2:13; Psa. 68:31; Isa. 18:1. See ETHIOPIA.

CUSHAN, poetic form of Cush, Hab. 3:7. See ETHIOPIA.

CUSHI. 1. A messenger, who brought tidings to David, 2 Sam. 18:21–32.

2. Father of Shelemiah, Jer. 36:14.

3. Father of Zephaniah, Zeph. 1:1.

CUTH, called also CUTHAH. A district of Asia, from which colonists were transported to Samaria, 2 Kin. 17:24–30; Ezra 4:10.

CUTTING the flesh for the dead, forbidden, Lev. 19:28; 21:5; Deut. 14:1; Jer. 16:6.

CYMBAL, a musical instrument. Of brass, 1 Chr. 15:19,28; 1 Cor. 13:1. Used in the tabernacle service, 2 Sam. 6:5; 1 Chr. 13: 8; 15:16,19,28; in the temple service, 2 Chr.

5:12,13; 1 Chr. 16:5,42; 25:1,6; Psa. 150:5. Used on special occasions : Day of atonement, 2 Chr. 29:25; laying of the foundation of the second temple, Ezra 3:10,11; dedication of the wall, Neh. 12:27,36.

CYPRESS. Isa. 44:14; Song 1:14 [marg.]; Song 4:13 [marg.]. *R. V.*, Henna.

CYPRUS. An island, Acts 21:3; 27:4. Barnabas born in, Acts 4:36. Persecuted Jews preached the gospel at, Acts 11:19,20. Visited by Barnabas and Saul, Acts 13:4–12. Barnabas and Mark visit, Acts 15:39. Mnason, a disciple of, Acts 21:16.

CYRENE. A city in Libya, Acts 2:10. Contained a synagogue, Acts 6:9. Simon and Lucius belonged to, Mark 15:21; Acts 11:20; 13:1.

CYRENIUS, governor of Syria, Luke 2:2.

CYRUS, king of Persia. Issues a decree for the emancipation of the Jews and rebuilding the temple, 2 Chr.36:22,23; Ezra 1; 3:7; 4:3; 5:13,14; 6:3. Prophecies concerning, Isa. 13:17–22; 21:2; 41:2; 44:28; 45:1–4,13; 46:11; 48:14,15.

D

DABAREH. See DABERATH.

DABBASHETH, a place on the boundary line of Zebulun, Josh. 19:11.

DABERATH, called also DABAREH. A town of Issachar, Josh. 19:12; 21:28. Assigned to the Levites, 1 Chr. 6:72.

DAGGER, a short sword, Judg. 3:16–22.

DAGON. An idol of the Philistines, Judg. 16:23; 1 Sam. 5. Temple of, 1 Chr. 10:10.

DAILY OFFERING. Sacrificial, Ex. 29:38–42; 30:7–9; Num. 28:3–8; Ezra 3:4–6; Ezek. 46:13–15; Dan. 9:21,26,27; 11:31; Acts 3:1.

See OFFERINGS.

FIGURATIVE : John 1:29,36; 1 Pet. 1:19.

DALAIAH. See DELAIAH.

DALMANUTHA, a town on the W. coast of the Sea of Galilee, Mark 8:10.

DALMATIA, a country on the eastern shore of the Adriatic, 2 Tim. 4:10.

DALPHON, son of Haman, Esth. 9:7.

DAMAGES AND COMPENSATION. Ex. 21:18. And if men strive together, and one smite another with a stone, or with *his* fist, and he die not, but keepeth *his* bed : 19. If he rise again, and walk abroad upon his staff, then shall he that smote *him* be quit : only he shall pay *for* the loss of his time, and shall cause *him* to be thoroughly healed.

22. If men strive, and hurt a woman with child, so that her fruit depart *from her*, and yet no mischief follow : he shall be surely punished, according as the woman's husband will lay upon him ; and he shall pay as the judges *determine*.

28. If an ox gore a man or a woman, that they die : then the ox shall be surely stoned, and his flesh shall not be eaten ; but the

owner of the ox *shall be* quit. 29. But if the ox were wont to push with his horn in time past, and it hath been testified to his owner, and he hath not kept him in, but that he hath killed a man or a woman; the ox shall be stoned, and his owner also shall be put to death. 30. If there be laid on him a sum of money, then he shall give for the ransom of his life whatsoever is laid upon him. 31. Whether he have gored a son, or have gored a daughter, according to this judgment shall it be done unto him. 32. If the ox shall push a manservant or a maidservant; he shall give unto their master thirty shekels of silver, and the ox shall be stoned.

33. And if a man shall open a pit, or if a man shall dig a pit, and not cover it, and an ox or an ass fall therein; 34. The owner of the pit shall make *it* good, *and* give money unto the owner of them; and the dead *beast* shall be his.

Lev. 6:1. And the LORD spake unto Moses, saying, 2. If a soul sin, and commit a trespass against the LORD, and lie unto his neighbour in that which was delivered him to keep, or in fellowship, or in a thing taken away by violence, or hath deceived his neighbour; 3. Or have found that which was lost, and lieth concerning it, and sweareth falsely; in any of all these that a man doeth, sinning therein: 4. Then it shall be, because he hath sinned, and is guilty, that he shall restore that which he took violently away, or the thing which he hath deceitfully gotten, or that which was delivered him to keep, or the lost thing which he found, 5. Or all that about which he hath sworn falsely; he shall even restore it in the principal, and shall add the fifth part more thereto, *and* give it unto him to whom it appertaineth, in the day of his trespass offering.

Deut. 22:13. If any man take a wife, and go in unto her, and hate her, 14. And give occasion of speech against her, and bring up an evil name upon her, and say, I took this woman, and when I came to her, I found her not a maid: 15. Then shall the father of the damsel, and her mother, take and bring forth *the tokens of* the damsel's virginity unto the elders of the city in the gate: 16. And the damsel's father shall say unto the elders, I gave my daughter unto this man to wife, and he hateth her; 17. And, lo, he hath given occasions of speech *against her*, saying, I found not thy daughter a maid; and yet these *are the tokens of* my daughter's virginity. And they shall spread the cloth before the elders of the city. 18. And the elders of that city shall take that man and chastise him; 19. And they shall amerce him in an hundred *shekels* of silver, and give *them* unto the father of the damsel, because he hath brought up an evil name upon a virgin of Israel: and she shall be his wife; he may not put her away all his days. 28. If a man find a damsel *that is* a virgin, which is not betrothed, and lay hold on her, and lie with her, and they be found;

29. Then the man that lay with her shall give unto the damsel's father fifty *shekels* of silver, and she shall be his wife; because he hath humbled her, he may not put her away all his days.

DAMARIS, a female convert of Athens, Acts 17:34.

DAMASCUS. An ancient city, Gen. 14:15; 15:2. Capital of Syria, 1 Kin. 20:34; Isa. 7:8; Jer. 49:23–29; Ezek. 47:16,17. Laid under tribute to David, 2 Sam. 8:5,6. Besieged by Rezon, 1 Kin. 11:23,24. Recovered by Jeroboam, 2 Kin. 14:28. Taken by king of Assyria, 2 Kin. 16:9. Walled, Jer. 49:27; 2 Cor. 11:33. Garrisoned, 2 Cor. 11:32. Luxury in, Amos, 3:12. Paul's experiences in, Acts 9; 22:5–16; 26:12–20; 2 Cor. 11:32; Gal. 1:17.

Prophecies concerning, Isa. 8:4; 17:1,2; Jer. 49:23–29; Amos 1:3,5; Zech. 9:1.

Wilderness of, 1 Kin. 19:15.

See SYRIA.

DAMNED. See WICKED, PUNISHMENT OF.

DAN. 1. Fifth son of Jacob and Bilhah, Gen. 30:6; 35:25. Descendants of, Gen. 46:23; Num. 26:42,43. See TRIBE OF, below. Blessed of Jacob, Gen. 49:16,17.

2. TRIBE OF: Census of, Num. 1:39; 26:42. 43. Inheritance of, according to the allotment of Joshua, Josh. 19:40–47; of Ezekiel. Ezek. 48:1. Position of, in journey and camp, during the exodus, Num. 2:25,31; 10: 25. Blessed by Moses, Deut. 33:22. Fail to conquer the Amorites, Judg. 1:34,35. Conquests by, Josh. 19:47; Judg. 18:27–29. Deborah upbraids, for cowardice, Judg. 5:17. Idolatry of, Judg. 18. Commerce of, Judg. 5:17; Ezek. 27:19.

See ISRAEL, TRIBES OF.

3. A city of the tribe of Dan. Called also LAISH, and LESHEM, Gen. 14:14; Deut. 34:1; Judg. 20:1; Jer. 8:16. Captured by the people of Dan, Josh. 19:47. Idolatry established at, Judg. 18; 1 Kin. 12:28,29; Amos 8:14. Captured by Ben-hadad, 1 Kin. 15:20; 2 Chr. 16:4.

DANCING. Ex. 15:20. And Miriam the prophetess, the sister of Aaron, took a timbrel in her hand; and all the women went out after her with timbrels and with dances.

Ex. 32:19. And it came to pass, as soon as he came nigh unto the camp, that he saw the calf, and the dancing: and Moses' anger waxed hot, and he cast the tables out of his hands, and brake them beneath the mount.

Judg. 11:34. And Jephthah came to Mispeh unto his house, and, behold, his daughter came out to meet him with timbrels and with dances: and she *was his* only child; beside her he had neither son nor daughter.

Judg. 21:19. Then they said, Behold, *there is* a feast of the LORD in Shiloh yearly *in a place* which *is* on the north side of Beth-el, on the east side of the highway that goeth up from Beth-el to Shechem, and on the south of Lebonah. 20. Therefore they commanded the children of Benjamin, saying, Go and lie in wait in the vineyards; 21. And see, and, behold, if the daughters of Shiloh come out to dance in dances, then come ye out of the vineyards, and catch you every man his wife of the daughters of Shiloh, and go to the land of Benjamin.

1 Sam. 18:6. And it came to pass as they came, when David was returned from the slaughter of the Philistine, that the women came out of all cities of Israel, singing and dancing, to meet king Saul, with tabrets, with joy, and with instruments of musick.

1 Sam. 21:11. And the servants of Achish said unto him, *Is* not this David the king of the land? did they not sing one to another of him in dances, saying, Saul hath slain his thousands, and David his ten thousands?

1 Sam. 30:16. And when he had brought him down, behold, *they were* spread abroad upon all the earth, eating and drinking, and ¹ dancing, because of all the great spoil that they had taken out of the land of the Philistines, and out of the land of Judah.   [¹ R. V. feasting]

2 Sam. 6:14. And David danced before the LORD with all *his* might; and David *was* girded with a linen ephod. 15. So David and all the house of Israel brought up the ark of the LORD with shouting, and with the sound of the trumpet. 16. And as the ark of the LORD came into the city of David, Michal Saul's daughter looked through a window, and saw king David leaping and dancing before the LORD; and she despised him in her heart.

Job 21:11. They send forth their little ones like a flock, and their children dance.

Psa. 30:11. Thou hast turned for me my mourning into dancing: thou hast put off my sackcloth, and girded me with gladness;

Psa. 149:3. Let them praise his name in the dance: let them sing praises unto him with the timbrel and harp.

Psa. 150:4. Praise him with the timbrel and dance: praise him with stringed instruments and organs.

Eccl. 3:4. A time to weep, and a time to laugh; a time to mourn, and a time to dance;

Jer. 31:4. Again I will build thee, and thou shalt be built, O virgin of Israel: thou shalt again be adorned with thy tabrets, and shalt go forth in the dances of them that make merry. 13. Then shall the virgin rejoice in the dance, both young men and old together: for I will turn their mourning into joy, and will comfort them, and make them rejoice from their sorrow.

Lam. 5:15. The joy of our heart is ceased; our dance is turned into mourning.

Matt. 11:17. And saying, We have piped unto you, and ye have not danced; we have mourned unto you, and ye have not lamented.

Luke 15:23. And bring hither the fatted calf, and kill *it*; and let us eat and be merry: 24. For this my son was dead, and is alive again; he was lost, and is found.

And they began to be merry. 25. Now his elder son was in the field: and as he came and drew nigh to the house, he heard musick and dancing.

Daughter of Herodias dances before Herod, Matt. 14:6; Mark 6:22. Idolatrous, Ex. 32:19, 25.

DANIEL. 1. A Jewish captive, called also BELTESHAZZAR. Educated at king's court, Dan. 1. Interprets visions, Dan. 2; 4; 5. Promotion and executive authority of, Dan. 2: 48, 49; 5:11, 29; 6:2. Conspiracy against, cast into the lions' den, Dan. 6.

Prophecies of, Dan. 4:8, 9; chapters 7-12; Matt. 24:15.

Abstinence of, Dan. 1:8-16. Wisdom of, Dan. 1:17; Ezek. 28:3. Devoutness of, Dan. 2:18; 6; 9; 10; 12; Ezek. 14:14. Courage and fidelity of, Dan. 4:27; 5:17-23; 6:10-23. Worshiped by Nebuchadnezzar, Dan. 2:6.

2. David's son. Called also CHILEAB, 2 Sam. 3:3; 1 Chr. 3:1.

3. A descendant of Ithamar, and a companion of Ezra, Ezra 8:2; Neh. 10:6.

DAN-JAAN, a place near the source of the Jordan, 2 Sam. 24:6.

DANNAH, a city in the mountains of Judah, Josh. 15:49.

DARA. See DARDA.

DARDA, called also DARA. A famous wise man, 1 Kin. 4:31; 1 Chr. 2:6.

DARIUS. 1. The Mede, king of Persia, Dan. 5:31; 6; 9:1.

2. King of Persia. Emancipates the Jews, Ezra 5; 6; Hag. 1:1, 15; Zech. 1:1.

3. The Persian, Neh. 12:22.

DARKNESS. Over the face of the earth, Gen. 1:2; Job 38:9; Jer. 4:23. Called NIGHT, Gen. 1:5. God creates, Isa. 45:7. Miraculous: In Egypt, Ex. 10:21, 22; Psa. 105:28; at Sinai, Ex. 20:21; Heb. 12:18; at the crucifixion, Matt. 27:45; Mark 15:33.

FIGURATIVE: Of judgments, Prov. 20: 20; Isa. 8:22; 13:10; Jer. 4:28; 13:16; Lam. 3:2; Ezek. 32:7, 8; Joel 2:2, 10; Amos 4:13; 5:18, 20; 8:9; Mic. 7:8; Matt. 24:29; Mark 13:24; Luke 23:45; Rev. 8:12; 9:2. Called outer darkness, Matt. 8:12; 22:13; 25:30. Of powers of evil, Luke 22:53; Eph. 6:12; Col. 1:13; 1 Thess. 5:5; Rev. 16:10.

OF SPIRITUAL BLINDNESS: Isa. 9:2. The people that walked in darkness have seen a great light: they that dwell in the land of the shadow of death, upon them hath the light shined. Matt. 4:16; Luke 1:79.

Isa. 42:16. And I will bring the blind by a way *that* they knew not; I will lead them in paths *that* they have not known: I will make darkness light before them, and crooked things straight. These things will I do unto them, and not forsake them.

Isa. 50:10. Who *is* among you that feareth the LORD, that obeyeth the voice of his servant, that walketh *in* darkness, and hath no light? let him trust in the name of the LORD, and stay upon his God.

Matt. 6:22. The light of the body is the eye: if therefore thine eye be single, thy whole body shall be full of light. 23. But if thine eye be evil, thy whole body shall be full of darkness. If therefore the light that is in thee be darkness, how great *is* that darkness!

Luke 11:34. The light of the body is the eye : . . . but when *thine eye* is evil, thy body also *is* full of darkness.

John 1:5. And the light shineth in darkness; and the darkness comprehended it not.

John 3:19. And this is the condemnation, that light is come into the world, and men loved darkness rather than light, because their deeds were evil. 20. For every one that doeth evil hateth the light, neither cometh to the light, lest his deeds should be reproved. 21. But he that doeth truth cometh to the light, that his deeds may be made manifest, that they are wrought in God.

John 8:12. Then spake Jesus again unto them, saying, I am the light of the world: he that followeth me shall not walk in darkness, but shall have the light of life.

John 11:9. Jesus answered, Are there not twelve hours in the day? If any man walk in the day, he stumbleth not, because he seeth the light of this world. 10. But if a man walk in the night, he stumbleth, because there is no light in him.

Acts 26:18. To open their eyes, *and* to turn *them* from darkness to light, and *from* the power of Satan unto God, that they may receive forgiveness of sins, and inheritance among them which are sanctified by faith that is in me.

Rom. 1:21. Became vain in their imaginations, and their foolish heart was darkened.

Rom. 13:12. The night is far spent, the day is at hand: let us therefore cast off the works of darkness, and let us put on the armour of light. 13. Let us walk honestly, as in the day; not in rioting and drunkenness, not in chambering and wantonness, not in strife and envying.

1 Cor. 4:5. Therefore judge nothing before the time, until the Lord come, who both will bring to light the hidden things of darkness, and will make manifest the counsels of the hearts: and then shall every man have praise of God.

2 Cor. 4:6. For God, who commanded the light to shine out of darkness, hath shined in our hearts, to *give* the light of the knowledge of the glory of God in the face of Jesus Christ.

2 Cor. 6:14. Be ye not unequally yoked together with unbelievers: for what fellowship hath righteousness with unrighteousness? and what communion hath light with darkness?

Eph. 5:8. For ye were sometimes darkness, but now *are ye* light in the Lord: walk as children of light: 11. And have no fellowship with the unfruitful works of darkness, but rather reprove *them.*

1 Thess. 5:4. But ye, brethren, are not in darkness, that that day should overtake you **as a thief.** 5. Ye are all the children of light,

and the children of the day: we are not of the night, nor of darkness.

1 Pet. 2:9. But ye *are* a chosen generation, a royal priesthood, an holy nation, a peculiar people; that ye should shew forth the praises of him who hath called you out of darkness into his marvellous light:

1 John 1:5. This then is the message which we have heard of him, and declare unto you, that God is light, and in him is no darkness at all. 6. If we say that we have fellowship with him, and walk in darkness, we lie, and do not the truth: 7. But if we walk in the light, as he is in the light, we have fellowship one with another, and the blood of Jesus Christ his Son cleanseth us from all sin.

1 John 2:8. Again, a new commandment I write unto you, which thing is true in him and in you: because the darkness is past, and the true light now shineth. 9. He that saith he is in the light, and hateth his brother, is in darkness even until now. 10. He that loveth his brother abideth in the light, and there is none occasion of stumbling in him. 11. But he that hateth his brother is in darkness, and walketh in darkness, and knoweth not whither he goeth, because that darkness hath blinded his eyes.

See BLINDNESS, SPIRITUAL.

The darkness of the Holy of Holies was symbolical of the dwelling place of Jehovah. See MOST HOLY PLACE, under the topic TABERNACLE. See also the following scriptures:

Ex. 19:16. And it came to pass on the third day in the morning, that there were thunders and lightnings, and a thick cloud upon the mount,

2 Sam. 22:10. He bowed the heavens also, and came down; and darkness *was* under his feet. 11. And he rode upon a cherub, and did fly: and he was seen upon the wings of the wind. 12. And he made darkness pavilions round about him, dark waters, *and* thick clouds of the skies.

2 Chr. 6:1. Then said Solomon, The LORD hath said that he would dwell in the thick darkness. 1 Kin. 8:12.

Psa. 18:11. He made darkness his secret place; his pavilion round about him *were* dark waters *and* thick clouds of the skies.

Psa. 97:2. Clouds and darkness *are* round about him: righteousness and judgment *are* the habitation of his throne.

Heb. 12:18. For ye are not come unto the mount that might be touched, and that burned with fire, nor unto blackness, and darkness, and tempest,

DARKON, a servant of Solomon, Ezra 2:56; Neh. 7:58.

DART, a light javelin, Num. 25:7; 1 Sam. 18:10; 2 Sam. 18:14; Job 41:29.

FIGURATIVE: Eph. 6:16.

DATE, a fruit, 2 Chr. 31:5 [marg.].

DATHAN, a conspirator against Moses, Num. 16:1–35; 26:9; Deut. 11:6; Psa. 106:17.

DAUGHTER. Forbidden to be wife of her mother's husband, Lev. 20:14. Sold in concubinage, Ex. 21:7-10. Given in marriage by parents, Judg. 1:12,13; 1 Sam. 17:25; 18:20,21. Property rights of, Num. 27:1-11; 36; Josh. 17:3-6; Ruth 4:3.

Used also for granddaughter, Gen. 36:2.

DAUGHTER-IN-LAW. FILIAL: INSTANCE OF, Ruth, Ruth 1:11-18; 4:15.

UNFILIAL: Prophecy of, Mic. 7:6; Matt. 10:35.

DAVID. 1. King of Israel. Genealogy of, Ruth 4:18-22; 1 Sam. 16:11; 17:12; 1 Chr. 2:3-15; Matt. 1:1-6; Luke 3:31-38. A shepherd, 1 Sam. 16:11. Kills a lion and a bear, 1 Sam. 17:34-36. Anointed king, while a youth, by the prophet Samuel, and inspired, 1 Sam. 16:1,13; Psa. 89:19-37. Chosen of God, Psa. 78:70.

Described to Saul, 1 Sam. 16:18. Detailed as armorbearer and musician at Saul's court, 1 Sam. 16:21-23. Slays Goliath, 1 Sam. 17. Love of Jonathan for, 1 Sam. 18:1-4. Popularity and discreetness of, 1 Sam. 18. Saul's jealousy of, 1 Sam. 18:8-30. Is defrauded of Merab, and given Michal to wife, 1 Sam. 18:17-27. Jonathan intercedes for, 1 Sam. 19:1-7. Probably writes Psalm 11 at this period of his life.

Conducts a campaign against, and defeats, the Philistines, 1 Sam. 19:8. Saul attempts to slay him; he escapes to Ramah, and dwells at Naioth, whither Saul pursues him, 1 Sam. 19:9-24. About this time writes Psalm 59. Returns, and Jonathan makes covenant with him, 1 Sam. 20. Escapes by way of Nob, where he obtains shewbread and Goliath's sword from Abimelech, 1 Sam. 21:1-6; Matt. 12:3,4; to Gath, 1 Sam. 21:10-15. At this time probably writes Psalms 34, 35, 52, 56, 120. Recruits an army of insurgents, goes to Moab, returns to Hareth, 1 Sam. 22. Probably writes Psalms 17, 35, 52, 58, 64, 109, 142. Saves Keilah, 1 Sam. 23:1-13. Makes second covenant with Jonathan, 1 Sam. 23:16-18. Goes to the wilderness of Ziph, is betrayed to Saul, 1 Sam. 23:13-26. Writes a psalm on the betrayal, Psalm 54, and probably Psalms 22, 31, 140. Saul is diverted from pursuit of, 1 Sam. 23: 27,28. At this time probably writes Psalm 12. Goes to En-gedi, 1 Sam. 23:29. Refrains from slaying Saul, 1 Sam. 24. Writes Psalm 57. Covenants with Saul, 1 Sam. 26. Marries Nabal's widow, Abigail, and Ahinoam, 1 Sam. 25. Dwells in the wilderness of Ziph, has opportunity to slay Saul, but takes his spear only, Saul is contrite, 1 Sam. 26. Flees to Achish and dwells in Ziklag, 1 Sam. 27. List of men who join him, 1 Chr. 12:1-22. Conducts an expedition against Amalekites, misstates the facts to Achish, 1 Sam. 27:8-12. At this time probably writes Psalm 141. Is refused permission to accompany the Philistines to battle against the Israelites, 1 Sam. 28:1,2; 29. Rescues the people of Ziklag, who had been captured by the Amalekites, 1 Sam. 30. Probably writes Psalm 13. Death and burial of Saul and his sons, 1 Sam. 31; 2

Sam. 21:1-14. Slays the murderer of Saul, 2 Sam. 1:1-16. Lamentation over Saul, 2 Sam. 1:17-27.

After dwelling one year and four months at Ziklag, 1 Sam. 27:7, goes to Hebron, and is anointed king by Judah, 2 Sam. 2:1-4,11; 5:5; 1 Kin. 2:11; 1 Chr. 3:4; 11:1-3. List of those who join him at Hebron, 1 Chr. 12: 23-40. Ish-bosheth, son of Saul, crowned, 2 Sam. chapters 2-4. David wages war against, and defeats, Ish-bosheth, 2 Sam. 2: 13-32; 3:4. Demands the restoration of Michal, his wife, 2 Sam. 3:14-16. Abner revolts from Ish-bosheth, and joins David, but is slain by Joab, 2 Sam. 3. Punishes Ish-bosheth's murderers, 2 Sam. 4.

Anointed king over all Israel, after reigning over Judah at Hebron seven years and six months, and reigns thirty-three years, 2 Sam. 2:11; 5:5; 1 Chr. 3:4; 11:1-3; 12:23-40; 29:27. Makes conquest of Jerusalem, 2 Sam. 5:6; 1 Chr. 11:4-8; Isa. 29:1. Builds a palace, 2 Sam. 5:11; 2 Chr. 2:3. Friendship of, with Hiram, king of Tyre, 2 Sam. 5:11; 1 Kin. 5:1. Prospered of God, 2 Sam. 5:10,12; 1 Chr. 11: 9. Fame of, 1 Chr. 14:17. Philistines make war against, and are defeated by him, 2 Sam. 5:17,25.

Assembles thirty thousand men to escort the ark to Jerusalem with music and thanksgiving, 2 Sam. 6:1-5. Uzzah is stricken when he attempts to steady the ark, 2 Sam. 6:6-11. David is terrified, and leaves the ark at the house of Obed-edom, 2 Sam. 6:9-11. After three months brings the ark to Jerusalem with dancing and great joy, 2 Sam. 6:12-16; 1 Chr. 13. Organized the tabernacle service, 1 Chr. 9:22; 15:16-24; 16:4-6,37-43. Offers sacrifice, distributes gifts, and blesses the people, 2 Sam. 6:17-19. Michal upbraids him for his religious enthusiasm, 2 Sam. 6: 20-23. Desires to build a temple, is forbidden, but receives promise that his seed should reign forever, 2 Sam. 7:12-16; 23:5; 1 Chr. 17:11-14; 2 Chr. 6:16; Psa. 89:3,4; 132: 11,12; Acts 15:16; Rom. 15:12. Interpretation and fulfillment of this prophecy, Acts 13:22,23. At this time, probably, writes Psalms 15, 16, 24, 101, 138. Conquers the Philistines, Moabites, and Syria, 2 Sam. 8.

Treats Mephibosheth, the lame son of Saul, with great kindness, 2 Sam. 9:6; 19:24-30. Sends commissioners with a message of sympathy to Hanun, son of the king of Ammon; the message misinterpreted, and commissioners treated with indignity; David retaliates by invading his kingdom, and defeating the combined armies of the Ammonites and Syrians, 2 Sam. 10; 1 Chr. 19. Probably writes Psalms 18, 20, 21.

Commits adultery with Bath-sheba, 2 Sam. 11:2-5. Wickedly causes the death of Uriah, 2 Sam. 11:6-25. Takes Bath-sheba to be his wife, 2 Sam. 11:26,27. Is rebuked by the prophet Nathan, 2 Sam. 12:1-14. Repents of his crime and confesses his guilt, Psa. 6; 32; 38; 39; 40; 51. Is chastised with grievous affliction on account of his crime,

Psa. 38; 41; 69. Death of his infant son by Bath-sheba, 2 Sam. 12:15-23. Solomon is born to, 2 Sam. 12:24,25.

Ammonites defeated and tortured, 2 Sam. 12:26-31. Amnon's crime, his murder by Absalom, and Absalom's flight, 2 Sam. 13. Absalom's return, 2 Sam. 14:1-24. Absalom's usurpation, 2 Sam. 14; 15. David's flight from Jerusalem, 2 Sam. 15:13-37. He probably writes, at this time, Psalms 5, 7, 26, 61, 63, 69, 70, 86, 143. Shimei curses him, 2 Sam. 16. Crosses the Jordan, 2 Sam. 17: 21-29. Absalom's defeat and death, 2 Sam. 18. Laments the death of Absalom, 2 Sam. 18:33; 19:1-4. Upbraided by Joab, 2 Sam. 19:5-7. David upbraids the priests for not showing loyalty amid the murmurings of the people against him, 2 Sam. 19:9-15. Shimei sues for clemency, 2 Sam. 19:16-23. Mephibosheth sues for the king's favor, 2 Sa..., 19:24-30. Barzillai rewarded, 2 Sam. 19:31-40. Judah accused by the ten tribes of stealing him away, 2 Sam. 19:41-43. Returns to Jerusalem, 2 Sam. 20:1-3. At this time, probably, composes Psalms 27, 66, 122, 144.

Sheba's conspiracy against David, and his death, 2 Sam. 20. Makes Amasa general, 2 Sam. 19:13. Amasa is slain, 2 Sam. 20:4-10. Consigns seven sons of Saul to the Gibeonites to be slain to atone for Saul's persecution of the Gibeonites, 2 Sam. 21:1-14. Buries Saul's bones, and his sons', 2 Sam. 21:12-14.

Defeats the Philistines, 2 Sam. 21:15-22; 1 Chr. 20:4-8. Takes the military strength of Israel without divine authority, and is reproved, 2 Sam. 24; 1 Chr. 21; 27:24. Probably composes Psalms 30, 131. Marries Abishag, 1 Kin. 1:1-4. Probably composes Psalms 19, 111.

Reorganizes the tabernacle service, 1 Chr. 22-26; 2 Chr. 7:6; 8:14; 23:18; 29:27-30; 35:15; Ezra 3:10; 8:20.

Adonijah usurps the sceptre, Solomon appointed to the throne, 1 Kin. 1; 1 Chr. 23:1. Delivers his charge to Solomon, 1 Kin. 2: 1-11; 1 Chr. 22:6-19; 28; 29. Probably composes Psalms 23, 145.

Last words of, 2 Sam. 23:1-7. Death of, 1 Kin. 2:10; 1 Chr. 29:28; Acts 2:29,30. Sepulchre of, Acts 2:29. Age of, at death, 2 Sam. 5:4,5; 1 Chr. 29:28. Length of reign, forty years, 1 Kin. 2:11; 1 Chr. 29:27,28.

Wives of, 2 Sam. 3:2-5; 11:3,27; 1 Chr. 3:5. Children born at Hebron, 2 Sam. 3:2-5; 1 Chr. 3:4; at Jerusalem, 2 Sam. 5:14-16; 1 Chr. 3:5-8; 14:4-7. Descendants of, 1 Chr. 3.

Civil and military officers of, 2 Sam. 8: 16-18. See CABINET.

Lists of his heroes, and of their exploits, 2 Sam. 23; 1 Chr. 11; 12:23-40.

Devoutness of, 1 Sam. 13:14; 2 Sam. 6:5, 14-18; 7:18-29; 8:11; 24:25; 1 Kin. 3:14; 1 Chr. 17:16-27; 29:10; 2 Chr. 7:17; Zech. 12:8; Psa. 6; 7; 11; 13; 17; 22; 26; 27:7-14; 28; 31; 35; 37; 38; 39; 40:11-17; 42; 43; 51; 54; 55; 56; 57; 59; 60; 61, 62; 64:1-6; 66; 69; 70; 71; 86; 101; 108; 120; 1-2; 140; 141; 142; 143; 144; Acts 13:22.

Justice in the administration of, 2 Sam. 8: 15; 1 Chr. 18:14. Discreetness of, 1 Sam. 18: 14,30. Meekness of, 1 Sam. 24:7; 26:11; 2 Sam. 16:11; 19:22,23. Merciful, 2 Sam. 19:23.

David as musician, 1 Sam. 16:21-23; 1 Chr. 15:16; 23:5; 2 Chr. 7:6; 29:26; Neh. 12:36; Amos 6:5; poet, 2 Sam. 22; see PSALMS OF DAVID; prophet, 2 Sam. 23:2-7; 1 Chr. 28:19; Matt. 22:41-46; Acts 2:25-38; 4:25.

Type of Christ, Psa. 2; 16; 18:43; 69:7-9, 20,21,26,29; 89:19-37. Jesus called son of, Matt. 9:27; 12:23; 15:22; 20:30,31; 21:9; 22:42; Mark 10:47,48; Luke 18:37,39.

Prophecies concerning him and his kingdom, Num. 24:17,19; 2 Sam. 7:11-16; 1 Chr. 17:9-14; 22; 2 Chr. 6:5-17; 13:5; 21:7; Psa. 89: 19-37; Isa. 9:7; 16:5; 22:20-25; Jer. 23:5; 33: 15-26; Luke 1:32,33.

Chronicles of, written by Samuel, Nathan, and Gad, 1 Chr. 29:29,30.

2. A prophetic name for Christ, Jer. 30: 9; Ezek. 34:23,24; 37:24,25; Hos. 3:5.

DAY. A creative period, Gen. 1:5,8,13, 19,23,31; 2:2. Divided into twelve hours, John 11:9. Prophetic, Dan. 8:14,26; 12:11,12; Rev. 9:15; 11:3; 12:6. Six working days ordained, Ex. 20:9; Ezek. 46:1. Sixth day of the week called preparation day, Mark 15:42; John 19:14,31,42. First day of the week called the Lord's day, Rev. 1:10. With the Lord as a thousand years, 2 Pet. 3:8.

Day's journey, eighteen or twenty miles, Ex. 3:18; 1 Kin. 19:4; Jonah 3:4. Sabbath day's journey, about two thousand paces, Acts 1:12. The seventh of the week ordained as a day of rest, see SABBATH.

Times of adversity called Day of the Lord, Isa. 2:12; 13:6,9; 34:8; Jer. 46:10; Lam. 2:22; Ezek. 30:3; Amos 5:18; Joel 2:1; Obad. 15; Zeph. 1:8,18; 2:2,3; Zech. 14:1.

JUDGMENT: Called DAY OF THE LORD, Mal. 4:5; 1 Cor. 5:5; 2 Cor. 1:14; 1 Thess. 5:2; 2 Pet. 3:10.

See JUDGMENT.

A figure of spiritual illumination, Prov. 4:18; 1 Thess. 5:8.

DAYSMAN, a mediator, Job 9:33.

DAYSTAR. Figurative of spiritual life, 2 Pet. 1:19.

DEACON, an ecclesiastic charged with the temporal affairs of the church. Ordained by the apostles, Acts 6:1-6. Qualifications of, 1 Tim. 3:8-13. The Greek word translated deacon signifies servant, and is so translated in Matt. 23:11; John 12:26. Also translated minister, Mark 10:43; 1 Cor. 3:5; 1 Thess. 3:2.

DEACONESS, Rom. 16:1 [R. V. marg.].

DEAD. Raised to life, instances of: Son of the widow of Zarephath, 1 Kin. 17: 17-23; Shunammite's son, 2 Kin. 4:32-37; young man laid in Elisha's sepulchre, 2 Kin. 13:21; widow's son, Luke 7:12-15; Jairus' daughter, Luke 8:49-55; Lazarus, John 11:43, 44; Dorcas, Acts 9:37-40; Eutychus, Acts 20: 9-12; see Heb. 11:35. Prepared for burial by washing, Acts 9:37; anointing, Matt. 26:

12; wrapping in linen, Matt. 27:59. Burned. See CREMATION.

Burnings of incense made for, 2 Chr. 16: 14; 21:19; Jer. 34:5.

See BURIAL; CREMATION; EMBALMING.

UNCLASSIFIED SCRIPTURES RELATING TO :

Job 3:13. For now should I have lain still and been quiet, I should have slept : then had I been at rest, 14. With kings and counsellors of the earth, which build desolate places for themselves; 15. Or with princes that had gold, who filled their houses with silver: 16. Or as an hidden untimely birth I had not been ; as infants *which* never saw light. 17. There the wicked cease *from* troubling ; and there the weary be at rest. 18. *There* the prisoners rest together; they hear not the voice of the oppressor. 19. The small and great are there ; and the servant *is* free from his master.

Job 14:11. *As* the waters fail from the sea, and the flood decayeth and drieth up: 12. So man lieth down, and riseth not : till the heavens *be* no more, they shall not awake, nor be raised out of their sleep. 13. O that thou wouldest hide me in the grave, that thou wouldest keep me secret, until thy wrath be past, that thou wouldest appoint me a set time, and remember me! 14. If a man die, shall he live *again?* all the days of my appointed time will I wait, till my change come. 15. Thou shalt call, and I will answer thee: thou wilt have a desire to the work of thine hands. 21. His sons come to honour, and he knoweth *it* not ; and they are brought low, but he perceiveth *it* not of them.

Job 17:13. If I wait, the grave *is* mine house : I have made my bed in the darkness. 14. I have said to corruption, Thou *art* my father : to the worm, *Thou art* my mother, and my sister. 15. And where *is* now my hope ? as for my hope, who shall see it? 16. They shall go down to the bars of the pit, when *our* rest together *is* in the dust.

Psa. 6:5. For in death *there is* no remembrance of thee : in the grave who shall give thee thanks ?

Psa. 30:9. What profit *is there* in my blood, when I go down to the pit ? Shall the dust praise thee ? shall it declare thy truth ?

Psa. 49:15. But God will redeem my soul from the power of the grave : for he shall receive me.

Psa. 88:10. Wilt thou shew wonders to the dead ? shall the dead arise *and* praise thee ? Selah. 11. Shall thy lovingkindness be declared in the grave ? *or* thy faithfulness in destruction? 12. Shall thy wonders be known in the dark ? and thy righteousness in the land of forgetfulness?

Psa. 115:17. The dead praise not the LORD, neither any that go down into silence.

Prov. 21:16. The man that wandereth out of the way of understanding shall remain in the congregation of the dead.

Eccl. 9:5. For the living know that they shall die: but the dead know not any thing,

neither have they any more a reward ; for the memory of them is forgotten. 6. Also their love, and their hatred, and their envy, is now perished ; neither have they any more a portion for ever in any *thing* that is done under the sun.

Ezek. 32:31. Pharaoh shall see them, and shall be comforted over all his multitude, *even* Pharaoh and all his army slain by the sword, saith the Lord GOD.

Dan. 12:2. And many of them that sleep in the dust of the earth shall awake, some to everlasting life, and some to shame *and* everlasting contempt.

Luke 9:30. And, behold, there talked with him two men, which were Moses and Elias : 31. Who appeared in glory, and spake of his decease which he should accomplish at Jerusalem.

Luke 16:19. There was a certain rich man, which was clothed in purple and fine linen, and fared sumptuously every day : 20. And there was a certain beggar named Lazarus, which was laid at his gate, full of sores, 21. And desiring to be fed with the crumbs which fell from the rich man's table : moreover the dogs came and licked his sores. 22. And it came to pass, that the beggar died, and was carried by the angels into Abraham's bosom : the rich man also died, and was buried ; 23. And in hell he lifted up his eyes, being in torments, and seeth Abraham afar off, and Lazarus in his bosom. 24. And he cried and said, Father Abraham, have mercy on me, and send Lazarus, that he may dip the tip of his finger in water, and cool my tongue ; for I am tormented in this flame. 25. But Abraham said, Son, remember that thou in thy lifetime receivedst thy good things, and likewise Lazarus evil things : but now he is comforted, and thou art tormented. 26. And beside all this, between us and you there is a great gulf fixed : so that they which would pass from hence to you cannot ; neither can they pass to us, that *would come* from thence. 27. Then he said, I pray thee therefore, father, that thou wouldest send him to my father's house : 28. For I have five brethren : that he may testify unto them, lest they also come into this place of torment. 29. Abraham saith unto him, They have Moses and the prophets ; let them hear them. 30. And he said, Nay, father Abraham : but if one went unto them from the dead, they will repent. 31. And he said unto him, If they hear not Moses and the prophets, neither will they be persuaded, though one rose from the dead.

Luke 20:35. But they which shall be accounted worthy to obtain that world, and the resurrection from the dead, neither marry, nor are given in marriage : 36. Neither can they die any more : for they are equal unto the angels ; and are the children of God, being the children of the resurrection.

Luke 23:43. And Jesus said unto him, Verily, I say unto thee, To day shalt thou be with me in paradise.

John 11:25. Jesus said unto her, I am the resurrection, and the life : he that believeth in me, though he ¹ were dead, yet shall he live : [¹ R. V. die]

See BURIAL; DEATH; MOURNING; RESURRECTION; RIGHTEOUS, PROMISES TO; WICKED, PUNISHMENT OF.

DEAD SEA, lies southeast of Jerusalem. Called SALT SEA, Gen. 14:3; Num. 34:12; SEA OF THE PLAIN. Deut. 3:17; 4:49; Josh. 3:16; EAST SEA, Joel 2:20; FORMER SEA, Zech. 14:8.

Prophecy concerning, Ezek. 47:7-10,18.

DEAFNESS. Law concerning, Lev. 19:14. Inflicted by God, Ex. 4:11. Miraculous cure of, Matt. 11:5; Mark 7:32; 9:25.

FIGURATIVE : Of moral insensibility, Isa. 6:10; 29:18; 35:5; Ezek. 12:2; Matt. 13:15; John 12:40; Acts 28:26,27.

See BLINDNESS, SPIRITUAL; CONSCIENCE, DEAD; IMPENITENCE; OBDURACY.

DEATH. INDEX OF SUB-TOPICS : *Miscellaneous Subjects : Unclassified Scriptures Relating to, p.* 280; *Preparation for, p.* 283; *Of the Righteous, p.* 284; *Scenes of, p.* 285; *Of the Wicked, p.* 290; *Spiritual, p.* 292; *Second Death, p.* 292; *Figurative of Regeneration, p.* 293.

CALLED GIVING UP THE GHOST, Gen. 25:8; 35:29; Lam. 1:19; Acts 5:10; KING OF TERRORS, Job 18:14; A CHANGE, Job 14:14. GOING TO THY FATHERS, Gen. 15:15; 25:8; 35:29; PUTTING OFF THIS TABERNACLE, 2 Pet. 1:14; REQUIRING THE SOUL, Luke 12:20; GOING THE WAY WHENCE THERE IS NO RETURN, Job 16:22; BEING GATHERED TO OUR PEOPLE, Gen. 49:33; GOING DOWN INTO SILENCE, Psa. 115:17; RETURNING TO DUST, Gen. 3:19; Psa. 104:29; BEING CUT DOWN, Job 14:2; FLEEING AS A SHADOW, Job 14:2; DEPARTING, Phil. 1:23.

CALLED SLEEP : Deut. 31:16. And the LORD said unto Moses, Behold, thou shalt sleep with thy fathers;

Job 7:21. Now shall I sleep in the dust; and thou shalt seek me in the morning, but I *shall* not *be.*

Job 14:12. So man lieth down, and riseth not : till the heavens *be* no more, they shall not awake, nor be raised out of their sleep.

Jer. 51:39. In their heat I will make their feasts, and I will make them drunken, that they may rejoice, and sleep a perpetual sleep, and not wake, saith the LORD.

Dan. 12:2. And many of them that sleep in the dust of the earth shall awake, some to everlasting life, and some to shame *and* everlasting contempt.

John 11:11. These things said he : and after that he saith unto them, Our friend Lazarus sleepeth ; but I go, that I may awake him out of sleep.

Acts 7:60. And he kneeled down, and cried with a loud voice, Lord, lay not this sin to their charge. And when he had said this, he fell asleep.

Acts 13:36. For David, after he had served his own generation by the will of God, fell on sleep, and was laid unto his fathers, and saw corruption :

1 Cor. 15:6. After that, he was seen of above five hundred brethren at once ; of whom the greater part remain unto this present, but some are fallen asleep. 18. Then they also which are fallen asleep in Christ are perished. 51. Behold, I shew you a mystery; We shall not all sleep, but we shall all be changed,

1 Thess. 4:14. For if we believe that Jesus died and rose again, even so them also which sleep in Jesus will God bring with him. 15. For this we say unto you by the word of the Lord, that we which are alive *and* remain unto the coming of the Lord shall not prevent them which are asleep.

EXEMPTION FROM : Enoch, Gen. 5:24; Heb. 11:5. Elijah, 2 Kin. 2. Promised to saints at the second coming of Christ, 1 Cor. 15:51; 1 Thess. 4:15,17. No death in heaven, Luke 20:36; Rev. 21:4.

DESIRED : Jer. 8:3; Rev. 9:6. By Moses, Num. 11:15; Elijah, 1 Kin. 19:4; Job, Job 3; 6:8-11; 7:1-3,15,16; 10:1; 14:13; Jonah, Jonah 4:8; Simeon, Luke 2:29; Paul, 2 Cor. 5:2,8; Phil. 1:20-23.

AS A JUDGMENT : Upon the Antediluvians, Gen. 6:7,11-13; Sodomites, Gen. 19:12, 13,24,25; Saul, 1 Chr. 10:13,14.

SYMBOLIZED : By the pale horse, Rev. 6:8; King of Terrors, Job 18:14.

APOSTROPHE TO : Hos. 13:14; 1 Cor. 15:55.

UNCLASSIFIED SCRIPTURES RELATING TO : Gen. 2:17. In the day that thou eatest thereof thou shalt surely die.

Gen. 3:19. Till thou return unto the ground; for out of it wast thou taken : for dust thou *art,* and unto dust shalt thou return.

Gen. 27:2. And he said, Behold now, I am old, I know not the day of my death :

Josh. 23:14. And, behold, this day I *am* going the way of all the earth :

1 Sam. 2:6. The LORD killeth, and maketh alive : he bringeth down to the grave, and bringeth up.

1 Sam. 20:2. And he said unto him, God forbid ; thou shalt not die : behold, my father will do nothing either great or small, but that he will shew it me : and why should my father hide this thing from me ? it *is* not *so.* 3. And David sware moreover, and said, Thy father certainly knoweth that I have found grace in thine eyes ; and he saith, Let not Jonathan know this, lest he be grieved : but truly *as* the LORD liveth, and *as* thy soul liveth, *there is* but a step between me and death.

2 Sam. 1:23. Saul and Jonathan *were* lovely and pleasant in their lives, and in their death they were not divided :

2 Sam. 14:14. We must needs die, and *are* as water spilt on the ground, which cannot be gathered up again ;

Job 3:13. For now should I have lain still and been quiet, I should have slept : then had I been at rest, 17. There the wicked cease *from* troubling ; and there the weary be at rest. 18. *There* the prisoners rest together; they hear not the voice of the oppressor. 19. The small and great are there; and the servant *is* free from his master.

Job 7:1. *Is there* not an appointed time to man upon earth? *are not* his days also like the days of an hireling? 8. The eye of him that hath seen me shall see me no *more:* thine eyes *are* upon me, and I *am* not. 9. *As* the cloud is consumed and vanisheth away: so he that goeth down to the grave shall come up no *more.* 10. He shall return no more to his house, neither shall his place know him any more. 21. Now shall I sleep in the dust; and thou shalt seek me in the morning, but I *shall* not *be.* Job 14:6.

Job 10:21. Before I go *whence* I shall not return, *even* to the land of darkness and the shadow of death; 22. A land of darkness, as darkness *itself; and* of the shadow of death, without any order, and *where* the light *is* as darkness.

Job 14:2. He cometh forth like a flower, and is cut down: he fleeth also as a shadow, and continueth not. 5. Seeing his days *are* determined, the number of his months *are* with thee, thou hast appointed his bounds that he cannot pass; 7. For there is hope of a tree, if it be cut down, that it will sprout again, and that the tender branch thereof will not cease. 8. Though the root thereof wax old in the earth, and the stock thereof die in the ground; 9. *Yet* through the scent of water it will bud, and bring forth boughs like a plant. 10. But man dieth, and wasteth away: yea, man giveth up the ghost, and where *is* he? 11. *As* the waters fail from the sea, and the flood decayeth and drieth up: 12. So man lieth down, and riseth not: till the heavens *be* no more, they shall not awake, nor be raised out of their sleep. 14. If a man die, shall he live *again?* all the days of my appointed time will I wait, till my change come. 19. Thou destroyest the hope of man. 20. Thou prevailest for ever against him, and he passeth: thou changest his countenance, and sendest him away. 21. His sons come to honour, and he knoweth *it* not; and they are brought low, but he perceiveth *it* not of them.

Job 16:22. When a few years are come, then I shall go the way *whence* I shall not return.

Job 17:13. If I wait, the grave *is* mine house: I have made my bed in the darkness. 14. I have said to corruption, Thou *art* my father: to the worm, *Thou art* my mother, and my sister. 16. They shall go down to the bars of the pit, when *our* rest together *is* in the dust.

Job 21:23. One dieth in his full strength, being wholly at ease and quiet. 25. And another dieth in the bitterness of his soul, and never eateth with pleasure. 26. They shall lie down alike in the dust, and the worms shall cover them. 32. Yet shall he be brought to the grave, and shall remain in the tomb. 33. The clods of the valley shall be sweet

unto him, and every man shall draw after him, as *there are* innumerable before him.

Job 30:23. For I know *that* thou wilt bring me *to* death, and *to* the house appointed for all living.

Job 34:14. If he set his heart upon man, *if* he gather unto himself his spirit and his breath; 15. All flesh shall perish together, and man shall turn again unto dust.

Job 36:18. Because *there is* wrath, *beware* lest he take thee away with *his* stroke: then a great ransom cannot deliver thee. 19. Will he esteem thy riches? *no,* not gold, nor all the forces of strength.

Job 38:17. Have the gates of death been opened unto thee? or hast thou seen the doors of the shadow of death?

Psa. 23:4. Yea, though I walk through the valley of the shadow of death, I will fear no evil: for thou *art* with me; thy rod and thy staff they comfort me.

Psa. 30:9. What profit *is there* in my blood, when I go down to the pit? Shall the dust praise thee? shall it declare thy truth? Psa. 6:5; 88:9–14; 115:17; Isa. 38:18.

Psa. 39:4. LORD, make me to know mine end, and the measure of my days, what it *is; that* I may know how frail I *am.* 13. O spare me, that I may recover strength, before I go hence, and be no more.

Psa. 49:7. None *of them* can by any means redeem his brother, nor give to God a ransom for him: 9. That he should still live for ever, *and* not see corruption. 10. For he seeth *that* wise men die, likewise the fool and the brutish person perish,

Psa. 68:20. Unto GOD the Lord *belong* the issues from death. Deut. 32:39.

Psa. 82:7. Ye shall die like men, and fall like one of the princes.

Psa. 89:48. What man *is he that* liveth, and shall not see death? shall he deliver his soul from the hand of the grave?

Psa. 90:3. Thou turnest man to destruction; and sayest, Return, ye children of men.

Psa. 103:14. He remembereth that we *are* dust. 15. *As for* man, his days *are* as grass: as a flower of the field, so he flourisheth. 16. For the wind passeth over it, and it is gone; and the place thereof shall know it no more.

Psa. 104:29. Thou hidest thy face, they are troubled: thou takest away their breath, they die, and return to their dust.

Psa. 143:3. For the enemy hath persecuted my soul; he hath smitten my life down to the ground; he hath made me to dwell in darkness, as those that have been long dead. Lam. 3:6.

Psa. 144:4. Man is like to vanity: his days *are* as a shadow that passeth away.

Psa. 146:4. His breath goeth forth, he returneth to his earth; in that very day his thoughts perish.

Eccl. 2:14. The wise man's eyes *are* in his head; but the fool walketh in darkness: and I myself perceived also that one event happeneth to them all. 15. Then said I in my heart, As it happeneth to the fool, so it happeneth even to me; and why was I then more wise? Then I said in my heart, that this also *is* vanity. 16. For *there is* no remembrance of the wise more than of the fool for ever; seeing that which now *is* in the days to come shall all be forgotten. And how dieth the wise *man?* as the fool. 17. Therefore I hated life; because the work that is wrought under the sun *is* grievous unto me: for all *is* vanity and vexation of spirit. 18. Yea, I hated all my labour which I had taken under the sun: because I should leave it unto the man that shall be after me.

Eccl. 3:2. A time to be born, and a time to die; 19. That which befalleth the sons of men befalleth beasts; even one thing befalleth them: as the one dieth, so dieth the other; yea, they have all one breath; 20. All go unto one place; all are of the dust, and all turn to dust again. 21. Who knoweth the spirit of man that goeth upward, and the spirit of the beast that goeth downward to the earth?

Eccl. 4:2. Wherefore I praised the dead which are already dead more than the living which are yet alive.

Eccl. 5:15. As he came forth of his mother's womb, naked shall he return to go as he came, and shall take nothing of his labour, which he may carry away in his hand. Job 1:21.

Eccl. 6:6. Yea, though he live a thousand years twice *told*, yet hath he seen no good: do not all go to one place? 10. That which hath been is named already, and it is known that it *is* man: neither may he contend with him that is mightier than he.

Eccl. 7:1. A good name *is* better than precious ointment; and the day of death than the day of one's birth. 2. *It is* better to go to the house of mourning, than to go to the house of feasting: for that *is* the end of all men; and the living will lay *it* to his heart. 15. All *things* have I seen in the days of my vanity: there is a just *man* that perisheth in his righteousness, and there is a wicked *man* that prolongeth *his life* in his wickedness.

Eccl. 8:8. *There is* no man that hath power over the spirit to retain the spirit; neither *hath he* power in the day of death: and *there is* no discharge in *that* war; neither shall wickedness deliver those that are given to it.

Eccl. 9:3. This *is* an evil among all *things* that are done under the sun, that *there is* one event unto all: yea, also the heart of the sons of men is full of evil, and madness *is* in their heart while they live, and after that *they* go to the dead. 5. For the living know that they shall die: but the dead know not any thing, neither have they any more a reward; for the memory of them is forgotten. 6. Also their love, and their hatred and their envy, is now perished; neither have they any more a portion for

ever in any *thing* that is done under the sun. 10. Whatsoever thy hand findeth to do, do *it* with thy might; for *there is* no work, nor device, nor knowledge, nor wisdom, in the grave, whither thou goest.

Eccl. 12:5. Man goeth to his long home, and the mourners go about the streets: 7. Then shall the dust return to the earth as it was: and the spirit shall return unto God who gave it.

Isa. 25:8. He will swallow up death [1 in victory; and the Lord God will wipe away tears from off all faces; [1 R. V. for ever]

Isa. 38:1. In those days was Hezekiah sick unto death. And Isaiah the prophet the son of Amoz came unto him, and said unto him, Thus saith the Lord, Set thine house in order: for thou shalt die, and not live. 10. I said in the cutting off of my days, I shall go to the gates of the grave: I am deprived of the residue of my years. 11. I said, I shall not see the Lord, *even* the Lord, in the land of the living: I shall behold man no more with the inhabitants of the world. 12. Mine age is departed, and is removed from me as a shepherd's tent: I have cut off like a weaver my life: he will cut me off with pining sickness: from day *even* to night wilt thou make an end of me. 13. I reckoned till morning, *that*, as a lion, so will he break all my bones: from day *even* to night wilt thou make an end of me.

Isa. 40:7. The grass withereth, the flower fadeth: because the spirit of the Lord bloweth upon it: surely the people *is* grass. 1 Pet. 1:24.

Isa. 51:12. I, *even* I, *am* he that comforteth you: who *art* thou, that thou shouldest be afraid of a man *that* shall die, and of the son of man *which* shall be made *as* grass;

Jer. 9:21. Death is come up into our windows, *and* is entered into our palaces, to cut off the children from without, *and* the young men from the streets.

Hos. 13:14. I will ransom them from the power of the grave; I will redeem them from death: O death, I will be thy plagues; O grave, I will be thy destruction: repentance shall be hid from mine eyes.

Zech. 1:5. Your fathers, where *are* they? and the prophets, do they live for ever?

Matt. 10:28. Fear not them which kill the body, but are not able to kill the soul:

Luke 20:34. And Jesus answering said unto them, The children of this world marry, and are given in marriage: 35. But they which shall be accounted worthy to obtain that world, and the resurrection from the dead, neither marry, nor are given in marriage: 36. Neither can they die any more: for they are equal unto the angels; and are the children of God, being the children of the resurrection. 37. Now that the dead are raised, even Moses shewed at the bush, when he calleth the Lord the God of Abraham, and the God of Isaac, and the God of Jacob. 38. For he is not a God of the dead, but of the living: for all live unto him.

Luke 23:39. And one of the malefactors which were hanged railed on him, saying, If thou be Christ, save thyself and us. 40. But the other answering rebuked him, saying, Dost not thou fear God, seeing thou art in the same condemnation? 41. And we indeed justly; for we receive the due reward of our deeds: but this man hath done nothing amiss. 42. And he said unto Jesus, Lord, remember me when thou comest into thy kingdom. 43. And Jesus said unto him, Verily I say unto thee, To day shalt thou be with me in paradise.

John 9:4. I must work the works of him that sent me, while it is day: the night cometh, when no man can work.

Rom. 5:12. Wherefore, as by one man sin entered into the world, and death by sin; and so death passed upon all men, for that all have sinned: 14. Nevertheless death reigned from Adam to Moses, even over them that had not sinned after the similitude of Adam's transgression, who is the figure of him that was to come.

1 Cor. 15:21. For since by man *came* death, by man *came* also the resurrection of the dead. 22. For as in Adam all die, even so in Christ shall all be made alive. 26. The last enemy *that* shall be destroyed *is* death. 55. O death, where *is* thy sting? O grave, where *is* thy victory? 56. The sting of death *is* sin; and the strength of sin *is* the law. 57. But thanks *be* to God, which giveth us the victory through our Lord Jesus Christ.

1 Tim. 6:7. For we brought nothing into *this* world, *and it is* certain we can carry nothing out.

2 Tim. 1:10. But is now made manifest by the appearing of our Saviour Jesus Christ, who hath abolished death, and hath brought life and ¹immortality to light through the gospel; [¹ R. V. incorruption]

Heb. 2:14. Forasmuch then as the children are partakers of flesh and blood, he also himself likewise took part of the same; that through death he might destroy him that had the power of death, that is, the devil: 15. And deliver them who through fear of death were all their lifetime subject to bondage.

Heb. 9:27. And as it is appointed unto men once to die, but after this the judgment:

Heb. 13:14. Here have we no continuing city, but we seek one to come.

Jas. 1:10. As the flower of the grass he shall pass away. 11. For the sun is no sooner risen with a burning heat, but it withereth the grass, and the flower thereof falleth, and the grace of the fashion of it perisheth: so also shall the rich man fade away in his ways.

1 Pet. 1:24. For all flesh *is* as grass, and all the glory of man as the flower of grass. The grass withereth, and the flower thereof falleth away:

Rev. 1:18. I *am* he that liveth, and was dead; and, behold, I am alive for evermore,

Amen; and have the keys of hell and of death.

Rev. 20:12. And I saw the dead, small and great, stand before God; and the books were opened: and another book was opened, which is *the book* of life: and the dead were judged out of those things which were written in the books, according to their works. 13. And the sea gave up the dead which were in it; and death and hell delivered up the dead which were in them: and they were judged every man according to their works. 14. And death and hell were cast into the lake of fire. This is the second death.

Rev. 21:4. And God shall wipe away all tears from their eyes; and there shall be no more death, neither sorrow, nor crying, neither shall there be any more pain: for the former things are passed away.

PREPARATION FOR: Deut. 32:29. O that they were wise, *that* they understood this, *that* they would consider their latter end!

2 Kin. 20:1. In those days was Hezekiah sick unto death. And the prophet Isaiah the son of Amoz came to him, and said unto him, Thus saith the LORD, Set thine house in order; for thou shalt die, and not live.

Psa. 39:4. LORD, make me to know mine end, and the measure of my days, what it *is*; *that* I may know how frail I *am*. 13. O spare me, that I may recover strength, before I go hence, and be no more.

Psa. 90:12. So teach *us* to number our days, that we may apply *our* hearts unto wisdom.

Eccl. 9:4. To him that is joined to all the living there is hope: for a living dog is better than a dead lion. 10. Whatsoever thy hand findeth to do, do *it* with thy might; for *there is* no work, nor device, nor knowledge, nor wisdom, in the grave, whither thou goest.

Eccl. 11:7. Truly the light *is* sweet, and a pleasant *thing it is* for the eyes to behold the sun: 8. But if a man live many years, *and* rejoice in them all; yet let him remember the days of darkness; for they shall be many.

Isa. 38:18. For the grave cannot praise thee, death can *not* celebrate thee: they that go down into the pit cannot hope for thy truth. 19. The living, the living, he shall praise thee, as I *do* this day: the father to the children shall make known thy truth.

Luke 12:35. Let your loins be girded about, and *your* lights burning; 36. And ye yourselves like unto men that wait for their lord, when he will return from the wedding; that when he cometh and knocketh, they may open unto him immediately. 37. Blessed *are* those servants, whom the lord when he cometh shall find watching:

John 9:4. I must work the works of him that sent me, while it is day: the night cometh, when no man can work.

Rom. 14:8. For whether we live, we live unto the Lord; and whether we die, we die unto the Lord: whether we live therefore, or die, we are the Lord's.

Phil. 1:21. For to me to live *is* Christ, and to die *is* gain.

Heb. 13:14. Here have we no continuing city, but we seek one to come.

Jas. 4:15. Ye *ought* to say, If the Lord will, we shall live, and do this, or that.

1 Pet. 1:17. And if ye call on the Father, who without respect of persons judgeth according to every man's work, pass the time of your sojourning *here* in fear:

OF THE RIGHTEOUS: Num. 23:10. Let me die the death of the righteous, and let my last end be like his!

2 Sam. 12:23. But now he is dead, wherefore should I fast? can I bring him back again? I shall go to him, but he shall not return to me.

2 Kin. 22:19. Because thine heart was tender, and thou hast humbled thyself before the LORD, when thou heardest what I spake against this place, and against the inhabitants thereof, that they should become a desolation and a curse, and hast rent thy clothes, and wept before me; I also have heard *thee*, saith the LORD. 20. Behold therefore, I will gather thee unto thy fathers, and thou shalt be gathered into thy grave in peace; and thine eyes shall not see all the evil which I will bring upon this place. And they brought the king word again.

Psa. 23:4. Though I walk through the valley of the shadow of death, I will fear no evil: for thou *art* with me; thy rod and thy staff they comfort me.

Psa. 31:5. Into thine hand I commit my spirit: thou hast redeemed me, O LORD God of truth.

Psa. 37:37. Mark the perfect *man*, and behold the upright: for the end of *that* man *is* peace.

Psa. 49:15. God will redeem my soul from the power of the grave: for he shall receive me.

Psa. 73:24. Thou shalt guide me with thy counsel, and afterward receive me *to* glory.

Psa. 116:15. Precious in the sight of the LORD *is* the death of his saints.

Prov. 14:32. The righteous hath hope in his death.

Eccl. 7:1. A good name *is* better than precious ointment; and the day of death than the day of one's birth.

Isa. 57:1. The righteous perisheth, and no man layeth *it* to heart: and merciful men *are* taken away, none considering that the righteous is taken away from the evil *to come*. 2. He shall enter into peace: they shall rest in their beds, *each one* walking in his uprightness.

Dan. 12:13. But go thou thy way till the end *be:* for thou shalt rest, and stand in thy lot at the end of the days.

Luke 2:29. Lord, now lettest thou thy servant depart in peace, according to thy word:

Luke 16:22. The beggar died, and was carried by the angels into Abraham's bosom:

Luke 23:43. To day shalt thou be with me in paradise.

John 11:11. These things said he: and after that he saith unto them, Our friend Lazarus sleepeth; but I go, that I may awake him out of sleep.

Acts 7:59. They stoned Stephen, calling upon *God*, and saying, Lord Jesus, receive my spirit.

Rom. 14:7. For none of us liveth to himself, and no man dieth to himself. 8. For whether we live, we live unto the Lord; and whether we die, we die unto the Lord: whether we live therefore, or die, we are the Lord's.

1 Cor. 3:21. All things are your's; 22. Whether Paul, or Apollos, or Cephas, or the world, or life, or death, or things present, or things to come; all are your's; 23. And ye are Christ's; and Christ *is* God's.

1 Cor. 15:51. Behold, I shew you a mystery; We shall not all sleep, but we shall all be changed, 52. In a moment, in the twinkling of an eye, at the last trump: for the trumpet shall sound, and the dead shall be raised incorruptible, and we shall be changed. 53. For this corruptible must put on incorruption, and this mortal *must* put on immortality. 54. So when this corruptible shall have put on incorruption, and this mortal shall have put on immortality, then shall be brought to pass the saying that is written, Death is swallowed up in victory. 55. O death, where *is* thy sting? O grave, where *is* thy victory? 56. The sting of death *is* sin; and the strength of sin *is* the law. 57. But thanks *be* to God, which giveth us the victory through our Lord Jesus Christ.

2 Cor. 1:9. But we had the sentence of death in ourselves, that we should not trust in ourselves, but in God which raiseth the dead: 10. Who delivered us from so great a death, and doth deliver: in whom we trust that he will yet deliver *us;*

2 Cor. 5:1. For we know that if our earthly house of *this* tabernacle were dissolved, we have a building of God, an house not made with hands, eternal in the heavens. 4. We that are in *this* tabernacle do groan, being burdened: not for that we would be unclothed, but clothed upon, that mortality might be swallowed up of life. 8. We are confident, *I say*, and willing rather to be absent from the body, and to be � present with the Lord. [1 R. V. at home]

Phil. 1:20. Christ shall be magnified in my body, whether *it be* by life, or by death. 21. To me to live *is* Christ, and to die *is* gain. 23. For I am in a strait betwixt two, having a desire to depart, and to be with Christ; which is far better: 24. Nevertheless to abide in the flesh *is* more needful for you.

1 Thess. 4:13. But I would not have you to be ignorant, brethren, concerning them which are asleep, that ye sorrow not, even as others which have no hope. 14. For if we believe that Jesus died and rose again, even so them also which sleep in Jesus will God bring with him.

1 Thess. 5:9. For God hath not appointed

us to wrath, but to obtain salvation by our Lord Jesus Christ, 10. Who died for us, that, whether we wake or sleep, we should live together with him.

2 Tim. 4:6. For I am now ready to be offered, and the time of my departure is at hand. 7. I have fought a good fight, I have finished *my* course, I have kept the faith: 8. Henceforth there is laid up for me a crown of righteousness,

Heb. 2:14. Forasmuch then as the children are partakers of flesh and blood, he also himself likewise took part of the same; that through death he might destroy him that had the power of death, that is, the devil; 15. And deliver them who through fear of death were all their lifetime subject to bondage.

Heb. 11:13. These all died in faith, not having received the promises, but having seen them afar off, and were persuaded of *them*, and embraced *them*, and confessed that they were strangers and pilgrims on the earth.

2 Pet. 1:11. For so an entrance shall be ministered unto you abundantly into the everlasting kingdom of our Lord and Saviour Jesus Christ. 14. Knowing that shortly I must put off *this* my tabernacle, even as our Lord Jesus Christ hath shewed me.

Rev. 14:13. And I heard a voice from heaven saying unto me, Write, Blessed *are* the dead which die in the Lord from henceforth: Yea, saith the Spirit, that they may rest from their labours: and their works do follow them.

ANTICIPATED : By Isaac : Gen. 27:1. And it came to pass, that when Isaac was old, and his eyes were dim, so that he could not see, he called Esau his eldest son, and said unto him, My son: and he said unto him, Behold, *here am* I. 2. And he said, Behold now, I am old, I know not the day of my death : 3. Now therefore take, I pray thee, thy weapons, thy quiver and thy bow, and go out to the field, and take me *some* venison ; 4. And make me savoury meat, such as I love, and bring *it* to me, that I may eat; that my soul may bless thee before I die. 22. And Jacob went near unto Isaac his father; and he felt him, and said, The voice *is* Jacob's voice, but the hands *are* the hands of Esau. 23. And he discerned him not, because his hands were hairy, as his brother Esau's hands: so he blessed him. 24. And he said, *Art* thou my very son Esau? And he said, I *am*.

25. And he said, Bring *it* near to me, and I will eat of my son's venison, that my soul may bless thee. And he brought *it* near to him, and he did eat: and he brought him wine, and he drank. 26. And his father Isaac said unto him, Come near now, and kiss me, my son. 27. And he came near, and kissed him: and he smelled the smell of his raiment, and blessed him, and said, See, the smell of my son *is* as the smell of a field which the LORD hath blessed: 28. Therefore God give thee of the dew of heaven,

and the fatness of the earth, and plenty of corn and wine : 29. Let people serve thee, and nations bow down to thee: be lord over thy brethren, and let thy mother's sons bow down to thee: cursed *be* every one that curseth thee, and blessed *be* he that blesseth thee. 30. And it came to pass, as soon as Isaac had made an end of blessing Jacob, and Jacob was yet scarce gone out from the presence of Isaac his father, that Esau his brother came in from his hunting. 31. And he also had made savoury meat, and brought it unto his father, and said unto his father, Let my father arise, and eat of his son's venison, that thy soul may bless me. 32. And Isaac his father said unto him, Who *art* thou? And he said, I *am* thy son, thy firstborn Esau. 33. And Isaac trembled very exceedingly, and said, Who? where *is* he that hath taken venison, and brought *it* me, and I have eaten of all before thou camest, and have blessed him? yea, *and* he shall be blessed. 34. And when Esau heard the words of his father, he cried with a great and exceeding bitter cry, and said unto his father, Bless me, *even* me also, O my father. 35. And he said, Thy brother came with subtilty, and hath taken away thy blessing. 36. And he said, Is not he rightly named Jacob? for he hath supplanted me these two times: he took away my birthright; and, behold, now he hath taken away my blessing. And he said, Hast thou not reserved a blessing for me? 37. And Isaac answered and said unto Esau, Behold, I have made him thy lord, and all his brethren have I given to him for servants; and with corn and wine have I sustained him: and what shall I do now unto thee, my son? 38. And Esau said unto his father, Hast thou but one blessing, my father? bless me, *even* me also, O my father. And Esau lifted up his voice, and wept. 39. And Isaac his father answered and said unto him, Behold, thy dwelling shall be the fatness of the earth, and of the dew of heaven from above ; 40. And by thy sword shalt thou live, and shalt serve thy brother ; and it shall come to pass when thou shalt have the dominion, that thou shalt break his yoke from off thy neck.

SCENES OF : OF JACOB : Gen. 49:1. And Jacob called unto his sons, and said, Gather yourselves together, that I may tell you *that* which shall befall you in the last days. 2. Gather yourselves together, and hear, ye sons of Jacob: and hearken unto Israel your father. 3. Reuben, thou *art* my firstborn, my might, and the beginning of my strength, the excellency of dignity, and the excellency of power: 4. Unstable as water, thou shalt not excel; because thou wentest up to thy father's bed; then defiledst thou *it :* he went up to my couch. 5. Simeon and Levi *are* brethren; instruments of cruelty *are in* their habitations. 6. O my soul, come not thou into their secret; unto their assembly, mine honour, be not thou united: for in their anger they slew a man, and in their selfwill they digged down a wall. 7. Cursed *be* their anger, for *it was* fierce; and their wrath, for it was cruel: I will divide them in Jacob, and scatter them in Israel. 8. Judah, thou *art he* whom thy brethren shall praise: thy hand *shall be* in the neck of thine enemies; thy father's children shall bow down before thee. 9. Judah *is* a lion's whelp: from the prey, my son, thou art gone up: he stooped down, he couched as a lion, and as an old lion; who shall rouse him up? 10. The sceptre shall not depart from Judah, nor a lawgiver from between his feet, until Shiloh come; and unto him *shall* the gathering of the people *be*. 11. Binding his foal unto the vine, and his ass's colt unto the choice vine; he washed his garments in wine, and his clothes in the blood of grapes: 12. His eyes *shall be* red with wine, and his teeth white with milk. 13. Zebulun shall dwell at the haven of the sea; and he *shall be* for an haven of ships; and his border *shall be* unto Zidon. 14. Issachar *is* a strong ass couching down between two burdens: 15. And he saw that rest *was* good, and the land that *it was* pleasant: and bowed his shoulder to bear, and became a servant unto tribute. 16. Dan shall judge his people, as one of the tribes of Israel. 17. Dan shall be a serpent by the way, an adder in the path, that biteth the horse heels, so that his rider shall fall backward. 18. I have waited for thy salvation, O LORD. 19. Gad, a troop shall overcome him: but he shall overcome at the last. 20. Out of Asher his bread *shall be* fat, and he shall yield royal dainties. 21. Naphtali *is* a hind let loose: he giveth goodly words. 22. Joseph *is* a fruitful bough, *even* a fruitful bough by a well; *whose* branches run over the wall: 23. The archers have sorely grieved him, and shot *at him*, and hated him: 24. But his bow abode in strength, and the arms of his hands were made strong by the hands of the mighty *God* of Jacob; (from thence *is* the shepherd, the stone of Israel:) 25. *Even* by the God of thy father, who shall help thee; and by the Almighty, who shall bless thee with blessings of heaven above, blessings of the deep that lieth under, blessings of the breasts, and of the womb: 26. The blessings of thy father have prevailed above the blessings of my progenitors unto the utmost bound of the everlasting hills: they shall be on the head of Joseph, and on the crown of the head of him that was separate from his brethren. 27. Benjamin shall ravin *as* a wolf: in the morning he shall devour the prey, and at night he shall divide the spoil. 28. All these *are* the twelve tribes of Israel: and this *is it* that their father spake unto them, and blessed them; every one according to his blessing he blessed them. 29. And he charged them, and said unto them, I am to be gathered unto my people: bury me with my fathers in the cave that *is* in the field of Ephron the Hittite. 30. In the cave that *is* in the field of Machpelah, which *is* before Mamre, in the land of Canaan, which

Abraham bought with the field of Ephron the Hittite for a possession of a burying-place. 31. There they buried Abraham and Sarah his wife; there they buried Isaac and Rebekah his wife; and there I buried Leah. 32. The purchase of the field and of the cave that *is* therein *was* from the children of Heth. 33. And when Jacob had made an end of commanding his sons, he gathered up his feet into the bed, and yielded up the ghost, and was gathered unto his people. Heb. 11:21.

OF AARON: Num. 20:23. And the LORD spake unto Moses and Aaron in mount Hor, by the coast of the land of Edom, saying. 24. Aaron shall be gathered unto his people: for he shall not enter into the land which I have given unto the children of Israel, because ye rebelled against my word at the water of Meribah. 25. Take Aaron and Eleazar his son, and bring them up unto mount Hor: 26. And strip Aaron of his garments, and put them upon Eleazar his son: and Aaron shall be gathered *unto his people*, and shall die there. 27. And Moses did as the LORD commanded: and they went up into mount Hor in the sight of all the congregation. 28. And Moses stripped Aaron of his garments, and put them upon Eleazar his son; and Aaron died there in the top of the mount: and Moses and Eleazar came down from the mount.

OF MOSES: Deut. 31:14. And the LORD said unto Moses, Behold, thy days approach that thou must die: call Joshua, and present yourselves in the tabernacle of the congregation, that I may give him a charge. And Moses and Joshua went, and presented themselves in the tabernacle of the congregation. 15. And the LORD appeared in the tabernacle in a pillar of a cloud: and the pillar of the cloud stood over the door of the tabernacle. 16. And the LORD said unto Moses, Behold, thou shalt sleep with thy fathers; and this people will rise up, and go a whoring after the gods of the strangers of the land, whither they go *to be* among them, and will forsake me, and break my covenant which I have made with them. 19. Now therefore write ye this song for you, and teach it the children of Israel: put it in their mouths, that this song may be a witness for me against the children of Israel. 21. And it shall come to pass, when many evils and troubles are befallen them, that this song shall testify against them as a witness: . . . . 22. Moses therefore wrote this song the same day, and taught it the children of Israel. 23. And he gave Joshua the son of Nun a charge, and said, Be strong and of a good courage: for thou shalt bring the children of Israel into the land which I sware unto them: and I will be with thee. 24. And it came to pass, when Moses had made an end of writing the words of this law in a book, until they were finished, 25. That Moses commanded the Levites, which bare the ark of the covenant of the Lord, saying, 26. Take this book of the law, and put it in the side of the ark of the covenant of the Lord your God, that it may be there for a witness against thee. 27. For I know thy rebellion, and thy stiff neck: behold, while I am yet alive with you this day, ye have been rebellious against the Lord; and how much more after my death? 28. Gather unto me all the elders of your tribes, and your officers, that I may speak these words in their ears, and call heaven and earth to record against them. 29. For I know that after my death ye will utterly corrupt *your-selves*, and turn aside from the way which I have commanded you; and evil will befall you in the latter days; because ye will do evil in the sight of the Lord, to provoke him to anger through the work of your hands. 30. And Moses spake in the ears of all the congregation of Israel the words of this song, until they were ended.

Deut. 32:1. Give ear, O ye heavens, and I will speak; and hear, O earth, the words of my mouth. 2. My doctrine shall drop as the rain, my speech shall distil as the dew, as the small rain upon the tender herb, and as the showers upon the grass: 3. Because I will publish the name of the Lord: ascribe ye greatness unto our God. 4. *He is* the Rock, his work *is* perfect: for all his ways *are* judgment: a God of truth and without iniquity, just and right *is* he. 5. They have corrupted themselves, their spot *is* not *the spot* of his children: *they are* a perverse and crooked generation. 6. Do ye thus requite the Lord, O foolish people and unwise? *is* not he thy father *that* hath bought thee? hath he not made thee, and established thee? 7. Remember the days of old, consider the years of many generations: ask thy father, and he will shew thee; thy elders and they will tell thee. 8. When the Most High divided to the nations their inheritance, when he separated the sons of Adam, he set the bounds of the people according to the number of the children of Israel. 9. For the Lord's portion *is* his people; Jacob *is* the lot of his inheritance. 10. He found him in a desert land, and in the waste howling wilderness; he led him about, he instructed him, he kept him as the apple of his eye. 11. As an eagle stirreth up her nest, fluttereth over her young, spreadeth abroad her wings, taketh them, beareth them on her wings: 12. *So* the Lord alone did lead him, and *there was* no strange god with him. 13. He made him ride on the high places of the earth, that he might eat the increase of the fields; and he made him to suck honey out of the rock, and oil out of the flinty rock; 14. Butter of kine, and milk of sheep, with fat of lambs, and rams of the breed of Bashan, and goats, with the fat of kidneys of wheat; and thou didst drink the pure blood of the grape. 15. But Jeshurun waxed fat, and kicked: thou art waxen fat, thou art grown thick, thou art

covered *with fatness;* then he forsook God *which* made him, and lightly esteemed the Rock of his salvation. 16. They provoked him to jealousy with strange *gods*, with abominations provoked they him to anger. 17. They sacrificed unto devils, not to God; to gods whom they knew not, to new *gods that* came newly up, whom your fathers feared not. 18. Of the Rock *that* begat thee thou art unmindful, and hast forgotten God that formed thee. 19. And when the Lord saw *it*, he abhorred *them*, because of the provoking of his sons, and of his daughters. 20. And he said, I will hide my face from them, I will see what their end *shall be:* for they *are* a very froward generation, children in whom *is* no faith. 21. They have moved me to jealousy with *that which is* not God; they have provoked me to anger with their vanities: and I will move them to jealousy with *those which are* not a people; I will provoke them to anger with a foolish nation. 22. For a fire is kindled in mine anger, and shall burn unto the lowest hell, and shall consume the earth with her increase, and set on fire the foundations of the mountains. 23. I will heap mischiefs upon them; I will spend mine arrows upon them. 24. *They shall be* burnt with hunger, and devoured with burning heat, and with bitter destruction: I will also send the teeth of beasts upon them, with the poison of serpents of the dust. 25. The sword without, and terror within, shall destroy both the young men and the virgin, the suckling *also* with the man of gray hairs. 26. I said, I would scatter them into corners, I would make the remembrance of them to cease from among men: 27. Were it not that I feared the wrath of the enemy, lest their adversaries should behave themselves strangely, *and* lest they should say, Our hand *is* high, and the Lord hath not done all this. 28. For they *are* a nation void of counsel, neither *is there any* understanding in them. 29. O that they were wise, *that* they understood this, *that* they would consider their latter end! 30. How should one chase a thousand, and two put ten thousand to flight, except their Rock had sold them, and the Lord had shut them up? 31. For their rock *is* not as our Rock, even our enemies themselves *being* judges. 32. For their vine *is* of the vine of Sodom, and of the fields of Gomorrah: their grapes *are* grapes of gall, their clusters *are* bitter: 33. Their wine *is* the poison of dragons, and the cruel venom of asps. 34. *Is* not this laid up in store with me, *and* sealed up among my treasures? 35. To me *belongeth* vengeance, and recompence; their foot shall slide in *due* time: for the day of their calamity *is* at hand, and the things that shall come upon them make haste. 36. For the Lord shall judge his people, and repent himself for his servants, when he seeth that *their* power is gone, and *there is* none shut up, or left. 37. And he shall say, Where *are* their gods, *their* rock in whom they trusted, 38. Which did eat the fat of their sacrifices. *and* drank the wine of their drink offerings? let them rise up and help you, *and* be your protection. 39. See now that I, *even* I, *am* he, and *there is* no god with me: I kill, and I make alive; I wound, and I heal: neither *is there any* that can deliver out of my hand. 40. For I lift up my hand to heaven, and say, I live for ever. 41. If I whet my glittering sword, and mine hand take hold on judgment; I will render vengeance to mine enemies, and will reward them that hate me. 42. I will make mine arrows drunk with blood, and my sword shall devour flesh; *and that* with the blood of the slain and of the captives, from the beginning of revenges upon the enemy. 43. Rejoice, O ye nations, *with* his people: for he will avenge the blood of his servants, and will render vengeance to his adversaries, and will be merciful unto his land, *and* to his people. 44. And Moses came and spake all the words of this song in the ears of the people, he, and Hoshea the son of Nun. 45. And Moses made an end of speaking all these words to all Israel: 46. And he said unto them, Set your hearts unto all the words which I testify among you this day, which he shall command your children to observe to do, all the words of this law. 47. For it *is* not a vain thing for you; because it *is* your life: and through this thing ye shall prolong *your* days in the land, whither ye go over Jordan to possess it. 48. And the LORD spake unto Moses that selfsame day, saying, 49. Get thee up into this mountain Abarim, *unto* mount Nebo, which *is* in the land of Moab, that *is* over against Jericho; and behold the land of Canaan, which I give unto the children of Israel for a possession: 50. And die in the mount whither thou goest up, and be gathered unto thy people; as Aaron thy brother died in mount Hor, and was gathered unto his people: 51. Because ye trespassed against me among the children of Israel at the waters of Meribah-Kadesh, in the wilderness of Zin; because ye sanctified me not in the midst of the children of Israel. 52. Yet thou shalt see the land before *thee*; but thou shalt not go thither unto the land which I give the children of Israel.

Deut. 33:1. And this *is* the blessing, wherewith Moses the man of God blessed the children of Israel before his death. 2. And he said, The LORD came from Sinai, and rose up from Seir unto them; he shined forth from mount Paran, and he came with ten thousands of saints: from his right hand *went* a fiery law for them. 3. Yea, he loved the people; all his saints *are* in thy hand: and they sat down at thy feet; *every one* shall receive of thy words. 4. Moses commanded us a law, *even* the inheritance of the congregation of Jacob. 5. And he was king in Jeshurun, when the heads of the people *and* the tribes of Israel were gathered together. 6. Let Reuben live, and not die; and let *not* his men be few. 7. And this *is the blessing* of Judah: and he said, Hear, LORD, the voice of Judah, and bring him unto his people: let his hands be sufficient for him; and be thou a help *to him* from his enemies. 8. And of Levi he said, *Let* thy Thummim and thy Urim *be* with thy holy one, whom thou didst prove at Massah, *and with* whom thou didst strive at the waters of Meribah; 9. Who said unto his father and to his mother, I have not seen him; neither did he acknowledge his brethren, nor knew his own children: for they have observed thy word, and kept thy covenant. 10. They shall teach Jacob thy judgments, and Israel thy law: they shall put incense before thee, and whole burnt sacrifice upon thine altar. 11. Bless, LORD, his substance, and accept the work of his hands: smite through the loins of them that rise against him, and of them that hate him, that they rise not again. 12. *And* of Benjamin he said, The beloved of the LORD shall dwell in safety by him; *and the LORD* shall cover him all the day long, and he shall dwell between his shoulders. 13. And of Joseph he said, Blessed of the LORD *be* his land, for the precious things of heaven, for the dew, and for the deep that coucheth beneath, 14. And for the precious fruits *brought forth* by the sun, and for the precious things put forth by the moon, 15. And for the chief things of the ancient mountains, and for the precious things of the lasting hills, 16. And for the precious things of the earth and fulness thereof, and *for* the good will of him that dwelt in the bush: let *the blessing* come upon the head of Joseph, and upon the top of the head of him *that was* separated from his brethren. 17. His glory *is like* the firstling of his bullock, and his horns *are like* the horns of unicorns: with them he shall push the people together to the ends of the earth: and they *are* the ten thousands of Ephraim, and they *are* the thousands of Manasseh. 18. And of Zebulun he said, Rejoice, Zebulun, in thy going out; and, Issachar, in thy tents. 19. They shall call the people unto the mountain; there they shall offer sacrifices of righteousness: for they shall suck *of* the abundance of the seas, and *of* treasures hid in the sand. 20. And of Gad he said, Blessed *be* he that enlargeth Gad: he dwelleth as a lion, and teareth the arm with the crown of the head. 21. And he provideth the first part for himself, because there, *in* a portion of the lawgiver, *was he* seated; and he came with the heads of the people, he executed the justice of the LORD, and his judgments with Israel. 22. And of Dan he said, Dan *is* a lion's whelp: he shall leap from Bashan. 23. And of Naphtali he said, O Naphtali, satisfied with favour, and full with the blessing of the LORD: possess thou the west and the south. 24. And of Asher he said, *Let* Asher *be* blessed with children;

let him be acceptable to his brethren, and let him dip his foot in oil. 25. Thy shoes *shall be* iron and brass; and as thy days, *so shall* thy strength *be.* 26. *There is* none like unto the God of Jeshurun, *who* rideth upon the heaven in thy help, and in his excellency on the sky. 27. The eternal God *is thy* refuge, and underneath *are* the everlasting arms: and he shall thrust out the enemy from before thee; and shall say, Destroy *them.* 28. Israel then shall dwell in safety alone: the fountain of Jacob *shall be* upon a land of corn and wine; also his heavens shall drop down dew. 29. Happy *art* thou, O Israel: who *is* like unto thee, O people saved by the LORD, the shield of thy help, and who *is* the sword of thy excellency! and thine enemies shall be found liars unto thee; and thou shalt tread upon their high places.

Deut. 34:1. And Moses went up from the plains of Moab unto the mountain of Nebo, to the top of Pisgah, that *is* over against Jericho: and the LORD shewed him all the land of Gilead, unto Dan, 2. And all Naphtali, and the land of Ephraim, and Manasseh, and all the land of Judah, unto the utmost sea, 3. And the south, and the plain of the valley of Jericho, the city of palm trees, unto Zoar. 4. And the LORD said unto him, This *is* the land which I sware unto Abraham, unto Isaac, and unto Jacob, saying, I will give it unto thy seed: I have caused thee to see *it* with thine eyes, but thou shalt not go over thither. 5. So Moses the servant of the LORD died there in the land of Moab, according to the word of the LORD. 6. And he buried him in a valley in the land of Moab, over against Beth-peor:

OF JOSHUA, Josh. 24:1–29.

OF SAMSON, Judg. 16:25–30.

OF ELI, 1 Sam. 4:12–18.

WIFE OF PHINEHAS, 1 Sam. 4:19–21.

OF DAVID: 1 Kin. 2:1. Now the days of David drew nigh that he should die; and he charged Solomon his son, saying, 2. I go the way of all the earth: be thou strong therefore, and shew thyself a man; 3. And keep the charge of the LORD thy God, to walk in his ways, to keep his statutes, and his commandments, and his judgments, and his testimonies, as it is written in the law of Moses, that thou mayest prosper in all that thou doest, and whithersoever thou turnest thyself: 4. That the LORD may continue his word which he spake concerning me, saying, If thy children take heed to their way, to walk before me in truth with all their heart and with all their soul, there shall not fail thee (said he) a man on the throne of Israel. 5. Moreover thou knowest also what Joab the son of Zeruiah did to me, *and* what he did to the two captains of the hosts of Israel, unto Abner the son of Ner, and unto Amasa the son of Jether, whom he slew, and shed the blood of war in peace, and put the blood of war upon his girdle that *was* about his loins, and in

his shoes that *were* on his feet. 6. Do therefore according to thy wisdom, and let not his hoar head go down to the grave in peace. 7. But shew kindness unto the sons of Barzillai the Gileadite, and let them be of those that eat at thy table: for so they came to me when I fled because of Absalom thy brother. 8. And, behold, *thou hast* with thee Shimei the son of Gera, a Benjamite of Bahurim, which cursed me with a grievous curse in the day when I went to Mahanaim: but he came down to meet me at Jordan, and I sware to him by the LORD, saying, I will not put thee to death with the sword. 9. Now therefore hold him not guiltless: for thou *art* a wise man, and knowest what thou oughtest to do unto him; but his hoar head bring thou down to the grave with blood. 10. So David slept with his fathers, and was buried in the city of David.

OF ZECHARIAH: 2 Chr. 24:22. Thus Joash the king remembered not the kindness which Jehoiada his father had done to him, but slew his son. And when he died, he said, The LORD look upon *it*, and require *it*.

OF JESUS: Matt. 27:34. They gave him vinegar to drink mingled with gall: and when he had tasted *thereof*, he would not drink. 35. And they crucified him, and parted his garments, casting lots: that it might be fulfilled which was spoken by the prophet, They parted my garments among them, and upon my vesture did they cast lots. 36. And sitting down they watched him there; 37. And set up over his head his accusation written, THIS IS JESUS THE KING OF THE JEWS. 38. Then were there two thieves crucified with him; one on the right hand, and another on the left. 39. And they that passed by reviled him, wagging their heads, 40. And saying, Thou that destroyest the temple, and buildest *it* in three days, save thyself. If thou be the Son of God, come down from the cross. 41. Likewise also the chief priests mocking *him*, with the scribes and elders, said, 42. He saved others; himself he cannot save. If he be the King of Israel, let him now come down from the cross, and we will believe him. 43. He trusted in God; let him deliver him now, if he will have him: for he said, I am the Son of God. 44. The thieves also, which were crucified with him, cast the same in his teeth. 45. Now from the sixth hour there was darkness over all the land unto the ninth hour. 46. And about the ninth hour Jesus cried with a loud voice, saying, Eli, Eli, lama sabachthani? that is to say, My God, my God, why hast thou forsaken me? 47. Some of them that stood there, when they heard *that*, said, This *man* calleth for Elias. 48. And straightway one of them ran, and took a spunge, and filled *it* with vinegar, and put *it* on a reed, and gave him to drink. 49. The rest said, Let be, let us see whether Elias will come to save him. 50. Jesus, when he had cried again with a loud voice, yielded up the ghost. 51. And, behold, the veil of the temple was rent in twain from the top to the bottom ; and the earth did quake, and the rocks rent ; 52. And the graves were opened ; and many bodies of the saints which slept arose, 53. And came out of the graves after his resurrection, and went into the holy city, and appeared unto many. Mark 15:23–38; Luke 23:27–49; John 19:16–30.

OF STEPHEN: Acts 7:59. And they stoned Stephen, calling upon *God*, and saying, Lord Jesus, receive my spirit. 60. And he kneeled down, and cried with a loud voice, Lord, lay not this sin to their charge. And when he had said this, he fell asleep.

OF PAUL: 2 Tim. 4:6. For I am now ready to be offered, and the time of my departure is at hand. 7. I have fought a good fight, I have finished *my* course, I have kept the faith ; 8. Henceforth there is laid up for me a crown of righteousness, which the Lord, the righteous judge, shall give me at that day : and not to me only, but unto all them also that love his appearing.

OF THE WICKED: Num. 16:30. But if the LORD make a new thing, and the earth open her mouth, and swallow them up, with all that *appertain* unto them, and they go down quick into the pit; then ye shall understand that these men have provoked the LORD.

1 Sam. 25:38. And it came to pass about ten days *after*, that the LORD smote Nabal, that he died.

2 Chr. 21:6. And he [Jehoram] wrought *that which was* evil in the eyes of the LORD. 20. Thirty and two years old was he when he began to reign, and he reigned in Jerusalem eight years, and departed without being desired. Howbeit they buried him in the city of David, but not in the sepulchres of the kings.

Job 4:21. Doth not their excellency *which is* in them go away ? they die, even without wisdom.

Job 18:14. His confidence shall be rooted out of his tabernacle, and it shall bring him to the king of terrors. 18. He shall be driven from light into darkness, and chased out of the world.

Job 20:4. Knowest thou *not* this of old, since man was placed upon earth, 5. That the triumphing of the wicked *is* short, and the joy of the hypocrite *but* for a moment ? 8. He shall fly away as a dream, and shall not be found : yea, he shall be chased away as a vision of the night. 11. His bones are full ¹ *of the sin* of his youth, which shall lie down with him in the dust. [¹ Omitted in R. V.]

Job 21:13. They spend their days in wealth, and in a moment go down to the grave. 17. How oft is the candle of the wicked put out ! and *how oft* cometh their destruction upon them ! *God* distributeth sorrows in his anger. 18. They are as stubble before the wind, and as chaff that the storm carrieth away. 23. One dieth in his full strength, being wholly at ease and quiet. 24. His breasts are full of milk, and his bones are

moistened with marrow. 25. And another dieth in the bitterness of his soul, and never eateth with pleasure. 26. They shall lie down alike in the dust, and the worms shall cover them.

Job 24:20. The worm shall feed sweetly on him ; he shall be no more remembered ; and wickedness shall be broken as a tree. 24. They are exalted for a little while, but are gone and brought low ; they are taken out of the way as all *other*, and cut off as the tops of the ears of corn.

Job 27:8. What *is* the hope of the hypocrite, though he hath gained, when God taketh away his soul ? 19. The rich man shall lie down, but he shall not be gathered ; he openeth his eyes, and he *is* not. 20. Terrors take hold on him as waters, a tempest stealeth him away in the night. 21. The east wind carrieth him away, and he departeth : and as a storm hurleth him out of his place. 22. For *God* shall cast upon him, and not spare : he would fain flee out of his hand. 23. *Men* shall clap their hands at him, and shall hiss him out of his place.

Job 34:20. In a moment shall they die, and the people shall be troubled at midnight, and pass away : and the mighty shall be taken away without hand.

Job 36:12. If they obey not, they shall perish by the sword, and they shall die without knowledge. 14. They die in youth, and their life *is* among the unclean. 18. Because *there is* wrath, *beware* lest he take thee away with *his* stroke : then a great ransom cannot deliver thee. 20. Desire not the night, when people are cut off in their place.

Psa. 37:1. Fret not thyself because of evildoers, neither be thou envious against the workers of iniquity. 2. They shall soon be cut down like the grass, and wither as the green herb. 9. Evildoers shall be cut off : 10. Yet a little while, and the wicked *shall not be :* yea, thou shalt diligently consider his place, and it *shall* not *be.* 35. I have seen the wicked in great power, and spreading himself like a green bay tree. 36. Yet he passed away, and, lo, he *was* not : yea, I sought him, but he could not be found.

Psa. 49:7. None *of them* can by any means redeem his brother, nor give to God a ransom for him : 9. That he should still live for ever, *and* not see corruption. 10. For he seeth *that* wise men die, likewise the fool and the brutish person perish, and leave their wealth to others. 14. Like sheep they are laid in the grave ; death shall feed on them ; and the upright shall have dominion over them in the morning ; and their beauty shall consume in the grave from their dwelling. 17. When he dieth he shall carry nothing away : his glory shall not descend after him. 19. He shall go to the generation of his fathers ; they shall never see light 20. Man *that is* in honour, and understandeth not, is like the beasts *that* perish.

Psa. 55:15. Let death seize upon them,

and let them go down quick into hell : for wickedness *is* in their dwellings, *and* among them. 23. Thou, O God, shalt bring them down into the pit of destruction : bloody and deceitful men shall not live out half their days ;

Psa. 58:9. Before your pots can feel the thorns, he shall take them away as with a whirlwind, both living, and in *his* wrath.

Psa. 73:3. For I was envious at the foolish, *when* I saw the prosperity of the wicked. 4. *There are* no bands in their death : but their strength *is* firm. 17. Until I went into the sanctuary of God ; *then* understood I their end. 18. Surely thou didst set them in slippery places : thou castedst them down into destruction. 19. How are they *brought* into desolation, as in a moment ! they are utterly consumed with terrors. 20. As a dream when *one* awaketh ; *so*, O Lord, when thou awakest, thou shalt despise their image.

Psa. 78:50. He made a way to his anger ; he spared not their soul from death, but gave their life over to the pestilence ;

Psa. 92:7. When the wicked spring as the grass, and when all the workers of iniquity do flourish ; *it is* that they shall be destroyed for ever :

Prov. 2:22. The wicked shall be cut off from the earth, and the transgressors shall be rooted out of it.

Prov. 5:22. His own iniquities shall take the wicked himself, and he shall be holden with the cords of his sins. 23. He shall die without instruction ;

Prov. 10:25. As the whirlwind passeth, so *is* the wicked no *more:* 27. The years of the wicked shall be shortened.

Prov. 11:7. When a wicked man dieth, *his* expectation shall perish : and the hope of unjust *men* perisheth. 10. When it goeth well with the righteous, the city rejoiceth : and when the wicked perish, *there is* shouting.

Prov. 13:9. The light of the righteous rejoiceth : but the lamp of the wicked shall be put out.

Prov. 14:32. The wicked is driven away in his wickedness : but the righteous hath hope in his death.

Prov. 21:16. The man that wandereth out of the way of understanding shall remain in the congregation of the dead.

Prov. 24:20. There shall be no reward to the evil *man ;* the candle of the wicked shall be put out.

Prov. 29:1. He, that being often reproved hardeneth *his* neck, shall suddenly be destroyed, and that without remedy. 16. When the wicked are multiplied, transgression increaseth :

Eccl. 8:10. I saw the wicked buried, who had come and gone from the place of the holy, and they were forgotten in the city where they had so done.

Isa. 14:11. Thy pomp is brought down to the grave, *and* the noise of thy viols : the worm is spread under thee, and the worms cover thee. 15. Thou shalt be brought down to hell, to the sides of the pit.

Isa. 17:14. And behold at eveningtide trouble : *and* before the morning he *is* not. This *is* the portion of them that spoil us, and the lot of them that rob us.

Isa. 26:14. *They are* dead, they shall not live ; *they are* deceased, they shall not rise : therefore hast thou visited and destroyed them, and made all their memory to perish.

Jer. 16:3. For thus saith the LORD concerning the sons and concerning the daughters that are born in this place, and concerning their mothers that bare them, and concerning their fathers that begat them in this land ; 4. They shall die of grievous deaths ; they shall not be lamented ; neither shall they be buried ; *but* they shall be as dung upon the face of the earth : and they shall be consumed by the sword, and by famine ; and their carcases shall be meat for the fowls of heaven, and for the beasts of the earth.

Ezek. 28:8. They shall bring thee down to the pit, and thou shalt die the deaths of *them that are* slain in the midst of the seas. 10. Thou shalt die the deaths of the uncircumcised by the hand of strangers : for I have spoken *it*, saith the Lord GOD.

Amos 9:10. All the sinners of my people shall die by the sword, which say, The evil shall not overtake nor prevent us.

Luke 12:20. But God said unto him, *Thou* fool, this night thy soul shall be required of thee : then whose shall those things be, which thou hast provided ?

Luke 16:22. The rich man also died, and was buried ; 23. And in hell he lift up his eyes, being in torments, and seeth Abraham afar off, and Lazarus in his bosom. 24. And he cried and said, Father Abraham, have mercy on me, and send Lazarus, that he may dip the tip of his finger in water, and cool my tongue ; for I am tormented in this flame. 25. But Abraham said, Son, remember that thou in thy lifetime receivedst thy good things, and likewise Lazarus evil things : but now he is comforted, and thou art tormented. 26. And beside all this, between us and you there is a great gulf fixed : so that they which would pass from hence to you cannot ; neither can they pass to us, that *would come* from thence. 27. Then he said, I pray thee therefore, father, that thou wouldest send him to my father's house : 28. For I have five brethren ; that he may testify unto them, lest they also come into this place of torment.

Acts 5:3. But Peter said, Ananias, why hath Satan filled thine heart to lie to the Holy Ghost, and to keep back *part* of the price of the land ? 4. Whiles it remained, was it not thine own ? and after it was sold, was it not in thine own power ? why hast thou conceived this thing in thine heart ? thou hast not lied unto men, but unto God. 5. And Ananias hearing these words fell down, and gave up the ghost: and great fear came on all them that heard these things. 6. And the young men arose, wound him up, and carried *him* out, and buried *him*. 7. And it was about the space of three hours after, when his wife, not knowing what was done, came in. 8. And Peter answered unto her, Tell me whether ye sold the land for so much? And she said, Yea, for so much. 9. Then Peter said unto her, How is it that ye have agreed together to tempt the Spirit of the Lord? behold, the feet of them which have buried thy husband *are* at the door, and shall carry thee out. 10. Then fell she down straightway at his feet, and yielded up the ghost: and the young men came in, and found her dead, and, carrying *her* forth, buried *her* by her husband.

1 Thess. 5:3. When they shall say, Peace and safety; then sudden destruction cometh upon them, as travail upon a woman with child; and they shall not escape.

SPIRITUAL: Luke 1:79. To give light to them that sit in darkness and *in* the shadow of death, to guide our feet into the way of peace.

John 5:24. Verily, verily, I say unto you, He that heareth my word, and believeth on him that sent me, hath everlasting life, and shall not come into condemnation; but is passed from death unto life. 25. Verily, verily, I say unto you, The hour is coming, and now is, when the dead shall hear the voice of the Son of God: and they that hear shall live. 26. For as the Father hath life in himself; so hath he given to the Son to have life in himself;

John 6:50. This is the bread which cometh down from heaven, that a man may eat thereof, and not die. 51. I am the living bread which came down from heaven: if any man eat of this bread, he shall live for ever: and the bread that I will give is my flesh, which I will give for the life of the world. 53. Then Jesus said unto them, Verily, verily, I say unto you, Except ye eat the flesh of the Son of man, and drink his blood, ye have no life in you.

John 11:26. And whosoever liveth and believeth in me shall never die. Believest thou this?

Rom. 5:12. Wherefore, as by one man sin entered into the world, and death by sin; and so death passed upon all men, for that all have sinned: 15. But not as the offence, so also *is* the free gift. For if through the offence of one many be dead, much more the grace of God, and the gift by grace, *which is* by one man, Jesus Christ, hath abounded unto many.

Rom. 7:11. Sin, taking occasion by the commandment, deceived me, and by it slew *me*.

Rom. 8:5. They that are after the flesh do mind the things of the flesh; 6. To be carnally minded *is* death; 12. Therefore, brethren, we are debtors, not to the flesh, to live after the flesh. 13. For if ye live after the flesh, ye shall die: but if ye through the

Spirit do mortify the deeds of the body, ye shall live.

2 Cor. 5:14. For the love of Christ constraineth us; because we thus judge, that if one died for all, ¹ then were all dead: [¹ R. V. therefore all died:]

Eph. 2:1. You *hath he quickened*, who were dead in trespasses and sins; 5. Even when we were dead in sins, hath quickened us together with Christ, (by grace ye are saved;) 6. And hath raised *us* up together, and made *us* sit together in heavenly *places* in Christ Jesus:

Eph. 4:18. Having the understanding darkened, being alienated from the life of God through the ignorance that is in them, because of the blindness of their heart:

Eph. 5:14. Wherefore he saith, Awake thou that sleepest, and arise from the dead, and Christ shall give thee light.

Col. 2:13. And you, being dead in your sins and the uncircumcision of your flesh, hath he quickened together with him, having forgiven you all trespasses;

1 Tim. 5:6. But she that liveth in pleasure is dead while she liveth.

1 Pet. 2:24. Who his own self bare our sins in his own body on the tree, that we, being dead to sins, should live unto righteousness: by whose stripes ye were healed.

1 John 5:12. He that hath the Son hath life; *and* he that hath not the Son of God hath not life.

See Depravity; Man, State of after the Fall; Reprobacy.

SECOND: Prov. 14:12. There is *a* way which seemeth right unto a man, but the end thereof *are* the ways of death.

Ezek. 18:4. The soul that sinneth, it shall die. 10. If he . . . . 13. Hath given forth upon usury, and hath taken increase: shall he then live? he shall not live: he hath done all these abominations; he shall surely die: his blood shall be upon him. 21. But if the wicked will turn from all his sins that he hath committed, and keep all my statutes, and do that which is lawful and right, he shall surely live, he shall not die. 23. Have I any pleasure at all that the wicked should die? saith the Lord God: *and* not that he should return from his ways, and live? 24. But when the righteous turneth away from his righteousness, and committeth iniquity, *and* doeth according to all the abominations that the wicked *man* doeth, shall he live? All his righteousness that he hath done shall not be mentioned: in his tresspass that he hath tresspassed, and in his sin that he hath sinned, in them shall he die.

Ezek. 33:8. When I say unto the wicked, O wicked *man*, thou shalt surely die: if thou dost not speak to warn the wicked from his way, that wicked *man* shall die in his iniquity; but his blood will I require at thine hand. 9. Nevertheless, if thou warn the wicked of his way to turn from it; if he do not turn from his way, he shall die in his iniquity; but thou hast delivered thy soul. 11. Say unto them, *As* I live, saith the Lord God,

I have no pleasure in the death of the wicked; but that the wicked turn from his way and live: turn ye, turn ye from your evil ways; for why will ye die, O house of Israel? 14. Again, when I say unto the wicked, Thou shalt surely die; if he turn from his sin, and do that which is lawful and right; 15. *If* the wicked restore the pledge, give again that he had robbed, walk in the statutes of life, without committing iniquity; he shall surely live, he shall not die. 16. None of his sins that he hath committed shall be mentioned unto him: he hath done that which is lawful and right; he shall surely live.

Matt. 7:13. Enter ye in at the strait gate: for wide *is* the gate, and broad *is* the way, that leadeth to destruction, and many there be which go in thereat:

Matt. 10:28. And fear not them which kill the body, but are not able to kill the soul: but rather fear him which is able to destroy both soul and body in hell.

Matt. 25:30. And cast ye the unprofitable servant into outer darkness: there shall be weeping and gnashing of teeth. 41. Then shall he say also unto them on the left hand, Depart from me, ye cursed, into everlasting fire, prepared for the devil and his angels: 46. And these shall go away into everlasting punishment: but the righteous into life eternal.

Mark 9:43. And if thy hand offend thee, cut it off: it is better for thee to enter into life maimed, than having two hands to go into hell, into the fire that never shall be quenched: 44. Where their worm dieth not, and the fire is not quenched. [Omitted in R. V.]

Rom. 1:32. Who knowing the judgment of God, that they which commit such things are worthy of death, not only do the same, but have pleasure in them that do them.

Rom. 6:16. Know ye not, that to whom ye yield yourselves servants to obey, his servants ye are to whom ye obey; whether of sin unto death, or of obedience unto righteousness? 21. What fruit had ye then in those things whereof ye are now ashamed? for the end of those things *is* death. 23. For the wages of sin *is* death; but the gift of God *is* eternal life through Jesus Christ our Lord.

Rom. 8:13. For if ye live after the flesh, ye shall die:

Rom. 9:22. *What* if God, willing to shew *his* wrath, and to make his power known, endured with much longsuffering the vessels of wrath fitted to destruction:

2 Thess. 1:9. Who shall be punished with everlasting destruction from the presence of the Lord, and from the glory of his power:

Jas. 1:15. Then when lust hath conceived, it bringeth forth sin; and sin, when it is finished, bringeth forth death.

Jas. 4:12. There is one lawgiver, who is able to save and to destroy:

2 Pet. 2:12. But these, as natural brute beasts made to be taken and destroyed, speak evil of the things that they understand not;

and shall utterly perish in their own corruption;

Rev. 2:11. He that hath an ear, let him hear what the Spirit saith unto the churches; He that overcometh shall not be hurt of the second death.

Rev. 19:20. And the beast was taken, and with him the false prophet that wrought miracles before him, with which he deceived them that had received the mark of the beast, and them that worshipped his image. These both were cast alive into a lake of fire burning with brimstone.

Rev. 20:14. And death and hell were cast into the lake of fire. This is the second death.

Rev. 21:8. But the fearful, and unbelieving, and the abominable, and murderers, and whoremongers, and sorcerers, and idolaters, and all liars, shall have their part in the lake which burneth with fire and brimstone: which is the second death.

See HELL; WICKED, PUNISHMENT OF.

FIGURATIVE OF REGENERATION: Rom. 6:2. How shall we, that are dead to sin, live any longer therein? 3. Know ye not, that so many of us as were baptized into Jesus Christ were baptized into his death? 4. Therefore we are buried with him by baptism into death: that like as Christ was raised up from the dead by the glory of the Father, even so we also should walk in newness of life. 5. For if we have been planted together in the likeness of his death, we shall be also *in the likeness* of *his* resurrection: 6. Knowing this, that our old man is crucified with *him*, that the body of sin might be destroyed, that henceforth we should not serve sin. 7. For he that is dead is freed from sin. 8. Now if we be dead with Christ, we believe that we shall also live with him: 9. Knowing that Christ being raised from the dead dieth no more; death hath no more dominion over him. 10. For in that he died, he died unto sin once: but in that he liveth, he liveth unto God. 11. Likewise reckon ye also yourselves to be dead indeed unto sin, but alive unto God through Jesus Christ our Lord.

Rom. 7:1. Know ye not, brethren, (for I speak to them that know the law,) how that the law hath dominion over a man as long as he liveth? 2. For the woman which hath an husband is bound by the law to *her* husband so long as he liveth; but if the husband be dead, she is loosed from the law of *her* husband. 3. So then if, while *her* husband liveth, she be married to another man, she shall be called an adulteress: but if *her* husband be dead, she is free from that law; so that she is no adulteress, though she be married to another man. 4. Wherefore, my brethren, ye also are become dead to the law by the body of Christ; that ye should be married to another, *even* to him who is raised from the dead, that we should bring forth fruit unto God. 5. For when we were in the flesh, the motions of sins, which were by the law, did work in our members to bring forth fruit unto death. 6. But now we are delivered from the law, that being dead wherein we were held; that we should serve in newness of spirit, and not *in* the old-ness of the letter. 7. What shall we say then? *Is* the law sin? God forbid. Nay, I had not known sin, but by the law: for I had not known lust, except the law had said, Thou shalt not covet. 8. But sin, taking occasion by the commandment, wrought in me all manner of concupiscence. For with-out the law sin *was* dead. 9. For I was alive without the law once: but when the commandment came, sin revived, and I died. 10. And the commandment, which *was ordained* to life, I found *to be* unto death. 11. For sin, taking occasion by the commandment, deceived me, and by it slew *me.*

Rom. 8:10. And if Christ *be* in you, the body *is* dead because of sin; but the Spirit *is* life because of righteousness. 11. But if the Spirit of him that raised up Jesus from the dead dwell in you, he that raised up Christ from the dead shall also quicken your mortal bodies by his Spirit that dwelleth in you.

Col. 2:20. Wherefore if ye be dead with Christ from the rudiments of the world, why, as though living in the world, are ye subject to ordinances.

See DEAD; REGENERATION.

DEBIR. 1. King of Eglon, Josh. 10:3–27. 2. A town in the mountains of Judah. Called also KIRJATH-SANNAH, and KIRJATH-SEPHER, which signifies a city of books, Josh. 15:15,16. Anakim expelled from, by Joshua, Josh. 11:21. Taken by Othniel, Josh. 15:15–17,49; Judg. 1:12,13. Allotted to the Aaronites, Josh. 21:15.

3. A place near the valley of Achor, Josh. 15:7.

DEBORAH. 1. Nurse to Rebecca, Gen. 24:59. Buried beneath an oak under Beth-el, Gen. 35:8.

2. The prophetess, a judge of Israel, Judg. 4:4,5; 5:7. Inspires Barak to defeat Sisera, Judg. 4:6–16. Triumphant song of, Judg. 5.

DEBT. Rom. 13:8. Owe no man any thing, but to love one another:

SECURITY FOR: Ex. 22:25. If thou lend money to *any of* my people *that is* poor by thee, thou shalt not be to him as an usurer, neither shalt thou lay upon him usury. 26. If thou at all take thy neighbour's raiment to pledge, thou shalt deliver it unto him by that the sun goeth down: 27. For that *is* his covering only, it *is* his raiment for his skin: wherein shall he sleep? and it shall come to pass, when he crieth unto me, that I will hear; for I *am* gracious.

Deut. 24:6. No man shall take the nether or the upper millstone to pledge: for he tak-eth *a man's* life to pledge.

10. When thou dost lend thy brother any thing, thou shalt not go into his house to fetch his pledge. 11. Thou shalt stand abroad,

and the man to whom thou dost lend shall bring out the pledge abroad unto thee. 12. And if the man *be* poor, thou shalt not sleep with his pledge: 13. In any case thou shalt deliver him the pledge again when the sun goeth down, that he may sleep in his own rai-ment, and bless thee: and it shall be right-eousness unto thee before the LORD thy God.

Neh. 5:3. *Some* also there were that said, We have mortgaged our lands, vineyards, and houses, that we might buy corn, be-cause of the dearth. 4. There were also that said, We have borrowed money for the king's tribute, *and that upon* our lands and vineyards.

Job 22:6. For thou hast taken a pledge from thy brother for nought, and stripped the naked of their clothing.

Job 24:9. They pluck the fatherless from the breast, and take a pledge of the poor.

Prov. 11:15. He that is surety for a stran-ger shall smart *for it:* and he that hateth suretiship is sure.

Prov. 22:26. Be not thou *one* of them that strike hands, *or* of them that are sureties for debts.

Amos 2:8. And they lay *themselves* down upon clothes laid to pledge by every altar, and they drink the wine of the condemned *in* the house of their god.

See DEBTOR; CREDITOR; SURETY.

DEBTOR, LAWS CONCERNING: Ex. 21:2. If thou buy an Hebrew servant, six years he shall serve: and in the seventh he shall go out free for nothing. 3. If he came in by himself, he shall go out by himself: if he were married, then his wife shall go out with him. 4. If his master have given him a wife, and she have born him sons or daughters; the wife and her children shall be her master's, and he shall go out by him-self. 5. And if the servant shall plainly say, I love my master, my wife, and my chil-dren; I will not go out free: 6. Then his master shall bring him unto the judges; he shall also bring him to the door, or unto the door post; and his master shall bore his ear through with an aul; and he shall serve him for ever.

Ex. 22:10. If a man deliver unto his neigh-bour an ass, or an ox, or a sheep, or any beast, to keep; and it die, or be hurt, or driven away, no man seeing *it:* 11. *Then* shall an oath of the LORD be between them both, that he hath not put his hand unto his neighbour's goods; and the owner of it shall accept *thereof*, and he shall not make *it* good. 12. And if it be stolen from him, he shall make restitution unto the owner there-of. 13. If it be torn in pieces, *then* let him bring it *for* witness, *and* he shall not make good that which was torn. 14. And if a man borrow *ought* of his neighbour, and it be hurt, or die, the owner thereof *being* not with it, he shall surely make *it* good. 15. *But* if the owner thereof *be* with it, he shall not make *it* good: if it *be* a hired *thing*, it came for his hire.

Lev. 25:14. And if thou sell ought unto thy neighbour, or buyest *ought* of thy neighbour's hand, ye shall not oppress one another: 15. According to the number of years after the jubile thou shalt buy of thy neighbour, *and* according unto the number of years of the fruits he shall sell unto thee: 16. According to the multitude of years thou shalt increase the price thereof, and according to the fewness of years thou shalt diminish the price of it: for *according* to the number *of the years* of the fruits doth he sell unto thee. 17. Ye shall not therefore oppress one another; but thou shalt fear thy God: for I *am* the LORD your God. 25. If thy brother be waxen poor, and hath sold away *some* of his possession, and if any of his kin come to redeem it, then shall he redeem that which his brother sold. 26. And if the man have none to redeem it, and himself be able to redeem it; 27. Then let him count the years of the sale therof, and restore the overplus unto the man to whom he sold it; that he may return unto his possession. 28. But if he be not able to restore *it* to him, then that which is sold shall remain in the hand of him that hath bought it until the year of jubile: and in the jubile it shall go out, and he shall return unto his possession. 29. And if a man sell a dwelling house in a walled city, then he may redeem it within a whole year after it is sold; *within* a full year may he redeem it. 30. And if it be not redeemed within the space of a full year, then the house that *is* in the walled city shall be established for ever to him that bought it throughout his generations: it shall not go out in the jubile. 31. But the houses of the villages which have no wall round about them shall be counted as the fields of the country: they may be redeemed, and they shall go out in the jubile. 32. Notwithstanding the cities of the Levites, *and* the houses of the cities of their possession, may the Levites redeem at any time. 33. And if a man purchase of the Levites, then the house that was sold, and the city of his possession, shall go out in *the year of* jubile: for the houses of the cities of the Levites *are* their possession among the children of Israel. 34. But the field of the suburbs of their cities may not be sold; for it *is* their perpetual possession. 35. And if thy brother be waxen poor, and fallen in decay with thee; then thou shalt relieve him: *yea, though he be* a stranger, or a sojourner; that he may live with thee. 36. Take thou no usury of him, or increase: but fear thy God; that thy brother may live with thee. 37. Thou shalt not give him thy money upon usury, nor lend him thy victuals for increase. 38. I *am* the LORD your God, which brought you forth out of the land of Egypt, to give you the land of Canaan, *and* to be your God. 39. And if thy brother *that dwelleth* by thee be waxen poor, and be sold unto thee; thou shalt not compel him to serve as a

bondservant: 40. *But* as an hired servant, *and* as a sojourner, he shall be with thee, *and* shall serve thee unto the year of jubile: 41. And *then* shall he depart from thee, *both* he and his children with him, and shall return unto his own family, and unto the possession of his fathers shall he return. 47. And if a sojourner or stranger wax rich by thee, and thy brother *that dwelleth* by him wax poor, and sell himself unto the stranger *or* sojourner by thee, or to the stock of the stranger's family: 48. After that he is sold he may be redeemed again; one of his brethren may redeem him: 49. Either his uncle, or his uncle's son, may redeem him, or *any* that is nigh of kin unto him of his family may redeem him; or if he be able, he may redeem himself. 50. And he shall reckon with him that bought him from the year that he was sold to him unto the year of jubile: and the price of his sale shall be according unto the number of years, according to the time of an hired servant shall it be with him. 51. If *there be* yet many years *behind*, according unto them he shall give again the price of his redemption out of the money that he was bought for. 52. And if there remain but few years unto the year of jubile, then he shall count with him, *and* according unto his years shall he give him again the price of his redemption. 53. *And* as a yearly hired servant shall he be with him: *and the other* shall not rule with rigour over him in thy sight. 54. And if he be not redeemed in these *years*, then he shall go out in the year of jubile, *both* he, and his children with him. 55. For unto me the children of Israel *are* servants; they *are* my servants whom I brought forth out of the land of Egypt: I *am* the LORD your God.

Neh. 10:31. We would leave the seventh year, and the exaction of every debt.

Matt. 5:25. Agree with thine adversary quickly, whiles thou art in the way with him; lest at any time the adversary deliver thee to the judge, and the judge deliver thee to the officer, and thou be cast into prison. 26. Verily I say unto thee, Thou shalt by no means come out thence, till thou hast paid the uttermost farthing. 40. And if any man will sue thee at the law, and take away thy coat, let him have *thy* cloke also.

Matt. 18:25. But forasmuch as he had not to pay, his lord commanded him to be sold, and his wife, and children, and all that he had, and payment to be made.

UNCLASSIFIED SCRIPTURES RELATING TO: 2 Kin. 4:1. Now there cried a certain woman of the wives of the sons of the prophets unto Elisha, saying, Thy servant my husband is dead; and thou knowest that thy servant did fear the LORD: and the creditor is come to take unto him my two sons to be bondmen. 2. And Elisha said unto her, What shall I do for thee? tell me, what hast thou in the house? And she said, Thine handmaid hath not any thing in the house, save a pot of oil. 3. Then he said, Go, borrow thee vessels abroad of all thy neighbours, *even* empty vessels; borrow not a few. 4. And when thou art come in, thou shalt shut the door upon thee and upon thy sons, and shalt pour out into all those vessels, and thou shalt set aside that which is full. 5. So she went from him, and shut the door upon her and upon her sons, who brought *the vessels* to her; and she poured out. 6. And it came to pass, when the vessels were full, that she said unto her son, Bring me yet a vessel. And he said unto her, *There is* not a vessel more. And the oil stayed. 7. Then she came and told the man of God. And he said, Go, sell the oil, and pay thy debt, and live thou and thy children of the rest.

Neh. 5:3. *Some* also there were that said, We have mortgaged our lands, vineyards, and houses, that we might buy corn, because of the dearth. 4. There were also that said, We have borrowed money for the king's tribute, *and that upon* our lands and vineyards. 5. Yet now our flesh *is* as the flesh of our brethren, our children as their children: and, lo, we bring into bondage our sons and our daughters to be servants, and *some* of our daughters are brought unto bondage *already:* neither *is it* in our power *to redeem them;* for other men have our lands and vineyards.

Job 20:18. That which he laboured for shall he restore, and shall not swallow *it* down: according to *his* substance *shall* the restitution *be*, and he shall not rejoice *therein.* 19. Because he hath oppressed *and* hath forsaken the poor; *because* he hath violently taken away an house which he builded not;

Matt. 18:23. Therefore is the kingdom of heaven likened unto a certain king, which would take account of his servants. 24. And when he had begun to reckon, one was brought unto him, which owed him ten thousand talents. 25. But forasmuch as he had not to pay, his lord commanded him to be sold, and his wife, and children, and all that he had, and payment to be made. 26. The servant therefore fell down, and worshipped him, saying, Lord, have patience with me, and I will pay thee all. 27. Then the lord of that servant was moved with compassion, and loosed him, and forgave him the debt. 28. But the same servant went out, and found one of his fellowservants, which owed him an hundred pence: and he laid hands on him, and took *him* by the throat, saying, Pay me that thou owest. 29. And his fellowservant fell down at his feet, and besought him, saying, Have patience with me, and I will pay thee all. 30. And he would not: but went and cast him into prison, till he should pay the debt. 31. So when his fellowservants saw what was done, they were very sorry, and came and told unto their lord all that was done. 32. Then his lord, after that he had called him, said unto him, O thou wicked

servant, I forgave thee all that debt, because thou desiredst me: 33. Shouldest not thou also have had compassion on thy fellowservant, even as I had pity on thee?

Luke 20:9. Then began he to speak to the people this parable; A certain man planted a vineyard, and let it forth to husbandmen, and went into a far country for a long time. 10. And at the season he sent a servant to the husbandmen, that they should give him of the fruit of the vineyard: but the husbandmen beat him, and sent *him* away empty. 11. And again he sent another servant: and they beat him also, and entreated *him* shamefully, and sent *him* away empty. 12. And again he sent a third: and they wounded him also, and cast *him* out. 13. Then said the lord of the vineyard, What shall I do? I will send my beloved son: it may be they will reverence *him* when they see him. 14. But when the husbandmen saw him, they reasoned among themselves, saying, This is the heir: come, let us kill him, that the inheritance may be ours. 15. So they cast him out of the vineyard, and killed *him.* What therefore shall the lord of the vineyard do unto them? 16. He shall come and destroy these husbandmen, and shall give the vineyard to others. And when they heard *it*, they said, God forbid.

See CREDITOR; DEBT; SURETY.

DECALOGUE. Written by God, Ex. 24:12; 31:18; 32:16; Deut. 5:22; 9:10; Hos. 8:12. Divine authority of, Ex. 20:1; 34:27,28; Deut. 5:4–22. Called WORDS OF THE COVENANT, Ex. 34:28; Deut. 4:13. TABLES OF TESTIMONY, Ex. 31:18; 34:29; 40:20.

See COMMANDMENTS.

Ex. 20:1. And God spake all these words, saying, 2. I *am* the LORD thy God, which have brought thee out of the land of Egypt, out of the house of bondage. 3. Thou shalt have no other gods before me. 4. Thou shalt not make unto thee any graven image, or any likeness *of any thing* that *is* in heaven above, or that *is* in the earth beneath, or that *is* in the water under the earth: 5. Thou shalt not bow down thyself to them, nor serve them: for I the LORD thy God *am* a jealous God, visiting the iniquity of the fathers upon the children unto the third and fourth *generation* of them that hate me; 6. And shewing mercy unto thousands of them that love me, and keep my commandments. 7. Thou shalt not take the name of the LORD thy God in vain: for the LORD will not hold him guiltless that taketh his name in vain. 8. Remember the sabbath day, to keep it holy. 9. Six days shalt thou labour, and do all thy work: 10. But the seventh day *is* the sabbath of the LORD thy God: *in it* thou shalt not do any work, thou, nor thy son, nor thy daughter, thy manservant, nor thy maidservant, nor thy cattle, nor thy stranger that *is* within thy gates: 11. For *in* six days the LORD made heaven and earth, the sea, and all that in them *is*, and rested the seventh day:

wherefore the LORD blessed the sabbath day, and hallowed it. 12. Honour thy father and thy mother: that thy days may be long upon the land which the LORD thy God giveth thee. 13. Thou shalt ¹ not kill. 14. Thou shalt not commit adultery. 15. Thou shalt not steal. 16. Thou shalt not bear false witness against thy neighbour. 17. Thou shalt not covet thy neighbour's house, thou shalt not covet thy neighbour's wife, nor his manservant, nor his maidservant, nor his ox, nor his ass, nor any thing that *is* thy neighbour's. [¹ R. V. do no murder]

Deut. 5:7. Thou shalt have none other gods before me. 8. Thou shalt not make thee *any* graven image, *or* any likeness *of any thing* that *is* in heaven above, or that *is* in the earth beneath, or that *is* in the waters beneath the earth: 9. Thou shalt not bow down thyself unto them, nor serve them: for I the LORD thy God *am* a jealous God, visiting the iniquity of the fathers upon the children unto the third and fourth *generation* of them that hate me, 10. And shewing mercy unto thousands of them that love me and keep my commandments. 11. Thou shalt not take the name of the LORD thy God in vain: for the LORD will not hold *him* guiltless that taketh his name in vain. 12. Keep the sabbath day to sanctify it, as the LORD thy God hath commanded thee. 13. Six days thou shalt labour, and do all thy work: 14. But the seventh day *is* the sabbath of the LORD thy God: *in it* thou shalt not do any work, thou, nor thy son, nor thy daughter, nor thy manservant, nor thy maidservant, nor thine ox, nor thine ass, nor any of thy cattle, nor thy stranger that *is* within thy gates: that thy manservant and thy maidservant may rest as well as thou. 15. And remember that thou wast a servant in the land of Egypt, and *that* the LORD thy God brought thee out thence through a mighty hand and by a stretched out arm: therefore the LORD thy God commanded thee to keep the sabbath day. 16. Honour thy father and thy mother, as the LORD thy God hath commanded thee; that thy days may be prolonged, and that it may go well with thee, in the land which the LORD thy God giveth thee. 17. Thou shalt not kill. 18. Neither shalt thou commit adultery. 19. Neither shalt thou steal. 20. Neither shalt thou bear false witness against thy neighbour. 21. Neither shalt thou desire thy neighbour's wife, neither shalt thou covet thy neighbour's house, his field, or his manservant, or his maidservant, his ox, or his ass, or any *thing* that *is* thy neighbour's.

Matt. 19:18. He saith unto him, Which? Jesus said, Thou shalt do no murder, Thou shalt not commit adultery, Thou shall not steal, Thou shalt not bear false witness, 19. Honour thy father and *thy* mother: and, Thou shalt love thy neighbour as thyself.

Matt. 22:34. But when the Pharisees had heard that he had put the Sadducees to silence, they were gathered together. 35. Then one of them, *which was* a lawyer, asked *him a question*, tempting him, and saying, 36. Master, which *is* the great commandment in the law? 37. Jesus said unto him, Thou shalt love the Lord thy God with all thy heart, and with all thy soul, and with all thy mind. 38. This is the first and great commandment. 39. And the second *is* like unto it, Thou shalt love thy neighbour as thyself. 40. On these two commandments hang all the law and the prophets.

Luke 10:25. And, behold, a certain lawyer stood up, and tempted him, saying, Master, what shall I do to inherit eternal life? 26. He said unto him, What is written in the law? how readest thou? 27. And he answering said, Thou shalt love the Lord thy God with all thy heart, and with all thy soul, and with all thy strength, and with all thy mind; and thy neighbour as thyself. 28. And he said unto him, Thou hast answered right: this do, and thou shalt live.

Rom. 13:8. Owe no man any thing, but to love one another: for he that loveth another hath fulfilled the law. 9. For this, Thou shalt not commit adultery, Thou shalt not kill, Thou shalt not steal, Thou shalt not bear false witness, Thou shalt not covet; and if *there be* any other commandment, it is briefly comprehended in this saying, namely, Thou shalt love thy neighbour as thyself. 10. Love worketh no ill to his neighbour: therefore love *is* the fulfilling of the law.

DECAPOLIS. Ten cities situated in one district on the east of the Sea of Galilee, Matt. 4:25; Mark 5:20; 7:31.

DECEIT. Is falsehood, Psa. 119:118. The tongue an instrument of, Rom. 3:13. Comes from the heart, Mark 7:22. Characteristic of the heart, Jer. 17:9. God abhors, Psa. 5:6. Forbidden, Prov. 24:28: 1 Pet. 3:10. Christ was perfectly free from, Isa. 53:9, with 1 Pet. 2:22.

Saints free from, Psa. 24:4; Zeph. 3:13; Rev. 14:5; purpose against, Job 27:4; avoid, Job 31:5; shun those addicted to, Psa. 101:7; pray for deliverance from those who use, Psa. 43:1; 120:2; delivered from those who use, Psa. 72:14; should beware of those who teach, Eph. 5:6; Col. 2:8; should lay aside, in seeking truth, 1 Pet. 2:1. Ministers should lay aside, 2 Cor. 4:2; 1 Thess. 2:3.

The wicked are full of, Rom. 1:29; devise, Psa. 35:20; 38:12; Prov. 12:5; utter, Psa. 10:7; 36:3; work, Prov. 11:18; increase in, 2 Tim. 3:13; use, to each other, Jer. 9:5; use, to themselves, Jer. 37:9; Obad. 3,7; delight in, Prov. 20:17.

False teachers are workers of, 2 Cor. 11:13; preach, Jer. 14:14; 23:26; impose on others by, Rom. 16:18; Eph. 4:14; sport themselves with, 2 Pet. 2:13. Hypocrites devise, Job 15:35. Hypocrites practise, Hos. 11:12. False witnesses use, Prov. 12:17. A characteristic of antichrist, 2 John 7. Characteristic of the apostasy, 2 Thess. 2:10.

Evil of: hinders knowledge of God, Jer. 9:6. Keeps from turning to God, Jer. 8:5. Leads to pride and oppression, Jer. 5:27,28, to lying, Prov. 14:25. Often accompanied by fraud and injustice, Psa. 10:7; 43:1. Hatred often concealed by, Prov. 26:24-26. The folly of fools is, Prov. 14:8. The kisses of an enemy are, Prov. 27:6. Blessedness of being free from, Psa. 24:4,5; 32:2. Punishment of, Psa. 55:23; Jer. 9:7-9.—*Bible Text Book.*

See CONFIDENCE, FALSE; DECEPTION; FALSEHOOD; FLATTERY; HYPOCRISY.

DECEPTION. INSTANCES OF: By Satan, Gen. 3:4. Abraham, in stating that Sarah was his sister, Gen. 12:13; 20:2. Isaac, in stating that his wife was his sister, Gen. 26:7. Jacob and Rebekah, in imposing Jacob on his father, and Jacob's impersonating Esau, Gen. 27:6-23. Jacob's sons, in entrapping the Shechemites, Gen. 34:13-31; in representing to their father that Joseph had been destroyed by wild beasts, Gen. 37:29-35. Joseph, in his ruse with his brethren, Gen. chapters 42-44. The Gibeonites, in misrepresenting their habitat, Josh. 9:3-15. Ehud deceives Eglon, and slays him, Judg. 3:15-30. Delilah deceives Samson, Judg. 16:4-20. David feigns madness, 1 Sam. 21:10-15. Amnon deceives Tamar by feigning sickness, 2 Sam. 13:6-14. Hushai deceives Absalom, 2 Sam. 16:15-19. Sanballat tries to deceive Nehemiah, Neh. 6. By Absalom, when he avenged his sister, 2 Sam. 13:24-28; when he began his conspiracy, 2 Sam. 15:7. The old prophet, 1 Kin. 13:18. Gehazi, 2 Kin. 5:20. Job's friends, Job 6:15. Doeg, Psa. 52:2. Herod, Matt. 2:8. Pharisees, Matt. 22:16. Chief priests, Mark 14:1. Lawyer, Luke 10:25. Ananias and Sapphira, Acts 5:1.

See DECEIT; HYPOCRISY; FALSEHOOD; FALSE WITNESS.

SELF: See CONFIDENCE, FALSE; FLATTERY.

DECISION. Deut. 30:19. I call heaven and earth to record this day against you, *that* I have set before you life and death, blessing and cursing: therefore choose life, that both thou and thy seed may live:

Josh. 23:8. But cleave unto the LORD your God, as ye have done unto this day.

Josh. 24:15. And if it seem evil unto you to serve the LORD, choose you this day whom ye will serve; whether the gods which your fathers served that *were* on the other side of the flood, or the gods of the Amorites, in whose land ye dwell: but as for me and my house, we will serve the LORD.

1 Sam. 12:20. And Samuel said unto the people, Fear not: ye have done all this wickedness: yet turn not aside from following the LORD, but serve the LORD with all your heart;

1 Kin. 18:21. And Elijah came unto all the people, and said, How long halt ye between two opinions? if the LORD be God, follow him: but if Baal, *then* follow him. And the people answered him not a word.

Psa. 37:34. Wait on the LORD, and keep his way, and he shall exalt thee to inherit the land:

Psa. 69:13. But as for me, my prayer *is* unto thee, O LORD, *in* an acceptable time: O God, in the multitude of thy mercy hear me, in the truth of thy salvation.

Prov. 4:25. Let thine eyes look right on, and let thine eyelids look straight before thee. 26. Ponder the path of thy feet, and let all thy ways be established. 27. Turn not to the right hand nor to the left: remove thy foot from evil.

Isa. 50:7. For the Lord GOD will help me; therefore shall I not be confounded: therefore have I set my face like a flint, and I know that I shall not be ashamed.

Matt. 24:13. He that shall endure unto the end, the same shall be saved. Mark 13:13; Matt. 10:22.

Matt. 25:23. Well done, good and faithful servant; thou hast been faithful over a few things, I will make thee ruler over many things: enter thou into the joy of thy lord.

Luke 7:23. Blessed is *he,* whosoever shall not be offended in me. Matt. 11:6.

John 8:31. Then said Jesus to those Jews which believed on him, If ye continue in my word, *then* are ye my disciples indeed;

John 15:4. Abide in me, and I in you. As the branch cannot bear fruit of itself, except it abide in the vine; no more can ye, except ye abide in me. 5. I am the vine, ye *are* the branches: He that abideth in me, and I in him, the same bringeth forth much fruit: for without me ye can do nothing. 7. If ye abide in me, and my words abide in you, ye shall ask what ye will, and it shall be done unto you. 9. Continue ye in my love.

Acts 11:23. Who, when he came, and had seen the grace of God, was glad, and exhorted them all, that with purpose of heart they would cleave unto the Lord.

Acts 13:43. Now when the congregation was broken up, many of the Jews and religious proselytes followed Paul and Barnabas: who, speaking to them, persuaded them to continue in the grace of God.

Acts 14:22. Confirming the souls of the disciples, *and* exhorting them to continue in the faith, and that we must through much tribulation enter into the kingdom of God.

Rom. 2:7. To them who by patient continuance in well doing seek for glory and honour and immortality, eternal life:

Rom. 8:38. For I am persuaded, that neither death, nor life, nor angels, nor principalities, nor powers, nor things present, nor things to come, 39. Nor height, nor depth, nor any other creature, shall be able to separate us from the love of God, which is in Christ Jesus our Lord.

Rom. 11:22. Behold therefore the goodness and severity of God: on them which fell, severity; but toward thee, goodness, if thou continue in *his* goodness: otherwise thou also shalt be cut off.

1 Cor. 15:58. Be ye stedfast, unmoveable, always abounding in the work of the Lord, forasmuch as ye know that your labour is not in vain in the Lord.

1 Cor. 16:13. Watch ye, stand fast in the faith, quit you like men, be strong.

Gal. 5:1. Stand fast therefore in the liberty wherewith Christ hath made us free, and be not entangled again with the yoke of bondage. 10. I have confidence in you through the Lord, that ye will be none otherwise minded:

Gal. 6:9. Let us not be weary in well doing: for in due season we shall reap, if we faint not.

Eph. 4:14. Be no more children, tossed to and fro, and carried about with every wind of doctrine, by the sleight of men, *and* cunning craftiness, whereby they lie in wait to deceive;

Eph. 6:13. Take unto you the whole armour of God, that ye may be able to withstand in the evil day, and having done all, to stand.

Phil. 1:27. Let your conversation be as it becometh the gospel of Christ: that whether I come and see you, or else be absent, I may hear of your affairs, that ye stand fast in one spirit, with one mind striving together for the faith of the gospel;

Phil. 4:1. Therefore, my brethren dearly beloved and longed for, my joy and crown, so stand fast in the Lord, *my* dearly beloved.

Col. 1:23. If ye continue in the faith grounded and settled, and *be* not moved away from the hope of the gospel, which ye have heard, *and* which was preached to every creature which is under heaven; whereof I Paul am made a minister;

1 Thess. 3:8. We live, if ye stand fast in the Lord. 13. To the end he may stablish your hearts unblameable in holiness before God, even our Father, at the coming of our Lord Jesus Christ with all his saints.

2 Thess. 2:15. Therefore, brethren, stand fast, and hold the traditions which ye have been taught, whether by word, or our epistle. 17. Comfort your hearts, and stablish you in every good word and work.

2 Thess. 3:13. Brethren, be not weary in well doing.

2 Tim. 1:13. Hold fast the form of sound words, which thou hast heard of me, in faith and love which is in Christ Jesus. 14. That good thing which was committed unto thee keep by the Holy Ghost which dwelleth in us.

2 Tim. 2:1. Thou therefore, my son, be strong in the grace that is in Christ Jesus. 3. Endure hardness, as a good soldier of Jesus Christ.

2 Tim. 3:14. Continue thou in the things which thou hast learned and hast been assured of, knowing of whom thou hast learned *them;*

Tit. 1:7. For a bishop must be blameless as the steward of God; 9. Holding fast the faithful word as he hath been taught, that he may be able by sound doctrine both to exhort and to convince the gainsayers.

Heb. 2:1. Therefore we ought to give the more earnest heed to the things which we have heard, lest at any time we should let *them* slip.

Heb. 3:6. But Christ as a son over his own house; whose house are we, if we hold fast the confidence and the rejoicing of the hope firm unto the end. 7. Wherefore as the Holy Ghost saith, To day if ye will hear his voice, 8. Harden not your hearts, as in the provocation, in the day of temptation in the wilderness: 14. We are made partakers of Christ, if we hold the beginning of our confidence stedfast unto the end;

Heb. 4:14. Seeing then that we have a great high priest, that is passed into the heavens, Jesus the Son of God, let us hold fast *our* profession.

Heb. 10:23. Let us hold fast the profession of *our* faith without wavering; (for he *is* faithful that promised;) 35. Cast not away therefore your confidence, which hath great recompence of reward.

Heb. 12:1. Seeing we also are compassed about with so great a cloud of witnesses, let us lay aside every weight, and the sin which doth so easily beset *us,* and let us run with patience the race that is set before us,

Heb. 13:9. Be not carried about with divers and strange doctrines. For *it is* a good thing that the heart be established with grace; 13. Let us go forth therefore unto him without the camp, bearing his reproach.

Jas. 1:4. Let patience have *her* perfect work, that ye may be perfect and entire, wanting nothing. 12. Blessed *is* the man that endureth temptation: for when he is tried, he shall receive the crown of life, which the Lord hath promised to them that love him. 25. Whoso looketh into the perfect law of liberty, and continueth *therein,* he being not a forgetful hearer, but a doer of the work, this man shall be blessed in his deed.

1 Pet. 1:13. Gird up the loins of your mind, be sober, and hope to the end for the grace that is to be brought unto you at the revelation of Jesus Christ;

1 Pet. 5:8. Be sober, be vigilant; because your adversary the devil, as a roaring lion, walketh about, seeking whom he may devour: 9. Whom resist stedfast in the faith,

2 Pet. 1:10. Give diligence to make your calling and election sure: for if ye do these things, ye shall never fall: 11. For so an entrance shall be ministered unto you abundantly into the everlasting kingdom of our Lord and Saviour Jesus Christ.

2 Pet. 3:17. Seeing ye know *these things*

before, beware lest ye also, being led away with the error of the wicked, fall from your own stedfastness. 18. Grow in grace, and *in* the knowledge of our Lord and Saviour Jesus Christ.

1 John 2:24. Let that therefore abide in you, which ye have heard from the beginning. If that which ye have heard from the beginning shall remain in you, ye also shall continue in the Son, and in the Father. 28. Little children, abide in him ; that, when he shall appear, we may have confidence, and not be ashamed before him at his coming.

2 John 8. Look to yourselves, that we lose not those things which we have wrought, but that we receive a full reward.

Jude 20. Building up yourselves on your most holy faith, . . . 21. Keep yourselves in the love of God.

Rev. 2:7. To him that overcometh will I give to eat of the tree of life, which is in the midst of the paradise of God. 10. Be thou faithful unto death, and I will give thee a crown of life. 11. He that overcometh shall not be hurt of the second death.

17. To him that overcometh will I give to eat of the hidden manna, and will give him a white stone, and in the stone a new name written, 25. That which ye have *already* hold fast till I come. 26. He that overcometh, and keepeth my works unto the end, to him will I give power over the nations :

Rev. 3:5. He that overcometh, the same shall be clothed in white raiment ; and I will not blot out his name out of the book of life, but I will confess his name before my Father, and before his angels. 11. Hold that fast which thou hast, that no man take thy crown. 12. Him that overcometh will I make a pillar in the temple of my God, and he shall go no more out : 21. To him that overcometh will I grant to sit with me in my throne, even as I also overcame, and am set down with my Father in his throne.

Rev. 15:2. I saw . . . them that had gotten the victory over the beast, and over his image, and over his mark, *and* over the number of his name, stand on the sea of glass, having the harps of God.

Rev. 21:7. He that overcometh shall inherit all things ; and I will be his God, and he shall be my son.

Rev. 22:11. He that is righteous, let him be righteous still : and he that is holy, let him be holy still.

See CHARACTER ; PERSEVERANCE ; STABILITY ; INDECISION ; INSTABILITY.

EXHORTATION TO: Josh. 1:7. Be thou strong and very courageous, that thou mayest observe to do according to all the law, which Moses my servant commanded thee : turn not from it *to* the right hand or *to* the left, that thou mayest prosper whithersoever thou goest.

1 Chr. 16:15. Be ye mindful always of his covenant ;

2 Chr. 19:11. Deal courageously, and the LORD shall be with the good.

Matt. 4:17. From that time Jesus began to preach, and to say, Repent : for the kingdom of heaven is at hand.

Matt. 6:24. No man can serve two masters : for either he will hate the one, and love the other ; or else he will hold to the one, and despise the other. Ye cannot serve God and mammon. Luke 16:13.

Matt. 10:32. Whosoever therefore shall confess me before men, him will I confess also before my Father which is in heaven.

Luke 9:59. He said unto another, Follow me. But he said, Lord, suffer me first to go and bury my father. 60. Jesus said unto him, Let the dead bury their dead : but go thou and preach the kingdom of God. Matt. 8:21,22.

61. And another also said, Lord, I will follow thee ; but let me first go bid them farewell, which are at home at my house. 62. And Jesus said unto him, No man, having put his hand to the plough, and looking back, is fit for the kingdom of God.

Luke 11:23. He that is not with me is against me : and he that gathereth not with me scattereth. Matt. 12:30.

Luke 12:8. Whosoever shall confess me before men, him shall the Son of man also confess before the angels of God :

Luke 17:32. Remember Lot's wife.

Col. 2:6. As ye have therefore received Christ Jesus the Lord, *so* walk ye in him : 7. Rooted and built up in him, and stablished in the faith, as ye have been taught, abounding therein with thanksgiving.

1 Tim. 6:11. But thou, O man of God, flee these things ; and follow after righteousness, godliness, faith, love, patience, meekness.

12. Fight the good fight of faith, lay hold on eternal life, whereunto thou art also called, and hast professed a good profession before many witnesses.

13. I give thee charge in the sight of God, who quickeneth all things, and *before* Christ Jesus, who before Pontius Pilate witnessed a good confession ;

14. That thou keep *this* commandment without spot, unrebukeable, until the appearing of our Lord Jesus Christ :

INSTANCES OF: ABEL : Heb. 11:4. By faith Abel offered unto God a more excellent sacrifice than Cain, by which he obtained witness that he was righteous, God testifying of his gifts : and by it he being dead yet speaketh.

ENOCH : Heb. 11:5. By faith Enoch was translated that he should not see death ; and was not found, because God had translated him : for before his translation he had this testimony, that he pleased God. 6. But without faith *it is* impossible to please *him :* for he that cometh to God must believe that he is, and *that* he is a rewarder of them that diligently seek him.

NOAH : Heb. 11:7. By faith Noah, being warned of God of things not seen as yet, moved with fear, prepared an ark to the saving of his house ; by the which he condemned the world, and became heir of the righteousness which is by faith.

ABRAHAM: Heb. 11:8. By faith Abraham, when he was called to go out into a place which he should after receive for an inheritance, obeyed; and he went out, not knowing whither he went. 17. By faith Abraham, when he was tried, offered up Isaac: and he that had received the promises offered up his only begotten *son*, 18. Of whom it was said, That in Isaac shall thy seed be called: 19. Accounting that God *was* able to raise *him* up, even from the dead; from whence also he received him in a figure.

JACOB: Gen. 28:20. If God will be with me, and will keep me in this way that I go, and will give me bread to eat, and raiment to put on, 21. So that I come again to my father's house in peace; then shall the LORD be my God:

JOSEPH: Gen. 39:9. How then can I do this great wickedness, and sin against God? *vs.* 7-20.

MOSES: Heb. 11:24. By faith Moses, when he was come to years, refused to be called the son of Pharaoh's daughter; 25. Choosing rather to suffer affliction with the people of God, than to enjoy the pleasures of sin for a season; 26. Esteeming the reproach of Christ greater riches than the treasures in Egypt: for he had respect unto the recompence of the reward.

Num. 12:7. My servant Moses . . . *is* faithful in all mine house. Heb. 3:5.

ISRAELITES: Ex. 19:7. And Moses came and called for the elders of the people, and laid before their faces all these words which the LORD commanded him. 8. And all the people answered together, and said, All that the LORD hath spoken we will do. And Moses returned the words of the people unto the LORD.

Ex. 24:3. And Moses came and told the people all the words of the LORD, and all the judgments: and all the people answered with one voice, and said, All the words which the LORD hath said will we do. 7. And he took the book of the covenant, and read in the audience of the people: and they said, All that the LORD hath said will we do, and be obedient.

Deut. 4:4. Ye that did cleave unto the LORD your God *are* alive every one of you this day.

Deut. 5:27. Go thou near, and hear all that the LORD our God shall say: and speak thou unto us all that the LORD our God shall speak unto thee; and we will hear *it*, and do *it*. Ex. 24:3,7; 19:8.

Deut. 26:17. Thou hast avouched the LORD this day to be thy God, and to walk in his ways, and to keep his statutes, and his commandments, and his judgments, and to hearken unto his voice: Deut. 29:12.

Josh. 22:34. The children of Reuben and the children of Gad called the altar *Ed:* for it *shall be* a witness between us that the LORD *is* God.

Josh. 24:21. And the people said unto Joshua, Nay; but we will serve the LORD. 22. And Joshua said unto the people, Ye *are* witnesses against yourselves that ye have chosen you the LORD, to serve him. And they said, *We are* witnesses. 23. Now therefore put away. *said he*, the strange gods which *are* among you, and incline your heart unto the LORD God of Israel. 24. And the people said unto Joshua, The LORD our God will we serve, and his voice will we obey. 25. So Joshua made a covenant with the people that day, and set them a statute and an ordinance in Shechem.

1 Kin. 19:18. I have left *me* seven thousand in Israel, all the knees which have not bowed unto Baal, and every mouth which hath not kissed him.

2 Chr. 11:16. Such as set their hearts to seek the LORD God of Israel came to Jerusalem, to sacrifice unto the LORD God of their fathers.

2 Chr. 13:10. As for us, the LORD *is* our God, and we have not forsaken him; 11. We keep the charge of the LORD our God;

2 Chr. 15:12. They entered into a covenant to seek the LORD God of their fathers with all their heart and with all their soul; 15. And all Judah rejoiced at the oath: for they had sworn with all their heart, and sought him with their whole desire; and he was found of them: 2 Chr. 23:16; 2 Kin. 11:17; 2 Chr. 29:10; Ezra 10:3-44; Neh. 9:38; Jer. 34:15.

Neh. 10:28. All they that had separated themselves from the people of the lands unto the law of God, their wives, their sons, and their daughters, every one having knowledge, and having understanding; 29. They clave to their brethren, their nobles, and entered into a curse, and into an oath, to walk in God's law, which was given by Moses the servant of God, and to observe and do all the commandments of the LORD our Lord, and his judgments and his statutes; *vs.* 1-39.

Psa. 50:5. Gather my saints together unto me: those that have made a covenant with me by sacrifice.

Jer. 42:5. The LORD be a true and faithful witness between us, if we do not even according to all things for the which the LORD thy God shall send thee to us. 6. Whether *it be* good, or whether *it be* evil, we will obey the voice of the LORD our God,

Jer. 50:5. They shall ask the way to Zion with their faces thitherward, *saying*, Come, and let us join ourselves to the LORD in a perpetual covenant *that* shall not be forgotten.

Hos. 11:12. Judah yet ruleth with God, and is faithful with the saints.

CALEB: Num. 14:24. But my servant Caleb, because he had another spirit with him, and hath followed me fully, him will I bring into the land whereinto he went; *vs.* 6-10,37, 38; Deut. 1:36; Josh. 14:14.

BALAAM: Num. 22:15. And Balak sent yet again princes, more, and more honourable than they. 16. And they came to Balaam, and said to him, Thus saith Balak the son of Zippor, Let nothing, I pray thee, hinder thee from coming unto me: 17. For I will promote thee unto very great honour, and I will do whatsoever thou sayest unto me: come therefore, I pray thee, curse me this people. 18. And Balaam answered and said unto the servants of Balak, If Balak would give me his house full of silver and gold, I cannot go beyond the word of the LORD my God, to do less or more.

PHINEHAS: Num. 25:7. And when Phinehas, the son of Eleazar, the son of Aaron the priest, saw *it*, he rose up from among the congregation, and took a javelin in his hand; 8. And he went after the man of Israel into the tent, and thrust both of them through, the man of Israel, and the woman through her belly. So the plague was stayed from the children of Israel. 9. And those that died in the plague were twenty and four thousand. 10. And the LORD spake unto Moses, saying, 11. Phinehas, the son of Eleazar, the son of Aaron the priest, hath turned my wrath away from the children of Israel, while he was zealous for my sake among them, that I consumed not the children of Israel in my jealousy. 12. Wherefore say, Behold, I give unto him my covenant of peace: 13. And he shall have it, and his seed after him, *even* the covenant of an everlasting priesthood; because he was zealous for his God, and made an atonement for the children of Israel.

JOSHUA: Josh. 24:15. As for me and my house, we will serve the LORD. 22. Ye *are* witnesses against yourselves that ye have chosen you the LORD, to serve him. And they said, *We are* witnesses. *vs.* 18–24.

GIDEON: Judg. 6:25. And it came to pass the same night, that the LORD said unto him, Take thy father's young bullock, even the second bullock of seven years old, and throw down the altar of Baal that thy father hath, and cut down the grove that *is* by it: 26. And build an altar unto the LORD thy God upon the top of this rock, in the ordered place, and take the second bullock, and offer a burnt sacrifice with the wood of the grove which thou shalt cut down. 27. Then Gideon took ten men of his servants, and did as the LORD had said unto him: and *so* it was, because he feared his father's household, and the men of the city, that he could not do *it* by day, that he did *it* by night. with *vs.* 28–40, and chapter 7.

RUTH: Ruth 1:16. Thy people *shall be* my people, and thy God my God:

SAUL: 1 Sam. 11:4. Then came the messengers to Gibeah of Saul, and told the tidings in the ears of the people: and all the people lifted up their voices, and wept. 5. And, behold, Saul came after the herd out of the field: and Saul said, What *aileth* the people that they weep? And they told him the tidings of the men of Jabesh. 6. And the Spirit of God came upon Saul when he heard those tidings, and his anger was kindled greatly. 7. And he took a yoke of oxen, and hewed them in pieces, and sent *them* throughout all the coasts of Israel by the hands of messengers, saying, Whosoever cometh not forth after Saul and after Samuel, so shall it be done unto his oxen. And the fear of the LORD fell on the people, and they came out with one consent.

ABIGAIL: 1 Sam. 25:18. Then Abigail made haste, and took two hundred loaves, and two bottles of wine, and five sheep ready dressed, and five measures of parched *corn*, and an hundred clusters of raisins, and two hundred cakes of figs, and laid *them* on asses. 19. And she said unto her servants, Go on before me; behold, I come after you. But she told not her husband Nabal. *vs.* 4–37.

DAVID: 1 Sam. 17:32. And David said to Saul, Let no man's heart fail because of him; thy servant will go and fight with this Philistine. 33. And Saul said to David, Thou art not able to go against this Philistine to fight with him: for thou *art but* a youth, and he a man of war from his youth. 34. And David said unto Saul, Thy servant kept his father's sheep, and there came a lion, and a bear, and took a lamb out of the flock: 35. And I went out after him, and smote him, and delivered *it* out of his mouth: and when he arose against me, I caught *him* by his beard, and smote him, and slew him. 36. Thy servant slew both the lion and the bear: and this uncircumcised Philistine shall be as one of them, seeing he hath defied the armies of the living God. 37. David said moreover, The LORD that delivered me out of the paw of the lion, and out of the paw of the bear, he will deliver me out of the hand of this Philistine. And Saul said unto David, Go, and the LORD be with thee. *vs.* 20–54.

2 Sam. 22:22. For I have kept the ways of the LORD, and have not wickedly departed from my God. 23. For all his judgments *were* before me: and *as for* his statutes, I did not depart from them. 24. I was also upright before him, and have kept myself from mine iniquity.

PSALMIST: Psa. 17:3. Thou hast proved mine heart; thou hast visited *me* in the night; thou hast tried me, *and* shalt find nothing; I am purposed *that* my mouth shall not transgress.

Psa. 26:6. I will wash mine hands in innocency: so will I compass thine altar, O LORD: 11. But as for me, I will walk in mine integrity:

Psa. 40:9. I have preached righteousness in the great congregation: lo, I have not refrained my lips, O LORD, thou knowest. 10. I have not hid thy righteousness within my heart; I have declared thy faithfulness and thy salvation: I have not concealed thy lovingkindness and thy truth from the great congregation.

Psa. 56:12. Thy vows *are* upon me, O God: I will render praises unto thee.

Psa. 66:16. Come *and* hear, all ye that fear God, and I will declare what he hath done for my soul.

Psa. 71:17. Hitherto have I declared thy wondrous works.

Psa. 86:11. I will walk in thy truth : unite my heart to fear thy name.

Psa. 101:2. I will behave myself wisely in a perfect way. O when wilt thou come unto me? I will walk within my house with a perfect heart. 3. I will set no wicked thing before mine eyes: I hate the work of them that turn aside; *it* shall not cleave to me.

Psa. 108:1. O God, my heart is fixed; I will sing and give praise, even with my glory. Psa. 57:7,8.

Psa. 116:9. I will walk before the LORD in the land of the living. 13. I will take the cup of salvation, and call upon the name of the LORD. 14. I will pay my vows unto the LORD now in the presence of all his people. 16. O LORD, truly I *am* thy servant; I *am* thy servant, *and* the son of thine handmaid:

Psa. 119:8. I will keep thy statutes: O forsake me not utterly. 30. I have chosen the way of truth: thy judgments have I laid *before me.* 31. I have stuck unto thy testimonies: 38. Stablish thy word unto thy servant, who *is devoted* to thy fear. 44. So shall I keep thy law continually for ever and ever. 45. And I will walk at liberty: for I seek thy precepts. 46. I will speak of thy testimonies also before kings, and will not be ashamed. 57. *Thou art* my portion, O LORD: I have said that I would keep thy words. 94. I *am* thine, save me; for I have sought thy precepts. 106. I have sworn, and I will perform *it,* that I will keep thy righteous judgments. 115. Depart from me, ye evildoers: for I will keep the commandments of my God. 125. I *am* thy servant; give me understanding, that I may know thy testimonies. 145. I cried with *my* whole heart; hear me, O LORD: I will keep thy statutes. 146. I cried unto thee; save me, and I shall keep thy testimonies. Psa. 143:12.

A PROPHET: 1 Kin. 13:8. And the man of God said unto the king, If thou wilt give me half thine house, I will not go in with thee, neither will I eat bread nor drink water in this place: 9. For so was it charged me by the word of the LORD, saying, Eat no bread, nor drink water, nor turn again by the same way that thou camest. 10. So he went another way, and returned not by the way that he came to Beth-el.

ELIJAH: 1 Kin. 18:22. Then said Elijah unto the people, I, *even* I only, remain a prophet of the LORD;

JEHOSHAPHAT: 1 Kin. 22:7. Jehoshaphat said, *Is there* not here a prophet of the LORD besides, that we might enquire of him? 2 Chr. 18:6.

NAAMAN: 2 Kin. 5:15. And he said, Behold, now I know that *there is* no God in all the earth, but in Israel: 17. Thy servant will henceforth offer neither burnt offering nor sacrifice unto other gods, but unto the LORD.

JEHU: 2 Kin. 9:18. So there went one on horseback to meet him, and said, Thus saith the king, Is it peace? And Jehu said, What hast thou to do with peace? turn thee behind me. And the watchman told, saying, The messenger came to them, but he cometh not again. 19. Then he sent out a second on horseback, which came to them, and said, Thus saith the king, Is it peace? And Jehu answered, What hast thou to do with peace? turn thee behind me. 20. And the watchman told, saying, He came even unto them, and cometh not again: and the driving *is* like the driving of Jehu the son of Nimshi; for he driveth furiously. *vs.* 11–37; chapter 10.

HEZEKIAH: 2 Kin. 18:6. He clave to the LORD, *and* departed not from following him, but kept his commandments, which the LORD commanded Moses. 2 Chr. 15:17.

JOSIAH: 2 Kin. 22:2. He did *that which was* right in the sight of the LORD, and walked in all the way of David his father, and turned not aside to the right hand or to the left.

2 Kin. 23:3. The king stood by a pillar, and made a covenant before the LORD, to walk after the LORD, and to keep his commandments and his testimonies and his statutes with all *their* heart and all *their* soul, to perform the words of this covenant that were written in this book. And all the people stood to the covenant. [2 Chr. 34:31.] 25. Like unto him was there no king before him, that turned to the LORD with all his heart, and with all his soul, and with all his might, according to all the law of Moses; neither after him arose there *any* like him.

NEHEMIAH: Neh. 6:11. Should such a man as I flee? and who *is there,* that, *being* as I *am,* would go into the temple to save his life? I will not go in. chapters 2; 4; 5; 6.

MORDECAI: Esth. 3:2. And all the king's servants, that *were* in the king's gate, bowed, and reverenced Haman: for the king had so commanded concerning him. But Mordecai bowed not, nor did *him* reverence. 3. Then the king's servants, which *were* in the king's gate, said unto Mordecai, Why transgressest thou the king's commandment?

ESTHER: Esth. 4:16. So will I go in unto the king, which *is* not according to the law: and if I perish, I perish.

JOB: Job 2:3. And the LORD said unto Satan, Hast thou considered my servant Job, that *there is* none like him in the earth, a perfect and an upright man, one that feareth God, and escheweth evil? and still he holdeth fast his integrity, although thou movedst me against him, to destroy him without cause.

Job 23:11. My foot hath held his steps, his way have I kept, and not declined. 12. Neither have I gone back from the commandment of his lips; I have esteemed the words of his mouth more than my necessary *food.*

MATTHEW: Matt. 9:9. And as Jesus passed forth from thence, he saw a man, named Matthew, sitting at the receipt of custom.

and he saith unto him, Follow me. And he arose, and followed him.

JOSEPH: Mark 15:43. Joseph of Arimathæa, . . . went in boldly unto Pilate, and craved the body of Jesus.

NATHANAEL: John 1:49. Nathanael . . . saith unto him, Rabbi, thou art the Son of God; thou art the King of Israel.

MARTHA: John 11:27. She saith unto him, Yea, Lord: I believe that thou art the Christ, the Son of God, which should come into the world.

THE DISCIPLES: Luke 18:28. Then Peter said, Lo, we have left all, and followed thee. John 6:68. Simon Peter answered him, Lord, to whom shall we go? thou hast the words of eternal life. 69. We believe, and are sure, that thou art ¹ that Christ, the Son of the living God.   [¹ R. V. the Holy One of]

Acts 2:42. They continued stedfastly in the apostles' doctrine and fellowship, and in breaking of bread, and in prayers.

PAUL: Acts 9:29. He spake boldly in the name of the Lord Jesus, and disputed against the Grecians:

Acts 26:6. I stand and am judged for the hope of the promise made of God unto our fathers:

Rom. 1:16. I am not ashamed of the gospel of Christ: for it is the power of God unto salvation to every one that believeth;

Phil. 1:20. In nothing I shall be ashamed, but *that* with all boldness, as always, *so* now also Christ shall be magnified in my body, whether *it be* by life, or by death. 21. For to me to live *is* Christ, and to die *is* gain.

Col. 2:5. Joying and beholding your order, and the stedfastness of your faith in Christ.

2 Tim. 4:7. I have fought a good fight, I have finished *my* course, I have kept the faith: 8. Henceforth there is laid up for me a crown of righteousness, which the Lord, the righteous judge, shall give me at that day: and not to me only, but unto all them also that love his appearing.

EPHESIANS: Rev. 2:2. I know thy works, and thy labour, and thy patience, . . . 3. And [how thou] hast borne, and hast patience, and for my name's sake hast laboured, and hast not fainted.

CHURCH OF SARDIS: Rev. 3:4. Thou hast a few names even in Sardis which have not defiled their garments; and they shall walk with me in white: for they are worthy. 8. Thou hast a little strength, and hast kept my word, and hast not denied my name. 10. Because thou hast kept the word of my patience, I also will keep thee from the hour of temptation, which shall come upon all the world,

SAINTS: Rev. 14:4. These are they which were not defiled with women; for they are virgins. These are they which follow the Lamb whithersoever he goeth.

See PERSEVERANCE; STABILITY; ZEAL, RELIGIOUS.

DECISION, VALLEY OF. Joel 3:14.

DECREES, of the Medes, irrevocable, Dan. 6:14,15.

Ecclesiastical, of the church at Jerusalem, Acts 16:4, with chapter 15:28,29.

DECREES. divine. See PREDESTINATION.

DEDAN. 1. Son of Raamah, Gen. 10:7; 1 Chr. 1:9.

2. Son of Jokshan, Gen. 25:3; 1 Chr. 1:32.

3. A country, probably bordering on Edom, Jer. 49:8; Ezek. 25:13; 27:15,20; 38:13.

DEDANIM, descendants of Dedan, Isa. 21:13.

DEDICATION. Law concerning dedicated things, Lev. 27; Num. 18:14; 1 Chr. 26: 26,27. Must be without blemish, Lev. 22: 18-23; Mal. 1:14. Not redeemable, Lev. 27: 28,29. Offering must be voluntary, Lev. 1: 3; 22:19. See OFFERINGS; VOWS.

Of the tabernacle, Num. 7. Solomon's temple, 1 Kin. 8; 2 Chr. 7:5. Second temple, Ezra 6:16,17. Of the wall of Jerusalem, Neh. 12:27-43. Of houses, Deut. 20:5. Of Samuel by his mother, 1 Sam. 1:11,22.

OF SELF. See CONSECRATION.

For instances of liberality in dedicated things, see LIBERALITY.

FEAST OF, John 10:22. See 1 Kin. 8:65; 2 Chr. 7:8-10.

DEED, to land, Jer. 32:12,14,44.

See LAND.

DEER, called also, FALLOW DEER, HART, HIND, ROEBUCK. Designated among the clean animals, to be eaten, Deut. 12:15; 14:5. Provided for Solomon's household, 1 Kin. 4: 23. Fleetness of, 2 Sam. 2:18; 1 Chr. 12:8; Prov. 6:5; Song 8:14; Isa. 35:6. Surefootedness of, 2 Sam. 22:34. Gentleness of, Prov. 5:19.

DEFENSE, an argument made before a court. Of Jeremiah, Jer. 26:12-16; Peter, Acts 4:8-13; 5:23-29; Stephen, Acts 7; Paul, Acts 22; 23:1-6; 24:10-21; 26:1-23.

Military defenses, see FORT; ARMIES.

DEFILEMENT. Laws relating to, Lev. 7:18-21; 11:43; 22:2-7. Caused by leprosy, Lev. 13:3,44-46; 14; 22:4-7; gonorrhea, Lev. 15:1-15; 22:4; copulation, Lev. 15:17; spermatorrhea, Lev. 15:16,17; childbirth, Lev. 12:2-8; Luke 2:22; menses, Lev. 15:19-33; 2 Sam. 11:4; touching the dead, Num. 19:11-22; 31:19,20; touching carcass of any unclean animal, Lev. 11:39,40; 17:15,16; 22:8; touching carcass of an unclean thing, Lev. 5:2-13; 11:8,24-28, 31-38; 14:46-57; 15:5-11; Deut. 23:10,11; slaying in battle, Num. 31:19,20. Contact with sinners falsely supposed to cause, John 18:28.

Of priests, Lev. 16:26,28; Num. 19:7-10; Ezek. 44:25,26.

Egyptian usage, concerning, Gen. 43:32.

See ABLUTION; PURIFICATION; UNCLEANNESS.

DEFORMITY. See BLEMISH.

DEGREES, or steps in the dial of Ahaz. 2 Kin. 20:9-11.

DEHAVITES, Ezra 4:9.

DEKAR, father of one of Solomon's purveyors, 1 Kin. 4:9.

DELAIAH. 1. Head of the twenty-third division of the priestly order, 1 Chr. 24:18.

2. A prince of Judah, Jer. 36:12,25.

3. A progenitor of certain Babylonish captives, Ezra 2:60; Neh. 7:62.

4. Father of a false prophet, Neh. 6:10.

5. A descendant of the royal line of Judah. Called also DALAIAH, 1 Chr. 3:24.

DELILAH, Samson's paramour, Judg. 16:4–18.

DELIVERANCE. See AFFLICTION; GOD, PROVIDENCE OF; PRAYER, ANSWERED.

DELIVERER, appellation of Jesus, Rom. 11:26.

DELUGE. See FLOOD.

DELUSION, SELF. See SELF-DELUSION.

DEMAGOGISM. INSTANCES OF: Absalom, 2 Sam. 15:2–6. Pilate, Matt. 27:17–26; Mark 15:15; Luke 23:13–24; John 18:38–40; 19:6–13. Felix, Acts 24:27. Herod, Acts 12:3.

DEMAS. A companion of Paul, Col. 4:14; Philem. 24. Deserts Paul, 2 Tim. 4:10.

DEMETRIUS. 1. A silversmith, noted for raising a riot, Acts 19:24–38.

2. A Christian mentioned in 3 John 12.

DEMONS. Worship of, Lev. 17:7; Deut. 32:17; 2 Chr. 11:15; Psa. 106:37; Matt. 4:9; Luke 4:7; 1 Cor. 10:20,21; 1 Tim. 4:1; Rev. 13:4. Worship of, forbidden, Lev. 17:7; Zech. 13:2; Rev. 9:20.

Possession by, instances of: Saul, 1 Sam. 16:14–23; 1 Sam. 18:10,11; 19:9,10. Two men of the Gergesenes, Matt. 8:28–34; Mark 5:2–20. The dumb man, Matt. 9:32,33. The blind and dumb man, Matt. 12:22; Luke, 11:14. The daughter of the Syrophenician, Matt. 15:22–29; Mark 7:25–30. The lunatic child, Matt. 17:14–18; Mark 9:17–27; Luke 9:37–42. The man in the synagogue, Mark 1:23–26; Luke 4:33–35. Mary Magdalene, Mark 16:9; Luke 8:2,3. The herd of swine, Matt. 8:30–32.

Cast out by Jesus, Matt. 4:24; 8:16; Mark 3:22; Luke 4:41.

Power over, given the disciples, Matt. 10:1; Mark 6:7; 16:17. Cast out by the disciples, Mark 9:38; Luke 10:17; by Peter, Acts 5:16; by Paul, Acts 16:16–18; 19:12; by Philip, Acts 8:7. Disciples could not expel, Mark 9:18, 28,29. Sceva's sons exorcise, Acts 19:13–16. Parable of the man repossessed, Matt. 12:43–45.

Jesus falsely accused of being possessed of, Mark 3:22–30; John 7:20; 8:48; 10:20.

Testify to the divinity of Jesus, Matt. 8:29; Mark 1:23,24; 3:11; 5:7; Luke 8:28; Acts 19:15.

Adversaries of men, Matt. 12:45. Sent to foment trouble between Abimelech and the Shechemites, Judg. 9:23. Messages given false prophets by, 1 Kin. 22:21–23.

Believe and tremble, Jas. 2:19. To be judged at the general judgment, Matt. 8:29, with 2 Pet. 2:4; Jude 6.

Punishment of, Matt. 8:29; 25:41; Luke 8:28; 2 Pet. 2:4; Jude 6; Rev. 12:7–9.

See SATAN.

DENS, used as places of refuge, Judg. 6:2; Heb. 11:38; Rev. 6:15.

DENYING JESUS. See JESUS, REJECTED.

DEPRAVITY OF MAN. Gen. 6:5. And GOD saw that the wickedness of man *was* great in the earth, and *that* every imagination of the thoughts of his heart *was* only evil continually. 6. And it repented the LORD that he had made man on the earth, and it grieved him at his heart. 7. And the LORD said, I will destroy man whom I have created from the face of the earth; both man, and beast, and the creeping thing, and the fowls of the air; for it repenteth me that I have made them. 8. But Noah found grace in the eyes of the LORD. 11. The earth also was corrupt before God, and the earth was filled with violence. 12. And God looked upon the earth, and, behold, it was corrupt; for all flesh had corrupted his way upon the earth. 13. And God said unto Noah, The end of all flesh is come before me; for the earth is filled with violence through them; and, behold, I will destroy them with the earth.

Gen. 8:21. The LORD said in his heart, I will not again curse the ground any more for man's sake; for the imagination of man's heart *is* evil from his youth;

Deut. 32:10. He found him in a desert land, and in the waste howling wilderness; he led him about, he instructed him, he kept him as the apple of his eye.

Job 4:17. Shall mortal man be more just than God? shall a man be more pure than his maker? 18. Behold, he put no trust in his servants; and his angels he charged with folly: 19. How much less *in* them that dwell in houses of clay, whose foundation *is* in the dust, *which* are crushed before the moth?

Job 9:2. How should man be just with God? 3. If he will contend with him, he cannot answer him one of a thousand. 20. If I justify myself, mine own mouth shall condemn me: *if I say,* I *am* perfect, it shall also prove me perverse. 29. *If* I be wicked, why then labour I in vain? 30. If I wash myself with snow water, and make my hands never so clean; 31. Yet shalt thou plunge me in the ditch, and mine own clothes shall abhor me.

Job 11:12. For vain man would be wise, though man be born *like* a wild ass's colt.

Job 14:4. Who can bring a clean *thing* out of an unclean? not one.

Job 15:14. What *is* man, that he should be clean? and *he which is* born of a woman, that he should be righteous? 15. Behold, he putteth no trust in his saints; yea, the heavens are not clean in his sight. 16. How much more abominable and filthy *is* man, which drinketh iniquity like water?

(20)

Job 25:4. How then can man be justified with God? or how can he be clean *that is* born of a woman? 5. Behold even to the moon, and it shineth not; yea, the stars are not pure in his sight. 6. How much less man, *that is* a worm? and the son of man, *which is* a worm?

Psa. 5:9. For *there is* no faithfulness in their mouth; their inward part *is* very wickedness; their throat *is* an open sepulchre; they flatter with their tongue.

Psa. 14:1. The fool hath said in his heart, *There is* no God. They are corrupt, they have done abominable works, *there is* none that doeth good. 2. The LORD looked down from heaven upon the children of men, to see if there were any that did understand, *and* seek God. 3. They are all gone aside, they are *all* together become filthy: *there is* none that doeth good, no, not one. Psa. 53:1-3.

Psa. 51:5. Behold, I was shapen in iniquity; and in sin did my mother conceive me.

Psa. 58:1. Do ye indeed speak righteousness, O congregation? do ye judge uprightly, O ye sons of men? 2. Yea, in heart ye work wickedness; ye weigh the violence of your hands in the earth. 3. The wicked are estranged from the womb: they go astray as soon as they be born, speaking lies. 4. Their poison *is* like the poison of a serpent: *they are* like the deaf adder *that* stoppeth her ear; 5. Which will not hearken to the voice of charmers, charming never so wisely.

Psa. 94:11. The LORD knoweth the thoughts of man, that they *are* vanity.

Psa. 130:3. If thou, LORD, shouldest mark iniquities, O Lord, who shall stand?

Psa. 143:2. And enter not into judgment with thy servant: for in thy sight shall no man living be justified.

Prov. 10:20. The heart of the wicked *is* little worth.

Prov. 20:6. Most men will proclaim every one his own goodness: but a faithful man who can find? 9. Who can say, I have made my heart clean, I am pure from my sin?

Prov. 21:8. The way of man *is* froward and strange:

Eccl. 7:20. *There is* not a just man upon earth, that doeth good, and sinneth not. 29. Lo, this only have I found, that God hath made man upright; but they have sought out many inventions. 2 Chr. 6:36.

Eccl. 8:11. Because sentence against an evil work is not executed speedily, therefore the heart of the sons of men is fully set in them to do evil.

Eccl. 9:3. The heart of the sons of men is full of evil, and madness *is* in their heart while they live, and after that *they go* to the dead.

Isa. 1:5. The whole head is sick, and the whole heart faint. 6. From the sole of the foot even unto the head *there is* no soundness in it; *but* wounds, and bruises, and putrifying sores: they have not been closed, neither bound up, neither mollified with ointment.

Isa. 42:6. I the LORD have called thee in righteousness, . . . for a light of the Gentiles; 7. To open the blind eyes, to bring out the prisoners from the prison, *and* them that sit in darkness out of the prison house.

Isa. 43:8. The blind people that have eyes, and the deaf that have ears.

Isa. 48:8. Yea, thou heardest not; yea, thou knewest not; yea, from that time *that* thine ear was not opened: for I knew that thou wouldest deal very treacherously, and wast called a transgressor from the womb.

Isa. 51:1. Hearken to me, ye that follow after righteousness, ye that seek the LORD: look unto the rock *whence* ye are hewn, and to the hole of the pit *whence* ye are digged.

Isa. 53:6. All we like sheep have gone astray; we have turned every one to his own way;

Isa. 64:6. We are all as an unclean *thing*, and all our righteousnesses *are* as filthy rags; and we all do fade as a leaf; and our iniquities, like the wind, have taken us away.

Jer. 2:22. Though thou wash thee with [1]nitre, and take thee much sope, *yet* thine iniquity is marked before me, saith the Lord GOD. 29. Wherefore will ye plead with me? ye all have transgressed against me, saith the LORD. [1 R. V. lye]

Jer. 6:7. As a fountain casteth out her waters, so she casteth out her wickedness: violence and spoil is heard in her; before me continually *is* grief and wounds.

Jer. 13:23. Can the Ethiopian change his skin, or the leopard his spots? *then* may ye also do good, that are accustomed to do evil.

Jer. 16:12. Behold, ye walk every one after the imagination of his evil heart, that they may not hearken unto me:

Jer. 17:9. The heart *is* deceitful above all *things*, and desperately [1]wicked: who can know it? [1 R. V. sick]

Ezek. 16:6. When I passed by thee, and saw thee polluted in thine own blood, I said unto thee *when thou wast* in thy blood, Live. Ezek. 37:1-3.

Ezek. 36:25. Then will I sprinkle clean water upon you, and ye shall be clean: from all your filthiness, and from all your idols, will I cleanse you. 26. A new heart also will I give you, and a new spirit will I put within you: and I will take away the stony heart out of your flesh, and I will give you an heart of flesh.

Hos. 6:7. They like [1]men have transgressed the covenant: there have they dealt treacherously against me. [1 R. V. Adam]

Hos. 14:9. Who *is* wise, and he shall understand these *things?* prudent, and he shall know them? for the ways of the LORD *are* right, and the just shall walk in them: but the transgressors shall fall therein.

Mic. 7:2. The good *man* is perished out of the earth; and *there is* none upright among men: they all lie in wait for blood; they hunt every man his brother with a net. 3. That they may do evil with both hands earnestly, the prince asketh, and the judge *asketh* for a reward; and the great *man*, he uttereth his mischievous desire: so they wrap it up. 4. The best of them *is* as a brier: the most upright *is sharper* than a thorn hedge: the day of thy watchmen *and* thy visitation cometh; now shall be their perplexity.

Matt. 7:17. Even so every good tree bringeth forth good fruit: but a corrupt tree bringeth forth evil fruit.

Matt. 12:34. O generation of vipers, how can ye, being evil, speak good things? for out of the abundance of the heart the mouth speaketh. 35. A good man out of the good treasure of the heart bringeth forth good things: and an evil man out of the evil treasure bringeth forth evil things.

Matt. 15:19. Out of the heart proceed evil thoughts, murders, adulteries, fornications, thefts, false witness, blaphemies: Mark 7: 21-23.

Luke 1:79. To give light to them that sit in darkness and *in* the shadow of death.

John 1:10. He was in the world, and the world was made by him, and the world knew him not. 11. He came unto his own, and his own received him not.

John 3:19. This is the condemnation, that light is come into the world, and men loved darkness rather than light, because their deeds were evil.

John 8:23. And he said unto them, Ye are from beneath; I am from above: ye are of this world;

John 14:17. The Spirit of truth; whom the world cannot receive, because it seeth him not, neither knoweth him:

Acts 8:23. For I perceive that thou art in the gall of bitterness, and *in* the bond of iniquity.

Rom. 2:1. Thou art inexcusable, O man, whosoever thou art that judgest: for wherein thou judgest another, thou condemnest thyself; for thou that judgest doest the same things.

Rom. 3:9. What then? are we better *than they?* No, in no wise: for we have before proved both Jews and Gentiles, that they are all under sin; 10. As it is written, There is none righteous, no, not one: 11. There is none that understandeth, there is none that seeketh after God. 12. They are all gone out of the way, they are together become unprofitable; there is none that doeth good, no, not one. 13. Their throat *is* an open sepulchre; with their tongues they have used deceit; the poison of asps *is* under their lips: 14. Whose mouth *is* full of cursing and bitterness: 15. Their feet *are* swift to shed blood: 16. Destruction and misery *are* in their ways: 17. And the way of peace have they not known: 18. There is no fear of God before their eyes. 19. Now we know that what things soever the law saith, it saith to them who are under the law: that every mouth

may be stopped, and all the world may become guilty before God. 23. For all have sinned, and come short of the glory of God;

Rom. 5:6. For when we were yet without strength, in due time Christ died for the ungodly.

12. Wherefore, as by one man sin entered into the world, and death by sin; and so death passed upon all men, for that all have sinned: 13. For until the law sin was in the world: but sin is not imputed when there is no law. 14. Nevertheless death reigned from Adam to Moses, even over them that had not sinned after the similitude of Adam's transgression.

Rom. 6:6. Knowing this that our old man is crucified with *him*, that the body of sin might be destroyed, that henceforth we should not serve sin. 19. As ye have yielded your members servants to uncleanness and to iniquity unto iniquity; even so now yield your members servants to righteousness unto holiness. 20. For when ye were the servants of sin, ye were free from righteousness. *v.* 17.

Rom. 7:5. When we were in the flesh, the motions of sins, which were by the law, did work in our members to bring forth fruit unto death. 11. Sin, taking occasion by the commandment, deceived me, and by it slew *me*. 13. Sin, that it might appear sin, working death in me by that which is good; that sin by the commandment might become exceeding sinful. 14. I am carnal, sold under sin. 15. For that which I do I allow not: for what I would, that do I not; but what I hate, that do I. 18. I know that in me (that is, in my flesh,) dwelleth no good thing: for to will is present with me; but *how* to perform that which is good I find not. 19. For the good that I would I do not: but the evil which I would not, that I do. 20. Now if I do that I would not, it is no more I that do it, but sin that dwelleth in me. 21. I find then a law, that, when I would do good, evil is present with me. 23. I see another law in my members, warring against the law of my mind, and bringing me into captivity to the law of sin which is in my members. 25. So then with the mind I myself serve the law of God; but with the flesh the law of sin.

Rom. 8:5. They that are after the flesh do mind the things of the flesh; 6. To be carnally minded *is* death; 7. The carnal mind *is* enmity against God: for it is not subject to the law of God, neither indeed can be. 8. So then they that are in the flesh cannot please God. 13. If ye live after the flesh, ye shall die: but if ye through the Spirit do mortify the deeds of the body, ye shall live.

Rom. 11:32. For God hath concluded them all in unbelief, that he might have mercy upon all.

1 Cor. 2:14. The natural man receiveth not the things of the Spirit of God: for they are foolishness unto him: neither can he know *them*, because they are spiritually discerned

1 Cor. 3:3. Ye are yet carnal: for whereas *there is* among you envying, and strife, and divisions, are ye not carnal, and walk as men?

1 Cor. 5:9. I wrote unto you in an epistle not to company with fornicators: 10. Yet not altogether with the fornicators of this world, or with the covetous, or extortioners, or with idolaters; for then must ye needs go out of the world.

2 Cor. 3:4. And such trust have we through Christ to God-ward: 5. Not that we are sufficient of ourselves to think any thing as of ourselves; but our sufficiency *is* of God;

2 Cor. 5:14. If one died for all, [1] then were all dead: [1 R. V. therefore all died:]

Gal. 3:10. As many as are of the works of the law are under the curse: 11. But that no man is justified by the law in the sight of God, *it is* evident: 22. The scripture hath concluded all under sin,

Gal. 5:17. The flesh lusteth against the Spirit, and the Spirit against the flesh: and these are contrary the one to the other: so that ye cannot do the things that ye would. 19. The works of the flesh are manifest, which are *these*: Adultery, fornication, uncleanness, lasciviousness, 20. Idolatry, witchcraft, hatred, variance, emulations, wrath, strife, seditions, heresies, 21. Envyings, murders, drunkenness, revellings, and such like:

Eph. 2:1. You *hath he quickened*, who were dead in trespasses and sins; 2. Wherein in time past ye walked according to the course of this world, according to the prince of the power of the air, the spirit that now worketh in the children of disobedience: 3. Among whom also we all had our conversation in times past in the lusts of our flesh, fulfilling the desires of the flesh and of the mind; and were by nature the children of wrath, even as others. 12. At that time ye were without Christ, being aliens from the commonwealth of Israel, and strangers from the covenants of promise, having no hope, and without God in the world: *v.* 11.

Eph. 4:17. This I say therefore, and testify in the Lord, that ye henceforth walk not as other Gentiles walk, in the vanity of their mind, 18. Having the understanding darkened, being alienated from the life of God through the ignorance that is in them, because of the blindness of their heart: 19. Who being past feeling have given themselves over unto lasciviousness, to work all uncleanness with greediness. 22. That ye put off concerning the former conversation the old man, which is corrupt according to the deceitful lusts;

Eph. 5:8. Ye were sometimes darkness, but now *are ye* light in the Lord: 14. Awake thou that sleepest, and arise from the dead,

Col. 1:13. Who hath delivered us from the power of darkness, 21. You, that were sometime alienated and enemies in *your* mind by wicked works,

Col. 2:13. You, being dead in your sins and the uncircumcision of your flesh, hath he quickened together with him,

Col. 3:5. Mortify therefore your members which are upon the earth; fornication, uncleanness, inordinate affection, evil concupiscence, and covetousness, which is idolatry: 7. In the which ye also walked some time, when ye lived in them.

2 Tim. 2:26. *That* they may recover themselves out of the snare of the devil, [1] who are taken captive by him at his will.

[1 R. V. having been taken captive by the Lord's servant unto the will of God]

Tit. 3:3. We ourselves also were sometimes foolish, disobedient, deceived, serving divers lusts and pleasures, living in malice and envy, hateful, *and* hating one another.

Jas. 3:2. In many things we [1] offend all.
[1 R. V. all stumble]

Jas. 4:5. Do ye think that the scripture saith in vain, The spirit that dwelleth in us lusteth to envy?

1 Pet. 1:18. Forasmuch as ye know that ye were not redeemed with corruptible things, . . . from your vain conversation *received* by tradition from your fathers;

1 Pet. 2:9. Ye should shew forth the praises of him who hath called you out of darkness into his marvellous light: 25. Ye were as sheep going astray;

1 John 1:8. If we say that we have no sin, we deceive ourselves, and the truth is not in us. 10. If we say that we have not sinned, we make him a liar, and his word is not in us.

1 John 2:16. All that *is* in the world, the lust of the flesh, and the lust of the eyes, and the pride of life, is not of the Father, but is of the world.

1 John 3:10. In this the children of God are manifest, and the children of the devil: whosoever doeth not righteousness is not of God, neither he that loveth not his brother.

1 John 5:19. The whole world lieth in wickedness.

Rev. 3:17. Thou sayest, I am rich, and increased with goods, and have need of nothing; and knowest not that thou art wretched, and miserable, and poor, and blind, and naked:

See FALL OF MAN; SIN.

DEPUTY, an officer who administers the functions of a superior in his absence, 1 Kin. 22:47; Acts 13:7,8; 18:12; 19:38.

DERBE, a city of Lycaonia. Paul flees to, Acts 14:6,20. Visited by Paul and Silas, Acts 16:1. Gaius born in, Acts 20:4.

DERISION, the wicked held in, by God, Psa. 2:4; Prov. 1:26.

INSTANCES OF: Sarah, when the angels gave her the promise of a child, Gen. 18:12. The evil children of Beth-el deride Elisha, 2 Kin. 2:23. The people of Israel scoff at Hezekiah, 2 Chr. 30:1-10.

See IRONY; SARCASM; SCOFFING.

DESERT, an arid region bearing only a sparse vegetation, Lev. 16:22; Deut. 8:15; Jer. 2:2,6; 17:6.

FIGURATIVE: Isa. 35:1.

DESIGN, in nature, evidence of, Job 12: 7-11; Prov. 16:4 [*R. V.*].

DESIRE. SPIRITUAL: Psa. 17:1. Hear the right, O LORD, attend unto my cry, give ear unto my prayer, *that goeth* not out of feigned lips.

Psa. 22:26. They shall praise the LORD that seek him: your heart shall live for ever.

Psa. 24:6. This *is* the generation of them that seek him, that seek thy face, O Jacob.

Psa. 25:5. Thou *art* the God of my salvation; on thee do I wait all the day. 15. Mine eyes *are* ever toward the LORD; for he shall pluck my feet out of the net.

Psa. 27:8. *When thou saidst,* Seek ye my face; my heart said unto thee, Thy face, LORD, will I seek. 14. Wait on the LORD: be of good courage, and he shall strengthen thine heart: wait, I say, on the LORD.

Psa. 33:20. Our soul waiteth for the LORD: he *is* our help and our shield.

Psa. 34:10. They that seek the LORD shall not want any good *thing.*

Psa. 37:4. Delight thyself also in the LORD; and he shall give thee the desires of thine heart. 7. Rest in the LORD, and wait patiently for him: 9. Those that wait upon the LORD, they shall inherit the earth. 34. Wait on the LORD, and keep his way, and he shall exalt thee to inherit the land:

Psa. 39:12. Hear my prayer, O LORD, and give ear unto my cry; hold not thy peace at my tears: for I *am* a stranger with thee, *and* a sojourner, as all my fathers *were.*

Psa. 40:1. I waited patiently for the LORD; 8. I delight to do thy will, O my God: yea, thy law *is* within my heart.

Psa. 42:1. As the hart panteth after the water brooks, so panteth my soul after thee, O God. 2. My soul thirsteth for God, for the living God: when shall I come and appear before God? 3. My tears have been my meat day and night, while they continually say unto me, Where *is* thy God? 4. When I remember these *things,* I pour out my soul in me: for I had gone with the multitude, I went with them to the house of God, with the voice of joy and praise, with a multitude that kept holyday. 5. Why art thou cast down, O my soul? and *why* art thou disquieted in me? hope thou in God: for I shall yet praise him *for* the help of his countenance. 6. O my God, my soul is cast down within me: therefore will I remember thee from the land of Jordan, and of the Hermonites, from the hill Mizar. 7. Deep calleth unto deep at the noise of thy waterspouts: all thy waves and thy billows are gone over me. 8. *Yet* the LORD will command his lovingkindness in the daytime, and in the night his song *shall be* with me, *and* my prayer unto the God of my life. 9. I will say unto God my rock, Why hast thou forgotten me? why go I mourning because of the oppression of the enemy? 10. *As* with a sword in my bones, mine enemies reproach me; while they say daily unto me, Where *is* thy God? 11. Why art thou cast down, O my soul? and why art

thou disquieted within me? hope thou in God: for I shall yet praise him, *who is* the health of my countenance, and my God.

Psa. 51:1. Have mercy upon me, O God, according to thy lovingkindness: according unto the multitude of thy tender mercies blot out my transgressions. 2. Wash me throughly from mine iniquity, and cleanse me from my sin. 3. For I acknowledge my transgressions: and my sin *is* ever before me. 4. Against thee, thee only, have I sinned, and done *this* evil in thy sight: that thou mightest be justified when thou speakest, *and* be clear when thou judgest. 5. Behold, I was shapen in iniquity; and in sin did my mother conceive me. 6. Behold, thou desirest truth in the inward parts: and in the hidden *part* thou shalt make me to know wisdom. 7. Purge me with hyssop, and I shall be clean: wash me, and I shall be whiter than snow. 8. Make me to hear joy and gladness; *that* the bones *which* thou hast broken may rejoice. 9. Hide thy face from my sins, and blot out all mine iniquities. 10. Create in me a clean heart, O God; and renew a right spirit within me. 11. Cast me not away from thy presence; and take not thy holy spirit from me. 12. Restore unto me the joy of thy salvation; and uphold me *with thy* free spirit. 13. *Then* will I teach transgressors thy ways; and sinners shall be converted unto thee. 14. Deliver me from bloodguiltiness, O God, thou God of my salvation: *and* my tongue shall sing aloud of thy righteousness. 15. O Lord, open thou my lips; and my mouth shall shew forth thy praise. 16. For thou desirest not sacrifice; else would I give *it:* thou delightest not in burnt offering. 17. The sacrifices of God *are* a broken spirit: a broken and a contrite heart, O God, thou wilt not despise.

Psa. 62:1. Truly my soul waiteth upon God: from him *cometh* my salvation.

Psa. 63:1. O God, thou *art* my God; early will I seek thee: my soul thirsteth for thee, my flesh longeth for thee in a dry and thirsty land, where no water is; 8. My soul followeth hard after thee: thy right hand upholdeth me.

Psa. 68:28. Strengthen, O God, that which thou hast wrought for us.

Psa. 69:3. Mine eyes fail while I wait for my God. 32. Your heart shall live that seek God.

Psa. 70:4. Let all those that seek thee rejoice and be glad in thee: and let such as love thy salvation say continually, Let God be magnified.

Psa. 81:10. I *am* the LORD thy God, which brought thee out of the land of Egypt: open thy mouth wide, and I will fill it.

Psa. 84:2. My soul longeth, yea, even fainteth for the courts of the LORD: my heart and my flesh crieth out for the living God.

Psa. 86:11. Teach me thy way, O LORD; I will walk in thy truth: unite my heart to fear thy name. 12. I will praise thee, O

Lord my God, with all my heart; and I will glorify thy name for evermore. 16. O turn unto me, and have mercy upon me; give thy strength unto thy servant, and save the son of thine handmaid. Psa. 9:1.

Psa. 94:19. In the multitude of my thoughts within me thy comforts delight my soul.

Psa. 105:4. Seek the LORD, and his strength: seek his face evermore.

Psa. 118:17. I shall not die, but live, and declare the works of the LORD.

Psa. 119:2. Blessed *are* they that keep his testimonies, *and that* seek him with the whole heart. 10. With my whole heart have I sought thee: O let me not wander from thy commandments. 20. My soul breaketh for the longing *that it hath* unto thy judgments at all times. [*v.* 19.] 40. Behold, I have longed after thy precepts: quicken me in thy righteousness. 77. Let thy tender mercies come unto me, that I may live: for thy law *is* my delight. 88. Quicken me after thy lovingkindness; so shall I keep the testimony of thy mouth. 116. Uphold me according unto thy word, that I may live: and let me not be ashamed of my hope. 117. Hold thou me up, and I shall be safe: and I will have respect unto thy statutes continually. 122. Be surety for thy servant for good: 133. Order my steps in thy word: and let not any iniquity have dominion over me. 149. Hear my voice according unto thy lovingkindness: O LORD, quicken me according to thy judgment. 156. Great *are* thy tender mercies, O LORD: quicken me according to thy judgments. *vs.* 107, 154, 159.

Psa. 123:1. Unto thee lift I up mine eyes, O thou that dwellest in the heavens. 2. Behold, as the eyes of servants *look* unto the hand of their masters, *and* as the eyes of a maiden unto the hand of her mistress; so our eyes *wait* upon the LORD our God, until that he have mercy upon us.

Psa. 130:5. I wait for the LORD, my soul doth wait, and in his word do I hope. 6. My soul *waiteth* for the Lord more than they that watch for the morning: *I say,* *more than* they that watch for the morning.

Psa. 143:5. I meditate on all thy works; I muse on the work of thy hands. 6. I stretch forth my hands unto thee: my soul *thirsteth* after thee, as a thirsty land.

Prov. 2:3. If thou criest after knowledge, *and* liftest up thy voice for understanding; 4 If thou seekest her as silver, and searchest for her as *for* hid treasures; 5. Then shalt thou understand the fear of the LORD, and find the knowledge of God.

Prov. 8:17. I love them that love me; and those that seek me early shall find me. 34. Blessed *is* the man that heareth me, watching daily at my gates, waiting at the posts of my doors.

Isa. 8:17. I will wait upon the LORD, that hideth his face from the house of Jacob, and I will look for him. 19. Should **not a people** seek unto their God?

Isa. 26:8. Yea, in the way of thy judgments, O LORD, have we waited for thee; the desire of *our* soul *is* to thy name, and to the remembrance of thee. 9. With my soul have I desired thee in the night; yea, with my spirit within me will I seek thee early:

Isa. 40:31. They that wait upon the LORD shall renew *their* strength; they shall mount up with wings as eagles;

Isa. 55:1. Ho, every one that thirsteth, come ye to the waters, and he that hath no money; come ye, buy, and eat; yea, come, buy wine and milk without money and without price. 2. Wherefore do ye spend money for *that which is* not bread? and your labor for *that which* satisfieth not? hearken diligently unto me, and eat ye *that which is* good, and let your soul delight itself in fatness. 6. Seek ye the LORD while he may be found, call ye upon him while he is near:

Jer. 29:13. Ye shall seek me, and find *me,* when ye shall search for me with all your heart. Deut. 4:29.

Lam. 3:25. The LORD *is* good unto them that wait for him, to the soul *that* seeketh him. 26. *It is* good that *a man* should both hope and quietly wait for the salvation of the LORD. 41. Let us lift up our heart with *our* hands unto God in the heavens.

Hos. 10:12. Sow to yourselves in righteousness, reap in mercy; break up your fallow ground: for *it is* time to seek the LORD, till he come and rain righteousness upon you.

Hab. 3:2. O LORD, revive thy work in the midst of the years, in the midst of the years make known; in wrath remember mercy.

Matt. 5:6. Blessed *are* they which do hunger and thirst after righteousness: for they shall be filled. Luke 6:21.

Luke 10:42. One thing is needful: and Mary hath chosen that good part, which shall not be taken away from her.

John 12:20. And there were certain Greeks . . . 21. The same came therefore to Philip, . . . saying, Sir, we would see Jesus.

Phil. 3:12. Not as though I had already attained, either were already perfect: but I follow after, if that I may apprehend that for which also I am apprehended of Christ Jesus. 13. Brethren, I count not myself to have apprehended: but *this* one thing *I do,* forgetting those things which are behind, and reaching forth unto those things which are before, 14. I press toward the mark for the prize of the high calling of God in Christ Jesus.

Heb. 11:6. He that cometh to God must believe that he is, and *that* he is a rewarder of them that diligently seek him.

See HUNGER, SPIRITUAL; THIRST, FIGURATIVE.

EVIL: See IMAGINATION; LUST.

DESPAIR. See DESPONDENCY.

DESPONDENCY. Num. 17:12. And the children of Israel spake unto Moses, saying, Behold, we die, we perish, we all perish.

13. Whosever cometh any thing near unto the tabernacle of the LORD shall die: shall we be consumed with dying?

Deut. 28:65. And among these nations shalt thou find no ease, neither shall the soul of thy foot have rest: but the LORD shall give thee there a trembling heart, and failing of eyes, and sorrow of mind: 66. And thy life shall hang in doubt before thee; and thou shalt fear day and night, and shalt have none assurance of thy life: 67. In the morning thou shalt say, Would God it were even! and at even thou shalt say, Would God it were morning! for the fear of thine heart wherewith thou shalt fear, and for the sight of thine eyes which thou shalt see.

Job 3:1. After this opened Job his mouth, and cursed his day. 2. And Job spake, and said, 3. Let the day perish wherein I was born, and the night *in which* it was said, There is a man child conceived. 4. Let that day be darkness; let not God regard it from above, neither let the light shine upon it. 5. Let darkness and the shadow of death stain it; let a cloud dwell upon it; let the blackness of the day terrify it. 6. *As for* that night, let darkness seize upon it; let it not be joined unto the days of the year, let it not come into the number of the months. 7. Lo, let that night be solitary; let no joyful voice come therein. 8. Let them curse it that curse the day, who are ready to raise up their mourning. 9. Let the stars of the twilight thereof be dark; let it look for light, but *have* none; neither let it see the dawning of the day: 10. Because it shut not up the doors of my *mother's* womb, nor hid sorrow from mine eyes. 11. Why died I not from the womb? *why* did I *not* give up the ghost when I came out of the belly? 12. Why did the knees prevent me? or why the breasts that I should suck? 13. For now should I have lain still and been quiet, I should have slept: then had I been at rest, 14. With kings and counsellors of the earth, which built desolate places for themselves; 15. Or with princes that had gold, who filled their houses with silver: 16. Or as an hidden untimely birth I had not been; as infants *which* never saw light. 17. There the wicked cease *from* troubling; and there the weary be at rest. 18. *There* the prisoners rest together; they hear not the voice of the oppressor. 19. The small and great are there; and the servant *is* free from his master. 20. Wherefore is light given to him that is in misery, and life unto the bitter *in* soul; 21. Which long for death, but it *cometh* not; and dig for it more than for hid treasures; 22. Which rejoice exceedingly, *and* are glad, when they can find the grave? 23. *Why is light given* to a man whose way is hid, and whom God hath hedged in? 24. For my sighing cometh before I eat, and my roarings are poured out like the waters. 25. For the thing which I greatly feared is come upon me, and that which I was afraid of is come unto me. 26. I was not in safety,

neither had I rest, neither was I quiet; yet trouble came.

Job 17:13. If I wait, the grave *is* mine house: I have made my bed in the darkness. 14. I have said to corruption, Thou *art* my father: to the worm, *Thou art* my mother, and my sister. 15. And where *is* now my hope? as for my hope, who shall see it? 16. They shall go down to the bars of the pit, when *our* rest together *is* in the dust.

Psa. 31:22. For I said in my haste, I am cut off from before thine eyes: nevertheless thou heardest the voice of my supplications when I cried unto thee.

Psa. 77:7. Will the Lord cast off for ever? and will he be favourable no more? 8. Is his mercy clean gone for ever? doth *his* promise fail for evermore? 9. Hath God forgotten to be gracious? hath he in anger shut up his tender mercies?

Prov. 13:12. Hope deferred maketh the heart sick: but *when* the desire cometh, *it is* a tree of life.

Isa. 2:19. And they shall go into the holes of the rocks, and into the caves of the earth, for fear of the LORD, and for the glory of his majesty, when he ariseth to shake terribly the earth.

Jer. 2:25. There is no hope: no; for I have loved strangers, and after them will I go.

Jer. 8:20. The harvest is past, the summer is ended, and we are not saved.

Jer. 18:12. And they said, There is no hope: but we will walk after our own devices, and we will every one do the imagination of his evil heart.

Lam. 3:1. I *am* the man *that* hath seen affliction by the rod of his wrath. 2. He hath led me, and brought *me into* darkness, but not *into* light. 3. Surely against me is he turned; he turneth his hand *against me* all the day. 4. My flesh and my skin hath he made old; he hath broken my bones. 5. He hath builded against me, and compassed *me* with gall and travail. 6. He hath set me in dark places, as *they that be* dead of old. 7. He hath hedged me about, that I cannot get out: he hath made my chain heavy. 8. Also when I cry and shout, he shutteth out my prayer. 9. He hath enclosed my ways with hewn stone, he hath made my paths crooked. 10. He *was* unto me *as* a bear lying in wait, *and as* a lion in secret places. 11. He hath turned aside my ways, and pulled me in pieces: he hath made me desolate. 12. He hath bent his bow, and set me as a mark for the arrow. 13. He hath caused the arrows of his quiver to enter into my reins. 14. I was a derision to all my people; *and* their song all the day. 15. He hath filled me with bitterness, he hath made me drunken with wormwood. 16. He hath also broken my teeth with gravel stones, he hath covered me with ashes. 17. And thou hast removed my soul far off from peace: I forgat prosperity. 18. And I said, My strength and my hope is perished from the LORD: 19. Remembering mine affliction and my misery, the wormwood and the gall. 20. My soul hath *them* still in remembrance, and is humbled in me. 21. This I recall to my mind, therefore have I hope.

Lam. 5:22. But thou hast utterly rejected us; thou art very wroth against us.

Hos. 10:8. The high places also of Aven, the sin of Israel, shall be destroyed: the thorn and the thistle shall come up on their altars; and they shall say to the mountains, Cover us; and to the hills, Fall on us.

Jonah 2:2. I cried by reason of mine affliction unto the LORD, and he heard me; out of the belly of hell cried I, *and* thou heardest my voice. 3. For thou hadst cast me into the deep, in the midst of the seas; and the floods compassed me about: all thy billows and thy waves passed over me. 4. Then I said, I am cast out of thy sight: yet I will look again toward thy holy temple.

Mic. 7:1. Woe is me! for I am as when they have gathered the summer fruits, as the grapegleanings of the vintage: *there is* no cluster to eat: my soul desireth the firstripe fruit. 2. The good *man* is perished out of the earth: and *there is* none upright among men: they all lie in wait for blood; they hunt every man his brother with a net. 3. That they may do evil with both hands earnestly, the prince asketh, and the judge *asketh* for a reward; and the great *man*, he uttereth his mischievous desire: so they wrap it up. 4. The best of them *is* as a brier: the most upright *is sharper* than a thorn hedge: the day of thy watchmen *and* thy visitation cometh; now shall be their perplexity. 5. Trust ye not in a friend, put ye not confidence in a guide: keep the doors of thy mouth from her that lieth in thy bosom. 6. For the son dishonoureth the father, the daughter riseth up against her mother, the daughter in law against her mother in law; a man's enemies *are* the men of his own house. 7. Therefore I will look unto the LORD; I will wait for the God of my salvation: my God will hear me.

Matt. 24:30. And then shall appear the sign of the Son of man in heaven: and then shall all the tribes of the earth mourn, and they shall see the Son of man coming in the clouds of heaven with power and great glory.

Luke 13:27. But he shall say, I tell you, I know you not whence ye are; depart from me, all *ye* workers of iniquity. 28. There shall be weeping and gnashing of teeth, when ye shall see Abraham, and Isaac, and Jacob, and all the prophets, in the kingdom of God, and you *yourselves* thrust out.

Luke 23:29. For, behold, the days are coming, in the which they shall say, Blessed *are* the barren, and the wombs that never bare, and the paps which never gave suck. 30. Then shall they begin to say to the mountains, Fall on us; and to the hills, Cover us.

Rev. 6:14. And the heaven departed as a scroll when it is rolled together: and every mountain and island were moved out of their places. 15. And the kings of the earth,

and the great men, and the rich men, and the chief captains, and the mighty men, and every bondman, and every free man, hid themselves in the dens and in the rocks of the mountains; 16. And said to the mountains and rocks, Fall on us, and hide us from the face of him that sitteth on the throne, and from the wrath of the Lamb: 17. For the great day of his wrath is come; and who shall be able to stand?

Rev. 9:5. And to them it was given that they should not kill them, but that they should be tormented five months: and their torment *was* as the torment of a scorpion, when he striketh a man. 6. And in those days shall men seek death, and shall not find it; and shall desire to die, and death shall flee from them.

See AFFLICTION; RESIGNATION; SORROW; SUFFERING.

INSTANCES OF: Cain, when God pronounced judgment upon him for the murder of Abel, Gen. 4:13,14. Hagar, when cast out of the household of Abraham on account of the jealousy of Sarah, Gen. 21:15, 16. Moses, when sent on his mission to the Israelites, Ex. 4:1,10,13; 6:12; at the Red Sea, Ex. 14:15; when the people lusted for flesh, Num. 11:15. The Israelites, on account of the cruel oppressions of the Egyptians, Ex. 6:9. Elijah, when he fled from Jezebel to the wilderness and sat under the juniper tree, and wished to die, 1 Kin. 19:4. Jonah, after he had preached to the Ninevites, Jonah 4:3,8. The mariners with Paul, Acts 27:20.

Job, see the above extracts from the Book of Job. Jeremiah, see the above extracts from the Lamentations of Jeremiah.

COMFORT IN: Isa. 35:3. Strengthen ye the weak hands, and confirm the feeble knees. 4. Say to them *that are* of a fearful heart, Be strong, fear not: behold, your God will come *with* vengeance, *even* God *with* a recompence; he will come and save you.

Luke 18:1. And he spake a parable unto them *to this end*, that men ought always to pray, and not to faint; 2. Saying, There was in a city a judge, which feared not God, neither regarded man: 3. And there was a widow in that city; and she came unto him, saying, Avenge me of mine adversary. 4. And he would not for a while: but afterward he said within himself, Though I fear not God, nor regard man; 5. Yet because this widow troubleth me, I will avenge her, lest by her continual coming she weary me. 6. And the Lord said, Hear what the unjust judge saith. 7. And shall not God avenge his own elect, which cry day and night unto him, though he bear long with them? 8. I tell you that he will avenge them speedily. Nevertheless, when the Son of man cometh, shall he find faith on the earth?

Heb. 12:12. Wherefore lift up the hands which hang down, and the feeble knees; 13. And make straight paths for your feet, lest that which is lame be turned out of the way; but let it rather be healed.

See AFFLICTION, CONSOLATION IN; RIGHTEOUS, PROMISES TO.

DESPOTISM. See GOVERNMENT, MONARCHICAL, TYRANNY IN.

DETECTIVES, Luke 20:20.

See SPIES.

DEUEL, called also REUEL. Captain of the tribe of Dan, Num. 1:14; 2:14; 7:42; 10:20.

DEVIL. See DEMON; SATAN.

DEVOTION, TO GOD. See RELIGION. For conspicuous instances of, let the student study ENOCH, NOAH, ABRAHAM, MOSES, DAVID'S later history, SOLOMON'S earlier life, JOSIAH, ASA, ISAIAH, ELIJAH, JEREMIAH, DANIEL, SHADRACH, MESHACH and ABED-NEGO.

TO JESUS. See PETER; JOHN; PAUL; MARY MAGDALENE.

For elaborated topics covering the subject, see LOVE OF MAN FOR GOD; CONSECRATION; ZEAL.

DEW. A merciful providence, Deut. 33: 13. Forms imperceptibly, 2 Sam. 17:12; in the night, Job 29:19. From the clouds, Prov. 3:20. Called the dew of heaven, Dan. 4:15. Absence of, 1 Kin. 17:1. Miraculous profusion and absence of, Judg. 6:36-40.

See METEOROLOGY.

FIGURATIVE: Psa. 110:3; Isa. 26:19; Hos. 6:4; 13:3; 14:5.

DIADEM. [R. V., mitre], Ezek. 21:26.

DIAL, a contrivance for indicating time by the sun's rays, 2 Kin. 20:11; Isa. 38:8.

DIAMOND, one of the jewels in the breastplate, Ex. 28:18; 39:11; Jer. 17:1; Ezek. 28:13.

DIANA, goddess of the Ephesians, Acts 19:24,27,28,35.

DIBLAIM, father of Hosea's wife, Hos. 1:3.

DIBLATH, an unknown place, Ezek. 6:14.

DIBON. 1. Called also DIBON-GAD and DIMON. A city on the northern banks of the Arnon, Num. 21:30. Israelites encamp at, Num. 33:45. Allotted to Gad and Reuben, Num. 32:3,34; Josh. 13:9,17. Taken by Moab, Isa. 15:2,9; Jer. 48:18,22.

2. A city in the tribe of Judah, Neh. 11: 25; probably identical with DIMONAH, Josh. 15:22.

DIBRI, father of Shelomith, Lev. 24:11.

DIDYMUS, surname of Thomas, John 11:16.

DIKLAH, son of Joktan, and name of a district inhabited by his descendants, Gen. 10:27.

DILEAN, a city of Judah, Josh. 15:38.

DILIGENCE. Jesus an example of, Mark 1:35; Luke 2:49.

Required by God in seeking him, 1 Chr. 22:19; Heb. 11:6; obeying him, Deut. 6:17; 11:13; hearkening to him, Isa. 55:2; striving after perfection, Phil. 3:13,14; cultivating Christian graces, 2 Pet. 1:5; keeping the soul, Deut. 4:9; keeping the heart, Prov. 4: 23; labors of love, Heb. 6:10-12; following

every good work, 1 Tim. 3:10; guarding against defilement, Heb. 12:15; seeking to be found spotless, 2 Pet. 3:14; making our calling sure, 2 Pet. 1:10; self-examination, Psa. 77:6; lawful business, Prov. 27:23; Eccl. 9:10; teaching religion, 2 Tim. 4:2; Jude 3; instructing children, Deut. 6:7; 11:19; discharging official duties, Deut. 19:18; saints should abound in, 2 Cor. 8:7.

Required in the service of God, John 9: 4; Gal. 6:9. Is not in vain, 1 Cor. 15:58. Preserves from evil, Ex. 15:26. Leads to assured hope, Heb. 6:11. God rewards, Deut. 11:14; Heb. 11:6.

In temporal matters leads to favor, Prov. 11:27; prosperity, Prov. 10:4; 13:4; honor, Prov. 12:24; 22:29.

FIGURATIVE: Prov. 6:6-8.

Exemplified: Ruth, Ruth 2:17. Hezekiah, 2 Chr. 31:21. Nehemiah and his helpers, Neh. 4:6. Psalmist, Psa. 119:60. Apostles, Acts 5:42. Apollos, Acts 18:25. Titus, 2 Cor. 8:22. Paul, 1 Thess. 2:9. Onesiphorus, 2 Tim. 1:17.—*Bible Text Book.*

See INDUSTRY; ZEAL; IDLENESS; SLOTHFULNESS.

DIMNAH, a Levitical city of Zebulun, Josh. 21:35.

DIMON. See DIBON, 1.

DIMONAH. See DIBON, 2.

DINAH. Daughter of Jacob and Leah, Gen. 30:21. Ravishment of, Gen. 34.

DINHABAH, a city of Edom, Gen. 36: 32; 1 Chr. 1:43.

DINNER, eaten at noon, Gen. 43:16.

See FEASTS.

DIONYSIUS, a convert of Paul, Acts 17:34.

DIOTREPHES, a false teacher, 3 John 9.

DIPLOMACY. 1 Cor. 9:20. And unto the Jews I became as a Jew, that I might gain the Jews; to them that are under the law, as under the law, that I might gain them that are under the law; 21. To them that are without law, as without law, (being not without law to God, but under the law to Christ,) that I might gain them that are without law. 22. To the weak became I as weak, that I might gain the weak: I am made all things to all *men*, that I might by all means save some. 23. And this I do for the gospel's sake, that I might be partaker thereof with *you.*

See TACT.

INSTANCES OF: Of Abimelech, Gen. 21: 22,23; 26:26-31. The Gibeonites, in securing a league with the Israelites through deception, Josh. 9:3-16. Of Jephthah, with the king of Moab, unsuccessful, Judg. 11:12-28. Of Abigail, 1 Sam. 25:23-31. Of Hiram, to secure the good will of David, 2 Sam. 5:11. Of Toi, to promote the friendship of David, 2 Sam. 8:10. David, in sending Hushai to Absalom's court, 2 Sam. 15:32-37; 16:15-19; 17:1-14. The wise woman of Abel, 2 Sam. 20:16-22. Absalom winning the people, 2 Sam. 15:2-6. Solomon, in his alliance with Hiram, 1 Kin. 5:1-12; 9:10-14,26,27; 10:11; **by**

intermarriage with other nations, 1 Kin. 1:1–
5. Ambassadors from Ben-hadad to Ahab,
1 Kin. 20:31–34. Jehoash purchases peace
from Hazael, 2 Kin. 12:18. Ahaz purchases
aid from the king of Assyria, 2 Kin. 16:7–9.
Rab-shakeh, in trying to induce Jerusalem
to capitulate by bombastic harangue, 2 Kin.
18:17–37; 19:1–13; Isa. 36:11–22. Sanballat, in
an attempt to prevent the rebuilding of Jerusalem by Nehemiah, Neh. 6.

The people of Tyre and Sidon, in securing
the favor of Herod, Acts 12:20–22. Paul, in arraying the Pharisees and Sadducees against
each other at his trial, Acts 23:6–10.

Ecclesiastical: Paul, in circumcising Timothy, Acts 16:3; in performing certain temple services to placate the Jews, Acts 21:20–
25, with Gal. 6:12.

Corrupt practices in: The officers of Nebuchadnezzar's court to secure the destruction of Daniel, Dan. 6:4–15.

DISBELIEF. See UNBELIEF.

DISCIPLE, a name given to the followers of any teacher. Of John the Baptist,
Matt. 9:14. Of Jesus, Matt. 10:1; 20:17; Acts 9:
26; 14:20; 21:4. The seventy sent forth, Luke
10:1. First called Christians at Antioch, Acts
11:26.

See APOSTLES; RIGHTEOUS.

DISCIPLESHIP, tests of, Matt. 10:32–
39; Luke 14:26,27,33; John 21:15–19.

See COMMANDMENTS.

DISCIPLINE, of armies, for disobedience of orders, Josh. 7:10–26; Judg. 21:5–12.
See ARMIES.

CHURCH DISCIPLINE: See CHURCH, DIS-
CIPLINE IN.

DISCONTENTMENT. See MURMUR-
ING. CONTENTMENT.

DISCOURAGEMENT. See DESPOND-
ENCY.

DISEASE. Sent from God, Lev. 14:34.
As judgments, Psa. 107:17; Isa. 3:17. IN-
STANCES OF: Upon the Egyptians, see
PLAGUES; upon Nabal, 1 Sam. 25:38; David's child, 2 Sam. 12:15; Gehazi, 2 Kin. 5:
27; Jeroboam, 2 Chr. 13:20; Jehoram, 2 Chr.
21:12–19; Uzziah, 2 Chr. 26:17–20.

Threatened as judgments, Lev. 26:16; Deut.
7:15; 28:22,27,28,35; 29:22.

Healing of, from God, Ex. 15:26; 23:25;
Deut. 7:15; 2 Chr. 16:12; Psa. 103:3; 107:20.
In answer to prayer: Of Hezekiah, 2 Kin.
20:1–11; Isa. 38:1–8; David, Psa. 21:4; 116:3–8.

Miraculous healing of, a sign to accompany the preaching of the word, Mark 16:18.
See MIRACLES.

Physicians employed for, 2 Chr. 16:12;
Jer. 8:22; Matt. 9:12; Mark 5:26; Luke 4:23.
Remedies used, Prov. 17:22; 20:30; Isa. 38:21;
Jer. 30:13; 46:11; poultices, 2 Kin. 20:7; oint-
ments, Isa. 1:6; Jer. 8:22; emulsions, Luke
10:34.

Of the sexual organs, Lev. 15; 22:4; Num.
5:2; Deut. 23:10. See CIRCUMCISION; MENSTRU-
ATION; GONORRHEA. Treatment of fractures,
Ezek. 30:21.

See AFFLICTION.

FIGURATIVE: Psa. 38:7; Isa. 1:6; Jer.
30:12.

Various kinds of: See ABORTION; AGUE;
ATROPHY; BLAIN; BLEMISH; BLINDNESS;
BOIL; CONGESTION; CONSUMPTION; DEAF-
NESS; DEMONS; DROPSY; DYSENTERY; DYS-
PEPSIA; EPILEPSY; FEVER; GONORRHEA;
GOUT; HEMORRHAGE; HEMORRHOIDS; IN-
SANITY; ITCH; LAMENESS; LEPROSY; MUR-
RAIN; PARALYSIS; PESTILENCE; SCAB: SCALL;
SCURVY; SPERMATORRHEA; STAMMERING; SUN-
STROKE; TUMOR; WORM.

Of the bowels. See BOWELS.

DISHAN, son of Seir, Gen. 36:21,30; 1
Chr. 1:38.

DISHON. 1. Son of Seir, Gen. 36:21,30;
1 Chr. 1:38.

2. Grandson of Seir, Gen. 36:25; 1 Chr.
1:41.

DISHONESTY. Lev. 6:2. If a soul sin,
and commit a trespass against the LORD,
and lie unto his neighbour in that which was
delivered him to keep, or in fellowship, or
in a thing taken away by violence, or hath
deceived his neighbour; 3. Or have found
that which was lost, and lieth concerning it,
and sweareth falsely; in any of all these
that a man doeth, sinning therein: 4. Then
it shall be, because he hath sinned, and is
guilty, that he shall restore that which he
took violently away, or the thing which he
hath deceitfully gotten, or that which was
delivered him to keep, or the lost thing
which he found, 5. Or all that about which
he hath sworn falsely; he shall even restore
it in the principal, and shall add the fifth
part more thereto, *and* give it unto him to
whom it appertaineth, in the day of his
trespass offering. 6. And he shall bring his
trespass offering unto the LORD, a ram
without blemish out of the flock, with
thy estimation, for a trespass offering,
unto the priest: 7. And the priest shall
make an atonement for him before the
LORD: and it shall be forgiven him for any
thing of all that he hath done in trespassing
therein.

Lev. 19:13. Thou shalt not defraud thy
neighbour, neither rob *him:* the wages of
him that is hired shall not abide with thee
all night until the morning.

35. Ye shall do no unrighteousness in
judgment, in meteyard, in weight, or in
measure. 36. Just balances, just weights,
a just ephah, and a just hin, shall ye have:
I *am* the LORD your God.

Deut. 25:13. Thou shalt not have in thy
bag divers weights, a great and a small. 14.
Thou shalt not have in thine house divers
measures, a great and a small. 15. *But* thou
shalt have a perfect and just weight, a perfect and just measure shalt thou have. 16.
For all that do such things, *and* all that do
unrighteously, *are* an abomination unto the
LORD thy God.

Job 24:2. *Some* remove the landmarks:
they violently take away flocks, and feed
thereof. 3. They drive away the ass of the

fatherless, they take the widow's ox for a pledge. 4. They turn the needy out of the way: the poor of the earth hide themselves together. 5. Behold, *as* wild asses in the desert, go they forth to their work; rising betimes for a prey: the wilderness *yieldeth* food for them *and* for *their* children. 6. They reap *every one* his corn in the field: and they gather the vintage of the wicked. 7. They cause the naked to lodge without clothing, that *they have* no covering in the cold. 8. They are wet with the showers of the mountains, and embrace the rock for want of a shelter. 9. They pluck the fatherless from the breast, and take a pledge of the poor. 10. They cause *him* to go naked without clothing, and they take away the sheaf *from* the hungry; 11. *Which* make oil within their walls, *and* tread *their* winepresses, and suffer thirst.

Psa. 37:21. The wicked borroweth, and payeth not again:

Psa. 50:18. When thou sawest a thief, then thou consentedst with him,

Psa. 62:10. Trust not in oppression, and become not vain in robbery:

Prov. 3:27. Withhold not good from them to whom it is due, when it is in the power of thine hand to do *it*. 28. Say not unto thy neighbour, Go, and come again, and to morrow I will give: when thou hast it by thee.

Prov. 11:1. A false balance *is* abomination to the Lord:

Prov. 20:10. Divers weights, *and* divers measures, both of them *are* alike abomination to the Lord. 14. *It is* naught, *it is* naught, saith the buyer: but when he is gone his way, then he boasteth. 17. Bread of deceit *is* sweet to a man; but afterwards his mouth shall be filled with gravel. 23. Divers weights *are* an abomination unto the Lord; and a false balance *is* not good.

Isa. 32:7. The instruments also of the churl *are* evil: he deviseth wicked devices to destroy the poor with lying words, even when the needy speaketh right.

Jer. 7:8. Behold, ye trust in lying words, that cannot profit. 9. Will ye steal, murder, and commit adultery, and swear falsely, and burn incense unto Baal, and walk after other gods whom ye know not; 10. And come and stand before me in this house, which is called by my name, and say, We are delivered to do all these abominations?

Jer. 9:4. Take ye heed every one of his neighbour, and trust ye not in any brother: for every brother will utterly supplant, and every neighbour will walk with slanders. 5. And they will deceive every one his neighbour, and will not speak the truth: they have taught their tongue to speak lies, *and* weary themselves to commit iniquity. 6. Thine habitation *is* in the midst of deceit; through deceit they refuse to know me, saith the Lord. 8. Their tongue *is as* an arrow shot out; it speaketh deceit · *one* speaketh peaceably

to his neighbour with his mouth, but in heart he layeth his weight.

Jer. 22:13. Woe unto him that buildeth his house by unrighteousness, and his chambers by wrong: *that* useth his neighbour's service without wages, and giveth him not for his work;

Ezek. 22:29. The people . . . used oppression, and exercised robbery, and have vexed the poor and needy; yea, they have oppressed the stranger wrongfully.

Hos. 4:1. The Lord hath a controversy with the inhabitants of the land, because *there is* no truth, nor mercy, nor knowledge of God in the land. 2. By swearing, and lying, and killing, and stealing, . . . they break out,

Hos. 12:7. The balances of deceit *are* in his hand: he loveth to oppress.

Amos 3:10. They know not to do right, saith the Lord, who store up violence and robbery in their palaces.

Amos 8:5. When will the new moon be gone, that we may sell corn? and the sabbath, that we may set forth wheat, making the ephah small, and the shekel great, and falsifying the balances by deceit?

Mic. 6:10. Are there yet the treasures of wickedness in the house of the wicked, and the scant measure *that is* abominable? 11. Shall I count *them* pure with the wicked balances, and with the bag of deceitful weights?

Nah. 3:1. Woe to the bloody city! it *is* all full of lies *and* robbery;

Zeph. 1:9. In the same day also will I punish all those . . . which fill their master's houses with violence and deceit.

Zech. 5:3. This *is* the curse that goeth forth over the face of the whole earth: for every one that stealeth shall be cut off *as* on this side according to it; and every one that sweareth shall be cut off *as* on that side according to it. 4. I will bring it forth, saith the Lord of hosts, and it shall enter into the house of the thief, . . . and it shall remain in the midst of his house, and shall consume it with the timber thereof and the stones thereof.

Luke 16:1. And he said also unto his disciples, There was a certain rich man, which had a steward; and the same was accused unto him that he had wasted his goods. 2. And he called him, and said unto him, How is it that I hear this of thee? give an account of thy stewardship; for thou mayest be no longer steward. 3. Then the steward said within himself, What shall I do? for my lord taketh away from me the stewardship: I cannot dig; to beg I am ashamed. 4. I am resolved what to do, that, when I am put out of the stewardship, they may receive me into their houses. 5. So he called every one of his lord's debtors *unto him*, and said unto the first, How much owest thou unto my lord? 6. And he said, An hundred measures of oil. And he said unto him, Take thy bill, and sit down quickly, and write fifty. 7. Then said he to another, And how much owest thou? And he said, An hundred measures of wheat. And he said unto him, Take thy bill, and write fourscore. 8. And the lord commended the unjust steward, because he had done wisely: for the children of this world are in their generation wiser than the children of light.

1 Thess. 4:6. That no *man* go beyond and defraud his brother in *any* matter: because that the Lord *is* the avenger of all such, as we also have forewarned you and testified.

Jas. 5:4. Behold, the hire of the labourers who have reaped down your fields, which is of you kept back by fraud, crieth: and the cries of them which have reaped are entered into the ears of the Lord of sabaoth.

INSTANCES OF: Abimelech's servants usurp a well of water, Gen. 21:25; 26:15–22. Jacob obtains his brother's birthright by unjust advantage, Gen. 25:29–33; steals his father's blessing, Gen. 27:6–29; Laban's flocks by skillful manipulation, Gen. 30:31–43. Rebekah's guile in Jacob's behalf, Gen. 27:6–17. Laban's treatment of Jacob, Gen. 29:21–30; 31:36–42. Rachel steals the household gods, Gen. 31:19. Simeon and Levi deceive the Shechemites, Gen. 34:15–31. Achan hides the wedge of gold and the Babylonish garment, Josh. 7:11–26. Micah steals eleven hundred pieces of silver, Judg. 17:2. Micah's priest steals his images, Judg. 18:14–21. Joab's guile in securing Absalom's return, 2 Sam. 14:2–20. Ahab usurps Naboth's vineyard,1 Kin. 21:2–16. Judas' hypocritical sympathy for the poor, John 12:6.

See DIPLOMACY; HYPOCRISY; INJUSTICE; TREASON.

DISOBEDIENCE TO GOD. DENUNCIATIONS AGAINST: Num. 14:11. And the LORD said unto Moses, How long will this people provoke me? and how long will it be ere they believe me, for all the signs which I have shewed among them? 12. I will smite them with the pestilence, and disinherit them, and will make of thee a greater nation and mightier than they. 22. Because all those men which have seen my glory, and my miracles, which I did in Egypt and in the wilderness, and have tempted me now these ten times, and have not hearkened to my voice; 23. Surely they shall not see the land which I sware unto their fathers, neither shall any of them that provoked me see it: 24. But my servant Caleb, because he had another spirit with him, and hath followed me fully, him will I bring into the land whereinto he went; and his seed shall possess it.

Num. 32:8. Thus did your fathers, when I sent them from Kadesh-barnea to see the land. 9. For when they went up unto the valley of Eshcol, and saw the land, they discouraged the heart of the children of Israel, that they should not go into the land which the LORD had given them. 10. And the LORD'S anger was kindled the same time, and he sware, saying, 11. Surely

none of the men that came up out of Egypt, from twenty years old and upward, shall see the land which I sware unto Abraham, unto Isaac, and unto Jacob; because they have not wholly followed me: 12. Save Caleb the son of Jephunneh the Kenezite, and Joshua the son of Nun: for they have wholly followed the LORD. 13. And the LORD'S anger was kindled against Israel, and he made them wander in the wilderness forty years, until all the generation, that had done evil in the sight of the LORD, was consumed.

Deut. 18:19. And it shall come to pass, *that* whosoever will not hearken unto my words which he shall speak in my name, I will require *it* of him.

Deut. 28:15. But it shall come to pass, if thou wilt not hearken unto the voice of the LORD thy God, to observe to do all his commandments and his statutes which I command thee this day; that all these curses shall come upon thee, and overtake thee: 16. Cursed *shalt* thou *be* in the city, and cursed *shalt* thou *be* in the field. 17. Cursed *shall be* thy basket and thy store. 18. Cursed *shall be* the fruit of thy body, and the fruit of thy land, the increase of thy kine, and the flocks of thy sheep. 19. Cursed *shalt* thou *be* when thou comest in, and cursed *shalt* thou *be* when thou goest out. 20. The LORD shall send upon thee cursing, vexation, and rebuke, in all that thou settest thine hand unto for to do, until thou be destroyed, and until thou perish quickly; because of the wickedness of thy doings, whereby thou hast forsaken me. 21. The LORD shall make the pestilence cleave unto thee, until he have consumed thee from off the land, whither thou goest to possess it. 22. The LORD shall smite thee with a consumption, and with a fever, and with an inflammation, and with an extreme burning, and with the sword, and with blasting, and with mildew; and they shall pursue thee until thou perish. 23. And thy heaven that *is* over thy head shall be brass, and the earth that *is* under thee *shall be* iron. 24. The LORD shall make the rain of thy land powder and dust: from heaven shall it come down upon thee, until thou be destroyed. 25. The LORD shall cause thee to be smitten before thine enemies: thou shalt go out one way against them, and flee seven ways before them; and shalt be removed into all the kingdoms of the earth. 26. And thy carcase shall be meat unto all fowls of the air, and unto the beasts of the earth, and no man shall fray *them* away. 27. The LORD will smite thee with the botch of Egypt, and with the emerods, and with the scab, and with the itch, whereof thou canst not be healed. 28. The LORD shall smite thee with madness, and blindness, and astonishment of heart: 29. And thou shalt grope at noonday, as the blind gropeth in darkness, and thou shall not prosper in thy ways: and thou shalt be only oppressed and spoiled evermore, and no man shall save *thee.* 30. Thou shalt betroth a wife, and another man shall lie with her: thou shalt build an house, and thou shalt not dwell therein: thou shalt plant a vineyard, and shalt not gather the grapes thereof. 31. Thine ox *shall be* slain before thine eyes, and thou shalt not eat thereof: thine ass *shall be* violently taken away from before thy face, and shall not be restored to thee: thy sheep *shall be* given unto thine enemies, and thou shalt have none to rescue *them.* 32. Thy sons and thy daughters *shall be* given unto another people, and thine eyes shall look, and fail *with longing* for them all the day long: and *there shall be* no might in thine hand. 33. The fruit of thy land, and all thy labours, shall a nation which thou knowest not eat up; and thou shalt be only oppressed and crushed alway: 34. So that thou shalt be mad for the sight of thine eyes which thou shalt see. 35. The LORD shall smite thee in the knees, and in the legs, with a sore botch that cannot be healed, from the sole of thy foot unto the top of thy head. 36. The LORD shall bring thee, and thy king which thou shalt set over thee, unto a nation which neither thou nor thy fathers have known; and there shalt thou serve other gods, wood and stone. 37. And thou shalt become an astonishment, a proverb, and a byword, among all nations whither the LORD shall lead thee. 38. Thou shalt carry much seed out into the field, and shalt gather *but* little in; for the locust shall consume it. 39. Thou shalt plant vineyards, and dress *them,* but shalt neither drink *of* the wine, nor gather *the grapes;* for the worms shall eat them. 40. Thou shalt have olive trees throughout all thy coasts, but thou shalt not anoint *thyself* with the oil; for thine olive shall cast *his fruit.* 41. Thou shalt beget sons and daughters, but thou shalt not enjoy them; for they shall go into captivity. 42. All thy trees and fruit of thy land shall the locust consume. 43. The stranger that *is* within thee shall get up above thee very high; and thou shalt come down very low. 44. He shall lend to thee, and thou shalt not lend to him: he shall be the head, and thou shalt be the tail. 45. Moreover all these curses shall come upon thee, and shall pursue thee, and overtake thee, till thou be destroyed; because thou hearkenedst not unto the voice of the LORD thy God, to keep his commandments and his statutes which he commanded thee: 46. And they shall be upon thee for a sign and for a wonder, and upon thy seed for ever. 47. Because thou servedst not the LORD thy God with joyfulness, and with gladness of heart, for the abundance of all *things;* 48. Therefore shalt thou serve thine enemies which the LORD shall send against thee, in hunger, and in thirst, and in nakedness, and in want of all *things:* and he shall put a yoke of iron upon thy neck,

until he have destroyed thee. 49. The LORD shall bring a nation against thee from far, from the end of the earth, *as swift* as the eagle flieth; a nation whose tongue thou shalt not understand; 50. A nation of fierce countenance, which shall not regard the person of the old, nor shew favour to the young: 51. And he shall eat the fruit of thy cattle, and the fruit of thy land, until thou be destroyed: which *also* shall not leave thee *either* corn, wine, or oil, *or* the increase of thy kine, or flocks of thy sheep, until he have destroyed thee. 52. And he shall besiege thee in all thy gates, until thy high and fenced walls come down, wherein thou trustedst, throughout all thy land: and he shall besiege thee in all thy gates throughout all thy land, which the LORD thy God hath given thee. 53. And thou shalt eat the fruit of thine own body, the flesh of thy sons and of thy daughters, which the LORD thy God hath given thee, in the siege, and in the straitness, wherewith thine enemies shall distress thee: 54. *So that* the man *that is* tender among you, and very delicate, his eye shall be evil toward his brother, and toward the wife of his bosom, and toward the remnant of his children which he shall leave: 55. So that he will not give to any of them of the flesh of his children whom he shall eat: because he hath nothing left him in the siege, and in the straitness, wherewith thine enemies shall distress thee in all thy gates. 56. The tender and delicate woman among you, which would not adventure to set the sole of her foot upon the ground for delicateness and tenderness, her eye shall be evil toward the husband of her bosom, and toward her son, and toward her daughter, 57. And toward her young one that cometh out from between her feet, and toward her children which she shall bear: for she shall eat them for want of all *things* secretly in the siege and straitness, wherewith thine enemy shall distress thee in thy gates. 58. If thou wilt not observe to do all the words of this law that are written in this book, that thou mayest fear this glorious and fearful name, THE LORD THY GOD; 59. Then the LORD will make thy plagues wonderful, and the plagues of thy seed, *even* great plagues, and of long continuance, and sore sicknesses, and of long continuance. 60. Moreover he will bring upon thee all the diseases of Egypt, which thou wast afraid of; and they shall cleave unto thee. 61. Also every sickness, and every plague, which *is* not written in the book of this law, them will the LORD bring upon thee, until thou be destroyed. 62. And ye shall be left few in number, whereas ye were as the stars of heaven for multitude; because thou wouldest not obey the voice of the LORD thy God. 63. And it shall come to pass, *that* as the LORD rejoiced over you to do you good, and to multiply you; so the LORD will rejoice over you to destroy you, and to bring you to nought; and ye shall be plucked from off the land whither thou goest to possess it. 64. And the LORD shall scatter thee among all people, from the one end of the earth even unto the other; and there thou shalt serve other gods, which neither thou nor thy fathers have known, *even* wood and stone. 65. And among these nations shalt thou find no ease, neither shall the sole of thy foot have rest: but the LORD shall give thee there a trembling heart, and failing of eyes, and sorrow of mind: 66. And thy life shall hang in doubt before thee; and thou shalt fear day and night, and shalt have none assurance of thy life: 67. In the morning thou shalt say, Would God it were even! and at even thou shalt say, Would God it were morning! for the fear of thine heart wherewith thou shalt fear, and for the sight of thine eyes which thou shalt see. 68. And the LORD shall bring thee into Egypt again with ships, by the way whereof I spake unto thee, Thou shalt see it no more again: and there ye shall be sold unto your enemies for bondmen and bondwomen, and no man shall buy *you*. Lev. 26:14–46.

PUNISHMENT OF: Of the Egyptians by plagues, see PLAGUES. See also SIN, PUNISHMENT OF.

INSTANCES OF: Of Adam and Eve, eating the forbidden fruit, Gen. 3:6–11. Of Lot, in refusing to go to the mountain, as commanded by the angels, Gen. 19:19,20. Of Lot's wife, in looking back upon Sodom, Gen. 19:26. Of Moses, in making excuses when commissioned to deliver Israel, Ex. 4:13,14; when he smote the rock, Num. 20: 11,23,24. Of Aaron, at the smiting of the rock by Moses, Num. 20:23,24. Of Pharaoh, in refusing to let the children of Israel go, Ex. 5:2; 7:13,22,23; 8:15,19,32; 9:12,34; 10:20, 27; 11:10; 14:8. Of the children of Israel, in gathering excessive quantities of manna, Ex. 16:19,20; in refusing to enter the promised land, Deut. 1:26, with Num. 14:1–10; Josh. 5:6; Psa. 106:24,25. Of Nadab and Abihu, in offering strange fire, Lev. 10:1,2. Of Balaam, in accompanying the messengers from Balak, Num. 22:22. Of Achan, in secreting the wedge of gold and the Babylonian garment, Josh. 7:15–26. Of Saul, in offering a sacrifice, 1 Sam. 13:13; in sparing Agag and the spoils of the Amalekites, 1 Sam. 15; 28: 18. Of David, in his adultery, and in the slaying of Uriah, 2 Sam. 12:9. Of Solomon, in building places for idolatrous worship, 1 Kin. 11:7–10. Of the prophet of Judah, in not keeping the commandment to deliver his message to Jeroboam without delay, 1 Kin. 13. Of a man of Israel, who refused to smite the prophet, 1 Kin. 20:35,36. Of Ahab, in suffering the king of Assyria to escape out of his hands, 1 Kin. 20:42. Of priests, in not performing their functions after the due order, 1 Chr. 15:13. Of the people of Judah, Jer. 43:7; in going to dwell in Egypt contrary to divine command, Jer. 44:12–14. Of Jonah, in refusing to deliver

the message to the Ninevites, Jonah 1. Of the blind men Jesus healed, and commanded not to publish their healing, Matt. 9:30,31. Of the leper whom Jesus healed, and commanded not to publish the fact, Mark 1:45. Of Paul, in going to Jerusalem contrary to repeated admonitions, Acts 21:4,10–14.

OF CHILDREN, see CHILDREN, COMMANDMENTS TO.

OF THE RIGHTEOUS, see COMMANDMENTS.

DISPERSION. Of the descendants of Noah, Gen. 10. After building the tower of Babel, Gen. 11:1–9; Deut. 32:8. Of the Jews, foretold, Jer. 16:15; 24:9; John 7:35 [*R. V.*].

DISPUTE, about property. See PROPERTY.

DISSEMBLING. INSTANCES OF: Joseph, Gen. 42:7–20; 43:26–34. David, 1 Sam. 21:13–15.

See DECEPTION; HYPOCRISY.

DISSENSION, in churches, 1 Cor. 1:10–13; 3:3,4; 11:18,19.

DISSIPATION, dangers of, Job 1:5.

See DRUNKENNESS.

DISTAFF, Prov. 31:19.

DITCH. FIGURATIVE, Prov. 23:27.

DIVINATION. See SORCERY.

DIVINITY OF CHRIST. See JESUS, DIVINITY OF.

DIVORCE. Ex. 21:7. And if a man sell his daughter to be a maidservant, she shall not go out as the menservants do. 8. If she please not her master, who hath betrothed her to himself, then shall he let her be redeemed: to sell her unto a strange nation he shall have no power, seeing he hath dealt deceitfully with her. 9. And if he have betrothed her unto his son, he shall deal with her after the manner of daughters. 10. If he take him another *wife;* her food, her raiment, and her duty of marriage, shall he not diminish. 11. And if he do not these three unto her, then shall she go out free without money.

Deut. 21:10. When thou goest forth to war against thine enemies, and the LORD thy God hath delivered them into thine hands, and thou hast taken them captive, 11. And seest among the captives a beautiful woman, and hast a desire unto her, that thou wouldest have her to thy wife; 12. Then thou shalt bring her home to thine house; and she shall shave her head, and pare her nails; 13. And she shall put the raiment of her captivity from off her, and shall remain in thine house, and bewail her father and her mother a full month: and after that thou shalt go in unto her, and be her husband, and she shall be thy wife. 14. And it shall be, if thou have no delight in her, then thou shalt let her go whither she will; but thou shalt not sell her at all for money, thou shalt not make merchandise of her, because thou hast humbled her.

Deut. 24:1. When a man hath taken a wife, and married her, and it come to pass that she find no favour in his eyes, because he hath found some uncleanness in her: then let him write her a bill of divorcement, and give *it* in her hand, and send her out of his house. 2. And when she is departed out of his house, she may go and be another man's *wife.* 3. And *if* the latter husband hate her, and write her a bill of divorcement, and giveth *it* in her hand, and sendeth her out of his house; or if the latter husband die, which took her *to be* his wife; 4. Her former husband, which sent her away, may not take her again to be his wife, after that she is defiled; for that *is* abomination before the LORD: and thou shalt not cause the land to sin, which the LORD thy God giveth thee *for* an inheritance.

Ezra 10:1. Now when Ezra had prayed, and when he had confessed, weeping and casting himself down before the house of God, there assembled unto him out of Israel a very great congregation of men and women and children: for the people wept very sore. 2. And Shechaniah the son of Jehiel, *one* of the sons of Elam, answered and said unto Ezra, We have trespassed against our God, and have taken strange wives of the people of the land: yet now there is hope in Israel concerning this thing. 3. Now therefore let us make a covenant with our God to put away all the wives, and such as are born of them, according to the counsel of my lord, and of those that tremble at the commandment of our God; and let it be done according to the law. 4. Arise; for *this* matter *belongeth* unto thee: we also *will be* with thee: be of good courage, and do *it.* 5. Then arose Ezra, and made the chief priests, the Levites, and all Israel, to swear that they should do according to this word. And they sware. 6. Then Ezra rose up from before the house of God, and went into the chamber of Johanan the son of Eliashib: and *when* he came thither, he did eat no bread, nor drink water: for he mourned because of the transgression of them that had been carried away. 7. And they made proclamation throughout Judah and Jerusalem unto all the children of the captivity, that they should gather themselves together unto Jerusalem; 8. And that whosoever would not come within three days, according to the counsel of the princes and the elders, all his substance should be forfeited, and himself separated from the congregation of those that had been carried away. 9. Then all the men of Judah and Benjamin gathered themselves together unto Jerusalem within three days. It *was* the ninth month, on the twentieth *day* of the month; and all the people sat in the street of the house of God, trembling because of *this* matter, and for the great rain. 10. And Ezra the priest stood up, and said unto them, Ye have transgressed, and have taken strange wives, to increase the trespass of Israel. 11. Now therefore make confession unto the LORD God of your fathers, and do his pleasure: and separate yourselves from the people of the land, and from the strange wives. 12. Then all

the congregation answered and said with a loud voice, As thou hast said, so must we do. 13. But the people *are* many, and *it is* a time of much rain, and we are not able to stand without, neither *is this* a work of one day or two: for we are many that have transgressed in this thing. 14. Let now our rulers of all the congregation stand, and let all them which have taken strange wives in our cities come at appointed times, and with them the elders of every city, and the judges thereof, until the fierce wrath of our God for this matter be turned from us. 15. Only Jonathan the son of Asahel and Jahaziah the son of Tikvah were employed about this *matter:* and Meshullam and Shabbethai the Levite helped them. 16. And the children of the captivity did so. And Ezra the priest, *with* certain chief of the fathers, after the house of their fathers, and all of them by *their* names, were separated, and sat down in the first day of the tenth month to examine the matter.

Neh. 13:23. In those days also saw I Jews *that* had married wives of Ashdod, of Ammon, *and* of Moab: 24. And their children spake half in the speech of Ashdod, and could not speak in the Jews' language, but according to the language of each people. 25. And I contended with them, and cursed them, and smote certain of them, and plucked off their hair, and made them swear by God, *saying,* Ye shall not give your daughters unto their sons, nor take their daughters unto your sons, or for yourselves. 26 Did not Solomon king of Israel sin by these things? yet among many nations was there no king like him, who was beloved of his God, and God made him king over all Israel: nevertheless even him did outlandish women cause to sin. 27. Shall we then hearken unto you to do all this great evil, to transgress against our God in marrying strange wives? 28. And *one* of the sons of Joiada, the son of Eliashib the high priest, *was* son in law to Sanballat the Horonite: therefore I chased him from me. 29. Remember them, O my God, because they have defiled the priesthood, and the covenant of the priesthood, and of the Levites. 30. Thus cleansed I them from all strangers, and appointed the wards of the priests and the Levites, every one in his business:

Jer. 3:1. They say, If a man put away his wife, and she go from him, and become another man's, shall he return unto her again? shall not that land be greatly polluted? but thou hast played the harlot with many lovers; yet return again to me, saith the LORD.

Mic. 2:9. The women of my people have ye cast out from their pleasant houses; from their children have ye taken away my glory for ever.

Mal. 2:14. Yet ye say, Wherefore? Because the LORD hath been witness between thee and the wife of thy youth, against whom thou hast dealt treacherously: yet *is* she thy companion, and the wife of thy covenant. 15. And did not he make one? Yet had he the residue of the spirit. And wherefore one? That he might seek a godly seed. Therefore take heed to your spirit, and let none deal treacherously against the wife of his youth. 16. For the LORD, the God of Israel, saith that he hateth putting away: for *one* covereth violence with his garment, saith the LORD of hosts: therefore take heed to your spirit, that ye deal not treacherously.

Matt. 5:31. It has been said, Whosoever shall put away his wife, let him give her a writing of divorcement: 32. But I say unto you, That whosoever shall put away his wife, saving for the cause of fornication, causeth her to commit adultery: and whosoever shall marry her that is divorced committeth adultery.

Matt. 19:3. The Pharisees also came unto him, tempting him, and saying unto him, Is it lawful for a man to put away his wife for every cause? 4. And he answered and said unto them, Have ye not read, that he which made *them* at the beginning made them male and female, 5. And said, For this cause shall a man leave father and mother, and shall cleave to his wife: and they twain shall be one flesh? 6. Wherefore they are no more twain, but one flesh. What therefore God hath joined together, let not man put asunder. 7. They say unto him, Why did Moses then command to give a writing of divorcement, and to put her away? 8. He saith unto them, Moses because of the hardness of your hearts suffered you to put away your wives: but from the beginning it was not so. 9. And I say unto you, Whosoever shall put away his wife, except *it be* for fornication, and shall marry another, committeth adultery: and whoso marrieth her which is put away doth commit adultery. 10. His disciples say unto him, If the case of the man be so with *his* wife, it is not good to marry. 11. But he said unto them, All *men* cannot receive this saying, save *they* to whom it is given. 12. For there are some eunuchs which were so born from *their* mother's womb: and there are some eunuchs, which were made eunuchs of men: and there be eunuchs, which have made themselves eunuchs for the kingdom of heaven's sake. He that is able to receive *it*, let him receive it. Mark 10:2.

Luke 16:18. Whosoever putteth away his wife, and marrieth another, committeth adultery: and whosoever marrieth her that is put away from *her* husband committeth adultery.

1 Cor. 7:10. And unto the married I command, *yet* not I, but the Lord, Let not the wife depart from *her* husband: 11. But and if she depart, let her remain unmarried, or be reconciled to *her* husband: and let not the husband put away *his* wife. 12. But to the rest speak I, not the Lord: If any brother hath a wife that believeth not, and she be

pleased to dwell with him, let him not put her away. 13. And the woman which hath an husband that believeth not, and if he be pleased to dwell with her, let her not leave him. 14. For the unbelieving husband is sanctified by the wife, and the unbelieving wife is sanctified by the husband: else were your children unclean; but now are they holy. 15. But if the unbelieving depart, let him depart. A brother or a sister is not under bondage in such *cases:* but God hath called us to peace. 16. For what knowest thou, O wife, whether thou shalt save *thy* husband? or how knowest thou, O man, whether thou shalt save *thy* wife? 17 But as God hath distributed to every man, as the Lord hath called every one, so let him walk. And so ordain I in all churches.

Disobedience of the wife to the husband, a sufficient cause for, in the Persian empire, Esth. 1:10–22.

See MARRIAGE.

FIGURATIVE: Isa. 50:1; 54:4; Jer. 3:8.

DOCTOR, a teacher, or master, Matt. 8: 19; Luke 2:46; 5:17; Acts 5:34; 1 Tim. 1:7.

See PHYSICIAN; DISEASE.

DOCTRINES. John 7:16. Jesus answered them, and said, My doctrine is not mine, but his that sent me. 17. If any man will do his will, he shall know of the doctrine [*R. V.*, teaching], whether it be of God, or *whether* I speak of myself.

Set forth by church councils, Acts 15:6–29.

FALSE: Matt. 5:19. Whosoever therefore shall break one of these least commandments, and shall teach men so, he shall be called the least in the kingdom of heaven:

Matt. 15:9. In vain they do worship me, teaching *for* doctrines the commandments of men. 13. Every plant, which my heavenly Father hath not planted, shall be rooted up.

Rom. 16:17. Now I beseech you, brethren, mark them which cause divisions and offences contrary to the doctrine which ye have learned; and avoid them. 18. For they that are such serve not our Lord Jesus Christ, but their own belly: and by good words and fair speeches deceive the hearts of the simple.

1 Cor. 3:11. For other foundation can no man lay than that is laid, which is Jesus Christ. 21. Therefore let no man glory in men. *vs.* 1–4.

1 Cor. 11:18. I hear that there be divisions among you; and I partly believe it. 19. For there must be also heresies among you, that they which are approved may be made manifest among you.

2 Cor. 2:17. We are not as many, which corrupt the word of God:

2 Cor. 11:3. I fear, lest by any means, as the serpent beguiled Eve through his subtilty, so your minds should be corrupted from the simplicity that is in Christ. 4. For if he that cometh preacheth another Jesus, whom we have not preached, or *if* ye receive another spirit, which ye have not received, or another gospel, which ye

have not accepted, ye might well bear with *him*.

Gal. 1:6. I marvel that ye are so soon removed from him that called you into the grace of Christ unto any other gospel: 7. Which is not another; but there be some that trouble you, and would pervert the gospel of Christ. 8. But though we, or an angel from heaven, preach any other gospel unto you than that which we have preached unto you, let him be accursed.

Eph. 4:14. Be no more children, tossed to and fro, and carried about with every wind of doctrine, by the sleight of men, *and* cunning craftiness, whereby they lie in wait to deceive;

Col. 2:4. This I say, lest any man should beguile you with enticing words. 8. Beware lest any man spoil you through philosophy and vain deceit, after the tradition of men, after the rudiments of the world, and not after Christ. 18. Let no man beguile you of your reward in a voluntary humility and worshipping of angels, intruding into those things which he hath not seen, vainly puffed up by his fleshly mind, 19. And not holding the Head, from which all the body by joints and bands having nourishment ministered, and knit together, increaseth with the increase of God. 20. Wherefore if ye be dead with Christ from the rudiments of the world, why, as though living in the world, are ye subject to ordinances, 21. (Touch not; taste not; handle not; 22. Which all are to perish with the using;) after the commandments and doctrines of men? 23. Which things have indeed a shew of wisdom in will worship, and humility, and neglecting of the body; not in any honour to the satisfying of the flesh.

1 Tim. 1:3. As I besought thee to abide still at Ephesus, when I went into Macedonia, that thou mightest charge some that they teach no other doctrine, 4. Neither give heed to fables and endless genealogies, which minister questions, rather than godly edifying which is in faith: *so do*. 6. From which some having swerved, have turned aside unto vain jangling; 7. Desiring to be teachers of the law; understanding neither what they say, nor whereof they affirm. 19. Holding faith and a good conscience; which some having put away concerning faith have made shipwreck:

1. Tim. 4:1. Now the Spirit speaketh expressly, that in the latter times some shall depart from the faith, giving heed to seducing spirits, and doctrines of devils; 2. Speaking lies in hypocrisy; having their conscience seared with a hot iron: 3. Forbidding to marry, *and commanding* to abstain from meats, 7. Refuse profane and old wives' fables, and exercise thyself *rather* unto godliness.

1 Tim. 6:3. If any man teach otherwise, and consent not to wholesome words, *even* the words of our Lord Jesus Christ, and to the doctrine which is according to godli-

ness; 4. He is proud, knowing nothing, but doting about questions and strifes of words, whereof cometh envy, strife, railings, evil surmisings, 5. Perverse disputings of men of corrupt minds, and destitute of the truth, supposing that ¹ gain is godliness: from such withdraw thyself. 20. O Timothy, keep that which is committed to thy trust, avoiding profane *and* vain babblings, and oppositions of science falsely so called: 21. Which some professing have erred concerning the faith. [¹ R. V. godliness is a way of gain]

2 Tim. 2:14. Of these things put *them* in remembrance, charging *them* before the Lord that they strive not about words to no profit, *but* to the subverting of the hearers. 16. Shun profane *and* vain babblings: for they will increase unto more ungodliness. 17. And their word will eat as doth a canker: of whom is Hymenæus and Philetus; 18. Who concerning the truth have erred, saying that the resurrection is past already; and overthrow the faith of some.

2 Tim. 3:6. Of this sort are they which creep into houses, and lead captive silly women laden with sins, led away with divers lusts, 7. Ever learning, and never able to come to the knowledge of the truth. 8. As Jannes and Jambres withstood Moses, so do these also resist the truth: men of corrupt minds, reprobate concerning the faith. 9. But they shall proceed no further: for their folly shall be manifest unto all *men*, as their's also was. 13. Evil men and seducers shall wax worse and worse, deceiving, and being deceived. 2 Tim. 4:3.

Tit. 1:10. For there are many unruly and vain talkers and deceivers, specially they of the circumcision: 11. Whose mouths must be stopped, who subvert whole houses, teaching things which they ought not, for filthy lucre's sake. 14. Not giving heed to Jewish fables, and commandments of men, that turn from the truth.

Tit. 3:10. A man that is an heretick after the first and second admonition reject; 11. Knowing that he that is such is subverted, and sinneth, being condemned of himself.

Heb. 13:9. Be not carried about with divers and strange doctrines. For *it is* a good thing that the heart be established with grace; not with meats, which have not profited them that have been occupied therein.

2 Pet. 2:1. There were false prophets also among the people, even as there shall be false teachers among you, who privily shall bring in ¹ damnable heresies, even denying the Lord that bought them, and bring upon themselves swift destruction. 2. Many shall follow their pernicious ways: by reason of whom the way of truth shall be evil spoken of. 3. Through covetousness shall they with feigned words make merchandise of you: whose judgment now of a long time lingereth not, and their damnation slumbereth not. 14. Beguiling unstable souls: an heart they have exercised with covetous

practices; cursed children: 15. Which have forsaken the right way, and are gone astray, following the way of Balaam *the son* of Bosor, who loved the wages of unrighteousness; 16. But was rebuked for his iniquity: 17. These are wells without water, clouds that are carried with a tempest; to whom the mist of darkness is reserved for ever. 18. When they speak great swelling *words* of vanity, they allure through the lusts of the flesh, *through much* wantonness, those that were clean escaped from them who live in error. 19. While they promise them liberty, they themselves are the servants of corruption: *vs.* 1–22.   [¹ R. V. **destructive**]

1 John 4:3. And every spirit that confesseth not ¹ that Jesus ¹ Christ is come in the flesh is not of God: and this is that *spirit* of antichrist, whereof ye have heard that it should come; and even now already is it in the world.   [¹ Omitted in R. V.]

2 John 7. Many deceivers are entered into the world, who confess not that Jesus Christ is come in the flesh. This is a deceiver and an antichrist. 9. Whosoever transgresseth, and abideth not in the doctrine of Christ, hath not God. 10. If there come any unto you, and bring not this doctrine, receive him not into *your* house, neither bid him God speed: 11. For he that biddeth him God speed is partaker of his evil deeds.

Jude 4. There are certain men crept in unawares, who were before of old ordained to this condemnation, ungodly men, turning the grace of our God into lasciviousness, and denying the only Lord God, and our Lord Jesus Christ. 11. Woe unto them! for they have gone in the way of Cain, and ran greedily after the error of Balaam for reward, and perished in the gainsaying of Core.

See MINISTERS, FALSE; SCHISM; TEACHERS, FALSE.

DODAI. See DODO.

DODANIM. Descendants of Noah, Gen. 10:4. Called RODANIM, 1 Chr. 1:7 [*R. V.*].

DODAVAH, a prophet, 2 Chr. 20:37.

DODO. 1. A descendant of Issachar, Judg. 10:1.

2. One of David's heroes, 2 Sam. 23:9; 1 Chr. 11:12. Called DODAI. 1 Chr. 27:4.

3. A Bethlehemite, 2 Sam. 23:24; 1 Chr. 11:26.

DOEG. An Edomite, present when Ahimelech helped David, 1 Sam. 21:7; 22:9,22; Psa. 52 [title]. Slew eighty-five priests, 1 Sam. 22:18,19.

DOER. OF THE WORD: Matt. 7:21. Not every one that saith unto me, Lord, Lord, shall enter into the kingdom of heaven; but he that doeth the will of my Father which is in heaven.

Matt. 12:50. For whosoever shall do the will of my Father which is in heaven, the same is my brother, and sister, and mother.

Luke 11:28. But he said, Yea rather, blessed *are* they that hear the word of God, and keep it.

Rom. 2:13. (For not the hearers of the law *are* just before God, but the doers of the law shall be justified. 14. For when the Gentiles, which have not the law, do by nature the things contained in the law, these, having not the law, are a law unto themselves: 15. Which shew the work of the law written in their hearts, their conscience also bearing witness, and *their* thoughts the mean while accusing or else excusing one another;)

2 Cor. 8:11. Now therefore perform the doing *of it;* that as *there was* a readiness to will, so *there may be* a performance also out of that which ye have.

Jas. 1:22. But be ye doers of the word, and not hearers only, deceiving your own selves. 23. For if any be a hearer of the word, and not a doer, he is like unto a man beholding his natural face in a glass. 24. For he beholdeth himself, and goeth his way, and straightway forgetteth what manner of man he was. 25. But whoso looketh into the perfect law of liberty, and continueth *therein,* he being not a forgetful hearer, but a doer of the work, this man shall be blessed in his deed. 26. If any man among you seem to be religious, and bridleth not his tongue, but deceiveth his own heart, this man's religion *is* vain. 27. Pure religion and undefiled before God and the Father is this, To visit the fatherless and widows in their affliction, *and* to keep himself unspotted from the world.

Jas. 4:11. If thou judge the law, thou art not a doer of the law, but a judge.

See HEARERS.

DOG. Price of, not to be brought into the sanctuary, Deut. 23:18. Shepherd dogs, Job 30:1. Habits of: Licking blood, 1 Kin. 21:19; 22:38; licking sores, Luke 16:21; returns to his vomit, Prov. 26:11; 2 Pet. 2:22; lapping of, Judg. 7:5. Dumb and sleeping, Isa. 56:10,11.

Greyhound, Prov. 30:31. Epithet of contempt, 1 Sam. 17:43; 24:14; 2 Sam. 3:8; 9:8; 16:9; 2 Kin. 8:13; Isa. 56:10,11; Matt. 15:26.

FIGURATIVE: Phil. 3:2; Rev. 22:15.

DOGMATISM. See COMMANDMENTS, OF MEN.

DOMICILE. RIGHTS OF: Deut. 24:10. When thou dost lend thy brother any thing, thou shalt not go into his house to fetch his pledge. 11. Thou shalt stand abroad, and the man to whom thou dost lend shall bring out the pledge abroad unto thee.

DOMINION. OF MAN: See MAN, DOMINION OF.

DONATIONS. See LIBERALITY.

DOOR. Posts of, sprinkled with the blood of the paschal lamb, Ex. 12:22; the law to be written on, Deut. 11:20. Hinges for, Prov. 26:14; made of gold, 1 Kin. 7:50. Doors of the temple made of two leaves, cherubim and flowers carved upon, covered with gold, 1 Kin. 6:31–35.

FIGURATIVE: Door of hope, Hos. 2:15; of opportunity, 1 Cor. 16:9; Rev. 3:8; closed, Matt. 25:10; Luke 13:25; Rev. 3:7.

DOORKEEPERS. Of the temple, 2 Kin. 25:18; of palaces, John 18:17.

DOPHKAH, camping place of the Israelites, Num. 33:12.

DOR. A town and district of Palestine, Josh. 11:2. Conquered by Joshua, Josh. 12: 23; 1 Kin. 4:11. Allotted to Manasseh, although situated in the territory of Asher, Josh. 17:11; Judg. 1:27.

DORCAS, called also TABITHA. A pious woman of Joppa, Acts 9:36-42.

DOTHAN. A district and town in Palestine, Gen. 37:17. Syrian army made blind at, 2 Kin. 6:13-19.

DOUBTING. Job 4:3. Behold, thou hast instructed many, and thou hast strengthened the weak hands. 4. Thy words have upholden him that was falling, and thou hast strengthened the feeble knees. 5. But now it is come upon thee, and thou faintest; it toucheth thee, and thou art troubled. 6. *Is* not *this* thy fear, thy confidence, thy hope, and the uprightness of thy ways?

Job 9:16. If I had called, and he had answered me; *yet* would I not believe that he had hearkened unto my voice. 17. For he breaketh me with a tempest, and multiplieth my wounds without cause. 18. He will not suffer me to take my breath, but filleth me with bitterness. 19. If *I speak* of strength, lo, *he is* strong: and if of judgment, who shall set me a time *to plead?* 20. If I justify myself, mine own mouth shall condemn me: *if I say,* I *am* perfect, it shall also prove me perverse. 21. *Though* I *were* perfect, *yet* would I not know my soul: I would despise my life. 22. This *is* one *thing,* therefore I said *it,* He destroyeth the perfect and the wicked. 23. If the scourge slay suddenly, he will laugh at the trial of the innocent.

Job 30:20. I cry unto thee, and thou dost not hear me: I stand up, and thou regardest me *not.* 21. Thou art become cruel to me: with thy strong hand thou opposest thyself against me. Job 3; 16; 17; 23:15-17.

Psa. 22:2. O my God, I cry in the daytime, but thou hearest not; and in the night season, and am not silent.

Psa. 31:22. I said in my haste, I am cut off from before thine eyes:

Psa. 42:5. Why art thou cast down, O my soul? and *why* art thou disquieted in me? hope thou in God: for I shall yet praise him *for* the help of his countenance. 6. O my God, my soul is cast down within me:

Psa. 49:5. Wherefore should I fear in the days of evil, *when* the iniquity of my heels shall compass me about?

Psa. 73:13. Verily I have cleansed my heart *in* vain, and washed my hands in innocency. 14. For all the day long have I been plagued, and chastened every morning. 15. If I say, I will speak thus; behold, I should offend *against* the generation of thy children. 16. When I thought to know this, it *was* too painful for me; 17. Until I went into the sanctuary of God;

Psa. 77:3. I remembered God, and was troubled: I complained, and my spirit was overwhelmed. 7. Will the Lord cast off for ever? and will he be favourable no more? 8. Is his mercy clean gone for ever? doth *his* promise fail for evermore? 9. Hath God forgotten to be gracious? hath he in anger shut up his tender mercies?

Prov. 24:10. *If* thou faint in the day of adversity, thy strength *is* small.

Isa. 40:27. Why sayest thou, O Jacob, and speakest, O Israel, My way is hid from the LORD, and my judgment is passed over from my God? 28. Hast thou not known? hast thou not heard, *that* the everlasting God, the LORD, the Creator of the ends of the earth, fainteth not, neither is weary? *there is* no searching of his understanding. Isa. 50:2.

Isa. 49:14. Zion said, The LORD hath forsaken me, and my Lord hath forgotten me. 15. Can a woman forget her sucking child, that she should not have compassion on the son of her womb? yea, they may forget, yet will I not forget thee.

Jer. 8:18. *When* I would comfort myself against sorrow, my heart *is* faint in me.

Jer. 15:18. Why is my pain perpetual, and my wound incurable, *which* refuseth to be healed? wilt thou be altogether unto me as a liar, *and as* waters *that* fail?

Jer. 45:3. Woe is me now! for the LORD hath added grief to my sorrow; I fainted in my sighing, and I find no rest.

Lam. 3:8. When I cry and shout, he shutteth out my prayer. 17. Thou hast removed my soul far off from peace: I forgat prosperity. 18. And I said, My strength and my hope is perished from the LORD:

Lam. 5:20. Wherefore dost thou forget us for ever, *and* forsake us so long time? Lam. chapters 1-5.

Hos. 10:3. We have no king, because we feared not the LORD; what then should a king do to us?

Matt. 8:26. And he said unto them, Why are ye fearful, O ye of little faith? Mark 4:40; Luke 8:25.

Matt. 14:31. Jesus . . . said unto him, O thou of little faith, wherefore didst thou doubt?

Matt. 17:17. Then Jesus answered and said, O faithless and perverse generation, how long shall I be with you? how long shall I suffer you? Mark 9:19; Luke 9:40.

Mark 4:38. They awake him, and say unto him, Master, carest thou not that we perish?

1 Pet. 1:6. Wherein ye greatly rejoice, though now for a season, if need be, ye are in heaviness through manifold temptations:

EXEMPLIFIED: Gen. 12:12. Therefore it shall come to pass, when the Egyptians shall see thee, that they shall say, This *is* his wife: and they will kill me, but they will save thee alive. 13. Say, I pray thee, thou *art* my sister: that it may be well with me for thy sake; and my soul shall live because of thee. Gen. 20:2, 11; 26:7.

Gen. 15:8. And he said, Lord GOD, whereby shall I know that I shall inherit it?

Gen. 18:12. Therefore Sarah laughed within herself, saying, After I am waxed old shall I have pleasure, my lord being old also? 13. And the LORD said unto Abraham, Wherefore did Sarah laugh, saying, Shall I of a surety bear a child, which am old? 14. Is any thing too hard for the LORD? At the time appointed I will return unto thee, according to the time of life, and Sarah shall have a son.

Gen. 19:30. And Lot went up out of Zoar, and dwelt in the mountain, and his two daughters with him; for he feared to dwell in Zoar: and he dwelt in a cave, he and his two daughters.

Ex. 3:11. And Moses said unto God, Who am I, that I should go unto Pharaoh, and that I should bring forth the children of Israel out of Egypt?

Ex. 4:1. And Moses answered and said, But, behold, they will not believe me, nor hearken unto my voice: for they will say, The LORD hath not appeared unto thee. 10. And Moses said unto the LORD, O my Lord, I am not eloquent, neither heretofore, nor since thou hast spoken unto thy servant: but I am slow of speech, and of a slow tongue. 13. And he said, O my Lord, send, I pray thee, by the hand of him whom thou wilt send.

Ex. 5:22. And Moses returned unto the LORD, and said, Lord, wherefore hast thou so evil entreated this people? why is it that thou hast sent me? 23. For since I came to Pharaoh to speak in thy name, he hath done evil to this people; neither hast thou delivered thy people at all.

Ex. 6:12. And Moses spake before the LORD, saying, Behold, the children of Israel have not hearkened unto me; how then shall Pharaoh hear me, who am of uncircumcised lips?

Ex. 14:10. And when Pharaoh drew nigh, the children of Israel lifted up their eyes, and, behold, the Egyptians marched after them; and they were sore afraid: and the children of Israel cried out unto the LORD. 11. And they said unto Moses, Because there were no graves in Egypt, hast thou taken us away to die in the wilderness? wherefore hast thou dealt thus with us, to carry us forth out of Egypt? 12. Is not this the word that we did tell thee in Egypt, saying, Let us alone, that we may serve the Egyptians? For it had been better for us to serve the Egyptians, than that we should die in the wilderness. 15. And the LORD said unto Moses, Wherefore criest thou unto me? speak unto the children of Israel, that they go forward:

Num. 11:21. And Moses said, The people, among whom I am, are six hundred thousand footmen: and thou hast said, I will give them flesh, that they may eat a whole month. 22. Shall the flocks and the herds be slain for them, to suffice them? or shall all the fish of the sea be gathered together for them, to suffice them?

Judg. 6:13. And Gideon said unto him, Oh my Lord, if the LORD be with us, why then is all this befallen us? and where be all his miracles which our fathers told us of, saying, Did not the LORD bring us up from Egypt? but now the LORD hath forsaken us, and delivered us into the hands of the Midianites. 15. And he said unto him, Oh my Lord, wherewith shall I save Israel? behold, my family is poor in Manasseh, and I am the least in my father's house.

1 Sam. 16:1. And the LORD said unto Samuel, How long wilt thou mourn for Saul, seeing I have rejected him from reigning over Israel? fill thine horn with oil, and go, I will send thee to Jesse the Beth-lehemite: for I have provided me a king among his sons. 2. And Samuel said, How can I go? if Saul hear it, he will kill me. And the LORD said, Take an heifer with thee, and say, I am come to sacrifice to the LORD.

1 Sam. 17:11. When Saul and all Israel heard those words of the Philistine, they were dismayed, and greatly afraid. 24. And all the men of Israel, when they saw the man, fled from him, and were sore afraid.

1 Sam. 22:3. And David went thence to Mizpeh of Moab: and he said unto the king of Moab, Let my father and my mother, I pray thee, come forth, and be with you, till I know what God will do for me. 4. And he brought them before the king of Moab: and they dwelt with him all the while that David was in the hold.

1 Kin. 18:7. And as Obadiah was in the way, behold, Elijah met him: and he knew him, and fell on his face, and said, Art thou that my lord Elijah? 8. And he answered him, I am: go, tell thy lord, Behold, Elijah is here. 9. And he said, What have I sinned, that thou wouldest deliver thy servant into the hand of Ahab, to slay me? 10. As the LORD thy God liveth, there is no nation or kingdom, whither my lord hath not sent to seek thee: and when they said, He is not there; he took an oath of the kingdom and nation, that they found thee not. 11. And now thou sayest, Go, tell thy lord, Behold, Elijah is here. 12. And it shall come to pass, as soon as I am gone from thee, that the Spirit of the LORD shall carry thee whither I know not; and so when I come and tell Ahab, and he cannot find thee, he shall slay me: but I thy servant fear the LORD from my youth. 13. Was it not told my lord what I did when Jezebel slew the prophets of the LORD, how I hid an hundred men of the LORD's prophets by fifty in a cave, and fed them with bread and water? 14. And now thou sayest, Go, tell thy lord, Behold, Elijah is here: and he shall slay me.

1 Kin. 19:13. And it was so, when Elijah heard it, that he wrapped his face in his mantle, and went out, and stood in the entering in of the cave. And, behold, there came a voice unto him, and said, What doest thou here, Elijah? 14. And he said, I have been very jealous for the LORD God of hosts: because the children of Israel have forsaken

thy covenant, thrown down thine altars, and slain thy prophets with the sword; and I, *even* I only, am left; and they seek my life, to take it away. 15. And the LORD said unto him. Go, return on thy way to the wilderness of Damascus: and when thou comest, anoint Hazael *to be* king over Syria: 16. And Jehu the son of Nimshi shalt thou anoint *to be* king over Israel: and Elisha the son of Shaphat of Abel-meholah shalt thou anoint *to be* prophet in thy room. 17. And it shall come to pass, *that* him that escapeth the sword of Hazael shall Jehu slay: and him that escapeth from the sword of Jehu shall Elisha slay. 18. Yet I have left *me* seven thousand in Israel, all the knees which have not bowed unto Baal, and every mouth which hath not kissed him.

2 Kin. 13:18. And he said, Take the arrows. And he took *them*. And he said unto the king of Israel, Smite upon the ground. And he smote thrice, and stayed. 19. And the man of God was wroth with him, and said, Thou shouldest have smitten five or six times; then hadst thou smitten Syria till thou hadst consumed *it:* whereas now thou shalt smite Syria *but* thrice.

Jer. 1:6. Then said I, Ah, Lord GOD! behold, I cannot speak: for I *am* a child.

Jer. 32:24. Behold the mounts, they are come unto the city to take it; and the city is given into the hand of the Chaldeans, that fight against it, because of the sword, and of the famine, and of the pestilence: and what thou hast spoken is come to pass; and, behold, thou seest *it*. 25. And thou hast said unto me, O Lord GOD, Buy thee the field for money, and take witnesses; for the city is given into the hand of the Chaldeans. Lam. chapters 1–5.

Matt. 8:23. And when he was entered into a ship, his disciples followed him. 24. And, behold, there arose a great tempest in the sea, insomuch that the ship was covered with the waves: but he was asleep. 25. And his disciples came to *him*, and awoke him, saying, Lord, save us: we perish. 26. And he saith unto them, Why are ye fearful, O ye of little faith? Then he arose, and rebuked the winds and the sea; and there was a great calm. 27. But the men marvelled, saying, What manner of man is this, that even the winds and the sea obey him!

Matt. 11:2. Now when John had heard in the prison the works of Christ, he sent two of his disciples, 3. And said unto him, Art thou he that should come, or do we look for another?

Matt. 14:29. And he said, Come. And when Peter was come down out of the ship, he walked on the water, to go to Jesus. 30. But when he saw the wind boisterous, he was afraid: and beginning to sink, he cried, saying, Lord, save me. 31. And immediately Jesus stretched forth *his* hand, and caught him, and said unto him, O thou of little faith, wherefore didst thou doubt?

Matt. 17:14. There came to him a *certain*

man, kneeling down to him, and saying, 15. Lord, have mercy on my son: for he is lunatick, and sore vexed: for ofttimes he falleth into the fire, and oft into the water. 16. And I brought him to thy disciples, and they could not cure him. 17. Then Jesus answered and said, O faithless and perverse generation, how long shall I be with you? how long shall I suffer you? bring him hither to me. 18. And Jesus rebuked the devil; and he departed out of him: and the child was cured from that very hour. 19. Then came the disciples to Jesus apart, and said, Why could not we cast him out? 20. And Jesus said unto them, Because of your unbelief: for verily I say unto you, If ye have faith as a grain of mustard seed, ye shall say unto this mountain, Remove hence to yonder place; and it shall remove; and nothing shall be impossible unto you. [21. Howbeit this kind goeth not out but by prayer and fasting. Mark 9:14–29.   [¹ Omitted in R. V.]

Matt. 28:17. And when they saw him, they worshipped him: but some doubted.

Mark 16:10. *And* she went and told them that had been with him, as they mourned and wept. 11. And they, when they had heard that he was alive, and had been seen of her, believed not.

John 14:8. Philip saith unto him, Lord, shew us the Father, and it sufficeth us. 9. Jesus saith unto him, Have I been so long time with you, and yet hast thou not known me, Philip? he that hath seen me hath seen the Father; and how sayest thou *then*,Shew us the Father? 10. Believest thou not that I am in the Father, and the Father in me? the words that I speak unto you I speak not of myself: but the Father that dwelleth in me, he doeth the works. 11. Believe me that I *am* in the Father, and the Father in me: or else believe me for the very works' sake.

Acts 9:13. Then Ananias answered, Lord, I have heard by many of this man, how much evil he hath done to thy saints at Jerusalem: 14. And here he hath authority from the chief priests to bind all that call on thy name.

See COWARDICE; MURMURING.

DOUGH. First of, offered to God, Num. 15:19–21; Neh. 10:37. Kneaded, Jer. 7:18; Hos. 7:4. Part of, for priest, Ezek. 44:30.

See BREAD; OVEN.

DOVE, TURTLE. Sent out from the ark by Noah, Gen. 8:8–11. Mourning of, Isa. 38:14; 59:11; Nah. 2:7. Domesticated, Isa. 60:8. Nests of, Jer. 48:28. Harmlessness of, typical of Christ's gentleness. Matt. 10:16. Sacrificial uses of, Gen. 15:9. Prescribed for purification: Of women, Lev. 12:6,8; Luke 2:24; of Nazarites, Num. 6:10; of lepers, Lev. 14:22. Burnt offering of, Lev. 1:14–17. Trespass offering of, for the impecunious, Lev. 5:7–10; 12:8. Sin offering, for those who touched any dead body, Num. 6:10. Market for, in the temple, Matt. 21:12; John 2:14.

SYMBOLICAL: Of the Holy Spirit, Matt. 3:16; Luke 3:22; John 1:32.

See PIGEON.

DOWRY. Ex. 22:16. And if a man entice a maid that is not betrothed, and lie with her, he shall surely endow her to be his wife. 17. If her father utterly refuse to give her unto him, he shall pay money according to the dowry of virgins.

Ruth 4:3. And he said unto the kinsman, Naomi, that is come again out of the country of Moab, selleth a parcel of land, which *was* our brother Elimelech's: 4. And I thought to advertise thee, saying, Buy *it* before the inhabitants, and before the elders of my people. If thou wilt redeem *it*, redeem *it:* but if thou will not redeem *it, then* tell me, that I may know: for *there is* none to redeem *it* beside thee; and I *am* after thee. And he said, I will redeem *it.* 5. Then said Boaz, What day thou buyest the field of the hand of Naomi, thou must buy *it* also of Ruth the Moabitess, the wife of the dead, to raise up the name of the dead upon his inheritance. 6. And the kinsman said, I cannot redeem *it* for myself, lest I mar mine own inheritance: redeem thou my right to thyself; for I cannot redeem *it.* 7. Now this *was the manner* in former time in Israel concerning redeeming and concerning changing, for to confirm all things; a man plucked off his shoe, and gave *it* to his neighbour: and this *was* a testimony in Israel. 8. Therefore the kinsman said unto Boaz, Buy *it* for thee. So he drew off his shoe. 9. And Boaz said unto the elders, and *unto* all the people, Ye *are* witnesses this day, that I have bought all that *was* Elimelech's, and all that *was* Chilion's and Mahlon's, of the hand of Naomi.

See WOMEN.

DOXOLOGY. See PRAISE.

DRAGON. Any terrible creature, as a venomous serpent, Deut. 32:33; Psa. 91:13; a sea serpent, Psa. 74:13; 148:7; Isa. 27:1; a jackal, Isa. 13:22; 34:13; 35:7; 43:20; Jer. 9:11; 10:22; 14:6; 49:33; 51:37; Mic. 1:8; Mal. 1:3.

A term applied to Pharaoh, Isa. 51:9; to Satan, Rev. 20:2.

Symbolical, Ezek. 29:3; 32:2; Rev. 12; 13; 16:13.

DRAM. Called also DRACHM. A Persian coin of differently estimated value, 1 Chr. 29:7; Ezra 2:69; 8:27; Neh. 7:70–72.

DRAMA. See PANTOMIME.

DRAWING, of pictures on tile, Ezek. 4:1.

DREAM. Evanescent, Job 20:8. Vanity of, Eccl. 5:3,7.

Revelations by, Num. 12:6; Job 33:15–17; Jer. 23:28; Joel 2:28; Acts 2:17. The dreams of the butler and baker, Gen. 40:8–23; Pharaoh, Gen. 41:1–36.

Interpreted by Joseph, Gen. 40:12,13,18, 19; 41:25–32; Daniel, Dan. 2:16–23,28–30; 4. Delusive, Isa. 29:7,8.

False prophets pretended to receive revelations through, Deut. 13:1–5; Jer. 23:25–32; 27:9; 29:8; Zech. 10:2.

See VISION.

INSTANCES OF: Of Abimelech, concerning Sarah, Gen. 20:3. Of Jacob, concerning the ladder, Gen. 28:12; the ring-straked cattle, Gen. 31:10–13; concerning his going down into Egypt, Gen. 46:2. Of Laban, concerning Jacob, Gen. 31:24. Of Joseph, concerning the sheaves, Gen. 37:5–10. Of the Midianite, concerning the cake of barley, Judg. 7:13. Of Solomon, concerning his choice of wisdom, 1 Kin. 3:3–15. Of Eliphaz, of a spirit speaking to him, Job 4:12–21. Of Daniel, concerning the four beasts, Dan. 7. Of Joseph, concerning Mary's innocence, Matt. 1: 20,21; concerning the flight into Egypt, Matt. 2:13; concerning the return into Palestine, Matt. 2:19–22. Of Pilate's wife, concerning Jesus, Matt. 27:19. Cornelius' vision, concerning Peter, Acts 10:3–6. Peter's vision of the unclean beasts, Acts 10:10–16. Paul's vision of the man in Macedonia, crying, "Come over into Macedonia," Acts 16:9; relating to his going to Rome, Acts 23:11; concerning the shipwreck, and the safety of all on board, Acts 27:23,24.

DRESS. Of fig leaves, Gen. 3:7. Of skins, Gen. 3:21. Of other materials, see HAIR; GOATS' HAIR; LEATHER; LINEN; SACKCLOTH; SILK; WOOL. Mixed materials in, forbidden, Deut. 22:11. Men forbidden to wear women's, and women forbidden to wear men's, Deut. 22:5. Rules with respect to women's, 1 Tim. 2:9,10; 1 Pet. 3:3. Not to be held over night as a pledge for debt, Ex. 22:26. Ceremonial purification of, Lev. 11:32; 13:47–59; Num. 31:20. Rending of, see MOURNING.

Of the head: Bonnets [*R. V.*, head-tires], prescribed by Moses, for the priests, Ex. 28: 40; 29:9; 39:28; by Ezekiel, Ezek. 44:18. Hats [turbans, *R. V.* margin], worn by men, Dan. 3:21. Bonnets [*R. V.*, head-tires], worn by women, Isa. 3:20; Ezek. 24:17,23. Hoods [turban, *R. V.*], Isa. 3:23. Kerchiefs, Ezek. 13:18,21.

Various articles of: Mantle, Ezra 9:3; 1 Kin. 19:13; 1 Chr. 15:27; Job 1:20; many colored, 2 Sam. 13:18; purple, John 19:2,5. Robe, Ex. 28:4; 1 Sam. 18:4. Shawls, Isa. 3: 22 [*R. V.*]. Embroidered coat, Ex. 28:4,40; 1 Sam. 2:19; Dan. 3:21. Sleeveless shirt, called coat, Matt. 5:40; Luke 6:29; John 19:23; Acts 9:39. Cloak, 2 Tim. 4:13; John 19:2,5. Hosen, Dan. 3:21. Skirts, Ezek. 5:3. Mufflers, Isa. 3:19. Wimples [satchels, *R. V.*], Isa. 3: 22. Sashes [*R. V.*], Isa. 3:20. See VAIL.

Changes of raiment, the folly of excessive, Job 27:16. Uniform vestments kept in store for worshipers of Baal, 2 Kin. 10:22,23; Zeph. 1:8; for wedding feasts, Matt. 22:11. Presents made of changes of raiment, Gen. 45:22; 1 Sam. 18:4; 2 Kin. 5:5; Esth. 6:8; Dan. 5:7. Vestments of priests, see PRIEST; of mourning, see MOURNING.

FIGURATIVE: Filthy, of unrighteousness, Isa. 64:6. Of righteousness and of iniquity, see COLOR, SYMBOLISM OF.

SYMBOLICAL: Filthy, of iniquity, Zech. 3:3,4.

DRINK, INTOXICATING, see ABSTINENCE, TOTAL; DRUNKARD; DRUNKENNESS; WINE.

DRINK OFFERING. See OFFERING.

DRIVING, rapid, by Jehu, 2 Kin. 9:20.

DROMEDARY, 1 Kin. 4:28; Esth. 8:10 [R. V., swift steeds]; Isa. 60:6.

DROPSY, Luke 14:2.

DROSS. FIGURATIVE: Psa. 119:119; Prov. 25:4; 26:23; Isa. 1:22; Ezek. 22:18,19.

DROUGHT. Gen. 31:40; 1 Kin. chapters 17,18; Jer. 14:1-6. Sent by God as a judgment, Deut. 28:23,24; 1 Kin. 8:35; 2 Chr. 6:26; 7:13; Hos. 13:15.

See FAMINE; METEOROLOGY; RAIN.

FIGURATIVE: Psa. 32:4; Isa. 44:3.

DRUNKARD. Deut. 21:20. And they shall say unto the elders of his city, This our son is stubborn and rebellious, he will not obey our voice; he is a glutton, and a drunkard. 21. And all the men of his city shall stone him with stones, that he die: so shalt thou put evil away from among you; and all Israel shall hear, and fear.

Psa. 69:12. They that sit in the gate speak against me; and I was the song of the drunkards.

Prov. 23:21. For the drunkard and the glutton shall come to poverty: and drowsiness shall clothe a man with rags.

Isa. 28:1. Woe to the crown of pride, to the drunkards of Ephraim, whose glorious beauty, is a fading flower, which are on the head of the fat valleys of them that are overcome with wine! 3. The crown of pride, the drunkards of Ephraim, shall be trodden under feet:

Joel 1:5. Awake, ye drunkards, and weep; and howl, all ye drinkers of wine, because of the new wine; for it is cut off from your mouth.

Nah. 1:10. For while they be folden together as thorns, and while they are drunken as drunkards, they shall be devoured as stubble fully dry.

1 Cor. 5:11. But now I have written unto you not to keep company, if any man that is called a brother be a fornicator, or covetous, or an idolater, or a railer, or a drunkard, or an extortioner; with such an one no not to eat.

1 Cor. 6:9. Know ye not that the unrighteous shall not inherit the kingdom of God? Be not deceived: neither fornicators, nor idolaters, nor adulterers, nor effeminate, nor abusers of themselves with mankind, 10. Nor thieves, nor covetous, nor drunkards, nor revilers, nor extortioners, shall inherit the kingdom of God.

See DRUNKENNESS.

DRUNKENNESS. Deut. 21:20. This our son . . . is a glutton and a drunkard. 21. And all the men of his city shall stone him with stones, that he die: so shalt thou put evil away from among you; and all Israel shall hear, and fear.

Deut. 29:19. And it come to pass, when he heareth the words of this curse, that he bless himself in his heart, saying, I shall have peace, though I walk in the imagination of mine heart, to | add drunkenness to thirst: 20. The LORD will not spare him, but then the anger of the LORD and his jealousies

shall smoke against that man, and all the curses that are written in this book shall lie upon him, and the LORD shall blot out his name from under heaven. 21. And the LORD shall separate him unto evil out of all the tribes of Israel, according to all the curses of the covenant that are written in this book of the law :   [¹ R. V. destroy the moist with the dry]

1 Sam. 1:14. How long wilt thou be drunken? put away thy wine from thee.

Psa. 69:12. I was the song of the drunkards.

Prov. 20:1. Wine is a mocker, strong drink is raging: and whosoever is deceived thereby is not wise.

Prov. 21:17. He that loveth wine . . . shall not be rich.

Prov. 23:20. Be not among winebibbers; 21. The drunkard and the glutton shall come to poverty: 29. Who hath woe? who hath sorrow? who hath contentions? who hath babbling? who hath wounds without cause? who hath redness of eyes? 30. They that tarry long at the wine; they that go to seek mixed wine. 31. Look not thou upon the wine when it is red, when it giveth his colour in the cup, when it moveth itself aright. 32. At the last it biteth like a serpent, and stingeth like an adder. 33. Thine eyes shall behold strange women, and thine heart shall utter perverse things. 34. Yea, thou shalt be as he that lieth down in the midst of the sea, or as he that lieth upon the top of a mast. 35. They have stricken me, shalt thou say, and I was not sick; they have beaten me, and I felt it not: when shall I awake? I will seek it yet again.

Prov. 31:4. It is not for kings, O Lemuel, it is not for kings to drink wine; nor for princes strong drink: 5. Lest they drink, and forget the law, and pervert the judgment of any of the afflicted. 6. Give strong drink unto him that is ready to perish, and wine unto those that be of heavy hearts. 7. Let him drink, and forget his poverty, and remember his misery no more.

Isa. 5:11. Woe unto them that rise up early in the morning, that they may follow strong drink; that continue until night, till wine inflame them! 12. And the harp, and the viol, the tabret, and pipe, and wine, are in their feasts: but they regard not the work of the LORD, neither consider the operation of his hands. 22. Woe unto them that are mighty to drink wine, and men of strength to mingle strong drink:

Isa. 19:14. The LORD hath mingled a perverse spirit in the midst thereof: and they have caused Egypt to err in every work thereof, as a drunken man staggereth in his vomit.

Isa. 24:9. They shall not drink wine with a song; strong drink shall be bitter to them that drink it. 11. There is a crying for wine in the streets; all joy is darkened, the mirth of the land is gone.

Isa. 28:1. Woe to the crown of pride, to the drunkards of Ephraim, whose glorious beauty *is* a fading flower, which *are* on the head of the fat valleys of them that are overcome with wine! 3. The crown of pride, the drunkards of Ephraim, shall be trodden under feet: 7. But they also have erred through wine, and through strong drink are out of the way; the priest and the prophet have erred through strong drink, they are swallowed up of wine, they are out of the way through strong drink; they err in vision, they stumble *in* judgment. 8. For all tables are full of vomit *and* filthiness, *so that there* is no place *clean*.

Isa. 56:12. Come ye, *say they*, I will fetch wine, and we will fill ourselves with strong drink; and to morrow shall be as this day, *and* much more abundant.

Jer. 25:27. Thus saith the LORD of hosts, the God of Israel; Drink ye, and be drunken, and spue, and fall, and rise no more, because of the sword which I will send among you.

Hos. 4:11. Whoredom and wine and new wine take away the heart.

Hos. 7:5. In the day of our king the princes have made *him* sick with bottles of wine; he stretched out his hand with scorners. 14. And they have not cried unto me with their heart, when they howled upon their beds: they assemble themselves for corn and wine, *and* they rebel against me.

Joel 1:5. Awake, ye drunkards, and weep; and howl, all ye drinkers of wine, because of the new wine; for it is cut off from your mouth.

Joel 3:3. And they have cast lots for my people; and have given a boy for an harlot, and sold a girl for wine, that they might drink.

Amos 2:8. And they lay *themselves* down upon clothes laid to pledge by every altar, and they drink the wine of the condemned *in* the house of their god. 12. But ye gave the Nazarites wine to drink; and commanded the prophets, saying, Prophesy not.

Amos 6:1. Woe to them *that are* at ease in Zion, . . . 6. That drink wine in bowls, and anoint themselves with the chief ointments: but they are not grieved for the affliction of Joseph.

Mic. 2:11. If a man walking in the spirit and falsehood do lie, *saying*, I will prophesy unto thee of wine and of strong drink; he shall even be the prophet of this people.

Nah. 1:10. For while *they be* folden together *as* thorns, and while they are drunken *as* drunkards, they shall be devoured as stubble fully dry.

Hab. 2:15. Woe unto him that giveth his neighbour drink, that [puttest thy bottle to *him*, and makest *him* drunken also, that thou mayest look on their nakedness! 16. Thou art filled with shame for glory: drink thou also, and let thy foreskin be uncovered: the cup of the LORD's right hand shall be turned unto thee, and shameful spewing *shall be* on thy glory. *v.* 17. [I R. V. addest thy venom thereto]

Matt. 24:49. And shall begin to smite *his*

fellowservants, and to eat and drink with the drunken; Luke 12:45.

Luke 21:34. Take heed to yourselves, lest at any time your hearts be overcharged with surfeiting, and drunkenness, and cares of this life, and *so* that day come upon you unawares.

Rom. 13:13. Let us walk honestly, as in the day; not in rioting and drunkenness, not in chambering and wantonness, not in strife and envying.

Gal. 5:19. Now the works of the flesh are manifest, which are *these:* Adultery, fornication, uncleanness, lasciviousness, 20. Idolatry, witchcraft, hatred, variance, emulations, wrath, strife, seditions, heresies, 21. Envyings, murders, drunkenness, revellings, and such like: of the which I tell you before, as I have also told *you* in time past, that they which do such things shall not inherit the kingdom of God.

Eph. 5:18. Be not drunk with wine, wherein is excess;

1 Thess. 5:7. They that be drunken are drunken in the night. 8. But let us, who are of the day, be sober,

FIGURATIVE: Isa. 28:8; 51:17,21–23; 63:6; Jer. 25:15,16,27,28; 51:7–9; Lam. 3:15; Ezek. 23:31–34; Hab. 2:15,16.

See ABSTINENCE; DRUNKARD; SOBRIETY; WINE.

INSTANCES OF: Noah, Gen. 9:21. Lot, Gen. 19:33. Nabal, 1 Sam. 25:36. Uriah, 2 Sam. 11:13. Amnon, 2 Sam. 13:28. Elah, 1 Kin. 16:9. Ben-hadad and his thirty-two confederate kings, 1 Kin. 20:16. Ahasuerus, Esth. 1:10,11. Belshazzar, Dan. 5:1–6.

FALSELY ACCUSED OF: Hannah, 1 Sam. 1:12–16. Jesus, Matt. 11:19. The Apostles, Acts 2:13–15.

DRUSILLA, wife of Felix, Acts 24:24.

DUKE. Title of the princes of Edom, Gen. 36:15–43; Ex. 15:15. 1 Chr. 1:51–54. Of the Midianites, Josh. 13:21.

DULCIMER, [R. V., marg., bagpipe], Dan. 3:5,10,15.

See MUSIC, INSTRUMENTS OF.

DUMAH. 1. Son of Ishmael, Gen. 25:14; 1 Chr. 1:30; Isa. 21:11,12.

2. A city of Canaan assigned to Judah, Josh. 15:52.

DUMB, stricken of God, Ex. 4:11; Luke 1:20,64; miraculous healing of, by Jesus, Matt. 9:32,33; 12:22; 15:30,31; Mark 7:37; 9:17,25,26.

See DEAFNESS.

DUNGEON, in prisons, Jer. 38:6; Lam. 3:53.

See PRISONS.

DURA, plain of, Dan. 3:1.

DUST. Man made from, Gen. 2:7; 3:19; 23; Eccl. 3:20. Casting of, in anger, 2 Sam. 16:13. Shaking from feet, Matt. 10:14; Acts 13:51. Put on the head in mourning, Josh. 7:6; 1 Sam. 4:12; 2 Sam. 1:2; 15:30; Job 2:12; 42:6.

DUTY, tribute levied on foreign commerce by Solomon, 1 Kin. 10:15.

DUTY. OF MAN TO GOD: Deut. 6:5. And thou shalt love the LORD thy God with all thine heart, and with all thy soul, and with all thy might.

Deut. 10:12. And now, Israel, what doth the LORD thy God require of thee, but to fear the LORD thy God, to walk in all his ways, and to love him, and to serve the LORD thy God with all thy heart and with all thy soul, 13. To keep the commandments of the LORD, and his statutes,

Deut. 11:1. Therefore thou shalt love the LORD thy God, and keep his charge, and his statutes, and his judgments, and his commandments, alway.

Deut. 30:15. See, I have set before thee this day life and good, and death and evil; 16. In that I command thee this day to love the LORD thy God, to walk in his ways, and to keep his commandments and his statutes and his judgments, that thou mayest live and multiply: and the LORD thy God shall bless thee in the land whither thou goest to possess it. 17. But if thine heart turn away, so that thou wilt not hear, but shalt be drawn away, and worship other gods, and serve them; 18. I denounce unto you this day, that ye shall surely perish, *and that* ye shall not prolong *your* days upon the land, whither thou passest over Jordan to go to possess it. 19. I call heaven and earth to record this day against you, *that* I have set before you life and death, blessing and cursing: therefore choose life, that both thou and thy seed may live: 20. That thou mayest love the LORD thy God, *and* that thou mayest obey his voice, and that thou mayest cleave unto him: for he *is* thy life, and the length of thy days: that thou mayest dwell in the land which the LORD sware unto thy fathers, to Abraham, to Isaac, and to Jacob, to give them.

Josh. 22:5. But take diligent heed to do the commandment and the law, which Moses the servant of the LORD charged you, to love the LORD your God, and to walk in all his ways, and to keep his commandments, and to cleave unto him, and to serve him with all your heart and with all your soul.

Josh. 23:11. Take good heed therefore unto yourselves, that ye love the LORD your God.

Psa. 31:23. O love the LORD, all ye his saints:

Prov. 23:26. My son, give me thine heart, and let thine eyes observe my ways.

Matt. 4:10. Then saith Jesus unto him, . . . It is written, Thou shalt worship the Lord thy God, and him only shalt thou serve.

Matt. 12:50. For whosoever shall do the will of my Father which is in heaven, the same is my brother, and sister, and mother.

Matt. 22:21. Then saith he unto them, Render therefore unto Cæsar the things which are Cæsar's; and unto God the things that are God's.

36. Master, which *is* the great commandment in the law? 37. Jesus said unto him, Thou shalt love the Lord thy God with all thy heart, and with all thy soul, and with all thy mind. 38. This is the first and great commandment. 39. And the second *is* like unto it, Thou shalt love thy neighbour as thyself. 40. On these two commandments hang all the law and the prophets.

Luke 17:10. When ye shall have done all those things which are commanded you, say, We are unprofitable servants: we have done that which was our duty to do.

Luke 21:3. Of a truth I say unto you, that this poor widow hath cast in more than they all: 4. For all these have of their abundance cast in unto the offerings of God: but she of her penury hath cast in all the living that she had.

John 4:34. Jesus saith unto them, My meat is to do the will of him that sent me, and to finish his work.

John 6:38. For I came down from heaven, not to do mine own will, but the will of him that sent me.

John 14:15. If ye love me, keep my commandments. 21. He that hath my commandments, and keepeth them, he it is that loveth me:

John 15:14. Ye are my friends, if ye do whatsoever I command you.

Acts 4:19. But Peter and John answered and said unto them, Whether it be right in the sight of God to hearken unto you more than unto God, judge ye. 20. For we cannot but speak the things which we have seen and heard.

Acts 5:29. Then Peter and the *other* apostles answered and said, We ought to obey God rather than men.

Jude 21. Keep yourselves in the love of God,

See COMMANDMENTS; FAITHFULNESS; OBEDIENCE.

OF MAN TO MAN: Lev. 19:18. Thou shalt love thy neighbour as thyself: I *am* the LORD.

Isa. 58:6. *Is* not this the fast that I have chosen? to loose the bands of wickedness, to undo the heavy burdens, and to let the oppressed go free, and that ye break every yoke? 7. *Is it* not to deal thy bread to the hungry, and that thou bring the poor that are cast out to thy house? when thou seest the naked, that thou cover him; and that thou hide not thyself from thine own flesh?

Matt. 7:12. Therefore all things whatsoever ye would that men should do to you, do ye even so to them: for this is the law and the prophets.

Matt. 25:34. Then shall the King say unto them on his right hand, Come, ye blessed of my Father, inherit the kingdom prepared for you from the foundation of the world: 35. For I was an hungred, and ye gave me meat: I was thirsty, and ye gave me drink: I was a stranger, and ye took me in: 36. Naked, and ye clothed me: I was sick, and ye visited me: I was in prison, and ye came unto me. 37. Then shall the righteous answer him, saying, Lord, when saw we thee an hungred and fed *thee?* or thirsty, and gave *thee* drink? 38. When saw we thee a stranger, and took *thee* in? or naked, and clothed *thee?* 39. Or when saw we thee sick, or in prison, and came unto thee? 40. And the King shall answer and say unto them, Verily I say unto you, Inasmuch as ye have done *it* unto one of the least of these my brethren, ye have done *it* unto me. 41. Then shall he say also unto them on the left hand, Depart from me, ye cursed, into everlasting fire, prepared for the devil and his angels: 42. For I was an hungred, and ye gave me no meat: I was thirsty, and ye gave me no drink: 43. I was a stranger, and ye took me not in: naked, and ye clothed me not: sick, and in prison, and ye visited me not. 44. Then shall they also answer him, saying, Lord, when saw we thee an hungred, or athirst, or a stranger, or naked, or sick, or in prison, and did not minister unto thee? 45. Then shall he answer them, saying, Verily I say unto you, Inasmuch as ye did *it* not to one of the least of these, ye did *it* not to me. 46. And these shall go away into everlasting punishment: but the righteous into life eternal.

Luke 10:25. And, behold, a certain lawyer stood up, and tempted him, saying, Master, what shall I do to inherit eternal life? 26. He said unto him, What is written in the law? how readest thou? 27. And he answering said, Thou shalt love the Lord thy God with all thy heart, and with all thy soul, and with all thy strength, and with all thy mind; and thy neighbour as thyself. 28. And he said unto him, Thou hast answered right: this do, and thou shalt live. 29. But he, willing to justify himself, said unto Jesus, And who is my neighbour? 30. And Jesus answering said, A certain *man* went down from Jerusalem to Jericho, and fell among thieves, which stripped him of his raiment, and wounded *him*, and departed, leaving *him* half dead. 31. And by chance there came down a certain priest that way: and when he saw him, he passed by on the other side. 32. And likewise a Levite, when he was at the place, came and looked *on him*, and passed by on the other side. 33. But a certain Samaritan, as he journeyed, came where he was: and when he saw him, he had compassion *on him*, 34. And went to *him*, and bound up his wounds, pouring in oil and wine, and set him on his own beast, and brought him to an inn, and took care of him. 35. And on the morrow when he departed, he took out two pence, and gave *them* to the host, and said unto him, Take care of him; and whatsoever thou spendest more, when I come again, I will repay thee. 36. Which now of these three, thinkest thou, was neighbour unto him that fell among the thieves? 37. And he said, He that shewed mercy on him. Then said Jesus unto him, Go, and do thou likewise.

See COMMANDMENTS; CHILDREN; HUSBAND; MINISTER, DUTIES OF; PARENTS; WIFE.

DWARFS, forbidden to be priests, Lev. 21:20.

DYEING, Ex. 25:5; 26:14; Isa. 63:1; Ezek. 23:15.

DYING. See DEATH.

DYSENTERY, Acts 28:8.

DYSPEPSIA, of Timothy, 1 Tim. 5:23.

E

EAGLE. Forbidden as food, Lev. 11:13; Deut. 14:12. Swift flight of, Deut. 28:49; Job 9:26; Prov. 30:19; Jer. 4:13; 49:22; Lam. 4:19. Nest of: Deut. 32:11; Job 39:27–30; Jer. 49:16. Bears her young on her wings, Ex. 19:4; Deut. 32:11. Long life of, Psa. 103:5. Bald, Mic. 1:16. Gier-eagle, Lev. 11:18.

FIGURATIVE: Ex. 19:4; Deut. 32:11; Jer. 48:40; Hos. 8:1.

SYMBOLICAL: Ezek. 1:10; 10:14; 17:3; Dan. 7:4; Rev. 4:7; 12:14.

EAR. Blood put upon, in consecration of priests, Ex. 29:20; Lev. 8:23; in cleansing lepers, Lev. 14:14,25. Anointed with oil in purifications, Lev. 14:17,28. Bored as a sign of servitude, Ex. 21:5,6.

See DEAFNESS.

FIGURATIVE: Anthropomorphic uses of: Psa. 17:6. Thou wilt hear me, O God: incline thine ear unto me *and hear*

Psa. 39:12. Give ear unto my cry;

Psa. 77:1. I cried unto God . . . and he gave ear unto me.

Psa. 80:1. Give ear, O Shepherd.

Psa. 84:8. Give ear, O God.

For more extended anthropomorphic uses, consult concordances.

EARNEST, a pledge or token, Psa. 86: 17; 2 Cor. 1:22; 5:5; Eph. 1:14.

See TOKEN.

EARNESTNESS. See ZEAL.

EAR-RING. Of gold, Prov. 25:12. Offering of, for the golden calf, Ex. 32:2,3; for the tabernacle, Ex. 35:22. Worn for idolatrous purposes, Gen. 35:4; Isa. 3:20.

EARTH. Primitive condition of, Gen. 1: 2,6,7; Job. 26:7; Psa. 104:5–9; Jer. 4:23. Design of, Isa. 45:18. Ancient notions concerning, 1 Sam. 2:8; Job 9:6; Rev. 7:1. Cursed of God, Gen. 3:17,18; Rom. 8:19–22. Circle of, Isa. 40:22. God's footstool, Isa. 66:1; Lam. 2:1. Given to man, Psa. 115:16. Early divisions of Gen. 10; 11; Deut. 32:8. Perpetuity of, Gen. 49:26; Deut. 33:15; Psa. 78:69; 104:5; Eccl. 1: 4; Hab. 3:6.

A new earth, Isa. 65:17; 66:22; Rev. 21:1.

CREATED BY GOD: Gen. 1:1. In the beginning God created the heaven and the earth.

2 Kin. 19:15. Thou hast made heaven and earth.

2 Chr. 2:12. Huram said moreover, Blessed *be* the LORD God of Israel, that made heaven and earth.

Neh. 9:6. Thou, *even* thou, *art* LORD alone; thou hast made heaven, the heaven of heavens, with all their host, the earth, and all *things* that *are* therein, the seas, and all that *is* therein, and thou preservest them all; and the host of heaven worshippeth thee.

Psa. 90:2. Before the mountains were brought forth, or ever thou hadst formed the earth and the world, even from everlasting to everlasting, thou *art* God.

Psa. 102:25. Of old hast thou laid the foundation of the earth:

Psa. 115:15. Ye *are* blessed of the LORD which made heaven and earth.

Psa. 146:6. Which made heaven, and earth, the sea, and all that therein *is:*

Prov. 8:22. The LORD possessed me in the beginning of his way, before his works of old. 23. I was set up from everlasting, from the beginning, or ever the earth was. 24. When *there were* no depths, I was brought forth; when *there were* no fountains abounding with water. 25. Before the mountains were settled, before the hills was I brought forth: 26. While as yet he had not made the earth, nor the fields, nor the highest part of the dust of the world.

Isa. 37:16. O LORD of hosts, God of Israel, that dwellest *between* the cherubims, thou *art* the God, *even* thou alone, of all the kingdoms of the earth: thou hast made heaven and earth.

Isa. 45:18. For thus saith the LORD that created the heavens; God himself that formed the earth and made it; he hath established it, he created it not in vain, he formed it to be inhabited: I *am* the LORD; and *there is* none else.

Jer. 10:12. He hath made the earth by his power, he hath established the world by his wisdom, and hath stretched out the heavens by his discretion.

Jer. 27:5. I have made the earth, the man and the beast that *are* upon the ground, by my great power and by my outstretched arm, and have given it unto whom it seemed meet unto me.

Jer. 32:17. Ah Lord GOD! behold, thou hast made the heaven and the earth by thy great power and stretched out arm, *and* there is nothing too hard for thee:

Jer. 51:15. He hath made the earth by his power, he hath established the world by his wisdom, and hath stretched out the heaven by his understanding.

John 17:24. Thou lovedst me before the foundation of the world.

2 Pet. 3:5. For this they willingly are ignorant of, that by the word of God the heavens were of old, and the earth standing out of the water and in the water:

Rev. 10:6. Sware by him that liveth for ever and ever, who created heaven, and the things that therein are, and the earth, and the things that therein are, and the sea, and the things which are therein, that there should be time no longer:

Rev. 14:7. Fear God, and give glory to him; for the hour of his judgment is come: and

worship him that made heaven, and earth, and the sea, and the fountains of waters.

BY CHRIST, John 1:3. All things were made by him; and without him was not any thing made that was made. 10. He was in the world, and the world was made by him, and the world knew him not.

Heb. 1:10. And, Thou, Lord, in the beginning hast laid the foundation of the earth; and the heavens are the works of thine hands:

See CREATION; GOD, CREATOR.

DESTRUCTION OF: Psa. 102:25. Of old hast thou laid the foundation of the earth: and the heavens *are* the work of thy hands. 26. They shall perish, but thou shalt endure; yea, all of them shall wax old like a garment; as a vesture shalt thou change them, and they shall be changed: 27. But thou *art* the same, and thy years shall have no end. Heb. 1:10–12.

Isa. 24:19. The earth is utterly broken down, the earth is clean dissolved, the earth is moved exceedingly. 20. The earth shall reel to and fro like a drunkard, and shall be removed like a cottage; and the transgression thereof shall be heavy upon it; and it shall fall, and not rise again.

Isa. 51:6. Lift up your eyes to the heavens, and look upon the earth beneath: for the heavens shall vanish away like smoke, and the earth shall wax old like a garment, and they that dwell therein shall die in like manner: but my salvation shall be for ever, and my righteousness shall not be abolished.

Matt. 5:18. Till heaven and earth pass, one jot or one tittle shall in no wise pass from the law, till all be fulfilled.

Matt. 24:3. And as he sat upon the mount of Olives, the disciples came unto him privately, saying, Tell us, when shall these things be? and what *shall be* the sign of thy coming, and of the end of the world? 14. And this gospel of the kingdom shall be preached in all the world for a witness unto all nations; and then shall the end come. 29. Immediately after the tribulation of those days shall the sun be darkened, and the moon shall not give her light, and the stars shall fall from heaven, and the powers of the heavens shall be shaken: 30. And then shall appear the sign of the Son of man in heaven: and then shall all the tribes of the earth mourn, and they shall see the Son of man coming in the clouds of heaven with power and great glory. 31. And he shall send his angels with a great sound of a trumpet, and they shall gather together his elect from the four winds, from one end of heaven to the other. 35. Heaven and earth shall pass away, but my words shall not pass away. 36. But of that day and hour knoweth no *man*, no, not the angels of heaven, but my Father only. 37. But as the days of Noe *were*, so shall also the coming of the Son of man be. 38. For as in the days that were before the flood they were eating and drinking, marrying and giving in marriage, until the day that Noe entered into the ark, 39. And knew not until the flood came, and took them all away; so shall also the coming of the Son of man be. Mark 13:24-37; Luke 21:26-36.

2 Pet. 3:10. But the day of the Lord will come as a thief in the night; in the which the heavens shall pass away with a great noise, and the elements shall melt with fervent heat, the earth also and the works that are therein shall be burned up. 11. *Seeing* then *that* all these things shall be dissolved, what manner *of persons* ought ye to be in *all* holy conversation and godliness, 12. Looking for and hasting unto the coming of the day of God, wherein the heavens being on fire shall be dissolved, and the elements shall melt with fervent heat? 13. Nevertheless we, according to his promise, look for new heavens and a new earth, wherein dwelleth righteousness.

Rev. 20:11. And I saw a great white throne, and him that sat on it, from whose face the earth and the heaven fled away; and there was found no place for them.

Rev. 21:1. And I saw a new heaven and a new earth: for the first heaven and the first earth were passed away; and there was no more sea.

EARTHENWARE. See POTTERY.

EARTHQUAKES. Job 9:6; Psa. 18:7; 46:2,3; 104:32; Jer. 4:24. As judgments, Psa. 18:15; 60:2; Isa. 13:13,14; 24:19,20; 29:6; Nah. 1:5. Prophecies of, Ezek. 38:19; Zech. 14:4; Matt. 24:7; Mark 13:8; Luke 21:11; Rev. 11:19.

INSTANCES OF: At Sinai, Ex. 19:18; Psa. 68:8; 77:18; 114:4-7; Heb.12:26. When Korah, Dathan, and Abiram were swallowed up, Num. 16:31,32. When Jonathan and his armorbearer attacked the garrison at Gibeah, 1 Sam. 14:15. When the Lord revealed himself to Elijah in the still small voice, 1 Kin. 19:11. In Canaan, in the days of Uzziah, king of Judah, Amos 1:1; Zech. 14:5. At the crucifixion of Jesus, Matt. 27:51. At the resurrection of Jesus, Matt. 28:2. When Paul and Silas were in prison at Philippi, Acts 16:26.

FIGURATIVE: Psa. 60:2.

SYMBOLICAL: Rev. 6:12-14; 11:13; 16:18,20.

EAST SEA. See DEAD SEA.

EAST WIND. See WIND.

EASTER [Passover, *R. V.*], Acts 12:4.

EATING. The host acting as waiter, Gen. 18:8. Favored guests served an extra portion, Gen. 43:34. Table used in, Judg. 1:7. Sitting at table, Ex. 32:6. Reclining on couches, Amos 6:4,7; Luke 7:37,38; John 13:25. Ablutions before, Matt. 15:2.

See FEASTS; FOOD; GLUTTONY.

EBAL. 1. Son of Joktan, 1 Chr. 1:22.

2. A Horite, Gen. 36:23; 1 Chr. 1:40.

3. A mountain of Ephraim. Half of the tribes of Israel stand on, to respond Amen to the curses of the law, Deut. 11:29; 27:

12,13; Josh. 8:33. Altar built on, Josh. 8:30.

See GERIZIM.

EBED. 1. Father of Gaal, Judg. 9:26-35.

2. A captive returned from Babylon, Ezra 8:6.

EBED-MELECH, an Ethiopian. Jeremiah rescued by, Jer. 38:7-13. Prophecy concerning, Jer.39:16-18.

EBENEZER. Name of a memorial stone, 1 Sam. 7:12. Philistines defeat the Israelites at, 1 Sam. 4. Philistines remove the ark from, 1 Sam. 5:1.

EBER, called also HEBER. 1. The probable founder of the Hebrew race, Gen. 10:21-25; 11:14; 1 Chr. 1:19,25; Luke 3:35. Prophecy concerning, Num. 24:24.

2. A Gadite, called HEBER, 1 Chr. 5:13.

3. A Benjamite, 1 Chr. 8:12.

4. A Benjamite of Jerusalem, 1 Chr. 8:22.

5. A priest, Neh. 12:20.

EBIASAPH, called also ASAPH. A son of Korah, 1 Chr. 6:23; 9:19; 26:1.

EBONY, a fossil. Merchandise in, Ezek. 27:15.

EBRONAH, the thirtieth camping place of the Israelites, Num. 33:34,35.

ECCLESIASTICISM. The Jewish, rebuked by Jesus, Matt. 9:10-13; 23:2-4,8-10, 13-35; Mark 9:49,50; to be overthrown, Matt. 21:19,20,28-44. Traditional rules of the Jewish, Matt. 15:1-20; Mark 7:2-23. See COMMANDMENTS OF MEN. Arrogance of, Matt. 12:2-7; 23:4.

See MINISTERS, FALSE; CHURCH; USURPATION, IN ECCLESIASTICAL AFFAIRS.

ECLIPSE. Of the sun and moon, Isa. 13:10; Ezek. 32:7,8; Joel 2:10,31; 3:15; Amos 8:9; Mic. 3:6; Matt. 24:29; Mark 13:24; Acts 2:20; Rev. 6:12,13; 8:12.

See SUN; MOON.

FIGURATIVE: Isa. 60:19.

ECONOMY, POLITICAL: See ECONOMICS; GOVERNMENT.

ECONOMICS. POLITICAL. Gen. 41:33-57. HOUSEHOLD, Prov. 24:27; 31:10-31; Eccl. 11:4-6; John 6:12,13.

See FAMILY; FRUGALITY; INDUSTRY.

ED, name of the altar, erected by the tribes, Reuben, Gad, and Manasseh at the fords of the Jordan, Josh. 22:34.

EDAR, a tower, Gen. 35:21; Mic. 4:8 [marg.].

EDEN. 1. The garden of Eden, Gen. 2:8-17; 3:23,24; 4:16; Isa. 51:3; Ezek. 28:13; 31:9, 16,18; 36:35; Joel 2:3.

2. A mart of costly merchandise, 2 Kin. 19:12; Isa. 37:12; Ezek. 27:23; Amos 1:5.

3. A Gershonite, 2 Chr. 29:12.

4. A Levite, 2 Chr. 31:15.

EDER, called also EDAR. 1. A place near Ephrath, Gen. 35:21.

2. A city of Judah, Josh. 15:21.

3. A grandson of Merari, 1 Chr.23:23; 24:30.

EDOM, signifies red. 1. A name of Esau, possibly on account of his being covered with red hair, Gen. 25:25,30; 36:1,8,19.

2. A name of the land occupied by the de-

scendants of Esau. It extended from the Elanitic Gulf to the Red Sea, and was called also IDUMEA, Gen. 32:3; 36:16,17,21; Jer. 40:11.

Noted for its wise men, Obad. 8. Sins of, Obad. 10–14. Prophecies concerning, Jer. 25:21–23; 27:1–11; Dan. 11:41.

See EDOMITES.

FIGURATIVE of the foes of Zion, Isa. 63:1. Wilderness of, 2 Kin. 3:8.

EDOMITES, called also EDOM. Descendants of Esau, Gen. 36. Kings of, Gen. 36:31–39; Num. 20:14; 1 Chr. 1:43–50; Ezek. 32:29; Amos 2:1. Dukes of, Gen. 36:9–43; Ex. 15:15; 1 Chr. 1:51–54. Land of, Gen. 32:3; Deut. 2:4,5,12.

Protected by divine command from desolation by the Israelites, Deut. 2:4–6; from being held in abhorrence by the Israelites, Deut. 23:7. Refuse to the Israelites passage through their country, Num. 20:18–21. Saul makes war against, 1 Sam. 14:47. David makes conquest of, 1 Kin. 11:14–16; 1 Chr. 18:11–13; garrisons, 2 Sam. 8:14; writes battle songs concerning his conquest of, Psa. 60:8,9; 108:9,10. Become confederates of Jehoshaphat, 2 Kin. 3:9,26. Ruled by a deputy king, 1 Kin. 22:47. The Lord delivers the army of, into the hands of Jehoshaphat, 2 Chr. 20:20,23. Revolt in the days of Joram, 2 Kin. 8:20–22; 2 Chr. 21:8–10. Amaziah, king of Judah, invades the territory of, 2 Kin. 14:5–7,10; 2 Chr. 25:11,12; 28:17. Join Babylon in war against the Israelites, Ezek. 35:5; Amos 1:9–11; Obad. 11–16. A Jewish prophet in Babylon denounces, Psa. 137:7; Ezek. 25:12–14; 35:3–10. Children of the third generation might be received into the congregation of Israel, Deut. 23:8. Prophecies concerning, Gen. 25:23; 27:29,37–40; Num. 24:18; Isa. 11:14; 21:11,12; 34; 63:1–4; Jer. 9:25,26; 27:1–11; 49:7–22; Lam. 4:21,22; Ezek. 25:12–14; 32:29,30,35; 36:5; Joel 3:19; Amos 1:11,12; 9:12; Obad. 1–21; Mal. 1:2–5.

EDREI, a town of Bashan. Allotted to Manasseh, Josh. 13:31. Joshua defeats Og at, Num. 21:33–35; Deut. 1:4; 3:1–3.

EDUCATION. See INSTRUCTION; TEACHERS; SCHOOLS; MATHEMATICS.

EGLAH, wife of David, 2 Sam. 3:5; 1 Chr. 3:3.

EGLAIM, city of Moab, Isa. 15:8.

EGLON. 1. King of Moab. Assassinated by Ehud, Judg. 3:12–30.

2. An ancient city of Canaan. Taken by Joshua. Josh. 10:23,35. Allotted to Judah, Josh. 15:39.

EGOTISM. See CONCEIT.

EGYPT. 1. The country of. Called RAHAB, Psa. 87:4; 89:10; LAND OF HAM, Psa. 105:23; 106:22. Limits of, Ezek. 29:10. Fertility of, Gen. 13:10. Productions of, Num. 11:5; Psa. 78:47; Prov. 7:16; Isa. 19: 5–9. Irrigation employed in, Deut. 11:10. Imports of, Gen. 37:25,36. Exports of, Prov. 7:16; Ezek. 27:7; of horses, 1 Kin. 10:28,29.

Famine in, Gen. 41; Acts 7:11. Armies of, Ex. 14:7; Isa. 31:1. Army of destroyed in the

Red Sea, Ex. 14:5–31; Isa. 43:17. Magi of, Gen. 41:8; Ex. 7:11; 1 Kin. 4:30; Acts 7:22. Priests of, Gen. 41:45: 47:22. Idols of, Ezek. 20:7,8.

Overflowed by the Nile, Amos 8:8; 9:5. Plagues in. See PLAGUES. Joseph's captivity in, and subsquent rule over, see JOSEPH. Civil war in, Isa. 19:2. The king acquires title to land of, Gen. 47:18–26. Abraham dwells in, Gen. 12:10–20; 13:1. Israelites in bondage in, see ISRAELITES. Joseph takes Jesus to, Matt. 2:13–20.

Prophecies against, Gen. 15:13,14; Isa. 19: 20:2–6; 45:14; Jer. 9:25,26; 43:8–13; 44:30; 46; Ezek. chapters 29–32; Hos. 8:13; Joel 3:11; Zech. 10:11.

See EGYPTIANS.

SYMBOLICAL, Rev. 11:8.

2. **RIVER, OR BROOK** [R.V.], **OF:** Perhaps identical with SIHOR, which see. A small stream flowing into the Mediterranean Sea, the western boundary of the land promised to the children of Israel, Gen. 15:18; Num. 34:5; Josh. 13:3; 15:4,47; 1 Kin. 8:65; 2 Kin. 24:7; Isa. 27:12; Ezek. 47:19; 48:28.

EGYPTIANS. Descendants of the Mizraim, Gen. 10:6,13,14. Wisdom of, 1 Kin. 4:30. The art of embalming the dead practised by, Gen 50:2,3,26. Hospitality of, to Abraham, Gen. 12:10–20. Slaves bought by, Gen. 37:36. Oppress the Israelites, Ex. chapters 1,2. Refuse to release the Israelites, Ex. chapters 5–10. Visited by plagues, Ex. chapters 7–12; Psa. 78:43–51; firstborn of, destroyed, Ex. 12:29; Psa. 78:51; 105:36; 136:10. Send the Israelites away, Ex. 12:29–36. Pursue Israelites, and the army of, destroyed, Ex. 14:5–30; Psa. 106:11; Heb. 11:29.

Abhorred shepherds, Gen. 46:34. Refused to eat with Hebrews, Gen. 43:32. Alliances with, forbidden to the Israelites, Isa. 30:2; 31:1; 36:6; Ezek, 17:15; 29:6. Eligible to membership in Israelitish congregation in the third generation, Deut. 23:7,8.

Invade the land of Israel: Under Shishak, 1 Kin. 14:25,26; 2 Chr. 12:2–9; Pharaohnechoh, 2 Kin. 23:29–35; 2 Chr. 35:20–24; 36: 3,4. Aid the Israelites against the Chaldeans, Jer. 37:5–11. Intermarry with the Jews, 1 Kin. 3:1.

An enthusiastic Egyptian instigated rebellion against Roman government, Acts 21:38.

Prophecies of dispersion and restoration of, Ezek. 29:12–15; 30:23,26. Conversion of, foretold, Isa. 19:18.

See EGYPT.

EHI. See EHUD.

EHUD. 1. A descendant of Benjamin, 1 Chr. 8:6. Called EHI, Gen. 46:21. Probably identical with AHIRAM, mentioned in Num. 26:38, and AHARAH, 1 Chr. 8:1, and AHOAH, v. 4, and AHIAH, v. 7, and AHER, 1 Chr. 7:12.

2. Son of Bilhan, 1 Chr. 7:10.

3. A Benjamite, the assassin of Eglon, Judg. 3:16.

EKER, son of Ram, 1 Chr. 2:27.

EKRON. One of the five chief cities of

the Philistines, Josh. 13:3. Conquered and
allotted to Judah, Josh. 15:11,45; Judg. 1:18.
Allotted to Dan, Josh. 19:43. The Ark of
God taken to, 1 Sam. 5:10. Temple of Baal-
zebub at, 2 Kin. 1:2.

Prophecies against, Jer. 25:20; Amos 1:8;
Zeph. 2:4; Zech. 9:5.

ELADAH, son of Ephraim, 1 Chr. 7:20.

ELAH. 1. A valley where David slew
Goliath, 1 Sam. 17:2,19; 21:9.

2. An Edomitish duke, Gen. 36:41; 1 Chr.
1:52.

3. Son of Caleb, 1 Chr. 4:15.

4. Father of Shimei, 1 Kin. 4:18.

5. Son and successor of Baasha, king of
Israel, 1 Kin. 16:6-14.

6. Father of Hoshea, 2 Kin. 15:30; 17:1.

7. A Benjamite chief, 1 Chr. 9:8.

ELAM. 1. A district southeast of Baby-
lon, on Persian Gulf, Gen. 14:1,9; Dan. 8:2.
Prophecies concerning, Isa. 11:11; 21:2; 22:6;
Jer. 25:25; 49:34-39; Ezek. 32:24. Jews from,
Acts 2:9.

See ELAMITES.

2. A Korhite Levite, 1 Chr. 26:3.

3. A Benjamite chief, 1 Chr. 8:24.

4. Designated as " the other Elam," Ezra
2:31; Neh. 7:34.

5. A Jewish captive, whose descendants,
to the number of twelve hundred and fifty-
four, returned from Babylon, Ezra 2:7; 8:7;
Neh. 7:12.

6. A Levite musician, Neh. 12:42.

7. One of the Israelitish chiefs with Nehemiah, Neh. 10:14.

ELAMITES. Descendants of Elam,
whose name was given to the district of
Elam, Gen. 10:22. Present at Pentecost,
Acts 2:9.

ELASAH. 1. Son of Helez, called ELEA-
SAH, 1 Chr. 2:39.

2. Son of Shaphan, Jer. 29:3.

3. Son of Pashur, Ezra 10:22.

ELATH, called also Eloth. A city of
Idumea, Deut. 2:8; 1 Kin. 9:26; 2 Chr. 8:17.
Conquest of, by Uzziah, 2 Chr. 26:2; by
the Syrians, 2 Kin. 16:6.

EL-BETH-EL, name of the altar erected
by Jacob where he had the vision of angels,
Gen. 35:7.

ELDAAH, a descendant of Abraham,
Gen. 25:4; 1 Chr. 1:33.

ELDAD, prophesies in the camp of the
Israelites, Num. 11:26-29.

ELDER. IN THE MOSAIC SYSTEM:
Equivalent to the title senator, in present
use. Elders, with delegated powers, were
authorized to act for their constituency,
Deut. 1:13,15.

See GOVERNMENT, MOSAIC.

IN THE CHRISTIAN CHURCH: Acts 11:29.
Then the disciples, every man according to
his ability, determined to send relief unto
the brethren which dwelt in Judæa: 30.
Which also they did, and sent it to the elders
by the hands of Barnabas and Saul.

Acts 14:23. And when they had ordained
them elders in every church, and had prayed

with fasting, they commended them to the
Lord, on whom they believed.

Acts 15:2. When therefore Paul and Barnabas had no small dissension and disputation with them, they determined that Paul
and Barnabas, and certain other of them,
should go up to Jerusalem unto the apostles
and elders about this question. [v. 4.] 5.
But there rose up certain of the sect of the
Pharisees which believed, saying, That it
was needful to circumcise them, and to command *them* to keep the law of Moses. 6.
And the apostles and elders came together
for to consider of this matter. 7. And when
there had been much disputing, Peter rose
up, and said unto them, Men *and* brethren,
ye know how that a good while ago God
made choice among us, that the Gentiles by
my mouth should hear the word of the gospel, and believe. 8. And God, which knoweth the hearts, bare them witness, giving
them the Holy Ghost, even as *he did* unto
us; 9. And put no difference between us
and them, purifying their hearts by faith.
10. Now therefore why tempt ye God, to put
a yoke upon the neck of the disciples, which
neither our fathers nor we were able to bear?
11. But we believe that through the grace
of the Lord Jesus Christ we shall be saved,
even as they. 12. Then all the multitude
kept silence, and gave audience to Barnabas
and Paul, declaring what miracles and
wonders God had wrought among the Gentiles by them. 13. And after they had held
their peace, James answered, saying, Men
and brethren, hearken unto me: 14. Simeon
hath declared how God at the first did visit
the Gentiles, to take out of them a people for
his name. 15. And to this agree the words
of the prophets; as it is written, 16. After
this I will return, and will build again the
tabernacle of David, which is fallen down;
and I will build again the ruins thereof, and
I will set it up: 17. That the residue of men
might seek after the Lord, and all the Gentiles, upon whom my name is called, saith
the Lord, who doeth all these things. 18.
Known unto God are all his works from the
beginning of the world. 19. Wherefore my
sentence is, that we trouble not them, which
from among the Gentiles are turned to God:
20. But that we write unto them, that they
abstain from pollutions of idols, and *from*
fornication, and *from* things strangled, and
from blood. 21. For Moses of old time hath
in every city them that preach him, being
read in the synagogues every sabbath day.
22. Then pleased it the apostles and elders,
with the whole church, to send chosen men
of their own company to Antioch with Paul
and Barnabas; *namely,* Judas surnamed
Barsabas, and Silas, chief men among the
brethren: 23. And they wrote *letters* by
them after this manner; The apostles and
elders and brethren *send* greeting unto the
brethren which are of the Gentiles in Antioch and Syria and Cilicia: 24. Forasmuch
as we have heard, that certain which went

out from us have troubled you with words, subverting your souls, saying, *Ye must* be circumcised, and keep the law : to whom we gave no *such* commandment : 25. It seemed good unto us, being assembled with one accord, to send chosen men unto you with our beloved Barnabas and Paul, 26. Men that have hazarded their lives for the name of our Lord Jesus Christ. 27. We have sent therefore Judas and Silas, who shall also tell *you* the same things by mouth. 28. For it seemed good to the Holy Ghost, and to us, to lay upon you no greater burden than these necessary things ; 29. That ye abstain from meats offered to idols, and from blood, and from things strangled, and from fornication : from which if ye keep yourselves, ye shall do well. Fare ye well. *vs.* 1–35.

Acts 16:4. And as they went through the cities, they delivered them the decrees for to keep, that were ordained of the apostles and elders which were at Jerusalem. 5. And so were the churches established in the faith, and increased in number daily.

Acts 20:17. And from Miletus he sent to Ephesus, and called the elders of the church. 28. Take heed therefore unto yourselves, and to all the flock, over the which the Holy Ghost hath made you overseers, to feed the church of God, which he hath purchased with his own blood. 29. For I know this, that after my departing shall grievous wolves enter in among you, not sparing the flock. 30. Also of your own selves shall men arise, speaking perverse things, to draw away disciples after them. 31. Therefore watch, and remember, that by the space of three years I ceased not to warn every one night and day with tears. 32. And now, brethren, I commend you to God, and to the word of his grace, which is able to build you up, and to give you an inheritance among all them which are sanctified.

Acts 21:18. And the *day* following Paul went in with us unto James ; and all the elders were present.

1 Tim. 4:14. Neglect not the gift that is in thee, which was given thee by prophecy, with the laying on of the hands of the presbytery.

1 Tim. 5:17. Let the elders that rule well be counted worthy of double honour, especially they who labour in the word and doctrine. 18. For the scripture saith, Thou shalt not muzzle the ox that treadeth out the corn. And, The labourer *is* worthy of his reward. 19. Against an elder receive not an accusation, but before two or three witnesses.

Tit. 1:5. For this cause left I thee in Crete, that thou shouldest set in order the things that are wanting, and ordain elders in every city, as I had appointed thee : 6. If any be blameless, the husband of one wife, having faithful children not accused of riot or unruly. 7. For a bishop must be blameless, as the steward of God ; not selfwilled, not soon angry, not given to wine, no striker, not

given to filthy lucre ; 8. But a lover of hospitality, a lover of good men, sober, just, holy, temperate ; 9. Holding fast the faithful word as he hath been taught, that he may be able by sound doctrine both to exhort and to convince the gainsayers.

Heb. 11:2. For by it the elders obtained a good report. [R. V. therein   had witness borne to them]

Jas. 5:14. Is any sick among you ? let him call for the elders of the church ; and let them pray over him, anointing him with oil in the name of the Lord : 15. And the prayer of faith shall save the sick, and the Lord shall raise him up ; and if he have committed sins, they shall be forgiven him.

1 Pet. 5:1. The elders which are among you I exhort, who am also an elder, and a witness of the sufferings of Christ, and also a partaker of the glory that shall be revealed : 2. Feed the flock of God which is among you, taking the oversight *thereof,* not by constraint, but willingly ; not for filthy lucre, but of a ready mind ; 3. Neither as being lords over *God's* heritage, but being ensamples to the flock. 4. And when the chief Shepherd shall appear, ye shall receive a crown of glory that fadeth not away. 5. Likewise, ye younger, submit yourselves unto the elder.

2 John 1. The elder unto the elect lady and her children. 3 John 1.

APOCALYPTIC VISION OF : Rev. 4:4,10; 5:5, 6,8,11,14; 7:11,13; 11:16; 14:3; 19:4.

See DEACON. Also see CHURCH. GOVERNMENT OF.

ELEAD, a descendant of Ephraim, 1 Chr. 7:21.

ELEALEH, a city of Moab. Taken by the Israelites, Num. 32:3,37. Repossessed by the Moabites, Isa. 15:4; 16:9.

ELEASAH. Name of two men, or of one man, uncertain which, called also ELASAH. Compare 1 Chr. 2:39; 8:37; 9:43, with Jer. 29:3, and Ezra 10:22.

ELEAZER. 1. Son of Aaron, Ex. 6:23; 28:1. Married a daughter of Putiel, who bore him Phinehas, Ex. 6:25. After the death of Nadab and Abihu is made chief of the tribe of Levi, Num. 3:32. Duties of, Num. 4:16.

Succeeds Aaron as high priest, Num. 20:26, 28; Deut. 10:6. Assists Moses in the census, Num. 26:63. With Joshua, divides Palestine, Num. 34:17. Death and burial of, Josh. 24:33. Descendants of, 1 Chr. 24:1–19.

2. An inhabitant of Kirjath-jearim who attended the ark, 1 Sam. 7:1,2.

3. A Merarite Levite, 1 Chr. 23:21,22; 24:28.

4. Son of Dodo, and one of David's distinguished heroes, 2 Sam. 23:9,10,13; 1 Chr. 11:12.

5. Son of Phinehas, Ezra 8:33; Neh. 12:42.

6. A returned Israelitish exile, Ezra 10:25.

ELECTION. OF RULERS : By lot, Neh. 11:1.

OF GRACE : John 15:16. Ye have not chosen me, but I have chosen you, and ordained you, that ye should go and bring forth fruit.

and *that* your fruit should remain : that whatsoever ye shall ask of the Father in my name, he may give it you.

John 17:6. I have manifested thy name unto the men which thou gavest me out of the world : thine they were, and thou gavest them me ; and they have kept thy word.

Eph. 1:4. According as he hath chosen us in him before the foundation of the world, that we should be holy and without blame before him in love :

Eph. 2:10. For we are his workmanship, created in Christ Jesus unto good works, which God hath before ordained that we should walk in them. .

2 Thess. 2:13. But we are bound to give thanks always to God for you, brethren beloved of the Lord, because God hath from the beginning chosen you to salvation through sanctification of the Spirit and belief of the truth :

Of Christ as Messiah, Isa. 42:1; 1 Pet. 2:6. Of good angels, 1 Tim. 5:21. Of Israel, Deut. 7:6; Isa. 45:4. Of ministers, Luke 6:13; Acts 9:15. Of churches, 1 Pet. 5:13.

See PREDESTINATION.

ELECTIONEERING. By Absalom, 2 Sam. 15:1-6. Adonijah, 1 Kin. 1:7.

ELEGY. David's, on Saul and Jonathan : 2 Sam. 1:17. And David lamented with his lamentation over Saul and over Jonathan his son : 19. The beauty of Israel is slain upon thy high places : how are the mighty fallen ! 20. Tell *it* not in Gath, publish *it* not in the streets of Askelon ; lest the daughters of the Philistines rejoice, lest the daughters of the uncircumcised triumph. 21. Ye mountains of Gilboa, *let there be* no dew, neither *let there be* rain, upon you, nor fields of offerings : for the shield of the mighty is vilely cast away, the shield of Saul, *as though he had* not *been* anointed with oil. 22. From the blood of the slain, from the fat of the mighty, the bow of Jonathan turned not back, and the sword of Saul returned not empty. 23. Saul and Jonathan *were* lovely and pleasant in their lives, and in their death they were not divided : they were swifter than eagles, they were stronger than lions. 24. Ye daughters of Israel, weep over Saul, who clothed you in scarlet, with *other* delights, who put on ornaments of gold upon your apparel. 25. How are the mighty fallen in the midst of the battle ! O Jonathan, *thou wast* slain in thine high places. 26. I am distressed for thee, my brother Jonathan : very pleasant hast thou been unto me : thy love to me was wonderful, passing the love of women. 27. How are the mighty fallen, and the weapons of war perished !

On Abner : 2 Sam. 3:33. And the king lamented over Abner, and said, Died Abner as a fool dieth ? 34. Thy hands *were* not bound, nor thy feet put into fetters : as a man falleth before wicked men, *so* fellest thou. And all the people wept again over him.

See the BOOK OF LAMENTATIONS. See also POETRY ; RHETORIC.

EL-ELOHE-ISRAEL, name of Jacob's altar at Salem, Gen. 33:20.

ELEPH, a town allotted to Benjamin, Josh. 18:28.

ELEPHANT, Job. 40:15 [marg. *A. V.*]. See IVORY.

ELHANAN. 1. A distinguished warrior in the time of David, who slew Lahmi, the brother of Goliath, the Gittite, 2 Sam. 21:19. Compare 1 Chr. 20:5.

2. Son of Dodo, one of David's heroes, 2 Sam. 23:24; 1 Chr. 11:26.

ELI. High priest, 1 Sam. 1:25; 2:11; 1 Kin. 2:27. Judge of Israel, 1 Sam. 4:18. Misjudges and rebukes Hannah, 1 Sam. 1:14. His benediction upon Hannah, 1 Sam. 1:17, 18; 2:20. Officiates when Samuel is presented at the tabernacle, 1 Sam. 1:24-28. Indulgent to his corrupt sons, 1 Sam. 2:22-25,29; 3:11-14. His solicitude for the ark, 1 Sam. 4:11-18. Death of, 1 Sam. 4:18.

Prophecies of judgments upon his house, 1 Sam. 2:27-36; 3, with 1 Kin. 2:27.

ELIAB. 1. A Reubenite, progenitor of Dathan and Abiram, Num. 26:8,9; 16:1,12; Deut. 11:6.

2. Son of Helon, Num. 1:9; 2:7; 7:24,29; 10:16.

3. Ancestor of Samuel, 1 Chr. 6:27. Called also ELIHU, 1 Sam. 1:1; and ELIEL, 1 Chr. 6:34.

4. Son of Jesse, and eldest brother of David, 1 Sam. 16:6; 17:13,28; 1 Chr. 2:13. A prince in the tribe of Judah, 1 Chr. 27:18.

5. A hero of the tribe of Gad, 1 Chr. 12:9.

6. A Levite, a porter and musician, 1 Chr. 15:18,20; 16:5.

ELIADA. 1. Son of David, 2 Sam. 5:16; 1 Chr. 3:8. Called BEELIADA, 1 Chr. 14:7.

2. A Benjamite, 2 Chr. 17:17.

ELIADAH, an Aramite, 1 Kin. 11:23.

ELIAH. See ELIJAH, No. 2.

ELIAHBA, one of David's heroes, 2 Sam. 23:32; 1 Chr. 11:33.

ELIAKIM. 1. Son of Melea, Luke 3:30.

2. Son of Hilkiah, deputy of Hezekiah, 2 Kin. 18:18; 19:2; Isa. 36:3,11,22; 37:2.

3. Original name of Jehoiakim, king of Judah, 2 Kin. 23:34; 2 Chr. 36:4.

4. Son of Abiud, Matt. 1:13. Probably same as SHECHANIAH, 1 Chr. 3:21.

5. A priest, Neh. 12:41.

ELIAM. 1. Father of Bath-sheba, 2 Sam. 11:3. Called AMMIEL, 1 Chr. 3:5.

2. One of David's valiant men, 2 Sam. 23:34. Called AHIJAH, 1 Chr. 11:36.

ELIAS. See ELIJAH.

ELIASAPH. 1. A chief of the tribe of Dan, Num. 1:14; 2:14; 7:42,47; 10:20.

2. Son of Lael, Num. 3:24.

ELIASHIB. 1. A priest, 1 Chr. 24:12.

2. Name of three Israelites, mentioned in Ezra 10:24,27,36.

3. High priest, Neh. 3:1; 12:10; 13:4-9,28.

4. Son of Elioenai, 1 Chr. 3:24.

ELIATHAH, a musician, 1 Chr. 25:4,27.

ELIDAD, a prince of Benjamin, Num. 34:21.

ELIEL. 1. A chief of Manasseh, 1 Chr. 5:24.

2. Son of Toah, 1 Chr. 6:34.

3. Two Benjamite chiefs, 1 Chr. 8:20,22.

4. Three of David's heroes, bearing the same name, 1 Chr. 11:46,47; 12:11.

5. Chief of Levites, 1 Chr. 15:9,11.

6. A Levite, who had charge of the temple, 2 Chr. 31:13.

ELIENAI, a Benjamite citizen of Jerusalem, 1 Chr. 8:20.

ELIEZER. 1. Abraham's servant, Gen. 15:2; 24.

2. Son of Becher, 1 Chr. 7:8.

3. Son of Moses, Ex. 18:4; 1 Chr. 23:15,17.

4. A priest, 1 Chr. 15:24.

5. Son of Zichri, 1 Chr. 27:16.

6. A prophet, 2 Chr. 20:37.

7. Son of Jorim, Luke 3:29.

8. A Jewish exile, Ezra 8:16.

9. A priest after the exile, Ezra 10:18.

10. A Levite, Ezra 10:23.

11. An Israelite after the exile, Ezra 10:31.

ELIHOENAI. 1. A Levite, 1 Chr. 26:3.

2. Son of Zerahiah, Ezra 8:4.

ELIHOREPH, son of Shisha, 1 Kin. 4:3.

ELIHU. 1. A Buzite and one of Job's three friends, Job, chapters 32-37.

2. Son of Tohu, 1 Sam. 1:1. Probably identical with ELIEL, 1 Chr. 6:34, and ELIAB, 1 Chr. 6:27.

3. A Manassite warrior, who joined David at Ziklag, 1 Chr. 12:20.

4. A porter of the temple, 1 Chr. 26:7.

5. A chief of the tribe of Judah, 1 Chr. 27:18. Possibly ELIAB, the oldest brother of David, 1 Sam. 16:6.

ELIJAH. 1. The Tishbite, a Gileadite and prophet, called ELIAS in the authorized version of the N. T. Persecuted by Ahab, 1 Kin. 17:2-7; 18:7-10. Escapes to the wilderness, where he is miraculously fed by ravens, 1 Kin. 17:1-7. By divine direction goes to Zarephath, where he is sustained in the household of a widow, whose meal and oil are miraculously increased, 1 Kin. 17:8-16. Returns, and sends a message to Ahab, 1 Kin. 18:1-16. Meets Ahab and directs him to assemble the prophets of Baal, 1 Kin. 18:17-20. Derisively challenges the priests of Baal to offer sacrifices, 1 Kin. 18:25-29. Slays the prophets of Baal, 1 Kin. 18:40. Escapes to the wilderness from the fierceness of Jezebel, 1 Kin. 19:1-18. Fasts forty days, 1 Kin. 19:8. Despondency and murmuring of, 1 Kin. 19:10,14. Consolation given to, 1 Kin. 19:11-18. Flees to the wilderness of Damascus; directed to anoint Hazael king over Syria, Jehu king over Israel, and Elisha to be a prophet in his own stead, 1 Kin. 19:9-21. Personal aspect of, 2 Kin. 1:8.

Piety of, 1 Kin. 19:10,14; Luke 1:17; Rom. 11:2; Jas. 5:17. His translation, 2 Kin. 2:11. Appears to Jesus at his transfiguration, Matt. 17:3,4; Mark 9:4; Luke 9:30. Anti-

(22)

type of John the Baptist, Matt. 11:14; 16:14; 17:10-12; Mark 9:12,13; Luke 1:17; John 1:21-25.

MIRACLES OF: Increases the oil of the widow of Zarephath, 1 Kin. 17:14-16. Raises from the dead the son of the woman of Zarephath, 1 Kin. 17:17-24. Causes rain after a drought of three and a half years, 1 Kin. 18:41-45; Jas. 5:17,18. Causes fire to consume the sacrifice, 1 Kin. 18:24,36-38. Calls fire down upon the soldiers of Ahaziah, 2 Kin. 1:10-12; Luke 9:54.

PROPHECIES OF: Foretells a drought, 1 Kin. 17:3; the destruction of Ahab and his house, 1 Kin. 21:17-29; 2 Kin. 9:25-37; the death of Ahaziah, 2 Kin. 1:2-17; the plague sent as a judgment upon the people in the time of Jehoram, king of Israel, 2 Chr. 21:12-15.

2. Called also ELIAH. A Benjamite chief, 1 Chr. 8:27.

3. A post-exile Jew, Ezra 10:21.

ELIKA, one of David's chiefs, 2 Sam. 23:25.

ELIM, second camp of the Israelites after crossing the Red Sea, Ex. 15:27; Num. 33:9.

ELIMELECH, with Naomi, his wife, and two sons, emigrate to Moab, Ruth 1:2,3; 2:1,2; 4:3,9.

ELIOENAI. See also ELIHOENAI.

1. Son of Becher, 1 Chr. 7:8.

2. A chief of Simeon, 1 Chr. 4:36.

3. A priest, Ezra 10:22. Possibly identical with one mentioned in Neh. 12:41, which see.

4. An Israelite, Ezra 10:27.

5. Son of Neariah, 1 Chr. 3:23,24.

ELIPHAL, a captain in David's army, 1 Chr. 11:35.

ELIPHALET. See ELIPHELET.

ELIPHAZ. 1. Son of Esau, Gen. 36:4, 10-16; 1 Chr. 1:35.

2. Friend of Job, Job 2:11; 4; 5; 22; 42:7-9.

ELIPHELEH, a Levite of the second degree, 1 Chr. 15:18,21.

ELIPHELET. 1. A distinguished warrior, 2 Sam. 23:34.

2. A son of David, 1 Chr. 3:6. Called ELPALET, 1 Chr. 14:5.

3. A son of David, probably identical with 2, above, 2 Sam. 5:16; 1 Chr. 3:8; 14:7. Called ELIPHALET in 2 Sam. 5:16; 1 Chr. 14:7.

4. A descendant of Saul, 1 Chr. 8:39.

5. A companion of Ezra, Ezra 8:13.

6. An Israelite, probably identical with No. 5, above, Ezra 10:33.

ELISABETH, wife of Zacharias and mother of John the Baptist, Luke 1:5-60.

ELISEUS, Luke 4:27. See ELISHA.

ELISHA, successor to the prophet Elijah. Elijah instructed to anoint, 1 Kin. 19:16. Called by Elijah, 1 Kin. 19:19. Ministers unto Elijah, 1 Kin. 19:21. Witnesses Elijah's translation, receives a double portion of his spirit, 2 Kin. 2:1-15; 3:11. Mocked by the children of Beth-el, 2 Kin. 2:23,24.

Causes the king to restore the property of the hospitable Shunammite, 2 Kin. 8:1-6. Instructs that Jehu be anointed king of Israel, 2 Kin. 9:1-3. Life of, sought by Jehoram, 2 Kin. 6:31-33. Death of, 2 Kin. 13: 14-20. Bones of, restore a dead man to life, 2 Kin. 13:21.

MIRACLES OF: Divides the Jordan, 2 Kin. 2:14. Purifies the waters of Jericho by casting salt into the fountain, 2 Kin. 2:19-22. Increases the oil of the woman whose sons were to be sold for debt, 2 Kin. 4:1-7. Raises from the dead the son of the Shunammite, 2 Kin. 4:18-37. Neutralizes the poison of the pottage, 2 Kin. 4:38-41. Increases the bread to feed one hundred men, 2 Kin. 4:42-44. Heals Naaman the leper, 2 Kin. 5:1-19; Luke 4:27. Sends leprosy as a judgment upon Gehazi, 2 Kin. 5:26,27. Recovers the ax that had fallen into a stream by causing it to float, 2 Kin. 6:6. Reveals the counsel of the king of Syria, 2 Kin. 6:12. Opens the eyes of his servant to see the hosts of the Lord, 2 Kin. 6:17. Brings blindness upon the army of Syria, 2 Kin. 6:18.

PROPHECIES OF: Foretells a son to the Shunammite woman, 2 Kin. 4:16; plenty to the starving in Samaria, 2 Kin. 7:1; death of the unbelieving prince, 2 Kin. 7:2; seven years' famine in the land of Canaan, 2 Kin. 8:1-3; death of Ben-hadad, king of Syria, 2 Kin. 8:7-10; elevation of Hazael to the throne, 2 Kin. 8:11-15; the victory of Jehoash over Syria, 13:14-19.

ELISHAH. A descendant of Noah, Gen. 10:4; 1 Chr. 1:7. Islands of the Mediterranean bear the name of, Ezek. 27:7.

ELISHAMA. 1. Grandfather of Joshua, Num. 1:10; 2:18; 7:48,53; 10:22; 1 Chr. 7:26.

2. A son of David, 2 Sam. 5:16; 1 Chr. 3:8; 14:7.

3. Another son of David, elsewhere called ELISHUA, which see. 1 Chr. 3:6.

4. A descendant of Judah, 1 Chr. 2:41.

5. Probably identical with No. 4, 2 Kin. 25:25; Jer. 41:1.

6. A secretary to Jehoiakim, Jer. 36:12, 20,21.

7. A priest sent by Jehoshaphat to teach the law, 2 Chr. 17:8.

ELISHAPHAT, a Jewish captain, 2 Chr. 23:1.

ELISHEBA, wife of Aaron, Ex. 6:23.

ELISHUA, a son of David, 2 Sam. 5:15; 1 Chr. 14:5. Called ELISHAMA, 1 Chr. 3:6.

ELIUD, an ancestor of Jesus, Matt. 1: 14,15.

ELIZAPHAN. 1. A Levite, Ex. 6:22; Lev. 10:4; Num. 3:30; 1 Chr. 15:8.

2. A prince of Zebulun, Num. 34:25.

3. Probably identical with 1, above, 2 Chr. 29:13.

ELIZUR, a chief of Reuben, Num. 1:5; 2:10; 7:30,35; 10:18.

ELKANAH. 1. Grandson of Korah, Ex. 6:24; 1 Chr. 6:23.

2. Father of Samuel; a descendant of pre-

ceding, 1 Sam. 1:1,4,8,19,21,23; 2:11,20; 1 Chr. 6:27,34.

3. A Levite, 1 Chr. 6:25,36.

4. Possibly identical with 3, above, 1 Chr. 6:26,35.

5. A Levite, 1 Chr. 9:16.

6. A Levite who joined David at Ziklag, 1 Chr. 12:6.

7. A doorkeeper for the ark, perhaps identical with 6, above, 1 Chr. 15:23.

8. A prince of Ahaz, 2 Chr. 28:7.

ELLASAR, a city of Chaldea. Its king invades Canaan, Gen. 14:1,9.

ELM, Hos. 4:13.

ELMODAM, an ancestor of Jesus, Luke 3:28.

ELNAAM, father of two distinguished warriors, 1 Chr. 11:46.

ELNATHAN. 1. Father of Nehushta, the mother of king Jehoiachin, 2 Kin. 24:8; Jer. 26:22; 36:12,25.

2. Name of three Levites in the time of Ezra, Ezra 8:16.

ELOI, Mark 15:34.

ELON. 1. Father-in-law of Esau, Gen. 26:34; 36:2.

2. A son of Zebulun, Gen. 46:14; Num. 26:26.

3. A town of Dan, Josh. 19:43.

4. A Hebrew judge, Judg. 12:11,12.

ELON-BETH-HANAN. A town of Dan, 1 Kin. 4:9. Perhaps identical with ELON in Josh. 19:43.

ELONITES, descendants of Elon, son of Zebulun, Num. 26:26.

ELOTH. See ELATH.

ELPAAL, a Benjamite, 1 Chr. 8:11,12, 18.

ELPALET. A son of David, 1 Chr. 14:5. Called ELIPHALET in 1 Chr. 3:6.

ELPARAN, a place in the wilderness of Paran, Gen. 14:6.

ELTEKEH, a city of Dan, Josh. 19:44; 21:23.

ELTEKON, a city of Judah, Josh. 15: 59.

ELTOLAD. A city of Judah, Josh. 15: 30; 19:4. Called TOLAD in 1 Chr. 4:29.

ELUL. Sixth month [September]. The Jews finish the wall of Jerusalem in, Neh. 6:15. Zerubbabel builds the temple in, Hag. 1:14,15.

ELUZAI, a Benjamite, 1 Chr. 12:5.

ELYMAS, a false prophet, punished with blindness, Acts 13:8,10.

ELZABAD. 1. A Gadite, 1 Chr. 12:12.

2. A Korhite, 1 Chr. 26:7.

ELZAPHAN. See ELIZAPHAN.

EMANCIPATION, of all Jewish servants, Ex. 21:2; Lev. 25:8-17,39-41; Deut. 15:12. Proclamation of: By Zedekiah, Jer. 34:8-11; by Cyrus, 2 Chr. 36:23; Ezra 1:1-4. See EXODUS; JUBILEE.

EMBALMING. Of Jacob, Gen. 50:2,3; of Joseph, Gen. 50:26; of Asa, 2 Chr. 16:14; of Jesus, Mark 15:46; 16:1; John 19:39,40.

EMBEZZLEMENT, Luke 16:1-7. See DISHONESTY; FRAUD.

EMBROIDERY. In blue and purple and scarlet on the curtains of the tabernacle, Ex. 26:1,36; 27:16; on the girdle and coat of the high priest, mingled with gold, Ex. 28: 4,39. On the garments of Sisera, Judg. 5:30. On the garments of princes, Ezek. 26:16. On the garments of women, Psa. 45:14; Ezek. 16:10,13,18. Bezaleel and Aholiab divinely inspired for, in the work of the tabernacle, Ex. 35:30–35; 38:22,23.

See Tapestry.

EMERALD, a precious stone. Color of the rainbow, Rev. 4:3. Merchandise of, in Tyre, Ezek. 27:16; 28:13. Set in the breast-plate, Ex. 28:18.

SYMBOLICAL: In the foundation of the holy city, Rev. 21:19.

EMERGENCY. Ex. 14:15. And the Lord said unto Moses, Wherefore criest thou unto me? speak unto the children of Israel, that they go forward:

Josh. 7:10. And the Lord said unto Joshua, Get thee up; wherefore liest thou thus upon thy face? 11. Israel hath sinned, and they have also transgressed my covenant which I commanded them: for they have even taken of the accursed thing, and have also stolen, and dissembled also, and they have put *it* even among their own stuff. 12. Therefore the children of Israel could not stand before their enemies, *but* turned *their* backs before their enemies, because they were accursed: neither will I be with you any more, except ye destroy the accursed from among you. 13. Up, sanctify the people, and say, Sanctify yourselves against to morrow: for thus saith the Lord God of Israel, *There is* an accursed thing in the midst of thee, O Israel: thou canst not stand before thine enemies, until ye take away the accursed thing from among you.

See Decision.

EMERODS. See Hemorrhoids.

EMIMS, a race of giants, Gen. 14:5; Deut. 2:10,11.

EMMANUEL, Matt. 1:23.

See Immanuel; Jesus.

EMMAUS, a village about threescore furlongs from Jerusalem. Appearance of Jesus in, after his resurrection, Luke 24:13.

EMMOR, Acts 7:16. See Hamor.

EMPLOYEE. Lev. 19:13. Thou shalt not defraud thy neighbour, neither rob *him:* the wages of him that is hired shall not abide with thee all night until the morning.

Lev. 25:6. And the sabbath of the land shall be meat for you; for thee, and for thy servant, and for thy maid, and for thy hired servant, and for thy stranger that sojourn-eth with thee,

Deut. 15:18. It shall not seem hard unto thee, when thou sendest him away free from thee; for he hath been worth a double hired servant to *thee,* in serving thee six years; and the Lord thy God shall bless thee in all that thou doest.

Deut. 24:14. Thou shalt not oppress an hired servant *that is* poor and needy, *whether he* be of thy brethren, or of thy strangers that *are* in thy land within thy gates: 15. At his day thou shalt give *him* his hire, neither shall the sun go down upon it; for he *is* poor, and setteth his heart upon it: lest he cry against thee unto the Lord, and it be sin unto thee.

Matt. 10:10. The workman is worthy of his meat.

Luke 10:7. The labourer is worthy of his hire.

Rom. 4:4. Now to him that worketh is the reward not reckoned of grace, but of debt.

1 Tim. 5:18. For the scripture saith, Thou shalt not muzzle the ox that treadeth out the corn. And, The labourer *is* worthy of his reward.

CHARACTER OF UNRIGHTEOUS: Job 7:1. *Is there* not an appointed time to man upon earth? *are not* his days also like the days of an hireling? 2. As a servant earnestly desir-eth the shadow, and as an hireling looketh for *the reward of* his work: 3. So am I made to possess months of vanity and wearisome nights are appointed to me.

Job 14:1. Man *that is* born of woman *is* of few days, and full of trouble. 6. Turn from him, that he may rest, till he shall accom-plish, as an hireling, his day.

Matt. 20:1. For the kingdom of heaven is like unto a man *that is* an householder, which went out early in the morning to hire labour-ers into his vineyard. 2. And when he had agreed with the labourers for a penny a day, he sent them into his vineyard. 3. And he went out about the third hour, and saw others standing idle in the marketplace, 4. And said unto them; Go ye also into the vineyard, and whatsoever is right I will give you. And they went their way. 5. Again he went out about the sixth and ninth hour, and did likewise. 6. And about the eleventh hour he went out, and found others stand-ing idle, and saith unto them, Why stand ye here all the day idle? 7. They say unto him, Because no man hath hired us. He saith unto them, Go ye also into the vineyard; and whatsoever is right, *that* shall ye re-ceive. 8. So when even was come, the lord of the vineyard saith unto his steward, Call the labourers, and give them *their* hire, be-ginning from the last unto the first. 9. And when they came that *were hired* about the eleventh hour, they received every man a penny. 10. But when the first came, they supposed that they should have received more; and they likewise received every man a penny. 11. And when they had received *it,* they murmured against the goodman of the house, 12. Saying, These last have wrought *but* one hour, and thou hast made them equal unto us, which have borne the burden and heat of the day. 13. But he answered one of them, and said, Friend, I do thee no wrong: didst not thou agree with me for a penny? 14. Take *that* thine *is,* and go thy way: I will give unto this last, even as unto thee. 15. Is it not lawful for me to do what I will with mine own ? Is thine eye evil, because I am good ?

Matt. 21:33. Hear another parable: There was a certain householder, which planted a vineyard, and hedged it round about, and digged a winepress in it, and built a tower, and let it out to husbandmen, and went into a far country: 34. And when the time of the fruit drew near, he sent his servants to the husbandmen, that they might receive the fruits of it. 35. And the husbandmen took his servants, and beat one, and killed another, and stoned another. 36. Again, he sent other servants more than the first: and they did unto them likewise. 37. But last of all he sent unto them his son, saying, They will reverence my son. 38. But when the husbandmen saw the son, they said among themselves, This is the heir; come, let us kill him, and let us seize on his inheritance. 39. And they caught *him*, and cast him out of the vineyard, and slew *him*. 40. When the lord therefore of the vineyard cometh, what will he do unto those husbandmen? 41. They say unto him, He will miserably destroy those wicked men, and will let out *his* vineyard unto other husbandmen, which shall render him the fruits in their seasons.

John 10:12. But he that is an hireling, and not the shepherd, whose own the sheep are not, seeth the wolf coming, and leaveth the sheep, and fleeth: and the wolf catcheth them, and scattereth the sheep. 13. The hireling fleeth, because he is an hireling, and careth not for the sheep.

KINDNESS TO: Ruth 2:4. And, behold, Boaz came from Beth-lehem, and said unto the reapers, The LORD *be* with you. And they answered him, The LORD bless thee.

Luke 15:17. And when he came to himself, he said, How many hired servants of my father's have bread enough and to spare, and I perish with hunger! 19. And am no more worthy to be called thy son: make me as one of thy hired servants.

OPPRESSIONS OF: Prov. 22:16. He that oppresseth the poor to increase his *riches*, *and* he that giveth to the rich, *shall* surely come to want.

Mal. 3:5. And I will come near to you to judgment; and I will be a swift witness against . . . those that oppress the hireling in *his* wages, the widow, and the fatherless, and that turn aside the stranger *from his right*,

Luke 15:15. And he went and joined himself to a citizen of that country; and he sent him into his fields to feed swine. 16. And he would fain have filled his belly with the husks that the swine did eat: and no man gave unto him.

Jas. 5:4. Behold, the hire of the labourers who have reaped down your fields, which is of you kept back by fraud, crieth: and the cries of them which have reaped are entered into the ears of the Lord of sabaoth.

See SERVANTS; EMPLOYER; MASTER.

EMPLOYER. Lev. 25:43. Thou shalt not rule over him with rigour: but shalt fear thy God.

Deut. 5:14. The sabbath of the LORD thy God: *in it* thou shalt not do any work, thou, nor thy son, nor thy daughter, nor thy manservant, nor thy maidservant, nor thine ox, nor thine ass, nor any of thy cattle, nor thy stranger that *is* within thy gates: that thy manservant and thy maidservant may rest as well as thou.

Deut. 24:14. Thou shalt not oppress an hired servant *that is* poor and needy, *whether he* be of thy brethren, or of thy strangers that *are* in thy land within thy gates: 15. At his day thou shalt give *him* his hire, neither shall the sun go down upon it; for he *is* poor, and setteth his heart upon it: lest he cry against thee unto the LORD, and it be sin unto thee. Lev. 19:13.

Job 31:13. If I did despise the cause of my manservant or of my maidservant, when they contended with me; 14. What then shall I do when God riseth up? and when he visiteth, what shall I answer him? 15. Did not he that made me in the womb make him?

Prov. 22:16. He that oppresseth the poor to increase his *riches*, *and* he that giveth to the rich, *shall* surely *come* to want.

Prov. 29:21. He that delicately bringeth up his servant from a child shall have him become *his* son at the length.

Jer. 22:13. Woe unto him . . . *that* useth his neighbour's service without wages, and giveth him not for his work;

Mal. 3:5. I will be a swift witness against . . . those that oppress the hireling in *his* wages,

Matt. 10:10. The workman is worthy of his meat.

Matt. 20:1. For the kingdom of heaven is like unto a man *that is* an householder, which went out early in the morning to hire labourers into his vineyard. 2. And when he had agreed with the labourers for a penny a day, he sent them into his vineyard. 3. And he went out about the third hour, and saw others standing idle in the marketplace, 4. And said unto them; Go ye also into the vineyard, and whatsoever is right I will give you. And they went their way. 5. Again he went out about the sixth and ninth hour, and did likewise. 6. And about the eleventh hour he went out, and found others standing idle, and saith unto them, Why stand ye here all the day idle? 7. They say unto him, Because no man hath hired us. He saith unto them, Go ye also into the vineyard; 1 and whatsoever is right, *that* shall ye receive. 8. So when even was come, the lord of the vineyard saith unto his steward, Call the labourers, and give them *their* hire, beginning from the last unto the first. 9. And when they came that *were hired* about the eleventh hour, they received every man a penny. 10. But when the first came, they supposed that they should have received more; and they likewise received every man a penny. 11. And when they had received *it*, they murmured against the goodman of the house, 12. Saying, These last have wrought *but* one hour, and thou hast made them equal unto us, which have borne the burden and heat of the day. 13. But he answered one of them, and said, Friend, I do thee no wrong: didst not thou agree with me for a penny? 14. Take *that* thine *is*, and go thy way: I will give unto this last, even as unto thee. 15. Is it not lawful for me to do what l will with mine own? Is thine eye evil, because I am good?   [1 Omitted in R. V.]

Luke 10:7. The labourer is worthy of his hire.

Rom. 4:4. Now to him that worketh is the reward not reckoned of grace, but of debt.

Eph. 6:9. Ye masters, do the same things unto them, forbearing threatening: knowing that your Master also is in heaven; neither is there respect of persons with him.

Col. 4:1. Masters, give unto *your* servants that which is just and equal; knowing that ye also have a Master in heaven.

1 Tim. 5:18. For the scripture saith, Thou shalt not muzzle the ox that treadeth out the corn. And, The labourer *is* worthy of his reward.

Philem. 15. For perhaps he therefore departed for a season, that thou shouldest receive him for ever; 16. Not now as a servant, but above a servant, a brother beloved, especially to me, but how much more unto thee, both in the flesh, and in the Lord?

Jas. 5:4. Behold, the hire of the labourers who have reaped down your fields, which is of you kept back by fraud, crieth: and the cries of them which have reaped are entered into the ears of the Lord of sabaoth. 5. Ye have lived in pleasure on the earth, and been wanton; ye have nourished your hearts, as in a day of slaughter.

See MASTER; EMPLOYER; LABOR; SERVANT.

EMULATION, Rom. 11:11. I say then, Have they stumbled that they should fall? God forbid: but *rather* through their fall salvation *is come* unto the Gentiles, for to provoke them to jealousy. 14. If by any means I may provoke to emulation *them which are* my flesh, and might save some of them.

2 Cor. 8:1. Moreover, brethren, we do you to wit of the grace of God bestowed on the churches of Macedonia; 2. How that in a great trial of affliction the abundance of their joy and their deep poverty abounded unto the riches of their liberality. 3. For to *their* power, I bear record, yea, and, beyond *their* power *they were* willing of themselves; 4. Praying us with much intreaty that we would receive the gift, and *take upon us* the fellowship of the ministering to the saints. 5. And *this they did*, not as we hoped, but

first gave their own selves to the Lord, and unto us by the will of God. 6. Insomuch that we desired Titus, that as he had begun, so he would also finish in you the same grace also. 7. Therefore, as ye abound in every *thing, in* faith, and utterance, and knowledge, and *in* all diligence, and *in* your love to us, *see* that ye abound in this grace also. 8. I speak not by commandment, but by occasion of the forwardness of others, and to prove the sincerity of your love.

2 Cor. 9:1. For as touching the ministering to the saints, it is superfluous for me to write to you: 2. For I know the forwardness of your mind, for which I boast of you to them of Macedonia, that Achaia was ready a year ago; and your zeal hath provoked very many. 3. Yet have I sent the brethren, lest our boasting of you should be in vain in this behalf; that, as I said, ye may be ready: 4. Lest haply if they of Macedonia come with me, and find you unprepared, we (that we say not, ye) should be ashamed in this same confident boasting. 5. Therefore I thought it necessary to exhort the brethren, that they would go before unto you, and make up beforehand your bounty, whereof ye had notice before, that the same might be ready, as *a matter of* bounty, and not as *of* covetousness.

Heb. 10:24. And let us consider one another to provoke unto love and to good works:

ILLUSTRATED: In Esau's marriages, Gen. 28:6-9. In Jacob's household, Gen. 30:1-24.

ENAM, a city of Judah, Josh. 15:34.

ENAN, a man of Naphtali, Num. 1:15; 2:29; 7:78,83; 10:27.

ENCHANTMENT. See MAGICIAN; SORCERY.

EN-DOR, a city of Manasseh, Josh. 17:11. The witch of, consulted by Saul, 1 Sam. 28: 7-25. Deborah triumphs at, over Sisera, Judg. 4; Psa. 83:10.

ENDURANCE. See PERSEVERANCE.

ENEAS. See ÆNEAS.

ENEGLAIM, a place near the Dead Sea, Ezek. 47:10.

ENEMY. Ex. 23:5. If thou see the ass of him that hateth thee lying under his burden, and wouldest forbear to help him, thou shalt surely help with him.

Job 31:29. If I rejoiced at the destruction of him that hated me, or lifted up myself when evil found him: 30. Neither have I suffered my mouth to sin by wishing a curse to his soul.

Psa. 35:1. Plead *my cause*, O LORD, with them that strive with me: fight against them that fight against me. 2. Take hold of shield and buckler, and stand up for mine help. 3. Draw out also the spear, and stop *the way* against them that persecute me: say unto my soul, I *am* thy salvation. 4. Let them be confounded and put to shame that seek after my soul: let them be turned back and brought to confusion that devise my hurt. 5. Let them be as chaff before he wind : and let the angel of the LORD chase *them*. 6. Let their way be dark and slippery : and let the angel of the LORD persecute them. 7. For without cause have they hid for me their net *in* a pit, *which* without cause they have digged for my soul. *vs*. 8-28.

Prov. 24:17. Rejoice not when thine enemy falleth, and let not thine heart be glad when he stumbleth : 18. Lest the LORD see *it*, and it displease him, and he turn away his wrath from him.

Prov. 25:21. If thine enemy be hungry, give him bread to eat ; and if he be thirsty, give him water to drink : 22. For thou shalt heap coals of fire upon his head, and the LORD shall reward thee.

Matt. 5:43. Ye have heard that it hath been said, Thou shalt love thy neighbour, and hate thine enemy. 44. But I say unto you, Love your enemies, bless them that curse you, do good to them that hate you, and pray for them which despitefully use you, and persecute you ; 45. That ye may be the children of your Father which is in heaven : for he maketh his sun to rise on the evil and on the good, and sendeth rain on the just and on the unjust. 46. For if ye love them which love you, what reward have ye ? do not even the publicans the same ? 47. And if ye salute your brethren only, what do ye more *than others ?* do not even the publicans so ? 48. Be ye therefore perfect, even as your Father which is in heaven is perfect.

Luke 6:27. But I say unto you which hear, Love your enemies, do good to them which hate you, 28. Bless them that curse you, and pray for them which despitefully use you. 29. And unto him that smiteth thee on the *one* cheek offer also the other ; and him that taketh away thy cloke forbid not *to take thy* coat also. 30. Give to every man that asketh of thee ; and of him that taketh away thy goods ask *them* not again. 31. And as ye would that men should do to you, do ye also to them likewise. 32. For if ye love them which love you, what thank have ye ? for sinners also love those that love them. 33. And if ye do good to them which do good to you, what thank have ye ? for sinners also do even the same. 34. And if ye lend *to them* of whom ye hope to receive, what thank have ye ? for sinners also lend to sinners, to receive as much again. 35. But love ye your enemies, and do good, and lend, hoping for nothing again ; and your reward shall be great, and ye shall be the children of the Highest : for he is kind unto the unthankful and *to* the evil. 36. Be ye therefore merciful, as your Father also is merciful.

Rom. 12:14. Bless them which persecute you : bless, and curse not. 20. Therefore if thine enemy hunger, feed him ; if he thirst, give him drink : for in so doing thou shalt heap coals of fire on his head.

The wickedness of David's, Psa. 56:5; 57:4,

6; 62:4; 69:4,9; 71:10; 102:8; 109:2-5; 129:1-3. His imprecations against, see PRAYER, IMPRECATORY.

Instances of forgiveness of : David, of Absalom, and co-conspirators, 2 Sam. 19:6,12.13. Jesus, of his persecutors, Luke 23:34. Stephen, of his murderers, Acts 7:60.

EN-GANNIM. 1. A city of Judah, Josh. 15:34.

2. A city of Issachar, Josh. 19:21; 21:29.

EN-GEDI, called HAZEZON-TAMAR. A city allotted to Judah, Josh. 15:62. Built by the Amorites, Gen. 14:7; 2 Chr. 20:2. Famous for its vineyards, Song 1:14.

Wilderness of, in the vicinity of the Dead Sea. David uses as a stronghold, 1 Sam. 23:29; 24. Cave of, 1 Sam. 24:3.

ENGINE, of war, 2 Chr. 26:15; Ezek. 26:9. See ARMIES; FORT.

ENGRAFTING. See GRAFTING.

ENGRAVING. In making idols, Ex. 32:4. On the stones set in the priest's breastplate, Ex. 28:9-11,21,36; 39:8-14; in the priest's girdle, Ex. 39:6; in the priest's crown, Ex. 39:30.

EN-HADDAH, a city of Issachar, Josh. 19:21.

EN-HAKKORE, a spring, miraculously supplied to Samson, Judg. 15:19.

EN-HAZOR, a city of Naphtali, Josh. 19:37.

EN-MISHPAT, ancient name of Kadesh, Gen. 14:7.

See KADESH.

ENOCH. 1. Eldest son of Cain, Gen. 4:17,18.

2. A city built by Cain, Gen. 4:17.

3. Father of Methuselah. Translation of, Gen. 5:18-24; Luke 3:37; Heb. 11:5; Jude 14. Called HENOCH, 1 Chr. 1:3.

ENON, a place E. of the Jordan. John baptized near, John 3:23.

ENOS, son of Seth, Gen. 4:26; 5:6-11; Luke 3:38. Called ENOSH, 1 Chr. 1:1.

ENQUIRING OF GOD. See AFFLICTION, PRAYER IN; PRAYER.

EN-RIMMON, a city of Judah, probably identical with AIN and RIMMON, Neh. 11:29.

EN-ROGEL, a spring near Jerusalem, Josh. 15:7; 18:16; 2 Sam. 17:17. A rebellious feast at, 1 Kin. 1:9.

EN-SHEMESH, a spring between Judah and Benjamin, Josh. 15:7; 18:17.

ENSIGN, Psa. 74:4; Isa. 5:26; 11:10,12; 18:3; 30:17; 31:9; Zech. 9:16.

See BANNER; STANDARD.

EN-TAPPUAH, a spring near Tappuah, Josh. 17:7.

ENTHUSIASM. INSTANCES OF : Gideon, Judg. chapters 6, 7; Jehu, 2 Kin. 9:1-14; 10:1-28.

See ZEAL.

ENUMERATION. See CENSUS.

ENVY. Job 5:2. For wrath killeth the foolish man, and envy slayeth the silly one. 3. I have seen the foolish taking root : but suddenly I cursed his habitation.

Psa. 37:1. Fret not thyself because of evil-doers, neither be thou envious against the workers of iniquity. 7. Fret not thyself because of him who prospereth in his way, because of the man who bringeth wicked devices to pass. Prov. 24:19.

Psa. 49:16. Be thou not afraid when one is made rich, when the glory of his house is increased;

Psa. 73:3. I was envious at the foolish, *when* I saw the prosperity of the wicked. *vs.* 17-20.

Psa. 112:10. The wicked shall see *it*, and be grieved; he shall gnash with his teeth, and melt away:

Prov. 3:31. Envy thou not the oppressor, and choose none of his ways.

Prov. 14:30. A sound heart *is* the life of the flesh: but envy the rottenness of the bones.

Prov. 23:17. Let not thine heart envy sinners:

Prov. 24:1. Be not thou envious against evil men, neither desire to be with them.

Prov. 27:4. Who *is* able to stand before envy?

Eccl. 4:4. Again, I considered all travail, and every right work, that for this a man is envied of his neighbour.

Song 8:6. Jealousy *is* cruel as the grave: the coals thereof *are* coals of fire, *which hath* a most vehement flame.

Isa. 26:11. They shall see, and be ashamed for *their* envy at the people;

Ezek. 35:11. Therefore, *as* I live, saith the Lord GOD, I will even do according to thine anger, and according to thine envy which thou hast used out of thy hatred against them;

Rom. 1:29. Being filled with all unrighteousness, fornication, wickedness, covetousness, maliciousness; full of envy, murder, debate, deceit, malignity;

Rom. 13:13. Let us walk honestly, as in the day; not in rioting and drunkenness, not in chambering and wantonness, not in strife and ¹ envying. [¹ R. V. jealousy]

1 Cor. 3:3. Whereas *there is* among you ¹ envying, and strife, and divisions, are ye not c rnal, and walk as men? [¹ R. V. jealousy]

1 Cor. 13:4. Charity envieth not;

2 Cor. 12:20. I fear, lest, when I come, I shall not find you such as I would, and *that* I shall be found unto you such as ye would not: lest *there be* debates, envyings, wraths, strifes, backbitings, whisperings, swellings, tumults:

Gal. 5:19. Now the works of the flesh are manifest, which are *these;* Adultery, fornication, uncleanness, lasciviousness, 20. Idolatry, witchcraft, hatred, variance, emulations, wrath, strife, seditions, heresies. 21. Envyings, murders, drunkenness, revellings, and such like: of the which I tell you before, as I have also told *you* in time past, that they which do such things shall not inherit the kingdom of God. 26. Let us not be desirous of vainglory, provoking one another, envying one another.

1 Tim. 6:4. Doting about questions and strifes of words, whereof cometh envy, strife, railings, evil surmisings, 5. Perverse disputings of men of corrupt minds, and destitute of the truth, supposing that ¹ gain is godliness: from such withdraw thyself. [¹ R. V. godliness is a way of gain]

Tit. 3:3. We ourselves also were sometimes foolish, disobedient, deceived, serving divers lusts and pleasures, living in malice and envy, hateful, *and* hating one another.

Jas. 3:14. If ye have bitter envying and strife in your hearts, glory not, and lie not against the truth. 16. Where envying and strife *is*, there *is* confusion and every evil work.

Jas. 4:5. Do ye think that the scripture saith in vain, The spirit that dwelleth in us lusteth to envy?

Jas. 5:9. Grudge not one against another, brethren, lest ye be condemned: behold, the judge standeth before the door.

1 Pet. 2:1. Laying aside all malice, and all guile, and hypocrisies, and envies, and all evil speakings,

INSTANCES OF: Cain, of Abel, Gen. 4:4-8. Sarah, of Hagar, Gen. 16:5,6; 21:9,10. Philistines, of Isaac, Gen. 26:14. Rachel, of Leah, Gen. 30:1. Leah, of Rachel, Gen. 30:15. Laban's sons, of Jacob, Gen. 31:1. Joseph's brethren, of Joseph, Gen. 37:4-11,19,20; Acts 7:9. Joshua, of Eldad and Medad, Num. 11:28-30. Miriam and Aaron, of Moses, Num. 12:1-10. Korah, Dathan, and Abiram, of Moses, Num. 16:3; Psa. 106:16-18. Saul, of David, 1 Sam. 18:8,9,29; 1 Sam. 20:31. Haman, of Mordecai, Esth. 5:13. The princes of Babylon, of Daniel, Dan. 6:4. Priests, of Jesus, Matt. 27:18; Mark 15:10; John 11:47. Jews, of Paul and Barnabas, Acts 13:45; 17:5.

EPAPHRAS, a co-laborer with Paul, Col. 1:7; 4:12; Philem. 23.

EPAPHRODITUS. A messenger of Paul, Phil. 2:25; 4:18. Sick at Rome, Phil. 2:26,27,30.

EPENETUS, a friend of Paul, Rom. 16:5.

EPHAH. 1. A son of Midian, Gen. 25:4; 1 Chr. 1:33; Isa. 60:6.

2. Caleb's concubine, 1 Chr. 2:46.

3. Son of Jahdai, 1 Chr. 2:47.

4. A measure of about three pecks. See MEASURE, DRY.

EPHAI, an Israelite, Jer. 40:8.

EPHER. 1. A son of Midian, Gen. 25:4; 1 Chr. 1:33.

2. Son of Ezra, 1 Chr. 4:17.

3. A chief of Manasseh, 1 Chr. 5:24.

EPHES-DAMMIN, a place in Judah, 1 Sam. 17:1.

EPHESIANS, Paul's letter to. See EPISTLE TO THE EPHESIANS. See also EPHESUS.

EPHESUS. Paul visits and preaches in, Acts 18:19-21; 19; 20:16-38. Apollos visits and preaches in, Acts 18:18-28. Sceva's sons attempt to expel a demon in, Acts 19:13-16. Timothy directed by Paul to remain at, 1 Tim. 1:3. Paul sends Tychicus to, 2 Tim. 4:12. Onesiphorus lives at, 2 Tim. 1:18. Church at, Rev. 1:11. See the

Epistle to the Ephesians. Apocalyptic message to, Rev. 2:1–7.

See Paul's Epistle to the Ephesians.

EPHLAL, a descendant of Pharez, 1 Chr. 2:37.

EPHOD. 1. A sacred vestment worn by the high priest. Described, Ex. 28:6–14, 31–35; 25:7. Making of, Ex. 39:2–26. Breastplate attached to, Ex. 28:22–29. Worn by Aaron, Ex. 39:5.

Used as an oracle, 1 Sam. 23:9,12; 30:7,8.

An inferior, was worn by the common priests, 1 Sam. 22:18; by Samuel, 1 Sam. 2:18; David, 2 Sam. 6:14. It was called COAT, Ex. 28:40; 29:8; 39:27; 40:14; Lev. 8:13; 10:5.

Made by Gideon, became an idolatrous snare to Israel, Judg. 8:27; 17:5; 18:14.

Prophecy concerning the absence of the Ephod from Israel, Hos. 3:4.

2. A man of Manasseh, Num. 34:23.

EPHRAIM. 1. Second son of Joseph, Gen. 41:52. Adopted by Jacob, Gen. 48:5. Blessed before Manasseh; prophecies concerning, Gen. 48:14–20. Descendants of, Num. 26:35–37; 1 Chr. 7:20–27. Mourns for his sons, 1 Chr. 7:21,22.

2. A tribe of Israel. Prophecy concerning, Gen. 49:25,26; Isa. 7; 9:18–21; 11:13; 28:1; Jer. 31; Hos. 5:14; Zech. 9:10; 10:7. Numbered at Sinai and in plains of Moab, Num. 1:33; 26:37. Place in camp and march, Num. 2:18,24; 10:22. Blessed by Moses, Deut. 33:13–17.

Territory allotted to, after the conquest of Canaan, Josh. 16:5–9; 17:9,10,15–18; 1 Chr. 7:28,29. Fail to expel the Canaanites, Josh. 16:10. Take Beth-el in battle, Judg. 1:22–25. Upbraid Gideon for not summoning them to join the war against the Midianites, Judg. 8:1. Join Gideon against the Midianites, Judg. 7:24,25. Their jealousy of Jephthah, Judg. 12:1. Defeated by him, Judg. 12:4–6. Receive Ish-bosheth as king, 2 Sam. 2:9. Jeroboam set up a golden calf in Beth-el, 1 Kin. 12:29. Revolt from house of David, 1 Kin. 12:25; 2 Chr. 10:16. Some of tribe join Judah under Asa, 2 Chr. 15:9. Chastise Ahaz and Judah, 2 Chr. 28:7. Join Hezekiah in reinstituting the passover, 2 Chr. 30:18. Join in the destruction of idolatrous forms in Jerusalem, 2 Chr. 31:1. Submit to the scepter of Josiah, 2 Chr. 34:1–6. Envied by other tribes, Isa. 11:13; Jer. 7:15; Ezek. 37:16,19; Hos. 13:1. Worshiped Baal, Hos. 13:1. Sin of, remembered by God, Hos. 13:12. Reallotment of territory to, by Ezekiel, Ezek. 48:5.

Name of, applied to the ten tribes, 2 Chr. 17:2; 25:6,7; Isa. 7:8,9; 11:12,13; 17:3; Jer. 31:18,20; Hos. 4:17; 5:3,5; 6:4,10; 8:11; 12:14. Tribe of, called JOSEPH, Rev. 7:8.

3. Mount of. A range of low mountains, Josh. 17:15–18. Joshua has his inheritance in, Judg. 2:9. Residence of Micah, Judg. 17:8. A place of hiding for Israelites, 1 Sam. 14:22. Sheba resides in, 2 Sam. 20:21. Noted

for rich pastures, Jer. 50:19. Prophecy concerning its conversion, Jer. 31:6.

4. A wood E. of the Jordan. Absalom slain in, 2 Sam. 18:6–17.

5. A gate of Jerusalem, 2 Kin. 14:13; 2 Chr. 25:23; Neh. 8:16; 12:39.

6. A city in the territory of Ephraim, 2 Chr. 13:19. Jesus escapes to, from the persecution of Caiaphas, John 11:54.

EPHRAIMITES. See EPHRAIM, 2.

EPHRAIN, a city in Benjamin, 2 Chr. 13:19. See EPHRAIM, 6.

EPHRATAH. 1. Called also EPHRATH. The ancient name of Beth-lehem-judah, Gen. 35:16,19; 48:7; Ruth 4:11; Psa. 132:6; Mic. 5:2.

2. Second wife of Caleb, mother of Hur, 1 Chr. 2:19,50; 4:4.

EPHRATH. See EPHRATAH.

EPHRON. 1. Son of Zohar, the Hittite. Sells to Abraham the field containing the cave Machpelah, Gen. 23:8–17; 25:9; 49:29,30; 50:13.

2. A mountain on the boundary line between Judah and Benjamin, Josh. 15:9.

EPIC, heroic poetry. Miriam's song, Ex. 15:1–19,21. Deborah's song, Judg. 5. David's war song, 2 Sam. 22.

See POETRY.

EPICUREANS. Reject John the Baptist, Matt. 11:18; Luke 7:33. Doctrines propagated by, familiar to Solomon, Eccl. 2:1–10; to Paul, 1 Cor. 15:32. Dispute with Paul, Acts 17:18.

See SENSUALISM.

EPILEPSY, Mark 9:17–22.

See DISEASE.

EPISTLES. From the church at Jerusalem to the Gentiles, Acts 15:23–29. Of Luke to Theophilus, Luke 1:1–4; Acts 1:1. Of Paul, see the books of ROMANS, CORINTHIANS, GALATIANS, EPHESIANS, PHILIPPIANS, COLOSSIANS, THESSALONIANS, TIMOTHY, and TITUS; of JAMES, PETER and JOHN, see books of the N. T., bearing their names.

See LETTERS.

EQUALITY, of men. See MAN, ALL MEN EQUAL.

EQUITY. See JUSTICE.

ER. 1. Son of Judah, Gen. 38:3,6,7; 46:12; Num. 26:19; 1 Chr. 2:3.

2. A son of Shelah, 1 Chr. 4:21.

3. An ancestor of Jesus, Luke 3:28.

ERAN, a grandson of Ephraim, Num. 26:36.

ERASTUS. 1. A friend of Paul, Acts 19:22; 2 Tim. 4:20.

2. Convert of Paul's, probably same as preceding, Rom. 16:23.

ERECH, a city of Shinar, Gen. 10:10.

ERI, a son of Gad, Gen. 46:16; Num. 26:16.

ERRORS, in teachers and doctrines. See TEACHERS, FALSE.

ESAIAS. See ISAIAH.

ESAR-HADDON, king of Assyria. Succeeds Sennacherib, 2 Kin. 19:37; Isa. 37:38. Called Asnapper, Ezra 4:2,10.

ESAU. Eldest of twin sons born to Isaac and Rebekah. Birth of, Gen. 25:19–26; 1 Chr. 1:34. Called Edom, Gen. 36:1,8. A hunter, Gen. 25:27,28. Beloved by Isaac, Gen. 25:27,28. Sells his birthright for a mess of pottage, Gen. 25:29-34; Mal. 1:2; Rom. 9: 13; Heb. 12:16. Marries a Hittite, Gen. 26: 34. His marriage to, a grief to Isaac and Rebekah, Gen. 26:35. Polygamy of, Gen. 26: 34; 28:9; 36:2,3. Is defrauded of his father's blessing by Jacob, Gen. 27; Heb. 11:20. Meets Jacob on the return of the latter from Ha-ran, Gen. 33:1. With Jacob, buries his fa-ther, Gen. 35:29. Descendants of, Gen. 36; 1 Chr. 1:35-57. Enmity of descendants of, toward descendants of Jacob, Obad. 10-14. Ancestor of Edomites, Jer. 49:8. Mount of Edom, called MOUNT OF ESAU, Obad. 8, 9,18,19,21. His name used to denote his de-scendants and their country, Deut. 2:5; Jer. 49:8,10; Obad. 6. Prophecies concerning, Obad. 18.

ESCAPE. NONE, FROM THE JUDG-MENTS OF GOD: Gen. 3:7. And the eyes of them both were opened, and they knew that they *were* naked; and they sewed fig leaves together, and made themselves aprons. 8. And they heard the voice of the LORD God walking in the garden in the cool of the day: and Adam and his wife hid themselves from the presence of the LORD God amongst the trees of the garden. 9. And the LORD God called unto Adam, and said unto him, Where *art* thou? 10. And he said, I heard thy voice in the garden, and I was afraid, because I *was* naked; and I hid myself. 11. And he said, Who told thee that thou *wast* naked? Hast thou eaten of the tree, whereof I commanded thee that thou shouldest not eat?

Gen. 4:9. And the LORD said unto Cain, Where *is* Abel thy brother? And he said, I know not: *Am* I my brother's keeper? 10. And he said, What hast thou done? the voice of thy brother's blood crieth unto me from the ground. 11. And now *art* thou cursed from the earth, which hath opened her mouth to receive thy brother's blood from thy hand.

Job 34:21. For his eyes *are* upon the ways of man, and he seeth all his goings. 22. *There is* no darkness, nor shadow of death, where the workers of iniquity may hide themselves.

Isa. 10:3. And what will ye do in the day of visitation, and in the desolation *which* shall come from far? to whom will ye flee for help, and where will ye leave your glory?

Matt. 23:33. Ye serpents, *ye* generation of vipers, how can ye escape the damnation of hell?

Rom. 2:3. And thinkest thou this, O man, that judgest them which do such things, and doest the same, that thou shalt escape the judgment of God?

1 Thess. 5:2. For yourselves know perfect-ly that the day of the Lord so cometh as a thief in the night. 3. For when they shall say, Peace and safety; then sudden destruc-tion cometh upon them, as travail upon a woman with child; and they shall not es-cape.

Heb. 2:2. For if the word spoken by angels was stedfast, and every transgression and disobedience received a just recompence of reward; 3. How shall we escape, if we neg-lect so great salvation; which at the first began to be spoken by the Lord, and was confirmed unto us by them that heard *him;*

Heb. 12:25. See that ye refuse not him that speaketh. For if they escaped not who re-fused him that spake on earth, much more *shall not* we *escape*, if we turn away from him that *speaketh* from heaven: 26. Whose voice then shook the earth: but now he hath promised, saying, Yet once more I shake not the earth only, but also heaven.

Rev. 6:15. And the kings of the earth, and the great men, and the rich men, and the chief captains, and the mighty men, and every bondman, and every free man, hid themselves in the dens and in the rocks of the mountains; 16. And said to the moun tains and rocks, Fall on us, and hide us from the face of him that sitteth on the throne, and from the wrath of the Lamb: 17. For the great day of his wrath is come; and who shall be able to stand?

See SIN, FRUITS OF, PUNISHMENT OF; JUDG-MENTS, NO ESCAPE FROM.

ESCHEAT. See CONFISCATION.

ESEK, a well dug by the servants of Isaac, Gen. 26:20.

ESH-BAAL. See ISH-BOSHETH.

ESHBAN, a son of Dishan or Dishon, Gen. 36:26; 1 Chr. 1:41.

ESHCOL. 1. An Amorite, and ally of Abraham, Gen. 14:13,24.

2. A valley or brook near Hebron, Num. 13:23,24; 32:9; Deut. 1:24.

ESHEAN, a city in Judah, Josh. 15:52.

ESHEK, a Benjamite, 1 Chr. 8:39.

ESHTAOL. A town of Judah, Josh. 15:33. Allotted to Dan, Josh. 19:41; Judg. 18:2,8,11. Samson moved by the spirit of the Lord near, Judg. 13:25. Samson buried near, Judg. 16:31.

ESHTEMOA. 1. Called also ESHTEMOH. A town of Canaan assigned to Judah, Josh. 15:50. Allotted to the Aaronites, Josh. 21:14; 1 Chr. 6:57. David shared spoil with, 1 Sam. 30:28.

2. A descendant of Ezra, 1 Chr. 4:17,19.

ESHTON, son of Mehir, 1 Chr. 4:11,12.

ESLI, an ancestor of Jesus, Luke 3:25.

ESROM, an ancestor of Jesus, Matt. 1:3; Luke 3:33.

ESTATE, vast landed, Isa. 5:8. See LAND.

ESTHER, called also HADASSAH. Niece of Mordecai, Esth. 2:7,15. Chosen queen, Esth. 2:17. Tells the king of the plot against his life, Esth. 2:22. Fasts on account of the decree to destroy the Israelites; accuses Ha-man to the king; intercedes for her people, Esth. chapters 4-9.

ETAM. 1. A village of Simeon, 1 Chr. 4:32.

2. A city in Judah. 2 Chr. 11:6.

3. A name in list of Judah's descendants,

but probably referring to No. 2, 1 Chr. 4:3.

4. A rock where Samson was bound and delivered to the Philistines, Judg. 15:8,11-13.

ETERNAL LIFE. See LIFE EVER-LASTING.

ETERNAL PUNISHMENT. See PUN-ISHMENT, ETERNAL.

ETERNITY. God inhabiteth, Isa. 57:15; Mic. 5:2; rules, Jer. 10:10.

See GOD, ETERNITY OF.

UNCLASSIFIED SCRIPTURES RELAT-ING TO: Psa. 30:12. O LORD my God, I will give thanks unto thee for ever.

Psa. 41:13. Blessed *be* the LORD God of Israel from everlasting, and to everlasting.

Psa. 72:17. His name shall endure for ever : his name shall be continued as long as the sun :

Psa. 90:2. Before the mountains were brought forth, or ever thou hadst formed the earth and the world, even from ever-lasting to everlasting, thou *art* God.

Psa. 110:4. The LORD hath sworn, and will not repent, Thou *art* a priest for ever after the order of Melchizedek.

Psa. 119:142. Thy righteousness *is* an ever-lasting righteousness, and thy law *is* the truth.

Matt. 6:13. ¹ For thine is the kingdom, and the power, and the glory, for ever.　　[¹ Omitted in R. V.]

Matt. 18:8. Wherefore if thy hand or thy foot offend thee, cut them off, and cast *them* from thee : it is better for thee to enter into life halt or maimed, rather than having two hands or two feet to be cast into everlasting fire.

2 Cor. 9:9. His righteousness remaineth for ever.

Jude 6. And the angels which kept not their first estate, but left their own habita-tion, he hath reserved in everlasting chains under darkness unto the judgment of the great day.

See LIFE, EVERLASTING ; PUNISHMENT, ETERNAL.

ETHAM, second camping place of Israel, Ex. 13:20; Num. 33:6,7.

ETHAN. 1. A renowned sage, 1 Kin. 4:31. See title, Psa. 89.

2. Son of Zerah, 1 Chr. 2:6,8.

3. Two Levites, 1 Chr. 6:42,44; 15:17,19.

ETHANIM. Seventh month [October]. Feast of Trumpets in, Lev. 23:23-25. Day of Atonement, on the tenth day of, Lev. 23:26-32. Feast of Tabernacles in, Lev. 23:33-43. Jubilee proclaimed on the tenth day of, Lev. 25:9. Temple dedicated in, 1 Kin. 8:2. Altar restored in, after the captivity, Ezra 3:1,6.

ETHBAAL, king of Sidon, 1 Kin. 16:31.

ETHER, a city of Caanan. Assigned to Judah, Josh. 15:42. Subsequently allotted to Simeon, Josh. 19:7. Called TOCHEN in 1 Chr. 4:32.

ETHIOPIA, a region in Africa, inhab-ited by the descendants of Ham. The inhab-itants of, black, Jer. 13:23. Within the

Babylonian empire, Esth. 1:1. Rivers of, Gen. 10:6; Isa. 18:1. Bordered Egypt on the S., Ezek. 29:10. Was called the land of Cush, mentioned in Gen. 10:6; 1 Chr. 1:9; Isa. 11:11. Warriors of, Jer. 46:9; 2 Chr. 12:3; Ezek. 38:5. Defeated by Asa, 2 Chr. 14:9-15; 16:8. Invaded Syria, 2 Kin. 19:9. Merchan-dise of, Isa. 45:14. Moses marries a woman of, Num. 12:1. Ebel-melech, at the court of Babylon, native of ; kindly treats Jeremiah, Jer. 38:7-13; 39:15-18. Candace, queen of, Acts 8:27. A eunuch from, becomes a disci-ple under the preaching of Philip, Acts 8:27-39. Prophecies concerning the conver-sion of, Psa. 68:31; 87:4; Isa. 45:14; Dan. 11:43. Desolation of, Isa. 18:1-6; 20:2-6; 43:3; Ezek. 30:4-9; Hab. 3:7; Zeph. 2:12.

ETHNAN, grandson of Ashur, 1 Chr. 4:7.

ETHNI, an ancestor of Asaph, 1 Chr. 6:41.

ETIQUETTE. See MANNERS.

EUBULUS, a friend of Paul, 2 Tim. 4:21.

EUCHARIST. Matt. 26:17. Now the first *day of* the *feast of* unleavened bread the disciples came to Jesus, saying unto him, Where wilt thou that we prepare for thee to eat the passover ? 18. And he said, Go into the city to such a man, and say unto him, The Master saith, My time is at hand : I will keep the passover at thy house with my dis-ciples. 19. And the disciples did as Jesus had appointed them ; and they made ready the passover. 20. Now when the even was come, he sat down with the twelve. 21. And as they did eat, he said, Verily I say unto you, that one of you shall betray me. 22. And they were exceeding sorrowful, and be-gan every one of them to say unto him, Lord, is it I ? 23. And he answered and said, He that dippeth *his* hand with me in the dish, the same shall betray me. 24. The Son of man goeth as it is written of him : but woe unto that man by whom the Son of man is betrayed ! it had been good for that man if he had not been born. 25. Then Judas, which betrayed him, answered and said, Master, is it I ? He said unto him, Thou hast said. 26. And as they were eating, Jesus took bread, and blessed *it*, and brake *it*, and gave *it* to the disciples, and said, Take, eat; this is my body. 27. And he took the cup, and gave thanks, and gave *it* to them, say-ing, Drink ye all of it ; 28. For this is my blood of the new testament, which is shed for many for the remission of sins. 29. But I say unto you, I will not drink henceforth of this fruit of the vine, until that day when I drink it new with you in my Father's kingdom. 30. And when they had sung an hymn, they went out into the mount of Olives. Mark 14:22-24; Luke 22:19,20; John 13:1-4.

Luke 13:26. Then shall ye begin to say, We have eaten and drunk in thy presence, and thou hast taught in our streets.

Acts 2:42. And they continued stedfastly in the apostles' doctrine and fellowship, and in breaking of bread, and in prayers. 46. And they, continuing daily with one **accord** in the temple, and breaking bread from house to house, did eat their meat with gladness and singleness of heart, 47. Praising God, and having favour with all the people.

Acts 20:7. And upon the first *day* of the week, when the disciples came together to break bread, Paul preached unto them, ready to depart on the morrow; and continued his speech until midnight.

1 Cor. 10:16. The cup of blessing which we bless, is it not the communion of the blood of Christ? The bread which we break, is it not the communion of the body of Christ? 17. For we *being* many are one bread, *and* one body: for we are all partakers of that one bread. 21. Ye cannot drink the cup of the Lord, and the cup of devils: ye cannot be partakers of the Lord's table, and of the table of devils. 22. Do we provoke the Lord to jealousy? are we stronger than he?

1 Cor. 11:20. When ye come together therefore into one place, *this* is not to eat the Lord's supper. 21. For in eating every one taketh before *other* his own supper: and one is hungry, and another is drunken. 22. What? have ye not houses to eat and to drink in? or despise ye the church of God, and shame them that have not? What shall I say to you? shall I praise you in this? I praise *you* not. 23. For I have received of the Lord that which also I delivered unto you, That the Lord Jesus the *same* night in which he was betrayed took bread: 24. And when he had given thanks, he brake *it*, and said, Take, eat: this is my body, which is broken for you: this do in remembrance of me. 25. After the same manner also *he took* the cup, when he had supped, saying, This cup is the new testament in my blood: this do ye, as oft as ye drink *it*, in remembrance of me. 26. For as often as ye eat this bread, and drink this cup, ye do shew the Lord's death till he come. 27. Wherefore whosoever shall eat this bread, and drink *this* cup of the Lord, unworthily, shall be guilty of the body and blood of the Lord. 28. But let a man examine himself, and so let him eat of *that* bread, and drink of *that* cup. 29. For he that eateth and drinketh unworthily, eateth and drinketh ¹ damnation to himself, not discerning the Lord's body. 30. For this cause many *are* weak and sickly among you, and many sleep. 31. For if we would judge ourselves, we should not be judged. 32. But when we are judged, we are chastened of the Lord, that we should not be condemned with the world. 33. Wherefore, my brethren, when ye come together to eat, tarry one for another. 34. And if any man hunger, let him eat at home: that ye come not together unto ¹ condemnation. And the rest will I set in order when I come.   [¹ R. V. judgment]

EUNICE, Timothy's mother, 2 Tim. 1:5. See Acts 16:1.

EUODIAS, a Christian woman of Philippi, Phil. 4:2.

EUNUCH. Matt. 19:12. Prohibited from certain privileges of the congregation, Deut.

23:1; Isa. 56:3–5. Influential court officials, Jer. 38:7–13; 52:25; Dan. 1:3. Those who voluntarily became (continent, probably) for the kingdom of heaven's sake, Matt. 19:12. Baptism of the Ethiopian, Acts 8:26–29.

EUPHRATES. A river in the garden of Eden, Gen. 2:14. The eastern limit of the kingdom of Israel, Gen. 15:18; Ex. 23:31; Deut. 1:7; 11:24; Josh. 1:4; 2 Sam. 8:3; 1 Kin. 4:21; 1 Chr. 5:9; 18:3. Pharaoh-nechoh, king of Egypt, made conquest to, 2 Kin. 24:7; Jer. 46:2–10. On the banks of, Jeremiah symbolically buries his girdle, Jer. 13:1–7. Casts the roll containing the prophecies against Babylon into, Jer. 51:59–64.

SYMBOLICAL: The inundations of, of the extension of the empire of Assyria, Isa. 8:6–8. In the symbolisms of the Apocalypse, Rev. 9:14; 16:12.

EUROCLYDON, a tempestuous wind, Acts 27:14.

EUTYCHUS, a young man of Troas, restored to life by Paul, Acts 20:9–11.

EVANGELISM. See MINISTERS, DUTIES OF; ZEAL.

EVAPORATION, Psa. 135:7; Jer. 10:13; 51:16; Amos. 5:8; 9:6.

EVE. Creation of, Gen. 1:26–28; 2:21–24. 1 Tim. 2:13. Named by Adam, Gen. 2:23; 3:20. Beguiled by Satan, Gen. 3; 2 Cor. 11:3; 1 Tim. 2:14. Clothed with fig leaves, Gen. 3:7; with skins, Gen. 3:21. Curse denounced against, Gen. 3:16. Messiah promised to, Gen. 3:15. Children of, Gen. 4:1,2,25; 5:3,4.

EVERLASTING FIRE. See FIRE, EVERLASTING.

EVERLASTING LIFE. See LIFE, EVERLASTING.

EVERLASTING PUNISHMENT. See PUNISHMENT, ETERNAL.

EVI, prince of Midian, slain, Num. 31:8; Josh. 13:21.

EVICTION, OF TENANTS, Matt. 21:41; Mark 12:9.

EVIDENCE. LAWS CONCERNING: Ex. 20:16. Thou shalt not bear false witness against thy neighbour.

Ex. 23:1. Thou shalt not raise a false report; put not thine hand with the wicked to be an unrighteous witness. 7. Keep thee far from a false matter; and the innocent and righteous slay thou not: for I will not justify the wicked.

Lev. 5:1. And if a soul sin, and hear the voice of swearing, and *is* a witness, whether he hath seen or known *of it;* if he do not utter *it*, then he shall bear his iniquity.

Lev. 24:14. Bring forth him that hath cursed without the camp; and let all that heard *him* lay their hands upon his head, and let all the congregation stone him.

Num. 35:30. Whoso killeth any person, the murderer shall be put to death by the mouth of witnesses: but one witness shall not testify against any person to cause *him* to die.

Deut. 17:6. At the mouth of two witnesses, or three witnesses, shall he that is worthy of death be put to death; *but* at the mouth of one witness he shall not be put to death. 7. The hands of the witnesses shall be first upon him to put him to death, and afterward the hands of all the people.

Deut. 19:15. One witness shall not rise up against a man for any iniquity, or for any sin, in any sin that he sinneth : at the mouth of two witnesses, or at the mouth of three witnesses, shall the matter be established. 16. If a false witness rise up against any man to testify against him *that which is* wrong ; 17. Then both the men, between whom the controversy *is*, shall stand before the LORD, before the priests and the judges, which shall be in those days ; 18. And the judges shall make diligent inquisition : and, behold, *if* the witness *be* a false witness, *and* hath testified falsely against his brother ; 19. Then shall ye do unto him, as he had thought to have done unto his brother : so shalt thou put the evil away from among you. 20. And those which remain shall hear, and fear, and shall henceforth commit no more any such evil among you. 21. And thine eye shall not pity ; *but* life *shall go* for life, eye for eye, tooth for tooth, hand for hand, foot for foot.

Prov. 24:28. Be not a witness against thy neighbour without cause ; and deceive *not* with thy lips.

Matt. 18:16. But if he will not hear *thee*, *then* take with thee one or two more, that in the mouth of two or three witnesses every word may be established.

Matt. 19:18. Jesus said, . . . Thou shalt not bear false witness.

Heb. 10:28. He that despised Moses' law died without mercy under two or three witnesses :

SELF-CRIMINATING: Josh. 7:19. And Joshua said unto Achan, My son, give, I pray thee, glory to the LORD God of Israel, and make confession unto him : and tell me now what thou hast done ; hide *it* not from me. 20. And Achan answered Joshua, and said, Indeed I have sinned against the LORD God of Israel, and thus and thus have I done : 21. When I saw among the spoils a goodly Babylonish garment, and two hundred shekels of silver, and a wedge of gold of fifty shekels weight, then I coveted them, and took them : and, behold, they *are* hid in the earth in the midst of my tent, and the silver under it.

See WITNESS ; FALSE WITNESS ; ACCUSATION, FALSE ; SELF-CRIMINATION.

EVIL, APPEARANCE OF, TO BE AVOIDED: Rom. 14:1. Him that is weak in the faith receive ye, *but* not to doubtful disputations. 2. For one believeth that he may eat all things : another, who is weak, eateth herbs. 3. Let not him that eateth despise him that eateth not ; and let not him which eateth not judge him that eateth : for God hath received him. 4. Who art thou that judgest another man's servant ? to his own master he standeth or falleth. Yea, he shall be holden up : for God is able to make him stand. 5. One man esteemeth one day above another : another esteemeth every day *alike*.

Let every man be fully persuaded in his own mind. 6. He that regardeth the day, regardeth *it* unto the Lord ; and he that regardeth not the day, to the Lord he doth not regard *it*. He that eateth, eateth to the Lord, for he giveth God thanks ; and he that eateth not, to the Lord he eateth not, and giveth God thanks. 7. For none of us liveth to himself, and no man dieth to himself. 8. For whether we live, we live unto the Lord ; and whether we die, we die unto the Lord : whether we live therefore, or die, we are the Lord's. 9. For to this end Christ both died, and rose, and revived, that he might be Lord both of the dead and living. 10. But why dost thou judge thy brother ? or why dost thou set at nought thy brother ? for we shall all stand before the judgment seat of Christ. 11. For it is written, *As* I live, saith the Lord, every knee shall bow to me, and every tongue shall confess to God. 12. So then every one of us shall give account of himself to God. 13. Let us not therefore judge one another any more : but judge this rather, that no man put a stumblingblock or an occasion to fall in *his* brother's way. 14. I know, and am persuaded by the Lord Jesus, that *there is* nothing unclean of itself : but to him that esteemeth any thing to be unclean, to him *it is* unclean. 15. But if thy brother be grieved with *thy* meat, now walkest thou not charitably. Destroy not him with thy meat, for whom Christ died. 16. Let not then your good be evil spoken of : 17. For the kingdom of God is not meat and drink ; but righteousness, and peace, and joy in the Holy Ghost. 18. For he that in these things serveth Christ *is* acceptable to God, and approved of men. 19. Let us therefore follow after the things which make for peace, and things wherewith one may edify another. 20. For meat destroy not the work of God. All things indeed *are* pure ; but *it is* evil for that man who eateth with offence. 21. *It is* good neither to eat flesh, nor to drink wine, nor *any thing* whereby thy brother stumbleth, or is offended, or is made weak. 22. Hast thou faith ? have *it* to thyself before God. Happy *is* he that condemneth not himself in that thing which he alloweth. 23. And he that doubteth is damned if he eat, because *he eateth* not of faith : for whatsoever *is* not of faith is sin.

1 Cor. 8:7. Howbeit *there is* not in every man that knowledge : for some with conscience of the idol unto this hour eat *it* as a thing offered unto an idol ; and their conscience being weak is defiled. 8. But meat commendeth us not to God : for neither, if we eat, are we the better ; neither, if we eat not, are we the worse. 9. But take heed lest by any means this liberty of your's become a stumblingblock to them that are weak. 10. For if any man see thee which hast knowledge sit at meat in the idol's temple, shall not the conscience of him

which is weak be emboldened to eat those things which are offered to idols; 11. And through thy knowledge shall the weak brother perish, for whom Christ died? 12. But when ye sin so against the brethren, and wound their weak conscience, ye sin against Christ. 13. Wherefore, if meat make my brother to offend, I will eat no flesh while the world standeth, lest I make my brother to offend.

1 Cor. 10:28. But if any man say unto you, This is offered in sacrifice unto idols, eat not for his sake that shewed it, and for conscience sake : ¹ for the earth *is* the Lord's, and the fulness thereof: 29. Conscience, I say, not thine own, but of the other : for why is my liberty judged of another *man's* conscience? 30. For if I by grace be a partaker, why am I evil spoken of for that for which I give thanks? 31. Whether therefore ye eat or drink, or whatsoever ye do, do all to the glory of God. 32. Give none offence, neither to the Jews, nor to the Gentiles, nor to the church of God : 33. Even as I please all *men* in all *things*, not seeking mine own profit, but the *profit* of many, that they may be saved.   [¹ Omitted in R. V.]

1 Thess. 4:11. Study to be quiet, and to do your own business, and to work with your own hands, as we commanded you; 12. That ye may walk honestly toward them that are without, and *that* ye may have lack of nothing.

1 Thess. 5:22. Abstain from all appearance of evil.

INSTANCES OF : Paul, in refusing to eat that which had been offered to idols, 1 Cor. 8:13. In supporting himself, 1 Cor. 9:7-23.

EVIL FOR EVIL. See RETALIATION.

EVIL FOR GOOD. Psa. 7:4. If I have rewarded evil unto him that was at peace with me; (yea, I have delivered him that without cause is mine enemy :) 5. Let the enemy persecute my soul, and take *it ;* yea, let him tread down my life upon the earth, and lay mine honour in the dust.

Psa. 35:12. They rewarded me evil for good *to* the spoiling of my soul.

Psa. 109:5. And they have rewarded me evil for good, and hatred for my love.

Prov. 17:13. Whoso rewardeth evil for good, evil shall not depart from his house.

INSTANCES OF : Joseph accuses his brethren of rendering, Gen. 44:4. Israelites, to Moses, Ex. 5:21; 14:11; 15:24; 16:2,3; 17:3,4. Nabal returns, to David, 1 Sam. 25:21: Saul returns, to David, 1 Sam. 19:1,4,5,10. David, to Uriah, 2 Sam. 11; to Joab, 1 Kin. 2:4,5,6.

See ENEMIES; GOOD FOR EVIL.

EVIL-MERODACH, son and successor of Nebuchadnezzar. Released Jehoiachin from prison, 2 Kin. 25:27-30; Jer. 52:31-34.

EVIL SPEAKING. See SPEAKING, EVIL.

EXALTATION. OF CHRIST : See JESUS, EXALTATION OF.

OF SELF : See SELF-EXALTATION.

EXAMPLE, BAD, ADMONITIONS

AGAINST : Lev. 18:2. Speak unto the children of Israel, and say unto them, I *am* the LORD your God. 3. After the doings of the land of Egypt, wherein ye dwelt, shall ye not do : and after the doings of the land of Canaan, whither I bring you, shall ye not do : neither shall ye walk in their ordinances.

Lev. 20:23. And ye shall not walk in the manners of the nation, which I cast out before you : for they committed all these things, and therefore I abhorred them.

Deut. 18:9. When thou art come into the land which the LORD thy God giveth thee, thou shalt not learn to do after the abominations of those nations.

2 Chr. 30:7. Be not ye like your fathers, and like your brethren, which trespassed against the LORD God of their fathers, *who* therefore gave them up to desolation, as ye see.

Prov. 22:24. Make no friendship with an angry man; and with a furious man thou shalt not go : 25. Lest thou learn his ways, and get a snare to thy soul.

Isa. 8:11. For the LORD spake thus to me with a strong hand, and instructed me that I should not walk in the way of this people,

Jer. 16:12. Ye have done worse than your fathers; for, behold, ye walk every one after the imagination of his evil heart, that they may not hearken unto me :

Jer. 17:1. The sin of Judah *is* written with a pen of iron, *and* with the point of a diamond : *it is* graven upon the table of their heart, and upon the horns of your altars; 2. Whilst their children remember their altars and their groves by the green trees upon the high hills.

Ezek. 20:18. But I said unto their children in the wilderness, Walk ye not in the statutes of your fathers, neither observe their judgments, nor defile yourselves with their idols :

Hos. 4:9. And there shall be, like people, like priest : and I will punish them for their ways, and reward them their doings.

15. Though thou, Israel, play the harlot, *yet* let not Judah offend; and come not ye unto Gilgal, neither go ye up to Beth-aven, nor swear, The LORD liveth.

Hos. 5:5. And the pride of Israel doth testify to his face : therefore shall Israel and Ephraim fall in their iniquity ; Judah also shall fall with them.

Zech. 1:4. Be ye not as your fathers, unto whom the former prophets have cried, saying, Thus saith the LORD of hosts; Turn ye now from your evil ways, and *from* your evil doings : but they did not hear, nor hearken unto me, saith the LORD.

Matt. 23:1. Then spake Jesus to the multitude, and to his disciples, 2. Saying, The scribes and the Pharisees sit in Moses' seat : 3. All therefore whatsoever they bid you observe, *that* observe and do; but do not ye after their works : for they say, and do not.

1 Cor. 8:9. But take heed lest by any means this liberty of your's become a

stumblingblock to them that are weak. 10. For if any man see thee which hath knowledge sit at meat in the idol's temple, shall not the conscience of him which is weak be emboldened to eat those things which are offered to idols; 11. And through thy knowledge shall the weak brother perish, for whom Christ died? 12. But when ye sin so against the brethren, and wound their weak conscience, ye sin against Christ. 13. Wherefore, if meat make my brother to offend, I will eat no flesh while the world standeth, lest I make my brother to offend.

1 Cor. 10:6. Now these things were our examples, to the intent we should not lust after evil things, as they also lusted.

Eph. 4:17. This I say therefore, and testify in the Lord, that ye henceforth walk not as other Gentiles walk, in the vanity of their mind.

3 John 11. Beloved, follow not that which is evil, but that which is good. He that doeth good is of God: but he that doeth evil hath not seen God.

See Influence.

GOOD, Neh. 5:8. And I said unto them, We, after our ability, have redeemed our brethren the Jews, which were sold unto the heathen; and will ye even sell your brethren? or shall they be sold unto us? Then held they their peace, and found nothing to answer. 9. Also I said, It is not good that ye do: ought ye not to walk in the fear of our God because of the reproach of the heathen our enemies? 10. I likewise, and my brethren, and my servants, might exact of them money and corn: I pray you, let us leave off this usury. 11. Restore, I pray you, to them, even this day, their lands, their vineyards, their oliveyards, and their houses, also the hundredth part of the money, and of the corn, the wine, and the oil, that ye exact of them. 12. Then said they, We will restore them, and will require nothing of them; so will we do as thou sayest. Then I called the priests, and took an oath of them, that they should do according to this promise. 13. Also I shook my lap, and said, So God shake out every man from his house, and from his labour, that performeth not this promise, even thus be he shaken out, and emptied. And all the congregation said, Amen, and praised the Lord. And the people did according to this promise. 14. Moreover from the time that I was appointed to be their governor in the land of Judah, from the twentieth year even unto the two and thirtieth year of Artaxerxes the king, that is, twelve years, I and my brethren have not eaten the bread of the governor. 15. But the former governors that had been before me were chargeable unto the people, and had taken of them bread and wine, beside forty shekels of silver; yea, even their servants bare rule over the people: but so did not I, because of the fear of God. 16. Yea, also I continued in the work of this wall, neither bought we any land: and all my servants

were gathered thither unto the work. 17. Moreover there were at my table an hundred and fifty of the Jews and rulers, beside those that came unto us from among the heathen that are about us. 18. Now that which was prepared for me daily was one ox and six choice sheep; also fowls were prepared for me, and once in ten days store of all sorts of wine: yet for all this required not I the bread of the governor, because the bondage was heavy upon this people. 19. Think upon me, my God, for good, according to all that I have done for this people.

Psa. 101:2. I will walk within my house with a perfect heart.

1 Thess. 1:6. And ye became followers of us, and of the Lord, having received the word in much affliction, with joy of the Holy Ghost: 7. So that ye were ensamples to all that believe in Macedonia and Achaia. 8. For from you sounded out the word of the Lord not only in Macedonia and Achaia, but also in every place your faith to God-ward is spread abroad; so that we need not to speak any thing.

1 Tim. 4:12. Let no man despise thy youth; but be thou an example of the believers, in word, in conversation, in charity, in spirit, in faith, in purity.

Tit. 2:7. In all things shewing thyself a pattern of good works: in doctrine shewing uncorruptness, gravity, sincerity, 8. Sound speech, that cannot be condemned; that he that is of the contrary part may be ashamed, having no evil thing to say of you.

Heb. 13:7. Remember them which have the rule over you, who have spoken unto you the word of God: whose faith follow, considering the end of their conversation:

Jas. 5:10. Take, my brethren, the prophets, who have spoken in the name of the Lord, for an example of suffering affliction, and of patience. 11. Behold, we count them happy which endure. Ye have heard of the patience of Job, and have seen the end of the Lord; that the Lord is very pitiful, and of tender mercy.

1 Pet. 2:11. Dearly beloved, I beseech you as strangers and pilgrims, abstain from fleshly lusts, which war against the soul; 12. Having your conversation honest among the Gentiles: that, whereas they speak against you as evildoers, they may by your good works, which they shall behold, glorify God in the day of visitation. 13. Submit yourselves to every ordinance of man for the Lord's sake: whether it be to the king, as supreme; 14. Or unto governors, as unto them that are sent by him for the punishment of evildoers, and for the praise of them that do well. 15. For so is the will of God, that with well doing ye may put to silence the ignorance of foolish men: 16. As free, and not using your liberty for a cloke of maliciousness, but as the servants of God. 17. Honour all men. Love the brotherhood. Fear God. Honour the king. 18. Servants,

be subject to *your* masters with all fear; not only to the good and gentle, but also to the froward. 19. For this *is* thankworthy, if a man for conscience toward God endure grief, suffering wrongfully. 20. For what glory *is it*, if, when ye be buffeted for your faults, ye shall take it patiently? but if, when ye do well, and suffer *for it*, ye take it patiently, this *is* acceptable with God. 21. For even hereunto were ye called: because Christ also suffered for us, leaving us an example, that ye should follow his steps: 22. Who did no sin, neither was guile found in his mouth: 23. Who, when he was reviled, reviled not again; when he suffered, he threatened not; but committed *himself* to him that judgeth righteously: 24. Who his own self bare our sins in his own body on the tree, that we, being dead to sins, should live unto righteousness: by whose stripes ye were healed. 25. For ye were as sheep going astray; but are now returned unto the Shepherd and Bishop of your souls.

1 Pet. 3:5. For after this manner in the old time the holy women also, who trusted in God, adorned themselves, being in subjection unto their own husbands: 6. Even as Sara obeyed Abraham, calling him lord: whose daughters ye are, as long as ye do well, and are not afraid with any amazement.

1 Pet. 5:3. Neither as being lords over *God's* heritage, but being ensamples to the flock.

See INFLUENCE.

GOD, OUR: Lev. 11:44. For I *am* the LORD your God: ye shall therefore sanctify yourselves, and ye shall be holy; for I *am* holy: neither shall ye defile yourselves with any manner of creeping thing that creepeth upon the earth.

Lev. 19:2. Speak unto all the congregation of the children of Israel, and say unto them, Ye shall be holy: for I the LORD your God *am* holy.

Matt. 5:48. Be ye therefore perfect, even as your Father which is in heaven is perfect.

Luke 6:36. Be ye therefore merciful, as your Father also is merciful.

Eph. 6:9. And, ye masters, do the same things unto them, forbearing threatening: knowing that your Master also is in heaven; neither is there respect of persons with him.

CHRIST, OUR: Mark 10:43. But so shall it not be among you: but whosoever will be great among you, shall be your minister: 44. And whosoever of you will be the chiefest, shall be servant of all. 45. For even the Son of man came not to be ministered unto, but to minister, and to give his life a ransom for many. Matt. 20:28.

Luke 22:27. For whether *is* greater, he that sitteth at meat, or he that serveth? *is* not he that sitteth at meat? but I am among you as he that serveth.

John 13:13. Ye call me Master and Lord: and ye say well; for *so* I am. 14. If I then, *your* Lord and Master, have washed your

feet; ye also ought to wash one another's feet. 15. For I have given you an example, that ye should do as I have done to you. 16. Verily, verily, I say unto you, The servant is not greater than his lord; neither he that is sent greater than he that sent him. 17. If ye know these things, happy are ye if ye do them. 34. A new commandment I give unto you, That ye love one another; as I have loved you, that ye also love one another.

Rom. 15:2. Let every one of us please *his* neighbour for *his* good to edification. 3. For even Christ pleased not himself; but, as it is written, The reproaches of them that reproached thee fell on me. 4. For whatsoever things were written aforetime were written for our learning, that we through patience and comfort of the scriptures might have hope. 5. Now the God of patience and consolation grant you to be likeminded one toward another according to Christ Jesus: 6. That ye may with one mind *and* one mouth glorify God, even the Father of our Lord Jesus Christ. 7. Wherefore receive ye one another, as Christ also received us to the glory of God.

2 Cor. 8:9. For ye know the grace of our Lord Jesus Christ, that, though he was rich, yet for your sakes he became poor, that ye through his poverty might be rich. With context.

2 Cor. 10:1. Now I Paul myself beseech you by the meekness and gentleness of Christ,

Eph. 5:1. Be ye therefore followers of God, as dear children; 2. And walk in love, as Christ also hath loved us, and hath given himself for us an offering and a sacrifice to God for a sweetsmelling savour.

Phil. 2:5. Let this mind be in you, which was also in Christ Jesus: 6. Who, being in the form of God, thought it not ¹ robbery to be equal with God: 7. But ² made himself of no reputation, and took upon him the form of a servant, and was made in the likeness of men: 8. And being found in fashion as a man, he humbled himself, and became obedient unto death, even the death of the cross. [R. V. ¹ a prize ² emptied himself, taking]

Col. 3:13. Forbearing one another, and forgiving one another, if any man have a quarrel against any: even as Christ forgave you, so also *do* ye.

Heb. 12:2. Looking unto Jesus the author and finisher of *our* faith; who for the joy that was set before him endured the cross, despising the shame, and is set down at the right hand of the throne of God. 3. For consider him that endured such contradiction of sinners against himself, lest ye be wearied and faint in your minds.

1 Pet. 2:21. For even hereunto were ye called: because Christ also suffered for us, leaving us an example, that ye should follow his steps:

1 Pet. 3:17. For *it is* better, if the will of God be so, that ye suffer for well doing, than

for evil doing. 18. For Christ also hath once suffered for sins, the just for the unjust, that he might bring us to God, being put to death in the flesh, but quickened by the Spirit:

1 Pet. 4:1. Forasmuch then as Christ hath suffered for us in the flesh, arm yourselves likewise with the same mind: for he that hath suffered in the flesh hath ceased from sin;

1 John 2:6. He that saith he abideth in him ought himself also so to walk, even as he walked.

1 John 3:16. Hereby perceive we the love ¹ *of God*, because he laid down his life for us: and we ought to lay down *our* lives for the brethren.   [¹ Omitted in R. V.]

Rev. 3:21. To him that overcometh will I grant to sit with me in my throne, even as I also overcame, and am set down with my Father in his throne.

PAUL, OUR: Acts 20:35. I have shewed you all things, how that so labouring ye ought to support the weak, and to remember the words of the Lord Jesus, how he said, It is more blessed to give than to receive.

1 Cor. 4:16. Wherefore I beseech you, be ye followers of me.

1 Cor. 7:7. For I would that all men were even as I myself. But every man hath his proper gift of God, one after this manner, and another after that. 8. I say therefore to the unmarried and widows, it is good for them if they abide even as I.

1 Cor. 11:1. Be ye followers of me, even as I also *am* of Christ.

Phil. 3:17. Brethren, be followers together of me, and mark them which walk so as ye have us for an ensample.

Phil. 4:9. Those things, which ye have both learned, and received, and heard, and seen in me, do: and the God of peace shall be with you.

2 Thess. 3:7. For yourselves know how ye ought to follow us: for we behaved not ourselves disorderly among you; 8. Neither did we eat any man's bread for nought; but wrought with labour and travail night and day, that we might not be chargeable to any of you: 9. Not because we have not power, but to make ourselves an ensample unto you to follow us. 10. For even when we were with you, this we commanded you, that if any would not work, neither should he eat.

1 Tim. 1:16. Howbeit for this cause I obtained mercy, that in me first Jesus Christ might shew forth all longsuffering, for a pattern to them which should hereafter believe on him to life everlasting.

2 Tim. 1:13. Hold fast the form of sound words, which thou hast heard of me, in faith and love which is in Christ Jesus.

See INFLUENCE.

EXCHANGERS. See MONEY CHANGERS.

EXCOMMUNICATION. See CHURCH, GOVERNMENT OF; RULES OF DISCIPLINE IN.

EXCUSES. Gen. 3:12. And the man said, The woman whom thou gavest *to be*

with me, she gave me of the tree, and I did eat. 13. And the LORD God said unto the woman, What *is* this *that* thou hast done? And the woman said, The serpent beguiled me, and I did eat.

Ex. 4:1. And Moses answered and said, But, behold, they will not believe me, nor hearken unto my voice: for they will say, The LORD hath not appeared unto thee. 10. And Moses said unto the LORD, O my Lord, I *am* not eloquent, neither heretofore, nor since thou hast spoken unto thy servant: but I *am* slow of speech, and of a slow tongue. 11. And the LORD said unto him, Who hath made man's mouth? or who maketh the dumb, or deaf, or the seeing, or the blind? have not I the LORD? 12. Now therefore go, and I will be with thy mouth, and teach thee what thou shalt say. 13. And he said, O my Lord, send, I pray thee, by the hand *of him whom* thou wilt send. 14. And the anger of the LORD was kindled against Moses, and he said, *Is* not Aaron the Levite thy brother? I know that he can speak well.

Ex. 32:22. And Aaron said, Let not the anger of my lord wax hot: thou knowest the people, that they *are set* on mischief. 23. For they said unto me, Make us gods, which shall go before us: for *as for* this Moses, the man that brought us up out of the land of Egypt, we wot not what is become of him. 24. And I said unto them, Whosoever hath any gold, let them break *it* off. So they gave *it* me: then I cast it into the fire, and there came out this calf.

Deut. 30:11. For this commandment which I command thee this day, it *is* not hidden from thee, neither *is* it far off. 12. It *is* not in heaven, that thou shouldest say, Who shall go up for us to heaven, and bring it unto us, that we may hear it, and do it? 13. Neither *is* it beyond the sea, that thou shouldest say, Who shall go over the sea for us, and bring it unto us, that we may hear it, and do it? 14. But the word *is* very nigh unto thee, in thy mouth, and in thy heart, that thou mayest do it.

Judg. 6:12. And the angel of the LORD appeared unto him, and said unto him, The LORD *is* with thee, thou mighty man of valour. 13. And Gideon said unto him, Oh my Lord, if the LORD be with us, why then is all this befallen us? and where *be* all his miracles which our fathers told us of, saying, Did not the LORD bring us up from Egypt? but now the LORD hath forsaken us, and delivered us into the hands of the Midianites. 14. And the LORD looked upon him, and said, Go in this thy might, and thou shalt save Israel from the hands of the Midianites: have not I sent thee? 15. And he said unto him, Oh my Lord, wherewith shall I save Israel? behold, my family *is* poor in Manasseh, and I *am* the least in my father's house. 16. And the LORD said unto him, Surely I will be with thee, and thou shalt smite the Midianites as one man. 17.

And he said unto him, If now I have found grace in thy sight, then shew me a sign that thou talkest with me.

1 Kin. 19:19. So he departed thence, and found Elisha the son of Shaphat, who *was* plowing *with* twelve yoke *of oxen* before him, and he with the twelfth: and Elijah passed by him, and cast his mantle upon him. 20. And he left the oxen, and ran after Elijah, and said, Let me, I pray thee, kiss my father and my mother, and *then* I will follow thee. And he said unto him, Go back again: for what have I done to thee? 21. And he returned back from him, and took a yoke of oxen, and slew them, and boiled their flesh with the instruments of the oxen, and gave unto the people, and they did eat. Then he arose, and went after Elijah, and ministered unto him.

2 Kin. 5:10. And Elisha sent a messenger unto him, saying, Go and wash in Jordan seven times, and thy flesh shall come again to thee, and thou shalt be clean. 11. But Naaman was wroth, and went away, and said, Behold, I thought, He will surely come out to me, and stand, and call on the name of the LORD his God, and strike his hand over the place, and recover the leper. 12. *Are* not Abana and Pharpar, rivers of Damascus, better than all the waters of Israel? may I not wash in them, and be clean? So he turned and went away in a rage. 13. And his servants came near, and spake unto him, and said, My father, *if* the prophet had bid thee *do some* great thing, wouldest thou not have done *it?* how much rather then, when he saith to thee, Wash, and be clean? 14. Then went he down, and dipped himself seven times in Jordan, according to the saying of the man of God: and his flesh came again like unto the flesh of a little child, and he was clean.

Jer. 1:1. The words of Jeremiah the son of Hilkiah, of the priests that *were* in Anathoth in the land of Benjamin: 4. Then the word of the LORD came unto me, saying, 5. Before I formed thee in the belly I knew thee; and before thou camest forth out of the womb I sanctified thee, *and* I ordained thee a prophet unto the nations. 6. Then said I, Ah, Lord GOD! behold, I cannot speak: for I *am* a child. 7. But the LORD said unto me, Say not, I *am* a child: for thou shalt go to all that I shall send thee, and whatsoever I command thee thou shalt speak. 8. Be not afraid of their faces: for I *am* with thee to deliver thee saith the LORD. 9. Then the LORD put forth his hand, and touched my mouth. And the LORD said unto me, Behold, I have put my words into thy mouth. 10. See, I have this day set thee over the nations and over the kingdoms, to root out, and to pull down, and to destroy, and to throw down, to build, and to plant.

Matt. 8:21. And another of his disciples said unto him, Lord, suffer me first to go and bury my father.

Luke 9:59. And he said unto another, Follow me. But he said, Lord, suffer me first to go and bury my father. 60. Jesus said unto him, Let the dead bury their dead: but go thou and preach the kingdom of God. 61. And another also said, Lord, I will follow thee; but let me first go bid them farewell, which are at home at my house. 62. And Jesus said unto him, No man, having put his hand to the plough, and looking back, is fit for the kingdom of God.

Luke 14:18. And they all with one *consent* began to make excuse. The first said unto him, I have bought a piece of ground, and I must needs go and see it: I pray thee have me excused. 19. And another said, I have bought five yoke of oxen, and I go to prove them: I pray thee have me excused. 20. And another said, I have married a wife, and therefore I cannot come.

Acts 24:25. And as he reasoned of righteousness, temperance, and judgment to come, Felix trembled, and answered, Go thy way for this time; when I have a convenient season, I will call for thee.

Rom. 1:20. For the invisible things of him from the creation of the world are clearly seen, being understood by the things that are made, *even* his eternal power and Godhead; so that they are without excuse:

Rom. 2:1. Therefore thou art inexcusable, O man, whosoever thou art that judgest: for wherein thou judgest another, thou condemnest thyself; for thou that judgest doest the same things.

EXECUTIONER, Gen. 37:36; Prov. 16: 14; Jer. 39:9 [marg.]; Dan. 2:14 [marg.]; Matt. 14:10.

See PUNISHMENT.

EXILE. Absalom, 2 Sam. 14:13,14,24. Ittai, 2 Sam. 15:19.

EXODUS. Of early tribes, Gen. 11:2. Of Israel from Egypt, see ISRAEL.

EXORCISM, casting out evil spirits by Sorcery, see SORCERY.

EXPEDIENCY. Rom. 14:14. I know, and am persuaded by the Lord Jesus, that *there is* nothing unclean of itself: but to him that esteemeth any thing to be unclean, to him *it is* unclean. 15. But if thy brother be grieved with *thy* meat, now walkest thou not charitably. Destroy not him with thy meat, for whom Christ died. 16. Let not then your good be evil spoken of: 17. For the kingdom of God is not meat and drink; but righteousness, and peace, and joy in the Holy Ghost. 18. For he that in these things serveth Christ *is* acceptable to God, and approved of men. 19. Let us therefore follow after the things which make for peace, and things wherewith one may edify another. 20. For meat destroy not the work of God. All things indeed *are* pure; but *it is* evil for that man who eateth with offence. 21. *It is* good neither to eat flesh, nor to drink wine, nor *any thing* whereby thy brother stumbleth, or is offended, or is made weak. 22. Hast thou faith? have *it* to thyself before God. Happy *is* he that condemneth not himself in that thing which he alloweth.

1 Cor. 6:12. All things are lawful unto me, but all things are not expedient: all things are lawful for me, but I will not be brought under the power of any.

1 Cor. 8:8. But meat commendeth us not to God: for neither, if we eat, are we the better; neither, if we eat not, are we the worse. 9. But take heed lest by any means this liberty of your's become a stumbling-block to them that are weak. 10. For if any man see thee which hast knowledge sit at meat in the idol's temple, shall not the conscience of him which is weak be emboldened to eat those things which are offered to idols; 11. And through thy knowledge shall the weak brother perish, for whom Christ died? 12. But when ye sin so against the brethren, and wound their weak conscience, ye sin against Christ. 13. Wherefore, if meat make my brother to offend, I will eat no flesh while the world standeth, lest I make my brother to offend.

1 Cor. 9:19. For though I be free from all *men*, yet have I made myself servant unto all, that I might gain the more. 20. And unto the Jews I became as a Jew, that I might gain the Jews; to them that are under the law, as under the law, that I might gain them that are under the law; 21. To them that are without law, as without law, (being not without law to God, but under the law to Christ,) that I might gain them that are without law. 22. To the weak became I as weak, that I might gain the weak: I am made all things to all *men*, that I might by all means save some. 23. And this I do for the gospel's sake, that I might be partaker thereof with *you*.

1 Cor. 10:23. All things are lawful for me, but all things are not expedient: all things are lawful for me, but all things edify not. 24. Let no man seek his own, but every man another's *wealth*. 25. Whatsoever is sold in the shambles, *that* eat, asking no question for conscience sake; 26. For the earth *is* the Lord's, and the fulness thereof. 27. If any of them that believe not bid you *to a feast*, and ye be disposed to go; whatsoever is set before you, eat, asking no question for conscience sake. 28. But if any man say unto you, This is offered in sacrifice unto idols, eat not for his sake that shewed it, and for conscience sake: for the earth *is* the Lord's, and the fulness thereof: 29. Conscience, I say, not thine own, but of the other: for why is my liberty judged of another *man's* conscience? 30. For if I by grace be a partaker, why am I evil spoken of for that for which I give thanks? 31. Whether therefore ye eat, or drink, or whatsoever ye do, do all to the glory of God. 32. Give none offence, neither to the Jews, nor to the Gentiles, nor to the church of God: 33. Even as I please all *men* in all *things*, not seeking mine own

profit, but the *profit* of many, that they may be saved.

See EVIL, APPEARANCE OF, TO BE AVOIDED; PRUDENCE.

EXPERIENCE, Solomon's, Eccl. 1:2.

RELIGIOUS, RELATING OF: See TESTIMONY, RELIGIOUS.

EXPERIMENT, in worldly pleasure, Solomon's, Eccl. 1; 2.

EXPIATION. See ATONEMENT.

EXPORTS. From Egypt: Of horses and chariots, and linen yarn, 1 Kin. 10:28,29; 2 Chr. 1:16,17; of corn, Gen. 42; 43. From Gilead: of spices, Gen. 37:25. From Ophir: of gold, 1 Kin. 10:11; 22:48; 1 Chr. 29:4. From Tarshish: of gold, 1 Kin. 10:22; ivory, apes, and peacocks, 1 Kin. 10:22; silver, iron, tin, lead, brass, slaves, Ezek. 27:12,13. From Arabia: of sheep and goats, Ezek. 27:21. Palestine: honey, Ezek. 27:17.

See IMPORTS; COMMERCE.

EXPOSTULATION. See REPROOF.

EXTERMINATION. See WAR OF.

EXTORTION. Psa. 109:11. Let the extortioner catch all that he hath; and let the strangers spoil his labour.

Isa. 16:4. Let mine outcasts dwell with thee, Moab; be thou a covert to them from the face of the spoiler: for the extortioner is at an end, the spoiler ceaseth, the oppressors are consumed out of the land.

Ezek. 22:12. In thee have they taken gifts to shed blood; thou hast taken usury and increase, and thou hast greedily gained of thy neighbours by extortion, and hast forgotten me, saith the Lord GOD.

Mic. 3:2. Who hate the good, and love the evil; who pluck off their skin from off them, and their flesh from off their bones; 3. Who also eat the flesh of my people, and flay their skin from off them; and they break their bones, and chop them in pieces, as for the pot, and as flesh within the caldron.

Matt. 23:25. Woe unto you, scribes and Pharisees, hypocrites! for ye make clean the outside of the cup and of the platter, but within they are full of extortion and excess.

Luke 18:11. The Pharisee stood and prayed thus with himself, God, I thank thee, that I am not as other men *are*, extortioners, unjust, adulterers, or even as this publican.

1 Cor. 5:10. Yet not altogether with the fornicators of this world, or with the covetous, or extortioners, or with idolaters; for then must ye needs go out of the world. 11. But now I have written unto you not to keep company, if any man that is called a brother be a fornicator, or covetous, or an idolater, or a railer, or a drunkard, or an extortioner; with such an one no not to eat.

1 Cor. 6:10. Nor thieves, nor covetous, nor drunkards, nor revilers, nor extortioners, shall inherit the kingdom of God.

See USURY.

INSTANCES OF: Jacob in demanding Esau's birthright for a mess of pottage, Gen. 25:31. Pharaoh in exacting of the Egyptians lands and persons, for corn, Gen. 47:13–26.

EXTRADITION. 1 Kin. 18:7. And as Obadiah was in the way, behold, Elijah met him: and he knew him, and fell on his face, and said, *Art* thou that my lord Elijah? 10. *As* the LORD thy God liveth, there is no nation or kingdom, whither my lord hath not sent to seek thee: and when they said, *He is* not *there;* he took an oath of the kingdom and nation, that they found thee not.

Jer. 26:21. And when Jehoiakim the king, with all his mighty men, and all the princes, heard his words, the king sought to put him to death: but when Urijah heard it, he was afraid, and fled, and went into Egypt; 22. And Jehoiakim the king sent men into Egypt, *namely,* Elnathan the son of Achbor, and *certain* men with him into Egypt. 23. And they fetched forth Urijah out of Egypt, and brought him unto Jehoiakim the king;

Acts 9:2. And desired of him letters to Damascus to the synagogues, that if he found any of this way, whether they were men or women, he might bring them bound unto Jerusalem. 14. And here he hath authority from the chief priests to bind all that call on thy name.

Acts 22:5. As also the high priest doth bear me witness, and all the estate of the elders: from whom also I received letters unto the brethren, and went to Damascus, to bring them which were there bound unto Jerusalem, for to be punished.

EXTRAVAGANCE. Prov. 21:17. He that loveth pleasure *shall be* a poor man: he that loveth wine and oil shall not be rich. 20. *There is* treasure to be desired and oil in the dwelling of the wise; but a foolish man spendeth it up.

Luke 16:19. There was a certain rich man, which was clothed in purple and fine linen, and fared sumptuously every day: See GLUTTONY.

EYE. ANTHROPOMORPHIC USES OF: Psa. 33:18. Behold, the eye of the LORD *is* upon them that fear him, upon them that hope in his mercy; 19. To deliver their soul from death, and to keep them alive in famine.

Psa. 34:15. The eyes of the LORD are on the righteous, Amos 9:8; 1 Pet. 3:12.

Psa. 121:3. He that keepeth thee will not slumber. 4. Behold, he that keepeth Israel shall neither slumber nor sleep. 5. The LORD *is* thy keeper:

Isa. 1:15. I will hide mine eyes from you: Isa. 3:8. Their doings . . . provoke the eyes of his glory.

Hab. 1:13. *Thou art* of purer eyes than to behold evil, and canst not look on iniquity: wherefore lookest thou upon them that deal treacherously, *and* holdest thy tongue when the wicked devoureth *the man that is* more righteous than he?

For additional anthropomorphic uses of, see ANTHROPOMORPHISMS.

FIGURATIVE: Of evil desire, never sat-

isfied, Prov. 27:20; Eccl. 1:8; 1 John 2:16. The offending, Matt. 5:29.

EYE FOR EYE. See RETALIATION.

EYELIDS, painted, Ezek. 23:40.

EZBAI, father of Naarai, 1 Chr. 11:37. Possibly identical with PAARAI in 2 Sam. 23:35.

EZBON. 1. A son of Gad, Gen. 46:16. Called OZNI in Num. 26:16.

2. Son of Bela, 1 Chr. 7:7.

EZEKIAS. See HEZEKIAH.

EZEKIEL, a priest. Time of his prophecy, Ezek. 1:1–3. Persecution of, Ezek. 3:25.

Visions of: of God's glory, Ezek. 1; 8; 10; 11; 22; of Jews' abominations, Ezek. 8:5,6; of their punishment, Ezek. 9:10; of the valley of dry bones, Ezek. 37:1–14; of a man with measuring line, Ezek. chapters 40–48; of the river, Ezek. 47:1–5.

Teaches by pantomime: Feigns dumbness, Ezek. 3:26; 24:27; 33:22; symbolizes the siege of Jerusalem by drawings on a tile, Ezek. 4; shaves himself, Ezek. 5:1–4; removes his stuff to illustrate the approaching Jewish captivity, Ezek. 12:3–7; sighs, Ezek. 21:6,7; employs a boiling pot to symbolize the destruction of Jerusalem, Ezek. 24:1–14; omits mourning at the death of his wife, Ezek. 24:16–27; prophesies by parable of an eagle, Ezek. 17:2–10. Other parables, Ezek. 15; 16; 19; 23.

Prophecies of, concerning various nations, Ezek. 25–29. His popularity, Ezek. 33:31,32.

EZEL. A stone near Saul's residence. David and Jonathan meet at, 1 Sam. 20:19.

EZEM, called also AZEM. A city of Simeon, Josh. 15:29; 19:3; 1 Chr. 4:29.

EZER. 1. Called also EZAR, a Horite duke, Gen. 36:21,27,30; 1 Chr. 1:38,42.

2. A son of Ephraim, 1 Chr. 7:21.

3. A priest, Neh. 12:42.

4. A man of Judah, 1 Chr. 4:4. Perhaps identical with the EZRA of 1 Chr. 4:17.

5. A Gadite warrior, 1 Chr. 12:9.

6. A Levite, Neh. 3:19.

EZION-GABER. Last encampment of Israel before coming to the "wilderness of Zin," Num. 33:35,36; Deut. 2:8. Solomon built a navy at, 1 Kin. 9:26. Solomon visits, 2 Chr. 8:17. Jehoshaphat built a navy at, 2 Chr. 20:36. Ships of Jehoshaphat wrecked at, 1 Kin. 22:48.

EZRA. 1. A famous scribe and priest, Ezra 7:1–5,6,10,21; Neh. 12:36. Appoints a fast, Ezra 8:21. Commissioned by Artaxerxes, returns to Jerusalem with a large company of Jews, Ezra 7:8. His charge to the priests, Ezra 8:29. Exhorts people to put away their heathen wives, Ezra 9; 10:1–17. Reads the law, Neh. 8. Reforms corruptions, Ezra 10; Neh. 13. Dedicates the wall of Jerusalem, Neh. 12:27–43.

2. A leading priest among the colonists under Zerubbabel, Neh. 12:1. Probably identical with AZARIAH in Neh. 10:2 and Ezra 7:1.

3. A descendant of Judah, 1 Chr. 4:17.

EZRI, an overseer of king David, 1 Chr. 27:26.

F

FABLE, 1 Tim. 1:4; 4:7; 2 Tim. 4:4; Tit. 1:14; 2 Pet. 1:16.

FACE. Character revealed in, Isa. 3:9. Transfigured: of Moses, Ex. 34:29–35; Jesus, Matt. 17:2, Luke 9:29. Covering of, Isa. 6:2. Disfiguring of, in fasting, Matt. 6:16.

FAINTING, Lam. 2:12; Dan. 8:27.

FAIR HAVENS, a harbor in Crete. Paul tarries at, on his way to Rome, Acts 27:8.

FAITH. 2 Sam. 22:31. *As for* God, his way *is* perfect; the word of the LORD *is* tried: he *is* a buckler to all them that trust in him.

Psa. 5:11. Let all those that put their trust in thee rejoice: let them ever shout for joy, because thou defendest them:

Psa. 7:1. O LORD my God, in thee do I put my trust: save me from all them that persecute me, and deliver me:

Psa. 9:9. The LORD also will be a refuge for the oppressed, a refuge in times of trouble. 10. And they that know thy name will put their trust in thee: for thou, LORD, hast not forsaken them that seek thee.

Psa. 18:30. He *is* a buckler to all those that trust in him.

Psa. 32:10. He that trusteth in the LORD, mercy shall compass him about.

Psa. 33:18. The eye of the LORD *is* upon them that fear him, upon them that hope in his mercy; 19 To deliver their soul from death, and to keep them alive in famine.

Psa. 34:8. O taste and see that the LORD *is* good blessed *is* the man *that* trusteth in him. 22. The LORD redeemeth the soul of his servants: and none of them that trust in him shall be desolate. *vs.* 1–8; Psa. 2:12.

Psa. 36:7. How excellent *is* thy lovingkindness, O God! therefore the children of men put their trust under the shadow of thy wings.

Psa. 40:4. Blessed *is* that man that maketh the LORD his trust.

Psa. 64:10. The righteous shall be glad in the LORD, and shall trust in him;

Psa. 78:7. That they might set their hope in God, and not forget the works of God, but keep his commandments: *vs.* 5–7.

Psa. 84:5. Blessed *is* the man whose strength *is* in thee: 12. O LORD of hosts, blessed *is* the man that trusteth in thee.

Psa. 112:5. A good man sheweth favour, and lendeth: he will guide his affairs with discretion. 7. He shall not be afraid of evil tidings: his heart is fixed, trusting in the LORD. 8. His heart *is* established, he shall not be afraid, until he see *his desire* upon his enemies.

Psa. 118:8. *It is* better to trust in the LORD than to put confidence in man. 9. *It is* better to trust in the LORD than to put confidence in princes.

Psa. 125:1. They that trust in the LORD *shall be* as mount Zion, *which* cannot be removed, *but* abideth for ever.

Psa. 147:11. The LORD taketh pleasure in them that fear him, in those that hope in his mercy.

Prov. 3:5. Trust in the LORD with all thine heart; and lean not unto thine own understanding.

Prov. 14:26. In the fear of the LORD *is* strong confidence: and his children shall have a place of refuge.

Prov. 22:19. That thy trust may be in the LORD, I have made known to thee this day,

Prov. 28:25. He that putteth his trust in the LORD shall be made fat.

Prov. 29:25. Whoso putteth his trust in the LORD shall be safe.

Prov. 30:5. He *is* a shield unto them that put their trust in him.

Isa. 10:20. The remnant of Israel . . . shall stay upon the LORD, the Holy One of Israel, in truth.

Isa. 14:32. The LORD hath founded Zion, and the poor of his people shall trust in it.

Isa. 26:3. Thou wilt keep *him* in perfect peace, *whose* mind *is* stayed *on thee:* because he trusteth in thee.

Isa. 30:15. Thus saith the Lord GOD, the Holy One of Israel; In returning and rest shall ye be saved; in quietness and in confidence shall be your strength:

Isa. 57:13. He that putteth his trust in me shall possess the land, and shall inherit my holy mountain;

Jer. 17:7. Blessed *is* the man that trusteth in the LORD, and whose hope the LORD is. 8. For he shall be as a tree planted by the waters, and *that* spreadeth out her roots by the river, and shall not see when heat cometh, but her leaf shall be green;

Jer. 39:18. I will surely deliver thee, and thou shalt not fall by the sword, but thy life shall be for a prey unto thee: because thou hast put thy trust in me, saith the LORD.

Nah. 1:7. The LORD *is* good, a strong hold in the day of trouble; and he knoweth them that trust in him.

Matt. 9:22. But Jesus turned him about, and when he saw her, he said, Daughter, be of good comfort; thy faith hath made thee whole. And the woman was made whole from that hour.

Matt. 21:21. Jesus answered and said unto them, Verily I say unto you, If ye have faith, and doubt not, ye shall not only do this *which is done* to the fig tree, but also if ye shall say unto this mountain, Be thou removed, and be thou cast into the sea: it shall be done. 22. And all things, whatsoever ye shall ask in prayer, believing, ye shall receive.

Mark 9:23. Jesus said unto him, If thou canst believe, all things *are* possible to him that believeth. 24. And straightway the father of the child cried out, and said with tears, Lord, I believe; help thou mine unbelief.

Mark 11:23. For verily I say unto you, That whosoever shall say unto this mountain, Be thou removed, and be thou cast into the sea; and shall not doubt in his heart, but shall believe that those things which he saith shall come to pass; he shall have whatsoever he saith. 24. Therefore I say unto you, What things soever ye desire, when ye pray, believe that ye receive *them*, and ye shall have *them*.

Luke 7:50. And he said to the woman, Thy faith hath saved thee; go in peace.

Luke 8:48. And he said unto her, Daughter, [1] be of good comfort: thy faith hath made thee whole; go in peace. 49. While he yet spake, there cometh one from the ruler of the synagogue's *house*, saying to him, Thy daughter is dead; trouble not the Master. 50. But when Jesus heard *it*, he answered him, saying, Fear not: believe only, and she shall be made whole. [1 Omitted in R. V.]

Luke 17:5. And the apostles said unto the Lord, Increase our faith.

Luke 18:8. When the Son of man cometh, shall he find faith on the earth?

John 11:25. Jesus said unto her, I am the resurrection, and the life: he that believeth in me, though he [1] were dead, yet shall he live: 26. And whosoever liveth and believeth in me shall never die. Believest thou this? 27. She saith unto him, Yea, Lord: I believe that thou art the Christ, the Son of God, which should come into the world. [R. V. die]

Acts 3:16. And his name through faith in his name hath made this man strong, whom ye see and know: yea, the faith which is by him hath given him this perfect soundness in the presence of you all.

Acts 13:48. As many as were ordained to eternal life believed.

Acts 26:18. That they may receive forgiveness of sins, and inheritance among them which are sanctified by faith that is in me.

Rom. 1:16. For I am not ashamed of the gospel of Christ: for it is the power of God unto salvation to every one that believeth; to the Jew first, and also to the Greek. 17. For therein is the righteousness of God revealed from faith to faith: as it is written, The just shall live by faith.

Rom. 4:1. What shall we say then that Abraham our father, as pertaining to the flesh, hath found? 2. For if Abraham were justified by works, he hath *whereof* to glory; but not before God. 3. For what saith the scripture? Abraham believed God, and it was counted unto him for righteousness. 4. Now to him that worketh is the reward not reckoned of grace, but of debt. 5. But to him that worketh not, but believeth on him that justifieth the ungodly, his faith is counted for righteousness. 6. Even as David also describeth the blessedness of the man, unto whom God imputeth righteousness without works, 7. *Saying*, Blessed *are* they whose iniquities are forgiven, and whose sins are covered. 8. Blessed *is* the man to whom the Lord will not impute sin. 9. *Cometh* this blessedness then upon the circumcision *only*, or upon the uncircumcision also? for we say that faith was reckoned to Abraham for righteousness. 10. How was it then reck-

oned? when he was in circumcision, or in uncircumcision? Not in circumcision, but in uncircumcision. 11. And he received the sign of circumcision, a seal of the righteousness of the faith which *he had yet* being uncircumcised: that he might be the father of all them that believe, though they be not circumcised: that righteousness might be imputed unto them also: 12. And the father of circumcision to them who are not of the circumcision only, but who also walk in the steps of that faith of our father Abraham, which *he had* being *yet* uncircumcised. 13. For the promise, that he should be the heir of the world, *was* not to Abraham, or to his seed, through the law, but through the righteousness of faith. 14. For if they which are of the law *be* heirs, faith is made void, and the promise made of none effect: 15. Because the law worketh wrath: for where no law is, *there is* no transgression. 16. Therefore *it is* of faith, that *it might be* by grace; to the end the promise might be sure to all the seed; not to that only which is of the law, but to that also which is of the faith of Abraham; who is the father of us all, 17. (As it is written, I have made thee a father of many nations,) before him whom he believed, *even* God, who quickeneth the dead, and calleth those things which be not as though they were. 18. Who against hope believed in hope, that he might become the father of many nations, according to that which was spoken, So shall thy seed be. 19. And being not weak in faith, he considered not his own body now dead, when he was about an hundred years old, neither yet the deadness of Sarah's womb: 20. He staggered not at the promise of God through unbelief; but was strong in faith, giving glory to God; 21. And being fully persuaded that, what he had promised, he was able also to perform. 22. And therefore it was imputed to him for righteousness. 23. Now it was not written for his sake alone, that it was imputed to him; 24. But for us also, to whom it shall be imputed, if we believe on him that raised up Jesus our Lord from the dead; 25. Who was delivered for our offences, and was raised again for our justification.

Rom. 5:1. Therefore being justified by faith, [1] we have peace with God through our Lord Jesus Christ: [1 R. V. let us]

Rom. 9:31. But Israel, which followed after the law of righteousness, hath not attained to the law of righteousness. 32. Wherefore? Because *they sought it* not by faith, but as it were by the works of the law. For they stumbled at that stumblingstone; 33. As it is written, Behold, I lay in Sion a stumblingstone and rock of offence: and whosoever believeth on him shall not be ashamed.

Rom. 10:6. But the righteousness which is of faith speaketh on this wise, Say not in thine heart, Who shall ascend into heaven? (that is, to bring Christ down *from above:*) 7. Or, Who shall descend into the deep? (that is, to bring up Christ again from the dead.) 8. But what saith it? The word is nigh thee, *even* in thy mouth, and in thy heart: that is, the word of faith, which we preach; 9. That if thou shalt confess with thy mouth the Lord Jesus, and shalt believe in thine heart that God hath raised him from the dead, thou shalt be saved. 10. For with the heart man believeth unto righteousness; and with the mouth confession is made unto salvation.

Rom. 11:20. Because of unbelief they were broken off, and thou standest by faith. 23. They also, if they abide not still in unbelief, shall be graffed in:

Rom. 15:13. The God of hope fill you with all joy and peace in believing, that ye may abound in hope, through the power of the Holy Ghost.

1 Cor. 1:21. It pleased God by the foolishness of preaching to save them that believe.

1 Cor. 2:5. Your faith should not stand in the wisdom of men, but in the power of God.

1 Cor. 12:8. To one is given by the Spirit the word of wisdom; to another the word of knowledge by the same Spirit; 9. To another faith by the same Spirit;

2 Cor. 1:24. Not for that we have dominion over your faith, but are helpers of your joy: for by faith ye stand.

Gal. 3:1. O foolish Galatians, who hath bewitched you, that ye should not obey the truth, before whose eyes Jesus Christ hath been evidently set forth, crucified among you? 2. This only would I learn of you, Received ye the Spirit by the works of the law, or by the hearing of faith? 3. Are ye so foolish? having begun in the Spirit, are ye now made perfect by the flesh? 4. Have ye suffered so many things in vain? if *it be* yet in vain. 5. He therefore that ministereth to you the Spirit, and worketh miracles among you, *doeth he it* by the works of the law, or by the hearing of faith? 6. Even as Abraham believed God, and it was accounted to him for righteousness. 7. Know ye therefore that they which are of faith, the same are the children of Abraham. 8. And the scripture, foreseeing that God would justify the heathen through faith, preached before the gospel unto Abraham, *saying*, In thee shall all nations be blessed. 9. So then they which be of faith are blessed with faithful Abraham. 10. For as many as are of the works of the law are under the curse: for it is written, Cursed *is* every one that continueth not in all things which are written in the book of the law to do them. 11. But that no man is justified by the law in the sight of God, *it is* evident: for, The just shall live by faith. 12. And the law is not of faith: but, The man that doeth them shall live in them. 13. Christ hath redeemed us from the curse of the law, being made a curse for us: for it is written, Cursed *is* every one that hangeth on a tree: 14. That the blessing of Abraham might come on the Gentiles through Jesus Christ; that we might receive the promise of the Spirit through faith. 15. Brethren, I speak after

the manner of men; Though *it be* but a man's covenant, yet *if it be* confirmed, no man disannulleth, or addeth thereto. 16. Now to Abraham and his seed were the promises made. He saith not, And to seeds, as of many; but as of one, And to thy seed, which is Christ. 17. And this I say, *that* the covenant, that was confirmed before of God in Christ, the law, which was four hundred and thirty years after, cannot disannul, that it should make the promise of none effect. 18. For if the inheritance *be* of the law, *it is* no more of promise: but God gave *it* to Abraham by promise. 19. Wherefore then *serveth* the law? It was added because of transgressions, till the seed should come to whom the promise was made; *and it was* ordained by angels in the hand of a mediator. 20. Now a mediator is not *a mediator* of one, but God is one. 21. *Is* the law then against the promises of God? God forbid: for if there had been a law given which could have given life, verily righteousness should have been by the law. 22. But the scripture hath concluded all under sin, that the promise by faith of Jesus Christ might be given to them that believe. 23. But before faith came, we were kept under the law, shut up unto the faith which should afterwards be revealed. 24. Wherefore the law was our schoolmaster *to bring us* unto Christ, that we might be justified by faith. 25. But after that faith is come, we are no longer under a schoolmaster. 26. For ye are all the children of God by faith in Christ Jesus. 27. For as many of you as have been baptized into Christ have put on Christ. 28. There is neither Jew nor Greek, there is neither bond nor free, there is neither male nor female: for ye are all one in Christ Jesus. 29. And if ye *be* Christ's, then are ye Abraham's seed, and heirs according to the promise.

Gal. 5:22. But the fruit of the Spirit is love, joy, peace, longsuffering, gentleness, goodness, [1] faith, [1 R. V. faithfulness]

Eph. 2:8. By grace are ye saved through faith; and that not of yourselves: *it is* the gift of God:

Eph. 6:16. Above all, taking the shield of faith, wherewith ye shall be able to quench all the fiery darts of the wicked.

Col. 1:23. If ye continue in the faith grounded and settled, and *be* not moved away from the hope of the gospel, which ye have heard,

Col. 2:12. Buried with him in baptism, wherein also ye are risen with *him* through the faith of the operation of God, who hath raised him from the dead.

1 Thess. 2:13. When ye received the word of God which ye heard of us, ye received *it* not *as* the word of men, but as it is in truth, the word of God, which effectually worketh also in you that believe.

1 Thess. 5:8. Putting on the breastplate of faith and love;

2 Thess. 2:13. God hath from the beginning chosen you to salvation through sanc-

tification of the Spirit and belief of the truth:

1 Tim. 1:5. The end of the commandment is charity out of a pure heart, and *of* a good conscience, and *of* faith unfeigned : 19. Holding faith, and a good conscience; which some having put away concerning faith have made shipwreck :

1 Tim. 2:15. She shall be saved in child-bearing, if they continue in faith and charity and holiness with sobriety.

1 Tim. 4:10. For therefore we both labour and suffer reproach, because we trust in the living God, who is the Saviour of all men, specially of those that believe.

1 Tim. 6:11. Follow after righteousness, godliness, faith, . . . 12. Fight the good fight of faith, lay hold on eternal life, whereunto thou art also called, and hast professed a good profession before many witnesses. 17. Charge them that are rich in this world, that they be not highminded, nor trust in uncertain riches, but in the living God, who giveth us richly all things to enjoy ;

2 Tim. 4:7. I have fought a good fight, I have finished *my* course, I have kept the faith : 8. Henceforth there is laid up for me a crown of righteousness, which the Lord, the righteous judge, shall give me at that day : and not to me only, but unto all them also that love his appearing.

Heb. 4:1. Let us therefore fear, lest, a promise being left *us* of entering into his rest, any of you should seem to come short of it. 2. For unto us was the gospel preached, as well as unto them : but the word preached did not profit them, not being mixed with faith in them that heard *it*. 3. For we which have believed do enter into rest, as he said, As I have sworn in my wrath, if they shall enter into my rest : although the works were finished from the foundation of the world. 4. For he spake in a certain place of the seventh *day* on this wise, And God did rest the seventh day from all his works. 5. And in this *place* again, If they shall enter into my rest. 6. Seeing therefore it remaineth that some must enter therein, and they to whom it was first preached entered not in because of [1]unbelief : 7. Again, he limiteth a certain day, saying in David, To day, after so long a time; as it is said, To day if ye will hear his voice, harden not your hearts. 8. For if Jesus had given them rest, then would he not afterward have spoken of another day. 9. There remaineth therefore a rest to the people of God. 10. For he that is entered into his rest, he also hath ceased from his own works, as God *did* from his. 11. Let us labour therefore to enter into that rest, lest any man fall after the same example of [1]unbelief.   [1 R. V. disobedience]

Heb. 6:1. Therefore leaving the principles of the doctrine of Christ, let us go on unto perfection ; not laying again the foundation of repentance from dead works, and of faith toward God. 7. For the earth which drinketh in the rain that cometh oft upon it, and bringeth forth herbs meet for them by whom

it is dressed, receiveth blessing from God: 12. That ye be not slothful, but followers of them who through faith and patience inherit the promises. 18. That by two immutable things, in which *it was* impossible for God to lie, we might have a strong consolation, who have fled for refuge to lay hold upon the hope set before us:

Heb. 10:35. Cast not away therefore your confidence, which hath great recompence of reward. 38. Now the just shall live by faith : but if *any man* draw back, my soul shall have no pleasure in him. 39. But we are not of them who draw back unto perdition ; but of them that believe to the saving of the soul.

Heb. 11:1. Faith is the [1]substance of things hoped for, the [2]evidence of things not seen. 2. For by it the elders obtained a good report. 3. Through faith we understand that the worlds were framed by the word of God, so that things which are seen were not made of things which do appear. 6. But without faith *it is* impossible to please *him:* for he that cometh to God must believe that he is, and *that* he is a rewarder of them that diligently seek him.   [R. V. [1]assurance [2]proving]

Heb. 13:5. He hath said, I will never leave thee, nor forsake thee. 6. So that we may boldly say, The Lord *is* my helper, and I will not fear what man shall do unto me.

Jas. 1:6. But let him ask in faith, nothing [1]wavering.   [1 R. V. doubting]

Jas. 2:1. My brethren, have not the faith of our Lord Jesus Christ, *the Lord* of glory, with respect of persons. 2. For if there come unto your assembly a man with a gold ring, in goodly apparel, and there come in also a poor man in vile raiment; 3. And ye have respect to him that weareth the gay clothing, and say unto him, Sit thou here in a good place; and say to the poor, Stand thou there, or sit here under my footstool: 4. Are ye not then partial in yourselves, and are become judges of evil thoughts ? 5. Hearken, my beloved brethren, Hath not God chosen the poor of this world rich in faith, and heirs of the kingdom which he hath promised to them that love him ? 6. But ye have despised the poor. Do not rich men oppress you, and draw you before the judgment seats ? 7. Do not they blaspheme that worthy name by the which ye are called ? 8. If ye fulfil the royal law according to the scripture, Thou shalt love thy neighbour as thyself, ye do well : 9. But if ye have respect to persons, ye commit sin, and are convinced of the law as transgressors. 10. For whosoever shall keep the whole law, and yet offend in one *point*, he is guilty of all. 11. For he that said, Do not commit adultery, said also, Do not kill. Now if thou commit no adultery, yet if thou kill, thou art become a transgressor of the law. 12. So speak ye, and so do, as they that shall be judged by the law of liberty. 13. For he shall have judgment without mercy, that hath shewed no mercy; and mercy rejoiceth against judgment. 14. What *doth it* profit, my brethren, though a man say he hath faith, and have not works? can faith save him? 15. If a brother or sister be naked, and destitute of daily food, 16. And one of you say unto them, Depart in peace, be *ye* warmed and filled; notwithstanding ye give them not those things which are needful to the body; what *doth it* profit? 17. Even so faith, if it hath not works, is dead, being alone. 18. Yea, a man may say, Thou hast faith, and I have works: shew me thy faith without thy works, and I will shew thee my faith by my works. 19. Thou believest that there is one God; thou doest well: the devils also believe, and tremble. 20. But wilt thou know, O vain man, that faith without works is dead? 21. Was not Abraham our father justified by works, when he had offered Isaac his son upon the altar? 22. Seest thou how faith wrought with his works, and by works was faith made perfect? 23. And the scripture was fulfilled which saith, Abraham believed God, and it was imputed unto him for righteousness: and he was called the Friend of God. 24. Ye see then how that by works a man is justified, and not by faith only. 25. Likewise also was not Rahab the harlot justified by works, when she had received the messengers, and had sent *them* out another way? 26. For as the body without the spirit is dead, so faith without works is dead also.

1 Pet. 1:5. Who are kept by the power of God through faith unto salvation ready to be revealed in the last time. 7. The trial of your faith, being much more precious than of gold that perisheth, though it be tried with fire, might be found unto praise and honour and glory at the appearing of Jesus Christ: 9. Receiving the end of your faith, *even* the salvation of *your* souls. 21. Who by him do believe in God, that raised him up from the dead, and gave him glory; that your faith and hope might be in God.

1 Pet. 3:5. The holy women also, who trusted in God, adorned themselves, being in subjection unto their own husbands:

1 John 3:21. Beloved, if our heart condemn us not, *then* have we confidence toward God.

1 John 5:4. Whatsoever is born of God overcometh the world: and this is the victory that overcometh the world, *even* our faith.

Rev. 22:7. Blessed *is* he that keepeth the sayings of the prophecy of this book.

See FAITH IN CHRIST.

ENJOINED: Ex. 14:13. Moses said unto the people, Fear ye not, stand still, and see the salvation of the LORD, which he will shew to you to day:

Deut. 20:1. When thou goest out to battle against thine enemies, and seest horses, and chariots, *and* a people more than thou, be not afraid of them: for the LORD thy God *is* with thee, which brought thee up out of the land of Egypt. Num. 21:34. Deut. 1:21-31;

3:2,22; 7:17-21; 31:23; Josh. 10:25; Judg. 6:14-16; 2 Kin. 19:6,7; 2 Chr. 20:15,17.

Deut. 31:8. The LORD, he *it is* that doth go before thee; he will be with thee, he will not fail thee, neither forsake thee: fear not, neither be dismayed. *vs.* 6-8.

Josh. 1:9. Have not I commanded thee? Be strong and of a good courage; be not afraid, neither be thou dismayed: for the LORD thy God *is* with thee whithersoever thou goest. *vs.* 5-9.

2 Chr. 15:7. Be ye strong therefore, and let not your hands be weak: for your work shall be rewarded.

2 Chr. 16:9. The eyes of the LORD run to and fro throughout the whole earth, to shew himself strong in the behalf of *them* whose heart *is* perfect toward him.

2 Chr. 20:20. Believe in the LORD your God, so shall ye be established; believe his prophets, so shall ye prosper.

2 Chr. 32:7. Be strong and courageous, be not afraid nor dismayed for the king of Assyria, nor for all the multitude that *is* with him: for *there be* more with us than with him: 8. With him *is* an arm of flesh; but with us *is* the LORD our God to help us, and to fight our battles.

Neh. 4:14. Be not ye afraid of them: remember the Lord, *which is* great and terrible.

Job 35:14. Although thou sayest thou shalt not see him, *yet* judgment *is* before him; therefore trust thou in him.

Psa. 4:5. Offer the sacrifices of righteousness, and put your trust in the LORD.

Psa. 27:14. Wait on the LORD: be of good courage, and he shall strengthen thine heart:

Psa. 31:19. How great *is* thy goodness, which thou hast laid up for them that fear thee; *which* thou hast wrought for them that trust in thee before the sons of men! 24. Be of good courage, and he shall strengthen your heart, all ye that hope in the LORD.

Psa. 37:3. Trust in the LORD, and do good; *so* shalt thou dwell in the land, and verily thou shalt be fed. 5. Commit thy way unto the LORD; trust also in him; and he shall bring *it* to pass. 7. Rest in the LORD, and wait patiently for him: 39. The salvation of the righteous *is* of the LORD: *he is* their strength in the time of trouble. 40. The LORD shall help them, and deliver them: he shall deliver them from the wicked, and save them, because they trust in him.

Psa. 55:22. Cast thy burden upon the LORD, and he shall sustain thee: he shall never suffer the righteous to be moved.

Psa. 62:8. Trust in him at all times; ye people, pour out your heart before him: God *is* a refuge for us.

Psa. 115:9. O Israel, trust thou in the LORD: he *is* their help and their shield. 11. Ye that fear the LORD, trust in the LORD: he *is* their help and their shield.

Psa. 130:7. Let Israel hope in the LORD: for with the LORD *there is* mercy, and with him *is* plenteous redemption.

Prov. 3:5. Trust in the LORD with all thine

heart; and lean not unto thine own understanding. 6. In all thy ways acknowledge him, and he shall direct thy paths. 24. When thou liest down, thou shalt not be afraid: yea, thou shalt lie down, and thy sleep shall be sweet. 25. Be not afraid of sudden fear, neither of the desolation of the wicked, when it cometh. 26. For the LORD shall be thy confidence, and shall keep thy foot from being taken.

Prov. 16:3. Commit thy works unto the LORD, and thy thoughts shall be established.

Isa. 26:4. Trust ye in the LORD for ever: for in the LORD Jehovah *is* everlasting strength: 20. Come, my people, enter thou into thy chambers, and shut thy doors about thee: hide thyself as it were for a little moment, until the indignation be overpast.

Isa. 35:3. Strengthen ye the weak hands, and confirm the feeble knees. 4. Say to them *that are* of a fearful heart, Be strong, fear not: behold, your God will come *with* vengeance, *even* God *with* a recompence; he will come and save you.

Isa. 37:6. Thus saith the LORD, Be not afraid of the words that thou hast heard, wherewith the servants of the king of Assyria have blasphemed me.

Isa. 41:10. Fear thou not: for I *am* with thee: be not dismayed; for I *am* thy God: I will strengthen thee; yea, I will help thee; yea, I will uphold thee with the right hand of my righteousness. 13. I the LORD thy God will hold thy right hand, saying unto thee, Fear not; I will help thee. 14. Fear not, thou worm Jacob, *and* ye men of Israel; I will help thee, saith the LORD, and thy redeemer, the Holy One of Israel.

Isa. 43:1. Thus saith the LORD that created thee, O Jacob, and he that formed thee, O Israel, Fear not: for I have redeemed thee, I have called *thee* by thy name; thou *art* mine. 2. When thou passest through the waters, I *will be* with thee; and through the rivers, they shall not overflow thee: when thou walkest through the fire, thou shalt not be burned; neither shall the flame kindle upon thee. 5. Fear not: for I *am* with thee: I will bring thy seed from the east, and gather thee from the west; 10. That ye may know and believe me, and understand that I *am* he:

Isa. 44:2. Thus saith the LORD that made thee, and formed thee from the womb, *which* will help thee; Fear not, O Jacob, my servant; and thou, Jesurun, whom I have chosen. 8. Fear ye not, neither be afraid: have not I told thee from that time, and have declared *it?* ye *are* even my witnesses. Is there a God beside me?

Isa. 50:10. Who *is* among you that feareth the LORD, that obeyeth the voice of his servant, that walketh *in* darkness, and hath no light? let him trust in the name of the LORD, and stay upon his God.

Jer. 42:11. Be not afraid of the king of Babylon, of whom ye are afraid; be not afraid of him, saith the LORD: for I *am* with

you to save you, and to deliver you from his hand.

Jer. 49:11. Leave thy fatherless children, I will preserve *them* alive; and let thy widows trust in me.

Joel 2:21. Fear not, O land; be glad and rejoice: for the LORD will do great things.

Joel 3:16. The LORD *will be* the hope of his people, and the strength of the children of Israel.

Hab. 2:3. For the vision *is* yet for an appointed time, . . . though it tarry, wait for it; because it will surely come, it will not tarry. 4. The just shall live by his faith.

Zeph. 3:16. In that day it shall be said to Jerusalem, Fear thou not: *and to* Zion, Let not thine hands be slack. 17. The LORD thy God in the midst of thee *is* mighty; he will save, he will rejoice over thee with joy; he will rest in his love, he will joy over **thee** with singing.

Zech. 8:9. Thus saith the LORD of hosts; Let your hands be strong, ye that hear in these days these words by the mouth of the prophets,

Zech. 9:12. Turn you to the strong hold, ye prisoners of hope: even to day do I declare *that* I will render double unto thee;

Matt. 6:25. Therefore I say unto you, [1] Take no thought for your life, what ye shall eat, or what ye shall drink; nor yet for your body, what ye shall put on. Is not the life more than meat, and the body than raiment? 26. Behold the fowls of the air: for they sow not, neither do they reap, nor gather into barns; yet your heavenly Father feedeth them. Are ye not much better than they? 27. Which of you by [2] taking thought can add one cubit unto his stature? 28. And why [3] take ye thought for raiment? Consider the lilies of the field, how they grow; they toil not, neither do they spin: 29. And yet I say unto you, That even Solomon in all his glory was not arrayed like one of these. 30. Wherefore, if God so clothe the grass of the field, which to day is, and to morrow is cast into the oven, *shall he* not much more *clothe* you, O ye of little faith? 31. [4] Therefore take no thought, saying, What shall we eat? or, What shall we drink? or, Wherewithal shall we be clothed? 32. (For after all these things do the Gentiles seek:) for your heavenly Father knoweth that ye have need of all these things. 33. But seek ye first the kingdom of God, and his righteousness; and all these things shall be added unto you. 34. [4] Take therefore no thought for the morrow: for the morrow [5] shall take thought for the things of itself. Sufficient unto the day *is* the evil thereof. Luke 12:22–32.

[R. V. [1] Be not anxious [2] being anxious [3] are ye anxious concerning [4] Be not therefore anxious [5] will be anxious for]

Matt. 17:18. And Jesus rebuked the devil; and he departed out of him: and the child was cured from that very hour. 19. Then came the disciples to Jesus apart, and said, Why could not we cast him out? 20. And

Jesus said unto them, Because of your unbelief: for verily I say unto you, If ye have faith as a grain of mustard seed, ye shall say unto this mountain, Remove hence to yonder place; and it shall remove; and nothing shall be impossible unto you. Mark 11:23,24.

Mark 1:15. Repent ye, and believe the gospel.

Mark 11:22. And Jesus answering saith unto them, Have faith in God.

Luke 12:32. Fear not, little flock; for it is your Father's good pleasure to give you the kingdom.

Luke 17:6. And the Lord said, If ye had faith as a grain of mustard seed, ye might say unto this sycamine tree, Be thou plucked up by the root, and be thou planted in the sea; and it should obey you.

INSTANCES OF: see after the following subtopic.

EXEMPLIFIED: Gen. 6:22. Thus did Noah; according to all that God commanded him, so did he.

Gen. 16:13. And she called the name of the LORD that spake unto her, Thou God seest me: for she said, Have I also here looked after him that seeth me?

Gen. 24:7. The LORD God of heaven, which took me from my father's house, and from the land of my kindred, and which spake unto me, and that sware unto me, saying, Unto thy seed will I give this land; 40. The LORD, before whom I walk, will send his angel with thee, and prosper thy way;

Gen. 48:21. And Israel said unto Joseph, Behold, I die: but God shall be with you, and bring you again unto the land of your fathers.

Gen. 50:20. But as for you, ye thought evil against me; *but* God meant it unto good, to bring to pass, as *it is* this day, to save much people alive. 24. And Joseph said unto his brethren, I die: and God will surely visit you, and bring you out of this land unto the land which he sware to Abraham, to Isaac, and to Jacob.

Ex. 15:2. The LORD *is* my strength and song, and he is become my salvation: he *is* my God, and I will prepare him an habitation; my father's God, and I will exalt him. 16. By the greatness of thine arm they shall be *as* still as a stone; till thy people pass over, O LORD, till the people pass over, *which* thou hast purchased. 17. Thou shalt bring them in, and plant them in the mountain of thine inheritance, *vs.* 1–19.

Ex. 18:11. Now I know that the LORD *is* greater than all gods: for in the thing wherein they dealt proudly *he was* above them.

Num. 10:29. And Moses said unto Hobab, the son of Raguel the Midianite, Moses' father in law, We are journeying unto the place of which the LORD said, I will give it you: come thou with us, and we will do thee good: for the LORD hath spoken good concerning Israel.

Num. 14:8. If the LORD delight in us, then he will bring us into this land, and give it us; 9. Only rebel not ye against the LORD, neither fear ye the people of the land; for they *are* bread for us: their defence is departed from them, and the LORD *is* with us: fear them not.

Josh. 14:12. If so be the LORD *will be* with me, then I shall be able to drive them out, as the LORD said.

1 Sam. 14:6. And Jonathan said to the young man that bare his armour, Come, and let us go over unto the garrison of these uncircumcised: it may be that the LORD will work for us: for *there is* no restraint to the LORD to save by many or by few.

1 Sam. 17:36. Thy servant slew both the lion and the bear: and this uncircumcised Philistine shall be as one of them, seeing he hath defied the armies of the living God. 37. David said moreover, The LORD that delivered me out of the paw of the lion, and out of the paw of the bear, he will deliver me out of the hand of this Philistine. And Saul said unto David, Go, and the LORD be with thee. 45. Then said David to the Philistine, Thou comest to me with a sword, and with a spear, and with a shield: but I come to thee in the name of the LORD of hosts, the God of the armies of Israel, whom thou hast defied. 46. This day will the LORD deliver thee into mine hand; and I will smite thee, and take thine head from thee; and I will give the carcases of the host of the Philistines this day unto the fowls of the air, and to the wild beasts of the earth; that all the earth may know that there is a God in Israel. 47. And all this assembly shall know that the LORD saveth not with sword and spear: for the battle *is* the LORD's, and he will give you into our hands.

2 Sam. 7:28. O Lord GOD, thou *art* that God, and thy words be true, and thou hast promised this goodness unto thy servant:

2 Sam. 23:5. He hath made with me an everlasting covenant, ordered in all *things,* and sure: for *this is* all my salvation, and all *my* desire,

2 Kin. 18:5. He [Hezekiah] trusted in the LORD God of Israel;

1 Chr. 28:20. And David said to Solomon his son, Be strong and of good courage, and do *it:* fear not, nor be dismayed: for the LORD God, *even* my God, *will be* with thee: he will not fail thee, nor forsake thee, until thou hast finished all the work for the service of the house of the LORD.

2 Chr. 13:10. But as for us, the LORD *is* our God, and we have not forsaken him; and the priests, which minister unto the LORD, *are* the sons of Aaron, and the Levites *wait* upon *their* business: 11. And they burn unto the LORD every morning and every evening burnt sacrifices and sweet incense: the shewbread also *set they in order* upon the pure table; and the candlestick of gold with the lamps thereof, to burn every evening: for we keep the charge of the LORD our God; but ye have forsaken him.

2 Chr. 14:11. And Asa cried unto the LORD his God, and said, LORD, *it is* nothing with thee to help, whether with many, or with them that have no power: help us, O LORD our God; for we rest on thee, and in thy name we go against this multitude.

2 Chr. 20:12. O our God, wilt thou not judge them? for we have no might against this great company that cometh against us; neither know we what to do: but our eyes *are* upon thee.

2 Chr. 32:7. *There be* more with us than with him: 8. With him is an arm of flesh; but with us *is* the LORD our God to help us, and to fight our battles. And the people rested themselves upon the words of Hezekiah king of Judah.

Ezra 8:22. The hand of our God *is* upon all them for good that seek him;

Neh. 1:10. These *are* thy servants and thy people, whom thou hast redeemed by thy great power, and by thy strong hand. *vs.* 8–10.

Neh. 2:20. The God of heaven, he will prosper us; therefore we his servants will arise and build:

Job 4:7. Remember, I pray thee, who *ever* perished, being innocent? or where were the righteous cut off? 8. Even as I have seen, they that plow iniquity, and sow wickedness, reap the same. 9. By the blast of God they perish, and by the breath of his nostrils are they consumed. 10. The roaring of the lion, and the voice of the fierce lion, and the teeth of the young lions, are broken. 11. The old lion perisheth for lack of prey, and the stout lion's whelps are scattered abroad. 12. Now a thing was secretly brought to me, and mine ear received a little thereof. 13. In thoughts from the visions of the night, when deep sleep falleth on men, 14. Fear came upon me, and trembling, which made all my bones to shake. 15. Then a spirit passed before my face; the hair of my flesh stood up: 16. It stood still, but I could not discern the form thereof: an image *was* before mine eyes, *there was* silence, and I heard a voice, *saying,* 17. Shall mortal man be more just than God? shall a man be more pure than his maker? 18. Behold, he put no trust in his servants; and his angels he charged with folly: 19. How much less *in* them that dwell in houses of clay, whose foundation *is* in the dust, *which* are crushed before the moth? 20. They are destroyed from morning to evening: they perish for ever without any regarding *it.* 21. Doth not their excellency *which is* in them go away? they die, even without wisdom.

Job 5:8. I would seek unto God, and unto God would I commit my cause: 9. Which doeth great things and unsearchable;

Job 10:12. Thou hast granted me life and favour, and thy visitation hath preserved my spirit.

Job 13:15. Though he slay me, yet will I trust in him. 16. He also *shall be* my salvation:

Job 14:15. Thou wilt have a desire to the work of thine hands.

Job 16:19. Behold, my witness *is* in heaven, and my record *is* on high.

Job 19:25. I know *that* my redeemer liveth, and *that* he shall stand at the latter *day* upon the earth: 26. And *though* after my skin *worms* destroy this *body,* yet in my flesh shall I see God: 27. Whom I shall see for myself, and mine eyes shall behold, and not another; *though* my reins be consumed within me.

Job 23:6. Will he plead against me with *his* great power? No; but he would put *strength* in me.

Job 42:2. I know that thou canst do every *thing,* and *that* no thought can be withholden from thee.

Psa. 3:3. Thou, O LORD, *art* a shield for me; my glory, and the lifter up of mine head. 5. I laid me down and slept; I awaked; for the LORD sustained me. 6. I will not be afraid of ten thousands of people, that have set *themselves* against me round about.

Psa. 4:3. The LORD hath set apart him that is godly for himself: the LORD will hear when I call unto him. 8. I will both lay me down in peace, and sleep: for thou, LORD, only makest me dwell in safety.

Psa. 6:8. The LORD hath heard the voice of my weeping. 9. The LORD hath heard my supplication; the LORD will receive my prayer.

Psa. 7:1. O LORD my God, in thee do I put my trust: 10. My defence *is* of God, which saveth the upright in heart.

Psa. 9:3. When mine enemies are turned back, they shall fall and perish at thy presence. 4. For thou hast maintained my right and my cause;

Psa. 11:1. In the LORD put I my trust: how say ye to my soul, Flee *as* a bird to your mountain?

Psa. 13:5. I have trusted in thy mercy; my heart shall rejoice in thy salvation.

Psa. 16:1. Preserve me, O God: for in thee do I put my trust. 2. *O my soul,* thou hast said unto the LORD, Thou *art* my Lord: 5. The LORD *is* the portion of mine inheritance and of my cup: thou maintainest my lot. 8. I have set the LORD always before me: because *he is* at my right hand, I shall not be moved. 11. Thou wilt shew me the path of life: in thy presence *is* fulness of joy;

Psa. 17:6. I have called upon thee, for thou wilt hear me, O God:

Psa. 18:1. I will love thee, O LORD, my strength. 2. The LORD *is* my rock, and my fortress, and my deliverer; my God, my strength, in whom I will trust; my buckler, and the horn of my salvation, *and* my high tower. 3. I will call upon the LORD, *who is worthy* to be praised: so shall I be saved from mine enemies. 18. They prevented me in the day of my calamity: but the LORD was my stay. 28. Thou wilt light my candle: the LORD my God will enlighten my darkness. 29. For by thee I have run through a troop; and by my God have I leaped over a wall. 2 Sam. 22:2-5.

Psa. 20:5. In the name of our God we will set up our banners: 6. Now know I that the LORD saveth his anointed; he will hear him from his holy heaven with the saving strength of his right hand. 7. Some trust in chariots, and some in horses: but we will remember the name of the LORD our God.

Psa. 21:7. The king trusteth in the LORD, and through the mercy of the most High he shall not be moved.

Psa. 22:4. Our fathers trusted in thee: they trusted, and thou didst deliver them. 5. They cried unto thee, and were delivered: they trusted in thee, and were not confounded.

Psa. 23:1. The LORD is my shepherd; I shall not want. vs. 1-6.

Psa. 25:1. Unto thee, O LORD, do I lift up my soul. 2. O my God, I trust in thee: 5. Lead me in thy truth, and teach me: for thou art the God of my salvation; on thee do I wait all the day. 15. Mine eyes are ever toward the LORD; for he shall pluck my feet out of the net. 20. O keep my soul, and deliver me: let me not be ashamed; for I put my trust in thee.

Psa. 26 1. I have trusted also in the LORD; therefore I shall not slide. 12. My foot standeth in an even place: in the congregations will I bless the LORD.

Psa. 27:1. The LORD is my light and my salvation: whom shall I fear? the LORD is the strength of my life; of whom shall I be afraid? 5. In the time of trouble he shall hide me in his pavilion: in the secret of his tabernacle shall he hide me; he shall set me up upon a rock. 6. And now shall mine head be lifted up above mine enemies round about me: 10. When my father and my mother forsake me, then the LORD will take me up.

Psa. 28:7. The LORD is my strength and my shield; my heart trusted in him, and I am helped:

Psa. 31:1. In thee, O LORD, do I put my trust; let me never be ashamed: 3. Thou art my rock and my fortress; therefore for thy name's sake lead me, and guide me. 4. Pull me out of the net that they have laid privily for me: for thou art my strength. 5. Into thine hand I commit my spirit: thou hast redeemed me, O LORD God of truth. 6. I trust in the LORD. 14. I trusted in thee, O LORD: I said, Thou art my God. 15. My times are in thy hand:

Psa. 32:7. Thou art my hiding place; thou shalt preserve me from trouble; thou shalt compass me about with songs of deliverance.

Psa. 33:20. Our soul waiteth for the LORD: he is our help and our shield. 21. Our heart shall rejoice in him, because we have trusted in his holy name. 22. Let thy mercy, O LORD, be upon us, according as we hope in thee.

Psa. 35:10. All my bones shall say, LORD, who is like unto thee, which deliverest the poor from him that is too strong for him, yea, the poor and the needy from him that spoileth him?

Psa. 38:9. Lord, all my desire is before thee; and my groaning is not hid from thee. 15. In thee, O LORD, do I hope: thou wilt hear, O Lord my God.

Psa. 39:7. Lord, what wait I for? my hope is in thee.

Psa. 40:3. And he hath put a new song in my mouth, even praise unto our God: many shall see it, and fear, and shall trust in the LORD. 4. Blessed is that man that maketh the LORD his trust, and respecteth not the proud, nor such as turn aside to lies. 17. I am poor and needy; yet the Lord thinketh upon me: thou art my help and my deliverer;

Psa. 41:12. Thou upholdest me in mine integrity, and settest me before thy face for ever.

Psa. 42:6. O my God, my soul is cast down within me: therefore will I remember thee . . . 8. The LORD will command his lovingkindness in the daytime, and in the night his song shall be with me, and my prayer unto the God of my life.

Psa. 43:5. Why art thou cast down, O my soul? and why art thou disquieted within me? hope in God: for I shall yet praise him, who is the health of my countenance, and my God. Psa. 42:5.

Psa. 44:5. Through thee will we push down our enemies: through thy name will we tread them under that rise up against us. 8. In God we boast all the day long, and praise thy name for ever.

Psa. 46:1. God is our refuge and strength, a very present help in trouble. 2. Therefore will not we fear, though the earth be removed, and though the mountains be carried into the midst of the sea; 3. Though the waters thereof roar and be troubled, though the mountains shake with the swelling thereof. 5. God is in the midst of her; she shall not be moved: God shall help her, and that right early. 7. The LORD of hosts is with us; the God of Jacob is our refuge.

Psa. 47:3. He shall subdue the people under us, and the nations under our feet. 4. He shall choose our inheritance for us,

Psa. 48:8. As we have heard, so have we seen in the city of the LORD of hosts, in the city of our God: God will establish it for ever. 14. This God is our God for ever and ever: he will be our guide even unto death.

Psa. 52:8. I trust in the mercy of God for ever and ever.

Psa. 54:4. Behold, God is mine helper: the Lord is with them that uphold my soul.

Psa. 55:16. I will call upon God; and the LORD shall save me. 17. Evening, and morning, and at noon, will I pray, and cry aloud: and he shall hear my voice.

Psa. 56:3. What time I am afraid, I will trust in thee. 4. In God I will praise his word, in God I have put my trust; I will not fear what flesh can do unto me. 8. Thou tellest my wanderings: put thou my tears into thy bottle: *are they* not in thy book? 9. When I cry *unto thee,* then shall mine enemies turn back: this I know; for God *is* for me. *v.* 11; Psa. 55:23.

Psa. 57:1. My soul trusteth in thee: yea, in the shadow of thy wings will I make my refuge, until *these* calamities be overpast. 2. I will cry unto God most high; unto God that performeth *all things* for me. 3. He shall send from heaven, and save me *from* the reproach of him that would swallow me up. God shall send forth his mercy and his truth.

Psa. 59:9. *Because of* his strength will I wait upon thee: for God *is* my defence. 10. The God of my mercy shall prevent me: God shall let me see *my desire* upon mine enemies. 17. Unto thee, O my strength, will I sing: for God *is* my defence, *and* the God of my mercy.

Psa. 60:9. Who will bring me *into* the strong city? who will lead me into Edom? 10. *Wilt* not thou, O God, *which* hadst cast us off? and *thou,* O God, *which* didst not go out with our armies? 12. Through God we shall do valiantly: for he *it is that* shall tread down our enemies. Psa. 108:10–13.

Psa. 61:2. From the end of the earth will I cry unto thee, when my heart is overwhelmed: lead me to the rock *that* is higher than I. 4. I will abide in thy tabernacle for ever: I will trust in the covert of thy wings. 6. Thou wilt prolong the king's life: *and* his years as many generations. 7. He shall abide before God for ever:

Psa. 62:1. Truly my soul waiteth upon God: from him *cometh* my salvation. 5. My soul, wait thou only upon God; for my expectation *is* from him. 6. He only *is* my rock and my salvation: *he is* my defence; I shall not be moved. 7. In God *is* my salvation and my glory: the rock of my strength, *and* my refuge, *is* in God.

Psa. 63:6. I remember thee upon my bed, *and* meditate on thee in the *night* watches. 7. Because thou hast been my help, therefore in the shadow of thy wings will I rejoice.

Psa. 66:9. Which holdeth our soul in life, and suffereth not our feet to be moved.

Psa. 67:6. God, *even* our own God, shall bless us.

Psa. 69:19. Thou hast known my reproach, and my shame, and my dishonour: mine adversaries *are* all before thee. 35. God will save Zion, and will build the cities of Judah: that they may dwell there, and have it in possession. 36. The seed also of his servants shall inherit it: and they that love his name shall dwell therein.

Psa. 70:5. Make haste unto me, O God: thou *art* my help and my deliverer:

Psa. 71:1. In thee, O LORD, do I put my trust: let me never be put to confusion. 3. Be thou my strong habitation, whereunto I may continually resort: thou hast given com-

mandment to save me; for thou *art* my rock and my fortress. 5. Thou *art* my hope, O Lord GOD: *thou art* my trust from my youth. 6. By thee have I been holden up from the womb: 7. I am as a wonder unto many; but thou *art* my strong refuge. 14. I will hope continually, and will yet praise thee more and more. 16. I will go in the strength of the Lord GOD: I will make mention of thy righteousness, *even* of thine only. 20. *Thou,* which hast shewed me great and sore troubles, shalt quicken me again, and shalt bring me up again from the depths of the earth. 21. Thou shalt increase my greatness, and comfort me on every side.

Psa. 73:23. I *am* continually with thee: thou hast holden *me* by my right hand. 24. Thou shalt guide me with thy counsel, and afterward receive me *to* glory. 26. My flesh and my heart faileth: *but* God *is* the strength of my heart, and my portion for ever. 28. *It is* good for me to draw near to God: I have put my trust in the Lord GOD,

Psa. 74:12. God *is* my King of old, working salvation in the midst of the earth.

Psa. 77:10. *I will remember* the years of the right hand of the most High. 11. I will remember the works of the LORD: surely I will remember thy wonders of old. 12. I will meditate also of all thy work, and talk of thy doings.

Psa. 86:2. O thou my God, save thy servant that trusteth in thee. 7. In the day of my trouble I will call upon thee: for thou wilt answer me.

Psa. 89:18. For the LORD *is* our defence: and the Holy One of Israel *is* our king. 26. Thou *art* my father, my God, and the rock of my salvation.

Psa. 90:1. LORD, thou hast been our dwelling place in all generations.

Psa. 91:1. He that dwelleth in the secret place of the most High shall abide under the shadow of the Almighty. 2. *He is* my refuge and my fortress: my God; in him will I trust. 9. Because thou hast made the LORD, *which is* my refuge, *even* the most High, thy habitation; 10. There shall no evil befall thee, neither shall any plague come nigh thy dwelling.

Psa. 92:10. My horn shalt thou exalt like *the horn of* an unicorn: I shall be anointed with fresh oil. 15. *He is* my rock, and *there is* no unrighteousness in him.

Psa. 94:14. For the LORD will not cast off his people, neither will he forsake his inheritance. 15. But judgment shall return unto righteousness: and all the upright in heart shall follow it. 17. Unless the LORD *had been* my help, my soul had almost dwelt in silence. 18. When I said, My foot slippeth; thy mercy, O LORD, held me up. 22. The LORD is my defence; and my God *is* the rock of my refuge.

Psa. 102:13. Thou shalt arise, *and* have mercy upon Zion: for the time to favour her, yea, the set time, is come.

Psa. 115:12. The LORD hath been mindful of us: he will bless *us;* he will bless the house of Israel; he will bless the house of Aaron. 13. He will bless them that fear the LORD, *both* small and great. 14. The LORD shall increase you more and more, you and your children.

Psa. 116:7. Return unto thy rest, O my soul; for the LORD hath dealt bountifully with thee.

Psa. 118:6. The LORD *is* on my side; I will not fear: what can man do unto me? 7. The LORD taketh my part with them that help me: therefore shall I see *my desire* upon them that hate me. 10. All nations compassed me about: but in the name of the LORD will I destroy them. 14. The LORD *is* my strength and song, and is become my salvation. 17. I shall not die, but live, and declare the works of the LORD.

Psa. 119:42. So shall I have wherewith to answer him that reproacheth me: for I trust in thy word. 43. And take not the word of truth utterly out of my mouth; for I have hoped in thy judgments. 57. *Thou art* my portion, O LORD: 74. I have hoped in thy word. 81. My soul fainteth for thy salvation: *but* I hope in thy word. 114. Thou *art* my hiding place and my shield: I hope in thy word. 151. Thou *art* near, O LORD; and all thy commandments *are* truth. 166. LORD, I have hoped for thy salvation,

Psa. 121:2. My help *cometh* from the LORD, which made heaven and earth. Psa. 124:8.

Psa. 130:5. I wait for the LORD, my soul doth wait, and in his word do I hope. 6. My soul *waiteth* for the Lord more than they that watch for the morning:

Psa. 138:7. Though I walk in the midst of trouble, thou wilt revive me: thou shalt stretch forth thine hand against the wrath of mine enemies, and thy right hand shall save me. 8. The LORD will perfect *that which* concerneth me: thy mercy, O LORD, *endureth* for ever:

Psa. 140:6. I said unto the LORD, Thou *art* my God: hear the voice of my supplications, O LORD. 7. O GOD the Lord, the strength of my salvation, thou hast covered my head in the day of battle. 12. I know that the LORD will maintain the cause of the afflicted, *and* the right of the poor.

Psa. 141:8. Mine eyes *are* unto thee, O GOD the Lord: in thee is my trust;

Psa. 142:3. When my spirit was overwhelmed within me, then thou knewest my path. 5. I cried unto thee, O LORD: I said, Thou *art* my refuge *and* my portion in the land of the living.

Psa. 143:8. In thee do I trust: cause me to know the way wherein I should walk; for I lift up my soul unto thee. 9. I flee unto thee to hide me.

Psa. 144:2. My goodness, and my fortress; my high tower, and my deliverer; my shield, and *he* in whom I trust; who subdueth my people under me. 10. *It is he* that giveth salvation unto kings: who delivereth David his servant from the hurtful sword.

Eccl. 11:1. Cast thy bread upon the waters: for thou shalt find it after many days.

Isa. 8:10. Take counsel together, and it shall come to nought; speak the word, and it shall not stand: for God *is* with us. 17. I will wait upon the LORD, that hideth his face from the house of Jacob, and I will look for him.

Isa. 12:2. Behold, God *is* my salvation; I will trust, and not be afraid: for the LORD JEHOVAH *is* my strength and *my* song; he also is become my salvation.

Isa. 25:9. Lo, this *is* our God; we have waited for him, and he will save us: this *is* the LORD; we have waited for him, we will be glad and rejoice in his salvation.

Isa. 26:1. We have a strong city; salvation will *God* appoint *for* walls and bulwarks. 8. In the way of thy judgments, O LORD, have we waited for thee; the desire of *our* soul *is* to thy name, and to the remembrance of thee.

Isa. 33:2. O LORD, be gracious unto us; we have waited for thee: 22. The LORD *is* our judge, the LORD *is* our lawgiver, the LORD *is* our king; he will save us.

Isa. 38:16. O Lord, by these *things men* live, and in all these *things is* the life of my spirit: so wilt thou recover me, and make me to live.

Isa. 50:7. For the Lord GOD will help me; therefore shall I not be confounded: therefore have I set my face like a flint, and I know that I shall not be ashamed. 8. *He is* near that justifieth me; who will contend with me? let us stand together: who *is* mine adversary? let him come near to me. 9. Behold, the Lord GOD will help me; who *is* he *that* shall condemn me? lo, they all shall wax old as a garment; the moth shall eat them up.

Isa. 63:16. Doubtless thou *art* our father, though Abraham be ignorant of us, and Israel acknowledge us not: thou, O LORD, *art* our father, our redeemer;

Isa. 64:8. Now, O LORD, thou *art* our father; we *are* the clay, and thou our potter; and we all *are* the work of thy hand.

Jer. 10:23. O LORD, I know that the way of man *is* not in himself: *it is* not in man that walketh to direct his steps.

Jer. 14:9. Thou, O LORD, *art* in the midst of us, and we are called by thy name; leave us not. 22. *Art* not thou he, O LORD our God? therefore we will wait upon thee: for thou hast made all these *things.*

Jer. 16:19. O LORD, my strength, and my fortress, and my refuge in the day of affliction,

Jer. 17:12. A glorious high throne from the beginning *is* the place of our sanctuary. 17. Thou *art* my hope in the day of evil.

Jer. 20:11. The LORD *is* with me as a mighty terrible one: therefore my persecutors shall stumble, and they shall not prevail:

Lam. 3:24. The LORD *is* my portion, saith my soul; therefore will I hope in him. *vs.* 25–32.

Dan. 3:16. Shadrach, Meshach, and Abednego, answered and said to the king, O Nebuchadnezzar, we *are* not careful to answer thee in this matter. 17. Our God whom we serve is able to deliver us from the burning fiery furnace, and he will deliver *us* out of thine hand, O king.

Dan. 6:16. *Now* the king spake and said unto Daniel, Thy God whom thou servest continually, he will deliver thee.

Jonah 2:2. I cried by reason of mine affliction unto the LORD, and he heard me; out of the belly of hell cried I, *and* thou heardest my voice. *vs.* 3–9.

Mic. 7:7. I will look unto the LORD; I will wait for the God of my salvation: my God will hear me. 8. Rejoice not against me, O mine enemy: when I fall, I shall arise; when I sit in darkness, the LORD *shall be* a light unto me. 9. I will bear the indignation of the LORD, because I have sinned against him, until he plead my cause, and execute judgment for me: he will bring me forth to the light, *and* I shall behold his righteousness. 20. Thou wilt perform the truth to Jacob, *and* the mercy to Abraham, which thou hast sworn unto our fathers from the days of old.

Hab. 1:12. *Art* thou not from everlasting, O LORD my God, mine Holy One? we shall not die.

Hab. 3:17. Although the fig tree shall not blossom, neither *shall* fruit *be* in the vines; the labour of the olives shall fail, and the fields shall yield no meat; the flock shall be cut off from the fold, and *there shall be* no herd in the stalls: 18. Yet I will rejoice in the LORD, I will joy in the God of my salvation. 19. The LORD God *is* my strength, and he will make my feet like hinds' *feet*, and he will make me to walk upon mine high places.

Zeph. 3:12. An afflicted and poor people, and they shall trust in the name of the LORD.

Luke 1:38. And Mary said, Behold the handmaid of the Lord; be it unto me according to thy word.

Luke 7:50. And he said to the woman, Thy faith hath saved thee; go in peace.

John 3:33. He that hath received his testimony hath set to his seal that God is true.

Acts 16:34. And when he had brought them into his house, he set meat before them, and rejoiced, believing in God with all his house.

Acts 24:14. But this I confess unto thee, that after the way which they call heresy, so worship I the God of my fathers, believing all things which are written in the law and in the prophets: 15. And have hope toward God, . . . that there shall be a resurrection of the dead, both of the just and unjust.

Acts 27:25. I believe God, that it shall be even as it was told me.

Rom. 8:18. I reckon that the sufferings of this present time *are* not worthy *to be compared* with the glory which shall be revealed in us. 28. And we know that all things work together for good to them that love God, to them who are the called according to *his* purpose. 38. I am persuaded, that neither death, nor life, nor angels, nor prin-

cipalities, nor powers, nor things present, nor things to come, 39. Nor height, nor depth, nor any other creature, shall be able to separate us from the love of God, which is in Christ Jesus our Lord.

Rom. 15:29. I am sure that, when I come unto you, I shall come in the fulness of the blessing of the gospel of Christ.

1 Cor. 9:26. I therefore so run, not as uncertainly; so fight I, not as one that beateth the air:

2 Cor. 1:10. Who delivered us from so great a death, and doth deliver: in whom we trust that he will yet deliver *us;*

2 Cor. 4:8. *We are* troubled on every side, yet not distressed; *we are* perplexed, but not in despair; 9. Persecuted, but not forsaken; cast down, but not destroyed; 13. We having the same spirit of faith, according as it is written, I believed, and therefore have I spoken; we also believe, and therefore speak; 16. For which cause we faint not; but though our outward man perish, yet the inward *man* is renewed day by day. 17. For our light affliction, which is but for a moment, worketh for us a far more exceeding *and* eternal weight of glory; 18. While we look not at the things which are seen, but at the things which are not seen:

2 Cor. 5:7. (We walk by faith, not by sight:)

Gal. 5:5. For we through the Spirit wait for the hope of righteousness by faith.

Phil. 1:19. For I know that this shall turn to my salvation through your prayer, and the supply of the Spirit of Jesus Christ. 20. According to my earnest expectation and *my* hope, that in nothing I shall be ashamed, but *that* with all boldness, as always, *so* now also Christ shall be magnified in my body, whether *it be* by life, or by death. 21. For to me to live *is* Christ, and to die *is* gain.

1 Tim. 4:10. We both labour and suffer reproach, because we trust in the living God, who is the Saviour of all men, specially of those that believe.

2 Tim. 1:12. For the which cause I also suffer these things: nevertheless I am not ashamed: for I know whom I have believed, and am persuaded that he is able to keep that which I have committed unto him against that day.

2 Tim. 2:11. *It is* a faithful saying: For if we be dead with *him*, we shall also live with *him;* 12. If we suffer, we shall also reign with *him:* if we deny *him*, he also will deny us: 13. If we believe not, *yet* he abideth faithful: he cannot deny himself.

Heb. 10:34. For ye had compassion of me in my bonds, and took joyfully the spoiling of your goods, knowing in yourselves that ye have in heaven a better and an enduring substance.

Heb. 11:4. By faith Abel offered unto God a more excellent sacrifice than Cain, by which he obtained witness that he was righteous, God testifying of his gifts: and by it he being dead yet speaketh. 5. By faith Enoch was translated that he should not see death; and was not found, because God had translated him: for before his translation he had this testimony, that he pleased God. 7. By faith Noah, being warned of God of things not seen as yet, moved with fear, prepared an ark to the saving of his house; by the which he condemned the world, and became heir of the righteousness which is by faith. 8. By faith Abraham, when he was called to go out into a place which he should after receive for an inheritance, obeyed; and he went out, not knowing whither he went. 9. By faith he sojourned in the land of promise, as in a strange country, dwelling in tabernacles with Isaac and Jacob, the heirs with him of the same promise: 10. He looked for a city which hath foundations, whose builder and maker is God. 11. Through faith also Sara herself received strength to conceive seed, and was delivered of a child when she was past age, because she judged him faithful who had promised. 13. These all died in faith, not having received the promises, but having seen them afar off, and were persuaded of them, and embraced them, and confessed that they were strangers and pilgrims on the earth. 14. For they that say such things declare plainly that they seek a country. 16. But now they desire a better country, that is, an heavenly: wherefore God is not ashamed to be called their God: for he hath prepared for them a city. 17. By faith Abraham, when he was tried, offered up Isaac: and he that had received the promises offered up his only begotten son, 18. Of whom it was said, That in Isaac shall thy seed be called: 19. Accounting that God was able to raise him up, even from the dead; from whence also he received him in a figure. 20. By faith Isaac blessed Jacob and Esau concerning things to come. 21. By faith Jacob, when he was a dying, blessed both the sons of Joseph; and worshipped, leaning upon the top of his staff. 22. By faith Joseph, when he died, made mention of the departing of the children of Israel; and gave commandment concerning his bones. 23. By faith Moses, when he was born, was hid three months of his parents, because they saw he was a proper child; and they were not afraid of the king's commandment. 24. By faith Moses, when he was come to years, refused to be called the son of Pharaoh's daughter; 25. Choosing rather to suffer affliction with the people of God, than to enjoy the pleasures of sin for a season; 26. Esteeming the reproach of Christ greater riches than the treasures in Egypt: for he had respect unto the recompence of the reward. 27. By faith he forsook Egypt, not fearing the wrath of the king: for he endured, as seeing him who is invisible. 28. Through faith he kept the passover, and the sprinkling of blood, lest he that destroyed the firstborn should touch them. 29. By faith they passed through the Red sea as by dry land: which the Egyptians assaying to do were drowned. 30. By faith

the walls of Jericho fell down, after they were compassed about seven days. 31. By faith the harlot Rahab perished not with them that believed not, when she had received the spies with peace. 32. And what shall I more say? for the time would fail me to tell of Gedeon, and of Barak, and of Samson, and of Jephthae; of David also, and Samuel, and of the prophets: 33. Who through faith subdued kingdoms, wrought righteousness, obtained promises, stopped the mouths of lions, 34. Quenched the violence of fire, escaped the edge of the sword, out of weakness were made strong, waxed valiant in fight, turned to flight the armies of the aliens. 35. Women received their dead raised to life again: and others were tortured, not accepting deliverance; that they might obtain a better resurrection: 36. And others had trial of cruel mockings and scourgings, yea, moreover of bonds and imprisonment: 37. They were stoned, they were sawn asunder, were tempted, were slain with the sword: they wandered about in sheepskins and goatskins; being destitute, afflicted, tormented; 38. (Of whom the world was not worthy:) they wandered in deserts, and in mountains, and in dens and caves of the earth. 39. And these all, having obtained a good report through faith, received not the promise:

Heb. 13:14. Here have we no continuing city, but we seek one to come.

2 Pet. 3:13. We, according to his promise, look for new heavens and a new earth, wherein dwelleth righteousness.

1 John 4:16. We have known and believed the love that God hath to us. God is love:

INSTANCES OF: Noah, in building the ark, Gen. 6:14–22; Heb. 11:7. Abraham, in forsaking the land of his nativity at the command of God, Gen. 12:1–4; believing the promise of many descendants, Gen. 12:7; 15:4–8; in the offering up of Isaac, Gen. 22:1–10; Rom. 4: 18–21; Heb. 11:8–19. Jacob, in blessing Joseph's sons, Heb. 11:21. Joseph, concerning God's providence in his being sold into Egypt, and the final deliverance of Israel, Gen. 50: 20; Heb. 11:22. Jochebed, in caring for Moses, Ex. 2:2; Heb. 11:23. Pharaoh's servants, who obeyed the Lord, Ex. 9:20. Moses, in espousing the cause of his people, Heb. 11: 24–28; at the death of Korah, Num. 16:28,29.

Israelites, when Aaron declared the mission of himself and Moses, Ex. 4:31; in the battle with the Canaanites, 1 Chr. 5:20, and other conquests, 2 Chr. 13:8–18. See MIRACLES OF MOSES. Caleb, in advising to take the land of promise, Num. 13:30; 14:6–9. Rahab, in hospitality to the spies, Josh. 2:9,11; Heb. 11:31. The spies, sent to reconnoiter Jericho, Josh. 2:24. Conquest of Jericho, Josh. 6. Manoah's wife, Judg. 13:23. Hannah, 1 Sam. 1. Jonathan, in smiting the Philistines, 1 Sam. 14:6. David, in smiting Goliath, 1 Sam. 17:37,46,47; in choosing to fall into the hands of the Almighty in his punishment for numbering Israel, 2 Sam. 24:14;

in believing God's promise, that his kingdom would be a perpetual kingdom, Acts 2:30. Elijah, in his controversy with the priests of Baal, 1 Kin. 18:32–38. Widow of Zarephath in feeding Elijah, 1 Kin. 17:13–15. Amaziah, in dismissing the Ephraimites in obedience to the command of God, and going alone to battle against the Edomites, 2 Chr. 25:7-10. Hezekiah, 2 Kin. 18:5; 19; 20:1–11. Daniel, in the lions' den, Dan. 6. The three Hebrews, who refused to worship Nebuchadnezzar's idol, Dan. 3:13–27. Ninevites, in obeying Jonah, Jonah 3:5. Ezra, in making the journey from Babylon to Jerusalem without a military escort, Ezra 8:22. Joseph, in obeying the vision about Mary and to flee into Egypt, Matt. 1:18–24; 2:13,14. Abel, Heb. 11:4. Eliphaz, in the overruling providence of God, that afflictions are for the good of the righteous, Job 5:6-27. Mordecai, in the deliverance of the Jews, Esth. 4:14. Simeon, when he saw Jesus in the temple, Luke 2:25-35. Conquests by, Heb. 11:32-34.

See FAITH, TRIAL OF, below; FAITH IN CHRIST, INSTANCES OF, below.

IN CHRIST: Matt. 7:24. Whosoever heareth these sayings of mine, and doeth them, I will liken him unto a wise man, which built his house upon a rock: 25. And the rain descended, and the floods came, and the winds blew, and beat upon that house; and it fell not: for it was founded upon a rock. Luke 6:46–49.

Matt. 8:2. And, behold, there came a leper and worshipped him, saying, Lord, if thou wilt, thou canst make me clean. 13. As thou hast believed, *so* be it done unto thee.

Matt. 9:22. But Jesus turned him about, and when he saw her, he said, Daughter, be of good comfort; thy faith hath made thee whole. 29. Then touched he their eyes, saying, According to your faith be it unto you.

Matt. 11:6. Blessed is *he*, whosoever shall not be offended in me. 28. Come unto me, all *ye* that labour and are heavy laden, and I will give you rest. 29. Take my yoke upon you, and learn of me; for I am meek and lowly in heart: and ye shall find rest unto your souls. 30. For my yoke *is* easy, and my burden is light.

Matt. 14:27. Jesus spake unto them, saying, Be of good cheer; it is I; be not afraid. John 6:20.

Matt. 15:28. Then Jesus answered and said unto her, O woman, great *is* thy faith: be it unto thee even as thou wilt.

Matt. 17:7. Jesus came and touched them, and said, Arise, and be not afraid.

Mark 9:23. Jesus said unto him, If thou canst believe, all things *are* possible to him that believeth.

Mark 16:16. He that believeth and is baptized shall be saved; but he that believeth not shall be damned.

Luke 7:9. When Jesus heard these things, he marvelled at him, and turned him about, and said unto the people that followed him, I say unto you, I have not found so great

faith, no, not in Israel. 50. And he said to the woman, Thy faith hath saved thee; go in peace.

Luke 8:50. When Jesus heard *it*, he answered him, saying, Fear not: believe only, and she shall be made whole. Mark 5:36.

Luke 17:6. If ye had faith as a grain of mustard seed, ye might say unto this sycamine tree, Be thou plucked up by the root, and be thou planted in the sea; and it should obey you.

Luke 18:42. Jesus said unto him, Receive thy sight: thy faith hath saved thee.

John 1:12. But as many as received him, to them gave he [1]power to become [2]the sons of God, *even* to them that believe on his name: [R. V. [1]the right [2]children]

John 3:14. And as Moses lifted up the serpent in the wilderness, even so must the Son of man be lifted up: 15. That whosoever believeth in him should not perish, but have eternal life. 16. For God so loved the world, that he gave his only begotten Son, that whosoever believeth in him should not perish, but have everlasting life. 18. He that believeth on him is not condemned: but he that believeth not is condemned already, because he hath not believed in the name of the only begotten Son of God. 36. He that believeth on the Son hath everlasting life: and he that [1]believeth not the Son shall not see life; but the wrath of God abideth on him. John 6:47. [[1] R. V. obeyeth

John 5:24. Verily, verily, I say unto you, He that heareth my word, and believeth on him that sent me, hath everlasting life, and shall not come into condemnation; but is passed from death unto life.

John 6:29. This is the work of God, that ye believe on him whom he hath sent. 35. He that cometh to me shall never hunger; and he that believeth on me shall never thirst. 45. Every man therefore that hath heard, and hath learned of the Father, cometh unto me.

John 7:38. He that believeth on me, as the scripture hath said, out of his belly shall flow rivers of living water.

John 9:35. Jesus . . . said unto him, Dost thou believe on the Son of God?

John 11:25. Jesus said unto her, I am the resurrection, and the life: he that believeth in me, though he [1]were dead, yet shall he live: 26. And whosoever liveth and believeth in me shall never die. Believest thou this? 40. Said I not unto thee, that, if thou wouldest believe, thou shouldest see the glory of God? [[1] R. V. die]

John 12:36. While ye have light, believe in the light, that ye may be the children of light. 44. Jesus cried and said, He that believeth on me, believeth not on me, but on him that sent me. 46. I am come a light into the world, that whosoever believeth on me should not abide in darkness.

John 13:7. What I do thou knowest not now; but thou shalt know hereafter. 20. He that receiveth whomsoever I send receiveth me; and he that receiveth me receiveth him that sent me.

John 14:1. Let not your heart be troubled: ye believe in God, believe also in me. 11. Or else believe me for the very works' sake. 12. He that believeth on me, the works that I do shall he do also; and greater *works* than these shall he do; because I go unto my Father.

John 16:27. For the Father himself loveth you, because ye have loved me, and have believed that I came out from God. 33. These things I have spoken unto you, that in me ye might have peace.

John 18:37. Every one that is of the truth heareth my voice.

John 20:27. And be not faithless, but believing. 29. Jesus saith unto him, Thomas, because thou hast seen me, thou hast believed: blessed *are* they that have not seen, and *yet* have believed. 31. But these are written, that ye might believe that Jesus is the Christ, the Son of God; and that believing ye might have life through his name.

Acts 3:16. His name through faith in his name hath made this man strong, whom ye see and know: yea, the faith which is by him hath given him this perfect soundness in the presence of you all.

Acts 10:43. To him give all the prophets witness, that through his name whosoever believeth in him shall receive remission of sins.

Acts 15:9. And put no difference between us and them, purifying their hearts by faith. 11. But we believe that through the grace of the Lord Jesus Christ we shall be saved, even as they.

Acts 16:31. Believe on the Lord Jesus Christ, and thou shalt be saved, and thy house.

Acts 20:21. Testifying both to the Jews, and also to the Greeks, repentance toward God, and faith toward our Lord Jesus Christ.

Acts. 26:18. That they may receive forgiveness of sins, and inheritance among them which are sanctified by faith that is in me.

Rom. 3:22. Even the righteousness of God *which is* by faith of Jesus Christ unto all and upon all them that believe: for there is no difference: 23. For all have sinned, and come short of the glory of God; 24. Being justified freely by his grace through the redemption that is in Christ Jesus: 25. Whom God hath set forth *to be* a propitiation through faith in his blood, to declare his righteousness for the remission of sins that are past, through the forbearance of God; 26. To declare, *I say*, at this time his righteousness: that he might be just, and the justifier of him which believeth in Jesus. 27. Where *is* boasting then? It is excluded. By what law? of works? Nay: but by the law of faith. 28. Therefore we conclude that a man is justified by faith without the deeds of the law.

Rom. 9:33. As it is written, Behold, I lay in Sion a stumblingstone and rock of offence: and whosoever believeth on him shall not be ashamed.

Rom. 10:4. For Christ *is* the end of the law for righteousness to every one that believeth. 9. If thou shalt confess with thy mouth the Lord Jesus, and shalt believe in thine heart that God hath raised him from the dead, thou shalt be saved.

Gal. 2:16. Knowing that a man is not justified by the works of the law, but by the faith of Jesus Christ, even we have believed in Jesus Christ, that we might be justified by the faith of Christ,

Gal. 3:1. O foolish Galatians, who hath bewitched you, that ye should not obey the truth, before whose eyes Jesus Christ hath been evidently set forth, crucified among you? 2. This only would I learn of you, Receive ye the Spirit by the works of the law, or by the hearing of faith? 3. Are ye so foolish? having begun in the Spirit, are ye now made perfect by the flesh? 4. Have ye suffered so many things in vain? If *it be* yet in vain. 5. He therefore that ministereth to you the Spirit, and worketh miracles among you, *doeth he it* by the works of the law, or by the hearing of faith? 6. Even as Abraham believed God, and it was accounted to him for righteousness. 7. Know ye therefore that they which are of faith, the same are the children of Abraham. 8. And the scripture, foreseeing that God would justify the heathen through faith, preached before the gospel unto Abraham, *saying*, In thee shall all nations be blessed. 9. So then they which be of faith are blessed with faithful Abraham. 10. For as many as are of the works of the law are under the curse: for it is written, Cursed *is* every one that continueth not in all things which are written in the book of the law to do them. 11. But that no man is justified by the law in the sight of God, *it is* evident: for, The just shall live by faith. 12. And the law is not of faith: but, The man that doeth them shall live in them. 13. Christ hath redeemed us from the curse of the law, being made a curse for us: for it is written, Cursed *is* every one that hangeth on a tree: 14. That the blessing of Abraham might come on the Gentiles through Jesus Christ; that we might receive the promise of the Spirit through faith. 15. Brethren, I speak after the manner of men; Though *it be* but a man's covenant, yet *if it be* confirmed, no man disannulleth, or addeth thereto. 16. Now to Abraham and his seed were the promises made. He saith not, And to seeds, as of many; but as of one. And to thy seed, which is Christ. 17. And this I say, *that* the covenant, that was confirmed before of God in Christ, the law, which was four hundred and thirty years after, cannot disannul, that it should make the promise of none effect. 18. For if the inheritance *be* of the law, *it is* no more of promise: but God gave *it* to Abraham by promise. 19. Wherefore then *serveth* the law? It was added because of transgressions, till the seed should come to whom the promise was made; *and it was* ordained by angels in the hand of a mediator. 20. Now a mediator is not *a mediator* of one, but God is one. 21. *Is* the law then against the promises of God? God forbid: for if there had been a law given which could have given life, verily righteousness should have been by the law. 22. But the scripture hath concluded all under sin, that the promise by faith of Jesus Christ might be given to them that believe. 23. But before faith came, we were kept under the law, shut up unto the faith which should afterwards be revealed. 24. Wherefore the law was our schoolmaster *to bring us* unto Christ, that we might be justified by faith. 25. But after that faith is come, we are no longer under a schoolmaster. 26. For ye are all the children of God by faith in Christ Jesus. 27. For as many of you as have been baptized into Christ have put on Christ. 28. There is neither Jew nor Greek, there is neither bond nor free, there is neither male nor female: for ye are all one in Christ Jesus. 29. And if ye *be* Christ's, then are ye Abraham's seed, and heirs according to the promise.

Gal. 5:6. In Jesus Christ neither circumcision availeth any thing, nor uncircumcision; but faith which worketh by love.

Eph. 1:12. That we should be to the praise of his glory, who first trusted in Christ. 13. In whom ye also *trusted*, after that ye heard the word of truth, the gospel of your salvation: in whom also after that ye believed, ye were sealed with that holy Spirit of promise. 14. Which is the earnest of our inheritance until the redemption of the purchased possession, unto the praise of his glory.

Eph. 3:12. In whom we have boldness and access with confidence by the faith of him. 17. That Christ may dwell in your hearts by faith;

Eph. 4:13. Till we all come in the unity of the faith, and of the knowledge of the Son of God, unto a perfect man, unto the measure of the stature of the fulness of Christ:

Phil. 3:9. Not having mine own righteousness, which is of the law, but that which is through the faith of Christ, the righteousness which is of God by faith:

Col. 2:7. Rooted and built up in him, and stablished in the faith.

1 Tim. 1:16. Howbeit for this cause I obtained mercy, that in me first Jesus Christ might shew forth all longsuffering, for a pattern to them which should hereafter believe on him to life everlasting.

2 Tim. 1:13. In faith and love which is in Christ Jesus.

2 Tim. 2:1. Be strong in the grace that is in Christ Jesus.

2 Tim. 3:15. From a child thou hast known the holy scriptures, which are able to make thee wise unto salvation through faith which is in Christ Jesus.

Heb. 4:16. Let us therefore come boldly unto the throne of grace, that we may obtain mercy, and find grace to help in time of need.

Heb 6:19. Which *hope* we have as an anchor of the soul, both sure and stedfast, and which entereth into that within the veil;

Heb. 10:22. Let us draw near with a true heart in full assurance of faith,

Heb. 12:2. Looking unto Jesus the author and finisher of *our* faith;

Heb. 13:7. Remember them which have the rule over you, who have spoken unto you the word of God: whose faith follow,

1 Pet. 1:8. In whom, though now ye see *him* not, yet believing, ye rejoice with joy unspeakable and full of glory:

1 Pet. 2:6. Behold, I lay in Sion a chief corner stone, elect, precious: and he that believeth on him shall not be confounded. 7. Unto you therefore which believe *he is* precious: Isa. 28:16.

2 Pet. 1:1. Simon Peter, a servant and an apostle of Jesus Christ, to them that have obtained like precious faith with us through the righteousness of God and our Saviour Jesus Christ:

1 John 3:23. This is his commandment, That we should believe on the name of his Son Jesus Christ,

1 John 5:4. This is the victory that overcometh the world, *even* our faith. 5. Who is he that overcometh the world, but he that believeth that Jesus is the Son of God? 10. He that believeth on the Son of God hath the witness in himself: . . . 13. Unto you [1] that believe on the name of the Son of God; that ye may know that ye have eternal life, [2] and that ye may believe on the name of the Son of God. [1 Omitted in R. V.   2 even unto you that]

14. This is the confidence that we have in him, that, if we ask any thing according to his will, he heareth us:

Jude 21. Keep yourselves in the love of God, looking for the mercy of our Lord Jesus Christ unto eternal life.

Rev. 1:17. Fear not; I am the first and the last:

Rev. 3:18. I counsel thee to buy of me gold tried in the fire, that thou mayest be rich; and white raiment, that thou mayest be clothed, . . . 20. Behold, I stand at the door, and knock: if any man hear my voice, and open the door, I will come in to him, and will sup with him, and he with me.

IN CHRIST, EXEMPLIFIED: Matt. 8:2. Lord, if thou wilt, thou canst make me clean.

Matt. 9:18. My daughter is even now dead: but come and lay thy hand upon her, and she shall live. 21. She said within herself, If I may but touch his garment, I shall be whole. [Mark. 5:28; Luke 8:48.] 28. Believe ye that I am able to do this? They said unto him, Yea, Lord.

Matt. 14:33. Then they that were in the ship came and worshipped him, saying, Of a truth thou art the Son of God.

Matt. 15:27. Truth, Lord: yet the dogs eat of the crumbs which fall from their masters' table. *vs.* 26,28; Mark 7:27-30.

Matt. 16:16. Simon Peter answered and said, Thou art the Christ, the Son of the living God.

Mark 9:24. And straightway the father of the child cried out, and said with tears, Lord, I believe; help thou mine unbelief. John 9:38.

Luke 5:5. Simon answering said unto him, Master, we have toiled all the night, and have taken nothing: nevertheless at thy word I will let down the net.

Luke 7:3. And when he heard of Jesus, he sent unto him the elders of the Jews, beseeching him that he would come and heal his servant. 4. And when they came to Jesus, they besought him instantly, saying, That he was worthy for whom he should do this: 5. For he loveth our nation, and he hath built us a synagogue. 6. Then Jesus went with them. And when he was now not far from the house, the centurion sent friends to him, saying unto him, Lord, trouble not thyself: for I am not worthy that thou shouldest enter under my roof: 7. Wherefore neither thought I myself worthy to come unto thee: but say in a word, and my servant shall be healed. 8. For I also am a man set under authority, having under me soldiers, and I say unto one, Go, and he goeth; and to another, Come, and he cometh; and to my servant, Do this, and he doeth it. 9. When Jesus heard these things, he marvelled at him, and turned him about, and said unto the people that followed him, I say unto you, I have not found so great faith, no, not in Israel. Matt. 8:5-10.

Luke 23:42. And he said unto Jesus, Lord, remember me when thou comest into thy kingdom.

John 4:29. Come, see a man, which told me all things that ever I did: is not this the Christ? 42. Now we believe, not because of thy saying: for we have heard him ourselves, and know that this is indeed the Christ, the Saviour of the world.

John 6:14. Then those men, when they had seen the miracle that Jesus did, said, This is of a truth that prophet that should come into the world. 68. Simon Peter answered him, Lord, to whom shall we go? thou hast the words of eternal life. 69. And we believe and are sure that thou art *that Christ, the Son of the living God.* [R. V. the Holy One of]

John 7:31. And many of the people believed on him, and said, When Christ cometh, will he do more miracles than these which this man hath done?

John 10:41. Many resorted unto him, and said, John did no miracle: but all things that John spake of this man were true. 42. And many believed on him there.

John 11:21. Martha said unto Jesus, Lord, if thou hadst been here, my brother had not died. 22. But I know, that even now, whatsoever thou wilt ask of God, God will give it thee. 27. I believe that thou art the Christ, the Son of God, which should come into the world. v. 32.

John 16:30. Now are we sure that thou knowest all things, and needest not that any man should ask thee: by this we believe that thou camest forth from God.

John 20:28. Thomas answered and said unto him; My Lord and my God.

Acts 8:37. *I believe that Jesus Christ Is the Son of God.* [Omitted in R. V.]

Acts 11:17. God gave them the like gift as he did unto us, who believed on the Lord Jesus Christ;

Rom. 7:24. O wretched man that I am! who shall deliver me from the body of this death? 25. I thank God through Jesus Christ our Lord.

Rom. 8:35. Who shall separate us from the love of Christ? shall tribulation, or distress, or persecution, or famine, or nakedness, or peril, or sword? 37. Nay, in all these things we are more than conquerors through him that loved us.

2 Cor. 12:9. Most gladly therefore will I rather glory in my infirmities, that the power of Christ may rest upon me. 10. Therefore I take pleasure in infirmities, in reproaches, in necessities, in persecutions, in distresses for Christ's sake:

Gal. 2:20. I am crucified with Christ: nevertheless I live; yet not I, but Christ liveth in me: and the life which I now live in the flesh I live by the faith of the Son of God, who loved me, and gave himself for me.

Phil. 4:13. I can do all things through Christ which strengtheneth me.

1 Tim. 1:14. The grace of our Lord was exceeding abundant with faith and love which is in Christ Jesus.

2 Tim. 1:12. I know whom I have believed, and am persuaded that he is able to keep that which I have committed unto him against that day.

2 Tim. 4:18. The Lord shall deliver me from every evil work, and will preserve me unto his heavenly kingdom:

INSTANCES OF FAITH IN CHRIST: The wise men of the east, Matt. 2:1,2,11. Peter, Matt. 4:18-22; Mark 1:16-20; Luke 5:4,5; John 6:68, 69. Andrew, Matt. 4:18-22; Mark 1:16-20, John 1:41. James and John, Matt. 4:21,22; Mark 1:19,20. The woman with the issue of blood, Matt. 9:21,22. Jairus, for the healing of his daughter, Matt. 9:18,23-25. Two blind men, Matt. 9:29,30. Blind Bartimæus and a fellow blind man, Matt. 20:30-34; Mark 10:46-52; Luke 18:35-42. The Samaritan leper, Luke 17:11-19. The sick of Gennesaret, Matt. 14:36; Mark 3:10; 6:54-56. Those who brought the paralytic to Jesus, Luke 5:18-20. The Syrophenician woman, Matt. 15:22-28; Mark 7:25-30. The woman who anointed Jesus' feet, Luke 7:36-50. Those who brought sick of palsy, Matt. 9:2. Philip, John 1:45,46. Nathanael, John 1:49. The Samaritans, who believed through the preaching of Jesus, John 4:39-42; through the preaching of Philip, Acts 8:9-12. The nobleman whose child was sick, John 4:46-53. Abraham, John 8:56. The blind man whom Jesus healed on the Sabbath, John 9:

13–38. Mary, the sister of Martha, Luke 10: 38–42; John 11:32. John the disciple, John 20:8. The disciples, through the miracle at Cana of Galilee, John 2:11. Jews at Jerusalem, John 2:23; 8:30; 11:45; 12:11. Three thousand at Pentecost, Acts 2:41. Five thousand, Acts 4:4. Multitudes, Acts 5:14. The cripple at Lystra, Acts 14:9. Stephen, Acts 6:8. Ethiopian eunuch, ¹ Acts 8:37. People of Lydda and Saron, Acts 9:35; of Joppa, Acts 9:42; of Antioch, Acts 11:21–24. Barnabas, Acts 11:24. Eunice, Lois, and Timothy, 2 Tim. 1:5; Acts 16:1. Lydia, Acts 16:14. Philippian jailer, Acts 16:31–34. Crispus, Acts 18:8. The Corinthians, Acts 18:8; 1 Cor. 15: 11. Jews at Rome, Acts 28:24. Ephesians, Eph. 1:13,15. Colossians, Col. 1:2,4. Thessalonians, 1 Thess. 1:6; 3:6–8; 2 Thess. 1:3,4. Philemon, Philem. 5. Church at Thyatira Rev. 2:19. [¹ Omitted in R. V.]

TRIAL OF: 1 Chr. 29:17. I know also, my God, that thou triest the heart, and hast pleasure in uprightness.

Psa. 26:2. Examine me, O LORD, and prove me; try my reins and my heart.

Psa. 81:7. I proved thee at the waters of Meribah.

Matt. 13:19. When any one heareth the word of the kingdom, and understandeth it not, then cometh the wicked one, and catcheth away that which was sown in his heart. This is he which received seed by the way side. 20. But he that received the seed into stony places, the same is he that heareth the word, and anon with joy receiveth it; 21. Yet hath he not root in himself, but dureth for a while: for when tribulation or persecution ariseth because of the word, by and by he is offended. 22. He also that received seed among the thorns is he that heareth the word; and the care of this world, and the deceitfulness of riches, choke the word, and he becometh unfruitful. Luke 8:13,14.

Matt. 24:21. For then shall be great tribulation, such as was not since the beginning of the world to this time, no, nor ever shall be. 22. And except those days should be shortened, there should no flesh be saved: but for the elect's sake those days shall be shortened. 23. Then if any man shall say unto you, Lo, here is Christ, or there; believe it not. 24. For there shall arise false Christs, and false prophets, and shall shew great signs and wonders; insomuch that, if it were possible, they shall deceive the very elect. 25. Behold, I have told you before.

2 Thess. 1:3. We are bound to thank God always for you, brethren, as it is meet, because that your faith groweth exceedingly, and the charity of every one of you all toward each other aboundeth: 4. So that we ourselves glory in you in the churches of God for your patience and faith in all your persecutions and tribulations that ye endure: 5. Which is a manifest token of the righteous judgment of God, that ye may be counted worthy of the kingdom of God, for which ye also suffer:

Heb. 6:13. For when God made promise to Abraham, because he could swear by no greater, he sware by himself. 14. Saying, Surely blessing I will bless thee, and multiplying I will multiply thee. 15. And so, after he had patiently endured, he obtained the promise.

Jas. 1:3. Knowing this, that the trying of your faith worketh patience. 12. Blessed is the man that endureth temptation: for when he ¹ is tried, he shall receive the crown of life, which the Lord hath promised to them that love him. [¹ R. V. hath been approved]

1 Pet. 1:7. That the trial of your faith, being much more precious than of gold that perisheth, though it be tried with fire, might be found unto praise and honour and glory at the appearing of Jesus Christ:

See TEMPTATION.

INSTANCES OF TRIAL OF : Noah, Gen. 6:14–22; Heb. 11:7. Abraham, when commanded to leave his native land and go he knew not whither, Gen. 12:1–4; Heb. 11:8; when commanded to offer Isaac, Gen. 22:1–19; Heb. 11: 17–19. Moses, when sent to Pharaoh, Ex. 3: 11,12; 4:10–17; Heb. 11:25–29; at the Red Sea, by the murmurings of the people, Ex. 14;15. Joshua and the children of Israel, in the method of taking Jericho, Josh. 6: Heb. 11:30. Gideon, when commanded to deliver Israel, Judg. 6:36–40; 7; Heb. 11:32. Job, by affliction and adversity, Job 1; 2. Ezra, in leaving Babylon without a military escort, Ezra 8:22. Daniel, when forbidden to pray to Jehovah, Dan. 6:4–23; Heb. 11:32,33. The three Hebrews, when commanded to worship the image, Dan. 3:8–30; Heb. 11:32–34.

The Syrophenician woman, Matt. 15:21–28; Mark 7:24–30. The two blind men who appealed to Jesus for sight, Matt. 9:28. The disciples, when Jesus came walking on the Sea of Galilee, Matt. 14:25–33.

The disciples: by the question of Jesus, as to who he was, Matt. 16:15–20; Luke 9:20,21; by their inability to cast out the evil spirit from the lunatic, Matt. 17:14–21; Mark 9:14–29; Luke 9:37–42; in the tempest at sea, Matt. 8:23–27; Mark 4:36–41; Luke 8:22–26. Of Philip, when questioned by Jesus as to how the multitude would be fed, John 6:5,6. Of Peter, when asked whether he loved Jesus, John 21:16,17. See AFFLICTION, DESIGN OF.

STRENGTHENED BY MIRACLES. See MIRACLES, DESIGN OF.

SUM TOTAL OF RELIGIOUS BELIEF AND LIFE: Rom. 1:8; Jude 3.

WEAK. See DOUBTING.

FAITHFULNESS. Psa. 12:1. Help, LORD; for the godly man ceaseth; for the faithful fail from among the children of men.

Psa. 31:23. O love the LORD, all ye his saints: for the LORD preserveth the faithful.

Prov. 20:6. A faithful man who can find?

Prov. 28:20. A faithful man shall abound with blessings:

Matt. 10:22. And ye shall be hated of all

men for my name's sake: but he that endureth to the end shall be saved.

Matt. 24:45. Who then is a faithful and wise servant, whom his lord hath made ruler over his household, to give them meat in due season? 46. Blessed *is* that servant, whom his lord when he cometh shall find so doing. 47. Verily I say unto you, That he shall make him ruler over all his goods. Luke 12:42–44.

Matt. 25:14. For *the kingdom of heaven is* as a man travelling into a far country, *who* called his own servants, and delivered unto them his goods. 15. And unto one he gave five talents, to another two, and to another one; to every man according to his several ability; and straightway took his journey. 16. Then he that had received the five talents went and traded with the same, and made *them* other five talents. 17. And likewise he that *had received* two, he also gained other two. 18. But he that had received one went and digged in the earth, and hid his lord's money. 19. After a long time the lord of those servants cometh, and reckoneth with them. 20. And so he that had received five talents came and brought other five talents, saying, Lord, thou deliveredst unto me five talents: behold, I have gained beside them five talents more. 21. His lord said unto him, Well done, *thou* good and faithful servant: thou hast been faithful over a few things, I will make thee ruler over many things: enter thou into the joy of thy lord. 22. He also that had received two talents came and said, Lord, thou deliveredst unto me two talents: behold, I have gained two other talents beside them. 23. His lord said unto him, Well done, good and faithful servant; thou hast been faithful over a few things, I will make thee ruler over many things: enter thou into the joy of thy lord. Luke 19:12–27.

Luke 16:10. He that is faithful in that which is least is faithful also in much: and he that is unjust in the least is unjust also in much. 11. If therefore ye have not been faithful in the unrighteous mammon, who will commit to your trust the true *riches?* 12. And if ye have not been faithful in that which is another man's, who shall give you that which is your own?

1 Cor. 4:2. Moreover it is required in stewards, that a man be found faithful.

Col. 3:22. Servants, obey in all things *your* masters according to the flesh: not with eyeservice, as menpleasers; but in singleness of heart, fearing God: Eph. 6:5–9.

Rev. 2:10. Be thou fai+hful unto death, and I will give thee a crown of life.

See OBEDIENCE, EXHORTATION TO; PERSEVERANCE; MINISTERS, FAITHFUL; REPROOF, FAITHFULNESS IN.

INSTANCES OF: Abraham, Gal. 3:9. Moses. Heb. 3:5. David, 2 Sam. 22:22–25. Elijah. 1 Kin. 19:10,14. Abijah, 2 Chr. 13:4–20. Jehoshaphat, 2 Chr. 20:1–30. Job, Job 1:21. 22; 2:9,10.

See HEZEKIAH; JOSIAH; JOASH; DANIEL.

OF GOD. See GOD, FAITHFULNESS OF.

FALCON, a carnivorous bird [*R. V.*], Lev. 11:14; Deut. 14:13.

FALL OF MAN. Gen. 3:1. Now the serpent was more subtil than any beast of the field which the LORD God had made. And he said unto the woman, Yea, hath God said, Ye shall not eat of every tree of the garden? 2. And the woman said unto the serpent, We may eat of the fruit of the trees of the garden: [Gen. 2:16.] 3. But of the fruit of the tree which *is* in the midst of the garden, God hath said, Ye shall not eat of it, neither shall ye touch it, lest ye die. [Gen. 2:17.] 4. And the serpent said unto the woman, Ye shall not surely die: 5. For God doth know that in the day ye eat thereof, then your eyes shall be opened, and ye shall be as gods, knowing good and evil. 6. And when the woman saw that the tree *was* good for food, and that it *was* pleasant to the eyes, and a tree to be desired to make *one* wise, she took of the fruit thereof, and did eat, and gave also unto her husband with her; and he did eat. 7. And the eyes of them both were opened, and they knew that they *were* naked; and they sewed fig leaves together, and made themselves aprons. 8. And they heard the voice of the LORD God walking in the garden in the cool of the day: and Adam and his wife hid themselves from the presence of the LORD God amongst the trees of the garden. 9. And the LORD God called unto Adam, and said unto him, Where *art* thou? 10. And he said, I heard thy voice in the garden, and I was afraid, because I *was* naked; and I hid myself. 11. And he said, Who told thee that thou *wast* naked? Hast thou eaten of the tree, whereof I commanded thee that thou shouldest not eat? 12. And the man said, The woman whom thou gavest *to be* with me, she gave me of the tree, and I did eat. 13. And the LORD God said unto the woman, What *is* this *that* thou hast done? And the woman said, The serpent beguiled me, and I did eat. 14. And the LORD God said unto the serpent, Because thou hast done this, thou *art* cursed above all cattle, and above every beast of the field; upon thy belly shalt thou go, and dust shalt thou eat all the days of thy life: 15. And I will put enmity between thee and the woman, and between thy seed and her seed; it shall bruise thy head, and thou shalt bruise his heel. 16. Unto the woman he said, I will greatly multiply thy sorrow and thy conception: in sorrow thou shalt bring forth children; and thy desire *shall be* to thy husband, and he shall rule over thee. 17. And unto Adam he said, Because thou hast hearkened unto the voice of thy wife, and hast eaten of the tree, of which I commanded thee, saying, Thou shalt not eat of it: cursed *is* the ground for thy sake; in sorrow shalt thou eat *of* it all the days of thy life; 18. Thorns also and thistles shall it bring forth to thee; and thou shalt eat the herb of the field; 19. In the sweat of thy face shalt thou eat bread, till thou return unto the ground; for out of it wast thou taken: for dust thou *art*, and unto dust shalt thou return.

Job 31:33. If I covered my transgressions as Adam, by hiding mine iniquity in my bosom:

Eccl. 7:29. Lo, this only have I found, that God hath made man upright; but they have sought out many inventions.

Isa. 43:27. Thy first father hath sinned, and thy teachers have transgressed against me.

Hos. 6:7. But they like men [Adam, *R. V.*] have transgressed the covenant:

Rom. 5:12. As by one man sin entered into the world, and death by sin; and so death passed upon all men, for that all have sinned: 14. Nevertheless death reigned from Adam to Moses, even over them that had not sinned after the similitude of Adam's transgression, who is the figure of him that was to come. 18. By the offence of one *judgment came* upon all men to condemnation; *vs.* 19,21.

1 Cor. 15:21. For since by man *came* death, by man *came* also the resurrection of the dead. 22. For as in Adam all die, even so in Christ shall all be made alive.

2 Cor. 11:3. The serpent beguiled Eve through his subtilty.

1 Tim. 2:14. Adam was not deceived, but the woman being deceived was in the transgression.

See DEPRAVITY.

FALSE ACCUSATION. See ACCUSATION; FALSE.

FALSE CONFIDENCE. In self, Deut. 29:19; 1 Kin. 20:11; Prov. 3:5; 23:4; 26:12; 28: 26; Isa. 5:21; Rom. 12:16; 2 Cor. 1:9. In outward resources, Psa. 20:7; 33:17; 44:6; 49:6; Prov. 11:28; Isa. 22:11; 31:1–3; Jer. 48:7; Zech. 4:6; Mark 10:24. In man, Psa. 33:16; 62:9; 118:8; 146:3,4; Isa. 2:22; Jer. 17:5; Hos. 5:13; 7:11.

INSTANCES OF: At Babel, Gen. 11:4. Sennacherib, in the siege of Jerusalem, 2 Kin. 19:23. Asa, in relying on Syria rather than on God, 2 Chr.16:7–9. Hezekiah, in the defenses of Jerusalem, Isa. 22:11. Peter, in asserting his devotion to Jesus, Matt. 26:35; Luke 22:33,34; John 13:37,38.

See CONFIDENCE, FALSE.

FALSEHOOD. Ex. 23:1. Thou shalt not raise a false report: put not thine hand with the wicked to be an unrighteous witness.

Lev. 6:2. If a soul sin, and commit a trespass against the LORD, and lie unto his neighbour in that which was delivered him to keep, or in fellowship, or in a thing taken away by violence, or hath deceived his neighbour; 3. Or have found that which was lost, and lieth concerning it, and sweareth falsely; in any of all these that a man doeth, sinning therein: 4. Then it shall be, because he hath sinned, and is guilty, that he shall restore that which he took violently

away, or the thing which he hath deceitfully gotten, or that which was delivered him to keep, or the lost thing which he found, 5. Or all that about which he hath sworn falsely; he shall even restore it in the principal, and shall add the fifth part more thereto, *and* give it unto him to whom it appertaineth, in the day of his trespass offering. 6. And he shall bring his trespass offering unto the LORD, a ram without blemish out of the flock, with thy estimation, for a trespass offering, unto the priest: 7. And the priest shall make an atonement for him before the LORD: and it shall be forgiven him for any thing of all that he hath done in trespassing therein.

Lev. 19:11. Ye shall not steal, neither deal falsely, neither lie one to another. 12. Ye shall not swear by my name falsely, 16. Thou shalt not go up and down *as* a talebearer among thy people: neither shalt thou stand against the blood of thy neighbour: Ex. 20:16.

Job 13:4. Ye *are* forgers of lies, ye *are* all physicians of no value.

Job 21:34. How then comfort ye me in vain, seeing in your answers there remaineth falsehood?

Job 27:4. My lips shall not speak wickedness, nor my tongue utter deceit.

Job 31:5. If I have walked with vanity, or if my foot hath hasted to deceit; 6. Let me be weighed in an even balance, that God may know mine integrity. 33. If I covered my transgressions as Adam, by hiding mine iniquity in my bosom:

Job 36:4. For truly my words *shall* not *be* false: he that is perfect in knowledge *is* with thee.

Psa. 5:6. Thou shalt destroy them that speak leasing: the LORD will abhor the bloody and deceitful man. 9. *There is* no faithfulness in their mouth; their inward part *is* very wickedness; their throat *is* an open sepulchre; they flatter with their tongue.

Psa. 10:7. His mouth is full of cursing and deceit and fraud: under his tongue *is* mischief and vanity.

Psa. 12:2. *With* flattering lips *and* with a double heart do they speak. 3. The LORD shall cut off all flattering lips.

Psa. 28:3. The workers of iniquity, which speak peace to their neighbours, but mischief *is* in their hearts.

Psa. 31:18. Let the lying lips be put to silence; which speak grievous things proudly and contemptuously against the righteous.

Psa. 34:13. Keep thy tongue from evil, and thy lips from speaking guile. 1 Pet. 3:10.

Psa. 36:3. The words of his mouth *are* iniquity and deceit:

Psa. 50:19. Thou givest thy mouth to evil, and thy tongue frameth deceit. 20. Thou sittest *and* speakest against thy brother; thou slanderest thine own mother's son.

Psa. 52:2. Thy tongue deviseth mischiefs; like a sharp razor, working deceitfully. **3.**

Thou lovest evil more than good; *and* lying rather than to speak righteousness. 4. Thou lovest all devouring words, O *thou* deceitful tongue. 5. God shall likewise destroy thee for ever.

Psa. 55:21. *The words* of his mouth were smoother than butter, but war *was* in his heart: his words were softer than oil, yet *were* they drawn swords. 23. But thou, O God, shalt bring them down into the pit of destruction: bloody and deceitful men shall not live out half their days;

Psa. 58:3. The wicked are estranged from the womb: they go astray as soon as they be born, speaking lies.

Psa. 59:12. *For* the sin of their mouth *and* the words of their lips let them even be taken in their pride: and for cursing and lying *which* they speak.

Psa. 62:4. They delight in lies: they bless with their mouth, but they curse inwardly.

Psa. 63:11. The mouth of them that speak lies shall be stopped.

Psa. 101:5. Whoso privily slandereth his neighbour, him will I cut off: 7. He that worketh deceit shall not dwell within my house: he that telleth lies shall not tarry in my sight.

Psa. 109:2. For the mouth of the wicked and the mouth of the deceitful are opened against me: they have spoken against me with a lying tongue.

Psa. 116:11. I said in my haste, All men *are* liars.

Psa. 119:29. Remove from me the way of lying: 69. The proud have forged a lie against me: 163. I hate and abhor lying:

Psa. 120:2. Deliver my soul, O LORD, from lying lips, *and* from a deceitful tongue. 3. What shall be done unto thee, thou false tongue? 4. Sharp arrows of the mighty, with coals of juniper.

Psa. 144:8. Whose mouth speaketh vanity, and their right hand *is* a right hand of falsehood. 11. Rid me, and deliver me from the hand of strange children, whose mouth speaketh vanity, and their right hand *is* a right hand of falsehood:

Prov. 2:12. To deliver thee from the way of the evil *man*, from the man that speaketh froward things; 13. Who leave the paths of uprightness, to walk in the ways of darkness; 14. Who rejoice to do evil, *and* delight in the frowardness of the wicked; 15. Whose ways *are* crooked, and *they* froward in their paths:

Prov 3:3. Let not mercy and truth forsake thee: bind them about thy neck; write them upon the table of thine heart:

Prov. 6:12. A naughty person, a wicked man, walketh with a froward mouth. 13. He winketh with his eyes, he speaketh with his feet, he teacheth with his fingers; 16. These six *things* doth the LORD hate: yea, seven *are* an abomination unto him: 17. A proud look, a lying tongue, and hands that shed innocent blood, 18. An heart that deviseth wicked imaginations, feet that be

swift in running to mischief, 19. A false witness *that* speaketh lies, and he that soweth discord among brethren.

Prov. 10:9. He that perverteth his ways shall be known. 10. He that winketh with the eye causeth sorrow: 18. He that hideth hatred *with* lying lips, and he that uttereth a slander, *is* a fool. 31. The mouth of the just bringeth forth wisdom: but the froward tongue shall be cut out.

Prov. 11:9. An hypocrite with *his* mouth destroyeth his neighbour:

Prov. 12:17. *He that* speaketh truth sheweth forth righteousness: but a false witness deceit. 19. A lying tongue *is* but for a moment. 20. Deceit *is* in the heart of them that imagine evil: 22. Lying lips *are* abomination to the LORD:

Prov. 13:5. A righteous *man* hateth lying: but a wicked *man* is loathsome, and cometh to shame.

Prov. 14:5. A faithful witness will not lie: but a false witness will utter lies. 8. The folly of fools *is* deceit. 25. A true witness delivereth souls: but a deceitful *witness* speaketh lies.

Prov. 17:4. A wicked doer giveth heed to false lips; *and* a liar giveth ear to a naughty tongue. 7. Excellent speech becometh not a fool: much less do lying lips a prince.

Prov. 19:5. A false witness shall not be unpunished, and *he that* speaketh lies shall not escape. [v. 9.] 22. A poor man *is* better than a liar. 28. An ungodly witness scorneth judgment:

Prov. 20:17. Bread of deceit *is* sweet to a man; but afterwards his mouth shall be filled with gravel.

Prov. 21:6. The getting of treasures by a lying tongue *is* a vanity tossed to and fro of them that seek death.

Prov. 26:18. As a mad *man* who casteth firebrands, arrows, and death, 19. So *is* the man *that* deceiveth his neighbour, and saith, Am not I in sport? 24. He that hateth dissembleth with his lips, and layeth up deceit within him; 25. When he speaketh fair, believe him not: for *there are* seven abominations in his heart. 26. *Whose* hatred is covered by deceit, his wickedness shall be shewed before the *whole* congregation. 28. A lying tongue hateth *those that are* afflicted by it:

Prov. 27:14. He that blesseth his friend with a loud voice, rising early in the morning, it shall be counted a curse to him.

Eccl. 5:6. Suffer not thy mouth to cause thy flesh to sin; neither say thou before the angel, that it *was* an error: wherefore should God be angry at thy voice, and destroy the work of thine hands?

Isa. 28:15. Because ye have said, We have made a covenant with death, and with hell are we at agreement; when the overflowing scourge shall pass through, it shall not come unto us: for we have made lies our refuge, and under falsehood have we hid ourselves:

Isa. 32:7. The instruments also of the chur]

are evil: he deviseth wicked devices to destroy the poor with lying words, even when the needy speaketh right.

Isa. 57:11. Of whom hast thou been afraid or feared, that thou hast lied, and hast not remembered me, nor laid *it* to thy heart?

Isa. 59:3. Your lips have spoken lies, your tongue hath muttered perverseness. 4. None calleth for justice, nor *any* pleadeth for truth: they trust in vanity, and speak lies; they conceive mischief, and bring forth iniquity. 12. For our transgressions are multiplied before thee, and our sins testify against us: for our transgressions *are* with us; and *as for* our iniquities, we know them; 13. In transgressing and lying against the LORD, and departing away from our God, speaking oppression and revolt, conceiving and uttering from the heart words of falsehood.

Isa. 63:8. He said, Surely they *are* my people, children *that* will not lie:

Jer. 7:8. Behold, ye trust in lying words, that cannot profit. 28. Truth is perished, and is cut off from their mouth.

Jer. 9:3. They bend their tongues *like* their bow *for* lies: but they are not valiant for the truth upon the earth; for they proceed from evil to evil, and they know not me, saith the LORD. 5. They will deceive every one his neighbour, and will not speak the truth: they have taught their tongue to speak lies, *and* weary themselves to commit iniquity. 6. Thine habitation *is* in the midst of deceit; through deceit they refuse to know me, saith the LORD. 8. Their tongue *is as* an arrow shot out: it speaketh deceit: *one* speaketh peaceably to his neighbour with his mouth, but in heart he layeth his wait.

Jer. 12:6. Even thy brethren, and the house of thy father, even they have dealt treacherously with thee; yea, they have called a multitude after thee: believe them not, though they speak fair words unto thee.

Jer. 50:36. A sword *is* upon the liars: and they shall dote: [ᴿ R. V. boasters]

Ezek. 22:9. In thee are men that carry tales to shed blood: and in thee they eat upon the mountains: in the midst of thee they commit lewdness.

Hos. 4:1. The LORD hath a controversy with the inhabitants of the land, because *there is* no truth . . . in the land. 2. By swearing, and lying, and killing, and stealing, and committing adultery, they break out, and blood toucheth blood.

Obad. 7. The men that were at peace with thee have deceived thee,

Mic. 6:12. The inhabitants thereof have spoken lies, and their tongue *is* deceitful in their mouth.

Nah. 3:1. Woe to the bloody city! it *is* all full of lies *and* robbery;

Zeph. 3:13. The remnant of Israel shall not do iniquity, nor speak lies; neither shall a deceitful tongue be found in their mouth: for they shall feed and lie down, and none shall make *them* afraid.

Matt. 25:44. Then shall they also answer him, saying, Lord, when saw we thee an hungred, or athirst, or a stranger, or naked, or sick, or in prison, and did not minister unto thee? 45. Then shall he answer them, saying, Verily I say unto you, Inasmuch as ye did *it* not to one of the least of these, ye did *it* not to me. 46. And these shall go away into everlasting punishment: but the righteous into life eternal.

John 8:44. Ye are of *your* father the devil, and the lusts of your father ye will do. He was a murderer from the beginning, and abode not in the truth, because there is no truth in him. When he speaketh a lie, he speaketh of his own: for he is a liar, and the father of it. 45. And because I tell *you* the truth, ye believe me not.

Eph. 4:25. Putting away lying, speak every man truth with his neighbour: 29. Let no corrupt communication proceed out of your mouth, but that which is good to the use of edifying, that it may minister grace unto the hearers.

Col. 3:9. Lie not one to another, seeing that ye have put off the old man with his deeds;

1 Tim. 1:9. The law is not made for a righteous man, but for the lawless and disobedient . . . 10. For liars, for perjured persons,

1 Tim. 4:2. Speaking lies in hypocrisy; having their conscience seared with a hot iron;

1 Pet. 3:16. Having a good conscience; that, whereas they speak evil of you, as of evildoers, they may be ashamed that falsely accuse your good conversation in Christ.

Rev. 21:8. All liars shall have their part in the lake which burneth with fire and brimstone: 27. And there shall in no wise enter into it [the holy city] any thing that . . . *maketh* a lie.

Rev. 22:15. Without *are* dogs, . . . and whosoever loveth and maketh a lie.

See ACCUSATION, FALSE; CONSPIRACY; DECEIT; DECEPTION; FALSE WITNESS; FLATTERY; HYPOCRISY; PERJURY; TEACHERS, FALSE.

INSTANCES OF: Satan, in deceiving Eve, Gen. 3:4,5; in impugning Job's motives for being righteous, Job 1:9,10; 2:4,5; in his false pretensions to Jesus, Matt. 4:8,9; Luke 4:6,7. Adam and Eve, in attempting to evade responsibility, Gen. 3:12,13. Cain, in denying knowledge of his brother, Gen. 4:9. Abraham, in denying that Sarah was his wife, Gen. 12:11-19; 20:2. Sarah, to the angels, denying her derisive laugh of unbelief, Gen. 18:15; in denying to the king of Gerar, that she was Abraham's wife, Gen. 20:5,16. Isaac, denying that Rebekah was his wife, Gen. 26:7-10. Rebekah and Isaac, in the conspiracy against Esau, Gen. 27:6-24,46. Jacob's sons, in the scheme to destroy the Shechemites by first having them circumcised, Gen. 34.

Joseph's brethren, in deceiving their father

into a belief that Joseph was killed by wild beasts, Gen. 37:29-35. Potiphar's wife, in falsely accusing Joseph, Gen. 39:14-17. Joseph, in the deception he carried on with his brethren, Gen. 42-44. Pharaoh, in dealing deceitfully with the Israelites, Ex. chapters 7-12.

Aaron, in attempting to shift responsibility for the making of the golden calf, Ex. 32:1-24. Rahab, in denying that the spies were in her house, Josh. 2:4-6. The Gibeonites, ambassadors, in the deception they perpetrated upon Joshua and the elders of Israel in leading them to believe that they came from a distant region, when in fact they dwelt in the immediate vicinity, Josh. 9. Ehud, in pretending to bear secret messages to Eglon, king of Moab, while his object was to assassinate him, Judg. 3:16-23. Sisera, who instructed Jael to mislead his pursuers, Judg. 4:20. Saul, in professing to Samuel to have obeyed the commandment to destroy all spoils of the Amalekites, when in fact he had not obeyed, 1 Sam. 15:1-26; in accusing Ahimelech of conspiring with David against himself, 1 Sam. 22:11-16. David lied to Ahimelech, professing to have a mission from the king, in order that he might obtain provisions and armor, 1 Sam. 21; in feigning madness, 1 Sam. 21:13-15; and other deceits with the Philistines, 1 Sam. 27:8-12; the falsehood he put in the mouth of Hushai, of friendship to Absalom, 2 Sam. 15:34-37.

Michal, in the false statement that David was sick, in order to save him from Saul's violence, 1 Sam. 19:12-17. The Amalekite who claimed to have slain Saul, 2 Sam. 1:10-12. Hushai, in false professions to Absalom, 2 Sam. 16:16-19; in his deceitful counsel to Absalom, 2 Sam. 17:7-14.

The wife of the Bahurimite who saved the lives of Hushai's messengers, sent to apprise David of the movements of Absalom's army, 2 Sam. 17:15-22. The murder, under false pretense: Of Adonijah, 1 Kin. 2:23, of Shimei, 1 Kin. 2:42,43; of Jeroboam's wife, 1 Kin. 14:2. The old prophet of Beth-el who misguided the prophet of Judah, 1 Kin. 13: 11-22; Jeroboam's wife, feigning herself another woman, 1 Kin. 14:5-7.

The conspirators against Naboth, 1 Kin. 21:7-13. Gehazi, when he ran after Naaman, and misrepresented that Elisha wanted a talent of silver and two changes of raiment, 2 Kin. 5:20-24. Hazael, servant of the king of Syria, lied to the king in misstating the prophet Elisha's message in regard to the king's recovery, 2 Kin. 8:7-15. Jehu lied to the worshipers of Baal in order to gain advantage over them, and destroy them, 2 Kin. 10:18-28. Zedekiah, in violating his oath of allegiance to Nebuchadnezzer, 2 Chr. 36:13, Ezek. 16:59; 17:15-20. Samaritans, in their efforts to hinder the rebuilding of the temple at Jerusalem, Ezra 4. Sanballat, in trying to obstruct the rebuilding of Jerusalem, Neh. 6. Haman, in his conspir-

acy against the Jews, Esth. 3:8. **Jeremiah's** adversaries, in accusing him of joining the Chaldeans, Jer. 37:13-15. Princes of Israel, when they went to Jeremiah for a vision from the Lord, Jer. 42:20.

Herod, to the wise men, in professing to desire to worship Jesus, Matt. 2:8.

Jews, in falsely accusing Jesus of being gluttonous and a winebibber, Matt. 11:19; in refusing to bear truthful testimony concerning John Baptist, Matt. 21:24-27; falsely accusing Jesus of blasphemy, when he remitted sin, Matt. 9:2-6; Mark 2:7; Luke 5:21; and announced that he was the Son of God, Matt. 26:65; Mark 14:64; John 10:33-38.

Peter, in denying Jesus, Matt. 26:69-75; Mark 14:68-71; Luke 22:56-62; John 18:25-27. The Roman soldiers, who said the disciples stole the body of Jesus, Matt. 28:13,15.

The disobedient son, who promised to work in the vineyard, but did not, Matt. 21: 30. Ananias and Sapphira falsely state that they had sold their land for a given sum, Acts 5:1-10.

Stephen's accusers, who falsely accused him of blaspheming Moses and God, Acts 6:11-14. Paul's traducers, falsely accusing him of treason to Cæsar, Acts 16:20,21; 17: 5-7; 24:5; 25:7,8. The Cretians are always liars, evil beasts, slow bellies, Tit. 1:12.

See ACCUSATION, FALSE; CONSPIRACY; FALSE WITNESS; HYPOCRISY; PERJURY; TEACHERS, FALSE.

FALSE TEACHERS. See TEACHERS, FALSE.

FALSE WITNESS: Ex. 20:16. Thou shalt not bear false witness against thy neighbour. Deut. 5:20; Matt. 19:18; Luke 18:20; Rom. 13:9. [R. V. omits, Thou shalt not bear false witness;]

Ex. 23:1. Thou shalt not raise a false report: put not thine hand with the wicked to be an unrighteous witness.

Lev. 6:3. Or have found that which was lost, and lieth concerning it, and sweareth falsely; in any of all these that a man doeth, sinning therein:

Lev. 19:11. Ye shall not steal, neither deal falsely, neither lie one to another.

12. Ye shall not swear by my name falsely, neither shalt thou profane the name of thy God: I am the LORD.

16. Thou shalt not go up and down as a talebearer among thy people: neither shalt thou stand against the blood of thy neighbour: I am the LORD. Ex. 20:16.

Deut. 19:16. If a false witness rise up against any man to testify against him that which is wrong; 17. Then both the men, between whom the controversy is, shall stand before the LORD, before the priests and the judges, which shall be in those days; 18. And the judges shall make diligent inquisition: and, behold, if the witness be a false witness, and hath testified falsely against his brother; 19. Then shall ye do unto him, as he had thought to have done unto his brother: so shalt thou put the evil away from among you. 20. And those which remain shall hear, and fear, and shall hence forth commit no more any such evil among you.

Psa. 27:12. False witnesses are risen up against me, and such as breathe out cruelty.

Psa. 35:11. False witnesses did rise up; they laid to my charge *things* that I knew not.

Prov. 6:16. These six *things* doth the LORD hate; yea, seven *are* an abomination unto him : 17. A proud look, a lying tongue, and hands that shed innocent blood, 18. An heart that deviseth wicked imaginations, feet that be swift in running to mischief, 19. A false witness *that* speaketh lies, and he that soweth discord among brethren.

Prov. 12:17. *He that* speaketh truth sheweth forth righteousness: but a false witness deceit.

Prov. 14:5. A faithful witness will not lie: but a false witness will utter lies. 8. The folly of fools *is* deceit. 25. A true witness delivereth souls: but a deceitful *witness* speaketh lies.

Prov. 18:5. *It is* not good to accept the person of the wicked, to overthrow the righteous in judgment.

Prov. 19:9. A false witness shall not be unpunished, and *he that* speaketh lies shall perish. 22. A poor man *is* better than a liar. 28. An ungodly witness scorneth judgment:

Prov. 21:28. A false witness shall perish:

Prov. 24:28. Be not a witness against thy neighbour without cause; and deceive *not* with thy lips.

Prov. 25:18. A man that beareth false witness against his neighbour *is* a maul, and a sword, and a sharp arrow.

Zech. 5:3. This *is* the curse that goeth forth over the face of the whole earth: for every one that stealeth shall be cut off *as* on this side according to it; and every one that sweareth shall be cut off *as* on that side according to it. 4. I will bring it forth, saith the LORD of hosts, and it shall enter into the house of the thief, and into the house of him that sweareth falsely by my name: and it shall remain in the midst of his house, and shall consume it with the timber thereof and the stones thereof.

Matt. 15:19. For out of the heart proceed evil thoughts, . . . false witness,

Luke 3:14. And the soldiers likewise demanded of him, saying, And what shall we do? And he said unto them, Do violence to no man, neither accuse *any* falsely; and be content with your wages.

1 Tim. 1:9. The law is not made for a righteous man, but for the lawless and disobedient, 10. . . . For liars, for perjured persons,

See PERJURY; FALSEHOOD; EVIDENCE, LAWS CONCERNING; WITNESS.

INSTANCES OF: Witnesses against Naboth, 1 Kin. 21:13; against Jesus, Matt. 26: 59-61; Mark 14:54-59; against Stephen, Acts 6:11,13; against Paul, Acts 16:20,21; 17:5-7; 24:5; 25:7,8.

FAMILIAR SPIRITS. Consulting of, forbidden, Lev. 19:31; 20:6,27; Deut. 18:10,11; vain, Isa. 8:19; 19:3. Those who consulted, to be cut off, Lev. 20:6,27.

INSTANCES OF THOSE WHO CONSULTED: Saul, 1 Sam. 28:3-25; 1 Chr. 10:13.

See DEMONS; NECROMANCY; WITCHCRAFT.

FAMILY. OF SAINTS: Blessed, Psa. 128:3,6. Should be taught God's word, Deut. 4:9,10. Worship God together, 1 Cor. 16:19. Be duly regulated, Prov. 31:27; 1 Tim. 3:4,5, 12. Live in unity, Gen. 45:24; Psa. 133:1. Live in mutual forbearance, Gen. 50:17-21; Matt. 18:21,22. Rejoice together before God, Deut. 14:26. Deceivers and liars should be removed from, Psa. 101:7. Warned against departing from God, Deut. 29:18. Punishment of irreligious, Jer. 10:25.

GOOD, EXEMPLIFIED: Abraham, Gen. 18:19. Jacob, Gen. 35:2. Joshua, Josh. 24: 15. David, 2 Sam. 6:20. Job, Job 1:5. Lazarus of Bethany, John 11:1-5. Cornelius, Acts 10:2,33. Lydia, Acts 16:15. Jailer of Philippi, Acts 16:31-34. Crispus, Acts 18:8. Lois, 2 Tim. 1:5.—*Bible Text Book.*

See CHILDREN; HUSBAND; WIFE; ORPHAN; WIDOW.

INSTITUTED: Gen. 2:23. And Adam said, This *is* now bone of my bones, and flesh of my flesh: she shall be called Woman, because she was taken out of Man. 24. Therefore shall a man leave his father and his mother, and shall cleave unto his wife: and they shall be one flesh.

GOVERNMENT OF: Gen. 3:16. Unto the woman he said, . . . thy desire *shall be* to thy husband, and he shall rule over thee.

Gen. 18:19. For I know him, that he will command his children and his household after him, and they shall keep the way of the LORD to do justice and judgment; that the LORD may bring upon Abraham that which he hath spoken of him.

Esth. 1:20. And when the king's decree which he shall make shall be published throughout all his empire, . . . all the wives shall give to their husbands honour, both to great and small. 22. That every man should bear rule in his own house.

1 Cor. 7:10. And unto the married I command, *yet* not I, but the Lord, Let not the wife depart from *her* husband :

1 Cor. 11:3. The head of the woman *is* the man; 7. The woman is the glory of the man. 8. For the man is not of the woman; but the woman of the man. 9. Neither was the man created for the woman; but the woman for the man.

Eph. 5:22. Wives, submit yourselves unto your own husbands, as unto the Lord. 23. For the husband is the head of the wife, even as Christ is the head of the church: and he is the saviour of the body. 24. Therefore as the church is subject unto Christ, so *let* the wives *be* to their own husbands in every thing.

Col. 3:18. Wives, submit yourselves unto your own husbands, as it is fit in the Lord.

1 Tim. 3:2. A bishop then must be blameless, the husband of one wife, vigilant, sober, of good behaviour, given to hospitality, apt to teach; 4. One that ruleth well his own house, having his children in subjection with all gravity; 5. (For if a man know not how to rule his own house, how shall he take care of the church of God?)

1 Pet. 3:1. Likewise, ye wives, *be* in subjection to your own husbands; 6. Even as Sara obeyed Abraham, calling him lord:

INFELICITY IN: Prov. 11:22. *As* a jewel of gold in a swine's snout, *so is* a fair woman which is without discretion.

Prov. 12:4. She that maketh ashamed *is* as rottenness in his bones.

Prov. 14:1. Every wise woman buildeth her house: but the foolish plucketh it down with her hands.

Prov. 15:17. Better *is* a dinner of herbs where love is, than a stalled ox and hatred therewith.

Prov. 18:19. A brother offended *is harder to be won* than a strong city: and *their* contentions *are* like the bars of a castle.

Prov. 19:13. A foolish son *is* the calamity of his father: and the contentions of a wife *are* a continual dropping.

Prov. 21:9. *It is* better to dwell in a corner of the housetop, than with a brawling woman in a wide house. [Prov. 25:24.] 19. *It is* better to dwell in the wilderness, than with a contentious and an angry woman.

Prov. 27:15. A continual dropping in a very rainy day and a contentious woman are alike. 16. Whosoever hideth her hideth the wind, and the ointment of his right hand, *which* bewrayeth *itself*. Prov. 19.13.

Prov. 30:21. For three things the earth is disquieted, . . . 23. For an odious *woman* when she is married; and an handmaid that is heir to her mistress.

INSTANCES OF INFELICITY IN: Of Abraham, on account of Hagar, Gen. 16:5; 21:10,11. Of Isaac, on account of disagreement between Jacob and Esau, Gen. 27:4–46. Of Jacob, bigamic jealousy between Leah and Rachel, Gen. 29:30–34; 30:1–25. Moses and Zipporah, Ex. 4:25,26. Elkanah, on account of bigamic feuds, 1 Sam. 1:4–7. David and Michal, 2 Sam. 6:16,20–23. Ahasuerus, on account of Vashti's refusing to appear before his drunken courtiers, Esth. 1:10–22.

PERSIAN, DOMESTIC CUSTOMS: Esth. 1:10–22.

See HAREM.

RELIGION OF THE: Gen. 12:7. And the LORD appeared unto Abram, and said, Unto thy seed will I give this land: and there builded he an altar unto the LORD, who appeared unto him. 8. And he removed from thence unto a mountain on the east of Beth-el, and pitched his tent, *having* Beth-el on the west, and Hai on the east: and there he builded an altar unto the LORD, and called upon the name of the LORD.

Gen. 13:3. And he went on his journeys from the south even to Beth-el, unto the place where his tent had been at the beginning, between Beth-el and Hai; 4. Unto the place of the altar, which he had made there at the first: and there Abram called on the name of the LORD.

Gen. 17:12. And he that is eight days old shall be circumcised among you, every man child in your generations, he that is born in the house, or bought with money of any stranger, which *is* not of thy seed. 13. He that is born in thy house, and he that is bought with thy money, must needs be circumcised: and my covenant shall be in your flesh for an everlasting covenant. 14. And the uncircumcised man child whose flesh of his foreskin is not circumcised, that soul shall be cut off from his people; he hath broken my covenant.

Gen. 18:19. For I know him, that he will command his children and his household after him, and they shall keep the way of the LORD, to do justice and judgment; that the LORD may bring upon Abraham that which he hath spoken of him.

Deut. 4:9. Only take heed to thyself, and keep thy soul diligently, lest thou forget the things which thine eyes have seen, and lest they depart from thy heart all the days of thy life: but teach them thy sons, and thy sons' sons; 10. *Specially* the day that thou stoodest before the LORD thy God in Horeb, when the LORD said unto me, Gather me the people together, and I will make them hear my words, that they may learn to fear me all the days that they shall live upon the earth, and *that* they may teach their children.

Deut. 11:19. And ye shall teach them your children, speaking of them when thou sittest in thine house, and when thou walkest by the way, when thou liest down, and when thou risest up. 20. And thou shalt write them upon the door posts of thine house, and upon thy gates:

Deut. 12:5. But unto the place which the LORD your God shall choose out of all your tribes to put his name there, *even* unto his habitation shall ye seek, and thither thou shalt come: 6. And thither ye shall bring your burnt offerings, and your sacrifices, and your tithes, and heave offerings of your hand, and your vows and your freewill offerings, and the firstlings of your herds and of your flocks: 7. And there ye shall eat before the LORD your God, and ye shall rejoice in all that ye put your hand unto, ye and your households, wherein the LORD thy God hath blessed thee. 11. Then there shall be a place which the LORD your God shall choose to cause his name to dwell there; thither shall ye bring all that I command you; your burnt offerings, and your sacrifices, your tithes, and the heave offering of your hand, and all your choice vows which ye vow unto the LORD: 12. And ye shall rejoice before the LORD your God, ye, and your sons, and your daughters, and your menservants, and your maidservants, and the Levite that *is* within your gates: forasmuch as he hath no part nor inheritance with you.

Josh. 24:15. But as for me and my house, we will serve the LORD.

Psa. 101:2. I will walk within my house with a perfect heart.

Jer. 7:18. The children gather wood, and the fathers kindle the fire, and the women knead *their* dough, to make cakes to the queen of heaven, and to pour out drink offerings unto other gods, that they may provoke me to anger.

Acts 10:1. There was a certain man in Cæsarea called Cornelius, a centurion of the band called the Italian *band.* 2. A devout *man*, and one that feared God with all his house, which gave much alms to the people, and prayed to God alway. 3. He saw in a vision evidently about the ninth hour of the day an angel of God coming in to him, and saying unto him, Cornelius. 4. And when he looked on him, he was afraid, and said, What is it, Lord? And he said unto him, thy prayers and thine alms are come up for a memorial before God. 5. And now send men to Joppa, and call for *one* Simon, whose surname is Peter: 6. He lodgeth with one Simon a tanner, whose house is by the sea side: he shall tell thee what thou oughtest to do. 33. Immediately therefore I sent to thee; and thou hast well done that thou art come. Now therefore are we all here present before God, to hear all things that are commanded thee of God.

44. While Peter yet spake these words, the Holy Ghost fell on all them which heard the word. 47. Can any man forbid water, that these should not be baptized, which have received the Holy Ghost as well as we? 48. And he commanded them to be baptized in the name of the Lord.

Acts 16:25. And at midnight Paul and Silas prayed, and sang praises unto God: and the prisoners heard them. 26. And suddenly there was a great earthquake, so that the foundations of the prison were shaken: and immediately all the doors were opened, and every one's bands were loosed. 27. And the keeper of the prison awaking out of his sleep, and seeing the prison doors open, he drew out his sword, and would have killed himself, supposing that the prisoners had been fled. 28. But Paul cried with a loud voice, saying, Do thyself no harm: for we are all here. 29. Then he called for a light, and sprang in, and came trembling, and fell down before Paul and Silas, 30. And brought them out, and said, Sirs, what must I do to be saved? 31. And they said, Believe on the Lord Jesus Christ, and thou shalt be saved, and thy house. 32. And they spake unto him the word of the Lord, and to all that were in his house. 33. And he took them the same hour of the night, and washed *their* stripes; and was baptized, he and all his, straightway. 34. And when he had brought them into his house, he set meat before them, and rejoiced, believing in God with all his house.

Acts 18:8. And Crispus, the chief ruler of the synagogue, believed on the Lord with all his house;

1 Cor. 1:16. And I baptized also the household of Stephanas:

FAMINE. Pharaoh forewarned of, in dreams, Gen. 41. Described, Deut. 28:53–57; Isa. 5:13; 9:18–21; 17:11; Jer. 5:17; 14:1–6; 48:33; Lam. 1:11,19; 2:11–22; 4:4–10; Joel 1:17–20. Sent as a judgment, Lev. 26:19–29; Deut. 28:23,24,38–42; 1 Kin. 17:1; 2 Kin. 8:1; 1 Chr. 21:12; Psa. 105:16; 107:33,34; Isa. 3:1–8; 14:30; Jer. 19:9; 14:15–22; 29:17,19; Lam. 5:4,5,10, Ezek. 4:16,17; 5:16,17; 14:13; Joel 1:15,16; Amos 4:6–9; 5:16,17; Hag. 1:10,11; Matt. 24:7; Luke 21:11; Rev. 6:5–8.

Cannibalism in, Deut. 28:53; 2 Kin. 6:28. Righteous delivered from, Job 5:20; Psa. 33:19; 37:19.

FIGURATIVE: Amos 8:11.

INSTANCES OF: In Canaan, Gen. 12:10; 26:1; 2 Sam. 21:1; 1 Kin. 17; 18:1; 2 Kin. 6:25–29; 7:4. In Jerusalem, from siege, 2 Kin. 25:3; Jer. 52:6. In Egypt, Gen. 41:53–57. Universal, Acts 11:28.

FAN, used for winnowing grain, Isa. 30:24; Jer. 15:7; 51:2; Matt. 3:12.

FARMING. See AGRICULTURE; VINEYARD.

FARTHING. This word is used to translate two different words in the Greek text: *assarion.* Matt. 10:29; Luke 12:6, a Roman coin worth, in American money, about 1½ cents; in English money, about 3 farthings; and *kodrantes*, Matt. 5:26; Mark 12:42, worth, in American money, about two-fifths of a cent; in English money, less than a farthing.

FASTING. Observed on occasions of public calamities, 2 Sam. 1:12; afflictions, Psa. 35:13; Dan. 6:18; private afflictions, 2 Sam. 12:16; approaching danger, Esth. 4:16; ordination of ministers, Acts 13:3; 14:23.

Accompanied by prayer, Dan. 9:3; confession of sin, 1 Sam. 7:6; Neh. 9:1,2; humiliation, Deut. 9:18; Neh. 9:1; reading of the Scriptures, Jer. 36:6.

Habitual: by John's disciples, Matt. 9:14; by Anna, Luke 2:37; by Pharisees, Matt. 9:14; Mark 2:18; Luke 18:12; by Cornelius, Acts 10:30; by Paul, 2 Cor. 6:5; 11:27.

In times of bereavement: of the people of Jabesh-gilead, for Saul and his sons, 1 Sam. 31:13; 1 Chr. 10:12; of David, at the time of Saul's death, 2 Sam. 1:12; of his child's sickness, 2 Sam. 12:16,21–23; of Abner's death, 2 Sam. 3:35.

Prolonged: for three weeks, by Daniel, Dan. 10:2,3; forty days, by Moses, Ex. 24:18; 34:28; Deut. 9:9,18; Elijah, 1 Kin. 19:8; Jesus, Matt. 4:2; Mark 1:12,13; Luke 4:1,2.

See HUMILIATION; HUMILITY.

UNCLASSIFIED SCRIPTURES RELATING TO: Ezra 8:21. Then I proclaimed a fast there, at the river of Ahava, that we might afflict ourselves before our God, to seek of him a right way for us, and for our little ones, and for all our substance. 22. For I was ashamed to require of the king a band of soldiers and horsemen to help us against the enemy in the way : because we had spoken unto the king, saying, The hand of our God *is* upon all them for good that seek him ; but his power and his wrath *is* against all them that forsake him. 23. So we fasted and besought our God for this : and he was intreated of us.

Psa. 35:13. But as for me, when they were sick, my clothing *was* sackcloth : I humbled my soul with fasting ;

Psa. 69:10. When I wept, *and chastened* my soul with fasting, that was to my reproach.

Isa. 58:3. Wherefore have we fasted, *say they*, and thou seest not ? *wherefore* have we afflicted our soul, and thou takest no knowledge ? Behold, in the day of your fast we find pleasure, and exact all your labours. 4. Behold, ye fast for strife and debate, and to smite with the fist of wickedness: ye shall not fast as *ye do this* day, to make your voice to be heard on high. 5. Is it such a fast that I have chosen ? a day for a man to afflict his soul ? *is it* to bow down his head as a bulrush, and to spread sackcloth and ashes *under him?* wilt thou call this a fast, and an acceptable day to the LORD ? 6. *Is* not this the fast that I have chosen ? to loose the bands of wickedness, to undo the heavy burdens, and to let the oppressed go free, and that ye break every yoke ? 7. *Is it* not to deal thy bread to the hungry, and that thou bring the poor that are cast out to thy house ? when thou seest the naked, that thou cover him ; and that thou hide not thyself from thine own flesh ?

Jer. 14:12. When they fast, I will not hear their cry ;

Dan. 10:2. In those days I Daniel was mourning three full weeks. 3. I ate no pleasant bread, neither came flesh nor wine in my mouth, neither did I anoint myself at all, till three whole weeks were fulfilled.

Joel 1:14. Sanctify ye a fast, call a solemn assembly, gather the elders *and* all the inhabitants of the land *into* the house of the LORD your God, and cry unto the LORD,

Joel 2:12. Therefore also now, saith the LORD, turn ye *even* to me with all your heart, and with fasting, and with weeping, and with mourning: 13. And rend your heart, and not your garments, and turn unto the LORD your God: for he *is* gracious and merciful, slow to anger, and of great kindness, and repenteth him of the evil.

Zech. 7:5. When ye fasted and mourned in the fifth and seventh *month*, even those seventy years, did ye at all fast unto me, *even* to me ?

Zech. 8:19. Thus saith the LORD of hosts ; The fast of the fourth *month*, and the fast of the fifth, and the fast of the seventh, and the fast of the tenth, shall be to the house of Judah joy and gladness, and cheerful feasts ; therefore love the truth and peace.

Matt. 6:16. When ye fast, be not, as the hypocrites, of a sad countenance : for they disfigure their faces, that they may appear

unto men to fast. Verily I say unto you, They have their reward. 17. But thou, when thou fastest, anoint thine head, and wash thy face ; 18. That thou appear not unto men to fast, but unto thy Father which is in secret : and thy Father, which seeth in secret, shall reward thee openly.

Matt. 9:14. Then came to him the disciples of John, saying, Why do we and the Pharisees fast oft, but thy disciples fast not ? 15. And Jesus said unto them, Can the children of the bridechamber mourn, as long as the bridegroom is with them ? but the days will come, when the bridegroom shall be taken from them, and then shall they fast.

Matt. 17:21. ¹ This kind goeth not out but by prayer and fasting.   [¹ Omitted in R. V.]

Acts 27:9. Now when much time was spent, and when sailing was now dangerous, because the fast was now already past, Paul admonished *them*, 33. And while the day was coming on, Paul besought *them* all to take meat, saying, This day is the fourteenth day that ye have tarried and continued fasting, having taken nothing. 34. Wherefore I pray you to take *some* meat : for this is for your health : for there shall not an hair fall from the head of any of you.

1 Cor. 7:5. That ye may give yourselves to ¹ fasting and prayer ;   [¹ Omitted in R. V.]

INSTANCES OF : Of the Israelites, in the conflict between the other tribes with the tribe of Benjamin, on account of the wrong suffered by a Levite's concubine. Judg. 20:26 ; when they went to Mizpeh for the ark, 1 Sam. 7:6. Of David, at the death of Saul, 2 Sam. 1:12 ; during the sickness of the child born to him by Bath-sheba, 2 Sam. 12:16–22 ; while interceding in prayer for his friends, Psa. 35: 13 ; in his zeal for Zion, Psa. 69:10 ; in prayer for himself and his adversaries, Psa. 109:4, 24. Of Ahab, when Elijah prophesied the destruction of himself and his house, 1 Kin. 21:27 ; with verses 20–29. Of Jehoshaphat, at the time of the invasion of the confederated armies of the Canaanites and Syrians, 2 Chr. 20:3. Of Ezra, on account of the idolatrous marriages of the Jews, Ezra 10:6. Of Nehemiah, on account of the desolation of Jerusalem and the temple, Neh. 1:4. Of the Jews, when Jeremiah prophesied against Judea and Jerusalem, Jer. 36:9 ; in Babylon, with prayer for divine deliverance and guidance, Ezra 8:21,23. Of Darius, when he put Daniel in the lions' den, Dan. 6:18. Of Daniel, on account of the captivity of the people, with prayer for their deliverance, Dan. 9:3 ; at the time of his vision, Dan. 10: 1–3. Ninevites, when Jonah preached to them, Jonah 3:5–10. By Paul, at the time of his conversion, Acts 9:9. Of the disciples, at the time of the consecration of Barnabas and Saul, Acts 13:2,3. Of the consecration of the elders, Acts 14:23.

FAT. Offered in sacrifice, Ex. 23:18 ; 29: 13,22 ; Lev. 1:8 ; 3:3–5,9–11,14–16 ; 4:8–10 ; 7:3–5 ; 8:16,25,26 ; 10:15 ; 17:6 ; 1 Sam. 2:15,16 ; Isa. 43:

24. Belonged to the Lord, Lev. 3:16. Forbidden as food, Lev. 3:16,17; 7:23. Idolatrous sacrifices of, Deut. 32:38.

FIGURATIVE: Gen. 45:18; 49:20; Psa. 37: 20; 81:16; Isa. 25:6.

FATHER. An idolatrous title of priests, Judg. 17:10. Forbidden to be used as a title among the disciples, Matt. 23:9. See PARENTS; GOD, FATHERHOOD OF.

FATHERHOOD. OF GOD. See GOD, FATHERHOOD OF.

FATHER-IN-LAW. Hospitable to son-in-law, a man of Bethlehem-judah, Judg. 19:3-9. Unjust, Laban to Jacob, Gen. 29: 21-23; 31:7,39-42.

FATHERLESS. See ORPHAN.

FATHOM, Acts 27:28.

FATTED CALF, Luke 15:23.

FAULT FINDING. See MURMURING; UNCHARITABLENESS.

FAVOR. See GOD, GRACE OF.

FAVORITISM. INSTANCES OF: Jacob, for Rachel, Gen. 29:30,34. Elkanah, for Hannah, 1 Sam. 1:4,5. Rebekah, for Jacob, Gen. 27:6-17. Jacob, for Joseph, Gen. 37:3,4. Joseph, for Benjamin, Gen. 43:34. Forbidden in parents, Deut. 21:15-17.

See PARTIALITY.

FEAR. See COWARDICE. Also FEAR OF GOD, below.

FEAR OF GOD. REVERENCE: Gen. 35:5. And they journeyed: and the terror of God was upon the cities that *were* round about them, and they did not pursue after the sons of Jacob.

Ex. 18:21. Moreover thou shalt provide out of all the people able men, such as fear God, men of truth, hating covetousness; and place *such* over them, *to be* rulers of thousands, *and* rulers of hundreds, rulers of fifties, and rulers of tens.

Ex. 20:18. And all the people saw the thunderings, and the lightnings, and the noise of the trumpet, and the mountain smoking: and when the people saw *it*, they removed, and stood afar off. 19. And they said unto Moses, Speak thou with us, and we will hear: but let not God speak with us, lest we die. 20. And Moses said unto the people, Fear not: for God is come to prove you, and that his fear may be before your faces, that ye sin not.

Lev. 22:32. Neither shall ye profane my holy name; but I will be hallowed among the children of Israel:

Deut. 4:10. The LORD said unto me, Gather me the people together, and I will make them hear my words, that they may learn to fear me . . . and *that* they may teach their children.

Deut. 5:29. O that there were such an heart in them, that they would fear me, and keep all my commandments always, that it might be well with them, and with their children for ever!

Deut. 6:2. That thou mightest fear the LORD thy God, to keep all his statutes and his commandments,

Deut. 10:12. Now, Israel, what doth the LORD thy God require of thee, but to fear the LORD thy God, to walk in all his ways, and to love him, and to serve the LORD thy God with all thy heart and with all thy soul, 20. Thou shalt fear the LORD thy God; him shalt thou serve, and to him shalt thou cleave, and swear by his name. 21. He *is* thy praise, and he *is* thy God, that hath done for thee these great and terrible things, which thine eyes have seen. Deut. 6:13; 13: 4; 14:23.

Deut. 28:49. The LORD shall bring a nation against thee from far, . . . 58. If thou wilt not observe to do all the words of this law that are written in this book, that thou mayest fear this glorious and fearful name, THE LORD THY GOD;

Josh. 4:24. That all the people of the earth might know the hand of the LORD, that it *is* mighty: that ye might fear the LORD your God for ever.

Josh. 24:14. Fear the LORD, and serve him in sincerity and in truth:

1 Sam. 2:30. Them that honour me I will honour, and they that despise me shall be lightly esteemed.

1 Sam. 12:14. If ye will fear the LORD, and serve him, and obey his voice, and not rebel against the commandment of the LORD, then shall both ye and also the king that reigneth over you continue following the LORD your God: 24. Only fear the LORD, and serve him in truth with all your heart: for consider how great *things* he hath done for you.

2 Sam. 23:3. The God of Israel said, the Rock of Israel spake to me, He that ruleth over men *must be* just, ruling in the fear of God.

1 Kin. 8:40. That they may fear thee all the days that they live in the land which thou gavest unto our fathers.

2 Kin. 17:36. The LORD, who brought you up out of the land of Egypt . . . him shall ye fear, and him shall ye worship, 39. The LORD your God ye shall fear; and he shall deliver you out of the hands of all your enemies. *v.* 28.

1 Chr. 16:30. Fear before him, all the earth:

2 Chr. 19:7. Let the fear of the LORD be upon you; take heed and do *it:* for *there is* no iniquity with the LORD our God. 9. Thus shall ye do in the fear of the LORD, faithfully, and with a perfect heart.

Ezra 10:3. Now therefore let us make a covenant with our God to put away all the wives, and such as are born of them, according to the counsel of my lord, and of those that tremble at the commandment of our God;

Neh. 5:9. I said, It *is* not good that ye do: ought ye not to walk in the fear of our God because of the reproach of the heathen our enemies?

Job 28:28. And unto man he said, Behold, the fear of the Lord, that *is* wisdom; and to depart from evil *is* understanding.

Job 37:24. Men do therefore fear him : he respecteth not any *that are* wise of heart.

Psa. 2:11. Serve the LORD with fear, and rejoice with trembling.

Psa. 4:4. Stand in awe, and sin not: commune with your own heart upon your bed, and be still.

Psa. 15:4. He honoureth them that fear the LORD.

Psa. 19:9. The fear of the LORD *is* clean, enduring for ever:

Psa. 22:23. Ye that fear the LORD, praise him: all ye the seed of Jacob, glorify him; and fear him, all ye the seed of Israel. 25. I will pay my vows before them that fear him.

Psa. 25:12. What man *is* he that feareth the LORD? him shall he teach in the way *that* he shall choose. 13. His soul shall dwell at ease; and his seed shall inherit the earth. 14. The secret of the LORD *is* with them that fear him; and he will shew them his covenant.

Psa. 31:19. *Oh* how great *is* thy goodness, which thou hast laid up for them that fear thee;

Psa. 33:8. Let all the earth fear the LORD : let all the inhabitants of the world stand in awe of him. 18. The eye of the LORD *is* upon them that fear him, upon them that hope in his mercy.

Psa. 34:7. The angel of the LORD encampeth round about them that fear him, and delivereth them. 9. O fear the LORD, ye his saints: for *there is* no want to them that fear him. 11. Come, ye children, hearken unto me: I will teach you the fear of the LORD.

Psa. 46:10. Be still, and know that I *am* God: I will be exalted among the heathen, I will be exalted in the earth.

Psa. 52:6. The righteous also shall see, and fear,

Psa. 60:4. Thou hast given a banner to them that fear thee, that it may be displayed because of the truth.

Psa. 64:9. All men shall fear, and shall declare the work of God; for they shall wisely consider of his doing.

Psa. 67:7. God shall bless us; and all the ends of the earth shall fear him.

Psa. 72:5. They shall fear thee as long as the sun and moon endure, throughout all generations.

Psa. 76:7. Thou, *even* thou, *art* to be feared : 11. Let all that be round about him bring presents unto him that ought to be feared.

Psa. 85:9. His salvation *is* nigh them that fear him; that glory may dwell in our land.

Psa. 86:11. Teach me thy way, O LORD; . . . unite my heart to fear thy name.

Psa. 89:7. God is greatly to be feared in the assembly of the saints, and to be had in reverence of all *them that are* about him.

Psa. 90:11. Who knoweth the power of thine anger? even according to thy fear, *so is* thy wrath.

Psa. 96:4. The LORD *is* great, and greatly to be praised: he *is* to be feared above all gods. 9. Fear before him, all the earth.

Psa. 99:1. The LORD reigneth; let the people tremble: he sitteth *between* the cherubims; let the earth be moved.

Psa. 102:15. The heathen shall fear the name of the LORD, and all the kings of the earth thy glory.

Psa. 103:11. As the heaven is high above the earth, *so* great is his mercy toward them that fear him. 13. Like as a father pitieth *his* children, *so* the LORD pitieth them that fear him. 17. The mercy of the LORD *is* from everlasting to everlasting upon them that fear him,

Psa. 111:5. He hath given meat unto them that fear him: 10. The fear of the LORD *is* the beginning of wisdom: Prov. 1:7; 9:10.

Psa. 112:1. Blessed *is* the man *that* feareth the LORD, *that* delighteth greatly in his commandments.

Psa. 115:11. Ye that fear the LORD, trust in the LORD: 13. He will bless them that fear the LORD, *both* small and great.

Psa. 118:4. Let them now that fear the LORD say, that his mercy *endureth* for ever.

Psa. 119:63. I *am* a companion of all *them* that fear thee, and of them that keep thy precepts. 74. They that fear thee will be glad when they see me; because I have hoped in thy word. 79. Let those that fear thee turn unto me, and those that have known thy testimonies. Psa. 66:16.

Psa. 128:1. Blessed *is* every one that feareth the LORD; that walketh in his ways. 4. Thus shall the man be blessed that feareth the LORD.

Psa. 130:4. *There is* forgiveness with thee, that thou mayest be feared.

Psa. 135:20. Ye that fear the LORD, bless the LORD.

Psa. 145:19. He will fulfil the desire of them that fear him: he also will hear their cry, and will save them.

Psa. 147:11. The LORD taketh pleasure in them that fear him,

Prov. 1:7. The fear of the LORD *is* the beginning of knowledge: *but* fools despise wisdom and instruction. Prov. 9:10.

Prov. 2:5. Then shalt thou understand the fear of the LORD,

Prov. 3:7. Fear the LORD and depart from evil.

Prov. 8:13. The fear of the LORD *is* to hate evil:

Prov. 10:27. The fear of the LORD prolongeth days:

Prov. 13:13. He that feareth the commandment shall be rewarded.

Prov. 14:2. He that walketh in his uprightness feareth the LORD: but *he that is* perverse in his ways despiseth him. 16. A wise *man* feareth, and departeth from evil: 26. In the fear of the LORD *is* strong confidence: 27. The fear of the LORD *is* a fountain of life, to depart from the snares of death.

Prov. 15:16. Better *is* little with the fear

of the LORD than great treasure and trouble therewith. 33. The fear of the LORD *is* the instruction of wisdom;

Prov. 16:6. By the fear of the LORD *men* depart from evil.

Prov. 19:23. The fear of the LORD *tendeth* to life: and *he that hath it* shall abide satisfied; he shall not be visited with evil.

Prov. 22:4. By humility *and* the fear of the LORD *are* riches, and honour, and life.

Prov. 23:17. *Be thou* in the fear of the LORD all the day long.

Prov. 24:21. My son, fear thou the LORD and the king:

Prov. 28:14. Happy *is* the man that feareth alway:

Prov. 31:30. A woman *that* feareth the LORD, she shall be praised.

Eccl. 3:14. I know that, whatsoever God doeth, it shall be for ever: nothing can be put to it, nor any thing taken from it: and God doeth *it*, that *men* should fear before him.

Eccl. 7:18. He that feareth God shall come forth from them all.

Eccl. 8:12. Surely I know that it shall be well with them that fear God, which fear before him:

Eccl. 12:13. Fear God, and keep his commandments: for this *is* the whole *duty* of man. Eccl. 5:7; 1 Pet. 2:17.

Isa. 2:10. Enter into the rock, and hide thee in the dust, for fear of the LORD, and for the glory of his majesty. 19. And they shall go into the holes of the rocks, and into the caves of the earth, for fear of the LORD, and for the glory of his majesty, when he ariseth to shake terribly the earth. 20. In that day a man shall cast his idols of silver, and his idols of gold, which they made *each one* for himself to worship, to the moles and to the bats; 21. To go into the clefts of the rocks, and into the tops of the ragged rocks, for fear of the LORD, and for the glory of his majesty, when he ariseth to shake terribly the earth.

Isa. 8:13. Sanctify the LORD of hosts himself; and *let* him *be* your fear, and *let* him *be* your dread.

Isa. 25:3. The strong people glorify thee, the city of the terrible nations shall fear thee.

Isa. 29:13. This people draw near *me* with their mouth, and with their lips do honour me, but have removed their heart far from me, and their fear toward me is taught by the precept of men: 23. They shall sanctify my name, and sanctify the Holy One of Jacob, and shall fear the God of Israel.

Isa. 33:6. The fear of the LORD *is* his treasure. 13. Hear, ye *that are* far off, what I have done; and, ye *that are* near, acknowledge my might.

Isa. 50:10. Who *is* among you that feareth the LORD, . . . let him trust in the name of the LORD, and stay upon his God.

Isa. 59:19. So shall they fear the name of the LORD from the west, and his glory from the rising of the sun.

Isa. 60:5. Then thou shalt see, and flow to-

gether, and thine heart shall fear, and be enlarged;

Jer. 5:22. Fear ye not me? saith the LORD: will ye not tremble at my presence, which have placed the sand *for* the bound of the sea by a perpetual decree, that it cannot pass it:

Jer. 10:7. Who would not fear thee, O King of nations? for to thee doth it appertain: forasmuch as among all the wise *men* of the nations, and in all their kingdoms, *there is* none like unto thee.

Jer. 32:39. I will give them one heart, and one way, that they may fear me for ever, for the good of them, and of their children after them: 40. I will put my fear in their hearts, that they shall not depart from me.

Jer. 33:9. They shall fear and tremble for all the goodness and for all the prosperity that I procure unto it.

Hos. 3:5. Afterward shall the children of Israel return, . . . and shall fear the LORD and his goodness in the latter days.

Mic. 7:16. The nations shall see and be confounded at all their might: they shall lay *their* hand upon *their* mouth, their ears shall be deaf. 17. They shall lick the dust like a serpent, they shall move out of their holes like worms of the earth: they shall be afraid of the LORD our God, and shall fear because of thee.

Zeph. 1:7. Hold thy peace at the presence of the Lord GOD:

Zeph. 3:7. I said, Surely thou wilt fear me, thou wilt receive instruction;

Zech. 2:13. Be silent, O all flesh, before the LORD: for he is raised up out of his holy habitation.

Mal. 1:6. A son honoureth *his* father, and a servant his master: if then I *be* a father, where *is* mine honour? and if I *be* a master, where *is* my fear? saith the LORD of hosts unto you, O priests, that despise my name.

Mal. 3:16. They that feared the LORD spake often one to another: and the LORD hearkened, and heard *it*, and a book of remembrance was written before him for them that feared the LORD, and that thought upon his name.

Mal. 4:2. Unto you that fear my name shall the Sun of righteousness arise with healing in his wings;

Matt. 10:28. And fear not them which kill the body, but are not able to kill the soul: but rather fear him which is able to destroy both soul and body in hell.

Luke 1:50. His mercy *is* on them that fear him from generation to generation.

Luke 12:5. I will forewarn you whom ye shall fear: Fear him, which after he hath killed hath power to cast into hell; yea, I say unto you, Fear him.

Luke 23:40. But the other answering rebuked him, saying, Dost not thou fear God, seeing thou art in the same condemnation?

Acts 10:35. In every nation he that feareth him, and worketh righteousness, is accepted with him.

Acts 13:16. Then Paul stood up, and beckoning with *his* hand said, Men of Israel, and ye that fear God, give audience. 26. Whosoever among you feareth God, to you is the word of this salvation sent.

Rom. 11:20. Be not highminded, but fear:

2 Cor. 7:1. Let us cleanse ourselves from all filthiness of the flesh and spirit, perfecting holiness in the fear of God.

Eph. 5:21. Submitting yourselves one to another in the fear of ¹ God.   [¹ R.V. Christ]

Eph. 6:5. Servants, be obedient to them that are *your* masters according to the flesh, with fear and trembling, in singleness of your heart, as unto Christ; 1 Pet. 2:18.

Phil. 2:12. Work out your own salvation with fear and trembling.

Col. 3:22. Servants, obey in all things *your* masters according to the flesh; not with eyeservice, as menpleasers; but in singleness of heart, fearing God:

Heb. 5:5. So also Christ, . . . 7. . . . Was heard in that he feared;

Heb. 12:28. Wherefore we receiving a kingdom which cannot be moved, let us have grace, whereby we may serve God acceptably with reverence and godly fear: 29. For our God *is* a consuming fire.

Jas. 2:19. Thou believest that there is one God; thou doest well: the devils also believe, and tremble.

1 Pet. 1:17. Pass the time of your sojourning *here* in fear:

1 Pet. 3:2. Your chaste conversation *coupled* with fear. 15. *Be* ready always to *give* an answer to every man that asketh you a reason of the hope that is in you with meekness and fear:

1 John 4:16. And we have known and believed the love that God hath to us. God is love; and he that dwelleth in love dwelleth in God, and God in him. 17. Herein is our love made perfect, that we may have boldness in the day of judgment: because as he is, so are we in this world. 18. There is no fear in love; but perfect love casteth out fear: because fear hath torment. He that feareth is not made perfect in love.

Rev. 11:18. That thou shouldest give reward unto thy servants the prophets, and to the saints, and them that fear thy name, small and great;

Rev. 14:7. Fear God, and give glory to him; for the hour of his judgment is come:

Rev. 19:5. Praise our God, all ye his servants, and ye that fear him, both small and great.

CONSPICUOUS INSTANCES OF THOSE WHO FEARED: Noah, in preparing the ark, Heb. 11:7. Abraham, tested in the offering of his son Isaac, Gen. 22:12. Jacob, in the vision of the ladder, and the covenant of God, Gen. 28:16,17; 42:18. The midwives of Egypt, in refusing to take the lives of the Hebrew children, Ex. 1: 17,21. The Egyptians, at the time of the plague of thunder and hail and fire, Ex. 9: 20. The nine and one-half tribes of Israel west of Jordan, Josh. 22:15-20. Phinehas, in turning away the anger of God at the time of the plague, Num. 25:11, with verses 6-15. Obadiah, in sheltering one hundred prophets against the wrath of Jezebel, 1 Kin. 18:3,4. Jehoshaphat, in proclaiming a feast, when the land was about to be invaded by the armies of the Ammonites and Moabites, 2 Chr. 20:3. Nehemiah, in his reform of the public administration, Neh. 5:15. Hanani, which qualified him to be ruler over Jerusalem, Neh. 7:2. Job, according to the testimony of Satan, Job 1:8. David, Psa. 5:7; 119:38. Hezekiah, in his treatment of the prophet Micah, who prophesied evil against Jerusalem, Jer. 26:19. Jonah, in the tempest, Jonah 1:9. The Jews, in obeying the voice of the Lord, Hag. 1:12. Levi, in receiving the covenant of life and peace, Hag. 1:5. The women at the sepulcher, Matt. 28:8. Cornelius, who feared God with all his house, Acts 10:2.

See CONVICTION OF SIN; FAITH.

CULTIVATED: Ex. 3:5. And he said, Draw not nigh hither: put off thy shoes from off thy feet; for the place whereon thou standest *is* holy ground.

Ex. 19:12. And thou shalt set bounds unto the people round about, saying, Take heed to yourselves, *that* ye go *not* up into the mount, or touch the border of it: whosoever toucheth the mount shall be surely put to death: 13. There shall not an hand touch it, but he shall surely be stoned, or shot through; whether *it be* beast or man, it shall not live: when the trumpet soundeth long, they shall come up to the mount.

Heb. 12:18. For ye are not come unto the mount that might be touched, and that burned with fire, nor unto blackness, and darkness, and tempest, 19. And the sound of a trumpet, and the voice of words; which *voice* they that heard intreated that the word should not be spoken to them any more: 20. (For they could not endure that which was commanded. And if so much as a beast touch the mountain, it shall be stoned, or thrust through with a dart: 21. And so terrible was the sight, *that* Moses said, I exceedingly fear and quake:) 22. But ye are come unto mount Sion, and unto the city of the living God, the heavenly Jerusalem, and to an innumerable company of angels, 23. To the general assembly and church of the firstborn, which are written in heaven, and to God the Judge of all, and to the spirits of just men made perfect, 24. And to Jesus the mediator of the new covenant, and to the blood of sprinkling, that speaketh better things than *that of* Abel.

GUILTY: Job 15:20. The wicked man travaileth with pain all *his* days, and the number of years is hidden to the oppressor. 21. A dreadful sound *is* in his ears: in prosperity the destroyer shall come upon him. 22. He believeth not that he shall return out of darkness, and he is waited for of the sword. 23. He wandereth abroad for bread, *saying,*

Where *is it?* he knoweth that the day of darkness is ready at his hand. 24. Trouble and anguish shall make him afraid; they shall prevail against him, as a king ready to the battle. 25. For he stretcheth out his hand against God, and strengtheneth himself against the Almighty.

Job 18:11. Terrors shall make him afraid on every side, and shall drive him to his feet.

Prov. 1:24. Because I have called, and ye refused; I have stretched out my hand, and no man regarded; 25. But ye have set at nought all my counsel, and would none of my reproof: 26. I also will laugh at your calamity; I will mock when your fear cometh; 27. When your fear cometh as desolation, and your destruction cometh as a whirlwind: when distress and anguish cometh upon you.

Prov. 10:24. The fear of the wicked, it shall come upon him:

Dan. 5:6. Then the king's countenance was changed, and his thoughts troubled him, so that the joints of his loins were loosed, and his knees smote one against another.

Jas. 2:19. The devils also believe, and tremble.

INSTANCES OF GUILTY FEAR: Adam and Eve, Gen. 3:8–13. The guards at Jesus' tomb, Matt. 28:4. Judas, Matt. 27:3–5. Devils, Jas. 2:19.

See CONVICTION, OF SIN.

A MOTIVE OF OBEDIENCE: Lev. 19:14. Thou shalt not curse the deaf, nor put a stumblingblock before the blind, but shalt fear thy God: I *am* the LORD. 32. Thou shalt rise up before the hoary head, and honour the face of the old man, and fear thy God: I *am* the LORD.

Lev. 25:17. Ye shall not therefore oppress one another; but thou shalt fear thy God: for I *am* the LORD your God. 36. Take thou no usury of him, or increase: but fear thy God; that thy brother may live with thee. 43. Thou shalt not rule over him with rigour; but shalt fear thy God.

Num. 32:15. For if ye turn away from after him, he will yet again leave them in the wilderness; and ye shall destroy all this people.

Deut. 6:13. Thou shalt fear the LORD thy God, and serve him, and shalt swear by his name. 14. Ye shall not go after other gods, of the gods of the people which *are* round about you; 15. (For the LORD thy God *is* a jealous God among you) lest the anger of the LORD thy God be kindled against thee, and destroy thee from off the face of the earth.

Deut. 7:4. For they will turn away thy son from following me, that they may serve other gods: so will the anger of the LORD be kindled against you, and destroy thee suddenly.

Deut. 8:5. Thou shalt also consider in thine heart, that, as a man chasteneth his son, *so* the LORD thy God chasteneth thee. 6. Therefore thou shalt keep the commandments of the LORD thy God, to walk in his ways, and to fear him.

Deut. 10:12. And now, Israel, what doth the LORD thy God require of thee, but to fear the LORD thy God, to walk in all his ways, and to love him, and to serve the LORD thy God with all thy heart and with all thy soul, 13. To keep the commandments of the LORD, and his statutes, which I command thee this day for thy good? 20. Thou shalt fear the LORD thy God; him shalt thou serve, and to him shalt thou cleave, and swear by his name.

Deut. 13:4. Ye shall walk after the LORD your God, and fear him, and keep his commandments, and obey his voice, and ye shall serve him, and cleave unto him. 6. If thy brother, the son of thy mother, or thy son, or thy daughter, or the wife of thy bosom, or thy friend, which *is* as thine own soul, entice thee secretly, saying, Let us go and serve other gods, which thou hast not known, thou, nor thy fathers; 7. *Namely,* of the gods of the people which *are* round about you, nigh unto thee, or far off from thee, from the *one* end of the earth even unto the *other* end of the earth; 8. Thou shalt not consent unto him, nor hearken unto him; neither shall thine eye pity him, neither shalt thou spare, neither shalt thou conceal him: 9. But thou shalt surely kill him; thine hand shall be first upon him to put him to death, and afterwards the hand of all the people. 10. And thou shalt stone him with stones, that he die; because he hath sought to thrust thee away from the LORD thy God, which brought thee out of the land of Egypt, from the house of bondage. 11. And all Israel shall hear, and fear, and shall do no more any such wickedness as this is among you.

Deut. 14:23. And thou shalt eat before the LORD thy God, in the place which he shall choose to place his name there, the tithe of thy corn, of thy wine, and of thine oil, and the firstlings of thy herds and of thy flocks; that thou mayest learn to fear the LORD thy God always.

Deut. 15:9. Beware that there be not a thought in thy wicked heart, saying, The seventh year, the year of release, is at hand; and thine eye be evil against thy poor brother, and thou givest him nought; and he cry unto the LORD against thee, and it be sin unto thee.

Deut. 17:11. According to the sentence of the law which they shall teach thee, and according to the judgment which they shall tell thee, thou shalt do: thou shalt not decline from the sentence which they shall shew thee, *to* the right hand, nor *to* the left. 12. And the man that will do presumptuously, and will not hearken unto the priest that standeth to minister there before the LORD thy God, or unto the judge, even that man shall die: and thou shalt put away the evil from Israel. 13. And all the people shall hear, and fear, and do no more presumptuously.

Deut. 19:16. If a false witness rise up against any man to testify against him *that which is* wrong; 17. Then both the men, between whom the controversy *is*, shall stand before the LORD, before the priests and the judges, which shall be in those days; 18. And the judges shall make diligent inquisition: and, behold, *if* the witness *be* a false witness, *and* hath testified falsely against his brother; 19. Then shall ye do unto him, as he had thought to have done unto his brother: so shalt thou put the evil away from among you. 20. And those which remain shall hear, and fear, and shall henceforth commit no more any such evil among you.

Deut. 21:18. If a man have a stubborn and rebellious son, which will not obey the voice of his father, or the voice of his mother, and *that*, when they have chastened him, will not hearken unto them: 19. Then shall his father and his mother lay hold on him, and bring him out unto the elders of his city, and unto the gate of his place; 20. And they shall say unto the elders of his city, This our son *is* stubborn and rebellious, he will not obey our voice; *he is* a glutton, and a drunkard. 21. And all the men of his city shall stone him with stones, that he die: so shalt thou put evil away from among you; and all Israel shall hear, and fear.

Deut. 28:14. And thou shalt not go aside from any of the words which I command thee this day, *to* the right hand, or *to* the left, to go after other gods to serve them. 15. But it shall come to pass, if thou wilt not hearken unto the voice of the LORD thy God, to observe to do all his commandments and his statutes which I command thee this day; that all these curses shall come upon thee, and overtake thee: 16. Cursed *shalt* thou *be* in the city, and cursed *shalt* thou *be* in the field. 17. Cursed *shall be* thy basket and thy store. 18. Cursed *shall be* the fruit of thy body, and the fruit of thy land, the increase of thy kine, and the flocks of thy sheep. 19. Cursed *shalt* thou *be* when thou comest in, and cursed *shalt* thou *be* when thou goest out. 20. The LORD shall send upon thee cursing, vexation, and rebuke, in all that thou settest thine hand unto for to do, until thou be destroyed, and until thou perish quickly; because of the wickedness of thy doings, whereby thou hast forsaken me. 21. The LORD shall make the pestilence cleave unto thee, until he have consumed thee from off the land, whither thou goest to possess it. 22. The LORD shall smite thee with a consumption, and with a fever, and with an inflammation, and with an extreme burning, and with the sword, and with blasting, and with mildew: and they shall pursue thee until thou perish. 23. And thy heaven that *is* over thy head shall be brass, and the earth that *is* under thee *shall be* iron. 24. The LORD shall make the rain of thy land

powder and dust: from heaven shall it come down upon thee, until thou be destroyed. 25. The LORD shall cause thee to be smitten before thine enemies: thou shalt go out one way against them, and flee seven ways before them: and shalt be removed into all the kingdoms of the earth. 26. And thy carcase shall be meat unto all fowls of the air, and unto the beasts of the earth, and no man shall fray *them* away. 27. The LORD will smite thee with the botch of Egypt, and with the emerods, and with the scab, and with the itch, whereof thou canst not be healed. 28. The LORD shall smite thee with madness, and blindness, and astonishment of heart: 29. And thou shalt grope at noonday, as the blind gropeth in darkness, and thou shalt not prosper in thy ways: and thou shalt be only oppressed and spoiled evermore, and no man shall save *thee*. 30. Thou shalt betroth a wife, and another man shall lie with her: thou shalt build an house, and thou shalt not dwell therein: thou shalt plant a vineyard, and shalt not gather the grapes thereof. 31. Thine ox *shall be* slain before thine eyes, and thou shalt not eat thereof: thine ass *shall be* violently taken away from before thy face, and shall not be restored to thee: thy sheep *shall be* given unto thine enemies, and thou shalt have none to rescue *them*. 32. Thy sons and thy daughters *shall be* given unto another people, and thine eyes shall look, and fail *with longing* for them all the day long: and *there shall be* no might in thine hand. 33. The fruit of thy land, and all thy labours, shall a nation which thou knowest not eat up; and thou shalt be only oppressed and crushed alway: 34. So that thou shalt be mad for the sight of thine eyes which thou shalt see. 35. The LORD shall smite thee in the knees, and in the legs, with a sore botch that cannot be healed, from the sole of thy foot unto the top of thy head. 36. The LORD shall bring thee, and thy king which thou shalt set over thee, unto a nation which neither thou nor thy fathers have known; and there shalt thou serve other gods, wood and stone. 37. And thou shalt become an astonishment, a proverb, and a byword, among all nations whither the LORD shall lead thee. 38. Thou shalt carry much seed out into the field, and shalt gather *but* little in; for the locust shall consume it. 39. Thou shalt plant vineyards, and dress *them*, but shalt neither drink *of* the wine, nor gather *the grapes*; for the worms shall eat them. 40. Thou shalt have olive trees throughout all thy coasts, but thou shalt not anoint *thyself* with the oil; for thine olive shall cast *his* *fruit*. 41. Thou shalt beget sons and daughters, but thou shalt not enjoy them; for they shall go into captivity. 42. All thy trees and fruit of thy land shall the locust consume. 43. The stranger that *is* within thee shall get up above thee very high; and thou shalt come down very low. 44. He shall lend to thee, and thou shalt not lend to him: he shall be the head, and thou shalt be the tail. 45. Moreover all these curses shall come upon thee, and shall pursue thee, and overtake thee, till thou be destroyed; because thou hearkenedst not unto the voice of the LORD thy God, to keep his commandments and his statutes which he commanded thee: 46. And they shall be upon thee for a sign and for a wonder, and upon thy seed for ever. 47. Because thou servedst not the LORD thy God with joyfulness, and with gladness of heart, for the abundance of all *things;* 48. Therefore shalt thou serve thine enemies which the LORD shall send against thee, in hunger, and in thirst, and in nakedness, and in want of all *things:* and he shall put a yoke of iron upon thy neck, until he have destroyed thee. 49. The LORD shall bring a nation against thee from far, from the end of the earth, *as swift* as the eagle flieth; a nation whose tongue thou shalt not understand; 50. A nation of fierce countenance, which shall not regard the person of the old, nor shew favour to the young: 51. And he shall eat the fruit of thy cattle, and the fruit of thy land, until thou be destroyed: which *also* shall not leave thee *either* corn, wine, or oil, *or* the increase of thy kine, or flocks of thy sheep, until he have destroyed thee. 52. And he shall besiege thee in all thy gates, until thy high and fenced walls come down, wherein thou trustedst, throughout all thy land: and he shall besiege thee in all thy gates throughout all thy land, which the LORD thy God hath given thee. 53. And thou shalt eat the fruit of thine own body, the flesh of thy sons and of thy daughters, which the LORD thy God hath given thee, in the siege, and in the straitness, wherewith thine enemies shall distress thee: 54. *So that* the man *that is* tender among you, and very delicate, his eye shall be evil toward his brother, and toward the wife of his bosom, and toward the remnant of his children which he shall leave: 55. So that he will not give to any of them of the flesh of his children whom he shall eat: because he hath nothing left him in the siege, and in the straitness, wherewith thine enemies shall distress thee in all thy gates. 56. The tender and delicate woman among you, which would not adventure to set the sole of her foot upon the ground for delicateness and tenderness, her eye shall be evil toward the husband of her bosom, and toward her son, and toward her daughter, 57. And toward her young one that cometh out from between her feet, and toward her children which she shall bear: for she shall eat them for want of all *things* secretly in the siege and straitness, wherewith thine enemy shall distress thee in thy gates. 58. If thou wilt not observe to do all the words of this law that are written in this book, that thou mayest fear this glorious and fear-

ful name, THE LORD THY GOD; 59. Then the LORD will make thy plagues wonderful, and the plagues of thy seed, *even* great plagues, and of long continuance, and sore sicknesses, and of long continuance. 60. Moreover he will bring upon thee all the diseases of Egypt, which thou wast afraid of; and they shall cleave unto thee. 61. Also every sickness, and every plague, which *is* not written in the book of this law, them will the LORD bring upon thee, until thou be destroyed. 62. And ye shall be left few in number, whereas ye were as the stars of heaven for multitude; because thou wouldest not obey the voice of the LORD thy God. 63. And it shall come to pass, *that* as the LORD rejoiced over you to do you good, and to multiply you; so the LORD will rejoice over you to destroy you, and to bring you to nought; and ye shall be plucked from off the land whither thou goest to possess it. 64. And the LORD shall scatter thee among all people, from the one end of the earth even unto the other; and there thou shalt serve other gods, which neither thou nor thy fathers have known, *even* wood and stone. 65. And among these nations shalt thou find no ease, neither shall the sole of thy foot have rest: but the LORD shall give thee there a trembling heart, and failing of eyes, and sorrow of mind: 66. And thy life shall hang in doubt before thee; and thou shalt fear day and night, and shalt have none assurance of thy life: 67. In the morning thou shalt say, Would God it were even! and at even thou shalt say, Would God it were morning! for the fear of thine heart wherewith thou shalt fear, and for the sight of thine eyes which thou shalt see. 68. And the LORD shall bring thee into Egypt again with ships, by the way whereof I spake unto thee, Thou shalt see it no more again: and there ye shall be sold unto your enemies for bondmen and bondwomen, and no man shall buy *you.*

Deut. 31:11. When all Israel is come to appear before the LORD thy God in the place which he shall choose, thou shalt read this law before all Israel in their hearing. 12. Gather the people together, men, and women, and children, and thy stranger that *is* within thy gates, that they may hear, and that they may learn, and fear the LORD your God, and observe to do all the words of this law: 13. And *that* their children, which have not known *any thing,* may hear, and learn to fear the LORD your God, as long as ye live in the land whither ye go over Jordan to possess it. Josh. 23:11–16.

1 Sam. 12:24. Only fear the LORD, and serve him in truth with all your heart: for consider how great *things* he hath done for you. 25. But if ye shall still do wickedly, ye shall be consumed, both ye and your king. *vs.* 14,15.

Job 13:21. Withdraw thine hand far from me: and let not thy dread make me afraid.

Job 31:1. I made a covenant with mine eyes; why then should I think upon a maid? 2. For what portion of God *is there* from above? and *what* inheritance of the Almighty frcm on high? 3. *Is* not destruction to the wicked? and a strange *punishment* to the workers of iniquity? 4. Doth not he see my ways, and count all my steps? 13. If I did despise the cause of my manservant or of my maidservant, when they contended with me; 14. What then shall I do when God riseth up? and when he visiteth, what shall I answer him? 15. Did not he that made me in the womb make him? and did not one fashion us in the womb? 23. For destruction *from* God *was* a terror to me, and by reason of his highness I could not endure.

Prov. 16:6. By the fear of the Lord *men* depart from evil.

Isa. 1:20. If ye refuse and rebel, ye shall be devoured with the sword: for the mouth of the Lord hath spoken *it*.

Jer. 4:4. Circumcise yourselves to the Lord, and take away the foreskins of your heart, ye men of Judah and inhabitants of Jerusalem: lest my fury come forth like fire, and burn that none can quench *it*, because of the evil of your doings.

Jer. 22:5. If ye will not hear these words, I swear by myself, saith the Lord, that this house shall become a desolation.

Matt. 10:28. Fear not them which kill the body, but are not able to kill the soul: but rather fear him which is able to destroy both soul and body in hell. Luke 12:4,5.

2 Cor. 5:10. We must all appear before the judgment seat of Christ; that every one may receive the things *done* in *his* body, according to that he hath done, whether *it be* good or bad. 11. Knowing therefore the terror of the Lord, we persuade men;

2 Tim. 4:1. I charge *thee* therefore before God, and the Lord Jesus Christ, who shall judge the quick and the dead at his appearing and his kingdom; 2. Preach the word; be instant in season, out of season; reprove, rebuke, exhort with all longsuffering and doctrine.

2 Pet. 3:10. The day of the Lord will come as a thief in the night; in the which the heavens shall pass away with a great noise, and the elements shall melt with fervent heat, the earth also and the works that are therein shall be burned up. 11. *Seeing* then *that* all these things shall be dissolved, what manner *of persons* ought ye to be in *all* holy conversation and godliness, 12. Looking for and hasting unto the coming of the day of God, wherein the heavens being on fire shall be dissolved, and the elements shall melt with fervent heat?

Rev. 14:9. And the third angel followed them, saying with a loud voice, If any man worship the beast and his image, and receive *his* mark in his forehead, or in his hand, 10. The same shall drink of the wine of the wrath of God, which is poured out without mixture into the cup of his indignation; and he shall be tormented with fire and brimstone in the presence of the holy angels, and in the presence of the Lamb:

See Punishment, Design of, to Secure Obedience ; Reward, a Motive for Faithfulness.

FEASTS. Ancient customs at: Men alone present at, Gen. 40:20; 43:32,34; 1 Sam. 9:22; Esth. 1:8; Mark 6:21; Luke 14:24; women alone, Esth. 1:9. Men and women attend, Ex. 32:6, with *vs.* 2,3; Dan. 5:1-3. Riddles propounded at, Judg. 14:12. Marriage feasts provided by the bridegroom, Judg. 14:10,17. Guests arranged according to age, Gen. 43: 33; rank, 1 Sam. 9:22; Luke 14:8-10. Reclined on couches, Amos 6:4,7; Luke 7:38; John 13:25. Served in one dish, Matt. 26:23. Were presided over by a governor, John 2: 8,9. Host served, Gen. 18:8. Wine served at, Esth. 5:6; 7:7. Music at, Isa. 5:12; Amos 6: 4,5; Luke 15:25. Dancing at, Matt. 14:6: Luke 15:25. Given by kings, 1 Sam. 20:5; 25:36; 2 Sam. 9:10; 1 Kin. 2:7; 4:22; 18:19; Esth. 1:3-8; Dan. 5:1-4. Drunkenness at, 1 Sam. 25:36; Esth. 1:10; Dan. 5:1-4.

Covenants ratified by, Gen. 26:28-30. Celebrations by: Birthdays, Gen. 40:20; Mark 6:21; coronations, 1 Kin. 1:25; 1 Chr. 12:38-40; national deliverances, Esth. 8:17; 9:17-19.

FIGURATIVE: Matt. 22:1-14; Luke 14:16-24; Rev. 19:9,17.

ANNUAL FESTIVALS: Instituted by Moses. Designated as Solemn Feasts; Num. 15:3; 2 Chr. 8:13; Lam. 2:6; Ezek. 46:9; Set Feasts, Num. 29:39; Ezra 3:5. Appointed Feasts, Isa. 1:14; Holy Convocations, Lev. 23:4. First and last days were Sabbatic, Lev. 23:39,40; Num. 28:18-25; 29:12,35; Neh. 8:1-18. Kept with rejoicing, Lev. 23:40; Deut. 16:11-14; 2 Chr. 30:21-26; Ezra 6:22; Neh. 8: 9-12,17; Psa. 42:4; 122:4; Isa. 30:29; Zech. 8: 19. Divine protection given during, Ex. 34:24.

The three principal, were Passover, Pentecost, Tabernacles. All males were required to attend, Ex. 23:17; 34:23; Deut. 16: 16; Psa. 42:4; 122:4; Ezek. 36:38; Luke 2:41; John 4:45; 7. Aliens permitted to attend, John 12:20; Acts 2:1-11. Attended by women, 1 Sam. 1:3,9; Luke 2:41. Observed: by Jesus, Matt. 26:17-20; Luke 2:41,42; 22:15; John 2:13,23; 5:1; 7:10; 10:22; by Paul, Acts 18:21; 19:21; 20:6,16; 24:11,17.

See for full treatment of annual feasts, Passover; Pentecost; Purim; Tabernacles; Trumpets.

FEET. Bells worn on, Isa. 3:16,18. Washing of, as an example, by Jesus, John 13:4-14. Sitting at, Deut. 33:3; Luke 10:39; Acts 22:3.

See Ablution.

FELIX, governor of Judæa. Paul tried before, Acts 23:24-35; 24. Trembles under Paul's preaching, Acts 24:25. Leaves Paul in bonds, Acts 24:26,27; 25:14.

FELLOWSHIP. INDEX OF SUB-TOPICS. *With God, p.* 391; *With Christ, p.* 391;

Of the Holy Spirit, p. 392; Of the Righteous, p. 393; With the Wicked, p. 395; With the Wicked Forbidden, p. 396; With the Wicked Exemplified, p. 397; Instances of Those Who Avoided Fellowship With the Wicked, p. 397.

Eccl. 4:9. Two *are* better than one; because they have a good reward for their labour. 10. For if they fall, the one will lift up his fellow: but woe to him *that is* alone when he falleth; for *he hath* not another to help him up. 11. Again, if two lie together, then they have heat: but how can one be warm *alone?* 12. And if one prevail against him, two shall withstand him; and a threefold cord is not quickly broken.

Amos 3:3. Can two walk together, except they be agreed?

See FRATERNITY; FELLOWSHIP.

WITH GOD: Gen. 5:22. And Enoch walked with God after he begat Methuselah three hundred years, and begat sons and daughters: 24. And Enoch walked with God: and he *was* not; for God took him.

Gen. 6:9. These *are* the generations of Noah: Noah was a just man *and* perfect in his generations, *and* Noah walked with God.

Ex. 29:45. And I will dwell among the children of Israel, and will be their God.

Ex. 33:14. And he said, My presence shall go *with thee*, and I will give thee rest. 15. And he said unto him, If thy presence go not *with me*, carry us not up hence. 16. For wherein shall it be known here that I and thy people have found grace in thy sight? *is it* not in that thou goest with us? so shall we be separated, I and thy people, from all the people that *are* upon the face of the earth. 17. And the LORD said unto Moses, I will do this thing also that thou hast spoken: for thou hast found grace in my sight, and I know thee by name.

Lev. 26:12. And I will walk among you, and will be your God, and ye shall be my people.

Isa. 57:15. For thus saith the high and lofty One that inhabiteth eternity, whose name *is* Holy; I dwell in the high and holy *place*, with him also *that is* of a contrite and humble spirit, to revive the spirit of the humble, and to revive the heart of the contrite ones.

Zech. 2:10. Sing and rejoice, O daughter of Zion: for, lo, I come, and I will dwell in the midst of thee, saith the LORD.

Mark 9:37. Whosoever shall receive one of such children in my name, receiveth me: and whosoever shall receive me, receiveth not me, but him that sent me.

John 14:23. Jesus answered and said unto him, If a man love me, he will keep my words: and my Father will love him, and we will come unto him, and make our abode with him.

John 17:21. That they all may be one; as thou, Father, *art* in me, and I in thee, that they also may be one in us: 23. I in them,

and thou in me, that they may be made perfect in one; and that the world may know that thou hast sent me, and hast loved them, as thou hast loved me.

2 Cor. 6:16. And what agreement hath the temple of God with idols? for ye are the temple of the living God; as God hath said, I will dwell in them, and walk in *them;* and I will be their God, and they shall be my people.

2 Cor. 13:11. Be perfect, be of good comfort, be of one mind, live in peace; and the God of love and peace shall be with you.

1 John 1:3. Truly our fellowship *is* with the Father, and with his Son Jesus Christ. 5. God is light, and in him is no darkness at all. 6. If we say that we have fellowship with him, and walk in darkness, we lie, and do not the truth: 7. But if we walk in the light, as he is in the light, we have fellowship one with another, and the blood of Jesus Christ his Son cleanseth us from all sin.

1 John 3:24. And he that keepeth his commandments dwelleth in him, and he in him. And hereby we know that he abideth in us, by the Spirit which he hath given us.

Rev. 21:3. And I heard a great voice out of heaven saying, Behold, the tabernacle of God *is* with men, and he will dwell with them, and they shall be his people, and God himself shall be with them, *and be* their God. 4. And God shall wipe away all tears from their eyes; and there shall be no more death, neither sorrow, nor crying, neither shall there be any more pain: for the former things are passed away.

See COMMUNION, WITH GOD.

WITH CHRIST: Matt. 12:48. But he answered and said unto him that told him, Who is my mother? and who are my brethren? 49. And he stretched forth his hand toward his disciples, and said, Behold my mother and my brethren! 50. For whosoever shall do the will of my Father which is in heaven, the same is my brother, and sister, and mother. Luke 8:21.

Matt. 18:20. For where two or three are gathered together in my name, there am I in the midst of them.

Mark 9:37. Whosoever shall receive one of such children in my name, receiveth me: and whosoever shall receive me, receiveth not me, but him that sent me.

Luke 24:32. And they said one to another, Did not our heart burn within us, while he talked with us by the way, and while he opened to us the scriptures?

John 6:53. Except ye eat the flesh of the Son of man, and drink his blood, ye have no life in you. 56. He that eateth my flesh, and drinketh my blood, dwelleth in me, and I in him. *vs.* 51-57.

John 14:20. At that day ye shall know that I *am* in my Father, and ye in me, and I in you. 21. He that hath my commandments, and keepeth them, he it is that loveth me: and he that loveth me shall be loved of my Father, and I will love him, and will manifest myself to him. 22. Judas saith unto him, not Iscariot, Lord, how is it that thou wilt manifest thyself unto us, and not unto the world? 23. Jesus answered and said unto him, If a man love me, he will keep my words: and my Father will love him, and we will come unto him, and make our abode with him.

John 15:4. Abide in me, and I in you. As the branch cannot bear fruit of itself, except it abide in the vine; no more can ye, except ye abide in me. 5. I am the vine, ye *are* the branches: He that abideth in me, and I in him, the same bringeth forth much fruit: for without me ye can do nothing. 7. If ye abide in me, and my words abide in you, ye shall ask what ye will, and it shall be done unto you. *vs.* 1-8.

John 17:21. That they all may be one; as thou, Father, *art* in me, and I in thee, that they also may be one in us: that the world may believe that thou hast sent me. 22. And the glory which thou gavest me I have given them; that they may be one, even as we are one: 23. I in them, and thou in me, that they may be made perfect in one; 26. I have declared unto them thy name, and will declare *it:* that the love wherewith thou hast loved me may be in them, and I in them.

Rom. 7:4. My brethren, ye also are become dead to the law by the body of Christ; that ye should be married to another, *even* to him who is raised from the dead, that we should bring forth fruit unto God. Psa. 45: 9-16; Song, chapters 1-8.

Rom. 8:1. *There is* therefore now no condemnation to them which are in Christ Jesus, . . . 10. If Christ *be* in you, the body *is* dead because of sin; but the Spirit *is* life because of righteousness. 17. If children, then heirs; heirs of God, and joint-heirs with Christ; if so be that we suffer with *him*, that we may be also glorified together.

Rom. 11:17. Thou, being a wild olive tree, wert graffed in among them, and with them partakest of the root and fatness of the olive tree;

Rom. 12:5. We, *being* many, are one body in Christ, and every one members one of another.

1 Cor. 1:9. God *is* faithful, by whom ye were called unto the fellowship of his Son Jesus Christ our Lord.

1 Cor. 6:13. Now the body *is* not for fornication, but for the Lord; and the Lord for the body. 14. And God hath both raised up the Lord, and will also raise up us by his own power. 15. Know ye not that your bodies are the members of Christ? 17. He that is joined unto the Lord is one spirit.

1 Cor. 10:16. The cup of blessing which we bless, is it not the communion of the blood of Christ? The bread which we break, is it not the communion of the body of Christ?

1 Cor. 12:12. As the body is one, and hath many members, and all the members of that one body, being many, are one body: so also *is* Christ. 27.. Now ye are the body of Christ, and members in particular.

2 Cor. 11:2. I have espoused you to one husband, that I may present *you as* a chaste virgin to Christ.

2 Cor. 13:5. Know ye not your own selves, how that Jesus Christ is in you, except ye be reprobates?

Eph. 5:30. We are members of his body, of his flesh, and of his bones. 32. This is a great mystery: but I speak concerning Christ and the church.

Col. 1:27. To whom God would make known what *is* the riches of the glory of this mystery among the Gentiles; which is Christ in you, the hope of glory:

Col. 3:3. For ye are dead, and your life is hid with Christ in God.

1 Thess. 5:9. God hath not appointed us to wrath, but to obtain salvation by our Lord Jesus Christ, 10. Who died for us, that whether we wake or sleep, we should live together with him.

Heb. 2:11. Both he that sanctifieth and they who are sanctified *are* all of one: for which cause he is not ashamed to call them brethren,

1 John 2:6. He that saith he abideth in him ought himself also so to walk, even as he walked. 24. If that which ye have heard from the beginning shall remain in you, ye also shall continue in the Son, and in the Father. 28. Little children, abide in him; that, when he shall appear, we may have confidence, and not be ashamed before him at his coming.

1 John 3:6. Whosoever abideth in him sinneth not: 24. He that keepeth his commandments dwelleth in him, and he in him. And hereby we know that he abideth in us, by the Spirit which he hath given us.

1 John 4:13. Hereby know we that we dwell in him, and he in us, because he hath given us of his Spirit.

1 John 5:12. He that hath the Son hath life; *and* he that hath not the Son of God hath not life. 20. And we know that the Son of God is come, and hath given us an understanding, that we may know him that is true, and we are in him that is true, *even* in his Son Jesus Christ.

2 John 9. He that abideth in the doctrine of Christ, he hath both the Father and the Son.

Rev. 3:20. Behold, I stand at the door, and knock: if any man hear my voice, and open the door, I will come in to him, and will sup with him, and he with me.

See COMMUNION.

OF THE HOLY SPIRIT: Rom. 8:9. But ye are not in the flesh, but in the Spirit, if so be that the Spirit of God dwell in you. Now if any man have not the Spirit of Christ, he is none of his.

1 Cor. 3:16. Know ye not that ye are the temple of God, and *that* the Spirit of God dwelleth in you?

2 Cor. 13:14. The grace of the Lord Jesus Christ, and the love of God, and

the communion of the Holy Ghost, *be* with you all.

See COMMUNION; HOLY SPIRIT.

OF THE RIGHTEOUS: Psa. 55:14. We took sweet counsel together, *and* walked unto the house of God in company.

Psa. 119:63. I *am* a companion of all *them* that fear thee, and of them that keep thy precepts.

Amos 3:3. Can two walk together, except they be agreed?

Mal. 3:16. Then they that feared the LORD spake often one to another: and the LORD hearkened, and heard *it*, and a book of remembrance was written before him for them that feared the LORD, and that thought upon his name.

Matt. 17:4. Then answered Peter, and said unto Jesus, Lord, it is good for us to be here: if thou wilt, let us make here three tabernacles; one for thee, and one for Moses, and one for Elias.

Matt. 20:25. But Jesus called them *unto* him, and said, Ye know that the princes of the Gentiles exercise dominion over them, and they that are great exercise authority upon them. 26. But it shall not be so among you: but whosoever will be great among you, let him be your minister; 27. And whosoever will be chief among you, let him be your servant: 28. Even as the Son of man came not to be ministered unto, but to minister, and to give his life a ransom for many.

Matt. 23:8. But be not ye called Rabbi: for one is your Master, *even* Christ; and all ye are brethren.

Mark 10:42. But Jesus called them *to him*, and saith unto them, Ye know that they which are accounted to rule over the Gentiles exercise lordship over them; and their great ones exercise authority upon them. 43. But so shall it not be among you: but whosoever will be great among you, shall be your minister: 44. And whosoever of you will be the chiefest, shall be servant of all. 45. For even the Son of man came not to be ministered unto, but to minister, and to give his life a ransom for many.

Luke 22:32. When thou art converted, strengthen thy brethren.

Luke 24:13. And, behold, two of them went that same day to a village called Emmaus, which was from Jerusalem *about* threescore furlongs. 14. And they talked together of all these things which had happened. 15. And it came to pass, that, while they communed *together* and reasoned, Jesus himself drew near, and went with them.

John 13:34. A new commandment I give unto you, That ye love one another; as I have loved you, that ye also love one another.

John 15:12. This is my commandment, That ye love one another, as I have loved you.

John 17:11. And now I am no more in the world, but these are in the world, and I come to thee. Holy Father, keep through thine own name those whom thou hast given me,

that they may be one, as we *are*. 21. That they all may be one; as thou, Father, *art* in me, and I in thee, that they also may be one in us: that the world may believe that thou hast sent me. 22. And the glory which thou gavest me I have given them; that they may be one, even as we are one: 23. I in them, and thou in me, that they may be made perfect in one; and that the world may know that thou hast sent me, and hast loved them, as thou hast loved me.

Acts 1:14. These all continued with one accord in prayer and supplication, with the women, and Mary the mother of Jesus, and with his brethren.

Acts 2:1. And when the day of Pentecost was fully come, they were all with one accord in one place. 42. And they continued stedfastly in the apostles' doctrine and fellowship, and in breaking of bread, and in prayers. 44. And all that believed were together, and had all things common; 45. And sold their possessions and goods, and parted them to all *men*, as every man had need. 46. And they, continuing daily with one accord in the temple, and breaking bread from house to house, did eat their meat with gladness and singleness of heart, 47. Praising God, and having favour with all the people. And the Lord added to the church daily such as should be saved.

Acts 17:4. And some of them believed, and consorted with Paul and Silas; and of the devout Greeks a great multitude, and of the chief women not a few.

Acts 20:35. I have shewed you all things, how that so labouring ye ought to support the weak, and to remember the words of the Lord Jesus, how he said, It is more blessed to give than to receive.

Rom. 1:12. That is, that I may be comforted together with you by the mutual faith both of you and me.

Rom. 14:1. Him that is weak in the faith receive ye, *but* not to doubtful disputations. 2. For one believeth that he may eat all things: another, who is weak, eateth herbs. 3. Let not him that eateth despise him that eateth not; and let not him which eateth not judge him that eateth: for God hath received him. 4. Who art thou that judgest another man's servant? to his own master he standeth or falleth. Yea, he shall be holden up: for God is able to make him stand. 10. But why dost thou judge thy brother? or why dost thou set at nought thy brother? for we shall all stand before the judgment seat of Christ. 13. Let us not therefore judge one another any more: but judge this rather, that no man put a stumblingblock or an occasion to fall in *his* brother's way. 14. I know, and am persuaded by the Lord Jesus, that *there is* nothing unclean of itself: but to him that esteemeth anything to be unclean, to him *it is* unclean. 15. But if thy brother be grieved with *thy* meat, now walkest thou not charitably. Destroy not him with thy meat, for whom Christ died. 16. Let not then your good be evil spoken of: for the kingdom of God is not meat and drink; but righteousness, and peace, and joy in the Holy Ghost. 18. For he that in these things serveth Christ *is* acceptable to God, and approved of men. 19. Let us therefore follow after the things which make for peace, and things wherewith one may edify another. 20. For meat destroy not the work of God. All things indeed *are* pure; but *it is* evil for that man who eateth with offence. 21. *It is* good neither to eat flesh, nor to drink wine, nor *any thing* whereby thy brother stumbleth, or is offended, or is made weak.

Rom. 15:1. We then that are strong ought to bear the infirmities of the weak, and not to please ourselves. 2. Let every one of us please *his* neighbour for *his* good to edification. 3. For even Christ pleased not himself: but, as it is written, The reproaches of them that reproached thee fell on me. 4. For whatsoever things were written aforetime were written for our learning, that we through patience and comfort of the scriptures might have hope. 5. Now the God of patience and consolation grant you to be likeminded one toward another according to Christ Jesus: 6. That ye may with one mind *and* one mouth glorify God, even the Father of our Lord Jesus Christ. 7. Wherefore receive ye one another, as Christ also received us to the glory of God.

1 Cor. 1:10. Now I beseech you, brethren, by the name of our Lord Jesus Christ, that ye all speak the same thing, and *that* there be no divisions among you; but *that* ye be perfectly joined together in the same mind and in the same judgment.

1 Cor. 10:16. The cup of blessing which we bless, is it not the communion of the blood of Christ? The bread which we break, is it not the communion of the body of Christ? 17. For we *being* many are one bread, *and* one body: for we are all partakers of that one bread.

1 Cor. 12:13. For by one Spirit are we all baptized into one body, whether *we be* Jews or Gentiles, whether *we be* bond or free; and have been all made to drink into one Spirit.

1 Cor. 16:19. The churches of Asia salute you. Aquila and Priscilla salute you much in the Lord, with the church that is in their house. 20. All the brethren greet you. Greet ye one another with an holy kiss.

Gal. 2:9. And when James, Cephas, and John, who seemed to be pillars, perceived the grace that was given unto me, they gave to me and Barnabas the right hands of fellowship; that we *should* go unto the heathen, and they unto the circumcision.

Gal. 6:2. Bear ye one another's burdens, and so fulfil the law of Christ. 10. As we have therefore opportunity, let us do good unto all *men*, especially unto them who are of the household of faith.

Eph. 2:14. For he is our peace, who hath **made** both one, and hath broken down the middle wall of partition *between us;* 15. Having abolished in his flesh the enmity, *even* the law of commandments *contained* in ordinances; for to make in himself of twain one new man, *so* making peace; 16. And that he might reconcile both unto God in one body by the cross, having slain the enmity thereby: 17. And came and preached peace to you which were afar off, and to them that were nigh. 18. For through him we both have access by one Spirit unto the Father. 19. Now therefore ye are no more strangers and foreigners, but fellowcitizens with the saints, and of the household of God; 20. And are built upon the foundation of the apostles and prophets, Jesus Christ himself being the chief corner *stone;* 21. In whom all the building fitly framed together groweth unto an holy temple in the Lord: 22. In whom ye also are builded together for an habitation of God through the Spirit.

Eph. 5:2. And walk in love, as Christ also hath loved us, and hath given himself for us an offering and a sacrifice to God for a sweetsmelling savour. 19. Speaking to yourselves in psalms and hymns and spiritual songs, singing and making melody in your heart to the Lord; 30. For we are members of his body, of his flesh, and of his bones.

Phil. 1:3. I thank my God . . . 5. For your fellowship in the gospel from the first day until now; 27. Only let your conversation be as it becometh the gospel of Christ: that whether I come and see you, or else be absent, I may hear of your affairs, that ye stand fast in one spirit, with one mind striving together for the faith of the gospel;

Phil. 2:1. If *there be* therefore any consolation in Christ, if any comfort of love, if any fellowship of the Spirit, if any bowels and mercies. 2. Fulfil ye my joy, that ye be likeminded, having the same love, *being* of one accord, of one mind.

Col. 2:2. That their hearts might be comforted, being knit together in love, and unto all riches of the full assurance of understanding, to the acknowledgment of the mystery of God, and of the Father, and of Christ;

Col. 3:16. Let the word of Christ dwell in you richly in all wisdom; teaching and admonishing one another in psalms and hymns and spiritual songs, singing with grace in your hearts to the Lord.

1 Thess. 4:18. Comfort one another with these words.

1 Thess. 5:11. Comfort yourselves together, and edify one another, even as also ye do. 14. We exhort you, brethren, warn them that are unruly, comfort the feebleminded, support the weak, be patient toward all *men*.

Heb. 3:13. Exhort one another daily, while it is called To day; lest any of you be hardened through the deceitfulness of sin.

Heb. 10:24. Let us consider one another to provoke unto love and to good works: 25. Not forsaking the assembling of ourselves together, as the manner of some *is;* but exhorting *one another:*

Heb. 13:1. Let brotherly love continue.

Jas. 5:16. Confess *your* faults one to another, and pray for one another, that ye may be healed.

1 Pet. 2:17. Love the brotherhood.

1 Pet. 3:8. Finally, *be ye* all of one mind, having compassion one of another, love as brethren, *be* pitiful, *be* courteous: 9. Not rendering evil for evil, or railing for railing: but contrariwise blessing; knowing that ye are thereunto called, that ye should inherit a blessing.

1 John 1:3. That which we have seen and heard declare we unto you, that ye also may have fellowship with us: 7. If we walk in the light, as he is in the light, we have fellowship one with another,

1 John 3:14. We know that we have passed from death unto life, because we love the brethren. He that loveth not *his* brother abideth in death.

1 John 4:7. Beloved, let us love one another: for love is of God: and every one that loveth is born of God, and knoweth God. 8. He that loveth not knoweth not God: for God is love. 11. Beloved, if God so loved us, we ought also to love one another. 12. No man hath seen God at any time. If we love one another, God dwelleth in us, and his love is perfected in us. 13. Hereby know we that we dwell in him, and he in us, because he hath given us of his Spirit.

See COMMUNION OF SAINTS.

WITH THE WICKED: Gen. 49:6. O my soul, come not thou into their secret; unto their assembly, mine honour, be not thou united:

Ex. 33:15. And he said unto him, If thy presence go not *with me,* carry us not up hence. 16. For wherein shall it be known here that I and thy people have found grace in thy sight? *is it* not in that thou goest with us? so shall we be separated, I and thy people, from all the people that *are* upon the face of the earth.

Ex. 34:13. But ye shall destroy their altars, break their images, and cut down their groves: 14. For thou shalt worship no other god: for the LORD, whose name *is* Jealous, *is* a jealous God: 15. Lest thou make a covenant with the inhabitants of the land, and they go a whoring after their gods, and do sacrifice unto their gods, and *one* call thee. and thou eat of his sacrifice : [Deut. 31:16,17.] 16. And thou take of their daughters unto thy sons, and their daughters go a whoring after their gods, and make thy sons go a whoring after their gods.

Num. 25:1. And Israel abode in Shittim, and the people began to commit whoredom with the daughters of Moab. 2. And they called the people unto the sacrifices of their gods: and the people did eat, and bowed down to their gods. 3. And Israel joined himself unto Baal-peor: and the anger of the LORD was kindled against Israel. 4. And the LORD said unto Moses, Take all the heads of the people, and hang them up before the LORD against the sun, that the fierce anger of the LORD may be turned away from Israel. 5. And Moses said unto the judges of Israel, Slay ye every one his men that were joined unto Baal-peor.

6. And, behold, one of the children of Israel came and brought unto his brethren a Midianitish woman in the sight of Moses, and in sight of all the congregation of the children of Israel, who *were* weeping *before* the door of the tabernacle of the congregation. 7. And when Phinehas, the son of Eleazar, the son of Aaron the priest, saw *it,* he rose up from among the congregation, and took a javelin in his hand; 8. And he went after the man of Israel into the tent, and thrust both of them through, the man of Israel, and the woman

Josh. 23:12. Else if ye do in any wise go back, and cleave unto the remnant of these nations, *even* these that remain among you, and shall make marriages with them, and go in unto them, and they to you: 13. Know for a certainty that the LORD your God will no more drive out *any of* these nations from before you: but they shall be snares and traps unto you, and scourges in your sides, and thorns in your eyes, until ye perish from off this good land which the LORD your God hath given you.

Ezra 6:21. And the children of Israel, which were come again out of captivity, and all such as had separated themselves unto them from the filthiness of the heathen of the land, to seek the LORD God of Israel, did eat, 22. And kept the feast of unleavened bread seven days with joy:

Ezra 9:14. Should we again break thy commandments, and join in affinity with the people of these abominations? wouldest not thou be angry with us till thou hadst consumed *us,* so that *there should be* no remnant nor escaping?

Psa. 6:8. Depart from me, all ye workers of iniquity; for the LORD hath heard the voice of my weeping.

Psa. 26:4. I have not sat with vain persons, neither will I go in with dissemblers. 5. I have hated the congregation of evil doers: and will not sit with the wicked.

Psa. 50:18. When thou sawest a thief, then thou consentedst with him, and hast been partaker with adulterers.

Psa. 102:7. I watch, and am as a sparrow alone upon the housetop. with *vs.* 6-8.

Prov. 28:19. He that tilleth his land shall have plenty of bread: but he that followeth after vain *persons* shall have poverty enough. chapter 12:11.

Prov. 29:24. Whoso is partner with a thief hateth his own soul: he heareth cursing, and bewrayeth *it* not.

1 Cor. 5:11. But now I have written unto you not to keep company, if any man that is called a brother be a fornicator, or covetous, or an idolater, or a railer, or a drunkard,

or an extortioner; with such an one no not to eat.

1 Cor. 15:33. Be not deceived: evil communications corrupt good manners.

2 Pet. 2:18. For when they speak great swelling *words* of vanity, they allure through the lusts of the flesh, *through much* wantonness, those that were clean escaped from them who live in error. 19. While they promise them liberty, they themselves are the servants of corruption: for of whom a man is overcome, of the same is he brought in bondage.

2 Pet. 3:17. Ye therefore, beloved, seeing ye know *these things* before, beware lest ye also, being led away with the error of the wicked, fall from your own stedfastness.

See the following sub-topics:

PUNISHMENT OF, Num. 33:56; Josh. 23:13; Judg. 2:3; 3:5–8; Ezra 9:7,14; Psa. 106:41,42; Rev. 2:16,22,23.

See COMPANY, EVIL; INFLUENCE.

WITH THE WICKED FORBIDDEN: Ex. 23:32. Thou shalt make no covenant with them, nor with their gods. 33. They shall not dwell in thy land, lest they make thee sin against me: for if thou serve their gods, it will surely be a snare unto thee.

Ex. 34:12. Take heed to thyself, lest thou make a covenant with the inhabitants of the land whither thou goest, lest it be for a snare in the midst of thee: Judg. 2:2.

Num. 16:26. And he spake unto the congregation, saying, Depart, I pray you, from the tents of these wicked men, and touch nothing of their's, lest ye be consumed in all their sins.

Deut. 7:2. And when the LORD thy God shall deliver them before thee; thou shalt smite them, *and* utterly destroy them; thou shalt make no covenant with them, nor shew mercy unto them: 3. Neither shalt thou make marriages with them; thy daughter thou shalt not give unto his son, nor his daughter shalt thou take unto thy son. 4. For they will turn away thy son from following me, that they may serve other gods: so will the anger of the LORD be kindled against you, and destroy thee suddenly. Deut. 12:30; Ezra 9:1,2.

Deut. 13:6. If thy brother, the son of thy mother, or thy son, or thy daughter, or the wife of thy bosom, or thy friend, which *is* as thine own soul, entice thee secretly, saying, Let us go and serve other gods, which thou hast not known, thou, nor thy fathers; 7. *Namely*, of the gods of the people which *are* round about you, nigh unto thee, or far off from thee, from the *one* end of the earth even unto the *other* end of the earth; 8. Thou shalt not consent unto him, nor hearken unto him; neither shall thine eye pity him, neither shalt thou spare, neither shalt thou conceal him: 9. But thou shalt surely kill him; thine hand shall be first upon him to put him to death, and afterwards the hand of all the people. 10. And thou shalt stone him with stones, that he die; because he hath sought to thrust thee away from the LORD thy God, which brought thee out of the land of Egypt, from the house of bondage. 11. And all Israel shall hear, and fear, and shall do no more any such wickedness as this is among you.

Josh. 23:6. Be ye therefore very courageous to keep and to do all that is written in the book of the law of Moses, that ye turn not aside therefrom *to* the right hand or *to* the left; 7. That ye come not among these nations, these that remain among you; neither make mention of the name of their gods, nor cause to swear *by them*, neither serve them, nor bow yourselves unto them: 13. Know for a certainty that the LORD your God will no more drive out *any of* these nations from before you; but they shall be snares and traps unto you, and scourges in your sides, and thorns in your eyes, until ye perish from off this good land which the LORD your God hath given you.

Ezra 9:12. Now therefore give not your daughters unto their sons, neither take their daughters unto your sons, nor seek their peace or their wealth for ever: that ye may be strong, and eat the good of the land, and leave *it* for an inheritance to your children for ever.

Ezra 10:11. Now therefore make confession unto the LORD God of your fathers, and do his pleasure: and separate yourselves from the people of the land, and from the strange wives.

Psa. 1:1. Blessed *is* the man that walketh not in the counsel of the ungodly, nor standeth in the way of sinners, nor sitteth in the seat of the scornful.

Prov. 1:10. My son, if sinners entice thee, consent thou not. 11. If they say, Come with us, let us lay wait for blood, let us lurk privily for the innocent without cause: 12. Let us swallow them up alive as the grave; and whole, as those that go down into the pit: 13. We shall find all precious substance, we shall fill our houses with spoil: 14. Cast in thy lot among us; let us all have one purse: 15. My son, walk not thou in the way with them; refrain thy foot from their path:

Prov. 4:14. Enter not into the path of the wicked, and go not in the way of evil *men*. 15. Avoid it, pass not by it, turn from it, and pass away.

Prov. 9:6. Forsake the foolish, and live; and go in the way of understanding.

Prov. 14:7. Go from the presence of a foolish man, when thou perceivest not *in him* the lips of knowledge.

Matt. 18:17. And if he shall neglect to hear them, tell *it* unto the church: but if he neglect to hear the church, let him be unto thee as an heathen man and a publican.

Rom. 16:17. Now I beseech you, brethren, mark them which cause divisions and offences contrary to the doctrine which ye have learned; and avoid them.

1 Cor. 5:9. I wrote unto you in an epistle not

to company with fornicators: 10. Yet not altogether with the fornicators of this world, or with the covetous, or extortioners, or with idolaters; for then must ye needs go out of the world. 11. But now I have written unto you not to keep company, if any man that is called a brother be a fornicator, or covetous, or an idolater, or a railer, or a drunkard, or an extortioner; with such an one no not to eat.

2 Cor. 6:14. Be ye not unequally yoked together with unbelievers: for what fellowship hath righteousness with unrighteousness? and what communion hath light with darkness? 15. And what concord hath Christ with Belial? or what part hath he that believeth with an infidel? 16. And what agreement hath the temple of God with idols? for ye are the temple of the living God; as God hath said, I will dwell in them, and walk in *them;* and I will be their God, and they shall be my people. 17. Wherefore come out from among them, and be ye separate, saith the Lord, and touch not the unclean *thing;* and I will receive you,

Eph. 5:11. And have no fellowship with the unfruitful works of darkness, but rather reprove *them.*

2 Thess. 3:6. Now we command you, brethren, in the name of our Lord Jesus Christ, that ye withdraw yourselves from every brother that walketh disorderly, and not after the tradition which he received of us. 14. And if any man obey not our word by this epistle, note that man, and have no company with him, that he may be ashamed. 15. Yet count *him* not as an enemy, but admonish *him* as a brother.

1 Tim. 6:3. If any man teach otherwise, and consent not to wholesome words, *even* the words of our Lord Jesus Christ, and to the doctrine which is according to godliness; 4. He is proud, knowing nothing, but doting about questions and strifes of words, whereof cometh envy, strife, railings, evil surmisings, 5. Perverse disputings of men of corrupt minds, and destitute of the truth, supposing that ¹ gain is godliness: from such withdraw thyself. [¹ R. V. godliness is a way of gain]

2 Tim. 3:2. For men shall be lovers of their own selves, covetous, boasters, proud, blasphemers, disobedient to parents, unthankful, unholy, 3. Without natural affection, trucebreakers, false accusers, incontinent, fierce, despisers of those that are good, 4. Traitors, heady, highminded, lovers of pleasures more than lovers of God; 5. Having a form of godliness, but denying the power thereof: from such turn away. 6. For of this sort are they which creep into houses, and lead captive silly women laden with sins, led away with divers lusts, 7. Ever learning, and never able to come to the knowledge of the truth.

2 Pet. 3:17. Ye therefore, beloved, seeing ye know *these things* before, beware lest ye also, being led away with the error of the wicked, fall from your own stedfastness.

2 John 9. Whosoever transgresseth, and abideth not in the doctrine of Christ, hath not God. He that abideth in the doctrine of Christ, he hath both the Father and the Son. 10. If there come any unto you, and bring not this doctrine, receive him not into *your* house, neither bid him God speed. 11. For he that biddeth him God speed is partaker of his evil deeds.

Rev. 18:1. And after these things I saw another angel come down from heaven, having great power; and the earth was lightened with his glory. 2. And he cried mightily with a strong voice, saying, Babylon the great is fallen, is fallen, and is become the habitation of devils, and the hold of every foul spirit, and a cage of every unclean and hateful bird. 3. For all nations have drunk of the wine of the wrath of her fornication, and the kings of the earth have committed fornication with her, and the merchants of the earth are waxed rich through the abundance of her delicacies. 4. And I heard another voice from heaven, saying, Come out of her, my people, that ye be not partakers of her sins, and that ye receive not of her plagues.

THE EVIL OF FELLOWSHIP WITH THE WICKED EXEMPLIFIED: By Solomon, 1 Kin. 11:1–8; Rehoboam, 1 Kin. 12:8,9; Jehoshaphat, 2 Chr. 18:3; 19:2; 20:35–37; Jehoram, 2 Chr. 21:6; Ahaziah, 2 Chr. 22:3–5; Israelites, Ezra 9:1,2; Israel, Ezek. 44:7; Judas Iscariot, Matt. 26:14–16.

INSTANCES OF THOSE WHO AVOIDED FELLOWSHIP WITH THE WICKED: Man of God, 1 Kin. 13:7–10. Nehemiah, Neh. 6:2–4; 10:29–31. David, Psa. 101:4–7; 119:115. Jeremiah, Jer. 15:17. Joseph of Arimathæa, Luke 23:51. Church of Ephesus, Rev. 2:6.

See COMPANY, EVIL; INFLUENCE, EVIL.

FENCE, Song 4:12. Made of stone walls, Num. 22:24; Psa. 62:3; Prov. 24:30,31; Isa. 5:2; Mic. 7:11. Hedge, Eccl. 10:8; Isa. 5:5; Nah. 3:17; Matt. 21:33; Prov. 15:19; Hos. 2:6.

FIGURATIVE: Ezek. 22:30.

FERRET, Lev. 11:30.

FERRYBOAT, 2 Sam. 19:18.

FESTIVALS See FEASTS.

FESTUS. Called also PORCIUS FESTUS, governor of Judæa, and successor to Felix, Acts 24:27. Tries Paul, Acts 25.

FETTERS. Used for securing prisoners, 2 Chr. 33:11; 36:6; Mark 5:4. Made of brass, Judg. 16:21; 2 Kin. 25:7. Made of iron. See CHAINS.

FEVER, Lev. 26:16; Deut. 28:22; Job 30:30; Psa. 22:15; Matt. 8:14; Acts 28:8.

FICKLENESS. See INSTABILITY.

FIG. Common to Palestine, Num. 13:23; Deut. 8:8; to Egypt, Psa. 105:33. Employed as a remedy, 2 Kin. 20:7; Isa. 38:21. Traffic in, Neh. 13:15. Dried and preserved, 1 Sam. 30:12. Cakes of, sent by Abigail to David, 1 Sam. 25:18–35. Aprons made of fig leaves, by Adam and Eve. Gen. 3:7.

FIGHT OF FAITH, 1 Tim. 6:12; 2 Tim.

4:7; Heb. 10:32; 11:34. See 2 Chr. 20:17.—*Bible Text Book.*

FIG TREE. In an allegory, Judg. 9:11. Jeremiah's parable of, Jer. 24:2,3. Barren, parable of, Luke 13:6–9; 21:29–31.

FIGURATIVE: Matt. 24:32; Rev. 6:13.

FIGURE. See FIGURATIVE under principal topics throughout the work. See also ALLEGORY; PANTOMIME; PARABLES; SYMBOLS; TYPES.

FILE, used for sharpening edged tools, 1 Sam. 13:21.

FINANCES. Methods of raising money. See TRIBUTE; TEMPLE; MONEY.

FINE, a penalty. Ex. 22:1. If a man shall steal an ox, or a sheep, and kill it, or sell it; he shall restore five oxen for an ox, and four sheep for a sheep. 4. If the theft be certainly found in his hand alive, whether it be ox, or ass, or sheep; he shall restore double. 7. If a man shall deliver unto his neighbour money or stuff to keep, and it be stolen out of the man's house; if the thief be found, let him pay double. 8. If the thief be not found, then the master of the house shall be brought unto the judges, *to see* whether he have put his hand unto his neighbour's goods. 9. For all manner of trespass, *whether it be* for ox, for ass, for sheep, for raiment, *or* for any manner of lost thing, which *another* challengeth to be his, the cause of both parties shall come before the judges; *and* whom the judges shall condemn, he shall pay double unto his neighbour.

Lev. 5:15. If a soul commit a trespass, and sin through ignorance, in the holy things of the LORD; then he shall bring for his trespass unto the LORD a ram without blemish out of the flocks, with thy estimation by shekels of silver, after the shekel of the sanctuary, for a trespass offering: 16. And he shall make amends for the harm that he hath done in the holy thing, and shall add the fifth part thereto, and give it unto the priest: and the priest shall make an atonement for him with the ram of the trespass offering, and it shall be forgiven him. Num. 5:5–8.

Lev. 6:5. Or all that about which he hath sworn falsely; he shall even restore it in the principal, and shall add the fifth part more thereto, *and* give it unto him to whom it appertaineth, in the day of his trespass offering. 6. And he shall bring his trespass offering unto the LORD, a ram without blemish out of the flock, with thy estimation, for a trespass offering, unto the priest:

Prov. 6:30. *Men* do not despise a thief, if he steal to satisfy his soul when he is hungry; 31. But *if* he be found, he shall restore sevenfold; he shall give all the substance of his house.

See DAMAGES.

FINGER, six on one hand, 2 Sam. 21:20.

FINGERBREADTH, a unit of measurement, Jer. 52:21.

FIR TREE. Wood of, used for building, 1 Kin. 6:15,34; Song 1:17. Ships made of, Ezek. 27:5. Instruments of music made of, 2 Sam. 6:5.

FIRE. Used as a signal in war, Jer. 6:1. Furnaces of, Dan. 3:6. Children caused to pass through, 2 Kin. 16:3; 17:17.

Miracles connected with: Miraculously descends upon, and consumes, Abraham's sacrifice, Gen. 15:17; David's, 1 Chr. 21:26; Elijah's, 1 Kin. 18:38; Solomon's, at dedication of the temple, 2 Chr. 7:1. Display of, in the plagues of Egypt, Ex. 9:24; at Elijah's translation, 2 Kin. 2:11. Consumes the conspirators with Korah, Dathan, and Abiram, Num. 16:35; the captains and their fifties, 2 Kin. 1:9–12.

Torture by, Lev. 21:9; Jer. 29:22; Ezek. 23: 25,47; Dan. 3.

Pillar of fire, Ex. 13:21,22; 14:19,24; 40:38; Num. 9:15–23.

See CLOUD, PILLAR OF.

FIGURATIVE: Of cleansing, Isa. 6:6,7; spiritual power, Psa. 104:4; Jer. 20:9; Matt. 3:11; Luke 3:16; judgments, Deut. 4:24; 32:22; Isa. 33:14; Jer. 23:29; Amos 1:4,7,10,12,14; 2:2; Mal. 3:2; Luke 12:49; Rev. 20:9; of the destruction of the wicked, Matt. 13:42,50; 25:41; Mark 9:48; Rev. 9:2; 21:8.

EVERLASTING FIRE, Isa. 33:14; Matt. 18:8; 25:41; Mark 9:48.

A SYMBOL: Of God's presence, Gen. 15:17; in the burning bush, Ex. 3:2; on Sinai, Ex. 19:18. Tongues of, on the apostles, Acts 2:3.

See ARSON.

FIREBRAND, used by Samson, Judg. 15:4.

FIGURATIVE: Prov. 26:18; Amos 4:11; Zech. 3:2.

FIREPAN, Ex. 38:3; 2 Kin. 25:15.

FIRKIN, about nine gallons, John 2:6.

FIRMAMENT, the expanse above the earth, Gen. 1:6–8,14–17,20; Psa. 19:1; Dan. 12:3.

FIRSTBORN, of man and beast, reserved to himself by God, Ex. 13:2,12–16; 22:29,30; 34:19,20; Lev. 27:26; Num. 3:13; 8: 17,18; Deut. 15:19–23; Neh. 10:36.

Redemption of, Ex. 13:13; 34:20; Lev. 27: 27; Num. 3:40–51; 18:15–17. Levites taken instead of firstborn of the families of Israel, Num. 3:12,40–45; 8:16–18.

Of Egyptians slain, Ex. 11:5; 12:12,29; 13: 15; Num. 33:4; Psa. 78:51; 105:36; 136:10. Of idolaters, sacrificed, Ezek. 20:26.

BIRTHRIGHT OF THE: Had precedence over other sons of the family, Gen. 4:7; a double portion of inheritance, Deut. 21:15–17; royal succession, 2 Chr. 21:3. Honorable distinction of, Ex. 4:22; Psa. 89: 27; Jer. 31:9; Rom. 8:29; Col. 1:15; Heb. 1:6; 12:23; Rev. 1:5. Sold by Esau, Gen. 25:29– 34; 27:36; Rom. 9:12,13; Heb. 12:16. Forfeited by Reuben, Gen. 49:3,4; 1 Chr. 5:1,2. Set aside: that of Manasseh, Gen. 48:15–20; 1 Chr. 5:1; Adonijah, 1 Kin. 2:15; Hosah's son, 1 Chr. 26:10.

See BIRTHRIGHT.

FIRST FRUITS. First ripe of fruits, grain, oil, wine, and first of fleece, required as an offering, Ex. 22:29; Lev. 2:12–16; Num. 18: 12; Deut. 18:4; 2 Chr. 31:5; Neh. 10:35,37,39; Prov. 3:9; Jer. 2:3; Rom. 11:16. Offerings of, must be free from blemish, Num. 18:12; presented at the tabernacle, Ex. 22:29; 23:19; 34:26; Deut. 26:3–10; belonged to the priests, Lev. 23:20; Num. 18:12,13; Deut. 18:3–5. Freewill offerings of, given to the prophets, 2 Kin. 4:42.

Wave offering of, Lev. 23:10–14,17. As a heave offering, Num. 15:20; Neh. 10:37; Ezek. 44:30. To be offered as a thank offering upon entrance into the Land of Promise, Deut. 26:3–10.

FIGURATIVE: Rom. 8:23; 11:16; 1 Cor. 15:20,23; James 1:18.

FIRSTLING. See FIRSTBORN.

FISH. Creation of, Gen. 1:20–22. Appointed for food, Gen. 9:2,3. Clean and unclean, Lev. 11:9–12; Deut. 14:9,10. Taken with nets, Eccl. 9:12; Hab. 1:14–17; Matt. 4: 21; Luke 5:2–6; John 21:6–8; hooks, Isa. 19: 8; Amos 4:2; Matt. 17:27; spears, Job 41:7.

Ponds for: in Heshbon, Song 7:4; in Egypt, Isa. 19:10. Traffic in, Neh. 13:16; John 21:13. Broiled, John 21:9–13; Luke 24: 42. Miracles connected with: Jonah swallowed by, Jonah 1:17; 2; Matt. 12:40; of the loaves and fishes, Matt. 14:19; 15:36; Luke 5:6; 9:13–17; coin obtained from mouth of, Matt. 17:27; great draught of, Luke 5:4–7; John 21:6; furnished to the disciples by Jesus after his resurrection, Luke 24:42; John 21:9–13.

FIGURATIVE: Ezek. 47:9,10.

FISHERMEN, certain apostles, Matt. 4:18–21; Mark 1:16,19; John 21:2,3.

FIGURATIVE: Jer. 16:16; Matt. 4:19.

FISH GATE, 2 Chr. 33:14; Neh. 3:3; Zeph. 1:10.

FISHHOOK, Amos 4:2.

FISHPOOL, Song 7:4.

FISH SPEAR, Job 41:7.

FITCH, Isa. 28:25–27; Ezek. 4:9.

FLAG. 1. [*R. V.*, bulrush.] Ex. 2:3,5; Job 8:11; Isa. 19:6; Jonah 2:5.

2. An ensign.

See ENSIGN.

FLAGON, erroneously translated [*A. V.*] flagon of wine, but more accurately cake of raisin [*R. V.*], Hos. 3:1; 2 Sam. 6:19; Song 2:15.

FLATTERY. Job 17:5. He that ↑ speaketh flattery to *his* friends, even the eyes of his children shall fail. [↑ R.V. denounceth his friends for a prey]

Job 32:21. Neither let me give flattering titles unto man. 22. For I know not to give flattering titles; *in so doing* my maker would soon take me away.

Psa. 5:8. Lead me, O LORD, in thy righteousness because of mine enemies; make thy way straight before my face. 9. For *there is* no faithfulness in their mouth; their inward part *is* very wickedness; their throat is an open sepulchre: they flatter with their tongue.

Psa. 12:2. They speak vanity every one with his neighbour: *with* flattering lips *and* with a double heart do they speak. 3. The LORD shall cut off all flattering lips. Psa. 5:9.

Psa. 36:2. For he flattereth himself in his own eyes, until his iniquity be found to be hateful.

Psa. 49:13. This their way *is* their folly: yet their posterity approve their sayings. 18. *Men* will praise thee, when thou doest well to thyself. Prov. 6:24.

Psa. 78:36. Nevertheless they did flatter him with their mouth, and they lied unto him with their tongues. Rom. 16:18.

Prov. 5:3. For the lips of a strange woman drop *as* an honeycomb, and her mouth *is* smoother than oil:

Prov. 7:5. That they may keep thee from the strange woman, from the stranger *which* flattereth with her words. 21. With her much fair speech she caused him to yield, with the flattering of her lips she forced him.

Prov. 14:20. The poor is hated even of his own neighbour: but the rich *hath* many friends.

Prov. 19:4. Wealth maketh many friends; 6. Many will intreat the favour of the prince: and every man *is* a friend to him that giveth gifts.

Prov. 20:19. Meddle not with him that flattereth with his lips.

Prov. 22:16. He that giveth to the rich, *shall* surely *come* to want.

Prov. 24:24. He that saith unto the wicked, Thou art righteous; him shall the people curse, nations shall abhor him:

Prov. 25:26. A righteous man falling down before the wicked *is as* a troubled fountain, and a corrupt spring.

Prov. 26:28. A lying tongue hateth *those that are* afflicted by it; and a flattering mouth worketh ruin.

Prov. 27:21. As the fining pot for silver, and the furnace for gold; so *is* a man to his praise.

Prov. 28:23. He that rebuketh a man afterwards shall find more favour than he that flattereth with the tongue.

Prov. 29:5. A man that flattereth his neighbour spreadeth a net for his feet.

Dan. 11:21. In his estate shall stand up a vile person, to whom they shall not give the honour of the kingdom: but he shall come in peaceably, and obtain the kingdom by flatteries. 34. Many shall cleave to them with flatteries.

Luke 6:26. Woe unto you, when all men shall speak well of you! for so did their fathers to the false prophets.

Gal. 1:10. Do I seek to please men? for if I yet pleased men, I should not be the servant of Christ.

1 Thess. 2:4. But as we were allowed of God to be put in trust with the gospel, even so we speak; not as pleasing men, but God, which trieth our hearts. 5. For neither at

any time used we flattering words, as ye know, nor a cloke of covetousness; God *is* witness: 6. Nor of men sought we glory, neither of you, nor *yet* of others,

Jude 16. Their mouth speaketh great swelling *words*, having men's persons in admiration because of advantage.

INSTANCES OF: By Jacob, Gen. 33:10. By Gideon, Judg. 8:1–3. By Mephibosheth, 2 Sam. 9:8. By woman of Tekoah, 2 Sam. 14:17–20. By Absalom, 2 Sam. 15:2–6. By Israel and Judah, 2 Sam. 19:41–43. By Adonijah, 1 Kin. 1:42. By Ahab, 1 Kin. 20: 4. By false prophets, 1 Kin. 22:13. By Darius's courtiers, Dan. 6:7. By Herodians, Luke 20:21. By Tyrians, Acts 12:22. Tertullus flatters Felix, Acts 24:2–4. Paul flatters Felix, Acts 24:10. By Agrippa, Acts 26:2,3.

FLAX. In Egypt, Ex. 9:31. In Palestine, Josh. 2:6. Linen made from, Prov. 31:13; Isa. 19:6; Hos. 2:5,9. Robes made of, Esth. 1: 16, Ezek. 40:3.

See LINEN.

FIGURATIVE: Smoking flax not quenched, Isa. 42:3; Matt. 12:20.

FLEA, 1 Sam. 24:14; 26:20.

FLESH. FIGURATIVE: Fruits of, Gal. 5:19–21. SYMBOLICAL: Body of Christ symbolized by the bread of the holy eucharist, John 6:51–63.

FLESHHOOK. Used in the tabernacle, Ex. 27:3; 38:3; Num. 4:14; 1 Sam. 2:13,14. Made of gold, 1 Chr. 28:17; of brass, 2 Chr. 4:16.

FLIES, Eccl. 10:1. Plague of, Ex. 8:21–31; Psa. 78:45; 105:31.

FIGURATIVE: Isa. 7:18.

FLINT, Deut. 8:15; 32:13; Psa. 114:8; Isa. 50:7; Ezek. 3:9.

FLOOD, the deluge. Foretold, Gen. 6: 13,17. History of, Gen. chapters 6–8. References to, Job 22:16; Psa. 90:5; Matt. 24:38; Luke 17:26,27; Heb. 11:7; 1 Pet. 3:20; 2 Pet. 2:5. The promise that it should not recur, Gen. 8:20,21; Isa. 54:9.

See METEOROLOGY.

FLOUR. See BARLEY; BREAD; OFFERING; WHEAT.

FLOWERS. See BOTANY.

FLUTE, Dan. 3:5,7,10,15.

See MUSIC, INSTRUMENTS OF.

FLY. See FLIES.

FOOD. ARTICLES OF: Milk, Gen. 49: 12; Prov. 27:27; butter, Deut. 32:14; 2 Sam. 17:29; cheese, 1 Sam. 17:18; Job 10:10; bread, Gen. 18:5; 1 Sam. 17:17; parched corn, Ruth 2:14; 1 Sam. 17:17; flesh, 2 Sam. 6:19; Prov. 9:2; fish, Matt. 7:10; Luke 24:42; herbs, Prov. 15:17; Rom. 14:2; Heb. 6:7; fruit, 2 Sam. 16: 2; dried fruit, 1 Sam. 25:18; 30:12; honey, Song 5:1; Isa. 7:15; oil, Deut. 12:17; Prov. 21: 17; Ezek. 16:13; vinegar, Num. 6:3; Ruth 2: 14; wine, 2 Sam. 6:19; John 2:3,10.

Prepared by females, Gen. 27:9; 1 Sam. 8: 13; Prov. 31:15. Thanks given before, Mark 8:6; Acts 27:35. A hymn sung after, Matt. **26:30.** Men and women did not partake to-

gether, Gen. 18:8,9; Esth. 1:3,9.—*Bible Text-Book.*

See BREAD; EATING; OVEN.

FROM GOD: Gen. 1:29. And God said, Behold, I have given you every herb bearing seed, which *is* upon the face of all the earth, and every tree, in the which *is* the fruit of a tree yielding seed; to you it shall be for meat. 30. And to every beast of the earth, and to every fowl of the air, and to every thing that creepeth upon the earth, wherein *there is* life, *I have given* every green herb for meat: and it was so.

Gen. 9:3. Every moving thing that liveth shall be meat for you; even as the green herb have I given you all things.

Gen. 48:15. And he blessed Joseph, and said, God, before whom my fathers Abraham and Isaac did walk, the God which fed me all my life long unto this day,

Psa. 23:5. Thou preparest a table before me in the presence of mine enemies: thou anointest my head with oil; my cup runneth over.

Psa. 103:5. Who satisfieth thy mouth with good *things; so that* thy youth is renewed like the eagle's.

Psa. 104:14. He causeth the grass to grow for the cattle, and herb for the service of man: that he may bring forth food out of the earth; 15. And wine *that* maketh glad the heart of man, *and* oil to make *his* face to shine, and bread *which* strengtheneth man's heart.

Psa. 111:5. He hath given meat unto them that fear him: he will ever be mindful of his covenant.

Psa. 136:25. Who giveth food to all flesh: for his mercy *endureth* for ever.

Psa. 145:15. The eyes of all wait upon thee; and thou givest them their meat in due season.

Psa. 147:9. He giveth to the beast his food, *and* to the young ravens which cry.

Prov. 30:8. Feed me with food convenient for me:

Isa. 3:1. For, behold, the Lord, the LORD of hosts, doth take away from Jerusalem and from Judah the stay and the staff, the whole stay of bread, and the whole stay of water,

Matt. 6:11. Give us this day our daily bread.

Rom. 14:14. I know, and am persuaded by the Lord Jesus, that *there is* nothing unclean of itself: but to him that esteemeth anything to be unclean, to him *it is* unclean. 21. *It is* good neither to eat flesh, nor to drink wine, nor *any thing* whereby thy brother stumbleth, [1] or is offended, or is made weak.   [1 Omitted in R. V.]

1 Tim. 4:3. *Commanding* to abstain from meats, which God hath created to be received with thanksgiving of them which believe and know the truth. 4. For every creature of God *is* good, and nothing to be refused, if it be received with thanksgiving: 5. For it is sanctified by the word of God and prayer.

THINGS PROHIBITED AS FOOD: Ex. 22:31. And ye shall be holy men unto me: neither shall ye eat *any* flesh *that is* torn of beasts in the field; ye shall cast it to the dogs.

Lev. 11:1. And the LORD spake unto Moses and to Aaron, saying unto them, 2. Speak unto the children of Israel, saying, These *are* the beasts which ye shall eat among all the beasts that *are* on the earth. 3. Whatsoever parteth the hoof, and is clovenfooted, *and* cheweth the cud, among the beasts, that shall ye eat. 4. Nevertheless these shall ye not eat of them that chew the cud, or of them that divide the hoof: *as* the camel, because he cheweth the cud, but divideth not the hoof; he *is* unclean unto you. 5. And the coney, because he cheweth the cud, but divideth not the hoof; he *is* unclean unto you. 6. And the hare, because he cheweth the cud, but divideth not the hoof; he *is* unclean unto you. 7. And the swine, though he divide the hoof, and be clovenfooted, yet he cheweth not the cud; he *is* unclean to you. 8. Of their flesh shall ye not eat, and their carcase shall ye not touch: they *are* unclean to you. 9. These shall ye eat of all that *are* in the waters: whatsoever hath fins and scales in the waters, in the seas, and in the rivers, them shall ye eat. 10. And all that have not fins and scales in the seas, and in the rivers, of all that move in the waters, and of any living thing which *is* in the waters, they *shall be* an abomination unto you: 11. They shall be even an abomination unto you; ye shall not eat of their flesh, but ye shall have their carcases in abomination. 12. Whatsoever hath no fins nor scales in the waters, that *shall be* an abomination unto you. 13. And these *are they which* ye shall have in abomination among the fowls; they shall not be eaten, they *are* an abomination: the eagle, and the ossifrage, and the ospray. 14. And the vulture, and the kite after his kind; 15. Every raven after his kind; 16. And the owl, and the nighthawk, and the cuckoo, and the hawk after his kind. 17. And the little owl, and the cormorant, and the great owl, 18. And the swan, and the pelican, and the gier eagle, 19. And the stork, the heron after her kind, and the lapwing, and the bat. 20. All fowls that creep, going upon *all* four, *shall be* an abomination unto you. 21. Yet these may ye eat of every flying creeping thing that goeth upon *all* four, which have legs above their feet, to leap withal upon the earth; 22. *Even* these of them ye may eat; the locust after his kind, and the bald locust after his kind, and the beetle after his kind, and the grasshopper after his kind. 23. But all *other* flying creeping things, which have four feet, *shall be* an abomination unto you. 24. And for these ye shall be unclean: whosoever toucheth the carcase of them shall be unclean until the even. 25. And whosoever beareth *ought* of the carcase of them shall wash his clothes, and be unclean until the even. 26. *The carcases* of every beast which divideth the hoof, and *is* not clovenfooted, nor cheweth the cud, *are* unclean unto you: every one that toucheth them shall be unclean. 27. And whatsoever goeth upon his paws, among all manner of beasts that go on *all* four, those *are* unclean unto you: whoso toucheth their carcase shall be unclean until the even. 28. And he that beareth the carcase of them shall wash his clothes, and be unclean until the even: they *are* unclean unto you. 29. These also *shall be* unclean unto you among the creeping things that creep upon the earth; the weasel, and the mouse, and the tortoise after his kind, 30. And the ferret, and the chameleon, and the lizard, and the snail, and the mole. 31. These *are* unclean to you among all that creep: whosoever doth touch them, when they be dead, shall be unclean unto the even. 32. And upon whatsoever *any* of them, when they are dead, doth fall, it shall be unclean; whether *it be* any vessel of wood, or raiment, or skin, or sack, whatsoever vessel *it be*, wherein *any* work is done, it must be put into water, and it shall be unclean until the even; so shall it be cleansed. 33. And every earthen vessel, whereinto *any* of them falleth, whatsoever *is* in it shall be unclean; and ye shall break it. 34. Of all meat which may be eaten, *that* on which *such* water cometh shall be unclean: and all drink that may be drunk in every *such* vessel shall be unclean. 35. And every *thing* whereupon *any part* of their carcase falleth shall be unclean; *whether it be* oven, or ranges for pots, they shall be broken down: *for* they *are* unclean, and shall be unclean unto you. 36. Nevertheless a fountain or pit *wherein there is* plenty of water, shall be clean: but that which toucheth their carcase shall be unclean. 37. And if *any part* of their carcase fall upon any sowing seed which is to be sown, it *shall be* clean. 38. But if *any* water be put upon the seed, and *any part* of their carcase fall thereon, it *shall be* unclean unto you. 39. And if any beast, of which ye may eat, die; he that toucheth the carcase thereof shall be unclean until the even. 40. And he that eateth of the carcase of it shall wash his clothes, and be unclean until the even: he also that beareth the carcase of it shall wash his clothes, and be unclean until the even. 41. And every creeping thing that creepeth upon the earth *shall be* an abomination; it shall not be eaten. 42. Whatsoever goeth upon the belly, and whatsoever goeth upon *all* four, or whatsoever hath more feet among all creeping things that creep upon the earth, them ye shall not eat; for they *are* an abomination. 43. Ye shall not make yourselves abominable with any creeping thing that creepeth, neither shall ye make yourselves unclean with them, that ye should be defiled thereby. 44. For I *am* the LORD your God: ye shall therefore sanctify yourselves, and ye shall be holy; for I *am* holy: neither shall ye defile yourselves with any manner of creeping thing that creepeth upon the earth. 45. For I *am* the LORD that bringeth you up out of the land of Egypt, to be your God: ye shall therefore be holy, for I *am* holy. 46. This *is* the law of the beasts, and of the fowl, and of every living creature that moveth in the waters, and of every creature that creepeth upon the earth: 47. To make a difference between the unclean and the clean, and between the beast that may be eaten and the beast that may not be eaten. Deut. 14.

Lev. 17:13. And whatsoever man *there be* of the children of Israel, or of the strangers that sojourn among you, which hunteth and catcheth any beast or fowl that may be eaten; he shall even pour out the blood thereof, and cover it with dust. 14. For *it is* the life of all flesh; the blood of it *is* for the life thereof: therefore I said unto the children of Israel, Ye shall eat the blood of no manner of flesh: for the life of all flesh *is* the blood thereof: whosoever eateth it shall be cut off. 15. And every soul that eateth that which died *of itself*, or that which was torn *with beasts, whether it be* one of your own country, or a stranger, he shall both wash his clothes, and bathe *himself* in water, and be unclean until the even: then shall he be clean.

FOOL. Psa. 5:5. The foolish shall not stand in thy sight: thou hatest all workers of iniquity.

Psa. 14:1. The fool hath said in his heart, *There is* no God. Psa. 53:1.

Psa. 74:18. The foolish people have blasphemed thy name. 22. Arise, O God, plead thine own cause: remember how the foolish man reproacheth thee daily.

Psa. 107:17. Fools because of their transgression, and because of their iniquities, are afflicted.

Prov. 1:7. The fear of the LORD *is* the beginning of knowledge: *but* fools despise wisdom and instruction. 22. How long, ye simple ones, will ye love simplicity? and the scorners delight in their scorning, and fools hate knowledge?

Prov. 3:35. Shame shall be the promotion of fools.

Prov. 9:6. Forsake the foolish, and live; and go in the way of understanding. 7. He that reproveth a scorner getteth to himself shame: and he that rebuketh a wicked *man getteth* himself a blot. 8. Reprove not a scorner, lest he hate thee: rebuke a wise man, and he will love thee.

13. A foolish woman *is* clamorous: *she is* simple, and knoweth nothing. 14. For she sitteth at the door of her house, on a seat in the high places of the city, 15. To call passengers who go right on their ways: 16. Whoso *is* simple, let him turn in hither: and *as for* him that wanteth understanding, she saith to him, 17. Stolen waters are sweet, and bread *eaten* in secret is pleasant.

Prov. 10:1. A foolish son *is* the heaviness of his mother.

8. A prating fool shall fall. *v.* 10.

13. A rod *is* for the back of him that is void of understanding.

14. Wise *men* lay up knowledge: but the mouth of the foolish *is* near destruction.

18. He that hideth hatred *with* lying lips, and he that uttereth a slander, *is* a fool.

23. *It is* as sport to a fool to do mischief: Prov. 14:1. Every wise woman buildeth her house: but the foolish plucketh it down with her hands.

7. Go from the presence of a foolish man, when thou perceivest not *in him* the lips of knowledge. 8. The wisdom of the prudent *is* to understand his way: but the folly of fools *is* deceit. 9. Fools make a mock at sin: but among the righteous *there is* favour.

15. The simple believeth every word:

Prov. 15:7. The lips of the wise disperse knowledge: but the heart of the foolish *doeth* not so.

20. A wise son maketh a glad father: but a foolish man despiseth his mother.

21. Folly *is* joy to *him that is* destitute of wisdom: but a man of understanding walketh uprightly.

Prov. 17:24. Wisdom *is* before him that hath understanding; but the eyes of a fool *are* in the ends of the earth. 25. A foolish son *is* a grief to his father, and bitterness to her that bare him.

Prov. 18:2. A fool hath no delight in understanding, but that his heart may discover itself.

6. A fool's lips enter into contention, and his mouth calleth for strokes.

7. A fool's mouth *is* his destruction, and his lips *are* the snare of his soul.

Prov. 19:13. A foolish son *is* the calamity of his father: and the contentions of a wife *are* a continual dropping.

Prov. 20:3. *It is* an honour for a man to cease from strife: but every fool will be meddling.

Prov. 21:20. *There is* treasure to be desired and oil in the dwelling of the wise; but a foolish man spendeth it up.

Prov. 26:3. A whip for the horse, a bridle for the ass, and a rod for the fool's back.

4. Answer not a fool according to his folly, lest thou also be like unto him.

5. Answer a fool according to his folly, lest he be wise in his own conceit.

6. He that sendeth a message by the hand of a fool cutteth off the feet, *and* drinketh damage.

7. The legs of the lame are not equal: so *is* a parable in the mouth of fools.

8. As he that bindeth a stone in a sling, so *is* he that giveth honour to a fool.

9. *As* a thorn goeth up into the hand of a drunkard, so *is* a parable in the mouth of fools.

10. The great *God* that formed all *things* both rewardeth the fool, and rewardeth transgressors.

11. As a dog returneth to his vomit, *so* a fool returneth to his folly.

12. Seest thou a man wise in his own conceit ? *there is* more hope of a fool than of him.

Prov. 29:9. *If* a wise man contendeth with a foolish man, whether he rage or laugh, *there is* no rest.

11. A fool uttereth all his mind : but a wise *man* keepeth it in till afterwards.

Eccl. 4:5. The fool foldeth his hands together, and eateth his own flesh.

Eccl. 7:9. Be not hasty in thy spirit to be angry : for anger resteth in the bosom of fools.

Eccl. 10:11. Surely the serpent will bite without enchantment ; and a babbler is no better.

12. The words of a wise man's mouth *are* gracious ; but the lips of a fool will swallow up himself.

13. The beginning of the words of his mouth *is* foolishness : and the end of his talk *is* mischievous madness.

14. A fool also is full of words : a man cannot tell what shall be ; and what shall be after him, who can tell him ?

15. The labour of the foolish wearieth every one of them, because he knoweth not how to go to the city.

Matt. 7:26. And every one that heareth these sayings of mine, and doeth them not, shall be likened unto a foolish man, which built his house upon the sand : 27. And the rain descended, and the floods came, and the winds blew, and beat upon that house ; and it fell : and great was the fall of it.

Tit. 3:3. For we ourselves also were sometimes foolish, disobedient, deceived, serving divers lusts and pleasures, living in malice and envy, hateful, *and* hating one another.

PARABLES OF: Of the foolish virgins, Matt. 25:1–13 ; of the rich fool, Luke 12:16–20.

FOOT. Washing the feet of the disciples by Jesus, John 13:4–16 ; by disciples, 1 Tim. 5:10.

See ABLUTIONS ; PURIFICATIONS.

For footwear, see SHOE.

FIGURATIVE : Matt. 18:8.

FOOTMAN, a runner before kings and princes, 1 Sam. 8:11 ; 2 Sam. 15:1 ; 1 Kin. 1:5.

FOOTSTOOL. FIGURATIVE : The earth is God's, Isa. 60:13 ; 66:1 ; Lam. 2:1 ; Acts 7:49.

FOREIGNER. FIGURATIVE : Eph. 2:19.

See ALIENS ; GENTILES ; STRANGERS.

FOREKNOWLEDGE OF GOD. See GOD, FOREKNOWLEDGE OF, WISDOM OF.

FOREMAN. See MASTER WORKMAN.

FOREORDINATION. See PREDESTINATION.

FORERUNNER. Figurative of Christ, Heb. 6:20.

FORGERY, by Jezebel, 1 Kin. 21:8.

FORGETTING GOD. A characteristic of the wicked, Prov. 2:17 ; Isa. 65:11. Backsliders guilty of, Jer. 2:32 ; 3:21.

Is forgetting his covenant, Deut. 4:23 ; 2

Kin. 17:38 ; works, Psa. 78:7,11 ; 106:13 ; benefits, Psa. 103:2 ; 106:7 ; word, Heb. 12:5 ; James 1:25 ; law, Psa. 119:153,176 ; Hos. 4:6 ; church, Psa. 137:5 ; past deliverances, Judg. 8:34 ; Psa. 78:42 ; power to deliver, Isa. 51:13–15.

Encouraged by false teachers, Jer. 23:27. Prosperity leads to, Deut. 8:12–14 ; Hos. 13:6. Trials should not lead to, Psa. 44:17–20. Resolve against, Psa. 119:16,93. Cautions against, Deut. 6:12 ; 8:11. Exhortation to those guilty of, Psa. 50:22.

Punishment of, Job 8:12,13 ; Psa. 9:17 ; Isa. 17:10,11 ; Ezek. 23:35 ; Hos. 8:14 ; threatened, Job 8:13 ; Psa. 9:17 ; 50:22 ; Isa. 17:10 ; Jer. 2: 32 ; Hos. 8:14.—*Bible Text-Book.*

See BACKSLIDERS ; FORSAKING GOD.

FORGIVENESS. OF ENEMIES : Ex. 23:4. If thou meet thine enemy's ox or his ass going astray, thou shalt surely bring it back to him again. 5. If thou see the ass of him that hateth thee lying under his burden, and wouldest forbear to help him, thou shalt surely help with him.

Prov. 19:11. The discretion of a man deferreth his anger ; and *it is* his glory to pass over a transgression.

Prov. 24:17. Rejoice not when thine enemy falleth, and let not thine heart be glad when he stumbleth : 29. Say not, I will do so to him as he hath done to me : I will render to the man according to his work.

Prov. 25:21. If thine enemy be hungry, give him bread to eat ; and if he be thirsty, give him water to drink : 22. For thou shalt heap coals of fire upon his head, and the LORD shall reward thee. Rom. 12:20.

Eccl. 7:21. Take no heed unto all words that are spoken ; lest thou hear thy servant curse thee :

Matt. 5:7. Blessed *are* the merciful : for they shall obtain mercy. 39. Resist not evil : but whosoever shall smite thee on thy right cheek, turn to him the other also. 40. And if any man will sue thee at the law, and take away thy coat, let him have *thy* cloke also. 41. And whosoever shall compel thee to go a mile, go with him twain. 43. It hath been said, Thou shalt love thy neighbour, and hate thine enemy. 44. But I say unto you, Love your enemies, bless them that curse you, do good to them that hate you, and pray for them which despitefully use you, and persecute you ; 45. That ye may be the children of your Father which is in heaven : for he maketh his sun to rise on the evil and on the good, and sendeth rain on the just and on the unjust. 46. For if ye love them which love you, what reward have ye ? do not even the publicans the same ? *vs.* 47, 48 ; Luke 6:27–34.

Matt. 6:12. Forgive us our debts, as we forgive our debtors. [Luke 11:4]. 14. If ye forgive men their trespasses, your heavenly Father will also forgive you : 15. But if ye forgive not men their trespasses, neither will your Father forgive your trespasses.

Matt. 18:21. Then came Peter to him, and said, Lord, how oft shall my brother sin against me, and I forgive him? till seven times? 22. Jesus saith unto him, I say not unto thee, Until seven times: but, Until seventy times seven. 23. Therefore is the kingdom of heaven likened unto a certain king, which would take account of his servants. 24. And when he had begun to reckon, one was brought unto him, which owed him ten thousand talents. 25. But forasmuch as he had not to pay, his lord commanded him to be sold, and his wife, and children, and all that he had, and payment to be made. 26. The servant therefore fell down, and worshipped him, saying, Lord, have patience with me, and I will pay thee all. 27. Then the lord of that servant was moved with compassion, and loosed him, and forgave him the debt. 28. But the same servant went out, and found one of his fellowservants, which owed him an hundred pence: and he laid hands on him, and took *him* by the throat, saying, Pay me that thou owest. 29. And his fellowservant fell down at his feet, and besought him, saying, Have patience with me, and I will pay thee all. 30. And he would not: but went and cast him into prison, till he should pay the debt. 31. So when his fellowservants saw what was done, they were very sorry, and came and told unto their lord all that was done. 32. Then his lord, after that he had called him, said unto him, O thou wicked servant, I forgave thee all that debt, because thou desiredst me: 33. Shouldest not thou also have had compassion on thy fellowservant, even as I had pity on thee? 34. And his lord was wroth, and delivered him to the tormentors, till he should pay all that was due unto him. 35. So likewise shall my heavenly Father do also unto you, if ye from your hearts forgive not every one his brother their trespasses.

Mark 11:25. When ye stand praying, forgive, if ye have ought against any: that your Father also which is in heaven may forgive you your trespasses.

Luke 6:35. Love ye your enemies, and do good, and lend, hoping for nothing again; and your reward shall be great, and ye shall be the children of the Highest: for he is kind unto the unthankful and *to* the evil. 36. Be ye therefore merciful, as your Father also is merciful. 37. Judge not, and ye shall not be judged: condemn not, and ye shall not be condemned: forgive, and ye shall be forgiven:

Luke 17:3. Take heed to yourselves: If thy brother trespass against thee, rebuke him; and if he repent, forgive him. 4. And if he trespass against thee seven times in a day, and seven times in a day turn again to thee, saying, I repent; thou shalt forgive him. Matt. 18:21,22.

Rom. 12:14. Bless them which persecute you: bless, and curse not. 17. Recompense to no man evil for evil. 19. Avenge not yourselves, but *rather* give place unto wrath: for it is written, Vengeance *is* mine; I will

repay, saith the Lord. 21. Be not overcome of evil, but overcome evil with good.

1 Cor. 4:12. Being reviled, we bless; being persecuted, we suffer it: 13. Being defamed, we intreat.

Eph. 4:32. Be ye kind one to another, tenderhearted, forgiving one another, even as God for Christ's sake hath forgiven you.

Col. 3:13. Forbearing one another, and forgiving one another, if any man have a quarrel against any: even as Christ forgave you, so also *do* ye.

Philem. 10. I beseech thee for my son Onesimus, . . . 18. If he hath wronged thee, or oweth *thee* ought, put that on mine account;

1 Pet. 3:9. Not rendering evil for evil, or railing for railing: but contrariwise blessing; knowing that ye are thereunto called, that ye should inherit a blessing.

See Enemy.

Instances of: Esau forgives Jacob, Gen. 33:4,11. Joseph, his brethren, Gen. 45:5-15; 50:19-21. Moses, the Israelites, Num. 12:1-13. David forgives Saul, 1 Sam. 24:10-12; 26:9,23; 2 Sam. 1:14-17; and Shimei, 2 Sam. 16:9-13; 19:23, with 1 Kin. 2:8,9. Solomon forgives Adonijah, 1 Kin. 1:53. The prophet of Judah forgives Jeroboam, 1 Kin. 13:3-6. Jesus forgives his enemies, Luke 23:34.

OF SINS. See Sin, Forgiveness of.

FORK, an agricultural implement, 1 Sam. 13:21.

See Fleshhook.

FORM. IN RELIGIOUS SERVICE: 1 Chr. 15:13. For because ye *did it* not at the first, the Lord our God made a breach upon us, for that we sought him not after the due order. 14. So the priests and the Levites sanctified themselves to bring up the ark of the Lord God of Israel.

2 Chr. 29:34. But the priests were too few, so that they could not flay all the burnt offerings: wherefore their brethren the Levites did help them, till the work was ended, and until the *other* priests had sanctified themselves: for the Levites *were* more upright in heart to sanctify themselves than the priests.

IRREGULARITY IN: 2 Chr. 30:2. For the king had taken counsel, and his princes, and all the congregation in Jerusalem, to keep the passover in the second month. 3. For they could not keep it at that time, because the priests had not sanctified themselves sufficiently, neither had the people gathered themselves together to Jerusalem. 4. And the thing pleased the king and all the congregation. 5. So they established a decree to make proclamation throughout all Israel, from Beer-sheba even to Dan, that they should come to keep the passover unto the Lord God of Israel at Jerusalem: for they had not done *it* of a long *time in such sort* as it was written. 17. For *there were* many in the congregation that were not sanctified: therefore the Levites had the charge of the killing of the passovers for every one *that was* not clean, to sanctif, *them* unto the

LORD. 18. For a multitude of the people, *even* many of Ephraim, and Manasseh, Issachar, and Zebulun, had not cleansed themselves, yet did they eat the passover otherwise than it was written. But Hezekiah prayed for them, saying, The good LORD pardon every one 19. *That* prepareth his heart to seek God, the LORD God of his fathers, though *he be* not *cleansed* according to the purification of the sanctuary. 20. And the LORD hearkened to Hezekiah, and healed the people.

Matt. 12:3. But he said unto them, Have ye not read what David did, when he was an hungred, and they that were with him; 4. How he entered into the house of God, and did eat the shewbread, which was not lawful for him to eat, neither for them which were with him, but only for the priests?

See CHURCH AND STATE.

FORMALISM. 1 Sam. 15:22. And Samuel said, Hath the LORD *as great* delight in burnt offerings and sacrifices, as in obeying the voice of the LORD? Behold, to obey *is* better than sacrifice, *and* to hearken than the fat of rams.

Psa. 50:8. I will not reprove thee for thy sacrifices or thy burnt offerings, *to have been* continually before me. 9. I will take no bullock out of thy house, *nor* he goats out of thy folds. 10. For every beast of the forest *is* mine, *and* the cattle upon a thousand hills. 11. I know all the fowls of the mountains: and the wild beasts of the field *are* mine. 12. If I were hungry, I would not tell thee: for the world *is* mine, and the fulness thereof. 13. Will I eat the flesh of bulls, or drink the blood of goats? 14. Offer unto God thanksgiving; and pay thy vows unto the most High: 15. And call upon me in the day of trouble: I will deliver thee, and thou shalt glorify me.

Psa. 51:16. For thou desirest not sacrifice; else would I give *it:* thou delightest not in burnt offering. 17. The sacrifices of God *are* a broken spirit: a broken and a contrite heart, O God, thou wilt not despise.

Psa. 69:30. I will praise the name of God with a song, and will magnify him with thanksgiving. 31. *This* also shall please the LORD better than an ox *or* bullock that hath horns and hoofs.

Eccl. 5:1. Keep thy foot when thou goest to the house of God, and be more ready to hear, than to give the sacrifice of fools: for they consider not that they do evil.

Isa. 1:11. To what purpose *is* the multitude of your sacrifices unto me? saith the LORD: I am full of the burnt offerings of rams, and the fat of fed beasts; and I delight not in the blood of bullocks, or of lambs, or of he goats. 12. When ye come to appear before me, who hath required this at your hand, to tread my courts? 13. Bring no more vain oblations; incense is an abomination unto me; the new moons and sabbaths, the calling of assemblies, I cannot away with; *it is* iniquity, even the solemn

meeting. 14. Your new moons and your appointed feasts my soul hateth: they are a trouble unto me; I am weary to bear *them.* 15. And when ye spread forth your hands, I will hide mine eyes from you: yea, when ye make many prayers, I will not hear: your hands are full of blood.

Isa. 29:13. Wherefore the Lord said, Forasmuch as this people draw near *me* with their mouth, and with their lips do honour me, but have removed their heart far from me, and their fear toward me is taught by the precept of men: 14. Therefore, behold, I will proceed to do a marvellous work among this people, *even* a marvellous work and a wonder: for the wisdom of their wise *men* shall perish, and the understanding of their prudent *men* shall be hid. 15. Woe unto them that seek deep to hide their counsel from the LORD, and their works are in the dark, and they say, Who seeth us? and who knoweth us? 16. Surely your turning of things upside down shall be esteemed as the potter's clay: for shall the work say of him that made it, He made me not? or shall the thing framed say of him that framed it, He had no understanding?

Jer. 6:20. To what purpose cometh there to me incense from Sheba, and the sweet cane from a far country? your burnt offerings *are* not acceptable, nor your sacrifices sweet unto me.

Jer. 14:12. When they fast, I will not hear their cry; and when they offer burnt offering and an oblation, I will not accept them: but I will consume them by the sword, and by the famine, and by the pestilence.

Hos. 6:6. For I desired mercy, and not sacrifice; and the knowledge of God more than burnt offerings.

Amos 5:21. I hate, I despise your feast days, and I will not smell in your solemn assemblies. 22. Though ye offer me burnt offerings and your meat offerings, I will not accept *them:* neither will I regard the peace offerings of your fat beasts. 23. Take thou away from me the noise of thy songs; for I will not hear the melody of thy viols.

Mic. 6:6. Wherewith shall I come before the LORD, *and* bow myself before the high God? shall I come before him with burnt offerings, with calves of a year old? 7. Will the LORD be pleased with thousands of rams, *or* with ten thousands of rivers of oil? shall I give my firstborn *for* my transgression, the fruit of my body *for* the sin of my soul?

Mal. 1:6. A son honoureth *his* father, and a servant his master: if then I *be* a father, where *is* mine honour? and if I *be* a master, where *is* my fear? saith the LORD of hosts unto you, O priests, that despise my name. And ye say, Wherein have we despised thy name? 8. And if ye offer the blind for sacrifice, *is it* not evil? and if ye offer the lame and sick, *is it* not evil? offer it now unto thy governor; will he be pleased with thee, or accept thy person? saith the LORD of hosts.

10. Who *is there* even among you that would shut the doors *for nought?* neither do ye kindle *fire* on mine altar for nought. I have no pleasure in you, saith the LORD of hosts, neither will I accept an offering at your hand. 13. Ye said also, Behold, what a weariness *is it!* and ye have snuffed at it, saith the LORD of hosts; and ye brought *that which was* torn, and the lame and the sick; thus·ye brought an offering: should I accept this of your hand? saith the LORD. 14. But cursed *be* the deceiver, which hath in his flock a male, and voweth, and sacrificeth unto the Lord a corrupt thing: for I *am* a great King, saith the LORD of hosts, and my name *is* dreadful among the heathen.

Matt. 9:13. But go ye and learn what *that* meaneth, I will have mercy, and not sacrifice: for I am not come to call the righteous, but sinners to repentance.

Matt. 12:7. But if ye had known what *this* meaneth, I will have mercy, and not sacrifice, ye would not have condemned the guiltless.

Matt. 15:8. This people draweth nigh unto me with their mouth, and honoureth me with *their* lips; but their heart is far from me. 9. But in vain they do worship me, teaching *for* doctrines the commandments of men.

Luke 13:24. Strive to enter in at the strait gate: for many, I say unto you, will seek to enter in, and shall not be able. 25. When once the master of the house has risen up, and hath shut to the door, and ye begin to stand without, and to knock at the door, saying, Lord, Lord, open unto us; and he shall answer and say unto you, I know you not whence ye are: 26. Then shall ye begin to say, We have eaten and drunk in thy presence, and thou hast taught in our streets. 27. But he shall say, I tell you, I know you not whence ye are; depart from me, all *ye* workers of iniquity.

Rom. 2:17. Behold, thou art called a Jew, and restest in the law, and makest thy boast of God, 18. And knowest *his* will, and approvest the things that are more excellent, being instructed out of the law; 19. And art confident that thou thyself art a guide of the blind, a light of them which are in darkness, 20. An instructor of the foolish, a teacher of babes, which hast the form of knowledge and of the truth in the law. 21. Thou therefore which teachest another, teachest thou not thyself? thou that preachest a man should not steal, dost thou steal? 22. Thou that sayest a man should not commit adultery, dost thou commit adultery? thou that abhorrest idols, dost thou commit sacrilege? 23. Thou that makest thy boast of the law, through breaking the law dishonourest thou God? 24. For the name of God is blasphemed among the Gentiles through you, as it is written. 25. For circumcision verily profiteth, if thou keep the law: but if thou be a breaker of the law,

thy circumcision is made uncircumcision. 26. Therefore if the uncircumcision keep the righteousness of the law, shall not his uncircumcision be counted for circumcision? 27. And shall not uncircumcision which is by nature, if it fulfil the law, judge thee, who by the letter and circumcision dost transgress the law? 28. For he is not a Jew, which is one outwardly; neither *is that* circumcision, which is outward in the flesh: 29. But he *is* a Jew, which is one inwardly; and circumcision *is that* of the heart, in the spirit, *and* not in the letter; whose praise *is* not of men, but of God.

1 Cor. 7:19. Circumcision is nothing, and uncircumcision is nothing, but the keeping of the commandments of God.

Phil. 3:4. Though I might also have confidence in the flesh. If any other man thinketh that he hath whereof he might trust in the flesh, I more: 5. Circumcised the eighth day, of the stock of Israel, *of* the tribe of Benjamin, an Hebrew of the Hebrews; as touching the law, a Pharisee; 6. Concerning zeal, persecuting the church; touching the righteousness which is in the law, blameless. 7. But what things were gain to me, those I counted loss for Christ.

2 Tim. 3:1. This know also, that in the last days perilous times shall come. 2. For men shall be lovers of their own selves, covetous, boasters, proud, blasphemers, disobedient to parents, unthankful, unholy, 3. Without natural affection, trucebreakers, false accusers, incontinent, fierce, despisers of those that are good, 4. Traitors, heady, highminded, lovers of pleasures more than lovers of God; 5. Having a form of godliness, but denying the power thereof: from such turn away.

See ORDINANCE; WORKS.

FORNICATION. See ADULTERY; LASCIVIOUSNESS.

FORT, a military defense. Field fortifications, Deut. 20:19,20; 2 Kin. 25:1; Ezek. 4:2; 17:17; 26:8. Defenses of cities, 2 Chr. 26:15; Isa. 25:12. See CASTLES; TOWERS; WALLS. Erected in vineyards and herding grounds, 2 Chr. 26:10; Isa. 5:2; Matt. 21:33; Mark 12:1; Luke 20:9. Caves used for, Judg. 6:2; 1 Sam. 23:29; Isa. 33:16.

FIGURATIVE: Of God's care, 2 Sam. 22: 2,3,47; Psa. 18:2; 31:3; 71:3; 91:2; 144:2; Prov. 18:10; Nah. 1:7.

FORTITUDE. See COURAGE.

FORTUNATUS, a Christian of Corinth, 1 Cor. 16:17.

FORTUNE, changes of. See illustrated in lives of Joseph, from slave to prime minister: Pharoah's butler and baker, Gen. 40: David, from shepherd boy to king, noting the vicissitudes. See also JEROBOAM; HAMAN; MORDECAI; ESTHER; JOB; DANIEL.

FORTUNE TELLING. See SORCERY.

FORTY. Remarkable coincidences in the number.

DAYS: Of rain, at the time of the flood,

Gen. 7:17; of flood, before sending forth the raven, Gen. 8:6. For embalming, Gen. 50:3. Of fasting: By Moses, Ex. 24:18; 34:28; Deut. 9:9,25; Elijah, 1 Kin. 19:8; Jesus, Matt. 4:2. Spies in the land of promise, Num. 13:25. Of probation, given to the Ninevites, Jonah 3:4. Christ's stay after the resurrection, Acts 1:3. Symbolical, Ezek. 4:6.

YEARS: Wanderings of the Israelites in the Wilderness, Ex. 16:35; Num. 14:34. Peace in Israel, Judg. 3:11; 5:31; 8:28. Egypt to be desolated, Ezek. 29:11; to be restored after, Ezek. 29:13.

STRIPES: Administered in punishing criminals, Deut. 25:3; 2 Cor. 11:24.

FOUNDING. See MOLDING.

FOUNTAIN. FIGURATIVE: Of divine grace, Psa. 36:9; Jer. 2:13; of the salvation of the gospel, Joel 3:18; Zech. 13:1; Rev. 7:17. The turgid, of the debasement of character, Prov. 25:26.

FOX. Dens of, Matt. 8:20; Luke 9:58. Samson uses, to burn the field of the Philistines, Judg. 15:4. Depredations of, Psa. 63:10; Song 2:15.

FIGURATIVE: Of unfaithful prophets, Ezek. 13:4. Of craftiness, Luke 13:32. Of heretics, Song 2:15.

FRACTURES, treatment of, Ezek. 30:21.

FRANKINCENSE. An ingredient of the sacred oil, Ex. 30:34. Used with showbread, Lev. 24:7; with meat offerings, Lev. 2:1,2,15,16; 6:15. Prohibited, in sin offerings when they consist of turtledoves or pigeons, Lev. 5:11; in making an offering of memorial, Num. 5:15. A perfume, Song 3:6. Commerce in, Rev. 18:11-13. Used as an incense, Isa. 43:23; 60:6; 66:3; Jer. 6:20. Gift of, Matt. 2:11.

FRATERNITY. Gen. 13:8. And Abram said unto Lot, Let there be no strife, I pray thee, between me and thee, and between my herdmen and thy herdmen; for we *be* brethren

Deut. 15:7. If there be among you a poor man of one of thy brethren within any of thy gates in thy land which the LORD thy God giveth thee, thou shalt not harden thine heart, nor shut thine hand from thy poor brother: 8. But thou shalt open thine hand wide unto him, and shalt surely lend him sufficient for his need, *in that* which he wanteth. 9. Beware that there be not a thought in thy wicked heart, saying, The seventh year, the year of release, is at hand; and thine eye be evil against thy poor brother, and thou givest him nought; and he cry unto the LORD against thee, and it be sin unto thee. 10. Thou shalt surely give him, and thine heart shall not be grieved when thou givest unto him: because that for this thing the LORD thy God shall bless thee in all thy works, and in all that thou puttest thine hand unto. 11. For the poor shall never cease out of the land: therefore I command thee, saying, Thou shalt open thine hand wide unto thy brother, to thy poor, and to thy needy, in thy land.

12. *And* if thy brother, an Hebrew man, or an Hebrew woman, be sold unto thee, and serve thee six years; then in the seventh year thou shalt let him go free from thee. 13. And when thou sendest him out free from thee, thou shalt not let him go away empty: 14. Thou shalt furnish him liberally out of thy flock, and out of thy floor, and out of thy winepress: *of that* wherewith the LORD thy God hath blessed thee thou shalt give unto him. 15. And thou shalt remember that thou wast a bondman in the land of Egypt, and the LORD thy God redeemed thee: therefore I command thee this thing to day.

Psa. 22:22. I will declare thy name unto my brethren:

Psa. 133:1. Behold, how good and how pleasant *it is* for brethren to dwell together in unity! 2. *It is* like the precious ointment upon the head, that ran down upon the beard, *even* Aaron's beard: that went down to the skirts of his garments; 3. As the dew of Hermon, *and as the dew* that descended upon the mountains of Zion: for there the LORD commanded the blessing, *even* life for evermore.

Zech. 11:14. Then I cut asunder mine other staff, *even* Bands, that I might break the brotherhood between Judah and Israel.

Mal. 2:10. Have we not all one father? hath not one God created us? why do we deal treacherously every man against his brother,

Matt. 5:22. Whosoever is angry with his brother without a cause shall be in danger of the judgment: and whosoever shall say to his brother, Raca, shall be in danger of the council: but whosoever shall say, Thou fool, shall be in danger of hell fire. 23. Therefore if thou bring thy gift to the altar, and there rememberest that thy brother hath ought against thee; 24. Leave there thy gift before the altar, and go thy way; first be reconciled to thy brother, and then come and offer thy gift.

Matt. 18:15. Moreover if thy brother shall trespass against thee, go and tell him his fault between thee and him alone: if he shall hear thee, thou hast gained thy brother. 16. But if he will not hear *thee, then* take with thee one or two more, that in the mouth of two or three witnesses every word may be established. 17. And if he shall neglect to hear them, tell *it* unto the church: but if he neglect to hear the church, let him be unto thee as an heathen man and a publican. 18. Verily I say unto you, Whatsoever ye shall bind on earth shall be bound in heaven: and whatsoever ye shall loose on earth shall be loosed in heaven.

21. Then came Peter to him, and said, Lord, how oft shall my brother sin against me, and I forgive him? till seven times? 22. Jesus saith unto him, I say not unto thee, Until seven times: but, Until seventy times seven.

35. So likewise shall my heavenly Father do also unto you, if ye from your hearts

forgive not every one his brother their trespasses.

Matt. 23:8. But be not ye called Rabbi: for one is your Master, *even* Christ; and all ye are brethren.

Matt. 25:40. And the King shall answer and say unto them, Verily I say unto you, Inasmuch as ye have done *it* unto one of the least of these my brethren, ye have done *it* unto me.

John 13:34. A new commandment I give unto you, That ye love one another; as I have loved you, that ye also love one another. chapter 15:12..

John 20:17. Jesus saith unto her, Touch me not; for I am not yet ascended to my Father: but go to my brethren, and say unto them, I ascend unto my Father, and your Father; and *to* my God, and your God.

Rom. 12:10. *Be* kindly affectioned one to another with brotherly love; in honour preferring one another;

1 Cor. 6:1. Dare any of you, having a matter against another, go to law before the unjust, and not before the saints? 2. Do ye not know that the saints shall judge the world? and if the world shall be judged by you, are ye unworthy to judge the smallest matters? 3. Know ye not that we shall judge angels? how much more things that pertain to this life? 4. If then ye have judgments of things pertaining to this life, set them to judge who are least esteemed in the church. 5. I speak to your shame. Is it so, that there is not a wise man among you? no, not one that shall be able to judge between his brethren? 6. But brother goeth to law with brother, and that before the unbelievers. 7. Now therefore there is utterly a fault among you, because ye go to law one with another. Why do ye not rather take wrong? why do ye not rather *suffer yourselves to* be defrauded? 8. Nay, ye do wrong, and defraud, and that *your* brethren.

1 Cor. 8:1. Now as touching things offered unto idols, we know that we all have knowledge. Knowledge puffeth up, but charity edifieth. 2. And if any man think that he knoweth any thing, he knoweth nothing yet as he ought to know. 3. But if any man love God, the same is known of him. 4. As concerning therefore the eating of those things that are offered in sacrifice unto idols, we know that an idol *is* nothing in the world, and that *there is* none other God but one. 5. For though there be that are called gods, whether in heaven or in earth, (as there be gods many, and lords many,) 6. But to us *there is but* one God, the Father, of whom *are* all things, and we in him; and one Lord Jesus Christ, by whom *are* all things, and we by him. 7. Howbeit *there is* not in every man that knowledge: for some with conscience of the idol unto this hour eat *it* as a thing offered unto an idol: and their conscience being weak is defiled. 8. But meat commendeth us not to God; for

neither, if we eat, are we the better; neither, if we eat not, are we the worse. 9. But take heed lest by any means this liberty of yours become a stumblingblock to them that are weak. 10. For if any man see thee which hast knowledge sit at meat in the idol's temple, shall not the conscience of him which is weak be emboldened to eat those things which are offered to idols; 11. And through thy knowledge shall the weak brother perish, for whom Christ died? 12. But when ye sin so against the brethren, and wound their weak conscience, ye sin against Christ. 13. Wherefore, if meat make my brother to offend, I will eat no flesh while the world standeth, lest I make my brother to offend.

Gal. 6:1. Brethren, if a man be overtaken in a fault, ye which are spiritual, restore such an one in the spirit of meekness; considering thyself, lest thou also be tempted. 2. Bear ye one another's burdens, and so fulfil the law of Christ.

1 Thess. 4:9. But as touching brotherly love ye need not that I write unto you: for ye yourselves are taught of God to love one another.

2 Thess. 3:14. And if any man obey not our word by this epistle, note that man, and have no company with him, that he may be ashamed. 15. Yet count *him* not as an enemy, but admonish *him* as a brother.

Heb. 13:1. Let brotherly love continue.

1 Pet. 1:22. Seeing ye have purified your souls in obeying the truth [1] through the Spirit unto unfeigned love of the brethren, *see that ye* love one another with a pure heart fervently: [1 Omitted in R. V.]

1 Pet. 2:17. Love the brotherhood.

1 Pet. 3:8. Finally, *be ye* all of one mind, having compassion one of another, love as brethren, *be* pitiful, *be* courteous:

2 Pet. 1:5. Add . . . 7. . . . To godliness brotherly kindness; and to brotherly kindness charity.

1 John 2:9. He that saith he is in the light, and hateth his brother, is in darkness even until now. 10. He that loveth his brother abideth in the light, and there is none occasion of stumbling in him. 11. But he that hateth his brother is in darkness, and walketh in darkness, and knoweth not whither he goeth, because that darkness hath blinded his eyes.

1 John 3:17. But whoso hath this world's good, and seeth his brother have need, and shutteth up his bowels *of compassion* from him, how dwelleth the love of God in him?

See BROTHER; CHURCH; FELLOWSHIP; FRIENDSHIP.

INSTANCES OF: The Nazarites, vows of, Num. 6:1-21; Lam. 4:7; Amos 2:11,12; Acts 21:24-31. See NAZARITES.

FRATRICIDE. INSTANCES OF: Cain, Gen. 4:8. Abimelech, Judg. 9:5. Absalom, 2 Sam. 13:28, 29. Solomon, 1 Kin. 2:23-25; Jehoram, 2 Chr. 21:4.

See HOMICIDE.

FRAUD. See DISHONESTY.

FREEDMEN, synagogue of, Acts 6:9. See EMANCIPATION.

FREEDOM, from servitude.

See EMANCIPATION; JUBILEE.

FREE-WILL. See BLESSINGS, CONTINGENT UPON OBEDIENCE.

FREE-WILL OFFERINGS. Lev. 22: 21,23; 23:38; Num. 29:39; Deut. 12:6,17; 2 Chr. 31:14; Ezra 3:5; 7:16; 8:28; Psa. 119: 108.

See BENEFICENCE; GIFTS; GIVING; LIBERALITY; OFFERINGS.

FRIENDS, Jesus calls his disciples, John 15:14, 15.

FALSE FRIENDS: Instances of: Pharaoh's butler false to Joseph, Gen. 40:23. Delilah to Samson, Judg. 16:1-20. The Ephraimite's wife, Judg. 19:1-2. David to Joab, 1 Kin. 2: 5,6; to Uriah, 2 Sam. 11. Ahithophel to David, 2 Sam. 15:12. David's friends to David, Psa. 35:11-16; 41:9; 55:12-14,20,21; 88:8,18. Judas, Matt. 26:48,49. Disciples, Matt. 26:56,58.

See HYPOCRISY.

FRIENDSHIP. Deut. 13:6. If thy brother, the son of thy mother, or thy son, or thy daughter, or the wife of thy bosom, or thy friend, which *is* as thine own soul, entice thee secretly, saying, Let us go and serve other gods, which thou hast not known, thou, nor thy fathers; 7. *Namely,* of the gods of the people which *are* round about you, nigh unto thee, or far off from thee, from the *one* end of the earth even unto the *other* end of the earth; 8. Thou shalt not consent unto him, nor hearken unto him; neither shall thine eye pity him, neither shalt thou spare, neither shalt thou conceal him: 9. But thou shalt surely kill him; thine hand shall be first upon him to put him to death, and afterwards the hand of all the people.

Job 6:14. To him that is afflicted pity *should be shewed* from his friend; but he forsaketh the fear of the Almighty. 15 My brethren have dealt deceitfully as a brook, *and* as the stream of brooks they pass away;

Job 16:2. I have heard many such things: miserable comforters *are* ye all. 20. My friends scorn me: *but* mine eye poureth out *tears* unto God.

Job 19:13. He hath put my brethren far from me, and mine acquaintance are verily estranged from me. 14. My kinsfolk have failed, and my familiar friends have forgotten me. 15. They that dwell in mine house, and my maids, count me for a stranger: I am an alien in their sight. 16. I called my servant, and he gave *me* no answer; I entreated him with my mouth. 17. My breath is strange to my wife, though I intreated for the children's *sake* of mine own body. 18. Yea, young children despised me: I arose, and they spake against me. 19. All my inward friends abhorred me: and they whom I loved are turned against me. 20. My bone cleaveth to my skin and to my flesh, and I am escaped with the skin of my teeth. 21. Have pity upon me, have pity upon me, O

ye my friends; for the hand of God hath touched me. 22. Why do ye persecute me as God, and are not satisfied with my flesh?

Psa. 35:13. But as for me, when they were sick, my clothing *was* sackcloth: I humbled my soul with fasting; and my prayer returned into mine own bosom. 14 I behaved myself as though *he had been* my friend or brother: I bowed down heavily, as one that mourneth *for his* mother.

Psa. 41:9. Yea, mine own familiar friend, in whom I trusted, which did eat of my bread, hath lifted up *his* heel against me.

Psa. 55:12. For *it was* not an enemy *that* reproached me; then I could have borne *it:* neither *was it* he that hated me *that* did magnify *himself* against me; then I would have hid myself from him: 13. But *it was* thou, a man mine equal, my guide, and mine acquaintance. 14. We took sweet counsel together, *and* walked unto the house of God in company.

Psa. 88:8. Thou hast put away mine acquaintance far from me; thou hast made me an abomination unto them: *I am* shut up, and I cannot come forth. 18. Lover and friend hast thou put far from me, *and* mine acquaintance into darkness.

Prov. 11:13. A talebearer revealeth secrets: but he that is of a faithful spirit concealeth the matter.

Prov. 17:9. He that covereth a transgression seeketh love; but he that repeateth a matter separateth *very* friends. 17. A friend loveth at all times, and a brother is born for adversity.

Prov. 18:24. A man *that hath* friends must shew himself friendly: and there is a friend *that* sticketh closer than a brother.

Prov. 22:24. Make no friendship with an angry man; and with a furious man thou shalt not go: 25. Lest thou learn his ways, and get a snare to thy soul. 26. Be not thou *one* of them that strike hands, or of them that are sureties for debts. 27. If thou hast nothing to pay, why should he take away thy bed from under thee?

Prov. 25:17. Withdraw thy foot from thy neighbour's house; lest he be weary of thee, and *so* hate thee. 19. Confidence in an unfaithful man in time of trouble *is like* a broken tooth, and a foot out of joint.

Prov. 27:6. Faithful *are* the wounds of a friend; but the kisses of an enemy *are* deceitful. 9. Ointment and perfume rejoice the heart: so *doth* the sweetness of a man's friend by hearty counsel. 10. Thine own friend, and thy father's friend, forsake not; neither go into thy brother's house in the day of thy calamity: *for* better *is* a neighbour *that is* near than a brother far off. 14. He that blesseth his friend with a loud voice, rising early in the morning, it shall be counted a curse to him. 17. Iron sharpeneth iron; so a man sharpeneth the countenance of his friend. 19. As in water face *answereth* to face, so the heart of man to man.

Eccl. 4:9. Two *are* better than one; because they have a good reward for their labour. 10. For if they fall, the one will lift up his fellow : but woe to him *that is* alone when he falleth; for *he hath* not another to help him up. 11. Again, if two lie together, then they have heat : but how can one be warm *alone?* 12. And if one prevail against him, two shall withstand him; and a threefold cord is not quickly broken.

Amos 3:3. Can two walk together, except they be agreed?

2 Tim. 4:16. At my first answer no man stood with me, but all *men* forsook me : *I pray God* that it may not be laid to their charge.

INSTANCES OF: Abraham and Lot, Gen. 14:14-16. Ruth and Naomi, Ruth 1:16,17. Samuel and Saul, 1 Sam. 15:35; 16:1. David and Jonathan, 1 Sam. 18:1-4; 20; 23:16-18; 2 Sam. 1:17-27; 9:1-13. David and Abiathar, 1 Sam. 22:23. David and Nahash, 2 Sam. 10:2. David and Hiram, 1 Kin. 5:1. David and Mephibosheth, 2 Sam. 9. David and Hushai, 2 Sam. 15:32-37; 16; 17:1-22. David and Ittai, 2 Sam. 15:19-21. Joram and Ahaziah, 2 Kin. 8:28,29; 9:16. Jehu and Jehonadab, 2 Kin. 10:15-27. Job and his three friends, Job 2:11-13. Daniel and his three companions, Dan. 2:49.

Mary, Martha, and Lazarus, and Jesus, Luke 10:38-42; John 11:1-46. The Marys, and Joseph of Arimathæa, for Jesus, Matt. 27:55-61; 28:1-8; Luke 24:10; John 20:11-18; Luke and Theophilus, Acts 1:1. Paul and his nephew, Acts 23:16. Paul, Priscilla, and Aquila, Rom. 16:3,4. Paul, Timothy, and Epaphroditus, Phil. 2:19,20,22,25.

FRINGES. Prescribed for vesture worn by the Israelites, Num. 15:38-41; Deut. 22:12. Made broad by the Pharisees, Matt. 23:5.

FROGS, plague of, Ex. 8:2-14; Psa. 78: 45; 105:30.

SYMBOLICAL : Rev. 16:13.

FRONTLETS. A leather band worn on the forehead, Ex. 13:6-16; Deut. 6:1-8; 11:18. See PHYLACTERY.

FRUGALITY. 1 Kin. 17:5. So he went and did according unto the word of the LORD: for he went and dwelt by the brook Cherith, that *is* before Jordan. 6. And the ravens brought him bread and flesh in the morning, and bread and flesh in the evening; and he drank of the brook. 10. So he arose and went to Zarephath. And when he came to the gate of the city, behold, the widow woman *was* there gathering of sticks: and he called to her, and said, Fetch me, I pray thee, a little water in a vessel, that I may drink. 11. And as she was going to fetch *it,* he called to her, and said, Bring me, I pray thee, a morsel of bread in thine hand. 12. And she said, *As* the LORD thy God liveth, I have not a cake, but an handful of meal in a barrel, and a little oil in a cruse : and, behold, I *am* gathering two sticks, that I may go in and dress it for me and my son, that we may eat it, and die.

13. And Elijah said unto her, Fear not; go *and* do as thou hast said : but make me thereof a little cake first, and bring *it* unto me, and after make for thee and for thy son.

Prov. 11:16. A gracious woman retaineth honour : and strong *men* retain riches.

Prov. 12:27. The slothful *man* roasteth not that which he took in hunting : but the substance of a diligent man *is* precious.

Prov. 13:22. A good *man* leaveth an inheritance to his children's children : and the wealth of the sinner *is* laid up for the just.

Prov. 21:17. He that loveth pleasure *shall be* a poor man : he that loveth wine and oil shall not be rich. 20. *There is* treasure to be desired and oil in the dwelling of the wise; but a foolish man spendeth it up.

Prov. 22:3. A prudent *man* foreseeth the evil, and hideth himself : but the simple pass on, and are punished.

Prov. 23:20. Be not among winebibbers; among riotous eaters of flesh : 21. For the drunkard and the glutton shall come to poverty : and drowsiness shall clothe *a man* with rags.

Prov. 31:27. She looketh well to the ways of her household, and eateth not the bread of idleness.

Matt. 14:20. And they did all eat, and were filled : and they took up of the fragments that remained twelve baskets full.

Matt. 15:37. And they did all eat, and were filled : and they took up of the broken *meat* that was left seven baskets full.

Mark 7:28. And she answered and said unto him, Yes, Lord : yet the dogs under the table eat of the children's crumbs.

Mark 14:4. And there were some that had indignation within themselves, and said, Why was this waste of the ointment made? 5. For it might have been sold for more than three hundred pence, and have been given to the poor. And they murmured against her.

Eph. 4:28. Let him that stole steal no more : but rather let him labour, working with *his* hands the thing which is good, that he may have to give to him that needeth.

See EXTRAVAGANCE; INDUSTRY.

INSTANCES OF : The provisions made by the Egyptians against famine, Gen. 41:48, 49,53,54. The gathering of manna, Ex. 16: 17,18,22-24.

FRUITS. NATURAL: Gen. 1:11. And God said, Let the earth bring forth grass, the herb yielding seed, *and* the fruit tree yielding fruit after his kind, whose seed *is* in itself, upon the earth : and it was so. 12. And the earth brought forth grass, *and* herb yielding seed after his kind, and the tree yielding fruit, whose seed *was* in itself, after his kind : and God saw that *it was* good. 27. So God created man in his *own* image, in the image of God created he him; male and female created he them. 28. And God blessed them, and God said unto them, Be fruitful, and multiply, and replenish the earth, and subdue it : 29. And God said,

Behold, I have given you every herb bearing seed, which *is* upon the face of all the earth, and every tree, in the which *is* the fruit of a tree yielding seed; to you it shall be for meat.

See under the respective headings of various fruit-producing trees.

SPIRITUAL: See RIGHTEOUSNESS, FRUITS OF; SIN, FRUITS OF.

FRUIT TREES, care for, Deut. 20:19,20.

FRYING PAN. Lev. 2:7; 7:9.

FUEL, for temple, how provided, Neh. 10:34; 13:30,31.

FUGITIVES, from servitude, not to be returned, Deut. 23:15,16.

INSTANCES OF: From slavery, Shimei's servants, 1 Kin. 2:39; Onesimus, Philem. 1. See EXODUS.

From justice: Moses, Ex. 2:15; Absalom, 2 Sam. 13:34–38.

From the wrath of the king: David, 1 Sam. 21:10; Jeroboam, 1 Kin. 11:40; Joseph, to Egypt, Matt. 2:13–15.

FULLER, Mal. 3:2; Mark 9:3.

FULLER'S FIELD. A spot near Jerusalem, 2 Kin. 18:17; Isa. 7:3; 36:2.

FUNERALS. See BURIAL; ELEGY.

FURLONG, one eighth of a mile, Luke 24:13; John 11:18; Rev. 21:16.

FURNACE. Uses of: For refining silver, Ezek. 22:22; Mal. 3:3; gold, Prov. 17:3. For melting lead and tin, Ezek. 22:20. For capital punishment, Shadrach, Meshach, and Abed-nego cast into, by Nebuchadnezzar, Dan. 3:6–26.

FIGURATIVE: Of affliction, Deut. 4:20; 1 Kin. 8:51; Psa. 12:6; Isa. 48:10; Jer. 11:4. Of lust, Hos. 7:4. Of hell, Mal. 4:1; Matt. 13:42, 50; Rev. 9:2.

FUTURE PUNISHMENT. See PUNISHMENT, ETERNAL.

G

GAAL, conspires against and is defeated by Abimelech, Judg. 9:26–41.

GAASH, a foothill of Mount Ephraim. Joshua's inheritance embraced, Josh. 24:30. Joshua buried on the north side of, Josh. 24:30; Judg. 2:9. Brooks of, 2 Sam. 23:30.

GABA, called also GEBA. A city of Canaan allotted to Benjamin, Josh. 18:24; Ezra 2:26; Neh. 7:30.

GABBAI, a Benjamite chief, Neh. 11:8.

GABBATHA, a place of judgment in Jerusalem, where Pilate passed sentence on Jesus, John 19:13.

GABRIEL, a messenger of God. Appeared to Daniel, Dan. 8:16; 9:21; to Zacharias, Luke 1:11–19; to Mary, Luke 1:26–29.

GAD. 1. Jacob's seventh son, Gen. 30:11; 35:26; Ex. 1:4. Children of, Gen. 46:16; Num. 26:15–18; 1 Chr. 5:11. Prophecy concerning, Gen. 49:19.

2. A tribe of Israel. Blessed by Moses, Deut. 33:20. Enumeration of, at Sinai, Num. 1:14,24,25; in the plains of Moab, Num. 26:15–18; in the reign of Jotham, 1 Chr. 5:11–17.

Place of, in camp and march, Num. 2:10,14, 16. Wealth of, in cattle, and spoils, Josh. 22:8; Num. 32:1. Petition for their portion of land E. of the Jordan, Num. 32:1–5; Deut. 3:12,16,17; 29:8. Boundaries of territory, Josh. 13:24–28; 1 Chr. 5:11. Aid in the conquest of the region W. of the Jordan, Num. 32:16–32; Josh. 4:12,13; 22:1–8. Erect a monument to signify the unity of the tribes E. of the Jordan with the tribes W. of the river, Josh. 22:10–14.

Disaffected toward Saul as king, and joined the faction under David in the wilderness of Hebron, 1 Chr. 12:8–15,37,38. Join the Reubenites in the war against the Hagarites, 1 Chr. 5:10,18–22. Smitten by the king of Syria, 2 Kin. 10:32,33. Carried into captivity to Assyria, 1 Chr. 5:26. Land of, occupied by the Ammonites, after the tribe is carried into captivity, Jer. 49:1. Reallotment of territory to, by Ezekiel, Ezek. 48:27,29.

3. A prophet of David, 2 Sam. 24:11. Bids David leave Adullam, 1 Sam. 22:5. Bears the divine message to David offering choice between three evils, for his presumption in numbering Israel, 2 Sam. 24:11–14; 1 Chr. 21:9–13. Bids David build an altar on threshing floor of Ornan, 2 Sam. 24:18,19; 1 Chr. 21:18,19. Assists David in arranging temple service, 2 Chr. 29:25. Writings of, 1 Chr. 29:29.

GADARENES, called also GERGESENES. Jesus visits and works miracles among, but is rejected, Matt. 8:28–34; Mark 5:1–19.

GADDI, a chief of Manasseh. One of the twelve spies who explored Canaan, Num. 13:11.

GADDIEL, a chief of Zebulun. One of the twelve spies, Num. 13:10.

GADI, father of Menahem, 2 Kin. 15:14,17.

GAHAM, son of Nahor, Gen. 22:24.

GAHAR, one of the Nethinim, Ezra 2:47; Neh. 7:49.

GAIUS. 1. A Macedonian, and a companion of Paul. Seized at Ephesus, Acts 19:29.

2. A man of Derbe, accompanied Paul from Macedonia, Acts 20:4.

3. A Corinthian, whom Paul baptized, Rom. 16:23; 1 Cor. 1:14.

4. Man to whom John's third epistle was addressed, 3 John.

GALAL. 1. A Levite, 1 Chr. 9:15.

2. Son of Jeduthun, 1 Chr. 9:16; Neh. 11:17.

GALATIA, a province of Asia Minor. Its churches visited by Paul, Acts 16:6; 18:23. Collection taken in, for Christians at Jerusalem, 1 Cor. 16:1. Peter's address to, 1 Pet. 1:1. Churches in, Gal. 1:1,2. See Paul's epistle to Galatians.

GALBANUM, a fragrant gum used in the sacred oil, Ex. 30:34.

GALEED, called also JEGAR-SAHADUTHA. The memorial of Jacob's and Laban's covenant, Gen. 31:47,48.

GALILEE. 1. The northern district of Palestine. A city of refuge in, Josh. 20:7; 21:32; 1 Chr. 6:76. Cities in, given to Hiram,

1 Kin. 9:11,12.   Taken by king of Assyria, 2 Kin. 15:29.   Prophecy concerning, Isa. 9:1; Matt. 4:15.   Called GALILEE OF THE NATIONS, Isa. 9:1.   Herod, tetrarch of, Mark 6:21; Luke 3:1; 23:6,7.   Jesus resides in, Matt. 17:22; 19:1; John 7:1,9.   Teaching and miracles of Jesus in, Matt. 4:23,25; 15:29–31;   Mark 1:14, 28,39; 3:7; Luke 4:14,44; 5:17; 23:5; John 1:43; 4:3,43–45; Acts 10:37.   People of, receive Jesus, John 4:45,53.   Disciples were chiefly from, Acts 1:11; 2:7.   Women from, ministered to Jesus, Matt. 27:55,56; Mark 15:41; Luke 23:49,55.   Jesus appeared to his disciples in, after his resurrection, Matt. 26:32; 28:7, 10, 16, 17; Mark 14:28; 16:7; John 21.

Routes from, to Judæa, Judg. 21:19; John 4:3–5.   Dialect of, Mark 14:70.   Called GENNESARET, Matt. 14:34; Mark 6:53.   Churches in, Acts 9:31.

2. Sea of.   Called SEA OF TIBERIAS, John 21:1; LAKE OF GENNESARET, Luke 5:1; SEA OF CHINNERETH, Num. 34:11; Deut. 3:17; Josh. 13:27; of CHINNEROTH, Josh. 12:3. Jesus calls disciples on the shore of, Matt. 4:18–22; Luke 5:1–11.   Jesus teaches from a ship on, Matt. 13:1–3.   Miracles of Jesus on, Matt. 8:24–32; 14:22–33; 17:27; Mark 4:37–39; Luke 5:1–9; 8:22–24; John 21:1–11.

GALL.   Any bitter or poisonous substance, as the bile, Job 16:13; venom of serpents, Job 20:14.

A bitter herb, Deut. 29:18.   Given Jesus, Psa. 69:21; Matt. 27:34.

FIGURATIVE: Gall of bitterness, Acts 8:23.

GALLERIES, in temple of Ezekiel's vision, Ezek. 42:3.

GALLIM, a town, probably in tribe of Benjamin, 1 Sam. 25:44; Isa. 10:30.

GALLIO, proconsul of Achaia.   Dismisses complaint of Jews against Paul, Acts 18:12–17.

GALLOWS.   Used for execution of criminals, Esth. 2:23; 5:14; 6:4; 7:9,10; 9:13,25. Reproach of being hanged upon, Gal. 3:13.   See PUNISHMENT.

GAMALIEL.   1. A celebrated teacher. Speech of, before the Sanhedrin, Acts 5:33–40.   Paul's teacher, Acts 22:3.

2. A captain of Manasseh, Num. 1:10; 2:20; 10:23.   Offering of, at dedication of tabernacle, Num. 7:54–59.

GAMES.   Foot races, 1 Cor. 9:24,26; Gal. 2:2; Phil. 2:16; Heb. 12:1.   Gladiatorial, 1 Cor. 4:9; 9:26; 15:32; 2 Tim. 4:7.

FIGURATIVE: Of the Christian life, 1 Cor. 9:24,26; Gal. 5:7; Phil. 2:16; 3:14; Heb. 12:1.   Of a successful ministry, Gal. 2:2; Phil. 2:16.   Fighting wild beasts, of spiritual conflict, 1 Cor. 4:9; 9:26; 15:32; 2 Tim. 4:7.

GAMMADIM, warriors or watchmen, Ezek. 27:11.

GAMUL, a priest in the time of David, 1 Chr. 24:17.

GARDEN, OF EDEN.   See EDEN.   Of Gethsemane.   See GETHSEMANE.

GAREB.   1. One of David's mighty men, 2 Sam. 23:38; 1 Chr. 11:40.

2. A hill, Jer. 31:39.

GARLANDS, Acts 14:13.

GARLIC, Num. 11:5.

GARMENT, of righteousness, Isa. 61:10; Matt. 22:11; 2 Cor. 5:3; Rev. 3:18; 7:14; 16:15; 19:8.

See DRESS; ROBE.

GARNER, Matt. 3:12.

GARRISON, a military camp, 1 Sam. 13:3; 14:1; 2 Sam. 8:6,14; 23:14.

GASHMU, called also GESHEM, A Samaritan, Neh. 6:1,6.

GATAM, grandson of Esau, Gen. 36:11, 16; 1 Chr. 1:36.

GATES.   Of cities, Deut. 3:5; Josh. 6:26; 1 Sam. 23:7; 2 Sam. 18:24; 2 Chr. 8:5.   Made of iron, Acts 12:10; wood, Neh. 1:3; brass, Psa. 107:16; Isa. 45:2.   Double doors, Isa. 45: 1; Ezek. 41:24.

The open square of, a place for idlers, Gen. 19:1; 1 Sam. 4:18; Psa. 69:12; Prov. 1:21; Jer. 17:19,20.   Religious services held at, Acts 14:13.   The law read at, Neh. 8.   Place for the transaction of public business, announcement of legal transactions, Gen. 23:10,16; conferences on public affairs, Gen. 34:20; holding courts of justice, Deut. 16:18; 21:19; 22: 15; Josh. 20:4; Ruth 4:1; 2 Sam. 15:2; Prov. 22:22; Zech. 8:16.   Place for public concourse, Gen. 23:10; Prov. 1:21; 8:3; Jer. 14:2; 22:2. Thrones of kings at, 1 Kin. 22:10; 2 Chr. 18:9; Jer. 38:7; 39:3.   Punishment of criminals outside of, Deut. 17:5; Jer. 20:2; Acts 7:58; Heb. 13:12.   Closed at night, Josh. 2:5,7; on the Sabbath, Neh. 13:19.   Guards at, 2 Kin. 7:17; Neh. 13:19,22.   Jails made in the towers of, Jer. 20:2.   Bodies of criminals exposed to view at, 2 Kin. 10:8.

FIGURATIVE: Of the people of a city, Isa. 3:26.   Of the gospel, Isa. 60:11.   Of the powers of hell, Matt. 16:18; of death, Job 38: 17; Psa. 9:13; of the grave, Isa. 38:10.   Of righteousness, Psa. 118:19.   Of salvation, Gen. 28:17; Psa. 24:7; 118:19,20; Isa. 26:2; Matt. 7:13.   Of death, Isa. 38:10.

SYMBOLICAL: Rev. 21:12,13,21,25.

GATH.   One of the five chief cities of the Philistines, Josh. 13:3; 1 Sam. 6:17; Amos 6: 2; Mic. 1:10.   Anakim, a race of giants, inhabitants of, Josh. 11:22.   Goliath dwelt in, 1 Sam. 17:4; 1 Chr. 20:5–8.   Obed-edom belonged to, 2 Sam. 6:10.   The ark taken to, 1 Sam. 5:8.   Inhabitants of, called GITTITES, Josh. 13:3.   David takes refuge at, 1 Sam. 21:10–15; 27:2–7.   Band of Gittites, attached to David, 2 Sam. 15:18–22.   Taken by David, 1 Chr. 18:1.   Shimei's servants come to, 1 Kin. 2:39–41.   Fortified by Rehoboam, 2 Chr. 11:8.   Taken, by Hazael, 2 Kin. 12:17. Recovered, by Jehoash, 2 Kin. 13:25.   Besieged, by Uzziah, 2 Chr. 26:6.   Called METHEGAMMAH, in 2 Sam. 8:1.

GATH-HEPHER, a city of Zebulun, 2 Kin. 14:25.

GATH-RIMMON.   1. A Levitical city of Dan, Josh 19:45.

2. A city of Manasseh, Josh. 21:24,25; 1 Chr. 6:69.   Called also BILEAM, 1 Chr. 6:70.

GAZA.   1. Called also AZZAH.   A city

of the Philistines, Josh. 13:3; Jer. 25:20. One of the border cities of the Canaanites, Gen. 10:19. A city of the Avim and Anakim, Deut. 2:23; Josh. 11:22. Allotted to Judah, Josh. 15:47; Judg. 1:18. A temple of Dagon, situated at, Judg. 16:23. Samson dies at, Judg. 16:21–31. On the western boundary of the kingdom of Israel in the time of Solomon, 1 Kin. 4:24. Smitten by Pharaoh, Jer. 47:1.

Prophecies relating to, Amos 1:6,7; Zeph. 2:4; Zech. 9:5.

Desert of, Acts 8:26–39.

2. A city of Ephraim, Judg. 6:4; 1 Chr. 7:28.

GAZATHITES, inhabitants of Gaza, Josh. 13:3. Called GAZITES, in Judg. 16:2.

GAZER, called also GEZER, 2 Sam. 5: 25; 1 Chr. 14:16.

GAZEZ. 1. A son of Caleb, 1 Chr. 2:46.

2. A grandson of Caleb, 1 Chr. 2:46.

GAZZAM, one of the Nethinim, Ezra 2: 48; Neh. 7:51.

GEBA, called also GABA. A city of Benjamin, assigned to the sons of Aaron, Josh. 21:17; 1 Sam. 13:3; 2 Sam. 5:25; 1 Kin. 15:22; 2 Kin. 23:8; 1 Chr. 6:60; 8:6; 2 Chr. 16: 6; Neh. 11:31; 12:29; Isa. 10:29; Zech. 14:10.

GEBAL. 1. A city south of Sidon. Given to Reuben, Josh. 13:5. People of, work for Solomon, 1 Kin. 5:18 [*R. V.*]. Shipbuilders in, Ezek. 27:9.

2. A district near the Dead Sea, Psa. 83:7.

GEBER, name of two men, officers of Solomon, 1 Kin. 4:13,19.

GEBIM, a city of Benjamin, Isa. 10:31.

GEDALIAH. 1. Governor appointed by Nebuchadnezzar after carrying the Jews into captivity, 2 Kin. 25:22–24. Jeremiah committed to the care of, Jer. 39:14; 40:5,6. Warned of the conspiracy of Ishmael by Johanan, and the captains of his army, Jer. 40: 13–16. Slain by Ishmael, 2 Kin. 25:25,26; Jer. 41:1–10.

2. A musician, 1 Chr. 25:3,9.

3. A priest, who divorced his Gentile wife after the exile, Ezra 10:18.

4. Ancestor of Zephaniah, Zeph. 1:1.

5. A prince who caused imprisonment of Jeremiah, Jer. 38:1.

GEDEON. See GIDEON.

GEDER. An ancient city of Canaan, Josh. 12:13. Possibly identical with GEDOR, 2 or 3.

GEDERAH, a city in plain of Judah, Josh. 15:36.

GEDEROTH, a city in plain of Judah, Josh. 15:41; 2 Chr. 28:18.

GEDEROTHAIM, a city in plain of Judah, Josh. 15:36.

GEDOR. 1. A city in mountains of Judah, Josh. 15:58.

2. The town of Jeroham, 1 Chr. 12:7. Possibly identical with GEDER, which see.

3. Valley of, taken by Simeonites, 1 Chr. 4:39.

See GEDER.

4. An ancestor of Saul, 1 Chr. 8:31; 9:37.

5. Either a place or a person, authorities disagree, 1 Chr. 4:4,18.

GEHAZI. Servant of Elisha, 2 Kin. 4: 12,29,31. Covetousness of, and the judgment of leprosy upon, 2 Kin. 5:20–27. Mentions to King Jehoram the miracles of Elisha, his master, 2 Kin. 8:4,5.

GEHENNA. See HELL.

GELILOTH. A place mentioned, Josh. 18:17, as marking the boundary of Benjamin. In Josh. 15:7, Gilgal is substituted.

GEMALLI, father of Ammiel, Num. 13:12.

GEMARIAH. 1. Son of Shaphan, Jer. 36:10–12,25.

2. An ambassador of Zedekiah to Nebuchadnezzar, Jer. 29:3.

GENEALOGY, Num. 1:18; 2 Chr. 12:15; Ezra 2:59; Neh. 7:5; Heb. 7:3. Of no spiritual significance, Matt. 3:9; 1 Tim. 1:4; Tit. 3:9.

From Adam to Noah, Gen. 4:16–22; 5; 1 Chr. 1:1–4; Luke 3:36–38; to Abraham, Gen. 11:10–32; 1 Chr. 1:4–27; Luke 3:34–38; to Jesus, Matt. 1:1–16; Luke 3:23–38. Of the descendants of Noah, Gen. 10; of Nahor, Gen. 22:20–24; of Abraham, by his wife Keturah, Gen. 25:1–4; 1 Chr. 1:32,33; of Ishmael, Gen. 25:12–16; 1 Chr. 1:28–31; of Esau, Gen. 36; 1 Chr.1:35–54; of Jacob, Gen. 35:23–26; Ex. 1:5; 6:14–27; Num. 26; 1 Chr. chapters 2–9; of Pharez to David, Ruth 4:18–22. Of the Jews who returned from the captivity, Ezra 7:1–5; 8:1–15; Neh. 7; 11:12. Of Joseph, Matt. 1; Luke 3:23–38.

GENERALS. Distinguished. See ABRAHAM; JOSHUA; SAUL; DAVID; JOAB; AMASA; GIDEON; BENAIAH; NAAMAN; JEPHTHAH; BEN-HADAD; SENNACHERIB. See CAPTAINS.

GENEROSITY. See LIBERALITY.

GENIUS, mechanical, a divine inspiration, Ex. 28:3; 31:2–11; 35:30–35; 36:1.

GENNESARET. See GALILEE.

GENTILES. UNCLASSIFIED SCRIPTURES RELATING TO: Jer. 10:2. Learn not the way of the heathen, and be not dismayed at the signs of heaven; for the heathen are dismayed at them. 3. For the customs of the people *are* vain:

Matt. 6:7. When ye pray, use not vain repetitions, as the heathen *do:* for they think that they shall be heard for their much speaking. 8. Be not ye therefore like unto them: 31. Therefore take no thought, saying, What shall we eat? or, What shall we drink? or, Wherewithal shall we be clothed? 32. (For after all these things do the Gentiles seek): for your heavenly Father knoweth that ye have need of all these things.

Acts 14:16. Who in times past suffered all nations to walk in their own ways.

Acts 17:4. And some of them believed, and consorted with Paul and Silas; and of the devout Greeks a great multitude, and of the chief women not a few. 16. Now, while Paul waited for them at Athens, his spirit was stirred in him, when he saw the city wholly given to idolatry. 17. Therefore disputed he in the synagogue with the Jews, and with the devout persons, and in the market daily with them that met with him. 22. Then Paul stood in the midst of Mars' hill, and said, Ye men of Athens, I perceive that in all things ye are too superstitious. 23. For as I passed by, and beheld your devotions, I found an altar with this inscription, TO THE UNKNOWN GOD. Whom therefore ye ignorantly worship, him declare I unto you. 24. God that made the world and all things therein, seeing that he is Lord of heaven and earth, dwelleth not in temples made with hands; 25. Neither is worshipped with men's hands, as though he needed anything, seeing he giveth to all life, and breath, and all things; 26. And hath made of one blood all nations of men for to dwell on all the face of the earth, and hath determined the times before appointed, and the bounds of their habitation; 27. That they should seek the Lord, if haply they might feel after him, and find him, though he be not far from every one of us:

Rom. 1:18. For the wrath of God is revealed from heaven against all ungodliness and unrighteousness of men, who hold the truth in unrighteousness; 19. Because that which may be known of God is manifest in them; for God hath shewed it unto them. 20. For the invisible things of him from the creation of the world are clearly seen, being understood by the things that are made, even his eternal power and Godhead; so that they are without excuse: 21. Because that, when they knew God, they glorified him not as God, neither were thankful; but became vain in their imaginations, and their foolish heart was darkened. 22. Professing themselves to be wise, they became fools, 23. And changed the glory of the uncorruptible God into an image made like to corruptible man, and to birds, and fourfooted beasts, and creeping things. 24. Wherefore God also gave them up to uncleanness through the lusts of their own hearts, to dishonour their own bodies between themselves: 25. Who changed the truth of God into a lie, and worshipped and served the creature more than the Creator, who is blessed for ever. Amen. 26. For this cause God gave them up unto vile affections: for even their women did change the natural use into that which is against nature: 27. And likewise also the men, leaving the natural use of the woman, burned in their lust one toward another; men with men working that which is unseemly, and receiving in themselves that recompence of their error which was meet. 28. And even as they did not like to retain God in their knowledge, God gave them over to a reprobate mind, to do those things which are not convenient; 29. Being filled with all unrighteousness, fornication, wickedness, covetousness, maliciousness; full of envy, murder, debate, deceit, malignity;

whisperers, 30. Backbiters, haters of God, despiteful, proud, boasters, inventors of evil things, disobedient to parents, 31. Without understanding, covenantbreakers, without natural affection, implacable, unmerciful: 32. Who knowing the judgment of God, that they which commit such things are worthy of death, not only do the same, but have pleasure in them that do them.

Rom. 2:1. Therefore thou art inexcusable, O man, whosoever thou art that judgest: for wherein thou judgest another, thou condemnest thyself; for thou that judgest doest the same things. 2. But we are sure that the judgment of God is according to truth against them which commit such things. 3. And thinkest thou this, O man, that judgest them which do such things, and doest the same, that thou shalt escape the judgment of God? 4. Or despisest thou the riches of his goodness and forbearance and longsuffering; not knowing that the goodness of God leadeth thee to repentance? 5. But after thy hardness and impenitent heart treasured up unto thyself wrath against the day of wrath and revelation of the righteous judgment of God; 6. Who will render to every man according to his deeds: 7. To them who by patient continuance in well doing seek for glory and honour and immortality, eternal life: 8. But unto them that are contentious, and do not obey the truth, but obey unrighteousness, indignation and wrath, 9. Tribulation and anguish, upon every soul of man that doeth evil, of the Jew first, and also of the Gentile; 10. But glory, honour, and peace, to every man that worketh good, to the Jew first, and also to the Gentile. 11. For there is no respect of persons with God. 12. For as many as have sinned without law shall also perish without law: and as many as have sinned in the law shall be judged by the law: 13. (For not the hearers of the law are just before God, but the doers of the law shall be justified. 14. For when the Gentiles, which have not the law, do by nature the things contained in the law, these, having not the law, are a law unto themselves: 15. Which shew the work of the law written in their hearts, their conscience also bearing witness, and their thoughts the mean while accusing or else excusing one another;)

1 Cor. 10:20. But I say, that the things which the Gentiles sacrifice, they sacrifice to devils, and not to God:

1 Cor. 12:2. Ye know that ye were Gentiles, carried away unto these dumb idols, even as ye were led.

Gal. 2:15. We who are Jews by nature, and not sinners of the Gentiles,

Eph. 2:12. At that time ye were without Christ, being aliens from the commonwealth of Israel, and strangers from the covenants of promise, having no hope, and without God in the world:

Eph. 4:17. This I say therefore, and testify in the Lord, that ye henceforth walk not as other Gentiles walk, in the vanity of their mind; 18. Having the understanding darkened, being alienated from the life of God through the ignorance that is in them, because of the blindness of their heart: 19. Who being past feeling have given themselves over unto lasciviousness, to work all uncleanness with greediness.

Eph. 5:12. It is a shame even to speak of those things which are done of them in secret.

1 Thess. 4:5. Not in the lust of concupiscence, even as the Gentiles which know not God:

1 Pet. 4:3. For the time past of *our* life may suffice us to have wrought the will of the Gentiles, when we walked in lasciviousness, lusts, excess of wine, revellings, banquetings, and abominable idolatries: 4. Wherein they think it strange that ye run not with *them* to the same excess of riot, speaking evil of *you:*

See IDOLATRY; MISSIONS.

PROPHECIES OF THE CONVERSION OF:
Gen. 12:3. In thee shall all families of the earth be blessed. *v.* 5.

Gen. 22:18. And in thy seed shall all the nations of the earth be blessed; because thou hast obeyed my voice.

Gen. 49:10. The sceptre shall not depart from Judah, nor a lawgiver from between his feet, until Shiloh come; and unto him *shall* the gathering of the people *be.*

Deut. 32:21. They have moved me to jealousy with *that which is* not God; they have provoked me to anger with their vanities: and I will move them to jealousy with *those which are* not a people; I will provoke them to anger with a foolish nation.

Psa. 2:8. Ask of me, and I shall give *thee* the heathen *for* thine inheritance, and the uttermost parts of the earth *for* thy possession.

Psa. 22:27. All the ends of the world shall remember and turn unto the LORD: and all the kindreds of the nations shall worship before thee. 28. For the kingdom *is* the LORD's: and he *is* the governor among the nations. 29. All *they that be* fat upon earth shall eat and worship: all they that go down to the dust shall bow before him: and none can keep alive his own soul. 30. A seed shall serve him; it shall be accounted to the Lord for a generation. 31. They shall come, and shall declare his righteousness unto a people that shall be born, that he hath done *this.*

Psa. 46:4. *There is* a river, the streams whereof shall make glad the city of God, the holy *place* of the tabernacles of the most High. 10. Be still, and know that I *am* God: I will be exalted among the heathen, I will be exalted in the earth.

Psa. 65:2. O thou that hearest prayer, unto thee shall all flesh come. 5. O God of our salvation; *who art* the confidence of all the ends of the earth, and of them that are afar off *upon* the sea:

Psa. 66:4. All the earth shall worship thee, and shall sing unto thee; they shall sing *to* thy name.

Psa. 68:31. Princes shall come out of Egypt; Ethiopia shall soon stretch out her hands unto God. 32. Sing unto God, ye kingdoms of the earth; O sing praises unto the Lord;

Psa. 72:8. He shall have dominion also from sea to sea, and from the river unto the ends of the earth. 9. They that dwell in the wilderness shall bow before him; and his enemies shall lick the dust. 10. The kings of Tarshish and of the isles shall bring presents: the kings of Sheba and Seba shall offer gifts. 11. Yea, all kings shall fall down before him: all nations shall serve him. 16. There shall be an handful of corn in the earth upon the top of the mountains; the fruit thereof shall shake like Lebanon: and *they* of the city shall flourish like grass of the earth. 19. Blessed *be* his glorious name for ever: and let the whole earth be filled *with* his glory; Amen, and Amen. *vs.* 1–20.

Psa. 86:9. All nations whom thou hast made shall come and worship before thee, O Lord; and shall glorify thy name.

Psa. 102:15. So the heathen shall fear the name of the LORD, and all the kings of the earth thy glory. 18. This shall be written for the generation to come: and the people which shall be created shall praise the LORD. 19. For he hath looked down from the height of his sanctuary; from heaven did the LORD behold the earth; 20. To hear the groaning of the prisoner; to loose those that are appointed to death; 21. To declare the name of the LORD in Zion, and his praise in Jerusalem; 22. When the people are gathered together, and the kingdoms, to serve the LORD.

Psa. 145:10. All thy works shall praise thee, O LORD; and thy saints shall bless thee. 11. They shall speak of the glory of thy kingdom, and talk of thy power;

Isa. 2:2. It shall come to pass in the last days, *that* the mountain of the LORD's house shall be established in the top of the mountains, and shall be exalted above the hills; and all nations shall flow unto it. 3. Many people shall go and say, Come ye, and let us go up to the mountain of the LORD, to the house of the God of Jacob; and he will teach us of his ways, and we will walk in his paths: for out of Zion shall go forth the law, and the word of the LORD from Jerusalem. 4. He shall judge among the nations, and shall rebuke many people: and they shall beat their swords into plowshares, and their spears into pruninghooks; nation shall not lift up sword against nation, neither shall they learn war any more. *v.* 5.

Isa. 9:2. The people that walked in darkness have seen a great light: they that dwell in the land of the shadow of death, upon them hath the light shined. 6. The government shall be upon his shoulder: and his name shall be called Wonderful, Counsellor, The mighty God, The everlasting Father, The Prince of Peace. 7. Of the increase of *his* government and peace *there shall be* no end, upon the throne of David, and upon his kingdom, to order it, and to establish it with judgment and with justice from henceforth even for ever. *vs.* 1–7.

Isa. 11:6. The wolf also shall dwell with the lamb, and the leopard shall lie down with the kid; and the calf and the young lion and the fatling together; and a little child shall lead them. 7. And the cow and the bear shall feed; their young ones shall lie down together: and the lion shall eat straw like the ox. 8. And the sucking child shall play on the hole of the asp, and the weaned child shall put his hand on the cockatrice' den. 9. They shall not hurt nor destroy in all my holy mountain: for the earth shall be full of the knowledge of the LORD, as the waters cover the sea. 10. And in that day there shall be a root of Jesse, which shall stand for an ensign of the people; to it shall the Gentiles seek: and his rest shall be glorious. *vs.* 1–10.

Isa. 18:7. In that time shall the present be brought unto the LORD of hosts of a people scattered and peeled, and from a people terrible from their beginning hitherto; a nation meted out and trodden under foot, whose land the rivers have spoiled, to the place of the name of the LORD of hosts, the mount Zion.

Isa. 24:16. From the uttermost part of the earth have we heard songs, *even* glory to the righteous.

Isa. 35:1. The wilderness and the solitary place shall be glad for them; and the desert shall rejoice, and blossom as the rose. 2. It shall blossom abundantly, and rejoice even with joy and singing: the glory of Lebanon shall be given unto it, the excellency of Carmel and Sharon, they shall see the glory of the LORD, *and* the excellency of our God. 5. The eyes of the blind shall be opened, and the ears of the deaf shall be unstopped.

6. Then shall the lame *man* leap as an hart, and the tongue of the dumb sing: for in the wilderness shall waters break out, and streams in the desert. 7. And the parched ground shall become a pool, and the thirsty land springs of water: in the habitation of dragons, where each lay, *shall be* grass with reeds and rushes. *vs.* 1–10.

Isa. 40:5. The glory of the LORD shall be revealed, and all flesh shall see *it* together: for the mouth of the LORD hath spoken *it*. *vs.* 4–11.

Isa. 42:1. Behold my servant, whom I uphold; mine elect, *in whom* my soul delighteth; I have put my spirit upon him: he shall bring forth judgment to the Gentiles. 4. He shall not fail nor be discouraged, till he have set judgment in the earth: and the isles shall wait for his law. *vs.* 1–12.

Isa. 45:8. Drop down, ye heavens, from above, and let the skies pour down righteousness: let the earth open, and let them bring forth salvation, and let righteousness spring up together; I the LORD have created it. 22. Look unto me, and be ye saved, all the ends of the earth: for I *am* God, and *there*

is none else. 23. I have sworn by myself, the word is gone out of my mouth *in* righteousness, and shall not return, That unto me every knee shall bow, every tongue shall swear. 24. Surely, shall *one* say, in the LORD have I righteousness and strength: *even* to him shall *men* come; *v.* 6.

Isa. 49:1. Listen, O isles, unto me; and hearken, ye people, from far; The LORD hath called me from the womb; from the bowels of my mother hath he made mention of my name. 5. And now, saith the LORD that formed me from the womb *to be* his servant, to bring Jacob again to him, Though Israel be not gathered, yet shall I be glorious in the eyes of the LORD, and my God shall be my strength. 6. And he said, It is a light thing that thou shouldest be my servant to raise up the tribes of Jacob, and to restore the preserved of Israel: I will also give thee for a light to the Gentiles, that thou mayest be my salvation unto the end of the earth. 18. Lift up thine eyes round about, and behold: all these gather themselves together, *and* come to thee. As I live, saith the LORD, thou shalt surely clothe thee with them all, as with an ornament, and bind them *on thee*, as a bride *doeth*. 19. For thy waste and thy desolate places, and the land of thy destruction, shall even now be too narrow by reason of the inhabitants, and they that swallowed thee up shall be far away. 20. The children which thou shalt have, after thou hast lost the other, shall say again in thine ears, The place *is* too strait for me: give place to me that I may dwell. 21. Then shalt thou say in thine heart, Who hath begotten me these, seeing I have lost my children, and am desolate, a captive, and removing to and fro? and who hath brought up these? Behold, I was left alone; these, where *had* they *been?* 22. Thus saith the Lord GOD, Behold, I will lift up mine hand to the Gentiles, and set up my standard to the people: and they shall bring thy sons in *their* arms, and thy daughters shall be carried upon *their* shoulders. 23. And kings shall be thy nursing fathers, and their queens thy nursing mothers: they shall bow down to thee with *their* face toward the earth, and lick up the dust of thy feet: and thou shalt know that I *am* the LORD: for they shall not be ashamed that wait for me.

Isa. 54:1. Sing, O barren, thou *that* didst not bear; break forth into singing, and cry aloud, thou *that* didst not travail with child: for more *are* the children of the desolate than the children of the married wife, saith the LORD. 2. Enlarge the place of thy tent, and let them stretch forth the curtains of thine habitations: spare not, lengthen thy cords, and strengthen thy stakes; 3. For thou shalt break forth on the right hand and on the left; and thy seed shall inherit the Gentiles, and make the desolate cities to be inhabited.

Isa. 55:5. Behold, thou shalt call a nation

that thou knowest not, and nations *that* knew not thee shall run unto thee, because of the LORD thy God, and for the Holy One of Israel; for he hath glorified thee.

Isa. 56:3. Neither let the son of the stranger, that hath joined himself to the LORD, speak, saying, The LORD hath utterly separated me from his people: neither let the eunuch say, Behold, I *am* a dry tree. 6. Also the sons of the stranger, that join themselves to the LORD, to serve him, and to love the name of the LORD, to be his servants, every one that keepeth the sabbath from polluting it, and taketh hold of my covenant; 7. Even them will I bring to my holy mountain, and make them joyful in my house of prayer: their burnt offerings and their sacrifices *shall be* accepted upon mine altar; for mine house shall be called an house of prayer for all people. 8. The Lord GOD which gathereth the outcasts of Israel saith, Yet will I gather *others* to him, beside those that are gathered unto him.

Isa. 60:1. Arise, shine; for thy light is come, and the glory of the LORD is risen upon thee. 3. The Gentiles shall come to thy light, and kings to the brightness of thy rising. 4. Lift up thy thine eyes round about, and see: all they gather themselves together, they come to thee: thy sons shall come from far, and thy daughters shall be nursed at *thy* side. 5. Then thou shalt see, and flow together, and thine heart shall fear, and be enlarged; because the abundance of the sea shall be converted unto thee, the forces of the Gentiles shall come unto thee. 8. Who *are* these *that* fly as a cloud, and as the doves to their windows? 9. Surely the isles shall wait for me, and the ships of Tarshish first, to bring thy sons from far, their silver and their gold with them, unto the name of the LORD thy God, and to the Holy One of Israel, because he hath glorified thee. 10. And the sons of strangers shall build up thy walls, and their kings shall minister unto thee: for in my wrath I smote thee, but in my favour have I had mercy on thee. 11. Therefore thy gates shall be open continually; they shall not be shut day nor night; that *men* may bring unto thee the forces of the Gentiles, and *that* their kings *may be* brought. 12. For the nation and kingdom that will not serve thee shall perish; yea, *those* nations shall be utterly wasted. 13. The glory of Lebanon shall come unto thee, the fir tree, the pine tree, and the box together, to beautify the place of my sanctuary; and I will make the place of my feet glorious. 14. The sons also of them that afflicted thee shall come bending unto thee; and all they that despised thee shall bow themselves down at the soles of thy feet; and they shall call thee, The city of the LORD, The Zion of the Holy One of Israel.

Isa. 65:1. I am sought of *them that* asked **not** *for me;* I am found of *them that* sought me not: I said, Behold me, behold me, unto a nation *that* was not called by my name.

Isa. 66:12. For thus saith the LORD, Behold, I will extend peace to her like a river, and the glory of the Gentiles like a flowing stream: then shall ye suck, ye shall be borne upon *her* sides, and be dandled upon *her* knees. 19. I will set a sign among them, and I will send those that escape of them unto the nations, *to* Tarshish, Pul, and Lud, that draw the bow, *to* Tubal, and Javan, *to* the isles afar off, that have not heard my fame, neither have seen my glory; and they shall declare my glory among the Gentiles. 23. It shall come to pass, *that* from one new moon to another, and from one sabbath to another, shall all flesh come to worship before me, saith the LORD. *vs.* 7–23.

Jer. 3:17. They shall call Jerusalem the throne of the LORD; and all the nations shall be gathered unto it, to the name of the LORD, to Jerusalem: neither shall they walk any more after the imagination of their evil heart.

Jer. 4:2. And thou shalt swear, The LORD liveth, in truth, in judgment, and in righteousness; and the nations shall bless themselves in him, and in him shall they glory.

Jer. 16:19. O LORD, my strength, and my fortress, and my refuge in the day of affliction, the Gentiles shall come unto thee from the ends of the earth, and shall say, Surely our fathers have inherited lies, vanity, and *things* wherein *there is* no profit. 20. Shall a man make gods unto himself, and they *are* no gods? 21. Therefore, behold, I will this once cause them to know, I will cause them to know mine hand and my might; and they shall know that my name *is* The LORD.

Ezek. 47:3. And when the man that had the line in his hand went forth eastward, he measured a thousand cubits, and he brought me through the waters; the waters *were* to the ancles. 4. Again he measured a thousand, and brought me through the waters; the waters *were* to the knees. Again he measured a thousand, and brought me through; the waters *were* to the loins. 5. Afterward he measured a thousand, *and it was* a river that I could not pass over: for the waters were risen, waters to swim in, a river that could not be passed over.

Dan. 2:35. And the stone that smote the image became a great mountain, and filled the whole earth. 44. In the days of these kings shall the God of heaven set up a kingdom, which shall never be destroyed: and the kingdom shall not be left to other people, *but* it shall break in pieces and consume all these kingdoms, and it shall stand for ever. *v.* 45.

Dan. 7:13. I saw in the night visions, and, behold, *one* like the Son of man came with the clouds of heaven, and came to the Ancient of days, and they brought him near before him. 14. And there was given him dominion, and glory, and a kingdom, that all people, nations, and languages, should serve him: his dominion *is* an everlasting dominion, which shall not pass away, and his kingdom *that* which shall not be destroyed.

Hos. 2:23. And I will sow her unto me in the earth; and I will have mercy upon her that had not obtained mercy; and I will say to *them which were* not my people, Thou *art* my people; and they shall say, *Thou art* my God.

Joel 2:28. And it shall come to pass afterward, *that* I will pour out my spirit upon all flesh; and your sons and your daughters shall prophesy, your old men shall dream dreams, your young men shall see visions: 29. And also upon the servants and upon the handmaids in those days will I pour out my spirit. 30. And I will shew wonders in the heavens and in the earth, blood, and fire, and pillars of smoke. 31. The sun shall be turned into darkness, and the moon into blood, before the great and terrible day of the LORD come. 32. And it shall come to pass, *that* whosoever shall call on the name of the LORD shall be delivered: for in mount Zion and in Jerusalem shall be deliverance, as the LORD hath said, and in the remnant whom the LORD shall call.

Amos 9:11. In that day will I raise up the tabernacle of David that is fallen, and close up the breaches thereof; and I will raise up his ruins, and I will build it as in the days of old: 12. That they may possess the remnant of Edom, and of all the heathen, which are called by my name, said the LORD that doeth this.

Mic. 4:3. He shall judge among many people, and rebuke strong nations afar off; and they shall beat their swords into plowshares, and their spears into pruninghooks: nation shall not lift up a sword against nation, neither shall they learn war any more. 4. But they shall sit every man under his vine and under his fig tree; and none shall make *them* afraid: for the mouth of the LORD of hosts hath spoken it.

Hag. 2:7. And I will shake all nations, and the desire of all nations shall come: and I will fill this house with glory, saith the LORD of hosts.

Zech. 2:10. Sing and rejoice, O daughter of Zion: for, lo, I come, and I will dwell in the midst of thee, saith the LORD. 11. And many nations shall be joined to the LORD in that day, and shall be my people: and I will dwell in the midst of thee, and thou shalt know that the LORD of hosts hath sent me unto thee.

Zech. 6:15. They *that are* far off shall come and build in the temple of the LORD,

Zech. 8:20. Thus saith the LORD of hosts; *It shall* yet *come to pass*, that there shall come people, and the inhabitants of many cities: 21. And the inhabitants of one *city* shall go to another, saying, Let us go speedily to pray before the LORD, and to seek the LORD of hosts: I will go also. 22. Yea, many people and strong nations shall come to seek

the LORD of hosts in Jerusalem, and to pray before the LORD. *vs.* 1-23.

23. Thus saith the LORD of hosts; In those days *it shall come to pass*, that ten men shall take hold out of all languages of the nations, even shall take hold of the skirt of him that is a Jew, saying, We will go with you: for we have heard *that* God *is* with you.

Zech. 9:1. When the eyes of man, as of all the tribes of Israel, *shall be* toward the LORD. 10. I will cut off the chariot from Ephraim, and the horse from Jerusalem, and the battle bow shall be cut off: and he shall speak peace unto the heathen: and his dominion *shall be* from sea *even* to sea, and from the river *even* to the ends of the earth. *vs.* 9–17.

Zech. 14:8. It shall be in that day, *that* living waters shall go out from Jerusalem; half of them toward the former sea, and half of them toward the hinder sea: in summer and in winter shall it be. 9. And the LORD shall be king over all the earth: in that day shall there be one LORD, and his name one. 16. Every one that is left of all the nations which came against Jerusalem shall even go up from year to year to worship the King, the LORD of hosts, and to keep the feast of tabernacles. *vs.* 8–21.

Mal. 1:11. For from the rising of the sun even unto the going down of the same my name *shall be* great among the Gentiles; and in every place incense *shall be* offered unto my name, and a pure offering: for my name *shall be* great among the heathen, saith the LORD of hosts.

Matt. 3:9. And think not to say within yourselves, We have Abraham to *our* father: for I say unto you, that God is able of these stones to raise up children unto Abraham.

Matt. 8:11. And I say unto you, That many shall come from the east and west, and shall sit down with Abraham, and Isaac, and Jacob, in the kingdom of heaven.

Matt. 12:17. That it might be fulfilled which was spoken by Esaias the prophet, saying, 18. Behold my servant, whom I have chosen; my beloved, in whom my soul is well pleased: I will put my spirit upon him, and he shall shew judgment to the Gentiles. 19. He shall not strive, nor cry; neither shall any man hear his voice in the streets. 20. A bruised reed shall he not break, and smoking flax shall he not quench, till he send forth judgment unto victory. 21. And in his name shall the Gentiles trust.

Matt. 19:30. But many *that are* first shall be last; and the last *shall be* first. Mark 10:31.

Luke 13:29. And they shall come from the east, and *from* the west, and from the north, and *from* the south, and shall sit down in the kingdom of God. 30. And, behold, there are last which shall be first, and there are first which shall be last.

Luke 21:24. And they shall fall by the edge of the sword, and shall be led away captive into all nations: and Jerusalem shall be trodden down of the Gentiles, until the times of the Gentiles be fulfilled.

John 10:16. And other sheep I have, which are not of this fold: them also I must bring, and they shall hear my voice; and there shall be one fold, *and* one shepherd.

Acts 9:15. But the Lord said unto him, Go thy way: for he is a chosen vessel unto me, to bear my name before the Gentiles, and kings, and the children of Israel:

See CHURCH; PROPHECIES CONCERNING PROSPERITY of.

CONVERSION OF: Acts 10:45. And they of the circumcision which believed were astonished, as many as came with Peter, because that on the Gentiles also was poured out the gift of the Holy Ghost.

Acts 11:1. And the apostles and brethren that were in Judæa heard that the Gentiles had also received the word of God. 2. And when Peter was come up to Jerusalem, they that were of the circumcision contended with him, 3. Saying, Thou wentest in to men uncircumcised, and didst eat with them. 4. But Peter rehearsed *the matter* from the beginning, and expounded *it* by order unto them, saying, 5. I was in the city of Joppa praying: and in a trance I saw a vision, A certain vessel descend, as it had been a great sheet, let down from heaven by four corners; and it came even to me: 6. Upon the which when I had fastened mine eyes, I considered, and saw fourfooted beasts of the earth, and wild beasts, and creeping things, and fowls of the air. 7. And I heard a voice saying unto me, Arise, Peter; slay and eat. 8. But I said, Not so, Lord: for nothing common or unclean hath at any time entered into my mouth. 9. But the voice answered me again from heaven, What God hath cleansed, *that* call not thou common. 10. And this was done three times: and all were drawn up again into heaven. 11. And, behold, immediately there were three men already come unto the house where I was, sent from Cæsarea unto me. 12. And the spirit bade me go with them, nothing doubting. Moreover these six brethren accompanied me, and we entered into the man's house: 13. And he shewed us how he had seen an angel in his house, which stood and said unto him, Send men to Joppa, and call for Simon, whose surname is Peter; 14. Who shall tell thee words, whereby thou and all thy house shall be saved. 15. And as I began to speak, the Holy Ghost fell on them, as on us at the beginning. 16. Then remembered I the word of the Lord, how that he said, John indeed baptized with water; but ye shall be baptized with the Holy Ghost. 17. Forasmuch then as God gave them the like gift as *he did* unto us, who believed on the Lord Jesus Christ; what was I, that I could withstand God? 18. When they heard these things, they held their peace, and glorified God, saying, Then hath God also to the Gentiles granted repentance unto life.

Acts 13:2. As they ministered to the Lord, and fasted, the Holy Ghost said, Separate me Barnabas and Saul for the work whereunto I have called them. 46. Then Paul and Barnabas waxed bold, and said, It was necessary that the word of God should first have been spoken to you: but seeing ye put it from you, and judge yourselves unworthy of everlasting life, lo, we turn to the Gentiles. 47. For so hath the Lord commanded us, *saying,* I have set thee to be a light of the Gentiles, that thou shouldest be for salvation unto the ends of the earth. 48. And when the Gentiles heard this, they were glad, and glorified the word of the Lord: and as many as were ordained to eternal life believed.

Acts 14:27. And when they were come, and had gathered the church together, they rehearsed all that God had done with them, and how he had opened the door of faith unto the Gentiles.

Acts 15:7. And when there had been much disputing, Peter rose up, and said unto them, Men *and* brethren, ye know how that a good while ago God made choice among us, that the Gentiles by my mouth should hear the word of the gospel, and believe. 8. And God, which knoweth the hearts, bare them witness, giving them the Holy Ghost, even as *he did* unto us; 9. And put no difference between us and them, purifying their hearts by faith. 12. Then all the multitude kept silence, and gave audience to Barnabas and Paul, declaring what miracles and wonders God had wrought among the Gentiles by them. 13. And after they had held their peace, James answered, saying, Men *and* brethren, hearken unto me: 14. Simeon hath declared how God at the first did visit the Gentiles, to take out of them a people for his name. 15. And to this agree the words of the prophet; as it is written, 16. After this I will return, and will build again the tabernacle of David, which is fallen down; and I will build again the ruins thereof, and I will set it up: 17. That the residue of men might seek after the Lord, and all the Gentiles, upon whom my name is called, saith the Lord, who doeth all these things. 18. Known unto God are all his works from the beginning of the world. 19. Wherefore my sentence is, that we trouble not them, which from among the Gentiles are turned to God: 20. But that we write unto them, that they abstain from pollutions of idols, and *from* fornication, and *from* things strangled, and *from* blood. 21. For Moses of old time hath in every city them that preach him, being read in the synagogues every sabbath day. 22. Then pleased it the apostles and elders, with the whole church, to send chosen men of their own company to Antioch with Paul and Barnabas; *namely,* Judas surnamed

Barsabas, and Silas, chief men among the brethren: 23. And they wrote *letters* by them after this manner; The apostles and elders and brethren *send* greeting unto the brethren which are of the Gentiles in Antioch and Syria and Cilicia: 24. Forasmuch as we have heard, that certain which went out from us have troubled you with words, subverting your souls, saying, *Ye must* be circumcised, and keep the law: to whom we gave no *such* commandment: 25. It seemed good unto us, being assembled with one accord, to send chosen men unto you with our beloved Barnabas and Paul, 26. Men that have hazarded their lives for the name of our Lord Jesus Christ. 27. We have sent therefore Judas and Silas, who shall also tell *you* the same things by mouth. 28. For it seemed good to the Holy Ghost, and to us, to lay upon you no greater burden than these necessary things; 29. That ye abstain from meats offered to idols, and from blood, and from things strangled, and from fornication: from which if ye keep yourselves, ye shall do well. Fare ye well. 30. So when they were dismissed, they came to Antioch: and when they had gathered the multitude together, they delivered the epistle: 31. *Which* when they had read, they rejoiced for the consolation.

Acts 18:4. And he reasoned in the synagogue every sabbath, and persuaded the Jews and the Greeks. 5. And when Silas and Timotheus were come from Macedonia, Paul was pressed in the spirit, and testified to the Jews *that* Jesus *was* Christ. 6. And when they opposed themselves, and blasphemed, he shook *his* raiment, and said unto them, Your blood *be* upon your own heads; I *am* clean: from henceforth I will go unto the Gentiles.

Acts 26:16. But rise, and stand upon thy feet: for I have appeared unto thee for this purpose, to make thee a minister and a witness both of these things which thou hast seen, and of those things in the which I will appear unto thee: 17. Delivering thee from the people, and *from* the Gentiles, unto whom now I send thee, 18. To open their eyes, *and* to turn *them* from darkness to light, and *from* the power of Satan unto God, that they may receive forgiveness of sins, and inheritance among them which are sanctified by faith that is in me.

Acts 28:28. Be it known therefore unto you, that the salvation of God is sent unto the Gentiles, and *that* they will hear it.

Rom. 1:5. By whom we have received grace and apostleship, for obedience to the faith among all nations, for his name: 6 Among whom are ye also the called of Jesus Christ: 7. To all that be in Rome, beloved of God, called *to be* saints: Grace to you and peace from God our Father, and the Lord Jesus Christ.

Rom. 9:22. *What* if God, willing to shew *his* wrath, and to make his power known, endured with much longsuffering the vessels of wrath fitted to destruction: 23. And that he might make known the riches of his glory on the vessels of mercy, which he had afore prepared unto glory, 24. Even us, whom he hath called, not of the Jews only, but also of the Gentiles? 25. As he saith also in Osee, I will call them my people, which were not my people, and her beloved, which was not beloved. 26. And it shall come to pass, *that* in the place where it was said unto them, Ye *are* not my people; there shall they be called the children of the living God. 27. Esaias also crieth concerning Israel, Though the number of the children of Israel be as the sand of the sea, a remnant shall be saved: 28. For he will finish the work, and cut *it* short in righteousness: because a short work will the Lord make upon the earth. 29. And as Esaias said before, Except the Lord of Sabaoth had left us a seed, we had been as Sodoma, and been made like unto Gomorrha. 30. What shall we say then? That the Gentiles, which followed not after righteousness, have attained to righteousness, even the righteousness which is of faith.

Rom. 10:19. But I say, Did not Israel know? First Moses saith, I will provoke you to jealousy by *them that are* no people, *and* by a foolish nation I will anger you. 20. But Esaias is very bold, and saith, I was found of them that sought me not: I was made manifest unto them that asked not after me.

Rom. 11:11. I say then, Have they stumbled that they should fall? God forbid: but *rather* through their fall salvation *is come* unto the Gentiles, for to provoke them to jealousy. 12. Now if the fall of them *be* the riches of the world, and the diminishing of them the riches of the Gentiles; how much more their fulness? 13. For I speak to you Gentiles, inasmuch as I am the apostle of the Gentiles, I magnify mine office: 17. And if some of the branches be broken off, and thou, being a wild olive tree, wert graffed in among them, and with them partakest of the root and fatness of the olive tree; 18. Boast not against the branches. But if thou boast, thou bearest not the root, but the root thee. 19. Thou wilt say then, The branches were broken off, that I might be graffed in. 20. Well; because of unbelief they were broken off, and thou standest by faith. Be not highminded, but fear: 21. For if God spared not the natural branches, *take heed* lest he also spare not thee.

Rom. 15:9. And that the Gentiles might glorify God for *his* mercy; as it is written, For this cause I will confess to thee among the Gentiles, and sing unto thy name. 10 And again he saith, Rejoice, ye Gentiles, with his people. 11. And again, Praise the Lord, all ye Gentiles; and laud him, all ye people. 12. And again, Esaias saith, There shall be a root of Jesse, and he that shall rise to reign over the Gentiles; in him shall the Gentiles ¹ trust. [¹ R. V. hope]

Gal. 1:15. But when it pleased God, who separated me from my mother's womb, and called me by his grace, 16. To reveal his Son in me, that I might preach him among the heathen; immediately I conferred not with flesh and blood:

Gal. 2:2. And I went up by revelation, and communicated unto them that gospel which I preach among the Gentiles, but privately to them which were of reputation, lest by any means I should run, or had run, in vain.

Gal. 3:14. That the blessing of Abraham might come on the Gentiles through Jesus Christ; that we might receive the promise of the Spirit through faith.

Eph. 3:1. For this cause I Paul, the prisoner of Jesus Christ for you Gentiles, 2. If ye have heard of the dispensation of the grace of God which is given me to you-ward: 3. How that by revelation he made known unto me the mystery; (as I wrote afore in few words, 4. Whereby, when ye read, ye may understand my knowledge in the mystery of Christ) 5. Which in other ages was not made known unto the sons of men, as it is now revealed unto his holy apostles and prophets by the Spirit; 6. That the Gentiles should be fellowheirs, and of the same body, and partakers of his promise in Christ by the gospel: 7. Whereof I was made a minister, according to the gift of the grace of God given unto me by the effectual working of his power. 8. Unto me, whom am less than the least of all saints, is this grace given, that I should preach among the Gentiles the unsearchable riches of Christ;

Col. 3:11. Where there is neither Greek nor Jew, circumcision nor uncircumcision, Barbarian, Scythian, bond nor free: but Christ is all, and in all.

1 Thess. 2:16. Forbidding us to speak to the Gentiles that they might be saved, to fill up their sins alway: for the wrath is come upon them to the uttermost.

1 Tim. 3:16. And without controversy great is the mystery of godliness: ¹ God was manifest in the flesh, justified in the Spirit, seen of angels, preached unto the Gentiles, believed on in the world, received up into glory. [¹ R. V. he who]

2 Tim. 1:11. Whereunto I am appointed a preacher, and an apostle, and a teacher of the Gentiles.

Rev. 11:15. The seventh angel sounded; and there were great voices in heaven, saying, The kingdoms of this world are become the kingdoms of our Lord, and of his Christ; and he shall reign for ever and ever.

Rev. 15:4. Who shall not fear thee, O Lord, and glorify thy name? for thou only art holy: for all nations shall come and worship before thee; for thy judgments are made manifest.

See MISSIONS. Also see CHURCH. PROPH-ECIES CONCERNING PROSPERITY OF; and

JESUS, KINGDOM OF, PROPHECIES CONCERNING.

GENTLENESS. OF CHRIST: Isa. 40: 11; 2 Cor. 10:1; Matt. 11:29.

See JESUS, COMPASSION OF, HUMILITY OF, MEEKNESS OF.

OF GOD: 2 Sam. 22:36; Psa. 18:35; Isa. 40:11.

See GOD, COMPASSION OF, LONG-SUFFERING OF.

Of Paul, 1 Thess. 2:7.

EXHORTATIONS TO: Gal. 5:22. But the fruit of the Spirit is love, joy, peace, long-suffering, gentleness,

2 Tim. 2:24. And the servant of the Lord must not strive; but be gentle unto all men, apt to teach, patient, 25. In meekness instructing those that oppose themselves; if God peradventure will give them repentance to the acknowledging of the truth; 26. And that they may recover themselves out of the snare of the devil, who are taken captive by him at his will.

Tit. 3:1. Put them in mind . . . 2. To speak evil of no man, to be no brawlers, but gentle, shewing all meekness unto all men.

Jas. 3:17. But the wisdom that is from above is first pure, then peaceable, gentle, and easy to be intreated, full of mercy and good fruits, without partiality, and without hypocrisy.

See HUMILITY; KINDNESS; MEEKNESS; PATIENCE.

GENUBATH, son of Hadad, 1 Kin. 11:20.

GEOLOGY. Gen. 1:9. And God said, Let the waters under the heaven be gathered together unto one place, and let the dry land appear: and it was so. 10. And God called the dry land Earth; and the gathering together of the waters called he Seas: and God saw that it was good.

1 Sam. 2:8. The pillars of the earth are the LORD's, and he hath set the world upon them.

2 Sam. 22:16. And the channels of the sea appeared, the foundations of the world were discovered, at the rebuking of the LORD, at the blast of the breath of his nostrils.

Job 12:8. Or speak to the earth, and it shall teach thee: and the fishes of the sea shall declare unto thee. 9. Who knoweth not in all these that the hand of the LORD hath wrought this?

Job 28:9. He putteth forth his hand upon the rock; he overturneth the mountains by the roots. 10. He cutteth out rivers among the rocks; and his eye seeth every precious thing. 11. He bindeth the floods from overflowing; and the thing that is hid bringeth he forth to light.

Psa. 18:15. Then the channels of waters were seen, and the foundations of the world were discovered at thy rebuke, O LORD, at the blast of the breath of thy nostrils.

Psa. 24:1. The earth is the LORD's, and the fulness thereof; the world, and they that dwell therein. 2. For he hath founded it upon the seas, and established it upon the floods.

Psa. 104:5. *Who* laid the foundations of the earth. *that* it should not be removed for ever. 6. Thou coveredst it with the deep as *with* a garment : the waters stood above the mountains. 7. At thy rebuke they fled; at the voice of thy thunder they hasted away. 8. They go up by the mountains; they go down by the valleys unto the place which thou hast founded for them. 9. Thou hast set a bound that they may not pass over; that they turn not again to cover the earth. 10. He sendeth the springs into the valleys, *which* run among the hills. 11. They give drink to every beast of the field : the wild asses quench their thirst. 12. By them shall the fowls of the heaven have their habitation, *which* sing among the branches. 13. He watereth the hills from his chambers : the earth is satisfied with the fruit of thy works.

Psa. 136:6. To him that stretched out the earth above the waters :

Prov. 30:4. Who hath ascended up into heaven, or descended? who hath gathered the wind in his fists? who hath bound the waters in a garment? who hath established all the ends of the earth? what *is* his name, and what *is* his son's name, if thou canst tell?

Jer. 31:37. Thus saith the LORD ; If heaven above can be measured, and the foundations of the earth searched out beneath, I will also cast off all the seed of Israel for all that they have done, saith the LORD.

Hab. 3:9. Thou didst cleave the earth with rivers.

2 Pet. 3:5. For this they willingly are ignorant of, that by the word of God the heavens were of old, and the earth standing out of the water and in the water: 6. Whereby the world that then was, being overflowed with water, perished: 7. But the heavens and the earth, which are now, by the same word are kept in store, reserved unto fire against the day of judgment and perdition of ungodly men.

See CREATION ; EARTH ; METEOROLOGY ; ASTRONOMY.

See also HOT SPRINGS.

GERA. Possibly the name of three men ; more probably of one. The son of Bela, Gen. 46:21; Judg. 3:15; 2 Sam. 16:5; 19:16,18; 1 Kin. 2:8; 1 Chr. 8:3,5,7.

GERAH. A weight equal to thirteen and seven tenths grains, Paris. Also a coin equivalent to about three cents American money, and three half-pence English money, Ex. 30:13; Lev. 27:25; Num. 3:47.

GERAR. 1. A city of the Philistines, Gen. 10:19. Abimelech, king of, Gen. 20:1; 26:6. Visited by Abraham, Gen. 20:1; by Isaac, Gen. 26:1; 2 Chr. 14:13,14.

2. A valley, Gen. 26:17-22.

GERGESENES. See GADARENES.

GERIZIM. Mount of blessing, Deut. 11: 29; 27:12; Josh. 8:33. Jotham addresses the Shechemites from, against the conspiracy of Abimelech, Judg. 9:7. Samaritans worship at, John 4:20.

GERSHOM. 1. Son of Moses, Ex. 2:22; 18:3; 1 Chr. 23:15,16; 26:24.

2. See GERSHON.

3. A descendant of Phinehas, Ezra 8:2.

4. A Levite, Judg. 18:30.

GERSHON, called also GERSHOM. Son of Levi, Gen. 46:11; Ex. 6:16,17; Num. 3:17-26; 4:22-28,38; 7:7; 10:17; 26:57; Josh. 21:6; 1 Chr. 6:1,16,17,20,43,62,71; 15:7; 23:6.

GESHAM, a descendant of Caleb, 1 Chr. 2:47.

GESHEM, called also GASHMU, an Arabian. Opposed Nehemiah in building Jerusalem, Neh. 2:19; 6:1-6.

GESHUR. 1. District E. of the sources of the Jordan. The inhabitants of, not subdued by the Israelites, Deut. 3:14; Josh. 13: 2-13; 1 Chr. 2:23. Inhabitants of one of the villages of, exterminated, and the spoils taken by David, 1 Sam. 27:8. David marries a princess of, 2 Sam. 3:3; 1 Chr. 3:2. Absalom takes refuge in, after the murder of Amnon, 2 Sam. 13:37,38; 15:8.

GETHSEMANE, a garden near Jerusalem. Jesus betrayed in, Matt. 26:36-50; Mark 14:32-46; Luke 22:39-49; John 18:1,2.

GEZER, called also GAZER, GAZARA, GAZERA, and GOB. A Canaanitish royal city; king of, defeated by Joshua, Josh. 10:33; 12:12. Canaanites not all expelled from, but made to pay tribute, Josh. 16:10; Judg. 1:29. Allotted to Ephraim, Josh. 16:3,10; 1 Chr. 7:28. Assigned to Levites, Josh. 2:21. Battle with Philistines at, 1 Chr. 20:4; 2 Sam. 21:18. Smitten by David, 1 Sam. 27:8. Fortified by Solomon, 1 Kin. 9:15-17.

GHOST, soul, Acts 5:5,10; 12:23.

See SPIRIT ; MAN, CREATED A SPIRIT.

GIAH, a place on the way to the wilderness of Gibeon, 2 Sam. 2:24.

GIANTS, Gen. 6:4.

See ANAKIM ; EMIMS ; GOLIATH ; ISHBI-BENOB ; OG ; REPHAIM ; ZAMZUMMIM.

GIBBAR, Ezra 2:20.

See GIBEON.

GIBBETHON. A city of Dan, Josh. 19:44. Allotted to the Levites, Josh. 21:23. Besieged by Israel, while in possession of Philistines, 1 Kin. 15:27; 16:15,17.

GIBEA, a descendant of Judah, 1 Chr. 2:49.

GIBEAH. 1. OF JUDAH, Josh. 15:57.

2. OF SAUL. Called also GIBEAH OF BENJAMIN. The people's wickedness, Judg. 19: 12-30; Hos. 9:9; 10:9. Destroyed by the Israelites, Judg. 20. The city of Saul, 1 Sam. 10: 26; 15:34; 22:6. The ark of the covenant conveyed to, by the Philistines, 1 Sam. 7:1; 2 Sam. 6:3. Deserted, Isa. 10:29.

3. Another town in Benjamin, called also GIBEATH, in Josh. 18:28.

4. GIBEAH IN THE FIELD, Judg. 20:31. Probably identical with GEBA, which see.

GIBEON. 1. A city of the Hivites, Josh. 9:3,17; 2 Sam. 21:2. The people of, adroitly draw Joshua into a treaty, Josh. 9. Made servants by the Israelites, when their sharp practice was discovered, Josh. 9:27. The sun stands still over, during Joshua's battle with the five confederated kings, Josh. 10:12–14. Allotted to Benjamin, Josh. 18:25. Assigned to the Aaronites, Josh. 21:17. The tabernacle located at, 1 Kin. 3:4; 1 Chr. 16:39; 21:29; 2 Chr. 1:2,3,13. Smitten by David, 1 Chr. 14:16. Seven sons of Saul slain at, to avenge the inhabitants of, 2 Sam. 21:1-9. Solomon worships at, and offers sacrifices, 1 Kin. 3:4 ; God appears to him in dreams, 1 Kin. 3:5; 9:2. Abner slays Asahel at, 2 Sam. 3:30. Ishmael, the son of Nethaniah, defeated at, by Johanan, Jer. 41:11-16.

2. Pool of, 2 Sam. 2:13; Jer. 41:12.

GIDDALTI, a son of Heman, 1 Chr. 25:4,29.

GIDDEL. 1. One of the Nethinim, Ezra 2:47; Neh. 7:49.

2. One of Solomon's servants, Ezra 2:56; Neh. 7:58.

GIDEON. Call of, by an angel, Judg. 6:11,14. His excuses, Judg. 6:15. Promises of the Lord to, Judg. 6:16. Angel attests the call to, by miracle, Judg. 6:21-24. He destroys the altar of Baal, and builds one to the Lord, Judg. 6:25-27. His prayer tests, Judg. 6:36-40. Leads an army against, and defeats the Midianites, Judg. 6:33-35; 7; 8:4-12. Ephraimites chide, for not inviting them to join in the campaign against the Midianites, Judg. 8:1-3. Avenges himself upon the people of Succoth, Judg. 8:14-17. Israel desires to make him king, he refuses, Judg. 8:22,23. Makes an ephod which becomes a snare to the Israelites, Judg. 8:24-27. Had seventy sons, Judg. 8:30. Death of, Judg. 8:32. Faith of, Heb. 11:32.

GIDEONI, father of Abidan, Num. 1:11; 2:22; 7:60,65; 10:24.

GIDOM, limit of pursuit after battle of Gibeah, Judg. 20:45.

GIFTS FROM GOD. SPIRITUAL : Christ, the Saviour, Isa. 42:6; 55:4; John 3:16; 4:10; 6:32,33. The Holy Spirit, the Comforter, see HOLY SPIRIT. Grace, Jas. 4:6. Wisdom, Prov. 2:6; Jas. 1:5. Repentance, Acts 11:18. Faith, Eph. 2:8; Phil. 1:29.

TEMPORAL : Food and raiment, Matt. 6:25,33. Ra n and fruitful seasons, Gen. 8:22; 27:28; Lev. 26:4,5; Isa. 30:23. Wisdom, 2 Chr. 1:12. Peace, Lev. 26:6; 1 Chr. 22:9.

To be used and enjoyed, Eccl. 3:13; 5:19,20; 1 Tim. 4:4,5. Should cause us to remember God, Deut. 8:18. All creatures partake of, Psa. 136:25; 145:15,16. Prayer for, Zech. 10:1; Matt. 6:11.

UNCLASSIFIED SCRIPTURES RELATING TO BOTH TEMPORAL AND SPIRITUAL: Psa. 4:7. Thou hast put gladness in my heart, more than in the time that their corn and their wine increased.

Psa. 21:2. Thou hast given him his heart's desire, and hast not withholden the request of his lips.

Psa. 34:10. The young lions do lack, and suffer hunger : but they that seek the LORD shall not want any good thing

Psa. 68:18. Thou hast ascended on high,

thou hast led captivity captive : thou hast received gifts for men ; 35. The God of Israel is he that giveth strength and power unto his people. Blessed be God. Psa. 29:11.

Psa. 84:11. For the LORD God is a sun and shield : the LORD will give grace and glory : no good thing will he withhold from them that walk uprightly.

Eccl. 2:26. For God giveth to a man that is good in his sight wisdom, and knowledge, and joy : but to the sinner he giveth travail, to gather and to heap up, that he may give to him that i good before God. This also is vanity and vexation of spirit.

Isa. 42:5. Thus saith God the LORD, he that created the heavens, and stretched them out ; he that spread forth the earth. and that which cometh out of it; he that giveth breath unto the people upon it, and spirit to them that walk therein :

Ezek. 11:19. And I will give them one heart, and I will put a new spirit within you ; and I will take the stony heart out of their flesh, and will give them an heart of flesh :

Dan. 2:21. He giveth wisdom unto the wise, and knowledge to them that know understanding : 22. He revealeth the deep and secret things : he knoweth what is in the darkness, and the light dwelleth with him. 23. I thank thee, and praise thee, O thou God of my fathers, who hast given me wisdom and might, and hast made known unto me now what we desired of thee : for thou hast now made known unto us the king's matter.

Matt. 11:28. Come unto me, all ye that labour and are heavy laden, and I will give you rest.

Matt. 25:14. For the kingdom of heaven is as a man travelling into a far country, who called his own servants, and delivered unto them his goods. 15. And unto one he gave five talents, to another two, and to another one ; to every man according to his several ability; and straightway took his journey. vs. 14-30.

John 6:27. Labour not for the meat which perisheth, but for that meat which endureth unto everlasting life, which the Son of man shall give unto you : for him hath God the Father sealed.

John 16:23. And in that day ye shall ask me nothing. Verily, verily, I say unto you, Whatsoever ye shall ask the Father in my name, he will give it you. 24. Hitherto have ye asked nothing in my name : ask, and ye shall receive, that your joy may be full.

John 17:22. And the glory which thou gavest me I have given them ;

Rom. 5:16. And not as it was by one that sinned, so is the gift : for the judgment was by one to condemnation, but the free gift is of many offences unto justification. 17. For if by one man's offence death reigned by one ; much more they which receive abundance of grace and of the gift of righteousness shall reign in life by one, Jesus Christ. 18. Therefore as by the offence of one *judgment came* upon all men to condemnation; even so by the righteousness of one *the free gift came* upon all men unto justification of life.

Rom. 6:23. For the wages of sin *is* death; but the gift of God *is* eternal life through Jesus Christ our Lord.

Rom. 8:32. He that spared not his own Son, but delivered him up for us all, how shall he not with him also freely give us all things?

Rom. 11:29. For the gifts and calling of God *are* without repentance.

Rom. 12:6. Having then gifts differing according to the grace that is given to us, whether prophecy, *let us prophesy* according to the proportion of faith; 7. Or ministry, *let us wait* on *our* ministering: or he that teacheth, on teaching; 8. Or he that exhorteth, on exhortation: he that giveth, *let him do it* with simplicity; he that ruleth, with diligence; he that sheweth mercy, with cheerfulness.

1 Cor. 1:5. That in every thing ye are enriched by him, in all utterance, and *in* all knowledge; 6. Even as the testimony of Christ was confirmed in you: 7. So that ye come behind in no gift;

1 Cor. 7:7. But every man hath his proper gift of God, one after this manner, and another after that.

1 Cor. 12:4. Now there are diversities of gifts, but the same Spirit. 5. And there are differences of administrations, but the same Lord. 6. And there are diversities of operations, but it is the same God which worketh all in all. 7. But the manifestation of the Spirit is given to every man to profit withal. 8. For to one is given by the Spirit the word of wisdom; to another the word of knowledge by the same Spirit; 9. To another faith by the same Spirit; to another the gifts of healing by the same Spirit; 10. To another the working of miracles; to another prophecy; to another discerning of spirits; to another *divers* kinds of tongues; to another the interpretation of tongues: 11. But all these worketh that one and the selfsame Spirit, dividing to every man severally as he will.

1 Cor. 13:2. And though I have *the gift of* prophecy, and understand all mysteries, and all knowledge; and though I have all faith, so that I could remove mountains, and have not charity, I am nothing.

Eph. 4:7. But unto every one of us is given grace according to the measure of the gift of Christ. 8. Wherefore he saith, When he ascended up on high, he led captivity captive, and gave gifts unto men.

1 Tim. 6:17. Charge them that are rich in this world, that they be not highminded, nor trust in uncertain riches, but in the living God, who giveth us richly all things to enjoy;

Jas. 1:17. Every good gift and every perfect gift is from above, and cometh down from the Father of lights, with whom is no variableness, neither shadow of turning.

1 Pet. 4:10. As every man hath received

the gift, *even so* minister the same one to another, as good stewards of the manifold grace of God.

2 Pet. 1:3. According as his divine power hath given unto us all things that *pertain* unto life and godliness.

See BLESSINGS FROM GOD.

GIHON. 1. A river in Egypt, Gen. 2:13. 2. Pools near Jerusalem, 1 Kin. 1:33,38,45. Hezekiah brings the waters of the upper pool by an aqueduct into the city of Jerusalem, 2 Chr. 32:4,30; 33:14; Neh. 2:13-15; 3:13-16; Isa. 7:3; 22:9-11; 36:2.

GILALAI, a priest and musician, Neh. 12:36.

GILBOA, a hill S. of Jezreel, where Saul was defeated by the Philistines, and died, 1 Sam. 28:4; 31:1-8; 1 Chr. 10:1-8.

GILEAD. 1. A region E. of the Jordan allotted to the tribes of Reuben and Gad and half tribe of Manasseh, Num. 32:1-30; Deut. 3:13; 34:1; 2 Kin. 10:33. Reubenites expel the Hagarites from, 1 Chr. 5:9,10,18-22. Ammonites make war against; defeated by Jephthah, Judg. 11; Amos 1:13. The prophet Elijah a native of, 1 Kin. 17:1. David retreats to, at the time of Absalom's rebellion, 2 Sam. 17:16,22,24. Pursued into, by Absalom, 2 Sam. 17:26. Absalom defeated and slain in the forests of, 2 Sam. 18:9.

Hazael, king of Syria, smites the land of, 2 Kin. 10:32,33; Amos 1:3. Invaded by Tiglath-pileser, king of Syria, 2 Kin. 15:29. A grazing country, Num. 32:1; 1 Chr. 5:9. Exported spices, balm, and myrrh, Gen. 37:25; Jer. 8:22; 46:11.

FIGURATIVE: Of prosperity, Jer. 22:6; 50:19.

2. A mountain, Judg. 7:3; Song 4:1; 6:5. Laban overtakes Jacob at, Gen. 31:21-25.

3. A city, Hos. 6:8; 12:11.

4. Grandson of Manasseh, Num. 26:29,30; 27:1; 36:1; Josh. 17:1,3; 1 Chr. 2:21,23; 7:14,17.

5. Father of Jephthah, Judg. 11:1,2.

6. A chief of Gad, 1 Chr. 5:14.

GILGAL. 1. Place of the first encampment of the Israelites W. of the Jordan, Josh. 4:19; 9:6; 10:6,43; 14:6. Monument erected in, to commemorate the passage of the Jordan by the children of Israel, Josh. 4:19-24. Circumcision renewed at, Josh. 5:2-9. Passover kept at, Josh. 5:10,11. Manna ceased at, after the passover, Josh. 5:12. Quarries at, Judg. 3:19. Eglon, king of Moab, resides and is slain at, Judg. 3:14-26. A judgment seat, where Israel, in that district, came to be judged by Samuel, 1 Sam. 7:16. Saul proclaimed king over all Israel at, 1 Sam. 11:15. An altar built at, and sacrifice offered, 1 Sam. 11:15; 13:4-15; 15:6-23. Agag, king of the Amalekites, slain at, by Samuel, 1 Sam. 15:33. Tribe of Judah assembles at, to proceed to the E. side of the Jordan to conduct king David back after the defeat of Absalom, 2 Sam. 19:14,15,40-43. A school of the prophets at, 2 Kin. 4:38-40.

Prophecies concerning, Hos. 4:15; 9:15; 12:11; Amos 4:4; 5:5.

2. A royal city in Canaan. Conquered by Joshua, Josh. 12:23.

GILOH, a town in Judah, Josh. 15:51; 2 Sam. 15:12.

GIMZO, a city of Judah, 2 Chr. 28:18.

GIN, a snare, Amos 3:5.

See SNARE.

GINATH, father of Tibni, 1 Kin. 16: 21,22.

GINNETHON, called also GINNETHO, a companion of Nehemiah, Neh. 10:6; 12: 4,16.

GIRDLE. Worn by the high priest, Ex. 28:4,39; 39:29; Lev. 8:7; 16:4; other priests, Ex. 28:40; 29:9; Lev. 8:13; women, Isa. 3:24. Embroidered, Ex. 28:8, 27,28; 29:5; Lev. 8:7. Made of linen, Prov. 31:24; of leather, 2 Kin. 1:8; Matt. 3:4. Traffic in, Prov. 31:24. Used to bear arms, 1 Sam. 18:4; 2 Sam. 20:8; 2 Kin. 3:21.

FIGURATIVE: Isa. 11:5; 22:21; Eph. 6:14. SYMBOLICAL: Jer. 13:1–11; Acts 21:11; Rev. 15:6.

GIRGASHITES. Land of, given to Abraham and his descendants, Gen. 15:21; Deut. 7:1; Josh. 3:10; Neh. 9:8. Delivered to the children of Israel, Josh. 24:11.

GISPA, called also GISPHA, an overseer of the Nethinim, Neh. 11:21.

GITTAH-HEPHER, a prolonged form of GATH-HEPHER, which see. Josh. 19:13.

GITTAIM, a place of which little is known, 2 Sam. 4:3; Neh. 11:33.

GITTITE. See GATH.

GITTITH. See MUSIC.

GIVING. RULES FOR: Matt. 6:1. Take heed that ye do not your alms before men, to be seen of them: otherwise ye have no reward of your Father which is in heaven. 2. Therefore when thou doest *thine* alms, do not sound a trumpet before thee, as the hypocrites do in the synagogues and in the streets, that they may have glory of men. Verily I say unto you, They have their reward. 3. But when thou doest alms, let not thy left hand know what thy right hand doeth: 4. That thine alms may be in secret: and thy Father which seeth in secret himself shall reward thee openly.

1 Cor. 16:2. Upon the first *day* of the week let every one of you lay by him in store, as [1] *God* hath prospered him, [1 R. V. he may prosper]

2 Cor. 8:11. Now therefore perform the doing *of it;* that as *there was* a readiness to will, so *there may be* a performance also out of that which ye have. 12. For if there be first a willing mind, *it is* accepted according to that a man hath, *and* not according to that he hath not. 14. But by an equality, *that* now at this time your abundance *may be a supply* for their want, that their abundance also may be *a supply* for your want: that there may be equality:

2 Cor. 9:6. But this *I say,* He which soweth sparingly shall reap also sparingly; and he which soweth bountifully shall reap also bountifully. 7. Every man according as he purposeth in his heart, *so let him give;* not grudgingly, or of necessity: for God loveth a cheerful giver.

See ALMS; BENEFICENCE; LIBERALITY.

GIZONITE, a man or town of Judah, 1 Chr. 11:34.

GLADIATOR, contend with wild beasts, 1 Cor. 15:32.

GLADNESS. See JOY.

GLASS. Job 28:17 [*R. V.*]. Symbolical: Rev. 21:18,21. Sea of, Rev. 15:2.

See MIRROR.

GLEANING. Laws concerning, Lev. 19:9,10; 23:22; Deut. 24:19,20.

See ORPHAN; STRANGER; WIDOW.

FIGURATIVE: Judg. 8:2; Isa. 17:6; Jer. 49:9; Mic. 7:1.

INSTANCES OF: Ruth in the field of Boaz, Ruth 2:2,3.

GLEDE, a carnivorous bird, Deut. 14:13.

GLORIFYING GOD. Commanded, 1 Chr. 16:28; Psa. 22:23; Isa. 42:12. Due to him, 1 Chr. 16:29; for his holiness, Psa. 99:9; Rev. 15:4; mercy and truth, Psa. 115:1; Rom. 15:9; faithfulness and truth, Isa. 25:1; wondrous works, Matt; 15:31; Acts 4:21; judgments, Isa. 25:3; Ezek. 28:22; Rev. 14:7; deliverances, Psa. 50:15; grace to others, Acts 11:18; 2 Cor. 9:13; Gal. 1:24.

Accomplished by: Relying on his promises, Rom. 4:20; praising him, Psa. 50:23; doing all to glorify him, 1 Cor. 10:31; dying for him, John 21:19; suffering for Christ, 1 Pet. 4:14,16; glorifying Christ, Acts 19:17; 2 Thess. 1:12; bringing forth fruits of righteousness, John 15:8; Phil. 1:11; patience in affliction, Isa. 24:15; faithfulness, 1 Pet. 4: 11. Required in body and spirit, 1 Cor. 6: 20. Shall be universal, Psa. 86:9; Rev. 5:13.

Saints: Should resolve on, Psa. 69:30; 118:28; unite in, Psa. 34:3; Rom. 15:6; persevere in, Psa. 86:12. All the blessings of God are designed to lead to, Isa. 60:21; 61:3. The holy example of the saints may lead others to, Matt. 5:16; 1 Pet. 2:12.

All, by nature, fail in, Rom. 3:23. The wicked averse to, Dan. 5:23; Rom. 1:21. Punishment for not, Dan. 5:23,30; Mal. 2:2; Acts 12:23; Rom. 1:21. Heavenly hosts engaged in, Rev. 4:11.

EXEMPLIFIED: By David, Psa. 57:5; the multitude, Matt. 9:8; 15:31; the virgin Mary, Luke 1:46; the angels, Luke 2:14; the shepherds, Luke 2:20; by Jesus, John 17:4; the man sick of the palsy, Luke 5:25; the woman with infirmity, Luke 13:13; the leper whom Jesus healed, Luke 17:15; the blind man, Luke 18:43; the centurion, Luke 23:47; the church at Jerusalem, Acts 11:18; the Gentiles at Antioch, Acts 13:48; Abraham, Rom. 4:20; Paul, Rom. 11:36.

GLORY. God is, to his people, Psa. 3:3; Zech. 2:5. Christ is, to his people, Isa. 60:1; Luke 2:32. The gospel ordained to be, to saints, 1 Cor. 2:7. Of the gospel exceeds that of the law, 2 Cor. 3:9,10. The joy of saints is full of, 1 Pet. 1:8.

SPIRITUAL: Is given by God, Psa. 84:11; is given by Christ, John 17:22; is the work of the Holy Ghost, 2 Cor. 3:18.

ETERNAL: Procured by the death of Christ, Heb. 2:10; accompanies salvation by Christ, 2 Tim. 2:10; inherited by saints, 1 Sam. 2:8; Psa. 73:24; Prov. 3:35; Col. 3:4; 1 Pet. 5:10; saints called to, 2 Thess. 2:14; 1 Pet. 5:10; saints prepared unto, Rom. 9:23; enhanced by afflictions, 2 Cor. 4:17; present afflictions not worthy to be compared with, Rom. 8:18; of the church shall be rich and abundant, Isa. 60:11–13; the bodies of saints shall be raised in, 1 Cor. 15:43; Phil. 3:21; saints shall be, of their ministers, 1 Thess. 2:19,20; afflictions of ministers are, to saints, Eph. 3:13.

TEMPORAL: Is given by God, Dan. 2:37; passeth away, 1 Pet. 1:24. The devil tries to seduce by, Matt. 4:8. Of hypocrites turned to shame, Hos. 4:7. Seek not, from man, Matt. 6:2; 1 Thess. 2:6. Of the wicked is in their shame, Phil. 3:19. Ends in destruction, Isa. 5:14.

OF GOD: Exhibited in Christ, John 1:14; 2 Cor. 4:6; Heb. 1:3. Ascribed to God, Gal. 1:5.

Exhibited in his name, Deut. 28:58; Neh. 9:5; his majesty, Job 37:22; Psa. 93:1; 104:1; 145:5,12; Isa. 2:10; his power, Ex. 15:1,6; Rom. 6:4; his works, Psa. 19:1; 111:3; his holiness, Ex. 15:11.

Described as great, Psa. 138:5; eternal, Psa. 104:31; rich, Eph. 3:16; highly exalted, Psa. 8:1; 113:4.

Exhibited to Moses, Ex. 34:5-7; with Ex. 33:18-23; Stephen, Acts 7:55; his church, Deut. 5:24; Psa. 102:16.

Enlightens the church, Isa. 60:1,2; Rev. 21:11,23. Saints desire to behold, Psa. 63:2; 90:16. God is jealous of, Isa. 42:8. The earth is full of, Isa. 6:3. The knowledge of, shall fill the earth, Hab. 2:14.—*Bible Text-Book.*

GLUTTONY. Ex. 16:20. Notwithstanding they hearkened not unto Moses; but some of them left of it until the morning, and it bred worms, and stank: and Moses was wroth with them. 21. And they gathered it every morning, every man according to his eating: and when the sun waxed hot, it melted. 27. And it came to pass, *that* there went out *some* of the people on the seventh day for to gather, and they found none.

Num. 11:32. And the people stood up all that day, and all *that* night, and all the next day, and they gathered the quails: he that gathered least gathered ten homers: and they spread *them* all abroad for themselves round about the camp. 33. And while the flesh *was* yet between their teeth, ere it was chewed, the wrath of the LORD was kindled against the people, and the LORD smote the people with a very great plague.

Deut. 21:20. And they shall say unto the elders of his city, This our son *is* stubborn and rebellious, he will not obey our voice; *he is* a glutton, and a drunkard. 21. And all the men of his city shall stone him with stones, that he die: so shalt thou put evil away from among you; and all Israel shall hear, and fear.

Prov. 23:21. For the drunkard and the glutton shall come to poverty: and drowsiness shall clothe *a man* with rags.

Prov. 30:21. For three *things* the earth is disquieted, and for four *which* it cannot bear: 22. For a servant when he reigneth; and a fool when he is filled with meat;

Eccl. 10:17. Blessed *art* thou, O land, when thy king *is* the son of nobles, and thy princes eat in due season, for strength, and not for drunkenness!

Isa. 22:13. And behold joy and gladness, slaying oxen, and killing sheep, eating flesh, and drinking wine: let us eat and drink; for to morrow we shall die.

Amos 6:4. That lie upon beds of ivory, and stretch themselves upon their couches, and eat the lambs out of the flock, and the calves out of the midst of the stall; 5. That chant to the sound of the viol, *and* invent to themselves instruments of musick, like David; 6. That drink wine in bowls, and anoint themselves with the chief ointments: but they are not grieved for the affliction of Joseph. 7. Therefore now shall they go captive with the first that go captive, and the banquet of them that stretched themselves shall be removed.

Luke 12:19. And I will say to my soul, Soul, thou hast much goods laid up for many years; take thine ease, eat, drink, *and* be merry. 20. But God said unto him, *Thou* fool, this night thy soul shall be required of thee: then whose shall those things be, which thou hast provided? 45. But and if that servant say in his heart, My lord delayeth his coming; and shall begin to beat the menservants and maidens, and to eat and drink, and to be drunken; 46. The lord of that servant will come in a day when he looketh not for *him,* and at an hour when he is not aware, and will cut him in sunder, and will appoint him his portion with the unbelievers.

Luke 21:34. And take heed to yourselves, lest at any time your hearts be overcharged with surfeiting, and drunkenness, and cares of this life, and *so* that day come upon you unawares.

Rom. 13:13. Let us walk honestly, as in the day; not in rioting and drunkenness, not in chambering and wantonness, not in strife and envying. 14. But put ye on the Lord Jesus Christ, and make not provision for the flesh, to *fulfil* the lusts *thereof.*

1 Cor. 15:32. If after the manner of men I have fought with beasts at Ephesus, what advantageth it me, if the dead rise not? let us eat and drink; for to morrow we die.

Phil. 3:19. Whose end *is* destruction, whose God *is their* belly, and *whose* glory *is* in their shame, who mind earthly things.

1 Pet. 4:3. For the time past of *our* life may suffice us to have wrought the will of the Gentiles, when we walked in lascivious-

ness, lusts, excess of wine, revellings, banquetings, and abominable idolatries:

Jude 12. These are spots in your feasts of charity, when they feast with you, feeding themselves without fear:

INSTANCES OF: Esau, Gen. 25:30–34, with Heb. 12:16,17. Israel, Num. 11:4, with Psa. 78:18. Sons of Eli, 1 Sam. 2:12–17. Belshazzar, Dan. 5:1.

GNASHING OF TEETH. Job. 16:9; Psa. 35:16; 37:12; 112:10; Lam. 2:16; Matt. 8:12; 13:42; 22:13; 24:51; 25:30; Luke 13:28. See TEETH.

GOAD, an instrument of torture. 1 Sam. 13:21. Six hundred men slain with, by Shamgar, a judge of Israel, Judg. 3:31.

FIGURATIVE: Of mental incentive, Eccl. 12:11.

GOAT. Designated as one of the clean animals to be eaten, Deut. 14:4, with Lev. 11:1–8. Used for food, Gen. 27:9; 1 Sam. 16:20; for the paschal feast, Ex. 12:5; 2 Chr. 35:7; as a sacrifice by Abraham, Gen. 15:9; by Gideon, Judg. 6:19; Manoah, Judg. 13:19. Milk of, used for food, Prov. 27:27. Hair of, used for clothing, Num. 31:20; pillows, 1 Sam. 19:13; curtains of the tabernacle, Ex. 26:7; 35:23; 36:14. Used for tents, see TABERNACLES. Regulations of Mosaic law required that a kid should not be killed for food before it was eight days old, Lev. 22:27, nor seethed in its mother's milk, Ex. 23:19. Numerous, Deut. 32:14; Song 4:1; 6:5; 1 Sam. 25:2; 2 Chr. 17:11. Wild, in Palestine, 1 Sam. 24:2; Psa. 104:18.

GOATH, a place near Jerusalem, Jer. 31:39.

GOB, also called GEZER, which see.

GOBLET. See CUP.

GOD. INDEX OF SUB-TOPICS: *Miscellany; Unclassified Scriptures Relating to, p. 427; Access to, p. 433; Compassion of, p. 434; Creator, p. 434; Creator of Man, p. 438; Eternity of, p. 439; Faithfulness of, p. 440; Fatherhood of, p. 443; Favor of, p. 448; Foreknowledge of, p. 448; Glory of, p. 448; Goodness of, p. 451; Grace of, p. 452; Guide, p. 455; Holiness of, p. 456; Human Forms and Appearance of, p. 457; Immutable, p. 457; Impartial, p. 458; Incomprehensible, p. 458; Infinite, p. 459; Invisible, p. 459; Jealous, p. 460; Judge, and His Justice, p. 460; Knowledge of, p. 465; Long-suffering, p. 467; Long-suffering of, Abused, p. 469; Love of, p. 469; Love of, Exemplified, p. 470; Mercy of, p. 474; Omnipotent, p. 480; Omnipresent, p. 480; Omniscient, p. 481; Perfection of, p. 481; Personality of, p. 481; Power of, p. 482; Presence of, p. 486; Preserver, p. 486; Providence of, p. 493; Providence of, Overruling Interpositions of the. p. 502; Providence of, Mysterious and Misinterpreted, p. 504; Righteousness of, p. 505; Saviour, p. 506; Self-existent, p. 509; Sovereign, p. 509; A Spirit, 512; Truth, p. 512; Ubiquitous, p. 513; Unchangeable, p. 513; Unity of, p. 513; Unsearchable, p. 514; Voice of, p. 514; Wisdom of, p. 514; Works of, p. 515.*

Appearances of: To Adam, Gen. 3:8–21; Abraham, Gen. 18:2–33; Jacob, at Beth-el, Gen. 35:7,9; Moses, in the flaming bush, Ex. 3:2; at Sinai, Ex. 19:16–24; 24:10; Moses and Joshua, Deut. 31:14,15; Israel, Judg. 2:1–5; Gideon, Judg. 6:11–24; Solomon, 1 Kin. 3:5; 9:2; 11:9; 2 Chr. 1:7–12; 7:12–22; Isaiah, Isa. 6:1–5; Ezekiel, Ezek. 1:26–28.

Name of: Proclaimed, Ex. 34:5,14; see Ex. 6:3; 15:3; Psa. 83:18; to be reverenced, Ex. 20:7; Deut. 5:11; 28:58; Psa. 111:9; Mic. 4:5; 1 Tim. 6:1; praised, Psa. 34:3; 72:17; not to be profaned, Ex. 20:7; Lev. 18:21; 19:12; 20:3; 21:6; 22:2,32; Deut. 5:11; Psa. 139:20; Prov. 30:9; Isa. 52:5; Rom. 2:24; Rev. 16:9; profaned, Psa. 139:20; Matt. 26:74. See BLASPHEMY; PERJURY.

Repentance attributed to: Gen. 6:6,7; Ex. 32:14; Judg. 2:18; 1 Sam. 15:35; 2 Sam. 24:16; 1 Chr. 21:15; Psa. 106:45; Jer. 26:19; Amos 7:3; Jonah 3:10. For other anthropomorphic scriptures, see ANTHROPOMORPHISMS.

Rejected: By Israel, 1 Sam. 8:7,8; Isa. 65:12; 66:4; Saul, 1 Sam. 15:26. See JESUS, REJECTED.

Comforter, Job 35:10. See AFFLICTION, CONSOLATION IN; HOLY SPIRIT. Covenant keeping. See COVENANT.

Anger of: See ANGER OF GOD. Attributes of. See each in alphabetical order below. Condescension of. See CONDESCENSION.

UNCLASSIFIED SCRIPTURES RELATING TO: Job 5:8. I would seek unto God, and unto God would I commit my cause: 9. Which doeth great things and unsearchable; marvellous things without number: 10. Who giveth rain upon the earth, and sendeth waters upon the fields: 11. To set up on high those that be low; that those which mourn may be exalted to safety. 12. He disappointeth the devices of the crafty, so that their hands cannot perform *their* enterprise. 13. He taketh the wise in their own craftiness: and the counsel of the froward is carried headlong. 14. They meet with darkness in the daytime, and grope in the noonday as in the night. 15. But he saveth the poor from the sword, from their mouth, and from the hand of the mighty. 16. So the poor hath hope, and iniquity stoppeth her mouth. 17. Behold, happy *is* the man whom God correcteth: therefore despise not thou the chastening of the Almighty: 18. For he maketh sore, and bindeth up: he woundeth, and his hands make whole. 19. He shall deliver thee in six troubles: yea, in seven there shall no evil touch thee. 20. In famine he shall redeem thee from death: and in war from the power of the sword.

Job 9:2. How should man be just with God? 3. If he will contend with him, he cannot answer him one of a thousand. 4. *He is* wise in heart, and mighty in strength: who hath hardened *himself* against him, and hath prospered? 5. Which removeth the mountains, and they know not: which overturneth them in his anger. 6. Which shaketh the earth out of her place, and the pillars thereof tremble. 7. Which commandeth the sun, and it riseth not; and sealeth up the stars. 8. Which alone spreadeth out the heavens, and treadeth upon the waves of the sea. 9. Which maketh Arcturus, Orion, and Pleiades, and the chambers of the south. 10. Which doeth great things past finding out; yea, and wonders without number. 11. Lo, he goeth by me, and I see *him* not: he passeth on also, but I perceive him not. 12. Behold, he taketh away, who can hinder him? who will say unto him, What doest thou? 13. *If* God will not withdraw his anger, the proud helpers do stoop under him. 14. How much less shall I answer him, *and* choose out my words *to reason* with him? 15. Whom, though I were righteous, *yet* would I not answer, *but* I would make supplication to my judge. 16. If I had called, and he had answered me; *yet* would I not believe that he had hearkened unto my voice. 17. For he breaketh me with a tempest, and multiplieth my wounds without cause. 18. He will not suffer me to take my breath, but filleth me with bitterness. 19. If *I speak* of strength, lo, *he is* strong: and if of judgment, who shall set me a time *to plead?* 20. If I justify myself, mine own mouth shall condemn me: *if I say*, I *am* perfect, it shall also prove me perverse. 21. *Though* I *were* perfect, *yet* would I not know my soul: I would despise my life. 22. This *is* one *thing*, therefore I said *it*, He destroyeth the perfect and the wicked. 23. If the scourge slay suddenly, he will laugh at the trial of the innocent. 24. The earth is given into the hand of the wicked: he covereth the faces of the judges thereof; if not, where, *and* who *is* he? 25. Now my days are swifter than a post: they flee away, they see no good. 26. They are passed away as the swift ships: as the eagle *that* hasteth to the prey. 27. If I say, I will forget my complaint, I will leave off my heaviness, and comfort *myself:* 28. I am afraid of all my sorrows, I know that thou wilt not hold me innocent. 29. *If* I be wicked, why then labour I in vain? 30. If I wash myself with snow water, and make my hands never so clean; 31. Yet shalt thou plunge me in the ditch, and mine own clothes shall abhor me. 32. For *he is* not a man, as I *am, that* I should answer him, *and* we should come together in judgment. 33. Neither is there any daysman betwixt us, *that* might lay his hand upon us both. 34. Let him take his rod away from me, and let not his fear terrify me: 35. *Then* would I speak, and not fear him; but *it is* not so with me.

Job 10:2. I will say unto God, Do not condemn me; shew me wherefore thou contendest with me. 3. *Is it* good unto thee that thou shouldest oppress, that thou shouldest depise the work of thine hands, and shine upon the counsel of the wicked? 4. Hast thou eyes of flesh? or seest thou as man seeth? 5. *Are* thy days as the days of man? *are* thy years as man's days, 6. That thou enquirest after mine iniquity, and searchest after my sin?

7. Thou knowest that I am not wicked; and *there is* none that can deliver out of thine hand. 8. Thine hands have made me and fashioned me together round about; yet thou dost destroy me. 9. Remember, I beseech thee, that thou hast made me as the clay; and wilt thou bring me into dust again? 10. Hast thou not poured me out as milk, and curdled me like cheese? 11. Thou hast clothed me with skin and flesh, and hast fenced me with bones and sinews. 12. Thou hast granted me life and favour, and thy visitation hath preserved my spirit. 13. And these *things* hast thou hid in thine heart: I know that this *is* with thee. 14. If I sin, then thou markest me, and thou wilt not acquit me from mine iniquity. 15. If I be wicked, woe unto me; and *if* I be righteous, *yet* will I not lift up my head. *I am* full of confusion; therefore see thou mine affliction; 16. For it increaseth. Thou huntest me as a fierce lion: and again thou shewest thyself marvellous upon me. 17. Thou renewest thy witnesses against me, and increasest thine indignation upon me; changes and war *are* against me. 18. Wherefore then hast thou brought me forth out of the womb? Oh that I had given up the ghost, and no eye had seen me!

Job 12:7. But ask now the beasts, and they shall teach thee; and the fowls of the air, and they shall tell thee: 8. Or speak to the earth, and it shall teach thee: and the fishes of the sea shall declare unto thee. 9. Who knoweth not in all these that the hand of the Lord hath wrought this? 10. In whose hand *is* the soul of every living thing, and the breath of all mankind. 11. Doth not the ear try words? and the mouth taste his meat? 12. With the ancient *is* wisdom; and in length of days understanding. 13. With him *is* wisdom and strength, he hath counsel and understanding. 14. Behold, he breaketh down, and it cannot be built again: he shutteth up a man, and there can be no opening. 15. Behold, he withholdeth the waters, and they dry up: also he sendeth them out, and they overturn the earth. 16. With him *is* strength and wisdom: the deceived and the deceiver *are* his. 17. He leadeth counsellors away spoiled, and maketh the judges fools. 18. He looseth the bond of kings, and girdeth their loins with a girdle. 19. He leadeth princes away spoiled, and overthroweth the mighty. 20. He removeth away the speech of the trusty, and taketh away the understanding of the aged.

Job 26:7. He stretcheth out the north over the empty place, *and* hangeth the earth upon nothing. 8. He bindeth up the waters in his thick clouds; and the cloud is not rent under them. 9. He holdeth back the face of his throne, *and* spreadeth his cloud upon it. 10. He hath compassed the waters with bounds, until the day and night come to an end. 11. The pillars of heaven tremble and are astonished at his reproof. 12. He divideth the sea with his power, and by his understanding he smiteth through the proud. 13. By his spirit he hath garnished the heavens; his hand hath formed the crooked serpent. 14. Lo, these *are* parts of his ways: but how little a portion is heard of him? but the thunder of his power who can understand?

Job 33:12. Behold, *in* this thou art not just: I will answer thee, that God is greater than man. 13. Why dost thou strive against him? for he giveth not account of any of his matters. 14. For God speaketh once, yea twice, *yet man* perceiveth it not. 15. In a dream, in a vision of the night, when deep sleep falleth upon men, in slumberings upon the bed; 16. Then he openeth the ears of men, and sealeth their instruction, 17. That he may withdraw man *from his* purpose, and hide pride from man. 18. He keepeth back his soul from the pit, and his life from perishing by the sword. 19. He is chastened also with pain upon his bed, and the multitude of his bones with strong *pain:* 20. So that his life abhorreth bread, and his soul dainty meat. 21. His flesh is consumed away, that it cannot be seen; and his bones *that* were not seen stick out. 22. Yea, his soul draweth near unto the grave, and his life to the destroyers. 23. If there be a messenger with him, an interpreter, one among a thousand, to shew unto man his uprightness: 24. Then he is gracious unto him, and saith, Deliver him from going down to the pit: I have found a ransom. 25. His flesh shall be fresher than a child's: he shall return to the days of his youth: 26. He shall pray unto God, and he will be favourable unto him: and he shall see his face with joy: for he will render unto man his righteousness. 27. He looketh upon men, and *if any* say, I have sinned, and perverted *that which was* right, and it profited me not; 28. He will deliver his soul from going into the pit, and his life shall see the light. 29. Lo, all these *things* worketh God oftentimes with man, 30. To bring back his soul from the pit, to be enlightened with the light of the living.

Job 34:10. Therefore hearken unto me, ye men of understanding: far be it from God, *that he should do* wickedness; and *from* the Almighty, *that he should commit* iniquity. 11. For the work of a man shall he render unto him, and cause every man to find according to *his* ways. 12. Yea, surely God will not do wickedly, neither will the Almighty pervert judgment. 13. Who hath given him a charge over the earth? or who hath disposed the whole world? 14. If he set his heart upon man, *if* he gather unto himself his spirit and his breath; 15. All flesh shall perish together, and man shall turn again unto dust. 16. If now *thou hast* understanding, hear this: hearken to the voice of my words. 17. Shall even he that hateth right govern? and wilt thou condemn him that is most just? 18. *Is it fit* to say to a king, *Thou art* wicked? *and* to princes, *Ye are* ungodly? 19. *How much less to him* that accepteth not the persons of princes, nor regardeth the rich more than the poor? for they all *are* the work

of his hands. 20. In a moment shall they die, and the people shall be troubled at midnight, and pass away: and the mighty shall be taken away without hand. 21. For his eyes *are* upon the ways of man, and he seeth all his goings. 22. *There is* no darkness, nor shadow of death, where the workers of iniquity may hide themselves. 23. For he will not lay upon man more *than right;* that he should enter into judgment with God. 24. He shall break in pieces mighty men without number, and set others in their stead. 25. Therefore he knoweth their works, and he overturneth *them* in the night, so that they are destroyed. 26. He striketh them as wicked men in the open sight of others; 27. Because they turned back from him, and would not consider any of his ways: 28. So that they cause the cry of the poor to come unto him, and he heareth the cry of the afflicted. 29. When he giveth quietness, who then can make trouble? and when he hideth *his* face who then can behold him? whether *it be done* against a nation, or against a man only: 30. That the hypocrite reign not, lest the people be ensnared.

Job 37:1. At this also my heart trembleth, and is moved out of his place. 2. Hear attentively the noise of his voice, and the sound *that* goeth out of his mouth. 3. He directeth it under the whole heaven, and his lightning unto the ends of the earth. 4. After it a voice roareth: he thundereth with the voice of his excellency; and he will not stay them when his voice is heard. 5. God thundereth marvellously with his voice; great things doeth he, which we cannot comprehend. 6. For he saith to the snow, Be thou *on* the earth; likewise to the small rain, and to the great rain of his strength. 7. He sealeth up the hand of every man; that all men may know his work. 8. Then the beasts go into dens, and remain in their places. 9. Out of the south cometh the whirlwind: and cold out of the north. 10. By the breath of God frost is given: and the breadth of the waters is straitened. 11. Also by watering he wearieth the thick cloud: he scattereth his bright cloud: 12. And it is turned round about by his counsels: that they may do whatsoever he commandeth them upon the face of the world in the earth. 13. He causeth it to come, whether for correction, or for his land, or for mercy. 14. Hearken unto this, O Job: stand still, and consider the wondrous works of God. 15. Dost thou know when God disposed them, and caused the light of his cloud to shine? 16. Dost thou know the balancings of the clouds, the wondrous works of him which is perfect in knowledge? 17. How thy garments *are* warm, when he quieteth the earth by the south *wind?* 18. Hast thou with him spread out the sky, *which is* strong, *and* as a molten looking glass? 19. Teach us what we shall say unto him; *for* we cannot order *our* speech by reason of darkness. 20. Shall it be told him that I speak? if a man speak, surely he shall be swallowed up. 21. And now *men* see not the bright light which *is* in the clouds: but the wind passeth, and cleanseth them. 22. Fair weather cometh out of the north: with God *is* terrible majesty. 23. *Touching* the Almighty, we cannot find him out: *he is* excellent in power, and in judgment, and in plenty of justice: he will not afflict. 24. Men do therefore fear him: he respecteth not any *that are* wise of heart.

Job 38:1. Then the Lord answered Job out of the whirlwind, and said, 2. Who *is* this that darkeneth counsel by words without knowledge? 3. Gird up now thy loins like a man; for I will demand of thee, and answer thou me. 4. Where wast thou when I laid the foundations of the earth? declare, if thou hast understanding. 5. Who hath laid the measures thereof, if thou knowest? or who hath stretched the line upon it? 6. Whereupon are the foundations thereof fastened? or who laid the corner stone thereof; 7. When the morning stars sang together, and all the sons of God shouted for joy? 8. Or *who* shut up the sea with doors, when it brake forth, *as if* it had issued out of the womb? 9. When I made the cloud the garment thereof, and thick darkness a swaddlingband for it, 10. And brake up for it my decreed *place*, and set bars and doors, 11. And said, Hitherto shalt thou come, but no further: and here shall thy proud waves be stayed? 12. Hast thou commanded the morning since thy days; *and* caused the dayspring to know his place; 13. That it might take hold of the ends of the earth, that the wicked might be shaken out of it? 14. It is turned as clay *to* the seal; and they stand as a garment. 15. And from the wicked their light is withholden, and the high arm shall be broken. 16. Hast thou entered into the springs of the sea? or hast thou walked in the search of the depth? 17. Have the gates of death been opened unto thee? or hast thou seen the doors of the shadow of death? 18. Hast thou perceived the breadth of the earth? declare if thou knowest it all. 19. Where *is* the way *where* light dwelleth? and *as for* darkness, where *is* the place thereof, 20. That thou shouldest take it to the bound thereof, and that thou shouldest know the paths *to* the house thereof? 21 Knowest thou *it*, because thou wast then born? or *because* the number of thy days *is* great? 22. Hast thou entered into the treasures of the snow? or hast thou seen the treasures of the hail, 23. Which I have reserved against the time of trouble, against the day of battle and war? 24. By what way is the light parted, *which* scattereth the east wind upon the earth? 25. Who hath divided a watercourse for the overflowing of waters, or a way for the lightning of thunder; 26. To cause it to rain on the earth, *where* no man *is; on* the wilderness, wherein *there is* no man; 27. To satisfy the desolate and waste *ground;* and to cause the bud of the tender herb to spring forth? 28. Hath the rain a father? or who hath begotten the drops of dew? 29. Out of whose womb came the ice? and the hoary frost of heaven, who hath gendered it? 30. The waters are hid as *with* a stone, and the face of the deep is frozen. 31. Canst thou bind the sweet influences of Pleiades, or loose the bands of Orion? 32. Canst thou bring forth Mazzaroth in his season? or canst thou guide Arcturus with his sons? 33. Knowest thou the ordinances of heaven? canst thou set the dominion thereof in the earth? 34. Canst thou lift up thy voice to the clouds, that abundance of waters may cover thee? 35. Canst thou send lightnings, that they may go, and say unto thee, Here we *are?* 36. Who hath put wisdom in the inward parts? or who hath given understanding to the heart? 37. Who can number the clouds in wisdom? or who can stay the bottles of heaven, 38. When the dust groweth into hardness, and the clods cleave fast together? 39. Wilt thou hunt the prey for the lion? or fill the appetite of the young lions, 40. When they couch in *their* dens, *and* abide in the covert to lie in wait? 41. Who provideth for the raven his food? when his young ones cry unto God, they wander for lack of meat.

Job 39:1. Knowest thou the time when the wild goats of the rock bring forth? *or* canst thou mark when the hinds do calve? 2. Canst thou number the months *that* they fulfil? or knowest thou the time when they bring forth? 3. They bow themselves, they bring forth their young ones, they cast out their sorrows. 4. Their young ones are in good liking, they grow up with corn; they go forth, and return not unto them. 5. Who hath sent out the wild ass free? or who hath loosed the bands of the wild ass? 6. Whose house I have made the wilderness, and the barren lands his dwellings. 7. He scorneth the multitude of the city, neither regardeth he the crying of the driver. 8. The range of the mountains *is* his pasture, and he searcheth after every green thing. 9. Will the unicorn be willing to serve thee, or abide by thy crib? 10. Canst thou bind the unicorn with his band in the furrow? or will he harrow the valleys after thee? 11. Wilt thou trust him, because his strength *is* great? or wilt thou leave thy labour to him? 12. Wilt thou believe him, that he will bring home thy seed, and gather *it into* thy barn? 13. *Gavest thou* the goodly wings unto the peacocks? or wings and feathers unto the ostrich? 14. Which leaveth her eggs in the earth, and warmeth them in dust, 15. And forgetteth that the foot may crush them, or that the wild beast may break them. 16. She is hardened against her young ones, as though *they were* not hers: her labour is in vain without fear; 17. Because God hath deprived her of wisdom, neither hath he imparted to her understanding. 18. What time she lifteth up herself on high, she scorneth the horse and his rider. 19. Hast thou given the horse strength? hast thou clothed his neck with thunder? 20. Canst thou make him afraid as a grasshopper? the glory of his nostrils *is* terrible. 21. He paweth in the valley, and rejoiceth in *his* strength: he goeth on to meet the armed men. 22. He mocketh at fear, and is not affrighted; neither turneth he back from the sword. 23. The quiver rattleth against him, the glittering spear and the shield. 24. He swalloweth the ground with fierceness and rage: neither believeth he that *it is* the sound of the trumpet. 25. He saith among the trumpets, Ha, ha; and he smelleth the battle afar off, the thunder of the captains, and the shouting. 26. Doth the hawk fly by thy wisdom, *and* stretch her wings toward the south? 27. Doth the eagle mount up at thy command, and make her nest on high? 28. She dwelleth and abideth on the rock, upon the crag of the rock, and the strong place. 29. From thence she seeketh the prey, *and* her eyes behold afar off. 30. Her young ones also suck up blood: and where the slain *are*, there *is* she.

Job 40:1. Moreover the LORD answered Job, and said, 2. Shall he that contendeth with the Almighty instruct *him?* he that reproveth God, let him answer it. 3. Then Job answered the LORD, and said, 4. Behold, I am vile; what shall I answer thee? I will lay mine hand upon my mouth. 5. Once have I spoken; but I will not answer: yea, twice; but I will proceed no further. 6. Then answered the LORD unto Job out of the whirlwind, and said, 7. Gird up thy loins now like a man: I will demand of thee, and declare thou unto me. 8. Wilt thou also disannul my judgment? wilt thou condemn me, that thou mayest be righteous? 9. Hast thou an arm like God? or canst thou thunder with a voice like him? 10. Deck thyself now *with* majesty and excellency; and array thyself with glory and beauty. 11. Cast abroad the rage of thy wrath: and behold every one *that is* proud, and abase him. 12. Look on every one *that is* proud, *and* bring him low; and tread down the wicked in their place. 13. Hide them in the dust together; *and* bind their faces in secret. 14. Then will I also confess unto thee that thine own right hand can save thee. 15. Behold now behemoth, which I made with thee; he eateth grass as an ox. 16. Lo now, his strength *is* in his loins, and his force *is* in the navel of his belly. 17. He moveth his tail like a cedar: the sinews of his stones are wrapped together. 18. His bones *are as* strong pieces of brass: his bones *are* like bars of iron. 19. He *is* the chief of the ways of God: he that made him can make his sword to approach *unto him.* 20. Surely the mountains bring him forth food, where all the beasts of the field play. 21. He lieth under the shady trees, in the covert of the reed, and fens. 22. The shady trees cover him *with* their shadow; the willows of the brook compass him about. 23. Behold, he drinketh up a river, *and* hasteth not: he trusteth that he

can draw up Jordan into his mouth. 24. He taketh it with his eyes: *his* nose pierceth through snares.

Job 41:1. Canst thou draw out leviathan with an hook? or his tongue with a cord *which* thou lettest down? 2. Canst thou put an hook into his nose? or bore his jaw through with a thorn? 3. Will he make many supplications unto thee? will he speak soft *words* unto thee? 4. Will he make a covenant with thee? wilt thou take him for a servant for ever? 5. Wilt thou play with him as *with* a bird? or wilt thou bind him for thy maidens? 6. Shall the companions make a banquet of him? shall they part him among the merchants? 7. Canst thou fill his skin with barbed irons? or his head with fish spears? 8. Lay thine hand upon him, remember the battle, do no more. 9. Behold, the hope of him is in vain: shall not *one* be cast down at the sight of him? 10. None *is so* fierce that dare stir him up: who then is able to stand before me? 11. Who hath prevented me, that I should repay *him? whatsoever is* under the whole heaven is mine. 12. I will not conceal his parts, nor his power, nor his comely proportion. 13. Who can discover the face of his garment? *or* who can come *to him* with his double bridle? 14. Who can open the doors of his face? his teeth *are* terrible round about. 15. *His* scales *are his* pride, shut up together *as with* a close seal. 16. One is so near to another, that no air can come between them. 17. They are joined one to another, they stick together, that they cannot be sundered. 18. By his neesings a light doth shine, and his eyes *are* like the eyelids of the morning. 19. Out of his mouth go burning lamps, *and* sparks of fire leap out. 20. Out of his nostrils goeth smoke. as *out* of a seething pot or caldron. 21. His breath kindleth coals, and a flame goeth out of his mouth. 22. In his neck remaineth strength, and sorrow is turned into joy before him. 23. The flakes of his flesh are joined together: they are firm in themselves; they cannot be moved. 24. His heart is as firm as a stone; yea, as hard as a piece of the nether *millstone.* 25. When he raiseth up himself, the mighty are afraid: by reason of breakings they purify themselves. 26. The sword of him that layeth at him cannot hold: the spear, the dart, nor the habergeon. 27. He esteemeth iron as straw, *and* brass as rotten wood. 28. The arrow cannot make him flee: slingstones are turned with him into stubble. 29. Darts are counted as stubble: he laugheth at the shaking of a spear. 30. Sharp stones *are* under him: he spreadeth sharp pointed things upon the mire. 31. He maketh the deep to boil like a pot: he maketh the sea like a pot of ointment. 32. He maketh a path to shine after him; *one* would think the deep *to be* hoary. 33. Upon earth there is not his like, who is made without fear. 34. He beholdeth all high *things:* he *is* a king over all the children of pride.

Job 42:1. Then Job answered the LORD, and

said, 2. I know that thou canst do every *thing*, and *that* no thought can be withholden from thee. 3. Who *is* he that hideth counsel without knowledge? therefore have I uttered that I understood not; things too wonderful for me, which I knew not. 4. Hear, I beseech thee, and I will speak: I will demand of thee, and declare thou unto me. 5. I have heard of thee by the hearing of the ear: but now mine eye seeth thee. 6. Wherefore I abhor *myself*, and repent in dust and ashes.

Psa. 8:3. When I consider thy heavens, the work of thy fingers, the moon and the stars, which thou hast ordained; 4. What is man, that thou art mindful of him? and the son of man, that thou visitest him? 5. For thou hast made him a little lower than the angels, and hast crowned him with glory and honour. 6. Thou madest him to have dominion over the works of thy hands; thou hast put all *things* under his feet:

Psa. 97:6. The heavens declare his righteousness, and all the people see his glory.

Psa. 104:1. Bless the LORD, O my soul. O LORD my God, thou art very great; thou art clothed with honour and majesty: 2. Who coverest *thyself* with light as *with* a garment: who stretchest out the heavens like a curtain: 3. Who layeth the beams of his chambers in the waters: who maketh the clouds his chariot: who walketh upon the wings of the wind: 4. Who maketh his angels spirits; his ministers a flaming fire: 5. *Who* laid the foundations of the earth, *that* it should not be removed for ever. 6. Thou coveredst it with the deep as *with* a garment: the waters stood above the mountains. 7. At thy rebuke they fled; at the voice of thy thunder they hasted away. 8. They go up by the mountains; they go down by the valleys unto the place which thou hast founded for them. 9. Thou hast set a bound that they may not pass over; that they turn not again to cover the earth. 10. He sendeth the springs into the valleys, *which* run among the hills. 11. They give drink to every beast of the field: the wild asses quench their thirst. 12. By them shall the fowls of the heaven have their habitation, *which* sing among the branches. 13. He watereth the hills from his chambers: the earth is satisfied with the fruit of thy works. 14. He causeth the grass to grow for the cattle, and herb for the service of man: that he may bring forth food out of the earth; 15. And wine *that* maketh glad the heart of man, *and* oil to make *his* face to shine, and bread *which* strengtheneth man's heart. 16. The trees of the LORD are full *of sap;* the cedars of Lebanon, which he hath planted; 17. Where the birds make their nests: *as for* the stork, the fir trees *are* her house. 18. The high hills *are* a refuge for the wild goats; *and* the rocks for the conies. 19. He appointed the moon for seasons: the sun knoweth his going down. 20. Thou makest darkness, and it is night:

wherein all the beasts of the forest do creep *forth*. 21. The young lions roar after their prey, and seek their meat from God. 22. The sun ariseth, they gather themselves together, and lay them down in their dens. 23. Man goeth forth unto his work and to his labour until the evening. 24. O LORD, how manifold are thy works! in wisdom hast thou made them all: the earth is full of thy riches. 25. *So is* this great and wide sea, wherein *are* things creeping innumerable, both small and great beasts. 26. There go the ships: *there is* that leviathan, *whom* thou hast made to play therein. 27. These wait all upon thee; that thou mayest give *them* their meat in due season. 28. *That* thou givest them they gather: thou openest thine hand, they are filled with good. 29. Thou hidest thy face, they are troubled: thou takest away their breath, they die, and return to their dust. 30. Thou sendest forth thy spirit, they are created: and thou renewest the face of the earth. 31. The glory of the LORD shall endure for ever: the LORD shall rejoice in his works. 32. He looketh on the earth, and it trembleth: he toucheth the hills, and they smoke.

Psa. 107:23. They that go down to the sea in ships, that do business in great waters; 24. These see the works of the LORD, and his wonders in the deep. 25. For he commandeth, and raiseth the stormy wind, which lifteth up the waves thereof. 26. They mount up to the heaven, they go down again to the depths: their soul is melted because of trouble.

Psa. 119:90. Thy faithfulness *is* unto all generations: thou hast established the earth, and it abideth. 91. They continue this day according to thine ordinances: for all *are* thy servants.

Psa. 135:6. Whatsoever the LORD pleased, *that* did he in heaven, and in earth, in the seas, and all deep places. 7. He causeth the vapours to ascend from the ends of the earth; he maketh lightnings for the rain; he bringeth the wind out of his treasuries.

Psa. 147:15. He sendeth forth his commandment *upon* earth: his word runneth very swiftly. 16. He giveth snow like wool: he scattereth the hoarfrost like ashes. 17. He casteth forth his ice like morsels: who can stand before his cold? 18. He sendeth out his word, and melteth them: he causeth his wind to blow, *and* the waters flow.

Psa. 148:3. Praise ye him, sun and moon: praise him, all ye stars of light. 4. Praise him, ye heavens of heavens, and ye waters that *be* above the heavens. 5. Let them praise the name of the LORD: for he commanded, and they were created. 6. He hath also stablished them for ever and ever: he hath made a decree which shall not pass.

Eccl. 3:14. I know that, whatsoever God doeth, it shall be for ever: nothing can be put to it, nor any thing taken from it: and God doeth *it*, that *men* should fear before him. 15. That which hath been is now; and that which is to be hath already been; and God requireth that which is past.

Isa. 2:19. And they shall go into the holes of the rocks, and into the caves of the earth, for fear of the LORD, and for the glory of his majesty, when he ariseth to shake terribly the earth.

Isa. 13:13. Therefore I will shake the heavens, and the earth shall remove out of her place, in the wrath of the LORD of hosts, and in the day of his fierce anger.

Isa. 29:6. Thou shalt be visited of the LORD of hosts with thunder, and with earthquake, and great noise, with storm and tempest, and the flame of devouring fire.

Isa. 48:13. Mine hand also hath laid the foundation of the earth, and my right hand hath spanned the heavens: *when* I call unto them, they stand up together.

Isa. 50:2. Wherefore, when I came, *was there* no man? when I called, *was there* none to answer? Is my hand shortened at all, that it cannot redeem? or have I no power to deliver? behold, at my rebuke I dry up the sea, I make the rivers a wilderness: their fish stinketh, because *there is* no water, and dieth for thirst. 3. I clothe the heavens with blackness, and I make sackcloth their covering.

Isa. 64:3. When thou didst terrible things *which* we looked not for, thou camest down, the mountains flowed down at thy presence.

Jer. 5:24. Neither say they in their heart, Let us now fear the LORD our God, that giveth rain, both the former and the latter, in his season: he reserveth unto us the appointed weeks of the harvest.

Jer. 10:2. Thus saith the LORD, Learn not the way of the heathen, and be not dismayed at the signs of heaven; for the heathen are dismayed at them. 13. When he uttereth his voice, *there is* a multitude of waters in the heavens, and he causeth the vapors to ascend from the ends of the earth; he maketh lightnings with rain, and bringeth forth the wind out of his treasures.

Jer. 31:35. Thus saith the LORD, which giveth the sun for a light by day, *and* the ordinances of the moon and of the stars for a light by night, which divideth the sea when the waves thereof roar; The LORD of hosts *is* his name: 36. If those ordinances depart from before me, saith the LORD. *then* the seed of Israel also shall cease from being a nation before me for ever. 37. Thus saith the LORD: If heaven above can be measured, and the foundations of the earth searched out beneath, I will also cast off all the seed of Israel for all that they have done, saith the LORD.

Jer. 33:20. Thus saith the LORD; If ye can break my covenant of the day, and my covenant of the night, and that there should not be day and night in their season; 21. *Then* may also my covenant be broken with David my servant, 25. Thus saith the LORD; If my covenant *be* not with day and night, *and if* I have not appointed the ordinances

of heaven and earth; 26. Then will I cast away the seed of Jacob, and David my servant, *so* that I will not take *any* of his seed *to be* rulers over the seed of Abraham, Isaac, and Jacob: for I will cause their captivity to return, and have mercy on them.

Jer. 51:16. When he uttereth *his* voice, *there is* a multitude of waters in the heavens; and he causeth the vapours to ascend from the ends of the earth: he maketh lightnings with rain, and bringeth forth the wind out of his treasures.

Dan. 2:21. And he changeth the times and the seasons:

Amos 5:8. *Seek him* that maketh the seven stars and Orion, and turneth the shadow of death into the morning, and maketh the day dark with night: that calleth for the waters of the sea, and poureth them out upon the face of the earth: The LORD *is* his name:

Nah. 1:3. The LORD *is* slow to anger, and great in power, and will not at all acquit *the wicked:* the LORD *hath* his way in the whirlwind and in the storm, and the clouds *are* the dust of his feet. 4. He rebuketh the sea, and maketh it dry, and drieth up all the rivers: Bashan languisheth, and Carmel, and the flower of Lebanon languisheth. 5. The mountains quake at him, and the hills melt, and the earth is burned at his presence, yea, the world, and all that dwell therein. 6. Who can stand before his indignation? and who can abide in the fierceness of his anger? his fury is poured out like fire, and the rocks are thrown down by him.

Rom. 1:19. Because that which may be known of God is manifest in them; for God hath shewed *it* unto them. 20. For the invisible things of him from the creation of the world are clearly seen, being understood by the things that are made, *even* his eternal power and Godhead;

ACCESS TO: Deut. 4:7. For what nation *is there so* great, who *hath* God *so* nigh unto them, as the LORD our God *is* in all *things that* we call upon him *for?*

Psa. 24:3. Who shall ascend into the hill of the LORD? or who shall stand in his holy place? 4. He that hath clean hands, and a pure heart; who hath not lifted up his soul unto vanity, nor sworn deceitfully.

Psa. 27:4. One *thing* have I desired of the LORD, that will I seek after; that I may dwell in the house of the LORD all the days of my life, to behold the beauty of the LORD, and to inquire in his temple.

Psa. 43:2. O send out thy light and thy truth: let them lead me; let them bring me unto thy holy hill, and to thy tabernacles.

Psa. 65:4. Blessed *is the man whom* thou choosest, and causest to approach *unto thee.* *that* he may dwell in thy courts: we shall be satisfied with the goodness of thy house, *even* of thy holy temple.

Psa. 145:18. The LORD *is* nigh unto all them that call upon him, to all that call him in truth. 19. He will fulfil the desire of them that fear him: he also will hear their cry, and will save them.

Isa. 55:3. Incline your ear, and come unto me: hear, and your soul shall live; and I will make an everlasting covenant with you, even the sure mercies of David.

Matt. 6:6. But thou, when thou prayest, enter into thy closet, and when thou hast shut thy door, pray to thy Father which is in secret; and thy Father which seeth in secret shall reward thee openly.

John 10:7. Then said Jesus unto them again, Verily, verily, I say unto you, I am the door of the sheep. 9. I am the door: by me if any man enter in, he shall be saved, and shall go in and out, and find pasture.

John 14:6. Jesus saith unto him, I am the way, the truth, and the life: no man cometh unto the Father, but by me.

Acts 14:27. And when they were come, and had gathered the church together, they rehearsed all that God had done with them, and how he had opened the door of faith unto the Gentiles.

Rom. 5:2. By whom also we have access by faith into this grace wherein we stand, and rejoice in hope of the glory of God.

Eph. 2:13. But now in Christ Jesus ye who sometimes were far off are made nigh by the blood of Christ. 18. For through him we both have access by one Spirit unto the Father.

Eph. 3:12. In whom we have boldness and access with confidence by the faith of him.

Col. 1:21. And you, that were sometime alienated and enemies in your mind by wicked works, yet now hath he reconciled 22. In the body of his flesh through death, to present you holy and unblameable and unreproveable in his sight.

Heb. 4:16. Let us therefore come boldly unto the throne of grace, that we may obtain mercy, and find grace to help in time of need.

Heb. 7:19. For the law made nothing perfect, but the bringing in of a better hope did; by the which we draw nigh unto God. 25. Wherefore he is able also to save them to the uttermost that come unto God by him, seeing he ever liveth to make intercession for them.

Heb. 10:19. Having therefore, brethren, boldness to enter into the holiest by the blood of Jesus, 22. Let us draw near with a true heart in full assurance of faith, having our hearts sprinkled from an evil conscience, and our bodies washed with pure water.

Heb. 11:6. But without faith it is impossible to please him: for he that cometh to God must believe that he is, and that he is a rewarder of them that diligently seek him

Jas. 4:8. Draw nigh to God, and he will draw nigh to you. Cleanse your hands, ye sinners; and purify your hearts, ye double minded.

1 Pet. 1:17. And if ye call on the Father,

who without respect of persons judgeth according to every man's work, pass the time of your sojourning here in fear:

1 Pet. 3:18. For Christ also hath once suffered for sins, the just for the unjust, that he might bring us to God, being put to death in the flesh, but quickened by the Spirit:

1 John 4:16. God is love; and he that dwelleth in love dwelleth in God, and God in him.

See PENITENTS; REPENTANCE; SEEKERS.

COMPASSION OF: See LONG SUFFERING OF; MERCY OF, below.

CREATOR: Gen. 1:1. In the beginning God created the heaven and the earth. 2. And the earth was without form, and void; and darkness was upon the face of the deep. And the Spirit of God moved upon the face of the waters. 3. And God said, Let there be light: and there was light. 4. And God saw the light, that it was good: and God divided the light from the darkness. 5. And God called the light Day, and the darkness he called Night. And the evening and the morning were the first day.

6. And God said, Let there be a firmament in the midst of the waters, and let it divide the waters from the waters. 7. And God made the firmament, and divided the waters which were under the firmament from the waters which were above the firmament: and it was so. 8. And God called the firmament Heaven. And the evening and the morning were the second day.

9. And God said, Let the waters under the heaven be gathered together unto one place, and let the dry land appear: and it was so. 10. And God called the dry land Earth; and the gathering together of the waters called he Seas: and God saw that it was good. 11. And God said, Let the earth bring forth grass, the herb yielding seed, and the fruit tree yielding fruit after his kind, whose seed is in itself, upon the earth: and it was so. 12. And the earth brought forth grass, and herb yielding seed after his kind, and the tree yielding fruit, whose seed was in itself, after his kind: and God saw that it was good. 13. And the evening and the morning were the third day.

14. And God said, Let there be lights in the firmament of the heaven to divide the day from the night; and let them be for signs, and for seasons, and for days, and years 15. And let them be for lights in the firmament of the heaven to give light upon the earth: and it was so. 16. And God made two great lights; the greater light to rule the day, and the lesser light to rule the night: he made the stars also. 17. And God set them in the firmament of the heaven to give light upon the earth, 18. And to rule over the day and over the night, and to divide the light from the darkness: and God saw that it was good. 19. And the evening and the morning were the fourth day.

20. And God said, Let the waters bring forth abundantly the moving creature that

hath life, and fowl *that* may fly above the earth in the open firmament of heaven.

21. And God created great whales, and every living creature that moveth, which the waters brought forth abundantly, after their kind, and every winged fowl after his kind: and God saw that *it was* good. 22. And God blessed them, saying, Be fruitful, and multiply, and fill the waters in the seas, and let fowl multiply in the earth. 23. And the evening and the morning were the fifth day.

24. And God said, Let the earth bring forth the living creature after his kind, cattle, and creeping thing, and beast of the earth after his kind: and it was so. 25. And God made the beast of the earth after his kind, and cattle after their kind, and every thing that creepeth upon the earth after his kind: and God saw that *it was* good.

26. And God said, Let us make man in our image, after our likeness: and let them have dominion over the fish of the sea, and over the fowl of the air, and over the cattle, and over all the earth, and over every creeping thing that creepeth upon the earth. 27. So God created man in his *own* image, in the image of God created he him; male and female created he them. 28. And God blessed them, and God said unto them, Be fruitful, and multiply, and replenish the earth, and subdue it: and have dominion over the fish of the sea, and over the fowl of the air, and over every living thing that moveth upon the earth.

31. And God saw every thing that he had made, and, behold, *it was* very good. And the evening and the morning were the sixth day.

Gen. 2:1. Thus the heavens and the earth were finished, and all the hosts of them. 2. And on the seventh day God ended his work which he had made: and he rested on the seventh day from all his work which he had made. 3. And God blessed the seventh day, and sanctified it: because that in it he had rested from all his work which God created and made. 4. These *are* the generations of the heavens and of the earth when they were created, in the day that the LORD God made the earth and the heavens. 7. And the LORD God formed man *of* the dust of the ground, and breathed into his nostrils the breath of life: and man became a living soul. Gen. 2:1-25.

Gen. 5:1. This *is* the book of the generations of Adam. In the day that God created man, in the likeness of God made he him; 2. Male and female created he them: and blessed them, and called their name Adam, in the day when they were created.

Gen. 9:6. Whoso sheddeth man's blood, by man shall his blood be shed: for in the image of God made he man.

Ex. 20:11. *In* six days the LORD made heaven and earth, the sea, and all that in them *is*, Psa. 146:6.

1 Sam. 2:8. The pillars of the earth *are*

the LORD's, and he hath set the world upon them.

2 Kin. 19:15. And Hezekiah prayed before the LORD, and said, O LORD God of Israel, which dwellest *between* the cherubims, thou art the God, *even* thou alone, of all kingdoms of the earth; thou hast made heaven and earth.

1 Chr. 16:26. For all the gods of the people *are* idols: but the LORD made the heavens.

Neh. 9:6. Thou hast made heaven, the heaven of heavens, with all their host, the earth, and all *things* that *are* therein, the seas, and all that *is* therein, and thou preservest them all.

Job 9:8. Which alone spreadeth out the heavens, and treadeth upon the waves of the sea. 9. Which maketh Arcturus, Orion, and Pleiades, and the chambers of the south.

Job 10:3. *Is it* good unto thee that thou shouldest oppress, that thou shouldest despise the work of thine hands, and shine upon the counsel of the wicked? 8. Thine hands have made me and fashioned me together round about; yet thou dost destroy me.

Job 12:7. But ask now the beasts, and they shall teach thee; and the fowls of the air, and they shall tell thee: 8. Or speak to the earth, and it shall teach thee: and the fishes of the sea shall declare unto thee. 9. Who knoweth not in all these that the hand of the LORD hath wrought this?

Job 26:7. He stretcheth out the north over the empty place, *and* hangeth the earth upon nothing. 13. By his spirit he hath garnished the heavens; his hand hath formed the crooked serpent. *vs.* 8-12.

Job 28:23. God understandeth the way thereof, and he knoweth the place thereof. 24. For he looketh to the ends of the earth, *and* seeth under the whole heaven; 25. To make the weight for the winds; and he weigheth the waters by measure. 26. When he made a decree for the rain, and a way for the lightning of the thunder:

Job 37:16. Dost thou know the balancings of the clouds, the wondrous works of him which is perfect in knowledge? 18. Hast thou with him spread out the sky, *which is* strong, *and* as a molten looking glass?

Job 38:4. Where wast thou when I laid the foundations of the earth? declare, if thou hast understanding. 7. When the morning stars sang together, and all the sons of God shouted for joy? 8. Or *who* shut up the sea with doors, when it brake forth, *as if* it had issued out of the womb? 9. When I made the cloud the garment thereof, and thick darkness a swaddlingband for it, 10. And brake up for it my decreed *place*, and set bars and doors. *vs.* 4-38.

Psa. 8:3. When I consider thy heavens, the work of thy fingers, the moon and the stars, which thou hast ordained;

Psa. 19:1. The heavens declare **the glory**

of God; and the firmament sheweth his handywork.   4. In them hath he set a tabernacle for the sun,

Psa. 24:1. The earth *is* the LORD's, and the fulness thereof; the world, and they that dwell therein.   2. For he hath founded it upon the seas, and established it upon the floods.

Psa. 33:6. By the word of the LORD were the heavens made; and all the host of them by the breath of his mouth.   7. He gathereth the waters of the sea together as an heap: he layeth up the depth in storehouses. 9. For he spake, and it was *done;* he commanded, and it stood fast.

Psa. 65:6. Which by his strength setteth fast the mountains; *being* girded with power:

Psa. 74:16. The day *is* thine, the night also *is* thine: thou hast prepared the light and the sun.   17. Thou hast set all the borders of the earth: thou hast made summer and winter.

Psa. 78:69. He built his sanctuary like high *palaces*, like the earth which he hath established for ever.

Psa. 89:11. The heavens *are* thine, the earth also *is* thine: *as for* the world and the fulness thereof, thou hast founded them. 12. The north and the south thou hast created them: 47. Remember how short my time is: wherefore hast thou made all men in vain?

Psa. 90:2. Before the mountains were brought forth, or ever thou hadst formed the earth and the world, even from everlasting to everlasting, thou *art* God.

Psa. 95:4. In his hand *are* the deep places of the earth: the strength of the hills *is* his also.   5. The sea *is* his, and he made it: and his hands formed the dry *land.*

Psa. 102:25. Of old hast thou laid the foundation of the earth: and the heavens *are* the work of thy hands.   Psa. 96:5.

Psa. 103:22. Bless the LORD, all his works in all places of his dominion:

Psa. 104:2. Who stretchest out the heavens like a curtain: 3. Who layeth the beams of his chambers in the waters: 5. *Who* laid the foundations of the earth, *that* it should not be removed for ever.   6. Thou coveredst it with the deep as *with* a garment: the waters stood above the mountains.   24. O LORD, how manifold are thy works! in wisdom hast thou made them all: the earth is full of thy riches.   30. Thou sendest forth thy spirit, they are created: and thou renewest the face of the earth.   *v.* 31.

Psa. 119:90. Thou hast established the earth, and it abideth.   91. They continue this day according to thine ordinances: for all *are* thy servants.

Psa. 121:2. My help *cometh* from the LORD, which made heaven and earth.

Psa. 124:8. Our help *is* in the name of the LORD, who made heaven and earth.

Psa. 136:5. To him that by wisdom made the heavens: 6. To him that stretched out the earth above the waters: 7. To him that made great lights: 8. The sun to rule by day: 9. The moon and stars to rule by night:

Psa. 146:5. Happy *is* he that *hath* the God of Jacob for his help, whose hope *is* in the LORD his God: 6. Which made heaven, and earth, the sea, and all that therein *is:* which keepeth truth for ever:

Psa. 148:5. Let them praise the name of the LORD: for he commanded, and they were created.   6. He hath also stablished them for ever and ever: he hath made a decree which shall not pass.

Prov. 3:19. The LORD by wisdom hath founded the earth; by understanding hath he established the heavens.

Prov. 8:26. While as yet he had not made the earth, nor the fields, nor the highest part of the dust of the world.   27. When he prepared the heavens, I *was* there: when he set a compass upon the face of the depth: 28. When he established the clouds above: when he strengthened the fountains of the deep: 29. When he gave to the sea his decree, that the waters should not pass his commandment: when he appointed the foundations of the earth:

Prov. 16:4. The LORD hath made all *things* for himself: yea, even the wicked for the day of evil.

Prov. 22:2. The rich and poor meet together: the LORD *is* the maker of them all.

Prov. 26:10. The great *God* that formed all *things* both rewardeth the fool, and rewardeth transgressors.

Prov. 30:4. Who hath gathered the wind in his fists? who hath bound the waters in a garment? who hath established all the ends of the earth?

Eccl. 3:11. He hath made every *thing* beautiful in his time: also he hath set the world in their heart, so that no man can find out the work that God maketh from the beginning to the end.

Eccl. 7:29. Lo, this only have I found, that God hath made man upright; but they have sought out many inventions.

Eccl. 11:5. As thou knowest not what *is* the way of the spirit, *nor* how the bones *do* grow in the womb of her that is with child: even so thou knowest not the works of God who maketh all.

Isa. 17:7. At that day shall a man look to his Maker, and his eyes shall have respect to the Holy One of Israel.

Isa. 37:16. O LORD of hosts, God of Israel, that dwellest *between* the cherubims, thou *art* the God, *even* thou alone, of all the kingdoms of the earth: thou hast made heaven and earth.

Isa. 40:12. Who hath measured the waters in the hollow of his hand, and meted out heaven with the span, and comprehended the dust of the earth in a measure, and weighed the mountains in scales, and the hills in a balance?   26. Lift up your eyes on high, and behold who hath created these *things*, that bringeth out their host by number: he calleth them all by names by the greatness of his might, for that *he is* strong in power; not one faileth. 28. Hast thou not known? hast thou not heard, *that* the everlasting God, the LORD, the Creator of the ends of the earth, fainteth not, neither is weary? *there is* no searching of his understanding.

Isa. 42:5. Thus saith God the LORD, he that created the heavens, and stretched them out; he that spread forth the earth, and that which cometh out of it;

Isa. 44:24. I *am* the LORD that maketh all *things;* that stretcheth forth the heavens alone; that spreadeth abroad the earth by myself;

Isa. 45:7. I form the light, and create darkness: I make peace, and create evil: I the LORD do all these *things.* 12. I have made the earth, and created man upon it: I, *even* my hands, have stretched out the heavens, and all their host have I commanded. 18. Thus saith the LORD that created the heavens; God himself that formed the earth and made it; he hath established it, he created it not in vain, he formed it to be inhabited:

Isa. 48:13. Mine hand also hath laid the foundation of the earth, and my right hand hath spanned the heavens: *when* I call unto them, they stand up together.

Isa. 51:13. And forgettest the LORD thy maker, that hath stretched forth the heavens, and laid the foundations of the earth; 16. And I have put my words in thy mouth, and I have covered thee in the shadow of mine hand, that I may plant the heavens, and lay the foundations of the earth, and say unto Zion, Thou *art* my people.

Isa. 66:2. For all those *things* hath mine hand made, and all those *things* have been, saith the LORD:

Jer. 5:22. Will ye not tremble at my presence, which have placed the sand *for* the bound of the sea by a perpetual decree, that it cannot pass it:

Jer. 10:12. He hath made the earth by his power, he hath established the world by his wisdom, and hath stretched out the heavens by his discretion. 16. The portion of Jacob *is* not like them: for he *is* the former of all *things;* and Israel *is* the rod of his inheritance: the LORD of hosts *is* his name. Jer. 51:19.

Jer. 27:5. I have made the earth, the man and the beast that *are* upon the ground, by my great power and by my outstretched arm, and have given it unto whom it seemed meet unto me.

Jer. 31:35. Thus saith the LORD, which giveth the sun for a light by day, *and* the ordinances of the moon and of the stars for a light by night, which divideth the sea when the waves thereof roar; The LORD of hosts *is* his name:

Jer. 32:17. Ah Lord GOD! behold, thou hast made the heaven and the earth by thy great power and stretched out arm, *and* there is nothing too hard for thee:

Jer. 33:2. Thus saith the LORD the maker thereof, the LORD that formed it, to establish it; the LORD *is* his name;

Jer. 51:15. He hath made the earth by his power, he hath established the world by his wisdom, and hath stretched out the heaven by his understanding. 16. When he uttereth *his* voice, *there is* a multitude of waters in the heavens; and he causeth the vapours to ascend from the ends of the earth: he maketh lightnings with rain, and bringeth forth the wind out of his treasures. Jer. 10:13.

Amos 4:13. For, lo, he that formeth the mountains, and createth the wind, and declareth unto man what *is* his thought, that maketh the morning darkness, and treadeth upon the high places of the earth, The LORD, The God of hosts, *is* his name.

Amos 5:8. *Seek him* that maketh the seven stars and Orion, and turneth the shadow of death into the morning, and maketh the day dark with night:

Amos 9:6. *It is* he that buildeth his stories in the heaven, and hath founded his troop in the earth; he that calleth for the waters of the sea, and poureth them out upon the face of the earth: The LORD *is* his name.

Jonah 1:9. And he said unto them, I *am* an Hebrew; and I fear the LORD, the God of heaven, which hath made the sea and the dry *land.*

Zech. 12:1. The burden of the word of the LORD for Israel, saith the LORD, which stretcheth forth the heavens, and layeth the foundation of the earth, and formeth the spirit of man within him.

Mark 10:6. But from the beginning of the creation God made them male and female.

Mark 13:19. For *in* those days shall be affliction, such as was not from the beginning of the creation which God created unto this time, neither shall be.

Acts 4:24. And when they heard that, they lifted up their voice to God with one accord, and said, Lord, thou *art* God, which hast made heaven, and earth, and the sea, and all that in them is:

Acts 7:50. Hath not my hand made all these things?

Acts 14:15. We . . . . preach unto you that ye should turn from these vanities unto the living God, which made heaven, and earth, and the sea, and all things that are therein:

Acts 17:24. God that made the world and all things therein, seeing that he is Lord of heaven and earth, dwelleth not in temples made with hands; 25. Neither is worshipped with men's hands, as though he needed any thing, seeing he giveth to all life, and breath, and all things; 26. And hath made of one blood all nations of men for to dwell on all the face of the earth, and hath determined the times before appointed, and the bounds of their habitation;

Rom. 1:20. For the invisible things of him from the creation of the world are clearly seen, being understood by the things that are made, *even* his eternal power and Godhead;

Rom. 11:36. Of him, and through him, and to him, *are* all things: to whom *be* glory for ever.

1 Cor. 8:6. To us *there is but* one God, the Father, of whom *are* all things, and we in him; and one Lord Jesus Christ, by whom *are* all things, and we by him.

2 Cor. 4:6. God who commanded the light to shine out of darkness, hath shined in our hearts,

2 Cor. 5:5. Now he that hath wrought us for the selfsame thing *is* God, who also hath given unto us the earnest of the Spirit. 18. All things are of God, 1 Cor. 11:12.

Eph. 3:9. And to make all *men* see what *is* the fellowship of the mystery, which from the beginning of the world hath been hid in God, who created all things 1 by Jesus Christ:

[1 Omitted in R. V.]

1 Tim. 6:13. I give thee charge in the sight of God, who quickeneth all things,

Heb. 1:1. God, ... 2. Hath in these last days spoken unto us by *his* Son, whom he hath appointed heir of all things, by whom also he made the worlds;

Heb. 2:10. For it became him, for whom *are* all things, and by whom *are* all things, in bringing many sons unto glory, to make the captain of their salvation perfect through sufferings.

Heb. 3:4. For every house is builded by some *man:* but he that built all things *is* God.

Heb. 11:3. Through faith we understand that the worlds were framed by the word of God, so that things which are seen were not made of things which do appear. 10 For he looked for a city which hath foundations, whose builder and maker *is* God.

Rev. 4:11. Thou art worthy, O Lord, to receive glory and honour and power: for thou hast created all things, and for thy pleasure they are and were created.

Rev. 10:6. And sware by him that liveth for ever and ever, who created heaven, and the things that therein are, and the earth, and the things that therein are, and the sea, and the things which are therein,

Rev. 14:7. Fear God, and give glory to him; . . . and worship him that made heaven, and earth, and the sea, and the fountains of waters.

CREATOR OF MAN: Gen. 1:26. God said, Let us make man in our image, after our likeness: 27. So God created man in his *own* image, in the image of God created he him; male and female created he them. Gen. 2:7.

Gen. 5:1. In the day that God created man, in the likeness of God made he him; 2. Male and female created he them; and blessed them, and called their name Adam, in the day when they were created.

Gen. 9:6. In the image of God made he man.

Ex. 4:11. Who hath made man's mouth? or who maketh the dumb, or deaf, or the seeing, or the blind? have not I the LORD?

Num. 16:22. And they fell upon their faces, and said, O God, the God of the spirits of all flesh, shall one man sin, and wilt thou be wroth with all the congregation? Num. 27:16.

Deut. 4:32. Since the day that God created man upon the earth,

Deut. 32:6. Do ye thus requite the LORD, O foolish people and unwise? *is* not he thy father *that* hath bought thee? hath he not made thee, and established thee? 15. But Jeshurun waxed fat, . . . then he forsook God *which* made him, and lightly esteemed the Rock of his salvation. 18. Of the Rock *that* begat thee thou art unmindful, and hast forgotten God that formed thee.

Job 10:8. Thine hands have made me and fashioned me together round about; 9. Thou hast made me as the clay; and wilt thou bring me into dust again? 11. Thou hast clothed me with skin and flesh, and hast fenced me with bones and sinews. 12. Thou hast granted me life and favour, and thy visitation hath preserved my spirit. Psa. 119:73.

Job 12:10. In whose hand *is* the soul of every living thing, and the breath of all mankind.

Job 27:3. All the while my breath *is* in me, and the spirit of God *is* in my nostrils;

Job 31:15. Did not he that made me in the womb make him? and did not one fashion us in the womb?

Job 33:4. The spirit of God hath made me, and the breath of the Almighty hath given me life.

Job 34:19. *How much less to him* that accepteth not the persons of princes, nor regardeth the rich more than the poor? for they all *are* the work of his hands.

Job 38:36. Who hath put wisdom in the inward parts? or who hath given understanding to the heart?

Psa. 33:15. He fashioneth their hearts alike; he considereth all their works.

Psa. 86:9. All nations whom thou hast made shall come and worship before thee, O Lord;

Psa. 94:9. He that planted the ear, shall he not hear? he that formed the eye, shall he not see?

Psa. 95:6. Let us kneel before the LORD our maker.

Psa. 100:3. Know ye that the LORD he *is* God: *it is* he *that* hath made us, and not we ourselves; *we are* his people, and the sheep of his pasture.

Psa. 139:13. Thou hast possessed my reins: thou hast covered me in my mother's womb.

Psa. 149:2. Let Israel rejoice in him that made him:

Prov. 16:4. The LORD hath made all *things* for himself: yea, even the wicked for the day of evil.

Prov. 20:12. The hearing ear, and the seeing eye, the LORD hath made even both of them.

Prov. 22:2. The rich and poor meet together: the LORD is the maker of them all.

Eccl. 11:5. Thou knowest not the works of God who maketh all.

Eccl. 12:1. Remember now thy Creator in the days of thy youth.

Isa. 42:5. He that giveth breath unto the people upon it, and spirit to them that walk therein.

Isa. 43:1. Thus saith the LORD that created thee, O Jacob, and he that formed thee, O Israel, 7. I have created him for my glory, I have formed him; yea, I have made him. 15. I am the LORD, your Holy One, the Creator of Israel, your King.

Isa. 44:2. The LORD that made thee, and formed thee from the womb, which will help thee; v. 24.

Isa. 45:12. I have made the earth, and created man upon it: 18. He created it not in vain, he formed it to be inhabited:

Isa. 51:13. Forgettest the LORD thy maker,

Isa. 64:8. Now, O LORD, thou art our father; we are the clay, and thou our potter; and we all are the work of thy hand.

Jer. 27:5. I have made the earth, the man and the beast that are upon the ground, by my great power and by my outstretched arm, and have given it unto whom it seemed meet unto me.

Dan. 5:23. The God in whose hand thy breath is, and whose are all thy ways, hast thou not glorified:

Zech. 12:1. The LORD, which stretcheth forth the heavens, . . . and formeth the spirit of man within him.

Mal. 2:10. Have we not all one father? hath not one God created us?

Acts 17:24. God that made the world and all things therein, 25. He giveth to all life, and breath, and all things; 26. And hath made of one blood all nations of men for to dwell on all the face of the earth, and hath determined the times before appointed, and the bounds of their habitation; 28. In him we live, and move, and have our being; as certain also of your own poets have said, For we are also his offspring. v. 29.

1 Cor. 12:18. Now hath God set the members, every one of them in the body, as it hath pleased him. 24. God hath tempered the body together, having given more abundant honour to that part which lacked: 25. That there should be no schism in the body;

1 Cor. 15:38. God giveth it a body as it hath pleased him, and to every seed his own body.

Heb. 12:9. Furthermore, we have had fathers of our flesh which corrected us, and we gave them reverence: shall we not much rather be in subjection unto the Father of spirits, and live?

1 Pet. 4:19. Wherefore, let them that suffer according to the will of God commit the keeping of their souls to him in well doing, as unto a faithful Creator.

See LIFE FROM GOD; MAN.

ETERNITY OF: Gen. 21:33. And Abraham planted a grove in Beer-sheba, and called there on the name of the LORD, the everlasting God. Rom. 16:26.

Ex. 3:15. The God of Abraham, the God of Isaac, and the God of Jacob, hath sent me unto you: this is my name for ever, and this is my memorial unto all generations.

Deut. 32:40. I lift up my hand to heaven, and say, I live for ever.

Deut. 33:27. The eternal God is thy refuge, and underneath are the everlasting arms:

1 Chr. 16:36. Blessed be the LORD God of Israel for ever and ever.

1 Chr. 29:10. Wherefore David blessed the LORD before all the congregation: and David said, Blessed be thou, LORD God of Israel our father, for ever and ever.

Neh. 9:5. Then the Levites, Jeshua, and Kadmiel, Bani, Hashabniah, Sherebiah, Hodijah, Shebaniah, and Pethahiah, said, Stand up and bless the LORD your God for ever and ever:

Job 36:26. Neither can the number of his years be searched out.

Psa. 9:7. But the LORD shall endure for ever:

Psa. 33:11. The counsel of the LORD standeth for ever, the thoughts of his heart to all generations.

Psa. 41:13. Blessed be the LORD God of Israel from everlasting, and to everlasting.

Psa. 55:19. God shall hear, and afflict them, even he that abideth of old.

Psa. 68:33. To him that rideth upon the heavens of heavens, which were of old; lo, he doth send out his voice, and that a mighty voice.

Psa. 90:1. LORD, thou hast been our dwelling place in all generations. 2. Before the mountains were brought forth, or ever thou hadst formed the earth and the world, even from everlasting to everlasting, thou art God. 4. A thousand years in thy sight are but as yesterday when it is past, and as a watch in the night.

Psa. 92:8. Thou, LORD, art most high for evermore.

Psa. 93:2. Thy throne is established of old: thou art from everlasting. Mic. 5:2.

Psa. 102:12. Thou, O LORD, shalt endure for ever; and thy remembrance unto all generations. 24. Thy years are throughout all generations. 25. Of old hast thou laid the foundations of the earth: and the heavens are the work of thy hands. 26. They shall perish, but thou shalt endure: yea, all of them shall wax old like a garment; as a vesture shalt thou change them, and they shall be changed: 27. But thou art the same, and thy years shall have no end.

Psa. 104:31. The glory of the LORD shall endure for ever:

Psa. 111:3. His righteousness endureth for ever.

Psa. 135:13. Thy name, O LORD, endureth for ever; and thy memorial, O LORD, throughout all generations.

Psa. 145:13. Thy kingdom *is* an everlasting kingdom, and thy dominion *endureth* throughout all generations.

Psa. 146:10. The LORD shall reign for ever, *even* thy God, O Zion, unto all generations. Ex. 15:18.

Prov. 8:23. I was set up from everlasting, from the beginning, or ever the earth was. 24. When *there were* no depths, I was brought forth; when *there were* no fountains abounding with water. 25. Before the mountains were settled, before the hills was I brought forth:

Isa. 26:4. Trust ye in the LORD for ever: for in the LORD JEHOVAH *is* everlasting strength:

Isa. 40:28. Hast thou not heard, *that* the everlasting God, the LORD, the Creator of the ends of the earth, fainteth not, neither is weary?

Isa. 41:4. Who hath wrought and done *it*, calling the generations from the beginning? I the LORD, the first, and with the last; I *am* he.

Isa. 43:13. Yea, before the day *was* I *am* he;

Isa. 44:6. I *am* the first, and I *am* the last; and beside me *there is* no God.

Isa. 46:4. *Even* to *your* old age I *am* he; and *even* to hoar hairs will I carry *you:* I have made, and I will bear;

Isa. 48:12. Hearken unto me, O Jacob and Israel, my called; I *am* he; I *am* the first, I also *am* the last.

Isa. 57:15. Thus saith the high and lofty One that inhabiteth eternity,

Isa. 63:16. Thy name *is* from everlasting.

Jer. 10:10. But the LORD *is* the true God, he is the living God, and an everlasting king:

Jer. 17:12. A glorious high throne from the beginning *is* the place of our sanctuary.

Lam. 5:19. Thou, O LORD, remainest for ever; thy throne from generation to generation. *v*. 3.

Dan. 4:34. And at the end of the days I Nebuchadnezzar lifted up mine eyes unto heaven, and mine understanding returned unto me, and I blessed the most High, and I praised and honoured him that liveth for ever, whose dominion *is* an everlasting dominion, and his kingdom *is* from generation to generation: *v*. 3.

Hab. 1:12. *Art* thou not from everlasting, O LORD my God, mine Holy One?

Hab. 3:6. He stood, and measured the earth: he beheld, and drove asunder the nations; and the everlasting mountains were scattered, the perpetual hills did bow: his ways *are* everlasting.

Rom. 1:20. The invisible things of him from the creation of the world are clearly seen, being understood by the things that are made, *even* his eternal power and Godhead;

Eph. 3:21. Unto him *be* glory in the church by Christ Jesus throughout all ages, world without end.

1 Tim. 1:17. Unto the King eternal, immortal, invisible, the only wise God, *be* honour and glory for ever and ever.

[† R. V. incorruptible]

1 Tim. 6:15. The blessed and only Potentate, the King of kings, and Lord of lords; 16. Who only hath immortality, dwelling in the light which no man can approach unto: whom no man hath seen, nor can see: to whom *be* honour and power everlasting.

Heb. 1:8. But unto the Son *he saith*, Thy throne, O God, *is* for ever and ever:

Heb. 9:14. How much more shall the blood of Christ, who through the eternal Spirit offered himself without spot to God,

2 Pet. 3:8. One day *is* with the Lord as a thousand years, and a thousand years as one day.

1 John 2:13. I write unto you, fathers, because ye have known him *that is* from the beginning.

Rev. 1:6. And hath made us kings and priests unto God and his Father; to him *be* glory and dominion for ever and ever.

Rev. 4:8. They rest not day and night, saying, Holy, holy, holy, Lord God Almighty, which was, and is, and is to come. 9. And when those beasts give glory and honour and thanks to him that sat on the throne, who liveth for ever and ever, *v*. 10; Rev. 1:4; 5:14; 11:17; 15:7.

Rev. 10:6. And sware by him that liveth for ever and ever, who created heaven, and the things that therein are, and the earth, and the things that therein are, and the sea, and the things which are therein, that there should be time no longer:

Rev. 16:5. And I heard the angel of the waters say, Thou art righteous, O Lord, which art, and wast, and shall be, because thou hast judged thus.

See GOD, SELF-EXISTENT.

FAITHFULNESS OF: Gen. 9:16. The bow shall be in the cloud; and I will look upon it, that I may remember the everlasting covenant between God and every living creature of all flesh that *is* upon the earth. *v*. 15; Gen. 6:18.

Gen. 21:1. The LORD visited Sarah as he had said, and the LORD did unto Sarah as he had spoken.

Gen. 24:27. Blessed *be* the LORD God of my master Abraham, who hath not left destitute my master of his mercy and his truth:

Gen. 28:15. I *am* with thee, and will keep thee in all *places* whither thou goest, and will bring thee again into this land; for I will not leave thee, until I have done *that* which I have spoken to thee of.

Gen. 32:10. I am not worthy of the least of all the mercies, and of all the truth, which thou hast shewed unto thy servant;

Ex. 6:4. I have also established my covenant with them, to give them the land of Canaan. 5. I have also heard the groaning of the children of Israel, whom the Egyptians keep in bondage; and I have remembered my covenant. Ex. 2:24.

Ex. 12:41. And it came to pass at the end

of the four hundred and thirty years, even the selfsame day it came to pass, that all the hosts of the LORD went out from the land of Egypt.

Ex. 34:6. And the LORD passed by before him, and proclaimed, The LORD, The LORD God, merciful and gracious, longsuffering, and abundant in goodness and truth,

Lev. 26:44. When they be in the land of their enemies, I will not cast them away, neither will I abhor them, to destroy them utterly, and to break my covenant with them: for I *am* the LORD their God. 45. But I will for their sakes remember the covenant of their ancestors,

Deut. 4:31. He will not forsake thee, neither destroy thee, nor forget the covenant of thy fathers which he sware unto them. Judg. 2:1.

Deut. 7:8. Because the LORD loved you, and because he would keep the oath which he had sworn unto your fathers, hath the LORD brought you out with a mighty hand, and redeemed you out of the house of bondmen, from the hand of Pharaoh king of Egypt. 9. Know therefore that the LORD thy God, he *is* God, the faithful God, which keepeth covenant and mercy with them that love him and keep his commandments to a thousand generations; Neh. 1:5.

Deut. 9:5. Not for thy righteousness, or for the uprightness of thine heart, dost thou go to possess their land: but . . . that he may perform the word which the LORD sware unto thy fathers,

Deut. 32:4. *He is* the Rock, his work *is* perfect: for all his ways *are* judgment: a God of truth, and without iniquity, just and right *is* he.

Josh. 23:14. Ye know in all your hearts and in all your souls, that not one thing hath failed of all the good things which the LORD your God spake concerning you; all are come to pass unto you, *and* not one thing hath failed thereof. Josh. 21:45.

1 Sam. 12:22. The LORD will not forsake his people for his great name's sake: because it hath pleased the LORD to make you his people.

2 Sam. 7:28. O Lord GOD, thou *art* that God, and thy words be true, and thou hast promised this goodness unto thy servant:

2 Sam. 23:5. Although my house *be* not so with God; yet he hath made with me an everlasting covenant, ordered in all *things*, and sure.

1 Kin. 8:23. Who keepest covenant and mercy with thy servants that walk before thee with all their heart: 24. Who hast kept with thy servant David my father that thou promisedst him: thou spakest also with thy mouth, and hast fulfilled *it* with thine hand, as *it is* this day. 56. Blessed *be* the LORD, that hath given rest unto his people Israel, according to all that he promised: there hath not failed one word of all his good promise, which he promised by the hand of Moses. *vs.* 15, 20; 2 Chr. 6:4-15.

2 Kin. 8:19. The LORD would not destroy Judah for David his servant's sake, as he promised him to give him alway a light, *and* to his children. 2 Chr. 21:7.

2 Kin. 13:23. The LORD was gracious unto them, and had compassion on them, and had respect unto them, because of his covenant with Abraham, Isaac, and Jacob, and would not destroy them, neither cast he them from his presence as yet.

1 Chr. 17:27. Now therefore let it please thee to bless the house of thy servant, that it may be before thee for ever: for thou blessest, O LORD, and *it shall be* blessed for ever.

1 Chr. 28:20. The LORD God, *even* my God, *will be* with thee; he will not fail thee, nor forsake thee, until thou hast finished all the work for the service of the house of the LORD. Deut. 31:6.

Ezra 9:9. For we *were* bondmen; yet our God hath not forsaken us in our bondage, but hath extended mercy unto us.

Neh. 9:7. Thou *art* the LORD the God, who didst choose Abram, . . . 8. And hast performed thy words; for thou *art* righteous: *v.* 32.

Psa. 9:10. And they that know thy name will put their trust in thee: for thou, LORD, hast not forsaken them that seek thee.

Psa. 18:30. *As for* God, his way *is* perfect: the word of the LORD is tried: he *is* a buckler to all those that trust in him. 2 Sam. 22:31.

Psa. 19:9. The judgments of the LORD *are* true *and* righteous altogether.

Psa. 25:10. All the paths of the LORD *are* mercy and truth unto such as keep his covenant and his testimonies.

Psa. 31:5. Into thine hand I commit my spirit: thou hast redeemed me, O LORD God of truth.

Psa. 33:4. The word of the LORD *is* right; and all his works *are done* in truth.

Psa. 36:5. Thy mercy, O LORD, *is* in the heavens; *and* thy faithfulness *reacheth* unto the clouds.

Psa. 37:28. The LORD loveth judgment, and forsaketh not his saints; they are preserved for ever:

Psa. 40:10. I have declared thy faithfulness and thy salvation: I have not concealed thy lovingkindness and thy truth from the great congregation.

Psa. 89:1. With my mouth will I make known thy faithfulness to all generations. 2. Thy faithfulness shalt thou establish in the very heavens. 5. The heavens shall praise . . . thy faithfulness also in the congregation of the saints. 8. O LORD God of hosts, who *is* a strong LORD like unto thee? or to thy faithfulness round about thee? 14. Mercy and truth shall go before thy face. 24. My faithfulness and my mercy *shall be* with him: 28. My mercy will I keep for him for evermore, and my covenant shall stand fast with him. 33. My lovingkindness will I not utterly take from him, nor suffer my faithfulness to fail. 34. My covenant will I not break, nor alter the thing that is gone out of my lips. 2 Sam. 7:14,15.

Psa. 92:1. *It is* a good thing to give thanks unto the LORD, and to sing praises unto thy name, O most High: 2. To shew forth thy lovingkindness in the morning, and thy faithfulness every night, 15. To shew that the LORD *is* upright: *he is* my rock, and *there is* no unrighteousness in him. *v.* 14.

Psa. 94:14. The LORD will not cast off his people, neither will he forsake his inheritance.

Psa. 98:3. He hath remembered his mercy and his truth toward the house of Israel:

Psa. 100:5. His truth *endureth* to all generations.

Psa. 103:17. The mercy of the LORD *is* from everlasting to everlasting upon them that fear him, and his righteousness unto children's children;

Psa. 105:8. He hath remembered his covenant for ever, the word *which* he commanded to a thousand generations. 42. He remembered his holy promise, *and* Abraham his servant.

Psa. 111:5. He will ever be mindful of his covenant. 7. The works of his hands *are* verity and judgment; all his commandments *are* sure. 8. They stand fast for ever and ever, *and are* done in truth and uprightness. 9. He sent redemption unto his people: he hath commanded his covenant for ever:

Psa. 117:2. The truth of the LORD *endureth* for ever.

Psa. 119:65. Thou hast dealt well with thy servant, O LORD, according unto thy word. 89. For ever, O LORD, thy word is settled in heaven. 90. Thy faithfulness *is* unto all generations:

Psa. 121:3. He will not suffer thy foot to be moved: he that keepeth thee will not slumber. 4. Behold, he that keepeth Israel shall neither slumber nor sleep.

Psa. 132:11. The LORD hath sworn *in* truth unto David; he will not turn from it;

Psa. 138:2 I will . . . praise thy name for thy lovingkindness and for thy truth: for thou hast magnified thy word above all thy name.

Psa. 146:6. Which keepeth truth for ever:

Isa. 11:5. And righteousness shall be the girdle of his loins, and faithfulness the girdle of his reins.

Isa. 25:1. *Thy* counsels of old *are* faithfulness *and* truth.

Isa. 42:16. And I will bring the blind by a way *that* they knew not; I will lead them in paths *that* they have not known: I will make darkness light before them, and crooked things straight. These things will I do unto them, and not forsake them.

Isa. 44:21. O Israel, thou shalt not be forgotten of me.

Isa. 49:7. Thus saith the LORD, the Redeemer of Israel, *and* his Holy One, to him whom man despiseth, to him whom the nation abhorreth, to a servant of rulers, Kings shall see and arise, princes also shall worship, because of the LORD that is faithful, *and* the Holy One of Israel, and he shall choose thee. 16. I have graven thee upon the palms of *my* hands; thy walls *are* continually before me.

Isa. 51:6. The heavens shall vanish away like smoke, and the earth shall wax old like a garment, and they that dwell therein shall die in like manner: but my salvation shall be for ever, and my righteousness shall not be abolished. 8. The moth shall eat them up like a garment, and the worm shall eat them like wool: but my righteousness shall be for ever, and my salvation from generation to generation.

Isa. 54:9. *As* I have sworn that the waters of Noah should no more go over the earth; so have I sworn that I would not be wroth with thee, nor rebuke thee. 10. For the mountains shall depart, and the hills be removed; but my kindness shall not depart from thee, neither shall the covenant of my peace be removed, saith the LORD that hath mercy on thee.

Isa. 65:16. He who blesseth himself in the earth shall bless himself in the God of truth; and he that sweareth in the earth shall swear by the God of truth;

Jer. 29:10. After seventy years be accomplished at Babylon I will visit you, and perform my good word toward you, in causing you to return to this place.

Jer. 31:36. If those ordinances depart from before me, saith the LORD, *then* the seed of Israel also shall cease from being a nation before me for ever. 37. If heaven above can be measured, and the foundations of the earth searched out beneath, I will also cast off all the seed of Israel for all that they have done, saith the LORD.

Jer. 32:40. I will make an everlasting covenant with them, that I will not turn away from them, to do them good;

Jer. 33:14. The days come, saith the LORD, that I will perform that good thing which I have promised unto the house of Israel and to the house of Judah. 20. If ye can break my covenant of the day, and my covenant of the night, and that there should not be day and night in their season; 21. *Then* may also my covenant be broken with David my servant. *vs.* 25,26.

Jer. 51:5. Israel *hath* not *been* forsaken, nor Judah of his God, of the LORD of hosts; though their land was filled with sin against the Holy One of Israel.

Lam. 3:23. Great *is* thy faithfulness.

Ezek. 16:60. I will remember my covenant with thee in the days of thy youth, and I will establish unto thee an everlasting covenant. *v.* 62.

Dan. 9:4. And I prayed unto the LORD my God, and made my confession, and said, O Lord, the great and dreadful God, keeping the covenant and mercy to them that love him, and to them that keep his commandments;

Hos. 2:19. I will betroth thee unto me for ever; yea, I will betroth thee unto me in righteousness, and in judgment, and in lovingkindness, and in mercies. 20. I will even betroth thee unto me in faithfulness:

Mic. 7:20. Thou wilt perform the truth to Jacob, *and* the mercy to Abraham, which thou hast sworn unto our fathers from the days of old.

Hag. 2:5. *According to* the word that I covenanted with you when ye came out of Egypt, so my spirit remaineth among you:

Zech. 9:11. By the blood of thy covenant I have sent forth thy prisoners out of the pit wherein *is* no water.

Matt. 24:34. This generation shall not pass, till all these things be fulfilled. *v.* 35.

Luke 1:54. He hath holpen his servant Israel, in remembrance of *his* mercy; 55. As he spake to our fathers, to Abraham, and to his seed for ever. 68. He hath visited and redeemed his people, 69. And hath raised up an horn of salvation for us in the house of his servant David; 70. As he spake by the mouth of his holy prophets, . . . 72. To perform the mercy *promised* to our fathers, and to remember his holy covenant; 73. The oath which he sware to our father Abraham,

John 8:26. He that sent me is true;

Acts 13:32. The promise which was made unto the fathers, 33. God hath fulfilled the same unto us their children, in that he hath raised up Jesus again;

Rom. 3:3. For what if some did not believe? shall their unbelief make the faith of God without effect? 4. God forbid: yea, let God be true, but every man a liar;

Rom. 11:2. God hath not cast away his people which he foreknew. 29. The gifts and calling of God *are* without repentance. *v.* 1.

Rom. 15:8. Jesus Christ was a minister of the circumcision for the truth of God, to confirm the promises *made* unto the fathers:

1 Cor. 1:9. God *is* faithful, by whom ye were called unto the fellowship of his Son Jesus Christ our Lord.

1 Cor. 10:13. God *is* faithful, who will not suffer you to be tempted above that ye are able;

2 Cor. 1:20. All the promises of God in him *are* yea, and in him Amen,

1 Thess. 5:24. Faithful *is* he that calleth you, who also will do *it.*

2 Tim. 2:13. If we believe not, *yet* he abideth faithful: he cannot deny himself. 19. The foundation of God standeth sure, having this seal, The Lord knoweth them that are his.

Tit. 1:2. In hope of eternal life, which God, that cannot lie, promised before the world began;

Heb. 6:10. God *is* not unrighteous to forget your work and labour of love, 13. For when God made promise to Abraham, be-

cause he could swear by no greater, he sware by himself, 14. Saying, Surely blessing I will bless thee, and multiplying I will multiply thee. 15. And so, after he had patiently endured, he obtained the promise. 16. For men verily swear by the greater: and an oath for confirmation *is* to them an end of all strife. 17. Wherein God, willing more abundantly to shew unto the heirs of promise the immutability of his counsel, confirmed *it* by an oath: 18. That by two immutable things, in which *it was* impossible for God to lie, we might have a strong consolation, who have fled for refuge to lay hold upon the hope set before us: 19. Which *hope* we have as an anchor of the soul, both sure and stedfast, and which entereth into that within the veil;

Heb. 10:22. Let us draw near with a true heart in full assurance of faith, having our hearts sprinkled from an evil conscience, and our bodies washed with pure water. 23. Let us hold fast the profession of *our* faith without wavering; (for he *is* faithful that promised;) 37. Yet a little while, and he that shall come will come, and will not tarry.

1 Pet. 4:19. Wherefore let them that suffer according to the will of God commit the keeping of their souls *to him* in well doing, as unto a faithful Creator.

2 Pet. 3:9. The Lord is not slack concerning his promise, as some men count slackness;

1 John 1:9. If we confess our sins, he is faithful and just to forgive us *our* sins, and to cleanse us from all unrighteousness.

Rev. 6:10. And they cried with a loud voice, saying, How long, O Lord, holy and true, dost thou not judge and avenge our blood on them that dwell on the earth?

Rev. 15:3. And they sing the song of Moses the servant of God, and the song of the Lamb, saying, Great and marvellous *are* thy works, Lord God Almighty; just and true *are* thy ways, thou King of saints.

FATHERHOOD OF: Ex. 4:22. And thou shalt say unto Pharaoh, Thus saith the Lord, Israel *is* my son, *even* my firstborn:

Deut. 14:1. Ye *are* the children of the Lord your God: ye shall not cut yourselves, nor make any baldness between your eyes for the dead.

Deut. 32:5. They have corrupted themselves, their spot *is* not *the spot* of his children: *they are* a perverse and crooked generation. 6. Do ye thus requite the Lord, O foolish people and unwise? *is* not he thy father *that* hath bought thee? hath he not made thee, and established thee?

2 Sam. 7:14. I will be his father, and he shall be my son. If he commit iniquity, I will chasten him with the rod of men, and with the stripes of the children of men:

1 Chr. 28:6. And he said unto me, Solomon thy son, he shall build my house and my courts: for I have chosen him *to be* my son, and I will be his father.

1 Chr. 29:10. Wherefore David blessed the LORD before all the congregation: and David said, Blessed *be* thou, LORD God of Israel our father, for ever and ever.

Psa. 68:5. A father of the fatherless, and a judge of the widows, *is* God in his holy habitation.

Psa. 89:26. He shall cry unto me, Thou *art* my father, my God, and the rock of my salvation.

Isa. 1:2. Hear, O heavens, and give ear, O earth: for the LORD hath spoken, I have nourished and brought up children, and they have rebelled against me.

Isa. 8:18. Behold, I and the children whom the LORD hath given me *are* for signs and for wonders in Israel from the LORD of hosts, which dwelleth in mount Zion.

Isa. 9:6. For unto us a child is born, unto us a son is given: and the government shall be upon his shoulder: and his name shall be called Wonderful, Counsellor, The mighty God, The everlasting Father, The Prince of Peace.

Isa. 63:16. Doubtless thou *art* our father, though Abraham be ignorant of us, and Israel acknowledge us not: thou, O LORD, *art* our father, our redeemer: thy name *is* from everlasting.

Isa. 64:8. But now, O LORD, thou *art* our father; we *are* the clay, and thou our potter; and we all *are* the work of thy hand.

Jer. 3:19. But I said, How shall I put thee among the children, and give thee a pleasant land, a goodly heritage of the hosts of nations? and I said, Thou shalt call me, My father; and shalt not turn away from me.

Hos. 1:10. *Ye are* the sons of the living God.

Hos. 11:1. When Israel *was* a child, then I loved him, and called my son out of Egypt.

Matt. 3:17. And lo a voice from heaven, saying, This is my beloved Son, in whom I am well pleased.

Matt. 5:45. That ye may be the children of your Father which is in heaven:

Matt. 6:4. That thine alms may be in secret: and thy Father which seeth in secret himself shall reward thee openly. [*v.* 6.] 8. Be not ye therefore like unto them: for your Father knoweth what things ye have need of, before ye ask him. 9. After this manner therefore pray ye: Our Father which art in heaven, Hallowed be thy name. Luke 11:2.

Matt. 7:11. If ye then, being evil, know how to give good gifts unto your children, how much more shall your Father which is in heaven give good things to them that ask him?

Matt. 10:20. For it is not ye that speak, but the Spirit of your Father which speaketh in you. 29. Are not two sparrows sold for a farthing? and one of them shall not fall on the ground without your Father. 32. Whosoever therefore shall confess me before men, him will I confess also before my Fa-

ther which is in heaven. 33. But whosoever shall deny me before men, him will I also deny before my Father which is in heaven.

Matt. 11:25. At that time Jesus answered and said, I thank thee, O Father, Lord of heaven and earth, because thou hast hid these things from the wise and prudent, and hast revealed them unto babes. 26. Even so, Father: for so it seemed good in thy sight. 27. All things are delivered unto me of my Father: and no man knoweth the Son, but the Father; neither knoweth any man the Father, save the Son, and *he* to whomsoever the Son will reveal *him*.

Matt. 12:50. For whosoever shall do the will of my Father which is in heaven, the same is my brother, and sister, and mother.

Matt. 13:43. Then shall the righteous shine forth as the sun in the kingdom of their Father.

Matt. 15:13. Every plant, which my heavenly Father hath not planted, shall be rooted up.

Matt. 16:17. Blessed art thou, Simon Barjona, for flesh and blood hath not revealed *it* unto thee, but my Father which is in heaven. 27. For the Son of man shall come in the glory of his Father with his angels;

Matt. 18:10. Take heed that ye despise not one of these little ones; for I say unto you, That in heaven their angels do always behold the face of my Father which is in heaven. 14. Even so it is not the will of your Father which is in heaven, that one of these little ones should perish. 19. Again I say unto you, That if two of you shall agree on earth as touching any thing that they shall ask, it shall be done for them of my Father which is in heaven.

Matt. 20:23. To sit on my right hand, and on my left, is not mine to give, but *it shall be given to them* for whom it is prepared of my Father.

Matt. 26:29. But I say unto you, I will not drink henceforth of this fruit of the vine, until that day when I drink it new with you in my Father's kingdom. 39. O my Father, if it be possible, let this cup pass from me: nevertheless not as I will, but as thou *wilt. v.* 42.

Mark 8:38. Whosoever therefore shall be ashamed of me and of my words in this adulterous and sinful generation, of him also shall the Son of man be ashamed, when he cometh in the glory of his Father with the holy angels.

Mark 11:25. And when ye stand praying, forgive, if ye have ought against any: that your Father also which is in heaven may forgive you your trespasses. ¹26. But if ye do not forgive, neither will your Father which is in heaven forgive your trespasses.   [¹ Omitted in R. V.]

Mark 13:32. But of that day and *that* hour knoweth no man, no, not the angels which are in heaven, neither the Son, but the Father.

Luke 2:49. And he said unto them, How

is it that ye sought me? wist ye not that I must be about my Father's business?

Luke 10:21. In that hour Jesus rejoiced in spirit, and said, I thank thee, O Father, Lord of heaven and earth, that thou hast hid these things from the wise and prudent, and hast revealed them unto babes: even so, Father; for so it seemed good in thy sight. 22. All things are delivered to me of my Father: and no man knoweth who the Son is, but the Father; and who the Father is, but the Son, and *he* to whom the Son will reveal *him*.

Luke 11:13. If ye then, being evil, know how to give good gifts unto your children: how much more shall *your* heavenly Father give the Holy Spirit to them that ask him?

Luke 22:29. And I appoint unto you a kingdom, as my Father hath appointed unto me;

Luke 23:46. And when Jesus had cried with a loud voice, he said, Father, into thy hands I commend my spirit: and having said thus, he gave up the ghost.

Luke 24:49. And, behold, I send the promise of my Father upon you: but tarry ye in the city of Jerusalem, until ye be endued with power from on high.

John 1:14. And the Word was made flesh, and dwelt among us, (and we beheld his glory, the glory as of the only begotten of the Father,) full of grace and truth. 18. No man hath seen God at any time; the only begotten Son, which is in the bosom of the Father, he hath declared *him*.

John 2:16. And said unto them that sold doves, Take these things hence; make not my Father's house an house of merchandise.

John 4:21. Jesus saith unto her, Woman, believe me, the hour cometh, when we shall neither in this mountain, nor yet at Jerusalem, worship the Father. 23. But the hour cometh, and now is, when the true worshippers shall worship the Father in spirit and in truth: for the Father seeketh such to worship him.

John 5:17. But Jesus answered them, My Father worketh hitherto, and I work. 18. Therefore the Jews sought the more to kill him, because he not only had broken the sabbath, but said also that God was his Father. making himself equal with God. 19. Then answered Jesus and said unto them, Verily, verily, I say unto you, The Son can do nothing of himself, but what he seeth the Father do: for what things soever he doeth, these also doeth the Son likewise. 20. For the Father loveth the Son, and sheweth him all things that himself doeth: and he will shew him greater works than these, that ye may marvel. 21. For as the Father raiseth up the dead and quickeneth *them;* even so the Son quickeneth whom he will. 22. For the Father judgeth no man, but hath committed all judgment unto the Son: 23. That all *men* should honour the Son, even as they honour the Father. He that honoureth not the Son honoureth not the Father which

hath sent him. 36. But I have greater witness than *that* of John: for the works which the Father hath given me to finish, the same works that I do, bear witness of me, that the Father hath sent me. 37. And the Father himself, which hath sent me, hath borne witness of me. Ye have neither heard his voice at any time, nor seen his shape. 43. I am come in my Father's name, and ye receive me not: if another shall come in his own name, him ye will receive.

John 6:27. Labour not for the meat which perisheth, but for that meat which endureth unto everlasting life, which the Son of man shall give unto you: for him hath God the Father sealed. 32. Then Jesus said unto them, Verily, verily, I say unto you, Moses gave you not that bread from heaven; but my Father giveth you the true bread from heaven. 44. No man can come to me, except the Father which hath sent me draw him: and I will raise him up at the last day. 45. It is written in the prophets, And they shall be all taught of God. Every man therefore that hath heard, and hath learned of the Father, cometh unto me. 46. Not that any man hath seen the Father, save he which is of God, he hath seen the Father.

John 8:19. Then said they unto him, Where is thy Father? Jesus answered, Ye neither know me, nor my Father: if ye had known me, ye should have known my Father also. 27. They understood not that he spake to them of the Father. 38. I speak that which I have seen with my Father: and ye do that which ye have seen with your father. 41. Ye do the deeds of your father. Then said they to him, We be not born of fornication; we have one Father, *even* God. 42. Jesus said unto them, If God were your Father, ye would love me: for I proceeded forth and came from God; neither came I of myself, but he sent me. 49. Jesus answered, I have not a devil; but I honour my Father, and ye do dishonour me.

John 10:15. As the Father knoweth me, even so know I the Father: and I lay down my life for the sheep. 29. My Father, which gave *them* me, is greater than all; and no *man* is able to pluck *them* out of my Father's hand. 30. I and *my* Father are one. 32. Jesus answered them, Many good works have I shewed you from my Father; for which of those works do ye stone me? 33. The Jews answered him, saying, For a good work we stone thee not; but for blasphemy: and because that thou, being a man, makest thyself God.

36. Say ye of him, whom the Father hath sanctified, and sent into the world, Thou blasphemest; because I said, I am the Son of God? 37. If I do not the works of my Father, believe me not. 38. But if I do, though ye believe not me, believe the works: that ye may know, and believe, that the Father *is* in me, and I in him.

John 12:26. If any man serve me, let him follow me; and where I am, there shall also my servant be : if any man serve me, him will *my* Father honour. 27. Now is my soul troubled; and what shall I say? Father, save me from this hour: but for this cause came I unto this hour. 28. Father, glorify thy name. Then came there a voice from heaven, *saying*, I have both glorified *it*, and will glorify *it* again.

50. And I know that his commandment is life everlasting : whatsoever I speak therefore, even as the Father said unto me, so I speak.

John 13:3. Jesus knowing that the Father had given all things into his hands, and that he was come from God, and went to God;

John 14:2. In my Father's house are many mansions : if *it were* not *so*, I would have told you. I go to prepare a place for you. 6. Jesus saith unto him, I am the way, the truth, and the life : no man cometh unto the Father, but by me. 7. If ye had known me, ye should have known my Father also: and from henceforth ye know him, and have seen him. 8. Philip saith unto him, Lord, shew us the Father, and it sufficeth us. 9. Jesus saith unto him, Have I been so long time with you, and yet hast thou not known me, Philip? he that hath seen me hath seen the Father ; and how sayest thou *then*, Shew us the Father? 10. Believest thou not that I am in the Father, and the Father in me? the words that I speak unto you I speak not of myself : but the Father that dwelleth in me, he doeth the works. 11. Believe me that I *am* in the Father, and the Father in me : or else believe me for the very works' sake. 12. Verily, verily, I say unto you, He that believeth on me, the works that I do shall he do also; and greater *works* than these shall he do ; because I go unto my Father. 13. And whatsoever ye shall ask in my name, that will I do, that the Father may be glorified in the Son. 16. And I will pray the Father, and he shall give you another Comforter, that he may abide with you for ever ; 20. At that day ye shall know that I *am* in my Father, and ye in me, and I in you. 21. He that hath my commandments, and keepeth them, he it is that loveth me : and he that loveth me shall be loved of my father, and I will love him, and will manifest myself to him. 23. Jesus answered and said unto him, If a man love me, he will keep my words : and my Father will love him, and we will come unto him, and make our abode with him. 24. He that loveth me not keepeth not my sayings : and the word which ye hear is not mine, but the Father's which sent me. 26. But the Comforter, *which is* the Holy Ghost, whom the Father will send in my name, he shall teach you all things, and bring all things to your remembrance, whatsoever I have said unto you. 31. But that the world may know that I love the Father ; and as the Father gave me commandment, even so I do.

John 15:8. Herein is my Father glorified, **that** ye bear much fruit ; so shall ye be my disciples. 9. As the Father hath loved me. so have I loved you : continue ye in my love. 10. If ye keep my commandments, ye shall abide in my love ; even as I have kept my Father's commandments, and abide in his love. 16. That whatsoever ye shall ask of the Father in my name, he may give it you. 23. He that hateth me hateth my Father also. 24. If I had not done among them the works which none other man did, they had not had sin : but now have they both seen and hated both me and my Father. 26. But when the Comforter is come, whom I will send unto you from the Father, *even* the Spirit of truth, which proceedeth from the Father, he shall testify of me :

John 16.3. And these things will they do unto you, because they have not known the Father, nor me. 10. Of righteousness, because I go to my Father, and ye see me no more ; 15. All things that the Father hath are mine : 23. Whatsoever ye shall ask the Father in my name, he will give *it* you. 25. These things have I spoken unto you in proverbs : but the time cometh, when I shall no more speak unto you in proverbs, but I shall shew you plainly of the Father. 26. At that day ye shall ask in my name : and I say not unto you, that I will pray the Father for you : 27. For the Father himself loveth you, because ye have loved me, and have believed that I came out from God. 28. I came forth from the Father, and am come into the world : again, I leave the world, and go to the Father.

John 17:1. These words spake Jesus, and lifted up his eyes to heaven, and said, Father, the hour is come ; glorify thy Son, that thy Son also may glorify thee : 5. And now, O Father, glorify thou me with thine own self with the glory which I had with thee before the world was. 11. Holy Father, keep through thine own name those whom thou hast given me, that they may be one, as we *are*. 21. That they all may be one ; as thou, Father, *art* in me. and I in thee, that they also may be one in us : that the world may believe that thou hast sent me. 24. Father, I will that they also, whom thou hast given me, be with me where I am ; that they may behold my glory, which thou hast given me : for thou lovedst me before the foundation of the world.

John 20:17. Jesus saith unto her, Touch me not ; for I am not yet ascended to my Father : but go to my brethren, and say unto them, I ascend unto my Father, and your Father ; and *to* my God, and your God. 21. Then said Jesus to them again, Peace *be* unto you : as *my* Father hath sent me, even so send I you.

Acts 1:4. Wait for the promise of the Father, which, *saith he*, ye have heard of me.

Acts 2:33. Therefore being by the right hand of God exalted, and having received **of** the Father the promise of the Holy Ghost, he hath shed forth this, which ye now **see** and hear.

Rom. 1:3. His son Jesus Christ our Lord, which was made of the seed of David according to the flesh; 4. And declared *to be* the Son of God with power, according to the spirit of holiness, by the resurrection from the dead: 7. To all that be in Rome, beloved of God, called *to be* saints: Grace to you and peace from God our Father and the Lord Jesus Christ. 1 Cor. 1:3; Gal. 1:3; Eph. 1:2; 6:23; Phil. 1:2; Col. 1:2; 1 Thess. 1:1; 2 Thess. 1:2; Tit. 1:4.

Rom. 8:15. For ye have not received the spirit of bondage again to fear; but ye have received the Spirit of adoption, whereby we cry, Abba, Father.

1 Cor 8:6. But to us *there is but* one God, the Father, of whom *are* all things, and we in him;

1 Cor. 15:24. Then *cometh* the end, when he shall have delivered up the kingdom to God even the Father;

2 Cor. 1:3. Blessed *be* God, even the Father of our Lord Jesus Christ, the Father of mercies, and the God of all comfort:

2 Cor. 6:18. And will be a Father unto you, and ye shall be my sons and daughters, saith the Lord Almighty.

Gal. 1:1. Paul, an apostle, (not of men, neither by man, but by Jesus Christ, and God the Father, who raised him from the dead;) 4. Who gave himself for our sins, that he might deliver us from this present evil world, according to the will of God and our Father:

Gal. 4:4. God sent forth his Son, made of a woman, 5. To redeem them that were under the law, that we might receive the adoption of sons. 6. And because ye are sons, God hath sent forth the Spirit of his Son into your hearts, crying, Abba, Father. 7. Wherefore thou art no more a servant, but a son; and if a son, then an heir [1] of God through Christ. [1 R. V. through God]

Eph. 1:3. Blessed *be* the God and Father of our Lord Jesus Christ, who hath blessed us with all spiritual blessings in heavenly *places* in Christ: 17. That the God of our Lord Jesus Christ, the Father of glory, may give unto you the spirit of wisdom and revelation in the knowledge of him:

Eph. 2:18. For through him we both have access by one Spirit unto the Father.

Eph. 3:14. For this cause I bow my knees unto the Father of our Lord Jesus Christ,

Eph. 4:6. One God and Father of all, who *is* above all, and through all, and in you all.

Eph. 5:20. Giving thanks always for all things unto God and the Father in the name of our Lord Jesus Christ;

Col. 1:3. We give thanks to God and the Father of our Lord Jesus Christ, praying always for you, 12. Giving thanks unto the Father, which hath made us meet to be partakers of the inheritance of the saints in light:

Col. 2:2. [1] The acknowledgment of the mystery of God, and of the Father, and of Christ; [1 R. V. that they may know the mystery of God, *even* Christ,]

Col. 3:17. And whatsoever ye do in word or deed, *do* all in the name of the Lord Jesus, giving thanks to God and the Father by him.

1 Thess. 1:1. Paul, and Silvanus, and Timotheus, unto the church of the Thessalonians *which is* in God the Father and *in* the Lord Jesus Christ: 3. Remembering without ceasing your work of faith, and labour of love, and patience of hope in our Lord Jesus Christ, in the sight of God and our Father;

1 Thess. 3:11. Now God himself and our Father, and our Lord Jesus Christ, direct our way unto you. 13. To the end he may stablish your hearts unblameable in holiness before God, even our Father,

2 Thess. 1:1. Paul, and Silvanus, and Timotheus, unto the church of the Thessalonians in God our Father and the Lord Jesus Christ: 2. Grace unto you, and peace, from God our Father and the Lord Jesus Christ.

2 Thess. 2:16. Now our Lord Jesus Christ himself, and God, even our Father, which hath loved us, and hath given *us* everlasting consolation and good hope through grace,

Heb. 1:5. For unto which of the angels said he at any time, . . . I will be to him a Father, and he shall be to me a Son? 6. And again, when he bringeth in the firstbegotten into the world, he saith, And let all the angels of God worship him.

Heb. 12:9. Shall we not much rather be in subjection unto the Father of spirits, and live?

Jas. 1:17. Every good gift and every perfect gift is from above, and cometh down from the Father of lights, 27. Pure religion and undefiled before God and the Father is this, To visit the fatherless and widows in their affliction, *and* to keep himself unspotted from the world.

Jas. 3:9. Therewith bless we God, even the Father;

1 Pet. 1:2. Elect according to the foreknowledge of God the Father, 3. Blessed *be* the God and Father of our Lord Jesus Christ, which according to his abundant mercy hath begotten us again unto a lively hope by the resurrection of Jesus Christ from the dead, 17. And if ye call on the Father, who without respect of persons judgeth according to every man's work, pass the time of your sojourning *here* in fear:

1 John 1:2. (For the life was manifested, and we have seen *it*, and bear witness, and shew unto you that eternal life, which was with the Father, and was manifested unto us;)

1 John 2:1. And if any man sin, we have an advocate with the Father, Jesus Christ the righteous: 13. I write unto you, little children, because ye have known the Father. 15. If any man love the world, the love of the Father is not in him. 22. Who is a liar but he that denieth that Jesus is the Christ? He is antichrist, that denieth the Father and the Son. 23. Whosoever

denieth the Son, the same hath not the Father: [but] he that acknowledgeth the Son hath the Father also. 24. If that which ye have heard from the beginning shall remain in you, ye also shall continue in the Son, and in the Father.

1 John 3:1. Behold, what manner of love the Father hath bestowed upon us, that we should be called the sons of God:

1 John 4:14. And we have seen and do testify that the Father sent the Son to be the Saviour of the world.

2 John 3. Grace be with you, mercy, and peace, from God the Father, and from the Lord Jesus Christ, the Son of the Father, in truth and love. 4. I rejoiced greatly that I found of thy children walking in truth, as we have received a commandment from the Father. 9. He that abideth in the doctrine of Christ, he hath both the Father and the Son.

Jude 1. Jude, the servant of Jesus Christ, and brother of James, to them that are sanctified by God the Father,

Rev. 1:5. Unto him that loved us, and washed us from our sins in his own blood, 6. And hath made us kings and priests unto God and his Father; to him be glory and dominion for ever and ever.

Rev. 3:5. He that overcometh, the same shall be clothed in white raiment; and I will not blot out his name out of the book of life, but I will confess his name before my Father, and before his angels.

Rev. 14:1. And I looked, and, lo, a Lamb stood on the mount Sion, and with him an hundred forty and four thousand, having his Father's name written in their foreheads.

See ADOPTION.

FAVOR OF : See GOD, GRACE OF.

FOREKNOWLEDGE OF : 1 Sam. 23:10. Then said David, O LORD God of Israel, thy servant hath certainly heard that Saul seeketh to come to Keilah, to destroy the city for my sake. 11. Will the men of Keilah deliver me up into his hand? will Saul come down, as thy servant hath heard? O LORD God of Israel, I beseech thee, tell thy servant. And the LORD said, He will come down. 12. Then said David, Will the men of Keilah deliver me and my men into the hand of Saul? And the LORD said, They will deliver thee up.

Isa. 42:9. Behold, the former things are come to pass, and new things do I declare : before they spring forth I tell you of them.

Isa. 44:7. And who, as I, shall call, and shall declare it, and set it in order for me, since I appointed the ancient people? and the things that are coming, and shall come, let them shew unto them.

Isa. 45:11. Thus saith the LORD, the Holy One of Israel, and his Maker, Ask me of things to come concerning my sons, and concerning the work of my hands command ye me.

Isa. 46:9. I am God, and there is none like me, 10. Declaring the end from the beginning, and from ancient times the things that are not yet done, saying, My counsel shall stand, and I will do all my pleasure :

Isa. 48:5. I have even from the beginning declared it to thee ; before it came to pass I shewed it thee: lest thou shouldest say, Mine idol hath done them ; and my graven image, and my molten image, hath commanded them. [v. 3.] 6. Thou hast heard, see all this ; and will not ye declare it ? I have shewed thee new things from this time, even hidden things, and thou didst not know them.

Jer. 1:5. Before I formed thee in the belly I knew thee ; and before thou camest forth out of the womb I sanctified thee, and I ordained thee a prophet unto the nations.

Dan. 2:28. But there is a God in heaven that revealeth secrets, and maketh known to the king Nebuchadnezzar what shall be in the latter days. Thy dream, and the visions of thy head upon thy bed, are these ; 29. As for thee, O king, thy thoughts came into thy mind upon thy bed, what should come to pass hereafter : and he that revealeth secrets maketh known to thee what shall come to pass.

Matt. 6:8. Your Father knoweth what things ye have need of, before ye ask him.

Matt. 24:36. But of that day and hour knoweth no man, no, not the angels of heaven, but my Father only.

Acts 15:18. Known unto God are all his works from the beginning of the world.

Rom. 8:29. For whom he did foreknow, he also did predestinate to be conformed to the image of his Son,

Rom. 11:2. God hath not cast away his people which he foreknew.

1 Pet. 1:2. Elect according to the foreknowledge of God the Father,

See GOD, KNOWLEDGE OF, WISDOM OF ; PREDESTINATION.

GLORY OF : Ex. 3:2. The angel of the LORD appeared unto him in a flame of fire out of the midst of a bush : and he looked, and, behold, the bush burned with fire, and the bush was not consumed.

Ex. 19:18. Sinai was altogether on a smoke, because the LORD descended upon it in fire : and the smoke thereof ascended as the smoke of a furnace, and the whole mount quaked greatly. vs. 16,19 ; Ex. 20:18,19 ; Deut. 4:11, 12,33,36 ; 5:5,24,25.

Ex. 24:10. They saw the God of Israel : and there was under his feet as it were a paved work of a sapphire stone, and as it were the body of heaven in his clearness. 17. And the sight of the glory of the LORD was like devouring fire on the top of the mount in the eyes of the children of Israel.

Ex. 33:20. Thou canst not see my face : for there shall no man see me, and live. 22. It shall come to pass, while my glory passeth by, that I will put thee in a clift of the rock, v. 23.

Ex. 34:5. The LORD descended in the cloud,

and stood with him there, and proclaimed the name of the LORD. *vs.* 29–35; Ex. 33:18,19.

Ex. 40:34. Then a cloud covered the tent of the congregation, and the glory of the LORD filled the tabernacle. 35. And Moses was not able to enter into the tent of the congregation, because the cloud abode thereon, and the glory of the LORD filled the tabernacle.

Deut. 10:17. The LORD your God *is* God of gods, and Lord of lords, a great God, a mighty, and a terrible, Deut. 7:21.

Deut. 28:58. That thou mayest fear this glorious and fearful name, THE LORD THY GOD;

Deut. 33:2. He shined forth from mount Paran, and he came with ten thousands of saints: 26. *There is* none like unto the God of Jeshurun, *who* rideth upon the heaven in thy help, and in his excellency on the sky.

1 Kin. 19:12. After the earthquake a fire; *but* the LORD *was* not in the fire: and after the fire a still small voice.

Job 9:32. *He is* not a man, as I *am, that* I should answer him, *and* we should come together in judgment. 33. Neither is there any daysman betwixt us, *that* might lay his hand upon us both.

Job 13:11. Shall not his excellency make you afraid? and his dread fall upon you?

Job 22:12. *Is* not God in the height of heaven? and behold the height of the stars, how high they are!

Job 25:3. Is there any number of his armies? and upon whom doth not his light arise?

Job 35:5. Look unto the heavens, and see; and behold the clouds *which* are higher than thou. 6. If thou sinnest, what doest thou against him? or *if* thy transgressions be multiplied, what doest thou unto him? 7. If thou be righteous, what givest thou him? or what receiveth he of thine hand?

Job 37:5. God thundereth marvellously with his voice; great things doeth he, which we cannot comprehend. 22. With God *is* terrible majesty. *v.* 4.

Psa. 8:9. O LORD, our Lord, how excellent *is* thy name in all the earth!

Psa. 18:9. He bowed the heavens also, and came down: and darkness *was* under his feet. 10. And he rode upon a cherub, and did fly: yea, he did fly upon the wings of the wind. 11. He made darkness his secret place; his pavilion round about him *were* dark waters *and* thick clouds of the skies. *vs.* 7–15; 2 Sam. 22.

Psa. 19:1. The heavens declare the glory of God; and the firmament sheweth his handywork. *vs.* 2–4.

Psa. 24:8. Who *is* this King of glory? The LORD strong and mighty, the LORD mighty in battle. 9. Lift up your heads, O ye gates; even lift *them* up, ye everlasting doors; and the King of glory shall come in. *v.* 10.

Psa. 29:2. Give unto the LORD the glory due unto his name; worship the LORD in the beauty of holiness. *vs.* 3,4.

Psa. 46:10. Be still, and know that I *am* God: I will be exalted among the heathen, I will be exalted in the earth.

Psa. 57:5. Be thou exalted, O God, above the heavens; *let* thy glory *be* above all the earth. *v.* 11.

Psa. 68:24. They have seen thy goings, O God; *even* the goings of my God, my King, in the sanctuary.

Psa. 72:18. Blessed *be* the LORD God, the God of Israel, who only doeth wondrous things. 19. And blessed *be* his glorious name for ever: and let the whole earth be filled *with* his glory;

Psa. 76:4. Thou *art* more glorious *and* excellent than the mountains of prey.

Psa. 96:3. Declare his glory among the heathen, his wonders among all people. 4. The LORD *is* great, and greatly to be praised: he *is* to be feared above all gods. 6. Honour and majesty *are* before him: strength and beauty *are* in his sanctuary. 7. Give unto the LORD, O ye kindreds of the people, give unto the LORD glory and strength. 1 Chr. 16:24,25.

Psa. 97:2. Clouds and darkness *are* round about him: righteousness and judgment *are* the habitation of his throne. 6. The heavens declare his righteousness, and all the people see his glory. 9. Thou, LORD, *art* high above all the earth: thou art exalted far above all gods. *vs.* 3–5.

Psa. 102:16. When the LORD shall build up Zion, he shall appear in his glory. 21. To declare the name of the LORD in Zion, and his praise in Jerusalem; 22. When the people are gathered together, and the kingdoms, to serve the LORD.

Psa. 104:31. The glory of the LORD shall endure for ever: the LORD shall rejoice in his works.

Psa. 106:8. He saved them for his name's sake, that he might make his mighty power to be known.

Psa. 113:4. The LORD *is* high above all nations, *and* his glory above the heavens.

Psa. 145:5. I will speak of the glorious honour of thy majesty, and of thy wondrous works. 11. They shall speak of the glory of thy kingdom, and talk of thy power; 12. To make known to the sons of men his mighty acts, and the glorious majesty of his kingdom.

Isa. 1:24. Therefore saith the Lord, the LORD of hosts, the mighty One of Israel,

Isa. 2:10. Enter into the rock, and hide thee in the dust, for fear of the LORD, and for the glory of his majesty.

Isa. 6:1. I saw also the Lord sitting upon a throne, high and lifted up, and his train filled the temple. 3. And one cried unto another, and said, Holy, holy, holy, *is* the LORD of hosts: the whole earth *is* full of his glory. *vs.* 1–5.

Isa. 12:6. Cry out and shout, thou inhabitant of Zion: for great *is* the Holy One of Israel in the midst of thee.

Isa. 24:23. The LORD of hosts shall reign

in mount Zion, and in Jerusalem, and before his ancients gloriously.

Isa. 26:15. Thou hast increased the nation: thou art glorified;

Isa. 28:5. In that day shall the LORD of hosts be for a crown of glory, and for a diadem of beauty, unto the residue of his people,

Isa. 29:23. When he seeth his children, the work of mine hands, in the midst of him, they shall sanctify my name, and sanctify the Holy One of Jacob, and shall fear the God of Israel.

Isa. 30:30. The LORD shall cause his glorious voice to be heard, and shall shew the lighting down of his arm, with the indignation of *his* anger, and *with* the flame of a devouring fire, *with* scattering, and tempest, and hailstones.

Isa. 33:5. The LORD is exalted; for he dwelleth on high: he hath filled Zion with judgment and righteousness. 10. Now will I rise, saith the LORD; now will I be exalted; now will I lift up myself.

Isa. 35:2. They shall see the glory of the LORD, *and* the excellency of our God.

Isa. 40:5. The glory of the LORD shall be revealed, and all flesh shall see *it* together:

Isa. 43:7. Every one that is called by my name: for I have created him for my glory, I have formed him; yea, I have made him. 21. This people have I formed for myself; they shall shew forth my praise.

Isa. 44:23. The LORD hath redeemed Jacob, and glorified himself in Israel.

Isa. 48:11. For mine own sake, *even* for mine own sake, will I do *it:* for how should my *name* be polluted? and I will not give my glory unto another. *v.* 9.

Isa. 49:3. Thou *art* my servant, O Israel, in whom I will be glorified. 26. All flesh shall know that I the LORD *am* thy Saviour and thy Redeemer, the mighty One of Jacob.

Isa. 52:10. The LORD hath made bare his holy arm in the eyes of all the nations; and all the ends of the earth shall see the salvation of our God.

Isa. 55:9. *As* the heavens are higher than the earth, so are my ways higher than your ways, and my thoughts than your thoughts.

Isa. 57:15. Thus saith the high and lofty One that inhabiteth eternity, whose name *is* Holy; I dwell in the high and holy *place.*

Isa. 60:1. Arise, shine; for thy light is come, and the glory of the LORD is risen upon thee. 2. For, behold, the darkness shall cover the earth, and gross darkness the people: but the LORD shall rise upon thee, and his glory shall be seen upon thee. 6. They shall shew forth the praises of the LORD. 19. But the LORD shall be unto thee an everlasting light, and thy God thy glory. 20. Thy sun shall no more go down; neither shall thy moon withdraw itself: for the LORD shall be thine everlasting light, and the days of thy mourning shall be ended. 21. Thy people also *shall be* all righteous: they shall inherit the land for ever, the branch

of my planting, the work of my hands, that I may be glorified.

Isa. 61:3. To appoint unto them that mourn in Zion, to give unto them beauty for ashes, the oil of joy for mourning, the garment of praise for the spirit of heaviness; that they might be called trees of righteousness, the planting of the LORD, that he might be glorified.

Isa. 62:3. Thou shalt also be a crown of glory in the hand of the LORD, and a royal diadem in the hand of thy God.

Isa. 63:12. That led *them* by the right hand of Moses with his glorious arm, dividing the water before them, to make himself an everlasting name? *v.* 14.

Isa. 66:1. The heaven *is* my throne, and the earth *is* my footstool: where *is* the house that ye build unto me? and where *is* the place of my rest? 2. For all those *things* hath mine hand made, 18. I will gather all the nations and tongues; and they shall come, and see my glory.

Jer. 13:11. That they might be unto me for a people, and for a name, and for a praise, and for a glory:

Jer. 17:12. A glorious high throne from the beginning *is* the place of our sanctuary.

Jer. 33:9. It shall be to me a name of joy, a praise and an honour before all the nations of the earth, which shall hear all the good that I do unto them:

Ezek. 1:26. Above the firmament that *was* over their heads *was* the likeness of a throne, as the appearance of a sapphire stone: and upon the likeness of the throne *was* the likeness as the appearance of a man above upon it. 27. And I saw as the colour of amber, as the appearance of fire round about within it, from the appearance of his loins even upward, and from the appearance of his loins even downward, I saw as it were the appearance of fire, and it had brightness round about. 28. As the appearance of the bow that is in the cloud in the day of rain, so *was* the appearance of the brightness round about. This *was* the appearance of the likeness of the glory of the LORD. And when I saw *it*, I fell upon my face, and I heard a voice of one that spake.

Ezek. 3:12. Then the spirit took me up, and I heard behind me a voice of a great rushing, *saying*, Blessed *be* the glory of the LORD from his place. 23. Then I arose, and went forth into the plain: and, behold, the glory of the LORD stood there, as the glory which I saw by the river of Chebar: and I fell on my face.

Ezek. 8:4. And, behold, the glory of the God of Israel *was* there, according to the vision that I saw in the plain.

Ezek. 20:14. I wrought for my name's sake, that it should not be polluted before the heathen, in whose sight I brought them out. 44. Ye shall know that I *am* the LORD, when I have wrought with you for my name's sake,

Ezek. 36:22. I do not *this* for your sakes, O house of Israel, but for mine holy name's sake, which ye have profaned among the heathen, whither ye went. 23. And I will sanctify my great name, which was profaned among the heathen, which ye have profaned in the midst of them; and the heathen shall know that I *am* the LORD, saith the Lord GOD, when I shall be sanctified in you before their eyes.

Ezek. 43:4. And the glory of the LORD came into the house by the way of the gate whose prospect *is* toward the east. 5. So the spirit took me up, and brought me into the inner court; and, behold, the glory of the LORD filled the house.

Hab. 3:3. His glory covered the heavens, and the earth was full of his praise. 4. And *his* brightness was as the light; he had horns *coming* out of his hand: and there *was* the hiding of his power. 5. Before him went the pestilence, and burning coals went forth at his feet. *v.* 6.

Matt. 6:9. Our Father which art in heaven, Hallowed be thy name. 13. Thine is the kingdom, and the power, and the glory, for ever.

Luke 2:14. Glory to God in the highest, and on earth peace, good will toward men.

John 8:50. I seek not mine own glory: there is one that seeketh and judgeth.

John 12:28. Father, glorify thy name. Then came there a voice from heaven, *saying*, I have both glorified *it*, and will glorify *it* again.

John 13:31. Now is the Son of man glorified, and God is glorified in him. 32. If God be glorified in him, God shall also glorify him in himself, and shall straightway glorify him.

John 14:13. Whatsoever ye shall ask in my name, that will I do, that the Father may be glorified in the Son.

John 17:1. Glorify thy Son, that thy Son also may glorify thee: 10. All mine are thine, and thine are mine; and I am glorified in them.

Acts 7:55. But he, being full of the Holy Ghost, looked up stedfastly into heaven, and saw the glory of God, and Jesus standing on the right hand of God,

Rom. 1:23. And changed the glory of the uncorruptible God into an image made like to corruptible man, and to birds, and four-footed beasts, and creeping things.

Rom. 11:36. Of him, and through him, and to him, *are* all things: to whom *be* glory for ever.

2 Cor. 1:20. All the promises of God in him *are* yea, and in him Amen, unto the glory of God by us.

2 Cor. 4:15. All things *are* for your sakes, that the abundant grace might through the thanksgiving of many redound to the glory of God.

Eph. 1:6. To the praise of the glory of his grace, wherein he hath made us accepted in the beloved. 12. We should be to the praise of his glory, who first trusted in Christ. 14. The redemption of the purchased possession, unto the praise of his glory.

Eph. 2:7. That in the ages to come he might shew the exceeding riches of his grace in *his* kindness toward us through Christ Jesus.

Eph. 3:21. Unto him *be* glory in the church by Christ Jesus throughout all ages, world without end.

Phil. 1:11. Being filled with the fruits of righteousness, which are by Jesus Christ, unto the glory and praise of God.

Phil. 2:11. Every tongue should confess that Jesus Christ *is* Lord, to the glory of God the Father.

Phil. 4:19. My God shall supply all your need according to his riches in glory by Christ Jesus.

1 Tim. 6:15. *Who is* the blessed and only Potentate, the King of kings, and Lord of lords; 16. Who only hath immortality, dwelling in the light which no man can approach unto; whom no man hath seen, nor can see: to whom *be* honour and power everlasting.

Heb. 12:18. For ye are not come unto the mount that might be touched, and that burned with fire, nor unto blackness, and darkness, and tempest, 19. And the sound of a trumpet, and the voice of words; which *voice* they that heard entreated that the word should not be spoken to them any more: 20. (For they could not endure that which was commanded, And if so much as a beast touch the mountain, it shall be stoned, or thrust through with a dart: 21. And so terrible was the sight, *that* Moses said, I exceedingly fear and quake:)

Jude 25. To the only wise God our Saviour, *be* glory and majesty, dominion and power, both now and ever.

Rev. 4:11. Thou art worthy, O Lord, to receive glory and honour and power: for thou hast created all things, and for thy pleasure they are and were created.

Rev. 15:8. The temple was filled with smoke from the glory of God, and from his power;

Rev. 21:10. And he carried me away in the spirit to a great and high mountain, and shewed me that great city, the holy Jerusalem, descending out of heaven from God, 11. Having the glory of God: 23. The city had no need of the sun, neither of the moon, to shine in it: for the glory of God did lighten it, and the Lamb *is* the light thereof.

See GLORY; PRAISE.

GOODNESS OF: Ex. 33:19. I will make all my goodness pass before thee,

Ex. 34:6. And the LORD passed by before him, and proclaimed, The LORD, The LORD God, merciful and gracious, longsuffering, and ¹ abundant in goodness and truth,

[¹ R. V. plenteous in mercy]

Deut. 30:9. And the LORD thy God will make thee plenteous in every work of thine hand, in the fruit of thy body, and in the fruit of thy cattle, and in the fruit of thy land, for good: for the LORD will again rejoice over thee for good, as he rejoiced over thy fathers:

2 Chr. 5:13. It came even to pass, as the trumpeters and singers *were* as one, to make one sound to be heard in praising and thanking the LORD; and when they lifted up *their* voice with the trumpets and cymbals and instruments of musick, and praised the LORD, *saying*, For *he is* good; for his mercy *endureth* for ever: that *then* the house was filled with a cloud, *even* the house of the LORD; chapter 7:3.

Psa. 8:4. What is man, that thou art mindful of him? and the son of man, that thou visitest him? *vs.* 1-9; Psa. 144:3.

Psa. 17:7. Shew thy marvellous lovingkindness, O thou that savest by thy right hand them which put their trust *in thee* from those that rise up *against them.*

Psa. 25:8. Good and upright *is* the LORD: *vs.* 9,10.

Psa. 33:5. The earth is full of the goodness of the LORD.

Psa. 34:8. O taste and see that the LORD *is* good:

Psa. 36:7. How excellent *is* thy lovingkindness, O God! therefore the children of men put their trust under the shadow of thy wings.

Psa. 52:1. The goodness of God *endureth* continually. 9. I will wait on thy name; for *it is* good before thy saints.

Psa. 68:19. Blessed *be* the Lord, *who* daily loadeth us *with benefits, even* the God of our salvation.

Psa. 69:16. Thy lovingkindness *is* good:

Psa. 73:1. Truly God *is* good to Israel, *even* to such as are of a clean heart.

Psa. 86:5. For thou, Lord, *art* good, and ready to forgive; and plenteous in mercy unto all them that call upon thee.

Psa. 100:5. The LORD *is* good; his mercy *is* everlasting;

Psa. 106:1. O give thanks unto the LORD; for *he is* good:

Psa. 107:8. Oh that *men* would praise the LORD *for* his goodness, and *for* his wonderful works to the children of men! 9. For he satisfieth the longing soul, and filleth the hungry soul with goodness. 43. Whoso *is* wise, and will observe these *things*, even they shall understand the lovingkindness of the LORD.

Psa. 118:29. O give thanks unto the LORD; for *he is* good: for his mercy *endureth* for ever. Psa. 135:3; 136:1; 1 Chr. 16:34.

Psa. 119:64. The earth, O LORD, is full of thy mercy: 68. Thou *art* good, and doest good;

Psa. 139:17. How precious also are thy thoughts unto me, O God! how great is the sum of them! 18. *If* I should count them, they are more in number than the sand: when I awake, I am still with thee.

Psa. 143:10. Thy spirit *is* good;

Psa. 145:7. They shall abundantly utter the memory of thy great goodness, 9. The LORD *is* good to all: and his tender mercies *are* over all his works.

Isa. 63:7. I will mention the lovingkindnesses of the LORD, *and* the praises of the LORD, according to all that the LORD hath bestowed on us, and the great goodness toward the house of Israel, which he hath bestowed on them according to his mercies, and according to the multitude of his lovingkindnesses.

Jer. 9:24. I *am* the LORD which exercise lovingkindness, judgment, and righteousness, in the earth: for in these *things* I delight, saith the LORD.

Lam. 3:25. The LORD *is* good unto them that wait for him, to the soul *that* seeketh him.

Hos. 3:5. The children of Israel . . . shall fear the LORD and his goodness in the latter days.

Nah. 1:7. The LORD *is* good, a strong hold in the day of trouble;

Matt. 7:11. If ye then, being evil, know how to give good gifts unto your children, how much more shall your Father which is in heaven give good things to them that ask him?

Matt. 19:17. And he said unto him, Why callest thou me good? *there is* none good but one, *that is*, God: Mark 10:18; Luke 18:19.

Luke 1:53. He hath filled the hungry with good things;

Luke 6:35. He is kind unto the unthankful and *to* the evil.

Rom. 2:4. Or despisest thou the riches of his goodness and forbearance and longsuffering; not knowing that the goodness of God leadeth thee to repentance?

Rom. 11:22. Behold therefore the goodness and severity of God: on them which fell, severity; but toward thee, goodness, if thou continue in *his* goodness: otherwise thou also shalt be cut off.

2 Thess. 1:11. Wherefore also we pray always for you, that our God would count you worthy of *this* calling, and fulfil all the good pleasure of *his* goodness, and the work of faith with power:

Tit. 3:4. The kindness and love of God our Saviour toward man appeared,

Jas. 1:5. If any of you lack wisdom, let him ask of God, that giveth to all *men* liberally, and upbraideth not; and it shall be given him. 17. Every good gift and every perfect gift is from above, and cometh down from the Father of lights,

1 John 4:8. God is love.

See GOD, GRACE OF, LONGSUFFERING OF, LOVE OF, MERCY OF.

GRACE OF: Gen. 6:8. Noah found grace in the eyes of the LORD. *v.* 9.

Gen. 18:26. And the LORD said, If I find in Sodom fifty righteous within the city, then I will spare all the place for their sakes, *vs.* 28,30,32.

Gen. 32:28. Thy name shall be called no more Jacob, but Israel: for as a prince hast thou power with God and with men, and hast prevailed.

Gen. 46:4. I will go down with thee into Egypt; and I will also surely bring thee up *again:*

Ex. 3:12. And he said, certainly I will be with thee; and this *shall be* a token unto thee, that I have sent thee: When thou hast brought forth the people out of Egypt, ye shall serve God upon this mountain.

Ex. 20:24. In all places where I record my name I will come unto thee, and I will bless thee.

Ex. 24:2. Moses alone shall come near the LORD: Ex. 20:21.

Ex. 33:11. The LORD spake unto Moses face to face, as a man speaketh unto his friend. 17. Thou hast found grace in my sight, and I know thee by name. 22. While my glory passeth by, . . . I will put thee in a clift of the rock, and will cover thee with my hand while I pass by: 23. And I will take away mine hand, and thou shalt see my back parts: but my face shall not be seen. *v.* 12.

Lev. 26:11. I will set my tabernacle among you: and my soul shall not abhor you. 12. And I will walk among you, and will be your God,

Num. 5:3. Their camps, in the midst whereof I dwell.

Num. 6:27. They shall put my name upon the children of Israel; and I will bless them.

Num. 14:14. Thou LORD *art* among this people, that thou LORD art seen face to face, and *that* thy cloud standeth over them, and *that* thou goest before them,

Num. 23:20. I have received *commandment* to bless: and he hath blessed; and I cannot reverse it. 21. He hath not beheld iniquity in Jacob, neither hath he seen perverseness in Israel: the LORD his God *is* with him, and the shout of a king *is* among them. Num. 22:12; 24:1.

Deut. 4:7. What nation *is there* so great, who *hath* God so nigh unto them, as the LORD our God *is* in all *things that* we call upon him *for?*

Deut. 33:23. Naphtali, satisfied with favour, and full with the blessing of the LORD:

Josh. 1:5. As I was with Moses, *so* I will be with thee: I will not fail thee, nor forsake thee. 9. The LORD thy God *is* with thee whithersoever thou goest. Deut. 31: 6,8.

1 Kin. 6:13. I will dwell among the children of Israel, and will not forsake my people Israel.

2 Chr. 15:2. The LORD *is* with you, while ye be with him; and if ye seek him, he will be found of you;

Job 10:12. Thou hast granted me life and favour, and thy visitation hath preserved my spirit.

Job 22:27. Thou shalt make thy prayer unto him, and he shall hear thee,

Job 29:3. When his candle shined upon my head, *and when* by his light I walked *through* darkness; 4. As I was in the days of my youth, when the secret of God *was*

upon my tabernacle; 5. When the Almighty *was* yet with me,

Psa. 3:8. Thy blessing *is* upon thy people.

Psa. 5:12. Thou, LORD, wilt bless the righteous; with favour wilt thou compass him as *with* a shield.

Psa. 11:7. The righteous LORD loveth righteousness; his countenance doth behold the upright.

Psa. 18:19. He brought me forth also into a large place; he delivered me, because he delighted in me. 25. With the merciful thou wilt shew thyself merciful; with an upright man thou wilt shew thyself upright; *v.* 26; 2 Sam. 22:20.

Psa. 24:4. He that hath clean hands, and a pure heart; 5. He shall receive the blessing from the LORD,

Psa. 25:14. The secret of the LORD *is* with them that fear him; and he will shew them his covenant.

Psa. 30:7. LORD, by thy favour thou hast made my mountain to stand strong:

Psa. 36:9. For with thee *is* the fountain of life: in thy light shall we see light.

Psa. 37:18. The LORD knoweth the days of the upright: 23. The steps of a *good* man are ordered by the LORD: and he delighteth in his way.

Psa. 41:11. By this I know that thou favourest me, because mine enemy doth not triumph over me. 12. And as for me, thou upholdest me in mine integrity, and settest me before thy face for ever.

Psa. 44:3. Neither did their own arm save them: but thy right hand, and thine arm, and the light of thy countenance, because thou hadst a favour unto them.

Psa. 46:7. The LORD of hosts *is* with us; the God of Jacob *is* our refuge.

Psa. 58:11. Verily there is a reward for the righteous:

Psa. 68:16. *This is* the hill *which* God desireth to dwell in; yea, the LORD will dwell *in it* for ever. 18. Thou hast received gifts for men; yea, *for* the rebellious also, that the LORD God might dwell *among them.*

Psa. 84:11. The LORD will give grace and glory:

Psa. 89:17. For thou *art* the glory of their strength: and in thy favour our horn shall be exalted.

Psa. 92:10. My horn shalt thou exalt like *the horn of* an unicorn: I shall be anointed with fresh oil. Psa. 75:10; 112:9.

Psa. 94:19. In the multitude of my thoughts within me thy comforts delight my soul.

Psa. 102:13. Thou shalt arise, *and* have mercy upon Zion: for the time to favour her, yea, the set time, is come.

Psa. 115:12. The LORD hath been mindful of us: he will bless *us;* he will bless the house of Israel; he will bless the house of Aaron. 13. He will bless them that fear the LORD, *both* small and great. *v.* 15.

Psa. 132:13. The LORD hath chosen Zion; he hath desired *it* for his habitation. 14. This *is* my rest for ever: here will I dwell; for I have desired it.

Psa. 147:11. The LORD taketh pleasure in them that fear him, in those that hope in his mercy.

Psa. 149:4. The LORD taketh pleasure in his people: he will beautify the meek with salvation.

Prov. 3:4. So shalt thou find favour and good understanding in the sight of God and man. 32. His secret *is* with the righteous. 35. The wise shall inherit glory: *v.* 23.

Prov. 8:35. Whoso findeth me findeth life, and shall obtain favour of the LORD.

Prov. 10:6. Blessings *are* upon the head of the just: 22. The blessing of the LORD, it maketh rich, and he addeth no sorrow with it. 24. The desire of the righteous shall be granted.

Prov. 11:20. They that are of a froward heart *are* abomination to the LORD: but *such as are* upright in *their* way *are* his delight. 27. He that diligently seeketh good procureth favour:

Prov. 12:2. A good *man* obtaineth favour of the LORD:

Prov. 14:9. Among the righteous *there is* favour.

Prov. 16:7. When a man's ways please the LORD, he maketh even his enemies to be at peace with him.

Isa. 28:5. In that day shall the LORD of hosts be for a crown of glory, and for a diadem of beauty,

Isa. 30:26. The light of the moon shall be as the light of the sun, and the light of the sun shall be sevenfold, as the light of seven days, in the day that the LORD bindeth up the breach of his people, and healeth the stroke of their wound.

Isa. 33:17. Thine eyes shall see the king in his beauty: 21. There the glorious LORD *will be* unto us a place of broad rivers *and* streams; *v.* 22.

Isa. 41:10. Fear thou not; for I *am* with thee: be not dismayed; for I *am* thy God: Isa. 43:5.

Isa. 43:21. This people have I formed for myself; they shall shew forth my praise.

Isa. 54:8. With everlasting kindness will I have mercy on thee, saith the LORD thy Redeemer.

Isa. 60:10. In my favour have I had mercy on thee.

Jer. 15:20. I *am* with thee to save thee and to deliver thee, saith the LORD.

Lam. 3:24. The LORD *is* my portion, saith my soul; therefore will I hope in him.

Ezek. 37:27. My tabernacle also shall be with them:

Ezek. 39:29. Neither will I hide my face any more from them: for I have poured out my spirit upon the house of Israel, saith the Lord GOD.

Ezek. 48:35. The name of the city from *that* day *shall be*, The LORD *is* there.

Hos. 14:4. I will love them freely: for mine anger is turned away from him.

Joel 2:27. Ye shall know that I *am* in the midst of Israel, and *that* I *am* the LORD your God, and none else: and my people shall never be ashamed. *v.* 26.

Joel 3:16: The LORD *will be* ¹ the hope of his people, and ² the strength of the children of Israel. 17. So shall ye know that I *am* the LORD your God dwelling in Zion, my holy mountain: *vs.* 20,21. [R. V. ¹ a refuge unto ² a strong hold]

Amos 3:2. You only have I known of all the families of the earth:

Zeph. 3:15. The king of Israel, *even* the LORD, *is* in the midst of thee: thou shalt not see evil any more. *v.* 17.

Hag. 1:13. I *am* with you, saith the LORD.

Zech. 2:5. For I, saith the LORD, will be unto her a wall of fire round about, and will be the glory in the midst of her.

Zech. 8:3. I am returned unto Zion, and will dwell in the midst of Jerusalem:

Zech. 9:16. And the LORD their God shall save them in that day as the flock of his people: for *they shall be as* the stones of a crown, lifted up as an ensign upon his land.

Luke 1:28. Hail, *thou that art* highly favoured, the Lord *is* with thee: ¹ blessed *art* thou among women. 30. Fear not, Mary: for thou hast found favour with God. 66. The hand of the Lord was with him [Jesus].
[¹ Omitted in R. V.]

Luke 2:52. Jesus increased in wisdom and stature, and in favour with God and man. 1 Sam. 2:26.

John 14:16. I will pray the Father, and he shall give you another Comforter, that he may abide with you for ever; 17. *Even* the Spirit of truth; . . . ye know him; for he dwelleth with you, and shall be in you. 18. I will not leave you comfortless: I will come to you. 19. Because I live, ye shall live also. 20. At that day ye shall know that I *am* in my Father, and ye in me, and I in you. 21. He that loveth me shall be loved of my Father, and I will love him, and will manifest myself to him. 23. My Father will love him, and we will come unto him, and make our abode with him.

John 15:15. I call you not servants; for the servant knoweth not what his lord doeth: but I have called you friends; for all things that I have heard of my Father I have made known unto you.

Acts 4:33. Great grace was upon them all.

Acts 10:35. In every nation he that feareth him, and worketh righteousness, is accepted with him.

Rom. 2:29. But he *is* a Jew, which is one inwardly; and circumcision *is that* of the heart, in the spirit, *and* not in the letter; whose praise *is* not of men, but of God.

1 Cor. 1:9. God *is* faithful, by whom ye were called unto the fellowship of his Son Jesus Christ our Lord.

1 Cor. 3:21. For all things are your's; 22. Whether Paul, or Apollos, or Cephas, or the world, or life, or death, or things present, or things to come; all are your's; 23. And ye are Christ's; and Christ *is* God's.

2 Cor. 4:15. For all things *are* for your sakes, that the abundant grace might through the thanksgiving of many redound to the glory of God.

2 Cor. 10:18. Not he that commendeth himself is approved, but whom the Lord commendeth.

Gal. 4:6. Because ye are sons, God hath sent forth the Spirit of his Son into your hearts, crying, Abba, Father.

Eph. 1:6. To the praise of the glory of his grace, wherein he hath made us accepted in the beloved.

Eph. 2:13. Now in Christ Jesus ye who sometimes were far off are made nigh by the blood of Christ. 14. He is our peace, 18. For through him we both have access by one Spirit unto the Father. 22. In whom ye also are builded together for an habitation of God through the Spirit. *v.* 19; Eph. 2:16.

Eph. 3:12. In whom we have boldness and access with confidence by the faith of him. Rom. 5:2.

Heb. 4:16. Let us therefore come boldly unto the throne of grace, that we may obtain mercy, and find grace to help in time of need.

Heb. 10:19. Having therefore, brethren, boldness to enter into the holiest by the blood of Jesus, 22. Let us draw near with a true heart in full assurance of faith,

Heb. 11:5. Before his translation he had this testimony, that he pleased God.

1 Pet. 2:9. But ye *are* a chosen generation, a royal priesthood, an holy nation, a peculiar people;

1 John 1:3. Truly our fellowship *is* with the Father, and with his Son Jesus Christ.

1 John 3:19. Hereby we know that we are of the truth, and shall assure our hearts before him.

1 John 4:17. Herein is our love made perfect, that we may have boldness in the day of judgment: because as he is, so are we in this world. 18. There is no fear in love; but perfect love casteth out fear: because fear hath torment. He that feareth is not made perfect in love.

Rev. 1:5. Unto him that loved us, and washed us from our sins in his own blood, 6. And hath made us kings and priests unto God and his Father; to him *be* glory and dominion for ever and ever.

Rev. 3:20. Behold, I stand at the door, and knock: if any man hear my voice, and open the door, I will come in to him, and will sup with him, and he with me. Rev.19:9.

Rev. 21:3. Behold, the tabernacle of God *is* with men, and he will dwell with them, and they shall be his people, and God himself shall be with them, *and be* their God.

See Grace.

Instances of Special Grace: To Enoch, Gen. 5:24. To Noah, Gen. 6:8. To Abraham, Gen. 12:2. To Jacob, Gen. 32:28; 46:4. To Moses, Ex. 3:12; 33:12,14. To Solomon, 1 Chr. 22:18.

GUIDE: Gen. 12:1. Now the Lord had said unto Abram, Get thee out of thy country, and from thy kindred, and from thy father's house, unto a land that I will shew thee:

Ex. 13:21. And the Lord went before them by day in a pillar of a cloud, to lead them the way; and by night in a pillar of fire, to give them light; to go by day and night:

Ex. 15:13. Thou in thy mercy hast led forth the people *which* thou hast redeemed: thou hast guided *them* in thy strength unto thy holy habitation.

Ex. 33:13. Now therefore, I pray thee, if I have found grace in thy sight, shew me now thy way, that I may know thee, that I may find grace in thy sight: and consider that this nation *is* thy people. 14. And he said, My presence shall go *with thee*, and I will give thee rest. 15. And he said unto him, If thy presence go not *with me*, carry us not up hence.

Num. 10:33. The ark of the covenant of the Lord went before them in the three days' journey, to search out a resting place for them.

Deut. 32:10. He found him in a desert land, and in the waste howling wilderness; he led him about, he instructed him, he kept him as the apple of his eye. 12. *So* the Lord alone did lead him, and *there was* no strange god with him.

2 Sam. 22:29. For thou *art* my lamp, O Lord: and the Lord will lighten my darkness.

2 Chr. 32:22. Thus the Lord saved Hezekiah and the inhabitants of Jerusalem from the hand of Sennacherib the king of Assyria, and from the hand of all *other*, and guided them on every side.

Neh. 9:19. Yet thou in thy manifold mercies forsookest them not in the wilderness: the pillar of the cloud departed not from them by day, to lead them in the way; neither the pillar of fire by night, to shew them light, and the way wherein they should go. 20. Thou gavest also thy good spirit to instruct them,

Psa. 5:8. Lead me, O Lord, in thy righteousness because of my enemies; make thy way straight before my face.

Psa. 23:2. He maketh me to lie down in green pastures: he leadeth me beside the still waters. 3. He restoreth my soul: he leadeth me in the paths of righteousness for his name's sake.

Psa. 25:5. Lead me in thy truth, and teach me: for thou *art* the God of my salvation; on thee do I wait all the day. 9. The meek will he guide in judgment: and the meek will he teach his way.

Psa. 27:11. Teach me thy way, O Lord, and lead me in a plain path, because of mine enemies.

Psa. 31:3. For thou *art* my rock and my fortress; therefore for thy name's sake lead me, and guide me.

Psa. 32:8. I will **instruct thee and teach**

thee in the way which thou shalt go: I will guide thee with mine eye.

Psa. 48:14. For this God *is* our God for ever and ever: he will be our guide *even* unto death.

Psa. 61:2. From the end of the earth will I cry unto thee, when my heart is overwhelmed: lead me to the rock *that* is higher than I.

Psa. 73:24. Thou shalt guide me with thy counsel, and afterward receive me *to* glory.

Psa. 78:52. But made his own people to go forth like sheep, and guided them in the wilderness like a flock.

Psa. 80:1. Give ear, O Shepherd of Israel, thou that leadest Joseph like a flock;

Psa. 107:7. And he led them forth by the right way, that they might go to a city of habitation.

Psa. 139:9. *If* I take the wings of the morning, *and* dwell in the uttermost parts of the sea; 10. Even there shall thy hand lead me, and thy right hand shall hold me. 24. And see if *there be any* wicked way in me, and lead me in the way everlasting.

Prov. 8:20. I lead in the way of righteousness, in the midst of the paths of judgment:

Isa. 40:11. He shall feed his flock like a shepherd: he shall gather the lambs with his arm, and carry *them* in his bosom, *and* shall gently lead those that are with young.

Isa. 42:16. And I will bring the blind by a way *that* they knew not: I will lead them in paths *that* they have not known: I will make darkness light before them, and crooked things straight. These things will I do unto them, and not forsake them.

Isa. 48:17. Thus saith the LORD, thy Redeemer, the Holy One of Israel; I *am* the LORD thy God which teacheth thee to profit, which leadeth thee by the way *that* thou shouldest go.

Isa. 55:4. Behold, I have given him *for* a witness to the people, a leader and commander to the people.

Isa. 57:18. I have seen his ways, and will heal him: I will lead him also, and restore comforts unto him and to his mourners.

Isa. 58:11. And the LORD shall guide thee continually, and satisfy thy soul in drought, and make fat thy bones: and thou shalt be like a watered garden, and like a spring of water, whose waters fail not.

Jer. 3:4. Wilt thou not from this time cry unto me, My father, thou *art* the guide of my youth?

Luke 1:79. To give light unto them that sit in darkness and *in* the shadow of death, to guide our feet into the way of peace.

John 10:3. To him the porter openeth; and the sheep hear his voice: and he calleth his own sheep by name, and leadeth them out. 4. And when he putteth forth his own sheep, he goeth before them, and the sheep follow him: for they know his voice.

John 16:13. Howbeit when he, the Spirit of truth, is come, he will guide you into all truth:

See GOD, PROVIDENCE OF.

HOLINESS OF: Ex. 3:5. Draw not nigh hither: put off thy shoes from off thy feet, for the place whereon thou standest *is* holy ground. Josh. 5:15.

Ex. 15:11. Who *is* like unto thee, O LORD, among the gods? who *is* like thee, glorious in holiness,

Lev. 19:2. Ye shall be holy: for I the LORD your God *am* holy. Lev. 11:44; 20:26; 21:8.

Deut. 32:4. *He is* the Rock, his work *is* perfect: for all his ways *are* judgment: a God of truth and without iniquity, just and right *is* he.

Josh. 24:19. And Joshua said unto the people, Ye cannot serve the LORD: for he *is* an holy God, he *is* a jealous God; he will not forgive your transgressions nor your sins.

1 Sam. 2:2. *There is* none holy as the LORD:

1 Sam. 6:20. Who is able to stand before this holy LORD God?

1 Chr. 16:10. Glory ye in his holy name: Psa. 105:3.

Job 4:17. Shall mortal man be more just than God? shall a man be more pure than his maker? *vs.* 18,19.

Job 6:10. I have not concealed the words of the Holy One.

Job 15:15. The heavens are not clean in his sight.

Job 25:5. Behold even to the moon, and it shineth not; yea, the stars are not pure in his sight.

Job 34:10. Far be it from God, *that he should do* wickedness; and *from* the Almighty, *that he should commit* iniquity.

Job 36:23. Who can say, Thou hast wrought iniquity?

Psa. 11:7. The righteous LORD loveth righteousness; his countenance doth behold the upright.

Psa. 18:30. *As for* God, his way *is* perfect:

Psa. 22:3. Thou *art* holy, *O thou* that inhabitest the praises of Israel.

Psa. 30:4. Sing unto the LORD, O ye saints of his, and give thanks at the remembrance of his holiness.

Psa. 33:4. The word of the LORD *is* right: and all his works *are done* in truth. 5. He loveth righteousness and judgment:

Psa. 36:6. Thy righteousness *is* like the great mountains;

Psa. 47:8. God sitteth upon the throne of his holiness.

Psa. 48:1. Great *is* the LORD, and greatly to be praised in the city of our God, *in* the mountain of his holiness. 10. Thy right hand is full of righteousness.

Psa. 60:6. God hath spoken in his holiness; Psa. 108:7.

Psa. 89:35. Once have I sworn by my holiness that I will not lie unto David.

Psa. 92:15. To shew that the LORD *is* upright: *he is* my rock, and *there is* no unrighteousness in him.

Psa. 99:3. Let them praise thy great and terrible name; ¹ *for* it *is* holy. 5. Exalt ye the LORD our God, and worship at his footstool · ¹ *for* he *is* holy. *v.* 9. [¹ R. V. Holy is he.]

Psa. 111:9. Holy and reverent *is* his name.

Psa. 119:142. Thy righteousness *is* an everlasting righteousness,

Psa. 145:17. The LORD *is* righteous in all his ways, and holy in all his works.

Prov. 9:10. The knowledge of the holy *is* understanding.

Isa. 5:16. God that is holy shall be sanctified in righteousness.

Isa. 6:3. Holy, holy, holy, *is* the LORD of hosts: the whole earth *is* full of his glory.

Isa. 12:6. Cry out and shout, thou inhabitant of Zion: for great *is* the Holy One of Israel in the midst of thee.

Isa. 29:19. The meek also shall increase *their* joy in the LORD, and the poor among men shall rejoice in the Holy One of Israel. 23. They shall sanctify my name, and sanctify the Holy One of Jacob, Isa. 41:14.

Isa. 43:14. Thus saith the LORD, your Redeemer, the Holy One of Israel; For your sake I have sent to Babylon, and have brought down all their nobles, and the Chaldeans, whose cry *is* in the ships. 15. I *am* the LORD, your Holy One, the creator of Israel, your King.

Isa. 45:19. I the LORD speak righteousness, I declare things that are right.

Isa. 47:4. Our redeemer, the LORD of hosts *is* his name, the Holy One of Israel.

Isa. 49:7. Thus saith the LORD, the Redeemer of Israel, *and* his Holy One, to him whom man despiseth, to him whom the nation abhorreth, to a servant of rulers, Kings shall see and arise, princes also shall worship, because of the LORD that is faithful, *and* the Holy One of Israel, and he shall choose thee.

Isa. 52:10. The LORD hath made bare his holy arm in the eyes of all the nations; Psa. 98:1.

Isa. 57:15. The high and lofty One that inhabiteth eternity, whose name *is* Holy;

Jer. 2:5. Thus saith the LORD, What iniquity have your fathers found in me, that they are gone far from me, and have walked after vanity, and are become vain?

Lam. 3:38. Out of the mouth of the most High proceedeth not evil and good?

Ezek. 39:7. So will I make my holy name known in the midst of my people Israel: and I will not *let them* pollute my holy name any more: and the heathen shall know that I *am* the LORD, the Holy One in Israel. *v.* 25; Ezek. 36:21,22.

Dan. 4:8. But at the last Daniel came in before me, whose name *was* Belteshazzar, according to the name of my God, and in whom *is* the spirit of the holy gods:

Hos. 11:9. I *am* God, and not man; the Holy One in the midst of thee:

Hab. 1:12. *Art* thou not from everlasting, O LORD my God, mine Holy One? 13. *Thou*

art of purer eyes than to behold evil, and canst not look on iniquity:

Matt. 5:48. Be ye therefore perfect, even as your Father which is in heaven is perfect.

Matt. 19:17. *There is* none good but one, *that is*, God: Mark 10:18; Luke 18:19.

Luke 1:49. Holy *is* his name.

John 7:28. Then cried Jesus in the temple as he taught, saying, Ye both know me, and ye know whence I am: and I am not come of myself, but he that sent me is true, whom ye know not.

John 17:11. Holy Father, keep through thine own name those whom thou hast given me,

Rom. 1:23. And changed the glory of the uncorruptible God into an image made like to corruptible man, and to birds, and four-footed beasts, and creeping things.

Heb. 1:8. But unto the Son *he saith*, Thy throne, O God, *is* for ever and ever: a sceptre of righteousness *is* the sceptre of thy kingdom.

Jas. 1:13. God cannot be tempted with evil, neither tempteth he any man:

1 Pet. 1:15. But as he which hath called you is holy, so be ye holy in all manner of ¹ conversation; 16. Because it is written, Be ye holy; for I am holy. [¹ R. V. living]

1 John 1:5. God is light, and in him is no darkness at all.

1 John 2:20. Ye have an unction from the Holy One,

Rev. 4:8. Holy, holy, holy, Lord God Almighty, which was, and is, and is to come.

Rev. 6:10. And they cried with a loud voice, saying, How long, O Lord, holy and true, dost thou not judge and avenge our blood on them that dwell on the earth?

Rev. 15:4. Who shall not fear thee, O Lord, and glorify thy name? for *thou* only *art* holy:

See SIN ALIENATES FROM GOD; GOD, PERFECTION OF, RIGHTEOUSNESS OF.

HUMAN FORMS AND APPEARANCE OF:

See ANTHROPOMORPHISMS.

IMMUTABLE: * Num. 23:19. God *is* not a man, that he should lie; neither the son of man, that he should repent: hath he said, and shall he not do *it?* or hath he spoken, and shall he not make it good? 20. Behold, I have received *commandment* to bless: and he hath blessed; and I cannot reverse it.

1 Sam. 15:29. The Strength of Israel will not lie nor repent: for he *is* not a man, that he should repent.

Job 23:13. He *is* in one *mind*, and who can turn him? and *what* his soul desireth, even *that* he doeth.

Psa. 33:11. The counsel of the LORD standeth for ever, the thoughts of his heart to all generations.

Psa. 119:89. For ever, O LORD, thy word is settled in heaven. 90. Thy faithfulness *is* unto all generations: thou hast established the earth, and it abideth. 91. They continue

*As deduced from the attributes, ETERNITY OF, KNOWLEDGE OF, AND SELF-EXISTENT, see each in its place.

this day according to thine ordinances: for all *are* thy servants.

Prov. 19:21. The counsel of the LORD, that shall stand.

Eccl. 3:14. Whatsoever God doeth, it shall be for ever: nothing can be put to it, nor anything taken from it:

Eccl. 7:13. Consider the work of God: for who can make *that* straight, which he hath made crooked?

Isa. 31:2. He also *is* wise, and will bring evil, and will not call back his words:

Isa. 40:28. Hast tnou not heard, *that* the everlasting God, the LORD, the Creator of the ends of the earth, fainteth not, neither is weary?

Isa. 59:1. The LORD's hand is not shortened, that it cannot save; neither his ear heavy, that it cannot hear:

Hos. 13:14. I will ransom them from the power of the grave; I will redeem them from death: O death, I will be thy plagues; O grave, I will be thy destruction: repentance shall be hid from mine eyes.

Mal. 3:6. I *am* the LORD, I change not; therefore ye sons of Jacob are not consumed.

Rom. 11:29. For the gifts and calling of God *are* without repentance.

Heb. 6:17. God, willing more abundantly to shew unto the heirs of promise the immutability of his counsel, confirmed *it* by an oath: 18. That by two immutable things, in which *it was* impossible for God to lie, we might have a strong consolation,

Jas. 1:17. Every good gift and every perfect gift is from above, and cometh down from the Father of lights, with whom is no variableness, neither shadow of turning.

IMPARTIAL: Deut. 10:17. For the LORD your God *is* God of gods, and Lord of lords, a great God, a mighty, and a terrible, which regardeth not persons, nor taketh reward:

Job 36:5. Behold, God *is* mighty, and despiseth not *any: he is* mighty in strength *and* wisdom.

Job 37:24. Men do therefore fear him: he respecteth not any *that are* wise of heart.

Acts 10:34. Then Peter opened *his* mouth, and said, Of a truth I perceive that God is no respecter of persons: 35. But in every nation he that feareth him, and worketh righteousness, is accepted with him.

Rom. 2:6. Who will render to every man according to his deeds: 11. For there is no respect of persons with God.

Gal. 2:6. But of these who seemed to be somewhat, (whatsoever they were, it maketh no matter to me: God accepteth no man's person:) for they who seemed *to be somewhat* in conference added nothing to me:

Eph. 6:8. Knowing that whatsoever good thing any man doeth, the same shall he receive of the Lord, whether *he be* bond or free.

Col. 3:25. But he that doeth wrong shall receive for the wrong which he hath done: and there is no respect of persons.

1 Pet. 1:17. And if ye call on the Father, who without respect of persons judgeth according to every man's work, pass the time of your sojourning *here* in fear.

INCOMPREHENSIBLE: Ex. 20:21. And the people stood afar off, and Moses drew near unto the thick darkness where God *was*.

Deut. 4:11. And ye came near and stood under the mountain; and the mountain burned with fire unto the midst of heaven, with darkness, clouds, and thick darkness.

Deut. 5:22. These words the LORD spake unto all your assembly in the mount out of the midst of the fire, of the cloud, and of the thick darkness, with a great voice: and he added no more.

1 Kin. 8:12. Then spake Solomon, The LORD said that he would dwell in the thick darkness.

Job 11:7. Canst thou by searching find out God? canst thou find out the Almighty unto perfection? 8. *It is* as high as heaven; what canst thou do? deeper than hell; what canst thcu know? 9. The measure thereof *is* longer than the earth, and broader than the sea.

Job 15:8. Hast thou heard the secret of God?

Job 37:1. At this also my heart trembleth, and is moved out of his place. 2. Hear attentively the noise of his voice, and the sound *that* goeth out of his mouth. 3. He directeth it under the whole heaven, and his lightning unto the ends of the earth. 4. After it a voice roareth: he thundereth with the voice of his excellency; and he will not stay them when his voice is heard. 5. God thundereth marvellously with his voice; great things doeth he, which we cannot comprehend. 6. For he saith to the snow, Be thou *on* the earth; likewise to the small rain, and to the great rain of his strength. 7. He sealeth up the hand of every man; that all men may know his work. 8. Then the beasts go into dens, and remain in their places. 9. Out of the south cometh the whirlwind: and cold out of the north. 10. By the breath of God frost is given: and the breadth of the waters is straitened. 11. Also by watering he wearieth the thick cloud: he scattereth his bright cloud: 12. And it is turned round about by his counsels: that they may do whatsoever he commandeth them upon the face of the world in the earth. 13. He causeth it to come, whether for correction, or for his land, or for mercy. 14. Hearken unto this, O Job: stand still, and consider the wondrous works of God. 15. Dost thou know when God disposed them, and caused the light of his cloud to shine? 16. Dost thou know the balancings of the clouds, the wondrous works of him which is perfect in knowledge? 17. How thy garments *are* warm, when he quieteth the earth by the south *wind?* 18. Hast thou with him spread out the sky, *which is* strong, *and* as a molten looking glass? 19. Teach us what we shall say unto him; *for* we cannot order *our* speech by reason of darkness. 20. Shall it be told him that I speak? if a man speak, surely he shall be swallowed up. 21. And now *men* see not the bright light which *is* in the clouds: but the wind passeth, and cleanseth them. 22. Fair weather cometh out of the north: with God *is* terrible majesty. 23. *Touching* the Almighty, we cannot find him out: *he is* excellent in power, and in judgment, and in plenty of justice: he will not afflict. 24. Men do therefore fear him: he respecteth not any *that are* wise of heart.

Psa. 18:11. He made darkness his secret place; his pavilion round about him *were* dark waters *and* thick clouds of the skies.

Psa. 97:2. Clouds and darkness *are* round about him: righteousness and judgment *are* the habitation of his throne.

Eccl. 3:11. No man can find out the work that God maketh from the beginning to the end.

Isa. 40:12. Who hath measured the waters in the hollow of his hand, and meted out heaven with the span, and comprehended the dust of the earth in a measure, and weighed the mountains in scales, and the hills in a balance? 13. Who hath directed the Spirit of the LORD, or *being* his counsellor hath taught him? 14. With whom took he counsel, and *who* instructed him, and taught him in the path of judgment, and taught him knowledge, and shewed to him the way of understanding? 15. Behold, the nations *are* as a drop of a bucket, and are counted as the small dust of the balance: behold, he taketh up the isles as a very little thing. 16. And Lebanon *is* not sufficient to burn, nor the beasts thereof sufficient for a burnt offering. 17. All nations before him *are* as nothing; and they are counted to him less than nothing, and vanity. 18. To whom then will ye liken God? or what likeness will ye compare unto him? 19. The workman melteth a graven image, and the goldsmith spreadeth it over with gold, and casteth silver chains. 20. He that *is* so impoverished that he hath no oblation chooseth a tree *that* will not rot; he seeketh unto him a cunning workman to prepare a graven image, *that* shall not be moved. 21. Have ye not known? have ye not heard? hath it not been told you from the beginning? have ye not understood from the foundations of the earth? 22. *It is* he that sitteth upon the circle of the earth, and the inhabitants thereof *are* as grasshoppers; and stretcheth out the heavens as a curtain, and spreadeth them out as a tent to dwell in: 23. That bringeth the princes to nothing; he maketh the judges of the earth as vanity. 24. Yea, they shall not be planted; yea, they shall not be sown: yea, their stock shall not take root in the earth: and he shall also blow upon them, and they shall wither, and the whirlwind shall take them away as stubble. 25. To whom then will ye liken me, or shall I be equal? saith the Holy One. 26. Lift up your eyes on high, and behold who hath created these *things*,

that bringeth out their host by number: he calleth them all by names by the greatness of his might, for that *he is* strong in power: not one faileth. 27. Why sayest thou, O Jacob, and speakest, O Israel, My way is hid from the LORD, and my judgment is passed over from my God? 28. Hast thou not known? hast thou not heard, *that* the everlasting God, the LORD, the Creator of the ends of the earth, fainteth not, neither is weary? *there is* no searching of his understanding. 29. He giveth power to the faint: and to *them that have* no might he increaseth strength. 30. Even the youths shall faint and be weary, and the young men shall utterly fall: 31. But they that wait upon the LORD shall renew *their* strength; they shall mount up with wings as eagles; they shall run, and not be weary; *and* they shall walk, and not faint.

Isa. 55:8. For my thoughts *are* not your thoughts, neither *are* your ways my ways, saith the LORD. 9. For *as* the heavens are higher than the earth, so are my ways higher than your ways, and my thoughts than your thoughts.

1 Cor. 2:16. For who hath known the mind of the Lord, that he may instruct him?

SYMBOLIZED: By the pillar of fire, Ex. 14:19,20. By the darkness of the Holy of Holies in the tabernacle, 1 Kin. 8:12; by the general structure of the Most Holy Place, see Lev. 16:2.

See GOD, UNSEARCHABLE.

INFINITE: 1 Kin. 8:27. Will God indeed dwell on the earth? behold, the heaven and heaven of heavens cannot contain thee; how much less this house that I have builded? 2 Chr. 2:6; 6:1,18.

Psa. 147:5. Great *is* our Lord, and of great power: his understanding *is* infinite.

Jer. 23:24. Do not I fill heaven and earth? saith the LORD.

See GOD, INCOMPREHENSIBLE, UBIQUITY OF, UNSEARCHABLE.

INVISIBLE: Ex. 20:21. And the people stood afar off, and Moses drew near unto the thick darkness where God *was*.

Ex. 33:20. Thou canst not see my face: for there shall no man see me, and live.

Deut. 4:11. And ye came near and stood under the mountain; and the mountain burned with fire unto the midst of heaven, with darkness, clouds, and thick darkness. 15. Ye saw no manner of similitude on the day *that* the LORD spake unto you in Horeb out of the midst of the fire:

Deut. 5:22. These words the LORD spake unto all your assembly in the mount out of the midst of the fire, of the cloud, and of the thick darkness, with a great voice: and he added no more.

1 Kin. 8:12. Then spake Solomon, The LORD said that he would dwell in the thick darkness.

Job 9:11. Lo, he goeth by me, and I see *him* not: he passeth on also, but I perceive him not.

Job 23:8. Behold, I go forward, but he *is* not *there;* and backward, but I cannot perceive him: 9. On the left hand, where he doth work, but I cannot behold *him:* he hideth himself on the right hand, that I cannot see *him:*

Psa. 18:11. He made darkness his secret place; his pavilion round about him *were* dark waters *and* thick clouds of the skies.

Psa. 97:2. Clouds and darkness *are* round about him: righteousness and judgment *are* the habitations of his throne.

John 1:18. No man hath seen God at any time; the only begotten Son, which is in the bosom of the Father, he hath declared *him.*

John 5:37. Ye have neither heard his voice at any time, nor seen his shape.

John 6:46. Not that any man hath seen the Father, save he which is of God, he hath seen the Father.

Rom. 1:20. The invisible things of him from the creation of the world are clearly seen, being understood by the things that are made, *even* his eternal power and Godhead;

Col. 1:13. Who hath delivered us from the power of darkness, and hath translated *us* into the kingdom of his dear Son: 14. In whom we have redemption through his blood, *even* the forgiveness of sins: 15. Who is the image of the invisible God, the firstborn of every creature:

1 Tim. 1:17. Now unto the King eternal, [1]immortal, invisible, the only wise God, *be* honour and glory for ever and ever.   [1 R. V. incorruptible]

1 Tim. 6:16. Who only hath immortality, dwelling in the light which no man can approach unto; whom no man hath seen, nor can see:

Heb. 11:27. By faith he [Moses] forsook Egypt, not fearing the wrath of the king: for he endured, as seeing him who is invisible.

1 John 4:12. No man hath seen God at any time.

See GOD, INCOMPREHENSIBLE, INFINITE, UNSEARCHABLE.

JEALOUS: Ex. 20:5. I the LORD thy God *am* a jealous God, 7. The LORD will not hold him guiltless that taketh his name in vain. Deut. 5:9,11.

Ex. 34:14. Thou shalt worship no other god: for the LORD, whose name *is* Jealous, *is* a jealous God: Deut. 6:15.

Deut. 4:24. The LORD thy God *is* a consuming fire, *even* a jealous God.

Deut. 29:20. The LORD will not spare him, but then the anger of the LORD and his jealousy shall smoke against that man,

Deut. 32:16. They provoked him to jealousy with strange *gods.* 21. They have moved me to jealousy with *that which is* not God; they have provoked me to anger with their vanities:

Josh. 24:19. Ye cannot serve the LORD: for he *is* an holy God; he *is* a jealous God; he will not forgive your transgressions nor your sins.

2 Chr. 16:7. And at that time Hannai the seer came to Asa king of Judah, and said unto him. Because thou hast relied on the king of Syria, and not relied on the LORD thy God, therefore is the host of the king of Syria escaped out of thine hand. 8. Were not the Ethiopians and the Lubims a huge host, with very many chariots and horsemen? yet, because thou didst rely on the LORD, he delivered them into thine hand. 9. For the eyes of the LORD run to and fro throughout the whole earth, to shew himself strong in the behalf of *them* whose heart *is* perfect toward him. Herein thou hast done foolishly: therefore from henceforth thou shalt have wars. 10. Then Asa was wroth with the seer, and put him in a prison house; for *he was* in a rage with him because of this *thing.* And Asa oppressed *some* of the people the same time.

Isa. 30:1. Woe to the rebellious children, saith the LORD, that take counsel, but not of me· and that cover with a covering, but not of my spirit, that they may add sin to sin: 2. That walk to go down into Egypt, and have not asked at my mouth; to strengthen themselves in the strength of Pharaoh, and to trust in the shadow of Egypt!

Isa. 31:1. Woe to them that go down to Egypt for help; and stay on horses, and trust in chariots, because *they are* many; and in horsemen, because they are very strong; but they look not unto the Holy One of Israel, neither seek the LORD! 3. Now the Eyptians *are* men, and not God; and their horses flesh, and not spirit. When the LORD shall stretch out his hand, both he that helpeth shall fall, and he that is holpen shall fall down, and they all shall fail together.

Ezek. 23:25. I will set my jealousy against thee,

Ezek. 36:5. Therefore thus saith the Lord GOD; Surely in the fire of my jealousy have I spoken against the residue of the heathen,

Ezek. 39:25. Now will I bring again the captivity of Jacob, and have mercy upon the whole house of Israel, and will be jealous for my holy name;

Joel 2:18. Then will the LORD be jealous for his land, and pity his people.

Nah. 1:2. God *is* jealous, and the LORD revengeth; the LORD revengeth, and *is* furious; the LORD will take vengeance on his adversaries,

Zech. 1:14. Thus saith the LORD of hosts; I am jealous for Jerusalem and for Zion with a great jealousy.

1 Cor. 10:22. Do we provoke the Lord to jealousy? are we stronger than he?

JUDGE, AND HIS JUSTICE: Gen. 16:5. And Sarai said unto Abram, My wrong *be* upon thee: . . . the LORD judge between me and thee.

Gen. 18:21. I will go down now, and see whether they have done altogether according to the cry of it, which is come unto me;

and if not, I will know. 25. That be far from thee to do after this manner, to slay the righteous with the wicked : and that the righteous should be as the wicked, that be far from thee : Shall not the Judge of all the earth do right ? v. 20.

Num. 16:22. And they fell upon their faces, and said, O God, the God of the spirits of all flesh, shall one man sin, and wilt thou be wroth with all the congregation ?

Deut. 10:17. For the LORD your God is God of gods, and Lord of lords, a great God, a mighty, and a terrible, which regardeth not persons, nor taketh reward : 2 Sam. 14:14; Rom. 2:11.

Deut. 32:4. He is the Rock, his work is perfect : for all his ways are judgment : a God of truth and without iniquity, just and right is he. 35. To me belongeth vengeance, and recompence ;

Josh. 24:19. Ye cannot serve the LORD : for he is an holy God; he is a jealous God; he will not forgive your transgressions nor your sins. Ex. 20:5; 34:7.

Judg. 11:27. The LORD the Judge be judge this day between the children of Israel and the children of Ammon.

1 Sam. 2:3. The LORD is a God of knowledge, and by him actions are weighed. 10. The adversaries of the LORD shall be broken to pieces; out of heaven shall he thunder upon them : the LORD shall judge the ends of the earth ;

1 Sam. 24:12. The LORD judge between me and thee, and the LORD avenge me of thee : but mine hand shall not be upon thee. 15. The LORD therefore be judge, and judge between me and thee, and see, and plead my cause, and deliver me out of thine hand.

2 Sam. 22:25. Therefore the LORD hath recompensed me according to my righteousness; according to my cleanness in his eye sight. 26. With the merciful thou wilt shew thyself merciful, and with the upright man thou wilt shew thyself upright. 27. With the pure thou wilt shew thyself pure; and with the froward thou wilt shew thyself unsavoury. Psa. 18:25,26.

1 Kin. 8:32. Hear thou in heaven, and do, and judge thy servants, condemning the wicked, to bring his way upon his head ; and justifying the righteous, to give him according to his righteousness. Judg. 9:56,57; 2 Chr. 6:22,23.

1 Chr. 16:33. Then shall the trees of the wood sing out at the presence of the LORD, because he cometh to judge the earth.

2 Chr. 19:7. There is no iniquity with the LORD our God, nor respect of persons, nor taking of gifts.

Neh. 9:33. Thou art just in all that is brought upon us; for thou hast done right, but we have done wickedly :

Job 4:17. Shall mortal man be more just than God ? shall a man be more pure than his maker ?

Job 8:3. Doth God pervert judgment ? or doth the Almighty pervert justice ?

Job 9:15. Whom, though I were righteous, yet would I not answer, but I would make supplication to my judge. 28. I know that thou wilt not hold me innocent.

Job 21:22. He judgeth those that are high.

Job 23:7. There the righteous might dispute with him; so should I be delivered for ever from my judge.

Job 31:13. If I did despise the cause of my manservant or of my maidservant, when they contended with me ; 14. What then shall I do when God riseth up ? and when he visiteth, what shall I answer him ? 15. Did not he that made me in the womb make him ? and did not one fashion us in the womb ?

Job 34:10. Far be it from God, that he should do wickedness; and from the Almighty, that he should commit iniquity. 11. For the work of a man shall he render unto him, and cause every man to find according to his ways. 12. Yea, surely God will not do wickedly, neither will the Almighty pervert judgment. 17. Shall even he that hateth right govern ? and wilt thou condemn him that is most just ? 19. Him that accepteth not the persons of princes, nor regardeth the rich more than the poor ? 23. He will not lay upon man more than right ; that he should enter into judgment with God.

Job 35:14. Thou sayest thou shalt not see him, yet judgment is before him ;

Job 36:3. I will fetch my knowledge from afar, and will ascribe righteousness to my Maker. 19. Will he esteem thy riches ? no, not gold, nor all the forces of strength.

Job 37:23. He is excellent in power, and in judgment, and in plenty of justice :

Psa. 7:9. The righteous God trieth the heart and reins. 11. God judgeth the righteous, and God is angry with the wicked every day. v. 8; Heb. 10:30.

Psa. 9:4. Thou hast maintained my right and my cause; thou satest in the throne judging right. 7. He hath prepared his throne for judgment. 8. And he shall judge the world in righteousness, he shall minister judgment to the people in uprightness.

Psa. 11:4. His eyes behold, his eyelids try, the children of men. 5. The LORD trieth the righteous : but the wicked and him that loveth violence his soul hateth. 7. The righteous LORD loveth righteousness; his countenance doth behold the upright.

Psa. 19:9. The judgments of the LORD are true and righteous altogether.

Psa. 26:1. Judge me, O LORD; for I have walked in mine integrity : I have trusted also in the LORD; therefore I shall not slide. 2. Examine me, O LORD, and prove me ; try my reins and my heart.

Psa. 33:5. He loveth righteousness and judgment : the earth is full of the goodness of the LORD.

Psa. 35:24. Judge me, O LORD my God, according to thy righteousness;

Psa. 43:1. Judge me, O God, and plead my

cause against an ungodly nation: O deliver me from the deceitful and unjust man.

Psa. 50:4. He shall call to the heavens from above, and to the earth, that he may judge his people. 6. The heavens shall declare his righteousness: for God *is* judge himself. Psa. 75:7.

Psa. 51:4. Against thee, thee only, have I sinned, and done *this* evil in thy sight: that thou mightest be justified when thou speakest, *and* be clear when thou judgest.

Psa. 58:11. Verily *there is* a reward for the righteous: verily he is a God that judgeth in the earth.

Psa. 62:12. Thou renderest to every man according to his work.

Psa. 67:4. Thou shalt judge the people righteously, and govern the nations upon earth.

Psa. 71:19. Thy righteousness also, O God, *is* very high, who hast done great things: O God, who *is* like unto thee!

Psa. 76:8. Thou didst cause judgment to be heard from heaven; the earth feared, and was still, 9. When God arose to judgment, to save all the meek of the earth.

Psa. 85:10. Mercy and truth are met together; righteousness and peace have kissed *each other*.

Psa. 89:14. Justice and judgment *are* the habitation of thy throne: mercy and truth shall go before thy face.

Psa. 90:8. Thou hast set our iniquities before thee, our secret *sins* in the light of thy countenance. 11. Who knoweth the power of thine anger? even according to thy fear, *so is* thy wrath.

Psa. 92:15. To shew that the LORD *is* upright: *he is* my rock, and *there is* no unrighteousness in him.

Psa. 94:1. O God, to whom vengeance belongeth, shew thyself. 2. Lift up thyself, thou judge of the earth: render a reward to the proud. 10. He that chastiseth the heathen, shall not he correct? Psa. 82:8.

Psa. 96:13. He cometh to judge the earth: he shall judge the world with righteousness, and the people with his truth. *v.* 10.

Psa. 97:2. Clouds and darkness *are* round about him: righteousness and judgment *are* the habitation of his throne.

Psa. 98:2. His righteousness hath he openly shewed in the sight of the heathen. *vs.* 3, 9.

Psa. 99:4. The king's strength also loveth judgment; thou dost establish equity, thou executest judgment and righteousness in Jacob. 8. Thou wast a God that forgavest them, though thou tookest vengeance of their inventions.

Psa. 103:6. The LORD executeth righteousness and judgment for all that are oppressed.

Psa. 111:7. The works of his hands *are* verity and judgment;

Psa. 119:137. Righteous *art* thou, O LORD, and upright *are* thy judgments.

Psa. 129:4. The LORD *is* righteous:

Psa. 135:14. For the LORD will judge his people, and he will repent himself concerning his servants.

Psa. 143:2. Enter not into judgment with thy servant: for in thy sight shall no man living be justified.

Psa. 145:17. The LORD *is* righteous in all his ways, and holy in all his works.

Prov. 11:31. The righteous shall be recompensed in the earth: much more the wicked and the sinner.

Prov. 16:2. All the ways of a man *are* clean in his own eyes; but the LORD weigheth the spirits.

Prov. 17:3. The fining pot *is* for silver, and the furnace for gold: but the LORD trieth the hearts.

Prov. 21:2. Every way of a man *is* right in his own eyes: but the LORD pondereth the hearts. 3. To do justice and judgment *is* more acceptable to the LORD than sacrifice.

Prov. 24:12. Doth not he that pondereth the heart consider *it?* and he that keepeth thy soul, doth *not* he know *it?* and shall *not* he render to *every* man according to his works?

Prov. 29:13. The poor and the deceitful man meet together: the LORD lighteneth both their eyes. 26. Many seek the ruler's favour; but *every* man's judgment *cometh* from the LORD.

Eccl. 3:15. That which hath been is now; and that which is to be hath already been; and God requireth that which is past. 17. God shall judge the righteous and the wicked: for *there is* a time there for every purpose and for every work.

Eccl. 11:9. Know thou, that for all these *things* God will bring thee into judgment.

Eccl. 12:14. God shall bring every work into judgment, with every secret thing, whether *it be* good, or whether *it be* evil.

Isa. 1:27. Zion shall be redeemed with judgment, and her converts with righteousness.

Isa. 3:13. The LORD standeth up to plead, and standeth to judge the people. 14. The LORD will enter into judgment with the ancients of his people, and the princes thereof:

Isa. 10:17. The light of Israel shall be for a fire, and his Holy One for a flame: and it shall burn and devour his thorns and his briers in one day; 18. And shall consume the glory of his forest, and of his fruitful field, both soul and body:

Isa. 26:7. Thou, most upright, dost weigh the path of the just.

Isa. 28:17. Judgment also will I lay to the line, and righteousness to the plummet: 21. The LORD shall rise up as *in* mount Perazim, he shall be wroth as *in* the valley of Gibeon, that he may do his work, his strange work; and bring to pass his act, his strange act.

Isa. 30:18. The LORD *is* a God of judgment: blessed *are* all they that wait for him. 27. Behold, the name of the LORD cometh from far, burning *with* his anger, and the burden *thereof is* heavy: his lips are full of indignation, and his tongue as a devouring fire: 30. The LORD shall cause his glorious voice to be heard, and shall shew the lighting down of his arm, with the indignation of *his* anger, and *with* the flame of a devouring fire, *with* scattering, and tempest, and hailstones.

Isa. 31:2. He also *is* wise, and will bring evil, and will not call back his words : but will arise against the house of the evildoers, and against the help of them that work iniquity.

Isa. 33:22. For the LORD *is* our judge, the LORD *is* our lawgiver, the LORD *is* our king ; he will save us.

Isa. 45:21. *There is* no God else beside me : a just God and a Saviour ;

Isa. 61:8. I the LORD love judgment, I hate robbery for burnt offering ; and I will direct their work in truth,

Jer. 9:24. I *am* the LORD which exercise lovingkindness, judgment, and righteousness, in the earth : for in these *things* I delight, saith the LORD.

Jer. 10:10. At his wrath the earth shall tremble, and the nations shall not be able to abide his indignation.

Jer. 11:20. O LORD of hosts, that judgest righteously, that triest the reins and the heart, let me see thy vengeance on them : Jer. 20:12.

Jer. 12:1. Righteous *art* thou, O LORD, when I plead with thee : yet let me talk with thee of *thy* judgments :

Jer. 32:19. Great in counsel, and mighty in work : for thine eyes *are* open upon all the ways of the sons of men : to give every one according to his ways, and according to the fruit of his doings :

Jer. 50:7. Their adversaries said, We offend not, because they have sinned against the LORD, the habitation of justice,

Jer. 51:10. The LORD hath brought forth our righteousness : come, and let us declare in Zion the work of the LORD our God.

Lam. 1:18. The LORD is righteous ; for I have rebelled against his commandment :

Ezek. 14:23. Ye shall know that I have not done without cause all that I have done in it, saith the Lord GOD.

Ezek. 18:25. Yet ye say, The way of the Lord is not equal. Hear now, O house of Israel ; Is not my way equal ? are not your ways unequal ? [*v.* 29.] 30. Therefore I will judge you, O house of Israel, every one according to his ways, saith the Lord GOD. Repent, and turn *yourselves* from all your transgressions ; so iniquity shall not be your ruin.

Ezek. 33:7. So thou, O son of man, I have set thee a watchman unto the house of Israel ; therefore thou shalt hear the word at my mouth, and warn them from me. 8. When I say unto the wicked, O wicked *man*, thou shalt surely die ; if thou dost not speak to warn the wicked from his way, that wicked *man* shall die in his iniquity ; but his blood will I require at thine hand. 9. Nevertheless, if thou warn the wicked of his way to return from it ; if he do not turn from his way, he shall die in his iniquity ; but thou hast delivered thy soul. 10. Therefore,

O thou son of man, speak unto the house of Israel ; Thus ye speak, saying, If our transgressions and our sins *be* upon us, and we pine away in them, how should we then live ? 11. Say unto them, *As* I live, saith the Lord GOD, I have no pleasure in the death of the wicked ; but that the wicked turn from his way and live : turn ye, turn ye from your evil ways ; for why will ye die, O house of Israel ? 12. Therefore, thou son of man, say unto the children of thy people, The righteousness of the righteous shall not deliver him in the day of his transgression : as for the wickedness of the wicked, he shall not fall thereby in the day that he turneth from his wickedness : neither shall the righteous be able to live for his *righteousness* in the day that he sinneth. 13. When I shall say to the righteous, *that* he shall surely live ; if he trust to his own righteousness, and commit iniquity, all his righteousness shall not be remembered : but for his iniquity that he hath committed, he shall die for it. 14. Again, when I say unto the wicked, Thou shalt surely die ; if he turn from his sin, and do that which is lawful and right ; 15. *If* the wicked restore the pledge, give again that he had robbed, walk in the statutes of life, without committing iniquity ; he shall surely live, he shall not die. 16. None of his sins that he hath committed shall be mentioned unto him : he hath done that which is lawful and right ; he shall surely live. 17. Yet the children of thy people say, The way of the Lord is not equal : but as for them, their way is not equal. 18. When the righteous turneth from his righteousness, and committeth iniquity, he shall even die thereby. 19. But if the wicked turn from his wickedness, and do that which is lawful and right, he shall live thereby.

Dan. 4:37. Now I Nebuchadnezzar praise and extol and honour the King of heaven, all whose works *are* truth, and his ways judgment : and those that walk in pride he is able to abase.

Dan. 7:9. The thrones were cast down, and the Ancient of days did sit, whose garment *was* white as snow, and the hair of his head like the pure wool : his throne *was like* the fiery flame, *and* his wheels *as* burning fire. 10. A fiery stream issued and came forth from before him : thousand thousands ministered unto him, and ten thousand times ten thousand stood before him : the judgment was set, and the books were opened.

Dan. 9:7. O Lord, righteousness *belongeth* unto thee, but unto us confusion of faces, as at this day ; 14. The LORD watched upon the evil, and brought it upon us : for the LORD our God *is* righteous in all his works which he doeth :

Hos. 10:10. *It is* in my desire that I should chastise them ;

Amos 8:7. The LORD hath sworn by the excellency of Jacob, Surely I will never forget any of their works.

Nah. 1:3. The LORD *is* slow to anger, and

great in power, and will not at all acquit *the wicked:* 6. Who can stand before his indignation? and who can abide in the fierceness of his anger? his fury is poured out like fire, and the rocks are thrown down by him.

Zeph. 3:5. The just LORD *is* in the midst thereof; he will not do iniquity: every morning doth he bring his judgment to light, he faileth not;

Mal. 3:5. I will come near to you to judgment; and I will be a swift witness against the sorcerers, and against the adulterers, and against false swearers, and against those that oppress the hireling in *his* wages, the widow, and the fatherless, and that turn aside the stranger *from his right*, and fear not me, saith the LORD of hosts. 18. Then shall ye return, and discern between the righteous and the wicked,

Acts 17:31. He hath appointed a day, in the which he will judge the world in righteousness by *that* man whom he hath ordained;

Rom. 1:32. Knowing the judgment of God, that they which commit such things are worthy of death,

Rom. 2:2. We are sure that the judgment of God is according to truth against them which commit such things. 5. But after thy hardness and impenitent heart treasurest up unto thyself wrath against the day of wrath and revelation of the righteous judgment of God; 6. Who will render to every man according to his deeds: 7. To them who by patient continuance in well doing seek for glory and honour and immortality, eternal life: 8. But unto them that are contentious, and do not obey the truth, but obey unrighteousness, indignation and wrath, 9. Tribulation and anguish, upon every soul of man that doeth evil, of the Jew first, and also of the Gentile; 10. But glory, honour, and peace, to every man that worketh good, to the Jew first, and also to the Gentile: 11. For there is no respect of persons with God. 12. For as many as have sinned without law shall also perish without law: and as many as have sinned in the law shall be judged by the law; 13. (For not the hearers of the law *are* just before God, but the doers of the law shall be justified. 14. For when the Gentiles, which have not the law, do by nature the things contained in the law, these, having not the law, are a law unto themselves: 15. Which shew the work of the law written in their hearts, their conscience also bearing witness, and *their* thoughts the mean while accusing or else excusing one another;) 16. In the day when God shall judge the secrets of men by Jesus Christ according to my gospel.

Rom. 3:4. Let God be true, but every man a liar; as it is written, That thou mightest be justified in thy sayings, and mightest overcome when thou art judged. 5. *Is* God unrighteous who taketh vengeance? (I speak as a man) 6. God forbid: for then how shall God judge the world? 26. To de-

clare, *I say,* at this time his righteousness that he might be just, and the justifier of him which believeth in Jesus.

Rom. 9:14. *Is there* unrighteousness with God? God forbid.

Rom. 11:22. Behold therefore the goodness and severity of God: on them which fell, severity; but toward thee, goodness, if thou continue in *his* goodness: otherwise thou also shalt be cut off.

Eph. 6:8. Whatsoever good thing any man doeth, the same shall he receive of the Lord, whether *he be* bond or free. 9. Your Master also is in heaven; neither is there respect of persons with him. Col. 3:25; Acts 10:34.

2 Thess. 1:4. So that we ourselves glory in you in the churches of God for your patience and faith in all your persecutions and tribulations that ye endure: 5. *Which is* a manifest token of the righteous judgment of God, that ye may be counted worthy of the kingdom of God, for which ye also suffer: 6. Seeing *it is* a righteous thing with God to recompense tribulation to them that trouble you;

Heb. 6:10. For God *is* not unrighteous to forget your work and labour of love, which ye have shewed toward his name, in that ye have ministered to the saints, and do minister.

Heb. 10:30. For we know him that hath said, Vengeance *belongeth* unto me, I will recompense, saith the Lord. And again, The Lord shall judge his people. 31. *It is* a fearful thing to fall into the hands of the living God.

Heb. 12:22. But ye are come unto mount Sion, . . . 23. . . . and to God the Judge of all, 29. For our God *is* a consuming fire. Deut. 4:24.

1 Pet. 1:17. And if ye call on the Father, who without respect of persons judgeth according to every man's work, pass the time of your sojourning *here* in fear.

2 Pet. 2:9. The Lord knoweth how to deliver the godly out of temptations, and to reserve the unjust unto the day of judgment to be punished:

1 John 1:9. If we confess our sins, he is faithful and just to forgive us *our* sins, and to cleanse us from all unrighteousness.

Jude 6. The angels which kept not their first estate, but left their own habitation, he hath reserved in everlasting chains under darkness unto the judgment of the great day.

Rev. 6:16. Fall on us, and hide us from the face of him that sitteth on the throne, and from the wrath of the Lamb: 17. For the great day of his wrath is come; and who shall be able to stand?

Rev. 11:18. Thy wrath is come, and the time of the dead, that they should be judged, and that thou shouldest give reward unto thy servants the prophets, and to the saints, and them that fear thy name, small and great; and shouldest destroy them which destroy the earth.

Rev. 15:3. Just and true *are* thy ways, thou King of saints.

Rev. 16:5. Thou art righteous, O Lord, which art, and wast, and shalt be, because thou hast judged thus. 6. For they have shed the blood of saints and prophets, and thou hast given them blood to drink; for they are worthy. 7. And I heard another out of the altar say, Even so, Lord God Almighty, true and righteous *are* thy judgments.

Rev. 18:8. Strong *is* the Lord God who judgeth her.

Rev. 19:2. True and righteous *are* his judgments: for he hath judged the great whore, which did corrupt the earth with her fornication, and hath avenged the blood of his servants at her hand.

See JESUS, JUDGE; GOVERNMENT, GOD IN; HOLINESS OF GOD, above; and RIGHTEOUSNESS OF, below; also JUDGMENT, GENERAL; JUDGMENTS; SIN, PUNISHMENT OF.

KING: See SOVEREIGN, below.

KNOWLEDGE OF: Gen. 16:13. Thou God seest me:

Ex. 3:7. I have surely seen the affliction of my people which *are* in Egypt, and have heard their cry by reason of their taskmasters; for I know their sorrows; *vs.* 3, 9, 19, 20; Ex. 6:1; 11:1; 14:3,4.

Num. 14:27. I have heard the murmurings of the children of Israel, which they murmur against me.

Deut. 2:7. He knoweth thy walking through this great wilderness: these forty years the LORD thy God *hath been* with thee;

Deut. 31:21. I know their imagination which they go about, even now, before I have brought them into the land which I sware.

1 Sam. 2:3. The LORD *is* a God of knowledge, and by him actions are weighed. Gen. 20:6.

1 Sam. 16:7. *The LORD seeth* not as man seeth; for man looketh on the outward appearance, but the LORD looketh on the heart.

2 Sam. 7:20. And what can David say more unto thee? for thou, Lord GOD, knowest thy servant.

1 Kin. 8:39. Then hear thou in heaven thy dwelling place, and forgive, and do. and give to every man according to his ways, whose heart thou knowest; (for thou, *even* thou only, knowest the hearts of all the children of men ;) 2 Chr. 6:30.

2 Kin. 19:27. I know thy abode, and thy going out, and thy coming in, and thy rage against me.

1 Chr. 28:9. The LORD searcheth all hearts, and understandeth all the imaginations of the thoughts:

1 Chr. 29:17. I know also, my God, that thou triest the heart, and hast pleasure in uprightness.

2 Chr. 16:9. The eyes of the LORD run to and fro throughout the whole earth, to shew

himself strong in the behalf of *them* whose heart *is* perfect toward him. Zech. 4:10.

Neh. 9:10. Thou knewest that they dealt proudly against them.

Job 11:11. For he knoweth vain men:

Job 12:13. With him *is* wisdom and strength, he hath counsel and understanding. 22. He discovereth deep things out of darkness, and bringeth out to light the shadow of death. *v.* 16.

Job 21:22. Shall *any* teach God knowledge? seeing he judgeth those that are high.

Job 22:13. And thou sayest, How doth God know? can he judge through the dark cloud? 14. Thick clouds *are* a covering to him, that he seeth not ; and he walketh in the circuit of heaven.

Job 23:10. He knoweth the way that I take:

Job 24:1. Why, seeing times are not hidden from the Almighty, do they that know him not see his days? 23. His eyes *are* upon their ways.

Job 26:6. Hell *is* naked before him, and destruction hath no covering.

Job 28:10. His eye seeth every precious thing. 24. He looketh to the ends of the earth, *and* seeth under the whole heaven;

Job 31:4. Doth not he see my ways, and count all my steps?

Job 34:21. His eyes *are* upon the ways of man, and he seeth all his goings. 22. *There is* no darkness, nor shadow of death, where the workers of iniquity may hide themselves. 25. He knoweth their works,

Job 36:4. He that is perfect in knowledge *is* with thee. 5. *He is* mighty in strength *and* wisdom.

Job 37:16. Dost thou know . . . the wondrous works of him which is perfect in knowledge?

Job 42:2. I know that thou canst do every *thing*, and *that* no thought can be withholden from thee.

Psa. 1:6. The LORD knoweth the way of the righteous:

Psa. 7:9. The righteous God trieth the hearts and reins.

Psa. 10:11. He hath said in his heart, God hath forgotten: he hideth his face; he will never see *it*. Psa. 94:7.

Psa. 11:4. His eyes behold, his eyelids try, the children of men.

Psa. 33:13. The LORD looketh from heaven ; he beholdeth all the sons of men. 14. From the place of his habitation he looketh upon all the inhabitants of the earth. 15. He considereth all their works.

Psa. 37:18. The LORD knoweth the days of the upright:

Psa. 38:9. Lord, all my desire *is* before thee; and my groaning is not hid from thee.

Psa. 44:21. Shall not God search this out? for he knoweth the secrets of the heart.

Psa. 66:7. His eyes behold the nations:

Psa. 69:19. Thou hast known my reproach, and my shame. and my dishonour : mine adversaries *are* all before thee.

Psa. 73:11. And they say, How doth God

know? and is there knowledge in the most High?

Psa. 92:5. O Lord, how great are thy works! *and* thy thoughts are very deep.

Psa. 94:9. He that planted the ear, shall he not hear? he that formed the eye, shall he not see? 10. He that teacheth man knowledge, *shall not he know?* 11. The Lord knoweth the thoughts of man, that they *are* vanity. 1 Cor. 3:20.

Psa. 103:14. He knoweth our frame; he remembereth that we *are* dust.

Psa. 104:24. O Lord, how manifold are thy works! in wisdom hast thou made them all: the earth is full of thy riches.

Psa. 119:168. All my ways *are* before thee.

Psa. 121:3. He that keepeth thee will not slumber. 4. Behold, he that keepeth Israel shall neither slumber nor sleep.

Psa. 136:5. To him that by wisdom made the heavens:

Psa. 139:1. O Lord, thou hast searched me, and known *me.* 2. Thou knowest my downsitting and mine uprising, thou understandest my thought afar off. 3. Thou compassest my path and my lying down, and art acquainted *with* all my ways. 4. For *there is* not a word in my tongue, *but,* lo, O Lord, thou knowest it altogether. 6. *Such* knowledge *is* too wonderful for me; it is high, I cannot *attain* unto it. 12. The darkness hideth not from thee; but the night shineth as the day: the darkness and the light *are* both alike *to thee.* 14. I will praise thee; for I am fearfully *and* wonderfully made: 15. My substance was not hid from thee, when I was made in secret, *and* curiously wrought in the lowest parts of the earth. 16. Thine eyes did see my substance, yet being unperfect; and in thy book all *my members* were written, *which* in continuance were fashioned, when *as yet there was* none of them. *vs.* 1-24.

Psa. 142:3. When my spirit was overwhelmed within me, then thou knewest my path.

Psa. 147:4. He telleth the number of the stars; he calleth them all by *their* names. 5. Great *is* our Lord, and of great power: his understanding *is* infinite. Isa. 40:26.

Prov. 3:19. The Lord by wisdom hath founded the earth; by understanding hath he established the heavens. 20. By his knowledge the depths are broken up, and the clouds drop down the dew.

Prov. 5:21. The ways of man *are* before the eyes of the Lord, and he pondereth all his goings.

Prov. 15:3. The eyes of the Lord *are* in every place, beholding the evil and the good. 11. Hell and destruction *are* before the Lord: how much more then the hearts of the children of men?

Prov. 16:2. The Lord weigheth the spirits.

Prov. 17:3. The fining pot *is* for silver, and the furnace for gold: but the Lord trieth the hearts.

Prov. 24:12. If thou sayest, Behold, we know it not; doth not he that pondereth the heart consider *it?* and he that keepeth thy soul, doth *not* he know *it?* Prov. 21:2.

Isa. 28:29. This also cometh forth from the Lord of hosts, *which* is wonderful in counsel, *and* excellent in working.

Isa. 29:15. Woe unto them that seek deep to hide their counsel from the Lord, and their works are in the dark, and they say, Who seeth us? and who knoweth us? 16. Shall the thing framed say of him that framed it, He had no understanding?

Isa. 37:28. But I know thy abode, and thy going out, and thy coming in, and thy rage against me.

Isa. 40:13. Who hath directed the Spirit of the Lord, or *being* his counsellor hath taught him? 14. With whom took he counsel, and *who* instructed him, and taught him in the path of judgment, and taught him knowledge, and shewed to him the way of understanding? 27. Why sayest thou, O Jacob, and speakest, O Israel, My way is hid from the Lord, and my judgment is passed over from my God? 28. *There is* no searching of his understanding.

Isa. 41:4. Who hath wrought and done *it,* calling the generations from the beginning? I the Lord, the first, and with the last; I *am* he.

Isa. 42:9. Behold, the former things are come to pass, and new things do I declare: before they spring forth I tell you of them.

Isa. 44:7. Who, as I, shall call, and shall declare it, and set it in order for me, since I appointed the ancient people? and the things that are coming, and shall come,

Isa. 45:4. I have even called thee by thy name: I have surnamed thee, though thou hast not known me. *v.* 21.

Isa. 46:10. Declaring the end from the beginning, and from ancient times *the things* that are not *yet* done, saying, My counsel shall stand, and I will do all my pleasure:

Isa. 48:5. I have even from the beginning declared *it* to thee; before it came to pass I shewed *it* thee; lest thou shouldest say, Mine idol hath done them, and my graven image, and my molten image, hath commanded them. 6. Thou hast heard, see all this; and will not ye declare *it?* I have shewed thee new things from this time, even hidden things, and thou didst not know them. *v.* 3.

Isa. 66:18. I *know* their works and their thoughts:

Jer. 5:3. O Lord, *are* not thine eyes upon the truth?

Jer. 10:7. Among all the wise *men* of the nations, and in all their kingdoms, *there is* none like unto thee.

Jer. 11:20. O Lord of hosts, that judgest righteously, that triest the reins and the heart, Jer. 20:12.

Jer. 17:10. I the Lord search the heart, *I* try the reins, even to give every man according to his ways, *and* according to the fruit of his doings.

Jer. 23:24. Can any hide himself in secret places that I shall not see him? saith the LORD. Do not I fill heaven and earth? saith the LORD.

Jer. 32:19. Great in counsel, and mighty in work: for thine eyes *are* open upon all the ways of the sons of men:

Jer. 51:15. He hath established the world by his wisdom, and hath stretched out the heaven by his understanding. Jer. 10:12.

Ezek. 9:9. Then said he unto me, The iniquity of the house of Israel and Judah *is* exceeding great, and the land is full of blood, and the city full of perverseness: for they say, The LORD hath forsaken the earth, and the LORD seeth not.

Ezek. 11:5. I know the things that come into your mind, *every one of* them.

Dan. 2:20. Wisdom and might are his: 22. He revealeth the deep and secret things: he knoweth what *is* in the darkness, and the light dwelleth with him. 28. There is a God in heaven that revealeth secrets, and maketh known to the king Nebuchadnezzar what shall be in the latter days.

Amos 4:13. He . . . that declareth unto man what *is* his thought,

Amos 9:2. Though they dig into hell, thence shall mine hand take them; though they climb up to heaven, thence will I bring them down: 3. And though they hide themselves in the top of Carmel, I will search and take them out thence; and though they be hid from my sight in the bottom of the sea, thence will I command the serpent, and he shall bite them: 4. And though they go into captivity before their enemies, thence will I command the sword, and it shall slay them:

Matt. 6:4. Thy Father which seeth in secret himself shall reward thee openly. 8. Your Father knoweth what things ye have need of, before ye ask him. 18. That thou appear not unto men to fast, but unto thy Father which is in secret: and thy Father, which seeth in secret, shall reward thee openly. 32. Your heavenly Father knoweth that ye have need of all these things.

Matt. 10:29. One of them shall not fall on the ground without your Father. 30. But the very hairs of your head are all numbered.

Matt. 24:36. Of that day and hour knoweth no *man*, no, not the angels of heaven, but my Father only. Mark 13:32.

Luke 16:15. God knoweth your hearts:

Acts 1:24. Thou, Lord, which knowest the hearts of all *men*, shew whether of these two thou hast chosen,

Acts 2:23. Him, being delivered by the determinate counsel and foreknowledge of God, ye have taken, and by wicked hands have crucified and slain:

Acts 15:8. God, which knoweth the hearts, bare them witness, 18. Known unto God are all his works from the beginning of the world.

Rom. 8:27. He that searcheth the hearts

. . . 29. Whom he did foreknow, he also did predestinate.

Rom. 11:33. O the depth of the riches both of the wisdom and knowledge of God! how unsearchable *are* his judgments, and his ways past finding out! 34. For who hath known the mind of the Lord? or who hath been his counsellor?

1 Cor. 1:25. The foolishness of God is wiser than men;

1 Cor. 2:7. But we speak the wisdom of God in a mystery, *even* the hidden *wisdom*, which God ordained before the world unto our glory:

1 Cor. 3:20. And again, The Lord knoweth the thoughts of the wise, that they are vain.

1 Cor. 8:3. If any man love God, the same is known of him.

Gal. 4:9. But now, after that ye have known God, or rather are known of God, how turn ye again to the weak and beggarly elements, whereunto ye desire again to be in bondage?

Eph. 1:8. Wherein he hath abounded toward us in all wisdom and prudence;

Eph. 3:10. To the intent that now unto the principalities and powers in heavenly *places* might be known by the church the manifold wisdom of God,

1 Thess. 2:4. Not as pleasing men, but God, which trieth our hearts.

1 Tim. 1:17. Now unto the King eternal, [1 immortal], invisible, the only wise God, *be* honour and glory for ever and ever. Rom. 16:27; Jude 25. [1 R. V. incorruptible]

2 Tim. 2:19. Nevertheless the foundation of God standeth sure, having this seal, The Lord knoweth them that are his.

Heb. 4:13. Neither is there any creature that is not manifest in his sight: but all things *are* naked and opened unto the eyes of him with whom we have to do.

1 Pet. 1:2. Elect according to the foreknowledge of God the Father,

1 John 1:5. God is light, and in him is no darkness at all.

1 John 3:20. If our heart condemn us, God is greater than our heart, and knoweth all things.

See FOREKNOWLEDGE OF GOD; WISDOM OF GOD.

LONGSUFFERING OF: Gen. 6:3. My spirit shall not always strive with man, for that he also *is* flesh: yet his days shall be an hundred and twenty years.

Gen. 15:16. They shall come hither again: for the iniquity of the Amorites *is* not yet full.

Ex. 34:6. And the LORD passed by before him, and proclaimed, The LORD, The LORD God, merciful and gracious, longsuffering, and abundant in goodness and truth,

Num. 14:18. The LORD *is* longsuffering, and of great mercy, forgiving iniquity and transgression,

Psa. 86:15. Thou, O Lord, *art* a God full of compassion, and gracious, longsuffering, and plenteous in mercy and truth.

Psa. 103:8. The LORD *is* merciful and

gracious, slow to anger, and plenteous in mercy. 9. He will not always chide: neither will he keep *his anger* for ever. 10. He hath not dealt with us after our sins; nor rewarded us according to our iniquities.

Isa. 5:1. Now will I sing to my wellbeloved a song of my beloved touching his vineyard. My wellbeloved hath a vineyard in a very fruitful hill: 2. And he fenced it, and gathered out the stones thereof, and planted it with the choicest vine, and built a tower in the midst of it, and also made a winepress therein: and he looked that it should bring forth grapes, and it brought forth wild grapes. 3. And now, O inhabitants of Jerusalem, and men of Judah, judge, I pray you, betwixt me and my vineyard. 4. What could have been done more to my vineyard, that I have not done in it? wherefore, when I looked that it should bring forth grapes, brought it forth wild grapes?

Isa. 30:18. And therefore will the LORD wait, that he may be gracious unto you, and therefore will he be exalted, that he may have mercy upon you:

Isa. 48:9. For my name's sake will I defer mine anger, and for my praise will I refrain for thee, that I cut thee not off. 11. For mine own sake, *even* for mine own sake, will I do *it:* for how should *my name* be polluted? and I will not give my glory unto another.

Jer. 7:13. And now, because ye have done all these works, saith the LORD, and I spake unto you, rising up early and speaking, but ye heard not; and I called you, but ye answered not; 23. But this thing commanded I them, saying, Obey my voice, and I will be your God, and ye shall be my people: and walk ye in all the ways that I have commanded you, that it may be well unto you. 24. But they hearkened not, nor inclined their ear, but walked in the counsels *and* in the [1 imagination] of their evil heart, and went backward, and not forward. 25. Since the day that your fathers came forth out of the land of Egypt unto this day I have even sent unto you all my servants the prophets, daily rising up early and sending *them:* Isa. 42:14; Jer. 11:7. ⁣　　[1 R. V. stubbornness]

Jer. 15:15. O LORD, thou knowest: remember me, and visit me, and revenge me of my persecutors; take me not away in thy longsuffering: know that for thy sake I have suffered rebuke.

Ezek. 20:17. Nevertheless mine eye spared them from destroying them, neither did I make an end of them in the wilderness.

Joel 2:13. And rend your heart, and not your garments, and turn unto the LORD your God: for he *is* gracious and merciful, slow to anger, and of great kindness, and repenteth him of the evil.

Hab. 1:2. O LORD, how long shall I cry, and thou wilt not hear! *even* cry out unto thee *of* violence, and thou wilt not save! 3. Why dost thou shew me iniquity, and cause *me* to behold grievance? for spoiling

and violence *are* before me: and there are *that* raise up strife and contention. 4. Therefore the law is slacked, and judgment doth never go forth: for the wicked doth compass about the righteous; therefore wrong judgment proceedeth.

Matt. 19:8. He saith unto them, Moses because of the hardness of your hearts suffered you to put away your wives: but from the beginning it was not so.

Matt. 21:33. Hear another parable: There was a certain householder, which planted a vineyard, and hedged it round about, and digged a winepress in it, and built a tower, and let it out to husbandmen, and went into a far country: 34. And when the time of the fruit drew near, he sent his servants to the husbandmen, that they might receive the fruits of it. 35. And the husbandmen took his servants, and beat one, and killed another, and stoned another. 36. Again, he sent other servants more than the first: and they did unto them likewise. 37. But last of all he sent unto them his son, saying, They will reverence my son. 38. But when the husbandmen saw the son, they said among themselves, This is the heir; come, let us kill him, and let us seize on his inheritance. 39. And they caught him, and cast *him* out of the vineyard, and slew *him*. 40. When the lord therefore of the vineyard cometh, what will he do unto those husbandmen? 41. They say unto him, He will miserably destroy those wicked men, and will let out *his* vineyard unto other husbandmen, which shall render him the fruits in their seasons. Mark 12:1-9; Luke 20: 9-16.

Matt. 23:37. O Jerusalem, Jerusalem, *thou* that killest the prophets, and stonest them which are sent unto thee, how often would I have gathered thy children together, even as a hen gathereth her chickens under *her* wings, and ye would not! Luke 13:34.

Luke 13:6. He spake also this parable; A certain *man* had a fig tree planted in his vineyard; and he came and sought fruit thereon, and found none. 7. Then said he unto the dresser of his vineyard, Behold, these three years I come seeking fruit on this fig tree, and find none: cut it down; why cumbereth it the ground? 8. And he answering said unto him, Lord, let it alone this year also, till I shall dig about it, and dung *it:* 9. And if it bear fruit, *well:* and if not, *then* after that thou shalt cut it down.

Acts 14:16. Who in times past suffered all nations to walk in their own ways.

Acts 17:30. And the times of this ignorance God winked at; but now commandeth all men every where to repent:

Rom. 2:4. Despisest thou the riches of his goodness and forbearance and longsuffering; not knowing that the goodness of God leadeth thee to repentance?

Rom. 3:25. Whom God hath set forth *to be* a propitiation through faith in his blood, to declare his righteousness for the remission of sins that are past, through the forbearance of God;

Rom. 9:22. *What* if God, willing to shew *his* wrath, and to make his power known, endured with much longsuffering the vessels of wrath fitted to destruction: 23. That he might make known the riches of his glory on the vessels of mercy, which he had afore prepared unto glory,

Rom. 15:5. Now the God of patience and consolation grant you to be likeminded one toward another according to Christ Jesus:

1 Pet. 3:20. The longsuffering of God waited in the days of Noah,

2 Pet. 3:9. The Lord is not slack concerning his promise, as some men count slackness; but is longsuffering to us-ward, not willing that any should perish, but that all should come to repentance. 15. And account *that* the longsuffering of our Lord *is* salvation;

Rev. 2:21. And I gave her space to repent of her fornication; and she repented not. 22. Behold, I will cast her into a bed, and them that commit adultery with her into great tribulation, except they repent of their deeds.

See LOVE OF; MERCY OF.

LONGSUFFERING OF, ABUSED: Neh. 9:28. But after they had rest, they did evil again before thee: therefore leftest thou them in the hand of their enemies, so that they had the dominion over them: yet when they returned, and cried unto thee, thou heardest *them* from heaven; and many times didst thou deliver them according to thy mercies; 29. And testifiedst against them, that thou mightest bring them again unto thy law: yet they dealt proudly, and hearkened not unto thy commandments, but sinned against thy judgments, (which if a man do, he shall live in them;) and withdrew the shoulder, and hardened their neck, and would not hear. 30. Yet many years didst thou forbear them, and testifiedst against them by thy spirit in thy prophets: yet would they not give ear: therefore gavest thou them into the hand of the people of the lands. 31. Nevertheless for thy great mercies' sake thou didst not utterly consume them, nor forsake them; for thou *art* a gracious and merciful God.

Prov. 1:24. Because I have called, and ye refused; I have stretched out my hand, and no man regarded; 25. But ye have set at naught all my counsel, and would none of my reproof: 26. I also will laugh at your calamity; I will mock when your fear cometh; 27. When your fear cometh as desolation, and your destruction cometh as a whirlwind; when distress and anguish cometh upon you.

Prov. 29:1. He, that being often reproved hardeneth *his* neck, shall suddenly be destroyed, and that without remedy.

Eccl. 8:11. Because sentence against an evil work is not executed speedily, therefore the heart of the sons of men is fully set in them to do evil.

Matt. 24:48. But and if that evil servant shall say in his heart, My lord delayeth his coming; 49. And shall begin to smite *his* fellowservants, and to eat and drink with the drunken; 50. The lord of that servant shall come in a day when he looketh not for *him*, and in an hour that he is not aware of, 51. And shall cut him asunder, and appoint *him* his portion with the hypocrites: there shall be weeping and gnashing of teeth.

Luke 13:6. He spake also this parable: A certain *man* had a fig tree planted in his vineyard; and he came and sought fruit thereon, and found none. 7. Then said he unto the dresser of his vineyard, Behold, these three years I come seeking fruit on this fig tree, and find none: cut it down; why cumbereth it the ground? 8. And he answering said unto him, Lord, let it alone this year also, till I shall dig about it, and dung *it:* 9. And if it bear fruit, *well:* and if not, *then* after that thou shalt cut it down.

LOVE OF: Deut. 4:37. Because he loved thy fathers, therefore he chose their seed after them, Deut. 9:29; 1 Kin. 8:51–53.

Deut. 7:7. The LORD did not set his love upon you, nor choose you, because ye were more in number than any people; for ye *were* the fewest of all people: 8. But because the LORD loved you, 13. And he will love thee, and bless thee, and multiply thee.

Deut. 10:15. The LORD had a delight in thy fathers to love them, and he chose their seed after them, 18. He doth execute the judgment of the fatherless and widow, and loveth the stranger, in giving him food and raiment.

Deut. 23:5. The LORD thy God turned the curse into a blessing unto thee, because the LORD thy God loved thee.

Deut. 33:3. Yea, he loved the people; all his saints *are* in thy hand: and they sat down at thy feet; *every one* shall receive of thy words. 12. The beloved of the LORD shall dwell in safety by him; *and the* LORD shall cover him all the day long, and he shall dwell between his shoulders.

2 Sam. 12:24. He called his name Solomon: and the LORD loved him. Neh. 13:26.

Job 7:17. What *is* man, that thou shouldest magnify him? and that thou shouldest set thine heart upon him?

Psa. 42:8. The LORD will command his lovingkindness in the daytime, and in the night his song *shall be* with me,

Psa. 47:4. He shall choose our inheritance for us, the excellency of Jacob whom **he** loved.

Psa. 63:3. Because thy lovingkindness *is* better than life, my lips shall praise thee.

Psa. 78:65. The LORD . . . 68. Chose **the** tribe of Judah, the mount Zion which he loved. *vs.* 61.62.

Psa. 89:33. My lovingkindness will I not utterly take from him, nor suffer **my faith**fulness to fail.

Psa. 103:13. Like as a father pitieth *his* children, *so* the LORD pitieth them that fear him.

Psa. 146:8. The LORD loveth the righteous: Prov. 15:9. He loveth him that followeth after righteousness.

Isa. 38:17. Behold, for peace I had great bitterness: but thou hast in love to my soul *delivered it* from the pit of corruption: for thou hast cast all my sins behind thy back.

Isa. 43:4. Since thou wast precious in my sight, thou hast been honourable, and I have loved thee: therefore will I give men for thee, and people for thy life.

Jer. 31:3. Yea, I have loved thee with an everlasting love: therefore with lovingkindness have I drawn thee.

Hos. 11:1. When Israel *was* a child, then I loved him, and called my son out of Egypt.

Mal. 1:2. I have loved you, saith the LORD.

John 3:16. God so loved the world, that he gave his only begotten Son, that whosoever believeth in him should not perish, but have everlasting life.

John 5:20. For the Father loveth the Son, and sheweth him all things that himself doeth: and he will shew him greater works than these, that ye may marvel.

John 14:21. He that loveth me shall be loved of my Father, and I will love him, and will manifest myself to him. 23. If a man love me, he will keep my words: and my Father will love him, and we will come unto him, and make our abode with him.

John 16:27. The Father himself loveth you, because ye have loved me, and have believed that I came out from God.

John 17:10. All mine are thine, and thine are mine; and I am glorified in them. 23. That the world may know that thou hast sent me, and hast loved them, as thou hast loved me. 26. That the love wherewith thou hast loved me may be in them, and I in them.

John 20:17. I ascend unto my Father, and your Father; and *to* my God and your God.

Rom. 1:7. Beloved of God, called *to be* saints: Grace to you and peace from God our Father.

Rom. 5:8. God commendeth his love toward us, in that, while we were yet sinners, Christ died for us.

Rom. 9:13. As it is written, Jacob have I loved, but Esau have I hated.

Rom. 11:28. As touching the election, *they are* beloved for the fathers' sakes.

2 Cor. 9 7. God loveth a cheerful giver.

2 Cor. 13:11. The God of love and peace shall be with you.

Eph. 2:4. God, who is rich in mercy, for his great love wherewith he loved us, 5. Even when we were dead in sins, hath quickened us together with Christ,

2 Thess. 2:16. God, even our Father, which hath loved us, and hath given *us* everlasting consolation and good hope through grace,

Tit. 3:4. But after that the kindness and love of God our Saviour toward man ap-

peared, 5. Not by works of righteousness which we have done, but according to his mercy he saved us, by the washing of regeneration, and renewing of the Holy Ghost;

Heb. 12:6. Whom the Lord loveth he chasteneth,

1 John 3:1. Behold, what manner of love the Father hath bestowed upon us,

1 John 4:8. He that loveth not knoweth not God; for God is love. 9. In this was manifested the love of God toward us, because that God sent his only begotten Son into the world, that we might live through him. 10. Herein is love, not that we loved God, but that he loved us, and sent his Son *to be* the propitiation for our sins. 12. God dwelleth in us, and his love is perfected in us. 13. Hereby know we that we dwell in him, and he in us, because he hath given us of his Spirit. 15. Whosoever shall confess that Jesus is the Son of God, God dwelleth in him, and he in God. 16. And we have known and believed the love that God hath to us. God is love; and he that dwelleth in love dwelleth in God, and God in him. 19. We love him, because he first loved us.

Jude 21. Keep yourselves in the love of God,

Rev. 3:12. Him that overcometh will I make a pillar in the temple of my God, and he shall go no more out: and I will write upon him the name of my God, and the name of the city of my God,

Rev. 14:1. With him an hundred forty *and* four thousand, having his Father's name written in their foreheads.

LOVE OF, EXEMPLIFIED: Gen. 17:7. I will establish my covenant between me and thee and thy seed after thee in their generations for an everlasting covenant, to be a God unto thee, and to thy seed after thee.

Ex. 3:6. I *am* the God of thy father, the God of Abraham, the God of Isaac, and the God of Jacob. Gen. 46:3.

Ex. 6:7. I will take you to me for a people, and I will be to you a God: Ex. 29: 45,46.

Ex. 19:4. Ye have seen what I did unto the Egyptians, and *how* I bare you on eagles' wings, and brought you unto myself. 5. Ye shall be a peculiar treasure unto me above all people: 6. Ye shall be unto me a kingdom of priests, and an holy nation.

Lev. 20:26. Ye shall be holy unto me: for I the LORD *am* holy, and have severed you from *other* people, that ye should be mine. *v.* 24.

Lev. 22:32. I will be hallowed among the children of Israel: I *am* the LORD which hallow you. 33. That brought you out of the land of Egypt, to be your God: Lev. 11: 44.45; 25:38. Num. 15:41.

Lev. 25:23. The land *is* mine; for ye *are* strangers and sojourners with me. 42. They *are* my servants, which I brought forth out of the land of Egypt: they shall not be sold as bondmen. *v.* 55.

Lev. 26:12. I will walk among you, and will be your God, and ye shall be my people.

Deut. 4:20. The LORD hath taken you, and brought you forth out of the iron furnace, *even* out of Egypt, to be unto him a people of inheritance, as *ye are* this day. 34. Hath God assayed to go *and* take him a nation from the midst of *another* nation . . . according to all that the LORD your God did for you in Egypt before your eyes? 37. Because he loved thy fathers, therefore he chose their seed after them, and brought thee out in his sight with his mighty power out of Egypt; Deut. 9:29; 1 Kin. 8: 51-53.

Deut. 7:7. The LORD did not set his love upon you, nor choose you, because ye were more in number than any people; for ye *were* the fewest of all people: 8. But because the LORD loved you, 13. And he will love thee, and bless thee, and multiply thee:

Deut. 10:15. The LORD had a delight in thy fathers to love them, and he chose their seed after them, *even* you above all people, as *it is* this day.

Deut. 14:2. Thou *art* an holy people unto the LORD thy God, and the LORD hath chosen thee to be a peculiar people unto himself, above all the nations that *are* upon the earth. Deut. 7:6.

Deut. 23:5. The LORD thy God turned the curse into a blessing unto thee, because the LORD thy God loved thee.

Deut. 26:18. The LORD hath avouched thee this day to be his peculiar people, as he hath promised thee, and that *thou* shouldest keep all his commandments; 19. And to make thee high above all nations which he hath made, in praise, and in name, and in honour; and that thou mayest be an holy people unto the LORD thy God, as he hath spoken.

Deut. 27:9. Take heed, and hearken, O Israel; this day thou art become the people of the LORD thy God.

Deut. 28:9. The LORD shall establish thee an holy people unto himself, as he hath sworn unto thee, if thou shalt keep the commandments of the LORD thy God, and walk in his ways. 10. And all people of the earth shall see that thou art called by the name of the LORD; Deut. 29:13.

Deut. 32:9. The LORD's portion *is* his people; Jacob *is* the lot of his inheritance. 10. He found him in a desert land, and in the waste howling wilderness; he led him about, he instructed him, he kept him as the apple of his eye. 11. As an eagle stirreth up her nest, fluttereth over her young, spreadeth abroad her wings, taketh them, beareth them on her wings: 12. *So* the LORD alone did lead him,

Deut. 33:3. Yea, he loved the people; all his saints *are* in thy hand: and they sat down at thy feet; *every one* shall receive of thy words. 12. The beloved of the LORD

shall dwell in safety by him; *and the LORD* shall cover him all the day long, and he shall dwell between his shoulders.

2 Sam. 7:23. What one nation in the earth *is* like thy people, *even* like Israel, whom God went to redeem for a people to himself, 24. For thou hast confirmed to thyself thy people Israel *to be* a people unto thee for ever: and thou, LORD, art become their God.

2 Sam. 12:24. He called his name Solomon: and the LORD loved him. Neh. 13:26.

Psa. 4:3. The LORD hath set apart him that is godly for himself:

Psa. 31:19. *Oh* how great *is* thy goodness, which thou hast laid up for them that fear thee; *which* thou hast wrought for them that trust in thee before the sons of men! 21. Blessed *be* the LORD: for he hath shewed me his marvellous kindness in a strong city.

Psa. 42:8. The LORD will command his lovingkindness in the daytime, and in the night his song *shall be* with me,

Psa. 47:4. He shall choose our inheritance for us, the excellency of Jacob whom he loved.

Psa. 48:9. We have thought of thy lovingkindness, O God, in the midst of thy temple. 14. This God *is* our God for ever and ever: he will be our guide *even* unto death.

Psa. 50:5. Gather my saints together unto me; those that have made a covenant with me by sacrifice. 7. Hear, O my people, and I will speak; O Israel, and I will testify against thee: I *am* God, *even* thy God.

Psa. 63:3. Because thy lovingkindness *is* better than life, my lips shall praise thee.

Psa. 73:1. Truly God *is* good to Israel, *even* to such as are of a clean heart.

Psa. 74:2. Remember thy congregation, *which* thou hast purchased of old; the rod of thine inheritance, *which* thou hast redeemed; this mount Zion, wherein thou hast dwelt.

Psa. 78:65. Then the Lord . . . 68. Chose the tribe of Judah, the mount Zion which he loved. *vs*. 61,62.

Psa. 81:13. Oh that my people had hearkened unto me, *and* Israel had walked in my ways!

Psa. 89:33. My lovingkindness will I not utterly take from him, nor suffer my faithfulness to fail.

Psa. 90:1. LORD, thou hast been our dwelling place in all generations.

Psa. 100:3. Know ye that the LORD he *is* God: *it is* he *that* hath made us, and not we ourselves; *we are* his people, and the sheep of his pasture. Psa. 79:13: 95:7.

Psa. 103:4. Who redeemeth thy life from destruction; who crowneth thee with lovingkindness and tender mercies:

Psa. 105:6. O ye seed of Abraham his servant, ye children of Jacob his chosen.

Psa. 114:2. Judah was his sanctuary, *and* Israel his dominion.

Psa. 135:4. The LORD hath chosen Jacob

unto himself, *and* Israel for his peculiar treasure.

Psa. 148:14. He also exalteth the horn of his people, the praise of all his saints; *even* of the children of Israel, a people near unto him.

Prov. 11:20. *Such as are* upright in *their* way *are* his delight.

Prov. 15:9. He loveth him that followeth after righteousness.

Isa. 5:7. The vineyard of the Lord of hosts *is* the house of Israel, and the men of Judah his pleasant plant:

Isa. 41:8. Thou, Israel, *art* my servant, Jacob whom I have chosen, the seed of Abraham my friend. 9. *Thou* whom I have taken from the ends of the earth, and called thee from the chief men thereof, and said unto thee, Thou *art* my servant; I have chosen thee, and not cast thee away. 10. Fear thou not; for I *am* with thee: be not dismayed; for I *am* thy God:

Isa. 43:1. Thus saith the Lord that created thee, O Jacob, and he that formed thee, O Israel, Fear not: for I have redeemed thee, I have called *thee* by thy name; thou *art* mine. 2. When thou passest through the waters, I *will be* with thee; and through the rivers, they shall not overflow thee: when thou walkest through the fire, thou shalt not be burned; neither shall the flame kindle upon thee. 3. For I *am* the Lord thy God, the Holy One of Israel, thy Saviour: I gave Egypt *for* thy ransom, Ethiopia and Seba for thee. 4. Since thou wast precious in my sight, thou hast been honourable, and I have loved thee: therefore will I give men for thee, and people for thy life. 7. Every one that is called by my name: for I have created him for my glory, I have formed him; yea, I have made him.

Isa. 44:1. Yet now hear, O Jacob my servant; and Israel, whom I have chosen: 2. Thus saith the Lord that made thee, and formed thee from the womb, *which* will help thee; Fear not, O Jacob, my servant; and thou, Jesurun, whom I have chosen. 21. I have formed thee; thou *art* my servant: O Israel, thou shalt not be forgotten of me. 22. I have blotted out, as a thick cloud, thy transgressions, and, as a cloud, thy sins: return unto me; for I have redeemed thee.

Isa. 48:12. Hearken unto me, O Jacob and Israel, my called;

Isa. 49:13. Sing, O heavens; and be joyful, O earth; and break forth into singing, O mountains: for the Lord hath comforted his people, and will have mercy upon his afflicted. 14. But Zion said, The Lord hath forsaken me, and my Lord hath forgotten me. 15. Can a woman forget her sucking child, that she should not have compassion on the son of her womb? yea, they may forget, yet will I not forget thee. 16. Behold, I have graven thee upon the palms of *my* hand; thy walls *are* continually before me. 17. Thy children shall make haste; thy destroyers and they that made thee waste shall go forth of thee.

Isa. 51:16. I have covered thee in the shadow of mine hand, that I may plant the heavens, and lay the foundations of the earth, and say unto Zion, Thou *art* my people.

Isa. 54:5. Thy Maker *is* thine husband; the Lord of hosts *is* his name; and thy Redeemer the Holy One of Israel; 6. The Lord hath called thee as a woman forsaken and grieved in spirit, and a wife of youth, when thou wast refused, saith thy God. 10. The mountains shall depart, and the hills be removed; but my kindness shall not depart from thee, neither shall the covenant of my peace be removed, saith the Lord that hath mercy on thee.

Isa. 62:4. Thou shalt no more be termed Forsaken; neither shall thy land any more be termed Desolate: but thou shalt be called Hephzi-bah, and thy land Beulah: for the Lord delighteth in thee, and thy land shall be married. 5. *As* the bridegroom rejoiceth over the bride, *so* shall thy God rejoice over thee.

Isa. 63:7. I will mention the lovingkindnesses of the Lord, *and* the praises of the Lord, according to all that the Lord hath bestowed on us, and the great goodness toward the house of Israel, which he hath bestowed on them according to his mercies, and according to the multitude of his lovingkindnesses. 8. For he said, Surely they *are* my people, children *that* will not lie: so he was their Saviour. 9. In all their affliction he was afflicted, and the angel of his presence saved them: in his love and in his pity he redeemed them; and he bare them, and carried them all the days of old.

Isa. 65:19. I will rejoice in Jerusalem, and joy in my people: and the voice of weeping shall be no more heard in her, nor the voice of crying.

Isa. 66:13. As one whom his mother comforteth, so will I comfort you;

Jer. 3:14. Turn, O backsliding children, saith the Lord; for I am married unto you: and I will take you one of a city, and two of a family, and I will bring you to Zion: 15. And I will give you pastors according to mine heart, which shall feed you with knowledge and understanding.

Jer. 10:16. The portion of Jacob *is* not like them: for he *is* the former of all *things*; and Israel *is* the rod of his inheritance: Jer. 51:19.

Jer. 12:7. I have forsaken mine house, I have left mine heritage; I have given the dearly beloved of my soul into the hand of her enemies.

Jer. 13:11. As the girdle cleaveth to the loins of a man, so have I caused to cleave unto me the whole house of Israel and the whole house of Judah, saith the Lord; that they might be unto me for a people, and for a name, and for a praise, and for a glory:

Jer. 15:16. I am called by thy name, O Lord God of hosts.

Jer. 31:3. Yea, I have loved thee with an

everlasting love: therefore with lovingkindness have I drawn thee. 14. I will satiate the soul of the priests with fatness, and my people shall be satisfied with my goodness, 32. I was an husband unto them, saith the LORD:

Jer. 32:41. I will rejoice over them to do them good, and I will plant them in this land assuredly with my whole heart and with my whole soul.

Ezek. 16:8. When I passed by thee, and looked upon thee, behold, thy time *was* the time of love; and I spread my skirt over thee, and covered thy nakedness: yea, I sware unto thee, and entered into a covenant with thee, saith the Lord GOD, and thou becamest mine. *vs.* 1-14.

Ezek. 34:31. Ye my flock, the flock of my pasture, *are* men, *and* I *am* your God, saith the LORD God.

Ezek. 37:27. My tabernacle also shall be with them: yea, I will be their God, and they shall be my people.

Hos. 2:19. I will betroth thee unto me for ever; yea, I will betroth thee unto me in righteousness, and in judgment, and in lovingkindness, and in mercies. 20. I will even betroth thee unto me in faithfulness: and thou shalt know the LORD. 23. I will say to *them which were* not my people, Thou *art* my people; and they shall say, *Thou art* my God. 1 Pet. 2:10.

Hos. 9:10. I found Israel like grapes in the wilderness; I saw your fathers as the firstripe in the fig tree at her first time:

Hos. 11:1. When Israel *was* a child, then I loved him, and called my son out of Egypt. 3. I taught Ephraim also to go, taking them ¹ by their arms; 4. I drew them with cords of a man, with bands of love: and I was to them as they that take off the yoke on their jaws, and I laid meat unto them. [¹ R. V. on my]

Zeph. 3:17. The LORD thy God in the midst of thee *is* mighty; he will save, he will rejoice over thee with joy; he will rest in his love, he will joy over thee with singing.

Hag. 2:23. In that day ... will I take thee, O Zerubbabel, my servant, ... and will make thee as a signet: for I have chosen thee, saith the LORD of hosts.

Zech. 1:14. Thus saith the LORD of hosts; I am jealous for Jerusalem and for Zion with a great jealousy.

Zech. 2:8. He that toucheth you toucheth the apple of his eye.

Zech. 8:8. They shall be my people, and I will be their God, in truth and in righteousness. Jer. 30:22.

Zech. 13:9. I will bring the third part through the fire, and will refine them as silver is refined, and will try them as gold is tried: they shall call on my name, and I will hear them: I will say, It *is* my people: and they shall say, The LORD *is* my God.

Mal. 1:2. I have loved you, saith the LORD. Yet ye say, Wherein hast thou loved us? *Was* not Esau Jacob's brother? saith the LORD: yet I loved Jacob. 3. And I hated Esau, and laid his mountains and his heritage waste for the dragons of the wilderness.

Mal. 3:16. The LORD hearkened, and heard *it*, and a book of remembrance was written before him for them that feared the LORD, and that thought upon his name. 17. They shall be mine, saith the LORD of hosts, in that day when I make up my jewels; and I will spare them, as a man spareth his own son that serveth him.

Matt. 18:11. ¹ For the Son of man is come to save that which was lost. 12. How think ye? if a man have an hundred sheep, and one of them be gone astray, doth he not leave the ninety and nine, and goeth into the mountains, and seeketh that which is gone astray? 13. And if so be that he find it, verily I say unto you, he rejoiceth more of that *sheep*, than of the ninety and nine which went not astray. 14. Even so it is not the will of your Father which is in heaven, that one of these little ones should perish.

[¹ Omitted in R. V.]

Luke 15:4. What man of you, having an hundred sheep, if he lose one of them, doth not leave the ninety and nine in the wilderness, and go after that which is lost, until he find it? 5. And when he hath found *it*, he layeth *it* on his shoulders, rejoicing. 6. And when he cometh home, he calleth together *his* friends and neighbours, saying unto them, Rejoice with me; for I have found my sheep which was lost. 7. I say unto you, that likewise joy shall be in heaven over one sinner that repenteth, more than over ninety and nine just persons, which need no repentance.

11. And he said, A certain man had two sons: 12. And the younger of them said to *his* father, Father, give me the portion of goods that falleth *to me*. And he divided unto them *his* living. 13. And not many days after the younger son gathered all together, and took his journey into a far country, and there wasted his substance with riotous living. 14. And when he had spent all, there arose a mighty famine in that land; and he began to be in want. 15. And he went and joined himself to a citizen of that country; and he sent him into his fields to feed swine. 16. And he would fain have filled his belly with the husks that the swine did eat: and no man gave unto him. 17. And when he came to himself, he said, How many hired servants of my father's have bread enough and to spare, and I perish with hunger! 18. I will arise and go to my father, and will say unto him, Father, I have sinned against heaven, and before thee, 19. And am no more worthy to be called thy son: make me as one of thy hired servants. 20. And he arose, and came to his father. But when he was yet a great way off, his father saw him, and had compassion, and ran, and fell on his neck, and kissed him. 21. And the son said unto him, Father, I have sinned against heaven, and

in thy sight, and am no more worthy to be called thy son. 22. But the father said to his servants, Bring forth the best robe, and put it on him; and put a ring on his hand, and shoes on his feet: 23. And bring hither the fatted calf, and kill it; and let us eat, and be merry: 24. For this my son was dead, and is alive again; he was lost, and is found. And they began to be merry. 25. Now his elder son was in the field: and as he came and drew nigh to the house, he heard musick and dancing. 26. And he called one of the servants, and asked what these things meant. 27. And he said unto him, Thy brother is come; and thy father hath killed the fatted calf, because he hath received him safe and sound.

John 14:21. He that loveth me shall be loved of my Father, and I will love him, 23. If a man love me, he will keep my words: and my Father will love him, and we will come unto him,

John 16:27. The Father himself loveth you, because ye have loved me, and have believed that I came out from God.

John 17:10. All mine are thine, and thine are mine; and I am glorified in them. 23. That the world may know that thou hast sent me, and hast loved them, as thou hast loved me. 26. That the love wherewith thou hast loved me may be in them, and I in them.

Rom. 1:7. To all that be in Rome, beloved of God, called to be saints: Grace to you and peace from God our Father,

Rom. 5:8. God commendeth his love toward us, in that, while we were yet sinners, Christ died for us.

Rom. 8:31. If God be for us, who can be against us? 32. He that spared not his own Son, but delivered him up for us all, how shall he not with him also freely give us all things? 39. Nor height, nor depth, nor any other creature, shall be able to separate us from the love of God, which is in Christ Jesus our Lord.

Rom. 11:28. As touching the election, they are beloved for the fathers' sakes.

1 Cor. 2:9. Eye hath not seen, nor ear heard, neither have entered into the heart of man, the things which God hath prepared for them that love him. Isa. 64:4.

1 Cor. 3:9. Ye are God's husbandry, ye are God's building.

1 Cor. 6:19. Know ye not that your body is the temple of the Holy Ghost which is in you, which ye have of God, and ye are not your own? 20. For ye are bought with a price: therefore glorify God in your body, and in your spirit, which are God's. 1 Cor. 7:23.

2 Cor. 5:18. And all things are of God, who hath reconciled us to himself by Jesus Christ, and hath given to us the ministry of reconciliation; 19. To wit, that God was in Christ, reconciling the world unto himself, not imputing their trespasses unto them: and hath committed unto us the word of

reconciliation. 20. Now then we are ambassadors for Christ, as though God did beseech you by us: we pray you in Christ's stead, be ye reconciled to God. 21. For he hath made him to be sin for us, who knew no sin; that we might be made the righteousness of God in him.

2 Cor. 6:16. Ye are the temple of the living God; as God hath said, I will dwell in them, and walk in them; and I will be their God, and they shall be my people.

2 Cor. 13:14. The love of God, and the communion of the Holy Ghost, be with you all.

Eph. 1:3. Blessed be the God and Father of our Lord Jesus Christ, who hath blessed us with all spiritual blessings in heavenly places in Christ: 4. According as he hath chosen us in him before the foundation of the world, that we should be holy and without blame before him in love: 5. Having predestinated us unto the adoption of children by Jesus Christ to himself, according to the good pleasure of his will. 6. To the praise of the glory of his grace, wherein he hath made us accepted in the beloved.

Col. 3:12. Put on therefore, as the elect of God, holy and beloved, bowels of mercies.

Heb. 11:16. God is not ashamed to be called their God: for he hath prepared for them a city.

Jas. 1:18. Of his own will begat he us with the word of truth, that we should be a kind of firstfruits of his creatures.

MERCY OF: Gen. 8:21, I will not again curse the ground any more for man's sake; for the imagination of man's heart is evil from his youth; neither will I again smite any more every thing living, as I have done.

Gen. 18:26. If I find in Sodom fifty righteous within the city, then I will spare all the place for their sakes. vs. 27-32.

Gen. 19:16. While he lingered, the men laid hold upon his hand, and upon the hand of his wife, and upon the hand of his two daughters; the LORD being merciful unto him: and they brought him forth, and set him without the city.

Ex. 15:13. Thou in thy mercy hast led forth the people which thou hast redeemed: thou hast guided them in thy strength unto thy holy habitation.

Ex. 20:2. I am the LORD thy God, . . . 6. . . . shewing mercy unto thousands of them that love me, and keep my commandments. 22. Ye have seen that I have talked with you from heaven. Deut. 5:10.

Ex. 22:27. It shall come to pass, when he crieth unto me, that I will hear; for I am gracious.

Ex. 25:17. Thou shalt make a mercy seat of pure gold: Psa. 80:1; Heb. 4:16.

Ex. 32:14. The LORD repented of the evil which he thought to do unto his people. 34. Behold, mine Angel shall go before thee:

Ex. 33:19. I will make all my goodness pass before thee, and I will proclaim the name of the LORD before thee; and will be gracious to whom I will be gracious, and will shew mercy on whom I will shew mercy.

Ex. 34:6. The Lord, the Lord God, merciful and gracious, longsuffering, and abundant in goodness and truth, 7. Keeping mercy for thousands, forgiving iniquity and transgression and sin,

Lev. 26:44. I will not cast them away, neither will I abhor them, to destroy them utterly, and to break my covenant with them: for I am the Lord their God. 45. But I will for their sakes remember the covenant of their ancestors, whom I brought forth out of the land of Egypt in the sight of the heathen, that I might be their God : vs. 40–43.

Num. 14:18. The Lord is longsuffering, and of great mercy, forgiving iniquity and transgression, 19. Pardon, I beseech thee, the iniquity of this people according unto the greatness of thy mercy, and as thou hast forgiven this people, from Egypt even until now. 20. And the Lord said, I have pardoned according to thy word :

Num. 16:48. He stood between the dead and the living; and the plague was stayed.

Num. 21:8. The Lord said unto Moses, Make thee a fiery serpent, and set it upon a pole: and it shall come to pass, that every one that is bitten, when he looketh upon it, shall live.

Deut. 4:31. (The Lord thy God is a merciful God ;) he will not forsake thee, neither destroy thee, nor forget the covenant of thy fathers which he sware unto them.

Deut. 5:29. O that there were such an heart in them, that they would fear me, and keep all my commandments always, that it might be well with them, and with their children for ever!

Deut. 7:9. Know therefore that the Lord thy God, he is God, the faithful God, which keepeth covenant and mercy with them that love him and keep his commandments to a thousand generations;

Deut. 32:29. O that they were wise, that they understood this, that they would consider their latter end! 36. The Lord shall judge his people, and repent himself for his servants, when he seeth that their power is gone, and there is none shut up, or left. 43. And will be merciful unto his land, and to his people.

Judg. 2:18. The Lord was with the judge, and delivered them out of the hand of their enemies all the days of the judge: for it repented the Lord because of their groanings by reason of them that oppressed them and vexed them. Ex. 2:24,25; Judg. 3:9,15.

Judg. 10:16. His soul was grieved for the misery of Israel.

2 Sam. 12:13. Nathan said unto David, The Lord also hath put away thy sin; thou shalt not die.

2 Sam. 14:14. Yet doth he devise means, that his banished be not expelled from him.

2 Sam. 24:14. Let us fall now into the hand of the Lord; for his mercies are great: 16.

When the angel stretched out his hand upon Jerusalem to destroy it, the Lord repented him of the evil, and said to the angel that destroyed the people, It is enough; stay now thine hand.

1 Kin. 8:23. There is no God like thee, in heaven above, or on earth beneath, who keepest covenant and mercy with thy servants that walk before thee with all their heart :

1 Kin. 11:39. I will for this afflict the seed of David, but not for ever.

2 Kin. 13:23. The Lord was gracious unto them, and had compassion on them, . . . and would not destroy them, neither cast he them from his presence as yet.

2 Kin. 14:26. The Lord saw the affliction of Israel, that it was very bitter: for there was not any shut up, nor any left, nor any helper for Israel. 27. And the Lord said not that he would blot out the name of Israel from under heaven: but he saved them by the hand of Jeroboam.

1 Chr. 16:34. O give thanks unto the Lord; for he is good; for his mercy endureth for ever.

2 Chr. 5:13. It came even to pass, as the trumpeters and singers were as one, to make one sound to be heard in praising and thanking the Lord; and when they lifted up their voice with the trumpets and cymbals and instruments of musick, and praised the Lord, saying, For he is good; for his mercy endureth for ever: that then the house was filled with a cloud, even the house of the Lord;

2 Chr. 7:3. And when all the children of Israel saw how the fire came down, and the glory of the Lord upon the house, they bowed themselves with their faces to the ground upon the pavement, and worshipped, and praised the Lord, saying, For he is good; for his mercy endureth for ever. 6. And the priests waited on their offices: the Levites also with instruments of musick of the Lord, which David the king had made to praise the Lord, because his mercy endureth for ever, 14. If my people, which are called by my name, shall humble themselves, and pray, and seek my face, and turn from their wicked ways; then will I hear from heaven, and will forgive their sin, and will heal their land.

2 Chr. 30:9. The Lord your God is gracious and merciful, and will not turn away his face from you, if ye return unto him.

2 Chr. 36:15. The Lord God of their fathers sent to them by his messengers, rising up betimes, and sending; because he had compassion on his people, and on his dwelling place : Jer. 7:25.

Ezra 9:9. For we were bondmen; yet our God hath not forsaken us in our bondage, but hath extended mercy unto us in the sight of the kings of Persia, to give us a reviving, to set up the house of our God, and to repair the desolations thereof, and to give us a wall in Judah and in Jerusalem. 13. Thou our God hast punished us less than our iniquities *deserve*, and hast given us *such* deliverance as this; *vs.* 7–14; Job 11:6.

Neh. 1:10. These *are* thy servants and thy people, whom thou hast redeemed by thy great power, and by thy strong hand.

Neh. 9:17. Thou *art* a God ready to pardon, gracious and merciful, slow to anger, and of great kindness, and forsookest them not. 27. In the time of their trouble, when they cried unto thee, thou heardest *them* from heaven; and according to thy manifold mercies thou gavest them saviours, who saved them out of the hand of their enemies. 28. When they returned, and cried unto thee, thou heardest *them* from heaven; and many times didst thou deliver them according to thy mercies; 29. And testifiedst against them, that thou mightest bring them again unto thy law: 30. Yet many years didst thou forbear them, and testifiedst against them by thy spirit in thy prophets: 31. For thy great mercies' sake thou didst not utterly consume them, nor forsake them; for thou *art* a gracious and merciful God. *vs.* 17–20; 2 Chr. 24:19.

Job 23:2. Even to day *is* my complaint bitter: my stroke is heavier than my groaning. 3. Oh that I knew where I might find him! *that* I might come *even* to his seat! 4. I would order *my* cause before him, and fill my mouth with arguments. 5. I would know the words *which* he would answer me, and understand what he would say unto me. 6. Will he plead against me with *his* great power? No; but he would put *strength* in me.

Job 24:12. Men groan from out of the city, and the soul of the wounded crieth out: yet God layeth not folly *to them*.

Job 33:14. For God speaketh once, yea twice, *yet man* perceiveth it not. 15. In a dream, in a vision of the night, when deep sleep falleth upon men, in slumberings upon the bed; 16. Then he openeth the ears of men, and sealeth their instruction, 17. That he may withdraw man *from his* purpose, and hide pride from man. 18. He keepeth back his soul from the pit, and his life from perishing by the sword. 19. He is chastened also with pain upon his bed, and the multitude of his bones with strong *pain:* 20. So that his life abhorreth bread, and his soul dainty meat. 21. His flesh is consumed away, that it cannot be seen; and his bones *that* were not seen stick out. 22. Yea, his soul draweth near unto the grave, and his life to the destroyers. 23. If there be a messenger with him, an interpreter, one among a thousand, to shew unto man his uprightness: 24. Then he is gracious unto him, and saith, Deliver him from going down to the pit: I have found a ransom. 25. His flesh shall be fresher than a child's: he shall return to the days of his youth: 26. He shall pray unto God, and he will be favourable unto him: and he shall see his face with joy: for he will render unto man his righteousness. 27. He looketh upon men, and *if any* say, I have sinned, and perverted

that which was right, and it profited me not; 28. He will deliver his soul from going into the pit, and his life shall see the light. 29. Lo, all these *things* worketh God oftentimes with man, 30. To bring back his soul from the pit, to be enlightened with the light of the living.

Psa. 18:50. Great deliverance giveth he to his king; and sheweth mercy to his anointed, to David, and to his seed for evermore.

Psa. 25:6. Remember, O Lord, thy tender mercies and thy lovingkindnesses; for they *have been* ever of old. 8. Good and upright *is* the Lord: therefore will he teach sinners in the way.

Psa. 30:5. His anger *endureth but* a moment; in his favour *is* life: weeping may endure for a night, but joy *cometh* in the morning.

Psa. 31:7. I will be glad and rejoice in thy mercy: for thou hast considered my trouble; thou hast known my soul in adversities;

Psa. 32:1. Blessed *is he whose* transgression *is* forgiven, *whose* sin *is* covered. 2. Blessed *is* the man unto whom the Lord imputeth not iniquity, 5. I said, I will confess my transgressions unto the Lord; and thou forgavest the iniquity of my sin.

Psa. 36:5. Thy mercy, O Lord, *is* in the heavens;

Psa. 50:21. These *things* hast thou done, and I kept silence;

Psa. 57:10. Thy mercy *is* great unto the heavens,

Psa. 62:12. Unto thee, O Lord, *belongeth* mercy:

Psa. 65:3. Iniquities prevail against me: *as for* our transgressions, thou shalt purge them away.

Psa. 69:16. Thy lovingkindness *is* good: turn unto me according to the multitude of thy tender mercies.

Psa. 78:38. But he, *being* full of compassion, forgave *their* iniquity, and destroyed *them* not; yea, many a time turned he his anger away, and did not stir up all his wrath. 39. For he remembered that they *were but* flesh; a wind that passeth away, and cometh not again. *vs.* 4–72; Psa. 106: 43–46.

Psa. 85:2. Thou hast forgiven the iniquity of thy people, thou hast covered all their sin. 3. Thou hast taken away all thy wrath: thou hast turned *thyself* from the fierceness of thine anger. 10. Mercy and truth are met together; righteousness and peace have kissed *each other*.

Psa. 86:5. Thou, Lord, *art* good, and ready to forgive; and plenteous in mercy unto all them that call upon thee. 13. Great *is* thy mercy toward me: and thou hast delivered my soul from the lowest hell. 15. Thou, O Lord, *art* a God full of compassion, and gracious, longsuffering, and plenteous in mercy and truth.

Psa. 89:2. Mercy shall be built up for ever: 14. Mercy and truth shall go before thy face. 28. My mercy will I keep for him for evermore,

Psa. 99:8. Thou answeredst them, O LORD our God : thou wast a God that forgavest them,

Psa. 100:5. The LORD *is* good ; his mercy *is* everlasting ;

Psa. 103:3. Who forgiveth all thine iniquities; who healeth all thy diseases; 8. The LORD *is* merciful and gracious, slow to anger, and plenteous in mercy. 9. He will not always chide : neither will he keep *his anger* for ever. 10. He hath not dealt with us after our sins; nor rewarded us according to our iniquities. 11. For as the heaven is high above the earth, *so* great is his mercy toward them that fear him. 12. As far as the east is from the west, *so* far hath he removed our transgressions from us. 13. Like as a father pitieth *his* children, *so* the LORD pitieth them that fear him. 14. For he knoweth our frame; he remembereth that we *are* dust. 17. The mercy of the LORD *is* from everlasting to everlasting upon them that fear him, and his righteousness unto children's children ;

Psa. 106:1. His mercy *endureth* for ever. Psa. 107:1; 136:3-26.

Psa. 108:4. Thy mercy *is* great above the heavens :

Psa. 111:4. The LORD *is* gracious and full of compassion.

Psa. 116:5. Gracious *is* the LORD, and righteous ; yea, our God *is* merciful.

Psa. 117:2. His merciful kindness is great toward us : Psa. 118:1-4,29.

Psa. 119:64. The earth, O LORD, is full of thy mercy: 156. Great *are* thy tender mercies, O LORD :

Psa. 130:3. If thou, LORD, shouldest mark iniquities, O Lord, who shall stand ? 4. *There is* forgiveness with thee, that thou mayest be feared. 7. Let Israel hope in the LORD: for with the LORD *there is* mercy, and with him *is* plenteous redemption. 8. And he shall redeem Israel from all his iniquities.

Psa. 135:14. He will repent himself concerning his servants.

Psa. 138:2. I will . . . praise thy name for thy lovingkindness and for thy truth :

Psa. 145:8. The LORD *is* gracious, and full of compassion; slow to anger, and of great mercy. 9. The LORD *is* good to all : and his tender mercies *are* over all his works.

Psa. 146:7. Which executeth judgment for the oppressed : which giveth food to the hungry. The LORD looseth the prisoners : 8. The LORD openeth *the eyes of* the blind : the LORD raiseth them that are bowed down :

Prov. 16:6. By mercy and truth iniquity is purged :

Prov. 28:13. He that covereth his sins shall not prosper : but whoso confesseth and forsaketh *them* shall have mercy.

Isa. 1:5. Why should ye be stricken any more ? 18. Come now, and let us reason together, saith the LORD : though your sins be as scarlet, they shall be as white as snow ; though they be red like crimson, they shall be as wool.

Isa. 6:7. Lo, this hath touched thy lips; and thine iniquity is taken away, and thy sin purged.

Isa. 12:1. O LORD, I will praise thee : though thou wast angry with me, thine anger is turned away, and thou comfortedst me.

Isa. 17:6. Yet gleaning grapes shall be left in it, as the shaking of an olive tree, two *or* three berries in the top of the uppermost bough, four *or* five in the outmost fruitful branches thereof, saith the LORD God of Israel. Isa. 24:13.

Isa. 54:9. For as I have sworn that the waters of Noah should no more go over the earth ; so have I sworn that I would not be wroth with thee, nor rebuke thee.

Isa. 55:7. Let the wicked forsake his way, and the unrighteous man his thoughts : and let him return unto the LORD, and he will have mercy upon him; and to our God, for he will abundantly pardon. 8. For my thoughts *are* not your thoughts, neither *are* your ways my ways, saith the LORD. 9. For *as* the heavens are higher than the earth, so are my ways higher than your ways, and my thoughts than your thoughts.

Isa. 57:11. Have not I held my peace even of old, and thou fearest me not ? 15. I dwell in the high and holy *place*, with him also *that is* of a contrite and humble spirit, to revive the spirit of the humble, and to revive the heart of the contrite ones. 16. I will not contend for ever, neither will I be always wroth : for the spirit should fail before me, and the souls *which* I have made. 18. I have seen his ways, and will heal him : I will lead him also, and restore comforts unto him and to his mourners. 19. I create the fruit of the lips; Peace, peace to *him that is* far off, and to *him that is* near, saith the LORD; and I will heal him.

Isa. 60:10. In my wrath I smote thee, but in my favour have I had mercy on thee.

Isa. 65:2. I have spread out my hands all the day unto a rebellious people, which walketh in a way *that was* not good, after their own thoughts ; 8. As the new wine is found in the cluster, and *one* saith, Destroy it not; for a blessing *is* in it : so will I do for my servants' sakes, that I may not destroy them all.

Jer. 2:9. Wherefore I will yet plead with you, saith the LORD, and with your children's children will I plead.

Jer. 3:12. Go and proclaim these words toward the north, and say, Return, thou backsliding Israel, saith the LORD; *and* I will not cause mine anger to fall upon you: for I *am* merciful, saith the LORD, *and* I will not keep *anger* for ever. 22. Return, ye backsliding children, *and* I will heal your backslidings. *vs.* 1-22.

Jer. 4:27. The whole land shall be desolate : yet will I not make a full end.

Jer. 5:10. Go ye up upon her walls, and destroy; but make not a full end:

Jer. 9:24. I *am* the LORD which exercise lovingkindness, judgment, and righteousness, in the earth: for in these *things* I delight, saith the LORD.

Jer. 29:11. I know the thoughts that I think toward you, saith the LORD, thoughts of peace, and not of evil, to give you an expected end.

Jer. 30:11. I *am* with thee, saith the LORD, to save thee: though I make a full end of all nations whither I have scattered thee, yet will I not make a full end of thee: but I will correct thee in measure, Jer. 46:28.

Jer. 31:20. *Is* Ephraim my dear son? *is he* a pleasant child? for since I spake against him, I do earnestly remember him still: therefore my bowels are troubled for him; I will surely have mercy upon him, saith the LORD. 34. I will forgive their iniquity, and I will remember their sin no more. 37. If heaven above can be measured, and the foundations of the earth searched out beneath, I will also cast off all the seed of Israel for all that they have done, saith the LORD.

Jer. 32:18. Thou shewest lovingkindness unto thousands,

Jer. 33:8. I will cleanse them from all their iniquity, whereby they have sinned against me; and I will pardon all their iniquities, whereby they have sinned, and whereby they have transgressed against me. 11. The voice of them that shall say, Praise the LORD of hosts: for the LORD *is* good; for his mercy *endureth* for ever: *and* of them that shall bring the sacrifice of praise into the house of the LORD. For I will cause to return the captivity of the land, as at the first, saith the LORD.

Jer. 36:3. Return every man from his evil way; that I may forgive their iniquity and their sin. *vs.* 6,7.

Jer. 50:20. The iniquity of Israel shall be sought for, and *there shall be* none; and the sins of Judah, and they shall not be found: for I will pardon them whom I reserve.

Jer. 51:5. Israel *hath* not *been* forsaken, nor Judah of his God, of the LORD of hosts; though their land was filled with sin against the Holy One of Israel.

Lam. 3:22. *It is of* the LORD's mercies that we are not consumed, because his compassions fail not. 23. *They are* new every morning: great *is* thy faithfulness. 31. The Lord will not cast off for ever: 32. But though he cause grief, yet will he have compassion according to the multitude of his mercies. 33. For he doth not afflict willingly nor grieve the children of men.

Ezek. 14:22. Therein shall be left a remnant that shall be brought forth, *both* sons and daughters: behold, they shall come forth unto you, and ye shall see their way and their doings: and ye shall be comforted concerning the evil that I have brought upon Jerusalem, *even* concerning all that I have brought upon it.

Ezek. 16:6. When I passed by thee, and saw thee polluted in thine own blood, I said unto thee *when thou wast* in thy blood, Live; yea, I said unto thee *when thou wast* in thy blood, Live. 42. So will I make my fury toward thee to rest, and my jealousy shall depart from thee, and I will be quiet, and will be no more angry. 63. I am pacified toward thee for all that thou hast done, saith the Lord GOD.

Ezek. 18:23. Have I any pleasure at all that the wicked should die? saith the Lord GOD: *and* not that he should return from his ways, and live? 31. Cast away from you all your transgressions, whereby ye have transgressed; and make you a new heart and a new spirit: for why will ye die, O house of Israel? 32. For I have no pleasure in the death of him that dieth, saith the Lord GOD: wherefore turn *yourselves*, and live ye.

Ezek. 20:17. Nevertheless mine eye spared them from destroying them, neither did I make an end of them in the wilderness. 42. Ye shall know that I *am* the LORD, when I shall bring you into the land of Israel, into the country *for* which I lifted up mine hand to give it to your fathers. *vs.* 11–44.

Ezek. 33:11. *As* I live, saith the Lord GOD, I have no pleasure in the death of the wicked; but that the wicked turn from his way and live: turn ye, turn ye from your evil ways; for why will ye die, O house of Israel?

Ezek. 36:25. Then will I sprinkle clean water upon you, and ye shall be clean: from all your filthiness, and from all your idols, will I cleanse you.

Dan. 4:22. It *is* thou, O king, that art grown and become strong: for thy greatness is grown, and reacheth unto heaven, and thy dominion to the end of the earth. 23. And whereas the king saw a watcher and an holy one coming down from heaven, and saying, Hew the tree down, and destroy it; yet leave the stump of the roots thereof in the earth, even with a band of iron and brass, in the tender grass of the field; and let it be wet with the dew of heaven, and *let* his portion *be* with the beasts of the field, till seven times pass over him; 24. This *is* the interpretation, O king, and this *is* the decree of the most High, which is come upon my lord the king: 25. That they shall drive thee from men, and thy dwelling shall be with the beasts of the field, and they shall make thee to eat grass as oxen, and they shall wet thee with the dew of heaven, and seven times shall pass over thee, till thou know that the most High ruleth in the kingdom of men, and giveth it to whomsoever he will. 26. And whereas they commanded to leave the stump of the tree roots; thy kingdom shall be sure unto thee, after that thou shalt have known that the heavens do rule. 27 Wherefore, O king, let my counsel be acceptable unto thee, and break off thy sins by righteousness, and thine iniquities by shewing mercy to the poor; if it may be a lengthening of thy tranquillity.

Dan. 9:4. O Lord, the great and dreadful God, keeping the covenant and mercy to them that love him, and to them that keep his commandments; 9. To the Lord our God *belong* mercies and forgivenesses, though we have rebelled against him;

Hos. 2:14. I will allure her, and bring her into the wilderness, and speak comfortably unto her. 23. I will sow her unto me in the earth; and I will have mercy upon her that had not obtained mercy;' *vs.* 14–23; Rom. 9: 15,18; 1 Pet. 2:10.

Hos. 11:8. How shall I give thee up, Ephraim? *how* shall I deliver thee, Israel? how shall I make thee as Admah? *how* shall I set thee as Zeboim? mine heart is turned within me, my repentings are kindled together. 9. I will not execute the fierceness of mine anger, I will not return to destroy Ephraim: for I *am* God, and not man; the Holy One in the midst of thee.

Hos. 14:4. I will heal their backsliding, I will love them freely: for mine anger is turned away from him. *vs.* 1–8.

Joel 2:13. Turn unto the Lord your God: for he *is* gracious and merciful, slow to anger, and of great kindness, and repenteth him of the evil. 18. Then will the LORD be jealous for his land, and pity his people.

Joel 3:21. I will cleanse their blood *that* I have not cleansed: for the LORD dwelleth in Zion.

Amos 7:3. The LORD repented for this: It shall not be, saith the LORD.

Jonah 4:2. I knew that thou *art* a gracious God, and merciful, slow to anger, and of great kindness, and repentest thee of the evil. 10. Then said the LORD, Thou hast had pity on the gourd, for the which thou hast not laboured, neither madest it grow; which came up in a night, and perished in a night: 11. Should not I spare Nineveh, that great city, wherein are more than sixscore thousand persons that cannot discern between their right hand and their left hand; and *also* much cattle?

Mic. 7:18. Who *is* a God like unto thee, that pardoneth iniquity, and passeth by the transgression of the remnant of his heritage? he retaineth not his anger for ever, because he delighteth *in* mercy. 19. He will turn again, he will have compassion upon us; he will subdue our iniquities; and thou wilt cast all their sins into the depths of the sea.

Nah. 1:3. The LORD *is* slow to anger, and great in power.

Zeph. 2:7. The LORD their God shall visit them, and [1] turn away their captivity.

[1 R. V. bring again]

Zech. 1:16. I am returned to Jerusalem with mercies: my house shall be built in it, saith the LORD of hosts, 17. The LORD shall yet comfort Zion, and shall yet choose Jerusalem,

Zech. 3:9. I will remove the iniquity of that land in one day.

Zech. 10:6. I will strengthen the house of Judah, and I will save the house of Joseph, and I will bring them again to place them; for I have mercy upon them: and they shall be as though I had not cast them off: for I *am* the LORD their God, and will hear them.

Mal. 3:6. I *am* the LORD, I change not; therefore ye sons of Jacob are not consumed.

Matt. 6:14. If ye forgive men their trespasses, your heavenly Father will also forgive you:

Matt. 18:11. [1] For the Son of man is come to save that which was lost. 12. How think ye? if a man have an hundred sheep, and one of them be gone astray, doth he not leave the ninety and nine, and goeth into the mountains, and seeketh that which is gone astray? 13. And if so be that he find it, verily I say unto you, he rejoiceth more of that *sheep*, than of the ninety and nine which went not astray. 14. Even so it is not the will of your Father which is in heaven, that one of these little ones should perish.

[1 Omitted in R. V.]

23. Therefore is the kingdom of heaven likened unto a certain king, which would take account of his servants. 24. And when he had begun to reckon, one was brought unto him, which owed him ten thousand talents. 25. But forasmuch as he had not to pay, his lord commanded him to be sold, and his wife, and children, and all that he had, and payment to be made. 26. The servant therefore fell down, and worshipped him, saying, Lord, have patience with me, and I will pay thee all. 27. Then the lord of that servant was moved with compassion, and loosed him, and forgave him the debt. Luke [1] 5:4–7.

Luke 1:50. His mercy *is* on them that fear him from generation to generation. 77. To give knowledge of salvation unto his people by the remission of their sins, 78. Through the tender mercy of our God; whereby the dayspring from on high hath visited us,

Luke 6:36. Be ye therefore merciful, as your Father also is merciful.

Acts 3:19. Repent ye therefore, and be converted, that your sins may be blotted out, when the times of refreshing shall come from the presence of the Lord;

Acts 17:30. The times of this ignorance God winked at; but now commandeth all men every where to repent:

Acts 26:18. To open their eyes, *and* to turn *them* from darkness to light, and *from* the power of Satan unto God, that they may receive forgiveness of sins,

Rom. 10:12. The same Lord over all is rich unto all that call upon him. 13. For whosoever shall call upon the name of the Lord shall be saved.

Rom. 11:32. God hath concluded them all

in unbelief, that he might have mercy upon all.

Rom. 15:9. That the Gentiles might glorify God for *his* mercy;

1 Cor. 15:10. By the grace of God I am what I am; and his grace which *was bestowed* upon me was not in vain;

2 Cor. 1:3. Blessed *be* God, even the Father of our Lord Jesus Christ, the Father of mercies, and the God of all comfort;

2 Cor. 4:15. All things *are* for your sakes, that the abundant grace might through the thanksgiving of many redound to the glory of God.

2 Cor. 12:9. My grace is sufficient for thee: for my strength is made perfect in weakness.

Eph. 1:6. To the praise of the glory of his grace, wherein he hath made us accepted in the beloved. 7. In whom we have redemption through his blood, the forgiveness of sins, according to the riches of his grace; 8. Wherein he hath abounded toward us in all wisdom and prudence;

Eph. 2:4. God, who is rich in mercy, for his great love wherewith he loved us, 5. Even when we were dead in sins, hath quickened us together with Christ, (by grace ye are saved;) 6. And hath raised *us* up together, and made *us* sit together in heavenly *places* in Christ Jesus: 7. That in the ages to come he might shew the exceeding riches of his grace in *his* kindness toward us through Christ Jesus.

1 Tim. 1:13. Who was before a blasphemer, and a persecutor, and injurious: but I obtained mercy, because I did *it* ignorantly in unbelief.

Tit. 3:5. Not by works of righteousness which we have done, but according to his mercy he saved us, by the washing of regeneration, and renewing of the Holy Ghost;

Heb. 4:16. Let us therefore come boldly unto the throne of grace, that we may obtain mercy, and find grace to help in time of need.

Heb. 8:12. I will be merciful to their unrighteousness, and their sins and their iniquities will I remember no more.

Jas. 2:13. For he shall have judgment without mercy, that hath shewed no mercy; and mercy rejoiceth against judgment.

Jas. 4:8. Draw nigh to God, and he will draw nigh to you.

Jas. 5:11. The Lord is very pitiful, and of tender mercy. 15. If he have committed sins, they shall be forgiven him.

1 Pet. 1:3. According to his abundant mercy hath begotten us again unto a lively hope by the resurrection of Jesus Christ from the dead,

1 Pet. 5:10. But the God of all grace, who hath called us unto his eternal glory by Christ Jesus, after that ye have suffered a while, make you perfect, stablish, strengthen, settle *you.*

2 Pet. 3:9. The Lord is not slack concerning his promise, as some men count slackness; but is longsuffering to us-ward, not willing that any should perish, but that all should come to repentance. 15. Account *that* the longsuffering of our Lord *is* salvation:

1 John 1:9. If we confess our sins, he is faithful and just to forgive us *our* sins, and to cleanse us from all unrighteousness.

Rev. 2:21. I gave her [the church at Thyatira] space to repent.

See Longsuffering of, Love of.

OMNIPOTENT: Gen. 17:1. I *am* the Almighty God; walk before me, and be thou perfect.

Gen. 18:14. Is any thing too hard for the Lord?

Job 42:2. I know that thou canst do every *thing,*

Isa. 26:4. In the Lord JEHOVAH *is* everlasting strength:

Matt. 19:26. With God all things are possible.

Luke 1:37. [1] For with God nothing shall be impossible.   [1 R. V. For no word from God shall be void of power]

Acts 26:8. Why should it be thought a thing incredible with you, that God should raise the dead?

Rev. 19:6. The Lord God omnipotent reigneth.

Rev. 21:22. And I saw no temple therein for the Lord God Almighty and the Lamb are the temple of it.

For uses of the term Almighty consult Concordances.

See Creator, above; Power of, Preserver, below.

OMNIPRESENT: Gen. 28:16. Surely the Lord is in this place; and I knew *it* not.

1 Kin. 8:27. Will God indeed dwell on the earth? behold, the heaven and the heaven of heavens cannot contain thee; how much less this house that I have builded? 2 Chr. 2:6; Acts 7:48,49.

Psa. 139:3. Thou compassest my path, and my lying down, 5. Thou hast beset me behind and before, and laid thine hand upon me. 7. Whither shall I go from thy spirit? or whither shall I flee from thy presence? 8. If I ascend up into heaven, thou *art* there: if I make my bed in hell, behold thou *art* there. 9. *If* I take the wings of the morning, *and* dwell in the uttermost parts of the sea; 10. Even there shall thy hand lead me, and thy right hand shall hold me.

Jer. 23:23. *Am* I a God at hand, saith the Lord, and not a God afar off? 24. Can any hide himself in secret places that I shall not see him? saith the Lord. Do not I fill heaven and earth? saith the Lord.

Acts 17:24. God that made the world and all things therein, seeing that he is Lord of heaven and earth, dwelleth not in temples made with hands; 27. That they should seek the Lord, if haply they might feel after him, and find him, though he be not far from every one of us: 28. For in him we live, and move, and have our being;

See Presence of, Ubiquitous.

OMNISCIENT : See KNOWLEDGE OF, WISDOM OF.

PERFECTION OF: Deut. 32:4. *He is* the Rock, his work *is* perfect: for all his ways *are* judgment: a God of truth and without iniquity, just and right *is* he.

2 Sam. 22:31. *As for* God, his way *is* perfect; the word of the LORD *is* tried : Psa. 18:30.

Matt. 5:48. Be ye therefore perfect, even as your Father which is in heaven is perfect.

Rom. 12:2. And be not conformed to this world : but be ye transformed by the renewing of your mind, that ye may prove what *is* that good, and acceptable, and perfect, will of God.

Jas. 1:17. Every good gift and every perfect gift is from above, and cometh down from the Father of lights, with whom is no variableness, neither shadow of turning.

See HOLINESS OF; JUDGE, AND HIS JUSTICE; KNOWLEDGE; WISDOM.

PERSONALITY OF: Ex. 8:10. That thou mayest know that *there is* none like unto the LORD our God. Ex. 3:14.

Ex. 15:11. Who *is* like unto thee, O LORD, among the gods? who *is* like thee, glorious in holiness, fearful *in* praises, doing wonders?

Ex. 20:3. Thou shalt have no other gods before me. Deut. 5:7.

Ex. 34:14. Thou shalt worship no other god : for the LORD, whose name *is* Jealous, *is* a jealous God :

Deut. 4:35. The LORD he *is* God ; *there is* none else beside him. 39. The LORD he *is* God in heaven above, and upon the earth beneath : *there is* none else.

Deut. 6:4. Hear, O Israel : The LORD our God *is* one LORD :

Deut. 10:17. The LORD your God *is* God of gods, and Lord of lords,

Deut. 32:12. The LORD alone did lead him, and *there was* no strange god with him. 39. See now that I, *even* I, *am* he, and *there is* no god with me :

Josh. 22:22. The LORD God of gods, the LORD God of gods, he knoweth,

Judg. 13:16. If thou wilt offer a burnt offering, thou must offer it unto the LORD.

1 Sam. 2:2. *There is* none holy as the LORD : for *there is* none beside thee : neither *is there* any rock like our God.

1 Sam. 7:3. Prepare your hearts unto the LORD, and serve him only :

2 Sam. 7:22. *There is* none like thee, neither *is there any* God beside thee,

2 Sam. 22:32. Who *is* God, save the LORD? and who *is* a rock, save our God ? Psa. 18:31.

1 Kin. 8:23. LORD God of Israel, *there is* no God like thee, in heaven above, or on earth beneath, 60. That all the people of the earth may know that the LORD *is* God, *and that there is* none else. 2 Chr. 6:14.

2 Kin. 17:36. Him shall ye fear, and him shall ye worship, and to him shall ye do sacrifice.

2 Kin. 19:15. Thou art the God, *even* thou alone, of all the kingdoms of the earth ;

thou hast made heaven and earth. Isa. 37:16; Psa. 86:10.

Ezra 1:3. The LORD God of Israel, (he *is* the God,)

Neh. 9:6. Thou, *even* thou, *art* LORD alone : ... and the host of heaven worshippeth thee.

Psa. 96:5. All the gods of the nations *are* idols : but the LORD made the heavens.

Isa. 40:25. To whom then will ye liken me, or shall I be equal ? saith the Holy One.

Isa. 42:8. I *am* the LORD: that *is* my name : and my glory will I not give to another, neither my praise to graven images.

Isa. 43:10. I *am* he : before me there was no God formed, neither shall there be after me. 11. I, *even* I, *am* the LORD ; and beside me *there is* no saviour.

Isa. 44:6. I *am* the first, and I *am* the last ; and beside me *there is* no God. 8. Is there a God beside me ? yea, *there is* no God ; I know not *any.*

Isa. 45:5. I *am* the LORD, and *there is* none else, *there is* no God beside me : 6. That they may know from the rising of the sun, and from the west, that *there is* none beside me. I *am* the LORD, and *there is* none else. 21. *There is* no God else beside me; a just God and a Saviour ; *there is* none beside me. *v.* 18.

Isa. 46:5. To whom will ye liken me, and make *me* equal, and compare me, that we may be like ? 9. I *am* God, and *there is* none else ; *I am* God, and *there is* none like me, Isa. 45:22.

Jer. 10:6. *There is* none like unto thee, O LORD; thou *art* great, and thy name *is* great in might. 7. Who would not fear thee, O King of nations? for to thee doth it appertain : forasmuch as among all the wise *men* of the nations, and in all their kingdoms, *there is* none like unto thee. 10. The LORD *is* the true God, he *is* the living God, and an everlasting king :

Jer. 14:22. Are there *any* among the vanities of the Gentiles that can cause rain ? or can the heavens give showers ? *art* not thou he, O LORD our God ?

Jer. 32:27. I *am* the LORD, the God of all flesh : is there any thing too hard for me ?

Hos. 13:4. Thou shalt know no god but me : for *there is* no saviour beside me.

Mal. 2:10. Have we not all one father ? hath not one God created us ?

Matt. 4:10. Thou shalt worship the Lord thy God, and him only shalt thou serve.

Matt. 23:9. Call no *man* your father upon the earth : for one is your Father, which is in heaven.

Mark 12:32. Well, Master, thou hast said the truth : for there is one God, and there is none other but he :

John 14:9. He that hath seen me hath seen the Father ; and how sayest thou *then,* Shew us the Father ?

John 17:3. And this is life eternal, that they might know thee the only true God,

Rom. 1:25. Who changed the truth of God into a lie, and worshipped and served the creature more than the Creator, who is blessed for ever.

Rom. 3:29. *Is he* the God of the Jews only? *is he* not also of the Gentiles? Yes, of the Gentiles also:

1 Cor. 8:4. *There is* none other God but one. 5. For though there be that are called gods, whether in heaven or in earth, (as there be gods many, and lords many,) 6. But to us *there is but* one God, the Father, of whom *are* all things, and we in him;

2 Cor. 4:4. In whom the god of this world hath blinded the minds of them which believe not, lest the light of the glorious gospel of Christ, who is the image of God, should shine unto them.

Gal. 3:20. Now a mediator is not *a mediator* of one, but God is one.

Eph. 4:6. One God and Father of all, who *is* above all, and through all, and in you all.

Col. 1:15. Who is the image of the invisible God, the firstborn of every creature:

1 Thess. 1:9. Ye turned to God from idols to serve the living and true God;

1 Tim. 2:5. *There is* one God, and one mediator between God and men, the man Christ Jesus;

Heb. 1:3. Who being the brightness of *his* glory, and the express image of his person, and upholding all things by the word of his power, when he had by himself purged our sins, sat down on the right hand of the Majesty on high;

See UNITY OF, below.

POWER OF: Ex. 15:3. The LORD is a man of war: the LORD is his name. 6. Thy right hand, O LORD, is become glorious in power: thy right hand, O LORD, hath dashed in pieces the enemy. 7. And in the greatness of thine excellency thou hast overthrown them that rose up against thee: 11. Who *is* like unto thee, O LORD, among the gods? who *is* like thee, glorious in holiness, fearful *in* praises, doing wonders? 12. Thou stretchedst out thy right hand, the earth swallowed them. *vs.* 8,10.

Num. 11:23. Is the LORD'S hand waxed short? thou shalt see now whether my word shall come to pass unto thee or not. Deut. 11:2.

Num. 23:20. I have received *commandment* to bless: and he hath blessed; and I cannot reverse it.

Deut. 3:24. O Lord GOD, thou hast begun to shew thy servant thy greatness, and thy mighty hand: for what God *is there* in heaven or in earth, that can do according to thy works, and according to thy might?

Deut. 7:21. The LORD thy God *is* among you, a mighty God and terrible.

Deut. 32:39. I kill, and I make alive; I wound, and I heal: neither *is there any* that can deliver out of my hand. Job 10:7.

Deut. 33:26. *There is* none like unto the God of Jeshurun, *who* rideth upon the heaven in thy help, and in his excellency on the sky. 27. The eternal God *is thy* refuge, and underneath *are* the everlasting arms:

Josh. 4:24. That all the people of the earth might know the hand of the LORD, that it *is* mighty:

1 Sam. 2:6. The LORD killeth, and maketh alive: he bringeth down to the grave, and bringeth up. 7. The LORD maketh poor, and maketh rich: he bringeth low, and lifteth up. 10. The adversaries of the LORD shall be broken to pieces; out of heaven shall he thunder upon them: *v.* 8.

1 Sam. 14:6. *There is* no restraint to the LORD to save by many or by few.

2 Sam. 22:13. Through the brightness before him were coals of fire kindled. 16. And the channels of the sea appeared, the foundations of the world were discovered, at the rebuking of the LORD, at the blast of the breath of his nostrils. Psa. 18.

1 Chr. 29:11. Thine, O LORD, *is* the greatness, and the power, and the glory, and the victory, and the majesty: 12. In thine hand *is* power and might; and in thine hand *it is* to make great, and to give strength unto all.

2 Chr. 14:11. And Asa cried unto the LORD his God, and said, LORD, *it is* nothing with thee to help, whether with many, or with them that have no power:

2 Chr. 16:9. The eyes of the LORD run to and fro throughout the whole earth, to shew himself strong in the behalf of *them* whose heart *is* perfect toward him,

2 Chr. 20:6. In thine hand *is there not* power and might, so that none is able to withstand thee?

2 Chr. 25:8. God hath power to help, and to cast down. 9. The LORD is able to give thee much more than this.

Ezra 8:22. The hand of our God *is* upon all them for good that seek him; but his power and his wrath *is* against all them that forsake him.

Neh. 1:10. Whom thou hast redeemed by thy great power, and by thy strong hand.

Job 9:4. *He is* wise in heart, and mighty in strength: who hath hardened *himself* against him, and hath prospered? 5. Which removeth the mountains, and they know not: which overturneth them in his anger. 6. Which shaketh the earth out of her place, and the pillars thereof tremble. 7. Which commandeth the sun, and it riseth not; and sealeth up the stars. 10. Which doeth great things past finding out; yea, and wonders without number. 12. He taketh away, who can hinder him? who will say unto him, What doest thou? 13. *If* God will not withdraw his anger, the proud helpers do stoop under him. 19. If *I speak* of strength, lo, *he is* strong: Job 5:9.

Job 11:10. If he cut off, and shut up, or gather together, then who can hinder him?

Job 12:14. He breaketh down, and it cannot be built again: he shutteth up a man, and there can be no opening. 16. With him *is* strength and wisdom: *v.* 15.

Job 14:20. Thou prevailest forever against him, and he passeth: thou changest his countenance, and sendest him away.

Job 23:13. He *is* in one *mind*, and who can turn him? and *what* his soul desireth, even *that* he doeth. 14. For he performeth *the thing that is* appointed for me:

Job 26:11. The pillars of heaven tremble and are astonished at his reproof. 14. The thunder of his power who can understand? *v.* 12.

Job 34:14. If he set his heart upon man, *if* he gather unto himself his spirit and his breath; 15. All flesh shall perish together, and man shall turn again unto dust.

Job 36:5. God *is* mighty, and depiseth not *any : he is* mighty in strength *and* wisdom. 22. Behold, God exalteth by his power: *vs.* 27-33.

Job 37:23. *Touching* the Almighty, we cannot find him out: *he is* excellent in power, and in judgment, and in plenty of justice: he will not afflict. *vs.* 1-22.

Job 38:8. *Who* shut up the sea with doors, when it brake forth, 11. And said, Hitherto shalt thou come, but no further: and here shall thy proud waves be stayed? *v.* 37.

Job 40:9. Hast thou an arm like God? or canst thou thunder with a voice like him?

Job 41:10. None *is so* fierce that dare stir him up: who then is able to stand before me? 11. Who hath prevented me, that I should repay *him?*

Jcb 42:2. I know that thou canst do every *thing,*

Psa. 21:13. Be thou exalted, Lord, in thine own strength: *so* will we sing and praise thy power.

Psa. 29:3. The voice of the Lord *is* upon the waters: the God of glory thundereth: the Lord *is* upon many waters. 4. The voice of the Lord *is* powerful; the voice of the Lord *is* full of majesty. 5. The voice of the Lord breaketh the cedars; *vs.* 6-9.

Psa. 33:9. He spake, and it was *done ;* he commanded, and it stood fast.

Psa. 46:6. The heathen raged, the kingdoms were moved: he uttered his voice, the earth melted.

Psa. 62:11. God hath spoken once; twice have I heard this; that power *belongeth* unto God.

Psa. 65:6. Which by his strength setteth fast the mountains; *being* girded with power: 7. Which stilleth the noise of the seas, the noise of their waves, and the tumult of the people.

Psa. 66:3. How terrible *art thou in* thy works! through the greatness of thy power shall thine enemies submit themselves unto thee. 7. He ruleth by his power for ever:

Psa. 68:33. Him that rideth upon the heavens of heavens, *which were* of old; lo, he doth send out his voice, *and that* a mighty voice. *vs.* 34,35.

Psa. 74:13. Thou didst divide the sea by thy strength: thou brakest the heads of the dragons in the waters. 15. Thou didst cleave the fountain and the flood: thou driedst up mighty rivers.

Psa. 76:6. At thy rebuke, O God of Jacob, both the chariot and horse are cast into a dead sleep. 7. Who may stand in thy sight when once thou art angry?

Psa. 77:14. Thou *art* the God that doest wonders: thou hast declared thy strength among the people. 16. The waters saw thee, O God, the waters saw thee; they were afraid: the depths also were troubled. 18. The voice of thy thunder *was* in the heaven: the lightnings lightened the world: the earth trembled and shook.

Psa. 78:26. He caused an east wind to blow in the heaven; and by his power he brought in the south wind. *vs.* 12-16,43-51.

Psa. 79:11. According to the greatness of thy power preserve thou those that are appointed to die;

Psa. 89:8. O Lord God of hosts, who *is* a strong Lord like unto thee? 9. Thou rulest the raging of the sea: when the waves thereof arise, thou stillest them. 13. Thou hast a mighty arm: strong is thy hand, *and* high is thy right hand.

Psa. 90:3. Thou turnest man to destruction; and sayest, Return, ye children of men.

Psa. 93:1. The Lord is clothed with strength, *wherewith* he hath girded himself: 4. The Lord on high *is* mightier than the noise of many waters, *yea, than* the mighty waves of the sea.

Psa. 97:3. A fire goeth before him, and burneth up his enemies round about. 4. His lightnings enlightened the world: the earth saw, and trembled. 5. The hills melted like wax at the presence of the Lord,

Psa. 104:7. At thy rebuke they fled; at the voice of thy thunder they hasted away. 9. Thou hast set a bound that they may not pass over; that they turn not again to cover the earth. 29. Thou hidest thy face, they are troubled: thou takest away their breath, they die, and return to their dust. 30. Thou sendest forth thy spirit, they are created: and thou renewest the face of the earth. 32. He looketh on the earth, and it trembleth: he toucheth the hills, and they smoke. Psa. 105; 114:3-8; 135:8-12; 136:10-22.

Psa. 106:8. He saved them for his name's sake, that he might make his mighty power to be known.

Psa. 107:25. He commandeth, and raiseth the stormy wind, which lifteth up the waves thereof. 29. He maketh the storm a calm, so that the waves thereof are still.

Psa. 111:6. He hath shewed his people the power of his works,

Psa. 114:7. Tremble, thou earth, at the presence of the Lord, at the presence of the God of Jacob; 8. Which turned the rock *into* a standing water, the flint into a fountain of waters.

Psa. 115:3. Our God *is* in the heavens: he hath done whatsoever he hath pleased.

Psa. 118:16. The right hand of the Lord is exalted: the right hand of the Lord doeth valiantly.

Psa. 135:6. Whatsoever the Lord pleased,

that did he in heaven, and in earth, in the seas, and all deep places.

Psa. 144:5. Bow thy heavens, O LORD, and come down : touch the mountains, and they shall smoke.

Psa. 145:6. *Men* shall speak of the might of thy terrible acts : and I will declare thy greatness. 16. Thou openest thine hand, and satisfiest the desire of every living thing.

Psa. 147:5. Great *is* our Lord, and of great power : 16. He giveth snow like wool : he scattereth the hoarfrost like ashes. 18. He sendeth out his word, and melteth them : he causeth his wind to blow, *and* the waters flow.

Psa. 148:5. He commanded, and they were created. 8. Fire, and hail ; snow, and vapours ; stormy wind fulfilling his word :

Prov. 21:30. *There is* no wisdom nor understanding nor counsel against the LORD.

Prov. 30:4. Who hath gathered the wind in his fists ? who hath bound the waters in a garment ? who hath established all the ends of the earth ?

Isa. 14:24. Surely as I have thought, so shall it come to pass ; and as I have purposed, *so* shall it stand : 27. The LORD of hosts hath purposed, and who shall disannul *it ?* and his hand *is* stretched out, and who shall turn it back ?

Isa. 17:13. The nations shall rush like the rushing of many waters : but *God* shall rebuke them, and they shall flee far off, and shall be chased as the chaff of the mountains before the wind, and like a rolling thing before the whirlwind. Psa. 2:4,5.

Isa. 19:1. The idols of Egypt shall be moved at his presence, and the heart of Egypt shall melt in the midst of it.

Isa. 23:11. He stretched out his hand over the sea, he shook the kingdoms :

Isa. 26:4. In the LORD JEHOVAH *is* everlasting strength :

Isa. 27:4. Who would set the briers *and* thorns against me in battle ? I would go through them, I would burn them together.

Isa. 31:3. When the LORD shall stretch out his hand, both he that helpeth shall fall, and he that is holpen shall fall down, and they all shall fail together.

Isa. 33:3. At the noise of the tumult the people fled ; at the lifting up of thyself the nations were scattered. 13. Hear, ye *that are* far off, what I have done ; and, ye *that are* near, acknowledge my might.

Isa. 40:12. Who hath measured the waters in the hollow of his hand, and meted out heaven with the span, and comprehended the dust of the earth in a measure, and weighed the mountains in scales, and the hills in a balance ? 22. He that sitteth upon the circle of the earth, and the inhabitants thereof *are* as grasshoppers ; that stretcheth out the heavens as a curtain, and spreadeth them out as a tent to dwell in : 24. He shall also blow upon them, and they shall wither, and the whirlwind shall take them away as stubble. 26. Lift up your eyes on high, and

behold who hath created these *things,* that bringeth out their host by number : he calleth them all by names by the greatness of his might, for that *he is* strong in power ; not one faileth. 28. Hast thou not heard, *that* the everlasting God, the LORD, the Creator of the ends of the earth, fainteth not, neither is weary ?

Isa. 43:13. *There is* none that can deliver out of my hand : I will work, and who shall let it ? 16. The LORD, which maketh a way in the sea, and a path in the mighty waters ; 17. Which bringeth forth the chariot and horse, the army and the power ;

Isa. 44:27. That saith to the deep, Be dry, and I will dry up thy rivers :

Isa. 46:10. My counsel shall stand, and I will do all my pleasure : 11. I have spoken *it,* I will also bring it to pass ; I have purposed *it,* I will also do it.

Isa. 48:13. Mine hand also hath laid the foundation of the earth, and my right hand hath spanned the heavens : *when* I call unto them, they stand up together.

Isa. 50:2. Is my hand shortened at all, that it cannot redeem ? or have I no power to deliver ? behold, at my rebuke I dry up the sea, I make the rivers a wilderness : 3. I clothe the heavens with blackness, and I make sackcloth their covering.

Isa. 51:10. *Art* thou not it which hath dried the sea, the waters of the great deep ; that hath made the depths of the sea a way for the ransomed to pass over ? *v.* 15.

Isa. 52:10. The LORD hath made bare his holy arm in the eyes of all the nations ;

Isa. 59:1. The LORD's hand is not shortened, that it cannot save : neither his ear heavy, that it cannot hear :

Isa. 60:16. Thou shalt know that I the LORD *am* thy Saviour and thy Redeemer, the mighty One of Jacob.

Isa. 63:12. With his glorious arm, dividing the water before them, to make himself an everlasting name ?

Jer. 5:22. Fear ye not me ? saith the LORD : . . . tremble at my presence, which have placed the sand *for* the bound of the sea by a perpetual decree, that it cannot pass it : and though the waves thereof toss themselves, yet can they not prevail ; though they roar, yet can they not pass over it ?

Jer. 10:6. *There is* none like unto thee, O LORD ; thou *art* great, and thy name *is* great in might. 12. He hath made the earth by his power, he hath established the world by his wisdom, and hath stretched out the heavens by his discretion. [chapter 51:15.] 13. When he uttereth his voice, *there is* a multitude of waters in the heavens, and he causeth the vapours to ascend from the ends of the earth ; he maketh lightnings with rain, and bringeth forth the wind out of his treasures.

Jer. 20:11. The LORD *is* with me as a mighty terrible one : therefore my persecutors shall stumble, and they shall not prevail :

Jer. 27:5. I have made the earth, the man and the beast that *are* upon the ground, by my great power and by my outstretched arm, and have given it unto whom it seemed meet unto me.

Jer. 32:17. Thou hast made the heaven and the earth by thy great power and stretched out arm, *and* there is nothing too hard for thee: 27. I *am* the LORD, the God of all flesh: is there any thing too hard for me?

Jer. 50:44. Who *is* like me? and who will appoint me the time? and who *is* that shepherd that will stand before me?

Dan. 2:20. Wisdom and might are his:

Dan. 3:17. Our God whom we serve is able to deliver us from the burning fiery furnace, and he will deliver *us* out of thine hand, O king.

Dan. 4:35. He doeth according to his will in the army of heaven, and *among* the inhabitants of the earth: and none can stay his hand, or say unto him, What doest thou?

Dan. 6:27. He delivereth and rescueth, and he worketh signs and wonders in heaven and in earth,

Joel 2:11. The LORD shall utter his voice before his army: for his camp *is* very great: for *he is* strong that executeth his word: for the day of the LORD *is* great and very terrible; and who can abide it?

Joel 3:16. The LORD also shall roar out of Zion, and utter his voice from Jerusalem; and the heavens and the earth shall shake: Amos 1:2.

Amos 4:13. He that formeth the mountains, and createth the wind, and declareth unto man what *is* his thought, that maketh the morning darkness, and treadeth upon the high places of the earth, The LORD, The God of hosts, *is* his name.

Amos 9:5. He that toucheth the land, and it shall melt, 6. *It is* he that buildeth his stories in the heaven, and hath founded his troop in the earth; he that calleth for the waters of the sea, and poureth them out upon the face of the earth:

Mic. 1:3. The LORD cometh forth out of his place, and will come down, and tread upon the high places of the earth. 4. And the mountains shall be molten under him, and the valleys shall be cleft, as wax before the fire, *and* as the waters *that are* poured down a steep place.

Nah. 1:3. The LORD *is* slow to anger, and great in power, . . . the Lord *hath* his way in the whirlwind and in the storm, and the clouds *are* the dust of his feet. 4. He rebuketh the sea, and maketh it dry, and drieth up all the rivers: 5. The mountains quake at him, and the hills melt, and the earth is burned at his presence, yea, the world, and all that dwell therein. 6. Who can stand before his indignation? and who can abide in the fierceness of his anger? his fury is poured out like fire, and the rocks are thrown down by him.

Hab. 3:6. He stood, and measured the earth: he beheld, and drove asunder the nations;

and the everlasting mountains were scattered, the perpetual hills did bow: 9. Thy bow was made quite naked, . . . Thou didst cleave the earth with rivers. 10. The mountains saw thee, *and* they trembled: the overflowing of the water passed by: the deep uttered his voice, *and* lifted up his hands on high. 11. The sun *and* moon stood still in their habitation: at the light of thine arrows they went, *and* at the shining of thy glittering spear. 15. Thou didst walk through the sea with thine horses, *through* the heap of great waters.

Zech. 9:14. The LORD shall be seen over them, and his arrow shall go forth as the lightning: and the Lord GOD shall blow the trumpet, and shall go with whirlwinds of the south.

Matt. 3:9. And think not to say within yourselves, We have Abraham to *our* father: for I say unto you, that God is able of these stones to raise up children unto Abraham.

Matt. 6:13. [1] Thine is the kingdom, and the power, [1 Omitted in R. V.]

Matt. 10:28. Fear him which is able to destroy both soul and body in hell.

Matt. 19:26. With God all things are possible. Mark 10:27: Luke 18:27.

Matt. 22:29. Ye do err, not knowing the scriptures, nor the power of God.

Mark 14:36. Father, all things *are* possible unto thee;

Luke 1:37. [1] With God nothing shall be impossible. 49. He that is mighty hath done to me great things; 51. He hath shewed strength with his arm; he hath scattered the proud in the imagination of their hearts.

[1 R. V. For no word from God shall be void of power]

Luke 11:20. If I with the finger of God cast out devils, no doubt the kingdom of God is come upon you.

Rom. 1:20. For the invisible things of him from the creation of the world are clearly seen, being understood by the things that are made, *even* his eternal power and Godhead;

Rom. 4:21. What he had promised, he was able also to perform.

1 Cor. 6:14. God hath both raised up the Lord, and will also raise up us by his own power.

2 Cor. 13:4. Though he was crucified through weakness, yet he liveth by the power of God.

Eph. 1:19. What *is* the exceeding greatness of his power to us-ward who believe, according to the working of his mighty power, 20. Which he wrought in Christ, when he raised him from the dead,

Eph. 3:20. Unto him that is able to do exceeding abundantly above all that we ask or think, according to the power that worketh in us, 21. Unto him *be* glory in the church by Christ Jesus throughout all ages, world without end.

Heb. 1:3. Who being the brightness of *his* glory, and the express image of his person, and upholding all things by the word of his power, when he had by himself purged our sins, sat down on the right hand of the Majesty on high;

Heb. 12:26. Whose voice then shook the earth: but now he hath promised, saying, Yet once more I shake not the earth only, but also heaven. 29. Our God is a consuming fire.

Jas. 4:12. One lawgiver, who is able to save and to destroy:

1 Pet. 1:5. Kept by the power of God through faith unto salvation, ready to be revealed in the last time.

Rev. 4:11. Thou art worthy, O Lord, to receive glory and honour and power: Rev. 5:13.

Rev. 11:17. Thou hast taken to thee thy great power, and hast reigned.

Rev. 19:1. I heard a great voice of much people in heaven, saying, Alleluia; Salvation, and glory, and honour, and power, unto the Lord our God: 6. The Lord God omnipotent reigneth.

See Omnipotent, above.

PRESENCE OF: Gen. 16:13. And she called the name of the Lord that spake unto her, Thou God seest me: for she said, Have I also here looked after him that seeth me?

Gen. 28:16. Surely the Lord is in this place; and I knew it not.

Ex. 20:24. In all places where I record my name I will come unto thee, and I will bless thee.

Deut. 4:34. Or hath God assayed to go and take him a nation from the midst of another nation, by temptations, by signs, and by wonders, and by war, and by a mighty hand, and by a stretched out arm, and by great terrors, according to all that the Lord your God did for you in Egypt before your eyes? 35. Unto thee it was shewed, that thou mightest know that the Lord he is God; there is none else beside him. 36. Out of heaven he made thee to hear his voice, that he might instruct thee: and upon earth he shewed thee his great fire; and thou heardest his words out of the midst of the fire. 39. Know therefore this day, and consider it in thine heart, that the Lord he is God in heaven above, and upon the earth beneath: Josh. 2:11.

1 Kin. 8:27. Will God indeed dwell on the earth? behold, the heaven and heaven of heavens cannot contain thee; how much less this house that I have builded? 2 Chr. 2:6; Acts 7:48,49.

Psa. 139:3. Thou compassest my path, and my lying down, 5. Thou hast beset me behind and before, and laid thine hand upon me. 7. Whither shall I go from thy spirit? or whither shall I flee from thy presence? 8. If I ascend up into heaven, thou art there: if I make my bed in hell, behold, thou art there. 9. If I take the wings of the morning, and dwell in the uttermost parts of the sea; 10. Even there shall thy hand lead me, and thy right hand shall hold me.

Isa. 57:15. Thus saith the high and lofty One that inhabiteth eternity, whose name is Holy; I dwell in the high and holy place, with him also that is of a contrite and humble spirit,

Isa. 66:1. The heaven is my throne, and the earth is my footstool: where is the house that ye build unto me? and where is the place of my rest?

Jer. 23:23. Am I a God at hand, saith the Lord, and not a God afar off? 24. Can any hide himself in secret places that I shall not see him? saith the Lord. Do not I fill heaven and earth? saith the Lord.

Jer. 32:18. The Great, the Mighty God, the Lord of hosts is his name; 19. Great in counsel, and mighty in work: for thine eyes are open upon all the ways of the sons of men: to give every one according to his ways, and according to the fruit of his doings:

Jonah 1:3. Jonah rose up to flee unto Tarshish from the presence of the Lord, and went down to Joppa; and he found a ship going to Tarshish: 4. But the Lord sent out a great wind into the sea,

Acts 17:24. God that made the world, and all things therein, seeing that he is Lord of heaven and earth, dwelleth not in temples made with hands; 27. That they should seek the Lord, if haply they might feel after him, and find him, though he be not far from every one of us: 28. For in him we live, and move, and have our being;

1 Cor. 12:6. There are diversities of operations, but it is the same God which worketh all in all.

Eph. 1:23. Him that filleth all in all.

See Omnipresent, above; Preserver, below.

PRESERVER: Gen. 14:20. Blessed be the most high God, which hath delivered thine enemies into thy hand.

Gen. 28:15. I am with thee, and will keep thee in all places whither thou goest, and will bring thee again into this land; for I will not leave thee, until I have done that which I have spoken to thee of. Gen. 31: 3,13.

Gen. 48:15. And he blessed Joseph, and said, God, before whom my fathers Abraham and Isaac did walk, the God which fed me all my life long unto this day, 16. The Angel which redeemed me from all evil, bless the lads;

Gen. 49:24. But his bow abode in strength, and the arms of his hands were made strong by the hands of the mighty God of Jacob; (from thence is the shepherd, the stone of Israel:) 25. Even by the God of thy father, who shall help thee; and by the Almighty, who shall bless thee with blessings of heaven above, blessings of the deep that lieth under, blessings of the breasts, and of the womb:

Ex. 6:6. I will bring you out from under the burdens of the Egyptians, and I will rid you out of their bondage, and I will redeem you with a stretched out arm, and with great judgments: 7. And I will take you to me for a people, and I will be to you a God: and ye shall know that I *am* the LORD your God, which bringeth you out from under the burdens of the Egyptians. Ex. 3:17.

Ex. 8:22. I will sever in that day the land of Goshen, in which my people dwell, that no swarms *of flies* shall be there; *v.* 23; Ex. 11:7.

Ex. 9:26. Only in the land of Goshen, where the children of Israel *were*, was there no hail.

Ex. 11:7. But against any of the children of Israel shall not a dog move his tongue, against man or beast: that ye may know how that the LORD doth put a difference between the Egyptians and Israel.

Ex. 12:13. And the blood shall be to you for a token upon the houses where ye *are*: and when I see the blood, I will pass over you, and the plague shall not be upon you to destroy *you*, when I smite the land of Egypt. 17. And ye shall observe *the feast of* unleavened bread; for in this selfsame day have I brought your armies out of the land of Egypt: therefore shall ye observe this day in your generations by an ordinance for ever. 23. When he seeth the blood upon the lintel, and on the two side posts, the LORD will pass over the door, and will not suffer the destroyer to come in unto your houses to smite *you*.

Ex. 13:21. The LORD went before them by day in a pillar of a cloud, to lead them the way; and by night in a pillar of fire, to give them light; to go by day and night: 22. He took not away the pillar of the cloud by day, nor the pillar of fire by night, *from* before the people.

Ex. 14:29. But the children of Israel walked upon dry *land* in the midst of the sea; and the waters *were* a wall unto them on their right hand, and on their left. 30. Thus the LORD saved Israel that day out of the hand of the Egyptians; and Israel saw the Egyptians dead upon the sea shore.

Ex. 15:2. The LORD *is* my strength and song, and he is become my salvation: 13. Thou in thy mercy hast led forth the people *which* thou hast redeemed: thou hast guided *them* in thy strength unto thy holy habitation. 16. Fear and dread shall fall upon them; by the greatness of thine arm. they shall be *as* still as a stone; till thy people pass over, O LORD, till the people pass over, *which* thou hast purchased. 17. Thou shalt bring them in, and plant them in the mountain of thine inheritance, *in* the place, O LORD, *which* thou hast made for thee to dwell in, *in* the sanctuary, O Lord, *which* thy hands have established.

Ex. 16:15. And when the children of Israel saw *it*, they said one to another, It *is* manna: for they wist not what it *was*. And Moses said unto them, This *is* the bread which the LORD hath given you to eat.

Ex. 19:4. I bare you on eagles' wings, and brought you unto myself.

Ex. 23:20. I send an Angel before thee, to keep thee in the way, and to bring thee into the place which I have prepared. *vs.* 21-31.

Ex. 34:24. I will cast out the nations before thee, and enlarge thy borders: neither shall any man desire thy land, when thou shalt go up to appear before the LORD thy God thrice in the year.

Num. 10:33. The ark of the covenant of the LORD went before them in the three days' journey, to search out a resting place for them.

Num. 23:23. Surely *there is* no enchantment against Jacob, neither *is there* any divination against Israel: according to this time it shall be said of Jacob and of Israel, What hath God wrought!

Deut. 1:30. The LORD your God which goeth before you, he shall fight for you, according to all that he did for you in Egypt before your eyes; 31. And in the wilderness, where thou hast seen how that the LORD thy God bare thee, as a man doth bear his son, in all the way that ye went, until ye came into this place.

Deut. 7:21. The LORD thy God *is* among you, a mighty God and terrible. 22. The LORD thy God will put out those nations before thee by little and little:

Deut. 9:3. The LORD thy God *is* he which goeth over before thee; *as* a consuming fire he shall destroy them, and he shall bring them down before thy face: so shalt thou drive them out, and destroy them quickly, as the LORD hath said unto thee.

Deut. 11:25. There shall no man be able to stand before you: *for* the LORD your God shall lay the fear of you and the dread of you upon all the land that ye shall tread upon,

Deut. 23:14. The LORD thy God walketh in the midst of thy camp, to deliver thee, and to give up thine enemies before thee;

Deut. 30:4. If *any* of thine be driven out unto the outmost *parts* of heaven, from thence will the LORD thy God gather thee, and from thence will he fetch thee: 20. He *is* thy life, and the length of thy days:

Deut. 31:3. The LORD thy God, he will go over before thee, *and* he will destroy these nations from before thee, and thou shalt possess them: *and* Joshua, he shall go over before thee, as the LORD hath said.

Deut. 32:10. He found him in a desert land, and in the waste howling wilderness; he led him about, he instructed him, he kept him as the apple of his eye.

Deut. 33:12. The beloved of the LORD shall dwell in safety by him; *and the LORD* shall cover him all the day long, and he shall dwell between his shoulders. 25. Thy shoes *shall be* iron and brass; and as thy days, *so shall* thy strength *be*. 26. *There is* none like unto the God of Jeshurun, *who* rideth upon the heaven in thy help, and in his excellency on the sky. 27. The eternal God *is thy* refuge, and underneath *are* the everlasting arms: and he shall thrust out the enemy from before thee; and shall say,

Destroy *them*. 28. Israel then shall dwell in safety alone: the fountain of Jacob *shall be* upon a land of corn and wine; also his heavens shall drop down dew. *v.* 29.

Josh. 23:10. One man of you shall chase a thousand: for the LORD your God, he *it is* that fighteth for you, as he hath promised you.

1 Sam. 2:6. The LORD killeth, and maketh alive: he bringeth down to the grave, and bringeth up. 9. He will keep the feet of his saints, and the wicked shall be silent in darkness; for by strength shall no man prevail.

1 Sam. 9:16. That he may save my people out of the hand of the Philistines: for I have looked upon my people, because their cry is come unto me.

2 Sam. 22:28. The afflicted people thou wilt save:

2 Kin. 20:6. I will deliver thee and this city out of the hand of the king of Assyria; and I will defend this city for mine own sake, and for my servant David's sake.

2 Chr. 16:9. The eyes of the LORD run to and fro throughout the whole earth, to shew himself strong in the behalf of *them* whose heart *is* perfect toward him.

2 Chr. 20:15. Be not afraid nor dismayed by reason of this great multitude; for the battle *is* not your's, but God's. 17. Ye shall not *need* to fight in this *battle:* set yourselves, stand ye *still*, and see the salvation of the LORD with you, O Judah and Jerusalem: fear not, nor be dismayed; to morrow go out against them: for the LORD *will be* with you.

Ezra 8:22. For I was ashamed to require of the king a band of soldiers and horsemen to help us against the enemy in the way: because we had spoken unto the king, saying, The hand of our God *is* upon all them for good that seek him; but his power and his wrath *is* against all them that forsake him. 23. So we fasted and besought our God for this: and he was entreated of us.

Neh. 9:6. Thou, *even* thou, *art* LORD alone; thou hast made heaven, the heaven of heavens, with all their host, the earth, and all *things* that *are* therein, the seas, and all that *is* therein, and thou preservest them all;

Job 1:10. Hast not thou made an hedge about him, and about his house, and about all that he hath on every side?

Job 4:7. Remember, I pray thee, who *ever* perished, being innocent? or where were the righteous cut off?

Job 5:11. To set up on high those that be low; that those which mourn may be exalted to safety. 18. He maketh sore, and bindeth up: he woundeth, and his hands make whole. 19. He shall deliver thee in six troubles: yea, in seven there shall no evil touch thee. 20. In famine he shall redeem thee from death: and in war from the power of the sword. 21. Thou shalt be hid from the scourge of the tongue: neither

shalt thou be afraid of destruction when it cometh. *vs.* 22–24.

Job 10:12. Thou hast granted me life and favour, and thy visitation hath preserved my spirit.

Job 11:18. And thou shalt be secure, because there is hope; yea, thou shalt dig *about thee, and* thou shalt take thy rest in safety. 19. Also thou shalt lie down, and none shall make *thee* afraid;

Job 22:25. The Almighty shall be thy defence, and thou shalt have plenty of silver.

Job 27:3. All the while my breath *is* in me, and the spirit of God *is* in my nostrils; 4. My lips shall not speak wickedness, nor my tongue utter deceit.

Job 33:18. He keepeth back his soul from the pit, and his life from perishing by the sword.

Job 36:7. He withdraweth not his eyes from the righteous: but with kings *are they* on the throne; yea, he doth establish them for ever, and they are exalted. 16. Even so would he have removed thee out of the strait *into* a broad place, where *there is* no straitness; and that which should be set on thy table *should be* full of fatness.

Psa. 1:6. The LORD knoweth the way of the righteous: but the way of the ungodly shall perish.

Psa. 3:3. But thou, O LORD, *art* a shield for me; my glory, and the lifter up of mine head.

Psa. 9:9. The LORD also will be a refuge for the oppressed, a refuge in times of trouble.

Psa. 10:17. LORD, thou hast heard the desire of the humble: thou wilt prepare their heart, thou wilt cause thine ear to hear: 18. To judge the fatherless and the oppressed, that the man of the earth may no more oppress.

Psa. 12:7. Thou shalt keep them, O LORD, thou shalt preserve them from this generation for ever.

Psa. 14:5. There were they in great fear: for God *is* in the generation of the righteous. 6. Ye have shamed the counsel of the poor, because the LORD *is* his refuge.

Psa. 17:7. Shew thy marvellous lovingkindness, O thou that savest by thy right hand them which put their trust *in thee* from those that rise up *against them*.

Psa. 18:17. He delivered me from my strong enemy, and from them which hated me: for they were too strong for me. 27. Thou wilt save the afflicted people;

Psa. 19:14. Let the words of my mouth, and the meditation of my heart, be acceptable in thy sight, O LORD, my strength, and my redeemer.

Psa. 25:8 Good and upright *is* the LORD: therefore will he teach sinners in the way. 9. The meek will he guide in judgment: and the meek will he teach his way. 12. What man *is* he that feareth the LORD? him shall he teach in the way *that* he shall choose.

Psa. 31:20. Thou shalt hide them in the secret of thy presence from the pride of man: thou shalt keep them secretly in a pavilion from the strife of tongues. **23.** O love the LORD, all ye his saints: *for* the LORD preserveth the faithful,

Psa. 32:6. Surely in the floods of great waters they shall not come nigh unto him. **8.** I will instruct thee and teach thee in the way which thou shalt go: I will guide thee with mine eye.

Psa. 34:15. The eyes of the LORD *are* upon the righteous, and his ears *are open* unto their cry. **17.** *The righteous* cry, and the LORD heareth, and delivereth them out of all their troubles. **19.** Many *are* the afflictions of the righteous: but the LORD delivereth him out of them all. **20.** He keepeth all his bones: not one of them is broken. *vs.* 21,22.

Psa. 37:17. The LORD upholdeth the righteous. **23.** The steps of a *good* man are ordered by the LORD: and he delighteth in his way. **24.** Though he fall, he shall not be utterly cast down: for the LORD upholdeth *him with* his hand. **28.** The LORD loveth judgment, and forsaketh not his saints; they are preserved for ever: **32.** The wicked watcheth the righteous and seeketh to slay him. **33.** The LORD will not leave him in his hand, nor condemn him when he is judged.

Psa. 41:1. Blessed *is* he that considereth the poor: the LORD will deliver him in time of trouble. **2.** The LORD will preserve him, and keep him alive ; *and* he shall be blessed upon the earth: and thou wilt not deliver him unto the will of his enemies. **3.** The LORD will strengthen him upon the bed of languishing: thou wilt make all his bed in his sickness.

Psa. 46:1. God *is* our refuge and strength, a very present help in trouble. **5.** God *is* in the midst of her; she shall not be moved: God shall help her, *and that* right early. **7.** The LORD of hosts *is* with us; the God of Jacob *is* our refuge.

Psa. 48:3. God is known in her palaces for a refuge.

Psa. 50:15. Call upon me in the day of trouble: I will deliver thee, and thou shalt glorify me.

Psa. 61:3. For thou hast been a shelter for me, *and* a strong tower from the enemy. **6.** Thou wilt prolong the king's life: *and* his years as many generations.

Psa. 68:6. God setteth the solitary in families: he bringeth out those which are bound with chains: **22.** I will bring *my people* again from the depths of the sea:

Psa. 72:14. He shall redeem their souls from deceit and violence: and precious shall their blood be in his sight.

Psa. 73:23. Nevertheless I *am* continually with thee: thou hast holden *me* by my right hand.

Psa. 80:1. Give ear, O Shepherd of Israel, thou that leadest Joseph like a flock;

Psa. 84:11. The LORD God *is* a sun and shield: the LORD will give grace and glory. no good *thing* will he withhold from them that walk uprightly.

Psa. 87:5. And of Zion it shall be said, . . . the highest himself shall establish her.

Psa. 91:1. He that dwelleth in the secret place of the most High shall abide under the shadow of the Almighty. **3.** Surely he shall deliver thee from the snare of the fowler, *and* from the noisome pestilence. **4.** He shall cover thee with his feathers, and under his wings shalt thou trust: his truth *shall be thy* shield and buckler. **7.** A thousand shall fall at thy side, and ten thousand at thy right hand; *but* it shall not come nigh thee. **9.** Because thou hast made the LORD, *which is* my refuge, *even* the most High, thy habitation ; **10.** There shall no evil befall thee, neither shall any plague come nigh thy dwelling. **14.** Because he hath set his love upon me, therefore will I deliver him: I will set him on high, because he hath known my name. **15.** He shall call upon me, and I will answer him: I *will be* with him in trouble; I will deliver him, and honour him. *vs.* 1–16.

Psa. 94:13. That thou mayest give him rest from the days of adversity,

Psa. 97:10. He preserveth the souls of his saints; he delivereth them out of the hand of the wicked.

Psa. 102:19. From heaven did the LORD behold the earth; **20.** To hear the groaning of the prisoner; to loose those that are appointed to death;

Psa. 103:2. Bless the LORD, O my soul, and forget not all his benefits: **3.** Who forgiveth all thine iniquities; who healeth all thy diseases; **4.** Who redeemeth thy life from destruction; who crowneth thee with lovingkindness and tender mercies; **5.** Who satisfieth thy mouth with good *things; so that* thy youth is renewed like the eagle's.

Psa. 107:9. He satisfieth the longing soul, and filleth the hungry soul with goodness. **10.** Such as sit in darkness and in the shadow of death, *being* bound in affliction and iron;

Psa. 112:4. Unto the upright there ariseth light in the darkness: *he is* gracious, and full of compassion, and righteous.

Psa. 115:10. O house of Aaron, trust in the LORD: he *is* their help and their shield.

Psa. 116:6. The LORD preserveth the simple: I was brought low, and he helped me.

Psa. 118:13. Thou hast thrust sore at me that I might fall: but the LORD helped me.

Psa. 121:3. He will not suffer thy foot to be moved: he that keepeth thee will not slumber. **4.** Behold, he that keepeth Israel shall neither slumber nor sleep. **7.** The LORD shall preserve thee from all evil: he shall preserve thy soul. **8.** The LORD shall preserve thy going out and thy coming in from this time forth, and even for evermore. *vs.* 5,6.

Psa. 124:1. If *it had not been* the LORD who was on our side, now may Israel say; **2.** If *it had not been* the LORD who was on our side, when men rose up against us : 3. Then they had swallowed us up quick, when their wrath was kindled against us : 4. Then the waters had overwhelmed us, the stream had gone over our soul : 5. Then the proud waters had gone over our soul. 6. Blessed *be* the LORD, who hath not given us *as* a prey to their teeth. 7. Our soul is escaped as a bird out of the snare of the fowlers : the snare is broken, and we are escaped. 8. Our help *is* in the name of the LORD, who made heaven and earth.

Psa. 125:1. They that trust in the LORD *shall be* as mount Zion, *which* cannot be removed, *but* abideth for ever. 2. *As* the mountains *are* round about Jerusalem, so the LORD *is* round about his people from henceforth even for ever. 3. For the rod of the wicked shall not rest upon the lot of the righteous ;

Psa. 127:1. Except the LORD build the house, they labour in vain that build it : except the LORD keep the city, the watchman waketh *but* in vain.

Psa. 145:14. The LORD upholdeth all that fall, and raiseth up all *those that be* bowed down. 19. He will fulfil the desire of them that fear him : he also will hear their cry, and will save them. 20. The LORD preserveth all them that love him : Prov. 22:12.

Psa. 146:7. The LORD looseth the prisoners : 8. The LORD openeth *the eyes of* the blind : the LORD raiseth them that are bowed down :

Psa. 147:2. The LORD doth build up Jerusalem : he gathereth together the outcasts of Israel. 3. He healeth the broken in heart, and bindeth up their wounds.

Prov. 2:7. *He is* a buckler to them that walk uprightly. 8. He keepeth the paths of judgment, and preserveth the way of his saints.

Prov. 3:6. In all thy ways acknowledge him, and he shall direct thy paths. 23. Then shalt thou walk in thy way safely, and thy foot shall not stumble. 24. When thou liest down, thou shalt not be afraid : yea, thou shalt lie down, and thy sleep shall be sweet.

Prov. 10:3. The LORD will not suffer the soul of the righteous to famish : 30. The righteous shall never be removed :

Prov. 11:8. The righteous is delivered out of trouble.

Prov. 12:3. The root of the righteous shall not be moved. 21. There shall no evil happen to the just : *v.* 13.

Prov. 14:26. In the fear of the LORD *is* strong confidence : and his children shall have a place of refuge.

Prov. 15:19. The way of the righteous *is* made plain.

Prov. 16:9. A man's heart deviseth his way : but the LORD directeth his steps. 33. The lot is cast into the lap ; but the whole disposing thereof *is* of the LORD.

Prov. 19:23. The fear of the LORD *tendeth* to life : and *he that hath it* shall

abide satisfied ; he shall not be visited with evil.

Prov. 20:22. Say not thou, I will recompense evil ; *but* wait on the LORD, and he shall save thee. 24. Man's goings *are* of the LORD ;

Prov. 21:31. The horse *is* prepared against the day of battle : but safety *is* of the LORD.

Prov. 24:16. A just *man* falleth seven times, and riseth up again :

Isa. 4:5. The LORD will create upon every dwelling place in mount Zion, and upon her assemblies, a cloud and smoke by day, and the shining of a flaming fire by night : for upon all the glory *shall be* a defence. 6. And there shall be a tabernacle for a shadow in the daytime from the heat, and for a place of refuge, and for a covert from storm and from rain.

Isa. 10:27. His burden shall be taken away from off thy shoulder, and his yoke from off thy neck,

Isa. 14:3. The LORD shall give thee rest from thy sorrow, and from thy fear, and from the hard bondage wherein thou wast made to serve,

Isa. 26:7. Thou, most upright, dost weigh the path of the just.

Isa. 27:3. I the LORD do keep it ; I will water it every moment : lest *any* hurt it, I will keep it night and day.

Isa. 30:21. Thine ears shall hear a word behind thee, saying, This *is* the way, walk ye in it, when ye turn to the right hand, and when ye turn to the left. 26. The light of the moon shall be as the light of the sun, and the light of the sun shall be sevenfold, as the light of seven days, in the day that the LORD bindeth up the breach of his people, and healeth the stroke of their wound.

Isa. 31:4. So shall the LORD of hosts come down to fight for mount Zion, and for the hill thereof. 5. As birds flying, so will the LORD of hosts defend Jerusalem ; defending also he will deliver *it ; and* passing over he will preserve *it.* 9. His princes shall be afraid of the ensign, saith the LORD, whose fire *is* in Zion, and his furnace in Jerusalem. *v.* 4.

Isa. 32:2. A man shall be as an hiding place from the wind, and a covert from the tempest ; as rivers of water in a dry place, as the shadow of a great rock in a weary land. 18. My people shall dwell in a peaceable habitation, and in sure dwellings, and in quiet resting places ;

Isa. 33:16. He shall dwell on high : his place of defence *shall be* the munitions of rocks : 20. Thine eyes shall see Jerusalem a quiet habitation, a tabernacle *that* shall not be taken down ; not one of the stakes thereof shall ever be removed, neither shall any of the cords thereof be broken.

Isa. 35:9. No lion shall be there, nor *any* ravenous beast shall go up thereon, it shall not be found there ; but the redeemed shall walk *there :*

Isa. 37:32. **Out of Jerusalem shall go forth**

a remnant, and they that escape out of mount Zion : the zeal of the LORD of hosts shall do this. 35. I will defend this city to save it for mine own sake, and for my servant David's sake.

Isa. 40:11. He shall feed his flock like a shepherd : he shall gather the lambs with his arm, and carry *them* in his bosom, *and* shall gently lead those that are with young. 29. He giveth power to the faint; and to *them that have* no might he increaseth strength. 31. They that wait upon the LORD shall renew *their* strength; they shall mount up with wings as eagles; they shall run, and not be weary; *and* they shall walk, and not faint.

Isa. 42:13. The LORD shall go forth as a mighty man, he shall stir up jealousy like a man of war : he shall cry, yea, roar; he shall prevail against his enemies. 16. I will bring the blind by a way *that* they knew not; I will lead them in paths *that* they have not known : I will make darkness light before them, and crooked things straight. These things will I do unto them, and not forsake them.

Isa. 43:2. When thou passest through the waters, I *will be* with thee; and through the rivers, they shall not overflow thee : when thou walkest through the fire, thou shalt not be burned; neither shall the flame kindle upon thee.

Isa. 45:2. I will go before thee, and make the crooked places straight : I will break in pieces the gates of brass, and cut in sunder the bars of iron : *v. 4.*

Isa. 46:4. And *even to your* old age I *am* he; and *even* to hoar hairs will I carry *you:* I have made, and I will bear; even I will carry, and will deliver *you. v. 3.*

Isa. 48:17. I *am* the LORD thy God which teacheth thee to profit, which leadeth thee by the way *that* thou shouldest go.

Isa. 49:9. They shall feed in the ways, and their pastures *shall be* in all high places. 10. They shall not hunger nor thirst; neither shall the heat nor sun smite them : for he that hath mercy on them shall lead them, even by the springs of water shall he guide them. 17. Thy children shall make haste; thy destroyers and they that made thee waste shall go forth of thee. 25. Even the captives of the mighty shall be taken away, and the prey of the terrible shall be delivered : for I will contend with him that contendeth with thee, and I will save thy children.

Isa. 51:9. Awake, awake, put on strength, O arm of the LORD; awake, as in the ancient days, in the generations of old. 10. *Art* thou not it which hath dried the sea, the waters of the great deep; that hath made the depths of the sea a way for the ransomed to pass over? 22. Thus saith thy Lord the LORD, and thy God *that* pleadeth the cause of his people, Behold, I have taken out of thine hand the cup of trembling, *even* the dregs of the cup of my fury; thou shalt no more drink it again :

Isa. 52:12. Ye shall not go out with haste, nor go by flight : for the LORD will go before you; and the God of Israel *will be* your rereward.

Isa. 54:14. In righteousness shalt thou be established : thou shalt be far from oppression; for thou shalt not fear : and from terror; for it shall not come near thee. 15. Behold, they shall surely gather together, *but* not by me : whosoever shall gather together against thee shall fall for thy sake. 17. No weapon that is formed against thee shall prosper; and every tongue *that* shall rise against thee in judgment thou shalt condemn. This *is* the heritage of the servants of the LORD, and their righteousness *is* of me, saith the LORD.

Isa. 57:14. Cast ye up, cast ye up, prepare the way, take up the stumblingblock out of the way of my people.

Isa. 58:11. The LORD shall guide thee continually, and satisfy thy soul in drought, and make fat thy bones : and thou shalt be like a watered garden, and like a spring of water, whose waters fail not.

Isa. 59:19. When the enemy shall come in like a flood, the Spirit of the LORD shall lift up a standard against him.

Isa. 63:9. In all their affliction he was afflicted, and the angel of his presence saved them : in his love and in his pity he redeemed them; and he bare them, and carried them all the days of old.

Jer. 2:3. Israel *was* holiness unto the LORD, *and* the firstfruits of his increase : all that devour him shall offend; evil shall come upon them, saith the LORD. 6. The LORD that brought us up out of the land of Egypt, that led us through the wilderness, through a land of deserts and of pits, through a land of drought, and of the shadow of death, through a land that no man passed through, and where no man dwelt? 20. For of old time I have broken thy yoke, *and* burst thy bands;

Jer. 3:4. Wilt thou not from this time cry unto me, My father, thou *art* the guide of my youth?

Jer. 11:4. I brought them forth out of the land of Egypt, from the iron furnace,

Jer. 30:7. It *is* even the time of Jacob's trouble; but he shall be saved out of it. 8. I will break his yoke from off thy neck, and will burst thy bonds, and strangers shall no more serve themselves of him : 11. I *am* with thee, saith the LORD, to save thee : though I make a full end of all nations whither I have scattered thee, yet will I not make a full end of thee : *v. 17.*

Jer. 31:9. They shall come with weeping, and with supplications will I lead them : I will cause them to walk by the rivers of waters in a straight way, wherein they shall not stumble : for I am a father to Israel, and Ephraim *is* my firstborn. 10. He that scattered Israel will gather him, and keep him, as a shepherd *doth* his flock. 28. Like as I have watched over them, to pluck up, and to break down, and to throw down, and to destroy, and to afflict; so will I watch over them, to build, and to plant, saith the LORD.

Ezek. 9:4. And the LORD said unto him, Go through the midst of the city, through the midst of Jerusalem, and set a mark upon the foreheads of the men that sigh and that cry for all the abominations that be done in the midst thereof. 6. But come not near any man upon whom *is* the mark; and begin at my sanctuary.

Ezek. 11:16. Thus saith the Lord GOD; . . . although I have scattered them among the countries, yet will I be to them as a little sanctuary in the countries where they shall come.

Ezek. 34:11. Behold, I, *even* I, will both search my sheep, and seek them out. 12. As a shepherd seeketh out his flock in the day that he is among his sheep *that are* scattered; so will I seek out my sheep, and will deliver them out of all places where they have been scattered in the cloudy and dark day. 15. I will feed my flock, and I will cause them to lie down, saith the Lord GOD. 16. I will seek that which was lost, and bring again that which was driven away, and will bind up *that which was* broken, and will strengthen that which was sick: 22. Therefore will I save my flock, and they shall no more be a prey; and I will judge between cattle and cattle. 31. And ye my flock, the flock of my pasture, *are* men, *and* I *am* your God, saith the Lord GOD. *vs.* 13,14.

Dan. 3:27. And the princes . . . saw these men, upon whose bodies the fire had no power, nor was an hair of their head singed, neither were their coats changed, nor the smell of fire had passed on them. 28. Nebuchadnezzar spake, and said, Blessed *be* the God of Shadrach, Meshach, and Abed-nego, who hath sent his angel, and delivered his servants that trusted in him,

Dan. 12:1. There shall be a time of trouble, such as never was since there was a nation *even* to that same time: and at that time thy people shall be delivered, every one that shall be found written in the book.

Hos. 2:18. In that day will I make a covenant for them with the beasts of the field, and with the fowls of heaven, and *with* the creeping things of the ground: and I will break the bow and the sword and the battle out of the earth, and will make them to lie down safely.

Hos. 13:10. I will be thy king: where *is any other* that may save thee in all thy cities?

Joel 2:18. Then will the LORD be jealous for his land, and pity his people.

Amos 5:8. The LORD *is* his name: 9. That [1] strengtheneth the spoiled against the strong, so that [2] the spoiled shall come against the fortress.

[R. V. [1] bringeth sudden destruction upon [2] destruction cometh upon]

Amos 9:9. I will sift the house of Israel among all nations, like as *corn* is sifted in a sieve, yet shall not the least grain fall upon the earth.

Mic. 2:13. Their king shall pass before them, and the LORD on the head of them.

Nah. 1:12. Though I have afflicted thee, I will afflict thee no more.

Zeph. 3:13. They shall feed and lie down, and none shall make *them* afraid. 15. The LORD hath taken away thy judgments, he hath cast out thine enemy: the king of Israel, *even* the LORD, *is* in the midst of thee: thou shalt not see evil any more. 17. The LORD thy God in the midst of thee *is* mighty; he will save, he will rejoice over thee with joy; he will rest in his love, he will joy over thee with singing. 19. At that time I will undo all that afflict thee: and I will save her that halteth, and gather her that was driven out; and I will get them praise and fame in every land where they have been put to shame. *v.* 20.

Zech. 2:5. I, saith the LORD, will be unto her a wall of fire round about, and will be the glory in the midst of her. 8. He that toucheth you toucheth the apple of his eye.

Zech. 4:6. Not by might, nor by power, but by my spirit, saith the LORD of hosts. 7. Who *art* thou, O great mountain? before Zerubbabel *thou shalt become* a plain: and he shall bring forth the headstone *thereof with* shoutings, *crying*, Grace, grace unto it. 10. Who hath despised the day of small things? for they shall rejoice, and shall see the plummet in the hand of Zerubbabel *with* those seven; they *are* the eyes of the LORD, which run to and fro through the whole earth.

Zech. 9:8. I will encamp about mine house because of the army, because of him that passeth by, and because of him that returneth: and no oppressor shall pass through them any more: for now have I seen with mine eyes. 14. The LORD shall be seen over them, and his arrow shall go forth as the lightning: and the Lord GOD shall blow the trumpet, and shall go with whirlwinds of the south. 15. The LORD of hosts shall defend them; 16. The LORD their God shall save them in that day as the flock of his people: for *they shall be as* the stones of a crown, lifted up as an ensign upon his land.

Zech. 12:8. In that day shall the LORD defend the inhabitants of Jerusalem; and he that is feeble among them at that day shall be as David; and the house of David *shall be* as God, as the angel of the LORD before them.

Matt. 4:6. If thou be the Son of God, cast thyself down: for it is written, He shall give his angels charge concerning thee: and in *their* hands they shall bear thee up, lest at any time thou dash thy foot against a stone.

Matt. 10:29. Are not two sparrows sold for a farthing? and one of them shall not fall on the ground without your Father. 30. But the very hairs of your head are all numbered. 31. Fear ye not therefore, ye are of more value than many sparrows. Luke 12: 6,7.

Matt. 24:22. For the elect's sake those days

shall be shortened. 31. He shall send his angels with a great sound of a trumpet, and they shall gather together his elect from the four winds, and from one end of heaven to the other. Mark 13:20.

Luke 18:7. Shall not God avenge his own elect, which cry day and night unto him, though he bear long with them? 8. I tell you that he will avenge them speedily.

Luke 21:18. There shall not an hair of your head perish.

Acts 17:28. In him we live, and move, and have our being;

Rom. 8:28. We know that all things work together for good to them that love God,

1 Cor. 10:13. God is faithful, who will not suffer you to be tempted above that ye are able; but will with the temptation also make a way to escape, that ye may be able to bear it.

2 Thess. 3:3. The Lord is faithful, who shall stablish you, and keep you from evil.

Heb. 1:14. Are they not all ministering spirits, sent forth to minister for them who shall be heirs of salvation?

Jas. 4:15. Ye ought to say, If the Lord will, we shall live, and do this, or that.

1 Pet. 3:12. The eyes of the Lord are over the righteous, and his ears are open unto their prayers: 13. Who is he that will harm you, if ye be followers of that which is good?

2 Pet. 2:9. The Lord knoweth how to deliver the godly out of temptation,

Rev. 3:10. I also will keep thee from the hour of temptation, which shall come upon all the world, to try them that dwell upon the earth.

Rev. 7:3. Hurt not the earth, neither the sea, nor the trees, till we have sealed the servants of our God in their foreheads.

Rev. 12:6. The woman fled into the wilderness, where she hath a place prepared of God, that they should feed her there a thousand two hundred and threescore days.

His Preserving Care Exemplified: To Noah and his family, at the time of the flood, Gen. 6:8,13-21; 7; 8:1,15,16. To Abraham and Sarah, in Egypt, Gen. 12:17; in Gerar, Gen. 20:3. To Lot, when Sodom was destroyed, Gen. 19. To Hagar, when Abraham cast her out, Gen. 21:17,19. To Jacob, when he fled from Laban, his father-in-law, Gen. 31:24,29; when he met Esau, Gen. 33:3-10; as he journeyed in the land of Canaan, Gen. 35:5. To Joseph, in Egypt, Gen. 39:2,21. To Moses, in his infancy, Ex. 2:1-10. To the Israelites, in bringing about their deliverance from bondage, Ex. 1:9-12; 2:23-25; 3:7-9; in exempting the land of Goshen from the plague of flies, Ex. 8:22; in preserving their cattle from the plague of murrain, Ex. 9:4-7; in exempting the land of Goshen from the plague of darkness, Ex. 10:21-23; in saving the firstborn, when the plague of death destroyed the firstborn of Egypt, Ex. 12:13,23; deliverance from Egypt, Ex. 13:3,17-22; 14; 19:4; Lev. 26:13; in the wilderness, Ex. 40:36-38; Num. 9:17-23; 10:33; 22:12; 23:8; Deut. 1:

31; 23:5. Victories over the Canaanites under Joshua, Josh. chapters 6-11; 24:11-13; under Othniel, Judg. 3:9-11; under Ehud, Judg. 3:15-30; under Shamgar, Judg. 3:31; under Deborah, Judg. 4:5; under Gideon, Judg. 7; 8:1-23; under Jephthah, Judg. 11: 29-40; on account of Samuel's intercession, 1 Sam. 7:7-10; under David, 1 Sam. 17:45-49; Ahab, 1 Kin. 20. Delivering the kingdom of Israel from Syria, 2 Sam. 8; delivering Israel by Jeroboam II., 2 Kin. 14:26,27; by Abijah, 2 Chr.13:4-18; in delivering from the oppressions of the king of Syria, 2 Kin. 13:2-5.

To the kingdom of Judah: In delivering from Egypt, 2 Chr. 12:2-12; the Ethiopian host, 2 Chr. 14:11-14; in giving peace with other nations, 2 Chr. 17; delivering them from the army of the Assyrians, 2 Kin. 19.

To David, 2 Sam. 7; 1 Chr. 11:13,14; Hezekiah, 2 Kin. 19; Job 1:9-12; 2:6; Jeremiah and Baruch, Jer. 36:26; Daniel and the three Hebrew captives, Dan. 2:18-23; 3:27; 6. Jonah, Jonah 1:17; the wise men of the east, Matt. 2:12; Jesus and his parents, Matt. 2:13, 19-22; Peter, Acts 12:3-17; Paul and Silas, Acts 16:26-39; Paul, Acts 27:24; 28:5,6, with Mark 16:18.

See Affliction, Comfort in; Faith; God; Saviour; Poor, God's Care of; God, Grace of.

See instances under the sub-topic Providence of.

PROVIDENCE OF: Gen. 1:29. And God; said, Behold, I have given you every herb bearing seed, which is upon the face of all the earth, and every tree, in the which is the fruit of a tree yielding seed; to you it shall be for meat. 30. To every beast of the earth, and to every fowl of the air, and to every thing that creepeth upon the earth, wherein there is life, I have given every green herb for meat:

Gen. 2:16. And the Lord God commanded the man, saying, Of every tree of the garden thou mayest freely eat:

Gen. 8:22. While the earth remaineth, seed time and harvest, and cold and heat, and summer and winter, and day and night shall not cease.

Gen. 9:1. God blessed Noah and his sons, and said unto them, Be fruitful, and multiply, and replenish the earth. 3. Every moving thing that liveth shall be meat for you; even as the green herb have I given you all things. v. 2.

Gen. 22:14. And Abraham called the name of that place Jehovah-jireh: 17. In blessing I will bless thee, and in multiplying I will multiply thy seed as the stars of the heaven, and as the sand which is upon the sea shore; and thy seed shall possess the gate of his enemies; Gen. 26:4,5.

Gen. 28:20. Jacob vowed a vow, saying, If God will be with me, and will keep me in this way that I go, and will give me bread to eat, and raiment to put on, 21. So that I come again to my father's house in peace: then shall the Lord be my God:

Gen. 49:24. His bow abode in strength, and the arms of his hands were made strong by the hands of the mighty *God* of Jacob; 25. *Even* by the God of thy father, who shall help thee; and by the Almighty, who shall bless thee with blessings of heaven above, blessings of the deep that lieth under, blessings of the breasts, and of the womb: *vs.* 11,12,20.

Ex. 23:22. If thou shalt indeed obey his voice, and do all that I speak; then I will be an enemy unto thine enemies, and an adversary unto thine adversaries.

Ex. 34:24. Neither shall any man desire thy land, when thou shalt go up to appear before the LORD thy God thrice in the year.

Lev. 25:20. And if ye shall say, What shall we eat the seventh year? behold, we shall not sow, nor gather in our increase: 21. Then I will command my blessing upon you in the sixth year, and it shall bring forth fruit for three years. 22. And ye shall sow the eighth year, and eat *yet* of old fruit until the ninth year; until her fruits come in ye shall eat *of* the old *store.*

Lev. 26:4. I will give you rain in due season, and the land shall yield her increase, and the trees of the field shall yield their fruit. 5. And your threshing shall reach unto the vintage, and the vintage shall reach unto the sowing time: and ye shall eat your bread to the full, and dwell in your land safely. 6. I will give peace in the land, and ye shall lie down, and none shall make *you* afraid: and I will rid evil beasts out of the land, neither shall the sword go through your land. 10. And ye shall eat old store, and bring forth the old because of the new.

Deut. 1:10. The LORD your God hath multiplied you, and, behold, ye *are* this day as the stars of heaven for multitude.

Deut. 2:7. The LORD thy God hath blessed thee in all the works of thy hand: he knoweth thy walking through this great wilderness: these forty years the LORD thy God *hath been* with thee; thou hast lacked nothing.

Deut. 4:4. Ye that did cleave unto the LORD your God *are* alive every one of you this day. *v.* 40; Num. 10:29; Deut. 6:2–25; 5:33; 12:28.

Deut. 5:29. O that there were such an heart in them, that they would fear me, and keep all my commandments always, that it might be well with them, and with their children for ever! Deut. 29:9.

Deut. 7:13. He will love thee, and bless thee, and multiply thee: he will also bless the fruit of thy womb, and the fruit of thy land, thy corn, and thy wine, and thine oil, the increase of thy kine, and the flocks of thy sheep, in the land which he sware unto thy fathers to give thee. 14. Thou shalt be blessed above all people: there shall not be male or female barren among you, or among your cattle. 15. And the LORD will take away from thee all sickness, and will put none of the evil diseases of Egypt, which

thou knowest, upon thee; *vs.* 16–24; Ex. 15:26; 23:25,26; Lev. 25:18,19; Deut. 6:2,3; 11:7,8; 13:17,18; 30:15–20.

Deut. 8:3. Man doth not live by bread only, but by every *word* that proceedeth out of the mouth of the LORD doth man live. 18. Remember the LORD thy God: for *it is* he that giveth thee power to get wealth, that he may establish his covenant which he sware unto thy fathers, as *it is* this day.

Deut. 10:18. He doth execute the judgment of the fatherless and widow, and loveth the stranger, in giving him food and raiment.

Deut. 11:12. A land which the LORD thy God careth for: the eyes of the LORD thy God *are* always upon it, from the beginning of the year even unto the end of the year. *vs.* 13–15.

Deut. 12:7. Ye shall eat before the LORD your God, and ye shall rejoice in all that ye put your hand unto, ye and your households, wherein the LORD thy God hath blessed thee.

Deut. 15:4. Save when there shall be no poor among you; for the LORD shall greatly bless thee in the land which the LORD thy God giveth thee *for* an inheritance to possess it: 5. Only if thou carefully hearken unto the voice of the LORD thy God, . . . 6. For the LORD thy God blesseth thee, as he promised thee: and thou shalt lend unto many nations, but thou shalt not borrow; and thou shalt reign over many nations, but they shall not reign over thee. Deut. 26:19; 28:2–13.

Deut. 29:5. I have led you forty years in the wilderness: your clothes are not waxen old upon you, and thy shoe is not waxen old upon thy foot. Deut. 8:4.

Deut. 32:11. As an eagle stirreth up her nest, fluttereth over her young, spreadeth abroad her wings, taketh them, beareth them on her wings: 12. *So* the LORD alone did lead him, and *there was* no strange god with him. 13. He made him ride on the high places of the earth, that he might eat the increase of the fields; and he made him to suck honey out of the rock, and oil out of the flinty rock; 14. Butter of kine, and milk of sheep, with fat of lambs, and rams of the breed of Bashan, and goats, with the fat of kidneys of wheat; and thou didst drink the pure blood of the grape. 47. It *is* not a vain thing for you; because it *is* your life: and through this thing ye shall prolong *your* days in the land, whither ye go over Jordan to possess it.

Josh. 1:8. This book of the law shall not depart out of thy mouth; . . . for then thou shalt make thy way prosperous, and then thou shalt have good success.

Ruth 1:6. She had heard in the country of Moab how that the LORD had visited his people in giving them bread.

1 Sam. 2:7. The LORD maketh poor, and maketh rich: he bringeth low, and lifteth up. 8. He raiseth up the poor out of the dust, *and* lifteth up the beggar from the dunghill, to set *them* among princes, and to make them inherit the throne of glory:

1 Sam. 14:6. And Jonathan said to the young man that bare his armour, Come, and let us go over unto the garrison of these uncircumcised: it may be that the LORD will work for us: for *there is* no restraint to the LORD to save by many or by few.

2 Sam. 7:8. I took thee from the sheep-cote, from following the sheep, to be ruler over my people, over Israel: 9. And I was with thee whithersoever thou wentest, and have cut off all thine enemies out of thy sight, and have made thee a great name, like unto the name of the great *men* that *are* in the earth. 1 Chr. 17:7,8.

1 Kin. 2:3. That thou mayest prosper in all that thou doest, and whithersoever thou turnest thyself: 4. That the LORD may continue his word which he spake concerning me, saying, If thy children take heed to their way, to walk before me in truth with all their heart and with all their soul, there shall not fail thee (said he) a man on the throne of Israel. 1 Kin. 9:4,5; 1 Chr. 22:9, 13; 2 Chr. 7:17,18; Psa. 132:9.

1 Chr. 28:8. Now therefore in the sight of all Israel the congregation of the LORD, and in the audience of our God, keep and seek for all the commandments of the LORD your God: that ye may possess this good land, and leave *it* for an inheritance for your children after you for ever.

1 Chr. 29:12. Both riches and honour *come* of thee, and thou reignest over all; and in thine hand *is* power and might; and in thine hand *it is* to make great, and to give strength unto all. 14. All things *come* of thee, and of thine own have we given thee. 16. O LORD our God, all this store that we have prepared to build thee an house for thine holy name *cometh* of thine hand, and *is* all thine own.

2 Chr. 1:12. Wisdom and knowledge is granted unto thee; and I will give thee riches, and wealth, and honour, such as none of the kings have had that *have been* before thee, neither shall there any after thee have the like.

2 Chr. 20:17. Ye shall not *need* to fight in this *battle:* set yourselves, stand ye *still*, and see the salvation of the LORD with you, O Judah and Jerusalem: fear not, nor be dismayed; to morrow go out against them: for the LORD *will be* with you. *vs.*3-30.

2 Chr. 30:9. If ye turn again unto the LORD, your brethren and your children *shall find* compassion before them that lead them captive, so that they shall come again into this land:

2 Chr. 31:10. Since *the people* began to bring the offerings into the house of the LORD, we have had enough to eat, and have left plenty: for the LORD hath blessed his people; and that which is left *is* this great store.

Ezra 8:22. For I was ashamed to require of the king a band of soldiers and horsemen to help us against the enemy in the way: because we had spoken unto the king, saying, The hand of our God *is* upon all them for good that seek him; but his power and his wrath *is* against all them that forsake him.

Neh. 9:25. They took strong cities, and a fat land, and possessed houses full of all goods, wells digged, vineyards, and olive-yards, and fruit trees in abundance: so they did eat, and were filled, and became fat, and delighted themselves in thy great goodness.

Job 5:6. Although affliction cometh not forth of the dust, neither doth trouble spring out of the ground; 7. Yet man is born unto trouble, as the sparks fly upward. 8. I would seek unto God, and unto God would I commit my cause: 9. Which doeth great things and unsearchable; marvellous things without number: 10. Who giveth rain upon the earth, and sendeth waters upon the fields: 11. To set up on high those that be low; that those which mourn may be exalted to safety.

Job 5:24. Thou shalt know that thy tabernacle *shall be* in peace; 25. Thou shalt know also that thy seed *shall be* great, and thine offspring as the grass of the earth. 26. Thou shalt come to *thy* grave in a full age, like as a shock of corn cometh in in his season.

Job 8:7. Though thy beginning was small, yet thy latter end should greatly increase. 20. God will not cast away a perfect *man* . . . 21. Till he fill thy mouth with laughing, and thy lips with rejoicing. *v.* 6.

Job 11:17. *Thine* age shall be clearer than the noonday; thou shalt shine forth, thou shalt be as the morning. 18. And thou shalt be secure, because there is hope; yea, thou shalt dig *about thee, and* thou shalt take thy rest in safety. 19. Also thou shalt lie down, and none shall make *thee* afraid; yea, many shall make suit unto thee.

Job 12:23. He increaseth the nations, and destroyeth them: he enlargeth the nations, and straiteneth them *again*.

Job 22:18. He filled their houses with good *things:* 24. Then shalt thou lay up gold as dust, and the *gold* of Ophir as the stones of the brooks. 25. Yea, the Almighty shall be thy defence, and thou shalt have plenty of silver. 28. Thou shalt also decree a thing, and it shall be established unto thee: and the light shall shine upon thy ways.

Job 29:5. When the Almighty *was* yet with me, *when* my children *were* about me; 19. My root *was* spread out by the waters, and the dew lay all night upon my branch. 20. My glory *was* fresh in me, and my bow was renewed in my hand.

Job 33:14. For God speaketh once, yea twice, *yet man* perceiveth it not. 15. In a dream, in a vision of the night, when deep sleep falleth upon men, in slumberings upon the bed; 16. Then he openeth the ears of men, and sealeth their instruction, 17. That he may withdraw man *from his* purpose, and hide pride from man. 18. He keepeth back his soul from the pit, and his life from perishing by the sword. 19. He is chastened also with pain upon his bed, and the multitude of his bones with strong *pain:* 20. So that his life abhorreth bread, and his soul dainty meat. 21. His flesh is consumed away, that it cannot be seen; and his bones *that* were not seen stick out. 22. Yea, his soul draweth near unto the grave, and his life to the destroyers. 23. If there be a messenger with him, an interpreter, one among a thousand, to shew unto man his uprightness: 24. Then he is gracious unto him, and saith, Deliver him from going down to the pit: I have found a ransom. 25. His flesh shall be fresher than a child's: he shall return to the days of his youth: 26. He shall pray unto God, and he will be favourable unto him: and he shall see his face with joy; for he will render unto man his righteousness. 27. He looketh upon men, and *if any* say, I have sinned, and perverted *that which was* right, and it profited me not; 28. He will deliver his soul from going into the pit, and his life shall see the light. 29. Lo, all these *things* worketh God oftentimes with man, 30. To bring back his soul from the pit, to be enlightened with the light of the living.

Job 36:11. If they obey and serve *him,* they shall spend their days in prosperity, and their years in pleasures.

Job 37:6. For he saith to the snow, Be thou *on* the earth; likewise to the small rain, and to the great rain of his strength. 7. He sealeth up the hand of every man; that all men may know his work. 8. Then the beasts go into dens, and remain in their places. 9. Out of the south cometh the whirlwind: and cold out of the north. 10. By the breath of God frost is given: and the breadth of the waters is straitened. 11. Also by watering he wearieth the thick cloud: he scattereth his bright cloud: 12. And it is turned round about by his counsels: that they may do whatsoever he commandeth them upon the face of the world in the earth. 13. He causeth it to come, whether for correction, or for his land, or for mercy. 14. Hearken unto this, O Job: stand still, and consider the wondrous works of God. 15. Dost thou know when God disposed them, and cause the light of his cloud to shine? 16. Dost thou know the balancings of the clouds, the wondrous works of him which is perfect in knowledge? 17. How thy garments *are* warm, when he quieteth the earth by the south *wind?* 18. Hast thou with him spread out the sky, *which is* strong, *and* as a molten looking glass? 19. Teach us what we shall say unto him; *for* we cannot order *our speech* by reason of darkness. 20. Shall it be told him that I speak? if a man speak, surely he shall be swallowed up. 21. And now *men* see not the bright light which *is* in

the clouds: but the wind passeth, and cleanseth them. 22. Fair weather cometh out of the north: with God *is* terrible majesty. 23. *Touching* the Almighty, we cannot find him out: *he is* excellent in power, and in judgment, and in plenty of justice: he will not afflict. 24. Men do therefore fear him: he respecteth not any *that are* wise of heart.

Job. 38:25. Who hath divided a watercourse for the overflowing of waters, or a way for the lightning of thunder; 26. To cause it to rain on the earth, *where* no man *is; on* the wilderness, wherein *there is* no man; 27. To satisfy the desolate and waste *ground;* and to cause the bud of the tender herb to spring forth? 41. Who provideth for the raven his food? when his young ones cry unto God, they wander for lack of meat.

Job 39:5. Who hath sent out the wild ass free? or who hath loosed the bands of the wild ass? 6. Whose house I have made the wilderness, and the barren lands his dwellings.

Psa. 21:3. Thou preventest him with the blessings of goodness: thou settest a crown of pure gold on his head. 4. He asked life of thee, *and* thou gavest *it* him, *even* length of days for ever and ever. 5. His glory *is* great in thy salvation: honour and majesty hast thou laid upon him.

Psa. 23:1. The LORD *is* my shepherd; I shall not want. 2. He maketh me to lie down in green pastures: he leadeth me beside the still waters. 3. He restoreth my soul: he leadeth me in the paths of righteousness for his name's sake. 4. Yea, though I walk through the valley of the shadow of death, I will fear no evil: for thou *art* with me; thy rod and thy staff they comfort me. 5. Thou preparest a table before me in the presence of mine enemies: thou anointest my head with oil; my cup runneth over. 6. Surely goodness and mercy shall follow me all the days of my life: and I will dwell in the house of the LORD for ever.

Psa. 33:12. Blessed *is* the nation whose God *is* the LORD; *and* the people *whom* he hath chosen for his own inheritance. 15. He fashioneth their hearts alike; he considereth all their works.

Psa. 34:7. The angel of the LORD encampeth round about them that fear him, and delivereth them. 9. O fear the LORD, ye his saints: for *there is* no want to them that fear him. 10. The young lions do lack, and suffer hunger: but they that seek the LORD shall not want any good *thing.*

Psa. 36:6. O LORD, thou preservest man and beast. 7. How excellent *is* thy lovingkindness, O God! therefore the children of men put their trust under the shadow of thy wings.

Psa. 37:3. Trust in the LORD, and do good; *so* shalt thou dwell in the land, and verily thou shalt be fed. 19. They shall not be ashamed in the evil time: and in the days of famine they shall be satisfied. 22. *Such as be* blessed of him shall inherit the earth;

25. I have been young, and *now* am old; yet have I not seen the righteous forsaken, nor his seed begging bread. **34.** Wait on the Lord, and keep his way, and he shall exalt thee to inherit the land:

Psa. 40:5. Many, O Lord my God, *are* thy wonderful works *which* thou hast done, and thy thoughts *which are* to us-ward: they cannot be reckoned up in order unto thee: *if* I would declare and speak *of them*, they are more than can be numbered.

Psa. 44:1. We have heard with our ears, O God, our fathers have told us, *what* work thou didst in their days, in the times of old. **2.** *How* thou didst drive out the heathen with thy hand, and plantedst them; *how* thou didst afflict the people, and cast them out. **3.** For they got not the land in possession by their own sword, neither did their own arm save them: but thy right hand, and thine arm, and the light of thy countenance, because thou hadst a favour unto them.

Psa. 65:9. Thou visitest the earth, and waterest it: thou greatly enrichest it with the river of God, *which* is full of water: thou preparest them corn, when thou hast so provided for it. **10.** Thou waterest the ridges thereof abundantly: thou settlest the furrows thereof: thou makest it soft with showers: thou blessest the springing thereof. **11.** Thou crownest the year with thy goodness; and thy paths drop fatness. **12.** They drop *upon* the pastures of the wilderness: and the little hills rejoice on every side. **13.** The pastures are clothed with flocks; the valleys also are covered over with corn; they shout for joy, they also sing.

Psa. 67:6. *Then* shall the earth yield her increase; *and* God, *even* our own God, shall bless us.

Psa. 68:6. God setteth the solitary in families: he bringeth out those which are bound with chains. **9.** Thou, O God, didst send a plentiful rain, whereby thou didst confirm thine inheritance, when it was weary. **10.** Thy congregation hath dwelt therein: thou, O God, hast prepared of thy goodness for the poor.

Psa. 69:35. God will save Zion, and will build the cities of Judah: that they may dwell there, and have it in possession. **36.** The seed also of his servants shall inherit it: and they that love his name shall dwell therein.

Psa. 71:6. By thee have I been holden up from the womb: thou art he that took me out of my mother's bowels: my praise *shall be* continually of thee. **7.** I am as a wonder unto many; but thou *art* my strong refuge. **15.** My mouth shall shew forth thy righteousness *and* thy salvation all the day; for I know not the numbers *thereof*.

Psa. 72:16. There shall be an handful of corn in the earth upon the top of the mountains; the fruit thereof shall shake like Lebanon: and *they* of the city shall flourish like grass of the earth.

Psa. 78:52. But made his own people to go forth like sheep, and guided them in the wilderness like a flock. **53.** And he led them on safely, so that they feared not: but the sea overwhelmed their enemies. **54.** And he brought them to the border of his sanctuary, *even to* this mountain, *which* his right hand had purchased. **55.** He cast out the heathen also before them, and divided them an inheritance by line, and made the tribes of Israel to dwell in their tents.

Psa. 81:16. He should have fed them also with the finest of the wheat: and with honey out of the rock should I have satisfied thee. *vs.* 13–15.

Psa. 85:12. Yea, the Lord shall give *that which is* good; and our land shall yield her increase.

Psa. 87:5. And of Zion it shall be said, This and that man was born in her: and the highest himself shall establish her.

Psa. 100:3. Know ye that the Lord he *is* God: *it is* he *that* hath made us, and not we ourselves; *we are* his people, and the sheep of his pasture.

Psa. 103:3. Who healeth all thy diseases; **4.** Who redeemeth thy life from destruction; who crowneth thee with lovingkindness and tender mercies; **5.** Who satisfieth thy mouth with good *things; so that* thy youth is renewed like the eagle's.

Psa. 104:10. He sendeth the springs into the valleys, *which* run among the hills. **11.** They give drink to every beast of the field: the wild asses quench their thirst. **12.** By them shall the fowls of the heaven have their habitation, *which* sing among the branches. **13.** He watereth the hills from his chambers: the earth is satisfied with the fruit of thy works. **14.** He causeth the grass to grow for the cattle, and herb for the service of man: that he may bring forth food out of the earth; **15.** And wine *that* maketh glad the heart of man, *and* oil to make *his* face to shine, and bread *which* strengtheneth man's heart. **16.** The trees of the Lord are full *of sap;* the cedars of Lebanon, which he hath planted; **17.** Where the birds make their nests: *as for* the stork, the fir trees *are* her house. **18.** The high hills *are* a refuge for the wild goats; *and* the rocks for the conies. **19.** He appointed the moon for seasons: the sun knoweth his going down. **24.** O Lord, how manifold are thy works! in wisdom hast thou made them all: the earth is full of thy riches. **25.** *So is* this great and wide sea, wherein *are* things creeping innumerable, both small and great beasts. **26.** There go the ships: *there is* that leviathan, *whom* thou hast made to play therein. **27.** These wait all upon thee; that thou mayest give *them* their meat in due season. **28.** *That* thou givest them they gather: thou openest thine hand, they are filled with good. **29.** Thou hidest thy face, they are troubled: thou takest away their breath, they die, and return to their dust. **30.** Thou sendest forth thy spirit, they are created: and thou renewest the face of the earth.

Psa. 105:14. He suffered no man to do them wrong: yea, he reproved kings for their sakes; 15. *Saying*, Touch not mine anointed, and do my prophets no harm. 16. Moreover he called for a famine upon the land: he brake the whole staff of bread. 17. He sent a man before them, *even* Joseph, *who* was sold for a servant: 18. Whose feet they hurt with fetters: he was laid in iron: 19. Until the time that his word came: the word of the LORD tried him. 20. The king sent and loosed him; *even* the ruler of the people, and let him go free. 21. He made him lord of his house, and ruler of all his substance: 22. To bind his princes at his pleasure; and teach his senators wisdom. 23. Israel also came into Egypt; and Jacob sojourned in the land of Ham. 24. And he increased his people greatly; and made them stronger than their enemies. 25. He turned their heart to hate his people, to deal subtilly with his servants. 26. He sent Moses his servant; *and* Aaron whom he had chosen. 27. They shewed his signs among them, and wonders in the land of Ham. 28. He sent darkness, and made it dark; and they rebelled not against his word. 29. He turned their waters into blood, and slew their fish. 30. Their land brought forth frogs in abundance, in the chambers of their kings. 31. He spake, and there came divers sorts of flies, *and* lice in all their coasts. 32. He gave them hail for rain, *and* flaming fire in their land. 33. He smote their vines also and their fig trees: and brake the trees of their coasts. 34. He spake, and the locusts came, and caterpillers, and that without number, 35. And did eat up all the herbs in their land, and devoured the fruit of their ground. 36. He smote also all the firstborn in their land, the chief of all their strength. 37. He brought them forth also with silver and gold: and *there was* not one feeble *person* among their tribes. 38. Egypt was glad when they departed: for the fear of them fell upon them. 39. He spread a cloud for a covering; and fire to give light in the night. 40. *The people* asked, and he brought quails, and satisfied them with the bread of heaven. 41. He opened the rock, and the waters gushed out; they ran in the dry places *like* a river. 42. For he remembered his holy promise, *and* Abraham his servant. 43. And he brought forth his people with joy, *and* his chosen with gladness: 44. And gave them the lands of the heathen: and they inherited the labour of the people; 45. That they might observe his statutes, and keep his laws. Praise ye the LORD. Acts 7:34–36.

Psa. 107:1. O give thanks unto the LORD, for *he is* good: for his mercy *endureth* for ever. 2. Let the redeemed of the LORD say so, whom he hath redeemed from the hand of the enemy; 3. And gathered them out of the lands, from the east, and from the west, from the north, and from the south. 4. They wandered in the wilderness in a solitary way; they found no city to dwell in. 5. Hungry and thirsty, their soul fainted in them. 6. Then they cried unto the LORD in their trouble, *and* he delivered them out of their distresses 7. And he led them forth by the right way, that they might go to a city of habitation. 8. Oh that *men* would praise the LORD *for* his goodness, and *for* his wonderful works to the children of men! 9. For he satisfieth the longing soul, and filleth the hungry soul with goodness. 10. Such as sit in darkness and in the shadow of death, *being* bound in affliction and iron; 11. Because they rebelled against the words of God, and contemned the counsel of the most High: 12. Therefore he brought down their heart with labour; they fell down, and *there was* none to help. 13. Then they cried unto the LORD in their trouble, *and* he saved them out of their distresses. 14. He brought them out of darkness and the shadow of death, and brake their bands in sunder. 15. Oh that *men* would praise the LORD *for* his goodness, and *for* his wonderful works to the children of men! 16. For he hath broken the gates of brass, and cut the bars of iron in sunder. 17. Fools because of their transgression, and because of their iniquities, are afflicted. 18. Their soul abhorreth all manner of meat; and they draw near unto the gates of death. 19. Then they cry unto the LORD in their trouble, *and* he saveth them out of their distresses. 20. He sent his word, and healed them, and delivered *them* from their destructions. 21. Oh that *men* would praise the LORD *for* his goodness, and *for* his wonderful works to the children of men! 22. And let them sacrifice the sacrifices of thanksgiving, and declare his works with rejoicing. 23. They that go down to the sea in ships, that do business in great waters; 24. These see the works of the LORD, and his wonders in the deep. 25. For he commandeth, and raiseth the stormy wind, which lifteth up the waves thereof. 26. They mount up to the heaven, they go down again to the depths: their soul is melted because of trouble. 27. They reel to and fro, and stagger like a drunken man, and are at their wit's end. 28. Then they cry unto the LORD in their trouble, and he bringeth them out of their distresses. 29. He maketh the storm a calm, so that the waves thereof are still. 30. Then are they glad because they be quiet; so he bringeth them unto their desired haven. 31. Oh that *men* would praise the LORD *for* his goodness, and *for* his wonderful works to the children of men! 32. Let them exalt him also in the congregation of the people, and praise him in the assembly of the elders. 33. He turneth rivers into a wilderness, and the watersprings into dry ground; 34. A fruitful land into barrenness, for the wickedness of them that dwell therein. 35. He turneth the wilderness into a standing water, and dry ground into watersprings. 36. And there he maketh the hungry to dwell, that they may prepare a city for habitation; 37. And sow the fields, and plant vineyards, which may yield fruits of increase. 38. He blesseth them also, so that they are multiplied greatly; and suffereth not their cattle to decrease. 39. Again, they are minished and brought low through oppression, affliction, and sorrow. 40. He poureth contempt upon princes, and causeth them to wander in the wilderness, *where there is* no way. 41. Yet setteth he the poor on high from affliction, and maketh *him* families like a flock. 42. The righteous shall see *it*, and rejoice: and all iniquity shall stop her mouth. 43. Whoso *is* wise, and will observe these *things*, even they shall understand the lovingkindness of the LORD.

Psa. 111:5. He hath given meat unto them that fear him: he will ever be mindful of his covenant.

Psa. 113:6. Who humbleth *himself* to behold *the things that are* in heaven, and in the earth! 7. He raiseth up the poor out of the dust, *and* lifteth the needy out of the dunghill; 8. That he may set *him* with princes, *even* with the princes of his people. 9. He maketh the barren woman to keep house, *and to be* a joyful mother of children.

Psa. 115:16. The earth hath he given to the children of men.

Psa. 116:1. I love the LORD, because he hath heard my voice *and* my supplications. 2. Because he hath inclined his ear unto me, therefore will I call upon *him* as long as I live. 3. The sorrows of death compassed me, and the pains of hell gat hold upon me: I found trouble and sorrow. 4. Then called I upon the name of the LORD; O LORD, I beseech thee, deliver my soul. 5. Gracious *is* the LORD, and righteous; yea, our God *is* merciful. 6. The LORD preserveth the simple: I was brought low, and he helped me. 7. Return unto thy rest, O my soul; for the LORD hath dealt bountifully with thee. 8. For thou hast delivered my soul from death, mine eyes from tears, *and* my feet from falling. 9. I will walk before the LORD in the land of the living. 10. I believe, therefore have I spoken: I was greatly afflicted: 11. I said in my haste, All men *are* liars. 12. What shall I render unto the LORD *for* all his benefits toward me? 13. I will take the cup of salvation, and call upon the name of the LORD. 14. I will pay my vows unto the LORD now in the presence of all his people. 15. Precious in the sight of the LORD *is* the death of his saints.

Psa. 118:5. I called upon the LORD in distress: the LORD answered me, *and set me* in a large place. 6. The LORD *is* on my side: I will not fear: what can man do unto me? 13. Thou hast thrust sore at me that I might fall: but the LORD helped me. 14. The LORD *is* my strength and song, and is become my salvation.

Psa. 127:1. Except the LORD build the house, they labour in vain that build it: except the LORD keep the city, the watchman waketh *but* in vain. *vs.* 2–5; Psa. 113:9.

Psa. 128:2. Thou shalt eat the labour of thine hands: happy *shalt* thou *be*, and *it shall be* well with thee. 3. Thy wife *shall be* as a fruitful vine by the sides of thine house: thy children like olive plants round about thy table. 4. Behold, that thus shall the man be blessed that feareth the LORD. 5. The LORD shall bless thee out of Zion: and thou shalt see the good of Jerusalem all the days of thy life. 6. Yea, thou shalt see thy children's children, *and* peace upon Israel.

Psa. 135:7. He causeth the vapours to ascend from the ends of the earth; he maketh lightnings for the rain; he bringeth the wind out of his treasuries. *vs.* 6–12.

Psa. 136:25. Who giveth food to all flesh: *vs.* 5–25.

Psa. 144:12. That our sons *may be* as plants grown up in their youth; *that* our daughters *may be* as corner stones, polished *after* the similitude of a palace: 13. *That* our garners *may be* full, affording all manner of store: *that* our sheep may bring forth thousands and ten thousands in our streets: 14. *That* our oxen *may be* strong to labour; *that there be* no breaking in, nor going out; that *there be* no complaining in our streets. 15. Happy *is that* people, that is in such a case: *yea*, happy *is that* people, whose God *is* the LORD.

Psa. 145:15. The eyes of all wait upon thee; and thou givest them their meat in due season. 16. Thou openest thine hand, and satisfiest the desire of every living thing.

Psa. 146:7. Which executeth judgment for the oppressed: which giveth food to the hungry. The LORD looseth the prisoners: 8. The LORD openeth *the eyes of* the blind: the LORD raiseth them that are bowed down: the LORD loveth the righteous: 9. The LORD preserveth the strangers; he relieveth the fatherless and widow: but the way of the wicked he turneth upside down.

Psa. 147:8. Who covereth the heaven with clouds, who prepareth rain for the earth, who maketh grass to grow upon the mountains. 9. He giveth to the beast his food, *and* to the young ravens which cry. 13. He hath strengthened the bars of thy gates; he hath blessed thy children within thee. 14. He maketh peace *in* thy borders, *and* filleth thee with the finest of the wheat.

Prov. 2:21. The upright shall dwell in the land, and the perfect shall remain in it.

Prov. 3:1. Let thine heart keep my commandments: 2. For length of days, and long life, and peace, shall they add to thee.

Prov. 10:22. The blessing of the LORD, it maketh rich, and he addeth no sorrow with it. 27. The fear of the LORD prolongeth days:

Prov. 11:10. When it goeth well with the righteous, the city rejoiceth: 11. By the blessing of the upright the city is exalted: 31. The righteous shall be recompensed in the earth:

Prov. 13:25. The righteous eateth to the satisfying of his soul:

Prov. 14:11. The tabernacle of the upright shall flourish. 19. The evil bow before the good; and the wicked at the gates of the righteous. 34. Righteousness exalteth a nation: Eccl. 2:26.

Prov. 15:6. In the house of the righteous *is* much treasure:

Prov. 16:7. When a man's ways please the LORD, he maketh even his enemies to be at peace with him. 9. A man's heart deviseth his way: but the LORD directeth his steps.

Prov. 28:10. The upright shall have good *things* in possession.

Eccl. 2:24. *There is* nothing better for a man, *than* that he should eat and drink, and that he should make his soul enjoy good in his labour. This also I saw, that it *was* from the hand of God. Eccl. 3:13.

Eccl. 5:19. Every man also to whom God hath given riches and wealth, and hath given him power to eat thereof, and to take his portion, and to rejoice in his labour; this *is* the gift of God.

Isa. 1:19. If ye be willing and obedient, ye shall eat the good of the land:

Isa. 25:4. For thou hast been a strength to the poor, a strength to the needy in his distress, a refuge from the storm, a shadow from the heat, when the blast of the terrible ones *is* as a storm *against* the wall.

Isa. 30:23. Then shall he give the rain of thy seed, that thou shalt sow the ground withal; and bread of the increase of the earth, and it shall be fat and plenteous: in that day shall thy cattle feed in large pastures. 26. Moreover the light of the moon shall be as the light of the sun, and the light of the sun shall be sevenfold, as the light of seven days, in the day that the LORD bindeth up the breach of his people, and healeth the stroke of their wounds. *vs.* 24,25.

Isa. 33:16. Bread shall be given him; his waters *shall be* sure.

Isa. 43:20. I give waters in the wilderness, *and* rivers in the desert, to give drink to my people, my chosen.

Isa. 46:3. Hearken unto me, O house of Jacob, and all the remnant of the house of Israel, which are born *by me* from the belly, which are carried from the womb: 4. And *even* to *your* old age I *am* he; and *even* to hoar hairs will I carry *you:* I have made, and I will bear; even I will carry, and will deliver *you.*

Isa. 48:17. Thus saith the LORD, thy Redeemer, the Holy One of Israel; I *am* the LORD thy God which teacheth thee to profit, which leadeth thee by the way *that* thou shouldest go. 21. They thirsted not *when* he led them through the deserts: he caused the waters to flow out of the rock for them: he clave the rock also, and the waters gushed out,

Isa. 51:2. Look unto Abraham your father, . . . I called him alone, and blessed him, and increased him.

Isa. 55:10. The rain cometh down, and the snow from heaven, and returneth not thither, but watereth the earth, and maketh it bring forth and bud, that it may give seed to the sower, and bread to the eater:

Isa. 61:9. Their seed shall be known among the Gentiles, and their offspring among the people: all that see them shall acknowledge them, that they *are* the seed *which* the LORD hath blessed.

Isa. 62:9. They that have gathered it shall eat it, and praise the LORD; and they that have brought it together shall drink it in the courts of my holiness.

Isa. 65:13. My servants shall eat, but ye shall be hungry: behold, my servants shall drink, but ye shall be thirsty: 23. They shall not labour in vain, nor bring forth for trouble; for they *are* the seed of the blessed of the LORD, and their offspring with them.

Jer. 5:24. Neither say they in their heart, Let us now fear the LORD our God, that giveth rain, both the former and the latter, in his season: he reserveth unto us the appointed weeks of the harvest.

Jer. 10:13. When he uttereth his voice *there is* a multitude of waters in the heavens, and he causeth the vapours to ascend from the ends of the earth; he maketh lightnings with rain, and bringeth forth the wind out of his treasures. Jer. 51:16.

Jer. 14:22. Are there *any* among the vanities of the Gentiles that can cause rain? or can the heavens give showers? *art* not thou he, O LORD our God? therefore we will wait upon thee: for thou hast made all these *things.*

Jer. 22:15. Did not thy father eat and drink, and do judgment and justice, *and* then *it was* well with him? 16. He judged the cause of the poor and needy; then *it was* well *with him:*

Jer. 27:6. The beasts of the field have I given him also to serve him.

Jer. 30:19. Out of them shall proceed thanksgiving and the voice of them that make merry: and I will multiply them, and they shall not be few; I will also glorify them, and they shall not be small.

Jer. 31:35. Thus saith the LORD, which giveth the sun for a light by day, *and* the ordinances of the moon and of the stars for a light by night, which divideth the sea when the waves thereof roar; The LORD of hosts *is* his name:

Jer. 33:11. The voice of joy, and the voice of gladness, the voice of the bridegroom, and the voice of the bride, the voice of them that shall say, Praise the LORD of hosts: for the LORD *is* good; for his mercy *endureth* for ever: *and* of them that shall bring the sacrifice of praise into the house of the LORD. For I will cause to return the captivity of the land, as at the first, saith the LORD.

Ezek. 36:9. For, behold, I *am* for you, and I will turn unto you, and ye shall be tilled and sown: 10. And I will multiply men upon you, all the house of Israel, *even* all of it: and the cities shall be inhabited, and the wastes shall be builded: 11. And I will multiply upon you man and beast; and they shall increase and bring fruit: and I will settle you after your old estates, and will do better *unto you* than at your beginnings: and ye shall know that I *am* the LORD. 30. I will multiply the fruit of the tree, and the increase of the field, that ye shall receive no more reproach of famine among the heathen. 36. Then the heathen that are left round about you shall know that I the LORD build the ruined *places, and* plant that that was desolate: I the LORD have spoken *it*, and I will do *it*. 38. As the holy flock, as the flock of Jerusalem in her solemn feasts; so shall the waste cities be filled with flocks of men: and they shall know that I *am* the LORD. *vs.* 28-38.

Dan. 5:18. The most high God gave Nebuchadnezzar thy father a kingdom, and majesty, and glory, and honour:

Dan. 6:20. And when he came to the den, he cried with a lamentable voice unto Daniel: *and* the king spake and said to Daniel, O Daniel, servant of the living God, is thy God, whom thou servest continually, able to deliver thee from the lions? 21. Then said Daniel unto the king, O king, live for ever. 22. My God hath sent his angel, and hath shut the lions' mouths, that they have not hurt me: forasmuch as before him innocency was found in me; and also before thee, O king, have I done no hurt.

Hos. 2:8. She did not know that I gave her corn, and wine, and oil, and multiplied her silver and gold,

21. And it shall come to pass in that day, I will ¹ hear, saith the LORD, I will ¹ hear the heavens, and they shall ¹ hear the earth; 22. And the earth shall ¹ hear the corn, and the wine, and the oil: and they shall ¹ hear Jezreel. [¹ R. V. answer]

Hos. 11:3. I taught Ephraim also to go, taking them ¹ by their arms; but they knew not that I healed them. [¹ R. V. on my]

Joel 2:21. Fear not, O land; be glad and rejoice: for the LORD will do great things. 23. Be glad then, ye children of Zion, and rejoice in the LORD your God: for he hath given you the former rain moderately, and he will cause to come down for you the rain, the former rain, and the latter rain in the first *month.* 26. Ye shall eat in plenty, and be satisfied, and praise the name of the LORD your God, that hath dealt wondrously with you: and my people shall never be ashamed. *vs.* 18-26.

Amos 4:7. And also I have withholden the rain from you, when *there were* yet three months to the harvest: and I caused it to rain upon one city, and caused it not to rain upon another city: one piece was **rained upon**, and the piece whereupon it

rained not withered. 8. So two *or* three cities wandered unto one city, to drink water; but they were not satisfied: yet have ye not returned unto me, saith the LORD. 9. I have smitten you with blasting and mildew: when your gardens and your vineyards and your fig trees and your olive trees increased the palmerworm devoured *them:* yet have ye not returned unto me, saith the LORD. 10. I have sent among you the pestilence after the manner of Egypt: your young men have I slain with the sword, and have taken away your horses; and I have made the stink of your camps to come up unto your nostrils: yet have ye not returned unto me, saith the LORD. 11. I have overthrown *some* of you, as God overthrew Sodom and Gomorrah, and ye were as a firebrand plucked out of the burning: yet have ye not returned unto me, saith the LORD. 12. Therefore thus will I do unto thee, O Israel: *and* because I will do this unto thee, prepare to meet thy God, O Israel.

Amos 9:13. The days come, saith the LORD, that the plowman shall overtake the reaper, and the treader of grapes him that soweth seed; and the mountains shall drop sweet wine, and all the hills shall melt.

Jonah 4:6. And the LORD God prepared a gourd, and made *it* to come up over Jonah, that it might be a shadow over his head, to deliver him from his grief.

Hag. 2:19. Is the secd yet in the barn? yea, as yet the vine, and the fig tree, and the pomegranate, and the olive tree, hath not brought forth: from this day will I bless *you.*

Zech. 3:7. Thus saith the LORD of hosts; If thou wilt walk in my ways, and if thou wilt keep my charge, then thou shalt also judge my house, and shalt also keep my courts, and I will give thee places to walk among these that stand by.

Zech. 8:12. ¹ The seed *shall* be prosperous; the vine shall give her fruit, and the ground shall give her increase, and the heavens shall give their dew: and I will cause the remnant of this people to possess all these *things.* [¹ R. V. there shall be the seed of peace]

Zech. 9:17. How great *is* his goodness, and how great *is* his beauty! corn shall make the young men cheerful, and new wine the maids.

Zech. 10:1. Ask ye of the LORD rain in the time of the latter rain; *so* the LORD shall make bright clouds, and give them showers of rain, to every one grass in the field.

Mal. 3:10. Bring ye all the tithes into the storehouse, that there may be meat in mine house, and prove me now herewith, saith the LORD of hosts, if I will not open you the windows of heaven, and pour you out a blessing, that *there shall* not *be* room enough *to receive it.* 12. All nations shall call you blessed: for ye shall be a delightsome land, saith the LORD of hosts. *v.* 11.

Matt. 5:5. Blessed *are* the meek: for they shall inherit the earth. 45. He maketh his sun to rise on the evil and on the good, and sendeth rain on the just and on the unjust.

Matt. 6:26. Behold the fowls of the air: for they sow not, neither do they reap, nor gather into barns; yet your heavenly Father feedeth them. Are ye not much better than they? 30. If God so clothe the grass of the field, which to day is, and to morrow is cast into the oven, *shall he* not much more *clothe* you, O ye of little faith? 31. Therefore take no thought, saying, What shall we eat? or, What shall we drink? or, Wherewithal shall we be clothed? 32. (For after all these things do the Gentiles seek:) for your heavenly Father knoweth that ye have need of all these things. 33. But seek ye first the kingdom of God, and his righteousness; and all these things shall be added unto you.

Matt. 10:29. Are not two sparrows sold for a farthing? and one of them shall not fall on the ground without your Father. 30. But the very hairs of your head are all numbered. [Luke 12:6,7,24–28.] 31. Fear ye not therefore, ye are of more value than many sparrows.

Luke 22:35. When I sent you without purse, and scrip, and shoes, lacked ye any thing? And they said, Nothing.

John 6:31. Our fathers did eat manna in the desert; as it is written, He gave them bread from heaven to eat.

Acts 14:17. He left not himself without witness, in that he did good, and gave us rain from heaven, and fruitful seasons, filling our hearts with food and gladness.

1 Cor. 2:9. But as it is written, Eye hath not seen, nor ear heard, neither have entered into the heart of man, the things which God hath prepared for them that love him.

1 Cor. 16:2. Upon the first *day* of the week let every one of you lay by him in store, as ¹ *God* hath prospered him.   [¹ R. V. he may prosper]

2 Cor. 9:8. And God *is* able to make all grace abound toward you; that ye, always having all sufficiency in all *things*, may abound to every good work: 9. (As it is written, He hath dispersed abroad; he hath given to the poor: his righteousness remaineth for ever. 10. Now he that ministereth seed to the sower both minister bread for *your* food, and multiply your seed sown, and increase the fruits of your righteousness;)

Instances of: Saving Noah, Gen. 7:1. The call of Abraham, Gen. 12:1. Protecting Abraham, Sarah, and Abimelech, Gen. 20:3–6. Deliverance of Lot, Gen. 19. Care of Isaac, Gen. 26:2,3. The mission of Joseph, Gen. 39: 2,3,23; 45:7,8; 50:20; Psa. 105:17–22. Warning Pharaoh of famine, Gen. 41. Delivering the Israelites, Ex. 3:8; 11:3; 13:18; Acts 7:34–36. The pillar of cloud, Ex. 13:21; 14:19,20. Dividing the Red Sea, Ex. 14:21. Delaying and destroying Pharaoh, Ex. 14:25–30. Purifying the waters of Marah, Ex. 15:25. Supplying manna and quail, Ex. 16:13–15; Num. 11:31, 32; water at Meribah, Num. 20:7–11; Neh. 9: 10–25. Protection of homes while at feasts,

Ex. 34:24. In the conquest of Canaan, Psa. 44: 2,3. Saving David's army, 2 Sam. 5:23–25. The revolt of the ten tribes, 1 Kin. 12:15,24; 2 Chr. 10:15. Fighting the battles of Israel, 2 Chr. 13:12,18; 14:9–14; 16:7–9; 20:15,17,22,23; 32:21,22. Restoring Manasseh after his conversion, 2 Chr. 33:12,13. Feeding Elijah and the widow, 1 Kin. 17; 19:1–8. In prospering Hezekiah, 2 Kin. 18:6,7; 2 Chr. 32:29; and Asa, 2 Chr. 14:6,7; and Jehoshaphat, 2 Chr. 17:3, 5; 20:30; and Uzziah, 2 Chr. 26:5–15; and Jotham, 2 Chr. 27:6; and Job, Job 1:10; 42: 10,12; and Daniel, Dan. 1:9. In turning the heart of the king of Assyria to favor the Jews, Ezra 6:22. In rescuing Jeremiah, Lam. 3:52–58, with Jer. 38:6–13. Restoration of the Jews, 2 Chr. 36:22,23; Ezra 1:1. Rescuing the Jews from Haman's plot, the Book of Esther. Rebuilding the walls of Jerusalem, Neh. 6: 16. Warning Joseph in dreams, Matt. 1:20; 2:13,19,20; and the wise men of the east, Matt. 2:12,13. Restoring Epaphroditus, Phil. 2:27. In the banishment of John to Patmos, Rev. 1:9.

See Goodness of; Preserver, above, and Overruling Interpositions of, below.

PROVIDENCE OF, OVERRULING INTERPOSITIONS OF THE: Gen. 50:20. As for you, ye thought evil against me; *but* God meant it unto good, to bring to pass, as *it is* this day, to save much people alive. Gen. 45:5–7; Psa. 105:17; Acts 7:9,10.

Ex. 14:4. I will harden Pharaoh's heart, that he shall follow after them; and I will be honoured upon Pharaoh, and upon all his host;

Num. 23:7. Balak the king of Moab hath brought me, . . . *saying*, Come, curse me Jacob, and come, defy Israel. 8. How shall I curse, whom God hath not cursed? or how shall I defy, *whom* the Lord hath not defied? 23. Surely *there is* no enchantment against Jacob, neither *is there* any divination against Israel: according to this time it shall be said of Jacob and of Israel, What hath God wrought! *vs.* 1–30; Num. 22:12–18; 24: 10–13.

Deut. 2:30. Sihon king of Heshbon would not let us pass by him: for the Lord thy God hardened his spirit, and made his heart obstinate, that he might deliver him into thy hand, as *appeareth* this day. Josh. 11:20.

Deut. 23:4. Because they met you not with bread and with water in the way, when ye came forth out of Egypt; and because they hired against thee Balaam the son of Beor of Pethor of Mesopotamia, to curse thee. 5. Nevertheless the Lord thy God would not hearken unto Balaam; but the Lord thy God turned the curse into a blessing unto thee, because the Lord thy God loved thee.

Judg. 9:23. God sent an evil spirit between Abimelech and the men of Shechem; 24. That the cruelty *done* to the threescore and ten sons of Jerubbaal might come, and their blood be laid upon Abimelech their brother, which slew them; and upon the men of Shechem, which aided him in the killing of his brethren.

1 Sam. 2:6. The LORD killeth, and maketh alive: he bringeth down to the grave, and bringeth up. 7. The LORD maketh poor. and maketh rich: he bringeth low, and lifteth up. 8. He raiseth up the poor out of the dust, *and* lifteth up the beggar from the dunghill, to set *them* among princes, and to make them inherit the throne of glory: for the pillars of the earth *are* the LORD's, and he hath set the world upon them. 9. He will keep the feet of his saints, and the wicked shall be silent in darkness; for by strength shall no man prevail.

2 Sam. 17:14. For the LORD had appointed to defeat the good counsel of Ahithophel, to the intent that the LORD might bring evil upon Absalom.

1 Kin. 12·15. The king hearkened not unto the people; for the cause was from the LORD, that he might perform his saying, which the LORD spake by Ahijah the Shilonite unto Jeroboam the son of Nebat. 1 Kin. 11:14–40; 2 Chr. 10:15.

1 Chr. 5:26. And the God of Israel stirred up the spirit of Pul king of Assyria, and the spirit of Tilgath-pilneser king of Assyria, and he carried them away, even the Reubenites, and the Gadites, and the half tribe of Manasseh, and brought them unto Halah, and Habor, and Hara, and to the river Gozan, unto this day.

2 Chr. 36:22. Now in the first year of Cyrus king of Persia, that the word of the LORD *spoken* by the mouth of Jeremiah might be accomplished, the LORD stirred up the spirit of Cyrus king of Persia, that he made a proclamation throughout all his kingdom, and *put it* also in writing, saying, 23. Thus saith Cyrus king of Persia, All the kingdoms of the earth hath the LORD God of heaven given me; and he hath charged me to build him an house in Jerusalem, which *is* in Judah. Who *is there* among you of all his people? The LORD his God *be* with him, and let him go up. Ezra 1:1.

Ezra 5:5. The eye of their God was upon the elders of the Jews, that they could not cause them to cease, till the matter came to Darius:

Ezra 6:22. The LORD had made them joyful, and turned the heart of the king of Assyria unto them, to strengthen their hands in the work of the house of God,

Neh. 6:16. And it came to pass, that when all our enemies heard *thereof*, and all the heathen that *were* about us saw *these things*, they were much cast down in their own eyes: for they perceived that this work was wrought of our God.

Esth. 7:10. So they hanged Haman on the gallows that he had prepared for Mordecai. Esth. 6:1–12; 9:25.

Esth. 9:1. Now in the twelfth month, that *is*, the month Adar, on the thirteenth day of the same, when the king's commandment and his decree drew near to be put in execu-

tion, in the day that the enemies of the Jews hoped to have power over them, (though it was turned to the contrary, that the Jews had rule over them that hated them;)

Job 5:12. He disappointeth the devices of the crafty, so that their hands cannot perform *their* enterprise. 13. He taketh the wise in their own craftiness: and the counsel of the froward is carried headlong. Isa. 8:9,10.

Psa. 17:13. Deliver my soul from the wicked, *which is* thy sword: 14. From men *which are* thy hand, O LORD,

Psa. 33:10. The LORD bringeth the counsel of the heathen to nought: he maketh the devices of the people of none effect.

Psa. 75:7. God *is* the judge: he putteth down one, and setteth up another.

Psa. 76:10. Surely the wrath of man shall praise thee: the remainder of wrath shalt thou restrain.

Psa. 127:1. Except the LORD build the house, they labour in vain that build it: except the LORD keep the city, the watchman waketh *but* in vain. 2. *It is* vain for you to rise up early, to sit up late, to eat the bread of sorrows: *for* so he giveth his beloved sleep.

Prov. 13:22. The wealth of the sinner *is* laid up for the just.

Prov. 14:19. The evil bow before the good; and the wicked at the gates of the righteous.

Prov. 16:7. When a man's ways please the LORD, he maketh even his enemies to be at peace with him. 33. The lot is cast into the lap; but the whole disposing thereof *is* of the LORD.

Prov. 19:21. *There are* many devices in a man's heart; nevertheless the counsel of the LORD, that shall stand.

Prov. 21:1. The king's heart *is* in the hand of the LORD, *as* the rivers of water: he turneth it whithersoever he will. 18. The wicked *shall be* a ransom for the righteous, and the transgressor for the upright.

Prov. 28:8. He that by usury and unjust gain increaseth his substance, he shall gather it for him that will pity the poor.

Eccl. 2:26. To the sinner he giveth travail, to gather and to heap up, that he may give to *him that is* good before God.

Eccl. 3:1. To every thing there *is* a season, and a time to every purpose under the heaven: 10. I have seen the travail, which God hath given to the sons of men to be exercised in it.

Isa. 10:5. O Assyrian, the rod of mine anger, and the staff in their hand is mine indignation. 6. I will send him against an hypocritical nation, and against the people of my wrath will I give him a charge, 7. Howbeit he meaneth not so, neither doth his heart think so; but *it is* in his heart to destroy and cut off nations not a few.

Isa. 13:3. I have commanded my sanctified ones, I have also called my mighty ones for mine anger, *even* them that rejoice in my highness. 4. The LORD of hosts mustereth the host of the battle. 5. They come from a far country, from the end of heaven, *even* the LORD, and the weapons of his indignation, to destroy the whole land.

Isa. 41:2. Who raised up the righteous *man* from the east, called him to his foot, gave the nations before him, and made *him* rule over kings? he gave *them* as the dust to his sword, *and* as driven stubble to his bow. 4. Who hath wrought and done *it*, calling the generations from the beginning? I the LORD, the first, and with the last; I *am* he.

Isa. 43:14. Thus saith the LORD, your redeemer, the Holy One of Israel; For your sake I have sent to Babylon, and have brought down all their nobles, and the Chaldeans, whose cry *is* in the ships.

Isa. 44:28. That saith of Cyrus, *He is* my shepherd, and shall perform all my pleasure: even saying to Jerusalem, Thou shalt be built; and to the temple, Thy foundation shall be laid.

Isa. 45:5. I *am* the LORD, and *there is* none else, *there is* no God beside me: I girded thee, though thou hast not known me: 6. That they may know from the rising of the sun, and from the west, that *there is* none beside me. I *am* the LORD, and *there is* none else. 13. I have raised him up in righteousness, and I will direct all his ways: he shall build my city, and he shall let go my captives, not for price nor reward, saith the LORD of hosts. *vs.* 1–5.

Isa. 48:14. The LORD hath loved him: he will do his pleasure on Babylon, and his arm *shall be on* the Chaldeans. 15. I, *even* I, have spoken: yea, I have called him: I have brought him, and he shall make his way prosperous.

Isa. 54:16. I have created the smith that bloweth the coals in the fire, and that bringeth forth an instrument for his work; and I have created the waster to destroy. 17. No weapon that is formed against thee shall prosper; and every tongue *that* shall rise against thee in judgment thou shalt condemn.

Jer. 51:20. Thou *art* my battle ax *and* weapons of war: for with thee will I break in pieces the nations, and with thee will I destroy kingdoms; 21. And with thee will I break in pieces the horse and his rider; and with thee will I break in pieces the chariot and his rider;

Jer. 52:3. For through the anger of the LORD it came to pass in Jerusalem and Judah, till he had cast them out from his presence, that Zedekiah rebelled against the king of Babylon.

Ezek. 21:26. Thus saith the Lord GOD; Remove the diadem, and take off the crown: this *shall* not *be* the same: exalt *him that is* low, and abase *him that is* high. 27. I will overturn, overturn, overturn, it: and it shall be no *more*, until he come whose right it is: and I will give it *him*.

Ezek. 29:19. Therefore thus saith the Lord GOD; . . . I will give the land of Egypt unto Nebuchadrezzar king of Babylon; and he shall take her multitude, and take her spoil, and take her prey; and it shall be the wages for his army. 20. I have given him the land of Egypt *for* his labour wherewith he served against it, because they wrought for me, saith the Lord GOD.

Dan. 11:27. Both these kings' hearts *shall be* to do mischief, and they shall speak lies at one table; but it shall not prosper: for yet the end *shall be* at the time appointed.

Acts 3:17. And now, brethren, I wot that through ignorance ye did *it*, as *did* also your rulers. 18. But those things, which God before had shewed by the mouth of all his prophets, that Christ should suffer, he hath so fulfilled.

Acts 5:38. And now I say unto you, Refrain from these men, and let them alone: for if this counsel or this work be of men, it will come to nought: 39. But if it be of God, ye cannot overthrow it; lest haply ye be found even to fight against God.

Rom. 1:10. Making request, if by any means now at length I might have a prosperous journey by the will of God to come unto you.

Rom. 8:28. All things work together for good to them that love God, to them who are the called according to *his* purpose.

1 Cor. 4:19. I will come to you shortly, if the Lord will,

1 Cor. 16:7. I trust to tarry a while with you, if the Lord permit.

Phil. 1:12. But I would ye should understand, brethren, that the things *which happened* unto me have fallen out rather unto the furtherance of the gospel; 19. For I know that this shall turn to my salvation through your prayer, and the supply of the Spirit of Jesus Christ,

Philem. 15. Perhaps he therefore departed for a season, that thou shouldest receive him for ever;

Jas. 4:15. For that ye *ought* to say, If the Lord will, we shall live, and do this, or that.

Rev. 17:17. For God hath put in their hearts to fulfil his will, and to agree, and give their kingdom unto the beast, until the words of God shall be fulfilled.

See GOODNESS OF. PRESERVER.

PROVIDENCE OF, MYSTERIOUS AND MISINTERPRETED: Job 10:15. If I be wicked, woe unto me; and *if* I be righteous, *yet* will I not lift up my head. *I am* full of confusion;

Job 12:6. The tabernacles of robbers prosper, and they that provoke God are secure; into whose hand God bringeth *abundantly*.

Job 21:7. Wherefore do the wicked live, become old, yea, are mighty in power?

Job 24:1. Why, seeing times are not hidden from the Almighty, do they that know him not see his days? *vs.* 1–12.

Job 33:13. Why dost thou strive against him? for he giveth not account of any of his matters.

Psa. 10:5. Thy judgments *are* far above out of his sight:

Psa. 73:2. But as for me, my feet were almost gone; my steps had well nigh slipped. 3. For I was envious at the foolish, *when* I saw the prosperity of the wicked. 13. Verily I have cleansed my heart *in* vain, and washed my hands in innocency. 14. For all the day long have I been plagued, and chastened every morning. 15. If I say, I will speak thus; behold, I should offend *against* the generation of thy children. 16. When I thought to know this, it *was* too painful for me; 17. Until I went into the sanctuary of God; *then* understood I their end. *vs.* 4,5,12.

Psa. 89:47. Wherefore hast thou made all men in vain?

Prov. 28:5. Evil men understand not judgment:

Eccl. 7:15. All *things* have I seen in the days of my vanity: there is a just *man* that perisheth in his righteousness, and there is a wicked *man* that prolongeth *his life* in his wickedness.

Eccl. 8:14. There be just *men*, unto whom it happeneth according to the work of the wicked; again, there be wicked *men*, to whom it happeneth according to the work of the righteous: *vs.* 12–17.

Eccl. 9:2. All *things come* alike to all: *there is* one event to the righteous, and to the wicked; to the good and to the clean, and to the unclean; to him that sacrificeth, and to him that sacrificeth not: as *is* the good, so *is* the sinner; *and* he that sweareth, as *he* that feareth an oath. 11. The race *is* not to the swift, nor the battle to the strong, neither yet bread to the wise, nor yet riches to men of understanding, nor yet favour to men of skill; but time and chance happeneth to them all.

Jer. 12:1. Righteous *art* thou, O LORD, when I plead with thee: yet let me talk with thee of *thy* judgments: Wherefore doth the way of the wicked prosper? *wherefore* are all they happy that deal very treacherously? 2. Thou hast planted them, yea, they have taken root: they grow, yea, they bring forth fruit: thou *art* near in their mouth, and far from their reins.

Jer. 50:7. Their adversaries said, We offend not, because they have sinned against the LORD,

Dan. 12:10. Many shall be purified, and made white, and tried; but the wicked shall do wickedly: and none of the wicked shall understand; but the wise shall understand.

Mic. 4:12. They know not the thoughts of the LORD, neither understand they his counsel: for he shall gather them as the sheaves into the floor.

Hab. 1:2. O LORD, how long shall I cry, and thou wilt not hear! *even* cry out unto thee *of* violence, and thou wilt not save! 3. Why dost thou shew me iniquity, and cause *me* to behold grievance? 11. Then shall *his* mind change, and he shall pass over, and

offend, *imputing* this his power unto his god. 13. Wherefore lookest thou upon them that deal treacherously, *and* holdest thy tongue when the wicked devoureth *the man that is* more righteous than he? 14. And makest men as the fishes of the sea, as the creeping things, *that have* no ruler over them?

Mal. 3:14. Ye have said, It *is* vain to serve God: and what profit *is it* that we have kept his ordinances, and that we have walked mournfully before the LORD of hosts? 15. And now we call the proud happy; yea, they that work wickedness are set up; yea, *they that* tempt God are even delivered.

See BLINDNESS, SPIRITUAL.

INSTANCES OF: Elijah's trials, 1 Kin. 19. Job's, Job 3:19–23, with chapters 1; 2. Israelites, Ex. 5:20–23.

RIGHTEOUSNESS OF: Judg. 5:11. *They that are delivered* from the noise of archers in the places of drawing water, there shall they rehearse the righteous acts of the LORD,

Ezra 9:15. O LORD God of Israel, thou *art* righteous:

Job 36:3. I will fetch my knowledge from afar, and will ascribe righteousness to my Maker.

Psa. 5:8. Lead me, O LORD, in thy righteousness because of mine enemies;

Psa. 7:9. The righteous God trieth the hearts and reins.

Psa. 48:10. Thy right hand is full of righteousness.

Psa. 50:6. And the heavens shall declare his righteousness: for God *is* judge himself.

Psa. 71:15. My mouth shall shew forth thy righteousness *and* thy salvation all the day; for I know not the numbers *thereof.* 19. Thy righteousness also, O God, *is* very high, who hast done great things: O God, who *is* like unto thee!

Psa. 72:1. Give the king thy judgments, O God, and thy righteousness unto the king's son.

Psa. 88:12. Shall thy wonders be known in the dark? and thy righteousness in the land of forgetfulness?

Psa. 89:16. In thy name shall they rejoice all the day: and in thy righteousness shall they be exalted.

Psa. 97:2. Clouds and darkness *are* round about him: righteousness and judgment *are* the habitation of his throne.

Psa. 111:3. His work *is* honourable and glorious: and his righteousness endureth for ever.

Psa. 112:4. *He is* gracious, and full of compassion, and righteous.

Psa. 116:5. Gracious *is* the LORD, and righteous; yea, our God *is* merciful.

Psa. 119:40. Behold, I have longed after thy precepts: quicken me in thy righteousness. 137. Righteous *art* thou, O LORD, and upright *are* thy judgments. 142. Thy righteousness *is* an everlasting righteousness, and thy law *is* the truth. 144. The righteousness of thy testimonies *is* everlasting: *v.* 172.

Psa. 143:1. Hear my prayer, O Lord, give ear to my supplications: in thy faithfulness answer me, *and* in thy righteousness.

Psa. 145:7. They shall abundantly utter the memory of thy great goodness, and shall sing of thy righteousness. 17. The Lord *is* righteous in all his ways, and holy in all his works.

Isa. 41:10. I will uphold thee with the right hand of my righteousness.

Isa. 51:8. My righteousness shall be for ever, and my salvation from generation to generation.

Isa. 56:1. Thus saith the Lord, Keep ye judgment, and do justice: for my salvation *is* near to come, and my righteousness to be revealed.

Jer. 4:2. And thou shalt swear, The Lord liveth, in truth, in judgment, and in righteousness;

Jer. 9:24. But let him that glorieth glory in this, that he understandeth and knoweth me, that I *am* the Lord which exercise lovingkindness, judgment, and righteousness, in the earth: for in these *things* I delight, saith the Lord.

Jer. 12:1. Righteous *art* thou, O Lord,

Lam. 3:34. To crush under his feet all the prisoners of the earth, 35. To turn aside the right of a man before the face of the most High, 36. To subvert a man in his cause, the Lord approveth not.

Dan. 9:7. O Lord, righteousness *belongeth* unto thee. 14. The Lord our God *is* righteous in all his works which he doeth:

Hos. 14:9. The ways of the Lord *are* right, and the just shall walk in them:

Mic. 7:9. He will bring me forth to the light, *and* I shall behold his righteousness.

Matt. 6:33. But seek ye first the kingdom of God, and his righteousness; and all these things shall be added unto you.

John 17:25. O righteous Father, the world hath not known thee: but I have known thee, and these have known that thou hast sent me.

Acts 17:31. Because he hath appointed a day, in the which he will judge the world in righteousness by *that* man whom he hath ordained;

Rom. 1:17. For therein is the righteousness of God revealed from faith to faith:

Rom. 3:4. God forbid: yea, let God be true, but every man a liar; as it is written, That thou mightest be justified in thy sayings, and mightest overcome when thou art judged. 5. But if our unrighteousness commend the righteousness of God, what shall we say? *Is* God unrighteous who taketh vengeance? (I speak as a man) 6. God forbid: for then how shall God judge the world? 21. But now the righteousness of God without the law is manifested, being witnessed by the law and the prophets: 22. Even the righteousness of God *which is* by faith of Jesus Christ unto all and upon

all them that believe: for there is no difference:

Rom. 9:14. What shall we say then? *Is there* unrighteousness with God? God forbid.

Rom. 10:3. For they being ignorant of God's righteousness, and going about to establish their own righteousness, have not submitted themselves unto the righteousness of God. 4. For Christ *is* the end of the law for righteousness to every one that believeth.

2 Tim. 4:8. Henceforth there is laid up for me a crown of righteousness, which the Lord, the righteous judge, shall give me at that day: and not to me only, but unto all them also that love his appearing.

1 Pet. 2:23. Who, when he was reviled, reviled not again; when he suffered, he threatened not; but committed *himself* to him that judgeth righteously:

2 Pet. 1:1. Simon Peter, a servant and an apostle of Jesus Christ, to them that have obtained like precious faith with us through the righteousness of God and our Saviour Jesus Christ:

1 John 2:1. And if any man sin, we have an advocate with the Father, Jesus Christ the righteous:

Rev. 16:5. And I heard the angel of the waters say, Thou art righteous, O Lord,

See Holiness of; Judge, and His Justice.

SAVIOUR: Gen. 48:16. The Angel which redeemed me from all evil, bless the lads;

Ex. 15:2. The Lord *is* my strength and song, and he is become my salvation:

Deut. 32:15. He forsook God *which* made him, and lightly esteemed the Rock of his salvation. 31. Their rock *is* not as our Rock, 39. I kill, and I make alive; I wound, and I heal:

Deut. 33:29. Happy *art* thou, O Israel: who *is* like unto thee, O people saved by the Lord, the shield of thy help, and who *is* the sword of thy excellency! *vs.* 25-29.

Job 33:24. He is gracious unto him, and saith, Deliver him from going down to the pit: I have found a ransom. 27. He looketh upon men, and *if any* say, I have sinned, and perverted *that which was* right, and it profited me not; 28. He will deliver his soul from going into the pit, and his life shall see the light. 29. Lo, all these *things* worketh God oftentimes with man. 30. To bring back his soul from the pit, to be enlightened with the light of the living.

Psa. 3:8. Salvation *belongeth* unto the Lord: thy blessing *is* upon thy people.

Psa. 18:30. He *is* a buckler to all those that trust in him. 31. For who *is* God save the Lord? or who *is* a rock save our God? 1 Sam. 2:2.

Psa. 19:14. Let the words of my mouth, and the meditation of my heart, be acceptable in thy sight, O Lord, my strength, and my redeemer.

Psa. 25:5. Thou *art* the God of my salvation; on thee do I wait all the day.

Psa. 27:1. The LORD is my light and my salvation; whom shall I fear? the LORD is the strength of my life; of whom shall I be afraid?

Psa. 28:8. The LORD is their strength, and he is the saving strength of his anointed.

Psa. 31:5. Into thine hand I commit my spirit: thou hast redeemed me, O LORD God of truth.

Psa. 33:18. The eye of the LORD is upon them that fear him, upon them that hope in his mercy; 19. To deliver their soul from death,

Psa. 34:22. The LORD redeemeth the soul of his servants: and none of them that trust in him shall be desolate.

Psa. 36:9. With thee is the fountain of life: in thy light shall we see light.

Psa. 37:39. The salvation of the righteous is of the LORD: he is their strength in the time of trouble. 40. The LORD shall help them, and deliver them: he shall deliver them from the wicked, and save them, because they trust in him.

Psa. 50:23. To him that ordereth his conversation aright will I shew the salvation of God.

Psa. 62:1. Truly my soul waiteth upon God: from him cometh my salvation. 6. He only is my rock and my salvation: he is my defence; I shall not be moved. 7. In God is my salvation and my glory: the rock of my strength, and my refuge, is in God. v. 2.

Psa. 65:5. O God of our salvation; who art the confidence of all the ends of the earth, and of them that are afar off upon the sea:

Psa. 68:19. Who daily loadeth us with benefits, even the God of our salvation. 20. He that is our God is the God of salvation; and unto GOD the Lord belong the issues from death.

Psa. 71:16. I will go in the strength of the Lord GOD: I will make mention of thy righteousness, even of thine only.

Psa. 74:12. God is my King of old, working salvation in the midst of the earth.

Psa. 76:8. The earth feared, and was still. 9. When God arose to judgment, to save all the meek of the earth.

Psa. 85:9. His salvation is nigh them that fear him; that glory may dwell in our land.

Psa. 88:1. O LORD God of my salvation, I have cried day and night before thee:

Psa. 96:2. Shew forth his salvation from day to day.

Psa. 98:2. The LORD hath made known his salvation: his righteousness hath he openly shewed in the sight of the heathen. 3. He hath remembered his mercy and his truth toward the house of Israel; all the ends of the earth have seen the salvation of our God.

Psa. 111:9. He sent redemption unto his people: he hath commanded his covenant for ever:

Psa. 118:14. The LORD is my strength and song, and is become my salvation. 21. I will

praise thee: for thou hast heard me, and art become my salvation. 27. God is the LORD, which hath shewed us light:

Psa. 121:7. The LORD shall preserve thee from all evil: he shall preserve thy soul.

Psa. 133:3. There the LORD commanded the blessing, even life for evermore. Psa. 145:9.

Psa. 149:4. The LORD taketh pleasure in his people: he will beautify the meek with salvation.

Isa. 12:2. Behold, God is my salvation; I will trust, and not be afraid: for the LORD JEHOVAH is my strength and my song; he also is become my salvation.

Isa. 25:4. Thou hast been a strength to the poor, a strength to the needy in his distress, a refuge from the storm, a shadow from the heat, when the blast of the terrible ones is as a storm against the wall. 9. Lo, this is our God; we have waited for him, and he will save us: this is the LORD; we have waited for him, we will be glad and rejoice in his salvation.

Isa. 26:1. In that day shall this song be sung in the land of Judah: We have a strong city; salvation will God appoint for walls and bulwarks.

Isa. 33:22. For the LORD is our judge, the LORD is our lawgiver, the LORD is our king; he will save us.

Isa. 35:4. Your God will come with vengeance, even God with a recompence; he will come and save you.

Isa. 41:14. Fear not, thou worm Jacob, and ye men of Israel; I will help thee, saith the LORD, and thy redeemer, the Holy One of Israel. Isa. 48:17.

Isa. 43:3. I am the LORD thy God, the Holy One of Israel, thy Saviour: I gave Egypt for thy ransom, 11. I, even I, am the LORD; and beside me there is no saviour. 12. I have declared, and have saved, and I have shewed, when there was no strange god among you: v. 14.

Isa. 44:22. I have blotted out, as a thick cloud, thy transgressions, and, as a cloud, thy sins: return unto me; for I have redeemed thee. 23. Break forth into singing, ye mountains, O forest, and every tree therein: for the LORD hath redeemed Jacob, and glorified himself in Israel. 24. The LORD, thy redeemer, and he that formed thee from the womb, v. 6.

Isa. 45:15. Verily thou art a God that hidest thyself, O God of Israel, the Saviour. 17. Israel shall be saved in the LORD with an everlasting salvation; ye shall not be ashamed nor confounded world without end. 21. There is no God else beside me; a just God and a Saviour; there is none beside me. 22. Look unto me, and be ye saved, all the ends of the earth: for I am God, and there is none else.

Isa. 46:12. Hearken unto me, ye stouthearted, that are far from righteousness: 13. I bring near my righteousness; it shall not be far off, and my salvation shall not tarry:

and I will place salvation in Zion for Israel my glory.

Isa. 47:4. *As for* our redeemer, the Lord of hosts *is* his name, the Holy One of Israel.

Isa. 49:25. I will save thy children.

Isa. 50:2. Wherefore, when I came, *was there* no man? when I called, *was there* none to answer? Is my hand shortened at all, that it cannot redeem? or have I no power to deliver?

Isa. 52:3. Ye have sold yourselves for nought; and ye shall be redeemed without money. 9. The Lord hath comforted his people, he hath redeemed Jerusalem. 10. The Lord hath made bare his holy arm in the eyes of all the nations; and all the ends of the earth shall see the salvation of our God.

Isa. 59:1. Behold, the Lord's hand is not shortened, that it cannot save; neither his ear heavy, that it cannot hear:

Isa. 60:16. Thou shalt know that I the Lord *am* thy Saviour and thy Redeemer, the mighty One of Jacob.

Isa. 63:8. He said, Surely they *are* my people, children *that* will not lie: so he was their Saviour. 16. Doubtless thou *art* our father, though Abraham be ignorant of us, and Israel acknowledge us not: thou, O Lord, *art* our father, our redeemer: thy name *is* from everlasting.

Jer. 3:23. In vain *is salvation hoped for* from the hills, *and from* the multitude of mountains: truly in the Lord our God *is* the salvation of Israel.

Jer. 8:22. *Is there* no balm in Gilead; *is there* no physician there? why then is not the health of the daughter of my people recovered?

Jer. 14:8. O the hope of Israel, the saviour thereof in time of trouble, why shouldest thou be as a stranger in the land,

Jer. 30:17. I will restore health unto thee, and I will heal thee of thy wounds, saith the Lord; because they called thee an Outcast, *saying*, This *is* Zion, whom no man seeketh after.

Jer. 33:6. I will bring it health and cure, and I will cure them, and will reveal unto them the abundance of peace and truth.

Jer. 50:34. Their Redeemer *is* strong; the Lord of hosts *is* his name: he shall throughly plead their cause,

Ezek. 37:23. I will save them out of all their dwellingplaces, wherein they have sinned, and will cleanse them: so shall they be my people, and I will be their God.

Hos. 1:7. I will have mercy upon the house of Judah, and will save them by the Lord their God,

Hos. 13:4. Thou shalt know no god but me: for *there is* no saviour beside me. 9. O Israel, thou hast destroyed thyself; ¹ but in me is thine help. [¹ R. V. that thou art against me, against thy]

Joel 3:16. The Lord *will be* ¹ the hope of his people, and ² the strength of the children of Israel. [R. V. ¹ a refuge unto ² a strong hold to]

Jonah 2:9. Salvation *is* of the Lord.

Zech. 9:11. By the blood of thy covenant

I have sent forth thy prisoners out of the pit wherein *is* no water. 12. Turn you to the strong hold, ye prisoners of hope: even to day do I declare *that* I will render double unto thee; 16. The Lord their God shall save them in that day as the flock of his people: for *they shall be as* the stones of a crown, lifted up as an ensign upon his land.

Luke 1:68. Blessed *be* the Lord God of Israel; for he hath visited and redeemed his people,

John 3:16. God so loved the world, that he gave his only begotten Son, that whosoever believeth in him should not perish, but have everlasting life. 17. For God sent not his Son into the world to condemn the world; but that the world through him might be saved.

John 6:39. This is the Father's will which hath sent me, that of all which he hath given me I should lose nothing, but should raise it up again at the last day.

Rom. 1:16. I am not ashamed of the gospel of Christ: for it is the power of God unto salvation to every one that believeth;

Rom. 6:23. The gift of God *is* eternal life through Jesus Christ our Lord.

Rom. 8:30. Whom he did predestinate, them he also called: and whom he called, them he also justified: and whom he justified, them he also glorified. 31. What shall we then say to these things? If God *be* for us, who *can be* against us? 32. He that spared not his own Son, but delivered him up for us all, how shall he not with him also freely give us all things?

1 Cor. 1:18. For the preaching of the cross is to them that perish foolishness; but unto us which are saved it is the power of God.

2 Cor. 5:18. All things *are* of God, who hath reconciled us to himself by Jesus Christ, and hath given to us the ministry of reconciliation;

Eph. 1:3. Blessed *be* the God and Father of our Lord Jesus Christ, who hath blessed us with all spiritual blessings in heavenly *places* in Christ: 5. Having predestinated us unto the adoption of children by Jesus Christ to himself, according to the good pleasure of his will,

1 Thess. 5:9. God hath not appointed us to wrath, but to obtain salvation by our Lord Jesus Christ,

2 Thess. 2:16. God, even our Father, which hath loved us, and hath given *us* everlasting consolation and good hope through grace, 17. Comfort your hearts, and stablish you in every good word and work.

1 Tim. 2:3. For this *is* good and acceptable in the sight of God our Saviour; 4. Who will have all men to be saved, and to come unto the knowledge of the truth.

1 Tim. 4:10. Therefore we both labour and suffer reproach, because we trust in the living God, who is the Saviour of all men, specially of those that believe.

2 Tim. 1:9. Who hath saved us, and called *us* with an holy calling, not according to

our works, but according to his own purpose and grace, which was given us in Christ Jesus before the world began,

Tit. 1:2. In hope of eternal life, which God, that cannot lie, promised before the world began: 3. But hath in due times manifested his word through preaching, which is committed unto me according to the commandment of God our Saviour;

Tit. 2:10. Not purloining, but shewing all good fidelity ; that they may adorn the doctrine of God our Saviour in all things. 11. For the grace of God that bringeth salvation hath appeared to all men,

Tit. 3:4. After that the kindness and love of God our Saviour toward man appeared, 5. Not by works of righteousness which we have done, but according to his mercy he saved us,

1 Pet. 1:5. Who are kept by the power of God through faith unto salvation ready to be revealed in the last time.

1 John 4:9. In this was manifested the love of God toward us, because that God sent his only begotten Son into the world, that we might live through him. 10. Herein is love, not that we loved God, but that he loved us, and sent his Son *to be* the propitiation for our sins.

1 John 5:11. And this is the record, that God hath given to us eternal life, and this life is in his Son.

Rev. 7:10. Salvation to our God which sitteth upon the throne, and unto the Lamb.

Rev. 19:1. Salvation, and glory, and honour, and power, unto the Lord our God :

See Preserver, above.

SELF-EXISTENT: Ex. 3:14. And God said unto Moses, I AM THAT I AM : and he said, Thus shalt thou say unto the children of Israel, I AM hath sent me unto you.

Deut. 32:40. For I lift up my hand to heaven, and say, I live for ever.

Job 35:6. If thou sinnest, what doest thou against him ? or *if* thy transgressions be multiplied, what doest thou unto him ? 7. If thou be righteous, what givest thou him ? or what receiveth he of thine hand ? 8. Thy wickedness *may hurt* a man as thou *art;* and thy righteousness *may profit* the son of man.

Isa. 44:6. Thus saith the Lord the King of Israel, and his redeemer the Lord of hosts ; I *am* the first, and I *am* the last; and beside me *there is* no God.

Jer. 10:10. But the Lord *is* the true God, he *is* the living God, and an everlasting king :

John 5:26. For as the Father hath life in himself ; so hath he given to the Son to have life in himself ;

Acts 17:24. God that made the world and all things therein, seeing that he is Lord of heaven and earth, dwelleth not in temples made with hands : 25. Neither is worshipped with men's hands, as though he

needed any thing, seeing he giveth to all life, and breath, and all things ;

See Eternity of, above.

SOVEREIGN: Gen. 14:18. And Melchizedek king of Salem brought forth bread and wine : and he *was* the priest of the most high God. [*v. 22.*] 19. And he blessed him, and said, Blessed *be* Abram of the most high God, possessor of heaven and earth : 20. And blessed be the most high God, which hath delivered thine enemies into thy hand.

Gen. 24:3. And I will make thee swear by the Lord, the God of heaven, and the God of the earth,

Ex. 8:22. To the end thou mayest know that I *am* the Lord in the midst of the earth.

Ex. 9:29. The thunder shall cease, neither shall there be any more hail ; that thou mayest know how that the earth *is* the Lord's.

Josh 3:11.

Ex. 15:18. The Lord shall reign for ever and ever.

Ex. 18:11. Now I know that the Lord *is* greater than all gods : for in the thing wherein they dealt proudly *he was* above them.

Num. 27:16. Let the Lord, the God of the spirits of all flesh, set a man over the congregation,

Deut. 2:19. I will not give thee of the land of the children of Ammon *any* possession ; because I have given it unto the children of Lot *for* a possession.

Deut. 4:39. Know therefore this day, and consider *it* in thine heart, that the Lord he *is* God in heaven above, and upon the earth beneath : *there is* none else.

Deut. 10:14. The heaven and the heaven of heavens *is* the Lord's thy God, the earth *also*, with all that therein *is*. 17. The Lord your God *is* God of gods, and Lord of lords, a great God, a mighty, and a terrible, which regardeth not persons, nor taketh reward. Ex. 19:5.

Deut. 32:8. When the Most High divided to the nations their inheritance, when he separated the sons of Adam, he set the bounds of the people according to the number of the children of Israel. 39. See now that I, *even* I, *am* he, and *there is* no god with me : I kill, and I make alive ; I wound, and I heal : neither *is there any* that can deliver out of my hand. 41. If I whet my glittering sword, and mine hand take hold on judgment ; I will render vengeance to mine enemies, and will reward them that hate me. 42. I will make mine arrows drunk with blood, and my sword shall devour flesh ; *and that* with the blood of the slain and of the captives, from the beginning of revenges upon the enemy. 43. Rejoice, O ye nations, *with* his people : for he will avenge the blood of his servants, and will render vengeance to his adversaries, and will be merciful unto his land, *and* to his people.

Josh. 2:11. The Lord your God, he *is* God in heaven above, and in earth beneath.

Josh. 3:11. Behold, the ark of the covenant

of the Lord of all the earth passeth over before you into Jordan.

1 Sam. 2:6. The LORD killeth, and maketh alive: he bringeth down to the grave, and bringeth up. 7. The LORD maketh poor, and maketh rich: he bringeth low, and lifteth up. 8. He raiseth up the poor out of the dust, *and* lifteth up the beggar from the dunghill, to set *them* among princes, and to make them inherit the throne of glory: for the pillars of the earth *are* the LORD's, and he hath set the world upon them.

2 Kin. 19:15. And Hezekiah prayed before the LORD, and said, O LORD God of Israel, which dwelleth *between* the cherubims, thou art the God, *even* thou alone, of all the kingdoms of the earth; thou hast made heaven and earth.

1 Chr. 29:11. Thine, O LORD, *is* the greatness, and the power, and the glory, and the victory, and the majesty: for all *that is* in the heaven and in the earth *is thine;* thine *is* the kingdom, O LORD, and thou art exalted as head above all. 12. Both riches and honour *come* of thee, and thou reignest over all; and in thine hand *is* power and might; and in thine hand *it is* to make great, and to give strength unto all.

2 Chr. 20:6. O LORD God of our fathers, *art* not thou God in heaven? and rulest *not* thou over all the kingdoms of the heathen? and in thine hand *is there not* power and might, so that none is able to withstand thee?

Neh. 9:6. Thou, *even* thou, *art* LORD alone; thou hast made heaven, the heaven of heavens, with all their host, the earth, and all *things* that *are* therein, the seas, and all that *is* therein, and thou preservest them all; and the host of heaven worshippeth thee.

Job 9:12. Behold, he taketh away, who can hinder him? who will say unto him, What doest thou?

Job 12:9. Who knoweth not in all these that the hand of the LORD hath wrought this? 10. In whose hand *is* the soul of every living thing, and the breath of all mankind. 16. With him *is* strength and wisdom: the deceived and the deceiver *are* his. 17. He leadeth counsellors away spoiled, and maketh the judges fools.

Job 25:2. Dominion and fear *are* with him, he maketh peace in his high places.

Job 33:13. Why dost thou strive against him? for he giveth not account of any of his matters.

Job 34:13. Who hath given him a charge over the earth? or who hath disposed the whole world? 24. He shall break in pieces mighty men without number, and set others in their stead. 33. *Should it be* according to thy mind? he will recompense it, whether thou refuse, or whether thou choose;

Job 36:23. Who hath enjoined him his way? or who can say, Thou hast wrought iniquity? *vs.* 1-33.

Job 41:11. *Whatsoever is* under the whole heaven is mine.

Psa. 10:16. The LORD *is* King for ever and ever: the heathen are perished out of his land.

Psa. 22:28. The kingdom *is* the LORD's: and he *is* the governor among the nations. 29. All *they that be* fat upon earth shall eat and worship: all they that go down to the dust shall bow before him: and none can keep alive his own soul.

Psa. 24:1. The earth *is* the LORD's, and the fulness thereof; the world, and they that dwell therein. 10. Who is this King of glory? The LORD of hosts, he *is* the King of glory. 1 Cor. 10:26.

Psa. 29:10. The LORD sitteth upon the flood; yea, the LORD sitteth King for ever.

Psa. 44:4. Thou art my King, O God: command deliverances for Jacob.

Psa. 47:2. The LORD most high *is* terrible; *he is* a great King over all the earth. 3. He shall subdue the people under us, and the nations under our feet. 7. God *is* the King of all the earth: sing ye praises with understanding. 8. God reigneth over the heathen: God sitteth upon the throne of his holiness.

Psa. 50:10. Every beast of the forest *is* mine, *and* the cattle upon a thousand hills. 11. I know all the fowls of the mountains: and the wild beasts of the field *are* mine. 12. If I were hungry, I would not tell thee: for the world *is* mine, and the fulness thereof.

Psa. 59:13. Let them know that God ruleth in Jacob unto the ends of the earth.

Psa. 65:5. O God of our salvation; *who art* the confidence of all the ends of the earth, and of them that are afar off *upon* the sea:

Psa. 66:7. He ruleth by his power for ever; his eyes behold the nations: let not the rebellious exalt themselves.

Psa. 67:4. O let the nations be glad and sing for joy: for thou shalt judge the people righteously, and govern the nations upon earth.

Psa. 74:12. For God *is* my King of old, working salvation in the midst of the earth.

Psa. 75:6. Promotion *cometh* neither from the east, nor from the west, nor from the south. 7. But God *is* the judge: he putteth down one, and setteth up another.

Psa. 76:11. Vow, and pay unto the LORD your God: let all that be round about him bring presents unto him that ought to be feared. 12. He shall cut off the spirit of princes: *he is* terrible to the kings of the earth.

Psa. 82:1. God standeth in the congregation of the mighty; he judgeth among the gods. 8. Arise, O God, judge the earth: for thou shalt inherit all nations.

Psa. 83:18. That *men* may know that thou, whose name alone *is* Jehovah, *art* the most high over all the earth.

Psa. 89:11. The heavens *are* thine, the earth also *is* thine: as *for* the world and the fulness thereof, thou hast founded them. 18. The LORD *is* our defence; and the Holy One of Israel *is* our king.

Psa. 93:1. The LORD reigneth, he is clothed

with majesty; the LORD is clothed with strength, *wherewith* he hath girded himself: the world also is stablished, that it cannot be moved. 2. Thy throne *is* established of old: thou *art* from everlasting.

Psa. 95:3. The LORD *is* a great God, and a great King above all gods. 4. In his hand *are* the deep places of the earth: the strength of the hills *is* his also. 5. The sea *is* his, and he made it: and his hands formed the dry *land.*

Psa. 96:10. Say among the heathen *that* the LORD reigneth: the world also shall be established that it shall not be moved: he shall judge the people righteously.

Psa. 97:1. The LORD reigneth; let the earth rejoice; let the multitude of isles be glad *thereof.* 2. Righteousness and judgment *are* the habitation of his throne. [*vs.* 5,9.] 9. Thou, LORD, *art* high above all the earth: thou art exalted far above all gods.

Psa. 98:6. With trumpets and sound of cornet make a joyful noise before the LORD, the King.

Psa. 99:1. The LORD reigneth; let the people tremble:

Psa. 103:19. The LORD hath prepared his throne in the heavens; and his kingdom ruleth over all.

Psa. 105:7. He *is* the LORD, our God: his judgments *are* in all the earth.

Psa. 113:4. The LORD *is* high above all nations, *and* his glory above the heavens.

Psa. 115:3. Our God *is* in the heavens: he hath done whatsoever he hath pleased. 16. The heaven, *even* the heavens, *are* the LORD's: but the earth hath he given to the children of men.

Psa. 135:5. For I know that the LORD *is* great, and *that* our Lord *is* above all g ds. 6. Whatsoever the LORD pleased, *that* did he in heaven, and in earth, in the seas, and all deep places.

Psa. 136:2. O give thanks unto the God of gods: for his mercy *endureth* for ever. 3. O give thanks to the Lord of lords: for his mercy *endureth* for ever.

Psa. 145:11. They shall speak of the glory of thy kingdom, and talk of thy power; 12. To make known to the sons of men his mighty acts, and the glorious majesty of his kingdom. 13. Thy kingdom *is* an everlasting kingdom, and thy dominion *endureth* throughout all generations.

Psa. 146:10. The LORD shall reign for ever, *even* thy God, O Zion, unto all generations. Isa. 52:7.

Eccl. 9:1. For all this I considered in my heart even to declare all this, that the righteous, and the wise, and their works, *are* in the hand of God:

Isa. 24:23. The LORD of hosts shall reign in mount Zion, and in Jerusalem, and before his ancients gloriously.

Isa. 33:22. For the LORD *is* our judge, the LORD *is* our lawgiver, the LORD *is* our King; he will save us.

Isa. 37:16. O LORD of hosts, God of Israel, that dwellest *between* the cherubims, thou *art* the God, *even* thou alone, of all the kingdoms of the earth: thou hast made heaven and earth.

Isa. 40:22. He that sitteth upon the circle of the earth, and the inhabitants thereof *are* as grasshoppers; 23. That bringeth the princes to nothing; he maketh the judges of the earth as vanity.

Isa. 43:15. I *am* the LORD, your Holy One, the creator of Israel, your King.

Isa. 44:6. Thus saith the LORD the King of Israel, and his redeemer the LORD of hosts: I *am* the first, and I *am* the last; and beside me *there is* no God.

Isa. 45:7. I form the light, and create darkness: I make peace, and create evil: I the LORD do all these *things.* 23. I have sworn by myself, the word is gone out of my mouth *in* righteousness, and shall not return, That unto me every knee shall bow, every tongue shall swear.

Isa. 54:5. For thy Maker *is* thine husband; The LORD of hosts is his name; and thy Redeemer the Holy One of Israel; The God of the whole earth shall he be called.

Jer. 10:10. The LORD *is* the true God, he *is* the living God, and an everlasting king: at his wrath the earth shall tremble, and the nations shall not be able to abide his indignation.

Jer. 18:6. O house of Israel, cannot I do with you as this potter? saith the LORD. Behold, as the clay *is* in the potter's hand, so *are* ye in mine hand, *vs.* 1–23.

Jer. 27:5. I have made the earth, the man and the beast that *are* upon the ground, by my great power and by my outstretched arm, and have given it unto whom it seemed meet unto me. 6. And now have I given all these lands into the hand of Nebuchadnezzar the king of Babylon, my servant; and the beasts of the field have I given him also to serve him. *v.* 7; Jer. 32:27,28.

Lam. 3:37. Who *is* he *that* saith, and it cometh to pass, *when* the Lord commanded *it* not? 38. Out of the mouth of the most High proceedeth not evil and good?

Lam. 5:19. Thou, O LORD, remainest for ever; thy throne from generation to generation.

Ezek. 16:50. And they were haughty, and committed abomination before me: therefore I took them away as I saw *good.*

Ezek. 17:24. All the trees of the field shall know that I the LORD have brought down the high tree, have exalted the low tree, have dried up the green tree, and have made the dry tree to flourish: I the LORD have spoken and have done *it.*

Ezek. 18:4. Behold, all souls are mine; as the soul of the father, so also the soul of the son is mine:

Dan. 2:20. Blessed be the name of God for ever and ever: for wisdom and might are his: 21. And he changeth the times and the seasons: he removeth kings, and setteth up kings: 47. The king answered unto Daniel, and said, Of a truth *it is*, that your God *is* a God of gods, and a Lord of kings,

Dan. 4:3. His kingdom *is* an everlasting kingdom, and his dominion *is* from generation to generation. 17. The most High ruleth in the kingdom of men, and giveth it to whoms ever he will, and setteth up over it the basest of men. 25. Thy dwelling shall be with the beasts of the field, . . . till thou know that the most High ruleth in the kingdom of men, and giveth it to whomsoever he will. 35. All the inhabitants of the earth *are* reputed as nothing: and he doeth according to his will in the army of heaven, and *among* the inhabitants of the earth: and none can stay his hand, or say unto him, What doest thou? 37. I Nebuchadnezzar praise and extol and honour the King of heaven, all whose works *are* truth, and his ways judgment: and those that walk in pride he is able to abase. *v.* 34.

Dan. 5:18. O thou king, the most high God gave Nebuchadnezzar thy father a kingdom, and majesty, and glory, and honour: 26. MENE; God hath numbered thy kingdom, and finished it. 27. TEKEL; Thou art weighed in the balances, and art found wanting. 28. PERES; Thy kingdom is divided, and given to the Medes and Persians.

Dan. 6:26. He *is* the living God, and stedfast for ever, and his kingdom *that* which shall not be destroyed, and his dominion *shall be even* unto the end.

Mic. 4:7. The LORD shall reign over them in mount Zion from henceforth, even for e er. 13. I will consecrate their gain unto the LORD, and their substance unto the Lord of the whole earth.

Hag. 2:8. The silver *is* mine, and the gold *is* mine, saith the LORD of hosts.

Mal. 1:14. I *am* a great King, saith the LORD of hosts, and my name *is* dreadful among the heathen.

Matt. 6:10. Thy kingdom come. Thy will be done in earth, as *it is* in heaven. 13. ¹ Thine is the kingdom, and the power, and the glory. for ever. [¹ Omitted in R. V.]

Matt. 11:25. At that time Jesus answered and said, I thank thee, O Father, Lord of heaven and earth, Luke 10:21.

Matt. 20:15. Is it not lawful for me to do what I will with mine own? Is thine eye evil, because I am good?

Luke 1:53. He hath filled the hungry with good things; and the rich he hath sent empty away.

John 10:29. My Father, which gave *them* me, is greater than all; and no *man* is able to pluck *them* out of my Father's hand.

John 19:11. Jesus answered, Thou couldest have no power *at all* against me, except it were given thee from above:

Acts 17:24. God that made the world and all things therein, seeing that he is Lord of heaven and earth, dwelleth not in temples made with hands; 25. Neither is worshipped with men's hands, as though he needed any thing, seeing he giveth to all life, and breath, and all things; 26. And hath made of one blood all nations of men for to dwell on all the face of the earth, and hath determined the times before appointed, and the bounds of their habitation;

Rom. 9:19. Thou wilt say then unto me, Why doth he yet find fault? For who hath resisted his will?

Rom. 14:11. *As* I live, saith the Lord, every knee shall bow to me, and every tongue shall confess to God.

Eph. 4:6. One God and Father of all, who *is* above all, and through all, and in you all.

1 Tim. 6:15. Which in his times he shall shew, *who is* the blessed and only Potentate, the King of kings, and Lord of lords; 16. Who only hath immortality, dwelling in the light which no man can approach unto; whom no man hath seen, nor can see: to whom *be* honour and power everlasting.

Heb. 1:3. Who being the brightness of *his* glory, and the express image of his person, and upholding all things by the word of his power, when he had by himself purged our sins, sat down on the right hand of the Majesty on high;

Jas. 4:12. There is one lawgiver, who is able to save and to destroy:

Rev. 1:6. And hath made us kings and priests unto God and his Father; to him *be* glory and dominion for ever and ever.

Rev. 4:11. Thou hast created all things, and for thy pleasure they are and were created.

Rev. 11:4. These are the two olive trees, and the two candlesticks standing before the God of the earth. 13. And the remnant were affrighted, and gave glory to the God of heaven. 17. Saying, We give thee thanks, O Lord God Almighty, which art, and wast, and art to come; because thou hast taken to thee thy great power, and hast reigned.

Rev. 19:6. And I heard as it were the voice of a great multitude, and as the voice of many waters, and as the voice of mighty thunderings, saying, Alleluia: for the Lord God omnipotent reigneth.

See GOD, POWER OF.

A SPIRIT: Num. 16:22. And they fell upon their faces, and said, O God, the God of the spirits of all flesh, Num. 27:16.

John 4:24. God *is* a Spirit: and they that worship him must worship *him* in spirit and in truth.

See HOLY SPIRIT; LIFE, SPIRITUAL.

TRUTH: Num. 23:19. God *is* not a man, that he should lie; neither the son of man, that he should repent: hath he said, and shall he not do *it?* or hath he spoken, and shall he not make it good?

Deut. 32:4. *He is* the Rock, his work *is* perfect: for all his ways *are* judgment: a God of truth and without iniquity, just and right *is* he.

1 Sam. 15:29. And also the Strength of Israel will not lie nor repent: for he *is* not a man, that he should repent.

Psa. 25:10. All the paths of the LORD *are*

mercy and truth unto such as keep his covenant and his testimonies.

Psa. 31:5. Into thine hand I commit my spirit: thou hast redeemed me, O LORD God of truth.

Psa. 33:4. For the word of the LORD *is* right; and all his works *are done* in truth.

Psa. 40:10. I have not hid thy righteousness within my heart; I have declared thy faithfulness and thy salvation: I have not concealed thy lovingkindness and thy truth from the great congregation.

Psa. 43:3. O send out thy light and thy truth: let them lead me; let them bring me unto thy holy hill, and to thy tabernacles.

Psa. 57:3. God shall send forth his mercy and his truth. 10. For thy mercy *is* great unto the heavens, and thy truth unto the clouds.

Psa. 71:22. I will also praise thee with the psaltery, *even* thy truth, O my God:

Psa. 86:11. Teach me thy way, O LORD; I will walk in thy truth: 15. But thou, O Lord, *art* a God full of compassion, and gracious, longsuffering, and plenteous in mercy and truth.

Psa. 89:14. Mercy and truth shall go before thy face.

Psa. 91:4. He shall cover thee with his feathers, and under his wings shalt thou trust: his truth *shall be thy* shield and buckler.

Psa. 100:5. For the LORD *is* good; his mercy *is* everlasting; and his truth *endureth* to all generations.

Psa. 117:2. The truth of the LORD *endureth* for ever.

Psa. 108:4. Thy truth *reacheth* unto the clouds.

Psa. 132:11. The LORD hath sworn *in* truth unto David; he will not turn from it;

Psa. 138:2. I will worship toward thy holy temple, and praise thy name for thy lovingkindness and for thy truth: for thou hast magnified thy word above all thy name.

Psa. 146:6. Which made heaven, and earth, the sea, and all that therein *is:* which keepeth truth for ever

Isa. 25:1. *Thy* counsels of old *are* faithfulness *and* truth.

Isa. 65:16. That he who blesseth himself in the earth shall bless himself in the God of truth; and he that sweareth in the earth shall swear by the God of truth; because the former troubles are forgotten, and because they are hid from mine eyes.

Jer. 10:10. The LORD *is* the true God, he *is* the living God, and an everlasting king ·

Dan. 4:37. Now I Nebuchadnezzar praise and extol and honour the King of heaven, all whose works *are* truth,

Dan. 9:13. As *it is* written in the law of Moses, all this evil is come upon us: yet made we not our prayer before the LORD our God, that we might turn from our iniquities, and understand thy truth.

John 8:26. But he that sent me is true; and I speak to the world those things which I have heard of him.

John 17:17. Sanctify them through thy truth: thy word is truth. 19. For their sakes I sanctify myself, that they also might be sanctified through the truth.

Rom. 3:4. Let God be true, but every man a liar; 7. If the truth of God hath more abounded through my lie unto his glory; why yet am I also judged as a sinner?

Tit. 1:2. In hope of eternal life, which God, that cannot lie, promised before the world began;

Rev. 6:10. And they cried with a loud voice, saying, How long, O Lord, holy and true, dost thou not judge and avenge our blood on them that dwell on the earth?

Rev. 15:3. And they sing . . . the song of the Lamb, saying, Great and marvellous *are* thy works, Lord God Almighty; just and true *are* thy ways, thou King of ¹ saints. [¹ R.V. the ages]

See FAITHFULNESS OF, JUDGE AND HIS JUSTICE, RIGHTEOUSNESS OF, above. See also TRUTH.

UBIQUITOUS: 1 Kin. 8:27. Will God indeed dwell on the earth? behold, the heaven and heaven of heavens cannot contain thee; how much less this house that I have builded? 2 Chr. 2:6; Acts 7:48,49.

Psa. 139:3. Thou compassest my path and my lying down, 5. Thou hast beset me behind and before, and laid thine hand upon me. 7. Whither shall I go from thy spirit? or whither shall I flee from thy presence? 8. If I ascend up into heaven, thou *art* there: if I make my bed in hell, behold thou *art there.* 9. *If* I take the wings of the morning, *and* dwell in the uttermost parts of the sea; 10. Even there shall thy hand lead me, and thy right hand shall hold me.

Jer. 23:23. *Am* I a God at hand, saith the LORD, and not a God afar off? 24. Can any hide himself in secret places that I shall not see him? saith the LORD. Do not I fill heaven and earth? saith the LORD.

See above ETERNITY OF, INFINITE, OMNIPRESENT, POWER OF, PRESENCE OF, PROVIDENCE OF.

UNCHANGEABLE. See IMMUTABLE.

UNITY OF: Deut. 6:4. Hear, O Israel: The LORD our God *is* one LORD: Mark 12:29.

1 Kin. 8:60. That all the people of the earth may know that the LORD *is* God *and that there is* none else.

1 Kin. 20:28. Thus saith the LORD, Because the Syrians have said, The LORD *is* God of the hills, but he *is* not God of the valleys, therefore will I deliver all this great multitude into thine hand, and ye shall know that I *am* the LORD.

Isa. 42:8. I *am* the LORD; that *is* my name: and my glory will I not give to another, neither my praise to graven images.

Mark 12:29. And Jesus answered him, The first of all the commandments *is*, Hear, O Israel; The Lord our God is one Lord: 32. And the scribe said unto him, Well, Master, thou hast said the truth: for there is one God; and there is none other but he:

John 17:3. And this is life eternal, that they might know thee the only true

God, and Jesus Christ, whom thou hast sent.

1 Cor. 8:4. As concerning therefore the eating of those things that are offered in sacrifice unto idols, we know that an idol *is* nothing in the world, and that *there is* none other God but one. 6. But to us *there is but* one God, the Father, of whom *are* all things, and we in him; and one Lord Jesus Christ, by whom *are* all things, and we by him.

Gal. 3:20. Now a mediator is not *a mediator* of one, but God is one.

1 Tim. 2:5. For *there is* one God, and one mediator between God and men, the man Christ Jesus.

Jas. 2:19. Thou believest that there is one God; thou doest well: the devils also believe, and tremble.

UNSEARCHABLE: Deut. 29:29. The secret *things belong* unto the LORD our God:

Judg. 13:18. And the angel of the LORD said unto him, Why askest thou thus after my name, seeing it *is* secret? Gen. 32:29.

1 Kin. 8:12. The LORD said that he would dwell in the thick darkness. 27. Will God indeed dwell on the earth? behold, the heaven and heaven of heavens cannot contain thee; how much less this house that I have builded? 2 Chr. 2:6; 6:1,18.

Job 5:8. Unto God would I commit my cause: 9. Which doeth great things and unsearchable; marvellous things without number: Job. 9:10.

Job 11:7. Canst thou by searching find out God? canst thou find out the Almighty unto perfection? 8. *It is* as high as heaven; what canst thou do? deeper than hell; what canst thou know? 9. The measure thereof *is* longer than the earth, and broader than the sea.

Job 26:9. He holdeth back the face of his throne, *and* spreadeth his cloud upon it. 14. Lo, these *are* parts of his ways: but how little a portion is heard of him? but the thunder of his power who can understand?

Job 36:26. Behold, God *is* great, and we know *him* not, neither can the number of his years be searched out.

Job 37:5. Great things doeth he, which we cannot comprehend. 23. *Touching* the Almighty, we cannot find him out:

Psa. 77:19. Thy way *is* in the sea, and thy path in the great waters, and thy footsteps are not known.

Psa. 92:5. O LORD, how great are thy works! *and* thy thoughts are very deep.

Psa. 97:2. Clouds and darkness *are* round about him:

Psa. 139:6. *Such* knowledge *is* too wonderful for me; it is high, I cannot *attain* unto it.

Psa. 145:3. Great *is* the LORD, and greatly to be praised; and his greatness *is* unsearchable.

Prov. 25:2. *It is* the glory of God to conceal a thing:

Prov. 30:4. Who hath ascended up into heaven, or descended? who hath gathered the wind in his fists? who hath bound the waters in a garment? who hath established all the ends of the earth? what *is* his name, and what *is* his son's name, if thou canst tell?

Eccl. 3:11. He hath made every *thing* beautiful in his time: also he hath set the world in their heart, so that no man can find out the work that God maketh from the beginning to the end.

Eccl. 7:24. That which is far off, and exceeding deep, who can find it out?

Eccl. 11:5. As thou knowest not what *is* the way of the spirit, *nor* how the bones *do grow* in the womb of her that is with child: even so thou knowest not the works of God who maketh all.

Isa. 40:28. *There is* no searching of his understanding.

Isa. 45:15. Verily thou *art* a God that hidest thyself, O God of Israel, the Saviour.

Isa. 55:8. For my thoughts *are* not your thoughts, neither *are* your ways my ways, saith the LORD. 9. For *as* the heavens are higher than the earth, so are my ways higher than your ways, and my thoughts than your thoughts.

Jer. 23:24. Do not I fill heaven and earth?

Nah. 1:3. The LORD *hath* his way in the whirlwind and in the storm, and the clouds *are* the dust of his feet.

Matt. 11:27. No man knoweth the Son, but the Father; neither knoweth any man the Father, save the Son, and *he* to whomsoever the Son will reveal *him*.

Rom. 11:33. O the depth of the riches both of the wisdom and knowledge of God! how unsearchable *are* his judgments, and his ways past finding out! 34. For who hath known the mind of the Lord? or who hath been his counsellor?

1 Cor. 2:10. The Spirit searcheth all things, yea, the deep things of God. 11. For what man knoweth the things of a man, save the spirit of man which is in him? even so the things of God knoweth no man, but the Spirit of God.

1 Cor. 2:16. For who hath known the mind of the Lord, that he may instruct him?

Eph. 3:8. Unto me, who am less than the least of all saints, is this grace given, that I should preach among the Gentiles the unsearchable riches of Christ;

See MYSTERIES.

VOICE OF: See ANTHROPOMORPHISM.

WISDOM OF: Ezra 7:25. And thou, Ezra, after the wisdom of thy God, that *is* in thine hand, set magistrates and judges,

Job 9:4. *He is* wise in heart, and mighty in strength:

Job 12:13. With him *is* wisdom and strength, he hath counsel and understanding. 16. With him *is* strength and wisdom: the deceived and the deceiver *are* his.

Psa. 104:24. O Lord, how manifold are thy works! in wisdom hast thou made them all: the earth is full of thy riches.

Psa. 136:5. Him that by wisdom made the heavens:

Psa. 147:5. Great *is* our Lord, and of great power: his understanding *is* infinite.

Prov. 3:19. The LORD by wisdom hath founded the earth; by understanding hath he established the heavens. 20. By his knowledge the depths are broken up, and the clouds drop down the dew.

Prov. 8:12. I wisdom dwell with prudence, and find out knowledge of witty inventions. 22. The LORD possessed me in the beginning of his way, before his works of old. 27. When he prepared the heavens, I *was* there; when he set a compass upon the face of the depth: 28. When he established the clouds above: when he strengthened the fountains of the deep: 29. When he gave to the sea his decree, that the waters should not pass his commandment: when he appointed the foundations of the earth: 30. Then I was by him, *as* one brought up *with him:* and I was daily *his* delight, rejoicing always before him; 31. Rejoicing in the habitable part of his earth; and my delights *were* with the sons of men.

Isa. 31:2. Yet he also *is* wise, and will bring evil, and will not call back his words:

Jer. 10:7. Among all the wise *men* of the nations, and in all their kingdoms, *there is* none like unto thee. 12. He hath made the earth by his power, he hath established the world by his wisdom, and hath stretched out the heavens by his discretion. Jer. 51:15.

Dan. 2:20. Wisdom and might are his: 21. He giveth wisdom unto the wise, and knowledge to them that know understanding: 22. He revealeth the deep and secret things: he knoweth what *is* in the darkness, and the light dwelleth with him. 28. There is a God in heaven that revealeth secrets, and maketh known to the king Nebuchadnezzar what shall be in the latter days.

Rom. 16:27. To God only wise, *be* glory through Jesus Christ for ever.

1 Cor. 1:24. But unto them which are called, both Jews and Greeks, Christ the power of God, and the wisdom of God. 25. The foolishness of God is wiser than men;

Eph. 1:8. He hath abounded toward us in all wisdom and prudence;

Eph. 3:10. That now unto the principalities and powers in heavenly *places* might be known by the church the manifold wisdom of God,

1 Tim. 1:17. Unto the King eternal, [1]immortal, invisible, the only wise God.

[1 R. V. incorruptible]

Rev. 7:12. Blessing, and glory, and wisdom, and thanksgiving, and honour, and power, and might, *be* unto our God for ever and ever.

See KNOWLEDGE OF, OMNISCIENT, above.

WORKS OF: Gen. 1:10. And God saw that *it was* good. *vs.* 18,21,25.

Deut. 32:4. *He is* the Rock, his work *is* perfect:

Psa. 26:7. That I may publish with the voice of thanksgiving, and tell of all thy wondrous works.

Psa. 33:4. For the word of the LORD *is* right; and all his works *are done* in truth.

Psa. 40:5. Many, O LORD my God, *are* thy wonderful works *which* thou hast done, and thy thoughts *which are* to us-ward: they cannot be reckoned up in order unto thee: *if* I would declare and speak *of them,* they are more than can be numbered.

Psa. 66:3. Say unto God, How terrible *art thou in* thy works! through the greatness of thy power shall thine enemies submit themselves unto thee.

Psa. 75:1. Unto thee, O God, do we give thanks, *unto thee* do we give thanks: for *that* thy name is near thy wondrous works declare.

Psa. 86:8. Among the gods *there is* none like unto thee, O Lord; neither *are there any works* like unto thy works.

Psa. 92:4. For thou, LORD, hast made me glad through thy work: I will triumph in the works of thy hands. 5. O LORD, how great are thy works! *and* thy thoughts are very deep.

Psa. 111:2. The works of the LORD *are* great, sought out of all them that have pleasure therein. 4. He hath made his wonderful works to be remembered: 6. He hath shewed his people the power of his works,

Psa. 118:17. I shall not die, but live, and declare the works of the LORD.

Psa. 136:4. To him who alone doeth great wonders: for his mercy *endureth* for ever. 5. To him that by wisdom made the heavens: for his mercy *endureth* for ever. 6. To him that stretched out the earth above the waters: for his mercy *endureth* for ever. 7. To him that made great lights: for his mercy *endureth* for ever: 8. The sun to rule by day: for his mercy *endureth* for ever: 9. The moon and stars to rule by night: for his mercy *endureth* for ever. *vs.* 1–26.

Psa. 139:14. I will praise thee; for I am fearfully *and* wonderfully made: marvellous *are* thy works: and *that* my soul knoweth right well.

Eccl. 3:11. He hath made every *thing* beautiful in his time: also he hath set the world in their heart, so that no man can find out the work that God maketh from the beginning to the end. 14. I know that, whatsoever God doeth, it shall be for ever: nothing can be put to it, nor any thing taken from it: and God doeth *it,* that *men* should fear before him.

See Job 9; and chapters 37–41; Psalms 8; 19; 89; 104; 111; 145; 147; 148; Jer. 10:12.

See CREATION; GOD, CREATOR; WORKS.

GODLESSNESS. Deut. 7:10. He will not be slack to him that hateth him, he will repay him to his face.

Deut. 32:15. He forsook God *which* made

him, and lightly esteemed the Rock of his salvation.

1 Sam. 2:30. They that despise me shall be lightly esteemed.

Job 8:11. Can the flag grow without water? 12. Whilst it *is* yet in his greenness, *and* not cut down, it withereth before any *other* herb. 13. So *are* the paths of all that forget God;

Job 35:10. None saith, Where *is* God my maker, who giveth songs in the night;

Psa. 2:2. The kings of the earth set themselves, and the rulers take counsel together, against the LORD, and against his anointed, 4. He that sitteth in the heavens shall laugh: the Lord shall have them in derision.

Psa. 9:17. The wicked shall be turned into hell, *and* all the nations that forget God.

Psa. 10:4. The wicked, through the pride of his countenance, will not seek *after God:* God *is* not in all his thoughts.

Psa. 14:2. The LORD looked down from heaven upon the children of men, to see if there were any that did understand, *and* seek God. 3. They are all gone aside, Psa. 53:2,3; Rom. 3:11,18.

Psa. 28:5. Because they regard not the works of the LORD, nor the operation of his hands, he shall destroy them, and not build them up. Isa. 5:12.

Psa. 36:1. The trangression of the wicked saith within my heart, *that there is* no fear of God before his eyes.

Psa. 50:22. Consider this, ye that forget God, lest I tear *you* in pieces, and *there be* none to deliver.

Psa. 52:7. Lo, *this is* the man *that* made not God his strength; but trusted in the abundance of his riches, *and* strengthened himself in his wickedness.

Psa. 53:4. Have the workers of iniquity no knowledge? who eat up my people *as* they eat bread: they have not called upon God.

Psa. 54:3. They have not set God before them.

Psa. 55:19. They have no changes, therefore they fear not God.

Psa. 86:14. The assemblies of violent *men* have sought after my soul; and have not set thee before them.

Prov. 14:2. He that walketh in his uprightness feareth the LORD: but *he that is* perverse in his ways despiseth him.

Isa. 1:3. The ox knoweth his owner, and the ass his master's crib: *but* Israel doth not know, my people doth not consider.

Isa. 17:10. Because thou hast forgotten the God of thy salvation, and hast not been mindful of the rock of thy strength, therefore shalt thou plant pleasant plants, and shalt set it with strange slips:

Isa. 22:11. Ye have not looked unto the maker thereof, neither had respect unto him that fashioned it long ago.

Isa. 30:1. Woe to the rebellious children, saith the LORD, that take counsel, but not of me; and that cover with a covering, but

not of my spirit, that they may add sin to sin: [*v. 2.*] 9. This *is* a rebellious people, lying children, children *that* will not hear the law of the LORD: 10. Which say to the seers, See not; and to the prophets, Prophesy not unto us right things, speak unto us smooth things, prophesy deceits: 11. Get you out of the way, turn aside out of the path, cause the Holy One of Israel to cease from before us. 12. Wherefore thus saith the Holy One of Israel, Because ye despise this word, and trust in oppression and perverseness, and stay thereon: 13. Therefore this iniquity shall be to you as a breach ready to fall, swelling out in a high wall, whose breaking cometh suddenly at an instant.

Isa. 31:1. Woe to them that go down to Egypt for help; and stay on horses, and trust in chariots, because *they are* many; and in horsemen, because they are very strong; but they look not unto the Holy One of Israel, neither seek the LORD!

Jer. 2:32. Can a maid forget her ornaments, *or* a bride her attire? yet my people have forgotten me days without number.

Dan. 5:23. But hast lifted up thyself against the Lord of heaven; . . . the God in whose hand thy breath *is*, and whose *are* all thy ways, hast thou not glorified:

Hos. 7:2. And they consider not in their hearts *that* I remember all their wickedness: now their own doings have beset them about; they are before my face. 3. They make the king glad with their wickedness, and the princes with their lies. 4. They *are* all adulterers, as an oven heated by the baker, *who* ceaseth from raising after he hath kneaded the dough, until it be leavened.

Mal. 2:17. Ye have wearied the LORD with your words. Yet ye say, Wherein have we wearied *him?* When ye say, Every one that doeth evil *is* good in the sight of the LORD, and he delighteth in them; or, Where *is* the God of judgment?

Mal. 3:8. Will a man rob God? Yet ye have robbed me. But ye say, Wherein have we robbed thee?

John 5:42. I know you, that ye have not the love of God in you. 44. How can ye believe, which receive honour one of another, and seek not the honour that *cometh* from God only?

John 15:23. He that hateth me, hateth my Father also. 24. But now have they both seen and hated both me and my Father. 25. They hated me without a cause.

Rom. 1:21. When they knew God, they glorified *him* not as God, neither were thankful; but became vain in their imaginations, and their foolish heart was darkened. 22. Professing themselves to be wise, they became fools, 28. As they did not like to retain God in *their* knowledge, God gave them over to a reprobate mind,

Rom. 8:6. For to be carnally minded *is* death; but to be spiritually minded *is* life and peace. 7. Because the carnal mind *is* enmity against God: for it is not subject to the law of God, neither indeed can be. 8. So then they that are in the flesh cannot please God.

Eph. 4:18. Having the understanding darkened, being alienated from the life of God through the ignorance that is in them, because of the blindness of their heart:

Col. 1:21. You, that were sometime alienated and enemies in *your* mind by wicked works,

Heb. 10:26. For if we sin wilfully after that we have received the knowledge of the truth, there remaineth no more sacrifice for sins, 27. But a certain fearful looking for of judgment and fiery indignation, which shall devour the adversaries.

Jas. 4:4. Know ye not that the friendship of the world is enmity with God? whosoever therefore will be a friend of the world is the enemy of God.

See IMPENITENCE; OBDURACY; PRAYERLESSNESS; REPROBACY; UNBELIEF; WICKED.

GODLINESS. See HOLINESS; RIGHTEOUSNESS.

GODLY. See RIGHTEOUS.

GODS. See IDOL; IDOLATRY; IMAGE.

GOG. 1. A Reubenite, 1 Chr. 5:4.

2. A Scythian prince. Prophecy against, Ezek. 38; 39; Rev. 20:8.

GOLAN, a town in Bashan. Given to Manasseh as a city of refuge, Deut. 4:43; Josh. 20:8. A Levitical city, Josh. 21:27; 1 Chr. 6:71.

GOLD. Exported from Havilah, Gen. 2: 11,12. From Ophir, 1 Kin. 9:28; 10:11; 1 Chr. 29:4; 2 Chr. 8:18; Job 22:24; Tarshish, 1 Kin. 22:48; Parvaim, 2 Chr. 3:6; Sheba, 1 Kin. 10: 10; 2 Chr. 9:9; Psa. 72:15; Uphaz, Jer. 10:9.

Refined, Job 28:19; 31:24; Prov. 8:19; 17:3; 27:21; Zech. 13:9; Mal. 3:3. Used in the arts: Beaten work, 2 Chr. 9:15; made into wire threads and wrought into embroidered tapestry, Ex. 39:3; apparel, Psa. 45:9,13; in ornamenting the priests' garments, Ex. 39; modeled into forms of fruits, Prov. 25:11; into ornaments, Gen. 24:22; Ex. 3:22; 11:2; 28:11; Num. 31:50,51; Song 1:10; 5:14; Ezek. 16:17; crowns made of, Ex. 25:25; 37:2-11; 39:30; Esth. 8:15; Psa. 21:3; Zech. 6:11; candlesticks made of, for the tabernacle, Ex. 25:31-38; 37:17-24; shields of, 1 Kin. 10:16,17; overlaying with, Ex. 25:11,13,24,28, with 1-40; 26:27,29; 30:5; 36:34,36,38; 37:2,4,11,15; 1 Kin. 6:20-22,28,30,32,35; bedsteads made of, Esth. 1:6. Wedge of, Josh. 7:21; Isa. 13:12.

Used as money, Gen. 44:8, with verse 1; 1 Chr. 21:25; Ezra 8:25-28; Isa. 13:17; 60:9; Ezek. 7:19; 28:4; Matt. 2:11; 10:9; Acts 3:6; 20:33; 1 Pet. 1:18. Solomon rich in, 1 Kin. 10:2,14,21.

Vessels and utensils made of, for the tabernacle, Ex. 25:26,29,38,39; 37:16; for the temple, 1 Chr. 18:11; 22:14,16; 29:2-7. Altar, lamps, and other articles made of, 1 Kin. 7:48,49-51; 2 Kin. 25:15; Jer. 52:19; Ezra 8:27; Dan. 5:3; see Overlaying with, above.

Belongs to God, Ezek. 16:17.

FIGURATIVE: Eccl. 12:6; Jer. 51:7; Lam. 4:1; 1 Cor. 3:12.

SYMBOLICAL: Dan. 2:32-45; Rev. 21:18,21.

See GOLDSMITH.

GOLDEN ALTAR. See ALTAR.

GOLDEN CANDLESTICK. See CANDLESTICK.

GOLDEN RULE. Lev. 19:18. Thou shalt love thy neighbour as thyself: I *am* the LORD. Rom. 13:9; Gal. 5:14.

Deut. 5:14. But the seventh day *is* the sabbath of the LORD thy God: *in it* thou shalt not do any work, thou, nor thy son, nor thy daughter, nor thy manservant, nor thy maidservant, nor thine ox, nor thine ass, nor any of thy cattle, nor thy stranger that *is* within thy gates; that thy manservant and thy maidservant may rest as well as thou. 15. And remember that thou wast a servant in the land of Egypt, and *that* the LORD thy God brought thee out thence through a mighty hand and by a stretched out arm: therefore the LORD thy God commanded thee to keep the sabbath day.

Matt. 7:12. Therefore all things whatsoever ye would that men should do to you, do ye even so to them: for this is the law and the prophets.

Luke 6:31. And as ye would that men should do to you, do ye also to them likewise.

GOLDSMITH, 2 Chr. 2:7,14; Neh. 3:8, 31,32; Isa. 40:19; 41:7; 46:6.

See GOLD.

GOLGOTHA, Hebrew name of the place where Jesus was crucified, Matt. 27:33; Mark 15:22; John 19:17.

See CALVARY.

GOLIATH, a giant champion of Gath. Defied armies of Israel and is slain by David, 1 Sam. 17; 21:9; 22:10. His sons, 2 Sam. 21:15-22; 1 Chr. 20:4-8.

GOMER. 1. Son of Japheth, Gen. 10:2,3; 1 Chr. 1:5,6.

2. A people descended from Gomer, Ezek. 38:6.

3. Wife, or concubine, of Hosea, Hos. 1:3.

GOMORRAH. One of the "cities of the plain," Gen. 10:19; 13:10. Its king defeated by Chedorlaomer, Gen. 14:2,8-11. Wickedness of, Gen. 18:20. Destroyed, Gen. 19:24-28; Deut. 29:23; 32:32; Isa. 1:9,10; 13:19; Jer. 23:14; 49:18; 50:40; Amos 4:11; Zeph. 2:9; Matt. 10:15; 1 Mark 6:11; Rom. 9:29; 2 Pet. 2:6; Jude 7.   [1 Reference to, omitted in R. V.]

GOOD AND EVIL. Choice between, by Adam and Eve, Gen. 3. Exhortation to choose between, Josh. 24:15. Conflict between, Rev. 16:13-21. Subjective conflict between, Rom. 7:9-25.

GONORRHEA, Lev. 15.

See DISEASES.

GOOD FOR EVIL. Matt. 5:44. But I say unto you, Love your enemies, bless them that curse you, do good to them that hate you, and pray for them which despitefully use you, and persecute you; 45. That ye may be the children of your Father which is in heaven: for he maketh his sun to rise on the evil and on the good, and sendeth rain on the just and on the unjust. 46. For if ye love them which love you, what reward have ye? do not even the publicans the same? 47. And if ye salute your brethren only, what do ye more *than others?* do not even the publicans so? 48. Be ye therefore perfect, even as your Father which is in heaven is perfect.

Luke 6:27. But I say unto you which hear, Love your enemies, do good to them which hate you, 28. Bless them that curse you, and pray for them which despitefully use you. 29. And unto him that smiteth thee on the *one* cheek offer also the other; and him that taketh away thy cloke forbid not *to take thy* coat also. 30. Give to every man that asketh of thee; and of him that taketh away thy goods ask *them* not again. 31. And as ye would that men should do to you, do ye also to them likewise. 32. For if ye love them which love you, what thank have ye? for sinners also love those that love them. 33. And if ye do good to them which do good to you, what thank have ye? for sinners also do even the same. 34. And if ye lend *to them* of whom ye hope to receive, what thank have ye? for sinners also lend to sinners, to receive as much again. 35. But love ye your enemies, and do good, and lend, hoping for nothing again; and your reward shall be great, and ye shall be the children of the Highest: for he is kind unto the unthankful and *to* the evil. 36. Be ye therefore merciful, as your Father also is merciful.

RETURNING: INSTANCES OF: Abraham, to Abimelech, Gen. 20:14–18. David, to Saul, 1 Sam. 24:17; 26. Elisha, to the Syrians, 2 Kin. 6:22,23. David, to his enemies, Psa. 35:12–14. Jesus, to his crucifiers, Luke 23:34. Stephen, Acts 7:60.

See GOLDEN RULE; EVIL FOR GOOD.

GOOD NEWS, Prov. 15:30; 25:25.

GOPHER WOOD, Noah's ark made of, Gen. 6:14.

GOSHEN. 1. A district in Egypt especially adapted to herds and flocks. Israelites dwelt in, Gen. 45:10; 46:28; 47. Exempted from plagues, Ex. 8:22; 9:26.

2. A town and district of Judah, Josh. 10: 41; 11:16; 15:51.

GOSPEL. Called GOSPEL OF THE KINGDOM, Matt. 4:23; 24:14; GOSPEL OF GOD, Rom. 1:1; 15:16; 1 Thess. 2:8; 1 Tim. 1:11; 1 Pet. 4: 17; GOSPEL OF JESUS CHRIST, Mark 1:1; GOSPEL OF CHRIST, Rom. 1:16; 1 Cor. 9:12,18; Gal. 1:7; Phil. 1:27; 1 Thess. 3:2; THE DISPENSATION OF THE GRACE OF GOD, Eph. 3:2; THE GRACE OF GOD, Acts 20:24; GOSPEL OF SALVATION, Eph. 1:13; GOSPEL OF PEACE, Eph. 6:15; THE KINGDOM OF GOD, Luke 16:16; GLORIOUS GOSPEL OF CHRIST, 2 Cor. 4:4; PREACHING OF JESUS CHRIST, Rom. 16:25; MYSTERY OF CHRIST, Eph. 3:4; MYSTERY OF THE GOSPEL, Eph. 6:19; WORD OF GOD, 1

Thess. 2:13; WORD OF CHRIST, Col. 3:16; WORD OF SALVATION, Acts 13:26; WORD OF RECONCILIATION, 2 Cor. 5:19; WORD OF TRUTH, Eph. 1:13; 2 Cor. 6:7; WORD OF FAITH, Rom. 10:8; WORD OF LIFE, Phil. 2:16; MINISTRATION OF THE SPIRIT, 2 Cor. 3:8; DOCTRINE ACCORDING TO GODLINESS, 1 Tim. 6:3; FORM OF SOUND WORDS, 2 Tim. 1:13.

Likened to a mustard seed, Matt. 13:31,32; Mark 4:30–33; Luke 13:18,19; good seed, Matt. 13:24–30,36–43; leaven, Matt. 13:33; a pearl of great price, Matt. 13:45,46; Luke 13:20,21; a treasure hidden in a field, Matt. 13:44; a householder, Matt. 20:1–16; a feast, Luke 14: 16–24.

UNCLASSIFIED SCRIPTURES RELATING TO: Psa. 46:4. *There is* a river, the streams whereof shall make glad the city of God, the holy *place* of the tabernacles of the Most High. 5. God *is* in the midst of her; she shall not be moved: God shall help her, *and that* right early.

Psa. 89:15. Blessed *is* the people that know the joyful sound:

Matt. 4:23. And Jesus went about all Galilee, teaching in their synagogues, and preaching the gospel of the kingdom, and healing all manner of sickness and all manner of disease among the people.

Matt. 11:4. Jesus answered and said unto them, Go and shew John again those things which ye do hear and see: 5. The blind receive their sight, and the lame walk, the lepers are cleansed, and the deaf hear, the dead are raised up, and the poor have the gospel preached to them. 6. And blessed is *he*, whosoever shall not be offended in me. Luke 7:22.

Matt. 13:17. For verily I say unto you, That many prophets and righteous *men* have desired to see *those things* which ye see, and have not seen *them;* and to hear *those things* which ye hear, and have not heard *them.*

Matt. 24:14. And this gospel of the kingdom shall be preached in all the world for a witness unto all nations; and then shall the end come.

Matt. 28:18. And Jesus came and spake unto them, saying, All power is given unto me in heaven and in earth. 19. Go ye therefore, and teach all nations, baptizing them in the name of the Father, and of the Son, and of the Holy Ghost: 20. Teaching them to observe all things whatsoever I have commanded you: and, lo, I am with you alway, *even* unto the end of the world.

Mark 1:14. Now after that John was put in prison, Jesus came into Galilee, preaching the gospel of the kingdom of God, 15. And saying, The time is fulfilled, and the kingdom of God is at hand: repent ye, and believe the gospel.

Mark 13:10. And the gospel must first be published among all nations. Mark 16:15.

Luke 1:67. And his father Zacharias was filled with the Holy Ghost, and prophesied, saying, 68. Blessed *be* the Lord God of Israel; for he hath visited and redeemed his people, 69. And hath raised up an horn of salvation for us in the house of his servant David; 70. As he spake by the mouth of his holy prophets, which have been since the world began: 71. That we should be saved from our enemies, and from the hand of all that hate us; 72. To perform the mercy *promised* to our fathers, and to remember his holy covenant; 73. The oath which he sware to our father Abraham, 74. That he would grant unto us, that we being delivered out of the hand of our enemies might serve him without fear, 75. In holiness and righteousness before him, all the days of our life. 76. And thou, child, shalt be called the prophet of the Highest: for thou shalt go before the face of the Lord to prepare his ways; 77. To give knowledge of salvation unto his people by the remission of their sins, 78. Through the tender mercy of our God; whereby the dayspring from on high hath visited us, 79. To give light to them that sit in darkness and *in* the shadow of death, to guide our feet into the way of peace.

Luke 2:10. And the angel said unto them, Fear not: for, behold, I bring you good tidings of great joy, which shall be to all people. 11. For unto you is born this day in the city of David a Saviour, which is Christ the Lord. 12. And this *shall be* a sign unto you; Ye shall find the babe wrapped in swaddling clothes, lying in a manger. 13. And suddenly there was with the angel a multitude of the heavenly host praising God, and saying, 14. Glory to God in the highest, and on earth peace, good will toward men. 34. This *child* is set for the fall and rising again of many in Israel;

Luke 4:18. The Spirit of the Lord *is* upon me, because he hath anointed me to preach the gospel to the poor; he hath sent me to heal the brokenhearted, to preach deliverance to the captives, and recovering of sight to the blind, to set at liberty them that are bruised, 19. To preach the acceptable year of the Lord.

Luke 10:23. And he turned him unto *his* disciples, and said privately, Blessed *are* the eyes which see the things that ye see: 24. For I tell you, that many prophets and kings have desired to see those things which ye see, and have not seen *them;* and to hear those things which ye hear, and have not heard *them.*

Luke 16:16. The law and the prophets *were* until John: since that time the kingdom of God is preached, and every man presseth into it. Acts 12:24; 19:20.

Luke 17:20. The kingdom of God cometh not with observation: 21. Neither shall they say, Lo here! or, lo there! for, behold, the kingdom of God is within you.

John 1:16. And of his fulness have all we received, and grace for grace. 17. For the law was given by Moses, *but* grace and truth came by Jesus Christ.

John 4:14. Whosoever drinketh of the water that I shall give him shall never thirst; but the water that I shall give him shall be in him a well of water springing up into everlasting life.

John 8:32. Ye shall know the truth, and the truth shall make you free.

John 12:35. Yet a little while is the light with you. Walk while ye have the light, lest darkness come upon you: 50. I know that his commandment is life everlasting:

John 17:7. All things whatsoever thou hast given me are of thee. 8. For I have given unto them the words which thou gavest me; and they have received *them,* and have known surely that I came out from thee, and they have believed that thou didst send me. John 13:20.

John 18:36. My kingdom is not of this world: if my kingdom were of this world, then would my servants fight, that I should not be delivered to the Jews: but now is my kingdom not from hence.

Acts 2:11. We do hear them speak in our tongues the wonderful works of God.

Acts 5:20. Go, stand and speak in the temple to the people all the words of this life.

Acts 10:36. The word which *God* sent unto the children of Israel, preaching peace by Jesus Christ:

Acts 13:32. We declare unto you glad tidings, how that the promise which was made unto the fathers, 33. God hath fulfilled the same unto us their children, in that he hath raised up Jesus again;

Acts 14:3. Long time therefore abode they speaking boldly in the Lord, which gave testimony unto the word of his grace, and granted signs and wonders to be done by their hands.

Acts 16:17. The same followed Paul and us, and cried, saying, These men are the servants of the most high God, which shew unto us the way of salvation.

Acts 20:24. But none of these things move me, neither count I my life dear unto myself, so that I might finish my course with joy, and the ministry, which I have received of the Lord Jesus, to testify the gospel of the grace of God. 32. And now, brethren, I commend you to God, and to the word of his grace, which is able to build you up, and to give you an inheritance among all them which are sanctified. chapter 14:3.

Rom. 1:16. For I am not ashamed of the gospel [1] of Christ: for it is the power of God unto salvation to every one that believeth; to the Jew first, and also to the Greek. 17. For therein is the righteousness of God revealed from faith to faith: as it is written, The just shall live by faith. [1 Omitted in R. V.]

Rom. 10:15. And how shall they preach, except they be sent? as it is written, How beautiful are the feet of them that preach the gospel of peace, and bring glad tidings of good things! 16. But they have not all obeyed the gospel. For Esaias saith, Lord, who hath believed our report? 17. So then faith *cometh* by hearing, and hearing by the word of God. 18. But I say, Have they not heard? Yes verily, their sound went into all the earth, and their words unto the ends of the world.

Rom. 15:29. And I am sure that, when I come unto you, I shall come in the fulness of the blessing of the gospel of Christ.

Rom. 16:25. To him that is of power to stablish you according to my gospel, and the preaching of Jesus Christ, according to the revelation of the mystery, which was kept secret since the world began, 26. But now is made manifest, and by the scriptures of the prophets, according to the commandment of the everlasting God, made known to all nations for the obedience of faith :

1 Cor. 1:18. The preaching of the cross is to them that perish foolishness; but unto us which are saved it is the power of God. 21. It pleased God by the foolishness of preaching to save them that believe. 24. Unto them which are called, both Jews and Greeks, Christ the power of God, and the wisdom of God. 25. Because the foolishness of God is wiser than men; and the weakness of God is stronger than men.

1 Cor. 2:4. My preaching *was* not with enticing words of man's wisdom, but in demonstration of the Spirit and of power : 5. That your faith should not stand in the wisdom of men, but in the power of God. 6. We speak wisdom among them that are perfect : yet not the wisdom of this world, nor of the princes of this world, that come to nought : 7. But we speak the wisdom of God in a mystery, *even* the hidden *wisdom*, which God ordained before the world unto our glory : 9. Eye hath not seen, nor ear heard, neither have entered into the heart of man, the things which God hath prepared for them that love him.

1 Cor. 4:20. The kingdom of God *is* not in word, but in power.

1 Cor. 9:16. For though I preach the gospel, I have nothing to glory of : for necessity is laid upon me; yea, woe is unto me, if I preach not the gospel! 17. For if I do this thing willingly, I have a reward : but if against my will, a dispensation *of the gospel* is committed unto me. 18. What is my reward then? *Verily* that, when I preach the gospel, I may make the gospel of Christ without charge, that I abuse not my power in the gospel.

1 Cor. 15:1. I declare unto you the gospel which I preached unto you, which also ye have received, and wherein ye stand; 2. By which also ye are saved, if ye keep in memory what I preached unto you, unless ye have believed in vain.

2 Cor. 3:6. The letter killeth, but the spirit giveth life. 7. But if the ministration of death, written *and* engraven in stones, was glorious, so that the children of Israel could not stedfastly behold the face of Moses for the glory of his countenance; which *glory* was to be done away: 8. How shall not the ministration of the spirit be rather glorious? 9. For if the ministration of condemnation *be* glory, much more doth the ministration of righteousness exceed in glory. 10. For even that which was made glorious had no glory in this respect, by reason of the glory that excelleth. 11. For if that which is done away *was* glorious, much more that which remaineth *is* glorious. 18. We all, with open face beholding as in a glass the glory of the Lord, are changed into the same image from glory to glory, *even* as by the Spirit of the Lord.

2 Cor. 4:3. But if our gospel be hid, it is hid to them that are lost: 4. In whom the god of this world hath blinded the minds of them which believe not, lest the light of the glorious gospel of Christ, who is the image of God, should shine unto them. 6. For God, who commanded the light to shine out of darkness, hath shined in our hearts, to *give* the light of the knowledge of the glory of God in the face of Jesus Christ.

2 Cor. 9:15. Thanks *be* unto God for his unspeakable gift.

2 Cor. 10:4. (For the weapons of our warfare *are* not carnal, but mighty through God to the pulling down of strong holds;) 5. Casting down imaginations, and every high thing that exalteth itself against the knowledge of God, and bringing into captivity every thought to the obedience of Christ;

Gal. 2:2. And I went up by revelation, and communicated unto them that gospel which I preach among the Gentiles, but privately to them which were of reputation, lest by any means I should run, or had run, in vain.

Gal. 3:8. And the scripture, foreseeing that God would justify the heathen through faith, preached before the gospel unto Abraham, *saying*, In thee shall all nations be blessed.

Eph. 1:13. In whom ye also *trusted*, after that ye heard the word of truth, the gospel of your salvation: in whom also after that ye believed, ye were sealed with that holy Spirit of promise, 14. Which is the earnest of our inheritance until the redemption of the purchased possession, unto the praise of his glory.

Eph. 3:8. That I should preach among the Gentiles the unsearchable riches of Christ; 9. And to make all *men* see what *is* the fellowship of the mystery, which from the beginning of the world hath been hid in God, who created all things [1]by Jesus Christ: 10. To the intent that now unto the principalities and powers in heavenly *places* might be known by the church the manifold wisdom of God, 11. According to the eternal purpose which he purposed in Christ Jesus our Lord: [1 Omitted in R. V.]

Eph. 6:15. And your feet shod with the preparation of the gospel of peace; 17. And take the helmet of salvation, and the sword of the Spirit, which is the word of God: 19. And for me, that utterance may be given unto me, that I may open my mouth boldly, to make known the mystery of the gospel, 20. For which I am an ambassador in bonds: that therein I may speak boldly, as I ought to speak.

Col. 1:5. The hope which is laid up for you in heaven, whereof ye heard before in the word of the truth of the gospel; 6. Which is come unto you, as *it is* in all the world; and bringeth forth fruit, as *it doth* also in you, since the day ye heard *of it*, and knew the grace of God in truth: 23. If ye continue in the faith grounded and settled, and *be* not moved away from the hope of the gospel, which ye have heard, *and* which was preached to every creature which is under heaven; 26. *Even* the mystery which hath been hid from ages and from generations, but now is made manifest to his saints: 27. To whom God would make known what *is* the riches of the glory of this mystery among the Gentiles; which is Christ in you, the hope of glory: 28. Whom we preach, warning every man, and teaching every man in all wisdom; that we may present every man perfect in Christ Jesus: 29. Whereunto I also labour, striving according to his working, which worketh in me mightily.

1 Thess. 1:5. For our gospel came not unto you in word only, but also in power, and in the Holy Ghost, and in much assurance; as ye know what manner of men we were among you for your sake.

1 Thess. 2:13. The word of God which ye heard of us, ye received *it* not *as* the word of men, but as it is in truth, the word of God,

2 Thess. 1:10. He shall come to be glorified in his saints, and to be admired in all them that believe (because our testimony among you was believed) in that day.

2 Thess. 2:10. Because they received not the love of the truth, that they might be saved. 14. Whereunto he called you by our gospel, to the obtaining of the glory of our Lord Jesus Christ.

1 Tim. 1:10. And if there be any other thing that is contrary to sound doctrine; 11. According to the glorious gospel of the blessed God, which was committed to my trust.

1 Tim. 2:4. Who will have all men to be saved, and to come unto the knowledge of the truth.

1 Tim. 3:16. Without controversy great is the mystery of godliness: ¹God was manifest in the flesh, justified in the Spirit, seen of angels, preached unto the Gentiles, believed on in the world, received up into glory.   [¹ R. V. he who]

1 Tim. 4:6. Nourished up in the words of faith and of good doctrine, whereunto thou hast attained.

2 Tim. 1:10. But is now made manifest by the appearing of our Saviour Jesus Christ, who hath abolished death, and hath brought life and ¹immortality to light through the gospel: [¹ R. V. incorruption]

2 Tim. 2:3. Thou therefore endure hardness, as a good soldier of Jesus Christ.

Heb. 4:2. For unto us was the gospel preached, as well as unto them: but the word preached did not profit them, not being mixed with faith in them that heard *it*.

Heb. 5:13. For every one that useth milk *is* unskilful in the word of righteousness:

Heb. 6:1. Leaving the principles of the doctrine of Christ, let us go on unto perfection;

Heb. 7:19. The law made nothing perfect, but the bringing in of a better hope *did ;* by the which we draw nigh unto God.

Jas. 1:18. Of his own will begat he us with the word of truth, 21. Wherefore . . . receive with meekness the ingrafted word, which is able to save your souls. 25. Whoso looketh into the perfect law of liberty, and continueth *therein*, he being not a forgetful hearer, but a doer of the work, this man shall be blessed in his deed.

1 Pet. 1:23. Being born again, not of corruptible seed, but of incorruptible, by the word of God, which liveth and abideth for ever. 25. The word of the Lord endureth for ever. And this is the word which by the gospel is preached unto you. Isa. 40:8.

1 Pet. 4:6. For for this cause was the gospel preached also to them that are dead, that they might be judged according to men in the flesh, but live according to God in the spirit.

1 Pet. 5:12. I have written briefly, exhorting, and testifying that this is the true grace of God wherein ye stand.

2 Pet. 1:16. We have not followed cunningly devised fables, when we made known unto you the power and coming of our Lord Jesus Christ, but were eyewitnesses of his majesty. 19. We have also a more sure word of prophecy; whereunto ye do well that ye take heed, as unto a light that shineth in a dark place, until the day dawn, and the day star arise in your hearts:

2 Pet. 2:2. And many shall follow their pernicious ways: by reason of whom the way of truth shall be evil spoken of. 21. For it had been better for them not to have known the way of righteousness, than, after they have known *it*, to turn from the holy commandment delivered unto them.

1 John 2:8. The darkness is past, and the true light now shineth.

Jude 3. It was needful for me to write unto you, and exhort *you* that ye should earnestly contend for the faith which was once delivered unto the saints.

Rev. 14:6. And I saw another angel fly in the midst of heaven, having the everlasting gospel to preach unto them that dwell on the earth, and to every nation, and kindred, and tongue, and people, 7. Saying with a loud voice, Fear God, and give glory to him; for the hour of his judgment is come: and worship him that made heaven, and earth, and the sea, and the fountains of waters.

CALLED THE NEW COVENANT: Jer. 31:31. Behold, the days come, saith the LORD, that I will make a new covenant with the house of Israel, and with the house of Judah : 32. Not according to the covenant that I made with their fathers in the day *that* I took them by the hand to bring them out of the land of Egypt; which my covenant they brake, although I was an husband unto them, saith the LORD : 33. But this *shall be* the covenant that I will make with the house of Israel; After those days, saith the LORD, I will put my law in their inward parts, and write it in their hearts; and will be their God, and they shall be my people. 34. And they shall teach no more every man his neighbour, and every man his brother, saying, Know the LORD : for they shall all know me, from the least of them unto the greatest of them, saith the LORD : for I will forgive their iniquity, and I will remember their sin no more.

Heb. 7:22. By so much was Jesus made a surety of a better ¹ testament.   [¹ R. V. covenant]

Heb. 8:6. But now hath he obtained a more excellent ministry, by how much also he is the mediator of a better covenant, which was established upon better promises. 7. For if that first *covenant* had been faultless, then should no place have been sought for the second. 8. For finding fault with them, he saith, Behold, the days come, saith the Lord, when I will make a new covenant with the house of Israel and with the house of Judah : 9. Not according to the covenant that I made with their fathers in the day when I took them by the hand to lead them out of the land of Egypt; because they continued not in my covenant, and I regarded them not, saith the Lord. 10. For this *is* the covenant that I will make with the house of Israel after those days, saith the Lord ; I will put my laws into their mind, and write them in their hearts : and I will be to them a God, and they shall be to me a people : 11. And they shall not teach every man his neighbour, and every man his brother, saying, Know the Lord : for all shall know me, from the least to the greatest. 12. For I will be merciful to their unrighteousness, and their sins and their iniquities will I remember no more. 13. In that he saith, A new *covenant*, he hath made the first old. Now that which decayeth and waxeth old *is* ready to vanish away.

Heb. 9:8. The Holy Ghost this signifying, that the way into the holiest of all was not yet made manifest, while as the first tabernacle was yet standing : 9. Which *was* a figure for the time then present, in which were offered both gifts and sacrifices, that could not make him that did the service perfect, as pertaining to the conscience; 10. *Which stood* only in meats and drinks, and divers washings, and carnal ordinances, imposed *on them* until the time of reformation. 11. But Christ being come an high priest of good things to come, by a greater and more per-

fect tabernacle, not made with hands, that is to say, not of this building; 12. Neither by the blood of goats and calves, but by his own blood he entered in once into the holy place, having obtained eternal redemption *for us*. 13. For if the blood of bulls and of goats, and the ashes of an heifer sprinkling the unclean, sanctifieth to the purifying of the flesh : 14. How much more shall the blood of Christ, who through the eternal Spirit offered himself without spot to God, purge your conscience from dead works to serve the living God? 15. And for this cause he is the mediator of the new testament, that by means of death, for the redemption of the transgressions *that were* under the first testament, they which are called might receive the promise of eternal inheritance.

Heb. 10:9. He taketh away the first, that he may establish the second.

Heb. 12:22. But ye are come unto mount Sion, and unto the city of the living God, the heavenly Jerusalem, and to an innumerable company of angels, 23. To the general assembly and church of the firstborn, which are written in heaven, and to God the Judge of all, and to the spirits of just men made perfect, 24. And to Jesus the mediator of the new covenant, and to the blood of sprinkling, that speaketh better things than *that of* Abel.

PROPHECIES RELATING TO: Psa. 46:4. *There is* a river, the streams whereof shall make glad the city of God, the holy *place* of the tabernacles of the most High.

Isa. 2:3. And many people shall go and say, Come ye, and let us go up to the mountain of the LORD, to the house of the God of Jacob ; and he will teach us of his ways, and we will walk in his paths : for out of Zion shall go forth the law, and the word of the LORD from Jerusalem. 4. And he shall judge among the nations, and shall rebuke many people : and they shall beat their swords into plowshares, and their spears into pruninghooks : nation shall not lift up sword against nation, neither shall they learn war any more. 5. O house of Jacob, come ye, and let us walk in the light of the LORD.

Isa. 4:2. In that day shall the branch of the LORD be beautiful and glorious, and the fruit of the earth *shall be* excellent and comely for them that are escaped of Israel. 3. And it shall come to pass, *that he that is* left in Zion, and *he that* remaineth in Jerusalem, shall be called holy, *even* every one that is written among the living in Jerusalem : 4. When the Lord shall have washed away the filth of the daughters of Zion, and shall have purged the blood of Jerusalem from the midst thereof by the spirit of judgment, and by the spirit of burning. 5. And the LORD will create upon every dwelling place of mount Zion, and upon her assemblies, a cloud and smoke by day, and the shining of a flaming fire by night : for upon all the glory *shall be* a defence. 6. And there shall be a tabernacle for a shadow in the daytime from the heat, and for a place of refuge, and for a covert from storm and from rain.

Isa. 9:2. The people that walked in darkness have seen a great light: they that dwell in the land of the shadow of death, upon them hath the light shined. 6. For unto us a child is born, unto us a son is given: and the government shall be upon his shoulder: and his name shall be called Wonderful, Counsellor, The mighty God, The everlasting Father, The Prince of Peace. 7. Of the increase of *his* government and peace *there shall be* no end, upon the throne of David, and upon his kingdom, to order it, and to establish it with judgment and with justice from henceforth even for ever. The zeal of the Lord of hosts will perform this.

Isa. 25:7. He will destroy in this mountain the face of the covering cast over all people, and the vail that is spread over all nations.

Isa. 29:18. In that day shall the deaf hear the words of the book, and the eyes of the blind shall see out of obscurity, and out of darkness. 24. They also that erred in spirit shall come to understanding, and they that murmured shall learn doctrine.

Isa. 32:3. The eyes of them that see shall not be dim, and the ears of them that' hear shall hearken.

Isa. 35:5. The eyes of the blind shall be opened, and the ears of the deaf shall be unstopped.

Isa. 40:9. O Zion, that bringest good tidings, get thee up into the high mountain; O Jerusalem, that bringest good tidings, lift up thy voice with strength; lift *it* up, be not afraid; say unto the cities of Judah, Behold your God!

Isa. 41:27. The first *shall say* to Zion, Behold, behold them: and I will give to Jerusalem one that bringeth good tidings.

Isa. 42:6. I the Lord have called thee in righteousness, and will hold thine hand, and will keep thee, and give thee for a covenant of the people, for a light of the Gentiles; 7. To open the blind eyes, to bring out the prisoners from the prison, *and* them that sit in darkness out of the prison house.

Isa. 43:18. Remember ye not the former things, neither consider the things of old. 19. Behold, I will do a new thing; now it shall spring forth; shall ye not know it? I will even make a way in the wilderness, *and* rivers in the desert. 20. The beast of the field shall honour me, the dragons and the owls: because I give waters in the wilderness, *and* rivers in the desert, to give drink to my people, my chosen. 21. This people have I formed for myself; they shall shew forth my praise.

Isa. 46:13. I bring near my righteousness; it shall not be far off, and my salvation shall not tarry: and I will place salvation in Zion for Israel my glory.

Isa. 49:13. Sing, O heavens; and be joyful, O earth; and break forth into singing, O mountains: for the Lord hath comforted his people, and will have mercy upon his afflicted.

Isa. 51:4. Hearken unto me, my people; and give ear unto me, O my nation: for a law shall proceed from me, and I will make my judgment to rest for a light of the people. 5. My righteousness *is* near; my salvation is gone forth, and mine arms shall judge the people; the isles shall wait upon me, and on mine arm shall they trust. 6. Lift up your eyes to the heavens, and look upon the earth beneath: for the heavens shall vanish away like smoke, and the earth shall wax old like a garment, and they that dwell therein shall die in like manner: but my salvation shall be for ever, and my righteousness shall not be abolished.

Isa. 52:7. How beautiful upon the mountains are the feet of him that bringeth good tidings, that publisheth peace; that bringeth good tidings of good, that publisheth salvation; that saith unto Zion, Thy God reigneth!

Isa. 55:1. Ho, every one that thirsteth, come ye to the waters, and he that hath no money; come ye, buy, and eat; yea, come, buy wine and milk without money and without price. 2. Wherefore do ye spend money for *that which is* not bread? and your labour for *that which* satisfieth not? hearken diligently unto me, and eat ye *that which is* good, and let your soul delight itself in fatness. 3. Incline your ear, and come unto me: hear, and your soul shall live; and I will make an everlasting covenant with you, *even* the sure mercies of David. 4. Behold, I have given him *for* a witness to the people, a leader and commander to the people. 5. Behold, thou shalt call a nation *that* thou knowest not, and nations *that* knew not thee shall run unto thee because of the Lord thy God, and for the Holy One of Israel; for he hath glorified thee.

Isa. 60:1. Arise, shine; for thy light is come, and the glory of the Lord is risen upon thee. 2. For, behold, the darkness shall cover the earth, and gross darkness the people: but the Lord shall arise upon thee, and his glory shall be seen upon thee. 3. And the Gentiles shall come to thy light, and kings to the brightness of thy rising. 4. Lift up thine eyes round about, and see: all they gather themselves together, they come to thee: thy sons shall come from far, and thy daughters shall be nursed at *thy* side. 5. Then thou shalt see, and flow together, and thine heart shall fear, and be enlarged; because the abundance of the sea shall be converted unto thee, the forces of the Gentiles shall come unto thee. 6. The multitude of camels shall cover thee, the dromedaries of Midian and Ephah; all they from Sheba shall come: they shall bring gold and incense; and they shall shew forth the praises of the Lord. 7. All the flocks of Kedar shall be gathered together unto thee, the rams of Nebaioth shall minister unto thee: they shall come up with acceptance on mine altar, and I will glorify the house of my glory. 8. Who *are* these *that* fly as a cloud, and as the doves to their windows ? 9. Surely the isles shall wait for me, and the ships of Tarshish first, to bring thy sons from far, their silver and their gold with them, unto the name of the LORD thy God, and to the Holy One of Israel, because he hath glorified thee. 10. And the sons of strangers shall build up thy walls, and their kings shall minister unto thee: for in my wrath I smote thee, but in my favour have I had mercy on thee. 11. Therefore thy gates shall be opened continually; they shall not be shut day nor night: that *men* may bring unto thee the forces of the Gentiles, and *that* their kings *may be* brought. 12. For the nation and kingdom that will not serve thee shall perish; yea, *those* nations shall be utterly wasted. 13. The glory of Lebanon shall come unto thee, the fir tree, the pine tree, and the box together, to beautify the place of my sanctuary ; and I will make the place of my feet glorious. 14. The sons also of them that afflicted thee shall come bending unto thee; and all they that despised thee shall bow themselves down at the soles of thy feet ; and they shall call thee, The city of the LORD, The Zion of the Holy One of Israel. 15. Whereas thou hast been forsaken and hated, so that no man went through *thee*, I will make thee an eternal excellency, a joy of many generations. 16. Thou shalt also suck the milk of the Gentiles, and shalt suck the breast of kings: and thou shalt know that I the LORD *am* thy Saviour and thy Redeemer, the mighty One of Jacob. 17. For brass I will bring gold, and for iron I will bring silver, and for wood brass, and for stones iron : I will also make thy officers peace, and thine exactors righteousness. 18. Violence shall no more be heard in thy land, wasting nor destruction within thy borders ; but thou shalt call thy walls Salvation, and thy gates Praise. 19. The sun shall be no more thy light by day ; neither for brightness shall the moon give light unto thee : but the LORD shall be unto thee an everlasting light, and thy God thy glory. 20. Thy sun shall no more go down ; neither shall thy moon withdraw itself: for the LORD shall be thine everlasting light, and the days of thy mourning shall be ended. 21. Thy people also *shall be* all righteous: they shall inherit the land for ever, the branch of my planting, the work of my hands, that I may be glorified. 22. A little one shall become a thousand, and a small one a strong nation: I the LORD will hasten it in his time.

Isa. 61:1. The Spirit of the Lord GOD *is* upon me; because the LORD hath anointed me to preach good tidings unto the meek; he hath sent me to bind up the brokenhearted, to proclaim liberty to the captives, and the opening of the prison to *them that are* bound ; 2. To proclaim the acceptable year of the LORD, and the day of vengeance of our God; to comfort all that mourn ; 3. To appoint unto them that mourn in Zion, to give unto them beauty for ashes, the oil of joy for mourning, the garment of praise for the spirit of heaviness ; that they might be called trees of righteousness, the planting of the LORD, that he might be glorified.

Ezek. 34:23. And I will set up one shepherd over them, and he shall feed them, *even* my servant David ; he shall feed them, and he shall be their shepherd. 24. And I the LORD will be their God, and my servant David a prince among them ; I the LORD have spoken *it*. 25. And I will make with them a covenant of peace, and will cause the evil beasts to cease out of the land : and they shall dwell safely in the wilderness, and sleep in the woods. 26. And I will make them and the places round about my hill a blessing ; and I will cause the shower to come down in his season ; there shall be showers of blessing. 27. And the tree of the field shall yield her fruit, and the earth shall yield her increase, and they shall be safe in their land, and shall know that I *am* the LORD, when I have broken the bands of their yoke, and delivered them out of the hand of those that served themselves of them. 28. And they shall no more be a prey to the heathen, neither shall the beast of the land devour them; but they shall dwell safely, and none shall make *them* afraid. 29. And I will raise up for them a plant of renown, and they shall be no more consumed with hunger in the land, neither bear the shame of the heathen any more. 30. Thus shall they know that I the LORD their God *am* with them, and *that* they, *even* the house of Israel, *are* my people, saith the Lord GOD. 31. And ye my flock, the flock of my pasture, *are* men, *and* I *am* your God, saith the Lord GOD.

Ezek. 47:8. These waters issue out toward the east country, and go down into the desert, and go into the sea : *which being* brought forth into the sea, the waters shall be healed. 12. By the river upon the bank thereof, on this side and on that side, shall grow all trees for meat, whose leaf shall not fade, neither shall the fruit thereof be consumed : it shall bring forth new fruit according to his months, because their waters they issued out of the sanctuary : and the fruit thereof shall be for meat, and the leaf thereof for medicine. *vs.* 1–12.

Joel 2:28. And it shall come to pass afterward, *that* I will pour out my spirit upon all flesh ; and your sons and your daughters shall prophesy, your old men shall dream dreams, your young men shall see visions: 29. And also upon the servants and upon the handmaids in those days will I pour out my spirit. 30. And I will shew wonders in the heavens and in the earth, blood, and fire, and pillars of smoke. 31. The sun shall be turned into darkness, and the moon into blood, before the great and the terrible day of the LORD come. 32. And it shall come to pass, *that* whosoever shall call on the name of the LORD shall be delivered: for in mount Zion and in Jerusalem shall be deliverance, as the LORD hath said, and in the remnant whom the LORD shall call.

Mic. 4:1. But in the last days it shall come to pass, *that* the mountain of the house of the LORD shall be established in the top of the mountains, and it shall be exalted above the hills; and people shall flow unto it. 2. And many nations shall come, and say, Come, and let us go up to the mountain of the LORD, and to the house of the God of Jacob; and he will teach us of his ways, and we will walk in his paths: for the law shall go forth of Zion, and the word of the LORD from Jerusalem. 3. And he shall judge among many people, and rebuke strong nations afar off; and they shall beat their swords into plowshares, and their spears into pruninghooks: nation shall not lift up a sword against nation, neither shall they learn war any more. 4. But they shall sit every man under his vine and under his fig tree; and none shall make *them* afraid: for the mouth of the LORD of hosts hath spoken *it*. 5. For all people will walk every one in the name of his god, and we will walk in the name of the LORD our God for ever and ever. 6. In that day, saith the LORD, will I assemble her that halteth, and I will gather her that is driven out, and her that I have afflicted; 7. And I will make her that halted a remnant, and her that was cast far off a strong nation: and the LORD shall reign over them in mount Zion from henceforth, even for ever.

Matt. 24:14. And this gospel of the kingdom shall be preached in all the world for a witness unto all nations; and then shall the end come.

See CHURCH, PROPHECIES CONCERNING; JESUS, KINGDOM OF, MISSION OF; KINGDOM OF HEAVEN.

GOSSIP. FORBIDDEN: Lev. 19:16. Thou shalt not go up and down *as* a talebearer among thy people:

Psa. 50:20. Thou sittest *and* speakest against thy brother; thou slanderest thine own mother's son.

Prov. 11:13. A talebearer revealeth secrets: but he that is of a faithful spirit concealeth the matter.

Prov. 20:19. He that goeth about *as* a talebearer revealeth secrets: therefore meddle not with him that flattereth with his lips.

Ezek. 22:9. In thee are men that carry tales to shed blood:

See SLANDER; SPEAKING, EVIL.

GOURD. Jonah's, believed to be a vine resembling the American squash, used in Assyria to cover booths, Jonah 4:6-10. The wild gourd mentioned 2 Kin. 4:39 is supposed to be a plant in appearance like the cucumber.

GOUT (?). 2 Chr. 16:12.

GOVERNMENT. Paternal functions of, Gen. 41:25-57. Civil service school provided by, Dan. 1:3-20. Maintains a system of public instruction, 2 Chr. 17:7-9.

Executive departments in. See CABINET; KING; RULER.

Judicial department in. See COURT; JUDGE; JUSTICE; LEVITE; PRIEST.

MOSAIC: ADMINISTRATIVE AND JUDICIAL SYSTEM: Ex. 18:13. And it came to pass on the morrow, that Moses sat to judge the people: and the people stood by Moses from the morning unto the evening. 14. And when Moses' father in law saw all that he did to the people, he said, What *is* this thing that thou doest to the people? Why sittest thou thyself alone, and all the people stand by thee from morning unto even? 15. And Moses said unto his father in law, Because the people come unto me to enquire of God: 16. When they have a matter, they come unto me; and I judge between one and another, and I do make *them* know the statutes of God, and his laws. 17. And Moses' father in law said unto him, The thing that thou doest *is* not good. 18. Thou wilt surely wear away, both thou, and this people that *is* with thee: for this thing *is* too heavy for thee; thou art not able to perform it thyself alone. 19. Hearken now unto my voice, I will give thee counsel, and God shall be with thee: Be thou for the people to God-ward, that thou mayest bring the causes unto God: 20. And thou shalt teach them ordinances and laws, and shalt shew them the way wherein they must walk, and the work that they must do. 21. Moreover thou shalt provide out of all the people able men, such as fear God, men of truth, hating covetousness; and place *such* over them, *to be* rulers of thousands, *and* rulers of hundreds, rulers of fifties, and rulers of tens. 22. And let them judge the people at all seasons: and it shall be, *that* every great matter they shall bring unto thee, but every small matter they shall judge: so shall it be easier for thyself, and they shall bear *the burden* with thee. 23. If thou shalt do this thing, and God command thee *so*, then thou shalt be able to endure, and all this people shall also go to their place in peace. 24. So Moses hearkened to the voice of his father in law, and did all that he had said. 25. And Moses chose able men out of all Israel, and made them heads over the people, rulers of thousands, rulers of hundreds, rulers of fifties, and rulers of tens. 26. And they judged the people at all seasons: the hard causes they brought unto Moses, but every small matter they judged themselves.

Num. 11:16. And the LORD said unto Moses, Gather unto me seventy men of the elders of Israel, whom thou knowest to be the elders of the people, and officers over them; and bring them unto the tabernacle of the congregation, that they may stand there with thee. 17. And I will come down and talk with thee there: and I will take of the spirit which *is* upon thee, and will put *it* upon them; and they shall bear the burden of the people with thee, that thou bear *it* not thyself alone. 24. And Moses went out, and told the people the words of the LORD, and gathered the seventy men of the elders of the people, and set them round about the tabernacle. 25. And the LORD came down in a cloud, and spake unto him, and took of the spirit that *was* upon him, and gave *it* unto the seventy elders : and it came to pass, that, when the spirit rested upon them, they prophesied, and did not cease.

Deut. 1:9. And I spake unto you at that time, saying, I am not able to bear you myself alone : 10. The LORD your God hath multiplied you, and, behold, ye *are* this day as the stars of heaven for multitude. 11. (The LORD God of your fathers make you a thousand times so many more as ye *are*, and bless you, as he hath promised you!) 12. How can I myself alone bear your cumbrance, and your burden, and your strife ? 13. Take you wise men, and understanding, and known among your tribes, and I will make them rulers over you. 14. And ye answered me, and said, The thing which thou hast spoken *is* good *for us* to do. 15. So I took the chief of your tribes, wise men, and known, and made them heads over you, captains over thousands, and captains over hundreds, and captains over fifties, and captains over tens, and officers among your tribes. 16. And I charged your judges at that time, saying, Hear *the causes* between your brethren, and judge righteously between *every* man and his brother, and the stranger *that is* with him. 17. Ye shall not respect persons in judgment ; *but* ye shall hear the small as well as the great ; ye shall not be afraid of the face of man ; for the judgment *is* God's : and the cause that is too hard for you, bring *it* unto me, and I will hear it.

POPULAR, BY A NATIONAL ASSEMBLY, OR ITS REPRESENTATIVES: Accepted, and agreed to, the law given by Moses, Ex. 19:7,8; 24:3, 7; Deut. 29:10-15. Refused to make conquest of Canaan, Num. 14:1-10. Chose, or ratified, the chief ruler, Num. 27:18-23; 1 Sam. 10:24, with 1 Sam. 8:4-22; 11:14,15; 2 Sam. 3:17-21; 5:1-3; 1 Chr. 29:22; 2 Chr. 23:3. Possessed veto power over the king's purposes, 1 Sam. 14:44,45. The court in certain capital cases, Num. 35:12,24,25.

THE DELEGATED, SENATORIAL COUNCIL: Closely associated with Moses and subsequent leaders, Ex. 3:16. Go, and gather the elders of Israel together, and say unto them, The LORD God of your fathers, the God of Abraham, of Isaac, and of Jacob, appeared unto me, saying, I have surely visited you, and *seen* that which is done to you in Egypt : 18. And they shall hearken to thy voice : and thou shalt come, thou and the elders of Israel, unto the king of Egypt, and ye shall say unto him, The LORD God of the Hebrews hath met with us : and now let us go, we beseech thee, three days' journey into the wilderness, that we may sacrifice to the LORD our God.

Ex. 4:29. And Moses and Aaron went and gathered together all the elders of the children of Israel : [Ex. 12:21; 17:5,6; 18:12; Lev.

9:1; Num. 16:25; Deut. 5:23.] 30. And Aaron spake all the words which the LORD had spoken unto Moses, and did the signs in the sight of the people. 31. And the people believed : and when they heard that the LORD had visited the children of Israel, and that he had looked upon their affliction, then they bowed their heads and worshipped.

Ex. 19:7. And Moses came and called for the elders of the people, and laid before their faces all these words which the LORD commanded him. 8. And all the people answered together, and said, All that the LORD hath spoken we will do. And Moses returned the words of the people unto the LORD.

Ex. 24:1. And he said unto Moses, Come up unto the LORD, thou, and Aaron, Nadab, and Abihu, and seventy of the elders of Israel ; and worship ye afar off. 14. And he said unto the elders, Tarry ye here for us, until we come again unto you : and, behold, Aaron and Hur *are* with you : if any man have any matters to do, let him come unto them.

Lev. 4:15. And the elders of the congregation shall lay their hands upon the head of the bullock before the LORD : and the bullock shall be killed before the LORD.

Num. 11:16. And the LORD said unto Moses, Gather unto me seventy men of the elders of Israel, whom thou knowest to be the elders of the people, and officers over them ; and bring them unto the tabernacle of the congregation, that they may stand there with thee. 17. And I will come down and talk with thee there : and I will take of the spirit which *is* upon thee, and will put *it* upon them ; and they shall bear the burden of the people with thee, that thou bear *it* not thyself alone. 18. And say thou unto the people, Sanctify yourselves against to morrow, and ye shall eat flesh : for ye have wept in the ears of the LORD, saying, Who shall give us flesh to eat ? for *it was* well with us in Egypt : therefore the LORD will give you flesh, and ye shall eat. 30. And Moses gat him into the camp, he and the elders of Israel.

Deut. 1:13. Take you wise men, and understanding, and known among your tribes, and I will make them rulers over you. 14. And ye answered me, and said, The thing which thou hast spoken *is* good *for us* to do. 15. So I took the chief of your tribes, wise men, and known, and made them heads over you, captains over thousands, and captains over hundreds, and captains over fifties, and captains over tens, and officers among your tribes.

Deut. 27:1. And Moses with the elders of Israel commanded the people, saying, Keep all the commandments which I command you this day.

Deut. 29:10. Ye stand this day all of you before the LORD your God ; your captains of your tribes, your elders, and your officers, *with* all the men of Israel, 11. Your little ones, your wives, and thy stranger that *is* in thy camp, from the hewer of thy wood unto the drawer of thy water : 12. That thou shouldest enter into covenant with the LORD thy God, and into his oath, which the LORD thy God maketh with thee this day: 13. That he may establish thee to day for a people unto himself, and *that* he may be unto thee a God, as he hath said unto thee, and as he hath sworn unto thy fathers, to Abraham, to Isaac, and to Jacob. 14. Neither with you only do I make this covenant and this oath; 15. But with *him* that standeth here with us this day before the LORD our God, and also with *him* that *is* not here with us this day:

Deut. 31:9. And Moses wrote this law, and delivered it unto the priests the sons of Levi, which bare the ark of the covenant of the LORD, and unto all the elders of Israel. 28. Gather unto me all the elders of your tribes, and your officers, that I may speak these words in their ears, and call heaven and earth to record against them.

Josh. 7:6. And Joshua rent his clothes, and fell to the earth upon his face before the ark of the LORD until the eventide, he and the elders of Israel, and put dust upon their heads.

Josh. 8:10. And Joshua rose up early in the morning, and numbered the people, and went up, he and the elders of Israel, before the people to Ai. 32. And he wrote there upon the stones a copy of the law of Moses, which he wrote in the presence of the children of Israel. 33. And all Israel, and their elders, and officers, and their judges, stood on this side the ark and on that side before the priests the Levites, which bare the ark of the covenant of the LORD, as well the stranger, as he that was born among them; half of them over against mount Gerizim, and half of them over against mount Ebal; as Moses the servant of the LORD had commanded before, that they should bless the people of Israel.

Josh. 23:2. And Joshua called for all Israel, *and* for their elders, and for their heads, and for their judges, and for their officers, and said unto them, I am old *and* stricken in age: 3. And ye have seen all that the LORD your God hath done unto all these nations because of you; for the LORD your God *is* he that hath fought for you. 6. Be ye therefore very courageous to keep and to do all that is written in the book of the law of Moses, that ye turn not aside therefrom *to* the right hand or *to* the left;

Josh. 24:1. And Joshua gathered all the tribes of Israel to Shechem, and called for the elders of Israel, and for their heads, and for their judges, and for their officers; and they presented themselves before God. 24. And the people said unto Joshua, The LORD our God will we serve, and his voice will we obey. 25. So Joshua made a covenant with the people that day, and set them a statute and an ordinance in Shechem.

Judg. 21:16. Then the elders of the congregation said, How shall we do for wives for them that remain, seeing the women are destroyed out of Benjamin? 17. And they

said, *There must be* an inheritance for them that be escaped of Benjamin, that a tribe be not destroyed out of Israel. *vs.* 18-25.

Acts 5:17. Then the high priest rose up, and all they that were with him, (which is the sect of the Sadducees,) and were filled with indignation, 18. And laid their hands on the apostles, and put them in the common prison. 21. And when they heard *that*, they entered into the temple early in the morning, and taught. But the high priest came, and they that were with him, and called the counsel together, and all the senate of the children of Israel, and sent to the prison to have them brought. with *vs.* 22-41.

MISCELLANY OF FACTS RELATING TO THE SENATE: Demands a king, 1 Sam. 8:4-10,19-22. Saul pleads to be honored before, 1 Sam. 15:30. Chooses David as king, 2 Sam. 3:17-21; 5:3; 1 Chr. 11:3. Closely associated with David, 2 Sam. 12:17; 1 Chr. 15:25; 21:16. Joins Absalom in his usurpation, 2 Sam. 17:4. David upbraids, 2 Sam. 19:11. Assists Solomon at the dedication of the temple, 1 Kin. 8:1-3; 2 Chr. 5:2-4. Counsels king Rehoboam, 1 Kin. 12:6-8,13. Counsels king Ahab, 1 Kin. 20:7,8. Josiah assembles to hear the law of the Lord, 2 Kin. 23:1; 2 Chr. 34: 29,31.

Legislates with Ezra in reforming certain marriages with the heathen, Ezra. 9:1; 10:8-14. Legislates in later times, Matt. 15:2,7-9; Mark 7:1-13. Sits as a court, Jer. 26:10-24. Constitutes, with priests and scribes, a court for the trial of both civil and ecclesiastical causes, Matt. 21:23; 26:3-5,57-68; 27:1,2; Mark 8:31; 14:43-65; 15:1; Luke 22:52-71; Acts 4:1-21; 6:9-15; 7:1-59. Unfaithful to the city, Lam. 1:19. Seeks counsel from prophets, Ezek. 8:1; 14:1; 20:1,3; Joel 1:14; 2:16. Corrupt, 1 Kin. 21:8-14; Ezek. 8:11,12; Matt. 26: 14,15; with chapter 27:3,4.

A similar senate existed among the Egyptians, Gen. 50:7, with Gen. 41:37,38; Ex. 10:1, 7; 12:30; 14:5; and among the Midianites and Moabites, Num. 22:4,7, and Gibeonites, Josh. 9:11.

EXECUTIVE OFFICERS OF TRIBES AND CITIES, CALLED, PRINCES OR NOBLES, MEMBERS OF THE NATIONAL ASSEMBLY, Num. 1:4-16,44; 7:2,3,10,11,18,24,54,84; 10:4; 16:2; 17:2,6; 27:2; 31:13,14; 32:2; 34:18-29; 36:1; Josh. 9:15-21; 17:4; 22:13-32; 1 Kin. 21:11-13; Neh. 3:9,12, 16,18,19.

THE MOSAIC JUDICIAL SYSTEM. See COURT; JUDGE; PRIEST; LEVITE; RULER; SANHEDRIN; SYNAGOGUE.

Forms and facts of government after the death of Moses and the princes who survived Moses. See ISRAEL, HISTORY OF, under the sub-topics JUDGES; KINGS.

CONSTITUTIONAL: See CONSTITUTION.

ECCLESIASTICAL: See CHURCH, GOVERNMENT OF; PRIESTS.

IMPERIAL: Gen. 14:1; Josh. 11:10; Esth. 1:1; Dan. 4:1; 6:1-3; Luke 2:1.

MONARCHICAL: Tyranny in, INSTANCE,

OF: By Saul, 1 Sam 22:6,12–19. By David, 2 Sam. 1:13–16; 4:9–12; 11:14–17. By Solomon, 1 Kin. 2:23–25,28–34,36–46; 12:1–16; 21:7–16; 2 Kin. 10. By Ahasuerus, Esth. chapters 2; 3. By Nebuchadnezzar, Dan. 1:10; 2:5–13; 5:19. By Herod, Mark 6:27,28. See ISRAEL, HISTORY OF, under the sub-topic KINGS. Also see ASSYRIA; BABYLON; CHALDEA; SYRIA.

Limited. See CONSTITUTION.

MUNICIPAL: Devolving on a local senate and executive officers, Deut. 19:12; 21:2–8,18–21; 22:13–21; 25:7–9; Josh. 20:4; Judg. 8:14–16; 11:5–11; Ruth 4:2–11; 1 Sam. 11:3; 16:4; 30:26; 1 Kin. 21:8–14; 2 Kin. 10:1–7; Ezra 10:8,14; Neh. 3:9,12,16,18,19; Lam. 5:14.

PATRIARCHAL: Gen. 27:29,37.

PROVINCIAL: Ezra 4:8,9; 5:3,6; 6:6; 8:36; Neh. 2:7,9; 5:14; Dan. 6:1–3; Matt. 27:2; 28:14; Luke 3:1; Acts 24:1. See HEROD; PILATE.

REPRESENTATIVE: Deut. 1:13–15; Josh. 9:11. See DELEGATED, SENATORIAL COUNCIL, above. Also see ELDER.

THEOCRATIC: Ex. 19:3. And Moses went up unto God, and the LORD called unto him out of the mountain, saying, Thus shalt thou say to the house of Jacob, and tell the children of Israel; 4. Ye have seen what I did unto the Egyptians, and *how* I bare you on eagles' wings, and brought you unto myself. 5. Now therefore, if ye will obey my voice indeed, and keep my covenant, then ye shall be a peculiar treasure unto me above all people: for all the earth *is* mine: 6. And ye shall be unto me a kingdom of priests, and an holy nation. These *are* the words which thou shalt speak unto the children of Israel. 7. And Moses came and called for the elders of the people, and laid before their faces all these words which the LORD commanded him. 8. And all the people answered together, and said, All that the LORD hath spoken we will do. And Moses returned the words of the people unto the LORD. Deut. 26:16–19.

Deut. 29:1. These *are* the words of the covenant, which the LORD commanded Moses to make with the children of Israel in the land of Moab, beside the covenant which he made with them in Horeb. 2. And Moses called unto all Israel, and said unto them, Ye have seen all that the LORD did before your eyes in the land of Egypt unto Pharaoh, and unto all his servants, and unto all his land; 3. The great temptations which thine eyes have seen, the signs, and those great miracles: 4. Yet the LORD hath not given you an heart to perceive, and eyes to see, and ears to hear, unto this day. 5. And I have led you forty years in the wilderness: your clothes are not waxen old upon you, and thy shoe is not waxen old upon thy foot. 6. Ye have not eaten bread, neither have ye drunk wine or strong drink: that ye might know that I *am* the LORD your God. 7. And when ye came unto this place, Sihon the king of Heshbon, and Og the king of Bashan, came out against us unto battle, and we smote them: 8. And we took their

land, and gave it for an inheritance unto the Reubenites, and to the Gadites, and to the half tribe of Manasseh. 9. Keep therefore the words of this covenant, and do them, that ye may prosper in all that ye do. 10. Ye stand this day all of you before the LORD your God; your captains of your tribes, your elders, and your officers, *with* all the men of Israel, 11. Your little ones, your wives, and thy stranger that *is* in thy camp, from the hewer of thy wood unto the drawer of thy water: 12. That thou shouldest enter into covenant with the LORD thy God, and into his oath, which the LORD thy God maketh with thee this day: 13. That he may establish thee to day for a people unto himself, and *that* he may be unto thee a God, as he hath said unto thee, and as he hath sworn unto thy fathers, to Abraham, to Isaac, and to Jacob.

1 Sam. 8:6. But the thing displeased Samuel, when they said, Give us a king to judge us. And Samuel prayed unto the LORD. 7. And the LORD said unto Samuel, Hearken unto the voice of the people in all that they say unto thee: for they have not rejected thee, but they have rejected me, that I should not reign over them.

See GOD IN, below. Also see RULERS; JUDGE; ELDER; CHURCH AND STATE.

CORRUPTION IN: 1 Kin. 21:5. But Jezebel his wife came to him, and said unto him, Why is thy spirit so sad, that thou eatest no bread? 6. And he said unto her, Because I spake unto Naboth the Jezreelite, and said unto him, Give me thy vineyard for money; or else, if it please thee, I will give thee *another* vineyard for it: and he answered, I will not give thee my vineyard. 7. And Jezebel his wife said unto him, Dost thou now govern the kingdom of Israel? arise, *and* eat bread, and let thine heart be merry: I will give thee the vineyard of Naboth the Jezreelite. 8. So she wrote letters in Ahab's name, and sealed *them* with his seal, and sent the letters unto the elders and to the nobles that *were* in his city, dwelling with Naboth. 9. And she wrote in the letters, saying, Proclaim a fast, and set Naboth on high among the people: 10. And set two men, sons of Belial, before him, to bear witness against him, saying, Thou didst blaspheme God and the king. And *then* carry him out, and stone him, that he may die. 11. And the men of his city, *even* the elders and the nobles who were the inhabitants in his city, did as Jezebel had sent unto them, *and* as it *was* written in the letters which she had sent unto them. 12. They proclaimed a fast, and set Naboth on high among the people. 13. And there came in two men, children of Belial, and sat before him: and the men of Belial witnessed against him, *even* against Naboth, in the presence of the people, saying, Naboth did blaspheme God and the king. Then they carried him forth out of the city, and stoned him with stones, that he died.

Prov. 25:5. Take away the wicked *from* before the king, and his throne shall be established in righteousness.

Mic. 3:1. And I said, Hear, I pray you, O heads of Jacob, and ye princes of the house of Israel; *Is it* not for you to know judgment? 2. Who hate the good, and love the evil; who pluck off their skin from off them, and their flesh from off their bones; 3. Who also eat the flesh of my people, and flay their skin from off them; and they break their bones, and chop them in pieces, as for the pot, and as flesh within the caldron. 4. Then shall they cry unto the LORD, but he will not hear them: he will even hide his face from them at that time, as they have behaved themselves ill in their doings. 9. Hear this, I pray you, ye heads of the house of Jacob, and princes of the house of Israel, that abhor judgment, and pervert all equity. 10. They build up Zion with blood, and Jerusalem with iniquity. 11. The heads thereof judge for reward, and the priests thereof teach for hire, and the prophets thereof divine for money: yet will they lean upon the LORD, and say, *Is* not the LORD among us? none evil can come upon us.

See CHURCH, CORRUPTION IN; COURT, CORRUPT.

INSTANCES OF: Pilate, in delivering Jesus to death to please the clamoring multitude, John 19:12-16; Matt. 27:24. Felix, who expected money from Paul, Acts 24:26. See RULERS, WICKED, INSTANCES OF.

DUTY OF CITIZENS TO: Matt. 22:17. Tell us therefore, What thinkest thou? Is it lawful to give tribute unto Cæsar, or not? 18. But Jesus perceived their wickedness, and said, Why tempt ye me, *ye* hypocrites? 19. Shew me the tribute money. And they brought unto him a penny. 20. And he saith unto them, Whose *is* this image and superscription? 21. They say unto him, Cæsar's. Then saith he unto them, Render therefore unto Cæsar the things which are Cæsar's; and unto God the things that are God's. Luke 20:25.

Rom. 13:1. Let every soul be subject unto the higher powers. For there is no power but of God: the powers that be are ordained of God. 2. Whosoever therefore resisteth the power, resisteth the ordinance of God: and they that resist shall receive to themselves damnation. 3. For rulers are not a terror to good works, but to the evil. Wilt thou then not be afraid of the power? do that which is good, and thou shalt have praise of the same: 4. For he is the minister of God to thee for good. But if thou do that which is evil, be afraid; for he beareth not the sword in vain: for he is the minister of God, a revenger to *execute* wrath upon him that doeth evil. 5. Wherefore *ye* must needs be subject, not only for wrath, but also for conscience sake. 6. For for this cause pay ye tribute also: for they are God's ministers, attending continually upon this very thing. 7. Render therefore to all their dues: tribute

to whom tribute *is due;* custom to whom custom; fear to whom fear; honour to whom honour.

Tit. 3:1. Put them in mind to be subject to principalities and powers, to obey magistrates, to be ready to every good work,

1 Pet. 2:13. Submit yourselves to every ordinance of man for the Lord's sake: whether it be to the king, as supreme; 14. Or unto governors, as unto them that are sent by him for the punishment of evildoers, and for the praise of them that do well. 15. For so is the will of God, that with well doing ye may put to silence the ignorance of foolish men: 16. As free, and not using *your* liberty for a cloke of maliciousness, but as the servants of God. 17. Honour all *men.* Love the brotherhood. Fear God. Honour the king.

See CITIZEN.

GOD IN: In appointment of Saul as king, 1 Sam. 9:15-17; 10:1. In Saul's rejection, 1 Sam. 15:26-28; Acts 13:22. In appointment of David, 1 Sam. 16:1,7,13; 2 Sam. 7:13-16; Psa. 89:19-37; Acts 13:22. In counseling Solomon, 1 Kin. 9:2-9. In magnifying him, 1 Chr. 29:25. In denouncing Solomon's wickedness, 1 Kin. 11:9-13. In raising adversaries against Solomon, 1 Kin. 11:14,23. In rending the Jewish nation in twain, 1 Kin. 11:13; 12:1-24; 2 Chr. 10:15; 11:4; 22:7. In blotting out the house of Jeroboam, 1 Kin. 14:7-16; 15:27-30. In appointment of kings, 1 Kin. 14:14; 16:1-4; 1 Chr. 28:4,5; 29:25; Psa. 22:28; Prov. 8:15,16; Dan. 2:20,21,37; 5:20-24. In destruction of nations, Amos 9:8. See THEOCRATIC, above. Also see GOD; SOVEREIGN.

UNCLASSIFIED SCRIPTURES RELATING TO GOD IN: Psa. 22:28. For the kingdom *is* the LORD's: and he *is* the governor among the nations.

Prov. 8:15. By me kings reign, and princes decree justice. 16. By me princes rule, and nobles, *even* all the judges of the earth.

Isa. 9:6. For unto us a child is born, unto us a son is given: and the government shall be upon his shoulder: and his name shall be called Wonderful, Counsellor, The mighty God, The everlasting Father, The Prince of Peace. 7. Of the increase of *his* government and peace *there shall be* no end, upon the throne of David, and upon his kingdom, to order it, and to establish it with judgment and with justice from henceforth even for ever. The zeal of the LORD of hosts will perform this.

Jer. 1:9. Then the LORD put forth his hand, and touched my mouth. And the LORD said unto me, Behold, I have put my words in thy mouth. 10. See, I have this day set thee over the nations and over the kingdoms, to root out, and to pull down, and to destroy, and to throw down, to build, and to plant.

Jer. 18:6. O house of Israel, cannot I do with you as this potter? saith the LORD. Behold, as the clay *is* in the potter's hand, so *are* ye in mine hand, O house of Israel. 7.

At what instant I shall speak concerning a nation, and concerning a kingdom, to pluck up, and to pull down, and to destroy *it;* 8. If that nation, against whom I have pronounced, turn from their evil, I will repent of the evil that I thought to do unto them. 9. And *at what* instant I shall speak concerning a nation, and concerning a kingdom, to build and to plant *it;* 10. If it do evil in my sight, that it obey not my voice, then I will repent of the good, wherewith I said I would benefit them.

Jer. 25:12. And it shall come to pass, when seventy years are accomplished, *that* I will punish the king of Babylon, and that nation, saith the Lord, for their iniquity, and the land of the Chaldeans, and will make it perpetual desolations. 13. And I will bring upon that land all my words which I have pronounced against it, *even* all that is written in this book, which Jeremiah hath prophesied against all the nations. 14. For many nations and great kings shall serve themselves of them also: and I will recompense them according to their deeds, and according to the works of their own hands. 15. For thus saith the Lord God of Israel unto me; Take the wine cup of this fury at my hand, and cause all the nations, to whom I send thee, to drink it. 16. And they shall drink, and be moved, and be mad, because of the sword that I will send among them. 17. Then took I the cup at the Lord's hand, and made all the nations to drink, unto whom the Lord had sent me: *vs.* 18–33.

Ezek. 21:25. And thou, profane wicked prince of Israel, whose day is come, when iniquity *shall have* an end, 26. Thus saith the Lord God; Remove the diadem, and take off the crown: this *shall* not *be* the same: exalt *him that is* low, and abase *him that is* high. 27. I will overturn, overturn, overturn, it: and it shall be no *more*, until he come whose right it is; and I will give it *him*.

Ezek. 29:19. Therefore thus saith the Lord God; Behold, I will give the land of Egypt unto Nebuchadrezzar king of Babylon; and he shall take her multitude, and take her spoil, and take her prey; and it shall be the wages for his army. 20. I have given him the land of Egypt *for* his labour wherewith he served against it, because they wrought for me, saith the Lord God.

Dan. 2:20. Daniel answered and said, Blessed be the name of God for ever and ever: for wisdom and might are his: 21. And he changeth the times and the seasons: he removeth kings, and setteth up kings: he giveth wisdom unto the wise, and knowledge to them that know understanding: 37. Thou, O king, *art* a king of kings: for the God of heaven hath given thee a kingdom, power, and strength, and glory.

Dan. 4:17. This matter *is* by the decree of the watchers, and the demand by the word of the holy ones: to the intent that the living may know that the most High ruleth in the kingdom of men, and giveth it to whomsoever he will, and setteth up over it the basest of men.

Dan. 5:18. O thou king, the most high God gave Nebuchadnezzar thy father a kingdom, and majesty, and glory, and honour: 19. And for the majesty that he gave him, all people, nations, and languages, trembled and feared before him: whom he would he slew; and whom he would he kept alive; and whom he would he set up; and whom he would he put down. 20. But when his heart was lifted up, and his mind hardened in pride, he was deposed from his kingly throne, and they took his glory from him: 21. And he was driven from the sons of men; and his heart was made like the beasts, and his dwelling *was* with the wild asses: they fed him with grass like oxen, and his body was wet with the dew of heaven; till he knew that the most high God ruled in the kingdom of men, and *that* he appointeth over it whomsoever he will. 22. And thou his son, O Belshazzar, hast not humbled thine heart, though thou knewest all this; 23. But hast lifted up thyself against the Lord of heaven; and they have brought the vessels of his house before thee, and thou, and thy lords, thy wives, and thy concubines, have drunk wine in them; and thou hast praised the gods of silver, and gold, of brass, iron, wood, and stone, which see not, nor hear, nor know: and the God in whose hand thy breath *is*, and whose *are* all thy ways, hast thou not glorified: 24. Then was the part of the hand sent from him; and this writing was written. 25. And this *is* the writing that was written, MENE, MENE, TEKEL, UPHARSIN. 26. This *is* the interpretation of the thing: MENE; God hath numbered thy kingdom, and finished it. 27. TEKEL; Thou art weighed in the balances, and art found wanting. 28. PERES; Thy kingdom is divided, and given to the Medes and Persians.

Dan. 10:13. But the prince of the kingdom of Persia withstood me one and twenty days: but, lo, Michael, one of the chief princes, came to help me; and I remained there with the kings of Persia.

Hos. 8:4. They have set up kings, but not by me: they have made princes, and I knew *it* not:

Amos 9:8. Behold, the eyes of the Lord God *are* upon the sinful kingdom, and I will destroy it from off the face of the earth: saving that I will not utterly destroy the house of Jacob, saith the Lord.

Hag. 2:21. Speak to Zerubbabel, governor of Judah, saying, I will shake the heavens and the earth; 22. And I will overthrow the throne of kingdoms, and I will destroy the strength of the kingdoms of the heathen; and I will overthrow the chariots, and those that ride in them; and the horses and their riders shall come down, every one by the sword of his brother.

John 19:10. Then saith Pilate unto him, Speakest thou not unto me? knowest thou not that I have power to crucify thee, and have power to release thee? 11. Jesus answered, Thou couldest have no power *at all* against me, except it were given thee from above: therefore he that delivered me unto thee hath the greater sin.

See GOD, SOVEREIGN; JESUS, KINGDOM OF.

GOZAN, a district of Mesopotamia. Israelites taken in captivity to, by the king of Assyria, after the conquest of Samaria, 1 Chr. 5:26; 2 Kin. 17:6; 18:11; 19:12.

GRACE OF GOD. Gen. 15:6. And he believed in the LORD; and he counted it to him for righteousness.

Gen. 20:6. And God said unto him in a dream, Yea, I know that thou didst this in the integrity of thy heart; for I also withheld thee from sinning against me: therefore suffered I thee not to touch her.

Deut. 7:6. For thou *art* an holy people unto the LORD thy God: the LORD thy God hath chosen thee to be a special people unto himself, above all people that *are* upon the face of the earth. 7. The LORD did not set his love upon you, nor choose you, because ye were more in number than any people; for ye *were* the fewest of all people: 8. But because the LORD loved you, and because he would keep the oath which he had sworn unto your fathers, hath the LORD brought you out with a mighty hand, and redeemed you out of the house of bondmen, from the hand of Pharaoh king of Egypt. 9. Know therefore that the LORD thy God, he *is* God, the faithful God, which keepeth covenant and mercy with them that love him and keep his commandments to a thousand generations;

Deut. 9:4. Speak not thou in thine heart, after that the LORD thy God hath cast them out from before thee, saying, For my righteousness the LORD hath brought me in to possess this land: but for the wickedness of these nations the LORD doth drive them out from before thee. 5. Not for thy righteousness, or for the uprightness of thine heart, dost thou go to possess their land: but for the wickedness of these nations the LORD thy God doth drive them out from before thee, and that he may perform the word which the LORD sware unto thy fathers, Abraham, Isaac, and Jacob. 6. Understand therefore, that the LORD thy God giveth thee not this good land to possess it for thy righteousness; for thou *art* a stiffnecked people.

Job 10:12. Thou hast granted me life and favour, and thy visitation hath preserved my spirit.

Job 22:2. Can a man be profitable unto God, as he that is wise may be profitable unto himself? 3. *Is it* any pleasure to the Almighty, that thou art righteous? or *is it* gain *to him*, that thou makest thy ways perfect?

Psa. 94:17. Unless the LORD *had been* my help, my soul had almost dwelt in silence.

18. When I said, My foot slippeth; thy mercy, O LORD, held me up. 19. In the multitude of my thoughts within me thy comforts delight my soul.

Psa. 138:3. In the day when I cried thou answeredst me, *and* strengthenedst me *with* strength in my soul.

Psa. 143:11. Quicken me, O LORD, for thy name's sake: for thy righteousness' sake bring my soul out of trouble.

Dan. 9:18. O my God, incline thine ear, and hear; open thine eyes, and behold our desolations, and the city which is called by thy name: for we do not present our supplications before thee for our righteousnesses, but for thy great mercies.

Dan. 10:18. Then there came again and touched me *one* like the appearance of a man, and he strengthened me, 19. And said, O man greatly beloved, fear not: peace *be* unto thee; be strong, yea, be strong. And when he had spoken unto me, I was strengthened, and said, Let my Lord speak; for thou hast strengthened me.

John 6:44. No man can come to me, except the Father which hath sent me draw him: and I will raise him up at the last day. 45. It is written in the prophets, And they shall be all taught of God. Every man therefore that hath heard, and hath learned of the Father, cometh unto me.

John 17:11. And now I am no more in the world, but these are in the world, and I come to thee. Holy Father, keep through thine own name those whom thou hast given me, that they may be one, as we *are*. 12. While I was with them in the world, I kept them in thy name: those that thou gavest me I have kept, and none of them is lost, but the son of perdition; that the scripture might be fulfilled. 15. I pray not that thou shouldest take them out of the world, but that thou shouldest keep them from the evil.

Acts 4:29. And now, Lord, behold their threatenings: and grant unto thy servants, that with all boldness they may speak thy word, 30. By stretching forth thine hand to heal; and that signs and wonders may be done by the name of thy holy child Jesus.

Acts 26:22. Having therefore obtained help of God, I continue unto this day, witnessing both to small and great,

Rom. 3:22. Even the righteousness of God *which is* by faith of Jesus Christ unto all and upon all them that believe: for there is no difference: 23. For all have sinned, and come short of the glory of God; 24. Being justified freely by his grace through the redemption that is in Christ Jesus:

Rom. 4:4. Now to him that worketh is the reward not reckoned of grace, but of debt. 5. But to him that worketh not, but believeth on him that justifieth the ungodly, his faith is counted for righteousness. 16. Therefore *it is* of faith, that *it might be* by grace; to the end the promise might be sure to all the seed;

Rom. 5:2. By whom also we have access by faith into this grace wherein we stand, and rejoice in hope of the glory of God. 6. For when we were yet without strength, in due time Christ died for the ungodly. 7. For scarcely for a righteous man will one die: yet peradventure for a good man some would even dare to die. 8. But God commendeth his love toward us, in that, while we were yet sinners, Christ died for us. 15. But not as the offence, so also *is* the free gift. For if through the offence of one many be dead, much more the grace of God, and the gift by grace, *which is* by one man, Jesus Christ, hath abounded unto many. 16. And not as *it was* by one that sinned, *so is* the gift: for the judgment *was* by one to condemnation, but the free gift *is* of many offences unto justification. 17. For if by one man's offence death reigned by one; much more they which receive abundance of grace and of the gift of righteousness shall reign in life by one, Jesus Christ. 18. Therefore as by the offence of one *judgment came* upon all men to condemnation; even so by the righteousness of one *the free gift came* upon all men unto justification of life. 19. For as by one man's disobedience many were made sinners, so by the obedience of one shall many be made righteous. 20. Moreover the law entered, that the offence might abound. But where sin abounded, grace did much more abound: 21. That as sin hath reigned unto death, even so might grace reign through righteousness unto eternal life by Jesus Christ our Lord.

Rom. 9:10. And not only *this;* but when Rebecca also had conceived by one, *even* by our father Isaac; 11. (For *the children* being not yet born, neither having done any good or evil, that the purpose of God according to election might stand, not of works, but of him that calleth;) 12. It was said unto her, The elder shall serve the younger. 13. As it is written, Jacob have I loved, but Esau have I hated. 14. What shall we say then? *Is there* unrighteousness with God? God forbid. 15. For he saith to Moses, I will have mercy on whom I will have mercy, and I will have compassion on whom I will have compassion. 16. So then *it is* not of him that willeth, nor of him that runneth, but of God that sheweth mercy.

Rom. 11:5. Even so then at this present time also there is a remnant according to the election of grace. 6. And if by grace, then *is it* no more of works: otherwise grace is no more grace. ¹ But if *it be* of works, then is it no more grace: otherwise work is no more work.

[¹ Omitted in R. V.]

1 Cor. 1:4. I thank my God always on your behalf, for the grace of God which is given you by Jesus Christ; 5. That in every thing ye are enriched by him, in all utterance, and *in* all knowledge; 6. Even as the testimony of Christ was confirmed in you: 7. So that ye come behind in no gift; wait-ing for the coming of our Lord Jesus Christ: 8. Who shall also confirm you unto the end, *that ye may be* blameless in the day of our Lord Jesus Christ.

1 Cor. 10:13. There hath no temptation taken you but such as is common to man: but God *is* faithful, who will not suffer you to be tempted above that ye are able; but will with the temptation also make a way to escape, that ye may be able to bear *it.*

1 Cor. 15:10. By the grace of God I am what I am: and his grace which *was bestowed* upon me was not in vain; but I laboured more abundantly than they all: yet not I, but the grace of God which was with me.

2 Cor. 1:12. Our rejoicing is this, the testimony of our conscience, that in simplicity and godly sincerity, not with fleshly wisdom, but by the grace of God, we have had our conversation in the world, and more abundantly to you-ward.

Gal. 1:15. But when it pleased God, who separated me from my mother's womb, and called *me* by his grace, 16. To reveal his Son in me, that I might preach him among the heathen; immediately I conferred not with flesh and blood:

Eph. 1:5. Having predestinated us unto the adoption of children by Jesus Christ to himself, according to the good pleasure of his will, 6. To the praise of the glory of his grace, wherein he hath made us accepted in the beloved. 7. In whom we have redemption through his blood, the forgiveness of sins, according to the riches of his grace; 8. Wherein he hath abounded toward us in all wisdom and prudence; 9. Having made known unto us the mystery of his will, according to his good pleasure which he hath purposed in himself: 11. In whom also we have obtained an inheritance, being predestinated according to the purpose of him who worketh all things after the counsel of his own will: 12. That we should be to the praise of his glory, who first trusted in Christ.

Eph. 2:8. By grace are ye saved through faith; and that not of yourselves: *it is* the gift of God: 9. Not of works, lest any man should boast.

Eph. 3:16. That he would grant you, according to the riches of his glory, to be strengthened with might by his Spirit in the inner man;

Eph. 4:7. But unto every one of us is given grace according to the measure of the gift of Christ.

Eph. 6:10. Finally, my brethren, be strong in the Lord, and in the power of his might.

Phil. 1:19. For I know that this shall turn to my salvation through your prayer, and the supply of the Spirit of Jesus Christ,

Phil. 2:13. For it is God which worketh in you both to will and to do of *his* good pleasure.

1 Thess. 1:1. Grace *be* unto you, and peace,

¹ from God our Father, and the Lord Jesus Christ.
1 Thess. 5:28; 2 Pet. 1:2.   [¹ Omitted in R. V.]

1 Tim. 1:14. And the grace of our Lord was exceeding abundant with faith and love which is in Christ Jesus.

2 Tim. 1:1. Paul, an apostle of Jesus Christ by the will of God, according to the promise of life which is in Christ Jesus. 9. Who hath saved us, and called us with an holy calling, not according to our works, but according to his own purpose and grace, which was given us in Christ Jesus before the world began.

Tit. 3:7. That being justified by his grace, we should be made heirs according to the hope of eternal life.

1 Pet. 1:5. Who are kept by the power of God through faith unto salvation ready to be revealed in the last time.

1 Pet. 4:10. As good stewards of the manifold grace of God.

1 Pet. 5:10. But the God of all grace, who hath called us unto his eternal glory by Christ Jesus, after that ye have suffered a while, make you perfect, stablish, strengthen, settle you.

Jude 1. Jude, the servant of Jesus Christ, and brother of James, to them that are sanctified by God the Father, and preserved in Jesus Christ, and called: 21. Keep yourselves in the love of God, looking for the mercy of our Lord Jesus Christ unto eternal life. 24. Now unto him that is able to keep you from falling, and to present you faultless before the presence of his glory with exceeding joy, 25. To the only wise God our Saviour, be glory and majesty, dominion and power, both now and ever.

Rev. 3:10. Because thou hast kept the word of my patience, I also will keep thee from the hour of temptation, which shall come upon all the world, to try them that dwell upon the earth.

See GOD, GRACE OF.

GROWTH IN: Psa. 84:7. They go from strength to strength, every one of them in Zion appeareth before God.

Prov. 4:18. But the path of the just is as the shining light, that shineth more and more unto the perfect day.

Phil. 1:6. Being confident of this very thing, that he which hath begun a good work in you will perform it until the day of Jesus Christ: 9. And this I pray, that your love may abound yet more and more in knowledge and in all judgment; 10. That ye may approve things that are excellent; that ye may be sincere and without offence till the day of Christ; 11. Being filled with the fruits of righteousness, which are by Jesus Christ, unto the glory and praise of God.

Phil. 3:12. Not as though I had already attained, either were already perfect: but I follow after, if that I may apprehend that for which also I am apprehended of Christ Jesus. 13. Brethren, I count not myself to have apprehended: but this one thing I do,

forgetting those things which are behind, and reaching forth unto those things which are before, 14. I press toward the mark for the prize of the high calling of God in Christ Jesus. 15. Let us therefore, as many as be perfect, be thus minded:

Col. 1:10. That ye might walk worthy of the Lord unto all pleasing, being fruitful in every good work, and increasing in the knowledge of God; 11. Strengthened with all might, according to his glorious power, unto all patience and longsuffering with joyfulness;

Col. 2:19. And not holding the Head, from which all the body by joints and bands having nourishment ministered, and knit together, increaseth with the increase of God.

1 Thess. 3:10. Night and day praying exceedingly that we might see your face, and might perfect that which is lacking in your faith? 12. And the Lord make you to increase and abound in love one toward another, and toward all men, even as we do toward you: 13. To the end he may stablish your hearts unblameable in holiness before God, even our Father, at the coming of our Lord Jesus Christ with all his saints.

2 Thess. 1:3. We are bound to thank God always for you, brethren, as it is meet, because that your faith groweth exceedingly, and the charity of every one of you all toward each other aboundeth;

Heb. 6:1. Therefore leaving the principles of the doctrine of Christ, let us go on unto perfection; not laying again the foundation of repentance from dead works, and of faith toward God, 2. Of the doctrine of baptisms, and of laying on of hands, and of resurrection of the dead, and of eternal judgment. 3. And this will we do, if God permit.

1 Pet. 2:1. Wherefore laying aside all malice, and all guile, and hypocrisies, and envies, and all evil speakings, 2. As newborn babes, desire the sincere milk of the word, that ye may grow thereby: 3. If so be ye have tasted that the Lord is gracious.

2 Pet. 3:18. But grow in grace, and in the knowledge of our Lord and Saviour Jesus Christ.

GRACES. Christian. Matt. 5:3. Blessed are the poor in spirit: for their's is the kingdom of heaven. 4. Blessed are they that mourn: for they shall be comforted. 5. Blessed are the meek: for they shall inherit the earth. 6. Blessed are they which do hunger and thirst after righteousness: for they shall be filled. 7. Blessed are the merciful: for they shall obtain mercy. 8. Blessed are the pure in heart: for they shall see God. 9. Blessed are the peacemakers: for they shall be called the children of God. 10. Blessed are they which are persecuted for righteousness' sake: for their's is the kingdom of heaven. 11. Blessed are ye, when men shall revile you, and persecute you, and shall say all manner of evil against you falsely, for my sake.

Rom. 5:3. And not only *so*, but we glory in tribulations also: knowing that tribulation worketh patience; 4. And patience, experience; and experience, hope: 5. And hope maketh not ashamed; because the love of God is shed abroad in our hearts by the Holy Ghost which is given unto us.

1 Cor. 13:1. Though I speak with the tongues of men and of angels, and have not charity, I am become *as* sounding brass, or a tinkling cymbal. 2. And though I have *the gift of* prophecy, and understand all mysteries, and all knowledge; and though I have all faith, so that I could remove mountains, and have not charity, I am nothing. 3. And though I bestow all my goods to feed *the poor*, and though I give my body to be burned, and have not charity, it profiteth me nothing. 4. Charity suffereth long, *and* is kind; charity envieth not; charity vaunteth not itself, is not puffed up, 5. Doth not behave itself unseemly, seeketh not her own, is not easily provoked, thinketh no evil; 6. Rejoiceth not in iniquity, but rejoiceth in the truth; 7. Beareth all things, believeth all things, hopeth all things, endureth all things. 8. Charity never faileth: but whether *there be* prophecies, they shall fail; whether *there be* tongues, they shall cease; whether *there be* knowledge, it shall vanish away. 13. And now abideth faith, hope, charity, these three; but the greatest of these *is* charity.

Gal. 5:22. But the fruit of the Spirit is love, joy, peace, longsuffering, gentleness, goodness, ¹faith, 23. Meekness, temperance: against such there is no law. [¹R. V. faithfulness]

2 Pet. 1:5. And beside this, giving all diligence, add to your faith virtue; and to virtue knowledge; 6. And to knowledge temperance; and to temperance patience; and to patience godliness; 7. And to godliness brotherly kindness; and to brotherly kindness charity. 8. For if these things be in you, and abound, they make *you that ye shall* neither *be* barren nor unfruitful in the knowledge of our Lord Jesus Christ. 9. But he that lacketh these things is blind, and cannot see afar off, and hath forgotten that he was purged from his old sins.

See CHARACTER; CHARITABLENESS; COURAGE; GENTLENESS; HOPE; KINDNESS; KNOWLEDGE; LONGSUFFERING; LOVE; MEEKNESS; MERCY; PATIENCE; PEACE; PERSEVERANCE; PURITY; RIGHTEOUSNESS, FRUITS OF; STABILITY; TEMPERANCE; WISDOM.

GRAFTING, Rom. 11:17–24.

GRANDFATHER, called FATHER, Gen. 10:21.

GRAPE. Cultivated in vineyards, by Noah, Gen. 9:20; the Canaanites, Num. 13:24; Deut. 6:11; Josh. 24:13; Edomites, Num. 20:17; Amorites, Num. 21:22; Isa. 16:8,9; Philistines, Judg. 15:5. Grown, at Abel, Judg. 11:33 [marg.]; Baal-hamon, Song 8:11; Carmel, 2 Chr. 26:10; En-gedi, Song 1:14; Jezreel, 1 Kin. 21:1; Lebanon, Hos. 14:7; Samaria, Jer. 31:5; Shechem, Judg. 9:27;

Shiloh, Judg. 21:20,21; Timnath, Judg. 14:5.

Culture of, Lev. 25:3,11; Deut. 28:39; 2 Chr. 26:10; Song 6:11; Isa. 5:1; Jer. 31:5.

Wine made of, Jer. 25:30. Wine of, forbidden to Nazarites, Num. 6:4. See NAZARITES. See VINE; VINEYARDS; WINE.

FIGURATIVE: Deut. 32:32; Psa. 128:3; Jer. 2:21; Ezek. 15; Hos. 10:1; Rev. 14:18–20.

FABLE OF, Judg. 9:12,13.

PARABLES OF THE VINE, Psa. 80:8–14; Ezek. 17:6–10; 19:10–14; John 15:1–5.

PROVERB OF, Ezek. 18:2.

See VINE; VINEYARDS; WINE.

GRASS. Created on the third creative day, Gen. 1:11. Mown, Psa. 72:6. God's care of, Matt. 6:30; Luke 12:28. On roofs of houses, Psa. 129:6.

FIGURATIVE: Psa. 90:5,6; Isa. 40:6; 1 Pet. 1:24; Jas. 1:10,11.

GRASSHOPPER, Num. 13:33; Eccl. 12:5; Isa. 40:22; Nah. 3:17.

See LOCUST.

GRATE, Ex. 27:4,5; 38:4,5.

GRATITUDE. See THANKFULNESS.

GRAVE. Prepared by Jacob, Gen. 50:5. Defilement from touching, Num. 19:16,18. Weeping at, 2 Sam. 3:32; John 11:31; 20:11. Of parents, honored, 2 Sam. 19:37. Welcomed, Job 3:20–22. Resurrection from: Of Lazarus, John 11:43,44; 12:17; of Jesus, Matt. 28:5,6; 1 Cor. 15:12–20; of saints after Jesus's resurrection, Matt. 27:52,53; of all the dead, foretold, John 5:28; 1 Cor. 15:22–54.

See BURIAL.

GRAVEL. FIGURATIVE: Prov. 20:17.

GRAVING. See ENGRAVING.

GREAT SEA. See MEDITERRANEAN SEA.

GREAVES, 1 Sam. 17:6.

GREECE. Inhabitants of, called Gentiles, Mark 7:26; John 7:35; Rom. 2:10; 3:9; 1 Cor. 10:32; 12:13; desire to see Jesus, John 12:20–23; marry among the Jews, Acts 16:1; accept the Messiah, Acts 17:2–4,12,34; persecute the early Christians, Acts 6:9–14; 9:29; 18:17. Gentiles called Greeks, Rom. 10:12; Gal. 3:28; Col. 3:11.

Schools of philosophy in Athens, Acts 19:9. Philosophy of, 1 Cor. 1:22,23. Poets of, Acts 17:28.

See ATHENS; EPICUREANS; STOICISM.

GREED. See COVETOUSNESS.

GREEK. Philosophy of, 1 Cor. 1:22,23. See GREECE.

GREYHOUND, Prov. 30:31.

GRIEF, attributed to the Holy Spirit, Eph. 4:30; Heb. 3:10,17.

See AFFLICTION; SORROW.

GRINDING. See MILL.

GROUND. Man made from, Gen. 2:7; 3:19,23; Job 4:19; 33:6. Animals from, Gen. 2:19. Vegetables from, Gen. 2:9.

Cursed, Gen. 3:17; 5:29.

GROVES [*R. V.* Asheroth, Asherah, Asherine, and in Gen. 21:33 tamarisk tree], probably an image or images of the Canaanitish goddess Asherah.

See ASHTORETH.

Forbidden to be established, Deut. 16:21; Isa. 1:29; 17:8; 27:9; Mic. 5:14. Worshiped by Israelites, Judg. 3:7; 1 Kin. 14:15,23; 15:13; 18:19; 2 Kin. 13:6; 17:10,16; 21:3–7; 2 Chr. 24: 18; Jer. 17:2.

Destroyed by Gideon, Judg. 6:28; Hezekiah, 2 Kin. 18:4; Josiah, 2 Kin. 23:14; 2 Chr. 34:3,4; Asa, 2 Chr. 14:3; Jehoshaphat, 2 Chr. 17:6; 19:3.

See IDOLATRY.

GUARD. See WATCHMAN.

GUDGODAH. A station of the Israelites in the wilderness, Deut. 10:7; probably identical with HOR-HAGIDGAD in Num. 33: 32,33.

GUEST. Salutations to, Gen. 18:2. Abraham's hospitality to, see HOSPITALITY. Rules for the conduct of, Prov. 23:1–3,6–8; 25:6,7,17; Luke 10:5–7; 14:7–11; 1 Cor. 10:27. See HOSPITALITY.

GUIDANCE. See GOD; GUIDE.

GUILE. See CONSPIRACY; DECEIT; FRAUD; HYPOCRISY.

GUILT. See CONVICTION; SIN; CONSCIENCE.

GUNI. 1. Son of Naphtali, Gen. 46:24; Num. 26:48; 1 Chr. 7:13.

2. Father of Abdiel, 1 Chr. 5:15.

GUR, place where Jehu slew Ahaziah, 2 Kin. 9:27.

GUR-BAAL, a town between Canaan and Arabia, 2 Chr. 26:7.

H

HAAHASHTARI, son of Naarah, 1 Chr. 4:6.

HABAIAH, a priest, whose descendants returned from captivity, Ezra 2:61; Neh. 7:63.

HABAKKUK. A prophet and poet, who prophesied after the destruction of Nineveh, probably, Hab. 1:1; 3:1. His hymn of praise of the majesty of God, Hab. 3.

HABAZINIAH, head of the family of Rechabites, Jer. 35:3.

HABERGEON, a part of the defensive armor of a soldier, Ex. 28:32; 39:23.

See BREASTPLATE.

HABOR, a river of Mesopotamia, 2 Kin. 17:6; 18:11; 1 Chr. 5:26.

HACHALIAH, father of Nehemiah, Neh. 1:1; 10:1.

HACHILAH, a hill in Judah where David and his followers hid from Saul, 1 Sam. 23:19; 26:3.

HACHMONI, father of Jehiel, 1 Chr. 11:11; 27:32.

HADAD. 1. A succcessor of Husham as king of Edom. Vanquished the Midianites on the field of Moab, Gen. 36:35; 1 Chr. 1:46.

2. A son of Ishmael, 1 Chr. 1:30. Called HADAR in Gen. 25:15.

3. Successor of Baal-hanan, king of Edom, 1 Chr. 1:50. Called HADAR in Gen. 36:39.

4. A prince of Edom. Adversary of Solomon, 1 Kin. 11:14–22,25.

HADADEZER, called also HADAREZER. King of Zobah, vanquished by David, 2 Sam.

8:3–13; 10:15–19; 1 Kin. 11:23; 1 Chr. 18:3–10; 19:6–19.

HADADRIMMON, a place in the valley of Megiddon, Zech. 12:11.

HADAR. See HADAD.

HADAREZER. See HADADEZER.

HADASHAH, a town in Judah, Josh. 15:37.

HADASSAH, Jewish name of Esther, Esth. 2:7.

See ESTHER.

HADATTAH, probably an adjective qualifying Hazor, making it equivalent to NEW HAZOR, Josh. 15:25.

HADES. 1. The unseen world, translated hell in *A. V.*, but in the *R. V.* the word Hades is retained, Matt. 11:23; 16:18; Luke 10:15; 16:23; Acts 2:27,31; Rev. 1:18; 6:8; 20:13,14.

See HELL.

2. **REALM, OR STATE, OF THE DEAD,** USUALLY EXPRESSED IN HEBREW BY SHEOL AND IN GREEK BY HADES: 2 Sam. 22:6. The sorrows of hell compassed me about; the snares of death prevented me;

Job 26:5. Dead *things* are formed from under the waters, and the inhabitants thereof.

Psa. 6:5. For in death *there is* no remembrance of thee: in the grave who shall give thee thanks?

Psa. 17:15. As for me, I will behold thy face in righteousness: I shall be satisfied, when I awake, with thy likeness.

Psa. 30:9. What profit *is there* in my blood, when I go down to the pit? Shall the dust praise thee? shall it declare thy truth?

Psa. 49:15. But God will redeem my soul from the power of the grave: for he shall receive me.

Psa. 86:13. For great *is* thy mercy toward me: and thou hast delivered my soul from the lowest hell.

Psa. 88:10. Wilt thou shew wonders to the dead? shall the dead arise *and* praise thee? 11. Shall thy lovingkindness be declared in the grave? *or* thy faithfulness in destruction? 12. Shall thy wonders be known in the dark? and thy righteousness in the land of forgetfulness?

Psa. 115:17. The dead praise not the LORD, neither any that go down into silence.

Psa. 116:3. The sorrows of death compassed me, and the pains of hell gat hold upon me: I found trouble and sorrow.

Prov. 15:24. The way of life *is* above to the wise, that he may depart from hell beneath.

Prov. 21:16. The man that wandereth out of the way of understanding shall remain in the congregation of the dead.

Prov. 27:20. Hell and destruction are never full; so the eyes of man are never satisfied.

Eccl. 9:4. For to him that is joined to all the living there is hope: for a living dog is better than a dead lion. 5. For the living know that they shall die: but the dead know not any thing, neither have they any more a reward; for the memory of them is forgotten. 6. Also their love, and their hatred, and their envy, is now perished; neither have they any more a portion for ever in any *thing* that is done under the sun.

Isa. 5:14. Therefore hell hath enlarged herself, and opened her mouth without measure: and their glory, and their multitude, and their pomp, and he that rejoiceth, shall descend into it.

Jonah 2:2. And said, I cried by reason of mine affliction unto the LORD, and he heard me; out of the belly of hell cried I, *and* thou heardest my voice.

Luke 23:42. And he said unto Jesus, Lord, remember me when thou comest into thy kingdom. 43. And Jesus said unto him, Verily I say unto thee, To day shalt thou be with me in paradise.

John 8:22. Then said the Jews, Will he kill himself? because he saith, Whither I go, ye cannot come.

2 Cor. 12:4. How that he was caught up into paradise, and heard unspeakable words, which it is not lawful for a man to utter.

See HELL; IMMORTALITY; PARADISE; RIGHTEOUS, FUTURE STATE OF; SPIRIT; WICKED, PUNISHMENT OF.

HADID, a city of Benjamin. Captives of, returned from Babylon, Ezra 2:33; Neh. 7:37; 11:34.

HADLAI, an Ephraimite, 2 Chr. 28:12.

HADORAM. 1. Descendant of Shem, Gen. 10:27; 1 Chr. 1:21.

2. Son of Ton, or Toi, 1 Chr. 18:10. Called JORAM, 2 Sam. 8:10.

3. Chief officer of the tribute under Rehoboam, 2 Chr. 10:18. Probably identical with ADONIRAM of 1 Kin. 4:6; 5:14; and ADORAM of 2 Sam. 20:24.

HADRACH, a district of Syria, Zech. 9:1.

HAGAB, one of the Nethinim, Ezra 2:46.

HAGABA, called also HAGABAH. One of the Nethinim, Ezra 2:45; Neh. 7:48.

HAGAR, a servant of Abraham and handmaid of Sarah. Given by Sarah to Abraham to be his wife, Gen. 16. Descendants of, Gen. 25:12–15; 1 Chr. 5:10,19–22; Psa. 83:6. Called AGAR, Gal. 4:24,25.

HAGGAI, one of the minor prophets. Urges the Jews to rebuild the temple, Ezra 5:1; 6:14. See the Book of Haggai.

HAGGERI, father of Mibhar, 1 Chr. 11:38.

HAGGI, son of Gad, Gen. 46:16; Num. 26:15.

HAGGIAH, a Levite, 1 Chr. 6:30.

HAGGITH, wife of David. Mother of Adonijah, 2 Sam. 3:4; 1 Kin. 1:5,11; 2:13; 1 Chr. 3:2.

HAI, Gen. 12:8; 13:3. See AI.

HAIL, Job 38:22; Hag. 2:17. Plague of, in Egypt, Ex. 9:18–29; Psa. 78:48; 105:32. Destroys army of the Amorites, Josh. 10:11. FIGURATIVE, Isa. 28:2; Rev. 8:7; 11:19; 16:21.

HAIR. Numbered, Matt. 10:30; Luke 12:7. Worn long by women, Isa. 3:24; Luke 7:38; 1 Cor. 11:5,6,15; 1 Tim. 2:9; 1 Pet. 3:3; Rev. 9:8; by Absalom, 2 Sam. 14:26. Worn short by men, 1 Cor. 11:14. Symbolical dividing of, Ezek. 5:1,2.

See BALDNESS; CAUL; LEPROSY; MOURNING; NAZARITE.

HAKKATAN, father of Johanan, Ezra 8:12.

HAKKOZ, a priest, 1 Chr. 24:10. Called Koz in Ezra 2:61; Neh. 3:4,21.

HAKUPHA, one of the Nethinim, Ezra 2:51; Neh. 7:53.

HALAH, a place to which Israelite captives were transported, 2 Kin. 17:6; 18:11; 1 Chr. 5:26.

HALAK, a mountain, the southern limit of Joshua's conquests, Josh. 11:17; 12:7.

HALF-HOMER, a measure of about seven or eight gallons.

See MEASURE, DRY.

HALHUL, a city in Judah, Josh. 15:58.

HALI, a border town of Asher, Josh. 19:25.

HALLELUJAH, an exclamatory expression of praise or adoration, Psa. 106:1; 111:1; 112:1; 113:1; 117:1; 135:1; 146:1,10; 147:1; 148:1; Rev. 19:1.

See PRAISE.

HALOHESH, called also HALLOHESH. Father of Shallum, Neh. 3:12. Sealed the covenant with Nehemiah, Neh. 10:24.

HAM. 1. Son of Noah, Gen. 5:32; 9:18,24; 1 Chr. 1:4. Provokes his father's wrath and is cursed by him, Gen. 9:18–27. His children, Gen. 10:6–20; 1 Chr. 1:8–16.

2. Patronymic of the descendants of Ham, 1 Chr. 4:40; Psa. 78:51; 105:23,27; 106:22.

3. Place where Chedorlaomer smote the Zuzims, Gen. 14:5.

HAMAN. Prime minister of Ahasuerus, Esth. 3:1. Plotted against Esther and the Jews, thwarted by Esther and Mordecai, hanged, Esth. chapters 3–9.

HAMATH, called also HEMATH. A city of upper Syria, Num. 13:21; 34:8; Josh. 13:5; 1 Kin. 8:65; Ezek. 47:16. Inhabited by Canaanites, Gen. 10:18. Prosperity of, Amos 6:2. David receives gifts of gold and silver from Toi, king of, 2 Sam. 8:9,10; 1 Chr. 18:3,9,10. Conquest of, by Jeroboam, 2 Kin. 14:25,28; by the Chaldeans, 2 Kin. 25:20,21. Israelites taken captive to, Isa. 11:11. Prophecy concerning, Jer. 49:23. Solomon builds store cities in, 2 Chr. 8:4.

HAMATH-ZOBAH, a town on the border of Palestine. Subdued by Solomon, 2 Chr. 8:3.

HAMMATH, a fortified city of Naphtali, Josh. 19:35.

See HAMMON; HAMMOTH-DOR.

HAMMEDATHA, father of Haman, Esth. 3:1,10; 8:5; 9:10,24.

HAMMELECH, name of a man, or possibly only an appellation, meaning "the king," Jer. 36:26; 38:6.

HAMMER, 1 Kin. 6:7; Isa. 41:7; Jer. 10:4.

FIGURATIVE: Jer. 23:29; 50:23.

HAMMOLEKETH, daughter of Machir, 1 Chr. 7:17,18.

HAMMON. 1. A city of Asher, Josh. 19:28.

2. A Levitical city of Naphtali, 1 Chr. 6: 76. Possibly identical with HAMMATH and HAMMOTH-DOR, which see.

HAMMOTH-DOR. A city of refuge of Naphtali, Josh. 21:32. Possibly identical with HAMMATH, Josh. 19:35. Called HAMMON, 1 Chr. 6:76.

HAMONAH, burial place of the multitudes of Gog, Ezek. 39:16.

HAMON-GOG, another name for HAMONAH, Ezek. 39:11,15.

HAMOR, father of Shechem. Jacob buys ground from, Gen. 33:19; Josh. 24:32; Judg. 9:28. Murdered by the sons of Jacob, Gen. 34:26; 49:6. Called EMMOR, Acts 7:16.

HAMUEL, a Simeonite, 1 Chr. 4:26.

HAMUL, son of Pharez, Gen. 46:12; Num. 26:21; 1 Chr. 2:5.

HAMUTAL, mother of Jehoahaz and Zedekiah, 2 Kin. 23:31; 24:18; Jer. 52:1.

HANAMEEL, cousin of JEREMIAH, to whom he sold a field in Anathoth, Jer. 32: 7-12.

HANAN. 1. Son of Shashak, 1 Chr. 8:23.

2. Son of Azel, 1 Chr. 8:38; 9:44.

3. One of David's mighty men, 1 Chr. 11:43.

4. One of the Nethinim, Ezra 2:46; Neh. 7:49.

5. A Levite, Neh. 8:7; 10:10. Probably identical with the one mentioned in Neh. 13:13.

6. A chief who sealed the covenant with Nehemiah, Neh. 10:22,26.

7. An officer in the temple, Jer. 35:2-10.

HANANEEL, name of a tower forming part of the wall of Jerusalem, Neh. 3:1; 12: 39; Jer. 31:38; Zech. 14:10.

HANANI. 1. Son of Heman, 1 Chr. 25: 4,25.

2. A prophet who rebuked Asa, king of Judah, 2 Chr. 16:7.

3. Father of Jehu the prophet, 1 Kin. 16: 1,7; 2 Chr. 19:2; 20:34. Possibly identical with 2.

4. A priest, Ezra 10:20.

5. A brother of Nehemiah and keeper of the gates of Jerusalem, Neh. 1:2; 7:2.

6. A priest and musician, Neh. 12:36.

HANANIAH. 1. Son of Heman, 1 Chr. 25:4,23.

2. A captain of Uzziah's army, 2 Chr. 26:11.

3. Father of Zedekiah, Jer. 36:12.

4. A prophet of Gibeon who uttered false prophecies in the temple during the reign of Zedekiah, Jer. 28.

5. Grandfather of Irijah, Jer. 37:13.

6. Son of Shashak, 1 Chr. 8:24.

7. Hebrew name of Shadrach, which see.

8. Son of Zerubbabel, 1 Chr. 3:19,21.

9. Son of Bebai, Ezra 10:28.

10. An apothecary and priest, Neh. 3:8.

11. Son of Shelemiah, Neh. 3:30.

12. A keeper of the gates of Jerusalem, Neh. 7:2.

13. One who sealed the covenant, Neh. 10:23.

14. A priest in time of Jehoiakim, Neh. 12:12,41.

HAND. Imposition of hands, Heb. 6:2; in consecration, Gen. 48:14; Ex. 29:10,15,19; Lev. 1:4; 3:2,8,13; 4:15,24,33; 16:21; in ordaining the Levites, Num. 8:10,11; Joshua, Num. 27:18-23; Deut. 34:9; Timothy, 1 Tim. 4:14; 2 Tim. 1:6; in healing, Mark 6:5; 7:32; 16:18; Luke 4:40; Acts 28:8; in blessing children, Matt. 19:13; Mark 10:16; in solemnizing testimony, Lev. 24:14. Lifted up in benediction, Lev. 9:22; Luke 24:50; in prayer, see PRAYER, ATTITUDES IN.

Ceremonial washing of, Matt. 15:2; Mark 7:2-5. See ABLUTIONS; CLEAN.

Symbolical of righteousness, Job 17:9. Washing of, a symbol of innocency, Deut. 21:6; Matt. 27:24.

Clasping of, in token of contract, Ezra 10: 19; Prov. 6:1; 17:18; Lam. 5:6; Ezek. 17:18; of friendship, 2 Kin. 10:15; Job 17:3. Right hand lifted up in swearing, Gen. 14:22; Psa. 106:26; Isa. 62:8; symbol of power, Isa. 23: 11; 41:10; place of honor, Psa. 45:9; 80:17.

FIGURATIVE: Matt. 5:30; 18:8; Mark 9:43. Anthropomorphic use of: Hand of the Lord waxed short, Num. 11:23; is mighty, Josh. 4:24; was heavy, 1 Sam. 5:6; against the Philistines, 1 Sam. 7:13; on Elijah, 1 Kin. 18:46; not shortened, Isa. 59:1; was with the early Christians, Acts 11:21. For extended anthropomorphisms consult concordances under the word hand.

See ANTHROPOMORPHISMS

HANDBREADTH, a measure, about four inches, Ex. 25:25; 1 Kin. 7:26; 2 Chr. 4:5; Psa. 39:5; Isa. 48:13; Ezek. 40:5,43; Jer. 52:21.

See SPAN, FINGERBREADTH.

HANDKERCHIEF, Acts 19:12.

HANES, a place in Egypt, Isa. 30:4.

HANGING. Capital punishment by, Gen. 40:19-22; Josh. 8:29; 2 Sam. 4:12; Esth. 7:10. The curse of death by, Deut. 21:22,23; Gal. 3:13.

See PUNISHMENT.

HANGINGS. See CURTAINS.

HANNAH, mother of Samuel. Her trials and prayer, and promise, 1 Sam. 1:1-18. Samuel born to, dedicates him to God, leaves him at the temple, 1 Sam. 1:19-28. Her hymn of praise, 1 Sam. 2:1-10. Visits Samuel at the temple from year to year, 1 Sam. 2:18,19. Children of, 1 Sam. 2:20,21.

HANNATHON, a city of Zebulun, Josh. 19:14.

HANNIEL. 1. A son of Ephod, appointed by Moses to divide the land among the several tribes, Num. 34:23.

2. A son of Ulla, called HANIEL in 1 Chr. 7:39.

HANOCH. 1. Son of Midian, Gen. 25:4. Called HENOCH, 1 Chr. 1:33.

2. Eldest son of Reuben, Gen. 46:9; Ex. 6:14; Num. 26:5; 1 Chr. 5:3.

HANUN, successor of Nahash as king of Ammon, dishonors David's ambassadors, 2 Sam. 10; 1 Chr. 19.

HAPHRAIM, a city of Issachar, Josh. 19:19.

HAPPINESS. OF THE WICKED: Limited to this life, Psa. 17:14; Luke 16:25; short, Job 20:5; uncertain, Luke 12:20; vain, Eccl. 2:1; 7:6.

Is derived from their wealth, Job 21:13; Psa. 52:7; their power, Job 21:7; Psa. 37:35; their worldly prosperity, Psa. 17:14; 73:3; 4,7; gluttony, Isa. 22:13; Hab. 1:16; drunkenness, Isa. 5:11; 56:12; vain pleasure, Job 21:12; Isa. 5:12; successful oppression, Hab. 1:15. Marred by jealousy, Esth. 5:13; often interrupted by judgments, Num. 11:33; Job 15:21; Psa. 73:18–20; Jer. 25:10,11. Leads to sorrow, Prov. 14:13. Leads to recklessness, Isa. 22:12. Sometimes a stumbling-block to saints, Psa. 73:3,16; Jer. 12:1; Hab. 1:13. Saints often permitted to see the end of, Psa. 73:17–20; envy not, Psa. 37:1. Woe against, Amos 6:1; Luke 6:25.

Illustrated, Psa. 37:35,36; Luke 12:16–20; 16:19–25.

Exemplified: Israel, Num. 11:33. Haman, Esth. 5:9–11. Belshazzar, Dan. 5:1. Herod, Acts 12:21–23.—*Bible Text-Book.*

OF THE RIGHTEOUS: Deut. 33:29. Happy *art* thou, O Israel: who *is* like unto thee, O people saved by the LORD, the shield of thy help, and who *is* the sword of thy excellency!

Job 5:17. Behold, happy *is* the man whom God correcteth: therefore despise not thou the chastening of the Almighty: 18. For he maketh sore, and bindeth up; he woundeth, and his hands make whole. 19. He shall deliver thee in six troubles: yea, in seven there shall no evil touch thee. 20. In famine he shall redeem thee from death: and in war from the power of the sword. 21. Thou shalt be hid from the scourge of the tongue: neither shalt thou be afraid of destruction when it cometh. 22. At destruction and famine thou shalt laugh: neither shalt thou be afraid of the beasts of the earth. 23. For thou shalt be in league with the stones of the field: and the beasts of the field shall be at peace with thee. 24. And thou shalt know that thy tabernacle *shall be* in peace; and thou shalt visit thy habitation, and shalt not sin. 25. Thou shalt know also that thy seed *shall be* great, and thine offspring as the grass of the earth. 26. Thou shalt come to *thy* grave in a full age, like as a shock of corn cometh in in his season. 27. Lo this, we have searched it, so it *is;* hear it, and know thou *it* for thy good.

Psa. 36:8. They shall be abundantly satisfied with the fatness of thy house; and thou shalt make them drink of the river of thy pleasures.

Psa. 40:8. I delight to do thy will, O my God: yea, thy law *is* within my heart.

Psa. 63:5. My soul shall be satisfied as *with* marrow and fatness; and my mouth shall praise *thee* with joyful lips:

Psa. 128:1. Blessed *is* every one that feareth the LORD; that walketh in his ways. 2. For thou shalt eat the labour of thine hands: happy *shalt* thou *be,* and *it shall be* well with thee.

Psa. 133:1. Behold, how good and how pleasant *it is* for brethren to dwell together in unity!

Psa. 144:15. Happy *is that* people, that is in such a case: *yea,* happy *is that* people, whose God *is* the LORD.

Psa. 146:5. Happy *is he* that *hath* the God of Jacob for his help, whose hope *is* in the LORD his God:

Prov. 3:13. Happy *is* the man *that* findeth wisdom, and the man *that* getteth understanding: 14. For the merchandise of it *is* better than the merchandise of silver, and the gain thereof than fine gold. 15. She *is* more precious than rubies: and all the things thou canst desire are not to be compared unto her. 16. Length of days *is* in her right hand; *and* in her left hand riches and honour. 17. Her ways *are* ways of pleasantness, and all her paths *are* peace. 18. She *is* a tree of life to them that lay hold upon her: and happy *is every* one that retaineth her.

Prov. 14:21. He that hath mercy on the poor, happy *is* he.

Prov. 16:20. Whoso trusteth in the LORD, happy *is* he.

Prov. 28:14. Happy *is* the man that feareth alway:

Prov. 29:18. He that keepeth the law, happy *is* he.

Eccl. 2:24. *There is* nothing better for a man, *than* that he should eat and drink, and *that* he should make his soul enjoy good in his labour. This also I saw, that it *was* from the hand of God. 25. For who can eat, or who else can hasten *hereunto,* more than I? 26. For *God* giveth to a man that *is* good in his sight wisdom, and knowledge, and joy: but to the sinner he giveth travail, to gather and to heap up, that he may give to *him that is* good before God. This also *is* vanity and vexation of spirit.

Eccl. 3:12. I know that *there is* no good in them, but for *a man* to rejoice, and to do good in his life. 13. And also that every man should eat and drink, and enjoy the good of all his labour, it *is* the gift of God. 22. Wherefore I perceive that *there is* nothing better, than that a man should rejoice in his own works; for that *is* his portion: for who shall bring him to see what shall be after him?

Isa. 12:2. Behold, God *is* my salvation; 1 will trust, and not be afraid: for the LORD JEHOVAH *is* my strength and *my* song; he also is become my salvation. 3. Therefore with joy shall ye draw water out of the wells of salvation.

Matt. 5:3. Blessed *are* the poor in spirit:

for their's is the kingdom of heaven. 4. Blessed *are* they that mourn : for they shall be comforted. 5. Blessed *are* the meek : for they shall inherit the earth. 6. Blessed *are* they which do hunger and thirst after righteousness : for they shall be filled. 7. Blessed *are* the merciful : for they shall obtain mercy. 8. Blessed *are* the pure in heart : for they shall see God. 9. Blessed *are* the peacemakers : for they shall be called the children of God. 10. Blessed *are* they which are persecuted for righteousness' sake : for their's is the kingdom of heaven. 11. Blessed are ye, when *men* shall revile you, and persecute *you*, and shall say all manner of evil against you falsely, for my sake. 12. Rejoice, and be exceeding glad : for great *is* your reward in heaven : for so persecuted they the prophets which were before you.

Rom. 5:2. By whom also we have access by faith into this grace wherein we stand, and rejoice in hope of the glory of God.

2 Cor. 12:10. Therefore I take pleasure in infirmities, in reproaches, in necessities, in persecutions, in distresses for Christ's sake : for when I am weak, then am I strong.

Phil. 4:7. And the peace of God, which passeth all understanding, shall keep your hearts and minds through Christ Jesus.

1 Pet. 3:14. But and if ye suffer for righteousness' sake, happy *are ye :* and be not afraid of their terror, neither be troubled :

1 Pet. 4:12. Beloved, think it not strange concerning the fiery trial which is to try you, as though some strange thing happened unto you : 13. But rejoice, inasmuch as ye are partakers of Christ's sufferings ; that, when his glory shall be revealed, ye may be glad also with exceeding joy.

See JOY ; PEACE ; PRAISE.

HARA, a place in Assyria. Israelitish captives carried to, 1 Chr. 5:26.

HARADAH, one of the camps of Israel, Num. 33:24,25.

HARAN. 1. Father of Lot and brother of Abraham, Gen. 11:26–31.

2. Son of Caleb, 1 Chr. 2:46.

3. A Levite, 1 Chr. 23:9.

4. Called also CHARRAN. A place in Mesopotamia to which Terah and Abraham migrated, Gen. 11:31 ; 12:4,5 ; Acts 7:4. Death of Terah at, Gen. 11:32. Abraham leaves, by divine command, Gen. 12:1–5. Jacob flees to, Gen. 27:43 ; 28:7 ; 29 ; returns from, with Rachel and Leah, Gen. 31:17–21. Conquest of, by king of Assyria, 2 Kin. 19:12. Merchants of, Ezek. 27:23. Idolatry in, Josh. 24:2,14 ; Isa. 37:12.

HARBONA, called also HARBONAH. A chamberlain of Ahasuerus, Esth. 1:10 ; 7:9.

HARE, forbidden as food, Lev. 11:6 ; Deut. 14:7.

HAREM, Persian household, Esth. 2:3, 13,14.

HAREPH, son of Caleb, 1 Chr. 2:51.

HARETH, a forest in which David found refuge from Saul, 1 Sam. 22:5.

HARHAIAH, father of Uzziel, Neh. 3:8.

HARHAS, grandfather of the husband of Huldah, the prophetess, 2 Kin. 22:14. Called HASRAH, 2 Chr. 34:22.

HARHUR, one of the Nethinim, Ezra 2:51 ; Neh. 7:53.

HARIM. 1. A priest, 1 Chr. 24:8.

2. An Israelite whose descendants returned from Babylon, Ezra 2:32,39 ; 10:31 ; Neh. 7:35,42.

3. The men who sealed the covenant, Neh. 10:5,27 ; 12:15.

HARIPH. 1. One of the exiles, Neh. 7:24. Probably the same with JORAH, Ezra 2:18.

2. One who sealed the covenant, Neh. 10:19.

HARLOT. Shamelessness of, Prov. 2:16 ; 7:11–27 ; 9:13–18. Machinations of, Prov. 7:10 ; 9:14–17 ; Isa. 23:15,16 ; Hos. 2:13. To be shunned, Prov. 5:3–20 ; 7:25–27. Hire of, not to be received at the temple, Deut. 23:18. Rahab, Josh. 2:3–6 ; 6:17,23,25 ; Heb. 11:31.

See ADULTERY ; HARLOTRY.

HARLOTRY, forbidden, Lev. 19:29 ; Deut. 23:17.

Punishment of, Lev. 21:9.

See ADULTERY ; WHOREDOM.

HAROD, a spring or well by which Gideon and his army camped, Judg. 7:1.

HAROEH, called also REAIAH. Son of Shobal, 1 Chr. 2:52 ; 4:2.

HAROSHETH, a town of Galilee. The home of Sisera, Judg. 4:2,13,16.

HARP, a stringed instrument of music, Isa. 38:20 ; Ezek. 33:32 ; Hab. 3:19. With three strings, 1 Sam. 18:6 [marg.] ; ten strings, Psa. 33:2 ; 92:3 ; 144:9 ; 150:4. Originated with Jubal, Gen. 4:21. Made of almug wood, 1 Kin. 10:12. David skilful in manipulating, 1 Sam. 16:16,23. Used in worship, 1 Sam. 10:5 ; 1 Chr. 16:5 ; 25:1–7 ; 2 Chr. 5:12,13 ; 29:25 ; Psa. 33:2 ; 43:4 ; 49:4 ; 57:8 ; 71:22 ; 81:2 ; 92:3 ; 98:5 ; 108:2 ; 147:7 ; 149:3 ; 150:3. Used, in national jubilees, after the triumph over Goliath, 1 Sam. 18:6 [marg.] ; over the armies of Ammon and Moab, 2 Chr. 20:28, with verses 20–29 ; when the new walls of Jerusalem were dedicated, Neh. 12:27,36. Used in festivities, Gen. 31:27 ; Job 21:11,12 ; Isa. 5:12 ; 23:16 ; 24:8 ; 30:32 ; Ezek. 26:13 ; Rev. 18:22 ; in mourning, Job 30:31. Discordant, 1 Cor. 14:7. Hung on the willows by the captive Jews, Psa. 137:2. Heard in heaven, in John's apocalyptic vision, Rev. 5:8 ; 14:2 ; 15:2. The symbol used in the psalmody to indicate when the harp was to be introduced in the music was Neginoth, see titles of Psa. 4 ; 6 ; 54 ; 55 ; 61 ; 67 ; 76.

See MUSIC, INSTRUMENTS OF.

HARROW, an agricultural implement used as an instrument of torture, 2 Sam. 12:31 ; 1 Chr. 20:3.

HARSHA, one of the Nethinim, Ezra 2:52 ; Neh. 7:54.

HART. See DEER.

HARUM, a descendant of Judah, 1 Chr. 4:8.

HARUMAPH, father of Jedaiah, Neh. 3:10.

HARUZ, father-in-law of King Manasseh, 2 Kin. 21:19.

HARVEST. Sabbath to be observed in, Ex. 34:21. Sabbath desecrated in, Neh. 13:15–22.

Of wheat at Pentecost, in Palestine, Ex. 34:22; Lev. 23:15–17; and before vintage, Lev. 26:5. Of barley, before wheat, Ex. 9:31,32. Celebrated with joy, Judg. 9:27; Isa. 9:3; 16:10; Jer. 48:33. Promises of plentiful, Gen. 8:22; Jer. 5:24; Joel 2:23,24.

FIGURATIVE: Job 24:6; Prov. 10:5; Jer. 8:20; Joel 3:13; Matt. 9:37; 13:39; Luke 10:2; Rev. 14:15.

See PENTECOST, FEAST OF; TABERNACLES, FEAST OF; FIRST FRUITS; REAPING; GLEANING.

HASADIAH, son of Zerubbabel, 1 Chr. 3:20.

HASENUAH, a Benjamite, 1 Chr. 9:7.

HASHABIAH. 1. Son of Amaziah, a Levite, 1 Chr. 6:45.

2. Son of Jeduthun, a Levite, 1 Chr. 25:3,19.

3. Son of Kemuel, 1 Chr. 26:30; 27:17.

4. A chief Levite, 2 Chr. 35:9.

5. Son of Bunni, 1 Chr. 9:14; Neh. 11:15.

6. Son of Mattaniah, a Levite, Neh. 11:22.

7. A chief priest who had charge of the bullion and other valuables of the temple, at Jerusalem, Ezra 8:24. Probably identical with the one mentioned in Neh. 12:21.

8. A Merarite Levite, Ezra 8:19.

9. A chief of the Levites, Neh. 3:17; 10:11; 12:24.

HASHABNAH, one who sealed the covenant, Neh. 10:25.

HASHABNIAH. 1. Father of Hattush, Neh. 3:10.

2. A Levite. Neh. 9:5.

HASHBADANA, a companion of Ezra, Neh. 8:4.

HASHEM, father of several members of David's guard, 1 Chr. 11:34.

HASHMONAH, a camp of the Israelites, Num. 33:29,30.

HASHUB. 1. Son of Pahath-moab, Neh. 3:11.

2. One of the captivity who assisted in repairing the wall of Jerusalem, Neh. 3:23.

3. Head of a family, Neh. 10:23.

4. Called also Hasshub. A Levite, 1 Chr. 9:14; Neh. 11:15.

HASHUBAH, a descendant of King Jehoiakim, 1 Chr. 3:20.

HASHUM. 1. Ancestor of certain Jews who returned from the captivity, Ezra 2:19; 10:33; Neh. 7:22.

2. A priest, Neh. 8:4.

3. A head of a family, Neh. 10:18.

HASHUPHA. See HASUPHA.

HASRAH. See HARHAS.

HASTE, in judgment, by Moses and the Israelites, Num. 32:1–19; Josh. 22:10–34. See RASHNESS.

HASUPHA, called also HASHUPHA. **A** Nethinim family, Ezra 2:43; Neh. 7:46.

HAT. See DRESS.

HATACH, a chamberlain in the court of Ahasuerus, Esth. 4:5,6,9,10.

HATHATH, a son of Othniel, 1 Chr. 4:13.

HATIPHA, one of the Nethinim, Ezra 2:54, Neh. 7:56.

HATITA, a porter of the temple, Ezra 2:42, Neh. 7:45.

HATRED, against iniquity, justified, Psa. 97:10; 101:3; 119:104,128,163; 139:21,22. Of God, Psa. 5:5; 45:7; Mal. 2:16.

SCRIPTURES RELATING TO: Lev.19:17. Thou shalt not hate thy brother in thine heart: thou shalt in any wise rebuke thy neighbour, and not suffer sin upon him.

Psa. 25:19. Consider mine enemies; for they are many; and they hate me with cruel hatred.

Psa. 35:19. Let not them that are mine enemies wrongfully rejoice over me: *neither* let them wink with the eye that hate me without a cause.

Prov. 10:12. Hatred stirreth up strifes: but love covereth all sins.

18. He that hideth hatred *with* lying lips, and he that uttereth a slander, *is* a fool.

Prov. 15:17. Better *is* a dinner of herbs where love is, than a stalled ox and hatred therewith.

Prov. 26:24. He that hateth dissembleth with his lips, and layeth up deceit within him; 25. When he speaketh fair, believe him not: for *there are* seven abominations in his heart. 26. *Whose* hatred is covered by deceit, his wickedness shall be shewed before the *whole* congregation.

Matt. 5:43. Ye have heard that it hath been said, Thou shalt love thy neighbour, and hate thine enemy. 44. But I say unto you, Love your enemies, bless them that curse you, do good to them that hate you, and pray for them which despitefully use you, and persecute you;

Matt. 6:15. If ye forgive not men their trespasses, neither will your Father forgive your trespasses.

Matt. 10:22. And ye shall be hated of all *men* for my name's sake: but he that endureth to the end shall be saved.

John 15:18. If the world hate you, ye know that it hated me before *it hated* you. 19. If ye were of the world, the world would love his own: but because ye are not of the world, but I have chosen you out of the world, therefore the world hateth you. 23. He that hateth me hateth my Father also. 24. If I had not done among them the works which none other man did, they had not had sin: but now have they both seen and hated both me and my Father. 25. But *this cometh to pass*, that the word might be fulfilled that is written in their law, They hated me without a cause.

John 17:14. I have given them thy word; and the world hath hated them, **because** they are not of the world, even as I am not of the world.

Gal. 5:19. The works of the flesh are manifest, . . . 20. . . . . Hatred, variance, emulations, wrath,

Eph. 4:31. Let all bitterness, and wrath, and anger, and clamour, and evil speaking, be put away from you, with all malice:

Col. 3:8. But now ye also put off all these; anger, wrath, malice, blasphemy, filthy communication out of your mouth.

1 John 2:9. He that saith he is in the light, and hateth his brother, is in darkness even until now. 11. He that hateth his brother is in darkness, and walketh in darkness, and knoweth not whither he goeth, because that darkness hath blinded his eyes.

1 John 3:10. Whosoever doeth not righteousness is not of God, neither he that loveth not his brother. 13. Marvel not, my brethren, if the world hate you. 14. We know that we have passed from death unto life, because we love the brethren. He that loveth not *his* brother abideth in death. 15. Whosoever hateth his brother is a murderer: and ye know that no murderer hath eternal life abiding in him.

1 John 4:20. If a man say, I love God, and hateth his brother, he is a liar: for he that loveth not his brother whom he hath seen, how can he love God whom he hath not seen?

See ENVY; JEALOUSY; MALICE; REVENGE.

HATTIL, a returned exile, Ezra 2:57; Neh. 7:59.

HATTUSH. 1. Son of Shemaiah, 1 Chr. 3:22.

2. A descendant of David, Ezra 8:2; Neh. 3:10; 10:4; 12:2.

3. A priest, Neh. 12:2.

HAUGHTINESS. See PRIDE.

HAURAN, a district probably S. of Damascus and E. of the Jordan, Ezek. 47:16,18.

HAVILAH. 1. Son of Cush, Gen. 10:7; 1 Chr. 1:9.

2. A son of Joktan, Gen. 10:29; 1 Chr. 1:23.

3. An unknown region, Gen. 2:11.

4. A district E. of Amalek, Gen. 25:18; 1 Sam. 15:7.

HAVOTH-JAIR, called also BASHAN-HAVOTH-JAIR in Deut. 3:14. Certain villages E. of the Jordan, Num. 32:41; Judg. 10:4.

HAWK, a carnivorous and unclean bird, Lev. 11:16; Deut. 14:15; Job 39:26.

HAY, Prov. 27:25; Isa. 15:6; 1 Cor. 3:12.

HAZAEL, king of Syria. Anointed king by Elijah, 1 Kin. 19:15. Conquests by, 2 Kin. 8:28,29; 9:14; 10:32,33; 12:17,18; 13:3,22; 2 Chr. 22:5,6. Conspires against, murders, and succeeds to the throne of Ben-hadad, 2 Kin. 8:8–15. Death of, 2 Kin. 13:24.

HAZAIAH, a man of Judah, Neh. 11:5.

HAZAR-ADDAR, called also ADAR, a place on the southern boundary of Canaan, Num. 34:4; Josh. 15:3.

HAZAR-ENAN, the N. E. boundary point of the promised land, Num. 34:9,10; Ezek. 47:17; 48:1.

HAZAR-GADDAH, a town in the southern district of Judah, Josh. 15:27.

HAZAR-HATTICON, a place on the boundary of Hauran, probably E. of Damascus, Ezek. 47:16.

HAZARMAVETH, son of Joktan, Gen. 10:26; 1 Chr. 1:20.

HAZAR-SHUAL, a town on the S. of Judah, Josh. 15:28; 19:3; 1 Chr. 4:28; Neh. 11:27.

HAZAR-SUSAH, called also HAZAR-SUSIM, a city of Judah, Josh. 19:5; 1 Chr. 4:31.

HAZEL, Gen. 30:37.

HAZELELPONI, daughter of Etam, 1 Chr. 4:3.

HAZERIM, a district in the S. of Canaan, Deut. 2:23.

HAZEROTH, a station in the journeyings of the children of Israel, Num. 11:35; 12:16; 33:17,18; Deut. 1:1.

HAZEZON-TAMAR, called also HAZAZON-TAMAR, ancient name of En-gedi, Gen. 14:7; 2 Chr. 20:2.

HAZIEL, a Levite, 1 Chr. 23:9.

HAZO, a son of Nahor, Gen. 22:22.

HAZOR. 1. A fortified city of Naphtali, Josh. 11:1,10,11,13; 12:19; 19:36; Judg. 4:2,17; 1 Sam. 12:9; 2 Kin. 15:29; Neh. 11:33.

2. A city in the S. of Judah, Josh. 15:23; 1 Kin. 9:15.

3. A place N. of Jerusalem, Neh. 11:33.

HAZOR-HADATTAH, a city of Judah, Josh. 15:25.

HEAD. Shaven when vows were taken, Acts 21:24. Diseases of, Isa. 3:17. Anointed, Lev. 14:18,29.

HEADBANDS, Isa. 3:20.

HEARERS. Ezek. 33:30. Also, thou son of man, the children of thy people still are talking against thee by the walls and in the doors of the houses, and speak one to another, every one to his brother, saying, Come, I pray you, and hear what is the word that cometh forth from the LORD. 31. And they come unto thee as the people cometh, and they sit before thee *as* my people, and they hear thy words, but they will not do them: for with their mouth they shew much love, *but* their heart goeth after their covetousness. 32. And, lo, thou *art* unto them as a very lovely song of one that hath a pleasant voice, and can play well on an instrument: for they hear thy words, but they do them not.

Matt. 7:24. Therefore whosoever heareth these sayings of mine, and doeth them, I will liken him unto a wise man, which built his house upon a rock: 25. And the rain descended, and the floods came, and the winds blew, and beat upon that house; and it fell not: for it was founded upon a rock. 26. And every one that heareth these sayings of mine, and doeth them not, shall be likened unto a foolish man, which built his house upon the sand: 27. And the rain descended, and the floods came, and the winds blew, and beat upon that house; and it fell: and great was the fall of it. Luke 6:49.

Matt. 13:14. And in them is fulfilled the prophecy of Esaias, which saith, By hearing ye shall hear, and shall not understand; and seeing ye shall see, and shall not perceive: 15. For this people's heart is waxed gross, and *their* ears are dull of hearing, and their eyes they have closed; lest at any time they should see with *their* eyes, and hear with *their* ears, and should understand with *their* heart, and should be converted, and I should heal them. 19. When any one heareth the word of the kingdom, and understandeth *it* not, then cometh the wicked *one*, and catcheth away that which was sown in his heart. This is he which received seed by the way side. 20. But he that received the seed into stony places, the same is he that heareth the word, and anon with joy receiveth it. 21. Yet hath he not root in himself, but dureth for a while: for when tribulation or persecution ariseth because of the word, by and by he is offended. 22. He also that received seed among the thorns is he that heareth the word; and the care of this world, and the deceitfulness of riches, choke the word, and he becometh unfruitful. 23. But he that received seed into the good ground is he that heareth the word, and understandeth *it;* which also beareth fruit, and bringeth forth, some an hundredfold, some sixty, some thirty. Luke 8:11–15.

Rom. 2:13. For not the hearers of the law *are* just before God, but the doers of the law shall be justified.

Jas. 1:19. Wherefore, my beloved brethren, let every man be swift to hear, slow to speak, slow to wrath: 22. But be ye doers of the word, and not hearers only, deceiving your own selves. 23. For if any be a hearer of the word, and not a doer, he is like unto a man beholding his natural face in a glass: 24. For he beholdeth himself, and goeth his way, and straightway forgetteth what manner of man he was. 25. But whoso looketh into the perfect law of liberty, and continueth *therein*, he being not a forgetful hearer, but a doer of the work, this man shall be blessed in his deed.

HEART, seat of the affections. **RENEWED:** Deut. 30:6; Psa. 51:10; Ezek. 11:19; 18:31; 36:26; Rom. 2:29; Eph. 4:23; Col. 3:10. Regenerated, John 3:3,7. Graciously affected of God, 1 Sam. 10:26; 1 Chr. 29:18; Ezra 6:22; 7:27; Prov. 16:1; 21:1; Jer. 20:9; Acts 16:14. Strengthened, Psa. 27:14; 112:8; 1 Thess. 3:13. Enlightened, 2 Cor. 4:6. Tried, 1 Chr. 29:17; Psa. 7:9; 26:2; Prov. 17:3; Jer. 11:20; 12:3; 20:12; 1 Thess. 2:4; Heb. 11:17; Rev. 2:2,10.

It should render to God obedience, Deut. 10:12; 11:13; 26:16; 1 Kin. 2:4; Psa. 119:1,12; Eph. 6:6; faith, Psa. 27:3; 112:7; ¹ Acts 8:37; Rom. 6:17; 10:10; trust, Prov. 3:5; love, Matt. 22:37; fear, Psa. 119:161; Jer. 32:40; fidelity, Neh. 9:8; zeal, 2 Chr. 17:16; Jer. 20:9. [¹ Omitted in R. V.]

It should seek God, 2 Chr. 19:3; 30:19; Ezra 7:10; Psa. 10:17; 84:2; be joyful, 1 Sam. 2:1; Psa. 4:7; 97:11; Isa. 65:14; Zech. 10:7; perfect,

1 Kin. 8:61; Psa. 101:2; upright, Psa. 97:11; 125:4; clean, Psa. 51:10; 73:1; pure, Psa. 24:4; Prov. 22:11; Matt. 5:8; 1 Tim. 1:5; 2 Tim. 2: 22; Jas. 4:8; 1 Pet. 1:22; sincere, Luke 8:15; Acts 2:46; Eph. 6:5; Col. 3:22; Heb. 10:22; repentant, Deut. 30:2; Psa. 34:18; 51:17; devout, 1 Sam. 1:13; Psa. 4:4; 9:1; 27:8; 77:6; 119:10,69, 145; wise, 1 Kin. 3:9,12; 4:29; Job 9:4; Prov. 8:10; 10:8; 11:29; 14:33; 23:15; tender, 1 Sam. 24:5; 2 Kin. 22:19; Job 23:16; Psa. 22:14; Eph. 4:32; holy, Psa. 66:18; 1 Pet. 3:15; compassionate, Jer. 4:19; Lam. 3:51; lowly, Matt. 11:29.

THE UNREGENERATE: Is full of iniquity, Gen. 6:5; 8:21; 1 Sam. 17:28; Prov. 6: 14,18; 11:20; Eccl. 8:11; 9:3; Jer. 4:14,18; 17:9; Rom. 1:21. Loves evil, Deut. 29:18; Psa. 95:10; Jer. 17:5. Is a fountain of evil, Matt. 12:34, 35; Mark 7:21. See DEPRAVITY. Is wayward, 2 Chr. 12:14; Psa. 101:4; Prov. 6:14; 11:20; 12: 8; 17:20; Jer. 5:23; Heb. 3:10; blind, Rom. 1: 21; Eph. 4:18. See BLINDNESS, SPIRITUAL. Is double, 1 Chr. 12:33; Psa. 12:2; Hos. 10:2; Jas. 1:6,8; Prov. 28:14; Isa. 9:9; 10:12; 46:12. See INSTABILITY. Is hard, Psa. 76:5; Ezek. 2: 4; 3:7; 11:19; 36:26; Mark 6:52; 10:5; 16:14; John 12:40; Rom. 1:21; 2:5. See IMPENITENCE; OBDURACY. Is deceitful, Jer. 17:9. Is proud, 2 Kin. 14:10; 2 Chr. 25:19; Psa. 101:5; Prov. 18: 12; 28:25; Jer. 48:29; 49:16. See PRIDE. Is subtle, Prov. 7:10. See HYPOCRISY. Is sensual, Ezek. 6:9; Hos. 13:6; Rom. 8:7. See LASCIVIOUSNESS. Is worldly, 2 Chr. 26:16; Dan. 5:20; Acts 8:21,22. Is judicially hardened, Ex. 4:21; Josh. 11:20; Isa. 6:10; Acts 28:26,27. Is malicious, Psa. 28:3; 140:2; Prov. 24:2; Eccl. 7:26; Ezek. 25:15. See MALICE. Is impenitent, Rom. 2:5. See IMPENITENCE. Is diabolical, John 13:2; Acts 5:3. Is covetous, Jer. 22:17; 2 Pet. 2:14. See COVETOUSNESS. Is foolish, Prov. 12:23; 22:15; Eccl. 9:3.

UNCLASSIFIED SCRIPTURES DESCRIPTIVE OF THE SEAT OF THE AFFECTIONS: Deut. 5:29. O that there were such an heart in them, that they would fear me, and keep all my commandments always, that it might be well with them, and with their children for ever!

Deut. 6:5. And thou shalt love the LORD thy God with all thine heart, and with all thy soul, and with all thy might. 6. And these words, which I command thee this day, shall be in thine heart:

1 Sam. 16:7. For *the* LORD *seeth* not as man seeth; for man looketh on the outward appearance, but the LORD looketh on the heart.

1 Chr. 28:9. And thou, Solomon my son, know thou the God of thy father, and serve him with a perfect heart and with a willing mind: for the LORD searcheth all hearts, and understandeth all the imaginations of the thoughts: if thou seek him, he will be found of thee; but if thou forsake him, he will cast thee off for ever.

2 Chr. 12:14. And he did evil, because he prepared not his heart to seek the LORD.

Psa. 22:26. Your heart shall live for ever.

Psa. 34:18. The LORD *is* nigh unto them that are of a broken heart; and saveth such as be of a contrite spirit.

Psa. 51:10. Create in me a clean heart, O God; and renew a right spirit within me. 17. The sacrifices of God *are* a broken spirit: a broken and a contrite heart, O God, thou wilt not despise.

Psa. 57:7. My heart is fixed, O God, my heart is fixed: I will sing and give praise. Psa. 112:7.

Prov. 4:23. Keep thy heart with all diligence; for out of it *are* the issues of life.

Prov. 14:30. A sound heart *is* the life of the flesh:

Prov. 15:13. A merry heart maketh a cheerful countenance: but by sorrow of the heart the spirit is broken. 14. The heart of him that hath understanding seeketh knowledge: but the mouth of fools feedeth on foolishness. 15. All the days of the afflicted *are* evil: but he that is of a merry heart *hath* a continual feast.

Prov. 16:1. The preparations of the heart in man, and the answer of the tongue, *is* from the LORD.

Prov. 20:9. Who can say, I have made my heart clean, I am pure from my sin?

Jer. 17:1. The sin of Judah *is* written with a pen of iron, *and* with the point of a diamond: *it is* graven upon the table of their heart, 9. The heart *is* deceitful above all *things*, and desperately ¹ wicked: who can know it? 10. I the LORD search the heart, *I* try the reins, even to give every man according to his ways, *and* according to the fruit of his doings. [¹ R. V. sick]

Matt. 5:8. Blessed *are* the pure in heart: for they shall see God.

Matt. 9:4. And Jesus knowing their thoughts said, Wherefore think ye evil in your hearts?

Matt. 12:33. Either make the tree good, and his fruit good; or else make the tree corrupt, and his fruit corrupt: for the tree is known by *his* fruit.

Matt. 15:18. But those things which proceed out of the mouth come forth from the heart; and they defile the man. 19. For out of the heart proceed evil thoughts, murders, adulteries, fornications, thefts, false witness, blasphemies: 20. These are *the things* which defile a man: but to eat with unwashen hands defileth not a man. Mark 7:21.

Matt. 23:26. *Thou* blind Pharisee, cleanse first that *which is* within the cup and platter, that the outside of them may be clean also.

Acts 8:22. Repent therefore of this thy wickedness, and pray God, if perhaps the thought of thine heart may be forgiven thee.

Rom. 2:5. But after thy hardness and impenitent heart treasurest up unto thyself wrath against the day of wrath and revelation of the righteous judgment of God: 14. For when the Gentiles, which have not the law, do by nature the things contained in the

law, these, having not the law, are a law unto themselves: 15. Which shew the work of the law written in their hearts, their conscience also bearing witness, and *their* thoughts the mean while accusing or else excusing one another; 16. In the day when God shall judge the secrets of men by Jesus Christ according to my gospel.

Heb. 3:8. Harden not your hearts, as in the provocation, in the day of temptation in the wilderness: *v.* 15.

INSTANCES OF HARDENED HEARTS: Pharoah, Ex. 4:21; 7:3,13,22; 8:15,32; 9:12, 34,35; 10:1,20,27; 11:9,10; 14:4,8,17. Sihon, Deut. 2:30. King of Canaan, Josh. 11:20. Others, 1 Sam. 6:6.

KNOWN TO GOD: Deut. 31:21. For I know their imagination which they go about, even now, before I have brought them into the land which I sware.

1 Sam. 16:7. *The LORD seeth* not as man seeth; for man looketh on the outward appearance, but the LORD looketh on the heart.

2 Sam. 7:20. And what can David say more unto thee? for thou, Lord GOD, knowest thy servant.

1 Kin. 8:39. Then hear thou in heaven thy dwelling place, and forgive, and do, and give to every man according to his ways, whose heart thou knowest; (for thou, *even* thou only, knowest the hearts of all the children of men;)

1 Chr. 28:9. And thou, Solomon my son, know thou the God of thy father, and serve him with a perfect heart and with a willing mind: for the LORD searcheth all hearts, and understandeth all the imaginations of the thoughts: if thou seek him, he will be found of thee; but if thou forsake him, he will cast thee off for ever.

Job 11:11. For he knoweth vain men: he seeth wickedness also; will he not then consider *it?*

Job 16:19. Also now, behold, my witness *is* in heaven, and my record *is* on high.

Job 31:4. Doth not he see my ways, and count all my steps?

Psa. 1:6. For the LORD knoweth the way of the righteous:

Psa. 44:21. Shall not God search this out? for he knoweth the secrets of the heart.

Psa. 51:10. Create in me a clean heart, O God; and renew a right spirit within me.

Psa. 94:11. The LORD knoweth the thoughts of man, that they *are* vanity.

Psa. 139:1. O LORD, thou hast searched me, and known *me.* 2. Thou knowest my downsitting and mine uprising, thou understandest my thought afar off. 3. Thou compassest my path and my lying down, and art acquainted *with* all my ways. 4. For *there is* not a word in my tongue, *but*, lo, O LORD, thou knowest it altogether. 5. Thou hast beset me behind and before, and laid thine hand upon me. 6. *Such* knowledge *is* too wonderful for me; it is high, I cannot *attain* unto it. 7. Whither shall I go from thy spirit? or whither shall I flee from thy presence? 8. If I ascend up into heaven, thou *art* there: if I make my bed in hell, behold thou *art there.* 9. *If* I take the wings of the morning, *and* dwell in the uttermost parts of the sea; 10. Even there shall thy hand lead me, and thy right hand shall hold me. 11. If I say, Surely the darkness shall cover me; even the night shall be light about me. 12. Yea, the darkness hideth not from thee; but the night shineth as the day: the darkness and the light *are* both alike *to thee.*

Prov. 5:21. For the ways of man *are* before the eyes of the LORD, and he pondereth all his goings.

Prov. 16:2. All the ways of a man *are* clean in his own eyes; but the LORD weigheth the spirits.

Prov. 21:2. Every way of a man *is* right in his own eyes: but the LORD pondereth the hearts.

Isa. 66:18. For I *know* their works and their thoughts:

Jer. 12:3. But thou, O LORD, knowest me: thou hast seen me, and tried mine heart toward thee:

Jer. 17:10. I the LORD search the heart, *I* try the reins, even to give every man according to his ways, *and* according to the fruit of his doings.

Ezek. 11:5. I know the things that come into your mind, *every one of* them. 19. And I will give them one heart, and I will put a new spirit within you; and I will take the stony heart out of their flesh, and will give them an heart of flesh: 20. That they may walk in my statutes, and keep mine ordinances, and do them: and they shall be my people, and I will be their God. 21. But *as for them* whose heart walketh after the heart of their detestable things and their abominations, I will recompense their way upon their own heads, saith the Lord GOD. Ezek. 36:25,26.

Luke 16:15. Ye are they which justify yourselves before men; but God knoweth your hearts:

Acts 1:24. And they prayed, and said, Thou, Lord, which knowest the hearts of all *men,* shew whether of these two thou hast chosen,

Acts 15:8. And God, which knoweth the hearts, bare them witness, giving them the Holy Ghost, even as *he did* unto us;

Rom. 8:27. And he that searcheth the hearts knoweth what *is* the mind of the Spirit, because he maketh intercession for the saints according to *the will of* God.

1 Cor. 3:20. The Lord knoweth the thoughts of the wise, that they are vain.

Heb. 4:12. For the word of God *is* quick, and powerful, and sharper than any two-edged sword, piercing even to the dividing asunder of soul and spirit, and of the joints and marrow, and *is* a discerner of the thoughts and intents of the heart.

Rev. 2:23. All the churches shall know that I am he which searcheth the reins and

hearts· and I will give unto every one of you according to your works.

CHANGE OF. INSTANCES OF: Saul, 1 Sam. 10:9. Solomon, 1 Kin. 3:11,12. Saul of Tarsus, Acts 9:1–18.

See REGENERATION; SANCTIFICATION.

HEARTH, Gen. 18:6; Isa. 30:14; Jer. 36: 22,23.

See BRAZIER.

HEAT, Jonah overcome with, Jonah 4:8. See SUNSTROKE.

HEATH, Jer. 17:6; 48:6.

HEATHEN. Under this head are grouped all who are not embraced under the Abrahamic covenant. Cast out of Canaan, Lev. 18:24,25: Psa.44:2; and their land given to Israel, Psa. 78:55; 105:44; 135:12; 136:21,22; Isa. 54:1–3. Excluded from the temple, Lam. 1:10.

Wicked Practices of. See IDOLATRY.

Divine revelations given to: Abimelech, Gen. 20:3–7; Pharaoh, Gen. 41:1–28; Balaam, Num. 22; Nebuchadnezzar, Dan. 4:1–18; Belshazzar, Dan. 5:5,24–29; Cyrus, 2 Chr. 36:23; Ezra 1:1–4; the Magi, Matt. 2:1–11; the centurion, Matt. 8:5–13; Luke 7:2–9; Cornelius, Acts 10:1–7.

Pious people among, Isa. 65:5; Acts 10:35. INSTANCES OF: Melchizedek, Gen. 14:18–20. Abimelech, Gen. 20. Balaam, Num. 22. Jethro, Ex. 18. Cyrus, Ezra 1:1–3. Eliphaz, Job 4. Bildad, Job 8. Zophar, Job 11. Elihu, Job 32. Nebuchadnezzar, after his restoration, Dan. 4. The Ninevites, Jonah 3:5–10. The Magi, Matt. 2:1–12. The centurion of Capernaum. Matt. 8:5–13; Luke 7:2–9; of Cæsarea, Acts 10.

See GENTILES.

HEAVE OFFERING. See OFFERINGS.

HEAVEN. GOD'S DWELLING PLACE: Deut. 26:15. Look down from thy holy habitation, from heaven, and bless thy people Israel, and the land which thou hast given us, as thou swarest unto our fathers, a land that floweth with milk and honey. Zech. 2:13; Isa. 63:15.

1 Kin. 8:30. Hear thou in heaven thy dwellingplace: and when thou hearest, forgive. *vs.* 39,43,49; 2 Chr. 6:18,21,27,30,33,35, 39; Jer. 23:24.

1 Chr. 16:31. Let the heavens be glad, and let the earth rejoice: and let *men* say among the nations, The LORD reigneth.

1 Chr. 21:26. He answered him from heaven 2 Chr. 7:14; Neh. 9:27.

2 Chr. 2:6. But who is able to build him an house, seeing the heaven and heaven of heavens cannot contain him? who *am* I then, that I should build him an house, save only to burn sacrifice before him?

2 Chr. 30:27. Then the priests the Levites arose and blessed the people: and their voice was heard, and their prayer came *up* to his holy dwelling place, *even* unto heaven.

Job 22:12. *Is* not God in the height of heaven? and behold the height of the stars, how high they are! 14. Thick clouds *are* a covering to him, that he seeth not; and he walketh in the circuit of heaven.

Psa. 2:4. He that sitteth in the heavens shall laugh : the Lord shall have them in derision.

Psa. 11:4. The LORD is in his holy temple, the LORD's throne is in heaven :

Psa. 20:6. Now know I that the LORD saveth his anointed ; he will hear him from his holy heaven with the saving strength of his right hand.

Psa. 33:13. The LORD looketh from heaven ; he beholdeth all the sons of men.

Psa. 102:19. For he hath looked down from the height of his sanctuary ; from heaven did the LORD behold the earth ;

Psa. 103:19. The LORD hath prepared his throne in the heavens ; and his kingdom ruleth over all. Psa. 135:6 ; Dan. 4:35.

Psa. 113:5. Who is like unto the LORD our God, who dwelleth on high,

Psa. 123:1. Unto thee lift I up mine eyes, O thou that dwellest in the heavens.

Eccl. 5:2. God is in heaven, and thou upon earth : therefore let thy words be few.

Isa. 57:15. For thus saith the high and lofty One that inhabiteth eternity, whose name is Holy ; I dwell in the high and holy place, with him also that is of a contrite and humble spirit, to revive the spirit of the humble, and to revive the heart of the contrite ones.

Isa. 63:15. Look down from heaven, and behold from the habitation of thy holiness and of thy glory :

Isa. 66:1. Thus saith the LORD, The heaven is my throne, and the earth is my footstool :

Lam. 3:41. Let us lift up our heart with our hands unto God in the heavens. 50. Till the LORD look down, and behold from heaven.

Dan. 5:23. But hast lifted up thyself against the Lord of heaven ;

Matt. 5:34. But I say unto you, Swear not at all ; neither by heaven ; for it is God's throne : 45. That ye may be the children of your Father which is in heaven :

Matt. 6:9. Our Father which art in heaven, Matt. 18:10,14 ; Mark 11:25,26.

Matt. 10:32. Whosoever therefore shall confess me before men, him will I confess also before my Father which is in heaven. 33. But whosoever shall deny me before men, him will I also deny before my Father which is in heaven.

Matt. 11:25. At that time Jesus answered and said, I thank thee, O Father, Lord of heaven and earth,

Matt. 12:50. For whosoever shall do the will of my Father which is in heaven, the same is my brother, and sister, and mother.

Matt. 16:17. And Jesus answered and said unto him, Blessed art thou, Simon Barjona : for flesh and blood hath not revealed it unto thee, but my Father which is in heaven.

Mark 16:19. So then after the Lord had spoken unto them, he was received up into heaven, and sat on the right hand of God.

(35)

Acts 7:49. Heaven is my throne,

Rom. 1:18. For the wrath of God is revealed from heaven against all ungodliness and unrighteousness of men ;

Heb. 8:1. Now of the things which we have spoken this is the sum : We have such an high priest, who is set on the right hand of the throne of the Majesty in the heavens ;

Rev. 8:1. And when he had opened the seventh seal, there was silence in heaven about the space of half an hour.

Rev. 12:7. And there was war in heaven : Michael and his angels fought against the dragon ; and the dragon fought and his angels, 8. And prevailed not ; neither was their place found any more in heaven. 9. And the great dragon was cast out, that old serpent, called the Devil, and Satan, which deceiveth the whole world : he was cast out into the earth, and his angels were cast out with him.

Rev. 21:22. And I saw no temple therein : for the Lord God Almighty and the Lamb are the temple of it. 23. And the city had no need of the sun, neither of the moon, to shine in it : for the glory of God did lighten it, and the Lamb is the light thereof. 24. And the nations of them which are saved shall walk in the light of it : and the kings of the earth do bring their glory and honour into it. 25. And the gates of it shall not be shut at all by day : for there shall be no night there. 26. And they shall bring the glory and honour of the nations into it. 27. And there shall in no wise enter into it any thing that defileth, neither whatsoever worketh abomination, or maketh a lie : but they which are written in the Lamb's book of life.

Rev. 22:1. And he shewed me a pure river of water of life, clear as crystal, proceeding out of the throne of God and of the Lamb. 2. In the midst of the street of it, and on either side of the river, was there the tree of life, which bare twelve manner of fruits, and yielded her fruit every month : and the leaves of the tree were for the healing of the nations. 3. And there shall be no more curse : but the throne of God and of the Lamb shall be in it : and his servants shall serve him : 4. And they shall see his face ; and his name shall be in their foreheads. 5. And there shall be no night there ; and they need no candle, neither light of the sun ; for the Lord God giveth them light ; and they shall reign for ever and ever.

THE FUTURE DWELLING PLACE OF THE RIGHTEOUS. Called A GARNER, Matt. 3:12 ; THE KINGDOM OF CHRIST AND OF GOD, Eph. 5:5 ; THE FATHER'S HOUSE, John 14:2 ; A HEAVENLY COUNTRY, Heb. 11:16 ; A REST, Heb. 4:9 ; Rev. 14:13 ; PARADISE, 2 Cor. 12:2,4.

The wicked excluded from, Gal. 5:21 ; Eph. 5:5 ; Rev. 22:15.

UNCLASSIFIED SCRIPTURES RELATING TO 2 Kin. 2:11. And Elijah went up by a whirlwind into heaven.

Job 3:17. There the wicked cease *from* troubling; and there the weary be at rest.

Psa. 16:11. In thy presence *is* fulness of joy; at thy right hand *there are* pleasures for evermore.

Psa. 17:15. As for me, I will behold thy face in righteousness: I shall be satisfied, when I awake, with thy likeness.

Psa. 23:6. I will dwell in the house of the LORD for ever.

Psa. 24:3. Who shall ascend into the hill of the LORD? or who shall stand in his holy place? 7. Lift up your heads, O ye gates; and be ye lift up, ye everlasting doors; and the King of glory shall come in.

Psa. 73:24. Thou shalt guide me with thy counsel, and afterward receive me *to* glory.

Isa. 33:17. Thine eyes shall see the king in his beauty: they shall behold the land that is very far off.

Dan. 12:3. They that be wise shall shine as the brightness of the firmament; and they that turn many to righteousness as the stars for ever and ever.

Mal. 3:17. They shall be mine, saith the LORD of hosts, in that day when I make up my jewels; and I will spare them, as a man spareth his own son that serveth him.

Matt. 5:3. Blessed *are* the poor in spirit: for their's is the kingdom of heaven. 8. Blessed *are* the pure in heart: for they shall see God. 12. Rejoice, and be exceeding glad: for great *is* your reward in heaven: 20. For I say unto you, That except your righteousness shall exceed *the righteousness* of the scribes and Pharisees, ye shall in no case enter into the kingdom of heaven.

Matt. 6:20. Lay up for yourselves treasures in heaven, where neither moth nor rust doth corrupt, and where thieves do not break through nor steal: Luke 12:33.

Matt. 8:11. Many shall come from the east and west, and shall sit down with Abraham, and Isaac, and Jacob, in the kingdom of heaven.

Matt. 13:30. Let both grow together until the harvest: and in the time of harvest I will say to the reapers, Gather ye together first the tares, and bind them in bundles to burn them: but gather the wheat into my barn. 43. Then shall the righteous shine forth as the sun in the kingdom of their Father. 49. So shall it be at the end of the world: the angels shall come forth, and sever the wicked from among the just, Matt. 3:12.

Matt. 18:10. Take heed that ye despise not one of these little ones; for I say unto you, That in heaven their angels do always behold the face of my Father which is in heaven.

Matt. 19:21. Jesus said unto him, If thou wilt be perfect, go *and* sell that thou hast, and give to the poor, and thou shalt have treasure in heaven: and come *and* follow me.

Matt. 25:34. Then shall the King say unto them on his right hand, Come, ye blessed of my Father, inherit the kingdom prepared for you from the foundation of the world: 46. And these shall go away into everlasting punishment: but the righteous into life eternal.

Luke 10:20. Rather rejoice, because your names are written in heaven.

Luke 12:32. Fear not, little flock; for it is your Father's good pleasure to give you the kingdom.

Luke 15:6. And when he cometh home, he calleth together *his* friends and neighbours, saying unto them, Rejoice with me; for I have found my sheep which was lost. 7. I say unto you, that likewise joy shall be in heaven over one sinner that repenteth, more than over ninety and nine just persons, which need no repentance. [*v.* 10.] 32. It was meet that we should make merry, and be glad: for this thy brother was dead and is alive again; and was lost, and is found.

Luke 16:22. The beggar died, and was carried by the angels into Abraham's bosom:

Luke 20:34. And Jesus answering said unto them, The children of this world marry, and are given in marriage: 35. But they which shall be accounted worthy to obtain that world, and the resurrection from the dead, neither marry, nor are given in marriage: [Matt. 22:30.] 36. Neither can they die any more: for they are equal unto the angels; and are the children of God, being the children of the resurrection.

Luke 22:29. I appoint unto you a kingdom, as my Father hath appointed unto me; 30. That ye may eat and drink at my table in my kingdom, and sit on thrones judging the twelve tribes of Israel.

Luke 23:43. Verily I say unto thee, To day shalt thou be with me in paradise.

John 5:28. Marvel not at this: for the hour is coming, in the which all that are in the grave shall hear his voice, 29. And shall come forth; they that have done good, unto the resurrection of life; and they that have done evil, unto the resurrection of damnation.

John 10:28. I give unto them eternal life; and they shall never perish, neither shall any *man* pluck them out of my hand.

John 12:26. Where I am, there shall also my servant be: if any man serve me, him will *my* Father honour.

John 13:36. Simon Peter said unto him, Lord, whither goest thou? Jesus answered him, Whither I go, thou canst not follow me now; but thou shalt follow me afterwards.

John 14:2. In my Father's house are many mansions: if *it were* not *so*, I would have told you. I go to prepare a place for you. 3. If I go and prepare a place for you, I will come again, and receive you unto myself; that where I am, *there* ye may be also.

John 17:22. And the glory which thou gavest me I have given them; 24. Father, I will that they also, whom thou hast given me, be with me where I am; that they may behold my glory,

Acts 7:55. He, being full of the Holy Ghost, looked up stedfastly into heaven, and saw the glory of God, and Jesus standing on the right hand of God, *v.* 56.

Rom. 5:17. For if by one man's offence death reigned by one; much more they which receive abundance of grace and of the gift of righteousness shall reign in life by one, Jesus Christ.

2 Cor. 5:1. For we know that if our earthly house of *this* tabernacle were dissolved, we have a building of God, an house not made with hands, eternal in the heavens.

2 Cor. 12:2. I knew a man in Christ above fourteen years ago, (whether in the body I cannot tell; or whether out of the body, I cannot tell: God knoweth;) such an one caught up to the third heaven. 3. And I knew such a man, (whether in the body, or out of the body, I cannot tell: God knoweth;) 4. How that he was caught up into paradise, and heard unspeakable words, which it is not lawful for a man to utter.

Eph. 1:18. That ye may know what is the hope of his calling, and what the riches of the glory of his inheritance in the saints,

Col. 1:5. For the hope which is laid up for you in heaven, whereof ye heard before in the word of the truth of the gospel; 6. Which is come unto you, as *it is* in all the world; and bringeth forth fruit, as *it doth* also in you, since the day ye heard *of it*, and knew the grace of God in truth: 12. Giving thanks unto the Father, which hath made us meet to be partakers of the inheritance of the saints in light:

Col. 3:4. When Christ, *who is* our life, shall appear, then shall ye also appear with him in glory.

1 Thess. 2:12. Walk worthy of God, who hath called you unto his kingdom and glory.

1 Thess. 4:17. We which are alive *and* remain shall be caught up together with them in the clouds, to meet the Lord in the air: and so shall we ever be with the Lord.

2 Thess. 1:7. To you who are troubled rest with us, when the Lord Jesus shall be revealed from heaven with his mighty angels,

2 Thess. 2:14. He called you by our gospel, to the obtaining of the glory of our Lord Jesus Christ.

Heb. 10:34. For ye had compassion on me in my bonds, and took joyfully the spoiling of your goods, knowing. in yourselves that ye have in heaven a better and an enduring substance.

Heb. 11:10. He looked for a city which hath foundations, whose builder and maker *is* God. 16. But now they desire a better *country*, that is, an heavenly: wherefore God is not ashamed to be called their God: for he hath prepared for them a city.

Heb. 12:22. Ye are come unto mount Sion, and unto the city of the living God, the heavenly Jerusalem, and to an innumerable company of angels, 23. To the general as-

sembly and church of the first-born, which are written in heaven, and to God the Judge of all, and to the spirits of just men made perfect, 24. And to Jesus the mediator of the new covenant, 28. We receiving a kingdom which cannot be moved, let us have grace,

Heb. 13:14. Here have we no continuing city, but we seek one to come.

1 Pet. 1:4. To an inheritance incorruptible, and undefiled, and that fadeth not away, reserved in heaven for you,

2 Pet. 1:11. An entrance shall be ministered unto you abundantly into the everlasting kingdom of our Lord and Saviour Jesus Christ.

2 Pet. 3:13. We, according to his promise, look for new heavens and a new earth, wherein dwelleth righteousness.

Rev. 2:7. To him that overcometh will I give to eat of the tree of life, which is in the midst of the paradise of God.

Rev. 3:21. To him that overcometh will I grant to sit with me in my throne, even as I also overcame, and am set down with my Father in his throne. Luke 12:8.

Rev. 4:4. Round about the throne *were* four and twenty seats: and upon the seats I saw four and twenty elders sitting, clothed in white raiment; and they had on their heads crowns of gold.

Rev. 5:9. They sung a new song, saying, Thou art worthy to take the book, and to open the seals thereof: for thou wast slain, and hast redeemed us to God by thy blood out of every kindred, and tongue, and people, and nation;

Rev. 7:9. Lo, a great multitude, which no man could number, of all nations, and kindreds, and people, and tongues, stood before the throne, and before the Lamb, clothed with white robes, and palms in their hands; 13. What are these which are arrayed in white robes? and whence came they? 14. These are they which came out of great tribulation, and have washed their robes, and made them white in the blood of the Lamb. 15. Therefore are they before the throne of God, and serve him day and night in his temple: and he that sitteth on the throne shall dwell among them. 16. They shall hunger no more, neither thirst any more; neither shall the sun light on them, nor any heat. 17. For the Lamb which is in the midst of the throne shall feed them, and shall lead them unto living fountains of waters: and God shall wipe away all tears from their eyes. Isa. 49:9,10.

Rev. 14:1. A Lamb stood on the mount Sion, and with him an hundred forty *and* four thousand, having his Father's name written in their foreheads. 2. And I heard a voice from heaven, as the voice of many waters, and as the voice of a great thunder: and I heard the voice of harpers harping with their harps: 3. And they sung as it were a new song before the throne, and before the four beasts, and the elders: and no man could learn that song but the hundred *and* forty *and* four thousand, which were redeemed from the earth.

Rev. 15:2. I saw as it were a sea of glass mingled with fire: and them that had gotten the victory over the beast, and over his image, and over his mark, *and* over the number of his name, stand on the sea of glass, having the harps of God.

Rev. 21:1. I saw a new heaven and a new earth: for the first heaven and the first earth were passed away; and there was no more sea. 2. And I John saw the holy city, new Jerusalem, coming down from God out of heaven, prepared as a bride adorned for her husband. 3. And I heard a great voice out of heaven saying, Behold, the tabernacle of God *is* with men, and he will dwell with them, and they shall be his people, and God himself shall be with them, *and be* their God. 4. And God shall wipe away all tears from their eyes; and there shall be no more death, neither sorrow, nor crying, neither shall there be any more pain: for the former things are passed away. 5. And he that sat upon the throne said, Behold, I make all things new. 9. Come hither, I will shew thee the bride, the Lamb's wife. 10. And he carried me away in the spirit to a great and high mountain, and shewed me that great city, the holy Jerusalem, descending out of heaven from God,

11. Having the glory of God: and her light *was* like unto a stone most precious, even like a jasper stone, clear as crystal; 18. The building of the wall of it was *of* jasper: and the city *was* pure gold, like unto clear glass. 19. And the foundations of the wall of the city *were* garnished with all manner of precious stones. 21. And the twelve gates *were* twelve pearls; every several gate was of one pearl: and the street of the city *was* pure gold, as it were transparent glass.

22. And I saw no temple therein: for the Lord God Almighty and the Lamb are the temple of it. 23. And the city had no need of the sun, neither of the moon, to shine in it: for the glory of God did lighten it, and the Lamb *is* the light thereof. 24. And the nations of them which are saved shall walk in the light of it: and the kings of the earth do bring their glory and honour into it.

25. And the gates of it shall not be shut at all by day: for there shall be no night there. 27. There shall in no wise enter into it any thing that defileth, neither *whatsoever* worketh abomination, or *maketh* a lie: but they which are written in the Lamb's book of life.

Rev. 22:1. He shewed me a pure river of water of life, clear as crystal, proceeding out of the throne of God and of the Lamb. 2. In the midst of the street of it, and on either side of the river, *was there* the tree of life, which bare twelve *manner of* fruits, *and* yielded her fruit every month: and the leaves of the tree *were* for the healing of the nations. 3. And there shall be no more

curse: but the throne of God and of the Lamb shall be in it; and his servants shall serve him:

4. And they shall see his face; and his name *shall be* in their foreheads. 5. And there shall be no night there; and they need no candle, neither light of the sun; for the Lord God giveth them light: and they shall reign for ever and ever.

See RIGHTEOUS, PROMISES TO.

THE PHYSICAL HEAVENS: Gen. 1:1. In the beginning God created the heaven and the earth. Job 37:18; Psa. 33:6; 136:5; Jer. 10:12.

Psa. 19:1. The heavens declare the glory of God; and the firmament sheweth his handywork.

Psa. 50:6. And the heavens shall declare his righteousness: for God *is* judge himself.

Psa. 68:33. To him that rideth upon the heavens of heavens, *which were* of old; lo, he doth send out his voice, *and that* a mighty voice.

Psa. 89:29. His seed also will I make *to endure* for ever, and his throne as the days of heaven.

Psa. 97:6. The heavens declare his righteousness, and all the people see his glory.

Psa. 103:11. For as the heaven is high above the earth, *so* great is his mercy toward them that fear him.

Psa. 113:4. The LORD *is* high above all nations, *and* his glory above the heavens.

Psa. 115:16. The heaven, *even* the heavens, *are* the LORD's:

Jer. 31:37. Thus saith the LORD; If heaven above can be measured, and the foundations of the earth searched out beneath, I will also cast off all the seed of Israel for all that they have done, saith the LORD.

Ezek. 1:1. Now it came to pass in the thirtieth year, in the fourth *month*, in the fifth *day* of the month, as I *was* among the captives by the river of Chebar, *that* the heavens were opened, and I saw visions of God.

Matt. 24:29. Immediately after the tribulation of those days shall the sun be darkened, and the moon shall not give her light, and the stars shall fall from heaven, and the powers of the heavens shall be shaken: 30. And then shall appear the sign of the Son of man in heaven: and then shall all the tribes of the earth mourn, and they shall see the Son of man coming in the clouds of heaven with power and great glory.

Acts 2:19. And I will shew wonders in heaven above, and signs in the earth beneath; blood, and fire, and vapour of smoke: 20. The sun shall be turned into darkness, and the moon into blood, before that great and notable day of the Lord come:

See Sub-topics, below.

PHYSICAL HEAVENS, CREATION OF: Gen. 1:1. In the beginning God created the heaven and the earth.

Gen. 2:1. Thus the heavens and the earth were finished, and all the host of them.

1 Chr. 16:26. For all the gods of the people *are* idols: but the LORD made the heavens.

2 Chr. 2:12. Huram said moreover, Blessed *be* the LORD God of Israel, that made heaven and earth,

Neh. 9:6. Thou, *even* thou, *art* LORD alone; thou hast made heaven, the heaven of heavens, with all their host, the earth, and all *things* that *are* therein, the seas, and all that *is* therein, and thou preservest them all; and the host of heaven worshippeth thee.

Job 9:8. Which alone spreadeth out the heavens, and treadeth upon the waves of the sea.

Psa. 8:3. When I consider thy heavens, the work of thy fingers, the moon and the stars, which thou hast ordained;

Psa. 19:1. The heavens declare the glory of God; and the firmament sheweth his handywork.

Psa. 33:6. By the word of the LORD were the heavens made; and all the host of them by the breath of his mouth. 9. For he spake, and it was *done;* he commanded, and it stood fast.

Psa. 148:4. Praise him, ye heavens of heavens, and ye waters that *be* above the heavens. 5. Let them praise the name of the LORD: for he commanded, and they were created. 6. He hath also stablished them for ever and ever: he hath made a decree which shall not pass.

Prov. 8:27. When he prepared the heavens, I *was* there: when he set a compass upon the face of the depth:

Isa. 37:16. O LORD of hosts, God of Israel, that dwellest *between* the cherubims, thou *art* the God, *even* thou alone, of all the kingdoms of the earth: thou hast made heaven and earth.

Isa. 40:22. *It is* he that sitteth upon the circle of the earth, and the inhabitants thereof *are* as grasshoppers; that stretcheth out the heavens as a curtain, and spreadeth them out as a tent to dwell in:

Isa. 42:5. Thus saith God the LORD, he that created the heavens, and stretched them out: chapter 45:18.

Isa. 45:12. I have made the earth, and created man upon it· I, *even* my hands, have stretched out the heavens, and all their host have I commanded.

Jer. 10:12. He hath made the earth by his power, he hath established the world by his wisdom, and hath stretched out the heavens by his discretion.

Jer. 32:17. Ah Lord GOD! behold, thou hast made the heaven and the earth by thy great power and stretched out arm, *and* there is nothing too hard for thee:

Jer. 51:15. He hath made the earth by his power, he hath established the world by his wisdom, and hath stretched out the heaven by his understanding.

Acts 4:24. Lord, thou *art* God, which hast made heaven, and earth, and the sea, and all that in them is: Acts 14:15.

Heb. 1:10. And, Thou, Lord, in the beginning hast laid the foundation of the earth;

and the heavens are the works of thine hands:

Rev. 10:6. And sware by him that liveth for ever and ever, who created heaven, and the things that therein are, and the earth, and the things that therein are, and the sea, and the things which are therein, that there should be time no longer:

Rev. 14:7. Saying with a loud voice, Fear God, and give glory to him; for the hour of his judgment is come: and worship him that made heaven, and earth, and the sea, and the fountains of waters.

See HEAVENS, NEW. See CREATION; GOD, CREATOR.

PHYSICAL HEAVENS, DESTRUCTION OF:
Job 14:12. So man lieth down, and riseth not: till the heavens *be* no more, they shall not awake, nor be raised out of their sleep.

Psa. 102:25. Of old hast thou laid the foundation of the earth: and the heavens *are* the work of thy hands. 26. They shall perish, but thou shalt endure: yea, all of them shall wax old like a garment; as a vesture shalt thou change them, and they shall be changed:

Isa. 34:4. And all the host of heaven shall be dissolved, and the heavens shall be rolled together as a scroll: and all their host shall fall down, as the leaf falleth off from the vine, and as a falling *fig* from the fig tree.

Isa. 51:6. Lift up your eyes to the heavens, and look upon the earth beneath: for the heavens shall vanish away like smoke, and the earth shall wax old like a garment, and they that dwell therein shall die in like manner: but my salvation shall be for ever, and my righteousness shall not be abolished.

Matt. 5:18. Till heaven and earth pass, one jot or one tittle shall in no wise pass from the law, till all be fulfilled.

Matt. 24:35. Heaven and earth shall pass away, but my words shall not pass away.

Heb. 1:10. And, Thou, Lord, in the beginning hast laid the foundation of the earth; and the heavens are the works of thine hands: 11. They shall perish; but thou remainest; and they all shall wax old as doth a garment; 12. And as a vesture shalt thou fold them up, and they shall be changed: but thou art the same, and thy years shall not fail.

2 Pet. 3:10. But the day of the Lord will come as a thief in the night; in the which the heavens shall pass away with a great noise, and the elements shall melt with fervent heat, the earth also and the works that are therein shall be burned up. 12. Looking for and hasting unto the coming of the day of God, wherein the heavens being on fire shall be dissolved, and the elements shall melt with fervent heat?

Rev. 6:12. And I beheld when he had opened the sixth seal, and, lo, there was a great earthquake; and the sun became black as sackcloth of hair, and the moon became as blood; 13. And the stars of heaven fell unto the earth, even as a fig tree casteth her untimely figs, when she is shaken of a mighty wind. 14. And the heaven departed as a scroll when it is rolled together ; and every mountain and island were moved out of their places.

Rev. 20:11. And I saw a great white throne, and him that sat on it, from whose face the earth and the heaven fled away ; and there was found no place for them.

Rev. 21:1. And I saw a new heaven and a new earth : for the first heaven and the first earth were passed away ; and there was no more sea. 4. For the former things are passed away.

NEW HEAVENS : Isa. 65:17. For, behold, I create new heavens and a new earth : and the former shall not be remembered, nor come into mind.

Isa. 66:22. For as the new heavens and the new earth, which I will make, shall remain before me, saith the LORD, so shall your seed and your name remain.

2 Pet. 3:13. Nevertheless we, according to his promise, look for new heavens and a new earth, wherein dwelleth righteousness.

Rev. 21:1. And I saw a new heaven and a new earth : for the first heaven and the first earth were passed away ; and there was no more sea. 2. And I John saw the holy city, new Jerusalem, coming down from God out of heaven, prepared as a bride adorned for her husband. 3. And I heard a great voice out of heaven saying, Behold, the tabernacle of God *is* with men, and he will dwell with them, and they shall be his people, and God himself will be with them, *and be* their God. 4. And God shall wipe away all tears from their eyes ; and there shall be no more death, neither sorrow, nor crying, neither shall there be any more pain : for the former things are passed away.

HEBER. 1. Head of a family in the tribe of Gad, 1 Chr. 5:13.

2. A Benjamite, 1 Chr. 8:22.

3. A son of Beriah, Gen. 46:17; Num. 26: 45; 1 Chr. 7:31,32; Luke 3:35.

4. Husband of Jael, Judg. 4:11,17,21; 5:24.

5. Son of Ezra, 1 Chr. 4:18.

6. A Benjamite, 1 Chr. 8:17.

HEBREW. A word supposed to be a corruption of the name of Eber, who was an ancestor of Abraham, Gen. 10:24; 11:14–26. See GENEALOGY. Applied to Abraham, Gen. 14:13; and his descendants, Gen. 39:14; 40:15; 43:32; Ex. 2:6; Deut. 15:12; 1 Sam. 4:9; 29:3; Jonah 1:9; Acts 6:1; 2 Cor. 11:22; Phil. 3:5. Used to denote the language of the Jews, John 5:2; 19:20; Acts 21:40; 22:2; 26:14; Rev. 9:11.

See ISRAELITES ; JEWS.

HEBRON. 1. A city of Asher, Josh. 19:28.

2. A city of Judah, S. of Jerusalem. When built, Num. 13:22. Fortified, 2 Chr. 11:10. Called KIRJATH-ARBA, Gen. 23:2; ARBA, Gen. 35:27; Josh. 15:13. Abraham dwells and Sarah dies at, Gen. 23:2. Hoham, king of, confederated with other kings of the Canaanites against Joshua, Josh. 10:3–39. Children of

Anakim dwell at, Num. 13:22; Josh. 11:21. Conquest of, by Caleb, Josh. 14:6–15; Judg. 1:10,20. A city of refuge, Josh. 20:7; 21:11, 13. David crowned king of Judah at, 2 Sam. 2:1–11; 3; of Israel, 2 Sam. 5:1–5. The burial place of Sarah, Gen. 23:2; Abner, 2 Sam. 3: 32; Ish-bosheth, 2 Sam. 4:12. The conspirators against Ish-bosheth hanged at, 2 Sam. 4: 12. Absalom made king at, 2 Sam. 15:9,10. Jews of the Babylonian captivity dwell at, Neh. 11:25.

Pool of, 2 Sam. 4:12.

3. Son of Kohath, Ex. 6:18; Num. 3:19; 1 Chr. 6:2,18; 23:12,19.

4. The patronymic of Mareshah, 1 Chr. 2 42,43; 15:9.

HEDGE. A fence, Job 1:10; Isa. 5:5; Jer. 49:3; Lam. 3:7; Ezek. 13:5; 22:30; Hos. 2:6; Mic. 7:4; Mark 12:1; of thorns, Prov. 15:19. People sheltered in, Luke 14:23.

See FENCE.

HEGAI, chamberlain of Ahasuerus, Esth. 2:3,8,15.

HEGIRA. See EXODUS.

HEIFER. When used as sacrifice, must be without blemish and must not have come under the yoke, Num. 19:2; Deut. 21:3. An atonement for murder, Deut. 21:1–9. The red heifer used for the water of separation, Num. 19; Heb. 9:13.

Used for draught, Judg. 14:18; for treading out wheat, Hos. 10:11. Tractable, Hos. 10:11. Intractable, Hos. 4:16.

See KINE ; OFFERING.

FIGURATIVE : Of backsliders, Hos. 4:16. Of the obedient, Hos. 10:11.

HEIR. Gal. 4:1,2.

Gen. 15:3. And Abram said, Behold, to me thou hast given no seed : and, lo, one born in my house is mine heir.

Gen. 21:10. Wherefore she said unto Abraham, Cast out this bondwoman and her son : for the son of this bondwoman shall not be heir with my son, *even* with Isaac. Gal. 4:30.

Gen. 25:5. And Abraham gave all that he had unto Isaac. 6. But unto the sons of the concubines, which Abraham had, Abraham gave gifts, and sent them away from Isaac his son, while he yet lived, eastward, unto the east country.

Lev. 25:45. Moreover of the children of the strangers that do sojourn among you, of them shall ye buy, and of their families that *are* with you, which they begat in your land : and they shall be your possession. 46. And ye shall take them as an inheritance for your children after you, to inherit *them for* a possession ; they shall be your bondmen for ever : but over your brethren the children of Israel, ye shall not rule one over another with rigour.

Num. 27:8. And thou shalt speak unto the children of Israel, saying, If a man die, and have no son, then ye shall cause his inheritance to pass unto his daughter. 9. And if he have no daughter, then ye shall give his inheritance unto his brethren. 10. And if he have no brethren, then ye shall give his inheritance unto his father's brethren. 11. And if his father have no brethren, then ye shall give his inheritance unto his kinsman that is next to him of his family, and he shall possess it: and it shall be unto the children of Israel a statute of judgment, as the LORD commanded Moses.

Num. 36:1. And the chief fathers of the families of the children of Gilead, the son of Machir, the son of Manasseh, of the families of the sons of Joseph, came near, and spake before Moses, and before the princes, the chief fathers of the children of Israel: 2. And they said, The LORD commanded my lord to give the land for an inheritance by lot to the children of Israel: and my lord was commanded by the LORD to give the inheritance of Zelophehad our brother unto his daughters. 3. And if they be married to any of the sons of the *other* tribes of the children of Israel, then shall their inheritance be taken from the inheritance of our fathers, and shall be put to the inheritance of the tribe whereunto they are received: so shall it be taken from the lot of our inheritance. 4. And when the jubile of the children of Israel shall be, then shall their inheritance be put unto the inheritance of the tribe whereunto they are received: so shall their inheritance be taken away from the inheritance of the tribe of our fathers. 5. And Moses commanded the children of Israel according to the word of the LORD, saying, The tribe of the sons of Joseph hath said well. 6. This *is* the thing which the LORD doth command concerning the daughters of Zelophehad, saying, Let them marry to whom they think best; only to the family of the tribe of their father shall they marry. 7. So shall not the inheritance of the children of Israel remove from tribe to tribe: for every one of the children of Israel shall keep himself to the inheritance of the tribe of his fathers. 8. And every daughter that possesseth an inheritance in any tribe of the children of Israel, shall be wife unto one of the family of the tribe of her father, that the children of Israel may enjoy every man the inheritance of his fathers. Josh. 17:3-6.

Deut. 21:15. If a man have two wives, one beloved, and another hated, and they have born him children, *both* the beloved and the hated; and *if* the firstborn son be her's that was hated: 16. Then it shall be, when he maketh his sons to inherit *that* which he hath, *that* he may not make the son of the beloved firstborn before the son of the hated, *which is indeed* the firstborn: 17. But he shall acknowledge the son of the hated *for* the firstborn, by giving him a double portion of all that he hath: for he *is* the beginning of his strength; the right of the firstborn *is* his.

Ruth 4:1. Then went Boaz up to the gate, and sat him down there: and, behold, the kinsman of whom Boaz spake came by; unto whom he said, Ho, such a one! turn aside, sit down here. And he turned aside, and sat down. 2. And he took ten men of the elders of the city, and said, Sit ye down here. And they sat down. 3. And he said unto the kinsman, Naomi, that is come again out of the country of Moab, selleth a parcel of land, which *was* our brother Elimelech's: 4. And I thought to advertise thee, saying, Buy *it* before the inhabitants, and before the elders of my people. If thou wilt redeem *it,* redeem *it:* but if thou wilt not redeem *it,* *then* tell me, that I may know: for *there is* none to redeem *it* beside thee; and I *am* after thee. And he said, I will redeem *it.* 5. Then said Boaz, What day thou buyest the field of the hand of Naomi, thou must buy *it* also of Ruth the Moabitess, the wife of the dead, to raise up the name of the dead upon his inheritance. 6. And the kinsman said, I cannot redeem *it* for myself, lest I mar mine own inheritance: redeem thou my right to thyself; for I cannot redeem *it.* 7. Now this *was the manner* in former time in Israel concerning redeeming and concerning changing, for to confirm all things: a man plucked off his shoe, and gave *it* to his neighbour: and this *was* a testimony in Israel. 8. Therefore the kinsman said unto Boaz, Buy *it* for thee. So he drew off his shoe. 9. And Boaz said unto the elders, and *unto* all the people, Ye *are* witnessess this day, that I have bought all that *was* Elimelech's, and all that *was* Chilion's and Mahlon's, of the hand of Naomi. 10. Moreover Ruth the Moabitess, the wife of Mahlon, have I purchased to be my wife, to raise up the name of the dead upon his inheritance, that the name of the dead be not cut off from among his brethren, and from the gate of his place: ye *are* witnesses this day. 11. And all the people that *were* in the gate, and the elders, said, *We are* witnesses. The LORD make the woman that is come into thine house like Rachel and like Leah, which two did build the house of Israel: and do thou worthily in Ephratah, and be famous in Beth-lehem: 12. And let thy house be like the house of Pharez, whom Tamar bare unto Judah, of the seed of which the LORD shall give thee of this young woman.

Eccl. 2:18. Yea, I hated all my labour which I had taken under the sun: because I should leave it unto the man that shall be after me. 19. And who knoweth whether he shall be a wise *man* or a fool? yet shall he have rule over all my labour wherein I have laboured, and wherein I have shewed myself wise under the sun. This *is* also vanity.

See INHERITANCE; BIRTHRIGHT; FIRSTBORN; ORPHAN; WILL.

FIGURATIVE: Rom. 8:14. For as many as are led by the Spirit of God, they are the sons of God. 15. For ye have not received the spirit of bondage again to fear; but ye have received the Spirit of adoption, whereby we cry, Abba, Father. 16. The Spirit itself beareth witness with our spirit, that we are the children of God: **17.** And if children, then heirs; heirs of God, and joint-heirs with Christ; if so be that we suffer with *him*, that we may be also glorified together.

Gal. 3:29. And if ye *be* Christ's, then are ye Abraham's seed, and heirs according to the promise.

Gal. 4:6. And because ye are sons, God hath sent forth the Spirit of his Son into your hearts, crying, Abba, Father. **7.** Wherefore thou art no more a servant, but a son; and if a son, then an heir ¹ of God through Christ.   [¹ R. V. through God]

Tit. 3:7. That being justified by his grace, we should be made heirs according to the hope of eternal life.

Jas. 2:5. Hearken, my beloved brethren, Hath not God chosen the poor of this world rich in faith, and heirs of the kingdom which he hath promised to them that love him?

See ADOPTION.

HELAH, a wife of Asher, 1 Chr. 4:5.

HELAM, a place E. of the Jordan, 2 Sam. 10:16,17.

HELBAH, a town of Asher, Judg. 1:31.

HELBON, a village near Damascus, noted for fine wines, Ezek. 27:18.

HELDAI. 1. The Netophathite. One of David's heroes, 1 Chr. 27:15. Called HELED, 1 Chr. 11:30; and HELEB, 2 Sam. 23:29.

2. An Israelite, Zech. 6:10.

HELEB. See HELDAI.

HELEK, son of Gilead, Num. 26:30; Josh. 17:2.

HELEM. 1. A descendant of Asher, 1 Chr. 7:35.

2. Probably same as HELDAI, Zech. 6:10,14.

HELEPH, town of Naphtali, Josh. 19:33.

HELEZ. 1. One of David's mighty men, 2 Sam. 23:26; 1 Chr. 11:27; 27:10.

2. A man of Judah, 1 Chr. 2:39.

HELI, father of Joseph, Luke 3:23.

HELKAI, a priest, Neh. 12:15.

HELKATH, called also HUKOK. A Levitical town, 1 Chr. 6:75; Josh. 19:25; 21:31.

HELKATH-HAZZURIM, a battle ground, 2 Sam. 2:16.

HELL. The word used in the King James Version of the *O. T.* to translate the Hebrew word sheol, signifying the unseen state, in Deut. 32:22; 2 Sam. 22:6; Job 11:8; 26:6; Psa. 9:17; 16:10; 18:5; 55:15; 86:13; 116:3; 139:8; Prov. 5:5; 7:27; 9:18; 15:11,24; 23:14; 27:20; Isa. 5:14; 14:9,15; 28:15,18; 57:9; Ezek. 31:16,17; 32:21, 27; Amos 9:2; Jonah 2:2; Hab. 2:5.

Translation of the Greek word hades in *N. T.* of King James Version, the unseen world, Matt. 11:23; 16:18; Luke 10:15; 16:23; Acts 2:27,31; Rev. 1:18; 6:8; 20:13,14; of the Greek word gehenna, signifying the place of torment, Matt. 5:22,29,30; 10:28; 18:9; 23:15, 33; Mark 9:43,45,47; Luke 12:5; Jas. 3:6; of the Greek word tartarus, signifying the infernal region, 2 Pet. 2:4.

Sheol is also translated grave in King James Version in Gen. 37:35; 42:38; 44:29, 31; 1 Sam. 2:6; 1 Kin. 2:6,9; Job 7:9; 14:13; 17:13; 21:13; 24:19; Psa. 6:5; 30:3; 31:17; 49:14,15;

88:3; 89:48; 141:7; Prov. 1:12; 30:16; Eccl. 9:10; Song 8:6; Isa. 14:11; 38:10,18; Ezek. 31:15; Hos. 13:14; pit, Num. 16:30,33; Job 17:16.

The English revisers insert the Hebrew word sheol in places where hell, grave, and pit were used in the *A. V.* as translations of the word sheol, except in Deut. 32:22; Psa. 55:15; 86:13; and in the prophetical books. The American revisers invariably use Sheol in the American text, where it occurs in the original.

THE FUTURE ABODE OF THE WICKED: Psa. 9:17. The wicked shall be turned into hell, *and* all the nations that forget God.

Prov. 5:5. Her feet go down to death; her steps take hold on hell.

Prov. 9:13. A foolish woman *is* clamorous: *she is* simple, and knoweth nothing. **14.** For she sitteth at the door of her house, on a seat in the high places of the city, **15.** To call passengers who go right on their ways: **16.** Whoso *is* simple, let him turn in hither: and *as for* him that wanteth understanding, she saith to him, **17.** Stolen waters are sweet, and bread *eaten* in secret is pleasant. **18.** But he knoweth not that the dead *are* there; *and that* her guests *are* in the depths of hell.

Prov. 15:24. The way of life *is* above to the wise, that he may depart from hell beneath.

Prov. 23:13. Withhold not correction from the child: for *if* thou beatest him with the rod, he shall not die. **14.** Thou shalt beat him with the rod, and shalt deliver his soul from hell.

Isa. 30:33. Tophet *is* ordained of old; yea, for the king it is prepared; he hath made *it* deep *and* large: the pile thereof *is* fire and much wood; the breath of the LORD, like a stream of brimstone, doth kindle it.

Isa. 33:14. The sinners in Zion are afraid; fearfulness hath surprised the hypocrites. Who among us shall dwell with devouring fire? who among us shall dwell with everlasting burnings?

Matt. 3:12. Whose fan *is* in his hand, and he will throughly purge his floor, and gather his wheat into the garner; but he will burn up the chaff with unquenchable fire.

Matt. 5:29. And if thy right eye offend thee, pluck it out, and cast *it* from thee: for it is profitable for thee that one of thy members should perish, and not *that* thy whole body should be cast into hell. *v.* 30.

Matt. 7:13. Wide *is* the gate, and broad *is* the way, that leadeth to destruction, and many there be which go in thereat: *v.* 14.

Matt. 8:11. And I say unto you, That many shall come from the east and west, and shall sit down with Abraham, and Isaac, and Jacob, in the kingdom of heaven. **12.** But the children of the kingdom shall be cast out into outer darkness: there shall be weeping and gnashing of teeth.

Matt. 10:28. Rather fear him which is able to destroy both soul and body in hell.

Matt. 13:30. Let both grow together until the harvest: and in the time of harvest I will say to the reapers, Gather ye together first the tares, and bind them in bundles to burn them: but gather the wheat into my barn. 38. The field is the world; the good seed are the children of the kingdom; but the tares are the children of the wicked *one;* 39. The enemy that sowed them is the devil; the harvest is the end of the world; and the reapers are the angels. 40. As therefore the tares are gathered and burned in the fire; so shall it be in the end of this world. 41. The Son of man shall send forth his angels, and they shall gather out of his kingdom all things that offend, and them which do iniquity; 42. And shall cast them into a furnace of fire: there shall be wailing and gnashing of teeth. 49. So shall it be at the end of the world: the angels shall come forth, and sever the wicked from among the just. 50. And shall cast them into the furnace of fire: there shall be wailing and gnashing of teeth.

Matt. 16:18. And I say also unto thee, That thou art Peter, and upon this rock I will build my church; and the gates of hell shall not prevail against it.

Matt. 18:8. Wherefore if thy hand or thy foot offend thee, cut them off, and cast *them* from thee: it is better for thee to enter into life halt or maimed, rather than having two hands or two feet to be cast into everlasting fire. 9. And if thine eye offend thee, pluck it out, and cast *it* from thee: it is better for thee to enter into life with one eye, rather than having two eyes to be cast into hell fire. 34. And his lord was wroth, and delivered him to the tormentors, till he should pay all that was due unto him. 35. So likewise shall my heavenly Father do also unto you, if ye from your hearts forgive not every one his brother their trespasses.

Matt. 22:13. Cast *him* into outer darkness; there shall be weeping and gnashing of teeth.

Matt. 25:28. Take therefore the talent from him, and give *it* unto him which hath ten talents. 29. For unto every one that hath shall be given, and he shall have abundance: but from him that hath not shall be taken away even that which he hath. 30. And cast ye the unprofitable servant into outer darkness: there shall be weeping and gnashing of teeth. 41. Then shall he say also unto them on the left hand, Depart from me, ye cursed, into everlasting fire, prepared for the devil and his angels: 46. These shall go away into everlasting punishment:

Mark 9:43. It is better for thee to enter into life maimed, than having two hands to go into hell, into the fire that never shall be quenched: ¹ 44. Where their worm dieth not, and the fire is not quenched. *vs.* 45–48. Matt. 5:29.

[¹ Omitted in R. V.]

Luke 3:17. Whose fan *is* in his hand, and he will throughly purge his floor, and will gather the wheat into his garner; but the chaff he will burn with fire unquenchable. Matt. 3:12.

Luke 16:23. In hell he lift up his eyes, being in torments, and seeth Abraham afar off, and Lazarus in his bosom. 24. And he cried and said, Father Abraham, have mercy on me, and send Lazarus, that he may dip the tip of his finger in water, and cool my tongue; for I am tormented in this flame. 26. Between us and you there is a great gulf fixed: so that they which would pass from hence to you cannot; neither can they pass to us, that *would come* from thence. *vs.* 25,28; Acts 1:25.

2 Thess. 1:9. Who shall be punished with everlasting destruction from the presence of the Lord, and from the glory of his power;

2 Pet. 2:4. If God spared not the angels that sinned, but cast *them* down to hell, and delivered *them* into chains of darkness, to be reserved unto judgment;

Jude 6. The angels which kept not their first estate, but left their own habitation, he hath reserved in everlasting chains under darkness unto the judgment of the great day. 23. And others save with fear, pulling *them* out of the fire; hating even the garment spotted by the flesh.

Rev. 9:1. To him was given the key of the bottomless pit. 2. And he opened the bottomless pit; and there arose a smoke out of the pit, as the smoke of a great furnace; and the sun and the air were darkened by reason of the smoke of the pit. Rev. 11.7.

Rev. 14:10. The same shall drink of the wine of the wrath of God, which is poured out without mixture into the cup of his indignation; and he shall be tormented with fire and brimstone in the presence of the holy angels, and in the presence of the Lamb: 11. The smoke of their torment ascendeth up for ever and ever: and they have no rest day nor night,

Rev. 19:20. And the beast was taken, and with him the false prophet . . . These both were cast alive into a lake of fire burning with brimstone.

Rev. 20:10. The devil that deceived them was cast into the lake of fire and brimstone, where the beast and the false prophet *are*, and shall be tormented day and night for ever and ever. 15. Whosoever was not found written in the book of life was cast into the lake of fire.

Rev. 21:8. But the fearful, and unbelieving, and the abominable, and murderers, and whoremongers, and sorcerers, and idolaters, and all liars, shall have their part in the lake which burneth with fire and brimstone: which is the second death. Rev. 2:11.

See WICKED, PUNISHMENT OF.

HELM, Acts 27:40; Jas. 3:4.

HELMET, a defensive headgear worn by soldiers, 1 Sam. 17:5,38; 2 Chr. 26:14; Jer. 46:4; Ezek. 23:24.

FIGURATIVE: Isa. 59:17; Eph. 6:17; 1 Thess. 5:8.

HELON, father of Eliab, Num. 1:9; 2:7; 7:24,29; 10:16.

HEMAM, a son of Lotan, Gen. 36:22. Called HOMAM, 1 Chr. 1:39.

HEMAN. 1. A man noted for wisdom, to whom Solomon is compared, 1 Kin. 4:31; 1 Chr. 2:6.

2. "The singer," a chief Levite, and musician, 1 Chr. 6:33; 15:17,19; 16:41. The king's seer, 1 Chr. 25:5. His sons and daughters temple musicians, 1 Chr. 6:33; 25:1-6. "Maschil of," title of Psalm 88.

HEMATH. 1. Another form for HAMATH, Amos 6:14.

2. An unknown person or place, 1 Chr.2:55.

HEMDAN, son of Dishon, Gen. 36:26.

HEMLOCK, a poisonous and bitter plant, Hos. 10:4; Amos 6:12.

See GALL.

HEMORRHAGE. Menstruation, Lev. 15:19; Matt. 9:20; Luke 8:43. A woman suffers twelve years, Mark 5:25-29.

See MENSTRUATION.

HEMORRHOIDS, a disease with which the Philistines were afflicted, 1 Sam. 5:6,12; 6:4; 5:11; Deut. 28:27.

See DISEASE; TUMOR.

HEN. FIGURATIVE: Matt. 23:37; Luke 13:34.

HENA, a city on the Euphrates, 2 Kin. 18:34; 19:13; Isa. 37:13.

HENADAD, a Levite, Ezra 3:9; Neh. 3:18,24; 10:9.

HEPHER. 1. Son of Gilead, and ancestor of Zelophehad, Num. 26:32,33; 27:1; Josh. 17:2,3.

2. Son of Naarah, 1 Chr. 4:6.

3. One of David's heroes, 1 Chr. 11:36.

4. A city west of the Jordan, Josh. 12:17; 1 Kin. 4:10.

HEPHZI-BAH. 1. Wife of Hezekiah, 2 Kin. 21:1.

2. A prophetic name of Jerusalem, Isa. 62:4.

HERALD. Isa. 40:3; Dan. 3:4. Signified by the word preacher, 1 Tim. 2:7; 2 Tim. 1:11; 2 Pet. 2:5. See *R.V.* [marg.].

HERBS, given for food, Gen. 1:29,30; Prov. 15:17.

See VEGETATION.

HEREDITY. Gen. 5:3. And Adam . . . begat *a son* in his own likeness, after his image;

Ex. 20:5. I the LORD thy God *am* a jealous God, visiting the iniquity of the fathers upon the children unto the third and fourth *generation* of them that hate me; [Ex. 34: 7; Num. 14:18.] 6. And shewing mercy unto thousands of them that love me, and keep my commandments.

Num. 14:33. And your children shall wander in the wilderness forty years, and bear your whoredoms, until your carcases be wasted in the wilderness.

Job 14:4. Who can bring a clean *thing* out of an unclean? not one.

Job 21:19. God layeth up his iniquity for his children:

Psa. 37:28. The seed of the wicked shall be cut off.

Psa. 51:5. Behold, I was shapen in iniquity; and in sin did my mother conceive me.

Psa. 58:3. The wicked are estranged from the womb: they go astray as soon as they be born, speaking lies.

Isa. 14:20. The seed of evildoers shall never be renowned. 21. Prepare slaughter for his children for the iniquity of their fathers; that they do not rise, nor possess the land, nor fill the face of the world with cities.

Isa. 48:8. A transgressor from the womb.

Isa. 65:6. Behold, *it is* written before me: I will not keep silence, but will recompense, even recompense into their bosom, 7. Your iniquities, and the iniquities of your fathers together, saith the LORD, which have burned incense upon the mountains, and blasphemed me upon the hills: therefore will I measure their former work into their bosom.

Jer. 31:29. In those days they shall say no more, The fathers have eaten a sour grape, and the children's teeth are set on edge. 30. But every one shall die for his own iniquity: every man that eateth the sour grape, his teeth shall be set on edge.

Jer. 32:18. Thou shewest lovingkindness unto thousands, and recompensest the iniquity of the fathers into the bosom of their children after them: the Great, the Mighty God, the LORD of hosts, *is* his name,

Ezek. 18:2. What mean ye, that ye use this proverb concerning the land of Israel, saying, The fathers have eaten sour grapes, and the children's teeth are set on edge?

Ezek. 18:19. Yet say ye, Why? doth not the son bear the iniquity of the father? When the son hath done that which is lawful and right, *and* hath kept all my statutes, and hath done them, he shall surely live. 20. The soul that sinneth, it shall die. The son shall not bear the iniquity of the father, neither shall the father bear the iniquity of the son:

Matt. 3:9. And think not to say within yourselves, We have Abraham to *our* father:

John 3:6. That which is born of the flesh is flesh; and that which is born of the Spirit is spirit. 7. Marvel not that I said unto thee, Ye must be born again.

John 9:2. And his disciples asked him, saying, Master, who did sin, this man, or his parents, that he was born blind?

Rom. 5:12. By one man sin entered into the world, and death by sin; and so death passed upon all men, for that all have sinned:

1 Cor. 15:22. As in Adam all die, even so in Christ shall all be made alive.

Eph. 2:3. By nature the children of wrath, even as others.

HERES, a mountain, Judg. 1:35.

HERESH, a Levite, 1 Chr. 9:15.

HERESY. Propagandism of, forbidden under severe penalties, Deut. 13; Tit. 3:10,11; 2 John 10,11. Teachers of, among early Christians, Acts 15:24; 2 Cor. 11:4; Gal. 1:7; 2:4; 2 Pet. 2; Jude 3-16; Rev. 2:2. Paul and Silas accused of, Acts 16:20,21,23. Paul accused of, Acts 18:13. Disavowed by Paul, Acts 24:13–16.

See TEACHERS, FALSE.

HERMAS, a Christian at Rome, Rom. 16:14.

HERMES, a Greek Christian, Rom. 16:14.

HERMOGENES, a Christian, who deserted Paul, 2 Tim. 1:15.

HERMON. A mountain in the N. of Palestine. Called SIRION, Deut. 3:8,9; Psa. 29:6; SION, Deut. 4:48; Psa.133:3; SHENIR, Deut. 3:9; 1 Chr. 5:23; Song 4:8.

HEROD. 1. King of Judah, Matt. 2. 2. Tetrarch of Galilee, Luke 3:1; 23:7. Incest of, Matt. 14:3,4; Mark 6:17–19. Beheads John the Baptist, Mark 6:16–28; Matt. 14:3–11. Desires to see Jesus, Luke 9:7,9; 23:8. Tyranny of, Luke 13:31,32. Jesus tried by, Luke 23:6–12,15; Acts 4:27. 3. Son of Aristobulus, Acts 12:1–23.

HERODIANS, a Jewish faction. Seek to entangle Jesus, Matt. 22:16; Mark 12:13. Conspire to slay Jesus, Mark 3:6; 12:13.

HERODIAS, daughter of Aristobulus, Matt. 14:3,6; Mark 6:17,19,22; Luke 3:19.

HERODION. A Roman Christian, Rom. 16:11.

HERON, Lev. 11:19; Deut. 14:18.

HESED, father of one of Solomon's officers, 1 Kin. 4:10.

HESHBON. A city of the Amorites, Num. 21:25–35; Deut. 1:4. Built by Reuben, Num. 32:37. Allotted to Gad, Josh. 21:38,39. Fish-pools at, Song 7:4. Prophecy concerning, Isa. 16:8; Jer. 48:2,34,35; 49:1–3.

HESHMON, a town in the S. of Judah, Josh. 15:27.

HETH, son of Canaan, and ancestor of the Hittites, Gen. 10:15; 23:3,5,7,10,16,18; 27:46; 49:32; 1 Chr. 1:13.

See HITTITES.

HETHLON, a place on the northern frontier of Palestine, Ezek. 47:15; 48:1.

HEZEKI, a Benjamite, 1 Chr. 8:17.

HEZEKIAH. 1. King of Judah, 2 Kin. 16:20; 18:1,2; 1 Chr. 3:13; 2 Chr. 29:1; Matt. 1:9. Religious zeal of, 2 Chr. 29; 30; 31. Purges the nation of idolatry, 2 Kin. 18:4; 2 Chr. 31:1; 33:3. Restores the true forms of worship, 2 Chr. 31:2–21. His piety, 2 Kin. 18:3,5,6; 2 Chr. 29:2; 31:20,21; 32:32; Jer. 26:19. Military operations of, 2 Kin. 18:19; 1 Chr. 4:39–43; 2 Chr. 32; Isa. 36:37. Sickness and restoration of, 2 Kin. 20:1–11; 2 Chr. 32:24; Isa. 38:1–8. His psalm of thanksgiving, Isa. 38:9–22. His lack of wisdom in showing his resources to commissioners of Babylon, 2 Kin. 20;12–19; 2 Chr. 32:25,26,31; Isa. 39. Prospered of God, 2 Kin. 18:7; 2 Chr. 32:27–30. Conducts the brook Gihon into Jerusalem, 2 Kin. 18:17; 20:20; 2 Chr. 32:4, 30; 33:14; Neh. 2:13–15; 3:13,16; Isa. 7:3; 22:9–11; 36:2. Scribes of, Prov. 25:1. Death and burial of, 2 Kin. 20:21; 2 Chr. 32:33. Prophecies concerning, 2 Kin. 19:20–34; 20:5, 6, 16–18; Isa. 38:5–8; 39:5–7; Jer. 26:18,19. 2. Son of Neariah, 1 Chr. 3:23.

3. One of the exiles, Ezra 2:16; Neh. 7:21; called Hizkijah, Neh. 10:17.

HEZION, grandfather of Ben-hadad, 1 Kin. 15:18.

HEZIR. 1. A Levite, 1 Chr. 24:15. 2. A prince of Judah, Neh. 10:20.

HEZRAI, called also HEZRO. A Carmelite, 2 Sam. 23:35; 1 Chr. 11:37.

HEZRO. See HEZRAI.

HEZRON. 1. Son of Pharez, Gen. 46:12. Ancestor of the Hezronites, Num. 26:6,21; 1 Chr. 2:5,9,18,21,24. 2. A son of Reuben, Gen. 46:9; Ex. 6:14; 1 Chr. 4:1; 5:3. Descendants of, called Hezronites, Num. 26:6.

HIDDAI. One of David's heroes, 2 Sam. 23:30. Called HURAI, 1 Chr. 11:32.

HIDDEKEL, ancient name of the River Tigris, Gen. 2:14; Dan. 10:4.

HIEL. Rebuilder of Jericho, 1 Kin. 16:34. In him was fulfilled the curse pronounced by Joshua, Josh. 6:26.

HIERAPOLIS. A city of Phrygia. Christians in, Col. 4:13.

HIGGAION. See MUSIC.

HIGH PLACES. A term used to describe places of worship, Gen. 12:8; 22:2,14; 31:54; 1 Sam. 9:12; 2 Sam. 24:25; 1 Kin. 3:2, 4; 18:30,38; 1 Chr. 16:39; 2 Chr. 1:3; 33:17. Signify a place of idolatrous worship, Num. 22:41; 1 Kin. 11:7; 12:31; 14:23; 15:14; 22:43; 2 Kin. 17:9,29; Jer. 7:31. Licentious practices at, Ezek. 16:24–43. The idolatrous, to be destroyed, Lev. 26:30; Num. 33:52. Asa destroys, 2 Chr. 14:3; Jehoshaphat, 2 Chr. 17:6; Hezekiah, 2 Kin. 18:4; Josiah, 2 Kin. 23:8.

See GROVES; IDOLATRY.

HIGH PRIEST. See PRIEST.

HIGHWAYS. FIGURATIVE: Prov. 16:17. The highway of the upright *is* to depart from evil: he that keepeth his way preserveth his soul.

Isa. 11:16. And there shall be an highway for the remnant of his people, which shall be left, from Assyria; like as it was to Israel in the day that he came up out of the land of Egypt.

Isa. 35:8. And an highway shall be there, and a way, and it shall be called The way of holiness; the unclean shall not pass over it; but it *shall be* for those: the wayfaring men, though fools, shall not err *therein*. 9. No lion shall be there, nor *any* ravenous beast shall go up thereon, it shall not be found there; but the redeemed shall walk *there*: 10. And the ransomed of the LORD shall return, and come to Zion with songs and everlasting joy upon their heads: they shall obtain joy and gladness, and sorrow and sighing shall flee away.

Isa. 40:3. The voice of him that crieth in the wilderness, Prepare ye the way of the LORD, make straight in the desert a highway for our God. 4. Every valley shall be exalted, and every mountain and hill shall be made low: and the crooked shall be made straight, and the rough places plain: Matt. 3:3.

Matt. 7:13. Enter ye in at the strait gate: for wide *is* the gate, and broad *is* the way, that leadeth to destruction, and many there be which go in thereat: 14. Because strait *is* the gate, and narrow *is* the way, which leadeth unto life, and few there be that find it.

See ROADS; WAY.

HILEN, a city of Judah. Assigned to the priests, 1 Chr. 6:58. Called HOLON, Josh. 15:51; 21:15.

HILKIAH. 1. Officer of Hezekiah, 2 Kin. 18:18,26,37; Isa. 22:20; 36:3,22.

2. High priest, 2 Kin. 22:4,8,10,12,14; 23: 4,24; 1 Chr. 6:13; 9:11; 2 Chr. 34:9,14,15,18, 20,22; Ezra 7:1; Jer. 29:3.

3. Name of two Levites, 1 Chr. 6:45; 26:11.

4. Two priests, Neh. 8:4; 12:7,21; Jer. 1:1.

HILLEL, father of Abdon, Judg. 12:13,15.

HILLS, perpetual, Gen. 49:26; Hab. 3:6.

HIN. A measure for liquids, containing one-sixth or one-seventh of a bath. Jewish authorities disagree as to the exact capacity. Probably equivalent to about one gallon one quart, or one gallon one and one-half quarts, Ex. 29:40; Lev 19:36; 23:13.

HIND. See DEER.

HINNOM. A valley W. and S.W. of Jerusalem, Josh. 15:8; 18:16; 2 Kin. 23:10; Neh. 11:30. Children offered in sacrifice in, 2 Chr. 28:3; 33:6; Jer.7:31,32; 19:2,4,6; 32:35. Possibly valley of vision identical with, Isa. 22:1,5.

See TOPHET.

HIPPOPOTAMUS, Job 40:15 [marg. R.V.].

HIRAH, an Adullamite, Gen. 38:1,12.

HIRAM. 1. Called HURAM, king of Tyre. Builds a house for David, 2 Sam. 5:11; 1 Chr. 14:1; 2 Chr. 2:3. Aids Solomon in building the temple, 1 Kin. 5; 2 Chr. 2:3–16. Dissatisfied with cities given by Solomon, 1 Kin. 9:11–13. Makes presents of gold and seamen to Solomon, 1 Kin. 9:14,26–28; 10:11.

2. Called also HURAM. An artificer sent by King Hiram to execute the artistic work of the interior of the temple, 1 Kin. 7:13–45; 2 Chr. 2:13; 4:11–16.

HIRELING, not to be oppressed, Mal.3:5. See SERVANT.

HISTORY, Job 8:8–10.

See BOOKS; books of Genesis, Joshua, Judges, Ruth, Samuel, Kings, Chronicles, Ezra, Nehemiah, Esther; ISRAEL, HISTORY OF; JESUS, LIFE OF.

HIRE, law concerning hired property, Ex. 22:14,15.

See WAGES; EMPLOYER; MASTER; SERVANT.

HITTITES. A tribe of Canaanites. Children of Heth, Gen. 10:15; 23:10. Sell a burying-ground to Abraham, Gen. 23. Esau intermarries with, Gen. 26:34; 36:2. Dwelling place of, Gen. 23:17–20; Num. 13:29; Josh. 1:4; Judg. 1:26. Their land given to the Israelites, Ex. 3:8; Deut. 7:1; Josh. 1:4. Conquered by Joshua, Josh. 9:1,2; chapters 10–12; 24:11. Intermarry with Israelites, Judg. 3:5–7; Ezra 9:1. Solomon intermarries with, 1 Kin. 11:1; Neh. 13:26. Pay tribute to

Solomon, 1 Kin. 9:20,21. Retain their own kings, 1 Kin. 10:29; 2 Kin. 7:6; 2 Chr. 1:17. Officers from, in David's army, 1 Sam. 26:6; 2 Sam. 11:3; 23:39.

HIVITES. A tribe of Canaanites, Gen. 10:17; 1 Chr. 1:15. Shechemites and Gibeonites were families of, Gen. 34:2; Josh. 9:7; 11:19. Esau intermarries with, Gen. 26:34; 36:2. Dwelling place of, Josh. 11:3; Judg. 3:3; 2 Sam. 24:7. Their land given to the Israelites, Ex. 23:23,28; Deut. 20:17; Judg. 3:5. Conquered by Joshua, Josh. 9:1; 12:8; 24:11. Pay tribute to Solomon, 1 Kin. 9:21; 2 Chr. 8:8.

HIZKIAH, an ancestor of Zephaniah, Zeph. 1:1.

HIZKIJAH, probably identical with HEZEKIAH, the exile, which see.

HOBAB, son of Raguel, Num. 10:29; Judg.4:11.

HOBAH, a place N. of Damascus, Gen. 14:15.

HOD, a son of Zophah, 1 Chr. 7:37.

HODAIAH, son of Elioenai, 1 Chr. 3:24.

HODAVIAH. 1. A chief of the half tribe of Manasseh, whose inheritance was E. of the Jordan, 1 Chr. 5:24.

2. A Benjamite, 1 Chr. 9:7.

3. A Levite, Ezra 2:40.

HODESH, wife of Shaharaim, 1 Chr. 8:9.

HODEVAH, a Levite, Neh. 7:43.

HODIAH, called also HODIJAH. 1. Wife of Ezra, 1 Chr. 4:19.

2. A Levite, Neh. 8:7; 9:5; 10:10,13.

3. An Israelitish chief, Neh. 10:18.

HOGLAH, a daughter of Zelophehad, Num. 26:33; 27:1; 36:11; Josh. 17:3.

HOHAM, king of Hebron, Josh. 10:3.

HOLIDAY. For rest. See SABBATH. One year in seven, Lev. 25:2–7.

See JUBILEE.

HOLINESS. Gen. 17:1. I *am* the Almighty God; walk before me, and be thou perfect.

Gen. 35:2. Put away the strange gods that *are* among you, and be clean, and change your garments:

Ex. 19:6. Ye shall be unto me a kingdom of priests, and an holy nation.

Ex. 22:31. And ye shall be holy men unto me: neither shall ye eat *any* flesh *that is* torn of beasts in the field; ye shall cast it to the dogs.

Ex. 39:30. And they made the plate of the holy crown *of* pure gold, and wrote upon it a writing, *like to* the engravings of a signet, HOLINESS TO THE LORD. Ex. 28:36.

Lev. 10:8. And the LORD spake unto Aaron, saying, 9. Do not drink wine nor strong drink, thou, nor thy sons with thee, when ye go into the tabernacle of the congregation, lest ye die: *it shall be* a statute for ever throughout your generations: 10. And that ye may put difference between holy and unholy, and between unclean and clean;

Lev. 11:44. For I *am* the LORD your God: ye shall therefore sanctify yourselves, and ye shall be holy; for I *am* holy: neither shall ye defile yourselves with any manner of creeping thing that creepeth upon the earth. 45. For I *am* the LORD that bringeth you up out of the land of Egypt, to be your God : ye shall therefore be holy, for I *am* holy. [Lev. 19:2; 20:7.] 47. To make a difference between the unclean and the clean, and between the beast that may be eaten and the beast that may not be eaten.

Lev. 20:26. And ye shall be holy unto me : for I the LORD *am* holy, and have severed you from *other* people, that ye should be mine.

Deut. 13:17. There shall cleave nought of the cursed thing to thine hand :

Deut. 14:2. Thou *art* an holy people unto the LORD thy God, and the LORD hath chosen thee to be a peculiar people unto himself. Deut. 26:19.

Deut. 18:13. Thou shalt be perfect with the LORD thy God.

Deut. 28:9. The LORD shall establish thee an holy people unto himself, as he hath sworn unto thee, if thou shalt keep the commandments of the LORD thy God, and walk in his ways.

Deut. 30:2. And shalt return unto the LORD thy God, and shalt obey his voice according to all that I command thee this day, thou and thy children, with all thine heart, and with all thy soul; 10. If thou shalt hearken unto the voice of the LORD thy God, to keep his commandments and his statutes which are written in this book of the law, *and* if thou turn unto the LORD thy God with all thine heart, and with all thy soul.

Josh. 7:12. Neither will I be with you any more, except ye destroy the accursed from among you. 13. Up, sanctify the people, and say, Sanctify yourselves against to morrow: for thus saith the LORD God of Israel, *There is* an accursed thing in the midst of thee, O Israel : thou canst not stand before thine enemies, until ye take away the accursed thing from among you.

Job 5:24. Thou shalt visit thy habitation, and shalt not sin.

Job 28:28. To depart from evil *is* understanding.

Job 36:21. Take heed, regard not iniquity : Psa. 4:4. Stand in awe, and sin not :

Psa. 24:3. Who shall ascend into the hill of the LORD? or who shall stand in his holy place ? 4. He that hath clean hands, and a pure heart; who hath not lifted up his soul unto vanity, nor sworn deceitfully. 5. He shall receive the blessing from the LORD, and righteousness from the God of his salvation. Psa. 15:1-5.

Psa. 32:2. Blessed *is* the man unto whom the LORD imputeth not iniquity, and in whose spirit *there is* no guile.

Psa. 37:27. Depart from evil, and do good ; and dwell for evermore.

Psa. 68:13. Though ye have lien among the pots, *yet shall ye be as* the wings of a dove covered with silver, and her feathers with yellow gold.

Psa. 73:1. Truly God *is* good to Israel, *even* to such as are of a clean heart.

Psa. 85:13. Righteousness shall go before him ; and shall set *us* in the way of his steps.

Psa. 94:15. Judgment shall return unto righteousness : and all the upright in heart shall follow it.

Psa. 97:10. Ye that love the LORD, hate evil : he preserveth the souls of his saints ;

Psa. 119:1. Blessed *are* the undefiled in the way, who walk in the law of the LORD. 2. Blessed *are* they that keep his testimonies, *and that* seek him with the whole heart. 3. They also do no iniquity : they walk in his ways.

Prov. 11:23. The desire of the righteous *is* only good : *but* the expectation of the wicked *is* wrath.

Prov. 12:5. The thoughts of the righteous *are* right, *but* the counsels of the wicked *are* deceit.

Prov. 16:17. The highway of the upright *is* to depart from evil : he that keepeth his way preserveth his soul.

Prov. 21:8. As *for* the pure, his work *is* right. 15. *It is* joy to the just to do judgment : 29. *As for* the upright, he directeth his way.

Prov. 22:1. A *good* name *is* rather to be chosen than great riches, *and* loving favour rather than silver and gold. Eccl. 7:1.

Isa. 4:3. *He that* remaineth in Jerusalem, shall be called holy, *even* every one that is written among the living in Jerusalem :

Isa. 26:2. Open ye the gates, that the righteous nation which keepeth the truth may enter in. 8. Yea, in the way of thy judgments, O LORD, have we waited for thee; the desire of *our* soul *is* to thy name, and to the remembrance of thee. 9. With my soul have I desired thee in the night; yea, with my spirit within me will I seek thee early : for when thy judgments *are* in the earth, the inhabitants of the world will learn righteousness.

Isa. 32:17. The work of righteousness shall be peace; and the effect of righteousness quietness and assurance for ever.

Isa. 35:8. And an highway shall be there, and a way, and it shall be called The way of holiness ; the unclean shall not pass over it; but it *shall be* for those : the wayfaring men, though fools, shall not err *therein*.

Isa. 51:7. Hearken unto me, ye that know righteousness, the people in whose heart *is* my law ;

Isa. 52:1. Awake, awake ; put on thy strength, O Zion ; put on thy beautiful garments, O Jerusalem, the holy city : for henceforth there shall no more come into thee the uncircumcised and the unclean. 11. Depart ye, go ye out from thence, touch no unclean *thing;* go ye out of the midst of her; be ye clean, that bear the vessels of the LORD.

Isa. 57:2. They shall rest in their beds, *each one* walking *in* his uprightness.

Isa. 60:1. Arise, shine ; for thy light is

come, and the glory of the LORD is risen upon thee. 21. Thy people also *shall be* all righteous:

Isa. 61:3. That they might be called trees of righteousness, the planting of the LORD, that he might be glorified. 9. And their seed shall be known among the Gentiles, and their offspring among the people: all that see them shall acknowledge them, that they *are* the seed *which* the LORD hath blessed. 10. I will greatly rejoice in the LORD, my soul shall be joyful in my God; for he hath clothed me with the garments of salvation, he hath covered me with the robe of righteousness, as a bridegroom decketh *himself* with ornaments, and as a bride adorneth *herself* with her jewels. 11. For as the earth bringeth forth her bud, and as the garden causeth the things that are sown in it to spring forth; so the Lord GOD will cause righteousness and praise to spring forth before all the nations.

Mic. 6:8. He hath shewed thee, O man, what *is* good; and what doth the LORD require of thee, but to do justly, and to love mercy, and to walk humbly with thy God?

Zeph. 2:3. Seek ye the LORD, all ye meek of the earth, which have wrought his judgment; seek righteousness, seek meekness:

Zech 8:3. Jerusalem shall be called a city of truth; and the mountain of the LORD of hosts the holy mountain,

Zech. 14:20. In that day shall there be upon the bells of the horses, HOLINESS UNTO THE LORD; and the pots in the LORD'S house shall be like the bowls before the altar. 21. Yea, every pot in Jerusalem and in Judah shall be holiness unto the LORD of hosts: . . . and in that day there shall be no more the Canaanite in the house of the LORD of hosts.

Matt. 5:6. Blessed *are* they which do hunger and thirst after righteousness: for they shall be filled. 8. Blessed *are* the pure in heart: for they shall see God. 29. If thy right eye offend thee, pluck it out, and cast *it* from thee: 30. If thy right hand offend thee, cut it off, and cast *it* from thee: for it is profitable for thee that one of thy members should perish, and not *that* thy whole body should be cast into hell. 48. Be ye therefore perfect, even as your Father which is in heaven is perfect.

Matt. 12:33. Either make the tree good, and his fruit good; or else make the tree corrupt, and his fruit corrupt: for the tree is known by *his* fruit.

Mark 9:49. For every one shall be salted with fire. ¹ and every sacrifice shall be salted with salt. 50. Salt *is* good: but if the salt have lost his saltness, wherewith will ye season it? [¹ Omitted in R. V.]

Luke 1:74. That he would grant unto us, that we . . . might serve him without fear, 75. In holiness and righteousness before him, all the days of our life.

Luke 6:45. A good man out of the good treasure of his heart bringeth forth that which is good; . . . for of the abundance of the heart his mouth speaketh.

John 1:47. Jesus saw Nathanael coming to him, and saith of him, Behold an Israelite indeed, in whom is no guile!

John 4:14. But whosoever drinketh of the water that I shall give him shall never thirst; but the water that I shall give him shall be in him a well of water springing up into everlasting life.

John 5:14. Afterward Jesus findeth him in the temple, and said unto him, Behold, thou art made whole: sin no more, lest a worse thing come unto thee.

John 6:35. And Jesus said unto them, I am the bread of life: he that cometh to me shall never hunger; and he that believeth on me shall never thirst.

John 15:19. If ye were of the world, the world would love his own: but because ye are not of the world, but I have chosen you out of the world, therefore the world hateth you.

John 17:23. I in them, and thou in me, that they may be made perfect in one;

Acts 24:16. And herein do I exercise myself, to have always a conscience void of offence toward God, and *toward* men.

Rom. 2:28. For he is not a Jew, which is one outwardly; neither *is that* circumcision, which is outward in the flesh: 29. But he *is* a Jew, which is one inwardly; and circumcision *is that* of the heart, in the spirit, *and* not in the letter; whose praise *is* not of men, but of God.

Rom. 6:1. What shall we say then? Shall we continue in sin, that grace may abound? 2. God forbid. How shall we, that are dead to sin, live any longer therein? 3. Know ye not, that so many of us as were baptized into Jesus Christ were baptized into his death? 4. Therefore we are buried with him by baptism into death: that like as Christ was raised up from the dead by the glory of the Father, even so we also should walk in newness of life. 5. For if we have been planted together in the likeness of his death, we shall be also *in the likeness* of *his* resurrection: 6. Knowing this, that our old man is crucified with *him*, that the body of sin might be destroyed, that henceforth we should not serve sin. 7. For he that is dead is freed from sin. 8. Now if we be dead with Christ, we believe that we shall also live with him: 9. Knowing that Christ being raised from the dead dieth no more; death hath no more dominion over him. 10. For in that he died, he died unto sin once: but in that he liveth, he liveth unto God. 11. Likewise reckon ye also yourselves to be dead indeed unto sin, but alive unto God through Jesus Christ our Lord. 12. Let not sin therefore reign in your mortal body, that ye should obey it in the lusts thereof. 13. Neither yield ye your members *as* instruments of unrighteousness unto sin: but yield yourselves unto God, as those that are alive from the dead, and your members *as* instruments of righteousness unto God. 14. For sin shall not have dominion over you: for ye are not under the law, but under grace. 15. What then? shall we sin, because we are not under the law, but under grace? God forbid. 16. Know ye not, that to whom ye yield yourselves servants to obey, his servants ye are to whom ye obey; whether of sin unto death, or of obedience unto righteousness? 17. But God be thanked, that ye were the servants of sin, but ye have obeyed from the heart that form of doctrine which was delivered you. 18. Being then made free from sin, ye became the servants of righteousness. 19. I speak after the manner of men because of the infirmity of your flesh: for as ye have yielded your members servants to uncleanness and to iniquity unto iniquity; even so now yield your members servants to righteousness unto holiness. 20. For when ye were the servants of sin, ye were free from righteousness. 21. What fruit had ye then in those things whereof ye are now ashamed? for the end of those things *is* death. 22. But now being made free from sin, and become servants to God, ye have your fruit unto holiness, and the end everlasting life. 23. For the wages of sin *is* death; but the gift of God *is* eternal life through Jesus Christ our Lord.

Rom. 7:4. Ye should be married to another, *even* to him who is raised from the dead, that we should bring forth fruit unto God. 6. We are delivered from the law, that being dead wherein we were held; that we should serve in newness of spirit, and not *in* the oldness of the letter.

Rom. 8:1. *There is* therefore now no condemnation to them which are in Christ Jesus, [1] who walk not after the flesh, but after the Spirit. 4. That the righteousness of the law might be fulfilled in us, who walk not after the flesh, but after the Spirit. 12. Brethren, we are debtors, not to the flesh, to live after the flesh. [1 Omitted in R. V.]

Rom. 11:16. For if the firstfruit *be* holy, the lump *is* also *holy:* and if the root *be* holy, so *are* the branches.

Rom. 12:1. I beseech you therefore, brethren, by the mercies of God, that ye present your bodies a living sacrifice, holy, acceptable unto God, *which is* your reasonable service. 2. And be not conformed to this world: but be ye transformed by the renewing of your mind, that ye may prove what *is* that good, and acceptable, and perfect, will of God. 9. Abhor that which is evil; cleave to that which is good.

Rom. 13:12. The night is far spent, the day is at hand: let us therefore cast off the works of darkness, and let us put on the armour of light. 13. Let us walk honestly as in the day; 14. Put ye on the Lord Jesus Christ, and make not provision for the flesh, to *fulfil* the lusts *thereof.*

Rom. 14:17. The kingdom of God is not meat and drink; but righteousness, and peace, and joy in the Holy Ghost.

Rom. 16:19. I would have you wise unto that which is good, and simple concerning evil.

1 Cor. 3:16. Know ye not that ye are the temple of God, and *that* the Spirit of God dwelleth in you? 17. If any man defile the temple of God, him shall God destroy; for the temple of God is holy, which *temple* ye are.

1 Cor. 5:7. Purge out therefore the old leaven, that ye may be a new lump, as ye are unleavened.

1 Cor. 6:12. All things are lawful unto me, but all things are not expedient: all things are lawful for me, but I will not be brought under the power of any. 13. The body *is* not for fornication, but for the Lord; and the Lord for the body. 19. What? know ye not that your body is the temple of the Holy Ghost *which is* in you, which ye have of God, and ye are not your own? 20. For ye are bought with a price: therefore glorify God in your body, and in your spirit, which are God's.

1 Cor. 7:23. Ye are bought with a price; be not ye the servants of men.

1 Cor. 8:12. When ye sin so against the brethren, and wound their weak conscience, ye sin against Christ.

1 Cor. 10:21. Ye cannot drink the cup of the Lord, and the cup of devils: ye cannot be partakers of the Lord's table, and of the table of devils. 31. Whether therefore ye eat, or drink, or whatsoever ye do, do all to the glory of God. 32. Give none offence, neither to the Jews, nor to the Gentiles, nor to the church of God:

1 Cor. 12:31. Covet earnestly the best gifts:

1 Cor. 15:34. Awake to righteousness, and sin not;

2 Cor. 6:14. Be ye not unequally yoked together with unbelievers: for what fellowship hath righteousness with unrighteousness? and what communion hath light with darkness? 15. And what concord hath Christ with Belial? or what part hath he that believeth with an infidel? 16. And what agreement hath the temple of God with idols? for ye are the temple of the living God; 17. Wherefore come out from among them, and be ye separate, saith the Lord, and touch not the unclean *thing;* and I will receive you,

2 Cor. 7:1. Let us cleanse ourselves from all filthiness of the flesh and spirit, perfecting holiness in the fear of God.

2 Cor. 10:3. Though we walk in the flesh, we do not war after the flesh: 5. Casting down imaginations, and every high thing that exalteth itself against the knowledge of God, and bringing into captivity every thought to the obedience of Christ;

2 Cor. 11:2. I have espoused you to one husband, that I may present *you as* a chaste virgin to Christ.

2 Cor. 13:7. I pray to God that ye do no evil; not that we should appear approved, but that ye should do that which is honest, 8. We can do nothing against the truth, but for the truth.

Gal. 2:17. If, while we seek to be justified by Christ, we ourselves also are found sinners, *is* therefore Christ the minister of sin? God forbid.

Gal. 5:22. The fruit of the Spirit is love, joy, peace, longsuffering, gentleness, goodness, ¹ faith, 23. Meekness, temperance: against such there is no law. 24. And they that are Christ's have crucified the flesh with the affections and lusts. 25. If we live in the Spirit, let us also walk in the Spirit.

[¹ R. V. faithfulness]

Gal. 6:15. ¹ In Christ Jesus neither circumcision availeth any thing, nor uncircumcision, but a new creature. [¹ Omitted in R. V.]

Eph. 1:4. He hath chosen us in him before the foundation of the world, that we should be holy and without blame before him in love: 13. In whom also after that ye believed ye were sealed with that holy Spirit of promise, 14. Which is the earnest of our inheritance until the redemption of the purchased possession, unto the praise of his glory.

Eph. 2:21. In whom all the building fitly framed together groweth unto an holy temple in the Lord: 22. In whom ye also are builded together for an habitation of God through the Spirit.

Eph. 4:20. Ye have not so learned Christ; 21. If so be that ye have heard him, and have been taught by him, as the truth is in Jesus: 22. That ye put off concerning the former conversation the old man, which is corrupt according to the deceitful lusts; 23. And be renewed in the spirit of your mind; 24. And that ye put on the new man, which after God is created in righteousness and true holiness.

Eph. 5:1. Be ye therefore followers of God, as dear children; 3. But fornication, and all uncleanness, or covetousness, let it not be once named among you, as becometh saints; 8. Ye were sometimes darkness, but now *are ye* light in the Lord: walk as children of light: 9. (For the fruit of the Spirit *is* in all goodness and righteousness and truth;) 10. Proving what is acceptable unto the Lord. 11. Have no fellowship with the unfruitful works of darkness, but rather reprove *them.*

Phil. 1:10. That ye may approve things that are excellent; that ye may be sincere and without offence till the day of Christ; 11. Being filled with the fruits of righteousness, which are by Jesus Christ, unto the glory and praise of God.

Phil. 2:15. Be blameless and harmless, the sons of God, without rebuke, in the midst of a crooked and perverse nation, among whom ye shine as lights in the world;

Phil. 4:8. Whatsoever things are true, whatsoever things *are* honest, whatsoever things

are just, whatsoever things *are* pure, whatsoever things *are* lovely, whatsoever things *are* of good report; if *there be* any virtue, and if *there be* any praise, think on these things.

Col. 1:22. To present you holy and unblameable and unreproveable in his sight:

Col. 3:5. Mortify therefore your members which are upon the earth; fornication, uncleanness, inordinate affection, evil concupiscence, and covetousness, which is idolatry: 6. For which things' sake the wrath of God cometh on the children of disobedience: 7. In the which ye also walked some time, when ye lived in them. 8. But now ye also put off all these; anger, wrath, malice, blasphemy, filthy communication out of your mouth. 9. Lie not one to another, seeing that ye have put off the old man with his deeds; 10. And have put on the new *man*, which is renewed in knowledge after the image of him that created him: 12. Put on therefore, as the elect of God, holy and beloved, bowels of mercies, kindness, humbleness of mind, meekness, longsuffering; 13. Forbearing one another, and forgiving one another, if any man have a quarrel against any: even as Christ forgave you, so also *do* ye. 14. And above all these things *put on* charity, which is the bond of perfectness. 15. And let the peace of God rule in your hearts, to the which also ye are called in one body; and be ye thankful.

1 Thess. 2:12. That ye would walk worthy of God, who hath called you unto his kingdom and glory.

1 Thess. 3:13. To the end he may stablish your hearts unblameable in holiness before God, even our Father, at the coming of our Lord Jesus Christ with all his saints.

1 Thess. 4:3. For this is the will of God, *even* your sanctification, that ye should abstain from fornication: 4. That every one of you should know how to possess his vessel in sanctification and honour; 7. For God hath not called us unto uncleanness, but unto holiness.

1 Thess. 5:5. Ye are all the children of light, and the children of the day: we are not of the night, nor of darkness. 22. Abstain from all appearance of evil. 23. And the very God of peace sanctify you wholly; and *I pray God* your whole spirit and soul and body be preserved blameless unto the coming of our Lord Jesus Christ.

2 Thess. 2:13. God hath from the beginning chosen you to salvation through sanctification of the Spirit and belief of the truth:

1 Tim. 1:5. The end of the commandment is charity out of a pure heart, and *of* a good conscience, and *of* faith unfeigned:

1 Tim. 4:8. Godliness is profitable unto all things, having promise of the life that now is, and of that which is to come. 12. Be thou an example of the believers, in word, in conversation, in charity, in spirit, in faith, in purity.

1 Tim. 5:22. Neither be partaker of other men's sins: keep thyself pure.

1 Tim. 6:6. Godliness with contentment is great gain. 11. O man of God, . . . follow after righteousness, godliness, faith, love, patience, meekness. 12. Fight the good fight of faith, lay hold on eternal life, whereunto thou art also called, and hast professed a good profession before many witnesses.

2 Tim. 2:19. Let every one that nameth the name of Christ depart from iniquity. 21. If a man therefore purge himself from these, he shall be a vessel unto honour, sanctified, and meet for the master's use, *and* prepared unto every good work. 22. Flee also youthful lusts: but follow righteousness, faith, charity, peace, with them that call on the Lord out of a pure heart. *vs.* 16,17.

2 Tim. 3:17. That the man of God may be perfect, throughly furnished unto all good works.

Tit. 1:15. Unto the pure all things *are* pure:

Tit. 2:9. Exhort servants . . . 10. . . . that they may adorn the doctrine of God our Saviour in all things. 12. Teaching us that, denying ungodliness and worldly lusts, we should live soberly, righteously, and godly, in this present world ;

Heb. 4:3. For we which have believed do enter into rest, as he said, As I have sworn in my wrath, if they shall enter into my rest: although the works were finished from the foundation of the world. 9. There remaineth therefore a rest to the people of God.

Heb. 10:22. Having our hearts sprinkled from an evil conscience, and our bodies washed with pure water.

Heb. 12:1. Let us lay aside every weight, and the sin which doth so easily beset *us*, and let us run with patience the race that is set before us, 14. Follow peace with all *men*, and ¹ holiness, without which no man shall see the Lord : 15. Looking diligently lest any man fail of the grace of God ; lest any root of bitterness springing up trouble *you*, and thereby many be defiled ; *v.* 10.   [¹ R. V. the sanctification]

Heb. 13:9. *It is* a good thing that the heart be established with grace ;

Jas. 1:21. Lay apart all filthiness and superfluity of naughtiness, 27. Pure religion and undefiled before God and the Father is this, To visit the fatherless and widows in their affliction, *and* to keep himself unspotted from the world.

Jas. 3:17. The wisdom that is from above is first pure, then peaceable, gentle, *and* easy to be intreated, full of mercy and good fruits, without partiality, and without hypocrisy.

Jas. 4:4. Whosoever therefore will be a friend of the world is the enemy of God.

1 Pet. 1:14. As obedient children, not fashioning yourselves according to the former lusts in your ignorance : 15. But as he which hath called you is holy, so be ye holy in all manner of ¹ conversation ; 16. Because it is written, Be ye holy; for I am holy.   [¹ R. V. living]

1 Pet. 2:1. Laying aside all malice, and all guile, and hypocrisies, and envies, and all evil speakings, 5. Ye also, as lively stones, are built up a spiritual house, an holy priest-

hood, to offer up spiritual sacrifices, acceptable to God by Jesus Christ. 9. Ye *are* a chosen generation, a royal priesthood, an holy nation, a peculiar people ; that ye should shew forth the praises of him who hath called you out of darkness into his marvellous light : 11. I beseech *you* as strangers and pilgrims, abstain from fleshly lusts, which war against the soul ; 12. Having your conversation honest among the Gentiles : that, whereas they speak against you as evildoers, they may by *your* good works, which they shall behold, glorify God in the day of visitation. 24. Who his own self bare our sins in his own body on the tree, that we, being dead to sins, should live unto righteousness:

1 Pet. 3:11. Let him eschew evil, and do good ; Psa. 34:14.

1 Pet. 4:1. Forasmuch then as Christ hath suffered for us in the flesh, arm yourselves likewise with the same mind : for he that hath suffered in the flesh hath ceased from sin ; 2. That he no longer should live the rest of *his* time in the flesh to the lusts of men, but to the will of God. 6. For for this cause was the gospel preached also to them that are dead, that they might be judged according to men in the flesh, but live according to God in the spirit. 7. The end of all things is at hand : be ye therefore sober, and watch unto prayer.

2 Pet. 1:5. Giving all diligence, add to your faith virtue ; and to virtue knowledge ; 6. And to knowledge temperance ; and to temperance patience ; and to patience godliness ; 7. And to godliness brotherly kindness ; and to brotherly kindness charity. 8. For if these things be in you, and abound, they make *you that ye shall* neither *be* barren nor unfruitful in the knowledge of our Lord Jesus Christ. *vs.* 2–4.

2 Pet. 3:11. *Seeing* then *that* all these things shall be dissolved, what manner *of persons* ought ye to be in *all* holy ¹ conversation and godliness, 12. Looking for and hasting unto the coming of the day of God, 14. Seeing that ye look for such things, be diligent that ye may be found of him in peace, without spot, and blameless.   [¹ R. V. living]

1 John 1:6. If we say that we have fellowship with him, and walk in darkness, we lie, and do not the truth : 7. But if we walk in the light, as he is in the light, we have fellowship one with another, and the blood of Jesus Christ his Son cleanseth us from all sin.

1 John 2:1. My little children, these things write I unto you, that ye sin not. 5. But whoso keepeth his word, in him verily is the love of God perfected : hereby know we that we are in him. 29. If ye know that he is righteous, ye know that every one that doeth righteousness is born of him.

1 John 3:3. And every man that hath this hope in him purifieth himself, even as he is pure. 6. Whosoever abideth in him sinneth not : whosoever sinneth hath not seen him, neither known him. 9. Whosoever is born

of God doth not commit sin; for his seed remaineth in him: and he cannot sin, because he is born of God. 10. In this the children of God are manifest, and the children of the devil: whosoever doeth not righteousness is not of God, neither he that loveth not his brother. *vs.* 7,8.

1 John 5:4. Whatsoever is born of God overcometh the world: and this is the victory that overcometh the world, *even* our faith. 5. Who is he that overcometh the world, but he that believeth that Jesus is the Son of God? 18. We know that whosoever is born of God sinneth not; but he that is begotten of God keepeth himself, and that wicked one toucheth him not. 21. Little children, keep yourselves from idols.

2 John 4. I rejoiced greatly that I found of thy children walking in truth, as we have received a commandment from the Father.

3 John 11. Follow not that which is evil, but that which is good. He that doeth good is of God: but he that doeth evil hath not seen God.

Rev. 14:4. These are they which were not defiled with women; for they are virgins. These are they which follow the Lamb whithersoever he goeth. These were redeemed from among men, *being* the firstfruits unto God and to the Lamb. 5. And in their mouth was found no guile: for they are without fault before the throne of God.

Rev. 18:4. Come out of her, my people, that ye be not partakers of her sins,

Rev. 19:8. To her was granted that she should be arrayed in fine linen, clean and white: for the fine linen is the righteousness of saints. See Desire, Spiritual; God, Holiness of; Righteousness; Sanctification; Sinlessness.

HOLM, a tree, Isa. 44:14. [*R.V.*]

HOLY DAY. See Holiday.

HOLY PLACE. See Tabernacle; Temple.

HOLY SPIRIT, Gen. 1:2. And the Spirit of God moved upon the face of the waters.

Gen. 6:3. And the Lord said, My spirit shall not always strive with man,

Gen. 41:38. And Pharaoh said unto his servants, Can we find *such a one* as this *is*, a man in whom the Spirit of God *is?*

Ex. 31:3. And I have filled him with the spirit of God, in wisdom, and in understanding, and in knowledge, and in all manner of workmanship, Ex. 35:31.

Num. 27:18. And the Lord said unto Moses, Take thee Joshua the son of Nun, a man in whom *is* the spirit, and lay thine hand upon him;

Neh. 9:20. Thou gavest also thy good spirit to instruct them,

Job 16:19. Also now, behold, my witness *is* in heaven, and my record *is* on high.

Job 32:8. But *there is* a spirit in man: and the inspiration of the Almighty giveth them understanding.

Job 33:4. The spirit of God hath made me,

and the breath of the Almighty hath given me life.

Psa. 51:11. Take not thy holy spirit from me. 12. And uphold me *with thy* free spirit.

Psa. 103:9. He will not always chide: neither will he keep *his anger* for ever.

Psa. 139:7. Whither shall I go from thy spirit? or whither shall I flee from thy presence?

Isa. 4:4. When the Lord shall have washed away the filth of the daughters of Zion, and shall have purged the blood of Jerusalem from the midst thereof by the spirit of judgment, and by the spirit of burning.

Isa. 6:8. Also I heard the voice of the Lord, saying, Whom shall I send, and who will go for us? Then said I, Here *am* I; send me.

Isa. 11:2. And the spirit of the Lord shall rest upon him, the spirit of wisdom and understanding, the spirit of counsel and might, the spirit of knowledge and of the fear of the Lord;

Isa. 28:6. And for a spirit of judgment to him that sitteth in judgment, and for strength to them that turn the battle to the gate.

Isa. 30:1. Woe to the rebellious children, saith the Lord, that take counsel, but not of me; and that cover with a covering, but not of my spirit, that they may add sin to sin:

Isa. 32:15. Until the spirit be poured upon us from on high,

Isa. 40:13. Who hath directed the Spirit of the Lord, or *being* his counsellor hath taught him?

Isa. 42:1. Behold my servant, whom I uphold; mine elect, *in whom* my soul delighteth: I have put my spirit upon him: he shall bring forth judgment to the Gentiles.

Isa. 44:3. I will pour water upon him that is thirsty, and floods upon the dry ground: I will pour my spirit upon thy seed, and my blessing upon thine offspring: 4. And they shall spring up *as* among the grass, as willows by the water courses.

Isa. 48:16. Come ye near unto me, hear ye this; I have not spoken in secret from the beginning; from the time that it was, there *am* I: and now the Lord God, and his Spirit, hath sent me.

Isa. 51:12. I, *even* I, *am* he that comforteth you; who *art* thou, that thou shouldest be afraid of a man *that* shall die, and of the son of man *which* shall be made *as* grass:

Isa. 54:13. And all thy children *shall be* taught of the Lord; and great *shall be* the peace of thy children.

Isa. 59:19. When the enemy shall come in like a flood, the Spirit of the Lord shall lift up a standard against him. 21. As for me, this *is* my covenant with them, saith the Lord; My spirit that *is* upon thee, and my words which I have put in thy mouth, shall not depart out of thy mouth, nor out of the mouth of thy seed, nor out of the mouth of thy seed's seed, saith the LORD, from henceforth and for ever.

Isa. 61:1. The Spirit of the Lord GOD *is* upon me; because the LORD hath anointed me to preach good tidings unto the meek; he hath sent me to bind up the brokenhearted, to proclaim liberty to the captives, and the opening of the prison to *them that are* bound; Luke 4:18.

Isa. 63:10. But they rebelled, and vexed his holy Spirit: 11. Where *is* he that brought them up out of the sea with the shepherd of his flock? where *is* he that put his holy Spirit within him? 14. As a beast goeth down into the valley, the Spirit of the LORD caused him to rest:

Ezek. 36:27. And I will put my spirit within you, and cause you to walk in my statutes, and ye shall keep my judgments, and do *them.*

Ezek. 37:9. Then said he unto me, Prophesy unto the wind, prophesy, son of man, and say to the wind, Thus saith the Lord GOD; Come from the four winds, O breath, and breathe upon these slain, that they may live. 14. And shall put my spirit in you, and ye shall live, and I shall place you in your own land: then shall ye know that I the LORD have spoken *it*, and performed *it*, saith the LORD.

Ezek. 39:29. Neither will I hide my face any more from them: for I have poured out my spirit upon the house of Israel, saith the Lord GOD.

Joel 2:28. And it shall come to pass afterward, *that* I will pour out my spirit upon all flesh: and your sons and your daughters shall prophesy, your old men shall dream dreams, your young men shall see visions: 29. And also upon the servants and upon the handmaids in those days will I pour out my spirit.

Mic. 2:7. O *thou that art* named the house of Jacob, is the spirit of the LORD straitened? *are* these his doings?

Mic. 3:8. But truly I am full of power by the spirit of the LORD, and of judgment, and of might,

Hag. 2:5. *According to* the word that I covenanted with you when ye came out of Egypt, so my spirit remaineth among you:

Zech. 4:6. Not by might, nor by power, but by my spirit, saith the LORD of hosts. *vs.* 1-7.

Zech. 12:10. I will pour upon the house of David, and upon the inhabitants of Jerusalem, the spirit of grace and of supplications:

Matt. 1:18. Now the birth of Jesus Christ was on this wise: When as his mother Mary was espoused to Joseph, before they came together, she was found with child of the Holy Ghost. *v.* 20.

Matt. 3:11. I indeed baptize you with water unto repentance: but . . . he shall baptize you with the Holy Ghost, and *with* fire: [John 1:33; Acts 11:16.] 16. And Jesus, when he was baptized, went up straightway out of the water: and lo, the heavens were opened unto him, and he saw the Spirit of God descending like a dove, and lighting upon him: 17. And lo a voice from heaven, saying, This is my beloved Son, in whom I am well pleased. Mark 1:10; Luke 3:22; John 1:32.

Matt. 4:1. Then was Jesus led up of the spirit into the wilderness to be tempted of the devil.

Matt. 10:20. For it is not ye that speak, but the Spirit of your Father which speaketh in you. Mark 13:11.

Matt. 12:28. But if I cast out devils by the Spirit of God, then the kingdom of God is come unto you.

Matt. 28:19. Baptizing them in the name of the Father, and of the Son, and of the Holy Ghost:

Mark 12:36. For David himself said by the Holy Ghost, The LORD said to my Lord, Sit thou on my right hand, till I make thine enemies thy footstool.

Mark 13:11. It is not ye that speak, but the Holy Ghost.

Luke 1:15. For he shall be great in the sight of the Lord, and shall drink neither wine nor strong drink; and he shall be filled with the Holy Ghost, even from his mother's womb. 35. And the angel answered and said unto her, The Holy Ghost shall come upon thee, and the power of the Highest shall overshadow thee: 67. And his father Zacharias was filled with the Holy Ghost,

Luke 2:25. And, behold, there was a man in Jerusalem, whose name *was* Simeon; and the same man *was* just and devout, waiting for the consolation of Israel: and the Holy Ghost was upon him. 26. And it was revealed unto him by the Holy Ghost, that he should not see death, before he had seen the Lord's Christ. 27. And he came by the Spirit into the temple:

Luke 11:13. If ye then, being evil, know how to give good gifts unto your children: how much more shall *your* heavenly Father give the Holy Spirit to them that ask him?

Luke 12:12. For the Holy Ghost shall teach you in the same hour what ye ought to say.

Luke 24:49. And, behold, I send the promise of my Father upon you: but tarry ye in the city of Jerusalem, until ye be endued with power from on high.

John 1:9. *That* was the true Light, which lighteth every man that cometh into the world.

John 3:5. Jesus answered, Verily, verily, I say unto thee, Except a man be born of water and *of* the Spirit, he cannot enter into the kingdom of God. 6. That which is born of the flesh is flesh; and that which is born of the Spirit is spirit. 34. For he whom God hath sent speaketh the words of God: for God giveth not the Spirit by measure *unto* him.

John 4:14. Whosoever drinketh of the water that I shall give him shall never thirst; but the water that I shall give him shall be in him a well of water springing up into everlasting life.

John 6:45. It is written in the prophets, And they shall be all taught of God. Every man therefore that hath heard, and hath learned of the Father, cometh unto me. 63. It is the spirit that quickeneth;

John 7:38. He that believeth on me, as the scripture hath said, out of his belly shall flow rivers of living water. 39. (But this spake he of the Spirit, which they that believe on him should receive: for the Holy Ghost was not yet *given;* because that Jesus was not yet glorified.)

John 14:16. I will pray the Father, and he shall give you another Comforter, that he may abide with you for ever; 17. *Even* the Spirit of truth; whom the world cannot receive, because it seeth him not, neither knoweth him: but ye know him; for he dwelleth with you, and shall be in you. 26. But the Comforter, *which is* the Holy Ghost, whom the Father will send in my name, he shall teach you all things, and bring all things to your remembrance, whatsoever I have said unto you.

John 15:26. When the Comforter is come, whom I will send unto you from the Father, *even* the Spirit of truth, which proceedeth from the Father, he shall testify of me:

John 16:7. Nevertheless I tell you the truth; It is expedient for you that I go away: for if I go not away, the Comforter will not come unto you; but if I depart, I will send him unto you. 8. And when he is come, he will reprove the world of sin, and of righteousness, and of judgment: 9. Of sin, because they believe not on me; 10. Of righteousness, because I go to my Father, and ye see me no more; 11. Of judgment, because the prince of this world is judged. 12. I have yet many things to say unto you, but ye cannot bear them now. 13. Howbeit when he, the Spirit of truth, is come, he will guide you into all truth: for he shall not speak of himself; but whatsoever he shall hear, *that* shall he speak: and he will shew you things to come. 14. He shall glorify me: for he shall receive of mine, and shall shew *it* unto you.

John 20:22. He breathed on *them,* and saith unto them, Receive ye the Holy Ghost:

Acts 1:2. Until the day in which he was taken up, after that he through the Holy Ghost had given commandments unto the apostles whom he had chosen: 5. For John truly baptized with water; but ye shall be baptized with the Holy Ghost not many days hence. 8. But ye shall receive power, after that the Holy Ghost is come upon you: 16. Men *and* brethren, this scripture must needs have been fulfilled, which the Holy Ghost by the mouth of David spake before concerning Judas, which was guide to them that took Jesus.

Acts 2:2. And suddenly there came a sound from heaven as of a rushing mighty wind, and it filled all the house where they were sitting. 3. And there appeared unto them cloven tongues like as of fire, and it sat upon each of them. 4. And they were all filled with the Holy Ghost, and began to speak with other tongues, as the Spirit gave them utterance. 33. Therefore being by the right hand of God exalted, and having received of the Father the promise of the Holy Ghost, he hath shed forth this, which ye now see and hear. 38. Then Peter said unto them, Repent, and be baptized . . . in the name of Jesus Christ for the remission of sins, and ye shall receive the gift of the Holy Ghost.

Acts 4:8. Then Peter, filled with the Holy Ghost, said unto them, Ye rulers of the people, and elders of Israel, 31. And when they had prayed, the place was shaken where they were assembled together; and they were all filled with the Holy Ghost, and they spake the word of God with boldness.

Acts 5:3. Ananias, why hath Satan filled thine heart to lie to the Holy Ghost? 4. Thou hast not lied unto men, but unto God. 9. Then Peter said unto her, How is it that ye have agreed together to tempt the Spirit of the Lord? 32. We are his witnesses . . . and *so is* also the Holy Ghost, whom God hath given to them that obey him.

Acts 6:5. They chose Stephen, a man full of faith and of the Holy Ghost,

Acts 7:51. Ye stiffnecked and uncircumcised in heart and ears, ye do always resist the Holy Ghost: as your fathers *did,* so *do* ye.

Acts 8:15. Who, when they were come down, prayed for them, that they might receive the Holy Ghost: 16. (For as yet he was fallen upon none of them: only they were baptized in the name of the Lord Jesus.) 17. Then laid they *their* hands on them, and they received the Holy Ghost. 18. And when Simon saw that through laying on of the apostles' hands the Holy Ghost was given, he offered them money, 19. Saying, Give me also this power, that on whomsoever I lay hands, he may receive the Holy Ghost.

Acts 9:31. Then had the churches rest . . . and walking in the fear of the Lord, and in the comfort of the Holy Ghost, were multiplied.

Acts 10:19. While Peter thought on the vision, the Spirit said unto him, Behold, three men seek thee. 20. Arise therefore, and get thee down, and go with them, doubting nothing: for I have sent them. 44. While Peter yet spake these words, the Holy Ghost fell on all them which heard the word. 45. And they of the circumcision which believed were astonished, as many as came with Peter, because that on the Gentiles also was poured out the gift of the Holy Ghost. 46. For they heard them speak with tongues, and magnify God. Then answered Peter, 47. Can any man forbid water, that these should not be baptized, which have received the Holy Ghost as well as we? Acts 11:17.

Acts 11:15. As I began to speak, the Holy Ghost fell on them, as on us at the beginning. 16. Then remembered I the word of the Lord, how that he said, John indeed baptized with water; but ye shall be baptized with the Holy Ghost.

24. He was a good man, and full of the Holy Ghost, and of faith.

Acts 13:2. As they ministered to the Lord, and fasted, the Holy Ghost said, Separate me Barnabas and Saul for the work whereunto I have called them. 4. So they, being sent forth by the Holy Ghost, departed unto Seleucia:

9. Then Saul, (who also *is called* Paul,) filled with the Holy Ghost,

52. The disciples were filled with joy, and with the Holy Ghost.

Acts 15:8. God, which knoweth the hearts, bare them witness, giving them the Holy Ghost, 28. For it seemed good to the Holy Ghost, and to us, to lay upon you no greater burden than these necessary things;

Acts 16:6. Now when they had gone throughout Phrygia and the region of Galatia, and were forbidden of the Holy Ghost to preach the word in Asia, 7 . . . They assayed to go into Bithynia: but the [1 Spirit] suffered them not. [1 R. V. Spirit of Jesus]

Acts 19:2. He said unto them, Have ye received the Holy Ghost since ye believed? And they said unto him, We have not so much as heard whether there be any Holy Ghost. 3. And he said unto them, Unto what then were ye baptized? And they said, Unto John's baptism. 4. Then said Paul, John verily baptized with the baptism of repentance, saying unto the people, that they should believe on him which should come after him, that is, on Christ Jesus. 5. When they heard *this*, they were baptized in the name of the Lord Jesus. 6. And when Paul had laid *his* hands upon them, the Holy Ghost came on them; and they spake with tongues, and prophesied.

Acts 20:28. Take heed . . . to all the flock, over the which the Holy Ghost hath made you overseers,

Rom. 1:4. And declared *to be* the Son of God with power, according to the spirit of holiness, by the resurrection from the dead:

Rom. 5:5. The love of God is shed abroad in our hearts by the Holy Ghost which is given unto us. *vs.* 3-5.

Rom. 8:1. *There is* therefore now no condemnation to them which are in Christ Jesus, [1 who walk not after the flesh, but after the spirit.] 2. For the law of the Spirit of life in Christ Jesus hath made me free from the law of sin and death. 4. That the righteousness of the law might be fulfilled in us, who walk not after the flesh, but after the Spirit. 9. But ye are not in the flesh, but in the Spirit, if so be that the

Spirit of God dwell in you. Now if any man have not the Spirit of Christ, he is none of his. 11. If the Spirit of him that raised up Jesus from the dead dwell in you, he that raised up Christ from the dead shall also quicken your mortal bodies by his Spirit that dwelleth in you. 13. If ye through the Spirit do mortify the deeds of the body, ye shall live. 14. For as many as are led by the Spirit of God, they are the sons of God. 15. For ye have not received the spirit of bondage again to fear; but ye have received the Spirit of adoption, whereby we cry, Abba, Father. 16. The Spirit [2 itself] beareth witness with our spirit, that we are the children of God: 23. And not only *they*, but ourselves also, which have the firstfruits of the Spirit, even we ourselves groan within ourselves, waiting for the adoption, *to wit*, the redemption of our body. 26. The Spirit also helpeth our infirmities: for we know not what we should pray for as we ought: but the Spirit itself maketh intercession for us with groanings which cannot be uttered. 27. And he that searcheth the hearts knoweth what *is* the mind of the Spirit, because he maketh intercession for the saints according to *the will of* God. *vs.* 1-27. [R. V. 1 Omitted. 2 himself.]

Rom. 9:1. I say the truth in Christ, I lie not, my conscience also bearing me witness in the Holy Ghost,

Rom. 14:17. For the kingdom of God is not meat and drink; but righteousness, and peace, and joy in the Holy Ghost.

Rom. 15:13. Now the God of hope fill you with all joy and peace in believing, that ye may abound in hope, through the power of the Holy Ghost. 16. That the offering up of the Gentiles might be acceptable, being sanctified by the Holy Ghost. 18. For I will not dare to speak of any of those things which Christ hath not wrought by me, to make the Gentiles obedient, by word and deed. 19. Through mighty signs and wonders, by the power of the Spirit of God; 30. Now I beseech you, brethren, for the Lord Jesus Christ's sake, and for the love of the Spirit, that ye strive together with me in *your* prayers to God for me;

1 Cor. 2:4. My speech and my preaching *was* not with enticing words of man's wisdom, but in demonstration of the Spirit and of power: 10. But God hath revealed *them* unto us by his Spirit: for the Spirit searcheth all things, yea, the deep things of God. [Rom. 11:33,34.] 11. For what man knoweth the things of a man, save the spirit of man which is in him? even so the things of God knoweth no man, but the Spirit of God. 12. Now we have received, not the spirit of the world, but the spirit which is of God; that we might know the things that are freely given to us of God. 13. Which things also we speak, not in the words which man's wisdom teacheth, but which the Holy Ghost teacheth; comparing spiritual things with spiritual. 14. But the natural man receiveth

not the things of the Spirit of God: for they are foolishness unto him: neither can he know *them*, because they are spiritually discerned.

1 Cor. 3:16. Know ye not that ye are the temple of God, and *that* the Spirit of God dwelleth in you? 1 Cor. 6:19.

1 Cor. 6:11. And such were some of you: but ye are washed, but ye are sanctified, but ye are justified in the name of the Lord Jesus, and by the Spirit of our God. 19. What? know ye not that your body is the temple of the Holy Ghost *which is* in you, which ye have of God, and ye are not your own?

1 Cor. 12:3. Wherefore I give you to understand, that no man speaking by the Spirit of God calleth Jesus accursed: and *that* no man can say that Jesus is the Lord, but by the Holy Ghost. 4. Now there are diversities of gifts, but the same Spirit. 5. And there are differences of administrations, but the same Lord. 6. And there are diversities of operations, but it is the same God which worketh all in all. 7. But the manifestation of the Spirit is given to every man to profit withal. 8. For to one is given by the Spirit the word of wisdom; to another the word of knowledge by the same Spirit; 9. To another faith by the same Spirit; to another the gifts of healing by the same Spirit; 10. To another the working of miracles; to another prophecy; to another discerning of spirits; to another *divers* kinds of tongues; to another the interpretation of tongues: 11. But all these worketh that one and the selfsame Spirit, dividing to every man severally as he will.

2 Cor. 1:22. Who hath also sealed us, and given the earnest of the Spirit in our hearts. 2 Cor. 5:5.

2 Cor. 3:3. *Forasmuch as ye are* manifestly declared to be the epistle of Christ ministered by us, written not with ink, but with the Spirit of the living God; not in tables of stone, but in fleshly tables of the heart. 6. Ministers of the new testament; not of the letter, but of the spirit: for the letter killeth, but the spirit giveth life. 8. How shall not the ministration of the spirit be rather glorious? 17. Now the Lord is that Spirit: and where the Spirit of the Lord *is*, there *is* liberty. 18. But we all, with open face beholding as in a glass the glory of the Lord, are changed into the same image from glory to glory, *even* as by the Spirit of the Lord.

2 Cor. 5:5. Now he that hath wrought us for the selfsame thing *is* God, who also hath given unto us the earnest of the Spirit.

2 Cor. 6:4. In all *things* approving ourselves as the ministers of God, . . . 6. . . . by the Holy Ghost,

2 Cor. 13:14. The grace of the Lord Jesus Christ, and the love of God, and the communion of the Holy Ghost, *be* with you all.

Gal. 3:2. Received ye the Spirit by the works of the law, or by the hearing of faith?

3. Are ye so foolish? having begun in the Spirit, are ye now made perfect by the flesh? 14. That we might receive the promise of the Spirit through faith.

Gal. 4:6. Because ye are sons, God hath sent forth the Spirit of his Son into your hearts, crying, Abba, Father.

Gal. 5:5. We through the Spirit wait for the hope of righteousness by faith. 16. Walk in the Spirit, and ye shall not fulfil the lust of the flesh. 17. For the flesh lusteth against the Spirit, and the Spirit against the flesh: and these are contrary the one to the other: so that ye cannot do the things that ye would. 18. But if ye be led of the Spirit, ye are not under the law. 22. But the fruit of the Spirit is love, joy, peace, longsuffering, gentleness, goodness, ¹faith, 23. Meekness, temperance: against such there is no law. 25. If we live in the Spirit, let us also walk in the Spirit. [¹ R. V. faithfulness]

Gal. 6:8. He that soweth to the Spirit shall of the Spirit reap life everlasting.

Eph. 1:12. That we should be to the praise of his glory, who first trusted in Christ. 13. In whom also after that ye believed, ye were sealed with that holy Spirit of promise, 14. Which is the earnest of our inheritance until the redemption of the purchased possession, unto the praise of his glory. 17. That the God of our Lord Jesus Christ, the Father of glory, may give unto you the spirit of wisdom and revelation in the knowledge of him:

Eph. 2:18. Through him [Jesus Christ] we both have access by one Spirit unto the Father. 22. In whom ye also are builded together for an habitation of God through the Spirit.

Eph. 3:5. Which in other ages was not made known unto the sons of men, as it is now revealed unto his holy apostles and prophets by the Spirit; 16. Strengthened with might by his Spirit in the inner man;

Eph. 4:3. Endeavouring to keep the unity of the Spirit in the bond of peace. 4. *There is* one body, and one Spirit, even as ye are called in one hope of your calling; 30. Grieve not the holy Spirit of God, whereby ye are sealed unto the day of redemption.

Eph. 5:9. (The fruit of the Spirit *is* in all goodness and righteousness and truth;) 18. And be not drunk with wine, wherein is excess; but be filled with the Spirit;

Eph. 6:17. And take the . . . sword of the Spirit, which is the word of God; 18. Praying always with all prayer and supplication in the Spirit,

Phil. 1:19. I know that this shall turn to my salvation through your prayer, and the supply of the Spirit of Jesus Christ,

Phil. 2:1. If *there be* . . . any fellowship of the Spirit,

Col. 1:8. Who also declared unto us your love in the Spirit.

1 Thess. 1:5. For our gospel came not unto you in word only, but also in power, and in the Holy Ghost, and in much assurance;

6. And ye became followers of us, and of the Lord, . . . with joy of the Holy Ghost:

1 Thess. 4:8. He therefore that despiseth, despiseth not man, but God, who hath also given unto us his holy Spirit. 9. But as touching brotherly love ye need not that I write unto you: for ye yourselves are taught of God to love one another.

1 Thess. 5:19. Quench not the Spirit.

2 Thess. 2:13. But we are bound to give thanks alway to God for you, brethren beloved of the Lord, because God hath from the beginning chosen you to salvation through sanctification of the Spirit and belief of the truth:

1 Tim. 4:1. Now the Spirit speaketh expressly, that in the latter times some shall depart from the faith, giving heed to seducing spirits, and doctrines of devils;

2 Tim. 1:7. God hath not given us the spirit of fear; but of power, and of love, and of a sound mind. 14. That good thing which was committed unto thee keep by the Holy Ghost which dwelleth in us.

Tit. 3:5. Not by works of righteousness which we have done, but according to his mercy he saved us, by the washing of regeneration, and renewing of the Holy Ghost: 6. Which he shed on us abundantly through Jesus Christ our Saviour;

Heb. 2:4. God also bearing *them* witness, both with signs and wonders, and with divers miracles, and gifts of the Holy Ghost, according to his own will?

Heb. 3:7. Wherefore as the Holy Ghost saith, To day if ye will hear his voice,

Heb. 6:4. For *it is* impossible for those who were once enlightened, and have tasted of the heavenly gift, and were made partakers of the Holy Ghost,

Heb. 9:14. How much more shall the blood of Christ, who through the eternal Spirit offered himself without spot to God, purge your conscience from dead works to serve the living God?

Heb. 10:15. *Whereof* the Holy Ghost also is a witness to us: 29. Of how much sorer punishment, suppose ye, shall he be thought worthy, who hath trodden under foot the Son of God, and hath counted the blood of the covenant, wherewith he was sanctified, an unholy thing, and hath done despite unto the Spirit of grace?

1 Pet. 1:2. Elect according to the foreknowledge of God the Father, through sanctification of the Spirit, unto obedience and sprinkling of the blood of Jesus Christ: 11. Searching what, or what manner of time the Spirit of Christ which was in them did signify, when it testified beforehand the sufferings of Christ, and the glory that should follow. 12. Unto whom it was revealed, that not unto themselves, but unto us they did minister the things, which are now reported unto you by them that have preached the gospel unto you with the Holy Ghost sent down from heaven; which things the angels desire to look into. 22. Seeing ye

have purified your souls in obeying the truth [1] through the Spirit unto unfeigned love of the brethren, *see that ye* love one another with a pure heart fervently: [1 Omitted in R. V.]

1 Pet. 3:18. Christ also hath once suffered for sins, . . . being put to death in the flesh, but quickened by the Spirit:

1 Pet. 4:14. If ye be reproached for the name of Christ, happy *are ye;* for the spirit of glory and of God resteth upon you:

2 Pet. 1:21. For the prophecy came not in old time by the will of man: but holy men of God spake *as they were* moved by the Holy Ghost.

1 John 2:20. But ye have an unction from the Holy One, and ye know all things.

1 John 3:24. Hereby we know that he abideth in us, by the Spirit which he hath given us.

1 John 4:2. Hereby know ye the Spirit of God: Every spirit that confesseth that Jesus Christ is come in the flesh is of God: 13. Hereby know we that we dwell in him, and he in us, because he hath given us of his Spirit.

1 John 5:6. It is the Spirit that beareth witness, because the Spirit is truth. [1] 7. For there are three that bear record in heaven, the Father, the Word, and the Holy Ghost: and these three are one. 8. And there are three that bear witness in earth, the spirit, and the water, and the blood: and these three agree in one.

[1 Omitted in R. V.]

Jude 19. These be they who separate themselves, sensual, having not the Spirit. 20. But ye, beloved, building up yourselves on your most holy faith, praying in the Holy Ghost,

Rev. 1:4. Grace *be* unto you, and peace, . . . from the seven Spirits which are before his throne; Rev. 4:5; 5:6.

Rev. 2:7. He that hath an ear, let him hear what the Spirit saith unto the churches; *vs.* 11,29.

Rev. 11:11. And after three days and an half the Spirit of life from God entered into them, and they stood upon their feet; and great fear fell upon them which saw them.

Rev. 14:13. And I heard a voice from heaven saying unto me, Write, Blessed *are* the dead which die in the Lord from henceforth: Yea, saith the Spirit, that they may rest from their labours; and their works do follow them.

Rev. 19:10. For the testimony of Jesus is the spirit of prophecy.

Rev. 22:17. The Spirit and the bride say, Come.

See GOD, A SPIRIT; INSPIRATION; WORD OF GOD, INSPIRATION OF.

INSPIRATION OF: INSTANCES OF: Joseph, Gen. 41:38. Bezaleel, Ex. 31:3; 35:31. The seventy elders, Num. 11:17. Balaam, Num. 24:2. Joshua, Num. 27:18.

The Judges: Othniel, Judg. 3:10; Gideon, Judg. 6:34: Jephthah, Judg. 11:29; Samson, Judg. 13:25; 14:6,19.

King David, 1 Chr. 28:11,12.

The prophets: Azariah, 2 Chr. 15:1; Zechariah, 2 Chr. 24:20; Zech. 1:1; Ezekiel, Ezek. 8:3; 11:1,5,24; Daniel, Dan. 4:8; Zacharias, Luke 1:67; Elizabeth, Luke 1:41; Simeon, Luke 2:25,26.

The disciples, Acts 6:3; 7:55; 8:29; 9:17; 10:45. See INSPIRATION.

SIN AGAINST: Isa. 63:10. They rebelled, and vexed his holy Spirit: therefore he was turned to be their enemy.

Matt. 12:31. The blasphemy *against* the *Holy* Ghost shall not be forgiven unto men. 32. And whosoever speaketh a word against the Son of man, it shall be forgiven him: but whosoever speaketh against the Holy Ghost, it shall not be forgiven him, neither in this world, neither in the *world* to come. Luke 12:10.

Mark 3:29. But he that shall blaspheme against the Holy Ghost hath never forgiveness, but is in ¹danger of eternal ²damnation. Luke 2:10; 1 John 5:16; Acts 5:9.

[R. V. ¹guilty   ²sin]

Acts 5:3. But Peter said, Ananias, why hath Satan filled thine heart to lie to the Holy Ghost, and to keep back *part* of the price of the land? 9. Then Peter said unto her, How is it that ye have agreed together to tempt the Spirit of the Lord? behold, the feet of them which have buried thy husband *are* at the door, and shall carry thee out.

Acts 7:51. Ye stiffnecked and uncircumcised in heart and ears, ye do always resist the Holy Ghost: as your fathers *did*, so *do* ye.

Acts 8:18. And when Simon saw that through laying on of the apostles' hands the Holy Ghost was given, he offered them money, 19. Saying, Give me also this power, that on whomsoever I lay hands, he may receive the Holy Ghost. 20. But Peter said unto him, Thy money perish with thee, because thou hast thought that the gift of God may be purchased with money. 21. Thou hast neither part nor lot in this matter: for thy heart is not right in the sight of God. 22. Repent therefore of this thy wickedness, and pray God, if perhaps the thought of thine heart may be forgiven thee.

Eph. 4:30. And grieve not the holy Spirit of God, whereby ye are sealed unto the day of redemption.

Heb. 10:29. Of how much sorer punishment, suppose ye, shall he be thought worthy, who . . . hath done despite unto the Spirit of grace?

WITHDRAWN FROM INCORRIGIBLE SINNERS: Gen. 6:3. And the LORD said, My spirit shall not always strive with man,

Deut. 32:30. How should one chase a thousand, and two put ten thousand to flight, except their Rock had sold them, and the LORD had shut them up?

Psa. 51:11. Cast me not away from thy presence; and take not thy holy spirit from me.

Prov. 1:24. Because I have called, and ye refused; I have stretched out my hand, and

no man regarded; 25. But ye have set at nought all my counsel, and would none of my reproof: 26. I also will laugh at your calamity; I will mock when your fear cometh; 27. When your fear cometh as desolation, and your destruction cometh as a whirlwind; when distress and anguish cometh upon you. 28. Then shall they call upon me, but I will not answer; they shall seek me early, but they shall not find me:

Jer. 7:29. Cut off thine hair, *O Jerusalem*, and cast *it* away, and take up a lamentation on high places; for the LORD hath rejected and forsaken the generation of his wrath.

Hos. 4:17. Ephraim *is* joined to idols: let him alone. 18. Their drink is sour: they have committed whoredom continually: her rulers *with* shame do love, Give ye.

Hos. 5:6. They shall go with their flocks and with their herds to seek the LORD; but they shall not find *him;* he hath withdrawn himself from them.

Hos. 9:12. Though they bring up their children, yet will I bereave them, *that there shall* not *be* a man *left:* yea, woe also to them when I depart from them!

Matt. 15:14. Let them alone: they be blind leaders of the blind. And if the blind lead the blind, both shall fall into the ditch.

Luke 13:7. Then said he unto the dresser of his vineyard, Behold, these three years I come seeking fruit on this fig tree, and find none: cut it down; why cumbereth it the ground?

Rom. 1:24. Wherefore God also gave them up to uncleanness, through the lusts of their own hearts, to dishonour their own bodies between themselves: 26. For this cause God gave them up unto vile affections: for even their women did change the natural use into that which is against nature: 28. And even as they did not like to retain God in *their* knowledge, God gave them over to a reprobate mind, to do those things which are not convenient;

See REPROBACY.

INSTANCES OF: Antediluvians, Gen. 6:3–7. People of Sodom, Gen. 19:13,24,25. Israelites, Num. 14:26–45; Deut. 1:42; 28:15–68; 31:17,18. Samson, Judg. 16:20. Saul, 1 Sam. 16:14; 18:10–12; 19:9–11; 20:30–33; 22:7–19; 28:15,16; 2 Sam. 7:15.

HOMAGE. Refused by Peter, Acts 10:26; Paul and Barnabas, Acts 14,11–18. By the angel seen by John in his vision, Rev. 19:10; 22:8,9. See WORSHIP. Rendered to kings, 1 Kin. 1:16,23,31; princes, Esth. 3:2,5.

HOMAM, called also HEMAN. An Edomite, Gen. 36,22; 1 Chr. 1:39.

HOME. See FAMILY.

HOMER, a measure.   See MEASURE.

HOMESTEAD. Mortgaged, Neh. 5:3. When alienable, and when inalienable, Lev. 25:25–34.

See LANDS.

HOMICIDE. ACCIDENTAL: Ex. 21:13. And if a man lie not in wait, but God deliver *him* into his hand; then I will appoint thee a place whither he shall flee. 28. If an ox gore a man or a woman, that they die: then the ox shall be surely stoned, and his flesh shall not be eaten; but the owner of the ox *shall be* quit. 29. But if the ox were wont to push with his horn in time past, and it hath been testified to his owner, and he hath not kept him in, but that he hath killed a man or a woman; the ox shall be stoned, and his owner also shall be put to death. 30. If there be laid on him a sum of money, then he shall give for the ransom of his life whatsoever is laid upon him. 31. Whether he have gored a son, or have gored a daughter, according to this judgment shall it be done unto him. 32. If the ox shall push a manservant or a maidservant; he shall give unto their master thirty shekels of silver, and the ox shall be stoned.

Num. 35:11. Then ye shall appoint you cities to be cities of refuge for you; that the slayer may flee thither, which killeth any person at unawares. 12. And they shall be unto you cities for refuge from the avenger; that the manslayer die not, until he stand before the congregation in judgment. 13. And of these cities which ye shall give, six cities shall ye have for refuge. 14. Ye shall give three cities on this side Jordan, and three cities shall ye give in the land of Canaan, *which* shall be cities of refuge. 15. These six cities shall be a refuge, *both* for the children of Israel, and for the stranger, and for the sojourner among them: that every one that killeth any person unawares may flee thither. 22. But if he thrust him suddenly without enmity, or have cast upon him any thing without laying of wait, 23. Or with any stone, wherewith a man may die, seeing *him* not, and cast *it* upon him, that he die, and *was* not his enemy, neither sought his harm: 24. Then the congregation shall judge between the slayer and the revenger of blood according to these judgments: 25. And the congregation shall deliver the slayer out of the hand of the revenger of blood, and the congregation shall restore him to the city of his refuge, whither he was fled: and he shall abide in it unto the death of the high priest, which was anointed with the holy oil. 26. But if the slayer shall at any time come without the border of the city of his refuge, whither he was fled; 27. And the revenger of blood find him without the borders of the city of his refuge, and .the revenger of blood kill the slayer; he shall not be guilty of blood: 28. Because he should have remained in the city of his refuge until the death of the high priest: but after the death of the high priest the slayer shall return into the land of his possession. 32. And ye shall take no satisfaction for him that is fled to the city of his refuge, that he should come again to dwell in the land, until the death of the priest. Deut. 4:41-43; 19:1-10.

Josh. 20:1. The LORD also spake unto Joshua, saying, 2. Speak to the children of Israel, saying, Appoint out for you cities of refuge, whereof I spake unto you by the hand of Moses: 3. That the slayer that killeth *any* person unawares *and* unwittingly may flee thither; and they shall be your refuge from the avenger of blood. 4. And when he that doth flee unto one of those cities shall stand at the entering of the gate of the city, and shall declare his cause in the ears of the elders of that city, they shall take him into the city unto them, and give him a place, that he may dwell among them. 5. And if the avenger of blood pursue after him, then they shall not deliver the slayer up into his hand; because he smote his neighbour unwittingly, and hated him not beforetime. 6. And he shall dwell in that city, until he stand before the congregation for judgment, *and* until the death of the high priest that shall be in those days: then shall the slayer return, and come unto his own city, and unto his own house, unto the city from whence he fled. 7. And they appointed Kedesh in Galilee in mount Naphtali, and Shechem in mount Ephraim, and Kirjath-arba, which *is* Hebron, in the mountain of Judah. 8. And on the other side Jordan by Jericho eastward, they assigned Bezer in the wilderness upon the plain out of the tribe of Reuben, and Ramoth in Gilead out of the tribe of Gad, and Golan in Bashan out of the tribe of Manasseh. 9. These were the cities appointed for all the children of Israel, and for the stranger that sojourneth among them, that whosoever killeth *any* person at unawares might flee thither, and not die by the hand of the avenger of blood, until he stood before the congregation.

FELONIOUS, OR MURDER: Gen. 4:9. And the LORD said . . . 10. What hast thou done? the voice of thy brother's blood crieth unto me from the ground. 11. And now *art* thou cursed from the earth, which hath opened her mouth to receive thy brother's blood from thy hand; *v.* 12.

Gen. 9:5. Surely your blood of your lives will I require; at the hand of every beast will I require it, and at the hand of man; at the hand of every man's brother will I require the life of man. 6. Whoso sheddeth man's blood, by man shall his blood be shed: for in the image of God made he man.

Gen. 49:7. Cursed *be* their anger, for *it was* fierce; and their wrath, for it was cruel: I will divide them in Jacob, and scatter them in Israel.

Ex. 20:13. Thou shalt ¹not kill.   Deut. 5:17; Rom. 13:9.   [¹ R. V. do no murder]

Ex. 21:29. But if the ox were wont to push with his horn in time past, and it hath been testified to his owner, and he hath not kept him in, but that he hath killed a man or a woman; the ox shall be stoned, and his owner also shall be put to death. 30. If there be laid on him a sum of money, then he shall give for the ransom of his life whatsoever is laid upon him. 31. Whether he have gored a son, or have gored a daughter, according to this judgment shall it be done unto him. 32. If the ox shall push a manservant or a maidservant; he shall give unto their master thirty shekels of silver, and the ox shall be stoned.

Num. 35:16. And if he smite him with an instrument of iron, so that he die, he *is* a murderer: the murderer shall surely be put to death. 17. And if he smite him with throwing a stone, wherewith he may die, and he die, he *is* a murderer: the murderer shall surely be put to death. 18. Or *if* he smite him with an hand weapon of wood, wherewith he may die, and he die, he *is* a murderer: the murderer shall surely be put to death. 19. The revenger of blood himself shall slay the murderer: when he meeteth him, he shall slay him. 20. But if he thrust him of hatred, or hurl at him by laying of wait, that he die; 21. Or in enmity smite him with his hand, that he die: he that smote *him* shall surely be put to death; *for* he *is* a murderer: the revenger of blood shall slay the murderer, when he meeteth him. 22. But if he thrust him suddenly without enmity, or have cast upon him any thing without laying of wait, 30. Whoso killeth any person, the murderer shall be put to death by the mouth of witnesses: but one witness shall not testify against any person *to cause him* to die. 31. Moreover ye shall take no satisfaction for the life of a murderer, which *is* guilty of death: but he shall be surely put to death.

Deut. 17:6. At the mouth of two witnesses, or three witnesses, shall he that is worthy of death be put to death; *but* at the mouth of one witness he shall not be put to death.

Deut. 21:1. If *one* be found slain in the land which the LORD thy God giveth thee to possess it, lying in the field, *and* it be not known who hath slain him: 2. Then thy elders and thy judges shall come forth, and they shall measure unto the cities which *are* round about him that is slain: 3. And it shall be, *that* the city *which is* next unto the slain man, even the elders of that city shall take an heifer, which hath not been wrought with, *and* which hath not drawn in the yoke; 4. And the elders of that city shall bring down the heifer unto a rough valley, which is neither eared nor sown, and shall strike off the heifer's neck there in the valley: 5. And the priests the sons of Levi shall come near; for them the LORD thy God hath chosen to minister unto him, and to bless in the name of the LORD; and by their word shall every controversy and every stroke be *tried:* 6. And all the elders of that city, *that are* next unto the slain *man,* shall wash their hands over the heifer that is beheaded in the valley: 7. And they shall answer and say, Our hands have not shed this blood, neither have our eyes seen *it.* 8. Be merciful, O LORD.

unto thy people Israel, whom thou hast redeemed, and lay not innocent blood unto thy people of Israel's charge. And the blood shall be forgiven them. 9. So shalt thou put away the *guilt of* innocent blood from among you, when thou shalt do *that which is* right in the sight of the LORD.

Deut. 22:8. When thou buildest a new house, then thou shalt make a battlement for thy roof, that thou bring not blood upon thine house, if any man fall from thence.

Deut. 27:24. Cursed *be* he that smiteth his neighbour secretly. 25. Cursed *be* he that taketh reward to slay an innocent person. And all the people shall say, Amen.

1 Kin. 21:19. Thus saith the LORD, Hast thou killed, and also taken possession? . . . In the place where dogs licked the blood of Naboth shall dogs lick thy blood, even thine.

2 Chr. 24:22. Thus Joash the king remembered not the kindness which Jehoiada his father had done to him, but slew his son. And when he died, he said, The LORD look upon *it,* and require *it.*

Job 24:14. The murderer rising with the light killeth the poor and needy, and in the night is as a thief. *vs.* 1–25.

Psa. 5:6. The LORD will abhor the bloody and deceitful man.

Psa. 9:12. When he maketh inquisition for blood, he remembereth them: he forgetteth not the cry of the humble.

Psa. 10:2. The wicked in *his* pride doth persecute the poor: 8. He sitteth in the lurking places of the villages: in the secret places doth he murder the innocent:

Psa. 26:9. Gather not my soul with sinners, nor my life with bloody men: 10. In whose hands *is* mischief.

Psa. 37:32. The wicked watcheth the righteous, and seeketh to slay him.

Psa. 38:12. They also that seek after my life lay snares *for me:*

Psa. 55:23. Thou, O God, shalt bring them down into the pit of destruction: bloody and deceitful men shall not live out half their days;

Psa. 94:3. LORD, . . . how long shall the wicked triumph? 6. They slay the widow and the stranger, and murder the fatherless.

Prov. 1:11. If they say, Come with us, let us lay wait for blood, let us lurk privily for the innocent without cause: 12. Let us swallow them up alive as the grave; and whole, as those that go down into the pit: 15. My son, walk not thou in the way with them; refrain thy foot from their path: 16. For their feet run to evil, and make haste to shed blood. Isa. 59:7.

Prov. 6:16. These . . . *things* doth the LORD hate: . . . 17. A proud look, a lying tongue, and hands that shed innocent blood,

Prov. 12:6. The words of the wicked *are* to lie in wait for blood:

Prov. 28:17. A man that doeth violence to the blood of *any* person shall flee to the pit; let no man stay him.

Isa. 26:21. The earth also shall disclose

her blood, and shall no more cover her slain.

Isa. 59:3. For your hands are defiled with blood, and your fingers with iniquity; your lips have spoken lies, your tongue hath muttered perverseness.

Jer. 2:34. In thy skirts is found the blood of the souls of the poor innocents: I have not found it by secret search, but upon all these. Jer. 19:4.

Jer. 7:9. Will ye steal, murder, . . . 10. And come and stand before me in this house, which is called by my name,

Jer. 22:3. Thus saith the LORD; Execute ye judgment and righteousness, and deliver the spoiled out of the hand of the oppressor: and do no wrong, do no violence to the stranger, the fatherless, nor the widow, neither shed innocent blood in this place.

Ezek. 22:9. In thee are men that carry tales to shed blood:

Ezek 35:6. As I live, saith the Lord GOD, I will prepare thee unto blood, and blood shall pursue thee: sith thou hast not hated blood, even blood shall pursue thee.

Hos. 1:4. For yet a little *while*, and I will avenge the blood of Jezreel upon the house of Jehu, and will cause to cease the kingdom of the house of Israel.

Hos. 4:1. The LORD hath a controversy with the inhabitants of the land, because *there is* no truth, nor mercy, . . . 2. By swearing, and lying, and killing, and stealing, and committing adultery, they break out, and blood toucheth blood. 3. Therefore shall the land mourn,

Hab. 2:10. Thou hast consulted shame to thy house by cutting off many people, and hast sinned *against* thy soul. 12. Woe to him that buildeth a town with blood,

Matt. 5:21. Ye have heard that it was said by them of old time, Thou shalt not kill; and whosoever shall kill shall be in danger of the judgment: 22. But I say unto you, That whosoever is angry with his brother without a cause shall be in danger of the judgment: and whosoever shall say to his brother, Raca, shall be in danger of the council: but whosoever shall say, Thou fool, shall be in danger of hell fire.

Matt. 15:19. Out of the heart proceed evil thoughts, murders, Mark 7:21.

Matt. 19:18. He saith unto him, Which? Jesus said, Thou shalt do no murder. Thou shalt not commit adultery, Thou shalt not steal, Thou shalt not bear false witness. Mark 10:19; Luke 18:20.

Gal. 5:19. Now the works of the flesh are manifest, which are *these;* [1]Adultery, fornication, uncleanness, lasciviousness, 20. Idolatry, witchcraft, hatred, variance, emulations, wrath, strife, seditions, heresies, 21. Envyings, [1]murders, drunkenness, revellings, and such like: of the which I tell you before, as I have also told *you* in time past, that they which do such things shall not inherit the kingdom of God. [1] Omitted in R. V.]

1 Tim. 1:9. Knowing this, that the law is not made for a righteous man, but for the lawless and disobedient, for the ungodly and for sinners, for unholy and profane, for murderers of fathers and murderers of mothers, for manslayers,

Jas. 2:11. For he that said, Do not commit adultery, said also, Do not kill. Now if thou commit no adultery, yet if thou kill, thou art become a transgressor of the law.

1 Pet. 4:15. Let none of you suffer as a murderer,

1 John 3:15. Whosoever hateth his brother is a murderer: and ye know that no murderer hath eternal life abiding in him. *v.* 12.

Rev. 9:21. Neither repented they of their murders,

Rev. 21:8. Murderers . . . shall have their part in the lake which burneth with fire and brimstone: which is the second death.

Rev. 22:15. Without *are* . . . murderers,

See CONSPIRACY; FRATRICIDE: PARRICIDE; PATRICIDE; REGICIDE; SUICIDE.

DAVID'S REPENTANCE FOR, AND CONFESSION OF, THE MURDER OF URIAH: Psa. 51:1. Have mercy upon me, O God, according to thy lovingkindness: according unto the multitude of thy tender mercies blot out my transgressions. 2. Wash me throughly from mine iniquity, and cleanse me from my sin. 3. For I acknowledge my transgressions: and my sin *is* ever before me. 4. Against thee, thee only, have I sinned, and done *this* evil in thy sight: that thou mightest be justified when thou speakest, *and* be clear when thou judgest. 5. Behold, I was shapen in iniquity; and in sin did my mother conceive me. 6. Behold, thou desirest truth in the inward parts: and in the hidden *part* thou shalt make me to know wisdom. 7. Purge me with hyssop, and I shall be clean: wash me, and I shall be whiter than snow. 8. Make me to hear joy and gladness; *that* the bones *which* thou hast broken may rejoice. 9. Hide thy face from my sins, and blot out all mine iniquities. 10. Create in me a clean heart, O God; and renew a right spirit within me. 11. Cast me not away from thy presence; and take not thy holy spirit from me. 12. Restore unto me the joy of thy salvation; and uphold me *with* *thy* free spirit. 13. *Then* will I teach transgressors thy ways; and sinners shall be converted unto thee. 14. Deliver me from bloodguiltiness, O God, thou God of my salvation: *and* my tongue shall sing aloud of thy righteousness, 15. O Lord, open thou my lips; and my mouth shall shew forth thy praise. 16. For thou desirest not sacrifice; else would I give *it:* thou delightest not in burnt offering. 17. The sacrifices of God *are* a broken spirit: a broken and a contrite heart, O God, thou wilt not despise.

INSTANCES OF FELONIOUS: By Cain, Gen. 4:8. Lamech, Gen. 4:23, 24. Simeon and Levi, Gen. 34:25-31. Pharaoh, Ex. 1:16, 22. Moses, Ex. 2:12. Ehud, Judg. 3:16-23. Jael, Judg. 4:21. Abimelech, Judg. 9:5, 18, 56. An Amalekite, 2 Sam. 1:16. Abner, 2 Sam. 2:18-24.

Joab, 2 Sam. 3:24-27; 2 Sam. 20:9,10; 1 Kin. 2:5. Solomon, 1 Kin. 2:23-46. Rechab and Baanah, 2 Sam. 4:5-8. David, 2 Sam. 11:14-17; 2 Sam. 12:9; Psa. 51:14. Of Amon, 2 Kin. 21:23. Absalom, 2 Sam. 13:22-29; Baasha, 1 Kin. 15:27-29. Zimri, 1 Kin. 16:9-11. Ahab and Jezebel, 1 Kin. 21:10-24; 2 Kin. 6:32. Hazael, 2 Kin. 8:15. Jehu, 2 Kin. 9:24-37; 2 Kin. 10:1-25. Athaliah, 2 Kin. 11:1. Of Joash by his servants, 2 Kin. 12:20,21. Menahem, 2 Kin. 15:16. Of Sennacherib, 2 Kin. 19:37; Isa. 37:38. Manasseh, 2 Kin. 21:16; 24:4. Jehoram, 2 Chr. 21:4. Joash, 2 Chr. 24:21. Amaziah's soldiers, 2 Chr. 25:12. Nebuchadnezzar, Jer. 39:6. Ishmael, Jer. 41:1-7. Ammonites, Amos, 1:13-15. Herod I., Matt. 2:16. Herod II., Matt. 14:10; Mark 6:27. Barabbas, Mark 15:7; Acts 3:14. Sanhedrin and Pilate, Matt. 26; 27. Sanhedrin, Acts 7:54-60. Herod, Acts 12:2,19. By raping, Judg. 19:25-28.

PUNISHMENT OF: Gen. 4:13. And Cain said unto the LORD, My punishment *is* greater than I can bear. 14. Behold, thou hast driven me out this day from the face of the earth; and from thy face shall I be hid; and I shall be a fugitive and a vagabond in the earth; and it shall come to pass, *that* every one that findeth me shall slay me. 15. And the LORD said unto him, Therefore whosoever slayeth Cain, vengeance shall be taken on him sevenfold. And the LORD set a mark upon Cain, lest any finding him should kill him.

Gen. 9:5. And surely your blood of your lives will I require; at the hand of every beast will I require it, and at the hand of man; at the hand of every man's brother will I require the life of man. 6. Whoso sheddeth man's blood, by man shall his blood be shed : for in the image of God made he man.

Gen. 27:43. Now therefore, my son, obey my voice; and arise, flee thou to Laban my brother to Haran; 44. And tarry with him a few days, until thy brother's fury turn away; 45. Until thy brother's anger turn away from thee, and he forget *that* which thou hast done to him : then I will send, and fetch thee from thence : why should I be deprived also of you both in one day?

Ex. 21:12. He that smiteth a man, so that he die, shall be surely put to death. 14. But if a man come presumptuously upon his neighbour, to slay him with guile; thou shalt take him from mine altar, that he may die.

Lev. 24:17. He that killeth any man shall surely be put to death.

Num. 35:16. And if he smite him with an instrument of iron, so that he die, he *is* a murderer : the murderer shall surely be put to death. 17. And if he smite him with throwing a stone, wherewith he may die, and he die, he *is* a murderer : the murderer shall surely be put to death. 18. Or *if* he smite him with a hand weapon of wood, wherewith he may die, and he die, he *is* a murderer : the murderer shall surely be put

to death. 19. The revenger of blood himself shall slay the murderer : when he meeteth him, he shall slay him. 20. But if he thrust him of hatred, or hurl at him by laying of wait, that he die; 21. Or in enmity smite him with his hand, that he die : he that smote *him* shall surely be put to death; *for* he *is* a murderer : the revenger of blood shall slay the murderer, when he meeteth him. 30. Whoso killeth any person, the murderer shall be put to death by the mouth of witnesses : but one witness shall not testify against any person *to cause him* to die. 31. Moreover ye shall take no satisfaction for the life of a murderer, which *is* guilty of death : but he shall be surely put to death. 32. And ye shall take no satisfaction for him that is fled to the city of his refuge, that he should come again to dwell in the land, until the death of the priest. 33. So ye shall not pollute the land wherein ye *are:* for blood it defileth the land : and the land cannot be cleansed of the blood that is shed therein, but by the blood of him that shed it.

Deut. 19:11. But if any man hate his neighbour, and lie in wait for him, and rise up against him, and smite him mortally that he die, and fleeth into one of these cities: 12. Then the elders of his city shall send and fetch him thence, and deliver him into the hand of the avenger of blood, that he may die. 13. Thine eye shall not pity him, but thou shalt put away *the guilt of* innocent blood from Israel, that it may go well with thee.

2 Sam. 12:9. Wherefore hast thou despised the commandment of the LORD, to do evil in his sight? thou hast killed Uriah the Hittite with the sword, and hast taken his wife *to be* thy wife, and hast slain him with the sword of the children of Ammon. 10. Now therefore the sword shall never depart from thine house; because thou hast despised me, and hast taken the wife of Uriah the Hittite to be thy wife. 11. Thus saith the LORD, Behold, I will raise up evil against thee out of thine own house, and I will take thy wives before thine eyes, and give *them* unto thy neighbour, and he shall lie with thy wives in the sight of this sun. 12. For thou didst *it* secretly : but I will do this thing before all Israel, and before the sun.

INSTANCES OF THE PUNISHMENT OF MURDERERS : Cain, Gen. 4:11-15. David, 2 Sam. 12:9,10. Joab, 1 Kin. 2:31-34. Haman, Esth. 7:10.

The murderer of Saul, 2 Sam. 1:15,16; of Ish-bosheth, 2 Sam. 4:11,12. The murderers of Joash. 2 Kin. 14:5.

HONESTY. Lev. 19:35. Ye shall do no unrighteousness in judgment, in meteyard, in weight, or in measure. 36. Just balances, just weights, a just ephah, and a just hin, shall ye have: I *am* the LORD your God, which brought you out of the land of Egypt.

Deut. 16:20. That which is altogether just shalt thou follow, that thou mayest live, and inherit the land which the LORD thy God giveth thee.

Deut. 25:13. Thou shalt not have in thy bag divers weights, a great and a small. 14. Thou shalt not have in thine house divers measures, a great and a small. 15. *But* thou shalt have a perfect and just weight, a perfect and just measure shalt thou have: that thy days may be lengthened in the land which the LORD thy God giveth thee. 16. For all that do such things, *and* all that do unrighteously, *are* an abomination unto the LORD thy God.

Job 27:6. My righteousness I hold fast, and will not let it go: my heart shall not reproach *me* so long as I live.

Psa. 7:3. O LORD my God, if I have done this; if there be iniquity in my hands; 4. If I have rewarded evil unto him that was at peace with me; (yea, I have delivered him that without cause is mine enemy :)

Psa. 15:5. *He that* putteth not out his money to usury, nor taketh reward against the innocent. He that doeth these *things* shall never be moved.

Psa. 24:4. He that hath clean hands, and a pure heart; who hath not lifted up his soul unto vanity, nor sworn deceitfully.

Prov. 4:25. Let thine eyes look right on, and let thine eyelids look straight before thee.

Prov. 11:1. A false balance *is* abomination to the LORD: but a just weight *is* his delight.

Prov. 12:22. Lying lips *are* abomination to the LORD: but they that deal truly *are* his delight.

Prov. 16:11. A just weight and balance *are* the LORD's: all the weights of the bag *are* his work.

Prov. 20:10. Divers weights, *and* divers measures, both of them *are* alike abomination to the LORD. *v.* 23.

Isa. 33:15. He that walketh righteously, and speaketh uprightly; he that despiseth the gain of oppressions, that shaketh his hands from holding of bribes, that stoppeth his ears from hearing of blood, and shutteth his eyes from seeing evil; 16. He shall dwell on high: his place of defence *shall be* the munitions of rocks: bread shall be given him; his waters *shall be* sure.

Ezek. 45:10. Ye shall have just balances, and a just ephah, and a just bath.

Mark 10:19. Thou knowest the commandments, Do not commit adultery, Do not kill, Do not steal, Do not bear false witness, Defraud not,

Luke 3:12. Then came also publicans to be baptized, and said unto him, Master, what shall we do? 13. And he said unto them, Exact no more than that which is appointed you.

Luke 6:31. As ye would that men should do to you, do ye also to them likewise. Matt. 7:12.

Acts 24:16. And herein do I exercise myself, to have always a conscience void of offence toward God, and *toward* men.

2 Cor. 4:1. Therefore seeing we have this ministry, as we have received mercy, we faint not; 2. But have renounced the hidden things of [1] dishonesty, not walking in craftiness, nor handling the word of God deceitfully; but by manifestation of the truth commending ourselves to every man's conscience in the sight of God.　　[1 R. V. shame]

2 Cor. 7:2. Receive us; we have wronged no man, we have corrupted no man, we have defrauded no man.

2 Cor. 8:21. Providing for honest things, not only in the sight of the Lord, but also in the sight of men.

Phil. 4:8. Brethren, whatsoever things are true, whatsoever things *are* honest, whatsoever things *are* just, . . . think on these things.

Col. 3:22. Not with eyeservice, as menpleasers; but in singleness of heart, fearing God:

1 Thess. 4:11. Study to be quiet, and to do your own business, and to work with your own hands, as we commanded you; 12. That ye may walk honestly toward them that are without, and *that* ye may have lack of nothing.

Heb. 13:18. Pray for us: for we trust we have a good conscience, in all things willing to live honestly.

1 Pet. 2:12. Having your conversation honest among the Gentiles: that, whereas they speak against you as evildoers, they may by *your* good works, which they shall behold, glorify God in the day of visitation.

INSTANCES OF: Jacob, returning money placed in the sacks, Gen. 43:12. The overseers of the temple repairs, 2 Kin. 12:15; 22: 4-7. Treasurers of the temple, Neh. 13:13.

See INTEGRITY; RIGHTEOUSNESS; DISHONESTY.

HONEY. Ex. 16:31; 2 Sam. 17:29; Prov. 25:27; Song 4:11; Isa. 7:15; Matt. 3:4; Luke 24:42. Not to be offered with sacrifices, Lev. 2:11. Found in rocks, Deut. 32:13; Psa. 81: 16; upon the ground, 1 Sam. 14:25. Samson's riddle concerning, Judg. 14:14. Sent as a present by Jacob to Egypt, Gen. 43:11. Plentiful in Palestine, Ex. 3:8; Lev. 20:24; Deut. 8:8; Ezek. 20:6; in Assyria, 2 Kin. 18: 32. An article of merchandise from Palestine, Ezek. 27:17.

HOOD, Isa. 3:23. See DRESS.

HOOF, parting of, one of the physical marks used for distinguishing clean and unclean animals, Lev. 11:3-8; Deut. 14:3-8.

HOOKS. For tabernacle, made of gold, Ex. 26:32,37; 36:36; silver, Ex. 27:10; 38:10-12,17,19. In the temple, seen in Ezekiel's vision, Ezek. 40:43. Used for catching fish, Ezek. 29:4. For pruning, Isa. 2:4; 18:5; Joel 3:10.

See FLESHHOOKS.

FIGURATIVE: Ezek. 38:4.

HOPE. Psa. 9:18. For the needy shall not always be forgotten: the expectation of the poor shall *not* perish for ever.

Psa. 16:9. Therefore my heart is glad, and

my glory rejoiceth: my flesh also shall rest in hope.

Psa. 31:24. Be of good courage, and he shall strengthen your heart, all ye that hope in the LORD.

Psa. 33:18. The eye of the LORD *is* upon them that fear him, upon them that hope in his mercy; 22. Let thy mercy, O LORD, be upon us, according as we hope in thee.

Psa. 38:15. In thee, O LORD, do I hope: thou wilt hear, O Lord my God.

Psa. 39:7. Now, Lord, what wait I for? my hope *is* in thee.

Psa. 43:5. Why art thou cast down, O my soul? and why art thou disquieted within me? hope in God: for I shall yet praise him, *who is* the health of my countenance, and my God.

Psa. 71:5. Thou *art* my hope, O Lord GOD: *thou art* my trust from my youth. 14. I will hope continually, and will yet praise thee more and more.

Psa. 78:5. For he established a testimony in Jacob, and appointed a law in Israel, which he commanded our fathers, that they should make them known to their children: 6. That the generation to come might know *them, even* the children *which* should be born; *who* should arise and declare *them* to their children: 7. That they might set their hope in God, and not forget the works of God, but keep his commandments:

Psa. 119:74. They that fear thee will be glad when they see me; because I have hoped in thy word. 81. My soul fainteth for thy salvation: *but* I hope in thy word. 116. Let me not be ashamed of my hope. 166. LORD, I have hoped for thy salvation,

Psa. 130:7. Let Israel hope in the LORD: for with the LORD *there is* mercy,

Psa. 146:5. Happy *is he* that *hath* the God of Jacob for his help, whose hope *is* in the LORD his God:

Prov. 10:28. The hope of the righteous *shall be* gladness:

Prov. 13:12. Hope deferred maketh the heart sick: but *when* the desire cometh, *it is* a tree of life.

Prov. 14:32. The righteous hath hope in his death.

Prov. 23:18. For surely there is an end; and thine expectation shall not be cut off.

Prov. 24:14. So *shall* the knowledge of wisdom *be* unto thy soul: when thou hast found *it*, then there shall be a reward, and thy expectation shall not be cut off.

Isa. 38:18. They that go down into the pit cannot hope for thy truth.

Jer. 17:7. Blessed *is* the man that trusteth in the LORD, and whose hope the LORD is.

Lam. 3:21. This I recall to my mind, therefore have I hope. 24. The LORD *is* my portion, saith my soul; therefore will I hope in him. 26. *It is* good that *a man* should both hope and quietly wait for the salvation of the LORD.

Hos. 2:15. I will give her . . . the valley of Achor for a door of hope:

Joel 3:16. The LORD *will be* [1] the hope of his people, and [2] the strength of the children of Israel. [R. V. [1] a refuge unto [2] and a strong hold to]

Zech. 9:12. Turn you to the strong hold, ye prisoners of hope:

Acts 23:6. Of the hope and resurrection of the dead I am called in question.

Acts 24:14. But this I confess unto thee, that after the way which they call heresy, so worship I the God of my fathers, believing all things which are written in the law and in the prophets: 15. And have hope toward God, which they themselves also allow, that there shall be a resurrection of the dead, both of the just and unjust.

Acts 26:6. I stand and am judged for the hope of the promise made of God unto our fathers: 7. Unto which *promise* our twelve tribes, instantly serving *God* day and night, hope to come. For which hope's sake, king Agrippa, I am accused of the Jews.

Acts 28:20. For the hope of Israel I am bound with this chain.

Rom. 4:18. Who against hope believed in hope, that he might become the father of many nations, according to that which was spoken, So shall thy seed be.

Rom. 5:2. By whom also we have access by faith into this grace wherein we stand, and rejoice in hope of the glory of God. 3. And not only *so*, but we glory in tribulations also: knowing that tribulation worketh patience; 4. And patience, experience; and experience, hope: 5. And hope maketh not ashamed; because the love of God is shed abroad in our hearts by the Holy Ghost which is given unto us.

Rom. 8:24. We are saved by hope: but hope that is seen is not hope: for what a man seeth, why doth he yet hope for? 25. But if we hope for that we see not, *then* do we with patience wait for *it*.

Rom. 12:12. Rejoicing in hope;

Rom. 15:4. That we through patience and comfort of the scriptures might have hope. 13. The God of hope fill you with all joy and peace in believing, that ye may abound in hope, through the power of the Holy Ghost.

1 Cor. 13:13. Now abideth faith, hope, charity,

1 Cor. 15:19. If in this life only we have hope in Christ, we are of all men most miserable.

2 Cor. 3:12. Seeing then that we have such hope, we use great plainness of speech:

Gal. 5:5. We through the Spirit wait for the hope of righteousness by faith.

Eph. 1:18. That ye may know what is the hope of his calling,

Eph. 4:4. Ye are called in one hope of your calling;

Phil. 1:20. According to my earnest expectation and *my* hope, that in nothing I shall be ashamed, but *that* with all boldness, as always, *so* now also Christ shall be magnified in my body, whether *it be* by life, or by death.

Col. 1:5. The hope which is laid up for you

in heaven, whereof ye heard before in the word of the truth of the gospel; 23. If ye continue in the faith grounded and settled, and *be* not moved away from the hope of the gospel, 27. To whom God would make known what *is* the riches of the glory of this mystery among the Gentiles; which is Christ in you, the hope of glory:

1 Thess. 1:3. Remembering without ceasing your work of faith, and labour of love, and patience of hope in our Lord Jesus Christ,

1 Thess. 5:8. For an helmet, the hope of salvation. Eph. 6:17.

2 Thess. 2:16. Our Father, which hath loved us, and hath given *us* everlasting consolation and good hope through grace,

1 Tim. 1:1. Paul, an apostle of Jesus Christ by the commandment of God our Saviour, and Lord Jesus Christ, *which is* our hope;

Tit. 1:2. In hope of eternal life, which God, that cannot lie, promised before the world began;

Tit. 2:13. Looking for that blessed hope, and the glorious appearing of the great God and our Saviour Jesus Christ;

Tit. 3:7. That being justified by his grace, we should be made heirs according to the hope of eternal life.

Heb. 3:6. But Christ as a son over his own house; whose house are we, if we hold fast the confidence and the rejoicing of the hope firm unto the end.

Heb. 6:11. And we desire that every one of you do shew the same diligence to the full assurance of hope unto the end: 18. That . . . we might have a strong consolation, who have fled for refuge to lay hold upon the hope set before us: 19. Which *hope* we have as an anchor of the soul, both sure and stedfast, and which entereth into that within the veil;

Heb. 11:1. Faith is the substance of things hoped for, the evidence of things not seen.

1 Pet. 1:3. Blessed *be* the God and Father of our Lord Jesus Christ, which according to his abundant mercy hath begotten us again unto a lively hope by the resurrection of Jesus Christ. . . . 13. . . . Gird up the loins of your mind, be sober, and hope to the end for the grace that is to be brought unto you at the revelation of Jesus Christ; 21. That your faith and hope might be in God.

1 Pet. 3:15. *Be* ready always to *give* an answer to every man that asketh you a reason of the hope that is in you with meekness and fear;

1 John 3:3. Every man that hath this hope in him purifieth himself, even as he is pure.

See FAITH.

OF THE WICKED: Job 8:13. The hypocrite's hope shall perish:

Job 11:20. But the eyes of the wicked shall fail, and they shall not escape, and their hope *shall be as* the giving up of the ghost.

Job 27:8. For what *is* the hope of the hypocrite, though he hath gained, when God taketh away his soul?

Job 31:24. If I have made gold my hope, or have said to the fine gold, *Thou art* my confidence; 28. For I should have ¹ denied the God *that is* above.   [¹ R. V. lied to]

Prov. 10:28. The hope of the righteous *shall be* gladness: but the expectation of the wicked shall perish.

Zech. 9:5. Ashkelon shall see *it*, and fear; Gaza also *shall see it*, and be very sorrowful, and Ekron; for her expectation shall be ashamed;

Eph. 2:12. That at that time ye were without Christ, being aliens from the commonwealth of Israel, and strangers from the covenants of promise, having no hope, and without God in the world:

HOPHNI. Son of Eli, 1 Sam. 1:3. Sin of, 1 Sam. 2:12–36; 3:11–14. Death of, 1 Sam. 4:4,11,17.

HOR, mountain on which Aaron died, Num. 20:22–29; 21:4; 33:38,39; 34:7,8; Deut. 32:50.

HORAM, king of Gezer, Josh. 10:33.

HOREB, a range of mountains of which Sinai is chief, Ex. 3:1; 17:6; 33:6; Deut. 1: 2,6,19; 4:10,15; 5:2; 9:8; 29:1; 1 Kin. 8:9; 19:8; 2 Chr. 5:10; Psa. 106:19; Mal. 4:4.

See SINAI.

HOREM, a fortification in Naphtali, Josh. 19:38.

HOR-HAGIDGAD, one of the stations of the Israelites in the wilderness, Num. 33: 32,33.

HORI. 1. Son of Lotan, Gen. 36:22,30; 1 Chr. 1:39.

2. A Simeonite, Num. 13:5.

HORMAH. A city S. W. of the Dead Sea, Num. 14:45; 21:1–3; Deut. 1:44. Taken by Judah and Simeon, Judg. 1:17; Josh. 12:14. Allotted to Simeon, Josh. 19:4; 1 Chr. 4:30. Within the territory allotted to Judah, Josh. 15:30; 1 Sam. 30:30.

HORN, used to hold the anointing oil, 1 Sam. 16:1; 1 Kin. 1:39. Used for a trumpet, see TRUMPET.

FIGURATIVE: Of divine protection, 2 Sam. 22:3. Of power, 1 Kin. 22:11; Psa. 89: 24; 92:10; 132:17.

SYMBOLICAL. Dan. 7:7–24; 8:3–9,20; Amos 6: 13; Mic. 4:13; Hab. 3:4; Zech. 1:18–21; Rev. 5:6; 12:3; 13:1,11; 17:3–16.

Horns of the altar, see ALTAR.

HORNET, or wasp, Ex. 23:28; Deut. 7: 20; Josh. 24:12.

HORONAIM, a town of Moab, Isa. 15: 5; Jer. 48:3,5,34.

HORONITE, Sanballat, the, Neh. 2:10, 19; 13:28.

HORSE. Description of : Great strength, Job 39:19–25; swifter than eagles, Jer. 4:13; snorting and neighing of, Isa. 5:28; Jer. 8:16; a vain thing for safety, Psa. 33:17; Prov. 21:31. Used by the Egyptians in war, Ex. 14:9; 15:19; the Israelites, 1 Kin. 22:4. Used for cavalry, 2 Kin. 18:23; Jer. 47:3; 51: 21. Egypt famous for, Isa. 31:1. Forbidden to kings of Israel, Deut. 17:16. Hamstrung by Joshua, Josh. 11:6,9; David, 2

Sam. 8:4. Israel reproved for keeping. Isa. 2:7; 31:1; Ezek. 17:15; Hos. 14:3. Exported from Egypt, 1 Kin. 10:28,29; 2 Chr. 9:25,28; from Babylon, Ezra 2:66; Neh. 7:68. Bits for, Jas. 3:3; bells for, Zech. 14:20; harness for, Jer. 46:4. Color of, Zech. 1:8. Commerce in, Rev. 18:13; see EXPORTED, above. Dedicated to religious uses, 2 Kin. 23:11.

SYMBOLICAL: Zech. 1:8; Rev. 6:2–8; 9:17; 19:11–21.

HORSE-LEECH, Prov. 30:15.

HORTICULTURE, encouraged, Lev. 19:23–25; Deut. 20:19,20.

See AGRICULTURE; GRAFTING; PRUNING.

HOSAH. 1. A city of Asher, Josh. 19:29.

2. A Levite, 1 Chr. 16:38; 26:10,11.

HOSANNA, a form of Jewish acclamation, Matt. 21:9,15; Mark 11:9,10; John 12:13.

HOSEA, one of the minor prophets. Called OSEE, Rom. 9:25. See book of Hosea.

HOSHAIAH. 1. One of the returned exiles, Neh. 12:32.

2. A distinguished Jewish captive, Jer. 42:1; 43:2.

HOSHAMA, son of Jeconiah, king of Judah, 1 Chr. 3:18.

HOSHEA. 1. Called also OSHEA. The original name of Joshua, Num. 13:8,16; Deut. 32:44.

2. A chief of Ephraim, 1 Chr. 27:20.

3. King of Israel. Assassinates Pekah and usurps the throne, 2 Kin. 15:30. Evil reign of, 2 Kin. 17:1,2. Becomes subject to Assyria, 2 Kin. 17:3. Conspires against Assyria and is imprisoned, 2 Kin. 17:4. Last king of Israel, 2 Kin. 17:6; 18:9–12; Hos. 10:3,7.

4. A Jewish exile, Neh. 10:23.

HOSPITALITY. Ex. 22:21. Thou shalt neither vex a stranger nor oppress him: for ye were strangers in the land of Egypt.

Ex. 23:9. Also thou shalt not oppress a stranger: for ye know the heart of a stranger, seeing ye were strangers in the land of Egypt.

Lev. 19:10. And thou shalt not glean thy vineyard, neither shalt thou gather *every* grape of thy vineyard; thou shalt leave them for the poor and stranger: I *am* the LORD your God. 33. And if a stranger sojourn with thee in your land, ye shall not vex him. 34. *But* the stranger that dwelleth with you shall be unto you as one born among you, and thou shalt love him as thyself; for ye were strangers in the land of Egypt: I *am* the LORD your God.

Lev. 24:22. Ye shall have one manner of law, as well for the stranger, as for one of your own country: for I *am* the LORD your God.

Deut. 10:18. He doth execute the judgment of the fatherless and widow, and loveth the stranger, in giving him food and raiment. 19. Love ye therefore the stranger: for ye were strangers in the land of Egypt.

Deut. 26:12. When thou hast made an end of tithing all the tithes of thine increase the third year, *which is* the year of tithing, and hast given *it* unto the Levite, the stranger, the fatherless, and the widow, that they

may eat within thy gates, and be filled; 13. Then thou shalt say before the LORD thy God, I have brought away the hallowed things out of *mine* house, and also have given them unto the Levite, and unto the stranger, to the fatherless, and to the widow, according to all thy commandments which thou hast commanded me: I have not transgressed thy commandments, neither have I forgotten *them:*

Deut. 27:19. Cursed *be* he that perverteth the judgment of the stranger, fatherless, and widow. And all the people shall say, Amen.

Prov. 9:1. Wisdom hath builded her house, she hath hewn out her seven pillars: 2. She hath killed her beasts; she hath mingled her wine; she hath also furnished her table. 3. She hath sent forth her maidens: she crieth upon the highest places of the city, 4. Whoso *is* simple, let him turn in hither: *as for* him that wanteth understanding, she saith to him, 5. Come, eat of my bread, and drink of the wine *which* I have mingled.

Prov. 23:6. Eat thou not the bread of *him that hath* an evil eye, neither desire thou his dainty meats: 7. For as he thinketh in his heart, so *is* he: Eat and drink, saith he to thee; but his heart *is* not with thee. 8. The morsel *which* thou hast eaten shalt thou vomit up, and lose thy sweet words.

Isa. 58:6. *Is* not this the fast that I have chosen? to loose the bands of wickedness, to undo the heavy burdens, and to let the oppressed go free, and that ye break every yoke? 7. *Is it* not to deal thy bread to the hungry, and that thou bring the poor that are cast out to thy house? when thou seest the naked, that thou cover him; and that thou hide not thyself from thine own flesh?

Matt. 22:2. The kingdom of heaven is like unto a certain king, which made a marriage for his son, 3. And sent forth his servants to call them that were bidden to the wedding: and they would not come. 4. Again, he sent forth other servants, saying, Tell them which are bidden, Behold, I have prepared my dinner: my oxen and *my* fatlings *are* killed, and all things *are* ready: come unto the marriage. 5. But they made light of *it*, and went their ways, one to his farm, another to his merchandise: 6. And the remnant took his servants, and entreated *them* spitefully, and slew *them*. 7. But when the king heard *thereof*, he was wroth: and he sent forth his armies, and destroyed those murderers, and burned up their city. 8. Then saith he to his servants, The wedding is ready, but they which were bidden were not worthy. 9. Go ye therefore into the highways, and as many as ye shall find, bid to the marriage. 10. So those servants went out into the highways, and gathered together all as many as they found, both bad and good: and the wedding was furnished with guests.

Matt. 25:34. Then shall the King say unto them on his right hand, Come, ye blessed of my Father, inherit the kingdom prepared for you from the foundation of the world: 35. For I was an hungred, and ye gave me meat: I was thirsty, and ye gave me drink: I was a stranger, and ye took me in: 36. Naked, and ye clothed me: I was sick, and ye visited me: I was in prison, and ye came unto me. 37. Then shall the righteous answer him, saying, Lord, when saw we thee an hungred, and fed *thee?* or thirsty, and gave *thee* drink? 38. When saw we thee a stranger, and took *thee* in? or naked, and clothed *thee?* 39. Or when saw we thee sick, or in prison, and came unto thee? 40. And the King shall answer and say unto them. Verily I say unto you, Inasmuch as ye have done *it* unto one of the least of these my brethren, ye have done *it* unto me. 41. Then shall he say also unto them on the left hand, Depart from me, ye cursed, into everlasting fire, prepared for the devil and his angels: 42. For I was an hungred, and ye gave me no meat: I was thirsty, and ye gave me no drink: 43. I was a stranger, and ye took me not in: naked, and ye clothed me not: sick, and in prison, and ye visited me not. 44. Then shall they also answer him, saying, Lord, when saw we thee an hungred, or athirst, or a stranger, or naked, or sick, or in prison, and did not minister unto thee? 45. Then shall he answer them, saying, Verily I say unto you, Inasmuch as ye did *it* not to one of the least of these, ye did *it* not to me. 46. And these shall go away into everlasting punishment: but the righteous into life eternal.

Luke 14:12. Then said he also to him that bade him, When thou makest a dinner or a supper, call not thy friends, nor thy brethren, neither thy kinsmen, nor *thy* rich neighbours; lest they also bid thee again, and a recompence be made thee. 13. But when thou makest a feast, call the poor, the maimed, the lame, the blind: 14. And thou shalt be blessed; for they cannot recompense thee: for thou shalt be recompensed at the resurrection of the just.

Rom. 12:13. Distributing to the necessity of saints; given to hospitality.

Rom. 16:1. I commend unto you Phebe our sister, which is a servant of the church which is at Cenchrea: 2. That ye receive her in the Lord, as becometh saints, and that ye assist her in whatsoever business she hath need of you: for she hath been a succourer of many, and of myself also.

1 Tim. 3:2. A bishop then must be blameless, the husband of one wife, vigilant, sober, of good behaviour, given to hospitality, apt to teach;

1 Tim. 5:10. Well reported of for good works; if she have brought up children, if she have lodged strangers, if she have washed the saints' feet, if she have relieved the afflicted, if she have diligently followed every good work.

Tit. 1:7. For a bishop must be blameless, as the steward of God; not selfwilled, not soon angry, not given to wine, no striker,

not given to filthy lucre; 8. But a lover of hospitality, a lover of good men, sober, just, holy, temperate;

Heb. 13:2. Be not forgetful to entertain strangers: for thereby some have entertained angels unawares.

1 Pet. 4:9. Use hospitality one to another without grudging. 10. As every man hath received the gift, *even so* minister the same one to another, as good stewards of the manifold grace of God. 11. If any man speak, *let him speak* as the oracles of God; if any man minister, *let him do it* as of the ability which God giveth;

3 John 5. Beloved, thou doest faithfully whatsoever thou doest to the brethren, and to strangers; 6. Which have borne witness of thy charity before the church: whom if thou bring forward on their journey after a godly sort, thou shalt do well: 7. Because that for his name's sake they went forth, taking nothing of the Gentiles. 8. We therefore ought to receive such, that we might be fellowhelpers to the truth.

See GUEST; STRANGERS.

INSTANCES OF: Pharaoh to Abraham. Gen. 12:16. Melchizedek to Abraham, Gen. 14: 18. Abraham to the angels, Gen. 18:1-8. Lot to the angel, Gen. 19:1-11. Abimelech to Abraham, Gen. 20:14,15. Sons of Heth to Abraham, Gen. 23:6,11. Laban to Abraham's servant, Gen. 24:31; to Jacob, Gen. 29:13,14. Isaac to Abimelech, Gen. 26:30. Joseph to his brethren, Gen. 43:31-34. Pharaoh to Jacob, Gen. 45:16-20; 47:7-12. Jethro to Moses, Ex. 2:20. Rahab to the spies, Josh. 2:1-16. Man of Gibeah to the Levite, Judg. 19:16-21. Pharaoh to Hadad, 1 Kin. 11:17,22. David to Mephibosheth, 2 Sam. 9:7-13. The widow of Zarephath to Elijah, 1 Kin. 17:10-24. The Shunammite to Elisha, 2 Kin. 4:8. Elisha to the Syrian spies, 2 Kin. 6:22. Job to strangers, Job 31:32. Martha to Jesus, Luke 10:38; John 12:1,2. Pharisees to Jesus, Luke 11:37,38. Zaccheus to Jesus, Luke 19:1-10. The tanner to Peter, Acts 10:6,23. Lydia to Paul and Silas, Acts 16:15. Publius to Paul, Acts 28:7; Phebe to Paul, Rom. 16:2. Onesiphorus to Paul, 2 Tim. 1:16. Gaius, 3 John 5-8.

REWARDED: INSTANCES OF: Rahab's, Josh. 6:17,22-25. Widow of Zarephath's, 1 Kin. 17:10-24.

See FEASTS; STRANGERS.

HOSTAGE, 2 Kin. 14:14; 2 Chr. 25:24.

HOTHAM, son of Heber, 1 Chr. 7:32.

HOTHAN, an Aroerite, 1 Chr. 11:44.

HOTHIR, son of Heman, 1 Chr. 25:4,28.

HOT SPRINGS, Gen. 36:24 [*R. V.*].

HOUGHING, of horses, Josh. 11:6,9; 2 Sam. 8:4; 1 Chr. 18:4.

HOURS. A division of time. Twelve, in the day, John 11:9; Matt. 20:3-12; 27:45,46; in the night, Acts 23:23.

SYMBOLICAL: Rev. 8:1; 9:15.

HOUSE. Built of stone, Lev. 14:40-45; Isa. 9:10; Amos 5:11; brick, Gen. 11:3; Ex. 1:11-14; Isa. 9:10; wood, Song 1:17; Isa. 9:10. Built into city walls, Josh. 2:15.

Used for worship, Acts 1:13,14; 12:12; Rom. 16:5; 1 Cor. 16:19; Col. 4:15; Philem. 2.

"A man's castle," Deut. 24:10,11.

ARCHITECTURE OF: Foundations of stone, 1 Kin. 5:17; 1 Kin. 7:9; Ezra 6:3; Jer. 51:26. Figurative: Psa. 87:1; Isa. 28:16; 48: 13; Rom. 15:20; 1 Cor. 3:11; Eph. 2:20; 1 Tim. 6:19; Heb. 6:1; Rev. 21:14. Corner stone, Job 38:6; Psa. 144:12. Figurative: Psa. 118: 22; Isa. 28:16; Eph. 2:20; 1 Pet. 2:6.

Porches, Judg. 3:23; 1 Kin. 7:6,7; courts, Esth. 1:5; summer apartment, Judg. 3:20, with Amos 3:15; 1 Kin. 17:19; inner chamber, 1 Kin. 22:25; chambers, Gen. 43:30; 2 Sam. 18:33; 2 Kin. 1:2; 4:10; Acts 1:13; 9:37; 20:8; guest chamber, Mark 14:14; pillars, Prov. 9:1; with courts, Neh. 8:16; lattice, Judg. 5:28; windows, Judg. 5:28; Prov. 7:6; ceiled and plastered, Dan. 5:5; hinges, Prov. 26:14.

Roofs, flat, Josh. 2:6; Judg. 16:27; 1 Sam. 9:25; 2 Sam. 11:2; 16:22; Isa. 15:3; 22:1; Matt. 24:17; Luke 12:3; battlements required in Mosaic law, Deut. 22:8. Prayer on, Acts 10:9. Altars on, 2 Kin. 23:12; Jer. 19:13; 32:29; Zeph. 1:5. Booths on, Neh. 8:16. Used as place to sleep, Josh. 2:8; Acts 10:9; as dwelling place, Prov. 21:9; 25:24.

Painted, Jer. 22:14; Ezek. 8:10,12. Chimneys of, Hos. 13:3. Texts of scripture on doorposts of, Deut. 6:9. Laws regarding sale of, Lev. 25:29–33; Neh. 5:3. Dedicated, Deut. 20:5; Psa. 30 [title].

FIGURATIVE: 2 Sam. 7:18; Psa. 23:6; 36:8; John 14:2; 2 Cor. 5:1; 1 Tim. 3:15; Heb. 3:2.

HOUSE OF GOD. A place of prayer, Matt. 21:13; Mark 11:17; Luke 19:46. Holy, Eccl. 5:1; Isa. 62:9; Ezek. 43:12; 1 Cor. 3:17. See SYNAGOGUE; TABERNACLE; TEMPLE.

HUKKOK, a place on the boundary line of Naphtali, Josh. 19:34.

HUKOK, see HELKATH.

HUL, son of Aram, Gen. 10:23; 1 Chr. 1:17.

HULDAH, a prophetess. Foretells the destruction of Jerusalem, 2 Kin. 22:14–20: 2 Chr. 34:22–28.

HUMAN SACRIFICE. See OFFERING, HUMAN.

HUMILIATION AND SELF-AFFLICTION. ENJOINED: Lev. 16:29. And *this* shall be a statute for ever unto you: *that* in the seventh month, on the tenth *day* of the month, ye shall afflict your souls, and do no work at all, *whether it be* one of your own country, or a stranger that sojourneth among you: 30. For on that day shall *the priest* make an atonement for you, to cleanse you, *that* ye may be clean from all your sins before the LORD. 31. It *shall be* a sabbath of rest unto you, and ye shall afflict your souls, by a statute for ever.

Lev. 23:26. And the LORD spake unto Moses, saying, 27. Also on the tenth *day* of this seventh month *there shall be* a day of atonement: it shall be an holy convocation unto you; and ye shall afflict your souls, and offer an offering made by fire unto the LORD. 28. And ye shall do no work in that same day: for it *is* a day of atonement, **to** make an atonement for you before the LORD your God. 29. For whatsoever soul *it be* that shall not be afflicted in that same day, he shall be cut off from among his people. 30. And whatsoever soul *it be* that doeth any work in that same day, the same soul will I destroy from among his people. 31. Ye shall do no manner of work: *it shall be* a statute for ever throughout your generations in all your dwellings. 32. It *shall be* unto you a sabbath of rest, and ye shall afflict your souls: in the ninth *day* of the month at even, from even unto even, shall ye celebrate your sabbath.

Ezra 8:21. Then I proclaimed a fast there, at the river of Ahava, that we might afflict ourselves before our God, to seek of him a right way for us, and for our little ones, and for all our substance. 22. For I was ashamed to require of the king a band of soldiers and horsemen to help us against the enemy in the way: because we had spoken unto the king, saying, The hand of our God *is* upon all them for good that seek him; but his power and his wrath *is* against all them that forsake him. 23. So we fasted and besought our God for this: and he was intreated of us.

2 Chr. 7:14. If my people, which are called by my name, shall humble themselves, and pray, and seek my face, and turn from their wicked ways; then will I hear from heaven, and will forgive their sin, and will heal their land.

See FASTING; HUMILITY.

HUMILITY. Deut. 9:7. Remember, *and* forget not, how thou provokedst the LORD thy God to wrath in the wilderness: *vs.*4–29.

Deut. 15:15. And thou shalt remember that thou wast a bondman in the land of Egypt, and the LORD thy God redeemed thee:

Job 5:11. To set up on high those that be low; that those which mourn may be exalted to safety.

Job 22:29. When *men* are cast down, then thou shalt say, *There is* lifting up; and he shall save the humble person.

Job 25:5. Behold even to the moon, and it shineth not; yea, the stars are not pure in his sight. 6. How much less man, *that is* a worm? and the son of man, *which is* a worm?

Psa. 9:12. He forgetteth not the cry of the humble.

Psa. 10:17. LORD, thou hast heard the desire of the humble: thou wilt prepare their heart, thou wilt cause thine ear to hear:

Psa. 22:6. But I *am* a worm, and no man; a reproach of men, and despised of the people. 26. The meek shall eat and be satisfied:

Psa. 25:9. The meek will he guide in judgment: and the meek will he teach his way.

Psa. 37:11. The meek shall inherit the earth; and shall delight themselves in the abundance of peace.

Psa. 69:32. The humble shall see *this, and* be glad: and your heart shall live that seek God.

Psa. 86:1. Bow down thine ear, O LORD, hear me: for I *am* poor and needy.

Psa. 131:1. Lord, my heart is not haughty, nor mine eyes lofty: neither do I exercise myself in great matters, or in things too high for me. 2. Surely I have behaved and quieted myself, as a child that is weaned of his mother: my soul *is* even as a weaned child.

Psa. 138:6. Though the LORD *be* high, yet hath he respect unto the lowly:

Psa. 147:6. The LORD lifteth up the meek:

Psa. 149:4. He will beautify the meek with salvation.

Prov. 3:34. Surely he scorneth the scorners: but he giveth grace unto the lowly.

Prov. 10:8. The wise in heart will receive commandments: but a prating fool shall fall.

Prov. 11:2. With the lowly *is* wisdom.

Prov. 12:15. He that hearkeneth unto counsel *is* wise.

Prov. 15:33. Before honour *is* humility.

Prov. 18:12.

Prov. 16:19. Better *it is to be* of an humble spirit with the lowly, than to divide the spoil with the proud.

Prov. 22:4. By humility *and* the fear of the LORD *are* riches, and honour, and life.

Prov. 25:6. Put not forth thyself in the presence of the king, and stand not in the place of great *men:* 7. For better *it is* that it be said unto thee, Come up hither; than that thou shouldest be put lower in the presence of the prince whom thine eyes have seen.

Prov. 27:2. Let another man praise thee, and not thine own mouth; a stranger, and not thine own lips.

Prov. 29:23. Honour shall uphold the humble in spirit.

Prov. 30:32. If thou hast done foolishly in lifting up thyself, or if thou hast thought evil, *lay* thine hand upon thy mouth.

Eccl. 5:2. Be not rash with thy mouth, and let not thine heart be hasty to utter *any* thing before God: for God *is* in heaven, and thou upon earth: therefore let thy words be few.

Isa. 29:19. The meek also shall increase *their* joy in the LORD, and the poor among men shall rejoice in the Holy One of Israel.

Isa. 51:1. Look unto the rock *whence* ye are hewn, and to the hole of the pit *whence* ye are digged. Deut. 32:7.

Isa. 57:15. I dwell in the high and holy *place,* with him also *that is* of a contrite and humble spirit, to revive the spirit of the humble, and to revive the heart of the contrite ones.

Isa. 66:2. To this *man* will I look, *even* to *him that is* poor and of a contrite spirit, and trembleth at my word.

Jer. 45:5. Seekest thou great things for thyself? seek *them* not:

Ezek. 16:63. Remember, and be confounded, and never open thy mouth any more because of thy shame, when I am pacified toward thee for all that thou hast done, saith the Lord GOD.

Mic. 6:8. What doth the LORD require of thee, but to . . . walk humbly with thy God?

Zeph. 3:11. I will take away out of the midst of thee them that rejoice in thy pride, and thou shalt no more be haughty because of my holy mountain. 12. I will also leave in the midst of thee an afflicted and poor people, and they shall trust in the name of the LORD.

Matt. 5:3. Blessed *are* the poor in spirit: for their's is the kingdom of heaven. Luke 6:20.

Matt. 11:29. Take my yoke upon you, and learn of me; for I am meek and lowly in heart: and ye shall find rest unto your souls.

Matt. 18:2. Jesus called a little child unto him, and set him in the midst of them, 3. And said, Verily I say unto you, Except ye be converted, and become as little children, ye shall not enter into the kingdom of heaven. 4. Whosoever therefore shall humble himself as this little child, the same is greatest in the kingdom of heaven. Mark 9:33-37; Luke 9:46-48.

Matt. 20:26. Whosoever will be great among you, let him be your minister; 27. And whosoever will be chief among you, let him be your servant: Mark 10:43,44; Luke 22:26.

Matt. 23:12. And whosoever shall exalt himself shall be abased; and he that shall humble himself shall be exalted. Luke 14:11.

Luke 1:52. He hath put down the mighty from *their* seats, and exalted them of low degree.

Luke 10:21. Thou hast hid these things from the wise and prudent, and hast revealed them unto babes:

Luke 14:10. When thou art bidden, go and sit down in the lowest room; that when he that bade thee cometh, he may say unto thee, Friend, Go up higher: *v.* 11: Prov. 25:6,7.

Luke 17:10. When ye shall have done all those things which are commanded you, say, We are unprofitable servants: we have done that which was our duty to do.

Luke 18:13. The publican, standing afar off, would not lift up so much as *his* eyes unto heaven, but smote upon his breast, saying, God be merciful to me a sinner. 14. I tell you, this man went down to his house justified *rather* than the other: for every one that exalteth himself shall be abased; and he that humbleth himself shall be exalted. Matt. 23:12.

Luke 22:24. And there was also a strife among them, which of them should be accounted the greatest. 25. And he said unto them, The kings of the Gentiles exercise lordship over them; and they that exercise authority upon them are called benefactors. 26. But ye *shall* not *be* so: but he that is greatest among you, let him be as the younger; and he that is chief, as he that doth serve. 27. For whether *is* greater, he that sitteth at meat, or he that serveth? *is* not he that sitteth at meat? but I am among you as he that serveth.

John 13:14. If I then, *your* Lord and

Master, have washed your feet; ye also ought to wash one another's feet. 15. For I have given you an example, that ye should do as I have done to you. 16. Verily, verily, I say unto you, The servant is not greater than his lord; neither he that is sent greater than he that sent him.

Rom. 11:18. Boast not against the branches. But if thou boast, thou bearest not the root, but the root thee. 20. Be not highminded, but fear: 25. For I would not, brethren, that ye should be ignorant of this mystery, lest ye should be wise in your own conceits: that blindness in part is happened to Israel, until the fulness of the Gentiles be come in.

Rom. 12:3. For I say, through the grace given unto me, to every man that is among you, not to think *of himself* more highly than he ought to think; but to think soberly, according as God hath dealt to every man the measure of faith. 10. In honour preferring one another; 16. Mind not high things, but condescend to men of low estate. Be not wise in your own conceits.

1 Cor. 1:28. Base things of the world, and things which are despised, hath God chosen, *yea*, and things which are not, to bring to nought things that are: 29. That no flesh should glory in his presence.

1 Cor. 2:1. And I, brethren, when I came to you, came not with excellency of speech or of wisdom, declaring unto you the testimony of God. 2. For I determined not to know any thing among you, save Jesus Christ, and him crucified. 3. And I was with you in weakness, and in fear, and in much trembling.

1 Cor. 3:18. If any man among you seemeth to be wise in this world, let him become a fool, that he may be wise.

1 Cor. 10:12. Let him that thinketh he standeth take heed lest he fall.

1 Cor. 13:4. Charity vaunteth not itself, is not puffed up,

2 Cor. 11:30. If I must needs glory, I will glory of the things which concern mine infirmities.

2 Cor. 12:5. Of such an one will I glory: yet of myself I will not glory, but in mine infirmities. 6. For though I would desire to glory, I shall not be a fool; for I will say the truth: but *now* I forbear, lest any man should think of me above that which he seeth me *to be*, or *that* he heareth of me. 7. And lest I should be exalted above measure through the abundance of the revelations, there was given to me a thorn in the flesh, the messenger of Satan to buffet me, lest I should be exalted above measure. 8. For this thing I besought the Lord thrice, that it might depart from me. 9. And he said unto me, My grace is sufficient for thee: for my strength is made perfect in weakness. Most gladly therefore will I rather glory in my infirmities, that the power of Christ may rest upon me. 10. Therefore I take pleasure in infirmities, in reproaches, in necessi-

ties, in persecutions, in distresses for Christ's sake: for when I am weak, then am I strong. 11. I am become a fool in glorying; ye have compelled me: for I ought to have been commended of you: for in nothing am I behind the very chiefest apostles, though I be nothing. 12. Truly the signs of an apostle were wrought among you in all patience, in signs, and wonders, and mighty deeds.

Gal. 5:26. Let us not be desirous of vain glory,

Gal. 6:14. But God forbid that I should glory, save in the cross of our Lord Jesus Christ, by whom the world is crucified unto me, and I unto the world.

Eph. 4:2. With all lowliness and meekness, with longsuffering, forbearing one another in love;

Eph. 5:21. Submitting yourselves one to another in the fear of [1] God. [1 R. V. Christ]

Phil. 2:3. *Let* nothing *be done* through strife or vainglory; but in lowliness of mind let each esteem other better than themselves. 4. Look not every man on his own things, but every man also on the things of others. 5. Let this mind be in you, which was also in Christ Jesus: 6. Who, being in the form of God, thought it not [1] robbery to be equal with God: 7. But [2] made himself of no reputation, and took upon him the likeness of a servant, and was made in the likeness of men: 8. And being found in fashion as a man, he humbled himself, and became obedient unto death, even the death of the cross. 9. Wherefore God also hath highly exalted him, and given him a name which is above every name: 10. That at the name of Jesus every knee should bow, of *things* in heaven, and *things* in earth, and *things* under the earth; 11. And *that* every tongue should confess that Jesus Christ *is* Lord, to the glory of God the Father. [R. V. [1a] prize [2] emptied himself, taking]

Col. 3:12. Put on therefore, as the elect of God, holy and beloved, . . . humbleness of mind, meekness,

Jas. 1:9. Let the brother of low degree rejoice in that he is exalted: 10. But the rich, in that he is made low: because as the flower of the grass he shall pass away. 19. Let every man be swift to hear, slow to speak, slow to wrath:

Jas. 3:1. Be not many masters, knowing that we shall receive the greater condemnation.

Jas. 4:6. God resisteth the proud, but giveth grace unto the humble. 10. Humble yourselves in the sight of the Lord, and he shall lift you up.

1 Pet. 5:3. Neither as being lords over *God's* heritage, but being ensamples to the flock. 5. Ye younger, submit yourselves unto the elder. Yea, all *of you* be subject one to another, and be clothed with humility: for God resisteth the proud, and giveth grace to the humble. 6. Humble yourselves therefore under the mighty hand of God, that he may exalt you in due time:

EXEMPLIFIED: Gen. 18:27. Behold now,

I have taken upon me to speak unto the Lord, which *am but* dust and ashes: *v.* 32.

Gen. 32:10. I am not worthy of the least of all the mercies, and of all the truth, which thou hast shewed unto thy servant;

Ex. 3:11. Who *am* I, that I should go unto Pharaoh, and that I should bring forth the children of Israel out of Egypt?

Ex. 4:10. O my Lord, I *am* not eloquent, neither heretofore, nor since thou hast spoken unto thy servant: but I *am* slow of speech, and of a slow tongue.

2 Sam. 7:18. Who *am* I, O Lord GOD? and what *is* my house, that thou hast brought me hitherto? 19. And this was yet a small thing in thy sight, O Lord GOD; but thou hast spoken also of thy servant's house for a great while to come. And *is* this the manner of man, O Lord GOD? 1 Chr. 17:17.

1 Kin. 3:7. And now, O LORD my God, thou hast made thy servant king instead of David my father: and I *am but* a little child: I know not *how* to go out or come in. 2 Chr. 1:10.

1 Chr. 29:14. Who *am* I, and what *is* my people, that we should be able to offer so willingly after this sort? for all things *come* of thee, and of thine own have we given thee.

2 Chr. 2:6. Who *am* I then, that I should build him an house, save only to burn sacrifice before him?

Ezra 9:13. Thou our God hast punished us less than our iniquities *deserve*,

Job 9:14. How much less shall I answer him, *and* choose out my words *to reason* with him? 15. Whom, though I were righteous, *yet* would I not answer, *but* I would make supplication to my judge. Job 10:15.

Job 33:6. I also am formed out of the clay.

Job 40:4. Behold, I am vile; what shall I answer thee? I will lay mine hand upon my mouth. 5. Once have I spoken; but I will not answer: yea, twice; but I will proceed no further.

Job 42:4. Hear, I beseech thee, and I will speak: 5. I have heard of thee by the hearing of the ear: but now mine eye seeth thee. 6. Wherefore I abhor *myself*, and repent in dust and ashes.

Psa. 8:3. When I consider thy heavens, . . . 4. What is man, that thou art mindful of him? and the son of man, that thou visitest him? Job 7:17,18; Psa. 144:3,4.

Psa. 73:22. So foolish *was* I, and ignorant: I was *as* a beast before thee.

Psa. 131:1. LORD, my heart is not haughty, nor mine eyes lofty: neither do I exercise myself in great matters, or in things too high for me. 2. Surely I have behaved and quieted myself, as a child that is weaned of his mother: my soul *is* even as a weaned child.

Psa. 141:5. Let the righteous smite me; *it shall be* a kindness: and let him reprove me; *it shall be* an excellent oil, *which* shall not break my head:

Prov. 30:2. Surely I *am* more brutish than *any* man, and have not the understanding of a man. 3. I neither learned wisdom, nor have the knowledge of the holy.

Isa. 6:5. Woe *is* me! for I am undone; because I *am* a man of unclean lips, and I dwell in the midst of a people of unclean lips: for mine eyes have seen the King, the LORD of hosts.

Isa. 38:15. I shall go softly all my years in the bitterness of my soul.

Jer. 1:6. Ah, Lord GOD! behold, I cannot speak: for I *am* a child.

Jer. 10:23. O LORD, I know that the way of man *is* not in himself: *it is* not in man that walketh to direct his steps. 24. O LORD, correct me, but with judgment; not in thine anger, lest thou bring me to nothing.

Dan. 2:30. This secret is not revealed to me for *any* wisdom that I have more than any living, Gen. 41:16; Acts 3:12.

Matt. 3:14. John forbade him, saying, I have need to be baptized of thee, and comest thou to me?

Matt. 15:27. Truth, Lord: yet the dogs eat of the crumbs which fall from their masters' table.

Matt. 25:37. Then shall the righteous answer him, saying, Lord, when saw we thee an hungred, and fed *thee?* or thirsty, and gave *thee* drink? 38. When saw we thee a stranger, and took *thee* in? or naked, and clothed *thee?* 39. Or when saw we thee sick, or in prison, and came unto thee? 40. And the King shall answer and say unto them, Verily I say unto you, Inasmuch as ye have done *it* unto one of the least of these my brethren, ye have done *it* unto me.

Luke 7:6. Lord, trouble not thyself: for I am not worthy that thou shouldest enter under my roof: 7. Wherefore neither thought I myself worthy to come unto thee: but say in a word, and my servant shall be healed. Matt. 8:8.

John 1:27. He it is, who coming after me is preferred before me, whose shoe's latchet I am not worthy to unloose.

John 3:29. He that hath the bride is the bridegroom: but the friend of the bridegroom, which standeth and heareth him, rejoiceth greatly because of the bridegroom's voice: this my joy therefore is fulfilled. 30. He must increase, but I *must* decrease.

Rom. 7:18. I know that in me (that is, in my flesh,) dwelleth no good thing:

1 Cor. 15:10. By the grace of God I am what I am: . . . I laboured more abundantly than they all: yet not I, but the grace of God which was with me.

2 Cor. 3:5. Not that we are sufficient of ourselves to think any thing as of ourselves; but our sufficiency *is* of God;

2 Cor. 12:7. And lest I should be exalted above measure through the abundance of the revelations, there was given to me a

thorn in the flesh, the messenger of Satan to buffet me, lest I should be exalted above measure.

Eph. 3:8. Unto me, who am less than the least of all saints, is this grace given,

Phil. 3:12. Not as though I had already attained, either were already perfect: but I follow after, if that I may apprehend that for which also I am apprehended of Christ Jesus. 13. Brethren, I count not myself to have apprehended:

Phil. 4:12. I know both how to be abased, and I know how to abound:

1 Tim. 1:15. This *is* a faithful saying, and worthy of all acceptation, that Christ Jesus came into the world to save sinners; of whom I am chief. 1 Cor. 15:9.

Rev. 4:10. The four and twenty elders fall down before him that sat on the throne, and worship him that liveth for ever and ever, and cast their crowns before the throne.

INSTANCES OF: Joseph, Gen. 41:16. David, 1 Sam. 18:18-23; 24:14; 26:20; 2 Sam. 7: 18-29; 1 Chr. 17:16-27. Mephibosheth, 2 Sam. 9:8. Ahab, 1 Kin. 21:29. Josiah, 2 Chr. 34:27; Elihu, Job 32:4-7. Isaiah, Isa. 6:5. Elisabeth, Luke 1:43. John the Baptist, Mark 1:7; Luke 3:16. Cornelius, Acts 10:33. Paul, Rom. 1:12; 16:7. Peter, Luke 5:8; 1 Pet. 5:1. John, Rev. 1:9.

HUMTAH, a city of Judah, Josh. 15:54.

HUNGER. Of Jesus, Matt. 4:2-4; 21:18; Mark 11:12; Luke 4:2-4; John 4:8. A stimulus to work, Prov. 16:26. No hunger in heaven, Rev. 7:16,17.

See FAMINE.

SPIRITUAL: Prov. 2:3. Yea, if thou criest after knowledge, *and* liftest up thy voice for understanding; 4. If thou seekest her as silver, and searchest for her as *for* hid treasures; 5. Then shalt thou understand the fear of the LORD, and find the knowledge of God.

Isa. 55:1. Ho, every one that thirsteth, come ye to the waters, and he that hath no money; come ye, buy, and eat; yea, come, buy wine and milk without money and without price. 2. Wherefore do ye spend money for *that which is* not bread? and your labour for *that which* satisfieth not? hearken diligently unto me, and eat ye *that which is* good, and let your soul delight itself in fatness.

Amos 8:11. Behold, the days come, saith the Lord GOD, that I will send a famine in the land, not a famine of bread, nor a thirst for water, but of hearing the words of the LORD: 12. And they shall wander from sea to sea, and from the north even to the east, they shall run to and fro to seek the word of the LORD, and shall not find *it*. 13. In that day shall the fair virgins and young men faint for thirst.

Matt. 5:6. Blessed *are* they which do hunger and thirst after righteousness: for they shall be filled.

Luke 6:21. Blessed *are ye* that hunger now: for ye shall be filled. Blessed *are ye* that weep now: for ye shall laugh.

1 Pet. 2:2. As newborn babes, desire the sincere milk of the word, that ye may grow thereby:

See DESIRE, SPIRITUAL; THIRST.

HUNTING. Authorized in the Mosaic law, Lev. 17:13. By Nimrod, Gen. 10:9. By Esau, Gen. 27:3,5,30,33. By Ishmael, Gen. 21:20. Of lion, Job 10:16. Fowling, 1 Sam. 26:20; Psa. 140:5; 141:9,10; Prov. 1:17; Eccl. 9:12; Lam. 3:52; Amos 3:5.

FIGURATIVE: Jer. 16:16.

HUPHAM, a Benjamite, Num. 26:39.

HUPPAH, a priest, 1 Chr. 24:13.

HUPPIM, a Benjamite, Gen. 46:21; 1 Chr. 7:12,15.

HUR. 1. An Israelite who assisted in supporting Moses's hands during battle, Ex. 17:10,12; 24:14.

2. A son of Caleb, Ex. 31:2; 35:30; 38:22; 1 Chr. 2:19,20; 2 Chr. 1:5.

3. A king of Midian, Num. 31:8; Josh 13:21.

4. Called Ben Hur, an officer of Solomon's commissary, 1 Kin. 4:8 [marg.].

5. Father of Caleb, 1 Chr. 2:50; 4:4.

6. A son of Judah, 1 Chr. 4:1.

7. A ruler, Neh. 3:9.

HURAI, one of David's guards, 1 Chr. 11:32.

HURAM. 1. Son of Bela, 1 Chr. 8:5.

2. King of Tyre. See HIRAM.

3. See HIRAM.

HURI, father of Abihail, 1 Chr. 5:14.

HUSBAND. Gen. 2:23. And Adam said, This *is* now bone of my bones, and flesh of my flesh: she shall be called Woman, because she was taken out of man. 24. Therefore shall a man leave his father and his mother, and shall cleave unto his wife: and they shall be one flesh. Matt. 19:5; Mark 10:7.

Num. 5:11. And the Lord spake unto Moses, saying, 12. Speak unto the children of Israel, and say unto them, If any man's wife go aside, and commit a trespass against him, 13. And a man lie with her carnally, and it be hid from the eyes of her husband, and be kept close, and she be defiled, and *there be* no witness against her, neither she be taken *with the manner*; 14. And the spirit of jealousy come upon him, and he be jealous of his wife, and she be defiled: or if the spirit of jealousy come upon him, and he be jealous of his wife, and she be not defiled: 15. Then shall the man bring his wife unto the priest, and he shall bring her offering for her, the tenth *part* of an ephah of barley meal; he shall pour no oil upon it, nor put frankincense thereon; for it *is* an offering of jealousy, an offering of memorial, bringing iniquity to remembrance. 16. And the priest shall bring her near, and set her before the LORD: 17. And the priest shall take holy water in an earthen vessel; and of the dust that is in the floor of the tabernacle the priest shall take, and put *it* into the water: 18. And the priest shall set the woman before the LORD, and uncover the woman's head, and put the offering of memorial in her hands, which *is* the jealousy offering: and the priest shall have in his hand the bitter water that causeth the curse: 19. And the priest shall charge her by an oath, and say unto the woman, If no man have lain with thee, and if thou hast not gone aside to uncleanness *with another* instead of thy husband, be thou free from this bitter water that causeth the curse: 20. But if thou hast gone aside *to another* instead of thy husband, and if thou be defiled, and some man have lain with thee beside thine husband: 21. Then the priest shall charge the woman with an oath of cursing, and the priest shall say unto the woman, The Lord make thee a curse and an oath among thy people, when the Lord doth make thy thigh to rot, and thy belly to swell; 22. And this water that causeth the curse shall go into thy bowels, to make *thy* belly to swell, and *thy* thigh to rot: And the woman shall say, Amen, amen. 23. And the priest shall write these curses in a book, and he shall blot *them* out with the bitter water: 24. And he shall cause the woman to drink the bitter water that causeth the curse: and the water that causeth the curse shall enter into her, *and become* bitter. 25. Then the priest shall take the jealousy offering out of the woman's hand, and shall wave the offering before the Lord, and offer it upon the altar: 26. And the priest shall take an handful of the offering, *even* the memorial thereof, and burn *it* upon the altar, and afterward shall cause the woman to drink the water. 27. And when he hath made her to drink the water, then it shall come to pass, *that* if she be defiled, and have done trespass against her husband, that the water that causeth the curse shall enter into her, *and become* bitter, and her belly shall swell, and her thigh shall rot: and the woman shall be a curse among her people. 28. And if the woman be not defiled, but be clean; then she shall be free, and shall conceive seed. 29. This *is* the law of jealousies, when a wife goeth aside *to another* instead of her husband, and is defiled; 30. Or when the spirit of jealousy cometh upon him, and he be jealous over his wife, and shall set the woman before the Lord, and the priest shall execute upon her all this law. 31. Then shall the man be guiltless from iniquity, and this woman shall bear her iniquity.

Deut. 22:13. If any man take a wife, and go in unto her, and hate her, 14. And give occasions of speech against her, and bring up an evil name upon her, and say, I took this woman, and when I came to her, I found her not a maid: 15. Then shall the father of the damsel, and her mother, take and bring forth *the tokens of* the damsel's virginity unto the elders of the city in the gate: 16. And the damsel's father shall say unto the elders, I gave my daughter unto this man to wife, and he hateth her; 17. And, lo, he hath given occasions of speech *against her*, saying, I found not thy daughter a maid; and yet these *are the tokens of* my daughter's virginity. And they shall spread the cloth before the elders of the city. 18. And the elders of that city shall take that man and chastise him; 19. And they shall amerce him in an hundred *shekels* of silver, and give *them* unto the father of the damsel, because he hath brought up an evil name upon a virgin of Israel: and she shall be his wife; he may not put her away all his days. 20. But if this thing be true, *and the tokens of* virginity be not found for the damsel: 21. Then they shall bring out the damsel to the door of her father's house, and the men of her city shall stone her with stones that she die; because she hath wrought folly in Israel, to play the whore in her father's house: so shalt thou put evil away from among you.

Deut. 24:5. When a man hath taken a new wife, he shall not go out to war, neither shall he be charged with any business: *but* he shall be free at home one year, and shall cheer up his wife which he hath taken.

Prov. 5:15. Drink waters out of thine own cistern, and running waters out of thine own well. 16. Let thy fountains be dispersed abroad, *and* rivers of waters in the streets. 17. Let them be only thine own, and not strangers' with thee. 18. Let thy fountain be blessed: and rejoice with the wife of thy youth. 19. *Let her be as* the loving hind and pleasant roe; let her breasts satisfy thee at all times; and be thou ravished always with her love.

Eccl. 9:9. Live joyfully with the wife whom thou lovest all the days of the life of thy vanity, which he hath given thee under the sun, all the days of thy vanity: for that *is* thy portion in *this* life, and in thy labour which thou takest under the sun.

Mal. 2:14. Yet ye say, Wherefore? Because the Lord hath been witness between thee and the wife of thy youth, against whom thou hast dealt treacherously: yet *is* she thy companion, and the wife of thy covenant. 15. And did not he make one? Yet had he the residue of the spirit. And wherefore one? That he might seek a godly seed. Therefore take heed to your spirit, and let none deal treacherously against the wife of his youth. 16. For the Lord, the God of Israel, saith that he hateth putting away: for *one* covereth violence with his garment, saith the Lord of hosts: therefore take heed to your spirit, that ye deal not treacherously.

1 Cor. 7:3. Let the husband render unto the wife due benevolence: and likewise also the wife unto the husband. 5. Defraud ye not one the other, except *it be* with consent for a time, that ye may give yourselves to fasting and prayer; and come together again, that Satan tempt you not for your incontinency.

1 Cor. 7:14. For the unbelieving husband is sanctified by the wife, and the unbelieving wife is sanctified by the husband; else were your children unclean, but now are

they holy. 16. For what knowest thou, O wife, whether thou shalt save *thy* husband? or how knowest thou, O man, whether thou shalt save *thy* wife. 33. But he that is married careth for the things that are of the world, how he may please *his* wife.

1 Cor. 11:3. But I would have you know, that the head of every man is Christ; and the head of the woman *is* the man; and the head of Christ *is* God.

Eph. 5:22. Wives, submit yourselves unto your own husbands, as unto the Lord. 23. For the husband is the head of the wife, even as Christ is the head of the church: and he is the saviour of the body. 24. Therefore as the church is subject unto Christ, so *let* the wives *be* to their own husbands in everything. 25. Husbands, love your wives. even as Christ also loved the church, and gave himself for it; 26. That he might sanctify and cleanse it with the washing of water by the word, 27. That he might present it to himself a glorious church, not having spot, or wrinkle, or any such thing; but that it should be holy and without blemish. 28. So ought men to love their wives as their own bodies. He that loveth his wife loveth himself. 29. For no man ever yet hated his own flesh; but nourisheth and cherisheth it, even as the Lord the church: 30. For we are members of his body, of his flesh, and of his bones. 31. For this cause shall a man leave his father and mother, and shall be joined unto his wife, and they two shall be one flesh. 32. This is a great mystery: but I speak concerning Christ and the church. 33. Nevertheless let every one of you in particular so love his wife even as himself; and the wife *see* that she reverence *her* husband.

Col. 3:18. Wives, submit youselves unto your own husbands, as it is fit in the Lord. 19. Husbands, love *your* wives, and be not bitter against them.

1 Tim. 5:8. But if any provide not for his own, and specially for those of his own house, he hath denied the faith, and is worse than an [1] infidel. [1 R. V. unbeliever]

1 Pet. 3:7. Likewise, ye husbands, dwell with *them* according to knowledge, giving honour unto the wife, as unto the weaker vessel, and as being heirs together of the grace of life; that your prayers be not hindered.

FAITHFUL: INSTANCES OF: Isaac, Gen. 24:67; Joseph, Matt. 1:19.

UNREASONABLE AND OPPRESSIVE: Ahasuerus, Esth. 1:10–22.

FIGURATIVE: Isa. 54:5,6; Jer. 3:14; 31:32; Hos. 2:19,20.

HUSBANDMAN, an agriculturist, Matt. 21:33–46; Mark 12:1-9; John 15:1; 1 Cor. 3:9.

See AGRICULTURE.

HUSBANDRY. See HUSBANDMAN; AGRICULTURE; ANIMALS.

HUSHAH. Son of Ezer, 1 Chr. 4:4. Probably called SHUAH, 1 Chr. 4:11.

HUSHAI, David's friend, 2 Sam. 15:32–37; 16:16–19; 17; 1 Chr. 27:33.

HUSHAM, a Temanite, Gen. 36:34,35; 1 Chr. 1:45,46.

HUSHIM. 1. Son of Dan, Gen. 46:23. Called SHUHAM, Num. 26:42.

2. A Benjamite, 1 Chr. 7:12.

3. Wife of Shaharaim, 1 Chr. 8:8,11.

HUSK, a pod, Num. 6:4; 2 Kin. 4:42. Eaten by the prodigal son, Luke 15:16.

HUZ. See UZ.

HUZZAB, probably a region E. of the Tigris, Nah. 2:7.

HYBRIDIZING, forbidden, Lev. 19:19.

HYGIENE, 1 Cor. 6:18; 9:25.

See SANITATION.

HYMENÆUS, a false teacher, 1 Tim. 1:20; 2 Tim. 2:17.

HYMN. See PSALMS; SONG.

HYPOCRISY. Job 8:13. The [1] hypocrite's hope shall perish: 14. Whose hope shall be cut off, and whose trust *shall be* a spider's web. 15. He shall lean upon his house, but it shall not stand: he shall hold it fast, but it shall not endure. [1 R. V. hope of the godless man]

Job 13:16. [1] An hypocrite shall not come before him. [1 R. V. For a godless man]

Job 15:31. Let not him that is deceived trust in vanity: for vanity shall be his recompence. 33. He shall shake off his unripe grape as the vine, and shall cast off his flower as the olive. 34. For the congregation of [1] hypocrites *shall be* desolate, and fire shall consume the tabernacles of bribery. [1 R. V. the godless]

Job 17:8. Upright *men* shall be astonied at this, and the innocent shall stir up himself against the [1] hypocrite. [1 R. V. godless]

Job 20:4. Knowest thou *not* this of old, since man was placed upon earth, 5. That the triumphing of the wicked *is* short, and the joy of the [1] hypocrite *but* for a moment? *vs.* 6–18. [1 R. V. godless]

Job 27:8. What *is* the hope of the [1] hypocrite, though he hath gained, when God taketh away his soul? 9. Will God hear his cry when trouble cometh upon him? 10. Will he delight himself in the Almighty? Will he always call upon God? *vs.* 13–18. [1 R. V. godless]

Job 31:33. If I covered my transgressions as Adam, by hiding mine iniquity in my bosom: 34. Did I fear a great multitude, or did the contempt of families terrify me, that I kept silence, *and* went not out of the door?

Job 34:30. That the [1] hypocrite reign not, lest the people be ensnared. [1 R. V. godless man]

Job 36:13. [1] The hypocrites in heart heap up wrath: they cry not when he bindeth them. 14. They die in youth, and their life *is* among the unclean. [1 R. V. They that are godless

Psa. 5:9. For *there is* no faithfulness in their mouth; their inward part *is* very wickedness; their throat *is* an open sepulchre; they flatter with their tongue.

Psa. 50:16. Unto the wicked God saith, What hast thou to do to declare my statutes, or *that* thou shouldest take my covenant in thy mouth? 17. Seeing thou hatest instruction, and castest my words behind thee.

Psa. 52:4. Thou lovest all devouring words. O thou deceitful tongue.

Psa. 55:12. It was not an enemy that reproached me; then I could have borne it: neither was it he that hated me that did magnify himself against me; then I would have hid myself from him: 13. But it was thou, a man mine equal, my guide, and mine acquaintance. 14. We took sweet counsel together, and walked unto the house of God in company. 20. He hath put forth his hands against such as be at peace with him: he hath broken his covenant. 21. The words of his mouth were smoother than butter, but war was in his heart: his words were softer than oil, yet were they drawn swords. 23. Thou, O God, shalt bring them down into the pit of destruction: bloody and deceitful men shall not live out half their days:

Psa. 78:34. When he slew them, then they sought him: and they returned and enquired early after God. 35. And they remembered that God was their rock, and the high God their redeemer. 36. Nevertheless they did flatter him with their mouth, and they lied unto him with their tongues. 37. For their heart was not right with him, neither were they stedfast in his covenant.

Psa. 101:7. He that worketh deceit shall not dwell within my house: he that telleth lies shall not tarry in my sight.

Prov. 7:10. And, behold, there met him a woman with the attire of an harlot, and subtil of heart. 11. (She is loud and stubborn; her feet abide not in her house: 12. Now is she without, now in the streets, and lieth in wait at every corner.) 13. So she caught him, and kissed him, and with an impudent face said unto him, 14. I have peace offerings with me; this day have I paid my vows. 15. Therefore came I forth to meet thee, diligently to seek thy face, and I have found thee. 16. I have decked my bed with coverings of tapestry, with carved works, with fine linen of Egypt. 17. I have perfumed my bed with myrrh, aloes, and cinnamon. 18. Come, let us take our fill of love until the morning: let us solace ourselves with loves. 19. For the goodman is not at home, he is gone a long journey: 20. He hath taken a bag of money with him, and will come home at the day appointed. 21. With her much fair speech she caused him to yield, with the flattering of her lips she forced him.

Prov. 11:9. An hypocrite with his mouth destroyeth his neighbour: but through knowledge shall the just be delivered.

Prov. 14:8. The wisdom of the prudent is to understand his way: but the folly of fools is deceit.

Prov. 15:8. The sacrifice of the wicked is an abomination to the LORD:

Prov. 20:14. It is naught, it is naught, saith the buyer: but when he is gone his way, then he boasteth.

Prov. 21:27. The sacrifice of the wicked is abomination: how much more, when he bringeth it with a wicked mind?

Prov. 23:6. Eat thou not the bread of him that hath an evil eye, neither desire thou his dainty meats: 7. For as he thinketh in his heart, so is he: Eat and drink, saith he to thee; but his heart is not with thee. 8. The morsel which thou hast eaten shalt thou vomit up, and lose thy sweet words.

Prov. 25:19. Confidence in an unfaithful man in time of trouble is like a broken tooth, and a foot out of joint.

Prov. 26:18. As a mad man who casteth firebrands, arrows, and death, 19. So is the man that deceiveth his neighbour, and saith, Am not I in sport? 23. Burning lips and a wicked heart are like a potsherd covered with silver dross. 24. He that hateth dissembleth with his lips, and layeth up deceit within him; 25. When he speaketh fair, believe him not: for there are seven abominations in his heart. 26. Whose hatred is covered by deceit, his wickedness shall be shewed before the whole congregation.

Isa. 1:13. Bring no more vain oblations; incense is an abomination unto me; the new moons and sabbaths, the calling of assemblies, I cannot away with; it is iniquity, even the solemn meeting. 15. And when ye spread forth your hands, I will hide mine eyes from you: yea, when ye make many prayers, I will not hear: your hands are full of blood. vs. 11-14. Isa. 66:3-5.

Isa. 9:17. The Lord shall have no joy in their young men, neither shall have mercy on their fatherless and widows: for every one is an hypocrite and an evildoer, and every mouth speaketh folly.

Isa. 10:6. I will send him against an hypocritical nation, and against the people of my wrath will I give him a charge, to take the spoil, and to take the prey, and to tread them down like the mire of the streets.

Isa. 29:13. This people draw near me with their mouth, and with their lips do honour me, but have removed their heart far from me, and their fear toward me is taught by the precept of men. [Matt. 15:8.] 15. Woe unto them that seek deep to hide their counsel from the LORD, and their works are in the dark, and they say, Who seeth us? and who knoweth us? 16. Surely your turning of things upside down shall be esteemed as the potter's clay:

Isa. 32:5. The vile person shall be no more called liberal, nor the churl said to be bountiful. 6. For the vile person will speak villany, and his heart will work iniquity, to practise hypocrisy, and to utter error against the LORD, to make empty the soul of the hungry, and he will cause the drink of the thirsty to fail.

Isa. 33:14. The sinners in Zion are afraid; fearfulness hath surprised the hypocrites.

Isa. 48:1. Hear ye this, O house of Jacob, which are called by the name of Israel, and are come forth out of the waters of Judah, which swear by the name of the LORD, and make mention of the God of Israel, *but* not in truth, nor in righteousness. 2. For they call themselves of the holy city, and stay themselves upon the God of Israel;

Isa. 58:2. They seek me daily, and delight to know my ways, as a nation that did righteousness, and forsook not the ordinance of their God: they ask of me the ordinances of justice; they take delight in approaching to God. 3. Wherefore have we fasted, *say they*, and thou seest not? *wherefore* have we afflicted our soul, and thou takest no knowledge? Behold, in the day of your fast ye find pleasure, and exact all your labours. 4. Behold, ye fast for strife and debate, and to smite with the fist of wickedness: ye shall not fast as *ye do this* day, to make your voice to be heard on high. 5. Is it such a fast that I have chosen? a day for a man to afflict his soul? *is it* to bow down his head as a bulrush, and to spread sackcloth and ashes *under him?* wilt thou call this a fast, and an acceptable day to the LORD?

Isa. 61:8. For I the LORD love judgment, I hate robbery for burnt offering;

Isa. 65:5. Which say, Stand by thyself, come not near to me; for I am holier than thou. These *are* a smoke in my nose, a fire that burneth all the day.

Jer. 3:10. Her treacherous sister Judah hath not turned unto me with her whole heart, but feignedly, saith the LORD. *v.* 11.

Jer. 5:2. Though they say, The LORD liveth; surely they swear falsely.

Jer. 6:20. To what purpose cometh there to me incense from Sheba, and the sweet cane from a far country? your burnt offerings *are* not acceptable, nor your sacrifices sweet unto me.

Jer. 7:4. Trust ye not in lying words, saying, The temple of the LORD, The temple of the LORD, The temple of the LORD, *are* these. 8. Ye trust in lying words, that cannot profit. 9. Will ye steal, murder, and commit adultery, and swear falsely, and burn incense unto Baal, and walk after other gods whom ye know not; 10. And come and stand before me in this house, which is called by my name, and say, We are delivered to do all these abominations?

Jer. 9:4. Take ye heed every one of his neighbour, and trust ye not in any brother: for every brother will utterly supplant, and every neighbour will walk with slanders. 8. Their tongue *is as* an arrow shot out; it speaketh deceit: *one* speaketh peaceably to his neighbour with his mouth, but in heart he layeth his wait.

Jer. 12:2. Thou hast planted them, yea, they have taken root: they grow, yea, they bring forth fruit: thou *art* near in their mouth, and far from their reins.

Jer. 17:9. The heart *is* deceitful above all *things*, and desperately ¹ wicked: who can know it? [¹ R. V. sick]

Jer. 42:20. Ye dissembled in your hearts, when ye sent me unto the LORD your God,

saying, Pray for us unto the LORD our God; and according unto all that the LORD our God shall say, so declare unto us, and we will do *it. vs.* 21,22.

Lam. 1:2. Among all her lovers she hath none to comfort *her:* all her friends have dealt treacherously with her, they are become her enemies.

Ezek. 14:7. Every one . . . which separateth himself from me, and setteth up his idols in his heart, and putteth the stumblingblock of his iniquity before his face, and cometh to a prophet to enquire of him concerning me; I the LORD will answer him by myself: 8. And I will set my face against that man, and will make him a sign and a proverb, and I will cut him off from the midst of my people; and ye shall know that I *am* the LORD. *v.* 4.

Ezek. 20:39. As for you, O house of Israel, thus saith the Lord GOD; Go ye, serve ye every one his idols, and hereafter *also*, if ye will not hearken unto me: but pollute ye my holy name no more with your gifts, and with your idols. Ezek. 5:11; Hos. 8:13; 9:4.

Ezek. 33:30. The children of thy people still are talking against thee by the walls and in the doors of the houses, and speak one to another, every one to his brother, saying, Come, I pray you, and hear what is the word that cometh forth from the LORD. 31. And they come unto thee as the people cometh, and they sit before thee *as* my people, and they hear thy words, but they will not do them: for with their mouth they shew much love, *but* their heart goeth after their covetousness. 32. And, lo, thou *art* unto them as a very lovely song of one that hath a pleasant voice, and can play well on an instrument: for they hear thy words, but they do them not.

Hos. 6:4. O Judah, what shall I do unto thee? for your goodness *is* as a morning cloud, and as the early dew it goeth away.

Hos. 7:14. They have not cried unto me with their heart, when they howled upon their beds: 16. They return, *but* not to the most High: they are like a deceitful bow:

Hos. 8:2. Israel shall cry unto me, My God, we know thee. 3. Israel hath cast off *the thing that is* good: the enemy shall pursue him.

Hos. 10:1. Israel *is* an empty vine, he bringeth forth fruit unto himself: 4. They have spoken words, swearing falsely in making a covenant:

Hos. 11:12. Ephraim compasseth me about with lies, and the house of Israel with deceit:

Amos 5:21. I hate, I despise your feast days, and I will not smell in your solemn assemblies. 23. Take thou away from me the noise of thy songs; for I will not hear the melody of thy viols. 24. But let judgment run down as waters, and righteousness as a mighty stream. *vs.* 22,25-27.

Obad. 7. The men that were at peace with thee have deceived thee, *and* prevailed against thee; *they that eat* thy bread have laid a wound under thee:

Mic. 3:11. The heads thereof judge for reward, and the priests thereof teach for hire, and the prophets thereof divine for money: yet will they lean upon the LORD, and say, *Is* not the LORD among us? none evil can come upon us.

Mic. 7:5. Trust ye not in a friend, put ye not confidence in a guide: keep the doors of thy mouth from her that lieth in thy bosom.

Zech. 7:5. When ye fasted and mourned in the fifth and seventh *month*, even those seventy years, did ye at all fast unto me, *even* to me? 6. And when ye did eat, and when ye did drink, did not ye eat *for yourselves*, and drink *for yourselves?*

Zech. 13:6. What *are* these wounds ¹ in thine hands? Then he shall answer, *Those* with which I was wounded *in* the house of my friends. [¹ R. V. between thine arms]

Mal. 1:6. If I *be* a master, where *is* my fear? saith the LORD of hosts unto you, O priests, that despise my name. And ye say, Wherein have we despised thy name? 7. Ye offer polluted bread upon mine altar; and ye say, Wherein have we polluted thee? In that ye say, The table of the LORD *is* contemptible. 8. And if ye offer the blind for sacrifice, *is it* not evil? and if ye offer the lame and sick, *is it* not evil? offer it now unto thy governor; will he be pleased with thee, or accept thy person? saith the LORD of hosts. 13. Ye said also, Behold, what a weariness *is it!* and ye have snuffed at it, saith the LORD of hosts; and ye brought *that which was* torn, and the lame, and the sick; thus ye brought an offering: should I accept this of your hand? saith the LORD. 14. But cursed *be* the deceiver, which hath in his flock a male, and voweth, and sacrificeth unto the Lord a corrupt thing: *vs.* 9-12.

Mal. 2:13. This have ye done again, covering the altar of the LORD with tears, with weeping, and with crying out, insomuch that he regardeth not the offering any more, or receiveth *it* with good will at your hand.

Mal. 3:14. Ye have said, It *is* vain to serve God: and what profit *is it* that we have kept his ordinance, and that we have walked mournfully before the LORD of hosts?

Matt. 3:7. O generation of vipers, who hath warned you to flee from the wrath to come? 8. Bring forth therefore fruits meet for repentance:

Matt. 6:1. Take heed that ye do not your alms before men, to be seen of them: otherwise ye have no reward of your Father which is in heaven. 2. Therefore when thou doest *thine* alms, do not sound a trumpet before thee, as the hypocrites do in the synagogues and in the streets, that they may have glory of men. Verily I say unto you, They have their reward. 5. When thou prayest, thou shalt not be as the hypocrites *are:* for they love to pray standing in the synagogues and in the corners of the streets,

that they may be seen of men. Verily I say unto you, They have their reward. 16. When ye fast, be not, as the hypocrites, of a sad countenance: for they disfigure their faces, that they may appear unto men to fast. Verily I say unto you, They have their reward.

24. No man can serve two masters: for either he will hate the one, and love the other; or else he will hold to the one, and despise the other. Ye cannot serve God and mammon.

Matt. 7:5. Thou hypocrite, first cast out the beam out of thine own eye; and then shalt thou see clearly to cast out the mote out of thy brother's eye. 15. Beware of false prophets, which come to you in sheep's clothing, but inwardly they are ravening wolves. 21. Not every one that saith unto me, Lord, Lord, shall enter into the kingdom of heaven; but he that doeth the will of my Father which is in heaven. 22. Many will say to me in that day, Lord, Lord, have we not prophesied in thy name? and in thy name have cast out devils? and in thy name done many wonderful works? 23. And then will I profess unto them, I never knew you: depart from me, ye that work iniquity. Luke 13:26,27.

Matt. 9:13. But go ye and learn what *that* meaneth, I will have mercy, and not sacrifice: for I am not come to call the righteous, but sinners to repentance.

Matt. 15:7. *Ye* hypocrites, well did Esaias prophesy of you, saying, 8. This people draweth nigh unto me with their mouth, and honoureth me with *their* lips; but their heart is far from me. [Mark 7:6.] 9. But in vain they do worship me, teaching *for* doctrines the commandments of men.

Matt. 16:3. ¹ O *ye* hypocrites, ye can discern the face of the sky; but can ye not *discern* the signs of the times? Luke 12:54-56.

[¹ Omitted in R. V.]

Matt. 21:28. But what think ye? A *certain* man had two sons; and he came to the first, and said, Son, go work to day in my vineyard. 29. He answered and said, I will not: but afterward he repented, and went. 30. And he came to the second, and said likewise. And he answered and said, I *go*, sir: and went not. 31. Whether of them twain did the will of *his* father? They say unto him, The first. Jesus saith unto them, Verily I say unto you, That the publicans and the harlots go into the kingdom of God before you. 32. For John came unto you in the way of righteousness, and ye believed him not; but the publicans and the harlots believed him: and ye, when ye had seen *it*, repented not afterward, that ye might believe him.

Matt. 22:12. Friend, how camest thou in hither not having a wedding garment? And he was speechless. 13. Then said the king to the servants, Bind him hand and foot, and take him away, and cast *him* into outer darkness; 18. Jesus perceived their wickedness, and said, Why tempt ye me, *ye hypocrites?*

Matt. 23:2. Saying, The scribes and the Pharisees sit in Moses' seat: 3 All therefore whatsoever they bid you observe, *that* observe and do; but do not ye after their works: for they say, and do not. 4. For they bind heavy burdens and grievous to be borne, and lay *them* on men's shoulders; but they *themselves* will not move them with one of their fingers. 5. All their works they do for to be seen of men: they make broad their phylacteries, and enlarge the borders of their garments, 6. And love the uppermost rooms at feasts, and the chief seats in the synagogues, 7. And greetings in the markets, and to be called of men, Rabbi, Rabbi. 8. But be not ye called Rabbi: for one is your Master, *even* Christ; and all ye are brethren. 9. And call no *man* your father upon the earth: for one is your Father, which is in heaven. 10. Neither be ye called masters: for one is your Master, *even* Christ. 11. But he that is greatest among you shall be your servant. 12. And whosoever shall exalt himself shall be abased; and he that shall humble himself shall be exalted. 13. But woe unto you, scribes and Pharisees, hypocrites! for ye shut up the kingdom of heaven against men: for ye neither go in *yourselves,* neither suffer ye them that are entering to go in. [1] 14. Woe unto you, scribes and Pharisees, hypocrites! for ye devour widows' houses, and for a pretence make long prayer: therefore ye shall receive the greater damnation. 15. Woe unto you, scribes and Pharisees, hypocrites! for ye compass sea and land to make one proselyte, and when he is made, ye make him twofold more the child of hell than yourselves. 16. Woe unto you, *ye* blind guides, which say, Whosoever shall swear by the temple, it is nothing; but whosoever shall swear by the gold of the temple, he is a debtor! 17. *Ye* fools and blind: for whether is greater, the gold, or the temple that sanctifieth the gold? 18. And, Whosoever shall swear by the altar, it is nothing; but whosoever sweareth by the gift that is upon it, he is guilty. 19. *Ye* fools and blind: for whether *is* greater, the gift, or the altar that sanctifieth the gift? 20. Whoso therefore shall swear by the altar, sweareth by it, and by all things thereon. 21. And whoso shall swear by the temple, sweareth by it, and by him that dwelleth therein. 22. And he that shall swear by heaven, sweareth by the throne of God, and by him that sitteth thereon. 23. Woe unto you, scribes and Pharisees, hypocrites! for ye pay tithe of mint and anise and cummin, and have omitted the weightier *matters* of the law, judgment, mercy, and faith: these ought ye to have done, and not to leave the other undone. 24. *Ye* blind guides, which strain [2] at a gnat, and swallow [3] a camel. 25. Woe unto you, scribes and Pharisees, hypocrites! for ye make clean the outside of the cup and of the platter, but within they are full of extortion and excess. 26. *Thou* blind Pharisee, cleanse first that *which is* within the cup and platter, that the outside of them may be clean also. 27. Woe unto you, scribes and Pharisees, hypocrites! for ye are like unto whited sepulchres, which indeed appear beautiful outward, but are within full of dead *men's* bones, and of all uncleanness. 28. Even so ye also outwardly appear righteous unto men, but within ye are full of hypocrisy and iniquity. 29. Woe unto you, scribes and Pharisees, hypocrites! because ye build the tombs of the prophets, and garnish the sepulchres of the righteous, 30. And say, If we had been in the days of our fathers, we would not have been partakers with them in the blood of the prophets. 31. Wherefore ye be witnesses unto yourselves, that ye are the children of them which killed the prophets. 32. Fill ye up then the measure of your fathers. 33. *Ye* serpents, *ye* generation of vipers, how can ye escape the damnation of hell? [R. V. 1 Omitted. 2 out the 3 the]

Matt. 24:50. The lord of that servant shall come in a day when he looketh not for *him,* and in an hour that he is not aware of, 51. And shall cut him asunder, and appoint *him* his portion with the hypocrites: there shall be weeping and gnashing of teeth.

Matt. 25:3. They that *were* foolish took their lamps, and took no oil with them: 41. Then shall he say also unto them on the left hand, Depart from me, ye cursed, into everlasting fire, prepared for the devil and his angels: 42. For I was an hungred, and ye gave me no meat: I was thirsty, and ye gave me no drink: 43. I was a stranger, and ye took me not in: naked, and ye clothed me not: sick, and in prison, and ye visited me not. 44. Then shall they also answer him, saying, Lord, when saw we thee an hungred, or athirst, or a stranger, or naked, or sick, or in prison, and did not minister unto thee? 45. Then shall he answer them, saying, Verily I say unto you, Inasmuch as ye did *it* not to one of the least of these, ye did *it* not to me.

Mark 7:7. Howbeit in vain do they worship me, teaching *for* doctrines the commandments of men. 8. For laying aside the commandment of God, ye hold the tradition of men, *as* the washing of pots and cups: and many other such like things ye do. Matt. 15:7-9.

Mark 12:38. And he said unto them in his doctrine, Beware of the scribes, which love to go in long clothing, and *love* salutations in the marketplaces, 39. And the chief seats in the synagogues, and the uppermost rooms at feasts: 40. Which devour widows' houses, and for a pretence make long prayers: these shall receive greater damnation.

Luke 6:46. Why call ye me, Lord, Lord, and do not the things which I say?

Luke 8:18. Whosoever hath not, from him

shall be taken even that which he seemeth to have.

Luke 11:39. And the Lord said unto him, Now do ye Pharisees make clean the outside of the cup and the platter; but your inward part is full of ravening and wickedness. 42. But woe unto you, Pharisees! for ye tithe mint and rue and all manner of herbs, and pass over judgment and the love of God: these ought ye to have done, and not to leave the other undone. 44. Woe unto you, scribes and Pharisees, hypocrites! for ye are as graves which appear not, and the men that walk over *them* are not aware *of them*. 52. Woe unto you, lawyers! for ye have taken away the key of knowledge: ye entered not in yourselves, and them that were entering in ye hindered. *vs. 39-52.*

Luke 12:1. Beware ye of the leaven of the Pharisees, which is hypocrisy. 2. For there is nothing covered, that shall not be revealed; neither hid, that shall not be known. Matt. 16:6, 12; Mark 8:15.

Luke 13:13. And he laid *his* hands on her: and immediately she was made straight, and glorified God. 14. And the ruler of the synagogue answered with indignation, because that Jesus had healed on the sabbath day, and said unto the people, There are six days in which men ought to work: in them therefore come and be healed, and not on the sabbath day. 15. The Lord then answered him, and said, *Thou* hypocrite, doth not each one of you on the sabbath loose his ox or *his* ass from the stall, and lead *him* away to watering? 16. And ought not this woman, being a daughter of Abraham, whom Satan hath bound, lo, these eighteen years, be loosed from this bond on the sabbath day? 17. And when he had said these things, all his adversaries were ashamed: and all the people rejoiced for all the glorious things that were done by him.

Luke 14:34. Salt *is* good: but if the salt have lost his savour, wherewith shall it be seasoned? *v.* 35; Mark 9:50.

Luke 16:13. No servant can serve two masters: for either he will hate the one, and love the other; or else he will hold to the one, and despise the other. Ye cannot serve God and mammon. 15. Ye are they which justify yourselves before men; but God knoweth your hearts: for that which is highly esteemed among men is abomination in the sight of God.

Luke 18:11. The Pharisee stood and prayed thus with himself, God, I thank thee, that I am not as other men *are*, extortioners, unjust, adulterers, or even as this publican. 12. I fast twice in the week, I give tithes of all that I possess.

Luke 20:46. Beware of the scribes, which desire to walk in long robes, and love greetings in the markets, and the highest seats in the synagogues, and the chief rooms at feasts; 47. Which devour widows' houses, and for a shew make long prayers: the same

shall receive greater ¹ damnation. Matt. 23:14; Mark 12:38-40. [¹ R. V. condemnation]

Luke 21:16. Ye shall be betrayed both by parents, and brethren, and kinsfolks, and friends; and *some* of you shall they cause to be put to death.

John 6:26. Ye seek me, not because ye saw the miracles, but because ye did eat of the loaves, and were filled. 70. Have not I chosen you twelve, and one of you is a devil?

John 7:19. Did not Moses give you the law, and *yet* none of you keepeth the law? Why go ye about to kill me?

John 15:2. Every branch in me that beareth not fruit he taketh away: 6. If a man abide not in me, he is cast forth as a branch, and is withered; and men gather them, and cast *them* into the fire, and they are burned.

Rom. 1:18. The wrath of God is revealed from heaven against all ungodliness and unrighteousness of men, who hold the truth in unrighteousness;

Rom. 2:1. Therefore thou art inexcusable, O man, whosoever thou art that judgest: for wherein thou judgest another, thou condemnest thyself; for thou that judgest doest the same things. 3. And thinkest thou this, O man, that judgest them which do such things, and doest the same, that thou shalt escape the judgment of God? 17. Behold, thou art called a Jew, and restest in the law, and makest thy boast of God, 18. And knowest *his* will, and approvest the things that are more excellent, being instructed out of the law; 19. And art confident that thou thyself art a guide of the blind, a light of them which are in darkness, 20. An instructor of the foolish, a teacher of babes, which hast the form of knowledge and of the truth in the law. 21. Thou therefore which teachest another, teachest thou not thyself? thou that preachest a man should not steal, dost thou steal? 22. Thou that sayest a man should not commit adultery, dost thou commit adultery? thou that abhorrest idols, dost thou commit sacrilege? 23. Thou that makest thy boast of the law, through breaking the law dishonourest thou God? 24. For the name of God is blasphemed among the Gentiles through you, as it is written. 25. For circumcision verily profiteth, if thou keep the law: but if thou be a breaker of the law, thy circumcision is made uncircumcision. 26. Therefore if the uncircumcision keep the righteousness of the law, shall not his uncircumcision be counted for circumcision? 27. And shall not uncircumcision which is by nature, if it fulfil the law, judge thee, who by the letter and circumcision dost transgress the law? 28. For he is not a Jew, which is one outwardly; neither *is that* circumcision, which is outward in the flesh: 29. But he *is* a Jew, which is one inwardly; and circumcision *is that* of the heart, in the spirit, *and* not in the letter; whose praise *is* not of men, but of God.

Rom. 9:6. They *are* not all Israel, which are of Israel : 7. Neither, because they are the seed of Abraham, *are they* all children :

Rom. 16:18. For they that are such serve not our Lord Jesus Christ, but their own belly ; and by good words and fair speeches deceive the hearts of the simple.

1 Cor. 13:1. Though I speak with the tongues of men and of angels, and have not charity, I am become *as* sounding brass, or a tinkling cymbal.

2 Cor. 4:2. But have renounced the hidden things of dishonesty, not walking in craftiness, nor handling the word of God deceitfully ; but by manifestation of the truth commending ourselves to every man's conscience in the sight of God.

2 Cor. 5:12. For we commend not ourselves again unto you, but give you occasion to glory on our behalf, that ye may have somewhat to *answer* them which glory in appearance, and not in heart.

Gal. 6:3. For if a man think himself to be something, when he is nothing, he deceiveth himself.

Phil. 3:2. Beware of dogs, beware of evil workers, beware of the concision. 18. Many walk, of whom I have told you often, and now tell you even weeping, *that they are* the enemies of the cross of Christ : 19. Whose end *is* destruction,

1 Tim. 4:2. Speaking lies in hypocrisy ; having their conscience seared with a hot iron ;

2 Tim. 3:5. Having a form of godliness, but denying the power thereof : 13. Evil men and seducers shall wax worse and worse, deceiving, and being deceived.

Tit. 1:16. They profess that they know God ; but in works they deny *him*, being abominable, and disobedient, and unto every good work reprobate.

Jas. 1:8. A double minded man *is* unstable in all his ways. [Jas. 4:8.] 22. Be ye doers of the word, and not hearers only, deceiving your own selves. 23. For if any be a hearer of the word, and not a doer, he is like unto a man beholding his natural face in a glass : 24. For he beholdeth himself, and goeth his way, and straightway forgetteth what manner of man he was. 26. If any man among you seem to be religious, and bridleth not his tongue, but deceiveth his own heart, this man's religion *is* vain.

Jas. 2:14. What *doth it* profit, my brethren, though a man say he hath faith, and have not works ? can faith save him ? 15. If a brother or sister be naked, and destitute of daily food, 16. And one of you say unto them, Depart in peace, be *ye* warmed and filled ; notwithstanding ye give them not those things which are needful to the body ; what *doth it* profit ? 17. Even so faith, if it hath not works, is dead, being alone. 18. Yea, a man may say, Thou hast faith, and I have works ; shew me thy faith without thy works, and I will shew thee my

faith by my works. 19. Thou believest that there is one God ; thou doest well : the devils also believe, and tremble. 20. But wilt thou know, O vain man, that faith without works is dead ? 21. Was not Abraham our father justified by works, when he had offered Isaac his son upon the altar ? 22. Seest thou how faith wrought with his works, and by works was faith made perfect ? 23. And the scripture was fulfilled which saith, Abraham believed God, and it was imputed unto him for righteousness : and he was called the friend of God. 24. Ye see then how that by works a man is justified, and not by faith only. 25. Likewise also was not Rahab the harlot justified by works, when she had received the messengers, and had sent *them* out another way ? 26. For as the body without the spirit is dead, so faith without works is dead also.

Jas. 3:17. But the wisdom that is from above is first pure, then peaceable, gentle, *and* easy to be intreated, full of mercy and good fruits, without partiality, and without hypocrisy.

1 Pet. 2:1. Laying aside all . . . hypocrisies, 16. As free, and not using *your* liberty for a cloke of maliciousness, but as the servants of God.

2 Pet. 2:1. There shall be false teachers among you, . . . 2. And many shall follow their pernicious ways ; by reason of whom the way of truth shall be evil spoken of. 3. Through covetousness shall they with feigned words make merchandise of you : whose judgment now of a long time lingereth not, and their damnation slumbereth not. 17. These are wells without water, clouds that are carried with a tempest ; to whom the mist of darkness is reserved for ever. 19. While they promise them liberty, they themselves are the servants of corruption : for of whom a man is overcome, of the same is he brought in bondage.

1 John 1:6. If we say that we have fellowship with him, and walk in darkness, we lie, and do not the truth : 10. If we say that we have not sinned, we make him a liar, and his word is not in us.

1 John 2:4. He that saith, I know him, and keepeth not his commandments, is a liar, and the truth is not in him. 9. He that saith he is in the light, and hateth his brother, is in darkness even until now. 19. They went out from us, but they were not of us : for if they had been of us, they would *no doubt* have continued with us : but *they went out*, that they might be made manifest that they were not all of us.

1 John 4:20. If a man say, I love God, and hateth his brother, he is a liar : for he that loveth not his brother whom he hath seen, how can he love God whom he hath not seen ?

Jude 12. These are spots in your feasts of charity, when they feast with you, feeding themselves without fear : clouds *they are* without water, carried about of winds; trees whose fruit withereth, without fruit, twice dead, plucked up by the roots; 13. Raging waves of the sea, foaming out their own shame; wandering stars, to whom is reserved the blackness of darkness for ever.

Rev. 2:9. *I know* the blasphemy of them which say they are Jews, and are not, but *are* the synagogue of Satan. Rev. 3:9.

Rev. 3:1. I know thy works, that thou hast a name that thou livest, and art dead.

See DECEIT; DECEPTION.·

INSTANCES OF: Jacob, in impersonating Esau and deceiving his father, Gen. 27. Jacob's sons, in deception of their father concerning Joseph, Gen. 37:29–35. Joseph's deception of his brethren, Gen. chapters 42–44. Pharaoh, Ex. 8:15,28,29,32; 9:27–35; 10:8–29. Balaam, Jude 11, with Num. chapters 22–24. Delilah, the wife of Samson, Judg. 16. Jael, Judg. 4:8–21. Ehud, Judg. 3:15–25. Rabshakeh, 2 Kin. 18:17–37. Ahaz, Isa. 7:12, with *vs.* 17–25. Johanan, Jer. 42:1–12,20,22. Ishmael, Jer. 41:6,7. The false prophets, Ezek. 13:1–23. Herod, Matt. 2:8. Judas, Matt. 26:25,48; John 12:5,6. Pilate, Matt. 27:24. Pharisees, Matt. 15:1–9; 22:18; Mark 12:13,14; John 8:4–9; 9:24; 19:15. The ruler, Luke 13:14–17. Spies sent to entrap Jesus, Luke 20:21. Priests and Levites, Luke 10: 31,32. Chief priests, John 18:28. Ananias and Sapphira, Acts 5:1–10. Simon Magus, Acts 8:18–23. Peter and other Christians at Antioch, Gal. 2:11–14. Judaizing Christians in Galatia, Gal. 6:13. False teachers at Ephesus, Rev. 2:2.

See CONSPIRACY; TREACHERY.

HYSSOP. An indigenous plant to western Asia and northern Africa, 1 Kin. 4:33. The Israelites used, in sprinkling the blood of the paschal lamb upon the lintels of their doors, Ex. 12:22; in sprinkling blood in purifications, Lev. 14:4,6,51,52; Heb. 9:19. Used in the sacrifices of separation, Num. 19:6. Used in giving Jesus vinegar on the cross, John 19:29.

FIGURATIVE: Of spiritual cleansing, Psa. 51:7.

I

I AM THAT I AM, a name of deity, Ex. 3:14; Rev. 1:4,11,17.

IBHAR, son of David, 2 Sam. 5:15; 1 Chr. 3:6; 14:5.

IBLEAM, a city of Manasseh, Josh. 17:11; Judg. 1:27; 2 Kin. 9:27.

IBNEIAH, a Benjamite, 1 Chr. 9:8.

IBNIJAH, a Benjamite, 1 Chr. 9:8.

IBRI, a Levite, 1 Chr. 24:27.

IBZAN, a Bethlehemite, and judge of Israel, Judg. 12:8–10.

ICE, Job 6:16; 38:29; Psa.147:17; Prov. 25:13.

I-CHABOD, son of Phinehas, and grandson of Eli, 1 Sam. 4:21; 14:3.

ICONIUM. A city of Asia Minor. Paul preaches in, Acts 13:51; 14:21,22; 16:2; is persecuted by the people of, Acts 14:1–6; 2 Tim. 3:11.

ICONOCLASM. Idols to be destroyed, Ex. 23:24; 34:13; Num. 33:52; Deut. 7:5,25,26; 12:1–4; Judg. 2:2; Jer. 50:2. Destroyed by Jacob, Gen. 35:2–4; Moses, Ex. 32:19,20; Gideon, Judg. 6:28–32; David, 2 Sam. 5:21; 1 Chr. 14:12; Jehu, 2 Kin. 10:26–28; Jehoiada, 2 Kin. 11:18; Hezekiah, 2 Kin. 18:3–6; Josiah, 2 Kin. 23:4–20; Asa, 2 Chr. 14:3–5; 15: 8–16; Jehoshaphat, 2 Chr. 17:6; 19:3; Jews, 2 Chr. 30:14; Manasseh, 2 Chr. 33:15.

See IDOLATRY.

IDALAH, a town of Zebulun, Josh. 19:15.

IDBASH, a descendant of Judah, 1 Chr. 4:3.

IDDO. 1. Father of Ahinadab, 1 Kin. 4:14.

2. A descendant of Gershom, 1 Chr. 6:21.

3. A son of Zechariah, 1 Chr. 27:21.

4. A prophet, 2 Chr. 9:29; 12:15; 13:22.

5. Ancestor of Zechariah, Ezra 5:1; 6:14; Zech. 1:1,7.

6. A priest, Neh. 12:4,16.

7. The chief of the Jews established at Casiphia, Ezra 8:17.

IDLENESS. Prov. 6:6. Go to the ant, thou sluggard; consider her ways, and be wise: 9. How long wilt thou sleep, O sluggard? when wilt thou arise out of thy sleep? 10. *Yet* a little sleep, a little slumber, a little folding of the hands to sleep: 11. So shall thy poverty come as one that travelleth, and thy want as an armed man. Prov. 24:33.

Prov. 10:4. He becometh poor that dealeth *with* a slack hand: 5. He that sleepeth in harvest *is* a son that causeth shame. 26. As vinegar to the teeth, and as smoke to the eyes, so *is* the sluggard to them that send him.

Prov. 12:9. *He that is* despised, and hath a servant, *is* better than he that honoureth himself, and lacketh bread. 24. The hand of the diligent shall bear rule: but the slothful shall be under tribute. 27. The slothful *man* roasteth not that which he took in hunting:

Prov. 13:4. The soul of the sluggard desireth, and *hath* nothing:

Prov. 14:23. In all labour there is profit: but the talk of the lips *tendeth* only to penury.

Prov. 15:19. The way of the slothful *man is* as an hedge of thorns:

Prov. 18:9. He also that is slothful in his work is brother to him that is a great waster.

Prov. 19:15. Slothfulness casteth into a deep sleep; and an idle soul shall suffer hunger. 24. A slothful *man* hideth his hand in *his* bosom, and will not so much as bring it to his mouth again.

Prov. 20:4. The sluggard will not plow by reason of the cold; *therefore* shall he beg in harvest, and *have* nothing. 13. Love not sleep, lest thou come to poverty:

Prov. 21:25. The desire of the slothful killeth him; for his hands refuse to labour. 26. He coveteth greedily all the day long:

Prov. 23:21. Drowsiness shall clothe *a* man with rags.

Prov. 24:30. I went by the field of the slothful, and by the vineyard of the man void of understanding; 31. And, lo, it was all grown over with thorns, *and* nettles had covered the face thereof, and the stone wall thereof was broken down. 33. *Yet* a little sleep, a little slumber, a little folding of the hands to sleep: 34. So shall thy poverty come *as* one that travelleth; and thy want as an armed man.

Prov. 26:13. The slothful *man* saith, *There is* a lion in the way; a lion *is* in the streets. [Prov. 22:13.] 14. *As* the door turneth upon his hinges, so *doth* the slothful upon his bed. 15. The slothful hideth his hand in *his* bosom; it grieveth him to bring it again to his mouth. 16. The sluggard *is* wiser in his own conceit than seven men that can render a reason.

Eccl. 4:5. The fool foldeth his hands together, and eateth his own flesh.

Eccl. 10:18. By much slothfulness the building decayeth; and through idleness of the hands the house droppeth through.

Isa. 56:10. His watchmen *are* blind: they are all ignorant, they *are* all dumb dogs, they cannot bark: sleeping, lying down, loving to slumber.

Ezek. 16:49. This was the iniquity of thy sister Sodom, pride, fulness of bread, and abundance of idleness was in her and in her daughters, Luke 19:20–25.

Matt. 20:6. And about the eleventh hour he went out, and found others standing idle, and saith unto them, Why stand ye here all the day idle? 7. They say unto him, Because no man hath hired us.

Acts 17:21. (All the Athenians and strangers which were there spent their time in nothing else, but either to tell, or to hear some new thing.)

2 Thess. 3:10. For even when we were with you, this we commanded you, that if any would not work, neither should he eat. 11. For we hear that there are some which walk among you disorderly, working not at all, but are busybodies.

1 Tim. 5:13. Withal they learn *to be* idle, wandering about from house to house; and not only idle, but tattlers also and busybodies, speaking things which they ought not.

See SLOTHFULNESS; INDUSTRY.

IDOL. Manufacture of, Ex. 20:4; 32:4, 20; Deut. 4:23; Isa. 40:19,20; 44:9–12,17; Hab. 2:18; Acts 19:24,25. Manufacture of, forbidden, Ex. 20:4; 34:17. Made of gold, Ex. 32: 3,4; Psa. 115:4–7; 135:15–17; Isa. 2:20; 30:22; 31:7; Hos. 8:4; silver, Isa. 2:20; 30:22; 31:7; Hos. 8:4; wood and stone, Lev. 26:1; Deut. 4:28; 2 Kin. 19:18; Isa. 37:19; 41:6; 44:13–19; Ezek. 20:32.

Coverings of, Isa. 30:22. Prayer to, unanswered, 1 Kin. 18:25–29; Isa. 16:12. Things offered to, not to be eaten, Ex. 34:15.

See ICONOCLASM.

IDOLATRY, WICKED PRACTICES OF:

Human sacrifices, Lev. 18:21; 20:2–5; Deut. 12:31; 18:10; 2 Kin. 3:26,27; 16:3; 17:17,18; 21:6; 23:10; 2 Chr. 28:3; 33:6; Psa. 106:37,38; Isa. 57:5; Jer. 7:31; 19:4–7; 32:35; Ezek. 16:20,21; 20:26,31; 23:37,39; Mic. 6:7; practices of, relating to the dead, Deut. 14:1; licentiousness of, Ex. 32:6,25; Num. 25:1–3; 1 Kin. 14: 24; 15:12; 2 Kin. 17:30;* 23:7; Ezek. 16:17; 23: 1–44; Hos. 4:12–14; Amos 2:8; Mic. 1:7; Rom. 1:24,26,27; 1 Cor. 10:7,8; 1 Pet. 4:3,4; Rev. 2: 14,20–22; 9:20,21; 14:8; 17:1–6.

OTHER CUSTOMS OF: Offered burnt offerings, Ex. 32:6; 1 Kin. 18:26; Acts 14:13; libations, Isa. 57:6; 65:11; Jer. 7:18; 19:13; 32: 29; 44:17,19,25; Ezek. 20:28; of wine, Deut. 32:38; of blood, Psa. 16:4; Zech. 9:7; meat offerings, Isa. 57:6; Jer. 7:18; 44:17; Ezek. 16:19; peace offerings, Ex. 32:6.

Incense burned on altars, 1 Kin. 12:33; 2 Chr. 30:14; 34:25; Isa. 65:3; Jer. 1:16; 11:12, 17; 44:3; 48:35; Ezek. 16:18; 23:41; Hos. 11:2. Prayers to idols, Judg. 10:14; Isa. 44:17; 45: 20; 46:7; Jonah 1:5. Praise, Judg. 16:24; Dan. 5:4.

Singing and dancing, Ex. 32:18,19. Music, Dan. 3:5–7. Cutting the flesh, 1 Kin. 18:28; Jer. 41:5. Kissing, 1 Kin. 19:18; Hos. 13:2; Job 31:27. Bowing, 1 Kin. 19:18; 2 Kin. 5:18. Tithes and gifts, 2 Kin. 23:11; Dan. 11:38; Amos 4:4,5.

ANNUAL FEASTS: 1 Kin. 12:32; Ezek. 18: 6,11,12,15; 22:9; Dan. 3:2,3.

OBJECTS OF: Sun, moon, and stars, Deut. 4:19; 2 Kin. 17:16; 21:3,5; 2 Chron. 33: 3,5; Job 31:26–28; Jer. 7:17–20; 8:2; Ezek. 8: 15,16; Zeph. 1:4,5; Acts 7:42. Images of angels, Col. 2:18; animals, Rom. 1:23. Gods of Egypt, Ex. 12:12. Golden calf, Ex. 32:4. Brazen serpent, 2 Kin. 18:4. Net and drag, Hab. 1:16. Pictures, Num. 33:52; Isa. 2:16. Pictures on walls, Ezek. 8:10. Earrings, Gen. 35:4.

See SHRINE.

DENUNCIATIONS AGAINST: Gen. 35:2. Then Jacob said unto his household, and to all that *were* with him, Put away the strange gods that *are* among you, and be clean, and change your garments:

Ex. 20:3. Thou shalt have no other gods before me. 4. Thou shalt not make unto thee any graven image, or any likeness *of any thing* that *is* in heaven above, or that *is* in the earth beneath, or that *is* in the water under the earth: 5. Thou shalt not bow down thyself to them, nor serve them: for I the LORD thy God *am* a jealous God, visiting the iniquity of the fathers upon the children unto the third and fourth *generation* of them that hate me; 6. And shewing mercy unto thousands of them that love me, and keep my commandments. 23. Ye shall not make with me gods of silver, neither shall ye make unto you gods of gold. Deut. 5:7–9.

Ex. 23:13. Make no mention of the name of other gods, neither let it be heard out of thy mouth. 1 Cor. 10:7.

*Succoth-benoth in the text implies unmentionable licentiousness.

Lev. 19:4. Turn ye not unto idols, nor make to yourselves molten gods: I *am* the LORD your God.

Lev. 26:1. Make you no idols nor graven image, neither rear you up a standing image, neither shall ye set up *any* image of stone in your land, to bow down unto it: for I *am* the LORD your God.   30. I will destroy your high places, and cut down your images, and cast your carcases upon the carcases of your idols, and my soul shall abhor you.   Deut. 16:21,22.

Deut. 4:15. Take ye therefore good heed unto yourselves; for ye saw no manner of similitude on the day *that* the LORD spake unto you in Horeb out of the midst of the fire: 16. Lest ye corrupt *yourselves,* and make you a graven image, the similitude of any figure, the likeness of male or female, 19. Lest thou... when thou seest the sun, and the moon, and the stars, *even* all the host of heaven, shouldest be driven to worship them, and serve them, which the LORD thy God hath divided unto all nations under the whole heaven.   *vs.* 15–23; Deut. 4:25–28; 11: 16,17,28;   28:15–68;   30:17,18;   31:16–21,29;   32: 15–26; 1 Kin. 9:6–9.

Deut. 12:31. Thou shalt not do so unto the LORD thy God: for every abomination to the LORD, which he hateth, have they done unto their gods; for even their sons and their daughters they have burnt in the fire to their gods.

Deut. 27:15. Cursed *be* the man that maketh *any* graven or molten image, an abomination unto the LORD, the work of the hands of the craftsman, and putteth *it* in *a* secret *place.*   Ex. 34:17.

1 Sam. 15:23. For rebellion *is as* the sin of witchcraft, and stubbornness *is as* iniquity and idolatry.   Because thou hast rejected the word of the LORD, he hath also rejected thee from *being* king.

Job 31:26. If I beheld the sun, when it shined, or the moon walking *in* brightness; 27. And my heart hath been secretly enticed, or my mouth hath kissed my hand: 28. This also *were* an iniquity *to be punished* by the judge: for I should have ¹denied the God *that is* above.   [¹ R. V. lied to]

Psa. 16:4. Their sorrows shall be multiplied *that* hasten *after* another *God:* their drink offerings of blood will I not offer, nor take up their names into my lips.

Psa. 44:20. If we have forgotten the name of our God, or stretched out our hands to a strange god;   21. Shall not God search this out?

Psa. 59:8. But thou, O LORD, shalt laugh at them; thou shalt have all the heathen in derision.

Psa. 79:6. Pour out thy wrath upon the heathen that have not known thee, and upon the kingdoms that have not called upon thy name.

Psa. 81:9. There shall no strange God be in thee; neither shalt thou worship any strange God.

Psa. 97:7. Confounded be all they that serve graven images, that boast themselves of idols:

Isa. 42:17. They shall be turned back, they shall be greatly ashamed, that trust in graven images, that say to the molten images, Ye *are* our gods.   Isa. 45:16.

Joel 3:12. Let the heathen be wakened, and come up to the valley of Jehoshaphat: for there will I sit to judge all the heathen round about.

Jonah 2:8. They that observe lying vanities forsake their own mercy.

Mic. 5:15. I will execute vengeance in anger and fury upon the heathen, such as they have not heard.

Hab. 1:16. They sacrifice unto their net, and burn incense unto their drag;

Acts 15:29. That ye abstain from meats offered to idols,   *v.* 20; 1 Cor. 8:1–13.

Acts 17:16. Now while Paul waited for them at Athens, his spirit was stirred in him, when he saw the city wholly given to idolatry.

Rom. 1:25. Who changed the truth of God into a lie, and worshipped and served the creature more than the Creator,

1 Cor. 6:9. Be not deceived: neither fornicators, nor idolaters, . . . 10. . . . shall inherit the kingdom of God.

1 Cor. 10:14. My dearly beloved, flee from idolatry.   20. But *I say,* that the things which the Gentiles sacrifice, they sacrifice to devils, and not to God: and I would not that ye should have fellowship with devils. *vs.* 21,22.

1 John 5:21. Little children, keep yourselves from idols.

Rev. 21:8. Idolaters . . . shall have their part in the lake which burneth with fire and brimstone: which is the second death.   Rev. 22:15.

See ICONOCLASM.

WARNINGS AGAINST, AND PUNISHMENTS OF: Deut. 17:2–5; 2 Chr. 28:23; Neh. 9:27–37; Psa. 78:58–64; 106:34–42; Isa. 1: 29–31; 2:6–22; 30:22; 57:3–13; 65:3–7; Jer. 1:15, 16; 3:1–11; 5:1–17; 7; 8:1,2,19; 13:9–27; 16; 17: 1–6; 18:13–15; 19; 22:9; 32:35; 44; 48:8; Ezek. 6; 7:19; 8:5–18; 9; 14:1–14; 16; 20; 22:4; 23; 44: 10–12; Hos. 1:2; 2:2–5; 4:12–19; 5:1–3; 8:5–14; 9:10; 10; 11:2; 12:11–14; 13:1–4; 14:8; Amos 3: 14; 4:4,5; 5:5; Mic. 1:1–9; 5:12–14; 6:16; Zeph. 1; Mal. 2:11–13.

PROPHECIES RELATING TO: Ex. 12:12. For I will pass through the land of Egypt this night, and will smite all the firstborn in the land of Egypt, both man and beast; and against all the gods of Egypt I will execute judgment: I *am* the LORD.   Num. 33:4.

Isa. 2:18. The idols he shall utterly abolish. 20. In that day a man shall cast his idols of silver, and his idols of gold, which they made *each one* for himself to worship, to the moles and to the bats;   Isa. 31:7.

Isa. 17:7. At that day shall a man look to his Maker, and his eyes shall have respect to the Holy One of Israel.   8. And he shall not look to the altars, the work of his hands, neither shall respect *that* which his fingers have made, either the groves, or the images.

Isa. 19:1. Behold, the LORD rideth upon a swift cloud, and shall come into Egypt: and the idols of Egypt shall be moved at his presence, and the heart of Egypt shall melt in the midst of it.

Isa. 27:9. When he maketh all the stones of the altar as chalkstones that are beaten in sunder, the groves and images shall not stand up.

Jer. 10:11. The gods that have not made the heavens and the earth, *even* they shall perish from the earth, 15. They *are* vanity, *and* the work of errors: in the time of their visitation they shall perish.

Jer. 51:44. And I will punish Bel in Babylon, and I will bring forth out of his mouth that which he hath swallowed up: and the nations shall not flow together any more unto him: 47. I will do judgment upon the graven images of Babylon: *v.* 52; Isa. 21:9.

Ezek. 43:7. And he said unto me, Son of man, the place of my throne, and the place of the soles of my feet, where I will dwell in the midst of the children of Israel for ever, and my holy name, shall the house of Israel no more defile, *neither* they, nor their kings, by their whoredom, nor by the carcases of their kings in their high places. 8. In their setting of their threshold by my thresholds, and their post by my posts, and the wall between me and them, they have even defiled my holy name by their abominations that they have committed: wherefore I have consumed them in mine anger. 9. Now let them put away their whoredom, and the carcases of their kings, far from me, and I will dwell in the midst of them for ever.

Hos. 10:2. Their heart is divided; now shall they be found faulty: he shall break down their altars, he shall spoil their images.

Mic. 5:13. Thy graven images also will I cut off, and thy standing images out of the midst of thee; and thou shalt no more worship the work of thine hands.

Zeph. 2:11. The Lord *will be* terrible unto them: for he will famish all the gods of the earth;

Zech. 13:2. I will cut off the names of the idols out of the land, and they shall no more be remembered: and also I will cause the prophets and the unclean spirit to pass out of the land.

FOLLY OF: Deut. 4:28. And there ye shall serve gods, the work of men's hands, wood and stone, which neither see, nor hear, nor eat, nor smell.

1 Kin. 18:27. Elijah mocked them, and said, Cry aloud: for he *is* a god; either he is talking, or he is pursuing, or he is in a journey, *or* peradventure he sleepeth, and must be awaked. Judg. 6:31; 1 Sam. 5:3,4.

2 Chr. 25:15. Wherefore the anger of the LORD was kindled against Amaziah, and he sent unto him a prophet, which said unto him, Why hast thou sought after the gods of the people, which could not deliver their own people out of thine hand? 1 Sam. 12:21; 2 Kin. 3:13; Isa. 16:12; 36:18.

2 Chr. 28:22. And in the time of his distress did he trespass yet more against the LORD: this *is that* king Ahaz. 23. For he sacrificed unto the gods of Damascus, which smote him: and he said, Because the gods of the kings of Syria help them, *therefore* will I sacrifice to them, that they may help me. But they were the ruin of him, and of all Israel.

Psa. 115:4. Their idols *are* silver and gold, the work of men's hands. 5. They have mouths, but they speak not: eyes have they, but they see not: 8. They that make them are like unto them; *so is* every one that trusteth in them. Psa. 96:5; 135:15–18; Isa. 2:8.

Isa. 40:12. Who hath measured the waters in the hollow of his hand, and meted out heaven with the span, and comprehended the dust of the earth in a measure, and weighed the mountains in scales, and the hills in a balance? 13. Who hath directed the Spirit of the LORD, or *being* his counsellor hath taught him? 14. With whom took he counsel, and *who* instructed him, and taught him in the path of judgment, and taught him knowledge, and shewed to him the way of understanding? 15. Behold, the nations *are* as a drop of a bucket, and are counted as the small dust of the balance: behold, he taketh up the isles as a very little thing. 16. And Lebanon *is* not sufficient to burn, nor the beasts thereof sufficient for a burnt offering. 17. All nations before him *are* as nothing; and they are counted to him less than nothing, and vanity. 18. To whom then will ye liken God? or what likeness will ye compare unto him? 19. The workman melteth a graven image, and the goldsmith spreadeth it over with gold, and casteth silver chains. 20. He that *is* so impoverished that he hath no oblation chooseth a tree *that* will not rot; he seeketh unto him a cunning workman to prepare a graven image, *that* shall not be moved. 21. Have ye not known? have ye not heard? hath it not been told you from the beginning? have ye not understood from the foundations of the earth? 22. *It is* he that sitteth upon the circle of the earth, and the inhabitants thereof *are* as grasshoppers; that stretcheth out the heavens as a curtain, and spreadeth them out as a tent to dwell in: 23. That bringeth the princes to nothing; he maketh the judges of the earth as vanity. 24. Yea, they shall not be planted; yea, they shall not be sown: yea, their stock shall not take root in the earth: and he shall also blow upon them, and they shall wither, and the whirlwind shall take them away as stubble. 25. To whom then will ye liken me, or shall I be equal? saith the Holy One. 26. Lift up your eyes on high, and behold who hath created these *things*, that bringeth out their host by number: he calleth them all by names by the greatness of his might, for that *he is* strong in power; not one faileth.

Isa. 41:23. Shew the things that are to come hereafter, that we may know that ye *are* gods . yea, do good, or do evil, that we may be dismayed, and behold *it* together. 24. Behold, ye *are* of nothing, and your work of nought: an abomination *is he that* chooseth you. *vs.* 26-29.

Isa. 44:19. None considereth in his heart, neither *is there* knowledge nor understanding to say, I have burned part of it in the fire; yea, also I have baked bread upon the coals thereof; I have roasted flesh, and eaten *it:* and shall I make th residue thereof an abomination? shall I fal down to the stock of a tree? *vs.* 9-20.

Isa. 45:20. They have no knowledge that set up the wood of their graven image, and pray unto a god *that* cannot save.

Isa. 46:1. Bel boweth down, Nebo stoopeth, their idols were upon the beasts, and upon the cattle: your carriages *were* heavy loaden; *they are* a burden to the weary *beast*. 2. They stoop, they bow down together; they could not deliver the burden, but themselves are gone into captivity. 6. They lavish gold out of the bag, and weigh silver in the balance, *and* hire a goldsmith; and he maketh it a god: they fall down, yea, they worship. 7. They bear him upon the shoulder, they carry him, and set him in his place, and he standeth; from his place shall he not remove: yea, *one* shall cry unto him, yet can he not answer, nor save him out of his trouble.

Isa. 47:13. Thou art wearied in the multitude of thy counsels. Let now the astrologers, the stargazers, the monthly prognosticators, stand up, and save thee from *these things* that shall come upon thee. 14. Behold, they shall be as stubble; the fire shall burn them; they shall not deliver themselves from the power of the flame: *there shall* not *be* a coal to warm at, *nor* fire to sit before it. *vs.* 12-15; 2 Kin. 19:18; Isa. 37:19; Zech. 10:2.

Isa. 57:13. When thou criest, let thy companies deliver thee; but the wind shall carry them all away; vanity shall take *them:*

Jer. 2:28. Where *are* thy gods that thou hast made thee? let them arise, if they can save thee in the time of thy trouble: for *according to* the number of thy cities are thy gods, O Judah. Deut. 32:37,38; Judg. 10:14.

Jer. 10:5. They *are* upright as the palm tree, but speak not: they must needs be borne, because they cannot go. Be not afraid of them; for they cannot do evil, neither also *is it* in them to do good. *vs.* 3-16; Jer. 48:13; 51:17; Hab. 2:18,19.

Jer. 11:12. Then shall the cities of Judah and inhabitants of Jerusalem go, and cry unto the gods unto whom they offer incense:

but they shall not save them at all in the time of their trouble.

Jer. 14:22. Are there *any* among the vanities of the Gentiles that can cause rain?

Jer. 16:19. O LORD, my strength, and my fortress, and my refuge in the day of affliction, the Gentiles shall come unto thee from the ends of the earth, and shall say, Surely our fathers have inherited lies, vanity, and *things* wherein *there is* no profit. 20. Shall a man make gods unto himself, and they *are* no gods?

Hos. 8:5. Thy calf, O Samaria, hath cast *thee* off; mine anger is kindled against them: how long *will it be* ere they attain to innocency? 6. For from Israel *was* it also: the workman made it; therefore it *is* not God: but the calf of Samaria shall be broken in pieces. Ex. 32:20; Psa. 106:20.

Acts 14:15. We also are men of like passions with you, and preach unto you that ye should turn from these vanities unto the living God,

Acts 17:22. Then Paul stood in the midst of Mars' hill, and said, Ye men of Athens, I perceive that in all things ye are too superstitious. 23. For as I passed by, and beheld your devotions, I found an altar with this inscription, TO THE UNKNOWN GOD. 29. We ought not to think that the Godhead is like unto gold, or silver, or stone, graven by art and man's device.

Rom. 1:22. Professing themselves to be wise, they became fools, 23. And changed the glory of the uncorruptible God into an image made like to corruptible man, and to birds, and fourfooted beasts, and creeping things.

1 Cor. 8:4. We know that an idol *is* nothing in the world, and that *there is* none other God but one. *with* 8:5; 10:19.

1 Cor. 12:2. Ye were Gentiles, carried away unto these dumb idols, even as ye were led.

Gal. 4:8. When ye knew not God, ye did service unto them which by nature are no gods.

Rev. 9:20. And the rest of the men which were not killed by these plagues yet repented not of the works of their hands, that they should not worship devils, and idols of gold, and silver, and brass, and stone, and of wood: which neither can see, nor hear, nor walk: Deut. 4:28; Dan. 5:23.

IDUMEA. See EDOM.

IFS, OF THE BIBLE. See BLESSINGS, CONTINGENT.

IGAL. 1. One of the spies sent to Canaan, Num. 13:7.

2. Called also JOEL. One of David's guards, 2 Sam. 23:36; 1 Chr. 11:38.

IGDALIAH, father of Hanan, Jer. 35:4.

IGEAL, son of Shemaiah, 1 Chr. 3:22.

IGNORANCE. Job 8:9. (For we *are but of* yesterday, and know nothing, because our days upon earth *are* a shadow:)

Job 11:7. Canst thou by searching find out God? canst thou find out the Almighty unto perfection? 8. *It is* as high as heaven; what canst thou do? deeper than hell; what canst thou know? 12. Vain man would be wise, though man be born *like* a wild ass's colt.

Job 28:12. Where shall wisdom be found? and where *is* the place of understanding? 13. Man knoweth not the price thereof; neither is it found in the land of the living. 20. Whence then cometh wisdom? and where *is* the place of understanding? 21. Seeing it is hid from the eyes of all living,

Job 36:26. God *is* great, and we know *him* not, neither can the number of his years be searched out. 29. Can *any* understand the spreadings of the clouds, *or* the noise of his tabernacle?

Job 37:5. God thundereth marvellously with his voice; great things doeth he, which we cannot comprehend. 15. Dost thou know when God disposed them, and caused the light of his cloud to shine? 16. Dost thou know the balancings of the clouds, the wondrous works of him which is perfect in knowledge? 19. Teach us what we shall say unto him; *for* we cannot order *our* speech by reason of darkness. 23. *Touching* the Almighty, we cannot find him out: chapters 38; 39.

Psa. 139:6. *Such* knowledge *is* too wonderful for me; it is high, I cannot *attain* unto it.

Prov. 7:6. For at the window of my house I looked through my casement, 7. And beheld among the simple ones, I discerned among the youths, a young man void of understanding, 8. Passing through the street near her corner; and he went the way to her house, 9. In the twilight, in the evening, in the black and dark night: 10. And, behold, there met him a woman *with* the attire of an harlot, and subtil of heart. 11. (She *is* loud and stubborn; her feet abide not in her house: 12. Now *is she* without, now in the streets, and lieth in wait at every corner.) 13. So she caught him, and kissed him, *and* with an impudent face said unto him, 14. *I have* peace offerings with me; this day have I paid my vows. 15. Therefore came I forth to meet thee, diligently to seek thy face, and I have found thee. 16. I have decked my bed with coverings of tapestry, with carved *works*, with fine linen of Egypt. 17. I have perfumed my bed with myrrh, aloes, and cinnamon. 18. Come, let us take our fill of love until the morning: let us solace ourselves with loves. 19. For the goodman *is* not at home, he is gone a long journey: 20. He hath taken a bag of money with him, *and* will come home at the day appointed. 21. With her much fair speech she caused him to yield, with the flattering of her lips she forced him. 22. He goeth after her straightway, as an ox goeth to the slaughter, or as a fool to the correction of the stocks; 23. Till a dart strike through his

liver; as a bird hasteth to the snare, and knoweth not that it *is* for his life.

Prov. 8:5. O ye simple, understand wisdom: and, ye fools, be ye of an understanding heart.

Prov. 9:14. For she sitteth at the door of her house, on a seat in the high places of the city, 15. To call passengers who go right on their ways: 16. Whoso *is* simple, let him turn in hither: and *as for* him that wanteth understanding, she saith to him, 17. Stolen waters are sweet, and bread *eaten* in secret is pleasant. 18. But he knoweth not that the dead *are* there; *and that* her guests *are* in the depths of hell.

Prov. 19:2. Also, *that* the soul *be* without knowledge, *it is* not good; and he that hasteth with *his* feet sinneth.

Prov. 20:24. Man's goings *are* of the Lord; how can a man then understand his own way?

Prov. 22:3. A prudent *man* foreseeth the evil, and hideth himself: but the simple pass on, and are punished. Prov. 27:12.

Prov. 27:1. Boast not thyself of to morrow; for thou knowest not what a day may bring forth.

Prov. 30:4. Who hath ascended up into heaven, or descended? who hath gathered the wind in his fists? who hath bound the waters in a garment? who hath established all the ends of the earth? what *is* his name, and what *is* his son's name, if thou canst tell?

Eccl. 3:11. He hath made every *thing* beautiful in his time: also he hath set the world in their heart, so that no man can find out the work that God maketh from the beginning to the end.

Eccl. 6:11. Seeing there be many things that increase vanity, what *is* man the better? 12. For who knoweth what *is* good for man in *this* life, all the days of his vain life which he spendeth as a shadow? for who can tell a man what shall be after him under the sun?

Eccl. 7:23. I said, I will be wise; but it *was* far from me. 24. That which is far off, and exceeding deep, who can find it out?

Eccl. 8:6. Because to every purpose there is time and judgment, therefore the misery of man *is* great upon him. 7. For he knoweth not that which shall be: for who can tell him when it shall be? 17. I beheld all the work of God, that a man cannot find out the work that is done under the sun: because though a man labour to seek *it* out, yet he shall not find *it*; yea farther; though a wise *man* think to know *it*, yet shall he not be able to find *it*.

Eccl. 9:12. For man also knoweth not his time: as the fishes that are taken in an evil net, and as the birds that are caught in the snare; so *are* the sons of men snared in an evil time, when it falleth suddenly upon them.

Eccl. 11:5. As thou knowest not what *is* the way of the spirit, *nor* how the bones *do grow* in the womb of her that is with child: even so thou knowest not the works of God who maketh all.

Jer. 10:23. O LORD, I know that the way of man *is* not in himself: *it is* not in man that walketh to direct his steps.

John 13:7. Jesus answered and said unto him, What I do thou knowest not now; but thou shalt know hereafter.

Acts 1:7. It is not for you to know the times or the seasons, which the Father hath put in his own power.

Acts 17:23. For as I passed by, and beheld your devotions, I found an altar with this inscription, TO THE UNKNOWN GOD. Whom therefore ye ignorantly worship, him declare I unto you. 30. And the times of this ignorance God winked at; but now commandeth all men everywhere to repent:

Rom. 8:24. For we are saved by hope: but hope that is seen is not hope: for what a man seeth, why doth he yet hope for? 25. But if we hope for that we see not, *then* do we with patience wait for *it*. 26. Likewise the Spirit also helpeth our infirmities: for we know not what we should pray for as we ought: but the Spirit itself maketh intercession for us with groanings which cannot be uttered.

1 Cor. 2:7. But we speak the wisdom of God in a mystery, *even* the hidden *wisdom*, which God ordained before the world unto our glory: 8. Which none of the princes of this world knew: for had they known *it*, they would not have crucified the Lord of glory. 9. But as it is written, Eye hath not seen, nor ear heard, neither have entered into the heart of man, the things which God hath prepared for them that love him. 10. But God hath revealed *them* unto us by his Spirit: for the Spirit searcheth all things, yea, the deep things of God.

1 Cor. 3:19. For the wisdom of this world is foolishness with God. For it is written, He taketh the wise in their own craftiness.

1 Cor. 13:9. We know in part, and we prophesy in part. 12. Now we see through a glass, darkly; but then face to face: now I know in part;

Jas. 1:5. If any of you lack wisdom, let him ask of God, that giveth to all *men* liberally, and upbraideth not; and it shall be given him. 6. But let him ask in faith, nothing ¹ wavering. For he that ² wavereth is like a wave of the sea driven with the wind and tossed. [R. V. ¹ doubting ² doubteth]

See KNOWLEDGE; WISDOM.

SINS OF: Gen. 20:1. And Abraham journeyed from thence toward the south country, and dwelt between Kadesh and Shur, and sojourned in Gerar. 2. And Abraham said of Sarah his wife, She *is* my sister: and Abimelech king of Gerar sent, and took Sarah. 3. But God came to Abimelech in a dream by night, and said to him, Behold, thou *art but* a dead man, for the woman which thou hast taken; for she *is* a man's

wife. 4. But Abimelech had not come near her: and he said, LORD, wilt thou slay also a righteous nation? 5. Said he not unto me, She *is* my sister? and she, even she herself said, He *is* my brother: in the integrity of my heart and innocency of my hands have I done this. 6. And God said unto him in a dream, Yea, I know that thou didst this in the integrity of thy heart; for I also withheld thee from sinning against me: therefore suffered I thee not to touch her. 7. Now therefore restore the man *his* wife; for he *is* a prophet, and he shall pray for thee, and thou shalt live: and if thou restore *her* not, know thou that thou shalt surely die, thou, and all that *are* thine.

Lev. 4:1. And the LORD spake unto Moses, saying, 2. Speak unto the children of Israel, saying, If a soul shall sin through ignorance against any of the commandments of the LORD *concerning things* which ought not to be done, and shall do against any of them: 3. If the priest that is anointed do sin according to the sin of the people; then let him bring for his sin, which he hath sinned, a young bullock without blemish unto the LORD for a sin offering. 4. And he shall bring the bullock unto the door of the tabernacle of the congregation before the LORD: and shall lay his hand upon the bullock's head, and kill the bullock before the LORD. 5. And the priest that is anointed shall take of the bullock's blood, and bring it to the tabernacle of the congregation: 6. And the priest shall dip his finger in the blood, and sprinkle of the blood seven times before the LORD, before the vail of the sanctuary. 7. And the priest shall put *some* of the blood upon the horns of the altar of sweet incense before the LORD, which *is* in the tabernacle of the congregation; and shall pour all the blood of the bullock at the bottom of the altar of the burnt offering, which *is at* the door of the tabernacle of the congregation. 8. And he shall take off from it all the fat of the bullock for the sin offering; the fat that covereth the inwards, and all the fat that *is* upon the inwards, 9. And the two kidneys, and the fat that *is* upon them, which *is* by the flanks, and the caul above the liver, with the kidneys, it shall he take away, 10. As it was taken off from the bullock of the sacrifice of peace offerings: and the priest shall burn them upon the altar of the burnt offering. 11. And the skin of the bullock, and all his flesh, with his head, and with his legs, and his inwards, and his dung, 12. Even the whole bullock shall he carry forth without the camp unto a clean place, where the ashes are poured out, and burn him on the wood with fire: where the ashes are poured out shall he be burnt. 13. And if the whole congregation of Israel sin through ignorance, and the thing be hid from the eyes of the assembly, and they have done *somewhat against* any of the commandments of the LORD *concerning things* which should not be done, and are guilty ; 14. When the sin, which they have sinned against it, is known, then the congregation shall offer a young bullock for the sin, and bring him before the tabernacle of the congregation. 15. And the elders of the congregation shall lay their hands upon the head of the bullock before the LORD : and the bullock shall be killed before the LORD. 16. And the priest that is anointed shall bring of the bullock's blood to the tabernacle of the congregation : 17. And the priest shall dip his finger *in some* of the blood, and sprinkle *it* seven times before the LORD, *even* before the vail. 18. And he shall put *some* of the blood upon the horns of the altar which *is* before the LORD, that *is* in the tabernacle of the congregation, and shall pour out all the blood at the bottom of the altar of the burnt offering, which *is at* the door of the tabernacle of the congregation. 19. And he shall take all his fat from him, and burn *it* upon the altar. 20. And he shall do with the bullock as he did with the bullock for a sin offering, so shall he do with this : and the priest shall make an atonement for them, and it shall be forgiven them. 21. And he shall carry forth the bullock without the camp, and burn him as he burned the first bullock : it *is* a sin offering for the congregation. 22. When a ruler hath sinned, and done *somewhat* through ignorance *against* any of the commandments of the LORD his God *concerning things* which should not be done, and is guilty ; 23. Or if his sin, wherein he hath sinned, come to his knowledge; he shall bring his offering, a kid of the goats, a male without blemish : 24. And he shall lay his hand upon the head of the goat, and kill it in the place where they kill the burnt offering before the LORD : it *is* a sin offering. 25. And the priest shall take of the blood of the sin offering with his finger, and put *it* upon the horns of the altar of burnt offering, and shall pour out his blood at the bottom of the altar of burnt offering. 26. And he shall burn all his fat upon the altar, as the fat of the sacrifice of peace offerings : and the priest shall make an atonement for him as concerning his sin, and it shall be forgiven him. 27. And if any one of the common people sin through ignorance, while he doeth *somewhat against* any of the commandments of the LORD *concerning things* which ought not to be done, and be guilty ; 28. Or if his sin, which he hath sinned, come to his knowledge ; then he shall bring his offering, a kid of the goats, a female without blemish, for his sin which he hath sinned. 29. And he shall lay his hand upon the head of the sin offering, and slay the sin offering in the place of the burnt offering. 30. And the priest shall take of the blood thereof with his finger, and put *it* upon the horns of the altar of burnt offering, and shall pour out all the blood thereof at the bottom of the

altar. 31. And he shall take away all the fat thereof, as the fat is taken away from off the sacrifice of peace offerings; and the priest shall burn *it* upon the altar for a sweet savour unto the LORD ; and the priest shall make an atonement for him, and it shall be forgiven him. 32. And if he bring a lamb for a sin offering, he shall bring it a female without blemish. 33. And he shall lay his hand upon the head of the sin offering, and slay it for a sin offering in the place where they kill the burnt offering. 34. And the priest shall take of the blood of the sin offering with his finger, and put *it* upon the horns of the altar of burnt offering, and shall pour out all the blood thereof at the bottom of the altar : 35. And he shall take away all the fat thereof, as the fat of the lamb is taken away from the sacrifice of the peace offerings; and the priest shall burn them upon the altar, according to the offerings made by fire unto the LORD : and the priest shall make an atonement for his sin that he hath committed, and it shall be forgiven him.

Lev. 5:4. If a soul swear, pronouncing with *his* lips to do evil, or to do good, whatsoever *it be* that a man shall pronounce with an oath, and it be hid from him ; when he knoweth *of it*, then he shall be guilty in one of these. 5. And it shall be, when he shall be guilty in one of these *things*, that he shall confess that he hath sinned in that *thing :* 6. And he shall bring his trespass offering unto the LORD for his sin which he hath sinned, a female from the flock, a lamb, or a kid of the goats, for a sin offering ; and the priest shall make an atonement for him concerning his sin. 7. And if he be not able to bring a lamb, then he shall bring for his trespass, which he hath committed, two turtledoves, or two young pigeons, unto the LORD ; one for a sin offering, and the other for a burnt offering. 8. And he shall bring them unto the priest, who shall offer *that* which *is* for the sin offering first, and wring off his head from his neck, but shall not divide *it* asunder : 9. And he shall sprinkle of the blood of the sin offering upon the side of the altar ; and the rest of the blood shall be wrung out at the bottom of the altar : it *is* a sin offering. 10. And he shall offer the second *for* a burnt offering, according to the manner : and the priest shall make an atonement for him for his sin which he hath sinned, and it shall be forgiven him. 11. But if he be not able to bring two turtledoves, or two young pigeons, then he that sinned shall bring for his offering the tenth part of an ephah of fine flour for a sin offering ; he shall put no oil upon it, neither shall he put *any* frankincense thereon : for it *is* a sin offering. 12. Then shall he bring it to the priest, and the priest shall take his handful of it, *even* a memorial thereof, and burn *it* on the altar, according to the offerings made by fire unto the LORD : it *is* a sin offering. 13. And the priest shall make an atonement for him as touching his sin that he hath sinned in one of these, and it shall be forgiven him: and *the remnant* shall be the priest's as a meat offering. 14. And the LORD spake unto Moses, saying, 15. If a soul commit a trespass, and sin through ignorance, in the holy things of the LORD; then he shall bring for his trespass unto the LORD a ram without blemish out of the flocks, with thy estimation by shekels of silver, after the shekel of the sanctuary, for a trespass offering: 16. And he shall make amends for the harm that he hath done in the holy thing, and shall add the fifth part thereto, and give it unto the priest: and the priest shall make an atonement for him with the ram of the trespass offering, and it shall be forgiven him. 17. And if a soul sin, and commit any of these things which are forbidden to be done by the commandments of the LORD; though he wist *it* not, yet is he guilty, and shall bear his iniquity. 18. And he shall bring a ram without blemish out of the flock, with thy estimation, for a trespass offering, unto the priest: and the priest shall make an atonement for him concerning his ignorance wherein he erred and wist *it* not, and it shall be forgiven him. 19. It *is* a trespass offering: he hath certainly trespassed against the LORD.

Lev. 22:14. And if a man eat *of* the holy thing unwittingly, then he shall put the fifth *part* thereof unto it, and shall give *it* unto the priest with the holy thing.

Num. 15:22. And if ye have erred, and not observed all these commandments, which the LORD hath spoken unto Moses, 23. *Even* all that the LORD hath commanded you by the hand of Moses, from the day that the LORD commanded *Moses*, and henceforward among your generations; 24. Then it shall be, if *ought* be committed by ignorance without the knowledge of the congregation, that all the congregation shall offer one young bullock for a burnt offering, for a sweet savour unto the LORD, with his meat offering, and his drink offering, according to the manner, and one kid of the goats for a sin offering. 25. And the priest shall make an atonement for all the congregation of the children of Israel, and it shall be forgiven them; for it *is* ignorance: and they shall bring their offering, a sacrifice made by fire unto the LORD, and their sin offering before the LORD, for their ignorance: 26. And it shall be forgiven all the congregation of the children of Israel, and the stranger that sojourneth among them; seeing all the people *were* in ignorance. 27. And if any soul sin through ignorance, then he shall bring a she goat of the first year for a sin offering. 28. And the priest shall make an atonement for the soul that sinneth ignorantly, when he sinneth by ignorance before the LORD, to make an atonement for him; and it shall be forgiven him. 29. Ye shall have one law for him that sin-

neth through ignorance, *both for* him that is born among the children of Israel, and for the stranger that sojourneth among them.

Ezek. 33:6. But if the watchman see the sword come, and blow not the trumpet, and the people be not warned; if the sword come, and take *any* person from among them, he is taken away in his iniquity; but his blood will I require at the watchman's hand. |chapter 3:18.| 8. When I say unto the wicked, O wicked *man*, thou shalt surely die; if thou dost not speak to warn the wicked from his way, that wicked *man* shall die in his iniquity; but his blood will I require at thine hand.

Ezek. 45:20. And so thou shalt do the seventh *day* of the month for every one that erreth, and for *him that is* simple: so shall ye ¹reconcile the house.   [¹ R. V. make atonement for]

Hos. 4:6. My people are destroyed for lack of knowledge: because thou hast rejected knowledge, I will also reject thee, that thou shalt be no priest to me: seeing thou hast forgotten the law of thy God, I will also forget thy children.

Luke 12:48. But he that knew not, and did commit things worthy of stripes, shall be beaten with few *stripes*. For unto whomsoever much is given, of him shall be much required: and to whom men have committed much, of him they will ask the more.

Luke 23:34. Then said Jesus, Father, forgive them; for they know not what they do.

John 16:2. They shall put you out of the synagogues: yea, the time cometh, that whosoever killeth you will think that he doeth God service.

Acts 3:14. But ye denied the Holy One and the Just, and desired a murderer to be granted unto you; 15. And killed the Prince of life, whom God hath raised from the dead; whereof we are witnesses. 17. And now, brethren, I wot that through ignorance ye did *it*, as *did* also your rulers.

1 Cor. 2:8. Which none of the princes of this world knew: for had they known *it*, they would not have crucified the Lord of glory.

Gal. 1:13. For ye have heard of my conversation in time past in the Jews' religion, how that beyond measure I persecuted the church of God, and wasted it: 14. And profited in the Jews' religion above many my equals in mine own nation, being more exceedingly zealous of the traditions of my fathers. 15. But when it pleased God, who separated me from my mother's womb, and called *me* by his grace, 16. To reveal his Son in me, that I might preach him among the heathen; immediately I conferred not with flesh and blood.

Eph. 4:18. Having the understanding darkened, being alienated from the life of God through the ignorance that is in them, because of the blindness of their heart: 19. Who being past feeling have given themselves over unto lasciviousness, to work all uncleanness with greediness.

1 Tim. 1:12. I thank Christ Jesus our Lord, who hath enabled me, for that he counted me faithful, putting me into the ministry; 13. Who was before a blasphemer, and a persecutor, and injurious: but I obtained mercy, because I did *it* ignorantly in unbelief.

INSTANCES OF PUNISHMENT OF SINS OF: Pharaoh, Gen. 12:11-17; Abimelech, Gen. 20:1-18.

IIM. 1. An encampment of the Israelites, Num. 33:45.

2. A town in the extreme S. of Judah, Josh. 15:29.

IJE-ABARIM, one of the later halting places of Israel, Num. 21:11; 33:44.

IJON, a town of Naphtali, 1 Kin. 15:20; 2 Kin. 15:29; 2 Chr. 16:4.

IKKESH, father of Ira, 2 Sam. 23:26; 1 Chr. 11:28; 27:9.

ILAI, an Ahohite, 1 Chr. 11:29.

ILLYRICUM, called also DALMATIA. Visited by Paul, Rom. 15:19; by Titus, 2 Tim. 4:10.

IMAGE. For idols.
See IDOLATRY.

FIGURATIVE: Man created in, of God, Gen. 1:26,27; 5:1; 9:6; Jas. 3:9. Regenerated into, Psa. 17:15; Rom. 8:29; 2 Cor. 3:18; Eph. 4:24; Col. 3:10; 1 John 3:1-3. Christ, of God, Col. 1:15; Heb. 1:3. Of jealousy, Ezek. 8:3,5.
See IDOL; IDOLATRY.

IMAGINATION. Gen. 6:5. And GOD saw that the wickedness of man *was* great in the earth, and *that* every imagination of the thoughts of his heart *was* only evil continually.

Gen. 8:21. And the LORD smelled a sweet savour; and the LORD said in his heart, I will not again curse the ground any more for man's sake; for the imagination of man's heart *is* evil from his youth; neither will I again smite any more every thing living, as I have done.

Deut. 29:19. And it come to pass, when he heareth the words of this curse, that he bless himself in his heart, saying, I shall have peace, though I walk in the imagination of mine heart, to add drunkenness to thirst: 20. The LORD will not spare him, but then the anger of the LORD and his jealousy shall smoke against that man, and all the curses that are written in this book shall lie upon him, and the LORD shall blot out his name from under heaven.

1 Chr. 28:9. And thou, Solomon my son, know thou the God of thy father, and serve him with a perfect heart and with a willing mind: for the LORD searcheth all hearts, and understandeth all the imaginations of the thoughts: if thou seek him, he will be found of thee; but if thou forsake him, he will cast thee off for ever.

Prov. 6:16. These six *things* doth the LORD hate; yea, seven *are* an abomination unto him: 17. A proud look, a lying tongue, and hands that shed innocent blood, 18. An heart that deviseth wicked imaginations, feet that be swift in running to mischief,

Matt. 5:28. Whosoever looketh on a woman to lust after her hath committed adultery with her already in his heart.

Rom. 1:21. When they knew God, they glorified *him* not as God, neither were thankful; but became vain in their imaginations, and their foolish heart was darkened.

2 Cor. 10:3. Though we walk in the flesh, we do not war after the flesh: 5. Casting down imaginations, and every high thing that exalteth itself against the knowledge of God, and bringing into captivity every thought to the obedience of Christ.

IMLA, called also IMLAH. **Father of** Michaiah the prophet, 2 Chr. 18:7,8.

IMMANUEL. A name of Jesus, Isa. 7:14. Called EMMANUEL, Matt. 1:23.
See JESUS, NAMES OF.

IMMER. 1. A family of priests, 1 Chr. 9:12; Ezra 2:37; 10:20; Neh. 7:40; 11:13.

2. Head of a division of priests, 1 Chr. 24:14.

3. Name of a man or town, Ezra 2:59; Neh. 7:61.

4. Father of Zadok, Neh. 3:29.

5. Father of Pashur, Jer. 20:1,2.

IMMORTALITY. Gen. 5:24. Enoch walked with God: and he *was* not; for God took him.

2 Sam. 12:23. But now he is dead, wherefore should I fast? can I bring him back again? I shall go to him, but he shall not return to me.

2 Kin. 2:11. And it came to pass, as they still went on, and talked, that, behold, *there appeared* a chariot of fire, and horses of fire, and parted them both asunder; and Elijah went up by a whirlwind into heaven.

Neh. 9:5. Stand up *and* bless the LORD your God for ever and ever: and blessed be thy glorious name, which is exalted above all blessing and praise.

Job 4:17. Shall mortal man be more just than God? shall a man be more pure than his maker? 18. Behold, he put no trust in his servants; and his angels he charged with folly: 19. How much less *in* them that dwell in houses of clay, whose foundation *is* in the dust, *which* are crushed before the moth? 20. They are destroyed from morning to evening: they perish for ever without any regarding *it*. 21. Doth not their excellency *which is* in them go away? they die, even without wisdom.

Job 14:13. O that thou wouldest hide me in the grave, that thou wouldest keep me secret, until thy wrath be past, that thou wouldest appoint me a set time, and remember me!

Psa. 16:10. For thou wilt not leave my soul in hell; neither wilt thou suffer thine Holy One to see corruption. 11. Thou wilt shew me the path of life: in thy presence *is* fulness of joy; at thy right hand *there are* pleasures for evermore.

Psa. 21:4. He asked life of thee, *and* thou gavest *it* him, *even* length of days for ever and ever.

Psa. 22:26. The meek shall eat and be satisfied: they shall praise the LORD that seek him: your heart shall live for ever.

Psa. 23:6. Surely goodness and mercy shall follow me all the days of my life: and I will dwell in the house of the LORD for ever.

Psa. 31:5. Into thine hand I commit my spirit: thou hast redeemed me, O LORD God of truth.

Psa. 36:9. For with thee *is* the fountain of life: in thy light shall we see light.

Psa. 37:18. The LORD knoweth the days of the upright: and their inheritance shall be for ever. 27. Depart from evil, and do good; and dwell for evermore.

Psa. 49:7. None *of them* can by any means redeem his brother, nor give to God a ransom for him: 8. (For the redemption of their soul *is* precious, and it ceaseth for ever:) 9. That he should still live for ever, *and* not see corruption.

Psa. 49:14. Like sheep they are laid in the grave; death shall feed on them; and the upright shall have dominion over them in the morning; and their beauty shall consume in the grave from their dwelling. 15. But God will redeem my soul from the power of the grave: for he shall receive me.

Psa. 73:26. My flesh and my heart faileth: *but* God *is* the strength of my heart, and my portion for ever.

Psa. 86:12. I will praise thee, O Lord my God, with all my heart: and I will glorify thy name for evermore.

Psa. 102:24. I said, O my God, take me not away in the midst of my days: thy years *are* throughout all generations. 25. Of old hast thou laid the foundation of the earth: and the heavens *are* the work of thy hands. 26. They shall perish, but thou shalt endure: yea, all of them shall wax old like a garment: as a vesture shalt thou change them, and they shall be changed: 27. But thou *art* the same, and thy years shall have no end. 28. The children of thy servants shall continue, and their seed shall be established before thee.

Psa. 121:8. The LORD shall preserve thy going out and thy coming in from this time forth, and even for evermore.

Psa. 133:3. As the dew of Hermon, *and as the dew* that descended upon the mountains of Zion: for there the LORD commanded the blessing, *even* life for evermore.

Psa. 145:1. I will extol thee, my God, O king; and I will bless thy name for ever and ever. 2. Every day will I bless thee; and I will praise thy name for ever and ever.

Prov. 14:32. The wicked is driven away in his wickedness: but the righteous hath hope in his death.

Eccl. 3:21. Who knoweth the spirit of man that goeth upward, and the spirit of the beast that goeth downward to the earth?

Eccl. 12:7. Then shall the dust return to the earth as it was: and the spirit shall return unto God who gave it.

Isa. 14:9. Hell from beneath is moved for thee to meet *thee* at thy coming: it stirreth up the dead for thee, *even* all the chief ones of the earth; it hath raised up from their thrones all the kings of the nations.

Isa. 25:8. He will swallow up death [1 in victory; [1 R. V. for ever]

Isa. 26:19. Thy dead *men* shall live, *together with* my dead body shall they arise. Awake and sing, ye that dwell in dust: for thy dew *is as* the dew of herbs, and the earth shall cast out the dead.

Isa. 38:18. For the grave cannot praise thee, death can *not* celebrate thee: they that go down into the pit cannot hope for thy truth. 19. The living, the living, he shall praise thee, as I *do* this day: the father to the children shall make known thy truth.

Ezek. 32:31. Pharaoh shall see them, and shall be comforted over all his multitude, *even* Pharaoh and all his army slain by the sword, saith the Lord GOD.

Dan. 12:2. And many of them that sleep in the dust of the earth shall awake, some to everlasting life, and some to shame *and* everlasting contempt. 3. And they that be wise shall shine as the brightness of the firmament; and they that turn many to righteousness as the stars for ever and ever.

Matt. 10:28. Fear not them which kill the body, but are not able to kill the soul: but rather fear him which is able to destroy both soul and body in hell.

Matt. 16:26. What is a man profited, if he shall gain the whole world, and lose his own soul? or what shall a man give in exchange for his soul?

Matt. 19:16. And, behold, one came and said unto him, Good Master, what good thing shall I do, that I may have eternal life? 17. And he said unto him, Why callest thou me good? *there is* none good but one, *that is*, God: but if thou wilt enter into life, keep the commandments. Luke 10:25–28.

Matt. 25:46. And these shall go away into everlasting punishment: but the righteous into life eternal.

Mark 10:30. But he shall receive an hundredfold now in this time, houses, and brethren, and sisters, and mothers, and children, and lands, with persecutions; and in the world to come eternal life.

Mark 12:26. And as touching the dead, that they rise: have ye not read in the book of Moses, how in the bush God spake unto him, saying, I *am* the God of Abraham, and the God of Isaac, and the God of Jacob? 27. He is not the God of the dead, but the God of the living: ye therefore do greatly err.

Luke 9:25. What is a man advantaged if he gain the whole world, and lose himself. or be cast away?

Luke 20:36. Neither can they **die any**

more: for they are equal unto the angels; and are the children of God, being the children of the resurrection. 37. Now that the dead are raised, even Moses shewed at the bush, when he calleth the Lord the God of Abraham, and the God of Isaac, and the God of Jacob. 38. For he is not a God of the dead, but of the living: for all live unto him.

John 3:14. And as Moses lifted up the serpent in the wilderness, even so must the Son of man be lifted up: 15. That whosoever believeth in him should not perish, but have eternal life. 16. For God so loved the world, that he gave his only begotten Son, that whosoever believeth in him should not perish, but have everlasting life. 36. He that believeth on the Son hath everlasting life: and he that believeth not the Son shall not see life; but the wrath of God abideth on him.

John 5:39. Search the scriptures [R. V., Ye search the scriptures]; for in them ye think ye have eternal life: and they are they which testify of me. 40. And ye will not come to me, that ye might have life.

John 6:39. And this is the Father's will which hath sent me, that of all which he hath given me I should lose nothing, but should raise it up again at the last day. 40. And this is the will of him that sent me, that every one which seeth the Son, and believeth on him, may have everlasting life: and I will raise him up at the last day. 44. No man can come to me, except the Father which hath sent me draw him: and I will raise him up at the last day. 47. Verily, verily, I say unto you, He that believeth on me hath everlasting life. 50. This is the bread which cometh down from heaven, that a man may eat thereof, and not die. 51. I am the living bread which came down from heaven; if any man eat of this bread, he shall live for ever: and the bread that I will give is my flesh, which I will give for the life of the world. 53. Then Jesus said unto them, Verily, verily, I say unto you, Except ye eat the flesh of the Son of man, and drink his blood, ye have no life in you. 54. Whoso eateth my flesh, and drinketh my blood, hath eternal life; and I will raise him up at the last day. 58. This is that bread which came down from heaven: not as your fathers did eat manna, and are dead: he that eateth of this bread shall live for ever.

John 10:28. And I give unto them eternal life; and they shall never perish, neither shall any *man* pluck them out of my hand.

John 11:25. Jesus said unto her, I am the resurrection, and the life: he that believeth in me, though he [1]were dead, yet shall he live: 26. And whosoever liveth and believeth in me shall never die. Believest thou this? [[1] R. V. die]

John 14:19. Yet a little while, and the world seeth me no more; but ye see me: because I live, ye shall live also.

John 17:2. As thou hast given him power over all flesh, that he should give eternal life to as many as thou hast given him. 3. And this is life eternal, that they might know thee the only true God, and Jesus Christ, whom thou hast sent.

Acts 20:32. And now, brethren, I commend you to God, and to the word of his grace, which is able to build you up, and to give you an inheritance among all them which are sanctified.

Acts 23:8. For the Sadducees say that there is no resurrection, neither angel, nor spirit: but the Pharisees confess both. 9. And there arose a great cry: and the scribes *that were* of the Pharisees' part arose, and strove, saying, We find no evil in this man: but if a spirit or an angel hath spoken to him, [1] let us not fight against God. [[1] Omitted in R. V.]

Acts 26:7. Unto which *promise* our twelve tribes, instantly serving *God* day and night, hope to come. For which hope's sake, king Agrippa, I am accused of the Jews. 8. Why should it be thought a thing incredible with you, that God should raise the dead? 18. To open their eyes, *and* to turn *them* from darkness to light, and *from* the power of Satan unto God, that they may receive forgiveness of sins, and inheritance among them which are sanctified by faith that is in me.

Rom. 2:7. To them who by patient continuance in well doing seek for glory and honour and immortality, eternal life:

Rom. 6:22. But now being made free from sin, and become servants to God, ye have your fruit unto holiness, and the end everlasting life. 23. For the wages of sin *is* death; but the gift of God *is* eternal life through Jesus Christ our Lord.

1 Cor. 15:12. Now if Christ be preached that he rose from the dead, how say some among you that there is no resurrection of the dead? 13. But if there be no resurrection of the dead, then is Christ not risen: 14. And if Christ be not risen, then *is* our preaching vain, and your faith *is* also vain. 15. Yea, and we are found false witnesses of God; because we have testified of God that he raised up Christ: whom he raised not up, if so be that the dead rise not. 16. For if the dead rise not, then is not Christ raised: 17. And if Christ be not raised, your faith *is* vain; ye are yet in your sins. 18. Then they also which are fallen asleep in Christ are perished. 19. If in this life only we have hope in Christ, we are of all men most miserable. 20. But now is Christ risen from the dead, *and* become the firstfruits of them that slept. 21. For since by man *came* death, by man *came* also the resurrection of the dead. 22. For as in Adam all die, even so in Christ shall all be made alive. 23. But every man in his own order: Christ the firstfruits; afterward they that are Christ's at his coming. 24. Then *cometh* the end, when he shall have delivered up the kingdom to God, even the Father; when he shall have put down all rule and all authority and power. 25. For he must reign,

till he hath put all enemies under his feet. 26. The last enemy *that* shall be destroyed *is* death. 27. For he hath put all things under his feet. But when he saith all things are put under *him*, *it is* manifest that he is excepted, which did put all things under him. 28. And when all things shall be subdued unto him, then shall the Son also himself be subject unto him that put all things under him, that God may be all in all. 29. Else what shall they do which are baptized for the dead, if the dead rise not at all? why are they then baptized for the dead? 30. And why stand we in jeopardy every hour? 31. I protest by your rejoicing which I have in Christ Jesus our Lord, I die daily. 32. If after the manner of men I have fought with beasts at Ephesus, what advantageth it me, if the dead rise not? let us eat and drink, for to morrow we die. 33. Be not deceived: evil communications corrupt good manners. 34. Awake to righteousness, and sin not; for some have not the knowledge of God: I speak *this* to your shame. 35. But some *man* will say, How are the dead raised up? and with what body do they come? 36. *Thou* fool, that which thou sowest is not quickened, except it die: 37. And that which thou sowest, thou sowest not that body that shall be, but bare grain, it may chance of wheat, or of some other *grain:* 38. But God giveth it a body as it hath pleased him, and to every seed his own body. 39. All flesh *is* not the same flesh: but *there is* one *kind of* flesh of men, another flesh of beasts, another of fishes, *and* another of birds. 40. *There are* also celestial bodies, and bodies terrestrial: but the glory of the celestial *is* one, and the *glory* of the terrestrial *is* another. 41. *There is* one glory of the sun, and another glory of the moon, and another glory of the stars: for *one* star differeth from *another* star in glory. 42. So also *is* the resurrection of the dead. It is sown in corruption; it is raised in incorruption: 43. It is sown in dishonour; it is raised in glory: it is sown in weakness; it is raised in power: 44. It is sown a natural body; it is raised a spiritual body. There is a natural body, and there is a spiritual body. 45. And so it is written, The first man Adam was made a living soul; the last Adam *was made* a quickening spirit. 46. Howbeit that *was* not first which is spiritual, but that which is natural; and afterward that which is spiritual. 47. The first man *is* of the earth, earthy: the second man *is* the Lord from heaven. 48. As *is* the earthy, such *are* they also that are earthy: and as *is* the heavenly, such *are* they also that are heavenly. 49. And as we have borne the image of the earthy, we shall also bear the image of the heavenly. 50. Now this I say, brethren, that flesh and blood cannot inherit the kingdom of God; neither doth corruption inherit incorruption. 51. Behold, I shew you a mystery; We shall not all sleep, but we shall all be changed,

52. In a moment, in the twinkling of an eye, at the last trump: for the trumpet shall sound, and the dead shall be raised incorruptible, and we shall be changed. 53. For this corruptible must put on incorruption, and this mortal *must* put on immortality. 54. So when this corruptible shall have put on incorruption, and this mortal shall have put on immortality, then shall be brought to pass the saying that is written, Death is swallowed up in victory. 55. O death, where *is* thy sting? O grave, where *is* thy victory?

Gal. 6:8. For he that soweth to his flesh shall of the flesh reap corruption; but he that soweth to the Spirit shall of the Spirit reap life everlasting.

Col. 1:5. For the hope which is laid up for you in heaven, whereof ye heard before in the word of the truth of the gospel; 6. Which is come unto you, as *it is* in all the world; and bringeth forth fruit, as *it doth* also in you, since the day ye heard *of it*, and knew the grace of God in truth:

1 Thess. 4:13. But I would not have you to be ignorant, brethren, concerning them which are asleep, that ye sorrow not, even as others which have no hope. 14. For if we believe that Jesus died and rose again, even so them also which sleep in Jesus will God bring with him. 15. For this we say unto you by the word of the Lord, that we which are alive *and* remain unto the coming of the Lord shall not prevent them which are asleep. 16. For the Lord himself shall descend from heaven with a shout, with the voice of the archangel, and with the trump of God: and the dead in Christ shall rise first: 17. Then we which are alive *and* remain shall be caught up together with them in the clouds, to meet the Lord in the air: and so shall we ever be with the Lord. 18. Wherefore comfort one another with these words.

1 Thess. 5:10. Who died for us, that, whether we wake or sleep, we should live together with him.

2 Thess. 1:7. And to you who are troubled rest with us, when the Lord Jesus shall be revealed from heaven with his mighty angels. 8. In flaming fire taking vengeance on them that know not God, and that obey not the gospel of our Lord Jesus Christ: 9. Who shall be punished with everlasting destruction from the presence of the Lord, and from the glory of his power;

2 Thess. 2:16. Now our Lord Jesus Christ himself, and God, even our Father, which hath loved us, and hath given *us* everlasting consolation and good hope through grace,

1 Tim. 4:8. Godliness is profitable unto all things, having promise of the life that now is, and of that which is to come.

1 Tim. 6:12. Fight the good fight of faith, lay hold on eternal life, whereunto thou art also called, . . . 19. Laying up in store

for themselves a good foundation against the time to come, that they may lay hold on [1] eternal life.   [1 R. V. the life which is life indeed]

2 Tim. 1:9. Who hath saved us, and called us with an holy calling, not according to our works, but according to his own purpose and grace, which was given us in Christ Jesus before the world began, 10. But is now made manifest by the appearing of our Saviour Jesus Christ, who hath abolished death, and hath brought life and [1] immortality to light through the gospel: [1 R. V. incorruption]

Tit. 1:2. In hope of eternal life, which God, that cannot lie, promised before the world began;

Tit. 3:7. That being justified by his grace, we should be made heirs according to the hope of eternal life.

Heb. 9:15. And for this cause he is the mediator of the new testament, that by means of death, for the redemption of the transgressions *that were* under the first testament, they which are called might receive the promise of eternal inheritance.

Heb. 10:34. For ye had compassion of me in my bonds, and took joyfully the spoiling of your goods, knowing in yourselves that ye have in heaven a better and an enduring substance.

Heb. 11:5. Enoch was translated that he should not see death; and was not found, because God had translated him: 10. For he [Abraham] looked for a city which hath foundations, whose builder and maker *is* God. 13. These all died in faith, not having received the promises, but having seen them afar off, and were persuaded of *them*, and embraced *them*, and confessed that they were strangers and pilgrims on the earth. 14. For they that say such things declare plainly that they seek a country. 15. And truly, if they had been mindful of that *country* from whence they came out, they might have had opportunity to have returned. 16. But now they desire a better *country*, that is, an heavenly: wherefore God is not ashamed to be called their God: for he hath prepared for them a city.

1 Pet. 1:3. Blessed *be* the God and Father of our Lord Jesus Christ, which according to his abundant mercy hath begotten us again unto a lively hope by the resurrection of Jesus Christ from the dead, 4. To an inheritance incorruptible, and undefiled, and that fadeth not away, reserved in heaven for you, 5. Who are kept by the power of God through faith unto salvation ready to be revealed in the last time.

1 John 2:17. The world passeth away, and the lust thereof: but he that doeth the will of God abideth for ever. 25. And this is the promise that he hath promised us, *even* eternal life.

1 John 5:13. That ye may know that ye have eternal life, [1] and that ye may believe on the name of the Son of God. [1 R. V. even unto you that]

Jude 21. Keep yourselves in the love of God, looking for the mercy of our Lord Jesus Christ unto eternal life.

Rev. 1:7. Behold, he cometh with clouds; and every eye shall see him, and they *also* which pierced him: and all kindreds of the earth shall wail because of him.

Rev. 3:4. Thou hast a few names even in Sardis which have not defiled their garments; and they shall walk with me in white: for they are worthy.

Rev. 22:5. And there shall be no night there; and they need no candle, neither light of the sun; for the Lord God giveth them light: and they shall reign for ever and ever.

See Resurrection; Righteous, Promises to; Wicked, Punishment of.

IMNA, son of Helem, 1 Chr. 7:35.

IMNAH. 1. Firstborn of Asher, 1 Chr. 7:30.

2. A Levite, 2 Chr. 31:14.

IMPENITENCE. Lev. 23:26. And the Lord spake unto Moses, saying, 27. Also on the tenth *day* of this seventh month *there shall be* a day of atonement: it shall be an holy convocation unto you; and ye shall afflict your souls, and offer an offering made by fire unto the Lord. 28. And ye shall do no work in that same day: for it *is* a day of atonement, to make an atonement for you before the Lord your God. 29. For whatsoever soul *it be* that shall not be afflicted in that same day, he shall be cut off from among his people.

Lev. 26:21. If ye walk contrary unto me, and will not hearken unto me; I will bring seven times more plagues upon you according to your sins. *vs.* 22-24.

Deut. 29:19. And it come to pass, when he heareth the words of this curse, that he bless himself in his heart, saying, I shall have peace, though I walk in the imagination of mine heart, to add drunkenness to thirst: 20. The Lord will not spare him, but then the anger of the Lord and his jealousy shall smoke against that man, and all the curses that are written in this book shall lie upon him, and the Lord shall blot out his name from under heaven. 21. And the Lord shall separate him unto evil out of all the tribes of Israel, according to all the curses of the covenant that are written in this book of the law:

1 Sam. 15:23. For rebellion *is as* the sin of witchcraft, and stubbornness *is as* iniquity and idolatry. Because thou hast rejected the word of the Lord, he hath also rejected thee from *being* king.

Job 9:2. How should man be just with God? 4. Who hath hardened *himself* against him, and hath prospered?

Job 24:13. They are of those that rebel against the light: they know not the ways thereof, nor abide in the paths thereof.

Job 33:14. God speaketh once, yea twice, *yet man* perceiveth it not.

Psa. 7:11. God is angry *with the wicked* every day. 12. If he turn not, he will whet his sword; he hath bent his bow, and made it ready. *v.* 13.

Psa. 10:3. For the wicked boasteth of his heart's desire, and blesseth the covetous, *whom* the LORD abhorreth.

Psa. 32:9. Be ye not as the horse, *or* as the mule, *which* have no understanding:

Psa. 50:17. Thou hatest instruction, and castest my words behind thee. 21. These *things* hast thou done, and I kept silence; . . . *but* I will reprove thee, and set *them* in order before thine eyes.

Psa. 52:1. Why boastest thou thyself in mischief, O mighty man? the goodness of God *endureth* continually.

7. Lo, *this is* the man *that* made not God his strength; but trusted in the abundance of his riches *and* strengthened himself in his wickedness.

Psa. 58:3. The wicked . . . go astray as soon as they be born, speaking lies. 4. *They are* like the deaf adder *that* stoppeth her ear; 5. Which will not hearken to the voice of charmers, charming never so wisely.

Psa. 68:21. God shall wound the head of his enemies, *and* the hairy scalp of such an one as goeth on still in his trespasses.

Psa. 78:8. A stubborn and rebellious generation; a generation *that* set not their heart aright, and whose spirit was not stedfast with God.

Psa. 81:11. My people would not hearken to my voice; and Israel would none of me. 12. So I gave them up unto their own hearts' lust: *and* they walked in their own counsels.

Psa. 82:5. They know not, neither will they understand; they walk on in darkness:

Psa. 95:8. Harden not your heart, as in the provocation, *and* as *in* the day of temptation in the wilderness. Heb. 3:8.

Psa. 106:24. Yea, they despised the pleasant land, they believed not his word: 25. But murmured in their tents, *and* hearkened not unto the voice of the LORD.

Psa. 107:11. They rebelled against the words of God, and contemned the counsel of the most High: 12. Therefore he brought down their heart with labour; they fell down, and *there was* none to help.

Prov. 1:24. Because I have called, and ye refused; I have stretched out my hand, and no man regarded; 25. But ye have set at nought all my counsel, and would none of my reproof: 26. I also will laugh at your calamity; I will mock when your fear cometh; 27. When your fear cometh as desolation, and your destruction cometh as a whirlwind; when distress and anguish cometh upon you. 28. Then shall they call upon me, but I will not answer; they shall seek me early, but they shall not find me: 29. For that they hated knowledge, and did not choose the fear of the LORD: 30. They would none of my counsel: they despised all my reproof. 31. Therefore shall they eat of the fruit of their own way, and be filled with their own devices.

Prov. 11:3. The perverseness of transgressors shall destroy them.

Prov. 15:10. Correction *is* grievous unto him that forsaketh the way: *and* he that hateth reproof shall die. 32. He that refuseth instruction despiseth his own soul:

Prov. 19:16. He that despiseth his ways shall die.

Prov. 21:29. A wicked man hardeneth his face:

Prov. 26:11. As a dog returneth to his vomit, *so* a fool returneth to his folly.

Prov. 28:13. He that covereth his sins shall not prosper: 14. He that hardeneth his heart shall fall into mischief.

Prov. 29:1. He, that being often reproved hardeneth *his* neck, shall suddenly be destroyed, and that without remedy.

Eccl. 8:11. Because sentence against an evil work is not executed speedily, therefore the heart of the sons of men is fully set in them to do evil. 13. But it shall not be well with the wicked, neither shall he prolong *his* days, *which are* as a shadow; because he feareth not before God.

Isa. 26:10. Let favour be shewed to the wicked, *yet* will he not learn righteousness; in the land of uprightness will he deal unjustly, and will not behold the majesty of the LORD.

Isa. 28:12. To whom he said, This *is* the rest *wherewith* ye may cause the weary to rest; and this *is* the refreshing: yet they would not hear.

Isa. 32:9. Rise up, ye women that are at ease; hear my voice, ye careless daughters; give ear unto my speech. 10. Many days and years shall ye be troubled, ye careless women: 11. Tremble, ye women that are at ease; be troubled, ye careless ones: strip you, and make you bare, and gird *sackcloth* upon *your* loins.

Isa. 42:22. This *is* a people robbed and spoiled; *they are* all of them snared in holes, and they are hid in prison houses: they are for a prey, and none delivereth; for a spoil, and none saith, Restore. 23. Who among you will give ear to this? *who* will hearken and hear for the time to come? 24. Who gave Jacob for a spoil, and Israel to the robbers? did not the LORD, he against whom we have sinned? for they would not walk in his ways, neither were they obedient unto his law. 25. Therefore he hath poured upon him the fury of his anger, and the strength of battle: and it hath set him on fire round about, yet he knew not; and it burned him, yet he laid *it* not to heart.

Isa. 46:12. Hearken unto me, ye stouthearted, that *are* far from righteousness: 13. I bring near my righteousness;

Isa. 48:4. I knew that thou *art* obstinate, and thy neck *is* an iron sinew, and thy brow brass; 8. Yea, thou heardest not: yea, thou knewest not; yea, from that time *that* thine ear was not opened: for I knew that thou wouldest deal very treacherously, and wast called a transgressor from the womb.

Isa. 57:11. Of whom hast thou been afraid or feared, that thou hast lied, and hast not remembered me, nor laid *it* to thy heart? have not I held my peace even of old, and thou fearest me not?

Isa. 65:12. Because when I called, ye did not answer: when I spake, ye did not hear; but did evil before mine eyes, and did choose *that* wherein I delighted not. 15. Ye shall leave your name for a curse unto my chosen: for the Lord GOD shall slay thee, Isa. 66:4.

Jer. 3:10. And yet for all this her treacherous sister Judah hath not turned unto me with her whole heart, but feignedly, saith the LORD. *vs.* 7-9.

Jer. 5:21. Hear now this, O foolish people, and without understanding; which have eyes, and see not; which have ears, and hear not: 22. Fear ye not me? saith the LORD: will ye not tremble at my presence, . . . 23. This people hath a revolting and a rebellious heart; they are revolted and gone. 24. Neither say they in their heart, Let us now fear the LORD our God, that giveth rain, both the former and the latter, in his season: he reserveth unto us the appointed weeks of the harvest.

Jer. 6:10. To whom shall I speak, and give warning, that they may hear? behold, their ear *is* uncircumcised, and they cannot hearken: behold, the word of the LORD is unto them a reproach; they have no delight in it. 16. Thus saith the LORD, Stand ye in the ways, and see, and ask for the old paths, where *is* the good way, and walk therein, and ye shall find rest for your souls. But they said, We will not walk *therein*. 17. I set watchmen over you, *saying*, Hearken to the sound of the trumpet. But they said, We will not hearken. 19. Hear, O earth; behold, I will bring evil upon this people, *even* the fruit of their thoughts, because they have not hearkened unto my words, nor to my law, but rejected it.

Jer. 7:13. I spake unto you, rising up early and speaking, but ye heard not; and I called you, but ye answered not; 14. Therefore will I do unto *this* house, which is called by my name, wherein ye trust, and unto the place which I gave to you and to your fathers, as I have done to Shiloh. 24. But they hearkened not, nor inclined their ear, but walked in the counsels *and* in the imagination of their evil heart, and went backward, and not forward. 28. But thou shalt say unto them, This *is* a nation that obeyeth not the voice of the LORD their God, nor receiveth correction: truth is perished, and is cut off from their mouth. *vs.* 13-34; Jer. 11: 8; 25:4; 26:4-6; 32:33; 35:14-17; Zech. 1:4.

Jer. 8:5. Why *then* is this people of Jerusalem slidden back by a perpetual backsliding? they hold fast deceit, they refuse to return. 6. I hearkened and heard, *but* they spake not aright: no man repented him of his wickedness, saying, What have I done? every one turned to his course, as the horse rusheth into the battle. 7. Yea, the stork in the heaven knoweth her appointed times; and the turtle and the crane and the swallow observe the time of their coming; but my people know not the judgment of the LORD. 20. The harvest is past, the summer is ended, and we are not saved. *vs.* 4-22.

Jer. 12:11. The whole land is made desolate, because no man layeth *it* to heart.

Jer. 13:17. If ye will not hear it, my soul shall weep in secret places for *your* pride, and mine eye shall weep sore, and run down with tears, because the LORD's flock is carried away captive. 27. Woe unto thee, O Jerusalem! wilt thou not be made clean? when *shall it* once *be? v.* 15; Jer. 19:15.

Jer. 14:10. Thus have they loved to wander, they have not refrained their feet, therefore the LORD doth not accept them; he will now remember their iniquity, and visit their sins. *vs.* 1-16.

Jer. 15:6. Thou hast forsaken me, saith the LORD, thou art gone backward: therefore will I stretch out my hand against thee, and destroy thee; I am weary with repenting. 7. And I will fan them with a fan in the gates of the land; I will bereave *them* of children, I will destroy my people, *since* they return not from their ways.

Jer. 16:12. Ye have done worse than your fathers; for, behold, ye walk every one after the imagination of his evil heart, that they may not hearken unto me:

Jer. 17:23. They obeyed not, neither inclined their ear, but made their neck stiff, that they might not hear, nor receive instruction.

Jer. 18:12. They said, There is no hope: but we will walk after our own devices, and we will every one do the imagination of his evil heart. Jer. 2:25.

Jer. 22:21. I spake unto thee in thy prosperity; *but* thou saidst, I will not hear. This *hath been* thy manner from thy youth, that thou obeyedst not my voice.

Jer. 29:19. Because they have not hearkened to my words, saith the LORD, which I sent unto them by my servants the prophets, rising up early and sending *them;* but ye would not hear, saith the LORD.

Jer. 44:10. They are not humbled *even* unto this day, neither have they feared, nor walked in my law, nor in my statutes, that I set before you and before your fathers. 16. *As for* the word that thou hast spoken unto us in the name of the LORD, we will not hearken unto thee. 17. But we will certainly do whatsoever thing goeth forth out of our own mouth, to burn incense unto the queen of heaven, as we have done, we, and our fathers, . . . for *then* we had plenty of victuals, and were well, and saw no evil.

Ezek. 2:5. They, whether they will hear, or whether they will forbear, (for they *are* a rebellious house,) yet shall know that there hath been a prophet among them.

Ezek. 3:5. For thou *art* not sent to a people of a strange speech and of an hard language, *but* to the house of Israel; 6. Not to many people of a strange speech and of an hard language, whose words thou canst not understand. Surely, had I sent thee to them, they would have hearkened unto thee. 7. But the house of Israel will not hearken unto thee; for they will not hearken unto me. for all the house of Israel *are* impudent and hardhearted. 19. If thou warn the wicked, and he turn not from his wickedness, nor from his wicked way, he shall die in his iniquity; 26. I will make thy tongue cleave to the roof of thy mouth, that thou shalt be dumb, and shalt not be to them a reprover: for they *are* a rebellious house. *vs.* 1-11; Ezek. 2:4; 33:9.

Ezek. 12:2. Thou dwellest in the midst of a rebellious house, which have eyes to see, and see not; they have ears to hear, and hear not: for they *are* a rebellious house.

Ezek. 20:8. But they rebelled against me, and would not hearken unto me: they did not every man cast away the abominations of their eyes, neither did they forsake the idols of Egypt: then I said, I will pour out my fury upon them, to accomplish my anger against them in the midst of the land of Egypt. 13. But the house of Israel rebelled against me in the wilderness: they walked not in my statutes, and they despised my judgments, which *if* a man do, he shall even live in them; and my sabbaths they greatly polluted: then I said, I would pour out my fury upon them in the wilderness, to consume them. 21. The children rebelled against me: they walked not in my statutes, neither kept my judgments to do them, which *if* a man do, he shall even live in them: they polluted my sabbaths: then I said, I would pour out my fury upon them,

Ezek. 33:4. Whosoever heareth the sound of the trumpet, and taketh not warning; if the sword come, and take him away, his blood shall be upon his own head. 5. He heard the sound of the trumpet, and took not warning: his blood shall be upon him.

Dan. 9:13. As *it is* written in the law of Moses, all this evil is come upon us; yet made we not our prayer before the LORD our God, that we might turn from our iniquities, and understand thy truth.

Hos. 4:17. Ephraim *is* joined to idols: let him alone.

Hos. 5:4. They will not frame their doings to turn unto their God: for the spirit of whoredoms *is* in the midst of them, and they have not known the LORD.

Hos. 7:13. Woe unto them! for they have fled from me: destruction unto them! because they have transgressed against me: though I have redeemed them, yet they have spoken lies against me. 15. Though I have bound *and* strengthened their arms, yet do they imagine mischief against me.

Hos. 11:2. *As* they called them, so they went from them: they sacrificed unto Baalim, and burned incense to graven images. 7. My people are bent to backsliding from me: though they called them to the most High, none at all would exalt *him*.

Zech. 7:11. They refused to hearken, and pulled away the shoulder, and stopped their ears, that they should not hear. 12. Yea, they made their hearts *as* an adamant stone, lest they should hear the law, and the words which the LORD of hosts hath sent in his spirit by the former prophets: therefore came a great wrath from the LORD of hosts. 13. Therefore it is come to pass, *that* as he cried, and they would not hear; so they cried, and I would not hear, saith the LORD of hosts: *vs.* 4-14.

Mal. 2:2. If ye will not hear, and if ye will not lay *it* to heart, to give glory unto my name, saith the LORD of hosts, I will even send a curse upon you, and I will curse your blessings: yea, I have cursed them already, because ye do not lay *it* to heart. 17. Ye have wearied the LORD with your words. Yet ye say, Wherein have we wearied *him?* When ye say, Every one that doeth evil *is* good in the sight of the LORD. and he delighteth in them; or, Where *is* the God of judgment?

Matt. 11:16. But whereunto shall I liken this generation? It is like unto children sitting in the markets, and calling unto their fellows, 17. And saying, We have piped unto you, and ye have not danced; we have mourned unto you, and ye have not lamented. 18. For John came neither eating nor drinking, and they say, He hath a devil. 19. The Son of man came eating and drinking, and they say, Behold a man gluttonous, and a winebibber, a friend of publicans and sinners. But wisdom is justified of her children. [Luke 7:35.] 20. Then began he to upbraid the cities wherein most of his mighty works were done, because they repented not: 21. Woe unto thee, Chorazin! woe unto thee. Bethsaida! for if the mighty works, which were done in you, had been done in Tyre and Sidon, they would have repented long ago in sackcloth and ashes. *vs.* 20 24; Matt. 12:41,42; Luke 10:13.

Matt. 13:15. For this people's heart is waxed gross, and *their* ears are dull of hearing, and their eyes they have closed; lest at any time they should see with *their* eyes, and hear with *their* ears, and should understand with *their* heart, and should be converted, and I should heal them.

Matt. 23:37. O Jerusalem, Jerusalem, *thou* that killest the prophets, and stonest them which are sent unto thee, how often would I have gathered thy children together, even as a hen gathereth her chickens under *her* wings, and ye would not! 38. Behold, your house is left unto you desolate. Luke 13:34.

Matt. 24:38. Marrying and giving in marriage, until the day that Noe entered into the ark, 39. And knew not until the flood came, and took them all away; so shall also the coming of the Son of man be. 48. If that evil servant shall say in his heart, My lord delayeth his coming; 49. And shall begin to smite *his* fellowservants, and to eat and drink with the drunken; 50. The lord of that servant shall come in a day when he looketh not for *him*, and in an hour that he is not aware of, 51. And shall cut him asunder, and appoint *him* his portion with the hypocrites:

Matt. 27:4. I have sinned in that I have betrayed the innocent blood. And they said, What *is that* to us? see thou *to that*. 25. Then answered all the people, and said, His blood *be* on us, and on our children.

Mark 3:5. He looked round about on them with anger, being grieved for the hardness of their hearts,

Luke 13:1. There were present at that season some that told him of the Galileans, whose blood Pilate had mingled with their sacrifices. 2. And Jesus answering said unto them, Suppose ye that these Galileans were sinners above all the Galileans, because they suffered such things? 3. I tell you, Nay: but, except ye repent, ye shall all likewise perish. *v.* 5.

Luke 16:31. And he said unto him, If they hear not Moses and the prophets, neither will they be persuaded, though one rose from the dead.

Acts 7:51. Ye stiffnecked and uncircumcised in heart and ears, ye do always resist the Holy Ghost: as your fathers *did, so do* ye.

Rom. 2:4. Despisest thou the riches of his goodness and forbearance and longsuffering; not knowing that the goodness of God leadeth thee to repentance? 5. After thy hardness and impenitent heart treasurest up unto thyself wrath against the day of wrath and revelation of the righteous judgment of God;

2 Cor. 12:21. *And* lest, when I come again, my God will humble me among you, and *that* I shall bewail many which have sinned already, and have not repented of the uncleanness and fornication and lasciviousness which they have committed.

Heb. 12:17. For ye know how that afterward, when he would have inherited the blessing, he was rejected: for he found no place of repentance, though he sought it carefully with tears.

Rev. 2:5. Remember therefore from whence thou art fallen, and repent, and do the first works; or else I will come unto thee quickly, and will remove thy candlestick out of his place, except thou repent. 16. Repent; or else I will come unto thee quickly, and will fight against them with the sword of my mouth. 21. I gave her space to repent of her fornication; and she repented not. 22. Behold I will cast her into a bed, and them that commit adultery with her into great tribulation, except they repent of their deeds.

Rev. 3:3. Remember therefore how thou hast received and heard, and hold fast, and repent. If therefore thou shalt not watch, I will come on thee as a thief, and thou shalt not know what hour I will come upon thee.

Rev. 9:20. And the rest of the men which were not killed by these plagues yet repented not of the works of their hands, that they should not worship devils, and idols of gold, and silver, and brass, and stone, and of wood: which neither can see, nor hear, nor walk: 21. Neither repented they of their murders, nor of their sorceries, nor of their fornication, nor of their thefts.

Rev. 16:9. And men were scorched with great heat, and blasphemed the name of God, which hath power over these plagues: and they repented not to give him glory. 21. And there fell upon men a great hail out of heaven, *every stone* about the weight of a talent: and men blasphemed God because of the plague of the hail; for the plague thereof was exceeding great.

See AFFLICTION, OBDURACY IN; BACKSLIDERS; BLINDNESS, SPIRITUAL; INFIDELITY; OBDURACY; UNBELIEF.

INSTANCES OF: Pharaoh, Ex. 9:30,34; 10: 27; 14:5-9. Israelites, Num. 14:22,23; 2 Kin. 17:14; 2 Chr. 24:19; 36:16,17; Neh. 9:16,17,29, 30; Jer. 36:31. Eli's sons, 1 Sam. 2:25. Amaziah, 2 Chr. 25:16. Manasseh, 2 Chr. 33:10. Amon, 2 Chr. 33:23. Zedekiah, 2 Chr. 36:12, 13; Jer. 37:2. Jehoiakim and his servants, Jer. 36:22-24. Belshazzar, Dan. 5:22,23. The rich young man, Matt. 19:22.

IMPORTS. Of Jerusalem: horses, chariots, and linen, 1 Kin. 10:28,29; 2 Chr. 1:16; gold, ivory, apes, peacocks, 2 Chr. 9:21. Of Egypt: spices, Gen. 37:25. Of Tyre, Ezek. 27:12-25.

See COMMERCE; EXPORTS; TRIBUTE.

IMPORTUNITY. See PRAYER.

IMPOSITION OF HANDS. See HANDS, IMPOSITION OF.

IMPRECATION. INSTANCES OF: Ruth, Ruth 1:17. Samuel, 1 Sam. 3:17. David, 2 Sam. 1:21; 3:28,29. Shimei, 2 Sam. 16:5,13. See PRAYER, IMPRECATORY.

IMPRISONMENT. Of Joseph, Gen. 39:20. Jeremiah, Jer. 38:6. John the Baptist, Matt. 11:2; 14:3. Apostles, Acts 5:18. Paul and Silas, Acts 16:24. Peter, Acts 12:4.

Of debtors, Matt. 5:26; 18:30.

See PRISON; PRISONERS; PUNISHMENTS.

IMRAH, a chief of the tribe of Asher, 1 Chr. 7:36.

IMRI. 1. A man of Judah, 1 Chr. 9:4. 2. Father of Zaccur, Neh. 3:2.

INCARNATION. See JESUS, INCARNATION OF.

INCENDIARISM. See ARSON.

INCENSE. Formula for compounding, Ex. 30:34,35. Uses of, Ex. 30:36-38; Lev. 16: 12; Num. 16:17,40,46; Deut. 33:10. Compounded by Bezaleel, Ex. 37:29; by priests, 1 Chr. 9:30. Offered morning and evening, Ex. 30:7,8; 2 Chr. 13:11; on the golden altar, Ex. 30:1-7; 40:5,27; 2 Chr. 2:4; 32:12; in making atonement, Lev. 16:12,13; Num. 16:46,47; Luke 1:10. Unlawfully offered by Nadab and Abihu, Lev. 10:1,2; Korah, Dathan, and Abiram, Num. 16:16-35; by Uzziah,

2 Chr. 26:16-21. Offered in idolatrous worship, 1 Kin. 12:33; Jer. 41:5; Ezek. 8:11. Presented by the wise men to Jesus, Matt. 2:11.

See ALTAR OF INCENSE.

FIGURATIVE: Of prayer, Psa. 141:2. Of praise, Mal. 1:11. Of an acceptable sacrifice, Eph. 5:2.

SYMBOLICAL· Of the prayers of saints, Rev. 5:8; 8:3,4.

INCEST. DEFINED AND FORBIDDEN: Lev. 18:6. None of you shall approach to any that is near of kin to him, to uncover *their* nakedness: I *am* the LORD. 7. The nakedness of thy father, or the nakedness of thy mother, shalt thou not uncover: she *is* thy mother; thou shalt not uncover her nakedness. 8. The nakedness of thy father's wife shalt thou not uncover: it *is* thy father's nakedness. 9. The nakedness of thy sister, the daughter of thy father, or daughter of thy mother, *whether she be* born at home, or born abroad, *even* their nakedness thou shalt not uncover. 10. The nakedness of thy son's daughter, or of thy daughter's daughter, *even* their nakedness thou shalt not uncover: for their's *is* thine own nakedness. 11. The nakedness of thy father's wife's daughter, begotten of thy father, she *is* thy sister, thou shalt not uncover her nakedness. 12. Thou shalt not uncover the nakedness of thy father's sister: she *is* thy father's near kinswoman. 13. Thou shalt not uncover the nakedness of thy mother's sister: for she *is* thy mother's near kinswoman. 14. Thou shalt not uncover the nakedness of thy father's brother, thou shalt not approach to his wife: she *is* thine aunt. 15. Thou shalt not uncover the nakedness of thy daughter in law: she *is* thy son's wife; thou shalt not uncover her nakedness. 16. Thou shalt not uncover the nakedness of thy brother's wife: it *is* thy brother's nakedness. 17. Thou shalt not uncover the nakedness of a woman and her daughter, neither shalt thou take her son's daughter, or her daughter's daughter, to uncover her nakedness; *for* they *are* her near kinswomen: it *is* wickedness. 18. Neither shalt thou take a wife to her sister, to vex *her*, to uncover her nakedness, beside the other in her life *time*.

Lev. 20:11. And the man that lieth with his father's wife hath uncovered his father's nakedness: both of them shall surely be put to death; their blood *shall be* upon them. 12. And if a man lie with his daughter in law, both of them shall surely be put to death: they have wrought confusion; their blood *shall be* upon them. 17. And if a man shall take his sister, his father's daughter, or his mother's daughter, and see her nakedness, and she see his nakedness; it *is* a wicked thing; and they shall be cut off in the sight of their people: he hath uncovered his sister's nakedness; he shall bear his iniquity. 19. And thou shalt not uncover the nakedness of thy mother's sister, nor of thy

father's sister: for he uncovereth his near kin: they shall bear their iniquity. 20. And if a man shall lie with his uncle's wife, he hath uncovered his uncle's nakedness: they shall bear their sin: they shall die childless. 21. And if a man shall take his brother's wife, it *is* an unclean thing: he hath uncovered his brother's nakedness; they shall be childless.

Deut. 22:30. A man shall not take his father's wife, nor discover his father's skirt.

Deut. 27:20. Cursed *be* he that lieth with his father's wife; because he uncovereth his father's skirt. And all the people shall say, Amen. 22. Cursed *be* he that lieth with his sister, the daughter of his father, or the daughter of his mother. And all the people shall say, Amen. 23. Cursed *be* he that lieth with his mother in law. And all the people shall say, Amen.

Ezek. 22:11. And one hath committed abomination with his neighbour's wife; and another hath lewdly defiled his daughter in law: and another in thee hath humbled his sister, his father's daughter.

1 Cor. 5:1. It is reported commonly *that there is* fornication among you, and such fornication as is not so much as named among the Gentiles, that one should have his father's wife.

INSTANCES OF: Lot with his daughters, Gen. 19:31-36. Abraham, Gen. 20:12,13. Nahor, Gen. 11:29. Reuben, Gen. 35:22; 49:4. Amram, Ex. 6:20. Judah, Gen. 38:16-18; 1 Chr. 2:4. Amnon, 2 Sam. 13:14. Absalom, 2 Sam. 16:21,22. Herod, Matt. 14:3,4; Mark 6:17,18; Luke 3:19. Israel, Amos 2:7.

Instances of marriage of near of kin: Isaac with Rebekah, Gen. 24:15,67. Jacob with Leah and Rachel, Gen. 29:23,30. Rehoboam, 2 Chr. 11:18.

INCINERATION. See CREMATION.

INCONSISTENCY. Matt. 7:3. And why beholdest thou the mote that is in thy brother's eye, but considerest not the beam that is in thine own eye? 4. Or how wilt thou say to thy brother, Let me pull out the mote out of thine eye; and, behold, a beam *is* in thine own eye? 5. Thou hypocrite, first cast out the beam out of thine own eye; and then shalt thou see clearly to cast out the mote out of thy brother's eye.

Matt. 23:3. All therefore whatsoever they bid you observe, *that* observe and do: but do not ye after their works: for they say, and do not. 4. For they bind heavy burdens and grievous to be borne, and lay *them* on men's shoulders; but they *them selves* will not move them with one of their fingers.

Rom. 2:1. Therefore thou art inexcusable, O man, whosoever thou art that judgest: for wherein thou judgest another, thou condemnest thyself; for thou that judgest doest the same things. 21. Thou therefore which teachest another, teachest thou not thyself? thou that preachest a man should not steal, dost thou steal? 22. Thou that sayest a man should not commit adultery, dost thou commit adultery? thou that abhorrest idols, dost thou commit sacrilege? 23. Thou that makest thy boast of the law, through breaking the law dishonourest thou God?

See DECEIT; DECEPTION; HYPOCRISY.

INSTANCES OF: Jehu, 2 Kin. 10:16-31. The Jews, in oppressing the poor, Neh. 5:9; in accusing Jesus of violating the Sabbath, John 7:22,23.

INDECISION. 1 Kin. 18:21. How long halt ye between two opinions? if the LORD *be* God, follow him: but if Baal, *then* follow him.

Hos. 10:2. Their heart is divided; now shall they be found faulty:

Matt. 6:24. No man can serve two masters: for either he will hate the one, and love the other; or else he will hold to the one, and despise the other. Ye cannot serve God and mammon.

Matt. 26:41. Watch and pray, that ye enter not into temptation: the spirit indeed *is* willing, but the flesh *is* weak.

Jas. 1:8. A double minded man *is* unstable in all his ways.

Jas. 4:17. To him that knoweth to do good, and doeth *it* not, to him it is sin.

See DECISION; INSTABILITY; LUKEWARMNESS.

INSTANCES OF: Moses at the Red Sea, Ex. 14:15. Joshua at Ai, Josh. 7:10. Esther, Esth. 5:8. Rulers, who believed in Jesus, John 12:42. Felix, Acts 24:25.

INDIA, probably the eastern limit of the kingdom of Ahasuerus, Esth. 1:1; 8:9.

INDICTMENTS. INSTANCES OF: Naboth on charge of blasphemy, 1 Kin. 21:13, with *vs.* 1-16. Jeremiah of treasonable prophecy, but of which he was acquitted, Jer. 26:1-24; a second indictment, Jer. 37:13-15. Three Hebrew captives on the charge of contumacy, Dan. 3:12, with *vs.* 1-28. Daniel of contumacy, Dan. 6:13 with *vs.* 1-24. Jesus, under two charges, first, of blasphemy, Matt. 26:61; Mark 14:58; Matt. 26:63-65; Mark 14:61-64; Luke 22:67-71; John 19:7; the second, of treason, Matt. 27:11,37; Mark 15:2,26; Luke 23:2,3,38; John 18:30,33; 19:12,19-22.

Stephen for blasphemy, Acts 6:11,13. Paul, Acts 17:7; 18:13; 24:5; 25:18,19,26,27. Paul and Silas, Acts 16:20,21.

Indictment quashed, Acts 18:14-16.

INDUSTRY. Gen. 2:15. The LORD God took the man, and put him into the garden of Eden to dress it and to keep it.

Ex. 23:12. Six days thou shalt do thy work, and on the seventh day thou shalt rest: Deut. 5:13.

Ex. 35:2. Six days shall work be done, but on the seventh day there shall be to you an holy day, a sabbath of rest to the LORD:

Prov. 10:4. He becometh poor that dealeth *with* a slack hand: but the hand of the diligent maketh rich. 5. He that gathereth in summer *is* a wise son:

Prov. 12:11. He that tilleth his land shall be satisfied with bread: 24. The hand of the diligent shall bear rule: but the slothful shall be under tribute. 27. The slothful *man* roasteth not that which he took in hunting: but the substance of a diligent man *is* precious.

Prov. 13:4. The soul of the sluggard desireth, and *hath* nothing: but the soul of the diligent shall be made fat. 11. He that gathereth by labour shall increase. 23. Much food *is in* the tillage of the poor:

Prov. 14:4. Where no oxen *are,* the crib *is* clean: but much increase *is* by the strength of the ox. 23. In all labour there is profit:

Prov. 16:26. He that laboureth laboureth for himself; for his mouth craveth it of him.

Prov. 20:13. Love not sleep, lest thou come to poverty; open thine eyes, *and* thou shalt be satisfied with bread.

Prov. 21:5. The thoughts of the diligent *tend* only to plenteousness; but of every one *that is* hasty only to want.

Prov. 22:29. Seest thou a man diligent in his business? he shall stand before kings; he shall not stand before mean *men.*

Prov. 27:23. Be thou diligent to know the state of thy flocks, *and* look well to thy herds: *vs.* 23-27.

Prov. 28:19. He that tilleth his land shall have plenty of bread:

Prov. 30:25. The ants *are* a people not strong, yet they prepare their meat in the summer; 26. The conies *are but* a feeble folk, yet make they their houses in the rocks; *vs.* 27,28.

Prov. 31:27. She looketh well to the ways of her household, and eateth not the bread of idleness. *vs.* 13-27.

Eccl. 1:3. What profit hath a man of all his labour which he taketh under the sun?

Eccl. 2:10. And whatsoever mine eyes desired I kept not from them, I withheld not my heart from any joy; for my heart rejoiced in all my labour: and this was my portion of all my labour. 11. Then I looked on all the works that my hands had wrought, and on the labour that I had laboured to do: and, behold, all *was* vanity and vexation of spirit, and *there was* no profit under the sun. 17. Therefore I hated life; because the work that is wrought under the sun *is* grievous unto me: for all *is* vanity and vexation of spirit. 18. Yea, I hated all my labour which I had taken under the sun: because I should leave it unto the man that shall be after me. 19. And who knoweth whether he shall be a wise *man* or a fool? yet shall he have rule over all my labour wherein I have laboured, and wherein I have shewed myself wise under the sun. This *is* also vanity. 20. Therefore I went about to cause my heart to despair of all the labour which I took under the sun. 21. For there is a man whose labour *is* in wisdom, and in knowledge, and in equity; yet to a man that hath not laboured therein shall he leave it *for* his portion. This also *is* vanity and a great evil. 22. For what hath man of all his labour, and of the vexation of his heart, wherein he hath laboured under the sun?

Eccl. 9:10. Whatsoever thy hand findeth to do, do *it* with thy might; for *there is* no work, nor device, nor knowledge, nor wisdom, in the grave, whither thou goest.

Eccl. 11:4. He that observeth the wind shall not sow; and he that regardeth the clouds shall not reap. 6. In the morning sow thy seed, and in the evening withhold not thine hand: for thou knowest not whether shall prosper, either this or that, or whether they both *shall be* alike good.

Rom. 12:11. ¹ Not slothful in business; **fervent** in spirit; serving the Lord;
[¹ R. V. In diligence not slothful]

Eph. 4:28. Let him that stole steal no more: but rather let him labour, working with *his* hands the thing which is good, that he may have to give to him that needeth.

1 Thess. 4:11. Study to be quiet, and to do your own business, and to work with your own hands, as we commanded you; 12. That ye may walk honestly toward them that are without, and *that* ye may have lack of nothing.

2 Thess. 3:10. For even when we were with you, this we commanded you, that if any would not work, neither should he eat. 11. For we hear that there are some which walk among you disorderly, working not at all, but are busybodies. 12. Now them that are such we command and exhort by our Lord Jesus Christ, that with quietness they work, and eat their own bread.

1 Tim. 5:8. If any provide not for his own, and specially for those of his own house, he hath denied the faith, and is worse than an infidel.

See FRUGALITY. Also see IDLENESS; SLOTHFULNESS.

INSTANCES OF: Jeroboam, 1 Kin. 11:28. Paul, Acts 18:3; 20:33,34; 2 Thess. 3:8.

INFANTICIDE, Ex. 1:15,16; Matt. 2:16–18; Acts 7:19.

INFANTS. See CHILDREN.

INFIDELITY. Gen. 3:1. Yea, hath God said, Ye shall not eat of every tree of the garden? *v.* 4.

Ex. 5:2. Pharaoh said, Who *is* the LORD, that I should obey his voice to let Israel go?

Ex. 14:11. And they said unto Moses, Because *there were* no graves in Egypt, hast thou taken us away to die in the wilderness? wherefore hast thou dealt thus with us, to carry us forth out of Egypt? *v.* 12; Ex. 16:3,7; Num. 14:27–34; 16:41; 21:5.

Ex. 17:7. And he called the name of the place Massah, and Meribah, because of the chiding of the children of Israel, and because they tempted the LORD, saying, Is the LORD among us, or not?

Num. 15:30. The soul that doeth *ought* presumptuously, *whether he be* born in the land, or a stranger, the same reproacheth the LORD; and that soul shall be cut off from among his people. *v.* 31.

Deut. 29:19. When he heareth the words of this curse, that he bless himself in his heart, saying, I shall have peace, though I walk in the imagination of mine heart, to add drunkenness to thirst: 20. The LORD will not spare him, but then the anger of the LORD and his jealousy shall smoke against that man, and all the curses that are written in this book shall lie upon him, and the LORD shall blot out his name from under heaven. *v.* 21.

Deut. 32:15. Jeshurun waxed fat, and kicked: thou art waxen fat, thou art grown thick, thou art covered *with fatness;* then he forsook God *which* made him, and lightly esteemed the Rock of his salvation.

1 Kin. 20:28. Because the Syrians have said, The LORD *is* God of the hills, but he *is* not God of the valleys, therefore will I deliver all this great multitude into thine hand, and ye shall know that I *am* the LORD.

1 Kin. 22:24. Zedekiah . . . went near, and smote Micaiah on the cheek, and said, Which way went the Spirit of the LORD from me to speak unto thee?

2 Kin. 2:23. There came forth little children out of the city, and mocked him, and said unto him, Go up, thou bald head; go up, thou bald head. *v.* 24.

2 Chr. 30:6. So the posts went with the letters from the king and his princes throughout all Israel and Judah, and according to the commandment of the king, saying, Ye children of Israel, turn again unto the LORD God of Abraham, Isaac, and Israel, and he will return to the remnant of you, that are escaped out of the hand of the kings of Assyria. 10. So the posts passed from city to city through the country of Ephraim and Manasseh even unto Zebulun: but they laughed them to scorn, and mocked them.

2 Chr. 32:15. Now therefore let not Hezekiah deceive you, nor persuade you on this manner, neither yet believe him: for no god of any nation or kingdom was able to deliver his people out of mine hand, and out of the hand of my fathers: how much less shall your God deliver you out of mine hand? *vs.* 16–19.

2 Chr. 36:16. They mocked the messengers of God, and despised his words, and misused his prophets, until the wrath of the LORD arose against his people, till *there was* no remedy.

Job 15:25. He stretcheth out his hand against God, and strengtheneth himself against the Almighty. 26. He runneth upon him, *even* on *his* neck, upon the thick bosses of his bucklers:

Job 21:14. They say unto God, Depart from us; for we desire not the knowledge of thy ways. 15. What *is* the Almighty, that we should serve him? and what profit should we have, if we pray unto him?

Job 22:13. Thou sayest, How doth God know? can he judge through the dark cloud? 14. Thick clouds *are* a covering to him, that he seeth not; and he walketh in the circuit of heaven. 17. Which said unto God, Depart from us: and what can the Almighty do for them?

Job 34:7. What man *is* like Job, *who* drinketh up scorning like water? 9. For he hath said, It profiteth a man nothing that he should delight himself with God. 17. Wilt thou condemn him that is most just? 18. *Is it fit* to say to a king, *Thou art* wicked? *and* to princes, *Ye are* ungodly? 19. *How much less to him* that accepteth not the persons of princes, nor regardeth the rich more than the poor? for they all *are* the work of his hands. 33. *Should it be* according to thy mind? he will recompense it, whether thou refuse, or whether thou choose;

Job 35:3. Thou saidst, What advantage will it be unto thee? *and*, What profit shall I have, *if I be cleansed* from my sin?

Job 36:23. Who hath enjoined him his way? or who can say, Thou hast wrought iniquity?

Psa. 1:1. Blessed *is* the man that walketh not in the counsel of the ungodly, nor standeth in the way of sinners, nor sitteth in the seat of the scornful.

Psa. 3:2. Many *there be* which say of my soul, *There is* no help for him in God.

Psa. 4:6. *There be* many that say, Who will shew us *any* good?

Psa. 10:11. He hath said in his heart, God hath forgotten: he hideth his face; he will never see *it*. 13. Wherefore doth the wicked contemn God? he hath said in his heart, Thou wilt not require *it*.

Psa. 12:3. The Lord shall cut off all flattering lips, *and* the tongue that speaketh proud things: 4. Who have said, With our tongue will we prevail; our lips *are* our own: who *is* lord over us?

Psa. 14:1. The fool hath said in his heart, *There is* no God. 6. Ye have shamed the counsel of the poor, because the Lord *is* his refuge. Psa. 53:1.

Psa. 42:3. My tears have been my meat day and night, while they continually say unto me, Where *is* thy God?

Psa. 50:21. These *things* hast thou done, and I kept silence; thou thoughtest that I was altogether *such an one* as thyself:

Psa. 59:7. Swords *are* in their lips: for who, *say they*, doth hear?

Psa. 64:5. They encourage themselves in an evil matter: they commune of laying snares privily; they say, Who shall see them?

Psa. 73:11. They say, How doth God know? and is there knowledge in the most High?

Psa. 78:19. Yea, they spake against God; they said, Can God furnish a table in the wilderness? *vs.* 20-22. Psa. 107:11,12.

Psa. 94:7. They say, The Lord shall not see, neither shall the God of Jacob regard *it*. 8. Understand, ye brutish among the people: and *ye* fools, when will ye be wise?

9. He that planted the ear, shall he not hear? he that formed the eye, shall he not see?

Psa. 106:24. They despised the pleasant land, they believed not his word: 25. But murmured in their tents, *and* hearkened not unto the voice of the Lord.

Prov. 1:22. How long, ye simple ones, will ye love simplicity? and the scorners delight in their scorning, and fools hate knowledge?

Prov. 3:34. Surely he scorneth the scorners:

Prov. 9:12. If thou be wise, thou shalt be wise for thyself: but *if* thou scornest, thou alone shalt bear *it*.

Prov. 14:6. A scorner seeketh wisdom, and *findeth it* not: 9. Fools make a mock at sin:

Prov. 19:29. Judgments are prepared for scorners,

Prov. 24:9. The scorner *is* an abomination to men.

Isa. 3:8. For Jerusalem is ruined, and Judah is fallen: because their tongue and their doings *are* against the Lord, to provoke the eyes of his glory.

Isa. 5:18. Woe unto them that draw iniquity with cords of vanity, and sin as it were with a cart rope: 19. That say, Let him make speed, *and* hasten his work, that we may see *it:* and let the counsel of the Holy One of Israel draw nigh and come, that we may know *it!* 24. As the fire devoureth the stubble, and the flame consumeth the chaff, *so* their root shall be as rottenness, and their blossom shall go up as dust: because they have cast away the law of the Lord of hosts, and despised the word of the Holy One of Israel. 25. Therefore is the anger of the Lord kindled against his people,

Isa. 10:15. Shall the ax boast itself against him that heweth therewith? *or* shall the saw magnify itself against him that shaketh it? as if the rod should shake *itself* against them that lift it up, *or* as if the staff should lift up *itself*, *as if it were* no wood.

Isa. 28:9. Whom shall he teach knowledge? and whom shall he make to understand doctrine? *them that are* weaned from the milk, *and* drawn from the breasts. 10. For precept *must be* upon precept, precept upon precept; line upon line, line upon line; here a little, *and* there a little: 14. Wherefore hear the word of the Lord, ye scornful men, that rule this people which *is* in Jerusalem. 15. Because ye have said, We have made a covenant with death, and with hell are we at agreement; when the overflowing scourge shall pass through, it shall not come unto us: for we have made lies our refuge, and under falsehood have we hid ourselves: 17. Judgment also will I lay to the line, and righteousness to the plummet: and the hail shall sweep away the refuge of lies, and the waters shall overflow the hiding place. 18. And your covenant with death shall be disannulled, and your agreement with hell shall not stand; when the overflowing scourge shall pass through, then ye shall be trodden down by it. 19. From the time that it goeth forth it shall take you: for morning by morning shall it pass over, by day and by night: and it shall be a vexation only *to* understand the report. 20. For the bed is shorter than that *a man* can stretch himself *on it:* and the covering narrower than that he can wrap himself *in it.* 21. For the LORD shall rise up as *in* mount Perazim, he shall be wroth as *in* the valley of Gibeon, that he may do his work, his strange work; and bring to pass his act, his strange act. 22. Now therefore be ye not mockers, lest your bands be made strong: for I have heard from the Lord GOD of hosts a consumption, even determined upon the whole earth.

Isa. 29:15. Woe unto them that seek deep to hide their counsel from the LORD, and their works are in the dark, and they say, Who seeth us? and who knoweth us? 16. Surely your turning of things upside down shall be esteemed as the potter's clay: for shall the work say of him that made it, He made me not? or shall the thing framed say of him that framed it, He had no understanding? 20. The scorner is consumed, and all that watch for iniquity are cut off:

Isa. 45:9. Woe unto him that striveth with his Maker! *Let* the potsherd *strive* with the potsherds of the earth. Shall the clay say to him that fashioneth it, What makest thou? or thy work, He hath no hands? 10. Woe unto him that saith unto *his* father, What begettest thou? or to the woman, What hast thou brought forth?

Isa. 47:10. Thou hast trusted in thy wickedness: thou hast said, None seeth me. Thy wisdom and thy knowledge, it hath perverted thee; and thou hast said in thine heart, I *am*, and none else beside me. 11. Therefore shall evil come upon thee; thou shalt not know from whence it riseth: and mischief shall fall upon thee; thou shalt not be able to put it off: and desolation shall come upon thee suddenly, *which* thou shalt not know.

Isa. 57:4. Against whom do ye sport yourselves? against whom make ye a wide mouth, *and* draw out the tongue? 11. And of whom hast thou been afraid or feared, that thou hast lied, and hast not remembered me, nor laid *it* to thy heart? have not I held my peace even of old, and thou fearest me not? *vs.* 5-10.

Jer. 2:31. O generation, see ye the word of the LORD. Have I been a wilderness unto Israel? a land of darkness? wherefore say my people, We are [1 lords]; we will come no more unto thee?   [1 R. V. broken loose]

Jer. 5:12. They have belied the LORD, and said, *It is* not he; neither shall evil come upon us; neither shall we see sword nor famine: 14. Wherefore thus saith the LORD God of hosts, Because ye speak this word, behold, I will make my words in thy mouth fire, and this people wood, and it shall devour them.

Jer. 17:15. They say unto me, Where *is* the word of the LORD? let it come now. Jer. 43:2.

Jer. 48:42. Moab shall be destroyed from *being* a people, because he hath magnified *himself* against the LORD. *v.*26.

Jer. 50:24. Thou art found, and also caught, because thou hast striven against the LORD. 29. According to all that she hath done, do unto her: for she hath been proud against the LORD, against the Holy One of Israel.

Lam. 1:7. Jerusalem remembered in the days of her affliction and of her miseries all her pleasant things that she had in the days of old, when her people fell into the hand of the enemy, and none did help her: the adversaries saw her, *and* did mock at her sabbaths.

Ezek. 9:9. Then said he unto me, The iniquity of the house of Israel and Judah *is* exceeding great, and the land is full of blood, and the city full of perverseness: for they say, The LORD hath forsaken the earth, and the LORD seeth not. 10. And as for me also, mine eye shall not spare, neither will I have pity, *but* I will recompense their way upon their head. Ezek. 8:12.

Ezek. 12:22. What *is* that proverb *that* ye have in the land of Israel, saying, The days are prolonged, and every vision faileth? Ezek. 11:3.

Ezek. 18:2. What mean ye, that ye use this proverb concerning the land of Israel, saying, The fathers have eaten sour grapes, and the children's teeth are set on edge? 29. Yet saith the house of Israel, The way of the Lord is not equal. O house of Israel, are not my ways equal? are not your ways unequal? Ezek. 33:17.

Ezek. 20:49. Ah Lord GOD! they say of me, Doth he not speak parables?

Ezek. 33:20. Yet ye say, The way of the Lord is not equal. O ye house of Israel, I will judge you every one after his ways. 30. The children of thy people still are talking against thee by the walls and in the doors of the houses, and speak one to another, every one to his brother, saying, Come, I pray you, and hear what is the word that cometh forth from the LORD.

Ezek. 36:2. Thus saith the Lord GOD; Because the enemy hath said against you, Aha, even the ancient high places are our's in possession:

Dan. 3:15. Who *is* that God that shall deliver you out of my hands?

Dan. 8:25. He shall magnify *himself* in his heart, . . . he shall also stand up against the Prince of princes; but he shall be broken without hand. *v.* 10. Dan. 7:25; 11:36,37.

Hos. 7:5. In the day of cur king the princes have made *him* sick with bottles of wine; 13. Woe unto them! for they have fled from me: destruction unto them! because they have transgressed against me: though I have redeemed them, yet they have spoken lies against me. 15. Though I have bound *and* strengthened their arms, yet do they imagine mischief against me.

Amos 5:18. Woe unto you that desire the day of the LORD! to what end *is* it for you? the day of the LORD *is* darkness, and not light.

Amos 7:16. Thou sayest, Prophesy not against Israel, and drop not *thy word* against the house of Isaac. 17. Therefore thus saith the LORD, . . . thou shalt die in a polluted land:

Mic. 7:10. Then *she that is* mine enemy shall see *it*, and shame shall cover her which said unto me, Where is the LORD thy God? mine eyes shall behold her: now shall she be trodden down as the mire of the streets.

Zeph. 1:12. I will search Jerusalem with candles, and punish the men that are settled on their lees: that say in their heart, The LORD will not do good, neither will he do evil.

Mal. 1:7. Ye offer polluted bread upon mine altar; and ye say, Wherein have we polluted thee? In that ye say, The table of the LORD *is* contemptible.

Mal. 3:13. Your words have been stout against me, saith the LORD. Yet ye say, What have we spoken *so much* against thee? 14. Ye have said, It *is* vain to serve God: and what profit *is it* that we have kept his ordinance, and that we have walked mournfully before the LORD of hosts?

Matt. 12:24. When the Pharisees heard *it*, they said, This *fellow* doth not cast out devils, but by Beelzebub the prince of the devils. Mark 3:22; Luke 11:15; 16:14.

Matt. 25:24. Then he which had received the one talent came and said, Lord, I knew thee that thou art an hard man, reaping where thou hast not sown, and gathering where thou hast not strawed: 25. And I was afraid, and went and hid thy talent in the earth: lo, *there* thou hast *that is* thine. 26. His lord answered and said unto him, *Thou* wicked and slothful servant, thou knewest that I reap where I sowed not, and gather where I have not strawed: 27. Thou oughtest therefore to have put my money to the exchangers, and *then* at my coming I should have received mine own with usury.

Matt. 27:39. And they that passed by reviled him, wagging their heads, 40. And saying, Thou that destroyest the temple, and buildest *it* in three days, save thyself. If thou be the Son of God, come down from the cross. 41. Likewise also the chief priests mocking *him*, with the scribes and elders, said, 42. He saved others; himself he cannot save. If he be the King of Israel, let him now come down from the cross, and we will believe him. 43. He trusted in God; let him deliver him now, if he will have him: for he said, I am the Son of God. 44. The thieves also, which were crucified with him, cast the same in his teeth.

Luke 4:23. And he said unto them, Ye will surely say unto me this proverb, Physician, heal thyself: whatsoever we have heard

done in Capernaum, do also here in thy country.

Luke 19:14. His citizens hated him, and sent a message after him, saying, We will not have this *man* to reign over us. 27. Those mine enemies, which would not that I should reign over them, bring hither, and slay *them* before me.

Acts 2:13. Others mocking said, These men are full of new wine.

Acts 13:45. When the Jews saw the multitudes, they were filled with envy, and spake against those things which were spoken by Paul, contradicting and blaspheming.

Acts 17:18. Then certain philosophers of the Epicureans, and of the Stoics, encountered him. And some said, What will this babbler say? other some, He seemeth to be a setter forth of strange gods: because he preached unto them Jesus, and the resurrection. 32. When they heard of the resurrection of the dead, some mocked:

Acts 23:8. The Sadducees say that there is no resurrection, neither angel, nor spirit: Matt. 22:23.

Rom. 9:20. Nay but, O man, who art thou that repliest against God? Shall the thing formed say to him that formed *it*, Why hast thou made me thus? 21. Hath not the potter power over the clay, of the same lump to make one vessel unto honour, and another unto dishonour? Rom. 3:5.

Heb. 10:29. Of how much sorer punishment, suppose ye, shall he be thought worthy, who hath trodden under foot the Son of God, and hath counted the blood of the covenant, wherewith he was sanctified, an unholy thing, and hath done despite unto the Spirit of grace?

2 Pet. 2:1. There shall be false teachers among you, who privily shall bring in ¹ damnable heresies, even denying the Lord that bought them, and bring upon themselves swift destruction. [¹ R. V. destructive]

2 Pet. 3:3. There shall come in the last days scoffers, walking after their own lusts, 4. And saying, Where is the promise of his coming? for since the fathers fell asleep, all things continue as *they were* from the beginning of the creation. *v.* 5.

Jude 4. There are certain men crept in unawares, who were before of old ordained to this condemnation, ungodly men, turning the grace of our God into lasciviousness, and denying the only Lord God, and our Lord Jesus Christ. 15. To execute judgment upon all, and to convince all that are ungodly among them of all their ungodly deeds which they have ungodly committed, and of all their hard *speeches* which ungodly sinners have spoken against him. 18. They told you there should be mockers in the last time, who should walk after their own ungodly lusts. *v.* 19.

See PRESUMPTION; SKEPTICISM; UNBE-LIEF.

INFIRMITY. PHYSICAL: Moses exempt from, Deut. 34:7; Caleb, Josh. 14:11.

See AFFLICTION; BLINDNESS; DEAFNESS; LAMENESS; OLD AGE; TASTE.

INFLUENCE. EVIL: 1 Kin. 11:3. And he had seven hundred wives, princesses, and three hundred concubines: and his wives turned away his heart. 4. For it came to pass, when Solomon was old, *that* his wives turned away his heart after other gods: and his heart was not perfect with the LORD his God, as *was* the heart of David his father.

1 Kin. 15:25. And Nadab the son of Jeroboam began to reign over Israel in the second year of Asa king of Judah, and reigned over Israel two years. 26. And he did evil in the sight of the LORD, and walked in the way of his father, and in his sin wherewith he made Israel to sin.

1 Kin. 21:25. But there was none like unto Ahab, which did sell himself to work wickedness in the sight of the LORD, whom Jezebel his wife stirred up.

1 Kin. 22:51. Ahaziah the son of Ahab began to reign over Israel in Samaria the seventeenth year of Jehoshaphat king of Judah, and reigned two years over Israel. 52. And he did evil in the sight of the LORD, and walked in the way of his father, and in the way of his mother, and in the way of Jeroboam the son of Nebat, who made Israel to sin: 53. For he served Baal, and worshipped him, and provoked to anger the LORD God of Israel, according to all that his father had done.

2 Kin. 8:16. And in the fifth year of Joram the son of Ahab king of Israel, Jehoshaphat *being* then king of Judah, Jehoram the son of Jehoshaphat king of Judah began to reign. 17. Thirty and two years old was he when he began to reign; and he reigned eight years in Jerusalem. 18. And he walked in the way of the kings of Israel, as did the house of Ahab: for the daughter of Ahab was his wife: and he did evil in the sight of the LORD. 25. In the twelfth year of Joram the son of Ahab king of Israel did Ahaziah the son of Jehoram king of Judah begin to reign. 26. Two and twenty years old *was* Ahaziah when he began to reign; and he reigned one year in Jerusalem. And his mother's name *was* Athaliah, the daughter of Omri king of Israel. 27. And he walked in the way of the house of Ahab, and did evil in the sight of the LORD, as *did* the house of Ahab: for he *was* the son in law of the house of Ahab.

2 Kin. 17:21. For he rent Israel from the house of David; and they made Jeroboam the son of Nebat king: and Jeroboam drave Israel from following the LORD, and made them sin a great sin. 22. For the children of Israel walked in all the sins of Jeroboam which he did; they departed not from them;

2 Kin. 21:9. But they hearkened not: and Manasseh seduced them to do more evil than did the nations whom the LORD destroyed before the children of Israel.

2 Chr. 21:5. Jehoram *was* thirty and two years old when he began to reign, and he reigned eight years in Jerusalem. 6. And he walked in the way of the kings of Israel, like as did the house of Ahab: for he had the daughter of Ahab to wife: and he wrought *that which was* evil in the eyes of the LORD.

2 Chr. 22:3. He also walked in the ways of the house of Ahab: for his mother was his counsellor to do wickedly. 4. Wherefore he did evil in the sight of the LORD like the house of Ahab: for they were his counsellors after the death of his father to his destruction. 5. He walked also after their counsel, and went with Jehoram the son of Ahab king of Israel to war against Hazael king of Syria at Ramoth-gilead: and the Syrians smote Joram.

2 Chr. 33:9. So Manasseh made Judah and the inhabitants of Jerusalem to err, *and* to do worse than the heathen, whom the LORD had destroyed before the children of Israel.

Prov. 22:24. Make no friendship with an angry man; and with a furious man thou shalt not go: 25. Lest thou learn his ways, and get a snare to thy soul.

Prov. 29:12. If a ruler hearken to lies, all his servants *are* wicked.

Jer. 17:1. The sin of Judah *is* written with a pen of iron, *and* with the point of a diamond: *it is* graven upon the table of their heart, and upon the horns of your altars; 2. Whilst their children remember their altars and their groves by the green trees upon the high hills.

Hos. 4:9. And there shall be, like people, like priest: and I will punish them for their ways, and reward them their doings.

Matt. 13:24. Another parable put he forth unto them, saying, The kingdom of heaven is likened unto a man which sowed good seed in his field: 25. But while men slept, his enemy came and sowed tares among the wheat, and went his way.

Luke 12:1. Beware ye of the leaven of the Pharisees, which is hypocrisy.

1 Cor. 5:6. Your glorying *is* not good. Know ye not that a little leaven leaveneth the whole lump? 7. Purge out therefore the old leaven, that ye may be a new lump, as ye are unleavened. For even Christ our passover is sacrificed for us: 8. Therefore let us keep the feast, not with old leaven, neither with the leaven of malice and wickedness; but with the unleavened *bread* of sincerity and truth.

Gal. 3:1. O foolish Galatians, who hath bewitched you, ¹ that ye should not obey the truth, before whose eyes Jesus Christ hath been evidently set forth, crucified among you?

[¹ Omitted in R. V.]

Gal. 5:7. Ye did run well; who did hinder you that ye should not obey the truth? 8. This persuasion *cometh* not of him that calleth you. 9. A little leaven leaveneth the whole lump.

2 Tim. 2:14. Of these things put *them* in remembrance, charging *them* before the Lord that they strive not about words to no

profit, *but* to the subverting of the hearers. 17. And their word will eat as doth a canker: of whom is Hymenæus and Philetus; 18. Who concerning the truth have erred, saying that the resurrection is past already; and overthrow the faith of some.

Heb. 12:15. Looking diligently lest any man fail of the grace of God; lest any root of bitterness springing up trouble *you*, and thereby many be defiled;

See EXAMPLE.

INSTANCES OF: Satan over Adam and Eve, Gen. 3:1-5. Eve over Adam, Gen. 3:6.

GOOD: 1 Sam. 19:1. And Saul spake to Jonathan his son, and to all his servants, that they should kill David. 2. But Jonathan Saul's son delighted much in David: and Jonathan told David, saying, Saul my father seeketh to kill thee: now therefore, I pray thee, take heed to thyself until the morning, and abide in a secret *place*, and hide thyself: 3. And I will go and stand beside my father in the field where thou *art*, and I will commune with my father of thee; and what I see, that I will tell thee. 4. And Jonathan spake good of David unto Saul his father, and said unto him, Let not the king sin against his servant, against David; because he hath not sinned against thee, and because his works *have been* to thee-ward very good: 5. For he did put his life in his hand, and slew the Philistine, and the LORD wrought a great salvation for all Israel: thou sawest *it*, and didst rejoice: wherefore then wilt thou sin against innocent blood, to slay David without a cause? 6. And Saul hearkened unto the voice of Jonathan: and Saul sware, *As* the LORD liveth, he shall not be slain.

1 Sam. 20:4. Then said Jonathan unto David, Whatsoever thy soul desireth, I will even do *it* for thee. 5. And David said unto Jonathan, Behold, to morrow *is* the new moon, and I should not fail to sit with the king at meat: but let me go, that I may hide myself in the field unto the third *day* at even. 6. If thy father at all miss me, then say, David earnestly asked *leave* of me that he might run to Beth-lehem his city: for *there is* a yearly sacrifice there for all the family. 7. If he say thus, It *is* well; thy servant shall have peace: but if he be very wroth, *then* be sure that evil is determined by him. 8. Therefore thou shalt deal kindly with thy servant; for thou hast brought thy servant into a covenant of the LORD with thee: notwithstanding, if there be in me iniquity, slay me thyself; for why shouldest thou bring me to thy father? 9. And Jonathan said, Far be it from thee: for if I knew certainly that evil were determined by my father to come upon thee, then would not I tell it thee?

1 Kin. 22:42. Jehoshaphat *was* thirty and five years old when he began to reign; and he reigned twenty and five years in Jerusalem. And his mother's name *was* Azubah the daughter of Shilhi. 43. And he walked in all the ways of Asa his father; he turned not aside from it, doing *that which was* right in the eyes of the LORD: nevertheless the high places were not taken away; *for* the people offered and burnt incense yet in the high places.

2 Kin. 15:1. In the twenty and seventh year of Jeroboam king of Israel began Azariah son of Amaziah king of Judah to reign. 2. Sixteen years old was he when he began to reign, and he reigned two and fifty years in Jerusalem. And his mother's name *was* Jecholiah of Jerusalem. 3. And he did *that which was* right in the sight of the LORD, according to all that his father Amaziah had done;

32. In the second year of Pekah the son of Remaliah king of Israel began Jotham the son of Uzziah king of Judah to reign. 33. Five and twenty years old was he when he began to reign, and he reigned sixteen years in Jerusalem. And his mother's name *was* Jerusha, the daughter of Zadok. 34. And he did *that which was* right in the sight of the LORD: he did according to all that his father Uzziah had done.

Matt. 5:13. Ye are the salt of the earth: but if the salt have lost his savour, wherewith shall it be salted? it is thenceforth good for nothing, but to be cast out, and to be trodden under foot of men. 14. Ye are the light of the world. A city that is set on an hill cannot be hid. 15. Neither do men light a candle, and put it under a bushel, but on a candlestick; and it giveth light unto all that are in the house. 16. Let your light so shine before men, that they may see your good works, and glorify your Father which is in heaven.

Mark 4:21. And he said unto them, Is a candle brought to be put under a bushel, or under a bed? and not to be set on a candlestick? 22. For there is nothing hid, which shall not be manifested; neither was any thing kept secret, but that it should come abroad.

Luke 11:33. No man, when he hath lighted a candle, putteth *it* in a secret place, neither under a bushel, but on a candlestick, that they which come in may see the light. 34. The light of the body is the eye: therefore when thine eye is single, thy whole body also is full of light; but when *thine eye* is evil, thy body also *is* full of darkness. 35. Take heed therefore that the light which is in thee be not darkness. 36. If thy whole body therefore *be* full of light, having no part dark, the whole shall be full of light, as when the bright shining of a candle doth give thee light.

John 7:38. He that believeth on me, as the scripture hath said, out of his belly shall flow rivers of living water.

1 Cor. 7:16. For what knowest thou, O wife, whether thou shalt save *thy* husband? or how knowest thou, O man, whether thou shalt save *thy* wife?

Phil. 2:15. That ye may be blameless and

harmless, the sons of God, without rebuke, in the midst of a crooked and perverse nation, among whom ye shine as lights in the world;

1 Thess. 1:7. Ye were ensamples to all that believe in Macedonia and Achaia. 8. For from you sounded out the word of the Lord not only in Macedonia and Achaia, but also in every place your faith to God-ward is spread abroad; so that we need not to speak any thing.

1 Tim. 6:1. Let as many servants as are under the yoke count their own masters worthy of all honour, that the name of God and *his* doctrine be not blasphemed.

Heb. 11:4. By faith Abel offered unto God a more excellent sacrifice than Cain, by which he obtained witness that he was righteous, God testifying of his gifts: and by it he being dead yet speaketh.

1 Pet. 2:11. Dearly beloved, I beseech *you* as strangers and pilgrims, abstain from fleshly lusts, which war against the soul; 12. Having your conversation honest among the Gentiles: that, whereas they speak against you as evildoers, they may by *your* good works, which they shall behold, glorify God in the day of visitation.

1 Pet. 3:1. Likewise, ye wives, *be* in subjection to your own husbands; that, if any obey not the word, they also may without the word be won by the conversation of the wives; 2. While they behold your chaste conversation *coupled* with fear. 15. But sanctify the Lord God in your hearts: and *be* ready always to *give* an answer to every man that asketh you a reason of the hope that is in you with meekness and fear: 16. Having a good conscience; that, whereas they speak evil of you, as of evildoers, they may be ashamed that falsely accuse your good conversation in Christ.

See EXAMPLE.

INSTANCES OF: Ezra, Ezra 10:1, with chapter 9. Nehemiah, Neh. chapters 4; 5. Hezekiah, 2 Chr. chapters 29-31. Josiah, 2 Kin. chapters 22:23; 2 Chr. chapters 34; 35. Manasseh, 2 Chr. 33:12-19.

POLITICAL: 1 Kin. 2:13. And Adonijah the son of Haggith came to Bath-sheba the mother of Solomon. And she said, Comest thou peaceably? And he said, Peaceably. 14. He said moreover, I have somewhat to say unto thee. And she said, Say on. 15. And he said, Thou knowest that the kingdom was mine, and *that* all Israel set their faces on me, that I should reign; howbeit the kingdom is turned about, and is become my brother's: for it was his from the LORD. 16. And now I ask one petition of thee, deny me not. And she said unto him, Say on. 17. And he said, Speak, I pray thee, unto Solomon the king, (for he will not say thee nay,) that he give me Abishag the Shunammite to wife. 18. And Bath-sheba said, Well; I will speak for thee unto the king.

2 Kin. 4:12. And he said to Gehazi his servant, Call this Shunammite. And when

he had called her, she stood before him. 13. And he said unto him, Say now unto her, Behold, thou hast been careful for us with all this care; what *is* to be done for thee? wouldest thou be spoken for to the king, or to the captain of the host? And she answered, I dwell among mine own people.

Neh. 6:17. Moreover in those days the nobles of Judah sent many letters unto Tobiah, and *the letters* of Tobiah came unto them. 18. For *there were* many in Judah sworn unto him, because he *was* the son in law of Shechaniah the son of Arah; and his son Johanan had taken the daughter of Meshullam the son of Berechiah. 19. Also they reported his good deeds before me, and uttered my words to him. *And* Tobiah sent letters to put me in fear.

Prov. 19:6. Many will intreat the favour of the prince: and every man *is* a friend to him that giveth gifts.

Prov. 29:26. Many seek the ruler's favour; but *every* man's judgment *cometh* from the LORD.

Dan. 5:10. *Now* the queen by reason of the words of the king and his lords came into the banquet house: *and* the queen spake and said, O king, live for ever: let not thy thoughts trouble thee, nor let thy countenance be changed · 11. There is a man in thy kingdom, in whom *is* the spirit of the holy gods; and in the days of thy father light and understanding and wisdom, like the wisdom of the gods, was found in him; whom the king Nebuchadnezzar thy father, the king, *I say*, thy father, made master of the magicians, astrologers, Chaldeans, *and* soothsayers; 12. Forasmuch as an excellent spirit, and knowledge, and understanding, interpreting of dreams, and shewing of hard sentences, and dissolving of doubts, were found in the same Daniel, whom the king named Belteshazzar: now let Daniel be called, and he will shew the interpretation.

Matt. 20:20. Then came to him the mother of Zebedee's children with her sons, worshipping *him*, and desiring a certain thing of him. 21. And he said unto her, What wilt thou? She saith unto him, Grant that these my two sons may sit, the one on thy right hand, and the other on the left, in thy kingdom. 22. But Jesus answered and said, Ye know not what ye ask. Are ye able to drink of the cup that I shall drink of, and to be baptized with the baptism that I am baptized with? They say unto him, We are able. 23. And he saith unto them, Ye shall drink indeed of my cup, and be baptized with the baptism that I am baptized with: but to sit on my right hand, and on my left, is not mine to give, but *it shall be given to them* for whom it is prepared of my Father. 24. And when the ten heard *it*, they were moved with indignation against the two brethren.

Acts 12:20. And Herod was highly displeased with them of Tyre and Sidon; but they came with one accord to him, and, having made Blastus the king's chamberlain their friend, desired peace; because their country was nourished by the king's *country.*

See POLITICS.

INGATHERING, FEAST OF: See TABERNACLES, FEAST OF.

INGRAFTING. See GRAFTING.

INGRATITUDE. OF MAN TO GOD: Num. 16:9. *Seemeth it but* a small thing unto you, that the God of Israel hath separated you from the congregation of Israel, to bring you near to himself to do the service of the tabernacle of the LORD, and to stand before the congregation to minister unto them? 10. And he hath brought thee near *to him,* and all thy brethren the sons of Levi with thee: and seek ye the priesthood also ?

Deut. 8:12. Lest *when* thou hast eaten and art full, and hast built goodly houses, and dwelt *therein ;* 13. And *when* thy herds and thy flocks multiply, and thy silver and thy gold is multiplied, and all that thou hast is multiplied ; 14. Then thine heart be lifted up, and thou forget the LORD thy God, which brought thee forth out of the land of Egypt, from the house of bondage; Deut. 6:11,12.

Deut. 28:47. Because thou servedst not the LORD thy God with joyfulness, and with gladness of heart, for the abundance of all *things ;* 48. Therefore shalt thou serve thine enemies which the LORD shall send against thee, in hunger, and in thirst, and in nakedness, and in want of all *things :*

Deut. 31:16. And the LORD said unto Moses, Behold, thou shalt sleep with thy fathers; and this people will rise up, and go a whoring after the gods of the strangers of the land, whither they go *to be* among them, and will forsake me,

Deut. 32:6. Do ye thus requite the LORD, O foolish people and unwise? *is* not he thy father *that* hath bought thee? hath he not made thee, and established thee? 15. But Jeshurun waxed fat, and kicked: thou art waxen fat, thou art grown thick, thou art covered *with fatness ;* then he forsook God *which* made him, and lightly esteemed the Rock of his salvation. 18. Of the Rock *that* begat thee thou art unmindful, and hast forgotten God that formed thee. *v.* 13.

Judg. 2:10. There arose another generation after them, which knew not the LORD, nor yet the works which he had done for Israel. 11. And the children of Israel did evil in the sight of the LORD, . . . 12. And they forsook the LORD God of their fathers, which brought them out of the land of Egypt, and followed other gods,

Judg. 8:34. And the children of Israel remembered not the LORD their God, who had delivered them out of the hands of all their enemies on every side: 35. Neither shewed they kindness to the house of Jerubbaal, *namely,* Gideon, according to all the goodness which he had shewed unto Israel.

Judg. 10:11. *Did* not *I deliver you* from the Egyptians, and from the Amorites, 13. Yet ye have forsaken me, and served other gods: wherefore I will deliver you no more. 14. Go and cry unto the gods which ye have chosen; let them deliver you in the time of your tribulation. Neh. 9:25,35; Psa. 106:7,21; Jer. 2:6,7.

1 Sam. 8:7. And the LORD said unto Samuel, Hearken unto the voice of the people in all that they say unto thee: for they have not rejected thee, but they have rejected me, that I should not reign over them. 8. According to all the works which they have done since the day that I brought them up out of Egypt even unto this day, wherewith they have forsaken me, and served other gods, so do they also unto thee.

1 Sam. 10:19. Ye have this day rejected your God, who himself saved you out of all your adversities and your tribulations ; and ye have said unto him, *Nay,* but set a king over us.

1 Sam. 15:17. When thou *wast* little in thine own sight, *wast* thou not *made* the head of the tribes of Israel, and the LORD anointed thee king over Israel ? 19. Wherefore then didst thou not obey the voice of the LORD, but didst fly upon the spoil, and didst evil in the sight of the LORD ?

2 Sam. 12:7. I delivered thee out of the hand of Saul ; 8. And I gave thee thy master's house, and thy master's wives into thy bosom, and gave thee the house of Israel and of Judah ; and if *that had been* too little, I would moreover have given unto thee such and such things. 9. Wherefore hast thou despised the commandment of the LORD, to do evil in his sight ? 2 Chr. 12:1.

1 Kin. 16:1. Then the word of the LORD came to Jehu the son of Hanani against Baasha, saying, 2. Forasmuch as I exalted thee out of the dust, and made thee prince over my people Israel; and thou hast walked in the way of Jeroboam, and hast made my people Israel to sin, to provoke me to anger with their sins; 3. Behold, I will take away the posterity of Baasha, and the posterity of his house ; and will make thy house like the house of Jeroboam the son of Nebat.

2 Chr. 26:15. His name spread far abroad for he was marvellously helped, till he was strong. 16. But when he was strong, his heart was lifted up to *his* destruction: for he transgressed against the LORD his God, and went into the temple of the LORD to burn incense upon the altar of incense.

2 Chr. 32:25. Hezekiah rendered not again according to the benefit *done* unto him; for his heart was lifted up: therefore there was wrath upon him, and upon Judah and Jerusalem.

Psa. 78:16. He brought streams also out of the rock, and caused waters to run down like rivers. 17. And they sinned yet more against him by provoking the most High in the wilderness. 27. He rained flesh also upon them as dust, and feathered fowls like as the sand of the sea: 28. And he let *it* fall in the midst of their camp, round about their habitations. 29. So they did eat, and were well filled : for he gave them their own desire; 30. They were not estranged from their lust. But while their meat *was* yet in their mouths, 31. The wrath of God came upon them, and slew the fattest of them, and smote down the chosen *men* of Israel. 32. For all this they sinned still, and believed not for his wondrous works.

Psa. 106:7. Our fathers understood not thy wonders in Egypt; they remembered not the multitude of thy mercies;

Isa. 1:2. I have nourished and brought up children, and they have rebelled against me.

Jer. 2:17. Hast thou not procured this unto thyself, in that thou hast forsaken the LORD thy God, when he led thee by the way ? 31. Have I been a wilderness unto Israel ? a land of darkness ? wherefore say my people, We are ¹ lords ; we will come no more unto thee ? [¹ R. V. broken loose]

Jer. 5:7. How shall I pardon thee for this ? thy children have forsaken me, and sworn by *them that are* no gods: when I had fed them to the full, they then committed adultery, 9. Shall I not visit for these *things?* saith the LORD: and shall not my soul be avenged on such a nation as this ? 24. Neither say they in their heart, Let us now fear the LORD our God, that giveth rain, both the former and the latter, in his season: he reserveth unto us the appointed weeks of the harvest.

Ezek. 16:17. Thou hast also taken thy fair jewels of my gold and of my silver, which I had given thee, and madest to thyself images of men, *vs.* 17-22.

Dan. 5:18. O thou king, the most high God gave Nebuchadnezzar thy father a kingdom, and majesty, and glory, and honour: 20. But when his heart was lifted up, and his mind hardened in pride, he was deposed from his kingly throne, and they took his glory from him: 21. And he was driven from the sons of men; ... till he knew that the most high God ruled in the kingdom of men, and *that* he appointeth over it whomsoever he will.

Hos. 2:8. She did not know that I gave her corn, and wine, and oil, and multiplied her silver and gold, *which* they prepared for Baal. 9. Therefore will I return, and take away my corn in the time thereof, and my wine in the season thereof, and will recover my wool and my flax *given* to cover her nakedness.

Hos. 4:7. As they were increased, so they sinned against me: *therefore* will I change their glory into shame.

Hos. 7:13. Woe unto them! for they have fled from me: destruction unto them! because they have transgressed against me: though I have redeemed them, yet they have spoken lies against me. 15. Though I have bound *and* strengthened their arms,

yet do they imagine mischief against me.

Hos. 11:1. When Israel was a child, then I loved him, ... 3. I taught Ephraim also to go, taking them ¹ by their arms; but they knew not that I healed them. [¹ R. V. on my]

Hos. 13:6. According to their pasture, so were they filled; they were filled, and their heart was exalted; therefore have they forgotten me.

Amos 3:1. O children of Israel, ... 2. You only have I known of all the families of the earth : therefore I will punish you for all your iniquities.

Mic. 6:3. O my people, what have I done unto thee ? and wherein have I wearied thee ? testify against me. 4. For I brought thee up out of the land of Egypt, and redeemed thee out of the house of servants;

Luke 17:17. Were there not ten cleansed ? but where *are* the nine ? 18. There are not found that returned to give glory to God, save this stranger.

John 1:11. He came unto his own, and his own received him not.

Rom. 1:21. Because that, when they knew God, they glorified *him* not as God, neither were thankful; but became vain in their imaginations, and their foolish heart was darkened.

2 Tim. 3:2. Men shall be lovers of their own selves, ... unthankful,

OF MAN TO MAN: Prov. 17:13; 2 Tim. 3:2.

INSTANCES OF: Laban to Jacob, Gen. 31. Pharaoh's butler to Joseph, Gen. 40:23. Israelites to Moses, Ex. 16:3; 17:2-4; Num. 16: 12-14; to Gideon, Judg. 8:35. Shechemites, Judg. 9:17,18. Men of Keilah to David, 1 Sam. 23:5-12. Saul to David, 1 Sam. 24. Nabal, 1 Sam. 25:21. David to Joab, 1 Kin. 2:5,6; with the history of Joab's services to David, see JOAB. David to Uriah, 2 Sam. 11:6-17. David's companions to David, Psa. 35:11-16; 38:20; 41:9; 109:4,5. Citizens, Eccl. 9:14-16. Joash, 2 Chr. 24:22. Jeremiah's enemies, Jer. 18:20.

INHERITANCE. Provisions for inheritance under Levirate marriages, Gen. 38: 7-11; Num. 36:6-9; Deut. 25:5-10; Ruth 3:1-8; 4:7-17.

UNCLASSIFIED SCRIPTURES RELATING TO: Gen. 15:3. And Abram said, Behold, to me thou hast given no seed: and, lo, one born in my house is mine heir.

Gen. 21:9. And Sarah saw the son of Hagar the Egyptian, which she had born unto Abraham, mocking. 10. Wherefore she said unto Abraham, Cast out this bondwoman and her son: for the son of this bondwoman shall not be heir with my son, *even* with Isaac. 11. And the thing was very grievous in Abraham's sight because of his son.

Gen. 24:36. And Sarah my master's wife bare a son to my master when she was old: and unto him hath he given all that he hath.

Gen. 25:5. And Abraham gave all that he had unto Isaac. 6. But unto the sons of the concubines, which Abraham had, Abraham gave gifts, and sent them away from Isaac his son, while he yet lived, eastward, unto the east country.

Gen. 48:21. And Israel said unto Joseph, Behold, I die; but God shall be with you, and bring you again unto the land of your fathers. 22. Moreover I have given to thee one portion above thy brethren, which I took out of the hand of the Amorite with my sword and with my bow.

Num. 27:6. And the LORD spake unto Moses, saying, 7. The daughters of Zelophehad speak right: thou shalt surely give them a possession of an inheritance among their father's brethren; and thou shalt cause the inheritance of their father to pass unto them. 8. And thou shalt speak unto the children of Israel, saying, If a man die, and have no son, then ye shall cause his inheritance to pass unto his daughter. 9. And if he have no daughter, then ye shall give his inheritance unto his brethren. 10. And if he have no brethren, then ye shall give his inheritance unto his father's brethren. 11. And if his father have no brethren, then ye shall give his inheritance unto his kinsman that is next to him of his family, and he shall possess it: and it shall be unto the children of Israel a statute of judgment, as the LORD commanded Moses.

Deut. 21:15. If a man have two wives, one beloved, and another hated, and they have born him children, *both* the beloved and the hated; and *if* the firstborn son be her's that was hated: 16. Then it shall be, when he maketh his sons to inherit *that* which he hath, *that* he may not make the son of the beloved firstborn before the son of the hated, *which is indeed* the firstborn: 17. But he shall acknowledge the son of the hated *for* the firstborn, by giving him a double portion of all that he hath: for he *is* the beginning of his strength; the right of the firstborn *is* his.

1 Kin. 21:3. And Naboth said to Ahab, The LORD forbid it me, that I should give the inheritance of my fathers unto thee.

2 Chr. 21:3. And their father gave them great gifts of silver, and of gold, and of precious things, with fenced cities in Judah: but the kingdom gave he to Jehoram; because he *was* the firstborn.

Job 42:15. And in all the land were no women found *so* fair as the daughters of Job: and their father gave them inheritance among their brethren.

Prov. 17:2. A wise servant shall have rule over a son that causeth shame, and shall have part of the inheritance among the brethren.

Prov. 20:21. An inheritance *may be* gotten hastily at the beginning; but the end thereof shall not be blessed.

Eccl. 2:18. Yea, I hated all my labour which I had taken under the sun: because I should leave it unto the man that shall be after me. 19. And who knoweth whether he shall be a wise *man* or a fool?

Jer. 32:6. And Jeremiah said, The word of the LORD came unto me, saying, 7. Behold, Hanameel the son of Shallum thine uncle shall come unto thee, saying, Buy thee my field that *is* in Anathoth: for the right of redemption *is* thine to buy *it*. 8. So Hanameel mine uncle's son came to me in the court of the prison according to the word of the LORD, and said unto me, Buy my field, I pray thee, that *is* in Anathoth, which *is* in the country of Benjamin: for the right of inheritance *is* thine, and the redemption *is* thine; buy *it* for thyself. Then I knew that this *was* the word of the LORD.

Ezek. 46:16. Thus saith the LORD GOD; If the prince give a gift unto any of his sons, the inheritance thereof shall be his sons'; it *shall be* their possession by inheritance. 17. But if he give a gift of his inheritance to one of his servants, then it shall be his to the year of liberty; after it shall return to the prince: but his inheritance shall be his sons' for them. 18. Moreover the prince shall not take of the people's inheritance by oppression, to thrust them out of their possession; *but* he shall give his sons inheritance out of his own possession: that my people be not scattered every man from his possession.

Luke 15:12. And the younger of them said to *his* father, Father, give me the portion of goods that falleth *to me*. And he divided unto them *his* living. 25. Now his elder son was in the field: and as he came and drew nigh to the house, he heard musick and dancing. 26. And he called one of the servants, and asked what these things meant. 27. And he said unto him, Thy brother is come; and thy father hath killed the fatted calf, because he hath received him safe and sound. 28. And he was angry, and would not go in: therefore came his father out, and entreated him. 29. And he answering said to *his* father, Lo, these many years do I serve thee, neither transgressed I at any time thy commandment; and yet thou never gavest me a kid, that I might make merry with my friends: 30. But as soon as this thy son was come, which hath devoured thy living with harlots, thou hast killed for him the fatted calf. 31. And he said unto him, Son, thou art ever with me, and all that I have is thine.

Gal. 3:15. Brethren, I speak after the manner of men; Though *it be* but a man's covenant, [marg., testament] yet *if it be* confirmed, no man disannulleth, or addeth thereto.

Heb. 9:16. For where a testament *is*, there must also of necessity be the death of the testator. 17. For a testament *is* of force after men are dead: otherwise it is of no strength at all while the testator liveth.

See WILL; HEIR.

FIGURATIVE: Psa. 37:29. The righteous shall inherit the land, and dwell therein for ever.

Acts 20:32. And now, brethren, I commend you to God, and to the word of his grace, which is able to build you up, and to give you an inheritance among all them which are sanctified.

Acts 26:18. To open their eyes, *and* to turn *them* from darkness to light, and *from* the power of Satan unto God, that they may receive forgiveness of sins, and inheritance among them which are sanctified by faith that is in me.

Rom. 8:16. The Spirit itself beareth witness with our spirit, that we are the children of God : 17. And if children, then heirs ; heirs of God, and joint-heirs with Christ ; if so be that we suffer with *him*, that we may be also glorified together.

Eph. 1:11. In whom also we have obtained an inheritance, being predestinated according to the purpose of him who worketh all things after the counsel of his own will : 12. That we should be to the praise of his glory, who first trusted in Christ. 13. In whom ye also *trusted*, after that ye heard the word of truth, the gospel of your salvation : in whom also after that ye believed, ye were sealed with that holy Spirit of promise, 14. Which is the earnest of our inheritance

Tit. 3:7. That being justified by his grace, we should be made heirs according to the hope of eternal life.

Heb. 1:14. Are they not all ministering spirits, sent forth to minister for them who shall be heirs of salvation ?

See FIRSTBORN ; HEIR ; WILL.

INHOSPITABLENESS. INSTANCES OF : Toward the Israelites : Edom, Num. 20: 18-21; Sihon, Num. 21:22,23; Ammonites and Moabites, Deut. 23:3-6. Men of Gibeah toward a Levite, Judg. 19:15. Nabal toward David, 1 Sam. 25:10-17. Samaritans toward Jesus, Luke 9:53.

See HOSPITALITY.

INJUSTICE. Ex. 22:21. Thou shalt neither vex a stranger, nor oppress him : 22. Ye shall not afflict any widow, or fatherless child.

Ex. 23:1. Thou shall not raise a false report : put not thine hand with the wicked to be an unrighteous witness.

2. Thou shalt not follow a multitude to *do* evil ; neither shalt thou speak in a cause to decline after many to wrest *judgment :* 3. Neither shalt thou countenance a poor man in his cause.

6. Thou shalt not wrest the judgment of thy poor in his cause. 7. Keep thee far from a false matter ; and the innocent and righteous slay thou not : for I will not justify the wicked.

Lev. 19:15. Ye shall do no unrighteousness in judgment : thou shalt not respect the person of the poor, nor honour the person of the mighty : *but* in righteousness shalt thou judge thy neighbour.

35. Ye shall do no unrighteousness in judgment, in meteyard, in weight, or in measure. 36. Just balances, just weights, a

just ephah, and a just hin, shall ye have : I *am* the LORD your God,

Deut. 16:19. Thou shalt not wrest judgment ; thou shalt not respect persons, neither take a gift : for a gift doth blind the eyes of the wise, and pervert the words of the righteous. 20. That which is altogether just shalt thou follow, that thou mayest live, and inherit the land which the LORD thy God giveth thee.

Deut. 24:17. Thou shalt not pervert the judgment of the stranger, *nor* of the fatherless ; nor take a widow's raiment to pledge : [Deut. 27:19.] 18. But thou shalt remember that thou wast a bondman in Egypt, and the LORD thy God redeemed thee thence : therefore I command thee to do this thing.

Job 16:16. My face is foul with weeping, and on my eyelids *is* the shadow of death ; 17. Not for *any* injustice in mine hands : also my prayer *is* pure.

Job 31:13. If I did despise the cause of my manservant or of my maidservant, when they contended with me ; 14. What then shall I do when God riseth up ? and when he visiteth, what shall I answer him ? 15. Did not he that made me in the womb make him ? and did not one fashion us in the womb ?

Psa. 12:5. For the oppression of the poor, for the sighing of the needy, now will I arise, saith the LORD ; I will set *him* in safety *from him that* puffeth at him.

Psa. 43:1. Judge me, O God, and plead my cause against an ungodly nation : O deliver me from the deceitful and unjust man.

Psa. 82:2. How long will ye judge unjustly, and accept the persons of the wicked ?

Prov. 11:7. When a wicked man dieth, *his* expectation shall perish : and the hope of unjust *men* perisheth.

Prov. 17:15. He that justifieth the wicked, and he that condemneth the just, even they both *are* abomination to the LORD.

Prov. 28:8. He that by usury and unjust gain increaseth his substance, he shall gather it for him that will pity the poor.

Prov. 29:27. An unjust man *is* an abomination to the just : and *he that is* upright in the way *is* abomination to the wicked.

Prov. 31:4. *It is* not for kings, O Lemuel, *it is* not for kings to drink wine ; nor for princes strong drink : 5. Lest they drink, and forget the law, and pervert the judgment of any of the afflicted.

Eccl. 3:16. And moreover I saw under the sun the place of judgment, *that* wickedness *was* there ; and the place of righteousness, *that* iniquity *was* there.

Eccl. 5:8. If thou seest the oppression of the poor, and violent perverting of judgment and justice in a province, marvel not at the matter : for *he that is* higher than the highest regardeth ; and *there be* higher than they.

Isa. 26:10. Let favour be shewed to the wicked, *yet* will he not learn righteousness ; in the land of uprightness will he deal unjustly, and will not behold the majesty of the LORD.

Jer. 22:3. Thus saith the LORD; Execute ye judgment and righteousness, and deliver the spoiled out of the hand of the oppressor: and do no wrong, do no violence to the stranger, the fatherless, nor the widow, neither shed innocent blood in this place. 4. For if ye do this thing indeed, then shall there enter in by the gates of this house kings sitting upon the throne of David, riding in chariots and on horses, he, and his servants, and his people. 5. But if ye will not hear these words, I swear by myself, saith the LORD, that this house shall become a desolation.

Lam. 3:34. To crush under his feet all the prisoners of the earth, 35. To turn aside the right of a man before the face of the most High, 36. To subvert a man in his cause, the Lord approveth not.

Amos 5:11. Forasmuch therefore as your treading *is* upon the poor, and ye take from him burdens of wheat: ye have built houses of hewn stone, but ye shall not dwell in them; ye have planted pleasant vineyards, but ye shall not drink wine of them. 12. For I know your manifold transgressions and your mighty sins: they afflict the just, they take a bribe, and they turn aside the poor in the gate *from their right.*

Zeph. 3:5. The unjust knoweth no shame.

Luke 3:14. And the soldiers likewise demanded of him, saying, And what shall we do? And he said unto them, Do violence to no man, neither accuse *any* falsely; and be content with your wages.

Luke 16:10. He that is unjust in the least is unjust also in much.

1 Thess. 4:7. That no *man* go beyond and defraud his brother in *any* matter: because that the Lord *is* the avenger of all such, as we also have forewarned you and testified.

Rev. 22:11. He that is unjust, let him be unjust still:

See COURTS; DISHONESTY; FRAUD; JUSTICE.

INK, Jer. 36:18; 2 Cor. 3:3; 2 John 12; 3 John 13.

INKHORN, Ezek. 9:2,3,11.

INN, Gen. 42:27; 43:21; Ex. 4:24; Luke 2: 7; 10:34.

INNOCENCY. Signified by washing the hands, Deut. 21:6; Psa. 26:6; Matt. 27:24. Found in Daniel, Dan. 6:22; Jeremiah, Jer. 2:35. Professed by Pilate, Matt. 27:24.

Contrasted with guilt, compare Gen. 2: 25; 3:7-11.

INNUENDO, Psa. 35:19; Prov. 6:13; 10:10. See ACCUSATION, FALSE.

INQUEST, Deut. 21:1-9.

INSANITY. Prov. 26:18. Feigned by David, 1 Sam. 21:13-15. Sent as a judgment from God, Deut. 28:28; Zech. 12:4. Nebuchadnezzar's, Dan. 4:32-34. Jesus accused of, Mark 3:21; John 10:20. Paul, Acts 26:24, 25. Cured by Jesus, Matt. 4:24; 17:15. Demoniacal: Saul, 1 Sam. 16:14; 18:10.

See DEMONS, POSSESSION BY.

INSCRIPTIONS. On gravestones, 2 Kin. 23:17. Over Jesus at the crucifixion, Matt. 27:37; Mark 15:26; Luke 23:38; John 19:19.

INSECTS, clean and unclean, Lev. 11: 21-25; Deut. 14:19.

See ANT; BEE; BEETLE; CANKERWORM; CATERPILLAR; FLEA; FLIES; GNAT; GRASSHOPPER; HORNET; HORSE-LEECH; LICE; LOCUST; MOTH; PALMERWORM; SCORPION; SNAIL; SPIDER; WORM.

INSINCERITY. See HYPOCRISY.

INSINUATION. See INNUENDO.

INSOMNIA. INSTANCES OF: Ahasuerus, Esth. 6:1. Nebuchadnezzar, Dan. 6:18.

INSPIRATION. Ex. 19:6. These *are* the words which thou shalt speak unto the children of Israel.

Ex. 25:21. And thou shalt put the mercy seat above upon the ark; and in the ark thou shalt put the testimony that I shall give thee. 22. And there I will meet with thee, and I will commune with thee from above the mercy seat, from between the two cherubims which *are* upon the ark of the testimony, of all *things* which I will give thee in commandment unto the children of Israel. Deut. 5:31.

Num. 11:16. And the LORD said unto Moses, Gather unto me seventy men of the elders of Israel, whom thou knowest to be the elders of the people, and officers over them; and bring them unto the tabernacle of the congregation, that they may stand there with thee. 17. And I will come down and talk with thee there: and I will take of the spirit which *is* upon thee, and will put *it* upon them; and they shall bear the burden of the people with thee, that thou bear *it* not thyself alone. 18. And say thou unto the people, Sanctify yourselves against to morrow, and ye shall eat flesh: for ye have wept in the ears of the LORD, saying, Who shall give us flesh to eat? for *it was* well with us in Egypt: therefore the LORD will give you flesh, and ye shall eat. 19. Ye shall not eat one day, nor two days, nor five days, neither ten days, nor twenty days; 20. *But* even a whole month, until it come out at your nostrils, and it be loathsome unto you: because that ye have despised the LORD which *is* among you, and have wept before him, saying, Why came we forth out of Egypt? 21. And Moses said, The people, among whom I *am*, *are* six hundred thousand footmen; and thou hast said, I will give them flesh, that they may eat a whole month. 22. Shall the flocks and the herds be slain for them, to suffice them? or shall all the fish of the sea be gathered together for them, to suffice them? 23. And the LORD said unto Moses, Is the LORD's hand waxed short? thou shalt see now whether my word shall come to pass unto thee or not. 24. And Moses went out, and told the people the words of the LORD, and gathered the seventy men of the elders of the people, and set them round about the tabernacle. 25.

And the LORD came down in a cloud, and spake unto him, and took of the spirit that *was* upon him, and gave *it* unto the seventy elders: and it came to pass, *that*, when the spirit rested upon them, they prophesied, and did not cease. 26. But there remained two *of the* men in the camp, the name of the one *was* Eldad, and the name of the other Medad: and the spirit rested upon them; and they *were* of them that were written, but went not out unto the tabernacle: and they prophesied in the camp. 28. And Joshua the son of Nun, the servant of Moses, *one* of his young men, answered and said, My lord Moses forbid them. 29. And Moses said unto him, Enviest thou for my sake? would God that all the LORD's people were prophets, *and* that the LORD would put his spirit upon them. Ex. 28:3; 31:3,6; 35:31; 36:1; Deut. 34:9; Job 32:8; Isa. 51:16; Jer. 1:9; Luke 1:15.

Luke 12:12. For the Holy Ghost shall teach you in the same hour what ye ought to say. Matt. 10:19; Mark 13:11; Luke 21:14,15.

2 Tim. 3:16. ¹ All scripture *is* given by inspiration of God, and *is* profitable for doctrine, for reproof, for correction, for instruction in righteousness:

[¹ R. V. Every scripture inspired of God *is* also profitable for teaching, for reproof, for correction, for instruction which is in righteousness]

Rev. 1:10. I was in the Spirit on the Lord's day, and heard behind me a great voice, as of a trumpet. 11. Saying, I am Alpha and Omega, the first and the last: and, What thou seest, write in a book, and send *it* unto the seven churches which are in Asia:

See PROPHECY; PROPHET; REVELATION; WORD OF GOD, INSPIRATION OF.

INSTABILITY. Gen. 49:3. Reuben, thou *art* my firstborn, my might, and the beginning of my strength, the excellency of dignity, and the excellency of power: 4. Unstable as water, thou shall not excel; because thou wentest up to thy father's bed; then defiledst thou *it*: he went up to my couch.

Ex. 8:15. But when Pharaoh saw that there was respite, he hardened his heart, and hearkened not unto them; as the LORD had said. *v.* 32.

Ex. 9:34. And when Pharaoh saw that the rain and the hail and the thunders were ceased, he sinned yet more, and hardened his heart, he and his servants. Ex. 10:8–11, 16-20; 14:5.

Ex. 32:8. They have turned aside quickly out of the way which I commanded them: they have made them a molten calf, and have worshipped it, and have sacrificed thereunto, and said, These *be* thy gods, O Israel, which have brought thee up out of the land of Egypt. 9. And the LORD said unto Moses, I have seen this people, and, behold, it *is* a stiffnecked people: 10. Now therefore let me alone, that my wrath may wax hot against them, and that I may con-

sume them: and I will make of thee a great nation. with Ex. 19:8; 24:3,7.

Judg. 2:17. And yet they would not hearken unto their judges, but they went a whoring after other gods, and bowed themselves unto them: they turned quickly out of the way which their fathers walked in, obeying the commandments of the LORD; *but* they did not so.

1 Kin. 18:21. And Elijah came unto all the people, and said, How long halt ye between two opinions? if the LORD *be* God, follow him: but if Baal, *then* follow him. And the people answered him not a word.

Psa. 106:12. Then believed they his words; they sang his praise. 13. They soon forgat his works; they waited not for his counsel:

Prov. 24:21. My son, fear thou the LORD and the king: *and* meddle not with them that are given to change: 22. For their calamity shall rise suddenly; and who knoweth the ruin of them both?

Prov. 27:8. As a bird that wandereth from her nest, so *is* a man that wandereth from his place.

Jer. 2:36. Why gaddest thou about so much to change thy way? thou also shalt be ashamed of Egypt, as thou wast ashamed of Assyria.

Hos. 6:4. O Ephraim, what shall I do unto thee? O Judah, what shall I do unto thee? for your goodness *is* as a morning cloud, and as the early dew it goeth away. 5. Therefore have I hewed *them* by the prophets; I have slain them by the words of my mouth: and thy judgments *are as* the light *that* goeth forth.

Matt. 6:24. No man can serve two masters: for either he will hate the one, and love the other: or else he will hold to the one, and despise the other. Ye cannot serve God and mammon.

Matt. 12:25. And Jesus knew their thoughts, and said unto them, Every kingdom divided against itself is brought to desolation; and every city or house divided against itself shall not stand:

Mark 4:14. The sower soweth the word. 15. And these are they by the way side, where the word is sown; but when they have heard, Satan cometh immediately, and taketh away the word that was sown in their hearts. 16. And these are they likewise which are sown on stony ground; who, when they have heard the word, immediately receive it with gladness; 17. And have no root in themselves, and so endure but for a time: afterward, when affliction or persecution ariseth for the word's sake, immediately they are offended. 18. And these are they which are sown among thorns; such as hear the word, 19. And the cares of this world, and the deceitfulness of riches, and the lusts of other things entering in, choke the word, and it becometh unfruitful. Matt. 13:20,21; Luke 8:13,14.

Luke 9:57. And it came to pass, that, as they went in the way, a certain *man* said unto him, Lord, I will follow thee whither-soever thou goest. 58. And Jesus said unto him, Foxes have holes, and birds of the air *have* nests; but the Son of man hath not where to lay *his* head. 59. And he said unto another, Follow me. But he said, Lord, suffer me first to go and bury my father. 60. Jesus said unto him, Let the dead bury their dead: but go thou and preach the kingdom of God. 61. And another also said, Lord, I will follow thee; but let me first go bid them farewell, which are at home at my house. 62. And Jesus said unto him, No man, having put his hand to the plough, and looking back, is fit for the kingdom of God. Matt. 8:19,20.

Luke 17:32. Remember Lot's wife.

John 5:35. He was a burning and a shining light: and ye were willing for a season to rejoice in his light.

Gal. 1:6. I marvel that ye are so soon removed from him that called you into the grace of Christ unto another gospel:

Gal. 4:9. But now, after that ye have known God, or rather are known of God, how turn ye again to the weak and beggarly elements, whereunto ye desire again to be in bondage? 10. Ye observe days, and months, and times, and years. 11. I am afraid of you, lest I have bestowed upon you labour in vain.

Eph. 4:14. That we *henceforth* be no more children, tossed to and fro, and carried about with every wind of doctrine, by the sleight of men, *and* cunning craftiness, whereby they lie in wait to deceive;

Heb. 13:9. Be not carried about with divers and strange doctrines. For *it is a* good thing that the heart be established with grace:

Jas. 1:6. Ask in faith, nothing wavering. For he that wavereth is like a wave of the sea driven with the wind and tossed. 7. For let not that man think that he shall receive any thing of the Lord. 8. A double minded man *is* unstable in all his ways.

Jas. 4:8. Draw nigh to God, and he will draw nigh to you. Cleanse *your* hands, *ye* sinners; and purify *your* hearts, *ye* double minded.

2 Pet. 2:14. Having eyes full of adultery, and that cannot cease from sin; beguiling unstable souls: an heart they have exercised with covetous practices; cursed children:

Rev. 2:4. I have *somewhat* against thee, because thou hast left thy first love.

Rev. 3:2. Be watchful, and strengthen the things which remain, that are ready to die: for I have not found thy words perfect before God. 15. I know thy works, that thou art neither cold nor hot: I would thou wert cold or hot. 16. So then because thou art lukewarm, and neither cold nor hot, I will spue thee out of my mouth.

See BACKSLIDING; HYPOCRISY; INDECISION.

INSTANCES OF: Reuben, Gen. 49:4. Saul, in his feelings toward David, 1 Sam. 18:19.

David, in yielding to lust, 2 Sam. 11:2–9. Solomon, in yielding to his idolatrous wives, 1 Kin. 11:1–8. Ephraim and Judah, Hos. 6:4. Lot's wife, Luke 17:32. Disciples of Jesus, John 6:66; Mark, Acts 15:38.

INSTINCT. Of animals, Prov. 1:17; Isa. 1:3. Of birds, Jer. 8:7.

See ANIMALS; BIRDS.

INSTRUCTION. From nature, Prov. 24:30–34; Eccl. 1:13–18; 3; 4:1; Matt. 6:25–30. See PARABLES. From the study of human nature, Eccl. chapters 3–12.

By Object Lessons: The pot of manna, Ex. 16:32. The pillar of twelve stones at the fords of the Jordan, Josh. 4:19–24. Fringes on the borders of garments, Num. 15:38,39. Symbolically wearing sackcloth and going barefoot, Isa. 20:2,3. The linen girdle, Jer. 13:1–11. Potter's vessel, Jer. 19:1–12. Basket of figs, Jer. 24. Bonds and yokes, Jer. 27:2–11; 28. Illustrations on a tile, Ezek. 4:1–3. Lying on one side in public view for a long period, Ezek. 4:4–8. Eating bread mixed with dung, Ezek. 4:9 17. Shaving the head, Ezek. 5. Moving household goods, Ezek. 12:3–16. Eating and drinking sparingly, Ezek. 12:18–20. Sighing, Ezek. 21:6,7. The boiling pot, Ezek. 24:1–14. Widowhood, Ezek. 24:16–27. Two sticks joined together, Ezek. 37:16–22. By symbols and parables. See SYMBOLS; PARABLES.

See PURIFICATIONS; FIRSTBORN; BEASTS, CLEAN and UNCLEAN; PASSOVER; PILLAR. See also Prov. 24:30–34.

UNCLASSIFIED SCRIPTURES RELATING TO: 2 Chr. 15:3. Now for a long season Israel *hath been* without the true God, and without a teaching priest, and without law.

2 Chr. 17:7. Also in the third year of his reign he sent to his princes, *even* to Benhail, and to Obadiah, and to Zechariah, and to Nethaneel, and to Michaiah, to teach in the cities of Judah. 8. And with them *he sent* Levites, *even* Shemaiah, and Nethaniah, and Zebadiah, and Asahel, and Shemiramoth, and Jehonathan, and Adonijah, and Tobijah, and Tob-adonijah, Levites: and with them Elishama and Jehoram, priests. 9. And they taught in Judah, and *had* the book of the law of the LORD with them, and went about throughout all the cities of Judah, and taught the people.

Ezra 7:10. For Ezra had prepared his heart to seek the law of the LORD, and to do *it*, and to teach in Israel statutes and judgments.

Psa. 50:17. Seeing thou hatest instruction, and castest my words behind thee.

Psa. 78:2. I will open my mouth in a parable: I will utter dark sayings of old: 3. Which we have heard and known, and our fathers have told us. 4. We will not hide *them* from their children, shewing to the generation to come the praises of the LORD, and his strength, and his wonderful works that he hath done. 5. For he established a testimony in Jacob, and appointed a law in Israel, which he commanded our **fathers,** that they should make them known to their children: 6. That the generation to come might know *them*, *even* the children *which* should be born; *who* should arise and declare *them* to their children: 7. That they might set their hope in God, and not forget the works of God, but keep his commandments: 8. And might not be as their fathers, a stubborn and rebellious generation; a generation *that* set not their heart aright, and whose spirit was not stedfast with God.

Psa. 119:12. Blessed *art* thou, O LORD: teach me thy statutes. *vs.* 3-125.

Psa. 143:8. Cause me to hear thy lovingkindness in the morning; for in thee do I trust: cause me to know the way wherein I should walk; for I lift up my soul unto thee. 10. Teach me to do thy will; for thou *art* my God: thy spirit *is* good; lead me into the land of uprightness.

Prov. 1:1. The proverbs of Solomon the son of David, king of Israel; 2. To know wisdom and instruction; to perceive the words of understanding; 3. To receive the instruction of wisdom, justice, and judgment, and equity; 4. To give subtilty to the simple, to the young man knowledge and discretion. 5. A wise *man* will hear, and will increase learning; and a man of understanding shall attain unto wise counsels: 6. To understand a proverb, and the interpretation; the words of the wise, and their dark sayings. 20. Wisdom crieth without; she uttereth her voice in the streets: 21. She crieth in the chief place of concourse, in the openings of the gates: in the city she uttereth her words, *saying*, 22. How long, ye simple ones, will ye love simplicity? and the scorners delight in their scorning, and fools hate knowledge? 23. Turn you at my reproof: Behold, I will pour out my spirit unto you, I will make known my words unto you. 24. Because I have called, and ye refused; I have stretched out my hand, and no man regarded; 25. But ye have set at nought all my counsel, and would none of my reproof: 26. I also will laugh at your calamity; I will mock when your fear cometh; 27. When your fear cometh as desolation, and your destruction cometh as a whirlwind; when distress and anguish cometh upon you. 28. Then shall they call upon me, but I will not answer; they shall seek me early, but they shall not find me: 29. For that they hated knowledge, and did not choose the fear of the LORD: 30. They would none of my counsel: they despised all my reproof.

Prov. 22:17. Bow down thine ear, and hear the words of the wise, and apply thine heart unto my knowledge. 18. For *it is a* pleasant thing if thou keep them within thee: they shall withal be fitted in thy lips. 19. That thy trust may be in the LORD, I have made known to thee this day, even to thee. 20. Have not I written to thee excellent things in counsels and knowledge, 21.

That I might make thee know the certainty of the words of truth; that thou mightest answer the words of truth to them that send unto thee?

Prov. 23:12. Apply thine heart unto instruction, and thine ears to the words of knowledge. 23. Buy the truth, and sell *it* not; *also* wisdom, and instruction, and understanding.

Prov. 24:30. I went by the field of the slothful, and by the vineyard of the man void of understanding; 31. And, lo, it was all grown over with thorns, *and* nettles had covered the face thereof, and the stone wall thereof was broken down. 32. Then I saw, *and* considered *it* well: I looked upon *it*, *and* received instruction. 33. *Yet* a little sleep, a little slumber, a little folding of the hands to sleep: 34. So shall thy poverty come *as* one that travelleth; and thy want as an armed man.

Jer. 32:33. And they have turned unto me the back, and not the face: though I taught them, rising up early and teaching *them*, yet they have not hearkened to receive instruction.

Dan. 1:3. And the king spake unto Ashpenaz the master of his eunuchs, that he should bring *certain* of the children of Israel, and of the king's seed, and of the princes: 4. Children in whom *was* no blemish, but well favoured, and skilful in all wisdom, and cunning in knowledge, and understanding science, and such as *had* ability in them to stand in the king's palace, and whom they might teach the learning and the tongue of the Chaldeans. 5. And the king appointed them a daily provision of the king's meat, and of the wine which he drank: so nourishing them three years, that at the end thereof they might stand before the king. 17. As for these four children, God gave them knowledge and skill in all learning and wisdom: and Daniel had understanding in all visions and dreams. 18. Now at the end of the days that the king had said he should bring them in, then the prince of the eunuchs brought them in before Nebuchadnezzar. 19. And the king communed with them; and among them all was found none like Daniel, Hananiah, Mishael, and Azariah: therefore stood they before the king. 20. And in all matters of wisdom *and* understanding, that the king inquired of them, he found them ten times better than all the magicians *and* astrologers that *were* in all his realm.

Luke 20:1. And it came to pass, *that* on one of those days, as he taught the people in the temple, and preached the gospel, the chief priests and the scribes came upon *him* with the elders, 2. And spake unto him, saying, Tell us, by what authority doest thou these things? or who is he that gave thee this authority?

Luke 21:37. And in the day time he was teaching in the temple; and at night he went out, and abode in the mount that is called *the mount* of Olives. 38. And all the people came early in the morning to him in the temple, for to hear him.

Rom. 2:18. And knowest *his* will, and approvest the things that are more excellent, being instructed out of the law;

1 Cor. 12:28. And God hath set some in the church, first apostles. secondarily prophets, thirdly teachers, after that miracles, then gifts of healings, helps, governments, diversities of tongues. 29. *Are* all apostles? *are* all prophets? *are* all teachers? *are* all workers of miracles?

Gal. 3:24. Wherefore the law was our schoolmaster *to bring us* unto Christ, that we might be justified by faith. 25. But after that faith is come, we are no longer under a schoolmaster.

Gal. 4:1. Now I say, *That* the heir, as long as he is a child, differeth nothing from a servant, though he be lord of all; 2. But is under tutors and governors until the time appointed of the father.

Eph. 4:11. And he gave some, apostles; and some, prophets; and some, evangelists; and some, pastors and teachers; 12. For the perfecting of the saints, for the work of the ministry, for the edifying of the body of Christ:

OF CHILDREN: Ex. 10:2. And that thou mayest tell in the ears of thy son, and of thy son's son, what things I have wrought in Egypt, and my signs which I have done among them; that ye may know how that I *am* the LORD.

Ex. 12:26. And it shall come to pass when your children shall say unto you, What mean ye by this service? 27. That ye shall say, It *is* the sacrifice of the LORD's passover, who passed over the houses of the children of Israel in Egypt, when he smote the Egyptians, and delivered our houses. chapter 13:14–16.

Ex. 13:8. And thou shalt shew thy son in that day, saying, *This is done* because of that *which* the LORD did unto me when I came forth out of Egypt. 9. And it shall be for a sign unto thee upon thine hand, and for a memorial between thine eyes, that the LORD's law may be in thy mouth: for with a strong hand hath the LORD brought thee out of Egypt. 10. Thou shalt therefore keep this ordinance in his season from year to year.

Deut. 4:9. Only take heed to thyself, and keep thy soul diligently, lest thou forget the things which thine eyes have seen, and lest they depart from thy heart all the days of thy life: but teach them thy sons, and thy sons' sons; 10. *Specially* the day that thou stoodest before the LORD thy God in Horeb, when the LORD said unto me, Gather me the people together, and I will make them hear my words, that they may learn to fear me all the days that they shall live upon the earth, and *that* they may teach their children.

Deut. 6:6. And these words, which I command thee this day, shall be in thine heart: 7. And thou shalt teach them diligently unto thy children, and shalt talk of them when thou sittest in thine house, and when thou walkest by the way, and when thou liest down, and when thou risest up. 8. And thou shalt bind them for a sign upon thine hand, and they shall be as frontlets between thine eyes. 9. And thou shalt write them upon the posts of thy house, and on thy gates.

Deut. 11:18. Therefore shall ye lay up these my words in your heart and in your soul, and bind them for a sign upon your hand, that they may be as frontlets between your eyes. 19. And ye shall teach them your children, speaking of them when thou sittest in thine house, and when thou walkest by the way, when thou liest down, and when thou risest up. 20. And thou shalt write them upon the door posts of thine house, and upon thy gates: 21. That your days may be multiplied, and the days of your children, in the land which the LORD sware unto your fathers to give them, as the days of heaven upon the earth.

Deut. 31:9. And Moses wrote this law, and delivered it unto the priests the sons of Levi, which bare the ark of the covenant of the LORD, and unto all the elders of Israel. 10. And Moses commanded them, saying, At the end of *every* seven years, in the solemnity of the year of release, in the feast of tabernacles. 11. When all Israel is come to appear before the LORD thy God in the place which he shall choose, thou shalt read this law before all Israel in their hearing. 12. Gather the people together, men, and women, and children, and thy stranger that *is* within thy gates, that they may hear, and that they may learn, and fear the LORD your God, and observe to do all the words of this law: 13. And *that* their children, which have not known *anything*, may hear, and learn to fear the LORD your God, as long as ye live in the land whither ye go over Jordan to possess it. Josh. 8:35.

Psa. 34:11. Come, ye children, hearken unto me: I will teach you the fear of the LORD.

Psa. 78:5. For he established a testimony in Jacob, and appointed a law in Israel, which he commanded our fathers, that they should make them known to their children: 6. That the generation to come might know *them, even* the children *which* should be born; *who* should arise and declare *them* to their children: 7. That they might set their hope in God, and not forget the works of God, but keep his commandments: 8. And might not be as their fathers, a stubborn and rebellious generation; a generation *that* set not their heart aright, and whose spirit was not stedfast with God.

Prov. 20:7. The just *man* walketh in his integrity: his children *are* blessed after him.

Prov. 22:6. Train up a child in the way he should go: and when he is old, he will not depart from it.

Isa. 38:19. The father to the children shall make known thy truth.

Acts 22:3. I am verily a man *which am* a Jew, born in Tarsus, *a city* in Cilicia, yet brought up in this city at the feet of Gamaliel, *and* taught according to the perfect manner of the law of the fathers, and was zealous toward God, as ye all are this day.

Eph. 6:4. And, ye fathers, provoke not your children to wrath: but bring them up in the nurture and admonition of the Lord.

2 Tim. 3:15. And that from a child thou hast known the holy scriptures, which are able to make thee wise unto salvation through faith which is in Christ Jesus.

See CHILDREN.

IN RELIGION: Ex. 13:11. And it shall be when the LORD shall bring thee into the land of the Canaanites, as he sware unto thee and to thy fathers, and shall give it thee, 12. That thou shalt set apart unto the LORD all that openeth the matrix, and every firstling that cometh of a beast which thou hast; the male *shall be* the LORD's. 13. And every firstling of an ass thou shalt redeem with a lamb; and if thou wilt not redeem it, then thou shalt break his neck: and all the firstborn of man among thy children shalt thou redeem. 14. And it shall be when thy son asketh thee in time to come, saying, What *is* this? that thou shalt say unto him, By strength of hand the LORD brought us out from Egypt, from the house of bondage: 15. And it came to pass, when Pharaoh would hardly let us go, that the LORD slew all the firstborn in the land of Egypt, both the firstborn of man, and the firstborn of beast: therefore I sacrifice to the LORD all that openeth the matrix, being males; but all the firstborn of my children I redeem. 16. And it shall be for a token upon thine hand, and for frontlets between thine eyes: for by strength of hand the LORD brought us forth out of Egypt.

Lev. 11:44. For I *am* the LORD your God: ye shall therefore sanctify yourselves, and ye shall be holy; for I *am* holy: neither shall ye defile yourselves with any manner of creeping thing that creepeth upon the earth. 45. For I *am* the LORD that bringeth you up out of the land of Egypt, to be your God: ye shall therefore be holy, for I *am* holy. 46. This *is* the law of the beasts, and of the fowl, and of every living creature that moveth in the waters, and of every creature that creepeth upon the earth: 47. To make a difference between the unclean and the clean,

Num. 15:38. Speak unto the children of Israel, and bid them that they make them fringes in the borders of their garments throughout their generations, and that they put upon the fringe of the borders a ribband of blue: 39. And it shall be unto you for a fringe, that ye may look upon it, and remember all the commandments of the LORD, and do them; and that ye seek not after your own heart and your own eyes, after which ye use to go a whoring:

Deut. 27:1. And Moses with the elders of Israel commanded the people, saying, Keep all the commandments which I command you this day. 2. And it shall be on the day when ye shall pass over Jordan unto the land which the LORD thy God giveth thee, that thou shalt set thee up great stones, and plaister them with plaister: 3. And thou shalt write upon them all the words of this law, when thou art passed over, that thou mayest go in unto the land which the LORD thy God giveth thee, a land that floweth with milk and honey; as the LORD God of thy fathers hath promised thee. [Josh. 4: 1-11.] 4. Therefore it shall be when ye be gone over Jordan, *that* ye shall set up these stones, which I command you this day, in mount Ebal, and thou shalt plaister them with plaister. 5. And there shalt thou build an altar unto the LORD thy God, an altar of stones: thou shalt not lift up *any* iron *tool* upon them. 6. Thou shalt build the altar of the LORD thy God of whole stones: and thou shalt offer burnt offerings thereon unto the LORD thy God: 7. And thou shalt offer peace offerings, and shalt eat there, and rejoice before the LORD thy God. 8. And thou shalt write upon the stones all the words of this law very plainly. 9. And Moses and the priests the Levites spake unto all Israel, saying, Take heed, and hearken, O Israel; this day thou art become the people of the LORD thy God. 10. Thou shalt therefore obey the voice of the LORD thy God, and do his commandments and his statutes, which I command thee this day. 11. And Moses charged the people the same day, saying, 12. These shall stand upon mount Gerizim to bless the people, when ye are come over Jordan; Simeon, and Levi, and Judah, and Issachar, and Joseph, and Benjamin: 13. And these shall stand upon mount Ebal to curse; Reuben, Gad, and Asher, and Zebulun, Dan, and Naphtali. 14. And the Levites shall speak, and say unto all the men of Israel with a loud voice, 15. Cursed *be* the man that maketh *any* graven or molten image, an abomination unto the LORD, the work of the hands of the craftsman, and putteth *it* in *a* secret *place*. And all the people shall answer and say, Amen. 16. Cursed *be* he that setteth light by his father or his mother. And all the people shall say, Amen. 17. Cursed *be* he that removeth his neighbour's landmark. And all the people shall say, Amen. 18. Cursed *be* he that maketh the blind to wander out of the way. And all the people shall say, Amen. 19. Cursed *be* he that perverteth the judgment of the stranger, fatherless, and widow. And all the people shall say, Amen. 20. Cursed *be* he that lieth with his father's wife; because he uncovereth his father's skirt. And all the people shall say, Amen. 21. Cursed *be* he that lieth with any manner of beast. And all the people shall say, Amen. 22. Cursed *be* he that lieth with his sister, the daughter of his father, or the daughter of his mother. And all the people shall say, Amen. 23. Cursed *be* he that lieth with his mother in law. And all the people shall say, Amen. 24. Cursed *be* he that smiteth his neighbour secretly. And all the people shall say, Amen. 25. Cursed *be* he that taketh reward to slay an innocent person. And all the people shall say, Amen. 26. Cursed *be* he that confirmeth not *all* the words of this law to do them. And all the people shall say, Amen.

Deut. 31:19. Now therefore write ye this song for you, and teach it the children of Israel: put it in their mouths, that this song may be a witness for me against the children of Israel.

Deut. 32:1. Give ear, O ye heavens, and I will speak; and hear, O earth, the words of my mouth. 2. My doctrine shall drop as the rain, my speech shall distil as the dew, as the small rain upon the tender herb, and as the showers upon the grass: 3. Because I will publish the name of the LORD: ascribe ye greatness unto our God. 4. *He is* the Rock, his work *is* perfect: for all his ways *are* judgment: a God of truth and without iniquity, just and right *is* he. 5. They have corrupted themselves, their spot *is* not *the spot* of his children: *they are* a perverse and crooked generation. 6. Do ye thus requite the LORD, O foolish people and unwise? *is* not he thy father *that* hath bought thee? hath he not made thee, and established thee? 7. Remember the days of old, consider the years of many generations: ask thy father, and he will shew thee; thy elders, and they will tell thee. 8. When the Most High divided to the nations their inheritance, when he separated the sons of Adam, he set the bounds of the people according to the number of the children of Israel. 9. For the LORD'S portion *is* his people; Jacob *is* the lot of his inheritance. 10. He found him in a desert land, and in the waste howling wilderness; he led him about, he instructed him, he kept him as the apple of his eye. 11. As an eagle stirreth up her nest, fluttereth over her young, spreadeth abroad her wings, taketh them, beareth them on her wings: 12. *So* the LORD alone did lead him, and *there was* no strange god with him. 13. He made him ride on the high places of the earth, that he might eat the increase of the fields; and he made him to suck honey out of the rock, and oil out of the flinty rock; 14. Butter of kine, and milk of sheep, with fat of lambs, and rams of the breed of Bashan, and goats, with the fat of kidneys of wheat; and thou didst drink the pure blood of the grape. 15. But Jeshurun waxed fat, and kicked: thou art waxen fat, thou art grown thick, thou art covered *with fatness;* then he forsook God *which* made him, and lightly esteemed the Rock of his salvation. 16. They provoked him to jealousy with **strange** *gods*, with abominations provoked

they him to anger. 17. They sacrificed unto devils, not to God; to gods whom they knew not, to new *gods that* came newly up, whom your fathers feared not. 18. Of the Rock *that* begat thee thou art unmindful, and hast forgotten God that formed thee. 19. And when the LORD saw *it*, he abhorred *them*, because of the provoking of his sons, and of his daughters. 20. And he said, I will hide my face from them, I will see what their end *shall be:* for they *are* a very froward generation, children in whom *is* no faith. 21. They have moved me to jealousy with *that which is* not God; they have provoked me to anger with their vanities: and I will move them to jealousy with *those which are* not a people; I will provoke them to anger with a foolish nation. 22. For a fire is kindled in mine anger, and shall burn unto the lowest hell, and shall consume the earth with her increase, and set on fire the foundations of the mountains. 23. I will heap mischiefs upon them; I will spend mine arrows upon them. 24. *They shall be* burnt with hunger, and devoured with burning heat, and with bitter destruction: I will also send the teeth of beasts upon them, with the poison of serpents of the dust. 25. The sword without, and terror within, shall destroy both the young man and the virgin, the suckling *also* with the man of gray hairs. 26. I said, I would scatter them into corners, I would make the remembrance of them to cease from among men: 27. Were it not that I feared the wrath of the enemy, lest their adversaries should behave themselves strangely, *and* lest they should say, Our hand *is* high, and the LORD hath not done all this. 28. For they *are* a nation void of counsel, neither *is there any* understanding in them. 29. O that they were wise, *that* they understood this, *that* they would consider their latter end! 30. How should one chase a thousand, and two put ten thousand to flight, except their Rock had sold them, and the LORD had shut them up? 31. For their rock *is* not as our Rock, even our enemies themselves *being* judges. 32. For their vine *is* of the vine of Sodom, and of the fields of Gomorrah: their grapes *are* grapes of gall, their clusters *are* bitter: 33. Their wine *is* the poison of dragons, and the cruel venom of asps. 34. *Is* not this laid up in store with me, *and* sealed up among my treasures? 35. To me *belongeth* vengeance, and recompence; their foot shall slide in *due* time: for the day of their calamity *is* at hand, and the things that shall come upon them make haste. 36. For the LORD shall judge his people, and repent himself for his servants, when he seeth that *their* power is gone, and *there is* none shut up, or left. 37. And he shall say, Where *are* their gods, *their* rock in whom they trusted, 38. Which did eat the fat of their sacrifices, *and* drank the wine of their drink offerings? let them rise up and help you, *and* be your protection.

39. See now that I, *even* I, *am* he, and *there is* no god with me : I kill, and I make alive; I wound, and I heal : neither *is there any* that can deliver out of my hand. 40. For I lift up my hand to heaven, and say, I live for ever. 41. If I whet my glittering sword, and mine hand take hold on judgment; I will render vengeance to mine enemies, and will reward them that hate me. 42. I will make mine arrows drunk with blood, and my sword shall devour flesh; *and that* with the blood of the slain and of the captives, from the beginning of revenges upon the enemy. 43. Rejoice, O ye nations, *with* his people : for he will avenge the blood of his servants, and will render vengeance to his adversaries, and will be merciful unto his land, *and* to his people. 44. And Moses came and spake all the words of this song in the ears of the people, he, and Hoshea the son of Nun. 45. And Moses made an end of speaking all these words to all Israel : 46. And he said unto them, Set your hearts unto all the words which I testify among you this day, which ye shall command your children to observe to do, all the words of this law. 47. For it *is* not a vain thing for you; because it *is* your life : and through this thing ye shall prolong *your* days in the land, whither ye go over Jordan to possess it.

2 Chr. 17:7. Also in the third year of his reign he sent to his princes, *even* to Benhail, and to Obadiah, and to Zechariah, and to Nethaneel, and to Michaiah, to teach in the cities of Judah. 8. And with them *he sent* Levites, *even* Shemaiah, and Nethaniah, and Zebadiah, and Asahel, and Shemiramoth, and Jehonathan, and Adonijah, and Tobijah, and Tob-adonijah, Levites; and with them Elishama and Jehoram, priests. 9. And they taught in Judah, and *had* the book of the law of the LORD with them, and went about throughout all the cities of Judah, and taught the people.

Neh. 8:7. Also Jeshua, and Bani, and Sherebiah, Jamin, Akkub, Shabbethai, Hodijah, Maaseiah, Kelita, Azariah, Jozabad, Hanan, Pelaiah, and the Levites, caused the people to understand the law : and the people *stood* in their place. 8. So they read in the book in the law of God distinctly, and gave the sense, and caused *them* to understand the reading.

Isa. 28:9. Whom shall he teach knowledge ? and whom shall he make to understand doctrine ? *them that are* weaned from the milk, *and* drawn from the breasts. 10. For precept *must be* upon precept, precept upon precept; line upon line, line upon line; here a little, *and* there a little :

Matt. 5:1. And seeing the multitudes, he went up into a mountain : and when he was set, his disciples came unto him : 2. And he opened his mouth, and taught them, saying, *vs.* 3–48; chapters 6; 7.

Luke 4:16. And he came to Nazareth, where he had been brought up : and, as his custom was, he went into the synagogue on the sabbath day, and stood up for to read. 17. And there was delivered unto him the book of the prophet Esaias. And when he had opened the book, he found the place where it was written, 18. The Spirit of the Lord *is* upon me, because he hath anointed me to preach the gospel to the poor; he hath sent me to heal the brokenhearted, to preach deliverance to the captives, and recovering of sight to the blind, to set at liberty them that are bruised, 19. To preach the acceptable year of the Lord. 20. And he closed the book, and he gave *it* again to the minister, and sat down. And the eyes of all them that were in the synagogue were fastened on him. 21. And he began to say unto them, This day is this scripture fulfilled in your ears.

Luke 24:27. And beginning at Moses and all the prophets, he expounded unto them in all the scriptures the things concerning himself.

John 7:14. Now about the midst of the feast Jesus went up into the temple, and taught. Mark 12:35; Luke 19:47; 20:1–18; John 8:2. See JESUS, CHRONOLOGICAL HISTORY OF.

Rom. 2:19. And art confident that thou thyself art a guide of the blind, a light of them which are in darkness, 20. An instructor of the foolish, a teacher of babes, which hast the form of knowledge and of the truth in the law.

Gal. 6:6. Let him that is taught in the word communicate unto him that teacheth in all good things.

See CHILDREN, INSTRUCTION OF; MINISTERS, DUTIES OF; TEACHER; SCHOOL.

IN MUSIC: See MUSIC.

INSTRUMENTALITY. See AGENCY.

INSTRUMENTS, MUSICAL: See MUSIC.

INSURGENTS, army of, David's, 1 Sam. 22:1.2.

INSURRECTION, Psa. 6:42. Described by David in Psa. 55. Led by Bichri, 2 Sam. 20; Absalom, see ABSALOM; Barabbas, Mark 15:7.

INTEGRITY. Gen. 18:19. For I know him, that he will command his children and his household after him, and they shall keep the way of the LORD, to do justice and judgment; that the LORD may bring upon Abraham that which he hath spoken of him.

Ex. 18:21. Moreover thou shalt provide out of all the people able men, such as fear God, men of truth, hating covetousness;

Deut. 16:19. Thou shalt not wrest judgment; thou shalt not respect persons, neither take a gift : for a gift doth blind the eyes of the wise, and pervert the words of the righteous. 20. That which is altogether just shalt thou follow, that thou mayest live, and inherit the land which the LORD thy God giveth thee.

Job 10:7. Thou knowest that I am not wicked;

Job 13:15. Though he slay me, yet will I trust in him: but I will maintain mine own ways before him. 18. Behold now, I have ordered *my* cause; I know that I shall be justified.

Job 16:17. Not for *any* injustice in mine hands: also my prayer *is* pure.

Job 27:4. My lips shall not speak wickedness, nor my tongue utter deceit. 5. God forbid that I should justify you: till I die I will not remove mine integrity from me. 6. My righteousness I hold fast, and will not let it go: my heart shall not reproach *me* so long as I live.

Job 29:14. I put on righteousness, and it clothed me: my judgment *was* as a robe and a diadem.

Job 31:1. I made a covenant with mine eyes; why then should I think upon a maid? 2. For what portion of God *is there* from above? and *what* inheritance of the Almighty from on high? 3. *Is* not destruction to the wicked? and a strange *punishment* to the workers of iniquity? 4. Doth not he see my ways, and count all my steps? 5. If I have walked with vanity, or if my foot hath hasted to deceit; 6. Let me be weighed in an even balance, that God may know mine integrity. 7. If my step hath turned out of the way, and mine heart walked after mine eyes, and if any blot hath cleaved to mine hands; 8. *Then* let me sow, and let another eat; yea, let my offspring be rooted out. 9. If mine heart have been deceived by a woman, or *if* I have laid wait at my neighbour's door; 10. *Then* let my wife grind unto another, and let others bow down upon her. 11. For this *is* an heinous crime; yea, it *is* an iniquity *to be punished by* the judges. 12. For it *is* a fire *that* consumeth to destruction, and would root out all mine increase. 13. If I did despise the cause of my manservant or of my maidservant, when they contended with me; 14. What then shall I do when God riseth up? and when he visiteth, what shall I answer him? 15. Did not he that made me in the womb make him? and did not one fashion us in the womb? 16. If I have withheld the poor from *their* desire, or have caused the eyes of the widow to fail; 17. Or have eaten my morsel myself alone, and the fatherless hath not eaten thereof; 18. (For from my youth he was brought up with me, as *with* a father, and I have guided her from my mother's womb;) 19. If I have seen any perish for want of clothing, or any poor without covering; 20. If his loins have not blessed me, and *if* he were *not* warmed with the fleece of my sheep: 21. If I have lifted up my hand against the fatherless, when I saw my help in the gate: 22. *Then* let mine arm fall from my shoulder blade, and mine arm be broken from the bone. 23. For destruction *from God was* a terror to me, and by reason of his highness I could not endure. 24. If I have made gold my hope, or have said to the fine gold, *Thou art* my confidence: 25. If I rejoiced because my wealth *was* great, and because mine hand had gotten much; 26. If I beheld the sun when it shined, or the moon walking *in* brightness; 27. And my heart hath been secretly enticed, or my mouth hath kissed my hand: 28. This also *were* an iniquity *to be punished by* the judge: for I should have denied the God *that is* above. 29. If I rejoiced at the destruction of him that hated me, or lifted up myself when evil found him: 30. Neither have I suffered my mouth to sin by wishing a curse to his soul. 31. If the men of my tabernacle said not, Oh that we had of his flesh! we cannot be satisfied. 32. The stranger did not lodge in the street: *but* I opened my doors to the traveller. 33. If I covered my transgressions as Adam, by hiding mine iniquity in my bosom: 34. Did I fear a great multitude, or did the contempt of families terrify me, that I kept silence, *and* went not out of the door? 35. Oh that one would hear me! behold, my desire *is, that* the Almighty would answer me, and *that* mine adversary had written a book. 36. Surely I would take it upon my shoulder, *and* bind it *as* a crown to me. 37. I would declare unto him the number of my steps; as a prince would I go near unto him. 38. If my land cry against me, or that the furrows likewise thereof complain; 39. If I have eaten the fruits thereof without money, or have caused the owners thereof to lose their life: 40. Let thistles grow instead of wheat, and cockle instead of barley. The words of Job are ended.

Psa. 7:3. O LORD my God, if I have done this; if there be iniquity in my hands; 4. If I have rewarded evil unto him that was at peace with me; (yea, I have delivered him that without cause is mine enemy:) 5. Let the enemy persecute my soul, and take *it;* 8. Judge me, O LORD, according to my righteousness, and according to mine integrity *that is* in me.

Psa. 15:1. LORD, who shall abide in thy tabernacle? who shall dwell in thy holy hill? 2. He that walketh uprightly, and worketh righteousness, and speaketh the truth in his heart. 3. *He that* backbiteth not with his tongue, nor doeth evil to his neighbour, nor taketh up a reproach against his neighbour. 4. In whose eyes a vile person is contemned; but he honoureth them that fear the LORD. *He that* sweareth to *his own* hurt, and changeth not. 5. *He that* putteth not out his money to usury, nor taketh reward against the innocent. He that doeth these *things* shall never be moved.

Psa. 17:3. Thou hast proved mine heart; thou hast visited *me* in the night; thou hast tried me, *and* shalt find nothing; I am purposed *that* my mouth shall not transgress.

Psa. 18:20. The LORD rewarded me according to my righteousness; according to the cleanness of my hands hath he recompensed me. 2 Sam. 22:21.

Psa. 24:3. Who shall ascend into the hill of the LORD? or who shall stand in his holy place? 4. He that hath clean hands, and a pure heart; who hath not lifted up his soul unto vanity, nor sworn deceitfully. 5. He shall receive the blessing from the LORD, and righteousness from the God of his salvation.

Psa. 26:1. Judge me, O LORD; for I have walked in mine integrity: I have trusted also in the LORD; *therefore* I shall not slide. 2. Examine me, O LORD, and prove me; try my reins and my heart. 3. I have walked in thy truth.

Psa. 69:4. I restored *that* which I took not away.

Psa. 73:15. If I say, I will speak thus; behold, I should offend *against* the generation of thy children. With *vs*. 2–22.

Psa. 119:121. I have done judgment and justice:

Prov. 2:2. Incline thine ear unto wisdom, *and* apply thine heart to understanding; 5. Then shalt thou understand the fear of the LORD, and find the knowledge of God. 9. Then shalt thou understand righteousness, and judgment, and equity; *yea*, every good path. Prov. 1:3.

Prov. 3:3. Let not mercy and truth forsake thee: bind them about thy neck; write them upon the table of thine heart: 4. So shalt thou find favour and good understanding in the sight of God and man.

Prov. 4:25. Let thine eyes look right on, and let thine eyelids look straight before thee. 26. Ponder the path of thy feet, and let all thy ways be established. 27. Turn not to the right hand nor to the left: remove thy foot from evil.

Prov. 10:9. He that walketh uprightly walketh surely:

Prov. 11:3. The integrity of the upright shall guide them: 5. The righteousness of the perfect shall direct his way:

Prov. 12:22. They that deal truly *are* his delight.

Prov. 14:30. A sound heart *is* the life of the flesh:

Prov. 15:21. A man of understanding walketh uprightly.

Prov. 16:11. A just weight and balance *are* the LORD's: all the weights of the bag *are* his work.

Prov. 19:1. Better *is* the poor that walketh in his integrity, than *he that is* perverse in his lips, and is a fool. Prov. 28:6.

Prov. 20:7. The just *man* walketh in his integrity: his children *are* blessed after him.

Prov. 21:3. To do justice and judgment *is* more acceptable to the LORD than sacrifice. 15. *It is* joy to the just to do judgment:

Prov. 22:11. He that loveth pureness of heart, *for* the grace of his lips the king *shall be* his friend.

Prov. 28:20. A faithful man shall abound with blessings:

Isa. 26:7. The way of the just *is* uprightness: thou, most upright, dost weigh the path of the just.

Isa. 33:15. He that walketh righteously, and speaketh uprightly; he that despiseth the gain of oppressions, that shaketh his hands from holding of bribes, that stoppeth his ears from hearing of blood, and shutteth his eyes from seeing evil; 16. He shall dwell on high: his place of defence *shall be* the munitions of rocks: bread shall be given him; his waters *shall be* sure.

Isa. 56:1. Thus saith the LORD, Keep ye judgment, and do justice:

Jer. 7:5. If ye throughly amend your ways and your doings; if ye throughly execute judgment between a man and his neighbour; 7. Then will I cause you to dwell in this place, in the land that I gave to your fathers, for ever and ever.

Ezek. 18:5. If a man be just, and do that which is lawful and right, 7. And hath not oppressed any, *but* hath restored to the debtor his pledge, hath spoiled none by violence, hath given his bread to the hungry, and hath covered the naked with a garment; 8. He *that* hath not given forth upon usury, neither hath taken any increase, *that* hath withdrawn his hand from iniquity, hath executed true judgment between man and man, 9. Hath walked in my statutes, and hath kept my judgments, to deal truly; he *is* just, he shall surely live, saith the Lord GOD.

Mic. 6:8. He hath shewed thee, O man, what *is* good; and what doth the LORD require of thee, but to do justly, and to love mercy, and to walk humbly with thy God?

Zech. 7:9. Thus speaketh the LORD of hosts, saying, Execute true judgment, and shew mercy and compassions every man to his brother:

Mal. 2:6. The law of truth was in his mouth, and iniquity was not found in his lips: he walked with me in peace and equity,

Luke 3:13. Exact no more than that which is appointed you. 14. Do violence to no man, neither accuse *any* falsely; and be content with your wages.

Luke 6:31. As ye would that men should do to you, do ye also to them likewise.

Luke 11:42. Woe unto you, Pharisees! for ye tithe mint and rue and all manner of herbs, and pass over judgment and the love of God: these ought ye to have done, and not to leave the other undone.

Luke 16:10. He that is faithful in that which is least is faithful also in much: and he that is unjust in the least is unjust also in much.

Acts 24:16. Herein do I exercise myself, to have always a conscience void of offence toward God, and *toward* men. Acts 23:1.

Rom. 9:1. I say the truth in Christ, I lie not, my conscience also bearing me witness in the Holy Ghost,

Rom. 13:5. *Ye* must needs be subject, not only for wrath, but also for conscience sake.

Rom. 14:5. One man esteemeth one day above another: another esteemeth every day *alike*. Let every man be fully persuaded in his own mind. 14. To him that esteemeth any thing to be unclean, to him *it is* unclean. 22. Hast thou faith? have *it* to thyself before God. Happy *is* he that condemneth not himself in that thing which he alloweth.

2 Cor. 4:2. But have renounced the hidden things of dishonesty, not walking in craftiness, nor handling the word of God deceitfully; but by manifestation of the truth commending ourselves to every man's conscience in the sight of God. 2 Cor. 5:11.

2 Cor. 7:2. We have wronged no man, we have corrupted no man, we have defrauded no man.

2 Cor. 8:21. Providing for honest things, not only in the sight of the Lord, but also in the sight of men.

Phil. 4:8. Finally, brethren, whatsoever things are true, whatsoever things *are* honest, whatsoever things *are* just, whatsoever things *are* pure, whatsoever things *are* lovely, whatsoever things *are* of good report; if *there be* any virtue, and if *there be* any praise, think on these things.

Col. 3:22. Servants, obey in all things *your* masters according to the flesh; not with eyeservice, as menpleasers; but in singleness of heart, fearing God: 23. And whatsoever ye do, do *it* heartily, as to the Lord, and not unto men; Eph. 6:6.

1 Thess. 2:4. As we were allowed of God to be put in trust with the gospel, even so we speak; not as pleasing men, but God, which trieth our hearts.

1 Tim. 1:5. The end of the commandment is charity out of a pure heart, and *of* a good conscience,

1 Tim. 3:9. Holding the mystery of the faith in a pure conscience.

Tit. 1:7. For a bishop must be blameless, as a steward of God: 8. A lover of hospitality, a lover of good men, sober, just, holy, temperate;

Heb. 13:18. We trust we have a good conscience, in all things willing to live honestly.

1 Pet. 2:12. Having your conversation honest among the Gentiles: that, whereas they speak against you as evildoers, they may by *your* good works, which they shall behold, glorify God in the day of visitation.

1 Pet. 3:16. Having a good conscience; that, whereas they speak evil of you, as of evildoers, they may be ashamed that falsely accuse your good conversation in Christ.

See CHARACTER; DISHONESTY; FRAUD; HONESTY; JUSTICE; RIGHTEOUSNESS.

INSTANCES OF: Pharaoh, when he learned that Sarah was Abraham's wife, Gen. 12:18. Abimelech, when warned of God that the woman he had taken into his household was Abraham's wife, Gen. 26:9-11. Jacob, in the care of Laban's property, Gen. 31:39. Joseph, in resisting Potiphar's wife, Gen. 39:8-12; innocent of the charge on which he was cast into the dungeon, Gen. 40:15. Jacob's sons, when accused by Jo

seph of robbery, Gen. 43:15-22; 44:7-16. The Egyptian midwives, when commanded to destroy the newborn babes of the Israelites, Ex. 1:17-21. Moses, in taking nothing from the Israelites in consideration of his services, Num. 16:15. Samuel, in exacting nothing from the people on account of services, 1 Sam. 12:4. David, in self-reproach for the cutting of Saul's skirt, 1 Sam. 24:5; in preventing foraging by his insurgent forces, 1 Sam. 25:15; in his conduct while in refuge with the Philistines, 1 Sam. 29:6,9, with *vs.* 1-11. Workmen, who repaired the temple, 2 Kin. 12:15; 22:7. Joab, when ordered by David to number the military forces of Israel, 1 Chr. 21:6. Priests, who received the offerings of gold and other gifts for the renewing of the temple under Ezra, Ezra 8:24-30. Nehemiah, reforming the civil service, and receiving no compensation for his own services, Neh. 5:14-19. The Rechabites, in keeping the Nazarite vows, Jer. 35:12-17. Daniel, in his abstemiousness, Dan. 1:8-20; in maintaining uprightness of character and consistent devoutness, Dan. 6:4. Joseph, the husband of Mary, in not jealously accusing her of immorality, Matt. 1:19. Zacchæus, in the administration of his wealth, Luke 19:8. Nathanael, in whom was no guile, John 1:47. Joseph, a counselor, Luke 23:50,51. Peter, when offered money by Simon Magus, Acts 8:18-23. Paul and Barnabas, when the people of Lystra desired to deify them, Acts 14:12-15.

INTEMPERANCE. See DRUNKARDS; DRUNKENNESS; WINE; ABSTINENCE; TEMPERANCE.

INTERCESSION. OF MAN WITH MAN: 1 Sam. 2:25. If one man sin against another, the judge shall judge him: but if a man sin against the LORD, who shall intreat for him?

INSTANCES OF: Reuben for Joseph, Gen. 37:21,22. Judah for Joseph, Gen. 37:26,27. Pharaoh's chief baker for Joseph, Gen. 41: 9-13, with Gen. 40:14. Jonathan for David, 1 Sam. 19:1-7. Abigail for Nabal, 1 Sam. 25:23-35. Joab for Absalom, 2 Sam. 14:1-24. Bath-sheba for Solomon, 1 Kin. 1:15-31; for Adonijah, 1 Kin. 2:13-25. Ebed-melech for Jeremiah, Jer. 38:7-13. Elisha offers to see the king for the Shunammite, 2 Kin. 4:13. The king of Syria for Naaman, 2 Kin. 5:6-8. Paul for Onesimus, Philem. 10-21.

OF MAN WITH GOD: Gen. 20:7. Now therefore restore the man *his* wife; for he *is* a prophet, and he shall pray for thee, and thou shalt live: and if thou restore *her* not, know thou that thou shalt surely die, thou, and all that *are* thine.

Ex. 28:12. And thou shalt put the two stones upon the shoulders of the ephod *for* stones of memorial unto the children of Israel: and Aaron shall bear their names before the LORD upon his two shoulders for a memorial. 29. And Aaron shall bear the names of the children of Israel in the breastplate of judgment upon his heart, when he goeth in unto the holy *place*, for a memorial before the LORD continually. 30. And thou shalt put in the breastplate of judgment the Urim and the Thummim; and they shall be upon Aaron's heart, when he goeth in before the LORD: and Aaron shall bear the judgment of the children of Israel upon his heart before the LORD continually. 38. And it shall be upon Aaron's forehead, that Aaron may bear the iniquity of the holy things, which the children of Israel shall hallow in all their holy gifts: and it shall be always upon his forehead, that they may be accepted before the LORD.

Ex. 32:9. And the LORD said unto Moses, I have seen this people, and, behold, it *is* a stiffnecked people: 10. Now therefore let me alone, that my wrath may wax hot against them, and that I may consume them: and I will make of thee a great nation. 11. And Moses besought the LORD his God, and said, LORD, why doth thy wrath wax hot against thy people, which thou hast brought forth out of the land of Egypt with great power, and with a mighty hand? 12. Wherefore should the Egyptians speak, and say, For mischief did he bring them out, to slay them in the mountains, and to consume them from the face of the earth? Turn from thy fierce wrath, and repent of this evil against thy people. 13. Remember Abraham, Isaac, and Israel, thy servants, to whom thou swarest by thine own self, and saidst unto them, I will multiply your seed as the stars of heaven, and all this land that I have spoken of will I give unto your seed, and they shall inherit *it* for ever. 14. And the LORD repented of the evil which he thought to do unto his people.

Num. 6:23. Speak unto Aaron and unto his sons, saying, On this wise ye shall bless the children of Israel, saying unto them, 24. The LORD bless thee, and keep thee: 25. The LORD make his face shine upon thee, and be gracious unto thee: 26. The LORD lift up his countenance upon thee, and give thee peace.

Num. 14:11. And the LORD said unto Moses, How long will this people provoke me? and how long will it be ere they believe me, for all the signs which I have shewed among them? 12. I will smite them with the pestilence, and disinherit them, and will make of thee a greater nation and mightier than they. 13. And Moses said unto the LORD, Then the Egyptians shall hear *it*,(for thou broughtest up this people in thy might from among them;) 14. And they will tell *it* to the inhabitants of this land: *for* they have heard that thou LORD *art* among this people, that thou LORD art seen face to face, and *that* thy cloud standeth over them, and *that* thou goest before them, by day-time in a pillar of a cloud, and in a pillar of fire by night. 15. Now *if* thou shalt kill *all* this people as one man, then the nations which have heard the fame of thee will speak, saying, 16. Because the LORD was

not able to bring this people into the land which he sware unto them, therefore he hath slain them in the wilderness. 17. And now, I beseech thee, let the power of my Lord be great, according as thou hast spoken, saying. 18. The LORD *is* longsuffering, and of great mercy, forgiving iniquity and transgression, and by no means clearing *the guilty*, visiting the iniquity of the fathers upon the children unto the third and fourth *generation*. 19. Pardon, I beseech thee, the iniquity of this people according unto the greatness of thy mercy, and as thou hast forgiven this people, from Egypt even until now. 20. And the LORD said, I have pardoned according to thy word: 21. But *as* truly *as* I live, all the earth shall be filled with the glory of the LORD.

Num. 16:46. And Moses said unto Aaron, Take a censer, and put fire therein from off the altar, and put on incense, and go quickly unto the congregation, and make an atonement for them: for there is wrath gone out from the LORD; the plague is begun. 47. And Aaron took as Moses commanded, and ran into the midst of the congregation; and, behold, the plague was begun among the people: and he put on incense, and made an atonement for the people. 48. And he stood between the dead and the living; and the plague was stayed. 49. Now they that died in the plague were fourteen thousand and seven hundred, beside them that died about the matter of Korah. 50. And Aaron returned unto Moses unto the door of the tabernacle of the congregation: and the plague was stayed.

Deut. 5:5. (I stood between the LORD and you at that time, to shew you the word of the LORD: for ye were afraid by reason of the fire, and went not up into the mount;)

Deut. 7:9. Know therefore that the LORD thy God, he *is* God, the faithful God, which keepeth covenant and mercy with them that love him and keep his commandments to a thousand generations;

Deut. 9:18. And I fell down before the LORD, as at the first, forty days and forty nights: I did neither eat bread, nor drink water, because of all your sins which ye sinned, in doing wickedly in the sight of the LORD, to provoke him to anger. 20. And the LORD was very angry with Aaron to have destroyed him: and I prayed for Aaron also the same time. 25. Thus I fell down before the LORD forty days and forty nights, as I fell down *at the first;* because the LORD had said he would destroy you. 26. I prayed therefore unto the LORD, and said, O Lord GOD, destroy not tny people and thine inheritance, which thou hast redeemed through thy greatness, which thou hast brought forth out of Egypt with a mighty hand. 27. Remember thy servants, Abraham, Isaac, and Jacob: look not unto the stubbornness of this people, nor to their wickedness, nor to their sin: 28. Lest the land whence thou broughtest us out say, Because the LORD was not able to bring them into the land which he promised them, and because he hated them, he hath brought them out to slay them in the wilderness. 29. Yet they *are* thy people and thine inheritance, which thou broughtest out by thy mighty power and by thy stretched out arm.

1 Sam. 7:5. And Samuel said, Gather all Israel to Mizpeh, and I will pray for you unto the LORD. 6. And they gathered together to Mizpeh, and drew water, and poured *it* out before the LORD, and fasted on that day, and said there, We have sinned against the LORD. And Samuel judged the children of Israel in Mizpeh. 7. And when the Philistines heard that the children of Israel were gathered together to Mizpeh, the lords of the Philistines went up against Israel. And when the children of Israel heard *it*, they were afraid of the Philistines. 8. And the children of Israel said to Samuel, Cease not to cry unto the LORD our God for us, that he will save us out of the hand of the Philistines.

1 Sam. 12:23. Moreover as for me, God forbid that I should sin against the LORD in ceasing to pray for you: but I will teach you the good and the right way:

1 Sam. 15:24. And Saul said unto Samuel, I have sinned: for I have transgressed the commandment of the LORD, and thy words: because I feared the people, and obeyed their voice. 25. Now therefore, I pray thee, pardon my sin, and turn again with me, that I may worship the LORD. 26. And Samuel said unto Saul, I will not return with thee: for thou hast rejected the word of the LORD, and the LORD hath rejected thee from being king over Israel. 30. Then he said, I have sinned: *yet* honour me now, I pray thee, before the elders of my people, and before Israel, and turn again with me, that I may worship the LORD thy God.

Job 1:5. And it was so, when the days of *their* feasting were gone about, that Job sent and sanctified them, and rose up early in the morning, and offered burnt offerings *according* to the number of them all: for Job said, It may be that my sons have sinned, and cursed God in their hearts. Thus did Job continually.

Job 9:32. For *he is* not a man, as I *am*, *that* I should answer him, *and* we should come together in judgment. 33. Neither is there any daysman betwixt us, *that* might lay his hand upon us both.

Job 16:21. Oh that one might plead for a man with God, as a man *pleadeth* for his neighbour!

Job 42:8. Therefore take unto you now seven bullocks and seven rams, and go to my servant Job, and offer up for yourselves a burnt offering; and my servant Job shall pray for you: for him will I accept: lest I deal with you *after your* folly, in that ye have not spoken of me *the thing which is*

right, like my servant Job. 9. So Eliphaz the Temanite and Bildad the Shuhite *and* Zophar the Naamathite went, and did according as the LORD commanded them: the LORD also accepted Job. 10. And the LORD turned the captivity of Job, when he prayed for his friends: also the LORD gave Job twice as much as he had before.

Psa. 122:6. Pray for the peace of Jerusalem: they shall prosper that love thee.

Isa. 62:6. I have set watchmen upon thy walls, O Jerusalem, *which* shall never hold their peace day nor night: ye that make mention of the LORD, keep not silence, 7. And give him no rest, till he establish, and till he make Jerusalem a praise in the earth.

Isa. 65:8. Thus saith the LORD, As the new wine is found in the cluster, and *one* saith, Destroy it not; for a blessing *is* in it: so will I do for my servants' sake, that I may not destroy them all.

Jer. 5:1. Run ye to and fro through the streets of Jerusalem, and see now, and know, and seek in the broad places thereof, if ye can find a man, if there be *any* that executeth judgment, that seeketh the truth; and I will pardon it.

Jer. 7:16. Therefore pray not thou for this people, neither lift up cry nor prayer for them, neither make intercession to me: for I will not hear thee.

Jer. 11:14. Therefore pray not thou for this people, neither lift up a cry or prayer for them: for I will not hear *them* in the time that they cry unto me for their trouble. chapter 14:11.

Jer. 15:1. Then said the LORD unto me, Though Moses and Samuel stood before me, *yet* my mind *could* not *be* toward this people: cast *them* out of my sight, and let them go forth.

Jer. 29:7. Seek the peace of the city whither I have caused you to be carried away captives, and pray unto the LORD for it:

Ezek. 22:30. And I sought for a man among them, that should make up the hedge, and stand in the gap before me for the land, that I should not destroy it: but I found none.

Matt. 8:5. And when Jesus was entered into Capernaum, there came unto him a centurion, beseeching him, 6. And saying, Lord, my servant lieth at home sick of the palsy, grievously tormented. 7. And Jesus said unto him, I will come and heal him. 8. The centurion answered and said, Lord, I am not worthy that thou shouldest come under my roof: but speak the word only, and my servant shall be healed. 9. For I am a man under authority, having soldiers under me: and I say to this *man*, Go, and he goeth; and to another, Come, and he cometh; and to my servant, Do this, and he doeth *it*. 10. When Jesus heard *it*, he marvelled, and said to them that followed, Verily I say unto you, I have not found so great faith, no, not in Israel. 11. And I say unto you, That many shall come from the east and west, and shall sit down with Abraham, and Isaac, and Jacob, in the kingdom of heaven. 12. But the children of the kingdom shall be cast out into outer darkness: there shall be weeping and gnashing of teeth. 13. And Jesus said unto the centurion, Go thy way; and as thou hast believed, so be it done unto thee. And his servant was healed in the selfsame hour.

Mark 6:55. And ran through that whole region round about, and began to carry about in beds those that were sick, where they heard he was. 56. And whithersoever he entered, into villages, or cities, or country, they laid the sick in the streets, and besought him that they might touch if it were but the border of his garment: and as many as touched him were made whole.

Eph. 6:18. Praying always with all prayer and supplication in the Spirit, and watching thereunto with all perseverance and supplication for all saints;

1 Tim. 2:1. I exhort therefore, that, first of all, supplications, prayers, intercessions, and giving of thanks, be made for all men; 2. For kings, and for all that are in authority;

Heb. 13:18. Pray for us:

Jas. 5:14. Is any sick among you? let him call for the elders of the church; and let them pray over him, anointing him with oil in the name of the Lord: 15. And the prayer of faith shall save the sick, and the Lord shall raise him up; and if he have committed sins, they shall be forgiven him. 16. Confess your faults one to another, and pray one for another, that ye may be healed. The effectual fervent prayer of a righteous man availeth much. 17. Elias was a man subject to like passions as we are, and he prayed earnestly that it might not rain: and it rained not on the earth by the space of three years and six months. 18. And he prayed again, and the heaven gave rain, and the earth brought forth her fruit. 19. Brethren, if any of you do err from the truth, and one convert him: 20. Let him know, that he which converteth the sinner from the error of his way shall save a soul from death, and shall hide a multitude of sins.

1 Pet. 2:5. Ye also, as lively stones, are built up a spiritual house, an holy priesthood, to offer up spiritual sacrifices, acceptable to God by Jesus Christ. v. 9.

1 John 5:16. If any man see his brother sin a sin which is not unto death, he shall ask, and he shall give him life for them that sin not unto death. There is a sin unto death: I do not say that he shall pray for it.

EXEMPLIFIED: Gen. 48:16. The Angel which redeemed me from all evil, bless the lads; and let my name be named on them, and the name of my fathers Abraham and Isaac; and let them grow into a multitude in the midst of the earth. vs. 15-20.

Ex. 32:31. Moses returned unto the Lord, and said, Oh, this people have sinned a great sin, and have made them gods of gold. 32. Yet now, if thou wilt forgive their sin—; and if not, blot me, I pray thee, out of thy book which thou hast written.

Ex. 34:9. If now I have found grace in thy sight, O Lord, let my Lord, I pray thee, go among us: for it is a stiffnecked people; and pardon our iniquity and our sin, and take us for thine inheritance.

Num. 10:35. Rise up, Lord, and let thine enemies be scattered; and let them that hate thee flee before thee. 36. Return, O Lord, unto the many thousands of Israel.

Num. 27:16. Let the Lord, the God of the spirits of all flesh, set a man over the congregation, 17. Which may go out before them, and which may go in before them, and which may lead them out, and which may bring them in; that the congregation of the Lord be not as sheep which have no shepherd.

Josh. 7:8. O Lord, what shall I say, when Israel turneth their backs before their enemies! 9. For the Canaanites and all the inhabitants of the land shall hear of it, and shall environ us round, and cut off our name from the earth: and what wilt thou do unto thy great name? vs. 7-26.

Judg. 5:31. Let all thine enemies perish, O Lord: but let them that love him be as the sun when he goeth forth in his might.

Ruth 2:12. The Lord recompense thy work, and a full reward be given thee of the Lord God of Israel, under whose wings thou art come to trust.

1 Sam. 1:17. Eli answered and said, Go in peace: and the God of Israel grant thee thy petition that thou hast asked of him.

1 Sam. 12:23. Moreover, as for me, God forbid that I should sin against the Lord in ceasing to pray for you:

2 Sam. 24:17. And David spake unto the Lord when he saw the angel that smote the people, and said, Lo, I have sinned, and I have done wickedly: but these sheep, what have they done? let thine hand, I pray thee, be against me, and against my father's house.

1 Kin. 8:29. That thine eyes may be open toward this house night and day, even toward the place of which thou hast said, My name shall be there: that thou mayest hearken unto the prayer which thy servant shall make toward this place. 38. What prayer and supplications soever be made by any man, or by all thy people Israel, which shall know every man the plague of his own heart, and spread forth his hands toward this house: 39. Then hear thou in heaven thy dwelling place, and forgive, and do, and give to every man according to his ways, whose heart thou knowest; 44. If thy people go out to battle against their enemy, whithersoever thou shalt send them, and shall pray unto the Lord toward the city which thou hast chosen, and toward the house that I have built for thy name: 45. Then hear thou in heaven their prayer and their supplication, and maintain their cause.

1 Chr. 29:18. O LORD God of Abraham, Isaac, and of Israel, our fathers, keep this for ever in the imagination of the thoughts of the heart of thy people, and prepare their heart unto thee: 19. Give unto Solomon my son a perfect heart, to keep thy commandments, thy testimonies, and thy statutes, and to do all *these things*, and to build the palace, *for* the which I have made provision.

2 Chr. 6:40. Now, my God, let, I beseech thee, thine eyes be open, and *let* thine ears *be* attent unto the prayer *that is made* in this place. 41. Now therefore arise, O LORD God, into thy resting place, thou, and the ark of thy strength: let thy priests, O LORD God, be clothed with salvation, and let thy saints rejoice in goodness.

2 Chr. 30:18. The good LORD pardon every one 19. *That* prepareth his heart to seek God, the LORD God of his fathers, though *he be* not *cleansed* according to the purification of the sanctuary.

Psa. 7:9. O let the wickedness of the wicked come to an end; but establish the just:

Psa. 12:1. Help, LORD; for the godly man ceaseth; for the faithful fail from among the children of men.

Psa. 20:1. The LORD hear thee in the day of trouble; the name of the God of Jacob defend thee; 2. Send thee help from the sanctuary, and strengthen thee out of Zion; 3. Remember all thy offerings, and accept thy burnt sacrifice; 4. Grant thee according to thine own heart, and fulfil all thy counsel.

Psa. 25:22. Redeem Israel, O God, out of all his troubles.

Psa. 28:9. Save thy people, and bless thine inheritance: feed them also, and lift them up for ever.

Psa. 36:10. O continue thy lovingkindness unto them that know thee; and thy righteousness to the upright in heart.

Psa. 51:18. Do good in thy good pleasure unto Zion: build thou the walls of Jerusalem.

Psa. 80:1. Give ear, O Shepherd of Israel, thou that leadest Joseph like a flock; thou that dwellest *between* the cherubims, shine forth. 2. Before Ephraim and Benjamin and Manasseh stir up thy strength, and come *and* save us. 14. Return, we beseech thee, O God of hosts: look down from heaven, and behold, and visit this vine; 15. And the vineyard which thy right hand hath planted, and the branch *that* thou madest strong for thyself. 17. Let thy hand be upon the man of thy right hand, upon the son of man *whom* thou madest strong for thyself. 19. Turn us again, O LORD God of hosts, cause thy face to shine; and we shall be saved.

Psa. 122:7. Peace be within thy walls, *and* prosperity within thy palaces. 8. For my brethren and companions' sakes, I will now say, Peace *be* within thee.

Psa. 125:4. Do good, O LORD, unto *those that be* good, and to *them that are* upright in their hearts.

Psa. 132:9. Let thy priests be clothed with righteousness; and let thy saints shout for joy. 10. For thy servant David's sake turn not away the face of thine anointed. *v.* 8.

Psa. 134:3. The LORD that made heaven and earth bless thee out of Zion.

Psa. 141:5. Let the righteous smite me; *it shall be* a kindness: and let him reprove me; *it shall be* an excellent oil, *which* shall not break my head: for yet my prayer also *shall be* in their calamities.

Isa. 62:1. For Zion's sake will I not hold my peace, and for Jerusalem's sake I will not rest, until the righteousness thereof go forth as brightness, and the salvation thereof as a lamp *that* burneth.

Isa. 63:17. O LORD, why hast thou made us to err from thy ways, *and* hardened our heart from thy fear? Return for thy servants' sake, the tribes of thine inheritance. 18. The people of thy holiness have possessed *it* but a little while: our adversaries have trodden down thy sanctuary. 19. We are *thine:* thou never barest rule over them; they were not called by thy name.

Isa. 64:8. But now, O LORD, thou *art* our Father; we *are* the clay, and thou our potter; and we all *are* the work of thy hand. 9. Be not wroth very sore, O LORD, neither remember iniquity for ever: behold, see, we beseech thee, we *are* all thy people. 10. Thy holy cities are a wilderness, Zion is a wilderness, Jerusalem a desolation. 11. Our holy and our beautiful house, where our fathers praised thee, is burned up with fire: and all our pleasant things are laid waste. 12. Wilt thou refrain thyself for these *things,* O LORD? wilt thou hold thy peace, and afflict us very sore?

Jer. 18:20. Shall evil be recompensed for good? for they have digged a pit for my soul. Remember that I stood before thee to speak good for them, *and* to turn away thy wrath from them.

Ezek. 9:8. And it came to pass, while they were slaying them, and I was left, that I fell upon my face, and cried, and said, Ah Lord GOD! wilt thou destroy all the residue of Israel in thy pouring out of thy fury upon Jerusalem? Ezek. 11:13.

Dan. 9:3. And I set my face unto the Lord God, to seek by prayer and supplications, with fasting, and sackcloth, and ashes: 4. And I prayed unto the LORD my God, and made my confession, and said, O Lord, the great and dreadful God, keeping the covenant and mercy to them that love him, and to them that keep his commandments; 5. We have sinned, and have committed iniquity, and have done wickedly, and have rebelled, even by departing from thy precepts and from thy judgments: 6. Neither have we hearkened unto thy servants the prophets, which spake in thy name to our kings, our princes, and our fathers, and to all the people of the land. 7. O Lord, righteousness *belongeth* unto thee, but unto us confusion of faces, as at this day; to the men of Judah, and to the inhabitants of Jerusalem, and unto all Israel, *that are* near, and *that are* far off, through all the countries whither thou hast driven them, because of their trespass that they have trespassed against thee. 8. O Lord, to us *belongeth* confusion of face, to our kings, to our princes, and to our fathers, because we have sinned against thee. 9. To the Lord our God *belong* mercies and forgiveness, though we have rebelled against him; 10. Neither have we obeyed the voice of the LORD our God, to walk in his laws, which he set before us by his servants the prophets. 11. Yea, all Israel have transgressed thy law, even by departing, that they might not obey thy voice; therefore the curse is poured upon us, and the oath that *is* written in the law of Moses the servant of God, because we have sinned against him. 12. And he hath confirmed his words, which he spake against us, and against our judges that judged us, by bringing upon us a great evil: for under the whole heaven hath not been done as hath been done upon Jerusalem. 13. As *it is* written in the law of Moses, all this evil is come upon us: yet made we not our prayer before the LORD our God, that we might turn from our iniquities, and understand thy truth. 14. Therefore hath the LORD watched upon the evil, and brought it upon us. for the LORD our God *is* righteous in all his works which he doeth: for we obeyed not his voice. 15. And now, O Lord our God, that hast brought thy people forth out of the land of Egypt with a mighty hand, and hast gotten thee renown, as at this day; we have sinned, we have done wickedly. 16. O Lord, according to all thy righteousness, I beseech thee, let thine anger and thy fury be turned away from thy city Jerusalem, thy holy mountain: because for our sins, and for the iniquities of our fathers, Jerusalem and thy people *are become* a reproach to all *that are* about us. 17. Now therefore, O our God, hear the prayer of thy servant, and his supplications, and cause thy face to shine upon thy sanctuary that is desolate, for the Lord's sake. 18. O my God, incline thine ear, and hear; open thine eyes, and behold our desolations, and the city which is called by thy name: for we do not present our supplications before thee for our righteousnesses, but for thy great mercies. 19. O Lord, hear; O LORD, forgive; O Lord, hearken and do; defer not, for thine own sake, O my God: for thy city and thy people are called by thy name.

Joel 2:17. Let the priests, the ministers of the LORD, weep between the porch and the altar, and let them say, Spare thy people, O LORD, and give not thine heritage to reproach,

Mic. 7:14. Feed thy people with thy rod, the flock of thine heritage, which dwell solitarily *in* the wood, in the midst of Carmel: let them feed *in* Bashan and Gilead, as in the days of old.

Matt. 5:44. Pray for them which despitefully use you, and persecute you;

Matt. 6:10. Thy kingdom come. Thy will be done in earth, as *it is* in heaven.

Acts 7:60. Lord, lay not this sin to their charge.

Acts 8:15. Who, when they were come down, prayed for them, that they might receive the Holy Ghost:

Rom. 1:9. Without ceasing I make mention of you always in my prayer;

Rom. 10:1. Brethren, my heart's desire and prayer to God for Israel is, that they might be saved.

1 Cor. 1:3. Grace *be* unto you, and peace, from God our Father, and *from* the Lord Jesus Christ. Gal. 1:3.

2 Cor. 9:10. He that ministereth seed to the sower both minister bread for *your* food, and multiply your seed sown, and increase the fruits of your righteousness; 14. By their prayer for you, which long after you for the exceeding grace of God in you.

2 Cor. 13:7. Now I pray to God that ye do no evil; not that we should appear approved, but that ye should do that which is honest, though we be as reprobates.

Gal. 6:16. As many as walk according to this rule, peace *be* on them, and mercy, and upon the Israel of God.

Eph. 1:15. Wherefore I also . . . 16. Cease not to give thanks for you, making mention of you in my prayers; 17. That the God of our Lord Jesus Christ, the Father of glory, may give unto you the spirit of wisdom and revelation in the knowledge of him: 18. The eyes of your understanding being enlightened; that ye may know what is the hope of his calling, and what the riches of the glory of his inheritance in the saints, 19. And what *is* the exceeding greatness of his power to us-ward who believe, according to the working of his mighty power, 1 Thess. 1:2.

Eph. 3:14. For this cause I bow my knees unto the Father of our Lord Jesus Christ, 15. Of whom the whole family in heaven and earth is named, 16. That he would grant you, according to the riches of his glory, to be strengthened with might by his Spirit in the inner man; 17. That Christ may dwell in your hearts by faith; that ye, being rooted and grounded in love, 18. May be able to comprehend with all saints what *is* the breadth, and length, and depth, and height; 19. And to know the love of Christ, which passeth knowledge, that ye might be filled with all the fulness of God.

Phil. 1:3. I thank my God upon every remembrance of you, 4. Always in every prayer of mine for you all making request with joy, 5. For your fellowship in the gospel from the first day until now; 9. This I pray, that your love may abound yet more and more in knowledge and *in* all judgment; *v.* 10.

Col. 1:3. We give thanks to God and the Father of our Lord Jesus Christ, praying always for you, 4. Since we heard of your faith in Christ Jesus, 9. For this cause we also, . . . do not cease to pray for you, and to desire that ye might be filled with the knowledge of his will in all wisdom and spiritual understanding;

Col. 2:1. For I would that ye knew what great conflict I have for you, and for them of Laodicea, and for as many as have not seen my face in the flesh; 2. That their hearts might be comforted, being knit together in love, and unto all riches of the full assurance of understanding, to the acknowledgment of the mystery of God, and of the Father, and of Christ; Col. 4:12.

1 Thess. 3;10. Night and day praying exceedingly that we might see your face, and might perfect that which is lacking in your faith? 12. The Lord make you to increase and abound in love one toward another, and toward all men, even as we do toward you : 13. To the end he may stablish your hearts unblameable in holiness before God, even our Father, at the coming of our Lord Jesus Christ with all his saints. 2 Tim. 1:3.

1 Thess. 5:23. The very God of peace sanctify you wholly; and I pray God your whole spirit and soul and body be preserved blameless unto the coming of our Lord Jesus Christ.

2 Thess. 1:11. We pray always for you, that our God would count you worthy of this calling, and fulfil all the good pleasure of his goodness, and the work of faith with power :

2 Thess. 2:16. Now our Lord Jesus Christ himself, and God, even our Father, which hath loved us, and hath given us everlasting consolation and good hope through grace, 17. Comfort your hearts, and stablish you in every good word and work.

2 Thess. 3:5. The Lord direct your hearts into the love of God, and into the patient waiting for Christ. 16. The Lord of peace himself give you peace always by all means. The Lord be with you all.

2 Tim. 1:18. The Lord grant unto him that he may find mercy of the Lord in that day:

2 Tim. 2:7. The Lord give thee understanding in all things.

2 Tim. 4:16. At my first answer no man stood with me, but all men forsook me: I pray God that it may not be laid to their charge.

Philem. 4. I thank my God, making mention of thee always in my prayers, 6. That the communication of thy faith may become effectual by the acknowledging of every good thing which is in you in Christ Jesus.

Heb. 13:20. The God of peace . . . 21. Make you perfect in every good work to do his will, working in you that which is wellpleasing in his sight, through Jesus Christ;

1 Pet. 5:10. The God of all grace, who hath called us unto his eternal glory by Christ Jesus, after that ye have suffered a while, make you perfect, stablish, strengthen, settle you.

See PRAYER, INTERCESSORY.

ADDITIONAL INSTANCES OF : Abraham, in behalf of Sodom, Gen. 18:23–32; in behalf of Abimelech, Gen. 20:17,18. Abraham's servant, in behalf of his master, Gen. 24:12. Jacob, in behalf of his children, Gen. 49. Moses, in behalf of Pharaoh, Ex. 8:12,13,30, 31; 9:33; 10:18,19. Moses, for Israel, Num. 16:20–22; 21:7; Deut. 33:6–17; Psa. 106:23; for Miriam, Num. 12:13–15. David, for Israel, 2 Sam. 24:17. Solomon, for Israel, 1 Kin. 8:29–53. Ezra, for Israel, Ezra 9:5–15. Nehemiah, in behalf of Judah and Jerusalem, Neh. 1:4–9. Asaph, for the church, Psa. 80; 83. Korah, for the church, Psa. 85:1–7. Jeremiah, for Israel, Jer. 14:7–22. Amos, for Israel, Amos 7:2–6. Syro-Phenician woman, for her daughter, Matt. 15:22. Disciples, in behalf of Peter's wife's mother, Luke 4:38,39. Parents, for lunatic son, Matt. 17:15; Mark 9:17–27. Others, who sought Jesus in behalf of the afflicted, Matt. 12:22; 15:22,30; 17:14–18; Mark 1:32; 2:3; Luke 5:18–20; John 4:47,49. Paul, for the church, Acts 20:32. Onesiphorus, 2 Tim. 1:16,18. For Paul, by the churches, Acts 14:26; 15:40.

SOLICITED : INSTANCES OF : By Pharaoh, of Moses, Ex. 8:8,28; 9:28; 10:17; 12:32; and by the Israelites, Num. 21:7. By Israel, of Samuel, 1 Sam. 12:19. By Jeroboam, of a prophet, 1 Kin. 13:6. By Hezekiah, of Isaiah, 2 Kin. 19:1–4. By Zedekiah, of Jeremiah, Jer. 37:3; and by Johanan, Jer. 42:1–6. By Daniel, of Shadrach, Meshach and Abed-nego, Dan. 2:17,18. By Darius, of the Jews, Ezra 6:10. By Simon Magus, of Peter, Acts 8:24. By Paul, of the churches, Rom. 15:30–32; 2 Cor. 1:11; Eph. 6:19,20; 1 Thess. 5:25; 2 Thess. 3:1; Heb. 13:18.

ANSWERED : INSTANCES OF : Of Moses, in behalf of Pharaoh, for the plague of frogs to be abated, Ex. 8:12,15; the plague of flies, Ex. 8:30–32; the plague of rain, thunder, and hail, Ex. 9:27–35; plague of locusts, Ex. 10:16–20; plague of darkness, Ex. 10:21–23. Of Moses, for the Israelites, during the battle with the Amalekites, Ex. 17:11–14; after the Israelites had made the golden calf, Ex. 32:11–14,31–34; Deut. 9:18–29; 10:10; Psa. 106:23; after the murmuring of the people, Ex. 33:15–17; when the fire of the Lord consumed the people, Num. 11:1,2; when the people murmured on account of the report of the spies, Num. 14:11–20; that the fiery serpents might be abated, Num. 21:4–9; that Miriam's leprosy might be healed, Num. 12:13; in behalf of Aaron, on account of his sin in making the golden calf, Deut. 9:20. Of Samuel, for deliverance from the oppressions of the Philistines, 1 Sam. 7:5–14. The prophet of Israel, for the restoration of Jeroboam's withered hand, 1 Kin. 13:1-6. Of Elijah, for the raising from the dead the son of the hospitable widow, 1 Kin. 17:20–23. Of Elisha, for the raising from the dead the son of the Shunammite woman, 2 Kin.

4:33-36. Of Isaiah, in behalf of Hezekiah and the people, to be delivered from Sennacherib, 2 Kin. 19.

INTERCESSIONAL INFLUENCE OF THE RIGHTEOUS: Gen. 18:26. And the LORD said, If I find in Sodom fifty righteous within the city, then I will spare all the place for their sakes. vs. 29,30,32.

Gen. 19:22. Haste thee, escape thither; for I cannot do any thing till thou be come thither.

Gen. 26:4. And I will make thy seed to multiply as the stars of heaven, and will give unto thy seed all these countries; and in thy seed shall all the nations of the earth be blessed; 5. Because that Abraham obeyed my voice, and kept my charge, my commandments, my statutes, and my laws. 24. And the LORD appeared unto him the same night, and said, I am the God of Abraham thy father: fear not, for I am with thee, and will bless thee, and multiply thy seed for my servant Abraham's sake.

1 Kin. 11:12. Notwithstanding in thy days I will not do it for David thy father's sake: but I will rend it out of the hand of thy son. 13. Howbeit I will not rend away all the kingdom; but will give one tribe to thy son for David my servant's sake, and for Jerusalem's sake which I have chosen. 34. Howbeit I will not take the whole kingdom out of his hand: but I will make him prince all the days of his life for David my servant's sake, whom I chose, because he kept my commandments and my statutes:

1 Kin. 15:4. Nevertheless for David's sake did the LORD his God give him a lamp in Jerusalem, to set up his son after him, and to establish Jerusalem:

2 Kin. 8:19. Yet the LORD would not destroy Judah for David his servant's sake, as he promised him to give him always a light, and to his children. 2 Chr. 21:7.

Psa. 103:17. But the mercy of the LORD is from everlasting to everlasting upon them that fear him, and his righteousness unto children's children; 18. To such as keep his covenant, and to those that remember his commandments to do them.

Isa. 37:35. For I will defend this city to save it for mine own sake, and for my servant David's sake.

Jer. 5:1. Run ye to and fro through the streets of Jerusalem, and see now, and know, and seek in the broad places thereof, if ye can find a man, if there be any that executeth judgment, that seeketh the truth; and I will pardon it.

Ezek. 14:14. Though these three men, Noah, Daniel, and Job, were in it, they should deliver but their own souls by their righteousness, saith the Lord GOD. vs. 18,20. 16. Though these three men were in it, as I live, saith the Lord GOD, they shall deliver neither sons nor daughters; they only shall be delivered, but the land shall be desolate.

Matt. 24:22. And except those days should be shortened, there should no flesh be saved:

but for the elect's sake those days shall be shortened.

Rom. 11:27. For this is my covenant unto them, when I shall take away their sins. 28. As concerning the gospel, they are enemies for your sakes: but as touching the election, they are beloved for the fathers' sakes.

Rev. 5:8. And when he had taken the book, the four beasts and four and twenty elders fell down before the Lamb, having every one of them harps, and golden vials full of odours, which are the prayers of saints.

Rev. 8:3. And another angel came and stood at the altar, having a golden censer; and there was given unto him much incense, that he should offer it with the prayers of all saints upon the golden altar which was before the throne. 4. And the smoke of the incense, which came with the prayers of the saints, ascended up before God out of the angel's hand.

See CHILDREN, OF THE RIGHTEOUS, BLESSED OF GOD; JESUS, MEDIATOR.

INTEREST. Income from loaning money, usually called usury in the scriptures, but not generally signifying unlawful or unjust rates.

Ex. 22:25. If thou lend money to any of my people that is poor by thee, thou shalt not be to him as an usurer, neither shalt thou lay upon him usury.

Lev. 25:36. Take thou no usury of him, or increase: but fear thy God; that thy brother may live with thee. 37. Thou shalt not give him thy money upon usury, nor lend him thy victuals for increase.

Deut. 23:19. Thou shalt not lend upon usury to thy brother; usury of money, usury of victuals, usury of any thing that is lent upon usury: 20. Unto a stranger thou mayest lend upon usury; but unto thy brother thou shalt not lend upon usury: that the LORD thy God may bless thee in all that thou settest thine hand to in the land whither thou goest to possess it.

Neh. 5:1. And there was a great cry of the people and of their wives against their brethren the Jews. 2. For there were that said, We, our sons, and our daughters, are many: therefore we take up corn for them, that we may eat, and live. 3. Some also there were that said, We have mortgaged our lands, vineyards, and houses, that we might buy corn, because of the dearth. 4. There were also that said, We have borrowed money for the king's tribute, and that upon our lands and vineyards. 5. Yet now our flesh is as the flesh of our brethren, our children as their children: and, lo, we bring into bondage our sons and our daughters to be servants, and some of our daughters are brought into bondage already: neither is it in our power to redeem them; for other men have our lands and vineyards. 6. And I was very angry when I heard their cry and these words. 7. Then I consulted with myself, and I rebuked the nobles, and the rulers, and said unto them, Ye exact usury, every one of his brother. And I set a great assembly against them. 8. And I said unto them, We after our ability have redeemed our brethren the Jews. which were sold unto the heathen; and will ye even sell your brethren? or shall they be sold unto us? Then held they their peace, and found nothing *to answer.* 9. Also I said, It *is* not good that ye do: ought ye not to walk in the fear of our God because of the reproach of the heathen our enemies: 10. I likewise, *and* my brethren, and my servants, might exact of them money and corn: I pray you, let us leave off this usury 11. Restore, I pray you, to them, even this day, their lands, their vineyards, their oliveyards, and their houses, also the hundredth *part* of the money, and of the corn, the wine, and the oil that ye exact of them. 12. Then said they, We will restore *them*, and will require nothing of them; so will we do as thou sayest. Then I called the priests, and took an oath of them, that they should do according to this promise. 13. Also I shook my lap, and said, So God shake out every man from his house, and from his labour, that performeth not this promise, even thus be he shaken out, and emptied. And all the congregation said, Amen, and praised the LORD. And the people did according to this promise.

Psa. 15:5. *He that* putteth not out his money to usury, nor taketh reward against the innocent. He that doeth these *things* shall never be moved.

Prov. 28:8. He that by usury and unjust gain increaseth his substance, he shall gather it for him that will pity the poor.

Isa. 24:2. And it shall be, as with the people, so with the priest; as with the servant, so with his master; as with the maid, so with her mistress; as with the buyer, so with the seller; as with the lender, so with the borrower; as with the taker of usury, so with the giver of usury to him.

Ezek. 18:8. He *that* hath not given forth upon usury, neither hath taken any increase, *that* hath withdrawn his hand from iniquity, hath executed true judgment between man and man, 9. Hath walked in my statutes, and hath kept my judgments, to deal truly; he *is* just, he shall surely live, saith the Lord GOD. 13. Hath given forth upon usury, and hath taken increase: shall he then live? he shall not live: he hath done all these abominations; he shall surely die; his blood shall be upon him. 17. *That* hath taken off his hand from the poor, *that* hath not received usury nor increase, hath executed my judgments, hath walked in my statutes; he shall not die for the iniquity of his father, he shall surely live.

Ezek. 22:12. In thee have they taken gifts to shed blood; thou hast taken usury and increase, and thou hast greedily gained of thy neighbours by extortion, and hast forgotten me, saith the Lord GOD.

See BORROWING; DEBT; DEBTORS; LENDING; MONEY.

INTERPRETATION. Of dreams, see DREAMS. Of foreign tongues, 1 Cor. 14:9-19, see TONGUES.

INTERPRETER. Of dreams, Gen. 40:8; 41:16; Dan. 2:18-30. Of languages, Gen. 42:23; 2 Chr. 32:31; Neh. 8:8; Job 33:23. In Christian churches, 1 Cor. 12:10,30; 14:5,13, 26-28.

FIGURATIVE: Job 33:23.

INTOLERANCE, religious. Exemplified by Cain, Gen. 4:8; Joshua, Num. 11:24-28; James and John, Mark 9:38,39; Luke 9:49; the Jews, in persecuting Jesus, see JESUS. HISTORY OF; and in persecuting the disciples, Acts 4:1-3,15-21; 17:13; and Stephen, Acts 6:9-15; 7:57-59; 8:1-3; and Paul, Acts 13:50; 17:5; 18:13; 21:28-31; 22:22, 23; 23:2.

Of idolatrous religions, taught by Moses, Ex. 22:20; Deut. 13; 17:1-7. Exemplified by Elijah, 1 Kin. 18:40; Jehu, 2 Kin. 10:18-31; by the Jews, at the time of the religious revival under the leadership of Azariah, 2 Chr. 15:12,13.

See PERSECUTION.

INTOXICANTS. See WINE.

INTOXICATION. See DRUNKENNESS; ABSTINENCE.

INTRIGUE. See CONSPIRACY.

INVECTIVE. See SATIRE.

INVENTION, Prov. 8:12. Of musical instruments: By Jubal, Gen. 4:21; by David, 1 Chr. 23:5; 2 Chr. 7:6; 29:26; Amos 6:5. The use of metals, Gen. 4:22. Engines of war, 2 Chr. 26:15.

INVESTIGATION, Eccl. 1:13-18; 2:1-12; 12:9-14.

IPHEDEIAH, a Benjamite, 1 Chr. 8:25.

IR, a Benjamite, 1 Chr. 7:12.

IRA. 1. A priest, 2 Sam. 20:26.

2. The Ithrite, one of David's heroes, 2 Sam. 23:38; 1 Chr. 11:40.

3. A Tekoite, one of David's heroes, 2 Sam. 23:26; 1 Chr. 11:28; 27:9.

IRAD, son of Enoch. Gen. 4:18.

IRAM, a duke of Edom, Gen. 36:43; 1 Chr. 1:54.

IRI, a son of Bela, 1 Chr. 7:7.

IRIJAH, a captain of the guard who imprisoned the prophet Jeremiah, Jer. 37: 13,14.

IR-NAHASH, whether a man or a town is not clear, 1 Chr. 4:12.

IRON. 1. First recorded use of, Gen. 4: 22. Ore of, Deut. 8:9; Job 28:2. Melted, Ezek. 22:20. Used in the temple, 1 Chr. 22:3; 29:2,7. Articles made of: Ax, 2 Kin. 6:6; 2 Chr. 18:10; Eccl. 10:10; Isa. 10:34; bedstead, Deut. 3:11; breastplate, Rev. 9:9; chariot, Josh. 17: 16,18; Judg. 1:19; 4:3; fetters, Psa. 105:18, 107:10,16; 149:8; file, Prov. 27:17; furnace, Deut. 4:20; 1 Kin. 8:51; Jer. 11:4; gate, Acts 12:10; harrow, 2 Sam. 12:31; horn, 1 Kin.

22:11; 2 Chr. 18:10; Mic. 4:13; idols, Dan. 2: 33; 5:4,23; pans, Ezek. 4:3; 27:19; pen, Job 19:24; Jer. 17:1; pillars, Jer. 1:18; rods for scourging, Psa. 2:9; Rev. 2:27; 12:5; 19:15; threshing instruments, Amos 1:3; tools, 1 Kin. 6:7; vessels, Josh. 6:24; weapons, Num. 35:16; 1 Sam. 17:7; Job 20:24; 41:7; yokes, Deut. 28:48; Jer. 28:13,14.

Stones of, Deut. 8:9; Job 28:2; Isa. 60:17. See STEEL.

FIGURATIVE: 2 Sam. 23:7; Jer. 15:12; 1 Tim. 4:2.

2. A city of Naphtali, Josh. 19:38.

IRONY. INSTANCES OF: Michal to David, 2 Sam. 6:20. Elijah to the priests of Baal, 1 Kin. 18:27. Job to his accusers, Job 12:2. Ezekiel to the prince of Tyre, Ezek. 28:3-5. Micaiah, 1 Kin. 22:15. Amos to the Samaritans, Amos 4:4. Jesus to Pharisees, Mark 2:17. Pharisees and Herodians to Jesus, Matt. 22:16. Roman soldiers to Jesus, Matt. 27:29; Mark 15:17-19; Luke 23:11; John 19:2,3. Pilate, calling Jesus king, Mark 15:19; John 19:15. Superscription of Pilate over Jesus, Matt. 27:37; Mark 15:26; Luke 23:38; John 19:19. Agrippa to Paul, Acts 26:28.

See SARCASM; SATIRE.

IRPEEL, a city of Benjamin, Josh. 18:27.

IRRIGATION, Deut. 11:10; Prov. 21: 1; Eccl. 2:6; Isa. 58:11.

FIGURATIVE: 1 Cor. 3:6,8.

IR-SHEMESH, a city of Dan, Josh. 19:41.

IRU, eldest son of Caleb, 1 Chr. 4:15.

ISAAC. 1. Miraculous son of Abraham, Gen.17:15-19; 18:1-15; 21:1-8; Josh.24:3; 1 Chr. 1:28; Gal.4:28; Heb.11:11. Ancestor of Jesus, Matt. 1:2. Offered in sacrifice by his father, Gen. 22:1-19; Heb. 11:17; Jas. 2:21. Is provided a wife from among his kindred, Gen. 24; 25:20. Abrahamic covenant confirmed in, Gen. 26:2-5; 1 Chr. 16:15-19. Dwells in the south country at the well Lahai-roi, Gen. 24:62; 25:11. With Ishmael, buries his father in the cave of Machpelah, Gen. 25: 9. Esau and Jacob born to, Gen. 25:19-26; 1 Chr. 1:34; Josh. 24:4. Dwells in Gerar, Gen. 26:7-11. Prospers, Gen. 26:12-14. Possesses large flocks and herds, Gen. 26:14. Digs wells, and is defrauded of them by the herdsmen of Abimelech, Gen. 26:15,21. Removes to the valley of Gerar, afterward called Beer-sheba, Gen. 26:22-33. His old age, last blessing upon his sons, Gen. 27:18-40. Death and burial of, Gen. 35:27-29; 49: 31. His filial obedience, Gen. 22:9. His peaceableness, Gen. 26:14-22. Was a prophet, Gen. 27:28,29,38,40; Heb. 11:20. His devoutness, Gen. 24:63; 25:21; 26:25; Matt. 8: 11; Luke 13:28. Prophecies concerning, Gen. 17:16-21; 18:10-14; 21:12; 26:2-5,24; Ex. 32: 13; 1 Chr. 16:16; Rom. 9:7.

2. A designation of the ten tribes, Amos 7:9.

ISAIAH, called also ESAIAS. Son of Amos, Isa. 1:1. Prophesies in the days of Uzziah, Jotham, Ahaz, and Hezekiah, kings

of Judah, Isa. 1:1; 6:1; 7:1,3; 14:27; 20:1; 36:1; 38:1; 39:1; at the time of the invasion by Tartan, of Assyria, Isa. 20:1. Symbolically wears sackcloth, and walks barefoot, as a sign to Israel, Isa. 20:2,3. Comforts and encourages Hezekiah and the people in the siege of Jerusalem by Rab-shakeh, 2 Kin. 18; 19; Isa. 37:6,7. Comforts Hezekiah in his affliction, 2 Kin. 20:1-11; Isa. 38. Performs the miracle of the returning shadow to confirm Hezekiah's faith, 2 Kin. 20:8-11. Reproves Hezekiah's folly in exhibiting his resources to the commissioners from Babylon, 2 Kin. 20:12-19; Isa. 39. Is chronicler of the times of Uzziah and Hezekiah, 2 Chr. 26:22; 32:32.

PROPHECIES, REPROOFS, AND EXHORTATIONS OF: Foretells punishment of the Jews for idolatry, and reproves self-confidence and distrust of God, Isa. 2:6-20. Foretells the destruction of the Jews, Isa. 3. Promises to the remnant restoration of divine favour, Isa. 4:2-6; 6. Delineates in the parable of the vineyard the ingratitude of the Jews, and reproves it, Isa. 5:1-10. Denounces existing corruptions, Isa. 5:8-30. Foretells the ill success of the plot of the Israelites and Syrians against Judah, Isa. 7:1-16. Denounces calamities against Israel and Judah, Isa. 7:16-25; 9:2-6. Foretells prosperity under Hezekiah, and the manifestation of the Messiah, Isa. 9:1-7. Denounces vengeance upon the enemies of Israel, Isa. 9:8-12. Denounces the wickedness of Israel, and foretells the judgments of God, Isa. 9:13-21. Denounces judgments against false prophets, Isa. 10:1-4. Foretells the destruction of Sennacherib's armies, Isa. 10:5-34; the restoration of Israel and the triumph of the Messiah's kingdom, Isa. 11. The burden of Babylon, Isa. 13; 14:1-28. Denunciation against the Philistines, Isa. 14:9-32. Burden of Moab, Isa. 15; 16. Burden of Damascus, Isa. 17. Obscure prophecy, supposed by some authorities to be directed against the Assyrians, by others against the Egyptians, and by others against the Ethiopians, Isa. 18. The burden of Egypt, Isa. 19; 20. Denunciations against Babylon, Isa. 21:1-10. Prophecy concerning Seir, Isa. 21: 11,12; Arabia, Isa. 21:13-17; concerning the conquest of Jerusalem, the captivity of Shebna, and the promotion of Eliakim, Isa. 22:1-22; the overthrow of Tyre, Isa. 23; the judgments upon the land, but that a remnant of the Jews would be saved, Isa. 25; 26: 27. Reproves Ephraim for his wickedness, and foretells the destruction by Shalmaneser, Isa. 28:1-5. Declares the glory of God upon the remnant who are saved, Isa. 28:5,6. Exposes the corruptions in Jerusalem and exhorts to repentance, Isa. 28:7-29. Foretells the invasion of Sennacherib, the distress of the Jews, and the destruction of the Assyrian army, Isa. 29:1-8. Denounces the hypocrisy of the Jews, Isa. 29:9-17. Promises a reformation, Isa. 29:18-24. Reproves the people for their confidence in

Egypt, and their contempt of God, Isa. 30:1-17; 31:1-6. Declares the goodness and long-suffering of God toward them, Isa. 30:18-26; chapters 32-35. Reproves the Jews for their spiritual blindness and infidelity, Isa. 42:18-25. Promises ultimate restoration of the Jews, Isa. 43:1-13. Foretells the ultimate destruction of Babylon, Isa. 43:14-17; 47. Exhorts the people to repent, Isa. 43:22-28. Comforts the church with promises, exposes the folly of idolatry, and their future deliverance from captivity by Cyrus, Isa. 44; 45: 1-5; 48:20. Foretells the conversion of the Gentiles, and triumph of the gospel, Isa. 45:5-25. Denounces the evils of idolatry, Isa. 46. Reproves the Jews for their idolatries and other wickedness, Isa. 48. Exhorts to sanctification, Isa. 56:1-8. Foretells calamities to Judah, Isa. 59:9-12, with chapters 57-59.

Foreshadows the person and the kingdom of the Messiah, Isa. chapters 32-35; 42; 45; 49-56; 59; vs. 15-21, and chapters 60-66.

ISCAH, daughter of Haran and sister of Lot, Gen. 11:29.

ISCARIOT. See JUDAS.

ISHBAH, father of Eshtemoa, 1 Chr. 4:17.

ISHBAK, son of Abraham and Keturah, Gen. 25:2; 1 Chr. 1:32.

ISHBI-BENOB, a giant warrior slain by Abishai, 2 Sam. 21:16.

ISH-BOSHETH. Son of Saul. Called ESH-BAAL in 1 Chr. 8:33; 9:39. Made king by Abner, 2 Sam. 2:8-10. Deserted by Abner, 2 Sam. 3:6-12. Restores Michal, David's wife, to David, 2 Sam. 3:14-16. Assassinated, 2 Sam. 4:5-8. Avenged by David, 2 Sam. 4:9-12.

ISHI. 1. A name of Deity, Hos. 2:16.

2. A son of Appaim, 1 Chr. 2:31.

3. A descendant of Judah, 1 Chr. 4:20.

4. A Simeonite, 1 Chr. 4:42.

5. One of the heads of Manasseh, 1 Chr. 5:24.

ISHIAH, one of the heads of Issachar, 1 Chr. 7:3; 24:21,25.

ISHIJAH, one of the sons of Harim, Ezra 10:31.

ISHMA, a descendant of Judah, 1 Chr. 4:3.

ISHMAEL. 1. Son of Abraham, Gen. 16:11,15,16; 1 Chr. 1:28. Prayer of Abraham for, Gen. 17:18,20. Circumcised, Gen. 17:23-26. Promised to be the father of a nation, Gen. 16:11,12; 17:20; 21:12,13,18. Sent away by Abraham, Gen. 21:6-21. With Isaac buries his father, Gen. 25:9. Children of, Gen. 25:12-18; 1 Chr. 1:29-31. Daughter of, marries Esau, Gen. 28:9; 36:2,3. Death of, Gen. 25:17,18.

2. Father of Zebadiah, 2 Chr. 19:11.

3. A son of Azel, 1 Chr. 8:38; 9:44.

4. One of the captains of hundreds, 2 Chr. 23:1.

5. A priest of the exile, Ezra 10:22.

6. A son of Nethaniah. Assassinated Gedaliah, governor of Judah under king of Babylon, and takes captive many Jews, Jer.

40:8-16; 41:1-11; 2 Kin. 25:23-25. Defeated by Johanan, and put to flight, Jer. 41:12-15.

ISHMAELITES. Region occupied by Gen. 25:18. Merchants of, buy Joseph, Gen 37:25-36; 39:1. Called MIDIANITES, Gen. 37:28,36; Judg. 8:24,26. Enemies to Israel, Psa. 83:6.

See ISHMAEL.

ISHMAIAH, a prince of Zebulun, 1 Chr. 27:19.

ISHMERAI, a chief Benjamite, 1 Chr. 8:18.

ISHOD, one of the tribe of Manasseh, 1 Chr. 7:18.

ISHPAN, a chief Benjamite, 1 Chr. 8:22.

ISH-TOB, a small state of Aram, 2 Sam. 10:6,8.

See TOB.

ISHUAH, called also ISUAH. Son of Asher, Gen. 46:17; 1 Chr. 7:30.

ISHUI, called also ISHUAI, ISUI, and JESUI. Son of Asher, Gen. 46:17; Num. 26:44; 1 Chr. 7:30.

2. Son of Saul, 1 Sam. 14:49.

ISLAND, prophecies concerning, Psa. 97:1; Isa. 11:11; 41:1,5; 49:1; Zeph. 2:11; Rev. 16:20.

ISMACHIAH, a Levite, 2 Chr. 31:13.

ISMAIAH, a Gibeonite who joined David at Ziklag, 1 Chr. 12:4.

ISPAH, a chief Benjamite, 1 Chr. 8:16.

ISRAEL. 1. A name given to Jacob, Gen. 32:24-32; 2 Kin. 17:34; Hos. 12:3,4.

2. A name of the Christ in prophecy, Isa. 49:3.

3. A name given to the descendants of Jacob, a nation. Called also ISRAELITES, and HEBREWS, Gen. 43:32; Ex. 1:15; 9:7; 10:3; 21:2; Lev. 23:42; Josh. 13:6, etc.; 1 Sam. 4:6; 13:3,19; 14:11,21; Phil. 3:5.

TRIBES OF ISRAEL were named after the sons of Jacob. In lists usually the names Levi and Joseph, two sons of Jacob, do not appear. The descendants of Levi were consecrated to the rites of religion, and the two sons of Joseph, Ephraim and Manasseh, were adopted by Jacob in Joseph's stead, Gen. 48:5; Josh. 14:4, and their names appear in the catalogues of tribes instead of those of Levi and Joseph, as follows: ASHER, BENJAMIN, DAN, EPHRAIM, GAD, ISSACHAR, JUDAH, MANASSEH, NAPHTALI, REUBEN, SIMEON, ZEBULUN.

Names of, seen in John's vision, on the gates of the New Jerusalem, Rev. 21:12.

Prophecies concerning, Gen. 15:5,13; 25:23; 26:4; 27:28,29,40; 48:19; 49; Deut. 33; of the multitude of, Gen. 13:16; 15:5; 22:17; 26:4; 28:14; of their captivity in Egypt, Gen. 15:13, 14; Acts 7:6,7.

Divided into families, each of which had a chief, Num. 25:14; 26; 36:1; Josh. 7:14; 1 Chr. chapters 4-8.

Number of, who went into Egypt, Gen 46:8-27; Ex. 1:5; Deut. 10:22; Acts 7:14. Number of, at the time of the exodus, Ex. 12:37, 38, with Gen. 47:27; Ex. 1:7-20; Psa. 105:24. Acts 7:17. Number of, fit for military service when they left Egypt, Ex. 12:37; at Sinai, by tribes, Num. 1:1-50; after the plague, Num. 26; when David numbered, 2 Sam. 24: 1-9; 1 Chr. 21:5,6; 27:23,24; after the captivity, Ezra 2:64; Neh. 7:66,67; in John's apocalyptic vision, Rev. 7:1-8.

Dwelt in Goshen, Gen. 46:28-34; 47:4-10, 27,28. Dwelt in Egypt four hundred and thirty years, Ex. 12:40,41, with Gen. 15:13; Acts 7:6; Gal. 3:17. Were enslaved and oppressed by the Egyptians, Ex. 1; 2; 5; Acts 7:18-36. Their groaning heard of God, Ex. 2:23-25. Moses commissioned as deliverer, Ex. 3:2-22; 4:1-17. The land of Egypt plagued on their account, see EGYPT. Exempt from the plagues, Ex. 8:22,23; 9:4-6,26; 10:23; 11:7; 12:13. Children were spared when the firstborn of the Egyptians were slain, Ex. 12:13,23. Instituted the passover, Ex. 12:1-28. Borrowed jewels from the Egyptians, Ex. 11:2,3; 12:35,36; Psa. 105:37. Urged by the Egyptians to depart, Ex. 12:31-39. Journey from Rameses to Succoth, Ex. 12:37-39. Made the journey by night, Ex. 12:42. The day of their deliverance to be a memorial, Ex. 12:42; 13:3-16. Led of God, Ex. 13:18,21,22. Providentially cared for, Deut. 8:3,4; 29:5,6; 34:7; Neh. 9:21; Psa. 105: 37. See MANNA; CLOUD, PILLAR OF.

Journey from Succoth to Etham, Ex. 13: 20; to Pi-hahiroth, Ex. 14:2; Num. 33:5-7. Pursued by the Egyptians, Ex. 14:5-31. Pass through the Red Sea, Ex. 14:19-22; Deut. 11: 4; Psa. 78; 105; 106; 107; 136. Order of march, Num. 2. Journey to Marah, Ex. 15: 23; Num. 33:8. Murmur on account of the bitter water, Ex. 15:23-25; water of, sweetened, Ex. 15:25. Journey to Elim, Ex. 15:27; Num. 33:9. For the itinerary, see Num. 33. Murmured for food, Ex. 16:2,3. Provided with manna and quails, Ex. 16:4-36. Murmured for want of water at Rephidim, Ex. 17:2-7; water miraculously supplied from the rock at Meribah, Ex. 17:5-7. Defeat the Amalekites, Ex. 17:13; Deut. 25:17, 18. Arrive at Sinai, Ex. 19:1; Num. 33:15. At the suggestion of Jethro, Moses's father-in-law, they organize a system of government, Ex. 18:25; Deut. 1:9-18. The message of God to them, requiring that they shall be obedient to his commandments, and as a reward they would be to him a holy nation, and their reply, Ex. 19:3-8. Sanctify themselves for receiving the law, Ex. 19:10-15. The law delivered to, Ex. 20; 21; 22; 23; 24: 1-4; 25; 26; 27; 28; 29; 30; 31; Lev. chapters 1-25; 27; Deut. 5; 15; 16. The people receive it and covenant obedience to it, Ex. 24:3,7. Idolatry of, Ex. 32; Deut. 9:17-21. The anger of the Lord in consequence, Ex. 32:9-14. Moses's indignation; breaks the tables of stone; enters the camp; commands the Levites; three thousand slain, Ex. 32:19-35. Visited by a plague, Ex. 32:35. Obduracy of, Ex. 33:3; 34:9; Deut. 9:12-29. God withdraws his presence, Ex. 33:1-3. The mourning of, when God refused to lead them, Ex. 33:4-10. Tables renewed, Ex 34. Pattern for the

tabernacle and the appurtenances, and forms of worship to be observed, Ex. chapters 25-31. Gifts consecrated for the creation of the tabernacle, Ex 35; 36:1-7; Num. 7. The erection of the tabernacle; the manufacture of the appurtenances, including the garments of the priests; and their sanctification, Ex. 36:8-38; chapters 37-40. First sacrifice offered by, under the law, Lev. 8:14-36; 9:8-24. Second passover observed, Num. 9:1-5. March out of the wilderness, Num. 10:11-36. For itinerary, see Num. 33. Order of camp and march, Num. 2. Arrive at the border of Canaan, Num. 12:16. Send twelve spies to view the land, Num. 13; 32:8; Deut. 1:22,25; Josh. 14:7. Return with a majority and minority report, Num. 13:26-33; 14:6-10. Murmuring over the report, Num. 14: 1-5. The judgment of God upon them in consequence of their unbelief and murmuring, Num. 14:13-39. Reaction, and their purpose to enter the land; are defeated by the Amalekites, Num. 14:40-45; Deut. 1:41-45. Abide at Kadesh, Deut. 1:46. Return to the wilderness, where they remain thirty-eight years, and all die except Joshua and Caleb, Num. 14:20-39. Rebellion of Korah, Dathan, and Abiram, Num. 16:1-40; Deut. 11:6. Murmur against Moses and Aaron; are plagued; fourteen thousand seven hundred die; plague stayed, Num. 16:41-50. Murmur for want of water in Meribah; the rock is smitten, Num. 20:1-13. Are refused passage through the country of Edom, Num. 20:14-21. The death of Aaron, Num. 20:22,29; 33:38, 39; Deut. 10:6. Defeat the Canaanites, Num. 21:1-3. Are scourged with serpents, Num. 21:4-9. Defeat the Amorites, Num. 21:21-32; Deut. 2:24-35, and the king of Baasha, Num. 21:33-35; Deut. 3:1-17. Arrive in the plains of Moab, at the fords of the Jordan, Num. 22:1; 33:48,49. Commit idolatry with the people of Moab, Num. 25:1-5. Visited by a plague in consequence; twenty-four thousand die, Num. 25:6-15; 26:1. The people numbered for the allotment of the land, Num. 26. The daughters of Zelophehad sue for an inheritance, Num. 27:1-11; Josh. 17:3-6. Conquest of the Midianites, Num. 31. Nations dread, Deut. 2:25. Renew the covenant, Deut. 29. Moses dies, and people mourn, Deut. 34. Joshua appointed leader, Num. 27:18-23. Deut. 31:23. See JOSHUA.

All who were numbered at Sinai perished in the wilderness except Caleb and Joshua, Num. 26:63,65; Deut. 2:14-16. Piety of those who entered Canaan, Josh. 23:8; Judg. 2:7-10; Jer. 2:2,3. Men chosen to allot the lands of Canaan among the tribes and families, Num. 34:17-29. Remove from Shittim to Jordan, Josh. 3:1. Cross Jordan, Josh. 4. Circumcision observed and passover celebrated, Josh. 5. Jericho taken, Josh. 6. Ai taken, Josh. 7 and 8. Make a league with the Gibeonites, Josh. 9. Defeat the five Amoritish kings, Josh. 10. Conquest of the land, Josh. 21:43-45, with Judg. 1. The land allotted, Josh. chapters 15-21.

Two and one-half tribes return from the west side of the Jordan; erect a memorial to signify the unity of the tribes; the memorial misunderstood; the controversy which followed; its amicable adjustment, Josh. 22. Joshua's exhortation immediately before his death, Josh. 23. Covenant renewed, death of Joshua, Josh. 24; Judg. 2:8,9. Religious fidelity during the life of Joshua, Josh. 24:31; Judg. 2:7.

UNDER THE JUDGES: Public affairs administered four hundred and fifty years by the judges, Judg. 2:16-19; Acts 13:20. The original inhabitants not fully expelled, Judg. 1:27-36; 3:1-7. Reproved by an angel for not casting out the original inhabitants, Judg. 2:1-5. People turn to idolatry, Judg. 2:10-23. Delivered for their idolatry to the king of Mesopotamia during eight years; their repentance and deliverance, Judg. 3:8-11. Renew their idolatry, and are put under tribute to the king of Moab during eighteen years; repent and are delivered by Ehud; eighty years of peace follow, Judg. 3:12-30. Shamgar resists a foray of the Philistines and delivers Israel, Judg. 3:31. People again do evil and are put under bonds for twenty years to the king of Syria, Judg. 4:1-3. Delivered by Deborah, a prophetess, and judged, Judg. 4; 5. Seven years of bondage to the Midianites; delivered by Gideon, Judg. 6; 7; 8:1-28; see GIDEON. Return to idolatry, Judg. 8:33, 34. Abimelech foments an inter-tribal war, Judg. 9. Judged by Tola twenty-three years, Judg. 10:1,2; by Jair twenty-two years, Judg. 10:3,4. People backslide, and are given over to the Philistines for chastisement eighteen years; repent and turn to the Lord; delivered by Jephthah, Judg. 10: 6-18; 11. Ephraimites go to war against other tribes; defeated by Jephthah, Judg. 12:1-7. Judged by Ibzan seven years, Judg. 12:8-10; by Elon ten years, Judg. 12:11,12; by Abdon eight years, Judg. 12:13-15. Backslide again and are chastised by the Philistines forty years, Judg. 13:1. Judged by Samson twenty years, Judg. 15:20, with chapters 13-16. Scandal of the Bethlehemite's concubine, and the consequent war between the Benjamites and the other tribes, Judg. chapters 19-21. Judged by Eli forty years, 1 Sam. 4:18, with chapters 1-4. Smitten by the Philistines at Eben-ezer, 1 Sam. 4:1,2,10,11. Demand a king, 1 Sam. 8:5-20; Hos. 13:10.

UNDER THE KINGS BEFORE THE SEPARATION INTO TWO KINGDOMS: Saul anointed king, 1 Sam. 10; 11:12-15; 12:13. Ammonites invade Israel, are defeated, 1 Sam. 11. Philistines smitten, 1 Sam. 14. Amalekites defeated, 1 Sam. 15. David anointed king, 1 Sam. 16:11-13. Goliath slain, 1 Sam. 17. Israel defeated by the Philistines, and Saul and his sons slain, 1 Sam. 31. See SAUL. David defeats the Amalekites, 1 Sam. 30; 2 Sam. 1:1; made king, 2 Sam. 2:4,11. Ish-bosheth made king, 2 Sam. 2:8-10.

The conflict between the two political factions, 2 Sam. 2:12-32; 3:1.

David made king over all Israel, 2 Sam. 5: 1-5. Conquests of David, 2 Sam. 8; Absalom's rebellion, 2 Sam. chapters 15-18. See DAVID.

Solomon anointed king, 1 Kin. 1:32-40. Temple built, 1 Kin. 6. Solomon's palace built, 1 Kin. 7. Solomon's death, 1 Kin. 11: 41-43. See SOLOMON.

THE REVOLT OF THE TEN TRIBES: Foreshadowing circumstances indicating the separation: Disagreement after Saul's death, 2 Sam. 2; 1 Chr. 12:23-40; 13. Lukewarmness of the ten tribes, and zeal of Judah for David in Absalom's rebellion, 2 Sam. 19: 41-43. The rebellion of Sheba, 2 Sam. 20. The two factions are distinguished as Israel and Judah during David's reign, 2 Sam. 21: 2. Providential, Zech. 11:14.

Revolt consummated under Rehoboam, son and successor of Solomon, 1 Kin. 12.

4. The name of the ten tribes that revolted from the house of David. Called also JACOB, Hos. 12:2.

List of the kings of Israel, and the period of time in which they reigned. For the facts of their reigns see under each name:
1. Jeroboam, twenty-two years.
2. Nadab, about two years.
3. Baasha, twenty-four years.
4. Elah, two years.
5. Zimri, seven days.
6. Omri, twelve years.
7. Ahab, twenty-two years.
8. Ahaziah, two years.
9. Jehoram, twelve years.
10. Jehu, twenty-eight years.
11. Jehoahaz, seventeen years.
12. Jehoash, sixteen years.
13. Jeroboam II. forty-one years.
14. Zachariah, six months.
15. Shallum, one month.
16. Menahem, ten years.
17. Pekahiah, two years.
18. Pekah, twenty years.
19. Hoshea, nine years.

The ten tribes carried captive to Assyria.

HISTORY OF: War continued between the two kingdoms all the days of Rehoboam and Jeroboam, 1 Kin. 14:30; and between Jeroboam and Abijam, 1 Kin. 15:7, and between Baasha and Asa, 1 Kin. 15:16,32. Famine prevails in the reign of Ahab, 1 Kin. 18:1-6. Israel, called also SAMARIA, invaded by, but defeats, Ben-hadad, king of Syria, 1 Kin. 20. Moab rebels, 2 Kin. 1:1; 3. Army of Syria invades Israel, but peacefully withdraws through the tact of the prophet Elisha, 2 Kin. 6:8-23. Samaria besieged, 2 Kin. 6:24-33; 7; city of, taken, and the people carried to Assyria, 2 Kin. 17. The land repeopled, 2 Kin. 17:24.

The remnant that remained after the able-bodied were carried into captivity affiliated with the kingdom of Judah, 2 Chr. 30:18-26; 34:6; 35:18.

PROPHECIES CONCERNING: Of captivity, famine, and judgments, 1 Kin. 14:15,16; 17:1; 20:13-28; 2 Kin. 7:1,2,17; 8:1; Isa. 7:8; 8:4-7; 9:8-21; 17:3-11; 28:1-8; Hos. 1:1-9; 2:1-

13; chapters 4; 8; 9; 10; 11:5,6; 12:7--14; 13; Amos 2:6–16; chapters 3–9.

Of restoration, Hos. 2:14–23; 11:9–11; 13:13,14; 14:8.

Of the reunion of the ten tribes and Judah, Jer. 3:18; Ezek. 37:16–22.

See the following:

5. **JUDAH.** The nation composed of the tribes of Judah and Benjamin, called JUDAH, Isa. 11:12,13; Jer. 4:3, and JEWS, [see JEWS,] ruled by the descendants of David.

In the historical books of the Kings and the Chronicles the nation is called JUDAH, but in the prophecies it is frequently referred to as ISRAEL, as in Isa. 8:14; 49:7.

List of rulers and the periods of time over which they reigned:

1. Rehoboam, seventeen years.
2. Abijah, or Abijam, three years.
3. Asa, forty-one years.
4. Jehoshaphat, twenty-five years.
5. Jehoram, eight years.
6. Ahaziah, one year.

Athaliah's usurpation, six years,

7. Joash, or Jehoash, forty years.
8. Amaziah, twenty-nine years.
9. Uzziah, or Azariah, fifty-two years.
10. Jotham, sixteen years.
11. Ahaz, sixteen years.
12. Hezekiah, twenty-nine years.
13. Manasseh, fifty-five years.
14. Amon, two years.
15. Josiah, thirty-one years.
16. Jehoahaz, Josiah's son, three months.
17. Jehoiakim, Josiah's son, eleven years.
18. Jehoiachin, or Jeconiah, Jehoiakim's son, three months.
19. Zedekiah, or Mattaniah, Josiah's son, eleven years.

For the history of the above kings see under each name.

Rehoboam succeeds Solomon. In consequence of his arbitrary policy ten tribes rebel, 1 Kin. 12. Other circumstances of his reign, 1 Kin. 14:21–31; 2 Chr. 10; 11; 12. Death of Rehoboam, 1 Kin. 14:31. Abijam's wicked reign, 1 Kin. 15:1–8; 2 Chr. 13; Asa's good reign, 1 Kin. 15:9–24; 2 Chr. 14; 15; 16. Asa makes a league with Ben-hadad, king of Syria, to make war against Israel, 1 Kin. 15:16–24. Jehoshaphat succeeds Asa, 1 Kin. 15:24; 2 Chr. 17; 18; 19; 20; 21:1; joins Ahab against the king of Syria, 1 Kin. 22. See JEHOSHAPHAT. Jehoram, called also JORAM, reigns in the stead of his father, Jehoshaphat, 2 Kin. 8:16–24; 2 Chr. 21. Edom revolts, 2 Kin. 8:20–22. Ahaziah, called also AZARIAH, 2 Chr. 22:6, and JEHOAHAZ, 2 Chr. 21:17; 25:23, succeeds Jehoram, 2 Kin. 8:24–29; 2 Chr. 22; slain by Jehu, 2 Kin. 9:27–29; 2 Chr. 22:8,9, Athaliah, his mother, succeeds him, 2 Kin. 11:1–16; 2 Chr. 22:10–12; 23:1–15. Jehoash, called also JOASH, succeeds Athaliah, 2 Kin. 11:21; 12:1–21; 2 Chr. 24. The temple repaired, 2 Kin. 12. Amaziah reigns, and Judah is invaded by the king of Israel; Jerusalem is taken and the sacred things of the temple carried away, 2 Kin. 14:1–20;

2 Chr. 25. Azariah, called also UZZIAH, succeeds him, 2 Kin. 14:21,22; 15:1–7; 2 Chr. 26. Jotham succeeds Uzziah, 2 Kin. 15:7,32–38; 2 Chr. 27. Rezin, king of Syria, invades Judah, 2 Kin. 15:37. Jotham is succeeded by Ahaz, 2 Kin. 16:1; 2 Chr. 28. Judah is invaded by kings of Samaria and Syria; Ahaz hires the king of Assyria to make war on the king of Syria, 2 Kin. 16:5–9. Ahaz changes the fashion of the altar in the temple, 2 Kin. 16:10–18. Hezekiah succeeds Ahaz, 2 Kin. 16:19,20; 2 Chr. chapters 29–32. His good reign, 2 Kin. 18:1–8. He revolts from the sovereignty of the king of Assyria, 2 Kin. 18:7. King of Assyria invades Judah, and blasphemes the God of Judah; his army overthrown, 2 Kin. 18:9–37; 19. Hezekiah's sickness and miraculous restoration, 2 Kin. 20. Succeeded by Manasseh, 2 Kin. 20:21; 2 Chr. 33:1–20. Manasseh's wicked reign, 2 Kin. 21:1–18. Amon succeeds Manasseh on the throne, 2 Kin. 21:18–26; 2 Chr. 33:20–25. Josiah succeeds Amon; the temple is repaired; the book of the law recovered; religious revival follows; and the king dies, 2 Kin. 22; 23:1–30; 2 Chr. 34; 35. Josiah is succeeded by Jehoahaz, who reigned three months, was dethroned by the king of Egypt, and the land put under tribute, 2 Kin. 23:30–35; 2 Chr. 36:1–3. Jehoiakim is elevated to the throne; becomes tributary to Nebuchadnezzar for three years; rebels; is conquered and carried to Babylon, 2 Kin. 24:1–6; 2 Chr. 36:4–8. Jehoiachin is made king; suffers invasion and is carried to Babylon, 2 Kin. 24:8–16; 2 Chr. 36:9,10. Zedekiah is made king by Nebuchadnezzar; rebels; Nebuchadnezzar invades Judah, takes Jerusalem, and carries the people to Babylon, despoiling the temple, 2 Kin. 24:17–20; 25; 2 Chr. 36:11–21. The poorest of the people were left to occupy the country, and were joined by fragments of the army of Judah, the dispersed Israelites in other lands, and the king's daughters, 2 Kin. 25:12,22,23; Jer. 39:10; 40:7–12; 52:16. Gedaliah appointed governor over, 2 Kin. 25: 22. His administration favorable to the people, 2 Kin. 25:23,24; Jer. 40:7–12. Conspired against and slain by Ishmael, 2 Kin. 25:25; Jer. 40:13–16; 41:1–3. Ishmael seeks to betray the people to the Ammonites, Jer. 41:1–18. The people, in fear, take refuge in Egypt, 2 Kin. 25:26; Jer. 41:14–18; 42:13–18.

CAPTIVITY OF: Great wickedness the cause of their adversity, Ezek. 5; 6; 7; 16; 23:22–44. Dwell in Babylon, Dan. 5:13; 6:13; Jer. 52:28–30; by the river Chebor, Ezek. 1:1; 10:15. Patriotism of, Psa. 137. Plotted against, by Haman, Esth. 3. Are saved by Esther, Esth. chapters 4–9. Cyrus decrees their restoration, 2 Chr. 36:22,23; Ezra 1:1–4. Cyrus directs the rebuilding of the temple, and the restoration of the vessels which had been carried to Babylon, 2 Chr. 36:23; Ezra 1:3–11. Proclamation renewed by Darius and Artaxerxes, Ezra 6:1–14. Ezra returns with seventeen hundred and fifty-four of the captivity to Jerusalem, Ezra 2. Temple rebuilt and dedicated, Ezra chapters 3–6. Artaxerxes issues proclamation to restore the temple service, Ezra 7. Priests and Levites authorized to return, Ezra 8. Corruptions among the returned captives; their reform, Ezra 9; 10.

Nehemiah is commissioned to lead the remainder of the captivity, forty-nine thousand nine hundred and forty-two, back to Canaan, Neh. 2; 7:5–67; Psa. 85; 87; 107; 126. Wall of Jerusalem rebuilt and dedicated, Neh. chapters 2–6; 12. The law read and expounded, Neh. 8. Solemn feast is kept; priests are purified; and the covenant sealed, Neh. chapters 8–10. One-tenth of the people, to be determined by lot, volunteer to dwell in Jerusalem, and the remaining nine parts dwell in other cities, Neh. 11. Catalogue of the priests and Levites who came up with Zerubbabel, Neh. 12. Nehemiah reforms various abuses, Neh. 13. Expect a Messiah, Luke 3:15. Many accept Jesus as the Christ, John 2:23; 10:42; 11:45; 12:11; Acts 21:20. Reject Jesus, see JESUS, REJECTED.

Rejected of God, Matt. 21:43; Luke 20:16. PROPHECIES CONCERNING: Of their rejection of the Messiah, Isa. 8:14,15; 49:5,7; 52:14; 53:1–3; Zech. 11; 13; Matt. 21:33; 22:1.

Of war and other judgments : Deut. 28:49–57; 2 Kin. 20:17,18; 21:12–15; 22:16,17; 23:26,27; Isa. 1:1–24; 3; 4:1; 5; 6:9–13; 7:17–25; 8:14–22; 9; 10:12; 22: 1–14; 28:14–22; 29:1–10; 30:1–17; 31:1–3; 32:9–14; Jer. 1:11–16; 4:5–31; 6; 7:8–34; 8; 9:9–26; 10:17–22; 11:9–23; 13:9–27; 14:14–18; 15:1–14; 16; 17:1–4; 18:15–17; 19; 20:5; 21:4–7; 22:24–30; 25:8–38; chapters 28; 34; 37; 38:1–3; 42:13–22; chapters 43; 44; 45; Lam. 5:6; Ezek. 4; 5; 11:7–12; chapters 12; 15; 16; 17; 19; 22:13–22; 23:22–35; 24; 33:21–29; Dan. 9:26–27; Joel 2:1–17; Amos 2:4,5; Mic. 2:10; 3; 4:8–10; Hab. 1:6–11; Zeph. 1; Zech. 11; 14:1–3; Mal. 4:1; Matt. 21:33,34; 23:35–38; 24:2,14–42; Mark 13:1–13; Luke 13:34,35; 19:43,44; 21:5–25; 23:28–31; Rev. 1:7.

Dispersion of : Isa. 24:1; Jer. 9:16; Hos. 9: 17; Joel 3:6,20; Amos 9:9; Ezek. 4:13; 5:10,12; 20:23; 36:19; Dan. 9:7; John 7:35; Acts 2:5.

Of blessing and restoration : Isa. 1:25–27; 2:1–5; 4:2–6; 11:11–13; 25; 26:1,2,12–19; 27:13; 29:18–24; 30:18–26; 32:15–20; 33:13–24; 35; 37: 31,32; 40:2,9; 41:27; 44; 49:13–23; 51; 52:1–12; 60; 61:4–9; 62; 66:5–22; Jer. 3:14–18; 4:3–18; 12:14–16; 23:3; 24:1–7; 29:1–14; 30:3–22; 32:36–44; 33; 44:28; Ezek. 14:22,23; 16:60–63; 20:40, 41; 36:1–38; 37:12,21; Dan. 11:30–45; 12:1; Joel 3; Amos 9:9–15; Obad. 17–21; Mic. 2:12, 13; 5:3; Zeph. 2:7; Zech. 1:14–21; 2; 8; 10:5–12; 12:1–14; 13; 14:3–21; Mal. 3:4; Rom. 11; 2 Cor. 3:16; Rev. 7:5.

ISRAELITES. See ISRAEL.

ISSACHAR. 1. Son of Jacob, Gen. 30: 18; Ex. 1:3; 1 Chr. 2:1. Jacob's prophetic benedictions upon, Gen. 49:14,15. In the time of David, 1 Chr. 7:2,5. See TRIBE OF, below.

2. **TRIBE OF :** Military forces of, taken at Sinai, Num. 1:28,29; 2:6; on the plains of

Moab, Num. 26:25. Moses's blessing upon, Deut. 33:18,19. Place in march and camp, Num. 2:3,5; 10:14,15. Parts of Canaan allotted to, Josh. 19:17–23, with Josh. 17:10,11.

Join Deborah and Barak in war against Sisera, Judg. 5:15. Insurgents from, joined David, 1 Chr. 12:32,40. Join with the kingdom of Judah after the conquest of the land by, 2 Chr. 30:18. For things common to all the tribes, see ISRAELITES, TRIBES OF.

ISSUE OF BLOOD, Matt. 9:20; Mark 5:25; Luke 8:43.

See HEMORRHAGE.

ITALY, Acts 27:1; Heb. 13:24. Aquila and Priscilla expelled from, Acts 18:2.

ITCH, Deut. 28:27.

ITHAI, called also ITTAI. One of David's valiant men, 2 Sam. 23:29; 1 Chr. 11:31.

ITHAMAR. Son of Aaron, Ex. 6:23; 28: 1; 1 Chr. 6:3. Intrusted with moneys of the tabernacle, Ex. 38:21. Charged with duties of the tabernacle, Num. 4:28; 7:8. Forbidden to lament the death of his brothers, Nadab and Abihu, Lev. 10:6,7. Descendants of, 1 Chr. 24:1–19.

ITHIEL. 1. A Benjamite, Neh. 11:7.

2. An unidentified person mentioned in Prov. 30:1.

ITHMAH, a Moabite, 1 Chr. 11:46.

ITHNAN, a town in the extreme S. of Judah, Josh. 15:23.

ITHRA, called also JETHER. Father of Amasa, 2 Sam. 17:25; 1 Chr. 2:17.

ITHRAN. 1. Son of Dishon, Gen. 36: 26; 1 Chr. 1:41.

2. Son of Zophah, 1 Chr. 7:37.

ITHREAM, son of David, 2 Sam. 3:5; 1 Chr. 3:3.

ITHRITES, patronymic of the family of Jether, 2 Sam. 23:38; 1 Chr. 2:53.

ITINERARY, of the Israelites, Num. 33; Deut. 10:6,7.

See ISRAEL.

ITTAH-KAZIN, a landmark in the boundary line of Zebulun, Josh. 19:13.

ITTAI. A chief of David, 2 Sam. 18:2; 1 Chr. 11:31. Supports David against Absalom, 2 Sam. 15:19–22; 18:2,5.

ITURÆA, small province in the N.W. of Palestine, Luke 3:1. See also 1 Chr. 1:31; 5:19.

IVAH. A district in Babylon conquered by the Assyrians, 2 Kin. 18:34; 19:13; Isa. 37:13.

IVORY. Song 5:14; 7:4; Ezek. 27:15. Exported from Tarshish, 1 Kin. 10:22; 2 Chr. 9:21; Chittim, Ezek. 27:6. Ahab's palace made of, 1 Kin. 22:39. Other houses made of, Psa. 45:8; Amos 3:15. Other articles made of : Stringed instruments, Psa. 45:8 [R. V.]; thrones, 1 Kin. 10:18; 2 Chr. 9:17; benches, Ezek. 27:6; beds, Amos 6:4; vessels, Rev. 18:12.

IZHAR, son of Kohath, Ex. 6:18,21; 1 Chr. 6:2,18,38; 23:12,18.

IZRAHIAH, grandson of Tola, 1 Chr.7:3.

IZRI, perhaps the same as ZERI. Leader of the fourth division of Levitical singers, 1 Chr. 25:11.

J

JAAKAN, called also AKAN and JAKAN. Son of Ezer, Gen. 36:27; Deut. 10:6; 1 Chr. 1:42.

JAAKOBAH, descendant of Simeon, 1 Chr. 4:36.

JAALA, called also JAALAH. One of the servants of Solomon returned from exile, Ezra 2:56; Neh. 7:58.

JAALAM, son of Esau, Gen. 36:5,14,18; 1 Chr. 1:35.

JAANAI, a Gadite chief, 1 Chr. 5:12.

JAARE-OREGIM, father of Elhanan, 2 Sam. 21:19.

JAASAU, of the family of Bani, Ezra 10:37.

JAASIEL, son of Abner, 1 Chr. 27:21.

JAAZANIAH. 1. Called also JEZANIAH. A captain who joined Gedaliah at Mizpah, 2 Kin. 25:23; Jer. 40:8; 42:1.

2. A Rechabite, Jer. 35:3.

3. An idolatrous zealot, Ezek. 8:11.

4. A wicked prince of Judah, Ezek. 11:1-13.

JAAZER, called also JAZER. A Levitical city of refuge in Gilead, allotted to Gad, and given to the Levites, Num. 21:32; 32:1, 3,35; Josh. 13:25; 21:39.

JAAZIAH, a descendant of Merari, 1 Chr. 24:26,27.

JAAZIEL, a Levite musician, 1 Chr. 15:18.

JABAL, son of Lamech. A shepherd, Gen. 4:20.

JABBOK. A stream on the E. of the Jordan, the northern boundary of the possessions of the Ammonites, Num. 21:24; Judg. 11:13; of the Reubenites and the Gadites, Josh. 12:2; Deut. 3:16. The northern boundary of the Amorites, Judg. 11:22.

JABESH-GILEAD. A city E. of the Jordan, Judg. 21:8-15. Besieged by the Ammonites, 1 Sam. 11:1-11. Saul and his sons buried at, 1 Sam. 31:11-13; 1 Chr. 10:11,12; 2 Sam. 2:4. Bones of Saul and his son removed from, by David, and buried at Zelah, 2 Sam. 21:12-14.

JABEZ. 1. A city of Judah, 1 Chr. 2:55.

2. The head of a family, 1 Chr. 4:9,10.

JABIN, names of two kings of Hazor, Josh. 11:1-14; Judg. 4:2,7,17,23,24; Psa. 83:9.

JABNEEL. 1. A city in Judah, Josh. 15:11.

2. A city of Naphtali, Josh. 19:33.

JABNEH, a Philistine city, 2 Chr. 26:6.

JACHAN, a Gadite, 1 Chr. 5:13.

JACHIN. 1. Son of Simeon, Gen. 46:10; Ex. 6:15; Num. 26:12. Called JARIB, 1 Chr. 4:24.

2. Name of a pillar, 1 Kin. 7:21; 2 Chr. 3:17. See BOAZ.

3. A priest, who returned from exile to Jerusalem, 1 Chr. 9:10; Neh. 11:10.

4. A priest, head of one of the courses, 1 Chr. 24:17.

JACINTH, a precious stone, Rev. 9:17; 21:20.

JACKAL, a carnivorous animal, Mal. 1:3 [R. V.].

JACOB. Son of Isaac, and twin brother of Esau, Gen. 25:24-26; Josh. 24:4; 1 Chr. 1:34; Acts 7:8. Ancestor of Jesus, Matt. 1:2. Given in answer to prayer, Gen. 25:21. Obtains Esau's birthright for a mess of pottage, Gen. 25:29-34; Heb. 12:16. Fraudulently obtains his father's blessing, Gen. 27:1-29; Heb. 11:20. Esau seeks to slay, escapes to Padan-aram, Gen. 27:41-46; 28:1-5; Hos. 12:12. His vision of the ladder, Gen. 28:10-22. God confirms the covenant of Abraham to, Gen. 28:13-22; 35:9-15; 1 Chr. 16:13-18.

Sojourns in Haran with his uncle, Laban, Gen. chapters 29; 30; Hos. 12:12. Serves fourteen years for Leah and Rachel, Gen. 29:15-30; Hos. 12:12. Sharp practice of, with the flocks and herds of Laban, Gen. 30:32-43. Dissatisfied with Laban's treatment and returns to the land of Canaan, Gen. 31. Meets angels of God on the journey, and calls the place Mahanaim, Gen. 32:1,2. Dreads to meet Esau; sends him presents; wrestles with an angel, Gen. 32. Name of, changed to Israel, Gen. 32:28; 35:10. Reconciliation of, with Esau, Gen. 33:4. Journeys to Succoth, Gen. 33:17; to Shalem, where he purchases a parcel of ground from Hamor, and erects an altar, Gen. 33:18-20. His daughter, Dinah, humbled, Gen. 34. Returns to Beth-el, where he builds an altar, and erects and dedicates a pillar, Gen. 35:1-7. Deborah, Rebekah's nurse, dies, and is buried at Beth-el, Gen. 35:8. Journeys to Ephrath; Benjamin is born to; Rachel dies, and is "buried in the way to Ephrath, which is Bethlehem," Gen. 35:16-19; 48:7. Erects a monument at Rachel's grave, Gen. 35:20. The incest of his son, Reuben, and his concubine, Bilhah, Gen. 35:22. List of the names of his twelve sons, Gen. 35:23-26. Returns to Arbah, the city of his father, Gen. 35:27. Dwells in the land of Canaan, Gen. 37:1. His partiality for his son, Joseph, and the consequent jealousy of his other sons, Gen. 37:3,4. Joseph's prophetic dream concerning, Gen. 37:9-11. His grief over the loss of Joseph, Gen. 37:34,35. Sends into Egypt to buy corn, Gen. 42:1,2; 43:1-14. His grief over the detention of Simeon, and the demand for Benjamin to be taken into Egypt, Gen. 42:36. His love for Benjamin, Gen. 43:14; 44:29. Hears that Joseph still lives, Gen. 45:26-28.

Removes to Egypt, Gen. 46:1-7; 1 Sam. 12:8; Psa. 105:23; Acts 7:14,15. List of his children and grandchildren who went down into Egypt, Gen. 46:8-27. Meets Joseph, Gen. 46:28-34. Pharaoh receives him, and is blessed by Jacob, Gen. 47:1-10. The land of Goshen assigned to, Gen. 47:11,12,27. Dwells in Egypt seventeen years, Gen. 47:28. Exacts a promise from Joseph to bury him with his fathers, Gen. 47:29-31. His benediction upon Joseph and his two sons, Gen. 48:15-22. Gives the land of the Amorites to Joseph, Gen. 48:22; John 4:5. His final prophetic benedictions upon his sons: Upon Reuben, Gen. 49:3,4; Simeon and Levi, Gen. 49:5-7; Judah, Gen. 49:8-12; Zebulun, Gen. 49:13; Issachar, Gen. 49:14,15; Dan, Gen. 49: 16-18; Gad, Gen. 49:19; Asher, Gen. 49:20; Naphtali, Gen. 49:21; Joseph, Gen. 49:22-26; Benjamin, 49:27. Charges his sons to bury him in the field of Machpelah, Gen. 49:29,30. Death of, Gen. 49:33. Body of, embalmed, Gen. 50:2. Forty days mourning for, Gen. 50:3. Burial of, Gen. 50:4-13. Descendants of, Gen. 29:31-35; 30:1-24; 35:18,22-26; 46:8-27; Ex. 1:1-5; 1 Chr. chapters 2-9.

Prophecies concerning himself and descendants, Gen. 25:23; 27:28,29; 28:10-15; Gen. 31:3; 35:9-13; 46:3; Deut. 1:8; Psa. 105:10,11. His wealth, Gen. 36:6,7. Well of, John 4:5-30.

JAEL, wife of Heber, and slayer of Sisera, Judg. 4:17-22; 5:6,24.

JAGUR, a town of Judah, Josh. 15:21.

JAHATH, name of four Levites, 1 Chr. 4:2; 23:10,11; 24:22; 2 Chr. 34:12.

JAHAZ, called also JAHAZA, JAHAZAH, and JAHZAH. A Levitical city in Reuben, taken from the Moabites, Josh. 13:18; 21:36; Isa. 15:4; Jer. 48:21. Sihon defeated at, Num. 21:23; Deut. 2:32; Judg. 11:20.

JAHAZIAH, a returned exile, Ezra 10:15.

JAHAZIEL. 1. A disaffected Israelite who joined David at Ziklag, 1 Chr. 12:4.

2. A priest, 1 Chr. 16:6.

3. Son of Hebron, 1 Chr. 23:19; 24:23.

4. A Levite, and prophet, 2 Chr. 20:14.

5. A chief, or the father of a chief, among the exiles, who returned from Babylon, Ezra 8:5.

JAHDAI, a descendant of Caleb, 1 Chr. 2:47.

JAHDIEL, head of a family of Manasseh, 1 Chr. 5:24.

JAHDO, son of Buz, 1 Chr. 5:14.

JAHLEEL, son of Zebulun, Gen. 46:14; Num. 26:26.

JAHMAI, son of Tola, 1 Chr. 7:2.

JAHZAH, a city of Reuben, 1 Chr. 6:78. See JAHAZ.

JAHZEEL, called also JAHZIEL. A son of Naphtali, Gen. 46:24; Num. 26:48; 1 Chr. 7:13.

JAHZERAH, a priest, 1 Chr. 9:12.

JAHZIEL, 1 Chr. 7:13. See JAHZEEL.

JAILER, of Philippi, converted, Acts 16:27-34.

JAIR. 1. Son of Manasseh. Founder of twenty-three cities in Gilead, Num. 32:41; Deut. 3:14; Josh. 13:30; 1 Kin. 4:13; 1 Chr. 2:22,23.

2. A judge of Israel, Judg. 10:3-5.

3. A Benjamite, Esth. 2:5.

4. Father of Elhanan, 1 Chr. 20:5.

JAIRUS. A ruler of the synagogue in Capernaum, Matt. 9:18. Daughter of, restored to life, Matt. 9:18,23-26; Mark 5:22-43; Luke 8:41-56.

JAKAN. See JAAKAN.

JAKEH, father of Agur, Prov. 30:1.

JAKIM. 1. A Benjamite, 1 Chr. 8:19.

2. Head of a sacerdotal division in the tabernacle service, 1 Chr. 24:12.

JALON, son of Ezra, 1 Chr. 4:17.

JAMBRES, an Egyptian magician, Ex. 7:11; 2 Tim. 3:8.

JAMES. 1. An apostle. Son of Zebedee and Salome, Matt. 4:21; 27:56. See SALOME. Brother of John, and a fisherman, Luke 5:10. Called to be an apostle, Matt. 4:21,22; 10:2; Mark 1:19,20; Luke 6:14; Acts 1:13. Surnamed Boanerges by Jesus, Mark 3:17. An intimate companion of Jesus, and present with him: At the great draught of fishes, Luke 5:10; the healing of Peter's mother-in-law, Mark 1:29; the raising of the daughter of Jairus, Mark 5:37; Luke 8:51; the transfiguration of Jesus, Matt. 17:1; Mark 9:2; Luke 9:28; in Gethsemane, Matt. 26:37; Mark 14:33. Asks Jesus concerning his second coming, Mark 13:3. Bigotry of, Luke 9:54. Civil ambitions of, Matt. 20:20-23; Mark 10:35-41. Present at the sea of Tiberias when Jesus revealed himself to the disciples after his resurrection, John 21:2; [1 Cor. 15:7 ?] Martyred, Acts 12:2.

2. An apostle. Son of Alphæus, Matt. 10:3; Mark 3:18; Luke 6:15; Acts 1:13; 12:17. Brother of Jesus, Matt. 13:55; 27:56; Mark 6:3; Luke 24:10; Gal. 1:19; 2:9,12. The brother of Judas, Luke 6:16; Jude 1, and of Joses, Mark 15:40. [Witness of Christ's resurrection, 1 Cor. 15:7 ?] Addresses the council at Jerusalem in favor of liberty for the Gentile converts, Acts 15:13-21. Disciples sent by, to Antioch, Gal. 2:12. Hears of the success attending Paul's ministry, Acts 21:18,19. Epistle of, Jas. 1:1.

3. Brother of Jesus,* Matt. 13:55; Mark 6:3; Gal. 1:19.

JAMIN. 1. Son of Simeon, Gen. 46:10; Ex. 6:15; Num. 26:12; 1 Chr. 4:24.

2. Descendant of Hezron, 1 Chr. 2:27.

3. A priest who expounded the law to the exiles who returned to Jerusalem, Neh. 8:7.

JAMLECH, descendant of Simeon, 1 Chr. 4:34.

JANNA, ancestor of Joseph, Luke 3:24.

JANNES, an Egyptian magician, Ex. 7:11; 2 Tim. 3:8.

JANOAH, a city of Naphtali, 2 Kin. 15:29.

JANOHAH, a city on the border of Ephraim, Josh. 16:6,7.

JANUM, a city of Judah, Josh. 15:53.

JAPHETH. Son of Noah, Gen. 5:32; 6:10; 9:18; 10:21. His life preserved at the time of the flood, Gen. 7:13; 9:18. Prudence of, on the occasion of Noah's drunkenness, Gen. 9:23,27. Descendants of, Gen. 10:2-5; 1 Chr. 1:5-7.

JAPHIA. 1. King of Lachish, Josh. 10:3.

2. A town of Zebulun, Josh. 19:12.

3. A son of David, 2 Sam. 5:15; 1 Chr. 3:7; 14:6.

---

* Whether this James is identical with James the son of Alphæus is one of the most difficult questions in the biographical history of the gospels. See 2 above. For full discussion of the subject the reader is referred to commentaries and biographical works.

JAPHLET, grandson of Beriah, 1 Chr. 7:33.

JAPHLETI, a place whose situation is unknown, Josh. 16:3.

JAPHO, a city of Dan, Josh. 19:46.

JARAH, son of Ahaz, 1 Chr. 9:42.

JAREB, king of Asshur, Hos. 5:13; 10:6.

JARED. 1. Called also JERED. A descendant of Seth, Gen. 5:15,16,18,19,20; 1 Chr. 1:2.

2. An ancestor of Jesus, Luke 3:37.

JARESIAH, son of Jeroham, 1 Chr. 8:27.

JARHA, an Egyptian, 1 Chr. 2:34,35.

JARIB. 1. Son of Simeon, 1 Chr. 4:24.

2. A chief among the captivity, Ezra 8:16.

3. A priest who married an idolatrous wife, Ezra 10:18.

JARMUTH. 1. A city in Judah, Josh. 10:3,5,23; 12:11; 15:35; Neh. 11:29.

2. A Levitical city in Issachar, Josh. 21:29.

JAROAH, a descendant of Gad, 1 Chr. 5:14.

JASHEN, father of one of David's heroes, 2 Sam. 23:32.

JASHOBEAM. 1. One of David's warriors, 2 Sam. 23:8; 1 Chr. 11:11; 27:2.

2. A Korhite Levite, 1 Chr. 12:6.

JASHUB. 1. Son of Issachar, Num. 26:24; 1 Chr. 7:1. Called JOB in Gen. 46:13.

2. Of the family of Bani, Ezra 10:29.

JASHUBI-LEHEM, a descendant of Shelah, 1 Chr. 4:22.

JASIEL, one of David's warriors, 1 Chr. 11:47.

JASON, a Christian at Thessalonica, Acts 17:5,6,7,9; and probably Paul's kinsman, mentioned in Rom. 16:21.

JASPER, a precious stone set in the high priest's breastplate, Ex. 28:20; 39:13; Ezek. 28:13; Rev. 4:3; 21:11,18,19.

JATHNIEL, son of Meshelemiah, 1 Chr. 26:2.

JATTIR, a Levitical city, Josh. 15:48; 21:14; 1 Sam. 30:27; 1 Chr. 6:57.

JAVAN. 1. Son of Japheth, Gen.10:2,4; 1 Chr. 1:5,7.

2. A city in Arabia in which the Phenicians traded, Ezek. 27:13,19.

JAVELIN, a heavy lance, Ezek. 39:9; used by Goliath [R. V.], 1 Sam. 17:6; by Saul, 1 Sam. 18:11; 19:9,10.

JAZER. 1. A city of refuge E. of the Jordan, Josh. 21:39. Taken from the Amorites, Num. 21:32; 32:1,3,35; Josh. 13:25.

2. Sea of, Jer. 48:32.

JAZIZ, a shepherd, 1 Chr. 27:31.

JEALOUSY. Prov. 6:34; 27:4; Eccl. 4:4; Song 8:6. Law concerning, when husband is jealous of his wife, Num. 5:12–31. Image of, Ezek. 8:3,4. Forbidden, Rom. 13:13 [R. V.].

Attributed to God, Ex. 20:5; 34:13,14; Num. 25:11; Deut. 29:20; 32:16,21; 1 Kin. 14:22; Psa. 78:58; 79:5; Isa. 30:1,2; 31:1,3; Ezek. 16:42; 23:25; 36:5,6; 38:19; Zeph. 1:18; 3:8; Zech. 1:14; 8:2; 1 Cor. 10:22. See ANTHROPOMORPHISMS.

A spirit of emulation, Rom. 10:19; 11:11. See EMULATION; ENVY.

FIGURATIVE: 2 Cor. 11:2.

INSTANCES OF : Cain, of Abel, Gen.4:5,6,8. Sarah, of Hagar, Gen. 16:5. Joseph's brethren, of Joseph, Gen. 37:4–11,18–28. Saul, of David, 1 Sam. 18:8–30; 19:8–24; 20:24–34. Joab, of Abner, 2 Sam. 3:24–27. Nathan, of Adonijah, 1 Kin. 1:24–26. Ephraimites, of Gideon, Judg. 8:1; of Jephthah, Judg. 12:1. The brother of the prodigal son, Luke 15:25–32. Sectional, between Israel and the tribe of Judah, 2 Sam. 19:41–43.

JEATERAI, descendant of Gershom, 1 Chr. 6:21.

JEBERECHIAH, father of Zechariah, Isa. 8:2.

JEBUS, called also JEBUSI. See JERUSALEM.

JEBUSITES. One of the tribes of Canaan, Deut. 7:1. Land of, given to Abraham and his descendants, Gen. 15:21; Ex. 3:8,17; 23:23,24; Deut. 20:17; Ex. 33:2; 34:10,11. Conquered by Joshua, Josh. chapters 10–12; and 24:11; by David, 2 Sam. 5:6–9. Jerusalem within the territory of,Josh.18:28. Not exterminated, but intermarry with the Israelites, Judg. 3:5,6; Ezra 9:1,2; 10:18–44. Pay tribute to Solomon, 1 Kin. 9:20,21.

JECAMIAH, son of Jeconiah, 1 Chr. 3:18.

JECHOLIAH, called also JECOLIAH. Mother of Azariah, 2 Kin. 15:2; 2 Chr. 26:3.

JECONIAH. See JEHOIACHIN.

JEDAIAH. 1. Descendant of Simeon, 1 Chr. 4:37.

2. A returned exile, Neh. 3:10.

3. A priest of the captivity, 1 Chr. 9:10; 24:7; Ezra 2:36; Neh. 7:39.

4. A priest who dwelt at Jerusalem after the return of the captivity, Neh. 11:10; 12:6, 19; Zech. 6:10,14.

5. Another priest, who returned from Babylon with Nehemiah, Neh. 12:7,21.

JEDIAEL. 1. Son of Benjamin, 1 Chr. 7:6,10,11.

2. Son of Shimri, 1 Chr. 11:45.

3. A Manassite chief, who joined David at Ziklag, 1 Chr. 12:20.

4. Son of Meshelemiah, 1 Chr. 26:2.

JEDIDAH, wife of Amon, 2 Kin. 22:1.

JEDIDIAH, a name given to Solomon, 2 Sam. 12:25.

JEDUTHUN. A musician of the temple, 1 Chr. 16:41; 25:1. Called ETHAN, 1 Chr. 6:44; 15:17. See titles of Psalms 39; 62; 77.

JEGAR-SAHADUTHA, called also GALEED. A heap of stones on Mount Gilead, Gen. 31:47,48.

JEHALELEEL, descendant of Judah, 1 Chr. 4:16.

JEHALELEL, a descendant of Merari, 2 Chr. 29:12.

JEHDEIAH. 1. Son of Shubael, 1 Chr. 24:20.

2. One of David's overseers, 1 Chr. 27: 30.

JEHEZEKEL, a priest, and head of

the twentieth division in the tabernacle service, 1 Chr. 24:16.

JEHIAH, a Levite, and doorkeeper of the ark, 1 Chr. 15:24.

JEHIEL. 1. A Levite porter, 1 Chr. 15:18. Probably identical with JEHIAH, above.

2. A Gershonite Levite, 1 Chr. 23:8; 29:8.

3. A companion of David's sons, 1 Chr. 27:32.

4. Son of Jehoshaphat, 2 Chr. 21:2.

5. Son of Heman, 2 Chr. 29:14.

6. A Levite overseer in the temple, 2 Chr. 31:13.

7. A priest who gave extraordinary offerings for the passover, 2 Chr. 35:8.

8. Father of Obadiah, Ezra 8:9.

9. Father of Shechaniah, Ezra 10:2.

10. Name of two priests who married idolatrous wives, Ezra 10:21,26.

JEHIELI, son of Laadan, 1 Chr. 26: 21,22.

JEHIZKIAH, son of Shallum, 2 Chr. 28:12.

JEHOADAH, son of Ahaz, 1 Chr. 8:36.

JEHOADDAN, mother of Amaziah, 2 Kin. 14:2; 2 Chr. 25:1.

JEHOAHAZ. 1. Son of Jehu, and king of Israel, 2 Kin. 10:35; 13:1–9.

2. Son of Jehoram, king of Judah, 2 Chr. 21:17. See AHAZIAH.

3. Called also SHALLUM. King of Judah, and successor of Josiah, 2 Kin. 23:30,31; 1 Chr. 3:15; 2 Chr. 36:1; Jer. 22:11. Wicked reign of, 2 Kin. 23:32. Pharaoh-nechoh, king of Egypt, invades the kingdom of, defeats him, and takes him captive to Egypt, 2 Kin. 23:33–35; 2 Chr. 36:3,4. Prophecies concerning, Jer. 22:10,11,12.

JEHOASH. 1. Called also JOASH. Successor of Jehoahaz, 2 Kin. 13:10–25. Defeats Amaziah, 2 Kin. 13:12; 14:8–15; 2 Chr. 25:17–24. Death of, 2 Kin. 13:13; 14:16.

2. King of Judah. See JOASH.

JEHOHANAN. 1. A porter of the tabernacle, 1 Chr. 26:3.

2. A military chief under Jehoshaphat, whose corps consisted of two hundred and eighty thousand men, 2 Chr. 17:15. Probably identical with a captain of a hundred, in 2 Chr. 23:1.

3. Son of Bebai, Ezra 10:28.

4. A priest among the exiles who returned from Babylon, Neh. 12:13.

5. A chorister in the temple, Neh. 12:42.

JEHOIACHIN. King of Judah and successor to Jehoiakim, 2 Kin. 24:6–8; 2 Chr. 36:8,9. Called JECONIAH, 1 Chr. 3:16; Jer. 24:1. Called CONIAH, Jer. 22:24; 37:1. Wicked reign of, 2 Kin. 24:9; 2 Chr. 36:9. Nebuchadnezzar invades his kingdom, takes him captive to Babylon, 2 Kin. 24:10–16; 2 Chr. 36:10; Esth. 2:6; Jer. 27:20; 29:1,2; Ezek. 1:2. Confined in prison thirty-seven years, 2 Kin. 25:27. Released from prison by Evil-merodach, and promoted above other kings, and honored until death, 2 Kin. 25:27–30; Jer. 52:31–34. Prophecies concerning, Jer.

22:24–30; 28:4. Sons of, 1 Chr. 3:17,18. Ancestor of Jesus, Matt. 1:12.

JEHOIADA. 1. Father of Benaiah, one of David's officers, 2 Sam. 8:18.

2. A high priest. Overthrows Athaliah, the usurping queen of Judah, and establishes Jehoash upon the throne, 2 Kin. 11; 2 Chr. 23. Salutary influence of, over Jehoash, 2 Kin. 12:2; 2 Chr. 24:2,22. Directs the repairs of the temple, 2 Kin. 12:4–16; 2 Chr. 24:4–14. Death of, 2 Chr. 24:15,16.

3. A priest who led three thousand seven hundred priests armed for war, 1 Chr. 12:27.

4. Son of Benaiah, 1 Chr. 27:34.

5. A returned exile, Neh. 3:6.

6. A priest mentioned in Jeremiah's letter to the captive Jews, Jer. 29:26.

JEHOIAKIM, called also ELIAKIM. King of Judah, 1 Chr. 3:15. Ancestor of Jesus, Matt. 1:11. Wicked reign and final overthrow of, 2 Kin. 23:34–37; 24:1–6; 2 Chr. 36:4–8; Jer. 22:13–19; 26:22,23; 36; Dan. 1:1,2. Dies, and is succeeded by his son, Jehoiachin, 2 Kin. 24:6.

JEHOIARIB, two priests bearing the same name, 1 Chr. 9:10; Neh. 11:10; 1 Chr. 24:7.

JEHONADAB. See JONADAB.

JEHONATHAN. 1. An overseer of David's storehouses, 1 Chr. 27:25.

2. A Levite sent to instruct the people in the law, 2 Chr. 17:8.

3. An obscure priest, Neh. 12:18.

JEHORAM. 1. King of Judah, 1 Kin. 22:50; 2 Kin. 8:16; 1 Chr. 3:11; 2 Chr. 21:5. Ancestor of Jesus, Matt. 1:8. Marries Athaliah, whose wicked counsels influence his reign for evil, 2 Kin. 8:18,19; 2 Chr. 21: 6–13.

Slays his brothers to strengthen himself in his sovereignty, 2 Chr. 21:4,13. Edom revolts from, 2 Kin. 8:20–22; 2 Chr. 21: 8–10. Philistines and Arabians invade his territory, 2 Chr. 21:16,17. Death of, 2 Chr. 21:18–20; 2 Kin. 8:24. Prophecy concerning, 2 Chr. 21:12–15.

2. A son of Ahab. See JORAM.

3. A priest commissioned to go through Israel and instruct the people in the law, 2 Chr. 17:8.

JEHOSHABEATH. See JEHOSHEBA.

JEHOSHAPHAT. 1. David's recorder, 2 Sam. 8:16; 20:24; 1 Kin. 4:3; 1 Chr. 18:15.

2. One of Solomon's commissariat officers, 1 Kin. 4:17.

3. King of Judah. Succeeds Asa, 1 Kin. 15:24; 22:41; 1 Chr. 3:10; 2 Chr. 17:1; Matt. 1: 8. Strengthens himself against Israel, 2 Chr. 17:2. Inaugurates a system of public instruction in the law, 2 Chr. 17:7–9. His wise reign, 1 Kin. 22:43; 2 Chr. 17:7–9; 19:3–11. His system of tribute, 2 Chr. 17:11. His military forces and armament, 2 Chr. 17:12–19. Joins Ahab in an invasion of Ramoth-gilead, 1 Kin. 22; 2 Chr. 18. Rebuked by the prophet Jehu, 2 Chr. 19:2. The allied forces of the Amorites, Moabites, and other tribes

invade his territory, and are defeated by, 2 Chr. 20. Builds ships for commerce with Tarshish, ships are destroyed, 1 Kin. 22:48, 49; 2 Chr. 20:35–37. Joins Jehoram, king of Israel, in an invasion of the land of Moab, defeats the Moabites, 2 Kin. 3. Makes valuable gifts to the temple, 2 Kin. 12:18. Death of, 1 Kin. 22:50; 2 Chr. 21:1. Religious zeal of, 1 Kin. 22:43,46; 2 Chr. 17:1–9; 19:20: 1–32; 22:9. Prosperity of, 1 Kin. 22:45,48; 2 Chr. chapters 17–20. Bequests of, to his children, 2 Chr. 21:2,3.

4. Father of Jehu, 2 Kin. 9:2,14.

5. A priest who assisted in bringing the ark from Obed-edom, 1 Chr. 15:24.

6. A valley. Called VALLEY OF DECISION, Joel 3:2,12,14.

JEHOSHEBA, called also JEHOSHAB-EATH. Daughter of Joram, 2 Kin. 11:2.

JEHOSHUA, a name sometimes given to one of the JOSHUAS, Num. 13:16.

JEHOSHUAH, a name of one of the JOSHUAS, 1 Chr. 7:27.

JEHOVAH-JIREH, Mount Moriah, in Jerusalem, where Abraham offered Isaac, Gen. 22:14.

JEHOVAH-NISSI, an altar, Ex. 17:15.

JEHOVAH-SHALOM, an altar built by Gideon, Judg. 6:24.

JEHOZABAD. 1. Son of Shomer, and one of the assassins of King Jehoash, 2 Kin. 12:21; 2 Chr. 24:26.

2. Son of Obed-edom, 1 Chr. 26:4.

3. A Benjamite chief who commanded one hundred and eighty thousand men, 2 Chr. 17:18.

JEHOZADAK, called also JOSEDECH and JOZADAK. A priest of the exile, 1 Chr. 6:14,15; Ezra 3:2,8; 5:2; 10:18; Neh. 12:26; Hag. 1:1,12,14; 2:2,4; Zech. 6:11.

JEHU. 1. The prophet who announced the wrath of Jehovah against Baasha, king of Israel, 1 Kin. 16:1,7,12; 2 Chr. 19:2; 20:34.

2. Son of Nimshi, king of Israel, 1 Kin. 19:16; 2 Kin. 9:1–14. Religious zeal of, in slaying idolaters, 2 Kin. 9:14–37; 10:1–28; 2 Chr. 22:8,9. His territory invaded by Hazael, king of Syria, 2 Kin. 10:32,33. Prophecies concerning, 1 Kin. 19:17; 2 Kin. 10:30; 15:12; Hos. 1:4. Death of, 2 Kin. 10:35.

3. Son of Obed, 1 Chr. 2:38.

4. Son of Josibiah, 1 Chr. 4:35.

5. A Benjamite, 1 Chr. 12:3.

JEHUBBAH, an Asherite, 1 Chr. 7:34.

JEHUCAL, called also JUCAL. Son of Shelemiah, Jer. 37:3; 38:1,4.

JEHUD, a city of Dan, Josh. 19:45.

JEHUDI, a Jew, Jer. 36:14,21,23.

JEHUDIJAH, wife of Ezra, 1 Chr. 4:18.

JEHUSH, a Benjamite, 1 Chr. 8:39.

JEIEL. 1. Called also JEHIEL. A Reubenite, 1 Chr. 5:7.

2. A Benjamite, 1 Chr. 9:35.

3 One of David's heroes, 1 Chr. 11:44.

4. A Levite, and chorister in the tabernacle service, 1 Chr. 15:18,21; 16:5.

5. A Levite, ancestor of Jehaziel, who encouraged Judah against their enemies, 2 Chr. 20:14.

6. A scribe during the reign of Uzziah, 2 Chr. 26:11.

7. A Levite who cleansed the temple, 2 Chr. 29:13.

8. A chief of the Levites who gave, with other chiefs, five thousand five hundred "small cattle" for sacrifice, 2 Chr. 35:9.

9. A son of Adonikam, an exile who returned to Jerusalem with Ezra, Ezra 8:13.

10. A priest who was defiled by marriage to an idolatrous woman, Ezra 10:43.

JEKABZEEL, a city in the S. of Judah, Neh. 11:25.

JEKAMEAM, son of Hebron, 1 Chr. 23:19; 24:23.

JEKAMIAH, a descendant of Jerahmeel, 1 Chr. 2:41.

JEKUTHIEL, son of Ezra, 1 Chr. 4:18.

JEMIMA, Job's daughter. Job 42:14.

JEMUEL, son of Simeon, Gen. 46:10; Ex. 6:15.

JEPHTHAH. A judge of Israel. Illegitimate, and therefore not entitled to inherit his father's property, Judg. 11:1,2. Escapes the violence of his half-brothers, dwells in the land of Tob, Judg. 11:3. Recalled from the land of Tob by the elders of Gilead, Judg. 11:5. Made captain of the host, Judg. 11:5–11; and made head of the land of Gilead, Judg. 11:7–11. His message to the king of the Ammonites, Judg. 11:12–28. Leads the host of Israel against the Ammonites, Judg. 11:29–33. His rash vow concerning his daughter, Judg. 11:31,34–40. Falsely accused by the Ephraimites, Judg. 12:1. Leads the army of the Gileadites against the Ephraimites, Judg. 12:4. Judges Israel six years,dies, and is buried in Gilead, Judg. 12:7. Faith of, Heb. 11:32.

JEPHUNNEH. 1. Father of Caleb, Num. 13:6.

2. An Asherite, 1 Chr. 7:38.

JERAH, son of Joktan, Gen. 10:26; 1 Chr. 1:20.

JERAHMEEL. 1. Son of Hezron, 1 Chr. 2:9.

2. Son of Kish, 1 Chr. 24:29.

3. An officer of Jehoiakim, king of Judah, Jer. 36:26.

JERED, son of Ezra. 1 Chr. 4:18.

JEREMAI, of the family of Hashum, Ezra 10:33.

JEREMIAH. 1. Of Libnah, grandfather of Jehoahaz, 2 Kin. 23:31; 24:18; Jer. 52:1.

2. A chief of Manasseh, 1 Chr. 5:24.

3. An Israelite who joined David at Ziklag, 1 Chr. 12:4.

4. Two Gadites who joined David at Ziklag, 1 Chr. 12:10,13.

5. The prophet. Jer. 1:1. A Rechabite, Jer. 35:3. A priest, Jer. 1:1. Call of, Jer. 1:4–19. Time of his prophecies, Jer. 3:6; 21:1; 24:1; 25:1–3; 26:1; 28:1; 32:1; 34:1; 45:1; 49:34. Letter to the captives in Babylon,

Jer. 29. Sorrow of, under persecution, Jer. 15:10,15; 17:15-18. Conspiracy against, Jer. 11:21-23; 18:18-23. Foretells the desolation of Jerusalem, Jer. 19. Pashur, the governor of the temple, scourges and casts him into prison, Jer. 20:1-3. Denounces Pashur, Jer. 20:3-6. His melancholy and murmuring against God, in consequence of persecution, Jer. 20:7-18. Imprisoned by Zedekiah, Jer. 32; 33:1; 37:15-21; 38:6-13; 39:15-18; Lam. 3: 53-55. Nebuchadnezzar directs the release of, Jer. 39:11-14; 40:1-4. Has a friend in Ahikam, Jer. 26:24. Ebed-melech, the Egyptian, intercedes with the king for him, and secures his release, Jer. 38:7-13.

Prophecies of, written by Baruch, Jer. 36:1-7,32; 45:1. Prophecies of, destroyed by Jehoiakim, Jer. 36:8-32. Book of the prophecies of, delivered to Seraiah, with a charge from Jeremiah, Jer. 51:59-64. Zedekiah seeks counsel from God by, Jer. 21:1,2; 37:3; 38:14. His intercession asked : By Johanan and all the people, Jer. 42:1-6; by Zedekiah, Jer. 37:3. Johanan carries Jeremiah into Egypt, Jer. 43:1-7. Foretells the conquest of Egypt by Babylon, Jer. 43:8-12. Prophecies of, studied by Daniel, Dan. 9:2. Celibacy of, Jer. 16:2. Purchases a field, Jer. 32:7-10. Lamentations of : Over Josiah, 2 Chr. 35:25; over the prosperity of the wicked, Jer. 12:1-6; over the desolation of God's heritage, Jer. 12:7-13; over Jerusalem, Jer. 4:14-18; 8; 9:1; 10:19-22; 18:11. See BOOK OF LAMENTATIONS. Dwells at Mizpah, Jer. 40:6. Prayers of, Jer. 14:7-9; 32:17-25. Zeal of, Jer. 15:16.

JEREMOTH. 1. A Benjamite, 1 Chr. 8:14.

2. One of the sons of Elam, Ezra 10:26.

3. One of the family of Zattu, Ezra 10:27.

JERIAH, called also JERIJAH. A descendant of Hebron, 1 Chr. 23:19; 24:23; 26:31.

JERIBAI, a valiant man of David's guard, 1 Chr. 11:46.

JERICHO. 1. A city E. of Jerusalem and near the Jordan, Num. 22:1; 26:3; Deut. 34:1. Called the CITY OF PALM TREES, Deut. 34:3. Situation of, pleasant, 2 Kin. 2:19. Rahab the harlot lived in, Josh. 2; Heb. 11:31. Joshua sees the "captain of the host" of the Lord near, Josh. 5:13-15. Besieged by Joshua seven days; fall and destruction of, Josh. 6; 24:11. Situated within the territory allotted to Benjamin, Josh. 18:12,21. The Kenites dwelt at, Judg. 1:16. King of Moab makes conquest of, and establishes his capital at, Judg. 3:13. Rebuilt by Hiel, 1 Kin. 16:34. Company of "the sons of the prophets," dwelt at, 2 Kin. 2:4,5,15, 18. Captives of Judah, taken by the king of Israel, released at, on account of the denunciation of the prophet Oded, 2 Chr. 28:7-15. Inhabitants of, taken captive to Babylon, return to, with Ezra and Nehemiah, Ezra 2:34; Neh. 7:36; assist in repairing the walls of Jerusalem, Neh. 3:2. Blind men healed at, by Jesus, Matt. 20:29-34;

Mark 10:46; Luke 18:35. Zacchæus dwelt at, Luke 19:1-10.

2. Plain of, 2 Kin. 25:5; Jer. 52:8.

3. Waters of, Josh. 16:1. Purified by Elisha, 2 Kin. 2:18-22.

JERIEL, son of Tola, 1 Chr. 7:2.

JERIMOTH. Called also JEREMOTH.

1. Son of Bela, 1 Chr. 7:7.

2. Son of Becher, 1 Chr. 7:8.

3. A disaffected Israelite, who denounced Saul and joined David at Ziklag, 1 Chr. 12:5.

4. Son of Mushi, 1 Chr. 23:23; 24:30.

5. Son of Heman, 1 Chr. 25:4.

6. A ruler of the tribe of Naphtali, 1 Chr. 27:19.

7. A son of David, 2 Chr. 11:18.

JERIOTH. Wife of Caleb. Probably identical with AZUBAH, 1 Chr. 2:18.

JEROBOAM : 1. First king of Israel after the revolt. Promoted by Solomon, 1 Kin. 11:28. Ahijah's prophecy concerning, 1 Kin. 11:29-39; 14:5-16. Flees to Egypt to escape from Solomon, 1 Kin. 11:26-40. Recalled from Egypt by the ten tribes on account of disaffection toward Rehoboam, and made king, 1 Kin. 12:1-20; 2 Chr. 10:12-19. Subverts the religion of Moses, 1 Kin. 12:25-33; 13:33,34; 14:9,16; 16:2,26,31; 2 Chr. 11:14; 13:8,9. Hand of, paralyzed, 1 Kin. 13:1-10. His wife sent to consult the prophet Ahijah concerning her child, 1 Kin. 14:1-18. His wars with Rehoboam, 1 Kin. 14:19,30; 15:6; 2 Chr. 11:1-4. His war with Abijah, 1 Kin. 15:7; 2 Chr. 13. Death of, 1 Kin. 14:20; 2 Chr. 13:20.

2. King of Israel. Successor to Jehoash, 2 Kin. 14:16,23. Makes conquest of Hamath and Damascus, 2 Kin. 14:25-28. Wicked reign of, 2 Kin. 14:24. Prophecies concerning, Amos 7:7-13. Death of, 2 Kin. 14:29. Genealogies written during his reign, 1 Chr. 5:17.

JEROHAM. 1. A Levite, and grandfather of Samuel, 1 Sam. 1:1; 1 Chr. 6:27,34.

2. A chief of the tribe of Benjamin, 1 Chr. 8:27.

3. A descendant of Benjamin, 1 Chr. 9:8.

4. A priest, and father of Adaiah, who dwelt in Jerusalem after the exile, 1 Chr. 9:12; Neh. 11:12.

5. Father of two Israelites who joined David at Ziklag, 1 Chr. 12:7.

6. The father of Azareel, 1 Chr. 27:22.

7. Father of Azariah, 2 Chr. 23:1.

JERUBBAAL. See GIDEON.

JERUEL, a wilderness in the S. of Judah, 2 Chr. 20:16.

JERUSALEM. Called JEBUS, Josh. 18: 28; Judg. 19:10; ZION, 1 Kin. 8:1; Zech. 9:13; CITY OF DAVID, 2 Sam. 5:7; Isa. 22:9; SALEM, Gen. 14:18; Psa. 76:2; ARIEL, Isa. 29:1; CITY OF GOD, Psa. 46:4; CITY OF THE GREAT KING, Psa. 48:2; CITY OF JUDAH, 2 Chr. 25:28; THE PERFECTION OF BEAUTY, THE JOY OF THE WHOLE EARTH, Lam. 2:15; THE THRONE OF THE LORD, Jer. 3:17; HOLY MOUNTAIN, Dan. 9:16,20; HOLY CITY, Neh. 11:1,18: Matt. 4:5; CITY OF SOLEMNITIES, Isa. 33:20: CITY OF TRUTH, Zech. 8:3; to be called "THE LORD

OUR RIGHTEOUSNESS," Jer. 33:16; JEHOVAH-SHAMMAH, Ezek. 48:35; [marg.] NEW JERUSALEM, Rev. 21:2,10–27.

Situation and appearance of, Psa. 122:3; 125:2; Song 6:4; Mic. 4:8. Walls of, Jer. 39:4.

Gates of : Old gate, fish gate, sheep gate, prison gate, Neh. 3:1,3,32; 12:39. Gate of Ephraim, 2 Chr. 25:23; Neh. 12:39. Gate of Benjamin, Jer. 37:13; Zech. 14:10; of Joshua, 2 Kin. 23:8. Old gate, Neh. 3:6; 12:39. Corner gate ; Zech. 14:10. Valley gate, Neh. 2: 13; 3:13. Dung gate, Neh. 2:13; 3:13; 12:31. Gate of the fountain, Neh. 2:14; 3:15; 12:37. Water gate, Neh. 3:26; 8:1; 12:37. Horse gate, Neh. 3:28. King's gate, 1 Chr. 9:18. Shallecheth, 1 Chr. 26:16. High gate, 2 Chr. 23:20. East gate, Neh. 3:29. Miphkad, Neh. 3:31. Middle gate, Jer. 39:3. First gate, Zech. 14:10.

Buildings : High priest's palace, John 18: 15. Castle, Acts 21:34. Stairs, Neh. 3:15.

Streets: East street, 2 Chr. 29:4. Street of the house of God, Ezra 10:9. Street of the Water gate of Ephraim gate, Neh. 8:16. Baker's street, Jer. 37:21.

Towers of. See HANANEEL ; MEAH ; MILLO ; OPHEL ; SILOAM.

Places in and around : Moriah, 2 Chr. 3:1. The sepulcher of Jesus, John 19: 41. See CALVARY ; GETHSEMANE ; OLIVES, MOUNT OF; JEHOSHAPHAT, VALLEY OF; TOPHET.

Measurement of, in Ezekiel's vision, Ezek. 45:6. Names of the gates of, in Ezekiel's vision, Ezek. 48:31–34.

The capital of David's kingdom by divine appointment, 1 Kin. 15:4; 2 Kin. 19:34; 2 Chr. 6:6; 12:13. To be called God's throne, Jer. 3:17. The chief Levites dwelt in. 1 Chr. 9:34. The high priest dwelt at, John 18:15. Annual feasts kept at, Ezek. 36:38, with Deut. 16:16, and Psa. 122:3–5; Luke 2:41; John 4:20; 5:1; 7:1–14; 12:20; Acts 18:21. Prayers of the Israelites made toward, 1 Kin. 8:38; Dan. 6:10. Beloved, Psa. 122:6; 137:1–7; Isa. 62:1–7. See COUNTRY, LOVE OF ; PATRIOTISM.

Oaths taken in the name of, Matt. 5:35.

Melchizedek ancient king and priest of, Gen. 14:18. King of, confederated with the four other kings of the Amorites, against Joshua and the hosts of Israel, Josh. 10:1–5. Confederated kings defeated, and the king of Jerusalem slain by Joshua, Josh. 10:15–26. Falls to Benjamin in the allotment of the land of Canaan, Josh. 18:28. Conquest of, made by David, 2 Sam. 5:7. The inhabitants of, not expelled, Josh. 15:63; Judg. 1:21. Conquest of Mount Zion in, made by David, 1 Chr. 11:4–6. The citadel of Mount Zion, occupied by David, and called the CITY OF DAVID, 2 Sam. 5:5–9; 1 Chr. 11:7. Ark brought to, by David, 2 Sam. 6:12–19. The threshing floor of Araunah within the citadel of, 2 Sam. 24:16. David purchases and erects an altar upon it, 2 Sam. 24:16–25. The city built around the citadel, 1 Chr. 11:8.

Fortified by Solomon, 1 Kin. 3:1; 9:15. The temple built within the citadel, see TEMPLE.

Captured and pillaged by : Shishak, king of Egypt, 1 Kin. 14:25,26; 2 Chr. 12:9; by Jehoash, king of Israel, 2 Kin. 14:13,14; 2 Chr. 25:23,24; Nebuchadnezzar, king of Babylon, 2 Kin. 24:8–16; 25:1–17; 2 Chr. 36:17–21; Jer. 1:3; 32:2; 39; 52:4–7,12–24; Lam. 1:5–8.

Walls of, restored and fortified : By Uzziah, 2 Chr. 26:9,10; by Jotham, 2 Chr. 27:3; Manasseh, 2 Chr. 33:14. Water supply brought in from the Gihon by Hezekiah. 2 Kin. 18:17; 20:20; 2 Chr. 32:3,4,30; Neh. 2:13–15; Isa. 7:3: 22:9–11; 36:2. Besieged : By Pekah, 2 Kin. 16:5; by the Philistines, 2 Chr. 21:16, 17; by Sennacherib, 2 Kin. 18:13–37; 19:20–37; 2 Chr. 32. Rebuilding of, ordered by proclamation of Cyrus, 2 Chr. 36:23; Ezra 1:1–4. Rebuilt by Nehemiah under the direction of Artaxerxes, Neh. chapters 2–6. Wall of, dedicated, Neh. 12:27–43. Temple restored, see TEMPLE.

Roman rulers resided at : Herod I., Matt. 2:3; Pontius Pilate, Matt. 27:2; Mark 15:1; Luke 23:1–7; John 18:28,29; Herod III., Acts 12:1–23.

Life and miracles of Jesus connected with, see JESUS, HISTORY OF.

Gospel first preached at, Mic. 4:2; Luke 24:47; Acts 1:4; 2:14. Pentecostal revival occurs at, Acts 2. Stephen martyred at, Acts 6:8–15; 7. Disciples persecuted and dispersed from, Acts 8:1–4; 11:19–21.

For personal incidents occurring therein, see biographies of individuals ; see also ISRAELITES.

Wickedness of, Luke 13:33,34. Catalogue of abominations in, Ezek. 22:3–12,25–30; 23; 33:25,26. Led Judah to sin, Mic. 1:5.

Prophecies against, Isa. 3:1–8; Jer. 9:11; 19:6,15; 21:10; 26:9,11; Dan. 9:2,27; Mic. 1: 1; 3:12; of pestilence, famine, and war in, Jer. 34:2; Ezek. 5:12; Joel 3:2,3; Amos 2:5; of the destruction of, Jer. 7:32–34; 26:18; 32: 29,31,32; Dan. 9:24–27. Destruction of, foretold by Jesus, Matt. 23:37,38; 24:15; Mark 13:14–23; Luke 13:35; 17:26–37; 19:41–44; 21: 20–24.

Prophecies of the rebuilding of, Isa. 44:28; Jer. 31:38–40; Ezek. 48:15–22; Dan. 9:25; Zech. 14:8–11. Of final restoration of, Joel 3:20,21; Zech. 2:2–5; 8.

HISTORICAL NOTICES OF : Melchizedek was ancient king of, Gen. 14:18.

JERUSHA, daughter of Zadok, 2 Kin. 15:33; 2 Chr. 27:1.

JESAIAH. 1. Called also JESHAIAH. Grandson of Zerubbabel, 1 Chr. 3:21.

2. Son of Jeduthun, 1 Chr. 25:3,15.

3. Grandson of Eliezer, 1 Chr. 26:25.

4. A Jew of the family of Elam, who returned from exile, Ezra 8:7.

5. A Levite who joined Ezra to return to Jerusalem, Ezra 8:19.

6. A Benjamite, detailed by lot to dwell in Jerusalem after the exile, Neh. 11:7.

JESHANAH, a city on the N. of Benjamin, 2 Chr. 13:19.

JESHARELAH, a Levite, choral leader, 1 Chr. 25:14.

JESHEBEAB, a priest, and head of the fourteenth course, 1 Chr. 24:13.

JESHER, son of Caleb, 1 Chr. 2:18.

JESHIMON. 1. A place in the Sinaitic peninsula, E. of the Jordan, Num. 21: 20; 23:28.

2. A place in the desert of Judah, 1 Sam. 23:24; 26:1.

JESHISHAI, a Gadite, 1 Chr. 5:14.

JESHOHAIAH, a descendant of Simeon, 1 Chr. 4:36.

JESHUA. 1. Called also JESHUAH. A priest, head of the ninth course, 1 Chr. 24:11. Nine hundred and seventy-three of his descendants returned from Babylon, Ezra 2:36; Neh. 7:39.

2. A Levite, had charge of the tithes, 2 Chr. 31:15. His descendants returned with Ezra from Babylon, Ezra 2:40; Neh. 7:43.

3. Called also JOSHUA. A priest who accompanied Zerubbabel from Babylon, Ezra 2:2; Neh. 7:7; 12:1. Descendants of, Neh. 12: 10. He rebuilt the altar, Ezra 3:2. Rebuilt the temple, Ezra 3:8–13. Contends with those who sought to defeat the rebuilding, Ezra 4:1–3; 5:1,2.

4. Father of Jozabad, Ezra 8:33.

5. Son of Pahath-moab, Ezra 2:6; Neh. 7:11.

6. Father of Ezer, Neh. 3:19.

7. A Levite who explained the law to the people when Ezra read it, Neh. 8:7; 12:8.

8. A Levite who sealed Nehemiah's covenant, Neh. 10:9.

9. A city of Judah, Neh. 11:26.

10. Joshua called, Neh. 8:17.

SYMBOLICAL: Prophecies concerning, Zech. 3; 6:9–15.

See JOSHUA.

JESHURUN, a name used poetically for Israel, Deut. 32:15; 33:5,26; Isa. 44:2.

JESIAH. 1. A disaffected Israelite who joined David at Ziklag, 1 Chr. 12:6.

2. A Kohathite Levite, 1 Chr. 23:20.

JESIMIEL, a descendant of Simeon, 1 Chr. 4:36.

JESSE. Father of David, Ruth 4:17; 1 Sam. 17:12. Ancestor of Jesus, Matt. 1:5,6. Samuel visits, under divine command, to select from his sons a successor to Saul, 1 Sam. 16:1–13. Saul asks, to send David to become a member of his court, 1 Sam. 16:19–23. Sons in Saul's army, 1 Sam. 17:13–28. Dwells with David in Moab, 1 Sam. 22:3,4. Descendants of, 1 Chr. 2:13–17.

JESTING. Foolish, forbidden, Eph. 5:4. See Matt. 12:36.

JESUI, a descendant of Asher, Num. 26:44.

JESUS, THE CHRIST. INDEX OF SUBTOPICS: *History of,* p. 654; *Miscellaneous Facts Concerning,* p. 657; *Unclassified Scriptures Relating to,* p. 657; *Ascension of,* p. 658; *Atonement by,* p. 658; *Attributes of,* p. 658; *Compassion of,* p. 658; *Confessing,* p. 659;

Creator, p. 659; *Death of,* p. 659; *Design of His Death,* p. 661; *Death of, Voluntary,* p. 664; *Denial of,* p. 665; *Divinity of,* p. 665; *Eternity of,* p. 667; *Exaltation of,* p. 667; *Example,* p. 668; *Faith in,* p. 670; *Genealogy of,* p. 670; *Holiness of,* p. 670; *Humanity of,* p. 671; *Humility of,* p. 673; *Incarnation of,* p. 673; *Intercession of,* p. 675; *Judge,* p. 675; *Justice of,* p. 676; *King,* p. 676; *Kingdom of,* p. 680; *Prophecies Concerning Its Universality,* p. 681; *Unclassified Prophecies Concerning the Kingdom of,* p. 686; *Secular Notions Concerning the Kingdom of,* p. 690; *Love of,* p. 691; *Mediation of,* p. 693; *Meekness of,* p. 695; *Messiah,* p. 696; *Miracles of,* p. 700; *Mission of,* p. 700; *Names of,* p. 703; *Obedience of,* p. 705; *Omnipotence of,* p. 705; *Omnipresence of,* p. 706; *Omniscience of,* p. 706; *Parables of,* p. 707; *Peccability of,* p. 708; *Perfections of,* p. 708; *Power of, to Forgive Sins,* p. 708; *Prayers of,* p. 708; *Preëxistence of,* p. 710; *Prescience of,* p. 710; *Priesthood of,* p. 711; *Promises of,* p. 711; *Prophecies Concerning,* p. 712; *Coming of,* p. 712; *Future Glory and Power of,* p. 715; *Prophet,* p. 716; *Received,* p. 716; *Redeemer,* p. 718; *Rejected,* p. 719; *Relation of, to the Father,* p. 722; *Resurrection of,* p. 726; *Revelations by,* p. 728; *Righteousness of,* p. 728; *Saviour,* p. 728; *Second Coming of,* p. 734; *Shepherd,* p. 737; *Son of God,* p. 737; *Son of Man,* p. 741; *Sovereignty of,* p. 741; *Sufferings of,* p. 741; *Prophecies Concerning,* p. 742; *Sympathy of,* p. 743; *Teacher,* p. 743; *Temptation of,* p. 744; *Unchangeable,* p. 744; *Union of, with the Righteous,* p. 744; *Worship of,* p. 744; *Zeal of,* p. 745.

HISTORY OF: Genealogy of, Matt. 1:1–17; Luke 3:23–38.

Facts before the birth of: The angel Gabriel appears to Mary [Nazareth], Luke 1:26–38. Mary visits Elisabeth [Hebron?], Luke 1:39–56. Mary's *magnificat* [Hebron?], Luke 1:46–55. An angel appears to Joseph concerning Mary, Matt. 1:18–25.

Birth of [Bethlehem], Luke 2:1–7.

Angels appear to the shepherds, Luke 2: 8–20.

Magi visit [Bethlehem], Matt. 2:1–12.

Circumcision of [Bethlehem], Luke 2:21. Is presented in the temple [Jerusalem], Luke 2:21–38.

Flight into, and return from, Egypt, Matt. 2:13–23.

Disputes with the doctors in the temple [Jerusalem], Luke 2:41–52.

Is baptized by John [Jordan], Matt. 3:13–17; Mark 1:9–11; Luke 3:21–23.

Temptation of [Desert of Judæa], Matt. 4: 1–11; Mark 1:12,13; Luke 4:1–13.

John's testimony concerning him, John 1:1–18.

Testimony of John the Baptist concerning [Bethabara], John 1:19–34.

Disciples adhere to, John 1:35–51.

Miracle at Cana of Galilee, John 2:1–12.

Drives the money changers from the temple [Jerusalem], John 2:13-25. Nicodemus comes to [Jerusalem], John 3:1-21.

Baptizes[Ænon], John 3:22, with chapter 4:2.

Returns to Galilee, Matt. 4:12; Mark 1:14; Luke 4:14; John 4:1-3.

Visits Sychar, and teaches the Samaritan woman, John 4:4-42.

Teaches in Galilee, Matt. 4:17; Mark 1:14, 15; Luke 4:14,15; John 4:43-45.

Heals a nobleman's son of Capernaum [Cana of Galilee], John 4:46-54.

Is rejected by the people of Nazareth, dwells at Capernaum, Matt. 4:13-16; Luke 4:16-31.

Chooses Peter, Andrew, James, and John as disciples, miracle of the draught of fishes [Capernaum], Matt. 4:18-22; Mark 1:16-20; Luke 5:1-11.

Preaches throughout Galilee, Matt. 4.23-25; Mark 1:35-39; Luke 4:42-44.

Heals a demoniac [Capernaum], Mark 1:21-28; Luke 4:31-37.

Heals Peter's mother-in-law [Capernaum], Matt. 8:14-17; Mark 1:29-34; Luke 4:38-41.

Heals a leper in Galilee, Matt. 8:2-4; Mark 1:40-45; Luke 5:12-16.

Heals a paralytic [Capernaum], Matt. 9:2-8; Mark 2:1-12; Luke 5:17-26.

Calls Matthew [Capernaum], Matt. 9:9; Mark 2:13,14; Luke 5:27,28.

Heals an impotent man at the pool of Bethesda on the Sabbath day, is persecuted, and makes his defense, John 5.

Defines the law of the Sabbath on the occasion of his disciples plucking the ears of corn [Capernaum], Matt. 12:1-8; Mark 2:23-28; Luke 6:1-5.

Heals a man having a withered hand [Capernaum], Matt. 12:9-14; Mark 3:1-6; Luke 6:6-11.

Withdraws from Capernaum to the Sea of Galilee, where he heals many, Matt. 12:15-21; Mark 3:7-12.

Goes up into a mountain, and calls and ordains twelve disciples [Galilee], Matt. 10:2-4; Mark 3:13-19; Luke 6:12-19.

Delivers the "Sermon on the Mount" [Galilee], Matt. 5; 6; 7; Luke 6:20-49.

Heals the servant of the centurion [near Capernaum], Matt. 8:5-13; Luke 7:1-10.

Raises from the dead the son of the widow of Nain, Luke 7:11-17.

Receives the message from John the Baptist [Galilee], Matt. 11:2-19; Luke 7:18-35.

Upbraids the unbelieving cities about Capernaum, Matt. 11:20-30.

Anointed by a sinful woman [Capernaum], Luke 7:36-50.

Preaches in the cities of Galilee, Luke 8:1-3.

Heals a demoniac, and denounces the scribes and Pharisees [Galilee], Matt. 12:22-37; Mark 3:19-30; Luke 11:14-26.

Replies to the scribes and Pharisees who seek a sign from him [Galilee], Matt. 12:38-45; Luke 11:16-36.

Denounces the Pharisees and other hypocrites [Galilee], Luke 11:37-54.

Discourses to his disciples [Galilee], Luke 12:1-59.

Parable of the barren fig tree [Galilee], Luke 13:6-9.

Parable of the sower [Sea of Galilee], Matt. 13:1-23; Mark 4:1-25; Luke 8:4-18.

Parable of the tares, and other teachings [Galilee], Matt. 13:24-53; Mark 4:26-34.

Crosses the Sea of Galilee, and stills the tempest, Matt. 8:18-27; Mark 4:35-41; Luke 8:22-25.

Miracle of the swine [Gadara], Matt. 8:28-33; Mark 5:1-21; Luke 8:26-40.

Returns to Capernaum, Matt. 9:1; Mark 5:21; Luke 8:40.

Eats with publicans and sinners, and discourses on fasting [Capernaum], Matt. 9:10-17; Mark 2:15-22; Luke 5:29-39.

Raises to life the daughter of Jairus, and heals the woman who has the issue of blood [Capernaum], Matt. 9:18-26; Mark 5:22-43 Luke 8:41-56.

Heals two blind men, and casts out a dumb spirit [Capernaum], Matt. 9:27-34.

Returns to Nazareth, Matt. 13:53-58; Mark 6:1-6.

Teaches in various cities in Galilee, Matt. 9:35-38.

Instructs his disciples, and empowers them to heal diseases and cast out unclean spirits, Matt. 10; Mark 6:6-13; Luke 9:1-6.

Herod falsely supposes him to be John, whom he had beheaded, Matt. 14:1,2,6-12; Mark 6:14-16,21-29; Luke 9:7-9.

The twelve return; he goes to the desert: multitudes follow him; he feeds five thousand [Sea of Galilee], Matt. 14:13-21; Mark 6:30-44; Luke 9:10-17; John 6:1-14.

Walks on the sea [Galilee], Matt. 14:22-36; Mark 6:45-56; John 6:15-21.

Teaches in the synagogue in Capernaum, John 6:22-65.

Disciples forsake him [Capernaum], John 6:66-71.

He justifies his disciples in eating without washing their hands [Capernaum], Matt. 15:1-20; Mark 7:1-23.

Heals the daughter of the Syro-phenician woman [Tyre and Sidon], Matt. 15:21-28; Mark 7:24-30.

Heals a dumb man [Decapolis], Matt. 15:29-31; Mark 7:31-37.

Feeds four thousand, Matt. 15:32-39; Mark 8:1-9.

Refuses to give a sign to the Pharisees [region of Magdala], Matt. 16:1-4; Mark 8:10-12.

Cautions his disciples against the leaven of hypocrisy [Sea of Galilee], Matt. 16:4-12; Mark 8:13-21.

Heals a blind man [Bethsaida], Mark 8:22-26.

Foretells his death and resurrection [near Cæsarea Philippi], Matt. 16:21-28; Mark 8:31-38; 9:1; Luke 9:21-27.

Is transfigured, Matt. 17:1-13; Mark 9:2-13; Luke 9:28-36.

Heals a demoniac [Cæsarea Philippi], Matt. 17:14-21; Mark 9:14-29; Luke 9:37-43.

Foretells his death and resurrection [Galilee], Matt. 17:22,23; Mark 9:30–32; Luke 9: 13–45.

Miracle of tribute money in the fish's mouth, Matt. 17:24–27.

Reproves the ambition of his disciples [Capernaum], Matt. 18:1–35; Mark 9:33–50; Luke 9:46–50.

Reproves the intolerance of his disciples, Mark 9:38,39; Luke 9:49,50.

Journeys to Jerusalem to attend the Feast of Tabernacles, passing through Samaria, Luke 9:51–62; John 7:2–11.

Commissions the seventy [Samaria], Luke 10:1–16.

Heals ten lepers, Luke 17:11–19.

Teaches in Jerusalem at the Feast of Tabernacles, John 7:14–53; 8.

Answers a lawyer, who tests his wisdom with the question, "What shall I do to inherit eternal life?" by the parable of the good Samaritan [Jerusalem], Luke 10:25–37.

Hears the report of the seventy [Jerusalem], Luke 10:17–24.

Teaches in the house of Mary, Martha, and Lazarus, in Bethany, Luke 10:38–42.

Teaches his disciples to pray, Luke 11:1–13.

Heals a blind man, who, because of his faith in Jesus, was excommunicated, John 9.

Teaches in Jerusalem, John 9:39–41; 10: 1–21.

Teaches in the temple at Jerusalem, at the Feast of Dedication, John 10:22–39.

Goes to Bethabara to escape violence from the rulers [E. of the Jordan], John 10:40–42; 11:3–16.

Returns to Bethany, and raises Lazarus from the dead, John 11:1–46.

Escapes to the city of Ephraim from the conspiracy led by Caiaphas, the high priest [Judæa], John 11:47–54.

Journeys toward Jerusalem to attend the passover; heals many who are diseased, and teaches the people [Peræa], Matt. 19:1,2; Mark 10:1; Luke 13:10–35.

Dines with a Pharisee on the Sabbath [Peræa], Luke 14:1–24.

Teaches the multitude the conditions of discipleship [Peræa], Luke 14:25–35.

Enunciates the parables of the lost sheep, the lost piece of silver, prodigal son, unjust steward [Peræa], Luke 15:1–32; 16:1–13.

Reproves the hypocrisy of the Pharisees [Peræa], Luke 16.

Enunciates the parable of the rich man and Lazarus [Peræa], Luke 16:19–31.

Teaches his disciples concerning offenses, meekness, and humility [Peræa], Luke 17: 1 10.

Teaches the Pharisees concerning the coming of his kingdom [Peræa], Luke 17:20–37.

Enunciates the parables of the unjust judge, and the Pharisee and publican praying in the temple [Peræa], Luke 18:1–14.

Interprets the law concerning marriage and divorce [Peræa], Matt. 19:3–12; Mark 10:2–12.

Blesses little children [Peræa], Matt. 19: 13–15; Mark 10:13–16; Luke 18:15–17.

Receives the rich young ruler, who asks what he shall do to inherit eternal life [Peræa], Matt. 19:16–22; Mark 10:17–22; Luke 18:18–24.

Enunciates the parable of the vineyard [Peræa], Matt. 20:1–16.

Foretells his death and resurrection [Peræa], Matt. 20:17–19; Mark 10:32–34; Luke 18:31–34.

Listens to the mother of James and John in behalf of her sons [Peræa], Matt. 20:20–28; Mark 10:35–45.

Heals two blind men at Jericho, Matt. 20: 29–34; Mark 10:46–50; Luke 18:35–43.

Visits Zacchæus, Luke 19:1–10.

Enunciates the parable of the pounds [Jericho], Luke 19:11–28.

Goes to Bethany six days before the passover, John 12:1–9.

Triumphal entry into Jerusalem, while the people throw palm branches in the way, Matt. 21:1–11; Mark 11:1–11; Luke 19:29–44; John 12:12–19.

Enters the temple, Matt. 21:12; Mark 11: 11; Luke 19:45.

Drives the money changers out of the temple, Matt. 21:12,13; Luke 19:45,46.

Heals the infirm in the temple, Matt. 21:14.

Teaches daily in the temple, Luke 19:47,48.

Performs the miracle of causing the barren fig tree to wither, Matt. 21:17–22; Mark 11:12–14,20–22.

Enunciates the parable of the two sons, Matt. 21:28–31; the parable of the wicked husbandmen, Matt. 21:33–46; Mark 12:1–12; Luke 20:9–19; of the marriage, Matt. 22:1–14; Luke 14:16–24.

Tested by the Pharisees and Herodians, and enunciates the duty of the citizen to his government, Matt. 22:15–22; Mark 12:13–17; Luke 20:20–26.

Tried by the Sadducees concerning the resurrection of the dead, Matt. 22:23–33; Mark 12:18–27; Luke 20:27–40; and by a lawyer, Matt. 22:34–40; Mark 12:28–34.

Exposes the hypocrisies of the scribes and Pharisees, Matt. 23; Mark 12:38–40; Luke 20: 45–47.

Extols the widow who casts two mites into the treasury, Mark 12:41–44; Luke 21: 1–4.

Verifies the prophecy of Isaiah concerning the unbelieving Jews, John 12:37–50.

Foretells the destruction of the temple, and of Jerusalem, Matt. 24; Mark 13; Luke 21:5–36.

Laments over Jerusalem, Matt. 23:37; Luke 19:41–44.

Enunciates the parables of the ten virgins and of the talents, Matt. 25:1–30.

Foretells the scenes of the day of judgment [Mount of Olives], Matt. 25:31–46.

Anointed with the box of precious ointment [Bethany], Matt. 26:6–13; Mark 14:3–9; John 12:1–8.

Last passover, and institution of the sacrament of the holy eucharist, Matt. 26:17-30; Mark 14:12-25; Luke 22:7-20.

Washes the disciples' feet, John 13:1-17.

Foretells his betrayal, Matt. 26:23; Mark 14:18-21; Luke 22:21; John 13:18.

Accuses Judas of his betrayal, Matt. 26:21-25; Mark 14:18-21; Luke 22:21-23; John 13:21-30.

Teaches his disciples, and comforts them with promises, and promises the gift of the Holy Spirit, John 14; 15; 16.

Last prayer [Jerusalem], John 17.

Repairs to Gethsemane [Mount of Olives], Matt. 26:30,36-46; Mark 14:26,32-42; Luke 22:39-46; John 18:1.

Is betrayed and apprehended [Gethsemane], Matt. 26:47-56; Mark 14:43-54,66-72; Luke 22:47-53; John 18:2-12.

Trial of, before Caiaphas [Jerusalem], Matt. 26:57,58,69-75; Mark 14:53,54,66-72; Luke 22:54-62; John 18:13-18,25-27.

Tried by the council, Matt. 26:59-68; Mark 14:55-65; Luke 22:63-71; John 18:19-21.

Led by the council to Pilate, Matt. 27:1,2, 11-14; Mark 15:1-5; Luke 23:1-5; John 18: 28-38.

Arraigned before Herod, Luke 23:6-12.

Tried before Pilate, Matt. 27:15-26; Mark 15:6-15; Luke 23:13-25; John 18:39,40; 19:1-16.

Mocked by the soldiers, Matt. 27:27-31; Mark 15:16-20.

Is led away to be crucified, Matt. 27:31-34; Mark 15:20-23; Luke 23:26-32; John 19:16,17.

Crucified, Matt. 27:35-56; Mark 15:24-41; Luke 23:33-49; John 19:18-30.

Taken from the cross and buried, Matt. 27:57-66; Mark 15:42-47; Luke 23:50-56; John 19:31-42.

Arises from the dead, Matt. 28:2-15; Mark 16:1-11; Luke 24:1-12; John 20:1-18.

Is seen by Mary Magdalene, Matt. 28:1-10; Mark 16:9; John 20:11-17; by Peter, Luke 24:34; 1 Cor. 15:5.

Appears to two disciples who journey to Emmaus, Mark 16:12,13; Luke 24:13-35.

Appears in the midst of the disciples, when Thomas is absent [Jerusalem], Mark 16:14-18; Luke 24:36-49; John 20:19-23; when Thomas was present [Jerusalem], John 20: 26-29; at the Sea of Galilee, Matt. 28:16; John 21:1-14; to the apostles and upwards of five hundred brethren on a mountain in Galilee, Matt. 28:16-20, with Acts 10:40-42. See also Acts 13:31; 1 Cor. 15:6,7.

Appears to James, and also to all the apostles [Jerusalem], Acts 1:3-8; 1 Cor. 15:7.

Ascends to heaven [Bethany], Mark 16: 19,20; Luke 24:50-53; Acts 1:9-12.

Appears to Paul, Acts 9:3-17; 18:9; 22:14, 18; 23:11; 26:16; 1 Cor. 9:1; 15:8.

Stephen's vision of, Acts 7:55,56.

Appears to John on Patmos, Rev. 1:10-18.

MISCELLANEOUS FACTS CONCERNING: Brethren of, Matt. 13:55; Mark 6:3; 1 Cor. 9: 5; Gal. 1:19. Sisters of, Matt. 13:56; Mark 6:3. Was with the Israelites in the wilderness, 1 Cor. 10:4,9; Heb. 11:26; Jude 5.

UNCLASSIFIED SCRIPTURES RELAT-

ING TO: John 6:35. And Jesus said unto them, I am the bread of life: he that cometh to me shall never hunger; and he that believeth on me shall never thirst. 41. The Jews then murmured at him, because he said, I am the bread which came down from heaven. 48. I am that bread of life. 50. This is the bread which cometh down from heaven, that a man may eat thereof, and not die. 51. I am the living bread which came down from heaven: if any man eat of this bread, he shall live for ever: and the bread that I will give is my flesh, which I will give for the life of the world. 53. Then Jesus said unto them, Verily, verily, I say unto you, Except ye eat the flesh of the Son of man, and drink his blood, ye have no life in you. 54. Whoso eateth my flesh, and drinketh my blood, hath eternal life; and I will raise him up at the last day. 55. For my flesh is meat indeed, and my blood is drink indeed. 56. He that eateth my flesh, and drinketh my blood, dwelleth in me, and I in him. 57. As the living Father hath sent me, and I live by the Father: so he that eateth me, even he shall live by me. 58. This is that bread which came down from heaven: . . . he that eateth of this bread shall live for ever.

John 8:12. Then spake Jesus again unto them, saying, I am the light of the world: he that followeth me shall not walk in darkness, but shall have the light of life.

John 10:9. I am the door: by me if any man enter in, he shall be saved, and shall go in and out, and find pasture. 10. The thief cometh not, but for to steal, and to kill, and to destroy: I am come that they might have life, and that they might have it more abundantly. 11. I am the good shepherd: the good shepherd giveth his life for the sheep. v. 14.

John 11:25. Jesus said unto her, I am the resurrection, and the life: he that believeth in me, though he [1] were dead, yet shall he live: [1 R. V. die]

John 14:6. Jesus saith unto him, I am the way, the truth, and the life: no man cometh unto the Father, but by me.

John 15:1. I am the true vine, and my Father is the husbandman. 5. I am the vine, ye are the branches: He that abideth in me, and I in him, the same bringeth forth much fruit: for without me ye can do nothing. 6. If a man abide not in me. he is cast forth as a branch, and is withered; and men gather them, and cast them into the fire, and they are burned. 7. If ye abide in me, and my words abide in you, ye shall ask what ye will, and it shall be done unto you.

Col. 3:4. When Christ, who is our life, shall appear, then shall ye also appear with him in glory.

2 Tim. 1:10. But is now made manifest by the appearing of our Saviour Jesus Christ, who hath abolished death, and hath brought life and [1] immortality to light through the gospel: [1 R. V. incorruption]

Rev. 1:18. *I am* he that liveth, and was dead; and, behold, I am alive for evermore, Amen; and have the keys of hell and of death.

Rev. 22:13. I am Alpha and Omega, the beginning and the end, the first and the last. Chapters 1–17.

ASCENSION OF: Psa. 47:5. God is gone up with a shout, the Lord with the sound of a trumpet.

Psa. 68:18. Thou hast ascended on high, thou hast led captivity captive: Eph. 4:8.

Mark 16:19. After the Lord had spoken unto them, he was received up into heaven, and sat on the right hand of God.

Luke 24:26. Ought not Christ to have suffered these things, and to enter into his glory? 50. He led them out as far as to Bethany, and he lifted up his hands, and blessed them, 51. And it came to pass, while he blessed them, he was parted from them, and carried up into heaven.

John 1:51. And he saith unto him, Verily, verily, I say unto you, Hereafter ye shall see heaven open, and the angels of God ascending and descending upon the Son of man.

John 6:62. *What* and if ye shall see the Son of man ascend up where he was before?

John 7:33. Then said Jesus unto them, Yet a little while am I with you, and *then* I go unto him that sent me. 34. Ye shall seek me, and shall not find *me:* and where I am, *thither* ye cannot come. 39. (But this spake he of the Spirit, which they that believed on him should receive: for the Holy Ghost was not yet *given;* because that Jesus was not yet glorified.)

John 14:2. I go to prepare a place for you. 3. And if I go and prepare a place for you, I will come again, and receive you unto myself; that where I am, *there* ye may be also. 4. And whither I go ye know, and the way ye know.

12. I go unto my Father. 28. Ye have heard how I said unto you, I go away, and come *again* unto you. If ye loved me, ye would rejoice, because I said, I go unto the Father: for my Father is greater than I.

John 16:5. Now I go my way to him that sent me; 7. It is expedient for you that I go away: for if I go not away, the Comforter will not come unto you; but if I depart, I will send him unto you. 10. I go to my Father, and ye see me no more; 16. A little while, and ye shall not see me: and again, a little while, and ye shall see me, [1]because I go to the Father. 25. The time cometh, when I shall no more speak unto you in proverbs, but I shall shew you plainly of the Father. 28. I came forth from the Father, and am come into the world: again, I leave the world, and go to the Father. [¹ Omitted in R. V.]

John 17:5. And now, O Father, glorify thou me with thine own self with the glory which I had with thee before the world was. 13. And now come I to thee; and these things I speak in the world, that they might have **my** joy fulfilled in themselves.

John 20:17. Touch me not; for I am **not** yet ascended to my Father:

Acts 1:9. When he had spoken these things, while they beheld, he was taken up; and **a** cloud received him out of their sight.

Acts 3:21. Whom the heaven must receive until the times of restitution of all things,

Eph. 1:20. Which he wrought in Christ, when he raised him from the dead, and set *him* at his own right hand in the heavenly *places,*

Eph. 4:8. Wherefore he saith, When he ascended up on high, he led captivity captive, and gave gifts unto men. 9. (Now that he ascended, what is it but that he also descended first into the lower parts of the earth? 10. He that descended is the same also that ascended up far above all heavens, that he might fill all things.)

1 Tim. 3:16. [1]God was manifest in the flesh, justified in the Spirit, seen of angels, preached unto the Gentiles, believed on in the world, received up into glory.   [¹ R. V. He who]

Heb. 1:3. When he had by himself purged our sins, sat down on the right hand of the Majesty on high;

Heb. 4:14. We have a great high priest, that is passed into the heavens, Jesus the Son of God,

Heb. 9:24. For Christ is not entered into the holy places made with hands, *which are* the figures of the true; but into heaven itself, now to appear in the presence of God for us:

See Exaltation of.

ATONEMENT BY: See Atonement.

ATTRIBUTES OF: See each one in its alphabetical order, below.

BIRTH OF: See Incarnation of.

COMPASSION OF: Isa. 40:11. He shall feed his flock like a shepherd: he shall gather the lambs with his arm, and carry *them* in his bosom, *and* shall gently lead those that are with young.

Isa. 42:3. A bruised reed shall he not break, and the smoking flax shall he not quench:

Isa. 63:9. In all their affliction he was afflicted, and the angel of his presence saved them: in his love and in his pity he redeemed them; and he bare them, and carried them all the days of old. *vs.* 7, 8.

Matt. 8:3. And Jesus put forth *his* hand, and touched him, saying, I will; be thou clean. And immediately his leprosy was cleansed. 16. When the even was come, they brought unto him many that were possessed with devils: and he cast out the spirits with *his* word, and healed all that were sick: 17. That it might be fulfilled which was spoken by Esaias the prophet, saying, Himself took our infirmities, and bare *our* sicknesses. Isa. 53:4.

Matt. 9:36. When he saw the multitudes, he was moved with compassion on them, because they fainted, and were scattered abroad, as sheep having no shepherd.

Matt. 14:14. Jesus went forth, and saw a great multitude, and was moved with compassion toward them, and he healed their sick.

Matt. 15:32. I have compassion on the multitude, because they continue with me now three days, and have nothing to eat: and I will not send them away fasting, lest they faint in the way.

Matt. 18:11. ¹ For the Son of man is come to save that which was lost. 12. How think ye? if a man have an hundred sheep, and one of them be gone astray, doth he not leave the ninety and nine, and goeth into the mountains, and seeketh that which is gone astray? 13. And if so be that he find it, verily I say unto you, he rejoiceth more of that *sheep*, than of the ninety and nine which went not astray. [¹ Omitted in R. V.]

Matt. 20:34. So Jesus had compassion *on them*, and touched their eyes: and immediately their eyes received sight, and they followed him.

Matt. 23:37. O Jerusalem, Jerusalem, *thou* that killest the prophets, and stonest them which are sent unto thee, how often would I have gathered thy children together, even as a hen gathereth her chickens under *her* wings, and ye would not!

Mark 6:34. And Jesus, when he came out, saw much people, and was moved with compassion toward them, because they were as sheep not having a shepherd: and he began to teach them many things.

Mark 8:2. I have compassion on the multitude, because they have now been with me three days, and have nothing to eat: 3. And if I send them away fasting to their own houses, they will faint by the way; for divers of them came from far.

Luke 7:13. When the Lord saw her, he had compassion on her, and said unto her, Weep not.

Luke 19:41. And when he was come near, he beheld the city, and wept over it, 42. Saying, If thou hadst known, even thou, at least in this thy day, the things *which belong* unto thy peace! but now they are hid from thine eyes.

John 11:34. And said, Where have ye laid him? They said unto him, Lord, come and see. 35. Jesus wept. 36. Then said the Jews, Behold how he loved him! 37. And some of them said, Could not this man, which opened the eyes of the blind, have caused that even this man should not have died? 38. Jesus therefore again groaning in himself cometh to the grave. It was a cave, and a stone lay upon it.

John 18:8. If therefore ye seek me, let these go their way: 9. That the saying might be fulfilled, which he spake, Of them which thou gavest me have I lost none.

2 Cor. 8:9. Ye know the grace of our Lord Jesus Christ, that, though he was rich, yet for your sakes he became poor, that ye through his poverty might be rich.

Heb. 4:15. We have not an high priest which cannot be touched with the feeling of our infirmities; but was in all points tempted like as *we are, yet* without sin.

See LOVE OF, below.

CONFESSING : See CONFESSION OF CHRIST; TESTIMONY, RELIGIOUS.

CREATOR : John 1:3. All things were made by him; and without him was not any thing made that was made. 10. He was in the world, and the world was made by him,

1 Cor. 8:6. *There is but* one God, the Father, of whom *are* all things, and we in him; and one Lord Jesus Christ, by whom *are* all things, and we by him.

Eph. 3:9. The fellowship of the mystery, which from the beginning of the world hath been hid in God, who created all things ¹ by Jesus Christ : [¹ Omitted in R. V.]

Col. 1:16. By him were all things created, that are in heaven, and that are in earth, visible and invisible, whether *they be* thrones, or dominions, or principalities, or powers: all things were created by him, and for him: 17. And he is before all things, and by him all things consist.

Heb. 1:2. Hath in these last days spoken unto us by *his* Son, whom he hath appointed heir of all things, by whom also he made the worlds; 10. And, Thou, Lord, in the beginning hast laid the foundation of the earth: and the heavens are the works of thine hands:

Rev. 3:14. And unto the angel of the church of the Laodiceans write; These things saith the Amen, the faithful and true witness, the beginning of the creation of God;

See PREEXISTENCE OF, below.

DEATH OF : Gen. 3:15. And I will put enmity between thee and the woman, and between thy seed and her seed; it shall bruise thy head, and thou shalt bruise his heel. Heb. 2:14.

Psa. 22:1. My God, my God, why hast thou forsaken me? *why art thou so* far from helping me, *and from* the words of my roaring? [Matt. 27:46.] 13. They gaped upon me *with* their mouths, *as* a ravening and a roaring lion. 16. They pierced my hands and my feet. 18. They part my garments among them, and cast lots upon my vesture. Luke 23:34; John 19:23, 24.

Psa. 34:20. He keepeth all his bones: not one of them is broken. John 19:36.

Psa. 69:21. They gave me also gall for my meat; and in my thirst they gave me vinegar to drink. [John 19:28-30; Matt. 27:34; Mark 15:23.] 26. They persecute *him* whom thou hast smitten; and they talk to the grief of those whom thou hast wounded. Matt. 27:34; Mark 15:23; John 19:29.

Psa. 109:25. I became also a reproach unto them: *when* they looked upon me they shaked their heads. Matt. 27:39.

Isa. 52:14. As many were astonied at thee; his visage was so marred more than any man, and his form more than the sons of men:

Isa. 53:7. He was oppressed, and he was afflicted, yet he opened not his mouth: he is brought as a lamb to the slaughter, and as a sheep before her shearers is dumb, so he openeth not his mouth. 8. He was taken from prison and from judgment: and who shall declare his generation? for he was cut off out of the land of the living: for the transgression of my people was he stricken. 9. And he made his grave with the wicked, and with the rich in his death; because he had done no violence, neither *was any* deceit in his mouth. 10. Yet it pleased the LORD to bruise him; he hath put *him* to grief: when thou shalt make his soul an offering for sin, he shall see *his* seed, he shall prolong *his* days, and the pleasure of the LORD shall prosper in his hand. 11. He shall see of the travail of his soul, *and* shall be satisfied: by his knowledge shall my righteous servant justify many; for he shall bear their iniquities. 12. Therefore will I divide him *a portion* with the great, and he shall divide the spoil with the strong; because he hath poured out his soul unto death: and he was numbered with the transgressors; and he bare the sin of many, and made intercession for the transgressors.

Dan. 9:26. And after threescore and two weeks shall Messiah be cut off, but not for himself: and the people of the prince that shall come shall destroy the city and the sanctuary; and the end thereof *shall be* with a flood, and unto the end of the war desolations are determined.

Zech. 12:9. It shall come to pass in that day, *that* I will seek to destroy all the nations that come against Jerusalem. 10. And I will pour upon the house of David, and upon the inhabitants of Jerusalem, the spirit of grace and of supplications: and they shall look upon me whom they have pierced, and they shall mourn for him, as one mourneth for *his* only *son*, and shall be in bitterness for him, as one that is in bitterness for *his* firstborn.

Zech. 13:6. *One* shall say unto him, What *are* these wounds ¹ in thine hands? Then he shall answer, *Those* with which I was wounded *in* the house of my friends. 7. Awake, O sword, against my shepherd, and against the man *that is* my fellow, saith the LORD of hosts: smite the shepherd, and the sheep shall be scattered. [¹ R.V. between thine arms]

Matt. 12:40. As Jonas was three days and three nights in the whale's belly: so shall the Son of man be three days and three nights in the heart of the earth. Luke 11:30.

Matt. 16:4. A wicked and adulterous generation seeketh after a sign; and there shall no sign be given unto it, but the sign of the prophet Jonas. 21. From that time forth began Jesus to shew unto his disciples, how that he must go unto Jerusalem, and suffer many things of the elders and chief priests and scribes, and be killed, and be raised again the third day. Luke 9:22.

Matt. 17:12. But I say unto you, That Elias is come already, and they knew him not, but have done unto him whatsoever they listed. Likewise shall also the Son of man

suffer of them. 13. Then the disciples understood that he spake unto them of John the Baptist. 22. And while they abode in Galilee, Jesus said unto them, The Son of man shall be betrayed into the hands of men: 23. And they shall kill him, and the third day he shall be raised again. And they were exceeding sorry.

Matt. 20:17. And Jesus going up to Jerusalem took the twelve disciples apart in the way, and said unto them, 18. Behold, we go up to Jerusalem; and the Son of man shall be betrayed unto the chief priests and unto the scribes, and they shall condemn him to death, 19. And shall deliver him to the Gentiles to mock, and to scourge, and to crucify *him:* and the third day he shall rise again. Mark 10:32,34.

Matt. 21:33. Hear another parable: There was a certain householder, which planted a vineyard, and hedged it round about, and digged a winepress in it, and built a tower, and let it out to husbandmen, and went into a far country: 34. And when the time of the fruit drew near, he sent his servants to the husbandmen, that they might receive the fruits of it. 35. And the husbandmen took his servants, and beat one, and killed another, and stoned another. 36. Again, he sent other servants more than the first: and they did unto them likewise. 37. But last of all he sent unto them his son, saying, They will reverence my son. 38. But when the husbandmen saw the son, they said among themselves, This is the heir; come, let us kill him, and let us seize on his inheritance. 39. And they caught him, and cast *him* out of the vineyard, and slew *him.*

Matt. 26:2. After two days is *the feast of* the passover, and the Son of man is betrayed to be crucified.

18. And he said, Go into the city to such a man, and say unto him, The Master saith, My time is at hand; I will keep the passover at thy house with my disciples.

Mark 8:31. And he began to teach them, that the Son of man must suffer many things, and be rejected of the elders, and *of* the chief priests, and scribes, and be killed, and after three days rise again.

Mark 9:31. For he taught his disciples, and said unto them, The Son of man is delivered into the hands of men, and they shall kill him; and after that he is killed, he shall rise the third day.

Mark 10:33. Behold, we go up to Jerusalem; and the Son of man shall be delivered unto the chief priests, and unto the scribes; and they shall condemn him to death, and shall deliver him to the Gentiles: 34. And they shall mock him, and shall scourge him, and shall spit upon him, and shall kill him: and the third day he shall rise again. Matt. 20:18,19; Luke 18:31-33.

Luke 2:34. Behold, this *child* is set for the fall and rising again of many in Israel; and for a sign which shall be spoken against; 35. (Yea, a sword shall pierce through thy own soul also,) that the thoughts of many hearts may be revealed.

Luke 9:22. Saying, The Son of man must suffer many things, and be rejected of the elders and chief priests and scribes, and be slain, and be raised the third day. 44. Let these sayings sink down into your ears: for the Son of man shall be delivered into the hands of men.

Luke 12:50. I have a baptism to be baptized with; and how am I straitened till it be accomplished!

Luke 17:25. First must he suffer many things, and be rejected of this generation.

Luke 22:15. With desire I have desired to eat this passover with you before I suffer: 37. This that is written must yet be accomplished in me, And he was reckoned among the transgressors: for the things concerning me have an end.

John 10:11. I am the good shepherd: the good shepherd giveth his life for the sheep. 15. I lay down my life for the sheep. 17. Therefore doth my Father love me, because I lay down my life, that I might take it again. 18. No man taketh it from me, but I lay it down of myself. I have power to lay it down, and I have power to take it again.

John 12:7. Let her alone: against the day of my burying hath she kept this. 32. I, if I be lifted up from the earth, will draw all *men* unto me. 33. This he said, signifying what death he should die. Matt. 26:12; Mark 14:9.

34. The people answered him, We have heard out of the law that Christ abideth for ever: and how sayest thou, The Son of man must be lifted up? who is this Son of man?

John 13:18. He that eateth bread with me hath lifted up his heel against me. 19. Now I tell you before it come, that, when it is come to pass, ye may believe that I am *he.* 21. Verily, verily, I say unto you, that one of you shall betray me. Matt. 26:21; Mark 14:18; Luke 22:21.

John 14:19. Yet a little while, and the world seeth me no more;

John 15:13. Greater love hath no man than this, that a man lay down his life for his friends.

John 16:20. Ye shall weep and lament, but the world shall rejoice: and ye shall be sorrowful, but your sorrow shall be turned into joy.

John 18:11. The cup which my Father hath given me, shall I not drink it?

Acts 26:22. Having therefore obtained help of God, I continue unto this day, witnessing both to small and great, saying none other things than those which the prophets and Moses did say should come: 23. That Christ should suffer, *and* that he should be the first that should rise from the dead, and should shew light unto the people, and to the Gentiles.

1 Cor. 1:17. For Christ sent me not to baptize, but to preach the gospel: not with wisdom of words, lest the cross of Christ should be made of none effect. 18. For the preaching of the cross is to them that perish, foolishness; but unto us which are saved, it is the power of God. 23. But we preach Christ crucified, unto the Jews a stumblingblock, and unto the Greeks foolishness; 24. But unto them which are called, both Jews and Greeks, Christ the power of God, and the wisdom of God.

1 Cor. 2:2. For I determined not to know anything among you, save Jesus Christ, and him crucified.

1 Cor. 15:3. For I delivered unto you first of all that which I also received, how that Christ died for our sins according to the scriptures; 4. And that he was buried, and that he rose again the third day according to the scriptures:

2 Cor. 4:10. Always bearing about in the body the dying of the Lord Jesus, that the life also of Jesus might be made manifest in our body. 11. For we which live are alway delivered unto death for Jesus' sake, that the life also of Jesus might be made manifest in our mortal flesh.

1 Thess. 4:14. For if we believe that Jesus died and rose again, even so them also which sleep in Jesus will God bring with him.

Rev. 5:12. Saying with a loud voice, Worthy is the Lamb that was slain to receive power, and riches, and wisdom, and strength, and honour, and glory, and blessing.

Rev. 13:8. And all that dwell upon the earth shall worship him, whose names are not written in the book of life of the Lamb slain from the foundation of the world.

For circumstances of the death of, see HISTORY OF, above.

DESIGN OF HIS DEATH: Gen: 3:15. I will put enmity between thee and the woman, and between thy seed and her seed; it shall bruise thy head, and thou shalt bruise his heel.

Isa. 53:4. Surely he hath borne our griefs, and carried our sorrows: yet we did esteem him stricken, smitten of God, and afflicted. 5. But he *was* wounded for our transgressions, *he was* bruised for our iniquities: the chastisement of our peace *was* upon him; and with his stripes we are healed. 6. All we like sheep have gone astray; we have turned every one to his own way; and the LORD hath laid on him the iniquity of us all. 8. He was cut off out of the land of the living: for the transgression of my people was he stricken. 10. It pleased the LORD to bruise him; he hath put *him* to grief: when thou shalt make his soul an offering for sin, he shall see *his* seed, he shall prolong *his* days, and the pleasure of the LORD shall prosper in his hand. 11. He shall see of the travail of his soul, *and* shall be satisfied: by his knowledge shall my righteous servant justify many; for he shall bear their iniquities. 12. Therefore will I divide him *a portion* with the great, and he shall divide the spoil with the strong; because he hath poured out his soul unto death: and he was numbered with the transgressors; and he bare the sin of many, and made intercession for the transgressors. *vs.* 1–12.

Dan. 9:24. Seventy weeks are determined upon thy people and upon thy holy city, to finish the transgression, and to make an end of sins, and to make reconciliation for iniquity, and to bring in everlasting righteousness, and to seal up the vision and prophecy, and to anoint the most Holy. 26. After three score and two weeks shall Messiah be cut off, but not for himself:

Zech. 9:11. By the blood of thy covenant I have sent forth thy prisoners out of the pit wherein *is* no water.

Zech. 13:1. There shall be a fountain opened to the house of David and to the inhabitants of Jerusalem for sin and for uncleanness.

Matt. 20:28. The Son of man came not to be ministered unto, but to minister, and to give his life a ransom for many. Mark 10:45.

Matt. 26:28. This is my blood of the new testament, which is shed for many for the remission of sins. Mark 14:24.

Luke 22:19. He took bread, and gave thanks, and brake *it*, and gave unto them, saying, This is my body which is given for you: this do in remembrance of me. 20. Likewise also the cup after supper, saying, This cup *is* the new [1] testament in my blood which is shed for you.	[1 R. V. covenant]

Luke 24:26. Ought not Christ to have suffered these things, and to enter into his glory?

John 1:29. Behold the Lamb of God, which taketh away the sin of the world.

John 3:14. As Moses lifted up the serpent in the wilderness, even so must the Son of man be lifted up: 15. That whosoever believeth in him should not perish, but have eternal life. 16. For God so loved the world, that he gave his only begotten Son, that whosoever believeth in him should not perish, but have everlasting life. 17. For God sent not his Son into the world to condemn the world; but that the world through him might be saved.

John 6:51. I am the living bread which came down from heaven: if any man eat of this bread, he shall live for ever: and the bread that I will give is my flesh, which I will give for the life of the world.

John 10:11. I am the good shepherd: the good shepherd giveth his life for the sheep. 15. I lay down my life for the sheep. 17. Therefore doth my Father love me, because I lay down my life, that I might take it again.

John 11:49. Ye know nothing at all, 50. Nor consider that it is expedient for us, that one man should die for the people, and that the whole nation perish not. 51. And this spake he not of himself: but being high priest that year, he prophesied that Jesus should die for that nation; 52. And not for that nation only, but that also he should gather together in one the children of God that were scattered abroad.

John 12:24. Except a corn of wheat fall into the ground and die, it abideth alone; but if it die, it bringeth forth much fruit. 31. Now is the judgment of this world: now shall the prince of this world be cast out. 32. And I, if I be lifted up from the earth, will draw all *men* unto me. 33. This he said, signifying what death he should die.

John 14:19. Yet a little while, and the world seeth me no more; but ye see me: because I live, ye shall live also.

John 15:13. Greater love hath no man than this, that a man lay down his life for his friends.

Acts 5:30. The God of our fathers raised up Jesus, whom ye slew and hanged on a tree. 31. Him hath God exalted with his right hand *to be* a Prince and a Saviour, for to give repentance to Israel, and forgiveness of sins.

Acts 20:28. The church of God, which he hath purchased with his own blood.

Acts 26:23. That Christ should suffer, *and* that he should be the first that should rise from the dead, and should shew light unto the people, and to the Gentiles.

Rom. 3:24. Justified freely by his grace through the redemption that is in Christ Jesus: 25. Whom God hath set forth *to be* a propitiation through faith in his blood, to declare his righteousness for the remission of sins that are past, through the forbearance of God;

Rom. 4:25. Who was delivered for our offences, and was raised again for our justification.

Rom. 5:6. When we were yet without strength, in due time Christ died for the ungodly. 7. Scarcely for a righteous man will one die: yet peradventure for a good man some would even dare to die. 8. But God commendeth his love toward us, in that, while we were yet sinners, Christ died for us. 9. Much more then, being now justified by his blood, we shall be saved from wrath through him. 10. For if, when we were enemies, we were reconciled to God by the death of his Son, much more, being reconciled, we shall be saved by his life. 11. We also joy in God through our Lord Jesus Christ, by whom we have now received the [1] atonement.	[1 R. V. reconciliation]

Rom. 6:3. Know ye not, that so many of us as were baptized into Jesus Christ were baptized into his death? 4. Therefore we are buried with him by baptism into death; that like as Christ was raised up from the dead by the glory of the Father, even so we also should walk in newness of life. 5. For if we have been planted together in the likeness of his death, we shall be also *in the likeness* of *his* resurrection. 9. Christ being raised from the dead dieth no more;

death hath no more dominion over him. 10. For in that he died, he died unto sin once:

Rom. 8:3. God sending his own Son in the likeness of sinful flesh, and for sin, condemned sin in the flesh: 32. He that spared not his own son, but delivered him up 'for us all, how shall he not with him also freely give us all things? 34. Who *is* he that condemneth? *It is* Christ that died, yea rather, that is risen again, who is even at the right hand of God, who also maketh intercession for us. 39. Nor height, nor depth, nor any other creature, shall be able to separate us from the love of God, which is in Christ Jesus our Lord.

Rom. 14:9. To this end Christ both died, and rose, and revived, that he might be Lord both of the dead and living. 15. Destroy not him with thy meat, for whom Christ died.

1 Cor. 5:7. Even Christ our passover is sacrificed for us:

1 Cor. 6:20. Ye are bought with a price: therefore glorify God in your body, and in your spirit, which are God's.

1 Cor. 8:11. Through thy knowledge shall the weak brother perish, for whom Christ died?

1 Cor. 15:3. Christ died for our sins according to the scriptures:

2 Cor. 5:14. The love of Christ constraineth us; because we thus judge, that if one died for all, 1 then were all dead: 15. And *that* he died for all, that they which live should not henceforth live unto themselves, but unto him which died for them, and rose again. 19. God was in Christ, reconciling the world unto himself, not imputing their trespasses unto them; and hath committed unto us the word of reconciliation. 21. He hath made him *to be* sin for us, who knew no sin; that we might be made the righteousness of God in him. [1 R. V. therefore all died;]

2 Cor. 8:9. Ye know the grace of our Lord Jesus Christ, that, though he was rich, yet for your sakes he became poor, that ye through his poverty might be rich.

Gal. 1:4. Who gave himself for our sins, that he might deliver us from this present evil world, according to the will of God and our Father:

Gal. 2:20. I am crucified with Christ: nevertheless I live; yet not I, but Christ liveth in me: and the life which I now live in the flesh I live by the faith of the Son of God, who loved me, and gave himself for me.

Gal. 3:13. Christ hath redeemed us from the curse of the law, being made a curse for us: for it is written, Cursed *is* every one that hangeth on a tree:

Gal. 4:4. When the fulness of the time was come, God sent forth his Son, made of a woman, made under the law, 5. To redeem them that were under the law, that we might receive the adoption of sons.

Eph. 1:6. He hath made us accepted in the beloved. 7. In whom we have redemption through his blood, the forgiveness of sins, according to the riches of his grace;

Eph. 2:13. Now in Christ Jesus ye who sometimes were far off are made nigh by the blood of Christ. 14. He is our peace, who hath made both one, and hath broken down the middle wall of partition *between us;* 15. Having abolished in his flesh the enmity, *even* the law of commandments *contained* in ordinances: for to make in himself of twain one new man, *so* making peace; 16. And that he might reconcile both unto God in one body by the cross, having slain the enmity thereby:

Eph. 5:2. Christ also hath loved us, and hath given himself for us an offering and a sacrifice to God for a sweetsmelling savour. 25. Christ also loved the church, and gave himself for it; 26. That he might sanctify and cleanse it with the washing of water by the word, 27. That he might present it to himself a glorious church, not having spot, or wrinkle, or any such thing; but that it should be holy and without blemish.

Col. 1:14. In whom we have redemption through his blood, *even* the forgiveness of sins: 20. Having made peace through the blood of his cross, by him to reconcile all things unto himself; by him, *I say,* whether *they be* things in earth, or things in heaven. 21. And you, that were sometime alienated and enemies in *your* mind by wicked works, yet now hath he reconciled 22. In the body of his flesh through death, to present you holy and unblameable and unreproveable in his sight:

Col. 2:14. Blotting out the handwriting of ordinances that was against us, which was contrary to us, and took it out of the way, nailing it to his cross; 15. *And* having spoiled principalities and powers, he made a show of them openly, triumphing over them in it.

1 Thess. 1:10. Whom he raised from the dead, *even* Jesus, which delivered us from the wrath to come.

1 Thess. 5:9. God hath not appointed us to wrath, but to obtain salvation by our Lord Jesus Christ, 10. Who died for us, that, whether we wake or sleep, we should live together with him.

1 Tim. 2:6. Who gave himself a ransom for all, to be testified in due time.

Tit. 2:14. Who gave himself for us, that he might redeem us from all iniquity, and purify unto himself a peculiar people, zealous of good works.

Heb. 1:3. Who, . . . when he had by himself purged our sins, sat down on the right hand of the Majesty on high;

Heb. 2:9. We see Jesus, who was made a little lower than the angels for the suffering of death, crowned with glory and honour; that he by the grace of God should taste death for every man. 10. To make the captain of their salvation perfect through sufferings. 14. As the children are partakers of flesh and blood, he also himself likewise took part of the same; that through death he might destroy him that had the power of death, that is, the devil; 15. And deliver them who through fear of death were all their lifetime subject to bondage. 18. In that he himself hath suffered being tempted, he is able to succour them that are tempted.

Heb. 7:27. Who needeth not daily, as those high priests, to offer up sacrifice, first for his own sins, and then for the people's: for this he did once, when he offered up himself.

Heb. 9:12. Neither by the blood of goats and calves, but by his own blood he entered in once into the holy place, having obtained eternal redemption *for us.* 13. For if the blood of bulls and of goats, and the ashes of an heifer sprinkling the unclean, sanctifieth to the purifying of the flesh: 14. How much more shall the blood of Christ, who through the eternal Spirit offered himself without spot to God, purge your conscience from dead works to serve the living God? 15. And for this cause he is the mediator of the new testament, that by means of death, for the redemption of the transgressions *that were* under the first testament, they which are called might receive the promise of eternal inheritance. 16. For where a testament *is*, there must also of necessity be the death of the testator. 17. For a testament *is* of force after men are dead: otherwise it is of no strength at all while the testator liveth. 25. Nor yet that he should offer himself often, as the high priest entereth into the holy place every year with the blood of others; 26. For then must he often have suffered since the foundation of the world: but now once in the end of the world hath he appeared to put away sin by the sacrifice of himself. 28. Christ was once offered to bear the sins of many;

Heb. 10:10. We are sanctified through the offering of the body of Jesus Christ once *for all.* 12. This man, after he had offered one sacrifice for sins for ever, sat down on the right hand of God; 14. By one offering he hath perfected for ever them that are sanctified. 17. Their sins and iniquities will I remember no more. 18. Now where remission of these *is, there is* no more offering for sin. 19. Having therefore, brethren, boldness to enter into the holiest by the blood of Jesus, 20. By a new and living way, which he hath consecrated for us, through the vail, that is to say, his flesh;

Heb. 12:2. Looking unto Jesus the author and finisher of *our* faith; who for the joy that was set before him endured the cross, despising the shame, and is set down at the right hand of the throne of God. 24. To Jesus, the mediator of the new covenant, and to the blood of sprinkling, that speaketh better things than *that of* Abel.

Heb. 13:11. The bodies of those beasts, whose blood is brought into the sanctuary by the high priest for sin, are burned without the camp. 12. Wherefore Jesus also,

that he might sanctify the people with his own blood, suffered without the gate.

1 Pet. 1:2. Elect according to the foreknowledge of God the Father, through sanctification of the Spirit, unto obedience and sprinkling of the blood of Jesus Christ: 18. Ye know that ye were not redeemed with corruptible things, *as* silver and gold, from your vain conversation *received* by tradition from your fathers; 19. But with the precious blood of Christ, as of a lamb without blemish and without spot: 20. Who verily was foreordained before the foundation of the world, but was manifest in these last times for you, 21. Who by him do believe in God, that raised him up from the dead, and gave him glory; that your faith and hope might be in God.

1 Pet. 2:21. Christ also suffered for us, leaving us an example, that ye should follow his steps: 24. Who his own self bare our sins in his own body on the tree, that we, being dead to sins, should live unto righteousness: by whose stripes ye were healed.

1 Pet. 3:18. Christ also hath once suffered for sins, the just for the unjust, that he might bring us to God, being put to death in the flesh, but quickened by the Spirit:

1 Pet. 4:1. Forasmuch then as Christ hath suffered for us in the flesh, arm yourselves likewise with the same mind:

1 John 1:7. The blood of Jesus Christ his Son cleanseth us from all sin.

1 John 2:2. He is the propitiation for our sins: and not for our's only, but also for *the sins of* the whole world.

1 John 3:16. Hereby perceive we [1] the love [1] *of God*, because he laid down his life for us:
[¹ Omitted in R. V.]

1 John 4:10. Herein is love, not that we loved God, but that he loved us, and sent his Son *to be* the propitiation for our sins.

Rev. 1:5. Unto him that loved us, and washed us from our sins in his own blood, 6. And hath made us kings and priests unto God and his Father;

Rev. 5:9. Thou wast slain, and hast redeemed us to God by thy blood out of every kindred, and tongue, and people, and nation; 10. And hast made us unto our God kings and priests: and we shall reign on the earth.

Rev. 7:14. These are they which came out of great tribulation, and have washed their robes, and made them white in the blood of the Lamb. 15. Therefore are they before the throne of God,

Rev. 13:8. And all that dwell upon the earth shall worship him, whose names are not written in the book of life of the Lamb slain from the foundation of the world.

See Atonement; Reconciliation; Satan, Kingdom of, to be Destroyed.

DEATH OF, VOLUNTARY: Isa. 50:6. I gave my back to the smiters, and my cheeks to them that plucked off the hair: I hid not my face from shame and spitting.

Isa. 53:12. He . . . poured out his soul unto death: and he was numbered with the transgressors; and he bare the sin of many, and made intercession for the transgressors.

Matt. 26:24. The Son of man goeth as it is written of him: 39. O my Father, if it be possible, let this cup pass from me: nevertheless not as I will, but as thou *wilt.* 42. O my Father, if this cup may not pass away from me, except I drink it, thy will be done. [Mark 14:36,39.] 53. Thinkest thou that I cannot now pray to my Father, and he shall presently give me more than twelve legions of angels? 54. But how then shall the scriptures be fulfilled, that thus it must be?

Luke 9:51. When the time was come that he should be received up, he stedfastly set his face to go to Jerusalem,

Luke 12:50. I have a baptism to be baptized with; and how am I straitened till it be accomplished! Luke 22:15.

Luke 22:42. Father, if thou be willing, remove this cup from me: nevertheless not my will, but thine, be done.

John 10:17. Therefore doth my Father love me, because I lay down my life, that I might take it again. 18. No man taketh it from me, but I lay it down of myself. I have power to lay it down, and I have power to take it again.

John 18:5. They answered him, Jesus of Nazareth. Jesus saith unto them, I am *he.* 8. I have told you that I am *he:* if therefore ye seek me, let these go their way: 11. Put up thy sword into the sheath: the cup which my Father hath given me, shall I not drink it?

John 19:11. Jesus answered, Thou couldest have no power *at all* against me, except it were given thee from above: therefore he that delivered me unto thee hath the greater sin.

Phil. 2:8. Being found in fashion as a man, he humbled himself, and became obedient unto death, even the death of the cross.

Heb. 7:27. Who needeth not daily, as those high priests, to offer up sacrifice, first for his own sins, and then for the people's: for this he did once, when he offered up himself.

Heb. 9:26. For then must he often have suffered since the foundation of the world: but now once in the end of the world hath he appeared to put away sin by the sacrifice of himself.

DENIAL OF: See JESUS, REJECTED.

DIVINITY OF: As Jehovah, Isa. 40:3, with Matt. 3:3; Jehovah of glory, Psa. 24:7,10, with 1 Cor. 2:8; Jas. 2:1; Jehovah our righteousness, Jer. 23:5,6, with 1 Cor. 1:30; Jehovah above all, Psa. 97:9, with John 3:31; Jehovah the first and the last, Isa. 44:6, with Rev. 1:17; Isa. 48:12–16, with Rev. 22:13; Jehovah's fellow and equal, Zech. 13:7; Phil. 2:6; Jehovah of hosts, Isa. 6:1–3, with John 12:41; Isa. 8:13,14, with 1 Pet. 2:8; Jehovah, Psa. 110:1, with Matt. 22:42–45; Jehovah the shepherd, Isa. 40:10,11; Heb. 13:20; Jehovah, for whose glory all things were created, Prov. 16:4, with Col. 1:16; Jehovah the messenger of the covenant, Mal. 3:1,

with Luke 7:27. Invoked as Jehovah, Joel 2:32, with 1 Cor. 1:2; as the eternal God and Creator, Psa. 102:24–27, with Heb. 1:8,10–12; the mighty God, Isa. 9:6; the great God and Saviour, Hos. 1:7, with Tit. 2:13; God over all, Rom. 9:5; God the Judge, Eccl. 12:14, with 1 Cor. 4:5; 2 Cor. 5:10; 2 Tim. 4:1; Emmanuel, Isa. 7:14, with Matt. 1:23; King of kings and Lord of lords, Dan. 10:17, with Rev. 1:5; 17:14; the Holy One, 1 Sam. 2:2, with Acts 3:14; the Lord from heaven, 1 Cor. 15:47; Lord of the sabbath, Gen. 2:3, with Matt. 12:8; Lord of all, Acts 10:36; Rom. 10:11–13; Son of God, Matt. 26:63–67; the only begotten Son of the Father, John 1:14, 18; 3:16,18; 1 John 4:9. His blood is called the blood of God, Acts 20:28. One with the Father, John 10:30,38; 12:45; 14:7–10; 17:10. As sending the Spirit equally with the Father, John 14:16, with John 15:26. As unsearchable equally with the Father, Prov. 30:4; Matt. 11:27. As Creator of all things, Isa. 40:28; John 1:3; Col. 1:16; supporter and preserver of all things, Neh. 9:6, with Col. 1:17; Heb. 1:3. Acknowledged by Old Testament saints, Gen. 17:1, with Gen. 48:15,16; 32:24–30, with Hos. 12:3–5; Judg. 6:22–24; 13:21,22; Job 19:25–27.—*Bible Text-Book.*

UNCLASSIFIED SCRIPTURES RELATING TO THE DIVINITY OF: Ex. 23:20. Behold, I send an Angel before thee, to keep thee in the way, and to bring thee into the place which I have prepared. 21. Beware of him, and obey his voice, provoke him not; for he will not pardon your transgressions: for my name *is* in him.

Psa. 24:10. Who is this King of glory? The LORD of hosts; he *is* the King of glory. 1 Cor. 2:8.

Psa. 45:6. Thy throne, O God, *is* for ever and ever. the sceptre of thy kingdom *is* a right sceptre. 7. Thou lovest righteousness, and hatest wickedness: therefore God, thy God, hath anointed thee with the oil of gladness above thy fellows. Heb. 1:8.

Isa. 6:1. I saw also the Lord sitting upon a throne, high and lifted up, and his train filled the temple. John 12:41.

Isa. 8:13. Sanctify the LORD of hosts himself; and *let* him *be* your fear, and *let* him *be* your dread. 14. And he shall be for a sanctuary; but for a stone of stumbling and for a rock of offence 1 Pet. 2:8.

Isa. 9:6. His name shall be called Wonderful, Counsellor, The mighty God, The everlasting Father, The Prince of Peace. Tit. 2:13.

Isa. 40:3. Prepare ye the way of the LORD, make straight in the desert a highway for our God. 9. Say unto the cities of Judah, Behold your God! 10. Behold, the Lord GOD will come with strong *hand,* and his arm shall rule for him: Matt. 3:3.

Mal. 3:1. The Lord, whom ye seek, shall suddenly come to his temple, even the messenger of the covenant, whom ye delight in: behold, he shall come, saith the LORD of hosts. Matt. 11:10.

Matt. 1:23. Behold, a virgin shall be with child, and shall bring forth a son, and they shall call his name Emmanuel, which being interpreted is, God with us. Isa. 7:14.

Matt. 8:29. And, behold, they cried out, saying, What have we to do with thee, Jesus, thou Son of God? art thou come hither to torment us before the time? Luke 8:28.

Matt. 9:6. But that ye may know that the Son of man hath power on earth to forgive sins, (then saith he to the sick of the palsy,) Arise, take up thy bed, and go unto thine house.

Matt. 22:43. How then doth David in spirit call him Lord, saying, 44. The LORD said unto my Lord, Sit thou on my right hand, till I make thine enemies thy footstool? 45. If David then call him Lord, how is he his son? Psa. 110:1.

Matt. 28:17. And when they saw him, they worshipped him: but some doubted. 18. And Jesus came and spake unto them, saying, All power is given unto me in heaven and in earth.

Mark 5:6. But when he saw Jesus afar off, he ran and worshipped him, 7. And cried with a loud voice, and said, What have I to do with thee, Jesus, *thou* Son of the most high God? I adjure thee by God, that thou torment me not.

Luke 4:12. And Jesus answering said unto him, It is said, Thou shalt not tempt the Lord thy God.

33. And in the synagogue there was a man which had a spirit of an unclean devil, and cried out with a loud voice, 34. Saying, Let *us* alone; what have we to do with thee, *thou* Jesus of Nazareth? art thou come to destroy us? I know thee who thou art; the Holy One of God.

Luke 9:43. And they were all amazed at the mighty power of God. But while they wondered every one at all things which Jesus did, he said unto his disciples, 44. Let these sayings sink down into your ears: for the Son of man shall be delivered into the hands of men.

John 1:1. In the beginning was the Word, and the Word was with God, and the Word was God, 2. The same was in the beginning with God.

John 5:17. Jesus answered them, My Father worketh hitherto, and I work. 18. Therefore the Jews sought the more to kill him, because he not only had broken the sabbath, but said also that God was his Father, making himself equal with God. 21. For as the Father raiseth up the dead, and quickeneth *them;* even so the Son quickeneth whom he will. 22. For the Father judgeth no man, but hath committed all judgment unto the Son: 23. That all *men* should honour the Son, even as they honour the Father. He that honoureth not the Son honoureth not the Father which hath sent him.

John 10:30. I and *my* Father are one. 31. Then the Jews took up stones again to stone him. 32. Jesus answered them, Many good works have I shewed you from **my** Father; for which of those works do **ye** stone me? 33. The Jews answered him, saying, For a good work we stone thee not; but for blasphemy; and because that thou, being a man, makest thyself God.

John 12:45. And he that seeth me seeth him that sent me.

John 20:28. Thomas answered and said unto him, My Lord and my God.

Acts 7:37. This is that Moses, which said unto the children of Israel, A prophet shall the Lord your God raise up unto you of your brethren, like unto me; him shall ye hear. 38. This is he, that was in the church in the wilderness with the angel which spake to him in the mount Sina, and *with* our fathers: who received the lively oracles to give unto us: 39. To whom our fathers would not obey, but thrust *him* from them, and in their hearts turned back again into Egypt,

Acts 20:28. Take heed . . . feed the church of God, which he hath purchased with his own blood.

Rom. 1:7. Grace to you, and peace, from God our Father and the Lord Jesus Christ. 1 Cor. 1:3; 2 Cor. 1:2; Col. 1:2; Phil. 1:2; 1 Thess. 1:1; 2 Thess. 1:1,2; 2 Tim. 1:2.

Rom. 9:5. Of whom as concerning the flesh Christ *came,* who is over all, God blessed for ever.

1 Cor. 8:6. But to us *there is but* one God, the Father, of whom *are* all things, and we in him: and one Lord Jesus Christ, by whom *are* all things, and we by him.

1 Cor. 10:9. Neither let us tempt Christ, as some of them also tempted, and were destroyed of serpents. Num. 21:6.

1 Cor. 15:47. The second man *is* the Lord from heaven.

Gal. 1:1. Paul, an apostle, (not of men, neither by man, but by Jesus Christ, and God the Father, who raised him from the dead ;) 3. Grace *be* to you and peace from God the Father, and *from* our Lord Jesus Christ.

Eph.1:2. Grace *be* to you, and peace, from God our Father, and *from* the Lord Jesus Christ.

Eph. 6:23. Peace *be* to the brethren, and love with faith, from God the Father and the Lord Jesus Christ.

Phil. 2:6. Who, being in the form of God, thought it not [1]robbery to be equal with God: *vs.* 5–11.   [1 R. V. a prize to be on an equality]

1 Thess. 3:11. Now God himself and our Father, and our Lord Jesus Christ, direct our way unto you.

2 Thess. 2:16. Now our Lord Jesus Christ himself, and God, even our Father, which hath loved us, and hath given *us* everlasting consolation and good hope through grace, 17. Comfort your hearts, and stablish you in every good word and work.

1 Tim. 3:16. And without controversy great is the mystery of godliness: [1]God was manifest in the flesh.   [1 R. V. He who]

Tit. 2:13. Looking for . . . the glorious appearing of the great God and our Saviour Jesus Christ;

Heb. 1:8. But unto the Son *he saith*, Thy throne, O God, *is* for ever and ever; a sceptre of righteousness *is* the sceptre of thy kingdom. 10. And, Thou, Lord, in the beginning hast laid the foundation of the earth; and the heavens are the works of thine hands: Psa.102:24–27; *vs.* 1–14, with Gen.1:1.

1 John 5:20. This is the true God and eternal life.

See Jesus, Creator; Judgment; Son of God; Son of Man; Trinity.

ETERNITY OF: Prov. 8:22. The Lord possessed me in the beginning of his way, before his works of old. 23. I was set up from everlasting, from the beginning, or ever the earth was. 24. When *there were* no depths, I was brought forth,; when *there were* no fountains abounding with water. 25. Before the mountains were settled, before the hills was I brought forth:

Isa. 9:6. For unto us a child is born, unto us a son is given: and the government shall be upon his shoulder: and his name shall be called Wonderful, Counsellor, The mighty God, The everlasting Father, The Prince of Peace.

Mic. 5:2. Out of thee shall he come forth unto me *that is* to be ruler in Israel; whose goings forth *have been* from of old, from everlasting.

Mark 12:36. For David himself said by the Holy Ghost, The Lord said to my Lord, Sit thou on my right hand, till I make thine enemies thy footstool. 37. David therefore himself calleth him Lord; and whence is he *then* his son? And the common people heard him gladly.

John 1:1. In the beginning was the Word, and the Word was with God, and the Word was God. 2. The same was in the beginning with God. 4. In him was life; 15. He that cometh after me is preferred before me: for he was before me.

John 6:62. *What* and if ye shall see the Son of man ascend up where he was before?

John 8:23. And he said unto them, Ye are from beneath; I am from above: ye are of this world; I am not of this world. 58. Before Abraham was, I am.

John 12:41. These things said Esaias, when he saw his glory, and spake of him.

John 17:5. And now, O Father, glorify thou me with thine own self with the glory which I had with thee before the world was. 24. Father, I will that they also, whom thou hast given me, be with me where I am; that they may behold my glory, which thou hast given me: for thou lovedst me before the foundation of the world. 25. O righteous Father, the world hath not known thee: but I have known thee, and these have known that thou hast sent me.

Eph. 3:21. Unto him *be* glory in the church by Christ Jesus throughout all ages, world without end.

Eph. 4:10. He that descended is the same also that ascended up far above all heavens, that he might fill all things.

Col. 1:17. He is before all things, and by him all things consist.

2 Tim. 1:9. Who hath saved us, and called *us* with an holy calling, not according to our works, but according to his own purpose and grace, which was given us in Christ Jesus before the world began,

Heb. 1:10. Thou, Lord, in the beginning hast laid the foundation of the earth; and the heavens are the works of thine hands: 11. They shall perish; but thou remainest; and they all shall wax old as doth a garment; 12. And as a vesture shalt thou fold them up, and they shall be changed: but thou art the same, and thy years shall not fail. Psa. 102:24–27.

Heb. 7:16. Made, not after the law of a carnal commandment, but after the power of an endless life. 24. But this *man*, because he continueth ever, hath an unchangeable priesthood. 25. Wherefore he is able also to save them to the uttermost that come unto God by him, seeing he ever liveth to make intercession for them. Heb. 6:20.

Heb. 13:8. Jesus Christ the same yesterday, and to day, and for ever.

1 Pet. 1:20. Who verily was foreordained before the foundation of the world, but was manifest in these last times for you,

1 John 1:1. That which was from the beginning, which we have heard, which we have seen with our eyes, which we have looked upon, and our hands have handled, of the Word of life; 2. (For the life was manifested, and we have seen *it*, and bear witness, and shew unto you that eternal life, which was with the Father, and was manifested unto us;)

1 John 2:13. I write unto you, fathers, because ye have known him *that is* from the beginning. I write unto you, young men, because ye have overcome the wicked one. I write unto you, little children, because ye have known the Father. 14. I have written unto you, fathers, because ye have known him *that is* from the beginning. I have written unto you, young men, because ye are strong, and the word of God abideth in you, and ye have overcome the wicked one.

Rev. 1:8. I am Alpha and Omega, the beginning and the ending, saith the Lord, which is, and which was, and which is to come, the Almighty. 11. [1]I am Alpha and Omega, the first and the last: 17. I am the first and the last: 18. I *am* he that liveth, and was dead; [1 Omitted in R. V.]

Rev. 5:13. And every creature which is in heaven, and on the earth, and under the earth, and such as are in the sea, and all that are in them, heard I saying, Blessing, and honour, and glory, and power, *be* unto him that sitteth upon the throne, and unto the Lamb for ever and ever. 14. And the four beasts said, Amen. And the four *and* twenty elders fell down and worshipped him that liveth for ever and ever.

See Preëxistence of, below.

EXALTATION OF: Psa. 2:8. Ask of me,

and I shall give *thee* the heathen *for* thine inheritance, and the uttermost parts of the earth *for* thy possession. 9. Thou shalt break them with a rod of iron; thou shalt dash them in pieces like a potter's vessel.

Psa. 24:7. Lift up your heads, O ye gates; and be ye lift up, ye everlasting doors; and the King of glory shall come in. *vs.* 8–10.

Psa. 68:18. Thou hast ascended on high, thou hast led captivity captive: Eph. 4:8.

Mark 16:19. After the Lord had spoken unto them, he was received up into heaven, and sat on the right hand of God.

Luke 22:69. Hereafter shall the Son of man sit on the right hand of the power of God.

Luke 24:26. Ought not Christ to have suffered these things, and to enter into his glory?

John 7:39. The Holy Ghost was not yet *given:* because that Jesus was not yet glorified.

John 13:31. Jesus said, Now is the Son of man glorified, and God is glorified in him. 32. If God be glorified in him, God shall also glorify him in himself, and shall straightway glorify him.

John 17:5. Now, O Father, glorify thou me with thine own self with the glory which I had with thee before the world was.

Acts 2:33. Being by the right hand of God exalted, and having received of the Father the promise of the Holy Ghost, he hath shed forth this, which ye now see and hear. 34. For David is not ascended into the heavens: but he saith himself, The LORD said unto my Lord, Sit thou on my right hand,

Acts 3:20. He shall send Jesus Christ, . . . 21. Whom the heaven must receive until the times of restitution of all things.

Acts 5:31. Him hath God exalted with his right hand *to be* a Prince and a Saviour, for to give repentance to Israel, and forgiveness of sins.

Acts 7:55. Looked up stedfastly into heaven, and saw the glory of God, and Jesus standing on the right hand of God, 56. And said, Behold, I see the heavens opened, and the Son of man standing on the right hand of God.

Rom. 8:17. And if children, then heirs; heirs of God, and joint-heirs with Christ; if so be that we suffer with *him,* that we may be also glorified together. 34. Who *is* he that condemneth? *It is* Christ that died, yea rather, that is risen again, who is even at the right hand of God, who also maketh intercession for us.

Eph. 1:20. He raised him from the dead, and set *him* at his own right hand in the heavenly *places,*

Eph. 4:10. He that descended is the same also that ascended up far above all heavens, that he might fill all things.

Phil. 2:9. Wherefore God also hath highly exalted him, and given him a name which is above every name: 10. That at the name of Jesus every knee should bow, of *things* in heaven, and *things* in earth, and *things*

under the earth; 11. And *that* every tongue should confess that Jesus Christ *is* Lord, to the glory of God the Father.

Col. 2:15. Having spoiled principalities and powers, he made a shew of them openly, triumphing over them in it.

Col. 3:1. Christ sitteth on the right hand of God.

1 Tim. 3:16. ¹ God was manifest in the flesh, . . . received up into glory. [¹ R.V. He who]

Heb. 1:3. When he had by himself purged our sins, sat down on the right hand of the Majesty on high;

Heb. 2:9. We see Jesus, who was made a little lower than the angels for the suffering of death, crowned with glory and honour;

Heb. 4:10. He that is entered into his rest, he also hath ceased from his own works, as God *did* from his. 14. We have a great high priest, that is passed into the heavens, Jesus the Son of God,

Heb. 6:20. The forerunner is for us entered, *even* Jesus, made an high priest for ever

Heb. 7:26. Such an high priest became us, *who is* holy, harmless, undefiled, separate from sinners, and made higher than the heavens;

Heb. 8:1. We have such an high priest, who is set on the right hand of the throne of the Majesty in the heavens;

Heb. 9:12. By his own blood he entered in once into the holy place, having obtained eternal redemption *for us.* 24. Christ is not entered into the holy places made with hands, *which are* the figures of the true; but into heaven itself, now to appear in the presence of God for us:

Heb. 10:12. After he had offered one sacrifice for sins for ever, sat down on the right hand of God; 13. From henceforth expecting till his enemies be made his footstool.

Heb. 12:2. Who for the joy that was set before him endured the cross, despising shame, and is set down at the right hand of the throne of God.

1 Pet. 3:22. Who is gone into heaven, and is on the right hand of God;

EXAMPLE, AN: Matt. 11:29. Take my yoke upon you, and learn of me; for I am meek and lowly in heart, and ye shall find rest unto your souls.

Matt. 20:28. Even as the Son of man came not to be ministered unto, but to minister, and to give his life a ransom for many.

Mark 10:43. But so shall it not be among you: but whosoever will be great among you, shall be your minister: 44. And whosoever of you will be the chiefest, shall be servant of all. 45. For even the Son of man came not to be ministered unto, but to minister, and to give his life a ransom for many.

Luke 22:26. But ye *shall* not *be* so: but he that is greatest among you, let him be as the younger; and he that is chief, as he that doth serve. 27. For whether *is* greater, he that sitteth at meat, or he that serveth? *is* not he that sitteth at meat? but I am among you as he that serveth.

John 10:4. He goeth before them, and the sheep follow him: for they know his voice.

John 13:13. Ye call me Master and Lord: and ye say well; for *so* I am. 14. If I then, *your* Lord and Master, have washed your feet; ye also ought to wash one another's feet. 15. For I have given you an example, that ye should do as I have done to you. 34. A new commandment I give unto you, That ye love one another; as I have loved you, that ye also love one another.

John 17:14. The world hath hated them, because they are not of the world, even as I am not of the world. 18. As thou hast sent me into the world, even so have I also sent them into the world. 21. That they all may be one; as thou, Father, *art* in me, and I in thee, that they also may be one in us: that the world may believe that thou hast sent me. 22. And the glory which thou gavest me I have given them; that they may be one, even as we are one:

Rom. 8:29. Whom he did foreknow, he also did predestinate *to be* conformed to the image of his Son,

Rom. 13:14. Put ye on the Lord Jesus Christ,

Rom. 15:2. Let every one of us please *his* neighbour for *his* good to edification. 3. For even Christ pleased not himself; 5. The God of patience and consolation grant you to be likeminded one toward another according to Christ Jesus: 7. Wherefore receive ye one another, as Christ also received us to the glory of God.

2 Cor. 4:10. Always bearing about in the body the dying of the Lord Jesus, that the life also of Jesus might be made manifest in our body.

2 Cor. 8:9. For ye know the grace of our Lord Jesus Christ, that, though he was rich, yet for your sakes he became poor, that ye through his poverty might be rich. with context.

2 Cor. 10:1. Now I Paul myself beseech you by the meekness and gentleness of Christ, who in presence *am* base among you, but being absent am bold toward you:

Gal. 3:27. For as many of you as have been baptized into Christ have put on Christ.

Gal. 6:2. Bear ye one another's burdens, and so fulfil the law of Christ.

Eph. 4:13. Till we all come in the unity of the faith, and of the knowledge of the Son of God, unto a perfect man, unto the measure of the stature of the fulness of Christ: 15 But speaking the truth in love, may grow up into him in all things, which is the head, *even* Christ: 24. Put on the new man, which after God is created in righteousness and true holiness. *v.* 32.

Eph. 5:2. Walk in love, as Christ also hath loved us, and hath given himself for us an offering and a sacrifice to God for a sweet-smelling savour.

Eph. 6:9. And, ye masters, do the same things unto them, forbearing threatening: knowing that your Master also is in heaven;

neither is there respect of persons with him.

Phil. 2:5. Let this mind be in you, which was also in Christ Jesus: 6. Who, being in the form of God, thought it not ¹robbery to be equal with God: 7. But ²made himself of no reputation, and took upon him the form of a servant, and was made in the likeness of men: 8. And being found in fashion as a man, he humbled himself, and became obedient unto death, even the death of the cross.
[R. V. ¹a prize ²emptied himself, taking]

Col. 3:10. Put on the new *man*, which is renewed in knowledge after the image of him that created him: 11. Christ *is* all, and in all. 13. Forbearing one another, and forgiving one another, if any man have a quarrel against any: even as Christ forgave you, so also *do* ye.

1 Thess. 1:6. Ye became followers of us, and of the Lord, having received the word in much affliction, with joy of the Holy Ghost:

Heb. 3:1. Holy brethren, partakers of the heavenly calling, consider the Apostle and High Priest of our profession, Christ Jesus;

Heb. 12:2. Looking unto Jesus the author and finisher of *our* faith, who for the joy that was set before him endured the cross, despising the shame, and is set down at the right hand of the throne of God. 3. For consider him that endured such contradiction of sinners against himself, lest ye be wearied and faint in your minds. 4. Ye have not yet resisted unto blood, striving against sin.

1 Pet. 1:15. As he which hath called you is holy, so be ye holy in all manner of ¹conversation; *v.* 16. [¹R. V. living]

1 Pet. 2:21. For even hereunto were ye called: because Christ also suffered for us, leaving us an example, that ye should follow his steps: 22. Who did no sin, neither was guile found in his mouth: 23. Who, when he was reviled, reviled not again; when he suffered, he threatened not; but committed *himself* to him that judgeth righteously: 24. Who his own self bare our sins in his own body on the tree, that we, being dead to sins, should live unto righteousness: by whose stripes ye were healed.

1 Pet. 3:17. For *it is* better, if the will of God be so, that ye suffer for well doing, than for evil doing. 18. For Christ also hath once suffered for sins, the just for the unjust, that he might bring us to God, being put to death in the flesh, but quickened by the Spirit:

1 John 2:6. He that saith he abideth in him ought himself also so to walk, even as he walked.

1 John 3:1. The world knoweth us not, because it knew him not. 2. Beloved, now are we the sons of God, and it doth not yet appear what we shall be: but we know that, when he shall appear, we shall be like him for we shall see him as he is. 3. Every man that hath this hope in him purifieth himself, even as he is pure. 16. Hereby perceive we

1 the love 1 of God, because he laid down his life for us: and we ought to lay down our lives for the brethren.   [1 Omitted in R. V.]

1 John 4:17. Herein is our love made perfect, that we may have boldness in the day of judgment: because as he is, so are we in this world.

Rev. 3:21. To him that overcometh will I grant to sit with me in my throne, even as I also overcame, and am set down with my Father in his throne.

Rev. 14:4. These are they which follow the Lamb whithersoever he goeth.

FAITH IN: See FAITH; SALVATION, CONDITIONS OF.

GENEALOGY OF: See JESUS, HISTORY OF, at beginning of the topic.

HEALING BY: See MIRACLES, p. 700.

HOLINESS OF: Psa. 45:7. Thou lovest righteousness, and hatest wickedness: Heb. 1:9.

Psa. 89:19. Then thou spakest in vision to thy holy one, and saidst, I have laid help upon one that is mighty; I have exalted one chosen out of the people.

Isa. 11:4. But with righteousness shall he judge the poor, and reprove with equity for the meek of the earth: and he shall smite the earth with the rod of his mouth, and with the breath of his lips shall he slay the wicked. 5. And righteousness shall be the girdle of his loins, and faithfulness the girdle of his reins.

Isa. 32:1. Behold, a king shall reign in righteousness,

Isa. 42:21. The LORD is well pleased for his righteousness' sake; he will magnify the law, and make it honourable.

Isa. 49:7. Thus saith the LORD, the Redeemer of Israel, and his Holy One, to him whom man despiseth, to him whom the nation abhorreth, to a servant of rulers, Kings shall see and arise, princes also shall worship, because of the LORD that is faithful, and the Holy One of Israel, and he shall choose thee.

Isa. 50:5. The Lord GOD hath opened mine ear, and I was not rebellious, neither turned away back.

Isa. 53:9. He had done no violence, neither was any deceit in his mouth.

Isa. 59:17. He put on righteousness as a breastplate, and an helmet of salvation upon his head; and he put on the garments of vengeance for clothing, and was clad with zeal as a cloke.

Jer. 23:5. I will raise unto David a righteous Branch,

Zech. 9:9. Behold, thy King cometh unto thee: he is just, and having salvation; lowly, and riding upon an ass, and upon a colt the foal of an ass.

Mark 1:24. Let us alone; what have we to do with thee, thou Jesus of Nazareth? art thou come to destroy us? I know thee who thou art, the Holy One of God.

Luke 1:35. That holy thing which shall be born of thee shall be called the Son of God.

Luke 4:34. I know thee who thou art; the Holy One of God.

Luke 23:40. But the other answering rebuked him, saying, Dost not thou fear God, seeing thou art in the same condemnation? 41. And we indeed justly; for we receive the due reward of our deeds: but this man hath done nothing amiss. 47. Now when the centurion saw what was done, he glorified God, saying, Certainly this was a righteous man.

John 5:30. My judgment is just; because I seek not mine own will, but the will of the Father which hath sent me.

John 7:18. He that seeketh his glory that sent him, the same is true, and no unrighteousness is in him.

John 8:46. Which of you convinceth me of sin?

John 14:30. The prince of this world cometh, and hath nothing in me.

Acts 3:14. But ye denied the Holy One and the Just, and desired a murderer to be granted unto you;

Acts 4:27. For of a truth against thy holy child Jesus, whom thou hast anointed, both Herod, and Pontius Pilate, with the Gentiles, and the people of Israel, were gathered together,

30. By stretching forth thine hand to heal; and that signs and wonders may be done by the name of thy holy child Jesus.

Acts 13:28. And though they found no cause of death in him, yet desired they Pilate that he should be slain. 35. Wherefore he saith also in another psalm, Thou shalt not suffer thine Holy One to see corruption.

2 Cor. 4:4. In whom the god of this world hath blinded the minds of them which believe not, lest the light of the glorious gospel of Christ, who is the image of God, should shine unto them.

2 Cor. 5:21. For he hath made him to be sin for us, who knew no sin: that we might be made the righteousness of God in him.

Heb. 1:9. Thou hast loved righteousness, and hated iniquity; therefore God, even thy God, hath anointed thee with the oil of gladness above thy fellows.

Heb. 4:15. We have not an high priest which cannot be touched with the feeling of our infirmities; but was in all points tempted like as we are, yet without sin.

Heb. 7:26. Such an high priest became us, who is holy, harmless, undefiled, separate from sinners, and made higher than the heavens; 27. Who needeth not daily, as those high priests, to offer up sacrifice, first for his own sins, and then for the people's: for this he did once, when he offered up himself. 28. For the law maketh men high priests which have infirmity; but the word of the oath, which was since the law, maketh the Son, who is consecrated for evermore.

Heb. 9:14. Christ, who through the eternal Spirit offered himself without spot to God,

1 Pet. 1:19. A lamb without blemish and without spot:

1 Pet. 2:22. Who did no sin, neither was guile found in his mouth:

1 John 2:29. If ye know that he is righteous, ye know that every one that doeth righteousness is born of him.

1 John 3:5. In him is no sin.

Rev. 3:7. And to the angel of the church in Philadelphia write; These things saith he that is holy, he that is true, he that hath the key of David, he that openeth, and no man shutteth; and shutteth, and no man openeth;

HUMANITY OF: Gen. 3:15. And I will put enmity between thee and the woman, and between thy seed and her seed; it shall bruise thy head, and thou shalt bruise his heel.

Deut. 18:15. The LORD thy God will raise up unto thee a Prophet from the midst of thee, of thy brethren, like unto me; unto him ye shall hearken; 16. According to all that thou desiredst of the LORD thy God in Horeb in the day of the assembly, saying, Let me not hear again the voice of the LORD my God, neither let me see this great fire any more, that I die not. 17. And the LORD said unto me, They have well *spoken that* which they have spoken. 18. I will raise them up a Prophet from among their brethren, like unto thee, and will put my words in his mouth; and he shall speak unto them all that I shall command him. 19. And it shall come to pass, *that* whosoever will not hearken unto my words which he shall speak in my name, I will require *it* of him.

Psa. 22:22. I will declare thy name unto my brethren: in the midst of the congregation will I praise thee.

Isa. 8:18. Behold, I and the children whom the LORD hath given me *are* for signs and for wonders in Israel from the LORD of hosts, which dwelleth in mount Zion.

Isa. 9:6. For unto us a child is born, unto us a son is given: and the government shall be upon his shoulder: and his name shall be called Wonderful, Counsellor, The mighty God, The everlasting Father, The Prince of Peace.

Dan. 7:13. I saw in the night visions, and, behold, *one* like the Son of man came with the clouds of heaven, and came to the Ancient of days, and they brought him near before him.

Matt. 16:27. For the Son of man shall come in the glory of his Father with his angels; and then he shall reward every man according to his works. 28. Verily I say unto you, There be some standing here, which shall not taste of death, till they see the Son of man coming in his kingdom.

Matt. 18:11. [1] For the Son of man is come to save that which was lost. [1 Omitted in R. V.]

Matt. 20:28. Even as the Son of man came not to be ministered unto, but to minister, and to give his life a ransom for many. 30. And, behold, two blind men sitting by the way side, when they heard that Jesus passed by, cried out, saying, Have mercy on us, O Lord, *thou* son of David. 31. And the multitude rebuked them, because they should hold their peace: but they cried the more, saying, Have mercy on us, O Lord, *thou* son of David.

Matt. 21:9. And the multitudes that went before, and that followed, cried, saying, Hosanna to the son of David: Blessed *is* he that cometh in the name of the Lord; Hosanna in the highest.

Matt. 26:2. Ye know that after two days is *the feast of* the passover, and the Son of man is betrayed to be crucified. 26. And as they were eating, Jesus took bread, and blessed *it*, and brake *it*, and gave *it* to the disciples, and said, Take, eat; this is my body. 27. And he took the cup, and gave thanks, and gave *it* to them, saying, Drink ye all of it; 28. For this is my blood of the new testament, which is shed for many for the remission of sins. 36. Then cometh Jesus with them unto a place called Gethsemane, and saith unto the disciples, Sit ye here, while I go and pray yonder. 37. And he took with him Peter and the two sons of Zebedee, and began to be sorrowful and very heavy. 38. Then saith he unto them, My soul is exceeding sorrowful, even unto death: tarry ye here, and watch with me. 39. And he went a little farther, and fell on his face, and prayed, saying, O my Father, if it be possible, let this cup pass from me: nevertheless, not as I will, but as thou *wilt*. 40. And he cometh unto the disciples, and findeth them asleep, and saith unto Peter, What, could ye not watch with me one hour? 41. Watch and pray, that ye enter not into temptation: the spirit indeed *is* willing, but the flesh *is* weak. 42. He went away again the second time, and prayed, saying, O my Father, if this cup may not pass away from me, except I drink it, thy will be done. 43. And he came and found them asleep again: for their eyes were heavy. 44. And he left them, and went away again, and prayed the third time, saying the same words. 45. Then cometh he to his disciples, and saith unto them, Sleep on now, and take *your* rest: behold, the hour is at hand, and the Son of man is betrayed into the hands of sinners.

Mark 14:34,42.

64. Jesus saith unto him, Thou hast said: nevertheless I say unto you, Hereafter shall ye see the Son of man sitting on the right hand of power, and coming in the clouds of heaven.

Mark 2:28. Therefore the Son of man is Lord also of the sabbath.

Mark 9:9. And as they came down from the mountain, he charged them that they should tell no man what things they had seen, till the Son of man were risen from the dead. 12. And he answered and told them, Elias verily cometh first, and restoreth all things; and how it is written of the Son of man, that he must suffer many things, and be set at nought.

Mark 10:33. *Saying*, Behold, we go up to Jerusalem; and the Son of man shall be delivered unto the chief priests, and unto the scribes; and they shall condemn him to death, and shall deliver him to the Gentiles: 45. For even the Son of man came not to be ministered unto, but to minister, and to give his life a ransom for many.

Mark 14:21. The Son of man indeed goeth, as it is written of him: but woe to that man by whom the Son of man is betrayed! good were it for that man if he had never been born. 62. And Jesus said, . . . ye shall see the Son of man sitting on the right hand of power, and coming in the clouds of heaven.

Luke 2:11. For unto you is born this day in the city of David a Saviour, which is Christ the Lord. 12. And this *shall be* a sign unto you; Ye shall find the babe wrapped in swaddling clothes, lying in a manger. 13. And suddenly there was with the angel a multitude of the heavenly host praising God, and saying, 14. Glory to God in the highest, and on earth peace, good will toward men.

Luke 5:24. But that ye may know that the Son of man hath power upon earth to forgive sins, (he said unto the sick of the palsy,) I say unto thee, Arise, and take up thy couch, and go into thine house.

Luke 17:22. And he said unto the disciples, The days will come, when ye shall desire to see one of the days of the Son of man, and ye shall not see *it*. 24. For as the lightning, that lighteneth out of the one *part* under heaven, shineth unto the other *part* under heaven; so shall also the Son of man be in his day.

Luke 18:31. Then he took *unto him* the twelve, and said unto them, Behold, we go up to Jerusalem, and all things that are written by the prophets concerning the Son of man shall be accomplished.

Luke 19:10. For the Son of man is come to seek and to save that which was lost.

Luke 21:36. Watch ye therefore, and pray always, that ye may be accounted worthy to escape all these things that shall come to pass, and to stand before the Son of man.

Luke 22:48. But Jesus said unto him, Judas, betrayest thou the Son of man with a kiss? 69. Hereafter shall the Son of man sit on the right hand of the power of God.

John 1:14. And the Word was made flesh, and dwelt among us, (and we beheld his glory, the glory as of the only begotten of the Father,) full of grace and truth.

John 5:27. And hath given him authority to execute judgment also, because he is the Son of man.

John 12:34. The people answered him, We have heard out of the law that Christ abideth for ever: and how sayest thou, The Son of man must be lifted up? who is this Son of man?

John 13:31. Therefore, when he was gone out, Jesus said, Now is the Son of man glorified, and God is glorified in him.

Acts 7:56. And said, Behold, I see the heavens opened, and the Son of man standing on the right hand of God.

Acts 17:31. Because he hath appointed a day, in the which he will judge the world in righteousness by *that* man whom he hath ordained; *whereof* he hath given assurance unto all *men*, in that he hath raised him from the dead.

Gal. 4:4. But when the fulness of the time was come, God sent forth his Son, made of a woman, made under the law,

Phil. 2:7. But [1] made himself of no reputation, and took upon him the form of a servant, and was made in the likeness of men: 8. And being found in fashion as a man, he humbled himself, and became obedient unto death, even the death of the cross. [1 R. V. emptied himself, taking]

1 Tim. 2:5. For *there is* one God, and one mediator between God and men, the man Christ Jesus;

Heb. 2:9. But we see Jesus, who was made a little lower than the angels for the suffering of death, crowned with glory and honour; that he by the grace of God should taste death for every man. 10. For it became him, for whom *are* all things, and by whom *are* all things, in bringing many sons into glory, to make the captain of their salvation perfect through sufferings. 14. Forasmuch then as the children are partakers of flesh and blood, he also himself likewise took part of the same; that through death he might destroy him that had the power of death, that is, the devil; 15. And deliver them who through fear of death were all their lifetime subject to bondage. 16. For verily he took not on *him the nature of* angels; but he took on *him* the seed of Abraham. 17. Wherefore in all things it behooved him to be made like unto *his* brethren, that he might be a merciful and faithful high priest in things *pertaining* to God, to make reconciliation for the sins of the people. 18. For in that he himself hath suffered being tempted, he is able to succour them that are tempted.

Heb. 10:12. But this man, after he had offered one sacrifice for sins for ever, sat down on the right hand of God.

1 John 4:2. Hereby know ye the Spirit of God: Every spirit that confesseth that Jesus Christ is come in the flesh is of God: 3. And every spirit that confesseth not [1] that Jesus [1 Christ is come in the flesh] is not of God: and this is that *spirit* of antichrist, whereof ye have heard that it should come; and even now already is it in the world. [1 Omitted in R. V.]

2 John 7. For many deceivers are entered into the world, who confess not that Jesus Christ is come in the flesh. This is a deceiver and an antichrist.

Rev. 1:13. And in the midst of the seven candlesticks *one* like unto the Son of man, clothed with a garment down to the foot, and girt about the paps with a golden girdle.

Rev. 14:14. And I looked, and behold a white cloud, and upon the cloud *one* sat like unto the Son of man, having on his head a golden crown, and in his hand a sharp sickle.

See JESUS, INCARNATION OF, HISTORY OF, RELATION OF, TO THE FATHER; PROPHECY CONCERNING THE COMING OF.

HUMILITY OF: Zech. 9:9. Lowly, and .iding upon an ass, and upon a colt the foal of an ass. Matt. 21:5.

Matt. 9:10. As Jesus sat at meat in the house, behold, many publicans and sinners came and sat down with him and his disciples. Mark 2:14; Luke 5:27,28.

Luke 22:27. For whether *is* greater, he that sitteth at meat, or he that serveth? *is* not he that sitteth at meat? but I am among you as he that serveth.

John 13:5. He poureth water into a bason, and began to wash the disciples' feet, and to wipe *them* with the towel wherewith he was girded. 14. If I then, *your* Lord and Master, have washed your feet; ye also ought to wash one another's feet.

Acts 8:32. The place of the scripture which he read was this, He was led as a sheep to the slaughter; and like a lamb dumb before his shearer, so opened he not his mouth: 33. In his humiliation his judgment was taken away: and who shall declare his generation? for his life is taken from the earth.

2 Cor. 8:9. For ye know the grace of our Lord Jesus Christ, that, though he was rich, yet for your sakes he became poor, that ye through his poverty might be rich.

2 Cor. 10:1. I Paul myself beseech you by the meekness and gentleness of Christ,

Phil. 2:7. [1 Made himself of no reputation, and took upon him] the form of a servant, and was made in the likeness of men: 8. And being found in fashion as a man, he humbled himself, and became obedient unto death, even the death of the cross. [1 R. V. emptied himself, taking]

See MEEKNESS OF, below; MEEKNESS.

IMPECCABILITY OF: See HOLINESS OF, above; TEMPTATION OF, below.

INCARNATION OF: Gen. 3:15. I will put enmity between thee and the woman, and between thy seed and her seed; it shall bruise thy head, and thou shalt bruise his heel.

Deut. 18:15. The LORD thy God will raise up unto thee a Prophet from the midst of ‘hee, of thy brethren, like unto me; unto him ye shall hearken; 16. According to all that thou desiredst of the LORD thy God in Horeb in the day of the assembly, saying, Let me not hear again the voice of the LORD my God, neither let me see this great fire any more, that I die not. 17. And the LORD said unto me, They have well *spoken that* which they have spoken. 18. I will raise them up a Prophet from among their brethren, like unto thee, and will put my words in his mouth; and he shall speak unto them all that I shall command him.

1 Chr. 5:2. Judah prevailed above his brethren and of him *came* the chief ruler; Psa. 2:7. The Lord hath said unto me,

Thou *art* my Son; this day have I begotten thee. Acts 13:33.

Psa. 40:7. Then said I, Lo, I come: in the volume of the book *it is* written of me, 8. I delight to do thy will, O my God:

Psa. 80:17. Let thy hand be upon the man of thy right hand, upon the son of man *whom* thou madest strong for thyself.

Psa. 89:19. Thou spakest in vision to thy holy one, and saidst, I have laid help upon *one that is* mighty; I have exalted *one* chosen out of the people.

Isa. 7:14. Therefore the Lord himself shall give you a sign; Behold, a virgin shall conceive, and bear a son, and shall call his name Immanuel. 15. Butter and honey shall he eat, that he may know to refuse the evil, and choose the good. 16. For before the child shall know to refuse the evil and choose the good, the land that thou abhorrest shall be forsaken of both her kings.

Isa. 9:6. For unto us a child is born, unto us a son is given: and the government shall be upon his shoulder; and his name shall be called Wonderful, Counsellor, The mighty God, The everlasting Father, The Prince of Peace.

Isa. 11:1. There shall come forth a rod out of the stem of Jesse, and a Branch shall grow out of his roots.

Isa. 32:2. And a man shall be as an hiding place from the wind, and a covert from the tempest; as rivers of water in a dry place, as the shadow of a great rock in a weary land.

Isa. 49:1. The LORD hath called me from the womb; from the bowels of my mother hath he made mention of my name. 5. And now, saith the LORD that formed me from the womb *to be* his servant, to bring Jacob again to him, Though Israel be not gathered, yet shall I be glorious in the eyes of the LORD, and my God shall be my strength.

Jer. 23:5. Behold, the days come, saith the LORD, that I will raise unto David a righteous Branch, and a King shall reign and prosper, and shall execute judgment and justice in the earth.

Mic. 5:2. But thou, Beth-lehem Ephratah, *though* thou be little among the thousands of Judah, *yet* out of thee shall he come forth unto me *that is* to be ruler in Israel; whose goings forth *have been* from of old, from everlasting. 3. Therefore will he give them up, until the time *that* she which travaileth hath brought forth: then the remnant of his brethren shall return unto the children of Israel. Matt. 2:5,6.

Matt. 1:1. The book of the generation of Jesus Christ, the son of David, the son of Abraham. 16. And Jacob begat Joseph the husband of Mary, of whom was born Jesus, who is called Christ. 17. So all the generations from Abraham to David *are* fourteen generations; and from David until the carrying away into Babylon *are* fourteen generations; and from the carrying away into Babylon unto Christ *are* fourteen generations. [Luke 3:23–38.] 18. The birth of Jesus Christ was on this wise: When as his mother Mary was espoused to Joseph, before they came together, she was found with child of the Holy Ghost. 23. Behold, a virgin shall be with child, and shall bring forth a son, and they shall call his name Emmanuel, which being interpreted is, God with us.

Matt. 8:20. The Son of man hath not where to lay *his* head.

Matt. 13:55. Is not this the carpenter's son? is not his mother called Mary? and his brethren, James, and Joses, and Simon, and Judas? 56. And his sisters, are they not all with us?

Matt. 22:45. If David then called him Lord, how is he his son?

Luke 1:26. And in the sixth month the angel Gabriel was sent from God unto a city of Galilee, named Nazareth. 27. To a virgin espoused to a man whose name was Joseph, of the house of David; and the virgin's name *was* Mary. 28. And the angel came in unto her, and said, Hail, *thou that art* highly favoured, the Lord *is* with thee: ¹ blessed *art* thou among women. 29. And when she saw *him*, she was troubled at his saying, and cast in her mind what manner of salutation this should be. 30. And the angel said unto her, Fear not, Mary: for thou hast found favour with God. 31. And, behold, thou shalt conceive in thy womb, and bring forth a son, and shalt call his name JESUS. 32. He shall be great, and shall be called the Son of the Highest: and the Lord God shall give unto him the throne of his father David; 33. And he shall reign over the house of Jacob for ever; and of his kingdom there shall be no end. 34. Then said Mary unto the angel, How shall this be, seeing I know not a man? 35. And the angel answered and said unto her, The Holy Ghost shall come upon thee, and the power of the Highest shall overshadow thee: therefore also that holy thing which shall be born of thee shall be called the Son of God. 38. And Mary said, Behold the handmaid of the Lord; be it unto me according to thy word. And the angel departed from her. 39. And Mary arose in those days, and went into the hill country with haste, into a city of Juda; 40. And entered into the house of Zacharias, and saluted Elisabeth. 41. And it came to pass, that, when Elisabeth heard the salutation of Mary, the babe leaped in her womb: and Elisabeth was filled with the Holy Ghost: 42. And she spake out with a loud voice, and said, Blessed *art* thou among women, and blessed *is* the fruit of thy womb. 43. And whence *is* this to me, that the mother of my Lord should come to me? 44. For, lo, as soon as the voice of thy salutation sounded in mine ears, the babe leaped in my womb for joy. 45. And blessed *is* she that be-

lieved: for there shall be a performance of those things which were told her from the Lord. 46. And Mary said, My soul doth magnify the Lord, 47. And my spirit hath rejoiced in God my Saviour. 48. For he hath regarded the low estate of his handmaiden: for, behold, from henceforth all generations shall call me blessed. 49. For he that is mighty hath done to me great things; and holy *is* his name. 50. And his mercy *is* on them that fear him from generation to generation. 51. He hath shewed strength with his arm; he hath scattered the proud in the imagination of their hearts. 52. He hath put down the mighty from *their* seats, and exalted them of low degree. 53. He hath filled the hungry with good things; and the rich he hath sent empty away. 54. He hath holpen his servant Israel, in remembrance of *his* mercy; 55. As he spake to our fathers, to Abraham, and to his seed for ever. 56. And Mary abode with her about three months, and returned to her own house.   [¹ Omitted in R. V.]

Luke 2:1. And it came to pass in those days, that there went out a decree from Cæsar Augustus, that all the world should be taxed. 2. (*And* this taxing was first made when Cyrenius was governor of Syria.) 3. And all went to be taxed, every one into his own city. 4. And Joseph also went up from Galilee, out of the city of Nazareth, into Judæa, unto the city of David, which is called Bethlehem; (because he was of the house and lineage of David:) 5. To be taxed with Mary his espoused wife, being great with child. 6. And so it was, that, while they were there, the days were accomplished that she should be delivered. 7. And she brought forth her firstborn son, and wrapped him in swaddling clothes, and laid him in a manger; because there was no room for them in the inn. 8. And there were in the same country shepherds abiding in the field, keeping watch over their flock by night. 9. And, lo, the angel of the Lord came upon them, and the glory of the Lord shone round about them; and they were sore afraid. 10. And the angel said unto them, Fear not: for, behold, I bring you good tidings of great joy, which shall be to all people. 11. For unto you is born this day in the city of David a Saviour, which is Christ the Lord. 12. And this *shall be* a sign unto you: Ye shall find the babe wrapped in swaddling clothes, lying in a manger. 13. And suddenly there was with the angel a multitude of the heavenly host praising God, and saying, 14. Glory to God in the highest, and on earth peace, good will toward men. 15. And it came to pass, as the angels were gone away from them into heaven, the shepherds said to one another, Let us now go even unto Bethlehem, and see this thing which is come to pass, which the Lord hath made known unto us. 16. And they came with haste and found Mary and Joseph, and the babe lying in a manger. 17. And when they had seen *it*, they made known abroad the saying which was told them concerning this child. 18. And all they that heard *it* wondered at those things which were told them by the shepherds. 19. But Mary kept all these things, and pondered *them* in her heart. 20. And the shepherds returned, glorifying and praising God for all the things that they had heard and seen, as it was told unto them. 21. And when eight days were accomplished for the circumcising of the child, his name was called JESUS, which was so named of the angel before he was conceived in the womb.

Luke 24:39. Behold my hands and my feet, that it is I myself: handle me, and see; for a spirit hath not flesh and bones, as ye see me have.

John 1:14. The Word was made flesh, and dwelt among us, (and we beheld his glory, the glory as of the only begotten of the Father,) full of grace and truth.

John 7:42. Hath not the scripture said, That Christ cometh of the seed of David, and out of the town of Bethlehem, where David was?

John 20:27. Reach hither thy finger, and behold my hands; and reach hither thy hand, and thrust *it* into my side: and be not faithless, but believing.

Acts 2:30. Knowing that God had sworn with an oath to him, that of the fruit of his loins, according to the flesh, he would raise up Christ to sit on his throne: 2 Sam. 7:12; Psa. 89:35,36.

Acts 3:22. Moses truly said unto the fathers, A prophet shall the Lord your God raise up unto you of your brethren, like unto me; Deut. 18:15–19.

Acts 13:23. Of this man's seed hath God according to *his* promise raised unto Israel a Saviour, Jesus:

Rom. 1:3. His Son Jesus Christ our Lord, which was made of the seed of David according to the flesh;

Rom. 8:3. For what the law could not do, in that it was weak through the flesh, God sending his own Son in the likeness of sinful flesh, and for sin, condemned sin in the flesh.

Rom. 9:5. Of whom as concerning the flesh Christ *came*, who is over all, God blessed for ever.

1 Cor. 15:47. The first man *is* of the earth, earthy: the second man *is* the Lord from heaven.

2 Cor. 5:16. Wherefore henceforth know we no man after the flesh: yea, though we have known Christ after the flesh, yet now henceforth know we *him* no more.

Gal. 3:16. To Abraham and his seed were the promises made. He saith not, And to seeds, as of many; but as of one, And to thy seed, which is Christ. Gen. 12:3; 17:7; 22:18.

Gal. 4:4. When the fulness of the time was come, God sent forth his Son, made of a woman, made under the law,

Phil. 2:7. ¹Made himself of no reputation, and took upon him the form of a servant, and was made in the likeness of men: 8. And being found in fashion as a man, he humbled himself, and became obedient unto death, even the death of the cross. [¹ R. V. emptied himself, taking]

Col. 1:15. Who is the image of the invisible God, the firstborn of every creature:

1 Tim. 3:16. Great is the mystery of godliness: ¹God was manifest in the flesh.

[¹ R. V. He who]

Heb. 1:3. Being the brightness of *his* glory, and the express image of his person, 6. And again, when he bringeth in the firstbegotten into the world, he saith, And let all the angels of God worship him.

Heb. 2:9. We see Jesus, who was made a little lower than the angels for the suffering of death, 14. As the children are partakers of flesh and blood, he also himself likewise took part of the same; 16. For verily ¹ he took not on *him the nature of* angels; but he took on *him* the seed of Abraham. 17. In all things it behoved him to be made like unto *his* brethren, that he might be a merciful and faithful high priest in things *pertaining* to God, to make reconciliation for the sins of the people. 18. For in that he himself hath suffered being tempted, he is able to succour them that are tempted. *vs.* 9–17.

[¹ R.V. not of angels doth he take hold, but he taketh hold of]

Heb. 7:14. *It is* evident that our Lord sprang out of Juda;

Heb. 10:5. Wherefore when he cometh into the world, he saith, Sacrifice and offering thou wouldest not, but a body hast thou prepared me:

1 John 1:1. That which was from the beginning, which we have heard, which we have seen with our eyes, which we have looked upon, and our hands have handled, of the Word of life; 2. (For the life was manifested, and we have seen *it*, and bear witness, and shew unto you that eternal life, which was with the Father, and was manifested unto us;) 3. That which we have seen and heard declare we unto you.

1 John 4:2. Hereby know ye the Spirit of God: Every spirit that confesseth that Jesus Christ is come in the flesh is of God: 3. And every spirit that confesseth not ¹that Jesus ¹ Christ is come in the flesh is not of God: and this is that *spirit* of antichrist, whereof ye have heard that it should come; and even now already is it in the world. [¹ R. V. omits.]

2 John 7. For many deceivers are entered into the world, who confess not that Jesus Christ is come in the flesh. This is a deceiver and an antichrist.

Rev. 22:16. I am the root and the offspring of David, *and* the bright and morning star.

See JESUS, HUMANITY OF, RELATION OF, TO THE FATHER.

INTERCESSION OF: See JESUS, MEDIATOR.

JUDGE: Psa. 72:2. He shall judge thy people with righteousness, and thy poor with judgment. 4. He shall judge the poor of the people, he shall save the children of the needy, and shall break in pieces the oppressor.

Psa. 75:2. When I shall receive the congregation I will judge uprightly.

Psa. 96:13. He cometh to judge the earth: he shall judge the world with righteousness, and the people with his truth.

Psa. 110:6. He shall judge among the heathen,

Isa. 2:4. He shall judge among the nations, and shall rebuke many people: Mic. 4:3.

Isa. 11:3. He shall not judge after the sight of his eyes, neither reprove after the hearing of his ears: 4. But with righteousness shall he judge the poor, and reprove with equity for the meek of the earth: and he shall smite the earth with the rod of his mouth, and with the breath of his lips shall he slay the wicked.

Mic. 5:1. They shall smite the judge of Israel with a rod upon the cheek.

Mal. 3:2. Who may abide the day of his coming? and who shall stand when he appeareth? for he *is* like a refiner's fire, and like fuller's sope: 3. He shall sit *as* a refiner and purifier of silver: and he shall purify the sons of Levi, and purge them as gold and silver, that they may offer unto the LORD an offering in righteousness.

Matt. 19:28. Jesus said unto them, Verily I say unto you, That ye which have followed me, in the regeneration when the Son of man shall sit in the throne of his glory, ye also shall sit upon twelve thrones, judging the twelve tribes of Israel.

Matt. 25:31. When the Son of man shall come in his glory, and all the holy angels with him, then shall he sit upon the throne of his glory: 32. And before him shall be gathered all nations : and he shall separate them one from another, as a shepherd divideth *his* sheep from the goats: 33. And he shall set the sheep on his right hand, but the goats on the left. 34. Then shall the King say unto them on his right hand, Come, ye blessed of my Father, inherit the kingdom prepared for you from the foundation of the world:

Luke 3:17. Whose fan *is* in his hand, and he will throughly purge his floor, and will gather the wheat into his garner; but the chaff he will burn with fire unquenchable. Matt. 3:12.

Acts 10:42. And he commanded us to preach unto the people, and to testify that it is he which was ordained of God *to be* the Judge of quick and dead.

Acts 17:31. He hath appointed a day, in the which he will judge the world in righteousness by *that* man whom he hath ordained; *whereof* he hath given assurance unto all *men*, in that he hath raised him from the dead.

Rom. 2:16. In the day when God shall judge the secrets of men by Jesus Christ according to my gospel.

Rom. 14:10. We shall all stand before the judgment seat of Christ.

1 Cor. 4:4. He that judgeth me is the Lord. 5. Judge nothing before the time, until the Lord come, who both will bring to light the hidden things of darkness, and will make manifest the counsels of the hearts:

2 Cor. 5:10. We must all appear before the judgment seat of Christ; that every one may receive the things *done* in *his* body, according to that he hath done, whether *it be* good or bad.

2 Tim. 4:1. I charge *thee* therefore before God, and the Lord Jesus Christ, who shall judge the quick and the dead at his appearing and his kingdom; 8. There is laid up for me a crown of righteousness, which the Lord, the righteous judge, shall give me at that day:

Jas. 5:9. Behold, the judge standeth before the door.

Rev. 2:23. I will kill her children with death; and all the churches shall know that I am he which searcheth the reins and hearts: and I will give unto every one of you according to your works.

See GOD, JUDGE.

JUSTICE OF: 2 Sam. 23:3. The God of Israel, said, the Rock of Israel spake to me, [1] He that ruleth over men [2] *must be* just, ruling in the fear of God.   [R. V. [1] One   [2] righteously, that ruleth]

Zech. 9:9. He *is* just, and having salvation :

Matt. 27:19. Have thou nothing to do with that [1] just man: [[1] R. V. righteous]

John 5:30. My judgment is [1] just; because I seek not mine own will, but the will of the Father which hath sent me.   [[1] R. V. righteous:]

Acts 3:14. But ye denied the Holy [1] One and the Just,   [[1] R. V. and Righteous One]

Acts 22:14. The God of our fathers hath [1] chosen thee, that thou shouldest know his will, and [2] see that Just One, and shouldest hear the voice of his mouth.   [R. V. [1] appointed thee to   [2] to see the Righteous One, and to hear a voice from]

See HOLINESS OF; JUDGE.

KING: Gen. 49:10. The sceptre shall not depart from Judah, nor a lawgiver from between his feet, until Shiloh come; and unto him *shall* the gathering of the people *be*.

Num. 24:17. I shall see him, but not now: I shall behold him, but not nigh: there shall come a Star out of Jacob, and a Sceptre shall rise out of Israel,

1 Sam. 2:10. He shall give strength unto his king, and exalt the horn of his anointed.

Psa. 2:6. Yet have I set my king upon my holy hill of Zion.

Psa. 18:43. Thou hast made me the head of the heathen: a people *whom* I have not known shall serve me. 44. As soon as they hear of me, they shall obey me: the strangers shall submit themselves unto me.

Psa. 24:8. Who *is* this King of glory? The LORD strong and mighty, the LORD mighty in battle. *vs.* 7–10.

Psa. 45:3. Gird thy sword upon *thy* thigh, O *most* mighty, with thy glory and thy majesty. 4. And in thy majesty ride prosperously because of truth and meekness *and* righteousness; and thy right hand shall teach thee terrible things. 5. Thine arrows *are* sharp in the heart of the king's enemies; *whereby* the people fall under thee. 6. Thy throne, O God, *is* for ever and ever: the sceptre of thy kingdom *is* a right sceptre. 7. Thou lovest righteousness, and hatest wickedness: therefore God, thy God, hath anointed thee with the oil of gladness above thy fellows. Song 1:4,12.

Psa. 72:5. They shall fear thee as long as the sun and moon endure, throughout all generations. 8. He shall have dominion also from sea to sea, and from the river unto the ends of the earth. 11. Yea, all kings shall fall down before him: all nations shall serve him.

Psa. 89:3. I have made a covenant with my chosen, I have sworn unto David my servant, 4. Thy seed will I establish for ever, and build up thy throne to all generations. 19. Thou spakest in vision to thy holy one, and saidst, I have laid help upon *one that is* mighty; I have exalted *one* chosen out of the people. 20. I have found David my servant; with my holy oil have I anointed him: 21. With whom my hand shall be established: mine arm also shall strengthen him. 23. And I will beat down his foes before his face, and plague them that hate him. 27. I will make him *my* firstborn, higher than the kings of the earth. 29. His seed also will I make *to endure* for ever, and his throne as the days of heaven. 36. His seed shall endure for ever, and his throne as the sun before me. 37. It shall be established for ever as the moon, and *as* a faithful witness in heaven.

Psa. 110:1. The Lord said unto my Lord, Sit thou at my right hand, until I make thine enemies thy footstool. 2. The Lord shall send the rod of thy strength out of Zion: rule thou in the midst of thine enemies.

Psa. 132:11. The Lord hath sworn *in* truth unto David; he will not turn from it; Of the fruit of thy body will I set upon thy throne. 17. There will I make the horn of David to bud: I have ordained a lamp for mine anointed. 18. His enemies will I clothe with shame: but upon himself shall his crown flourish.

Isa. 6:1. I saw also the Lord sitting upon a throne, high and lifted up, and his train filled the temple. *vs.* 2,3; John 12:41.

Isa. 9:6. The government shall be upon his shoulder: and his name shall be called Wonderful, Counsellor, The mighty God, The everlasting Father, The Prince of Peace. 7. Of the increase of *his* government and peace *there shall be* no end, upon the throne of David, and upon his kingdom, to order it, and to establish it with judgment and with justice from henceforth even for ever.

Isa. 11:10. In that day there shall be a root of Jesse, which shall stand for an ensign of the people; to it shall the Gentiles seek:

Isa. 32:1. Behold, a king shall reign in righteousness,

Isa. 33:17. Thine eyes shall see the king in his beauty:

Isa. 40:10. Behold, the Lord God will come with strong *hand*, and his arm shall rule for him: behold, his reward *is* with him, and his work before him.

Isa. 52:7. How beautiful upon the mountains are the feet of him that bringeth good tidings, that publisheth peace; that bringeth good tidings of good, that publisheth salvation; that saith unto Zion, Thy God reigneth! 13. Behold, my servant shall deal prudently, he shall be exalted and extolled, and be very high.

Jer. 23:5. Behold, the days come, saith the Lord, that I will raise unto David a righteous Branch, and a King shall reign and prosper, and shall execute judgment and justice in the earth. 6. In his days Judah shall be saved, and Israel shall dwell safely: and this *is* his name whereby he shall be called, THE LORD OUR RIGHTEOUSNESS.

Jer. 30:9. They shall serve the Lord their God, and David their king, whom I will raise up unto them.

Jer. 33:17. For thus saith the Lord; David shall never want a man to sit upon the throne of the house of Israel;

Ezek. 37:24. And David my servant *shall be* king over them; and they all shall have one shepherd: they shall also walk in my judgments, and observe my statutes, and do them. 25. And they shall dwell in the land that I have given unto Jacob my servant, wherein your fathers have dwelt; and they shall dwell therein, *even* they, and their children, and their children's children for ever: and my servant David *shall be* their prince for ever.

Dan. 2:35. The stone that smote the image became a great mountain, and filled the whole earth. 44. And in the days of these kings shall the God of heaven set up a kingdom, which shall never be destroyed: and the kingdom shall not be left to other people, *but* it shall break in pieces and consume all these kingdoms, and it shall stand for ever.

Dan. 7:13. Behold, *one* like the Son of man came with the clouds of heaven, and came to the Ancient of days, and they brought him near before him. 14. And there was given him dominion, and glory, and a kingdom, that all people, nations, and languages, should serve him: his dominion *is* an everlasting dominion, which shall not pass away, and his kingdom *that* which shall not be destroyed.

Dan. 8:23. A king of fierce countenance, and understanding dark sentences, shall stand up. 25. He shall also stand up against the Prince of princes; but he shall be broken without hand.

Dan. 9:25. From the going forth of the commandment to restore and to build Jerusalem unto the Messiah the Prince *shall be* seven weeks, and threescore and two weeks:

Hos. 3:5. Afterward shall the children of Israel return, and seek the LORD their God, and David their king; and shall fear the LORD and his goodness in the latter days.

Mic. 5:2. Out of thee shall he come forth unto me *that is* to be ruler in Israel; whose goings forth *have been* from of old, from everlasting. 4. And he shall stand and feed in the strength of the LORD, in the majesty of the name of the LORD his God; and they shall abide: for now shall he be great unto the ends of the earth.

Zech. 6:13. He shall bear the glory, and shall sit and rule upon his throne;

Zech. 9:9. Rejoice greatly, O daughter of Zion; shout, O daughter of Jerusalem: behold, thy King cometh unto thee: he *is* just, and having salvation; lowly, and riding upon an ass, and upon a colt the foal of an ass. 10. And he shall speak peace unto the heathen: and his dominion *shall be* from sea *even* to sea, and from the river *even* to the ends of the earth.

Matt. 2:2. Where is he that is born King of the Jews? for we have seen his star in the east, and are come to worship him. 6. And thou Bethlehem, *in* the land of Juda, art not the least among the princes of Juda: for out of thee shall come a Governor, that shall rule my people Israel.

Matt. 3:12. Whose fan *is* in his hand, and he will throughly purge his floor, and gather his wheat into the garner; but he will burn up the chaff with unquenchable fire. Luke 3:17.

Matt. 12:6. In this place is *one* greater than the temple.

Matt. 13:41. The Son of man shall send forth his angels, and they shall gather out of his kingdom all things that offend, and them which do iniquity.

Matt. 19:28. In the regeneration when the Son of man shall sit in the throne of his glory, ye also shall sit upon twelve thrones,

Matt. 21:5. Behold, thy King cometh unto thee, meek, and sitting upon an ass, and a colt the foal of an ass.

Matt. 25:31. When the Son of man shall come in his glory, and all the holy angels with him, then shall he sit upon the throne of his glory: 32. And before him shall be gathered all nations: and he shall separate them one from another, as a shepherd divideth *his* sheep from the goats: 33. And he shall set the sheep on his right hand, but the goats on the left. 34. Then shall the King say unto them on his right hand, Come, ye blessed of my Father,

Matt. 26:64. Hereafter shall ye see the Son of man sitting on the right hand of power, and coming in the clouds of heaven. Mark 14:62; Luke 22:69.

Matt. 27:11. And Jesus stood before the governor: and the governor asked him,

saying, Art thou the King of the Jews? And Jesus said unto him, Thou sayest.

Matt. 28:18. And Jesus came and spake unto them, saying, All power is given unto me in heaven and in earth.

Luke 1:32. He shall be great, and shall be called the Son of the Highest: and the Lord God shall give unto him the throne of his father David: 33. He shall reign over the house of Jacob for ever; and of his kingdom there shall be no end.

Luke 2:11. Unto you is born this day in the city of David a Saviour, which is Christ the Lord.

Luke 10:22. All things are delivered to me of my Father: Matt. 11:27.

Luke 19:27. Those mine enemies, which would not that I should reign over them, bring hither, and slay *them* before me. 38. Blessed *be* the King that cometh in the name of the Lord: peace in heaven, and glory in the highest.

Luke 22:29. I appoint unto you a kingdom, as my Father hath appointed unto me; 30. That ye may eat and drink at my table in my kingdom, and sit on thrones judging the twelve tribes of Israel.

Luke 23:42. He said unto Jesus, Lord, remember me when thou comest into thy kingdom.

John 1:49. Nathanael answered and saith unto him, Rabbi, thou art the Son of God; thou art the King of Israel.

John 3:31. He that is of the earth is earthly, and speaketh of the earth: he that cometh from heaven is above all.

John 12:13. Hosanna: Blessed *is* the King of Israel that cometh in the name of the Lord. 15. Fear not, daughter of Sion: behold, thy King cometh, sitting on an ass's colt. Matt. 21:5.

John 13:3. Jesus knowing that the Father had given all things into his hands, and that he was come from God, and went to God;

John 18:36. My kingdom is not of this world: if my kingdom were of this world, then would my servants fight, that I should not be delivered to the Jews: but now is my kingdom not from hence. 37. Pilate therefore said unto him, Art thou a king then? Jesus answered, Thou sayest that I am a king. To this end was I born,

John 19:19. Pilate wrote a title, and put *it* on the cross. And the writing was, JESUS OF NAZARETH THE KING OF THE JEWS.

Acts 2:30. Knowing that God had sworn with an oath to him, that of the fruit of his loins, according to the flesh, he would raise up Christ to sit on his throne;

Acts 3:15. And killed the Prince of life, whom God hath raised from the dead;

Acts 5:31. Him hath God exalted with his right hand *to be* a Prince and a Saviour,

Acts 10:36. The word which *God* sent unto the children of Israel, preaching peace by Jesus Christ: (he is Lord of all:)

Rom. 9:5. Christ *came*, who is over all, God blessed for ever.

Rom. 14:9. To this end Christ both died, and rose, and revived, that he might be Lord both of the dead and living.

1 Cor. 15:23. But every man in his own order : Christ the firstfruits ; afterward they that are Christ's at his coming. 24. Then *cometh* the end, when he shall have delivered up the kingdom to God, even the Father ; when he shall have put down all rule and all authority and power. 25. For he must reign, till he hath put all enemies under his feet. 26. The last enemy *that* shall be destroyed *is* death. 27. For he hath put all things under his feet. But when he saith all things are put under *him, it is* manifest that he is excepted, which did put all things under him. 28. And when all things shall be subdued unto him, then shall the Son also himself be subject unto him that put all things under him, that God may be all in all.

Eph. 1:20. Which he wrought in Christ, when he raised him from the dead, and set *him* at his own right hand in the heavenly *places*, 21. Far above all principality, and power, and might, and dominion, and every name that is named, not only in this world, but also in that which is to come : 22. And hath put all *things* under his feet, and gave him *to be* the head over all *things* to the church,

Phil. 2:9. God also hath highly exalted him, and given him a name which is above every name : 10. That at the name of Jesus every knee should bow, of *things* in heaven, and *things* in earth, and *things* under the earth ; 11. And *that* every tongue should confess that Jesus Christ *is* Lord, to the glory of God the Father.

1 Tim. 6:15. *Who is* the blessed and only Potentate, the King of kings, and Lord of lords ; 16. Who only hath immortality, dwelling in the light which no man can approach unto ; whom no man hath seen, nor can see ; to whom *be* honour and power everlasting.

2 Tim. 4:8. There is laid up for me a crown of righteousness, which the Lord, the righteous judge, shall give me at that day :

Heb. 2:7. Thou madest him a little lower than the angels : thou crownedst him with glory and honour, and didst set him over the works of thy hands : 8. Thou hast put all things in subjection under his feet. For in that he put all in subjection under him, he left nothing *that is* not put under him.

Heb. 10:12. But this man, after he had offered one sacrifice for sins for ever, sat down on the right hand of God ; 13. From henceforth expecting till his enemies be made his footstool.

1 Pet. 3:22. Who is gone into heaven, and is on the right hand of God ; angels and authorities and powers being made subject unto him.

Rev. 1:5. Jesus Christ, *who is* the faithful witness, *and* the first begotten of the dead, and the prince of the kings of the earth. Unto him that loved us, and washed us from our sins in his own blood, 6. And hath made us kings and priests unto God and his Father ; to him *be* glory and dominion for ever and ever. Amen. 7. Behold, he cometh with clouds ; and every eye shall see him, and they *also* which pierced him : and all kindreds of the earth shall wail because of him. 18. *I am* he that liveth, and was dead ; and, behold, I am alive for evermore, Amen ; and have the keys of hell and of death.

Rev. 3:7. These things saith he that is holy, he that is true, he that hath the key of David, he that openeth, and no man shutteth ; and shutteth, and no man openeth ; 14. These things saith the Amen, the faithful and true witness, the beginning of the creation of God ; 21. To him that overcometh will I grant to sit with me in my throne, even as I also overcame, and am set down with my Father in his throne. Isa. 22:22.

Rev. 5:5. The Lion of the tribe of Juda, the Root of David, hath prevailed to open the book, and to loose the seven seals thereof. 12. Worthy is the Lamb that was slain to receive power, and riches, and wisdom, and strength, and honour, and glory, and blessing.

Rev. 6:2. And I saw, and behold a white horse : and he that sat on him had a bow ; and a crown was given unto him : and he went forth conquering, and to conquer. 15. And the kings of the earth, and the great men, and the rich men, and the chief captains, and the mighty men, and every bondman, and every free man, hid themselves in the dens and in the rocks of the mountains ; 16. And said to the mountains and rocks, Fall on us, and hide us from the face of him that sitteth on the throne, and from the wrath of the Lamb : 17. For the great day of his wrath is come ; and who shall be able to stand ?

Rev. 11:15. The kingdoms of this world are become *the kingdoms* of our Lord, and of his Christ : and he shall reign for ever and ever.

Rev. 12:10. And I heard a loud voice saying in heaven, Now is come salvation, and strength, and the kingdom of our God, and the power of his Christ :

Rev. 14:14. Behold a white cloud, and upon the cloud *one* sat like unto the Son of man, having on his head a golden crown, and in his hand a sharp sickle.

Rev. 17:14. These shall make war with the Lamb, and the Lamb shall overcome them : for he is Lord of lords, and King of kings:

Rev. 19:11. I saw heaven opened, and behold a white horse ; and he that sat upon him *was* called Faithful and True, and in righteousness he doth judge and make war. 12. His eyes *were* as a flame of fire, and on his head *were* many crowns ; and he had a name written, that no man knew, but he himself. 15. Out of his mouth goeth a sharp sword, that with it he should smite the nations: and he shall rule them with a rod of iron: and he treadeth the winepress of the fierceness and wrath of Almighty God. 16. He hath on *his* vesture and on his thigh a name written, KING OF KINGS, AND LORD OF LORDS.

Rev. 20:4. I saw thrones, and they sat upon them, and judgment was given unto them: and *I saw* the souls of them that were beheaded for the witness of Jesus, and for the word of God, and which had not worshipped the beast, neither his image, neither had received *his* mark upon their foreheads, or in their hands; and they lived and reigned with Christ a thousand years. 6. Blessed and holy *is* he that hath part in the first resurrection: on such the second death hath no power, but they shall be priests of God and of Christ, and shall reign with him a thousand years.

See CHURCH, PROPHECIES CONCERNING.

KINGDOM OF: ITS NATURE. Matt. 13:24. Another parable put he forth unto them, saying, The kingdom of heaven is likened unto a man which sowed good seed in his field: 25. But while men slept, his enemy came and sowed tares among the wheat, and went his way. 26. But when the blade was sprung up, and brought forth fruit, then appeared the tares also. 27. So the servants of the householder came and said unto him, Sir, didst not thou sow good seed in thy field? from whence then hath it tares? 28. He said unto them, An enemy hath done this. The servants said unto him, Wilt thou then that we go and gather them up? 29. But he said, Nay; lest while ye gather up the tares, ye root up also the wheat with them. 30. Let both grow together until the harvest: and in the time of harvest I will say to the reapers, Gather ye together first the tares, and bind them in bundles to burn them: but gather the wheat into my barn. 31. Another parable put he forth unto them, saying, The kingdom of heaven is like to a grain of mustard seed, which a man took, and sowed in his field: 32. Which indeed is the least of all seeds: but when it is grown, it is the greatest among herbs, and becometh a tree, so that the birds of the air come and lodge in the branches thereof. 33. Another parable spake he unto them; The kingdom of heaven is like unto leaven, which a woman took, and hid in three measures of meal, till the whole was leavened. 34. All these things spake Jesus unto the multitude in parables; and without a parable spake he not unto them: 35. That it might be fulfilled which was spoken by the prophet, saying, I will open my mouth in parables; I will utter things which have been kept secret from the foundation of the world. 36. Then Jesus sent the multitude away, and went into the house: and his disciples came unto him, saying, Declare unto us the parable of the tares of the field. 37. He answered and said unto them, He that soweth the good seed is the Son of man; 38. The field is the world; the good seed are the children of the kingdom; but the tares are the children of the wicked one; 39. The enemy that sowed them is the devil; the harvest is the end of the world; and the reapers are the angels. 40. As therefore the tares are gathered and burned in the fire; so shall it be in the end of this world. 41. The Son of man shall send forth his angels, and they shall gather out of his kingdom all things that offend, and them which do iniquity; 42. And shall cast them into a furnace of fire: there shall be wailing and gnashing of teeth. 43. Then shall the righteous shine forth as the sun in the kingdom of their Father. Who hath ears to hear, let him hear. 44. Again, the kingdom of heaven is like unto treasure hid in a field; the which when a man hath found, he hideth, and for joy thereof goeth and selleth all that he hath, and buyeth that field. 45. Again, the kingdom of heaven is like unto a merchant man, seeking goodly pearls: 46. Who, when he had found one pearl of great price, went and sold all that he had, and bought it. 47. Again, the kingdom of heaven is like unto a net, that was cast into the sea, and gathered of every kind: 48. Which, when it was full, they drew to shore, and sat down, and gathered the good into vessels, but cast the bad away. 49. So shall it be at the end of the world: the angels shall come forth, and sever the wicked from among the just, 50. And shall cast them into the furnace of fire: there shall be wailing and gnashing of teeth. 51. Jesus saith unto them, Have ye understood all these things? They say unto him, Yea, Lord.

Matt. 18:3. And said, Verily I say unto you, Except ye be converted, and become as little children, ye shall not enter into the kingdom of heaven. 4. Whosoever therefore shall humble himself as this little child, the same is greatest in the kingdom of heaven.

Luke 17:21. Neither shall they say, Lo here! or, lo there! for, behold, the kingdom of God is within you.

John 8:23. And he said unto them, Ye are from beneath; I am from above: ye are of this world; I am not of this world.

John 18:36. Jesus answered, My kingdom is not of this world: if my kingdom were of this world, then would my servants fight, that I should not be delivered to the Jews: but now is my kingdom not from hence. 37. Pilate therefore said unto him, Art thou a king then? Jesus answered, Thou sayest that I am a king. To this end was I born, and for this cause came I into the world, that I should bear witness unto the truth. Every one that is of the truth heareth my voice.

2 Cor. 5:16. Wherefore henceforth know we no man after the flesh: yea, though we

have known Christ after the flesh, yet now henceforth know we *him* no more. 17. Therefore if any man *be* in Christ, *he is* a new creature: old things are passed away; behold, all things are become new. 2 Cor. 10:3. For though we walk in the flesh, we do not war after the flesh: 4. (For the weapons of our warfare *are* not carnal, but mighty through God to the pulling down of strong holds;) 5. Casting down imaginations, and every high thing that exalteth itself against the knowledge of God, and bringing into captivity every thought to the obedience of Christ;

See below, UNCLASSIFIED PROPHECIES CONCERNING, p. 686.

PROPHECIES CONCERNING UNIVERSALITY OF THE KINGDOM OF: Gen. 12:3. In thee shall all families of the earth be blessed.

Gen. 49:10. The sceptre shall not depart from Judah, nor a lawgiver from between his feet, until Shiloh come; and unto him *shall* the gathering of the people *be*.

Deut. 32:21. I will move them to jealousy with *those which are* not a people; I will provoke them to anger with a foolish nation.

Psa. 2:8. Ask of me, and I shall give *thee* the heathen *for* thine inheritance, and the uttermost parts of the earth *for* thy possession.

Psa. 22:27. All the ends of the world shall remember and turn unto the LORD: and all the kindreds of the nations shall worship before thee. 28. For the kingdom *is* the LORD'S: and he *is* the governor among the nations. 29. All *they that be* fat upon earth shall eat and worship: all they that go down to the dust shall bow before him: and none can keep alive his own soul. 30. A seed shall serve him; it shall be accounted to the Lord for a generation. 31. They shall come, and shall declare his righteousness unto a people that shall be born, that he hath done *this*.

Psa. 47:8. God reigneth over the heathen: God sitteth upon the throne of his holiness.

Psa. 65:2. O thou that hearest prayer, unto thee shall all flesh come.

Psa. 66:4. All the earth shall worship thee, and shall sing unto thee; they shall sing *to* thy name.

Psa. 68:31. Princes shall come out of Egypt; Ethiopia shall soon stretch out her hands unto God. 32. Sing unto God, ye kingdoms of the earth; O sing praises unto the Lord;

Psa. 72:5. They shall fear thee as long as the sun and moon endure, throughout all generations. 8. He shall have dominion also from sea to sea, and from the river unto the ends of the earth. 9. They that dwell in the wilderness shall bow before him; and his enemies shall lick the dust. 10. The kings of Tarshish and of the isles shall bring presents: the kings of Sheba and Seba shall offer gifts. 11. Yea, all kings shall fall down before him: all nations shall serve

him. 16. There shall be an handful of corn in the earth upon the top of the mountains; the fruit thereof shall shake like Lebanon: and *they* of the city shall flourish like grass of the earth. 17. His name shall endure for ever: his name shall be continued as long as the sun: and *men* shall be blessed in him: all nations shall call him blessed. 19. Blessed *be* his glorious name for ever: and let the whole earth be filled *with* his glory; Amen, and Amen.

Psa. 85:10. Mercy and truth are met together; righteousness and peace have kissed *each other*. 11. Truth shall spring out of the earth; and righteousness shall look down from heaven. 12. Yea, the LORD shall give *that which is* good; and our land shall yield her increase.

Psa. 86:9. All nations whom thou hast made shall come and worship before thee, O Lord; and shall glorify thy name.

Psa. 87:1. His foundation *is* in the holy mountains. 2. The LORD loveth the gates of Zion more than all the dwellings of Jacob. 3. Glorious things are spoken of thee, O city of God. Selah. 4. I will make mention of Rahab and Babylon to them that know me: behold Philistia, and Tyre, with Ethiopia; this *man* was born there. 5. And of Zion it shall be said, This and that man was born in her: and the highest himself shall establish her.

Psa. 89:25. I will set his hand also in the sea, and his right hand in the rivers. 29. His seed also will I make *to endure* for ever, and his throne as the days of heaven. 36. His seed shall endure for ever, and his throne as the sun before me. 37. It shall be established for ever as the moon, and *as* a faithful witness in heaven. *vs.* 1-37.

Psa. 96:11. Let the heavens rejoice, and let the earth be glad; let the sea roar, and the fulness thereof. 12. Let the field be joyful, and all that *is* therein: then shall all the trees of the wood rejoice 13. Before the LORD: for he cometh, for he cometh to judge the earth: he shall judge the world with righteousness, and the people with his truth. *vs.* 1-13.

Psa. 102:13. Thou shalt arise, *and* have mercy upon Zion: for the time to favour her, yea, the set time, is come. 14. For thy servants take pleasure in her stones, and favour the dust thereof. 15. So the heathen shall fear the name of the LORD, and all the kings of the earth thy glory. 16. When the LORD shall build up Zion, he shall appear in his glory.

Psa. 110:1. The LORD said unto my Lord, Sit thou at my right hand, until I make thine enemies thy footstool. 2. The LORD shall send the rod of thy strength out of Zion: rule thou in the midst of thine enemies. 3. Thy people *shall be* willing in the day of thy power, in the beauties of holiness from the womb of the morning: thou hast the dew of thy youth. 4. The LORD hath sworn, and will not repent, Thou *art* a priest for ever after the order of Melchizedek. 5. The Lord at thy right hand shall strike through kings in the day of his wrath. 6. He shall judge among the heathen, he shall fill *the places* with the dead bodies; he shall wound the heads over many countries.

Psa. 113:3. From the rising of the sun unto the going down of the same the LORD's name *is* to be praised.

Psa. 138:4. All the kings of the earth shall praise thee, O LORD, when they hear the words of thy mouth. 5. Yea, they shall sing in the ways of the LORD: for great *is* the glory of the LORD.

Psa. 145:10. All thy works shall praise thee, O LORD; and thy saints shall bless thee. 11. They shall speak of the glory of thy kingdom, and talk of thy power;

Isa. 2:2. It shall come to pass in the last days, *that* the mountain of the LORD's house shall be established in the top of the mountains, and shall be exalted above the hills; and all nations shall flow unto it. 3. Many people shall go and say, Come ye, and let us go up to the mountain of the LORD, to the house of the God of Jacob; and he will teach us of his ways, and we will walk in his paths: for out of Zion shall go forth the law, and the word of the LORD from Jerusalem. 4. He shall judge among the nations, and shall rebuke many people: and they shall beat their swords into plowshares, and their spears into pruninghooks: nation shall not lift up sword against nation, neither shall they learn war any more. *v.* 5.

Isa. 4:2. In that day shall the branch of the LORD be beautiful and glorious, and the fruit of the earth *shall be* excellent and comely for them that are escaped of Israel. 3. And it shall come to pass *that he that is* left in Zion, and *he that* remaineth in Jerusalem, shall be called holy, *even* every one that is written among the living in Jerusalem:

Isa. 9:7. Of the increase of *his* government and peace *there shall be* no end, upon the throne of David, and upon his kingdom, to order it, and to establish it with judgment and with justice from henceforth even for ever. *vs.* 1–7.

Isa. 11:6. The wolf also shall dwell with the lamb, and the leopard shall lie down with the kid; and the calf and the young lion and the fatling together; and a little child shall lead them. 7. And the cow and the bear shall feed; their young ones shall lie down together: and the lion shall eat straw like the ox. 8. And the sucking child shall play on the hole of the asp, and the weaned child shall put his hand on the cockatrice' den. 9. They shall not hurt nor destroy in all my holy mountain: for the earth shall be full of the knowledge of the LORD, as the waters cover the sea. 10. And in that day there shall be a root of Jesse, which shall stand for an ensign of the people; to it shall the Gentiles seek: and his rest shall be glorious. *vs.* 1–10.

Isa. 24:16. From the uttermost part of the earth have we heard songs, *even* glory to the righteous.

Isa. 25:6. And in this mountain shall the LORD of hosts make unto all people a feast of fat things, a feast of wines on the lees, of fat things full of marrow, of wines on the lees well refined. 7. And he will destroy in this mountain the face of the covering cast over all people, and the vail that is spread over all nations. 8. He will swallow up death in victory; and the Lord GOD will wipe away tears from off all faces; and the rebuke of his people shall he take away from off all the earth: for the LORD hath spoken *it*.

Isa. 29:18. In that day shall the deaf hear the words of the book, and the eyes of the blind shall see out of obscurity, and out of darkness. 19. The meek also shall increase *their* joy in the LORD, and the poor among men shall rejoice in the Holy One of Israel.

Isa. 32:15. Until the spirit be poured upon us from on high, and the wilderness be a fruitful field, and the fruitful field be counted for a forest. 16. Then judgment shall dwell in the wilderness, and righteousness remain in the fruitful field. 17. And the work of righteousness shall be peace; and the effect of righteousness quietness and assurance for ever.

Isa. 35:1. The wilderness and the solitary place shall be glad for them; and the desert shall rejoice, and blossom as the rose. 2. It shall blossom abundantly, and rejoice even with joy and singing: the glory of Lebanon shall be given unto it, the excellency of Carmel and Sharon; they shall see the glory of the LORD, *and* the excellency of our God.

Isa. 40:5. The glory of the LORD shall be revealed, and all flesh shall see *it* together: for the mouth of the LORD hath spoken *it*. *vs.* 4–11.

Isa. 42:3. He shall bring forth judgment unto truth. 4. He shall not fail nor be discouraged, till he have set judgment in the earth: and the isles shall wait for his law.

Isa. 45:8. Drop down, ye heavens, from above, and let the skies pour down righteousness: let the earth open, and let them bring forth salvation, and let righteousness spring up together; I the LORD have created it. 23. I have sworn by myself, the word is gone out of my mouth *in* righteousness, and shall not return, That unto me every knee shall bow, every tongue shall swear. 24. Surely, shall *one* say, In the LORD have I righteousness and strength: *even* to him shall *men* come:

Isa. 49:12. Behold, these shall come from far; and, lo, these from the north and from the west; and these from the land of Sinim. 18. Lift up thine eyes round about, and behold: all these gather themselves together, *and* come to thee. *As* I live, saith the LORD, thou shalt surely clothe thee with them all, as with an ornament, and bind them *on thee*, as a bride *doeth*. *vs.* 1–26.

Isa. 51:6. Lift up your eyes to the heavens, and look upon the earth beneath: for the heavens shall vanish away like smoke, and the earth shall wax old like a garment, and they that dwell therein shall die in like manner: but my salvation shall be for ever, and my righteousness shall not be abolished. 8. For the moth shall eat them up like a garment, and the worm shall eat them like wool: but my righteousness shall be for ever, and my salvation from generation to generation.

Isa. 53:10. When thou shalt make his soul an offering for sin, he shall see *his* seed, he shall prolong *his* days, and the pleasure of the LORD shall prosper in his hand. 11. He shall see of the travail of his soul, *and* shall be satisfied: by his knowledge shall my righteous servant justify many; for he shall bear their iniquities. 12. Therefore will I divide him *a portion* with the great, and he shall divide the spoil with the strong;

Isa. 54:1. Sing, O barren, thou *that* didst not bear; break forth into singing, and cry aloud, thou *that* didst not travail with child: for more *are* the children of the desolate than the children of the married wife, saith the LORD. 2. Enlarge the place of thy tent, and let them stretch forth the curtains of thine habitations; spare not, lengthen thy cords, and strengthen thy stakes; 3. For thou shalt break forth on the right hand and on the left; and thy seed shall inherit the Gentiles, and make the desolate cities to be inhabited.

Isa. 55:5. Behold, thou shalt call a nation *that* thou knowest not, and nations *that* knew not thee shall run unto thee because of the LORD thy God, and for the Holy One of Israel; for he hath glorified thee. 10. For as the rain cometh down, and the snow from heaven, and returneth not thither, but watereth the earth, and maketh it bring forth and bud, that it may give seed to the sower, and bread to the eater: 11. So shall my word be that goeth forth out of my mouth: it shall not return unto me void, but it shall acomplish that which I please, and it shall prosper *in the thing* whereto I sent it. 12. Ye shall go out with joy, and be led forth with peace: the mountains and the hills shall break forth before you into singing, and all the trees of the field shall clap *their* hands. 13. Instead of the thorn shall come up the fir tree, and instead of the brier shall come up the myrtle tree: and it shall be to the LORD for a name, for an ever-lasting sign *that* shall not be cut off.

Isa. 56:7. Mine house shall be called an house of prayer for all people. 8. The Lord GOD which gathereth the outcasts of Israel saith, Yet will I gather *others* to him, be-side those that are gathered unto him. *vs.* 3–8.

Isa. 59:19. So shall they fear the name of the LORD from the west, and his glory from

the rising of the sun. When the enemy shall come in like a flood, the Spirit of the LORD shall lift up a standard against him. *vs.* 19–21.

Isa. 60:1. Arise, shine; for thy light is come, and the glory of the LORD is risen upon thee. 2. For, behold, the darkness shall cover the earth, and gross darkness the people: but the LORD shall arise upon thee, and his glory shall be seen upon thee. 3. The Gentiles shall come to thy light, and kings to the brightness of thy rising. 4. Lift up thine eyes round about, and see: all they gather themselves together, they come to thee: thy sons shall come from far, and thy daughters shall be nursed at *thy* side. 5. Then thou shalt see, and flow to-gether, and thine heart shall fear and be enlarged; because the abundance of the sea shall be converted unto thee, the forces of the Gentiles shall come unto thee. 7. All the flocks of Kedar shall be gathered to-gether unto thee, the rams of Nebaioth shall minister unto thee: they shall come up with acceptance on mine altar, and I will glorify the house of my glory. 8. Who *are* these *that* fly as a cloud, and as the doves to their windows? 9. Surely the isles shall wait for me, and the ships of Tarshish first, to bring thy sons from far, their silver and their gold with them, unto the name of the LORD thy God, and to the Holy One of Israel, because he hath glorified thee.

Isa. 66:12. Behold, I will extend peace to her like a river, and the glory of the Gen-tiles like a flowing stream: then shall ye suck, ye shall be borne upon *her* sides, and be dandled upon *her* knees. 19. I will set a sign among them, and I will send those that escape of them unto the nations, *to* Tarshish, Pul, and Lud, that draw the bow, *to* Tubal, and Javan, *to* the isles afar off, that have not heard my fame, neither have seen my glory; and they shall declare my glory among the Gentiles. 23. It shall come to pass, *that* from one new moon to another, and from one sabbath to another, shall all flesh come to worship before me, saith the LORD. *vs.* 7–23.

Jer. 3:17. At that time they shall call Jerusalem the throne of the LORD; and all the nations shall be gathered unto it, to the name of the LORD, to Jerusalem: neither shall they walk any more after the imagina-tion of their evil heart.

Jer. 4:2. The nations shall bless themselves in him, and in him shall they glory.

Jer. 16:19. The Gentiles shall come unto thee from the ends of the earth, and shall say, Surely our fathers have inherited lies, vanity, and *things* wherein *there is* no profit. 20. Shall a man make gods unto himself, and they *are* no gods? 21. Therefore, be-hold, I will this once cause them to know, I will cause them to know mine hand and my might; and they shall know that my name *is* The LORD.

Jer. 31:34. They shall teach no more every

man his neighbour, and every man his brother, saying, Know the LORD: for they shall all know me, from the least of them unto the greatest of them, saith the LORD: for I will forgive their iniquity, and I will remember their sin no more.

Jer. 33:22. As the host of heaven cannot be numbered, neither the sand of the sea measured: so will I multiply the seed of David my servant,

Ezek. 17:22. I will also take of the highest branch of the high cedar, and will set *it*; I will crop off from the top of his young twigs a tender one, and will plant *it* upon an high mountain and eminent: 23. In the mountain of the height of Israel will I plant it: and it shall bring forth boughs, and bear fruit, and be a goodly cedar: and under it shall dwell all fowl of every wing; in the shadow of the branches thereof shall they dwell.

Ezek. 47:3. When the man that had the line in his hand went forth eastward, he measured a thousand cubits, and he brought me through the waters; the waters *were* to the ancles. 4. Again he measured a thousand, and brought me through the waters; the waters *were* to the knees. Again he measured a thousand, and brought me through; the waters *were* to the loins. 5. Afterwards he measured a thousand; *and it was* a river that I could not pass over: for the waters were risen, waters to swim in, a river that could not be passed over. 7. Now when I had returned, behold, at the bank of the river *were* very many trees on the one side and on the other. 8. Then said he unto me, These waters issue out toward the east country, and go down into the desert, and go into the sea: *which being* brought forth into the sea, the waters shall be healed. 9. And it shall come to pass, *that* every thing that liveth, which moveth, whithersoever the rivers come, shall live: and there shall be a very great multitude of fish, because these waters shall come thither: for they shall be healed; and every thing shall live whither the river cometh. 12. And by the river upon the bank thereof, on this side and on that side, shall grow all trees for meat, whose leaf shall not fade, neither shall the fruit thereof be consumed: it shall bring forth new fruit according to his months, because their waters they issued out of the sanctuary: and the fruit thereof shall be for meat, and the leaf thereof for medicine. *vs.* 1-12.

Dan. 2:35. And the stone that smote the image became a great mountain, and filled the whole earth. 44. In the days of these kings shall the God of heaven set up a kingdom, which shall never be destroyed: and the kingdom shall not be left to other people, *but* it shall break in pieces and consume all these kingdoms, and it shall stand for ever.

Dan. 7:13. I saw in the night visions, and, behold, *one* like the Son of man came with the clouds of heaven, and came to the Ancient of days, and they brought him near

before him. 14. And there was given him dominion, and glory, and a kingdom, that all people, nations, and languages, should serve him: his dominion *is* an everlasting dominion, which shall not pass away, and his kingdom *that* which shall not be destroyed. 18. But the saints of the most High shall take the kingdom, and possess the kingdom for ever, even for ever and ever. 22. Until the Ancient of days came, and judgment was given to the saints of the most High; and the time came that the saints possessed the kingdom. 27. The kingdom and dominion, and the greatness of the kingdom under the whole heaven, shall be given to the people of the saints of the most High, whose kingdom *is* an everlasting kingdom, and all dominions shall serve and obey him.

Dan. 12:4. Seal the book, *even* to the time of the end: many shall run to and fro, and knowledge shall be increased.

Joel 2:28. And it shall come to pass afterward, *that* I will pour out my spirit upon all flesh; and your sons and your daughters shall prophesy, your old men shall dream dreams, your young men shall see visions: 29. And also upon the servants and upon the handmaids in those days will I pour out my spirit.

Mic. 4:1. But in the last days it shall come to pass, *that* the mountain of the house of the LORD shall be established in the top of the mountains, and it shall be exalted above the hills; and people shall flow unto it. 2. And many nations shall come, and say, Come, and let us go up to the mountain of the LORD, and to the house of the God of Jacob; and he will teach us of his ways, and we will walk in his paths: for the law shall go forth of Zion, and the word of the LORD from Jerusalem. 3. He shall judge among many people, and rebuke strong nations afar off; and they shall beat their swords into plowshares, and their spears into pruninghooks: nation shall not lift up a sword against nation, neither shall they learn war any more. 4. But they shall sit every man under his vine and under his fig tree; and none shall make *them* afraid: for the mouth of the LORD of hosts hath spoken *it*.

Hab. 2:14. The earth shall be filled with the knowledge of the glory of the LORD, as the waters cover the sea.

Zeph. 2:11. The LORD *will be* terrible unto them: for he will famish all the gods of the earth; and *men* shall worship him, every one from his place, *even* all the isles of the heathen.

Zeph. 3:9. Then will I turn to the people a pure language, that they may all call upon the name of the LORD, to serve him with one consent.

Hag. 2:7. And I will shake all nations, and the [1] desire of all nations shall come: and I will fill this house with glory, saith the LORD of hosts. 8. The silver *is* mine, and the gold *is* mine, saith the LORD of hosts. 9.

The glory of this latter house shall be greater than of the former, saith the LORD of hosts: and in this place will I give peace, saith the LORD of hosts.   [¹ R. V. desirable things]

Zech. 2:10. Sing and rejoice, O daughter of Zion: for, lo, I come, and I will dwell in the midst of thee, saith the LORD. 11. And many nations shall be joined to the LORD in that day, and shall be my people: and I will dwell in the midst of thee, and thou shalt know that the LORD of hosts hath sent me unto thee.

Zech. 4:10. Who hath despised the day of small things? for they shall rejoice, and shall see the plummet in the hand of Zerubbabel *with* those seven; they *are* the eyes of the LORD, which run to and fro through the whole earth.

Zech. 6:15. They *that are* far off shall come and build in the temple of the LORD,

Zech. 8:20. *It shall* yet *come to pass*, that there shall come people, and the inhabitants of many cities: 21. And the inhabitants of one *city* shall go to another, saying, Let us go speedily to pray before the LORD, and to seek the LORD of hosts: I will go also. 22. Yea, many people and strong nations shall come to seek the LORD of hosts in Jerusalem, and to pray before the LORD. 23. Thus saith the LORD of hosts; In those days *it shall come to pass*, that ten men shall take hold out of all languages of the nations, even shall take hold of the skirt of him that is a Jew, saying, We will go with you: for we have heard *that* God *is* with you.

Zech. 9:1. The eyes of man, as of all the tribes of Israel, *shall be* toward the LORD. 10. I will cut off the chariot from Ephraim, and the horse from Jerusalem, and the battle bow shall be cut off: and he shall speak peace unto the heathen: and his dominion *shall be* from sea *even* to sea, and from the river *even* to the ends of the earth.

Zech. 14:8. It shall be in that day, *that* living waters shall go out from Jerusalem; half of them toward the former sea, and half of them toward the hinder sea: in summer and in winter shall it be. 9. And the LORD shall be king over all the earth: in that day shall there be one LORD, and his name one. 16. Every one that is left of all the nations which came against Jerusalem shall even go up from year to year to worship the King, the LORD of hosts, and to keep the feasts of tabernacles. 20. In that day shall there be upon the bells of the horses, HOLINESS UNTO THE LORD; and the pots in the LORD's house shall be like the bowls before the altar. 21. Yea, every pot in Jerusalem and in Judah shall be holiness unto the LORD of hosts: and all they that sacrifice shall come and take of them, and seethe therein: and in that day there shall be no more the Canaanite in the house of the LORD of hosts.

Mal. 1:11. From the rising of the sun even unto the going down of the same my name *shall be* great among the Gentiles; and in every place incense *shall be* offered unto my name, and a pure offering: for my name *shall be* great among the heathen, saith the LORD of hosts.

Matt. 8:11. Many shall come from the east and west, and shall sit down with Abraham, and Isaac, and Jacob, in the kingdom of heaven.

Matt. 13:31. The kingdom of heaven is like to a grain of mustard seed, which a man took, and sowed in his field: 32. Which indeed is the least of all seeds: but when it is grown, it is the greatest among herbs, and becometh a tree, so that the birds of the air come and lodge in the branches thereof. 33. The kingdom of heaven is like unto leaven, which a woman took, and hid in three measures of meal, till the whole was leavened.

Mark 13:10. And the gospel must first be published among all nations.

Luke 1:33. And he shall reign over the house of Jacob for ever; and of his kingdom there shall be no end.

Luke 2:10. And the angel said unto them, Fear not, for, behold, I bring you good tidings of great joy, which shall be to all people.

John 3:30. He must increase, but I *must* decrease.

John 10:16. Other sheep I have, which are not of this fold: them also I must bring, and they shall hear my voice; and there shall be one fold, *and* one shepherd.

John 12:31. Now is the judgment of this world: now shall the prince of this world be cast out. 32. And I, if I be lifted up from the earth, will draw all *men* unto me.

Acts 2:34. For David is not ascended into the heavens: but he saith himself, The LORD said unto my lord, Sit thou on my right hand, 35. Until I make thy foes thy footstool.

1 Cor. 15:24. Then *cometh* the end, when he shall have delivered up the kingdom to God, even the Father; when he shall have put down all rule and all authority and power. 25. For he must reign, till he hath put all enemies under his feet. 26. The last enemy *that* shall be destroyed *is* death. 27. For he hath put all things under his feet. But when he saith all things are put under *him, it is* manifest that he is excepted, which did put all things under him. 28. And when all things shall be subdued unto him, then shall the Son also himself be subject unto him that put all things under him, that God may be all in all.

Eph. 1:10. That in the dispensation of the fulness of times he might gather together in one all things in Christ, both which are in heaven, and which are on earth; *even* in him:

Phil. 2:10. That at the name of Jesus every knee should bow, of *things* in heaven, and *things* in earth, and *things* under the earth; 11. And *that* every tongue should confess that Jesus Christ *is* Lord, to the glory of God the Father.

Heb. 8:11. And they shall not teach every

man his neighbour, and every man his brother, saying, Know the Lord : for all shall know me, from the least to the greatest.

Heb. 10:13. From henceforth expecting till his enemies be made his footstool.

Heb. 12:23. To the general assembly and church of the firstborn, which are written in heaven, and to God the Judge of all, and to the spirits of just men made perfect, 24. And to Jesus the mediator of the new covenant, and to the blood of sprinkling, that speaketh better things than *that of* Abel. 27. This *word*, Yet once more, signifieth the removing of those things that are shaken, as of things that are made, that those things which cannot be shaken may remain. 28. Wherefore we receiving a kingdom which cannot be moved, let us have grace, whereby we may serve God acceptably with reverence and godly fear :

Rev. 5:9. They sung a new song, saying, Thou art worthy to take the book, and to open the seals thereof : for thou wast slain, and hast redeemed us to God by thy blood out of every kindred, and tongue, and people, and nation ; 10. Hast made us unto our God kings and priests : and we shall reign on the earth. 13. Every creature which is in heaven, and on the earth, and under the earth, and such as are in the sea, and all that are in them, heard I saying, Blessing, and honour, and glory, and power, *be* unto him that sitteth upon the throne, and unto the Lamb for ever and ever. 14. And the four beasts said, Amen. And the four *and* twenty elders fell down and worshipped him that liveth for ever and ever.

Rev. 6:2. I saw, and behold a white horse : and he that sat on him had a bow ; and a crown was given unto him : and he went forth conquering, and to conquer.

Rev. 11:15. The seventh angel sounded ; and there were great voices in heaven, saying, The kingdoms of this world are become *the kingdoms* of our Lord, and of his Christ ; and he shall reign for ever and ever.

Rev. 12:10. I heard a loud voice saying in heaven, Now is come salvation, and strength, and the kingdom of our God, and the power of his Christ : for the accuser of our brethren is cast down, which accused them before our God day and night.

Rev. 14:6. I saw another angel fly in the midst of heaven, having the everlasting gospel to preach unto them that dwell on the earth, and to every nation, and kindred, and tongue, and people,

Rev. 15:4. Who shall not fear thee, O Lord, and glorify thy name ? for *thou* only *art* holy : for all nations shall come and worship before thee ; for thy judgments are made manifest.

Rev. 17:14. These shall make war with the Lamb, and the Lamb shall overcome them : for he is Lord of lords, and King of kings : and they that are with him *are* called, and chosen, and faithful.

Rev. 19:6. And I heard as it were the voice of a great multitude, and as the voice of many waters, and as the voice of mighty thunderings, saying, Alleluia : for the Lord God omnipotent reigneth. 11. And I saw heaven opened, and behold a white horse ; and he that sat upon him *was* called Faithful and True, and in righteousness he doth judge and make war. 12. His eyes *were* as a flame of fire, and on his head *were* many crowns ; and he had a name written, that no man knew, but he himself. 13. And he *was* clothed with a vesture dipped in blood ; and his name is called The Word of God. 14. And the armies *which were* in heaven followed him upon white horses, clothed in fine linen, white and clean. 15. And out of his mouth goeth a sharp sword, that with it he should smite the nations : and he shall rule them with a rod of iron : and he treadeth the winepress of the fierceness and wrath of Almighty God. 16. And he hath on *his* vesture and on his thigh a name written, KING OF KINGS, AND LORD OF LORDS. 17. And I saw an angel standing in the sun ; and he cried with a loud voice, saying to all the fowls that fly in the midst of heaven, Come and gather yourselves together unto the supper of the great God ; 18. That ye may eat the flesh of kings, and the flesh of captains, and the flesh of mighty men, and the flesh of horses, and of them that sit on them, and the flesh of all *men, both* free and bond, both small and great. 19. And I saw the beast, and the kings of the earth, and their armies, gathered together to make war against him that sat on the horse, and against his army. 20. And the beast was taken, and with him the false prophet that wrought miracles before him, with which he deceived them that had received the mark of the beast, and them that worshipped his image. These both were cast alive into a lake of fire burning with brimstone. 21. And the remnant were slain with the sword of him that sat upon the horse, which *sword* proceedeth out of his mouth : and all the fowls were filled with their flesh.

Rev. 20:1. And I saw an angel come down from heaven, having the key of the bottomless pit and a great chain in his hand. 2. And he laid hold on the dragon, that old serpent, which is the Devil, and Satan, and bound him a thousand years, 3. And cast him into the bottomless pit, and shut him up, and set a seal upon him, that he should deceive the nations no more, till the thousand years should be fulfilled : and after that he must be loosed a little season.

UNCLASSIFIED PROPHECIES CONCERNING KINGDOM OF : Gen. 22:18. And in thy seed shall all the nations of the earth be blessed ; because thou hast obeyed my voice.

Gen. 49:10. The sceptre shall not depart from Judah, nor a lawgiver from between his feet, until Shiloh come ; and unto him *shall* the gathering of the people *be*.

Psa. 2:9. Thou shalt break them with a

rod of iron; thou shalt dash them in pieces like a potter's vessel.

Psa. 46:9. He maketh wars to cease unto the end of the earth; he breaketh the bow, and cutteth the spear in sunder; he burneth the chariot in the fire.

Psa. 67:1. God be merciful unto us, and bless us; *and* cause his face to shine upon us; 2. That thy way may be known upon earth, thy saving health among all nations. 3. Let the people praise thee, O God; let all the people praise thee. 4. O let the nations be glad and sing for joy: for thou shalt judge the people righteously, and govern the nations upon earth. 5. Let the people praise thee, O God; let all the people praise thee. 6. *Then* shall the earth yield her increase; *and* God, *even* our own God, shall bless us. 7. God shall bless us; and all the ends of the earth shall fear him.

Psa. 72:12. For he shall deliver the needy when he crieth; the poor also, and *him* that hath no helper.

Isa. 2:2. And it shall come to pass in the last days, *that* the mountain of the Lord's house shall be established in the top of the mountains, and shall be exalted above the hills; and all nations shall flow unto it. 3. And many people shall go and say, Come ye, and let us go up to the mountain of the Lord, to the house of the God of Jacob; and he will teach us of his ways, and we will walk in his paths: for out of Zion shall go forth the law, and the word of the Lord from Jerusalem. 4. And he shall judge among the nations, and shall rebuke many people: and they shall beat their swords into plowshares, and their spears into pruning-hooks: nation shall not lift up sword against nation, neither shall they learn war any more.

Isa. 9:5. For every battle of the warrior *is* with confused noise, and garments rolled in blood; but *this* shall be with burning *and* fuel of fire.

Isa. 11:1. And there shall come forth a rod out of the stem of Jesse, and a Branch shall grow out of his roots: 2. And the spirit of the Lord shall rest upon him, the spirit of wisdom and understanding, the spirit of counsel and might, the spirit of knowledge and of the fear of the Lord; 3. And shall make him of quick understanding in the fear of the Lord: and he shall not judge after the sight of his eyes, neither reprove after the hearing of his ears: 4. But with righteousness shall he judge the poor, and reprove with equity for the meek of the earth: and he shall smite the earth with the rod of his mouth, and with the breath of his lips shall he slay the wicked. 5. And righteousness shall be the girdle of his loins, and faithfulness the girdle of his reins. 6. The wolf also shall dwell with the lamb, and the leopard shall lie down with the kid; and the calf and the young lion and the fatling together; and a little child shall lead them. 7. And the cow and the bear shall feed; their young ones shall lie down together: and the lion shall eat straw like the ox. 8. And the sucking child shall play on the hole of the asp, and the weaned child shall put his hand on the cockatrice' den. 9. They shall not hurt nor destroy in all my holy mountain: for the earth shall be full of the knowledge of the Lord, as the waters cover the sea. 10. And in that day there shall be a root of Jesse, which shall stand for an ensign of the people; to it shall the Gentiles seek: and his rest shall be glorious. 11. And it shall come to pass in that day, *that* the Lord shall set his hand again the second time to recover the remnant of his people, which shall be left, from Assyria, and from Egypt, and from Pathros, and from Cush, and from Elam, and from Shinar, and from Hamath, and from the islands of the sea. 12. And he shall set up an ensign for the nations, and shall assemble the outcasts of Israel, and gather together the dispersed of Judah from the four corners of the earth. 13. The envy also of Ephraim shall depart, and the adversaries of Judah shall be cut off: Ephraim shall not envy Judah, and Judah shall not vex Ephraim.

Isa. 25:6. And in this mountain shall the Lord of hosts make unto all people a feast of fat things, a feast of wines on the lees, of fat things full of marrow, of wines on the lees well refined.

Isa. 35:1. The wilderness and the solitary place shall be glad for them; and the desert shall rejoice, and blossom as the rose. 2. It shall blossom abundantly, and rejoice even with joy and singing: the glory of Lebanon shall be given unto it, the excellency of Carmel and Sharon, they shall see the glory of the Lord, *and* the excellency of our God. 3. Strengthen ye the weak hands, and confirm the feeble knees. 4. Say to them *that are* of a fearful heart, Be strong, fear not: behold, your God will come *with* vengeance, *even* God *with* a recompence; he will come and save you. 5. Then the eyes of the blind shall be opened, and the ears of the deaf shall be unstopped. [Matt. 11:5.] 6. Then shall the lame *man* leap as an hart, and the tongue of the dumb sing: for in the wilderness shall waters break out, and streams in the desert. 7. And the parched ground shall become a pool, and the thirsty land springs of water: in the habitation of dragons, where each lay, *shall be* grass with reeds and rushes. 8. And an highway shall be there, and a way, and it shall be called The way of holiness; the unclean shall not pass over it; but it *shall be* for those: the wayfaring men, though fools, shall not err *therein*. 9. No lion shall be there, nor *any* ravenous beast shall go up thereon, it shall not be found there; but the redeemed shall walk *there*: 10. And the ransomed of the Lord shall return, and come to Zion with songs and everlasting joy upon their heads: they shall obtain joy and gladness, and sorrow and sighing shall flee away.

Isa. 42:1. Behold my servant, whom I uphold; mine elect, *in whom* my soul delighteth; I have put my spirit upon him: he shall bring forth judgment to the Gentiles. 2. He shall not cry, nor lift up, nor cause his voice to be heard in the street. [Matt. 12:18-21.] 3. A bruised reed shall he not break, and the smoking flax shall he not quench: he shall bring forth judgment unto truth. 4. He shall not fail nor be discouraged, till he have set judgment in the earth: and the isles shall wait for his law. 5. Thus saith God the LORD, he that created the heavens, and stretched them out; he that spread forth the earth, and that which cometh out of it; he that giveth breath unto the people upon it, and spirit to them that walk therein: 6. I the LORD have called thee in righteousness, and will hold thine hand, and will keep thee, and give thee for a covenant of the people, for a light of the Gentiles; 7. To open the blind eyes, to bring out the prisoners from the prison, *and* them that sit in darkness out of the prison house. 18. Hear, ye deaf; and look, ye blind, that ye may see. 19. Who *is* blind, but my servant? or deaf, as my messenger *that* I sent? who *is* blind as *he that is* perfect, and blind as the LORD's servant? 20. Seeing many things, but thou observest not; opening the ears, but he heareth not. 21. The LORD is well pleased for his righteousness' sake; he will magnify the law, and make *it* honourable.

Isa. 45:14. Thus saith the LORD, The labour of Egypt, and merchandise of Ethiopia and of the Sabeans, men of stature, shall come over unto thee, and they shall be thine: they shall come after thee; in chains they shall come over, and they shall fall down unto thee, they shall make supplication unto thee, *saying*, Surely God *is* in thee; and *there is* none else, *there is* no God.

Isa. 49:5. And now, saith the LORD that formed me from the womb *to be* his servant, to bring Jacob again to him, Though Israel be not gathered, yet shall I be glorious in the eyes of the LORD, and my God shall be my strength. 18. Lift up thine eyes round about, and behold: all these gather themselves together, *and* come to thee. As I live, saith the LORD, thou shalt surely clothe thee with them all, as with an ornament, and bind them *on thee*, as a bride *doeth*. 19. For thy waste and thy desolate places, and the land of thy destruction, shall even now be too narrow by reason of the inhabitants, and they that swallowed thee up shall be far away. 20. The children which thou shalt have, after thou hast lost the other, shall say again in thine ears, The place *is* too strait for me: give place to me that I may dwell. 21. Then shalt thou say in thine heart, Who hath begotten me these, seeing I have lost my children, and am desolate, a captive, and removing to and fro? and who hath brought up these? Behold, I was left alone; these, where *had* they *been?* 22. Thus saith the Lord GOD, Behold, I will lift up mine hand to the Gentiles, and set up my standard to the people: and they shall bring thy sons in *their* arms, and thy daughters shall be carried upon *their* shoulders. 23. And kings shall be thy nursing fathers, and their queens thy nursing mothers: they shall bow down to thee with *their* face toward the earth, and lick up the dust of thy feet; and thou shalt know that I *am* the LORD: for they shall not be ashamed that wait for me.

Isa. 55:1. Ho, every one that thirsteth, come ye to the waters, and he that hath no money; come ye, buy, and eat; yea, come, buy wine and milk without money and without price. 2. Wherefore do ye spend money for *that which is* not bread? and your labour for *that which* satisfieth not? hearken diligently unto me, and eat ye *that which is* good, and let your soul delight itself in fatness. 3. Incline your ear, and come unto me: hear, and your soul shall live; and I will make an everlasting covenant with you, *even* the sure mercies of David. 4. Behold, I have given him *for* a witness to the people, a leader and commander to the people. 5. Behold, thou shalt call a nation *that* thou knowest not, and nations *that* knew not thee shall run unto thee because of the LORD thy God, and for the Holy One of Israel: for he hath glorified thee. 6. Seek ye the LORD while he may be found, call ye upon him while he is near: 7. Let the wicked forsake his way, and the unrighteous man his thoughts: and let him return unto the LORD, and he will have mercy upon him; and to our God, for he will abundantly pardon. 8. For my thoughts *are* not your thoughts, neither *are* your ways my ways, saith the LORD. 9. For *as* the heavens are higher than the earth, so are my ways higher than your ways, and my thoughts than your thoughts. 10. For as the rain cometh down, and the snow from heaven, and returneth not thither, but watereth the earth, and maketh it bring forth and bud, that it may give seed to the sower, and bread to the eater; 11. So shall my word be that goeth forth out of my mouth: it shall not return unto me void, but it shall accomplish that which I please, and it shall prosper *in the thing* whereto I sent it. 12. For ye shall go out with joy, and be led forth with peace: the mountains and the hills shall break forth before you into singing, and all the trees of the field shall clap *their* hands. 13. Instead of the thorn shall come up the fir tree, and instead of the brier shall come up the myrtle tree: and it shall be to the LORD for a name, for an everlasting sign *that* shall not be cut off.

Isa. 62:11. Behold, the LORD hath proclaimed unto the end of the world, Say ye to the daughter of Zion, Behold, thy salvation cometh; behold, his reward *is* with him, and his work before him. Matt. 21:4,5.

Isa. 65:17. For, behold, I create new heavens and a new earth: and the former shall not be remembered, nor come into mind. 18. But be ye glad and rejoice for ever *in that* which I create: for, behold, I create Jerusalem a rejoicing, and her people a joy. 19. And I will rejoice in Jerusalem, and joy in my people: and the voice of weeping shall be no more heard in her, nor the voice of crying. 20. There shall be no more thence an infant of days, nor an old man that hath not filled his days: for the child shall die an hundred years old; but the sinner *being* an hundred years old shall be accursed. 21. And they shall build houses, and inhabit *them;* and they shall plant vineyards, and eat the fruit of them. 22. They shall not build, and another inhabit; they shall not plant, and another eat: for as the days of a tree *are* the days of my people, and mine elect shall long enjoy the work of their hands. 23. They shall not labour in vain, nor bring forth for trouble; for they *are* the seed of the blessed of the LORD, and their offspring with them. 24. And it shall come to pass, that before they call, I will answer; and while they are yet speaking, I will hear. 25. The wolf and the lamb shall feed together, and the lion shall eat straw like the bullock: and dust *shall be* the serpent's meat. They shall not hurt nor destroy in all my holy mountain, saith the LORD.

Isa. 66:19. And I will set a sign among them, and I will send those that escape of them unto the nations, *to* Tarshish, Pul, and Lud, that draw the bow, *to* Tubal, and Javan, *to* the isles afar off, that have not heard my fame, neither have seen my glory; and they shall declare my glory among the Gentiles.

Jer. 3:14. Turn, O backsliding children, saith the LORD; for I am married unto you: and I will take you one of a city, and two of a family, and I will bring you to Zion: 15. And I will give you pastors according to mine heart, which shall feed you with knowledge and understanding. 16. And it shall come to pass, when ye be multiplied and increased in the land, in those days, saith the LORD, they shall say no more, The ark of the covenant of the LORD: neither shall it come to mind; neither shall they remember it; neither shall they visit *it;* neither shall *that* be done any more. 17. At that time they shall call Jerusalem the throne of the LORD; and all the nations shall be gathered unto it, to the name of the LORD, to Jerusalem: neither shall they walk any more after the imagination of their evil heart. 18. In those days the house of Judah shall walk with the house of Israel, and they shall come together out of the land of the north to the land that I have given for an inheritance unto your fathers. 19. But I said, How shall I put thee among the children, and give thee a pleasant land, a goodly heritage of the hosts of nations? and I said, Thou shalt call me, My father; and shalt not turn away from me.

Dan. 2:44. And in the days of these kings shall the God of heaven set up a kingdom, which shall never be destroyed: and the kingdom shall not be left to other people, *but* it shall break in pieces and consume all these kingdoms, and it shall stand for ever.

Dan. 7:9. I beheld till the thrones were cast down, and the Ancient of days did sit, whose garment *was* white as snow, and the hair of his head like the pure wool: his throne *was like* the fiery flame, *and* his wheels *as* burning fire. 10. A fiery stream issued and came forth from before him: thousand thousands ministered unto him, and ten thousand times ten thousand stood before him: the judgment was set, and the books were opened. 11. I beheld then because of the voice of the great words which the horn spake: I beheld *even* till the beast was slain, and his body destroyed, and given to the burning flame. 12. As concerning the rest of the beasts, they had their dominion taken away: yet their lives were prolonged for a season and time. 13. I saw in the night visions, and, behold, *one* like the Son of man came with the clouds of heaven, and came to the Ancient of days, and they brought him near before him. 14. And there was given him dominion, and glory, and a kingdom, that all people, nations, and languages, should serve him: his dominion *is* an everlasting dominion, which shall not pass away, and his kingdom *that* which shall not be destroyed. 27. And the kingdom and dominion, and the greatness of the kingdom under the whole heaven, shall be given to the people of the saints of the most High, whose kingdom *is* an everlasting kingdom, and all dominions shall serve and obey him.

Hos. 2:18. And in that day will I make a covenant for them with the beasts of the field, and with the fowls of heaven, and *with* the creeping things of the ground: and I will break the bow and the sword and the battle out of the earth, and will make them to lie down safely. 23. I will say to *them which were* not my people, Thou *art* my people; and they shall say, *Thou art* my God.

Amos 9:11. In that day will I raise up the tabernacle of David that is fallen, and close up the breaches thereof: and I will raise up his ruins, and I will build it as in the days of old. 12. That they may possess the remnant of Edom, and of all the heathen, which are called by my name, saith the LORD that doeth this.

Mic. 4:1. But in the last days it shall come to pass, *that* the mountain of the house of the LORD shall be established in the top of the mountains, and it shall be exalted above the hills; and people shall flow unto it. 2. And many nations shall come, and say, Come, and let us go up to the mountain of the LORD, and to the house of the God of Jacob; and he will teach us of his ways, and we will walk in his paths: for the law shall go forth of Zion, and the word of the LORD from Jerusalem. 3. And he shall judge among many people, and rebuke strong nations afar off; and they shall beat their swords into plowshares, and their spears into pruninghooks: nation shall not lift up a sword against nation, neither shall they learn war any more. 4. But they shall sit every man under his vine and under his fig tree; and none shall make *them* afraid: for the mouth of the LORD of hosts hath spoken *it*. 5. For all people will walk every one in the name of his god, and we will walk in the name of the LORD our God for ever and ever. 6. In that day, saith the LORD, will I assemble her that halteth, and I will gather her that is driven out, and her that I have afflicted; 7. And I will make her that halted a remnant, and her that was cast far off a strong nation: and the LORD shall reign over them in mount Zion from henceforth, even for ever.

Zech. 8:20. Thus saith the LORD of hosts: *It shall* yet *come to pass,* that there shall come people, and the inhabitants of many cities: 21. And the inhabitants of one *city* shall go to another, saying, Let us go speedily to pray before the LORD, and to seek the LORD of hosts: I will go also. 22. Yea, many people and strong nations shall come to seek the LORD of hosts in Jerusalem, and to pray before the LORD. 23. Thus saith the LORD of hosts; In those days *it shall come to pass,* that ten men shall take hold out of all languages of the nations, even shall take hold of the skirt of him that is a Jew, saying, We will go with you: for we have heard *that* God *is* with you.

Zech. 9:9. Rejoice greatly, O daughter of Zion; shout, O daughter of Jerusalem: behold, thy King cometh unto thee: he *is* just, and having salvation; lowly, and riding upon an ass, and upon a colt the foal of an ass.

Zech. 11:12. And I said unto them, If ye think good, give *me* my ¹price; and if not, forbear. So they weighed for my ¹price thirty *pieces* of silver. 13. And the LORD said unto me, Cast it unto the potter: a goodly price that I was prised at of them. And I took the thirty *pieces* of silver, and cast them to the potter in the house of the LORD. Matt. 26:15; 27:3–10. [¹ R. V. hire]

Zech. 13:7. Awake, O sword, against my shepherd, and against the man *that is* my fellow, saith the LORD of hosts: smite the shepherd, and the sheep shall be scattered: Matt. 26:31.

Mal. 3:1. Behold, I will send my messenger, and he shall prepare the way before me: and the Lord, whom ye seek, shall suddenly come to his temple, even the messenger of the covenant, whom ye delight in: behold, he shall come, saith the LORD of hosts. Matt. 11:10.

Matt. 12:29. How can one enter into a strong man's house, and spoil his goods, except he first bind the strong man? and then he will spoil his house.

Matt. 16:28. Verily I say unto you, There be some standing here, which shall not taste of death, till they see the Son of man coming in his kingdom.

Matt. 28:18. And Jesus came and spake unto them, saying, All power is given unto me in heaven and in earth.

Luke 1:32. He shall be great, and shall be called the Son of the Highest: and the Lord God shall give unto him the throne of his father David: 33. And he shall reign over the house of Jacob for ever; and of his kingdom there shall be no end.

Luke 22:29. And I appoint unto you a kingdom, as my Father hath appointed unto me; 30. That ye may eat and drink at my table in my kingdom, and sit on thrones judging the twelve tribes of Israel.

Heb. 1:8. But unto the Son *he saith,* Thy throne, O God, *is* for ever and ever: a sceptre of righteousness *is* the sceptre of thy kingdom.

2 Pet. 1:11. For so an entrance shall be ministered unto you abundantly into the everlasting kingdom of our Lord and Saviour Jesus Christ.

See JESUS, MESSIAH; PSALMS, MESSIANIC.

SECULAR NOTIONS CONCERNING THE KINGDOM OF: Matt. 18:1. At the same time came the disciples unto Jesus, saying, Who is the greatest in the kingdom of heaven? 2. And Jesus called a little child unto him, and set him in the midst of them, 3. And said, Verily I say unto you, Except ye be converted, and become as little children, ye shall not enter into the kingdom of heaven. Luke 9:46–48.

Matt. 20:20. Then came to him the mother of Zebedee's children with her sons, worshipping *him,* and desiring a certain thing of him. 21. And he said unto her, What wilt thou? She saith unto him, Grant that these my two sons may sit, the one on thy right hand, and the other on the left, in thy kingdom. 22. But Jesus answered and said, Ye know not what ye ask. Are ye able to drink of the cup that I shall drink of, and to be baptized with the baptism that I am baptized with? They say unto him, We are able. 23. And he saith unto them, Ye shall drink indeed of my cup, and be baptized with the baptism that I am baptized with: but to sit on my right hand, and on my left, is not mine to give, but *it shall be given to them* for whom it is prepared of my Father. Mark 10:35–40.

Mark 11:9. And they that went before, and they that followed, cried, saying, Hosanna; Blessed *is* he that cometh in the name of the Lord: 10. Blessed *be* the kingdom of our father David, that cometh in the name of the Lord: Hosanna in the highest.

John 6:15. When Jesus therefore perceived that they would come and take him by force, to make him a king, he departed again into a mountain himself alone.

Acts 1:6. When they therefore were come together, they asked of him, saying, Lord, wilt thou at this time restore again the kingdom to Israel? 7. And he said unto them, It is not for you to know the times or the seasons, which the Father hath put in his own power.

LOVE OF: Psa. 69:9. For the zeal of thine house hath eaten me up;

Psa. 72:14. He shall redeem their soul from deceit and violence: and precious shall their blood be in his sight.

Prov. 8:17. I love them that love me; and those that seek me early shall find me. 31. My delights *were* with the sons of men.

Isa. 40:11. He shall feed his flock like a shepherd: he shall gather the lambs with his arm, and carry *them* in his bosom, *and* shall gently lead those that are with young.

Isa. 42:3. A bruised reed shall he not break, and the smoking flax shall he not quench:

Isa. 63:9. In all their affliction he was afflicted, and the angel of his presence saved them: in his love and in his pity he redeemed them; and he bare them, and carried them all the days of old. *vs.* 7,8.

Mic. 5:4. He shall stand and feed in the strength of the LORD, in the majesty of the name of the LORD his God; and they shall abide:

Matt. 8:17. Himself took our infirmities, and bare *our* sicknesses. Isa. 53:4.

Matt. 9:36. When he saw the multitudes, he was moved with compassion on them, because they fainted, and were scattered abroad, as sheep having no shepherd.

Matt. 12:49. And he stretched forth his hand toward his disciples, and said, Behold my mother and my brethren! 50. For whosoever shall do the will of my Father which is in heaven, the same is my brother, and sister, and mother. Mark 3:31–35; Luke 8:19–21.

Matt. 14:14. Jesus went forth, and saw a great multitude, and was moved with compassion toward them, and he healed their sick.

Matt. 15:32. I have compassion on the multitude, because they continue with me now three days, and have nothing to eat: and I will not send them away fasting, lest they faint in the way.

Matt. 18:6. But whoso shall offend one of these little ones which believe in me, it were better for him that a millstone were hanged about his neck, and *that* he were drowned in the depth of the sea. 10. Take heed that ye despise not one of these little ones; for I say unto you, That in heaven their angels do always behold the face of my Father which is in heaven. Mark 9:37, 42; Luke 9:48.

Matt. 18:11. [1] For the Son of man is come to save that which was lost. 12. How think ye? if a man have an hundred sheep, and one of them be gone astray, doth he not leave the ninety and nine, and goeth into the mountains, and seeketh that which is gone astray? 13. And if so be that he find

it, verily I say unto you, he rejoiceth more of that *sheep*, than of the ninety and nine which went not astray. [1 Omitted in R. V.]

Matt. 23:37. O Jerusalem, Jerusalem, *thou* that killest the prophets, and stonest them which are sent unto thee, how often would I have gathered thy children together, even as a hen gathereth her chickens under *her* wings, and ye would not!

Matt. 28:10. Then said Jesus unto them, Be not afraid: go tell my brethren that they go into Galilee, and there shall they see me.

Mark 8:12. He sighed deeply in his spirit, and saith, Why doth this generation seek after a sign?

Mark 9:36. He took a child, and set him in the midst of them: and when he had taken him in his arms, he said unto them, 37. Whosoever shall receive one of such children in my name, receiveth me: Matt. 18:2–5; Luke 9:48.

Mark 10:13. They brought young children to him, that he should touch them: and *his* disciples rebuked those that brought *them*. 14. But when Jesus saw *it*, he was much displeased, and said unto them, Suffer the little children to come unto me, and forbid them not: for of such is the kingdom of God. 16. And he took them up in his arms, put *his* hands upon them, and blessed them. 21. Jesus beholding him [the rich young ruler] loved him, Matt. 19:13–15; Luke 18:15,16.

Luke 7:13. When the Lord saw her, he had compassion on her, and said unto her, Weep not.

Luke 22:31. And the Lord said, Simon, Simon, behold, Satan hath desired *to have* you, that he may sift *you* as wheat: 32. But I have prayed for thee, that thy faith fail not: and when thou art converted, strengthen thy brethren.

Luke 23:28. Jesus turning unto them said, Daughters of Jerusalem, weep not for me, but weep for yourselves, and for your children.

Luke 24:38. He said unto them, Why are ye troubled? and why do thoughts arise in your hearts? 39. Behold my hands and my feet, that it is I myself: handle me, and see; for a spirit hath not flesh and bones, as ye see me have. 40. And when he had thus spoken, he shewed them *his* hands and *his* feet.

John 10:3. The sheep hear his voice: and he calleth his own sheep by name, and leadeth them out. 4. And when he putteth forth his own sheep, he goeth before them, and the sheep follow him: for they know his voice. 11. I am the good shepherd: the good shepherd giveth his life for the sheep. 14. I am the good shepherd, and know my *sheep*, and am known of mine. 15. I lay down my life for the sheep. 16. And other sheep I have, which are not of this fold: them also I must bring, and they shall hear my voice; and there shall be one fold, *and* one shepherd.

John 11:5. Jesus loved Martha, and her sister, and Lazarus. 33. When Jesus therefore saw her weeping, and the Jews also weeping which came with her, he groaned in the spirit, and was troubled, 34. And said, Where have ye laid him? They said unto him, Lord, come and see. 35. Jesus wept. 36. Then said the Jews, Behold how he loved him!

John 13:1. Jesus . . . having loved his own which were in the world . . . loved them unto the end. 23. There was leaning on Jesus' bosom one of his disciples, whom Jesus loved. 34. A new commandment I give unto you, That ye love one another; as I have loved you, that ye also love one another.

John 14:1. Let not your heart be troubled: ye believe in God, believe also in me. 2. In my Father's house are many mansions: if *it were* not *so,* I would have told you. I go to prepare a place for you. 3. And if I go and prepare a place for you, I will come again, and receive you unto myself; that where I am, *there* ye may be also. 18. I will not leave you comfortless: I will come to you. 21. He that loveth me shall be loved of my Father, and I will love him, and will manifest myself to him. 27. Peace I leave with you, my peace I give unto you: not as the world giveth, give I unto you. Let not your heart be troubled, neither let it be afraid.

John 15:9. As the Father hath loved me, so have I loved you: continue ye in my love. 10. If ye keep my commandments, ye shall abide in my love; 11. These things have I spoken unto you, that my joy might remain in you, and *that* your joy might be full. 12. This is my commandment, That ye love one another, as I have loved you. 13. Greater love hath no man than this, that a man lay down his life for his friends. 15. I call you not servants; for the servant knoweth not what his lord doeth: but I have called you friends; for all things that I have heard of my Father I have made known unto you.

John 17:12. While I was with them in the world, I kept them in thy name: those that thou gavest me I have kept, and none of them is lost, 15. I pray not that thou shouldest take them out of the world, but that thou shouldest keep them from the evil. 19. For their sakes I sanctify myself, that they also might be sanctified through the truth.

John 18:8. I have told you that I am *he:* if therefore ye seek me, let these go their way: 9. That the saying might be fulfilled, which he spake, Of them which thou gavest me have I lost none.

John 19:26. When Jesus therefore saw his mother, and the disciple standing by, whom he loved, he saith unto his mother, Woman, behold thy son! 27. Then saith he to the disciple, Behold thy mother!

John 20:17. Go to my brethren, and say unto them, I ascend unto my Father, and your Father; and *to* my God, and your God. 27. Then saith he to Thomas, reach hither thy finger, and behold my hands; and reach hither thy hand, and thrust *it* into my side: and be not faithless, but believing.

John 21:15. Jesus saith to Simon Peter, Simon, *son* of Jonas, lovest thou me more than these? He saith unto him, Yea, Lord; thou knowest that I love thee. 16. He saith to him again . . . Lovest thou me? . . . 17. He saith unto him the third time, Simon, *son* of Jonas, lovest thou me? Peter was grieved because he said unto him the third time, Lovest thou me? And he said unto him, Lord, thou knowest all things; thou knowest that I love thee. Jesus saith unto him, Feed my sheep.

Acts 9:4. Saul, Saul, why persecutest thou me? 5. And he said, Who art thou, Lord? And the Lord said, I am Jesus whom thou persecutest:

Acts 10:38. Who went about doing good, and healing all that were oppressed of the devil;

Rom. 8:35. Who shall separate us from the love of Christ? *shall* tribulation; or distress, or persecution, or famine, or nakedness, or peril, or sword? 37. Nay, in all these things we are more than conquerors through him that loved us. 38. Neither death, nor life, nor angels, nor principalities, nor powers, nor things present, nor things to come, 39. Nor height, nor depth, nor any other creature, shall be able to separate us from the love of God, which is in Christ Jesus our Lord.

Rom. 15:3. Even Christ pleased not himself; but, as it is written, The reproaches of them that reproached thee fell on me.

2 Cor. 5:13. Whether we be beside ourselves, *it is* to God: or whether we be sober, *it is* for your cause. 14. For the love of Christ constraineth us:

2 Cor. 8:9. Ye know the grace of our Lord Jesus Christ, that, though he was rich, yet for your sakes he became poor, that ye through his poverty might be rich.

Gal. 2:20. The life which I now live in the flesh I live by the faith of the Son of God, who loved me, and gave himself for me.

Eph. 3:17. That ye, being rooted and grounded in love, 18. May be able to comprehend with all saints what *is* the breadth, and length, and depth, and height; 19. And to know the love of Christ, which passeth knowledge,

Eph. 5:2. Walk in love, as Christ also hath loved us, and hath given himself for us an offering and a sacrifice to God for a sweetsmelling savour. 25. Christ also loved the church, and gave himself for it; 29. No man ever yet hated his own flesh; but nourisheth and cherisheth it, even as the Lord the church: 30. For we are members of his body, of his flesh, and of his bones.

2 Thess. 2:13. But we are bound to give

thanks alway to God for you, brethren beloved of the Lord, because God hath from the beginning chosen you to salvation through sanctification of the Spirit and belief of the truth:

Heb. 2:11. Both he that sanctifieth and they who are sanctified *are* all of one: for which cause he is not ashamed to call them brethren, 18. In that he himself hath suffered being tempted, he is able to succour them that are tempted.

Heb. 4:15. We have not an high priest which cannot be touched with the feeling of our infirmities; but was in all points tempted like as *we are, yet* without sin.

1 John 3:16. Hereby perceive we [1] the love [1] *of God*, because he laid down his life for us:
[1 Omitted in R. V.]

Rev. 1:5. Unto him that loved us, and washed us from our sins in his own blood,

Rev. 3:9. I will make them to come and worship before thy feet, and to know that I have loved thee. 19. As many as I love, I rebuke and chasten:

See COMPASSION OF, above.

MEDIATION OF: Deut. 18:18. I will raise them up a Prophet from among their brethren, like unto thee, and will put my words in his mouth; and he shall speak unto them all that I shall command him.

Psa. 110:4. The LORD hath sworn, and will not repent, Thou *art* a priest for ever after the order of Melchizedek.

Isa. 53:10. Yet it pleased the LORD to bruise him; he hath put *him* to grief: when thou shalt make his soul an offering for sin, he shall see *his* seed, he shall prolong *his* days, and the pleasure of the LORD shall prosper in his hand. 11. He shall see of the travail of his soul, *and* shall be satisfied: by his knowledge shall my righteous servant justify many; for he shall bear their iniquities. 12. Therefore will I divide him *a portion* with the great, and he shall divide the spoil with the strong; because he hath poured out his soul unto death: and he was numbered with the transgressors; and he bare the sin of many, and made intercession for the transgressors.

Zech. 1:12. Then the angel of the LORD answered and said, O LORD of hosts, how long wilt thou not have mercy on Jerusalem and on the cities of Judah, against which thou hast had indignation these threescore and ten years? 13. And the LORD answered the angel that talked with me *with* good words *and* comfortable words.

Zech. 6:13. He shall be a priest upon his throne; and the counsel of peace shall be between them both.

Matt. 18:20. For where two or three are gathered together in my name, there am I in the midst of them.

Luke 22:31. And the Lord said, Simon, Simon, behold, Satan hath desired *to have* you, that he may sift *you* as wheat: 32. But I have prayed for thee, that thy faith fail not:

Luke 23:33. And when they were come to the place which is called Calvary, there they crucified him, 34. Then said Jesus, Father, forgive them; for they know not what they do.

John 14:6. I am the way, the truth, and the life: no man cometh unto the Father, but by me. 13. And whatsoever ye shall ask in my name, that will I do, that the Father may be glorified in the Son. 14. If ye shall ask any thing in my name, I will do *it*. 16. And I will pray the Father, and he shall give you another Comforter, that he may abide with you for ever;

John 16:23. Verily, verily, I say unto you, Whatsoever ye shall ask the Father in my name, he will give *it* you. 24. Hitherto have ye asked nothing in my name: ask, and ye shall receive, that your joy may be full. 26. At that day ye shall ask in my name: and I say not unto you, that I will pray the Father for you:

John 17:9. I pray . . . for them which thou hast given me; for they are thine. 11. Holy Father, keep through thine own name those whom thou hast given me, that they may be one, as we *are*. 15. I pray not that thou shouldest take them out of the world, but that thou shouldest keep them from the evil. 16. They are not of the world, even as I am not of the world. 17. Sanctify them through thy truth: thy word is truth. 20. Neither pray I for these alone, but for them also which shall believe on me through their word; 21. That they all may be one; as thou, Father, *art* in me, and I in thee, that they also may be one in us: that the world may believe that thou hast sent me. 22. And the glory which thou gavest me I have given them; that they may be one, even as we are one: *vs.* 1-26.

John 20:31. But these are written, that ye might believe that Jesus is the Christ, the Son of God; and that believing ye might have life through his name.

Rom. 1:8. I thank my God through Jesus Christ for you all.

Rom. 5:1. Therefore being justified by faith, [1] we have peace with God through our Lord Jesus Christ: 2. By whom also we have access by faith into this grace wherein we stand, and [2] rejoice in hope of the glory of God.
[R. V. [1] let us   [2] let us rejoice]

Rom. 6:23. The gift of God *is* eternal life through Jesus Christ our Lord.

Rom. 8:34. Who *is* he that condemneth? *It is* Christ that died, yea rather, that is risen again, who is even at the right hand of God, who also maketh intercession for us.

Rom. 16:27. To God only wise, *be* glory through Jesus Christ for ever. Amen.

1 Cor. 6:11. But ye are washed, but ye are sanctified, but ye are justified in the name of the Lord Jesus, and by the Spirit of our God.

1 Cor. 15:57. But thanks *be* to God, which

giveth us the victory through our Lord Jesus Christ.

2 Cor. 1:20. For all the promises of God in him *are* yea, and in him Amen, unto the glory of God by us.

Gal. 4:7. Wherefore thou art no more a servant, but a son; and if a son, then an heir [1] of God through Christ.   [1 R. V. through God]

Eph. 2:13. But now in Christ Jesus ye who sometimes were far off are made nigh by the blood of Christ. 14. For he is our peace, who hath made both one, and hath broken down the middle wall of partition *between us;* 15. Having abolished in his flesh the enmity, *even* the law of commandments *contained* in ordinances; for to make in himself of twain one new man, *so* making peace; 16. And that he might reconcile both unto God in one body by the cross, having slain the enmity thereby: 17. And came and preached peace to you which were afar off, and to them that were nigh. 18. For through him we both have access by one Spirit unto the Father.

Eph. 3:12. In whom we have boldness and access with confidence by the faith of him.

Eph. 4:32. And be ye kind one to another, tenderhearted, forgiving one another, even as God for Christ's sake hath forgiven you.

Eph. 5:20. Giving thanks always for all things unto God and the Father in the name of our Lord Jesus Christ;

Col. 3:17. Whatsoever ye do in word or deed, *do* all in the name of the Lord Jesus, giving thanks to God and the Father by him.

1 Tim. 2:1. I exhort therefore, that, first of all, supplications, prayers, intercessions, *and* giving of thanks, be made for all men; 3. For this *is* good and acceptable in the sight of God our Saviour; 5. For *there is* one God, and one mediator between God and men, the man Christ Jesus;

Heb. 2:17. In all things it behoved him to be made like unto *his* brethren, that he might be a merciful and faithful high priest in things *pertaining* to God, to make reconciliation for the sins of the people.

Heb. 3:1. Consider the Apostle and High Priest of our profession, Christ Jesus; 2. Who was faithful to him that appointed him, as also Moses *was faithful* in all his house.

Heb. 4:14. Seeing then that we have a great high priest, that is passed into the heavens, Jesus the Son of God, let us hold fast *our* profession. 15. For we have not an high priest which cannot be touched with the feeling of our infirmities; but was in all points tempted like as *we are,* yet without sin.

Heb. 5:5. Christ glorified not himself to be made an high priest; but he that said unto him, Thou art my Son, to day have I begotten thee. 6. As he saith also in another *place,* Thou *art* a priest for ever after the order of Melchisedec. 10. Called of God an high priest after the order of Melchisedec.

Heb. 6:19. Within the veil; 20. Whither the forerunner is for us entered, *even* Jesus, made an high priest for ever after the order of Melchisedec. Heb. 7:21.

Heb. 7:1. Melchisedec, king of Salem, priest of the most high God, ... 3. Without father, without mother, without descent, having neither beginning of days, nor end of life; but made like unto the Son of God; abideth a priest continually. 19. For the law made nothing perfect, but the bringing in of a better hope *did;* by the which we draw nigh unto God. 24. But this *man,* because he continueth ever, hath an unchangeable priesthood. 25. Wherefore he is able also to save them to the uttermost that come unto God by him, seeing he ever liveth to make intercession for them. 26. For such an high priest became us, *who is* holy, harmless, undefiled, separate from sinners, and made higher than the heavens; 27. Who needeth not daily, as those high priests, to offer up sacrifice, first for his own sins, and then for the people's: for this he did once, when he offered up himself. 28. For the law maketh men high priests which have infirmity; but the word of the oath, which was since the law, *maketh* the Son, who is consecrated for evermore.

Heb. 8:1. Now of the things which we have spoken *this is* the sum: We have such an high priest, who is set on the right hand of the throne of the Majesty in the heavens; 2. A minister of the sanctuary, and of the true tabernacle, which the Lord pitched, and not man. 6. He obtained a more excellent ministry, by how much also he is the mediator of a better covenant, which was established upon better promises.

Heb. 9:11. Christ being come an high priest of good things to come, by a greater and more perfect tabernacle, not made with hands, that is to say, not of this building; 12. Neither by the blood of goats and calves, but by his own blood he entered in once into the holy place, having obtained eternal redemption *for us.* 15. For this cause he is the mediator of the new testament, that by means of death, for the redemption of the transgressions *that were* under the first testament, they which are called might receive the promise of eternal inheritance. 24. Christ is not entered into the holy places made with hands, *which are* the figures of the true; but into heaven itself, now to appear in the presence of God for us: *vs.* 11–28. See Rev. 8:3, 4.

Heb. 10:11. Every priest standeth daily ministering and offering oftentimes the same sacrifices, which can never take away sins: 12. But this man, after he had offered one sacrifice for sins for ever, sat down on the right hand of God; 19. Having therefore, brethren, boldness to enter into the holiest by the blood of Jesus, 20. By a new and living way, which he hath consecrated for us, through the veil, that is to say, his flesh; 21. And *having* an high priest over the house of God; *vs.* 1–21.

Heb. 12:24. Jesus the mediator of the new covenant, and to the blood of sprinkling, that speaketh better things than *that of* Abel.

Heb. 13:15. By him therefore let us offer the sacrifice of praise to God continually, that is, the fruit of *our* lips giving thanks to his name.

1 Pet. 2:5. Ye also, as lively stones, are built up a spiritual house, an holy priesthood, to offer up spiritual sacrifices, acceptable to God by Jesus Christ.

1 John 2:1. If any man sin, we have an advocate with the Father, Jesus Christ the righteous: 2. And he is the propitiation for our sins: and not for our's only, but also for *the sins of* the whole world. 12. I write unto you, little children, because your sins are forgiven you for his name's sake.

Typified: Moses, Deut. 5:5; Gal. 3:19. Aaron, Num. 16:48.

See INTERCESSION.

MEEKNESS OF: Psa. 45:4. And in thy majesty ride prosperously because of truth and meekness *and* righteousness;

Isa. 42:2. He shall not cry, nor lift up, nor cause his voice to be heard in the street.

Isa. 50:5. The LORD GOD hath opened mine ear, and I was not rebellious, neither turned away back. 6. I gave my back to the smiters, and my cheeks to them that plucked off the hair: I hid not my face from shame and spitting.

Isa. 52:13. Behold, my servant shall deal prudently, he shall be exalted and extolled, and be very high.

Isa. 53:7. He was oppressed, and he was afflicted, yet he opened not his mouth: he is brought as a lamb to the slaughter, and as a sheep before her shearers is dumb, so he openeth not his mouth. Acts 8:32.

Matt. 11:29. Learn of me; for I am meek and lowly in heart:

Matt. 12:19. He shall not strive, nor cry; neither shall any man hear his voice in the streets. 20. A bruised reed shall he not break, and smoking flax shall he not quench, till he send forth judgment unto victory.

Matt. 21:5. Tell ye the daughter of Sion, Behold, thy King cometh unto thee, meek, and sitting upon an ass, and a colt the foal of an ass.

Matt. 26:49. Forthwith he came to Jesus, and said, Hail, master; and kissed him. 50. And Jesus said unto him, Friend, wherefore art thou come? 51. And, behold, one of them which were with Jesus stretched out *his* hand, and drew his sword, and struck a servant of the high priest's, and smote off his ear. 52. Then said Jesus unto him, Put up again thy sword into his place: for all they that take the sword shall perish with the sword. 53. Thinkest thou that I cannot now pray to my Father, and he shall presently give me more than twelve legions of angels?

54. But how then shall the scriptures be fulfilled, that thus it must be? 55. In that same hour said Jesus to the multitudes, Are ye come out as against a thief with swords and staves for to take me? I sat daily with you teaching in the temple, and ye laid no hold on me. 56. But all this was done, that the scriptures of the prophets might be fulfilled. Then all the disciples forsook him, and fled. 57. And they that had laid hold on Jesus led *him* away to Caiaphas the high priest, where the scribes and the elders were assembled. 58. But Peter followed him afar off unto the high priest's palace, and went in, and sat with the servants, to see the end. 59. Now the chief priests, and elders, and all the council, sought false witness against Jesus, to put him to death: 60. But found none: yea, though many false witnesses came, *yet* found they none. At the last came two false witnesses. 61. And said, This *fellow* said, I am able to destroy the temple of God, and to build it in three days. 62. And the high priest arose, and said unto him, Answerest thou nothing? what *is it which* these witness against thee? 63. But Jesus held his peace.

Matt. 27:12. When he was accused of the chief priests and elders, he answered nothing. 13. Then said Pilate unto him, Hearest thou not how many things they witness against thee? 14. He answered him to never a word; insomuch that the governor marvelled greatly.

Mark 2:6. But there were certain of the scribes sitting there and reasoning in their hearts, 7. Why doth this *man* thus speak blasphemies? who can forgive sins but God only? 8. And immediately when Jesus perceived in his spirit that they so reasoned within themselves, he said unto them, Why reason ye these things in your hearts? 9. Whether is it easier to say to the sick of the palsy, *Thy* sins be forgiven thee; or to say, Arise, and take up thy bed, and walk? 10. But that ye may know that the Son of man hath power on earth to forgive sins, (he saith to the sick of the palsy,) 11. I say unto thee, Arise, and take up thy bed, and go thy way into thine house.

Luke 22:27. I am among you as he that serveth.

Luke 23:34. Then said Jesus, Father, forgive them; for they know not what they do.

John 8:48. The Jews . . . said unto him, Say we not well that thou art a Samaritan, and hast a devil? 49. Jesus answered, I have not a devil; but I honour my Father, and ye do dishonour me. 50. And I seek not mine own glory:

John 13:5. He poureth water into a bason, and began to wash the disciples' feet, and to wipe *them* with the towel wherewith he was girded. 14. If I then, *your* Lord and master, have washed your feet; ye also ought to wash one another's feet.

2 Cor. 10:1. Now I Paul myself beseech you by the meekness and gentleness of Christ,

Phil. 2:7. Made himself of no reputation, and took upon him the form of a servant, and was made in the likeness of men: 8. And being found in fashion as a man, he humbled himself, and became obedient unto death, even the death of the cross.

Heb. 12:2. Looking unto Jesus the author and finisher of *our* faith; who for the joy that was set before him endured the cross, despising the shame, and is set down at the right hand of the throne of God. 3. For consider him that endureth such contradiction of sinners against himself, lest ye be wearied and faint in your minds.

1 Pet. 2:23. Who, when he was reviled, reviled not again; when he suffered, he threatened not; but committed *himself* to him that judgeth righteously:

See HUMILITY OF, above; MEEKNESS.

MESSIAH: MESSIANIC PSALMS: Psa. 2:1. Why do the heathen rage, and the people imagine a vain thing? 2. The kings of the earth set themselves, and the rulers take counsel together, against the LORD, and against his anointed, *saying*, 3. Let us break their bands asunder, and cast away their cords from us. 4. He that sitteth in the heavens shall laugh: the Lord shall have them in derision. 5. Then shall he speak unto them in his wrath, and vex them in his sore displeasure. 6. Yet have I set my king upon my holy hill of Zion. 7. I will declare the decree: the LORD hath said unto me, Thou *art* my Son; this day have I begotten thee. 8. Ask of me, and I shall give *thee* the heathen *for* thine inheritance, and the uttermost parts of the earth *for* thy possession. 9. Thou shalt break them with a rod of iron; thou shalt dash them in pieces like a potter's vessel. 10. Be wise now therefore, O ye kings: be instructed, ye judges of the earth. 11. Serve the LORD with fear, and rejoice with trembling. 12. Kiss the Son, lest he be angry, and ye perish *from* the way, when his wrath is kindled but a little. Blessed *are* all they that put their trust in him.

Psa. 16:7. I will bless the LORD, who hath given me counsel: my reins also instruct me in the night seasons. 8. I have set the LORD always before me: because *he is* at my right hand, I shall not be moved. 9. Therefore my heart is glad, and my glory rejoiceth: my flesh also shall rest in hope. 10. For thou wilt not leave my soul in hell; neither wilt thou suffer thine Holy One to see corruption. 11. Thou wilt shew me the path of life: in thy presence *is* fulness of joy; at thy right hand *there are* pleasures for evermore.

Psa. 67:1. God be merciful unto us, and bless us; *and* cause his face to shine upon us; Selah. 2. That thy way may be known upon earth, thy saving health among all nations. 3. Let the people praise thee, O God; let all the people praise thee. 4. O let the nations be glad and sing for joy: for thou shalt judge the people righteously, and govern the nations upon earth. Selah. 5. Let the people praise thee, O God; let all the people praise thee. 6. *Then* shall the earth yield her increase; *and* God, *even* our own God, shall bless us. 7. God shall bless us; and all the ends of the earth shall fear him.

Psa. 68:28. Thy God hath commanded thy strength: strengthen, O God, that which thou hast wrought for us. 29. Because of thy temple at Jerusalem shall kings bring presents unto thee. 30. Rebuke the company of spearmen, the multitude of the bulls, with the calves of the people, *till every one* submit himself with pieces of silver: scatter thou the people *that* delight in war. 31. Princes shall come out of Egypt; Ethiopia shall soon stretch out her hands unto God. 32. Sing unto God, ye kingdoms of the earth; O sing praises unto the Lord; 33. To him that rideth upon the heavens of heavens, *which were* of old; lo, he doth send out his voice, *and that* a mighty voice. 34. Ascribe ye strength unto God: his excellency *is* over Israel, and his strength *is* in the clouds. 35. O God, *thou art* terrible out of thy holy places: the God of Israel *is* he that giveth strength and power unto *his* people. Blessed *be* God.

Psa. 69:1. Save me, O God; for the waters are come in unto *my* soul. 2. I sink in deep mire, where *there is* no standing: I am come into deep waters, where the floods overflow me. 3. I am weary of my crying: my throat is dried: mine eyes fail while I wait for my God. 4. They that hate me without a cause are more than the hairs of mine head: they that would destroy me, *being* mine enemies wrongfully, are mighty: then I restored *that* which I took not away. 5. O God, thou knowest my foolishness; and my sins are not hid from thee. 6. Let not them that wait on thee, O Lord GOD of hosts, be ashamed for my sake: let not those that seek thee be confounded for my sake, O God of Israel. 7. Because for thy sake I have borne reproach; shame hath covered my face. 8. I am become a stranger unto my brethren, and an alien unto my mother's children. 9. For the zeal of thine house hath eaten me up; and the reproaches of them that reproached thee are fallen upon me. 10. When I wept, *and chastened* my soul with fasting, that was to my reproach. 11. I made sackcloth also my garment; and I became a proverb to them. 12. They that sit in the gate speak against me: and I *was* the song of the drunkards. 13. But as for me, my prayer *is* unto thee, O LORD, *in* an acceptable time: O God, in the multitude of thy mercy hear me, in the truth of thy salvation. 14. Deliver me out of the mire, and let me not sink: let me be delivered from them that hate me, and out of the deep waters. 15. Let not the waterflood overflow me, neither let the deep swallow me up, and let not the pit shut her mouth upon me. 16. Hear me, O LORD; for thy lovingkindness *is* good : turn unto me according to the multitude of thy tender mercies. 17. And hide not thy face from thy servant; for I am in trouble : hear me speedily. 18. Draw nigh unto my soul, *and* redeem it : deliver me because of mine enemies. 19. Thou hast known my reproach, and my shame, and my dishonour : mine adversaries *are* all before thee. 20. Reproach hath broken my heart; and I am full of heaviness : and I looked *for some* to take pity, but *there was* none ; and for comforters, but I found none. 21. They gave me also gall for my meat; and in my thirst they gave me vinegar to drink. 22. Let their table become a snare before them : and *that which should have been* for *their* welfare, *let it become* a trap. 23. Let their eyes be darkened, that they see not; and make their loins continually to shake. 24. Pour out thine indignation upon them, and let thy wrathful anger take hold of them. 25. Let their habitation be desolate ; *and* let none dwell in their tents. 26. For they persecute *him* whom thou hast smitten ; and they talk to the grief of those whom thou hast wounded. 27. Add iniquity unto their iniquity : and let them not come into thy righteousness. 28. Let them be blotted out of the book of the living, and not be written with the righteous. 29. But I *am* poor and sorrowful : let thy salvation, O God, set me up on high. 30. I will praise the name of God with a song, and will magnify him with thanksgiving. 31. *This* also shall please the LORD better than an ox *or* bullock that hath horns and hoofs. 32. The humble shall see *this, and* be glad : and your heart shall live that seek God. 33. For the LORD heareth the poor, and despiseth not his prisoners. 34. Let the heaven and earth praise him, the seas, and every thing that moveth therein. 35. For God will save Zion, and will build the cities of Judah : that they may dwell there, and have it in possession. 36. The seed also of his servants shall inherit it : and they that love his name shall dwell therein.

Psa. 72:1. Give the king thy judgments, O God, and thy righteousness unto the king's son. 2. He shall judge thy people with righteousness, and thy poor with judgment. 3. The mountains shall bring peace to the people, and the little hills, by righteousness. 4. He shall judge the poor of the people, he shall save the children of the needy, and shall break in pieces the oppressor. 5. They shal fear thee as long as the sun and moon endure, throughout all generations. 6. He shall come down like rain upon the mown grass : as showers *that* water the earth. 7. In his days shall the righteous flourish ; and abundance of peace so long as the moon endureth. 8. He shall have dominion also from sea to sea, and from the river unto the ends of the earth. 9. They that dwell in the wilderness shall bow before him ; and his enemies shall lick the dust. 10. The kings of Tarshish and of

the isles shall bring presents : the kings of Sheba and Seba shall offer gifts. 11. Yea, all kings shall fall down before him : all nations shall serve him. 12. For he shall deliver the needy when he crieth ; the poor also, and *him* that hath no helper. 13. He shall spare the poor and needy, and shall save the souls of the needy. 14. He shall redeem their soul from deceit and violence : and precious shall their blood be in his sight. 15. And he shall live, and to him shall be given of the gold of Sheba : prayer also shall be made for him continually ; *and* daily shall he be praised. 16. There shall be an handful of corn in the earth upon the top of the mountains ; the fruit thereof shall shake like Lebanon : and *they* of the city shall flourish like grass of the earth. 17. His name shall endure for ever : his name shall be continued as long as the sun : and *men* shall be blessed in him : all nations shall call him blessed. 18. Blessed *be* the LORD God, the God of Israel, who only doeth wondrous things. 19. And blessed *be* his glorious name for ever : and let the whole earth be filled *with* his glory ; Amen, and Amen.

Psa. 93:1. The LORD reigneth, he is clothed with majesty ; the LORD is clothed with strength, *wherewith* he hath girded himself : the world also is stablished, that it cannot be moved. 2. Thy throne *is* established of old : thou *art* from everlasting. 3. The floods have lifted up, O LORD, the floods have lifted up their voice ; the floods lift up their waves. 4. The LORD on high *is* mightier than the noise of many waters, *yea, than* the mighty waves of the sea. 5. Thy testimonies are very sure : holiness becometh thine house, O LORD, for ever.

Psa. 96:1. O sing unto the LORD a new song : sing unto the LORD, all the earth. 2. Sing unto the LORD, bless his name ; shew forth his salvation from day to day. 3. Declare his glory among the heathen, his wonders among all people. 4. For the LORD *is* great, and greatly to be praised : he *is* to be feared above all gods. 5. For all the gods of the nations *are* idols : but the LORD made the heavens. 6. Honour and majesty *are* before him : strength and beauty *are* in his sanctuary. 7. Give unto the LORD, O ye kindreds of the people, give unto the LORD glory and strength. 8. Give unto the LORD the glory *due unto* his name : bring an offering, and come into his courts. 9. O worship the LORD in the beauty of holiness : fear before him, all the earth. 10. Say among the heathen *that* the LORD reigneth : the world also shall be established that it shall not be moved : he shall judge the people righteously. 11. Let the heavens rejoice, and let the earth be glad ; let the sea roar, and the fulness thereof. 12 Let the field be joyful, and all that *is* therein : then shall all the trees of the wood rejoice 13. Before the LORD : for he cometh, for he cometh to judge the earth : he shall judge the world with righteousness, and the people with his truth.

Psa. 97:1. The LORD reigneth; let the earth rejoice; let the multitude of isles be glad *thereof.* 2. Clouds and darkness *are* round about him: righteousness and judgment *are* the habitation of his throne. 3. A fire goeth before him, and burneth up his enemies round about. 4. His lightnings enlightened the world: the earth saw, and trembled. 5. The hills melted like wax at the presence of the LORD, at the presence of the Lord of the whole earth. 6. The heavens declare his righteousness, and all the people see his glory. 7. Confounded be all they that serve graven images, that boast themselves of idols: worship him, all *ye* gods. 8. Zion heard, and was glad; and the daughters of Judah rejoiced because of thy judgments, O LORD. 9. For thou, LORD, *art* high above all the earth: thou art exalted far above all gods. 10. Ye that love the LORD, hate evil: he preserveth the souls of his saints; he delivereth them out of the hand of the wicked. 11. Light is sown for the righteous, and gladness for the upright in heart. 12. Rejoice in the LORD, ye righteous; and give thanks at the remembrance of his holiness.

Psa. 98:1. O sing unto the LORD a new song; for he hath done marvellous things: his right hand, and his holy arm, hath gotten him the victory. 2. The LORD hath made known his salvation: his righteousness hath he openly shewed in the sight of the heathen. 3. He hath remembered his mercy and his truth toward the house of Israel: all the ends of the earth have seen the salvation of our God. 4. Make a joyful noise unto the LORD, all the earth: make a loud noise, and rejoice, and sing praise. 5. Sing unto the LORD with the harp; with the harp, and the voice of a psalm. 6. With trumpets and sound of cornet make a joyful noise before the LORD, the King. 7. Let the sea roar, and the fulness thereof; the world, and they that dwell therein. 8. Let the floods clap *their* hands: let the hills be joyful together 9. Before the LORD; for he cometh to judge the earth: with righteousness shall he judge the world, and the people with equity.

Psa. 99:1. The LORD reigneth; let the people tremble: he sitteth *between* the cherubim; let the earth be moved. 2. The LORD is great in Zion; and he *is* high above all the people. 3. Let them praise thy great and terrible name; *for* it *is* holy. 4. The king's strength also loveth judgment; thou dost establish equity, thou executest judgment and righteousness in Jacob. 5. Exalt ye the LORD our God, and worship at his footstool; *for* he *is* holy. 6. Moses and Aaron among his priests, and Samuel among them that call upon his name; they called upon the LORD, and he answered them. 7. He spake unto them in the cloudy pillar: they kept his testimonies, and the ordinance

that he gave them. 8. Thou answeredst them, O LORD our God: thou wast a God that forgavest them, though thou tookest vengeance of their inventions. 9. Exalt the LORD our God, and worship at his holy hill; for the LORD our God *is* holy.

Psa. 110:1. The LORD said unto my Lord, Sit thou at my right hand, until I make thine enemies thy footstool. 2. The LORD shall send the rod of thy strength out of Zion: rule thou in the midst of thine enemies. 3. Thy people *shall be* willing in the day of thy power, in the beauties of holiness from the womb of the morning: thou hast the dew of thy youth. 4. The LORD hath sworn, and will not repent, Thou *art* a priest for ever after the order of Melchizedek. 5. The Lord at thy right hand shall strike through kings in the day of his wrath. 6. He shall judge among the heathen, he shall fill *the places* with the dead bodies; he shall wound the heads over many countries. 7. He shall drink of the brook in the way: therefore shall he lift up the head.

Psa. 118:19. Open to me the gates of righteousness: I will go into them, *and* I will praise the LORD: 20. This gate of the LORD, into which the righteous shall enter. 21. I will praise thee: for thou hast heard me, and art become my salvation. 22. The stone *which* the builders refused is become the head *stone* of the corner. 23. This is the LORD'S doing; it *is* marvellous in our eyes. 24. This *is* the day *which* the LORD hath made; we will rejoice and be glad in it. 25. Save now, I beseech thee, O LORD: O LORD, I beseech thee, send now prosperity. 26. Blessed *be* he that cometh in the name of the LORD: we have blessed you out of the house of the LORD. 27. God *is* the LORD, which hath shewed us light: bind the sacrifice with cords, *even* unto the horns of the altar. 28. Thou *art* my God, and I will praise thee: *thou art* my God, I will exalt thee. 29. O give thanks unto the LORD; for *he is* good: for his mercy *endureth* for ever.

OTHER SCRIPTURES RELATING TO HIS MESSIAHSHIP: Dan. 9:25. From the going forth of the commandment to restore and to build Jerusalem unto the Messiah the Prince *shall be* seven weeks, and threescore and two weeks: 26. And after threescore and two weeks shall Messiah be cut off, but not for himself:

Matt. 11:3. Art thou he that should come, or do we look for another? 4. Jesus answered and said unto them, Go and shew John again those things which ye do hear and see: 5. The blind receive their sight, and the lame walk, the lepers are cleansed, and the deaf hear, the dead are raised up, and the poor have the gospel preached to them. 6. And blessed is *he*, whosoever shall not be offended in me.

Matt. 16:15. He saith unto them, But whom say ye that I am? 16. And Simon Peter answered and said, Thou art the Christ, the Son of the living God.

Matt. 26:63. I adjure thee by the living God, that thou tell us whether thou be the Christ, the Son of God. 64. Jesus saith unto him, Thou hast said: nevertheless I say unto you, Hereafter shall ye see the Son of man sitting on the right hand of power, and coming in the clouds of heaven.

Luke 2:28. Then took he him up in his arms, and blessed God, and said, 29. Lord, now lettest thou thy servant depart in peace, according to thy word: 30. For mine eyes have seen thy salvation, 31. Which thou hast prepared before the face of all people; 32. A light to lighten the Gentiles, and the glory of thy people Israel. 38. She [Anna] coming in that instant gave thanks likewise unto the Lord, and spake of him to all them that looked for redemption in Jerusalem.

Luke 20:41. How say they that Christ is David's son? 42. And David himself saith in the book of Psalms, The LORD said unto my Lord, Sit thou on my right hand, 43. Till I make thine enemies thy footstool. 44. David therefore calleth him Lord, how is he then his son? Matt. 22:42–45; Mark 12:35–37.

Luke 24:25. O fools, and slow of heart to believe all that the prophets have spoken: 26. Ought not Christ to have suffered these things, and to enter into his glory? 27. And beginning at Moses and all the prophets, he expounded unto them in all the scriptures the things concerning himself.

John 1:41. We have found the Messias, which is, being interpreted, the Christ. 45. We have found him, of whom Moses in the law, and the prophets, did write, Jesus of Nazareth, the son of Joseph.

John 4:25. The woman saith unto him, I know that Messias cometh, which is called Christ: when he is come, he will tell us all things. 26. Jesus saith unto her, I that speak unto thee am *he*. 29. Come, see a man, which told me all things that ever I did: is not this the Christ? 42. Now we believe, not because of thy saying: for we have heard *him* ourselves, and know that this is indeed the Christ, the Saviour of the world.

John 5:33. Ye sent unto John, and he bare witness unto the truth. 36. I have greater witness than *that* of John: for the works which the Father hath given me to finish, the same works that I do, bear witness of me, that the Father hath sent me. 37. The Father himself, which hath sent me, hath borne witness of me. Ye have neither heard his voice at any time, nor seen his shape. 39. Search [Ye search, *R. V.*] the scriptures; for in them ye think ye have eternal life: and they are they which testify of me. 46. Had ye believed Moses, ye would have believed me: for he wrote of me.

John 6:27. Labour not for the meat which perisheth, but for that meat which endureth unto everlasting life, which the Son of

man shall give unto you: for him hath God the Father sealed.

John 8:14. Though I bear record of myself, *yet* my record is true: for I know whence I came, and whither I go; 17. It is also written in your law, that the testimony of two men is true. 18. I am one that bear witness of myself, and the Father that sent me beareth witness of me. 25. Then said they unto him, Who art thou? And Jesus saith unto them, Even *the same* that I said unto you from the beginning. 28. When ye have lifted up the Son of man, then shall ye know that I am *he*, and *that* I do nothing of myself; but as my Father hath taught me, I speak these things. 56. Your Father Abraham rejoiced to see my day: and he saw *it*, and was glad.

John 13:19. I tell you before it come, that, when it is come to pass, ye may believe that I am *he*.

Acts 3:18. Those things, which God before hath shewed by the mouth of all his prophets, that Christ should suffer, he hath so fulfilled. 20. He shall send Jesus Christ, which before was preached unto you: 24. All the prophets from Samuel and those that follow after, as many as have spoken, have likewise foretold of these days.

Acts 4:26. The kings of the earth stood up, and the rulers were gathered together against the Lord, and against his Christ. 27. For of a truth against thy holy child Jesus, whom thou hast anointed, both Herod, and Pontius Pilate, with the Gentiles, and the people of Israel, were gathered together, Psa. 2:2.

Acts 9:22. Saul . . . confounded the Jews which dwelt at Damascus, proving that this is very Christ.

Acts 13:27. Their rulers, because they knew him not, nor yet the voices of the prophets which are read every sabbath day, they have fulfilled *them* in condemning *him*.

Acts 17:2. And Paul, as his manner was, went in unto them, and three sabbath days reasoned with them out of the scriptures, 3. Opening and alleging, that Christ must needs have suffered, and risen again from the dead; and that this Jesus, whom I preach unto you, is Christ.

Acts 26:6. I stand and am judged for the hope of the promise made of God unto our fathers: 7. Unto which *promise* our twelve tribes, instantly serving *God* day and night, hope to come. 22. Witnessing both to small and great, saying none other things than those which the prophets and Moses did say should come: 23. That Christ should suffer, *and* that he should be the first that should rise from the dead, and should shew light unto the people, and to the Gentiles.

Acts 28:23. He expounded and testified the kingdom of God, persuading them concerning Jesus, both out of the law of Moses, and *out of* the prophets,

Rom. 1:1. Paul, a servant of Jesus Christ, . . . separated unto the gospel of God, 2. (Which he had promised afore by his prophets in the holy scriptures,) 3. Concerning his Son Jesus Christ our Lord, which was made of the seed of David according to the flesh ;

1 Cor. 15:3. I delivered unto you first of all that which I also received, how that Christ died for our sins according to the scriptures ;

1 Pet. 1:10. Of which salvation the prophets have inquired and searched diligently, who prophesied of the grace *that should come* unto you : 11. Searching what, or what manner of time the Spirit of Christ which was in them did signify, when it testified beforehand the sufferings of Christ, and the glory that should follow.

2 Pet. 1:16. We have not followed cunningly devised fables, when we made known unto you the power and coming of our Lord Jesus Christ, but were eyewitnesses of his majesty. 17. For he received from God the Father honour and glory, when there came such a voice to him from the excellent glory, This is my beloved Son, in whom I am well pleased. 18. And this voice which came from heaven we heard, when we were with him in the holy mount.

1 John 5:6. This is he that came by water and blood, *even* Jesus Christ ; not by water only, but by water and blood. And it is the Spirit that beareth witness, because the Spirit is truth. [1] 7. For there are three that bear record in heaven, the Father, the Word, and the Holy Ghost: and these three are one. 8. And there are three that bear witness in earth, the spirit, and the water, and the blood : and these three agree in one. 9. If we receive the witness of men, the witness of God is greater: for this is the witness of God which he hath testified of his Son.

[1 Omitted in R. V.]

See KING, above ; DIVINITY OF.

MIRACLES OF : Water made wine, John 2:1–11.

Heals the nobleman's son, John 4:46–54.

First miraculous draught of fishes, Luke 5:1–11.

Demoniac in the synagogue healed, Mark 1:23–26 ; Luke 4:33–36.

Heals Simon's wife's mother, Matt. 8:14, 15 ; Mark 1:29–31 ; Luke 4:38,39.

Heals diseases in Galilee, Matt. 4:23,24 ; Mark 1:34.

Miracles at Jerusalem, John 2:23.

Cleanses the leper, Matt. 8:1–4 ; Mark 1: 40–45 ; Luke 5:12–16.

Heals the paralytic, Matt. 9:1–8 ; Mark 2: 1–12 ; Luke 5:17–26.

Heals the impotent man, John 5:1–16.

Restores the withered hand, Matt. 12:9–13 ; Mark 3:1–5 ; Luke 6:6–11.

Heals multitudes from Judah, Jerusalem, and coasts of Tyre and Sidon, Luke 6:17–19.

Heals the centurion's servant, Matt. 8:5–13 ; Luke 7:1–10.

Heals demoniacs, Matt. 8:16,17 ; Luke 4: 40,41.

Raises the widow's son, Luke 7:11–16.

Heals in Galilee, Luke 7:21,22.

Heals a demoniac, Matt. 12:22–37 ; Mark 3:19–30 ; Luke 11:14,15,17–23.

Stills the tempest, Matt. 8:23–27 ; Mark 4: 35–41 ; Luke 8:22–25 ; Matt. 14:32.

Healing of the diseased in the land of Gennesaret, Matt. 14:34–36.

The demoniacs in Gadara healed, Matt. 8:28–34 ; Mark 5:1–20 ; Luke 8:26–39.

Raises Jairus's daughter, Matt. 9:18,19, 23–26 ; Mark 5:22–24, 35–43 ; Luke 8:41,42, 49–56.

Heals the woman with the issue of blood, Matt. 9:20–22 ; Mark 5:25–34 ; Luke 8:43–48.

Opens the eyes of two blind men in the house, Matt. 9:27–31.

A devil cast out and a dumb man cured, Matt. 9:32,33.

Five thousand fed, Matt. 14:15–21 ; Mark 6:35–44 ; Luke 9:12–17 ; John 6:5–14.

Heals sick in Galilee, Matt. 14:14.

Walking on the sea, Matt. 14:22–33 ; Mark 6:45–52 ; John 6:14–21.

The daughter of the Syrophenician healed, Matt. 15:21–28 ; Mark 7:24–30.

Healing of lame, blind, dumb, and maimed, near the Sea of Galilee, Matt. 15:30.

Four thousand fed, Matt. 15:32–39 ; Mark 8:1–9.

One deaf and dumb cured, Mark 7:31–37.

One blind cured, Mark 8:22–36.

Lunatic child healed, Matt. 17:14–21 ; Mark 9:14–29 ; Luke 9:37–43.

Piece of money in the fish's mouth, Matt. 17:24–27.

The ten lepers cured, Luke 17:11–19.

Opening the eyes of one born blind, John 9.

Raising of Lazarus, John 11:1–54.

Woman with the spirit of infirmity cured, Luke 13:10–17.

The dropsy cured, Luke 14:1–6.

Two blind men cured near Jericho, Matt. 20:29–34 ; Mark 10:46–52 ; Luke 18:35–43.

The fig tree blighted, Matt. 21:17–22 ; Mark 11:12–14,20–24.

Healing of Malchus's ear, Luke 22:49–51.

Second draught of fishes, John 21:6.

Not particularly described, Matt. 4:23,24 ; 14:14 ; 15:30 ; Mark 1:34 ; Luke 6:17–19 ; 7:21, 22 ; John 2:23 ; 3:2. Resurrection, Matt. 28:6 ; Mark 16:6 ; Luke 24:6 ; John 20:1–18. Holds the vision of his disciples, that they should not recognize him, Luke 24:16,31,35. His appearances and disappearances, Luke 24:15, 31,36–45 ; John 20:19,26. Opening the understanding of his disciples, Luke 24:45. His ascension, Luke 24:51 ; Acts 1:9.

See MIRACLES.

MISSION OF : 2 Sam. 23:3. The God of Israel said. the Rock of Israel spake to me, He that ruleth over men *must be* just, ruling in the fear of God. 4. And *he shall be* as the light of the morning, *when* the sun riseth, *even* a morning without clouds ; *as* the tender grass *springing* out of the earth by clear shining after rain.

Isa. 42:6. I the LORD have called thee in righteousness, and will hold thine hand, and will keep thee, and give thee for a covenant of the people, for a light of the Gentiles ; 7. To open the blind eyes, to bring out the prisoners from the prison, *and* them that sit in darkness out of the prison house.

Isa. 61:1. The Spirit of the Lord GOD *is* upon me ; because the LORD hath anointed me to preach good tidings unto the meek ; he hath sent me to bind up the brokenhearted, to proclaim liberty to the captives, and the opening of the prison to *them that are* bound ; 2. To proclaim the acceptable year of the LORD, and the day of vengeance of our God ; to comfort all that mourn ; 3. To appoint unto them that mourn in Zion, to give unto them beauty for ashes, the oil of joy for mourning, the garment of praise for the spirit of heaviness ; that they might be called trees of righteousness, the planting of the LORD, that he might be glorified.

Dan. 9:24. Seventy weeks are determined upon thy people and upon thy holy city, to finish the transgression, and to make an end of sins, and to make reconciliation for iniquity, and to bring in everlasting righteousness, and to seal up the vision and prophecy, and to anoint the most Holy. 27. And he shall confirm the covenant with many for one week : and in the midst of the week he shall cause the sacrifice and the oblation to cease, and for the overspreading of abominations he shall make *it* desolate, even until the consummation, and that determined shall be poured upon the desolate.

Mic. 5:2. But thou, Beth-lehem Ephratah, *though* thou be little among the thousands of Judah, *yet* out of thee shall he come forth unto me *that is* to be ruler in Israel ; whose goings forth *have been* from of old, from everlasting.

Zech. 13:1. In that day there shall be a fountain opened to the house of David and to the inhabitants of Jerusalem for sin and for uncleanness.

Mal. 3:2. But who may abide the day of his coming ? and who shall stand when he appeareth ? for he *is* like a refiner's fire, and like fullers' sope : 3. And he shall sit *as* a refiner and purifier of silver : and he shall purify the sons of Levi, and purge them as gold and silver, that they may offer unto the LORD an offering in righteousness.

Matt. 1:21. For he shall save his people from their sins.

Matt. 3:11. I indeed baptize you with water unto repentance : but he that cometh after me is mightier than I, whose shoes I am not worthy to bear : he shall baptize you with the Holy Ghost, and *with* fire : 12. Whose fan *is* in his hand, and he will throughly purge his floor, and gather his wheat into the garner ; but he will burn up the chaff with unquenchable fire.

Matt. 4:23. And Jesus went about all Gal-

ilee, teaching in their synagogues, and preaching the gospel of the kingdom, and healing all manner of sickness and all manner of disease among the people.

Matt. 5:17. Think not that I am come to destroy the law, or the prophets : I am not come to destroy, but to fulfil.

Matt. 9:13. I am not come to call the righteous, but sinners 1 to repentance. Luke 5:30–32. [1 Omitted in R. V.]

Matt. 10:34. Think not that I am come to send peace on earth : I came not to send peace, but a sword. 35. For I am come to set a man at variance against his father, and the daughter against her mother, and the daughter in law against her mother in law. 36. And a man's foes *shall be* they of his own household. Luke 12:49–53 ; Mic. 7:6.

Matt. 15:24. But he answered and said, I am not sent but unto the lost sheep of the house of Israel.

Matt. 18:11. 1 For the Son of man is come to save that which was lost. [Luke 19:10.] 12. How think ye ? if a man have an hundred sheep, and one of them be gone astray, doth he not leave the ninety and nine, and goeth into the mountains, and seeketh that which is gone astray ? 13. And if so be that he find it, verily I say unto you, he rejoiceth more of that *sheep,* than of the ninety and nine which went not astray. 14. Even so it is not the will of your Father which is in heaven, that one of these little ones should perish. Luke 15:3–7. [1 Omitted in R. V.]

Matt. 20:28. Even as the Son of man came not to be ministered unto, but to minister, and to give his life a ransom for many. Mark 10:45.

Mark 1:38. And he said unto them, Let us go into the next towns, that I may preach there also : for therefore came I forth. Luke 4:43.

Mark 2:15. As Jesus sat at meat in his house, many publicans and sinners sat also together with Jesus and his disciples ; for there were many, and they followed him. 16. And when the scribes and Pharisees saw him eat with publicans and sinners, they said unto his disciples, How is it that he eateth and drinketh with publicans and sinners ? 17. When Jesus heard *it,* he saith unto them, They that are whole have no need of the physician, but they that are sick : I came not to call the righteous, but sinners to repentance. 18. And the disciples of John and the Pharisees used to fast : and they come and say unto him, Why do the disciples of John and of the Pharisees fast, but thy disciples fast not ? 19. And Jesus said unto them, Can the children of the bridechamber fast, while the bridegroom is with them ? as long as they have the bridegroom with them, they cannot fast. 20. But the days will come, when the bridegroom shall be taken away from them, and then shall they fast in those days. 21. No man also seweth a piece of new cloth on an old garment : else the new piece that filled it up taketh away from the old, and the rent is made worse   22. And no man putteth new wine into old bottles: else the new wine doth burst the bottles, and the wine is spilled, and the bottles will be marred: but new wine must be put into new bottles.

Luke 1:78. Through the tender mercy of our God; whereby the dayspring from on high hath visited us,   79. To give light to them that sit in darkness and *in* the shadow of death, to guide our feet into the way of peace.

Luke 2:30. For mine eyes have seen thy salvation,   31. Which thou hast prepared before the face of all people;   32. A light to lighten the Gentiles, and the glory of thy people Israel.   34. And Simeon blessed them, and said unto Mary his mother, Behold, this *child* is set for the fall and rising again of many in Israel; and for a sign which shall be spoken against;   35. (Yea, a sword shall pierce through thy own soul also;) that the thoughts of many hearts may be revealed.   38. And she coming in that instant gave thanks likewise unto the Lord, and spake of him to all them that looked for redemption in Jerusalem.

Luke 4:18. The Spirit of the Lord *is* upon me, because he hath anointed me to preach the gospel to the poor; he hath sent me to heal the brokenhearted, to preach deliverance to the captives, and recovering of sight to the blind, to set at liberty them that are bruised,   19. To preach the acceptable year of the Lord.   43. And he said unto them, I must preach the kingdom of God to other cities also: for therefore am I sent.

Luke 8:1. And it came to pass afterward, that he went throughout every city and village, preaching and shewing the glad tidings of the kingdom of God: and the twelve *were* with him.

Luke 9:56. ¹ The Son of man is not come to destroy men's lives, but to save *them*.   [Omitted in R. V.]

Luke 12:49. I am come to send fire on the earth; and what will I, if it be already kindled?   50. But I have a baptism to be baptized with; and how am I straitened till it be accomplished!   51. Suppose ye that I am come to give peace on earth? I tell you, Nay; but rather division: 52. For from henceforth there shall be five in one house divided, three against two, and two against three.   53. The father shall be divided against the son, and the son against the father; the mother against the daughter, and the daughter against the mother; the mother in law against her daughter in law, and the daughter in law against her mother in law.

Luke 24:26. Ought not Christ to have suffered these things, and to enter into his glory?   46. And said unto them, Thus it is written, and thus it behoved Christ to suffer, and to rise from the dead the third day: 47. And that repentance and remission of sins should be preached in his name among all nations, beginning at Jerusalem.

John 3:13. And no man hath ascended up to heaven, but he that came down from heaven, *even* the Son of man which is in heaven.   14. And as Moses lifted up the serpent in the wilderness, even so must the Son of man be lifted up: 15. That whosoever believeth in him should not perish, but have eternal life.   16. For God so loved the world, that he gave his only begotten Son, that whosoever believeth in him should not perish, but have everlasting life.   17. For God sent not his Son into the world to condemn the world; but that the world through him might be saved.

John 4:34. My meat is to do the will of him that sent me, and to finish his work.

John 6:51. I am the living bread which came down from heaven; if any man eat of this bread, he shall live forever: and the bread that I will give is my flesh, which I will give for the life of the world.

John 8:12. I am the light of the world: he that followeth me shall not walk in darkness, but shall have the light of life.

John 9:39. And Jesus said, For judgment I am come into this world, that they which see not might see; and that they which see might be made blind.

John 10:10. I am come that they might have life, and that they might have *it* more abundantly.

John 11:50. Nor consider (ye) that it is expedient for us, that one man should die for the people, and that the whole nation perish not.   51. Being high priest that year, he prophesied that Jesus should die for that nation;   52. And not for that nation only, but that also he should gather together in one the children of God that were scattered abroad.

John 12:27. Father, save me from this hour: but for this cause came I unto this hour.   46. I am come a light into the world, that whosoever believeth on me should not abide in darkness.   47. I came not to judge the world, but to save the world.

John 18:37. To this end was I born, and for this cause came I into the world, that I should bear witness unto the truth.

Acts 5:31. Him hath God exalted with his right hand *to be* a Prince and a Saviour, for to give repentance to Israel, and forgiveness of sins.

Acts 10:43. To him give all the prophets witness, that through his name whosoever believeth in him shall receive remission of sins.

Acts 26:23. That Christ should suffer, *and* that he should be the first that should rise from the dead, and should shew light unto the people, and to the Gentiles.

Rom. 4:25. Who was delivered for our offences, and was raised again for our justification.

Rom. 5:6. For when we were yet without strength, in due time Christ died for the ungodly.   7. For scarcely for a righteous man will one die: yet peradventure for a good man some would even dare to die. 8. But God commendeth his love toward us, in that, while we were yet sinners, Christ died for us.

Rom. 8:3. For what the law could not do, in that it was weak through the flesh, God sending his own Son in the likeness of sinful flesh, and for sin, condemned sin in the flesh: 4. That the righteousness of the law might be fulfilled in us, who walk not after the flesh, but after the Spirit.

Rom. 10:4. For Christ *is* the end of the law for righteousness to every one that believeth.

Rom. 14:9. For to this end Christ both died, and rose, and revived, that he might be Lord both of the dead and living. 15. Destroy not him with thy meat, for whom Christ died.

Rom. 15:8. Now I say that Jesus Christ was a minister of the circumcision for the truth of God, to confirm the promises *made* unto the fathers: 9. And that the Gentiles might glorify God for *his* mercy; as it is written, For this cause I will confess to thee among the Gentiles, and sing unto thy name.

2 Cor. 5:14. For the love of Christ constraineth us; because we thus judge, that if one died for all, ¹then were all dead: 15. And *that* he died for all, that they which live should not henceforth live unto themselves, but unto him which died for them, and rose again. [¹ R. V. therefore all died;]

Gal. 1:3. Grace *be* to you and peace from God the Father, and *from* our Lord Jesus Christ, 4. Who gave himself for our sins, that he might deliver us from this present evil world, according to the will of God and our Father:

Gal. 4:4. But when the fulness of the time was come, God sent forth his Son, made of a woman, made under the law, 5. To redeem them that were under the law, that we might receive the adoption of sons.

Eph. 4:10. He that descended is the same also that ascended up far above all heavens, that he might fill all things.

1 Tim. 1:15. This *is* a faithful saying, and worthy of all acceptation, that Christ Jesus came into the world to save sinners:

Heb. 2:9. But we see Jesus, who was made a little lower than the angels for the suffering of death, crowned with glory and honour; that he by the grace of God should taste death for every man. 14. Forasmuch then as the children are partakers of flesh and blood, he also himself likewise took part of the same; that through death he might destroy him that had the power of death, that is, the devil; 15. And deliver them who through fear of death were all their lifetime subject to bondage. 18. For in that he himself hath suffered being tempted, he is able to succour them that are tempted.

Heb. 9:26. For then must he often have suffered since the foundation of the world: but now once in the end of the world hath he appeared to put away sin by the sacrifice of himself.

1 John 3:5. And ye know that he was manifested to take away our sins; and in him is no sin. 8. For this purpose the Son of God was manifested, that he might destroy the works of the devil.

1 John 4:10. Herein is love, not that we loved God, but that he loved us, and sent his Son *to be* the propitiation for our sins.

NAMES, APPELLATIONS, AND TITLES OF: Adam, 1 Cor. 15:45. Advocate, 1 John, 2:1. Almighty, Rev. 1:8. Alpha and Omega, Rev. 1:8. Amen, Rev. 3:14. Angel, Gen. 48:16; Ex. 23:20,21. Angel of his presence, Isa. 63:9. Anointed, Psa. 2:2. Apostle, Heb. 3:1. Arm of the Lord, Isa. 51:9,10. Author and finisher of our faith, Heb. 12:2.

Beginning and end of the creation of God, Rev. 3:14; 22:13. Beloved, Eph. 1:6. Bishop, 1 Pet. 2:25. Blessed and only Potentate, 1 Tim. 6:15. Branch, Jer. 23:5; Zech. 3:8. Bread of life, John 6:48. Bridegroom, Matt. 9:15. Bright and morning star, Rev. 22:16. Brightness of the Father's glory, Heb. 1:3.

Captain of the Lord's host, Josh. 5:14. Captain of salvation, Heb. 2:10. Carpenter, Mark 6:3. Carpenter's son, Matt. 13:55. Chief Shepherd, 1 Pet. 5:4. Chief corner stone, 1 Pet. 2:6. Chiefest among ten thousand, Song 5:10. Child, Isa. 9:6; Luke 2:27,43. Chosen of God, 1 Pet. 2:4. Christ, Matt. 1:16; Luke 9:20. The Christ, Matt. 16:20; Mark 14:61. Christ, a King, Luke 23:2. Christ Jesus, Acts 19:4; Rom. 3:24; 8:1; 1 Cor. 1:2; 1 Cor. 1:30; Heb. 3:1; 1 Pet. 5:10,14. Christ Jesus our Lord, 1 Tim. 1:12; Rom. 8:39. Christ of God, Luke 9:20. Christ, the chosen of God, Luke 23:35. Christ the Lord, Luke 2:11; Christ the power of God, 1 Cor. 1:24. Christ the wisdom of God, 1 Cor. 1:24. Christ, the Son of God, Acts 9:20. Christ, Son of the Blessed, Mark 14:61. Commander, Isa. 55:4. Consolation of Israel, Luke 2:25. Corner stone, Eph. 2:20. Counsellor, Isa. 9:6. Covenant of the people, Isa. 42:6.

David, Jer. 30:9. Daysman, Job 9:33. Dayspring, Luke 1:78. Day star, 2 Pet. 1:19. Deliverer, Rom. 11:26. ¹Desire of all nations, Hag. 2:7. Door, John 10:7. [¹ R. V. desirable things]

Elect, Isa. 42:1. Emmanuel, Isa. 7:14. Ensign, Isa. 11:10. Eternal life, 1 John 5:20. Everlasting Father, Isa. 9:6.

Faithful and True, Rev. 19:11. Faithful witness, Rev. 1:5. Faithful and true witness, Rev. 3:14. Finisher of faith, Heb. 12:2. First and last, Rev. 1:17; 2:8; 22:13. First begotten, Heb. 1:6. First begotten of the dead, Rev. 1:5. Firstborn, Psa. 89:27. Foundation, Isa. 28:16. Fountain, Zech. 13:1. Forerunner, Heb. 6:20. Friend of sinners, Matt. 11:19.

Gift of God, John 4:10. Glory of Israel, Luke 2:32. God, John 1:1. God blessed for ever, Rom. 9:5. God manifest in the flesh, 1 Tim. 3:16. God of Israel, the Saviour, Isa. 45:15. God of the whole earth, Isa. 54:5. God our Saviour, 1 Tim. 2:3. God's dear Son, Col. 1:13. God with us, Matt. 1:23. Good Master, Matt. 19:16. Governor, Matt.

2:6. Great shepherd of the sheep, Heb. 13:20.

Head of the church, Eph. 5:23. Heir of all things, Heb. 1:2. High priest, Heb. 4:14. Head of every man, 1 Cor. 11:3. Head of the church, Col. 1:18. Head of the corner, Matt. 21:42. Holy child Jesus, Acts 4:30. Holy one, Psa. 16:10; Acts 3:14. Holy one of God, Mark 1:24. Holy one of Israel, Isa. 41:14; 54:5. Holy thing, Luke 1:35. Hope [our], 1 Tim. 1:1. Horn of salvation, Luke 1:69.

I Am, John 8:58. Image of God, Heb. 1:3. Israel, Isa. 49:3.

Jehovah, Isa. 40:3. Jehovah's fellow, Zech. 13:7. Jesus, Matt. 1:21. Jesus Christ, Matt. 1:1; John 1:17; 17:3; Acts 2:38; 4:10; 9:34; 10:36; 16:18; Rom. 1:1,3,6; 2:16; 5:15,17; 6:3; 1 Cor. 1:1,4; 1 Cor. 2:2; 2 Cor. 1:19; 4:6; 13:5; Gal. 2:16; Phil. 1:8; 2:11; 1 Tim. 1:15; Heb. 13:8; 1 John 1:7; 2:1. Jesus Christ our Lord, Rom. 1:3; 6:11,23; 1 Cor. 1:9; 7:25. Jesus Christ our Saviour, Tit. 3:6. Jesus of Nazareth, Mark 1:24; Luke 24:19. Jesus of Nazareth, King of the Jews, John 19:19. Jesus, the King of the Jews, Matt. 27:37. Jesus, the Son of God, Heb. 4:14. Jesus, the Son of Joseph, John 6:42. Judge, Acts 10:42. Just man, Matt. 27:19. Just one, Acts 3:14; 7:52; 22:14. Just person, Matt. 27:24.

King, Matt. 21:5. King of Israel, John 1:49. King of the Jews, Matt. 2:2. King of saints, Rev. 15:3. King of kings, 1 Tim. 6:15; Rev. 17:14. King of glory, Psa. 24:7-10. King of Zion, Matt. 21:5. King over all the earth, Zech. 14:9.

Lamb, Rev. 5:6,8; 6:16; 7:9,10,17; 12:11; 13:8,11; 14:1,4; 15:3; 17:14; 19:7,9; 21:9,14,22, 23,27. Lamb of God, John 1:29. Lawgiver, Isa. 33:22. Leader, Isa. 55:4. Life, John 14:6. Light, John 8:12. Light, everlasting, Isa. 60:20. Light of the world, John 8:12. Light to the Gentiles, Isa. 42:6. Light, true, John 1:9. Living bread, John 6:51. Living stone, 1 Pet. 2:4. Lion of the tribe of Judah, Rev. 5:5. Lord, Rom. 1:3. Lord of lords, Rev. 17:14; 19:16. Lord of all, Acts 10:36. Lord our righteousness, Jer. 23:6. Lord God Almighty, Rev. 15:3. Lord from heaven, 1 Cor. 15:47. Lord and Saviour Jesus Christ, 2 Pet. 1:11; 3:18. Lord Christ, Col. 3:24. Lord Jesus, Acts 7:59; Col. 3:17; 1 Thess. 4:2. Lord Jesus Christ, Acts 11:17; 16:31; 20:21; Rom. 5:1,11; 13:14. Lord Jesus Christ our Saviour, Tit. 1:4. Lord of glory, Jas. 2:1. Lord of Hosts, Isa. 44:6. Lord, mighty in battle, Psa. 24:8. Lord of the dead and living, Rom. 14:9. Lord of the sabbath, Mark 2:28. Lord over all, Rom. 10:12. Lord's Christ, Luke 2:26. Lord, strong and mighty, Psa. 24:8. Lord, the, our righteousness, Jer. 23:6. Lord, your holy one, Isa. 43:15. Lord, your redeemer, Isa. 43:14.

Man Christ Jesus, 1 Tim. 2:5. Man of sorrows, Isa. 53:3. Master, Matt. 23:8. Mediator, 1 Tim. 2:5. Messenger of the covenant, Mal. 3:1. Messiah, John 1:41. Messiah the Prince, Dan. 9:25. Mighty God, Isa. 9:6.

Mighty one of Israel, Isa. 30:29. Mighty one of Jacob, Isa. 49:26. Mighty to save, Isa. 63:1. Minister of the sanctuary, Heb. 8:2. Morning star, Rev. 22:16. Most holy, Dan. 9:24. Most mighty, Psa. 45:3.

Nazarene, Matt. 2:23.

Offspring of David, Rev. 22:16. Only begotten, John 1:14. Only begotten of the Father, John 1:14. Only begotten Son, John 1:18. Only wise God, our Saviour, Jude 25.

Passover, 1 Cor. 5:7. Plant of renown, Ezek. 34:29. Potentate, 1 Tim. 6:15. Power of God, 1 Cor. 1:24. Physician, Matt. 9:12. Precious corner stone, Isa. 28:16. Priest, Heb. 7:17. Prince, Act 5:31. Prince of life, Acts 3:15. Prince of peace, Isa. 9:6. Prince of the kings of the earth, Rev. 1:5. Prophet, Deut. 18:15,18; Matt. 21:11; Luke 24:19. Propitiation, 1 John 2:2.

Rabbi, John 1:49. Rabboni, John 20:16. Ransom, 1 Tim. 2:6. Redeemer, Isa. 59:20. Resurrection and life, John 11:25. Redemption, 1 Cor. 1:30. Righteous branch, Jer. 23:5. Righteous judge, 2 Tim. 4:8. Righteous servant, Isa. 53:11. Righteousness, 1 Cor. 1:30. Rock, 1 Cor. 10:4. Rock of offence, 1 Pet. 2:8. Root of David, Rev. 5:5; 22:16. Root of Jesse, Isa. 11:10. Rose of Sharon, Song 2:1. Ruler in Israel, Mic. 5:2.

Salvation, Luke 2:30. Sanctification, 1 Cor. 1:30. Sanctuary, Isa. 8:14. Saviour. Luke 2:11. Saviour, Jesus Christ, 2 Tim. 1:10; Tit. 2:13; 2 Pet. 1:1. Saviour of the body, Eph. 5:23. Saviour of the world, 1 John 4:14. Sceptre, Num. 24:17. Second man, 1 Cor. 15:47. Seed of David, 2 Tim. 2:8. Seed of the woman, Gen. 3:15. Servant, Isa. 42:1. Servant of rulers, Isa. 49:7. Shepherd, Mark 14:27. Shepherd and bishop of souls, 1 Pet. 2:25. Shepherd, chief, 1 Pet. 5:4. Shepherd, good, John 10:11. Shepherd, great, Heb. 13:20. Shepherd of Israel, Psa. 80:1. Shiloh, Gen. 49:10. Son of the Father, 2 John 3. Son of God, see JESUS, SON OF GOD. Son of Man, see JESUS, SON OF MAN. Son of the blessed, Mark 14:61. Son of the highest, Luke 1:32. Son of David, Matt. 9:27. Star, Num. 24:17. Sun of righteousness, Mal. 4:2. Surety, Heb. 7:22. Stone, Matt. 21:42. Stone of stumbling, 1 Pet. 2:8. Sure foundation, Isa. 28:16.

Teacher, John 3:2. True God, 1 John 5:20. True vine, John 15:1. Truth, John 14:6.

Unspeakable gift, 2 Cor. 9:15.

Very Christ, Acts 9:22. Vine, John 15:1.

Way, John 14:6. Which is, which was, which is to come, Rev. 1:4. Wisdom, Prov. 8:12. Wisdom of God, 1 Cor. 1:24. Witness, Isa. 55:4; Rev. 1:5. Wonderful, Isa. 9:6. Word, John 1:1. Word of God, Rev. 19:13. Word of life, 1 John 1:1.

Those who use his name must depart from evil, 2 Tim. 2:19.

IN HIS NAME. 1 Cor. 6:11; Phil. 2:9; Col. 3:17; Rev. 19:16. Prayer, John 14:13; 16:23, 24,26; Eph. 5:20; Col. 3:17; Heb. 13:15. Miracles performed, Acts 3:6; 4:10; 19:13; baptism, Matt. 28:19; Acts 2:38. **Preaching,** Luke 24:

47. Faith, Matt. 12:21; John 1:12; 2:23. Remission of sins, Luke 24:47; Acts 10:43; 1 John 2:12. Life, John 20:31. Salvation, Acts 4:12; 10:43.

See INTERCESSION OF, above; and PRIESTHOOD OF, below.

OBEDIENCE OF: Psa. 40:8. I delight to do thy will, O my God; yea, thy law *is* within my heart.

Isa. 11:5. Righteousness shall be the girdle of his loins, and faithfulness the girdle of his reins.

Isa. 42:21. The LORD is well pleased for his righteousness' sake; he will magnify the law, and make *it* honourable.

Isa. 50:5. The Lord GOD hath opened mine ear, and I was not rebellious, neither turned away back. 6. I gave my back to the smiters, and my cheeks to them that plucked off the hair: I hid not my face from shame and spitting.

Matt. 3:15. And Jesus answering said unto him, Suffer *it to be so* now: for thus it becometh us to fulfil all righteousness.

Matt. 26:39. O my Father, if it be possible, let this cup pass from me: nevertheless not as I will, but as thou *wilt*. 42. He went away again the second time, and prayed, saying, O my Father, if this cup may not pass away from me, except I drink it, thy will be done. Mark 14:36; Luke 22:42.

Luke 2:49. Wist ye not that I must be ¹ about my Father's business? [¹ R. V. in my Father's house]

John 4:34. Jesus saith unto them, My meat is to do the will of him that sent me, and to finish his work.

John 5:30. I can of mine own self do nothing: as I hear, I judge: and my judgment is just; because I seek not mine own will, but the will of the Father which hath sent me. 36. But I have greater witness than *that* of John: for the works which the Father hath given me to finish, the same works that I do, bear witness of me, that the Father hath sent me.

John 6:38. For I came down from heaven, not to do mine own will, but the will of him that sent me.

John 7:18. He that seeketh his glory that sent him, the same is true, and no unrighteousness is in him.

John 8:29. I do always those things that please him. 46. Which of you convinceth me of sin? 55. I know him, and keep his saying.

John 9:4. I must work the works of him that sent me, while it is day: the night cometh, when no man can work.

John 14:31. But that the world may know that I love the Father; and as the Father gave me commandment, even so I do.

John 15:10. Even as I have kept my Father's commandments, and abide in his love.

John 17:4. I have glorified thee on the earth: I have finished the work which thou gavest me to do.

John 19:30. When Jesus therefore had received the vinegar, he said, It is finished: and he bowed his head, and gave up the ghost.

Phil. 2:8. And being found in fashion as a man, he humbled himself, and became obedient unto death, even the death of the cross.

Heb. 5:8. Though he were a Son, yet learned he obedience by the things which he suffered;

Heb. 10:7. Then said I, Lo, I come (in the volume of the book it is written of me) to do thy will, O God. 8. Above when he said, Sacrifice and offering and burnt offerings and *offering* for sin thou wouldest not, neither hadst pleasure *therein;* which are offered by the law: 9. Then said he, Lo, I come to do thy will, O God.

OMNIPOTENCE OF: Psa. 45:3. Gird thy sword upon *thy* thigh, O *most* mighty, with thy glory and thy majesty. 4. And in thy majesty ride prosperously because of truth and meekness *and* righteousness; and thy right hand shall teach thee terrible things. 5. Thine arrows *are* sharp in the heart of the king's enemies; *whereby* the people fall under thee.

Psa. 110:3. Thy people *shall be* willing in the day of thy power,

Isa. 9:6. The government shall be upon his shoulder: and his name shall be called Wonderful, Counsellor, The mighty God, The everlasting Father, The Prince of Peace.

Isa. 40:10. Behold, the Lord GOD will come with strong *hand*, and his arm shall rule for him: behold, his reward *is* with him, and his work before him.

Isa. 50:2. Is my hand shortened at all, that it cannot redeem? or have I no power to deliver? behold, at my rebuke I dry up the sea, I make the rivers a wilderness: their fish stinketh, because *there is* no water, and dieth for thirst. 3. I clothe the heavens with blackness, and I make sackcloth their covering. *v. 4.*

Isa. 63:1. Who *is* this that cometh from Edom, with dyed garments from Bozrah? this *that is* glorious in his apparel, travelling in the greatness of his strength? I that speak in righteousness, mighty to save.

Matt. 8:3. Jesus put forth *his* hand, and touched him, saying, I will; be thou clean. And immediately his leprosy was cleansed. 16. And he cast out the spirits with *his* word, and healed all that were sick: 27. The men marvelled, saying, What manner of man is this, that even the winds and the sea obey him!

Matt. 10:1. When he had called unto *him* his twelve disciples, he gave them power *against* unclean spirits, to cast them out, and to heal all manner of sickness and all manner of disease. Mark 6:7; Luke 9:1.

Matt. 12:13. Then saith he to the man, Stretch forth thine hand. And he stretched *it* forth; and it was restored whole, like as the other. 28. If I cast out devils by the Spirit of God, then the kingdom of God is come unto you. 29. Or else how can one enter into a strong man's house, and spoil his goods, except he first bind the strong man? and then he will spoil his house. Mark 3:27; Luke 11:20–22.

Matt. 28:18. Jesus came and spake unto them, saying, All power is given unto me in heaven and in earth.

Luke 5:17. The power of the Lord was *present* to heal them. .

John 2:19. Jesus answered and said unto them, Destroy this temple, and in three days I will raise it up.

John 5:21. As the Father raiseth up the dead, and quickeneth *them;* even so the Son quickeneth whom he will. 28. Marvel not at this: for the hour is coming, in the which all that are in the graves shall hear his voice. 29. And shall come forth;

John 10:17. Therefore doth my Father love me, because I lay down my life, that I might take it again. 18. No man taketh it from me, but I lay it down of myself. I have power to lay it down, and I have power to take it again. 28. I give unto them eternal life; and they shall never perish, neither shall any *man* pluck them out of my hand.

John 17:1. These words spake Jesus, and lifted up his eyes to heaven, and said, Father, the hour is come; glorify thy Son, that thy Son also may glorify thee: 2. As thou hast given him [1] power over all flesh, that he should give eternal life to as many as thou hast given him.   [[1] R. V. authority]

Phil. 3:20. . . . we look for the Saviour, the Lord Jesus Christ: 21. [1] Who shall change our vile body, that it may be fashioned like unto his glorious body, according to the working whereby he is able even to subdue all things unto himself.

[[1] R. V. who shall fashion anew the body of our humiliation, that it may be conformed to the body of his glory]

Col. 1:17. And he is before all things, and by him all things consist.

2 Thess. 1:9. Who shall be punished with everlasting destruction from the presence of the Lord, and from the glory of his power;

1 Tim. 6:16. To whom *be* honour and power everlasting.

Heb. 1:3. Who being the brightness of *his* glory, and the express image of his person, and upholding all things by the word of his power, when he had by himself purged our sins, sat down on the right hand of the Majesty on high;

Heb. 7:25. He is able also to save them to the uttermost that come unto God by him,

2 Pet. 1:16. We have not followed cunningly devised fables, when we made known unto you the power and coming of our Lord Jesus Christ,

Rev. 1:8. I am Alpha and Omega, the beginning and the ending, saith the Lord, which is, and which was, and which is to come, the Almighty.

Rev. 3:7. These things saith he that is holy, he that is true, he that hath the key of David, he that openeth, and no man shutteth; and shutteth, and no man openeth;

Rev. 5:12. Worthy is the Lamb that was slain to receive power, and riches, and wisdom, and strength, and honour, and glory, and blessing.

See Miracles of.

OMNIPRESENCE OF: Matt. 18:20. Where two or three are gathered together in my name, there am I in the midst of them.

Matt. 28:20. Lo, I am with you alway, *even* unto the end of the world.

John 3:13. No man hath ascended up to heaven, but he that came down from heaven, *even* the Son of man which is in heaven.

Eph. 1:23. Him that filleth all in all.

OMNISCIENCE OF: Prov. 8:14. Counsel *is* mine, and sound wisdom: I *am* understanding; I have strength. 15. By me kings reign, and princes decree justice. 16. By me princes rule, and nobles, *even* all the judges of the earth.

Isa. 11:2. The spirit of the Lord shall rest upon him, the spirit of wisdom and understanding, the spirit of counsel and might, the spirit of knowledge and of the fear of the Lord; 3. And shall make him of quick understanding in the fear of the Lord: and he shall not judge after the sight of his eyes, neither reprove after the hearing of his ears:

Isa. 50:4. The Lord God hath given me the tongue of the learned, that I should know how to speak a word in season to *him that is* weary: he wakeneth morning by morning, he wakeneth mine ear to hear as the learned.

Matt. 9:4. And Jesus knowing their thoughts said, Wherefore think ye evil in your hearts?

Matt. 11:27. All things are delivered unto me of my Father: and no man knoweth the Son, but the Father; neither knoweth any man the Father, save the Son, and *he* to whomsoever the Son will reveal *him.*

Matt. 12:25. And Jesus knew their thoughts, and said unto them, Every kingdom divided against itself is brought to desolation; and every city or house divided against itself shall not stand:

Matt. 13:54. And when he was come into his own country, he taught them in their synagogue, insomuch that they were astonished, and said, Whence hath this *man* this wisdom, and *these* mighty works?

Matt. 22:18. But Jesus perceived their wickedness, and said, Why tempt ye me, *ye* hypocrites?

Matt. 24:25. Behold, I have told you before.

Matt. 26:46. Behold, he is at hand that doth betray me. Mark 14:42.

Mark 2:8. Immediately when Jesus perceived in his spirit that they so reasoned within themselves, he said unto them, Why reason ye these things in your hearts?

Mark 5:30. Jesus, immediately knowing in himself that virtue had gone out of him, turned him about in the press. and said, Who touched my clothes?

Luke 2:40. The child grew, and waxed strong in spirit, filled with wisdom: and the grace of God was upon him. 47. And all that heard him were astonished at his understanding and answers. 52. Jesus increased in wisdom and stature, and in favour with God and man.

Luke 5:22. When Jesus perceived their thoughts, he answering said unto them, What reason ye in your hearts?

Luke 6:8. He knew their thoughts,

Luke 9:46. Then there arose a reasoning among them, which of them should be greatest. 47. Jesus, perceiving the thought of their heart, took a child, and set him by him, 48. And said unto them, Whosoever shall receive this child in my name receiveth me: and whosoever shall receive me receiveth him that sent me: for he that is least among you all, the same shall be great.

Luke 22:10. When ye are entered into the city, there shall a man meet you, bearing a pitcher of water; follow him into the house where he entereth in. 11. And ye shall say unto the goodman of the house, The Master saith unto thee, Where is the guestchamber, where I shall eat the passover with my disciples? 12. And he shall shew you a large upper room furnished: there make ready. 13. And they went, and found as he had said unto them: Mark 14:13–15.

John 1:48. Nathanael saith unto him, Whence knowest thou me? Jesus answered and said unto him, Before that Philip called thee, when thou wast under the fig tree, I saw thee.

John 2:24. Jesus did not commit himself unto them, because he knew all *men*, 25. And needed not that any should testify of man: for he knew what was in man.

John 3:32. What he hath seen and heard, that he testifieth;

John 4:16. Jesus saith unto her, Go, call thy husband, and come hither. 17. The woman answered and said, I have no husband. Jesus said unto her, Thou hast well said, I have no husband: 18. For thou hast had five husbands; and he whom thou now hast is not thy husband: in that saidst thou truly. 19. The woman saith unto him, Sir, I perceive that thou art a prophet. 28. The woman then left her waterpot, and went her way into the city, and saith to the men, 29. Come, see a man, which told me all things that ever I did: is not this the Christ?

John 5:30. I can of mine own self do nothing: as I hear, I judge: and my judgment is just; because I seek not mine own will, but the will of the Father which hath sent me. 42. I know you, that ye have not the love of God in you.

John 6:64. Jesus knew from the beginning who they were that believed not, and who should betray him.

John 8:16. Yet if I judge, my judgment is true: for I am not alone, but I and the Father that sent me.

John 13:1. Jesus knew that his hour was come that he should depart out of this world unto the Father, 3. Jesus knowing that the Father had given all things into his hands, and that he was come from God, and went to God; 10. Jesus saith to him, . . . Ye are clean, but not all. 11. He knew who should betray him; therefore said he, Ye are not all clean.

John 16:30. Now are we sure that thou knowest all things, and needest not that any man should ask thee: 32. Behold, the hour cometh, yea, is now come, that ye shall be scattered, every man to his own, and shall leave me alone:

John 17:1. These words spake Jesus, and lifted up his eyes to heaven, and said, Father, the hour is come; glorify thy Son, that thy Son also may glorify thee:

John 18:4. Jesus therefore, knowing all things that should come upon him, went forth, and said unto them, Whom seek ye?

John 21:17. Peter . . . said unto him, Lord, thou knowest all things; thou knowest that I love thee.

Acts 1:24. They prayed, and said, Thou, Lord, which knowest the hearts of all *men*, shew whether of these two thou hast chosen,

Col. 2:3. In whom are hid all the treasures of wisdom and knowledge.

Rev. 2:18. These things saith the Son of God, who hath his eyes like unto a flame of fire, 23. All the churches shall know that I am he which searcheth the reins and hearts: and I will give unto every one of you according to your works.

Rev. 5:5. Behold, the Lion of the tribe of Juda, the Root of David, hath prevailed to open the book, and to loose the seven seals thereof. 12. Worthy is the Lamb that was slain to receive power, and riches, and wisdom,

PARABLES OF: The wise and foolish builders, Matt. 7:24–27; Luke 6:47,49.

Two debtors, Luke 7:41–47.

The rich fool, Luke 12:16–21.

The servants waiting for their Lord, Luke 12:35–40.

Barren fig tree, Luke 13:6–9.

The sower, Matt. 13:3–9,18–23; **Mark** 4:1–9,14–20; Luke 8:5–8,11–15.

The tares, Matt. 13:24–30,36–43.

Seed growing secretly, Mark 4:26–29.

Mustard seed, Matt. 13:31,32; Mark 4:30–32; Luke 13:18,19.

Leaven, Matt. 13:33; Luke 13:20,21.

Hid treasure, Matt. 13:44.

Pearl of great price, Matt. 13:45,46.

Drawnet, Matt. 13:47–50.

Unmerciful servant, Matt. 18:23–35.

Good Samaritan, Luke 10:30–37.

Friend at midnight, Luke 11:5–8.

Good shepherd, John 10:1–16.

Great supper, Luke 14:15–24.

Lost sheep, Luke 15:3-7; Matt. 18:12-14.

Lost piece of money, Luke 15:8-10.

The prodigal and his brother, Luke 15: 11-32.

The unjust steward, Luke 16:1-9.

Rich man and Lazarus, Luke 16:19-31.

Importunate widow, Luke 18:1-8.

Pharisee and publican, Luke 18:9-14.

Laborers in the vineyard, Matt. 20:1-16.

The pounds, Luke 19:11-27.

The two sons, Matt. 21:28-32.

Wicked husbandmen, Matt. 21:33-44; Mark 12:1-12; Luke 20:9-18.

Marriage of the king's son, Matt. 22:1-14.

Fig tree leafing, Matt. 24:32; Mark 13:28,29.

Man taking a far journey, Mark 13:34-37.

Ten virgins, Matt. 25:1-13.

Talents, Matt. 25:14-30.

The vine, John 15:1-5.

PASSION OF: See Sufferings of.

PECCABILITY OF: See Temptation of.

PERFECTIONS OF: Not classified under foregoing topics: Psa. 45:2. Thou art fairer than the children of men: grace is poured into thy lips:

Isa. 11:5. And righteousness shall be the girdle of his loins, and faithfulness the girdle of his reins.

Isa. 49:2. And he hath made my mouth like a sharp sword; in the shadow of his hand hath he hid me, and made me a polished shaft; in his quiver hath he hid me;

Isa. 53:9. He had done no violence, neither *was any* deceit in his mouth.

Ezek. 34:29. I will raise up for them a plant of renown,

Mic. 5:4. He shall stand and feed in the strength of the Lord, in the majesty of the name of the Lord his God;

Hag. 2:7. And I will shake all nations, and the [1] desire of all nations shall come :

[1 R. V. desirable things]

Matt. 12:41. Behold, a greater than Jonas is here. 42. A greater than Solomon is here.

Matt. 27:3. Then Judas, which had betrayed him, when he saw that he was condemned, repented himself, and brought again the thirty pieces of silver to the chief priests and elders, 4. Saying, I have sinned in that I have betrayed the innocent blood.

Luke 3:16. One mightier than I cometh, the latchet of whose shoes I am not worthy to unloose. Matt. 3:11; Mark 1:7,8.

Luke 23:41. This man hath done nothing amiss.

John 1:14. We beheld his glory, the glory as of the only begotten of the Father, full of grace and truth. 18. The only begotten Son, which is in the bosom of the Father,

John 5:30. My judgment is just; because I seek not mine own will, but the will of the Father which hath sent me. 34. I receive not testimony from man. 41. I receive not honour from men.

John 7:18. He that speaketh of himself seeketh his own glory: but he that seeketh his glory that sent him, the same is true, and no unrighteousness is in him.

Acts 13:28. They found no cause of death *in him,*

1 Cor. 1:24. Christ the power of God, and the wisdom of God.

1 Cor. 15:45. The last Adam *was made* a quickening spirit. 47. The second man *is* the Lord from heaven.

2 Cor. 1:19. The Son of God, Jesus Christ, . . . was not yea and nay, but in him was yea.

2 Cor. 4:4. Christ, who is the image of God,

2 Cor. 5:21. For he hath made him *to be* sin for us, who knew no sin; that we might be made the righteousness of God in him.

Eph. 3:8. That I should preach among the Gentiles the unsearchable riches of Christ;

Col. 1:19. It pleased *the Father* that in him should all fulness dwell;

2 Thess. 3:3. But the Lord is faithful, who shall stablish you, and keep *you* from evil.

2 Tim. 2:13. He abideth faithful: he cannot deny himself.

Heb. 1:3. Who being the brightness of *his* glory, and the express image of his person,

Heb. 2:10. For it became him, for whom *are* all things, and by whom *are* all things, in bringing many sons unto glory, to make the captain of their salvation perfect through sufferings.

Heb. 3:2. Who was faithful to him that appointed him,

PERSECUTIONS OF: See Persecutions.

POWER OF, TO FORGIVE SINS: Matt. 9:2. Jesus seeing their faith said unto the sick of the palsy; Son, be of good cheer; thy sins be forgiven thee. 6. But that ye may know that the Son of man hath power on earth to forgive sins, (then saith he to the sick of the palsy,) Arise, take up thy bed, and go unto thine house. Mark 2:5,10; Luke 5:20,24.

Luke 7:47. Her sins, which are many, are forgiven; for she loved much: 48. And he said unto her, Thy sins are forgiven. 49. They that sat at meat with him began to say within themselves, Who is this that forgiveth sins also? 50. He said to the woman, Thy faith hath saved thee; go in peace.

Acts 5:31. Him hath God exalted with his right hand *to be* a Prince and a Saviour, for to give repentance to Israel, and forgiveness of sins.

Col. 3:13. As Christ forgave you, so also *do* ye.

See Divinity of.

PRAYERS OF: Matt. 11:25. I thank thee, O Father, Lord of heaven and earth, because thou hast hid these things from the wise and prudent, and hast revealed them unto babes. 26. Even so, Father: for so it seemed good in thy sight.

Matt. 14:23. He went up into a mountain apart to pray: and when the evening was come, he was there alone. Mark 6:46.

Matt. 15:36. And he took the seven loaves

and the fishes, and gave thanks, and brake *them*,

Matt. 19:13. Then were there brought unto him little children, that he should put *his* hands on them, and pray:

Matt. 26:26. And as they were eating, Jesus took bread, and blessed *it*, and brake *it*, and gave *it* to the disciples, and said, Take, eat; this is my body. 27. And he took the cup, and gave thanks, [1 Cor. 11:24.] 36. Then cometh Jesus with them unto a place called Gethsemane, and saith unto the disciples, Sit ye here, while I go and pray yonder. 39. And he went a little farther, and fell on his face, and prayed, saying, O my Father, if it be possible, let this cup pass from me: nevertheless not as I will, but as thou *wilt*. 42. He went away again the second time, and prayed, saying, O my Father, if this cup may not pass away from me, except I drink it, thy will be done. 44. And he left them, and went away again, and prayed the third time, saying the same words. Mark. 14:32–39.

Matt. 27:46. Jesus cried with a loud voice, saying, Eli, Eli, lama sabachthani? That is to say, My God, my God, why hast thou forsaken me?

Mark 1:35. In the morning, rising up a great while before day, he went out, and departed into a solitary place, and there prayed.

Mark 6:41. When he had taken the five loaves and the two fishes, he looked up to heaven, and blessed, and brake the loaves,

Luke 3:21. Jesus also being baptized, and praying, the heaven was opened,

Luke 5:16. He withdrew himself into the wilderness, and prayed.

Luke 6:12. He went out into a mountain to pray, and continued all night in prayer to God.

Luke 9:18. As he was alone praying, his disciples were with him: 28. He took Peter and John and James, and went up into a mountain to pray. 29. And as he prayed, the fashion of his countenance was altered, and his raiment *was* white *and* glistering.

Luke 11:1. As he was praying in a certain place, when he ceased, one of his disciples said unto him, Lord, teach us to pray, as John also taught his disciples.

Luke 22:32. I have prayed for thee, that thy faith fail not: 41. And he was withdrawn from them about a stone's cast, and kneeled down, and prayed, 42. Saying, Father, if thou be willing, remove this cup from me: nevertheless not my will, but thine, be done. 43. There appeared an angel unto him from heaven, strengthening him. 44. Being in an agony he prayed more earnestly: and his sweat was as it were great drops of blood falling down to the ground.

Luke 23:34. Then said Jesus, Father, forgive them; for they know not what they do. 46. When Jesus had cried with a loud voice, he said, Father, into thy hands I commend my spirit: and having said thus, he gave up the ghost.

John 11:41. Jesus lifted up *his* eyes, and said, Father, I thank thee that thou hast heard me. 42. And I knew that thou hearest me always: but because of the people which stand by I said *it*, that they may believe that thou hast sent me.

John 12:27. Now is my soul troubled; and what shall I say? Father, save me from this hour: but for this cause came I unto this hour. 28. Father, glorify thy name. Then came there a voice from heaven, *saying*, I have both glorified *it*, and will glorify *it* again.

John 17:1. These words spake Jesus, and lifted up his eyes to heaven, and said, Father, the hour is come; glorify thy Son, that thy Son also may glorify thee: 2. As thou hast given him power over all flesh, that he should give eternal life to as many as thou hast given him. 3. And this is life eternal, that they might know thee the only true God, and Jesus Christ, whom thou hast sent. 4. I have glorified thee on the earth: I have finished the work which thou gavest me to do. 5. And now, O Father, glorify thou me with thine own self with the glory which I had with thee before the world was. 6. I have manifested thy name unto the men which thou gavest me out of the world: thine they were, and thou gavest them me; and they have kept thy word. 7. Now they have known that all things whatsoever thou hast given me are of thee. 8. For I have given unto them the words which thou gavest me; and they have received *them*, and have known surely that I came out from thee, and they have believed that thou didst send me. 9. I pray for them: I pray not for the world, but for them which thou hast given me: for they are thine. 10. And all mine are thine, and thine are mine; and I am glorified in them. 11. And now I am no more in the world, but these are in the world, and I come to thee. Holy Father, keep through thine own name those whom thou hast given me, that they may be one, as we *are*. 12. While I was with them in the world, I kept them in thy name: those that thou gavest me I have kept, and none of them is lost, but the son of perdition; that the scripture might be fulfilled. 13. And now come I to thee; and these things I speak in the world, that they might have my joy fulfilled in themselves. 14. I have given them thy word; and the world hath hated them, because they are not of the world, even as I am not of the world. 15. I pray not that thou shouldest take them out of the world, but that thou shouldest keep them from the evil. 16. They are not of the world, even as I am not of the world. 17. Sanctify them through thy truth: thy word is truth. 18. As thou hast sent me into the world, even so have I also sent them into the world. 19. And for their sakes I sanctify myself, that they also might be sanctified through the truth. 20. Neither pray I for these alone, but for them also which shall believe on me through their word; 21. That they all may be one; as thou, Father, *art* in me, and I in thee, that they also may be one in us: that the world may believe that thou hast sent me. 22. And the glory which thou gavest me I have given them; that they may be one, even as we are one: 23. I in them, and thou in me, that they may be made perfect in one; and that the world may know that thou hast sent me, and hast loved them, as thou hast loved me. 24. Father, I will that they also, whom thou hast given me, be with me where I am; that they may behold my glory, which thou hast given me: for thou lovedst me before the foundation of the world. 25. O righteous Father, the world hath not known thee: but I have known thee, and these have known that thou hast sent me. 26. And I have declared unto them thy name, and will declare *it:* that the love wherewith thou hast loved me **may** be in them, and I in them.

Heb. 5:7. Who in the days of his flesh, when he had offered up prayers and supplications with strong crying and tears unto him that was able to save him from death, and was heard in that he feared;

See CHRIST; HIGH PRIEST; JESUS, MEDIATOR.

PREËXISTENCE OF: Gen. 1:26. And God said, Let us make man in our image, after our likeness: and let them have dominion over the fish of the sea, and over the fowl of the air, and over the cattle, and over all the earth, and over every creeping thing that creepeth upon the earth.

Psa. 102:25. Of old hast thou laid the foundation of the earth: and the heavens *are* the work of thy hands. 26. They shall perish, but thou shalt endure: yea, all of them shall wax old like a garment; as a vesture shalt thou change them, and they shall be changed: 27. But thou *art* the same, and thy years shall have no end. with Heb. 1:8-12.

Prov. 8:22. The LORD possessed me in the beginning of his way, before his works of old. 23. I was set up from everlasting, from the beginning, or ever the earth was. 24. When *there were* no depths, I was brought forth; when *there were* no fountains abounding with water. 25. Before the mountains were settled, before the hills was I brought forth: 26. While as yet he had not made the earth, nor the fields, nor the highest part of the dust of the world. 27. When he prepared the heavens, I *was* there: when he set a compass upon the face of the depth: 28. When he established the clouds above: when he strengthened the fountains of the deep: 29. When he gave to the sea his decree, that the waters should not pass his commandment: when he appointed the foundations of the earth: 30. Then I was by him, *as* one brought up *with him:* and

I was daily *his* delight, rejoicing always before him; 31. Rejoicing in the habitable part of his earth; and my delights *were* with the sons of men. 32. Now therefore hearken unto me, O ye children: for blessed *are they that* keep my ways. 33. Hear instruction, and be wise, and refuse it not. 34. Blessed *is* the man that heareth me, watching daily at my gates, waiting at the posts of my doors. 35. For whoso findeth me findeth life, and shall obtain favour of the LORD. 36. But he that sinneth against me wrongeth his own soul: all they that hate me love death.

John 1:1. In the beginning was the Word, and the Word was with God, and the Word was God. 2. The same was in the beginning with God. 3. All things were made by him; and without him was not any thing made that was made.

John 3:13. And no man hath ascended up to heaven, but he that came down from heaven, *even* the Son of man which is in heaven.

John 6:62. *What* and if ye shall see the Son of man ascend up where he was before?

John 8:56. Your father Abraham rejoiced to see my day: and he saw *it*, and was glad. 57. Then said the Jews unto him, Thou art not yet fifty years old, and hast thou seen Abraham? 58. Jesus said unto them, Verily, verily, I say unto you, Before Abraham was, I am.

John 17:5. And now, O Father, glorify thou me with thine own self with the glory which I had with thee before the world was.

Rom. 11:36. For of him, and through him, and to him, *are* all things: to whom *be* glory for ever.

1 Cor. 8:6. But to us *there is but* one God, the Father, of whom *are* all things, and we in him; and one Lord Jesus Christ, by whom *are* all things, and we by him.

Phil. 2:5. Let this mind be in you, which was also in Christ Jesus: 6. Who, being in the form of God, thought it not [1] robbery to be equal with God: 7. But [2] made himself of no reputation, and took upon him the form of a servant, and was made in the likeness of men: [R. V. [1] a prize   [2] emptied himself, taking]

Col. 1:15. Who is the image of the invisible God, the firstborn of every creature; 16. For by him were all things created, that are in heaven, and that are in earth, visible and invisible, whether *they be* thrones, or dominions, or principalities, or powers: all things were created by him, and for him: 17. And he is before all things, and by him all things consist.

Heb. 1:1. God, who at sundry times and in divers manners spake in time past unto the fathers by the prophets, 2. Hath in these last days spoken unto us by *his* Son, whom he hath appointed heir of all things, by whom also he made the worlds;

Heb. 2:9. But we see Jesus, who was **made** a little lower than the angels for the suffering of death, crowned with glory and honour; that he by the grace of God should taste death for every man. 14. Forasmuch then as the children are partakers of flesh and blood, he also himself likewise took part of the same; that through death he might destroy him that had the power of death, that is, the devil; 15. And deliver them who through fear of death were all their lifetime subject to bondage. 16. For verily he took not on *him the nature of* angels; but he took on *him* the seed of Abraham.

Rev. 4:11. Thou art worthy, O Lord, to receive glory and ·honour and power: for thou hast created all things, and for thy pleasure they are and were created.

See above, ETERNITY OF, CREATOR, INCARNATION OF, OMNIPOTENCE OF, OMNIPRESENCE OF, OMNISCIENCE OF.

PRESCIENCE OF: See OMNISCIENCE OF.

PRIESTHOOD OF: Appointed and called by God, Heb. 3:1,2; 5:4,5; after the order of Melchizedek, Psa. 110:4, with Heb. 5:6; 6:20; 7:15,17; superior to Aaron and the Levitical priests, Heb. 7:11,16,22; 8:1,2,6. Consecrated with an oath, Heb. 7:20,21. Has an unchangeable priesthood, Heb. 7:23,28. Is of unblemished purity, Heb. 7:26,28; faithful, Heb. 3:2. Needed no sacrifice for himself, Heb. 7:27.

Offered himself a sacrifice, Heb. 9:14,26. His sacrifice superior to all others, Heb. 9:13, 14,23. Offered sacrifice but once, Heb. 7:27. Made reconciliation, Heb. 2:17. Obtained redemption for us, Heb. 9:12. Entered into heaven, Heb. 4.14; 10:12. Sympathizes with saints, Heb. 2:18; 4:15. Intercedes, Heb. 7:25; 9:24. Blesses, Num. 6:23–26, with Acts 3:26. On his throne, Zech. 6:13. Appointment of, an encouragement to steadfastness, Heb. 4:14.

Typified: Melchizedek, Gen. 14:18–20. Aaron and his sons, Ex. 40:12–15.—*Bible Text-Book.*

PROMISES OF: PROPHETIC: Matt. 19:28. Ye which have followed me, in the regeneration when the Son of man shall sit in the throne of his glory, ye also shall sit upon twelve thrones, judging the twelve tribes of Israel. 29. And every one that hath forsaken houses, or brethren, or sisters, or father, or mother, or wife, or children, or lands, for my name's sake, shall receive an hundredfold, and shall inherit everlasting life.

Mark 10:29. And Jesus answered and said, Verily I say unto you, There is no man that hath left house, or brethren, or sisters, or father, or mother, or wife, or children, or lands, for my sake, and the gospel's, 30. But he shall receive an hundredfold now in this time, houses, and brethren, and sisters, and mothers, and children, and lands, with persecutions; and in the world to come eternal life. Luke 18:29,30.

Luke 22:29. And I appoint unto you a kingdom, as my Father hath appointed unto me; 30. That ye may eat and drink at my table in my kingdom, and sit on thrones judging the twelve tribes of Israel.

Luke 23:43. And Jesus said unto him, Verily I say unto thee, To day shalt thou be with me in paradise.

Luke 24:49. And, behold, I send the promise of my Father upon you: but tarry ye in the city of Jerusalem, until ye be endued with power from on high.

John 5:25. Verily, verily, I say unto you, The hour is coming, and now is, when the dead shall hear the voice of the Son of God: and they that hear shall live. 26. For as the Father hath life in himself; so hath he given to the Son to have life in himself; 27. And hath given him authority to execute judgment also, because he is the Son of man. 28. Marvel not at this: for the hour is coming, in the which all that are in the graves shall hear his voice, 29. And shall come forth; they that have done good, unto the resurrection of life; and they that have done evil, unto the resurrection of damnation.

John 6:54. Whoso eateth my flesh, and drinketh my blood, hath eternal life; and I will raise him up at the last day. 57. As the living Father hath sent me, and I live by the Father: so he that eateth me, even he shall live by me. 58. This is that bread which came down from heaven: not as your fathers did eat manna, and are dead: he that eateth of this bread shall live for ever.

John 7:39. (But this spake he of the Spirit, which they that believe on him should receive: for the Holy Ghost was not yet *given;* because that Jesus was not yet glorified.)

John 12:25. He that loveth his life shall lose it: and he that hateth his life in this world shall keep it unto life eternal. 26. If any man serve me, let him follow me; and where I am, there shall also my servant be: if any man serve me, him will *my* Father honour.

John 14:16. I will pray the Father, and he shall give you another Comforter, that he may abide with you for ever; 26. But the Comforter, *which is* the Holy Ghost, whom the Father will send in my name, he shall teach you all things, and bring all things to your remembrance, whatsoever I have said unto you.

John 15:26. But when the Comforter is come, whom I will send unto you from the Father, *even* the Spirit of truth, which proceedeth from the Father, he shall testify of me: 27. And ye also shall bear witness, because ye have been with me from the beginning.

John 16:7. Nevertheless I tell you the truth; It is expedient for you that I go away: for if I go not away, the Comforter will not come unto you; but if I depart, I will send him unto you. 8. And when he is come, he will reprove the world of sin, and of righteousness, and of judgment: 9. Of sin, because they believe not on me; 10. Of righteousness, because I go to my Father, and ye see me no more; 11. Of judgment, because the prince of this world is judged. 12. I have yet many things to say unto you, but ye cannot bear them now. 13. Howbeit when he, the Spirit of truth, is come, he will guide you into all truth: for he shall not speak of himself; but whatsoever he shall hear, *that* shall he speak: and he will shew you things to come. 14. He shall glorify me: for he shall receive of mine, and shall shew *it* unto you. 15. All things that the Father hath are mine: therefore said I, that he shall take of mine, and shall shew *it* unto you. 16. A little while, and ye shall not see me: and again, a little while, and ye shall see me, because I go to the Father. 20. Verily, verily, I say unto you, That ye shall weep and lament, but the world shall rejoice: and ye shall be sorrowful, but your sorrow shall be turned into joy. 21. A woman when she is in travail hath sorrow, because her hour is come: but as soon as she is delivered of the child, she remembereth no more the anguish, for joy that a man is born into the world. 22. And ye now therefore have sorrow: but I will see you again, and your heart shall rejoice, and your joy no man taketh from you. 23. And in that day ye shall ask me nothing. Verily, verily, I say unto you, Whatsoever ye shall ask the Father in my name, he will give *it* you. 24. Hitherto have ye asked nothing in my name: ask, and ye shall receive, that your joy may be full. 25. These things have I spoken unto you in proverbs: but the time cometh, when I shall no more speak unto you in proverbs, but I shall shew you plainly of the Father. 26. At that day ye shall ask in my name: and I say not unto you, that I will pray the Father for you: 33. These things I have spoken unto you, that in me ye might have peace. In the world ye shall have tribulation: but be of good cheer; I have overcome the world.

Acts 1:4. And, being assembled together with *them*, commanded them that they should not depart from Jerusalem, but wait for the promise of the Father, which, *saith he*, ye have heard of me. 5. For John truly baptized with water; but ye shall be baptized with the Holy Ghost not many days hence. 6. When they therefore were come together, they asked of him, saying, Lord, wilt thou at this time restore again the kingdom to Israel? 7. And he said unto them, It is not for you to know the times or the seasons, which the Father hath put in his own power. 8. But ye shall receive power, after that the Holy Ghost is come upon you: and ye shall be witnesses unto me both in Jerusalem, and in all Judæa, and in Samaria, and unto the uttermost part of the earth.

PROPHECIES CONCERNING: Coming of:
Gen. 3:15. And I will put enmity between thee and the woman, and between thy seed and her seed; it shall bruise thy head, and thou shalt bruise his heel.

Gen. 12:3. In thee shall all families of the earth be blessed.

Gen. 49:10. The sceptre shall not depart from Judah, nor a lawgiver from between his feet, until Shiloh come; and unto him *shall* the gathering of the people *be*.

Deut. 32:18. Of the Rock *that* begat thee thou art unmindful, and hast forgotten God that formed thee.

1 Sam. 2:10. The adversaries of the Lord shall be broken to pieces; out of heaven shall he thunder upon them: the Lord shall judge the ends of the earth; and he shall give strength unto his king, and exalt the horn of his anointed.

Job 19:25. For I know *that* my redeemer liveth, and *that* he shall stand at the latter *day* upon the earth:

Psa. 21:5. His glory *is* great in thy salvation: honour and majesty hast thou laid upon him. 6. For thou hast made him most blessed for ever: thou hast made him exceeding glad with thy countenance. 7. For the king trusteth in the Lord, and through the mercy of the most High he shall not be moved.

Psa. 40:6. Sacrifice and offering thou didst not desire; mine ears hast thou opened: burnt offering and sin offering hast thou not required. 7. Then said I, Lo, I come: in the volume of the book *it is* written of me, 8. I delight to do thy will, O my God: yea, thy law *is* within my heart. 9. I have preached righteousness in the great congregation: lo, I have not refrained my lips, O Lord, thou knowest. 10. I have not hid thy righteousness within my heart; I have declared thy faithfulness and thy salvation: I have not concealed thy lovingkindness and thy truth from the great congregation.

Psa. 68:18. Thou hast ascended on high, thou hast led captivity captive: thou hast received gifts for men;

Psa. 118:22. The stone *which* the builders refused is become the head *stone* of the corner. 23. This is the Lord's doing; it *is* marvellous in our eyes. 24. This *is* the day *which* the Lord hath made; we will rejoice and be glad in it. 26. Blessed *be* he that cometh in the name of the Lord: we have blessed you out of the house of the Lord.

Isa. 11:1. And there shall come forth a rod out of the stem of Jesse, and a Branch shall grow out of his roots: [Rom. 15:12.] 2. And the spirit of the Lord shall rest upon him, the spirit of wisdom and understanding, the spirit of counsel and might, the spirit of knowledge and of the fear of the Lord; 3. And shall make him of quick understanding in the fear of the Lord: and he shall not judge after the sight of his eyes, neither reprove after the hearing of his ears: 4. But with righteousness shall he judge the poor, and reprove with equity for the meek of the earth: and he shall smite the earth with the rod of his mouth, and with the breath of his lips shall he slay the wicked. 5. And righteousness shall be the girdle of his loins, and faithfulness the girdle of his reins. 6. The wolf also shall dwell with the lamb, and the leopard shall lie down with the kid; and the calf and the young lion and the fatling together; and a little child shall lead them.   7. And the cow and the bear shall feed; their young ones shall lie down together: and the lion shall eat straw like the ox.   8. And the sucking child shall play on the hole of the asp, and the weaned child shall put his hand on the cockatrice' den.   9. They shall not hurt nor destroy in all my holy mountain: for the earth shall be full of the knowledge of the LORD, as the waters cover the sea.   10. And in that day there shall be a root of Jesse, which shall stand for an ensign of the people; to it shall the Gentiles seek: and his rest shall be glorious.   *vs.* 11–16.

Isa. 28:16. Therefore thus saith the Lord GOD, Behold, I lay in Zion for a foundation a stone, a tried stone, a precious corner *stone*, a sure foundation: he that believeth shall not make haste.

Isa. 40:3. The voice of him that crieth in the wilderness, Prepare ye the way of the LORD, make straight in the desert a highway for our God.   [Luke 3:4.]   11. He shall feed his flock like a shepherd: he shall gather the lambs with his arm, and carry *them* in his bosom, *and* shall gently lead those that are with young.

Isa. 42:1. Behold my servant, whom I uphold; mine elect, *in whom* my soul delighteth: I have put my spirit upon him: he shall bring forth judgment to the Gentiles. 2. He shall not cry, nor lift up, nor cause his voice to be heard in the street.   3. A bruised reed shall he not break, and the smoking flax shall he not quench: he shall bring forth judgment unto truth.   4. He shall not fail nor be discouraged, till he have set judgment in the earth: and the isles shall wait for his law.

Isa. 49:1. Listen, O isles, unto me: and hearken, ye people, from far; The LORD hath called me from the womb; from the bowels of my mother hath he made mention of my name.   2. And he hath made my mouth like a sharp sword; in the shadow of his hand hath he hid me, and made me a polished shaft; in his quiver hath he hid me; 3. And said unto me, Thou *art* my servant, O Israel, in whom I will be glorified.   4. Then I said, I have laboured in vain, I have spent my strength for nought, and in vain: *yet* surely my judgment *is* with the LORD, and my work with my God.   5. And now, saith the LORD that formed me from the womb *to be* his servant, to bring Jacob again to him, Though Israel be not gathered, yet shall I be glorious in the eyes of the LORD, and my God shall be my strength.   6. And he said, It is a light thing that thou shouldest be my servant to raise up the tribes of Jacob, and to restore the preserved of Israel: I will also give thee for a light to the Gentiles, that thou mayest be my salvation unto the end of the earth.   7. Thus saith the LORD, the Redeemer of Israel, *and* his Holy One,

to him whom man despiseth, to him whom the nation abhorreth, to a servant of rulers, Kings shall see and arise, princes also shall worship, because of the LORD that is faithful, *and* the Holy One of Israel, and he shall choose thee.   8. Thus saith the LORD, In an acceptable time have I heard thee, and in a day of salvation have I helped thee: and I will preserve thee, and give thee for a covenant of the people, to establish the earth, to cause to inherit the desolate heritages; 9. That thou mayest say to the prisoners, Go forth; to them that *are* in darkness, Shew yourselves. They shall feed in the ways, and their pastures *shall be* in all high places. 10. They shall not hunger nor thirst; neither shall the heat nor sun smite them: for he that hath mercy on them shall lead them, even by the springs of water shall he guide them.   11. And I will make all my mountains a way, and my highways shall be exalted.   12. Behold, these shall come from far: and, lo, these from the north and from the west; and these from the land of Sinim. *vs.* 13–26; Isa. 53.   See p. 743.

Isa. 55:3. Incline your ear, and come unto me: hear, and your soul shall live; and I will make an everlasting covenant with you, *even* the sure mercies of David.   4. Behold, I have given him *for* a witness to the people, a leader and commander to the people.   5. Behold, thou shalt call a nation *that* thou knowest not, and nations *that* knew not thee shall run unto thee because of the LORD thy God, and for the Holy One of Israel; for he hath glorified thee.

Isa. 56:1. Thus saith the LORD, Keep ye judgment, and do justice: for my salvation *is* near to come, and my righteousness to be revealed.

Isa. 59:16. And he saw that *there was* no man, and wondered that *there was* no intercessor: therefore his arm brought salvation unto him; and his righteousness, it sustained him.   17. For he put on righteousness as a breastplate, and an helmet of salvation upon his head; and he put on the garments of vengeance *for* clothing, and was clad with zeal as a cloke.   18. According to *their* deeds, accordingly he will repay, fury to his adversaries, recompence to his enemies; to the islands he will repay recompence.   20. And the Redeemer shall come to Zion, and unto them that turn from transgression in Jacob, saith the LORD.

Isa. 62:10. Go through, go through the gates; prepare ye the way of the people; cast up, cast up the highway; gather out the stones; lift up a standard for the people. 11. Behold, the LORD hath proclaimed unto the end of the world, Say ye to the daughter of Zion, Behold, thy salvation cometh; behold, his reward *is* with him, and his work before him.

Jer. 23:5. Behold, the days come, saith the LORD, that I will raise unto David a righteous Branch, and a King shall reign and prosper, and shall execute judgment and justice in the earth.   6. In his days Judah shall be saved, and Israel shall dwell safely: and this *is* his name whereby he shall be called, THE LORD OUR RIGHTEOUSNESS.

Jer. 33:15. In those days, and at that time, will I cause the Branch of righteousness to grow up unto David; and he shall execute judgment and righteousness in the land. 16. In those days shall Judah be saved, and Jerusalem shall dwell safely: and this *is the name* wherewith she shall be called, The LORD our righteousness.   17. For thus saith the LORD; David shall never want a man to sit upon the throne of the house of Israel; 18. Neither shall the priests the Levites want a man before me to offer burnt offerings, and to kindle meat offerings, and to do sacrifice continually.

Dan. 7:13. I saw in the night visions, and, behold, *one* like the Son of man came with the clouds of heaven, and came to the Ancient of days, and they brought him near before him.   14. And there was given him dominion, and glory, and a kingdom, that all people, nations, and languages, should serve him: his dominion *is* an everlasting dominion, which shall not pass away, and his kingdom *that* which shall not be destroyed.

Dan. 9:24. Seventy weeks are determined upon thy people and upon thy holy city, to finish the transgression, and to make an end of sins, and to make reconciliation for iniquity, and to bring in everlasting righteousness, and to seal up the vision and prophecy, and to anoint the most Holy. 25. Know therefore and understand, *that* from the going forth of the commandment to restore and to build Jerusalem unto the Messiah the Prince *shall be* seven weeks, and threescore and two weeks: the street shall be built again, and the wall, even in troublous times.   26. And after threescore and two weeks shall Messiah be cut off, but not for himself: and the people of the prince that shall come shall destroy the city and the sanctuary; and the end thereof *shall be* with a flood, and unto the end of the war desolations are determined. 27. And he shall confirm the covenant with many for one week: and in the midst of the week he shall cause the sacrifice and the oblation to cease, and for the overspreading of abominations he shall make *it* desolate, even until the consummation, and that determined shall be poured upon the desolate.

Hag. 2:7. And I will shake all nations, and the ¹ desire of all nations shall come: and I will fill this house with glory, saith the LORD of hosts.   [¹ R. V. desirable things]

Zech. 3:8. Hear now, O Joshua the high priest, thou, and thy fellows that sit before thee: for they *are* men wondered at: for, behold, I will bring forth my servant the BRANCH.

Zech. 9:9. Rejoice greatly, O daughter of Zion; shout, O daughter of Jerusalem: behold, thy King cometh unto thee: he *is* just, and having salvation; lowly, and riding upon an ass, and upon a colt the foal of an ass.

Zech. 13:1. In that day there shall be a fountain opened to the house of David and to the inhabitants of Jerusalem for sin and for uncleanness.

Mal. 3:1. Behold, I will send my messenger, and he shall prepare the way before me: and the Lord, whom ye seek, shall suddenly come to his temple, even the messenger of the covenant, whom ye delight in: behold, he shall come, saith the LORD of hosts.   2. But who may abide the day of his coming? and who shall stand when he appeareth? for he *is* like a refiner's fire, and like fullers' sope: 3. And he shall sit *as* a refiner and purifier of silver: and he shall purify the sons of Levi, and purge them as gold and silver, that they may offer unto the LORD an offering in righteousness.

Mal. 4:2. But unto you that fear my name shall the Sun of righteousness arise with healing in his wings; and ye shall go forth, and grow up as calves of the stall.

Matt. 1:20. But while he thought on these things, behold, the angel of the Lord appeared unto him in a dream, saying, Joseph, thou son of David, fear not to take unto thee Mary thy wife: for that which is conceived in her is of the Holy Ghost. 21. And she shall bring forth a son, and thou shalt call his name JESUS: for he shall save his people from their sins.   22. Now all this was done, that it might be fulfilled which was spoken of the Lord by the prophet, saying,   23. Behold, a virgin shall be with child, and shall bring forth a son, and they shall call his name Emmanuel, which being interpreted is, God with us.

Luke 1:26. And in the sixth month the angel Gabriel was sent from God unto a city of Galilee, named Nazareth, 27. To a virgin espoused to a man whose name was Joseph, of the house of David; and the virgin's name *was* Mary.   28. And the angel came in unto her, and said, Hail, *thou that art* highly favoured, the Lord *is* with thee: ¹ blessed *art* thou among women.   29. And when she saw *him*, she was troubled at his saying, and cast in her mind what manner of salutation this should be.   30. And the angel said unto her, Fear not, Mary: for thou hast found favour with God. 31. And, behold, thou shalt conceive in thy womb, and bring forth a son, and shalt call his name JESUS.   32. He shall be great, and shall be called the Son of the Highest; and the Lord God shall give unto him the throne of his father David: 33. And he shall reign over the house of Jacob for ever; and of his kingdom there shall be no end.   34. Then said Mary unto the angel, How shall this be, seeing I know not a man? 35. And the angel answered and said unto her, The Holy Ghost shall come upon thee, and the power of the Highest shall overshadow thee : therefore also that holy thing which shall be born of thee shall be called the Son of God. 36. And, behold, thy cousin Elisabeth, she hath also conceived a son in her old age : and this is the sixth month with her, who was called barren. 37. For with God nothing shall be impossible. 41. And it came to pass, that, when Elisabeth heard the salutation of Mary, the babe leaped in her womb ; and Elisabeth was filled with the Holy Ghost: 42. And she spake out with a loud voice, and said, Blessed *art* thou among women, and blessed *is* the fruit of thy womb. 43. And whence *is* this to me, that the mother of my Lord should come to me ? 44. For, lo, as soon as the voice of thy salutation sounded in mine ears, the babe leaped in my womb for joy. 45. And blessed *is* she that believed : for there shall be a performance of those things which were told her from the Lord.   [¹ Omitted in R. V.]

Luke 2:26. And it was revealed unto him by the Holy Ghost, that he should not see death, before he had seen the Lord's Christ. 31. Which thou hast prepared before the face of all people ; 32. A light to lighten the Gentiles, and the glory of thy people Israel. 34. And Simeon blessed them, and said unto Mary his mother, Behold, this *child* is set for the falling and rising again of many in Israel; and for a sign which shall be spoken against; 35. (Yea, a sword shall pierce through thy own soul also,) that the thoughts of many hearts may be revealed. 38. And she coming in that instant gave thanks likewise unto the Lord, and spake of him to all them that looked for redemption in Jerusalem.

John 8:56. Your father Abraham rejoiced to see my day: and he saw *it*, and was glad.

Acts 3:22. For Moses truly said unto the fathers, A Prophet shall the Lord your God raise up unto you of your brethren, like unto me ; him shall ye hear in all things whatsoever he shall say unto you. 23. And it shall come to pass, *that* every soul, which will not hear that Prophet, shall be destroyed from among the people. 24. Yea, and all the prophets from Samuel and those that follow after, as many as have spoken, have likewise foretold of these days.

Rom. 1:2. (Which he had promised afore by his prophets in the holy scriptures,) 3. Concerning his Son Jesus Christ our Lord,

Heb. 7:16. Who is made, not after the law of a carnal commandment, but after the power of an endless life.

Heb. 10:9. Then said he, Lo, I come to do thy will, O God. He taketh away the first, that he may establish the second.

See JESUS, KINGDOM OF, PROPHECIES CONCERNING; CHURCH, PROPHECIES CONCERNING.

PROPHECIES CONCERNING THE FUTURE GLORY AND POWER OF: Mark 14:62. And Jesus said, I am : and ye shall see the Son of man sitting on the right hand of power, and coming in the clouds of heaven.

1 Pet. 3:22. Who is gone into heaven, and is on the right hand of God ; angels and authorities and powers being made subject unto him.

Jude 14. Behold, the Lord cometh with ten thousand of his saints, 15. To execute judgment upon all, and to convince all that are ungodly among them of all their ungodly deeds which they have ungodly committed, and of all their hard *speeches* which ungodly sinners have spoken against him.

Rev. 1:5. Jesus Christ, *who is* the faithful witness, *and* the first begotten of the dead, and the prince of the kings of the earth. Unto him that loved us, and washed us from our sins in his own blood, 6. And hath made us kings and priests unto God and his Father; to him *be* glory and dominion for ever and ever. Amen. 7. Behold, he cometh with clouds; and every eye shall see him, and they *also* which pierced him : and all kindreds of the earth shall wail because of him. 18. *I am* he that liveth, and was dead; and, behold, I am alive for evermore, Amen; and have the keys of hell and of death.

Rev. 2:23. I will kill her children with death; and all the churches shall know that I am he which searcheth the reins and hearts: and I will give unto every one of you, according to your works.

Rev. 3:7. These things saith he that is holy, he that is true, he that hath the key of David, he that openeth, and no man shutteth; and shutteth, and no man openeth ; 14. These things saith the Amen, the faithful and true witness, the beginning of the creation of God ; 21. To him that overcometh will I grant to sit with me in my throne, even as I also overcame, and am set down with my Father in his throne. Isa. 22:22.

Rev. 5:5. The Lion of the tribe of Juda, the Root of David, hath prevailed to open the book, and to loose the seven seals thereof. 12. Worthy is the Lamb that was slain to receive power, and riches, and wisdom, and strength, and honour, and glory, and blessing.

Rev. 6:16. And said to the mountains and rocks, Fall on us, and hide us from the face of him that sitteth on the throne, and from the wrath of the Lamb: 17. For the great day of his wrath is come; and who shall be able to stand ?

Rev. 7:9. After this I beheld, and, lo, a great multitude, which no man could number, of all nations, and kindreds, and people, and tongues, stood before the throne, and before the Lamb, clothed with white robes, and palms in their hands; 10. And cried with a loud voice, saying, Salvation to our God which sitteth upon the throne, and unto the Lamb. 11. And all the angels stood round about the throne, and *about* the elders and the four beasts, and fell before the throne on their faces, and worshipped God, 12. Saying, Amen: Blessing, and glory, and wisdom, and thanksgiving, and honour, and power, and might, *be* unto our God for ever and ever.   Amen.   13. And one of the elders answered, saying unto me, What are these which are arrayed in white robes? and whence came they?   14. And I said unto him, Sir, thou knowest, And he said to me, These are they which came out of great tribulation, and have washed their robes, and made them white in the blood of the Lamb.   15. Therefore are they before the throne of God, and serve him day and night in his temple: and he that sitteth on the throne shall dwell among them.   16. They shall hunger no more, neither thirst any more; neither shall the sun light on them, nor any heat.   17. For the Lamb which is in the midst of the throne shall feed them, and shall lead them unto living fountains of waters: and God shall wipe away all tears from their eyes.

Rev. 11:15. The kingdoms of this world are become *the kingdoms* of our Lord, and of his Christ; and he shall reign for ever and ever.

Rev. 12:10. Now is come salvation, and strength, and the kingdom of our God, and the power of his Christ: for the accuser of our brethren is cast down,

Rev. 14:14. Behold a white cloud, and upon the cloud *one* sat like unto the Son of man, having on his head a golden crown, and in his hand a sharp sickle.

Rev. 17:14. These shall make war with the Lamb, and the Lamb shall overcome them: for he is Lord of lords, and King of kings:

Rev. 19:11. I saw heaven opened, and behold a white horse; and he that sat upon him *was* called Faithful and True, and in righteousness he doth judge and make war. 12. His eyes *were* as a flame of fire, and on his head *were* many crowns; and he had a name written, that no man knew, but he himself.   15. Out of his mouth goeth a sharp sword, that with it he should smite the nations: and he shall rule them with a rod of iron: and he treadeth the winepress of the fierceness and wrath of Almighty God. 16. He hath on *his* vesture and on his thigh a name written, KING OF KINGS, AND LORD OF LORDS.

Rev. 20:4. I saw thrones, and they sat upon them, and judgment was given unto them: and *I saw* the souls of them that were beheaded for the witness of Jesus, and for the word of God, and which had not worshipped the beast, neither his image, neither had received *his* mark upon their foreheads, or in their hands; and they lived and reigned with Christ a thousand years. 6. Blessed and holy *is* he that hath part in the first resurrection: on such the second death hath no power, but they shall be priests of God and of Christ, and shall reign with him a thousand years.

See above, EXALTATION OF, KINGDOM OF.

PROPHET: Foretold, Isa. 52:7; Nah.

1:15.   Anointed with the Holy Ghost, Isa. 42:1; 61:1, with Luke 4:18; John 3:34.   Reveals God, Matt. 11:27; John 3:2,13,34; 17:6, 14,26; Heb. 1:1,2.   Declared his doctrine to be that of the Father, John 8:26,28; 12:49,50; 14:10,24; 15:15; 17:8,26.   Foretold things to come, Matt. 24:3–35; Luke 19:41–44.   Faithful, Luke 4:43; John 17:8; Heb. 3:2; Rev. 1:5; 3:14. Abounded in wisdom, Luke 2:40,47,52; Col. 2:3.   Mighty in deed and word, Matt. 13:54; Mark 1:27; Luke 4:32; John 7:46.   Unostentatious in his teaching, Isa. 42:2; Matt. 12:17–20.   God commands us to hear, Deut. 18:15; Acts 3:22.   God will severely visit neglect of, Deut. 18:10; Acts 3:23; Heb. 2:3.

Deut. 18:15. The LORD thy God will raise up unto thee a Prophet from the midst of thee, of thy brethren, like unto me; unto him ye shall hearken;   18. I will raise them up a Prophet from among their brethren, like unto thee, and will put my words in his mouth; and he shall speak unto them all that I shall command him.   Acts 3:22,23; 7:37.

Matt. 21:11. And the multitude said, This is Jesus the prophet of Nazareth of Galilee. 46. But when they sought to lay hands on him, they feared the multitude, because they took him for a prophet.

Luke 7:16. They glorified God, saying, That a great prophet is risen up among us; and, That God hath visited his people.   39. Now when the Pharisee which had bidden him saw *it*, he spake within himself, saying, This man, if he were a prophet, would have known who and what manner of woman *this is* that toucheth him: for she is a sinner.

Luke 13:33. Nevertheless I must walk to day, and to morrow, and the *day* following: for it cannot be that a prophet perish out of Jerusalem.

Luke 24:19. And he said unto them, What things? And they said unto him, Concerning Jesus of Nazareth, which was a prophet mighty in deed and word before God and all the people:

John 3:2. Rabbi, we know that thou art a teacher come from God: for no man can do these miracles that thou doest, except God be with him.

John 4:19. The woman saith unto him, Sir, I perceive that thou art a prophet.

John 6:14. Then those men, when they had seen the miracle that Jesus did, said, This is of a truth that prophet that should come into the world.

John 7:40. Many of the people therefore, when they heard this saying, said, Of a truth this is the Prophet.

John 9:17. They say unto the blind man again, What sayest thou of him, that he hath opened thine eyes? He said, He is a prophet.

RECEIVED: Matt. 4:24. And his fame went throughout all Syria: and they brought unto him all sick people that were taken with divers diseases and torments, and those which were possessed with devils, and those which were lunatick, and those that had the palsy; and he healed them. 25. And there followed him great multitudes of people from Galilee, and *from* Decapolis. and *from* Jerusalem, and *from* Judæa, and *from* beyond Jordan. Matt. 8:1; 19:1,2; Mark 10:1; 3:7; 5:21.

Matt. 7:28. When Jesus had ended these sayings, the people were astonished at his doctrine: 29. For he taught them as *one* having authority, and not as the scribes. Mark 1:22; Luke 4:32.

Matt. 9:8. When the multitudes saw *it*, they marvelled, and glorified God, which had given such power unto men. 27. Two blind men followed him, crying, and saying, *Thou* son of David, have mercy on us. 33. The multitudes marvelled, saying, It was never so seen in Israel.

Matt. 12:23. And all the people were amazed, and said, Is not this the son of David?

Matt. 13:2. Great multitudes were gathered together unto him, so that he went into a ship, and sat; and the whole multitude stood on the shore. 54. And when he was come into his own country, he taught them in their synagogue, insomuch that they were astonished, and said, Whence hath this *man* this wisdom, and *these* mighty works? Mark 4:1; 6:2.

Matt. 14:33. Came and worshipped him, saying, Of a truth thou art the Son of God. Mark 6:51,52.

Matt. 16:1. The Pharisees also with the Sadducees came, and tempting desired him that he would shew them a sign from heaven. 14. Some *say that thou art* John the Baptist; some, Elias; and others, Jeremias, or one of the prophets. Matt. 12:38; Mark 8:11,28; Luke 9:19; 11:16.

Matt. 21:8. A very great multitude spread their garments in the way; others cut down branches from the trees and strawed *them* in the way. 9. And the multitudes that went before, and that followed, cried, saying, Hosanna to the son of David: Blessed *is* he that cometh in the name of the Lord; Hosanna in the highest. 10. And when he was come into Jerusalem, all the city was moved, saying, Who is this? [Mark 11:8–10; Luke 19:36–38; John 12:12,13.] 11. And the multitude said, This is Jesus the prophet of Nazareth of Galilee. 15. When the chief priests and scribes saw the wonderful things that he did, and the children crying in the temple, and saying, Hosanna to the son of David; they were sore displeased.

Matt. 27:54. When the centurion, and they that were with him, watching Jesus, saw the earthquake, and those things that were done, they feared greatly, saying, Truly this was the Son of God. Mark 15:39; Luke 23:47.

Mark 1:37. When they had found him, they said unto him, All *men* seek for thee. 45. But he went out, and began to publish

it much, and to blaze abroad the matter, insomuch that Jesus could no more openly enter into the city, but was without in desert places: and they came to him from every quarter.

Mark 2:2. Many were gathered together, insomuch that there was no room to receive *them*, no, not so much as about the door: and he preached the word unto them. 12. They were all amazed, and glorified God, saying, We never saw it on this fashion. 15. As Jesus sat at meat in his house, many publicans and sinners sat also together with Jesus and his disciples: for there were many, and they followed him. Mark 1:33.

Mark 3:20. The multitude cometh together again, so that they could not so much as eat bread. 21. When his friends heard *of it*, they went out to lay hold on him: for they said, He is beside himself.

Mark 5:42. They were astonished with a great astonishment. Luke 8:56.

Mark 6:33. The people saw them departing, and many knew him, and ran afoot thither out of all cities, and outwent them, and came together unto him. 55. And ran through that whole region round about, and began to carry about in beds those that were sick, where they heard he was. 56. And whithersoever he entered, into villages, or cities, or country, they laid the sick in the streets, and besought him that they might touch if it were but the border of his garment: Matt. 14:13,35; Luke 9:11; John 6:2.

Mark 7:37. And were beyond measure astonished, saying, He hath done all things well: he maketh both the deaf to hear, and the dumb to speak. Matt. 15:31.

Mark 12:37. The common people heard him gladly.

Luke 4:14. There went out a fame of him through all the region round about. 15. And he taught in their synagogues, being glorified of all. 22. All bare him witness, and wondered at the gracious words which proceeded out of his mouth. And they said, Is not this Joseph's son? 36. They were all amazed, and spake among themselves, saying, What a word *is* this! for with authority and power he commandeth the unclean spirits, and they come out. 37. And the fame of him went out into every place of the country round about. 42. The people sought him, and came unto him, and stayed him, that he should not depart from them. Mark 1:27.

Luke 5:1. As the people pressed upon him to hear the word of God, 17. And it came to pass on a certain day, as he was teaching, that there were Pharisees and doctors of the law sitting by, which were come out of every town of Galilee, and Judæa, and Jerusalem: 19. When they could not find by what *way* they might bring him in because of the multitude, they went upon the housetop, and let him down through the tiling, with *his* couch, into the midst before Jesus. 26. They were all amazed, and they glorified

God, and were filled with fear, saying, We have seen strange things to day.

Luke 6:17. He came down with them, and stood in the plain, and the company of his disciples, and a great multitude of people out of all Judæa and Jerusalem, and from the sea coast of Tyre and Sidon, which came to hear him, and to be healed of their diseases; 18. And they that were vexed with unclean spirits: and they were healed. 19. And the whole multitude sought to touch him: for there went virtue out of him, and healed *them* all.

Luke 7:16. There came a fear on all: and they glorified God, saying, That a great prophet is risen up among us; and, That God hath visited his people. 17. And this rumour of him went forth throughout all Judæa, and throughout all the region round about. 18. And the disciples of John shewed him of all these things. 29. All the people that heard *him*, and the publicans, justified God, being baptized with the baptism of John.

Luke 12:1. There were gathered together an innumerable multitude of people, insomuch that they trode one upon another,

Luke 13:17. All the people rejoiced for all the glorious things that were done by him.

Luke 18:43. Immediately he received his sight, and followed him, glorifying God: and all the people, when they saw *it*, gave praise unto God.

Luke 19:37. When he was come nigh, even now at the descent of the mount of Olives, the whole multitude of the disciples began to rejoice and praise God with a loud voice for all the mighty works that they had seen; 47. But the chief priests and the scribes and the chief of the people sought to destroy him, 48. And could not find what they might do: for all the people were very attentive to hear him. Mark 11:18.

Luke 21:38. And all the people came early in the morning to him in the temple, for to hear him. John 8:2.

Luke 23:27. There followed him a great company of people, and of women, which also bewailed and lamented him.

John 2:11. This beginning of miracles did Jesus in Cana of Galilee, and manifested forth his glory; and his disciples believed on him. 23. When he was in Jerusalem at the passover, in the feast *day*, many believed in his name, when they saw the miracles which he did.

John 7:31. Many of the people believed on him, and said, When Christ cometh, will he do more miracles than these which this *man* hath done? 40. Many of the people therefore, when they heard this saying, said, Of a truth this is the Prophet. 41. Others said, This is the Christ. But some said, Shall Christ come out of Galilee? 42. Hath not the scripture said, That Christ cometh of the seed of David, and out of the town of Bethlehem, where David was? 43. So there was a division among the people because of him.

44. And some of them would have taken him; but no man laid hands on him. 46. Never man spake like this man.

John 8:30. As he spake these words, many believed on him.

John 9:17. They say unto the blind man again, What sayest thou of him, that he hath opened thine eyes? He said, He is a prophet. 24. Give God the praise: we know that this man is a sinner. 25. He answered and said, Whether he be a sinner *or no*, I know not: one thing I know, that, whereas I was blind, now I see. 29. We know that God spake unto Moses: *as for* this *fellow*, we know not from whence he is. 30. Ye know not from whence he is, and *yet* he hath opened mine eyes. 33. If this man were not of God, he could do nothing.

John 10:41. Many resorted unto him, and said, John did no miracle: but all things that John spake of this man were true. 42. And many believed on him there.

John 11:37. Some of them said, Could not this man, which opened the eyes of the blind, have caused that even this man should not have died? 45. Many of the Jews which came to Mary, and had seen the things which Jesus did, believed on him. 46. But some of them went their ways to the Pharisees, and told them what things Jesus had done. 47. Then gathered the chief priests and the Pharisees a council, and said, What do we? for this man doeth many miracles. 48. If we let him thus alone, all *men* will believe on him:

John 12:9. Much people of the Jews therefore knew that he was there: and they came not for Jesus' sake only, but that they might see Lazarus also, whom he had raised from the dead. 11. Because that by reason of him many of the Jews went away, and believed on Jesus. 18. For this cause the people also met him, for that they heard that he had done this miracle. 19. The Pharisees therefore said among themselves, Perceive ye how ye prevail nothing? behold, the world is gone after him. 20. There were certain Greeks among them that came up to worship at the feast: 21. The same came therefore to Philip, which was of Bethsaida of Galilee, and desired him, saying, Sir, we would see Jesus. 34. We have heard out of the law that Christ abideth for ever: and how sayest thou, The Son of man must be lifted up? who is this Son of man? 42. Nevertheless among the chief rulers also many believed on him; but because of the Pharisees they did not confess *him*, lest they should be put out of the synagogue:

INSTANCES OF: By Matthew, Matt. 9:9,10. Peter and other disciples, Mark 1:16-20; Luke 5:3-11. Zacchæus, Luke 19:1-10. Philip, John 1:43,45. Nathanael, John 1:45-50. Three thousand at Pentecost, Acts 2:41; 4:4. The eunuch, Acts 8:27-39.

See FAITH IN CHRIST, INSTANCES OF.

REDEEMER: See JESUS, SAVIOUR; REDEMPTION.

REJECTED: Psa. 2:1. Why do the heathen rage, and the people imagine a vain thing? 2. The kings of the earth set themselves, and the rulers take counsel together, against the LORD, and against his anointed, *saying*, 3. Let us break their bonds asunder, and cast away their cords from us.

Psa. 118:22. The stone *which* the builders refused is become the head *stone* of the corner. Luke 20:17,18.

Isa. 8:14. And he shall be for a sanctuary; but for a stone of stumbling and for a rock of offence to both the houses of Israel, for a gin and for a snare to the inhabitants of Jerusalem.

Isa. 49:4. I have laboured in vain, I have spent my strength for nought, and in vain:

Isa. 50:1. Thus saith the LORD, Where *is* the bill of your mother's divorcement, whom I have put away? or which of my creditors *is it* to whom I have sold you? Behold, for your iniquities have ye sold yourselves, and for your transgressions is your mother put away. 2. Wherefore, when I came, *was there* no man? when I called, *was there* none to answer? Is my hand shortened at all, that it cannot redeem? or have I no power to deliver? behold, at my rebuke I dry up the sea, I make the rivers a wilderness: their fish stinketh, because *there is* no water, and dieth for thirst. 3. I clothe the heavens with blackness, and I make sackcloth their covering. 4. The Lord GOD hath given me the tongue of the learned, that I should know how to speak a word in season to *him that is* weary: he wakeneth morning by morning, he wakeneth mine ear to hear as the learned. 5. The Lord GOD hath opened mine ear, and I was not rebellious, neither turned away back. 6. I gave my back to the smiters, and my cheeks to them that plucked off the hair: I hid not my face from shame and spitting. 7. For the Lord GOD will help me; therefore shall I not be confounded: therefore have I set my face like a flint, and I know that I shall not be ashamed. 8. *He is* near that justifieth me; who will contend with me? let us stand together: who *is* mine adversary? let him come near to me. 9. Behold, the Lord GOD will help me; who *is* he *that* shall condemn me? lo, they all shall wax old as a garment; the moth shall eat them up. 10. Who *is* among you that feareth the LORD, that obeyeth the voice of his servant, that walketh *in* darkness, and hath no light? let him trust in the name of the LORD, and stay upon his God. 11. Behold, all ye that kindle a fire, that compass *yourselves* about with sparks: walk in the light of your fire, and in the sparks *that* ye have kindled. This shall ye have of mine hand; ye shall lie down in sorrow.

Isa. 53:1. Who hath believed our report? and to whom is the arm of the LORD revealed? 2. For he shall grow up before him as a tender plant, and as a root out of a dry ground: he hath no form nor comeliness; and when we shall see him, *there is* no beauty that we should desire him. 3. He is despised and rejected of men; a man of sorrows, and acquainted with grief: and we hid as it were *our* faces from him; he was despised, and we esteemed him not. 4. We did esteem him stricken, smitten of God, and afflicted.

Matt. 7:26. Every one that heareth these sayings of mine, and doeth them not, shall be likened unto a foolish man, which built his house upon the sand: 27. And the rain descended, and the floods came, and the winds blew, and beat upon that house; and it fell: and great was the fall of it. Luke 6:46–49.

Matt. 8:12. The children of the kingdom shall be cast out into outer darkness: there shall be weeping and gnashing of teeth. 34. And, behold, the whole city came out to meet Jesus: and when they saw him, they besought *him* that he would depart out of their coasts. Mark 5:17; Luke 8:37.

Matt. 10:14. Whosoever shall not receive you, nor hear your words, when ye depart out of that house or city, shake off the dust of your feet. 15. Verily I say unto you, It shall be more tolerable for the land of Sodom and Gomorrha in the day of judgment, than for that city. 33. But whosoever shall deny me before men, him will I also deny before my Father which is in heaven.

Matt. 11:16. Whereunto shall I liken this generation? It is like unto children sitting in the markets, and calling unto their fellows, 17. And saying, We have piped unto you, and ye have not danced; we have mourned unto you, and ye have not lamented. 18. For John came neither eating nor drinking, and they say, He hath a devil. 19. The Son of man came eating and drinking, and they say, Behold a man gluttonous, and a winebibber, a friend of publicans and sinners. Luke 7:31–35.

Matt. 12:38. Then certain of the scribes and of the Pharisees answered, saying, Master, we would see a sign from thee. 39. But he answered and said unto them, An evil and adulterous generation seeketh after a sign; and there shall no sign be given to it, but the sign of the prophet Jonas: 40. For as Jonas was three days and three nights in the whale's belly; so shall the Son of man be three days and three nights in the heart of the earth. 41. The men of Nineveh shall rise in judgment with this generation, and shall condemn it: because they repented at the preaching of Jonas; and, behold, a greater than Jonas *is* here. 42. The queen of the south shall rise up in the judgment with this generation, and shall condemn it; for she came from the uttermost parts of the earth to hear the wisdom of Solomon; and, behold, a greater than Solomon *is* here. 43. When the unclean spirit is gone out of a man, he walketh through dry places, seeking rest, and findeth none. 44. Then he saith, I will return into my house from whence I came out; and when he is come, he findeth *it* empty, swept, and garnished. 45. Then goeth he, and taketh with himself seven other spirits more wicked than himself, and they enter in and dwell there: and the last *state* of that man is worse than the first. Even so shall it be also unto this wicked generation.

Matt. 13:13. Therefore speak I to them in parables: because they seeing, see not; and hearing they hear not, neither do they understand. 58. He did not many mighty works there because of their unbelief. *vs.* 3–14; Isa. 6:9,10.

Matt. 17:17. Jesus answered and said, O faithless and perverse generation, how long shall I be with you? how long shall I suffer you?

Matt. 21:32. John came unto you in the way of righteousness, and ye believed him not; but the publicans and the harlots believed him: and ye, when ye had seen *it*, repented not afterward, that ye might believe him.

38. But when the husbandmen saw the son, they said among themselves, This is the heir; come, let us kill him, and let us seize on his inheritance. 39. And they caught him, and cast *him* out of the vineyard, and slew *him*. 40. When the lord therefore of the vineyard cometh, what will he do unto those husbandmen? 41. They say unto him, He will miserably destroy those wicked men, and will let out *his* vineyard unto other husbandmen, which shall render him the fruits in their seasons. 42. Jesus saith unto them, Did ye never read in the scriptures, The stone which the builders rejected, the same is become the head of the corner: this is the Lord's doing, and it is marvellous in our eyes? 43. Therefore say I unto you, The kingdom of God shall be taken from you, and given to a nation bringing forth the fruits thereof. 44. And whosoever shall fall on this stone shall be broken: but on whomsoever it shall fall, it will grind him to powder. 45. And when the chief priests and Pharisees had heard his parables, they perceived that he spake of them. Mark 12:1–12; Luke 20:9–18.

Matt. 26:31. Then saith Jesus unto them, All ye shall be offended because of me this night: for it is written, I will smite the shepherd, and the sheep of the flock shall be scattered abroad. 32. But after I am risen again, I will go before you into Galilee. 33. Peter answered and said unto him, Though all *men* shall be offended because of thee, *yet* will I never be offended. 34. Jesus said unto him, Verily I say unto thee, That this night, before the cock crow, thou shalt deny me thrice. 35. Peter said unto him, Though I should die with thee, yet will I not deny thee. Likewise also said all the disciples. 69. Now Peter sat without in the palace: and a damsel came unto him, saying, Thou also wast with Jesus of Galilee. 70. But he denied before *them* all, saying, I know not

what thou sayest. 71. And when he was gone out into the porch, another *maid* saw him, and said unto them that were there, This *fellow* was also with Jesus of Nazareth. 72. And again he denied with an oath, I do not know the man. 73. And after a while came unto *him* they that stood by, and said to Peter, Surely thou also art *one* of them; for thy speech bewrayeth thee. 74. Then began he to curse and to swear, *saying,* I know not the man. And immediately the cock crew. 75. And Peter remembered the word of Jesus, which said unto him, Before the cock crow, thou shalt deny me thrice. And he went out, and wept bitterly. Mark 14:27–31, 66–72; Luke 22:31–34, 54–62; John 18:15–27.

Mark 6:3. Is not this the carpenter, the son of Mary, the brother of James, and Joses, and of Juda, and Simon? and are not his sisters here with us? And they were offended at him. 4. But Jesus said unto them, A prophet is not without honour, but in his own country, and among his own kin, and in his own house. 5. And he could there do no mighty work, save that he laid his hands upon a few sick folk, and healed *them*. 6. And he marvelled because of their unbelief. And he went round about the villages, teaching.

Mark 16:16. He that believeth not shall be [1] damned.   [1 R. V. condemned]

Luke 7:30. But the Pharisees and lawyers rejected the counsel of God against themselves, being not baptized of him. 34. The Son of man is come eating and drinking; and ye say, Behold a gluttonous man, and a winebibber, a friend of publicans and sinners!

Luke 10:16. He that heareth you heareth me; and he that despiseth you despiseth me; and he that despiseth me despiseth him that sent me.

Luke 11:23. He that is not with me is against me; and he that gathereth not with me scattereth. 24. When the unclean spirit is gone out of a man, he walketh through dry places, seeking rest; and finding none, he saith, I will return unto my house whence I came out. 25. And when he cometh, he findeth *it* swept and garnished. 26. Then goeth he, and taketh *to him* seven other spirits more wicked than himself; and they enter in, and dwell there: and the last *state* of that man is worse than the first.

Luke 13:34. O Jerusalem, Jerusalem, which killest the prophets, and stonest them that are sent unto thee; how often would I have gathered thy children together, as a hen *doth gather* her brood under *her* wings, and ye would not!

Luke 14:16. Then said he unto him, A certain man made a great supper, and bade many: 17. And sent his servant at supper time to say to them that were bidden, Come; for all things are now ready. 18. And they all with one *consent* began to make excuse. The first said unto him, I have bought a piece of ground, and I must needs go and see it: I pray thee have me excused. 19. And another said, I have bought five yoke of oxen, and I go to prove them: I pray thee have me excused. 20. And another said, I have married a wife, and therefore I cannot come. 21. So that servant came, and shewed his lord these things. Then the master of the house being angry said to his servant, Go out quickly into the streets and lanes of the city, and bring in hither the poor, and the maimed, and the halt, and the blind. 22. And the servant said, Lord, it is done as thou hast commanded, and yet there is room. 23. And the lord said unto the servant, Go out into the highways and hedges, and compel *them* to come in, that my house may be filled. 24. For I say unto you, That none of those men which were bidden shall taste of my supper. Matt. 22:2–13.

Luke 17:25. But first must he suffer many things, and be rejected of this generation.

Luke 19:42. If thou hadst known, even thou, at least in this thy day, the things *which belong* unto thy peace! but now they are hid from thine eyes.

Luke 22:67. Art thou the Christ? tell us. And he said unto them, If I tell you, ye will not believe:

Luke 24:25. O fools, and slow of heart to believe all that the prophets have spoken: *vs.* 11,15–25,37–39.

John 1:11. He came unto his own, and his own received him not.

John 3:11. We speak that we do know, and testify that we have seen; and ye receive not our witness. 12. If I have told you earthly things, and ye believe not, how shall ye believe if I tell you *of* heavenly things? 18. He that believeth not is condemned already, because he hath not believed in the name of the only begotten Son of God. 19. And this is the condemnation, that light is come into the world, and men loved darkness rather than light, because their deeds were evil. 32. And what he hath seen and heard, that he testifieth; and no man receiveth his testimony.

John 5:38. And ye have not his word abiding in you: for whom he hath sent, him ye believe not. 40. And ye will not come to me, that ye might have life. 43. I am come in my Father's name, and ye receive me not: if another shall come in his own name, him ye will receive.

John 6:36. Ye also have seen me, and believe not. 60. Many therefore of his disciples, when they had heard *this*, said, This is an hard saying; who can hear it? 61. When Jesus knew in himself that his disciples murmured at it, he said unto them, Doth this offend you? 62. *What* and if ye shall see the Son of man ascend up where he was before? 63. It is the spirit that quickeneth; the flesh profiteth nothing: the words that I speak unto you, *they* are spirit, and *they* are life. 64. But there are some of you that believe not. For Jesus knew from the beginning who they were that believed not, and who should betray him. 65. And he said, Therefore said I unto you, that no man can come unto me, except it were given unto him of my Father. 66. From that *time* many of his disciples went back, and walked no more with him. 67. Then said Jesus unto the twelve, Will ye also go away? 68. Then Simon Peter answered him, Lord, to whom shall we go? thou hast the words of eternal life.

John 7:3. His brethren therefore said unto him, Depart hence, and go into Judæa, that thy disciples also may see the works that thou doest. 4. For *there is* no man *that* doeth any thing in secret, and he himself seeketh to be known openly. If thou do these things, shew thyself to the world. 5. For neither did his brethren believe in him. 12. There was much murmuring among the people concerning him: for some said, He is a good man: others said, Nay; but he deceiveth the people. 13. Howbeit no man spake openly of him for fear of the Jews. 15. The Jews marvelled, saying, How knoweth this man letters, having never learned? 25. Then said some of them of Jerusalem, Is not this he, whom they seek to kill? 26. But, lo, he speaketh boldly, and they say nothing unto him. Do the rulers know indeed that this is the very Christ? 27. Howbeit we know this man whence he is: but when Christ cometh, no man knoweth whence he is.

John 8:13. The Pharisees therefore said unto him, Thou bearest record of thyself; thy record is not true. 21. Then said Jesus again unto them, I go my way, and ye shall seek me, and shall die in your sins: whither I go, ye cannot come. 22. Then said the Jews, Will he kill himself? because he saith, Whither I go, ye cannot come. 24. If ye believe not that I am *he*, ye shall die in your sins. 30. As he spake these words, many believed on him. [with *vs.* 25–29.] 45. Because I tell *you* the truth, ye believe me not. 46. If I say the truth, why do ye not believe me? 47. He that is of God heareth God's words: ye therefore hear *them* not, because ye are not of God. 53. Art thou greater than our father Abraham, which is dead? and the prophets are dead: whom makest thou thyself?

John 9:16. Therefore said some of the Pharisees, This man is not of God, because he keepeth not the sabbath day. Others said, How can a man that is a sinner do such miracles? And there was a division among them. 17. They say unto the blind man again, What sayest thou of him, that he hath opened thine eyes? He said, He is a prophet. 24. Give God the praise: we know that this man is a sinner.

John 10:20. Many of them said, He hath a devil, and is mad; why hear ye him? 21. Others said, These are not the words of him that hath a devil. Can a devil open the eyes of the blind? 24. Then came the Jews round about him, and said unto him, How long dost thou make us to doubt? If thou be the Christ, tell us plainly. 33. For a good work we stone thee not; but for blasphemy; and because that thou, being a man, makest thyself God.

John 11:46. But some of them went their ways to the Pharisees, and told them what things Jesus had done. 47. Then gathered the chief priests and the Pharisees a council, and said, What do we? for this man doeth many miracles. 48. If we let him thus alone, all *men* will believe on him:

John 12:37. But though he had done so many miracles before them, yet they believed not on him: 48. He that rejecteth me, and receiveth not my words, hath one that judgeth him: the word that I have spoken, the same shall judge him in the last day.

John 15:18. If the world hate you, ye know that it hated me before *it hated* you. 20. Remember the word that I said unto you, The servant is not greater than his lord. If they have persecuted me, they will also persecute you; if they have kept my saying, they will keep your's also. 24. If I had not done among them the works which none other man did, they had not had sin: but now have they both seen and hated both me and my Father.

Acts 13:46. Then Paul and Barnabas waxed bold, and said, It was necessary that the word of God should first have been spoken to you: but seeing ye put it from you, and judge yourselves unworthy of everlasting life, lo, we turn to the Gentiles.

Acts 18:5. And when Silas and Timotheus were come from Macedonia, Paul was pressed in the spirit, and testified to the Jews *that* Jesus *was* Christ. 6. And when they opposed themselves, and blasphemed, he shook *his* raiment, and said unto them, Your blood *be* upon your own heads; I *am* clean: from henceforth I will go unto the Gentiles.

Acts 22:18. They will not receive thy testimony concerning me.

Acts 28:24. And some believed the things which were spoken, and some believed not. 25. And when they agreed not among themselves, they departed, after that Paul had spoken one word, Well spake the Holy Ghost by Esaias the prophet unto our fathers, 27. For the heart of this people is waxed gross, and their ears are dull of hearing, and their eyes have they closed; lest they should see with *their* eyes, and hear with *their* ears, and understand with *their* heart, and should be converted, and I should heal them.

Rom. 3:3. For what if some did not believe? shall their unbelief make the faith of God without effect?

Rom. 9:31. Israel, which followed after the law of righteousness, hath not attained to the law of righteousness. 32. Wherefore? Because *they sought it* not by faith, but as it were by the works of the law.

Rom. 10:16. They have not all obeyed the gospel. For Esaias saith, Lord, who hath believed our report? 21. But to Israel he saith, All day long I have stretched forth my hands unto a disobedient and gainsaying people.

1 Cor. 1:18. For the preaching of the cross is to them that perish, foolishness; but unto us which are saved it is the power of God. 23. But we preach Christ crucified, unto the Jews a stumblingblock, and unto the Greeks foolishness;

2 Tim. 2:12. If we suffer, we shall also reign with *him:* if we deny *him*, he also will deny us:

Heb. 6:6. If they shall fall away, to renew them again unto repentance; seeing they crucify to themselves the Son of God afresh, and put *him* to an open shame.

Heb. 10:29. Of how much sorer punishment, suppose ye, shall he be thought worthy, who hath trodden under foot the Son of God, and hath counted the blood of the covenant, wherewith he was sanctified, an unholy thing, and hath done despite unto the Spirit of grace?

1 Pet. 2:4. A living stone, disallowed indeed of men, but chosen of God, *and* precious, 7. Unto them which be disobedient, the stone which the builders disallowed, the same is made the head of the corner, 8. And a stone of stumbling, and a rock of offence, *even to them* which stumble at the word, being disobedient: whereunto also they were appointed.

2 Pet. 2:1. But there were false prophets also among the people, even as there shall be false teachers among you, who privily shall bring in damnable heresies, even denying the Lord that bought them, and bring upon themselves swift destruction.

1 John 2:22. Who is a liar but he that denieth that Jesus is the Christ? He is antichrist, that denieth the Father and the Son. 23. Whosoever denieth the Son, the same hath not the Father:

2 John 1:7. For many deceivers are entered into the world, who confess not that Jesus Christ is come in the flesh. This is a deceiver and an antichrist.

Jude 4. For there are certain men crept in unawares, who were before of old ordained to this condemnation, ungodly men, turning the grace of our God into lasciviousness, and denying the only Lord God, and our Lord Jesus Christ.

RELATION OF, TO THE FATHER: Psa. 110:1. The Lord said unto my Lord, Sit thou at my right hand, until I make thine enemies thy footstool.

Isa. 42:1. Behold my servant, whom I uphold; mine elect, *in whom* my soul delighteth; I have put my spirit upon him:

Isa. 49:5. And now, saith the Lord that formed me from the womb *to be* his servant, to bring Jacob again to him, Though Israel be not gathered, yet shall I be glorious in the eyes of the LORD, and my God shall be my strength. 6. And he said, It is a light thing that thou shouldest be my servant to raise up the tribes of Jacob, and to restore the preserved of Israel: I will also give thee for a light to the Gentiles, that thou mayest be my salvation unto the end of the earth.

Isa. 61:1. The Spirit of the Lord GOD *is* upon me; because the LORD hath anointed me to preach good tidings unto the meek; he hath sent me to bind up the broken-hearted,

Mic. 5:4. He shall stand and feed in the strength of the LORD, in the majesty of the name of the LORD his God; and they shall abide:

Matt. 20:23. And he saith unto them, Ye shall drink indeed of my cup, ¹ and be baptized with the baptism that I am baptized with: but to sit on my right hand, and on my left, is not mine to give, but *it shall be given to them* for whom it is prepared of my Father.
(¹ Omitted in R. V.)

Matt. 26:39. And he went a little farther, and fell on his face, and prayed, saying, O my Father, if it be possible, let this cup pass from me: nevertheless, not as I will, but as thou *wilt*.

Mark 10:40. But to sit on my right hand and on my left hand is not mine to give; but *it shall be given to them* for whom it is prepared.

Mark 13:32. But of that day and *that* hour knoweth no man, no, not the angels which are in heaven, neither the Son, but the Father.

John 1:1. In the beginning was the Word, and the Word was with God, and the Word was God. 2. The same was in the beginning with God. 14. And the Word was made flesh, and dwelt among us, (and we beheld his glory, the glory as of the only begotten of the Father,) full of grace and truth.

John 3:34. For he whom God hath sent speaketh the words of God: for God giveth not the Spirit by measure *unto him.* 35. The Father loveth the Son, and hath given all things into his hand.

John 4:34. Jesus saith unto them, My meat is to do the will of him that sent me, and to finish his work.

John 5:19. Then answered Jesus and said unto them, Verily, verily, I say unto you, The Son can do nothing of himself, but what he seeth the Father do: for what things soever he doeth, these also doeth the Son likewise. 20. For the Father loveth the Son, and sheweth him all things that himself doeth: and he will shew him greater works than these, that ye may marvel. 21. For as the Father raiseth up the dead, and quickeneth *them;* even so the Son quickeneth whom he will. 22. For the Father judgeth no man, but hath committed all judgment unto the Son: 23. That all *men* should honour the Son, even as they honour the Father.

He that honoureth not the Son honoureth not the Father which hath sent him. 24. Verily, verily, I say unto you, He that heareth my word, and believeth on him that sent me, hath everlasting life, and shall not come into condemnation; but is passed from death unto life. 25. Verily, verily, I say unto you, The hour is coming, and now is, when the dead shall hear the voice of the Son of God: and they that hear shall live. 26. For as the Father hath life in himself; so hath he given to the Son to have life in himself; 27. And hath given him authority to execute judgment also, because he is the Son of man. 28. Marvel not at this: for the hour is coming, in the which all that are in the graves shall hear his voice, 29. And shall come forth; they that have done good, unto the resurrection of life; and they that have done evil, unto the resurrection of damnation. 30. I can of mine own self do nothing: as I hear, I judge: and my judgment is just; because I seek not mine own will, but the will of the Father which hath sent me. 31. If I bear witness of myself, my witness is not true. 37. And the Father himself, which hath sent me, hath borne witness of me. Ye have neither heard his voice at any time, nor seen his shape. 45. Do not think that I will accuse you to the Father: there is *one* that accuseth you, *even* Moses, in whom ye trust.

John 6:32. Then Jesus said unto them, Verily, verily, I say unto you, Moses gave you not that bread from heaven; but my Father giveth you the true bread from heaven. 33. For the bread of God is he which cometh down from heaven, and giveth life unto the world. 38. For I came down from heaven, not to do mine own will, but the will of him that sent me. 39. And this is the Father's will which hath sent me, that of all which he hath given me I should lose nothing, but should raise it up again at the last day. 40. And this is the will of him that sent me, that every one which seeth the Son, and believeth on him, may have everlasting life: and I will raise him up at the last day. 44. No man can come to me, except the Father which hath sent me draw him: and I will raise him up at the last day. 45. It is written in the prophets, And they shall be all taught of God. Every man therefore that hath heard, and hath learned of the Father, cometh unto me. 46. Not that any man hath seen the Father, save he which is of God, he hath seen the Father.

John 7:16. Jesus answered them, and said, My doctrine is not mine, but his that sent me. 28. Then cried Jesus in the temple as he taught, saying, Ye both know me, and ye know whence I am: and I am not come of myself, but he that sent me is true, whom ye know not. 29. But I know him: for I am from him, and he hath sent me. 33. Then said Jesus unto them, Yet a little while am I with you, and *then* I go unto him that sent me.

John 8:16. And yet if I judge, my judgment is true : for I am not alone, but I and the Father that sent me. 19. Then said they unto him, Where is thy Father? Jesus answered, Ye neither know me, nor my Father : if ye had known me, ye should have known my Father also. 28. Then said Jesus unto them, When ye have lifted up the Son of man, then shall ye know that I am *he*, and *that* I do nothing of myself; but as my Father hath taught me, I speak these things. 29. And he that sent me is with me : the Father hath not left me alone; for I do always those things that please him. 38. I speak that which I have seen with my Father : and ye do that which ye have seen with your father. 40. But now ye seek to kill me, a man that hath told you the truth, which I have heard of God : this did not Abraham. 42. Jesus said unto them, if God were your Father, ye would love me : for I proceeded forth and came from God; neither came I of myself, but he sent me. 49. Jesus answered, I have not a devil; but I honour my Father, and ye do dishonour me. 54. Jesus answered, If I honour myself, my honour is nothing : it is my Father that honoureth me; of whom ye say, that he is your God : 55. Yet ye have not known him; but I know him : and if I should say, I know him not, I shall be a liar like unto you : but I know him, and keep his saying.

John 9:4. I must work the works of him that sent me, while it is day : the night cometh, when no man can work.

John 10:15. As the Father knoweth me, even so know I the Father : and I lay down my life for the sheep. 18. No man taketh it from me, but I lay it down of myself. I have power to lay it down, and I have power to take it again. This commandment have I received of my Father. 25. Jesus answered them, I told you, and ye believed not : the works that I do in my Father's name, they bear witness of me. 29. My Father, which gave *them* me, is greater than all ; and no *man* is able to pluck *them* out of my Father's hand. 30. I and *my* Father are one. 32. Jesus answered them, Many good works have I shewed you from my Father; for which of those works do ye stone me ? 33. The Jews answered him, saying, For a good work we stone thee not; but for blasphemy; and because that thou, being a man, makest thyself God. 36. Say ye of him, whom the Father hath sanctified, and sent into the world, Thou blasphemest; because I said, I am the Son of God ? 37. If I do not the works of my Father, believe me not. 38. But if I do, though ye believe not me, believe the works; that ye may know, and believe, that the Father *is* in me, and I in him.

John 11:41. Then they took away the stone *from the place* where the dead was laid. And Jesus lifted up *his* eyes, and said, Father, I thank thee that thou hast heard me. 42. And I knew that thou hearest me always : but because of the people which stand by I said *it*, that they may believe that thou hast sent me.

John 12:44. Jesus cried and said, He that believeth on me, believeth not on me, but on him that sent me. 49. For I have not spoken of myself; but the Father which sent me, he gave me a commandment, what I should say, and what I should speak. 50. And I know that his commandment is life everlasting; whatsoever I speak therefore, even as the Father said unto me, so I speak.

John 14:7. If ye had known me, ye should have known my Father also : and from henceforth ye know him, and have seen him. 9. Jesus saith unto him, Have I been so long time with you, and yet hast thou not known me, Philip ? he that hath seen me hath seen the Father; and how sayest thou *then*, Shew us the Father ? 10. Believest thou not that I am in the Father, and the Father in me ? the words that I speak unto you I speak not of myself : but the Father that dwelleth in me, he doeth the works. 11. Believe me that I *am* in the Father, and the Father in me : or else believe me for the very works' sake. 12. Verily, verily, I say unto you, He that believeth on me, the works that I do shall he do also ; and greater *works* than these shall he do; because I go unto my Father. 13. And whatsoever ye shall ask in my name, that will I do, that the Father may be glorified in the Son. 14. If ye shall ask any thing in my name, I will do *it*. 20. At that day ye shall know that I *am* in my Father, and ye in me, and I in you. 24. He that loveth me not keepeth not my sayings : and the word which ye hear is not mine, but the Father's which sent me. 28. Ye have heard how I said unto you, I go away, and come *again* unto you. If ye loved me, ye would rejoice, because I said, I go unto the Father : for my Father is greater than I. 31. But that the world may know that I love the Father : and as the Father gave me commmandment, even so I do. Arise, let us go hence.

John 15:9. As the Father hath loved me, so have I loved you : continue ye in my love. 10. If ye keep my commandments, ye shall abide in my love ; even as I have kept my Father's commandments, and abide in his love. 15. Henceforth I call you not servants; for the servant knoweth not what his lord doeth : but I have called you friends; for all things that I have heard of my Father I have made known unto you. 23. He that hateth me hateth my Father also. 24. If I had not done among them the works which none other man did, they had not had sin : but now have they both seen and hated both me and my Father. 25. But *this cometh to pass*, that the word might be fulfilled that is written in their law, They hated me without a cause. 26. But when the Comforter is come, whom I will send unto you from the Father, *even* the Spirit of truth, which proceedeth from the Father, he shall testify of me :

John 16:5. But now I go my way to him that sent me; and none of you asketh me, Whither goest thou? 10. Of righteousness, because I go to my Father, and ye see me no more; 15. All things that the Father hath are mine: therefore said I, that he shall take of mine, and shall shew *it* unto you. 23. And in that day ye shall ask me nothing. Verily, verily, I say unto you, Whatsoever ye shall ask the Father in my name, he will give *it* you. 25. These things have I spoken unto you in proverbs: but the time cometh, when I shall no more speak unto you in proverbs, but I shall shew you plainly of the Father. 27. For the Father himself loveth you, because ye have loved me, and have believed that I came out from God. 28. I came forth from the Father, and am come into the world; again, I leave the world, and go to the Father. 32. Behold, the hour cometh, yea, is now come, that ye shall be scattered, every man to his own, and shall leave me alone: and yet I am not alone, because the Father is with me.

John 17:1. These words spake Jesus, and lifted up his eyes to heaven, and said, Father, the hour is come; glorify thy Son, that thy Son also may glorify thee: 2. As thou hast given him power over all flesh, that he should give eternal life to as many as thou hast given him. 3. And this is life eternal, that they might know thee the only true God, and Jesus Christ, whom thou hast sent. 4. I have glorified thee on the earth: I have finished the work which thou gavest me to do. 5. And now, O Father, glorify thou me with thine own self with the glory which I had with thee before the world was. 6. I have manifested thy name unto the men which thou gavest me out of the world: thine they were, and thou gavest them me; and they have kept thy word. 7. Now they have known that all things whatsoever thou hast given me are of thee. 8. For I have given unto them the words which thou gavest me; and they have received *them*, and have known surely that I came out from thee, and they have believed that thou didst send me. 9. I pray for them: I pray not for the world, but for them which thou hast given me; for they are thine. 10. And all mine are thine, and thine are mine; and I am glorified in them. 11. And now I am no more in the world, but these are in the world, and I come to thee. Holy Father, keep through thine own name those whom thou hast given me, that they may be one, as we *are*. 12. While I was with them in the world, I kept them in thy name: those that thou gavest me I have kept, and none of them is lost, but the son of perdition; that the scripture might be fulfilled. 13. And now come I to thee: and these things I speak in the world, that they might have my joy fulfilled in themselves. 14. I have given them thy word; and the world hath hated them, because they are not of the world, even as I am not of the world.

15. I pray not that thou shouldest take them out of the world, but that thou shouldest keep them from the evil. 16. They are not of the world, even as I am not of the world. 17. Sanctify them through thy truth: thy word is truth. 18. As thou hast sent me into the world, even so have I also sent them into the world. 19. And for their sakes I sanctify myself, that they also might be sanctified through the truth. 20. Neither pray I for these alone, but for them also which shall believe on me through their word; 21. That they all may be one; as thou, Father, *art* in me, and I in thee, that they also may be one in us: that the world may believe that thou hast sent me. 22. And the glory which thou gavest me I have given them; that they may be one, even as we are one: 23. I in them, and thou in me, that they may be made perfect in one; and that the world may know that thou hast sent me, and hast loved them, as thou hast loved me. 24. Father, I will that they also, whom thou hast given me, be with me where I am; that they may behold my glory, which thou hast given me: for thou lovedst me before the foundation of the world. 25. O righteous Father, the world hath not known thee: but I have known thee, and these have known that thou hast sent me. 26. And I have declared unto them thy name, and will declare *it:* that the love wherewith thou hast loved me may be in them, and I in them.

Acts 2:33. Therefore being by the right hand of God exalted, and having received of the Father the promise of the Holy Ghost, he hath shed forth this, which ye now see and hear. 36. Therefore let all the house of Israel know assuredly, that God hath made that same Jesus, whom ye have crucified, both Lord and Christ.

Acts 10:38. How God anointed Jesus of Nazareth with the Holy Ghost and with power: who went about doing good, and healing all that were oppressed of the devil; for God was with him.

Acts 13:37. He, whom God raised again, saw no corruption.

Rom. 1:4. Declared *to be* the Son of God with power, according to the spirit of holiness, by the resurrection from the dead:

Rom. 8:32. He that spared not his own Son, but delivered him up for us all,

1 Cor. 1:30. Of him are ye in Christ Jesus, who of God is made unto us wisdom, and righteousness, and sanctification, and redemption:

1 Cor. 3:23. And ye are Christ's; and Christ *is* God's.

1 Cor. 11:3. The head of Christ *is* God.

1 Cor. 15:24. Then *cometh* the end, when he shall have delivered up the kingdom to God, even the Father; when he shall have put down all rule and all authority and power. 27. For he hath put all things under his feet. But when he saith all things are put under *him*, *it is* manifest that he is

excepted, which did put all things under him. 28. And when all things shall be subdued unto him, then shall the Son also himself be subject unto him that put all things under him, that God may be all in all.

2 Cor. 4:4. In whom the god of this world hath blinded the minds of them which believe not, lest the light of the glorious gospel of Christ, who is the image of God, should shine unto them. 6. For God, who commanded the light to shine out of darkness, hath shined in our hearts, to *give* the light of the knowledge of the glory of God in the face of Jesus Christ.

Eph. 1:17. That the God of our Lord Jesus Christ, the Father of glory, may give unto you the spirit of wisdom and revelation in the knowledge of him: 20. Which he wrought in Christ, when he raised him from the dead, and set *him* at his own right hand in the heavenly *places*, 21. Far above all principality, and power, and might, and dominion, and every name that is named, not only in this world, but also in that which is to come: 22. And hath put all *things* under his feet, and gave him *to be* the head over all *things* to the church,

Phil. 2:6. Who, being in the form of God, thought it not ¹ robbery to be equal with God: 11. And *that* every tongue should confess that Jesus Christ *is* Lord, to the glory of God the Father.   [¹ R. V. a prize]

Col. 1:15. Who is the image of the invisible God, the firstborn of every creature: 19. For it pleased *the Father* that in him should all fulness dwell;

1 Thess. 5:18. In every thing give thanks: for this is the will of God in Christ Jesus concerning you.

Heb. 1:2. Hath in these last days spoken unto us by *his* Son, whom he hath appointed heir of all things, by whom also he made the worlds; 3. Who being the brightness of *his* glory, and the express image of his person, and upholding all things by the word of his power, when he had by himself purged our sins, sat down on the right hand of the Majesty on high;

Heb. 2:9. But we see Jesus, who was made a little lower than the angels for the suffering of death, crowned with glory and honour; that he by the grace of God should taste death for every man.

Heb. 3:2. Who was faithful to him that appointed him, as also Moses *was faithful* in all his house.

Heb. 5:5. So also Christ glorified not himself to be made an high priest; but he that said unto him, Thou art my Son, to day have I begotten thee. 6. As he saith also in another *place*, Thou *art* a priest for ever after the order of Melchisedec. 7. Who in the days of his flesh, when he had offered up prayers and supplications with strong crying and tears unto him that was able to save him from death, and was heard in that he feared; 8. Though he were a Son,

yet learned he obedience by the things which he suffered; 9. And being made perfect, he became the author of eternal salvation unto all them that obey him; 10. Called of God an high priest after the order of Melchisedec.

1 Pet. 1:21. Who by him do believe in God, that raised him up from the dead, and gave him glory; that your faith and hope might be in God.

1 Pet. 2:4. To whom coming, *as unto* a living stone, disallowed indeed of men, but chosen of God, *and* precious, 23. Who, when he was reviled, reviled not again; when he suffered, he threatened not; but committed *himself* to him that judgeth righteously:

2 Pet. 1:17. For he received from God the Father honour and glory, when there came such a voice to him from the excellent glory, This is my beloved Son, in whom I am well pleased.

1 John 4:9. In this was manifested the love of God toward us, because that God sent his only begotten Son into the world, that we might live through him. 10. Herein is love, not that we loved God, but that he loved us, and sent his Son *to be* the propitiation for our sins. 14. And we have seen and do testify that the Father sent the Son *to be* the Saviour of the world.

Rev. 2:27. And he shall rule them with a rod of iron; as the vessels of a potter shall they be broken to shivers: even as I received of my Father.

Rev. 3:12. Him that overcometh will I make a pillar in the temple of my God, and he shall go no more out: and I will write upon him the name of my God, and the name of the city of my God, *which is* new Jerusalem, which cometh down out of heaven from my God: and *I will write upon him* my new name. 21. To him that overcometh will I grant to sit with me in my throne, even as I also overcame, and am set down with my Father in his throne.

See DIVINITY OF, HUMANITY OF, SON OF GOD.

RESURRECTION OF: Psa. 2:7. The LORD hath said unto me, Thou *art* my Son; this day have I begotten thee. Acts 13:33.

Psa. 16:9. My flesh also shall rest in hope. 10. For thou wilt not leave my soul in hell; neither wilt thou suffer thine Holy One to see corruption.

Matt. 12:40. As Jonas was three days and three nights in the whale's belly; so shall the Son of man be three days and three nights in the heart of the earth.

Matt. 16:4. A wicked and adulterous generation seeketh after a sign; and there shall no sign be given unto it, but the sign of the prophet Jonas. 21. From that time forth began Jesus to shew unto his disciples, how that he must go unto Jerusalem, . . . and be killed, and be raised again the third day. Matt. 17:23; Luke 9:22,31; 24:7.

Matt. 20:19. Shall deliver him to the Gentiles to mock, and to scourge, and to crucify *him:* and the third day he shall rise again. Mark 10:34.

Matt. 26:32. But after I am risen again, I will go before you into Galilee. Mark 14:28.

Matt. 27:52. And the graves were opened; and many bodies of the saints which slept arose, 53. And came out of the graves after his resurrection, and went into the holy city, and appeared unto many. 63. Sir, we remember that that deceiver said, while he was yet alive, After three days I will rise again. Mark 8:31.

Matt. 28:6. He is not here: for he is risen, as he said. Come, see the place where the Lord lay. 7. And go quickly, and tell his disciples that he is risen from the dead; and, behold, he goeth before you into Galilee; there shall ye see him: lo, I have told you. Mark 16:6,7; Luke 24:5-7; John 20:1-18.

Mark 9:9. And as they came down from the mountain, he charged them that they should tell no man what things they had seen, till the Son of man were risen from the dead. 10. And they kept that saying with themselves, questioning one with another what the rising from the dead should mean.

Luke 18:33. And they shall scourge *him*, and put him to death: and the third day he shall rise again.

Luke 24:46. Thus it is written, and thus it behoved Christ to suffer, and to rise from the dead the third day:

John 2:19. Jesus answered and said unto them, Destroy this temple, and in three days I will raise it up. 21. He spake of the temple of his body. *v.* 22; Mark 14:58.

John 12:23. The hour is come, that the Son of man should be glorified.

John 16:16. A little while, and ye shall not see me: and again, a little while, and ye shall see me, because I go to the Father. 22. And ye now therefore have sorrow: but I will see you again, and your heart shall rejoice, and your joy no man taketh from you.

Acts 1:3. To whom also he shewed himself alive after his passion by many infallible proofs, being seen of them forty days, and speaking of the things pertaining to the kingdom of God: 22. Must one be ordained to be a witness with us of his resurrection.

Acts 2:24. Whom God hath raised up, having loosed the pains of death: because it was not possible that he should be holden of it. 31. He seeing this before spake of the resurrection of Christ, that his soul was not left in hell, neither his flesh did see corruption. 32. This Jesus hath God raised up, whereof we all are witnesses. Psa. 16:9,10.

Acts 3:15. And killed the Prince of life, whom God hath raised from the dead; whereof we are witnesses.

Acts 4:10. Be it known unto you all, and to all the people of Israel, that by the name of Jesus Christ of Nazareth, whom ye crucified, whom God raised from the dead, *even* by him doth this man stand here before you whole. 33. And with great power gave the

apostles witness of the resurrection of the Lord Jesus: and great grace was upon them all.

Acts 5:30. The God of our fathers raised up Jesus, whom ye slew and hanged on a tree. 31. Him hath God exalted with his right hand *to be* a Prince and a Saviour, for to give repentance to Israel, and forgiveness of sins. 32. And we are his witnesses of these things; and *so is* also the Holy Ghost, whom God hath given to them that obey him.

Acts 10:40. Him God raised up the third day, and shewed him openly; 41. Not to all the people, but unto witnesses chosen before of God, *even* to us, who did eat and drink with him after he rose from the dead.

Acts 13:30. God raised him from the dead: 31. And he was seen many days of them which came up with him from Galilee to Jerusalem, who are his witnesses unto the people. 32. And we declare unto you glad tidings, how that the promise which was made unto the fathers, 33. God hath fulfilled the same unto us their children, in that he hath raised up Jesus again; as it is also written in the second psalm, Thou art my Son, this day have I begotten thee. 34. And as concerning that he raised him up from the dead, *now* no more to return to corruption, he said on this wise, I will give you the sure mercies of David. Psa. 2:7.

Acts 17:2. And Paul, as his manner was, went in unto them, and three sabbath days reasoned with them out of the scriptures, 3. Opening and alleging, that Christ must needs have suffered, and risen again from the dead; and that this Jesus, whom I preach unto you, is Christ.

31. He will judge the world in righteousness by *that* man whom he hath ordained; *whereof* he hath given assurance unto all *men*, in that he hath raised him from the dead.

Acts 26:23. That Christ should suffer, *and* that he should be the first that should rise from the dead, *v.* 26.

Rom. 1:4. Declared *to be* the Son of God with power, according to the spirit of holiness, by the resurrection from the dead:

Rom. 4:24. But for us also, to whom it shall be imputed, if we believe on him that raised up Jesus our Lord from the dead; 25. Who was delivered for our offences, and was raised again for our justification.

Rom. 5:10. If, when we were enemies, we were reconciled to God by the death of his Son, much more, being reconciled, we shall be saved by his life.

Rom. 6:4. Christ was raised up from the dead by the glory of the Father, 5. If we have been planted together in the likeness of his death, we shall be also *in the likeness* of *his* resurrection: 9. Christ being raised from the dead dieth no more; death hath no more dominion over him. 10. For in that he died, he died unto sin once: but in that he liveth, he liveth unto God.

Rom. 8:11. But if the Spirit of him that

raised up Jesus from the dead dwell in you, he that raised up Christ from the dead shall also quicken your mortal bodies by his Spirit that dwelleth in you. 34. Who *is* he that condemneth? *It is* Christ that died, yea rather, that is risen again, who is even at the right hand of God,

Rom. 10:9. If thou shalt confess with thy mouth the Lord Jesus, and shalt believe in thine heart that God hath raised him from the dead, thou shalt be saved.

1 Cor. 6:14. God hath both raised up the Lord, and will also raise up us by his own power.

1 Cor. 15:3. For I delivered unto you first of all that which I also received, how that Christ died for our sins according to the scriptures; 4. That he was buried, and that he rose again the third day according to the scriptures: 20. Now is Christ risen from the dead, *and* become the firstfruits of them that slept. 21. For since by man *came* death, by man *came* also the resurrection of the dead. 22. For as in Adam all die, even so in Christ shall all be made alive. 23. But every man in his own order: Christ the first-fruits; afterward they that are Christ's at his coming. *vs.* 5-8,12-20.

2 Cor. 4:10. Always bearing about in the body the dying of the Lord Jesus, that the life also of Jesus might be made manifest in our body. 11. For we which live are alway delivered unto death for Jesus' sake, that the life also of Jesus might be made manifest in our mortal flesh. 14. Knowing that he which raised up the Lord Jesus shall raise up us also by Jesus, and shall present *us* with you.

2 Cor. 5:15. And *that* he died for all, that they which live should not henceforth live unto themselves, but unto him which died for them, and rose again.

2 Cor. 13:4. Though he was crucified through weakness, yet he liveth by the power of God.

Gal. 1:1. Paul, an apostle, (not of men, neither by man, but by Jesus Christ, and God the Father, who raised him from the dead;)

Eph. 1:20. Which he wrought in Christ, when he raised him from the dead, and set *him* at his own right hand in the heavenly *places,*

Phil. 3:10. That I may know him, and the power of his resurrection,

Col. 1:18. The firstborn from the dead; that in all *things* he might have the preeminence.

Col. 2:12. Buried with him in baptism, wherein also ye are risen with *him* through the faith of the operation of God, who hath raised him from the dead.

1 Thess. 1:10. And to wait for his Son from heaven, whom he raised from the dead, *even* Jesus, which delivered us from the wrath to come.

1 Thess. 4:14. For if we believe that Jesus died and rose again, even so them also which sleep in Jesus will God bring with him.

2 Tim. 2:8. Remember that Jesus Christ of the seed of David was raised from the dead according to my gospel:

Heb. 13:20. The God of peace, that brought again from the dead our Lord Jesus,

1 Pet. 1:3. Blessed be the God and Father of our Lord Jesus Christ, which according to his abundant mercy hath begotten us again unto a lively hope by the resurrection of Jesus Christ from the dead, 21. Who by him do believe in God, that raised him up from the dead, and gave him glory;

1 Pet. 3:18. For Christ also hath once suffered for sins, the just for the unjust, that he might bring us to God, being put to death in the flesh, but quickened by the Spirit: 21. The like figure whereunto *even* baptism doth also now save us . . . by the resurrection of Jesus Christ:

Rev. 1:5. And from Jesus Christ, *who is* the faithful witness, *and* the first begotten of the dead, 18. *I am* he that liveth, and was dead; and, behold, I am alive for evermore, Amen; and have the keys of hell and of death.

See RESURRECTION.

REVELATIONS BY: Concerning his kingdom: Matt. 8:11,12; Luke 13:28,29; Matt. 10: 23,34; 13:24-50; 16:18,28; Mark 9:1; Luke 9: 27; Matt. 21:43,44; 24:14; Mark 16:17,18; Luke 12:40-53; 13:24-35; 17:20-37; John 4:21,23; 5: 25-29; 6:39,54; 12:35; 13:19; 14:29; 16:4; his rejection by the Jews, Matt. 21:33-44; Luke 17:25; his betrayal, Matt. 26:21,23-25; crucifixion, John 3:14; 8:28; 12:32; judgments upon the Jews, Matt. 23:37-39; 25; Mark 11: 12-14; Luke 23:28-31; the destruction of the temple, and Jerusalem, Matt. 24; Mark 13; Luke 19:41-48; the destruction of Capernaum, Matt. 11:23; Luke 10:15.

Concerning persecutions of Christians, Matt. 23:34-36; his being forsaken by his disciples, John 16:32. Concerning Lazarus, John 11:4,11,23,40. Concerning Peter, John 21:18-23; fame of the woman who anointed his head, Matt. 26:13; Mark 14:8,9. Antichrist, Matt. 24:4,5,23-26; Mark 13:5,6,21-23; Luke 17:23,24; 21:8.

Concerning his death and resurrection, Matt. 12:39,40; 16:21; 17:22,23; 20:18,19; 26:2, 21,23,24,45,46; Mark 8:31; 9:31; 10:32-34; Luke 9:22-24; 18:31-33; John 2:19; 12:7,23; 13:18-27,36-38; 16:32; ascension, John 7:33,34; 8:21; 12:8; 13:33; 16:10,16.

RIGHTEOUSNESS OF: See HOLINESS OF, above.

SALVATION BY: See SAVIOUR, below.

SAVIOUR: Gen. 12:3. In thee shall all families of the earth be blessed.

Gen. 49:18. I have waited for thy salvation, O LORD.

2 Sam. 23:6. But *the sons* of Belial *shall be* all of them as thorns thrust away, because they cannot be taken with hands: 7. But the man *that* shall touch them must be fenced with iron and the staff of a spear; and they shall be utterly burned with fire in the *same* place

Job 33:23. If there be a messenger with him, an interpreter, one among a thousand, to shew unto man his uprightness : 24. Then he is gracious unto him, and saith, Deliver him from going down to the pit : I have found a ransom.

Psa. 14:7. Oh that the salvation of Israel *were come* out of Zion !

Psa. 72:4. He shall judge the poor of the people, he shall save the children of the needy, and shall break in pieces the oppressor. 12. For he shall deliver the needy when he crieth ; the poor also, and *him* that hath no helper. 13. He shall spare the poor and needy, and shall save the souls of the needy. 14. He shall redeem their soul from deceit and violence : and precious shall their blood be in his sight. 17. *Men* shall be blessed in him : all nations shall call him blessed.

Psa. 80:17. Let thy hand be upon the man of thy right hand, upon the son of man *whom* thou madest strong for thyself.

Psa. 89:19. Then thou spakest in vision to thy holy one, and saidst, I have laid help upon *one that is* mighty : I have exalted *one* chosen out of the people.

Isa. 8:14. He shall be for a sanctuary ;

Isa. 28:16. Thus saith the Lord God, Behold, I lay in Zion for a foundation a stone, a tried stone, a precious corner *stone*, a sure foundation : he that believeth shall not make haste.

Isa. 32:2. A man shall be as an hiding place from the wind, and a covert from the tempest : as rivers of water in a dry place, as the shadow of a great rock in a weary land.

Isa. 40:10. The Lord God will come with strong *hand*, and his arm shall rule for him : behold, his reward *is* with him, and his work before him. 11. He shall feed his flock like a shepherd : he shall gather the lambs with his arm, and carry *them* in his bosom, *and* shall gently lead those that are with young.

Isa. 42:6. I the Lord have called thee in righteousness, and will hold thine hand, and will keep thee, and give thee for a covenant of the people, for a light of the Gentiles ; 7. To open the blind eyes, to bring out the prisoners from the prison, *and* them that sit in darkness out of the prison house.

Isa. 49:6. It is a light thing that thou shouldest be my servant to raise up the tribes of Jacob, and to restore the preserved of Israel : I will also give thee for a light to the Gentiles, that thou mayest be my salvation unto the end of the earth. 8. Thus saith the Lord, In an acceptable time have I heard thee, and in a day of salvation have I helped thee : and I will preserve thee, and give thee for a covenant of the people, to establish the earth, to cause to inherit the desolate heritages ; 9. That thou mayest say to the prisoners, Go forth ; to them that *are* in darkness, Shew yourselves. Acts 13:47.

Isa. 50:2. Wherefore, when I came, *was* there no man ? when I called, *was there* none to answer ? Is my hand shortened at all, that it cannot redeem ? or have I no power to deliver ? 8. *He is* near that justifieth me ; who will contend with me ? let us stand together : who *is* mine adversary ? let him come near to me. 9. Behold, the Lord God will help me ; who *is* he *that* shall condemn me ?

Isa. 53:10. It pleased the Lord to bruise him ; he hath put *him* to grief : when thou shalt make his soul an offering for sin, he shall see *his* seed, he shall prolong *his* days, and the pleasure of the Lord shall prosper in his hand. 11. He shall see of the travail of his soul, *and* shall be satisfied : by his knowledge shall my righteous servant justify many ; for he shall bear their iniquities.

Isa. 59:16. He saw that *there was* no man, and wondered that *there was* no intercessor : therefore his arm brought salvation unto him ; and his righteousness, it sustained him. 17. For he put on righteousness as a breastplate, and an helmet of salvation upon his head ; and he put on the garments of vengeance *for* clothing, and was clad with zeal as a cloke. 20. The Redeemer shall come to Zion, and unto them that turn from transgression in Jacob, saith the Lord.

Isa. 61:1. The Spirit of the Lord God *is* upon me ; because the Lord hath anointed me to preach good tidings unto the meek ; he hath sent me to bind up the brokenhearted, to proclaim liberty to the captives, and the opening of the prison to *them that are* bound ; 2. To proclaim the acceptable year of the Lord, and the day of vengeance of our God ; to comfort all that mourn ; 3. To appoint unto them that mourn in Zion, to give unto them beauty for ashes, the oil of joy for mourning, the garment of praise for the spirit of heaviness ; that they might be called trees of righteousness, the planting of the Lord, that he might be glorified.

Isa. 62:11. The Lord hath proclaimed unto the end of the world, Say ye to the daughter of Zion, Behold, thy salvation cometh ; behold, his reward *is* with him, and his work before him.

Isa. 63:1. Who *is* this that cometh from Edom, with dyed garments from Bozrah ? this *that is* glorious in his apparel, travelling in the greatness of his strength ? I that speak in righteousness, mighty to save. 5. I looked, and *there was* none to help ; and I wondered that *there was* none to uphold : therefore mine own arm brought salvation unto me ; and my fury, it upheld me. 8. He said, Surely they *are* my people, children *that* will not lie : so he was their Saviour. 9. In all their affliction he was afflicted, and the angel of his presence saved them : in his love and in his pity he redeemed them ; and he bare them, and carried them all the days of old.

Jer. 23:5. Behold, the days come, saith the Lord, that I will raise unto David a righteous Branch, and a King shall reign and prosper, and shall execute judgment and justice in the earth. 6. In his days Judah shall be saved, and Israel shall dwell safely: and this *is* his name whereby he shall be called, THE LORD OUR RIGHTEOUSNESS. Jer. 33:15,16.

Ezek. 34:23. I will set up one shepherd over them, and he shall feed them, *even* my servant David; he shall feed them, and he shall be their shepherd.

Hag. 2:7. The [1]desire of all nations shall come: [1 R. V. desirable things]

Zech. 4:7. He shall bring forth the headstone *thereof with* shoutings, *crying*, Grace, grace unto it.

Zech. 9:9. Shout, O daughter of Jerusalem: behold, thy king cometh unto thee: he *is* just, and having salvation;

Mal. 4:2. Unto you that fear my name shall the Sun of righteousness arise with healing in his wings; and ye shall go forth, and grow up as calves of the stall.

Matt. 1:21. Thou shalt call his name JESUS: for he shall save his people from their sins.

Matt. 15:24. I am not sent but unto the lost sheep of the house of Israel.

Matt. 18:11. [1] The Son of man is come to save that which was lost. 12. How think ye? if a man have an hundred sheep, and one of them be gone astray, doth he not leave the ninety and nine, and goeth into the mountains, and seeketh that which is gone astray? 13. And if so be that he find it, verily I say unto you, he rejoiceth more of that *sheep,* than of the ninety and nine which went not astray. Luke 15:1-6. [1 Omitted in R. V.]

Luke 1:68. Blessed *be* the Lord God of Israel; for he hath visited and redeemed his people, 69. And hath raised up an horn of salvation for us in the house of his servant David; 70. As he spake by the mouth of his holy prophets, which have been since the world began: 71. That we should be saved from our enemies, and from the hand of all that hate us; 72. To perform the mercy *promised* to our fathers, and to remember his holy covenant; 73. The oath which he sware to our father Abraham, 74. That he would grant unto us, that we being delivered out of the hand of our enemies might serve him without fear, 75. In holiness and righteousness before him, all the days of our life. 76. And thou, child, shalt be called the prophet of the Highest: for thou shalt go before the face of the Lord to prepare his ways; 77. To give knowledge of salvation unto his people by the remission of their sins,

Luke 2:11. Unto you is born this day in the city of David a Saviour, which is Christ the Lord. 30. Mine eyes have seen thy salvation. 31. Which thou hast prepared before the face of all people; 32. A light to lighten the Gentiles, and the glory of thy people Israel. 34. And Simeon blessed them, and said unto Mary his mother, Behold, this *child* is set for the fall and rising

again of many in Israel; and for a sign which shall be spoken against;

Luke 5:31. Jesus . . . said unto them, They that are whole need not a physician; but they that are sick. 32. I came not to call the righteous, but sinners to repentance. Matt. 9:12,13.

Luke 9:56. [1] The Son of man is not come to destroy men's lives, but to save *them.* [1 Omitted in R. V.]

Luke 19:10. The Son of man is come to seek and to save that which was lost. Luke 15:4-10.

John 1:9. *That* was the true Light, which lighteth every man that cometh into the world. 29. The next day John seeth Jesus coming unto him, and saith, Behold, the Lamb of God, which taketh away the sin of the world.

John 3:16. God so loved the world, that he gave his only begotten Son, that whosoever believeth in him should not perish, but have everlasting life. 17. God sent not his Son into the world to condemn the world; but that the world through him might be saved.

John 4:14. Whosoever drinketh of the water that I shall give him shall never thirst; but the water that I shall give him shall be in him a well of water springing up into everlasting life. 42. And said unto the woman, Now we believe, not because of thy saying: for we have heard *him* ourselves, and know that this is indeed the Christ, the Saviour of the world.

John 5:26. As the Father hath life in himself; so hath he given to the Son to have life in himself; 33. Ye sent unto John, and he bare witness unto the truth. 34. But I receive not testimony from man: but these things I say, that ye might be saved. 40. And ye will not come to me, that ye might have life.

John 6:27. Labour not for the meat which perisheth, but for that meat which endureth unto everlasting life, which the Son of man shall give unto you: for him hath God the Father sealed. 32. My Father giveth you the true bread from heaven. 33. For the bread of God is he which cometh down from heaven, and giveth life unto the world. 35. I am the bread of life: he that cometh to me shall never hunger; and he that believeth on me shall never thirst. 37. Him that cometh to me I will in no wise cast out. 39. And this is the Father's will which hath sent me, that of all which he hath given me I should lose nothing, but should raise it up again at the last day. 51. I am the living bread which came down from heaven; if any man eat of this bread, he shall live for ever: and the bread that I will give is my flesh, which I will give for the life of the world. 53. Then Jesus said unto them, Verily, verily, I say unto you, Except ye eat the flesh of the Son of man, and drink his blood, ye have no life in you. 54. Whoso eateth my flesh, and drinketh my blood, hath eternal life; and I will raise him up at the last day. 55. For my flesh is meat indeed, and my blood is drink indeed. 56. He that eateth my flesh, and drinketh my blood, dwelleth in me, and I in him. 57. As the living Father hath sent me, and I live by the Father: so he that eateth me, even he shall live by me. 58. This is that bread which came down from heaven: not as your fathers did eat manna, and are dead: he that eateth of this bread shall live for ever. 68. Simon Peter answered him, Lord, to whom shall we go? thou hast the words of eternal life.

John 7:37. In the last day, that great *day* of the feast, Jesus stood and cried, saying, If any man thirst, let him come unto me and drink. 38. He that believeth on me, as the scripture hath said, out of his belly shall flow rivers of .living water. 39. (But this spake he of the Spirit, which they that believe on him should receive: for the Holy Ghost was not yet *given;* because that Jesus was not yet glorified.)

John 8:12. I am the light of the world: he that followeth me shall not walk in darkness, but shall have the light of life.

John 9:5. As long as I am in the world, I am the light of the world. 39. For judgment I am come into this world, that they which see not might see;

John 10:7. I am the door of the sheep. 9. I am the door: by me if any man enter in, he shall be saved, and shall go in and out, and find pasture. 10. I am come that they might have life, and that they might have *it* more abundantly. 11. I am the good shepherd: the good shepherd giveth his life for the sheep. 14. I am the good shepherd, and know my *sheep*, and am known of mine. 15. As the Father knoweth me, even so know I the Father: and I lay down my life for the sheep. 16. And other sheep I have, which are not of this fold: them also I must bring, and they shall hear my voice; and there shall be one fold, *and* one shepherd. 27. My sheep hear my voice, and I know them, and they follow me: 28. And I give unto them eternal life; and they shall never perish, neither shall any *man* pluck them out of my hand.

John 11:25. Jesus said unto her, I am the resurrection, and the life: he that believeth in me, though he [1] were dead, yet shall he live: 26. And whosoever liveth and believeth in me shall never die. Believest thou this? 27. She saith unto him, Yea, Lord: I believe that thou art the Christ, the Son of God, which should come into the world.   [1 R. V. die]

John 12:47. I came not to judge the world, but to save the world.

John 14:6. I am the way, the truth, and the life: no man cometh unto the Father, but by me. 19. Because I live, ye shall live also.

John 16:33. Be of good cheer, I have overcome the world.

John 17:2. As thou hast given him power over all flesh, that he should give eternal life to as many as thou hast given him. 3. This is life eternal, that they might know thee the only true God, and Jesus Christ, whom thou hast sent.

Acts 3:26. God, having raised up his [1] Son Jesus, sent him to bless you, in turning away every one of you from his iniquities.
                                        [1 R. V. Servant.]

Acts 4:12. Neither is there salvation in any other: for there is none other name under heaven given among men, whereby we must be saved.

Acts 5:31. Him hath God exalted with his right hand *to be* a Prince and a Saviour, for to give repentance to Israel, and forgiveness of sins.

Acts 13:23. Of this man's seed hath God according to *his* promise raised unto Israel a Saviour, Jesus: 38. Be it known unto you therefore, men *and* brethren, that through this man is preached unto you the forgiveness of sins: 39. And by him all that believe are justified from all things, from which ye could not be justified by the law of Moses.

Acts 15:11. We believe that through the grace of the Lord Jesus Christ we shall be saved,

Acts 16:31. Believe on the Lord Jesus Christ, and thou shalt be saved, and thy house.

Rom. 3:24. Being justified freely by his grace through the redemption that is in Christ Jesus: 25. Whom God hath set forth *to be* a propitiation through faith in his blood, to declare his righteousness for the remission of sins that are past, through the forbearance of God; 26. To declare, *I say*, at this time his righteousness: that he might be just, and the justifier of him which believeth in Jesus.

Rom. 4:25. Who was delivered for our offences, and was raised again for our justification.

Rom. 5:1. Therefore being justified by faith, [1] we have peace with God through our Lord Jesus Christ: 6. For when we were yet without strength, in due time Christ died for the ungodly. 8. But God commendeth his love toward us, in that, while we were yet sinners, Christ died for us. 9. Much more then, being now justified by his blood, we shall be saved from wrath through him. 10. For if, when we were enemies, we were reconciled to God by the death of his Son, much more, being reconciled, we shall be saved by his life. 11. And not only *so*, but we also joy in God through our Lord Jesus Christ, by whom we have now received the [2] atonement.   [R. V. 1 let us   2 reconciliation]

15. But not as the offence, so also *is* the free gift. For if through the offence of one many be dead, much more the grace of God, and the gift by grace, *which is* by one man, Jesus Christ, hath abounded unto many. 17. For if by one man's offence death reigned by one; much more they which receive abundance of grace and of the gift of righteousness shall reign in life

by one, Jesus Christ. 18. By the righteousness of one *the free gift came* upon all men unto justification of life. 19. For as by one man's disobedience many were made sinners, so by the obedience of one shall many be made righteous. 21. As sin hath reigned unto death, even so might grace reign through righteousness unto eternal life by Jesus Christ our Lord.

Rom. 6:23. The gift of God *is* eternal life through Jesus Christ our Lord.

Rom. 8:2. For the law of the Spirit of life in Christ Jesus hath made me free from the law of sin and death.

Rom. 10:9. If thou shalt confess with thy mouth the Lord Jesus, and shalt believe in thine heart that God hath raised him from the dead, thou shalt be saved. 11. For the scripture saith, Whosoever believeth on him shall not be ashamed.

Rom. 15:7. Christ also received us to the glory of God. 8. Jesus Christ was a minister of the circumcision for the truth of God, to confirm the promises *made* unto the fathers: 9. And that the Gentiles might glorify God for *his* mercy;

1 Cor. 1:30. Of him are ye in Christ Jesus, who of God is made unto us wisdom, and righteousness, and sanctification, and redemption:

1 Cor. 3:11. Other foundation can no man lay than that is laid, which is Jesus Christ.

1 Cor. 6:11. Ye are washed, but ye are sanctified, but ye are justified in the name of the Lord Jesus, and by the Spirit of our God.

1 Cor. 10:3. And did all eat the same spiritual meat; 4. And did all drink the same spiritual drink: for they drank of that spiritual Rock that followed them: and that Rock was Christ.

1 Cor. 15:17. If Christ be not raised, your faith *is* vain; ye are yet in your sins. 57. Thanks *be* to God, which giveth us the victory through our Lord Jesus Christ.

2 Cor. 5:18. All things *are* of God, who hath reconciled us to himself by Jesus Christ, and hath given to us the ministry of reconciliation; 19. To wit, that God was in Christ, reconciling the world unto himself, not imputing their trespasses unto them; and hath committed unto us the word of reconciliation. 21. For he hath made him *to be* sin for us, who knew no sin; that we might be made the righteousness of God in him.

Gal. 1:3. Grace *be* to you and peace from God the Father, and *from* our Lord Jesus Christ, 4. Who gave himself for our sins, that he might deliver us from this present evil world, according to the will of God and our Father:

Gal. 2:20. I am crucified with Christ: nevertheless I live; yet not I, but Christ liveth in me: and the life which I now live in the flesh I live by the faith of the Son of God, who loved me, and gave himself for me.

Gal. 4:7. Thou art no more a servant, but

a son; and if a son, then an heir [1] of God through Christ.   [1 R. V. through God]

Eph. 1:10. That in the dispensation of the fulness of times he might gather together in one all things in Christ, both which are in heaven, and which are on earth; *even* in him: 11. In whom also we have obtained an inheritance,

Eph. 2:7. That in the ages to come he might shew the exceeding riches of his grace in *his* kindness toward us through Christ Jesus. 13. But now in Christ Jesus ye who sometime were far off are made nigh by the blood of Christ. 14. For he is our peace, who hath made both one, and hath broken down the middle wall of partition *between us;* 15. Having abolished in his flesh the enmity, *even* the law of commandments *contained* in ordinances; for to make in himself of twain one new man, *so* making peace; 16. And that he might reconcile both unto God in one body by the cross, having slain the enmity thereby: 17. And came and preached peace to you which were afar off, and to them that were nigh. 18. For through him we both have access by one Spirit unto the Father. 20. And are built upon the foundation of the apostles and prophets, Jesus Christ himself being the chief corner *stone;*

Eph. 4:8. When he ascended up on high, he led captivity captive, and gave gifts unto men.

Eph. 5:2. Walk in love, as Christ also hath loved us, and hath given himself for us an offering and a sacrifice to God for a sweet-smelling savour. 14. Wherefore he saith, Awake thou that sleepest, and arise from the dead, and Christ shall give thee light. 23. Christ is the head of the church: and he is the saviour of the body.

25. Husbands, love your wives, even as Christ also loved the church, and gave himself for it; 26. That he might sanctify and cleanse it with the washing of water by the word,

Phil. 3:20. For our conversation is in heaven; from whence also we look for the Saviour, the Lord Jesus Christ:

Col. 1:12. Giving thanks unto the Father, . . . 13. Who hath delivered us from the power of darkness, and hath translated *us* into the kingdom of his dear Son: 14. In whom we have redemption through his blood, *even* the forgiveness of sins: 27. Christ in you, the hope of glory: 28. Whom we preach, warning every man, and teaching every man in all wisdom; that we may present every man perfect in Christ Jesus:

Col. 2:8. Beware lest any man spoil you through philosophy, . . . and not after Christ. 10. Ye are complete in him, which is the head of all principality and power:

Col. 3:3. Ye are dead, and your life is hid with Christ in God. 4. When Christ, *who is* our life, shall appear, then shall ye also appear with him in glory. 11. Christ *is* all, and in all.

1 Thess. 1:10. And to wait for his Son from heaven, whom he raised from the dead, *even* Jesus, which delivered us from the wrath to come.

1 Thess. 5:9. For God hath not appointed us to wrath, but to obtain salvation by our Lord Jesus Christ, 10. Who died for us, that, whether we wake or sleep, we should live together with him.

2 Thess. 1:12. That the name of our Lord Jesus Christ may be glorified in you, and ye in him, according to the grace of our God and the Lord Jesus Christ.

1 Tim. 1:1. Paul, an apostle of Jesus Christ by the commandment of God our Saviour, and Lord Jesus Christ, *which is* our hope; 15. This *is* a faithful saying, and worthy of all acceptation, that Christ Jesus came into the world to save sinners;

2 Tim. 1:1. According to the promise of life which is in Christ Jesus, 9. Who hath saved us, and called *us* with an holy calling, not according to our works, but according to his own purpose and grace, which was given us in Christ Jesus before the world began, 10. But is now made manifest by the appearing of our Saviour Jesus Christ, who hath abolished death, and hath brought life and [1] immortality to light through the gospel: 12. I know whom I have believed, and am persuaded that he is able to keep that which I have committed unto him against that day. [1 R. V. incorruption]

2 Tim. 2:10. Therefore I endure all things for the elect's sakes, that they may also obtain the salvation which is in Christ Jesus with eternal glory.

2 Tim. 3:15. And that from a child thou hast known the holy scriptures, which are able to make thee wise unto salvation through faith which is in Christ Jesus.

Tit. 1:4. To Titus, *mine* own son after the common faith: Grace, mercy, *and* peace, from God the Father and the Lord Jesus Christ our Saviour.

Tit. 2:13. Looking for that blessed hope, and the glorious appearing of the great God and our Saviour Jesus Christ; 14. Who gave himself for us, that he might redeem us from all iniquity, and purify unto himself a peculiar people, zealous of good works.

Heb. 2:3. How shall we escape, if we neglect so great salvation; which at the first began to be spoken by the Lord, and was confirmed unto us by them that heard *him*; 17. In all things it behoved him to be made like unto *his* brethren, that he might be a merciful and faithful high priest in things *pertaining* to God, to make reconciliation for the sins of the people.

Heb. 5:9. Being made perfect, he became the author of eternal salvation unto all them that obey him;

Heb. 7:22. By so much was Jesus made a surety of a better testament. 25. He is able also to save them to the uttermost that come unto God by him, seeing he ever liveth to make intercession for them.

Heb. 13:10. We have an altar, whereof they have no right to eat which serve the tabernacle. 20. The God of peace, that brought again from the dead our Lord Jesus, that great shepherd of the sheep, through the blood of the everlasting covenant,

1 Pet. 1:3. Blessed *be* the God and Father of our Lord Jesus Christ, which according to his abundant mercy hath begotten us again unto a lively hope by the resurrection of Jesus Christ from the dead, 18. Forasmuch as ye know that ye were not redeemed with corruptible things, *as* silver and gold, from your vain conversation *received* by tradition from your fathers; 19. But with the precious blood of Christ, as of a lamb without blemish and without spot:

1 Pet. 2:4. To whom coming, *as unto* a living stone, disallowed indeed of men, but chosen of God, *and* precious, 5. Ye also, as lively stones, are built up a spiritual house, an holy priesthood, to offer up spiritual sacrifices, acceptable to God by Jesus Christ. 6. Wherefore also it is contained in the scripture, Behold, I lay in Sion a chief corner stone, elect, precious: and he that believeth on him shall not be confounded. 7. Unto you therefore which believe *he is* precious: . . . the stone which the builders disallowed, the same is made the head of the corner, 25. Ye were as sheep going astray; but are now returned unto the Shepherd and Bishop of your souls.

1 Pet. 3:18. For Christ also hath once suffered for sins, the just for the unjust, that he might bring us to God, being put to death in the flesh, but quickened by the Spirit: 21. The like figure whereunto *even* baptism doth also now save us (not the putting away of the filth of the flesh, but the answer of a good conscience toward God), by the resurrection of Jesus Christ:

1 Pet. 5:10. The God of all grace, who hath called us unto his eternal glory by Christ Jesus,

2 Pet. 1:3. His divine power hath given unto us all things that *pertain* unto life and godliness, through the knowledge of him that hath called us to glory and virtue: 11. For so an entrance shall be ministered unto you abundantly into the everlasting kingdom of our Lord and Saviour Jesus Christ.

2 Pet. 2:20. For if after they have escaped the pollutions of the world through the knowledge of the Lord and Saviour Jesus Christ, they are again entangled therein, and overcome, the latter end is worse with them than the beginning.

1 John 3:5. Ye know that he was manifested to take away our sins; 8. For this purpose the Son of God was manifested, that he might destroy the works of the devil.

1 John 4:9. In this was manifested the love of God toward us, because that God sent his only begotten Son into the world,

that we might live through him. 10. Herein is love, not that we loved God, but that he loved us, and sent his Son *to be* the propitiation for our sins. 14. We have seen and do testify that the Father sent the Son *to be* the Saviour of the world.

1 John 5:11. This is the record, that God hath given to us eternal life, and this life is in his Son. 12. He that hath the Son hath life; *and* he that hath not the Son of God hath not life. 13. These things have I written unto you ¹ that believe on the name of the Son of God; that ye may know that ye have eternal life, ² and that ye may believe on the name of the Son of God. 20. We know that the Son of God is come, and hath given us an understanding, that we may know him that is true, and we are in him that is true, *even* in his Son Jesus Christ. This is the true God, and eternal life.

[R. V. ¹ Omitted.   ² even unto you that]

Jude 1. To them that are sanctified by God the Father, and preserved in Jesus Christ,

Rev. 2:7. To him that overcometh will I give to eat of the tree of life, which is in the midst of the paradise of God.

Rev. 3:18. I counsel thee to buy of me gold tried in the fire, that thou mayest be rich; and white raiment, that thou mayest be clothed, and *that* the shame of thy nakedness do not appear; and anoint thine eyes with eyesalve, that thou mayest see.

Rev. 5:5. And one of the elders saith unto me, Weep not: behold, the Lion of the tribe of Juda, the Root of David, hath prevailed to open the book, and to loose the seven seals thereof. 6. And I beheld, and, lo, in the midst of the throne and of the four beasts, and in the midst of the elders, stood a Lamb as it had been slain, having seven horns and seven eyes, which are the seven Spirits of God sent forth into all the earth. 7. And he came and took the book out of the right hand of him that sat upon the throne. 8. And when he had taken the book, the four beasts and four *and* twenty elders fell down before the Lamb, having every one of them harps, and golden vials full of odours, which are the prayers of saints. 9. And they sung a new song, saying, Thou art worthy to take the book, and to open the seals thereof: for thou wast slain, and hast redeemed us to God by thy blood out of every kindred, and tongue, and people, and nation; 10. And hast made us unto our God kings and priests: and we shall reign on the earth. 11. And I beheld, and I heard the voice of many angels round about the throne, and the beasts and the elders: and the number of them was ten thousand times ten thousand, and thousands of thousands; 12. Saying with a loud voice, Worthy is the Lamb that was slain to receive power, and riches, and wisdom, and strength, and honour, and glory, and blessing. 13. And every creature which is in heaven, and on the earth, and under the earth, and such as are in the sea, and

all that are in them, heard I saying, Blessing, and honour, and glory, and power, *be* unto him that sitteth upon the throne, and unto the Lamb for ever and ever. 14. And the four beasts said, Amen. And the four *and* twenty elders fell down and worshipped him that liveth for ever and ever.

Rev. 7:10. Salvation to our God which sitteth upon the throne, and unto the Lamb.

Rev. 14:4. These are they which follow the Lamb whithersoever he goeth. These were redeemed from among men, *being* the firstfruits unto God and to the Lamb.

Rev. 21:27. There shall in no wise enter into it any thing that defileth, . . . but they which are written in the Lamb's book of life.

Rev. 22:1. He shewed me a pure river of water of life, clear as crystal, proceeding out of the throne of God and of the Lamb. 2. In the midst of the street of it, and on either side of the river, *was there* the tree of life, which bare twelve *manner of* fruits, *and* yielded her fruit every month: and the leaves of the tree *were* for the healing of the nations.

See DEATH OF, ITS DESIGN, above; FAITH IN.

See ASCENSION OF.

SECOND COMING OF: Job 19:25. I know *that* my redeemer liveth, and *that* he shall stand at the latter *day* upon the earth: 26. And *though* after my skin *worms* destroy this *body*, yet in my flesh shall I see God:

Matt. 16:27. The Son of man shall come in the glory of his Father with his angels; and then he shall reward every man according to his works. 28. There be some standing here, which shall not taste of death, till they see the Son of man coming in his kingdom. Mark 9:1; Luke 9:27.

Matt. 23:39. For I say unto you, Ye shall not see me henceforth, till ye shall say, Blessed *is* he that cometh in the name of the Lord.

Matt. 24:3. And as he sat upon the mount of Olives, the disciples came unto him privately, saying, Tell us, when shall these things be? and what *shall be* the sign of thy coming, and of the end of the world? 27. As the lightning cometh out of the east, and shineth even unto the west; so shall also the coming of the Son of man be. 30. Then shall appear the sign of the Son of man in heaven: and then shall all the tribes of the earth mourn, and they shall see the Son of man coming in the clouds of heaven with power and great glory. 31. And he shall send his angels with a great sound of a trumpet, and they shall gather together his elect from the four winds, from one end of heaven to the other.

37. As the days of Noe *were*, so shall also the coming of the Son of man be. 38. As in the days that were before the flood they were eating and drinking, marrying and giving in marriage, until the day that Noe entered into the ark, 39. And knew not

until the flood came, and took them all away; so shall also the coming of the Son of man be.

42. Watch therefore: for ye know not what hour your Lord doth come. 43. If the goodman of the house had known in what watch the thief would come, he would have watched, and would not have suffered his house to be broken up. 44. Therefore be ye also ready: for in such an hour as ye think not the Son of man cometh. *vs.* 1-51; Mark 13:1-37; Luke 21:5-35; 17:22-37; 12:40.

Matt. 25:6. At midnight there was a cry made, Behold, the bridegroom cometh; go ye out to meet him. 10. While they went to buy, the bridegroom came; and they that were ready went in with him to the marriage: and the door was shut. 13. Watch therefore, for ye know neither the day nor the hour wherein the Son of man cometh. 19. After a long time the lord of those servants cometh, and reckoneth with them. 31. When the Son of man shall come in his glory, and all the holy angels with him, then shall he sit upon the throne of his glory: *vs.* 1-13,31-46.

Matt. 26:64. Hereafter shall ye see the Son of man sitting on the right hand of power, and coming in the clouds of heaven.

Mark 13:27. Then shall he send his angels, and shall gather together his elect from the four winds, from the uttermost part of the earth to the uttermost part of heaven. 32. But of that day and *that* hour knoweth no man, no, not the angels which are in heaven, neither the Son, but the Father. 35. Watch ye therefore: for ye know not when the master of the house cometh, at even, or at midnight, or at the cockcrowing, or in the morning: 36. Lest coming suddenly he find you sleeping. Matt. 24:36.

Mark 14:62. Ye shall see the Son of man sitting on the right hand of power, and coming in the clouds of heaven.

Luke 9:26. Whosoever shall be ashamed of me and of my words, of him shall the Son of man be ashamed, when he shall come in his own glory, and *in his* Father's, and of the holy angels. Mark 8:38.

Luke 12:37. Blessed *are* those servants, whom the lord when he cometh shall find watching: verily I say unto you, that he shall gird himself, and make them to sit down to meat, and will come forth and serve them. 38. And if he shall come in the second watch, or come in the third watch, and find *them* so, blessed are those servants. 39. And this know, that if the goodman of the house had known what hour the thief would come, he would have watched, and not have suffered his house to be broken through. 40. Be ye therefore ready also: for the Son of man cometh at an hour when ye think not.

Luke 17:30. Even thus shall it be in the day when the Son of man is revealed.

Luke 18:8. Nevertheless when the Son of man cometh, shall he find faith on the earth?

Luke 19:12. A certain nobleman went into a far country to receive for himself a kingdom, and to return. 13. And he called his ten servants, and delivered them ten pounds, and said unto them, Occupy till I come. 15. And it came to pass, that when he was returned, having received the kingdom, then he commanded these servants to be called unto him,

Luke 21:27. Then shall they see the Son of man coming in a cloud with power and great glory. 28. And when these things begin to come to pass, then look up, and lift up your heads; for your redemption draweth nigh. 29. And he spake to them a parable; Behold the fig tree, and all the trees; 30. When they now shoot forth, ye see and know of your own selves that summer is now nigh at hand. 31. So likewise ye, when ye see these things come to pass, know ye that the kingdom of God is nigh at hand. 32. Verily I say unto you, This generation shall not pass away, till all be fulfilled. 33. Heaven and earth shall pass away: but my words shall not pass away. 34. And take heed to yourselves, lest at any time your hearts be overcharged with surfeiting, and drunkenness, and cares of this life, and *so* that day come upon you unawares. 35. For as a snare shall it come on all them that dwell on the face of the whole earth. 36. Watch ye therefore, and pray always, that ye may be accounted worthy to escape all these things that shall come to pass, and to stand before the Son of man.

John 14:3. If I go and prepare a place for you, I will come again, and receive you unto myself; that where I am, *there* ye may be also. 18. I will not leave you comfortless: I will come to you.

28. Ye have heard how I said unto you, I go away, and come *again* unto you. If ye loved me, ye would rejoice, because I said, I go unto the Father: for my Father is greater than I. 29. And now I have told you before it come to pass, that, when it is come to pass, ye might believe.

Acts 1:11. This same Jesus, which is taken up from you into heaven, shall so come in like manner as ye have seen him go into heaven.

Acts 3:20. He shall send Jesus Christ, which before was preached unto you: 21. Whom the heaven must receive until the times of restitution of all things, which God hath spoken by the mouth of all his holy prophets since the world began.

1 Cor. 1:7. So that ye come behind in no gift; waiting for the coming of our Lord Jesus Christ: 8. Who shall also confirm you unto the end, *that ye may be* blameless in the day of our Lord Jesus Christ.

1 Cor. 4:5. Judge nothing before the time, until the Lord come, who both will bring to light the hidden things of darkness, and will make manifest the counsels of the hearts:

1 Cor. 11:26. As often as ye eat this bread,

and drink this cup, ye do shew the Lord's death till he come.

1 Cor. 15:23. Christ the firstfruits; afterward they that are Christ's at his coming.

Phil. 3:20. Our conversation is in heaven; from whence also we look for the Saviour, the Lord Jesus Christ: 21. Who shall change our vile body, that it may be fashioned like unto his glorious body, according to the working whereby he is able even to subdue all things unto himself.

Phil. 4:5. The Lord is at hand.

Col. 3:4. When Christ, who is our life, shall appear, then shall ye also appear with him in glory.

1 Thess. 1:10. And to wait for his Son from heaven, whom he raised from the dead, even Jesus,

1 Thess. 2:19. What is our hope, or joy, or crown of rejoicing? Are not even ye in the presence of our Lord Jesus Christ at his coming?

1 Thess. 3:13. To the end he may stablish your hearts unblameable in holiness before God, even our Father, at the coming of our Lord Jesus Christ with all his saints.

1 Thess. 4:15. For this we say unto you by the word of the Lord, that we which are alive and remain unto the coming of the Lord shall not prevent them which are asleep. 16. For the Lord himself shall descend from heaven with a shout, with the voice of the archangel, and with the trump of God: and the dead in Christ shall rise first: 17. Then we which are alive and remain shall be caught up together with them in the clouds, to meet the Lord in the air: and so shall we ever be with the Lord.

1 Thess. 5:2. Yourselves know perfectly that the day of the Lord so cometh as a thief in the night. 3. For when they shall say, Peace and safety; then sudden destruction cometh upon them, as travail upon a woman with child; and they shall not escape. 23. I pray God your whole spirit and soul and body be preserved blameless unto the coming of our Lord Jesus Christ.

2 Thess. 1:7. To you who are troubled rest with us, when the Lord Jesus shall be revealed from heaven with his mighty angels, 8. In flaming fire taking vengeance on them that know not God, and that obey not the gospel of our Lord Jesus Christ: 9. Who shall be punished with everlasting destruction from the presence of the Lord, and from the glory of his power; 10. When he shall come to be glorified in his saints, and to be admired in all them that believe (because our testimony among you was believed) in that day.

2 Thess. 2:1. We beseech you, brethren, by the coming of our Lord Jesus Christ, and by our gathering together unto him, 2. That ye be not soon shaken in mind, or be troubled, neither by spirit, nor by word, nor by letter as from us, as that the day of Christ is at hand. 3. Let no man deceive you by any means: for that day shall not

come, except there come a falling away first, and that man of sin be revealed, the son of perdition; 5. Remember ye not, that, when I was yet with you, I told you these things? 8. Then shall that Wicked be revealed, whom the Lord shall consume with the spirit of his mouth, and shall destroy with the brightness of his coming:

2 Thess. 3:5. The Lord direct your hearts into the love of God, and into the ¹patient waiting for Christ.   [¹R. V. patience of]

1 Tim. 6:14. Keep this commandment without spot, unrebukeable, until the appearing of our Lord Jesus Christ: 15. Which in his times he shall shew, who is the blessed and only Potentate, the King of kings, and Lord of lords;

2 Tim. 4:1. I charge thee therefore before God, and the Lord Jesus Christ, who shall judge the quick and the dead at his appearing and his kingdom; 8. Henceforth there is laid up for me a crown of righteousness, which the Lord, the righteous judge, shall give me at that day: and not to me only, but unto all them also that love his appearing.

Tit. 2:13. Looking for that blessed hope, and the glorious appearing of the great God and our Saviour Jesus Christ;

Heb. 9:28. So Christ was once offered to bear the sins of many; and unto them that look for him shall he appear the second time without sin unto salvation.

Jas. 5:7. Be patient therefore, brethren, unto the coming of the Lord. Behold, the husbandman waiteth for the precious fruit of the earth, and hath long patience for it, until he receive the early and latter rain. 8. Be ye also patient; stablish your hearts: for the coming of the Lord draweth nigh. 9. Behold, the judge standeth before the door.

1 Pet. 1:7. That the trial of your faith ... might be found unto praise and honour and glory at the appearing of Jesus Christ: 13. Wherefore gird up the loins of your mind, be sober, and hope to the end for the grace that is to be brought unto you at the revelation of Jesus Christ;

1 Pet. 4:13. But rejoice, inasmuch as ye are partakers of Christ's sufferings; that, when his glory shall be revealed, ye may be glad also with exceeding joy.

1 Pet. 5:4. When the chief Shepherd shall appear, ye shall receive a crown of glory that fadeth not away.

2 Pet. 1:16. We have not followed cunningly devised fables, when we made known unto you the power and coming of our Lord Jesus Christ,

2 Pet. 3:3. Knowing this first, that there shall come in the last days scoffers, walking after their own lusts, 4. And saying, Where is the promise of his coming? for since the fathers fell asleep, all things continue as they were from the beginning of the creation. 10. But the day of the Lord will come as a thief in the night; in the which the heavens shall pass away with a great noise, and the elements shall melt with fervent

heat, the earth also and the works that are therein shall be burned up. 11. *Seeing* then *that* all these things shall be dissolved, what manner *of persons* ought ye to be in *all* holy conversation and godliness. 12. Looking for and hasting unto the coming of the day of God, wherein the heavens being on fire shall be dissolved, and the elements shall melt with fervent heat? *vs.* 3, 4, 8–14.

1 John 2:28. Little children, abide in him; that, when he shall appear, we may have confidence, and not be ashamed before him at his coming.

1 John 3:2. But we know that, when he shall appear, we shall be like him; for we shall see him as he is.

Jude 14. Enoch also, the seventh from Adam, prophesied of these, saying, Behold, the Lord cometh with ten thousands of his saints, 15. To execute judgment upon all.

Rev. 1:7. Behold, he cometh with clouds; and every eye shall see him, and they *also* which pierced him: and all kindreds of the earth shall wail because of him.

Rev. 3:11. Behold, I come quickly: hold that fast which thou hast, that no man take thy crown.

Rev. 16:15. Behold I come as a thief.

Rev. 22:12. Behold, I come quickly; and my reward *is* with me, to give every man according as his work shall be. 20. He which testifieth these things saith, Surely I come quickly. Amen. Even so, come, Lord Jesus.

See MILLENNIUM.

SHEPHERD: JESUS THE TRUE: Foretold, Gen. 49:24; Isa. 40:11; Ezek. 34:23; 37:24. The chief, 1 Pet. 5:4. The good, John 10: 11, 14. The great, Mic. 5:4; Heb. 13:20.

His sheep he knows, John 10:14, 27. He calls, John 10:3. He gathers, Isa. 40:11; John 10:16. He guides, Psa. 23:3; John 10: 3, 4. He feeds, Psa. 23:1, 2; John 10:9. He cherishes tenderly, Isa. 40:11. He protects and preserves, Jer. 31:10; Ezek. 34:10; Zech. 9:16; John 10:28. He laid down his life for, Zech. 13:7; Matt. 26:31; John 10:11, 15; Acts 20:28. He gives eternal life to, John 10:28. Typified: David, 1 Sam. 16:11.—*Bible Text-Book.*

SON OF GOD: Psa. 2:7. I will declare the decree: the LORD hath said unto me, Thou *art* my Son; this day have I begotten thee.

Psa. 89:26. He shall cry unto me, Thou *art* my father, my God, and the rock of my salvation. 27. Also I will make him *my* firstborn, higher than the kings of the earth.

Matt. 3:17. Lo a voice from heaven, saying, This is my beloved Son, in whom I am well pleased. Mark 1:11; Luke 3:22.

Matt. 4:3. And when the tempter came to him, he said, If thou be the Son of God, command that these stones be made bread. 6. And saith unto him, If thou be the Son of God, cast thyself down: for it is written, He shall give his angels charge concerning thee: and in *their* hands they shall bear

thee up, lest at any time thou dash thy foot against a stone.

Matt. 10:40. He that receiveth me receiveth him that sent me.

Matt. 11:27. All things are delivered unto me of my Father: and no man knoweth the Son, but the Father; neither knoweth any man the Father, save the Son, and *he* to whomsoever the Son will reveal *him*. Luke 10:22.

Matt. 14:33. Then they that were in the ship came and worshipped him, saying, Of a truth thou art the Son of God.

Matt. 15:13. Every plant, which my heavenly Father hath not planted, shall be rooted up.

Matt. 16:15. He saith unto them, But whom say ye that I am? 16. And Simon Peter answered and said, Thou art the Christ, the Son of the living God. 17. And Jesus answered and said unto him, Blessed art thou, Simon Bar-jona: for flesh and blood hath not revealed *it* unto thee, but my Father which is in heaven.

Matt. 17:5. While he yet spake, behold, a bright cloud overshadowed them: and behold a voice out of the cloud, which said, This is my beloved Son, in whom I am well pleased; hear ye him. Mark 9:7; Luke 9:35; 2 Pet. 1:17.

Matt. 18:10. Take heed that ye despise not one of these little ones; for I say unto you, That in heaven their angels do always behold the face of my Father which is in heaven. 19. Again I say unto you, That if two of you shall agree on earth as touching any thing that they shall ask, it shall be done for them of my Father which is in heaven.

Matt. 20:23. To sit on my right hand, and on my left, is not mine to give, but *it shall be given to them* for whom it is prepared of my Father.

Matt. 21:37. But last of all he sent unto them his son, saying, They will reverence my son. Luke 20:13.

Matt. 26:53. Thinkest thou that I cannot now pray to my Father, and he shall presently give me more than twelve legions of angels? 63. And the high priest answered and said unto him, I adjure thee by the living God, that thou tell us whether thou be the Christ, the Son of God. 64. Jesus saith unto him, Thou hast said: nevertheless I say unto you, Hereafter shall ye see the Son of man sitting on the right hand of power, and coming in the clouds of heaven.

Matt. 27:43. He trusted in God; let him deliver him now, if he will have him: for he said, I am the Son of God. 54. Now when the centurion, and they that were with him, watching Jesus, saw the earthquake, and those things that were done, they feared greatly, saying, Truly this was the Son of God.

Mark 1:1. The beginning of the gospel of Jesus Christ, the Son of God;

Mark 3:11. And unclean spirits, when

they saw him, fell down before him, and cried, saying, Thou art the Son of God.

Mark 5:7. And cried with a loud voice, and said, What have I to do with thee, Jesus, *thou* Son of the most high God? I adjure thee by God, that thou torment me not. Luke 8:28.

Mark 14:61. Again the high priest asked him, and said unto him, Art thou the Christ, the Son of the Blessed? 62. And Jesus said, I am: and ye shall see the Son of man sitting on the right hand of power, and coming in the clouds of heaven.

Mark 15:39. And when the centurion, which stood over against him, saw that he so cried out, and gave up the ghost, he said, Truly this man was the Son of God.

Luke 1:32. He shall be great, and shall be called the Son of the Highest; and the Lord God shall give unto him the throne of his father David: 35. The Holy Ghost shall come upon thee, and the power of the Highest shall overshadow thee: therefore also that holy thing which shall be born of thee shall be called the Son of God.

Luke 4:3. And the devil said unto him, If thou be the Son of God, command this stone that it be made bread. 9. And he brought him to Jerusalem, and set him on a pinnacle of the temple, and said unto him, If thou be the Son of God, cast thyself down from hence:

41. And devils also came out of many, crying out, and saying, Thou art Christ the Son of God. And he rebuking *them* suffered them not to speak: for they knew that he was Christ.

Luke 9:35. And there came a voice out of the cloud, saying, This is my beloved Son: hear him.

Luke 10:22. All things are delivered to me of my Father: and no man knoweth who the Son is, but the Father; and who the Father is, but the Son, and *he* to whom the Son will reveal *him*.

Luke 22:29. I appoint unto you a kingdom, as my Father hath appointed unto me; 70. Then said they all, Art thou then the Son of God? And he said unto them, Ye say that I am. Mark 14:61.

John 1:1. In the beginning was the Word, and the Word was with God, and the Word was God. 2. The same was in the beginning with God. 14. The Word was made flesh, and dwelt among us (and we beheld his glory, the glory as of the only begotten of the Father,) full of grace and truth. 18. No man hath seen God at any time; the only begotten Son, which is in the bosom of the Father, he hath declared *him*. 34. I saw, and bare record that this is the Son of God. 49. Nathanael answered and saith unto him, Rabbi, thou art the Son of God; thou art the King of Israel. 50. Jesus answered and said unto him, Because I said unto thee, I saw thee under the fig tree, believest thou? thou shalt see greater things than these.

John 3:16. For God so loved the world,

that he gave his only begotten Son, that whosoever believeth in him should not perish, but have everlasting life. 17. For God sent not his Son into the world to condemn the world; but that the world through him might be saved. 18. He that believeth on him is not condemned: but he that believeth not is condemned already, because he hath not believed in the name of the only begotten Son of God. 34. He whom God hath sent speaketh the words of God: for God giveth not the Spirit by measure *unto him.* 35. The Father loveth the Son, and hath given all things into his hand. 36. He that believeth on the Son hath everlasting life: and he that believeth not the Son shall not see life; but the wrath of God abideth on him.

John 5:19. The Son can do nothing of himself, but what he seeth the Father do: for what things soever he doeth, these also doeth the Son likewise. 20. The Father loveth the Son, and sheweth him all things that himself doeth: and he will shew him greater works than these, 21. As the Father raiseth up the dead, and quickeneth *them;* even so the Son quickeneth whom he will. 23. All *men* should honour the Son, even as they honour the Father. He that honoureth not the Son honoureth not the Father which hath sent him. 26. As the Father hath life in himself; so hath he given to the Son to have life in himself; 27. And hath given him authority to execute judgment also, because he is the Son of man. 30. I can of mine own self do nothing: as I hear, I judge: and my judgment is just; because I seek not mine own will, but the will of the Father which hath sent me. 32. There is another that beareth witness of me; and I know that the witness which he witnesseth of me is true. 36. The works which the Father hath given me to finish, the same works that I do, bear witness of me, that the Father hath sent me. 37. The Father himself, which hath sent me, hath borne witness of me. Ye have neither heard his voice at any time, nor seen his shape.

John 6:27. Him hath God the Father sealed. 38. I came down from heaven, not to do mine own will, but the will of him that sent me. 40. And this is the will of him that sent me, that every one which seeth the Son, and believeth on him, may have everlasting life: and I will raise him up at the last day. 46. Not that any man hath seen the Father, save he which is of God, he hath seen the Father. 57. The living Father hath sent me, and I live by the Father: 69. We believe and are sure that thou art [1]that Christ, the Son of the living God.   [1 R. V. the Holy One of]

John 7:16. My doctrine is not mine, but his that sent me. 28. I am not come of myself, but he that sent me is true, whom ye know not. 29. But I know him: for I am from him, and he hath sent me.

John 8:16. I am not alone, but I and the Father that sent me. 19. Then said they unto him, Where is thy Father? Jesus answered, Ye neither know me, nor my Father: if ye had known me, ye should have known my Father also. 26. He that sent me is true; and I speak to the world those things which I have heard of him. 27. They understood not that he spake to them of the Father. 28. When ye have lifted up the Son of man, then shall ye know that I am *he*, and *that* I do nothing of myself; but as my Father hath taught me, I speak these things. 29. And he that sent me is with me: the Father hath not left me alone; for I do always those things that please him. 38. I speak that which I have seen with my Father: 40. But now ye seek to kill me, a man that hath told you the truth, which I have heard of God: 42. If God were your Father, ye would love me: for I proceeded forth and came from God; neither came I of myself, but he sent me. 49. I honour my Father, and ye do dishonour me. 54. If I honour myself, my honour is nothing: it is my Father that honoureth me;

John 9:35. Jesus . . . said unto him, Dost thou believe on the Son of God? 36. He answered and said, Who is he, Lord, that I might believe on him? 37. Jesus said unto him, Thou hast both seen him, and it is he that talketh with thee.

John 10:15. As the Father knoweth me, even so know I the Father: 17. Therefore doth my Father love me, because I lay down my life, that I might take it again. 18. This commandment have I received of my Father. 29. My Father, which gave *them* me, is greater than all; and no *man* is able to pluck *them* out of my Father's hand. 30. I and *my* Father are one. 36. Say ye of him, whom the Father hath sanctified, and sent into the world, Thou blasphemest; because I said, I am the Son of God? 37. If I do not the works of my Father, believe me not. 38. But if I do, though ye believe not me, believe the works: that ye may know, and believe, that the Father *is* in me, and I in him.

John 11:4. When Jesus heard *that*, he said, This sickness is not unto death, but for the glory of God, that the Son of God might be glorified thereby. 27. She saith unto him, Yea, Lord: I believe that thou art the Christ, the Son of God, which should come into the world. 41. Father, I thank thee that thou hast heard me.

John 12:49. I have not spoken of myself; but the Father which sent me, he gave me a commandment, what I should say, and what I should speak. 50. And I know that his commandment is life everlasting: whatsoever I speak therefore, even as the Father said unto me, so I speak.

John 13:3. Jesus knowing that the Father had given all things into his hands, and that he was come from God, and went to God;

John 14:7. If ye had known me, ye should have known my Father also: and from henceforth ye know him, and have seen him. 9. He that hath seen me hath seen the Father; and how sayest thou *then*, Shew us the Father? 10. Believest thou not that I am in the Father, and the Father in me? the words that I speak unto you I speak not of myself: but the Father that dwelleth in me, he doeth the works. 11. Believe me that I *am* in the Father, and the Father in me: 13. Whatsoever ye shall ask in my name, that will I do, that the Father may be glorified in the Son. 16. I will pray the Father, and he shall give you another Comforter, that he may abide with you for ever; 20. At that day ye shall know that I *am* in my Father, and ye in me, and I in you. 24. The word which ye hear is not mine, but the Father's which sent me. 28. If ye love me, ye would rejoice, because I said, I go unto the Father: for my Father is greater than I. 31. That the world may know that I love the Father; and as the Father gave me commandment, even so I do.

John 15:1. I am the true vine, and my Father is the husbandman. 8. Herein is my Father glorified, that ye bear much fruit; so shall ye be my disciples. 9. As the Father hath loved me, so have I loved you: continue ye in my love. 10. If ye keep my commandments, ye shall abide in my love: even as I have kept my Father's commandments, and abide in his love. 23. He that hateth me hateth my Father also. 24. Now have they both seen and hated both me and my Father.

John 16:5. I go my way to him that sent me; 15. All things that the Father hath are mine: 27. The Father himself loveth you, because ye have loved me, and have believed that I came out from God. 28. I came forth from the Father, and am come into the world: again, I leave the world, and go to the Father. 32. I am not alone, because the Father is with me.

John 17:1. Father, the hour is come; glorify thy Son, that thy Son also may glorify thee: *vs.* 1-26.

John 19:7. The Jews answered him, We have a law, and by our law he ought to die, because he made himself the Son of God.

John 20:17. I am not yet ascended to my Father: but go to my brethren, and say unto them, I ascend unto my Father, and your Father; and *to* my God, and your God. 21. As *my* Father hath sent me, even so send I you. 31. But these are written, that ye might believe that Jesus is the Christ, the Son of God; and that believing ye might have life through his name.

Acts 3:13. The God of our fathers, hath glorified his Son Jesus;

Acts 13:33. God hath fulfilled the same unto us their children, in that he hath raised up Jesus again; as it is also written in the second psalm, Thou art my Son, this day have I begotten thee.

Rom. 1:3. Concerning his Son Jesus Christ our Lord, which was made of the seed of

David acccording to the flesh; 4. And declared *to be* the Son of God with power, according to the Spirit of holiness, by the resurrection from the dead : 9. For God is my witness, whom I serve with my spirit in the gospel of his Son, that without ceasing I make mention of you always in my prayers;

Rom. 8:3. For what the law could not do, in that it was weak through the flesh, God sending his own Son in the likeness of sinful flesh, and for sin, condemned sin in the flesh : 29. For whom he did foreknow, he also did predestinate *to be* conformed to the image of his Son, that he might be the firstborn among many brethren. 32. He that spared not his own Son, but delivered him up for us all,

1 Cor. 1:9. God *is* faithful, by whom ye were called unto the fellowship of his Son Jesus Christ our Lord.

1 Cor. 15:24. Then cometh the end, when he shall have delivered up the kingdom to God, even the Father ; 27. He hath put all things under his feet. But when he saith all things are put under *him*, *it is* manifest that he is excepted, which did put all things under him. 28. And when all things shall be subdued unto him, then shall the Son also himself be subject unto him that put all things under him, that God may be all in all.

2 Cor. 1:3. Blessed *be* God, even the Father of our Lord Jesus Christ, 19. For the Son of God, Jesus Christ, who was preached among you by us, *even* by me and Silvanus and Timotheus, was not yea and nay, but in him was yea.

Gal. 1:16. To reveal his Son in me, that I might preach him among the heathen ;

Gal. 4:4. When the fulness of the time was come, God sent forth his Son, made of a woman, made under the law,

Eph. 1:3. Blessed *be* the God and Father of our Lord Jesus Christ,

Eph. 3:14. For this cause I bow my knees unto the Father of our Lord Jesus Christ,

Col. 1:3. We give thanks to God and the Father of our Lord Jesus Christ, praying always for you, 15. Who is the image of the invisible God, the firstborn of every creature : 19. It pleased *the Father* that in him should all fulness dwell ;

Col. 3:17. And whatsoever ye do in word or deed, *do* all in the name of the Lord Jesus, giving thanks to God and the Father by him.

1 Thess. 1:10. And to wait for his Son from heaven, whom he raised from the dead, *even* Jesus, which delivered us from the wrath to come.

Heb. 1:1. God . . . 2. Hath in these last days spoken unto us by *his* Son, whom he hath appointed heir of all things, by whom also he made the worlds ; 3. Who being the brightness of *his* glory, and the express image of his person, and upholding all things by the word of his power, when he had by himself purged our sins, sat down on the right hand of the Majesty on high ; 5. For unto which of the angels said he at any time, Thou art my Son, this day have I begotten thee ? And again, I will be to him a Father, and he shall be to me a Son ?

Heb. 4:14. Seeing then that we have a great high priest, that is passed into the heavens, Jesus the Son of God, let us hold fast *our* profession.

Heb. 5:5. Christ glorified not himself to be made an high priest ; but he that said unto him, Thou art my Son, to day have I begotten thee. 8. Though he were a Son, yet learned he obedience by the things which he suffered ; 10. Called of God an high priest after the order of Melchisedec.

Heb. 6:6. They crucify to themselves the Son of God afresh, and put *him* to an open shame.

Heb. 7:3. Without father, without mother, without descent, having neither beginning of days, nor end of life ; but made like unto the Son of God ; abideth a priest continually.

Heb. 10:29. Of how much sorer punishment, suppose ye, shall he be thought worthy, who hath trodden under foot the Son of God, and hath counted the blood of the covenant, wherewith he was sanctified, an unholy thing, and hath done despite unto the Spirit of grace ?

1 John 1:7. But if we walk in the light, as he is in the light, we have fellowship one with another, and the blood of Jesus Christ his Son cleanseth us from all sin.

1 John 2:22. Who is a liar but he that denieth that Jesus is the Christ ? He is antichrist, that denieth the Father and the Son. 23. Whosoever denieth the Son, the same hath not the Father : [*but*] *he that acknowledgeth the Son hath the Father also.* 24. Let that therefore abide in you, which ye have heard from the beginning. If that which ye have heard from the beginning shall remain in you, ye also shall continue in the Son, and in the Father.

1 John 3:8. For this purpose the Son of God was manifested, that he might destroy the works of the devil. 23. And this is his commandment, That we should believe on the name of his Son Jesus Christ, and love one another, as he gave us commandment.

1 John 4:9. God sent his only begotten Son into the world, that we might live through him. 10. Herein is love, not that we loved God, but that he loved us, and sent his Son *to be* the propitiation for our sins. 14. And we have seen and do testify that the Father sent the Son *to be* the Saviour of the world.

1 John 5:5. Who is he that overcometh the world, but he that believeth that Jesus is the Son of God ? 9. This is the witness of God which he hath testified of his Son. 10. He that believeth on the Son of God hath the witness in himself ; he that believeth not God hath made him a liar ; because he

believeth not the record that God gave of his Son. 13. These things have I written unto you [1] that believe on the name of the Son of God; that ye may know that ye have eternal life, and that ye may believe on the name of the Son of God. 20. And we know that the Son of God is come, and hath given us an understanding, that we may know him that is true, and we are in him that is true, *even* in his Son Jesus Christ. This is the true God, and eternal life. [1 Omitted in R. V.]

2 John 3. Grace be with you, mercy, *and* peace, from God the Father, and from the Lord Jesus Christ, the Son of the Father, in truth and love.

Rev. 2:18. And unto the angel of the church in Thyatira write; These things saith the Son of God, who hath his eyes like unto a flame of fire, and his feet *are* like fine brass;

See DIVINITY OF, above; RELATION OF, TO THE FATHER, above.

SON OF MAN: See HUMANITY OF, above.

SOVEREIGNTY OF: See JESUS, KING; SUFFERINGS OF.

SUFFERINGS OF: Matt. 26:38. Then saith he unto them, My soul is exceeding sorrowful, even unto death: tarry ye here, and watch with me. 39. And he went a little farther, and fell on his face, and prayed, saying, O my Father, if it be possible, let this cup pass from me: nevertheless not as I will, but as thou *wilt*. 40. And he cometh unto the disciples, and findeth them asleep, and saith unto Peter, What, could ye not watch with me one hour? 41. Watch and pray, that ye enter not into temptation: the spirit indeed *is* willing, but the flesh *is* weak. 42. He went away again the second time, and prayed, saying, O my Father, if this cup may not pass away from me, except I drink it, thy will be done. 43. And he came and found them asleep again: for their eyes were heavy. 44. And he left them, and went away again, and prayed the third time, saying the same words. 45. Then cometh he to his disciples, and saith unto them, Sleep on now, and take *your* rest: behold, the hour is at hand, and the Son of man is betrayed into the hands of sinners.

Matt. 27:24. When Pilate saw that he could prevail nothing, but *that* rather a tumult was made, he took water, and washed *his* hands before the multitude, saying, I am innocent of the blood of this just person: see ye *to it*. 25. Then answered all the people, and said, His blood *be* on us, and on our children. 26. Then released he Barabbas unto them: and when he had scourged Jesus, he delivered *him* to be crucified. 27. Then the soldiers of the governor took Jesus into the common hall, and gathered unto him the whole band *of soldiers*. 28. And they stripped him, and put on him a scarlet robe. 29. And when they had platted a crown of thorns, they put *it* upon his head, and a reed in his right hand:

and they bowed the knee before him, and mocked him, saying, Hail, King of the Jews! 30. And they spit upon him, and took the reed, and smote him on the head. 31. And after that they had mocked him, they took the robe off from him, and put his own raiment on him, and led him away to crucify *him*. 32. And as they came out, they found a man of Cyrene, Simon by name: him they compelled to bear his cross. 33. And when they were come unto a place called Golgotha, that is to say, a place of a skull, 34. They gave him vinegar to drink mingled with gall: and when he had tasted *thereof*, he would not drink. 35. And they crucified him, and parted his garments, casting lots: that it might be fulfilled which was spoken by the prophet, They parted my garments among them, and upon my vesture did they cast lots. 36. And sitting down they watched him there; 37. And set up over his head his accusation written, THIS IS JESUS THE KING OF THE JEWS. 38. Then were there two thieves crucified with him, one on the right hand, and another on the left. 39. And they that passed by reviled him, wagging their heads, 40. And saying, Thou that destroyest the temple, and buildest *it* in three days, save thyself. If thou be the Son of God, come down from the cross. 41. Likewise also the chief priests mocking *him*, with the scribes and elders, said, 42. He saved others; himself he cannot save. If he be the King of Israel, let him now come down from the cross, and we will believe him. 43. He trusted in God; let him deliver him now, if he will have him: for he said, I am the Son of God. 44. The thieves also, which were crucified with him, cast the same in his teeth. 45. Now from the sixth hour there was darkness over all the land unto the ninth hour. 46. And about the ninth hour Jesus cried with a loud voice, saying, Eli, Eli, lama sabachthani? that is to say, My God, my God, why hast thou forsaken me? 47. Some of them that stood there, when they heard *that*, said, This *man* calleth for Elias. 48. And straightway one of them ran, and took a sponge, and filled *it* with vinegar, and put *it* on a reed, and gave him to drink. 49. The rest said, Let be, let us see whether Elias will come to save him. 50. Jesus, when he had cried again with a loud voice, yielded up the ghost. Mark 14; 15; Luke 22; 23; John 18; 19.

Mark 15:34. At the ninth hour Jesus cried with a loud voice, saying, Eloi, Eloi, lama sabachthani? which is, being interpreted, My God, my God, why hast thou forsaken me?

Luke 2:34. Behold, this *child* is set for . . . a sign which shall be spoken against;

Luke 4:28. All they in the synagogue, when they heard these things, were filled with wrath, 29. And rose up, and thrust him out of the city, and led him unto the brow of the hill whereon their city was built, that they might cast him down headlong.

Luke 22:44. Being in an agony he prayed more earnestly: and his sweat was as it were great drops of blood falling down to the ground.

Luke 24:46. And said unto them, Thus it is written, and thus it behoved Christ to suffer, and to rise from the dead the third day:

John 4:6. Jesus therefore, being wearied with *his* journey, sat thus on the well:

John 11:33. When Jesus therefore saw her weeping, and the Jews also weeping which came with her, he groaned in the spirit, and was troubled, 35. Jesus wept.

John 12:27. Now is my soul troubled; and what shall I say? Father, save me from this hour: but for this cause came I unto this hour.

John 18:11. The cup which my Father hath given me, shall I not drink it?

John 19:28. Jesus knowing that all things were now accomplished, that the scripture might be fulfilled, saith, I thirst.

Acts 3:18. But those things, which God before had shewed by the mouth of all his prophets, that Christ should suffer, he hath so fulfilled.

Acts 17:3. Opening and alleging, that Christ must needs have suffered, and risen again from the dead; and that this Jesus, whom I preach unto you, is Christ.

2 Cor. 1:5. For as the sufferings of Christ abound in us, so our consolation also aboundeth by Christ.

Phil. 2:7. Made himself of no reputation, and took upon him the form of a servant, and was made in the likeness of men: 8. And being found in fashion as a man, he humbled himself, and became obedient unto death, even the death of the cross.

Phil. 3:10. That I may know him, and the power of his resurrection, and the fellowship of his sufferings, being made conformable unto his death;

Heb. 2:9. But we see Jesus, who was made a little lower than the angels for the suffering of death,

Heb. 4:15. For we have not an high priest which cannot be touched with the feeling of our infirmities; but was in all points tempted like as *we are, yet* without sin.

Heb. 5:7. Who in the days of his flesh, when he had offered up prayers and supplications with strong crying and tears unto him that was able to save him from death, and was heard in that he feared; 8. Though he were a Son, yet learned he obedience by the things which he suffered;

Heb. 12:2. Looking unto Jesus the author and finisher of *our* faith; who for the joy that was set before him endured the cross, despising the shame, and is set down at the right hand of the throne of God. 3. For consider him that endured such contradiction of sinners against himself, lest ye be wearied and faint in your minds.

1 Pet. 1:11. Searching what, or what manner of time the Spirit of Christ which was

in them did signify, when it testified beforehand the sufferings of Christ, and the glory that should follow.

1 Pet. 2:21. For even hereunto were ye called: because Christ also suffered for us, leaving us an example, that ye should follow his steps: 22. Who did no sin, neither was guile found in his mouth: 23. Who, when he was reviled, reviled not again; when he suffered, he threatened not; but committed *himself* to him that judgeth righteously:

1 Pet. 4:1. Forasmuch then as Christ hath suffered for us in the flesh, arm yourselves likewise with the same mind: for he that hath suffered in the flesh hath ceased from sin;

Rev. 5:6. And I beheld, and, lo, in the midst of the throne and of the four beasts, and in the midst of the elders, stood a Lamb as it had been slain,

Rev. 19:13. He *was* clothed with a vesture dipped in blood: and his name is called The Word of God.

See Death of, above; Persecution.

Prophecies Concerning: Psa. 22:6. I *am* a worm, and no man; a reproach of men, and despised of the people. 7. All they that see me laugh me to scorn: they shoot out the lip, they shake the head, *saying,* 8. He trusted on the Lord *that* he would deliver him: let him deliver him, seeing he delighted in him. 11. Be not far from me; for trouble *is* near; for *there is* none to help. 12. Many bulls have compassed me: strong *bulls* of Bashan have beset me round. 13. They gaped upon me *with* their mouths, *as* a ravening and a roaring lion. 17. I may tell all my bones: they look *and* stare upon me. 18. They part my garments among them, and cast lots upon my vesture. [Matt. 27:35; Mark 15:24; Luke 23:34; John 19:23.] 19. But be not thou far from me, O Lord: O my strength, haste thee to help me. 20. Deliver my soul from the sword; my darling from the power of the dog: 21. Save me from the lion's mouth: for thou hast heard me from the horns of the unicorns.

Psa. 69:7. For thy sake I have borne reproach; shame hath covered my face. 8. I am become a stranger unto my brethren, and an alien unto my mother's children. 9. For the zeal of thine house hath eaten me up; and the reproaches of them that reproached thee are fallen upon me. 20. Reproach hath broken my heart; and I am full of heaviness: and I looked *for some* to take pity, but *there was* none; and for comforters, but I found none.

Psa. 109:25. I became also a reproach unto them: *when* they looked upon me they shaked their heads.

Isa. 50:6. I gave my back to the smiters, and my cheeks to them that plucked off the hair: I hid not my face from shame and spitting.

Isa. 52:13. Behold, my servant shall deal

prudently, he shall be exalted and extolled, and be very high. 14. As many were astonied at thee; his visage was so marred more than any man, and his form more than the sons of men:

Isa. 53:1. Who hath believed our report? and to whom is the arm of the LORD revealed? [John 12:38.] 2. For he shall grow up before him as a tender plant, and as a root out of a dry ground: he hath no form nor comeliness; and when we shall see him, *there is* no beauty that we should desire him. 3. He is despised and rejected of men; a man of sorrows, and acquainted with grief: and we hid as it were *our* faces from him; he was despised, and we esteemed him not. 4. Surely he hath borne our griefs, and carried our sorrows: yet we did esteem him stricken, smitten of God, and afflicted. 5. But he *was* wounded for our transgressions, *he was* bruised for our iniquities: the chastisement of our peace *was* upon him; and with his stripes we are healed. 6. All we like sheep have gone astray; we have turned every one to his own way; and the LORD hath laid on him the iniquity of us all. 7. He was oppressed, and he was afflicted, yet he opened not his mouth: he is brought as a lamb to the slaughter, and as a sheep before her shearers is dumb, so he openeth not his mouth. 8. He was taken from prison and from judgment: and who shall declare his generation? for he was cut off out of the land of the living: for the transgression of my people was he stricken. 9. And he made his grave with the wicked, and with the rich in his death; because he had done no violence, neither *was any* deceit in his mouth. 10. Yet it pleased the LORD to bruise him; he hath put *him* to grief: when thou shalt make his soul an offering for sin, he shall see *his* seed, he shall prolong *his* days, and the pleasure of the LORD shall prosper in his hand. 11. He shall see of the travail of his soul, *and* shall be satisfied: by his knowledge shall my righteous servant justify many; for he shall bear their iniquities. 12. Therefore will I divide him *a portion* with the great, and he shall divide the spoil with the strong; because he hath poured out his soul unto death: and he was numbered with the transgressors; and he bare the sin of many, and made intercession for the transgressors. Luke 22:37.

Mic. 5:1. They shall smite the judge of Israel with a rod upon the cheek.

Zech. 11:12. And I said unto them, If ye think good, give *me* my ¹ price; and if not, forbear. So they weighed for my ¹ price thirty *pieces* of silver. 13. And the LORD said unto me, Cast it unto the potter: a goodly price that I was prised at of them. And I took the thirty *pieces* of silver, and cast them to the potter in the house of the LORD. [¹ R. V. hire]

Zech. 13:6. And *one* shall say unto him, What *are* these wounds ¹ in thine hands? Then

he shall answer, *Those* with which I was wounded *in* the house of my friends. 7. Awake, O sword, against my shepherd, and against the man *that is* my fellow, saith the LORD of hosts: smite the shepherd, and the sheep shall be scattered: and I will turn mine hand upon the little ones.

[¹ R. V. between thine arms]

Matt. 16:21. From that time forth began Jesus to shew unto his disciples, how that he must go unto Jerusalem, and suffer many things of the elders and chief priests and scribes, and be killed, and be raised again the third day.

Matt. 17:12. But I say unto you, That Elias is come already, and they knew him not, but have done unto him whatsoever they listed. Likewise shall also the Son of man suffer of them. 22. And while they abode in Galilee, Jesus said unto them, The Son of man shall be betrayed into the hands of men: 23. And they shall kill him, and the third day he shall be raised again. And they were exceeding sorry.

Matt. 20:17. And Jesus going up to Jerusalem took the twelve disciples apart in the way, and said unto them, 18. Behold, we go up to Jerusalem; and the Son of man shall be betrayed unto the chief priests and unto the scribes, and they shall condemn him to death, 19. And shall deliver him to the Gentiles to mock, and to scourge, and to crucify *him:* and the third day he shall rise again. Mark 10:32–34; Luke 18: 31–33.

Mark 8:31. And he began to teach them, that the Son of man must suffer many things, and be rejected of the elders, and *of* the chief priests, and scribes, and be killed, and after three days rise again.

Luke 2:34. And Simeon blessed them, and said unto Mary his mother, Behold, this *child* is set for the fall and rising again of many in Israel; and for a sign which shall be spoken against; 35. (Yea, a sword shall pierce through thy own soul also,) that the thoughts of many hearts may be revealed.

Luke 9:22. Saying, The Son of man must suffer many things, and be rejected of the elders and chief priests and scribes, and be slain, and be raised the third day.

1 Pet. 1:11. Searching what, or what manner of time the Spirit of Christ which was in them did signify, when it testified beforehand the sufferings of Christ, and the glory that should follow.

SYMPATHY OF: See COMPASSION OF; LOVE OF.

TEACHER: Matt. 4:23. And Jesus went about all Galilee, teaching in their synagogues, and preaching the gospel of the kingdom,

Matt. 7:29. For he taught them as *one* having authority, and not as the scribes.

Matt. 11:1. And it came to pass, when Jesus had made an end of commanding his twelve disciples, he departed thence to teach and to preach in their cities.

Matt. 21:23. And when he was come into the temple, the chief priests and the elders of the people came unto him as he was teaching, and said, By what authority doest thou these things? and who gave thee this authority?

Matt. 22:16. And they sent out unto him their disciples with the Herodians, saying, Master, we know that thou art true, and teachest the way of God in truth, neither carest thou for any *man:* for thou regardest not the person of men. Mark 12:14; Luke 20:21.

Matt. 23:8. But be not ye called Rabbi: for one is your Master, *even* Christ; and all ye are brethren.

Matt. 26:55. In that same hour said Jesus to the multitudes, Are ye come out as against a thief with swords and staves for to take me? I sat daily with you teaching in the temple, and ye laid no hold on me.

Mark 4:1. And he began again to teach by the sea side: and there was gathered unto him a great multitude, so that he entered into a ship, and sat in the sea; and the whole multitude was by the sea on the land. Matt. 5:1.

Luke 4:15. And he taught in their synagogues, being glorified of all.

Luke 6:6. And it came to pass also on another sabbath, that he entered into the synagogue and taught: and there was a man whose right hand was withered.

Luke 23:5. And they were the more fierce, saying, He stirreth up the people, teaching throughout all Jewry, beginning from Galilee to this place.

John 3:2. The same came to Jesus by night, and said unto him, Rabbi, we know that thou art a teacher come from God:

Acts 1:1. The former treatise have I made, O Theophilus, of all that Jesus began both to do and teach,

TEMPTATION OF: Isa. 7:16. For before the child shall know to refuse the evil, and choose the good, the land that thou abhorrest shall be forsaken of both her kings.

Matt. 4:1. Then was Jesus led up of the spirit into the wilderness to be tempted of the devil. 2. And when he had fasted forty days and forty nights, he was afterward an hungred. 3. And when the tempter came to him, he said, If thou be the Son of God, command that these stones be made bread. 4. But he answered and said, It is written, Man shall not live by bread alone, but by every word that proceedeth out of the mouth of God. 5. Then the devil taketh him up into the holy city, and setteth him on a pinnacle of the temple. 6. And saith unto him, If thou be the Son of God, cast thyself down: for it is written, He shall give his angels charge concerning thee: and in *their* hands they shall bear thee up, lest at any time thou dash thy foot against a stone. 7. Jesus said unto him, It is written again, Thou shalt not tempt the Lord thy God. 8. Again, the devil taketh him up into an ex-

ceeding high mountain, and sheweth him all the kingdoms of the world, and the glory of them; 9. And saith unto him, All these things will I give thee, if thou wilt fall down and worship me. 10. Then saith Jesus unto him, Get thee hence, Satan: for it is written, Thou shalt worship the Lord thy God, and him only shalt thou serve. 11. Then the devil leaveth him, and, behold, angels came and ministered unto him. Mark 1:12,13; Luke 4:1–13.

Luke 22:28. Ye are they which have continued with me in my temptations.

John 14:30. The prince of this world cometh, and hath nothing in me.

Heb. 2:18. For in that he himself hath suffered being tempted, he is able to succour them that are tempted.

Heb. 4:15. For we have not an high priest which cannot be touched with the feeling of our infirmities; but was in all points tempted like as *we are, yet* without sin.

TYPES OF: See TYPES.

UNCHANGEABLE: Heb. 13:8. Jesus Christ the same yesterday, and to day, and for ever.

UNION OF, WITH THE RIGHTEOUS: See RIGHTEOUS, UNION OF, WITH CHRIST.

WISDOM OF: See OMNISCIENCE OF, above.

WORSHIP OF: Josh. 5:14. And he said, Nay; but *as* captain of the host of the LORD am I now come. And Joshua fell on his face to the earth, and did worship, and said unto him, What saith my lord unto his servant? 15. And the captain of the LORD's host said unto Joshua, Loose thy shoe from off thy foot; for the place whereon thou standest *is* holy. And Joshua did so.

Psa. 45:11. He *is* thy Lord; and worship thou him. 17. I will make thy name to be remembered in all generations: therefore shall the people praise thee for ever and ever.

Matt. 2:2. Saying, Where is he that is born King of the Jews? for we have seen his star in the east, and are come to worship him. 11. And when they were come into the house, they saw the young child with Mary his mother, and fell down, and worshipped him:

Matt. 9:18. While he spake these things unto them, behold, there came a certain ruler, and worshipped him, saying, My daughter is even now dead: but come and lay thy hand upon her, and she shall live.

Matt. 14:33. Then they that were in the ship came and worshipped him, saying, Of a truth thou art the Son of God.

Matt. 15:25. Then came she and worshipped him, saying, Lord, help me.

Matt. 20:20. Then came to him the mother of Zebedee's children with her sons, worshipping *him,* and desiring a certain thing of him.

Matt. 28:9. Jesus met them, saying, All hail. And they came and held him by the feet, and worshipped him. 16. Then the eleven disciples went away into Galilee, into a mountain where Jesus had appointed them. 17. And when they saw him, they worshipped him: but some doubted.

Mark 3:11. And unclean spirits, when they saw him, fell down before him, and cried, saying, Thou art the Son of God.

Mark 5:6. But when he saw Jesus afar off, he ran and worshipped him, 7. And cried with a loud voice, and said, What have I to do with thee, Jesus, *thou* Son of the most high God? I adjure thee by God, that thou torment me not.

Mark 11:9. They that went before, and they that followed, cried, saying, Hosanna; Blessed *is* he that cometh in the name of the Lord: 10. Blessed *be* the kingdom of our father David, that cometh in the name of the Lord: Hosanna in the highest. Matt. 21:9; John 12:13.

Luke 4:41. And devils also came out of many, crying out, and saying, Thou art Christ the Son of God. And he rebuking *them* suffered them not to speak: for they knew that he was Christ.

Luke 5:8. When Simon Peter saw *it*, he fell down at Jesus' knees, saying, Depart from me; for I am a sinful man, O Lord.

Luke 23:42. He said unto Jesus, Lord, remember me when thou comest into thy kingdom.

Luke 24:52. They worshipped him, and returned to Jerusalem with great joy:

John 5:23. All *men* should honour the Son, even as they honour the Father. He that honoureth not the Son honoureth not the Father which hath sent him.

John 9:38. And he said, Lord, I believe. And he worshipped him.

Acts 7:59. They stoned Stephen, calling upon *God*, and saying, Lord Jesus, receive my spirit. 60. And he kneeled down, and cried with a loud voice, Lord, lay not this sin to their charge. And when he had said this, he fell asleep. Acts 1:24.

1 Cor. 1:2. With all that in every place call upon the name of Jesus Christ our Lord, both their's and our's:

2 Cor. 12:8. I besought the Lord thrice, that it might depart from me. 9. And he said unto me, My grace is sufficient for thee: for my strength is made perfect in weakness.

Phil. 2:10. At the name of Jesus every knee should bow, of *things* in heaven, and *things* in earth, and *things* under the earth; 11. And *that* every tongue should confess that Jesus Christ *is* Lord, to the glory of God the Father.

1 Tim. 1:12. And I thank Christ Jesus our Lord, who hath enabled me, for that he counted me faithful, putting me into the ministry;

Heb. 1:6. When he bringeth in the first-begotten into the world, he saith, And let all the angels of God worship him.

2 Pet. 3:18. But grow in grace, and *in* the knowledge of our Lord and Saviour Jesus Christ. To him *be* glory both now and for ever. Amen.

Rev. 5:8. The four beasts and four *and* twenty elders fell down before the Lamb, having every one of them harps, and golden vials full of odours, which are the prayers of saints. 9. And they sung a new song, saying, Thou art worthy to take the book, and to open the seals thereof: 12. Worthy is the Lamb that was slain to receive power, and riches, and wisdom, and strength, and honour, and glory, and blessing. 13. And every creature which is in heaven, and on the earth, and under the earth, and such as are in the sea, and all that are in them, heard I saying, Blessing, and honour, and glory, and power, *be* unto him that sitteth upon the throne, and unto the Lamb for ever and ever. 14. And the four beasts said, Amen. And the four *and* twenty elders fell down and worshipped him that liveth for ever and ever.

Rev. 7:10. Salvation to our God which sitteth upon the throne, and unto the Lamb.

ZEAL OF: Psa. 69:9. The zeal of thine house hath eaten me up;

Isa. 59:17. He put on the garments of vengeance *for* clothing, and was clad with zeal as a cloke.

Matt. 4:23. Jesus went about all Galilee, teaching in their synagogues, and preaching the gospel of the kingdom, and healing all manner of sickness and all manner of disease among the people. Matt. 9:35; Mark 6:6.

Mark 3:20. The multitude cometh together again, so that they could not so much as eat bread. 21. And when his friends heard *of* it, they went out to lay hold on him: for they said, He is beside himself.

Luke 2:49. He said unto them, How is it that ye sought me? wist ye not that I must be about my Father's business?

Luke 4:43. I must preach the kingdom of God to other cities also: for therefore am I sent. Mark 1:38.

Luke 8:1. He went throughout every city and village, preaching and shewing the glad tidings of the kingdom of God:

Luke 9:51. When the time was come that he should be received up, he stedfastly set his face to go to Jerusalem,

Luke 12:50. I have a baptism to be baptized with; and how am I straitened till it be accomplished!

Luke 13:32. And he said unto them, Go ye, and tell that fox, Behold, I cast out devils, and I do cures to day and to morrow, and the third *day* I shall be perfected. 33. Nevertheless I must walk to day, and to morrow, and the *day* following:

John 2:17. His disciples remembered that it was written, The zeal of thine house hath eaten me up.

John 4:32. He said unto them, I have meat to eat that ye know not of. 34. My meat is to do the will of him that sent me, and to finish his work.

John 9:4. I must work the works of him that sent me, while it is day: the night cometh, when no man can work.

Acts 10:38. Who went about doing good, and healing all that were oppressed of the devil; for God was with him.

Rom. 15:3. Even Christ pleased not himself; but, as it is written, The reproaches of them that reproached thee fell on me.

1 Tim. 6:13. I give thee charge in the sight of God, . . . and ' fore Christ Jesus, who before Pontius Pilate witnessed a good confession;

JETHER. 1. Son of Gideon, Feared to slay the Midianitish kings, Judg. 8:20.

2. An Ishmaelite who married David's sister, 1 Kin. 2:5,32; 1 Chr. 2:17. Called ITHRA, 2 Sam. 17:25.

3. A son of Jada, 1 Chr. 2:32.

4. A son of Ezra, 1 Chr. 4:17.

5. A chief of the line of Asher, 1 Chr. 7:38.

JETHETH, a duke of Esau, Gen. 36: 40; 1 Chr. 1:51.

JETHLAH, a city of Dan, Josh. 19:42.

JETHRO, called RAGUEL and REUEL. A priest of Midian. Moses spent forty years of exile with, and married his daughter, Ex. 2:15–22; 3:1; 4:18; Num. 10:29.

JETUR, son of Ishmael, Gen. 25:15; 1 Chr. 1:31.

JEUEL, a descendent of Zerah, 1 Chr. 9:6.

JEUSH. 1. Son of Esau, Gen. 36:5,14, 18; 1 Chr. 1:35.

2. A Benjamite, 1 Chr. 7:10.

3. A Gershonite Levite, 1 Chr. 23:10,11.

4. Son of Rehoboam, 2 Chr. 11:19.

JEUZ, head of a Benjamite family, 1 Chr. 8:10.

JEWELS. Betrothal presents of, Gen. 24:53. Borrowed from Egyptians by Israelites, Ex. 3:22; 11:2; 12:35. Dedicated to the tabernacle, Ex. 35:22; Num. 31:50–52. Regarded by Jacob as obnoxious to holiness, Gen. 35:4; Ex. 33:4–6; Isa. 3:18–21. Tokens of love, Ezek. 16:11–13. Worn by men, Ezek. 23:42.

FIGURATIVE: Prov. 20:15; Mal. 3:17.

See BRACELET; CHAIR; EARRINGS; MUFFLER; PEARL; RING; SEAL; STONE, PRECIOUS.

JEWS. A corrupted form, doubtless, of Judah, and applied to the people of the kingdom of Judah and Benjamin, 2 Kin. 16:6; 25:25; 2 Chr. 32:18. After the dissolution of the kingdom of Israel the name was applied to all Israelites, as well as to those of the two tribes.

See ISRAEL.

JEZANIAH. See JAAZANIAH.

JEZEBEL. Daughter of Ethbaal, a Zidonian, and wife of Ahab, 1 Kin. 16:31. Was an idolatress and persecuted the prophets of God, 1 Kin. 18:4,13,19; 2 Kin. 3:2,13; 9:7,22. Vowed to kill Elijah, 1 Kin. 19:1–3. Wickedly accomplishes the death of Naboth, 1 Kin. 21:5–16. Death of, foretold, 1 Kin. 21:23; 2 Kin. 9:10. Death of, at the hand of Jehu, 2 Kin. 9:30–37.

FIGURATIVE: Rev. 2:20.

JEZER, son of Naphtali, Gen. 46:24; Num. 26:49; 1 Chr. 7:13.

JEZIAH, an Israelite who married an idolatrous wife, Ezra 10:25.

JEZIEL, a disaffected Israelite who joined David at Ziklag, 1 Chr. 12:3.

JEZLIAH, a Benjamite, 1 Chr. 8:18.

JEZOAR, son of Helah, 1 Chr. 4:7.

JEZRAHIAH, a leader of the choir, Neh. 12:42.

JEZREEL. 1. A city in the S. of Judah, Josh. 15:56; 1 Sam. 25:43; 27:3; 29:1,11.

2. A city of Issachar, Josh. 19:18; 2 Sam. 2:9. Ahab's residence in, 1 Kin. 18:45,46; 21:1. Naboth's vineyard in, 1 Kin. 21:1. Joram's residence in, 2 Kin. 8:29. Jehu kills King Ahab, his wife, and friends at, 2 Kin. 9:15–37; 10:11. Prophecies concerning, Hos. 1:4,5,11.

3. A valley, Josh. 17:16. Place of Gideon's battle with the Midianites, Judg. 6:33. Place of the defeat of the Israelites under Saul and Jonathan, 1 Sam. 29:1,11; 31:1–6; 2 Sam. 4:4.

4. A descendant of Etam, 1 Chr. 4:3.

5. Figurative of Israel, Hos. 1:4,5,11.

JIBSAM, son of Tola, 1 Chr. 7:2.

JIDLAPH, son of Nahor, Gen. 22:22.

JIMNAH, called also JIMNA. Son of Asher, Gen. 46:17; Num. 26:44.

JIPHTAH, a city of Judah, Josh. 15:43.

JIPHTHAH-EL, a valley in Zebulun, Josh. 19:14,27.

JOAB. 1. Son of David's sister, 1 Chr. 2:16. Commander of David's army, 2 Sam. 8:16; 20:23; 1 Chr. 11:6; 18:15; 27:34. Dedicated spoils of his battles, 1 Chr. 26:28. Defeated the Jebusites, 1 Chr. 11:6. Defeats and slays Abner, 2 Sam. 2:13–32; 3:27; 1 Kin. 2:5. Destroys all the males in Edom, 1 Kin. 11:16. (See Psa. 60, title.) Defeats the Ammonites, 2 Sam. 10:7–14; 1 Chr. 19:6–15. Captures Rabbah, 2 Sam. 11:1,15–25; 12:26–29; 1 Chr. 20:1,2.

Procures the return of Absalom to Jerusalem, 2 Sam. 14:1–24. Barley field of, burned by Absalom, 2 Sam. 14:29–33. Pursues and kills Absalom, 2 Sam. 18. Censures David for lamenting the death of Absalom, 2 Sam. 19:1–8. Replaced by Amasa as commander of David's army, 2 Sam. 17: 25; 19:13. Kills Amasa, 2 Sam. 20:8–13; 1 Kin. 2:5. Causes Sheba to be put to death, 2 Sam. 20:16–22. Opposes the numbering of the people, 2 Sam. 24:3; 1 Chr. 21:3. Numbers the people, 2 Sam. 24:4–9; 1 Chr. 21:4,5; 27:23,24. Supports Adonijah as successor to David, 1 Kin. 1:7; 2:28. Slain by Benaiah, under Solomon's order, 1 Kin. 2:29–34.

2. A grandson of Kenaz, 1 Chr. 4:14.

3. An Israelite (or the name of two Israelites) whose descendants returned from Babylon to Jerusalem, Ezra 2:6; 8:9; Neh. 7:11.

4. "House of Joab," 1 Chr. 2:54. Probably identical with 1.

JOAH. 1. Son of Asaph, 2 Kin. 18:18,26; Isa. 36:3,11,22.

2. A descendant of Gershom, 1 Chr. 6:21; 2 Chr. 29:12.

3. A son of Obed-edom, 1 Chr. 26:4.

4. A Levite, who repaired the temple, 2 Chr. 34:8.

JOAHAZ, father of Joah, 2 Chr. 34:8.

JOANNA. 1. Wife of Chuza, the steward of Herod Agrippa, and a disciple of Jesus, Luke 8:3; 24:10.

2. An ancestor of Jesus, Luke 3:27.

JOASH. 1. Son of Becher, 1 Chr. 7:8.

2. Keeper of the stores of oil, 1 Chr. 27:28.

3. Father of Gideon, Judg. 6:11,29,31; 7: 14; 8:13,29-32.

4. Son of Ahab, king of Israel, 1 Kin. 22:26; 2 Chr. 18:25.

5. Called also JEHOASH. Son of Ahaziah and king of Judah. Saved from his grandmother by Jehosheba, his aunt, and hidden for six years, 2 Kin. 11:1-3; 2 Chr. 22:11,12. Anointed king by the priest, Jehoiada, 2 Kin. 11:12-21; 2 Chr. 23. Righteousness of, under influence of Jehoiada, 2 Kin. 12:2; 2 Chr. 24: 2. Repaired the temple, 2 Kin. 12:4-16; 2 Chr. 24:4-14,27. Wickedness of, after Jehoiada's death, 2 Chr. 24:17-22. Procured peace from Hazael, king of Syria, by gift of dedicated treasures from the temple, 2 Kin. 12:17,18; 2 Chr. 24:23,24. Prophecy against, 2 Chr. 24:19,20. Put Jehoiada's son to death, 2 Chr. 24:20-22; Matt. 23:35. Diseases of, 2 Chr. 24:25. Conspired against and slain, 2 Kin. 12:20,21; 2 Chr. 24:25,26.

6. A king of Israel. See JEHOAHAZ.

7. A descendant of Shelah, 1 Chr. 4:22.

8. One of David's officers, 1 Chr. 12:3.

JOB. 1. A man who dwelt in Uz, Job 1:1. Righteousness of, Job 1:1,5,8; 2:3; Ezek. 14:14,20. Riches of, Job 1:3. Trial of, by affliction of Satan, Job 1:13-19; 2:7-10. Fortitude of, Job 1:20-22; 2:10; Jas. 5:11. Visited by Eliphaz, Bildad, and Zophar as comforters, Job 2:11-13. Complaints of, and replies by his three friends to, Job chapters 3-37. Replied to by God, Job chapters 38-41. Submission of, to God, Job 40:3-5; 42:1-6. Later blessings and riches of, Job 42:10-16. Death of, Job 42:16,17.

2. See JASHUB.

JOBAB. 1. Son of Joktan, Gen. 10:29; 1 Chr. 1:23.

2. A king of Edom, Gen. 36:33,34; 1 Chr. 1:44,45.

3. A king of Madon, Josh. 11:1.

4. Name of two Benjamites of whom little is known, 1 Chr. 8:9,18.

JOCHEBED. Mother of Miriam, Aaron, and Moses, Ex. 6:20; Num. 26:59. Nurses Moses when he is adopted by Pharaoh's daughter, Ex. 2:1-9.

JOED, a Benjamite, Neh. 11:7.

JOEL. 1. Son of Samuel, 1 Sam. 8:2; 1 Chr. 6:33; 15:17. Called VASHNI, 1 Chr. 6:28.

2. A Simeonite, 1 Chr. 4:35.

3. A Reubenite, 1 Chr. 5:4,8.

4. A Gadite, 1 Chr. 5:12.

5. A Kohathite Levite, 1 Chr. 6:36.

6. Descendant of Issachar, 1 Chr. 7:3.

7. One of David's valiant men, 1 Chr. 11:

38. Called "IGAL, son of Nathan," 2 Sam. 23:36.

8. Name of two Gershonites, 1 Chr. 15: 7,11; 23:8; 26:22.

9. Prince of Manasseh, 1 Chr. 27:20.

10. A Kohathite who assisted in the cleansing of the temple, 2 Chr. 29:12.

11. One of Nebo's family, Ezra 10:43.

12. Son of Zichri, Neh. 11:9.

13. One of the twelve minor prophets, probably lived in the days of Uzziah, Joel 1:1; Acts 2:16. Declares the terribleness of God's judgments, Joel 1; 2:1-11. Exhorts to repentance, Joel 1:12-32. Denounces judgments against the enemies of God, Joel 3:1-17. Sets forth the blessings of the church, Joel 3:18-21.

JOELAH, son of Jeroham, 1 Chr. 12:7.

JOEZER, a Korhite, who joined David at Ziklag, 1 Chr. 12:6.

JOGBEHAH, a place in Gad, Num. 32: 35; Judg. 8:11.

JOGLI, a prince of Dan, Num. 34:22.

JOHA. 1. A Benjamite, 1 Chr. 8:16.

2. One of David's valiant men, 1 Chr. 11:45.

JOHANAN. 1. A Jewish captain, 2 Kin. 25:22-24. Warns Gedaliah against Ishmael, Jer. 40:13-16. Ishmael defeated by, Jer. 41:11-15. Sought prayers of Jeremiah, Jer. 42:2,3. Disobeyed Jeremiah and took him to Egypt, Jer. 43:1-7.

2. Son of Josiah, 1 Chr. 3:15.

3. A son of Elioenai, 1 Chr. 3:24.

4. A Levite, 1 Chr. 6:9,10.

5. Two Israelites who joined David at Ziklag, 1 Chr. 12:4,12.

6. An Ephraimite, 2 Chr. 28:12.

7. A returned exile, Ezra 8:12.

8. A priest, Ezra 10:6; Neh. 12:22,23. Probably identical with Jonathan, Neh. 12:11.

9. Son of Tobiah the Ammonite, Neh. 6:18.

JOHN. 1. The Baptist: Prophecies concerning, Isa. 40:3; Mal. 4:5,6; Luke 1:11-17. Miraculous birth of, Luke 1:11-20,57-65. Dwells in the desert, Matt. 3:1; Mark 1:4; Luke 1:80; 3:2,3. Mission of, Matt. 17:11; Mark 1:2-8; Luke 1:15-17,76-79; 3:4-6; John 1:7,8,15,22-28,31-34; 5:32-35; Acts 13:24,25; 19:4. Ministry of, Matt. 3:1-3; Mark 1:4; Luke 3:2,3; John 1:6-8. His influence upon the public mind, Matt. 3:5,6; 14:5; 21:32; Mark 1:5; 11:32; Luke 3:7,15; 20:6; John 1:35-40. Testifies to the messiahship of Jesus, Matt. 3:11,12; Mark 1:7,8; Luke 3: 16,17; John 1:15,26-36; 3:23-36; 5:32,33; 10:41; Acts 13:25. Teaches his disciples to pray, Luke 11:1; to fast, Luke 5:33. The baptism which he taught, see BAPTISM. Baptizes Jesus, Matt. 3:13-16; Mark 1:9-11; Luke 3: 21,22; John 1:32. The testimony of Jesus concerning, John 5:32-35; Matt. 17:12,13; 21: 32; Mark 9:13; see below, Jesus discourses upon. His ministry not attested by miracles, John 10:41. Reproves Herod on account of his incest; Herod imprisons him; beheads him, Matt. 4:12; 14:1-12; Mark 6:16-29; 9:13; Luke 3:18-20. Sends two disciples to Jesus, Matt. 11:2–6; Luke 7:18–23. Herod falsely supposes Jesus to be, Matt. 14:1,2; 16:14; Mark 6:14,16; Luke 9:19. Character of, Mark 6:20; John 5:35. Jesus discourses upon, Matt. 11:7–19; Luke 7:24–33. Affected probably by the doctrines of the stoics, Matt. 11:18; Mark 1:6; Luke 1:80. A Nazarite, Matt. 11:18; Luke 1:15; 7:33.

2. The Apostle: Intimately associated with Jesus, John 13:23–26; 21:20; is present when Jesus performs the following miracles: Healing of Peter's mother-in-law, Matt. 8: 14,15; Mark 1:30,31; Luke 4:38,39; raising of the daughter of Jairus, Mark 5:37; Luke 8:51; the two draughts of fishes, Luke 5:10; John 21:1–7; transfiguration, Matt. 17:1; Mark 9:2; Luke 9:28. Is present with Jesus in the garden, Matt. 26:37; Mark 14:33; Luke 22:39. Intolerance of, Mark 9:38; Luke 9:49,50,54–56. Civil ambitions of, Matt. 20:20–24; Mark 10:35–41. Prepares the passover, Matt. 26: 18,19; Mark 14:13–16; Luke 22:8–13. Present at the trial of Jesus before the high priest, John 18:15,16; at the crucifixion, John 19:26, 27; at the sepulcher, John 20:2–8; when Jesus manifested himself at the Sea of Galilee, John 21; with Peter in the temple, Acts 3:1–11. Dwells in Jerusalem, Acts 1:13. Is intrusted with the care of Mary, mother of Jesus, John 19:26. Imprisoned by the rulers of the Jews, Acts 4:1–19. Sent by the church with the commission to Samaria, Acts 8:14–17. A pillar of the church, Gal. 2:9. Writes to the churches, see the EPISTLES OF JOHN. Writes his apocalyptic vision from Patmos, Rev. 1:9. Prophecy concerning, Rev. 10:11.

3. A kinsman of Annas the high priest, Acts 4:6.

4. Whose surname was Mark. See MARK.

JOIADA, son and successor of Eliashib in the high priesthood, Neh. 12:10,11,22; 13: 28.

JOIAKIM, a high priest, Neh. 12:10,12,26.

JOIARIB. 1. A returned exile, Ezra 8:16.

2. A descendant of Judah, Neh. 11:5.

3. A priest who returned from Babylon, Neh. 12:6,19.

4. See JEHOIARIB.

JOKDEAM, a city of Judah. Josh. 15:56.

JOKIM, a descendant of Shelah, 1 Chr. 4:22.

JOKMEAM, a Levitical city of Ephraim, 1 Chr. 6:68.

JOKNEAM, a Levitical city of Zebulun, Josh. 12:22; 19:11; 21:34.

See JOKMEAM.

JOKSHAN, son of Abraham, by Keturah, Gen. 25:2,3,6; 1 Chr. 1:32.

JOKTAN, son of Eber, Gen. 10:25,26,29; 1 Chr. 1:19,20,23.

JOKTHEEL. 1. A city of Judah, Josh. 15:38.

2. A name given by Amaziah to Selah, a stronghold of Edom, 2 Kin. 14:7; 2 Chr. 25:11:

12. Called rock in Judg. 1:36.

JONADAB. 1. Nephew of David. His complicity with Amnon in his rape of Tamar,

2 Sam. 13:3–5. Comforts David on death of Amnon, 2 Sam. 13:32–35.

2. Called also JEHONADAB. A Rechabite and companion of Jehu, 2 Kin. 10:15–23. His sons refuse to drink wine in obedience to his command, Jer. 35:5–10,16–19.

See RECHABITES.

JONAH, called also JONAS. A prophet of Israel, 2 Kin. 14:25. Sent by God to warn Nineveh, Jonah 1:1,2. Disobedience and punishment of, Jonah 1:3–17. Repentance and deliverance of, Jonah 2; Matt. 12:40. Brought Ninevites to repentance, Jonah 3; Matt. 12:41. Displeased with God's mercy to Nineveh; reproved, Jonah 4. Is a sign, Matt. 16:4; Luke 11:29,30.

JONAN, an ancestor of Christ, Luke 3:30.

JONAS. 1. See JONAH.

2. Father of Peter, John 21:15–17. Called JONA, John 1:42.

JONATHAN. 1. A Levite of Bethlehem, who becomes a priest for Micah; accepts idolatry; joins the Danites, Judg. 17: 7–13; 18:1–30.

2. Son of Saul, 1 Sam. 14:49. Victory of, over the Philistine garrison of Geba, 1 Sam. 13:3,4,16; over Philistines at Michmash, 1 Sam. 14:1–18. Under Saul's curse pronounced against any who might take food before he was avenged of his enemies, 1 Sam. 14:24–30, 43. Rescued by the people, 1 Sam. 14:43–45. Love of, for David, 1 Sam. 18:1–4; 19:1–7; 20; 23:16–18. Killed in battle with Philistines, 1 Sam. 31:2,6; 1 Chr. 10:2; 2 Sam. 21:12–14. Buried by inhabitants of Jabesh-gilead, 1 Sam. 31:11–13. Mourned by David, 2 Sam. 1:12,17–27. Son of, cared for by David, 2 Sam. 4:4; 9; 1 Chr. 8:34.

3. Son of Abiathar, 2 Sam. 15:27. Acts as spy for David, 2 Sam. 15:27,28; 17:17–22. Informs Adonijah of Solomon's succession to David, 1 Kin. 1:42–48.

4. Nephew of David, slays a giant, and becomes one of David's chief warriors, 2 Sam. 21:21; 1 Chr. 20:7.

5. One of David's heroes, 2 Sam. 23:32; 1 Chr. 11:34.

6. A son of Jada, 1 Chr. 2:32,33.

7. Secretary of the cabinet of David, 1 Chr. 27:32.

8. Father of Ebed, Ezra 8:6.

9. Son of Asahel, Ezra 10:15.

10. Called also JOHANAN. A descendant of Jeshua, Neh. 12:11,22.

11. Name of two priests, Neh. 12:14,35.

12. A scribe, Jer. 37:15,20; 38:26.

13. Son of Kareah, Jer. 40:8.

JOPPA. A seaport, Josh. 19:46. Exports from, 2 Chr. 2:16; Ezra 3:7. Passenger traffic from, Jonah 1:3. Peter performs a miracle at, Acts 9:36–43; has a vision of a sheet let down from heaven at, Acts 10:9–18.

JORAH, a returned exile, Ezra 2:18.

JORAI, a Gadite, 1 Chr. 5:13.

JORAM. 1. A son of Toi, 2 Sam. 8:9,10. Called HADORAM, 1 Chr. 18:10.

2. Called also JEHORAM. King of Israel, 2 Kin 1:17; 3:1. King of Syria sends Naaman

to, that he may be healed of his leprosy, 2 Kin. 5:1-27. Has war with the king of Syria, 2 Kin. 6:8-23; 7; 8:28,29; 2 Chr. 22:5,6. Inquires for the particulars concerning Elisha's miracles, 2 Kin. 8:4,5. Slain by Jehu, 2 Kin. 9:14-26.

JORDAN. A river in Palestine. Empties into the Dead Sea, Josh. 15:5. Fords of, Gen. 32:10; Josh. 2:7; Judg. 3:28; 7:24; 8:4; 10: 9; 12:5,6; 2 Sam. 2:29; 17:22,24; 19:15,31; 1 Chr. 19:17. Swelling of, at harvest time, Josh. 3:15; Jer. 12:5; and in the early spring, 1 Chr. 12:15. The waters of, miraculously separated for the passage of the Israelites, Josh. 3; 4; 5:1; Psa. 114:3; of Elijah, 2 Kin. 2: 6-8; of Elisha, 2 Kin. 2:14. Crossed by a ferryboat, 2 Sam. 19:18. Naaman washes in, for the healing of his leprosy, 2 Kin. 5:10-14. John the Baptist baptizes in, Matt. 3:6; Mark 1:5; baptizes Jesus in, Matt. 3:13; Mark 1:9.

PLAIN OF: Gen. 13:10-12. Israelites camped in, Num. 22:1; 26:3,63. Solomon's foundry in, 1 Kin. 7:46; 2 Chr. 4:17.

JORIM, an ancestor of Jesus, Luke 3:29.

JORKOAM, descendant of Caleb, 1 Chr. 2:44.

JOSABAD, a famous archer who joined David at Ziklag, 1 Chr. 12:4.

JOSAPHAT. See JEHOSHAPHAT.

JOSE, an ancestor of Jesus, Luke 3:29.

JOSEDECH. See JEHOZADAK.

JOSEPH. 1. Son of Jacob, Gen. 30:24. Personal appearance of, Gen. 39:6. His father's favorite child, Gen. 33:2; 37:3,4,35; 48:22; 1 Chr. 5:2; John 4:5. His father's partiality for, excites the jealousy of his brethren, Gen. 37:4,11,18-28; Psa. 105:17; Acts 7:9. His prophetic dreams of his fortunes in Egypt, Gen. 37:5-11. Sold into Egypt, Gen. 37:27,28. Is falsely reported to his father as killed by wild beasts, Gen. 37:29-35. Is bought by Potiphar, an officer of Pharaoh, Gen. 37: 36. Is prospered of God, Gen. 39:2-5,21,23. Is falsely accused, and cast into prison; is delivered by the friendship of another prisoner, Gen. 39; 40; Psa. 105:18. Is an interpreter of dreams: of the two prisoners, Gen. 40:5-23; of Pharaoh, Gen. 41:1-37. His name is changed to Zaphnath-paaneah, Gen. 41:45. Is promoted to authority next to Pharaoh at thirty years of age, Gen. 41:37-46; Psa. 105:19-22. Takes to wife the daughter of the priest of On, Gen. 41:45. Provides against the years of famine, Gen. 41:46-57. Exports the produce of Egypt to other countries, Gen. 41:57. Sells the stores of food to the people of Egypt, exacting of them all their money, flocks and herds, lands and lives, Gen. 47:13-26. Exempts the priests from the exactions, Gen. 47:22,26.

His father sends down into Egypt to buy corn, Gen. 42; 43; 44. Reveals himself to his brethren; sends for his father; provides the land of Goshen for his people; and sustains them during the famine, Gen. chapters 45; 46; 47:1-12. His two sons, Gen. 41:50,52. See EPHRAIM; MANASSEH. Mourns the death of his father, Gen. 50:1-14. Exacts a pledge

from his brethren to convey his remains to Canaan, Gen. 50:24,25; Heb. 11:22, with Ex. 13:19; Josh. 24:32; Acts 7:16. Death of, Gen. 50:22-26.

Kindness of heart, Gen. 40:7,8. His integrity, Gen. 39:7-12; humility, Gen. 41:16; 45:7-9; wisdom, Gen. 41:33-57; piety, Gen. 41:51. 52; faith, Gen. 45:5-8. Was a prophet, Gen. 41:38,39; 50:25; Ex. 13:19. God's providence with, Gen. 39:2-5; Psa. 105:17-22. His sons conjointly called JOSEPH, Deut. 33:13-17. Descendants of, Gen. 46:20; Num. 26:28-37.

2. Father of Igal the spy, Num. 13:7.

3. Of the sons of Asaph, 1 Chr. 25:2,9.

4. A returned exile, Ezra 10:42.

5. A priest, Neh. 12:14.

6. Husband of Mary, Matt. 13:55; Mark 6: 3; Matt. 1:18-25; Luke 1:27. His genealogy, Matt. 1:1-16; Luke 3:23-38. An angel appears and testifies to the innocency of his betrothed, Matt. 1:19-24. Dwells at Nazareth, Luke 2:4. Belongs to the city of Bethlehem, Luke 2:4. Goes to Bethlehem to be enrolled, Luke 2:1-4. Jesus born to, Matt. 1: 25; Luke 2:7. Presents Jesus in the temple, Luke 2:22-39. Returns to Nazareth, Luke 2: 39. Warned in a dream to escape to Egypt in order to save the child's life, Matt. 2:13-15. Warned in a dream to return to Nazareth, Matt. 2:19-23. Attends the annual feast at Jerusalem with his family, Luke 2:42-51.

7. Of Arimathæa. Begs the body of Jesus for burial in his own tomb, Matt. 27:57-60; Mark 15:42-47; Luke 23:50-56; John 19:38-42.

8. Three ancestors of Joseph, Luke 3:24, 26,30.

9. Called also BARSABAS, surnamed JUSTUS. One of the two persons nominated in place of Judas, Acts 1:21,22,23.

10. A designation of the ten tribes of Israel, Amos 5:6.

JOSES. 1. One of the brethren of Jesus, Matt. 13:55; 27:56; Mark 6:3; 15:40,47.

2. A Levite, surnamed Barnabas by the apostles, Acts 4:36.

JOSHAH, a descendant of Simeon, 1 Chr. 4:34.

JOSHAPHAT, one of David's valiant men, 1 Chr. 11:43.

JOSHAVIAH, one of David's bodyguard, 1 Chr. 11:46.

JOSHBEKASHAH, son of Heman, 1 Chr. 25:4,24.

JOSHUA. 1. Called also JEHOSHUA, and JEHOSHUAH, and OSHEA. Son of Nun, Num. 13:8; 1 Chr. 7:27. Intimately associated with Moses, Ex. 24:13; 32:17; 33:11. A religious zealot, Num. 11:28. Sent with others to view the promised land, Num. 13:8. Makes favorable report, Num. 14:6-10. Rewarded for his courage and fidelity, Num. 14:30,38; 32:12. Commissioned, ordained, and charged with the responsibilities of Moses's office, Num. 27:18-23; Deut. 1:38; 3:28; 31:3,7,23; 34:9. Divinely inspired, Num. 27:18; Deut. 34:9; Josh. 1:5,9; 3:7; 8:8. His life miraculously preserved when he made a favorable report of the land, Num.

14:10. Promises to, Josh. 1:5-9. Leads the people into the land of Canaan, Josh. chapters 1-4; Acts 7:45; Heb. 4:8. Renews circumcision of the children of Israel; reëstablishes the passover; has a vision of the angel of God, Josh. 5. Besieges and takes Jericho, Josh. 6. Takes Ai, Josh. 7; 8. Makes a league with the Gibeonites, Josh. 9:3-27. The kings of the six nations of the Canaanites confederate against him, Josh. 9:1,2; make war upon the Gibeonites; are defeated and slain, Josh. 10. Defeats seven other kings, Josh. 10:28-43. Makes conquest of Hazor, Josh. 11. Completes the conquest of the whole land, Josh. 11:23. List of the kings whom Joshua smote, Josh. 12. Allots the land, Josh. chapters 13-19. Sets the tabernacle up in Shiloh, Josh. 18:1. Sets apart cities of refuge, Josh. 20; forty-eight cities for the Levites, Josh. 21. Exhortation of, before his death, Josh. 23;24. Survives the Israelites who refused to enter Canaan, Num. 26:63-65. His portion of the land, Josh. 19:49,50. Death and burial of, Josh. 24:29,30. Esteem in which he was held, Josh. 1:16-18. Faith of, Josh. 6:16. Military genius of, as exhibited at the defeat of the Amalekites, Ex. 17:13; at Ai, Josh. 8; in Gibeon, Josh. 10; at Hazor, Josh. 11. Age of, at death, Judg. 2:8.

2. An Israelite, 1 Sam. 6:14,18.

3. A governor of Jerusalem, 2 Kin. 23:8.

4. Called also JESHUA. The high priest of the captivity, Ezra 2:2. Assists Zerubbabel in restoring the temple, Ezra 3; 4:1-6; 5; Hag. 1:1,12-14; 2:2.

SYMBOLICAL: Of the restoration of the church, Zech. 3; 6:9-15.

JOSIAH. 1. King of Judah, 2 Kin. 21: 24-26; 22:1; 1 Chr. 3:14; 2 Chr. 33:25. Ancestor of Jesus, Matt. 1:10,11. Slain in battle with Pharaoh-nechoh, 2 Kin. 23:29,30; 2 Chr. 35:20-24. Lamentations for, 2 Chr. 35: 25. Piety of: exemplified in his repairing the temple, 2 Kin. 22:3-7; 2 Chr. 34:1-4. Solicitude when the copy of the law was discovered and read to him, 2 Kin. 22:8-20; 2 Chr. 34:14-33; in keeping a solemn passover, 2 Kin. 23:21-23; 2 Chr. 35:1-19. Called Josias, Matt. 1:10,11. Prophecies concerning, 1 Kin. 13:1-3. Destroys the altar and high places of idolatry, 2 Kin. 23:3-20,24,25.

2. Son of Zephaniah, Zech. 6:10.

JOSIAS. See JOSIAH, 1.

JOSIBIAH, a Simeonite, 1 Chr. 4:35.

JOSIPHIAH, father of a chief, Ezra 8:10.

JOT, vowel point in Hebrew, Matt. 5:18.

JOTBAH. A place in Judah, 2 Kin. 21: 19. Called JOTBATH in Deut. 10:7.

JOTBATHAH, the twentieth encampment of Israel, Num. 33:33,34.

JOTHAM. 1. Son of Gideon, Judg. 9:5, 57. Rebukes the Shechemites in the parable of the trees, Judg. 9:7-21.

2. Son of Azariah, king of Judah, 2 Kin. 15:5-7,32,38; 1 Chr. 3:12; 2 Chr. 26:21-23; 27. Piety of, 2 Chr. 27. The moral condition of

Israel during his reign, Hos. 4. Ancestor of Jesus, Matt. 1:9.

3. Son of Jahdai, 1 Chr. 2:47.

JOY. Attributed to God, Deut. 28:63; 30:9; Jer. 32:41. In heaven, Luke 15:10-32.

UNCLASSIFIED SCRIPTURES RELATING TO: Deut. 12:18. Thou shalt rejoice before the LORD thy God in all that thou puttest thine hands unto.

1 Sam. 2:1. My heart rejoiceth in the LORD, mine horn is exalted in the LORD: my mouth is enlarged over mine enemies: because I rejoice in thy salvation.

1 Chr. 16:27. Glory and honour *are* in his presence; strength and gladness *are* in his place.

2 Chr. 7:10. On the three and twentieth day of the seventh month he sent the people away into their tents, glad and merry in heart for the goodness that the LORD had shewed unto David, and to Solomon, and to Israel his people.

Ezra 6:22. And kept the feast of unleavened bread seven days with joy: for the LORD had made them joyful, and turned the heart of the king of Assyria unto them, to strengthen their hands in the work of the house of God, the God of Israel.

Neh. 8:10. Then he said unto them, Go your way, eat the fat, and drink the sweet, and send portions unto them for whom nothing is prepared: for *this* day *is* holy unto our Lord: neither be ye sorry; for the joy of the LORD is your strength. 12. And all the people went their way to eat, and to drink, and to send portions, and to make great mirth, because they had understood the words that were declared unto them.

Neh. 12:43. Also that day they offered great sacrifices, and rejoiced: for God had made them rejoice with great joy: the wives also and the children rejoiced: so that the joy of Jerusalem was heard even afar off.

Job 8:21. Till he fill thy mouth with laughing, and thy lips with rejoicing.

Job 22:21. Acquaint now thyself with him, and be at peace: thereby good shall come unto thee. 26. Then shalt thou have thy delight in the Almighty, and shalt lift up thy face unto God.

Job 33:26. He shall pray unto God, and he will be favourable unto him: and he shall see his face with joy: for he will render unto man his righteousness.

Psa. 2:11. Serve the LORD with fear, and rejoice with trembling.

Psa. 4:7. Thou hast put gladness in my heart, more than in the time *that* their corn and their wine increased.

Psa. 5:11. Let all those that put their trust in thee rejoice: let them ever shout for joy, because thou defendest them: let them also that love thy name be joyful in thee.

Psa. 9:2. I will be glad and rejoice in thee: I will sing praise to thy name, O thou most High.

Psa. 13:5. My heart shall rejoice in thy salvation. Psa. 9:14.

Psa. 16:5. The LORD *is* the portion of mine inheritance and of my cup: thou maintainest my lot. 6. The lines are fallen unto me in pleasant *places;* yea, I have a goodly heritage. 8. I have set the LORD always before me: because *he is* at my right hand, I shall not be moved. 9. Therefore my heart is glad, and my glory rejoiceth: my flesh also shall rest in hope. 11. Thou wilt shew me the path of life: in thy presence *is* fulness of joy; at thy right hand *there are* pleasures for evermore.

Psa. 17:15. As for me, I will behold thy face in righteousness: I shall be satisfied, when I awake, with thy likeness.

Psa. 19:8. The statutes of the LORD *are* right, rejoicing the heart:

Psa. 20:5. We will rejoice in thy salvation, and in the name of our God we will set up *our* banners:

Psa. 21:1. The king shall joy in thy strength, O LORD; and in thy salvation how greatly shall he rejoice! 6. Thou hast made him most blessed for ever: thou hast made him exceeding glad with thy countenance.

Psa. 28:7. The LORD *is* my strength and my shield; my heart trusted in him, and I am helped: therefore my heart greatly rejoiceth; and with my song will I praise him.

Psa. 30:5. Weeping may endure for a night, but joy *cometh* in the morning. 11. Thou hast turned for me my mourning into dancing: thou hast put off my sackcloth, and girded me with gladness. *v.* 12.

Psa. 32:11. Be glad in the LORD, and rejoice, ye righteous: and shout for joy, all *ye that are* upright in heart. *vs.* 1,2.

Psa. 33:21. Our heart shall rejoice in him, because we have trusted in his holy name.

Psa. 35:9. My soul shall be joyful in the LORD: it shall rejoice in his salvation.

Psa. 36:8. They shall be abundantly satisfied with the fatness of thy house; and thou shalt make them drink of the river of thy pleasures.

Psa. 40:16. Let all those that seek thee rejoice and be glad in thee: let such as love thy salvation say continually, The LORD be magnified. Psa. 70:4.

Psa. 42:4. I had gone with the multitude, I went with them to the house of God, with the voice of joy and praise,

Psa. 43:4. Then will I go unto the altar of God, unto God my exceeding joy: yea, upon the harp will I praise thee, O God my God.

Psa. 45:15. With gladness and rejoicing shall they be brought: they shall enter into the king's palace.

Psa. 46:4. *There is* a river, the streams whereof shall make glad the city of God,

Psa. 51:8. Make me to hear joy and gladness; *that* the bones *which* thou hast broken may rejoice. 12. Restore unto me the joy of thy salvation.

Psa. 53:6. When God bringeth back the captivity of his people, Jacob shall rejoice, *and* Israel shall be glad. Psa. 14:7.

Psa. 63:5. My soul shall be satisfied as *with* marrow and fatness; and my mouth shall praise *thee* with joyful lips: 6. When I remember thee upon my bed, *and* meditate on thee in the *night* watches. 7. Because thou hast been my help, therefore in the shadow of thy wings will I rejoice. 11. The king shall rejoice in God; every one that sweareth by him shall glory:

Psa. 64:10. The righteous shall be glad in the LORD, and shall trust in him; and all the upright in heart shall glory.

Psa. 68:3. Let the righteous be glad; let them rejoice before God: yea, let them exceedingly rejoice.

Psa. 69:32. The humble shall see *this, and* be glad:

Psa. 71:23. My lips shall greatly rejoice when I sing unto thee; and my soul, which thou hast redeemed.

Psa. 85:6. Wilt thou not revive us again: that thy people may rejoice in thee?

Psa. 89:15. Blessed *is* the people that know the joyful sound: they shall walk, O LORD, in the light of thy countenance. 16. In thy name shall they rejoice all the day: and in thy righteousness shall they be exalted.

Psa. 97:11. Light is sown for the righteous, and gladness for the upright in heart. 12. Rejoice in the LORD, ye righteous;

Psa. 100:1. Make a joyful noise unto the LORD, all ye lands. 2. Serve the LORD with gladness: come before his presence with singing.

Psa. 104:34. My meditation of him shall be sweet: I will be glad in the LORD.

Psa. 105:3. Glory ye in his holy name: let the heart of them rejoice that seek the LORD. 43. He brought forth his people with joy, *and* his chosen with gladness:

Psa. 119:1. Blessed *are* the undefiled in the way, who walk in the law of the LORD. 2. Blessed *are* they that keep his testimonies, *and that* seek him with the whole heart. 14. I have rejoiced in the way of thy testimonies, as *much as* in all riches. 16. I will delight myself in thy statutes: I will not forget thy word. 55. I have remembered thy name, O LORD, in the night, 111. Thy testimonies have I taken as an heritage for ever: for they *are* the rejoicing of my heart. 162. I rejoice at thy word, as one that findeth great spoil. 165. Great peace have they which love thy law: and nothing shall offend them.

Psa. 126:5. They that sow in tears shall reap in joy. 6. He that goeth forth and weepeth, bearing precious seed, shall doubtless come again with rejoicing, bringing his sheaves *with him.*

Psa. 132:16. I will also clothe her priests with salvation: and her saints shall shout aloud for joy.

Psa. 138:5. They shall sing in the ways of the LORD:

Psa. 149:2. Let Israel rejoice in him that made him: let the children of Zion be joyful in their King. 5. Let the saints be joyful in glory: let them sing aloud upon their beds.

Prov. 10:28. The hope of the righteous *shall be* gladness:

Prov. 13:9. The light of the righteous rejoiceth:

Prov. 19:23. The fear of the LORD *tendeth* to life: and *he that hath it* shall abide satisfied;

Prov. 29:6. The righteous doth sing and rejoice. Prov. 28:12.

Eccl. 2:26. For *God* giveth to a man that *is* good in his sight wisdom, and knowledge, and joy: but to the sinner he giveth travail, to gather and to heap up, that he may give to *him that is* good before God.

Isa. 9:3. They joy before thee according to the joy in harvest, *and* as *men* rejoice when they divide the spoil.

Isa. 12:1. And in that day thou shalt say, O LORD, I will praise thee: though thou wast angry with me, thine anger is turned away, and thou comfortedst me. 2. Behold, God *is* my salvation; I will trust, and not be afraid: for the LORD JEHOVAH *is* my strength and *my* song; he also is become my salvation. 3. Therefore with joy shall ye draw water out of the wells of salvation. 4. And in that day shall ye say, Praise the LORD, call upon his name, declare his doings among the people, make mention that his name is exalted. 5. Sing unto the LORD; for he hath done excellent things: this *is* known in all the earth. 6. Cry out and shout, thou inhabitant of Zion: for great *is* the Holy One of Israel in the midst of thee.

Isa. 25:9. Lo, this *is* our God; we have waited for him, and he will save us: this *is* the LORD; we have waited for him, we will be glad, and rejoice in his salvation.

Isa. 29:19. The meek also shall increase *their* joy in the LORD, and the poor among men shall rejoice in the Holy One of Israel.

Isa. 30:29. Ye shall have a song, as in the night, *when* a holy solemnity is kept; and gladness of heart, as when one goeth with a pipe to come into the mountain of the LORD, to the mighty One of Israel.

Isa. 35:1. The wilderness and the solitary place shall be glad for them; and the desert shall rejoice, and blossom as the rose. 2. It shall blossom abundantly, and rejoice even with joy and singing: 10. And the ransomed of the LORD shall return, and come to Zion with songs and everlasting joy upon their heads: they shall obtain joy and gladness, and sorrow and sighing shall flee away.

Isa. 41:16. Thou shalt rejoice in the LORD, *and* shalt glory in the Holy One of Israel.

Isa. 44:23. Sing, O ye heavens; for the LORD hath done *it:* shout, ye lower parts of the earth: break forth into singing, ye mountains, O forest, and every tree therein: for the LORD hath redeemed Jacob, and glorified himself in Israel. Isa. 49:13; 52:9.

Isa. 51:11. The redeemed of the LORD shall return, and come with singing unto Zion; **and everlasting joy** *shall be* upon their head: they shall obtain gladness and joy; *and* sorrow and mourning shall flee away. Isa. 56:7.

Isa. 55:12. Ye shall go out with joy, and be led forth with peace: the mountains and the hills shall break forth before you into singing, and all the trees of the field shall clap *their* hands.

Isa. 61:3. To appoint unto them that mourn in Zion, to give unto them beauty for ashes, the oil of joy for mourning, the garment of praise for the spirit of heaviness; 7. *For* confusion they shall rejoice in their portion: therefore in their land they shall possess the double: everlasting joy shall be unto them. 10. I will greatly rejoice in the LORD, my soul shall be joyful in my God; for he hath clothed me with the garments of salvation, he hath covered me with the robe of righteousness, as a bridegroom decketh *himself* with ornaments, and as a bride adorneth *herself* with her jewels.

Isa. 65:14. My servants shall sing for joy of heart, 18. Be ye glad and rejoice for ever *in that* which I create: for, behold, I create Jerusalem a rejoicing, and her people a joy. 19. And I will rejoice in Jerusalem, and joy in my people: and the voice of weeping shall be no more heard in her, nor the voice of crying.

Isa. 66:10. Rejoice ye with Jerusalem, and be glad with her, all ye that love her: rejoice for joy with her, all ye that mourn for her: 11. That ye may suck, and be satisfied with the breasts of her consolations; that ye may milk out, and be delighted with the abundance of her glory. 12. Behold, I will extend peace to her like a river, and the glory of the Gentiles like a flowing stream: 14. Your heart shall rejoice, and your bones shall flourish like an herb: and the hand of the LORD shall be known toward his servants,

Jer. 15:16. Thy words were found, and I did eat them; and thy word was unto me the joy and rejoicing of mine heart: for I am called by thy name, O LORD God of hosts.

Jer. 31:12. They shall come and sing in the height of Zion, and shall flow together to the goodness of the LORD, for wheat, and for wine, and for oil, and for the young of the flock and of the herd: and their soul shall be as a watered garden; and they shall not sorrow any more at all 13. Then shall the virgin rejoice in the dance, both young men and old together: for I will turn their mourning into joy, and will comfort them, and make them rejoice from their sorrow. 14. And I will satiate the soul of the priests with fatness, and my people shall be satisfied with my goodness, saith the LORD. 25. I have satiated the weary soul, and I have replenished every sorrowful soul. 26. Upon this I awaked, and beheld; and my sleep was sweet unto me.

Jer. 33:6. I will bring it health and cure, and I will cure them, and will reveal unto them the abundance of peace and truth. 11.

The voice of joy, and the voice of gladness, the voice of the bridegroom, and the voice of the bride, the voice of them that shall say, Praise the LORD of hosts: for the LORD *is* good; for his mercy *endureth* for ever: *and* of them that shall bring the sacrifice of praise into the house of the LORD.

Joel 2:23. Be glad then, ye children of Zion, and rejoice in the LORD your God:

Nah. 1:15. Behold upon the mountains the feet of him that bringeth good tidings, that publisheth peace!

Hab. 3:18. I will rejoice in the LORD, I will joy in the God of my salvation.

Zeph. 3:14. Sing, O daughter of Zion; shout, O Israel; be glad and rejoice with all the heart, O daughter of Jerusalem.

Hag. 2:9. In this place will I give peace, saith the LORD of hosts.

Zech. 2:10. Sing and rejoice, O daughter of Zion: for, lo, I come, and I will dwell in the midst of thee, saith the LORD.

Zech. 9:9. Rejoice greatly, O daughter of Zion; shout, O daughter of Jerusalem: behold, thy King cometh unto thee:

Zech. 10:7. And *they of* Ephraim shall be like a mighty *man*, and their heart shall rejoice as through wine: yea, their children shall see *it*, and be glad; their heart shall rejoice in the LORD.

Matt. 25:21. His lord said unto him, Well done, *thou* good and faithful servant: thou hast been faithful over a few things, I will make thee ruler over many things: enter thou into the joy of thy lord.

Luke 1:47. And my spirit hath rejoiced in God my Saviour.

Luke 2:10. And the angel said unto them, Fear not: for, behold, I bring you good tidings of great joy, which shall be to all people.

Luke 6:22. Blessed are ye, when men shall hate you, and when they shall separate you *from their company*, and shall reproach *you*, and cast out your name as evil, for the Son of man's sake. 23. Rejoice ye in that day, and leap for joy: for, behold, your reward *is* great in heaven: for in the like manner did their fathers unto the prophets.

Luke 10:20. But rather rejoice, because your names are written in heaven.

Luke 15:6. And when he cometh home, he calleth together *his* friends and neighbours, saying unto them, Rejoice with me; for I have found my sheep which was lost. 7. I say unto you, that likewise joy shall be in heaven over one sinner that repenteth, more than over ninety and nine just persons, which need no repentance. 8. Either what woman having ten pieces of silver, if she lose one piece, doth not light a candle, and sweep the house, and seek diligently till she find *it?* 10. Likewise, I say unto you, there is joy in the presence of the angels of God over one sinner that repenteth.

Matt. 18:13. 22. But the father said to his servants, Bring forth the best robe, and put *it* on him; and put a ring on his hand, and shoes on *his* feet: 23. And bring hither the fatted calf, and kill *it;* and let us eat, and be merry: 24. For this my son was dead, and is alive again; he was lost, and is found. And they began to be merry. 25. Now his elder son was in the field: and as he came and drew nigh to the house, he heard musick and dancing. 26. And he called one of the servants, and asked what these things meant. 27. And he said unto him, Thy brother is come; and thy father hath killed the fatted calf, because he hath received him safe and sound. 28. And he was angry, and would not go in: therefore came his father out, and entreated him. 29. And he answering said to *his* father, Lo, these many years do I serve thee, neither transgressed I at any time thy commandment: and yet thou never gavest me a kid, that I might make merry with my friends: 30. But as soon as this thy son was come, which hath devoured thy living with harlots, thou hast killed for him the fatted calf. 31. And he said unto him, Son, thou art ever with me, and all that I have is thine. 32. It was meet that we should make merry, and be glad: for this thy brother was dead, and is alive again; and was lost, and is found.

Luke 24:52. And they worshipped him, and returned to Jerusalem with great joy: 53. And were continually in the temple, praising and blessing God.

John 15:11. These things have I spoken unto you, that my joy might remain in you, and *that* your joy might be full. *vs.* 10-32.

John 16:20. Verily, verily, I say unto you, That ye shall weep and lament, but the world shall rejoice: and ye shall be sorrowful, but your sorrow shall be turned into joy. 22. I will see you again, and your heart shall rejoice, and your joy no man taketh from you. 24. Hitherto have ye asked nothing in my name: ask, and ye shall receive, that your joy may be full. 33. These things I have spoken unto you, that in me ye might have peace. In the world ye shall have tribulation: but be of good cheer; I have overcome the world.

John 17:13. These things I speak in the world, that they might have my joy fulfilled in themselves.

Acts 2:28. Thou hast made known to me the ways of life; thou shalt make me full of joy with thy countenance.

Acts 8:8. There was great joy in that city. 39. And when they were come up out of the water, the Spirit of the Lord caught away Philip, that the eunuch saw him no more: and he went on his way rejoicing.

Acts 13:52. The disciples were filled with joy, and with the Holy Ghost.

Acts 16:25. At midnight Paul and Silas prayed, and sang praises unto God: 34. And when he had brought them into his house, he set meat before them, and rejoiced, believing in God with all his house.

Rom. 5:2. By whom also we have access by faith into this grace wherein we stand,

and rejoice in hope of the glory of God. 11. And not only *so*, but we also joy in God through our Lord Jesus Christ, by whom we have now received the atonement.

Rom. 12:12. Rejoicing in hope;

Rom. 14:17. The kingdom of God is not meat and drink; but righteousness, and peace, and joy in the Holy Ghost.

Rom. 15:13. Now the God of hope fill you with all joy and peace in believing, that ye may abound in hope, through the power of the Holy Ghost.

2 Cor. 1:12. For our rejoicing is this, the testimony of our conscience, 24. Not for that we have dominion over your faith, but are helpers of your joy:

2 Cor. 6:10. As sorrowful, yet alway rejoicing; as poor, yet making many rich; as having nothing, and *yet* possessing all things.

2 Cor. 7:4. I am filled with comfort, I am exceeding joyful in all our tribulation.

2 Cor. 8:2. In a great trial of affliction the abundance of their joy and their deep poverty abounded unto the riches of their liberality.

2 Cor. 12:10. Therefore I take pleasure in infirmities, in reproaches, in necessities, in persecutions, in distresses for Christ's sake: for when I am weak, then am I strong.

Gal. 5:22. The fruit of the Spirit is love, joy, peace,

Eph. 5:18. Be filled with the Spirit; 19. Speaking to yourselves in psalms and hymns and spiritual songs, singing and making melody in your heart to the Lord;

Phil. 3:3. For we are the circumcision, which worship God in the spirit, and rejoice in Christ Jesus, and have no confidence in the flesh.

Phil. 4:4. Rejoice in the Lord alway: *and* again I say, Rejoice.

Col. 1:11. Strengthened with all might, according to his glorious power, unto all patience and longsuffering with joyfulness;

1 Thess. 1:6. And ye became followers of us, and of the Lord, having received the word in much affliction, with joy of the Holy Ghost:

1 Thess. 5:16. Rejoice evermore.

Heb. 10:34. For ye had compassion of me in my bonds, and took joyfully the spoiling of your goods, knowing in yourselves that ye have in heaven a better and an enduring substance.

Jas. 1:2. My brethren, count it all joy when ye fall into divers temptations;

Jas. 5:13. Is any ¹ merry? let him sing ² psalms.   [R. V. ¹ cheerful   ² praise]

1 Pet. 1:8. Whom having not seen, ye love; in whom, though now ye see *him* not, yet believing, ye rejoice with joy unspeakable and full of glory:

1 Pet. 4:13. But rejoice, inasmuch as ye are partakers of Christ's sufferings; that, when his glory shall be revealed, ye may be glad also with exceeding joy.

1 John 1:4. And these things write we unto you, that your joy may be full.

Jude 24. Now unto him that is able to keep you from falling, and to present *you* faultless before the presence of his glory with exceeding joy,

INSTANCES OF: Of Moses and the Israelites, when Pharaoh and his army were destroyed, Ex. 15:1-22. Of Deborah and the Israelites, when Sisera was overthrown, Judg. 5. Of Jephthah's daughter, when he returned from his victory over the Ammonites, Judg. 11:34. Of Hannah, when Samuel was born, 1 Sam. 2:1-11. Of Naomi, when Boaz showed kindness to Ruth, Ruth 2:20; 4:14. Of the Israelites: When Saul was presented as their king, 1 Sam. 10:24; when David slew Goliath, 1 Sam. 18:6,7; when they repaired to David to Hebron to make him king, 1 Chr. 12:40; when they took the ark from Kirjath-jearim, 1 Chr. 13:8; when they brought the ark from the house of Obededom to Jerusalem, 1 Chr. 15:16,25,28; when they made gifts to the house of God, 1 Chr. 29:9; when they kept the dedication of the temple, and the feast of tabernacles under Ezra. Ezra 6:16,22. Of the Jews, after hearing, anew, the word of God, Neh. 8:9-18; when they turned away from idolatry, 2 Chr. 15:14,15; 23:18,21; 29:30,36; 30:21,23,26; when the wall of Jerusalem was dedicated, Neh. 12:43; when the foundation of the second temple was laid, Ezra 3:11-13.

Of David, over the offerings of the princes and people for the house of God, 1 Chr. 29: 10-19. Jews, over the hanging of Haman, Esth. 8:15,16, with 7:10.

Of Elisabeth, when Mary visited her, Luke 1:5-44. Of Mary, when she visited Elisabeth, Luke 1:46-56. Of Zecharias, when John was born, Luke 1:67-79. Of angels, when Jesus was born, Luke 2:13,14. Of the shepherds, when they saw the infant Jesus, Luke 2:20. Of the Magi, Matt. 2:10. Of Simeon, when Jesus was presented in the temple, Luke 2:28-32. Of the disciples, because the devils were subject to them, Luke 10:17. Of the father, when his prodigal son returns, Luke 15:20-32. Of angels, when sinners repent, Luke 15:7,10. Of the disciples, when Jesus triumphantly entered Jerusalem, Matt. 21:8,9; Mark 11: 8-10. Of the women who returned from the Lord's sepulcher, Matt. 28:8. The disciple, after the resurrection of Jesus, Luke 24:41. Of the disciples in the temple after the ascension of Jesus, Luke 24:53. Of the disciples in the temple because they had received the gift of the Holy Ghost, Acts 2: 46,47. Of the impotent man, healed by Peter, Acts 3:8. Of Paul, when he went up to Jerusalem, Acts 20:22-24. Of Paul and Silas, in the jail at Philippi, Acts 16:25. Of Rhoda, when she heard Peter at the gate, Acts 12:14. Of the disciples at Jerusalem, when Peter told them about the conversion of Cornelius and other Gentiles, Acts 11:18. Of Barnabas, when he saw the success of the gospel at Antioch, Acts 11:22,23. Of Paul and the Corinthians, because the excommunicated member repented, 2 Cor. 1: 24; 2:3. Of Paul and Titus, because of the hospitality of the Corinthians, 2 Cor. 7:13, with 8:6; Rom. 15:32; 1 Cor. 16:18. Of the Macedonians, when they made a contribution for the Christians at Jerusalem, 2 Cor. 8:2. Of Paul, when he prayed for the Philippians, Phil. 1:4. Of Thessalonians, when they believed Paul's gospel, 1 Thess. 1:6. Of Paul, rejoicing over his converts, 1 Thess. 2:19,20; 3:9; Philem. 7. Of early Christians, when they believed in Jesus, 1 Pet. 1:8,9.

OF THE WICKED: Job 20:5. That the triumphing of the wicked *is* short, and the joy of the hypocrite *but* for a moment?

Prov. 14:13. Even in laughter the heart is sorrowful; and the end of that mirth *is* heaviness.

Prov. 15:21. Folly *is* joy to *him that is* destitute of wisdom:

Eccl. 2:10. And whatsoever mine eyes desired I kept not from them, I withheld not my heart from any joy; for my heart rejoiced in all my labour: and this was my portion of all my labour.

Eccl. 7:6. For as the crackling of thorns under a pot, so *is* the laughter of the fool: this also *is* vanity.

Eccl. 11:8. But if a man live many years, *and* rejoice in them all; yet let him remember the days of darkness; for they shall be many. All that cometh *is* vanity. 9. Rejoice, O young man, in thy youth; and let thy heart cheer thee in the days of thy youth, and walk in the ways of thine heart, and in the sight of thine eyes: but know thou, that for all these *things* God will bring thee into judgment.

Isa. 16:10. And gladness is taken away, and joy out of the plentiful field; and in the vineyards there shall be no singing. neither shall there be shouting: the treaders shall tread out no wine in *their* presses; I have made *their vintage* shouting to cease.

Jas. 4:9. Be afflicted, and mourn, and weep: let your laughter be turned to mourning, and *your* joy to heaviness.

See HAPPINESS; PRAISE; THANKSGIVING.

JOZABAD. 1. Two men of Manasseh, 1 Chr. 12:20.

2. Two Levites, 2 Chr. 31:13; 35:9.

3. Son of Jeshua, Ezra 8:33.

4. A priest, Ezra 10:22.

5. Three Levites, Ezra 10:23; Neh. 8:7; 11:16.

6. One of David's famous warriors, 1 Chr. 12:4.

JOZACHAR. One of the two servants of Joash, king of Judah, who slew him in Millo, 2 Kin. 12:21. Called ZABAD, 2 Chr. 24:26.

JOZADAK. See JEHOZADAK.

JUBAL, inventor of musical instruments, Gen. 4:21.

JUBILEE. Called ACCEPTABLE YEAR OF THE LORD, Isa. 61:2. THE YEAR OF LIBERTY, Ezek. 46:17.

LAWS CONCERNING: Lev. 25:8. And thou shalt number seven sabbaths of years unto thee, seven times seven years; and the space of the seven sabbaths of years shall be unto thee forty and nine years. 9. Then shalt thou cause the trumpet of the jubile to sound on the tenth *day* of the seventh month, in the day of atonement shall ye make the trumpet sound throughout all your land. 10. And ye shall hallow the fiftieth year, and proclaim liberty throughout *all* the land unto all the inhabitants thereof: it shall be a jubile unto you; and ye shall return every man unto his possession, and ye shall return every man unto his family. 11. A jubile shall that fiftieth year be unto you: ye shall not sow, neither reap that which groweth of itself in it, nor gather *the* grapes in it of thy vine undressed. 12. For it *is* the jubile; it shall be holy unto you: ye shall eat the increase thereof out of the field. 13. In the year of this jubile ye shall return every man unto his possession. 14. And if thou sell ought unto thy neighbour, or buyest *ought* of thy neighbour's hand, ye shall not oppress one another: 15. According to the number of years after the jubile thou shalt buy of thy neighbour, *and* according unto the number of years of the fruits he shall sell unto thee: 16. According to the multitude of years thou shalt increase the price thereof, and according to the fewness of years thou shalt diminish the price of it: for *according* to the number *of the years* of the fruits doth he sell unto thee. 17. Ye shall not therefore oppress one another: but thou shalt fear thy God: for I *am* the LORD your God. 18. Wherefore ye shall do my statutes, and keep my judgments, and do them; and ye shall dwell in the land in safety. 19. And the land shall yield her fruit, and ye shall eat your fill, and dwell therein in safety. 20. And if ye shall say, What shall we eat the seventh year? behold, we shall not sow, nor gather in our increase: 21. Then I will command my blessing upon you in the sixth year, and it shall bring forth fruit for three years. 22. And ye shall sow the eighth year, and eat *yet* of old fruit until the ninth year; until her fruits come in ye shall eat *of* the old *store.* 23. The land shall not be sold for ever: for the land *is* mine; for ye *are* strangers and sojourners with me. 24. And in all the land of your possession ye shall grant a redemption for the land. 25. If thy brother be waxen poor, and hath sold away *some* of his possession, and if any of his kin come to redeem it, then shall he redeem that which his brother sold. 26. And if the man have none to redeem it, and himself be able to redeem it; 27. Then let him count the years of the sale thereof, and restore the overplus unto the man to whom he sold it; that he may return unto his possession. 28. But if he be not able to restore *it* to him, then that which is sold shall remain in the hand of him that hath bought it until the year of jubile; and in the jubile it shall go out, and he shall return unto his possession. 29. And if a man sell a dwelling house in a walled city, then he may redeem it within a whole year after it is sold; *within* a full year may he redeem it. 30. And if it be not redeemed within the space of a full year, then the house that *is* in the walled city shall be established for ever to him that bought it throughout his generations: it shall not go out in the jubile. 31. But the houses of the villages which have no wall round about them shall be counted as the fields of the country: they may be redeemed, and they shall go out in the jubile. 32. Notwithstanding the cities of the Levites, *and* the houses of the cities of their possession, may the Levites redeem at any time. 33. And if a man purchase of the Levites, then the house that was sold, and the city of his possession, shall go out in *the year of* jubile: for the houses of the cities of the Levites *are* their possession among the children of Israel. 34. But the field of the suburbs of their cities may not be sold: for it *is* their perpetual possession. 35. And if thy brother be waxen poor, and fallen in decay with thee; then thou shalt relieve him: *yea, though he be* a stranger, or a sojourner, that he may live with thee. 36. Take thou no usury of him, or increase: but fear thy God; that thy brother may live with thee. 37. Thou shalt not give him thy money upon usury, nor lend him thy victuals for increase. 38. I *am* the LORD your God, which brought you forth out of the land of Egypt, to give you the land of Canaan, *and* to be your God. 39. And if thy brother *that dwelleth* by thee be waxen poor, and be sold unto thee; thou shalt not compel him to serve as a bondservant: 40. *But* as an hired servant, *and* as a sojourner, he shall be with thee, *and* shall serve thee unto the year of jubile: 41. And *then* shall he depart from thee, *both* he and his children with him, and shall return unto his own family, and unto the possession of his fathers shall he return. 42. For they *are* my servants, which I brought forth out of the land of Egypt: they shall not be sold as bondmen. 43. Thou shalt not rule over him with rigour; but shalt fear thy God. 44. Both thy bondmen, and thy bondmaids, which thou shalt have, *shall be* of the heathen that are round about you; of them shall ye buy bondmen and bondmaids. 45. Moreover of the children of the strangers that do sojourn among you, of them shall ye buy, and of their families that *are* with you, which they begat in your land: and they shall be your possession. 46. And ye shall take them as an inheritance for your children after you, to inherit *them for* a possession; they shall be your bondmen for ever: but over your brethren the children of Israel, ye shall not rule one over another with rigour. 47. And if a sojourner or stranger wax rich by thee, and thy brother *that dwelleth* by him wax poor, and sell himself unto the stranger *or* sojourner by thee, or to the stock of the stranger's family:

48. After that he is sold he may be redeemed again; one of his brethren may redeem him: 49. Either his uncle, or his uncle's son, may redeem him, or *any* that is nigh of kin unto him of his family may redeem him; or if he be able, he may redeem himself. 50. And he shall reckon with him that bought him from the year that he was sold to him unto the year of jubile: and the price of his sale shall be according unto the number of years, according to the time of an hired servant shall it be with him. 51. If *there be* yet many years *behind*, according unto them he shall give again the price of his redemption out of the money that he was bought for. 52. And if there remain but few years unto the year of jubile, then he shall count with him, *and* according unto his years shall he give him again the price of his redemption. 53. *And* as a yearly hired servant shall he be with him: *and the other* shall not rule with rigour over him in thy sight. 54. And if he be not redeemed in these *years*, then he shall go out in the year of jubile, *both* he, and his children with him. 55. For unto me the children of Israel *are* servants; they *are* my servants whom I brought forth out of the land of Egypt: I *am* the LORD your God.

Lev. 27:17. If he sanctify his field from the year of jubile, according to thy estimation it shall stand. 18. But if he sanctify his field after the jubile, then the priest shall reckon unto him the money according to the years that remain, even unto the year of the jubile, and it shall be abated from thy estimation. 19. And if he that sanctified the field will in any wise redeem it, then he shall add the fifth *part* of the money of thy estimation unto it, and it shall be assured to him. 20. And if he will not redeem the field, or if he have sold the field to another man, it shall not be redeemed any more. 21. But the field, when it goeth out in the jubile, shall be holy unto the LORD, as a field devoted; the possession thereof shall be the priest's. 22. And if *a man* sanctify unto the LORD a field which he hath bought, which *is* not of the fields of his possession; 23. Then the priest shall reckon unto him the worth of thy estimation, *even* unto the year of the jubile: and he shall give thine estimation in that day, *as* a holy thing unto the LORD. 24. In the year of the jubile the field shall return unto him of whom it was bought, *even* to him to whom the possession of the land *did belong*.

Num. 36:4. And when the jubile of the children of Israel shall be, then shall their inheritance be put unto the inheritance of the tribe whereunto they are received: so shall their inheritance be taken away from the inheritance of the tribe of our fathers.

See SABBATIC YEAR.

JUDAH. 1. Son of Jacob, Gen. 35:23. Intercedes for Joseph's life when his brethren were about to slay him, and proposes that they sell him to the Ishmaelites, Gen. 37:26,27.   Takes two wives, Gen. 38:1-6.

Dwells at Chezib, Gen. 38:5. His incest with his daughter-in-law, Gen. 38:12-26. Goes down into Egypt for corn, Gen. 43:1-10; 44:14-34; 46:28. Prophetic benediction of his father upon, Gen. 49:8-12. The ancestor of Jesus, Matt. 1:2,3; Rev. 5:5.

2. Tribe of: Prophecies concerning, Gen. 49:10. Enrollment of the military forces of, at Sinai, Num. 1:26,27; 2:4; at Bezek, 1 Sam. 11:8; 2 Sam. 24:9; in the plain of Moab, Num. 26:22. Place of, in camp and march, Num. 2:3,9; 10:14. By whom commanded, Num. 2:3. Moses' benediction upon, Deut. 33:7. Commissioned of God to lead in the conquest of the promised land, Judg. 1:1-3, with verses 4-21. Make David king, 2 Sam. 2:1-11; 5:4,5. Upbraided by David for lukewarmness toward him after Absalom's defeat, 2 Sam. 19:11-15. Accused by the other tribes of stealing the heart of David, 2 Sam. 19:41-43. Loyal to David at the time of the insurrection led by Sheba, 2 Sam. 20:1,2. Is accorded the birthright forfeited by Reuben, 1 Chr. 5:1,2; 28:4; Psa. 60:7. Loyal to the house of David at the time of the revolt of the ten tribes, 1 Kin. 12:20. Inheritance of, Josh. 15; 18:5; 19:1,9.

3. Name of two exiled priests, Ezra 10:23; Neh. 12:8.

4. A Benjamite, Neh. 11:9.

5. A prince or priest who assisted in the dedication of the walls of Jerusalem, Neh. 12:34,36.

JUDAISM. 1. The religion of the Jews. To yield place to the Gospel, Matt. 3:8,9; 5:17-19,21-44; 9:16,17.

2. A corrupt form of Christianity, Acts 15:1; 21:20-25; Gal. chapters 3-6.

See TEACHERS, FALSE.

JUDAS. 1. Surnamed Iscariot. Chosen as an apostle, Matt. 10:4; Mark 3:19; Luke 6:16; Acts 1:17. Treasurer of the disciples, John 12:6; 13:29. His covetousness exemplified by his protest against the breaking of the box of ointment, John 12:4-6; by his bargain to betray Jesus for a sum of money, Matt. 26:14-16; Mark 14:10,11; Luke 22:3-6; John 13:2. His apostasy, John 17:12. Betrays the Lord, Matt. 26:47-50; Mark 14:43-45; Luke 22:47-49; John 18:2-5; Acts 1:16-25. Returns the money to the rulers of the Jews, Matt. 27:3-10. Hangs himself, Matt. 27:5; Acts 1:18. Prophecies concerning, Matt. 26:21-25; Mark 14:18-21; Luke 22:21-23; John 13:18-26; 17:12; Acts 1:16,20, with Psa. 41:9; 109:8; Zech. 11:12,13.

2. One of the brethren of Jesus, Matt. 13:55; Mark 6:3.

3. Brother of James and writer of the Epistle of Jude, Luke 6:16; Acts 1:13; Jude 1.

4. An apostle, probably identical with LEBBÆUS, or THADDÆUS, John 14:22.

5. Of Galilee, who stirred up a sedition among the Jews soon after the birth of Jesus, Acts 5:37.

6. A disciple who entertained Paul, Acts 9:11.

7. Surnamed BARSABAS. A Christian sent to Antioch with Paul and Barnabas, Acts 15:22-32.

JUDEA. 1. Called also JUDAH and JUDÆA. The southern division of Palestine. It extended from the Jordan and Dead Sea to the Mediterranean, and from Shiloh on the N. to the wilderness on the S., Matt. 4:25; Luke 5:17; John 4:47,54. In Luke 1:5 the term applies to all Palestine. In Matt. 19:1, Mark 10:1, and Luke 23:5 it applies to the territory E. of Jordan.

2. Wilderness of. Called Beth-arabah, Josh. 15:6,61. Assigned to Benjamin, Josh. 18:22. John the Baptist preaches in, Matt. 3:1; Luke 3:3.

JUDGE. Appointed by Persians, Ezra 7:25. Kings and other rulers as, 2 Sam. 8:15; 15:2; 1 Kin. 3:16-28; 10:9; 2 Kin. 8:1-6; Psa. 72:1-4; Matt. 27:11-26; Acts 23:34,35; 24; 25:11,12. Priests and Levites as, Deut. 17:9; 2 Chr. 19:8; Ezek. 44:23,24; Matt. 26:57-62. Women as: Deborah, Judg. 4:4.

Held circuit courts, 1 Sam. 7:16.

See COURTS; JUSTICE; WITNESS.

CHARACTER OF, AND PRECEPTS RELATING TO: Ex. 18:21. Moreover thou shalt provide out of all the people able men, such as fear God, men of truth, hating covetousness; and place *such* over them, *to be* rulers of thousands, *and* rulers of hundreds, rulers of fifties, and rulers of tens: 22. And let them judge the people at all seasons: and it shall be, *that* every great matter they shall bring unto thee, but every small matter they shall judge: so shall it be easier for thyself, and they shall bear *the burden* with thee.

Ex. 22:9. For all manner of trespass, *whether it be* for ox, for ass, for sheep, for raiment, *or* for any manner of lost thing, which *another* challengeth to be his, the cause of both parties shall come before the judges; *and* whom the judges shall condemn, he shall pay double unto his neighbour. 28. Thou shalt not revile the gods, nor curse the ruler of thy people.

Lev. 19:15. Ye shall do no unrighteousness in judgment; thou shalt not respect the person of the poor, nor honour the person of the mighty: *but* in righteousness shalt thou judge thy neighbour.

Deut. 1:12. How can I myself alone bear your cumbrance, and your burden, and your strife? 13. Take you wise men, and understanding, and known among your tribes, and I will make them rulers over you. 14. And ye answered me, and said, The thing which thou hast spoken *is* good *for us* to do. 15. So I took the chief of your tribes, wise men, and known, and made them heads over you, captains over thousands, and captains over hundreds, and captains over fifties, and captains over tens, and officers among your tribes. 16. And I charged your judges at that time, saying, Hear *the causes* between your brethren, and judge righteously between *every* man and his brother, and the stranger *that is* with him. 17. Ye shall not respect persons in judgment; *but* ye shall hear the small as well as the great; ye shall not be afraid of the face of man; for the judgment *is* God's: and the cause that is too hard for you, bring *it* unto me, and I will hear it.

Deut. 16:18. Judges and officers shalt thou make thee in all thy gates, which the LORD thy God giveth thee, throughout thy tribes: and they shall judge the people with just judgment. 19. Thou shalt not wrest judgment; thou shalt not respect persons, neither take a gift: for a gift doth blind the eyes of the wise, and pervert the words of the righteous. 20. That which is altogether just shalt thou follow, that thou mayest live, and inherit the land which the LORD thy God giveth thee.

Deut. 17:8. If there arise a matter too hard for thee in judgment, between blood and blood, between plea and plea, and between stroke and stroke, *being* matters of controversy within thy gates: then shalt thou arise, and get thee up into the place which the LORD thy God shall choose; 9. And thou shalt come unto the priests the Levites, and unto the judge that shall be in those days, and enquire; and they shall shew thee the sentence of judgment: 10. And thou shalt do according to the sentence, which they of that place which the LORD shall choose shall shew thee; and thou shalt observe to do according to all that they inform thee: 11. According to the sentence of the law which they shall teach thee, and according to the judgment which they shall tell thee, thou shalt do: thou shalt not decline from the sentence which they shall shew thee, *to* the right hand, nor *to* the left.

Deut. 19:16. If a false witness rise up against any man to testify against him *that which is* wrong; 17. Then both the men, between whom the controversy *is,* shall stand before the LORD, before the priests and the judges, which shall be in those days; 18. And the judges shall make diligent inquisition: and, behold, *if* the witness *be* a false witness, *and* hath testified falsely against his brother; 19. Then shall ye do unto him, as he had thought to have done unto his brother: so shalt thou put the evil away from among you.

Deut. 25:1. If there be a controversy between men, and they come unto judgment, that *the judges* may judge them; then they shall justify the righteous, and condemn the wicked. 2. And it shall be, if the wicked man *be* worthy to be beaten, that the judge shall cause him to lie down, and to be beaten before his face, according to his fault, by a certain number. 3. Forty stripes he may give him, *and* not exceed: lest, *if* he should exceed, and beat him above these with many stripes, then thy brother should seem vile unto thee.

1 Sam. 2:25. If one man sin against another, the judge shall judge him: but if a man sin against the LORD, who shall intreat for him?

1 Sam. 8:3. And his sons walked not in his ways, but turned aside after lucre, and took bribes, and perverted judgment.

1 Kin. 3:9. Give therefore thy servant an understanding heart to judge thy people, that I may discern between good and bad: for who is able to judge this thy so great a people?

2 Chr. 19:5. And he set judges in the land throughout all the fenced cities of Judah, city by city, 6. And said to the judges, Take heed what ye do: for ye judge not for man, but for the LORD, who *is* with you in the judgment. 7. Wherefore now let the fear of the LORD be upon you; take heed and do *it:* for *there is* no iniquity with the LORD our God, nor respect of persons, nor taking of gifts. 8. Moreover in Jerusalem did Jehoshaphat set of the Levites, and *of* the priests, and of the chief of the fathers of Israel, for the judgment of the LORD, and for controversies, when they returned to Jerusalem. 9. And he charged them, saying, Thus shall ye do in the fear of the LORD, faithfully, and with a perfect heart. 10. And what cause soever shall come to you of your brethren that dwell in their cities, between blood and blood, between law and commandment, statutes and judgments, ye shall even warn them that they trespass not against the LORD, and *so* wrath come upon you, and upon your brethren: this do, and ye shall not trespass.

Psa. 58:1. Do ye indeed speak righteousness, O congregation? do ye judge uprightly, O ye sons of men? 2. Yea, in heart ye work wickedness; ye weigh the violence of your hands in the earth.

Psa. 72:1. Give the king thy judgments, O God, and thy righteousness unto the king's son. 2. He shall judge thy people with righteousness, and thy poor with judgment. 4. He shall judge the poor of the people, he shall save the children of the needy, and shall break in pieces the oppressor. *vs.* 12–14.

Psa. 82:2. How long will ye judge unjustly, and accept the persons of the wicked? 3. Defend the poor and fatherless: do justice to the afflicted and needy. 4. Deliver the poor and needy: rid *them* out of the hand of the wicked.

Prov. 24:23. These *things* also *belong* to the wise. *It is* not good to have respect of persons in judgment.

Isa. 5:22. Woe unto *them that are* mighty to drink wine, and men of strength to mingle strong drink: 23. Which justify the wicked for reward, and take away the righteousness of the righteous from him!

Isa. 28:5. In that day shall the LORD of hosts be for a crown of glory, and for a diadem of beauty, unto the residue of his people, 6. And for a spirit of judgment to him that sitteth in judgment, and for strength to them that turn the battle to the gate.

Ezek. 44:24. In controversy they shall stand in judgment; *and* they shall judge it according to my judgments: and they shall keep my laws and my statutes in all mine assemblies; and they shall hallow my sabbaths.

Dan. 9:12. And he hath confirmed his words, which he spake against us, and against our judges that judged us, by bringing upon us a great evil:

Mic. 7:3. That they may do evil with both hands earnestly, the prince asketh, and the judge *asketh* for a reward; and the great *man*, he uttereth his mischievous desire: so they wrap it up.

Zeph. 3:3. Her princes within her *are* roaring lions; her judges *are* evening wolves; they gnaw not the bones till the morrow.

John 7:24. Judge not according to the appearance, but judge righteous judgment.

See JUSTICE; COURTS.

CORRUPT: INSTANCES OF: Eli's sons, 1 Sam. 2:12-17,22-25. Samuel's sons, 1 Sam. 8:1-5. The judges of Jezreel, 1 Kin. 21:8-13. Pilate, Matt. 27:24; Mark 15:15, with 19-24. Felix, Acts 24:26,27.

GOD AS: See GOD, JUDGE.

JUDGES OF ISRAEL: During the time when the land was ruled by judges, Judg. 2:16-19; Acts 13:20. 1. Othniel, Judg. 3:9-11.
2. Ehud, Judg. 3:15-30.
3. Shamgar, Judg. 3:31.
4. Deborah, Judg. 4; 5.
5. Gideon, Judg. 6:11-40; 7; 8.
6. Abimelech, Judg. 9:1-54.
7. Tola, Judg. 10:1,2.
8. Jair, Judg. 10:3-5.
9. Jephthah, Judg. 11; 12:1-7.
10. Ibzan, Judg. 12:8-10.
11. Elon, Judg. 12:11,12.
12. Abdon, Judg. 12:13,14.
13. Samson, Judg. chapters 13-16.
Eli judged Israel, 1 Sam. 4:18. Samuel as judge, 1 Sam. 7:6,15-17. The sons of Samuel, 1 Sam. 8:1-5.

JUDGING. See UNCHARITABLENESS.

JUDGMENT. THE GENERAL: 1 Chr. 16:33. Then shall the trees of the wood sing out at the presence of the LORD, because he cometh to judge the earth.

Job 14:17. My transgression *is* sealed up in a bag, and thou sewest up mine iniquity.

Job 21:30. The wicked is reserved to the day of destruction? they shall be brought forth to the day of wrath.

Job 31:13. If I did despise the cause of my manservant or of my maidservant, when they contended with me; 14. What then shall I do when God riseth up? and when he visiteth, what shall I answer him? 15. Did not he that made me in the womb make him? and did not one fashion us in the womb?

Psa. 9:7. But the LORD shall endure for ever: he hath prepared his throne for judgment.

Psa. 50:3. Our God shall come, and shall not keep silence: a fire shall devour before him, and it shall be very tempestuous round about him. 4. He shall call to the heavens from above, and to the earth, that he may judge his people. 5. Gather my saints together unto me; those that have made a covenant with me by sacrifice. 6. And the heavens shall declare his righteousness: for God *is* judge himself.

Psa. 96:13. The LORD: for he cometh, for he cometh to judge the earth: he shall judge the world with righteousness, and the people with his truth. Psa. 98:9.

Eccl. 3:17. I said in mine heart, God shall judge the righteous and the wicked: for *there is* a time there for every purpose and for every work.

Eccl. 11:9. Rejoice, O young man, in thy youth; and let thy heart cheer thee in the days of thy youth, and walk in the ways of thine heart, and in the sight of thine eyes: but know thou, that for all these *things* God will bring thee into judgment.

Eccl. 12:14. God shall bring every work into judgment, with every secret thing, whether *it be* good, or whether *it be* evil.

Ezek. 18:20. The soul that sinneth, it shall die. The son shall not bear the iniquity of the father, neither shall the father bear the iniquity of the son: the righteousness of the righteous shall be upon him, and the wickedness of the wicked shall be upon him. 21. But if the wicked will turn from all his sins that he hath committed, and keep all my statutes, and do that which is lawful and right, he shall surely live, he shall not die. 22. All his transgressions that he hath committed, they shall not be mentioned unto him: in his righteousness that he hath done he shall live. 23. Have I any pleasure at all that the wicked should die? saith the Lord GOD: *and* not that he should return from his ways, and live? 24. But when the righteous turneth away from his righteousness, and committeth iniquity, *and* doeth according to all the abominations that the wicked *man* doeth, shall he live? All his righteousness that he hath done shall not be mentioned: in his trespass that he hath trespassed, and in his sin that he hath sinned, in them shall he die. 25. Yet ye say, The way of the Lord is not equal. Hear now, O house of Israel; Is not my way equal? are not your ways unequal? 26. When a righteous *man* turneth away from his righteousness, and committeth iniquity, and dieth in them; for his iniquity that he hath done shall he die. 27. Again, when the wicked *man* turneth away from his wickedness that he hath committed, and doeth that which is lawful and right, he shall save his soul alive. 28. Because he considereth, and turneth away from all his transgressions that he hath committed, he shall surely live, he shall not die.

Dan. 7:9. I beheld till the thrones were cast down, and the Ancient of days did sit, whose garment *was* white as snow, and the hair of his head like the pure wool: his throne *was like* the fiery flame, *and* his wheels *as* burning fire. 10. A fiery stream issued and came forth from before him: thousand thousands ministered unto him, and ten thousand times ten thousand stood before him: the judgment was set, and the books were opened.

Amos 4:12. Therefore thus will I do unto thee, O Israel: *and* because I will do this unto thee, prepare to meet thy God, O Israel.

Matt. 3:12. Whose fan *is* in his hand, and he will throughly purge his floor, and gather his wheat into the garner; but he will burn up the chaff with unquenchable fire. Luke 3:17.

Matt. 7:22. Many will say to me in that day, Lord, Lord, have we not prophesied in thy name? ánd in thy name have cast out devils? and in thy name done many wonderful works? 23. And then will I profess unto them, I never knew you: depart from me, ye that work iniquity.

Matt. 8:29. And, behold, they cried out, saying, What have we to do with thee, Jesus, thou Son of God? art thou come hither to torment us before the time? With 2 Pet. 2:4; Jude 6.

Matt. 11:22. It shall be more tolerable for Tyre and Sidon at the day of judgment, than for you. Matt. 10:15.

Matt. 12:36. Every idle word that men shall speak, they shall give account thereof in the day of judgment. 37. For by thy words thou shalt be justified, and by thy words thou shalt be condemned. 41. The men of Nineveh shall rise in judgment with this generation, and shall condemn it: because they repented at the preaching of Jonas; and, behold, a greater than Jonas *is* here. 42. The queen of the south shall rise up in the judgment with this generation, and shall condemn it: for she came from the uttermost parts of the earth to hear the wisdom of Solomon; and, behold, a greater than Solomon *is* here. Luke 11:31,32.

Matt. 13:30. In the time of harvest I will say to the reapers, Gather ye together first the tares, and bind them in bundles to burn them: but gather the wheat into my barn. 40. As therefore the tares are gathered and burned in the fire; so shall it be in the end of this world. 41. The Son of man shall send forth his angels, and they shall gather out of his kingdom all things that offend, and them which do iniquity; 42. And shall cast them into a furnace of fire: there shall be wailing and gnashing of teeth. 43. Then shall the righteous shine forth as the sun in the kingdom of their Father. 49. So shall it be at the end of the world: the angels shall come forth, and sever the wicked from among the just, 50. And shall cast them into the furnace of fire: there shall be wailing and gnashing of teeth.

Matt. 16:27. The Son of man shall come in the glory of his Father with his angels; and then he shall reward every man according to his works. Mark 8:38.

Matt. 22:13. Then said the king to the servants, Bind him hand and foot, and take him away, and cast *him* into outer darkness; there shall be weeping and gnashing of teeth. *vs.* 11–13.

Matt. 23:14. [1] Woe unto you, scribes and Pharisees, hypocrites! for ye devour widows' houses, and for a pretence make long prayer: therefore ye shall receive the greater damnation. [1 Omitted in R. V.]

Matt. 25:1. Then shall the kingdom of heaven be likened unto ten virgins, which took their lamps, and went forth to meet the bridegroom. 2. And five of them were wise, and five *were* foolish. 3. They that *were* foolish took their lamps, and took no oil with them: 4. But the wise took oil in their vessels with their lamps. 5. While the bridegroom tarried, they all slumbered and slept. 6. And at midnight there was a cry made, Behold, the bridegroom cometh: go ye out to meet him. 7. Then all those virgins arose, and trimmed their lamps. 8. And the foolish said unto the wise, Give us of your oil; for our lamps are gone out. 9. But the wise answered, saying, *Not so;* lest there be not enough for us and you: but go ye rather to them that sell, and buy for yourselves. 10. And while they went to buy, the bridgroom came; and they that were ready went in with him to the marriage: and the door was shut. 11. Afterward came also the other virgins, saying, Lord, Lord, open to us. 12. But he answered and said, Verily I say unto you, I know you not. 13. Watch therefore, for ye know neither the day nor the hour wherein the Son of man cometh. 14. For *the kingdom of heaven is* as a man travelling into a far country, *who* called his own servants, and delivered unto them his goods. [Luke 19: 12–26.] 15. And unto one he gave five talents, to another two, and to another one; to every man according to his several ability; and straightway took his journey. 16. Then he that had received the five talents went and traded with the same, and made *them* other five talents. 17. And likewise he that *had received* two, he also gained other two. 18. But he that had received one went and digged in the earth, and hid his lord's money. 19. After a long time the lord of those servants cometh, and reckoneth with them. 20. And so he that had received five talents came and brought other five talents, saying, Lord, thou deliveredst unto me five talents: behold, I have gained beside them five talents more. 21. His lord said unto him, Well done, *thou* good and faithful servant: thou hast been faithful over a few things, I will make thee ruler over many things: enter thou into the joy of thy lord. 22. He also that had received two talents came and said, Lord, thou deliveredst unto me two talents: behold, I have gained two other talents beside them. 23. His lord said unto him, Well done, good and faithful servant; thou hast been faithful over a few things, I will make thee ruler over many things: enter thou into the joy of thy lord. 24. Then he which had received the one talent came and said, Lord, I knew thee that thou art an hard man, reaping where thou hast not sown, and gathering where thou hast not strawed: 25. And I was afraid, and went and hid thy talent in the earth: lo, *there* thou hast *that is* thine. 26. His lord answered and said unto him, *Thou* wicked and slothful servant, thou knewest that I reap where I sowed not, and gather where I have not strawed: 27. Thou oughtest therefore to have put my money to the exchangers, and *then* at my coming I should have received mine own with usury. 28. Take therefore the talent from him, and give *it* unto him which hath ten talents. 29. For unto every one that hath shall be given, and he shall have abundance: but from him that hath not shall be taken away even that which he hath. 30. And cast ye the unprofitable servant into outer darkness: there shall be weeping and gnashing of teeth. 31. When the Son of man shall come in his glory, and all the holy angels with him, then shall he sit upon the throne of his glory: 32. And before him shall be gathered all nations: and he shall separate them one from another, as a shepherd divideth *his* sheep from the goats: 33. And he shall set the sheep on his right hand, but the goats on the left. 34. Then shall the King say unto them on his right hand, Come, ye blessed of my Father, inherit the kingdom prepared for you from the foundation of the world: 35. For I was an hungred, and ye gave me meat: I was thirsty, and ye gave me drink: I was a stranger, and ye took me in: 36. Naked, and ye clothed me: I was sick, and ye visited me: I was in prison, and ye came unto me. 37. Then shall the righteous answer him, saying, Lord, when saw we thee an hungred, and fed *thee?* or thirsty, and gave *thee* drink? 38. When saw we thee a stranger, and took *thee* in? or naked, and clothed *thee?* 39. Or when saw we thee sick, or in prison, and came unto thee? 40. And the King shall answer and say unto them, Verily I say unto you, Inasmuch as ye have done *it* unto one of the least of these my brethren, ye have done *it* unto me. 41. Then shall he say also unto them on the left hand, Depart from me, ye cursed, into everlasting fire, prepared for the devil and his angels. 42. For I was an hungred, and ye gave me no meat: I was thirsty, and ye gave me no drink: 43. I was a stranger, and ye took me not in: naked, and ye clothed me not: sick, and in prison, and ye visited me not. 44. Then shall they also answer him, saying, Lord, when saw we thee an hungred, or athirst, or a stranger, or naked, or sick, or in prison, and did not minister unto thee? 45. Then shall he answer them, saying, Verily I say unto you, Inasmuch as ye did *it* not to one of the least of these, ye did *it* not to me. 46. And these

shall go away into everlasting punishment: but the righteous into life eternal.

Mark 4:22. For there is nothing hid, which shall not be manifested; neither was anything kept secret, but that it should come abroad.

Mark 13:32. But of that day and *that* hour knoweth no man, no, not the angels which are in heaven, neither the Son, but the Father.

Luke 10:10. But into whatsoever city ye enter, and they receive you not, go your ways out into the streets of the same, and say, 11. Even the very dust of your city, which cleaveth on us, we do wipe off against you: notwithstanding be ye sure of this, that the kingdom of God is come nigh unto you. 12. But I say unto you, that it shall be more tolerable in that day for Sodom, than for that city. 13. Woe unto thee, Chorazin! woe unto thee, Bethsaida! for if the mighty works had been done in Tyre and Sidon, which have been done in you, they had a great while ago repented, sitting in sackcloth and ashes. 14. But it shall be more tolerable for Tyre and Sidon at the judgment, than for you.

Luke 12:2. For there is nothing covered, that shall not be revealed; neither hid, that shall not be known. 3. Therefore whatsoever ye have spoken in darkness shall be heard in the light; and that which ye have spoken in the ear in closets shall be proclaimed upon the housetops. 4. And I say unto you my friends, Be not afraid of them that kill the body, and after that have no more that they can do. 5. But I will forewarn you whom ye shall fear: Fear him, which after he hath killed hath power to cast into hell; yea, I say unto you, Fear him.

Luke 13:24. Strive to enter in at the strait gate: for many, I say unto you, will seek to enter in, and shall not be able. 25. When once the master of the house is risen up, and hath shut to the door, and ye begin to stand without, and to knock at the door, saying, Lord, Lord, open unto us; and he shall answer and say unto you, I know you not whence ye are: 26. Then shall ye begin to say, We have eaten and drunk in thy presence, and thou hast taught in our streets. 27. But he shall say, I tell you, I know you not whence ye are; depart from me, all *ye* workers of iniquity. 28. There shall be weeping and gnashing of teeth, when ye shall see Abraham, and Isaac, and Jacob, and all the prophets, in the kingdom of God, and you *yourselves* thrust out. 29. And they shall come from the east, and *from* the west, and from the north, and *from* the south, and shall sit down in the kingdom of God.

Luke 20:45. Then in the audience of all the people he said unto his disciples, 46. Beware of the scribes, which desire to walk in long robes, and love greetings in the markets, and the highest seats in the synagogues, and the chief rooms at feasts; 47. Which devour widows' houses, and for a shew make long prayers: the same shall receive **greater** [1] damnation.   [1 R. V. condemnation]

John 5:22. For the Father judgeth no man, but hath committed all judgment unto the Son:

John 12:48. He that rejecteth me, and receiveth not my words, hath one that judgeth him: the word that I have spoken, the same shall judge him in the last day.

Acts 2:19. And I will shew wonders in heaven above, and signs in the earth beneath; blood, and fire, and vapour of smoke: 20. The sun shall be turned into darkness, and the moon into blood, before that great and notable day of the Lord come: 21. And it shall come to pass, *that* whosoever shall call on the name of the Lord shall be saved.

Acts 10:42. And he commanded us to preach unto the people, and to testify that it is he which was ordained of God *to be* the Judge of quick and dead.

Acts 17:31. He hath appointed a day, in the which he will judge the world in righteousness by *that* man whom he hath ordained; *whereof* he hath given assurance unto all *men*, in that he hath raised him from the dead.

Acts 24:25. As he reasoned of righteousness, temperance, and judgment to come, Felix trembled,

Rom. 2:5. But after thy hardness and impenitent heart treasurest up unto thyself wrath against the day of wrath and revelation of the righteous judgment of God; 6. Who will render to every man according to his deeds: 7. To them who by patient continuance in well doing seek for glory and honour and immortality, eternal life: 8. But unto them that are contentious, and do not obey the truth, but obey unrighteousness, indignation, and wrath, 9. Tribulation and anguish, upon every soul of man that doeth evil; of the Jew first, and also of the Gentile: 10. But glory, honour, and peace, to every man that worketh good; to the Jew first, and also to the Gentile: 12. For as many as have sinned without law shall also perish without law; and as many as have sinned in the law shall be judged by the law; 13. (For not the hearers of the law *are* just before God, but the doers of the law shall be justified. 14. For when the Gentiles, which have not the law, do by nature the things contained in the law, these, having not the law, are a law unto themselves: 15. Which shew the work of the law written in their hearts, their conscience also bearing witness, and *their* thoughts the mean while accusing or else excusing one another;) 16. In the day when God shall judge the secrets of men by Jesus Christ according to my gospel.

Rom. 14:10. But why dost thou judge thy brother? or why dost thou set at nought thy brother? for we shall all stand before the judgment seat of Christ. 11. *As* I live, saith the Lord, every knee shall bow to me, and every tongue shall confess to God. 12. So then every one of us shall give account of himself to God.

1 Cor. 3:13. Every man's work shall be made manifest: for the day shall declare it, because it shall be revealed by fire; and the fire shall try every man's work of what sort it is.

1 Cor. 4:5. Judge nothing before the time, until the Lord come, who both will bring to light the hidden things of darkness, and will make manifest the counsels of the hearts: and then shall every man have praise of God.

1 Cor. 6:2. Do ye not know that the saints shall judge the world? and if the world shall be judged by you, are ye unworthy to judge the smallest matters?

2 Cor. 5:10. We must all appear before the judgment seat of Christ; that every one may receive the things *done* in *his* body, according to that he hath done, whether *it be* good or bad.

2 Thess. 1:7. To you who are troubled rest with us, when the Lord Jesus shall be revealed from heaven with his mighty angels, 8. In flaming fire taking vengeance on them that know not God, and that obey not the gospel of our Lord Jesus Christ.

2 Tim. 4:1. I charge *thee* therefore before God, and the Lord Jesus Christ, who shall judge the quick and the dead at his appearing and his kingdom; 8. Henceforth there is laid up for me a crown of righteousness, which the Lord, the righteous judge, shall give me at that day: and not to me only, but unto all them also that love his appearing.

Heb. 6:2. Of the doctrine of baptisms, and of laying on of hands, and of resurrection of the dead, and of eternal judgment.

Heb. 9:27. It is appointed unto men once to die, but after this the judgment:

Heb. 10:27. A certain fearful looking for of judgment and fiery indignation, which shall devour the adversaries.

1 Pet. 4:5. Who shall give account to him that is ready to judge the quick and the dead. 7. The end of all things is at hand: be ye therefore sober, and watch unto prayer.

2 Pet. 2:4. God spared not the angels that sinned, but cast *them* down to hell, and delivered *them* into chains of darkness, to be reserved unto judgment; 9. The Lord knoweth how to . . . reserve the unjust unto the day of judgment to be punished:

2 Pet. 3:7. The heavens and the earth, which are now, by the same word are kept in store, reserved unto fire against the day of judgment and perdition of ungodly men. 10. The day of the Lord will come as a thief in the night; in the which the heavens shall pass away with a great noise, and the elements shall melt with fervent heat, the earth also and the works that are therein shall be burned up. 11. *Seeing* then *that* all these things shall be dissolved, **what**

manner *of persons* ought ye to be in all holy conversation and godliness, 12. Looking for and hasting unto the coming of the day of God, wherein the heavens being on fire shall be dissolved, and the elements shall melt with fervent heat?

1 John 4:17. Herein is our love made perfect, that we may have boldness in the day of judgment.

Jude 6. The angels which kept not their first estate, but left their own habitation, he hath reserved in everlasting chains under darkness unto the judgment of the great day. 14. Behold, the Lord cometh with ten thousands of his saints, 15. To execute judgment upon all, and to convince all that are ungodly among them of all their ungodly deeds which they have ungodly committed, and of all their hard *speeches* which ungodly sinners have spoken against him. 24. Him that is able to . . . present *you* faultless before the presence of his glory with exceeding joy,

Rev. 1:7. Behold, he cometh with clouds; and every eye shall see him, and they *also* which pierced him: and all kindreds of the earth shall wail because of him.

Rev. 6:15. The kings of the earth, and the great men, and the rich men, and the chief captains, and the mighty men, and every bondman, and every freeman, hid themselves in the dens and in the rocks of the mountains; 16. And said to the mountains and rocks, Fall on us, and hide us from the face of him that sitteth on the throne, and from the wrath of the Lamb: 17. For the great day of his wrath is come; and who shall be able to stand?

Rev. 11:18. The nations were angry, and thy wrath is come, and the time of the dead, that they should be judged, and that thou shouldest give reward unto thy servants the prophets, and to the saints, and them that fear thy name, small and great; and shouldest destroy them which destroy the earth.

Rev. 20:11. I saw a great white throne, and him that sat on it, from whose face the earth and the heaven fled away; and there was found no place for them. 12. And I saw the dead, small and great, stand before God; and the books were opened: and another book was opened, which is *the book* of life: and the dead were judged out of those things which were written in the books, according to their works. 13. And the sea gave up the dead which were in it; and death and hell delivered up the dead which were in them: and they were judged every man according to their works. 14. And death and hell were cast into the lake of fire. This is the second death. 15. And whosoever was not found written in the book of life was cast into the lake of fire.

Rev. 22:12. Behold, I come quickly; and my reward *is* with me, to give every man according as his work shall be.

ACCORDING TO OPPORTUNITY AND WORKS: Gen. 4:7. If thou doest well, shalt thou not be accepted? and if thou doest not well, sin lieth at the door.

Job 34:11. For the work of a man shall he render unto him, and cause every man to find according to *his* ways.

Prov. 11:31. The righteous shall be recompensed in the earth; much more the wicked and the sinner.

Prov. 12:14. The recompence of a man's hands shall be rendered unto him.

Prov. 24:11. If thou forbear to deliver *them that are* drawn unto death, and *those that are* ready to be slain; 12. If thou sayest, Behold, we knew it not; doth not he that pondereth the heart consider it? and he that keepeth thy soul, doth *not* he know *it?* and shall *not* he render to *every* man according to his works? Psa. 62:12; 2 Tim. 4:14.

Isa. 3:10. Say ye to the righteous, that *it shall be* well *with him:* for they shall eat the fruit of their doings. 11. Woe unto the wicked! *it shall be* ill *with him:* for the reward of his hands shall be given him.

Isa. 5:15. The mean man shall be brought down, and the mighty man shall be humbled, and the eyes of the lofty shall be humbled: 16. But the Lord of hosts shall be exalted in judgment, and God that is holy shall be sanctified in righteousness.

Isa. 24:2. It shall be, as with the people, so with the priest; as with the servant, so with his master; as with the maid, so with her mistress; as with the buyer, so with the seller; as with the lender, so with the borrower; as with the taker of usury, so with the giver of usury to him.

Isa. 59:18. According to *their* deeds, accordingly he will repay, fury to his adversaries, recompence to his enemies; to the islands he will repay recompence.

Jer. 17:10. I the Lord search the heart, *I* try the reins, even to give every man according to his ways, *and* according to the fruit of his doings. 11. *As* the partridge sitteth *on eggs,* and hatcheth *them* not; *so* he that getteth riches, and not by right, shall leave them in the midst of his days, and at his end shall be a fool.

Jer. 32:19. Thine eyes *are* open upon all the ways of the sons of men: to give every one according to his ways, and according to the fruit of his doings:

Ezek. 7:3. Now *is* the end *come* upon thee, and I will send mine anger upon thee, and will judge thee according to thy ways, and will recompense upon thee all thine abominations. 4. And mine eye shall not spare thee, neither will I have pity: but I will recompense thy ways upon thee, and thine abominations shall be in the midst of thee: and ye shall know that I *am* the Lord. 27. I will do unto them after their way, and according to their deserts will I judge them; and they shall know that I *am* the Lord.

Ezek. 9:4. And the Lord said unto him, Go through the midst of the city, through the midst of Jerusalem, and set a mark upon the foreheads of the men that sigh and that cry for all the abominations that be done in the midst thereof. 5. And to the others he said in mine hearing, Go ye after him through the city, and smite: let not your eye spare, neither have ye pity: 6. Slay utterly old *and* young, both maids, and little children, and women: but come not near any man upon whom *is* the mark; and begin at my sanctuary.

Ezek. 16:59. For thus saith the Lord God; I will even deal with thee as thou hast done, which hast despised the oath in breaking the covenant.

Ezek. 18:4. Behold, all souls are mine; as the soul of the father, so also the soul of the son is mine: the soul that sinneth, it shall die. [*vs.* 5-9.] 19. Yet say ye, Why? doth not the son bear the iniquity of the father? When the son hath done that which is lawful and right, *and* hath kept all my statutes, and hath done them, he shall surely live. 20. The soul that sinneth, it shall die. The son shall not bear the iniquity of the father, neither shall the father bear the iniquity of the son: the righteousness of the righteous shall be upon him, and the wickedness of the wicked shall be upon him. 21. But if the wicked will turn from all his sins that he hath committed, and keep all my statutes, and do that which is lawful and right, he shall surely live, he shall not die. 22. All his transgressions that he hath committed, they shall not be mentioned unto him: in his righteousness that he hath done he shall live. 23. Have I any pleasure at all that the wicked should die? saith the Lord God: *and* not that he should return from his ways, and live? 24. But when the righteous turneth away from his righteousness, and committeth iniquity, *and* doeth according to all the abominations that the wicked *man* doeth, shall he live? All his righteousness that he hath done shall not be mentioned: in his trespass that he hath trespassed, and in his sin that he hath sinned, in them shall he die. 25. Yet ye say, The way of the Lord is not equal. Hear now, O house of Israel; Is not my way equal? are not your ways unequal? 26. When a righteous *man* turneth away from his righteousness, and committeth iniquity, and dieth in them; for his iniquity that he hath done shall he die. 27. Again, when the wicked *man* turneth away from his wickedness that he hath committed, and doeth that which is lawful and right, he shall save his soul alive. 28. Because he considereth, and turneth away from all his transgressions that he hath committed, he shall surely live, he shall not die. 29. Yet saith the house of Israel, The way of the Lord is not equal. O house of Israel, are not my ways equal? are not your ways unequal? 30. Therefore I will judge you, O house of Israel, every one according to his ways, saith the Lord God. Repent, and turn *yourselves* from all your transgressions; so iniquity shall not be your

ruin. 31. Cast away from you all your transgressions, whereby ye have transgressed; and make you a new heart and a new spirit: for why will ye die, O house of Israel? 32. For I have no pleasure in the death of him that dieth, saith the Lord God: wherefore turn *yourselves*, and live ye.

Ezek. 33:18. When the righteous turneth from his righteousness, and committeth iniquity, he shall even die thereby. 19. But if the wicked turn from his wickedness, and do that which is lawful and right, he shall live thereby. 20. Yet ye say, The way of the Lord is not equal. O ye house of Israel, I will judge you every one after his ways.

Ezek. 39:24. According to their uncleanness and according to their transgressions have I done unto them, and hid my face from them.

Hos. 4:9. There shall be, like people, like priest: and I will punish them for their ways, and reward them their doings. Hos. 12:2.

Amos 3:2. You only have I known of all the families of the earth: therefore I will punish you for all your iniquities.

Zech. 1:6. But my words and my statutes, which I commanded my servants the prophets, did they not take hold of your fathers? and they returned and said, Like as the Lord of hosts thought to do unto us, according to our ways, and according to our doings, so hath he dealt with us.

Matt. 10:14. Whosoever shall not receive you, nor hear your words, when ye depart out of that house or city, shake off the dust of your feet. 15. It shall be more tolerable for the land of Sodom and Gomorrha in the day of judgment, than for that city. Matt. 11:24; Mark 6:11; Luke 9:5; 10:12-15.

Matt. 12:37. By thy words thou shalt be justified, and by thy words thou shalt be condemned.

Matt. 23:14. [1] Woe unto you, scribes and Pharisees, hypocrites! for ye devour widows' houses, and for a pretence make long prayer: therefore ye shall receive the greater damnation. Luke 20:47.

[1 Omitted in R. V.]

Mark 14:21. The Son of man indeed goeth, as it is written of him: but woe to that man by whom the Son of man is betrayed! good were it for that man if he had never been born.

Luke 11:49. Therefore also said the wisdom of God, I will send them prophets and apostles, and *some* of them they shall slay and persecute: 50. That the blood of all the prophets, which was shed from the foundation of the world, may be required of this generation; *v.* 51.

Luke 12:47. That servant, which knew his lord's will, and prepared not *himself*, neither did according to his will, shall be beaten with many *stripes*. 48. But he that knew not, and did commit things worthy of stripes, shall be beaten with few *stripes*. For unto whomsoever much is given, of him shall be much required: and to whom men have committed much, of him they will ask the more. [See parable of the vineyard, Isa. 5: 1-6. Of the husbandman, Isa. 28:24-28. Of the wicked husbandmen, Matt. 21:33-36. Of the talents, Matt. 25:14-30.]

Luke 13:6. He spake also this parable; A certain *man* had a fig tree planted in his vineyard; and he came and sought fruit thereon, and found none. 7. Then said he unto the dresser of his vineyard, Behold, these three years I come seeking fruit on this fig tree, and find none: cut it down; why cumbereth it the ground? 8. And he answering said unto him, Lord, let it alone this year also, till I shall dig about it, and dung *it:* 9. And if it bear fruit, *well:* and if not, *then* after that thou shalt cut it down.

Luke 19:12. He said therefore, A certain nobleman went into a far country to receive for himself a kingdom, and to return. 13. And he called his ten servants, and delivered them ten pounds, and said unto them, Occupy till I come. 14. But his citizens hated him, and sent a message after him, saying, We will not have this *man* to reign over us. 15. And it came to pass, that when he was returned, having received the kingdom, then he commanded these servants to be called unto him, to whom he had given the money, that he might know how much every man had gained by trading. 16. Then came the first, saying, Lord, thy pound hath gained ten pounds. 17. And he said unto him, Well, thou good servant: because thou hast been faithful in a very little, have thou authority over ten cities. 18. And the second came, saying, Lord, thy pound hath gained five pounds. 19. And he said likewise to him, Be thou also over five cities. 20. And another came, saying, Lord, behold, *here is* thy pound, which I have kept laid up in a napkin: 21. For I feared thee, because thou art an austere man: thou takest up that thou layest not down, and reapest that thou didst not sow. 22. And he saith unto him, Out of thine own mouth will I judge thee, *thou* wicked servant. Thou knewest that I was an austere man, taking up that I laid not down, and reaping that I did not sow: 23. Wherefore then gavest not thou my money into the bank, that at my coming I might have required mine own with usury? 24. And he said unto them that stood by, Take from him the pound, and give *it* to him that hath ten pounds. 25. (And they said unto him, Lord, he hath ten pounds.) 26. For I say unto you, That unto every one which hath shall be given; and from him that hath not, even that he hath shall be taken away from him. 27. But those mine enemies, which would not that I should reign over them, bring hither, and slay *them* before me.

Luke 21:1. And he looked up, and saw the rich men casting their gifts into the treasury. 2. And he saw also a certain poor widow casting in thither two mites. 3. And

he said, Of a truth I say unto you, that this poor widow hath cast in more than they all: 4. For all these have of their abundance cast in unto the offerings of God: but she of her penury hath cast in all the living that she had.

John 3:19. This is the condemnation, that light is come into the world, and men loved darkness rather than light, because their deeds were evil. 20. For every one that doeth evil hateth the light, neither cometh to the light, lest his deeds should be reproved.

John 5:45. Do not think that I will accuse you to the Father: there is *one* that accuseth you, *even* Moses, in whom ye trust.

John 9:41. Jesus said unto them, If ye were blind, ye should have no sin: but now ye say, We see; therefore your sin remaineth.

John 12:48. He that rejecteth me, and receiveth not my words, hath one that judgeth him: the word that I have spoken, the same shall judge him in the last day.

John 15:22. If I had not come and spoken unto them, they had not had sin: but now they have no cloke for their sin. 24. If I had not done among them the works which none other man did, they had not had sin: but now have they both seen and hated both me and my Father.

Rom. 2:5. But after thy hardness and impenitent heart treasurest up unto thyself wrath against the day of wrath and revelation of the righteous judgment of God; 6. Who will render to every man according to his deeds: 7. To them who by patient continuance in well doing seek for glory and honour and immortality, eternal life: 8. But unto them that are contentious, and do not obey the truth, but obey unrighteousness, indignation and wrath, 9. Tribulation and anguish, upon every soul of man that doeth evil, of the Jew first, and also of the Gentile; 10. Glory, honour, and peace, to every man that worketh good, to the Jew first, and also to the Gentile: 11. For there is no respect of persons with God. 12. As many as have sinned without law shall also perish without law: and as many as have sinned in the law shall be judged by the law; 27. Shall not uncircumcision which is by nature, if it fulfil the law, judge thee, who by the letter and circumcision dost transgress the law?

1 Cor. 3:8. Every man shall receive his own reward according to his own labour. 13. Every man's work shall be made manifest: for the day shall declare it, because it shall be revealed by fire; and the fire shall try every man's work of what sort it is. 14. If any man's work abide which he hath built thereupon, he shall receive a reward. 15. If any man's work shall be burned, he shall suffer loss: but he himself shall be saved; yet so as by fire. *v.* 12.

1 Cor. 4:5. Therefore judge nothing before the time, until the Lord come, who both

will bring to light the hidden things of darkness, and will make manifest the counsels of the hearts: and then shall every man have praise of God.

2 Cor. 2:15. For we are unto God a sweet savour of Christ, in them that are saved, and in them that perish: 16. To the one *we are* the savour of death unto death; and to the other the savour of life unto life.

2 Cor. 11:15. Therefore *it is* no great thing if his ministers also be transformed as the ministers of righteousness; whose end shall be according to their works.

Gal. 6:5. Every man shall bear his own burden. 6. Let him that is taught in the word communicate unto him that teacheth in all good things. 7. Be not deceived; God is not mocked; for whatsoever a man soweth, that shall he also reap. 8. For he that soweth to his flesh shall of the flesh reap corruption; but he that soweth to the Spirit shall of the Spirit reap life everlasting. 9. And let us not be weary in well doing: for in due season we shall reap, if we faint not. 10. As we have therefore opportunity, let us do good unto all *men*, especially unto them who are of the household of faith.

Eph. 6:7. With good will doing service, as to the Lord, and not to men: 8. Knowing that whatsoever good thing any man doeth, the same shall he receive of the Lord, whether *he be* bond or free.

Col. 3:25. He that doeth wrong shall receive for the wrong which he hath done: and there is no respect of persons.

1 Tim. 1:13. Who was before a blasphemer, and a persecutor, and injurious: but I obtained mercy, because I did *it* ignorantly in unbelief.

Heb. 2:2. If the word spoken by angels was stedfast, and every transgression and disobedience received a just recompence of reward; 3. How shall we escape, if we neglect so great salvation;

Heb. 10:26. If we sin wilfully after that we have received the knowledge of the truth, there remaineth no more sacrifice for sins, 27. But a certain fearful looking for of judgment and fiery indignation, which shall devour the adversaries. 28. He that despised Moses' law died without mercy under two or three witnesses: 29. Of how much sorer punishment, suppose ye, shall he be thought worthy, who hath trodden under foot the Son of God, and hath counted the blood of the covenant, wherewith he was sanctified, an unholy thing, and hath done despite unto the Spirit of grace? 30. For we know him that hath said, Vengeance *belongeth* unto me, I will recompense, saith the Lord. And again, The Lord shall judge his people.

Heb. 12:25. If they escaped not who refused him that spake on earth, much more *shall not* we *escape*, if we turn away from him that *speaketh* from heaven:

Jas. 2:12. So speak ye, and so do, as they that shall be judged by the law of liberty.

13. He shall have judgment without mercy, that hath shewed no mercy;

1 Pet. 1:17. And if ye call on the Father, who without respect of persons judgeth according to every man's work, pass the time of your sojourning *here* in fear:

2 Pet. 2:20. For if after they have escaped the pollutions of the world through the knowledge of the Lord and Saviour Jesus Christ, they are again entangled therein, and overcome, the latter end is worse with them than the beginning. 21. It had been better for them not to have known the way of righteousness, than, after they have known *it*, to turn from the holy commandment delivered unto them.

Rev. 2:23. All the churches shall know that I am he which searcheth the reins and hearts: and I will give unto every one of you according to your works.

Rev. 20:12. And I saw the dead, small and great, stand before God; and the books were opened: and another book was opened, which is *the book* of life: and the dead were judged out of those things which were written in the books, according to their works. 13. And the sea gave up the dead which were in it; and death and hell delivered up the dead which were in them: and they were judged every man according to their works.

See GOD, JUDGE; JESUS, JUDGE; PUNISHMENT, ACCORDING TO DEEDS.

JUDGMENT-HALL. See PRETORIUM.

JUDGMENT-SEAT, Matt. 27:19; Acts 18:12; 25:10. Of Christ, Rom. 14:10.

JUDGMENTS. On the serpent, Gen. 3:14,15. Eve, Gen. 3:16; Adam, Gen. 3:17–19. Cain, Gen. 4:11–15; the Antediluvians, Gen. chapters 6,7; Sodomites, Gen. 19:23–25; Egyptians, the plagues and overthrow, Ex. chapters 7–14; Nadab and Abihu, Lev. 10: 1–3; Miriam, Num. 12:1–15.

Upon the Israelites: For worshiping Aaron's calf, Ex. 32:35; for murmuring, Num. 11:1,33,34; 14:22,23,32,35–37; 21:6; 25:4, 5,9. The forty years' wandering a judgment, Num. 14:26–39; 26:63–65; Deut. 2:14–17; delivered into the hands of the Assyrians, 2 Kin. 17:6–41; Chaldeans, 2 Chr. 36:14–21.

Upon the Canaanites, Lev. 18:25; Deut. 7; 12:29–32, with the conquest of, by Joshua. See CANAANITES.

Upon Abimelech, Judg. 9:52–57; Uzzah, 2 Sam. 6:7; Hananiah, the false prophet, Jer. 28:15,16,17; Eli's house, 1 Sam. 2:27–36, with chapter 4:10–22; the prophet of Judah, for disobedience, 1 Kin. 13:1–24; Zimri, 1 Kin. 16:18,19; Gehazi, 2 Kin. 5:27; Sennacherib, 2 Kin. 19:35–37.

Denounced against Solomon, 1 Kin. 11:9–14,23; Jeroboam, 1 Kin. 14:7–15; Ahab and Jezebel, 1 Kin. 21:19–24; Ahaziah, 2 Chr. 22: 7–9; Manasseh, 2 Chr. 33:11.

Denounced against disobedience, Lev. 26: 14–39; Deut. 28:15–68; 29; 32:19–43.

Misunderstood, Jer. 16:10; Joel 2:17. No escape from, Ex. 20:7; 34:7; Isa. 2:10,12–19,21;

Ezek. 14:13,14; Amos 5:16-20; 9:1-4; Matt. 23:33; Heb. 2:1-3; 10:28,29; 12:25; Rev. 6:16, 17. See ESCAPE. Executed by human instrumentality, Jer. 51:2. Delayed, Psa. 10: 6; 50:21; 55:19. See PUNISHMENT, DELAYED.

See CHASTISEMENT; PUNISHMENT; SIN, PUNISHMENT OF.

DESIGN OF: Ex. 14:17. And I, behold, I will harden the hearts of the Egyptians, and they shall follow them: and I will get me honour upon Pharaoh, and upon all his host, upon his chariots, and upon his horsemen. 18. And the Egyptians shall know that I am the LORD, when I have gotten me honour upon Pharaoh, upon his chariots, and upon his horsemen. 31. And Israel saw that great work which the LORD did upon the Egyptians: and the people feared the LORD, and believed the LORD, and his servant Moses.

Lev. 10:3. Then Moses said unto Aaron, This is it that the LORD spake, saying, I will be sanctified in them that come nigh me, and before all the people I will be glorified.

Deut. 29:22. So that the generation to come of your children that shall rise up after you, and the stranger that shall come from a far land, shall say, when they see the plagues of that land, and the sicknesses which the LORD hath laid upon it; 23. And that the whole land thereof is brimstone, and salt, and burning, that it is not sown, nor beareth, nor any grass groweth therein, like the overthrow of Sodom and Gomorrah, Admah, and Zeboim, which the LORD overthrew in his anger, and in his wrath: 24. Even all nations shall say, Wherefore hath the LORD done thus unto this land? what meaneth the heat of this great anger? 25. Then men shall say, Because they have forsaken the covenant of the LORD God of their fathers, which he made with them when he brought them forth out of the land of Egypt: 26. For they went and served other gods, and worshipped them, gods whom they knew not, and whom he had not given unto them: 27. And the anger of the LORD was kindled against this land, to bring upon it all the curses that are written in this book: 28. And the LORD rooted them out of their land in anger, and in wrath, and in great indignation, and cast them into another land, as it is this day.

Psa. 9:16. The LORD is known by the judgment which he executeth: the wicked is snared in the work of his own hands. 20. Put them in fear, O LORD: that the nations may know themselves to be but men.

Psa. 59:13. Consume them in wrath, consume them, that they may not be: and let them know that God ruleth in Jacob unto the ends of the earth.

Psa. 83:16. Fill their faces with shame; that they may seek thy name, O LORD. 17. Let them be confounded and troubled for ever; yea, let them be put to shame, and perish: 18. That men may know that thou,

whose name alone is JEHOVAH, art the most high over all the earth.

Isa. 26:9. With my soul have I desired thee in the night; yea, with my spirit within me will I seek thee early: for when thy judgments are in the earth, the inhabitants of the world will learn righteousness.

Isa. 64:1. Oh that thou wouldest rend the heavens, that thou wouldest come down, that the mountains might flow down at thy presence. 2. As when the melting fire burneth, the fire causeth the waters to boil, to make thy name known to thine adversaries, that the nations may tremble at thy presence!

Ezek. 11:10. Ye shall fall by the sword; I will judge you in the border of Israel; and ye shall know that I am the LORD. 11. This city shall not be your caldron, neither shall ye be the flesh in the midst thereof; but I will judge you in the border of Israel: 12. And ye shall know that I am the LORD: for ye have not walked in my statutes, neither executed my judgments, but have done after the manners of the heathen that are round about you.

Ezek. 12:16. But I will leave a few men of them from the sword, from the famine, and from the pestilence; that they may declare all their abominations among the heathen whither they come; and they shall know that I am the LORD.

Ezek. 14:7. For every one of the house of Israel, or of the stranger that sojourneth in Israel, which separateth himself from me, and setteth up his idols in his heart, and putteth the stumblingblock of his iniquity before his face, and cometh to a prophet to inquire of him concerning me; I the LORD will answer him by myself: 8. And I will set my face against that man, and will make him a sign and a proverb, and I will cut him off from the midst of my people; and ye shall know that I am the LORD.

Ezek. 21:3 And say to the land of Israel, Thus saith the LORD; Behold, I am against thee, and will draw forth my sword out of his sheath, and will cut off from thee the righteous and the wicked. 4. Seeing then that I will cut off from thee the righteous and the wicked, therefore shall my sword go forth out of his sheath against all flesh from the south to the north: 5. That all flesh may know that I the LORD have drawn forth my sword out of his sheath: it shall not return any more.

Ezek. 25:5. And I will make Rabbah a stable for camels, and the Ammonites a couching place for flocks; and ye shall know that I am the LORD. 7. Behold, therefore, I will stretch out mine hand upon thee, and will deliver thee for a spoil to the heathen; and I will cut thee off from the people, and I will cause thee to perish out of the countries: I will destroy thee; and thou shalt know that I am the LORD. 11. And I will execute judgments upon Moab; and they shall know that I am the LORD.

Ezek. 26:6. And her daughters which are

in the field shall be slain by the sword; and they shall know that I *am* the LORD.

Ezek. 29:9. And the land of Egypt shall be desolate and waste; and they shall know that I *am* the LORD: because he hath said, The river *is* mine, and I have made *it*. 16. And it shall be no more the confidence of the house of Israel, which bringeth *their* iniquity to remembrance, when they shall look after them: but they shall know that I *am* the Lord GOD.

Ezek. 30:8. And they shall know that I *am* the LORD, when I have set a fire in Egypt, and *when* all her helpers shall be destroyed. 25. But I will strengthen the arms of the king of Babylon, and the arms of Pharaoh shall fall down; and they shall know that I *am* the LORD, when I shall put my sword into the hand of the king of Babylon, and he shall stretch it out upon the land of Egypt. 26. And I will scatter the Egyptians among the nations, and disperse them among the countries; and they shall know that I *am* the LORD.

Ezek. 33:29. Then shall they know that I *am* the LORD, when I have laid the land most desolate because of all their abominations which they have committed.

Ezek. 38:22. And I will plead against him with pestilence and with blood; and I will rain upon him, and upon his bands, and upon the many people that *are* with him, an overflowing rain, and great hailstones, fire, and brimstone. 23. Thus will I magnify myself, and sanctify myself; and I will be known in the eyes of many nations, and they shall know that I *am* the LORD.

Dan. 4:17. This matter *is* by the decree of the watchers, and the demand by the word of the holy ones: to the intent that the living may know that the most High ruleth in the kingdom of men, and giveth it to whomsoever he will, and setteth up over it the basest of men. 24. This *is* the interpretation, O king, and this *is* the decree of the most High, which is come upon my lord the king: 25. That they shall drive thee from men, and thy dwelling shall be with the beasts of the field, and they shall make thee to eat grass as oxen, and they shall wet thee with the dew of heaven, and seven times shall pass over thee, till thou know that the most High ruleth in the kingdom of men, and giveth it to whomsoever he will. 26. And whereas they commanded to leave the stump of the tree roots; thy kingdom shall be sure unto thee, after that thou shalt have known that the heavens do rule. 34. And at the end of the days I Nebuchadnezzar lifted up mine eyes unto heaven, and mine understanding returned unto me, and I blessed the most High, and I praised and honoured him that liveth for ever, whose dominion *is* an everlasting dominion, and his kingdom *is* from generation to generation:

Rom. 9:17. For the scripture saith unto Pharaoh, Even for this same purpose have I raised thee up, that I might shew my power in thee, and that my name might be declared throughout all the earth. 22. *What* if God, willing to shew *his* wrath, and to make his power known, endured with much longsuffering the vessels of wrath fitted to destruction:

1 Cor. 10:6. Now these things were our examples, to the intent we should not lust after evil things, as they also lusted. 11. Now all these things happened unto them for ensamples: and they are written for our admonition, upon whom the ends of the world are come.

Rev. 2:23. And I will kill her children with death; and all the churches shall know that I am he which searcheth the reins and hearts: and I will give unto every one of you according to your works.

See AFFLICTIONS, DESIGN OF.

See also CHASTISEMENT; PUNISHMENT; SIN, PUNISHMENT OF.

JUDITH. A wife of Esau, Gen. 26:34. Called AHOLIBAMAH, Gen. 36:2.

JULIA, a Christian woman in Rome, Rom. 16:15.

JULIUS, a centurion, Acts 27:1,3,43.

JUNIA, a kinsman of Paul, Rom. 16:7.

JUNIPER, a tree, 1 Kin. 19:4,5; Job 30:4; Psa. 120:4.

JUPITER, a Greek and Roman deity, Acts 14:12,13; 19:35.

JURISDICTION. See CHURCH AND STATE.

JURY. Of ten men, Ruth 4:2. Of seventy men, elders (senators), Num. 11:16, 17,24,25.

JUSHAB-HESED, son of Zerubbabel, 1 Chr. 3:20.

JUSTICE. Ex. 23:1. Thou shalt not raise a false report: put not thine hand with the wicked to be an unrighteous witness. 2. Thou shalt not follow a multitude to *do* evil; neither shalt thou speak in a cause to decline after many to wrest *judgment:* 3. Neither shalt thou countenance a poor man in his cause. 6. Thou shalt not wrest the judgment of thy poor in his cause. 7. Keep thee far from a false matter; and the innocent and righteous slay thou not: for I will not justify the wicked. 8. And thou shalt take no gift: for the gift blindeth the wise, and perverteth the words of the righteous.

Lev. 19:13. Thou shalt not defraud thy neighbour, neither rob *him:* the wages of him that is hired shall not abide with thee all night until the morning. 14. Thou shalt not curse the deaf, nor put a stumblingblock before the blind, but shalt fear thy God: I *am* the LORD. 15. Ye shall do no unrighteousness in judgment; thou shalt not respect the person of the poor, nor honour the person of the mighty: *but* in righteousness shalt thou judge thy neighbour.

Deut. 16:18. Judges and officers shalt thou make thee in all thy gates, which the LORD thy God giveth thee, throughout thy tribes:

and they shall judge the people with just judgment. 19. Thou shalt not wrest judgment; thou shalt not respect persons, neither take a gift: for a gift doth blind the eyes of the wise, and pervert the words of the righteous. 20. That which is altogether just shalt thou follow, that thou mayest live, and inherit the land which the LORD thy God giveth thee.

Deut. 25:1. If there be a controversy between men, and they come unto judgment, that *the judges* may judge them; then they shall justify the righteous, and condemn the wicked. 2. And it shall be, if the wicked man *be* worthy to be beaten, that the judge shall cause him to lie down, and to be beaten before his face, according to his fault, by a certain number. 3. Forty stripes he may give him, *and* not exceed: lest, *if* he should exceed, and beat him above these with many stripes, then thy brother should seem vile unto thee. 4. Thou shalt not muzzle the ox when he treadeth out *the corn.*

Ezra 7:26. And whosoever will not do the law of thy God, and the law of the king, let judgment be executed speedily upon him, whether *it be* unto death, or to banishment, or to confiscation of goods, or to imprisonment.

Psa. 72:1. Give the king thy judgments, O God, and thy righteousness unto the king's son. 2. He shall judge thy people with righteousness, and thy poor with judgment.

Psa. 82:2. How long will ye judge unjustly, and accept the persons of the wicked? 3. Defend the poor and fatherless: do justice to the afflicted and needy. 4. Deliver the poor and needy: rid *them* out of the hand of the wicked.

Prov. 17:15. He that justifieth the wicked, and he that condemneth the just, even they both *are* abomination to the LORD.

26. To punish the just *is* not good, *nor* to strike princes for equity.

Prov. 18:5. *It is* not good to accept the person of the wicked, to overthrow the righteous in judgment.

17. *He that is* first in his own cause *seemeth* just; but his neighbour cometh and searcheth him.

Prov. 20:8. A king that sitteth in the throne of judgment scattereth away all evil with his eyes.

Prov. 22:27. If thou hast nothing to pay, why should he take away thy bed from under thee?

Prov. 24:23. These *things* also *belong* to the wise. *It is* not good to have respect of persons in judgment.

Prov. 28:21. To have respect of persons *is* not good: for for a piece of bread *that* man will transgress.

Prov. 29:26. Many seek the ruler's favour: but *every* man's judgment *cometh* from the LORD.

Eccl. 3:16. And moreover I saw under the sun the place of judgment, *that* wickedness *was* there; and the place of righteousness,

that iniquity *was* there. 17. I said in mine heart, God shall judge the righteous and the wicked: for *there is* a time there for every purpose and for every work.

Eccl. 5:8. If thou seest the oppression of the poor, and violent perverting of judgment and justice in a province, marvel not at the matter: for *he that is* higher than the highest regardeth; and *there be* higher than they.

Eccl. 7:7. Surely oppression maketh a wise man mad; and a gift destroyeth the heart.

Isa. 1:17. Learn to do well; seek judgment, relieve the oppressed, judge the fatherless, plead for the widow.

Isa. 56:1. Thus saith the LORD, Keep ye judgment, and do justice: for my salvation *is* near to come, and my righteousness to be revealed.

Isa. 59:14. And judgment is turned away backward, and justice standeth afar off: for truth is fallen in the street, and equity cannot enter. 15. Yea, truth faileth; and he *that* departeth from evil maketh himself a prey: and the LORD saw *it*, and it displeased him that *there was* no judgment.

Jer. 22:1. Thus saith the LORD; Go down to the house of the king of Judah, and speak there this word, 2. And say, Hear the word of the LORD, O king of Judah, that sittest upon the throne of David, thou, and thy servants, and thy people that enter in by these gates: 3. Thus saith the LORD; Execute ye judgment and righteousness, and deliver the spoiled out of the hand of the oppressor: and do no wrong, do no violence to the stranger, the fatherless, nor the widow, neither shed innocent blood in this place. 4. For if ye do this thing indeed, then shall there enter in by the gates of this house kings sitting upon the throne of David, riding in chariots and on horses, he, and his servants, and his people.

Lam. 3:35. To turn aside the right of a man before the face of the most High, 36. To subvert a man in his cause, the Lord approveth not.

Amos 5:7. Ye who turn judgment to wormwood, and leave off righteousness in the earth, 11. Forasmuch therefore as your treading *is* upon the poor, and ye take from him burdens of wheat: ye have built houses of hewn stone, but ye shall not dwell in them; ye have planted pleasant vineyards, but ye shall not drink wine of them. 12. For I know your manifold transgressions and your mighty sins: they afflict the just, they take a bribe, and they turn aside the poor in the gate *from their right.*

Mic. 7:3. That they may do evil with both hands earnestly, the prince asketh, and the judge *asketh* for a reward; and the great *man*, he uttereth his mischievous desire: so they wrap it up.

Hab. 1:4. Therefore the law is slacked, and judgment doth never go forth: for the wicked doth compass about the righteous; therefore wrong judgment proceedeth.

Zech. 8:16. These *are* the things that ye shall do ; Speak ye every man the truth to his neighbour ; execute the judgment of truth and peace in your gates :

Matt. 5:23. Therefore if thou bring thy gift to the altar, and there rememberest that thy brother hath aught against thee ; 24. Leave there thy gift before the altar, and go thy way ; first be reconciled to thy brother, and then come and offer thy gift.

Matt. 12:7. But if ye had known what *this* meaneth, I will have mercy, and not sacrifice, ye would not have condemned the guiltless.

John 7:24. Judge not according to the appearance, but judge righteous judgment. 51. Doth our law judge *any* man, before it hear him, and know what he doeth ?

1 Cor. 13:6. Rejoiceth not in iniquity, but rejoiceth in the truth ;

See COURTS ; JUDGES ; WITNESS ; LAWYERS.

JUSTIFICATION. Gen. 15:6. He believed the LORD ; and he counted it to him for righteousness. Rom. 4:3.

Psa. 32:2. Blessed *is* the man unto whom the LORD imputeth not iniquity, Rom. 4:6.

Psa. 71:16. I will go in the strength of the Lord GOD : I will make mention of thy righteousness, *even* of thine only.

Psa. 89:16. In thy name shall they rejoice all the day : and in thy righteousness shall they be exalted.

Isa. 42:21. The LORD is well pleased for his righteousness' sake ; he will magnify the law, and make *it* honourable.

Isa. 45:24. Surely, shall one say, in the LORD have I righteousness and strength : *even* to him shall *men* come ; 25. In the LORD shall all the seed of Israel be justified, and shall glory.

Isa. 46:12. Hearken unto me, ye stouthearted, that *are* far from righteousness : 13. I bring near my righteousness ; it shall not be far off, and my salvation shall not tarry : and I will place salvation in Zion for Israel my glory.

Isa. 50:8. *He is* near that justifieth me ; who will contend with me ? let us stand together : who *is* mine adversary ? let him come near to me.

Isa. 51:5. My righteousness *is* near ; my salvation is gone forth, and mine arms shall judge the people ; the isles shall wait upon me, and on mine arm shall they trust. 6. Lift up your eyes to the heavens, and look upon the earth beneath : for the heavens shall vanish away like smoke, and the earth shall wax old like a garment, and they that dwell therein shall die in like manner : but my salvation shall be for ever, and my righteousness shall not be abolished.

Isa. 53:11. He shall see of the travail of his soul, *and* shall be satisfied : by his knowledge shall my righteous servant justify many ; for he shall bear their iniquities.

Isa. 54:17. No weapon that is formed against thee shall prosper ; and every tongue *that* shall rise against thee in judgment thou shalt condemn. This *is* the heritage of the servants of the LORD, and their righteousness *is* of me, saith the LORD.

Isa. 56:1. Thus saith the LORD, Keep ye judgment, and do justice : for my salvation *is* near to come, and my righteousness to be revealed.

Isa. 61:10. My soul shall be joyful in my God ; for he hath clothed me with the garments of salvation, he hath covered me with the robe of righteousness, as a bridegroom decketh *himself* with ornaments, and as a bride adorneth *herself* with her jewels.

Jer. 23:6. In his days Judah shall be saved, and Israel shall dwell safely ; and this *is* his name whereby he shall be called, THE LORD OUR RIGHTEOUSNESS.

Zech. 3:4. Take away the filthy garments from him. And unto him he said, Behold, I have caused thine iniquity to pass from thee, and I will clothe thee with ¹ change of raiment.　[1 R. V. rich apparel]

John 5:24. He that heareth my word, and believeth on him that sent me, hath everlasting life, and shall not come into condemnation ; but is passed from death unto life.

Acts 13:39. By him all that believe are justified from all things, from which ye could not be justified by the law of Moses.

Rom. 1:16. For I am not ashamed of the gospel of Christ : for it is the power of God unto salvation to every one that believeth ; to the Jew first, and also to the Greek. 17. For therein is the righteousness of God revealed from faith to faith : as it is written, The just shall live by faith. Hab. 2:4 ; Gal. 3:11.

Rom. 2:13. For not the hearers of the law *are* just before God, but the doers of the law shall be justified.

Rom. 3:21. The righteousness of God without the law is manifested, being witnessed by the law and the prophets ; 22. Even the righteousness of God *which is* by faith of Jesus Christ unto all and upon all them that believe : for there is no difference : 24. Being justified freely by his grace through the redemption that is in Christ Jesus : 25. Whom God hath set forth *to be* a propitiation through faith in his blood, to declare his righteousness for the remission of sins that are past, through the forbearance of God ; 26. To declare, I say, at this time his righteousness : that he might be just, and the justifier of him which believeth in Jesus. 28. Therefore we conclude that a man is justified by faith without the deeds of the law. 30. *It is* one God, which shall justify the circumcision by faith, and uncircumcision through faith.

Rom. 4:5. But to him that worketh not, but believeth on him that justifieth the ungodly, his faith is counted for righteousness. 6. Even as David also describeth the blessedness of the man, unto whom God imputeth righteousness without works, 7. *Saying,* Blessed *are* they whose iniquities are forgiven, and whose sins are covered. 8. Blessed *is* the man to whom the Lord will not impute sin. 9. *Cometh* this blessedness then upon the circumcision *only*, or upon the uncircumcision also? for we say that faith was reckoned to Abraham for righteousness. 10. How was it then reckoned? when he was in circumcision, or in uncircumcision? Not in circumcision, but in uncircumcision. 11. And he received the sign of circumcision, a seal of the righteousness of the faith which *he had yet* being uncircumcised: that he might be the father of all them that believe, though they be not circumcised; that righteousness might be imputed unto them also: 12. And the father of circumcision to them who are not of the circumcision only, but who also walk in the steps of that faith of our father Abraham, which *he had* being *yet* uncircumcised. 13. For the promise, that he should be the heir of the world, *was* not to Abraham, or to his seed, through the law, but through the righteousness of faith. 14. For if they which are of the law *be* heirs, faith is made void, and the promise made of none effect: 15. Because the law worketh wrath: for where no law is, *there is* no transgression. 16. Therefore *it is* of faith, that *it might be* by grace; to the end the promise might be sure to all the seed; not to that only which is of the law, but to that also which is of the faith of Abraham; who is the father of us all, 17. (As it is written, I have made thee a father of many nations,) before him whom he believed, *even* God, who quickeneth the dead, and calleth those things which be not as though they were. 18. Who against hope believed in hope, that he might become the father of many nations, according to that which was spoken, So shall thy seed be. 19. And being not weak in faith, he considered not his own body now dead, when he was about an hundred years old, neither yet the deadness of Sarah's womb: 20. He staggered not at the promise of God through unbelief; but was strong in faith, giving glory to God; 21. And being fully persuaded that, what he had promised, he was able also to perform. 22. And therefore it was imputed to him for righteousness. 23. Now it was not written for his sake alone, that it was imputed to him; 24. But for us also, to whom it shall be imputed, if we believe on him that raised up Jesus our Lord from the dead; 25. Who was delivered for our offences, and was raised again for our justification.

Rom. 5:1. Being justified by faith, [1] we have peace with God through our Lord Jesus Christ: 9. Much more then, being now justified by his blood, we shall be saved from [2] wrath through him. 11. We also joy in God through our Lord Jesus Christ, by whom we have now received the atonement. 16. And not as *it was* by one that sinned, *so is* the gift: for the judgment *was* by one to condemnation, but the free gift *is* of many offences unto justification. 17. For if by one man's offence death reigned by one;

much more they which receive abundance of grace and of the gift of righteousness shall reign in life by one, Jesus Christ. 18. Therefore as by the offence of one *judgment came* upon all men to condemnation; even so by the righteousness of one *the free gift came* upon all men unto justification of life. 21. That as sin hath reigned unto death, even so might grace reign through righteousness unto eternal life by Jesus Christ our Lord. *vs.* 12-21. [1 R. V. let us   2 wrath of God]

Rom. 6:22. But now being made free from sin, and become servants to God, ye have your fruit unto holiness, and the end everlasting life.

Rom. 7:4. Wherefore, my brethren, ye also are become dead to the law by the body of Christ; that ye should be married to another, *even* to him who is raised from the dead, that we should bring forth fruit unto God. *vs.* 1-25.

Rom. 8:1. *There* is therefore now no condemnation to them which are in Christ Jesus, [1] who walk not after the flesh, but after the Spirit. 30. Whom he called, them he also justified: and whom he justified, them he also glorified. 31. What shall we then say to these things? If God *be* for us, who *can be* against us? 33. Who shall lay any thing to the charge of God's elect? *It is* God that justifieth. 34. Who *is* he that condemneth? *It is* Christ that died, yea rather, that is risen again, who is even at the right hand of God, who also maketh intercession for us. [1 Omitted in R. V.]

Rom. 9:30. The Gentiles, which followed not after righteousness, have attained to righteousness, even the righteousness which is of faith. 31. Israel, which followed after the law of righteousness, hath not attained to the law of righteousness. 32. Wherefore? Because *they sought it* not by faith, but as it were by the works of the law.

Rom. 10:4. Christ *is* the end of the law for righteousness to every one that believeth. 5. For Moses describeth the righteousness which is of the law, That the man which doeth those things shall live by them. 6. But the righteousness which is of faith speaketh on this wise, 8. The word is nigh thee, *even* in thy mouth, and in thy heart: that is, the word of faith, which we preach; 9. That if thou shalt confess with thy mouth the Lord Jesus, and shalt believe in thine heart that God hath raised him from the dead, thou shalt be saved. 10. For with the heart man believeth unto righteousness; and with the mouth confession is made unto salvation. 11. For the scripture saith, Whosoever believeth on him shall not be ashamed. *vs.* 1-21.

1 Cor. 1:30. But of him are ye in Christ Jesus, who of God is made unto us wisdom, and righteousness, and sanctification, and redemption:

1 Cor. 6:11. And such were some of you: but ye are washed, but ye are sanctified, but ye are justified in the name of the Lord Jesus, and by the Spirit of our God.

2 Cor. 5:19. To wit, that God was in Christ, reconciling the world unto himself, not imputing their trespasses unto them; and hath committed unto us the word of reconciliation. 21. He hath made him *to be* sin for us, who knew no sin; that we might be made the righteousness of God in him.

Gal. 2:16. A man is not justified by the works of the law, but by the faith of Jesus Christ, even we have believed in Jesus Christ, that we might be justified by the faith of Christ, and not by the works of the law: for by the works of the law shall no flesh be justified. *vs.* 14-21.

Gal. 3:8. The scripture, foreseeing that God would justify the heathen through faith, preached before the gospel unto Abraham, *saying*, In thee shall all nations be blessed. 9. So then they which be of faith are blessed with faithful Abraham. [*v.* 6.] 21. If there had been a law given which could have given life, verily righteousness should have been by the law. 22. But the scripture hath concluded all under sin, that the promise by faith of Jesus Christ might be given to them that believe. 24. The law was our schoolmaster *to bring us* unto Christ, that we might be justified by faith. Gal. 4:21-31.

Gal. 5:4. Christ is become of no effect unto you, whosoever of you are justified by the law; ye are fallen from grace. 5. For we through the Spirit wait for the hope of righteousness by faith. 6. For in Jesus Christ neither circumcision availeth any thing, nor uncircumcision; but faith which worketh by love.

Eph. 6:14. Stand therefore, having your loins girt about with truth, and having on the breastplate of righteousness;

Phil. 3:8. That I may win Christ, 9. And be found in him, not having mine own righteousness, which is of the law, but that which is through the faith of Christ, the righteousness which is of God by faith:

Col. 2:13. And you, being dead in your sins and the uncircumcision of your flesh, hath he quickened together with him, having forgiven you all trespasses; 14. Blotting out the handwriting of ordinances that was against us, which was contrary to us, and took it out of the way, nailing it to his cross;

Tit. 3:7. Being justified by his grace, we should be made heirs according to the hope of eternal life.

Heb. 11:4. By faith Abel offered unto God a more excellent sacrifice than Cain, by which he obtained witness that he was righteous, God testifying of his gifts: 7. By faith Noah, being warned of God of things not seen as yet, moved with fear, prepared an ark to the saving of his house; by the which he condemned the world, and became heir of the righteousness which is by faith.

Jas. 2:20. But wilt thou know, O vain man, that faith without works is dead? 21. Was not Abraham our father justified by works, when he had offered Isaac his son upon the altar? 22. Seest thou how faith wrought with his works, and by works was faith made perfect? 23. And the scripture was fulfilled which saith, Abraham believed God, and it was imputed unto him for righteousness: and he was called the Friend of God. 26. For as the body without the spirit is dead, so faith without works is dead also.

KINDRED SUBJECTS TO: See ADOPTION; FORGIVENESS; REGENERATION; SANCTIFICATION; SIN, CONFESSION OF, FORGIVENESS OF.

JUSTUS. 1. A disciple nominated with Matthias to succeed Judas Iscariot, Acts 1:23.

2. A believer in Corinth, Acts 18:7.

3. Called also JESUS. A disciple in Rome, Col. 4:11.

JUTTAH, a Levitical city in Judah, Josh. 15:55; 21:16.

K

KABZEEL, a city of Judah, Josh. 15:21; 2 Sam. 23:20; 1 Chr. 11:22.

KADESH, called also KADESH-BARNEA. A city on the southern boundary of Palestine, Josh. 15:3. Smitten by Chedorlaomer, Gen. 14:7. Abraham dwells by the wells near, Gen. 20:1 with 14:7; 16:14. Israel encamps at, Num. 12:16; 13:26; 20:1; 33:36. Canaanites defeated at, Josh. 10:41.

KADMIEL. 1. A Levite, Ezra 2:40; 3:9; Neh. 7:43; 12:8,24.

2. A Levite who assisted in leading the devotions of the people, Neh. 9:4,5; 10:9.

KALLAI, a priest, Neh. 12:20.

KANAH. 1. A brook dividing Ephraim from Manasseh, Josh. 16:8; 17:9.

2. A town in Asher, Josh. 19:28.

KAREAH, called also CAREAH. Father of Johanan, 2 Kin. 25:23; Jer. 40:8,13; 41:11, 13,14,16.

KARKAA, a city of Judah, Josh. 15:3.

KARKOR, a city in Gad, Judg. 8:10.

KARTAH, a city of Zebulun, Josh. 21: 34.

KARTAN, a Levitical city in Naphtali, Josh. 21:32.

KATTATH, a city in Zebulun, Josh. 19:15.

KEDAR. 1. Son of Ishmael, Gen. 25:13; 1 Chr. 1:29.

2. A nomadic clan of the Ishmaelites, Psa. 120:5; Song 1:5; Isa. 21:16; 42:11; 60:7; Jer. 49:28. Flocks of, Isa. 60:7; Jer. 49:28. Princes and commerce of, Ezek. 27:21.

KEDEMAH, son of Ishmael, Gen. 25: 15; 1 Chr. 1:31.

KEDEMOTH. A city of Moab, allotted to Reuben and the Merarite Levites, Josh. 13:18; 1 Chr. 6:79. Encircled by a wilderness of same name, Deut. 2:26.

KEDESH. 1. A city of Judah, Josh. 15: 23. Possibly identical with KADESH-BARNEA.

2. Called also KISHION and KISHON. A

Canaanite city taken by Joshua, Josh. 12: 22; 19:20; 21:28; 1 Chr. 6:72.

3. Called also KEDESH-NAPHTALI. A city of refuge, Josh. 20:7; 21:32. Home of Barak and Heber, Judg. 4:6,9,11. Captured by Tiglath-pileser, 2 Kin. 15:29.

KEHELATHAH, an encampment of Israel. Num. 33:22,23.

KEILAH. 1. One of a group of nine cities in the southern part of Palestine allotted to Judah, Josh. 15:44. Philistines make a predatory excursion against, after harvest, 1 Sam. 23:1. David rescues, 1 Sam. 23:2–13. Rulers of, aid in restoring the wall of Jerusalem after the captivity, Neh. 3:17,18.

2. A descendant of Caleb, 1 Chr. 4:19.

KELAIAH, called also KELITA. A Levite who divorced his Gentile wife after the captivity, and assisted Ezra in expounding the law, Ezra 10:23; Neh. 8:7; 10:10.

KEMUEL. 1. Son of Nahor, Gen. 22: 21.

2. A prince of Ephraim, Num. 34:24.

3. A Levite, 1 Chr. 27:17.

KENAN. See CAINAN.

KENATH, called also NOBAH. A city of Gilead, Num. 32:42; 1 Chr. 2:23.

KENAZ. 1. Grandson of Esau, Gen. 36:11,15; 1 Chr. 1:36.

2. A duke of Edom, Gen. 36:42; 1 Chr. 1:53.

3. Brother of Caleb, Josh. 15:17; Judg. 1: 13; 3:9,11; 1 Chr. 4:13.

4. Grandson of Caleb, 1 Chr. 4:15.

KENITES. 1. A Canaanitish tribe whose country was given to Abraham, Gen. 15:19; Num. 24:21-23.

2. The descendants of Jethro, a Midianite, father-in-law of Moses. Join the Israelites and dwell at Jericho, Judg. 1:16; 4:11; 1 Chr. 2:55; later in the wilderness of Judah, Judg. 1:16,17. Jael, one of the, betrays and slays Sisera, Judg. 4:17-21.

KENIZZITES,an Edomitish tribe whose land was promised to Abraham, Gen. 15:19.

KERCHIEF. See HANDKERCHIEF.

KEREN-HAPPUCH, youngest daughter of Job, Job 42:14.

KERIOTH. 1. A city of Judah, Josh. 15:25.

2. Called also KIRIOTH. A city of Moab, Jer. 48:24,41; Amos 2:2.

KETURAH, wife or concubine of Abraham, Gen. 25:1-4; 1 Chr. 1:32.

KEY, Judg. 3:25. A symbol of authority, Isa. 22:22; Matt. 16:19; Rev. 1:18; 3:7; 9:1; 20:1.

FIGURATIVE: Luke 11:52.

KEZIA, second daughter of Job, Job 42:14.

KEZIZ, a valley and city of Benjamin, Josh. 18:21.

KIBROTH-HATTAAVAH, a station where the Israelites were miraculously fed with quails, Num. 11:31-35; 33:16,17; Deut. 9:22.

KIBZAIM, a Levitical city in Ephraim, Josh. 21:22.

KIDNAPPING, forbidden, Ex. 21:16; Deut. 24:7.

INSTANCE OF: Judg. 21:20-23.

KIDNEY, burnt offering of the, Ex. 29:13,22; Lev. 3; 4:9,10; 7:4,5; 8:16; 9:10; Deut. 32:14.

KIDRON, called also CEDRON. A valley and stream between Jerusalem and the Mount of Olives, 1 Kin. 2:37; Neh. 2:15; Jer. 31:40. David flees from Absalom across, 2 Sam. 15:23. Destruction of idols at, by Asa, Josiah, and the Levites, 1 Kin. 15:13; 2 Kin. 23:6,12; 2 Chr. 29:16. Source of, closed by Hezekiah, 2 Chr. 32:4. Jesus crossed, on the night of his agony, John 18:1.

KILLING. See HOMICIDE.

KINAH, a city of Judah, Josh. 15:22.

KINDNESS. Lev.19:34. *But* the stranger that dwelleth with you shall be unto you as one born among you, and thou shalt love him as thyself; for ye were strangers in the land of Egypt:

Deut. 22:1. Thou shalt not see thy brother's ox or his sheep go astray, and hide thyself from them: thou shalt in any case bring them again unto thy brother. *vs.* 2-4.

Psa. 112:5. A good man sheweth favor, and lendeth:

Prov. 14:21. He that despiseth his neighbour sinneth: but he that hath mercy on the poor, happy *is* he.

Prov. 19:22. The desire of a man *is* his kindness:

Prov. 31:26. In her tongue *is* the law of kindness.

Isa. 11:13. The envy also of Ephraim shall depart, and the adversaries of Judah shall be cut off: Ephraim shall not envy Judah, and Judah shall not vex Ephraim.

Zech. 7:9. Thus speaketh the LORD of hosts, saying, Execute true judgment, and shew mercy and compassions every man to his brother: 10. And oppress not the widow, nor the fatherless, the stranger, nor the poor; and let none of you imagine evil against his brother in your heart.

Matt. 5:7. Blessed *are* the merciful: for they shall obtain mercy. 42. Give to him that asketh thee, and from him that would borrow of thee turn not thou away. Luke 6:30.

Matt. 25:34. Then shall the King say unto them on his right hand, Come, ye blessed of my Father, inherit the kingdom prepared for you from the foundation of the world: 35. For I was an hungred, and ye gave me meat: I was thirsty, and ye gave me drink: I was a stranger, and ye took me in: 36. Naked, and ye clothed me: I was sick, and ye visited me: I was in prison, and ye came unto me.

Luke 6:34. And if ye lend *to them* of whom ye hope to receive, what thank have ye? for sinners also lend to sinners, to receive as much again. 35. But love ye your enemies, and do good, and lend, hoping for nothing again; and your reward shall be great, and ye shall be the children of the

Highest: for he is kind unto the unthankful and *to* the evil.

Acts 20:35. I have shewed you all things, how that so labouring ye ought to support the weak, and to remember the words of the Lord Jesus, how he said, It is more blessed to give than to receive.

Rom. 12:15. Rejoice with them that do rejoice, and weep with them that weep.

Rom. 15:1. We then that are strong ought to bear the infirmities of the weak, and not to please ourselves. 2. Let every one of us please *his* neighbour for *his* good to edification. 5. The God of patience and consolation grant you to be likeminded one toward another according to Christ Jesus:

1 Cor. 13:4. Charity suffereth long, *and* is kind; charity envieth not; charity vaunteth not itself, is not puffed up, 5. Doth not behave itself unseemly, seeketh not her own, is not easily provoked, thinketh no evil; 6. Rejoiceth not in iniquity, but rejoiceth in the truth; 7. Beareth all things, believeth all things, hopeth all things, endureth all things.

Gal. 6:1. Brethren, if a man be overtaken in a fault, ye which are spiritual, restore such an one in the spirit of meekness; considering thyself, lest thou also be tempted. 2. Bear ye one another's burdens, and so fulfil the law of Christ. 10. As we have therefore opportunity, let us do good unto all *men*, especially unto them who are of the household of faith.

Eph. 4:32. And be ye kind one to another, tenderhearted, forgiving one another, even as God for Christ's sake hath forgiven you.

Col. 3:12. Put on therefore, as the elect of God, holy and beloved, bowels of mercies, kindness, humbleness of mind, meekness, longsuffering; 14. And above all these things, *put on* charity, which is the bond of perfectness.

1 Tim. 5:9. Let not a widow be taken into the number under threescore years old, having been the wife of one man, 10. Well reported of for good works; if she have brought up children, if she have lodged strangers, if she have washed the saints' feet, if she have relieved the afflicted, if she have diligently followed every good work.

Heb. 5:2. Who can have compassion on the ignorant, and on them that are out of the way; for that he himself also is compassed with infirmity.

1 Pet. 3:8. *Be ye* all of one mind, having compassion one of another, love as brethren, *be* pitiful, *be* courteous: *v. 9.*

1 Pet. 4:8. Above all things have fervent charity among yourselves: for charity shall cover the multitude of sins.

2 Pet. 1:7. And to godliness, brotherly kindness; and to brotherly kindness, charity.

1 John 3:17. But whoso hath this world's good, and seeth his brother have need, and shutteth up his bowels *of compassion* from him, how dwelleth the love of God in him?

18. My little children, let us not love in word, neither in tongue; but in deed and in truth.

INSTANCES OF: Pharaoh to Jacob, Gen. 45:16-20; 47:5,6. Pharaoh's daughter to Moses, Ex. 2:6-10. Rahab to the spies, Josh. 2:6-16. David to Mephibosheth, 2 Sam. 9:1-13. Joab to Absalom, 2 Sam. 14: 1-24. Ahab to Ben-hadad, 1 Kin. 20:32-34. Elisha to the woman whose son he restored to life, 2 Kin. 8:1. Evil-merodach to Jehoiachin, 2 Kin. 25:28-30. Jehoshabeath to Joash, 2 Chr. 22:11. Jews to the people, Neh. 5:8-19. Mordecai to Esther, Esth. 2:7. Nebuchadrezzar to Jeremiah, Jer. 39:11,12.

Joseph to Mary, Matt. 1:19. Centurion to his servant, Luke 7:2-6. Jews to Mary and Martha, John 11:19,33. John to Mary, John 19:27. Felix to Paul, Acts 24:23. Julius to Paul, Acts 27:3,43. Onesiphorus to Paul, 2 Tim. 1:16-18.

KINE, Pharaoh's dream of, Gen. 41:2-7, 26-30.

See CATTLE.

FIGURATIVE: Amos 4:1.

KING. Called KING OF KINGS, Ezra 7:12; Ezek. 26:7; Dan. 2:37. Divinely authorized, Deut. 17:15; 1 Sam. 9:16,17; 16:12; 1 Chr. 22: 10; 2 Chr. 2:11,12; Prov. 8:15; Dan. 2:21,37; 4:17; 5:20; Hos. 8:4; 13:11.

How chosen: By divine appointment, Saul, 1 Sam. 10:1; David and the Davidic dynasty, 1 Sam. 16:1-13. Hereditary succession, 2 Sam. 7:12-16; 1 Kin. 1:28-30; 2 Chr. 21:3,4; Psa. 89:35-37. See ISRAEL; KINGS OF JUDAH. Not hereditary, 1 Chr. 1:43-51. See ISRAEL; KINGS OF ISRAEL, after the revolt. By lot, 1 Sam. 10:20,21. Modes of induction into office: By anointing. See ANOINTING. By proclamation, 2 Sam. 15:10; 1 Kin. 1:33,34; 2 Kin. 9:13; 11:12; by an oath, 2 Kin. 11:4. Ceremonial recognition of: Prostration, 1 Sam. 25:41; 2 Sam. 9:6,8; 1 Kin. 1:23,31,47; obeisance, 1 Kin. 1:16; kneeling before, Matt. 27:29; salutation to: "O king, live forever," Dan. 2:4; 6:6,21.

Acts as Judge, 2 Sam. 8:15; 15:2; 1 Kin. 10:9; 2 Kin. 8:1-6; Psa. 72:1-4; 122:5; Acts 25:11,12,20. Precepts concerning, Deut. 17: 14-19; Prov. 31:4,5; Ezek. 46:16-18. Obedience to, enjoined, Eccl. 8:2-5. Rights and duties of, Prov. 25:2,5,6,15; 29:4,12,14; Jer. 21:12. Exercise executive clemency, 1 Sam. 11:13. Constitutional restrictions of, Deut. 17:18-20; 1 Sam. 10:24,25; 2 Sam. 5:3; 2 Kin. 11:12,17; 2 Chr. 23:11; Jer. 34:8-11; Dan. 6: 12-15. Influenced by popular opinion: Saul, 1 Sam. 14:45; 15:24; David, 2 Chr. 20:21; Hezekiah, 2 Chr. 30:2; Zedekiah, Jer. 38:19, 24-27; Herod, Matt. 14:5; Acts 12:2,3; Pilate, John 19:6-13.

Religious duties of, Ezek. 45:9-25; 46:2,4-8. Deification of, Ezek. 28:2,9. Loyalty to, enjoined, Prov. 16:14,15; Eccl. 10:20. Influence of queens over: Bath-sheba, 1 Kin. 1:28-34; Jezebel, 1 Kin. 18:4,13; 19:1-3; 21:5-16; Esther, Esth. 5:1-8. Respect due to, Job 34:18; Isa. 8:21; Matt. 22:21; Mark 12:17.

Emoluments of : Confiscations of property, 2 Sam. 16:4; 1 Kin. 21:1-16. Spoils, 2 Sam. 12:30; 1 Chr. 26:27; 2 Chr. 24:23. Tariff on imports, and internal revenue on merchandise, 1 Kin. 10:15-29. Tribute, 2 Sam. 20:24; 1 Kin. 12:18; 2 Chr. 17:11. Poll tax, Matt. 17: 24-27. Presents, 1 Sam. 10:27; 16:20; 2 Sam. 8:2; 1 Kin. 10:2, 10, 25; 2 Chr. 9:24; Psa. 72:10. Commissary of, 1 Kin. 4:7-19,27,28; 1 Chr. 27:25-31; 2 Chr. 26:10; 32:28,29.

Extensive studs of, Judg. 12:14; 1 Kin. 1: 33; 4:26; 10:25; 2 Chr. 9:24,25; Esth. 6:8.

Chief officers of : Captain of the host, 2 Sam. 8:16; 1 Kin. 4:4; recorder, 2 Sam. 8:16; 20:24; 1 Kin. 4:3; scribe, 2 Sam. 8:17; 20:25; 1 Kin. 4:3; chief priests, 2 Sam. 8:17; 20:25; 1 Kin. 4:2; chief of the bodyguard, 2 Sam. 8:18; 15:18; 20:23; 1 Chr. 11:25; collector of tribute, 2 Sam. 20:24; chief ruler, 2 Sam. 20:26; 1 Kin. 4:5; Esth. 3:1,2; 8:1,2,15; 10:3; counselor, 1 Kin. 4:5; provincial governors, Dan. 6:1-3.

Subordinate officers of : Governor of the household, 1 Kin. 4:6; 2 Chr. 28:7; keeper of the wardrobe, 2 Kin. 22:14; 2 Chr. 34:22.

Drunkenness of, forbidden, Prov. 31:4,5. Drunken, instances of, Hos. 7:5; Baasha, 1 Kin. 16:9; Ben-hadad, 1 Kin. 20:16; Belshazzar, Dan. 5:1-4,23; Ahasuerus, Esth. 1: 7,10; 5:6; 7:2.

Prayer for, Ezra 6:10. Prayer for, enjoined, 1 Tim. 2:1,2.

Decrees of, irrevocable, Esth. 8:8; Dan. 6: 8,9,12-15.

Chronicles of, kept, 1 Kin. 11:41; 14:19; 2 Kin. 21:25; 1 Chr. 9:1; 27:24; 29:29; 2 Chr. 9:29; 12:15; 20:34; 26:22; 32:32; Ezra 5:17; Esth. 6:1.

See GOVERNMENT ; RULERS.

For the kings of Israel, before and after the revolt of the ten tribes, see ISRAEL.

KINGDOM OF HEAVEN. Likened to a man who sowed good seed, Matt. 13:24-30,38-43; Mark 4:26-29; to a grain of mustard seed, Matt. 13:31,32; Mark 4:30,31; Luke 13:18,19; to leaven, Matt. 13:33; Luke 13:21; to a treasure, Matt. 13:44; to a pearl, Matt. 13: 45; to a net, Matt. 13:47-50; to a king who called his servants to a reckoning, Matt. 18:23-35; to a householder, Matt. 20:1-16; to a king who made a marriage feast for his son, Matt. 22:2-14; Luke 14:16-24; to ten virgins, Matt. 25:1-13; to a man traveling into a far country, who called his servants, and delivered to them his goods, Matt. 25: 14-30; Luke 19:12-27.

" My kingdom is not of this world," John 18:36.

Children of the, Matt. 18:3; 19:14; Mark 10:14; Luke 18:16. Rich cannot enter, Matt. 19:23,24; Mark 10:23-25; Luke 18:24,25,29,30. Keys of, Matt. 16:19. Glad tidings of, Luke 8:1. Mysteries of, Luke 8:10. Is not meat and drink, Rom. 14:17.

See CHURCH ; JESUS, KINGDOM OF.

KINGDOM OF SATAN, Matt. 12:26.

KING'S DALE, Gen. 14:17; 2 Sam. 18:18.

KIR. The inhabitants of Damascus carried into captivity to, by the king of Assyria,

2 Kin. 16:9. Prophecies concerning, Isa. 22: 6; Amos 1:5; 9:7.

KIR-HARASETH, called also KIRHARESH, KIR-HARESETH, and KIR-HERES. A city of Moab, 2 Kin. 3:25; Isa. 16:7,11; Jer. 48:31,36. Called KIR OF MOAB, Isa. 15:1.

KIRIATHAIM. See KIRJATHAIM.

KIRJATHAIM, 1. Called also KIRIATHAIM. A city of Reuben, Num. 32:37; Josh. 13:19. Prophecies concerning, Jer. 48:1,23; Ezek. 25:9.

2. A Levitical city in Naphtali, 1 Chr. 6:76.

KIRJATH-ARBA, an early name of HEBRON, Gen. 23:2; Josh. 14:15; Judg. 1:10.

KIRJATH-HUZOTH, a residence of Balak, Num. 22:39.

KIRJATH-JEARIM, called also BAALAH, one of the four cities of the Gibeonites. Inhabitants of, not smitten, on account of the covenant made by the Israelites with the Gibeonites, but put under servitude, Josh. 9:17, with verses 3-27.

In the territory allotted to Judah, Josh. 15:9,60; 18:14. The Philistines bring the ark to, 1 Sam. 6:21, with verses 1-21; ark remains twenty years at, 1 Sam. 7:1,2; 1 Chr. 13:5,6. David brings the ark from, 2 Sam. 6:1-11; 1 Chr. 13:5-8; 2 Chr. 1:4. Inhabitants of, who were taken into captivity to Babylon, returned, Ezra 2:25; Neh. 7:29. Urijah, the prophet, an inhabitant of, Jer. 26:20.

KIRJATH-SANNAH, a city of Judah, Josh. 15:49.
See DEBIR.

KIRJATH-SEPHER, Josh. 15:15,16.
See DEBIR.

KISH. 1. Father of Saul, 1 Sam. 9:1-3; 10:21; 2 Sam. 21:14. Called CIS in Acts 13:21.

2. A Benjamite, 1 Chr. 8:30; 9:36.

3. A Levite, 1 Chr. 23:21,22; 24:29.

4. A Levite, 2 Chr. 29:12.

5. Great grandfather of Mordecai, Esth. 2:5.

KISHI, called also KUSHAIAH. Father of Ethan, a chief assistant in the temple music, 1 Chr. 6:44; 15:17.

KISHION. See KEDESH.

KISHON, called also KISON. A noted river of Palestine emptying into the Mediterranean near the northern base of Mount Carmel ; Sisera defeated at, and his army destroyed in, Judg. 4:7,13; 5:21; Psa. 83:9. Prophets of Baal destroyed by Elijah at, 1 Kin. 18:40.

KISS. Of affection, Gen. 27:26,27; 31:55; 33:4; 48:10; 50:1; Ex. 18:7; Ruth 1:14; 2 Sam. 14:33; 19:39; Luke 15:20; Acts 20:37. The feet of Jesus kissed by the penitent woman, Luke 7:38. Deceitful, Prov. 27:6; of Joab when he slew Amasa, 2 Sam. 20:9,10; of Judas, when he betrayed Jesus, Matt. 26:48. Luke 22:48. Holy, Rom. 16:16; 2 Cor. 13:12; 1 Thess. 5:26; 1 Pet. 5:14.

KITE, a bird forbidden as food, Lev. 11:14; Deut. 14:13.

KITHLISH, a city of Judah, Josh. 15:40.

KITRON, a city of Zebulun, Judg. 1:30.

KITTIM. See CHITTIM.

KNEADING-TROUGH. Ex. 8:3; 12:34; Deut. 28:5,17 [marg.].

KNIFE. An edged tool used by Abraham in offering Isaac, Gen. 22:6. Of the temple, returned from Babylon, Ezra 1:9. Used for sharpening pens, Jer. 36:23. Self-flagellation with, in idolatrous worship, 1 Kin. 18:28.

KNOWLEDGE. Of good and evil, Gen. 2:9,17; 3:22. Is power, Prov. 3:20; 24:5. Desire for, 1 Kin. 3:9; Psa. 119:66; Prov. 2; 3; 12:1; 15:14; 18:15. Rejected, Hos. 4:6. Those who reject are destroyed, Hos. 4:6. Fools hate, Prov. 1:22,29. A divine gift, 1 Cor. 12:8. Is pleasant, Prov. 2:10. Shall be increased, Dan. 12:4.

The earth shall be full of, Isa. 11:9. Fear of the Lord is the beginning of, Prov. 1:7. Of more value than gold, Prov. 8:10. The priest's lips should keep, Mal. 2:7.

Of salvation, Luke 1:77. Key of, Luke 11:52. Now we know in part, 1 Cor. 13:9-12. Of God more than burnt offering, Hos. 6:6. Of Christ, Phil. 3:8.

See WISDOM.

KOA, a symbolical term in Ezek. 23:23.

KOHATH. Son of Levi, Gen. 46:11; Ex. 6:16. Grandfather of Moses, Aaron, and Miriam, Num. 26:58,59. Father of the Kohathites, one of the divisions of the Levites, Ex. 6:18; Num. 3:19,27.

See LEVITES.

KOLAIAH. 1. A Benjamite and ancestor of Sallu, Neh. 11:7.

2. Father of the false prophet Ahab, Jer. 29:21.

KORAH. 1. A son of Esau, Gen. 36:5, 14,18.

2. A Korhite Levite, Ex. 6:18,21,24; jealous of Moses, leads two hundred and fifty princes in an insurrection, and is swallowed up in the earth, Num. 16; 26:9,10; Deut. 11:6; Psa. 106:17; Jude 11.

3. Son of Hebron, 1 Chr. 2:43.

4. Son of Kohath, and head of the family of sacred musicians among the Levites, 1 Chr. 6:22.

See titles to Psalms 42; 45; 46; 47; 48; 87; 88.

KORE. 1. A Korahite, 1 Chr. 9:19; 26:1.

2. A Levite, keeper of the east gate, 2 Chr. 31:14.

KORHITES, a division of the Levites. See LEVITES.

KOZ, called also HAKKOZ. Head of the seventh division priests, 1 Chr. 24:10. Descendants of, excluded from priesthood because of defective genealogies, Ezra 2:61; Neh. 7:63; repair walls of Jerusalem, Neh. 3:4,21.

KUSHAIAH. See KISHI.

L

LAADAH, son of Shelah, 1 Chr. 4:21.

LAADAN. 1. A descendant of Ephraim, 1 Chr. 7:26.

2. A Levite, called also LIBNI, 1 Chr. 6:17; 23:7-9; 26:21.

LABAN. Son of Bethuel, Gen. 28:5. Brother of Rebekah, Gen. 22:23; 24:15,29. Receives the servant of Abraham, Gen. 24:29-33. Receives Jacob, and gives him his daughters in marriage, Gen. 29:12-30. Jacob becomes his servant, Gen. 29:15-20,27; 30:27-43. Outwitted by Jacob, Gen. 30:37-43; 31:1-21. Pursues Jacob, overtakes him at Mount Gilead, and covenants with him, Gen. 31:22-55.

LABOR. Gen. 3:19. In the sweat of thy face shalt thou eat bread, till thou return unto the ground; for out of it wast thou taken: for dust thou *art*, and unto dust shalt thou return.

Ex. 20:9. Six days shalt thou labour, and do all thy work: 10. But the seventh day *is* the sabbath of the LORD thy God: *in it* thou shalt not do any work, thou, nor thy son, nor thy daughter, thy manservant, nor thy maidservant, nor thy cattle, nor thy stranger that *is* within thy gates: 11. For *in* six days the LORD made heaven and earth, the sea, and all that in them *is*, and rested the seventh day: wherefore the LORD blessed the sabbath day, and hallowed it.

Ex. 23:12. Six days thou shalt do thy work, and on the seventh day thou shalt rest: that thine ox and thine ass may rest, and the son of thy handmaid, and the stranger, may be refreshed.

Ex. 34:21. Six days thou shalt work, but on the seventh day thou shalt rest: in earing time and in harvest thou shalt rest. Lev. 23:3.

Lev. 19:13. Thou shalt not defraud thy neighbour, neither rob *him:* the wages of him that is hired shall not abide with thee all night until the morning.

Deut. 24:14. Thou shalt not oppress an hired servant *that is* poor and needy, *whether he be* of thy brethren, or of thy strangers that *are* in thy land within thy gates: 15. At his day thou shalt give *him* his hire, neither shall the sun go down upon it; for he *is* poor, and setteth his heart upon it: lest he cry against thee unto the LORD, and it be sin unto thee.

Deut. 25:4. Thou shalt not muzzle the ox when he treadeth out *the corn.* 1 Cor. 9:9; 1 Tim. 5:18.

Eccl. 5:12. The sleep of a labouring man *is* sweet, whether he eat little or much: but the abundance of the rich will not suffer him to sleep.

Jer. 22:13. Woe unto him that buildeth his house by unrighteousness, and his chambers by wrong; *that* useth his neighbour's service without wages, and giveth him not for his work:

Mal. 3:5. And I will come near to you to judgment; and I will be a swift witness against the sorcerers, and against the adulterers, and against false swearers, and against those that oppress the hireling in *his* wages,

Matt. 20:1. For the kingdom of heaven is like unto a man *that is* an householder, which went out early in the morning to hire labourers into his vineyard. 2. And when he had agreed with the labourers for a penny a day, he sent them into his vineyard. 3. And he went out about the third hour, and saw others standing idle in the market-place. 4. And said unto them; Go ye also into the vineyard, and whatsoever is right I will give you. And they went their way. 5. Again he went out about the sixth and ninth hour, and did likewise. 6. And about the eleventh hour he went out, and found others standing idle, and saith unto them, Why stand ye here all the day idle? 7. They say unto him, Because no man hath hired us. He said unto them; Go ye also into the vineyard; ¹and whatsoever is right, *that* shall ye receive. 8. So when even was come, the lord of the vineyard saith unto his steward, Call the labourers, and give them *their* hire, beginning from the last unto the first. 9. And when they came that *were hired* about the eleventh hour, they received every man a penny. 10. But when the first came, they supposed that they should have received more; and they likewise received every man a penny. 11. And when they had received *it*, they murmured against the goodman of the house, 12. Saying, These last have wrought *but* one hour, and thou hast made them equal unto us, which have borne the burden and heat of the day. 13. But he answered one of them, and said, Friend, I do thee no wrong: didst not thou agree with me for a penny? 14. Take *that* thine *is*, and go thy way: I will give unto this last, even as unto thee. 15. Is it not lawful for me to do what I will with mine own? Is thine eye evil, because I am good?   [¹ Omitted in R. V.]

Luke 10:7. The labourer is worthy of his hire.

Acts 20:35. I have shewed you all things, how that so labouring ye ought to support the weak, and to remember the words of the Lord Jesus, how he said, It is more blessed to give than to receive.

Eph. 4:28. Let him that stole steal no more: but rather let him labour, working with *his* hands the thing which is good, that he may have to give to him that needeth.

1 Thess. 4:11. Study to be quiet, and to do your own business, and to work with your own hands, as we commanded you; 12. That ye may walk honestly toward them that are without, and *that* ye may have lack of nothing.

2 Thess. 3:7. Yourselves know how ye ought to follow us: for we behaved not ourselves disorderly among you; 8. Neither did we eat any man's bread for nought; but wrought with labour and travail night and day, that we might not be chargeable to any of you: 9. Not because we have not power, but to make ourselves an ensample unto you to follow us. 10. For even when

we were with you, this we commanded you, that if any would not work, neither should he eat. 11. For we hear that there are some which walk among you disorderly, working not at all, but are busybodies. 12. Now them that are such we command and exhort by our Lord Jesus Christ, that with quietness they work, and eat their own bread. 13. But ye, brethren, be not weary in well doing.

Jas. 5:4. Behold, the hire of the labourers who have reaped down your fields, which is of you kept back by fraud, crieth: and the cries of them which have reaped are entered into the ears of the Lord of sabaoth.

See EMPLOYEE; EMPLOYER; IDLENESS; INDUSTRY; MASTER; SERVANT.

LACE, Ex. 39:31.

LACHISH. A city. King of, besieges Gibeon, Josh. 10:5. Captured by Joshua, Josh. 10:31,32. Allotted to Judah, Josh. 15:39. Fortified by Rehoboam, 2 Chr. 11:9. Assassination of Amaziah at, 2 Kin. 14:19. Besieged by Sennacherib, 2 Kin. 18:13-17; 19:8; 2 Chr. 32:9; by Nebuchadnezzar, Jer. 34:7. Prophecy concerning, Mic. 1:13.

LACHRYMATORY, Psa. 56:8.

LADDER, in Jacob's vision, Gen. 28:12.

LAHAD, a descendant of Judah, 1 Chr. 4:2.

LAHAI-ROI, called also BEER-LAHAI-ROI. A well near Kadesh. Hagar fled to, Gen. 16:7-14. Isaac dwells at, Gen. 24:62; 25:11.

LAHMAM, a city of Judah, Josh. 15:40.

LAHMI. Brother of Goliath. Slain by Elhanan, 2 Sam. 21:19; 1 Chr. 20:5.

LAISH. 1. Called also LESHEM. See DAN.

2. A native of Gallim, 1 Sam. 25:44; 2 Sam. 3:15.

3. A town near Jerusalem, Isa. 10:30.

LAKE, of fire, Rev. 19:20; 20:10,14,15; 21:8.

LAKUM, a city in Naphtali, Josh. 19:33.

LAMA SABACHTHANI, the dying wail of Jesus, Matt. 27:46; Mark 15:34. See Psa. 22:1.

LAMB. Offering of, Ex. 29:38-41; Lev. 3:7; 4:32; 5:6; 22:23; 23:12; Num. 6:12; 7:15,21; 28:3-8. Not to be seethed in its mother's milk, Ex. 23:19.

LAMB OF GOD, an appellation of Jesus, John 1:29; Rev. 6:16; 7:9,10,14,17; 12:11; 13:8; 14:1,4; 15:3; 17:14; 19:7; 21:9,14,22,23,27; 22:1,3.

LAMECH. 1. Father of Jabal, Jubal, and Tubal-cain, Gen. 4:18-24.

2. Son of Methuselah, and father of Noah, lived 777 years, Gen. 5:25-31; 1 Chr. 1:3. Ancestor of Jesus, Luke 3:36.

LAMENESS. Disqualified priests from exercising the priestly office, Lev. 21:18. Disqualified animals for sacrificial uses, Deut. 15:21. Hated by David, 2 Sam. 5:8. Healed by Jesus, Matt. 11:5; 15:31; 21:14; Luke 7:22; by Peter, Acts 3:2-11.

FIGURATIVE: Heb. 12:13.

LAMENTATIONS. Of David, Psa.

60:1–3. Of Jeremiah, see the Book of Lamentations. Of Ezekiel, Ezek. 19; 28:12–19.

See ELEGY.

LAMP. Miraculously appeared at Abraham's sacrifice, Gen. 15:17. For the tabernacle, Ex. 25:31–40; 37:17–22.

Kept burning at night in the tabernacle and cared for by priests, Ex. 27:20,21; Lev. 24:2–4.

FIGURATIVE: Job 18:6; Psa. 119:105; Prov. 13:9; 20:20; Isa. 62:1; Jer. 25:10; Zeph. 1:12; Matt. 6:22; 2 Pet. 1:19; Rev. 21:23.

SYMBOLICAL: Rev. 4:5; 8:10. See CANDLESTICK.

LANCE. See JAVELIN; SPEAR.

LAND. Appeared on third creative day, Gen. 1:9. Original title to, from God, Gen. 13:14–17; 15:7; Ex. 23:31; Lev. 25:23. Bought and sold, Gen. 23:3–18; 33:19; Acts 4:34; 5:1–8.

Sale and redemption of, laws concerning, Lev. 25:15,16,23–33; 27:17–24; Num. 36:4; Jer. 32:7–16,25,44; Ezek. 46:18. Conveyance of, by written deeds and other forms, Gen. 23: 3–20; Ruth 4:3–8,11; Jer. 32:9–14; witnessed, Gen. 23:10,11; Ruth 4:9–11; Jer. 32:9–14.

Sold for debt, Neh. 5:3–5. Rights in, alienated, 2 Kin. 8:1–6. Leased, Luke 20:9–16; Matt. 21:33–41.

Priests' part in, Gen. 47:22; Ezek. 48:10. King's part in, Ezek. 48:21. Widow's dower in, Ruth 4:3–9. Unmarried woman's rights in, Num. 27:1–11; 36:1–11.

To rest every seventh year for the benefit of the poor, Ex. 23:11. Products of, for all, Eccl. 5:9. Monopoly of, Gen. 47:20–26; Isa. 5:8; Mic. 2:1,2. See MORTGAGE.

Rules for apportioning Canaan among the tribes. See CANAAN; also Ezek. 47:22.

LANDMARKS, protected from fraudulent removal, Deut. 19:14; 27:17; Job 24:2; Prov. 22:28; 23:10; Hos. 5:10.

LANGUAGE. Unity of, Gen. 11:1,6. Confusion of, Gen. 11:1–9; 10:5,20,31. Dialects of the Jews, Judg. 12:6; Matt. 26:73. Many spoken at Jerusalem, John 19:20; Acts 2:8–11. Speaking in unknown, in religious assemblies, forbidden, 1 Cor. 14:2–28.

Gift of, Mark 16:17; Acts 2:7,8; 10:46; 19:6; 1 Cor. 12:10; 14.

Mentioned in scripture: Of Ashdod, Neh. 13:24; Chaldee, Dan. 1:4; Egyptian, Acts 2:10; Psa. 114:1; Greek, Luke 23:38; Acts 21:37; Latin, Luke 23:38; John 19:20; Lycaonia, Acts 14:11; Parthia and other lands, Acts 2:9–11; Syria, 2 Kin. 18:26; Ezra 4:7; Dan. 2:4.

LANTERN, John 18:3.

LAODICEA. A Phrygian city. Paul's concern for, Col. 2:1. Epaphras's zeal for, Col. 4:13. Epistle to the Colossians to be read in, Col. 4:15,16. Message to, through John, Rev. 1:11; 3:14–22.

LAPIDARY, one who cuts precious stones, Ex. 31:5; 35:33.

LAPIDOTH, husband of Deborah, Judg. 4:4.

LAPWING, a bird forbidden as food, Lev. 11:19; Deut. 14:18.

LARCENY. See THEFT.

LASCIVIOUSNESS. Ex. 32:6. And they rose up early on the morrow, and offered burnt offerings, and brought peace offerings; and the people sat down to eat and to drink, and rose up to play.

Prov. 2:16. To deliver thee from the strange woman, *even* from the stranger *which* flattereth with her words; 17. Which forsaketh the guide of her youth, and forgetteth the covenant of her God. 18. For her house inclineth unto death, and her paths unto the dead.

Prov. 5:3. For the lips of a strange woman drop *as* an honeycomb, and her mouth *is* smoother than oil: 4. But her end is bitter as wormwood, sharp as a twoedged sword. 5. Her feet go down to death; her steps take hold on hell. 8. Remove thy way far from her, and come not nigh the door of her house: 9. Lest thou give thine honour unto others, and thy years unto the cruel: 10. Lest strangers be filled with thy wealth; and thy labours *be* in the house of a stranger; 11. And thou mourn at the last, when thy flesh and thy body are consumed, 12. And say, How have I hated instruction, and my heart despised reproof; 13. And have not obeyed the voice of my teachers, nor inclined mine ear to them that instructed me!

Prov. 7:6. For at the window of my house I looked through my casement, 7. And beheld among the simple ones, I discerned among the youths, a young man void of understanding, 8. Passing through the street near her corner; and he went the way to her house, 9. In the twilight, in the evening, in the black and dark night: 10. And, behold, there met him a woman *with* the attire of an harlot, and subtil of heart. 11. (She *is* loud and stubborn; her feet abide not in her house: 12. Now *is she* without, now in the streets, and lieth in wait at every corner.) 13. So she caught him, and kissed him, *and* with an impudent face said unto him, 14. *I have* peace offerings with me; this day have I paid my vows. 15. Therefore came I forth to meet thee, diligently to seek thy face, and I have found thee. 16. I have decked my bed with coverings of tapestry, with carved *works*, with fine linen of Egypt. 17. I have perfumed my bed with myrrh, aloes, and cinnamon. 18. Come, let us take our fill of love until the morning: let us solace ourselves with loves. 19. For the goodman *is* not at home, he is gone a long journey: 20. He hath taken a bag of money with him, *and* will come home at the day appointed. 21. With her much fair speech she caused him to yield, with the flattering of her lips she forced him. 22. He goeth after her straightway, as an ox goeth to the slaughter, or as a fool to the correction of the stocks; 23. Till a dart strike through his liver; as a bird hasteth to the snare, and knoweth not that *it is* for his life. 24. Hearken unto me now therefore, O ye children, and attend to the words of my mouth. 25. Let not thine heart decline to her ways, go not astray in her paths. 26. For she hath cast down many wounded: yea, many strong *men* have been slain by her. 27. Her house *is* the way to hell, going down to the chambers of death.

Prov. 9:13. A foolish woman *is* clamorous: *she is* simple, and knoweth nothing. 14. For she sitteth at the door of her house, on a seat in the high places of the city, 15. To call passengers who go right on their ways: 16. Whoso *is* simple, let him turn in hither: and *as for* him that wanteth understanding, she saith to him, 17. Stolen waters are sweet, and bread *eaten* in secret is pleasant. 18. But he knoweth not that the dead *are* there; *and that* her guests *are* in the depths of hell.

Prov. 20:16. Take his garment that is surety *for* a stranger: and ¹ take a pledge of him for a strange woman.

[¹ R. V. hold him in pledge that is surety for strangers]

Prov. 30:18. There be three *things which* are too wonderful for me, yea, four which I know not: 19. The way of an eagle in the air; the way of a serpent upon a rock; the way of a ship in the midst of the sea; and the way of a man with a maid. 20. Such *is* the way of an adulterous woman; she eateth, and wipeth her mouth, and saith, I have done no wickedness.

Joel 3:3. And they have cast lots for my people; and have given a boy for an harlot, and sold a girl for wine, that they might drink.

Mark 7:21. For from within, out of the heart of men, proceed evil thoughts, adulteries, fornications, murders, 22. Thefts, covetousness, wickedness, deceit, lasciviousness, an evil eye, blasphemy, pride, foolishness: 23. All these evil things come from within, and defile the man.

Rom. 1:22. Professing themselves to be wise, they became fools, 23. And changed the glory of the uncorruptible God into an image made like to corruptible man, and to birds, and fourfooted beasts, and creeping things. 24. Wherefore God also gave them up to uncleanness through the lusts of their own hearts, to dishonour their own bodies between themselves: 25. Who changed the truth of God into a lie, and worshipped and served the creature more than the Creator, who is blessed for ever. Amen. 26. For this cause God gave them up unto vile affections: for even their women did change the natural use into that which is against nature: 27. And likewise also the men, leaving the natural use of the woman, burned in their lust one toward another; men with men working that which is unseemly, and receiving in themselves that recompence of their error which was meet. 28. And even as they did not like to retain God in *their* knowledge, God gave them over to a reprobate mind, to do those things which are not convenient; 29. Being filled with all unrighteousness, ¹ fornication, wickedness,

[¹ Omitted in R. V.]

Rom. 7:8. But sin, taking occasion by the commandment, wrought in me all manner of ¹ concupiscence. [¹ R. V. coveting]

Rom. 13:13. Let us walk honestly, as in the day; not in rioting and drunkenness, not in chambering and wantonness, not in strife and envying.

1 Cor. 6:9. Know ye not that the unrighteous shall not inherit the kingdom of God? Be not deceived: neither fornicators, nor idolaters, nor adulterers, nor effeminate, nor abusers of themselves with mankind, 10. Nor thieves, nor covetous, nor drunkards, nor revilers, nor extortioners, shall inherit the kingdom of God. 13. Meats for the belly, and the belly for meats: but God shall destroy both it and them. Now the body *is* not for fornication, but for the Lord; and the Lord for the body. 15. Know ye not that your bodies are the members of Christ? shall I then take the members of Christ, and make *them* the members of an harlot? God forbid. 16. What? know ye not that he which is joined to an harlot is one body? for two, saith he, shall be one flesh. 17. But he that is joined unto the Lord is one spirit. 18. Flee fornication. Every sin that a man doeth is without the body; but he that committeth fornication sinneth against his own body.

1 Cor. 9:27. But I keep under my body, and bring *it* into subjection: lest that by any means, when I have preached to others, I myself should be a castaway.

2 Cor. 12:21. I shall bewail many which have sinned already, and have not repented of the uncleanness and fornication and lasciviousness which they have committed.

Gal. 5:19. Now the works of the flesh are manifest, which are *these;* Adultery, fornication, uncleanness, lasciviousness, 20. Idolatry, witchcraft, hatred, variance, emulations, wrath, strife, seditions, heresies, 21. Envyings, murders, drunkenness, revellings, and such like: of the which I tell you before, as I have also told *you* in time past, that they which do such things shall not inherit the kingdom of God.

Eph. 4:17. This I say therefore, and testify in the Lord, that ye henceforth walk not as other Gentiles walk, in the vanity of their mind, 18. Having the understanding darkened, being alienated from the life of God through the ignorance that is in them, because of the blindness of their heart. 19. Who being past feeling have given themselves over unto lasciviousness, to work all uncleanness with greediness.

Eph. 5:5. For this ye know, that no whoremonger, nor unclean person, nor covetous man, who is an idolater, hath any inheritance in the kingdom of Christ and of God.

Col. 3:5. Mortify therefore your members which are upon the earth; fornication, uncleanness, inordinate affection, evil concupiscence, and covetousness, which is idolatry:

1 Thess. 4:5. Not in the lust of concupis-

cence, even as the Gentiles which know not God:

2 Tim. 3:6. For of this sort are they which creep into houses, and lead captive silly women laden with sins, led away with divers lusts,

1 Pet. 4:2. That he no longer should live the rest of *his* time in the flesh to the lusts of men, but to the will of God. 3. For the time past of *our* life may suffice us to have wrought the will of the Gentiles, when we walked in lasciviousness, lusts, excess of wine, revellings, banquetings, and abominable idolatries:

Jude 4. For there are certain men crept in unawares, who were before of old ordained to this condemnation, ungodly men, turning the grace of our God into lasciviousness, and denying the only Lord God, and our Lord Jesus Christ. 7. Even as Sodom and Gomorrah, and the cities about them in like manner, giving themselves over to fornication, and going after strange flesh, are set forth for an example, suffering the vengeance of eternal fire.

See ADULTERY; IDOLATRY, LICENTIOUS PRACTICES OF; INCEST; LUST; RAPE; SENSUALITY; SODOMY; WHORE; WHOREDOM.

FIGURATIVE: Ezek. 16:15-59. See WHOREDOMS.

INSTANCES OF: Sodomites, Gen. 19:5. Lot's daughters, Gen. 19:30-38. Judah, Gen. 38:15,16. The Gibeahites, Judg. 19:22-25. Eli's sons, 1 Sam. 2:22. David, 2 Sam. 5:13; 11:2-27. Amnon, 2 Sam. 13:1-14. Solomon, 1 Kin. 11:1-3. Rehoboam, 2 Chr. 11:21-23. Persian kings, Esth. 2:3,13,14,19.

LASEA, a city of Crete, Acts 27:8.

LASHA, a place at the southern extremity of Canaan, Gen. 10:19.

LASHARON, king of, killed by Joshua, Josh. 12:18.

LATIN, Luke 23:38; John 19:20.

LAUGHTER. A time for, Eccl. 3:4. Attributed to God, Psa. 37:13; 59:8; Prov. 1:26.

See HAPPINESS; JOY.

LAVER. Directions for making, Ex. 30:18-20. Situation of, in the tabernacle, tent of the congregation, and the altar, Ex. 40:7. Sanctified, Ex. 30:28; 40:11; Lev. 8:11. Used for washing, Ex. 40:30-32.

Brazen, made by Solomon for the temple, 1 Kin. 7:23-26,30,38,39; 2 Chr. 4:2-14. Altered by Ahaz, 2 Kin. 16:17. Broken and carried to Babylon by the Chaldeans, 2 Kin. 25:13,16; Jer. 52:17,20.

FIGURATIVE: Rev. 4:6; 15:2, in connection with Ex. 38:8; 1 Kin. 7:23.

LAW. Psa. 19:7. The law of the LORD *is* perfect, converting the soul: the testimony of the LORD *is* sure, making wise the simple. 8. The statutes of the LORD *are* right, rejoicing the heart: the commandment of the LORD *is* pure, enlightening the eyes. 9. The fear of the LORD *is* clean, enduring for ever: the judgments of the LORD *are* true *and* righteous altogether.

Psa. 119:1. Blessed *are* the undefiled in the way, who walk in the law of the LORD. 2. Blessed *are* they that keep his testimonies, *and that* seek him with the whole heart. 3. They also do no iniquity: they walk in his ways. 4. Thou hast commanded *us* to keep thy precepts diligently. 5. O that my ways were directed to keep thy statutes! 6. Then shall I not be ashamed, when I have respect unto all thy commandments. 7. I will praise thee with uprightness of heart, when I shall have learned thy righteous judgments. 8. I will keep thy statutes: O forsake me not utterly.

Prov. 28:4. They that forsake the law praise the wicked: but such as keep the law contend with them. 5. Evil men understand not judgment: but they that seek the LORD understand all *things.*

Matt. 22:21. Then saith he unto them, Render therefore unto Cæsar the things which are Cæsar's; and unto God the things that are God's. Luke 20:22-25.

Luke 16:17. It is easier for heaven and earth to pass, than one tittle of the law to fail.

Rom. 2:14. For when the Gentiles, which have not the law, do by nature the things contained in the law, these, having not the law, are a law unto themselves: 15. Which shew the work of the law written in their hearts, their conscience also bearing witness, and *their* thoughts the mean while accusing or else excusing one another;

Rom. 7:7. I had not known sin, but by the law: for I had not known lust, except the law had said, Thou shall not covet. 12. The law *is* holy, and the commandment holy, and just, and good. 14. We know that the law is spiritual:

Rom. 13:10. Love worketh no ill to his neighbour: therefore love *is* the fulfilling of the law.

1 Tim. 1:5. The end of the commandment is charity out of a pure heart, and *of* a good conscience, and *of* faith unfeigned: 8. But we know that the law *is* good, if a man use it lawfully; 9. Knowing this, that the law is not made for a righteous man, but for the lawless and disobedient, for the ungodly, and for sinners, for unholy and profane, for murderers of fathers and murderers of mothers, for manslayers, 10. For whoremongers, for them that defile themselves with mankind, for menstealers, for liars, for perjured persons, and if there be any other thing that is contrary to sound doctrine;

Jas. 1:25. But whoso looketh into the perfect law of liberty, and continueth *therein,* he being not a forgetful hearer, but a doer of the work, this man shall be blessed in his deed.

1 John 3:4. Whosoever committeth sin transgresseth also the law: for sin is the transgression of the law.

1 John 5:3. This is the love of God, that we keep his commandments: and his commandments are not grievous.

See LITIGATION; COMMANDMENTS; DUTY TO GOD.

OF MOSES: Contained in the books, Exodus, Leviticus, Numbers, and Deuteronomy. Given at Sinai, Ex. 19; Deut. 1:1; 4: 10-13,44-46; 33:2; Hab. 3:3. Received by the disposition of angels, Deut. 33:2; Psa. 68:17; Acts 7:53; Gal. 3:19; Heb. 2:2. Was given because of transgressions until the Messiah come, Gal. 3:19. Engraved on stone, Ex. 20:3-17, with 24:12; 31:18; 32:16; 34:29; 40:20; Deut. 4:13; 5:4-22: 9:10. See TABLES; COMMANDMENTS. Preserved in the Ark of the Covenant, Ex. 25:16; Deut. 31:9,26. Found by Hilkiah in the house of the Lord, 2 Kin. 22:8. Engraved upon monuments, Deut. 27:2-8; Josh. 8:30-35. To be written on door posts, Deut. 6:9; 11:20; on frontlets for the forehead, and parchment for the hand, Ex. 13:9,16; Deut. 6:4-9; 11:18-21. Children instructed in. See CHILDREN; INSTRUCTION. Expounded by the priests and Levites, Lev. 10:11; Deut. 33:10; 2 Chr. 35:3; princes, priests, and Levites publicly taught, Ezra 7:10; Neh. 8:1-18; from city to city, 2 Chr. 17:7-10; in synagogues, Luke 4:16:32; Acts 13:14-52; 15: 21, with 9:20; 14:1; 17:1-3; 18:4,26. Expounded to the assembled nation at the feast of tabernacles in the sabbatic year, Deut. 31: 10-13. Renewed by Moses, 4:44-46.

Curses of, responsively read by Levites and people at Ebal and Gerizim, Deut. 27:12-26; Josh. 8:33-35. Formed a constitution on which the civil government of the Israelites was founded, and according to which rulers were required to rule, Deut. 17:18-20; 2 Kin. 11:12; 2 Chr. 23:11. See GOVERNMENT, CONSTITUTIONAL. Divine authority for, Ex. 19:16-24; 20:1-17; 24:12-18; 31:18; 32:15,16; 34:1-4,27,28; Lev. 26:46; Deut. 4:10-13,36; 5:1-22; 9:10; 10:1-5; 33:2-4; 1 Kin. 8:9; Ezra 7:6; Neh. 1:7; 8:1; 9:14; Psa. 78:5; 103:7; Isa. 33:22; Mal. 4:4; Acts 7:38,53; Gal. 3:19; Heb. 9:18-21.

Prophecies in, of the Messiah, Luke 24:44; John 1:45; 5:46; 12:34; Acts 26:22,23; 28:23; Rom. 3:21,22. See JESUS, PROPHECIES CONCERNING. Epitomized by Jesus, Matt. 22:40; Mark 12:29-33; Luke 10:27.

Book of found by Hilkiah in the temple, 2 Kin. 22:8; 2 Chr. 34:14.

TEMPORARY: Jer. 3:16. And it shall come to pass, when ye be multiplied and increased in the land, in those days, said the LORD, they shall say no more, The ark of the covenant of the LORD: neither shall it come to mind: neither shall they remember it; neither shall they visit *it;* neither shall *that* be done any more.

Dan. 9:27. And he shall confirm the covenant with many for one week; and in the midst of the week he shall cause the sacrifice and the oblation to cease, and for the overspreading of abominations he shall make *it* desolate, even until the consummation, and that determined shall be poured upon the desolate.

Matt. 5:17. Think not that I am come to destroy the law, or the prophets: I am not come to destroy, but to fulfil. 18. For verily I say unto you, Till heaven and earth pass, one jot or one tittle shall in no wise pass from the law, till all be fulfilled. 19. Whosoever therefore shall break one of these least commandments, and shall teach men so, he shall be called the least in the kingdom of heaven: but whosoever shall do and teach *them,* the same shall be called great in the kingdom of heaven. 20. For I say unto you, That except your righteousness shall exceed *the righteousness* of the scribes and Pharisees, ye shall in no case enter into the kingdom of heaven. 21. Ye have heard that it was said by them of old time, Thou shalt not kill; and whosoever shall kill shall be in danger of the judgment: 22. But I say unto you, That whosoever is angry with his brother without a cause shall be in danger of the judgment: and whosoever shall say to his brother, Raca, shall be in danger of the council: but whosoever shall say, Thou fool, shall be in danger of hell fire. 23. Therefore if thou bring thy gift to the altar, and there rememberest that thy brother hath ought against thee; 24. Leave there thy gift before the altar, and go thy way; first be reconciled to thy brother, and then come and offer thy gift. 25. Agree with thine adversary quickly, whiles thou art in the way with him; lest at any time the adversary deliver thee to the judge, and the judge deliver thee to the officer, and thou be cast into prison. 26. Verily I say unto thee, Thou shalt by no means come out thence, till thou hast paid the uttermost farthing. 27. Ye have heard that it was said by them of old time, Thou shalt not commit adultery: 28. But I say unto you, That whosoever looketh on a woman to lust after her hath committed adultery with her already in his heart. 29. And if thy right eye offend thee, pluck it out, and cast *it* from thee: for it is profitable for thee that one of thy members should perish, and not *that* thy whole body should be cast into hell. 30. And if thy right hand offend thee, cut it off, and cast *it* from thee: for it is profitable for thee that one of thy members should perish, and not *that* thy whole body should be cast into hell. 31. It hath been said, Whosoever shall put away his wife, let him give her a writing of divorcement: 32. But I say unto you, That whosoever shall put away his wife, saving for the cause of fornication, causeth her to commit adultery: and whosoever shall marry her that is divorced committeth adultery. 33. Again, ye have heard that it hath been said by them of old time, Thou shalt not forswear thyself, but shalt perform unto the Lord thine oaths: 34. But I say unto you, Swear not at all; neither by heaven; for it is God's throne: 35. Nor by the earth; for it is his footstool: neither by Jerusalem; for it is the city of the great King. 36. Neither shalt thou swear by thy head, because thou canst not make one hair white or black. 37. But let your communication be, Yea, yea; Nay, nay: for whatsoever is more than these cometh of evil. 38. Ye have heard that it hath been said, An eye for an eye, and a tooth for a tooth: 39. But I say unto you, That ye resist not evil: but whosoever shall smite thee on thy right cheek, turn to him the other also. 40. And if any man will sue thee at the law, and take away thy coat, let him have *thy* cloke also. 41. And whosoever shall compel thee to go a mile, go with him twain. 42. Give to him that asketh thee, and from him that would borrow of thee turn not thou away. 43. Ye have heard that it hath been said, Thou shalt love thy neighbour, and hate thine enemy. 44. But I say unto you, Love your enemies, bless them that curse you, do good to them that hate you, and pray for them which despitefully use you, and persecute you; 45. That ye may be the children of your Father which is in heaven: for he maketh his sun to rise on the evil and on the good, and sendeth rain on the just and on the unjust.

Luke 16:16. The law and the prophets *were* until John: since that time the kingdom of God is preached, and every man presseth into it. 17. And it is easier for heaven and earth to pass, than one tittle of the law to fail.

John 1:17. For the law was given by Moses, *but* grace and truth came by Jesus Christ.

John 4:20. Our fathers worshipped in this mountain; and ye say, that in Jerusalem is the place where men ought to worship. 21. Jesus saith unto her, Woman, believe me, the hour cometh, when ye shall neither in this mountain, nor yet at Jerusalem, worship the Father. 22. Ye worship ye know not what: we know what we worship: for salvation is of the Jews. 23. But the hour cometh, and now is, when the true worshippers shall worship the Father in spirit and in truth: for the Father seeketh such to worship him. 24. God *is* a Spirit: and they that worship him must worship *him* in spirit and in truth.

John 8:35. And the servant abideth not in the house for ever: *but* the Son abideth ever. with Gal. 4:30, 31, below.

Acts 6:14. For we have heard him say, that this Jesus of Nazareth shall destroy this place, and shall change the customs which Moses delivered us.

Acts 10:28. And he said unto them, Ye know how that it is an unlawful thing for a man that is a Jew to keep company, or come unto one of another nation; but God hath shewed me that I should not call any man common or unclean.

Acts 13:39. And by him all that believe are justified from all things, from which ye could not be justified by the law of Moses.

Acts 15:1. And certain men which came down from Judæa taught the brethren, *and* said, Except ye be circumcised after the manner of Moses, ye cannot be saved. 2. When therefore Paul and Barnabas had no

small dissension and disputation with them, they determined that Paul and Barnabas, and certain other of them, should go up to Jerusalem unto the apostles and elders about this question. 3. And being brought on their way by the church, they passed through Phenice and Samaria, declaring the conversion of the Gentiles: and they caused great joy unto all the brethren. 4. And when they were come to Jerusalem, they were received of the church, and *of* the apostles and elders, and they declared all things that God had done with them. 5. But there rose up certain of the sect of the Pharisees which believed, saying, That it was needful to circumcise them, and to command *them* to keep the law of Moses. 6. And the apostles and elders came together for to consider of this matter. 7. And when there had been much disputing, Peter rose up, and said unto them, Men *and* brethren, ye know how that a good while ago God made choice among us, that the Gentiles by my mouth should hear the word of the gospel, and believe. 8. And God, which knoweth the hearts, bare them witness, giving them the Holy Ghost, even as *he did* unto us; 9. And put no difference between us and them, purifying their hearts by faith. 10. Now therefore why tempt ye God, to put a yoke upon the neck of the disciples, which neither our fathers nor we were able to bear? 11. But we believe that through the grace of the Lord Jesus Christ we shall be saved, even as they. 12. Then all the multitude kept silence, and gave audience to Barnabas and Paul, declaring what miracles and wonders God had wrought among the Gentiles by them. 13. And after they had held their peace, James answered, saying, Men *and* brethren, hearken unto me: 14. Simeon hath declared how God at the first did visit the Gentiles, to take out of them a people for his name. 15. And to this agree the words of the prophets; as it is written, 16. After this I will return, and will build again the tabernacle of David, which is fallen down; and I will build again the ruins thereof, and I will set it up: 17. That the residue of men might seek after the Lord, and all the Gentiles, upon whom my name is called, saith the Lord, who doeth all these things. 18. Known unto God are all his works from the beginning of the world. 19. Wherefore my sentence is, that we trouble not them, which from among the Gentiles are turned to God: 20. But that we write unto them, that they abstain from pollutions of idols, and *from* fornication, and *from* things strangled, and *from* blood. 21. For Moses of old time hath in every city them that preach him, being read in the synagogues every sabbath day. 22. Then pleased it the apostles and elders, with the whole church, to send chosen men of their own company to Antioch with Paul and Barnabas; *namely*, Judas surnamed Barsabas, and Silas, chief men among the brethren: 23. And they wrote *letters* by them after this manner; The apostles and elders and brethren *send* greeting unto the brethren which are of the Gentiles in Antioch and Syria and Cilicia: 24. Forasmuch as we have heard, that certain which went out from us have troubled you with words, subverting your souls, saying, *Ye must* be circumcised, and keep the law: to whom we gave no *such* commandment: 25. It seemed good unto us, being assembled with one accord, to send chosen men unto you with our beloved Barnabas and Paul, 26. Men that have hazarded their lives for the name of our Lord Jesus Christ. 27. We have sent therefore Judas and Silas, who shall also tell *you* the same things by mouth. 28. For it seemed good to the Holy Ghost, and to us, to lay upon you no greater burden than these necessary things; 29. That ye abstain from meats offered to idols, and from blood, and from things strangled, and from fornication: from which if ye keep yourselves, ye shall do well.

Acts 21:20. And when they heard *it*, they glorified the Lord, and said unto him, Thou seest, brother, how many thousands of Jews there are which believe; and they are all zealous of the law: 21. And they are informed of thee, that thou teachest all the Jews which are among the Gentiles to for sake Moses, saying that they ought not to circumcise *their* children, neither to walk after the customs. 22. What is it therefore? the multitude must needs come together: for they will hear that thou art come. 23. Do therefore this that we say to thee: We have four men which have a vow on them; 24. Them take, and purify thyself with them, and be at charges with them, that they may shave *their* heads: and all may know that those things, whereof they were informed concerning thee, are nothing; but *that* thou thyself also walkest orderly, and keepest the law. 25. As touching the Gentiles which believe, we have written *and* concluded that they observe no such thing, save only that they keep themselves from *things* offered to idols, and from blood, and from strangled, and from fornication.

Rom. 3:1. What advantage then hath the Jew? or what profit *is there* of circumcision? 2. Much every way: chiefly, because that unto them were committed the oracles of God.

Rom. 7:1. Know ye not, brethren, (for I speak to them that know the law,) how that the law hath dominion over a man as long as he liveth? 2. For the woman which hath an husband is bound by the law to *her* husband so long as he liveth; but if the husband be dead, she is loosed from the law of *her* husband. 3. So then if, while *her* husband liveth, she be married to another man, she shall be called an adulteress: but if her husband be dead, she is free from that law; so that she is no adulteress, though she be married to another man. 4. Wherefore, my brethren, ye also are become dead to the law by the body of Christ; that ye should be married to another, *even* to him who is raised from the dead, that we should bring forth fruit unto God. 5. For when we were in the flesh, the motions of sins, which were by the law, did work in our members to bring forth fruit unto death. 6. But now we are delivered from the law, that being dead wherein we were held; that we should serve in newness of spirit, and not *in* the oldness of the letter.

Rom. 8:3. For what the law could not do, in that it was weak through the flesh, God sending his own Son in the likeness of sinful flesh, and for sin, condemned sin in the flesh:

Rom. 10:4. For Christ *is* the end of the law for righteousness to every one that believeth.

2 Cor. 3:7. But if the ministration of death, written *and* engraven in stones, was glorious, so that the children of Israel could not stedfastly behold the face of Moses for the glory of his countenance; which *glory* was to be done away: 8. How shall not the ministration of the spirit be rather glorious? 9. For if the ministration of condemnation *be* glory, much more doth the ministration of righteousness exceed in glory. 10. For even that which was made glorious had no glory in this respect, by reason of the glory that excelleth. 11. For if that which is done away *was* glorious, much more that which remaineth *is* glorious. 12. Seeing then that we have such hope, we use great plainness of speech: 13. And not as Moses, *which* put a vail over his face, that the children of Israel could not stedfastly look to the end of that which is abolished: 14. But their minds were blinded: for until this day remaineth the same vail untaken away in the reading of the old testament; which *vail* is done away in Christ.

Gal. 2:3. But neither Titus, who was with me, being a Greek, was compelled to be circumcised: 4. And that because of false brethren unawares brought in, who came in privily to spy out our liberty which we have in Christ Jesus, that they might bring us into bondage: 5. To whom we gave place by subjection, no, not for an hour; that the truth of the gospel might continue with you. 6. But of these who seemed to be somewhat, (whatsoever they were, it maketh no matter to me: God accepteth no man's person:) for they who seemed *to be somewhat* in conference added nothing to me: 7. But contrariwise, when they saw that the gospel of the uncircumcision was committed unto me, as *the gospel* of the circumcision *was* unto Peter; 8. (For he that wrought effectually in Peter to the apostleship of the circumcision, the same was mighty in me toward the Gentiles:) 9. And when James, Cephas, and John, who seemed to be pillars, perceived the grace that was given unto me, they gave to me and Barnabas the right hands of fellowship;

that we *should go* unto the heathen, and they unto the circumcision.

Gal. 4:30. Nevertheless what saith the scripture? Cast out the bondwoman and her son: for the son of the bondwoman shall not be heir with the son of the freewoman. 31. So then, brethren, we are not children of the bondwoman, but of the free.

Eph. 2:15. Having abolished in his flesh the enmity, *even* the law of commandments *contained* in ordinances; for to make in himself of twain one new man, *so* making peace;

Col. 2:14. Blotting out the handwriting of ordinances that was against us, which was contrary to us, and took it out of the way, nailing it to his cross; 15. *And* having spoiled principalities and powers, he made a shew of them openly, triumphing over them in it. 16. Let no man therefore judge you in meat, or in drink, or in respect of an holyday, or of the new moon, or of the sabbath *days:* 17. Which are a shadow of things to come; but the body *is* of Christ. 18. Let no man beguile you of your reward in a voluntary humility and worshipping of angels, intruding into those things which he hath not seen, vainly puffed up by his fleshly mind, 19. And not holding the Head, from which all the body by joints and bands having nourishment ministered, and knit together, increaseth with the increase of God. 20. Wherefore if ye be dead with Christ from the rudiments of the world, why, as though living in the world, are ye subject to ordinances, 21. (Touch not; taste not; handle not; 22. Which all are to perish with the using;) after the commandments and doctrines of men? 23. Which things have indeed a shew of wisdom in will worship, and humility, and neglecting of the body; not in any honour to the satisfying of the flesh.

Heb. 8:4. For if he were on earth, he should not be a priest, seeing that there are priests that offer gifts according to the law: 5. Who serve unto the example and shadow of heavenly things, as Moses was admonished of God when he was about to make the tabernacle: for, See, saith he, *that* thou make all things according to the pattern shewed to thee in the mount. 6. But now hath he obtained a more excellent ministry, by how much also he is the mediator of a better covenant, which was established upon better promises. 7. For if that first *covenant* had been faultless, then should no place have been sought for the second. 8. For finding fault with them, he saith, Behold, the days come, saith the Lord, when I will make a new covenant with the house of Israel and with the house of Judah: 9. Not according to the covenant that I made with their fathers in the day when I took them by the hand to lead them out of the land of Egypt; because they continued not in my covenant, and I regarded them not, saith the Lord. 10. For this *is* the covenant that

I will make with the house of Israel after those days, saith the Lord; I will put my laws into their mind, and write them in their hearts: and I will be to them a God, and they shall be to me a people: 11. And they shall not teach every man his neighbour, and every man his brother, saying, Know the Lord: for all shall know me, from the least to the greatest. 12. For I will be merciful to their unrighteousness, and their sins and their iniquities will I remember no more. 13. In that he saith, A new *covenant,* he hath made the first old. Now that which decayeth and waxeth old *is* ready to vanish away.

Heb. 9:8. The Holy Ghost this signifying, that the way into the holiest of all was not yet made manifest, while as the first tabernacle was yet standing. 9. Which *was* a figure for the time then present, in which were offered both gifts and sacrifices, that could not make him that did the service perfect, as pertaining to the conscience; 10. *Which* stood only in meats and drinks, and divers washings, and carnal ordinances, imposed *on them* until the time of reformation. 11. But Christ being come an high priest of good things to come, by a greater and more perfect tabernacle, not made with hands, that is to say, not of this building; 12. Neither by the blood of goats and calves, but by his own blood he entered in once into the holy place, having obtained eternal redemption *for us.* 13. For if the blood of bulls and of goats, and the ashes of an heifer sprinkling the unclean, sanctifieth to the purifying of the flesh: 14. How much more shall the blood of Christ, who through the eternal Spirit offered himself without spot to God, purge your conscience from dead works to serve the living God? 15. And for this cause he is the mediator of the new testament, that by means of death, for the redemption of the transgressions *that were* under the first testament, they which are called might receive the promise of eternal inheritance. 16. For where a testament *is,* there must also of necessity be the death of the testator. 17. For a testament *is* of force after men are dead: otherwise it is of no strength at all while the testator liveth. 18. Whereupon neither the first *testament* was dedicated without blood. 19. For when Moses had spoken every precept to all the people according to the law, he took the blood of calves and of goats, with water, and scarlet wool, and hyssop, and sprinkled both the book, and all the people. 20. Saying, This *is* the blood of the testament which God hath enjoined unto you. 21. Moreover he sprinkled with blood both the tabernacle, and all the vessels of the ministry. 22. And almost all things are by the law purged with blood: and without shedding of blood is no remission. 23. *It was* therefore necessary that the patterns of things in the heavens should be purified with these; but the heavenly things themselves with better sacrifices than these. 24. For Christ is not entered into the holy places made with hands, *which are* the figures of the true ; but into heaven itself, now to appear in the presence of God for us:

Heb. 10:1. For the law having a shadow of good things to come, *and* not the very image of the things, can never with those sacrifices which they offered year by year continually make the comers thereunto perfect. 2. For then would they not have ceased to be offered? because that the worshippers once purged should have had no more conscience of sins. 3. But in those *sacrifices there is* a remembrance again *made* of sins every year. 4. For *it is* not possible that the blood of bulls and of goats should take away sins. 5. Wherefore when he cometh into the world, he saith, Sacrifice and offering thou wouldest not, but a body hast thou prepared me: 6. In burnt offerings and *sacrifices* for sin thou hast had no pleasure. 7. Then said I, Lo, I come (in the volume of the book it is written of me,) to do thy will, O God. 8. Above when he said, Sacrifice and offering and burnt offerings and *offering* for sin thou wouldest not, neither hadst pleasure *therein;* which are offered by the law; 9. Then said he, Lo, I come to do thy will, O God. He taketh away the first, that he may establish the second. 10. By the which will we are sanctified through the offering of the body of Jesus Christ once *for all.* 11. And every priest standeth daily ministering and offering oftentimes the same sacrifices, which can never take away sins: 12. But this man, after he had offered one sacrifice for sins for ever, sat down on the right hand of God; 13. From henceforth expecting till his enemies be made his footstool. 14. For by one offering he hath perfected for ever them that are sanctified. 15. *Whereof* the Holy Ghost also is a witness to us: for after that he had said before, 16. This *is* the covenant that I will make with them after those days, saith the Lord, I will put my laws into their hearts, and in their minds will I write them; 17. And their sins and iniquities will I remember no more. 18. Now where remission of these *is, there is* no more offering for sin.

Heb. 11:40. God having provided some better thing for us, that they without us should not be made perfect.

Heb. 12:18. For ye are not come unto the mount that might be touched, and that burned with fire, nor unto blackness, and darkness, and tempest, 19. And the sound of a trumpet, and the voice of words; which *voice* they that heard intreated that the word should not be spoken to them any more: 27. And this *word,* Yet once more, signifieth the removing of those things that are shaken, as of things that are made, that those things which cannot be shaken may remain.

LAWSUITS, to be avoided, Prov. 25:8-10; Matt. 5:25,26; 1 Cor. 6:1-8.

See ACTIONS AT LAW ; ADJUDICATION ; ARBITRATION ; COMPROMISE ; COURTS ; JUSTICE.

LAWYER. One versed in the Mosaic law. Test Jesus with questions, Matt. 22: 35; Luke 10:25-37. Jesus' satire against, Luke 11:45-52. Zenas, a, Tit. 3:13.

See LITIGATION.

LAYING ON OF HANDS. See HANDS, IMPOSITION OF.

LAZARUS. 1. Brother of Mary and Martha. Sickness and death of, John 11:1-14. Resurrection of, John 11:38-44; 12:17,18. Supped with Jesus, John 12:1,2,9. Plotted against by the chief priests, John 12:10,11.

LAZINESS. See SLOTHFULNESS.

LEAD. A mineral, Ex. 15:10. Purified by fire, Num. 31:22; Jer. 6:29; Ezek. 22:18,20. Used in making inscriptions on stone, Job 19:24. Lead-founder, Jer. 6:29; Ezek. 22:18, 20. Trade in, Ezek. 27:12. Used for weighing, Zech. 5:7,8.

LEADERSHIP. INSTANCES OF: ABRAHAM, MOSES, JOSHUA, GIDEON, DEBORAH. See each respectively.

LEAGUE. See ALLIANCES ; TREATY.

LEAH. Daughter of Laban, Gen. 29:16. Married to Jacob, Gen. 29:23-26. Children of, Gen. 29:31-35; 30:9-13,17-21. Flees with Jacob, Gen. 31:4,14,17; 33:2-7. "Builder of the house of Israel," Ruth 4:11.

LEARNING. See INSTRUCTION ; KNOWLEDGE.

LEASE, of real estate, Matt. 21:33-41; Mark 12:1-9; Luke 20:9-16. See LAND.

LEASING, falsifying, Psa. 4:2.

LEATHER. Girdles of, 2 Kin. 1:8; Matt. 3:4. Tanning of, Acts 9:43; 10:5,6. Called skin, Gen. 3:21; Mark 1:6; hide, Lev. 8:17.

LEAVEN. For bread, Ex. 12:34,39; Hos. 7:4; Matt. 13:33. Leavened bread used with peace offering, Lev. 7:13; Amos 4:5; with wave offering, Lev. 23:15-17. Leavened bread forbidden with meat offerings, Lev. 2:11; 6:17; 10:12; Ex. 23:18; 34:25; at the passover, Ex. 12:19,20; 13:3,4,7; 23:18; with blood, Ex. 23:18; 34:25.

A type of sin, 1 Cor. 5:6-8.

FIGURATIVE: Of the hypocrisy of the Pharisees, Matt. 16:6-12; Mark 8:15; Luke 12:1. Of other evils, 1 Cor. 5:6-8; Gal. 5:9. Parable of, Matt. 13:33; Luke 13:21.

LEBANAH, called also LEBANA. One of the Nethinim, Ezra 2:45; Neh. 7:48.

LEBANON. A mountain range. Northern boundary of the land of Canaan, Deut. 1:7; 3:25; 11:24; Josh. 1:4; 9:1. Early inhabitants of, Judg. 3:3. Snow of, Jer. 18:14. Streams of, Song 4:15. Cedars of, Judg. 9:15; 2 Kin. 19:23; 2 Chr. 2:8; Psa. 29:5; 104: 16; Isa. 2:13; 14:8; Ezek. 27:5. Other trees of, 2 Kin. 19:23; 2 Chr. 2:8. Flower of, Nah. 1:4. Beasts of, Isa. 40:16. Fertility and productiveness of, Hos. 14:5-7. "House of the forest of." 1 Kin. 7:2-5. Valley of, Josh. 11:17; 12:7. Tower of, Song 7:4. Solomon had cities of store in, 1 Kin. 9:19.

FIGURATIVE: Isa. 29:17; Jer. 22:6.

LEBAOTH, a city of Simeon, Josh. 15: 32. See BETH-LEBAOTH.

LEBBÆUS, surnamed THADDÆUS. One of the twelve apostles, Matt. 10:3.

LEBONAH, a city on the highway from Beth-el to Shechem, Judg. 21:19.

LECAH, a town or person in Judah, 1 Chr. 4:21.

LEEK, Num. 11:5.

LEES, settlings of wine, Psa. 75:8; Isa. 25:6; Jer. 48:11; Zeph. 1:12.

LEFT-HANDED, Judg. 3:15; 20:16.

LEGENDS. "Holiness to the LORD," engraved on the high priest's mitre, Ex. 28:36; 39:30; on bells of horses, on pots and bowls, Zech. 14:20. "This is Jesus, the King of the Jews, " Matt. 27:37. Precepts written on door posts and gates, and worn on the hand and forehead. Deut. 6:6-9; 11:18-20; Isa. 57:8.

LEHABIM, a Mizraite people, Gen. 10: 13; 1 Chr. 1:11.

LEHI, a district of Judah, where Samson slew a thousand Philistines with the jawbone of an ass, Judg. 15:9-19.

LEGION. Of angels, Matt. 26:53. Devils, Mark 5:9,15.

LEGISLATION, class, forbidden, Ex. 12:49; Lev. 24:22; Num. 9:14; 15:15,29; Gal. 3:28.

Supplemental, concerning Sabbath-breaking, Num. 15:32-35; inheritance, Num. 27: 1-11. See GOVERNMENT; LAW.

LEGS, of the crucified broken, John 19: 31,32.

LEMUEL. A king. Probably refers to Solomon, Prov. 31:1,4.

LENDING. Ex. 22:25. If thou lend money to *any of* my people *that is* poor by thee, thou shalt not be to him as a usurer, neither shalt thou lay upon him usury. 26. If thou at all take thy neighbour's raiment to pledge, thou shalt deliver it unto him by that the sun goeth down: 27. For that *is* his covering only, it *is* his raiment for his skin: wherein shall he sleep? and it shall come to pass, when he crieth unto me, that I will hear; for I *am* gracious.

Lev. 25:35. If thy brother be waxen poor, and fallen in decay with thee; then thou shalt relieve him: *yea, though he be* a stranger, or a sojourner; that he may live with thee. 36. Take thou no usury of him, or increase: but fear thy God; that thy brother may live with thee. 37. Thou shalt not give him thy money upon usury, nor lend him thy victuals for increase.

Deut. 15:1. At the end of *every* seven years thou shalt make a release. 2. And this *is* the manner of the release: Every creditor that lendeth *ought* unto his neighbour shall release *it;* he shall not exact *it* of his neighbour, or of his brother; because it is called the LORD's release. 3. Of a foreigner thou mayest exact *it again:* but *that* which is thine with thy brother thine hand shall release; 4. Save when there shall be no poor among you; for the LORD shall greatly bless thee in the land which the

LORD thy God giveth thee *for* an inheritance to possess it: 5. Only if thou carefully hearken unto the voice of the LORD thy God, to observe to do all these commandments which I command thee this day. 6. For the LORD thy God blesseth thee, as he promised thee: and thou shalt lend unto many nations, but thou shalt not borrow; and thou shalt reign over many nations, but they shall not reign over thee. 7. If there be among you a poor man of one of thy brethren within any of thy gates in thy land which the LORD thy God giveth thee, thou shalt not harden thine heart, nor shut thine hand from thy poor brother: 8. But thou shalt open thine hand wide unto him, and shalt surely lend him sufficient for his need, *in that* which he wanteth. 9. Beware that there be not a thought in thy wicked heart, saying, The seventh year, the year of release, is at hand; and thine eye be evil against thy poor brother, and thou givest him nought; and he cry unto the LORD against thee, and it be sin unto thee. 10. Thou shalt surely give him, and thine heart shall not be grieved when thou givest unto him: because that for this thing the LORD thy God shall bless thee in all thy works, and in all that thou puttest thine hand unto. 11. For the poor shall never cease out of the land: therefore I command thee, saying, Thou shalt open thine hand wide unto thy brother, to thy poor, and to thy needy, in thy land.

Deut. 23:19. Thou shalt not lend upon usury to thy brother; usury of money, usury of victuals, usury of any thing that is lent upon usury: 20. Unto a stranger thou mayest lend upon usury; but unto thy brother thou shalt not lend upon usury: that the LORD thy God may bless thee in all that thou settest thine hand to in the land whither thou goest to possess it.

Deut. 24:6. No man shall take the nether or the upper millstone to pledge: for he taketh *a man's* life to pledge. 10. When thou dost lend thy brother any thing, thou shalt not go into his house to fetch his pledge. 11. Thou shall stand abroad, and the man to whom thou dost lend shall bring out the pledge abroad unto thee. 12. And if the man *be* poor, thou shalt not sleep with his pledge: 13. In any case thou shalt deliver him the pledge again when the sun goeth down, that he may sleep in his own raiment, and bless thee: and it shall be righteousness unto thee before the LORD thy God. 17. Thou shalt not pervert the judgment of the stranger, *nor* of the fatherless; nor take a widow's raiment to pledge:

Neh. 5:1. And there was a great cry of the people and of their wives against their brethren the Jews. 2. For there were that said, We, our sons, and our daughters, *are* many: therefore we take up corn *for them,* that we may eat, and live. 3. *Some* also there were that said, We have mortgaged our land, vineyards, and houses, that we might buy corn, because of the dearth. 4.

There were also that said, We have borrowed money for the king's tribute, *and that upon* our lands and vineyards. 5. Yet now our flesh *is* as the flesh of our brethren, our children as their children: and, lo, we bring into bondage our sons and our daughters to be servants, and *some* of our daughters are brought into bondage *already:* neither *is it* in our power *to redeem them;* for other men have our lands and vineyards. 6. And I was very angry when I heard their cry and these words. 7. Then I consulted with myself, and I rebuked the nobles, and the rulers, and said unto them, Ye exact usury, every one of his brother. And I set a great assembly against them. 8. And I said unto them, We after our ability have redeemed our brethren the Jews, which were sold unto the heathen; and will ye even sell your brethren? or shall they be sold unto us? Then held they their peace, and found nothing *to answer.* 9. Also I said, It *is* not good that ye do: ought ye not to walk in the fear of our God because of the reproach of the heathen our enemies? 10. I likewise, *and* my brethren, and my servants, might exact of them money and corn: I pray you, let us leave off this usury. 11. Restore, I pray you, to them, even this day, their lands, their vineyards, their oliveyards, and their houses, also the hundredth *part* of the money, and of the corn, the wine, and the oil, that ye exact of them. 12. Then said they, We will restore *them,* and will require nothing of them; so will we do as thou sayest. Then I called the priests, and took an oath of them, that they should do according to this promise. 13. Also I shook my lap, and said, So God shake out every man from his house, and from his labour, that performeth not this promise, even thus be he shaken out, and emptied. And all the congregation said, Amen, and praised the LORD. And the people did according to this promise.

Psa. 37:25. I have been young, and *now* am old: yet have I not seen the righteous forsaken, nor his seed begging bread. 26. *He is* ever merciful, and lendeth; and his seed *is* blessed.

Psa. 112:5. A good man sheweth favour, and lendeth: he will guide his affairs with discretion.

Prov. 19:17. He that hath pity upon the poor lendeth unto the LORD; and that which he hath given will he pay him again.

Prov. 22:7. The rich ruleth over the poor, and the borrower *is* servant to the lender.

Prov. 28:8. He that by usury and unjust gain increaseth his substance, he shall gather it for him that will pity the poor.

Isa. 24:1. Behold, the LORD maketh the earth empty, and maketh it waste, and turneth it upside down, and scattereth abroad the inhabitants thereof. 2. And it shall be, as with the people, so with the priest; as with the servant, so with his master; as with the maid, so with her mistress; as with the buyer, so with the seller; as with the lender, so with the borrower; as with the taker of usury, so with the giver of usury to him.

Ezek. 18:13. Hath given forth upon usury, and hath taken increase: shall he then live? he shall not live: he hath done all these abominations; he shall surely die; his blood shall be upon him.

Matt. 5:42. Give to him that asketh thee, and from him that would borrow of thee turn not thou away.

Luke 6:34. And if ye lend *to them* of whom ye hope to receive, what thank have ye? for sinners also lend to sinners, to receive as much again. 35. But love ye your enemies, and do good, and lend, hoping for nothing again; and your reward shall be great, and ye shall be the children of the Highest: for he is kind unto the unthankful and *to* the evil.

See BORROWING; INTEREST; MONEY.

LENTILES, Gen. 25:34; 2 Sam. 17:28; 23:11; Ezek. 4:9.

LEOPARD. A carnivorous animal, Song 4:8. Fierceness of, Jer. 5:6; 13:23; Hos. 13:7; Hab. 1:8.

FIGURATIVE: Dan. 7:6. Taming of, the triumph of the gospel, Isa. 11:6.

LEPROSY, Law concerning, Lev. 13; 14; 22:4; Num. 5:1-3; 12:14; Deut. 24:8; Matt. 8:4; Luke 5:14; 17:14. Sent as a judgment: On Miriam, Num. 12:1-10; Gehazi, 2 Kin. 5:27; Uzziah, 2 Chr. 26:20,21. Entailed, 2 Kin. 5:27. Isolation of lepers, Lev. 13:46; Num. 5:2; 12:14; 2 Kin. 15:5; 2 Chr. 26:21. Separate burial of, 2 Chr. 26:23.

Instances of leprosy not mentioned above: Four lepers outside Samaria, 2 Kin. 7:3; Azariah, 2 Kin. 15:5; Simon, Mark 14:3.

HEALED: Miriam, Num. 12:13,14; Naaman, 2 Kin. 5:8-14; by Jesus, Matt. 8:3; Mark 1:40-42; Luke 5:13; 17:12-14.

Disciples empowered to heal, Matt. 10:8.

LESHEM, called also LAISH. See DAN.

LETTERS. Written by David to Joab, 2 Sam. 11:14; king of Syria to king of Israel, 2 Kin. 5:5,6; Rabshakeh to Hezekiah, Isa. 37:9-14; King of Babylon to Hezekiah, Isa. 39:1; Sennacherib to Hezekiah, 2 Kin. 19:14. Of Artaxerxes to Nehemiah, Neh. 2:7-9. Open letter from Sanballat to Nehemiah, Neh. 6:5. Luke to Theophilus, the books of Luke and Acts, Acts 1:1. Claudius Lysias to Felix, Acts 23:25-30. Letters of intercession by Paul and Philemon in behalf of Onesimus, Philem. 1; of recommendation, 2 Cor. 3:1.

LETUSHIM, a son of Dedan, Gen. 25:3.

LEUMMIM, a son of Dedan, Gen. 25:3.

LEVI. Son of Jacob, Gen. 29:34; 35:23; 1 Chr. 2:1. Avenges the seduction of Dinah, Gen. 34; 49:5-7. Jacob's prophecy regarding, Gen. 49:5-7. His age at death, Ex. 6:16. Descendants of, made ministers of religion. See LEVITES.

LEVIATHAN. Possibly a crocodile, Job 41; Psa. 104:26. The crooked [*R. V.*] serpent, Isa. 27:1.

FIGURATIVE: Psa. **74:14.**

LEVITES. The descendants of Levi. Set apart as ministers of religion, Num. 1: 47-54; 3:6-16; 16:9; 26:57-62; Deut. 10:8; 1 Chr. 15:2. Substituted in the place of the firstborn, Num. 3:12,41-45; 8:14,16-18; 18:6. Religious zeal of, Ex. 32:26-28; Deut. 33:9, 10; Mal. 2:4,5. Consecration of, Num. 8:6-21. Sedition among, led by Korah, Dathan, Abiram, and On, on account of jealousy toward Moses and Aaron, Num. 16, with 4:19,20.

Three divisions of, each having the name of one of its progenitors, Gershon, Kohath, and Merari, Num. 3:17. Gershonites and their duties, Num. 3:18-26; 4:23-26; 10:17. Ruling chief over the Gershonites was the second son of the ruling high priest, Num. 4:28. Kohathites, consisting of the families of the Amramites, Izeharites, Hebronites, Uzzielites, Num. 3:27; 4:18-20. Of the Amramites, Aaron and his family were set apart as priests, Ex. 28:1; 29:9; Num. 3:38; 8:1-14; 17; 18:1; the remaining families appointed to take charge of the ark, table, candlestick, altars, and vessels of the sanctuary, the hangings, and all the service, Num. 3:27-32; 4:2-15. The chief over the Kohathites was the oldest son of the ruling high priest, Num 3:32; 1 Chr. 9:20. Merarites, Num. 3:20,33-37; 4: 31-33; 7:8; 10:17; 1 Chr. 6:19,29,30; 23:21-23. The chief over the Merarites was the second son of the ruling high priest, Num. 4:33.

Place of, in camp and march, Num. 1:50-53; 2:17; 3:23-35. Cities assigned to, in the land of Canaan, Josh. 21. Lodged in the chambers of the temple, 1 Chr. 9:27,33; Ezek. 40:44. Resided also in villages outside of Jerusalem, Neh. 12:29.

Age of, when inducted into office, Num. 4:3,30,47; 8:23-26; 1 Chr. 23:3,24,27; Ezra 3:8; when retired from office, Num. 4:3,47; 8:25,26.

Functions of: Had charge of the tabernacle in camp and on the march, Num. 1: 50-53; 3:6-9,21-37; 4:1-15,17-49; 8:19,22; 18: 3-6; and of the temple, 1 Chr. 9:27-29; 23: 2-32; Ezra 8:24-34.

Bore the ark of the covenant, Deut. 10:8; 1 Chr. 15:2,26,27. Ministered before the ark, 1 Chr. 16:4. Custodians and administrators of the tithes and other offerings, 1 Chr. 9:26-29; 26:28; 29:8; 2 Chr. 24:5,11; 31:11-19; 34:9; Ezra 8:29,30,33; Neh. 12:44. Prepared the shewbread, 1 Chr. 23:28,29. Assisted the priests in preparing the sacrifice, 2 Chr. 29:12-36; 2 Chr. 35:1-18. Killed the passover for the children of the captivity, Ezra 6:20,21. Teachers of the law, Deut. 33: 10; 2 Chr. 17:8,9; 30:22; 35:3; Neh. 8:7-13; Mal. 2:6,7. Were judges, Deut.17:9; 1 Chr. 23:4; 26: 29; 2 Chr. 19:8-11; Neh. 11:16. See JUDGES.

Were scribes of the sacred books. See SCRIBES. Pronounced the blessings of the law in the responsive service at Mount Gerizim, Deut. 27:12; Josh. 8:33. Were porters of the doors. See PORTERS. Were overseers in building and the repairs of the temple, 1 Chr. 23:2-4; Ezra 3:8,9. Were musicians of the temple service. See MUSIC. Supervised weights and measures, 1 Chr. 23:29.

List of those who returned from captivity, Ezra 2:40-63; 7:7; 8:16-20; Neh. 7:43-73; 12. Sealed the covenant with Nehemiah, Neh. 10:9-28.

Emoluments of: In lieu of landed inheritance, forty-eight cities with suburbs were assigned to them, Num. 35:2-8, with 18:24 and 26:62; Deut. 10:9; 12:12,18,19; 14:27-29; 18:1-8; Josh. 13:14; 14:3; 18:7; 1 Chr. 6:54-81; 13:2; 2 Chr. 23:2; Ezek. 34:1-5. Assigned to, by families, Josh. 21:4-40. Suburbs of their cities were inalienable for debt, Lev. 25:32-34. Tithes and other offerings, Num. 18:24,26-32; Deut. 18:1-8; 26:11-13; Josh. 13: 14; Neh. 10:38,39; 12:44,47. First fruits, Neh. 12:44,47. Spoils of war, including captives, Num. 31:30,42-47. See TITHES. Tithes withheld from, Neh. 13:10-13; Mal. 3:10. Pensioned, 2 Chr. 31:16-18. Owned lands, Deut. 18:8, with 1 Kin. 2:26. Land allotted to, by Ezekiel, Ezek. 48:13,14.

Enrollment of, at Sinai, Num. 1:47-49; 2:33; 3:14-39; 4:2,3; 26:57-62; 1 Chr. 23:3-5. Degraded from the Levitical office by Jeroboam, 2 Chr. 11:13-17; 13:9-11. Loyal to the ruler, 2 Kin. 11:7-11; 2 Chr. 23:7.

Intermarry with Canaanites, Ezra 9:1,2; 10:23,24. Exempt from enrollment for military duty, Num. 1:47-54, with 1 Chr. 12:26. Subordinate to the sons of Aaron, Num. 3:9; 8:19; 18:6.

Prophecies concerning, Jer. 33:18; Ezek. 44:10-14; Mal. 3:3; of their repentance of the crucifixion of the Messiah, Zech. 12:10-13. John's vision concerning, Rev. 7:7.

LEX TALIONIS. See RETALIATION.

LIARS. All men liars, Psa. 116:11. Satan a, John 8:44,55. Prohibited the Kingdom of Heaven, Rev. 21:8.

See DECEIT; DECEPTION; FALSEHOOD; HYPOCRISY.

LIBERALITY. Ex. 22:29. Thou shalt not delay *to offer* the first of thy ripe fruits, and of thy liquors: the firstborn of thy sons shalt thou give unto me. 30. Likewise shalt thou do with thine oxen, *and* with thy sheep: Ex. 13:2,12.

Ex. 23:15. Thou shalt keep the feast of unleavened bread: (thou shalt eat unleavened bread seven days, as I commanded thee, in the time appointed of the month Abib: for in it thou camest out from Egypt: and none shall appear before me empty:) Ex. 34:20.

Ex. 25:1. And the LORD spake unto Moses, saying. 2. Speak unto the children of Israel, that they bring me an offering: of every man that giveth it willingly with his heart ye shall take my offering. 3. And this *is* the offering which ye shall take of them; gold, and silver, and brass, 4. And blue, and purple, and scarlet, and fine linen, and goats' *hair*. 5. And rams' skins dyed red, and badgers' skins, and shittim wood, 6. Oil for the light, spices for anointing oil, and for sweet incense. 7. Onyx stones, and stones to be set in the ephod, and in the breastplate. 8. And let them make me a sanctuary; that I may dwell among them.

Ex. 35:4. And Moses spake unto all the congregation of the children of Israel, saying, This *is* the thing which the LORD commanded, saying, 5. Take ye from among you an offering unto the LORD: whosoever *is* of a willing heart, let him bring it, an offering of the LORD; gold, and silver, and brass, 6. And blue, and purple, and scarlet, and fine linen, and goats' *hair*, 7. And rams' skins dyed red, and badgers' skins, and shittim wood, 8. And oil for the light, and spices for anointing oil, and for the sweet incense, 9. And onyx stones, and stones to be set for the ephod, and for the breastplate, 10. And every wise hearted among you shall come, and make all that the LORD hath commanded; 11. The tabernacle, his tent, and his covering, his taches, and his boards, his bars, his pillars, and his sockets; 12. The ark, and the staves thereof, *with* the mercy seat, and the vail of the covering; 13. The table, and his staves, and all his vessels, and the shewbread, 14. The candlestick also for the light, and his furniture, and his lamps, with the oil for the light; 15. And the incense altar, and his staves, and the anointing oil, and the sweet incense, and the hanging for the door at the entering in of the tabernacle, 16. The altar of burnt offering, with his brazen grate, his staves, and all his vessels, the laver and his foot; 17. The hangings of the court, his pillars, and their sockets, and the hanging for the door of the court; 18. The pins of the tabernacle, and the pins of the court, and their cords, 19. The cloths of service, to do service in the holy *place*, the holy garments for Aaron the priest, and the garments of his sons, to minister in the priest's office. 20. And all the congregation of the children of Israel departed from the presence of Moses. 21. And they came, every one whose heart stirred him up, and every one whom his spirit made willing, *and* they brought the LORD's offering to the work of the tabernacle of the congregation, and for all his service, and for the holy garments. 22. And they came, both men and women, as many as were willing hearted, *and* brought bracelets, and earrings, and rings, and tablets, all jewels of gold: and every man that offered, *offered* an offering of gold unto the LORD. 23. And every man, with whom was found blue, and purple, and scarlet, and fine linen, and goats' *hair*, and red skins of rams, and badgers' skins, brought *them*. 24. Every one that did offer an offering of silver and brass brought the LORD's offering: and every man, with whom was found shittim wood for any work of the service, brought *it*. 25. And all the women that were wise hearted did spin with their hands, and brought that which they had spun, *both* of blue, and of purple, *and* of scarlet, and of fine linen. 26. And all the women whose heart stirred them up in wisdom spun goats' *hair*. 27. And the rulers brought onyx stones, and stones to be set, for the ephod, and for the breastplate; 28. And spice, and oil for the light, and for the anointing oil, and for the sweet incense. 29. The children of Israel brought a willing offering unto the LORD, every man and woman, whose heart made them willing to bring for all manner of work, which the LORD had commanded to be made by the hand of Moses.

Ex. 36:3. And they received of Moses all the offering, which the children of Israel had brought for the work of the service of the sanctuary, to make it *withal*. And they brought yet unto him free offerings every morning. 4. And all the wise men, that wrought all the work of the sanctuary, came every man from his work which they made; 5. And they spake unto Moses, saying, The people bring much more than enough for the service of the work, which the LORD commanded to make. 6. And Moses gave commandment, and they caused it to be proclaimed throughout the camp, saying, Let neither man nor woman make any more work for the offering of the sanctuary. So the people were restrained from bringing.

Ex. 38:8. And he made the laver *of* brass, and the foot of it *of* brass, of the lookingglasses [mirrors, *R. V.*] of *the women* assembling, which assembled *at* the door of the tabernacle of the congregation.

Lev. 19:5. If ye offer a sacrifice of peace offerings unto the LORD, ye shall offer it at your own will. Lev. 22:29; Num. 35:8.

Deut. 12:11. Then there shall be a place which the LORD your God shall choose to cause his name to dwell there; thither shall ye bring all that I command you; your burnt offerings, and your sacrifices, your tithes, and the heave offering of your hand, and all your choice vows which ye vow unto the LORD: 12. And ye shall rejoice before the LORD your God, ye, and your sons, and your daughters, and your menservants, and your maidservants, and the Levite that *is* within your gates; forasmuch as he hath no part nor inheritance with you. 17. Thou mayest not eat within thy gates the tithe of thy corn, or of thy wine, or of thy oil, or the firstlings of thy herds or of thy flock, nor any of thy vows which thou vowest, nor thy freewill offerings, or heave offering of thine hand: 18. But thou must eat them before the LORD thy God in the place which the LORD thy God shall choose, thou, and thy son, and thy daughter, and thy manservant, and thy maidservant, and the Levite that *is* within thy gates: and thou shalt rejoice before the LORD thy God in all that thou puttest thine hands unto. 19. Take heed to thyself that thou forsake not the Levite as long as thou livest upon the earth.

Deut. 14:27. And the Levite that *is* within

thy gates; thou shalt not forsake him; for he hath no part nor inheritance with thee. 28. At the end of three years thou shalt bring forth all the tithe of thine increase the same year, and shalt lay *it* up within thy gates: 29. And the Levite, (because he hath no part nor inheritance with thee,) and the stranger, and the fatherless, and the widow, which *are* within thy gates, shall come, and shall eat and be satisfied; that the LORD thy God may bless thee in all the work of thine hand which thou doest.

Deut. 15:7. If there be among you a poor man of one of thy brethren within any of thy gates in thy land which the LORD thy God giveth thee, thou shalt not harden thine heart, nor shut thine hand from thy poor brother: 8. But thou shalt open thine hand wide unto him, and shalt surely lend him sufficient for his need, *in that* which he wanteth. 9. Beware that there be not a thought in thy wicked heart, saying, The seventh year, the year of release, is at hand; and thine eye be evil against thy poor brother, and thou givest him nought; and he cry unto the LORD against thee, and it be sin unto thee. 10. Thou shalt surely give him, and thine heart shall not be grieved when thou givest unto him: because that for this thing the LORD thy God shall bless thee in all thy works, and in all that thou puttest thine hand unto. 11. For the poor shall never cease out of the land: therefore I command thee, saying, Thou shalt open thine hand wide unto thy brother, to thy poor, and to thy needy, in thy land. 12. *And* if thy brother, an Hebrew man, or an Hebrew woman, be sold unto thee, and serve thee six years; then in the seventh year thou shalt let him go free from thee. 13. And when thou sendest him out free from thee, thou shalt not let him go away empty: 14. Thou shalt furnish him liberally out of thy flock, and out of thy floor, and out of thy winepress: *of that* wherewith the LORD thy God hath blessed thee thou shalt give unto him. 15. And thou shalt remember that thou wast a bondman in the land of Egypt, and the LORD thy God redeemed thee: therefore I command thee this thing to day. 16. And it shall be, if he say unto thee, I will not go away from thee; because he loveth thee and thine house, because he is well with thee; 17. Then thou shalt take an awl, and thrust *it* through his ear unto the door, and he shall be thy servant for ever. And also unto thy maidservant thou shalt do likewise. 18. It shall not seem hard unto thee, when thou sendest him away free from thee; for he hath been worth a double hired servant *to thee*, in serving thee six years: and the *LORD* thy God shall bless thee in all that thou doest.

Deut. 16:10. Thou shalt keep the feast of weeks unto the LORD thy God with a tribute of a freewill offering of thine hand, which thou shalt give *unto the LORD thy God*, according as the LORD thy God hath blessed thee: 17. Every man *shall give* as he is able, according to the blessing of the LORD thy God which he hath given thee.

Deut. 18:1. The priests the Levites, *and* all the tribe of Levi, shall have no part nor inheritance with Israel: they shall eat the offerings of the LORD made by fire, and his inheritance. 2. Therefore shall they have no inheritance among their brethren: the LORD *is* their inheritance, as he hath said unto them. 3. And this shall be the priest's due from the people, from them that offer a sacrifice, whether *it be* ox or sheep; and they shall give unto the priest the shoulder, and the two cheeks, and the maw. 4. The firstfruit *also* of thy corn, of thy wine, and of thine oil, and the first of the fleece of thy sheep, shalt thou give him. 5. For the LORD thy God hath chosen him out of all thy tribes, to stand to minister in the name of the LORD, him and his sons for ever. 6. And if a Levite come from any of thy gates out of all Israel, where he sojourned, and come with all the desire of his mind unto the place which the LORD shall choose; 7. Then he shall minister in the name of the LORD his God, as all his brethren the Levites *do*, which stand there before the LORD. 8. They shall have like portions to eat, beside that which cometh of the sale of his patrimony.

Deut. 24:19. When thou cuttest down thine harvest in thy field, and hast forgot a sheaf in the field, thou shalt not go again to fetch it: it shall be for the stranger, for the fatherless, and for the widow: that the LORD thy God may bless thee in all the work of thine hands. 20. When thou beatest thine olive tree, thou shalt not go over the boughs again: it shall be for the stranger, for the fatherless, and for the widow. 21 When thou gatherest the grapes of thy vineyard, thou shalt not glean *it* afterward: it shall be for the stranger, for the fatherless, and for the widow. 22. And thou shalt remember that thou wast a bondman in the land of Egypt: therefore I command thee to do this thing.

2 Sam. 24:24. And the king said unto Araunah, Nay; but I will surely buy *it* of thee at a price: neither will I offer burnt offerings unto the LORD my God of that which doth cost me nothing. So David bought the threshingfloor and the oxen for fifty shekels of silver.

1 Chr. 22:19. Now set your heart and your soul to seek the LORD your God; arise therefore, and build ye the sanctuary of the LORD God, to bring the ark of the covenant of the LORD, and the holy vessels of God, into the house that is to be built to the name of the LORD.

1 Chr. 28:10. Take heed now: for the LORD hath chosen thee to build an house for the sanctuary: be strong, and do *it*. 20. And David said to Solomon his son, Be strong and of good courage and do *it:* fear not, nor be dismayed: for the LORD God, *even* my God, *will be* with thee; he will not

fail thee, nor forsake thee, until thou hast finished all the work for the service of the house of the LORD.

1 Chr. 29:5. Who *then* is willing to consecrate his service this day unto the LORD?

2 Chr. 15:7. Be ye strong therefore, and let not your hands be weak: for your work shall be rewarded. 18. And he brought into the house of God the things that his father had dedicated, and that he himself had dedicated, silver, and gold, and vessels.

Ezra 1:2. Thus saith Cyrus king of Persia, The LORD God of heaven hath given me all the kingdoms of the earth; and he hath charged me to build him an house at Jerusalem, which *is* in Judah. 3. Who *is there* among you of all his people? his God be with him, and let him go up to Jerusalem, which *is* in Judah, and build the house of the LORD God of Israel, (he *is* the God,) which *is* in Jerusalem. 4. And whosoever remaineth in any place where he sojourneth, let the men of his place help him with silver, and with gold, and with goods, and with beasts, beside the freewill offering for the house of God that *is* in Jerusalem.

Psa. 41:1. Blessed *is* he that considereth the poor: the LORD will deliver him in time of trouble. 2. The LORD will preserve him, and keep him alive; *and* he shall be blessed upon the earth: and thou wilt not deliver him unto the will of his enemies. 3. The LORD will strengthen him upon the bed of languishing: thou wilt make all his bed in his sickness.

Psa. 76:11. Vow, and pay unto the LORD your God: let all that be round about him bring presents unto him that ought to be feared.

Psa. 112:5. A good man sheweth favour, and lendeth: he will guide his affairs with discretion. 9. He hath dispersed, he hath given to the poor; his righteousness endureth for ever; his horn shall be exalted with honour.

Psa. 132:1. LORD, remember David, *and* all his afflictions: 2. How he sware unto the LORD, *and* vowed unto the mighty *God* of Jacob; 3. Surely I will not come into the tabernacle of my house, nor go up into my bed; 4. I will not give sleep to mine eyes, *or* slumber to mine eyelids, 5. Until I find out a place for the LORD, an habitation for the mighty *God* of Jacob.

Prov. 3:9. Honour the LORD with thy substance, and with the firstfruits of all thine increase: 10. So shall thy barns be filled with plenty, and thy presses shall burst out with new wine.

Prov. 11:24. There is that scattereth, and yet increaseth; 25. The liberal soul shall be made fat: and he that watereth shall be watered also himself.

Prov. 13:7. There is that maketh himself rich, yet *hath* nothing: *there is* that maketh himself poor, yet *hath* great riches.

Prov. 14:21. He that despiseth his neighbour sinneth: but he that hath mercy on the poor, happy *is* he.

Prov. 19:6. Many will intreat the favour of the prince: and every man *is* a friend to him that giveth gifts. 17. He that hath pity upon the poor lendeth unto the LORD; and that which he hath given will he pay him again.

Prov. 21:26. He coveteth greedily all the day long: but the righteous giveth and spareth not.

Prov. 22:9. He that hath a bountiful eye shall be blessed; for he giveth of his bread to the poor.

Prov. 28:27. He that giveth unto the poor shall not lack:

Prov. 31:20. She stretcheth out her hand to the poor; yea, she reacheth forth her hands to the needy.

Eccl. 11:1. Cast thy bread upon the waters: for thou shalt find it after many days. 2. Give a portion to seven and also to eight; for thou knowest not what evil shall be upon the earth.

Isa. 32:8. The liberal deviseth liberal things; and by liberal things shall he stand.

Isa. 60:7. All the flocks of Kedar shall be gathered together unto thee, the rams of Nebaioth shall minister unto thee: they shall come up with acceptance on mine altar, and I will glorify the house of my glory. 9. Surely the isles shall wait for me, and the ships of Tarshish first, to bring thy sons from far, their silver and their gold with them, unto the name of the LORD thy God, 17. For brass I will bring gold, and for iron I will bring silver, and for wood brass, and for stones iron: I will also make thy officers peace, and thine exactors righteousness.

Hag. 1:8. Go up to the mountain, and bring wood, and build the house; and I will take pleasure in it, and I will be glorified, saith the LORD.

Hag. 2:18. *Even* from the day that the foundation of the LORD's temple was laid, consider *it.* 19. Is the seed yet in the barn? yea, as yet the vine, and the fig tree, and the pomegranate, and the olive tree, hath not brought forth: from this day will I bless *you.*

Mal. 3:10. Bring ye all the tithes into the storehouse, that there may be meat in mine house, and prove me now herewith, saith the LORD of hosts, if I will not open you the windows of heaven, and pour you out a blessing, that *there shall* not *be room* enough *to receive it.* 11. And I will rebuke the devourer for your sakes, and he shall not destroy the fruits of your ground; neither shall your vine cast her fruit before the time in the field, saith the LORD of hosts. 12. And all nations shall call you blessed: for ye shall be a delightsome land, saith the LORD of hosts.

Matt. 6:1. Take heed that ye do not your alms before men, to be seen of them: otherwise ye have no reward of your Father which is in heaven. 2. Therefore when thou doest *thine* alms, do not sound a trumpet before thee, as the hypocrites do in the synagogues and in the streets, that they may have glory of men. Verily I say unto you, They have their reward. 3. But when thou doest alms, let not thy left hand know what thy right hand doeth: 4. That thine alms may be in secret: and thy Father which seeth in secret himself shall reward thee openly.

Matt. 19:21. Jesus said unto him, If thou wilt be perfect, go *and* sell that thou hast, and give to the poor, and thou shalt have treasure in heaven: and come *and* follow me. 22. But when the young man heard that saying, he went away sorrowful: for he had great possessions.

Matt. 25:34. Then shall the King say unto them on his right hand, Come, ye blessed of my Father, inherit the kingdom prepared for you from the foundation of the world: 35. For I was an hungred, and ye gave me meat: I was thirsty, and ye gave me drink: I was a stranger, and ye took me in: 36. Naked, and ye clothed me: I was sick, and ye visited me: I was in prison, and ye came unto me. 37. Then shall the righteous answer him, saying, Lord, when saw we thee an hungred, and fed *thee?* or thirsty, and gave *thee* drink? 38. When saw we thee a stranger, and took *thee* in? or naked, and clothed *thee?* 39. Or when saw we thee sick, or in prison, and came unto thee? 40. And the King shall answer and say unto them, Verily I say unto you, Inasmuch as ye have done *it* unto one of the least of these my brethren, ye have done *it* unto me.

Luke 3:10. And the people asked him, saying, What shall we do then? 11. He answereth and saith unto them, He that hath two coats, let him impart to him that hath none; and he that hath meat, let him do likewise.

Luke 6:38. Give, and it shall be given unto you; good measure, pressed down, and shaken together, and running over, shall men give into your bosom. For with the same measure that ye mete withal it shall be measured to you again. Matt. 5:42.

Luke 11:41. But rather give alms of such things as ye have:

Luke 12:33. Sell that ye have, and give alms; provide yourselves bags which wax not old, a treasure in the heavens that faileth not, where no thief approacheth, neither moth corrupteth. 34. For where your treasure is, there will your heart be also.

Luke 16:9. Make to yourselves friends of the mammon of unrighteousness; that, when ye fail, they may receive you into everlasting habitations.

Acts 10:4. And when he looked on him, he was afraid, and said, What is it, Lord? And he said unto him, Thy prayers and thine alms are come up for a memorial before God.

Acts 20:35. I have shewed you all things, how that so labouring ye ought to support the weak, and to remember the words of the Lord Jesus, how he said, It is more blessed to give than to receive.

Rom. 12:8. He that giveth, *let him do it* with ¹ simplicity; 13. Distributing to the necessity of saints; given to hospitality. [¹ R. V. liberality]

Rom. 15:27. It hath pleased them verily; and their debtors they are. For if the Gentiles have been made partakers of their spiritual things, their duty is also to minister unto them in carnal things.

1 Cor. 13:3. And though I bestow all my goods to feed *the poor*, and though I give my body to be burned, and have not charity, it profiteth me nothing.

1 Cor. 16:1. Concerning the collection for the saints, as I have given order to the churches of Galatia, even so do ye. 2. Upon the first *day* of the week let every one of you lay by him in store, as ¹ *God* hath prospered him, that there be no gatherings when I come. 3. And when I come, whomsoever ye shall approve by *your* letters, them will I send to bring your liberality unto Jerusalem. [¹ R. V. he may prosper]

2 Cor. 8:7. Therefore, as ye abound in every *thing*, *in* faith, and utterance, and knowledge, and *in* all diligence, and *in* your love to us, *see* that ye abound in this grace also. 9. Ye know the grace of our Lord Jesus Christ, that, though he was rich, yet for your sakes he became poor, that ye through his poverty might be rich. 11. Now therefore perform the doing *of it;* that as *there was* a readiness to will, so *there may be* a performance also out of that which ye have. 12. If there be first a willing mind, *it is* accepted according to that a man hath, *and* not according to that he hath not. 13. *I mean* not that other men be eased, and ye burdened: 14. But by an equality, *that* now at this time your abundance *may be a supply* for their want, that their abundance also may be *a supply* for your want: that there may be equality: 24. Shew ye to them, and before the churches, the proof of your love, and of our boasting on your behalf. *vs.* 8,15.

2 Cor. 9:6. He which soweth sparingly shall reap also sparingly; and he which soweth bountifully shall reap also bountifully. 7. Every man according as he purposeth in his heart, *so let him give;* not grudgingly, or of necessity: for God loveth a cheerful giver. 8. God *is* able to make all grace abound toward you; that ye, always having all sufficiency in all *things*, may abound to every good work: [*v.* 9.] 10. He that ministereth seed to the sower both minister bread for *your* food, and multiply your seed sown, and increase the fruits of your righteousness; 11. Being enriched in every thing to all bountifulness, which causeth through us thanksgiving to God. 12. The administration of this service not only supplieth the want of the saints, but is

abundant also by many thanksgivings unto God; *v.* 13.

Eph. 4:28. Let him that stole steal no more: but rather let him labour, working with *his* hands the thing which is good, that he may have to give to him that needeth.

1 Tim. 5:16. If any man or woman that believeth have widows, let them relieve them, and let not the church be charged; that it may relieve them that are widows indeed.

1 Tim. 6:17. Charge them that are rich in this world, that they be not highminded, nor trust in uncertain riches, but in the living God, who giveth us richly all things to enjoy; 18. That they do good, that they be rich in good works, ready to distribute, willing to communicate; 19. Laying up in store for themselves a good foundation against the time to come, that they may lay hold on [1] eternal life.   [1 R. V. the life which is life indeed]

Philem. 14. But without thy mind would I do nothing; that thy benefit should not be as it were of necessity, but willingly.

Heb. 6:10. For God *is* not unrighteous to forget your work and labour of love, which ye have shewed toward his name, in that ye have ministered to the saints, and do minister.

Heb. 13:16. To do good and to communicate forget not: for with such sacrifices God is well pleased.

1 John 3:17. But whoso hath this world's good, and seeth his brother have need, and shutteth up his bowels *of compassion* from him, how dwelleth the love of God in him? 18. My little children, let us not love in word, neither in tongue; but in deed and in truth.

See ALMS; BENEFICENCE; CHARITABLENESS; MINISTERS, EMOLUMENTS OF; GIVING; POOR, DUTY TO; RICH; RICHES; TITHES.

INSTANCES OF: King of Sodom to Abraham, Gen. 14:21. Jacob, Gen. 28:22. Pharaoh to Joseph's people, Gen. 45:18-20. Israelites at the erection of the tabernacle, Ex. 35:21-29; 36:3-7; 38:8; Num. 7; 31:48-54; Josh. 18:1. Reubenites, Josh. 22:24-29. David, 2 Sam. 7:2; 1 Chr. 17:1; 2 Sam. 8:11; 1 Kin. 7:51; 8:17,18; 1 Chr. 21:24: 22; 26:26; 28: 2; 29:2-5,17; Psa. 132:1-5. Barzillai and others to David, 2 Sam. 17:27-29; 19:32. Araunah for sacrifice, 2 Sam. 24:22,23. Joab to David, 2 Sam. 12:26-28.

Israelites' offerings for the temple, 1 Chr. 29:6-9,16,17. Samuel, 1 Chr. 26:27,28. Solomon, 1 Kin. 4:29; 5:4,5; 2 Chr. 2:1-6; 1 Kin. 6; 7:51; 8:13. Queen of Sheba to Solomon, 1 Kin. 10:10. Asa and Abijam, 1 Kin. 15:15. Elisha toward Elijah, 1 Kin. 19:21. Jehoshaphat, 2 Kin. 12:18. Joash and his people, 2 Kin. 12:4-14; 2 Chr. 24:4-14. David, 1 Chr. 16:3. Hezekiah, 2 Chr. 29; 30:1-12; 31: 1-10,21. Manasseh, 2 Chr. 33:16. Josiah, 2 Kin. 22:3-6; 2 Chr. 34:8-13; 35:1-19.

Jews after the captivity, Ezra 1:5,6; 2:68, 69; 3:2-9; 5:2-6; 6:14-22; 8:25-35; Neh. 3; 4:6; 6:3; 7:70-72; 10:32-39; 13:12,31; Hag. 1:12-14; 2:18,19. Cyrus, Ezra 1:2-4,7-11; 3:7; 5:13-15;

6:3. Darius, Ezra 6:7-12. Artaxerxes, Ezra 7:13-27; 8:24-36. The Magi, Matt. 2:11. Centurion, Luke 7:4,5. Mary Magdalene, Luke 8:2,3. The good Samaritan, Luke 10:33-35. Poor widow, Luke 21:2-4. Christians in Jerusalem, Acts 2:44,45; 4:32-37; in Antioch, Acts 11:29; at Philippi, Phil. 4:18; Corinth, 2 Cor. 8:19; 9:1-13; Macedonia, 2 Cor. 8:1-4. People of Melita to Paul, Acts 28:10.

LIBERTINES, freedmen, Acts 6:9.

LIBERTY. Proclaimed in the year of jubilee, Lev. 25:10; Jer. 34:8,15-17. Political, Judg. 17:6; 21:25; Acts 22:28.

See JUBILEE.

FIGURATIVE: Isa. 61:1; 63:4; Luke 4:18; John 8:32,33,36; Gal. 3:28; Eph. 6:8; Col. 3:11.

LIBNAH. 1. A station of the Israelites in the desert, Num. 33:20.

2. A city of Judah, captured by Joshua, Josh. 10:29-32,39; 12:15. Allotted to the priests, Josh. 21:13; 1 Chr. 6:57. Sennacherib besieged; his army defeated near, 2 Kin. 19: 8,35; Isa. 37:8-36.

LIBNI. 1. Son of Gershon, Ex. 6:17; Num. 3:18; 1 Chr. 6:17,20. Descendants called LIBNITES, Num. 3:21; 26:58.

2. Grandson of Merari, 1 Chr. 6:29.

LIBYA. Region N. of Egypt, Ezek. 30:5; 38:5; Acts 2:10. Called also LUBIM and PHUT, which see.

LIBYANS, the inhabitants of Libya, Jer. 46:9; Dan. 11:43.

LICE, plague of, Ex. 8:16-19; Psa. 105:31.

LICENTIOUSNESS. See ADULTERY; LASCIVIOUSNESS.

LIFE. INDEX OF SUB-TOPICS: *Miscellany of Minor Sub-Topics, p.*793; *Brevity and Uncertainty of, p.* 793; *Everlasting, p.* 795; *From God, p.* 796; *Long, p.* 797; *Spiritual, p.* 797.

MISCELLANY OF MINOR SUB-TOPICS: Breath of, Gen. 2:7. Called SPIRIT OF GOD, Job 27:3. Tree of, Gen. 2:9; 3:22,24; Prov. 3:18; 13:12; Rev. 2:7. SACREDNESS OF, an inference from what is taught in the law concerning murder. See HOMICIDE.

Long life promised to obedient children, Ex. 20:12; Deut. 5:16; to those who keep the commandments, Deut. 4:40; 22:7.

Vanity of, Eccl. chapters 1-7. Hated, Eccl. 2:17. To be hated for Christ's sake, Luke 14:26. What shall a man give in exchange for, Matt. 16:26; Mark 8:37. He that loseth it shall save it, Matt. 10:39; 16:25,26; Luke 9:24; John 12:25.

Weary of: Job, Job 3; 7:1-3; 10:18-20. Jeremiah, Jer. 20:14-18; Elijah, 1 Kin. 19:1-8; Jonah, Jonah 4:8,9. See SUICIDE.

Life of Christ, a ransom, Matt. 20:28; Mark 10:45; 1 Tim. 2:6. See SPIRITUAL, below.

BREVITY AND UNCERTAINTY OF: Gen. 47:9. The days of the years of my pilgrimage *are* an hundred and thirty years: few and evil have the days of the years of my life been,

1 Sam. 20:3. Truly *as* the LORD liveth, and *as* thy soul liveth, *there is* but a step between me and death.

2 Sam. 14:14. We must needs die, and *are* as water spilt on the ground, which cannot be gathered up again;

1 Chr. 29:15. We *are* strangers before thee, and sojourners, as *were* all our fathers: our days on the earth *are* as a shadow, and *there is* none abiding.

Job 4:19. Them that dwell in houses of clay, whose foundation *is* in the dust, *which* are crushed before the moth? 20. They are destroyed from morning to evening: they perish for ever without any regarding *it.* 21. Doth not their excellency *which is* in them go away? they die, even without wisdom.

Job 7:6. My days are swifter than a weaver's shuttle, and are spent without hope. 7. O remember that my life *is* wind: mine eye shall no more see good. 8. The eye of him that hath seen me shall see me no *more:* thine eyes *are* upon me, and I *am* not. 9. *As* the cloud is consumed and vanisheth away, so he that goeth down to the grave shall come up no *more.* 10. He shall return no more to his house, neither shall his place know him any more. *v.* 17.

Job 8:9. (We *are but of* yesterday, and know nothing, because our days upon earth *are* a shadow:)

Job 9:25. Now my days are swifter than a post: they flee away, they see no good. 26. They are passed away as the swift ships: as the eagle *that* hasteth to the prey.

Job 10:9. Remember, I beseech thee, that thou hast made me as the clay; and wilt thou bring me into dust again? 20. *Are* not my days few? cease *then, and* let me alone, that I may take comfort a little, 21. Before I go *whence* I shall not return, *even* to the land of darkness and the shadow of death;

Job 13:12. Your remembrances *are* like unto ashes, your bodies to bodies of clay. 25. Wilt thou break a leaf driven to and fro? and wilt thou pursue the dry stubble? 28. He, as a rotten thing, consumeth, as a garment that is moth eaten. Gen. 18:27.

Job 14:1. Man *that is* born of a woman *is* of few days, and full of trouble. 2. He cometh forth like a flower, and is cut down: he fleeth also as a shadow, and continueth not.

Job 17:1. My breath is corrupt, my days are extinct, the graves *are ready* for me.

Psa. 22:29. None can keep alive his own soul.

Psa. 39:4. LORD, make me to know mine end, and the measure of my days, what it *is; that* I may know how frail I *am.* 5. Behold, thou hast made my days *as* an handbreadth; and mine age *is* as nothing before thee: verily every man at his best state *is* altogether vanity. 6. Surely every man walketh in a vain shew: surely they are disquieted in vain: he heapeth up *riches,* and knoweth not who shall gather them. 11. When thou with rebukes dost correct man for iniquity, thou makest his

beauty to consume away like a moth: surely every man *is* vanity.

Psa. 78:39. He remembered that they *were but* flesh; a wind that passeth away, and cometh not again.

Psa. 89:47. Remember how short my time is: wherefore hast thou made all men in vain? 48. What man *is he that* liveth, and shall not see death? shall he deliver his soul from the hand of the grave?

Psa. 90:3. Thou turnest man to destruction; and sayest, Return, ye children of men. 5. Thou carriest them away as with a flood; they are *as* a sleep: in the morning *they are* like grass *which* groweth up. 6. In the morning it flourisheth, and groweth up; in the evening it is cut down, and withereth. 9. All our days are passed away in thy wrath: we spend our years as a tale *that is told.* 10. The days of our years *are* threescore years and ten; and if by reason of strength *they be* fourscore years, yet *is* their strength labour and sorrow; for it is soon cut off, and we fly away.

Psa. 102:11. My days *are* like a shadow that declineth; and I am withered like grass.

Psa. 103:14. He knoweth our frame; he remembereth that we *are* dust. 15. *As for* man, his days *are* as grass: as a flower of the field, so he flourisheth. 16. For the wind passeth over it, and it is gone; and the place thereof shall know it no more.

Psa. 144:4. Man is like to vanity: his days *are* as a shadow that passeth away. *v.* 3.

Psa. 146:4. His breath goeth forth, he returneth to his earth; in that very day his thoughts perish.

Prov. 27:1. Boast not thyself of to morrow; for thou knowest not what a day may bring forth.

Eccl. 1:4. *One* generation passeth away, and *another* generation cometh: but the earth abideth for ever.

Eccl. 6:12. Who knoweth what *is* good for man in *this* life, all the days of his vain life which he spendeth as a shadow? for who can tell a man what shall be after him under the sun?

Isa. 2:22. Cease ye from man, whose breath *is* in his nostrils: for wherein is he to be accounted of?

Isa. 38:12. Mine age is departed, and is removed from me as a shepherd's tent: I have cut off like a weaver my life: he will cut me off with pining sickness: from day *even* to night wilt thou make an end of me.

Isa. 40:6. All flesh *is* grass, and all the goodliness thereof *is* as the flower of the field: 7. The grass withereth, the flower fadeth: because the spirit of the LORD bloweth upon it: surely the people *is* grass. 24. Yea, they shall not be planted; yea, they shall not be sown: yea, their stock shall not take root in the earth: and he shall also blow upon them, and they shall wither, and the whirlwind shall take them away as stubble. 1 Pet. 1:24.

Isa. 51:8. The moth shall eat them up like a garment, and the worm shall eat them like wool: 12. Who *art* thou, that thou shouldest be afraid of a man *that* shall die, and of the son of man *which* shall be made *as* grass;

Isa. 64:6. We all do fade as a leaf;

Luke 12:20. But God said unto him, *Thou* fool, this night thy soul shall be required of thee: then whose shall those things be, which thou hast provided?

Jas. 1:10. As the flower of the grass he shall pass away. 11. For the sun is no sooner risen with a burning heat, but it withereth the grass, and the flower thereof falleth, and the grace of the fashion of it perisheth: so also shall the rich man fade away in his ways.

Jas. 4:14. Ye know not what *shall be* on the morrow. For what *is* your life? It is even a vapour, that appeareth for a little time, and then vanisheth away. *v.* 15.

See DEATH.

EVERLASTING: Psa. 21:4. He asked life of thee, *and* thou gavest *it* him, *even* length of days for ever and ever.

Psa. 121:8. The LORD shall preserve thy going out and thy coming in from this time forth, and even for evermore.

Psa. 133:3. The LORD commanded the blessing, *even* life for evermore.

Isa. 25:8. He will swallow up death in victory;

Dan. 12:2. And many of them that sleep in the dust of the earth shall awake, some to everlasting life, and some to shame *and* everlasting contempt.

Matt. 19:16. And, behold, one came and said unto him, Good Master, what good thing shall I do, that I may have eternal life? 17. And he said unto him, Why callest thou me good? *there is* none good but one, *that is,* God: but if thou wilt enter into life, keep the commandments. 18. He saith unto him, Which? Jesus said, Thou shalt do no murder, Thou shalt not commit adultery, Thou shalt not steal, Thou shalt not bear false witness, 19. Honour thy father and *thy* mother: and, Thou shalt love thy neighbour as thyself. 20. The young man saith unto him, All these things have I kept from my youth up: what lack I yet? 21. Jesus said unto him, If thou wilt be perfect, go *and* sell that thou hast, and give to the poor, and thou shalt have treasure in heaven: and come *and* follow me. [Luke 18:18.] 29. And every one that hath forsaken houses, or brethren, or sisters, or father, or mother, or wife, or children, or lands, for my name's sake, shall receive an hundredfold, and shall inherit everlasting life. Mark 10:30.

Matt. 25:46. And these shall go away into everlasting punishment: but the righteous into life eternal.

Luke 18:30. Who shall not receive manifold more in this present time, and in the world to come life everlasting.

Luke 20:36. Neither can they die any more: for they are equal unto the angels; and are the children of God, being the children of the resurrection.

John 3:14. And as Moses lifted up the serpent in the wilderness, even so must the Son of man be lifted up: 15. That whosoever believeth in him should not perish, but have eternal life. 16. For God so loved the world, that he gave his only begotten Son, that whosoever believeth in him should not perish, but have everlasting life.

John 4:14. But whosoever drinketh of the water that I shall give him shall never thirst; but the water that I shall give him shall be in him a well of water springing up into everlasting life.

John 5:24. Verily, verily, I say unto you, He that heareth my word, and believeth on him that sent me, hath everlasting life, and shall not come into condemnation; but is passed from death unto life. 25. Verily, verily, I say unto you, The hour is coming, and now is, when the dead shall hear the voice of the Son of God: and they that hear shall live. 29. And shall come forth; they that have done good, unto the resurrection of life; and they that have done evil, unto the resurrection of damnation. 39. Search [Ye search, *R. V.*] the scriptures; for in them ye think ye have eternal life:

John 6:27. Labour not for the meat which perisheth, but for that meat which endureth unto everlasting life, which the Son of man shall give unto you: for him hath God the Father sealed. 40. And this is the will of him that sent me, that every one which seeth the Son, and believeth on him, may have everlasting life: and I will raise him up at the last day. 47. Verily, verily, I say unto you, He that believeth on me hath everlasting life.

50. This is the bread which cometh down from heaven, that a man may eat thereof, and not die. 51. I am the living bread which came down from heaven: if any man eat of this bread, he shall live for ever: and the bread that I will give is my flesh, which I will give for the life of the world. 52. The Jews therefore strove among themselves, saying, How can this man give us *his* flesh to eat? 53. Then Jesus said unto them, Verily, verily, I say unto you, Except ye eat the flesh of the Son of man, and drink his blood, ye have no life in you. 54. Whoso eateth my flesh, and drinketh my blood, hath eternal life; and I will raise him up at the last day. 55. For my flesh is meat indeed, and my blood is drink indeed. 56. He that eateth my flesh, and drinketh my blood, dwelleth in me, and I in him. 57. As the living Father hath sent me, and I live by the Father; so he that eateth me, even he shall live by me. 58. This is that bread which came down from heaven: not as your fathers did eat manna, and are dead: he that eateth of this bread shall live for ever. 68. Then Simon Peter answered him, Lord, to whom shall we go? thou hast the words of eternal life.

John 10:10. I am come that they might have life, and that they might have *it* more abundantly. 27. My sheep hear my voice, and I know them, and they follow me: 28. And I give unto them eternal life;

John 12:25. He that loveth his life shall lose it; and he that hateth his life in this world shall keep it unto life eternal. 50. And I know that his commandment is life everlasting:

John 17:2. As thou hast given him power over all flesh, that he should give eternal life to as many as thou hast given him. 3. And this is life eternal, that they might know thee the only true God, and Jesus Christ, whom thou hast sent.

Acts 13:46. Then Paul and Barnabas waxed bold, and said, It was necessary that the word of God should first have been spoken to you: but seeing ye put it from you, and judge yourselves unworthy of everlasting life, lo, we turn to the Gentiles. 48. And when the Gentiles heard this, they were glad, and glorified the word of the Lord: and as many as were ordained to eternal life believed.

Rom. 2:7. To them who by patient continuance in well doing seek for glory and honour and immortality, eternal life:

Rom. 5:21. That as sin hath reigned unto death, even so might grace reign through righteousness unto eternal life by Jesus Christ our Lord.

Rom. 6:22. But now being made free from sin, and become servants to God, ye have your fruit unto holiness, and the end everlasting life. 23. For the wages of sin *is* death; but the gift of God *is* eternal life through Jesus Christ our Lord.

1 Cor. 15:53. This corruptible must put on incorruption, and this mortal *must* put on immortality. 54. So when this corruptible shall have put on incorruption, and this mortal shall have put on immortality, then shall be brought to pass the saying that is written, Death is swallowed up in victory.

2 Cor. 5:1. For we know that, if our earthly house of *this* tabernacle were dissolved, we have a building of God, an house not made with hands, eternal in the heavens.

Gal. 6:8. For he that soweth to his flesh shall of the flesh reap corruption; but he that soweth to the Spirit shall of the Spirit reap life everlasting.

1 Tim. 1:16. Howbeit for this cause I obtained mercy, that in me first Jesus Christ might shew forth all longsuffering, for a pattern to them which should hereafter believe on him to life everlasting.

1 Tim. 4:8. Godliness is profitable unto all things, having promise of the life that now is, and of that which is to come.

1 Tim. 6:12. Fight the good fight of faith, lay hold on eternal life, whereunto thou art also called, and hast professed a good profession before many witnesses. *v.* 19.

2 Tim. 1:10. Our Saviour Jesus Christ, who hath abolished death, and hath brought life and [1] immortality to light through the gospel: [1 R. V. incorruption]

Tit. 1:2. In hope of eternal life, which God, that cannot lie, promised before the world began;

Tit. 3:7. Being justified by his grace, we should be made heirs according to the hope of eternal life.

1 John 2:25. And this is the promise that he hath promised us, *even* eternal life.

1 John 3:15. Ye know that no murderer hath eternal life abiding in him.

1 John 5:11. And this is the record, that God hath given to us eternal life, and this life is in his Son. 12. He that hath the Son hath life; *and* he that hath not the Son of God hath not life. 13. These things have I written unto you [1] that believe on the name of the Son of God; that ye may know that ye have eternal life, [2] and that ye may believe on the name of the Son of God. 20. And we know that the Son of God is come, and hath given us an understanding, that we may know him that is true; and we are in him that is true, *even* in his Son Jesus Christ. This is the true God, and eternal life.

[R. V. [1] Omitted. [2] even unto you that]

Jude 21. Keep yourselves in the love of God, looking for the mercy of our Lord Jesus Christ unto eternal life.

Rev. 1:18. *I am* he that liveth, and was dead; and, behold, I am alive for evermore, Amen; and have the keys of hell and of death.

See IMMORTALITY.

FROM GOD: Gen. 2:7. The LORD God formed man *of* the dust of the ground, and breathed into his nostrils the breath of life; and man became a living soul.

Deut. 8:3. Man doth not live by bread only, but by every *word* that proceedeth out of the mouth of the LORD doth man live.

Deut. 30:20. That thou mayest love the LORD thy God, *and* that thou mayest obey his voice, and that thou mayest cleave unto him: for he *is* thy life, and the length of thy days: that thou mayest dwell in the land which the LORD sware unto thy fathers, to Abraham, to Isaac, and to Jacob, to give them.

Deut. 32:39. See now that I, *even* I, *am* he, and *there is* no god with me: I kill, and I make alive; I wound, and I heal: neither *is there any* that can deliver out of my hand. 40. For I lift up my hand to heaven, and say, I live for ever.

1 Sam. 2:6. The LORD killeth, and maketh alive: he bringeth down to the grave, and bringeth up.

Job 27:3. All the while my breath *is* in me, and the spirit of God *is* in my nostrils;

Job 34:14. If he set his heart upon man, *if* he gather unto himself his spirit and his breath; 15. All flesh shall perish together, and man shall turn again unto dust.

Psa. 22:29. None can keep alive his own soul.

Psa. 30:3. O LORD, thou hast brought up my soul from the grave: thou hast kept me alive, that I should not go down to the pit.

Psa. 68:20. Unto GOD the Lord *belong* the issues from death.

Psa. 104:30. Thou sendest forth thy spirit, they are created: and thou renewest the face of the earth.

Eccl. 12:7. Then shall the dust return to the earth as it was: and the spirit shall return unto God who gave it.

Isa. 38:16. O Lord, by these *things men* live, and in all these *things is* the life of my spirit: so wilt thou recover me, and make me to live. 17. Behold, for peace I had great bitterness: but thou hast in love to my soul *delivered it* from the pit of corruption: for thou hast cast all my sins behind thy back. 18. For the grave cannot praise thee, death can *not* celebrate thee: they that go down into the pit cannot hope for thy truth. 19. The living, the living, he shall praise thee, as I *do* this day: the father to the children shall make known thy truth. 20. The LORD *was ready* to save me: therefore we will sing my songs to the stringed instruments all the days of our life in the house of the LORD.

Acts 17:25. He giveth to all life, and breath, and all things; 26. And hath made of one blood all nations of men for to dwell on all the face of the earth, and hath determined the times before appointed, and the bounds of their habitation; 28. For in him we live, and move, and have our being; as certain also of your own poets have said, For we are also his offspring.

Rom. 4:17. God, who quickeneth the dead, and calleth those things which be not as though they were.

1 Tim. 6:13. I give thee charge in the sight of God, who quickeneth all things,

Jas. 4:15. For that ye *ought* to say, If the Lord will, we shall live, and do this, or that.

LONG: See LONGEVITY.

SPIRITUAL: John 3:3. Jesus answered and said unto him, Verily, verily, I say unto thee, Except a man be born again, he cannot see the kingdom of God. 4. Nicodemus saith unto him, How can a man be born when he is old? can he enter the second time into his mother's womb, and be born? 5. Jesus answered, Verily, verily, I say unto thee, Except a man be born of water and *of* the Spirit, he cannot enter into the kingdom of God. 6. That which is born of the flesh is flesh; and that which is born of the Spirit is spirit. 7. Marvel not that I said unto thee, Ye must be born again. 8. The wind bloweth where it listeth, and thou hearest the sound thereof, but canst not tell whence it cometh, and whither it goeth: so is every one that is born of the Spirit. 9. Nicodemus answered and said unto him, How can these things be? 10. Jesus answered and said unto him, Art thou a master of Israel, and knowest not these things? 11. Verily, verily, I say unto thee, We speak that we do know, and testify that we have seen; and ye receive not our witness. 12. If I have told you earthly

things, and ye believe not, how shall ye believe, if I tell you *of* heavenly things? 13. And no man hath ascended up to heaven, but he that came down from heaven, *even* the Son of man which is in heaven. 14. And as Moses lifted up the serpent in the wilderness, even so must the Son of man be lifted up: 15. That whosoever believeth in him should not perish, but have eternal life. 16. For God so loved the world, that he gave his only begotten Son, that whosoever believeth in him should not perish, but have everlasting life.

John 5:24. Verily, verily, I say unto you, He that heareth my word, and believeth on him that sent me, hath everlasting life, and shall not come into condemnation; but is passed from death unto life. 25. Verily, verily, I say unto you, The hour is coming, and now is, when the dead shall hear the voice of the Son of God: and they that hear shall live. 26. For as the Father hath life in himself; so hath he given to the Son to have life in himself; 40. And ye will not come to me, that ye might have life.

John 6:27. Labour not for the meat which perisheth, but for that meat which endureth unto everlasting life, which the Son of man shall give unto you: for him hath God the Father sealed. 33. For the bread of God is he which cometh down from heaven, and giveth life unto the world. 35. And Jesus said unto them, I am the bread of life: he that cometh to me shall never hunger; and he that believeth on me shall never thirst. 40. And this is the will of him that sent me, that every one which seeth the Son, and believeth on him, may have everlasting life: and I will raise him up at the last day. 47. Verily, verily, I say unto you, He that believeth on me hath everlasting life.

John 10:10. The thief cometh not, but for to steal, and to kill, and to destroy: I am come that they might have life, and that they might have *it* more abundantly.

John 11:25. Jesus said unto her. I am the resurrection, and the life: he that believeth in me though he ¹ were dead, yet shall he live: 26. And whosoever liveth and believeth in me shall never die. [¹ R. V. die]

John 14:6. Jesus saith unto him, I am the way, the truth, and the life: no man cometh unto the Father, but by me.

John 17:2. As thou hast given him power over all flesh, that he should give eternal life to as many as thou hast given him. 3. And this is life eternal, that they might know thee the only true God, and Jesus Christ, whom thou hast sent.

John 20:31. But these are written, that ye might believe that Jesus is the Christ, the Son of God; and that believing ye might have life through his name.

Rom. 6:4. Therefore we are buried with him by baptism into death: that like as Christ was raised up from the dead by the glory of the Father, even so we also should walk in newness of life. 5. For if we **have** been planted together in the likeness of his death, we shall be also *in the likeness* of *his* resurrection: 8. Now if we be dead with Christ, we believe that we shall also live with him: 11. Likewise reckon ye also yourselves to be dead indeed unto sin, but alive unto God through Jesus Christ our Lord. 13. Neither yield ye your members *as* instruments of unrighteousness unto sin: but yield yourselves unto God, as those that are alive from the dead, and your members *as* instruments of righteousness unto God. 22. But now being made free from sin, and become servants to God, ye have your fruit unto holiness, and the end everlasting life. 23. For the wages of sin *is* death: but the gift of God *is* eternal life through Jesus Christ our Lord.

Rom. 8:10. And if Christ *be* in you, the body *is* dead because of sin; but the Spirit *is* life because of righteousness.

1 John 1:1. That which was from the beginning, which we have heard, which we have seen with our eyes, which we have looked upon, and our hands have handled, of the Word of life: 2. (For the life was manifested, and we have seen *it*, and bear witness, and shew unto you that eternal life, which was with the Father, and was manifested unto us;)

LIGHT. Created, Gen. 1:3–5; Psa. 74:16; Isa. 45:7; 2 Cor. 4:6. Miraculous, Matt. 17:2; Acts 9:3.

FIGURATIVE AND SYMBOLICAL: 1 Kin. 11:36. And unto his son will I give one tribe, that David my servant may have a light alway before me in Jerusalem, the city which I have chosen me to put my name there.

Psa. 27:1. The LORD *is* my light and my salvation; whom shall I fear? the LORD *is* the strength of my life; of whom shall I be afraid?

Psa. 119:105. Thy word *is* a lamp unto my feet, and a light unto my path. 130. The entrance of thy words giveth light; it giveth understanding unto the simple.

Prov. 6:23. For the commandment *is* a lamp; and the law *is* light;

Eccl. 2:13. Then I saw that wisdom excelleth folly, as far as light excelleth darkness.

Isa. 8:20. To the law and to the testimony: if they speak not according to this word, *it* is because *there is* no light in them.

Isa. 49:6. I will also give thee for a light to the Gentiles, that thou mayest be my salvation unto the end of the earth.

Isa. 58:8. Then shall thy light break forth as the morning, and thine health shall spring forth speedily: and thy righteousness shall go before thee; the glory of the LORD shall be thy rereward.

Isa. 60:19. The sun shall be no more thy light by day; neither for brightness shall the moon give light unto thee: but the LORD shall be unto thee an everlasting light, and thy God thy glory. 20. Thy sun shall no more go down; neither shall thy moon with-

draw itself: for the LORD shall be thine everlasting light, and the days of thy mourning shall be ended.

Matt. 4:16. The people which sat in darkness saw great light; and to them which sat in the region and shadow of death light is sprung up.

Matt. 5:14. Ye are the light of the world. A city that is set on a hill cannot be hid. 16. Let your light so shine before men, that they may see your good works, and glorify your Father which is in heaven.

Luke 2:32. A light to lighten the Gentiles, and the glory of thy people Israel.

Luke 11:34. The light of the body is the eye: therefore when thine eye is single, thy whole body also is full of light; but when *thine eye* is evil, thy body also *is* full of darkness.

Luke 16:8. And the lord commended the unjust steward, because he had done wisely: for the children of this world are in their generation wiser than the children of light.

John 1:4. In him was life; and the life was the light of men. 5. And the light shineth in darkness; and the darkness comprehended it not. 7. The same came for a witness, to bear witness of the Light, that all *men* through him might believe. 8. He was not that Light, but *was sent* to bear witness of that Light. 9. *That* was the true Light, which lighteth every man that cometh into the world.

John 3:19. And this is the condemnation, that light is come into the world, and men loved darkness rather than light, because their deeds were evil. 20. For every one that doeth evil hateth the light, neither cometh to the light, lest his deeds should be reproved. 21. But he that doeth truth cometh to the light, that his deeds may be made manifest, that they are wrought in God.

John 5:35. He was a burning and a shining light: and ye were willing for a season to rejoice in his light.

John 8:12. Then spake Jesus again unto them, saying, I am the light of the world: he that followeth me shall not walk in darkness, but shall have the light of life.

John 9:5. As long as I am in the world, I am the light of the world.

John 12:35. Then Jesus said unto them, Yet a little while is the light with you. Walk while ye have the light, lest darkness come upon you: for he that walketh in darkness knoweth not whither he goeth. 36. While ye have light, believe in the light, that ye may be the children of light. These things spake Jesus, and departed, and did hide himself from them.

Acts 26:18. To open their eyes, *and* to turn *them* from darkness to light, and *from* the power of Satan unto God, that they may receive forgiveness of sins, and inheritance among them which are sanctified by faith that is in me.

Eph. 5:8. For ye were sometimes **darkness,**

but now *are ye* light in the Lord: walk as children of light: 14. Awake thou that sleepest, and arise from the dead, and Christ shall give thee light.

Phil. 2:15. That ye may be blameless and harmless, the sons of God, without rebuke, in the midst of a crooked and perverse nation, among whom ye shine as lights in the world;

1 Thess. 5:5. Ye are all the children of light, and the children of the day: we are not of the night, nor of darkness.

1 Tim. 6:16. Who only hath immortality, dwelling in the light which no man can approach unto;

Jas. 1:17. Every good gift and every perfect gift is from above, and cometh down from the Father of lights, with whom is no variableness, neither shadow of turning.

1 Pet. 2:9. But ye *are* a chosen generation, a royal priesthood, an holy nation, a peculiar people; that ye should shew forth the praises of him who hath called you out of darkness into his marvellous light:

2 Pet. 1:19. We have also a more sure word of prophecy; whereunto ye do well that ye take heed, as unto a light that shineth in a dark place, until the day dawn, and the daystar arise in your hearts:

1 John 1:5. This then is the message which we have heard of him, and declare unto you, that God is light, and in him is no darkness at all. 7. But if we walk in the light, as he is in the light, we have fellowship one with another, and the blood of Jesus Christ his Son cleanseth us from all sin.

Rev. 21:23. And the city had no need of the sun, neither of the moon, to shine in it: for the glory of God did lighten it, and the Lamb *is* the light thereof.

LIGHTNING, Job 28:26; 37:3; 38:25,35; Psa. 18:14; 77:18; 78:48; 97:4; 135:7; 144:6; Jer. 10:13; 51:16; Ezek. 1:13,14; Dan. 10:6; Nah. 2:4; Zech. 9:14; 10:1; Matt. 24:27; 28:3; Luke 10:18; Rev. 4:5; 8:5; 11:19; 16:18.

LIGN-ALOE, a tree, not identified by naturalists, Num. 24:6.

LIGURE, a precious stone, Ex. 28:19; 39:12.

LILY. The principal chapiters of the temple ornamented with carvings of, 1 Kin. 7:19,22,26. Molded on the rim of the molten laver in the temple, 1 Kin. 7:26; 2 Chr. 4:5. Lessons of trust gathered from, Matt. 6:28-30; Luke 12:27.

FIGURATIVE: Of the lips of the beloved, Song 5:13.

LIME, Isa. 33:12; Amos 2:1.

LINEN. Exported from Egypt, 1 Kin. 10:28; Ezek. 27:7; from Syria, Ezek. 27:16. Curtains of the tabernacle made of, Ex. 26:1; 27:9. Vestments of priests made of, Ex. 28:5-8,15,39-42. Livery of royal households made of, Gen. 41:42; Esth. 8:15. Garments for men made of, Gen. 41:42; Ezek. 9:2; Luke 16:19; for women, Isa. 3:23; Ezek. 16:10-13. Bedding made of, Prov. 7:16. Mosaic law forbade its being mingled with wool, Lev.

19:19; Deut. 22:11. The body of Jesus wrapped in, Mark 15:46; John 20:5.

FIGURATIVE: Pure and white, of righteousness, Rev. 15:6; 19:8,14.

LINUS, a Christian at Rome, 2 Tim. 4:21.

LION. King of beasts, Mic. 5:8. Fierceness of, Job 4:10; 28:8; Psa. 7:2; Prov. 22:13; Jer. 2:15; 49:19; 50:44; Hos. 13:8. The roaring of, Psa. 22:13; Prov. 20:2. Strength of, Prov. 30:30; Isa. 38:13; Joel 1:6. Instincts of, in taking prey, Psa. 10:9; 17:12; Lam. 3:10; Amos 3:4; Nah. 2:12. Lair of, in the jungles, Jer. 4:7; 25:38. The bases in the temple ornamented by mouldings of, 1 Kin. 7:29,36. Twelve statues of, on the stairs leading to Solomon's throne, 1 Kin. 10:19,20. Samson's riddle concerning, Judg. 14:14,18. Proverb of, Eccl. 9:4. Parable of, Ezek. 19:1-9. Kept in captivity, Dan. 6. Sent as judgment upon the Samaritans, 2 Kin. 17:25,26. Slain by Samson, Judg. 14:5-9; David, 1 Sam. 17:34,36; Benaiah, 2 Sam. 23:20; saints, Heb. 11:33. Disobedient prophet slain by, 1 Kin. 13:24-28; an unnamed person slain by, 1 Kin. 20:36. Used for the torture of criminals, Dan. 6:16-24; 7:12; 2 Tim. 4:17.

FIGURATIVE: Of a ruler's wrath, Prov. 19:12; Jer. 5:6; 50:17; Hos. 5:14; of Satan, 1 Pet. 5:8; of divine judgments, Isa. 15:9.

SYMBOLICAL: Gen. 49:9; Isa. 29:1 [marg.]; Ezek. 1:10; 10:14; Dan. 7:4; Rev. 4:7; 5:5; 9:8,17; 13:2.

LITIGATION, to be avoided, Matt. 5:25; Luke 12:58; 1 Cor. 6:1-8.

See ACTIONS AT LAW: ADJUDICATION; ARBITRATION; COMPROMISE.

LITTER, an Oriental contrivance for carrying persons, Isa. 66:20.

LIVER. Superstitious rites with, Ezek. 21:21.

LIVERY, of seizin. See LAND, CONVEYANCE OF.

LIZARD, Lev. 11:30; Prov. 30:28 [*R. V.*].

LO-AMMI, a symbolical name given to a son of Hosea, Hos. 1:9.

LOAVES. Miracle of the five, Matt. 14:15-21; 16:9; Luke 9:12-17; of the seven, Matt. 15:34-38; 16:10.

See BREAD.

LOBBYING, Ezra 4:4,5.

See DIPLOMACY; INFLUENCE, POLITICAL.

LOCK, Judg. 3:23-25; Neh. 3:13,14; Song 5:5.

LOCUST. Authorized as food, Lev. 11:22; used as, Matt. 3:4; Mark 1:6. Plague of, Ex. 10:1-19; Psa. 105:34,35. Devastation by, Deut. 28:38; 1 Kin. 8:37; 2 Chr. 7:13; Isa. 33:4; Joel 1:4-7; Rev. 9:7-10. Sun obscured by, Joel 2:2,10. Instincts of, Prov. 30:27.

In *A. V.* often inaccurately translated grasshopper, as in Judg. 6:5; 7:12; Job 39:20; Jer. 46:23.

See GRASSHOPPER.

FIGURATIVE: Jer. 46:23 [*R. V.*].

SYMBOLICAL: Rev. 9:3-10.

LOD. A city in Benjamin, 1 Chr. 8:12; Ezra 2:33; Neh. 7:37; 11:35. Called LYDDA, Acts 9:38.

LO-DEBAR. A city in Manasseh, 2 Sam. 9:4,5; 17:27. Home of Mephibosheth, the lame son of Jonathan, 2 Sam. 9:3-5.

LOG, a measure for liquids, holding about a pint, Lev. 14:10,12,15,24.

LOIS, grandmother of Timothy, commended by Paul for her faith, 2 Tim. 1:5.

LONGEVITY. Gen. 6:3. And the LORD said, My spirit shall not always strive with man, for that he also *is* flesh: yet his days shall be an hundred and twenty years.

Ex. 20:12. Honour thy father and thy mother: that thy days may be long upon the land which the LORD thy God giveth thee.

1 Kin. 3:11. And God said unto him, Because thou hast asked this thing, and hast not asked for thyself long life; neither hast asked riches for thyself, nor hast asked the life of thine enemies; but hast asked for thyself understanding to discern judgment; 12. Behold, I have done according to thy words: lo, I have given thee a wise and an understanding heart; so that there was none like thee before thee, neither after thee shall any arise like unto thee. 13. And I have also given thee that which thou hast not asked, both riches, and honour: so that there shall not be any among the kings like unto thee all thy days. 14. And if thou wilt walk in my ways, to keep my statutes and my commandments, as thy father David did walk, then I will lengthen thy days.

Job 5:26. Thou shalt come to *thy* grave in a full age, like as a shock of corn cometh in in his season.

Psa. 21:4. He asked life of thee, *and* thou gavest *it* him, *even* length of days for ever and ever.

Psa. 34:11. Come, ye children, hearken unto me: I will teach you the fear of the LORD. 12. What man *is he that* desireth life, *and* loveth *many* days, that he may see good? 13. Keep thy tongue from evil, and thy lips from speaking guile.

Psa. 90:10. The days of our years *are* threescore years and ten; and if by reason of strength *they be* fourscore years, yet *is* their strength labour and sorrow; for it is soon cut off, and we fly away.

Psa. 91:16. With long life will I satisfy him, and shew him my salvation.

Prov. 3:1. My son, forget not my law; but let thine heart keep my commandments: 2. For length of days, and long life, and peace, shall they add to thee. 16. Length of days *is* in her right hand; *and* in her left hand riches and honour.

Prov. 9:11. For by me thy days shall be multiplied, and the years of thy life shall be increased.

Prov. 10:27. The fear of the LORD prolongeth days: but the years of the wicked shall be shortened.

Isa. 65:20. There shall be no more thence an infant of days, nor an old man that hath not filled his days: for the child shall die an hundred years old; but the sinner *being* an hundred years old shall be accursed.

1 Pet. 3:10. For he that will love life, and see good days, let him refrain his tongue from evil, and his lips that they speak no guile: 11. Let him eschew evil, and do good; let him seek peace, and ensue it.

See OLD AGE.

INSTANCES OF: Adam, 930 years, Gen. 5:5. Seth, 912 years, Gen. 5:8. Enos, 905 years, Gen. 5:11. Cainan, 910 years, Gen. 5:14. Mahalaleel, 895 years, Gen. 5:17. Jared, 962 years, Gen. 5:20. Enoch, 365 years, Gen. 5:23. Methuselah, 969 years, Gen. 5:27. Lamech, 777 years, Gen. 5:31. Noah, 950 years, Gen. 9:29. Shem, Gen. 11:11. Arphaxad, Gen. 11:13. Salah, Gen. 11:15. Eber, Gen. 11:17. Peleg, Gen. 11:19. Reu, Gen. 11:21. Serug, Gen. 11:23. Nahor, Gen. 11:25. Terah, 205 years, Gen. 11:32. Sarah, 127 years, Gen. 23:1. Abraham, 175 years, Gen. 25:7. Isaac, 180 years, Gen. 35:28. Jacob, 147 years, Gen. 47:28. Joseph, 110 years, Gen. 50:26. Amram, 137 years, Ex. 6:20. Aaron, 123 years, Num. 33:39. Moses, 120 years, Deut. 31:2; 34:7. Joshua, 110 years, Josh. 24:29. Eli, 98 years, 1 Sam. 4:15. Barzillai, 80 years, 2 Sam. 19:32. Job, Job 42:16. Jehoiada, 130 years, 2 Chr. 24:15. Anna, Luke 2:36,37. Paul, Philem. 1:9.

LONGSUFFERING. 1 Cor. 13:4. Charity suffereth long, *and* is kind; 7. Beareth all things, believeth all things, hopeth all things, endureth all things.

2 Cor. 6:4. But in all *things* approving ourselves as the ministers of God, in much patience, in afflictions, in necessities, in distresses, 5. In stripes, in imprisonments, in tumults, in labours, in watchings, in fastings; 6. By pureness, by knowledge, by longsuffering, by kindness, by the Holy Ghost,

Gal. 5:22. But the fruit of the Spirit is love, joy, peace, longsuffering, gentleness, goodness, [1] faith,   [1 R. V. faithfulness]

Eph. 4:1. I therefore, the prisoner of the Lord, beseech you that ye walk worthy of the vocation wherewith ye are called, 2. With all lowliness and meekness, with longsuffering, forbearing one another in love;

Col. 1:11. Strengthened with all might, according to his glorious power, unto all patience and longsuffering with joyfulness;

Col. 3:12. Put on therefore, as the elect of God, holy and beloved, bowels of mercies, kindness, humbleness of mind, meekness, longsuffering; 13. Forbearing one another, and forgiving one another, if any man have a quarrel against any: even as Christ forgave you, so also *do* ye.

1 Tim. 1:16. Howbeit for this cause I obtained mercy, that in me first Jesus Christ might shew forth all longsuffering, for a pattern to them which should hereafter believe on him to life everlasting.

2 Tim. 3:10. But thou hast fully known my doctrine, manner of life, purpose, faith, longsuffering, charity, patience,

2 Tim. 4:2. Preach the word; be instant

in season, out of season; reprove, rebuke, exhort with all longsuffering and doctrine.

See CHARITABLENESS; GOD, LONGSUFFERING OF; PATIENCE.

LOOKING-GLASS. See MIRROR.

LORD, a prince, Josh. 13:3; Judg. 3:3; 1 Sam. 5:8; 6:4.

See GOD; JESUS.

LORD'S DAY. See SABBATH.

LORD'S PRAYER, Matt. 6:9-13; Luke 11:2-4.

LORD'S SUPPER. See EUCHARIST.

LOST SHEEP, parable of, Matt. 18:12, 13; Luke 15:4-7.

LOST, THE. See WICKED, PUNISHMENT OF.

LO-RUHAMAH, Hosea's daughter, Hos. 1:6-8.

LOT, THE. Prov. 16:33; 18:18; Isa. 34:17; Joel 3:3. The scapegoat chosen by, Lev. 16:8-10.

The land of Canaan divided among the tribes by, Num. 26:55; Josh. 15; 18:10; 19:51; 21; 1 Chr. 6:61,65; Ezek. 45:1; 47:22; 48:29; Mic. 2:5; Acts 13:19. Saul chosen king by, 1 Sam. 10:20,21. Priests and Levites designated by, for sanctuary service, 1 Chr. 24:5-31; 26:13; Neh. 10:34; Luke 1:9. Used after the captivity, Neh. 11:1. An apostle chosen by, Acts 1:26. Achan's guilt ascertained by, Josh. 7:14-18; Jonathan's, 1 Sam. 14:41,42; Jonah's, Jonah 1:7. Used to fix the time for the execution of condemned persons, Esth. 3:7; 9:24. The garments of Jesus divided by, Psa. 22:18; Matt. 27:35; Mark 15:24; John 19:23,24.

LOT. 1. Feast of. See PURIM.

2. The son of Haran. Accompanies Terah from Ur of the Chaldees to Haran, Gen. 11:31. Migrates with Abraham to the land of Canaan, Gen. 12:4. Accompanies Abraham to Egypt; returns with him to Beth-el, Gen. 13:1-3. Rich in flocks, and herds, and servants; separates from Abraham, and locates in Sodom, Gen. 13:5-14. Taken captive by Chedorlaomer; rescued by Abraham, Gen. 14:1-16. Providentially saved from destruction in Sodom, Gen, 19; Luke 17:28,29. Righteous, 2 Pet. 2:7,8. Disobediently protests against going to the mountains, and chooses Zoar, Gen. 19:17-22. His wife disobediently longs after Sodom, and becomes a pillar of salt, Gen. 19:26; Luke 17:32. Commits incest with his daughters, Gen. 19:30-38. Descendants of, see AMMONITES; MOABITES.

LOVE. OF CHILDREN FOR PARENTS: See CHILDREN.

OF GOD: See GOD. LOVE OF.

OF MAN FOR GOD: Ex. 20:6. Shewing mercy unto thousands of them that love me, and keep my commandments. Deut. 5:10.

Deut. 6:5. And thou shalt love the LORD thy God with all thine heart, and with all thy soul, and with all thy might.

Deut. 7:9. Know therefore that the LORD thy God, he *is* God, the faithful God, which keepeth covenant and mercy with them that love him and keep his commandments to a thousand generations;

Deut. 10:12. What doth the LORD thy God require of thee, but to fear the LORD thy God, to walk in all his ways, and to love him, and to serve the LORD thy God with all thy heart and with all thy soul,

Deut. 11:1. Therefore thou shalt love the LORD thy God, and keep his charge, and his statutes.

Deut. 13:3. The LORD your God proveth you, to know whether ye love the LORD your God with all your heart and with all your soul.

Deut. 30:6. The LORD thy God will circumcise thine heart, and the heart of thy seed, to love the LORD thy God with all thine heart, and with all thy soul, that thou mayest live. *vs.* 16,20.

Josh. 22:5. Take diligent heed to . . . love the LORD your God, and to walk in all his ways, and to keep his commandments, and to cleave unto him, and to serve him with all your heart and with all your soul. Deut. 11:1,13,22.

Josh. 23:11. Take good heed therefore unto yourselves, that ye love the LORD your God.

Psa. 18:1. I will love thee, O LORD, my strength.

Psa. 31:23. O love the LORD, all ye his saints:

Psa. 37:4. Delight thyself also in the LORD; and he shall give thee the desires of thine heart.

Psa. 45:10. Forget also thine own people, and thy father's house; 11. So shall the king greatly desire thy beauty: for he *is* thy Lord; and worship thou him. See Song of Solomon.

Psa. 63:5. My soul shall be satisfied as *with* marrow and fatness; and my mouth shall praise *thee* with joyful lips: 6. When I remember thee upon my bed, *and* meditate on thee in the *night* watches.

Psa. 69:35. For God will save Zion, and will build the cities of Judah: that they may dwell there, and have it in possession. 36. The seed also of his servants shall inherit it: and they that love his name shall dwell therein.

Psa. 73:25. Whom have I in heaven *but* thee? and *there is* none upon earth *that* I desire beside thee. 26. My flesh and my heart faileth: *but* God *is* the strength of my heart, and my portion for ever.

Psa. 91:14. Because he hath set his love upon me, therefore will I deliver him: I will set him on high, because he hath known my name.

Psa. 97:10. Ye that love the LORD, hate evil:

Psa. 116:1. I love the LORD, because he hath heard my voice *and* my supplications.

Psa. 145:20. The LORD preserveth all them that love him:

Prov. 8:17. I love them that love me; and those that seek me early shall find me.

Prov. 23:26. My son, give me thine heart, and let thine eyes observe my ways.

Isa. 56:6. The sons of the stranger, that

join themselves to the LORD, to serve him, and to love the name of the LORD, to be his servants, every one that keepeth the sabbath from polluting it, and taketh hold of my covenant. 7. Even them will I bring to my holy mountain, and make them joyful in my house of prayer: their burnt offerings and their sacrifices *shall be* accepted upon mine altar;

Jer. 2:2. Go and cry in the ears of Jerusalem, saying, Thus saith the LORD; I remember thee, the kindness of thy youth, the love of thine espousals, when thou wentest after me in the wilderness, in a land *that was* not sown. 3. Israel *was* holiness unto the LORD, *and* the firstfruits of his increase:

Mark 12:29. Jesus answered him, The first of all the commandments *is*, Hear, O Israel; The Lord our God is one Lord: 30. And thou shalt love the Lord thy God with all thy heart, and with all thy soul, and with all thy mind, and with all thy strength: this *is* the first commandment. 32. And the scribe said unto him, Well, Master, thou hast said the truth: for there is one God; and there is none other but he: 33. To love him with all the heart, and with all the understanding, and with all the soul, and with all the strength, and to love *his* neighbour as himself, is more than all whole burnt offerings and sacrifices. Matt. 22:37,38.

Luke 11:42. Ye tithe mint and rue, and all manner of herbs, and pass over judgment and the love of God: these ought ye to have done, and not to leave the other undone.

John 5:42. But I know you, that ye have not the love of God in you.

Rom. 5:5. And hope maketh not ashamed; because the love of God is shed abroad in our hearts by the Holy Ghost which is given unto us.

Rom. 8:28. And we know that all things work together for good to them that love God,

1 Cor. 8:3. But if any man love God, the same is known of him.

Phil. 1:9. I pray, that your love may abound yet more and more in knowledge and *in* all judgment;

2 Thess. 3:5. The Lord direct your hearts into the love of God, and into the patient waiting for Christ.

2 Tim. 1:7. God hath not given us the spirit of fear; but of power, and of love, and of a sound mind.

1 John 2:5. Whoso keepeth his word, in him verily is the love of God perfected: hereby know we that we are in him. 15. If any man love the world, the love of the Father is not in him.

1 John 3:17. Whoso hath this world's good, and seeth his brother have need, and shutteth up his bowels *of compassion* from him, how dwelleth the love of God in him? 18. My little children, let us not love in word, neither in tongue; but in deed and in truth.

1 John 4:12. If we love one another, God dwelleth in us, and his love is perfected in us. 16. We have known and believed the love that God hath to us. God is love; and he that dwelleth in love dwelleth in God, and God in him. 17. Herein is our love made perfect, that we may have boldness in the day of judgment: because as he is, so are we in this world. 18. There is no fear in love; but perfect love casteth out fear: because fear hath torment. He that feareth is not made perfect in love. 19. We love him, because he first loved us. 20. If a man say, I love God, and hateth his brother, he is a liar: for he that loveth not his brother whom he hath seen, how can he love God whom he hath not seen? 21. And this commandment have we from him, That he who loveth God love his brother also.

1 John 5:1. Whosoever believeth that Jesus is the Christ is born of God: and every one that loveth him that begat loveth him also that is begotten of him. 2. By this we know that we love the children of God, when we love God, and keep his commandments. 3. For this is the love of God, that we keep his commandments:

2 John 6. This is love, that we walk after his commandments.

Jude 21. Keep yourselves in the love of God,

OF MAN FOR JESUS: Matt. 10:37. He that loveth father or mother more than me is not worthy of me: and he that loveth son or daughter more than me is not worthy of me. *v.* 38.

Matt. 25:34. Then shall the King say unto them on his right hand, Come, ye blessed of my Father, inherit the kingdom prepared for you from the foundation of the world: 35. For I was an hungred, and ye gave me meat: I was thirsty, and ye gave me drink: I was a stranger, and ye took me in: 36. Naked, and ye clothed me: I was sick, and ye visited me: I was in prison, and ye came unto me. 37. Then shall the righteous answer him, saying, Lord, when saw we thee an hungred, and fed *thee?* or thirsty, and gave *thee* drink? 38. When saw we thee a stranger, and took *thee* in? or naked, and clothed *thee?* 39. Or when saw we thee sick, or in prison, and came unto thee? 40. And the King shall answer and say unto them, Verily I say unto you, Inasmuch as ye have done *it* unto one of the least of these my brethren, ye have done *it* unto me.

Matt. 27:55. And many women were there beholding afar off, which followed Jesus from Galilee, ministering unto him: 56. Among which was Mary Magdalene, and Mary the mother of James and Joses, and the mother of Zebedee's children. 57. When the even was come, there came a rich man of Arimathæa, named Joseph, who also himself was Jesus' disciple: 58. He went to Pilate, and begged the body of Jesus. Then Pilate commanded the body to be delivered. 59. And when Joseph had taken the body, he wrapped it in a clean linen cloth, 60. And laid it in his own new tomb, which he had hewn out in the rock : and he rolled a great stone to the door of the sepulchre, and departed. 61. And there was Mary Magdalene, and the other Mary, sitting over against the sepulchre.

Mark 9:41. Whosoever shall give you a cup of water to drink in my name, because ye belong to Christ, verily I say unto you, he shall not lose his reward.

Luke 2:29. Lord, now lettest thou thy servant depart in peace, according to thy word : 30. For mine eyes have seen thy salvation,

Luke 7:47. Her sins, which are many, are forgiven ; for she loved much : but to whom little is forgiven, *the same* loveth little.

John 8:42. Jesus said unto them, If God were your Father, ye would love me: for I proceeded forth and came from God ; neither came I of myself, but he sent me.

John 14:15. If ye love me, keep my commandments. 21. He that hath my commandments, and keepeth them, he it is that loveth me : and he that loveth me shall be loved of my Father, and I will love him, and will manifest myself to him. 23. If a man love me, he will keep my words: and my Father will love him, and we will come unto him, and make our abode with him. 28. . . . If ye loved me, ye would rejoice, because I said, I go unto the Father:

John 15:9. As the Father hath loved me, so have I loved you ; continue ye in my love.

John 16:27. The Father himself loveth you, because ye have loved me,

John 17:26. And I have declared unto them thy name, and will declare *it :* that the love wherewith thou hast loved me may be in them, and I in them.

John 21:17. Lord, thou knowest all things; thou knowest that I love thee.

Acts 21:13. I am ready not to be bound only, but also to die at Jerusalem for the name of the Lord Jesus.

1 Cor. 16:22. If any man love not the Lord Jesus Christ, let him be Anathema Maran-atha.

2 Cor. 5:8. We are confident, *I say*, and willing rather to be absent from the body, and to be present with the Lord. [*v.* 6.] 14. The love of Christ constraineth us ; because we thus judge, that if one died for all, ¹ then were all dead : 15. And *that* he died for all, that they which live should not henceforth live unto themselves, but unto him which died for them, and rose again.   [¹ R. V. therefore all died ;]

Gal. 5:6. In Jesus Christ neither circumcision availeth any thing, nor uncircumcision ; but faith which worketh by love. 22. The fruit of the Spirit is love,

Gal. 6:14. God forbid that I should glory, save in the cross of our Lord Jesus Christ, by whom the world is crucified unto me, and I unto the world.

Eph. 3:17. That Christ may dwell in your hearts by faith ; that ye, being rooted and grounded in love, 18. May be able to comprehend with all saints what *is* the breadth, and length, and depth, and height ; 19. And to know the love of Christ, which passeth knowledge, that ye might be filled with all the fulness of God.

Eph. 4:15. Speaking the truth in love, may grow up into him in all things, which is the head, *even* Christ :

Eph. 6:24. Grace *be* with all them that love our Lord Jesus Christ in sincerity.

Phil. 1:9. I pray, that your love may abound yet more and more in knowledge and *in* all judgment ;

Phil. 1:23. For I am in a strait betwixt two, having a desire to depart, and to be with Christ ; which is far better : *vs.* 20,21.

Phil. 3:7. What things were gain to me, those I counted loss for Christ. 8. Yea doubtless, and I count all things *but* loss for the excellency of the knowledge of Christ Jesus my Lord : for whom I have suffered the loss of all things, and do count them *but* dung, that I may win Christ,

Col. 1:8. Who also declared unto us your love in the Spirit.

2 Thess. 3:5. The Lord direct your hearts into the love of God, and into the ¹ patient waiting for Christ.   [¹ R. V. patience of]

2 Tim. 1:13. Hold fast the form of sound words, . . . in faith and love which is in Christ Jesus.

2 Tim. 4:8. Henceforth there is laid up for me a crown of righteousness, which the Lord, the righteous judge, shall give me at that day : and not to me only, but unto all them also that love his appearing.

Philem. 5. Hearing of thy love and faith, which thou hast toward the Lord Jesus, and toward all saints ;

Heb. 6:10. God *is* not unrighteous to forget your work and labour of love, which ye have shewed toward his name, in that ye have ministered to the saints, and do minister.

Jas. 1:12. Blessed *is* the man that endureth temptation: for when he is tried, he shall receive the crown of life, which the Lord hath promised to them that love him.

Jas. 2:5. Hearken, my beloved brethren, Hath not God chosen the poor of this world rich in faith, and heirs of the kingdom which he hath promised to them that love him ?

1 Pet. 1:8. Whom having not seen, ye love ; in whom, though now ye see *him* not, yet believing, ye rejoice with joy unspeakable and full of glory :

1 Pet. 2:7. Unto you therefore which believe *he is* precious :

Rev. 2:4. Nevertheless I have *somewhat* against thee, because thou hast left thy first love.

INSTANCES OF LOVE FOR JESUS: Mary, Matt. 26:6-13; John 12:3-8; Luke 10:39. Peter, Matt. 17:4; John 13:37; 18:10; 20:3-6; 21:7. Thomas, John 11:16. The disciples, Mark 16:10; Luke 24:17-41; John 20:20. Mary Magdalene and other disciples,

Matt. 27:55,56,61; 28:1-9; Luke 8:2,3; 23:27, 55,56; 24:1-10; John 20:1,2,11-18. A man of Gadara out of whom Jesus cast an evil spirit, Mark 5:18. Joseph of Aramathæa, Matt. 27:57-60. Nicodemus, John 19:39,40. Women of Jerusalem, Luke 23:27.

OF MAN FOR MAN: Lev. 19:18. Thou shalt love thy neighbour as thyself: I *am* the LORD. 34. *But* the stranger that dwelleth with you shall be unto you as one born among you, and thou shalt love him as thyself; for ye were strangers in the land of Egypt:

Deut. 10:19. Love ye therefore the stranger: for ye were strangers in the land of Egypt.

Psa. 133:1. Behold, how good and how pleasant *it is* for brethren to dwell together in unity! 2. *It is* like the precious ointment upon the head, that ran down upon the beard, *even* Aaron's beard: that went down to the skirts of his garments; 3. As the dew of Hermon, *and as the dew* that descended upon the mountains of Zion: for there the LORD commanded the blessing, *even* life for evermore.

Prov. 10:12. Hatred stirreth up strifes: but love covereth all sins.

Prov. 15:17. Better *is* a dinner of herbs where love is, than a stalled ox and hatred therewith.

Prov. 17:9. He that covereth a transgression seeketh love; but he that repeateth a matter separateth *very* friends. 17. A friend loveth at all times, and a brother is born for adversity.

Song 8:6. Love *is* strong as death: jealousy *is* cruel as the grave; the coals thereof *are* coals of fire, *which hath* a most vehement flame. 7. Many waters cannot quench love, neither can the floods drown it: if a man would give all the substance of his house for love, it would utterly be contemned.

Matt. 5:41. Whosoever shall compel thee to go a mile, go with him twain. 42. Give to him that asketh thee, and from him that would borrow of thee turn not thou away. *vs.* 41-47.

Matt. 10:41. He that receiveth a prophet in the name of a prophet shall receive a prophet's reward; and he that receiveth a righteous man in the name of a righteous man shall receive a righteous man's reward. 42. And whosoever shall give to drink unto one of these little ones a cup of cold *water* only in the name of a disciple, verily I say unto you, He shall in no wise lose his reward.

Matt. 19:19. Thou shalt love thy neighbour as thyself. Gal. 5:14.

Matt. 25:34. Come, ye blessed of my Father, inherit the kingdom prepared for you from the foundation of the world: 35. For I was an hungred, and ye gave me meat: I was thirsty, and ye gave me drink: I was a stranger, and ye took me in: 36. Naked, and ye clothed me: I was sick, and ye visited me: I was in prison, and ye came unto me. 37. Then shall the righteous an-

swer him, saying, Lord, when saw we thee an hungred, and fed *thee?* or thirsty, and gave *thee* drink? 38. When saw we thee a stranger, and took *thee* in? or naked and clothed *thee?* 39. Or when saw we thee sick, or in prison, and came unto thee? 40. And the King shall answer and say unto them, Verily I say unto you, Inasmuch as ye have done *it* unto one of the least of these my brethren, ye have done *it* unto me. *vs.* 34-40.

Mark 9:41. Whosoever shall give you a cup of water to drink in my name, because ye belong to Christ, verily I say unto you, he shall not lose his reward.

Mark 12:30. And thou shalt love the Lord thy God with all thy heart, and with all thy soul, and with all thy mind, and with all thy strength: this *is* the first commandment. 31. And the second *is* like, *namely* this, Thou shalt love thy neighbour as thyself. There is none other commandment greater than these. 32. And the scribe said unto him, Well, Master, thou hast said the truth: for there is one God; and there is none other but he: 33. And to love him with all the heart, and with all the understanding, and with all the soul, and with all the strength, and to love *his* neighbour as himself, is more than all whole burnt offerings and sacrifices.

Luke 6:31. As ye would that men should do to you, do ye also to them likewise. 32. If ye love them which love you, what thank have ye? for sinners also love those that love them. 33. And if ye do good to them which do good to you, what thank have ye? for sinners also do even the same. 34. And if ye lend *to them* of whom ye hope to receive, what thank have ye? for sinners also lend to sinners, to receive as much again. 35. But love ye your enemies, and do good, and lend, hoping for nothing again; and your reward shall be great, and ye shall be the children of the Highest: for he is kind unto the unthankful and *to* the evil. Matt. 7:12.

Luke 10:36. Which now of these three, thinkest thou, was neighbour unto him that fell among the thieves? 37. And he said, He that shewed mercy on him. Then said Jesus unto him, Go, and do thou likewise. *vs.* 30-37.

John 13:14. If I then, *your* Lord and Master, have washed your feet; ye also ought to wash one another's feet. 15. I have given you an example, that ye should do as I have done to you. 34. A new commandment I give unto you, That ye love one another; as I have loved you, that ye also love one another. 35. By this shall all *men* know that ye are my disciples, if ye have love one to another.

John 15:12. This is my commandment, That ye love one another, as I have loved you. 13. Greater love hath no man than this, that a man lay down his life for his friends. *v.* 17.

Rom. 12:9. *Let* love be without dissimulation. 10. *Be* kindly affectioned one to another with brotherly love; in honour preferring one another;

Rom. 13:8. Owe no man any thing, but to love one another: for he that loveth another hath fulfilled the law. 9. For this, Thou shalt not commit adultery, Thou shalt not kill, Thou shalt not steal, Thou shalt not bear false witness, Thou shalt not covet; and if *there be* any other commandment, it is briefly comprehended in this saying, namely, Thou shalt love thy neighbour as thyself. 10. Love worketh no ill to his neighbour: therefore love *is* the fulfilling of the law.

1 Cor. 8:1. Knowledge puffeth up, but charity edifieth.

1 Cor. 13:1. Though I speak with the tongues of men and of angels, and have not charity, I am become *as* sounding brass, or a tinkling cymbal. 2. And though I have *the gift of* prophecy, and understand all mysteries, and all knowledge; and though I have all faith, so that I could remove mountains, and have not charity, I am nothing. 3. And though I bestow all my goods to feed *the poor*, and though I give my body to be burned, and have not charity, it profiteth me nothing. 4. Charity suffereth long, *and* is kind; charity envieth not; charity vaunteth not itself, is not puffed up, 5. Doth not behave itself unseemly, seeketh not her own, is not easily provoked, thinketh no evil; 6. Rejoiceth not in iniquity, but rejoiceth in the truth; 7. Beareth all things, believeth all things, hopeth all things, endureth all things. 8. Charity never faileth: but whether *there be* prophecies, they shall fail; whether *there be* tongues, they shall cease; whether *there be* knowledge, it shall vanish away. 9. For we know in part, and we prophesy in part. 10. But when that which is perfect is come, then that which is in part shall be done away. 11. When I was a child, I spake as a child: I understood as a child, I thought as a child; but when I became a man, I put away childish things. 12. For now we see through a glass, darkly; but then face to face: now I know in part; but then shall I know even as also I am known. 13. And now abideth faith, hope, charity, these three; but the greatest of these *is* charity.

1 Cor. 14:1. Follow after charity,

1 Cor. 16:14. Let all your things be done with charity.

2 Cor. 8:7. Therefore, as ye abound in every *thing, in* faith, and utterance, and knowledge, and *in* all diligence, and *in* your love to us, *see* that ye abound in this grace also. 8. I speak not by commandment, but by occasion of the forwardness of others, and to prove the sincerity of your love.

Gal. 5:13. For, brethren, ye have been called unto liberty; only *use* not liberty for an occasion to the flesh, but by love serve one another. 22. But the fruit of the Spirit is love, joy, peace, longsuffering, gentleness, goodness, ¹faith, 26. Let us not be desirous of vain glory, provoking one another, envying one another. [¹ R. V. faithfulness]

Eph. 5:2. **Walk in love,** as Christ also hath loved us, and hath given himself for us an offering and a sacrifice to God for a sweetsmelling savour.

Phil. 1:9. I pray, that your love may abound yet more and more in knowledge and *in* all judgment;

Phil. 2:2. Fulfil ye my joy, that ye be likeminded, having the same love, *being* of one accord, of one mind.

Col. 2:2. That their hearts might be comforted, being knit together in love,

Col. 3:12. Put on therefore, as the elect of God, holy and beloved, bowels of mercies, kindness, humbleness of mind, meekness, longsuffering; 13. Forbearing one another, and forgiving one another, if any man have a quarrel against any: even as Christ forgave you, so also *do* ye. 14. Above all these things *put on* charity, which is the bond of perfectness.

1 Thess. 1:3. Remembering without ceasing your work of faith, and labour of love,

1 Thess. 3:12. The Lord make you to increase and abound in love one toward another, and toward all *men*, even as we *do* toward you:

1 Thess. 4:9. As touching brotherly love ye need not that I write unto you: for ye yourselves are taught of God to love one another.

1 Tim. 1:5. The end of the commandment is charity out of a pure heart, and *of* a good conscience, and *of* faith unfeigned: 14. The grace of our Lord was exceeding abundant with faith and love which is in Christ Jesus.

1 Tim. 2:15. Notwithstanding she shall be saved in childbearing, if they continue in faith and charity and holiness with sobriety.

1 Tim. 4:12. Let no man despise thy youth; but be thou an example of the believers, in word, in conversation, in charity,

1 Tim. 6:2. They that have believing masters, let them not despise *them*, because they are brethren; but rather do *them* service, because they are faithful and beloved, partakers of the benefit. 11. Follow after righteousness, godliness, faith, love, patience, meekness.

2 Tim. 2:22. Flee also youthful lusts: but follow righteousness, faith, charity,

Tit. 3:15. Greet them that love us in the faith.

Philem. 12. Receive him [Onesimus], that is, mine own bowels: 16. Not now as a servant, but above a servant, a brother beloved, specially to me, but how much more unto thee, both in the flesh, and in the Lord?

Heb. 10:24. And let us consider one another to provoke unto love and to good works:

Jas. 2:8. If ye fulfil the royal law according

to the scripture, Thou shalt love thy neighbour as thyself, ye do well:

1 Pet. 1:22. Seeing ye have purified your souls in obeying the truth [1]through the Spirit unto unfeigned love of the brethren, [1 see that] ye love one another [2]with a pure heart fervently: [R. V. 1 Omitted.   2 from the]

1 Pet. 2:17. Honour all *men*. Love the brotherhood.

1 Pet. 3:8. *Be ye* all of one mind, having compassion one of another, love as brethren, *be* pitiful, *be* courteous: *v.* 9.

1 Pet. 4:8. Have fervent charity among yourselves: for charity shall cover the multitude of sins.

2 Pet. 1:7. And to godliness brotherly kindness; and to brotherly kindness charity.

1 John 2:10. He that loveth his brother abideth in the light, and there is none occasion of stumbling in him. *vs.* 9,11.

1 John 3:11. This is the message that ye heard from the beginning, that we should love one another. 14. We know that we have passed from death unto life, because we love the brethren. He that loveth not *his* brother abideth in death. 16. Hereby perceive we [1]the love [1 of God], because he laid down his life for us: and we ought to lay down *our* lives for the brethren. 17. But whoso hath this world's good, and seeth his brother have need, and shutteth up his bowels *of compassion* from him, how dwelleth the love of God in him? 18. My little children, let us not love in word, neither in tongue; but in deed and in truth. 23. Love one another, as he gave us commandment. *v.* 19.   [1 Omitted in R. V.]

1 John 4:7. Let us love one another: for love is of God; and every one that loveth is born of God, and knoweth God. 11. If God so loved us, we ought also to love one another. 12. If we love one another, God dwelleth in us, and his love is perfected in us. 20. If a man say, I love God, and hateth his brother, he is a liar: for he that loveth not his brother whom he hath seen, how can he love God whom he hath not seen? 21. And this commandment have we from him, That he who loveth God love his brother also.

1 John 5:1. Whosoever believeth that Jesus is the Christ is born of God: and every one that loveth him that begat loveth him also that is begotten of him. 2. By this we know that we love the children of God, when we love God, and keep his commandments.

2 John 5. And now I beseech thee, lady, not as though I wrote a new commandment unto thee, but that which we had from the beginning, that we love one another.

EXEMPLIFICATION OF THE LOVE OF MAN FOR MAN: Ex. 32:31. And Moses returned unto the LORD, and said, Oh, this people have sinned a great sin, and have made them gods of gold. 32. Yet now, if thou wilt forgive their sin—; and if not, blot me, I pray thee, out of thy book which thou hast written.

Psa. 133:1. Behold, how good and how pleasant *it is* for brethren to dwell together in unity! *vs.* 2,3.

Prov. 24:17. Rejoice not when thine enemy falleth, and let not thine heart be glad when he stumbleth: 18. Lest the LORD see *it*, and it displease him, and he turn away his wrath from him.

Matt. 5:41. Whosoever shall compel thee to go a mile, go with him twain. 42. Give to him that asketh thee, and from him that would borrow of thee turn not thou away.

Matt. 10:41. He that receiveth a prophet in the name of a prophet shall receive a prophet's reward; and he that receiveth a righteous man in the name of a righteous man shall receive a righteous man's reward. 42. And whosoever shall give to drink unto one of these little ones a cup of cold *water* only in the name of a disciple, verily I say unto you, He shall in no wise lose his reward.

Matt. 25:34. Come, ye blessed of my Father, inherit the kingdom prepared for you from the foundation of the world: 35. For I was an hungred, and ye gave me meat: I was thirsty, and ye gave me drink: I was a stranger, and ye took me in: 36. Naked, and ye clothed me: I was sick, and ye visited me: I was in prison, and ye came unto me. 37. Then shall the righteous answer him, saying, Lord, when saw we thee an hungred, and fed *thee?* or thirsty, and gave *thee* drink? 38. When saw we thee a stranger, and took *thee* in? or naked, and clothed *thee?* 39. Or when saw we thee sick, or in prison, and came unto thee? 40. And the King shall answer and say unto them, Verily I say unto you, Inasmuch as ye have done *it* unto one of the least of these my brethren, ye have done *it* unto me. *vs.* 34–40.

Mark 9:41. Whosoever shall give you a cup of water to drink in my name, because ye belong to Christ, verily I say unto you, he shall not lose his reward.

Luke 10:25. And, behold, a certain lawyer stood up, and tempted him, saying, Master, what shall I do to inherit eternal life? 26. He said unto him, What is written in the law? how readest thou? 27. And he answering said, Thou shalt love the Lord thy God with all thy heart, and with all thy soul, and with all thy strength, and with all thy mind: and thy neighbour as thyself. 28. And he said unto him, Thou hast answered right: this do, and thou shalt live. 29. But he, willing to justify himself, said unto Jesus, And who is my neighbour? 30. And Jesus answering said, A certain *man* went down from Jerusalem to Jericho, and fell among thieves, which stripped him of his raiment, and wounded *him*, and departed, leaving *him* half dead. 31. And by chance there came down a certain priest that way: and when he saw him, he passed by on the other side. 32. And likewise a Levite, when he was at the place, came and looked *on him*, and passed by on the other side. 33. But a certain Samaritan, as he journeyed, came where he was: and when he saw him, he had compassion *on him*, 34. And went to *him*, and bound up his wounds, pouring in oil and wine, and set him on his own beast, and brought him to an inn, and took care of him. 35. And on the morrow when he departed, he took out two pence, and gave *them* to the host, and said unto him, Take care of him; and whatsoever thou spendest more, when I come again, I will repay thee. 36. Which now of these three, thinkest thou, was neighbour unto him that fell among the thieves? 37. And he said, He that shewed mercy on him. Then said Jesus unto him, Go, and do thou likewise.

Acts 20:26. I take you to record this day, that I *am* pure from the blood of all *men*. 27. For I have not shunned to declare unto you all the counsel of God. 31. Watch, and remember, that by the space of three years I ceased not to warn every one night and day with tears.

Acts 26:29. And Paul said, I would to God, that not only thou, but also all that hear me this day, were both almost, and altogether such as I am, except these bonds.

Rom. 1:12. That I may be comforted together with you by the mutual faith both of you and me.

Rom. 5:7. Scarcely for a righteous man will one die: yet peradventure for a good man some would even dare to die.

Rom. 9:3. I could wish that myself were accursed from Christ for my brethren, my kinsmen according to the flesh: *vs.* 1,2.

Rom. 12:15. Rejoice with them that do rejoice, and weep with them that weep. 16. *Be* of the same mind one toward another. Mind not high things, but condescend to men of low estate.

Rom. 14:19. Follow after the things which make for peace, and things wherewith one may edify another. 21. *It is* good neither to eat flesh, nor to drink wine, nor *any thing* whereby thy brother stumbleth, ¹ or is offended, or is made weak. [¹ Omitted in R. V.]

Rom. 15:1. We then that are strong ought to bear the infirmities of the weak, and not to please ourselves. 2. Let every one of us please *his* neighbour for *his* good to edification. 5. The God of patience and consolation grant you to be likeminded one toward another according to Christ Jesus: 7. Receive ye one another, as Christ also received us to the glory of God. 14. I myself also am persuaded of you, my brethren, that ye also are full of goodness, filled with all knowledge, able also to admonish one another. 15. Nevertheless, brethren, I have written the more boldly unto you in some sort, as putting you in mind, because of the grace that is given to me of God, 24. I trust to see you in my journey, and to be brought on my way thitherward by you, if first I be somewhat filled with your *company*. 32. That I may come unto you with joy by the will of God, and may with you be refreshed.

Rom. 16:1. I commend unto you Phebe our sister, which is a servant of the church which is at Cenchrea: 2. That ye receive her in the Lord, as becometh saints, and that ye assist her in whatsoever business she hath need of you: for she hath been a succourer of many, and of myself also. 8. Greet Amplias my beloved in the Lord. 19. Your obedience is come abroad unto all *men*. I am glad therefore on your behalf: *vs.* 1-16; Col. 4:7.

1 Cor. 1:4. I thank my God always on your behalf, for the grace of God which is given you by Jesus Christ;

1 Cor. 4:14. I write not these things to shame you, but as my beloved sons I warn *you*. 15. For though ye have ten thousand instructors in Christ, yet *have ye* not many fathers: for in Christ Jesus I have begotten you through the gospel. 16. Wherefore I beseech you, be ye followers of me.

1 Cor. 8:13. If meat make my brother to offend, I will eat no flesh while the world standeth, lest I make my brother to offend.

1 Cor. 10:24. Let no man seek his own, but every man another's *wealth*.

2 Cor. 1:3. Blessed *be* God, ... 4. Who comforteth us in all our tribulation, that we may be able to comfort them which are in any trouble, by the comfort wherewith we ourselves are comforted of God. 5. For as the sufferings of Christ abound in us, so our consolation also aboundeth by Christ. 6. And whether we be afflicted, *it is* for your consolation and salvation, which is effectual in the enduring of the same sufferings which we also suffer: or whether we be comforted, *it is* for your consolation and salvation. 14. Ye have acknowledged us in part, that we are your rejoicing, even as ye also *are* our's in the day of the Lord Jesus. *vs.* 23,24.

2 Cor. 2:4. Out of much affliction and anguish of heart I wrote unto you with many tears; not that ye should be grieved, but that ye might know the love which I have more abundantly unto you. *vs.* 1-17.

2 Cor. 3:2. Ye are our epistle written in our hearts, known and read of all men:

2 Cor. 4:5. For we preach not ourselves, but Christ Jesus the Lord; and ourselves your servants for Jesus' sake.

2 Cor. 6:4. But in all *things* approving ourselves as the ministers of God, in much patience, in afflictions, in necessities, in distresses, 5. In stripes, in imprisonments, in tumults, in labours, in watchings, in fastings; 6. By pureness, by knowledge, by longsuffering, by kindness, by the Holy Ghost, by love unfeigned, 11. O *ye* Corinthians, our mouth is open unto you, our heart is enlarged. 12. Ye are not straitened in us, but ye are straitened in your own bowels. 13. Now for a recompence in the same, (I speak as unto *my* children,) be ye also enlarged.

2 Cor. 7:1. Having therefore these promises, dearly beloved, let us cleanse ourselves from all filthiness of the flesh and spirit, perfecting holiness in the fear of God.

2. Receive us; we have wronged no man, we have corrupted no man, we have defrauded no man. 3. I speak not *this* to condemn *you:* for I have said before, that ye are in our hearts to die and live with *you.* 4. Great *is* my boldness of speech toward you, great *is* my glory of you: 7. And not by his coming only, but by the consolation wherewith he was comforted in you, when he told us your earnest desire, your mourning, your fervent mind toward me; so that I rejoiced the more. 12. Though I wrote unto you, *I did it* not for his cause that had done the wrong, nor for his cause that suffered wrong, but that our care for you in the sight of God might appear unto you.

2 Cor. 11:2. I am jealous over you with godly jealousy: for I have espoused you to one husband, that I may present *you as* a chaste virgin to Christ.

2 Cor. 12:14. The third time I am ready to come to you; and I will not be burdensome to you: for I seek not your's, but you: for the children ought not to lay up for the parents, but the parents for the children. 15. I will very gladly spend and be spent for you; though the more abundantly I love you, the less I be loved. 16. But be it so, I did not burden you: nevertheless, being crafty, I caught you with guile. 19. *We do* all things, dearly beloved, for your edifying. 20. For I fear, lest, when I come, I shall not find you such as I would, and *that* I shall be found unto you such as ye would not: 21. *And* lest, when I come again, my God will humble me among you, and *that* I shall bewail many which have sinned already,

2 Cor. 13:9. We are glad, when we are weak, and ye are strong: and this [1] also we wish, *even* your [2] perfection. [R. V. [1] we also pray for [2] perfecting]

Gal. 4:11. I am afraid of you, lest I have bestowed upon you labour in vain. 12. Brethren, I beseech you, be as I *am;* for I *am* as ye *are:* ye have not injured me at all. 13. Ye know how through infirmity of the flesh I preached the gospel unto you at the first. 14. And my temptation which was in my flesh ye despised not, nor rejected; but received me as an angel of God, *even* as Christ Jesus. 15. Where is then the blessedness ye spake of? for I bear you record, that, if *it had been* possible, ye would have plucked out your own eyes, and have given them to me. 16. Am I therefore become your enemy, because I tell you the truth? 19. My little children, of whom I travail in birth again until Christ be formed in you, 20. I desire to be present with you now, and to change my voice; for I stand in doubt of you. *vs.* 11–20.

Gal. 6:1. If a man be overtaken in a fault, ye which are spiritual, restore such an one in the spirit of meekness; considering thyself, lest thou also be tempted. 2. Bear ye one another's burdens, and so fulfil the law of Christ. 10. As we have therefore opportunity, let us do good unto all *men*, especially unto them who are of the household of faith.

Eph. 3:13. I desire that ye faint not at my tribulations for you, which is your glory.

Eph. 4:2. With all lowliness and meekness, with longsuffering, forbearing one another in love; 32. Be ye kind one to another, tenderhearted, forgiving one another, even as God for Christ's sake hath forgiven you.

Eph. 6:22. Whom I have sent unto you for the same purpose, that ye might know our affairs, and *that* he might comfort your hearts. *v.* 24.

Phil. 1:3. I thank my God upon every remembrance of you, 4. Always in every prayer of mine for you all making request with joy, 5. For your fellowship in the gospel from the first day until now; 7. I have you in my heart; inasmuch as both in my bonds, and in the defence and confirmation of the gospel, ye all are partakers of my grace. 8. For God is my record, how greatly I long after you all in the bowels of Jesus Christ. 23. For I am in a strait betwixt two, having a desire to depart, and to be with Christ; which is far better: 24. Nevertheless to abide in the flesh *is* more needful for you. 25. And having this confidence, I know that I shall abide and continue with you all for your furtherance and joy of faith; 26. That your rejoicing may be more abundant in Jesus Christ for me by my coming to you again.

Phil. 2:19. I trust in the Lord Jesus to send Timotheus shortly unto you, that I also may be of good comfort, when I know your state.

Phil. 3:18. Many walk, of whom I have told you often, and now tell you even weeping, *that they are* the enemies of the cross of Christ:

Phil. 4:1. My brethren dearly beloved and longed for, my joy and crown, so stand fast in the Lord, *my* dearly beloved.

Col. 1:3. We give thanks to God and the Father of our Lord Jesus Christ, praying always for you, 4. Since we heard of your faith in Christ Jesus, and of the love *which* ye have to all the saints, 24. Who now rejoice in my sufferings for you, and fill up that which is behind of the afflictions of Christ in my flesh for his body's sake, which is the church: 28. Whom we preach, warning every man, and teaching every man in all wisdom; that we may present every man perfect in Christ Jesus: 29. Whereunto I also labour, striving according to his working, which worketh in me mightily.

Col. 2:1. I would that ye knew what great conflict I have for you, and *for* them at Laodicea, and *for* as many as have not seen my face in the flesh; 5. Though I be absent in the flesh, yet am I with you in the spirit, joying and beholding your order, and the stedfastness of your faith in Christ.

1 Thess. 1:3. Remembering without ceasing your work of faith, and labour of love, and patience of hope in our Lord Jesus Christ, in the sight of God and our Father; 4. Knowing, brethren beloved, your election of God.

1 Thess. 2:7. We were gentle among you, even as a nurse cherisheth her children: 8. So being affectionately desirous of you, we were willing to have imparted unto you, not the gospel of God only, but also our own souls, because ye were dear unto us. 11. Ye know how we exhorted and comforted and charged every one of you, as a father *doth* his children, 12. That ye would walk worthy of God, who hath called you unto his kingdom and glory. 17. We, brethren, being taken from you for a short time in presence, not in heart, endeavoured the more abundantly to see your face with great desire. 18. Wherefore we would have come unto you, even I Paul, once and again; but Satan hindered us. 19. What *is* our hope, or joy, or crown of rejoicing? *Are* not even ye in the presence of our Lord Jesus Christ at his coming? 20. For ye are our glory and joy.

1 Thess. 3:5. When I could no longer forbear, I sent to know your faith, lest by some means the tempter have tempted you, and our labour be in vain. 7. Brethren, we were comforted over you in all our affliction and distress by your faith: 8. For now we live, if ye stand fast in the Lord. 9. For what thanks can we render to God again for you, for all the joy wherewith we joy for your sakes before our God; 10. Night and day praying exceedingly that we might see your face, and might perfect that which is lacking in your faith? 12. The Lord make you to increase and abound in love one toward another, and toward all *men*, even as we *do* toward you:

1 Thess. 5:8. But let us, who are of the day, be sober, putting on the breastplate of faith and love; 11. Comfort yourselves together, and edify one another, even as also ye do. 14. Now we exhort you, brethren, warn them that are unruly, comfort the feebleminded, support the weak, be patient toward all *men*.

2 Thess. 1:4. We ourselves glory in you in the churches of God for your patience and faith in all your persecutions and tribulations that ye endure:

1 Tim. 1:5. The end of the commandment is charity out of a pure heart, and *of* a good conscience, and *of* faith unfeigned:

1 Tim. 5:9. Let not a widow. be taken into the number under threescore years old, having been the wife of one man, 10. Well reported of for good works; if she have . . . lodged strangers, if she have washed the saints' feet, if she have relieved the afflicted, if she have diligently followed every good work.

1 Tim. 6:2. They that have believing masters, let them not despise *them*, because they are brethren; but rather do *them* service, because they are faithful and beloved, partakers of the benefit. 11. Follow after righteousness, godliness, faith, love, patience, meekness.

2 Tim. 1:3. I thank God, whom I serve

from *my* forefathers with pure conscience, that without ceasing I have remembrance of thee in my prayers night and day; 4. Greatly desiring to see thee, being mindful of thy tears, that I may be filled with joy; 8. Be not thou therefore ashamed of the testimony of our Lord, nor of me his prisoner:

2 Tim. 2:10. I endure all things for the elect's sakes, that they may also obtain the salvation which is in Christ Jesus with eternal glory.

Philem. 8. Though I might be much bold in Christ to enjoin thee that which is convenient, 9. Yet for love's sake I rather beseech *thee*, being such an one as Paul the aged, and now also a prisoner of Jesus Christ. 12. Whom I have sent again: thou therefore receive him, that is, mine own bowels: 16. Not now as a servant, but above a servant, a brother beloved, specially to me, but how much more unto thee, both in the flesh, and in the Lord? 17. If thou count me therefore a partner, receive him as myself. 18. If he hath wronged thee, or oweth *thee* aught, put that on mine account; 19. I Paul have written *it* with mine own hand, I will repay *it:* albeit I do not say to thee how thou owest unto me even thine own self besides. 20. Yea, brother, let me have joy of thee in the Lord: refresh my bowels in the Lord. 21. Having confidence in thy obedience I wrote unto thee, knowing that thou wilt also do more than I say.

Heb. 5:2. Who can have compassion on the ignorant, and on them that are out of the way; for that he himself also is compassed with infirmity.

Heb. 6:9. Beloved, we are persuaded better things of you, and things that accompany salvation, though we thus speak. 10. For God *is* not unrighteous to forget your work and labour of love, which ye have shewed toward his name, in that ye have ministered to the saints, and do minister.

Heb. 13:1. Let brotherly love continue. 2. Be not forgetful to entertain strangers: for thereby some have entertained angels unawares. 3. Remember them that are in bonds, as bound with them; *and* them which suffer adversity, as being yourselves also in the body. 22. I beseech you, brethren, suffer the word of exhortation: for I have written a letter unto you in few words.

Jas. 1:27. Pure religion and undefiled before God and the Father is this, To visit the fatherless and widows in their affliction, *and* to keep himself unspotted from the world.

See FRATERNITY.

INSTANCES OF: Abraham for Lot, Gen. 14: 14-16. Naomi, Ruth, and Boaz, Ruth chapters 1-3. David and Jonathan, 1 Sam. 20. David's subjects, 2 Sam. 15:30; 17:27-29. Obadiah for the prophets, 1 Kin. 18:4. Jehoshabeath for Joash, 2 Chr. 22:11. Nehemiah for Israelites, Neh. 5:10-15. Mordecai for Esther, Esth. 2:7. Job's friends, Job 42: 11. Centurion for his servant, Luke 7:2-6. Roman Christians for Paul, Acts 28:15.

OF MONEY: The root of evil, 1 Tim. 6:10. See Riches.

OF PARENTS FOR CHILDREN: See Parents.

See also Brother; Fraternity; Friendship.

LOVEFEASTS, assemblies of Christian fellowship, 2 Pet. 2:13; Jude 12.

LOVERS. INSTANCES OF: Isaac for Rebekah, Gen. 24:67. Jacob for Rachel, Gen. 29:20,30. Shechem for Dinah, Gen. 34:3,12. Boaz for Ruth, Ruth chapters 2–4.

LOYALTY. Enjoined, Ex. 22:28; Num. 27:20; Ezra 6:10; 7:26; Job 34:18; Prov. 24:21; Eccl. 8:2; 10:4; Rom. 13:1; Tit. 3:1. Enforced, Ezra 10:8; Prov. 17:11. Disloyalty, 2 Pet. 2:10.

See Patriotism.

INSTANCES OF: Israelites, Josh. 1:16–18; 2 Sam. 3:36,37; 15:23,30: 18:3; 21:17; 1 Chr. 12:38. David, 1 Sam. 24:6–10; 26:6–16; 2 Sam. 1:14. Uriah, 2 Sam. 11:9. Ittai, 2 Sam. 15:21. Hushai, 2 Sam. 17:15,16. David's soldiers, 2 Sam. 18:12,13; 23:15,16. Joab, 2 Sam. 19:5,6. Barzillai, 2 Sam. 19:32. Jehoiada, 2 Kin. 11:4–12. Mordecai, Esth. 2:21–23.

LUBIMS. Inhabitants of northern Africa, 2 Chr. 12:3; 16:8. The region they inhabited was called Phut in Ezek. 27:10; Nah. 3:9. See Phut. Called Libya, Acts 2:10.

LUCAS, fellow-laborer of Paul, Philem. 24.

See Luke.

LUCIFER, Nebuchadnezzar called, Isa. 14:12.

LUCIUS. 1. A Christian at Antioch, Acts 13:1.

2. A kinsman of Paul, Rom. 16:21.

LUD, a son of Shem, Gen. 10:22; 1 Chr. 1:17.

LUDIM. 1. Son of Mizraim, Gen. 10:13; 1 Chr. 1:11.

2. Descendants of Ludim, Gen. 10:13. Warriors, Isa. 66:19; Jer. 46:9; Ezek. 27:10; 30:5.

LUHITH, a city of Moab, Isa. 15:5; Jer. 48:5.

LUKE. A disciple. A physician, Col. 4:14. Wrote to Theophilus, Luke 1:1–4; Acts 1:1,2. Accompanies Paul in his tour of Asia and Macedonia, Acts 16:10-13; 20:5,6; to Jerusalem, Acts 21:1-18; to Rome, Acts 27; 28; 2 Tim. 4:11; Phiiem. 24.

LUKEWARMNESS. FIGURATIVE: Jer. 9:3. They are not valiant for the truth upon the earth;

Ezek. 13:5. Ye have not gone up into the gaps, neither made up the hedge for the house of Israel to stand in the battle in the day of the Lord.

Ezek. 16:30. How weak is thine heart, saith the Lord God, seeing thou doest all these *things*,

Hos. 6:4. O Ephraim, what shall I do unto thee? O Judah, what shall I do unto thee? for your goodness *is* as a morning cloud, and as the early dew it goeth away.

Hos. 10:2. Their heart is divided; now shall they be found faulty: he shall break

down their altars, he shall spoil their images.

Hag. 1:2. Thus speaketh the Lord of hosts, saying, This people say, The time is not come, the time that the Lord's house should be built. *vs.* 4–11; Hag. 2:15,16.

Matt. 26:41. The spirit indeed *is* willing, but the flesh *is* weak.

Rev. 2:4. Nevertheless I have *somewhat* against thee, because thou hast left thy first love.

Rev. 3:2. Be watchful, and strengthen the things which remain, that are ready to die: for I have not found thy works perfect before God. 15. I know thy works, that thou art neither cold nor hot: I would thou wert cold or hot. 16. So then because thou art lukewarm, and neither cold nor hot, I will spue thee out of my mouth.

See Backsliding; Blindness, Spiritual.

INSTANCES OF: The Reubenites, when Deborah called on them to assist Sisera, Judg. 5:16. The Jews under Nehemiah, Neh. 3:5; 13:11. The church at Pergamos, Rev. 2:14–16; Thyatira, Rev. 2:20–24; Sardis, Rev. 3:1–3; Laodicea, Rev. 3:14–16.

LUNACY. See Insanity; Demons.

LUST. Evil desire. Gen. 3:6. And when the woman saw that the tree *was* good for food, and that it *was* pleasant to the eyes, and a tree to be desired to make *one* wise, she took of the fruit thereof, and did eat, and gave also unto her husband with her; and he did eat.

Ex. 20:17. Thou shalt not covet thy neighbour's house, thou shalt not covet thy neighbour's wife, nor his manservant, nor his maidservant, nor his ox, nor his ass, nor any thing that *is* thy neighbour's.

Job 31:9. If mine heart have been deceived by a woman, or *if* I have laid wait at my neighbour's door; 10. *Then* let my wife grind unto another, and let others bow down upon her. 11. For this *is* an heinous crime; yea, it *is* an iniquity *to be punished by* the judges. 12. For it *is* a fire *that* consumeth to destruction, and would root out all mine increase.

Psa. 81:12. So I gave them up unto their own hearts' lust: *and* they walked in their own counsels.

Prov. 6:24. To keep thee from the evil woman, from the flattery of the tongue of a strange woman. 25. Lust not after her beauty in thine heart; neither let her take thee with her eyelids.

Matt. 5:28. But I say unto you, That whosoever looketh on a woman to lust after her hath committed adultery with her already in his heart.

Mark 4:19. And the cares of this world, and the deceitfulness of riches, and the lusts of other things entering in, choke the word, and it becometh unfruitful.

John 8:44. Ye are of *your* father the devil, and the lusts of your father ye will do.

1 Cor. 9:27. But I keep under my body,

and bring *it* into subjection: lest that by any means, when I have preached to others, I myself should be a castaway.

1 Cor. 10:6. Now these things were our examples, to the intent we should not lust after evil things, as they also lusted. 7. Neither be ye idolaters, as *were* some of them; as it is written, The people sat down to eat and drink, and rose up to play.

Eph. 4:22. That ye put off concerning the former conversation the old man, which is corrupt according to the deceitful lusts;

1 Tim. 6:9. But they that will be rich fall into temptation and a snare, and *into* many foolish and hurtful lusts, which drown men in destruction and perdition.

2 Tim. 2:22. Flee also youthful lusts:

2 Tim. 4:3. For the time will come when they will not endure sound doctrine; but after their own lusts shall they heap to themselves teachers, having itching ears; 4. And they shall turn away *their* ears from the truth, and shall be turned unto fables.

Tit. 2:12. Teaching us that, denying ungodliness and worldly lusts, we should live soberly, righteously, and godly, in this present world;

Jas. 1:14. But every man is tempted, when he is drawn away of his own lust, and enticed. 15. Then when lust hath conceived, it bringeth forth sin: and sin, when it is finished, bringeth forth death.

Jas. 4:1. From whence *come* wars, and fightings among you? *come they* not hence, *even* of your lusts that war in your members? 2. Ye lust, and have not: ye kill, and desire to have, and cannot obtain: ye fight and war, yet ye have not, because ye ask not. 3. Ye ask, and receive not, because ye ask amiss, that ye may consume *it* upon your lusts.

1 Pet. 2:11. Dearly beloved, I beseech *you* as strangers and pilgrims, abstain from fleshly lusts, which war against the soul;

1 Pet. 4:3. For the time past of *our* life may suffice us to have wrought the will of the Gentiles, when we walked in lasciviousness, lusts, excess of wine, revellings, banquetings, and abominable idolatries:

2 Pet. 2:18. For when they speak great swelling *words* of vanity, they allure through the lusts of the flesh, *through much* wantonness, those that were clean escaped from them who live in error.

2 Pet. 3:3. Knowing this first, that there shall come in the last days scoffers, walking after their own lusts,

1 John 2:16. For all that *is* in the world, the lust of the flesh, and the lust of the eyes, and the pride of life, is not of the Father, but is of the world. 17. And the world passeth away, and the lust thereof: but he that doeth the will of God abideth for ever.

Jude 16. These are murmurers, complainers, walking after their own lusts; and their mouth speaketh great swelling *words*, having men's persons in admiration because of advantage. 18. How that they told you there

should be mockers in the last time, who should walk after their own ungodly lusts.

See ADULTERY; COVETOUSNESS; INCEST; LASCIVIOUSNESS; SENSUALITY; SODOMY.

LYCAONIA. A province of Asia Minor. Paul visits towns of, Acts 14:6-21; 16:1,2.

LYCIA. A province of Asia Minor. Paul visits, Acts 27:5.

LYDDA, called also LOD. A city of Benjamin, 1 Chr. 8:12; Ezra 2:33; Neh. 11:35. Peter heals Æneas in, Acts 9:32-35.

LYDIA. 1. A woman of Thyatira, who with her household was converted through the preaching of Paul, Acts 16:14,15. Entertains Paul and Silas, Acts 16:15,40.

2. Incorrectly put for LUD, Ezek. 30:5.

LYING, lying spirit from God, 1 Kin. 22:21-23; 2 Chr. 18:20-22.

See FALSEHOOD; HYPOCRISY.

LYSANIAS, a tetrarch, Luke 3:1.

LYSIAS, chief captain of Roman troops in Jerusalem, Acts 24:7,22.

See CLAUDIUS LYSIAS.

LYSTRA. One of two cities of Lycaonia, to which Paul and Barnabas fled from persecutions in Iconium, Acts 14:6-23; 2 Tim. 3:11. Church of, elders ordained for, by Paul and Barnabas, Acts 14:23. Timothy a resident of, Acts 16:1-4.

M

MAACHAH. 1. Son of Nahor, Gen. 22:24.

2. Called also MAACAH. Mother of Absalom, 2 Sam. 3:3; 1 Chr. 3:2.

3. Called also MAOCH. Father of Achish, 1 Sam. 27:2; 1 Kin. 2:39.

4. Called also MICHAIAH. Mother of Abijam and grandmother of Asa, 1 Kin. 15:2, 10-13; 2 Chr. 11:20-23; 13:2; 15:16.

5. Wife of Machir, 1 Chr. 7:15,16.

6. Concubine of Caleb, 1 Chr. 2:48.

7. Wife of Jehiel, 1 Chr. 8:29; 9:35.

8. Father of Hanan, 1 Chr. 11:43.

9. Father of Shephatiah, 1 Chr. 27:16.

10. Called also MAACAH and MAACHATHI. A small kingdom E. of Bashan, Deut. 3:14; Josh. 12:5; 2 Sam. 10:6,8; 1 Chr. 19:6,7.

MAADAI, a returned exile, Ezra 10:34.

MAADIAH, a priest, Neh. 12:5.

MAAI, a priest, Neh. 12:36.

MAALEH-ACRABBIM, an acclivity on the S. border of Judah, Josh. 15:3.

See AKRABBIM.

MAARATH, a city of Judah, Josh. 15:59.

MAASEIAH. 1. A Levite musician, 1 Chr. 15:18,20.

2. A captain of hundreds, 2 Chr. 23:1.

3. An officer of Uzziah, 2 Chr. 26:11.

4. Son of Ahaz. Slain by Zichri, 2 Chr. 28:7.

5. Governor of Jerusalem, 2 Chr. 34:8.

6. The name of a number of priests of the exile, Ezra 10:18,21,22; Neh. 8:4,7; 12:41,42; Jer. 21:1; 29:25; 37:3.

7. A returned exile, Ezra 10:30.

8. Father of Azariah, Neh. 3:23.

9. One who sealed the covenant, Neh. 10:25.

10. A descendant of Pharez, Neh. 11:5.

11. A Benjamite, Neh. 11:7.

12. Father of a false prophet; Jer. 29:21.

13. An officer of the temple, Jer. 35:4.

14. Grandfather of Baruch, Jer. 32:12; 51:59.

MAASIAI, a priest, 1 Chr. 9:12.

MAATH, an ancestor of Jesus, Luke 3:26.

MAAZ, a son of Ram, 1 Chr. 2:27.

MAAZIAH. 1. A priest, 1 Chr. 24:18.

2. A priest who sealed the covenant with Nehemiah, Neh. 10:8.

MACEDONIA. A country in southeastern Europe. Paul has a vision concerning, Acts 16:9; preaches in, at Philippi, Acts 16:12; revisits, Acts 20:1-6; 2 Cor. 2:13; 7:5. Church at, sends contributions to the poor in Jerusalem, Rom. 15:26; 2 Cor. 8:1-5. Timothy visits, Acts 19:22. Disciples in, Acts 19:23; 27:2.

MACHBANAI, a Gadite warrior, 1 Chr. 12:13.

MACHI, a Gadite, Num. 13:15.

MACHIR. 1. One of the sons of Manasseh, Gen. 50:23. Father of the Machirites, Num. 26:29; 36:1. The land of Gilead allotted to, Num. 32:39,40; Deut 3:15; Josh. 13:31. Certain cities of Bashan given to, Josh. 13:31; 17:1.

2. A man of Lo-debar who took care of Jonathan's lame son, Mephibosheth, 2 Sam. 9:4,5; 17:27.

MACHNADEBAI, a Jew, Ezra 10:40.

MACHPELAH, the burying place of Sarah, Abraham, Isaac, Rebekah, Leah, and Jacob, Gen. 23:9,17-20; 25:9; 49:30,31; 50:13; Acts 7:16.

MADAI, son of Japheth, Gen. 10:2; 1 Chr. 1:5.

MADMANNAH, a city of Judah, Josh. 15:31.

MADMENAH, a city of Benjamin, Isa. 10:31.

MADNESS. See INSANITY.

MADON, a Canaanitish city, Josh. 11:1; 12:19.

MAGDALA. A city of Galilee. Christ visits, Matt. 15:39.

MAGI, the wise men who visited Jesus, Matt. 2:1-12.

MAGIC. See ASTROLOGY; MAGICIAN; NECROMANCY; SORCERY; WITCHCRAFT.

MAGICIAN. A person who claims to understand and explain mysteries by magic, Dan. 1:20. Failed to interpret Pharaoh's dreams, Gen. 41:8,24; Nebuchadnezzar's, Dan. 2:2-13; 4:7. Wrought apparent miracles, Ex. 7:11,12,22; 8:7,18.

MAGISTRATE. An officer of civil law, Judg. 18:7; Ezra 7:25; Luke 12:11,58; Acts 16:20,22,35,38. Obedience to, enjoined, Tit. 3:1.

See GOVERNMENT; RULERS.

MAGNA CHARTA, of the Israelites. See CONSTITUTION.

MAGNANIMITY. INSTANCES OF: Joshua and the elders of Israel to the Gibeonites who had deceived the Israelites, Josh. 9:3-27. Of Moses, see MOSES. David to Saul, 1 Sam. 24:3-11. Ahab to Benhadad, 1 Kin. 20:32-34.

See CHARITABLENESS.

MAGNIFICAT, of Mary, Luke 1:46-55.

MAGOG. Son of Japheth, Gen. 10:2; 1 Chr. 1:5. Prophecy concerning, Ezek. 38:2; 39:6.

Symbolical of the enemies of God, Rev. 20:8.

MAGOR-MISSABIB, a symbolical name given by Jeremiah to Pashur, Jer. 20: 3-6.

MAGPIASH, a person or family, Neh. 10:20.

MAHALAH, grandson of Manasseh, 1 Chr. 7:18.

MAHALALEEL. 1. Called also MALELEEL. Son of Cainan, Gen. 5:12-17; 1 Chr. 1:2; Luke 3:37.

2. A man of Judah, Neh. 11:4.

MAHALATH. 1. Called also BASHEMATH. Daughter of Ishmael, Gen. 28:9; 36:3.

2. A granddaughter of David, 2 Chr. 11: 18.

3. See MUSIC.

MAHANAIM. The place where Jacob had the vision of angels, Gen. 32:2. The town of, allotted to Gad, Josh. 13:26,30. One of the Levitical cities, Josh. 21:38. Ishbosheth establishes himself at, when made king over Israel, 2 Sam. 2:8-12. David lodges at, at the time of Absalom's rebellion, 2 Sam. 17:27-29; 1 Kin. 2:8.

MAHANEH-DAN, an encampment of the Danites, Judg. 13:25; 18:12.

MAHARAI, one of David's warriors, 2 Sam. 23:28; 1 Chr. 11:30; 27:13.

MAHATH, name of two descendants of Kohath, 1 Chr. 6:35; 2 Chr. 29:12; 31:13.

MAHAZIOTH, son of Heman, 1 Chr. 25:4,30.

MAHER-SHALAL-HASH-BAZ, a symbolical name, Isa. 8:1-4.

MAHLAH. One of the daughters of Zelophehad. Special legislation in regard to the inheritance of, Num. 26:33; 27:1-7; 36:1-12; Josh. 17:3,4.

MAHLI. 1. Son of Merari, Ex. 6:19; 1 Chr. 6:19; Ezra 8:18.

2. Son of Mushi, 1 Chr. 6:47; 23:23; 24:30.

MAHLON, son of Naomi, and first husband of Ruth, Ruth 1:2,5; 4:9,10.

MAHOL, father of Heman, Chalcol, and Darda, 1 Kin. 4:31.

MAIDEN. See VIRGIN; SERVANT.

MAIL. 1. Information, public or private. Carried by post, Esth. 3:13; 8:10.

2. Armor, 1 Sam. 17:5. See ARMOR.

MAJESTY, name of God, Heb. 1:3; 8:1. See GOD.

MAJORITY AND MINORITY REPORTS, of the spies, Num. 13:26-33; 14. 6-10.

MAKAZ, a place in Judah, 1 Kin. 4:9.

MAKHELOTH, an encampment of Israel, Num. 33:25,26.

MAKKEDAH. A city in Judah, conquered by Joshua, Josh. 10:28; 12:16. Five kings of the Amorites hide in a cave of, and are slain by Joshua, Josh. 10:5,16-27.

MAKTESH, a district where merchants traded, Zeph. 1:11.

MALACHI. Last of the minor prophets, Mal. 1:1. Reproves the church for its impiety, Mal. 1; 2; 3:7-15. Foretells the coming of the Messiah, Mal. 3:1-6; the judgments on the wicked and consolations of the righteous, Mal. 4:1-3; the coming of the forerunner of the Messiah, Mal. 4:4-6.

MALCHAM. 1. A Benjamite, 1 Chr. 8:9.

2. An idol, Zeph. 1:5.

MALCHIAH. Called also MALCHIJAH.

1. A Gershonite, 1 Chr. 6:40.

2. Called also MELCHIAH. An Aaronite, 1 Chr. 9:12; Neh. 11:12; Jer. 21:1; 38:1.

3. Head of a division of priests, 1 Chr. 24:9.

4. Name of three exiles, Ezra 10:25,31.

5. A son of Rechab who repaired the dung gate of Jerusalem, Neh. 3:14.

6. A Jew who helped repair the walls of Jerusalem, Neh. 3:31.

7. A Jew who stood by Ezra when he read the book of the law to the people, Neh. 8:4.

8. A priest who sealed the covenant with Nehemiah, Neh. 10:3.

9. A priest appointed to assist in dedicating the walls of Jerusalem, Neh. 12:42.

MALCHIEL, son of Beriah, Gen. 46:17; Num. 26:45; 1 Chr. 7:31.

MALCHIRAM, son of Jeconiah, 1 Chr. 3:18.

MALCHUS, servant of the high priest; Peter assaults in Gethsemane; healed by Jesus, Matt. 26:51; Mark 14:47; Luke 22:50, 51; John 18:10.

MALEFACTOR, crucified with Jesus, Matt. 27:38-44; Luke 23:32-39.

MALFEASANCE IN OFFICE. INSTANCES OF: The lessees of the vineyard, in one of the parables of Jesus, Mark 12:1-8; Luke 20:9-15. The steward mentioned in one of the parables of Jesus, Luke 16:1-7.

MALICE. Gen. 3:15. And I will put enmity between thee and the woman, and between thy seed and her seed; it shall bruise thy head, and thou shalt bruise his heel.

Lev. 19:14. Thou shalt not curse the deaf, nor put a stumblingblock before the blind, but shalt fear thy God: 17. Thou shalt not hate thy brother in thine heart: 18. Thou shalt not avenge, nor bear any grudge against the children of thy people, but thou shalt love thy neighbour as thyself:

Deut. 27:17. Cursed *be* he that removeth his neighbour's landmark. 18. Cursed *be* he that maketh the blind to wander out of the way.

Deut. 32:32. For their vine *is* of the vine of Sodom, and of the fields of Gomorrah: their grapes *are* grapes of gall, their clusters *are* bitter: 33. Their wine *is* the poison of dragons, and the cruel venom of asps.

2 Kin. 6:21. And the king of Israel said unto Elisha, when he saw them, My father, shall I smite *them?* shall I smite *them?* 22. And he answered, Thou shalt not smite *them:* wouldest thou smite those whom thou hast taken captive with thy sword and with thy bow? set bread and water before them, that they may eat and drink, and go to their master.

Job 31:29. If I rejoiced at the destruction of him that hated me, or lifted up myself when evil found him: 30. Neither have I suffered my mouth to sin by wishing a curse to his soul.

Psa. 4:2. O ye sons of men, how long *will ye turn* my glory into shame?

Psa. 7:14. He travaileth with iniquity, and hath conceived mischief, and brought forth falsehood. 15. He made a pit, and digged it, and is fallen into the ditch *which* he made. 16. His mischief shall return upon his own head, and his violent dealing shall come down upon his own pate. Job 15:35.

Psa. 10:7. His mouth is full of cursing and deceit and fraud: under his tongue *is* mischief and vanity. 8. He sitteth in the lurking places of the villages: in the secret places doth he murder the innocent: his eyes are privily set against the poor. 9. He lieth in wait secretly as a lion in his den: he lieth in wait to catch the poor: he doth catch the poor, when he draweth him into his net. 10. He croucheth, *and* humbleth himself, that the poor may fall by his strong ones. 14. Thou hast seen *it;* for thou beholdest mischief and spite, to requite *it* with thy hand:

Psa. 21:11. They intended evil against thee: they imagined a mischievous device, *which* they are not able *to perform.*

Psa. 22:7. All they that see me laugh me to scorn: they shoot out the lip, they shake the head, *saying,* 8. He trusted on the LORD *that* he would deliver him: let him deliver him, seeing he delighted in him.

Psa. 35:15. But in mine adversity they rejoiced, and gathered themselves together: *yea,* the abjects gathered themselves together against me, and I knew *it* not; they did tear *me,* and ceased not: 16. With hypocritical mockers in feasts, they gnashed upon me with their teeth. 19. Let not them that are mine enemies wrongfully rejoice over me: *neither* let them wink with the eye that hate me without a cause. 20. For they speak not peace: but they devise deceitful matters against *them that are* quiet in the land. 21. Yea, they opened their mouth wide against me, *and* said, Aha, aha, our eye hath seen *it.*

Psa. 38:16. For I said, *Hear me,* lest *otherwise* they should rejoice over me: when my foot slippeth, they magnify *themselves* against me. 19. Mine enemies *are* lively, *and* they are strong: and they that hate me wrongfully are multiplied.

Psa. 41:5. Mine enemies speak evil of me, When shall he die, and his name perish? 6. And if he come to see *me*, he speaketh vanity: his heart gathereth iniquity to itself; *when* he goeth abroad, he telleth *it*. 7. All that hate me whisper together against me : against me do they devise my hurt. 8. An evil disease, *say they*, cleaveth fast unto him : and *now* that he lieth he shall rise up no more.

Psa. 55:3. They cast iniquity upon me, and in wrath they hate me. 10. Day and night they go about it upon the walls thereof : mischief also and sorrow *are* in the midst of it. 11. Wickedness *is* in the midst thereof : deceit and guile depart not from her streets.

Psa. 56:5. Every day they wrest my words : all their thoughts *are* against me for evil. 6. They gather themselves together, they hide themselves, they mark my steps, when they wait for my soul.

Psa. 57:4. My soul *is* among lions : *and* I lie *even among* them that are set on fire, *even* the sons of men, whose teeth *are* spears and arrows, and their tongue a sharp sword. 6. They have prepared a net for my steps ; my soul is bowed down : they have digged a pit before me, into the midst whereof they are fallen *themselves*.

Psa. 59:3. Lo, they lie in wait for my soul: the mighty are gathered against me ; not *for* my transgression, nor *for* my sin, O Lord. 4. They run and prepare themselves without *my* fault : 6. They return at evening: they make a noise like a dog, and go round about the city. 7. Behold, they belch out with their mouth : swords *are* in their lips : for who, *say they*, doth hear?

Psa. 62:3. How long will ye imagine mischief against a man? ye shall be slain all of you : as a bowing wall *shall ye be, and as* a tottering fence. 4. They only consult to cast *him* down from his excellency : they delight in lies : they bless with their mouth, but they curse inwardly.

Psa. 64:2. Hide me from the secret counsel of the wicked ; from the insurrection of the workers of iniquity : 3. Who whet their tongue like a sword, *and* bend *their bows to shoot* their arrows, *even* bitter words : 4. That they may shoot in secret at the perfect: suddenly do they shoot at him, and fear not. 5. They encourage themselves *in* an evil matter : they commune of laying snares privily ; they say, Who shall see them? 6. They search out iniquities ; they accomplish a diligent search : both the inward *thought* of every one *of them*, and the heart, *is* deep.

Psa. 69:4. They that hate me without a cause are more than the hairs of mine head: they that would destroy me, *being* mine enemies wrongfully, are mighty : 10. When I wept, *and chastened* my soul with fasting, that was to my reproach. 11. I made sack-cloth also my garment; and I became a proverb to them. 12. They that sit in the gate speak against me ; and I *was* the song of the drunkards. 26. They persecute *him* whom thou hast smitten ; and they talk to the grief of those whom thou hast wounded.

Psa. 70:2. Let them be ashamed and confounded that seek after my soul: let them be turned backward, and put to confusion, that desire my hurt. 3. Let them be turned back for a reward of their shame that say, Aha, aha.

Psa. 71:10. Mine enemies speak against me ; and they that lay wait for my soul take counsel together, 11. Saying, God hath forsaken him : persecute and take him ; for *there is* none to deliver *him*. *vs.* 13,24.

Psa. 74:20. The dark places of the earth are full of the habitations of cruelty.

Psa. 86:14. O God, the proud are risen against me, and the assemblies of violent *men* have sought after my soul ;

Psa. 102:8. Mine enemies reproach me all the day ; *and* they that are mad against me are sworn against me.

Psa. 109:2. For the mouth of the wicked and the mouth of the deceitful are opened against me : they have spoken against me with a lying tongue. 3. They compassed me about also with words of hatred ; and fought against me without a cause. 4. For my love they are my adversaries : but I *give myself unto* prayer. 5. And they have rewarded me evil for good, and hatred for my love. 16. Because that he remembered not to shew mercy, but persecuted the poor and needy man, that he might even slay the broken in heart. 17. As he loved cursing, so let it come unto him : as he delighted not in blessing, so let it be far from him. 18. As he clothed himself with cursing like as with his garment, so let it come into his bowels like water, and like oil into his bones.

Psa. 119:150. They draw nigh that follow after mischief: they are far from thy law. *v.* 78.

Psa. 140:1. Deliver me, O Lord, from the evil man : preserve me from the violent man ; 2. Which imagine mischiefs in *their* heart; continually are they gathered together *for* war. 3. They have sharpened their tongues like a serpent; adders' poison *is* under their lips. Selah. 4. Keep me, O Lord, from the hands of the wicked; preserve me from the violent man ; who have purposed to overthrow my goings.

Prov. 4:16. They sleep not, except they have done mischief; and their sleep is taken away, unless they cause *some* to fall. 17. For they eat the bread of wickedness, and drink the wine of violence.

Prov. 6:14. Frowardness *is* in his heart, he deviseth mischief continually; he soweth discord. 15. Therefore shall his calamity come suddenly; suddenly shall he be broken without remedy. 18. An heart that deviseth wicked imaginations, feet that be swift in running to mischief, 19. A false witness *that* speaketh lies, and he that soweth discord among brethren. *v.* 16.

Prov. 10:6. Violence covereth the mouth of the wicked. 12. Hatred stirreth up strifes:

Prov. 11:17. *He that is* cruel troubleth his own flesh.

Prov. 12:10. The tender mercies of the wicked *are* cruel.

Prov. 14:17. A man of wicked devices is hated. 22. Do they not err that devise evil?

Prov. 15:17. Better *is* a dinner of herbs where love is, than a stalled ox and hatred therewith.

Prov. 16:30. He shutteth his eyes to devise froward things: moving his lips he bringeth evil to pass.

Prov. 17:5. Whoso mocketh the poor reproacheth his Maker: *and* he that is glad at calamities shall not be unpunished.

Prov. 20:22. Say not thou, I will recompense evil; *but* wait on the LORD, and he shall save thee.

Prov. 21:10. The soul of the wicked desireth evil: his neighbour findeth no favour in his eyes.

Prov. 24:8. He that deviseth to do evil shall be called a mischievous person. 17. Rejoice not when thine enemy falleth, and let not thine heart be glad when he stumbleth: 18. Lest the LORD see *it*, and it displease him, and he turn away his wrath from him. 29. Say not, I will do so to him as he hath done to me: I will render to the man according to his work.

Prov. 26:2. As the bird by wandering, . . . so the curse causeless shall not come. 27. Whoso diggeth a pit shall fall therein: and he that rolleth a stone, it will return upon him.

Prov. 28:10. Whoso causeth the righteous to go astray in an evil way, he shall fall himself into his own pit:

Prov. 30:14. *There is* a generation, whose teeth *are as* swords, and their jaw teeth *as* knives, to devour the poor from off the earth, and the needy from *among* men.

Isa. 29:20. For the terrible one is brought to nought, and the scorner is consumed, and all that watch for iniquity are cut off: 21. That make a man an offender for a word, and lay a snare for him that reproveth in the gate, and turn aside the just for a thing of nought.

Isa. 32:6. The vile person will speak villany, and his heart will work iniquity, to practise hypocrisy, and to utter error against the LORD, to make empty the soul of the hungry, and he will cause the drink of the thirsty to fail.

Isa. 59:4. None calleth for justice, nor *any* pleadeth for truth: they trust in vanity, and speak lies; they conceive mischief, and bring forth iniquity. 5. They hatch cockatrice' eggs, and weave the spider's web: he that eateth of their eggs dieth, and that which is crushed breaketh out into a viper. 6. Their webs shall not become garments, nei-

ther shall they cover themselves with their works: their works *are* works of iniquity and the act of violence *is* in their hands. *v.* 7.

Jer. 20:10. I heard the defaming of many, fear on every side. Report, *say they*, and we will report it. All my familiars watched for my halting, *saying*, Peradventure he will be enticed, and we shall prevail against him, and we shall take our revenge on him.

Lam. 4:3. Even the sea monsters draw out the breast, they give suck to their young ones: the daughter of my people *is become* cruel, like the ostriches in the wilderness. 4. The tongue of the sucking child cleaveth to the roof of his mouth for thirst: the young children ask bread, *and* no man breaketh *it* unto them.

Ezek. 18:18. Because he cruelly oppressed, spoiled his brother by violence and did *that* which *is* not good among his people, lo, even he shall die in his iniquity.

Ezek. 25:3. And say unto the Ammonites, Hear the word of the Lord GOD; Thus saith the Lord GOD; Because thou saidst, Aha, against my sanctuary, when it was profaned; and against the land of Israel, when it was desolate; and against the house of Judah, when they went into captivity; 6. Because thou hast clapped *thine* hands, and stamped with the feet, and rejoiced in heart with all thy despite against the land of Israel; 7. Behold, therefore I will stretch out mine hand upon thee, and will deliver thee for a spoil to the heathen; 12. Thus saith the Lord GOD; Because that Edom hath dealt against the house of Judah by taking vengeance, and hath greatly offended, and revenged himself upon them; 15. Because the Philistines have dealt by revenge, and have taken vengeance with a despiteful heart, to destroy *it* for the old hatred; 17. I will execute great vengeance upon them with furious rebukes;

Ezek. 26:2. Because that Tyrus hath said against Jerusalem, Aha, she is broken *that was* the gates of the people: she is turned unto me: I shall be replenished, *now* she is laid waste: 3. Therefore thus saith the Lord GOD; Behold, I am against thee, O Tyrus, and will cause many nations to come up against thee, as the sea causeth his waves to come up.

Amos 1:11. Thus saith the LORD; For three transgressions of Edom, and for four, I will not turn away *the punishment* thereof; because he did pursue his brother with the sword, and did cast off all pity, and his anger did tear perpetually, and he kept his wrath for ever:

Mic. 2:1. Woe to them that devise iniquity, and work evil upon their beds! when the morning is light, they practise it, because it is in the power of their hand.

Zech. 8:17. Let none of you imagine evil in your hearts against his neighbour; and love no false oath: for all these *are things* that I hate, saith the LORD. Zech. 7:10.

Matt. 5:38. Ye have heard that it hath been said, An eye for an eye, and a tooth for a tooth: 39. But I say unto you, That ye resist not evil: but whosoever shall smite thee on thy right cheek, turn to him the other also. 40. And if any man will sue thee at the law, and take away thy coat, let him have *thy* cloke also. 41. And whosoever shall compel thee to go a mile, go with him twain. Luke 6:29.

Matt. 6:15. If ye forgive not men their trespasses, neither will your Father forgive your trespasses.

Matt. 18:28. But the same servant went out, and found one of his fellowservants, which owed him an hundred pence: and he laid hands on him, and took *him* by the throat, saying, Pay me that thou owest. 29. And his fellowservant fell down at his feet, and besought him, saying, Have patience with me, and I will pay thee all. 30. And he would not: but went and cast him into prison, till he should pay the debt. 31. So when his fellowservants saw what was done, they were very sorry, and came and told unto their lord all that was done. 32. Then his lord, after that he had called him, said unto him, O thou wicked servant, I forgave thee all that debt, because thou desiredst me: 33. Shouldest not thou also have had compassion on thy fellowservant, even as I had pity on thee? 34. And his lord was wroth, and delivered him to the tormentors, till he should pay all that was due unto him. 35. So likewise shall my heavenly Father do also unto you, if ye from your hearts forgive not every one his brother their trespasses.

Matt. 26:52. All they that take the sword shall perish with the sword.

Mark 15:10. For he knew that the chief priests had delivered him for envy.

John 8:44. Ye are of *your* father the devil, and the lusts of your father ye will do. He was a murderer from the beginning, and abode not in the truth, because there is no truth in him. When he speaketh a lie, he speaketh of his own: for he is a liar, and the father of it.

John 18:22. And when he had thus spoken, one of the officers which stood by struck Jesus with the palm of his hand, saying, Answerest thou the high priest so? 23. If I have spoken evil, bear witness of the evil: but if well, why smitest thou me?

Acts 23:12. And when it was day, certain of the Jews banded together, and bound themselves under a curse, saying that they would neither eat nor drink till they had killed Paul. 13. And they were more than forty which had made this conspiracy. 14. And they came to the chief priests and elders, and said, We have bound ourselves under a great curse, that we will eat nothing until we have slain Paul.

Rom. 1:29. Being filled with all unrighteousness, fornication, wickedness, covetousness, maliciousness; full of envy, murder, debate, deceit, malignity; whisperers, 30.

Backbiters, haters of God, despiteful, proud, boasters, inventors of evil things, disobedient to parents, 31. Without understanding, covenantbreakers, without natural affection, implacable, unmerciful: 32. Who knowing the judgment of God, that they which commit such things are worthy of death, not only do the same, but hath pleasure in them that do them.

Rom. 12:19. Avenge not yourselves, but *rather* give place unto wrath; for it is written, Vengeance *is* mine; I will repay, saith the Lord.

1 Cor. 5:8. Therefore let us keep the feast, not with old leaven, neither with the leaven of malice and wickedness; but with the unleavened *bread* of sincerity and truth.

1 Cor. 14:20. Brethren, be not children in understanding: howbeit in malice be ye children, but in understanding be men.

Gal. 5:19. Now the works of the flesh are manifest, which are *these*, Adultery, fornication, uncleanness, lasciviousness, 20. Idolatry, witchcraft, hatred, variance, emulations, wrath, strife, seditions, heresies, 21. Envyings, murders, drunkenness, revellings, and such like: of the which I tell you before, as I have also told *you* in time past, that they which do such things shall not inherit the kingdom of God.

Eph. 4:31. Let all bitterness, and wrath, and anger, and clamour, and evil speaking, be put away from you, with all malice:

Phil. 1:15. Some indeed preach Christ even of envy and strife; and some also of good will: 16. The one preach Christ of contention, not sincerely, supposing to add affliction to my bonds:

Col. 3:8. But now ye also put off all these; anger, wrath, malice. blasphemy, filthy communication out of your mouth.

1 Thess. 5:15. See that none render evil for evil unto any *man;*

Tit. 3:3. We ourselves also were sometimes . . . living in malice and envy, hateful, *and* hating one another.

Jas. 1:21. Wherefore lay apart all filthiness and superfluity of naughtiness, and receive with meekness the engrafted word, which is able to save your souls.

Jas. 2:13. He shall have judgment without mercy, that hath shewed no mercy;

1 Pet. 2:1. Wherefore laying aside all malice, and all guile, and hypocrisies, and envies, and all evil speakings,

1 Pet. 3:9. Not rendering evil for evil, or railing for railing:

1 John 2:9. He that saith he is in the light, and hateth his brother, is in darkness even until now. 11. He that hateth his brother is in darkness, and walketh in darkness, and knoweth not whither he goeth, because that darkness hath blinded his eyes.

1 John 3:10. In this the children of God are manifest, and the children of the devil: whosoever doeth not righteousness is not of God, neither he that loveth not his brother. 13. Marvel not, my brethren, if the world

FOUR THOUSAND QUESTIONS AND ANSWERS

ON THE

OLD AND NEW TESTAMENTS.

INTENDED TO OPEN UP THE SCRIPTURES

FOR THE USE OF STUDENTS AND SUNDAY-SCHOOL TEACHERS.

THE FALL. (Gen. 2, 3.)

1. *Where did God place man when he had created him?*—In the garden of Eden, near the river Euphrates. Gen. 2: 8.

2. *What is a garden?*—A piece of ground enclosed and planted for the production of trees and flowers, of fruits and other food.

3. *What description have we given to us of this garden?*—That God made to grow in it the tree of life, the tree of knowledge of good and evil, and every tree that is pleasant to the sight and good for food. Gen. 2: 9.

4. *How was it watered?*—By a river, that flowed afterward in four rivers or channels to the sea. Gen. 2: 10-14.

5. *Can any of those rivers be now traced?*—The Euphrates only.

6. *Was man idle in the garden of Eden, or did God employ him there?*—He was put into the garden to dress it and keep it (Gen. 2: 15); so that it was a duty and a blessing, even in Paradise, to be employed.

7. *How was the garden refreshed, before man was placed there to tend it?*—By a mist from the earth. Gen. 2: 6.

8. *Did God permit man to pluck and eat the fruit of this garden?*—He was allowed freely to eat of every tree. Gen. 2: 16.

9. *Were there any restrictions to this permission?*—An exception was made of the tree of knowledge of good and evil, under the penalty of death. Gen. 2: 17. Thus was a trial made of obedience and love, and a gracious warning given.

10. *Were they forbidden to eat of the tree of life?*—They were not.

11. *What do we conclude from this?*—That they were intended to live forever.

12. *Did man obey God's command?*—He did not.

13. *What did he do?*—He ate the forbidden fruit.

14. *Who was the first transgressor?*—Eve.

15. *How came it about?*—The devil, in the form of a serpent, deceived her by a lie. Gen. 3: 1-6.

16. *What did the devil promise Eve?*—That they should not surely die, but be as gods, knowing good and evil. Gen. 3: 4, 5.

17. *Was she disappointed?*—Satan's words proved false, for there is no truth in him. They fell under sentence of death; and Satan showed himself a liar and a murderer from the beginning. John 8: 44.

18. *What foolish plan did they adopt to hide their shame?*—They hid themselves amongst the trees of the garden, knowing the evil they had done.

19. *Can any place conceal us from God's eye?*—None.

O Lord, thou hast searched me, and known me. Thou knowest my downsitting and mine uprising, thou understandest my thought afar off. Thou compassest my path and my lying down, and art acquainted with all my ways. For there is not a word in my tongue, but, lo, O Lord, thou knowest it altogether. Thou hast beset me behind and before, and laid thine hand upon me. Such knowledge is too wonderful for me; it is high, I cannot attain unto it. Whither shall I go from thy Spirit? or whither shall I flee from thy presence? If I ascend up into heaven, thou art there; if I make my bed in hell, behold, thou art there. If I take the wings of the morning, and dwell in the uttermost parts of the sea; even there shall thy hand lead me, and thy right hand shall hold me. If I say, Surely the darkness shall cover me; even the night shall be light about me. Yea, the darkness hideth not from thee: but the night shineth as the day: the darkness and the light are both alike to thee. Ps. 139 : 1-12.

20. *What is it that makes us fear to meet God?*—The consciousness that we have sinned, and that he knows it.

21. *What do we do when we commit sin?*—We generally try to hide our wrong-doings even from ourselves.

22. *What ought we to do?*—To confess and be truly sorry for our sin; to come to God, through Christ, for the pardon of it, and to forsake it.

If we say that we have no sin, we deceive ourselves, and the truth is not in us. If we confess our sins, he is faithful and just to forgive us our sins, and to cleanse us from all unrighteousness. If we say that we have not sinned, we make him a liar, and his word is not in us. My little children, these things write I unto you that ye sin not. And if any man sin, we have an advocate with the Father, Jesus Christ the righteous, and he is the propitiation for our sins; and not for ours only, but also for the sins of the whole world. 1 John 1 : 8-2 : 2.

He that covereth his sins shall not prosper; but whoso confesseth and forsaketh them shall have mercy. Prov. 28 : 13.

23. *Can we provide a covering for our sin?*—No: for our very best deeds are imperfect and defiled. We are all as an unclean thing, and all our righteousnesses are as filthy rags. Isa. 64: 6.

24. *Has God taken pity on us and given us a robe of righteousness?*—I will greatly rejoice in the Lord, my soul shall be joyful in my God; for he hath clothed me with the garments of salvation, he hath covered me with the robe of righteousness, as a bridegroom decketh himself with ornaments, and as a bride adorneth herself with her jewels. Isa. 61: 10 *Where is this further spoken of?*—Even the righteousness of God which is by faith of Jesus Christ unto all, and upon all them that believe. Rom. 3 : 22.

25. *How was it made known to our first parents?*—It was included in the intimation of a Saviour, conveyed in the promise that the seed of the woman should bruise the serpent's head. Gen. 3: 15; and see No. 26.

26. *How did God cloth their bodies?*—In coats of skin. Gen. 3 : 21.

27. *What is it supposed was done with the bodies of the animals thus slain?*—That they were offered in sacrifice to God, as types or representations of the future sacrifice of Christ. Gen. 4 : 4.

28. *How did this represent the great atonement that Jesus afterward accomplished?*—By the shedding of blood, without which there is no remission of sins. Heb. 9 : 22.

29. *Did God give them any direct promise of this blessed Person?* See No. 25.

30. *Was the devil disappointed?*—Yes, he failed in ruining man for ever.

31. *Who got the curse?*—Satan, whose head or power was to be bruised or crushed. Gen. 3 : 15. Man also suffered, in a less degree, by being driven out of Eden, and condemned to laborious toil, and at last to bodily death. Gen. 3 : 17-19, 23, 24.

32. *For whose sake was the ground cursed?*—For man's sake. Gen. 3 : 17.

33. *How was man to feel this?*—By the weeds it brought forth, and the labor it required.

34. *Was there any special punishment to the woman for being first in the transgression?*—In personal suffering.

35. *Was there not also a special mercy granted to her?*—That she should be the ancestress of Christ. Gen. 3 : 15.

36. *Did they continue in the garden of Eden?*—No.

37. *Why not?*—Lest they should eat of the tree of life, and live for ever upon earth. Gen. 3 : 22.

38. *Is the tree of life ever mentioned again in Scripture? Where?*—In Rev. 22 : 1, 2, as standing by the river of the water of life, in the heavenly Jerusalem; Rev. 21 : 2, in the midst of the paradise of God. Rev. 2 : 7.

39. *Who will again eat of it?*—They that do God's commandments, and that overcome in the battle with Satan and with sin. Rev. 22 : 14; 2 : 7.

40. *How did God guard the gate of Eden?*—By cherubim or angels and a flaming sword. Gen. 3 : 24.

41. *Are the cherubim again mentioned in Scripture? Where?*—In the vision of Ezekiel, chapters 1 and 10, and in the account of the tabernacle and the temple, etc., twenty-one places altogether.

42. *Why did Adam name his wife Eve?*—Because she was the mother of all living, and the word means "living." Gen. 3 : 20.

CAIN AND ABEL. (Gen. 4.)

1. *What was the name of Adam's first child?*—Cain. Gen. 4 : 1.

2. *What is the meaning of the name?*—Got or obtained.

3. *Whom did Eve suppose him to be?*—The seed or child or Saviour promised.

4. *Was she disappointed?*—Yes; he became a wicked man and a murderer.

5. *What name did she give her second son?*—Abel, or Vanity.

6. *What did this show?*—That her expectations had declined.

7. *Did he prove as bad as his brother?*—No; his works were righteous. 1 John 3 : 12.

8. *What difference do we observe in the offerings of the two brothers?*—Cain offered of the fruit of the ground, and Abel the firstlings of his flock. Gen. 4 : 3, 4.

9. *How does this give us their characters?*—Cain showed indifference or self-will, and Abel obedience and faith.

By faith Abel offered unto God a more excellent sacrifice than Cain, by which he obtained witness that he was righteous, God testifying of his gifts and by it he being dead yet speaketh. Heb. 11 : 4.

10. *Will God receive us in any other way than the way he has appointed?*—He will not.

11. *How is that?*—Jesus saith, I am the way, the truth, and the life: no man cometh unto the Father, but by me. John 14 : 6.

12. *How did the slain lamb represent Jesus?*—In being without blemish and without spot (1 Pet. 1 : 19), and in having its blood shed; for without shedding of blood is no remission of sin. Heb. 9 : 22.

13. *What did John the Baptist say of Jesus?*—Behold! the Lamb of God, which taketh away the sin of the world. John 1 : 29.

14. *What proof did God give that the sacrifice was accepted?*—Probably the consuming it by fire from heaven, as Elijah's was consumed on Carmel. 1 Kings 18 : 38.

15. *How did Cain act when he found that his own way did not please God?*—He was very angry. Gen. 4 : 5.

16. *How should he have acted?*—He should have offered, in penitence and faith, the sacrifice that God required. Gen. 4 : 7.

17. *Did not sin lie at his own door, then, seeing God had provided a way to remove it?*—It did (Gen. 4 : 7), and led to greater guilt and sin.

18. *What awful act did Cain's jealousy of his brother lead to?*—The murder of his brother, his only brother.

19. *What fearful lie did he tell?*—He told the all-seeing God that he knew not where his murdered brother was.

20. *What did God say had cried to him?*—His brother's blood.

21. *In John 8 : 44 the devil is called a murderer. What is said of Cain in 1 John 3 : 10-12?*—In this the children of God are manifest, and the children of the devil: whosoever doeth not righteousness is not of God, neither he that loveth not his brother. For this is the message that ye heard from the beginning, that we should love one another. Not as Cain, who was of that wicked one and slew his brother. And wherefore slew he him? Because his own works were evil, and his brother's righteous.

22. *Did Cain procure for himself Satan's portion—a curse?*—See Gen. 4 : 11, 12.

23. *What did Cain feel when God's curse lighted on him?*—That his punishment was greater than he could bear, as any one might kill him.

24. *Did God in mercy mitigate Cain's punishment?*—He set a mark upon him to prevent his being killed.

25. *What is meant by Cain's going from God's presence?*—He perhaps never heard him again, or saw him in the form he used to take, or felt his Spirit within him. He left the place where his worship was held, and the place where his glory may have appeared. Gen. 3 : 24.

26. *When God takes vengeance into his own hand, will he let any one else perform it?*—God, to whom vengeance belongeth, says, Vengeance is mine; I will repay. Rom. 12 : 19; Ps. 94 : 1.

27. *Is there a day of reckoning coming?*—It is appointed unto men once to die, and after that the judgment. Heb. 9 : 27.

THE ANTEDILUVIAN PATRIARCHS. (Gen. 5.)

1. *What is the allotted age of man now?*—Threescore years and ten. Ps. 90 : 10.

2. *Could we then have imagined it possible for men to have lived so long as the patriarchs, if the Bible had not informed us?*—We could not.

3. Place all these lives in a row. in long lines measured by 100 years, and say which lived the longest.

	100	200	300	400	500	600	700	800	900
Adam									
Seth									
Enos									
Cainan									
Mahalaleel									
Jared									
Enoch									
Methuselah									
Lamech									
Noah									

4. How is it that Enoch's is so much shorter than the others?—Because God took him to himself before he had lived half the usual time. It is a blessing to us, in life and in death, to live near unto God.

5. What does the apostle, in Heb. 11 : 5, say of Enoch?—By faith Enoch was translated, that he should not see death.

6. What remarkable prophecy of Enoch's does the apostle Jude repeat?—Behold, the Lord cometh with ten thousands of his saints.

7. To which coming of the Lord does it refer? To the first or second?—The second.

8. Is that second coming spoken of in other parts of the Bible? If so, where?—In 1 Thess 4 : 16, 17, and fifty other places at least.

9. When Jesus came the first time, was it to execute vengeance? If not, what was the object?—God sent not his Son into the world to condemn the world; but that the word through him might be saved. John 3 : 17.

10. What will be the design of the Lord's second coming?—To judge the world.

11. What remarkable likeness is there between the prophecy of God's first prophet and God's last prophet?—Each foretold the coming of our Lord.

12. What did John say?—Behold, he cometh with clouds; and every eye shall see him, and they also which pierced him: and all kindreds of the earth shall wail because of him. Even so, Amen. Rev. 1 : 7.

13. Who guided those who wrote the Bible?—The Holy Ghost.

> For the prophecy came not in old time by the will of man: but holy men of God spake as they were moved by the Holy Ghost. 2 Pet. 1 : 21.

14. Do we know when the Lord Jesus is coming?—Watch, therefore: for ye know not what hour your Lord doth come. Matt. 24 : 42.

15. What effect should this uncertainty as to our knowledge have upon us?—The day of the Lord will come as a thief in the night. Wherefore, beloved, seeing that ye look for such things, be diligent that ye may be found of him in peace, without spot and blameless. Pet. 3 : 10, 14.

16. Was Enoch ready when he was caught up?—Yes, quite.

17. With whom was he walking in communion?—With God. "Oh for a closer walk with God!"

18. What is said in Amos 3 : 3?—Can two walk together, except they be agreed?

19. Who are our companions?—We should choose, as often as we can, those whom we believe to be walking with God and who can help us to do so.

20. Do we delight in being alone with him, or do we shrink from him?—We must be alone with him in death; and it is our wisdom and comfort to be much alone with him in life.

21. What solemn warning does God give in Heb. 3 : 7, 8?—As the Holy Ghost saith, To-day if ye will hear his voice, harden not your hearts.

THE FLOOD. (Gen. 5, 6.)

1. What do we read of Cain's descendants in Gen. 4 : 17-23?—That Cain had a son Enoch, and built a city, etc.

2. Were they as good as they were skillful?—No, they shared the general corruption, and would probably be worse, from their ancestor's separation from the people of God and the presence of the Lord. Gen. 4 : 16; 6 : 5.

3. What was the name of the son that God gave Adam in the place of Abel, whom Cain slew?—Seth. Gen. 4 : 25.

4. Did the children of Seth keep themselves separate from Cain's children?—Yes. They called themselves by the name of the Lord. Gen. 4 : 26, margin.

5. When God looked down from heaven, what did he see?—The great wickedness of man. Gen. 6 : 5.

6. What did he resolve to do?—To destroy both man and beast. Gen. 6 : 7.

7. Did he find one faithful family?—Yes. Gen. 6 : 8, 18.

8. Whose was that?—Noah's.

9. What is Noah said to be in 2 Pet. 2 : 5?—A preacher of righteousness.

10. When did Noah preach to these wicked people?—While the ark was preparing. 1 Pet. 3 : 20.

11. What does the book of Jonah show us?—That if man had repented, God would have spared.

> God saw their works, that they turned from their evil way: and God repented of the evil, that he had said that he would do unto them; and he did it not. Jonah 3 : 10.

12. Did these sinners repent at the preaching of Noah?—No.

13. What was the consequence?—The flood came, and took them all away. Matt. 24 : 39; Gen. 7 : 21-23.

14. How were Noah and his family preserved?—In the ark, which Noah built at God's command.

15. What is a type?—A thing that represents another thing, or has some points of resemblance to it, or is intended to foreshow it.

16. Of whom was the ark, in which Noah and his family were saved, a type?—Of Christ.

17. How?—As an appointed means of saving man from destruction.

18. Of what was the flood a type?—Of the future destruction of the world.

> The world that then was, being overflowed with water, perished: but the heavens and the earth, which are now, by the same word are kept in store, reserved unto fire against the day of judgment and perdition of ungodly men. 2 Pet. 3 : 6, 7.

19. Does this concern us at all?—Yes; as both living and dead will need a Saviour at that day.

20. What opportunity does God give us of fleeing into a place of safety?—He spares our lives, and gives us Bibles and preachers and teachers, to show us the way of salvation.

21. Has he provided a secure place of dependence? What is it?—God himself, in Christ, is our refuge.

> A man shall be as an hiding-place from the wind, and a covert from the tempest; as rivers of water in a dry place, as the shadow of a great rock in a weary land. Isa. 32 : 2.

> For this shall every one that is godly pray unto thee in a time when thou mayest be found: surely in the floods of great waters they shall not come nigh unto him. Thou art my hiding-place; thou shalt preserve me from trouble; thou shalt compass me about with songs of deliverance. Ps. 32 : 6, 7.

> Thou art my hiding-place and my shield: I hope in thy word. Ps. 119 : 114.

22. What does the Holy Spirit say to us in 2 Cor. 6 : 2?—That now is the accepted time; now is the day of salvation.

23. *Can there be a time when even God shall forget to be gracious?*—Yes; as when, in the parable of the ten virgins, the door was shut. Matt. 25 : 10.

NOAH. (Gen. 7, 8, 9.)

1. *How long was the ark building?*—Perhaps a great part of the time that Noah was preaching, or of the one hundred and twenty years mentioned in Gen. 6 : 3.

2. *How old were Noah and his sons when they went into the ark?*—Noah, six hundred years (Gen. 7 : 6), and his sons about one hundred. Gen. 5 : 32 ; 11 : 10.

3. *Who shut them in?*—God himself. Gen. 7 : 16.

4. *What went into the ark with them?*—(Besides their wives) seven, or two, of every living creature. Gen. 7 : 2, 3, 7-9, 13-16.

5. *How long did it continue raining?*—Forty days and nights. Gen. 7 : 12.

6. *How long did the waters continue?*—One hundred and fifty days. Gen. 7 : 24.

7. *How did Noah ascertain when the waters had abated?*—By sending out a dove, which returned with an olive-leaf in its mouth; and which, when sent out again, did not return at all. Gen. 8 : 10-12.

8. *Why did not the raven return to the ark?*—It probably often went forth and returned, as the words "to and fro" are explained in the margin to mean. Gen. 8 : 7. But if it met with floating carcasses, it might not come in for food.

9. *Of what is that an emblem?*—Perhaps of the carnal heart, content with the corrupt enjoyments of the world.

10. *And is there anything to be learnt from the opposite conduct of the dove?*—The privilege of the soul, unsatisfied with the world, returning to Christ Jesus as its rest.

11. *What does the Lord Jesus say in Matt. 11 : 28-30?*—Come unto me, all ye that labor and are heavy laden, and I will give you rest. Take my yoke upon you, and learn of me; for I am meek and lowly in heart: and ye shall find rest unto your souls. For my yoke is easy, and my burden is light.

12. *What was Noah's first act when he came forth from the ark?*—He built an altar, and offered a sacrifice. Gen. 8 : 20.

13. *What was the burnt-offering?*—A bullock, sheep, goat, turtle-dove or young pigeon. Lev. 1.

14. *Did God accept it?*—It pleased him, as a sweet savor or smell. Gen. 8 : 21.

15. *What promise did God give Noah at that time?*—That he would not again curse the ground any more for man's sake, etc. Gen. 8 : 21-23 ; 9 : 2.

16, 17. *Did God condescend to give him a token? What was it?*—He said that the rainbow should be a token or remembrance of his covenant or promise. Gen. 9 : 8-17.

18. *Does it remain?*—Yes.

19. *When does it appear?*—Whenever the sun shines upon rain.

20. *Did God make any change in man's food at that time?*—He gave him animal food, in addition to his former vegetable food. Gen. 9 : 3.

21. *Under what restriction?*—That the blood should not be used with the flesh. Gen. 9 : 4.

22. *Why was not blood to be eaten?*—Because it was a type of the blood of Christ; and to restrain blood-thirsty cruelty to man or beast. Gen. 5 : 16.

23. *What evil use did Noah afterward make of the fruits of the earth?*—He once became drunk with wine. Gen. 9 : 21.

24. *Does the Bible cover up and hide the sins of God's people?*—No, it mentions them whenever it seemed to the wisdom of God to be desirable to do so.

25. *What does the Psalmist say of God's word in Ps.*

119 : 140?*—That it is "very pure." Many books and magazines and newspapers in our days are very impure, and are written to please the impure.

26. *Which of Noah's sons brought a curse on his posterity by his conduct to his father on this occasion?*—Ham.

27. *Do the effects of this curse continue to the present time? Where?*—Yes: in Africa, which was peopled by the descendants of Ham, and is the chief scene of the horrible traffic in slaves.

28. *Show the fulfillment of Shem's blessing?*—God's people, the Jews, and Christ himself descended from Shem.

29. *Describe how Japheth has been enlarged?*—By his descendants, the Greeks and Romans, and by many Gentile nations sprung from him.

30. *How old was Noah when he died?*—Nine hundred and fifty years. Gen. 9 : 29.

THE TOWER OF BABEL. (Gen. 10, 11.)

1. *What mighty nations have their origin given in these chapters?*—The Chaldeans, Assyrians, and Canaanites.

2. *Were the genealogies and histories of all these nations continued in the Bible?*—No.

3. *Why was one family singled out for this special honor?*—Because out of it came Jesus Christ.

4. *What great event happened in the days of Peleg?*—The scattering of mankind over all the earth. Gen. 11 : 9. Unto Eber were born two sons: the name of the one was Peleg—i. e., division (margin), because in his days the earth was divided. 1 Chron. 1 : 19.

5. *Why did God thus divide or scatter men?*—To restrain them from building the tower of Babel.

6. *What motive had these men in building the tower?*—To form a conspicuous gathering-point, in defiance of the divine intention.

7. *Of what did they compose it?*—Of bricks, joined together with mortar of slime or mud that dried hard.

8. *Are there any remains of the materials of which it was built yet in existence? Where?*—Yes, in the ruins of Babylon.

9. *Where did Shem's family remove to?*—Some of them from Upper and Middle Asia to Canaan.

10. *Which of Abraham's ancestors were alive when he was born?*—Nahor and Terah.

11. *How old was Shem when Abram was born?*—Four hundred and fifty-two years [B. C. 2448-1996]. Gen. 5 : 32 ; 11 : 27.

12. *How many years did Shem live after Abram was born?*—One hundred and forty-nine years [B. C. 1996-1847]. Gen. 11 : 10, 11.

13. *What was the name of Abram's father?*—Terah. Gen. 11 : 26.

14. *How many years had he lived with Noah?*—One hundred and twenty-eight years. Gen. 5 : 29 ; 11 : 24.

15. *Was Noah alive when Abram was born?*—No; he died two years before. Gen. 9 : 29.

16. *Was Adam alive when Noah was born?*—No; he died one hundred and twenty-six years before.

17. *Was Adam alive when Lamech was born?*—Yes.

18. *How many years did they live together?*—Fifty-six.

19. *How many years before Noah did Adam die?*—One hundred and twenty-six years before Noah was born.

20. *Do we not see by this how nearly Adam and Abram were contemporaries, although the world was nearly twenty hundred years old when Abram was born?*—There were only Lamech, Noah and Terah between them.

ABRAHAM. (Gen. 11-22.)

1. *What was the name of Abram's father?*—Terah. Gen. 11 : 26.

2. *Where was Abram born?*—In Ur of the Chaldees. Gen. 11:28.

3. *Did his father die there?*—No.

4. *To what land did his father remove?*—To Haran, on the way to Canaan.

5. *Which of Abram's brothers died before they left their native land?*—Haran. Gen. 11:28.

6. *Did he leave a son, and what was his name?*—Lot. Gen. 11:27.

7. *Did this grandson accompany Terah and Abram to Haran?*—Yes. Gen. 11:31.

8. *Where did Terah die?*—In Haran. Gen. 11:32.

CHAPTER 12.

9. *After his father's death, did Abram stay in Haran?*—No.

10. *Why did he remove?*—Because God told him so to do.

11. *Who went with him?*—Sarai his wife, and Lot and their servants.

12. *What relation was Lot to Abram?*—His nephew.

13. *Where are Ur, Haran and Canaan?*—Ur is in Chaldea, to the south-east of Babylon; Haran is in Mesopotamia, between Nineveh and Tarsus; and Canaan is on the eastern shore of the Mediterranean Sea, and is now called Palestine or the Holy Land.

14. *Where did Abram first settle, and what was his first act in the land of Canaan?*—At Sichem, in the plain of Moreh, near Samaria, where he built an altar to God, who appeared to him.

15. *What remarkable circumstance in the history of Jacob happened there?*—Jacob buried under an oak there the idols and earrings taken from his household. Gen. 35:4.

16. *What acts of Joshua's again distinguished this spot when he first subdued Canaan?*—His assembling of the tribes of Israel to renew their covenant with God; his appointing Shechem one of the cities of refuge; his reading the law between Mounts Gerizim and Ebal. Josh. 24:1, 25, 26; 20:7; 8:33.

17. *At what place did he rear the tabernacle, and at his death make a covenant with Israel?*—At *Shiloh*, near Sichem. Josh. 18:1. At Shechem. See No. 16.

18. *What event in the New Testament yet further endears the spot to us?*—Our Lord's conversation at Sychar with the woman of Samaria as he sat wearied upon Jacob's well. John 4:5-42.

19. *Did Abram continue to live at Sichem? Why?*—He removed to the neighborhood of Bethel, being doubtless directed by God to enter farther into the land. Gen. 12:8, 9; 13:17.

20. *What sin was Abram guilty of in Egypt?*—Of want of truthfulness and faith respecting Sarai his wife. Gen. 12:11-20.

21. *What does this teach us?*—We have before proved, both Jews and Gentiles, that they are all under sin; as it is written, There is none righteous, no, not one. Rom. 3:9, 10.

CHAPTER 13.

22. *Was Abram a rich or poor man?*—He was very rich. Gen. 13:2.

23. *How had Lot prospered?*—Very much. Gen. 13:5.

24. *What was the result?*—A quarrel between the herdmen of the two. Gen. 13:6, 7.

25. *How did Abram behave on this occasion?*—He proposed that they should part, and gave Lot the choice of the land. Gen. 13:8, 9.

26. *Do you think Lot behaved as well as Abram in this affair?*—He made no liberal offer in return, and thought more of the goodness of the pasture than of the character of the people. When choosing a family or place to reside in, we should know whether God is feared in it, and his truth faithfully taught.

27. *Had Lot cause to repent his choice?*—He suffered constant distress of mind, and at length narrowly escaped with his life, with the loss of his wife and of many of his family, and of most or all of his substance. Gen. 19:15-29.

Delivered just Lot, vexed with the filthy conversation of the wicked; for that righteous man dwelling among them, in seeing and hearing, vexed his righteous soul from day to day with their unlawful deeds. 2 Pet. 2:7, 8.

28. *Why? What kind of people did he go to sojourn amongst?*—Exceedingly wicked. Gen. 13:13.

29. *After this separation how did God manifest himself to Abram?*—He repeated to him his promises. Gen. 13:14-17.

CHAPTER 14.

30. *What doleful news did Abram soon hear of Lot?*—That Lot and his goods had been carried away in a war with Sodom and Gomorrah. Gen. 14:12, 13.

31. *How did Abram act?*—He armed his men and went in pursuit. Gen. 14:14.

32. *Was he successful? Give an account of the expedition?*—He divided his men, and attacked the enemy by night on several sides at once, routing them and recovering the prisoners and their goods. Gen. 14:15, 16.

33. *Who met Abram on his return?*—Melchizedek, king of Salem. Gen. 14:18.

34. *Where must Melchizedek have lived? Trace Abram's resting-place and the field of battle, and see what spot is between the two.*—At the present Jerusalem, which is between Dan and Mamre. Gen. 13:18.

35. *Is this mysterious person ever alluded to again in Scripture? Where?*—Heb. 6:20; 7:1-3.

36. *Of whom was he a type?*—Of Christ, in being both King and Priest; and also in his eternity, nothing being told us of his birth and death.

37. *What is a type?*—See page 2. Gen. 4:4.

38. *How did Abram behave after the battle, when urged by the king of Sodom to take part of the spoil?*—He declined taking anything but some food for his men. Gen. 14:21-24.

CHAPTER 15.

39. *What wonderful prophecy does this chapter record?*—That Abram's seed or descendants should be in number as the stars. Gen. 15:5.

40. *Had Abram at this time any children?*—No. Gen. 15:3.

41. *To what did God compare the number of his seed?*—See No. 39.

42. *Did Abram believe the Lord?*—Yes.

43. *What was his faith accounted or reckoned?*—For righteousness. Gen. 15:6.

44. *Is faith, then, very precious in the estimation of God?*—Yes, for his Son's sake.

45. *What is faith?*—That belief in Christ, as our own Saviour, which unites us to him, and makes us righteous before God in and through him.

46. *Does this account concern us?*—Now, it was not written for his sake alone, that it was imputed to him; but for us also, to whom it shall be imputed, if we believe on Him that raised up Jesus our Lord from the dead; who was delivered for our offences, and was raised again for our justification. Rom. 4:23-25.

47. *How much land did God promise to Abram?*—From a river in or near Egypt to the Euphrates. Gen. 15:18-21.

CHAPTER 16.

48. Who was Hagar? — One of Sarai's waiting-maids. Gen. 16:1.

49. Why did Abram take her to be his wife? —That Sarai might, by her, have children that would be reckoned as her own, and from whom the Messiah might come. Gen. 16:2.

50. Did Sarai use her kindly? —Hagar, when likely to have children, despised her mistress, and Sarai dealt hardly with her. Gen. 16:4-6.

51. What did Hagar do? —She ran away.

52. Did the Lord approve of Hagar running away from her mistress? —No; he ordered her to return and submit herself. Gen. 16:9.

Servants, be subject to your masters with all fear; not only to the good and gentle, but also to the froward. For this is thankworthy, if a man for conscience toward God endure grief, suffering wrongfully. For what glory is it, if, when ye be buffeted for your faults, ye shall take it patiently? but if, when ye do well, and suffer for it, ye take it patiently, this is acceptable with God. 1 Pet. 2:18-20.

53. What did God promise her? —That he would multiply her seed exceedingly; and the Arabians have sprung from her. Gen. 16:10.

54. After she returned what event happened? —She had a son.

55. What name was given to Hagar's son? —Abram called him Ishmael.

56. How old was Abram when Ishmael was born? —Eighty-six.

CHAPTER 17.

57. When Abram was ninety-nine years of age, what further covenant did God enter into with him? —He renewed his promise that he should have a great posterity, and covenanted to be his God, and to be *their* God. Gen. 17:1-8.

58. How did Abram show his love to Ishmael? —He prayed that he might live before God, or be favored by him. Gen. 17:18.

59. Did God accept Abram's prayer? —He blessed Ishmael, and promised to make him a great nation. Gen. 17:20.

60. Who was to be the promised seed? —Isaac, who was not yet born, and with whom God established his covenant. Gen. 17:19.

61. How long did God fix for the fulfillment of his promise to Abram and his wife? —A whole year. Gen. 17:21.

62. How did the Lord alter their names? —From Abram, or "high father," to Abraham, or, "multitude of nations;" and from Sarai, "my princess," to Sarah, or "princess of a multitude."

63. What does the name Abraham signify? —See No. 62.

64. What does Sarah's name express? —See No. 62.

65. How old was Ishmael when he was circumcised? —Thirteen.

CHAPTER 18.

66. Where was Mamre? —Near Hebron, in Judah. Gen. 13:18.

67. What remarkable event happened to Abraham there? —Three angels or heavenly visitors appeared to him in the form of men.

68. What is said of this visit in Heb. 13:2? —Be not forgetful to entertain strangers; for thereby some have entertained angels unawares.

69. Did Abraham at first know whom he was entertaining? How did he find it out? —He took them at first for ordinary travelers, but found out, by what one of them said, that they were angels and the Son of God. Gen. 18:10, 14.

70. What is Abraham called in Isa. 41:8? —The friend of God. James 2:23.

71. How did Sarah displease the Lord at this time? —By laughing within herself at the unlikelihood of what he said.

72. What was she tempted to do when the Lord expressed his displeasure? —To deny that she had laughed.

73. When the three heavenly visitors had eaten with Abraham, did they all depart from him together? —The Angel, Son of God, remained, and the other two angels went toward Sodom. Gen. 18:22.

74. Who stayed, and who went? —See No. 73.

75. To what place did those who departed go? —See No. 73.

76. Why did they visit Sodom? —To destroy it and to rescue Lot.

77. How came Abraham to know the purpose of their visit to Sodom? —From what the Lord said to him. Gen. 18:20, 21.

78. Did Abraham venture to plead for the city? How? —By six times asking the Lord to spare it if there were fifty, forty-five, forty, thirty, twenty, and even ten, righteous persons in it. Gen. 18:23-32.

79. Did God permit him to go on as long as he would? How did the Lord reply? —The Lord put no check upon his intercession, and consented to do all that he asked.

80. What should this teach us? —To persevere in prayer. Men ought always to pray, and not to faint. Luke 18:1.

Who can tell if God will turn and repent, and turn away from his fierce anger, that we perish not? And God saw their works, that they turned from their evil way; and God repented of the evil that he had said that he would do unto them; and he did it not. But it displeased Jonah exceedingly, and he was very angry. And he prayed unto the Lord, and said, I pray thee, O Lord, was not this my saying, when I was yet in my country? Therefore I fled before unto Tarshish: for I knew that thou art a gracious God, and merciful, slow to anger, and of great kindness, and repentest thee of the evil. Jonah 3:9, 10-4:1, 2.

81. Who has turned away the righteous anger of God from us, and yet pleads our cause? —If any man sin, we have an Advocate with the Father, Jesus Christ the righteous: and he is the propitiation for our sins: and not for ours only, but also for the sins of the whole world. 1 John 2:1, 2.

CHAPTER 19.

82. Where did Lot dwell? —In Sodom.

83. What is said of him in 2 Pet. 2:9? —The Lord knoweth how to deliver the godly out of temptations, and to reserve the unjust unto the day of judgment to be punished.

84. What happened to him one evening as he sat in the gate of the city? —Two angels came to him. Gen. 18:22; 19:1.

85. Who did those persons prove to be? —See No. 84.

86. For what did they visit Sodom? —To destroy it and to rescue Lot.

87. Did they find it as wicked as they expected? —It could hardly be worse than it was. Gen. 18:21.

88. In what way did they punish the men who wished to get into Lot's house? —They struck them blind. Gen. 19:11.

89. How many of Lot's family believed the warning and fled with him? —His wife and two daughters. Gen. 19:16.

90. Did all these eventually escape? Describe the circumstances of Lot's wife? —The daughters escaped, but his wife looked back and became a pillar of salt. Gen. 19:26.

91. How are we reminded of this in the New Testament? —In the days of Lot they did eat, they drank, they bought, they sold, they planted, they builded; but the same day that Lot went out of Sodom it rained fire and brimstone from heaven and destroyed them all. Even thus shall it be in the day when the Son of man is revealed. In that day, he which shall be on the housetop, and his stuff in the house, let him not come down to take it away: and he that is in the field, let him likewise not return back. Remember Lot's wife. Luke 17 : 28-32.

92. *Does there remain any relic of this awful event at the present day?*—The Dead Sea, with its deadly waters.

93. *Of what is the overthrow of Sodom and Gomorrah a type?*—Of the future destruction of the world by fire.

94. *What did the angel say to Lot when he pleaded for Zoar?*—That he would not overthrow it. Gen. 19 : 20-22.

95. *What does that teach us?*—The Lord is not slack concerning his promise, as some men count slackness; but is long-suffering to us-ward, not willing that any should perish, but that all should come to repentance. 2 Pet. 3 : 9.

CHAPTER 20.

96. *Into what disgraceful fault were Abraham and Sarah again betrayed at Gerar?*—Untruthfulness and distrust, in concealing that they were man and wife.

97. *How did God preserve them?*—By warning Abimelech in a dream.

98. *How did Abimelech behave?*—He immediately restored to Abraham his wife (whom he had intended to marry) and made him a handsome present.

99. *Did not Sarah deserve the reproof which Abimelech gave her?*—She needed the reproof that her husband was her proper protector.

100. *How did the Lord put honor on Abraham?*—He heard his prayer for Abimelech and his family.

CHAPTER 21.

101. *When did God perform his promise to Sarah?*—At the end of the year, the time fixed. Gen. 21 : 2.

102. *By what name was this child of promise called?*—Isaac, meaning "laughter" or "joy."

103. *What circumstance occurred on the day Isaac was weaned?*—Abraham made a great feast. Gen. 21 : 8.

104. *What did Sarah wish Abraham to do?*—To send away Hagar and Ishmael. Gen. 21 : 9, 10.

105. *Who confirmed Sarah's wish?*—God himself, to carry out his purposes as to both Isaac and Ishmael. Gen. 21 : 12, 13.

106. *How did Abraham act?*—He sent them away provided with bread and water, and doubtless commended to the care of God. Gen. 21 : 14.

107. *What became of Hagar and Ishmael?*—They lived at last in the wilderness of Paran, in Arabia Petræa. Gen. 21 : 14-21.

108. *Who at the present day are the descendants of Ishmael?*—The Arabs.

109. *Who was Abraham's rightful heir and child of promise?*—Isaac. Gen. 21 : 1-3, 12.

110. *What testimony to Abraham's God, by a stranger, does this chapter record?*—King Abimelech said that God was with Abraham in all that he did. Gen. 21 : 22.

111. *What is the meaning of the word Beersheba?*—The "well of the oath." Gen. 21 : 31.

112. *Where was Abraham sojourning at this time?*—In the land of the Philistines. Gen. 21 : 34.

113. *Were the Philistines always friendly with Abraham's posterity, or the reverse? Is there any instance in Scripture?*—They were frequently at war with each other, as in the days of Samson and of David and Goliath.

CHAPTER 22.

114. *What was the greatest trial that Abraham's faith experienced?*—The command of God to make a burnt-offering of his only son Isaac, whom he loved.

115. *What is said of this act in Heb. 11 : 17-19?*—By faith Abraham, when he was tried, offered up Isaac; and he that had received the promises offered up his only begotten son, of whom it was said, That in Isaac shall thy seed be called: accounting that God was able to raise him up, even from the dead; from whence also he received him in a figure.

116. *What proof did Abraham give of his prompt obedience?*—He arose early in the morning and set out.

117. *Did he tell his son what he was about to do with him?*—No.

118. *When Isaac inquired for the lamb, what was Abraham's reply?*—That God would provide one. Gen. 22 : 8.

119. *To whom did Abraham allude?*—To Jesus Christ, the Lamb of God, which taketh away the sins of the world. "Your father Abraham rejoiced to see my day; he saw it, and was glad."—John 1 : 29; 8 : 56.

120. *When Isaac knew his father's intention, did he resist it?*—No.

121. *Was he able to have done so? How old was he at this time?*—Yes, as he was twenty-five years old.

122. *What is said of the Lord Jesus Christ when he was offered a sacrifice for sin?*—That he did it of himself.

Therefore doth my Father love me, because I lay down my life, that I might take it again. No man taketh it from me, but I lay it down of myself. I have power to lay it down, and I have power to take it again. This commandment have I received of my Father.—Let this mind be in you, which was also in Christ Jesus: who, being in the form of God, thought it not robbery to be equal with God: but made himself of no reputation, and took upon him the form of a servant, and was made in the likeness of men: and being found in fashion as a man, he humbled himself, and became obedient unto death, even the death of the cross. Wherefore God also hath highly exalted him, and given him a name which is above every name: that at the name of Jesus every knee should bow, of things in heaven, and things in earth, and things under the earth. John 10 : 17, 18; Phil. 2 : 5-10.

123. *Does the ram caught in the thicket and offered as a substitute for Isaac present a type?*—The ram would be without blemish, and Christ was without sin. He hath made Him to be sin for us who knew no sin, that we might be made the righteousness of God in him. 2 Cor. 5 : 21.

124. *By what name did Abraham call the place where this occurred? And what was the meaning of it?*—Jehovah-jireh, "the Lord will see or provide."

125. *Is Mount Moriah mentioned again in Scripture?*—Yes, in 2 Chron. 3 : 1. Then Solomon began to build the house of the Lord at Jerusalem in Mount Moriah, where the Lord appeared unto David, his father, in the place that David had prepared in the threshing-floor of Ornan the Jebusite. [But this is not now considered to be the same mountain.]

126. *What magnificent building stood on that mount?*—Solomon's temple.

127. *Give the account why this place was chosen for that building.*—See 125.

128. *What beautiful edifice now stands there?*—The mosque of Omar, a Mohammedan place of worship.

129. *What do the Jews feel when they see this?*—Doubtless deep grief, as they often visit a place near it called "the place of wailing."

130. *What special covenant did the Lord renew with Abraham at this time?*—That in Abraham's seed should all the nations of the earth be blessed. Gen. 22 : 15-18.

131 *Why is Nahor's posterity mentioned here?*—

Because one of them was Rebekah, Isaac's future wife.

ISAAC AND REBEKAH. (Gen. 23, 24.)

1. *How old was Sarah when she died?*—One hundred and twenty-seven years.

2. *Where did Abraham bury her?*—In the cave of Machpelah, near Mamre, Hebron or Kirjath-arba. Gen 23 : 2, 19.

3. *How did he obtain possession of this burying-place?*—By purchase from Ephron the Hittite. Gen. 23 : 3-18.

4. *What did that show?*—That Abraham had no land of his own. Gen. 23 : 4.

5. *How old was Isaac when his mother died?*—About thirty-seven.

6. *How many years did he live solitary and alone before he married?*—Forty years from his birth, and latterly near the well Lahai-roi, in the south country. Gen. 23 : 62.

7. *How did his father obtain a wife for him?*—He sent his steward to his own kindred in Mesopotamia for the purpose, after pledging him not to seek for one among the heathen around him. Gen. 24 : 2, 3, 4, 10. Be ye not unequally yoked together with unbelievers. Only in the Lord. 2 Cor. 6 : 14; 1 Cor. 7 : 39.

8. *Whom did Abraham send on this important mission?*—See No. 7.

9. *What was the name of this "eldest servant" of Abraham's house?*—Eliezer of Damascus. Gen. 15 : 2.

10. *How did this servant act?*—With prudence, prayerfulness, diligence and courtesy. Gen. 24 : 5-26.

11. *Did he succeed in his mission?*—He was led by God's providence to the house of Abraham's nephew, Bethuel, and obtained his daughter, Rebekah. Gen. 24 : 15, 51.

12. *Whom did he bring?*—See No. 11.

13. *What did he give to his young master's intended bride?*—Golden earrings, bracelets, jewels of silver and gold, and raiment, according to the custom of those lands and times. Gen. 24 : 22, 30, 53.

14. *How did he describe his master's possessions?*—That the Lord had greatly blessed him, and given him flocks and herds, silver and gold, etc. Gen. 24 : 35.

15. *Was she willing to leave her home on his report?*—She was. Gen. 24 : 58.

16. *Did she find it all true?*—Doubtless she did. Gen. 13 : 2.

17. *Who came out to meet her?*—Isaac himself. Gen. 24 : 62, 63.

18. *Where did he take her, and how did he feel toward her?*—To his mother's tent, and she became his wife, and he loved her. Gen. 24 : 67.

19. *Is this interesting account a type of spiritual things?*—Now all these things happened unto them for ensamples; and they are written for our admonition, upon whom the ends of the world are come. For whatsoever things were written aforetime were written for our learning, that we through patience and comfort of the Scriptures might have hope. 1 Cor. 10 : 11: Rom. 15 : 4.

20. *Of whom is Abraham the type here?*—Of God the Father.

21. *Of whom is Rebekah the type?*—Of his Church and people.

22. *Of whom is Eliezer the type?*—Of God's Spirit, who finds those who are far from him, and brings them to him.

23. *Of whom is Isaac the type?*—Of Christ, the Bridegroom of the Church.

24. *And of what great event is the closing scene the type?*—Of the Church, the bride of Christ, being presented to him spotless at the last day

25. *How are we interested in this?*—We must each of us be found by him, and given to him, and adorned and sanctified by him, if we seek to live with him eternally.

JACOB AND ESAU. (Gen. 25, 26, 27.)

1. *Whom did Abraham marry after Sarah's death?* Keturah. Gen. 25 : 1.

2. *How many children had she?*—Six.

3. *How did he portion them?*—He made them gifts.

4. *To whom did he leave his great riches?*—To Isaac

5. *How old was Abraham when he died?*—One hundred and seventy-five years.

6. *Who buried him?*—Isaac and Ishmael.

7. *By what title are Ishmael's twelve sons called?*—Princes.

8. *What was Isaac's occupation, although his father's heir?*—That of a herdsman and shepherd.

9. *Of whom is he a type in this?*—Of Christ, who humbled himself, though Lord of all.

10. *How many sons had Isaac?*—Two—Esau and Jacob. Gen. 25 : 26.

11. *Were they born before Abraham's death?*—Yes, fifteen years. *Is there not a proof of this in the New Testament?*

By faith Abraham, when he was called to go out into a place which he should after receive for an inheritance, obeyed; and he went out, not knowing whither he went. By faith he sojourned in the land of promise, as in a strange country, dwelling in tabernacles with Isaac and Jacob, the heirs with him of the same promise. Heb. 11 : 8, 9.

12. *What was the difference personally between those two boys?*—Esau was red or hairy, and Jacob smooth. Gen. 25 : 25; 27 : 11.

13. *Did they grow up alike? Describe them?*—Esau was a skillful hunter, and Jacob a quiet man, fond of home. Gen. 25 : 27.

14. *Which was the first born?*—Esau.

15. *Did he value his birthright? The proof.*—He sold it, when hungry and faint, to Jacob for a dish of potted beans or other food. So thousands, for present pleasure, will risk or lose their souls.

16. *To whom did he sell it, and for what?*—See No. 15.

CHAPTER 26.

17. *What was Isaac's character?*—His conduct in this chapter entitles him to the character of a peacemaker. Gen. 26 : 14-31.

Blessed are the peacemakers: for they shall be called the children of God. Matt. 5 : 9.

18. *What covenant did God renew with Isaac?*—The covenant he had made with Abraham. Gen. 26 : 2-5

19. *What direction did God give Isaac as to his place of sojourn?*—That he should not go down into Egypt, but dwell among the Philistines at Gerar. Gen. 26 : 1, 2, 6.

20. *How did he act there?*—He was guilty of the same weakness and sin about his wife as Abraham was. Gen. 26 : 7-11.

21. *How did the Philistines behave toward Isaac?*—They envied his prosperity, and maliciously stopped up his old wells and claimed possession of his new ones. Gen. 26 : 14-21.

22. *Did he return evil for evil?*—No; he removed more than once out of their way.

23. *Whom did Esau choose as his wives?*—Judith and Bashemath, Hittites. Gen. 26 : 34.

24. *Did his parents approve his choice?*—No; they were grieved by it.

CHAPTER 27.

25. *What was it the custom of the ancient patriarchs to do before their death?*—To bless their children.

26. *Which son did Isaac consider his first-born?*—Esau. Gen. 27 : 1-4.

27. *How had he forfeited that honor?*—By selling it to his brother. Gen. 25: 29–34.

28. *Did Jacob allow Esau to obtain the blessing of the birthright?*—No; he pretended to be Esau, to prevent it.

29. *Did he go the right way to work?*—No; he should have left it to God to secure him the blessing in his own time and way.

30. *Who shared his sin with him?*—His mother told him how to act.

31. *How did Esau feel when he found that he had lost his blessing?*—He was in great distress of mind.

32. *Had he not voluntarily sold it to Jacob some years before?*—Yes; about forty-five years before.

33. *Whom had he then to blame?*—Chiefly himself.

34. *Whom shall we have to blame if we, like Esau, despise God's blessing now?*—Ourselves alone.

35. *What lesson should Esau's bitter grief teach us?*—To earnestly seek God's blessing, and to carefully cherish it.

JACOB. (Gen. 28–35.)

1. *What was Jacob's general character?*—One of artifice and deceit.

2. *Did God then choose him for his natural goodness?*—No; there is no one whom he can choose on this account.

I will have compassion on whom I will have compassion. So then it is not of him that willeth, nor of him that runneth, but of God that showeth mercy. Rom. 9: 15, 16.

3. *What should this teach us?*—That, as we all have sinned, it is only by the faith that unites us to Christ that we can be righteous before God.

For all have sinned, and come short of the glory of God; being justified freely by his grace through the redemption that is in Christ Jesus; whom God hath set forth to be a propitiation through faith in his blood, to declare his righteousness for the remission of sins that are past, through the forbearance of God; therefore being justified by faith, we have peace with God through our Lord Jesus Christ. Rom. 4: 23–25; 5: 1.

4. *How did Esau treat Jacob after Jacob had obtained the blessing?*—He hated him and determined to kill him. Gen. 27: 41.

5. *What did Jacob's parents resolve to do?*—To send him to Haran out of Esau's way, and to get a wife among the daughters of Laban. Gen. 27: 42–28: 2.

6. *What remarkable thing occurred to Jacob on his way to Syria?*—He had a vision by night, and a renewal of God's promise and blessing. Gen. 28: 10–15.

7. *Did he fully understand it? Can you explain his feelings?*—He could not fully understand what he saw, but seems to have felt that fear and awe which sinners must feel in the presence of a holy God.

8. *Can we see the meaning?*—We, happily, are taught to see *Christ* as the ladder of communication between heaven and earth.

Hereafter ye shall see heaven open, and the angels of God ascending and descending upon the Son of man. John 1: 51.

9. *Whom did the latter typify?*—See No. 8.

10. *How did Jesus unite heaven and earth?*—By his birth, death, resurrection and ascension, as God and man in one.

11. *What promise did Jacob make at this place?*—That the Lord should be his God, and that he would devote to him a tenth of all that he should give him. Gen. 28: 20–22.

CHAPTERS 29, 30, 31.

12. *Whom did Jacob first see when he got to Syria?*—The servants of Laban, and then Rachel his daughter. Gen. 29: 3–5, 9.

13. *How did his uncle Laban receive him?*—With kindness and affection. Gen. 29: 13, 14.

14. *What did he promise him?*—That he should have Rachel for his wife, in return for seven years' service.

15. *Did Laban afterward fulfill his promise?*—No; he gave him Leah instead.

16. *How many wives had Jacob?*—Both Rachel and Leah; and afterward their handmaids Bilhah and Zilpah by their mistresses' desire, and according to the custom of the time. See Gen. 16: 2.

17. *How many years did Jacob serve Laban before he allowed him to have any cattle for his wages?*—Fourteen years. *Gen. 30: 26–30.

18. *Did Jacob succeed in obtaining large possessions of flocks and herds?*—Yes. Gen. 30: 43.

19. *How did the sons of Laban feel when they observed this?*—They were displeased at the success of his plan.

20. *What did Jacob and his wives resolve to do?*—Jacob, at the command of God, resolved to return to Canaan, and Rachel and Leah resolved to go with him. Gen. 31: 3, 14–16.

21. *What wicked act was Rachel guilty of?*—Of stealing her father's images. Gen. 31: 19.

22. *What did it prove?*—That she and her father still worshiped heathen gods as well as the true God.

Joshua said unto all the people, Thus saith the Lord God of Israel, Your fathers dwelt on the other side of the flood in old time, even Terah, the father of Abraham, and the father of Nachor: and they served other gods. Josh. 24: 2.

23. *What did Laban do when he found Jacob had left him?*—He pursued him.

24. *How did God protect Jacob from Laban's anger?*—By warning Laban in a dream.

25. *How did the interview between Laban and Jacob terminate?*—It ended peacefully and well. Gen. 31: 44, 55.

CHAPTER 32.

26. *What is the meaning of the word Mahanaim?*—Two hosts or camps. Gen. 32: 1, 2.

27. *Why was the place so called?*—Because a company of angels met Jacob there.

28. *How ought Jacob to have felt when he saw this angelic guard?*—That he was secure against all harm.

The angel of the Lord encampeth round about them that fear him, and delivereth them. Ps. 34: 7.

29. *How did he feel when he heard his brother Esau was coming to meet him?*—He was greatly afraid and distressed. Gen. 32: 7.

30. *How did Jacob act?*—He divided his people and flocks into two bands. Gen. 32: 7, 8.

31. *What occurred to Jacob before he went over the brook?*—A heavenly Being wrestled with him during the night.

32. *How long did the Angel wrestle with Jacob?*—Until break of day.

33. *What name did Jacob give to the place where this occurred?*—Peniel, or "the face of God."

34. *Why did he so call it?*—Because he had seen God face to face. Gen. 32: 30.

35. *Whom, then, may we suppose that wondrous Person to be with whom he wrestled?*—The Son of God; as no man hath seen God himself, who is a Spirit, at any time. John 4: 24; 1 John 4: 12.

36. *What spiritual act does this typify?*—Prayer, in which, if real, we have communion or intercourse of spirit with God.

37. *Are we interested in it?*—It encourages earnest perseverance in prayer.

He spake a parable unto them to this end, that men ought always to pray, and not to faint; saying, There was in a city a judge, which feared not God, neither regarded man; and there was a widow in that city, and she came unto him, saying, Avenge me of mine adversary. And he would not for a while; but afterward he said within himself, Though I fear not God, nor regard man; yet because this widow troubleth me, I will avenge her, lest by her continual coming she weary me. And the Lord said, Hear what the unjust judge saith. And shall not God avenge his own elect, which cry day and night unto him, though he bear long with them? I tell you that he will avenge them speedily. Luke 18 : 1–8.

So run, that ye may obtain. 1 Cor. 9 : 24.

CHAPTERS 33, 34, 35.

38. *How did Jacob and Esau meet?*—In brotherly affection and peace, in answer to Jacob's prayer.

39. *Where did Jacob pitch his tent and make booths for his cattle when he got into Canaan?*—At Succoth. Gen. 33 : 17.

40. *Name the two instances in Scripture where this purchase is afterward referred to?*—His purchase at Shalem, a city of Shechem, is referred to in John 4 : 5, 6, and Acts 7 : 15, 16. Gen. 33 : 18, 19.

Then cometh he to a city of Samaria, which is called Sychar, near to the parcel of ground that Jacob gave to his son Joseph. Now Jacob's well was there. So Jacob went down into Egypt, and died, he and our fathers, and were carried over into Sychem, and laid in the sepulchre that [he, like] Abraham bought for a sum of money of the sons of Emmor the father of Sychem.

41. *What two mountains was Shechem situate between?*—Gerizim and Ebal.

42. *Where was the tabernacle first reared in the land of Canaan?*—At Gilgal on the Jordan. (Not the Gilgal in Shechem.)

43. *Where did Joshua make his solemn covenant with Israel before his death?*—Joshua gathered all the tribes of Israel to Shechem, and called for the elders of Israel, and for their heads, and for their judges, and for their officers; and they presented themselves before God. Josh. 24 : 1.

44. *Where was the first idol temple built in Israel?*—In Shechem. 1 Kings 12 : 25–33.

45. *What act of treachery was Simeon and Levi guilty of to Shechem, the founder of this city?*—They slew him when, through their own contrivance, he was unprepared to resist them. Gen. 34 : 13, 25, 26.

46. *What did God at this time desire Jacob to do?*—To go and live at Bethel. Gen. 35 : 1.

47. *How did Jacob prepare for this journey?*—By calling upon his people to put away their idols, and be clean and change their garments.

48. *How did God preserve him from the anger of the inhabitants of the land? What proof is there that God's care of his people is the same now as then?*—By making the inhabitants afraid of him and of his God. He preserveth the souls of his saints; he delivereth them out of the hand of the wicked. Gen. 35 : 5 ; Ps. 97 : 10.

49. *What sorrowful event happened at Bethel?*—The death of Rebekah's nurse. Gen. 35 : 8.

50. *What peculiar name did God confirm, and what special blessing did he give, to Jacob at this place?*—The name of Israel and the gift of the land of Canaan. Gen. 35 : 9–12.

51. *What great loss did Jacob sustain when near Bethlehem?*—The death of Rachel. Gen. 35 : 19.

52. *How many children had Jacob at this time?*—Twelve. Gen. 35 : 22–26.

53. *How far south did Jacob travel?*—To Mamre, near Hebron.

54. *Who resided there?*—Isaac.

55. *How many years did Jacob live with his father before his father died?*—About three years.

56. *Who united together to bury Isaac?*—Esau and Jacob

JACOB AND HIS SONS. (Gen. 37.)

1. *To which son did Jacob show a great partiality?*—To Joseph. Gen. 37 : 3.

2. *Why did Jacob feel this, and how did he show it?*—Because he was the son of his old age. By making him a coat of many colors.

3. *What character did the other sons of Jacob display?*—An envious and malicious one.

4. *Why did they hate Joseph?*—Because of their father's special love to him.

5. *Did he deserve it? Had his dreams anything to do with it? What were they?*—No. Yes. That his brothers' sheaves made obeisance to his, and that the sun, moon and eleven stars did the same to him.

6. *How did Joseph's father feel when he heard one of the dreams?*—He was surprised at the dream, but doubtless felt it was from God. Gen. 37 : 11.

7. *How did Joseph get into his brethren's power?*—On Jacob sending him to them to see if they were well. Gen. 37 : 14.

8. *What did they do with him?*—They threw him into a pit. Gen. 37 : 24.

9. *How old was Joseph at this time?*—Sixteen.

10. *What story did they make up to their father?*—That they had found his coat bloody, and that he had been killed by a wild beast.

11. *What difference was there in Reuben's behavior toward Joseph to the rest of his brethren?*—He dissuaded them from killing him. Gen. 37 : 21, 22.

12. *How did Jacob receive the news?*—He mourned and refused to be comforted.

13. *How did the Midianites dispose of Joseph?*—They took him out of the pit and sold him to some Ishmaelites. Gen. 37 : 28.

14. *What connection was there between Abraham and the Midianites?*—Midian was a son of Keturah, his second wife. Gen. 25 : 1, 2.

15. *What connection was there between Moses and the Midianites?*—He lived among them and took his wife thence. Ex. 2 : 15, 21.

16. *What connection was there between Balaam and the Midianites?*—He lived among them and was killed in battle by the Israelites.

17. *What event in Gideon's history was connected with the Midianites?*—The appearance to him of the angel Son of God before he fought against and overthrew them. Judg. 6, 7.

JOSEPH IN EGYPT. (Gen. 39, 40, 41.)

1. *To whom did the Ishmaelites sell Joseph?*—To Potiphar, captain of Pharaoh's guard. Gen. 39 : 1.

2. *What office did Potiphar appoint Joseph to fill?*—Overseer of his house. Gen. 39 : 4.

3. *How was God's favor manifested to Joseph in this situation?*—By everything prospering under his care. Gen. 39 : 2–5.

4. *Was he not deprived of his situation by false accusation?*—Yes, through the wickedness of his master's wife, who was embittered against him by his virtue and his fear of God. Gen. 39 : 7–18.

5. *What unjust punishment was suffered by Joseph?*—He was put in prison.

6. *Did the Lord forsake him?*—He was with him and showed him mercy.

7. *How did the keeper of the prison behave to Joseph?*—He gave him the entire charge of the prison.

8. *What kind of prison was this? Who were principally confined there?*—A prison connected with Potiphar's house, and in which state prisoners were kept.

9. *What remarkable circumstance occurred to two of those prisoners?*—They had dreams which troubled them.

10. *How did Joseph assist them in their perplexity?*—He interpreted their dreams. Gen. 40.

11. *Were his words found true? Name the result.*—The chief butler was restored, and the chief baker was hanged, as Joseph had foretold.

12. *How did Pharaoh's butler behave to Joseph?*—He forgot his promise to get Joseph released.

13. *What brought his dream again to his mind?*—A dream which Pharaoh had. Gen. 41: 1-13.

14. *Could the magicians of Egypt interpret Pharaoh's dream?*—They could not. Gen. 41: 8.

15. *For whom did he send?*—For Joseph, whom the butler had named.

16. *Did Joseph take the honor of interpretation to himself, or confess God's power before the king?*—He said, It is not in me; *God* shall give Pharaoh an answer of peace. Gen. 41: 16.

17. *Name a king who was smitten with worms and died because he gave* not *God the glory?*—Herod Agrippa, king of Judea. Acts 12: 23.

18. *Name another king who was driven from men, and was for seven years like a beast, because he gave not glory to God?*—Nebuchadnezzar, who said, Is not this great Babylon, that I have built for the house of the kingdom by the might of my power, and for the honor of my majesty? While the word was in the king's mouth, there fell a voice from heaven, saying, O King Nebuchadnezzar, to thee it is spoken, The kingdom is departed from thee. And they shall drive thee from men, and thy dwelling shall be with the beasts of the field: they shall make thee to eat grass as oxen, and seven times shall pass over thee, until thou know that the Most High ruleth in the kingdom of men, and giveth it to whomsoever he will. Dan. 4: 30-32.

19. *How was the latter part of verse 30 in 1 Sam. 2 fulfilled in Joseph's case?*—By his being made ruler over all Egypt. He had honored God by his resistance of temptation and his faithfulness to his duties, and now God honored *him*. Them that honor *me* I will honor. Gen. 41: 43.

20. *How old was Joseph at this time?*—Thirty. Gen. 41: 46.

21. *What name did Pharaoh give Joseph, and what is the meaning of it?*—Zaphnath-paaneah, a "revealer of secrets," or "the man to whom secrets are revealed."

22. *What were the names of Joseph's wife and his two sons?*—Asenath, Manasseh and Ephraim. 41: 45, 51, 52.

23. *What did Joseph do during the seven years of plenty?*—He laid up the food in the cities. Gen. 41: 48.

24. *When the people cried to Pharaoh for bread, to whom did he send them?*—To Joseph. Gen. 41: 55.

25. *Was this great famine confined to the land of Egypt?*—It was over all the face of the earth, or all that part of it. Gen. 41: 56, 57.

JACOB AND HIS SONS IN EGYPT. (Gen. 42–50.)

1. *Where was Jacob living at this time?*—In Canaan. Gen. 42: 5.

2. *Did the famine extend to the land of Canaan?*—Yes. Gen. 42: 5.

3. *How did they procure bread?*—Ten of Jacob's sons went to buy corn in Egypt. Gen. 42: 3.

4. *How did Joseph behave to his brethren when he saw them?*—He made himself strange to them and spoke roughly to them, but not from a spirit of revenge. Gen. 42: 7.

5. *Did they recognize him?*—No. Gen. 42: 8.

6. *How did Jacob feel when they returned and told him the news?*—He felt that all things were against him, and that he should lose Benjamin also. But all things

work together for good to them that love God. Gen. 42: 36, 38; Rom. 8: 28.

7. *Whom did they take with them on their second journey?*—Benjamin. Gen. 43: 15.

8. *What proof have we in this chapter of the truth of Num. 13: 21-27?*—The fruits, honey and spices they took with them. Gen. 43: 11.

They went up and searched the land. And they ascended by the south, and came unto Hebron. And they came unto the brook of Eshcol, and cut down from thence a branch with one cluster of grapes, and they bare it between two upon a staff: and they brought of the pomegranates and of the figs. And they went and came to Moses and to Aaron; and brought back word unto them and unto all the congregation, and showed them the fruit of the land. And they told him and said, We came unto the land whither thou sentest us, and surely it floweth with milk and honey; and this is the fruit of it.

9. *How did Joseph feel when he saw Benjamin stand among his brethren?*—His love was greatly excited, and he retired to weep. Gen. 43: 30, 31.

10. *What closer relationship was there between Joseph and Benjamin than between Joseph and his other brothers?*—They had the same mother, Rachel. Gen. 30: 22-24; 35: 16-18.

11. *What effect did Joseph's kindness have on them?*—They wondered at it. Gen. 43: 33.

12. *What was Joseph's intention in all this treatment?*—To make them conscious of their sin and sorry for it, and to better carry out his plans.

13. *Did it have the effect he desired?*—It had. Gen. 42: 21; 44: 16.

14. *How did Judah behave at this trying time?*—He begged that Benjamin might be allowed to go back with the rest, and offered to remain himself behind as surety for his return. Gen. 44: 18, 33.

15. *Of whom was he a type in this?*—Of Jesus Christ, our Substitute, who suffered in our stead.

16. *How was Joseph's tender heart affected by all this?*—He could bear it no longer, but wept aloud, and told them he was Joseph their brother. Gen. 45: 1-4.

17. *How did they feel when they knew this mighty prince was their own brother?*—They could not answer him for fear. Gen. 45: 3.

18. *What proofs did he give them of it?*—He gave proofs of his love and power by the rich presents he made them and the promise of a home and plenty in Egypt. Gen. 45: 17-23.

19. *Did Joseph and his father ever meet again?*—They met in Egypt, whither Jacob and all his family had come. Gen. 46: 29.

20. *How?*—See No. 19.

21. *What proof have we in this of the truth of Rom. 8: 28?*—What Jacob thought to be against him proved to be for his good. (See No. 6.)

22. *Where in the land of Egypt did Jacob and his family dwell?*—In the land of Goshen. Gen. 47: 1.

23. *Had the Egyptians any particular antipathy to shepherds?*—They disliked shepherds and cattle-dealers from foreign lands for slaughtering their sacred animals, or from having formerly invaded and plundered their country.

24. *Why?*—See No. 23.

25. *Was Jacob introduced to Pharaoh?*—Yes, and gave him his blessing. Gen. 47: 7.

26. *What proof have we in Jacob's remark to Pharaoh of the truth of Ps. 90?*—The longest life is but short to look back on.

For all our days are passed away in thy wrath: we spend our years as a tale that is told. The days of our years are threescore years and ten; and if by reason of strength they be fourscore years, yet is their strength labor and sorrow; for it is soon cut off, and we fly away. Ps. 90: 9, 10.

27. *What peculiar blessing did Jacob give to the sons of Joseph?*—He placed his right hand on the younger instead of the elder. Gen. 48 : 17-19.

28. *In his prophetical blessing of his twelve sons, to whom did he give the birthright?*—Gen. 48 : 8.

Now the sons of Reuben the first-born of Israel (for he was the first-born; but, forasmuch as he defiled his father's bed, his birthright was given unto the sons of Joseph the son of Israel: and the genealogy is not to be reckoned after the birthright. For Judah prevailed above his brethren, and of him came the chief ruler; but the birthright was Joseph's). 1 Chron. 5 : 1, 2.

29. *What was the special blessing of Judah?*—That ut of his family the Messiah should come. Gen. 49 : 10.

30. *How was this fulfilled?*—Our Lord sprang out of Juda. Heb. 7 : 14.

The book of the generation of Jesus Christ, the son of David, the son of Abraham. Abraham begat Isaac; and Isaac begat Jacob; and Jacob begat Judas and his brethren; and Judas begat Phares. Matt. 1 : 1-3.

31. *To whom is allusion made in chap. 49, verse 24, in Joseph's blessing? Compare Num. 13 : 8, 16 with Num. 27 : 15-23.*—To Joshua.

Of the tribe of Ephraim, Oshea the son of Nun. And Moses called Oshea the son of Nun Jehoshua. And Moses spake unto the Lord, saying, Let the Lord, the God of the spirits of all flesh, set a man over the congregation, which may go out before them, and which may go in before them, and which may lead them out, and which may bring them in; that the congregation of the Lord be not as sheep which have no shepherd. And the Lord said unto Moses, Take thee Joshua the son of Nun, a man in whom is the spirit, and lay thine hand upon him: and set him before Eleazar the priest, and before all the congregation; and give him a charge in their sight. And thou shalt put some of thine honor upon him, that all the congregation of the children of Israel may be obedient. And he shall stand before Eleazar the priest, who shall ask counsel for him after the judgment of Urim before the Lord: at his word shall they go out, and at his word they shall come in, both he and all the children of Israel with him, even all the congregation. And Moses did as the Lord commanded him; and he took Joshua, and set him before Eleazar the priest, and before all the congregation; and he laid his hands upon him, and gave him a charge, as the Lord commanded by the hand of Moses.

32. *How was Joshua in this a type of Jesus?*—As Joshua led the Israelites in the wilderness and into the promised land, so Jesus is the guide of his people upon earth and the means of their entrance into heaven.

Then said Jesus unto them again, Verily, verily, I say unto you, I am the door of the sheep. All that ever came before me are thieves and robbers: but the sheep did not hear them. I am the door: by me if any man enter in, he shall be saved, and shall go in and out, and find pasture. My sheep hear my voice, and I know them, and they follow me. John 10 : 7-9, 27.

33. *What other Joshua was a type of Jesus under the double figure of a branch and a stone?*—And he showed me Joshua the high priest standing before the angel of the Lord. And the angel of the Lord protested unto Joshua, saying, Thus saith the Lord of hosts; If thou wilt walk in my ways, and if thou wilt keep my charge, then thou shalt also judge my house, and shalt also keep my courts, and I will give thee places to walk among these that stand by. Hear now, O Joshua the high priest, thou, and thy fellows that sit before thee: for they are men wondered at; for, behold, I will bring forth my servant the BRANCH. For behold the stone that I have laid before Joshua; upon one stone shall be seven eyes: behold, I will engrave the graving thereof, saith the Lord of hosts, and I will remove the iniquity of that land in one day. Zech. 3 : 1, 6-9.

34. *What does Isaiah prophesy of this stone?*—Thus saith the Lord God, Behold, I lay in Zion for a foundation a stone, a tried stone, a precious cornerstone, a sure foundation. Isa. 28 : 16.

35. *Give the texts in which the Lord Jesus speaks of himself under this figure?*—Jesus saith unto them, Did ye never read in the Scriptures, The stone which the builders rejected, the same is become the head of the corner: and whosoever shall fall on this stone shall be broken: but on whomsoever it shall fall, it will grind him to powder. Matt. 21 : 42, 44; Mark 12 : 10; Luke 20 : 17, 18.

36. *Find the text in which the apostle Peter speaks of the Lord Jesus under this figure?*—To whom coming, as unto a living stone, disallowed indeed of men, but chosen of God, and precious, ye also, as lively stones, are built up a spiritual house, an holy priesthood, to offer up spiritual sacrifices, acceptable to God by Jesus Christ. Wherefore also it is contained in the Scripture, Behold, I lay in Sion a chief cornerstone, elect, precious: and he that believeth on him shall not be confounded. Unto you therefore which believe he is precious: but unto them which be disobedient, the stone which the builders disallowed, the same is made the head of the corner, and a stone of stumbling, and a rock of offence, even to them which stumble at the word, being disobedient: whereunto also they were appointed. 1 Pet. 2 : 4-8.

37. *Where was Jacob buried?*—In the cave of Machpelah. Gen. 50 : 13.

38. *What fears had Joseph's brethren after their father's death?*—That Joseph would ill-treat them and punish them. Gen. 50 : 15.

39. *How did Joseph behave to them?*—He comforted them and spoke kindly to them.

40. *Of whom were Joseph and his brethren types in this transaction?*—Of Christ and his forgiving love.

41. *When was Joseph buried?*—Not until the Israelites reached Canaan, above two hundred years after his death. Gen. 50 : 26.

And the bones of Joseph, which the children of Israel brought up out of Egypt, buried they in Shechem, in a parcel of ground which Jacob bought of the sons of Hamor, the father of Shechem, for an hundred pieces of silver. Josh. 24 : 32.

JOSEPH'S HISTORY.

1. *What great peculiarity marks the Bible histories?*—Their reference to our Lord Jesus Christ.

2. *Of whose history can this pre-eminently be said?*—Of Joseph's.

3. *To whom must we look to enlighten our minds when studying God's word?*—To God the Holy Spirit; saying, Open thou mine eyes, that I may behold wondrous things out of thy law. Ps. 119 : 18; 2 Pet. 1 : 20, 21.

4. *What did Jesus say in John 5 : 39?*—Search the Scriptures; for in them ye think ye have eternal life: and they are they which testify of me.

5. *And how did he upbraid the two disciples whom he overtook going to Emmaus?*—O fools, and slow of heart to believe all that the prophets have spoken! Luke 24 : 26.

6. *Is it not, then, our duty to seek for Jesus even so far back as the writings of Moses?*—They drank of that spiritual Rock that followed them; and that Rock was Christ. 1 Cor. 10 : 4.

7. *Who wrote Genesis?*—Moses.

8. *How was Joseph a type of Jesus, when he was at home, clothed in a beautiful robe, the darling of his father?*—In that Jesus shared his Father's glory and enjoyed his love.

Thou lovedst me before the foundation of the world. John 17 : 24.

9. *How was Joseph a type in going out to see after the welfare of his brethren?*—In Jesus graciously visiting his brethren in human nature.

The Son of man is come to seek and to save that which was lost. Luke 19 : 10.

10. *How in their treatment of him?*—In being sold by Judas and delivered to death by the Jews.

He came unto his own, and his own received him not. John 1 : 11.

When the husbandmen saw the son, they said among themselves, This is the heir; come, let us kill him, and let us seize on his inheritance. Matt. 21 : 38.

11. *How in his dreams?*—In his prophecies of his future kingdom and glory. Matt. 25 : 31, 32.

12. *How in the false accusations brought against him?*—In his freedom from blame. Matt. 26 : 59, 60.

13. *How in being committed to prison?*—They laid hands on Jesus, and took him. Matt. 26 : 50.

14. *How in leaving that prison and being exalted?*—God hath made that same Jesus, whom ye have crucified, both Lord and Christ. Acts 2 : 36.

15. *How in his feeding and blessing his brethren and all who came to him?*—In being the Bread of life.

16. *How in Pharaoh transferring all his power to him?*—The Father committed all judgment unto the Son. John 5 : 22.

17. *How in his returning good for evil?*—Jesus died for his persecutors, and prayed for them to the last.

JOB.

1. *Who was Job?*—A very rich man in the north of Arabia who worshiped the true God. Job 1 : 3.

2. *When was he supposed to live?*—Probably about the time of Isaac.

3. *Why? Do we gather anything from his not mentioning God's wonders in Egypt and the Red Sea?*—From the age to which he lived, said to be two hundred years; from the very early customs alluded to in the book, as the worship of the sun, moon and stars, the use of engraving for writing, and the reckoning of riches by cattle, that they had not then occurred, or Job would certainly have heard of them and spoken of them. Job 21 : 26–28; 19 : 23, 24; 1 : 3.

4. *Can you give any proof from the fact that as head of the family he offered sacrifices?*—After God's appointment of priests he would not have done this.

5. *How is he supposed to have obtained his knowledge of the true God?*—By tradition, or knowledge passed down by word of mouth from one generation to another, and perhaps by direct revelation from God, like Adam and Moses.

6. *What proof of the truth of 1 Pet. 5 : 8 does the history of Job supply?*—Satan's plots against Job. Your adversary the devil, as a roaring lion, walketh about, seeking whom he may devour. Job 1 : 6–12; 2 : 1–7.

7. *Where is Satan called "the accuser of the brethren"?*—Rev. 12 : 10.

8. *What high terms of praise did the Lord use when speaking of Job to Satan?*—Job 1 : 8.

9. *And how did the Lord afterward, to Ezekiel, mention him?*—He classed him with Noah and Daniel.

Through these three men, Noah, Daniel, and Job, were in it, they should deliver but their own souls by their righteousness, saith the Lord God. Ezek. 14 : 14.

10. *In what way did the Lord first try this good man?*—By suffering him to be deprived in one day of his children, servants and goods. Job 1.

11. *Did he fail?*—He submitted to God's will, and blessed him in memorable words. Job 1 : 21.

12. *Did Satan again have permission to hurt him?*—Yes, by bodily suffering. Job 2 : 4–8.

13. *Did he continue steadfast?*—He seems to have uttered no complaint against God. Job 2 : 8.

14. *How did his wife afflict him?*—By tempting him to curse God, that he might die. Job 2 : 9.

15. *Did this prove too much for him?*—No; he again expressed his submission to the will of God. Job 2 : 10.

16. *Who came to comfort him?*—His three principal friends. Job 2 : 11.

17. *What relation is Eliphaz supposed to have been to Esau?*—These are the names of Esau's sons; Eliphaz the son of Adah the wife of Esau. . . . And the sons of Eliphaz were Teman, Omar, Zepho and Gatam, and Kenaz. Gen. 36 : 10, 11. Eliphaz seems to have been an Idumean or Arabian name.

18. *In what way did Job fail?*—He cursed his birth, though not his God, and sometimes showed a self-righteous spirit. Job 3.

My face is foul with weeping, and on my eyelids is the shadow of death; not for any injustice in mine hands: also my prayer is pure. Job 16 : 16, 17.

19. *Did not his friends suppose that all his misfortunes had come upon him in consequence of sin?*—They did. Job 4 : 7, 8.

20. *If Job, instead of justifying himself, had appealed unto God, would it not have shown a better knowledge?*—Yes, for it is easy to form a too favorable judgment of our own selves.

21. *How did the Lord Jesus Christ act when he was wrongfully accused?*—He answered not a word. Matt. 27 : 12–14.

22. *Who is the only perfect man that ever lived?*—The man Christ Jesus.

23. *How did Job feel when God himself spoke to him at last?*—Deeply humbled. *What did Job say?*—Then Job answered the Lord, and said, Behold I am vile; what shall I answer thee? I will lay my hand upon my mouth. Job 40 : 3, 4.

24. *Did the Lord condemn him?*—No; he accepted or forgave him. Job 42 : 9.

25. *How did the Lord pass over the error of Job's three friends in their condemnation of Job?*—In consideration of their sacrifice and of Job's prayer. Job 42 : 7–9.

26. *How did the Lord disappoint Satan and bless Job's latter end?*—He gave him a family again, and twice as much substance as he had before. Job 42 : 10, 12, 13.

27. *How old was Job when he died?*—About two hundred years. Job 42 : 16.

PHARAOH AND MOSES. (Ex. 1 : 2.)

1. *How did the Egyptians behave to the children of Israel after the death of Joseph?*—They enslaved and oppressed them. Ex. 1 : 8–14.

2. *Did the children of Israel multiply and increase very rapidly?*—They did. Ex. 1 : 12.

3. *Why should this have made the Egyptians afraid?*—Lest they should join their enemies. Ex. 1 : 10.

4. *How were the children of Israel employed by the Egyptians?*—In making bricks and other field-service. Ex. 1 : 14.

5. *What cruel device did Pharaoh resolve on to destroy the male children of Israel?*—To employ the Hebrew nurses to do so. Ex. 1 : 16.

6. *Who was Moses?*—The second son of Amram and Jochebed of the tribe of Levi. Ex. 2 : 1; 6 : 20.

7. *What plan did his mother adopt to spare his life?*—She hid him in a floating basket among the flags growing by a river-side. Ex. 2 : 2, 3.

8. *How did her design succeed?*—The child was found by Pharaoh's daughter, who took charge of it. Ex. 2 : 5–10.

9. *Whom had his mother set to watch the little ark?*—His sister Miriam. Ex. 2:4; 15:20.

10. *When the princess sought a nurse for the child, whom did Miriam fetch?*—His mother. Ex. 2:7-9.

11. *What blessing did this ensure to Moses?*—The tenderest care, and perhaps also the knowledge of the true God.

12. *What proof does this give us of the truth of Isa. 46:10?*—My counsel shall stand, and I will do all my pleasure.

There is no wisdom nor understanding nor counsel against the Lord. Prov. 21:30.

13. *With whom did Moses join himself—with the Egyptians or the Hebrews?*—By faith Moses, when he was come to years, refused to be called the son of Pharaoh's daughter; choosing rather to suffer affliction with the people of God. Heb. 11:24, 25.

14. *Did they receive him graciously?*—Who made thee a ruler and a judge over us? Wilt thou kill me as thou diddest the Egyptian yesterday? Acts 7:27, 28.

15. *What was Moses obliged to do?*—To leave Egypt. Ex. 2:11-15.

16. *To what land did he flee?*—To Midian.

17. *What occurred to him there?*—He married a daughter of the priest or prince of Midian. Ex. 2:16-21.

18. *How long did he stay there?*—Forty years. Acts 7:30.

19. *How many sons had he? What were their names and his wife's name?*—Two—Gershom and Eliezer; Zipporah. Ex. 2:22; 18:3, 4; 2:21.

The Burning Bush. (Ex. 3, 4.)

1. *How was Moses employed when the Lord appeared to him?*—In keeping his father-in-law's flock. Ex. 3:1.

2. *What wondrous sight attracted the attention of Moses?*—A burning bush unconsumed. Ex. 3:2.

3. *Whose voice addressed him from the midst of the fire?*—The voice of the Son of God, God's messenger, and yet God himself. Ex. 3:2, 4.

4. *What commission did the Lord give to Moses?*—To go to Pharaoh and bring the Israelites out of Egypt. Ex. 3:10.

5. *Was Moses willing to undertake it?*—He said they would not believe that God had appeared to him. Ex. 4:1.

6. *What excuses did he make?*—See No. 5.

7. *How did the Lord show him that it was not his own might or power in which he was to go to Pharaoh?*—He changed Moses' rod into a serpent and made his hand leprous, and restored them again. Ex. 4:2-8.

8. *Did this remove his scruples?*—He then objected that he was too poor a speaker to deliver God's message. Ex. 4:10.

9. *How did the Lord graciously meet his weakness?*—He promised to teach him what to say. Ex. 4:12.

10. *Whom did the Lord appoint his helper?*—His brother Aaron, who could speak well. Ex. 4:14-16.

11. *What solemn rite had Moses neglected to perform on his sons in the land of Midian?*—Circumcision. Ex. 4:25.

12. *What punishment had God enjoined on those who neglected it?*—The uncircumcised man-child shall be cut off from his people; he hath broken my covenant (by loss of privileges or by death). Gen. 17:14.

13. *Did not the sons of Moses narrowly escape?*—They were doubtless in imminent danger of punishment, with Moses himself. Ex. 4:24-26.

14. *Who met Moses on his return to Egypt?*—Aaron, by command of God. Ex. 4:27.

15. *How did the poor afflicted Israelites receive the message?*—They believed it, and worshiped God. Ex. 4:31.

The Plagues of Egypt. (Ex. 5-11.)

1. *Who was the king of Egypt now?*—Pharaoh.

2. *Was it the same Pharaoh who had ordered the little children to be killed?*—No; it was one who lived one hundred and forty years later.

3. *Did he treat the children of Israel more mercifully than the former king?*—Though he did not order their male offspring to death like the former king, he was very cruel to them.

4. *How did he receive Moses and Aaron when they went in to him?*—He abused them for interfering with the people's work. Ex. 5:2-4.

5. *What was the result?*—Heavier work was laid upon them. Ex. 5:6-9.

6. *Whom did the children of Israel blame for this?*—Moses and Aaron. Ex. 5:20, 21.

7. *Of whom was Pharaoh, in his daring rebellion, a type?*—Of the great rebel Satan. Jude 6.

8. *What was the first plague?*—The river Nile turned into blood. Ex. 7.

9. *In what respect was this a peculiar trial to the Egyptians?*—Because the yearly overflowing of the Nile was most valuable for their land, and they worshiped the river as a god, and much of their food was fish.

10. *What were the second and third plagues?*—Frogs and lice. Ex. 8.

11. *How far were the magicians permitted to follow Moses and Aaron?*—So far as to turn water into blood and to bring frogs. Ex. 7, 8.

12. *What did they say when they could go no farther?*—That the miracles of Moses were the finger of God. Ex. 8:19.

13. *What was the next plague?*—Swarms of flies or hurtful insects. Ex. 8:24.

14. *How did God mark the distinction between the Egyptians and Israelites in this?*—He suffered none in the land of Goshen, where the Israelites dwelt.

15. *Did this influence Pharaoh to let the Israelites go?*—No (Ex. 8:32), though he gave way a little at first. Ex. 8:28.

16. *What was the fifth plague?*—A murrain upon cattle, horses, asses, camels and sheep. Ex. 9.

17. *What painful attack on man and beast did God send next?*—Boils and blains, or sores. Ex. 9:9.

18. *Did any of these move the haughty king?*—No. Ex. 9:7, 12.

19. *What merciful provision did God make in the seventh plague for those who believed in his word?*—He warned them to remove their cattle to a place of shelter. Ex. 9:19.

20. *Why was this plague peculiarly terrible to the Egyptians?*—Because they were not accustomed to either hail or rain. Deut. 11:10, 11.

21. *Why was it that all these judgments had no effect on Pharaoh?*—Because his heart was hardened, or he hardened his own heart, as it is expressed in Ex. 8:15, 32; 9:34, 35, so that God gave him up to his own wicked heart, as he is said in Rom. 1:28, 21, 20 to have given up the Gentiles to a reprobate mind, their foolish heart being darkened, and they themselves without excuse.

Let no man say when he is tempted, I am tempted of God: for God cannot be tempted with evil, neither tempteth he any man. James 1:13.

22. *Is it not an awful thing when God gives a man over to his own hardened heart?*—If we sin willfully after that we have received the knowledge of the truth, there remaineth no more sacrifice for sins, but a certain fearful looking-for of judgment and fiery indignation, which shall devour the adversaries. Heb. 10:26, 27.

23. *What was the eighth plague?*—Locusts. Ex. 10.

24. What appearance must the land of Egypt have presented at this time?—The land was darkened by them, and every green thing eaten up. Ex. 10:15.

25. What was the ninth plague?—Thick darkness for three days. Ex. 10:21-23.

26. What solemn interview had Moses with Pharaoh during this awful darkness?—When Pharaoh bade Moses see his face no more. Ex. 10:28.

27. What was the last plague?—The destruction of first-born.

THE PASSOVER. (Ex. 12–14.)

1. What did God command the Israelites to do before he brought the last plague on the Egyptians?—To have the passover sacrifice and feast. Ex. 12.

2. Of whom was the lamb a type?—Of Christ the Lamb of God, slain from the foundation of the world. John 1:29; Rev. 13:8.

3. In how many ways was the paschal lamb a type of Him whom it prefigured?—In its gentleness and unblemished innocence, and in its being slain without a bone being broken; and in other respects besides.

4. What divine ordinance in the Christian Church still commemorates the Passover?—The Lord's Supper.

5. When was it instituted?—The evening before our blessed Saviour suffered.

6. What does it set forth?—The sacrifice of the death of Christ, and the benefits we receive thereby.

7. Wherein does "the mass" of the Romish Church differ from "the Lord's Supper" in the Protestant churches?—In the mass the priest professes every time to offer Christ himself as a sacrifice for sin, while the Lord's Supper is a remembrance of his perfect sacrifice made once for all.

8. Which is most in harmony with the word of God?—We are sanctified through the offering of the body of Jesus Christ once for all. For by one offering he hath perfected for ever them that are sanctified. Heb. 10:10, 14.

9. What is the meaning of the word Passover?—It refers to the destroying angel *passing over* the blood-sprinkled doorposts of the children of Israel. Ex. 12:23.

10. How were the Israelites preserved from the destroying angel?—By striking the lintels and doorposts of their houses with the blood of the slain lamb. Ex. 12:22.

11. Why was not the blood sprinkled on the doorway?—Lest any should trample on so sacred a thing.

> Of how much sorer punishment, suppose ye, shall he be thought worthy who hath trodden under foot the Son of God, and hath counted the blood of the covenant, wherewith he was sanctified, an unholy thing, and hath done despite unto the Spirit of grace! Heb. 10:29.

12. How was the bread to be prepared?—Without leaven (or yeast or sour paste) to raise it. Ex. 12:15.

13. What does the apostle Paul declare this to be a type of, in 1 Cor. 5:7, 8?—Of purity and sincerity.

14. What did the bitter herbs signify?—The bitterness of Egyptian bondage, of true sorrow for sin and of Christ's cup of suffering. Ps. 69:20, 21.

15. If any Israelite had despised the means of safety, what would have been the consequence?—He would have lost his first-born child.

16. And what will be our state if we despise the hiding-place which God has provided for us?—We shall be destroyed by the storm of God's just wrath.

17. Is God's salvation merely a safety from his wrath, or does he provide ample blessing for the soul that trusts in him?—He provides not only escape from hell, but a home in heaven—eternal life begun below and perfected above.

18. What part of this type is a proof of this?—The feast upon the slaughtered lamb.

19. Give some other parts of Scripture where the gospel provision is compared to a feast.—Isa. 25:6; Rev 19:9.

20. How did Pharaoh act when he found the threatened vengeance of God had descended on him?—He ordered the Israelites to depart. Ex. 12:31, 32.

21. How did God recompense the Israelites for all that they had suffered at the hands of the Egyptians?—By disposing the Egyptians to give them gold and silver and raiment. Ex. 12:35, 36; Rom. 12:17-21.

22. In what way did the Israelites obey the king's mandate?—They hurried away with their flocks and herds and hastily-prepared food. Ex. 12:37-39.

23. Did they remember Joseph's wish at this time?—They took his bones with them. Ex. 13:19.

24. Did Pharaoh quietly allow them to go?—He pursued them to bring them back. Ex. 14:5-9.

25. How did the children of Israel feel when they heard that Pharaoh was pursuing them?—They were terribly afraid. Ex. 14:10.

26. What had the Israelites to guide them as to the way they should take?—A pillar of cloud and of fire. Ex. 14:19, 20, 24.

27. What speech did Israel make to Moses when they saw the sea before them and the host of Pharaoh behind?—That they had better have remained in Egypt. Ex. 14:11, 12.

28. Did God reward them as they deserved for this wicked speech? What did he do?—He made a way for them through the sea. Ex. 14:16.

29. Which got on the fastest—Pharaoh in his chariots or Israel on foot?—Israel on foot, as God took off the chariot-wheels. Ex. 14:25.

30. How did the Lord hinder the Egyptians?—See No. 29.

31. How did God keep the hosts separate all the night?—By the pillar of cloud, which kept the Egyptians in darkness and prevented them from moving on. Ex. 14:20.

32. Ought we ever to doubt a God who can help his people in any difficulty?—If God be for us, who can be against us? Rom. 8:31.

33. What happened as soon as Israel was safely over the sea?—The Egyptians were overwhelmed by the returning waters. Ex. 14:27, 28.

THE SONG OF MOSES. (Ex. 15:1-21.)

1. What is the passage through the Red Sea a type of?—The introduction of believers by baptism into covenant with God. 1 Cor. 10:1-4.

2. What is baptism a type of?—Of having done with sin on being given to God. Rom. 6:1-4.

3. What did Jesus call his death?—A baptism.

> I have a baptism to be baptized with; and how am I straitened till it be accomplished! Luke 12:50.

4. Is the song of Moses ever again mentioned in Scripture?—Rev. 15:2, 3.

5. Of whom is Pharaoh a type in these verses?—Of the enemies of God.

6. What is said of Pharaoh in Rom. 9:17?—Even for this same purpose have I raised thee up, that I might show my power in thee.

7. What will be the end of all God's enemies?—To be subdued by Christ.

> For David saith, The Lord said unto my Lord, Sit thou on my right hand, until I make thy foes thy footstool. Acts 2:34, 35.

8. Which is the last enemy that is to be destroyed?—Death. 1 Cor. 15:26.

9. What song may the Christian sing even now in prospect of that victory?—Death is swallowed up in victory. 1 Cor. 15:54-57.

10. *Through whom is the conquest obtained?*—Heb. 2:14, 15; 1 Cor. 15:57.

THEIR JOURNEY BEGUN. (Ex. 15:22–27.)

1. *How many days did Israel travel in the wilderness before they found water?*—Three. Ex. 15:22.

2. *And when they found water, of what kind was it?*—Bitter. Ex. 15:23.

3. *How did the children of Israel bear this disappointment?*—They murmured against Moses. Ex. 15:24.

4. *What is this world compared to?*—A wilderness.

5. *Are the journeyings of the children of Israel calculated to teach us any useful lessons?*—Not to expect perfect comfort in our pilgrimage here below—to follow God's guidance, and to cheerfully submit to all his dealings with us on our heavenward way.

6. *Are not young people apt to think that this world is a resting-place?*—They forget that youth and health may not last them long.

7. *What does God's word say in Mic. 2:10?*—Arise ye, and depart; for this is not your rest: because it is polluted, it shall destroy you, even with a sore destruction.

8. *There is one thing that can turn the bitter waters of earthly sorrow into sweetness; what is it?*—Seeing a Father's hand overruling all our affairs.

9. *Where did Israel next encamp?*—At Elim. Ex. 15:27.

10. *What blessing had the Lord in store for them there?* —Plenty of water.

11. *Is it not God's way ever to bring good out of evil?* —Who fed thee in the wilderness with manna, which thy fathers knew not, that he might humble thee, and that he might prove thee, to do thee good at thy latter end. Deut. 8:16.

THE MANNA. (Ex. 16.)

1. *How were the Israelites fed in the wilderness?*—With manna.

2. *What was manna?*—A small round thing, like a frozen drop of dew, miraculously sent by God, and able to be made into bread. Ex. 16:14, 15, 23, 31.

3. *How often were they to gather it?*—Every day except the Sabbath-day.

4. *What provision did the Lord make for sanctifying the Sabbath-day, and resting on it?*—A double quantity of manna the day before. Ex. 16:22–30.

5. *Were the children of Israel obedient to the Lord in this arrangement? How did they act?*—Some of them went out to gather on the Sabbath-day. Ex. 16:27.

6. *Who was it that declared himself to be the true bread that came down from heaven?*—I am the living bread which came down from heaven. John 6:51.

7. *Were the Israelites satisfied with God's provision?*—Our soul loatheth this light bread. Num. 21:5.

8. *What is said in 2 Tim. 3:16?*—All Scripture is given by inspiration of God.

9. *What instruction ought we to gain from reading about the sins of Israel?*—To watch against falling into the same sins ourselves.

As in water face answereth to face, so the heart of man to man. Prov. 27:19.

10. *What provision has God made for the life of our souls?*—His Son, his Spirit and his word.

11. *Are we satisfied with this, or do we prefer earthly pleasures?*—We are prone to love this present world.

12. *Compare Matt. 7:1, 2 and 1 Cor. 10:11, 12.*—Judge not, that ye be not judged. For with what judgment ye judge, ye shall be judged: and with what measure ye mete, it shall be measured to you again. All these things are written for our admonition. Wherefore let him that thinketh he standeth, take heed lest he fall.

THE SMITTEN ROCK. (Ex. 17:1–7.)

1. *What are those who travel in deserts constantly liable to?*—The want of water.

2. *How were the Israelites supplied?*—From a stream that flowed from a rock in Horeb on Moses striking it with his rod. Ex. 17:6.

3. *Of whom is the smitten rock a beautiful type?*—That rock was Christ. 1 Cor. 10:4.

4. *What did Jesus say to the woman of Samaria?*—But whosoever drinketh of the water that I shall give him shall never thirst; but the water that I shall give him shall be in him a well of water springing up into everlasting life. John 4:14.

5. *At the feast of tabernacles, which was a feast commemorative of the sojourn of Israel in the desert, they used to pour out water in remembrance of the smitten rock; when Jesus was present at this ceremony, what did he cry aloud?* —If any man thirst, let him come unto me and drink. John 7:37.

6. *Have you obeyed that command?*—Let the conscience of each reply. If you have not yet come, come now.

7. *What excuse will you have to offer if you refuse to obey?*—None at all. Prov. 1:20–31; Rev. 22:17.

THE BATTLE WITH AMALEK. (Ex. 17:8–16.)

1. *What is prayer?*—Prayer is the simplest words of the mouth and the earnest desire of the heart, taught by the Holy Spirit and presented through Jesus Christ.

2. *Why do we pray to God?*—Because he is willing to help us, and no one else can.

3. *How did God teach Israel this at Rephidim?*—By giving them victory over the Amalekites in answer to Moses' prayer. Ex. 17:8–11.

4. *Who were the Amalekites?*—Descendants of Esau, to the south of Palestine.

5. *Was it not very cruel to come out and fight Israel when they were so weak?*—They thought now was their opportunity, but they forgot that God was on Israel's side.

6. *Was not God angry with them for this?*—God sentenced them to constant war, and at last to destruction. Ex. 17:14, 16.

7. *Which army obtained victory?*—The Israelites'.

8. *How was this?*—By Moses' continued prayer. Ex. 17:12.

9. *Of whom was Moses a type when he thus interceded for Israel?*—Of Christ, who ever lives to make intercession for us in heaven.

10. *Of whom was Joshua a type while leading on the battle?*—Of the great Captain of our salvation.

11. *What foes has the Christian to contend with?*—The temptations of his own evil heart, of Satan and of sinners around him.

12. *How can he overcome?*—In the strength of the Lord God.

13. *What is the meaning of Jehovah-nissi?*—"The Lord, my banner." Ex. 17:15.

14. *If this be the banner of the Christian, what is his armor?*—Eph. 6:10–18.

Be strong in the Lord, and in the power of his might. Put on the whole armor of God, that ye may be able to stand against the wiles of the devil. Eph. 6:10, 11.

THE COVENANT OF WORKS. (Ex. 19–24.)

1. *What is the human heart most prone to?*—Sin.

2. *What does this show?*—The heart is deceitful above all things, and desperately wicked: who can know it? Jer. 17:9.

3. *How did God teach this to Israel, and through them to us?*—By practical lessons which showed them their

weakness and wickedness, and their need of a better righteousness than their own, and of a greater sacrifice than the blood of bulls and goats. Gal. 3 : 24.

4. *What is the law?*—The term here refers to the Ten Commandments, and to others that immediately follow.

5. *Under what circumstances did God give the law?* —From the top of Mount Sinai, amidst thunder and lightning, clouds and darkness, trumpet-blast and earthquake. Ex. 19.

6. *Where is Sinai?*—In the wilderness, near the Red Sea.

7. *Could Israel bear the presence of God?*—They could not endure the light of God's presence in their consciences. Our God is a consuming fire. Heb. 12 : 20, 21, 29.

8. *Why not?*—See No. 7.

9. *Who went up into the thick darkness where God was?*—Moses. Ex. 19 : 20; 20 : 21.

10. *When he came forth with God's message to them, what did they promise to do?*—All the words which God had said. Ex. 24 : 3.

11. *Were they able to perform their promise?*—No.

12. *Why?*—From the sinfulness of their own hearts.

13. *Are we able to keep God's holy law now?*—No.

14. *What refuge, then, have we from God's wrath?*— Christ hath redeemed us from the curse of the law, being made a curse for us. Gal. 3 : 13.

THE COVENANT BROKEN. (Ex. 32.)

1. *How long was Moses upon the mount with God?*— Forty days and nights. Ex. 24 : 18.

2. *What awful proof did Israel give of their inability to keep the law, of their forgetfulness of God, and of their own evil hearts while Moses was on the mount?*—They made and worshiped a golden calf, probably after some idol in Egypt. Ex. 32 : 1–6.

3. *When was Moses made acquainted with their sin?* —God told him while he was on the mount. Ex. 32 : 7, 8.

4. *Did he plead for them with God?*—Yes, and his prayer was heard. Ex. 32 : 11–14.

5. *Who was waiting on the side of the mount for Moses when he came down?*—Joshua. Ex. 32 : 17.

6. *What sight did they see?*—The calf, and the people dancing about it. Ex. 32 : 19.

7. *What did Moses do?*—He broke the stone tables, as they had broken the law, and he destroyed the golden calf. Ex. 32 : 19, 20.

8. *Although Joshua was not in the transgression of making the calf, which of Israel's leaders was?*—Aaron. Ex. 32 : 2–5.

9. *Was not his excuse a vain one?*—Yes; and sinners now by silly falsehoods strive in vain to hide their sins.

10. *Why was this painful history recorded?*—For our instruction; see 1 Cor. 10 : 1–12.

THE SECOND GIVING OF THE LAW. (Ex. 32 : 30–55; 33 and 34.)

1. *Who interceded for Israel at this awful time?*— Moses. Ex. 32 : 30–32.

2. *What testimony did Moses bear against them?*— That they had sinned a great sin. Ex. 32 : 30.

3. *Whom did Moses associate with himself in this act?* —Joshua, Abraham, Isaac and Jacob. Ex. 24 : 13; 32 : 13.

4. *What proof did the Lord give to Moses that he had accepted him?*—Allowing him to see something of his glory and proclaiming to him his name. Ex. 33 : 16; 34 : 7.

5. *How was the law given the second time?*—By Moses taking two fresh tables of stone up the mount, and God's writing upon them the Ten Commandments. Ex. 34 : 1, 4, 28.

6. *How long was Moses in the mount this time?*— Forty days and forty nights. Deut. 10 : 10.

7. *What wonderful manifestation was there on the face of Moses that he been with God, and had spoken to him face to face?*—His face shone brightly. Ex. 33 : 11; 34 : 29, 30.

And there arose not a prophet since in Israel like unto Moses, whom the Lord knew face to face. Deut. 34 : 10.

8. *How did the children of Israel feel when they saw this?*—They were afraid to come near him. Ex. 34 : 30.

9. *What was this a type of?*—Of the blindness of their minds, which prevented them from seeing the truth then, and which prevents them still.

Their minds were blinded: for until this day remaineth the same veil untaken away in the reading of the Old Testament; which veil is done away in Christ. 2 Cor. 3 : 14.

THE TABERNACLE. (Ex. 35–40.)

1. *How did Moses obtain the instruction to make the tabernacle?*—From God himself and a pattern shown him on the mount. Ex. 25 : 9, 40.

2. *What is a tabernacle?*—A tent.

3. *Whom did God specially endow with skill to perform this work?*—Bezaleel and Aholiab and other wise-hearted men. Ex. 36 : 1.

4. *Where did Moses get the materials?*—From the free offerings of the people. Ex. 35 : 21; 36 : 3–7.

5. *Did the women assist? In what?*—Yes. In spinning. Ex. 35 : 22, 25, 26.

*6. *What solemn injunction did Moses receive?*—To make the tabernacle and its furniture according to the patterns God had shown him. Ex. 25 : 40; 26 : 30; Heb. 8 : 5.

7. *What expression, used eight times in the fortieth chapter of Exodus, shows that Moses fulfilled the work that God gave him to do?*—As the Lord commanded Moses.

8. *When was the tabernacle reared?*—On the first day (of the first month) of the second year of the sojourn in the wilderness. Ex. 40 : 17.

9. *Of whom is the tabernacle a type?*—Of Jesus Christ, the "true" and "perfect tabernacle." John 2 : 19–21; Heb. 8 : 2; 9 : 11.

10. *Are our bodies compared to a tabernacle and temple?*—Yes; to a tabernacle, to be taken down, in 2 Cor. 5 : 1, and to a temple of the Holy Ghost, to be kept holy, in 1 Cor. 6 : 19.

11. *In what respect was the tabernacle in the wilderness a type of Jesus?*—As the way to the Father's presence. Heb. 9 : 8, 9, 11, 12.

12. *What was its outward appearance?*—Plain, from its badger-skins covering. Ex. 26 : 14. As Christ had no outward beauty. Isa. 53 : 2, 3.

His visage was so marred more than any man, and his form more than the sons of men. Isa. 52 : 14.

13. *Was the inside different? How was this a type of Jesus?*—Yes; it was richly adorned with gold and silver and embroidery. Ex. 31 and 36. So He who was "altogether lovely" (Song of Sol. 5 : 16) pleased his heavenly Father.

Lo a voice from heaven, saying, This is my beloved Son, in whom I am well pleased. Matt. 3 : 17.

A cloud overshadowed them: and a voice came out of the cloud, saying, This is my beloved Son: hear him. Mark 9 : 7.

The centurion said, Truly this man was the Son of God. Mark 15 : 39.

The officers answered, Never man spake like this man. John 7 : 46.

14. *To what did Jesus compare himself in John 10 and 14 : 6 ?*—To the door of the sheepfold and to a road or way. (See No. 11.)

I am the way, the truth, and the life; no man cometh unto the Father, but by me.

15. *How was the brazen altar a type of Jesus ?*—Because it bore the sacrificial fires which consumed the victims.

16. *Who first kindled the fire on this altar ?*—God himself. Lev. 9 : 24.

17. *What is fire a type of ?*—It is the element of purification Ezek. 21 : 31, 32; 22 : 31; Heb. 12 : 29.

18. *What do we deserve ?*—We cannot possibly conceive the exceeding sinfulness of our estrangement from our Father.

19. *Who was the Sin-bearer in our stead ?*—Christ Jesus.

He was wounded for our transgressions, he was bruised for our iniquities: the chastisement of our peace was upon him; and with his stripes we are healed. Isa. 53 : 5.

Even Jesus, which delivered us from the wrath to come. 1 Thess. 1 : 10.

20. *Suppose any Israelite had refused to bring his offering to this altar, what would have been the consequence ?*—He would have remained unclean and deprived of the privilege of worshiping.

21. *Suppose we refuse to lay our sins on Jesus, what will be the consequence ?*—They will remain upon ourselves, and the wrath of God will abide upon us.

22. *What stood next to the brazen altar in the outer court ?*—The laver. Ex. 38 : 8.

23. *What was its use ?*—For the priests to wash their feet. Ex. 30 : 18-21.

24. *What was the laver a type of ?*—Of the word and Spirit of God, which cleanse and restore our souls.

25. *Of what was the laver made ?*—Of brass, taken from the looking-glasses, or plates of polished metal, which the women used.

26. *How does the apostle James allude to this in the first chapter of his Epistle ?*—Whoso looketh into the perfect law of liberty, and continueth therein, he being not a forgetful hearer, but a doer of the work, this man shall be blessed in his deed.

27. *Is the word of God ever compared to water ?*—Christ also loved the Church, and gave himself for it, that he might sanctify and cleanse it with the washing of water by the word. Eph. 5 : 25, 26.

28. *Where else is the word of God alluded to as a cleansing process ?*—Not by works of righteousness which we have done, but according to his mercy he saved us, by the washing of regeneration, and renewing of the Holy Ghost. Tit. 3 : 5. Except a man be born of water and of the Spirit, he cannot enter into the kingdom of God. John 3 : 5. Of his own will begat he us with the word of truth, that we should be kind of first-fruits of his creatures. James 1 : 18.

29. *How did Jesus (the Word of God) declare we must be cleansed ?*—By himself.

If I wash thee not, thou hast no part with me. John 13 : 8.

30. *What objects presented themselves when the doorway curtain of the tabernacle was drawn aside ?*—The altar of incense, the table of shewbread, the golden candlestick and the curtain or veil of the holy of holies.

31. *What did Jesus say of himself in John 9 : 5 ?*—As long as I am in the world, I am the light of the world.

32. *What is said of the Lord's people in Matt. 5 : 14-16 ?*—Ye are the light of the world. A city that is set on a hill cannot be hid.

33. *Under what figure is prayer represented in Rev. 8 : 3, 4 ?*—The smoke of burning incense.

34. *What did the Lord Jesus style himself in John 6 : 35 ?*—I am the bread of life: he that cometh to me shall never hunger; and he that believeth on me shall never thirst.

35. *Who were permitted to go in and minister in this holy place ?*—The priests went always into the first tabernacle, accomplishing the service of God. Heb. 9 : 6.

36. *Who alone might go into the most holy place ?*—But into the second went the high priest alone once every year, not without blood, which he offered for himself and for the errors of the people. Heb. 9 : 7.

37. *How often might he go in ?*—See No. 36.

38. *Of what is the most holy place a type ?*—Of the immediate presence of God.

39. *Who has entered there ?*—Seeing then that we have a great High Priest, that is passed into the heavens, Jesus the Son of God, let us hold fast our profession. Heb. 4 : 14.

40. *What happened to the beautiful veil of the temple when the Lord Jesus was crucified ?*—It was rent in twain from the top to the bottom.

41. *If man had rent it, would it have been done in the same way ? How ?*—It would have been rent from the bottom.

42. *What did this show ?*—The rending of the veil showed that the way into heaven was now open. Heb. 10 : 19-22.

43. *What stood in the most holy place ?*—The ark of the covenant.

44. *Of what was the ark composed ?*—Of shittim-wood, overlaid with gold. Ex. 25 : 10, 11.

45. *How did it represent the glory of Jesus ?*—By the mercy-seat and cherubim above it. Ex. 25 : 17-22.

46. *What was preserved in the ark ?*—The golden pot that had manna, and Aaron's rod that budded, and the tables of the covenant. Heb. 9 : 4.

47. *What was the budding rod a type of ?*—The resurrection of the dead. 1 Cor. 15 : 42.

48. *What was this incorruptible manna a type of ?*—Being born again, not of corruptible seed, but of incorruptible, by the word of God, which liveth and abideth for ever. 1 Pet. 1 : 23; Acts 2 : 31, 32.

49. *Where in the Revelation is this incorruptible manna alluded to ?*—To him that overcometh will I give to eat of the hidden manna. Rev. 2 : 17.

50. *What proof have we that Jesus has gone into heaven with a human body ?*—Behold my hands and my feet, that it is I myself: handle me, and see; for a spirit hath not flesh and bones as ye see me have. And when he had thus spoken, he showed them his hands and his feet. And while they yet believed not for joy, and wondered, he said unto them, Have ye here any meat? And they gave him a piece of a broiled fish, and of an honeycomb. And he took it, and did eat before them. And he led them out as far as to Bethany, and he lifted up his hands, and blessed them. And it came to pass, while he blessed them, he was parted from them, and carried up into heaven. Luke 24 : 39-43, 50, 51.

51. *What hope have we to rest on that we shall share that glory with him ?*—To him that overcometh will I grant to sit with me in my throne, even as I also overcame, and am set down with my Father in his throne Rev. 3. 21.

The Sacrifices and Offerings. (Lev. and Num. 19.)

1. *What is the principal thing treated of in the book of Leviticus ?*—Access to God by a purified worshiper.

2. *Name the four principal offerings.*—The burnt-offering, the sin-offering, the trespass-offering and the peace-offering.

3. *What characterized the burnt-offering?*—It was a male without blemish from the herd or the flock, or a turtle-dove or young pigeon; the blood of the beast being sprinkled about, and its body cut up and burnt on the altar. Lev. 1.

4. *In what did the sin-offering and the trespass-offering differ from the burnt-offering?*—In the sin-offering having the blood sprinkled and poured out on and under the altar, and having the fat, and not the whole animal, burnt upon it; and in the trespass-offering being allowed to be of the female sex, and being on account of *special* rather than *general* sin. The sin-offering referred rather to atonement, and the burnt-offering to self-dedication. Lev. 4, 5, 6.

5. *What was there different to both these in the peace-offering?*—The peace-offering, whether from the herd or the flock, was an expression of thankfulness to God for his gifts. Lev. 3; 7: 11-38.

6. *What difference was there between the meat- (or food-) and the burnt-offering?*—The meat-offering, of flour, oil and wine, was also a sacrifice of thanksgiving. Lev. 2.

7. *Who was prefigured by all these sacrifices?*—Jesus Christ, the *great* Atonement and the great self-devoted Sacrifice.

8. *What is said in Heb. 10: 1-18?*—The sacrifice of Christ's body, once offered, hath for ever taken away sins.

9. *Where was Moses when God gave him the instruction about sacrifices?*—On Mount Sinai. Ex. 24: 18; 32: 15.

10. *What special type of Jesus was there in the cleansing of the leper?*—Christ brings near those who were far off, as the leper was obliged to be kept; and Christ was slain for us, like the one bird, and rose to heaven for us like the other. Lev. 14.

But now in Christ Jesus ye who sometimes were far off are made nigh by the blood of Christ. Eph. 2: 13. Who was delivered for our offences, and raised again for our justification. Rom. 4: 25.

11. *What was the leprosy in the house a type of?*—Corruption. Lev. 14.

Flesh and blood cannot inherit the kingdom of God; neither doth corruption inherit incorruption. 1 Cor. 15: 50.

12. *Name some of the ceremonies which took place on the great day of atonement.*—Aaron the high priest made sin-offerings for himself and for the people, and sprinkled the blood upon the mercy-seat in the most holy place; confessed the sins of the people over the scapegoat, and sent it away into the wilderness; and offered burnt-offerings for himself and for the people. Lev. 16.

13. *What is the meaning of the word "atonement"?*—Reconciliation, or setting at one again, by a sacrifice in another's stead.

14. *Who atoned for our sins?*—Jesus Christ, who suffered in our place the punishment of our sins.

15. *How did the scapegoat set this forth?*—It bore the sins of Israel, as Christ bears ours.

16. *Have not you and I committed sin?*—Every day of our lives.

17. *Should we not ask ourselves where is our sin?*—It is the most important question we can ask ourselves.

18. *Where must it be—either by faith laid on Jesus, or where?*—Still resting on ourselves, with all its burden and its curse.

19. *What was the ceremony connected with the red heifer?*—The heifer was slain and burnt, and its blood was sprinkled before the tabernacle.

20. *What was the appointed use of the ashes of the red heifer?*—They were mixed with water and sprinkled upon persons who in various ways had become unclean, and as a token of purification for sin.

21. *Who was again prefigured in this type?*—How much more shall the blood of Christ, who through the eternal Spirit offered himself without spot to God, purge your conscience from dead works to serve the living God! Heb. 9: 14.

THE FEASTS. (Lev. 23.)

1. *What is a type?*—A thing that represents another thing, or has some points of resemblance to it, or is intended to foreshow it.

2. *Why did God teach us so much truth in this way?*—To make it clearer to our minds.

3. *How do we teach little children?*—By pictures, imitations, comparisons and tales.

4. *What is God's way of pardoning sin?*—Accepting on behalf of every one who believes the punishment which Jesus bore in his stead.

5. *How has he shown this to us?*—By his accepting the sacrifices which referred to Christ.

6. *What is faith?*—Trusting in Christ as our own Saviour.

7. *How is faith in the Lord Jesus shown us in the typical sacrifices of the Old Testament?*—Because they could have no value in themselves, but only as referring to Him that was to come.

8. *What does this chapter especially describe to us?*—The Jewish feasts.

9. *Which is the first "feast" spoken of?*—The Sabbath.

10. *How often was it to be kept?*—Every seventh day

11. *When was the keeping of the Sabbath first enjoined?*—In the garden of Eden, when God first sanctified it or set it apart for holy use. (See also Ex. 16 and 20.)

God blessed the seventh day, and sanctified it: because that in it he had rested from all his work which God created and made. Gen. 2: 3.

12. *Why is it here called a "feast?"*—Because it is a day of sacred rest. (And see No. 14.)

13. *Does the word "feast" in this chapter mean a time of eating and drinking?*—No; but of meeting together for a holy, happy purpose. Lev. 23: 4.

14. *What is the meaning of the word "festival?"*—A time of joyful worship.

15. *Does not God always unite happiness or joy with religion?*—He does.

If thou turn away thy foot from the sabbath, from doing thy pleasure on my holy day; and call the sabbath a delight, the holy of the Lord, honorable; and shalt honor him, not doing thine own ways, nor finding thine own pleasure, nor speaking thine own words: then shalt thou delight thyself in the Lord; and I will cause thee to ride upon the high places of the earth, and feed thee with the heritage of Jacob thy father: for the mouth of the Lord hath spoken it. Isa. 58: 13, 14.

16. *If it be not so to us, what is the cause?*—We have either no religion at all, or not enough to make us happy.

17. *Of what was the Jewish Sabbath a type?*—Of the rest of heaven. Heb. 4: 8-11.

18. *How can our souls, even in this world, "enter into rest"?*—We may enjoy the rest of a steadfast faith, an anchored hope and an abiding peace.

19. *Which was the second feast or festival spoken of?*—The feast of the Passover or of unleavened bread. Lev 23: 5, 6.

20. *When was that kept? How often?*—It began on the fifteenth day of the first month, about our March or April. Once a year.

21. *How was it kept?*—By the sacrifice of a lamb, the use of unleavened bread and offering the first-fruits of the early harvest. (But see No. 24.)

22. *When was this instituted?*—When the Israelites came out of Egypt.

23 *What did the Passover teach them, and what must it teach us?*—To remember their deliverance by blood, and to look for our own deliverance by the same means.

24. *What feast or festival came next?*—The offering of the first-fruits of the harvest at Pentecost.

25. *What ceremony were they to perform with the first sheaf?*—The priest was to wave it before the Lord. Lev. 23 : 10, 11.

26. *What did "waving" it mean?*—An act of worship of the Lord of the whole earth.

27. *Whom did that first sheaf represent?*—Now is Christ risen from the dead, and become the first-fruits of them that slept. 1 Cor. 15 : 20.

28. *Did Jesus compare himself to wheat when speaking of his death?*—The hour is come, that the Son of man should be glorified. Verily, verily, I say unto you, Except a corn of wheat fall into the ground and die, it abideth alone: but if it die, it bringeth forth much fruit.

29. *What were the Israelites to do fifty days after they had brought in the first-fruits?*—To offer a new meat-offering to the Lord. Lev. 15 : 15–21.

30. *Of what was this a type?*—This feast was a type of the outpouring of the Holy Ghost, fifty days after Christ our Passover was sacrificed for us, when the apostles received the first-fruits of the Spirit, and presented to God the first-fruit converts of the Christian Church. Acts 2.

31. *What festival was held on the first day of the seventh month?*—The feast of trumpets. Lev. 15 : 23–25.

32. *Of what was this a type?*—Of the call to repentance and of the preaching of the gospel.

Cry aloud, spare not, lift up thy voice like a trumpet, and show my people their transgression, and the house of Jacob their sins. Isa. 58 : 1.

Go ye into all the world, and preach the gospel to every creature. Mark 16 : 15.

33. *How many days after this festival of trumpets was the great day of atonement kept?*—Nine days.

34. *What remarkable ceremonies took place on this day?*—Aaron the high priest made sin-offerings for himself and for the people, and sprinkled the blood upon the mercy-seat in the most holy place; confessed the sins of the people over the scapegoat, and sent it away into the wilderness; and offered burnt-offerings for himself and for the people. Lev. 16.

35. *Are we not very prone to excuse ourselves when looking into our own sinful hearts?*—The heart is deceitful above all things, and desperately wicked: who can know it? Jer. 17 : 9.

36. *Where shall we best discover God's estimate of sin?*—In those parts of Scripture which contain his denunciations against it, his punishments of it, and (above all) his provision, in both the Old and New Testaments, for the pardon and removal of it.

37. *What other ceremony took place on this day, mentioned in this chapter and not in the sixteenth chapter?*—The blowing of a trumpet on the first day of the month. Lev. 23 : 24.

38. *Where is this more fully described?*—Lev. 25 : 9.

39. *Of what were the trumpets made?*—Of silver. Num. 10 : 2.

40. *Of what was the jubilee a type?*—It was typical of our redemption by Christ from the slavery of sin and Satan, and of our restoration to the glorious liberty of the children of God.

41. *How are we interested in it?*—See No. 40.

42. *How many days after the day of atonement did the feast of tabernacles occur?*—Five days. Lev. 23 : 34.

43. *What ceremonies marked this festival?*—The offering of sacrifices and the dwelling in booths.

44. *How many days did they keep it?*—Eight days.

45. *What is this festival a type of?*—Of heaven. Rev. 21 : 3, 4.

46. *What does the twenty-ninth chapter of Numbers tell of?*—Of the offerings at the feasts of trumpets and tabernacles and on the day of atonement.

47. *Is the feast of tabernacles ever mentioned in the New Testament?*—Now the Jews' feast of tabernacles was at hand. In the last day, that great day of the feast, Jesus stood and cried, saying, If any man thirst, let him come unto me and drink. John 7 : 2, 37.

48. *At what time of the year was King Solomon's temple dedicated?*—Solomon kept the feast seven days in the seventh month, and all Israel with him, a very great congregation, from the entering in of Hamath unto the river of Egypt. 2 Chron. 7 : 8, 10.

49. *And when was the second temple dedicated?*—The children of the Captivity kept the Passover upon the fourteenth day of the first month. Ezra 6 : 19.

50. *Of what were those buildings a type?*—Of the Lord God Almighty and the Lamb, who are the temple of heaven. Rev. 21 : 22. (And see Rev. 21 : 3, 4, above—No. 45.)

THE NUMBERING OF THE ISRAELITES AND DEPARTURE FROM SINAI. (Num. 1–4, 7–10.)

1. *What do these chapters describe?*—The numbering of the people, the duties of the priests and Levites, the offerings for the tabernacle, the marchings of the Israelites, etc.

2. *How long had the children of Israel remained at Sinai?*—About eleven months.

3. *Tell me some of the most remarkable events that had occurred there?*—The giving of the law, the worship of the golden calf, the making of the tabernacle, and the punishment of Nadab and Abihu.

4. *How long was it after they left Egypt that the tabernacle was first set up?*—About ten months. Ex. 40 : 2.

5. *What rite did they celebrate on the fourteenth of the first month?*—The Passover. Num. 9 : 1–5.

6. *What did God command Moses to do on the first of the second month?*—To number the people. Num. 1 : 1–3.

7. *Whom did God accept for his service instead of the first-born?*—The Levites. Num. 3 : 12; 8 : 16.

8. *Did the numbers tell out exactly the same?*—The first-born were two hundred and seventy-three more. Num. 3 : 46.

9. *How was the difference arranged?*—Five shekels (or about $2.75) each was paid to Aaron for them. Num. 8.

10. *How were the children of Israel to encamp and to march on their journey?*—Each tribe was to march and encamp by itself, in a fixed order and place, the Levites in the midst. Num. 2.

11. *Who provided the wagons to carry the tabernacle?*—The princes or heads of the tribes. Num. 7 : 2, 3.

12. *Why had not the sons of Kohath any wagon allotted to them?*—Because their burdens were carried on their shoulders.

13. *What part of the tabernacle did they carry?*—The holy things of the tabernacle. Num. 4 : 2–15.

14. *What did each of the princes of Israel offer as a gift to the service of the tabernacle?*—Gold and silver vessels and animals for sacrifice. Num. 7.

15. *What direction did the Lord give Moses as to making trumpets?*—That they should be of silver, and be used for assembling and for marching in journeys or in war. Num. 10 : 1–10.

16. *On which day did the cloud move?*—On the twentieth day of the second month of the second year. Num. 10 : 11.

17. *Of what was the moving of the cloud to inform the Israelites?*—That they were to proceed on their journey. Num. 9 : 17.

18. *When the first alarm of the trumpets was given.*

which tribes marched first?—Judah, Issachar and Zebulun.

19. *How many encamped on the east of the tabernacle?* The above three. Num. 2:3–9.

20. *What immediately followed these three tribes?*—The tabernacle. Num. 10:17; 7:7, 8.

21. *Which three tribes followed these wagons?*—Reuben, Simeon and Gad. Num. 10:18–20.

22. *What part of the tabernacle went next?*—The sanctuary. Num. 10:21.

23. *Name the six tribes that followed.*—Ephraim, Manasseh and Benjamin; Dan, Asher and Naphtali.

24. *Whom did Moses entreat to accompany them?*—Hobab, his father-in-law. Num. 10:29.

25. *Did he not at first refuse?*—He did. Num. 10:30.

26. *What proofs have we afterward that he changed his mind and went with the Israelites into the promised land?*—The children of the Kenite, Moses' father-in-law, went up out of the city of palm trees with the children of Judah into the wilderness of Judah, which lieth in the south of Arad; and they went and dwelt among the people. Judg. 1:16. Now Heber the Kenite, which was of the children of Hobab the father-in-law of Moses, had severed himself from the Kenites, and pitched his tent unto the plain of Zaanaim, which is by Kedesh. Judg. 4:11.

27. *To what family did Jonadab, mentioned in 2 Kings 10 and Jer. 35, belong?*—To the Kenites, that came of Hemath, the father of Rechab. 1 Chron. 2:55; 2 Kings 10:15.

28. *When all was ready for marching what beautiful prayer did Moses offer?*—Rise up, Lord, and let thine enemies be scattered; and let them that hate thee flee before thee. Num. 10:35.

29. *And what when the ark rested again?*—Return, O Lord, unto the many thousands of Israel. Num. 10:36.

TRANSGRESSIONS. (Num. 11.)

1. *By what were the children of Israel in the wilderness chiefly distinguished?*—By their repeated rebellions against God. Heb. 3:8–12; Ps. 106:7, 8, 13–46.

2. *Of what should their sad history warn us?*—Of the sad consequences of sin.

3. *On what did the Lord feed Israel while at Sinai?*—On manna.

4. *Ought they not, then, to have trusted God on their journey? Did they?*—They ungratefully and discontentedly desired a change of food. Num. 11:1–6.

5. *How were they punished?*—Many of them were destroyed by fire· and others were diseased by the quails that were sent in answer to their demand for *flesh* to eat.

6. *Did not Moses feel their continual provocation too much for him?*—He complained to God of the burden it was to him. Num. 11:11–15.

7. *How did the Lord assist him?*—He appointed seventy elders to assist him. Num. 11:16, 17.

8. *How did Joshua show his affection for his master and zeal for his honor?*—By telling him of two men who seemed to be unlawfully exercising the authority of Moses in the camp. Num. 11:26–28.

9. *What was Moses' beautiful reply?*—Enviest thou for my sake? Would God that all the Lord's people were prophets (or true teachers), and that the Lord would put his Spirit upon them!

10. *How did the people behave when they had got the food they coveted?*—They probably indulged in it to excess, forgetting the warning in Num. 11:20.

11. *How did the Lord punish them for their sin?*—The quails produced a disease or plague among them. Num. 11:19, 20, 33. See No. 5.

12. *What lessons should we reap from their trans-*

gressions?—With many of them God was not well pleased, for they were overthrown in the wilderness. Now these things were our examples, to the intent we should not lust after evil things, as they also lusted. 1 Cor. 10:5, 6.

MIRIAM'S SIN AND PUNISHMENT. (Num. 12.)

1. *What affecting proof have we here that Rom. 3:10 is true?*—The sin of Miriam and Aaron shows that there is none righteous, no, not one.

2. *What was the sin of Miriam and Aaron?*—They claimed equal authority with Moses himself. Num. 12:2.

3. *What special favor had God given to Moses?*—More friendly conversation with himself and a near view of his glory. Num. 12:8.

4. *Ought any one aspire to a station in which God has not placed him?*—St. Paul said: I have learned, in whatsover state I am, therewith to be content; and, Godliness with contentment is great gain. For we brought nothing into this world, and it is certain we can carry nothing out. And having food and raiment, let us be therewith content. 1 Tim. 6:6–8.

5. *What special proof did God give of his displeasure?*—He made Miriam a leper. Num. 12:10.

6. *Who pleaded for Miriam?*—Aaron with Moses, and Moses with God. Num. 12:11, 13.

7. *How did the Lord mitigate her punishment?*—By removing her disease in seven days. Num. 12:14, 15.

8. *Of what was her punishment the type?*—Of the loathsomeness of sin in the eyes of God.

9. *In what way did the Lord permit the whole camp to sympathize with Miriam?*—By not requiring them to go on their way until she was restored.

THE REPORT OF THE SPIES.

1. *Where were the children of Israel at this time?*—In the wilderness of Paran. Ex. 12:16; 13:3.

2. *Was it far from the land of Canaan?*—One end of it was near to Judah.

3. *What did God command Moses to do?*—To send men to search the land of Canaan. Num. 13:2.

4. *Whom did Moses select for this errand?*—Heads of the tribes.

5. *What change did he make in the name of one of them?*—He called Oshea, the son of Nun, Jehoshua or Joshua. Num. 13:16.

6. *Give the meaning of the name before and after the change, and then say of whom he was the type.*—"Help" before, and "help of Jehovah" or "Saviour" after—a type of Christ the Saviour.

7. *To whom did Jacob refer in Gen. 49:24?*—To Joseph, another type of Christ.

8. *How long were they in searching the land?*—Forty days.

9. *What report did they bring?*—That the land flowed with milk and honey, but that the inhabitants were giants and the cities great and walled. Num. 13:26–28, 31–33.

10. *Did all the twelve join in the cowardly report?*—All but Caleb and Joshua. Num. 13:30; 14:6–9.

11. *What effect did this have on the people?*—They were in great distress, and proposed returning to Egypt. Num. 14:1–4.

12. *How did Moses and Aaron act?*—They fell on their faces in humiliation and intercessory prayer. Num. 14:5.

13. *What did Caleb and Joshua say?*—That the Lord was with Israel, and that they had nothing to fear from the inhabitants of the land. Num. 14:6–9.

14. *Who appeared at the moment when they were about to be stoned?*—God himself in his glory. Num. 14:10.

15. *What did he propose to Moses?*—To disinherit

Israel, and to make of Moses a mightier nation than theirs. Num. 14 : 11, 12.

16. *Did Moses accept this great honor?*—No; he pleaded for their pardon instead.

17. *What special mercy did the Lord promise to Caleb and Joshua?*—That they alone should enter the land of Canaan. Num. 14 : 30.

18. *How did he punish the ten rebels?*—They died of the plague. Num. 14 : 37.

19. *What punishment did the Lord lay on the whole congregation?*—To wander forty years in the wilderness till they died. Num. 14 : 33.

20. *Of what foolish act were they guilty next day?*—They entered the land before the time.

21. *How were they punished?*—They were attacked and driven back. Num. 14 : 40–45.

THE SABBATH-BREAKER, THE SIN OF KORAH, AND THE BUDDING ROD. (Num. 15, 16, 17.)

1. *Of what sin was a man found guilty about this time?*—Of gathering sticks upon the Sabbath-day. Num. 15 : 32.

2. *What did they do with him?*—They brought him to Moses. Num. 15 : 33.

3. *How was he punished?*—He was stoned to death by God's command. Num. 15 : 35, 36.

4. *Had not God already declared his mind about this sin?*—Ye shall keep the sabbath therefore; for it is holy unto you: every one that defileth it shall surely be put to death; for whosoever doeth any work therein, that soul shall be cut off from among his people. Ex. 31 : 14.

5. *Had he here said how the man was to be put to death?*—He had not.

6. *Does this not show us that Moses acted in everything immediately under the Lord's direction?*—It does. Num. 15 : 34, 35.

7. *What did the Lord order the people to make, that they might keep in remembrance his commandments?*—A blue fringed ribbon on the borders of their garments. Num. 15 : 38–40.

8. *Who was Korah?*—A Levite. Num. 16 : 8.

9. *Who were Dathan and Abiram, On and Peleth?*—Of the tribe of Reuben. Num. 16 : 1.

10. *What sin did they commit?*—They rebelled against the authority of Moses and Aaron. Num. 16 : 3.

11. *Had they not lately had a warning of this very sin in Miriam's case?*—The very same. Num. 12.

12. *What did Moses propose for these men to do, to prove whether God accepted them as priests or not?*—That they should come to the tabernacle, burning incense, to see if God would accept them. Num. 16 : 7, 18.

13. *In what way did God at once manifest his displeasure?*—By commanding Moses and Aaron and the congregation to keep away from the rebellious company and their habitations (Num. 16 : 20–24), when the earth opened and swallowed them up. Num. 16 : 31–33.

14. *How did the two hundred and fifty men who had thus transgressed die?*—A fire from the Lord consumed them. Num. 16 : 35.

15. *Did this still the murmurings of the people?*—The people then charged Moses and Aaron with killing the people of the Lord. Num. 16 : 41.

16. *What happened the next day?*—See No. 15.

17. *How did God again appear to vindicate the honor of his own appointed priesthood?*—Above fourteen thousand were struck dead by the plague. Num. 16 : 49.

18. *What did Moses command Aaron to do to avert the judgment he felt was about to fall on the people?*—To burn incense and make an atonement. Num. 16 : 46.

19. *Did God accept the service and own the act?*—He immediately stopped the plague. Num. 16 : 47, 48.

20. *Of whom was Aaron the type?*—Of Christ, our ever-living Intercessor.

21. *And of what was incense the type?*—The prayers of saints. Rev. 5 : 8.

22. *What was done with the censers of the rebels?*—They were beaten into plates to cover the altar, as a memorial of their sin. Num. 16 : 38–40.

23. *How did the Lord himself show whom he had chosen?*—By causing Aaron's rod to bud. Ex. 17 : 1–10.

24. *And what proof has he given to us that Jesus "is able to save to the uttermost" all that put their trust in him?*—By raising him from the dead. Acts 17 : 31.

25. *Of what was the budding rod a type?*—Of the resurrection and eternal life of Christ.

26. *Why is resurrection a proof that Jesus is the Son of God?*—Because he laid down his life and took it again by his divine power. Acts 2.

27. *Could any one less than God atone for sin?*—No, for sin is against God. "Thanks be unto God for his unspeakable gift!"

THE SIN OF MOSES AND AARON; AARON AND MIRIAM'S DEATH. (Num. 20.)

1. *Where did Miriam die?*—At Kadesh, in the desert of Zin. Num. 20 : 1.

2. *What trial of their faith did the children of Israel have here?*—The want of water. Num. 20 : 2.

3. *How did they behave?*—They reproached Moses for it. Num. 20 : 2–5.

4. *What did the Lord command Moses to do?*—To speak to the rock before the people, and it should give forth water.

5. *How did Moses in this matter dishonor the Lord?*—He spoke as if he and Aaron, by their own power, would bring the water out; and he also struck the rock. Num. 20 : 10, 11.

6. *What punishment did he and Aaron bring upon themselves for this sin?*—They were not allowed to enter the promised land. Num. 20 : 12.

7. *How many times did Moses mention this in his after writings?*—Five times: Num. 27 : 14; Deut. 1 : 37; 3 : 26; 31 : 2; 32 : 51.

8. *Did the Lord alter his purpose?*—No.

9. *How did the Edomites behave at this time to the children of Israel?*—They ungraciously refused them a passage through their land. Num. 20 : 14–21.

10. *From whom had the Edomites descended?*—From "Esau, who was Edom." Gen. 36 : 1.

11. *Why were they called by this name?*—Esau was called Edom, or "red," from the red pottage he got from Jacob. Gen. 25 : 30.

12. *What event happened at Mount Hor?*—The death of Aaron. Num. 20 : 22–29.

13. *What solemnity attended it?*—The removal, first, of his priestly robes, and putting them on Eleazar his son.

14. *What mark of respect did the children of Israel pay to the memory of Aaron?*—They mourned for him thirty days.

15. *Of whom was Aaron a type?*—Of Jesus our great High Priest.

16. *What is the meaning of consecrated?*—Set apart for the service of God.

17. *How was Aaron a type of Jesus in this?*—Jesus was anointed by the Holy Ghost, sanctified or set apart for his atoning and interceding work.

18. *What is the meaning of the name Christ?*—Anointed.

19. *Where is Jesus spoken of as Intercessor?*—Jesus, . . . because he continueth ever, hath an unchangeable priesthood. Wherefore he is able also to save them

to the uttermost that come unto God by him, seeing he ever liveth to make intercession for them. Heb. 7 : 22, 24. 25.

20. *Which of the apostles had a vision of Jesus dressed in priestly garments?*—John, in Rev. 1 : 12, 13.

21. *How is the Lord Jesus described in Heb. 4 : 14 16?*—As a great High Priest. Seeing, then, that we have a great High Priest that is passed into the heavens, Jesus the Son of God.

22. *Read Ps. 89 : 15 and 119 : 103, and say what part of Aaron's robe set these forth?*—The "golden bells and the pomegranates" "upon the hem" of it. Blessed is the people that know the joyful sound! they shall walk, O Lord, in the light of thy countenance. How sweet are thy words unto my taste! yea, sweeter than honey to my mouth. Ex. 28 : 34.

23. *Is the perfume of Aaron's garments ever spoken of in connection with the Lord Jesus?*—All thy garments smell of myrrh, and aloes, and cassia, out of the ivory palaces, whereby they have made thee glad. Ps. 45 : 8.

24. *In how many respects does the priesthood of the Lord Jesus excel the priesthood of Aaron?*—In its divinity and duration, Christ being God and a Priest for ever.

25. *What higher order of priesthood is compared to the priesthood of the Lord Jesus Christ?*—The priesthood of Melchizedek, which *seemed* to be everlasting, nothing being said in Scripture of his birth and death. Heb. 5, 6, 7.

THE BRAZEN SERPENT. (Num. 21 : 1–9.)

1. *Who came and fought with Israel?*—King Arad, the Canaanite.

2. *Which army was victorious?*—The Israelites'.

3. *How came it about?*—Because they made a vow unto God to destroy the Canaanites if he gave them the victory.

4. *Why were the people obliged to take such a long way round?*—To avoid the land of Edom. Num. 20 : 21.

5. *How did they meet this trouble?*—They were much discouraged, and complained of the want of bread and water.

6. *How did the Lord punish them?*—By means of fiery serpents—fiery in their color or their bite.

7. *What remedy was Moses commanded to prepare?*—A serpent of brass upon a pole, that the people might look upon it and live.

8. *Of whom was this a type?*—Of Christ.

9. *How?*—As the sinner may look upon him crucified, and live.

10. *Of what wicked spirit are the serpents a type?*—Of that old serpent, the devil.

11. *Are we all in the same danger?*—We are.

12. *What is our remedy?*—To look unto Christ by faith.

13. *What is faith?*—Faith in Christ is looking to him, fleeing to him, coming to him, apprehending or laying hold on him, trusting in him, leaning upon him.

BALAAM. (Num. 21 : 10–35; 22–26; and 31 : 1–8.)

1. *How far had the children of Israel got on their journey?*—To the wilderness before Moab.

2. *Where was Moab?*—On the east side on the Jordan.

3 *What interesting event had occurred at Beer?*—A supply of water, followed by a song of praise.

4. *What two mighty kings did the children of Israel conquer and slay at this time?*—Sihon, king of the Amorites, and Og, king of Bashan. Num. 21 : 23, 24, 33–35.

5. *What description is given of Og in Deuteronomy?* That he was a giant.

For only Og king of Bashan remained of the remnant of giants; behold, his bedstead was a bedstead of iron; is it not in Rabbath of the children of Ammon? nine cubits was the length thereof, and four cubits the breadth of it, after the cubit of a man Deut. 3 : 11.

6. *How many times in the Psalms are these conquest spoken of?*—Twice: Ps. 135 : 11 and 136 : 19, 20.

7. *What was the name of the king of Moab?*—Balak Num. 22 : 4.

8. *How did he feel when he saw the host of Israel?*—He was greatly alarmed. Num. 22 : 2–6.

9. *Who was Balaam?*—A noted heathen soothsayer, or pretended prophet, who lived by the Euphrates in Mesopotamia, and who sometimes received revelations from God. Num. 22 : 5; 24 : 1, 2.

10. *Why did Balak desire so much to see him?*—To get him to curse the Israelites, so that he might overcome them. Num. 22 : 6.

11. *Did Balaam desire to go?*—Yes, as the rewards that were offered him tempted his covetousness.

12. *What hindered him?*—The command of God Num. 22 : 12.

13. *Did God permit him to have his own way?*—Yes. Num. 22 : 20.

14. *Did that show that God was pleased with the errand?*—No; but it gave him an opportunity of showing his power over him in a more public and striking manner. Num. 23 : 7–12.

15. *How did God show his disapprobation?*—By sending his angel to stop him on his way. Num. 22 : 22.

16. *Did God send Balaam back, or permit him to go on?*—He let him go on. Num. 22 : 35.

17. *Had Balaam any power when he got there?*—Only to say what God told him. Num. 22 : 38.

18. *Did he try by divination to accomplish Balak's wish?*—Yes, while Balak offered sacrifice. Num. 23 : 3, 15, 23; 24 : 1.

19. *Did it succeed?*—No; God made him utter a blessing instead of a curse. Num. 23 : 8–10, 20–24; 24 : 2–9.

20. *How did Balak feel when he found he had brought a blessing instead of a curse on his enemies?*—He was angry with Balaam. Num. 24 : 10.

21. *When Balaam found that he could not prevail by enchantment, did he yield himself to the power of God?*—Yes. Num. 24 : 13, 14.

22. *What beautiful prophecy did he utter of the glory of the Lord Jesus?*—I see him, but not now (not as already come); I behold him, etc. Num. 24 : 17.

23. *How did he show he was a bad man?*—By his infamous advice to Balak to tempt the children of Israel to sin.

24. *What was his end?*—He was killed by the Israelites in battle with the Midianites. Num. 31 : 8.

25. *Of whom is he a type?*—Of the enemies of God.

26. *Is he mentioned in the New Testament?*—Woe unto them! for they have gone in the way of Cain, and run greedily after the error of Balaam for reward. Jude 11.

THE CITIES OF REFUGE. (Num. 26 and 27; 31–35.)

1. *What does chap. 26 record?*—The numbering of the Israelites.

2. *After the numbering how many men were left of those who came out of Egypt with Moses?*—Only two, Caleb and Joshua. Num. 26 : 65.

3. *How was this?*—God had said that all the rest should die in the wilderness. Num. 26 : 65.

4. *What lesson should it teach us?*—To beware of unbelief. Heb. 3 : 7–19.

5. *What kind arrangement did the Lord make for one family when all the men of it were dead?*—That the property of the father should go to his daughters. Num. 27 : 1–11.

6. *What petition did Moses present to the Lord at the end of chap. 27?*—That he would provide him a successor. Num. 27 : 15–17.

7. *Whom did the Lord appoint?*—Joshua.

8. *Of which tribe was Joshua?*—Ephraim. 1 Chron. 7 : 22–27.

9. *How does Jacob allude to him and to the Lord Jesus (of whom Joshua was a type) in Gen. 49 : 24?*—His bow abode in strength, and the arms of his hands were made strong by the hands of the mighty God of Jacob (from thence is the shepherd, the stone of Israel).

10. *What does chap. 31 describe?*—The defeat of the Midianites.

11. *How was the spoil to be purified?*—By fire or by water.

12. *To what is the judgment of the last day compared?*—1 Cor. 3 : 13–15.

13. *Which of the children of Israel had their inheritance on the east of the Jordan?*—Reuben, Gad and half the tribe of Manasseh. Num. 32.

14. *What do chaps. 33 and 34 describe?*—The forty-two stages of the journey through the wilderness, and the boundaries of Canaan, and the officers appointed to divide it.

15. *How many cities out of the tribes of Israel were to be given to the Levites?*—Forty-eight. Num. 35 : 7.

16. *For what purpose were six of these cities to be separated?*—For cities of refuge. Num. 35 : 6.

17. *Who had the privilege of fleeing thither?*—Any one who had accidentally killed another. Num. 35 : 11, 12, 24–28.

18. *Was there any protection to be afforded to the murderer?*—No. Num. 35 : 16–21.

19. *In what relationship did the "revenger of blood" stand to the slain person?*—Next of kin.

20. *How many witnesses were necessary to prove the wicked deed?*—Two.

21. *What event released the manslayer from the city of refuge, and permitted him to go at large again without fear of death?*—The death of the high priest. Num. 35 : 25.

22. *Of whom were those cities of refuge a type?*—Of Christ, the sinner's refuge from Satan and the wrath to come.

23. *Can you describe where those cities of refuge stood?*—Three on the east of Jordan, in the tribes of Reuben, Gad and Manasseh; and three on the west, in Galilee, Samaria and Judah. Deut. 4 : 41–43.

And they appointed Kedesh in Galilee in Mount Naphtali, and Shechem in Mount Ephraim, and Kirjath-arba, which is Hebron, in the mountain of Judah. Josh. 20 : 7.

24. *Were they in valleys or on hills?*—On hills.

25. *Why was this?*—So as to be more easily seen.

26. *Of whom is the manslayer a type?*—Of Satan, the great enemy of souls.

27. *How can we be said to be manslayers?*—By the self-destruction of sin.

O Israel, thou hast destroyed thyself; but in me is thine help. Hos. 13 : 9.

28. *Who is represented by the way to those cities?*—Jesus Christ.

I am the way, the truth, and the life; no man cometh unto the Father, but by me. John 14 : 6.

By a new and living way, which he hath consecrated for us, through the veil, that is to say, his flesh. Heb. 10 : 20.

29. *Of what is the avenger a type?*—Of the law, which requires us to do or die. Rom. 3 : 9–19; Gal. 3 : 22–24.

30. *Are we all conscious of our danger?*—Sinners are dead in sin, and both wise and foolish often slumber and sleep.

31. *Who must arouse us?*—Christ, by his awakening and enlightening Spirit. John 16 : 7–9; Eph. 5 : 13, 14.

32. *Are there any hinderances in the way?*—None from Christ himself.

Come unto me, all ye that labor and are heavy laden, and I will give you rest. Matt. 11 : 28.

33. *To what is allusion made in Ps. 9 : 9; 57 : 1; 59 : 16; 61 : 4; 62 : 7, 8; 71 : 7; 91 : 1, 2; 142 : 4, 5?*—To the refuge we have in God, through Christ.

The Lord also will be a refuge for the oppressed, a refuge in times of trouble. Ps. 9 : 9.

Be merciful unto me, O God, be merciful unto me: for my soul trusteth in thee: yea, in the shadow of thy wings will I make my refuge, until these calamities be overpast. Ps. 57 : 1.

DEUTERONOMY. (Deuteronomy.)

1. *When was the book of Deuteronomy written?*—A little before Moses' death. Deut. 1 : 3.

2. *Where were Moses and the children of Israel at this time?*—In the land of Moab, on the east of Jordan. Deut. 1 : 1, 4, 5.

3. *Of what is the book of Deuteronomy a summary?*—Of much of the history and the laws contained in the three foregoing books.

4. *Of whom does Moses speak in Deut. 18 : 15–19 as "the prophet"?*—Of Jesus Christ. Acts 3 : 20–22.

5. *What beautiful ceremony does he bid them perform when they should get into the promised land?*—To bring a basket of first-fruits to the priest as a thank-offering to God. Deut. 26 : 1–11.

6. *What was the name of the two mountains on which the blessing and the curse were to be written?*—Gerizim and Ebal. Deut. 27 : 1–8, 11–13.

7. *What fearful prophecy and warning did Moses utter?*—Curses of pestilence, drought, war, famine and other evils for disobedience of God's law. Deut. 28–30.

8. *In what way (chap. 31) did the Lord signally set apart Joshua to the office of leader?*—By appearing to him in the tabernacle in the pillar of cloud. Deut. 31 : 14, 15.

9. *In what way did Moses preserve what he said to them?*—By writing it and delivering it to the priests (Deut. 31 : 9), to be put in the ark of the covenant. Deut. 31 : 24–26.

10. *What special song was he commanded to write and rehearse before them?*—That contained in Deut. 32 : 1–43; 31 : 19.

11. *Who assisted him in the task?*—Joshua. Deut. 32 : 44.

12. *What did the Lord command Moses to do immediately after he had finished this work?*—To go up Mount Nebo and die. Deut. 32 : 48–52.

13. *In pronouncing his dying blessing on the tribes of Israel which did he single out for peculiar honor?*—Levi and Ephraim and Manasseh.

14. *What spot on earth was appointed by God to be the place of the death of Moses?*—The top of Pisgah. Deut. 34 : 1.

15. *What splendid prospect did the Lord give him ere he died?*—A great part or the whole of the land of Canaan. Deut. 32 : 2–4.

16. *In what did Moses differ from any other prophet?*—In God's speaking to him (as if) face to face. Deut. 34 : 10.

17. *How old was Moses when he died?*—One hundred and twenty years. Deut. 34 : 7.

18. *What special power was manifested in the preservation of his bodily strength?*—The power of God. who

prolonged his life and strength so much beyond the usual seventy years.

JOSHUA. (Josh. 1–4.)

1. *Who was Joshua?*—The son of Nun, of the tribe of Ephraim.

2. *Of whom is he a type?*—Of Christ, the Leader and the Conqueror.

3. *Of what is Canaan a type?*—Of heaven.

4. *Of what is the wilderness a type?*—Of the world.

5. *Of what is the river Jordan a type?*—Of death.

6. *Of what was the ark a type?*—Of Christ, by whom we pass safely through the Jordan of death.

7. *Of what were the stones that they took from the river a type?*—Of memories in heaven, of mercies and deliverances on earth.

8. *When Jesus was born in Bethlehem, did he come as a warrior?*—No.

9. *To what coming, then, does this type refer?*—His coming to judgment.

10. *Where is the Lord's second coming spoken of as a day of terror to his enemies?*—Behold, he cometh with clouds; and every eye shall see him, and they also which pierced him: and all kindreds of the earth shall wail because of him. Rev. 1 : 7.

11. *To what glorious prospect have the followers of Jesus to look forward?*—The final triumph of Christ over all his and our enemies. Rev. 19 : 19–21.

THE TAKING OF JERICHO—THE SCARLET LINE. (Josh. 2, 5 and 6.)

1. *Where did the city of Jericho stand?*—Near the west side of the Jordan.

2. *How did Joshua endeavor to ascertain the strength of the city?*—By sending two spies.

3. *How were these men treated in Jericho?*—They were sheltered in the house of Rahab from the king of Jericho's messengers.

4. *What promise did they make to the woman who had sheltered them?*—To save the lives and property of her family on the taking of the city. Josh. 2 : 12–14.

5. *Did she avail herself of the token they gave?*—She did. Josh. 2 : 17–21.

6. *What effect had their report on the people?*—They were doubtless much encouraged.

7. *What remarkable events happened on the plains of Jericho?*—The keeping of the Passover, the ceasing of the manna, the appearance of a heavenly Being to Joshua.

8. *Who appeared to Joshua when he was under the walls of Jericho?*—The Son of God.

9. *Did Joshua perceive, at first, who it was?*—No; he merely saw an armed man.

10. *How did he find it out?*—By his saying he was Captain of the Lord's host.

11. *What directions did the Lord give him as to the taking of the city?*—To march round it with the ark and blowing of trumpets, and at last with a shout. Josh. 6 : 3–5.

12. *Did he and Israel obey the Lord?*—Yes. Josh. 6 : 8–16, 20.

13. *What was the result?*—The wall fell down flat, and the city was taken and destroyed. Josh. 6 : 20, 21, 24.

14. *Did Rahab perish with the slain?*—She was brought away safely. Josh. 6 : 23.

15. *What was her preservation?*—Her faith and the scarlet-cord token that she had been directed to use.

By faith the harlot Rahab perished not with them that believed not, when she had received the spies with peace. Heb. 11 : 31.

16. *Of what is the destruction of Jericho a type?*—Of the destruction of all the enemies of God.

17. *Are we interested in this?*—Yes, as sinners.

18. *How?*—We are exposed to God's wrath, and deeply interested to know how we may be saved.

19. *What does the Bible tell us must be our safeguard in the day of wrath.* Rev. 7 : 13, 14.

20. *Can we trust that word?*—He is faithful that promised. Heb. 10 : 23.

21. *Had Rahab any reason to regret her faith in the word of the spies?*—No.

22. *Are there many ways of escape, or only one?*—There is none other Name under heaven given among men whereby we must be saved. Acts 4 : 12.

23. *Perhaps Rahab had been scoffed at for her scarlet line; did that deter her from trusting in it?*—No.

24. *Should the laugh and jeer of the world hinder us from trusting to the blood of Jesus for safety?*—The believer will enter into eternal joy, when the laughter ends in weeping and gnashing of teeth.

25. *Was Rahab alone saved?*—Her near relatives and her goods were saved with her. Josh. 6 : 22, 23.

26. *If we know a place of safety, should not we tell others of the same?*—It is our duty and privilege to do so.

27. *How can we do so?*—By telling them of Jesus Christ, and getting them to read and hear about him; and by living ourselves as those should do who know him and love him and enjoy him.

ACHAN'S SIN, AND THE TAKING OF AI. (Josh. 7 and 8.)

1. *What special command was given to Israel at the destruction of Jericho?*—To bring the silver and the gold into the treasury of the Lord. Josh. 6 : 18, 19.

2. *Who transgressed this command?*—Achan.

3. *What punishment did this sin bring on all Israel?*—A defeat by the men of Ai. Josh. 7.

4. *How was the offender discovered?*—By drawing lots under the guidance of God. Josh. 7 : 16–18.

5. *To what honored tribe did he belong?*—Judah. Josh. 7 : 1.

6. *Did this preserve him?*—No; honor and privilege often increase guilt.

7. *What awful punishment was necessary to cleanse Israel from the sin Achan had brought on them?*—The destruction of himself and his family and goods by stoning and by fire. Josh. 7 : 24, 25.

8. *What view of God's character does this history give us?*—His hatred of sin especially of "covetousness, which is idolatry;" and his severity to the impenitent sinner: "our God is a consuming fire." Heb. 12 : 29.

9. *Will the riches of the sinner avail when God brings him into judgment?*—Nothing at all.

10. *Can we hide our sins from God?*—O Lord, thou hast searched me, and know me. Thou knowest my downsitting and mine uprising, thou understandest my thought afar off. Thou compassest my path and my lying down, and art acquainted with all my ways. Ps. 139 : 1–3.

11. *When Achan's sin was wiped away, did God again give victory to Israel?*—The city of Ai was taken and destroyed. Josh. 8.

12. *Who bore the wrath of God and the punishment due to our sin?*—Our Lord Jesus Christ.

13. *Can God again smile on us?*—Yes, in Christ Jesus, in whom he is "well pleased."

14. *After the destruction of Ai what solemn act of obedience did Joshua perform?*—He wrote the law upon stone, and read its blessings and its curses on Mounts Gerizim and Ebal. Josh. 8 : 30–35.

15. *Where in the land of Canaan were those two mountains situated?*—Near Samaria.

16. *For what was Joshua remarkable as well as courage?*—For obedience to the will of God.

17. *Of whom was he a type in this?*—Of Christ. Heb. 10 : 7.

THE GIBEONITES. (Josh. 9.)

1. *How did the Gibeonites act when they saw the victories of the Israelites?*—They sent to Joshua messengers, who pretended that the Gibeonites did not live in Canaan, so that Joshua might be at liberty to spare them.

2. *Did they deceive Joshua and the elders of Israel?*—Yes. Josh. 9 : 15.

3. *How came Joshua to fail in this particular?*—Because he had not asked God's direction. Josh. 9 : 14.

4. *Who was the only Person who never failed?*—Christ, who knew the hearts of men.

5. *Were the Gibeonites spared?*—Yes.

6. *Why?*—Because of the league made with them, confirmed by oath. Josh. 9 : 16, 19.

7. *Was the Lord jealous when an oath was made in his name?*—Yes, very. Num. 30 : 2.

8. *What proof have we of this in the case of the Gibeonites in the after-history of Israel?*—2 Sam. 21 : 1, 2.

9. *To what service were the Gibeonites appointed?*—To be hewers of wood and drawers of water. Josh. 9 : 21.

THE BATTLE OF THE FIVE KINGS. (Josh. 10.)

1. *What did the rest of the kings of Canaan do when they found that the Gibeonites had made peace with Israel?*—Five of them joined in war against Gibeon.

2. *To whom did the Gibeonites appeal?*—To Joshua. Josh. 10 : 6.

3. *Who fought for and with Israel?*—God did. Josh. 10 : 10, 11.

4. *What signal proofs did the Lord give of this in the battle with those kings?*—Showering heavy hailstones upon their enemies, and miraculously prolonging the light of the sun and of the moon upon the scene of battle and pursuit. Josh. 10 : 11-14.

5. *Is this ever after referred to in Scripture?*—The sun and moon stood still in their habitation: at the light of thine arrows they went, and at the shining of thy glittering spear. Hab. 3 : 11.

6. *Of what battle is this the type?*—Of the spiritual warfare in every converted heart.

THE FINAL BATTLE WITH THE KINGS OF CANAAN. (Josh. 11.)

1. *What commandment had the Lord given relative to the destruction of the Canaanites?*—Ex. 34 : 11-13; Deut. 7 : 1, 2.

2. *Why did the Lord thus deal with these nations?*—Their wickedness had reached its height.
The iniquity of the Amorites is not yet full. Gen. 15 : 16.
Thou shalt not learn to do after the abominations of those nations. Deut. 18 : 9.

3. *How is the host that mustered against Joshua described?*—As being numerous as the sand upon the seashore. Josh. 11 : 4.

4. *What great advantage had they over Israel?*—The possession of chariots and horses.

5. *And yet which conquered?*—The Israelites, completely. Josh. 11 : 8.

6. *How was this?*—If God be for us, who can be against us? Rom. 8 : 31.
The Lord is on my side; I will not fear: what can man do unto me? Ps. 118 : 6-9.

7. *What did Joshua do with the city of Hazor?*—He burnt it with fire.

8. *Why Hazor in particular?*—Because it was the head of all the kingdoms he had fought with.

9. *Was this the last battle that Joshua fought?*—No; he had a long war afterward, till he took the whole land. Josh. 11 : 15-23.

DIVIDING THE LAND, AND DEATH OF JOSHUA. (Josh. 12-24.)

1. *What did Joshua begin so soon as the land had rest from war?*—To divide it among the tribes.

2. *Where was the tabernacle set up?*—At Shiloh. Josh. 18 : 1.

3. *In which tribe was this?*—Ephraim.

4. *How many men did Joshua appoint to survey the land?*—Three men from each of the last seven tribes. Josh. 18 : 4.

5. *How was it divided?*—By lot before the Lord. Josh. 18 : 6.

6. *How were their portions registered?*—In a book. Josh. 18 : 9.

7. *Describe the position of all the tribes on the map.*—Asher, half-Manasseh, Ephraim and Dan down the west coast, but Ephraim reaching to the Jordan; Naphtali, Zebulon, Issachar, Benjamin and Judah by the west border of the sea of Chinnereth, the Jordan and the Dead Sea; and Simeon below; half-Manasseh, Gad and Reuben on the east borders.

8. *In which tribe had Joshua his inheritance?*—Ephraim.

9. *Why?*—Because of his own choice. Josh. 19 : 49, 50.

10. *What portion had Caleb?*—Hebron. Josh. 14 : 12-14.

11. *Why?*—Because he chose it; and as he had wholly followed the Lord, Joshua confirmed his choice.

12. *What was the next thing they did after dividing the land?*—They appointed the cities of refuge.

13. *Which tribe was it that had no portion of the land set apart for them?*—Levi.

14. *How were they provided for?*—Forty-eight cities were assigned to them by the tribes.

15. *How many tribes had their inheritance on the east of Jordan?*—Reuben, Gad and half-Manasseh. Num. 32 : 33.

16. *What part of these tribes passed over Jordan with their brethren?*—The armed men. Josh. 1 : 14.

17. *When did they return home to their families again?*—After the end of the war and the division of the land. Josh. 22.

18. *What unexpected act did they do which alarmed their brethren?*—They built an altar of their own to the Lord. Josh. 22 : 10.

19. *How did they explain it?*—They had not built it for burnt-offering or sacrifice, but to remind them, and their children after them, of their connection with the true altar. Josh. 22 : 26, 27.

20. *Was it satisfactory?*—Quite. Josh. 22 : 30-33.

21. *To what age had Joshua lived?*—About one hundred and nine years.

22. *What was the last act he performed?*—He gave the elders of Israel (Josh. 23) a short history of their nation, and a solemn exhortation to renew their covenant with God. Josh. 24.

23. *What solemn covenant did Israel enter into with him?*—That they would serve idols no more. (Josh. 24 : 16-24.)

24. *Where did they make this covenant?*—At Shechem. Josh. 24 : 1.

25. *Where was Shechem?*—In Ephraim, or Samaria.

26. *What token of remembrance did Joshua set up there?*—A stone of witness. Josh. 24 : 26, 27.

27. *How old was Joshua when he died?*—One hundred and ten years.

28. *Where was he buried?*—In Mount Ephraim. Josh. 24 : 30.

29. *What other illustrious person was buried in Mount Ephraim?*—Eleazar. Josh. 24 : 33.

THE JUDGES.—BOCHIM, OR ISRAEL'S FAILURE. (Judg. 1, 2.)

1. *What is the meaning of the word Bochim?*—"Weepers." Judg. 2 : 5, marg.

2. *Why was the place so called?*—Because the Israelites wept there.

3. *What caused the weeping of Israel?*—Sorrow for the sin for which an angel had rebuked them. Judg. 2 : 1–4.

4. *How had they transgressed?*—By neglecting their covenant to make no league with the Canaanites, but to throw down their altars.

5. *Ought not the affecting history of Israel to lead us to look into our own hearts?*—That is what we should do whenever we read or hear of the sins or the faults of others.

6. *If we do, what shall we see there?*—The seeds of the same sins.

7. *Does God kindly admonish us as he did them?*—Take heed, brethren, lest there be in any of you an evil heart of unbelief, in departing from the living God. But exhort one another daily, while it is called to-day, lest any of you be hardened through the deceitfulness of sin. Heb. 3 : 12, 13.

8. *Where?*—See No. 7.

9. *When we try ourselves by God's standard are we justly condemned?*—We know that what things soever the law saith, it saith to them who are under the law: that every mouth may be stopped, and all the world may become guilty before God.

10. *To whom must we look for deliverance when the sins of our hearts, like the foes in Canaan, rise against us?*—To Christ our Saviour, whose blood and Spirit can remove the guilt and power of sin.

OTHNIEL, EHUD, SHAMGAR, DEBORAH AND BARAK. (Judg. 3–5.)

1. *Whom did the Lord first raise up as Israel's deliverer?*—Othniel. Judg. 3 : 9.

2. *To what great warrior was he related?*—To Caleb, who was probably his brother.

3. *How many years had the land rest?*—Forty. Judg. 3 : 11.

4. *When the children of Israel did evil again, to whom did the Lord deliver them?*—To Eglon, king of Moab, for eighteen years. Judg. 3 : 12–14.

5. *When they again repented, did God hear their prayer?*—Yes.

6. *Whom did he raise up to save them?*—Ehud, a Benjamite. Judg. 3 : 15.

7. *What was there remarkable about him?*—He was eft-handed.

8. *How did this bring about the king of Moab's death?*—It enabled Ehud to stab him in an unexpected manner. Judg. 3 : 21.

9. *Did Israel avail themselves of his death to go against the Moabites?*—Yes. Judg. 3 : 27, 28.

10. *How many did they slay?*—About ten thousand men. Judg. 3 : 29.

11. *Who was Israel's third deliverer?*—Shamgar. Judg. 3 : 31.

12. *What marvelous feat of strength is recorded of him?*—He slew six hundred Philistines with an ox-goad.

13. *What city was it in the north of Canaan that Joshua utterly destroyed?*—Hazor. Josh. 11 : 10, 11.

14. *By whom was it rebuilt?*—By Solomon. 1 Kings 9 : 15.

15. *Of what is this a proof?*—Of its importance as a fortress, and of disregard of the will of God.

16. *Who was judge at this time, and prophetess also?*—Deborah. Judg. 4 : 4.

17. *Who was Barak?*—A leader of the tribes of Zebulon and Naphtali. Judg. 4 : 6, 10.

18. *Which appeared to have the most courage, Deborah or Barak?*—Deborah, as Barak would not venture to fight without her. Judg. 4 : 8.

19. *How was Barak reproved for his faint-heartedness?*—By being told that the enemy's general would be given into the hands of a woman. Judg. 4 : 9.

20. *What kind of army did the Canaanitish general muster?*—Nine hundred chariots of iron formed part of it. Judg. 4 : 13.

21. *What was that general's name?*—Sisera. Judg. 4 : 7.

22. *How came it that Israel conquered such a host?*—The power of God was with them. Judg. 4 : 14, 15.

23. *Who was Jael?*—The wife of Heber. Judg. 4 : 17

24. *From what family had Heber, Jael's husband, descended?*—The Kenites and Hobab. Judg. 4 : 11.

25. *Was that an Israelitish family?*—No; the Kenites were one of the families or nations promised to Abraham's seed, but *Hobab's* family was settled in Israel.

26. *Was this why Sisera took shelter in their tent?*—He took shelter with them because they were at peace with Jabin his master. Judg. 4 : 17.

27. *Which side of the battle did Heber favor?*—The Israelites'. Judg. 4 : 11.

28. *What proof did his wife give of this?*—She killed Sisera. Judg. 4 : 21.

29. *Which side did the Lord take?*—The Israelites'. Judg. 4 : 14, 15. (No. 22.)

30. *As this battle is a type of the spiritual warfare that goes on in the soul, what should we do with an enemy to God that we may find hiding in our bosoms?*—Overcome and destroy it.

31. *Who delivered Sisera into Jael's hand?*—The Lord himself. Judg. 4 : 9.

32. *Who helps us if we desire to conquer our evil passions?*—The grace of God is sufficient for us.

33. *To what evil in our hearts can we compare Sisera with his nine hundred chariots of iron?*—To our chief evil passion or temptation, whatever it may be.

34. *To whom did Deborah and Barak give the glory of the victory in their beautiful song?*—To God. Judg. 5 : 2.

35. *What fearful curse did they pronounce on those who would not assist in this battle?*—Read Judg. 5 : 23.

36. *And what will be our condemnation if we are indifferent to those momentous concerns?*—We shall suffer with the enemies of God, as those who are not with him are against him.

GIDEON. (Judg. 6–8.)

1. *How came it after this that Israel got into trouble again?*—They did evil in the sight of the Lord. Judg. 6 : 1.

2. *Whom did the Lord permit to be their scourge at this time?*—The Midianites and the Amalekites. Judg. 6 : 3.

3. *To what miserable plight were the Israelites reduced?*—They were left without food. Judg. 6 : 4.

4. *On which side of Israel did these two nations lie?*—The Midianites on the south-east, and the Amalekites on the south-west.

5. *Where was Gaza?*—In the land of the Philistines.

6. *What means did the children of Israel at last use*

to free themselves from their great affliction?—They cried unto the Lord. Judg. 6 : 7.

7. *Did the Lord hear them?*—He sent a prophet to them, and afterward a deliverer, Gideon. Judg. 6 : 7–12.

8. *Who was Gideon? Of what tribe and family?*—A warrior, of the tribe of Manasseh and family of the Abiezrites.

9. *Who appeared to him?*—An angel (Judg. 6 : 11), or, rather, the Angel Son of God. Judg. 6 : 14.

10. *What was he doing?*—Threshing wheat.

11. *Did he at first know who addressed him?*—No; he did not address his visitor at first as God. Judg. 6 : 13, 17.

12. *How did he find it out?*—By the divine Angel's causing fire out of the rock to consume the food set before him (Judg. 6 : 21), and also by the language he used. Judg. 6 : 16.

13. *What were his feelings?*—Those of deep humility and conscious sinfulness. Judg. 6 : 22.

14. *Had he any cause for fear?*—Doubtless he was an Israelite indeed in whom was no guile, and as such he had nothing to fear.

15. *What makes man in general afraid of God?*—The consciousness of unrepented sin. Gen. 3 : 9, 10.

16. *What has the Lord provided to remove our fear, of which Gideon's offering was a type?*—The accepted sacrifice of Christ.

17. *Who has power to speak " peace " to the soul?*—He who said to the sick of the palsy, "Thy sins be forgiven thee."

18. *What was Gideon's first act of faith?*—To throw down the altar of Baal. Judg. 6 : 25–30.

19. *Did he get killed for fulfilling God's will?*—No; Joash his father prevented it by wisely saying that if Baal were a god he could punish him himself. Judg. 6 : 31, 32.

20. *How was his own father's heart influenced by the act?*—See No. 19.

21. *How does God reward those who honor his word?*—He says, "Them that honor me I will honor."

22. *What name of honor did Gideon get for this act?*—Jerubbaal, or "let *Baal* plead" against him. Judg. 6 : 32.

23. *Describe the army that was at this time gathered against Israel?*—The Midianites, Amalekites and other eastern nations. Judg. 6 : 33.

24. *What mighty power rested on Gideon at this time?*—The Spirit of the Lord. Judg. 6 : 34.

25. *Was he entirely without fear?*—No, for he asked God to give him a private token of his power. Judg. 6 : 36–40.

26. *How did he prove that God was a hearer and answerer of prayer?*—By the sign of the wet fleece on the dry ground, and of the dry fleece on the wet ground.

27. *Does God change, or is he as near to us and as ready to hear us as he was near to Gideon and ready and willing to hear him?*—Every good gift and every perfect gift is from above, and cometh down from the Father of lights, with whom is no variableness, neither shadow of turning. James 1 : 17. Jesus Christ, the same yesterday, and to-day, and for ever. Heb. 13 : 8.

28. *When Gideon blew his trumpet, how many came after him?*—Thirty-two thousand. Judg. 6 : 34; 7 : 3.

29. *Did the Lord intend to use so many to destroy the enemy?*—No, not even ten thousand.

30. *What sign did the Lord give to Gideon whereby he should know how many and which he had chosen?*—Their two different ways of taking or drinking water on a particular occasion. Judg. 7 : 4, 5.

31. *How many remained with Gideon after this selection?*—Three hundred men, who took the water in the quicker manner.

32. *How many were sent to their homes again?*—Nine thousand seven hundred.

33. *Must this not have been a great trial to Gideon's faith?*—No doubt it was. 1 Pet. 1 : 7.

34. *Did it fail?*—No, for God strengthened it. Judg 7 : 7, 9, 14; Heb. 11 : 32–34.

35. *What great encouragement did the Lord give Gideon just before he and his three hundred men went down to battle?*—A dream of one of the soldiers. Judg. 7 : 13, 14.

36. *What effect had this man's dream on Gideon?*—He praised God, and immediately prepared his men. Judg. 7 : 15, 16.

37. *What effect did it have on his own people?*—The same as on Gideon himself. Judg. 7 : 14, 20.

38. *Is the Lord ever at a loss for means to effect his purpose?*—Never.

39. *What plan was adopted to surprise the enemy?*—The unusual one of suddenly blowing trumpets and exposing a line of lights all round the enemy's camp in the middle of the night. Judg. 7 : 16–20.

40. *Did it answer? Why?*—Yes, because God was trusted in, and God blessed it.

41. *Of what were the lamps and pitchers a type?*—Of God's faithful ministers, and the light of truth they possess and hold forth.

We have this treasure in earthen vessels, that the excellency of the power may be of God, and not of us. 2 Cor. 4 : 7.

42. *Does God always work by means?*—He does, and we in our difficulties should use both prayer and means.

43. *Who tells us that he is " the light of the world "?*—Jesus Christ, in John 8 : 12.

44. *Whom does God appoint to hold up that light?*—His ministers especially, by their preaching and their example.

45. *Are not all Christians charged to do it?*—They are in Christ's sermon on the mount.

Ye are the light of the world. Matt. 5 : 14.

46. *Whose mighty power is it that must accompany the word for it to be effectual?*—The Spirit of truth. John 16 : 13.

47. *Why had Gideon's trumpets and his lamps such a wonderful effect on the enemy?*—Because God worked with them and by them, and made the Midianites slay each other. Judg. 7 : 22.

48. *On whom must we depend if we are to overcome and conquer our spiritual foes?*—On the same almighty power.

49. *Was Gideon conqueror?*—Yes, completely. Judg. 7 : 22–25.

50. *Shall we be?*—We certainly shall.

If God be for us, who can be against us? Rom. 8 : 31
I can do all things through Christ which strengtheneth me. Phil. 4 : 13.

51. *How was Gideon treated after this victory by his fellow-countrymen when he was faint and weary?*—They refused food to him and his men. Judg. 8 : 4–6.

52. *Did they afterward desire to honor him?*—They wished him to be their king. Judg. 8 : 22.

53. *Would he accept the kingly office?*—He declined it, as God had not yet appointed that form of government for Israel. Judg. 8 : 23.

54. *Yet what did he desire of them?*—The golden earrings taken from their enemies. Judg. 8 : 24–26.

55. *What effect did this have on his family?*—Gideon made the earrings into an ephod (an important part of the dress of the high priest as an intercessor with God. Ex. 28), and kept it in his city of Ophrah, where the people paid it some idolatrous worship, and brought temptation and punishment upon his family. Judg. 8 : 27.

ABIMELECH, OR THE CONTRAST. (Judg. 9.)

1. *Who was Abimelech?*—A son of Gideon. Judg. 9:1.

2. *Was his course an honorable one, like that of his father?*—No; he basely plotted to be made king. Judg. 9:2.

3. *Of what awful crime was he guilty?*—He slew his brethren. Judg. 9:5.

4. *Did either escape?*—Jotham alone.

5. *What parable did Jotham utter?*—He spoke of the useful trees, as the olive, the fig and the vine, refusing to be placed over the rest; and of the worthless bramble, as the only one that desired it. Judg. 9:8-15.

6. *Can you explain the meaning of this simile as it respects Abimelech?*—That part of it which speaks of the bramble represents the character and end of Abimelech. Judg. 9:52-57.

7. *Of what are the olive, vine and fig tree types?*—Together they are types of useful, amiable, wise and humble-minded men.

8. *Was it fulfilled? How?*—The parable was fulfilled in the foolish choice of Abimelech by the Shechemites, in the violent quarrels between them, and the destruction of both. Judg. 9:15, 20, 23, 49, 52, 54.

9. *Where did all this shameful scene take place?*—At Shechem.

10. *What remarkable events had rendered this spot peculiarly hallowed?*—The visit of Abraham on reaching Canaan, the reading of the law (Josh. 9), and the renewal of the covenant. Josh. 24.

11. *How did it stand with regard to the two mountains of blessing and cursing spoken of in Deut. 27 and in Josh. 8?*—In a narrow plain between them.

12. *How near was it to Shiloh, where the tabernacle was pitched?*—About twenty miles.

13. *What must an idol temple built on this spot be a proof of?*—That the Israelites had not yet conquered the whole country and destroyed its idols. Judg. 9:4-6.

14. *Has Jotham's parable anything to do with us?*—Yes, for all Scripture is given by inspiration of God. Tim. 3:16.

15. *Who in Scripture are compared to fruit trees?*—God's own people.

I am the vine, ye are the branches. John 15:5.

16. *Who are represented by the bramble?*—The wicked.

17. *What is expected of fruit trees?*—That they should bring forth fruit.

18. *What has the bramble or thorn to expect?*—To be burned. Isa. 30:12; 2 Sam. 23:6, 7.

19. *How is the hypocrite known from the true Christian?*—Ye shall know them by their fruits. Do men gather grapes of thorns, or figs of thistles? Matt. 7:16.

20. *What should our prayer be?*—Search me, O God, nd know my heart. Ps. 139:23.

TOLA, JAIR, JEPHTHAH, IBZAN, ELON AND ABDON. (Judg. 10-12.)

1. *Give me the name of the next judge of Israel.*—Tola. Judg. 10:1.

2. *How long did he judge Israel?*—Twenty-three years.

3. *Who succeeded him?*—Jair.

4. *How is his family described?*—As riding on ass-colts as deputy-judges. Judg. 5:10; 10:4.

5. *From whom did he get this inheritance?*—The children of Machir the son of Manasseh went to Gilead and took it, and dispossessed the Amorite which was in it. And Moses gave Gilead unto Machir the son of Manasseh; and he dwelt therein. And Jair the son of Manasseh went and took the small towns thereof, and called them Havoth-jair. Num. 32:39-41.

6. *How long did he judge Israel?*—Twenty-two years.

7. *How many idols are enumerated here which Israel at this time worshiped?*—Baalim and Ashtaroth, and the gods of five nations besides. Judg. 10:6.

8. *What had God commanded Israel with respect to this awful sin?*—Ye shall make you no idols nor graven image, neither rear you up a standing image, neither shall ye set up any image of stone in your land, to bow down unto it: for I am the Lord your God. Lev. 26:1, 14, 17.

9. *How did he punish them?*—By delivering them into the hands of the Philistines and Ammonites for eighteen years. Judg. 10:7, 8.

10. *When they prayed to the Lord did he hear them?*—No; he charged them with their ingratitude and idolatry. Judg. 10:10-14.

11. *Did he at once deliver them?*—See No. 10.

12. *Did he convince them of their sin?*—Yes; they confessed their guilt. Judg. 10:15.

13. *When God had convinced them of their sin, and they were humbled on account of it, did they forsake it?*—Yes; they put away their strange gods.

14. *How?*—See No. 13.

15. *What did the Lord then feel for them?*—His soul was grieved for their misery.

16. *Who was Jephthah?*—A great warrior of Gilead. Judg. 11:1.

17. *On which side of the land of Israel was the land of the Ammonites?*—On the east.

18. *Where was Gilead?*—In the neighboring tribe of Gad.

19. *Why did the men of Gilead choose Jephthah to be their captain?*—Because he was likely to lead them to victory.

20. *On what conditions did Jephthah accept the office?*—That he should be their head on his return. Judg. 11:9.

21. *What vow did Jephthah make before he went to battle?*—That if he were victorious, whoever came forth first out of his house to meet him on his return should be given up (like Samuel) to God's service for life, and that he would offer to the Lord a burnt-offering besides. Judg. 11:30, 31.

22. *Who came out first to meet him?*—His daughter and only child. Judg. 11:34.

23. *What did Jephthah feel and say when he saw his only child?*—He was deeply distressed, and told her of his vow. Judg. 11:35.

24. *What was her beautiful answer?*—That as God had given him victory he must do to her according to his vow. Judg. 11:36.

25. *What law of God was there to regulate what Jephthah said under these circumstances?*—That the subject of the vow might be redeemed by a payment in money. Lev. 27:2-5.

26. *What difference was there between "a vow" and a "devoted thing"?*—A thing devoted by some more solemn consecration than a vow could not be redeemed.

27. *For how much did Jephthah redeem his daughter if he did not slay her for an offering?*—About $5 or $15, according to her age.

28. *Why do we think he redeemed her?*—Because her friends went every year to lament her separation from them or to talk with her. Judg. 11:40, margin.

29. *Why was it a great grief for any woman in Israel to be childless?*—Because she might be the mother or ancestress of the Messiah, the promised seed of the woman that was to bruise the serpent's head. Gen. 3:15.

30. *Do you think that Jephthah valued the honor which he had sought, of being the head of his tribe, after this mournful event?*—Probably not, as it had cost him the

society of his only child; but he would still value the office of *judge* conferred on him by God.

31. *Can any honor or pleasure in this world give satisfaction in itself?*—No; nothing in the world that is passing away.

32. *What proof did Jephthah give of his knowledge of the Scripture history when he met the king of Ammon before the battle?*—He told him how it was that the Israelites became possessed of the land that the king was unlawfully claiming from them. Judg. 11 : 12–28.

33. *Where must our strength lie when we go against our spiritual foes?*—In the Lord and the power of his might. Eph. 6 : 10.

34. *What weapons did the Lord Jesus Christ use when he met Satan?*—The sword of the Spirit, the word of God. Eph. 6 : 17. It is written. Matt. 4 : 4, 7, 10.

35. *What is "the word of God" called in Heb. 4 : 12?*—Quick (or living) and powerful, and sharper than any two-edged sword.

36. *By what shall we be judged at the last day?*—The word that Christ has spoken.

37. *What painful circumstance arose from the jealousy of the Ephraimites?*—A quarrel with Jephthah, whom they had before unkindly treated, and a consequent defeat by him in battle with great slaughter. Judg. 12 : 1, 6.

38. *How long did Jephthah hold his honors?*—Six years.

39. *Who judged Israel after Jephthah?*—Ibzan.

40. *For how long?*—Seven years.

41. *Who succeeded Ibzan?*—Elon.

42. *How long did he judge Israel?*—Ten years.

43. *Who followed Elon?*—Abdon.

44. *How many sons and nephews had he?*—Seventy sons and nephews or grandsons.

45. *Was not this considered a great honor in Israel?*—Yes, as increasing the likelihood of being the ancestor of the Messiah.

46. *Why?*—See No. 45.

47. *What higher honor had Jephthah than even being the ancestor of the Messiah?*—The honor of being named with David and Samuel and the prophets in the roll of heroes and martyrs in the cause of God. Heb. 11 : 32.

SAMSON. (Judg. 13–17.)

1. *Who was Samson?*—One of the tribe of Dan. Judg. 13 : 1.

2. *What remarkable circumstance took place before his birth?*—The angel of the Lord appearing to his mother, and telling her that she should have a son, who should be a Nazarite unto God, and deliver Israel from the Philistines. Judg. 13 : 2–5.

3. *What was the name of Samson's father?*—Manoah. Judg. 13 : 2.

4. *Did he not seem to have some doubts lest his wife had been mistaken?*—Perhaps so, as he desired some further instruction. Judg. 13 : 8.

5. *Did the angel appear a second time?*—He did.

6. *Did he alter anything he had said before?*—He did not.

7. *What should this teach us?*—The truth: I am the Lord, I change not. Mal. 3 : 6.

8. *Which seemed to have the greatest faith, Manoah or his wife?*—His wife.

9. *How do you prove this?*—By Judg. 13 : 22, 23.

10. *How did Manoah and his wife know that their visitor was an angel?*—By the words he spoke, and by his ascending in the flame. Judg. 13 : 18–20.

11. *Did the angel ever appear to them again after the birth of Samson?*—No.

12. *What was there remarkable about Samson?*—His very great strength.

13. *What was a Nazarite?*—A person "separated unto the Lord." Num. 6 : 2–21.

14. *What special gift rested on Samson?*—The Spirit of the Lord. Judg. 13 : 25; 14 : 6.

15. *Where did Samson's strength lie? was it in his hair?*—No.

16. *Was it in his limbs?*—No.

17. *What was it that made the lamp and pitchers in Gideon's hand so effective?*—The power of God.

18. *What power rested on Deborah and Barak?*—See No. 17.

19. *What gave Jephthah the victory?*—See No. 17.

20. *Did the same power rest on Samson?*—Yes.

21. *Was Samson ever restored to the possession of his strength again?*—Yes, just before his death. Judg, 16 : 30.

22. *Name all his wonderful feats of strength, and say which was the greatest.*—He tore a young lion like a kid (Judg. 14 : 5, 6); he slew thirty Philistines (Judg. 14 : 19), and afterward one thousand (Judg. 15 : 15); he carried away the gates of Gaza (Judg. 16 : 3); he broke the green withs and new ropes with which he had been bound (Judg. 16 : 9); he carried away the beam of a weaving-machine to which his hair had been secured (Judg. 16 : 14); he pulled down a large building by its two pillars on the heads of the Philistines (Judg. 16 : 29, 30), the last and greatest feat of all.

23. *Does God still hear and answer prayer?*—He does, as every true Christian can bear witness.

24. *Of whom was Samson a type?*—Of Christ, in some of the special circumstances of his birth, and in his being devoted to God's service.

25. *In what respect particularly?*—As Christ triumphed in his death over Satan and his hosts.

26. *How did Samson, in type, show the resurrection of Jesus?*—In the recovery of his strength in spite of his enemies.

27. *Whom did the Lord Jesus meet single-handed? and who is called in Scripture a "roaring lion"?*—The devil. Matt. 4 and 1 Pet. 5–8.

28. *By what name is the Lord Jesus called in Isa. 9 : 6?*—"The mighty God."

29. *Where is the Lord Jesus, in prophecy, described as treading the wine-press of the wrath of God alone?*—In Isa. 63 : 3.

30. *Who is spoken of as bringing salvation alone?*—Jesus Christ.

> He saw that there was no man, and wondered that there was no intercessor: therefore his arm brought salvation unto him; and his righteousness, it sustained him. Isa. 59 : 16.

31. *On whom must we then depend for salvation?*—Jesus Christ.

> Neither is there salvation in any other: for there i none other Name under heaven given among men whereby we must be saved. Acts 4 : 12.

THE STORY OF MICAH, AND THE CLOSE OF THE JUDGES. (Judg. 17–21.)

1. *When a man does "that which is right in his own eyes" what is he sure to do?*—Wrong, for there is a way that seemeth right unto a man, but the end thereof are the ways of death. Prov. 16 : 25; Judg. 17 : 6.

2. *What standard has God given us by which we may judge ourselves?*—His holy word.

> To the law and to the testimony: if they speak not according to this word, it is because there is no light in them. Isa. 8 : 20.

3. *What proof do Micah and his mother give that by doing "that which was right in their own eyes" they did wrong?*—They both committed idolatry, and Micah committed theft. Judg. 17 : 2, 3, 5.

4. *Which commandments of God's law did Micah break?*—The second and the eighth.

5. *Why was it wrong to take a Levite for his priest?*—The duties of the Levites were at the tabernacle in Shiloh; and none of them could be priests but those called by God.

He hath brought thee near to him, and all thy brethren the sons of Levi with thee; and seek ye the priesthood also? Num. 16:10.

6. *Were Micah and his mother the only idolaters in Israel?*—No; the Danites also. Judg. 18:30.

7. *What relation had these Danites to Samson?*—Some of them came from Zorah and Eshtaol, where Samson had been. Judg. 13:25.

8. *To what part of Israel did they remove and settle?*—To Laish, in the tribe of Naphtali.

9. *Of what crimes were they guilty?*—Of robbery, murder and idolatry. Judg. 18:17, 27, 30.

10. *Do you think if you had lived in their days you would have done better?*—Probably not.

Are we better than they? No, in no wise. Rom. 3:9.

11. *Have we the same law to be our guide as they had?*—The same law, and the teaching of the prophets, of our Lord and of his apostles besides.

12. *What is the word of God compared to in Heb. 4:12?*—A "two-edged sword;" so thoroughly does it pierce our hearts and expose our sin.

13. *By what shall we be judged at the last day?*—"The word that" Christ has "spoken," including the whole Bible spoken by his Spirit.

14. *Is the Scripture our appointed rule, and is it sufficient?*—Yes; it thoroughly furnishes all the instruction we need. 2 Tim. 3:16, 17.

15. *What will be our condemnation if we neglect it?*—Eternal punishment. Luke 16:20-31.

BOAZ, OR THE REDEEMER. (Ruth.)

1. *Who was Elimelech?*—A man of Bethlehem-judah. Ruth 1:1, 2.

2. *What were the names of his wife and of his two sons?*—Naomi, and Mahlon and Chilion.

3. *Where did this family live?*—In the country of Moab. Ruth 1:1, 2.

4. *At what time did they live?*—In the days of the judges. Ruth 1:1.

5. *What event happened in Israel that drove them to sojourn in Moab?*—A famine.

6. *Of what was this a proof?*—Of the disobedience and idolatry of the people. Deut. 28:15-18.

7. *Whom did the sons marry?*—Orpah and Ruth, women of Moab. Ruth 1:4.

8. *Did they prosper and have long life?*—Both the sons soon died. Ruth 1:5.

9. *What became of Naomi after the death of her husband and sons?*—She returned to Judah, as the famine had ceased. Ruth 1:6, 7.

10. *What difference was there in the behavior of her daughters-in-law toward her?*—Both were distressed at the idea of parting with her, and said they would go with her, but only Ruth went.

11. *Did God accept this stranger who determined to forsake her people and her gods and trust in him?*—He did, and showed her much favor.

12. *And is God the same now as he was then?*—Yes; he receives all who receive Christ.

Peter said, Of a truth I perceive that God is no respecter of persons. Acts 10:34.

13. *What is the meaning of the name Naomi?*—"Pleasant." Ruth 1:20, margin.

14. *To what name did Naomi wish hers changed, and why?*—To Mara, or "bitter," because of the sorrows she had suffered.

15. *What rich and noble relative had the poor widow Naomi in her native place?*—Boaz. Ruth 2:1.

16. *Whose field did Ruth happen to glean in?*—His field. Ruth 2:2.

17. *Did Boaz notice Ruth? In what manner?*—He told her to glean his fields until the end of harvest, and gave orders for her refreshment and protection, and for a plentiful gleaning. Ruth 2:4-17, 21.

18. *What description can you give of Boaz, besides that he was rich and noble?*—He was a kind-hearted and a good man who honored God. Ruth 2:8-12.

19. *What effect did his kindness have on Naomi when she heard of it?*—She blessed God for his goodness, and told Ruth how to claim Boaz as her kinsman in the manner which the custom of the country allowed. Ruth 2:19, 20; 3:1-4.

20. *Did Ruth do as her mother-in-law bade her?*—She did. Ruth 2:5-7.

Children, obey your parents in the Lord: for this is right. Honor thy father and mother; which is the first commandment with promise; that it may be well with thee, and thou mayest live long on the earth. Eph. 6:1-3.

21. *What did this prove?*—That she knew the privileges of filial obedience.

22. *Did Boaz answer the high expectation that Naomi had of him?*—Yes; he behaved both well and kindly to his virtuous relation, and promised to do a kinsman's duty to her according to the law. Ruth 2:8-17.

23. *Was he the nearest relative that Naomi had?*—He was not. Ruth 2:12; 4:1.

24. *On whom did the duty of kinsman or redeemer fall?*—If brethren dwell together, and one of them die, and have no child, the wife of the dead shall not marry without unto a stranger: her husband's brother shall go in unto her, and take her to him to wife, and perform the duty of an husband's brother unto her. And it shall be that the first-born which she beareth shall succeed in the name of his brother which is dead, that his name be not put out of Israel. And if the man like not to take his brother's wife, then let his brother's wife go up to the gate unto the elders, and say, My husband's brother refuseth to raise up to his brother a name in Israel, he will not perform the duty of my husband's brother. Then the elders of his city shall call him, and speak unto him: and if he stand to it, and say, I like not to take her; then shall his brother's wife come unto him in the presence of the elders, and loose his shoe from off his foot, and spit in his face, and shall answer and say, So shall it be done unto that man that will not build up his brother's house. And his name shall be called in Israel, The house of him that hath his shoe loosed. Deut. 25:5-10.

25. *Did the nearest kinsman perform his duty to Naomi?*—No; he declined doing it. Ruth 4:1-6.

26. *What was the custom in such cases?*—For the person who gave up his right to hand his shoe, as a token of such giving up, to the person who took his place. Ruth 4:7.

27. *Who stepped in and took his place?*—Boaz. Ruth 4:9, 10.

28. *What blessing did the elders of Israel pronounce upon Ruth when she became the wife of Boaz?*—They prayed that God would bless her with many children, that she might be an ancestress of the Messiah. Ruth 4:11, 12.

29. *Do you think Naomi wished her name changed to Mara now?*—Certainly not.

30. *What should this teach us?*—To trust God that all will at length be well.

Oh taste and see that the Lord is good: blessed is the man that trusteth in him. Many are the afflictions of the righteous; but the Lord delivereth him out of them all. Ps. 34 : 8, 19.

31. *What was the name of the son whom God gave to Ruth?*—Obed. Ruth 4 : 17.

32. *What were the names* of his son *and of his grandson?*—Jesse and David.

33. *What relation, then, was Ruth to David?*—Great-grandmother.

34. *Of what glorious Person was Ruth, then, the ancestress?*—Of Christ.

35. *What is the meaning of the name Boaz?*—Strength" or "Swiftness."

36. *Of whom was Boaz a type?*—Of Christ.

37. *In what particular character was Boaz the type of the Lord Jesus?*—In that of brother, kinsman and redeemer.

38. *Refer to some texts to show the Lord Jesus as a Redeemer.*—

1st. As being of the human family:
When the fullness of the time was come, God sent forth his Son, made of a woman, made under the law, to redeem them that were under the law, that we might receive the adoption of sons. Gal. 4 : 4, 5.

2d. That he is not ashamed to call us brethren:
Both He that sanctifieth and they who are sanctified are all of one; for which cause he is not ashamed to call them brethren. Heb. 2 : 11.

3d. The price paid for our redemption:
Ye know that ye were not redeemed with corruptible things, as silver and gold, from your vain conversation received by tradition from your fathers; but with the precious blood of Christ, as of a lamb without blemish and without spot. 1 Pet. 1 : 18, 19.

4th. Give a proof of our poverty:
Thou sayest, I am rich, and increased with goods, and have need of nothing; and knowest not that thou art wretched, and miserable, and poor, and blind, and naked: I counsel thee to buy of me gold tried in the fire, that thou mayest be rich; and white raiment, that thou mayest be clothed. Rev. 3 : 17, 18.

5th. Give a proof of the Lord's riches:
The unsearchable riches of Christ. Eph. 3 : 8.

6th. Give a proof that he is heir of all things:
God, who at sundry times and in divers manners spake in time past unto the fathers by the prophets, hath in these last days spoken unto us by his Son, whom he hath appointed heir of all things. Heb. 1 : 1, 2.

7th. That he hath taken the Church to be his Bride:
Christ loved the church, and gave himself for it: that he might sanctify and cleanse it with the washing of water by the word, that he might present it to himself a glorious church, not having spot, or wrinkle, or any such thing. Eph. 5 : 26, 27.

8th. That he has not only purchased her to himself, but that he is Lord of all creation:
Jesus Christ: he is Lord of all. Acts 10 : 36.

9th. That though now his people are poor and weak and despised, the great Redeemer will come and claim his and their rightful inheritance:
I go to prepare a place for you. And if I go and prepare a place for you, I will come again, and receive you unto myself; that where I am, there ye may be also. John 14 : 2, 3.

39. *Was the "Redeemer" also the "revenger of blood"?*—It was the nearest relation in both cases.

40. *Will the Lord Jesus, when he comes again, fulfill that double character?*—The Lord Jesus shall be revealed from heaven with his mighty angels, in flaming fire taking vengeance on them that know not God, and that obey not the gospel of our Lord Jesus Christ; who shall be punished with everlasting destruction from the presence of the Lord, and from the glory of his power; when he shall come to be glorified in his saints, and to be admired in all them that believe. 2 Thess. 1 : 7-10.

41. *On whom will he execute justice?*—See No. 40.

42. *What effect should this solemn truth have on our minds?*—It should stir us up to flee at once to Jesus, our Redeemer, from the wrath to come.

43. *In Rev. 5 : 5 the Lord Jesus is called "the root of David;" to whom could that refer?*—As God, Christ was David's root or source; as man, he was his son. In Boaz, his type, he may also have been David's Redeemer or root.

44. *Why is the Lord Jesus called "the root of David," or Redeemer, in the same chapter as he is represented as the slain lamb?*—Because he redeemed us, not only as our kinsman in the human nature, but as the sacrificed Lamb of God.
Thou wast slain, and hast redeemed us to God by thy blood out of every kindred, and tongue, and people, and nation. Rev. 5 : 9.

45. *Compare Acts 20 : 28; Eph. 1 : 7; Heb. 9 : 11-14; 1 Pet. 1 : 18-25, and say if there be any excuse for those who neglect this great salvation.*—No, for redemption through the blood of Jesus is now plainly revealed and preached to us.

ELI AND SAMUEL. (1 Sam. 1–3.)

1. *Who was Eli?*—The priest—*i. e.* high priest. 1 Sam. 1 : 9.

2. *By whom was the priesthood in Israel appointed?*—By God himself.
This is the thing that thou shalt do unto them to hallow them, to minister unto me in the priest's office: Take one bullock, and two rams without blemish, etc. Ex. 29 : 1.

3. *Who was the first high priest?*—Aaron.

4. *Who ought to have succeeded him in the high priesthood?*—His sons Nadab and Abihu. Lev. 10.

5. *Which of Aaron's sons was high priest at his father's death?*—Eleazar.
Take Aaron and Eleazar his son, and bring them up unto Mount Hor; and strip Aaron of his garments, and put them upon Eleazar his son; and Aaron shall be gathered unto his people, and shall die there. Num. 20 : 25, 26.

6. *From whom had Eli descended?*—From Ithamar, Aaron's younger son.

7. *Did his sons walk in the way of their father Eli?*—No; they were very wicked. 1 Sam. 2 : 12-17.

8. *What sin was Eli guilty of that brought upon him God's anger?*—Only mildly reproving his wicked sons when he should have restrained them with the authority of a father. 1 Sam. 2 : 23, 24; 3 : 13, 14.

9. *Who was Elkanah?*—A Levite of Mount Ephraim. 1 Sam. 1 : 1.

10. *What were the names of his wives?*—Hannah and Peninnah.

11. *Which did he love the most?*—Hannah. 1 Sam. 1 : 5.

12. *What great trial had Hannah?*—Not having any child. 1 Sam. 1 : 10, 11.

13. *To whom did she tell her sorrow?*—To God in prayer.

14. *What did Eli suppose when he saw her lips moving in silent prayer?*—That she was drunken. 1 Sam. 1 : 13.

15. *When he found that he was mistaken, what did he say?*—Read 1 Sam. 1 : 17.

16. *Did this comfort Hannah's heart? and had she her desire?*—Her countenance was no more sad, and a child was born to her. 1 Sam. 1 : 18, 20.

17. *What name did she give the child?*—Samuel.

18. *What is the meaning of that name?*—"Asked of God."

19. *Why did she not go up with her husband to worship the next year?*—She preferred waiting until her child was old enough to remain altogether in the house of

the Lord to be his servant, according to her vow. 1 Sam. 1 : 22, 11.

20. *By whose command used the children of Israel to go up to Shiloh to worship?*—By God's command.

21. *How many times a year were all the men to appear before the Lord?*—Three times. Ex. 23 : 17.

22. *Which feast must this have been when the women met as well?*—The Passover, to which women sometimes went.

Now his parents went to Jerusalem every year at the feast of the passover. Luke 2 : 41.

23. *At what time of the year was this feast held?*—About the end of March or beginning of April.

24. *Did Hannah do with the child as she had promised?*—She did. 1 Sam. 1 : 24-28.

25. *How old was he when his mother took him up and dedicated him to the Lord?*—He "was young," perhaps six years old. 1 Sam. 1 : 24, margin.

26. *Why was it wrong of Eli's sons to take any part of the sacrifice they liked? Which part had God appointed for the priest's use?*—Because God had assigned them a particular part, the breast and the right shoulder. Lev. 7 : 31-34.

27. *What had God commanded relative to the fat of his sacrifices?*—Read Lev. 3 : 14-17.

28. *What condemnation did Eli's sons bring on themselves by eating the fat of the sacrifices?*—Whosoever eateth the fat of the beast, of which men offer an offering made by fire unto the Lord, even the soul that eateth it shall be cut off from his people. Lev. 7 : 25.

29. *Did the Lord send any messenger to warn Eli of the sin his sons were committing?*—He sent a man of God, a prophet. 1 Sam. 2 : 27-36.

30. *Is there any rule by which we may know if we are doing the will of God or not? What is it?*—Thy word is a lamp unto my feet and a light unto my path. Ps. 119 : 105.

31. *Did Eli regard this awful message?*—Perhaps not sufficiently, as another awful message was sent to him some years afterward; or it may have been too late and his sons become thoroughly hardened in sin. 1 Sam. 2 : 25.

32. *What manifest token did the Lord give that he had accepted the gift of Hannah and chosen her son as a prophet of his own?*—God gave him a special call and message. 1 Sam. 3 : 4-14, 20, 21.

33. *How old was Samuel when this occurred?*—About twelve, but some think he was much older.

34. *Had Eli instructed Samuel in the knowledge of God before this time?*—No doubt Eli had made him acquainted with God's law, and explained to him the tabernacle service; but Samuel had no experience yet of God's special way of making himself and his word or will known to his prophets. 1 Sam. 3 : 7.

35. *Are there any children now who, though often seen God's house, yet know him not?*—It is to be feared there are but very few of them who know God, so as to love and obey him, as Samuel did.

36. *When God called to Samuel, what did he answer?*—Speak, for thy servant heareth. 1 Sam. 3 : 10.

37. *Have you answered God's call to you?*—If not, he is calling to you now as you listen to his word—calling you to be his child, and to give him your heart. Ask him, for his dear Son's sake, to help you to obey the call. Give yourself to him *now.*

38. *What solemn message did the Lord give Samuel concerning Eli's house?*—That he would punish it for ever. 1 Sam. 3 : 11-14.

39. *Did the Lord continue to manifest himself to Samuel rather than to Eli?*—He did. 1 Sam. 3 : 19-21.

40. *What did this show?*—That God honors those who honor him, dishonors those who dishonor him. 1 Sam. 2 : 30.

THE TAKING OF THE ARK. (1 Sam. 4–7.)

1. *Who were Israel's greatest enemies at this time?*—The Philistines.

2. *What sinful act did Israel resort to when they found themselves smitten before the enemy?*—They brought the ark from its place at Shiloh. 1 Sam. 4 : 3-5.

3. *What effect did it have on the Philistines?*—They were afraid at first, but roused each other to a great effort. 1 Sam. 4 : 7-9.

4. *Of what was this a proof?*—That God was not with Israel, though the ark was.

Go not up, for the Lord is not among you; that ye be not smitten before your enemies. Num. 14 : 42.

5. *What was the fate of the ark, and of those who carried it?*—The ark was taken, and Eli's sons were slain. 1 Sam. 4 : 11.

6. *How did Eli bear the tidings?*—He fell back and died. 1 Sam. 4 : 18.

7. *What sorrowful event happened to the wife of Phinehas?*—She died in childbirth. 1 Sam. 4 : 19-22.

8. *What name did she give her son ere she died?*—Ichabod.

9. *What is the meaning of that name?*—"No glory."

10. *Why did she choose it?*—Because the glory had departed from Israel, the ark being taken.

11. *What did the Philistines do with the ark?*—They set it beside their idol Dagon. 1 Sam. 5 : 1, 2.

12. *What happened to their idol?*—It fell on its face before the ark. 1 Sam. 5 : 3, 4.

13. *Did this convince them of the sin of idolatry?*—Not at all.

14. *Whose office is it to open our minds to receive the truth?*—The Holy Spirit, who convinces of sin.

When he, the Spirit of truth, is come, he will guide you into all truth. John 16 : 13.

15. *Had they not full opportunity, living actually within the land of Israel, to know about the true God?*—Yes, but like thousands among ourselves now, they did not take advantage of it, and so they perished in their sins.

I said not unto the seed of Jacob, Seek ye me in vain : I the Lord speak righteousness, I declare things that are right. Look unto me, and be ye saved, all the ends of the earth : for I am God, and there is none else. Isa. 45 : 19, 22.

16. *What does David say about idols in Ps. 115?*—Their idols are silver and gold, the work of men's hands. They have mouths, but they speak not: eyes have they, but they see not: they have ears, but they hear not: noses have they, but they smell not: they have hands, but they handle not: feet have they, but they walk not: neither speak they through their throat. They that make them are like unto them; so is every one that trusteth in them.

17. *What proof did Dagon give of this in this history?*—He could not take care of himself. 1 Sam. 5 : 3, 4.

18. *What calamities did God's presence bring on his enemies?*—A painful disease and a plague of mice, and a deadly destruction besides. 1 Sam. 5 : 6, 9, 11, 12; 6 : 4, 5.

19. *What did they resolve to do?*—To send back the ark with a trespass-offering. 1 Sam. 6 : 2, 3.

20. *What test did they employ to ascertain if indeed the God of Israel had brought on them all these miseries?*—They yoked to the cart that carried the ark two cows, to see if they would go to the land of Israel without their calves. 1 Sam. 6 : 7-12.

21. *Who had power over the affections of these kine in making them go opposite to their natural feelings?*—God alone.

For every beast of the forest is mine, and the cattle upon a thousand hills. Ps. 50 : 10.

22. *How was the ark received?*—With joy (1 Sam. 6 :

13) and a sacrifice of thanksgiving to God. 1 Sam. 6: 14, 15.

23. *Of what act of impiety were the men of Beth-she-mesh guilty?*—Of looking into the ark (1 Sam. 6 : 19), which caused God to slay fifty thousand and seventy men.

24. *Why was this act of theirs inexcusable?*—They shall not go in to see when the holy things are covered, lest they die. Num. 4 : 20.

25. *Was the ark taken back again to Shiloh? If not, where was it taken?*—To Kirjath-jearim. 1 Sam. 7 : 1.

26. *How long did it remain there?*—Twenty years (1 Sam. 7 : 2), until the repentance of Israel.

27. *Who afterward removed it? and where did it go?*—David removed it to Mount Zion. 2 Sam. 6 : 2-17.

28. *Did Israel repent of their sins?*—They did, at the call of Samuel. 1 Sam. 7 : 3-6.

29. *To whom did they apply?*—To Samuel, to pray for their delivery from the Philistines. 1 Sam. 7 : 8.

30. *What did he do for them?*—He offered a sacrifice and cried unto the Lord.

31. *What proof did the Lord give that he accepted their sacrifice and heard their prayer?*—He caused a great thunder-storm and a defeat of the Philistines. 1 Sam. 7 : 10.

32. *Of what use could the offering of that lamb be to them?*—Because it typified or referred to Jesus, "the Lamb of God, which taketh away the sin of the world." John 1 : 29.

33. *Is Samuel mentioned among those who had faith in Him who was to come?*—Yes, in Heb. 11 : 32.

34. *Why is the Lord Jesus said (Rev. 13 : 8) to be "the Lamb slain from the foundation of the world"?*—Because we are redeemed with the precious blood of Christ, as of a lamb without blemish and without spot: who verily was foreordained before the foundation of the world, but was manifest in these last times for you. 1 Pet. 1 : 19, 20.

35. *Are there many ways by which we can be saved?*—There is one God, and one Mediator between God and men, the man Christ Jesus; who gave himself a ransom for all, to be testified in due time. 1 Tim. 2 : 5, 6. Neither is there salvation in any other: for there is none other Name under heaven given among men, whereby we must be saved. Acts 14 : 12.

36. *What memorial did Samuel set up in remembrance of this deliverance?*—A stone called Eben-ezer, or "the stone of help." 1 Sam. 7 : 12.

37. *What three characters did Samuel unite in his person?*—Priest, prophet or teacher, and judge.

38. *Of whom was he thus a type?*—Of our Lord Jesus Christ. Deut. 18 : 18, 19; 1 Sam. 2 : 35; Gen. 18 : 25; Rev. 19 : 11; 20 : 11, 12; Matt. 25 : 31, etc.

39. *If we believe that Jesus will ere long be our Judge, as he was the Priest to atone for us and the Prophet and Advocate to pray for and instruct us, what ought we to do?*—Seek ye the Lord while he may be found, call ye upon him while he is near: let the wicked forsake his way, and the unrighteous man his thoughts: and let him return unto the Lord, and he will have mercy upon him; and to our God, for he will abundantly pardon. Isa. 55 : 6, 7.

SAUL. (1 Sam. 9–31.)

1. *Who was Saul?*—Son of Kish. 1 Sam. 9.

2. *Of which tribe was he?*—Benjamin.

3. *What was there remarkable about his person?*—He was very tall and very handsome. 1 Sam. 9 : 2.

4. *What power did God allow to rest upon him?*—His Spirit, as he did to Balaam—in his gifts, but not his graces; in his enlightening, but not his converting power. 1 Sam. 10 : 10.

5. *Are there not some characters more difficult to un-*derstand than others?—There are, as the tares of the East resemble the wheat, and the sheep the goats.

6. *What contradictions do there appear in Saul's character?*—In many things he honored Samuel and honored God, but he mixed his religion with superstition, and was proud, disobedient and self-willed.

7. *How can we come to a conclusion in so judging?*—No man can serve two masters; for either he will hate the one, and love the other; or else he will hold to the one, and despise the other. Ye cannot serve God and mammon. Matt. 6 : 24.

8. *What made the children of Israel first think of having a king?*—Because Samuel was old, and his sons were unfit to help him or succeed him. 1 Sam. 8 : 5, 20.

9. *How did Samuel feel about it?*—He was displeased with their so dishonoring and disobeying God. 1 Sam. 8 : 6.

10. *How was he comforted?*—By prayer, and direction from God. 1 Sam. 8 : 6, 7.

11. *In what spirit did the Lord give them a king?*—In anger: "I gave thee a king in mine anger." Hos. 13 : 11.

12. *How did God establish the kingdom in his hand?*—By a victory over the Ammonites. 1 Sam. 11 : 11-15.

13. *Did Saul follow up this victory?*—He next attacked the Philistines. 1 Sam. 13.

14. *Who was Jonathan?*—Saul's son.

15. *What marked difference was there between him and his father?*—He was of a modest and affectionate disposition, and loved David.

16. *Who obtained the victory recorded in 1 Sam. 13 : 3?*—Jonathan.

17. *Who reaped the honor of it?*—Saul. 1 Sam. 13 : 3, 4.

18. *Was it not unworthy of Saul to take the glory that did not belong to him?*—It was.

19. *How did Saul again show his mean spirit in this same chapter?*—By retiring to Gilgal, leaving Jonathan and his men exposed to the enemy. 1 Sam. 13 : 2, 4.

20. *What did Samuel say to Saul when he came?*—He reproved him for offering a sacrifice to God without the high priest. 1 Sam. 13 : 13.

21. *What proof does this chapter give us of the degraded state into which Israel had fallen?*—The Philistines did not allow them arms, or even a smith to sharpen their tools. 1 Sam. 13 : 19, 20.

22. *What glorious victory does 1 Sam. 14 : 4-23, 31 record?*—Over the Philistines between Michmash and Aijalon.

23. *Who was the brave warrior here?*—Jonathan. 1 Sam. 14 : 4-14.

24. *How did Saul nearly spoil the victory of that day?*—By pledging his people to eat nothing all day until the battle was won. 1 Sam. 14 : 24.

25. *Was not an oath a very sacred thing?*—When thou shalt vow a vow unto the Lord thy God, thou shalt not be slack to pay it: for the Lord thy God will surely require it of thee; and it would be sin in thee. But if thou shalt forbear to vow, it shall be no sin in thee. Deut. 23 : 21, 22.

26. *What proof can you give of this in 2 Sam. 21 : 7?*—King David spared Mephibosheth, the son of Jonathan the son of Saul because of the Lord's oath that was between them, between David and Jonathan the son of Saul.

27. *Was not that transaction another proof of Saul's cowardly disposition? Who were the Gibeonites?*—It was cowardly of Saul to kill those who trusted to the Israelites' oath, and were not prepared to defend themselves. 2 Sam. 21 : 2. They were Amorites who had

deceived the Israelites, but whom they had promised not to kill. Josh. 9.

28. *What great touchstone has God given to try man by?*—Not every one that saith unto me, Lord, Lord, shall enter into the kingdom of heaven; but he that doeth the will of my Father which is in heaven. Matt. 7 : 21.

29. *What test of obedience did God require from Saul?*—That in fighting with the Amalekites he should destroy their sheep and oxen also. 1 Sam. 15 : 3.

30. *How did he act?*—He spared the best of them. 1 Sam. 15 : 9.

31. *How did Samuel feel?*—He was grieved. 1 Sam. 15 : 11.

32. *How did Samuel act?*—He told Saul that he should be no longer king. 1 Sam. 15 : 23.

33. *How did Saul's real character come out in this transaction?*—He showed himself more anxious to please his people for his *own* honor than for the honor of God. 1 Sam. 15 : 30.

34. *What accident happened to Samuel's garment as he turned away from Saul?*—It was rent. 1 Sam. 15 : 27.

35. *What prophecy did Samuel utter in connection with it?*—That God had rent his kingdom from him, and had given it to a better man. 1 Sam. 15 : 28.

36. *When did Saul next see Samuel?*—When Saul prophesied before him in Ramah, whither Saul had gone to see *him* (1 Sam. 19 : 24), and afterward when Samuel came and appeared to *Saul*, by God's permission, at the summons of the witch of Endor. 1 Sam. 28 : 3–20.

37. *What proof does that transaction give us that God never alters the word that he has once spoken?*—Because Samuel repeated and confirmed God's former judgment against him. 1 Sam. 28 : 17.

38. *Was not the woman surprised at what she herself had been permitted to do?*—She cried out from fear. 1 Sam. 28 : 12.

39. *In whose keeping are the spirits of the departed dead?*—They are all in the keeping of God—the blessed in paradise with Christ, and the wicked with Satan in their own place.

40. *Suppose any could return to us again, could they add to the testimony of Scripture?*—They could only confirm it.

If they hear not Moses and the prophets, neither will they be persuaded, though one rose from the dead. Luke 16 : 31.

DAVID. (1 Sam. 16.)

1. *Who was David?*—The youngest son of Jesse, a Bethlehemite. 1 Sam. 16 : 1.

2. *What prophecy was spoken of the tribe of Judah by Jacob?*—Judah, thou art he whom thy brethren shall praise: thy hand shall be in the neck of thine enemies; thy father's children shall bow down before thee. Gen. 49 : 8.

3. *Why did the Lord reject Saul from being king?*—Because he had not obeyed his commands. 1 Sam. 15 : 11, 23.

4. *Whom did he choose in his place?*—David. 1 Sam. 16 : 1, 11–13.

5. *Who was appointed to anoint David?*—Samuel. 1 Sam. 16 : 1.

6. *Why had the Lord chosen Saul?*—On account merely of his being a tall and a noble-looking man; God being displeased with the Israelites' *asking* for a king. 1 Sam. 9 : 2.

7. *Did the same rule apply to David?*—No; he was chosen rather on account of his qualities of mind and heart. 1 Sam. 16 : 6, 7.

8. *How was Samuel taught this?*—By being told to reject Jesse's elder sons.

9. *What occupation was David following at this time?*—Keeping sheep. 1 Sam. 16 : 11.

10. *What deplorable loss did Saul sustain when the Spirit of the Lord rested upon David?*—The Spirit departed from himself. 1 Sam. 16 : 14.

11. *What evil power took possession of Saul?*—An evil spirit, by permission of God.

12. *In what way did he obtain comfort?*—By having some one to play to him on the harp. 1 Sam. 16 : 16.

13. *Who was selected as his minstrel?*—David. 1 Sam. 16 : 18–23.

14. *What did this prove?*—The guiding providence of God.

15. *As David was then a shepherd, what psalm may we suppose he sang on his harp to the king?*—Perhaps the twenty-third.

16. *What effect did David's sweet harp have on the king?*—He was soothed and refreshed, but Jesus Christ and his Spirit, alone, can give our troubled conscience peace.

DAVID AND GOLIATH. (1 Sam. 17.)

1. *Did David continue to live with Saul?*—No; he returned to his father's sheep. 1 Sam. 17 : 15.

2. *Did his intercourse with Saul's court unfit him for a shepherd life?*—By the grace of God, it seems not to have done so.

3. *Where were David's brothers at this time?*—The three eldest went with Saul to battle. 1 Sam. 17 : 13.

4. *What did Jesse desire David to do?*—To take his brothers a present, and see how they fared. 1 Sam. 17 : 17, 18.

5. *Who were Israel's greatest enemies at this time?*—The Philistines.

6. *What had these enemies particularly to encourage them to fight at this time?*—The giant Goliath was on their side. 1 Sam. 17 : 4–11.

7. *What did David do when he got to the camp?*—He asked who Goliath was, and what was to be the reward for killing him. 1 Sam. 17 : 26.

8. *What effect did David's questions have on his brothers?*—Eliab thought him proud and presumptuous, and was angry with him. 1 Sam. 17 : 28.

9. *How did David answer them?*—Meekly and calmly. 1 Sam. 17 : 29.

10. *For what pleasing traits of character was David always remarkable?*—Gentleness, patience and forbearance.

11. *What was he called?*—A man after God's own heart. Acts 13 : 22.

12. *Give some texts in which God commends a meek and gentle spirit?*—I therefore, the prisoner of the Lord, beseech you that ye walk worthy of the vocation wherewith ye are called, with all lowliness and meekness, with long-suffering, forbearing one another in love. Eph. 4 : 1, 2. Put on therefore, as the elect of God, holy and beloved, bowels of mercies, kindness, humbleness of mind, meekness, long-suffering; forbearing one another, and forgiving one another, if any man have a quarrel against any: even as Christ forgave you, so also do ye. Col. 3 : 12, 13.

13. *What is said to be "of great price" in the Lord's estimation?*—The ornament of a meek and quiet spirit. 1 Pet. 3 : 4.

14. *Who was the most meek and gentle Being who ever lived?*—Christ also suffered for us, leaving us an example, that ye should follow his steps: who did no sin, neither was guile found in his mouth: who, when he was reviled, reviled not again; when he suffered, he threatened not; but committed himself to Him that judgeth righteously. 1 Pet. 2 : 21–23.

15. *Of whom are we commanded to "learn"?*—Of Jesus Christ.

Take my yoke upon you, and learn of me; for I am meek and lowly in heart. Matt. 11 : 29.

16. *Did David gain the information that he sought?*—He did. 1 Sam. 17 : 25-27.

17. *What was the result?*—David undertook to fight with the Philistine. 1 Sam. 17 : 32.

18. *How did Saul wish to prepare David?*—With Saul's own armor. 1 Sam. 17 : 38.

19. *Did he use the armor?*—No, because he was unaccustomed to it.

20. *What preparation did David make?*—He only took his staff and sling and five stones in a bag. 1 Sam. 17 : 40.

21. *What was the result of the engagement?*—The giant was killed by the first stone slung. 1 Sam. 17 : 49.

22. *Was only the giant slain?*—The Philistines fled, and many of them were slain.

23. *What did David do with the head and armor of Goliath?*—He brought the head to Saul and to Jerusalem, and put the armor in his tent.

24. *How was it that David had such power?*—Because he trusted in the Lord his God.

25. *Is his act of faith mentioned in Heb. 11?*—Yes, in verse 32.

DAVID AND JONATHAN. (1 Sam. 17 : 55-58; 18, 19, 20.)

1. *What remarkable question did Saul ask Abner when David went to fight the giant?*—Whose son David was. 1 Sam. 17 : 55.

2. *Was Abner able to answer Saul's question?*—He was not.

3. *How did they ascertain who the young conqueror was?*—Saul ascertained it from David's own mouth.

4. *Which of Saul's sons standing by felt his soul knit to David?*—Jonathan. 1 Sam. 18 : 1.

5. *What touching proof did he give of his love?*—He gave him his robes and some of his arms, though the scarceness of arms had made them especially valuable. Compare 1 Sam. 18 : 4 with 1 Sam. 13 : 22.

6. *What joyful song did the women sing when they went to meet the conquerors after the battle?*—Saul has slain his thousands, and David his ten thousands. 1 Sam. 18 : 7.

7. *What effect did this have on Saul?*—It made him jealous and angry.

8. *How did David behave himself?*—Wisely. 1 Sam. 18 : 14.

9. *Did Saul remember his promise to give his daughter in marriage to the man who should slay Goliath?*—No; he gave her to another man. 1 Sam. 18 : 17-19.

10. *What artful design did he form to get David slain?*—He required him to kill one hundred Philistines as the price of his daughter Michal, hoping he would have been killed himself. 1 Sam. 18 : 25.

11. *Did it succeed?*—No; David slew two hundred, and was unhurt.

12. *What was Saul obliged to do?*—To give him his daughter Michal for his wife. 1 Sam. 18 : 27.

13. *Did Saul's daughter love David?*—Yes. 1 Sam. 18 : 20, 28.

14. *How did she prove this?*—By letting him down from a window, that he might escape her father's rage. 1 Sam. 19 : 12-17.

15. *Why was David obliged to flee?*—Because Saul designed to kill him. 1 Sam. 19 : 1, 15.

16. *Would Jonathan believe this?*—No. 1 Sam. 20 : 1, 2; 19 : 4-7.

17. *Where did David first escape to?*—To Samuel, in Ramah. 1 Sam. 19 : 18.

18. *What wonderful power did God exercise over the* messengers sent to take David?*—The power of his Spirit, causing them to prophesy like Samuel's prophets. 1 Sam. 19 : 20, 21.

19. *Did David venture into Saul's presence again?*—He seems to have done so at Naioth in Ramah. 1 Sam. 19 : 22-24; 20 : 5.

20. *How did Jonathan assure himself that his father desired David's death?*—By what David said. 1 Sam. 20 : 3.

21. *When he discovered it, what course did he take?*—He promised to tell David of Saul's designs. 1 Sam. 20 : 9.

22. *What beautiful covenant did they make together?*—That Jonathan should warn David, and that David should be kind to Jonathan and his children. 1 Sam. 19 : 12-17, 23.

23. *Where did they each go afterward?*—David to his former hiding-place, and Jonathan to his father. 1 Sam. 20 : 19; 19 : 2.

DAVID A FUGITIVE. (1 Sam. 21-31.)

1. *Whither did David flee?*—To Nob.

2. *What did he obtain there?*—Some bread.

3. *Did he do this honorably?*—No; he pretended he was on the king's business. 1 Sam. 21 : 2.

4. *What made him tell a lie?*—Want of food, and fear that the priest would not give it him.

5. *Did not this show a want of faith in the living God who had hitherto so wonderfully preserved him?*—It did.

6. *To what place did he next proceed?*—To Gath. 1 Sam. 21 : 10.

7. *Did he act more consistently there?*—No; he pretended to be mad, that he might escape being imprisoned. 1 Sam. 21 : 11-13.

8. *What does this show us?*—That even the best men often fall into weakness and sin through their forgetfulness of God.

9. *Where did he go when he left Achish?*—To the cave Adullam. 1 Sam. 22 : 1.

10. *Who came to him there?*—Every one that was discontented or in debt or distress. 1 Sam. 22 : 2.

11. *What kind care did he take of his father and his mother?*—He got the king of Moab to receive and protect them. 1 Sam. 22 : 3, 4.

12. *Why were they obliged to leave their native place, Bethlehem?*—Because the garrison of the Philistines was then in Bethlehem. 2 Sam. 23 : 14; 1 Chron. 11 : 15, 16.

13. *Who joined David here?*—Jonathan, in the wilderness of Ziph. 1 Sam. 23 : 15, 16.

14. *Is there any description given of his men?*—Three mighty chiefs are there mentioned who slew great numbers of the Philistines; and thirty other valiant men, among whom Abishai and Benaiah are especially noted for their exploits. 2 Sam. 23; 1 Chron. 11.

15. *What proof of love did his men give him at this time?*—Three of them broke through the host of the Philistines to fetch him water from a favorite well. 2 Sam. 23 : 16; 1 Chron. 11 : 18.

16. *How did he show the tenderness of his heart in return?*—By declining to drink what had been obtained at so great a risk of his men's lives, and by pouring out the water in thankfulness to God.

17. *What are courage and tenderness, united, a proof of?*—Of a truly manly character.

18. *What cowardly act was Saul again guilty of toward the priests who had helped David?*—He ordered them to be slain. 1 Sam. 22 : 17.

19. *How did David and his noble little band of warriors employ themselves?*—In fighting with the Philistines, and rescuing the inhabitants of Keilah. 1 Sam. 23 : 1-5.

20. *When Saul heard it, what did he resolve to do?*—

To besiege Keilah and take David prisoner. 1 Sam. 23:7, 8.

21. *How did the Lord deliver David when Saul had nearly taken him?*—By causing the Philistines to invade the land, David having first prayed for direction, and Jonathan having given him encouragement from God. 1 Sam. 23 : 27, 28, 10, 16.

22. *Did Saul again go after David?*—Yes, in the wilderness of Engedi. 1 Sam. 24 : 1, 2.

23. *How did David behave when the Lord put Saul in his power?*—He would not kill him nor allow his men to do so. 1 Sam. 24 : 4–7.

24. *What effect did this have on Saul?*—He wept and spoke kindly to David. 1 Sam. 24 : 8–22.

25. *What treatment did David at this time meet with from Nabal?*—He refused to give food to David and his men, though they had taken nothing from him all the time they had been hiding and in want of provisions near him. 1 Sam. 25 : 1–13.

26. *How did Nabal's wife act?*—She went to him with a supply of food. 1 Sam. 25 : 14–31.

27. *What proof did she give of the high honor in which she held David (though an exile) at her husband's death?*—She became his wife. 1 Sam. 25 : 39–42.

28. *Did Saul again seek after David?*—Yes, in the wilderness of Ziph. 1 Sam. 26 : 1, 2.

29. *How did David revenge himself?*—By again sparing Saul's life. 1 Sam. 26 : 7–12.

> Dearly beloved, avenge not yourselves, but rather give place unto wrath: for it is written, Vengeance is mine; I will repay, saith the Lord. Therefore if thine enemy hunger, feed him; if he thirst, give him drink: for in so doing thou shalt heap coals of fire on his head. Be not overcome of evil, but overcome evil with good. Rom. 12 : 19–21.

30. *With what heathen did David again join himself?*—With Achish, king of Gath. 1 Sam. 27.

31. *Was this right?*—No; it was contrary to God's commandments to Moses and Joshua.

32. *What difficulties did David bring upon himself by this unholy alliance?*—He was invited by Achish to join him in fighting against the Israelites. 1 Sam. 28 : 1, 2.

33. *Where was David when the last decisive battle between Saul and the Philistines was fought?*—At Ziklag.

34. *To which side did David offer himself and his men?*—To Achish. 1 Sam. 29 : 8.

35. *Is it not likely he would have gone over to the side of Israel?*—No doubt.

36. *How did God preserve him from so very dangerous a position?*—By inducing the Philistine leaders to object to his being with them. 1 Sam. 29 : 4, 5.

37. *What event happened to him and his men while they were absent from Ziklag?*—The Amalekites burnt the city, and carried away the women and children captive. 1 Sam. 30 : 1, 2.

38. *Did they recover their treasures?*—Yes.

39. *How?*—They pursued and slew the Amalekites, and recovered all, after David had laid his trouble before God and obtained direction from him. 1 Sam. 30 : 6–20.

40. *What did he do with the spoil that they won?*—He divided it among all his men who had taken part in the pursuit or fight. 1 Sam. 30 : 21–25.

41. *What tremendous battle was happening in Israel while David and his men were thus employed?*—A battle with the Philistines in Mount Gilboa. 1 Sam. 31 : 1.

DAVID KING IN HEBRON. (2 Sam. 1–4.)

1. *How was David employed when the news came to him of the death of Saul and Jonathan?*—He was returned to Ziklag. 2 Sam. 1 : 1.

2. *What effect did the death of Saul have on David?*—He mourned for him and wept. 2 Sam. 1 : 12.

3. *How did Saul die?*—By his own hand, after being wounded by the Philistines. 1 Sam. 31 : 3, 4.

4. *What did David do to the young man who by his own confession had killed Saul?*—He ordered one of his soldiers to kill him. 2 Sam. 1 : 14–16.

5. *What touching record did David leave of his love to Saul and Jonathan?*—A song of lamentation. 2 Sam. 1 : 17–27.

6. *Did David at once go and possess the kingdom How did he act?*—Yes; after seeking direction from God, he went up to Hebron, and was there anointed king. 2 Sam. 2 : 1–4.

7. *Which tribe first acknowledged David's claim?*—Judah.

8. *What act of unnecessary bloodshed took place at Gibeon?*—A battle between the men of Judah and the men of Israel, who had Ishbosheth, a son of Saul, for their king. 2 Sam. 2 : 8–17.

9. *Which were victorious, Joab's men or Abner's?*—Joab's.

10. *What happened to Asahel, Joab's brother?*—He was killed by Abner. 2 Sam. 2 : 18–23.

11. *How long did the war continue between the houses of Saul and David?*—About two years. 2 Sam. 2 : 10; 3 : 1.

12. *What event turned the scale on David's side?*—Abner's deserting Israel on account of a quarrel with Ishbosheth, and offering to make terms with David. 2 Sam. 3 : 6–20.

13. *Did David receive Abner?*—Yes, with hospitality and honor. 2 Sam. 3 : 20.

14. *How did Joab like this?*—He blamed David for it. 2 Sam. 3 : 24, 25.

15. *What did Joab do?*—He killed Abner in revenge for the death of Asahel. 2 Sam. 3 : 27.

16. *What course did David take when he heard this?*—He called upon all the people to mourn with him for Abner. 2 Sam. 3 : 31.

17. *What traits of character does David's conduct display?*—Tenderness of heart and readiness to forgive.

18. *Did David approve of Joab's conduct?*—No; as Abner was no longer a rebel, and as Joab had killed him deceitfully and revengefully in time of peace.

19. *Why did he not punish him?*—Because he had not the power. 2 Sam. 3 : 39.

20. *Who was Zeruiah?*—The mother of Abishai, Joab and Asahel.

21. *Of what act of treachery were the servants of Ishbosheth guilty?*—They killed their master. 2 Sam. 4 : 2, 5–8.

22. *Did not the death of Ishbosheth clear the way to David's ascent to the throne of Israel?*—It did, as no one else was seeking to be king.

23. *Did David on this account reward the murderers How did he act toward them?*—So far from rewarding them for their treachery and infidelity, he ordered them to be slain.

DAVID AND THE ARK OF GOD. (2 Sam. 5 and 6, and 1 Chron. 14, 15, 16.)

1. *How old was David when all Israel came to anoint him king?*—Thirty. 2 Sam. 5 : 4.

2. *What was David's first conquest?*—The stronghold of Zion. Sam. 2 : 5, 7.

3. *What was there about this city that renders it so remarkable and makes it of peculiar interest to us?*—The temple in which our Lord so often taught was built there.

4. *What king made presents to David?*—Hiram, king of Tyre. 2 Sam. 5 : 11.

5. *Where was Tyre?*—To the north of Canaan, on the borders of the Mediterranean Sea.

6. *For what was Tyre remarkable?*—For its manufacture of purple dresses and for its commerce.

7. *Did the Philistines treat David as Hiram had? How did they act when they heard he was king?*—No; they went to fight against him. 2 Sam. 5:18.

8. *What did the Philistines take with them to battle?*—Images of their gods. 2 Sam. 5:21.

9. *How was David guided?*—By God, whose direction he had sought. 2 Sam. 5:19.

10. *Which host conquered?*—David's. 2 Sam. 5:20.

11. *What became of the gods of the Philistines?*—David burnt them. 2 Sam. 5:21.

12. *What was David's next act?*—To bring the ark from Kirjath-jearim. 2 Sam. 6:2, 3.

13. *How came the ark to be at Kirjath-jearim?*—Because God had not yet directed it to be removed thence.

14. *Where was the tabernacle at this time?*—In Gibeon. Scott on 2 Sam. 6:17.

15. *In whose house had the ark been kept?*—In the house of Abinadab. 1 Sam. 7:1.

16. *In what way did they bring it?*—In a new cart. 2 Sam. 6:3.

17. *What happened to Uzzah?*—He died by the hand of God for thoughtlessly and rashly taking hold of so sacred a thing as the ark when it seemed about to fall. 2 Sam. 6:6, 7.

18. *How did David feel?*—He was displeased, and afraid to go farther. 2 Sam. 6:8-10.

19. *What did he do with the ark then?*—He placed it in the house of Obed-edom the Gittite. 2 Sam. 6:10.

20. *How ought the ark to have been brought?*—By hand, with staves. Num. 4:15.

21. *How many months had elapsed before David had courage to fetch the ark?*—Three. 2 Sam. 6:11.

22. *What induced him then to do it?*—The blessing that rested upon those who had the charge of it. 2 Sam. 6:12.

23. *How was it accomplished this time?*—The Levites bore the ark with staves upon their shoulders. 1 Chron. 15:2, 15.

24. *Why was Michal, David's wife, offended with David?*—Because of his dancing to the music before the ark. 2 Sam. 6:20.

25. *What did David's manner really express?*—Religious joy and humble thankfulness.

26. *Of whom in his humility was David a type?*—Of Christ, the lowly one of heart.

27. *Where did David place the ark?*—In a tent on Mount Zion, in the city of David. 1 Sam. 7:1, 3; 16:1.

28. *Was he satisfied with this? What did he desire to do?*—No; he desired to build for the ark a house of cedar. 1 Sam. 17:1.

29. *Did the Lord permit him to do it?*—No.

30. *How did the Lord make his will known to David?*—By Nathan the prophet. 1 Sam. 7:3-15.

31. *What did David feel? and what did he say?*—He felt deeply humble and very unworthy of God's promised blessings, and prayed to God to confirm his word. 1 Sam. 7:16-27.

32. *In whom was David's house to be confirmed for ever?*—In Jesus Christ, as Zacharias declared in Luke 1:68-70.

33. *Was the claim of Jesus as "son of David" acknowledged when he was on earth? When?*—Yes, when he rode into Jerusalem.

And the multitudes that went before, and that followed, cried saying, Hosanna to the son of David! Matt. 21:9.

34. *When does Jesus call himself "the offspring of David"?*—In Rev. 22:16.

35. *Has he yet sat on David's throne?*—No; we see not yet all things put under him. Heb. 2:8.

36. *Where is it said "I will give to him the throne of his father David"?*—The Lord God shall give unto him the throne of his father David: and he shall reign over the house of Jacob for ever; and of his kingdom there shall be no end. Luke 1:32, 33.

37. *When will this be fulfilled?*—When Christ returns to judge and reign.

DAVID'S CONQUEST—HIS SIN. (2 Sam. 8-12; 1 Chron. 18-20.)

1. *What had God's promise been of the boundary of Israel's possession?*—"From the river of Egypt unto the river Euphrates."

2. *What conquests did David make which fulfilled this?*—The conquest of the Philistines, Moabites, Ammonites and Syrians. 2 Sam. 8:1, 2, 6, 12, 14; 10:19.

3. *What splendid armor had the Syrians?*—Golden shields. 2 Sam. 8:7.

4. *What did David do with the spoil that he took in battle?*—He gave the gold and silver and brass for the ornament and service of the tabernacle. 2 Sam. 8:10, 11.

5. *How did he arrange his kingdom?*—He made Joab commander-in-chief; Jehoshaphat, historian; Zadok and Ahimelech, priests; and his own sons and others, judges and officers. 2 Sam. 8:15-18.

6. *Did he forget his friend Jonathan in this his prosperity? What proof did he give?*—No; he inquired after the family of Saul, and gave Saul's land and a place at his own table to Mephibosheth, son of Jonathan. 2 Sam. 9.

7. *How often was it customary for kings to go forth to battle?*—"At the return of the year," or in spring.

8. *Whom did David send to besiege Rabbah?*—Joab. 2 Sam. 11:1.

9. *Where was David?*—At Jerusalem.

10. *Why did David send Uriah with a letter to Joab, telling him to put him in the front of the battle?*—In order that he might be killed. 2 Sam. 11:15.

11. *Why did David wish the brave Uriah to die?*—That he might get possession of his wife, with whom he had committed adultery.

12. *Was not this a very awful sin?*—Yes; it was adding *murder* to his other shocking sin.

13. *Whom did the Lord send to convince David of his sin?*—Nathan the prophet. 2 Sam. 12:1.

14. *How did he do it?*—By a parable.

15. *Did the Lord pardon David?*—Yes, and said he should not die. 2 Sam. 12:13.

16. *Did he not say also that in his feelings as a father he would chastise him for it?*—Yes, by the death of his child; and he was also punished by Absalom's rebellion. 2 Sam. 12:14.

17. *How did David feel?*—It is believed that his deep sorrow for his sin is expressed in the fifty-first Psalm.

18. *Did the Israelites conquer Rabbah?*—Yes. 2 Sam 12:26.

19. *What message did Joab send to David?*—That he should come and have the honor of completing the conquest of the city himself. 2 Sam. 12:27, 28.

20. *Although David got the honor of conquering Rabbah, and had the crown placed on his head, do you think he felt happy in it when the brave Uriah had died under the walls?*—No; he said his sin was ever before him. Ps. 51:3.

21. *What signal proof did the Lord give to David of his full and free forgiveness?*—By giving him another child. 2 Sam. 12:24.

22. *What was the name of this child?*—Solomon.

23. *What was the meaning of the name?*—"Peaceable."

24. *What name did Nathan the prophet add to this? and what did it mean?*—Jedidiah, "Beloved of the Lord." 2 Sam. 12 : 25.

25. *Through whom must we obtain forgiveness of our sins?*—Through Jesus Christ.

26. *Is there any limit to God's forgiving grace?*—No; he will abundantly pardon. Isa. 55 : 7.

27. *What did Jesus say to the woman whom he forgave when on earth?*—" Neither do I condemn thee: go and sin no more." John 8 : 11.

DAVID AND ABSALOM. (2 Sam. 13–22.)

1. *Who was Absalom?*—A son of David. 2 Sam. 13 : 1.

2. *Why did he flee away to Geshur?*—Because he had killed his half-brother Ammon for outraging his sister Tamar. 2 Sam. 13 : 28, 32, 37.

3. *How long did he stay there?*—Three years.

4. *Who brought him back again?*—Joab, who by a kind contrivance had gotten David's leave. 2 Sam. 14 : 23.

5. *How did he repay his father's kindness?*—By making a conspiracy against him. 2 Sam. 15.

6. *What punishment had the Lord said should spring from David's own house?*—The sword and other evils. 2 Sam. 12 : 10, 11.

7. *Why?*—Because of his taking Uriah's wife.

8. *How did Absalom steal away the people's affections from David?*—By artful speeches and promises and civilities. 2 Sam. 15 : 2–6.

9. *When David heard of the conspiracy, what did he do?*—He fled from Jerusalem. 2 Sam. 15 : 13–16.

10. *Who went with him?*—All his household and six hundred men from Gath. 2 Sam. 15 : 16–18.

11. *What famous counselor followed Absalom?*—Ahithophel. 2 Sam. 15 : 31.

12. *Who managed by an artifice to set his counsel aside?*—Hushai, David's friend. 2 Sam. 15 : 32–37; 17 : 1–14.

13. *Whose advice did Absalom follow?*—Hushai's. 2 Sam. 17 : 14.

14. *What effect did this have on Ahithophel?*—He hanged himself. 2 Sam. 17 : 23.

15. *Why did Hushai give this advice?*—That he might secure David's escape.

16. *Who slew Absalom?*—Joab.

17. *How was it done?*—As Absalom hung from an oak tree by his hair, which had become entangled as he rode under it. 2 Sam. 18 : 9–15.

18. *What command had David given about Absalom to his captains?*—That they should deal gently with him for his sake. 2 Sam. 18 : 5.

19. *Did Joab seem to care for this?*—Not at all. 2 Sam. 18 : 11, 14.

20. *How did David feel, and what did he say, when Absalom was slain?*—He was deeply distressed, and said, "Would God I had died for thee, O Absalom, my son, my son!" 2 Sam. 18 : 33; 19 : 1–4.

21. *Of what sin was Absalom guilty?*—Rebellion against his father and against his king.

22. *Of whom, in both these particulars, was he a type?*—Of Satan, the rebel against God, and the angel of light.

23. *Describe Absalom's person?*—He was the handsomest man in the country, and was remarkable for his long, flowing hair. 2 Sam. 14 : 25, 26.

24. *What does the Lord say about pride in Proverbs?*—Pride, and arrogancy, and the evil way, and the froward mouth, do I hate. 8 : 13. When pride cometh, then cometh shame: but with the lowly is wisdom. 11 : 2. Pride goeth before destruction, and an haughty spirit before a fall. 16 : 18.

25. *Was peace at once again restored to Israel?*—It was. 2 Sam. 19 : 9, 14.

26. *Whom had David appointed captain of his host instead of Joab?*—Amasa. 2 Sam. 19 : 13.

27. *How did Joab act on hearing this?*—He killed him. 2 Sam. 20 : 9, 10.

28. *What relation was Amasa to David?*—Nephew, as son of his sister Abigail.

29. *Did David again spare Joab from punishment?*—Yes; he continued to be commander-in-chief. 2 Sam. 20 : 23.

30. *Who quelled the insurrection?*—Joab. 2 Sam. 28 : 14.

31. *What was a famine in Israel a sign of?*—National guilt. Deut. 28.

Heaven is shut up, and there is no rain, because they have sinned against thee. 1 Kings 8 : 35.

32. *What were David's feelings when a famine of three years visited Israel?*—Doubtless he felt compassion for his suffering people, and believed that the famine was a visitation of God. 2 Sam. 21.

33. *Of whom did he inquire?*—Of the Lord. 2 Sam. 21 : 1.

34. *What was the Lord's reply?*—That the famine was in consequence of the guilt incurred by the nation when Saul and his people slew the Gibeonites. 2 Sam. 21 : 1, 2.

35. *What expiation did the Gibeonites require?*—The death of seven of Saul's sons. 2 Sam. 21 : 6.

36. *What touching proof of a mother's love did Rizpah give?*—She watched the bodies of her sons night and day, to prevent their being torn by birds or beasts. 2 Sam. 21 : 10.

37. *What old enemies of David's again showed themselves?*—The Philistines. 2 Sam. 21 : 15.

38. *What proof have we of David's declining strength and of the faithful love of his followers?*—He was faint in battle, and Abishai preserved his life, and his people said he should no longer go out with them to battle. 2 Sam. 21 : 15–17.

39. *What is the twenty-second chapter of 2 Samuel about?*—It is David's psalm of thanksgiving for deliverance from his enemies.

DAVID'S TRANSGRESSION, HIS LAST ARRANGEMENTS, AND DEATH. (2 Sam. 24; 1 Chron. 21–29; 1 Kings 1, 2.)

1. *By whom was David tempted to number Israel?*—Satan. 1 Chron. 21 : 1.

2. *What is Satan called in 1 Pet. 5 : 8?*—A roaring lion, walking about seeking whom he may devour.

3. *Who remonstrated with David?*—Joab. 2 Sam. 24 : 3.

4. *Did not David's heart smite him after he had don it?*—Yes; he said he had sinned greatly and don very foolishly. 2 Sam. 24 : 10.

5. *What was God's promise to Abraham as to the number of Israel?*—That it should be very great, like the number of the stars.

6. *Whom did the Lord commission to reprove David?*—The prophet Gad. 2 Sam. 24 : 11.

7. *What did he offer him?*—The choice of one of three punishments.

8. *Which did David choose? and why?*—Famine or pestilence, rather than war; the immediate hand of God, rather than the hand of man.

9. *At what spot did the destroying angel stop?*—The threshing-floor of Araunah. 2 Sam. 24 : 16.

10. *What event had occurred on that hill about eight hundred years before?*—The offering up of Isaac (in the opinion of some).

11. *Of what was that circumstance a type?*—Of the sacrifice of Christ as the atonement for sin.

12. *How did David know that the Lord had accepted his offering?*—By the plague being stayed. 2 Sam. 24:25.

13. *By whose authority did he consecrate the threshing-floor of Araunah?*—By the authority of the prophet Gad. 2 Sam. 24:18.

14. *Why did he not go up to the tabernacle at Gibeon?*—Because he was afraid of meeting the angel again at the place of God's special presence. 1 Chron. 21:29, 30.

15. *What preparations did he make for the future building of the temple?*—Hewn stone, gold, silver, iron, brass and cedar. 1 Chron. 22:2-5, 14-16.

16. *What solemn charge did David give to Solomon concerning the temple?*—To build it, as David himself had desired to do. 1 Chron. 22:6-16.

17. *What other arrangements did David make?*—He divided the priests and Levites and other officers into orders, and fixed their duties. 1 Chron. 23:23-27.

18. *Who showed David the pattern of the future temple?*—God himself, by his Spirit. 1 Chron. 28:12, 19.

19. *Did any one besides David contribute toward the future glory of the temple?*—The chiefs and the people. 1 Chron. 29:6-9.

20. *Whom did David make king over Israel before he died?*—Solomon. 1 Chron. 23:1.

21. *Who had aspired to be king?*—Adonijah, one of David's sons. 1 Kings 1:5, 6.

22. *What charge did David give to Solomon concerning Joab and Shimei?*—That they should receive the punishment due to their guilt. 1 Kings 2:5, 6, 8, 9.

23. *What were the last words of David?*—Now bless the Lord your God. 1 Chron. 29:20.

24. *How old was David when he died?*—Seventy.

25. *How many years had he reigned in Hebron? how many over all Israel?*—David was thirty years old when he began to reign, and he reigned forty years. In Hebron he reigned over Judah seven years and six months; and in Jerusalem he reigned thirty-and-three years over all Israel and Judah. 2 Sam. 5:4, 5.

26. *In what respect was David a man after God's own heart?*—In the general character of his life, and in his being a type of Christ, his own beloved Son.

DAVID A TYPE OF CHRIST.

1. *What is the meaning of the name Christ?*—"Anointed."

2. *Was David made king at the time he was anointed?*—He was not at the time of his first anointing by Samuel.

3. *Tell how this circumstance is typical of the Lord Jesus Christ?*—Because, though Christ's kingdom began when he was anointed with the Holy Ghost and commenced his ministry on earth, his great universal reign has not yet taken place.

4. *What was David before he was called from his father's house?*—A keeper of sheep.

5. *What wild beasts did he fight with and kill?*—A lion and a bear.

6. *Of whom are those beasts a type?*—Of Satan the roaring lion. 1 Pet. 5:8.

7. *Who is "the Good Shepherd" who gives "his life for the sheep"?*—Jesus Christ. John 10:11.

8. *What was David's conduct to his father?*—That of a faithful, devoted and obedient son. 1 Sam. 17:20, 34, 35.

9. *Of whom is it recorded, "This is my beloved Son in whom I am well pleased"?*—Of Jesus Christ. Matt. 3:17.

10. *In what relative position did David stand to Saul?*—In that of servant to a master.

11. *What ought a servant to be?*—Honest, diligent, faithful and zealous, as serving God as well as man.

12. *How did David behave himself while serving Saul?*—Faithfully in duty and forbearing under provocation.

13. *Of whom is it recorded "I delight to do thy will, O my God"?*—Of Christ in the name of David. Ps. 40:8.

14. *Did David bear any other characters? Was he a prophet?*—Many. Yes.

15. *Did he speak of Jesus in the Psalms?*—Constantly, but especially in Psalms 22 and 110.

All things must be fulfilled, which were written in the law of Moses, and in the prophets, and in the psalms, concerning me. Luke 24:44.

16. *When did the Lord Jesus quote from the Psalms?*—Jesus saith unto them, Yea, have ye never read, Out of the mouth of babes and sucklings thou hast perfected praise? (Matt. 21:16; Ps. 8:2); Jesus cried with a loud voice, saying, Eli, Eli, lama Sabacthani? that is to say, My God, my God, why hast thou forsaken me? (Matt. 27:46; Ps. 22:1); and in other places.

17. *Of whom, then, as Psalmist, is David a type?*—Of Christ.

18. *Was not David a warrior, a captain and a leader?*—He was.

19. *What Scriptures show that the Lord Jesus was all these?*—Behold, I have given him for a witness to the people, a leader and commander to the people. Isa. 55:4; Rev. 19:13-15. The Captain of . . . salvation. Heb. 2:10.

20. *Where was David born?*—Doubtless at Bethlehem, where Jesse his father lived. 1 Sam. 17:12-15.

21. *Where was Jesus born?*—At Bethlehem. Matt. 2:1.

22. *Was the kingship of David acknowledged at once?*—No; Saul and his son Ishbosheth opposed or rebelled against him.

23. *Were there not a few who did recognize David as the anointed of God, even in his adversity? Name them.*—Samuel, Jonathan, Ahimelech, Gad, the Adullamites, Abiathar, Abigail, Joab, Abishai, Asahel and others.

24. *Were there any who owned the glory of Jesus when he was here in abasement?*—There were his apostles and disciples, and many women who ministered unto him.

25. *Did not the followers of David dearly love him?*—They did.

26. *Did they not even risk their lives for his sake?*—Many of them did in battle, and three of them to only get him some water for his thirst.

27. *And what is the feeling of those who own Jesus as their Lord and Master?*—A feeling, more or less warm and strong, of devoted, self-denying love.

28. *What did David feel toward them?*—A tender and grateful love.

29. *How did Jesus testify his estimation of love shown to him?*—Whosoever shall give to drink unto one of these little ones a cup of cold water only in the name of a disciple, verily I say unto you, he shall in no wise lose his reward. Matt. 10:42. Inasmuch as ye have done it unto one of the least of these my brethren, ye have done it unto me. Matt. 25:40.

30. *Did David conquer other nations, and rule beyond the limits of the twelve tribes of Israel?*—He conquered the Syrians, Ammonites and others.

31. *By what name is Jesus called in Rev. 19:16?*—KING OF KINGS AND LORD OF LORDS.

32. *What earthly throne is said to be everlasting?*—David's.

Thine house and thy kingdom shall be established for ever before thee: thy throne shall be established for ever. 2 Sam. 7:16.

33. *Of whom must that be spoken?*—Of Christ, the King.

34. *To whom does the parable in Luke 19 : 12–27 refer?*—The parable of the returned nobleman calling his servants to account refers to Christ coming again in his kingdom.

35. *Ought we not, then, to examine our hearts to see who is reigning there?*—Yes; for if he is not ruling over our affections now, we shall not be partakers of his kingdom hereafter.

36. *Have we not each some talent we shall be called to an account for?*—Yes; we all have time and influence, and more or less of means and abilities, to use for God's glory.

37. *Will you not have to give an account of even this lesson?*—Yes, and of every sermon we hear.

38. *What should you, then, strive to do?*—To remember what we hear, and, by the grace of God, to live and act according to it.

39. *Was David's reign a type of the peaceful reign of the Lord Jesus?*—No; he had been a man of war.

40. *Which king's reign is a type of it?*—Solomon's.

41. *What is the meaning of the name Solomon?*—"Peaceable."

SOLOMON. (1 Kings 1–11; 1 Chron. 21–29; 2 Chron. 1–9.)

1. *Of whom was Solomon a type?*—Of Christ, his peaceful reign being like the final kingdom of the Prince of Peace.

2. *Whose son was he?*—David's.

3. *What did the children cry of Jesus in the temple when he was on earth?*—Hosanna to the son of David! Matt. 21 : 15.

4. *Read John 6 : 15, and say what temporal honor the people wished to force upon Jesus?*—Jesus perceived that they would come and take him by force, to make him a king.

5. *Was the Lord Jesus rightful heir to David's throne on earth?*—Yes.

6. *Would he consent to take it from their hands?*—No.

7. *From whom will the Lord Jesus receive his kingdom?*—From God the Father in the appointed time.

8. *What did these same people do to the Lord Jesus very soon afterward?*—They derided his claim to be king and clamored for his crucifixion.

9. *When will Jesus take to himself his great power and reign?*—At the day of judgment. Rev. 11 : 15–18.

10. *Is this coming glory prophesied of in Scripture?*—In 2 Thess. 1 : 7–10, and other places.

11. *What was the first thing that Solomon did when he came to the throne—that is, after his father's death?*—He put Joab and Shimei (among others) to death. 1 Kings 2 : 28–46.

12. *Who had previously condemned them?*—David. 1 Kings 2 : 5, 6, 8, 9.

13. *How will our final award be settled?*—He that believeth and is baptized shall be saved; but he that believeth not shall be damned. Mark 16 : 16. Look to yourselves, that we lose not those things which we have wrought, but that we receive a full reward. 2 John 8.

14. *Who will be our Judge?*—God, in Christ.

15. *How does the Lord judge?*—Man looketh on the outward appearance, but the Lord looketh on the heart. 1 Sam. 16 : 7.

16. *By what standard shall we be judged?*—He that rejecteth me, and receiveth not my words, hath one that judgeth him: the word that I have spoken, the same shall judge him in the last day. John 12 : 48.

17. *Did Jesus judge men when he was on earth?*—No. If any man hear my words, and believe not, I judge

him not: for I came not to judge the world, but to save the world. John 12 : 47.

18. *To what time does the Lord Jesus defer the judgment?*—To the last day. John 12 : 48.

19. *Were not David in deferring the judgment, and Solomon in executing it, great types of this?*—Yes.

20. *Have sinners any hope from the circumstance that God delays judgment?*—None at all, if they remain impenitent.

21. *Say what merciful reason the apostle Peter gives for delay in the last chapter of his Second Epistle?*—The Lord is not slack concerning his promise, as some men count slackness; but is long-suffering to us-ward, not willing that any should perish, but that all should come to repentance.

22. *Can you give some texts where the certainty of the judgment-day is spoken of?*—Behold, the Lord cometh with ten thousands of his saints, to execute judgment upon all. Jude 14, 15. When the Son of man shall come in his glory, and all the holy angels with him, then shall he sit upon the throne of his glory; and before him shall be gathered all nations; and he shall separate them one from another, as a shepherd divideth his sheep from the goats; and he shall set the sheep on his right hand, but the goats on the left. And these shall go away into everlasting punishment; but the righteous into life eternal. Matt. 25 : 31–36, 46. Behold, he cometh with clouds; and every eye shall see him, and they also which pierced him; and all kindreds of the earth shall wail because of him. Rev. 1 : 7.

23. *Can you give a description of it?*—I saw a great white throne, and him that sat on it, from whose face the earth and the heaven fled away; and there was found no place for them. And I saw the dead, small and great, stand before God; and the books were opened; and another book was opened, which is the book of life; and the dead were judged out of those things which were written in the books, according to their works. And the sea gave up the dead which were in it; and death and hell delivered up the dead which were in them; and they were judged every man according to their works. And death and hell were cast into the lake of fire. This is the second death. And whosoever was not found written in the book of life was cast into the lake of fire. Rev. 20 : 11–15.

24. *Will it be of any use for us to run to "the altar" (as Joab did) then?*—No; the day of salvation will have past, there will remain no more sacrifice for sin, and the mountains and rocks will be no shelter from the wrath of the Lamb.

25. *Of whom is the altar a type?*—Of Christ, the refuge now from the wrath to come.

26. *When should we flee to Jesus and lay hold of his righteousness?*—"Now is the accepted time." 2 Cor 6 : 2.

27. *Who was Solomon's queen?*—Pharaoh's daughter. 1 Kings 3 : 1.

28. *Had Egypt been a friend or enemy to Israel in former time?*—An enemy and oppressor for a long time after Joseph's death.

29. *Was it not remarkable that Solomon should choose a bride from Egypt?*—Yes, but she is supposed to have embraced the Jewish religion.

30. *Of whom was Solomon's bride a type?*—Of the Church, the bride of Christ. Rev. 19 : 7, 8.

31. *For whom did the Lord Jesus die? Was it for angels?*—Forasmuch, then, as the children are partakers of flesh and blood, he also himself likewise took part of the same. Heb. 2 : 14.

32. *By taking on himself our nature, to what place of dignity has he raised his people?*—To be "heirs of God, and joint-heirs with Christ" (Rom. 8 : 17), and "to sit with" him "in" his "throne." Rev. 3 : 21.

24*

33. *By whose command did Solomon build the temple?* —By command of God. 1 Kings 5 : 5.

34. *Who had prepared greatly for this before him?*—David. 1 Chron. 22.

35. *Why was not David permitted to build the temple?* —Because he had "been a man of war." 1 Chron. 28 : 3.

36. *To whom had the pattern been shown?*—To David "by the Spirit" of God. 1 Chron. 28 : 11, 12.

37. *Who selected the place on which the temple was to be built?*—David. 1 Chron. 21 : 28–22 : 2.

38. *On what mountain was it built?*—Moriah. 2 Chron. 3 : 1.

39. *What wondrous act of faith had taken place on that mountain about eight hundred years before?*—It has been supposed that Abraham offered up Isaac on this spot.

40. *What is on that mountain* now?—The Turkish mosque or church of Omar.

41. *Who provided Solomon with timber, etc.?*—Hiram, king of Tyre. 1 Kings 5 : 1, 8–10.

42. *Was this a gift to Solomon, or did he pay for it?* —Solomon paid wages and supplied food to Hiram's men (1 Kings 5 : 6, 9), and gave him twenty cities in Galilee. 1 Kings 9 : 11.

43. *Was anything done in Lebanon besides felling the trees?*—Stone was hewn from the quarries. 1 Kings 5 : 17.

44. *Was the stone also prepared before it came to the temple?*—Yes. 1 Kings 5 : 18.

45. *Of what was this a type?*—Of the preparation of God's people to be "the temple of the living God" (2 Cor. 6 : 16), built upon the foundation of the apostles and prophets, Jesus Christ himself being the chief corner-stone. Eph. 2 : 20.

46. *What is said in Matt. 25 : 10 about being* ready? —While they went to buy, the bridegroom came ; and they that were ready went in with him to the marriage ; and the door was shut.

47. *Can you see any resemblance between the state of these virgins in the parable and the trees of Lebanon in the time of Solomon?*—Both were fit and ready for the service for which they were required.

48. *What tree does the woodman select when he seeks timber?*—A tree of the proper kind of wood, straight, sound and of sufficient size.

49. *What becomes of small wood, brambles, brushwood, etc.?*—They are burned.

50. *What warning word should we allow to have influence over us?*—Be ye also ready, for in such an hour as ye think not the Son of man cometh. Matt. 24 : 44.

51. *How was Solomon's temple dedicated?*—There was a solemn feast, the bringing in of the ark, Solomon's prayer and blessing, and a sacrifice of peace-offerings. 1 Kings 8.

52. *Who was raised up above all the people?*—Solomon.

53. *Who blessed them?*—Solomon.

54. *Of whom was he a type in this?*—Of Christ.

55. *Who will be gathered together when God's spiritual temple, formed of living stones, is reared?*—God's holy people.

If any man defile the temple of God, him shall God destroy ; for the temple of God is holy, which temple ye are. 1 Cor. 3 : 17.

Ye also, as lively stones, are built up a spiritual house, an holy priesthood, to offer up spiritual sacrifices, acceptable to God by Jesus Christ. 1 Pet. 2 : 5.

56. *Who is the foundation and chief corner-stone of that glorious building?*—"Jesus Christ himself." Eph. 2 : 20.

57. *Will it do to build good works or human merit on this foundation?*—We cannot add to or extend the foundation ; we can only build upon it the spiritual house, the . . . holy temple.

58. *What are all such vain things compared to in 1 Cor. 3 : 11–17?*—To "wood, hay and stubble."

59. *What remarkable dream did Solomon have immediately after his father's death?*—That God asked him what he should give him. 1 Kings 3 : 5.

60. *What did he ask for?*—Wisdom to govern his people well. 1 Kings 3 : 9.

61. *What did God promise to give him that he did* not ask for?—Riches and honor. 1 Kings 3 : 13.

62. *Describe Solomon's grandeur?*—He had an immense daily provision for his household, and thousands of chariot-horses and riders. 1 Kings 4 : 22, 23, 26.

63. *What queen, having heard of it from afar, came to visit Solomon?*—The queen of Sheba in Arabia. 1 Kings 10.

64. *Was she disappointed?*—No ; she said that half had not been told her. 1 Kings 10 : 7.

65. *What testimony did she leave behind her?*—She testified to the blessedness of those who served the living God.

66. *Has the glory of the Lord Jesus been exaggerated?* —No ; it exceeds all that is revealed to us on earth.

Eye hath not seen, nor ear heard, neither have entered into the heart of man, the things which God hath prepared for them that love him. But God hath revealed them unto us by his Spirit. 1 Cor. 2 : 9, 10.

67. *When the Lord Jesus compared himself with Solomon, and spoke about the queen of Sheba, what did he say?*—The queen of the south shall rise up in the judgment with this generation, and shall condemn it ; for she came from the uttermost parts of the earth to hear the wisdom of Solomon ; and, behold, a greater than Solomon is here. Matt. 12 : 42.

68. *How and by what means may we hope to share that glory by and by?*—By giving him our faith and love and service now.

69. *What is the best proof we can give that we believe the Bible to be true?*—Believing in the Saviour it reveals to us, obeying the commands it gives us, and making it known, as far as we can, to every creature.

PROVERBS.

1. *Who wrote the book of Proverbs?*—Solomon. Prov. 1 : 1.

2. *To whom is the book addressed?*—To his son Rehoboam.

3. *How many chapters does Solomon take in addressing his son before the Proverbs begin?*—Nine.

CHAPTER 1.

4. *What does Solomon say is the beginning of wisdom?* —The fear of the Lord. Prov. 1 : 7.

5. *What does he say is an ornament of grace to the neck of a child?*—Obedience to the instructions of his father and mother. Prov. 1 : 8, 9.

6. *How does he warn his son against sinners?*—To keep out of their way. Prov. 1 : 10–19.

7. *Whom does Solomon mean when he says, "Wisdom crieth without"?*—Jesus Christ.

Of him are ye in Christ Jesus, who of God is made unto us wisdom, and righteousness, and sanctification, and redemption. 1 Cor. 1 : 30.

The Son of man came eating and drinking, and they say, Behold a man gluttonous, and a winebibber, a friend of publicans and sinners. But wisdom is justified of her children. Matt. 11 : 19.

8. *Which is the only book that can be said to be "wisdom"?*—The Book, the Bible.

Therefore also said the wisdom of God, I will send them prophets and apostles, and some of them they shall slay and persecute. Luke 11 : 49.

9. *What has the Lord Jesus promised to "pour out" on those who "turn at his reproof"?*—He has said that our heavenly Father will give the Holy Spirit to them that ask him. Luke 11 : 13.

10. And what has he said will be the condemnation of those who refuse when he calls?—To be judged by his word at the last day. John 12 : 48.

11. What is written in 2 Cor. 6 : 2?—Behold, now is the day of salvation.

CHAPTER 2.

12. What reward is promised those who seek diligently after the Lord Jesus, the true "Wisdom"?—That they shall find him.

13. What blessings will they enjoy?—Pardon, peace, grace, hope, joy.

14. From what will it preserve them?—True wisdom preserves from the ways and society of the wicked, from all folly and sin, and from all real evil.

15. Who rejoices to do evil?—The ungodly man. Prov. 2 : 12–14.

16. Who has promised to be the "guide of youth"?—God, who thus invites the young to come unto him:

Wilt thou not from this time cry unto me, My Father, thou art the guide of my youth? Jer. 2 : 4.

17. What great contrast is there in this chapter between the upright and the wicked?—The upright shall dwell in the land, and the perfect shall remain in it. But the wicked shall be cut off from the earth, and the transgressors shall be rooted out of it. Prov. 2 : 21, 22.

CHAPTER 3.

18. How can we write anything on the tablets of our heart?—By fixing it in our memory and our affections.

19. How can we hope that God will direct our path?—If we seek and trust his guidance rather than our own. Prov. 3 : 5, 6.

20. Why should we not be weary of God's correction?—Because it is a sure token of his wisdom and love. Prov. 3 : 11, 12.

21. Can you tell me some of the ways in which God corrects us?—By sickness, losses, disappointments, and many things that are called accidents or misfortunes.

22. Which does it make us, "happy" or unhappy, to find Jesus (the true "Wisdom")?—Happy, as we have then a treasure we can never lose.

23. How did Solomon estimate wisdom?—Above riches and honor.

24. What does the apostle Peter say about the value of the blood shed by the Lord Jesus?—That it is "precious." 1 Pet. 1 : 19.

25. What is the Lord Jesus to those who believe in him?—"Precious." 1 Pet. 2 : 7.

26. What is the Lord Jesus called in Matt. 13 : 44–46?—A treasure and a pearl of great price.

27. What are "wisdom's" ways called?—"Ways of pleasantness and peace." Prov. 3 : 17.

28. What does the Lord Jesus himself say of those in Matt. 11 : 28–30?—Come unto me, all ye that labor and are heavy laden, and I will give you rest. Take my yoke upon you, and learn of me; for I am meek and lowly in heart: and ye shall find rest unto your souls. For my yoke is easy, and my burden is light.

29. Who is here spoken of as "the tree of life"?—Jesus Christ, the true Wisdom. Prov. 3 : 18.

30. Where was that tree first planted?—In the garden of Eden. Gen. 2 : 8, 9.

31. Will any one have a right to taste it again?—Yes.

Blessed are they that do his commandments, that they may have right to the tree of life, and may enter in through the gates into the city. Rev. 22 : 14.

To him that overcometh will I give to eat of the tree of life, which is in the midst of the paradise of God. Rev. 2 : 7.

32. By whom did the Lord create the heaven and the earth?—By Jesus Christ.

In the beginning was the Word, and the Word was with God, and the Word was God. All things were made by him; and without him was not any thing made that was made. John 1 : 1, 3.

Who is the image of the invisible God, the first-born of every creature; for by him were all things created that are in heaven, and that are in earth, visible and invisible, whether they be thrones, or dominions, or principalities, or powers: all things were created by him, and for him. Col. 1 : 15, 16.

33. Have those anything to fear who put their trust in the Lord? Why not?—No. Because God has promised it. Prov. 3 : 21–26, 5, 6.

34. Is there any charge in this chapter to be benevolent?—Prov. 3 : 9, 10, 27, 28.

35. Who is an abomination to the Lord?—The froward or self-willed. Prov. 3 : 32.

36. What will be the glorious destiny of "the wise"?—To inherit glory. Prov. 3 : 35.

37. Does this mean earthly or heavenly wisdom?—Heavenly, as much of the wisdom of *this* world is really folly and ends in shame.

CHAPTER 4.

38. What description does Solomon give of his father and mother in this chapter?—That his father wisely instructed him, and his mother tenderly loved him Prov. 4 : 3, 4.

39. Who was Solomon's father?—David.

40. What was his mother's name?—Bathsheba.

41. What instructions did David give him?—Prov. 4 : 4–19.

42. What great contrast is there in the eighteenth and nineteenth verses between "the just" and "the wicked"?—The way of the just is light, and of the wicked dark.

43. Can you give any examples from the New Testament where wickedness is compared to darkness?—This is the condemnation, that light is come into the world, and men loved darkness rather than light, because their deeds were evil. John 3 : 19. Have no fellowship with the unfruitful works of darkness, but rather reprove them. Eph. 5 : 11. The night is far spent, the day is at hand: let us therefore cast off the works of darkness, and let us put on the armor of light. Rom. 13 : 12.

44. What does the Lord Jesus call himself in John 8 : 12?—The light of the world.

45. What does Jesus command in Matt. 5 : 16?—Let your light so shine before men, that they may see your good works, and glorify your Father which is in heaven.

46. What does Solomon say of "wisdom" in the seventh and two following verses?—(Read them.)

47. Who is intended by wisdom? Who is it that shall give us the promised "crown of glory"?—Jesus Christ.

Blessed is the man that endureth temptation; for when he is tried, he shall receive the crown of life, which the Lord hath promised to them that love him. James 1 : 12.

When the chief Shepherd shall appear, ye shall receive a crown of glory that fadeth not away. 1 Pet. 5 : 4.

Looking unto Jesus, the author and finisher of our faith. Heb. 12 : 2.

Henceforth there is laid up for me a crown of righteousness, which the Lord, the righteous judge, shall give me at that day; and not to me only, but unto all them also that love his appearing. 2 Tim. 4 : 8.

48. What does Solomon say about the heart in this chapter at the twenty-third verse?—(Read it.)

49. What does the prophet Jeremiah say about the heart?—The heart is deceitful above all things, and desperately wicked: who can know it? Jer. 17 : 9.

50. What did the Lord Jesus say about the heart when he was on earth?—Out of the heart proceed evil thoughts, murders, adulteries, fornications, thefts, false witness, blasphemies. Matt. 15 : 19.

51. *Repeat David's prayer respecting his heart.*—Create in me a clean heart, O God; and renew a right spirit within me. Ps. 51 : 10.

52. *Whose office alone is it to search the heart?*—I the Lord search the heart, I try the reins, even to give every man according to his ways, and according to the fruit of his doings. Jer. 17 : 10. The Lord seeth not as man seeth; for man looketh on the outward appearance, but the Lord looketh on the heart. 1 Sam. 16 : 7. Shall not God search this out? for he knoweth the secrets of the heart. Ps. 44 : 21. If thou sayest, Behold, we knew it not; doth not he that pondereth the heart consider it? and he that keepeth thy soul, doth not he know it? and shall not he render to every man according to his works? Ps. 24 : 12. O Lord of hosts, that triest the righteous, and seest the reins and the heart. Jer. 20 : 12.

53. *Who promises to renew the heart?*—I will give them one heart, and I will put a new spirit within you; and I will take the stony heart out of their flesh, and will give them an heart of flesh. Ezek. 11 : 19. A new heart also will I give you, and a new spirit will I put within you; and I will take away the stony heart out of your flesh, and I will give you an heart of flesh. Ezek. 36 : 26.

CHAPTERS 5, 6, 7.

54. *By what endearing title does Solomon address the youth in these chapters?*—The title of "son."

55. *What encouragement have we to regard God as our Father in Heb. 12 : 5-7?*—Because he there speaks tenderly to his afflicted people as children.

Ye have forgotten the exhortation which speaketh unto you as unto children, My son, despise not thou the chastening of the Lord, nor faint when thou art rebuked of him; for whom the Lord loveth he chasteneth, and scourgeth every son whom he receiveth. If ye endure chastening, God dealeth with you as with sons; for what son is he whom the father chasteneth not?

56. *To what little insect are we referred as an example in Prov. 6 : 6-8?*—To the ant.

57. *What has a lazy person to expect?*—Poverty and want. Prov. 6 : 9-11.

58. *Name the seven things that the Lord hates?*—See Prov. 6 : 16-19.

59. *How can we bind a thing continually on our heart?*—By thinking earnestly or affectionately upon it. Prov. 6 : 20, 27; 7 : 2, 3.

60. *Is there any blessing attached to a child who is obedient to his parents?*—Guidance in life and preservation from sin and harm are here promised. Prov. 6 : 20, etc.

61. *Which is the only commandment among the Ten Commandments which has a promise joined with it?*—The fifth.

62. *To what are a parent's instructions compared in Prov. 6 : 23?*—To a lamp or light.

63. *Where else is the word of God compared, as in this sense, to a lamp?*—In Ps. 119 : 105.

Thy word is a lamp unto my feet, and a light unto my path.

CHAPTERS 8, 9.

64. *Whom does Solomon mean when he says, "Wisdom cries, she standeth"?*—Christ Jesus, who is wisdom for us and in us.

Of him are ye in Christ Jesus, who of God is made unto us wisdom, and righteousness, and sanctification, and redemption. 1 Cor. 1 : 30.

65. *What does "Wisdom" say in chap. 8 : 6?*—Hear.

66. *What did the Lord Jesus say, when on earth, in Matt. 11 : 15; 13 : 9?*—He that hath ears to hear, let him hear.

67. *What does "Wisdom" say in chap. 8 : 7?*—"My mouth shall speak truth."

68. *What does the Lord Jesus say in John 14 : 6?*—"I am the truth."

69. *To what does Solomon compare "wisdom"?*—To gold and rubies. Prov. 8 : 11, 19.

70. *What did St. Paul, in his letter to the Philippians, consider all things when compared with Christ Jesus?*—I count all things but loss for the excellency of the knowledge of Christ Jesus my Lord; for whom I have suffered the loss of all things, and do count them but dung, that I may win Christ. Phil. 3 : 8.

71. *Does "the fear of the Lord" (Prov. 8 : 13) mean hating God, or hating what he disapproves of?*—It means hating what he disapproves of through love to him, and consequent fear of offending him.

72. *What does the Lord hate?*—Pride and all other sin. Prov. 8 : 13.

73. *If God hates pride, how ought we to feel toward that sin in ourselves?*—We should hate it too.

74. *By whom do kings and princes rule?*—By the KING OF KINGS AND LORD OF LORDS. Rev. 19 : 16.

75. *What encouragement does Jesus give to the young to seek him?*—Prov. 8 : 32, 33. Suffer the little children to come unto me, and forbid them not: for of such is the kingdom of God. And he took them up in his arms, put his hands upon them, and blessed them. Mark 10 : 14, 16.

76. *What blessings are promised to those who choose him for their portion?*—Constant guidance upon earth and a lasting treasure in heaven.

77. *Where was the Lord Jesus when God created the world?*—With God, as being God himself. Prov. 8 : 27-31.

78. *Had the Lord Jesus existed before that time?*—Yes, from everlasting. Prov. 8 : 22-26.

79. *Did Jesus even then take pleasure in his people?*—He did.

We love him, because he first loved us. 1 John 4 : 19.

80. *How does Jesus invite us to him?*—Come unto me, all ye that labor and are heavy laden, and I will give you rest. Matt. 11 : 28.

81. *What remarkable comparison is there between Prov. 9 : 1-5 and Matt. 22 : 1-14?*—The sameness of the feast or provision of religious truth then and now, and of the welcome to it.

82. *Who spreads the feast? and who are invited to come?*—Christ in each case spreads the feast, and all the needy are invited to come.

83. *Is not religion a personal thing?*—Yes; the word in the singular number here betoken this. Prov. 8 : 34, 35; 9 : 12. No mere union, by sacraments or profession, with a Christian Church will save our souls. We should be able to say with St. Paul in Gal. 2 : 20, he "loved me and gave himself for me."

84. *Whose fault will it be if those who are thus invited, warned and counseled are lost at last?*—Their own; and this consciousness of willful folly, as well as sin, will be a gnawing worm of anguish that will never die.

ECCLESIASTES.

1. *By whom was Ecclesiastes written?*—By Solomon.

2. *What is the meaning of the term Ecclesiastes?*—The "Preacher."

3. *Had Solomon any means of knowing the subject on which he wrote? How?*—He had personal experience and divine teaching.

4. *What was the result of his great knowledge?*—That all is vanity under the sun. Eccles. 1 : 2, 3.

5. *Was there anything that Solomon found under the sun sufficient to satisfy his soul?*—Nothing.

6. *What is the meaning of that term, "under the sun"?*—Things that relate to this world alone.

7. *Where, then, must we look for solid happiness?*—To the world to come.

8. *What will be the end of "everything under the sun"?*—The day of the Lord will come as a thief in the ight; in the which the heavens shall pass away with great noise, and the elements shall melt with fervent heat, the earth also and the works that are therein shall be burned up. 2 Pet. 3 : 10. All the host of heaven shal' be dissolved, and the heavens shall be rolled together as a scroll: and all their host shall fall down, as the leaf falleth off from the vine, and as a falling fig from the fig tree. Isa. 34 : 4. And the heaven departed as a scroll when it is rolled together; and every mountain and island were moved out of their places. Rev. 6 : 14.

9. *Where should we then lay up our treasure?*—Lay up for yourselves treasures in heaven, where neither moth nor rust doth corrupt, and where thieves do not break through nor steal; for where your treasure is, there will your heart be also. Matt. 6 : 20, 21.

10. *Did Solomon wish to impress this truth on us?*—He did.

11. *What arguments does he use in Eccles. 12 to urge this in early life?*—The approach of old age and of death. Eccles. 12 : 1–7.

12. *What does he say is the conclusion of the whole matter?*—Let us hear the conclusion of the whole matter: Fear God, and keep his commandments; for this is the whole duty of man. For God shall bring every work into judgment, with every secret thing, whether it be good, or whether it be evil. Eccles. 12 : 13, 14.

13. *Which, then, is the wisest and happiest person—he who lives in pleasure or he who lives to God?*—He who lives to God.

14. *What was the apostle Paul's estimate of present things and things to come?*—I reckon that the sufferings of this present time are not worthy to be compared with the glory which shall be revealed in us. Rom. 8 : 18. For our light affliction, which is but for a moment, worketh for us a far more exceeding and eternal weight of glory; while we look not at the things which are seen, but at the things which are not seen: for the things which are seen are temporal; but the things which are not seen are eternal. 2 Cor. 4 : 17, 18.

15. *What does Luke 16 : 19–25 teach us?*—The parable of the rich man and Lazarus shows us the sad end of those who have only earthly riches when they come to die.

16. *Can we venture to have a little of this world first, and hope for heaven after?*—No. Luke 12 : 16–21.

17. *What was the apostle James's estimate of all that might be enjoyed "under the sun"?*—Go to now, ye rich men, weep and howl for your miseries that shall come upon you. Your riches are corrupted, and your garments are moth-eaten. Your gold and silver is cankered; and the rust of them shall be a witness against you, and shall eat your flesh as it were fire. Ye have heaped treasure together for the last days. James 5 : 1–3.

18. *Was it not the prospect of resurrection and the coming of the Lord that also sustained the apostle Paul?*—It was.

I protest by your rejoicing which I have in Christ Jesus our Lord, I die daily. If after the manner of men I have fought with beasts at Ephesus, what advantageth it me if the dead rise not? let us eat and drink, for to-morrow we die. 1 Cor. 15 : 31, 32.

19. *Seeing life is uncertain, and death sure, what ought we to do?*—Forsake our wicked way, and "seek the Lord while he may be found." Isa. 55 : 6, 7.

REHOBOAM. (1 Kings 11 and 12.)

1. *What great sin was Solomon guilty of in his latter days?*—Idolatry, through the influence of his wives. 1 Kings 11 : 4.

2. *What did the Lord say to Solomon about this?*—That he would take away the greater part of his kingdom from his family. 1 Kings 11 : 11–13.

3. *To what "covenant" did the Lord refer?*—When thy days be fulfilled, and thou shalt sleep with thy fathers, I will set up thy seed after thee, which shall proceed out of thy bowels, and I will establish his kingdom. He shall build an house for my name, and I will stablish the throne of his kingdom for ever. I will be his father, and he shall be my son. 2 Sam. 7 : 12–14.

4. *Had Solomon broken this covenant?*—Yes, by his idolatry.

5. *What were the consequences?*—The stirring up of enemies after a long reign of peace.

6. *How many adversaries did the Lord raise up against Solomon?*—Hadad the Edomite, Rezon the Syrian, and Jeroboam his servant.

7. *Whom had Solomon to blame for this?*—Himself alone, for his folly and sin.

8. *Whom have we to blame for punishment if we sin against God?*—Ourselves alone.

9. *How long did Solomon reign?*—Forty years.

10. *Who succeeded him?*—Rehoboam his son.

11. *Was he a wise or a foolish king?*—A foolish one. 1 Kings 12.

12. *What is the proof?*—His following the advice of young men instead of old and experienced ones. 1 Kings 12 : 6–14.

13. *What opinion do young people often form of their elders?*—They often and foolishly think that their elders are behind the times, and are not so wise as they are themselves.

14. *What ought Rehoboam's history teach us?*—To value and follow the advice of older and wiser relations and friends.

THE KINGS OF ISRAEL—JEROBOAM'S DYNASTY. (1 Kings 11 : 26–43 ; 12–16.)

1. *Who was Jeroboam?*—Son of Nebat and servant of Solomon. 1 Kings 11 : 26.

2. *What was the name of the prophet who foretold his honors?*—Ahijah. 1 Kings 11 : 29.

3. *How did he do this?*—By tearing Jeroboam's outer garment into twelve pieces and giving him ten.

4. *When was this prophecy fulfilled?*—At the revol of the ten tribes. 1 Kings 12 : 16.

5. *How was it brought about?*—Through Rehoboam's refusing to listen to his people's complaint, by the advice of his young and ignorant companions. 1 Kings 12 : 16.

6. *How much of Israel did Jeroboam reign over?*—Ten tribes. 1 Kings 12 : 21.

7. *What wicked means did he use to keep the ten tribes under his rule?*—Setting up idol-worship in Bethel and Dan. 1 Kings 12 : 28, 29.

8. *Where was Bethel?*—In the tribe of Benjamin.

9. *What remarkable circumstance happened to Jacob there before he went to Syria?*—His dream of the ladder between earth and heaven.

10. *How did Jacob distinguish the place when he returned from Syria? Who was buried there?*—He built there an altar. Gen. 35 : 7. Deborah, Rebekah's nurse. Gen. 25 : 8.

11. *Is Bethel mentioned before Jacob's time?*—Abra-

ham is said, in Gen. 12 : 8, to have encamped near Bethel.

12. *Was not Jeroboam very wickedly wise to choose a place of such interest for his idol?*—He was.

13. *What state must Israel have been in that Jeroboam could so easily turn them to idolatry?*—In a very ungodly state.

14. *How is it that Satan's temptations so easily prevail over us?*—Because we do not sufficiently "watch and pray."

15. *Had God's law forbidden idolatry?*—Repeatedly.

16. *Have we any excuse for sin?*—No, as we have the word of God to go to, and the voice of conscience and the striving of the Spirit within us.

17. *Is there any point on which God has left us in doubt of his mind and will?*—None at all, as, besides *particular* directions, we have *general* ones that include all cases.

18. *Where must we go to learn God's will?*—To his holy word.

19. *What will be our condemnation if we do not?*—Eternal punishment if we willfully and habitually neglect it.

20. *Had the Israelites any excuse for idolatry, even though their king commanded it, when they had God's written law?*—They had no excuse at all.

21. *There was one of Jeroboam's family, though young in years, who feared the Lord; who was he?*—Abijah. 1 Kings 14 : 13.

22. *What did his parents do when they feared he would die?*—His mother went to Ahijah the prophet to have him cured. 1 Kings 14 : 1–4.

23. *Why did they not go to the calf at Bethel to save the child?*—Because they had no real confidence in their idol-god.

24. *Was it of any use that Jeroboam's wife disguised herself to the prophet?*—No; God knew it, and made it known to him. 1 Kings 14 : 5.

25. *Can we hide anything from God?*—There is not a word in my tongue, but, lo, O Lord, thou knowest it altogether. Thou hast beset me behind and before, and laid thine hand upon me. Whither shall I go from thy spirit? or whither shall I flee from thy presence? Ps. 139 : 4, 5, 7, etc.

26. *What promises has God given to encourage little children to love him?*—I love them that love me; and those that seek me early shall find me. Prov. 8 : 17.

27. *Does not this show that even a little child in a wicked family who tries to serve God is not unnoticed by him?*—God's noticing Abijah shows this.

28. *How many of Jeroboam's race came to the crown of Israel?*—Only Nadab his son. 1 Kings 15 : 25–30.

29. *In what disgraceful state was Elah (the last of Jeroboam's family) when he was slain?*—He was drunk. 1 Kings 16 : 9.

30. *By whom was he slain?*—By his servant Zimri.

THE DISOBEDIENT PROPHET. (1 Kings 13 and 2 Kings 23 : 15–18.)

1. *Did God suffer the sinful idolatry of Israel to go unrebuked?*—No.

2. *Whom did the Lord send to them?*—A prophet. 1 Kings 13 : 2, 3.

3. *How far did he go obediently to the Lord?*—To Bethel only. 1 Kings 13 : 1, 9, 10.

4. *Who was standing by the altar at Bethel when he got there?*—Jeroboam.

5. *Was the prophet afraid to deliver his message?*—No. 1 Kings 13 : 2, 3.

6. *When the king heard it, what did he do?*—He put out his hand to seize the prophet. 1 Kings 13 : 4.

7. *Was not this a very daring act? How was it punished?*—It was defying God. His arm was stiffened and dried up.

8. *How was the king's arm recovered?*—By the prophet's prayer.

9. *Did the man of God go home with the king and take refreshment with him?*—No, for God had told him not to do so. 1 Kings 13 : 7–9.

10. *Who tempted the man of God to turn aside?*—An old prophet. 1 Kings 13 · 11–19.

11. *Ought he to have rested on God's word spoken to him, or believed this old prophet's word?*—If there arise among you a prophet, or a dreamer of dreams, and giveth thee a sign or a wonder, and the sign or the wonder come to pass, whereof he spake unto thee, saying, Let us go after other gods, which thou hast not known, and let us serve them; thou shalt not hearken unto the words of that prophet, or that dreamer of dreams: for the Lord your God proveth you, to know whether ye love the Lord your God with all your heart and with all your soul. Deut. 13 : 1–3.

12. *Did God use the lips of the old prophet again to really speak his word?*—Yes. 1 Kings 13 : 20–22.

13. *Must not this have been heavy tidings to the disobedient one?*—It must indeed. How careful should we be to exactly obey!

14. *How was the prophecy fulfilled?*—He was killed by a lion. 1 Kings 13 : 24.

15. *Did God quite cast off the man of God for this act of disobedience?*—No; he preserved his body for burial, and took care that his prophecy was fulfilled.

16. *How did the old prophet feel toward him?*—He mourned for him and buried him, and wished to be laid beside him. 1 Kings 13 : 29–31.

17. *What mark of respect also did Josiah, the king of Judah, pay to his memory in after years?*—He "let no man move his bones." 2 Kings 23 : 18.

THE KINGS OF ISRAEL—ZIMRI, OMRI AND AHAB. (1 Kings 16–22.)

1. *Who was Zimri?*—One of the captains of Elah, son of Baasha. 1 Kings 16 : 8, 9.

2. *What vengeance did he execute on the wicked family of Jeroboam?*—He killed Elah, the third successor of Jeroboam.

3. *How long did Zimri reign?*—About seven days. 1 Kings 16 : 15–19.

4. *What was his end?*—He burnt himself in his house when surrounded by his enemies.

5. *Who reigned over Israel next?*—Omri. 1 Kings 16 : 16.

6. *Who was he? and how long did he reign?*—He was commander of the army, and reigned twelve years. 1 Kings 16 : 23.

7. *What city did he purchase and make the chief cit of Israel?*—Samaria. 1 Kings 16 : 24.

8. *What was the name of his son?*—Ahab.

9. *How was Ahab distinguished above the kings that went before him?*—In wickedness. 1 Kings 16 : 30.

10. *What was the name of his wife? and whose daughter was she?*—Jezebel, daughter of the king of Zidon. 1 Kings 16 : 31.

11. *What new idol-worship was she the means of bringing in?*—The worship of Baal.

12. *What is recorded of Jericho in his reign?*—That it was rebuilt by Hiel. 1 Kings 16 : 34.

13. *Of what prophecy was this the fulfillment?*—Joshua adjured them at that time, saying, Cursed be the man before the Lord that riseth up and buildeth this city Jericho: he shall lay the foundation thereof in his first-born, and in his youngest son shall he set up the gates of it (Josh. 6 : 26)—*i. e.*, he should lose all his children during the building of it.

14. *Can God's word ever fall to the ground?*—No; all must come to pass.

15. *Are there any prophecies yet to be fulfilled?*—Many in the book of Revelation and elsewhere as to the conversion and restoration of the Jews, the second coming and kingdom of Christ, the last judgment and other events.

16. *Are we interested in them?*—We are eternally in many of them.

17. *In what state should we at all times be found?*—Watching and ready, as we "know not what hour" our "Lord doth come." Matt. 24: 42, 44.

ELIJAH DURING FAMINE. (1 Kings 17.)

1. *Who was Elijah?*—A prophet of Gilead.

2. *Where was Gilead?*—On the east of Jordan.

3. *What was Elijah commissioned to tell Ahab?*—That there should be neither dew nor rain.

4. *Why did God send a famine on the land?*—It shall come to pass, if thou wilt not hearken unto the voice of the Lord thy God, to observe to do all his commandments and his statutes which I command thee this day; that all these curses shall come upon thee, and overtake thee: cursed shalt thou be in the city, and cursed shalt thou be in the field. Cursed shall be thy basket and thy store. Cursed shall be the fruit of thy body, and the fruit of thy land, the increase of thy kine, and the flocks of thy sheep. Deut. 28: 15–18.

5. *Where did God promise to provide for Elijah? and how?*—By the brook Cherith, and by means of ravens.

6. *When the brook dried up, where did the Lord command Elijah to go?*—To Zarephath (1 Kings 17: 9), where a widow would sustain him.

7. *In what sorrowful employment did Elijah find the woman engaged?*—In gathering sticks to dress her last meal.

8. *Did she seem aware of the wonderful miracle that was wrought day by day?*—No.

9. *What should this teach us?*—To beware of not observing and not being thankful for the good providence of God.

10. *How did the Lord convince her that he was the living God?*—By Elijah's restoring her dead child to life.

11. *Did she confess it at last?*—Yes. 1 Kings 17: 24.

12. *What proof have we that God is the living God?*—His word by St. Paul that "he giveth to all life and breath and all things," and that "in him we live and move and have our being."

13. *Is not the written word of God to us now what the spoken word was by the prophets then?*—Yes; "we have a more sure word of prophecy," to which we should "take heed." 2 Pet. 1: 19.

ELIJAH ON CARMEL. (1 Kings 18.)

1. *Were Israel at this time idolaters, or worshipers of the true God?*—Idolaters—worshipers of Baal.

2. *Were all Israel worshipers of Baal?*—No; seven thousand of them were not.

3. *Who was Obadiah?*—Governor or steward of Ahab's house.

4. *What kind act had he performed when Jezebel, the wicked queen, slew the Lord's prophets?*—He had hid and fed them.

5. *How many years had the famine lasted when Elijah stood before Ahab?*—Above two years. 1 Kings 18: 1.

6. *What did Ahab accuse Elijah of doing?*—Of being the cause of Israel's trouble.

7. *Who was really to blame?*—Ahab himself and the other idolaters.

8. *How did Elijah propose to decide the point as to who was the living God?*—By observing upon whose sacrifice the fire came down from heaven. 1 Kings 18: 24.

9. *How does Isaiah describe idols?*—He heweth him down cedars, and taketh the cypress and the oak: he burneth part thereof in the fire; with part thereof he eateth flesh; he roasteth roast, and is satisfied: yea, he warmeth himself, and saith, Aha, I am warm, I have seen the fire: and the residue thereof he maketh a god, even his graven image: he falleth down unto it, and worshipeth it, and prayeth unto it, and saith, Deliver me; for thou art my god. Isa. 44: 14, 16, 17.

10. *How does the Psalmist describe them?*—Their idols are silver and gold, the work of men's hands. They have mouths, but they speak not: eyes have they, but they see not: they have ears, but they hear not: noses have they, but they smell not: they have hands, but they handle not: feet have they, but they walk not: neither speak they through their throat. They that make them are like unto them; so is every one that trusteth in them. Ps. 115: 4–8.

11. *Was it of any use for Baal's priests to cry to him?*—None at all.

12. *How did Elijah mock them?*—By telling them to cry aloud, as their god might be asleep. 1 Kings 18: 27.

13. *Did he give them time enough to make a fair trial?*—Yes, from morni g till evening. 1 Kings 18: 26, 29.

14. *About what time in the day was it when Elijah built his altar to the true God?*—About evening. 1 Kings 18: 29, 30.

15 *Of what use was the trench he had made round the altar?*—That the water might not escape.

16. *Why did he drench the sacrifice with water?*—To show the power of the fire.

17. *How was the power of God manifested?*—By the fire drying up the water and burning the wet bullock and wood and stone.

18. *What effect did it have on the people?*—They fell on their faces and cried out that Jehovah was the true God. 1 Kings 18: 39.

19. *What became of Baal's priests?*—They were taken and slain.

20. *What did Elijah venture to promise Ahab even before there was any appearance of it?*—Abundance of rain.

21. *On what did Elijah's faith rest?*—On the promise of God. 1 Kings 18: 1.

22. *What is faith?*—"The substance" or realizing "of things hoped for," "the evidence" or assurance "of things not seen." Heb. 11: 1.

23. *How many times had Elijah to ask ere the promised blessing came?*—Seven or eight times.

24. *What should this teach us?*—Always to pray, and not to faint. Luke 18. 1–7.

25. *How was the Lord's power again manifested on Elijah, although he had had a day of such extraordinary energy?*—In enabling him to run before Ahab's chariot.

26. *Was Elijah like one of us, or was he a supernatural being?*—Elias was a man subject to like passions (or infirmities) as we are (a human being like ourselves), and he prayed earnestly that it might not rain; and it rained not on the earth by the space of three years and six months. And he prayed again, and the heaven gave rain, and the earth brought forth her fruit. James 5: 17, 18.

27. *Is God as much the hearer and answerer of prayer now as he was then?*—He is always the same.

ELIJAH IN THE DESERT. (1 Kings 19.)

1. *What proof did Elijah give that he was "a man subject to like passions with us"?*—In his weakness of body and mind he requested that he might die. 1 Kings 19: 4.

2. *To what place did he flee for fear of Jezebel?*—To Beersheba. 1 Kings 19: 3.

3. *What kind care did the Lord take of him there?*—An angel brought him bread and water.

4. Was he more than once invited to eat ?—Yes, twice. 1 Kings 19 : 7.

5. For how long did that food sustain him?—Forty days.

6. When he was revived, to what place did he go?—To Mount Horeb.

7. Is it the Lord's will that his servants should be idle?—No; he has always work for every one to do.

8. What did the Lord say to Elijah?—What doest thou here, Elijah?

9. Is this not a striking proof that it is not the Lord's will that people should live shut up in monasteries or live as lonely hermits ?—It is.

10. Can any former work excuse them from future service ?—Not while the means are in their power.

11. What is God's way of speaking to his people? Is it in the fire, wind and earthquake, or how ?—He sometimes speaks in the louder voice of suffering and distress, but more frequently in the gentler one of his Spirit's whisper to the heart.

12. Where can we hear his "still small voice" ?—All Scripture is given by inspiration of God, and is profitable for doctrine, for reproof, for correction, for instruction in righteousness : that the man of God may be perfect, thoroughly furnished unto all good works. 2 Tim. 3 : 16, 17. God, who at sundry times and in divers manners spake in time past unto the fathers by the prophets, hath in these last days spoken unto us by his Son. Heb. 1 : 1, 2. We have also a more sure word of prophecy; whereunto ye do well that ye take heed, as unto a light that shineth in a dark place. 2 Pet. 1 : 19.

13. What effect should it have on us?—It should dispose us to say, with Eli, "Speak, Lord, for thy servant heareth." 1 Sam. 3 : 9.

14. Can any supposed mystery in the dealings of God be an excuse for neglect of duty ?—No; we must do our part, and leave God to explain in his own time.

15. What further work did the Lord give Elijah to do?—To anoint two kings and a prophet. 1 Kings 19 : 15, 16.

16. What effect did the casting of Elijah's mantle on Elisha have?—It made him leave his work and his home for the service to which God had called him.

17. Did Elisha wait till Elijah was taken up? or did he follow him at once?—He followed him at once.

18. What does the Lord say in Prov. 8 : 17 to encourage young people to follow him?—"Those that seek me early shall find me."

AHAB'S PUBLIC AND PRIVATE CHARACTER. (1 Kings 20 and 21.)

1. What was Ahab's character in the sight of God?—He did more to provoke him than all the kings of Israel before him. 1 Kings 16 : 33.

2. Had God at this time given up Israel?—No; he still warned them by his prophets.

3. Were there other prophets at this time in Israel besides Elijah ?—Yes, there were false prophets, as well as true.

4. Who were Israel's greatest enemies at this time ?—The Syrians.

5. What was the capital city of Syria?—Damascus.

6. Who was king of Syria at this time?—Benhadad.

7. What did he purpose to do to Israel?—To destroy Samaria. 1 Kings 20 : 10.

8. How did the Lord frustrate his design?—By means of the household servants of Ahab's princes when Benhadad and his royal allies were drunk.

9. Was Ahab grateful for this?—Probably not.

10. How did the Lord show his displeasure?—By bringing the Syrians to attack him again. 1 Kings 20 · 26, 42.

11. Who was Naboth?—The owner of a vineyard near Ahab's palace in Jezreel. 1 Kings 21.

12. Why did he not like to let Ahab have his vineyard?—Because he was forbidden by the law to part with what had come to him from his fathers.

The land shall not be sold for ever; for the land is mine; for ye are strangers and sojourners with me. And in all the land of your possession ye shall grant a redemption for the land. Lev. 25 : 23, 24.

13. What wicked act did Jezebel stir Ahab up to do?—To kill Naboth and take his vineyard.

14. Did God suffer this to go unpunished ?—No.

15. Who was sent to Ahab?—Elijah.

16. How did Ahab salute him?—As his enemy who had found him out, for his conscience pricked him. 1 Kings 21 : 20.

17. What fearful prediction did he utter?—That God would destroy Ahab's family, and that the dogs should eat the flesh of Jezebel and lick his own blood.

18. How did Ahab receive the tidings?—He showed the outward signs of repentance and humbled himself before God.

19. What proof is there in this place of the truth of Jonah 4 : 2 ?—God delayed the punishment.

I knew that thou art a gracious God, and merciful, slow to anger, and of great kindness, and repentest thee of the evil.

THE KINGS OF JUDAH—ABIJAH, ASA AND JEHOSHAPHAT. (2 Chron. 13-17.)

1. Who succeeded Rehoboam as king of Judah ?—Abijah his son. 2 Chron. 12 : 16.

2. What was his mother's name? and whose daughter was she ?—Michaiah, daughter of Uriel.

3. What beautiful testimony did he bear against Israel's idolatry ?—That they had forsaken God and his altars, and made themselves golden calves. 2 Chron. 13 : 8-11.

4. To whom did the army of Judah cry when they were in danger?—To God. 2 Chron. 13 : 14.

5. What was the result ?—They gained the battle, because they relied upon God.

6. Who followed Abijah on the throne of Judah?—Asa his son. 2 Chron. 14 : 1.

7. What was Asa's character in God's estimation?—He did what was good and right.

8. What proof did he give of his heart being right with God when he first came to the throne?—He destroyed the idols and their places of worship.

9. Was his early reign prosperous?—Yes, his land was at peace.

10. How did he behave when the vast army from Ethiopia came up against him?—He prayed to God and fought in his name.

11. What was the result?—The Ethiopians fled.

12. Is God the same as he was then?—The same now and for ever.

13. Does he hear and answer prayer now as he did then?—Yes, as every one, whether young or old, can testify who really prays.

14. What encouragement did the Lord give Asa by the mouth of Azariah the prophet?—That God would be with him as long as he was with God, or obedient to him. 2 Chron. 15 : 1-7.

15. What similar promise is given to us in Prov. 8 ?—"I love them that love me." Prov. 8 : 17.

16. What effect did it have on the king and people?—He put down idolatry, and the people made a covenant to seek the Lord with all their heart (2 Chron. 15 : 8-15), and God gave them peace.

17. Did this happy state of things continue to the end of Asa's reign? How did he behave when Baasha king of Israel came against him?—It continued to the thirty-fifth year of his reign, when, instead of going for help to God, he sent to the king of Syria. 2 Chron. 16 : 1-4.

18. *Did the Lord suffer this to go unnoticed?*—No; he sent Hanani to reprove him.

19. *What did the prophet say to Asa?*—He reminded him of God's readiness to help his people, and told him that henceforth he should have wars.

20. *How did Asa receive the reproof?*—He was enraged, and put the prophet in prison.

21. *How was he punished?*—He suffered and died of a painful disease.

22. *Are any of our actions hidden from God?*—The ways of man are before the eyes of the Lord, and he pondereth all his goings. Prov. 5 : 21. The eyes of the Lord are in every place, beholding the evil and the good. Prov. 15 : 3. Mine eyes are upon all their ways: they are not hid from my face, neither is their iniquity hid from mine eyes. Jer. 16 : 17. If I say, Surely the darkness shall cover me; even the night shall be light about me. Yea, the darkness hideth not from thee; but the night shineth as the day: the darkness and the light are both alike to thee. Ps. 139 : 11, 12.

23. *Who succeeded Asa on the throne of Judah?*—Jehoshaphat his son. 2 Chron. 17 : 1.

24. *What character did he bear?*—He sought the God of his father and walked in his commandments.

25. *What beautiful testimony is continually given to David?*—That he was a pattern in his general conduct for others to imitate.

26. *Was Jehoshaphat's a prosperous reign?*—Yes, he was long without war, and became a very great king, and had riches and honor in abundance.

27. *Describe his army?*—(Read 2 Chron. 17 : 14-19.)

MICAIAH. (2 Chron. 18 and 1 Kings 22.)

1. *What was the great error of Jehoshaphat's life?*—Making an alliance with Ahab.

2. *Was Ahab glad to make the compact?*—Yes; he made a feast for Jehoshaphat and his servants.

3. *Who were the enemies that still fought against Israel?*—The Syrians.

4. *What place had they taken?*—Ramoth-gilead.

5. *Where was it?*—In the tribe of Gad on the east of Jordan.

6. *What did Jehoshaphat require before he would go up to fight?*—That the will of God should be known.

7. *What did all Ahab's prophets say?*—That he might go, and God would be with him. 2 Chron. 18 : 5.

8. *Was the king of Judah satisfied?*—No.

9. *Whom did he wish to consult?*—Micaiah.

10. *Why did not Ahab like Micaiah?*—Because he always prophesied evil unto him.

11. *Was it not very foolish of Ahab to be satisfied with lies?*—Very.

12. *When are we like Ahab in this?*—When we let our own ignorant, selfish and sinful wishes influence our conduct and our prayers.

13. *What is the only sure test of truth?*—God's word.

14. *What does the Psalmist say in Ps. 119 : 105, 140?*—"Thy word is a lamp unto my feet, and a light unto my path" . . . "is very pure."

15. *What did Jehoshaphat's love of truth prove him to be?*—A true servant of God.

16. *What wonderful vision did Micaiah describe?*—Of God upon his throne, and the host of heaven around him, and of an evil spirit going forth to entice Ahab to his fall.

17. *Is there in Scripture any other display of what occurs in the unseen world?*—In Job 1 and Isa. 6 etc.

18. *How did Ahab reward the faithful prophet?*—He put him in prison.

19. *What did Ahab do to prevent his prediction from coming true?*—He disguised himself, that he might not be known.

20. *What narrow escape had Jehoshaphat in the battle?*—The Syrians mistook him for Ahab, and surrounded him.

21. *By whom was he delivered?*—By God, who caused them to leave him.

22. *Can any circumstances be too difficult for the Lord to overrule?*—None.

23. *How was Ahab killed?*—By an arrow shot at random.

24. *How was Elijah's prediction in 1 Kings 21 : 19 fulfilled?*—The dogs licked up his blood in his chariot.

25. *Was it of any use that Ahab disguised himself in the battle?*—None at all.

26. *Can we hide ourselves from God?*—We cannot.

27. *What during his life did Ahab build?*—Some cities, an ivory house and a sepulchre.

28. *Have these works rendered his name honorable?*—No.

29. *What alone is true honor?*—That which comes from God.

ELIJAH AND THE LIVING GOD. (2 Kings 1 and 2.)

1. *Which of Ahab's sons succeeded his father?*—Ahaziah. 1 Kings 22 : 40.

2. *What character did he bear?*—He was wicked and idolatrous. 1 Kings 22 : 52, 53.

3. *What accident befell him?*—He fell from an upper room. 2 Kings 1 : 2.

4. *What means did he take for his recovery?*—He sent to an idol-god. 2 Kings 1 : 2.

5. *What testimony did Elijah bear to this impiety?*—He said that he should not recover.

6. *What course did Ahaziah take?*—He sent soldiers to take him.

7. *What befell his messengers?*—They were consumed by fire from heaven.

8. *Did all share alike?*—The last party was spared in answer to their leader's prayer.

9. *Was Elijah induced to alter his denunciation against the king?*—No.

10. *Who reigned in Israel after Ahaziah? and what relation was he to that king?*—Jehoram. His brother. 2 Kings 1 : 17; 3 : 1.

11. *What peculiar testimony did Elijah bear all through his life?*—Against idolatry and for the honor of God.

12. *Was not Elijah privileged to manifest this in his departure from this world?*—God's glory was shown in the miracle wrought and in the translation to heaven.

13. *How did that event take place?*—In a whirlwind, by a chariot and horses of fire. 2 Kings 2 : 11.

14. *Who was permitted to witness it?*—Elisha.

15. *What favor was Elijah permitted to grant Elisha ere he was parted from him?*—To ask what he should do for him.

16. *What did Elisha request?*—A double portion of Elijah's spirit.

17. *How often in Elijah's history is his mantle mentioned?*—Three times. 1 Kings 19 : 13, 19 and 2 Kings 2 : 8.

18. *Of what is Elijah's mantle a type?*—Of the Holy Spirit.

19. *How did Elisha use it?*—To divide the waters of Jordan.

20. *Of what is the parting of Jordan a type?*—Of the opening of the way to heaven,

21. *How many times before this had Jordan been miraculously divided?*—Twice—when Israel entered Canaan, and when Elijah crossed before his death.

22. *How did the other prophets recognize the superiority of Elisha?*—By the spirit of Elijah resting upon him. 2 Kings 2 : 15.

23. *How did they manifest their unbelief?*—By proposing to send men to search for Elijah.

24. *Did Elisha yield?*—He did, at last.

25. *What proof did Elisha at once give that he, like Elijah, was the prophet of the living God?*—By healing the unwholesome water.

26. *What proof of Israel's impiety did the little children give?*—They mocked Elisha.

27. *What did they mean by "Go up"?*—Go up to heaven, like Elijah.

28. *How were they punished?*—They were killed by bears.

29. *Does this not show that even the faults of little children are noticed by God?*—It does. He sees and hates all sin.

30. *How did Jesus when on earth manifest his love for little children?*—By calling them to him and blessing them.

31. *And what does the Lord say in Prov. 8 : 17?*—Those that seek me early shall find me.

JEHOSHAPHAT. (2 Kings 3; 2 Chron. 19, 20.)

1. *Did the Lord suffer the evil confederacy which Jehoshaphat had made with Ahab to go unnoticed?*—No.

2. *Whom did the Lord send to warn the king?*—Hanani the seer.

3. *How did the Lord show his displeasure when Jehoshaphat joined affinity with Ahaziah, Ahab's son, in sending ships to go to Tarshish?*—The ships were wrecked. 1 Kings 22 : 48.

4. *When Ahaziah afterward wished his servants to go with Jehoshaphat's, what was his conduct?*—He refused. 1 Kings 22 : 49.

5. *Was Joram (son of Ahab) a better man than either his brother Ahaziah or his father?*—He was better in putting away the image of Baal, but in other respects he was very wicked. 2 Kings 3 : 2, 3.

6. *Did Jehoshaphat consent to go to battle with him?*—He did. 2 Kings 3 : 7.

7. *Whom did they go to fight?*—The Moabites.

8. *What other king went with them?*—The king of Edom. 2 Kings 3 : 9.

9. *What signal honor did the prophet Elisha put upon Jehoshaphat?*—He told Jehoram that he would not have noticed him but for Jehoshaphat's sake. 2 Kings 3 : 14.

10. *Why had Elisha been sent for?*—To know from him whether the Moabites would be defeated or not.

11. *How did the Lord appear for them?*—He deceived the Moabites, by the miraculous appearance of reddened water, with the belief that the armies of the three kings had destroyed one another. 2 Kings 3 : 16, 20–23.

12. *What frightful sacrifice did the king of Moab offer to propitiate his gods?*—His eldest son as a burnt-offering. 2 Kings 3 : 27.

13. *How did the king of Moab soon after try to revenge this defeat?*—By making war against Jehoshaphat. 2 Chron. 20 : 1.

14. *What kings joined with him?*—The Ammonites and others.

15. *How did Jehoshaphat feel?*—He was afraid. 2 Chron. 20 : 3.

16. *What did he do?*—He proclaimed a fast and prayed to God before the people.

17. *Who was Jahaziel?*—A Levite.

18. *What gracious message did the Lord send by him?*—That he would destroy their enemies without a battle.

19. *Did Jehoshaphat and his people believe the message that thus came to them from God?*—Yes, and united together in praising God.

20. *Does not God always honor faith in himself?*—He does.

21. *What is said of faith in Heb. 11 : 1?*—That it "is the substance of things hoped for, the evidence of things not seen."

22. *What is the message that God has given us of his Son which it is necessary for us to believe if we would be saved?*—That "the blood of Jesus Christ his Son cleanseth us from all sin." 1 John 1 : 7.

23. *Did Jehoshaphat and his people wait till after the victory before they began to praise, or did they begin before the fight?*—They praised God as soon as his promise was given.

24. *How did this prove their faith in God's word?*—It showed that they realized what would come to pass. Heb. 11 : 1.

25. *What is said of praise in Ps. 50 : 23?*—That it honors God.

Whoso offereth praise glorifieth me: and to him that ordereth his conversation aright will I show the salvation of God.

26. *What spoils did they gain?*—Abundance of riches and jewels. 2 Chron. 20 : 25.

27. *Of what is this a type?*—Of the treasure in heaven of those who conquer on earth in the victory of faith.

28. *What effect did this great conquest have on the nations around?*—The fear of God was upon them, and they troubled Jehoshaphat no more. 2 Chron. 20 : 29, 30.

29. *With whom is Jehoshaphat compared as to goodness?*—With Asa his father.

30. *What great abomination did he, notwithstanding all his excellence, leave in the land?*—The high places of the heathen gods.

31. *Which of his sons did Jehoshaphat make king during his own life?*—Jehoram.

32. *How long did Jehoram enjoy this honor before his father's death?*—About a year. Compare 2 Kings 1 : 17 with 2 Kings 3 : 1; 8 : 16; and 2 Chron. 20 : 31.

33. *How old was Jehoshaphat when he died? and how long had he reigned?*—Sixty years old, having reigned twenty-five.

ELISHA'S MIRACLES—THE WATERS OF JERICHO. (2 Kings 2.)

1. *Which was the last city Elijah and Elisha visited ere Elijah ascended to heaven?*—Jericho. 2 Kings 2 : 4.

2. *Did Elijah ascend near this place?*—Yes, by Jordan.

3. *By whom was Jericho chiefly inhabited at this time?*—By students in the schools of the prophets.

4. *Did Elisha return there?*—Yes. 2 Kings 2 : 18.

5. *How long did he stay there?*—Only a short time. 2 Kings 2 : 23, 25.

6. *What caused the waters of this place to be barren?*—The curse of God.

7. *By whom, and when, had the curse on Jericho been pronounced?*—By Joshua, after the taking of the city.

8. *What was Elisha permitted to do?*—To make the water good.

9. *How did he do it?*—By casting a little salt into it, accompanied by the healing power of God.

10. *Of what was salt a type in Scripture?*—Of divine grace in the heart and life. "Ye are the salt of the earth." Matt. 5 : 13.

11. *What peculiar quality has salt besides its being savory?*—Of preserving things from corruption.

12. *Of what, then, is it a symbol?*—Of divine grace.

13. *Were not the children of Israel commanded to use salt with their sacrifices?*—Every oblation of thy meat.

offering shalt thou season with salt; neither shalt thou suffer the salt of the covenant of thy God to be lacking from thy meat-offering: with all thine offerings thou shalt offer salt. Lev. 2 : 13.

14. *How was this salt, thus used in the sacrifices, a type of the Lord Jesus Christ?*—See 1 Tim. 3 : 16; Phil. 2 : 5–8.

15. *By whom must the curse pronounced on this earth be removed?*—Christ hath redeemed us from the curse of the law, being made a curse for us; for it is written, Cursed is every one that hangeth on a tree. Gal. 3 : 13.

THE WIDOW'S OIL. (2 Kings 4 : 1–7.)

1. *Who cried to Elisha?*—The wife of one of the sons of the prophets.

2. *Why did she cry to him?*—Because he was the chief of the prophets.

3. *What was her trouble?*—That a creditor of her late husband had taken her two sons for bondmen for the debt.

4. *What plea had she to offer?*—That her husband had been a servant of God.

5. *What did he command her to do?*—To borrow several empty vessels and fill them from her pot of oil.

6. *When did the oil stop running?*—Only when there were no more vessels to fill.

7. *Of what is oil in the Scripture a type?*—Of the Holy Spirit.

8. *What does the Lord promise us if we ask for this blessed gift?*—If ye then, being evil, know how to give good gifts unto your children, how much more shall your heavenly Father give the Holy Spirit to them that ask him! Luke 11 : 13.

9. *Is there any limit to God's supply? or can we receive this heavenly gift according to the empty vessel we bring to receive it?*—There is no limit in God, but only in ourselves. He says, "Open thy mouth wide, and I will fill it." Ps. 81 : 10.

10. *How must our debt be paid?*—By Jesus Christ, wholly and alone.

11. *After our "debt" is paid on whom must we depend for the life of our souls?*—On Jesus still.

12. *Where was Shunem?*—In the tribe of Issachar.

13. *How was Elisha entertained by a rich woman there?*—She and her husband set apart a room, to be for his use whenever he came that way, because she knew him to be a holy man of God. 2 Kings 4 : 8–10.

14. *What kind gift did the Lord bestow upon her for Elisha's sake?*—A child when she had none.

15. *What happened to this child?*—He died by a sunstroke.

16. *Where was Elisha at the time?*—At Mount Carmel. 2 Kings 4 : 25.

17. *How did the poor mother act?*—She set off quickly to Elisha.

18. *What was her reply when Elisha inquired after the welfare of her household?*—"It is well." 2 Kings 4 : 26.

19. *What did this prove?*—Her resignation to God's will and her assurance of her child being in heaven.

20. *What means did Elisha at first use to recover the child?*—His servant laid Elisha's staff upon the child. 2 Kings 4 : 31.

21. *Did the Lord permit it to be effectual?*—No.

22. *What did Elisha then do?*—Elisha prayed, and then stretched himself upon the child, and he revived.

23. *Can God work as well without means as with them?*—He can.

24. *How does the Lord usually act?*—By means.

25. *What did the restoration of this child prove Elisha to have been?*—A true prophet and servant of God.

THE MEAL AND THE CORN. (2 Ki. 4 : 38–44.)

1. *What was the Lord Jesus manifested to destroy?*—"The works of the devil." 1 John 3 : 8.

2. *What was Satan's first great work?*—Bringing sin and death into the world by Adam's fall.

3. *By what means did the Lord Jesus destroy it?*—By his own death.

As the children are partakers of flesh and blood, he also himself likewise took part of the same; that through death he might destroy him that had the power of death, that is, the devil; and deliver them who through fear of death were all their lifetime subject to bondage. Heb. 2 : 14, 15.

4. *In what respect were the miracles Elisha was allowed to perform similar to the mission of the Lord Jesus?*—In restoring or creating health and life.

5. *How did the miracle of the meal thrown into the pot of wild gourds show this?*—It was an instance of a cause of death being taken away.

6. *What great distinction was there between the idols Israel at this time worshiped and Jehovah?*—They were without power and without life, and were worshiped with unholy rites, and by the *sacrifice*, instead of the *service*, of human lives.

7. *Is not death Satan's greatest triumph?*—Yes, the death or ruin of the soul.

The wages of sin is death. Rom. 6 : 23.

In Adam all die. 1 Cor. 15 : 22.

8. *In what, then, will the power of the Lord Jesus be the most manifestly seen?*—In triumphing over death.

Death is swallowed up in victory. Thanks be to God, which giveth us the victory through our Lord Jesus Christ! 1 Cor. 15 : 54, 57.

9. *What other alone attribute of Jehovah is ascribed to the Lord Jesus?*—Creation.

Who is the image of the invisible God, the first-born of every creature: for by him were all things created, that are in heaven, and that are in earth, visible and invisible, whether they be thrones, or dominions, or principalities, or powers: all things were created by him, and for him: and he is before all things, and by him all things consist. Col. 1 : 15–17.

In the beginning was the Word, and the Word was with God, and the Word was God. The same was in the beginning with God. All things were made by him; and without him was not any thing made that was made. John 1 : 1–3.

When he prepared the heavens, I was there: when he set a compass upon the face of the depth: when he established the clouds above: when he strengthened the fountains of the deep: when he gave to the sea his decree, that the waters should not pass his commandment: when he appointed the foundations of the earth. Prov. 8 : 27–29.

By the word of the Lord were the heavens made; and all the host of them by the breath of his mouth. Ps. 33 : 6.

God . . . created all things by Jesus Christ. Eph. 3 : 9.

10. *How did Elisha attempt to teach Israel, by using this power given to him, that he was the prophet of the living God?*—By doing miracles connected with the preservation or restoration of life, and by praying to God as the living God.

11. *Were any of the miracles that the Lord Jesus wrought when on earth similar to this?*—The turning the water into wine and healing various diseases.

12. *Had the miracles of Elisha the effect of winning Israel back from their fearful idolatry?*—No.

13. *What was the Lord's merciful design in sending Elisha with such signs and wonders to his people?*—To bring them back to himself, and save them from the punishment due to their guilt.

14. *Did the miracles of the Lord Jesus convince the children of Israel in his day that he was "God manifest in the flesh"?*—No; their hearts were so hardened in willful ignorance, self-righteousness and sin that they would not believe.

15. *Should not this check the feeling that may arise in our hearts that if we had seen a miracle we should cer-*

tainly have believed?—Yes; it should make us deeply thankful if God has given us to believe.

Abraham saith unto him, They have Moses and the prophets; let them hear them. And he said, Nay, Father Abraham: but if one went unto them from the dead they will repent. And he said unto him, If they hear not Moses and the prophets, neither will they be persuaded, though one rose from the dead. Luke 16: 29–31.

16. *What does the apostle Peter call the word of God?* —"A more sure word of prophecy, . . . that came not in old time by the will of man; but" was spoken by "holy men of God, . . . moved by the Holy Ghost." 2 Pet. 1: 16–21.

NAAMAN. (2 Kings 5.)

1. *With what loathsome disease was Naaman afflicted?* —Leprosy.

2. *Who was he?*—Commander of the army of the king of Syria.

3. *What did the little captive maid recommend her master to do?*—She wished he was with Elisha, as he would cure him. 2 Kings 5: 3.

4. *Did he go?*—Yes.

5. *How did Elisha receive him?*—He sent a message to him to wash in Jordan and be clean. 2 Kings 5: 10.

6. *What had Naaman expected?*—That Elisha would come to him and in a solemn manner call upon God to heal him.

7. *Was he induced to try the remedy?*—Yes; his pride and anger yielded to the wise advice of those about him.

8. *What was the result?*—He was perfectly cured.

9. *Is there any lesson to be gained by us in this history?*—Yes, humbleness of mind.

10. *Of what is leprosy a type in Scripture?*—Of sin.

11. *How must sin be put away?*—There shall be a fountain opened to the house of David and to the inhabitants of Jerusalem for sin and for uncleanness (Zech. 13:1)—the fountain of the cleansing blood of Christ, sprinkled on the heart by faith.

12. *To whom does the prophet in that verse refer?*—To Jesus Christ, who "washed us from our sins in his own blood." Rev. 1: 5.

These are they which came out of great tribulation, and have washed their robes, and made them white in the blood of the Lamb. Rev. 7: 14.

How much more shall the blood of Christ, who through the eternal Spirit offered himself without spot to God, purge your conscience from dead works to serve the living God! Heb. 9: 14.

13. *How do we get this good news?*—By the gospel.

14. *Are we, like Naaman, desiring some other way than God's appointed way?*—By nature we expect and try to wholly or partly save ourselves.

15. *If so, in what state must we still remain?*—Diseased and dead.

16. *Will God say any more to us than he has said—"Wash and be clean"?*—No; the gospel invitation is the same. Come, and rest. Believe, and live.

17. *If so, why do we hesitate?*—From unbelief, pride, sloth and love of sin and the world.

18. *What was the blessed result of Naaman's falling in with God's simple plan?*—A perfect cure.

19. *What will be the thrice-blessed result to us if we are washed and cleansed in the blood of Jesus?*—Complete salvation.

20. *Ought each of us to tell what we know of the efficacy of this precious fountain?*—We ought to do so, for the glory of God and the good of man.

21. *If a little captive maid could be the means of such blessing to an earthly master, is there not something that each of us can do to spread the knowledge of a Saviour's*

worth among the heathen of our day?—Some can give themselves, and all a portion of their money and their time, their influence and their prayers.

GEHAZI. (2 Kings 5: 20–27.)

1. *What dreadful sins did covetousness lead Elisha's servant to commit?*—Lying and tempting God's Spirit.

2. *What is said of covetousness in 1 Tim. 6: 9, 10?*— They that will be rich fall into temptation and a snare, and into many foolish and hurtful lusts, which drown men in destruction and perdition. For the love of money is the root of all evil; which while some coveted after, they have erred from the faith, and pierced themselves through with many sorrows.

3. *What proof does Gehazi's example afford us of the truth of Rom. 2: 28, 29; Gal. 6: 15?*—He was evidently, amidst all his religious privileges, an unconverted man.

He is not a Jew, which is one outwardly; neither is that circumcision which is outward in the flesh: but he is a Jew, which is one inwardly; and circumcision is that of the heart, in the spirit, and not in the letter; whose praise is not of men, but of God. Rom. 2: 28, 29.

For in Christ Jesus neither circumcision availeth any thing, nor uncircumcision, but a new creature. Gal. 6: 15.

4. *Can any outward rite or ceremony, any family connection or outward recognition by the people of God, make us indeed and of a truth "a member of Christ, a child of God and an inheritor of the kingdom of heaven"?*—It cannot.

5. *What is necessary?*—Except a man be born again, he cannot see the kingdom of God. John 3: 3.

6. *How is this new birth described in 2 Cor. 5: 17?*— If any man be in Christ, he is a new creature; old things are passed away; behold, all things are become new.

7. *What is it called in James 1: 18?*—Of his own will begat he us with the word of truth, that we should be a kind of first-fruits of his creatures.

8. *What was Gehazi compelled from this day and forward to do?*—To live apart.

The leper in whom the plague is, his clothes shall be rent, and his head bare, and he shall put a covering upon his upper lip, and shall cry, Unclean, unclean! All the days wherein the plague shall be in him he shall be defiled; he is unclean; he shall dwell alone; without the camp shall his habitation be. Lev. 13: 45, 46.

9. *What blessed contrast to this had Naaman experienced?*—The being brought near.

At that time ye were without Christ, having no hope, and without God in the world: but now in Christ Jesus ye who sometimes were far off are made nigh by the blood of Christ. Eph. 2: 12, 13.

10. *Ought we not to examine ourselves, lest we should be deceived in so momentous a question?*—Yes, both as to our hearts and lives.

11. *How did David do this in Ps. 51: 10; 139: 23, 24?*—He prayed for "a clean heart;" and said, "Search me, O God, and know my heart: try me, and know my thoughts: and see if there be any wicked way in me, and lead me in the way everlasting."

12. *Can we do better than follow his example, seeing our Master is omniscient, and can see our most secret actions, even as Elisha was permitted to know Gehazi's secret sin?*—We cannot; and we should do it at once, before our heart gets hard.

13. *Why is God's estimate of us so much more correct than the estimate man forms of us?*—The Lord seeth not as man seeth; for man looketh on the outward appearance, but the Lord looketh on the heart. 1 Sam 16: 7

ELISHA MANIFESTING THE LORD'S ATTRI-
BUTES. (2 Kings 6, 7, 8 : 1–6.)

1. *What signal proof did Elisha give of God's omnipotent power? What is the meaning of "omnipotent"?*
—Making an iron axe-head to swim. 2 Kings 6. All-
powerful, or able to do everything.

2. *Why was it remarkable that iron should swim?*—
Because when not hollow it is much heavier than
water.

3. *What proof did Elisha next give of God's omniscient power?*—By knowing from God and telling the
king of Syria's designs. 2 Kings 6 : 9.

4. *What is the meaning of "omniscience"?*—Knowing
everything.

5. *How was the king of Syria affected by this?*—He
was much troubled, and suspected his own people of
betraying him.

6. *What means did he use to prevent it?*—He sent a
host of men to take him.

7. *Who was king of Israel at this time?*—Jehoram.
2 Kings 3 : 1.

8. *How did Elisha's servant feel when he saw the host
of Syrians?*—He was greatly afraid.

9. *Why was not Elisha equally frightened?*—Because
he had confidence in God.

10. *Are not the people of God always as safe as Elisha was, whether they see it or not?*—They are safe from
all harm that God does not permit.

The angel of the Lord encampeth round about them
that fear him, and delivereth them. Ps. 34 : 7.

The chariots of God are twenty thousand, even thousands of angels: the Lord is among them, as in Sinai,
in the holy place. Ps. 68 : 17.

11. *How did this wonderful circumstance manifest
God's omnipresence?*—Without that attribute he would
not have known of Elisha's danger, or been ready to
help him.

12. *By what means did Elisha lead this host from
Dothan to Samaria?*—By blinding them.

13. *Did it quite baffle the Syrians at that time?*—Yes;
they came no more.

14. *Was the king of Israel (Joram) taught by this the
wondrous power that rested on his favored land? What
course did he take toward Elisha when the Syrians came
against him and besieged Samaria?*—It seems not. He
threatened to kill him.

15. *How did Elisha receive the king's messenger?*—
He ordered him to be shut out.

16. *Dia Joram himself go down with the executioner?*
—He did.

17. *How did Elisha receive the king? and what did he
promise him?*—He called upon him to hear the word
of the Lord, and promised him plenty.

18. *Who accompanied the king?*—One of his lords.

19. *What unbelieving speech did he make?*—That unless God were to make windows in heaven the promise
could not be fulfilled.

20. *Was not this a very fearful famine?*—Yes, for a
woman fed upon her own child. 2 Kings 6 : 29.

21. *Was that any reason why God could not do what
he had promised?*—None at all.

22. *How was the wondrous change of events brought
about?*—By making the Syrians fancy they heard the
noise of a great host, God caused them to fly for their
lives and leave all their provisions behind.

23. *Have we not here a proof of God's faithfulness
and mercy?*—Yes—of his faithfulness to his promise,
and of his mercy to his people.

24. *How was the prediction respecting the nobleman
fulfilled?*—He was trodden to death by the crowd as
they rushed out of the city for food.

25. *Have we not here a display of God's justice?*—
We have—a striking one.

26. *How many attributes of God has this Scripture lesson displayed?*—Five—his omnipotence, omniscience, faithfulness, mercy and justice.

27. *How does the remaining history of the Shunammite
woman show God's providence?*—She had the land that
she had left restored to her on her return. 2 Kings
8 : 6.

JEHU. (2 Kings 8 : 7–15 ; 9, 10.)

1. *Of whom is it said, "He putteth down one and setteth up another" king?*—Of God. Ps. 77 : 7.

2. *Whom did Elisha anoint king of Syria?*—Elisha
told Hazael that he should be king. 2 Kings 8 : 13.

3. *Was he chosen by God for his goodness?*—No.

4. *Was he not greatly shocked when Elisha told him
what he would do?*—He was. 2 Kings 8 : 13.

5. *Ought not this exhibition of the evil of man's nature
make us cry out as in Ps. 2 : 10, 11?*—It should.

Create in me a clean heart, O God; and renew a
right spirit within me. Cast me not away from thy
presence; and take not thy Holy Spirit from me.

6. *Whom had the Lord already appointed king of
Israel?*—Jehu. 1 Kings 19 : 16.

7. *Who anointed him?*—A young prophet sent by
Elisha. 1 Kings 9 : 1–6.

8. *Who was Jehu? and where was he at this time?*—
A captain in the army, at Ramoth-gilead.

9. *Where was Joram (king of Israel) at this time?*—
At Jezreel. 1 Kings 9 : 15.

10. *Who was visiting Joram?*—Ahaziah, king of Judah. 1 Kings 9 : 16.

11. *Was Jehu long in executing God's vengeance?*—
No; he set about it instantly.

12. *Had not the time arrived to which God had postponed it?*—It had.

Seest thou how Ahab humbleth himself before me?
because he humbleth himself before me, I will not
bring the evil in his days; but in his son's days will
I bring the evil upon his house. 1 Kings 21 : 29.

13. *What now delays God's threatened vengeance on
this apostate earth?*—The long-suffering of God.

The Lord is not slack concerning his promise, as
some men count slackness; but is long-suffering to
usward, not willing that any should perish, but that
all should come to repentance. 2 Pet. 3 : 9.

14. *Did Jezebel (Joram's mother), Ahab's wicked wife,
escape? How was she slain?*—No. She was thrown
down from a window and killed. 2 Kings 9 : 33.

15. *What had been predicted of her? and by whom?*
—Elijah had prophesied (1 Kings 21 : 23) that the
dogs should eat her flesh in Jezreel.

16. *Of whom is Jezebel the type?*—Of any wicked
Church or people that has cast off the true love and
worship of God. Rev. 2 : 20–22; 17, 18, 19 : 1–3.

17. *What did Ahaziah king of Judah get by being
found in such company?*—He was killed also. 2 Kings
9 : 27.

18. *What warning does the Lord give his people now
in Rev. 18 : 4?*—Come out of her, my people, that ye
be not partakers of her sins, and that ye receive not
of her plagues.

19. *What was Jehu's character?*—He showed great
zeal for the outward worship of God, but was in other
respects a wicked man.

20. *Having executed God's vengeance on the king and
his mother, how did he act toward the rest of Ahab's family?*—He had them all beheaded.

21. *What family relationship did there exist at this
time between the royal families of Judah and Israel?*—
Jehoram was Ahaziah's uncle.

22. *In what calamity did this involve the former?*—
Ahaziah's family were slain. 2 Kings 10 : 13, 14.

23. *How did Jehu treat Baal's worshipers?*—He had
them all slain. 2 Kings 10 : 23–25.

24. *Whom did he meet on the way?*—Jehonadab, son of Rechab. 2 Kings 10:15.

25. *To what family did this man belong?*—The Kenites.

26. *Is he ever mentioned in Scripture again?*—In Jer. 35, where is also mentioned his command to his family and descendants to drink no wine.

27. *Did Jehu thoroughly destroy Baal-worship in Israel?*—Yes. 2 Kings 10:28.

28. *What promise did the Lord make to him for thus fulfilling his will?*—That his children for four generations should sit on the throne of Israel. 2 Kings 10:30.

29. *Did he destroy the calves of Bethel as well as Baal, or leave that cursed idolatry in the land?*—He left that idolatry still.

30. *Then Jehu, after all, fell short of the worship of the true God?*—Very far short.

31. *What fearful lesson does this teach us?*—To be thoroughly sound in our Christian profession, lest, like the fig tree with leaves but no fruit, we be discovered and destroyed at the last. Mark 11:13, 20.

32. *What does the Lord find on us? Are we bearing fruit, or is there nothing on us but the leaves of an empty profession?*—Let the conscience of each answer as in the sight of God.

33. *How long did Jehu reign? and who succeeded him?*—Twenty-eight years. 2 Kings 10:36. Jehoahaz, his son. 2 Kings 13:1.

JEHU'S DYNASTY; ELISHA'S DEATH. (2 Kings 13, 14, 15 : 1–12.)

1. *What character did Jehoahaz bear?*—He was a wicked man. 2 Kings 13:2.

2. *How did the Lord punish Israel?*—By delivering them into the hands of the king of Syria.

3. *What effect did this have upon the king?*—He prayed to God for relief, and was heard, but idolatry still continued in the land.

4. *How long did he reign? and who succeeded him?*—Seventeen years. Joash, his son.

5. *Was he a better king? Describe him.*—He was no better, but walked, like his father, in Jeroboam's sins.

6. *What sorrowful event happened in this reign?*—The death of Elisha.

7. *When Joash heard of the prophet's illness, what did he do?*—He came and wept over him, and praised him.

8. *What symbolical prophecy did the prophet cause the king to act at this interview?*—Shooting, and striking the ground with arrows, as a token of success against the Syrians.

9. *What miraculous event took place in connection with Elisha's remains?*—A dead man revived when his body touched them.

10. *Where was Moab situated?*—On the south-east of the Dead Sea.

11. *Where was Elisha's grave, supposing he was buried in the inheritance of his fathers?*—At Abel-meholah in Simeon, where his father lived.

12. *Was Elisha's prophecy fulfilled in the days of Joash (called also Jehoash)?*—Joash defeated the Syrians thrice, as Elisha had said.

13. *How came Israel and Judah to go to war in this reign?*—Because the king of Judah challenged the king of Israel to do so. 2 Kings 14:8.

14. *What insolent message did Joash send to Amaziah?*—He proudly replied that he would crush him as a wild beast does a thistle.

15. *On which side did victory turn?*—On Israel's side.

16. *How long did Joash (or Jehoash) reign?*—Sixteen years. 2 Kings 13:10.

17. *Who succeeded Joash on the throne of Israel?*—Jeroboam his son. 2 Kings 14:16.

18. *How many years did he reign?*—Forty-one. 2 Kings 14:23.

19. *Of what character was he, morally?*—He did evil in the sight of the Lord.

20. *What kind of king and warrior was he?*—He was successful in war, and recovered some border-lands which Israel had lost.

21. *How came it that Jeroboam was so victorious?*—Because of God's pity and promise. 2 Kings 14:25-27.

22. *How many prophets besides Jonah prophesied in this reign?*—Four—Isaiah, Hosea, Joel and Amos.

23. *Who succeeded Jeroboam II.?*—Zachariah his son.

24. *Was his a long or short reign?*—Only six months. 2 Kings 15:8.

25. *How did he come by his death?*—He was killed by Shallum. 2 Kings 15:10.

26. *What promise had the Lord given Jehu?*—That his sons should be kings of Israel for four generations.

27. *How was this fulfilled?*—In the succession of Jehoahaz, Joash, Jeroboam and Zachariah.

28. *What is said in Isa. 46:9, 10?*—I am God, and there is none like me, declaring the end from the beginning, and from ancient times the things that are not yet done, saying, My counsel shall stand, and I will do all my pleasure.

JONAH, HOSEA AND AMOS.

JONAH.

1. *Is there any prophesying of Jonah's recorded besides the book called by his name?*—The prophecy of the reconquest by Jeroboam. 2 Kings 14:25.

2. *Why is he generally styled "the disobedient prophet"?*—Because he fled away when ordered by God to go to Nineveh.

3. *Against whom was he commanded to prophesy?*—Against the Ninevites.

4. *How is Nineveh described in Scripture?*—An exceeding great city, of three days' journey (or sixty miles) round.

5. *Do the vast ruins lately discovered confirm or contradict this Scripture testimony?*—They strongly confirm it.

6. *Why did Jonah shrink from his errand?*—From fear of being killed, or of seeming to be a false prophet if God's threatenings were mercifully unfulfilled, or from a dislike to prophesy to a mere heathen nation.

7. *Is it of any use for man to refuse to fulfill the will of God?*—None.

Woe unto him that striveth with his Maker! Let the potsherd strive with the potsherds of the earth. Shall the clay say to him that fashioneth it, What makest thou? or thy work, He hath no hands? Isa. 45:9.

That saith of Cyrus, He is my shepherd, and shall perform all my pleasure. Isa. 44:28.

8. *How did the Lord overtake Jonah in his rebellion?*—By a storm at Sea.

9. *What did the mariners strive to do?*—To save their lives by calling on their gods and lightening the ship, and rowing hard to reach the land.

10. *Was it of any use?*—No.

11. *How did Jonah own God's righteous dealing?*—By telling them of his flight, and that the storm was on his account.

12. *When thrown overboard, how did God preserve him?*—By means of a great fish he had prepared.

13. *Is Jehovah God ever at a loss to fulfill his purposes?*—Never.

14. *How did Jonah feel when in the fish's belly?*—Cast out of God's sight.

15. *How was Jonah's case a fulfillment of Ps. 139?*—He found it impossible to flee from God's presence.

If I take the wings of the morning, and dwell in the uttermost parts of the sea; even there shall thy hand lead me, and thy right hand shall hold me. Ps. 139: 9, 10.

16. *If the Lord could hear Jonah from the depths of the sea, can we be in any circumstances beyond the reach of his arm to save?*—Never.

17. *When the Lord again commanded Jonah to go to Nineveh, did he obey?*—He did. Jonah 3.

18. *What was the result of his preaching?*—The king and people believed God, and repented and turned from their evil way.

19. *How did Jonah like this?*—He was very angry that his threatening was not fulfilled, fearing, perhaps, that he would not be considered a true prophet, and that the Israelites would not repent when they saw that Nineveh was spared.

20. *How did the Lord comfort and reprove Jonah?*—By giving him a shade from the heat, and by rebuking his anger at its loss.

21. *Is not God's mercy to the Ninevites a pledge to us of his mercy and his grace?*—It is, if *our* repentance is as deep and sincere.

22. *How may it be that these poor heathen may rise in condemnation against us at the last day?*—If we do not repent under the teaching and preaching of God's word.

23. *But how much are our privileges greater than theirs?*—God hath in these last days spoken unto us by his Son. Heb. 1: 2. Therefore we ought to give the more earnest heed to the things which we have heard, lest at any time we should let them slip. Heb. 2: 1.

24. *Where is Nineveh?*—On the river Tigris, in the ancient Assyria, and near the modern towns of Mosul and Bagdad.

25. *What attribute of the Lord's glorious character does his conduct toward Nineveh display?*—His wonderful mercy.

26. *Where is Nineveh first mentioned in Scripture?*—In Gen. 10: 11, where Asshur is said to have built it.

27. *How old must this great city have been when Jonah prophesied against it?*—About fifteen hundred years.

HOSEA.

28. *Who was Hosea?*—A prophet, son of Beeri.

29. *In whose reigns did he prophesy?*—In the reigns of Uzziah, Jotham, Ahaz and Hezekiah, kings of Judah, and in the reign of Jeroboam, son of Joash, king of Israel.

30. *What touching expostulation does the Lord address to Israel in Hos. 11: 8?*—How shall I give thee up, Ephraim? how shall I deliver thee, Israel? how shall I make thee as Admah? how shall I set thee as Zeboim? mine heart is turned within me, my repentings are kindled together.

31. *Who is meant by Ephraim?*—Israel.

32. *Why is the name of Ephraim given to Israel?*—Because the tribe of Ephraim was the chief part of the kingdom of Israel.

33. *What idolatries of Israel are alluded to in Hos. 13?*—The worship of Baal and the golden calves.

34. *What beautiful invitation is given in Hos. 14: 1, 2?*—O Israel, return unto the Lord thy God; for thou hast fallen by thine iniquity. Take with you words, and turn to the Lord: say unto him, Take away all iniquity, and receive us graciously.

35. *Does the Lord only address such gracious words to Israel as a nation, or may we believe them spoken to us?*—"For our sakes, no doubt, this is written," as sinners in every age and of every country need the same mercy and the same invitation. 1 Cor. 9: 9, 10.

AMOS.

36. *Who was Amos?*—A native of Tekoah in Judah and a prophet.

37. *What was his occupation when the Lord called him to be a prophet?*—That of a herdsman or shepherd.

38. *Against how many nations does he prophesy before he utters his denunciations against Israel?*—Against six—Syria, Philistia, Tyre, Edom, Ammon and Moab.

39. *Into what two sins of Israel does Amos 2: 12 give us an insight?*—Drunkenness and rejection of God' word and prophets.

40. *How does Amos 3: 12 show us that according to our privileges so will our punishment be?*—You only have I known of all the families of the earth: therefore I will punish you for all your iniquities.

41. *Point out our Lord's parables that more fully explain this.*—The wicked husbandmen (Matt. 21: 33), the marriage-feast (Matt. 22), and our Lord's denunciation against Capernaum. Matt. 11: 23.

42. *What prophecy against the altar of Bethel does Amos 3 also contain?*—In the day that I shall visit the transgressions of Israel upon him I will also visit the altars of Bethel; and the horns of the altar shall be cut off, and fall to the ground.

43. *When was this fulfilled? and by whom?*—About one hundred and sixty years after, by Josiah.

The altar that was at Bethel, and the high place which Jeroboam the son of Nebat, who made Israel to sin, had made, both that altar and the high place he brake down, and burned the high place, and stamped it small to powder, and burned the grove. 2 Kings 23: 15.

44. *What great similarity is there between Amos 4 and Deut. 28?*—Amos 4 seems to be a fulfillment of the curses of drought, famine and pestilence pronounced in Deut. 28 upon their national sins.

45. *What prophecy is there in the lamentation of Amos (chap. 5) that Stephen quotes in Acts 7?*—Vs. 25-27; Acts 7: 42, 43.

46. *What proofs of Israel's luxury at this time (in the reign of Jeroboam II.) does Amos 6 give us?*—(Read vs. 4-6.)

47. *What did Amaziah the priest of Bethel send and say to Jeroboam when Amos had uttered these prophecies?*—That Amos was conspiring against him. Amos 7: 10.

48. *What did he advise Amos to do? and why?*—To go into Judah to live and to prophesy, as Bethel was the king's court.

49. *What sins of Israel does Amos 8 set forth?*—Dishonesty, oppression and neglect of God's word. Vs. 5, 6, 11, 12.

50. *After the fearful denunciations of chaps. 8 and 9, what predictions of after glory does the last chapter close with?*—The restoration of Israel to their own land in plenty and peace.

51. *By whom must "the fallen tabernacle of David" be reared?*—By Jesus Christ.

He shall be great, and shall be called the Son of the Highest: and the Lord God shall give unto him the throne of his father David: and he shall reign over the house of Jacob for ever; and of his kingdom there shall be no end. Luke 1: 32, 33.

THE LAST KINGS OF ISRAEL. (2 Kings 15-17.)

1. *Who slew Zachariah, the last of Jehu's dynasty?*—Shallum. 2 Kings 15: 10.

2. *How long did he reign?*—A month.

3. *Who destroyed him?*—Menahem.

4. *How long did Menahem reign?*—Ten years. 2 Kings 15: 17.

5. *What kind of king was he?*—A wicked one.

6. *Who fought against him?*—Pul, king of Assyria.

7. *Who succeeded Menahem?*—Pekahiah his son.

8. *How long did Pekahiah reign?*—Two years.

9. *Who slew him?*—Pekah, one of his captains.

10. *How long did Pekah reign?*—Twenty years.

11. *Which was the last king of Israel?*—Hoshea.

12. *How long did he reign?*—Nine years. 2 Kings 17:1.

13. *Which of the kings of Assyria came against him?*—Shalmaneser.

14. *Did Israel conquer, or the Assyrians?*—The Assyrians.

15. *How was this?*—The Lord shall bring thee, and thy king which thou shalt set over thee, unto a nation which neither thou nor thy fathers have known; and there shalt thou serve other gods, wood and stone. Moreover, all these curses shall come upon thee, and shall pursue thee, and overtake thee, till thou be destroyed; because thou hearkenedst not unto the voice of the Lord thy God, to keep his commandments and his statutes which he commanded thee. Deut. 28:36, 45.

16. *Had not God often warned them of their danger?*—Yes, by his prophets.

17. *Will not all God's threatenings be fulfilled, as well as his promises?*—They will.

18. *What has God said in his word shall be the punishment of impenitent sinners?*—"Except ye repent, ye shall all likewise perish." Luke 3:13.

19. *If we slight the word of God as Israel did of old, what must we expect?*—Punishment—as a nation, here; and as individuals, here and hereafter, now and for ever.

20. *Have we a remedy? What is it?*—To "return unto the Lord, and he will have mercy upon" us. Isa. 55:6, 7.

21. *To what places was Israel carried captive?*—To places in Media and Mesopotamia.

22. *Who were brought in to fill the depopulated cities?*—People from Babylon and the regions around it. 2 Kings 17:24.

23. *What was the result?*—A mixture of the worship of God and of idols. 2 Kings 17:33.

JORAM (OR JEHORAM) TO AMAZIAH, KINGS OF JUDAH. (2 Chron. 21–25.)

1. *Whose son was Joram (Jehoram) king of Judah?*—Son of Jehoshaphat. 2 Chron. 21:1.

2. *Which of Israel's kings reigned at the same time?*—Ahaziah, and afterward Jehoram. 2 Kings 1:17, 18.

3. *Whose daughter was Joram's wife?*—Ahab's. 2 Chron. 21:6.

4. *What effect did this unholy alliance have on the king?*—It led him into the sins of Ahab's house. 2 Chron. 21:6.

5. *How many years did Joram reign jointly with his father?*—About two. 2 Kings 8:16.

6. *What was the first wicked thing he did after his father was dead and he reigned alone?*—He killed his brothers. 2 Chron. 21:4.

7. *What kingdom revolted from under the sway of Judah in this reign?*—Edom, and the city of Libnah.

8. *What message came to him from God by the hand of Elijah the prophet?*—Of a great plague or affliction for his family and people, and a mortal disease for himself.

9. *By what death did he die?*—By a long and painful illness.

10. *How long had he reigned?*—Eight years.

11. *Who succeeded him?*—Ahaziah his son.

12. *By what three names is this king called?*—Ahaziah, Jehoahaz and Azariah. 2 Chron. 21:17; 22:1. 6.

13. *By which is he more generally called?*—Ahaziah. 2 Kings 9.

14. *Which of Joram's sons was he?*—The youngest.

15. *Why did not Joram's eldest son reign?*—Because he had been killed with his brothers.

16. *What did this prove?*—That Elijah's message had come true.

17. *To what untimely end did this king of Judah come?*—He was killed, with Joram, by order of Jehu.

18. *How did it happen?*—He had gone under the guidance of God to visit Joram. 2 Kings 8:29; 2 Chron. 22:7.

19. *What was the name of Ahaziah's mother?*—Athaliah.

20. *When she saw her son was dead, what cruel act did she exercise toward his children, her own grandchildren?*—She had them all but one destroyed.

21. *Name her father and mother.*—Ahab and Jezebel.

22. *When we see how much evil the good Jehoshaphat brought on his family by his alliance with Ahab, should it not make us most careful as to the company we keep?*—It should indeed.

> Be not deceived: evil communications corrupt good manners. 1 Cor. 15:33.
>
> Be not deceived: God is not mocked: for whatsoever a man soweth, that shall he also reap. For he that soweth to his flesh shall of the flesh reap corruption; but he that soweth to the Spirit shall of the Spirit reap life everlasting. Gal. 6:7, 8.

23. *How was one grandchild unexpectedly preserved?*—He was hid by Jehoshabeath. 2 Chron. 22:11.

24. *What relation was the good Jehoshabeath to the little boy?*—His aunt.

25. *How long did the wicked Athaliah keep the throne?*—Six years. 2 Chron. 22:12.

26. *What was her end?*—She was slain when Joash, the lawful king, was raised to the throne.

27. *How old was the young king when he began to reign?*—Seven.

28. *How long did he continue to do well?*—During the life of Jehoiada the priest, about twenty-eight years.

29. *What good service did he do the temple of God during Jehoiada's life?*—He repaired and refitted it. 2 Chron. 24:4–14.

30. *To what commandment by Moses did the king refer as to the contribution to the Lord's service?*—And the Lord spake unto Moses, saying, When thou takest the sum of the children of Israel after their number, then shall they give every man a ransom for his soul unto the Lord, when thou numberest them: that there be no plague among them, when thou numberest them. This they shall give, every one that passeth among them that are numbered, half a shekel after the shekel of the sanctuary (a shekel is twenty gerahs): an half shekel shall be the offering of the Lord. Every one that passeth among them that are numbered, from twenty years old and above, shall give an offering unto the Lord. The rich shall not give more, and the poor shall not give less than half a shekel, when they give an offering unto the Lord, to make an atonement for your souls. And thou shalt take the atonement money of the children of Israel, and shalt appoint it for the service of the tabernacle of the congregation; that it may be a memorial unto the children of Israel before the Lord, to make an atonement for your souls. Ex. 30:11–16.

31. *How old was the good Jehoiada when he died?*—One hundred and thirty years. 2 Chron. 24:15.

32. *What honor did they show his remains?*—They buried him among the kings.

33. *How did Joash behave after his uncle's death?*—He worshiped idols.

34. *Whom did the Lord send to warn him of his sins?*—Zechariah the son of Jehoiada.

35. *What did Joash cause to be done to him?*—To be stoned to death.

36. *What did Zechariah say in dying?*—"The Lord look upon it, and require it."

37. *Is his death alluded to in the New Testament?*—That upon you may come all the righteous blood shed upon the earth, from the blood of righteous Abel unto the blood of Zacharias son of Barachias, whom ye slew between the temple and the altar. Matt. 23 : 35.

38. *How did the Lord punish Judah for their idolatry?*—By the Syrian army.

39. *How did he punish this wicked king?*—By great diseases.

40. *In what way did he die?*—He was killed by his own servants.

41. *How long did he reign?*—Forty years. 2 Chron. 24 : 1.

42. *Who succeeded him?*—Amaziah his son.

43. *Was Amaziah a better man than his father?*—Probably not, as his heart was not right toward God, and as, after reigning well for some time, he fell into idolatry.

44. *How did God try his faith?*—By telling him to trust him to replace the loss of one hundred talents which he had paid for the hire of an Israelitish army. 2 Chron. 25 : 6–10.

45. *Did he continue to serve the Lord?*—No. 2 Chron. 25 : 14, 27.

46. *What new idolatry did he introduce?*—The gods of Edom. 2 Chron. 25 : 14, 20.

47. *How was he punished for this?*—By defeat in war and by conspiracy at home.

48. *How did he die?*—He was killed by his own people.

49. *How long did he reign?*—Twenty-nine years.

50. *Which king of Israel reigned at the same time?*—Joash or Jehoash.

51. *What battle did these two kings fight?*—The battle of Bethshemesh.

52. *Which was victorious? Why?*—Joash, because of Amaziah's idolatry.

53. *Does not this show us that all our actions are noticed by God?*—Yes, and that he punishes idolatry, boasting and all other sin.

UZZIAH, JOTHAM AND AHAZ, KINGS OF JUDAH. (2 Chron. 26–32.)

1. *Who was Uzziah?*—Amaziah's son.

2. *How old was he when he began to reign?*—Sixteen.

3. *By what other name is he called?*—Azariah. 2 Kings 15 : 1.

4. *What king was reigning in Israel at this time?*—Jeroboam II.

5. *How many prophets prophesied in the reign of Uzziah?*—Five—Isaiah, Hosea, Joel, Amos and Jonah.

6. *What is said of Uzziah in 2 Chron. 26 : 5?*—That while he sought the Lord he prospered.

7. *How was this manifested in the early part of his reign?*—By great success in war. 2 Chron. 26 : 6–15.

8. *By whose influence was he kept in the right way?*—By the influence of Zechariah, a man of God.

9. *What effect did prosperity have on him?*—It lifted up his heart.

10. *What does it mean by his heart being lifted up?*—That he was proud and presumptuous.

11. *What does the Lord say about pride in the Scripture?*—That it "goeth before destruction." Prov. 16 : 18.

12. *To what act of impiety did Uzziah's pride prompt him?*—To burn incense like a priest.

13. *How was it punished?*—By being smitten with leprosy.

14. *What effect did his punishment have on him?*—It made him go and live alone.

15. *Of what was leprosy a type?*—Of sin.

16. *How was leprosy under the Mosaic law cleansed?*—The priest shall go forth out of the camp; and the priest shall look, and, behold, if the plague of leprosy be healed in the leper, then shall the priest command to take for him that is to be cleansed two birds alive and clean, and cedar-wood, and scarlet, and hyssop; and the priest shall command that one of the birds be killed in an earthen vessel over running water: as for the living bird, he shall take it, and the cedar-wood, and the scarlet, and the hyssop, and shall dip them and the living bird in the blood of the bird that was killed over the running water; and he shall sprinkle upon him that is to be cleansed from the leprosy seven times, and shall pronounce him clean, and shall let the living bird loose into the open field. Lev. 14 : 3–7.

17. *Who was typified by the bird that was slain, and by the living bird?*—The Saviour and the sinner.

18. *How many instances are recorded in Scripture of persons being punished by leprosy?*—Three—those of Miriam, Gehazi and Uzziah.

19. *What great deprivations did Uzziah suffer in consequence of this malady?*—He was cut off from the house of the Lord, from the honors of a king and from all human society.

20. *How had Uzziah occupied himself?*—In war, in building cities and towers, in digging wells, and in keeping much cattle; also in cultivating fruitful fields. *How many years did he reign?*—Fifty-two years.

21. *Who shared the government with him when he was laid aside, and succeeded him on the throne of Judah?*—Jotham his son.

22. *How old was Jotham when he began to reign?*—Twenty-five. 2 Chron. 27 : 1.

23. *How is his character described?*—"He did that which was right in the sight of the Lord."

24. *How does 2 Chron. 27 : 6 give us the secret of his prosperity?*—It says that "he prepared (or established) his ways before God." So Joshua and David had a fixed purpose or plan to serve the Lord.

25. *How long did he reign?*—Sixteen years.

26. *Who followed Jotham?*—Ahaz his son.

27. *Was he not a very different king?*—Yes; "he did not right in the sight of the Lord."

28. *In whose ways did he walk?*—In those of the kings of Israel.

29. *Who was king of Israel at this time?*—Pekah.

30. *Did Ahaz go on in this sad career without warning?*—No; he was warned by the prophets.

31. *Which of the prophets prophesied in his reign?*—Isaiah, Hosea and Micah.

32. *How does Isaiah, in his first chapter, describe the state of Israel and Judah at this time?*—Ah sinful nation, a people laden with iniquity, a seed of evil-doers, children that are corrupters: they have forsaken the Lord, they have provoked the Holy One of Israel unto anger, they are gone away backward.

33. *How are the daughters of Judah described in the end of his third chapter?*—The daughters of Zion are haughty, and walk with stretched-forth necks and wanton eyes, walking and mincing as they go, and making a tinkling with their feet.

34. *What idol-worship did Ahaz again introduce?*—Of Baal and the gods of Syria. 2 Chron. 28 : 2, 23.

35. *What cruel heathen practice did he exercise on his son?*—He burnt his children in sacrifice. 2 Chron. 28 : 3.

36. *What enemies came against Judah as a punishment for their sins?*—Pekah and Rezin.

37. *Who was Pekah?*—King of Israel.

38. *Who was Rezin?*—King of Syria.

39. *What encouragement did the Lord give by his prophet Isaiah concerning these kings?*—Take heed, and be quiet; fear not, neither be faint-hearted for the two tails of these smoking fire-brands, for the fierce anger of Rezin with Syria, and of the son of Remaliah. Isa. 7 : 4.

40. *When Ahaz declared he would not ask a sign of God, was that from reverence or disregard?*—From disregard.

41. *How did his seeking aid from the king of Assyria against his foes, and not from the Lord, decide this?*—It showed he was determined to take his own course.

42. *What was the consequence of his seeking to the Assyrians?*—Embarrassment instead of support. 2 Chron. 28 : 20.

43. *How did he strip the temple of God to pay the Assyrian king?*—He took away much of its brass (or copper) work. 2 Kings 16 : 17, 18.

44. *Did he, after all, obtain the help he desired?*—He did not.

45. *Which were the most prosperous kings, those who served the Lord, or those who forsook him?*—Those who served the Lord.

46. *What effect had chastisement on him?*—He sinned yet more against the Lord. 2 Chron. 28 : 23.

47. *What did this prove him not to be?*—It proved him not to be a son of God, or he would have profited by his fatherly chastisement.

If ye endure chastening, God dealeth with you as with sons; for what son is he whom the father chasteneth not? Heb. 12 : 7.

48. *How many years did he reign?*—Sixteen years.

49. *Was he buried among the good kings of Judah?*—No 2 Chron. 28 : 27.

ISAIAH, MICAH AND NAHUM.

1. *Who was Isaiah?*—A prophet, the son of Amoz.

2. *In whose reigns did he prophesy?*—In those of "Uzziah, Jotham, Ahaz and Hezekiah, kings of Judah."

3. *Is any part of his book historical? how much?*—Yes, about four chapters, chaps. 36–39.

4. *What great and glorious Person was he privileged to announce?*—The Messiah.

Unto us a Child is born, unto us a Son is given: and the government shall be upon his shoulder: and his name shall be called Wonderful, Counselor, The Mighty God, The Everlasting Father, The Prince of Peace. Of the increase of his government and peace there shall be no end, upon the throne of David, and upon his kingdom, to order it, and to establish it with judgment and with justice from henceforth even for ever. Isa. 9 : 6, 7.

5. *What prophecy of Isaiah's is quoted in Matt. 1 : 23?*—Therefore the Lord himself shall give you a sign: Behold, a virgin shall conceive, and bear a son, and shall call his name Immanuel. Isa. 7 : 14.

6. *How many titles does Isaiah attribute to the Lord Jesus in Isa. 9 : 6, 7?*—Five.

7. *To whom does Isaiah attribute the term "Wonderful" in Isa. 28 : 29?*—To Jehovah himself.

The Lord of hosts, which is wonderful in counsel, and excellent in working.

8. *Who, then, must the Lord Jesus Christ be?*—God.

9. *Are there any other texts of Scripture that plainly show him forth to be "the Mighty God"?*—"The great God and our Saviour Jesus Christ." Tit. 2 : 13.

I am Alpha and Omega, the beginning and the ending, saith the Lord, which is, and which was, and which is to come, the Almighty. Rev. 1 : 8.

10. *How does John 10 : 30 prove that the Lord Jesus is "the Everlasting Father"?*—God is called "the everlasting God" in Rom. 16 : 26, and Jesus says in John 10 : 30, "I and my Father are one."

11. *To which character of the Lord Jesus does the* apostle *Paul allude in Eph. 2 : 14?*—"He is our peace" —"The Prince of Peace."

12. *When will the "government be on the shoulder" of the Lord Jesus?*—When his reign of one thousand years begins. Rev. 19 : 11-16.

13. *Is there any earthly throne which he is promised?*—"The throne of David."

14. *What power does the Lord Jesus exercise now?*—The power which, as God, he exercises by the Holy Spirit. Matt. 28 : 18.

15. *Where is the Lord Jesus now?*—On the throne of God in heaven.

David is not ascended into the heavens: but he saith himself, The Lord said unto my Lord, Sit thou on my right hand, until I make thy foes thy footstool. Therefore let all the house of Israel know assuredly, that God hath made that same Jesus, whom ye have crucified, both Lord and Christ. Acts 2 : 34-36.

Behold, I see the heavens opened, and the Son of man standing on the right hand of God. Acts 7 : 56.

To him that overcometh will I grant to sit with me in my throne, even as I also overcame, and am set down with my Father in his throne. Rev. 3 : 21.

16. *Under what name is the Lord Jesus spoken of in Isa. 11 : 1?*—"A Rod out of the stem of Jesse, and a Branch . . . out of his roots."

17. *Who was Jesse?*—The father of David.

18. *Who was the root of Jesse (that is, his forefather)?*—Christ, as David's Lord.

19. *From what "stem of Jesse" did the Lord Jesus spring?*—From David, whose father was Jesse and great-grandfather Boaz. Ruth 4 : 16, 17.

20. *Where does the Lord Jesus call himself "the root and offspring of David"?*—Rev. 22 : 16.

21. *What is the Lord Jesus called in Rev. 5 : 5?*—The Lion of the tribe of Juda, the root of David.

22. *Of what is the lion expressive?*—Of strength.

23. *What is the meaning of the name Boaz?*—"In strength."

24. *What connection have all these passages together?*—They all unite in describing Christ.

25. *How does Isaiah describe the kingly power of the Lord Jesus in Isa. 32 : 1?*—"Behold, a King shall reign in righteousness."

26. *Under what character does he represent the Lord Jesus in the second verse of that chapter?*—A man shall be as an hiding-place from the wind, and a covert from the tempest; as rivers of water in a dry place, as the shadow of a great rock in a weary land.

27. *Can his kingly glory be a joy to us unless we know him first as a "hiding-place"?*—No.

28. *What part of Isaiah did the Lord Jesus read when he was on earth, when "the eyes of all in the synagogue were fastened on him"?*—Isa. 61 : 1, 2. The Spirit of the Lord is upon me, because he hath anointed me to preach the gospel to the poor; he hath sent me to heal the broken-hearted, to preach deliverance to the captives, and recovering of sight to the blind, to set at liberty them that are bruised, to preach the acceptable year of the Lord. Luke 4 : 18, 19.

29. *What did he say when he closed the book?*—This day is this scripture fulfilled in your ears. Luke 4 : 21.

30. *How often does the Lord (that is, Jehovah) call himself by the name of Jesus (that is, Saviour) in the book of Isaiah?*—Four times or more—as, "I am the Lord thy God, the Holy One of Israel, thy Saviour" (Isa. 43 : 3); "a just God and a Saviour." Isa. 45 : 21.

31. *How often does he speak of himself as "Redeemer"?*—Directly and indirectly, nine times or more—as, "I will help thee, saith the Lord, and thy Redeemer, the Holy One of Israel" (Isa. 41 : 14); "And all flesh shall know that I the Lord am thy Saviour and thy Redeemer, the mighty One of Jacob." Isa. 49 : 26.

32. *What part of Isaiah's prophecy was the eunuch reading when Philip overtook him?*—Isa. 53 : 7, 8. The

place of the scripture which he read was this, He was led as a lamb to the slaughter; and like a lamb dumb before his shearer, so opened he not his mouth: in his humiliation his judgment was taken away: and who shall declare his generation? for his life is taken from the earth. Acts 8 : 32, 33.

33. *Who was intended by the term "lamb"?*—Jesus Christ.

John seeth Jesus coming unto him, and saith, Behold the Lamb of God, which taketh away the sin of the world. John 1 : 29.

Worthy is the Lamb that was slain. Rev. 5 : 12.

The Lamb slain from the foundation of the world. Rev. 13 : 8.

A Lamb stood on the Mount Sion. Rev. 14 : 1.

The song of the Lamb. Rev. 15 : 3.

34. *Give the fulfillment of the prophecy (Isa. 53) in each particular.—*

Verse 1:

Though he had done so many miracles before them, yet they believed not on him. John 12 : 37.

Verse 2:

He made himself of no reputation, and took upon him the form of a servant, and was made in the likeness of men. Phil. 2 : 7.

Verse 3:

Is not this the carpenter, the son of Mary? Mark 6 : 3.

Out of Galilee ariseth no prophet. John 7 : 52.

Thou art a Samaritan, and hast a devil. John 8 : 48.

He came unto his own, and his own received him not. John 1 : 11.

Verse 4:

He cast out the spirits with his word, and healed all that were sick. Matt. 8 : 16.

Verses 5 and 6:

Christ died for our sins according to the Scriptures. 1 Cor. 15 : 3.

Verse 7:

When he was accused of the chief priests and elders, he answered nothing. Matt. 27 : 12.

Verse 8:

And when they had bound him, they led him away, and delivered him to Pontius Pilate the governor: and when he had scourged Jesus, he delivered him to be crucified. Matt. 27 : 2, 26.

Verse 9:

There were also two other, malefactors, led with him to be put to death.

There came a rich man of Arimathea, named Joseph: he went to Pilate, and begged the body of Jesus. Then Pilate commanded the body to be delivered. Matt. 27 : 57, 58.

Verses 10 and 11:

Lo, a Lamb stood on the mount Sion, and with him an hundred forty and four thousand, having his Father's name written in their foreheads. These were redeemed from among men, being the first-fruits unto God and to the Lamb. And in their mouth was found no guile: for they are without fault before the throne of God. Rev. 14 : 1, 4, 5.

Verse 12:

Forasmuch then as the children are partakers of flesh and blood, he also himself likewise took part of the same: that through death he might destroy him that had the power of death, that is, the devil. Heb. 2 : 14.

And with him they crucify two thieves: the one on his right hand, and the other on his left. And the scripture was fulfilled, which saith, And he was numbered with the transgressors. Mark 15 : 27, 28.

35. *Compare Isa. 63 : 1-3 with Rev. 19 : 13, 15, and tell of whom the prophecies speak.*—He was clothed with a vesture dipped in blood: and his name is called The Word of God. And he treadeth the winepress of the fierceness and wrath of Almighty God.

36. *Are we concerned in this?*—Yes, for as sinners we are enemies of God.

37. *Then what should we do now?*—We should come at once by faith to Christ our Saviour, and be cleansed by his atoning blood.

38. *Are there not many gracious invitations to sinners throughout the book of Isaiah?*—Come now, and let us reason together, saith the Lord: though your sins be as scarlet, they shall be as white as snow; though they be red like crimson, they shall be as wool. Isa. 1 : 18. Ho, every one that thirsteth, come ye to the waters, and he that hath no money; come ye, buy, and eat; yea, come, buy wine and milk without money and without price. Isa. 55 : 1.

39. *Were there not many special promises to the Gentiles?*—Yes, as in chaps. 9, 11, 35, 42, 49, 60, 65.

40. *Who are the Gentiles?*—All who are not Jews.

41. *To whom are the principal prophecies in this book addressed?*—To the Jews.

42. *How are the sins of Israel described in Isa. 1 and elsewhere?*—Thy princes are rebellious, and companions of thieves; every one loveth gifts, and followeth after rewards: they judge not the fatherless, neither doth the cause of the widow come unto them. Isa. 1 : 23. The vineyard of the Lord of hosts is the house of Israel, and the men of Judah his pleasant plant: and he looked for judgment, but behold oppression; for righteousness, but behold a cry. Isa. 5 : 7.

43. *What glorious promises are addressed to God's favored people?*—As for me, this is my covenant with them, saith the Lord; My spirit that is upon thee, and my words which I have put in thy mouth, shall not depart out of thy mouth, nor out of the mouth of thy seed, nor out of the mouth of thy seed's seed, saith the Lord, from henceforth and for ever. Isa. 59 : 21. The Lord shall comfort Zion: he will comfort all her waste places; and he will make her wilderness like Eden, and her desert like the garden of the Lord. Isa. 51 : 3. Awake, awake; put on thy strength, O Zion; put on thy beautiful garments, O Jerusalem, the holy city: for henceforth there shall no more come into thee the uncircumcised and the unclean. Isa. 52 : 1.

44. *How does Isaiah describe their idolatry in Isa. 44?*—He heweth him down cedars, and taketh the cypress and the oak, which he strengtheneth for himself among the trees of the forest: he planteth an ash, and the rain doth nourish it. Then shall it be for a man to burn: for he will take thereof, and warm himself; yea, he kindleth it, and baketh bread; yea, he maketh a god, and worshipeth it; he maketh it a graven image, and falleth down thereto. He burneth part thereof in the fire; with part thereof he eateth flesh; he roasteth roast, and is satisfied: yea, he warmeth himself, and saith, Aha, I am warm, I have seen the fire: and the residue thereof he maketh a god, even his graven image: he falleth down unto it, and worshipeth it, and prayeth unto it, and saith Deliver me; for thou art my god.

45. *Under what beautiful symbol does he describe God's care of Israel in chap. 5?*—A husbandman's care of his vineyard.

What could have been done more to my vineyard, that I have not done in it? wherefore, when I looked that it should bring forth grapes, brought it forth wild grapes?

46. *What touching images does he use to portray God's love to his people in chaps. 49 : 14, 16; 54 : 5-8; 66 : 13?*—As one whom his mother comforteth, so will I comfort you.

47. *Are there not many fearful denunciations against the wicked in this prophecy?*—There are, as in 1 : 28:

The destruction of the transgressors and of the sinners shall be together, and they that forsake the Lord shall be consumed. And the strong shall be as tow, and the maker of it as a spark, and they shall both burn together, and none shall quench them.

48. What nations then flourishing did Isaiah specially prophesy against by name?—Assyria, Babylon, Palestine, Moab, Israel, Ethiopia, Egypt, Arabia, Tyre, Jerusalem, the Jews.

49. Take each in succession, and tell us as nearly as you can their present state.—Assyria is now in a very low state, under Turkish rule.

Babylon is so utterly destroyed that travelers have passed over its place without knowing it.

Palestine, generally, is in an uncultivated, thinly-peopled, oppressed and half-barbarous state.

Moab is in the same condition.

Israel is described under Palestine, above.

Ethiopia is in the same condition.

Egypt is in an improving state, but probably far less populous and less richly cultivated than of old.

Arabia is still chiefly inhabited by wandering tribes, whose hand is against every man.

Tyre is reduced to a mere fishing-village.

Jerusalem is in the hands of Mohammedans, and shares the fate of Judah and Israel and Palestine at large.

50. To what period does this wonderful prophecy extend?—To the end of time.

Behold, I create new heavens and a new earth; and the former shall not be remembered, nor come into mind. Isa. 65 : 17.

51. What glorious vision did Isaiah see which prepared him to do the Lord's service?—In the year that King Uzziah died I saw also the Lord sitting upon a throne, high and lifted up, and his train filled the temple. Above it stood the seraphims. Then flew one of the seraphims unto me, having a live coal in his hand, which he had taken with the tongs from off the altar: and he laid it upon my mouth, and said, Lo, this hath touched thy lips; and thine iniquity is taken away, and thy sin purged. Also I heard the voice of the Lord, saying, Whom shall I send, and who will go for us? Isa. 6 : 1, 2, 6–8.

52. In whose reign did he see that vision?—In Uzziah's.

53. Do you find anything similar to it in the book of Revelation?—I was in the spirit: and, behold, a throne was set in heaven, and One sat on the throne. Rev. 4 : 2.

54. What effect did the sight of God's glory have on Isaiah?—He deeply felt his sinfulness.

Then said I, Woe is me! for I am undone; because I am a man of unclean lips, and I dwell in the midst of a people of unclean lips: for mine eyes have seen the King, the Lord of hosts. Isa. 6 : 5.

55. What was Job's expression when God spoke to him?—I have heard of thee by the hearing of the ear: bu. now mine eye seeth thee. Wherefore I abhor myself, and repent in dust and ashes. Job 42 : 5, 6.

56. What alone can remove the terror which all men as sinners must feel in the presence of God?—"The blood of Jesus Christ his Son, that cleanseth us from all sin." 1 John 1 : 7.

57. What removed Isaiah's terror?—The live coal touching his lips.

58. How could a coal touching his lips remove sin?—As a token of God's grace.

59. What does "an altar" imply?—A sacrifice.

60. In the vision of the apostle John, Rev. 6 (which corresponds with Isaiah's), who is seen there as the slain sacrifice on the altar?—Jesus Christ, the "Lamb as it had been slain." Rev. 5 : 6.

61. What preparation, then, do we require ere we can dare to meet Jehovah's presence and glory?—To be cleansed by the blood of Christ, and made one with him by a living faith.

62. Is there any hinderance to our obtaining it?—None whatever.

Ho, every one that thirsteth, come ye to the waters, and he that hath no money; come ye, buy, and eat; yea, come, buy wine and milk without money and without price. Seek ye the Lord while he may be found, call ye upon him while he is near: let the wicked forsake his way, and the unrighteous man his thoughts: and let him return unto the Lord, and he will have mercy upon him; and to our God, for he will abundantly pardon. Isa. 55 : 1, 6, 7.

The Spirit and the bride say, Come. And let him that heareth say, Come. And let him that is athirst come. And whosoever will, let him take the water of life freely. Rev. 22 : 17.

MICAH.

63. In whose reigns did Micah prophesy?—In the reigns of Jotham, Ahaz and Hezekiah, kings of Judah.

64. What prophecy of his is referred to in Jer. 26 : 18?—Micah the Morasthite prophesied in the days of Hezekiah king of Judah, and spake to all the people of Judah, saying, Thus saith the Lord of hosts: Zion shall be ploughed like a field, and Jerusalem shall become heaps, and the mountain of the house as the high places of a forest.

65. Where is it found in his book? and how has it been fulfilled?—Mic. 3 : 12. The site of the temple was really ploughed over by a Roman emperor; and Jerusalem has at different times been made heaps in the various sieges it has sustained.

66. In what state does he declare Samaria will be?—"As an heap of the field." Mic. 1 : 6.

67. What sins of Israel are enumerated in Mic. 3, 6, 7?—Cruelty, oppression and idolatry.

68. What promises for the latter days does Mic. 4 : 1-4 record?—The restoration of Zion and the reign of peace.

69. What glorious Person is prophesied of in Mic. 5 : 2?—Jesus Christ.

70. Where was Jesus born?—At Bethlehem.

71. Where is Bethlehem first mentioned in the Bible?—In Gen. 35 : 19 : "Rachel died, and was buried in the way to Ephrath, which is Bethlehem."

72. Where did Rahab (who was saved in Jericho) live?—At Bethlehem after her marriage.

73. Whose wife was she?—Salmon's.

74. Whose mother was she?—Boaz's.

75. Where did Ruth live?—At Bethlehem. Ruth 1 : 1, 2, 19, 22.

76. Where was David born?—At Bethlehem.

77. What striking proof of love did three of his mighty men give when David desired a draught of water from the well at Bethlehem?—The three mighty men brake through the host of the Philistines, and drew water out of the well of Bethlehem that was by the gate, and took it, and brought it to David. 2 Sam. 23 : 16.

78. To what glorious event did the prophet allude when he spoke of Bethlehem's glory?—To the birth of Jesus.

79. Read Prov. 8 : 22, 23; John 1 : 1; Col. 1 : 17, and say to whom they refer.—The Lord possessed me in the beginning of his way, before his works of old. I was set up from everlasting, from the beginning, or ever the earth was. Prov. 8 : 23, 23. In the beginning was the Word. John 1 : 1. And he is before all things, and by him all things consist (Col. 1 : 17): viz., Jesus Christ.

80. Of whom alone can it be said in the words of Micah, "Whose goings forth have been from of old, even from everlasting"?—Of God.

81. Who, then, must the Lord Jesus be?—God.

NAHUM.

82. *Against whom did Nahum utter his prophecy?*—Against the inhabitants of Nineveh.

83. *Josephus says Nahum prophesied in the reign of Jotham king of Judah; how long was this after Jonah's prophecy?*—About sixty years.

84. *In which reign of the kings of Israel did Jonah preach at Nineveh?*—Jeroboam II.'s.

85. *In which tribe did Nahum live?*—Simeon, as some think.

86. *How long after Nahum's prophecy was his prediction fulfilled?*—About one hundred years.

HEZEKIAH, KING OF JUDAH. (2 Chron. 29–32.)

1. *Who reigned after Ahaz?*—Hezekiah.

2. *How old was Hezekiah when he began to reign?*—Twenty-five.

3. *Into what state of neglect does 2 Chron. 29: 3, 7 show that the temple of God had fallen?*—Into even a filthy state. 2 Chron. 29: 5.

4. *What did Hezekiah do to set up the worship of God again?*—He called upon the priests and Levites to assist.

5. *Did the priests, Levites and people respond to the call?*—Yes, very heartily. 2 Chron. 29: 12–17, 28–35.

6. *What proof does the end of 2 Chron. 29 give that it was so?*—The abundance of the sacrifices and offerings that were made.

7. *Was his reformation confined to Judah, or did he desire to extend it to all Israel?*—He invited all Israel and Judah to join in a solemn Passover.

8. *In what state was the kingdom of Israel at this time?*—In a sad and idolatrous state under the reign of Hoshea. 2 Kings 17.

9. *How were Hezekiah's messengers received?*—They were laughed at and mocked. 2 Chron. 30: 10.

10. *Were there any who responded to his appeal?*—Several came from Asher, Manasseh and Zebulun.

11. *What beautiful prayer did Hezekiah offer for these?*—That the good Lord would pardon every one who had prepared his heart to seek him, though he was not clean according to the temple laws.

12. *Did the Lord accept it?*—He did. 2 Chron. 30: 20.

13. *What proof does 2 Chron. 30: 23 give us that the service of God, when sincerely engaged in, and not as an empty form, is pleasant?*—They kept the holy feast a second week.

14. *How long had it been since there had been such a Passover as this?*—Not since the time of Solomon, three hundred years before.

15. *How does David describe his pleasure in the Lord's service?*—How amiable are thy tabernacles, O Lord of hosts! My soul longeth, yea, even fainteth for the courts of the Lord; my heart and my flesh crieth out for the living God. Ps. 84: 1, 2. I was glad when they said unto me, Let us go into the house of the Lord. Ps. 122: 1.

16. *What effect did this joy in the Lord have on the people with regard to the idols of the land?*—They destroyed them all. 2 Chron. 31.

17. *What is said in Prov. 27: 19?*—As in water face answereth to face, so the heart of man to man.

18. *Can we not, then, try our hearts, and ascertain their state by knowing if the service of God is our joy?*—We can do so, and ought to do so.

19. *If not, in what condition are we?*—In a state of condemnation and death.

20. *What was the next proof the people gave that their hearts were right with God?*—The abundance of their offerings for the service of God. 2 Chron. 31: 5–7.

21. *How did Zaccheus manifest the same feeling?*—Zaccheus said unto the Lord; Behold, Lord, the half

of my goods I give to the poor; and if I have taken any thing from any man by false accusation, I restore him fourfold. Luke 19: 8.

22. *How can we show our love to his service?*—By giving to it, as far as we can, our money and our time.

23. *Read Prov. 23: 26, and say how Hezekiah, in the twenty-first verse of this chapter, fulfilled this.*—"My son, give me thine heart." He did every work for God with all his heart.

24. *Who was Hezekiah's father?*—Ahaz.

25. *What foolish compact had he made with the king of Assyria?*—He bought his help against his enemies by robbing God's house.

26. *Did it prosper?*—No; he was distressed by him, and not helped. 2 Chron. 28: 19–21.

27. *How was Hezekiah made to feel this?*—Sennacherib, the succeeding king, was tempted to attack him.

28. *What did Hezekiah do when the king of Assyria came against him?*—He fortified Jerusalem and cut off the water from the enemy's camp.

29. *On whom did he depend for succor?*—On God alone. 2 Chron. 32: 8.

30. *How did the people feel when Hezekiah cheered them?*—They rested on his words.

31. *What did Sennacherib do to endeavor to shake their confidence in God?*—He boasted of his victories in other lands.

32. *Did he succeed?*—No; the people held their peace. 2 Kings 18: 36.

33. *Who was the exalted prophet of Israel at this time?*—Isaiah.

34. *To whom did Hezekiah send? and what did he himself do?*—He sent to Isaiah, and went into the temple for prayer to God. 2 Kings 19: 1, 2.

35. *How did the Lord appear for his people at this time?*—He promised them the departure and death of Sennacherib. 2 Kings 19: 6, 7.

36. *Was the king of Assyria aware that God was fighting against him? or did he make another attempt on Jerusalem?*—He made another attempt.

37. *Did he address Hezekiah by word of mouth, as before, or send a letter to him?*—He sent a letter.

38. *What did Hezekiah do with the letter?*—He spread it before the Lord in prayer.

39. *Where should we go when in trouble?*—Direct to God.

40. *Is God now the hearer and answerer of prayer, as he was then?*—He is, as every true child of God can testify.

41. *What was Hezekiah's prayer?*—That God would save them for his own glory. 2 Kings 19: 15–19.

42. *By whom did the Lord answer his prayer?*—Isaiah.

43. *How was this wonderful deliverance effected?*—By means of an angel of God, who struck the Assyrian army with death.

44. *What was Sennacherib's miserable end?*—He was killed by his own sons.

45. *What mighty city was the capital of the Assyrian empire?*—Nineveh.

46. *Are there any proofs in the present day of this Assyrian king's conquests and final defeat?*—The ruins of Nineveh have lately been exposed to view, and letters and figures been met with, carved upon slabs of stone, which thoroughly confirm the Bible account.

47. *What is next recorded of Hezekiah?*—That he was "sick unto death." 2 Kings 20: 1.

48. *Did he die of this illness? or was he restored? and how?*—He was restored to health in answer to prayer and by God's blessing on the means which Isaiah ordered to be used. 2 Kings 20: 3–7.

49. *Was there any part of Hezekiah's history that was dishonorable to him?*—Yes; he made a display to the king of Babylon's messengers of all his treasures.

50. *Of what sin was he guilty?*—Of pride. "A proud heart is sin." Prov. 21 : 4.

51. *How does the Lord estimate pride of heart?*—Every one that is proud in heart is an abomination to the Lord; though hand join in hand, he shall not be unpunished. Prov. 16 : 5. Him that hath an high look and a proud heart will not I suffer. Ps. 101 : 5.

52. *What fearful prediction was Isaiah commissioned to take to him?*—That all his treasures should in a future age be carried away to Babylon. 2 Kings 20 : 17, 18.

53. *How did Hezekiah receive the reproof?*—He humbly submitted to the will of God.

54. *What did this prove him to be?*—A true son God.

Ye have forgotten the exhortation which speaketh unto you as unto children, My son, despise not thou the chastening of the Lord, nor faint when thou art rebuked of him: for whom the Lord loveth he chasteneth, and scourgeth every son whom he receiveth. If ye endure chastening, God dealeth with you as with sons; for what son is he whom the father chasteneth not? Heb. 12 : 5-7.

55. *Name the benefits in a domestic way that Hezekiah conferred on Jerusalem?*—He erected various public buildings and brought water from a distance.

56. *How much of Hezekiah's history is written in the book of Isaiah?*—Nearly the whole.

57. *How long did he reign?*—Twenty-nine years. 2 Kings 18 : 2.

58. *Where did they bury him?*—In the chief sepulchre of the kings.

MANASSEH AND AMON, KINGS OF JUDAH.
(2 Chron. 33.)

1. *Whose son was Manasseh?*—Hezekiah's.

2. *Was he a good king like his father? Describe his character as given in the first seven verses of this chapter.*—No; he restored idolatry and witchcraft, and set up idols even in the temple itself.

3. *How was he punished by the Lord for this?*—He was carried captive to Babylon.

4. *What effect did captivity have on him?*—It brought him, by the grace of God, to penitence and prayer.

5. *Did the Lord hear and answer his prayer?*—Yes; he restored him to his kingdom.

6. *How did Manasseh act on his return to his kingdom?*—He put away idolatry throughout all Judah.

7. *What encouragement does his history give to us?*—That if we confess and forsake our sins, he will abundantly pardon.

8. *Is God as compassionate now as he was then?*—Yes, as thousands of true penitents can thankfully declare.

9. *Are we to dare to sin because God is merciful?*—Shall we continue in sin, that grace may abound? God forbid. How shall we, that are dead to sin, live any longer therein? Rom. 6 : 1, 2.

10. *Are we to dare to postpone repentance because God is merciful?*—No.

Now is the accepted time; now is the day of salvation. 2 Cor. 6 : 2.

11. *How does the apostle Paul say that he obtained mercy?*—Through the free grace of Christ.

I thank Christ Jesus our Lord, who hath enabled me, for that he counted me faithful, putting me into the ministry; who was before a blasphemer, and a persecutor, and injurious: but I obtained mercy, because I did it ignorantly in unbelief. 1 Tim. 1 : 12, 13.

12. *Does the apostle give any other reason for this favor?*—That he might be a pattern for the encouragement of penitent sinners in all time,

This is a faithful saying, and worthy of all acceptation, that Christ Jesus came into the world to save sinners; of whom I am chief. Howbeit for this cause I obtained mercy, that in me first Jesus Christ might show forth all long-suffering, for a pattern to them which should hereafter believe on him to life everlasting. 1 Tim 1 : 15, 16.

13. *Is not the invitation so free that none need doubt?*—It is to "every one"—"whosoever will."

Ho, every one that thirsteth, come ye to the waters, and he that hath no money; come ye, buy, and eat; yea, come, buy wine and milk without money and without price. Isa. 55 : 1.

And the Spirit and the bride say, Come. And let him that heareth say, Come. And let him that is athirst come. And whosoever will, let him take the water of life freely. Rev. 22 : 17.

14. *Will not Manasseh rise up in the judgment and condemn us if we should plead that we are too great sinners for God to save us?*—He may do so.

15. *How long did Manasseh reign?*—Fifty-five years.

16. *Who succeeded him?*—Amon his son.

17. *Did Amon follow his father's steps in the end or the beginning of his reign?*—He followed, throughout his reign, his father's steps in the *beginning* of his reign.

18. *How long did Amon reign?*—Two years.

19. *What was his melancholy end?*—He was killed by his own servants.

JOEL, HABAKKUK AND ZEPHANIAH.
JOEL.

1. *Is it known when Joel prophesied by his own writings?*—No, not at all distinctly.

2. *How do we gather from his prophecy that he wrote it in a time of famine?*—He speaks of the devourings by locusts and of the want of pasture, corn, wine and figs. Joel 1 : 4-20.

3. *Of what was a famine in Israel ever a proof?*—Of God's anger against sin.

4. *What does he call on the people to do?*—To fast, repent and pray.

5. *To what solemn event does he call attention in his second chapter?*—To the day of judgment.

6. *What does the apostle Peter say about "the day of the Lord"?*—The day of the Lord will come as a thief in the night; in the which the heavens shall pass away with a great noise, and the elements shall melt with fervent heat, the earth also and the works that are therein shall be burned up. Seeing then that all these things shall be dissolved, what manner of persons ought ye to be in all holy conversation and godliness? 2 Pet. 3 : 10, 11.

7. *Is this important "day" ever mentioned elsewhere in Scripture?*—As in the days that were before the flood they were eating and drinking, marrying and giving in marriage, until the day that Noe entered into the ark, and knew not until the flood came, and took them all away; so also shall the coming of the Son of man be. Matt. 24 : 38, 39.

8. *To what period does it refer?*—To the day of judgment.

9. *Are we at all interested in that solemn event?*—Yes.

10. *How?*—Because we shall all stand before the judgment-seat of Christ.

11. *Ought we not to be prepared for it?*—We ought indeed.

12. *How can we be?*—By being in Christ, and clothed with his righteousness by faith. Phil. 3 : 7-11.

13. *In what part of the book of the Acts does the apostle Peter quote this prophecy in reference to the miraculous gift of tongues?*—In Acts 2 : 16-21 he quotes Joel 2 : 28-32.

14. *What proof does Joel 3 give us that this prophet wrote after the days of Jehoshaphat, and probably very near the Captivity?*—Because he mentions the valley of Jehoshaphat, and because his referring to the cap-

tivity of *Judah* only (in v. 1) makes it probable that his prophecy was written *after* the captivity of *Israel*.

15. *With what glorious and consoling promises does the prophecy close?*—Those of the future glory of Jerusalem and of the Church in 3 : 16–21.

HABAKKUK.

16. *What proof does Hab. 1 : 6 give us that Habakkuk wrote before the Captivity?*—Because he there prophesies its coming.

17. *Who were the Chaldeans?*—The inhabitants of Babylon and the surrounding country.

18. *What threatenings respecting them had Isaiah given to Hezekiah?*—That they would come and carry away all his treasures.

19. *What prediction does Habakkuk record in Hab. 2?*—That in due time God would destroy the Chaldean power.

20. *What promise is given in verse 14 of this chapter?* —The earth shall be filled with the knowledge of the glory of the Lord, as the waters cover the sea.

21. *Which verse in this prophecy answers the important question, "How can man be justified before God"?*— Hab. 2 : 4. "The just shall live by his faith."

22. *How many times, and where, is this emphatic verse quoted in the New Testament?*—Three times—Rom. 1 : 17; Gal. 3 : 11; Heb. 10 : 38.

23. *Can you tell me what great Reformer was converted to God by it?*—Martin Luther.

24. *What contrast is displayed in verses 18–20 of this chapter?*—Between dumb idols and the true God.

25. *To what great event in past history does the opening of Hab. 3 refer?*—To the giving of the law on Mount Sinai.

26. *To what event is reference made in verses 8 and 15?*—To the passing of the Red Sea.

27. *To what event in verse 11?*—To Joshua's victory at Gibeon.

28. *How does the prophet express his confidence in God?*—In the beautiful words of verses 17, 18.

ZEPHANIAH.

29. *In whose reign did Zephaniah prophesy?*— Josiah's.

30. *How does the first chapter show the abominations of the land before Josiah's reformation?*—It speaks of the idolatry and indifference to God that prevailed. Zeph. 1 : 5, 12.

31. *Against how many nations besides Judah is this prophecy uttered?*—Five others—Philistia, Moab, Ammon, Ethiopia and Assyria.

32. *What proof is there in this book that Nahum's prophecy against Nineveh had not been fulfilled in the early part of Josiah's reign?*—Its desolation is spoken of as yet to come. Zeph. 2 : 13.

33. *With what glorious promises of Israel's restoration does the prophecy close?*—With those of Zeph. 3 : 8–20, and especially verses 10–13, and the expression of God's joy and love in verse 17.

JOSIAH, KING OF JUDAH. (2 Chron. 34, 35, and 2 Kings 22, 23.)

1. *How old was Josiah when he ascended the throne of Judah?*—Eight.

2. *Whose son was he?*—Amon's.

3. *What character did he bear?*—He did that which was right in the sight of the Lord.

4. *How soon did he begin to manifest his piety?*—At the age of fifteen. 2 Chron. 34 : 3.

5. *What was the first reformation he effected?*—The removal of everything connected with idol-worship.

6. *What wonderful discovery was made in cleansing the temple?*—A book of the law.

7. *What did this prove?*—That it had been neglected and despised.

8. *What effect did the reading of God's word have on the young king?*—He was shocked and alarmed by the national guilt and danger.

9. *To whom did he send to inquire the will of God concerning his people?*—To Huldah the prophetess.

10. *Did God alter the word that had gone forth out of his mouth?*—No. 2 Chron. 24 : 24, 25.

11. *How did he comfort Josiah notwithstanding?*—B promising that his judgments should not take plac during Josiah's life.

12. *What effect did this message have on Josiah?*—He caused the book of the law to be publicly read, and induced the people to renew their covenant with God.

13. *How does 2 Chron. 35 : 3 show us that the ark had been taken out of the temple?*—By relating Josiah's order that it should be put in again.

14. *What multiplied idolatries does 2 Kings 23 show had gained footing in Judah at this time?*—The worship of Baal and the abominations of Sidon, Moab and Ammon.

15. *How did Josiah deal with them all?*—He destroyed and defiled them.

16. *What remarkable prophecy had gone before of this young king?*—And, behold, there came a man of God out of Judah by the word of the Lord unto Bethel: and Jeroboam stood by the altar to burn incense. And he cried against the altar in the word of the Lord, and said, O altar, altar, thus saith the Lord; Behold, a child shall be born unto the house of David, Josiah by name; and upon thee shall he offer the priests of the high places that burn incense upon thee, and men's bones shall be burnt upon thee. 1 Kings 13 : 1, 2.

17. *Did he fulfill it?*—Yes, exactly. 2 Chron. 34 : 5.

18. *Could all Josiah's goodness turn away God's wrath from Judah?*—No. 2 Kings 24 : 3, 4.

19. *What was Josiah's end?*—He was killed in battle.

20. *How did this come about?*—He had attacked the king of Egypt as he was going against the king of Assyria.

21. *Was not this the only failure recorded of this good and pious king?*—It was.

22. *Must not their transgressions have reached a fearful height, seeing even Josiah's reformation could not purge the land?*—They must indeed.

23. *How was the news of his death received by his people?*—With deep and universal mourning.

24. *Which famous prophet is named as mourning for him?*—Jeremiah. 2 Chron. 35 : 25.

The breath of our nostrils, the anointed of the Lord, was taken in their pits, of whom we said, Under his shadow we shall live among the heathen. Lam. 4 : 20

25. *Where was Josiah slain?*—At Megiddo.

26. *How does Zechariah the prophet, who lived above seventy years after this, refer to this grievous lamentation over Josiah?*—In that day shall there be a great mourning in Jerusalem, as the mourning of Hadadrimmon in the valley of Megiddon. Zech. 12 : 11.

27. *How long had this good king reigned?*—Thirty-one years.

JEREMIAH AND THE LAST KINGS OF JUDAH. (Jer., 2 Kings 23 to 25 and 2 Chron. 36.)

1. *In whose reign is Jeremiah first mentioned?*—Josiah's.

2. *In which year of his reign did this prophecy commence?*—The thirteenth. Jer. 1 : 2.

3. *Was this before or after Josiah's reformation?*—The fifth year after.

4. *How did Jeremiah at first feel when he found the Lord had appointed him to the prophet's office?*—Timid and unfitted, like a child.

5. *By what promises did the Lord comfort him?*—That he would be with him to deliver him. Jer. 1: 8, 19.

6. *What office did Jeremiah hold by birthright? and which was his native city?*—A priest. Anathoth, in Benjamin. Jer. 1: 1.

7. *How does Jer. 2 display Judah's sin at this time?*—It shows their worship of Baal and other gods. Jer. : 20-28.

8. *How does the prophet beautifully describe the contrast between God's service and idolatry in chap. 2: 13?*—My people have committed two evils; they have forsaken me the fountain of living waters, and hewed them out cisterns, broken cisterns, that can hold no water.

9. *May we not ask ourselves here, On which are we resting?*—Yes, for our deceitful hearts may have many Idols.

10. *Although there may be no open idolatry in the land, what objects can the heart set up and do homage to rather than God?*—Riches, pleasures, fame and many more.

11. *What is the result of this heart-idolatry?*—"Evil and bitter" in the end. Jer. 2: 19.

12. *Compare Jer. 2: 21 with Isa. 5 and Ps. 80, and describe God's people under this figure.*—Like a vineyard, or a vine, they are tenderly sheltered, nourished, and trained, are wisely instructed and restrained, and bear rich and abundant fruit.

13. *Who has revealed himself to us as the only "true Vine"?*—Jesus Christ.

I am the true vine, and my Father is the husbandman. John 15: 1.

14. *Have we any hope of participation in its blessings?*—We are all *invited* to partake; and if we have a true faith in Christ, we *do* partake *now*.

15. *How does chap. 3: 22 describe the reformation under Josiah? also chap. 4: 1-4?*—They speak of the return of the Jews from their evil ways.

16. *Name some of the sins of Judah set forth in chap. 5; also chap. 6: 13.*—Adultery, covetousness, fraud, corruption and oppression, and general rebellion against God.

17. *What coming judgment is foretold in chap. 6: 1-9?*—War and siege.

18. *Why?*—Because of their wickedness. Jer. 6: 7.

19. *Where did the Lord command Jeremiah to stand when he uttered this prophecy?*—In the gates or principal places of assembly. Jer. 17: 19.

20. *Was Jeremiah the only prophet whom the Lord had sent to warn Israel?*—No; they had constantly had warning prophets in time past. Jer. 7: 25, 26.

21. *Did the Lord at this time (the reign of Josiah) give the people any encouragement to obey him?*—Yes; another invitation was given, with promises of blessing. Jer. 17: 19-27.

22. *Which of Josiah's sons succeeded him on the throne?*—Jehoahaz. 2 Chron. 36.

23. *How old was he when he began to reign? and how long did he reign?*—Twenty-three. Three months.

24. *How was it that his reign was so short? and where did he die?*—He was put down from his throne by the king of Egypt, and carried away into Egypt, and died there. Jer. 22: 11, 12.

25. *Who reigned next?*—Eliakim.

26. *What relation was he to Josiah?*—Son.

27. *Into what name did the king of Egypt change Eliakim's?*—Jehoiakim.

28. *How old was he when he began to reign? and how long did he reign?*—Twenty-five. Eleven years.

29. *What tax had he to pay Pharaoh-Nechoh?*—Silver and gold. 2 Kings 23: 35.

30. *What prophecy against Egypt and this king did Jeremiah utter (Jer. 46)? and when was it fulfilled?*—Their conquest, by Nebuchadnezzar (2 Kings 24: 7). About eight years after.

31. *What prophecy was Jeremiah commanded to utter in this (Jehoiakim's) reign?*—That the Jews should be punished for their guilt if they did not repent. Jer. 26; 7; 9.

32. *What special charge was given to the prophet as to where he was to stand and how he was to perform the mission?*—He was to stand in the court of the Lord's house, and to speak to all who came thither from all parts of Judah to worship. Jer. 26.

33. *How did the people receive the message?*—They gathered together against Jeremiah.

34. *What did they wish to do to Jeremiah?*—To put him to death.

35. *How was he rescued from them?*—By Ahikam.

36. *What wicked act of Jehoiakim's does the sixteenth chapter record?*—He killed the prophet Urijah.

37. *What pleasing contrast is given to this in Hezekiah's history?*—Hezekiah hearkened to the prophecy of Micah, and besought the Lord.

38. *Read Jer. 7, 8, 9, 10, and say where Jeremiah uttered the prophecies recorded in them.*—In the gateway of the temple.

39. *What sins of Israel do they reveal?*—Robbery, murder, adultery, false-swearing and idolatry.

40. *What coming judgments do they record?*—The captivity of the people and desolation of the land.

41. *How does the Lord plead with them?*—With tender reproach.

42. *To what does he compare them?*—To a horse rushing headlong into battle. Jer. 8: 6.

43. *What bitter lamentation does the prophet utter in chap. 8: 20?*—"The harvest is past, the summer is ended, and we are not saved."

44. *Has that word any warning to us?*—It solemnly applies to many of us year after year.

45. *How does the prophet bewail the state of things in chap. 9: 1, 2?*—In most pathetic words. Read them.

46. *Of what event which is not recorded either in the Kings or Chronicles does chap. 14 complain?*—Of dearth.

47. *Of what was a dearth in Israel always a sign?*—Of national guilt. Deut. 28.

48. *What honorable testimony does the Lord give to Moses and Samuel in chap. 15?*—That they were holy men of prayer.

49. *When was Moses intercessor for Israel?*—After they had made the golden calf.

50. *When was Samuel intercessor for Israel?*—When the Philistines were going to attack them. 1 Sam 7: 9.

51. *How did the Lord comfort Jeremiah in chap. 15?*—By promising him kind treatment and deliverance. Vs. 11, 21.

52. *How does the Lord describe the sin of Judah in chap. 17: 1?*—As graven deeply on their hearts.

53. *To what does the Lord in chap. 17 compare the man who trusts for salvation in his fellow-men?*—To the heath in the desert, that cannot thrive.

54. *What blessed contrast does the Lord give of the man who rests alone on Christ for salvation?*—He is like a tree by the water-side, fruitful and ever green. Jer. 17: 7, 8.

55. *Should we not ask ourselves, On what is our hope resting?*—We should, if we would be safe for a single hour.

Neither is there salvation in any other: for there is none other Name under heaven given among men, whereby we must be saved. Acts 4: 12.

56. *Is not the same simile used in Ps. 1 : 1–4 ?*—Yes.

Blessed is the man that walketh not in the counsel of the ungodly, nor standeth in the way of sinners, nor sitteth in the seat of the scornful. But his delight is in the law of the Lord; and in his law doth he meditate day and night. And he shall be like a tree planted by the rivers of water, that bringeth forth his fruit in his season; his leaf also shall not wither; and whatsoever he doeth shall prosper. The ungodly are not so: but are like the chaff which the wind driveth away.

57. *Does not chap. 17 also supply a beautiful prayer for us to utter ?*—"Heal me, O Lord, and I shall be ealed; save me, and I shall be saved." V. 14.

58. *To what does the Lord compare himself and Israel in chap. 18 ?*—To a potter moulding clay, and dealing with it as he wills.

59. *What sign did the Lord bid Jeremiah show them? and what was the meaning of it ?*—The breaking of a potter's vessel as a token of the ruin of Israel. Chap. 19.

60. *What misery did Jeremiah bring on himself by thus faithfully proclaiming God's word ?*—He was put in the stocks. Jer. 20.

61. *What did Pashur bring upon himself by this ?*—Captivity in Babylon.

62. *Was not the good Jeremiah sometimes tempted to keep back God's word ?*—Yes, when he saw it was so badly received. Jer. 20 : 8, 9.

63. *Was there not a mighty power over him that he could not withstand ?*—Yes; God was stronger than he. Jer. 20 : 7.

64. *How did Jeremiah comfort himself in the Lord ?*—By remembering that God was with him. Jer. 20 : 11–13.

65. *Of whom does Jeremiah speak in chap. 23 : 5, 6 ?*—Of Jesus Christ.

66. *How many other prophets spoke of Christ as a "Branch" ?*—Two.

There shall come forth a rod out of the stem of Jesse, and a Branch shall grow out of his roots. Isa. 11 : 1.

Thus speaketh the Lord of hosts, saying, Behold the man whose name is The BRANCH; and he shall grow up out of his place, and he shall build the temple of the Lord. Zech. 6 : 12.

67. *Where, besides this place, is Jesus spoken of as "King" ?*—

Yet have I set my king upon my holy hill of Zion. I will declare the decree: the Lord hath said unto me, Thou art my Son: this day have I begotten thee. Ps. 2 : 6, 7.

All this was done, that it might be fulfilled which was spoken by the prophet, saying, Tell ye the daughter of Sion, Behold, thy King cometh unto thee. Matt. 21 : 4, 5.

These shall make war with the Lamb, and the Lamb shall overcome them: for he is the Lord of lords, and King of kings. Rev. 17 : 14.

68. *By what name will Jesus be called when he comes again as King of Israel ?*—"The Lord our Righteousness." Jer. 23 : 6.

69. *What does St. Paul say in 1 Cor. 1 : 31 and in Phil. 3 : 8 ?*—He that glorieth, let him glory in the Lord. "Christ Jesus my Lord."

70. *Read Jer. 35, and say what Jeremiah was commanded to do.*—To give the Rechabites wine.

71. *Who were the Rechabites ?*—Descendants of Rechab.

When he (Jehu) was departed thence, he lighted on Jehonadab the son of Rechab coming to meet him. 2 Kings 10 : 15.

These are the Kenites that came of Hemath, the father of the house of Rechab. 1 Chron. 2 : 55.

72. *Who were the Kenites ?*—The children of the Kenite, Moses' father-in-law, went up out of the city of palm trees with the children of Judah into the wilderness of Judah, which lieth in the south of Arad; and they went and dwelt among the people. Judg. 1 : 16.

73. *Is not this a proof that Moses's father-in-law did go with him after all ?*—It is.

74. *How was this tribe distinguished from Israel ?*—By separate origin and abode.

75. *What excellent virtue had they practiced ?*—Abstinence from wine.

76. *What is said of drunkards in the Bible ?*—

They shall say unto the elders of his city, This our son is stubborn and rebellious, he will not obey our voice; he is a glutton, and a drunkard. And all the men of his city shall stone him with stones, that he die. Deut. 21 : 20, 21.

Hear thou, my son, and be wise, and guide thine heart in the way. Be not among winebibbers; among riotous eaters of flesh: for the drunkard and the glutton shall come to poverty. Who hath woe? who hath sorrow? who hath contentions? who hath babbling? who hath wounds without cause? who hath redness of eyes? they that tarry long at the wine; they that go to seek mixed wine. Look not thou upon the wine when it is red, when it giveth his color in the cup, when it moveth itself aright. At the last it biteth like a serpent, and stingeth like an adder. Prov. 23 : 19–21, 29–32.

Nor thieves, nor covetous, nor drunkards, shall inherit the kingdom of God. 1 Cor. 6 : 10.

77. *What great honor did the Lord set on temperanc and obedience in chap. 35 ?*—The preservation of the family of the Rechabites when others were cut off.

78. *Who was the strongest man ?*—Samson.

79. *Did he ever taste wine and strong drink ?*—No.

80. *What was a Nazarite ?*—One who devoted himself to the service of God, and also abstained from wine.

81. *What command did the Lord give to Aaron and his sons after the death of Nadab and Abihu ?*—Do not drink wine nor strong drink, thou, nor thy sons with thee, when ye go into the tabernacle of the congregation, lest ye die: it shall be a statute for ever throughout your generations. Lev. 10 : 9.

82. *Is it not therefore supposed that Nadab and Abihu were drunk when they offered the strange fire ?*—Yes.

83. *What does the apostle Paul say about drunkenness in Rom. 13 : 13; Gal. 5 : 21; Eph. 5 : 18 ?*—Let us walk honestly as in the day; not in rioting and drunkenness, envyings, murders, revellings, and such like: of the which I tell you before, as I have also told you in time past, that they which do such things shall not inherit the kingdom of God. Be not drunk with wine, wherein is excess.

84. *Read Jer. 25 : 9, and tell me who was to come up against Judah and take it.*—Nebuchadrezzar, king of Babylon.

85. *How long was the Captivity to last ?*—Seventy years. Jer. 25 : 12.

86. *What was to happen at the end of it ?*—Babylon was to be destroyed. Jer. 25 : 12–14.

87. *How long was this special prophecy uttered before it was fulfilled? In which year of Jehoiakim was it uttered ?*—About eighteen years. The fourth.

88. *After Jeremiah had spoken these words, what did the Lord command him to do ?*—To write them in a roll or book. Jer. 36.

89. *Whom did Jeremiah employ to write it ?*—Baruch.

90. *Who read it to the people ?*—Baruch.

91. *To whom did Michaiah desire the roll to be read ?*—The princes.

92. *When the princes heard it, to whom did they wish it to be read ?*—The king.

93. *Why did they tell Jeremiah and Baruch to go and hide themselves ?*—Lest the king should seize them.

94. *How did King Jehoiakim receive the message?
Did he allow it all to be read to him?*—With anger
and contempt. Only three or four leaves.

95. *What did he do with it?*—He cut it and burnt it.

96. *Could he by this destroy the word of God?*—Certainly not.

97. *What was Jeremiah commanded to do?*—To write
the words in another roll.

98. *What punishment did the king bring on himself by
this act?*—His dead body was cast out unburied, and
his family ceased to reign on the throne of Judah. Jer.
36 : 30 ; 22.

99. *Did his determination not to hear God's word
hinder it from being fulfilled?*—No, not at all.

100. *Who was in that roll predicted, and who did
come up against Judah and carry Jehoiakim's son captive to Babylon? And how was Jehoiakim himself to
be disgraced?*—Nebuchadrezzar. Jer. 36 : 2 ; 22 : 25 ;
39 : 1. By being left without burial. Jer. 22 : 18, 19.

101. *What kind promise did the Lord give Baruch at
this time of trouble because he had done the Lord's work?*
—That he would save his life in the desolation of the
land. Jer. 45.

102. *Who succeeded Jehoiakim?*—His son.

103. *By how many names is this king called?*—
Jehoiachim (2 Kings 24 : 8), Jeconiah (1 Chron. 3 :
16) and Coniah. Jer. 22 : 24.

104. *How old was he when his father died?*—Eight
years.

105. *How soon after was he carried to Babylon?*—
About three months. 2 Chron. 36 : 9, 10.

106. *Had not the Lord foretold this in Jer. 36 : 30?*
—Yes. Jer. 22 : 25.

107. *When Nebuchadrezzar carried this young prince
captive to Babylon, whom did he make king over the remnant of Judah? and how did he change his name?*—His
uncle, Mattaniah. Zedekiah.

108. *What relation was Zedekiah to the good Josiah?*
—Brother.

109. *What did Nebuchadrezzar carry away with the
young prince and his mother from Jerusalem?*—The
treasures and ornaments of the temple.

110. *What character did he bear in the Lord's sight?*
—He did evil in God's sight. 2 Chron. 36 : 12.

111. *What prediction did Jeremiah utter to King
Zedekiah of the complete and entire destruction of Jerusalem?*—That by sword, famine and pestilence its
people should be consumed. Jer. 24.

112. *How do chaps. 11 and 12 show the sins of
Judah at this time?*—By describing their idolatry and
their persecution of the prophet.

113. *Which was Jeremiah's native city?*—Anathoth.

114. *How was he treated there?*—They plotted to
kill him.

115. *Read Jer. 24, and say to what the captives now
in Babylon were compared, and to what Zedekiah and
those left in Judah were compared, and why?*—The
former to good figs, and the latter to bad, the one
being penitent, and the other not.

116. *What comforting letter was Jeremiah commanded
to write to the former?*—That they should seek God and
nd him, and be restored to their own land. Jer. 29.

117. *Who withstood Jeremiah's words?*—Shemaiah.

118. *How did the Lord punish him?*—By shortening
nis life and cutting off his seed.

119. *Read Jer. 27, and say by what beautiful simile
did the Lord show that he had given the nations to the
king of Babylon.*—By bonds and yokes upon the
prophet's neck.

120. *Who prophesied in opposition to Jeremiah?*—
Hananiah. Jer. 28.

121. *What symbol did he make with the yoke which
was on the neck of Jeremiah?*—He broke it, as if God
would break Nebuchadrezzar's yoke.

122. *Did the Lord suffer such impiety to pass? What
message did he send to Hananiah by Jeremiah?*—No.
That he should die the same year.

123. *When was it accomplished?*—In the seventh
month.

124. *What should this teach us?*—All flesh is as
grass, and all the glory of man as the flower of grass.
The grass withereth, and the flower thereof falleth
away : but the word of the Lord endureth for ever.
1 Pet. 1 : 24, 25.

125. *Did Zedekiah believe that it was God's will t
bow Judah beneath the yoke of the king of Babylon?*—
He sent to Jeremiah to know.

126. *What message did the Lord send to Zedekiah or
this subject?*—That those who escaped the pestilence
and famine should fall by the king of Babylon's
sword. Jer. 21.

127. *Read Jer. 34, and say what transgression the
people of Judah again fell into, which brought wrath
upon them.*—They again enslaved their released bond-servants, contrary to the law.

128. *What special prophecy against Zedekiah was
there in chap. 34?*—That he should be carried captive to Babylon.

129. *What army did Zedekiah get to help him against
the Chaldeans?*—The Egyptians. Jer. 37.

130. *Did it prosper, or was it only for a time that the
Chaldeans withdrew?*—Only for a time.

131. *While they were away, what did Jeremiah desire
to do?*—To return to his own land. Jer. 37 : 12.

132. *Why was he persecuted? and what did the princes
do with him?*—Because they thought he was deserting
to the Chaldeans. They put him into prison.

133. *Who released Jeremiah?*—Zedekiah.

134. *Did the kindness of the king tempt Jeremiah to
alter God's word to him?*—No. Jer. 38 : 1, 3.

135. *How did the king permit the princes to treat the
prophet?*—He allowed them to imprison him again.

136. *Who stood up and spoke for Jeremiah?*—Ebed-melech.

137. *How did he rescue him?*—He raised him by
cords from the dungeon-pit.

138. *Did the king's kindness again to Jeremiah tempt
him to swerve from the truth? What did he tell the
king?*—No. That if he stayed in the city it would be
taken and burnt. Jer. 38 : 18.

139. *Did the king believe him and obey the word of
the Lord?*—No ; he stayed till it was too late. Jer.
39 : 2, 4, 8.

140. *Where was Jeremiah when the city was taken?*—
In the court of the prison. Jer. 38 : 28.

141. *What kind deliverance did the Lord grant to
Ebed-melech in remembrance of his kindness to Jeremiah in the pit?*—From the Chaldeans. Jer. 39 : 16-18.

142. *What should this teach us?*—To always show
special kindness to God's own people. Matt. 25 : 34
-36.

He that receiveth you receiveth me, and he that re-ceiveth me receiveth Him that sent me. And whoso-ever shall give to drink unto one of these little ones
a cup of cold water only in the name of a disciple,
verily I say unto you, he shall in no wise lose his re-ward. Matt. 10 : 40, 42.

143. *How did Nebuchadrezzar treat Zedekiah?*—He
put out his eyes, after killing his sons in his sight, and
imprisoned him in Babylon for life. Jer. 52 : 10,
11.

144. *How was the loss of Zedekiah's eyesight foretold
by the prophet Ezekiel?*—This burden concerneth the
prince in Jerusalem, and all the house of Israel that
are among them. They shall remove and go into
captivity. And the prince that is among them shall
bear upon his shoulder in the twilight, and shall go

forth: he shall cover his face, that he see not the ground with his eyes. And I will bring him to Babylon to the land of the Chaldeans; yet shall he not see it, though he shall die there. Ezek. 12:10–13.

145. *How did the Chaldeans treat Jeremiah?*—By order of the king he was kindly sent back, according to his wish, to his own land. Jer. 39, 40.

146. *What comforting promises did the Lord give his people ere they were carried away captive?*—Of return to their own land, and of the coming of the Messiah, the Lord our Righteousness. Jer. 32, 33.

147. *When were these uttered?*—About five hundred and ninety years before Christ.

148. *Whom did the king of Babylon leave as governor in Judah?*—Gedaliah. 2 Kings 25; Jer. 40.

149. *What happened to him?*—He was killed by Ishmael and others. Jer. 40, 41.

150. *What was the sad result of his death?*—The carrying away as prisoners those under his charge. Jer. 41:10.

151. *Whither did the people purpose to bend their steps for fear the Chaldeans should revenge his death?*—Toward Egypt. Jer. 41:17, 18.

152. *What did the people pretend to desire after they had made up their minds to go down into Egypt?*—Direction from God. Jer. 42:2, 3; 43:1–7.

153. *Did they not prove this by their conduct?*—Yes, they showed their hypocrisy by going into Egypt, notwithstanding Jeremiah's warning against it.

154. *Did they take Jeremiah and Baruch with them, or leave them behind?*—They took them with them. Jer. 43:6, 7.

155. *Had Jeremiah any message from the Lord to his rebellious people in Egypt?*—He threatened them with destruction for their idolatry. Jer. 44.

156. *What abominable idolatry does this chapter reveal?*—Burning incense to the queen of heaven and to other gods. Jer. 44.

157. *Were the people better off in Egypt than in Judea?*—No, as its conquest by Nebuchadnezzar was foretold. Jer. 46.

158. *Against how many foreign countries did Jeremiah prophesy?*—Against ten or more, as Egypt, Philistia, Moab, Ammon, Edom, Damascus, Kedar, Hazor, Elam and Babylon. Jer. 50, 51.

159. *What other book did Jeremiah write besides his prophecy?*—The Lamentations.

160. *Where is it supposed Jeremiah died?*—In Egypt, by the hands of the Jews.

Ezekiel.

1. *Who was Ezekiel?*—A priest and prophet.

2. *Where was he when he saw the wonderful vision his first chapter records?*—By the river Chebar.

3. *How came he there?*—With the Jews carried captive to Babylon.

4. *How old was he at this time?*—In his thirtieth year, according to some. Ezek. 1:1.

5. *How long had he been in captivity?*—Above four years. Ezek. 1:2.

6. *Who was the Jehoiachin whose captivity is here spoken of?*—King of Judah.

7. *Who had carried them captive?*—Nebuchadnezzar.

8. *Where was the river Chebar?*—In Mesopotamia.

9. *Where are the cherubim first spoken of in the Bible?*—In Gen. 3, in Eden.

10. *For what were they placed in Eden?*—To guard the tree of life.

11. *What was always associated with the cherubim?*—The glory of God. Ezek. 1:28; 3:23; 43:2.

12. *Where is God said to dwell in Ps. 80:1; 99:1?*—Between the cherubim.

13. *Mention other texts to show that the cherubim are always symbols of God's promise?*—"He rode upon a cherub, and did fly." Ps. 18:10.

14. *When it was said (Gen. 4:16) "Cain went out from the presence of the Lord," from what symbol of his presence is it supposed he departed?*—From the cherubim.

15. *How were the carved cherubim in the tabernacle and Solomon's temple connected with the glory of the Lord?*—Because they were over the mercy-seat, where the glory of the Lord was seen.

16. *Where did God say he would meet his people?*—"Above the mercy-seat between the cherubim." Ezek. 25:22.

17. *Have we any record of this?*—When Moses was gone into the tabernacle of the congregation to speak with him, then he heard the voice of one speaking unto him from off the mercy-seat that was upon the ark of testimony, from between the two cherubim: and he spake unto him. Num. 7:89.

18. *Are the cherubim ever spoken of in the New Testament?*—Not by that name.

19. *Are not the seraphim seen by Isaiah (chap. 6) the same in appearance as the cherubim?*—Very much the same.

20. *In how many respects are the "cherubim" of Ezekiel, the "seraphim" of Isaiah and the "living creatures" (translated "beasts") in Rev. 4, alike?*—In having wings.

21. *Do we not learn by Isa. 6:3 and Rev. 4:8 that in God's presence all is holiness?*—Yes, as these winged beings are there described as saying, "Holy, holy, holy . . . Lord of hosts, . . . Lord God Almighty." "God sitteth upon the throne of his holiness." Ps. 47:8.

22. *What is said in Heb. 12:14 and Rev. 21:27?*—"Without" "holiness" "no man shall see the Lord." "There shall in no wise enter into it any thing that defileth."

23. *How, then, can guilty sinners hope to be admitted there?*—By having their robes washed and made "white in the blood of the Lamb." Rev. 7:9–17.

24. *Ought we not to be very anxious to know if we have on that spotless robe?*—We ought indeed.

25. *What became of that man who ventured into the feast without the wedding-garment?*—He was cast "into darkness," to "weeping and gnashing of teeth." Matt. 22.

26. *What was that garment meant to represent?*—"The righteousness of saints." Rev. 19:7, 8.

27. *How does the Lord in Ezek. 2 describe the children of Israel to whom he sent Ezekiel to prophesy?*—As "most rebellious."

28. *How did the Lord prepare the prophet for his mission?*—By encouraging and warning him not to fear. Ezek. 3.

29. *How was the destruction of Jerusalem (which had not then taken place) described by Ezekiel?*—Under the figure of a siege, with tokens of severe famine. Ezek. 4.

30. *How long after Jehoiachin's captivity was Jerusalem taken by Nebuchadnezzar?*—About eleven years. 2 Kings 25.

31. *How was the utter dispersion of Israel described in Ezek. 5, 6, 7?*—God said they should be scattered "into all the winds."

32. *How was Ezekiel transported to Jerusalem?*—In a vision by the Spirit of God. Ezek. 8:3.

33. *What abominations did the Lord reveal to him there?*—Those of the vilest idolatry. Ezek. 8–11.

34. *Whose captivity is predicted in Ezek. 12? and how is the loss of his eyesight foretold?*—Zedekiah's. When it is said that he should die at Babylon without seeing it.

35. *What great honor does the Lord put on Noah, Daniel and Job in Ezek. 14? and which of these three was living at this time?*—By distinguishing them as eminently righteous men. Daniel.

36. *To what does the Lord compare the inhabitants of Jerusalem in Ezek. 15 and 16?*—To a useless vine-branch and to a neglected infant.

37. *To what is Nebuchadnezzar compared in Ezek. 17?*—To a great eagle.

38. *How does God show in Ezek. 18: 19, 20 that the son shall not be punished for his father's sins?*—"The son shall not bear the iniquity of the father."

39. *Which of the kings of Judah are spoken of under the figures of the young lions?*—Jehoahaz and Jehoiakim. Ezek. 19; 2 Chron. 36.

40. *To what animal did Jacob, in blessing his sons, compare the tribe of Judah?*—"A lion's whelp." Gen. 49: 9.

41. *Is the Lord Jesus ever spoken of under this symbol?*—Yes, as the Lion of the tribe of Judah. Rev. 5: 5.

42. *How does Ezek. 21: 21, 22 show us the manner in which the ancient Chaldeans divined?*—By casting lots with arrows bearing the names of their enemies' cities to be attacked, and by observing the appearances of the entrails of their sacrifices.

43. *Against how many nations besides Israel did Ezekiel prophesy?*—Eight—Ammon, Moab, Edom, Philistia, Tyre, Zidon, Egypt and Assyria.

44. *Read Ezek. 33: 8, and say what is the "watchman's" duty.*—To warn the wicked to turn from his evil way.

45. *What is the duty of those who have the alarm sounded in their ears?*—To turn at once from their evil ways.

46. *Does this concern us?*—Quite as much as it concerned them.

47. *What will be our condemnation if warned to flee from the wrath to come, and we disregard it?*—The worm of remorse that never dies, and the fire that is never quenched.

48. *Against whom is the prophecy in Ezek. 34 uttered?*—Against the priests, prophets or religious teachers.

49. *Who is the Good Shepherd?*—Jesus Christ. Ezek. 34: 23.

50. *By what name is that glorious Person spoken of in chap. 34: 29?*—A plant of renown.

51. *Are there any promises of future blessing in Ezekiel's prophecy?*—Yes, of the restoration of Israel to their own land, and of great spiritual blessings, like a resurrection of the dead. Ezek. 36: 37.

52. *What remarkable vision did the prophet see?*—A valley of dry bones revived into an army of living men.

53. *In what state are our souls by nature?*—Dead in sin. Eph. 2: 1.

54. *By what means is life imparted to them?*—By being "born again" "of the Spirit." John 3: 1-8.

55. *What means was the prophet to use to waken these dry bones?*—To prophesy or preach and pray.

56. *And what means are constantly being used to rouse us?*—The teaching and preaching of God's word and prayer for his blessing upon it.

57. *If "dry bones" can live, are we not without excuse?*—Yes, for our blessed Lord says, Ask, and it shall be given you; seek, and ye shall find; knock, and it shall be opened unto you. For every one that asketh receiveth; and he that seeketh findeth; and to him that knocketh it shall be opened unto you. Luke 11: 9, 10.

58. *What vision did Ezekiel see in the twenty-fifth year of the captivity of Judah?*—Of a glorious temple, and of healing waters issuing from it. Ezek. 40-48.

59. *To what place was he in vision transported to see it?*—To a mountain in the land of Israel.

60. *As Jerusalem has never been built by this pattern, to what must it refer?*—To the future spiritual glory of Israel and the Church.

61. *What great similarity is there between Ezek. 47 and Rev. 22?*—The waters issuing from the temple are like the pure river of water of life, clear as crystal, proceeding out of the throne of God and of the Lamb. And as in Ezekiel's vision there were on the bank of the river fruitful and healing trees, so in John's vision.

62. *When and why was the "tree of life" prohibited?*—At Adam's fall and spiritual death, lest he should live again without the atoning and restoring blood of Christ.

63. *Will it ever be tasted again?*—It will.

64. *By whom?*—By "him that overcometh." Rev. 2: 7.

65. *How can we "overcome"?*—"By the blood of the Lamb." Rev. 12: 11.

66. *What beautiful ceremony ere the children of Israel left Egypt teaches us the value of the blood of Christ?*—The sprinkling about their doors of the blood of a lamb, to preserve them from the destroying angel's hand.

67. *Of what was the "scarlet line" which Rahab hung out from her window, when Jericho was taken and she was spared, a type?*—Of the saving blood of Christ.

68. *Shall not we be without excuse if we neglect to take refuge in Jesus?*—We shall indeed.

If ye know these things, happy are ye if ye do them. John 13: 17.

DANIEL DURING THE BABYLONIAN DYNASTY. (Dan. 1-4, 5, 7, 8.)

1. *When was Daniel taken to Babylon?* — With Jehoiakim, king of Judah.

2. *Where was Babylon?*—On the Euphrates, in Chaldea.

3. *What relationship did Jehoiakim bear to the good Josiah?*—He was his son.

4. *Was Daniel also of the royal family of Judah?*—He was. Dan 1: 3.

5. *How came he to Babylon?*—With the captives Nebuchadnezzar made.

6. *Who was Nebuchadnezzar?*—King of Babylon.

7. *What commandment did he give respecting the royal captives of Judah?*—That some of the choicest and cleverest of them should be specially prepared for the king's service.

8. *Why did Daniel object to eat the king's food?*—It shall be a perpetual statute for your generations throughout all your dwellings that ye eat neither fat nor blood. Lev. 3: 17.

9. *What was the result of the experiment that David requested might be tried on them?*—They looked better than those who ate the king's food. Dan. 1: 15.

10. *How does this prove the truth of 1 Sam. 2: 28-30?*—It shows that God "will honor" those who obey and "honor" him.

11. *What astonishing proof did Daniel give Nebuchadnezzar in Dan. 2 that God had endowed him with divine knowledge?*—By telling him the dream that he had forgotten.

12. *What was the dream?*—That he had seen a great image, with a golden head, struck and destroyed by a stone, which became a great mountain. Dan. 2: 31.

13. *Did Daniel take the honor to himself, or give it to God?*—He gave it to God. Dan. 2: 19-23, 28.

14. *How did Daniel interpret this dream?*—Who did he say was the "head of gold"?—Nebuchadnezzar himself. Dan. 2: 38.

15. *In what position did Nebuchadnezzar stand to the*

other kingdoms of the earth at this time?—He was a king of kings in glory and power. Dan. 2 : 37.

16. *What kingdom was represented by the "breast and arms of silver"?*—The kingdom of the Medes and Persians.

17. *In what respect were the two arms of the image a graphic representation of this kingdom?*—They showed their united power.

18. *What kingdom did "the belly and thighs" (or "sides," see margin) "of brass" represent?*—The Macedonian or Grecian kingdom.

19. *In what respect was "brass" an appropriate symbol for this power?*—It was gained and held by force of arms, and was less splendid than the other kingdoms before it in outward show.

20. *How did the fourth kingdom differ from the former ones?*—In strength.

21. *When might this kingdom be said to be an "iron" power?*—When it conquered the kingdom of Greece and other lands.

22. *When was it in an enfeebled state?*—When it joined the conquered nations to maintain its power.

23. *What power was to be greater than all these kingdoms, and crumble them into atoms?*—The kingdom of Christ.

24. *What does it mean when it says it was "cut out without hands"?*—Because it was formed by the power of God, without the help of man. Isa. 63 : 1-6.

25. *When was this kingdom to be set up?*—In the days of one of these kingdoms or kings. Dan. 2 : 44.

26. *At what time, as represented in this image, was Jesus born?*—Under the iron or Roman kingdom.

27. *What effect did the wonderful interpretation of this dream have on Nebuchadnezzar?*—He worshiped Daniel as the messenger of God.

28. *To what was Daniel promoted?*—To be ruler over the whole province of Babylon.

29. *About whom did he make request when himself in power?*—About Shadrach, Meshach and Abed-nego, that they should have a share in the government of the province.

30. *How was the faith of these three friends of Daniel tried? What did the king command them to do?*—By Nebuchadnezzar's setting up a great image of gold, to be worshiped by all his people. Dan. 3. To fall down and worship with the rest.

31. *Were they able to do this? Why not?*—No. Because they could worship only the one true God.

32. *What was the consequence?*—They were cast into a burning fiery furnace.

33. *Who walked with them in the furnace?*—The Son of God.

34. *What happened to the men that threw them in?*—They were killed by the flames.

35. *Were the three servants of God injured?*—Not at all, nor even their clothes touched.

36. *What effect did this wonderful deliverance have on Nebuchadnezzar?*—He blessed and honored God, and promoted his three faithful servants.

37. *What had been God's promise, by the mouth of his servant the prophet Jeremiah, to those who went down into Babylon?*—Seek the peace of the city whither I have caused you to be carried away captives, and pray unto the Lord for it: for in the peace thereof shall ye have peace. Jer. 29 : 7.

38. *Was not this the fulfillment of it?*—Doubtless it was.

39. *And is not God as faithful to his word now as he was then?*—He is, as every day's experience of his people proves.

40. *Can God see into man's heart?*—Yes; "the Lord looketh on the heart." 1 Sam. 16 : 7.

41. *Did the Lord see the heart of Nebuchadnezzar humbled by what he had beheld of the true God, or still proud?*—He saw the pride within.

42. *What dream did he give the king to warn him?*—A vision of a lofty and flourishing tree hewn down. with its stump left for seven years among the grass and beasts of the field. Dan. 4.

43. *Who interpreted this dream to Nebuchadnezzar?*—Daniel.

44. *Did the king take warning? How was his pride humbled?*—No. Dan. 4 : 30. By his being deprived of reason and made a companion of beasts. Dan. 4 : 33.

45. *What was the effect of this on the king?*—At the end of seven years his reason returned, and he acknowledged and praised God.

46. *Is there any account given in the book of Daniel of Evil-merodach, Nebuchadnezzar's son?*—No.

47. *Where must we turn to read about him?*—It came to pass in the seven and thirtieth year of the captivity of Jehoiachin king of Judah, that Evil-merodach king of Babylon in the first year of his reign lifted up the head of Jehoiachin king of Judah, and brought him forth out of prison, and spake kindly unto him, and set his throne above the throne of the kings that were with him in Babylon. Jer. 52 : 31, 32.

48. *Who was this Jehoiachin? and when was he carried captive? Give his other names.*—King of Judah. In the first year of his reign. Jeconiah and Coniah.

49. *What wonderful vision does Dan. 7 record?*—Of four great beasts that came up from the sea.

50. *In which year of Belshazzar's reign did this happen?*—The first.

51. *Who was Belshazzar?*—King of Babylon.

52. *What kingdom was represented by the first of these four beasts?*—The kingdom of Babylon.

53. *Do we see anything similar to this on the Nineveh sculptures lately discovered?*—Yes; many winged lions are there portrayed.

54. *What was the second beast like?*—A bear.

55. *What kingdom did that symbolize?*—The kingdom of the Medes and Persians.

56. *What was the third beast like?*—A leopard.

57. *How did the "four wings" symbolize this power?*—Because the Grecian conquests were rapid as a bird's flight.

58. *Who were represented by these four wings?*—The kings of the four parts into which the Grecian kingdom was divided.

59. *What was the fourth beast like?*—It was terrible and strong, and had iron teeth and ten horns.

60. *In what respect was this kingdom "diverse" from the others?*—In having horns.

61. *Who is the representative of that fourth or final power now? What "wears out the saints of the Most High"?*—The pope of Rome. The popish system, as far as it has any remaining power.

62. *How long is it to continue?*—Till about the time when our Lord returns.

63. *Who is meant by "the Ancient of Days"?*—The eternal God.

64. *When will his throne of judgment be set?*—When the millennium begins and God puts down his enemies' power.

65. *What glorious Person, under the name "Son of man," is introduced in this chapter?*—Jesus Christ.

66. *What "kingdom" is spoken of that "the saints of God" are to take and possess for ever and for ever?*—The kingdom of Christ to the end of time.

67. *When the Lord Jesus came on the earth the first time, did he come as a conqueror?*—No, as a servant.

68. *When will he come to reign?*—When the number

of his people is complete, and the time has come "which the Father has put in his own power." Acts 1:7.

69. *What vision of Daniel's does Dan. 8 set forth?*—Of the ram and he-goat.

70. *In what year of Belshazzar's reign did this take place?*—The third.

71. *Do these two beasts represent any of the kingdoms of the former visions?*—Yes—the ram the Median and Persian, and the goat the Grecian.

72. *Whom do the two horns of the first of these two beasts symbolize?*—The separate Median and Persian powers.

73. *Do not the four horns of the second beast in this vision mean the same as the four wings of the fowl in the third beast of the former vision? In what respect are they similar?*—Yes. They both correspond in numbers to the four kingdoms into which the Grecian was divided.

74. *Is the "little horn" of this vision the same as "the little horn" of the former vision?*—No.

75. *What erroneous form of religion does "the little horn" of the first vision symbolize?*—The popish one.

76. *What other great error or false religion does "the little horn" of the second vision symbolize?*—The Mohammedan one.

77. *Is there any limit put to the rule of these false religions?*—Yes; in periods obscurely expressed, but which seem likely to end together about the present time. Dan. 7:25; 8:14.

78. *Has not God purposely hidden the time when they shall come to an end?*—He has, in order that all may watch in every age.

Heaven and earth shall pass away, but my words shall not pass away. But of that day and hour knoweth no man, no, not the angels of heaven, but my Father only. Matt. 24:35, 36.

79. *What effect did these visions have on Daniel?*—He fainted and was greatly distressed.

80. *How soon after this were they fulfilled?*—They began to be fulfilled by the overthrow of Babylon by the Medes and Persians in about sixteen years.

81. *What impious act of profanity was King Belshazzar guilty of the very night in which his kingdom was taken?*—Drinking out of the gold and silver vessels of the temple. Dan. 5.

82. *How was it that he did not know that destruction was so near?*—He was bent on sinful pleasure, and probably refused to know and understand.

83. *Who took the city? and how?*—Darius, the king of the Medes. By turning the river into another channel, and so entering the city by surprise through the open gates.

84. *Which of the beasts of Daniel's visions, and what part of Nebuchanezzar's image, were symbols of this conquering power?*—The bear and ram and the silver breast and arms.

85. *How did God reveal to Belshazzar his impending fate just before it fell on him?*—By an awful handwriting on the wall.

86. *Who came in and reminded the king of Daniel?*—The queen.

87. *What did the mystic handwriting on the wall predict? Mene? Tekel? Peres?*—MENE: God hath numbered thy kingdom, and finished it. TEKEL: Thou art weighed in the balances, and art found wanting. PERES: Thy kingdom is divided, and given to the Medes and Persians. Dan. 5:26-28.

88. *And if "Tekel" were said to us, what would be our hope, our refuge?*—Jesus Christ alone, in whom his people are complete.

89. *Who has satisfied God's justice, and whose righteousness must avail for us?*—Christ has fully paid our debt, and his righteousness is sufficient for us.

90. *Of whom alone can it be said, "Thou art weighed in the balances and not found wanting"?*—He "who did no sin" (1 Pet. 2:22), but "is holy, harmless, undefiled." Heb. 7:36.

91. *How will his righteousness avail for us?*—As perfect in itself, and performed and offered in our stead.

As by one man's disobedience many were made sinners, so by the obedience of one shall many be made righteous. Rom. 5:19.

The wages of sin is death; but the gift of God is eternal life through Jesus Christ our Lord. Rom. 6:23.

There is therefore now no condemnation to them which are in Christ Jesus, who walk not after the flesh, but after the Spirit. Rom. 8:1.

92. *What empty honor did Belshazzar put upon Daniel when he had interpreted the handwriting?*—A chain of gold and higher rank.

93. *How soon after it was Belshazzar slain?*—The same night.

94. *Who was associated with Darius in taking Babylon?*—Cyrus, his nephew and son-in-law.

95. *How long before this had his name been mentioned by the prophet Isaiah?*—About one hundred and seventy years.

That saith to the deep, Be dry, and I will dry up thy rivers. That saith of Cyrus, He is my shepherd, and shall perform all my pleasure. Thus saith the Lord to his anointed, to Cyrus, whose right hand I have holden, to subdue nations before him; and I will loose the loins of kings, to open before him the two-leaved gates; and the gates shall not be shut. Isa. 44:27, 28; 45:1.

96. *How does this prophecy describe the manner of taking Babylon?*—Compare No. 83 with Isa. 44:27, 28; 45:1.

97. *Of what spiritual power is Babylon the type?*—Of the popish or any other apostate, false and persecuting Church. Rev. 17, 18.

98. *By what majestic figure is the destruction of that spiritual power represented?*—A mighty angel took up a stone like a great millstone, and cast it into the sea, saying, Thus with violence shall that great city Babylon be thrown down, and shall be found no more at all. Rev. 18.

99. *Did not the prophet Jeremiah use a similar symbol when he predicted the fall of the natural Babylon?*—It shall be, when thou hast made an end of reading this book, that thou shalt bind a stone to it, and cast it into the middle of the Euphrates; and thou shalt say, Thus shall Babylon sink, and shall not rise from the evil that I will bring upon her. Jer. 51:63, 64.

100. *What is the present state of the natural Babylon?*—A huge mass of brick and stone and earth, so mingled together that travelers have passed over the site without knowing it.

101. *Are we not sure that God's word will be fulfilled on the spiritual Babylon as it has on the natural?*—We are, for Christ says, Heaven and earth shall pass away, but my words shall not pass away. Matt. 24:35.

102. *What command, then, should those who are in error take heed to?*—Come out of her, my people, that ye be not partakers of her sins, and that ye receive not of her plagues. Rev. 18:4.

103. *And how can we be preserved from error?*—Thy word is a lamp unto my feet, and a light unto my path. Psa. 119:105. From a child thou hast known the Holy Scriptures, which are able to make thee wise unto salvation through faith which is in Christ Jesus. 2 Tim. 3:15.

DANIEL UNDER THE MEDO-PERSIAN DYNASTY. (Dan. 6, 9-12.)

1. *What relationship was there between Darius and Cyrus?*—Cyrus was nephew and son-in-law to Darius.

2. How are these two kings described in Daniel's vision, chap. 8?—As the ram with two horns. Dan. 8: 3, 20.

3. Which was the most powerful king?—Cyrus the Persian.

4. Which reigned over Babylon first?—Darius. Dan. 5: 31; 6: 28.

5. What feelings did Daniel's prosperity excite in the minds of the king's other princes?—Jealousy, envy and malice.

6. How did they try first to find an occasion against him?—Out of his manner of performing the duties of his office.

7. What unwilling testimony did they bear to his excellence of character and uprightness?—That they could find in him no error or fault.

8. What trap did they lay for him?—They obtained a royal decree that no one should offer a petition or prayer for thirty days to any one but the king.

9. Did he forsake the worship of his God when he knew the consequences?—No.

10. Why did Daniel pray so publicly, when Jesus said, "Enter thy closet and shut the door"?—He desired in this case to show that he was not ashamed of his duty to God.

If they return to thee with all their heart and with all their soul in the land of their captivity, whither they have carried them captives, and pray toward their land, which thou gavest unto their fathers, and toward the city which thou hast chosen, and toward the house which I have built for thy name: then hear thou from the heavens, even from thy dwelling-place, their prayer and their supplications, and maintain their cause, and forgive thy people which have sinned against thee. 2 Chron. 6: 38, 39.

11. Had Daniel heard these words of the Lord Jesus?—No; he lived many years before the Christian era.

12. Under what dispensation did Daniel live?—The old and strict one of the law.

13. What was his act, then?—was it ostentation or devout prayer?—Devout prayer.

14. How did the king feel when he found what his edict had involved?—He was much displeased with himself.

15. Why would not the king alter the decree?—Because of a foolish law of the Medes that no decree of the king could be changed.

16. What became of Daniel in the den?—He was unhurt.

17. Was it because the lions were not hungry?—No.

18. How do you prove this?—By the fury with which they devoured those who immediately after were cast into the den.

19. How were Daniel's enemies punished by the king?—With the same dreadful punishment they had intended for him.

20. What effect had this wonderful deliverance on the king?—He ordered reverence to be paid to the God of Daniel throughout his kingdom.

21. Was not all this overruled of God for the benefit of the poor captive Jews in Babylon?—It was.

22. What was God's promise to those who went into captivity?—That he would "bring" them "again into the place whence" he had "caused" them "to be carried away captive." Jer. 29: 14; 28.

23. How long had the Lord declared the captivity in Babylon should last?—"Seventy years." Dan. 29: 10.

24. How did Daniel feel as he found the time drawing near for the return of the people to the land of their fathers?—Anxious, probably, to hasten it on. Dan. 9.

25. How did Daniel seek to obtain the Lord's mind?—By prayer and fasting and confession of sin. Dan. 9.

26. How soon was his prayer answered?—Before it was finished. Dan. 9: 20.

27. What remarkable contrast is there between the time of the answer to these petitions and the one recorded in Dan. 10?—The one in Dan. 10 was not answered until twenty-one days after, though God had heard and accepted it. Ver. 2, 12, 13.

28. In what gracious way does the Lord allude to Daniel's prayers in Ezekiel's prophecy?—Son of man, when the land sinneth against me by trespassing grievously, then will I stretch out mine hand upon it, and will break the staff of the bread thereof, and will send famine upon it, and will cut off man and beast from it: though these three men, Noah, Daniel, and Job, were in it, they should deliver but their own souls by their righteousness, saith the Lord God. Ezek. 14: 13, 14.

29. Which three principal prophets were contemporaries?—Jeremiah, Ezekiel and Daniel, for about ten years.

30. It was at "the time of the evening sacrifice" that God answered Daniel's prayer. What other signal answer to prayer did God give at the same hour in Ahab's reign?—The fire to consume Elijah's sacrifice. 1 Kings 18: 29, 38.

31. What revelation of God's future will concerning Israel does chap. 9 give?—The end of the Jewish sacrifices and the destruction of their city and temple. Ver. 24–27.

32. Of what glorious Person does this chapter speak?—Of the Messiah.

33. Reckoning a day for a year, how soon might the Jews of that day anticipate his coming?—In rather less than four hundred and ninety years.

34. Did Jesus come exactly when he was by Daniel's prophecy expected?—Yes, when Simeon and others were looking for him.

35. What is the meaning of the name Messiah?—"Anointed."

36. How is the death of Christ set forth in this prophecy?—He was to be cut off, but not for himself. Dan. 9: 26.

37. If he was to be "cut off," but "not for himself," for whom did he die?—Instead of fallen men, that they might not die for ever.

38. Who was sent to Daniel to give him this revelation?—Gabriel. Dan. 9: 21.

39. In how many other places in Scripture is this angel spoken of?—In Dan. 8: 16, and in Luke 1: 19, 26 as appearing to Zacharias and Mary.

40. What is said of angels in Heb. 1: 13, 14 and in Ps. 103: 20?—To which of the angels said he at any time, Sit on my right hand, until I make thine enemies thy footstool? Are they not all ministering spirits, sent forth to minister for them who shall be heirs of salvation?—Bless the Lord, ye his angels, that excel in strength, that do his commandments, hearkening unto the voice of his word.

41. How was Daniel employed when the next heavenly messenger was sent to him?—In fasting, humiliation and prayer. Dan. 10: 2, 3, 12.

42. Is the Lord always the hearer and answerer of prayer?—Always, but in his own good time and way.

43. How long was Daniel kept without an answer to this prayer?—Twenty-one days.

44. Was it because God had not heard him?—No, but because he had reason for delay. Dan. 10: 12.

45. Who is said to be "the prince of the power of the air"?—"The spirit that now worketh in the children of disobedience." Eph. 2: 2.

46. Whom are we to resist?—Put on the whole armor of God, that ye may be able to stand against the wiles of the devil. For we wrestle not against flesh and blood, but against principalities, against powers, against the rulers of the darkness of this world, against spiritual wickedness in high places. Eph. 6: 11, 12.

47. *Does not this chapter (Dan. 10) reveal to us the conflict that goes on unseen by us?*—Yes, in verse 13.

48. *What do Job 2, 1 Kings 22 and Rev. 12 : 7–9 also show?*—They show, by expressions about Job and Ahab and their tempters, and about Michael and Satan, that there is a perpetual conflict between the powers of good and evil for dominion over the soul of man.

49. *How do we also get a sight of angelic agency, good and bad, in Jude 9?*—Michael the archangel, when, contending with the devil, he disputed about the body of Moses.

50. *Who may we suppose was the glorious Being who appeared to Daniel, and strengthened him to receive this final revelation?*—The glorious Being who appeared to Daniel in chap. 10 : 5 was doubtless the Son of God, and his hand, or that of an angel, afterward gave him strength. Dan. 10 : 10.

51. *To what extended period did it reach?*—Until the second coming of Christ. Dan. 12.

52. *What blessed promise is given in Dan. 12 : 3?*—They that be wise shall shine as the brightness of the firmament; and they that turn many to righteousness as the stars for ever and ever.

53. *Although much of this prophecy is to be understood by history, may we not join with the prophet, chap. 12 : 8?*—We may indeed exclaim or humbly inquire, "What shall be the end of these things?"

54. *Where is Daniel supposed to have died?*—At Susa, in Persia, after having been previously governor of Judæa. Compare Dan. 10 : 1, 4 with Ezra 1.

55. *What solemn announcement does Dan. 12 : 2 give?*—Many of them that sleep in the dust of the earth shall awake, some to everlasting life, and some to shame and everlasting contempt.

56. *Will it not in the present life be decided on which side we shall stand?*—It will.

If the tree fall toward the south, or toward the north in the place where the tree falleth, there it shall be. Eccles. 11 : 3.

57. *What, then, ought we to do?*—We ought to come to Christ now, that we may be his in the hour of death and at the day of judgment.

EZRA, HAGGAI, ZECHARIAH AND ESTHER.

1. *In whose reign did the Jews return from their seventy years' captivity?*—In the reign of Cyrus, king of Persia.

2. *By which prophet had this captivity been foretold?*—By Jeremiah (chap. 25 : 11): "These nations shall serve the king of Babylon seventy years."

3. *Why had that exact time been fixed?*—See 2 Chron. 36 : 20, 21; Lev. 26 : 33–35.

Them that had escaped from the sword carried he away to Babylon: where they were servants to him and his sons until the reign of the kingdom of Persia: to fulfill the word of the Lord by the mouth of Jeremiah, until the land had enjoyed her sabbaths: for as long as she lay desolate she kept sabbath to fulfill threescore and ten years.

I will scatter you among the heathen, and will draw out a sword after you: and your land shall be desolate, and your cities waste. Then shall the land enjoy her sabbaths, as long as it lieth desolate, and ye be in your enemies' land; even then shall the land rest, and enjoy her sabbaths. As long as it lieth desolate it shall rest: because it did not rest in your sabbaths, when ye dwelt upon it.

4. *How often ought Israel, according to God's command, to have put aside a year for rest to the land?*—Every seventh year.

In the seventh year shall be a sabbath of rest unto the land, a sabbath for the Lord: thou shalt neither sow thy field, nor prune thy vineyard. Lev. 25 : 4.

5. *Of how many sabbatical years, or years of rest, had*

Israel robbed the Lord?—About one hundred and twenty-three—from the entry into Canaan to the removal to Babylon.

6. *Which attribute of God does this display?*—His exact and unfailing justice.

7. *Ought the unerring justice of God (Eccles. 12 : 14) to make us afraid?*—Yes, for God shall bring every work into judgment, with every secret thing, whether it be good, or whether it be evil.

8. *What remedy is there for this fear?*—Refuge in Christ.

As it is appointed unto men once to die, but after this the judgment: so Christ was once offered to bear the sins of many. Heb. 9 : 27, 28.

9. *If Israel was judged by God's law, by what shall we be judged?*—This is the condemnation, that light is come into the world, but men loved darkness rather than light, because their deeds were evil.

He that rejecteth me, and receiveth not my words, hath one that judgeth him: the word that I have spoken, the same shall judge him in the last day. John 12 : 48.

10. *Ought we not, then, to study God's word, that we may know and do his will?*—Yes; it is as needful for us as our food, and happily always within our reach.

For this commandment which I command thee this day, it is not hidden from thee, neither is it far off. It is not in heaven, that thou shouldest say, Who shall go up for us to heaven, and bring it unto us, that we may hear it, and do it? Neither is it beyond the sea, that thou shouldest say, Who shall go over the sea for us, and bring it unto us, that we may hear it, and do it? But the word is very nigh unto thee, in thy mouth, and in thy heart, that thou mayest do it. Deut. 30 : 11–14.

11. *How did David esteem God's word?*—I rejoice at thy word, as one that findeth great spoil. How sweet are thy words unto my taste! yea, sweeter than honey to my mouth! Thy word is a lamp unto my feet, and a light unto my path. Therefore I love thy commandments above gold; yea, above fine gold. Mine eyes prevent the night watches, that I might meditate in thy word. Ps. 119 : 162, 103, 105, 127, 148.

12. *What proof was there in King Josiah's reign that the cause of Israel's apostasy was disregard of God's word?*—Great is the wrath of the Lord that is poured out upon us, because our fathers have not kept the word of the Lord, to do after all that is written in this book. 2 Chron. 34 : 21.

13. *What "books" did Daniel study (Dan. 9) when he found out God's will concerning Israel?*—Probably the books of Jeremiah, Chronicles, Deuteronomy, etc.

14. *What proof is there in Ezra 1 : 1 that God puts honor on his own word?*—The proclamation by Cyrus is there said to be owing to God's word by Jeremiah.

15. *Who was Cyrus?*—King of the Persians.

16. *Which prophet had prophesied of this king by name?*—Isaiah.

Thus saith the Lord to his anointed, to Cyrus, whose right hand I have holden, to subdue nations before him. Isa. 45 : 1.

17. *How long had that been uttered before the event?*—About one hundred and seventy years before the taking of Babylon.

18. *What edict concerning the captive Jews did Cyrus issue?*—That they should return to Judæa and rebuild the temple.

19. *Who was at this time prince of Judah?*—Shezbazzar.

20. *Who was the head of the tribe of Levi, and by birth high priest?*—Jeshua, or Joshua. Ez. 2 : 40; 3 : 2.

21. *How many returned to Judæa when this decree was published?*—42,360, besides 7337 servants. Ez. 2 : 1, 64, 65.

22. *What did they bring with them?*—The gold and silver vessels of the temple. Ez. 1 : 9–11.

23. *In which month of the year did they return?*—The seventh. Ez. 3 : 1.

24. *What feast fell on the fifteenth day of that month?*—The feast of tabernacles.

25. *Did they keep it?*—Yes. Ez. 3 : 4.

26. *What was there remarkable about this feast?*—The living in booths.

Ye shall take you on the first day the boughs of goodly trees, branches of palm trees, and the boughs of thick trees, and willows of the brook; and ye shall rejoice before the Lord your God seven days. Lev. 23 : 40.

27. *How far did they get in building the temple before they were interrupted?*—The foundation was laid. Ez. 3 : 11; 4 : 4.

28. *Who were their enemies?*—The Samaritans.

29. *By what means did the Lord rouse them to their duty?*—By Haggai and Zechariah, the prophets. Ez. 5.

30. *Who was Haggai?*—A prophet.

31. *How does his first chapter show us that the Jews were more anxious to build their own houses than the temple of the Lord?*—Is it time for you, O ye, to dwell in your ceiled houses, and this house lie waste? Hag. 1 : 4.

32. *Is not worldly ease our besetting sin also?*—It is.

33. *What effect ought the word of the Lord to have on us?*—To make us diligent and obedient.

34. *What effect had it on Zerubbabel the prince of Judah, and Joshua the high priest?*—The Lord stirred up the spirit of Zerubbabel the son of Shealtiel, governor of Judah, and the spirit of Joshua the son of Josedech, the high priest, and the spirit of all the remnant of the people; and they came and did work in the house of the Lord of hosts, their God. Hag. 1 : 14.

35. *To whom did the prophet refer in Hag. 2 : 6, 7?*—To Christ, as "the desire of all nations."

36. *When the foundation of this new temple was laid, the people who had seen the former temple wept, yet the Lord says (Hag. 2 : 9) that the glory of the latter house shall exceed the former. How was this to be?*—Because Christ would glorify it by his presence.

37. *What promises did the Lord give to the Jews in connection with the building of his house?*—That he would be with them, and give them glory and peace. Hag. 2 : 4, 9.

38. *And what blessing may we expect if we too work for him?*—Grace, mercy and peace, and as many other blessings as he sees good.

39. *To whom does the silver and the gold belong?*—To God, to give and to take away.

40. *What must we say if we offer of our substance to the Lord?*—Thine, O Lord, is the greatness, and the power, and the glory, and the victory, and the majesty; for all that is in the heaven and in the earth is thine; thine is the kingdom, O Lord, and thou art exalted as head above all. Both riches and honor come of thee, and thou reignest over all; and in thine hand is power and might: and in thine hand it is to make great, and to give strength unto all. Now therefore, our God, we thank thee, and praise thy glorious name. But whom am I, and what is my people, that we should be able to offer so willingly after this sort? for all things come of thee, and of thine own have we given thee. 1 Chron. 29 : 11–14.

41. *By what other prophet were they stirred up?*—By Zechariah.

42. *In which king's reign did these prophets utter their message?*—Darius's.

43. *Was this the same Darius who put Daniel into the den of lions?*—No.

44. *Whom does chap. 3 of this book (Zechariah) reveal to us as the hidden adversary of Israel?*—Satan.

45. *What does the apostle Paul tell us of this wily foe in Eph. 6 : 11–17?*—That he is a wicked spirit, ruling "the darkness of this world," working by "wiles" and casting "fiery darts."

46. *What is Satan called in Rev. 12 : 9, 10?*—The great dragon, that old serpent, called the devil, and Satan, which deceiveth the whole world: the accuser of our brethren, which accused them before our God day and night.

47. *What glorious Person did the Lord speak of to comfort his people under the name of "the Branch"?*—Jesus Christ. Zech. 3 : 8; 6 : 12.

48. *Who was destined to crush the head of "the old serpent"?*—The seed of Eve. Gen. 3 : 15.

49. *What special promises to Zerubbabel does Zech. 4 contain?*—The grace and help of the Holy Spirit and the providential care of God.

50. *What further prophecy of the Lord Jesus is there in Zech. 9 : 9?*—Rejoice greatly, O daughter of Zion; shout, O daughter of Jerusalem: behold, thy King cometh unto thee; he is just, and having salvation; lowly, and riding upon an ass, and upon a colt the foal of an ass.

51. *When was this fulfilled?*—When Jesus entered Jerusalem riding on an ass.

52. *To what fountain does Zech. 13 refer?*—To the blood of Jesus Christ, that cleanseth from all sin.

53. *To what does the Lord Jesus compare himself in John 10 : 11, etc.?*—To a good shepherd.

54. *Of whom does "the Lord of hosts" speak when he says (Zech. 13 : 7), "Awake, O sword, against my shepherd, against the man that is my fellow"?*—Of Jesus Christ.

55. *How was "the man" Christ Jesus God's fellow or equal?*—As himself also almighty and eternal God.

56. *When was this prophecy of the smitten shepherd and the scattered sheep fulfilled?*—When Jesus was crucified and his disciples fled.

57. *What prophecy is there in Zech. 14 : 4 of the second coming of the Lord Jesus?*—"His feet shall stand in that day upon the Mount of Olives."

58. *From what part of Judea did the Lord Jesus ascend to heaven?*—"From the mount called Olivet." Acts 1 : 12.

59. *What did the angels say to his disciples who had seen him go into heaven?*—This same Jesus, which is taken up from you into heaven, shall so come in like manner as ye have seen him go into heaven. Acts 1 : 11.

60. *In verse 8 of this chapter (Zech. 14) living waters are spoken of; where else in Scripture are these described?*—In Ezek. 47 : 1–12, as issuing "out of the sanctuary;" in Joel 3 : 18, as coming "forth of the house of the Lord;" in Rev. 22 : 1, as "proceeding out of the throne of God and of the Lamb."

61. *What glorious promises does this prophecy contain of future blessings in store for Israel?*—That God would bring them again to their own land (Zech. 10 : 6–12), and would dwell among them (Zech. 2 : 10–12), and pour his Spirit upon them (Zech. 12 : 6–14), and that they should be holiness unto the Lord (Zech. 14 : 16–21), and be a blessing. Zech. 8 : 3–23.

62. *Must not these have been peculiarly comforting to the poor Jews in their impoverished state?*—They must indeed.

63. *What effect did it have on them?*—They began to build the house of God, and prospered and finished it. Ez. 5 : 2; 6 : 14.

64. *How did they withstand their adversaries?*—Through "the eye of their God" upon them. Ez. 5 : 5.

65. *What new edict did they obtain from the king?*—That the Persian governors should furnish them

supplies for the building and the sacrifices. Zech. 6: 6–12.

66. *How had this been brought about?*—Through the discovery of the former decree of Cyrus. Ez. 5: 3; 6: 5.

67. *When was the temple finished?*—In the sixth year of King Darius, and about the year 515. B. C.

68. *How was it dedicated?*—With special sacrifices and the keeping of the Passover. Ez. 6: 16–22.

69. *Who is the Artaxerxes mentioned in Ez. 6: 14, and again in Ez. 7: 1?*—Artaxerxes Longimanus, son of Xerxes.

70. *By what other name is he called in the book of Esther?*—Xerxes, or Artaxerxes; a previous one, of Ez. 4: 7, is in Esther called Ahasuerus.

71. *How came a Jewish damsel to be his wife?*—Ahasuerus's former wife had been divorced, and Esther had been chosen in her place from many who had been taken to the king by his command. Esth. 1: 9; 2: 1–17.

72. *What was the name of Esther's uncle?*—Mordecai.

73. *What kind of relationship had he sustained toward her?*—That of father since her parents' death.

74. *Where was the Persian court held at this time?*—At Shushan (or Susa) in Persia.

75. *Who was the Jews' great enemy at this time?*—Haman.

76. *From whom had he descended?*—From Agag, king of Amalek.

77. *Would not this account for his great antipathy to the Jews?*—Yes, as his ancestors had been almost destroyed by them. 1 Sam. 15.

78. *What had the Lord decreed concerning Amalek?*—The Lord said unto Moses, Write this for a memorial in a book, and rehearse it in the ears of Joshua; for I will utterly put out the remembrance of Amalek from under heaven. And Moses built an altar, and called the name of it Jehovah-nissi: for he said, Because the Lord hath sworn that the Lord will have war with Amalek from generation to generation. Ex. 17: 14–16.

79. *Would this not account for Mordecai refusing to bow down to him?*—It would, as he was thus numbered among the enemies of God.

80. *How did Haman attempt to wreak his vengeance on the Jews?*—By destroying all of them throughout the kingdom.

81. *How did the Lord prevent this?*—By means of Esther, the Jewish queen. Esth. 4.

82. *What did the king command to be read before him to amuse his waking hours?*—The history of his reign. Esth. 6: 1.

83. *Must not Haman have been woefully disappointed when the honor he intended for himself was placed on Mordecai?*—Yes; such is often the mortification of malice and pride.

84. *How did Esther obtain the deliverance of her kindred?*—By petitioning the king.

85. *Was it not likely that she was raised to the throne of Persia with this intent?*—Yes, extremely likely. Esth. 4: 14.

86. *Is the Lord ever at a loss for means to accomplish his purposes?*—Never.

87. *What feast was ever after celebrated among the Jews to commemorate this deliverance?*—The feast of Purim. Esth. 9: 26.

88. *Why was it so called?*—Because their enemies had cast *Pur*, or the lot, as to the time of destroying them. Esth. 9: 24: 3: 6, 7.

89. *To what dignity was Mordecai raised in the Persian court?*—The highest dignity under the king. Esth. 10: 3.

90. *Will not this account for the great favor shown to the Jews at Jerusalem by the Persian king?*—It will.

91. *Who was Ezra?*—A priestly descendant of Aaron and a writer of the law. Ez. 7: 1–5, 11.

92. *Is it supposed that he went up to Jerusalem in the reign of Cyrus, or not till that of Artaxerxes (Longimanus)?* In that of Artaxerxes Longimanus.

93. *What was his object in going to Jerusalem?*—To carry back the treasures of the temple (Ez. 7: 19) and royal gifts for the temple service.

94. *What kind letter and munificent gift was he the bearer of from the Persian king?*—A letter empowering the Jews to return to Jerusalem, and exempting many of them from tribute and custom; and a gift of silver and gold and other needful things. Ez. 7: 11–26; 8: 26, 27.

95. *Whose unseen Hand is beheld here, and whom did Ezra acknowledge in the last verses of this chapter (Ez. 7)?*—The hand of God, God having put it into the king's heart.

96. *How does Ezra describe his journey from Babylon to Judea?*—That they set out with fasting and prayer, and arrived in safety. Ez. 8: 21–23, 31, 32.

97. *What proof have we in Ez. 8: 23 of the truth of 1 Kings 8: 46–49; 9: 3?*—The prayer of the penitent captives was heard.

98. *What did Ezra and his company take up with them?*—The royal gifts for the service of the temple.

99. *What act of worship did they perform when they arrived in Judæa?*—They offered a burnt-offering. Ez. 8: 35.

100. *What sinful act was Ezra made acquainted with by the princes of Judah?*—Of the Jews intermarrying with the people of the land. Ez. 9.

101. *How did Ezra receive this mournful information?*—He was greatly distressed.

102. *Did he justify these acts before the Lord, or confess the sin to him?*—He confessed it with the deepest humiliation.

103. *What effect did his faithfulness have on the people?*—They were truly penitent and distressed, and put away their wives. Ez. 10: 1, 19.

104. *How did they bring about the desired reformation?*—They made a covenant with God and with each other, and a public proclamation.

105. *Were there many in this trespass?*—Many. Ez. 10: 13.

106. *Were the priests included in the number?*—Yes. Ez. 10: 18.

107. *What had been the Lord's special command on this point?*—(See Ex. 34: 12–16.)

Take heed to thyself, lest thou make a covenant with the inhabitants of the land whither thou goest, lest it be for a snare in the midst of thee: but ye shall destroy their altars, break their images, and cut down their groves: for thou shalt worship no other god: for the Lord, whose name is Jealous, is a jealous God: lest thou make a covenant with the inhabitants of the land, and they go a-whoring after their gods, and do sacrifice unto their gods, and one call thee, and thou eat of his sacrifice; and thou take of their daughters unto thy sons, and their daughters go a-whoring after their gods, and make thy sons go a-whoring after their gods.

NEHEMIAH AND MALACHI.

1. *Was Ezra left alone to reform the people, or did he soon obtain a companion in the good work?*—God sent him a fellow-worker. Neh. 8: 9.

2. *Who was this?*—Nehemiah. Neh. 1.

3. *What office had he held in the Persian court?*—That of king's cupbearer. Neh. 1: 11.

4. *Why did he wish to give up so high an appointment?*—That he might return to Judæa to assist in the rebuilding of the temple.

5. *What means did he adopt to obtain his desire?*—Prayer to God. Neh. 1: 11; 2: 4.

6. *Can God, then, hear the desire of the heart, as well as the words of the mouth?*—He can, for he is a discerner of the thoughts and intents of the heart. Neither is there any creature that is not manifest in his sight: but all things are naked and opened unto the eyes of Him with whom we have to do. Heb. 4: 12, 13. When Jesus perceived their thoughts, he answering said unto them, What reason ye in your hearts? Luke 5: 22; 6: 8; 9: 47; 11: 17.

7. *Did the king grant his request?*—He did. Neh. 2: 6.

8. *Had Nehemiah gone unprepared into the king's presence, or had he sought the Lord by prayer?*—He had offered humble and earnest prayer.

9. *What promise had he pleaded in prayer?*—God's promise to his people by Moses, that if they returned in penitence and obedience to him, he would restore them to their land. Neh. 1: 8, 9.

10. *May not we too depend on God, that what he has promised to us he will perform?*—We always and confidently may, for "He is faithful that promised."

11. *What does Nehemiah's example encourage us to do?*—To be "instant in prayer."

12. *What king was this before whom Nehemiah was so "sore afraid"?*—Artaxerxes Longimanus.

13. *What was the name of his queen?*—Uncertain—not Vashti or Esther.

14. *What was Nehemiah's particular request to the king?*—That he would send him into Judæa to rebuild his city. Neh. 2: 5.

15. *Whom had the king sent with Nehemiah?*—Ezra. Ez. 7: 12, 13.

16. *How did the Jews' enemies feel when they understood Nehemiah's errand?*—They were much displeased. Neh. 2: 10, 19; 4: 1, 7.

17. *What was Nehemiah's first act after he got to Jerusalem?*—He privately examined the ruins by night. Neh. 2: 12-15.

18. *In what state did he find the wall?*—Everywhere broken down.

19. *Who assisted him in repairing it?*—The high priest, the priests and many of the rulers, merchants and others. Neh. 3.

20. *Were they all regular masons and builders?*—No; some were goldsmiths (ver. 32) and apothecaries (ver. 8).

21. *Who are spoken of in Neh. 3: 12?*—The daughters of a ruler, as giving their help.

22. *Should not this teach us that in the Lord's work all can assist?*—Yes, and that all should feel glad and honored to do so.

23. *What did Paul say in Acts 9: 6?*—"Lord, what wilt thou have me to do?"

24. *What honorable mention is made of a "ruler" and his daughters" assisting in the good work, contrasted with what is said of "the nobles of Tekoah" in Neh. 3:?*—The "nobles put not their necks to the work of their Lord." (See No. 21, ver. 12.)

25. *Is it not so in the present day?*—"Not many noble are called." 1 Cor. 1: 26.

26. *When the enemies of the Jews saw the wall of Jerusalem progressing, what did they wish to do?*—To stop the work. Neh. 4: 11.

27. *What reproachful thing did they say of the work?*—"If a fox go up, he shall even break down their stone wall." Neh. 4: 3.

28. *Did they succeed in hindering the work?*—No.

29. *How did Nehemiah meet the danger?*—By prayer and faith, and by being armed and watchful. Neh. 4: 9-23.

30. *What great zeal and self-denial does Neh. 23 record?*—Their not putting off their clothes at night.

31. *What great abuse did Nehemiah set himself to rectify?*—The requiring usury, or excessive interest, for the loan of money to the famished and distressed. Neh. 5.

32. *Were the people willing to do as he said?*—Yes, and did it at once. Neh. 5: 12, 13.

33. *What example did Nehemiah himself set them?*—He declined receiving his own allowance, to spare the poor.

34. *How was it that he was so disinterested?*—From "fear of God." Neh. 5: 15.

35. *To whom did he look for recompense?*—From God. Neh. 5: 19.

36. *Was not the eye of Moses fixed on the same blessed object?*—It was.

By faith Moses, when he was come to years, refused to be called the son of Pharaoh's daughter; choosing rather to suffer affliction with the people of God, than to enjoy the pleasures of sin for a season; esteeming the reproach of Christ greater riches than the treasures in Egypt: for he had respect unto the recompense of the reward. Heb. 11: 24-26.

37. *What was the sustaining power that upheld the apostle Paul in his arduous course?*—His expectation of "a crown of righteousness" to be given him "at that day." 2 Tim. 4: 6-8.

38. *Does not the apostle Peter remind us that it is that same blessed period to which we must look?*—When the chief Shepherd shall appear, ye shall receive a crown of glory that fadeth not away. 1 Pet. 5: 4.

39. *What does Matt. 25 tell us about that time?*—That those who serve God and his people upon earth, shall, when Christ returns in his glory, enter into eternal life and the joy of their Lord. Vs. 19-23, 31-40, 46.

40. *Ought we not, then, to examine ourselves, to see whether we are getting our reward here or waiting for it hereafter?*—Yes, as it is of *hypocrites* that it is said (Matt. 6: 2, 5, 16), "They *have* their reward," and have no other and better to come.

41. *What wicked device did Sanballat and his companions next try to put the good Nehemiah in fear?*—They invited him to a meeting in order to get him into their hands, and they sent him a false prophet to induce him to leave his work. Neh. 6.

42. *Did they succeed?*—No.

43. *On whom did Nehemiah depend?*—Upon God. Neh. 6: 9.

44. *Was any one ever disappointed who put his trust in God?*—Never.

45. *How long was the wall building?*—Fifty-two days. Neh. 6: 15.

46. *What prophecy of Daniel was connected with the building of this wall?*—Know therefore and understand, that from the going forth of the commandment to restore and to build Jerusalem unto the Messiah the Prince shall be seven weeks, and threescore and two weeks: the street shall be built again, and the wall, even in troublous times. Dan. 9: 25.

47. *Whom did Nehemiah appoint to the charge of Jerusalem, and why?*—I gave my brother Hanani, and Hananiah the ruler of the palace, charge over Jerusalem: for he was a faithful man, and feared God above many. Neh. 7: 2.

48. *What did God put into the heart of Nehemiah to do after this?*—To make a register of the families that returned from Babylon. Neh. 7: 5.

49. *Why was the preservation of the genealogies of the children of Israel so important?*—To show the fulfillment in Christ of the promise to Abraham, that in his seed should all the nations of the earth be blessed (Dan. 22: 18) and of the promise to David, that God would raise up a king to sit for ever on his throne. Acts 2: 29, 30; Luke 1: 30-33.

50. *What further arrangement was completed by the*

seventh month?—The settling of the Israelites in their cities. Neh. 7:73.

51. *What special feast was to be kept in that month?*—The feast of tabernacles. Neh. 8:14–18.

52. *Of what was it symbolical?*—The booths were in remembrance of the tents in the wilderness. Luke 23:43.

Speak unto the children of Israel, saying, The fifteenth day of this seventh month shall be the feast of tabernacles for seven days unto the Lord. On the first day shall be an holy convocation: ye shall do no servile work therein. Seven days ye shall offer an offering made by fire unto the Lord: on the eighth day shall be an holy convocation unto you: and ye shall offer an offering made by fire unto the Lord: it is a solemn assembly; and ye shall do no servile work therein. Ye shall dwell in booths seven days. Lev. 23:34–36, 42.

53. *When will be its great antitype?*—I saw a new heaven and a new earth: for the first heaven and the first earth were passed away; and there was no more sea. And I John saw the holy city, new Jerusalem, coming down from God out of heaven, prepared as a bride adorned for her husband. And I heard a great voice out of heaven saying, Behold, the tabernacle of God is with men, and he will dwell with them, and they shall be his people, and God himself shall be with them, and be their God. Rev. 21:1–3.

54. *Who read the law to Israel at this solemn feast?*—Ezra himself.

55. *Does not Neh. 8:8 show that their seventy years' residence in a foreign land had made them forget their mother-tongue, Hebrew?*—Yes, as distinct reading and explanation were required.

56. *What effect did the reading of the law have on the people?*—They wept, from mingled feelings of sorrow and of joy. Neh. 8:9.

57. *How did Ezra encourage the people?*—He said the joy of the Lord was their strength. Neh. 8:10.

58. *What does Neh. 9 record?*—A solemn fast, with reading of the law and confession of sin.

59. *What further arrangements do Neh. 10 and 11 set forth?*—The entering into a covenant with God for obedience to his law and as to the offerings for his service, and the selecting the inhabitants of the city and country.

60. *How was the wall dedicated?*—With music and thanksgiving and great joy. Neh. 12:27–43.

61. *How long did this reformation last?*—During the days of Zerubbabel and Nehemiah. Neh. 12:47.

62. *When had Nehemiah returned to the king of Persia, his master?* (*Neh. 13*).—In the thirty-second year of Artaxerxes' reign. Neh. 5:14.

63. *When he returned to Jerusalem again, did he find the government going on prosperously?*—No.

64. *What evils did he discover?*—Abuse and neglect of the house of God, Sabbath-breaking and heathen marriages.

65. *How did he correct them?*—He cleansed the temple and made new treasurers of its funds, and closed the city gates against Sabbath traffic, and put an end to marriage of heathen wives.

66. *Had not the Sabbath-day been the great token of the covenant between the Lord and Israel?*—It had. Isa. 58:13, 14; Ezek. 20:12–20.

Speak thou also unto the children of Israel, saying, Verily, my sabbaths ye shall keep: for it is a sign between me and you throughout your generations; that ye may know that I am the Lord that doth sanctify you. It is a sign between me and the children of Israel for ever: for in six days the Lord made heaven and earth, and on the seventh day he rested, and was refreshed. Ex. 31:13, 17.

67. *Will God suffer his laws to be trampled on without punishment?*—No, as we see in the case of the Jews' neglect to keep their seventh years of rest.

Them that had escaped from the sword carried he away to Babylon; to fulfill the word of the Lord by the mouth of Jeremiah, until the land had enjoyed her sabbaths; for as long as she lay desolate she kept sabbath, to fulfill threescore and ten years. 2 Chron. 36:20, 21.

68. *What command did the Lord give about marrying heathen wives?*—Thou shalt smite them, and utterly destroy them; thou shalt make no covenant with them, nor show mercy unto them; neither shalt thou make marriages with them: thy daughter thou shalt not give unto his son, nor his daughter shalt thou take unto thy son. For they will turn away thy son from following me, that they may serve other gods. Deut. 7:2–4.

69. *Did not Nehemiah vigorously root out this evil?*—He did. Neh. 13:25, 28, 30.

70. *Where is Nehemiah supposed to have ended his days?*—At Babylon, as cupbearer to the king. Neh. 1:11; 13:6.

71. *After his death, what further evils does the prophecy of Malachi record?*—Scanty and mean sacrifices and offerings to God. Mal. 1.

72. *Does not chap. 2:1–11 of this prophecy show us that the sin which Nehemiah had with such zeal cleansed away a few years before, the priests had fallen into again?*—Yes; they seemed to have married heathen wives. Mal. 1:1–11.

73. *Had they not made it an excuse for putting away their wives?*—Yes. Mal. 2:14–16.

74. *Would God wink at this sin?*—No, for he hateth putting away.

75. *Of whom does Mal. 3:1 speak?*—Of John the Baptist.

76. *How is he described?*—As God's messenger, to prepare his way.

77. *Does not this chapter reveal yet further Israel's sin at that time?*—Yes, it speaks of their adultery, false swearing, oppression of the poor and robbery of God. Mal. 3:5–9.

78. *Were there any faithful ones left among this general corruption?*—Yes, some that feared God, and met together to speak about him for their mutual comfort and help, and who were all written down in his book of remembrance. Mal. 3:16, 17.

79. *What awful day does the prophet speak of in Mal. 4:1, 5?*—The great and dreadful day of judgment.

80. *Is this "day" mentioned in any other part of Scripture?*—Yes, in Joel 2:31 as "the great and terrible day of the Lord."

81. *Who have need to fear the terror of "that day"?*—"Scoffers" who walk "after their own lust." 2 Pet. 3:3.

And the kings of the earth, and the great men, and the rich men, and the chief captains, and the mighty men, and every bondman, and every free man, hid themselves in the dens and in the rocks of the mountains; and said to the mountains and rocks, Fall on us, and hide us from the face of Him that sitteth on the throne, and from the wrath of the Lamb. Rev. 6:15, 16.

For the great day of his wrath is come; and who shall be able to stand?

82. *With what feelings may those who "fear the Lord" look forward to it?*—With solemn awe, with humble hope, with calm peace and thankful joy.

83. *Who is spoken of under the figure of the "Sun of Righteousness"?*—Our Lord Jesus Christ.

84. *To whom does Deborah allude in her song in Judg. 5:31?*—To Jesus Christ, "the sun" going "forth in his might."

85. *Did not David look forward to the same blessed Person in his "last words"?*—Yes, as the light of the morning, when the sun riseth. 2 Sam. 23:4.

86. *Should we not ask ourselves, Are we ready for his appearing?*—Yes, day by day, knowing the time, that now it is high time to awake out of sleep: for now is our salvation nearer than when we believed. The night is far spent, the day is at hand: let us therefore cast off the works of darkness, and let us put on the armor of light. Rom. 13: 11, 12.

87. *How can we know that we are ready?*—By knowing that we are in Christ by faith; for as it is appointed unto men once to die, but after this the judgment: so Christ was once offered to bear the sins of many; and unto them that look for him shall he appear the second time without sin unto salvation. Heb. 9: 27, 28.

88. *What in Rev. 19: 8 is the bride's dress said to be in which she appears to meet the Lord?*—To her was granted that she should be arrayed in fine linen, clean and white; for the fine linen is the righteousness of saints (even the righteousness of Christ).

89. *Whose righteousness must we be clothed in if we sit down at the marriage-supper of the Lamb?*—"Not" our "own righteousness, which is of the law, but that which is through the faith of Christ, the righteousness which is of God by faith." Phil. 3: 9.

90. *How can we procure this?*—"Through Jesus Christ our Saviour." Tit. 3: 5-7.

91. *What right have we to obtain it?*—A perfect right through Christ by faith. "And the Spirit and the bride say, Come. And whosoever will" may come. Rev. 22: 17.

THE NEW TESTAMENT.

LUKE 1.

1. *Who was the evangelist Luke?*—The writer of a Gospel and of the Acts of the Apostles, a physician, and said to have been born at Antioch in Syria.

2. *Was he a personal disciple of our Lord?*—This is not known.

3. *Who was Theophilus?*—A Gentile of rather high rank, and a Christian. Acts 1: 1.

4. *How much of Palestine was under Herod's jurisdiction?*—Judæa. Luke 1: 5.

5. *What is meant by the courses of the priests?*—They were "divided by lot" "in the service of the house of the Lord." 1 Chron. 24: 1-19.

6. *Does not the word "temple" in verse 9 signify rather the holy place?*—It does, for God says to Moses, "Thou shalt make an altar to burn incense upon," "and thou shalt put it" "before the mercy-seat." Ex. 30: 1, 6-8.

7. *What was our Lord's testimony to John the Baptist at a later period?*—That "he was a burning and a shining light." John 5: 35.

8. *What prophecy agrees with verse 17?*—Behold, I will send you Elijah the prophet before the coming of the great and dreadful day of the Lord: and he shall turn the heart of the fathers to the children, and the heart of the children to their fathers, lest I come and smite the earth with a curse. Mal. 4: 5, 6.

9. *How much older was John the Baptist than our Lord?*—About six months. V. 36.

10. *Is there not a connection between verses 28 and 38?*—The angel said to Mary, "The Lord is with thee," and Mary replied, "Behold the handmaid of the Lord."

11. *Whom does Mary speak of as God my Saviour?*—Of God the Father, who designed the salvation of man, and sent his Son to execute it.

12. *What was the oath unto Abraham?*—The angel of the Lord called unto Abraham out of heaven, and said, By myself, have I sworn, saith the Lord, for because thou hast done this thing, and hast not withheld thy son, thine only son: that in blessing I will bless thee, and in multiplying I will multiply thy seed as the stars of the heaven, and as the sand which is upon the sea-shore; and thy seed shall possess the gate of his enemies: and in thy seed shall all the nations of the earth be blessed; because thou hast obeyed my voice. Gen. 22: 15-18.

13. *To what do we owe the remission of our sins?*—To the righteousness and death of Christ, "through the tender mercy of our God." Vs. 77, 78.

14. *How do we know that the way of life is light and peace?*—By the word of God (v. 79), and by the experience of our own minds and hearts.

MATTHEW 1: 18-25.

15. *How do we know it was the same angel as appeared to Mary?*—Because he is spoken of in v. 20 as "the angel of the Lord."

16. *What is the meaning of being saved from our sins?*—Being saved from the power and guilt and punishment of them, and made "holy and unblamable and unreprovable in" God's "sight." Col. 1: 22.

LUKE 2.

17. *Who was Cæsar Augustus?*—The first emperor of Rome.

18. *What does the term "all the world" include?*—The Roman empire, which then included nearly all the known or civilized world.

19. *How do the angels speak of Jesus to the shepherds?*—As "a Saviour," "Christ the Lord." V. 11.

20. *Is there not a sign of the poverty of Joseph and Mary in the offering they presented?*—There is.

When the days of her purifying are fulfilled, for a son, or for a daughter, she shall bring a lamb of the first year for a burnt-offering, and a young pigeon, or a turtledove, for a sin-offering, unto the door of the tabernacle of the congregation, unto the priest: who shall offer it before the Lord, and make an atonement for her; and she shall be cleansed from the issue of her blood. This is the law for her that hath borne a male or a female. And if she be not able to bring a lamb, then she shall bring two turtles, or two young pigeons; the one for the burnt-offering, and the other for a sin-offering: and the priest shall make an atonement for her, and she shall be clean. Lev. 12: 6-8.

21. *Is Simeon of verse 25 the same person as in Acts 15: 14?*—No; the Simeon of the Acts was Simon Peter.

22. *Who are the Gentiles?*—All nations but the Jews.

23. *How does the compulsory taxation of Luke 2: 1 agree with the boast of the Jews in John 8: 33?*—It does not agree at all, but shows the falseness of their boast.

24. *What was the feast of the Passover?*—Observe the month of Abib, and keep the passover unto the Lord thy God: for in the month of Abib the Lord thy God brought thee forth out of Egypt by night. Thou shalt therefore sacrifice the passover unto the Lord thy God, of the flock and the herd, in the place which the Lord shall choose to place his name there. Thou shalt eat no leavened bread with it. Deut. 16: 1-3.

MATTHEW 2: 1-12.

25. *Who were the wise men?*—Some Magi from the East, who studied the stars and the supposed influence of the stars on human affairs.

26. *Why was all Jerusalem troubled, instead of welcoming their promised King?*—Many were afraid lest he should overthrow the reigning king.

He came unto his own, and his own received him not. John 1:11.

27. *What proof of the overruling providence of God is there in verse 12?*—The special warning by a dream.

28. *Why was the term "Nazarene" a reproach?*—Because of the contempt in which Nazareth was held by the educated Jews.

LUKE 3 (MATTHEW 3, MARK 1).

29. *Who was Tiberius Cæsar?*—The second emperor of Rome.

30. *What was the Roman title of Pontius Pilate?*—Governor. Luke 3:1.

31. *What was the special feature of John's preaching?*—Repentance for remission or pardon of sin through the coming Messiah, and baptism as the outward sign and public profession.

32. *What is repentance?*—Not only sorrow for sin, but a total change of mind and heart.

33. *Who is addressed in Mark 1:2; Mal. 3:1; Isa. 40:3?*—Jesus Christ is addressed in Mark 1:2, and referred to in Mal. 3:1: "Behold, I will send my messenger, and he shall prepare the way before me;" and in Isa. 40:3: "The voice of him that crieth in the wilderness, Prepare ye the way of the Lord."

34. *Was John's preaching successful?*—Yes; people from all parts of Judæa confessed and were baptized. Matt. 3:5; Mark 1:5.

35. *Whither should we flee from the wrath to come?*—To Christ, our perfect and only Shield.

36. *What is the fruit of true repentance?*—Ceasing "to do evil," willfully and habitually, any more. Isa. 1:16.

37. *What solemn warning is contained in Luke 3:9?*—Now also the axe is laid unto the root of the trees: every tree therefore which bringeth not forth good fruit is hewn down and cast into the fire.

38. *How does John's reply in Luke 3:11 illustrate the second great commandment?*—By teaching kindness and self-denial for each other's good.

39. *What were the publicans?*—Jewish collectors of Roman taxes.

40. *Why were they so odious to their countrymen?*—Because they farmed the taxes, and made as much out of them as possible for their own benefit.

41. *What is the meaning of the word Christ?*—"Anointed." Luke 4:18.

42. *What was the difference between John's baptism and the Lord's?*—The baptism ordained by our Lord was "into the name of the Father, and of the Son, and of the Holy Ghost," and was accompanied by the grace of the Holy Spirit to those who believed. "John truly baptized with water; but ye shall be baptized with the Holy Ghost not many days hence." Acts 1:5. As took place at Pentecost and in the house of Cornelius. Acts 2:2–4; 11:15.

43. *What is the meaning of baptism with fire?*—The purifying fire of the Holy Spirit, or some searching and exposing power.

Every man's work shall be made manifest: for the day shall declare it, because it shall be revealed by fire: and the fire shall try every man's work of what sort it is. 1 Cor. 3:13.

44. *What is the allusion to the use of the fan?*—The final separation by Christ of the righteous and the wicked, as the winnowing-fan divides the chaff from the wheat.

45. *What proof of our Lord having no need of repentance is found in Luke 3:22?*—The approving voice of the holy and omniscient God.

LUKE 4 (MATTHEW 4, MARK 1).

46. *How did the Lord Jesus ascertain the will of God concerning himself from day to day?*—By constant filial communion with the Father.

47. *What is the devil called in Mark 1:13?*—Satan.

48. *What is the meaning of the two terms?*—Satan means "adversary" or "enemy," and devil, "accuser."

49. *What proof of the divine authority of the Pentateuch is in Luke 4:4?*—Its being quoted by Christ.

50. *What does "living by every word of God" signify?*—Trusting his promises and keeping his commands.

51. *What is the meaning of the word "tempt" in Luke 4:12?*—Presumptuously try or provoke.

52. *Was it an empty boast of the devil in Luke 4:6?*—Not altogether, as he is called "the god of this world" (Eph. 2:2) and "the prince of the power of the air." 2 Cor. 4:4.

53. *What relation is there between our Lord's temptation and John 2:16?*—They both show that there can be no fellowship between Christ and Satan, and between God's service and the world's.

JOHN 1.

54. *Why is our Lord called the Word?*—Because he is the revelation of God. V. 18.

55. *What proof of his divinity is there in verse 1, and again in verse 2, and again in verse 3?*—He is stated to be "God," and to have been "in the beginning," and to have "made" "all things."

56. *What is the glad hope of eternal life called in verse 4?*—"The light of men" in Christ.

57. *How do we know the gospel is free to all?*—Because Christ, like the light, reaches all, "that all through him might believe." Vs. 7, 9.

58. *Who are meant by "his own"?*—The Jews. V. 11.

59. *What great change takes place in us when we truly believe?*—We become new creatures in Christ, even "sons of God."

60. *Who effects this change?*—"God" himself through Christ, by the Holy Spirit. V. 13.

61. *Out of whose fullness do we receive every grace?*—Out of the fullness of Christ.

62. *Trace the connection between verses 18 and 1?*—Christ, as the word of God, declares him or makes him known.

63. *What was the difference between priests and Levites?*—The priests were descendants of Aaron, and the chief officers of the temple; the Levites, of other families of the tribe, and the assistants of the priests.

64. *Who was Elias?*—"Elijah the prophet."

65. *Why was he expected to reappear?*—Because Malachi prophesied that he should come. Mal. 4:5.

66. *Who was meant by "that prophet"?*—Christ, who, like Moses, was a mediator and teacher.

The Lord thy God will raise up unto thee a prophet from the midst of thee of thy brethren; like unto me Deut. 18:15.

67. *Why did John call Jesus the "Lamb of God"?*—Because he was the spotless sacrifice and gift of God.

68. *What further proof of the freeness of the gospel is there in verse 29?*—He "taketh away the sin of the world."

69. *What language is the word "rabbi"?*—Hebrew.

70. *In what estimation was Nazareth commonly held?*—It was much despised—more even than Galilee in general, whose inhabitants were looked down upon by the more civilized Jews.

71. *Can we too often use Philip's invitation?*—No. Having seen and known Jesus ourselves, we should say unto all who inquire, and all who doubt, and all who pass by, "Come and see."

72. *What is an "Israelite indeed"?*—One who sincerely inquires or believes.

Truly, God is good to Israel, even to such as are of a clean heart. Ps. 73 : 1.

For he is not a Jew, which is one outwardly; neither is that circumcision, which is outward in the flesh: but he is a Jew, which is one inwardly; and circumcision is that of the heart, in the spirit, and not in the letter; whose praise is not of men, but of God. Rom. 2 : 28, 29.

73. *What proof of our Lord's divinity does verse 48 contain?*—He saw Nathanael, by his all-seeing power, when he thought he was alone in prayer.

74. *What is the meaning of the word "Israel"?*—"A prince of God." Gen. 32 : 28, margin.

Thy name shall be called no more Jacob, but Israel: for as a prince hast thou power with God and with men, and hast prevailed.

75. *Compare verse 51 with Gen. 28 : 12 and Heb. 1 : 14.*—Christ is the ladder of communication between heaven and earth, between earth and heaven; and angels were messengers and servants to Jacob of old and to Christ upon earth, and are "ministering spirits" "to the heirs of salvation" now.

JOHN 2.

76. *Is not the Passover generally called the Lord's Passover?*—It is, in many parts of the Old Testament.

77. *For what purpose were the animals brought to the temple?*—To be sold as offerings and sacrifices to God, and for the food of the priests and people.

78. *What temple did our Lord refer to in verse 19?*—The temple of his own body.

79. *How does this verse illustrate John 10 : 18?*—Each verse shows his "power to take again" the body or life he had laid down.

80. *Who built the temple that was then standing?*—Ezra and Nehemiah.

81. *What proof of the omniscience of Jesus is in verse 25?*—"He knew what was in man."

JOHN 3.

82. *Who were the Pharisees?*—A sect of the Jews who "trusted in themselves that they were righteous, and despised others." Luke 18 : 9, 10.

83. *What recent miracles does Nicodemus refer to?*—Those related or referred to in John 2 : 2, 7-11, 23.

84. *Is there any exception to the necessity for the new birth?*—None.

85. *By whom are we born again?*—By the Holy Spirit.

86. *Who are the "we" of verse 11?*—Jesus and the Father.

87. *What fresh proof of the freeness of the gospel is there in verses 15 and 16?*—Jesus saying, that "whosoever believeth in him" shall "have everlasting life."

88. *What proof of salvation being a present blessing is there in verse 18?*—The saying of Jesus, that "He that believeth on him is not condemned," but (v. 30) "hath everlasting life."

89. *Why do we reject the Light of life?*—Because we love sin, or darkness, better.

90. *Who is the great Example of verse 21?*—Jesus himself.

91. *Who is the "bride" of verse 29?*—The Church or people of Christ.

92. *What is the meaning of the expression "set to his seal"?*—Shown his belief.

93. *What are the terrible consequences of unbelief?*—Being "condemned already" and under the abiding "wrath of God." Vs. 18, 36.

MARK 6 (MATTHEW 14, LUKE 3).

94. *Why was John imprisoned?*—Because of his faithful boldness in respect to Herod's unlawful marriage with his brother's wife. Mark 6 : 17, 18.

95. *Did not Herod's respect for John greatly add to his criminality?*—It did, as it showed that his conscience told him John was right.

JOHN 4.

96. *Why must Jesus "needs go through Samaria"?*—Because it lay between. Vs. 3, 4.

97. *When was the parcel of ground sold to Jacob?*—Jacob bought it on his return from Laban, and probably gave it to Joseph as part of his dying blessing. Josh. 24 : 32.

98. *Why had the Jews no dealings with the Samaritans?*—Because they did not come to Jerusalem to worship. V. 20.

99. *Who were the Samaritans?*—Colonists from Assyria who worshiped God, but not like the Jews.

100. *Is not the freeness of the gospel again brought out in verse 10?*—Yes; the Samaritan woman, living in open sin, was welcome to the living water of the Spirit if she asked.

101. *What are the soul-satisfying effects of faith?*—The grace and comfort of the Holy Spirit. Vs. 13, 14.

102. *What proof of omniscience is there in this narrative?*—Jesus knowing the history of the woman's life. V. 18.

103. *What is the true worship which alone is acceptable to God?*—The worship of the heart. Vs. 23, 24.

104. *Compare verses 31-34 with Matt. 4 : 4.*—God's word is the food of the soul.

105. *What simple act of faith is recorded in verse 50?*—The nobleman's instant belief that Jesus had cured his child.

LUKE 4 (MATTHEW 4, MARK 1).

106. *Who are the "broken-hearted," verse 18?*—Those whose hearts are broken or crushed under godly sorrow for sin.

107. *What is the captivity referred to?*—To Satan, who leads his victims captive at his will.

108. *What is it to be blind to the truth?*—To be unwilling, and so unable, to see and receive it.

109. *Why is it called "the acceptable year of the Lord"?*—The time of grace (compared to the jubilee year), when God is ready to hear and to forgive. Isa. 1 : 18, etc.

110. *Why did our Lord not read the remainder of the verse?*—Because "the day of vengeance" was not yet come.

111. *Will not the time come when the rest of the sentence will be fulfilled?*—The day of the Lord will come as a thief in the night: in the which the heavens shall pass away with a great noise, and the elements shall melt with fervent heat, the earth also and the works that are therein shall be burned up. Seeing then that all these things shall be dissolved, what manner of persons ought ye to be in all holy conversation and godliness, looking for and hasting unto the coming of the day of God? 2 Pet. 3 : 10-12.

112. *Why did they wonder in verse 22?*—Because they knew him only as a Nazarene carpenter's son.

113. *Why did our Lord's declaration in verses 24-27 so excite their wrath?*—Because of their Jewish pride and contempt for all other people.

114. *Was Sarepta a Jewish town?*—No, a city of Sidon, in Phœnicia.

115. *Was Naaman a Jew?*—No, a Syrian.

LUKE 5 (MATTHEW 4, MARK 1).

116. *What proof of the power of Jesus does the draught of fishes show?*—By bringing the fish in great numbers where there were none the night before.

117. *Did not Peter's exclamation show how much he realized the divinity of our Lord?*—Yes; it made him deeply feel his own sinfulness in the presence of Christ's holiness and power.

118. *In what sense was Peter henceforth to catch men?*—By drawing them out of the world to Christ in the gospel net.

119. *What act of faith is recorded of the disciples?*—Their letting down their net, after a night of fruitless toil, at Jesus' word.

MARK 1 : 29 (MATTHEW 8, LUKE 4).

120. *How do we see the completeness of the cure of Peter's wife's mother?*—She was able to wait upon them immediately.

121. *Why did they wait for sunset?*—Because it was the Sabbath-day. Mark 1 : 32.

122. *Why did not Jesus allow the devils to speak?*—Perhaps because (as in the case of Paul and the female soothsayer) they might make it appear he was in league with them. Acts 16 : 16–18.

123. *Who is the great Example of fervent prayer?*—Jesus, whose long and earnest prayers by day or night, and especially before great duties and events, are often named.

124. *What is meant by "all Syria" in Matt. 4 : 24?*—That part of it which adjoined the Holy Land.

125. *Was there any need for the "if" in the leper's appeal, Mark 1 : 40?*—No; and Christ is as willing now, as he is able now, to cleanse us from all sin.

126. *How could Jesus touch the leper without being himself rendered unclean?*—By his divine purity.

Command the children of Israel, that they put out of the camp every leper; that they defile not their camps, in the midst whereof I dwell. Num. 5 : 2, 3.

127. *Is it not a proof of the immaculate purity of our Lord?*—Yes; we may conclude that, as he could not be defiled without, he must have been equally undefiled within.

128. *What offering was required by the law?*—Two lambs, doves or pigeons, with flour and oil. Lev. 14 : 10, 21, 22.

MARK 2 (LUKE 5, MATTHEW 9).

129. *What proof of the connection between sin and suffering is there in Mark 2 : 5?*—Jesus saying to the sick of the palsy, "Thy sins be forgiven thee."

130. *Why was not our Lord's forgiveness of sins blasphemy?*—Because he was God himself. Isa. 43 : 25.

131. *What other proof of his Godhead does Mark 2 : 8 contain?*—His knowledge of the people's thoughts.

132. *Why does Matthew, in chap. 9, verse 9, call himself by his common name, while in Mark and Luke he is called Levi?*—He calls himself Matthew from humility: he is called by his new name of Levi from respect.

JOHN 5.

133. *What proof of the connection between sin and suffering is there in verse 14?*—The warning of Jesus to the sick man to sin no more, lest a worse disease or thing should happen unto him.

134. *Does not verse 17 show that God cannot rest until redemption is accomplished?*—Yes; all his works, in providence and grace, show him to have that end in view.

135. *Compare verse 18 with Phil. 2 : 6.*—Christ Jesus is there said to be "in the form of God" and "to be equal with God."

136. *Who is to be the Judge of all? and why?*—Christ is to be the Judge, that he may have equal honor with God. V. 23.

137. *Why is the verb in the present tense before "everlasting life," and in the future tense before "condemnation"?*—Because the everlasting life of believers is already begun, while condemnation is reserved for those who will not believe.

138. *What is the terrible alternative of resurrection unto life?*—Resurrection to damnation, to "shame and everlasting contempt." Dan. 12 : 2.

139. *What is a fatal stumbling-block to faith?*—The preference of honor from men to honor from God.

140. *What confirmation of the inspiration of the Pentateuch is there in verse 46?*—Jesus quoting it as written of himself.

141. *What is the abiding testimony against the Jews' unbelief?*—The writings of Moses and the prophets, which testify of Christ.

MATTHEW 12 (MARK 2, LUKE 6).

142. *Were the disciples justified in taking the growing corn?*—They were.

When thou comest into the standing corn of thy neighbor, then thou mayest pluck the ears with thine hand; but thou shalt not move a sickle unto thy neighbor's standing corn. Deut. 23.

143. *How did the priests profane the Sabbath and remain blameless?*—They appeared to do so by killing the sacrifices on that day as on other days.

In the first day shall be an holy convocation; ye shall do no manner of servile work therein: but ye shall off r a sacrifice made by fire for a burnt-offering unto the Lord; two young bullocks, and one ram, and seven lambs. Num. 28 : 18, 19.

144. *What is taught of the nature of the Sabbath in Mark 2 : 27?*—That "the sabbath was made for man, and not man for the sabbath;" the day being appointed, even in Paradise, as a day of rest; and being now a blessed season of rest of body and mind from earthly care and pleasure and toil—a time of special regard to the interests of our immortal souls, and of kind offices to the souls and bodies of our fellow-men.

145. *What was the shew-bread?*—An important offering.

Thou shalt take fine flour, and bake twelve cakes thereof. And thou shalt set them in two rows, six on a row, upon the pure table before the Lord. And thou shalt put pure frankincense upon each row, that it may be on the bread for a memorial, even an offering made by fire unto the Lord. Every sabbath he shall set it in order before the Lord continually, being taken from the children of Israel by an everlasting covenant. And it shall be Aaron's and his sons'; and they shall eat it in the holy place: for it is most holy unto him of the offerings of the Lord made by fire by a perpetual statute. Lev. 24 : 5–9.

146. *What is meant by a "bruised reed" and "smoking flax"?*—The conscience-stricken and spiritually distressed and the weak in faith.

MATTHEW 5 (LUKE 6).

147. *To whom was the sermon on the mount addressed?*—To the disciples of Jesus.

148. *Who are "the poor in spirit"?*—The humble-minded.

149. *What is the "mourning" referred to?*—Mourning for sin and for the low state of the Church. Isa 61 : 2, 3.

150. *What is meekness?*—Patience under provocation, after the example of Christ, "who, when he was reviled, reviled not again." 1 Pet. 2 : 23.

151. *What is it to hunger and thirst after anything?*—To greatly long for it and to seek and strive to obtain it.

152. *Who are the "merciful"?*—Those who are kind to the poor, the "hungry" and the "afflicted." Isa. 58 : 10, 11.

153. *What is it to be "pure in heart"?*—To have that "holiness without which no man shall see the Lord." Heb. 12 : 14.

154. *Why are the "peacemakers" so distinguished?*—Because of the difficulty of making and keeping peace, and as Christ is the Prince of peace.

If it be possible, as much as lieth in you, live peaceably with all men. Rom. 12 : 18.

155. *How does our Lord connect his disciples with himself in Matt. 5 : 11?*—By promising them a blessing upon all that they endured for his sake.

156. *What great lesson of mutual forgiveness does Matt. 5 : 23–26 contain?*—That we should come to the worship and service of God in peace and reconciliation with our fellow-men.

157. *What rule against trifling with evil is contained in Matt. 5 : 29, 30?*—That we should make any sacrifice to be free from sin.

158. *What lesson against procrastination is there in Matt. 5 : 25?*—We may learn, if we are living in enmity toward God, our Judge, to be earnest in seeking reconciliation with him, through Christ, while we have time.

159. *What lesson of the largeness of the love of God have we in Matt. 5 : 45 and Luke 6 : 35?*—"He is kind" to "the unthankful" and "evil," and pours his daily blessings alike upon the wicked and the good.

160. *Compare Matt. 5 : 48 with Luke 6 : 36.*—We should strive to be like our heavenly Father in holiness and mercy.

MATTHEW 6.

161. *Does not the first precept commend itself to our consciences?*—It does, or should do. The eye and favor of God should be our chief thought and aim.

162. *Compare the reward of verse 2 with that of verse 4.*—The hypocrite's reward is the present and fleeting one of honor from men, while the true Christian's reward (besides peace and blessing upon earth) is the eternal one of glory in heaven.

163. *What encouragement for our imperfect petitions is there in verse 8?*—That our heavenly Father knows what we have need of before we ask.

164. *How do the first words of the Lord's Prayer adapt it to the whole family of man?*—They show that we have "all one Father."

165. *What is it to "hallow" anything?*—To treat it as holy.

166. *How are we taught that we must render practical obedience to the will of God?*—By the standard of the obedience of the angels in heaven. V. 10.

167. *Does not verse 11 refer to the daily supply of manna?*—It does, and teaches us not to be over-thoughtful about to-morrow's supply.

168. *What striking condition is added to the petition for forgiveness of our trespasses?*—That we should forgive those who have trespassed against us.

169. *Give an example of the sort of temptation intended here.*—The tempting or trying of the faith of Abraham by requiring Isaac's life. Gen. 22 : 1.

170. *How can we judge whether we love God?*—By thinking where our chief treasure is, whether on earth or in heaven. V. 21.

171. *Who takes care of our lives?*—Our heavenly Father. Vs. 26, 30, 32, 33.

MATTHEW 7 (LUKE 6).

172. *What lesson of self-examination do the first five verses convey?*—Lest we should condemn our neighbor, while we are worse ourselves.

173. *What is the meaning of the strait gate?*—The narrow entrance into heaven, which, "though wide enough for any sinner, is too strait for any sin."

174. *Is there any immediate sign of danger in the broad road?*—No, not to the eye of the thoughtless worldly man.

175. *Should not our Lord's declaration in Matt. 7 : 14 excite us to make diligent search?*—Yes, that we are among the few in the narrow way.

176. *What lesson do we learn about our conduct in Matt. 7 : 16 and following verses?*—That we shall be judged by our conduct, rather than our profession—by our fruits rather than our leaves.

LUKE 7 (MATTHEW 8).

177. *What was the particular feature of the centurion's faith?*—It was humble and strong, and was the faith of a Gentile, and not of a Jew.

178. *What practical answer did Jesus give to John the Baptist's messengers?*—That they were to conclude he was the Messiah from the miracles he did and the prophecies he fulfilled. Luke 7 : 21.

179. *How does our Lord sum up his reference to the greatness of John the Baptist?*—By saying that the least of those in the kingdom of Christ were greater even than John.

180. *What does Luke 7 : 35 refer to?*—To the wisdom of God, as shown in the conduct of Christ and of John, being seen and acknowledged by all God's people.

MATTHEW 11 : 20.

181. *May we not apply these woes to our own country and time?*—Yes, with still greater truth.

182. *What state of heart is specially inculcated in verses 25–30?*—Humility, teachableness and meekness.

183. *What blessing is vouchsafed to those who take Christ's yoke upon them?*—The blessing of rest in Christ from self-righteous and worldly labors and cares.

LUKE 7 : 36.

184. *In what manner did they sit at table?*—They reclined on sofas round it.

185. *What was the reason for the omission of providing water for his feet?*—Abraham offered water for his visitors' feet (Gen. 18 : 4), but Simon had invited Jesus from curiosity alone, and did not care to show him respect.

LUKE 12 : 14 (MATTHEW 12, MARK 3).

186. *What was Beelzebub?*—The fly-god of Ekron, in Philistia. 2 Kings 1 : 2.

187. *What proof of our Lord's omniscience is there in Luke 11 : 17–20?*—His knowing the people's thoughts.

MATTHEW 12 : 31–37 (MARK 3).

188. *Who will judge our words?*—Christ, at the day of judgment, even every idle word.

189. *How do we see that the closest family relationships are subordinate to discipleship?*—By Christ's saying that those who did his Father's will were to him as brother and sister and mother. Matt. 12 : 46–50.

LUKE 11 : 37.

190. *Who were the scribes and lawyers?*—Persons who copied and explained the law.

LUKE 12 : 1.

191. *What is "the leaven" of the Pharisees?*—Their bad principles and influence and hypocrisy. Matt. 16 : 6.

192. *Whom does Christ advise us to fear? and why?*—God, who has power to cast into hell. Luke 12 : 5.

193. *What proof of God's overruling providence have we in verse 6?*—Even sparrows not being forgotten by him.

194. *What blessing is promised to the confession of Christ?*—Those who are not afraid or ashamed to acknowledge Christ upon earth will be acknowledged by him before all the angels at the last day.

195. *Against what are we warned in verses 17–20?*—Against the love of the riches and pleasures of the world.

196. *What does the soul's "being required" mean?*—Being called away from earth to its great account.

197. *What is it to be "rich toward God"?*—To be full of love to him and of good works for his sake.

198. *What is it to have a treasure in the heavens?*—To have Christ there as our own Saviour, and all his riches as our own through him.

199. *What great event is involved in the exhortation to "watch"?*—The sudden coming of our Lord.

200. *What responsibility is attached to knowing the Lord's will?*—The doing it.

201. *What is the meaning of verse 49?*—It may refer to the "fire" of "the Holy Ghost," "the spirit of burning" (Isa. 4 : 4), and to the gospel of peace being made an occasion of burning hatred among the families and nations of men. Matt. 3 : 11.

LUKE 13.

202. *What is the call to repentance in verses 1-9?*—The sudden death of others and the gracious sparing of our own lives are solemn calls upon us to repent, lest we likewise perish.

MATTHEW 13 (MARK 4, LUKE 8).

203. *Who are they that receive the gospel?*—Those who truly receive it are those who receive it into their hearts, as seed into good ground, and show its effects in their lives. V. 8.

204. *What is the fate of the tares?*—To be burned.

205. *What is meant by the harvest?*—The judgment-day. V. 30.

206. *What is meant by the barn?*—The heavenly treasure-house and home.

207. *Who are the reapers?*—The angels.

208. *How are the tares described?*—As the children of the wicked one. V. 38.

MATTHEW 8 (MARK 4, LUKE 8).

209. *What proof have we in Matt 8 : 20 of the poverty of our Lord?*—He had not where to lay his head.

210. *What do we learn from our Lord's calling the conduct of the disciples before the stilling of the tempest an act of little faith?*—That we ought to have strong faith at all times in his goodness and power.

MARK 5 (MATTHEW 8, LUKE 8).

211. *Was it lawful for the Jews to trade in swine?*—It was not.

212. *How does Mark 5 : 17 illustrate John 3 : 19?*—It shows that they did not wish their evil deeds to be brought to light.

LUKE 5 : 29 (MATTHEW 9, MARK 2).

213. *Compare Luke 5 : 30 with 1 Tim 1 : 15.*—Jesus ate and drank with "sinners," because he came into the world to "seek" and "save" them.

214. *Of what material were the wine-bottles made?*—Of skins or leather.

MARK 5 : 22 (MATTHEW 9, LUKE 8).

215. *What was the reason of the poor woman's timid and almost stealthy manner of approaching Christ?*—Because a person with her disease was ordered to be kept separate, and was considered unclean.

216. *What was the difference between the touch of the thronging multitude and that of the woman?*—Hers was the touch of faith.

217. *Ought the death of the little girl to have made them give up hope after having applied to Jesus?*—No, for Jesus was coming, and He who could cure could also restore to life.

218. *What is death called in Mark 5 : 39?*—A "sleep," from which Jesus could "awake." John 11 : 11.

219. *Was the life thus miraculously restored independent of natural circumstances for its preservation?*—No; Jesus ordered her something to eat.

MATTHEW 9 : 27.

220. *What was the proof of the faith of the blind men?*—They acknowledged Jesus to be Christ, the Son of David; and they prayed and persevered.

221. *May we not secure the same blessing if we use the same means?*—We may.

MARK 6 (MATTHEW 13).

222. *Why did Jesus refrain from doing his mighty works?*—Because of their obstinate unbelief.

223. *What ought to be the effect of our Lord's miracles on us?*—To strengthen our faith. Mark 6 : 6.

224. *To what are sheep having no shepherd exposed?*—To be "scattered" and destroyed: and we, who are by nature as "sheep going astray," should be deeply thankful to Him who came to seek and to save. Matt. 9 : 36: Isa. 53 : 6.

225. *Is the harvest yet all gathered in?*—No; the invitation of the gospel is still, "Whosoever will, let him take the water of life freely."

MATTHEW 10 (MARK 6, LUKE 9).

226. *Compare Matt. 10 : 8 with Acts 20 : 33-35?*—The words, "Freely ye have received, freely give," and "It is more blessed to give than to receive," convey the same truth.

227. *Who would provide for the destitute disciples?*—Christ undertook to provide for them.

228. *Why are Sodom and Gomorrah used to point the terrors of the Lord's denunciation?*—Because the privileges and opportunities of Sodom and Gomorrah were not so great as those of cities of our Lord's time and of our own.

229. *What is the end spoken of in Matt. 10 : 22?*—The end of life.

230. *Compare Matt. 10 : 36 with Mic. 7 : 6.*—The words are almost exactly the same, showing the hostility to true religion in every age.

231. *Is taking the cross only the endurance of petty vexations, or does it represent the preliminary of ignominy and death?*—It includes every trial, small or great, that God appoints.

232. *What is the meaning of finding life in Matt. 10 : 39?*—Saving one's earthly life by giving up Christ.

233. *What encouragement have we for active love to the Lord's people?*—Christ's assurance that the giver of even a cup of cold water to one of his disciples shall not lose his reward.

MARK 6 : 14 (MATTHEW 14, LUKE 9).

234. *What was the testimony of Herod's conscience when he heard of our Lord's miracles?*—That they were done by John, whom he had beheaded, and who (he believed) had risen from the dead.

235. *Who was Herodias?*—His brother Philip's wife.

236. *Why does Herodias say "by and by"?*—Because she knew that John's prison was at some distance.

237. *Was John imprisoned at the place where these festivities were held?*—No—at Machærus, on the Dead Sea.

238. *Ought the disciples to have been so surprised at our Lord's walking on the water?*—No; they ought to have remembered his former miracles. Mark 6 : 52.

239. *What was the power that enabled Peter to walk on the water?*—The power of Christ, that gave him faith and help. Matt. 14 : 28-31.

240. *What was Peter's cause of failure?*—His faith being weak and giving way. Matt. 14 : 31.

241. *Was Jesus ready to save?*—Yes, immediately. Matt. 14: 31.

JOHN 6 : 22.

242. *How did our Lord rebuke the insincerity of those who came seeking him?*—By telling them that they came for the sake of the loaves he had fed them with.

243. *What is the meaning of the "meat which perisheth"?*—Worldly comforts and riches.

244. *What is the meaning of the word "sealed" in verse 27?*—Stamped or approved as his own by the miracles he wrought.

245. *Does not verse 28 show how ready we are to bring our works before God?*—In verse 28 they asked what they should do.

246. *Does not verse 29 show the true simplicity of the way of life?*—Yes; it is only to "repent and believe" (Mark 1 : 15), when all good works will follow.

247. *What was the nature of the Jews' demand in verse 30 after beholding his mighty miracles?*—A dissatisfied and unbelieving one.

248. *What bread were the Jews willing to accept?*—Bread from heaven.

249. *Is there not in Jesus what will completely satisfy the soul?*—Yes; he is the bread of life, that satisfies all hunger and thirst. V. 35.

250. *What gracious assurance of acceptance have we in coming to Christ?*—That he "will in no wise cast out." V. 37.

251. *How many times does our Lord repeat the promise of the resurrection in this chapter?*—Four times. Vs. 39, 40, 44, 54.

252. *How do we know that everlasting life may be our present possession?*—From Jesus saying that "he that believeth on" him "hath everlasting life." Vs. 47–51.

253. *Do not many now fall into the same mistake as the Jews of old in supposing the Lord's literal body was intended?*—Yes; papists and their imitators believe that the consecrated bread they eat is the body of Christ, who is in heaven. The true Protestant feeds daily and hourly upon Christ himself, but only by faith. V. 53.

254. *What antidote have we to this error in verse 63?*—The lesson that it is the Spirit only that gives life to what is written.

MARK 7 (MATTHEW 15).

255. *Did the traditions of the elders always correspond with the law of God?*—No; they made it of no effect. Mark 7 : 7-13.

256. *What lesson of the necessity of sincerity in dealing with God do verses 6 and 7 contain?*—The warning that he knows the heart, and that all hypocritical worship is "vain."

257. *What is the sentence passed upon false teachers in Matt. 15 : 14?*—That they and their followers would perish together.

258. *Do we really believe that our hearts are the abodes of all these terrible evils?*—If we did, we should keep our hearts with more diligence than we do. Mark 7: 21-23.

259. *Were Tyre and Sidon Jewish cities?*—No; they were on the sea-coast, to the north-west.

260. *Who were meant by the "children" in Mark 7: 27?*—The Jews. Matt. 15: 24, 26.

261. *Is there any limit to the power of faith?*—No; it takes hold of the power of God. Mark 7 : 29

262. *Why did Jesus sigh?*—He was oppressed with their unbelief. Mark 7 : 34.

263. *What does the word "Ephphatha" show us of the dialect in which our Lord usually conversed?*—That it was Syriac he spoke. Mark 5 : 41.

MARK 8 (MATTHEW 15 AND 16).

264. *Were not the doubts of the disciples wonderful after their experience of the previous miracles?*—They were indeed, but we do just the same.

265. *May we not learn a lesson from their unbelief?*—Yes, to trust God, at all times, to give us whatever is good for us.

266. *Compare Matt. 16 : 18, 19 ; 1 Cor. 3 : 11 ; Acts 4 :11, 12 ; and Eph. 2 : 20.*—The true Church is built, not on Peter himself, as the papists suppose, but on the truth contained in what he had said about Christ, even upon the foundation of the apostles and prophets, Jesus Christ himself being the chief corner-stone. Neither is there salvation in any other : for there is none other Name under heaven given among men, whereby we must be saved. For other foundation can no man lay than that which is laid, which is Jesus Christ.

267. *What remarkable rebuke was addressed to Peter soon after his noble confession?*—"Get thee behind me, Satan !"

268. *What is the meaning of the word "savorest"?*—Likest or mindest.

269. *What explanation of Mark 8 : 36 is found in Luke 5 : 25 ?*—What is a man advantaged if he gain the whole world, and lose himself or be cast away.

MARK 9 (MATTHEW 17, LUKE 9).

270. *Is there any other testimony to Jesus as the "beloved Son," Mark 9 : 7?*—Yes, at his baptism. Matt. 3 : 17.

271. *What are we enjoined to do in Mark 9 : 7?*—To hear him.

272. *Whom did our Lord mean when he said, "Elias is indeed come"?*—John the Baptist.

273. *Why were the people amazed?*—Because of the remaining glory of his appearance. V. 15; compare v. 3.

274. *Why could not the disciples cure the demoniac?*—From want of faith and prayer. Mark 9 : 18, 19, 23, 24, 29.

275. *Compare Mark 9 : 19 with Num. 14 : 11, 27.*—They contain the same complaint of unbelief, notwithstanding "all the signs which" God had "showed among them."

276. *Did not the poor father's faith almost fail?*—Yes; he doubted Jesus' power. Mark 9 : 22.

277. *How did Jesus strengthen it?*—By telling him that "all things were possible to him that believeth."

278. *Where does Jesus foretell his death and resurrection besides Mark 9 : 31?*—In John 2 : 19, 21, when he spoke of raising up the temple of his body in three days.

MATTHEW 17 : 24 (MARK 9).

279. *What was this tribute-money?*—"Half a shekel," or about thirty cents, "for the offering of the Lord" or the service of the temple. Ex. 30 : 13; 2 Chron. 24 : 9.

280. *What is the meaning of "prevented"?*—"Anticipated" what Peter was going to say.

281. *What lesson of considerateness does the Lord of all teach us?*—Not to give needless offence, especially in little matters.

282. *What do we learn from the "piece of money" being the exact amount claimed for Peter and our Lord?*—Perhaps that Jesus had miraculously brought the exact coin required into the fish's mouth.

MARK 9 : 33 (MATTHEW 18, LUKE 9).

283. *What lesson did our Lord teach in Mark 9 . 35-37?*—Humility.

284. *What great reward is promised to those who learn this lesson?*—All the blessings that follow from receiving Christ and being his.

285. *Is not all intolerance discouraged in Mark 9 : 39?*—Yes; when we feel assured of any one that he is a true servant of Christ, we should not disown him because he does not agree on all religious subjects with ourselves.

286. *Are great deeds done for Christ the only ones accepted by him?*—No; even the giving of a cup of water for Christ's sake shall have its reward.

287. *What further lesson have we against all persecution?*—That any one who willfully injures a young, weak or lowly believer in Jesus is liable to a greater punishment than even loss of life. Mark 9 : 42.

288. *How are we to deal with our sins?*—To give them up, and every help or temptation to them, at any cost.

289. *Are any of them to be tenderly dealt with?*—No; all of them firmly, promptly and decidedly.

MATTHEW 18 : 10.

290. *How do we see the care of our Lord over the least of his disciples?*—By his appointing angels to watch over them.

291. *Are there any exceptions to verse 11?*—No; all are lost, and all may be saved.

292. *What condition of the sheep led to the exercise of the Shepherd's love?*—Their being gone astray.

293. *How does our Lord inculcate the duty of mutual forbearance and forgiveness?*—By calling upon the injured to strive to gain over the offender by a quiet appeal to him when alone.

294. *To whom in another Gospel was the promise in verse 18 given?*—To the disciples generally, and not to Peter only. John 20 : 23; Matt. 16 : 19.

295. *Is there any limitation to the two blessed promises in verses 19, 20?*—Only that what we ask of God must be "according to his will." 1 John 5 : 14.

296. *What was the utmost extent of forgiveness that seemed possible to Peter?*—Forgiving seven times.

297. *Did the estimate of Jesus agree with him?*—No; he ordered us to forgive seventy times seven.

298. *In the parable, verse 23, what was the amount of the debt, at £187 10 each talent?*—Nearly ten million dollars.

299. *Does not this show the incalculable claims that God has upon us for breaches of only the first commandment?*—It may well do so.

300. *Do we not also see the entire freeness of the divine forgiveness?*—Yes, as compassion alone forgave the debt.

301. *Are we not called upon to imitate the long-suffering of God?*—We are indeed; and if we know ourselves forgiven by him, we shall certainly do so.

302. *Where do we learn that the merciful God is also a God of judgment?*—In the same parable, by his sentence on the ungrateful and unforgiving servant. V. 34.

JOHN 7.

303. *What was the "feast of tabernacles"?*—In the fifteenth day of the seventh month, when ye have gathered in the fruit of the land, ye shall keep a feast unto the Lord seven days: and ye shall take you on the first day the boughs of goodly trees, branches of palm trees, and the boughs of thick trees, and willows of the brook; and ye shall rejoice before the Lord your God seven days. Lev. 23 : 39, 40.

304. *What hidden motives influenced the relatives of Jesus in their advice to our Lord?*—To bring him into danger and expose him if he were a deceiver, and to cause him to proclaim himself as king for their worldly benefit if he were really the Messiah.

LUKE 9 : 51.

305. *Why is the term "steadfastly" used?*—Because Jesus knew all the sufferings that would come upon him.

306. *What example of meekness did our Lord show?*—By not punishing the Samaritans for their inhospitable conduct.

307. *Who are the dead that are to bury their dead?*—The dead in sin.

308. *Why is it particularly hurtful to look back while ploughing?*—Because you may lose the right course.

LUKE 10.

309. *Do not the directions to the Seventy show the daily and hourly care of the Master?*—Yes, for their bodily comfort as well as for their ministerial success.

310. *How was Capernaum exalted to heaven?*—As a prosperous city, that had enjoyed the privilege of Christ's preaching.

311. *What proof have we in verse 16 of the union between Christ and his people?*—His saying that the hearing or despising of his ministers was the hearing or despising of himself.

LUKE 17 : 11.

312. *Why did the lepers stand "afar off"?*—Because they were obliged by law to keep separate from others.

313. *Why were they to show themselves to the priests?*—First, to know if they were lepers; and afterward, to know if they were healed. Lev. 13 : 2.

314. *Was their cleansing previous to or after they had acted in faith?*—After they had showed their faith by calling upon Jesus for mercy.

315. *Did the ingratitude of the nine hinder their blessing?*—It did not make Jesus recall their cure.

JOHN 7 : 11.

316. *Why were the people afraid of the Jews?*—"Lest they should be put out of the synagogue," or excommunicated, if they confessed themselves followers of Christ. Acts 5 : 13.

317. *What remarkable connection is there between obedience and the knowledge of right doctrine?*—The man who really desires to do God's will shall understand the truth and meaning of his word. V. 17.

318. *Whom did the people mean by the "very Christ"?*—The true Messiah.

319. *What was the hinderance of verse 34?*—Insincerity and worldly motives.

320. *Who are the "dispersed"?*—The scattered Israelites. V. 35.

321. *Could the Jews bear to think that the gospel was to be preached to the Gentiles?*—No; they were too jealous, selfish and proud to think it.

322. *What is it to come to Jesus and drink?*—To receive him as our Saviour, and so to satisfy all the longings of the thirsty soul.

323. *Who was referred to as "the prophet"?*—The one that Moses said God would "raise up" like unto himself. Deut. 18 : 15, 18.

324. *What is meant by "the law" in verse 49?*—The law of Moses and the writings of the prophets.

325. *Had not the interview with Jesus strengthened the faith of Nicodemus?*—Yes, for he took Jesus' part. Vs. 50, 51.

326. *Was Galilee held in honor by the Jews?*—No; it was despised.

327. *Where was the search to be made?*—In the Scriptures, which spoke (Isa. 9:1, 2) of "Galilee" as a land of "darkness." V. 52.

JOHN 8.

328. *What striking instance of the power of conscience when under the eye of the Judge of all the earth is there in verse 9?*—The sinful accusers of the adulterous woman going out of his presence, every one.

329. *In what condition are they who walk without th*

Light of life?—In darkness now, and in the way to "blackness of darkness for ever."

330. *What is it to "judge after the flesh"?*—To judge by outward appearances and worldly notions.

331. *How are we to know God the Father?*—In and through Jesus Christ. V. 19.

332. *What does our Lord mean by being "lifted up"?*—Being raised on the cross.

333. *How is verse 29 full of blessing?*—It shows how completely our blessed Saviour is accepted by God, and what grace and help his people may have through him.

334. *How did verse 33 agree with the payment to the Roman emperor?*—Not at all, being an idle boast of the Jews.

335. *What were the works of Abraham?*—The "obedience of faith," which should have led the Jews to believe and obey Christ.

336. *Who alone can say, "Who convinceth me of sin"?*—Jesus only.

337. *What example of grace is there in verse 49?*—The gentleness of Jesus' reply to so shameful an accusation.

338. *Is death of the body referred to in verse 51?*—No—the death or ruin of the soul, "the second or everlasting death."

339. *How did Abraham see the "day of Christ"?*—By the far-seeing eye of faith, looking at the promises of God.

340. *Why did the Jews say "fifty years old"?*—Because "his visage was so marred" by privation and suffering that he looked older than he was. Isa. 52 : 14.

341. *What does our Lord mean by "I am"?*—That he was *always* in being, from all eternity; as God called himself to Moses, "I AM." Ex. 3 : 14.

342. *Why did he not say "I was"?*—Because "I am" is a stronger expression of eternal being, and also made him equal with God.

Luke 10 : 20.

343. *Is anything to be reserved in obeying the two great commandments?*—No; they require the love of the whole heart.

344. *What is the lesson taught by the parable?*—How to reduce to practice God's commands, and how far we must always fall short of entire obedience to his will. We shall never *do* and live; we must *believe* and live.

345. *What is the "one thing needful"?*—To come to Christ for salvation of the soul. V. 42.

346. *What is the true cause of rejoicing?*—That we have found Christ, and have our names written in heaven. V. 20.

347. *What was the cause of our Lord's joy?*—The bringing of his humble disciples to the saving knowledge of the truth.

Luke 11.

348. *Compare verses 2-4 with Matt. 6 : 9-13?*—We may use our Lord's Prayer, or pray in our own words after its manner, placing the concerns of God before our own.

349. *How should we use importunity in prayer?*—By feeling and speaking earnestly and perseveringly, as those who will not be denied whatever it may be God's will to grant.

John 9.

350. *What did our Lord mean by verse 3.*—That the blindness gave an opportunity of showing the power of God.

351. *What does our Lord mean by day and night?*—Life as the time of working for God, and death as the rest from our labor.

352. *What is meant by expulsion from the synagogue?*—Not allowing attendance at the chief place of religious meeting, and so bringing disgrace and distress, and some social privations besides.

353. *What proof of our Lord's divine nature is there in verses 36-38?*—His allowing himself to be worshiped as the Son of God.

John 10.

354. *What sort of sheepfolds were in use in Palestine?*—Uncovered enclosures in the pasture-grounds for the protection of the sheep at night.

355. *What is promised to those who 'enter in by 'the door?*—Those ministers and teachers who are called and qualified by the Holy Spirit may expect a blessing on their work.

356. *What was our Lord's solemn object in coming into the world?*—To lay down his life in order to give life. Vs. 15, 10.

357. *How is the atonement taught in verses 11, 15-18?*—By Jesus saying that he laid down his "life for the sheep," or in their stead, that they might live.

358. *What was the feast of the dedication?*—It was kept in memory of God's delivery of the temple from King Antiochus. 1 Mac. 4 : 52-59; 2 Mac. 10 : 5-8.

359. *What is the security of the Lord's true people?*—His own assurance that they shall never perish. Vs. 27, 28.

360. *Why cannot the Scripture be broken?*—Because it is the word of God.

361. *What is the special use of miracles?*—To prove a commission from God, and to give divine authority to what is spoken in his name. Vs. 22-42.

John 11.

362. *What interesting fact about sickness do we learn in verse 4?*—That the sickness of God's people is for his glory.

363. *What is taught us about the right use of opportunity in verses 9, 10?*—That time and opportunity will soon be at an end.

364. *How is death spoken of?*—As a sleep in the case of the people of God, as they will awake and arise to a new and spiritual life.

365. *What does Thomas mean in verse 16?*—That he expected Jesus would be killed by the Jews.

366. *How was Jesus himself the resurrection and the life?*—Because his people, by their union with him, have a glorious resurrection to eternal life.

367. *Who are the dead spoken of in verse 25?*—"The dead in Christ." 1 Thess. 4 : 16.

368. *Who are the living who shall never die?*—Those who "are alive" at "the coming of the Lord." 1 Thess. 4 : 17.

369. *What proof of our Lord's true humanity is there in verse 35?*—His weeping at the grave.

370. *Are not Caiaphas and Balaam examples of unbelieving prophets?*—Yes; God merely "put a word in Balaam's mouth," for he "loved the wages of unrighteousness," and he afterward died in battle among the enemies of God. Num. 33 : 5, 16; 2 Pet. 2 : 15.

Luke 13 : 10.

371. *Does not the readiness of the poor woman to glorify God after being healed account for the omission of any mention of her previous faith?*—No doubt it does.

372. *Who is said to be the author of such affliction?*—Satan. V. 16.

373. *What constitutes the inability of verse 24?*—No want of power or will on the part of God, but a want of will in man from long indulgence in sin—an inability from not casting off all sin or from coming too late.

374. *Is there not a limit to the day of grace?*—Yes;

"*now* is the accepted time." Every day's continuance in an unconverted state, every day's indulgence in a sinful world, only makes the heart more hard.

375. *Who are they that will be rejected?*—Those who neglect or refuse to be received and saved.

376. *What is the meaning of verse 30?*—The Jews, who were the first to receive the light of the truth, give place to the Gentiles, who were the last.

377. *What does our Lord mean in verse 33?*—That he would be safe for the short time he remained in Galilee.

378. *Compare verse 35 with Luke 19 : 38.*—The disciples used these words as Jesus afterward entered into Jerusalem. The whole verse (35) may also be a prophecy of the present unbelief and future conversion of the Jews.

LUKE 14.

379. *What might be lawfully done on the Sabbath-day?*—Works of necessity and mercy.

380. *How do we know that this lesson of humility may be applied to ourselves?*—By our consciousness of the natural pride of our own hearts. V. 11.

381. *Who are meant by the invited guests? and to whom was the offer of mercy conveyed on their rejection of it?*—The Jews. The Gentiles. Vs. 16–24.

382. *Were not the excuses made by the guests very hollow?*—Yes; they showed their worldly minds.

383. *What comforting assurance is there in verse 22?*—There is always room at the gospel feast and in the heavenly mansions for all who will come.

384. *Is it an easy thing to be a disciple of Jesus?*—No; it requires a readiness to sacrifice not only our sins, but our affections and our lives, to the love of God and the salvation of our souls. Vs. 26, 27.

LUKE 15.

385. *What important truth does verse 2 contain?*—That it is the blessed character of Christ that he receives sinners coming to him with the burden of their sins.

386. *How do we learn our preciousness in the sight of God?*—By the joy in heaven that a repenting sinner creates. Vs. 7, 10.

387. *To what extremity was the prodigal son reduced in the service of sin and Satan?*—He had spent all, and was perishing with hunger, and no man gave unto him.

388. *Can we be said to be in our right mind when we are afar off from God?*—No; our hearts and minds are willfully blinded and deceived, and the grace of God alone can bring us to ourselves. V. 17.

389. *What difference is there between what the prodigal intended to say and what he actually said?*—He intended, in the deep penitence of his heart, to have asked to be one of his father's servants.

390. *Did the father's love give him time to say the rest?*—No; and so ready is our *heavenly* Father to welcome his repenting and returning sons.

391. *How is the sinner returning to God described?*—As dead and lost, and then alive and found. V. 32.

LUKE 16.

392. *What principle did the unjust steward act upon?*—Upon the worldly and sinful one of making friends by any means, whether good or bad.

393. *What is meant by serving mammon?*—Seeking riches or the favor of the world.

394. *Does God's judgment of human affairs correspond with our judgment of them?*—No, for he judges by the heart. V. 15.

395. *What is the lesson to be learned from the parable of the rich man and Lazarus?*—To take care, if we are rich, to make a good use of our riches, and, whether rich or poor, to have a treasure in heaven.

396. *What responsibility is connected with the possession of the Scriptures?*—To "search" them, "receive" them and obey them, as "able to save" our "souls." V. 31.

LUKE 17.

397. *What measure of faith was required to do the mighty works mentioned in verse 6?*—A very small measure, as it takes hold of the omnipotence of God.

398. *Does obedience warrant self-exaltation?*—No; at the best we can but do our duty, and can never repay God's mercy. Vs. 9, 10.

399. *What is the meaning of the kingdom of God being "within" us?*—It means God's rule in the hearts of his people, producing "righteousness and peace and joy in the Holy Ghost." Rom. 14 : 17.

400. *Will there be any remarkable difference in the state of society at the time of the coming judgment?*—It will be still the same as in former judgments, though a larger proportion of persons (vs. 34–36) may now be in the number of the saved. Vs. 26, etc.

401. *What is the lesson of Lot's wife?*—To escape for our lives, and not to look back to the world.

LUKE 18.

402. *What does the parable of the importunate widow teach?*—That we should continue to pray and never faint.

403. *Notice the solemn observation at the end of verse 8.*—There will be such "a falling away first" that faith in Christ as a Saviour, or the faith that looks for his coming, will scarcely be found.

404. *What should we learn from the parable of the Pharisee and the publican?*—To be penitently humble, instead of self-righteously proud.

405. *What state of the heart is acceptable in God's sight?*—The sacrifices of God are a broken spirit; a broken and a contrite heart, O God, thou wilt not despise. Ps. 51 : 17. For thus saith the high and lofty One that inhabiteth eternity, whose name is Holy; I dwell in the high and holy place, with him also that is of a contrite and humble spirit, to revive the spirit of the humble, and to revive the heart of the contrite ones. Isa. 57 :15. The Lord is nigh unto them that are of a broken heart; and saveth such as be of a contrite spirit. Ps. 34 :18.

406. *What is the teaching in verse 17?*—To humbly accept God's way of salvation by faith, however lowering to human pride.

407. *Was not our Lord's question in verse 19 put with the hope of eliciting a confession of his personal Godhead?*—Yes, the ruler does not seem to have looked upon Jesus as more than man.

408. *Is the possession of wealth always a blessing?*—No; it is always a temptation and snare, often our ruin, and very seldom a blessing. Vs. 22, 23.

409. *How do we learn the deep-rooted nature of covetousness?*—By our Lord's description of the extreme difficulty of a rich man's entering into the kingdom of God. Vs. 25, 26.

410. *What is to be understood by the "world to come"?*—The state or time after death. V. 30.

MATTHEW 20 (MARK 10, LUKE 18).

411. *What does the parable of the householder teach as to God's sovereignty?*—"That God is debtor unto no man," and gives to all as he thinks fit.

412. *What is true humility?*—Being ready to be last of all and servant of all. Matt. 20 : 26.

413. *How did the blind men prove the sincerity of their faith?*—By their persevering prayers to Jesus as the Christ, the son of David. Matt. 20 : 31.

LUKE 19.

414. *How did our Lord respond to the faith of Zaccheus?*—By noticing him and making himself a guest at his house. V. 5.

415. *What do we learn of the practices of the tax-gatherers?*—That they were in the habit of taking more than was due. V. 8.

416. *For what did Jesus come into the world?*—To seek and to save the lost. V. 10.

417. *What is the object of the parable of the nobleman?*—To impress upon us the duty of using our time and talents and opportunities to God's glory and in remembrance of our final account.

418. *How did our Lord assert his divine authority?*—By telling his disciples to say, concerning the colt, that the *Lord* had need of it. V. 31.

419. *What special miracle was the occasion of the exultation of the people?*—Vs. 37, 38. The people that was with him when he called Lazarus out of his grave, and raised him from the dead, bare record. For this cause the people also met him, for that they heard that he had done this miracle. John 12 : 17, 18.

420. *How may we learn the convincing nature of the miracles of our Lord?*—By our Lord's assertion that if *men* did not acknowledge them, the very *stones* would cry out. V. 40.

421. *How was our Lord's prophecy about Jerusalem fulfilled?*—In its destruction by the Romans within forty years after.

422. *What remarkable act of authority is recorded in verse 45 and in Mark 11 : 15, 16?*—Jesus sending the buyers and sellers and money-changers out of the temple.

MARK 11 : 20 (MATTHEW 21).

423. *What is declared to be the power of faith?*—The obtaining whatever we desire that is according to God's will. Mark 11 : 22–24.

424. *Is a spirit of forgiveness important to our success in prayer?*—It is indispensable. Mark 11 : 25, 26.

MARK 12 (MATTHEW 21, LUKE 20).

425. *Who are the husbandmen, who are the servants, and who the son in this parable?*—The Jews generally, and especially their rulers and teachers; the prophets; and Christ himself.

426. *What was the snare laid for Jesus in Mark 12 : 14, 15?*—A question designed to bring an answer that would almost certainly offend against either the Jewish law or the Roman.

427. *Upon what single word in Mark 12 : 26 does the Lord's argument depend?*—The word "am," which signified that though dead they were still existing as departed spirits when he spoke.

428. *Who was the living example of the fulfillment of these two great commandments?*—Jesus himself. Mark 12 : 30, 31.

429. *What testimony to the inspiration of the Scriptures is in Mark 12 : 36?*—It is said that David spoke "by the Holy Ghost." Ps. 110 : 1.

MATTHEW 23 (MARK 12, LUKE 20).

430. *How does our Lord distinguish between profession and practice?*—By saying of the scribes and Pharisees, "they say, and do not."

431. *What are phylacteries?*—Slips of parchment, with texts of Scripture upon them, which the Pharisees wore as charms, or "preservatives," as the word means; probably taking the idea from Ex. 13 : 15, 16; Num. 15 : 38, 39.

432. *What is the difference between the long prayers of the Pharisees and the "pray without ceasing" of the apostle?*—The long prayers of the Pharisees were made for a pretence, to obtain the character of being holy men, while the injunction of the apostle was to encourage and maintain a constant *spirit* of prayer.

433. *What feature in the character of the scribes and Pharisees is most prominent in our Lord's denunciations?*—Their woeful hypocrisy.

MARK 12 : 41.

434. *How is the truth that the Lord looks on the heart illustrated by the widow's mite?*—Because he would not have commended the gift if he had not known the motive with which it was given.

JOHN 12 : 20.

435. *Who were the Greeks?*—Persons from Greece who had embraced the Jewish faith.

436. *What connection is there between their wish to see Jesus and his declaration in verse 23?*—Jesus meant that they must be prepared for his death and for any trials which that event might bring upon his followers.

437. *Why must a grain of wheat die before it can be fruitful?*—Because it contains the germ of life of the new plant, which it must yield up.

438. *For what cause did our Lord come to the hour of his self-sacrifice?*—Because he had willingly given himself up to die for the salvation of men and his own final glory. Vs. 27, 28; compare verses 24, 32.

439. *What is meant by "all men" in verse 32?*—People of all kinds and of all nations.

I beheld, and, lo, a great multitude, which no man could number, of all nations, and kindreds, and people, and tongues, stood before the throne, and before the Lamb, clothed with white robes, and palms in their hands. Rev. 7 : 9.

440. *What is the great sin of the human race?*—Not believing on Christ, and obstinately rejecting him. Vs. 37, etc.

MATTHEW 24 (MARK 13, LUKE 21).

441. *Who built the temple then standing?*—The Jews, under Ezra and Nehemiah.

442. *When was it destroyed?*—About forty years after Christ's death.

443. *By whom?*—By the Romans, under Titus.

444. *Is the universal success of the gospel promised in Matt. 24 : 14?*—No; only its universal *preaching* as a testimony of Christ; and this seems to be now nearly fulfilled.

445. *What was the "abomination of desolation"?*—The banners of the desolating and destroying Roman armies surrounding Jerusalem. Luke 21 : 20.

446. *Would not many who heard this prophecy be alive at its accomplishment thirty-seven years later?*—They would. Matt. 24 : 34.

447. *What are we enjoined to do while prophecy is fulfilling?*—To watch. Matt. 24 : 42, etc.; Mark 13 : 37.

MATTHEW 25.

448. *Is there any special lesson to be learnt from verse 5?*—That even the Lord's own people may slumber and sleep.

449. *Also from the time at which the cry breaks forth, "Behold, the Bridegroom cometh!"?*—That our Lord, instead of being faithfully and lovingly looked for, will be generally unexpected when he comes.

450. *What is the lesson taught by the parable of the talents?*—To impress upon us the duty of using our time and talents and opportunities to God's glory and in remembrance of our final account.

451. *Will any people be exempted from the final judgment?*—No; all nations will be assembled and judged. V. 32.

452. *What oneness of Christ and his disciples is there in verses 35, 40?*—His regarding what is done or undone to one of his least disciples as done or undone **to himself.**

453. *How may we judge whether we are serving Christ?* —By our feeling and conduct toward his humble disciples. V. 45.

MATTHEW 26 (MARK 14, LUKE 22).

454. *Where do we learn that the Jews at first proposed the private assassination of Jesus?*—From Matt. 26 : 4.

455. *What remarkable act of living faith is recorded in Matt. 26 : 7?*—The woman's pouring a box of precious ointment upon Jesus' head in anticipation, by faith, of his burial.

456. *Who was this woman?*—Mary, the sister of Lazarus. John 12 : 3.

457. *What is to be understood by Mary's "doing this for the burial of Jesus"?*—It was usual to anoint the dead, and Mary wished perhaps to do now what she might not be able to do after.

458. *Did not Judas show his estimate of his Master by the price he demanded for his betrayal?*—Yes; it was the compensation-money for a servant killed by an ox. Ex. 21 : 32.

459. *What had the disciples to prepare for the Passover?*—The lamb, with unleavened bread, bitter herbs, wine, and a sauce made of dates, raisins, and other things, from which Judas received the sop.

460. *What lesson of true humility do we learn from Luke 22 : 26–28 and John 13 : 1, etc.?*—To be as willing to serve as to rule, and to be ready to render any offices of kindness to our brethren and sisters in Christ.

JOHN 13 (MATTHEW 26, MARK 14, LUKE 22).

461. *What all-important declaration does Jesus make in John 13 : 8?*—He said to Peter, "If I wash thee not, thou hast no part with me."

462. *From what must we be washed before we can have part with Jesus?*—From all our sins in his own blood.

463. *Is not the reality of our complete forgiveness shown in John 13 : 10?*—Yes; all past guilt is washed away by a look of living faith, and our robes are clean and white.

464. *What is the meaning of leaning on Jesus' bosom?* —Being the nearest to him in the order of reclining **at** the feast.

465. *Did John ask Jesus so as to be heard by the rest or in a whisper?*—In a whisper.

466. *Compare John 13, verses 34 and 35, with verse 1.*—And learn to love as Christ did, and to love unto the end.

467. *What is the true test of discipleship?*—Love one to another. John 13 : 35.

468. *Was there not a wide difference between Peter's profession and his practice?*—Yes, a sad difference when he denied him in his hour of utmost need; but he repented under his Lord's forgiving look, and long afterward he died a martyr for his sake. John 13 : 38.

LUKE 22 : 19 (MATTHEW 26, MARK 14, 1 CORINTHIANS 11).

469. *What is the object of the Lord's Supper?*—That we may remember our Lord's death till he come, and that our souls may be strengthened and refreshed as we feed together upon him in loving fellowship and faith.

JOHN 14.

470. *What is meant by the Father's house?*—Our home in heaven.

471. *How must we come to the Father?*—By Christ, the only way.

472. *How do we know that our Lord was a perfect* manifestation *of the Father?*—By Christ's assertion to Philip that whoever had **seen him** had seen the Father. Vs. 7, etc.

473. *Who will answer our petitions?*—Our heavenly Father if we ask in Jesus' name. V. 14.

474. *Who was the promised Comforter?*—The Holy Ghost. V. 26.

475. *Was the Holy Ghost a temporary gift?*—No; to abide with us for ever.

476. *Why cannot the world receive him?*—Because it knows him not, nor Christ, through whom he comes.

477. *How can we judge whether we love Christ?*—By our prevailing obedience to his commands, by the witness of the Spirit within us that we love Him who first loved us. Vs. 21, 23.

478. *What enabled the evangelists to remember the sayings and doings of the Lord?*—The teaching of the Holy Ghost. V. 26.

479. *Does Christ mean that his disciples shall have peace on earth when he gave them his peace?*—No; he told them they should have tribulation without, but peace within. John 16 : 33.

480. *Who only could say with truth that he had yielded no allegiance to the prince of this world?*—Jesus Christ. V. 30.

481. *Who is the prince of this world?*—Satan, who rules over the evil spirits of the air and in the hearts of men.

JOHN 15.

482. *In what condition only can we bring forth fruit?* —By being united to Christ and abiding in him by **a** living faith. V. 5.

483. *What will be the consequence of our not bearing fruit?*—Eternal misery in separation from God and Christ, as dead leaves are cast forth and burned. V. 6.

484. *What is the token of being Christ's friends?*— The doing whatsoever he commands. V. 14.

485. *Are we to be surprised by the hatred of the world?* —No, for it first hated our Lord, who was perfect goodness and perfect love.

486. *Is love of the world compatible with love to our Lord?*—No; there can be no true love for a holy Saviour and an unholy world. V. 19.

487. *What sin is referred to in verses 22 and 24?*— The sin of seeing Christ's miracles and hearing his words, and yet rejecting both God and him.

JOHN 16.

488. *Compare verse 2 with Acts 26 : 9–11.*—Saul thought when in his unconverted state that he ought to persecute the followers of Christ.

489. *What was the "little while" in verse 16?*—Jesus was separated a little while from his disciples by his death, and was with them again a little while after his resurrection.

490. *What was the proof that satisfied the unbelieving disciples?*—Jesus knowing their wish or thought, and telling them plainly that he was going back to his Father. Vs. 19, 30.

491. *What is our consolation in trouble?*—That Christ has overcome the world, and that in him we may have peace. V. 33.

JOHN 17.

492. *What "hour" did Jesus refer to in verse 11?*— The time of his death upon the cross.

493. *What is "life eternal"?*—To truly know God as our reconciled Father in Jesus Christ. Union with Christ is life eternal already begun.

494. *Can we at the end of our life use the words of our Lord in verse 4?*—No; we all of us fall short of doing

the work for God, and so of bringing him the glory that we might.

495. *Must we not rather use the words of Isa. 53 : 6?* —Yes; we have indeed too much "turned every one to his own way."

496. *Who was the son of perdition?*—Judas, who was fast falling into ruin and perdition.

497. *How do we know that believers of the present day were included in the Lord's petition ?*—Because they believe through the word of the apostles handed down in the New Testament, and through the preaching and teaching of a succession of Christ's people from that day to this. V. 20.

JOHN 18 : 19 (MATTHEW 26, MARK 14, LUKE 22).

498. *Why did the high priest question Jesus as to his disciples?*—To know the number and rank of his followers.

499. *Does not John 18 : 28 contain an illustration of the parable of the mote and beam?*—Yes; the people shrunk from entering a heathen court, as they thought it would defile them, and so unfit them to eat the Passover; and yet they did not shrink from the far greater guilt of causing Jesus' death. Matt. 7 : 5.

500. *Does John 18 : 30 show the hollowness of the accusations of the Jews?*—Yes, as they did not dare to bring any particular charge against him.

501. *How did John 18, verses 31 and 32, show in what manner our Lord would be put to death?*—The Jews put to death by stoning, but as they were now under Roman government, Jesus would suffer by the Roman form of crucifixion.

502. *To whom did our Lord appear first after his resurrection?*—To Mary Magdalene and Mary the mother of James. Matt. 28 : 1, 5; 27 : 56.

503. *To whom was his second appearance?*—To Mary Magdalene. John 20 : 11-18.

504. *To whom was his third appearance?*—To Peter. 1 Cor. 15 : 5.

505. *To whom was Jesus' fourth appearance?*—To two disciples on the way to Emmaus. Luke 14 : 13.

506. *To whom was the fifth appearance?*—To an evening assembly of the apostles or disciples. John 20 : 19; 1 Cor. 15 : 5.

507. *What were the circumstances of the sixth?*—Jesus appeared again to the disciples, and made himself especially known to Thomas. John 20 : 24.

508. *To whom was the seventh manifestation?*—To some of the disciples and to Nathanael at the Sea of Tiberias. John 21 : 1.

509. *How many saw the Lord upon his eighth appearance?*—The apostles and about five hundred brethren at once.

510. *Where?*—On a mountain in Galilee.

511. *To whom was our Lord's ninth appearance?*— To James. 1 Cor. 15 : 7.

512. *Who witnessed the final appearance?*—"All the apostles," by whom he had been "seen forty days." 1 Cor. 15 : 7; Acts 1 : 4.

513. *What was our Lord's last act upon earth?*—To give the disciples his blessing. Luke 24 : 50, 51.

ACTS 1.

514. *Who wrote the Acts?*—St. Luke.

515. *What is the meaning of "passion"?*—Suffering.

516. *What were some of the infallible proofs?*—The wounds in his hands and his side, which he allowed Thomas to feel. John 20 : 26-28.

517. *What were the "things pertaining to the kingdom of God"?*—The prophecies concerning himself, and the preaching the Gospel "among all nations, beginning at Jerusalem." Luke 24 : 45-49

518. *Find an example of baptism with the Holy Ghost.* —His descent upon the assembly in the house of Cornelius. Acts 11 : 15.

519. *How did the disciples understand the kingdom of God?*—The restoring the kingdom to Israel, with Christ as king. Vs. 3, 6.

520. *What proof have we in verse 11 that Jesus is the "same yesterday, to-day and for ever"?*—The testimony of the angels that he would come again "in like manner as" the disciples had seen him go.

521. *How far was the Mount of Olives from Jerusalem?*—About a mile.

522. *What proof of the inspiration of the Psalms is there in verse 16?*—The assertion of Peter that the Holy Ghost spake by David.

523. *Compare verse 17 with Matt. 7 : 22, 23.*—"Many will say to me in that day, Lord, Lord, have we not prophesied in thy name? and in thy name have cast out devils? and in thy name done many wonderful works? and then will I profess unto them, I never knew you; depart from me, ye that work iniquity."

524. *What was this "reward of iniquity"?*—Thirty pieces of silver. Matt. 26 : 15.

525. *Who are "these men" of verse 21?*—The seventy disciples. Luke 10 : 1.

526. *Compare verse 14 with the selection of David.*— David was chosen by "the Lord," who "looketh on the heart."

527. *What awful illustration of Ps. 17 is there in verse 15?*—The doom of Judas.

The wicked shall be turned into hell, and all the nations that forget God.

ACTS 2.

528. *What was the day of Pentecost?*—"Seven Sabbaths," or "fifty days," from the Passover. Luke 18 : 15, 16.

529. *How was it that there were Jews "out of every nation"?*—Because they were scattered "among all people," as God had said they should be, for their sins. Deut. 28 : 64.

530. *Compare verse 7 with chap. 1 : 11.*—In both verses the disciples are called Galileans.

531. *At what time was the "third hour of the day"?*— At nine A. M. V. 15.

532. *What is probably the "day" referred to in verse 20?*—The destruction of Jerusalem.

533. *Why is it not likely to be the day of final judgment?*—Because at that day it will be too late to call and be saved. V. 21.

534. *Why was it not possible Jesus should be holden of death?*—Because of his divine power, and of the necessity of his body's rising again to prove his Godhead and complete his work.

535. *What blessed hope in connection with our Lord's resurrection is there in 1 Cor. 6 : 14?*—That "God" "will also raise up us by his own power."

536. *Can we learn anything of the pious dead from verse 34?*—That they are not yet "ascended into the heavens."

537. *What is the meaning of "pricked in their heart"?* —Having the conscience convinced of sin, and being brought to say with the jailer, "What must I do to be saved?" Acts 16 : 30.

538. *What does "had all things common" mean?*— Voluntarily brought all their goods into one common stock. V. 44.

539. *What is "singleness of heart"?*—Sincerity.

ACTS 3.

540. *What time was the ninth hour?*—Three P. M.

541. *Compare verse 12 with John 15 : 5; 2 Cor. 3 : 5.*—Peter knew that "without" Christ he could "do nothing," and that his "sufficiency" was "of God."

542. *Refer to Pilate's efforts to save Jesus.*—Pilate said more than once that he found no fault in Jesus. Luke 23 : 4, 14, 16, 20, 22 ; John 19 : 4, 6, 12, 15.

543. *Compare verse 15 with 2 Tim. 1 : 10.*—Christ, "the Prince of Life," "brought life and immortality to light."

544. *Was the "ignorance" excusable?*—No; it was *willful* ignorance that made them guilty. V. 17.

545. *How does verse 19 prove this?*—By showing that they had sin which needed to be blotted out.

546. *Who was the prophet predicted by Moses?*—Jesus Christ, to despise whom would be to despise God who sent him. Vs. 22, 23 ; Luke 10 : 16.

Acts 4.

547. *Why were the Sadducees particularly grieved?*—Because they believed there was "no resurrection." Acts 23 : 8.

548. *How does verse 8 fulfill the promise in Luke 12 : 11, 12?*—Because Christ had promised that when brought before rulers "the Holy Ghost" should teach his disciples what to say.

549. *Compare verse 12 with 1 John 5 : 11, 12.*—This is the record, that God hath given to us eternal life, and this life is in his Son. He that hath the Son hath life; and he that hath not the Son of God hath not life.

550. *How does verse 13 explain 1 Cor. 1 : 27?*—It is an instance of God's choosing the "weak" and seemingly "foolish" things of the world to confound the "mighty" and "the wise."

551. *What general principle is laid down in verse 19?*—That "we ought to obey God, rather than men." Acts 5 : 29.

552. *How did Hezekiah act when he was overwhelmed with threatenings?*—Like the apostles (vs. 23–30), he brought his trouble before the Lord in prayer. Isa. 37 : 14–17.

Acts 5.

553. *What was the heinousness of the sin of Ananias?* —His lying not only unto men, but unto God.

554. *What is the devil called in John 8 : 44?*—"A liar and the father of" lies.

555. *How did they tempt the Holy Spirit?*—By trying his knowledge, as if he might not know, and as if he were "altogether such an one as" themselves. Ps. 50 : 21.

556. *Compare verse 28 with Matt. 27 : 25.*—Then answered all the people, and said, His blood be on us and on our children.

557. *What examples of the principles laid down in verse 29 are there?*—When Shadrach, Meshach and Abed-nego refused to worship the image, and when Daniel persevered in prayer to God. Dan. 3 : 18; 6 : 10.

558. *Who was one of Gamaliel's pupils?*—Paul. Acts 22 : 3.

Acts 6.

559. *What was the meaning of "serving tables"?*—Attending to the distribution of food.

560. *What did the laying on of the apostles' hands signify?*—The setting apart of the chosen men for their work.

561. *Compare verse 7 with Isa. 55 : 10, 11.*—In the latter place we read:

As the rain cometh down, and the snow from heaven, and returneth not thither, but watereth the earth, and maketh it bring forth and bud, that it may give seed to the sower, and bread to the eater: so shall my word be that goeth forth out of my mouth: it shall not return unto me void, but it shall accomplish that which I please, and it shall prosper in the thing whereto I sent it.

562. *What promise was fulfilled in verse 10?*—I will give you a mouth and wisdom, which all your adversaries shall not be able to gainsay nor resist. Luke 21 : 15.

Acts 8.

563. *Who was Saul?*—A young Jew and bigoted Pharisee.

564. *To whose death was he consenting?*—Stephen's.

565. *Did the apostles leave Jerusalem at that time in consequence of the persecution?*—No; while others were scattered they remained.

566. *How did the persecution defeat its own object?*—The scattered ones everywhere preached the word. V. 4.

567. *What was Simon's intention in offering Peter money?*—That he might have the power of giving the Holy Ghost. V. 19.

568. *In what did Peter declare that Simon had no part?*—In the religion of Christ, which he professed to believe.

Acts 9.

569. *What proof of the oneness of Christ and his disciples is there in verse 4?*—Christ's treating the persecution of his disciples as the persecution of himself.

570. *What proof of Saul's immediate conversion is there in verses 5, 6?*—His addressing Jesus as his Lord, and asking what he would have him to do.

571. *What was the most striking proof of the great change that had taken place in Saul?*—His praying.

572. *How did Ananias, in obedience to the vision, immediately address the persecutor Saul?*—As "Brother Saul."

573. *Where did Saul obtain the ability to preach with the power of verse 22?*—"By the revelation of Jesus Christ." Gal. 1 : 11, 12.

574. *Why had the churches rest at that time?*—The loss of the leadership of Saul had checked persecution for a while.

Acts 10.

575. *What is a centurion?*—An officer in the Roman army.

576. *What assurance that God notices our actions and keeps account of them is there in verse 4?*—Cornelius' prayers and alms were remembered by God.

577. *What proof is there in verse 6 that the Lord knows where all his disciples are dwelling?*—The angel told Cornelius where Peter lodged.

578. *Why was the housetop convenient for prayer?*—The houses there have flat roofs surrounded by a parapet wall.

579. *What did the variety mentioned in verse 12 signify?*—The "redeemed" unto God "out of every kindred and tongue and people and nation." Rev. 5 : 9.

580. *What did Peter mean by "unclean"?*—Forbidden to be eaten by the law.

581. *Compare verse 15 with Eph. 2 : 14.*—Showing Christ, "our peace," making Jew and Gentile "one."

582. *Why was the vision thrice repeated?*—Because, like the subject of Pharaoh's dream, "the thing" referred to was "established by God," who would "shortly bring it to pass." Gen. 41 : 32.

583. *What proof of an overruling Providence is there in verse 20?*—The men who came to Peter were sent by God.

584. *Were not the Jews very slow to realize the calling in of the Gentiles?*—Yes; even believers in Jesus "were astonished" to find that "God also to the Gentiles" had "granted repentance unto life." V. 45, and Acts 11 : 18.

Acts 11.

585. *What name was given to the disciples at Antioch?*—Christians. V. 26.

ACTS 12.

586. *Which was strongest—the prison or the prayer of the Church?*—Prayer. V. 5.

587. *Was there any sign of hurry in Peter's deliverance?*—No; he had time to dress. V. 8.

588. *What other remarkable instance of the same deliberation is there in John 10 : 7?*—Our Lord's grave-clothes being neatly folded up.

589. *Ought not the fact recorded in verse 12 to have prevented the unbelief of verse 15?*—Yes, but we are always slow in expecting answers to our prayers.

590. *What is the meaning of the word "examined" in verse 19?*—Scourged them to make them confess the truth. Acts 22 : 24.

591. *What example of pride is there in verses 21-23?* —Herod's being pleased with the gross flattery of his people, and being instantly and dreadfully punished by God.

592. *Compare verse 23 with Dan. 4 : 37.*—I Nebuchadnezzar praise and extol and honor the King of heaven, all whose works are truth, and his ways judgment: and those that walk in pride he is able to abase.

593. *What is the usual result of persecution?*—To defeat its own purpose. V. 24.

ACTS 13.

594. *What illustration of the custom of the synagogue have we in verse 15?*—It was the custom for any one present to be allowed to read or speak, as Jesus did at Nazareth and Paul at Antioch. Luke 4 : 16.

595. *What is the gospel message called in verses 26, 32, 38?*—"The word" of "salvation," "glad tidings" and "forgiveness of sins."

596. *Was the gospel at this time preached only to the Jews?*—Yes; hitherto only to the Jews. Vs. 42-48.

597. *What should be the result of the reception of the gospel?*—The being "filled with joy and with the Holy Ghost." V. 52.

ACTS 14.

598. *What was the condition of healing?*—The sufferer's faith, as Jesus elsewhere "did not many mighty works" "because of their unbelief." V. 9; Matt. 13 : 58.

599. *Should Christians expect to escape trouble?*—No; it is only "through much tribulation" that we can "enter into the kingdom of God." V. 22.

600. *How do we as Gentiles enter the family of God?* —By the door of faith. V. 27.

ACTS 15.

601. *What was the effect upon Paul and Barnabas by the corruption of the gospel mentioned in verses 1, 5?*— They firmly withstood it. V. 2.

602. *What was the witness of God to the disciples?*— The giving them the Holy Ghost. V. 8.

603. *How is the Jewish ceremonial law spoken of?*— As "a yoke" that it was difficult "to bear." V. 10.

604. *Why did they so strenuously resist the rite of circumcision?*—For as many as are of the works of the law are under the curse: for it is written, Cursed is every one that continueth not in all things which are written in the book of the law to do them. Gal. 3 : 10. For whosoever shall keep the whole law, and yet offend in one point, he is guilty of all. James 2 : 10.

605. *Who was Simeon?*—Simon Peter. Vs. 14, 7.

606. *What conclusion did the apostles come to?*—To lay upon the disciples no greater burden of Jewish ceremonial law than the abstaining from some things that were chiefly connected with polluted idol-worship. V. 20.

ACTS 16.

607. *Are our hearts naturally inclined to receive the gospel?*—No; God must open our hearts. V. 14.

608. *What is the meaning of "divination" and "soothsaying"?*—Pretended knowledge of future events and fortune-telling.

609. *Compare verse 17 with Luke 4 : 33, 34.*—There was a man which had a spirit of an unclean devil, and cried out with a loud voice, saying, Let us alone; what have we to do with thee, thou Jesus of Nazareth? art thou come to destroy us? I know thee who thou art; the Holy One of God.

610. *How does verse 19 show that the deliverance from the evil spirit was a reality?*—The "masters saw that the hope of their gains was gone."

611. *What did the keeper of the prison fear?*—Death, which Peter's keepers had suffered. V. 27; Acts 12 : 19.

612. *What was the privilege of being a Roman?*—Not to be bound or punished without a regular trial.

613. *Compare verse 40 with 2 Cor. 1 : 3-6?*—In the latter place we read:

Blessed be God, even the Father of our Lord Jesus Christ, the Father of mercies, and the God of all comfort: who comforteth us in all our tribulation, that we may be able to comfort them which are in any trouble, by the comfort wherewith we ourselves are comforted of God. For as the sufferings of Christ abound in us, so our consolation also aboundeth by Christ. And whether we be afflicted, it is for your consolation and salvation, which is effectual in the enduring of the same sufferings which we also suffer: or whether we be comforted, it is for your consolation and salvation.

ACTS 17.

614. *What is the supreme authority in religious controversies?*—"The Scriptures." Vs. 2, 3, 11; Acts 18 : 28.

615. *What proof is there in verse 7 of the subjection of the Jews to the Gentile power?*—Their being under the decrees of the Roman emperor, Claudius Cæsar.

616. *And does not this same verse illustrate John 1 : 11?*—Yes; here, as in his native land, Christ's own people, the Jews, "received him not."

617. *What was it that distinguished the Bereans?*— Their readiness to receive the word preached, and their daily searching of the Scriptures respecting it.

618. *What was Athens remarkable for at that time?* —All the Athenians and strangers which were there spent their time in nothing else but either to tell or to hear some new thing.

619. *Who is to be the final Judge of all men?*—God, by Jesus Christ. V. 31.

620. *Who appoints the day of judgment?*—God himself.

621. *Did the Athenians believe in a future life?*— Very few of them did.

ACTS 18.

622. *Were the Jews in favor with the Romans?*—No; they had been expelled from Rome. V. 2.

623. *Is manual labor necessarily undignified?*—No; Paul was obliged to work as a tentmaker for the support of himself and those that were with him. Acts 20 : 34.

624. *Was there not a limit to the apostle's forbearance?* —Yes; he was not bound to cast "pearls before swine." Vs. 5, 6.

625. *Why did the Greeks beat Sosthenes rather than Paul?*—Because Paul was a Roman citizen.

626. *Was the Mosaic economy superseded at this time?* —Yes, but Paul might have had reasons that are not mentioned for complying with the custom at that time. V. 21.

627. *What is the meaning of "mighty in the Scriptures," as distinguished from "eloquence"?*—Well acquainted with them, and enabled to understand them and to teach from them by the Holy Ghost.

ACTS 19.

628. *What example of practical repentance do verses 18, 19 show?*—The fortune-tellers and others burning the books that were the means of their profits and of their sin.

629. *Was the worship of Diana a costly service?*—Yes; her temple was filled with ornaments and gifts, and sin and error are usually more costly than holiness and truth. V. 27.

630. *Why did the disciples hinder Paul?*—Lest he should be injured by the crowd. V. 30.

631. *Were the Jews held in honor at Ephesus?*—No, as they despised all idolatry. V. 34.

632. *Was not the testimony of the Jews to the one God the cause of the uproar?*—Yes.

633. *What were the deputies?*—Judges appointed by the Romans. V. 38.

634. *By whom were the assembly in danger of being called to account?*—The Roman governor.

ACTS 20.

635. *How far was Miletus from Ephesus?*—Thirty-six miles.

636. *What country is meant by Asia?*—A part of Asia Minor or Turkey in Asia, about Ionia and Smyrna, was so called. V. 18.

637. *Notice the holy fortitude of verse 14.*—So Jesus steadfastly set his face to go up to Jerusalem. Acts 21:13.

638. *What did Paul mean by being "pure from the blood of all men"?*—That as he had faithfully taught the whole truth of God, his hearers had only themselves to blame if they rejected it and were lost. V. 27.

When I say unto the wicked, Thou shalt surely die; and thou givest him not warning, nor speakest to warn the wicked from his wicked way, to save his life; the same wicked man shall die in his iniquity; but his blood will I require at thine hand. Ezek. 3:18.

639. *Who appoints the ministry of the Church?*—Whatever human means are used, true ministers are made by the Holy Ghost alone. V. 28.

640. *Compare verse 33 with 1 Sam. 12:3.*—In the latter place we read:

Behold, here I am; witness against me before the Lord, and before his anointed: whose ox have I taken? or whose ass have I taken? or whom have I defrauded? whom have I oppressed? or of whose hand have I received any bribe to blind mine eyes therewith? and I will restore it you.

ACTS 21.

641. *What is the meaning of "took up our carriages"?*—Took our baggage or things carried. V. 15.

642. *Of what nation were the soldiers who rescued Paul?*—They were Romans.

643. *What was the nature of the double chain put upon Paul?*—Being chained to "two soldiers," as Peter was. Acts 12:6.

ACTS 22.

644. *What was it that so provoked the Jews?*—Paul's speaking of being sent to the Gentiles. Vs. 21, 22.

645. *How were the thongs used when not employed for binding prisoners?*—In scourging them to extort the truth. V. 24.

ACTS 23.

646. *What form of unbelief were Sadducees subject to?*—Denying the resurrection.

647. *Was the danger from the bigotry of the Jews unimportant?*—No; it was thought prudent to give Paul nearly five hundred soldiers as a guard. V. 23.

648. *How far was Cæsarea from Jerusalem?*—About sixty miles.

ACTS 24.

649. *Which address to Felix was the most truthful?*—The simpler words of Paul, as Felix's government was "a mean, cruel and profligate" one.

650. *Did Paul spare the conscience of Felix?*—No; he touched it till he trembled. V. 25.

651. *How does the effect of Paul's reasoning upon Felix illustrate Heb. 4:12?*—It shows that the word of God is quick and powerful, and sharper than any two-edged sword, piercing even to the dividing asunder of soul and spirit, and of the joints and marrow, and is a discerner of the thoughts and intents of the heart.

652. *What mercenary motive influenced Felix?*—The hope of a bribe from Paul to release him.

653. *In what did the two governors agree?*—In desiring to please the Jews, and so to keep them at peace. V. 27; Acts 25:9.

ACTS 25.

654. *To what privilege of Roman citizenship did Paul appeal?*—That of having his cause heard by Cæsar.

655. *Who was the Cæsar referred to?*—The Roman emperor Nero.

656. *Who was King Agrippa?*—The second Herod Agrippa, and Jewish king or viceroy of the country to the north and east of Galilee.

657. *What invaluable modern privilege does verse 27 foreshadow?*—The habeas corpus act, which prevents a long imprisonment without trial.

ACTS 26.

658. *What great results are to follow the preaching of the gospel?*—The turning the Gentiles "from darkness to light." V. 18.

659. *What must be added to repentance and turning to God?*—Works consistent with it. V. 20.

660. *Why did Festus accuse Paul of insanity?*—Because he had spoken of a resurrection of the dead.

ACTS 27.

661. *Why did the soldiers advise the killing of the prisoners?*—Lest, like Peter's keepers, they should be put to death if they escaped. V. 42; Acts 12:19.

ACTS 28.

662. *What is the meaning of the term "barbarous"?*—Strange.

663. *To what did the barbarians refer when they said, "Vengeance suffereth him not to live"?*—Vengeance is here a sort of proper name of a mythological deity.

664. *In what way did the soldier "keep" Paul?*—By a chain to himself. Vs. 16, 20.

MISSIONARY JOURNEYS OF ST. PAUL

AND

HIS VOYAGE TO ROME.

FIRST MISSIONARY JOURNEY.

ANTIOCH. Antioch, on the Orontes, was capital of the Roman province of Syria. A mixed body of Jewish and Greek converts formed an early Christian congregation there, which attracted the attention of the church in Jerusalem. It sent Barnabas to Antioch to encourage the congregation. Barnabas went to Tarsus to seek Paul as a helper, whom he knew by experience in Jerusalem as a man with special qualification for missionary work in Gentile fields. They returned to Antioch together (A. D. 43), and that city soon became a center of interest and progress in the church, the brethren being first called Christians there. At Antioch the Holy Ghost said: "Separate me Barnabas and Saul for the work whereunto I have called them. And when they had fasted and prayed, and laid their hands on them, they sent them away." Acts, 13:1-5. Thus called, and in company with John Mark, they started (A. D. 45) down the valley of the Orontes to

SELEUCIA, the port of Antioch. Here they took ship and embarked for

CYPRUS, landing on the east side of the island at Salamis, then a flourishing city with a large Jewish population. At

SALAMIS they preached in the synagogue, and then made a missionary tour of the island, finally arriving at

PAPHOS. This was the capital city and residence of the Proconsul, Sergius Paulus. Here also resided one Elymas, skilled in lore and magic, who tried to refute the doctrine of the missionaries and was struck blind. Sergius was converted. Acts 13:11, 12. Saul (now Paul) and his companions set sail from Paphos to the southern shores of Asia, and, probably landing at Attalia, went to

PERGA, a coast town of the province of Pamphylia. Here John Mark left his companions and returned to Jerusalem, Acts 13:37-39. After leaving Perga they crossed the Taurus range and arrived at

ANTIOCH IN PISIDIA, situated on the Anthius. It was a strong Roman colony and bulwark, with a large Jewish population, and a center of commerce between Ephesus and the East. Here, on the first Sabbath after their arrival, Paul preached his first recorded sermon to Jews, Acts 13:16-41. On the next Sabbath he preached to Gentiles, Acts 13:46-48. He incurred the hostility of the Jews, who could not understand how he could preach the same gospel to Jew and Gentile. They raised a persecution against the apostles, who were expelled by the rulers of the city. Crossing the hills to

ICONIUM, a trading city on the commercial highway between Ephesus and the East, they preached in the synagogue for a time, making many converts, Acts 14:3. But here, as at Antioch in Pisidia, they found a divided multitude, which rose up against them and threatened to stone them. They fled into Lycaonia, crossed the plain and the ridge which separates the Phrygian from the Lycaonian region of Galatia, and arrived at

LYSTRA, a small town peopled by very superstitious inhabitants. Here Paul healed a cripple, and the people at once said the gods had come among them. They called Paul Mercury, and Barnabas Jupiter, and the apostles had to intercede with priests and people to prevent them from worshiping them. Shortly afterwards a mob, influenced by Jews from Antioch and Iconium, stoned Paul and dragged him out of the city, leaving him for dead, Acts 14:19. But he recovered and fled with his companion over the plain, a distance of twenty-seven miles, to

DERBE, a small town on the edge of the Roman province, away from the highway, and near a pass called the "Cilician Gates." Here they rested for a time, preaching the word and teaching many, Acts 14:21. Thence they returned through Lystra, Iconium and Antioch, evidently not preaching much, but giving their attention to the organization of new churches and the appointment of elders for the same, in whose charge they left them. They then recrossed the mountains to Perga, where they preached again. Proceeding thence, about sixteen miles westward, they reached the harbor of

ATTALIA, where they took ship and sailed away for

ANTIOCH, the Syrian capital, from which they started. Here they made a report of their work to a full assembly of the church, and abode there "no little time with the disciples," Acts 14:27, 28 (R. V.)

COUNCIL AT JERUSALEM. Soon after the return of Paul and Barnabas to Antioch a dispute arose among the brethren over the free admission of Gentiles to the church without subscribing to the Jewish laws and customs. Peter was a visitor there and ate with Gentiles, but he wavered when he heard certain teachers sent out by James advocating that circumcision was necessary to salvation. Acts 15:24; Gal. 2:12. Paul and Barnabas adhered to the doctrine that circumcision was not necessary to salvation. To relieve the strained situation at Antioch, the church there sent Paul and Barnabas as delegates to Jerusalem to consult with the elders and apostles respecting the vexed question. On their journey thither they passed through Phœnicia and Samaria, advocating, as opportunity occurred, their doctrine of free acceptance of Gentile converts. On arriving in Jerusalem a general meeting of the church was convened, before which Paul and Barnabas laid an account of their work and the cause and object of their mission. The disputed question was referred to a special Council, which finally decided that Gentile converts need not subscribe to the Jewish law of circumcision, provided they abstained from idolatry, fornication, strangled flesh and blood. This decision was promulgated in writing to the churches in Antioch, Syria and Cilicia. Judas Barnabas and Silas were sent to Antioch to explain and confirm it in person. After seeing that the decision was generally received as satisfactory, Judas went back to Jerusalem and Silas stayed in Antioch. The date of the Council at Jerusalem is fixed by some chronologists as A. D. 48, or three years after Paul started on his first missionary journey. Other chronologists fix the date of Paul's first journey at A. D. 48, and that of the Council at A. D. 50.

PAUL'S SECOND MISSIONARY JOURNEY.

ANTIOCH. In or about the year A. D. 49 (some say A. D. 51) Paul suggested to Barnabas at Antioch that they should revisit the brethren in the churches they had founded, Acts 15 : 36. Barnabas assented, but wished to take John Mark along. Paul objected, because Mark had deserted them in Pamphylia. Thereupon Barnabas and Mark set sail for Cyprus, while Paul took Silas (Silvanus) and began a journey by land, Acts 15 : 37–41. Their mission was to preach, teach, convert, reconfirm, and organize new churches, but they had a special object in acquainting all their hearers with the decision and decree of the Council at Jerusalem, which was a vindication of the doctrine of Paul and Barnabas respecting the free admission of Gentiles into the Christian communion. In their passage through Syria they did not read and explain the decree of the Council, because that work was attended to from the capital, Antioch. Neither did they read it in passing through Cilicia, because it was part of the province of Syria. Crossing the Taurus ranges, they came to

DERBE and **LYSTRA**, in Lycaonia. At the latter place Paul found a disciple and a probably previous convert, named Timothy, son of a Greek father and Jewish mother, whom he circumcised in order to satisfy Jewish prejudices, and took along with him as companion, Acts 16 : 1 ; 2 Tim. 1 : 5. Passing through

PHRYGIA and **GALATIA**, Acts 16 : 6, visiting churches and delivering the decree of the Jerusalem Council, they crossed the frontier of the province and entered Asia. Forbidden by the Holy Spirit to preach in Asia, they turned northward, intending to enter the province of Bithynia. But when they came to a point on their way opposite to

MYSIA, Acts 16 : 7 (R. V.), the Holy Spirit suffered them not to go on into Bithynia. They, therefore, passed westward through Mysia, not preaching in the province, and came to

ALEXANDRIA TROAS. This was an important port town and a Roman colony, upon the Ægean Sea. Here Paul first met Luke, "the beloved physician," and here he witnessed the vision of a man calling him to come over into Macedonia, Acts 16 : 9. Taking Luke along, they sailed for Macedonia, touching at

SAMOTHRACIA, a lofty island in the Ægean, at one of whose anchorages they spent a night. On the next day they sailed past Thasos and reached

NEAPOLIS, the seaport of Thrace, and now the port and town of Kavalla. Thence they proceeded across the Pharsalian plain to

PHILIPPI, which was a Roman colony of Macedonia, Acts 16 : 11, 12. Here, on the Sabbath, they preached by the river side, outside of the city, Acts 16 : 13. One Lydia, of Thyatira, a seller of purple, was here converted and baptized. Paul cast the divining spirit out of a slave girl whose owners, seeing their gains cut off, caught Paul and Silas and drew them into the market-place before the magistrates. The charge brought against them was that they were Jews teaching customs not lawful for Romans to receive and observe. Being condemned without hearing, the magistrates tore off their clothes and ordered them to be scourged and thrown into prison. During the night they were miraculously delivered, and the jailor and his household were converted and baptized, Acts 16 : 14–40. After staying awhile at Lydia's house, Paul and Silas and Timothy (Luke seems to have been left behind) journeyed to

AMPHIPOLIS, a small city of Macedonia, thirty-three miles southwest of Philippi, and three miles from the seacoast. Passing through this and Apollonia they came to

THESSALONICA. This city, still known as Salonika, was the metropolis of Macedonia. There was a synagogue there, and Paul remained some time preaching and teaching. He made many converts, male and female, among the Grecian inhabitants, and worked for his own living, receiving only urgent supplies from the brethren in Philippi. Acts 17 : 1–4 ; Phil. 4 : 15, 16. Paul's success here roused the unbelieving Jews and the rabble and precipitated a riot, during which the house of Jason, where Paul lodged, was assaulted. Jason and some of the brethren were dragged before the rulers (politarchs) on the charge of treason against the Emperor, and were put under bonds to keep the peace. The brethren sent Paul and Silas away by night, Acts 17 : 5–10, to

BEREA, a city of Macedonia, on the eastern slope of the Olympian range. Here Paul preached successfully to both Greeks and Jews. But when the Jews of Thessalonica heard of his success they came and stirred up the people, and compelled the brethren to send Paul away to the seacoast, supposedly to Dium. Silas and Timothy remained. Acts 17 : 10–14. Paul's escort from Berea brought him by sea to

ATHENS, then a free Roman city of Achaia. After a little time Silas and Timothy joined him here. At Athens Paul preached in the synagogue, reasoned much with the Jews, and was brought by the philosophers before the Areopagus council to be heard. When he came to speak of the resurrection he was interrupted and mocked, and he departed from among them, Acts 17 : 22–33. From Athens he went to

CORINTH, capital of the Roman province of Achaia, and emporium of a rich commerce between the East and West. Here Paul lodged with Aquila, and wrought with him at the trade of tent-making, and here Silas and Timothy, who had been sent from Athens back to Macedonia, rejoined him. Paul resided at Corinth for a year and a half, preaching vigorously in the synagogue, making many notable converts, and writing his Epistles to the Thessalonians. Incurring the hostility of the Jews, they brought Paul before the Proconsul, Gallio, on the charge that he was persuading men to worship God contrary to the law. Gallio refused to hear the accusers on a question of words and names and their law, and drove them from the judgment seat. After this, Paul sailed with Aquila and Priscilla from

CENCHREA, which is the eastern port of Corinth, to

EPHESUS. He was now on his return journey, and his ship did but little more than touch at Ephesus. However, Paul preached in the synagogue there, and, leaving his traveling companions, sailed on to

CÆSAREA, the political capital of Palestine, on the shores of the Mediterranean. Thence he journeyed overland to

JERUSALEM, where he saluted the church, and probably joined in the Passover ceremonies, which fell on March 22d, A. D. 53. On leaving Jerusalem he went to

ANTIOCH, where he remained for some time, Acts 18 : 23. Some authors say that during this residence at Antioch Paul wrote the Epistle to the Galatians, but others place the date at four years later, or A. D. 58.

PAUL'S THIRD MISSIONARY JOURNEY.

ANTIOCH. After a sojourn of some length at Antioch, Paul, accompanied by Timothy and, probably, Titus, began his third missionary journey by visiting the churches of

GALATIA and **PHRYGIA.** No details of this visit are given, but the inference from 1 Cor. 16 : 1, 2 is that he exhorted the brethren to contribute to the wants of the poorer brethren in Judea. Leaving these regions, he went to

EPHESUS, the seat of government of Roman Asia, and remarkable for its wealth, beauty of architecture, learning, idolatries and superstitions. Here Paul re-baptized twelve men who had been baptized only unto John's baptism, Acts 19: 2-7. He then went into the synagogue and preached regularly for three months, after which he taught for two years in the school of one Tyrannus, refuting the many errors of idolatry, sorcery and paganism. It was probably during this period that churches were established at Collossæ, Laodicea, Pergamos and other places by Timothy and his helpers. Paul wrought many miracles at Ephesus, and his preaching so interfered with the trade of the image-makers that one Demetrius, who was at the head of his craft, called the tradesmen together in angry council. They rushed over into the theatre, where Alexander, the coppersmith, was called upon to harangue the crowd; but when it was found that he was a Jew his voice was drowned by shouts of "Great is Diana of the Ephesians." The town clerk succeeded in appeasing and dismissing the mob, though not until Paul had passed through great danger, Acts 19: 23-41; 2 Cor. 1: 8. In the end Paul was compelled to leave Ephesus after a stay of at least two years and three months, during which time he wrote his Epistle to the Corinthians. On leaving Ephesus he sailed along the coast to

TROAS, where he expected to meet Titus, but was disappointed, 2 Cor. 2: 12, 13. Being anxious to learn of the effect of his letter to the Corinthians, he hastened onward to Macedonia and to

PHILIPPI, where he met Titus, and was greatly relieved to find that the state of the church in Corinth was excellent, 2 Cor. 7: 4-13. He spent some time in Macedonia, during which he wrote his Second Epistle to the Corinthians, probably at Philippi, and made a short tour into Illyricum, on the eastern shore of the Adriatic, north of Macedonia, Rom. 15: 19. On the approach of the winter (perhaps that of A. D. 57) he went down to Achaia, and took up his abode at

CORINTH, where he spent three months, and where he was met by Luke. During his stay there he wrote his Epistles to the Galatians and Romans. His intention was to sail thence to Jerusalem with the offerings to the poor, but it was frustrated by the discovery of a plot to kill him, and by the need of a hasty escape overland through Macedonia to

PHILIPPI. At Philippi Paul sent most of his traveling companions in advance to Troas, while he remained behind with Luke to keep the Feast of the Passover, Acts 20: 6. Then they set sail, and in five days arrived at

TROAS, where they joined their companions. On the last Sabbath of their stay here, and while Paul was preaching at midnight in an upper room, one Eutychus fell from a window and was taken up dead. Paul miraculously restored him to life, and returned to the room and to the breaking of bread till daybreak, Acts 20: 6-12. Paul then left Troas on foot for

ASSOS, a seaport of Mysia, opposite Lesbos, whither his companions had preceded him by sea. Here they all took ship, and on the first day reached

MITYLENE, the chief town of the island of Lesbos. The next day they anchored off Chios, Acts 20: 15, and the day following put in at

TROGYLLIUM, a promontory on the main land opposite the island of Samos. The next day they touched at

MILETUS, the ancient capital of Ionia. Here he called together the Ephesian elders, and delivered to them a solemn parting address, Acts 20: 18-35. Sailing thence, they passed Coos and Rhodes, and reached

PATARA, a seaport of Lycia. Here they changed vessels, and took passage on one sailing direct to Syria. They then sailed past Cyprus and reached

TYRE, the famous seaport of Phœnicia. There the ship was bound to unload cargo, and Paul went ashore and spent seven days with the Christians of Tyre, Acts 21: 3, 4. After exchanging prayerful farewells on the seashore, the voyage was continued to

PTOLEMAIS, now called Acre. Here the voyage came to an end, and after remaining one day they set out on foot for

CÆSAREA, to find shelter and rest in the house of Philip the Evangelist, Acts 21: 8. Here they tarried many days, and were visited by Agabus, a Judean prophet, who bound his feet and hands in Paul's girdle, and prophesied his imprisonment in Jerusalem, if he dared to go there, Acts 21: 10-14. Whereupon they all implored Paul not to go, but in vain. Accompanied by certain disciples of Cæsarea, and by one Mnason, of Cyprus, an old disciple with whom they were to lodge, they set out overland for

JERUSALEM. Here they were welcomed by the brethren, on their arrival, and on the next day were formally received by a full assembly of apostles and elders. Paul delivered an address, in which he recounted his missionary efforts since his last visit to Jerusalem. The address was well received by all but the Judaizing sect in the church. These advised him to prove his observance of the Jewish law by taking charge of four Jewish Christians, who were under a vow, by purifying himself with them in the Temple, and by paying their expenses, Acts 21: 20-25. This Paul undertook to do, but before the necessary seven days were ended the Asiatic Jews stirred up the mob against him, and he would have been torn to pieces but for the timely arrival of a body of soldiers under their captain, Claudius Lysias, who extricated him and eventually sent him to Cæsarea to Felix, the Governor. Acts 21: 27-40; 22, 23.

PAUL'S VOYAGE TO ROME AND SUBSEQUENT MISSIONARY WORK.

CÆSAREA. When Felix learned that Paul was a Cilician he ordered him to be kept in Herod's judgment hall. In a few days Ananias, the high priest, with some members of the Sanhedrim and Tertullus, a lawyer, came down to Cæsarea to charge Paul with being a leader of the Nazarenes and a profaner of the Temple. Paul defended himself, and Felix postponed judgment till he could send for the captain, Claudius Lysias, and hear the whole matter of the mob, the rescue and the arrest in Jerusalem from his own lips. Meanwhile, Felix had interviews with Paul of such a serious nature as to make the cruel Governor tremble. He delayed trial of Paul, and hoped to get a ransom for his release. Thus two years passed, when Felix was succeeded by Porcius Festus as Procurator.

On the accession of Festus, the Jews besought him to bring Paul to Jerusalem for trial, intending to kill him on the way. Festus said he would hear the case at Cæsarea, and went down there. Paul claimed the rights of a Roman citizen, refused to be heard before Festus, and made his appeal directly to Rome and the Emperor. Just after this Herod Agrippa II., King of Chalcis, arrived, and Festus consulted with him about Paul's case. They agreed that his appeal to Rome must be respected, and they sent Paul to Rome, at the first opportunity, in company with other prisoners, Acts 26: 1. He embarked at Cæsarea in a ship of Adramytium. The prisoners were in charge of Julius, a Roman centurion. The ship first touched at

SIDON, where Paul was permitted to go on shore and see his friends. They then sailed under the lee (along the north side) of

CYPRUS, and then across the sea which is over (off) Cilicia and Pamphylia to

MYRA, then a flourishing seaport of Lycia. Here they took one of the large ships which carried corn from Alexandria to Rome, and after sailing slowly for many days, owing to adverse winds, they came over against

CNIDUS, a promontory of Caria, at the extreme southwest of Asia Minor. Here the wind checked their direct course, and they were driven southward to

SALMONE, the eastern promontory of the island of Crete. Rounding it, they worked their way slowly along under shelter of the southern coast of the island to the roadstead of

FAIR HAVENS, about five miles east of the town of Lasæa. Here Paul advised them to winter, but the harbor being incommodious, an effort was made to reach

PHŒNIX (R. V.), PHENICE (A. V.), another harbor of Crete, looking to the southwest and northwest, Acts 27:1-13. But when the ship rounded Cape Matala it was caught by the stormy northeast wind called Euroclydon, Acts 27:14, (Euraquilo, R. V.,) beating down from the Cretan mountains, and was driven under the lee of

CLAUDA (A. V.), CAUDA (R. V.), an island southwest of Crete. It was with great difficulty that they rescued the ship's boats, and the ship itself had to be stayed with ropes about its frame, Acts 27:16, 17. Fearing they should be driven into the

SYRTIS, or "great quicksands" north of Lybia, they lowered the gear and drifted slowly before the wind through

ADRIA, or the sea lying between Malta, Italy, Greece and Crete. On the first day they lightened ship by throwing the freight overboard, and on the next crew and passengers joined in ridding the ship of its spare gear. Then they drifted in despair, but for the promises of Paul that the ship would eventually be saved, until the fourteenth day at midnight, when the sound of breakers was heard. Four anchors were thrown out of the stern, and daylight was anxiously awaited. The ship was then further lightened of cargo and run aground on a creek, where two seas met, of the island of

MALTA, MELITA. The passengers escaped safely to land, and were treated kindly by the inhabitants. Paul, while placing a stick on a fire, was bitten by a viper. The venom had no effect on him, whereupon the inhabitants regarded him as a god. He requited the kindness of Publius, the chief man, by curing his father of a fever, and he healed many of diseases. After a three months' stay at Malta they sailed for Rome in a ship called The Twin Brothers (Castor and Pollux), and soon reached

SYRACUSE, the chief port and city of Sicily. Here they stayed for three days, and from thence shaped a course toward the straits of Messina. But the wind being adverse, they were compelled, after making a circuit, Acts 28:13, to put into

REGIUM, at the extreme southwest of Italy, where they remained one day. Next day they reached

PUTEOLI, on the northern shore of the Bay of Naples, and at that time the harbor for the corn fleets of Alexandria. Here Paul rested seven days with the Christian brethren he found. The journey was now overland and by the celebrated Appian Way to

APPII FORUM, which was about forty-three miles south of Rome. Here a company of brethren met Paul, whom, when he saw, "he thanked God and took courage," Acts 28:15. Ten miles further on they came to

THE THREE TAVERNS, where another company of brethren greeted him. Then they went on to

ROME, where the centurion delivered his prisoners to the chief of the guard. Paul was allowed to live in his own hired house, in company with a soldier who guarded him. He remained in Rome for two years, preaching the kingdom of God, and teaching the things concerning the Lord Jesus Christ with all confidence, Acts 28:31, and writing his Epistles to Philemon, Colossians and Ephesians. Near the end of A. D. 61 he was tried and acquitted.

After his acquittal, his career, for a time, is not distinct, but he probably passed through Macedonia to Philippi, Phil. 2:24, and then through Troas to Ephesus. From the latter place he may have visited the churches of Colossæ, Laodicea and Pergamum, Phile. 22. Some say he may even have gone to Spain, and then returned to Macedonia, where he wrote the First Epistle to Timothy, 1 Tim. 1:3, to whom he had committed the care of the Ephesian church. Coming back to Ephesus, he wrote the Epistle to Titus, in which, Tit. 3:12, he said he intended to winter in

NICOPOLIS. Whether he wintered at Nicopolis is not certainly known, but he went from Ephesus to Miletus, where Trophimus took sick, and thence to Corinth, where Erastus remained. 2 Tim. 4:20. He was placed under arrest a second time and carried to

ROME. This time he was treated more harshly than before, 2 Tim. 1:8; 2:9. During his imprisonment, and when deserted by all his companions except Luke, he wrote his last and most pathetic Epistle to Timothy, in which he gave up hope of acquittal and recognized that "the time of my departure is come." According to the traditions, he suffered martyrdom in the reign of Nero by being beheaded with the sword. The date, according to some authorities, was A. D. 66, and according to others A. D. 68.

hate you. 14. He that loveth not *his* brother abideth in death. 15. Whosoever hateth his brother is a murderer: and ye know that no murderer hath eternal life abiding in him.

1 John 4:20. If a man say, I love God, and hateth his brother, he is a liar: for he that loveth not his brother whom he hath seen, how can he love God whom he hath not seen?

3 John 10. Wherefore, if I come, I will remember his deeds which he doeth, prating against us with malicious words: and not content therewith, neither doth he himself receive the brethren, and forbiddeth them that would, and casteth *them* out of the church.

See CONSPIRACY; HATRED; HOMICIDE; JEALOUSY; REVENGE.

INSTANCES OF: Cain toward Abel, Gen. 4:8. Ishmael toward Sarah, Gen. 21:9. Sarah toward Hagar, Gen. 21:10. Philistines toward Isaac, Gen. 26. Esau toward Jacob, Gen. 27:41. Joseph's brethren toward Joseph, Gen. 37; 42:21. Potiphar's wife toward Joseph, Gen. 39:14-20. Ammonites toward the Israelites, Deut. 23:3,4. Saul toward David, 1 Sam. 18:8-29; 19; 20:30-33; 22:6-18; 23:7-23; 26:18. David toward Michal, 2 Sam. 6:21-23; toward Joab, 1 Kin. 2:5,6; Shimei, 1 Kin. 2:8,9. Shimei toward David, 2 Sam. 16:5-8. Ahithophel toward David, 2 Sam. 17:1-3. Jezebel toward Elijah, 1 Kin. 19:1,2. Ahaziah toward Elijah, 2 Kin. 1. Jehoram toward Elisha, 2 Kin. 6:31. Samaritans toward the Jews, Ezra 4; Neh. 2:10; 4; 6. Haman toward Mordecai, Esth. 3:5-15; 5:9-14. Jeremiah's enemies, Jer. 26:8-11; 38. Nebuchadrezzar toward Zedekiah, Jer. 52: 10,11. Daniel's enemies, Dan. 6:4-9. Herodias toward John, Matt. 14:3-10; Mark 6: 24-28. Herod toward Jesus, Luke 23:11. The Jews toward Jesus, Matt. 27:18; Mark 12:12; 15:10; Luke 11:53,54. James and John toward the Samaritans, Luke 9:54. Jews toward Paul, Acts 17:5; 23:12; 25:3. Masters of the sorcerous damsel toward Paul, Acts 16:19-24.

MALINGERING. INSTANCE OF: David feigning madness, 1 Sam. 21:13-15.

MALLOTHI, son of Heman, a singer, 1 Chr. 25:4,26.

MALLOWS, a plant. Job 30:4.

MALLUCH. 1. A Merarite Levite, 1 Chr. 6:44.

2. Son of Bani, who divorced his Gentile wife after the captivity, Ezra 10:29.

3. One of the family of Harim, who divorced his Gentile wife after the captivity, Ezra 10:32.

4. A priest who sealed the covenant with Nehemiah, Neh. 10:4; 12:2.

5. A chief of the people who sealed the covenant with Nehemiah, Neh. 10:27.

MAMMON, wealth, Matt. 6:24; Luke 16: 9,11,13.

See RICH; RICHES.

MAMRE. 1. A plain near Hebron. Abraham resides in, Gen, 13:18; 14:13. Entertains three angels, and is promised a son, Gen. 18: 1-15. Isaac dwells in, Gen. 35:27.

2. An Amorite and confederate of Abraham, Gen. 14:13,24.

MAN. INDEX OF SUB-TOPICS: *Created*, p. 817; *Created in the Image of God*, p. 818; *Design of the Creation of*, p. 818; *Dominion of*, p. 818; *Duty of*, p. 819; *Equality of*, p. 819; *Ignorance of*, p. 819; *Immortal*, p. 819; *Insignificance of*, p. 819; *Little Lower than the Angels*, p.819; *Mortal*, p. 820; *Spirit*, p. 820; *State of, after the Fall*, p 821; *State of, before the Fall*, p. 821; *Young Men*, p. 821.

CREATED: Gen. 1:26. And God said, Let us make man in our image, after our likeness: and let them have dominion over the fish of the sea, and over the fowl of the air, and over the cattle, and over all the earth, and over every creeping thing that creepeth upon the earth. 27. So God created man in his *own* image, in the image of God created he him; male and female created he them.

Gen. 2:7. And the LORD God formed man *of* the dust of the ground, and breathed into his nostrils the breath of life; and man became a living soul.

Gen. 5:1. This *is* the book of the generations of Adam. In the day that God created man, in the likeness of God made he him; 2. Male and female created he them; and blessed them, and called their name Adam, in the day when they were created.

Deut. 4:32. For ask now of the days that are passed, which were before thee, since the day that God created man upon the earth, and *ask* from the one side of heaven unto the other, whether there hath been *any such thing* as this great thing *is*, or hath been heard like it?

Job 4:17. Shall mortal man be more just than God? shall a man be more pure than his maker?

Job 10:2. I will say unto God, Do not condemn me; shew me wherefore thou contendest with me. 3. *Is it* good unto thee that thou shouldest oppress, that thou shouldest despise the work of thine hands, and shine upon the counsel of the wicked? 8. Thine hands have made me and fashioned me together round about; yet thou dost destroy me. 9. Remember, I beseech thee, that thou hast made me as the clay; and wilt thou bring me into dust again?

Job 31:15. Did not he that made me in the womb make him? and did not one fashion us in the womb?

Job 33:4. The Spirit of God hath made me, and the breath of the Almighty hath given me life.

Job 34:19. *How much less to him* that accepteth not the persons of princes, nor regardeth the rich more than the poor? for they all *are* the work of his hands.

Job 35:10. But none saith, Where *is* God my maker, who giveth songs in the night;

Psa. 8:5. For thou hast made him a little lower than [1]the angels, and hast crowned him with glory and honour. [1 R. V. God]

Psa. 100:3. Know ye that the LORD he *is*

God: *it is* he *that* hath made us, and not we ourselves; *we are* his people, and the sheep of his pasture.

Psa. 119:73. Thy hands have made me and fashioned me:

Psa. 138:8. The LORD will perfect *that which* concerneth me: thy mercy, O LORD, *endureth* for ever: forsake not the works of thine own hands.

Psa. 139:14. I will praise thee; for I am fearfully *and* wonderfully made: marvellous *are* thy works; and *that* my soul knoweth right well.

Eccl. 7:29. Lo, this only have I found, that God hath made man upright;

Isa. 17:7. At that day shall a man look to his Maker, and his eyes shall have respect to the Holy One of Israel.

Isa. 42:5. Thus saith God the LORD, he that created the heavens, and stretched them out; he that spread forth the earth, and that which cometh out of it; he that giveth breath unto the people upon it, and spirit to them that walk therein:

Isa. 43:7. *Even* every one that is called by my name: for I have created him for my glory, I have formed him; yea, I have made him.

Isa. 45:12. I have made the earth, and created man upon it: I, *even* my hands, have stretched out the heavens, and all their host have I commanded.

Isa. 64:8. But now, O LORD, thou *art* our Father; we *are* the clay, and thou our potter; and we all *are* the work of thy hand.

Jer. 27:5. I have made the earth, the man and the beast that *are* upon the ground, by my great power and by my outstretched arm, and have given it unto whom it seemed meet unto me.

Zech. 12:1. The burden of the word of the LORD for Israel, saith the LORD, which stretcheth forth the heavens, and layeth the foundation of the earth, and formeth the spirit of man within him.

Mal. 2:10. Have we not all one father? hath not one God created us?

Mark 10:6. But from the beginning of the creation God made them male and female.

Heb. 2:7. Thou madest him a little lower than the angels; thou crownedst him with glory and honour, and didst set him over the works of thy hands:

See CREATED IN THE IMAGE OF GOD, below.

CREATED IN THE IMAGE OF GOD: Gen. 1:26. And God said, Let us make man in our image, after our likeness: and let them have dominion over the fish of the sea, and over the fowl of the air, and over the cattle, and over all the earth, and over every creeping thing that creepeth upon the earth. 27. So God created man in his *own* image, in the image of God created he him; male and female created he them.

Gen. 9:6. Whoso sheddeth man's blood, by man shall his blood be shed: for in the image of God made he man.

Eccl. 7:29. Lo, this only have I found, that

God hath made man upright; but they have sought out many inventions.

1 Cor. 11:7. For a man indeed ought not to cover *his* head, forasmuch as he is the image and glory of God: but the woman is the glory of the man.

1 Cor. 15:48. As *is* the earthy, such *are* they also that are earthy: and as *is* the heavenly, such *are* they also that are heavenly. 49. And as we have borne the image of the earthy, we shall also bear the image of the heavenly.

Jas. 3:9. Therewith bless we God, even the Father; and therewith curse we men, which are made after the similitude of God.

DESIGN OF THE CREATION OF: Psa. 8:6. Thou madest him to have dominion over the works of thy hands; thou hast put all *things* under his feet: 7. All sheep and oxen, yea, and the beasts of the field; 8. The fowl of the air, and the fish of the sea, *and whatsoever* passeth through the paths of the seas.

Prov. 16:4. The LORD hath made all *things* for himself: yea, even the wicked for the day of evil.

Isa. 43:7. *Even* every one that is called by my name: for I have created him for my glory,

DOMINION OF: Gen. 1:26. And God said, Let us make man in our image, after our likeness: and let them have dominion over the fish of the sea, and over the fowl of the air, and over the cattle, and over all the earth, and over every creeping thing that creepeth upon the earth. 28. And God blessed them, and God said unto them, Be fruitful, and multiply, and replenish the earth, and subdue it: and have dominion over the fish of the sea, and over the fowl of the air, and over every living thing that moveth upon the earth.

Gen. 2:19. And out of the ground the LORD God formed every beast of the field, and every fowl of the air; and brought *them* unto Adam to see what he would call them: and whatsoever Adam called every living creature, that *was* the name thereof. 20. And Adam gave names to all cattle, and to the fowl of the air, and to every beast of the field; but for Adam there was not found a help meet for him.

Gen. 9:2. And the fear of you and the dread of you shall be upon every beast of the earth, and upon every fowl of the air, upon all that moveth *upon* the earth, and upon all the fishes of the sea; into your hand are they delivered. 3. Every moving thing that liveth shall be meat for you; even as the green herb have I given you all things.

Jer. 27:6. And now have I given all these lands into the hand of Nebuchadnezzar the king of Babylon, my servant; and the beasts of the field have I given him also to serve him. Jer. 28:14.

Dan. 2:38. And wheresoever the children of men dwell, the beasts of the field and the fowls of the heaven hath he given into thine hand, and hath made thee ruler over them all.

Heb. 2:7. Thou madest him a little lower than the angels; thou crownedst him with glory and honour, and didst set him over the works of thy hands: 8. Thou hast put all things in subjection under his feet. For in that he put all in subjection under him, he left nothing *that is* not put under him. But now we see not yet all things put under him.

DUTY OF: See Duty; Neighbor.

EQUALITY OF: Job 31:13. If I did despise the cause of my manservant or of my maidservant, when they contended with me; 14. What then shall I do when God riseth up? and when he visiteth, what shall I answer him? 15. Did not he that made me in the womb make him? and did not one fashion us in the womb?

Psa. 33:13. The Lord looketh from heaven; he beholdeth all the sons of men. 14. From the place of his habitation he looketh upon all the inhabitants of the earth. 15. He fashioneth their hearts alike; he considereth all their works.

Prov. 22:2. The rich and poor meet together: the Lord *is* the maker of them all.

Matt. 20:25. But Jesus called them *unto him*, and said, Ye know that the princes of the Gentiles exercise dominion over them, and they that are great exercise authority upon them. 26. But it shall not be so among you: but whosoever will be great among you, let him be your minister; 27. And whosoever will be chief among you, let him be your servant: 28. Even as the Son of man came not to be ministered unto, but to minister, and to give his life a ransom for many.

Matt. 23:8. But be not ye called Rabbi: for one is your Master, *even* Christ; and all ye are brethren. 11. But he that is greatest among you shall be your servant.

Mark 10:42. But Jesus called them *to him*, and saith unto them, Ye know that they which are accounted to rule over the Gentiles exercise lordship over them; and their great ones exercise authority upon them. 43. But so shall it not be among you: but whosoever will be great among you, shall be your minister: 44. And whosoever of you will be the chiefest, shall be servant of all.

Acts 10:28. And he said unto them, Ye know how that it is an unlawful thing for a man that is a Jew to keep company, or come unto one of another nation; but God hath shewed me that I should not call any man common or unclean.

Act 17:26. And hath made of one blood all nations of men for to dwell on all the face of the earth, and hath determined the times before appointed, and the bounds of their habitation;

Gal. 3:28. There is neither Jew nor Greek, there is neither bond nor free, there is neither male nor female: for ye are all one in Christ Jesus.

See Race, Unity of.

IGNORANCE OF: See Ignorance.

IMMORTAL: See Immortality.

INSIGNIFICANCE OF: Job 4:18. Behold, he put no trust in his servants; and his angels he charged with folly: 19. How much less *in* them that dwell in houses of clay, whose foundation *is* in the dust, *which* are crushed before the moth?

Job 15:14. What *is* man, that he should be clean? and *he which is* born of a woman, that he should be righteous?

Job 22:2. Can a man be profitable unto God, as he that is wise may be profitable unto himself? 3. *Is it* any pleasure to the Almighty, that thou art righteous? or *is it* gain *to him*, that thou makest thy ways perfect? 4. Will he reprove thee for fear of thee? Will he enter with thee into judgment? 5. *Is* not thy wickedness great? and thine iniquities infinite?

Job 25:4. How then can man be justified with God? or how can he be clean *that is* born of a woman? 5. Behold even to the moon, and it shineth not; yea, the stars are not pure in his sight. 6. How much less man, *that is* a worm? and the son of man, *which is* a worm?

Job 35:2. Thinkest thou this to be right, *that* thou saidst, My righteousness *is* more than God's? 3. For thou saidst, What advantage will it be unto thee? *and*, What profit shall I have, *if I be cleansed* from my sin? 4. I will answer thee, and thy companions with thee. 5. Look unto the heavens, and see; and behold the clouds *which* are higher than thou. 6. If thou sinnest, what doest thou against him? or *if* thy transgressions be multiplied, what doest thou unto him? 7. If thou be righteous, what givest thou him? or what receiveth he of thine hand? 8. Thy wickedness *may hurt* a man as thou *art;* and thy righteousness *may profit* the son of man.

Job 38:4. Where wast thou when I laid the foundations of the earth? declare, if thou hast understanding. 12. Hast thou commanded the morning since thy days; *and* caused the dayspring to know his place; 13. That it might take hold of the ends of the earth, that the wicked might be shaken out of it.

Psa. 8:3. When I consider thy heavens, the work of thy fingers, the moon and the stars, which thou hast ordained; 4. What is man, that thou art mindful of him? and the son of man, that thou visitest him?

Psa. 144:3. Lord, what *is* man, that thou takest knowledge of him! *or* the son of man, that thou makest account of him! 4. Man is like to vanity: his days *are* as a shadow that passeth away.

LITTLE LOWER THAN THE ANGELS: Job 4:18. Behold, he put no trust in his servants; and his angels he charged with folly: 19. How much less *in* them that dwell in houses of clay, whose foundation *is* in the dust, *which* are crushed before the moth? 20. They are destroyed from morning to evening: they perish for ever without any regarding *it*. 21. Doth not their excellency *which is* in them go away? they die, even without wisdom.

Psa. 8:5. For thou hast made him a little lower than [1] the angels, and hast crowned him with glory and honour.   [1 R. V. God]

Heb. 2:7. Thou madest him a little lower than the angels: thou crownedst him with glory and honour, and didst set him over the works of thy hands: 8. Thou hast put all things in subjection under his feet. For in that he put all in subjection under him, he left nothing *that is* not put under him. But now we see not yet all things put under him.

MORTAL: Job 4:17. Shall mortal man be more just than God? shall a man be more pure than his maker?

Eccl. 2:14. The wise man's eyes *are* in his head; but the fool walketh in darkness: and I myself perceived also that one event happeneth to them all. 15. Then said I in my heart, As it happeneth to the fool, so it happeneth even to me; and why was I then more wise? Then I said in my heart, that this also *is* vanity.

Eccl. 3:20. All go unto one place; all are of the dust, and all turn to dust again.

1 Cor. 15:21. For since by man *came* death, by man *came* also the resurrection of the dead. 22. For as in Adam all die, even so in Christ shall all be made alive.

Heb. 9:27. And as it is appointed unto men once to die, but after this the judgment:

See Death.

SPIRIT: Job 4:19. Them that dwell in houses of clay, whose foundation *is* in the dust, *which* are crushed before the moth?

Job 32:8. But *there is* a spirit in man: and the inspiration of the Almighty giveth them understanding.

Psa. 31:5. Into thine hand I commit my spirit: thou hast redeemed me, O Lord God of truth.

Prov. 20:27. The spirit of man *is* the candle of the Lord,

Eccl. 1:8. The eye is not satisfied with seeing, nor the ear filled with hearing.

Eccl. 3:21. Who knoweth the spirit of man that goeth upward, and the spirit of the beast that goeth downward to the earth?

Eccl. 12:7. Then shall the dust return to the earth as it was: and the spirit shall return unto God who gave it.

Isa. 26:9. With my soul have I desired thee in the night; yea, with my spirit within me will I seek thee early: for when thy judgments *are* in the earth, the inhabitants of the world will learn righteousness.

Zech. 12:1. The burden of the word of the Lord for Israel, saith the Lord, which

stretcheth forth the heavens, and layeth the foundation of the earth, and formeth the spirit of man within him.

Matt. 4:4. But he answered and said, It is written, Man shall not live by bread alone, but by every word that proceedeth out of the mouth of God.

Matt. 10:28. And fear not them which kill the body, but are not able to kill the soul: but rather fear him which is able to destroy both soul and body in hell.

Matt. 26:41. The spirit indeed *is* willing, but the flesh *is* weak. Mark 14:38; Luke 22:40.

Luke 23:46. And when Jesus had cried with a loud voice, he said, Father, into thy hands I commend my spirit: and having said thus, he gave up the ghost.

Luke 24:39. For a spirit hath not flesh and bones, as ye see me have.

John 3:3. Jesus answered and said unto him, Verily, verily, I say unto thee, Except a man be born again, he cannot see the kingdom of God. 4. Nicodemus saith unto him, How can a man be born when he is old? can he enter the second time into his mother's womb, and be born? 5. Jesus answered, Verily, verily, I say unto thee, Except a man be born of water and *of* the Spirit, he cannot enter into the kingdom of God. 6. That which is born of the flesh is flesh; and that which is born of the Spirit is spirit. 7. Marvel not that I said unto thee, Ye must be born again. 8. The wind bloweth where it listeth, and thou hearest the sound thereof, but canst not tell whence it cometh, and whither it goeth: so is every one that is born of the Spirit.

John 4:24. God *is* a Spirit: and they that worship him must worship *him* in spirit and in truth.

Acts 7:59. And they stoned Stephen, calling upon *God*, and saying, Lord Jesus, receive my spirit.

Rom. 1:9. For God is my witness, whom I serve with my spirit in the gospel of his Son, that without ceasing I make mention of you always in my prayers;

Rom. 2:29. But he *is* a Jew, which is one inwardly; and circumcision *is that* of the heart, in the spirit, *and* not in the letter; whose praise *is* not of men, but of God.

Rom. 7:14. For we know that the law is spiritual: but I am carnal, sold under sin. 15. For that which I do, I allow not: for what I would, that do I not; but what I hate, that do I. 16. If then I do that which I would not, I consent unto the law that *it is* good. 17. Now then it is no more I that do it, but sin that dwelleth in me. 18. For I know that in me (that is, in my flesh,) dwelleth no good thing: for to will is present with me; but *how* to perform that which is good I find not. 19. For the good that I would, I do not: but the evil which I would not, that I do. 20. Now if I do that I would not, it is no more I that do it, but sin that dwelleth in me. 21. I find then a law, that, when I would do good, evil is present with me. 22. For I delight in the law of God after the inward man: 23. But I see another law in my members, warring against the law of my mind, and bringing me into captivity to the law of sin which is in my members. 24. O wretched man that I am! who shall deliver me from the body of this death? 25. I thank God through Jesus Christ our Lord. So then with the mind I myself serve the law of God; but with the flesh the law of sin.

1 Cor. 2:11. For what man knoweth the things of a man, save the spirit of man which is in him? even so the things of God knoweth no man, but the Spirit of God.

1 Cor. 6:20. Glorify God in your body, [1 and in your spirit, which are God's.   [1 Omitted in R. V.]

1 Cor. 7:34. The unmarried woman careth for the things of the Lord, that she may be holy both in body and in spirit:

1 Cor. 14:14. For if I pray in an *unknown* tongue, my spirit prayeth, but my understanding is unfruitful.

2 Cor. 4:6. For God, who commanded the light to shine out of darkness, hath shined in our hearts, to *give* the light of the knowledge of the glory of God in the face of Jesus Christ. 7. But we have this treasure in earthen vessels, 16. For which cause we faint not; but though our outward man perish, yet the inward *man* is renewed day by day.

2 Cor. 5:1. For we know that if our earthly house of *this* tabernacle were dissolved, we have a building of God, an house not made with hands, eternal in the heavens. 2. For in this we groan, earnestly desiring to be clothed upon with our house which is from heaven: 3. If so be that being clothed we shall not be found naked. 4. For we that are in *this* tabernacle do groan, being burdened: not for that we would be unclothed, but clothed upon, that mortality might be swallowed up of life. 5. Now he that hath wrought us for the selfsame thing *is* God, who also hath given unto us the earnest of the Spirit. 6. Therefore *we are* always confident, knowing that, whilst we are at home in the body, we are absent from the Lord: 7. (For we walk by faith, not by sight:) 8. We are confident, *I say,* and willing rather to be absent from the body, and to be present with the Lord. 9. Wherefore we labour, that, whether present or absent, we may be accepted of him.

Eph. 3:16. That he would grant you, according to the riches of his glory, to be strengthened with might by his Spirit in the inner man;

Eph. 4:4. *There is* one body, and one Spirit, even as ye are called in one hope of your calling;

1 Thess. 5:23. And the very God of peace sanctify you wholly; and *I pray God* your whole spirit and soul and body be preserved blameless unto the coming of our Lord Jesus Christ.

Heb. 4:12. For the word of God *is* quick, and powerful, and sharper than any twoedged sword, piercing even to the dividing asunder of soul and spirit, and of the joints and marrow, and *is* a discerner of the thoughts and intents of the heart.

Jas. 2:26. For as the body without the spirit is dead, so faith without works is dead also.

STATE OF, AFTER THE FALL: See DEPRAVITY.

STATE OF, BEFORE THE FALL: See above, CREATED IN THE IMAGE OF GOD.

YOUNG MEN: See YOUNG MEN.

MANAEN, an associate of Herod in his youth, and a Christian teacher, Acts 13:1.

MANAHATH. 1. Son of Shobal, Gen. 36:23; 1 Chr. 1:40.

2. A city in Benjamin, 1 Chr. 8:6.

MANASSEH. 1. Son of Joseph and Asenath, Gen. 41:50,51; 46:20; adopted by Jacob on his deathbed, Gen. 48:1,5–20. Called MANASSES, Rev. 7:6.

2. Tribe of. Descendants of Joseph. The two sons of Joseph, Ephraim and Manasseh, were reckoned among the primogenitors of the twelve tribes, taking the places of Joseph and Levi.

Adopted by Jacob, Gen. 48:5. Prophecy concerning, Gen. 49:25,26. Enumeration of, Num. 1:34,35; 26:29–34. Place of, in camp and march, Num. 2:18,20; 10:22,23. Blessing of Moses on, Deut. 33:13–17. Inheritance of one-half of tribe east of Jordan, Num. 32: 33,39–42. One-half of tribe west of Jordan, Josh. 16:9; 17:5–11. The eastern half assist in the conquest of the country west of the Jordan, Deut. 3:18–20; Josh. 1:12–15; 4:12,13. Join the other eastern tribes in erecting a monument to testify to the unity of all Israel; misunderstood; make satisfactory explanation, Josh. 22. Join Gideon in war with the Midianites, Judg. 6;7. Malcontents of, join David, 1 Chr. 12:19,31. Smitten by Hazael, 2 Kin. 10:33. Return from captivity, 1 Chr. 9:3. Reallotment of territory to, by Ezekiel, Ezek. 48:4. Affiliate with the Jews in the reign of Hezekiah, 2 Chr. 30. Incorporated into kingdom of Judah, 2 Chr. 15: 9; 34:6,7.

See ISRAEL, TRIBES OF.

3. [MOSES, *R. V.*] Father of Gershom, Judg. 18:30.

4. King of Judah. History of, 2 Kin. 21: 1–18; 2 Chr. 33:1–20.

5. Two Jews who put away their Gentile wives after the captivity, Ezra 10:30,33.

MANDRAKE, Gen. 30:14–16; Song 7:13.

MANEH. A weight. Rendered pound, 1 Kin. 10:17; Ezra 2:69; Neh. 7:71,72. Equal to one hundred shekels, 1 Kin. 10:17, with 2 Chr. 9:16.

See WEIGHTS.

MANGER. Luke 2:7,12,16. Rendered stall, Luke 13:15.

MANNA. Ex. 16:4–35; Num. 11:6–10; Deut. 8:3,16; Josh. 5:12; Neh. 9:20; Psa. 78: 24; John 6:31,49,58. Preserved in the ark of the testimony, Ex. 16:33; Heb. 9:4.

FIGURATIVE: John 6:48–51; 1 Cor. 10:3; Rev. 2:17.

MANNERS. Social customs. Obeisance to strangers, Gen. 18:2; 19:1. Standing while guests eat, Gen. 18:8; in presence of superiors, Gen. 31:35; Job 29:8; of the aged, Lev. 19:32. Courteousness enjoined, 1 Pet. 3:8. Rules for guests, Prov. 23:1,2; 1 Cor. 10:27.

See SALUTATIONS.

MANOAH, a Danite of Zorah and father of Samson, Judg. 13:2–24.

MANSERVANT. See SERVANT.

MANSION. FIGURATIVE: John 14:2.

MANSLAUGHTER. See FRATRICIDE; HOMICIDE; REGICIDE.

MANSLAYER. See HOMICIDE; CITIES OF REGUGE.

MANTLE. Rent in token of grief, Ezra 9:3; Job 1:20; 2:12. Of Elijah, 1 Kin. 19:19; 2 Kin. 2:8,13,14.

See DRESS.

MANURE. Used as fertilizer, Isa. 25:10; Luke 13:8; 14:34,35.

MAON. A city allotted to Judah, Josh. 15:55. Dwelling place of Nabal, 1 Sam. 25:2. David with his insurgents encamps near, 1 Sam. 23:24,25. Uzziah engages in war against the people of, called Mehunims, 2 Chr. 26:7.

MARAH, the first station of the Israelites, where Moses made the bitter waters sweet, Ex. 15:22–25; Num. 33:8,9.

MARALAH, a landmark on the boundary of Zebulun, Josh. 19:11.

MARBLE. In the temple, 1 Chr. 29:2. Pillars of, Esth. 1:6; Song 5:15. Merchandise of, Rev. 18:12. Mosaics of, Esth. 1:6.

MARESHAH 1. A city of Judah, Josh. 15:44; 2 Chr. 11:8; 14:9,10. Birthplace of Eliezer the prophet, 2 Chr. 20:37. Prophecy concerning, Mic. 1:15.

2. Father of Hebron, 1 Chr. 2:42.

3. A son of, or possibly a city founded by, Laadah, 1 Chr. 4:21.

MARINER. 1 Kin. 9:27; 2 Chr. 8:18; Isa. 42:10; Ezek. 27:27. Perils of, Psa. 107: 23–30; Jonah 1:5; Acts 27:17–44. Cowardice of, Acts 27:30.

See SHIP; COMMERCE.

MARK. A nephew of Barnabas, Col. 4: 10. A disciple of Jesus, Acts 12:12,25; 13:5, 13. Paul and Barnabas contend concerning, Acts 15:36–39. A convert of Peter, 1 Pet. 5:13. Fellow-worker with Paul at Rome, Col. 4:10,11; 2 Tim. 4:11; Philem. 24.

MARKET. A place for general merchandise. Held at gates. See GATES. Judgment seat at, Acts 16:19. Traffic of, in Tyre, consisted of horses, horsemen, mules, horns, ivory, and ebony, emeralds, purple, broidered wares, linen, coral, agate, honey, balm, wine, wool, oil, cassia, calamus, charioteers' clothing, lambs, rams, goats, precious stones, and gold, spices, and costly apparel, Ezek. 27:13–25.

See GATES.

MAROTH, a city of Judah. Mic. 1:12.

MARRIAGE. Consanguineous, Abraham and Sarah, Gen. 11:29; 12:13; 20:3,9–16. Isaac and Rebekah, Gen. 24:3,4,67; 28:2. Jacob and his wives, Gen. 29:15–30; see below, in the elaborated text. Levirate (the brother required to marry a brother's widow), Gen. 38:8,11; Deut. 25:5–10; Ruth 4:5; Matt. 22:24; Mark 12:19–23; Luke 20:28.

Parents contract for their children: Hagar selects a wife for Ishmael, Gen. 21:21; Abraham for Isaac, Gen. 24; Laban arranges for his daughters' marriage, Gen. 29; Samson asks his parents to procure him a wife, Judg. 14:2. Parents' consent required in the Mosaic law, Ex. 22:17. Presents given to parents to secure their favor, Gen. 24:53; 34:12; Deut. 22:29; 1 Sam. 18:25; Hos. 3:2. Nuptial feasts, Gen. 29:22; Judg. 14:12; Esth. 2:18; Matt. 22:11,12. Jesus present at, John 2:1–5. Ceremony attested by witnesses, Ruth 4:1–11; Isa. 8:1–3. Bridegroom exempt one year from military duty, Deut. 24:5. Bridal ornaments, Isa. 49:18; Jer. 2:32. Bridal presents, Gen. 24:53; Psa. 45:12. Herald preceded the bridegroom, Matt. 25:6. Wedding robes adorned with jewels, Isa. 61:10.

Wives obtained by purchase, Gen. 29:20; Ruth 4:10; Hos. 3:2; 12:12; by kidnapping, Judg. 21:21–23. Given by Kings, 1 Sam. 17: 25; 18:17,21. Daughters given in, as rewards of valor, Judg. 1:12; 1 Sam. 17:25; 18:27.

Wives taken by edict, Esth. 2:2–4,8–14. David gave one hundred Philistine foreskins for a wife, 2 Sam. 3:14.

Wives among the Israelites must be Israelites, Ex. 34:16; Deut. 7:3,4; 1 Chr. 23:22; Ezra 9:1,2,12; Neh. 10:30; 13:26,27; Mal. 2:11; 1 Cor. 7:39; 2 Cor. 6:14. Betrothal a quasi-marriage, Matt. 1:18; Luke 1:27. Betrothal made with the spirit, Ezek. 16:8. Celibacy deplored, Judg. 11:38; Isa. 4:1; Jer. 16:9; advised, 1 Cor. 7:7,8,24–40.

Obligations under, inferior to duty to God, Deut. 13:6–10; Matt. 19:29; Luke 14:26.

Not binding after death, Matt. 22:29,30; Mark 12:24,25.

See BRIDE; BRIDEGROOM.

UNCLASSIFIED SCRIPTURES RELATING TO: Gen. 2:23. And Adam said, This *is* now bone of my bones, and flesh of my flesh: she shall be called Woman, because she was taken out of Man. 24. Therefore shall a man leave his father and his mother, and shall cleave unto his wife: and they shall be one flesh. 1 Cor. 6:16.

Ex. 22:16. And if a man entice a maid that is not betrothed, and lie with her, he shall surely endow her to be his wife. 17. If her father utterly refuse to give her unto him, he shall pay money according to the dowry of virgins.

Lev. 18: 6. None of you shall approach to any that is near of kin to him, to uncover *their* nakedness: I *am* the LORD. 7. The nakedness of thy father, or the nakedness of thy mother, shalt thou not uncover: she *is* thy mother; thou shalt not uncover her nakedness. 8. The nakedness of thy father's wife shalt thou not uncover: it *is* thy father's nakedness. [Deut. 22:30.] 9. The nakedness of thy sister, the daughter of thy father, or daughter of thy mother, *whether she be* born at home, or born abroad, *even* their nakedness thou shalt not uncover. 10. The nakedness of thy son's daughter, or of thy daughter's daughter, *even* their nakedness thou shalt not uncover: for theirs *is* thine own nakedness. 11. The nakedness of thy father's wife's daughter, begotten of thy father, she *is* thy sister, thou shalt not uncover her nakedness. 12. Thou shalt not uncover the nakedness of thy father's sister: she *is* thy father's near kinswoman. 13. Thou shalt not uncover the nakedness of thy mother's sister: for she *is* thy mother's near kinswoman. 14. Thou shalt not uncover the nakedness of thy father's brother, thou shalt not approach to his wife: she *is* thine aunt. 15. Thou shalt not uncover the nakedness of thy daughter in law: she *is* thy son's wife; thou shalt not uncover her nakedness. 16. Thou shalt not uncover the nakedness of thy brother's wife: it *is* thy brother's nakedness. 17. Thou shalt not uncover the nakedness of a woman and her daughter; neither shalt thou take her son's daughter, or her daughter's daughter, to uncover her nakedness; *for* they *are* her near kinswomen: it *is* wickedness. 18. Neither shalt thou take a wife to her sister, to vex *her*, to uncover her nakedness, beside the other in her life *time*.

Lev. 20:14. And if a man take a wife and her mother, it *is* wickedness: they shall be burnt with fire, both he and they; that there be no wickedness among you. 17. And if a man shall take his sister, his father's daughter, or his mother's daughter, and see her nakedness, and she see his nakedness; it *is* a wicked thing; and they shall be cut off in the sight of their people: he hath uncovered his sister's nakedness: he shall bear his iniquity. 19. And thou shalt not uncover the nakedness of thy mother's sister, nor of thy father's sister: for he uncovereth his near kin: they shall bear their iniquity. 20. And if a man shall lie with his uncle's wife, he hath uncovered his uncle's nakedness: they shall bear their sin; they shall die childless. 21. And if a man shall take his brother's wife, it *is* an unclean thing: he hath uncovered his brother's nakedness; they shall be childless.

Lev. 21:1. And the LORD said unto Moses, Speak unto the priests the sons of Aaron, and say unto them, 7. They shall not take a wife *that is* a whore, or profane; neither shall they take a woman put away from her husband: for he *is* holy unto his God. 13. And he shall take a wife in her virginity. 14. A widow, or a divorced woman, or profane, *or* an harlot, these shall he not take: but he shall take a virgin of his own people to wife. 15. Neither shall he profane his

seed among his people: for I the LORD do sanctify him.

Num. 36:8. And every daughter, that possesseth an inheritance in any tribe of the children of Israel, shall be wife unto one of the family of the tribe of her father, that the children of Israel may enjoy every man the inheritance of his fathers.

Deut. 21:10. When thou goest forth to war against thine enemies, and the LORD thy God hath delivered them into thine hands, and thou hast taken them captive, 11. And seest among the captives a beautiful woman, and hast a desire unto her, that thou wouldest have her to thy wife; 12. Then thou shalt bring her home to thine house; and she shall shave her head, and pare her nails; 13. And she shall put the raiment of her captivity from off her, and shall remain in thine house, and bewail her father and her mother a full month: and after that thou shalt go in unto her, and be her husband, and she shall be thy wife. 14. And it shall be, if thou have no delight in her, then thou shalt let her go whither she will; but thou shalt not sell her at all for money, thou shalt not make merchandise of her, because thou hast humbled her.

Deut. 24:1. When a man hath taken a wife, and married her, and it come to pass that she find no favour in his eyes, because he hath found some uncleanness in her: then let him write her a bill of divorcement, and give *it* in her hand, and send her out of his house. 2. And when she is departed out of his house, she may go and be another man's *wife*. 3. And *if* the latter husband hate her, and write her a bill of divorcement, and giveth *it* in her hand, and sendeth her out of his house; or if the latter husband die, which took her *to be* his wife; 4. Her former husband, which sent her away, may not take her again to be his wife, after that she is defiled; for that *is* abomination before the LORD: and thou shalt not cause the land to sin, which the LORD thy God giveth thee *for* an inheritance. 5. When a man hath taken a new wife, he shall not go out to war, neither shall he be charged with any business: *but* he shall be free at home one year, and shall cheer up his wife which he hath taken.

Prov. 18:22. *Whoso* findeth a wife findeth a good *thing*, and obtaineth favour of the LORD.

Prov. 21:9. *It is* better to dwell in a corner of the housetop, than with a brawling woman in a wide house. 19. *It is* better to dwell in the wilderness, than with a contentious and an angry woman.

Jer. 29:6. Take ye wives, and beget sons and daughters; and take wives for your sons, and give your daughters to husbands, that they may bear sons and daughters; that ye may be increased there, and not diminished.

Hos. 2:19. And I will betroth thee unto me for ever; yea, I will betroth thee unto me in righteousness, and in judgment, and in lovingkindness, and in mercies. 20. I will even betroth thee unto me in faithfulness: and thou shalt know the LORD.

Mal. 2:13. And this have ye done again, covering the altar of the LORD with tears, with weeping, and with crying out, insomuch that he regardeth not the offering any more, or receiveth it with good will at your hand. 14. Yet ye say, Wherefore? Because the LORD hath been witness between thee and the wife of thy youth, against whom thou hast dealt treacherously: yet is she thy companion, and the wife of thy covenant. 15. And did not he make one? Yet had he the residue of the spirit. And wherefore one? That he might seek a godly seed. Therefore take heed to your spirit, and let none deal treacherously against the wife of his youth. 16. For the LORD, the God of Israel, saith that he hateth putting away: for one covereth violence with his garment, saith the LORD of hosts: therefore take heed to your spirit, that ye deal not treacherously.

Matt. 5:31. It hath been said, Whosoever shall put away his wife, let him give her a writing of divorcement: 32. But I say unto you, That whosoever shall put away his wife, saving for the cause of fornication, causeth her to commit adultery: and whosoever shall marry her that is divorced committeth adultery.

Mark 6:17. For Herod himself had sent forth and laid hold upon John, and bound him in prison for Herodias' sake, his brother Philip's wife: for he had married her. 18. For John had said unto Herod, It is not lawful for thee to have thy brother's wife.

Mark 10:2. And the Pharisees came to him, and asked him, Is it lawful for a man to put away his wife? tempting him. 3. And he answered and said unto them, What did Moses command you? 4. And they said, Moses suffered to write a bill of divorcement, and to put her away. 5. And Jesus answered and said unto them, For the hardness of your heart he wrote you this precept. 6. But from the beginning of the creation God made them male and female. 7. For this cause shall a man leave his father and mother, and cleave to his wife; 8. And they twain shall be one flesh: so then they are no more twain, but one flesh. 9. What therefore God hath joined together, let not man put asunder. 10. And in the house his disciples asked him again of the same matter. 11. And he saith unto them, Whosoever shall put away his wife, and marry another, committeth adultery against her. 12. And if a woman shall put away her husband, and be married to another, she committeth adultery. Matt. 19:2-9.

Luke 16:18. Whosoever putteth away his wife, and marrieth another, committeth adultery: and whosoever marrieth her that is put away from her husband committeth adultery.

Rom. 7:1. Know ye not, brethren, (for I speak to them that know the law,) how that the law hath dominion over a man as long as he liveth? 2. For the woman which hath an husband is bound by the law to her husband so long as he liveth; but if the husband be dead, she is loosed from the law of her husband. 3. So then if, while her husband liveth, she be married to another man, she shall be called an adulteress: but if her husband be dead, she is free from that law; so that she is no adulteress, though she be married to another man.

1 Cor. 7:1. Now concerning the things whereof ye wrote unto me: It is good for a man not to touch a woman. 2. Nevertheless, to avoid fornication, let every man have his own wife, and let every woman have her own husband. 3. Let the husband render unto the wife due benevolence: and likewise also the wife unto the husband. 4. The wife hath not power of her own body, but the husband: and likewise also the husband hath not power of his own body, but the wife. 5. Defraud ye not one the other, except it be with consent for a time, that ye may give yourselves to fasting and prayer; and come together again, that Satan tempt you not for your incontinency. 6. But I speak this by permission, and not of commandment. 7. For I would that all men were even as I myself. But every man hath his proper gift of God, one after this manner, and another after that. 8. I say therefore to the unmarried and widows, It is good for them if they abide even as I. 9. But if they cannot contain, let them marry: for it is better to marry than to burn. 10. And unto the married I command, yet not I, but the Lord, Let not the wife depart from her husband: 11. But and if she depart, let her remain unmarried, or be reconciled to her husband: and let not the husband put away his wife. 12. But to the rest speak I, not the Lord: If any brother hath a wife that believeth not, and she be pleased to dwell with him, let him not put her away. 13. And the woman which hath an husband that believeth not, and if he be pleased to dwell with her, let her not leave him. 14. For the unbelieving husband is sanctified by the wife, and the unbelieving wife is sanctified by the husband: else were your children unclean; but now are they holy. 15. But if the unbelieving depart, let him depart. A brother or a sister is not under bondage in such cases: but God hath called us to peace. 16. For what knowest thou, O wife, whether thou shalt save thy husband? or how knowest thou, O man, whether thou shalt save thy wife? 17. But as God hath distributed to every man, as the Lord hath called every one, so let him walk. And so ordain I in all churches. 18. Is any man called being circumcised? let him not become uncircumcised. Is any called in uncircumcision? let him not be circumcised. 19. Circumcision

is nothing, and uncircumcision is nothing, but the keeping of the commandments of God. 20. Let every man abide in the same calling wherein he was called. 21. Art thou called *being* a servant? care not for it: but if thou mayest be made free, use *it* rather. 22. For he that is called in the Lord, *being* a servant, is the Lord's freeman: likewise also he that is called, *being* free, is Christ's servant. 23. Ye are bought with a price; be not ye the servants of men. 24. Brethren, let every man, wherein he is called, therein abide with God. 25. Now concerning virgins I have no commandment of the Lord: yet I give my judgment, as one that hath obtained mercy of the Lord to be faithful. 26. I suppose therefore that this is good for the present distress, *I say*, that *it is* good for a man so to be. 27. Art thou bound unto a wife? seek not to be loosed. Art thou loosed from a wife? seek not a wife. 28. But and if thou marry, thou hast not sinned; and if a virgin marry, she hath not sinned. Nevertheless such shall have trouble in the flesh: but I spare you. 29. But this I say, brethren, the time *is* short: it remaineth, that both they that have wives be as though they had none; 30. And they that weep, as though they wept not; and they that rejoice, as though they rejoiced not; and they that buy, as though they possessed not; 31. And they that use this world, as not abusing *it:* for the fashion of this world passeth away. 32. But I would have you without carefulness. He that is unmarried careth for the things that belong to the Lord, how he may please the Lord: 33. But he that is married careth for the things that are of the world, how he may please *his* wife. 34. There is difference *also* between a wife and a virgin. The unmarried woman careth for the things of the Lord, that she may be holy both in body and in spirit: but she that is married careth for the things of the world, how she may please *her* husband. 35. And this I speak for your own profit; not that I may cast a snare upon you, but for that which is comely, and that ye may attend upon the Lord without distraction. 36. But if any man think that he behaveth himself uncomely toward his virgin, if she pass the flower of *her* age, and need so require, let him do what he will, he sinneth not: let them marry. 37. Nevertheless he that standeth stedfast in his heart, having no necessity, but hath power over his own will, and hath so decreed in his heart that he will keep his virgin, doeth well. 38. So then he that giveth *her* in marriage doeth well; but he that giveth *her* not in marriage doeth better. 39. The wife is bound by the law as long as her husband liveth; but if her husband be dead, she is at liberty to be married to whom she will; only in the Lord. 40. But she is happier if she so abide, after my judgment: and I think also that I have the Spirit of God.

1 Cor. 9:5. Have we not power to lead about a sister, a wife, as well as other apostles, and *as* the brethren of the Lord, and Cephas?

1 Cor. 11:11. Nevertheless neither is the man without the woman, neither the woman without the man, in the Lord. 12. For as the woman *is* of the man, even so *is* the man also by the woman; but all things of God.

1 Tim. 3:2. A bishop then must be blameless, the husband of one wife, 12. Let the deacons be the husbands of one wife, ruling their children and their own houses well.

1 Tim. 4:1. Now the Spirit speaketh expressly, that in the latter times some shall depart from the faith, giving heed to seducing spirits, and doctrines of devils; 3. Forbidding to marry,

1 Tim. 5:14. I will therefore that the younger women marry, bear children, guide the house, give none occasion to the adversary to speak reproachfully.

Heb. 13:4. Marriage *is* honourable in all, and the bed undefiled: but whoremongers and adulterers God will judge.

FIGURATIVE: Isa. 54:5; 62:4,5; Jer. 3: 14; 31:32; Hos. 1:2; 2:19,20; Eph. 5:30-32; Rev. 19:7-9. Parables from, Matt. 22:2; 25:1-10.

See DIVORCE; HUSBAND; WIFE.

MARS' HILL, a hill in Athens, Acts 17:19-34.

MARTHA. Sister of Mary and Lazarus, John 11:1. Ministers to Jesus, Luke 10:38-42; John 12:2. Beloved by Jesus, John 11:5.

See LAZARUS; MARY.

MARTYRDOM. Psa. 44:22. Yea, for thy sake are we killed all the day long; we are counted as sheep for the slaughter. Rom. 8:36.

Matt. 10:21. And the brother shall deliver up the brother to death, and the father the child: and the children shall rise up against *their* parents, and cause them to be put to death. 22. And ye shall be hated of all *men* for my name's sake: but he that endureth to the end shall be saved. [Mark 13:12; Luke 21:16,17.] 39. He that findeth his life shall lose it: and he that loseth his life for my sake shall find it. Matt. 16:25; John 12:25.

Matt. 23:34. Wherefore, behold, I send unto you prophets, and wise men, and scribes: and *some* of them ye shall kill and crucify; and *some* of them shall ye scourge in your synagogues, and persecute *them* from city to city: [Luke 11:50.] 35. That upon you may come all the righteous blood shed upon the earth, from the blood of righteous Abel unto the blood of Zacharias son of Barachias, whom ye slew between the temple and the altar.

Matt. 24:9. Then shall they deliver you up to be afflicted, and shall kill you: and ye shall be hated of all nations for my name's sake.

Luke 9:24. For whosoever will save his

life shall lose it: but whosoever will lose his life for my sake, the same shall save it. John 12:25.

1 Cor. 13:3. And though I bestow all my goods to feed *the poor*, and though I give my body to be burned, and have not charity, it profiteth me nothing.

Rev. 6:9. And when he had opened the fifth seal, I saw under the altar the souls of them that were slain for the word of God, and for the testimony which they held: 10. And they cried with a loud voice, saying, How long, O Lord, holy and true, dost thou not judge and avenge our blood on them that dwell on the earth? 11. And white robes were given unto every one of them: and it was said unto them, that they should rest yet for a little season, until their fellow-servants also and their brethren, that should be killed as they *were*, should be fulfilled.

Rev. 11:7. And when they shall have finished their testimony, the beast that ascendeth out of the bottomless pit shall make war against them, and shall overcome them, and kill them. 8. And their dead bodies *shall lie* in the street of the great city, which spiritually is called Sodom and Egypt, where also our Lord was crucified. 9. And they of the people and kindreds and tongues and nations shall see their dead bodies three days and an half, and shall not suffer their dead bodies to be put in graves. 10. And they that dwell upon the earth shall rejoice over them, and make merry, and shall send gifts one to another; because these two prophets tormented them that dwelt on the earth. 11. And after three days and an half the Spirit of life from God entered into them, and they stood upon their feet; and great fear fell upon them which saw them. 12. And they heard a great voice from heaven saying unto them, Come up hither. And they ascended up to heaven in a cloud; and their enemies beheld them.

Rev. 12:11. And they overcame him by the blood of the Lamb, and by the word of their testimony; and they loved not their lives unto the death.

Rev. 16:6. For they have shed the blood of saints and prophets, and thou hast given them blood to drink: for they are worthy.

Rev. 17:6. And I saw the woman drunken with the blood of the saints, and with the blood of the martyrs of Jesus: and when I saw her, I wondered with great admiration. See PERSECUTION.

INSTANCES OF: Abel, Gen. 4:3-8. Prophets slain by Jezebel, 1 Kin. 18:4,13. Zechariah, 2 Chr. 24:21,22. John the Baptist, Mark 6:18-28. Jesus, see JESUS. Stephen, Acts 7:58-60. James the apostle, Acts 12:2. The prophets, Matt. 22:6; 23:35; Rom. 11:3; 1 Thess. 2:15; Heb. 11:32-37.

MARY. 1. The mother of Jesus, Matt. 1:16; Luke 1:26-38; 2:5-19. Visits her cousin Elisabeth, Luke 1:39-56. Attends the feast at Jerusalem with her husband and her

son, starts on the return, misses Jesus, seeks and finds him in the temple, Luke 2:48-51. Is present with Jesus at a marriage in Cana of Galilee, John 2:1-10. Seeks Jesus when he is teaching in a house, Matt. 12:46,47; Mark 3:31; Luke 8:19. Present at the cross, John 19:25-27. Is committed to the care of John, John 19:27. Dwells with the disciples in Jerusalem, Acts 1:14. Prophecies concerning, Isa. 7:14; Luke 2:35.

2. Magdalene. Possessed of devils, delivered by Jesus, Mark 16:9; Luke 8:2,3. Present at the crucifixion, Matt. 27:56; Mark 15:40; John 19:25; at the sepulcher, Matt. 27:61; 28:1-7; Mark 15:47; 16:1-7; Luke 23:55, 56; 24:1-7; John 20:1,11-13. Recognizes Jesus after the resurrection, Matt. 28:8-10; Mark 16:9; John 20:14-18.

3. Sister of Mary the mother of Jesus and wife of Cleophas, John 19:25. Mother of James and Joses, Matt. 27:56; Mark 15:40; John 19:25. At the sepulcher, Matt. 27:61; Mark 15:47. Assists in preparing the body of Jesus for burial, Matt. 28:1; Mark 16:1. A witness of the resurrection, Luke 24:10.

4. Sister of Lazarus. Sits at Jesus' feet for instruction, Luke 10:38-42. Beloved of Jesus, John 11:1,5. Anoints Jesus, Matt. 26:7-13; Mark 14:3-9; John 11:2; 12:3.

5. Mother of Mark and sister of Barnabas, Acts 12:12; Col. 4:10.

6. A Christian woman in Rome, Rom. 16:6.

MASCHIL. See MUSIC.

MASH, son of Aram, Gen. 10:23.

MASHAL, called also MISHAL and MISHEAL. A Levitical city in Asher, Josh. 19:26; 21:30; 1 Chr. 6:74.

MASKING, by Tamar, Gen. 38:14.

MASON. A trade in the time of David, 2 Sam. 5:11; of later times, 2 Kin. 12:12; 22:6; 1 Chr. 14:1; Ezra 3:7.

MASREKAH, a place in Edom, Gen. 36:36; 1 Chr. 1:47.

MASSA, son of Ishmael, Gen. 25:14; 1 Chr. 1:30.

MASSACRE. Authorized by Moses, Deut. 20:13,16. Decree to destroy the Jews, Esth. 3.

INSTANCES OF: Inhabitants of Heshbon, Deut. 2:34; of Bashan, Deut. 3:6; of Ai, Josh. 8:24-26; of Hazor, Josh. 11:11,12; of the cities of the seven kings, Josh. 10:28-40. Midianites, Num. 31:7,8. Prophets of Baal, 1 Kin. 18:40. Worshipers of Baal, 2 Kin. 10:18-28. Sons of Ahab, 2 Kin. 10:1-8. Seed royal of Athaliah, 2 Kin. 11:1. Inhabitants of Tiphsah, 2 Kin. 15:16. Edomites, 2 Kin. 14:7.

See CAPTIVE.

MASSAH, an encampment of the Israelites, Ex. 17:7.

See MERIBAH.

MASTER. Jesus called, Matt. 8:19; 10:25; 23:8; 26:18,25,49; Mark 14:45; Luke 8:24; John 13:13,14. Jesus prohibited the appellation, Matt. 23:8.

SCRIPTURES RELATING TO MASTERS OF SERVANTS: Ex. 21:20. And if a man smite his servant, or his maid, with a rod, and he die under his hand; he shall be surely punished. 21. Notwithstanding, if he continue a day or two, he shall not be punished: for he *is* his money. 26. And if a man smite the eye of his servant, or the eye of his maid, that it perish; he shall let him go free for his eye's sake. 27. And if he smite out his manservant's tooth, or his maidservant's tooth; he shall let him go free for his tooth's sake.

Lev. 19:13. Thou shalt not defraud thy neighbour, neither rob *him:* the wages of him that is hired shall not abide with thee all night until the morning.

Lev. 25:43. Thou shalt not rule over him with rigour; but shalt fear thy God.

Deut. 5:14. The seventh day *is* the sabbath of the LORD thy God: *in it* thou shalt not do any work, thou, nor thy son, nor thy daughter, nor thy manservant, nor thy maidservant, nor thine ox, nor thine ass, nor any of thy cattle, nor thy stranger that *is* within thy gates; that thy manservant and thy maidservant may rest as well as thou.

Deut. 24:14. Thou shalt not oppress an hired servant *that is* poor and needy, *whether he be* of thy brethren, or of thy strangers that *are* in thy land within thy gates: 15. At his day thou shalt give *him* his hire, neither shall the sun go down upon it; for he *is* poor, and setteth his heart upon it: lest he cry against thee unto the LORD, and it be sin unto thee. Lev. 19:13.

Job. 31:13. If I did despise the cause of my manservant or of my maidservant, when they contended with me; 14. What then shall I do when God riseth up? and when he visiteth, what shall I answer him? 15. Did not he that made me in the womb make him? and did not one fashion us in the womb?

Prov. 22:16. He that oppresseth the poor to increase his *riches, and* he that giveth to the rich, *shall* surely *come* to want.

Prov. 29:12. If a ruler hearken to lies, all his servants *are* wicked. 21. He that delicately bringeth up his servant from a child shall have him become *his* son at the length.

Jer. 22:13. Woe unto him that buildeth his house by unrighteousness, and his chambers by wrong; *that* useth his neighbour's service without wages, and giveth him not for his work;

Mal. 3:5. And I will come near to you to judgment; and I will be a swift witness against . . . those that oppress the hireling in *his* wages.

Rom. 4:4. Now to him that worketh is the reward not reckoned of grace, but of debt.

Eph. 6:9. Ye masters, do the same things unto them, forbearing threatening: knowing that your Master also in his heaven; neither is there respect of persons with him.

Col. 4:1. Masters, give unto *your* servants that which is just and equal; knowing that ye also have a Master in heaven.

1 Tim. 5:18. For the scripture saith, Thou shalt not muzzle the ox that treadeth out the corn. And, The labourer *is* worthy of his reward.

Philem. 10. I beseech thee for my son Onesimus, whom I have begotten in my bonds: 11. Which in time past was to thee unprofitable, but now profitable to thee and to me: 12. Whom I have sent again: thou therefore receive him, that is, mine own bowels: 13. Whom I would have retained with me, that in thy stead he might have ministered unto me in the bonds of the gospel: 14. But without thy mind would I do nothing; that thy benefit should not be as it were of necessity, but willingly. 15. For perhaps he therefore departed for a season, that thou shouldest receive him for ever; 16. Not now as a servant, but above a servant, a brother beloved, specially to me, but how much more unto thee, both in the flesh, and in the Lord?

Jas. 5:4. Behold, the hire of the labourers who have reaped down your fields, which is of you kept back by fraud, crieth: and the cries of them which have reaped are entered into the ears of the Lord of sabaoth.

See SERVANT.

GOOD: INSTANCES OF: Abraham, Gen. 18:19; Job, Job 31:13–15; the centurion, Luke 7:2.

UNJUST: INSTANCES OF: Sarah to Hagar, Gen. 16:6. Laban to Jacob, Gen. 31:7; Potiphar's wife to Joseph, Gen. 39:7–20.

MASTER WORKMAN, Prov. [R. V.] 8:30; 1 Cor. 3:10.

INSTANCES OF: Tubal-cain, Gen. 4:22; Bezaleel, Ex. 31:2–11; 35:30–35; Hiram, 1 Kin. 7:13–50; 2 Chr. 2:13,14; 4:11–18. See ART.

MATERIALISM, Acts 23:8. See INFIDELITY.

MATRED, mother of Mehetabel, Gen. 36:39; 1 Chr. 1:50.

MATRI, a Benjamite, 1 Sam. 10:21.

MATTAN. 1. A priest of Baal slain in the idol temple at Jerusalem, 2 Kin. 11:18; 2 Chr. 23:17.

2. Father of Shephatiah, Jer. 38:1.

MATTANAH, a station of Israel, Num. 21:18,19.

MATTANIAH. 1. Original name of Zedekiah, king of Judah, 2 Kin. 24:17. See ZEDEKIAH.

2. A Levite of the sons of Asaph. 2 Chr. 20:14; Neh. 12:8.

3. Son of Heman, who had charge of the ninth division of musicians, 1 Chr. 25:4,16.

4. Descendant of Asaph, who assisted in purifying the temple, 2 Chr. 29:13.

5. Four Israelites who divorced their Gentile wives after the captivity, Ezra 10: 26,27,30,37.

6. A Levite, father of Zaccur, Neh. 13:13.

MATTATHA, an ancestor of Jesus, Luke 3:31.

MATTATHAH, one of the family of Hashum, Ezra 10:33.

MATTATHIAS, an ancestor of Jesus, Luke 3:25.26.

MATTENAI. 1. Two Israelites who put away their Gentile wives after the captivity, Ezra 10:33,37.

2. A priest in the time of Joiakim, Neh. 12:19.

MATTHAN, an ancestor of Jesus, Matt. 1:15.

MATTHAT. 1. Father of Heli, and ancestor of Joseph, Luke 3:24.

2. Father of Jorim, and ancestor of Joseph, Luke 3:29.

MATTHEW, called also LEVI. A receiver of customs. Becomes a disciple of Jesus, Matt. 9:9,10; 10:3; Mark 2:14,15; 3:18; Luke 5:27–29; 6:15; Acts 1:13.

MATTHIAS, surnamed JUSTUS. Chosen as an apostle in the place of Judas, Acts 1:15–26.

MATTITHIAH. 1. A Levite who had charge of the baked offerings, 1 Chr. 9:31.

2. A Levite musician, 1 Chr. 15:18,21; 16:5.

3. A chief of the fourteenth division of temple musicians, 1 Chr. 25:3,21.

4. An Israelite who divorced his Gentile wife after the captivity, Ezra 10:43.

5. A prince who stood by Ezra when he read the law to the people, Neh. 8:4.

MATTOCK, 1 Sam. 13:20,21; Isa. 7:25.

MAUL, Prov. 25:18.

MAZZAROTH, probably signs of the zodiac, see Job 38:32 [*R. V.*].

See MUSIC.

MEAH, a tower in Jerusalem, Neh. 3:1; 12:39.

MEAL. See EATING; FOOD.

MEASURE. The following modern equivalents of ancient measurements are based upon the latest researches, and are probably as nearly correct as is possible at this time:

DRY: 1. Bushel, about a peck, Matt. 5:15; Mark 4:21; Luke 11:33.

2. Cab, or kab, about two quarts, 2 Kin. 6:25.

3. Cor, equal to one homer or ten ephahs, equal to about eleven and one-ninth bushels, 1 Kin. 4:22; 5:11; 2 Chr. 2:10; 27:5; Ezra 7:22.

4. Ephah, equal to three seah, and in liquid, to a bath, containing about a bushel and a half, Ex. 16:36; Lev. 5:11; 6:20; 19:36; Num. 5:15; 28:5; Judg. 6:19; Ruth 2:17; 1 Sam. 1:24; 17:17; Isa. 5:10; Ezek. 45:10,11,13,24; 46:5,7,11,14; Amos 8:5; Zech. 5:6–10.

5. Half-homer, about five and a half bushels, Hos. 3:2.

6. Homer, about eleven bushels, equal to a cor or ten ephahs, Lev. 27:16; Num. 11:32; Isa. 5:10; Ezek. 45:11–14; Hos. 3:2.

7. Omer, about one bushel, Ex. 16:16,18, 22,32,33,36.

8. Seah, about a peck and a half, Gen. 18:6; 1 Sam. 25:18; 1 Kin. 18:32; 2 Kin. 7:1,16,18.

9. Tenth deal, about a gallon, equal to one-tenth of an ephah, Ex. 29:40; Lev. 14:10,21; 23:13,17; 24:5; Num. 15:4,6,9; 28:9,12,13,20,21, 28,29; 29:3,4,9,10,14,15.

LIQUID: 1. Bath, about eight gallons and a half, 1 Kin. 7:26,38; 2 Chr. 2:10; 4:5; Ezra 7:22; Isa. 5:10; Ezek. 45:10,11,14; Luke 16:6.

2. Firkin, nearly nine gallons, John 2:6.

3. Hin, about a gallon and a half, Ex. 29:40; 30:24; Lev. 19:36; 23:13; Num. 15:4–10; 28:5,7,14; Ezek. 4:11; 45:24; 46:5,7,11,14.

4. Log, about a pint, one-twelfth of a hin, Lev. 14:10,12,15,21,24.

See WEIGHTS.

LINEAR: 1. Finger, Jer. 52:21.

2. Handbreadth, Ex. 25:25; 37:12; 1 Kin. 7:26; 2 Chr. 4:5; Psa. 39:5; Ezek. 40:5,43; 43:13.

3. Span, Ex. 28:16; 1 Sam. 17:4; Isa. 40:12; 48:13; Lam. 2:20; Ezek. 43:13.

4. Cubit, the length of the forearm. See CUBIT.

5. Reed, probably six cubits, Ezek. 40:5.

6. Fathom, Acts 27:28.

7. Pace, 2 Sam. 6:13.

8. Furlong, Luke 24:13.

9. Mile, probably nine-tenths of an English mile, Matt. 5:41.

10. Sabbath day's journey, two thousand paces, Acts 1:12.

MUST BE JUST: Lev. 19:35. Ye shall do no unrighteousness in judgment, in meteyard, in weight, or in measure. 36. Just balances, just weights, a just ephah, and a just hin, shall ye have: I *am* the LORD your God, which brought you out of the land of Egypt.

Deut. 25:13. Thou shalt not have in thy bag divers weights, a great and a small. 14. Thou shalt not have in thine house divers measures, a great and a small. 15. *But* thou shalt have a perfect and just weight, a perfect and just measure shalt thou have: that thy days may be lengthened in the land which the LORD thy God giveth thee. 16. For all that do such things, *and* all that do unrighteously, *are* an abomination unto the LORD thy God.

Prov. 11:1. A false balance *is* abomination to the LORD: but a just weight *is* his delight.

Prov. 16:11. A just weight and balance *are* the LORD's: all the weights of the bag *are* his work.

Prov. 20:10. Divers weights, *and* divers measures, both of them *are* alike abomination to the LORD. 23. Divers weights *are* an abomination unto the LORD; and a false balance *is* not good.

Hos. 12:7. *He is* a merchant, the balances of deceit *are* in his hand: he loveth to oppress. 8. And Ephraim said, Yet I am become rich, I have found me out substance: *in* all my labours they shall find none iniquity in me that *were* sin. 9. And I *that am* the LORD thy God from the land of Egypt will yet make thee to dwell in tabernacles, as in the days of the solemn feast.

Mic. 6:10. Are there yet the treasures of

wickedness in the house of the wicked, and the scant measure *that is* abominable? 11. Shall I count *them* pure with the wicked balances, and with the bag of deceitful weights? 12. For the rich men thereof are full of violence, and the inhabitants thereof have spoken lies, and their tongue *is* deceitful in their mouth.

See DISHONESTY; INTEGRITY.

MEAT OFFERING. See OFFERINGS, MEAT.

MEBUNNAI, one of David's guards, 2 Sam. 23:27.

MECHANIC, Prov. [*R. V.*] 8:30; 1 Cor. 3:10.

INSTANCES OF: Tubal-cain, Gen. 4:22. Bezaleel, Ex. 31:2–11; 35:30–35. Hiram, 1 Kin. 7:13–50; 2 Chr. 2:13,14; 4:11–18.

See ART.

MEDAD, one of the seventy elders who did not go to the tabernacle with Moses, but prophesied in the camp, Num. 11:26–29.

MEDAN, son of Abraham and Keturah, Gen. 25:2; 1 Chr. 1:32.

MEDDLING. See BUSYBODY; TALE-BEARER.

MEDEBA. A city of Moab, Num. 21:30. An idolatrous high place, Isa. 15:2. Allotted to Reuben, Josh. 13:9,16. David defeats army and the Ammonites at, 1 Chr. 19:7–15.

MEDES. Inhabitants of Media. Israelites distributed among, when carried to Assyria, 2 Kin. 17:6; 18:11. Palace in the Babylonian province of, Ezra 6:2. An essential part of the Medo-Persian empire, Esth. 1: 1–19. Supremacy of, in the Chaldean empire, Dan. 5:28,31; 9:1; 11:1.

MEDIA. See MEDES.

MEDIATION. See INTERCESSION; JESUS, MEDIATOR.

MEDICINE. Prov. 17:22. A merry heart doeth good *like* a medicine: but a broken spirit drieth the bones.

Isa. 1:6. From the sole of the foot even unto the head *there is* no soundness in it; *but* wounds, and bruises, and putrifying sores: they have not been closed, neither bound up, neither mollified with ointment.

Isa. 38:21. For Isaiah had said, Let them take a lump of figs, and lay *it* for a plaister upon the boil, and he shall recover.

Jer. 8:22. *Is there* no balm in Gilead; *is there* no physician there? why then is not the health of the daughter of my people recovered?

Jer. 30:13. *There is* none to plead thy cause, that thou mayest be bound up: thou hast no healing medicines.

Jer. 46:11. Go up into Gilead, and take balm, O virgin, the daughter of Egypt: in vain shalt thou use many medicines; *for* thou shalt not be cured.

Jer. 51:8. Babylon is suddenly fallen and destroyed: howl for her; take balm for her pain, if so be she may be healed. 9. We would have healed Babylon, but she is not healed: forsake her, and let us go every one into his own country: for her judgment

reacheth unto heaven, and is lifted up *even* to the skies.

Ezek. 47:12. And by the river upon the the bank thereof, on this side and on that side, shall grow all trees for meat, whose leaves shall not fade, neither shall the fruit thereof be consumed: it shall bring forth new fruit according to his months, because their waters they issued out of the sanctuary: and the fruit thereof shall be for meat, and the leaf thereof for medicine.

Luke 10:34. And went to *him,* and bound up his wounds, pouring in oil and wine, and set him on his own beast, and brought him to an inn, and took care of him.

Rev. 22:2. In the midst of the street of it, and on either side of the river, *was there* the tree of life, which bare twelve *manner of* fruits, *and* yielded her fruit every month: and the leaves of the tree *were* for the healing of the nations.

See DISEASES; PHYSICIAN.

MEDITATION. Josh. 1:8. This book of the law shall not depart out of thy mouth; but thou shalt meditate therein day and night, that thou mayest observe to do according to all that is written therein: for then thou shalt make thy way prosperous, and then thou shalt have good success.

Psa. 1:2. But his delight *is* in the law of the LORD, and in his law doth he meditate day and night.

Psa. 4:4. Stand in awe, and sin not: commune with your own heart upon your bed, and be still.

Psa. 19:14. Let the words of my mouth, and the meditation of my heart, be acceptable in thy sight, O LORD, my strength, and my redeemer.

Psa. 39:3. My heart was hot within me, while I was musing the fire burned: *then* spake I with my tongue,

Psa. 49:3. My mouth shall speak of wisdom; and the meditation of my heart *shall be* of understanding.

Psa. 63:5. My soul shall be satisfied as *with* marrow and fatness; and my mouth shall praise *thee* with joyful lips: 6. When I remember thee upon my bed, *and* meditate on thee in the *night* watches.

Psa. 73:12. Behold, these *are* the ungodly, who prosper in the world; they increase *in* riches. 13. Verily I have cleansed my heart *in* vain, and washed my hands in innocency. 14. For all the day long have I been plagued, and chastened every morning. 15. If I say, I will speak thus; behold, I should offend *against* the generation of thy children. 16. When I thought to know this, it *was* too painful for me; 17. Until I went into the sanctuary of God; *then* understood I their end. 18. Surely thou didst set them in slippery places: thou castedst them down into destruction. 19. How are they *brought* into desolation, as in a moment! they are utterly consumed with terrors. 20. As a dream when *one* awaketh; *so,* O Lord, when thou awakest, thou shalt despise their image.

21. Thus my heart was grieved, and I was pricked in my reins. 22. So foolish *was* I, and ignorant:

Psa. 77:10. And I said, This *is* my infirmity: *but I will remember* the years of the right hand of the most High. 11. I will remember the works of the LORD: surely I will remember thy wonders of old. 12. I will meditate also of all thy work, and talk of thy doings.

Psa. 104:34. My meditation of him shall be sweet: I will be glad in the LORD.

Psa. 119:11. Thy word have I hid in mine heart, that I might not sin against thee. 15. I will meditate in thy precepts, and have respect unto thy ways. 16. I will delight myself in thy statutes: I will not forget thy word. 23. Princes also did sit *and* speak against me: *but* thy servant did meditate in thy statutes. 48. My hands also will I lift up unto thy commandments, which I have loved; and I will meditate in thy statutes. 55. I have remembered thy name, O LORD, in the night, and have kept thy law. 59. I thought on my ways, and turned my feet unto thy testimonies. 78. Let the proud be ashamed; for they dealt perversely with me without a cause: *but* I will meditate in thy precepts. 97. O how love I thy law! it *is* my meditation all the day. 98. Thou through thy commandments hast made me wiser than mine enemies· 99. I have more understanding than all my teachers: for thy testimonies *are* my meditation. 148. Mine eyes prevent the *night* watches, that I might meditate in thy word.

Psa. 139:17. How precious also are thy thoughts unto me, O God! how great is the sum of them! 18. *If* I should count them, they are more in number than the sand: when I awake, I am still with thee.

Psa. 143:5. I remember the days of old; I meditate on all thy works; I muse on the work of thy hands.

1 Tim. 4:13. Till I come, give attention to reading, to exhortation, to doctrine. 14. Neglect not the gift that is in thee, which was given thee by prophecy, with the laying on of the hands of the presbytery. 15. Meditate upon these things; give thyself wholly to them; that thy profiting may appear to all.

INSTANCE OF: Isaac, Gen. 24:63.

MEDITERRANEAN SEA. Mentioned in scripture as the great sea, Num. 34:6,7; Josh. 1:4; 9:1; 15:12,47; 23:4; Ezek. 47:10,15, 20; 48:28; Sea of the Philistines, Ex. 23:31; Sea of Joppa, Ezra 3:7; the hinder sea, Zech. 14:8; the uttermost sea, Deut. 11:24; the utmost sea, Joel 2:20.

MEEKNESS. Psa. 22:26. The meek shall eat and be satisfied: they shall praise the LORD that seek him: your heart shall live for ever.

Psa. 25:9. The meek will he guide in judgment: and the meek will he teach his way.

Psa. 37:11. But the meek shall inherit the earth; and shall delight themselves in the abundance of peace.

Psa. 76:8. Thou didst cause judgment to be heard from heaven; the earth feared, and was still, 9. When God arose to judgment, to save all the meek of the earth.

Psa. 147:6. The LORD lifteth up the meek: he casteth the wicked down to the ground.

Psa. 149:4. For the LORD taketh pleasure in his people: he will beautify the meek with salvation.

Prov. 14:29. *He that is* slow to wrath *is* of great understanding:

Prov. 15:1. A soft answer turneth away wrath: 18. *He that is* slow to anger appeaseth strife.

Prov. 16:32. *He that is* slow to anger *is* better than the mighty; and he that ruleth his spirit than he that taketh a city.

Prov. 17:1. Better *is* a dry morsel, and quietness therewith, than an house full of sacrifices *with* strife.

Prov. 19:11. The discretion of a man deferreth his anger; and *it is* his glory to pass over a transgression.

Prov. 20:3. *It is* an honour for a man to cease from strife.

Prov. 25:15. By long forbearing is a prince persuaded, and a soft tongue breaketh the bone.

Prov. 29:8. Wise *men* turn away wrath.

Eccl. 7:8. The patient in spirit *is* better than the proud in spirit.

Eccl. 10:4. If the spirit of the ruler rise up against thee, leave not thy place: for yielding pacifieth great offences.

Isa. 11:4. But with righteousness shall he judge the poor, and reprove with equity for the meek of the earth: and he shall smite the earth with the rod of his mouth, and with the breath of his lips shall he slay the wicked.

Isa. 29:19. The meek also shall increase *their* joy in the LORD, and the poor among men shall rejoice in the Holy One of Israel.

Lam. 3:28. He sitteth alone and keepeth silence, because he hath borne *it* upon him. 29. He putteth his mouth in the dust; if so be there may be hope. 30. He giveth *his* cheek to him that smiteth him: he is filled full with reproach.

Amos 3:3. Can two walk together, except they be agreed?

Zeph. 2:3. Seek ye the LORD, all ye meek of the earth, which have wrought his judgment: seek righteousness, seek meekness:

Matt. 5:5. Blessed *are* the meek: for they shall inherit the earth. 9. Blessed *are* the peacemakers: for they shall be called the children of God. 38. Ye have heard that it hath been said, An eye for an eye, and a tooth for a tooth: 39. But I say unto you, That ye resist not evil: but whosoever shall smite thee on thy right cheek, turn to him the other also. 40. And if any man will sue thee at the law, and take away thy coat, let him have *thy* cloke also. [Luke 6:29.] 41. And whosoever shall compel thee to go a mile, go with him twain. 42. Give to him that asketh thee, and from him that would borrow of thee turn not thou away.

Matt. 11:29. Take my yoke upon you, and learn of me; for I am meek and lowly in heart: and ye shall find rest unto your souls.

Matt. 27:13. Then said Pilate unto him, Hearest thou not how many things they witness against thee? 14. And he answered him to never a word; insomuch that the governor marvelled greatly.

Mark 9:50. Salt *is* good: but if the salt have lost his saltness, wherewith will ye season it? Have salt in yourselves, and have peace one with another.

Rom. 12:14. Bless them which persecute you: bless, and curse not. 18. If it be possible, as much as lieth in you, live peaceably with all men.

Rom. 14:19. Let us therefore follow after the things which make for peace, and things wherewith one may edify another.

1 Cor. 6:7. Now therefore there is utterly a fault among you, because ye go to law one with another. Why do ye not rather take wrong? why do ye not rather *suffer your-selves to* be defrauded?

1 Cor. 7:15. But if the unbelieving depart, let him depart. A brother or a sister is not under bondage in such *cases:* but God hath called us to peace.

1 Cor. 10:32. Give none offence, neither to the Jews, nor to the Gentiles, nor to the church of God:

1 Cor. 13:4. Charity suffereth long, *and* is kind; charity envieth not; charity vaunt-eth not itself, is not puffed up, 5. Doth not behave itself unseemly, seeketh not her own, is not easily provoked, thinketh no evil; 7. Beareth all things, believeth all things, hopeth all things, endureth all things.

2 Cor. 10:1. Now I Paul myself beseech you by the meekness and gentleness of Christ, who in presence *am* base among you, but being absent am bold toward you:

2 Cor. 13:11. Be perfect, be of good comfort, be of one mind, live in peace; and the God of love and peace shall be with you.

Gal. 5:22. The fruit of the Spirit is love, joy, peace, longsuffering, gentleness, goodness, [1]faith, 23. Meekness, temperance: against such there is no law. 26. Let us not be desirous of vain glory, provoking one another, envying one another.   [1 R. V. faithfulness]

Gal. 6:1. Brethren, if a man be overtaken in a fault, ye which are spiritual, restore such an one in the spirit of meekness; considering thyself, lest thou also be tempted.

Eph. 4:1. I therefore, the prisoner of the Lord, beseech you that ye walk worthy of the vocation wherewith ye are called, 2. With all lowliness and meekness, with long-suffering, forbearing one another in love;

Phil. 2:14. Do all things without murmurings and disputings: 15. That ye may be blameless and harmless, the sons of God, without rebuke, in the midst of a crooked

and perverse nation, among whom ye shine as lights in the world;

Col. 3:12. Put on therefore, as the elect of God, holy and beloved, bowels of mercies, kindness, humbleness of mind, meekness, longsuffering; 13. Forbearing one another, and forgiving one another, if any man have a quarrel against any: even as Christ forgave you, so also *do* ye.

1 Thess. 5:14. Now we exhort you, brethren, . . . be patient toward all *men.* 15. See that none render evil for evil unto any *man;* but ever follow that which is good, both among yourselves, and to all *men.*

2 Thess. 3:5. The Lord direct your hearts into the love of God, and into the [1]patient waiting for Christ.   [1 R. V. patience of]

1 Tim. 3:2. A bishop then must be blameless, the husband of one wife, vigilant, sober, of good behaviour, given to hospitality, apt to teach; 3. Not given to wine, no striker, not greedy of filthy lucre; but patient, not a brawler, not covetous;

1 Tim. 6:11. Follow after righteousness, godliness, faith, love, patience, meekness. 12. Fight the good fight of faith, lay hold on eternal life, whereunto thou art also called, and hast professed a good profession before many witnesses.

2 Tim. 2:24. The servant of the Lord must not strive; but be gentle unto all *men,* apt to teach, patient, 25. In meekness instructing those that oppose themselves;

Tit. 2:2. That the aged men be sober, grave, temperate, sound in faith, in charity, in patience. 9. *Exhort* servants to be obedient unto their own masters, *and* to please *them* well in all *things;* not answering again;

Tit. 3:2. To speak evil of no man, to be no brawlers, *but* gentle, shewing all meekness unto all men.

Heb. 10:36. Ye have need of patience, that, after ye have done the will of God, ye might receive the promise.

Heb. 12:14. Follow peace with all *men,*

Jas. 1:4. Let patience have *her* perfect work, that ye may be perfect and entire, wanting nothing. 19. Wherefore, my beloved brethren, let every man be swift to hear, slow to speak, slow to wrath: 21. Wherefore lay apart all filthiness and superfluity of naughtiness, and receive with meekness the engrafted word, which is able to save your souls.

Jas. 3:13. Who *is* a wise man and endued with knowledge among you? let him shew out of a good conversation his works with meekness of wisdom. 17. The wisdom that is from above is first pure, then peaceable, gentle, *and* easy to be intreated, full of mercy and good fruits, without partiality, and without hypocrisy. 18. And the fruit of righteousness is sown in peace of them that make peace.

1 Pet. 2:18. Servants, *be* subject to *your* masters with all fear; not only to the good and gentle, but also to the froward. 19. For this *is* thankworthy, if a man for conscience

toward God endure grief, suffering wrongfully. 20. For what glory *is it*, if, when ye be buffeted for your faults, ye shall take it patiently? but if, when ye do well, and suffer *for it*, ye take it patiently, this *is* acceptable with God. 21. For even hereunto were ye called: because Christ also suffered for us, leaving us an example, that ye should follow his steps: 22. Who did no sin, neither was guile found in his mouth: 23. Who, when he was reviled, reviled not again; when he suffered, he threatened not; but committed *himself* to him that judgeth righteously:

1 Pet. 3:4. But *let it be* the hidden man of the heart, in that which is not corruptible, *even the ornament* of a meek and quiet spirit, which is in the sight of God of great price. 11. Let him eschew evil, and do good; let him seek peace, and ensue it. 15. *Be* ready always to *give* an answer to every man that asketh you a reason of the hope that is in you with meekness and fear: Psa. 34:14.

2 Pet. 1:5. And beside this, giving all diligence, add to your faith virtue; and to virtue knowledge; 6. And to knowledge temperance; and to temperance patience; and to patience godliness; 7. And to godliness brotherly kindness; and to brotherly kindness charity.

Jude 9. Yet Michael the archangel, when contending with the devil he disputed about the body of Moses, durst not bring against him a railing accusation, but said, The Lord rebuke thee.

INSTANCES OF: Abraham, Gen. 13:8. Isaac, Gen. 26:20–22. Moses, Ex. 2:13; 14: 13,14; 15:24; 16:7,8; 17:2; Num. 12:3; 16:4–11. Gideon, Judg. 8:2,3. Hannah, 1 Sam. 1:13–16. Saul, 1 Sam. 10:27. David, 1 Sam. 17: 29; 2 Sam. 16:9–14; Psa. 38:13,14; 120:5–7. Paul, Acts 21:20–26; 1 Thess. 2:7; 2 Tim. 4: 16. The Thessalonians, 2 Thess. 1:4. Job, Jas. 5:11. The angel, Jude 9. For the meekness of Jesus, see below.

See HUMILITY; KINDNESS; PATIENCE.

OF JESUS: Isa. 42:1. Behold my servant, whom I uphold; mine elect, *in whom* my soul delighteth; I have put my spirit upon him: he shall bring forth judgment to the Gentiles. 2. He shall not cry, nor lift up, nor cause his voice to be heard in the street. 3. A bruised reed shall he not break, and the smoking flax shall he not quench: he shall bring forth judgment unto truth. 4. He shall not fail nor be discouraged, till he have set judgment in the earth: and the isles shall wait for his law. Matt. 12:19,20.

Isa. 53:7. He was oppressed, and he was afflicted, yet he opened not his mouth: he is brought as a lamb to the slaughter, and as a sheep before her shearers is dumb, so he openeth not his mouth.

Matt. 26:47. And while he yet spake, lo, Judas, one of the twelve, came, and with him a great multitude with swords and staves, from the chief priests and elders of the people. 48. Now he that betrayed him gave them a sign, saying, Whomsoever I shall kiss, that same is he: hold him fast. 49. And forthwith he came to Jesus, and said, Hail, master; and kissed him. 50. And Jesus said unto him, Friend, wherefore art thou come? Then came they, and laid hands on Jesus, and took him. 51. And, behold, one of them which were with Jesus stretched out *his* hand, and drew his sword, and struck a servant of the high priest's, and smote off his ear. 52. Then said Jesus unto him, Put up again thy sword into his place: for all they that take the sword shall perish with the sword. 53. Thinkest thou that I cannot now pray to my Father, and he shall presently give me more than twelve legions of angels? 54. But how then shall the scriptures be fulfilled, that thus it must be?

See JESUS, HUMILITY OF.

MEGIDDO, called also MEGIDDON, and probably ARMAGEDDON. A city in Issachar, situated on the southern edge of the plain of Esdraelon, Josh. 17:11; 1 Chr. 7:29. Conquest of, by Joshua, Josh. 12:21. Walled by Solomon, 1 Kin. 9:15; included in one of Solomon's commissary districts, 1 Kin. 4:12. Ahaziah dies at, 2 Kin. 9:27. Valley of, Deborah defeats Sisera in, Judg. 5:19. Josiah slain at, by Pharaoh-nechoh, 2 Kin. 23: 29,30; 2 Chr. 35:22–24. Prophecy concerning, Zech. 12:11.

MEHETABEEL, a person whose grandson tried to intimidate Nehemiah, Neh. 6:10.

MEHETABEL, wife of Hadar, Gen. 36:39; 1 Chr. 1:50.

MEHIDA, a person whose descendants returned from Babylon, Ezra 2:52; Neh. 7:54.

MEHIR, son of Chelub, 1 Chr. 4:11.

MEHOLATHITE, an inhabitant of a city in Issachar, 1 Sam. 18:19; 2 Sam. 21:8.

MEHUJAEL, son of Irad, Gen. 4:18.

MEHUMAN, a chamberlain of Ahasuerus, Esth. 1:10.

MEHUNIM, called also MEUNIM. A person whose descendants returned from exile, Ezra 2:50; Neh. 7:52.

ME-JARKON, a city in Dan, Josh. 19: 46.

MEKONAH, a city in Judah, Neh. 11: 28.

MELATIAH, a Gibeonite who assisted in repairing the wall of Jerusalem, Neh. 3:7.

MELCHI. 1. Ancestor of Jesus, Luke 3:24.

2. Remote ancestor of Jesus, Luke 3:28.

MELCHESEDEC. See MELCHIZEDEK.

MELCHISHUA, called also MALCHISHUA. Son of king Saul, 1 Sam. 14:49; 31:2; 1 Chr. 8:33; 9:39; 10:2.

MELCHIZEDEK. King of Salem, Gen. 14:18–20; Psa. 110:4. A priest and type of Christ, Heb. 5:6,10; 6:20; 7:1–21.

MELECH, son of Micah, 1 Chr. 8:35; 9: 41.

MELICU, a priest, Neh. 12:14.

MELITA, an island in the Mediterranean. Paul shipwrecked on the coast of, Acts 28:1–10.

MELON. Num. 11:5.

MELZAR, the steward whom the prince of the eunuchs set over Daniel and the three Hebrew children, Dan. 1:11–16.

MEMORIAL. Passover, Ex. 12:14. See PASSOVER. Firstborn set apart as a, Ex. 13: 12–16. Pot of manna, Ex. 16:32–34. Feast of tabernacles, Lev. 23:43. Shoulder stones of the ephod, Ex. 28:12.

Lord's supper, Luke 22:19; 1 Cor. 11:24–26. See PILLAR.

MEMPHIS, called also NOPH. A celebrated city of Egypt, Hos. 9:6. Prophecies concerning, Isa. 19:13; Jer. 2:16; 46:14,19; Ezek. 30:16.

MEMUCAN, one of the seven princes of Ahasuerus who counsels the king to divorce Queen Vashti, Esth. 1:14–21.

MENAHEM, king of Israel, 2 Kin. 15: 13–22.

MENAN, an ancestor of Jesus, Luke 3:31.

MENE, Dan. 5:25,26.

MENSES. See MENSTRUATION.

MENSTRUATION. Law relating to, Lev. 15:19–30; 20:18; Ezek. 18:6. Cessation of, in old age, Gen. 18:11. Immunities of women during, Gen. 31:35. Of animals, Jer. 2:24. Uncleanness of, Isa. 30:22.

FIGURATIVE: Isa. 30:22; Lam. 1:17; Ezek. 36:17.

MEONENIM, a place in Ephraim, Judg. 9:37.

MEONOTHAI, father of Ophrah, 1 Chr. 4:14.

MEPHAATH, a Levitical city in Reuben, Josh. 13:18; 21:37; 1 Chr. 6:79; Jer. 48:21.

MEPHIBOSHETH. 1. Son of Saul by Rizpah, whom David surrendered to the Gibeonites to be slain, 2 Sam. 21:8,9.

2. Son of Jonathan, 2 Sam. 4:4. Called MERIB-BAAL, 1 Chr. 8:34; 9:40. Was lame, 2 Sam. 4:4. David entertains him at his table, 2 Sam. 9:1–7; 21:7. Property restored to, 2 Sam. 9:9,10. His ingratitude to David at the time of Absalom's usurpation, 2 Sam. 16:1–4; 19:24–30. Property of, confiscated, 2 Sam. 16:4; 19:29,30.

MERAB. Daughter of King Saul, 1 Sam. 14:49. Betrothed to David by Saul, 1 Sam. 18:17,18; but given to Adriel to wife, 1 Sam. 18:19.

MERAIAH, a priest, Neh. 12:12.

MERAIOTH. 1. A high priest of the line of Eleazar, 1 Chr. 6:6,7,52; Ezra 7:3. Probably identical with the priest of same name in 1 Chr. 9:11; Neh. 11:11.

2. A priest in the time of Joiakim, Neh. 12:15.

MERARI. Son of Levi, Gen. 46:11. Head of the Merarite Levites, Num. 3:17,33–35. See LEVITES.

MERATHAIM, probably a poetical name for Chaldea, Jer. 50:21.

MERCENARIES. See SOLDIERS.

MERCHANDISE. See COMMERCE.

MERCHANT, Gen. 23:16; 37:28; 1 Kin. 10:15,28; 2 Chr. 9:14; Neh. 3:32; 13:20; Job 41:6; Song 3:6; Isa. 23:2; 47:15; Ezek. 17:4; 27:13,17,21–36; 38:13; Hos. 12:7; Nah. 3:16; Matt. 13:45; Rev. 18:3,11,23.

See COMMERCE.

MERCURIUS, Mercury. Paul taken for, in Lycaonia, Acts 14:11,12.

MERCY. 2 Sam. 22:26. With the merciful thou wilt shew thyself merciful, *and* with the upright man thou wilt shew thyself upright.

Psa. 18:25. With the merciful thou wilt shew thyself merciful;

Psa. 37:25. I have been young, and *now* am old; yet have I not seen the righteous forsaken, nor his seed begging bread. 26. *He is* ever merciful, and lendeth; and his seed *is* blessed.

Psa. 85:10. Mercy and truth are met together; righteousness and peace have kissed *each other.*

Prov. 3:3. Let not mercy and truth forsake thee: bind them about thy neck; write them upon the table of thine heart: 4. So shalt thou find favour and good understanding in the sight of God and man.

Prov. 11:17. The merciful man doeth good to his own soul: but *he that is* cruel troubleth his own flesh.

Prov. 12:10. A righteous *man* regardeth the life of his beast: but the tender mercies of the wicked *are* cruel.

Prov. 14:21. He that despiseth his neighbour sinneth: but he that hath mercy on the poor, happy *is* he. 22. Do they not err that devise evil? but mercy and truth *shall be* to them that devise good. 31. He that oppresseth the poor reproacheth his Maker: but he that honoureth him hath mercy on the poor.

Prov. 20:28. Mercy and truth preserve the king: and his throne is upholden by mercy.

Prov. 21:21. He that followeth after righteousness and mercy findeth life, righteousness, and honour.

Hos. 4:1. Hear the word of the LORD, ye children of Israel: for the LORD hath a controversy with the inhabitants of the land, because *there is* no truth, nor mercy, nor knowledge of God in the land.

Hos. 12:6. Therefore turn thou to thy God: keep mercy and judgment, and wait on thy God continually.

Mic. 6:8. He hath shewed thee, O man, what *is* good; and what doth the LORD require of thee, but to do justly, and to love mercy, and to walk humbly with thy God?

Matt. 5:7. Blessed *are* the merciful: for they shall obtain mercy.

Matt. 23:23. Woe unto you, scribes and Pharisees, hypocrites! for ye pay tithe of mint and anise and cummin, and have omitted the weightier *matters* of the law, judgment, mercy, and faith: these ought ye to have done, and not to leave the other undone.

Luke 6:36. Be ye therefore merciful, as your Father also is merciful.

Rom. 12:8. He that sheweth mercy, with cheerfulness.

Col. 3:12. Put on therefore, as the elect of God, holy and beloved, bowels of mercies, kindness, humbleness of mind, meekness, longsuffering; 13. Forbearing one another, and forgiving one another, if any man have a quarrel against any: even as Christ forgave you, so also *do* ye.

Jas. 2:13. For he shall have judgment without mercy, that hath shewed no mercy; and mercy rejoiceth against judgment.

See GOD, MERCY OF; KINDNESS.

INSTANCES OF: The prison keeper, to Joseph, Gen. 39:21–23. Joshua to Rahab, Josh. 6:25. The Israelites to the man of Beth-el, Judg. 1:23–26. David to Saul, 1 Sam. 24:10–13,17.

MERCY SEAT. Description of, Ex. 25:17–22. Placed on the ark of the testimony, Ex. 26:34; 30:6; 31:7; 40:20; Heb. 9:5. Materials of, to be a freewill offering, Ex. 35:4–12. Made by Bezaleel, Ex. 37:1,6–9.

Sprinkled with blood, Lev. 16:14,15. The shekinah upon, Ex. 25:22; 30:6,36; Lev. 16:2; Num. 7:89; 17:4; 1 Sam. 4:4; 2 Sam. 6:2; 2 Kin. 19:15; 1 Chr. 13:6; Psa. 80:1; Psa. 99:1; Isa. 37:16; Heb. 4:16.

In Solomon's temple, 1 Chr. 28:11.

See TABERNACLE.

MERED, son of Ezra, 1 Chr. 4:17,18.

MEREMOTH. 1. A priest who was appointed to weigh and register gold and silver vessels brought to Jerusalem, Ezra 8:33; Neh. 3:4,21.

2. A Jew who divorced his Gentile wife after the captivity, Ezra 10:36.

3. A priest who sealed the covenant with Nehemiah, Neh. 10:5; 12:3.

MERES, one of the princes of Persia, Esth. 1:14.

MERIBAH. 1. A place in Rephidim, where Moses struck a rock and brought forth water, Ex. 17:1–7.

2. Meribah-kadesh, fountain in the desert of Zin, Num. 20:13,24.

MERIB-BAAL. See MEPHIBOSHETH.

MERIT. Personal. See GRACE.

MERODACH, a Babylonian idol, Jer. 50:2.

MERODACH - BALADAN, called BERODACH-BALADAN, king of Persia. Sends congratulatory letters and a present to Hezekiah, 2 Kin. 20:12; Isa. 39:1.

MEROM. The district near the springs of Jordan. Joshua conquered the confederacy of kings under Jabin, king of Hazor, near, Josh. 11:5–7.

MEROZ. A place N. of Mount Tabor. Deborah and Barak curse the inhabitants of, in their song of triumph, Judg. 5:23.

MESHA. 1. King of Moab. Tributary to Ahab, 2 Kin. 3:4,5.

2. Son of Caleb, 1 Chr. 2:42.

3. A place in possession of the Joktanites, Gen. 10:30.

4. A Benjamite, 1 Chr. 8:9.

MESHACH, a name given by the chief eunuch to Mishael, one of the three Hebrew children, Dan. 1:7; 2:49; 3:12–30.

MESHECH. 1. Called also MESECH. Son of Japheth, Gen. 10:2; 1 Chr. 1:5.

2. Son of Shem, 1 Chr. 1:17.

3. A tribe, Psa. 120:5.

4. The Moschi, Ezek. 27:13; 32:26; 38:2,3.

MESHELEMIAH, a gatekeeper of the temple, 1 Chr. 9:21; 26:1,2,9.

MESHEZABEEL. 1. Ancestor of Meshullam, Neh. 3:4.

2. A person who sealed the covenant, Neh. 10:21; 11:24.

MESHILLEMITH, a priest, 1 Chr. 9:12.

MESHILLEMOTH. 1. Father of an Ephraimite who protested against the attempt of the Israelites to enslave their captive brethren, 2 Chr. 28:12,13.

2. A priest, Neh. 11:13.

MESHOBAB, a Simeonite, 1 Chr. 4:34.

MESHULLAM. 1. Grandfather of Shaphan, 2 Kin. 22:3.

2. A son of Zerubbabel, 1 Chr. 3:19.

3. A Gadite of Bashan, 1 Chr. 5:13.

4. Three Benjamites, 1 Chr. 8:17; 9:7,8.

5. An Aaronite, 1 Chr. 9:11; Neh. 11:11.

6. A priest, 1 Chr. 9:12.

7. A Kohathite and overseer of the temple repairs, 2 Chr. 34:12.

8. A chief who returned with Ezra, Ezra 8:16.

9. A returned exile, Ezra 10:15.

10. Son of Bani who divorced his Gentile wife, Ezra 10:29.

11. Two persons who rebuilt portions of the wall, Neh. 3:4,6,30.

12. A prince who stood by Ezra when he read the law to the people, Neh. 8:4.

13. Two priests who signed the covenant, Neh. 10:7,20.

14. A Benjamite, Neh. 11:7.

15. Two priests who returned with Zerubbabel from Babylon, Neh. 12:13,16,33.

16. A Levite, Neh. 12:25.

MESHULLEMETH, wife of Manasseh and mother of Amon, 2 Kin. 21:19.

MESOPOTAMIA. The country between the Tigris and the Euphrates. Abraham a native of, Acts 7:2. Nahor dwelt in, Gen. 24:10. People who dwelt in, called Syrians, Gen. 25:20. Balaam from, Deut. 23:4. The children of Israel subjected to, eight years under the judgments of God, Judg. 3:8; delivered from, by Othniel, Judg. 3:9,10. Chariots hired from, by the Ammonites, 1 Chr. 19:6,7. People of, present at Pentecost, Acts 2:9.

See BABYLON; CHALDEA.

MESSENGER, FIGURATIVE: Hag. 1: 13; Mal. 2:7; 3:1; 4:5,6; Matt. 11:10; Mark 1:2; Luke 7:27. Of Satan, 2 Cor. 12:7.

MESSIAH. See JESUS.

METAL. See BRASS (copper); GOLD; IRON; LEAD; SILVER; TIN.

METAPHOR, Jesus spoke in, Mark 4:11. See PARABLES.

METEOROLOGY AND CELESTIAL PHENOMENA. Gen. 2:5. The LORD God had not caused it to rain upon the earth, and *there was* not a man to till the ground. 6. But there went up a mist from the earth, and watered the whole face of the ground.

Gen. 27:39. And Isaac his father answered and said unto him, Behold, thy dwelling shall be the fatness of the earth, and the dew of heaven from above;

Job 9:7. Which commandeth the sun, and it riseth not; and sealeth up the stars.

Job 26:7. He stretcheth out the north over the empty place, *and* hangeth the earth upon nothing. 8. He bindeth up the waters in his thick clouds; and the cloud is not rent under them. 11. The pillars of heaven tremble and are astonished at his reproof.

Job 27:20. Terrors take hold on him as waters, a tempest stealeth him away in the night. 21. The east wind carrieth him away, and he departeth: and as a storm hurleth him out of his place.

Job 28:24. For he looketh to the ends of the earth, *and* seeth under the whole heaven; 25. To make the weight for the winds; and he weigheth the waters by measure. 26. When he made a decree for the rain, and a way for the lightning of the thunder: 27. Then did he see it, and declare it; he prepared it, yea, and searched it out.

Job 29:19. The dew lay all night upon my branch.

Job 36:27. For he maketh small the drops of water: they pour down rain according to the vapour thereof; 28. Which the clouds do drop *and* distil upon man abundantly. 29. Also can *any* understand the spreadings of the clouds, *or* the noise of his tabernacle? 30. Behold, he spreadeth his light upon it, and covereth the bottom of the sea. 31. For by them judgeth he the people; he giveth meat in abundance. 32. With clouds he covereth the light; and commandeth it *not to shine* by *the cloud* that cometh betwixt. 33. The noise thereof sheweth concerning it, the cattle also concerning the vapour.

Job 37:6. For he saith to the snow, Be thou *on* the earth; likewise to the small rain, and to the great rain of his strength. 7. He sealeth up the hand of every man; that all men may know his work. 8. Then the beasts go into dens, and remain in their places. 9. Out of the south cometh the whirlwind: and cold out of the north. 10. By the breath of God frost is given: and the breadth of the waters is straitened. 11. Also by watering he wearieth the thick cloud: he scattereth his bright cloud: 12. And it is turned round about by his counsels: that they may do whatsoever he commandeth them upon the face of the world in the earth. 13. He causeth it to come, whether for correction, or for his land, or for mercy. 14. Hearken unto this, O Job: stand still,

and consider the wondrous works of God. 15. Dost thou know when God disposed them, and caused the light of his cloud to shine? 16. Dost thou know the balancings of the clouds, the wondrous works of him which is perfect in knowledge? 17. How thy garments *are* warm, when he quieteth the earth by the south *wind?* 18. Hast thou with him spread out the sky, *which is* strong, *and* as a molten looking glass? 19. Teach us what we shall say unto him; *for* we cannot order *our speech* by reason of darkness. 20. Shall it be told him that I speak? if a man speak, surely he shall be swallowed up. 21. And now *men* see not the bright light which *is* in the clouds: but the wind passeth, and cleanseth them. 22. Fair weather cometh out of the north: with God *is* terrible majesty.

Job 38:9. When I made the cloud the garment thereof, and thick darkness a swaddlingband for it, [with *vs.* 8–11.] 22. Hast thou entered into the treasures of the snow? or hast thou seen the treasures of the hail, 24. By what way is the light parted, *which* scattereth the east wind upon the earth? 25. Who hath divided a watercourse for the overflowing of waters, or a way for the lightning of thunder; 26. To cause it to rain on the earth *where* no man *is; on* the wilderness, wherein *there is* no man; 27. To satisfy the desolate and waste *ground;* 28. Hath the rain a father? or who hath begotten the drops of dew? 29. Out of whose womb came the ice? and the hoary frost of heaven, who hath gendered it? 31. Canst thou bind the sweet influences of Pleiades, or loose the bands of Orion? 32. Canst thou bring forth Mazzaroth in his season? or canst thou guide Arcturus with his sons? 33. Knowest thou the ordinances of heaven? canst thou set the dominion thereof in the earth? 34. Canst thou lift up thy voice to the clouds, that abundance of waters may cover thee? 35. Canst thou send lightnings, that they may go, and say unto thee, Here we *are?* 37. Who can number the clouds in wisdom? or who can stay the bottles of heaven,

Psa. 18:8. There went up a smoke out of his nostrils, and fire out of his mouth devoured: coals were kindled by it. 9. He bowed the heavens also, and came down: and darkness *was* under his feet. 10. And he rode upon a cherub, and did fly: yea, he did fly upon the wings of the wind. 11. He made darkness his secret place; his pavilion round about him *were* dark waters *and* thick clouds of the skies. 12. At the brightness *that was* before him his thick clouds passed, hail *stones* and coals of fire. 13. The LORD also thundered in the heavens, and the Highest gave his voice; hail *stones* and coals of fire. 14. Yea, he sent out his arrows, and scattered them; and he shot out lightnings, and discomfited them. 15. Then the channels of waters were seen, and the foundations of the world were discovered at thy rebuke, O Lord, at the blast of the breath of thy nostrils.

Psa. 19:2. Day unto day uttereth speech, and night unto night sheweth knowledge. 3. *There is* no speech nor language, *where* their voice is not heard. 4. Their line is gone out through all the earth, and their words to the end of the world. In them hath he set a tabernacle for the sun, 5. Which *is* as a bridegroom coming out of his chamber, *and* rejoiceth as a strong man to run a race. 6. His going forth *is* from the end of the heaven, and his circuit unto the ends of it: and there is nothing hid from the heat thereof.

Psa. 29:3. The voice of the Lord *is* upon the waters: the God of glory thundereth: the Lord *is* upon many waters. 4. The voice of the Lord *is* powerful; the voice of the Lord *is* full of majesty. 5. The voice of the Lord breaketh the cedars; yea, the Lord breaketh the cedars of Lebanon. 6. He maketh them also to skip like a calf; Lebanon and Sirion like a young unicorn. 7. The voice of the Lord divideth the flames of fire. 8. The voice of the Lord shaketh the wilderness; the Lord shaketh the wilderness of Kadesh. 9. The voice of the Lord maketh the hinds to calve, and discovereth the forests: and in his temple doth every one speak of *his* glory. 10. The Lord sitteth upon the flood; yea, the Lord sitteth King for ever.

Psa. 65:8. They also that dwell in the uttermost parts are afraid at thy tokens: thou makest the outgoings of the morning and evening to rejoice. 9. Thou visitest the earth, and waterest it: thou greatly enrichest it with the river of God, *which* is full of water: thou preparest them corn, when thou hast so provided for it. 10. Thou waterest the ridges thereof abundantly: thou settlest the furrows thereof: thou makest it soft with showers: thou blessest the springing thereof. 11. Thou crownest the year with thy goodness; and thy paths drop fatness. 12. They drop *upon* the pastures of the wilderness: and the little hills rejoice on every side.

Psa. 104:2. Who coverest *thyself* with light as *with* a garment: who stretchest out the heavens like a curtain: 3. Who layeth the beams of his chambers in the waters: who maketh the clouds his chariot: who walketh upon the wings of the wind: 7. At thy rebuke they fled; at the voice of thy thunder they hasted away. 13. He watereth the hills from his chambers: the earth is satisfied with the fruit of thy works. 19. He appointed the moon for seasons: the sun knoweth his going down. 20. Thou makest darkness, and it is night:

Psa. 147:7. Sing unto the Lord with thanksgiving; sing praise upon the harp unto our God: 8. Who covereth the heaven with clouds, who prepareth rain for the earth,

Psa. 148:7. Praise the Lord from the

earth, ye dragons, and all deeps: 8. Fire, and hail; snow, and vapour; stormy wind fulfilling his word:

Prov. 25:23. The north wind ¹ driveth away rain: [¹ R. V. bringeth forth]

Prov. 26:1. As snow in summer, and as rain in harvest, so honour is not seemly for a fool.

Prov. 30:4. Who hath ascended up into heaven, or descended? who hath gathered the wind in his fists? who hath bound the waters in a garment? who hath established all the ends of the earth? what *is* his name, and what *is* his son's name, if thou canst tell?

Eccl. 1:6. The wind goeth toward the south, and turneth about unto the north; it whirleth about continually, and the wind returneth again according to his circuits. 7. All the rivers run into the sea; yet the sea *is* not full: unto the place from whence the rivers come, thither they return again.

Eccl. 11:3. If the clouds be full of rain, they empty *themselves* upon the earth:

Isa. 5:5. And now go to: I will tell you what I will do to my vineyard: I will take away the hedge thereof, and it shall be eaten up; *and* break down the wall thereof, and it shall be trodden down: 6. And I will lay it waste: it shall not be pruned, nor digged; but there shall come up briers and thorns: I will also command the clouds that they rain no rain upon it.

Isa. 13:13. Therefore I will shake the heavens, and the earth shall remove out of her place, in the wrath of the Lord of hosts, and in the day of his fierce anger.

Isa. 24:18. For the windows from on high are open, and the foundations of the earth do shake.

Isa. 50:3. I clothe the heavens with blackness, and I make sackcloth their covering.

Jer. 4:11. At that time shall it be said to this people and to Jerusalem, A dry wind of the high places in the wilderness toward the daughter of my people, not to fan, nor to cleanse, 12. *Even* a full wind from those *places* shall come unto me: now also will I give sentence against them.

Jer. 10:13. When he uttereth his voice, *there is* a multitude of waters in the heavens, and he causeth the vapours to ascend from the ends of the earth; he maketh lightnings with rain, and bringeth forth the wind out of his treasures.

Jer. 51:16. When he uttereth *his* voice, *there is* a multitude of waters in the heavens; and he causeth the vapours to ascend from the ends of the earth: he maketh lightnings with rain, and bringeth forth the wind out of his treasures.

Dan. 2:21. And he changeth the times and the seasons:

Hos. 6:4. O Ephraim, what shall I do unto thee? O Judah, what shall I do unto thee? for your goodness *is* as a morning cloud, and as the early dew it goeth away.

Hos. 8:7. For they have sown the wind, and they shall reap the whirlwind:

Hos. 13:15. Though he be fruitful among *his* brethren, an east wind shall come, the wind of the LORD shall come up from the wilderness, and his spring shall become dry, and his fountain shall be dried up:

Joel 2:30. And I will shew wonders in the heavens and in the earth, blood, and fire, and pillars of smoke. 31. The sun shall be turned into darkness, and the moon into blood, before the great and the terrible day of the LORD come.

Amos 9:6. *It is* he that buildeth his stories in the heaven, and hath founded his troop in the earth; he that calleth for the waters of the sea, and poureth them out upon the face of the earth: The LORD *is* his name.

Nah. 1:3. The LORD *hath* his way in the whirlwind and in the storm, and the clouds *are* the dust of his feet.

Matt. 8:24. And, behold, there arose a great tempest in the sea, insomuch that the ship was covered with the waves: but he was asleep. 25. And his disciples came to *him*, and awoke him, saying, Lord, save us: we perish. 26. And he saith unto them, Why are ye fearful, O ye of little faith? Then he arose, and rebuked the winds and the sea; and there was a great calm. 27. But the men marvelled, saying, What manner of man is this, that even the winds and the sea obey him! Luke 8:24,25.

Matt. 16:2. He answered and said unto them, When it is evening, ye say, *It will be* fair weather: for the sky is red. 3. And in the morning, *It will be* foul weather to day: for the sky is red and lowring. O *ye* hypocrites, ye can discern the face of the sky; but can ye not *discern* the signs of the times?

Matt. 24:27. For as the lightning cometh out of the east, and shineth even unto the west; so shall also the coming of the Son of man be. 29. Immediately after the tribulation of those days shall the sun be darkened, and the moon shall not give her light, and the stars shall fall from heaven, and the powers of the heavens shall be shaken:

Matt. 27:45. Now from the sixth hour there was darkness over all the land unto the ninth hour. Luke 23:44,45.

Luke 12:54. And he said also to the people, When ye see a cloud rise out of the west, straightway ye say, There cometh a shower; and so it is. 55. And when ye *see* the south wind blow, ye say, There will be heat; and it cometh to pass. 56. *Ye* hypocrites, ye can discern the face of the sky and of the earth; but how is it that ye do not discern this time?

Luke 21:25. And there shall be signs in the sun, and in the moon, and in the stars;

John 3:8. The wind bloweth where it listeth, and thou hearest the sound thereof, but canst not tell whence it cometh, and whither it goeth:

Acts 2:19. And I will shew wonders in heaven above, and signs in the earth beneath; blood, and fire, and vapour of smoke: 20. The sun shall be turned into darkness,

and the moon into blood, before that great and notable day of the Lord come:

Jas. 5:17. Elias was a man subject to like passions as we are, and he prayed earnestly that it might not rain: and it rained not on the earth by the space of three years and six months. 18. And he prayed again, and the heaven gave rain, and the earth brought forth her fruit.

2 Pet. 2:17. These are wells without water, clouds that are carried with a tempest; to whom the mist of darkness is reserved for ever.

Jude 12. These are spots in your feasts of charity, when they feast with you, feeding themselves without fear: clouds *they are* without water, carried about of winds;

Rev. 6:12. And I beheld when he had opened the sixth seal, and, lo, there was a great earthquake; and the sun became black as sackcloth of hair, and the moon became as blood; 13. And the stars of heaven fell unto the earth, even as a fig tree casteth her untimely figs, when she is shaken of a mighty wind. 14. And the heaven departed as a scroll when it is rolled together; and every mountain and island were moved out of their places.

Rev. 7:1. And after these things I saw four angels standing on the four corners of the earth, holding the four winds of the earth, that the wind should not blow on the earth, nor on the sea, nor on any tree.

Rev. 8:5. And the angel took the censer, and filled it with fire of the altar, and cast *it* into the earth: and there were voices, and thunderings, and lightnings, and an earthquake. 7. The first angel sounded, and there followed hail and fire mingled with blood, and they were cast upon the earth: and the third part of trees was burnt up, and all green grass was burnt up. 10. And the third angel sounded, and there fell a great star from heaven, burning as it were a lamp, and it fell upon the third part of the rivers, and upon the fountains of waters; 12. And the fourth angel sounded, and the third part of the sun was smitten, and the third part of the moon, and the third part of the stars; so as the third part of them was darkened, and the day shone not for a third part of it, and the night likewise.

Rev. 9:1. And the fifth angel sounded, and I saw a star fall from heaven unto the earth: and to him was given the key of the bottomless pit. 2. And he opened the bottomless pit; and there arose a smoke out of the pit, as the smoke of a great furnace; and the sun and the air were darkened by reason of the smoke of the pit.

Rev. 11:6. These have power to shut heaven, that it rain not in the days of their prophecy: and have power over waters to turn them to blood, and to smite the earth with all plagues, as often as they will.

Rev. 16:21. And there fell upon men a great hail out of heaven, *every stone* about the weight of a talent: and men blasphemed

God because of the plague of the hail; for the plague thereof was exceeding great.

PHENOMENA OF: The deluge, Gen. 7;8. Fire from heaven on the cities of the plain, Gen. 19:24,25. Plagues of hail, thunder, and lightning in Egypt, Ex. 9:22–29; Psa. 78:17–23; of darkness, Ex. 10:22,23. East wind that divided the Red Sea, Ex. 14:21; that brought the quails, Num. 11:31,32; Psa. 78:26–28. Pillar of cloud and fire, see PILLAR. Sun stood still, Josh. 10:12,13. Dew on Gideon's fleece, Judg. 6:36–40. Stars in their courses fought against Sisera, Judg. 5:20. Stones from heaven, Josh. 10:11. Fire from heaven at Elijah's command, 2 Kin. 1:10–14. The whirlwind which carried Elijah to heaven, 2 Kin. 2:1,11.

Wind under God's control, Psa. 107:25. East wind, Psa. 48:7. Rain, formation of, Psa. 135:6,7. Dew, copious, Psa. 133:3. Rain in answer to Samuel's prayer, 1 Sam. 12:16–18; Elijah's prayer, 1 Kin. 18:41–45. Rain discomfits the Philistine army, 1 Sam. 7:10. Wind destroyed Job's children, Job 1:18,19. Darkness at the crucifixion, Matt. 27:45; Luke 23:44,45. The autumnal weather on the Mediterranean, Acts 27:9–14,20.

See ASTRONOMY; DEW; HAIL; RAIN.

SYMBOLICAL: Used in the Revelation of John, Rev. 6:12–14; 7:1; 8:3–12; 9:1,2,17–19; 10:1–6; 11:6; 12:1–4,7–9; 14; 15:1–4; 16:8,17–21; 19:11–18; 20:11; 21:1.

METHEG-AMMAH, a place in Philistia, 2 Sam. 8:1.

METHUSAEL, father of Lamech, Gen. 4:18.

METHUSELAH, son of Enoch and grandfather of Noah, Gen. 5:21–27; 1 Chr. 1:3.

MEZAHAB, grandfather of Mehetabel, Gen. 36:39; 1 Chr. 1:50.

MIAMIN. 1. A Jew who divorced his Gentile wife after the captivity, Ezra 10:25.

2. A priest who returned with Zerubbabel from Babylon, Neh. 12:5.

MIBHAR, one of David's valiant men, 1 Chr. 11:38.

MIBSAM. 1. Son of Ishmael, Gen. 25:13; 1 Chr. 1:29.

2. Son of Shallum, 1 Chr. 4:25.

MIBZAR, chief of Edom, Gen. 36:42; 1 Chr. 1:53.

MICAH. 1. An Ephraimite. His robbery and idolatry, Judg. 17;18.

2. Head of a family of Reuben, 1 Chr. 5:5.

3. Called also MICHA. Son of Mephibosheth, 2 Sam. 9:12; 1 Chr. 8:34,35; 9:40,41.

4. Called also MICHAH. A Kohathite, 1 Chr. 23:20; 24:24,25.

5. Father of Abdon, 2 Chr. 34:20.

6. One of the minor prophets, Jer. 26:18, 19; Mic. 1:1,14,15. Denounces the idolatry of his times, Mic. 1; the oppressions of the covetous, Mic. 2:1–11. Foretells the restoration of Israel, Mic. 2:12,13; the injustice of judges and falsehoods of false prophets, Mic. 3. Prophesies the coming of the Messiah, Mic. 4; 5. Denounces the oppressions,

frauds, and other abominations, Mic. 6. Laments the state of Zion, and foretells the triumphs, righteousness, and the mercies of God, Mic. 7.

MICAIAH, a prophet who reproved King Ahab, 1 Kin. 22:8–28; 2 Chr. 18:4–27.

MICE. See MOUSE.

MICHA. 1. See MICAH, 3.

2. A Levite, Neh. 10:11; 11:17,22.

MICHAEL. 1. An Asherite, Num. 13:13.

2. Two Gadites, 1 Chr. 5:13,14.

3. A Gershonite Levite, 1 Chr. 6:40.

4. A descendant of Issachar, 1 Chr. 7:3.

5. A Benjamite, 1 Chr. 8:16.

6. A captain of the thousands of Manasseh who joined David at Ziklag, 1 Chr. 12:20.

7. Father of Omri, 1 Chr. 27:18.

8. Son of Jehoshaphat. Slain by his brother, Jehoram, 2 Chr. 21:2–4.

9. Father of Zebadiah, Ezra 8:8.

10. The Archangel. His message to Daniel, Dan. 10:13,21; 12:1. Contention with the devil, Jude 9. Fights with the dragon, Rev. 12:7.

MICHAIAH. 1. Father of Achbor, 2 Kin. 22:12.

2. See MAACHAH, 4.

3. A prince sent by Jehoshaphat to teach the law in the cities of Judah, 2 Chr. 17:7.

4. A priest of the family of Asaph, Neh. 12:35,41.

5. Son of Gemariah. Who expounds to the princes the prophecies of Jeremiah read by Baruch to the people, Jer. 36:11–14.

MICHAL, daughter of Saul. Given to David as a reward for slaying Goliath, 1 Sam. 18:22–28. Rescues David from death, 1 Sam. 19:9–17. Saul forcibly separates them and she is given in marriage to Phalti, 1 Sam. 25:44. David recovers, to himself, 2 Sam. 3:13–16. Ridicules David on account of his religious zeal, 2 Sam. 6:16,20–23.

MICHMAS. See MICHMASH.

MICHMASH. A city of Benjamin, 1 Sam. 13:5. People of the captivity return to, and dwell in, Ezra 2:27; Neh. 11:31. Prophecy concerning the king of Assyria storing his baggage at, Isa. 10:28. Is garrisoned by Saul, 1 Sam. 13:2. Philistines smitten at, by Jonathan, 1 Sam 14:31.

MICHMETHAH, a city between Ephraim and Manasseh, Josh. 16:6; 17:7.

MICHRI, a Benjamite, 1 Chr. 9:8.

MICHTAM. See MUSIC.

MIDDIN, a city of Judah, Josh. 15:61.

MIDIAN, son of Abraham by Keturah, Gen. 25:2,4; 1 Chr. 1:32,33.

MIDIANITES. Descendants of Midian, son of Abraham by Keturah, Gen. 25:1,2,4; 1 Chr. 1:32,33. Called ISHMAELITES, Gen. 37:25,28; Judg. 8:24. Were merchantmen, Gen. 37:28. Buy Joseph and sell him to Potiphar, Gen. 37:28,36. Defeated by the Israelites under Phinehas; five of their kings slain; the women taken captives: cities burned; and rich spoils taken, Num. 31. Defeated by

Gideon, Judg. chapters 6–8. Owned multitudes of camels, and dromedaries, and large quantities of gold, Isa. 60:6. A snare to the Israelites, Num. 25:16–18. Prophecies concerning, Isa. 60:6; Hab. 3:7.

MIDWIFERY, Gen. 35:17; Ex. 1:15–21; Ezek. 16:4.

MIGDAL-EL, a city of Naphtali, Josh. 19:38.

MIGDAL-GAD, a city of Judah, Josh. 15:37.

MIGDOL. 1. A place near the Red Sea where the Israelites encamped, Ex. 14:2; Num. 33:7,8.

2. A city on the northeastern border of lower Egypt, Jer. 44:1; 46:14.

MIGRON. A city in Benjamin. Saul encamps near, under a pomegranate tree, 1 Sam. 14:2. Prophecy concerning, Isa. 10:28.

MIJAMIN. 1. A priest in the time of David, 1 Chr. 24:9.

2. A priest who sealed the covenant with Nehemiah, Neh. 10:7.

MIKLOTH. 1. A Benjamite of Jerusalem, 1 Chr. 8:32; 9:37,38.

2. A ruler in the reign of David, 1 Chr. 27:4.

MIKNEIAH, a doorkeeper of the temple, and musician, 1 Chr. 15:18,21.

MILALAI, a priest who took part in the dedication of the walls of Jerusalem, Neh. 12:36.

MILCAH. 1. Wife of Nahor and mother of Bethuel, Gen. 11:29; 22:20–23; 24:15,24,47.

2. Daughter of Zelophehad. Special legislation in regard to the inheritance of, Num. 26:33; 27:1–7; 36:1–12; Josh. 17:3,4.

MILCOM. See Molech.

MILDEW, Deut. 28:22; Amos 4:9; Hag. 2:17.

MILE, Matt. 5:41.

MILETUS, called also Miletum. A seaport in Asia Minor. Paul visits, Acts 20:15; and sends to Ephesus for the elders of the church, and addresses them at, Acts 20:17–38. Trophimus left sick at, 2 Tim. 4:20.

MILITARY INSTRUCTION, of children, 2 Sam. 1:18.

See Armies.

MILK. Used for food, Gen. 18:8; Judg. 4:19; Song 5:1; Ezek. 25:4; 1 Cor. 9:7. Of goats, Prov. 27:27; sheep, Deut. 32:14; Isa. 7:21,22; camels, Gen. 32:15; cows, Deut. 32:14; 1 Sam. 6:7,10. Churned, Prov. 30:33. Kid not to be seethed in its mother's, Ex. 23:19; Deut. 14:21.

FIGURATIVE: Ex. 3:8,17; 13:5; 33:3; Num. 13:27; Deut. 26:9,15; Isa. 55:1; 60:16; Jer. 11:5; 32:22; Ezek. 20:6; Joel 3:18; 1 Cor. 3:2; Heb. 5:12,13; 1 Pet. 2:2.

MILL. Jer. 25:10. Upper and nether stones of, Deut. 24:6; Job 41:24; Isa. 47:2. Used in Egypt, Ex. 11:5. Operated by women, Matt. 24:41; and captives, Judg. 16:21; Lam. 5:13. Manna ground in, Num. 11:8. Sound of, to cease, Rev. 18:22.

See Millstone.

MILLENNIUM. Isa. 65:17. For, behold, I create new heavens and a new earth: and the former shall not be remembered, nor come into mind. 18. But be ye glad and rejoice for ever in that which I create: for, behold, I create Jerusalem a rejoicing, and her people a joy. 19. And I will rejoice in Jerusalem, and joy in my people: and the voice of weeping shall be no more heard in her, nor the voice of crying. 20. There shall be no more thence an infant of days, nor an old man that hath not filled his days: for the child shall die an hundred years old: but the sinner being an hundred years old shall be accursed. 21. And they shall build houses, and inhabit them; and they shall plant vineyards, and eat the fruit of them. 22. They shall not build, and another inhabit; they shall not plant, and another eat: for as the days of a tree are the days of my people, and mine elect shall long enjoy the work of their hands. 23. They shall not labour in vain, nor bring forth for trouble; for they are the seed of the blessed of the Lord, and their offspring with them. 24. And it shall come to pass, that before they call, I will answer; and while they are yet speaking, I will hear. 25. The wolf and the lamb shall feed together, and the lion shall eat straw like the bullock: and dust shall be the serpent's meat. They shall not hurt nor destroy in all my holy mountain, saith the Lord.

Zeph. 3:11. In that day shalt thou not be ashamed for all thy doings, wherein thou hast transgressed against me: for then I will take away out of the midst of thee them that rejoice in thy pride, and thou shalt no more be haughty because of my holy mountain. 12. I will also leave in the midst of thee an afflicted and poor people, and they shall trust in the name of the Lord. 13. The remnant of Israel shall not do iniquity, nor speak lies; neither shall a deceitful tongue be found in their mouth: for they shall feed and lie down, and none shall make them afraid.

Zech. 9:9. Rejoice greatly, O daughter of Zion; shout, O daughter of Jerusalem: behold, thy King cometh unto thee: he is just, and having salvation; lowly, and riding upon an ass, and upon a colt the foal of an ass. 10. And I will cut off the chariot from Ephraim, and the horse from Jerusalem, and the battle bow shall be cut off: and he shall speak peace unto the heathen: and his dominion shall be from sea even to sea, and from the river even to the ends of the earth.

Zech. 14:16. And it shall come to pass, that every one that is left of all the nations which came against Jerusalem shall even go up from year to year to worship the King, the Lord of hosts, and to keep the feast of tabernacles. 17. And it shall be, that whoso will not come up of all the families of the earth unto Jerusalem to worship the King, the Lord of hosts, even upon them shall be no rain. 18. And if the family of Egypt go not up, and come not, that *have* no *rain;* there shall be the plague, wherewith the LORD will smite the heathen that come not up to keep the feast of tabernacles. 19. This shall be the punishment of Egypt, and the punishment of all nations that come not up to keep the feast of tabernacles. 20. In that day there shall be upon the bells of the horses, HOLINESS UNTO THE LORD; and the pots in the LORD's house shall be like the bowls before the altar. 21. Yea, every pot in Jerusalem and in Judah shall be holiness unto the LORD of hosts: and all they that sacrifice shall come and take of them, and seethe therein: and in that day there shall be no more the Canaanite in the house of the LORD of hosts.

Matt. 16:18. And I say also unto thee, That thou art Peter, and upon this rock I will build my church; and the gates of hell shall not prevail against it. 19. And I will give unto thee the keys of the kingdom of heaven: and whatsoever thou shalt bind on earth shall be bound in heaven; and whatsoever thou shalt loose on earth shall be loosed in heaven.

Matt. 26:29. But I say unto you, I will not drink henceforth of this fruit of the vine, until that day when I drink it new with you in my Father's kingdom. Mark 14:25.

Heb. 8:11. And they shall not teach every man his neighbour, and every man his brother, saying, Know the Lord: for all shall know me, from the least to the greatest.

Rev. 14:6. And I saw another angel fly in the midst of heaven, having the everlasting gospel to preach unto them that dwell on the earth, and to every nation, and kindred, and tongue, and people,

Rev. 20:1. And I saw an angel come down from heaven, having the key of the bottomless pit and a great chain in his hand. 2. And he laid hold on the dragon, that old serpent, which is the Devil, and Satan, and bound him a thousand years, 3. And cast him into the bottomless pit, and shut him up, and set a seal upon him, that he should deceive the nations no more, till the thousand years should be fulfilled: and after that he must be loosed a little season. 4. And I saw thrones, and they sat upon them, and judgment was given unto them: and *I saw* the souls of them that were beheaded for the witness of Jesus, and for the word of God, and which had not worshipped the beast, neither his image, neither had received *his* mark upon their foreheads, or in their hands; and they lived and reigned with Christ a thousand years. 5. But the rest of the dead lived not again until the thousand years were finished. This *is* the first resurrection. 6. Blessed and holy *is* he that hath part in the first resurrection: on such the second death hath no power, but they shall be priests of God

and of Christ, and shall reign with him a thousand years. *vs.* 7–15.

See CHURCH, PROPHECIES CONCERNING; JESUS, KINGDOM OF; SECOND COMING OF.

MILLET, Ezek. 4:9.

MILLO. 1. The house of Millo, possibly a clan at Shechem, Judg. 9:6,20.

2. A name given to part of the citadel of Jerusalem, 2 Sam. 5:9; 1 Chr. 11:8. King Solomon raises a levy to repair, 1 Kin. 9:15, 24; 11:27. Repaired by King Hezekiah, 2 Chr. 32:5. King Joash murdered at, 2 Kin. 12:20.

MILLSTONE. Not to be taken in pledge, Deut. 24:6. Probably used in executions by drowning, Matt. 18:6; Mark 9:42; Luke 17:2. Abimelech killed by one being hurled upon him, Judg. 9:53. Figurative of the hard heart, Job 41:24.

MINCING, Isa. 3:16.

MINERALS. See ADAMANT; AGATE; ALABASTER; AMETHYST: BERYL; BRIMSTONE; CHALCEDONY; CHALK; CHRYSOLYTE: CHRYSOPRASUS; COPPER; CORAL; DIAMOND; FLINT; GOLD; IRON; JACINTH; JASPER: LEAD; LIME; MARBLE; NITRE; PITCH; SALT: SAPPHIRE; SARDIUS; SARDONYX; SILVER; SLIME; STONE; TIN; TOPAZ.

See STONES, PRECIOUS.

MINIAMIN. 1. A Levite who assisted in the distribution of the sacred offerings in the time of Hezekiah, 2 Chr. 31:15.

2. A priest who came from Babylon with Zerubbabel, Neh. 12:17,41.

MINISTER. An officer in civil government. Joseph, Gen. 41:40-44; Ira, 2 Sam. 20:26; Zabud, 1 Kin. 4:5; Ahithophel, 1 Chr. 27:33; Zebadiah, 2 Chr. 19:11; Elkanah, 2 Chr. 28:7; Haman, Esth. 3:1; Mordecai, Esth. 10:3, with chapters 8; 9; Daniel, Dan. 2:48; 6:1-3.

See CABINET.

MINISTER, a sacred teacher.

INDEX OF SUB-TOPICS: *Miscellany of Minor Sub-Topics: Call of,* p. 841; *Character and Qualifications of,* p. 843; *Charge Delivered to,* p. 849; *Courage of,* p. 854; *Duties of,* p. 854; *Duties of the Church to,* p. 860; *Emoluments of,* p. 861; *Faithful, Instances of,* p. 862; *False and Corrupt,* p. 862; *Hospitality to,* p. 869; *Ordination of,* p. 869; *Prayer for, Enjoined; Exemplified,* p. 869; *Promises to, and Joys of,* p. 869; *Success Attending,* p. 870; *Trials and Persecutions of,* p. 870; *Zealous,* p. 872.

Called: AMBASSADORS FOR CHRIST, 2 Cor. 5:20; ANGELS OF THE CHURCH, Rev. 1:20; 2:1; APOSTLES, Luke 6:13; Rev. 18:20; APOSTLES OF JESUS CHRIST, Tit. 1:1;

DEFENDERS OF THE FAITH, Phil. 1:7;

ELDERS, 1 Tim. 5:17; 1 Pet. 5:1; EVANGELISTS, Eph. 4:11; 2 Tim. 4:5;

FISHERS OF MEN, Matt. 4:19; Mark 1:17;

LABORERS, Matt. 9:38, with Philem. 1; LABORERS IN THE GOSPEL OF CHRIST, 1 Thess. 3:2; LIGHTS, John 5:35;

MEN OF GOD, Deut. 33:1; 1 Tim. 6:11; MESSENGERS OF THE CHURCH, 2 Cor. 8:23. MESSENGERS OF THE LORD OF HOSTS, Mal. 2:7;

MINISTERS OF GOD, Isa. 61:6; 2 Cor. 6:4; OF THE LORD, Joel 2:17; CHRIST, Rom. 15:16; 1 Cor.4:1; OF THE SANCTUARY, Ezek. 45:4; OF THE GOSPEL, Eph. 3:7; Col. 1:23; OF THE WORD, Luke 1:2; OF THE NEW TESTAMENT, 2 Cor. 3:6; OF THE CHURCH, Col. 1:24,25; OF RIGHTEOUSNESS, 2 Cor. 11:15;

OVERSEERS, Acts 20:28;

PASTORS, Jer. 3:15; John 21:16–18; Eph. 4:11. PREACHERS, Rom. 10:14; 1 Tim. 2:7; PREACHERS OF RIGHTEOUSNESS, 2 Pet. 2:5;

SERVANTS OF GOD, Tit. 1:1; Jas. 1:1; OF THE LORD, 2 Tim. 2:24; OF JESUS CHRIST, Phil. 1:1; Jude 1; OF THE CHURCH, 2 Cor. 4:5; SHEPHERDS, Jer. 23:4; SOLDIERS OF CHRIST, Phil. 2:25; 2 Tim. 2:3,4; STARS, Rev. 1:20; 2:1; STEWARDS OF GOD, Tit. 1:7; OF THE GRACE OF GOD, 1 Pet. 4:10; OF THE MYSTERIES OF GOD, 1 Cor. 4:1.

TEACHERS, Isa. 30:20; Eph. 4:11;

WATCHMEN, Isa. 62:6; Ezek. 33:7; WITNESSES, Acts 1:8; 5:32; 26:16; WORKERS TOGETHER WITH GOD, 2 Cor. 6:1.

Likened to sowers, Psa. 126:6; Matt. 13:3–8; Mark 4:3–20; Luke 8:5–8.

Teachers of schools, 1 Sam. 19:20; 2 Kin. 2:3,5,15; 4:38; 2 Chr. 15:3; 17:7–9; Acts 13:1.

Hired, Judg. 18:4. Exempt from taxation, Ezra 7:24. Non-partisan in politics, 2 Sam. 15:24–27.

Influential in public affairs: Designate kings, 1 Sam. 9:15,16; 10:1; 16:1–13; recommend civil and military appointments, 2 Kin. 4:13. Expostulate with rulers: Samuel with Saul, 1 Sam. 13:11–14; 15:10–31; Nathan with David, 2 Sam. 12:1–14; Elijah with Ahab, 1 Kin. 18:17,18.

Tact of, 1 Cor. 9:20–23; 10:23,28–33; 2 Cor. 12:16. Recreations for, Mark 6:31,32,45. Take leave of congregations, Acts 20:17–38. Personal bearing of, Tit. 2:7,8. Preach without ecclesiastical authority, Gal. 1:15–24; 2:1–9. Patience of, Jas. 5:10. Work of, will be tried, 1 Cor. 3:12–15. Responsibility of, Ezek. 3:17–21; 33:8; Matt. 10:14–40; Acts 18:6; 20:26,27. Speaking evil of, forbidden, Jude 8–10.

Marriage of, Lev. 21:7–15; Matt. 8:14; 1 Cor. 9:5; 1 Tim. 3:2,12; Tit. 1:5–7. Incorruptible: Balaam, Num. 22:18,37,38; 23:8,12; 24:12–14, with 2 Pet. 2:15,16; Micaiah, 1 Kin. 22:13,14; Peter, Acts 8:18–23.

Love of, for the church, exemplified by Paul, Phil. 1:7; 1 Thess. 1:2–4; 2:8,11. Kindness to: Ebed-melech to Jeremiah, Jer. 38:7–13. Fear of, 1 Sam. 16:4. Ensamples to the flock, Phil. 3:17; 2 Thess. 3:9; 1 Tim. 4:12; 1 Pet. 5:3. Intolerance of, Matt. 15:23; 19:13; Mark 10:13; Luke 18:15. Message of, rejected, Ezek. 33:30–33. Inconsistent, Matt. 27:3–7. God's care of, 1 Kin. 17:1–16; 19:1–18; Isa. 30:20; Matt. 10:29–31; Luke 12:6,7. Their calling glorious, 2 Cor. 3:7–11. Discouragements of, Isa. 53:1; Ezek. 3:8,9,14; Hab. 1:2,3; Matt. 13:57; Mark 6:3,4; Luke 4:24; John 4:44. Defended, Jer. 26:16–19. Beloved, Acts 20:37,38; 21:5,6.

Sent forth two and two: Disciples, Mark 6:7. Paul and Barnabas, Acts 13:2,3. Judas and Silas, Acts 15:27. Barnabas and Mark, Acts 15:37,39. Paul and Silas, Acts 15:40. Paul and Timothy, Acts 16:1–4. Paul and Titus, 2 Cor. 8:19,23. Timothy and Erastus, Acts 19:22. Titus and a companion, 2 Cor. 12:18.

See TRIALS AND PERSECUTIONS OF, below.

CALL OF: Ex. 28:1. And take thou unto thee Aaron thy brother, and his sons with him, from among the children of Israel, that he may minister unto me in the priest's office, even Aaron, Nadab and Abihu, Eleazar and Ithamar, Aaron's sons.

Num. 3:5. And the LORD spake unto Moses, saying, 6. Bring the tribe of Levi near, and present them before Aaron the priest, that they may minister unto him. 7. And they shall keep his charge, and the charge of the whole congregation before the tabernacle of the congregation, to do the service of the tabernacle. 8. And they shall keep all the instruments of the tabernacle of the congregation, and the charge of the children of Israel, to do the service of the tabernacle. 9. And thou shalt give the Levites unto Aaron and to his sons: they are wholly given unto him out of the children of Israel. 10. And thou shalt appoint Aaron and his sons, and they shall wait on their priest's office: and the stranger that cometh nigh shall be put to death. 11. And the LORD spake unto Moses, saying, 12. And I, behold, I have taken the Levites from among the children of Israel instead of all the firstborn that openeth the matrix among the children of Israel: therefore the Levites shall be mine; 13. Because all the firstborn are mine; for on the day that I smote all the firstborn in the land of Egypt I hallowed unto me all the firstborn in Israel, both man and beast: mine shall they be: I am the LORD.

1 Sam. 3:4. The LORD called Samuel: and he answered, Here am I. 5. And he ran unto Eli, and said, Here am I; for thou calledst me. And he said, I called not; lie down again. And he went and lay down. 6. And the LORD called yet again, Samuel. And Samuel arose and went to Eli, and said, Here am I; for thou didst call me. And he answered, I called not, my son; lie down again. 7. Now Samuel did not yet know the LORD, neither was the word of the LORD yet revealed unto him. 8. And the LORD called Samuel again the third time. And he arose and went to Eli, and said, Here am I; for thou didst call me. And Eli perceived that the LORD had called the child. 9. Therefore Eli said unto Samuel, Go, lie down: and it shall be, if he call thee, that thou shalt say, Speak, LORD; for thy servant heareth. So Samuel went and lay down in his place. 10. And the LORD came, and stood, and called as at other times, Samuel, Samuel. Then Samuel answered, Speak; for thy servant heareth.

1 Kin. 19:16. Elisha the son of Shaphat of

Abel-meholah shalt thou anoint *to be* prophet in thy room. 19. So he departed thence, and found Elisha the son of Shaphat, who *was* plowing *with* twelve yoke *of* oxen before him, and he with the twelfth: and Elijah passed by him, and cast his mantle upon him.

1 Chr. 23:13. Aaron was separated, that he should sanctify the most holy things, he and his sons for ever, to burn incense before the LORD, to minister unto him, and to bless in his name for ever.

Isa. 6:8. Also I heard the voice of the Lord, saying, Whom shall I send, and who will go for us? Then said I, Here *am* I; send me. 9. And he said, Go, and tell this people, Hear ye indeed, but understand not; and see ye indeed, but perceive not. 10. Make the heart of this people fat, and make their ears heavy, and shut their eyes; lest they see with their eyes, and hear with their ears, and understand with their heart, and convert, and be healed.

Jer. 1:5. Before I formed thee in the belly I knew thee; and before thou camest forth out of the womb I sanctified thee, *and* I ordained thee a prophet unto the nations.

Amos 2:11. And I raised up of your sons for prophets, and of your young men for Nazarites. *Is it* not even thus, O ye children of Israel? saith the LORD.

Jonah 1:1. Now the word of the LORD came unto Jonah the son of Amittai, saying, 2. Arise, go to Nineveh, that great city, and cry against it; for their wickedness is come up before me. chapter 3:1,2.

Matt. 4:18. And Jesus, walking by the sea of Galilee, saw two brethren, Simon called Peter, and Andrew his brother, casting a net into the sea: for they were fishers. 19. And he saith unto them, Follow me, and I will make you fishers of men. 20. And they straightway left *their* nets, and followed him. 21. And going on from thence, he saw other two brethren, James *the son* of Zebedee, and John his brother, in a ship with Zebedee their father, mending their nets; and he called them. 22. And they immediately left the ship and their father, and followed him. Mark 1:17–20.

Matt. 9:9. And as Jesus passed forth from thence, he saw a man, named Matthew, sitting at the receipt of custom: and he saith unto him, Follow me. And he arose, and followed him. Mark 2:14.

Luke 10:1. After these things the Lord appointed other seventy also, and sent them two and two before his face into every city and place, whither he himself would come. 2. Therefore said he unto them, The harvest truly *is* great, but the labourers *are* few: pray ye therefore the Lord of the harvest, that he would send forth labourers into his harvest.

John 1:43. The day following Jesus would go forth into Galilee, and findeth Philip, and saith unto him, Follow me.

Acts 13:2. As they ministered to the Lord, and fasted, the Holy Ghost said, Separate me Barnabas and Saul for the work whereunto I have called them. 3. And when they had fasted and prayed, and laid *their* hands on them, they sent *them* away.

Acts 20:24. But none of these things move me, neither count I my life dear unto myself, so that I might finish my course with joy, and the ministry, which I have received of the Lord Jesus, to testify the gospel of the grace of God.

Acts 22:12. And one Ananias, a devout man according to the law, having a good report of all the Jews which dwelt *there*, 13. Came unto me, and stood, and said unto me, Brother Saul, receive thy sight. And the same hour I looked up upon him. 14. And he said, The God of our fathers hath chosen thee, that thou shouldest know his will, and see that Just One, and shouldest hear the voice of his mouth. 15. For thou shalt be his witness unto all men of what thou hast seen and heard.

Acts 26:14. And when we were all fallen to the earth, I heard a voice speaking unto me, and saying in the Hebrew tongue, Saul, Saul, why persecutest thou me? *it is* hard for thee to kick against the pricks. 15. And I said, Who art thou, Lord? And he said, I am Jesus whom thou persecutest. 16. But rise, and stand upon thy feet: for I have appeared unto thee for this purpose, to make thee a minister and a witness both of these things which thou hast seen, and of those things in the which I will appear unto thee; 17. Delivering thee from the people, and *from* the Gentiles, unto whom now I send thee. 18. To open their eyes, *and* to turn *them* from darkness to light, and *from* the power of Satan unto God, that they may receive forgiveness of sins, and inheritance among them which are sanctified by faith that is in me.

Rom. 1:1. Paul, a servant of Jesus Christ, called *to be* an apostle, separated unto the gospel of God,

Rom. 10:14. How then shall they call on him in whom they have not believed? and how shall they believe in him of whom they have not heard? and how shall they hear without a preacher? 15. And how shall they preach, except they be sent? as it is written, How beautiful are the feet of them that preach the gospel of peace, and bring glad tidings of good things!

1 Cor. 1:1. Paul, called *to be* an apostle of Jesus Christ through the will of God, and Sosthenes *our* brother, [2 Cor. 1:1; Col. 1:1.] 27. But God hath chosen the foolish things of the world to confound the wise; and God hath chosen the weak things of the world to confound the things which are mighty; 28. And base things of the world, and things which are despised, hath God chosen, *yea*, and things which are not, to bring to nought things that are:

1 Cor. 9:16. For though I preach the gospel, I have nothing to glory of: for neces-

sity is laid upon me; yea, woe is unto me, if I preach not the gospel! 17. For if I do this thing willingly, I have a reward: but if against my will, a dispensation *of the gospel* is committed unto me. 18. What is my reward then? *Verily* that, when I preach the gospel, I may make the gospel of Christ without charge, that I abuse not my power in the gospel. 19. For though I be free from all *men*, yet have I made myself servant unto all, that I might gain the more.

2 Cor. 5:18. And all things *are* of God, who hath reconciled us to himself by Jesus Christ, and hath given to us the ministry of reconciliation; 19. To wit, that God was in Christ, reconciling the world unto himself, not imputing their trespasses unto them; and hath committed unto us the word of reconciliation. 20. Now then we are ambassadors for Christ, as though God did beseech *you* by us: we pray *you* in Christ's stead, be ye reconciled to God.

Gal. 1:15. But when it pleased God, who separated me from my mother's womb, and called *me* by his grace, 16. To reveal his Son in me, that I might preach him among the heathen; immediately I conferred not with flesh and blood:

Eph. 3:7. Whereof I was made a minister, according to the gift of the grace of God given unto me by the effectual working of his power. 8. Unto me, who am less than the least of all saints, is this grace given, that I should preach among the Gentiles the unsearchable riches of Christ;

Eph. 4:11. And he gave some, apostles; and some, prophets; and some, evangelists; and some, pastors and teachers; 12. For the perfecting of the saints, for the work of the ministry, for the edifying of the body of Christ:

Col. 1:25. Whereof I am made a minister, according to the dispensation of God which is given to me for you, to fulfil the word of God; 26. *Even* the mystery which hath been hid from ages and from generations, but now is made manifest to his saints: 27. To whom God would make known what *is* the riches of the glory of this mystery among the Gentiles; which is Christ in you, the hope of glory: 28. Whom we preach, warning every man, and teaching every man in all wisdom; that we may present every man perfect in Christ Jesus: 29. Whereunto I also labour, striving according to his working, which worketh in me mightily.

Col. 4:17. And say to Archippus, Take heed to the ministry which thou hast received in the Lord, that thou fulfil it.

1 Tim. 1:12. And I thank Christ Jesus our Lord, who hath enabled me, for that he counted me faithful, putting me into the ministry; 13. Who was before a blasphemer, and a persecutor, and injurious: but I obtained mercy, because I did *it* ignorantly in unbelief. 14. And the grace of our Lord was exceeding abundant with faith and love which is in Christ Jesus.

1 Tim. 2:7. Whereunto I am ordained a preacher, and an apostle, (I speak the truth in Christ, *and* lie not;) a teacher of the Gentiles in faith and verity. 2 Tim. 1:11.

Tit. 1:3. But hath in due times manifested his word through preaching, which is committed unto me according to the commandment of God our Saviour;

Heb. 5:4. And no man taketh this honour unto himself, but he that is called of God, as *was* Aaron.

See PRIESTS; LEVITES; CALL, PERSONAL; EXCUSES.

CHARACTER AND QUALIFICATIONS OF: Lev. 10:3. Then Moses said unto Aaron, This *is it* that the LORD spake, saying, I will be sanctified in them that come nigh me, and before all the people I will be glorified. And Aaron held his peace. 4. And Moses called Mishael and Elzaphan, the sons of Uzziel the uncle of Aaron, and said unto them, Come near, carry your brethren from before the sanctuary out of the camp. 5. So they went near, and carried them in their coats out of the camp; as Moses had said. 6. And Moses said unto Aaron, and unto Eleazar and unto Ithamar, his sons, Uncover not your heads, neither rend your clothes; lest ye die, and lest wrath come upon all the people: but let your brethren, the whole house of Israel, bewail the burning which the LORD hath kindled. 7. And ye shall not go out from the door of the tabernacle of the congregation, lest ye die: for the anointing oil of the LORD *is* upon you. And they did according to the word of Moses. 8. And the LORD spake unto Aaron, saying, 9. Do not drink wine nor strong drink, thou, nor thy sons with thee, when ye go into the tabernacle of the congregation, lest ye die: *it shall be* a statute for ever throughout your generations: 10. And that ye may put difference between holy and unholy, and between unclean and clean; 11. And that ye may teach the children of Israel all the statutes which the LORD hath spoken unto them by the hand of Moses.

Lev. 21:6. They shall be holy unto their God, and not profane the name of their God: for the offerings of the LORD made by fire, *and* the bread of their God, they do offer: therefore they shall be holy. 2 Chr. 29:11.

Num. 16:9. *Seemeth it but* a small thing unto you, that the God of Israel hath separated you from the congregation of Israel, to bring you near to himself to do the service of the tabernacle of the LORD, and to stand before the congregation to minister unto them? 10. And he hath brought thee near *to him*, and all thy brethren the sons of Levi with thee: and seek ye the priesthood also?

Deut. 32:1. Give ear, O ye heavens, and I will speak; and hear, O earth, the words of my mouth. 2. My doctrine shall drop as the rain, my speech shall distil as the dew, as the small rain upon the tender herb, and as the showers upon the grass: 3. Because I will publish the name of the LORD: ascribe ye greatness unto our God.

1 Sam. 2:35. I will raise me up a faithful priest, *that* shall do according to *that* which *is* in mine heart and in my mind:

1 Sam. 12:7. Now therefore stand still, that I may reason with you before the LORD of all the righteous acts of the LORD, which he did to you and to your fathers.

2 Chr. 6:41. Let thy priests, O LORD God, be clothed with salvation, and let thy saints rejoice in goodness.

Ezra 7:10. For Ezra had prepared his heart to seek the law of the LORD, and to do *it*, and to teach in Israel statutes and judgments.

Psa. 68:11. The Lord gave the word: ¹great *was* the company of those that published *it*.

[¹ R. V. the women that publish the tidings are a great host]

Prov. 11:30. The fruit of the righteous *is* a tree of life; and he that winneth souls *is* wise.

Isa. 6:5. Then said I, Woe *is* me! for I am undone; because I *am* a man of unclean lips, and I dwell in the midst of a people of unclean lips: for mine eyes have seen the King, the LORD of hosts. 6. Then flew one of the seraphims unto me, having a live coal in his hand, *which* he had taken with the tongs from off the altar: 7. And he laid *it* upon my mouth, and said, Lo, this hath touched thy lips; and thine iniquity is taken away, and thy sin purged. 8. Also I heard the voice of the Lord, saying, Whom shall I send, and who will go for us? Then said I, Here *am* I; send me.

Isa. 32:20. Blessed *are* ye that sow beside all waters, that send forth *thither* the feet of the ox and the ass.

Isa. 52:11. Be ye clean, that bear the vessels of the LORD.

Jer. 1:7. But the LORD said unto me, Say not, I *am* a child: for thou shalt go to all that I shall send thee, and whatsoever I command thee thou shalt speak. 8. Be not afraid of their faces: for I *am* with thee to deliver thee, saith the LORD.

Jer. 3:15. I will give you pastors according to mine heart, which shall feed you with knowledge and understanding.

Jer. 20:9. But *his word* was in mine heart as a burning fire shut up in my bones, and I was weary with forbearing, and I could not *stay*.

Ezek. 34:2. Thus saith the Lord GOD unto the shepherds; Woe *be* to the shepherds of Israel that do feed themselves! should not the shepherds feed the flocks? *vs.* 1-31.

Mal. 2:6. The law of truth was in his mouth, and iniquity was not found in his lips: he walked with me in peace and equity, and did turn many away from iniquity. 7. For the priest's lips should keep knowledge, and they should seek the law at his mouth: for he *is* the messenger of the LORD of hosts.

Matt. 10:16. Behold, I send you forth as sheep in the midst of wolves: be ye therefore wise as serpents, and harmless as doves. 17. But beware of men: for they will deliver you up to the councils, and they will scourge you in their synagogues; 18. And ye shall be brought before governors and kings for my sake, for a testimony against them and the Gentiles. 19. But when they deliver you up, take no thought how or what ye shall speak: for it shall be given you in that same hour what ye shall speak. 20. For it is not ye that speak, but the Spirit of your Father which speaketh in you. 22. And ye shall be hated of all *men* for my name's sake: but he that endureth to the end shall be saved. 23. But when they persecute you in this city, flee ye into another: for verily I say unto you, Ye shall not have gone over the cities of Israel, till the Son of man be come. 24. The disciple is not above *his* master, nor the servant above his lord.

Matt. 11:25. At that time Jesus answered and said, I thank thee, O Father, Lord of heaven and earth, because thou hast hid these things from the wise and prudent, and hast revealed them unto babes. [Luke 10:21.] 26. Even so, Father: for so it seemed good in thy sight.

Matt. 13:51. Jesus saith unto them, Have ye understood all these things? They say unto him, Yea, Lord. 52. Then said he unto them, Therefore every scribe *which is* instructed unto the kingdom of heaven is like unto a man *that is* an householder, which bringeth forth out of his treasure *things* new and old.

Matt. 20:25. But Jesus called them *unto him*, and said, Ye know that the princes of the Gentiles exercise dominion over them, and they that are great exercise authority upon them. 26. But it shall not be so among you: but whosoever will be great among you, let him be your minister; 27. And whosoever will be chief among you, let him be your servant: 28. Even as the Son of man came not to be ministered unto, but to minister, and to give his life a ransom for many. Luke 22:27; John 13:14,15.

Matt. 23:8. Be not ye called Rabbi: for one is your Master, *even* Christ; and all ye are brethren. 9. And call no *man* your father upon the earth: for one is your Father, which is in heaven. 10. Neither be ye called masters: for one is your Master, *even* Christ. 11. But he that is greatest among you shall be your servant.

Luke 6:39. And he spake a parable unto them; Can the blind lead the blind? shall they not both fall into the ditch?

Luke 12:42. And the Lord said, Who then is that faithful and wise steward, whom *his* lord shall make ruler over his household, to give *them their* portion of meat in due season? 43. Blessed *is* that servant, whom his lord when he cometh shall find so doing. 44. Of a truth I say unto you, that he will make him ruler over all that he hath. Matt. 24:45.

Luke 24:49. And, behold, I send the promise of my Father upon you: but tarry ye in the city of Jerusalem, until ye be endued with power from on high.

John 3:27. A man can receive nothing, except it be given him from heaven. 34. For he whom God hath sent speaketh the words of God: for God giveth not the Spirit by measure *unto him.*

John 4:36. He that reapeth receiveth wages, and gathereth fruit unto life eternal: that both he that soweth and he that reapeth may rejoice together. 37. And herein is that saying true, One soweth, and another reapeth. 38. I sent you to reap that whereon ye bestowed no labour: other men laboured, and ye are entered into their labours.

John 10:2. He that entereth in by the door is the shepherd of the sheep. 3. To him the porter openeth; and the sheep hear his voice: and he calleth his own sheep by name, and leadeth them out. 4. And when he putteth forth his own sheep, he goeth before them, and the sheep follow him: for they know his voice. 5. And a stranger will they not follow, but will flee from him: for they know not the voice of strangers. 11. I am the good shepherd: the good shepherd giveth his life for the sheep. 12. But he that is an hireling, and not the shepherd, whose own the sheep are not, seeth the wolf coming, and leaveth the sheep, and fleeth: and the wolf catcheth them, and scattereth the sheep. 13. The hireling fleeth, because he is an hireling, and careth not for the sheep. 14. I am the good shepherd, and know my *sheep,* and am known of mine. 15. As the Father knoweth me, even so know I the Father: and I lay down my life for the sheep.

John 13:13. Ye call me Master and Lord: and ye say well; for *so* I am. 14. If I then, *your* Lord and Master, have washed your feet; ye also ought to wash one another's feet. 15. For I have given you an example, that ye should do as I have done to you. 16. Verily, verily, I say unto you, The servant is not greater than his lord; neither he that is sent greater than he that sent him. 17. If ye know these things, happy are ye if ye do them.

John 15:20. Remember the word that I said unto you, The servant is not greater than his lord. If they have persecuted me, they will also persecute you; if they have kept my saying, they will keep your's also. 21. But all these things will they do unto you for my name's sake, because they know not him that sent me.

John 17:16. They are not of the world, even as I am not of the world. 17. Sanctify them through thy truth: thy word is truth. 18. As thou hast sent me into the world, even so have I also sent them into the world. 20. Neither pray I for these alone, but for them also which shall believe on me through their word;

Acts 1:8. But ye shall receive power, after that the Holy Ghost is come upon you: and ye shall be witnesses unto me both in Jerusalem, and in all Judæa, and in Samaria, and unto the uttermost part of the earth.

Acts 4:8. Then Peter, filled with the Holy Ghost, said unto them, Ye rulers of the people, and elders of Israel, 31. And when they had prayed, the place was shaken where they were assembled together; and they were all filled with the Holy Ghost, and they spake the word of God with boldness.

Acts 6:3. Wherefore, brethren, look ye out among you seven men of honest report, full of the Holy Ghost and wisdom, whom we may appoint over this business. 4. But we will give ourselves continually to prayer, and to the ministry of the word.

Acts 20:22. And now, behold, I go bound in the spirit unto Jerusalem, not knowing the things that shall befall me there: 23. Save that the Holy Ghost witnesseth in every city, saying that bonds and afflictions abide me. 24. But none of these things move me, neither count I my life dear unto myself, so that I might finish my course with joy, and the ministry, which I have received of the Lord Jesus, to testify the gospel of the grace of God.

Rom. 2:21. Thou therefore which teachest another, teachest thou not thyself? thou that preachest a man should not steal, dost thou steal? 22. Thou that sayest a man should not commit adultery, dost thou commit adultery? thou that abhorrest idols, dost thou commit sacrilege? 23. Thou that makest thy boast of the law, through breaking the law dishonourest thou God?

1 Cor. 1:23. But we preach Christ crucified, unto the Jews a stumblingblock, and unto the Greeks foolishness; 27. But God hath chosen the foolish things of the world to confound the wise; and God hath chosen the weak things of the world to confound the things which are mighty; 28. And base things of the world, and things which are despised, hath God chosen, *yea,* and things which are not, to bring to nought things that are: 29. That no flesh should glory in his presence. 30. But of him are ye in Christ Jesus, who of God is made unto us wisdom, and righteousness, and sanctification, and redemption:

1 Cor. 2:2. For I determined not to know any thing among you, save Jesus Christ, and him crucified.

1 Cor. 3:7. So then neither is he that planteth any thing, neither he that watereth; but God that giveth the increase. 8. Now he that planteth and he that watereth are one: and every man shall receive his own reward according to his own labour. 9. For we are labourers together with God: ye are God's husbandry, *ye are* God's building. 10. According to the grace of God which is given unto me, as a wise masterbuilder, I have laid the foundation, and another

buildeth thereon. But let every man take heed how he buildeth thereupon.

1 Cor. 4:10. We *are* fools for Christ's sake, but ye *are* wise in Christ; we *are* weak, but ye *are* strong; ye *are* honourable, but we *are* despised. 11. Even unto this present hour we both hunger, and thirst, and are naked, and are buffeted, and have no certain dwellingplace; 12. And labour, working with our own hands: being reviled, we bless; being persecuted, we suffer it: 13. Being defamed, we intreat: we are made as the filth of the world, *and are* the offscouring of all things unto this day.

1 Cor. 9:16. For though I preach the gospel, I have nothing to glory of: for necessity is laid upon me; yea, woe is unto me, if I preach not the gospel! 17. For if I do this thing willingly, I have a reward: but if against my will, a dispensation *of the gospel* is committed unto me. 18. What is my reward then? *Verily* that, when I preach the gospel, I may make the gospel of Christ without charge, that I abuse not my power in the gospel. 19. For though I be free from all *men*, yet have I made myself servant unto all, that I might gain the more. 20. And unto the Jews I became as a Jew, that I might gain the Jews; to them that are under the law, as under the law, that I might gain them that are under the law; 21. To them that are without law, as without law, (being not without law to God, but under the law to Christ,) that I might gain them that are without law. 22. To the weak became I as weak, that I might gain the weak: I am made all things to all *men*, that I might by all means save some. 23. And this I do for the gospel's sake, that I might be partaker thereof with *you*. 27. But I keep under my body, and bring *it* into subjection: lest that by any means, when I have preached to others, I myself should be a castaway.

1 Cor. 15:10. But by the grace of God I am what I am: and his grace which *was bestowed* upon me was not in vain; but I laboured more abundantly than they all: yet not I, but the grace of God which was with me.

2 Cor. 2:15. For we are unto God a sweet savour of Christ, in them that are saved, and in them that perish: 16. To the one *we are* the savour of death unto death; and to the other the savour of life unto life. And who *is* sufficient for these things? 17. For we are not as many, which corrupt the word of God: but as of sincerity, but as of God, in the sight of God speak we in Christ.

2 Cor. 3:6. Who also hath made us able ministers of the new testament; not of the letter, but of the spirit: for the letter killeth, but the spirit giveth life. 7. But if the ministration of death, written *and* engraven in stones, was glorious, so that the children of Israel could not stedfastly behold the face of Moses for the glory of his countenance; which *glory* was to be done away; 8.

How shall not the ministration of the spirit be rather glorious? 9. For if the ministration of condemnation *be* glory, much more doth the ministration of righteousness exceed in glory. 10. For even that which was made glorious had no glory in this respect, by reason of the glory that excelleth.

2 Cor. 4:1. Therefore seeing we have this ministry, as we have received mercy, we faint not; 2. But have renounced the hidden things of dishonesty, not walking in craftiness, nor handling the word of God deceitfully, but by manifestation of the truth commending ourselves to every man's conscience in the sight of God. 3. But if our gospel be hid, it is hid to them that are lost: 4. In whom the god of this world hath blinded the minds of them which believe not, lest the light of the glorious gospel of Christ, who is the image of God, should shine unto them. 5. For we preach not ourselves, but Christ Jesus the Lord; and ourselves your servants for Jesus' sake. 6. For God, who commanded the light to shine out of darkness, hath shined in our hearts, to *give* the light of the knowledge of the glory of God in the face of Jesus Christ. 7. But we have this treasure in earthen vessels, that the excellency of the power may be of God, and not of us. 8. *We are* troubled on every side, yet not distressed; *we are* perplexed, but not in despair; 9. Persecuted, but not forsaken; cast down, but not destroyed; 10. Always bearing about in the body the dying of the Lord Jesus, that the life also of Jesus might be made manifest in our body.

2 Cor. 5:11. Knowing therefore the terror of the Lord, we persuade men; but we are made manifest unto God; and I trust also are made manifest in your consciences. 18. And all things *are* of God, who hath reconciled us to himself by Jesus Christ, and hath given to us the ministry of reconciliation; 19. To wit, that God was in Christ, reconciling the world unto himself, not imputing their trespasses unto them; and hath committed unto us the word of reconciliation. 20. Now then we are ambassadors for Christ, as though God did beseech *you* by us: we pray *you* in Christ's stead, be ye reconciled to God.

2 Cor. 6:3. Giving no offence in any thing, that the ministry be not blamed: 4. But in all *things* approving ourselves as the ministers of God, in much patience, in afflictions, in necessities, in distresses, 5. In stripes, in imprisonments, in tumults, in labours, in watchings, in fastings; 6. By pureness, by knowledge, by longsuffering, by kindness, by the Holy Ghost, by love unfeigned, 7. By the word of truth, by the power of God, by the armour of righteousness on the right hand and on the left,

2 Cor. 10:1. Now I Paul myself beseech you by the meekness and gentleness of Christ, who in presence *am* base among you, but being absent am bold toward you:

2. But I beseech *you*, that I may not be bold when I am present with that confidence, wherewith I think to be bold against some, which think of us as if we walked according to the flesh. 8. For though I should boast somewhat more of our authority, which the Lord hath given us for edification, and not for your destruction, I should not be ashamed:

2 Cor. 13:10. Therefore I write these things being absent, lest being present I should use sharpness, according to the power which the Lord hath given me to edification, and not to destruction.

Gal. 2:8. (For he that wrought effectually in Peter to the apostleship of the circumcision, the same was mighty in me toward the Gentiles:)

Gal. 6:17. From henceforth let no man trouble me: for I bear in my body the marks of the Lord Jesus.

Phil. 3:17. Brethren, be followers together of me, and mark them which walk so as ye have us for an ensample.

1 Thess. 2:3. For our exhortation *was* not of deceit, nor of uncleanness, nor in guile: 4. But as we were allowed of God to be put in trust with the gospel, even so we speak; not as pleasing men, but God, which trieth our hearts. 5. For neither at any time used we flattering words, as ye know, nor a cloak of coveteousness; God *is* witness: 6. Nor of men sought we glory, neither of you, nor *yet* of others, when we might have been burdensome, as the apostles of Christ. 7. But we were gentle among you, even as a nurse cherisheth her children: 8. So being affectionately desirous of you, we were willing to have imparted unto you, not the gospel of God only, but also our own souls, because ye were dear unto us. 9. For ye remember, brethren, our labour and travail: for labouring night and day, because we would not be chargeable unto any of you, we preached unto you the gospel of God. 10. Ye *are* witnesses, and God *also*, how holily and justly and unblameably we behaved ourselves among you that believe: 11. As ye know how we exhorted and comforted and charged every one of you, as a father *doth* his children, 12. That ye would walk worthy of God, who hath called you unto his kingdom and glory.

1 Tim. 3:1. This *is* a true saying, If a man desire the office of a bishop, he desireth a good work. 2. A bishop then must be blameless, the husband of one wife, vigilant, sober, of good behaviour, given to hospitality, apt to teach; 3. Not given to wine, no striker, not greedy of filthy lucre; but patient, not a brawler, not coveteous; 4. One that ruleth well his own house, having his children in subjection with all gravity; 5. (For if a man know not how to rule his own house, how shall he take care of the church of God?) 6. Not a novice, lest being lifted up with pride he fall into the condemnation of the devil. 7. Moreover he must have a

good report of them which are without; lest he fall into reproach and the snare of the devil. 8. Likewise *must* the deacons *be* grave, not doubletongued, not given to much wine, not greedy of filthy lucre; 9. Holding the mystery of the faith in a pure conscience. 10. And let these also first be proved; then let them use the office of a deacon, being *found* blameless. 11. Even so *must their* wives *be* grave, not slanderers, sober, faithful in all things. 12. Let the deacons be the husbands of one wife, ruling their children and their own houses well. 13. For they that have used the office of a deacon well purchase to themselves a good degree, and great boldness in the faith which is in Christ Jesus. 15. If I tarry long, that thou mayest know how thou oughtest to behave thyself in the house of God,

1 Tim. 5:17. Let the elders that rule well be counted worthy of double honour, especially they who labour in the word and doctrine. 21. I charge *thee* before God, and the Lord Jesus Christ, and the elect angels, that thou observe these things without preferring one before another, doing nothing by partiality.

1 Tim. 6:11. O man of God, flee these things; and follow after righteousness, godliness, faith, love, patience, meekness. 13. I give thee charge in the sight of God, who quickeneth all things, and *before* Christ Jesus, who before Pontius Pilate witnessed a good confession; 14. That thou keep *this* commandment without spot, unrebukeable, until the appearing of our Lord Jesus Christ: 20. O Timothy, keep that which is committed to thy trust, avoiding profane *and* vain babblings, and oppositions of science falsely so called: 21. Which some professing have erred concerning the faith.

2 Tim. 1:6. Wherefore I put thee in remembrance that thou stir up the gift of God, which is in thee by the putting on of my hands. 7. For God hath not given us the spirit of fear; but of power, and of love, and of a sound mind. 8. Be not thou therefore ashamed of the testimony of our Lord, nor of me his prisoner: but be thou partaker of the afflictions of the gospel according to the power of God; 13. Hold fast the form of sound words, which thou hast heard of me, in faith and love which is in Christ Jesus. 14. That good thing which was committed unto thee keep by the Holy Ghost which dwelleth in us.

2 Tim. 2:1. Thou therefore, my son, be strong in the grace that is in Christ Jesus. 2. And the things that thou hast heard of me among many witnesses, the same commit thou to faithful men, who shall be able to teach others also. 3. Thou therefore endure hardness, as a good soldier of Jesus Christ. 4. No man that warreth entangleth himself with the affairs of *this* life; that he may please him who hath chosen him to be a soldier. 5. If a man also strive for

masteries, *yet* is he not crowned, except he strive lawfully. 6. The husbandman that laboureth must be first partaker of the fruits. 7. Consider what I say; and the Lord give thee understanding in all things. 14. Of these things put *them* in remembrance, charging *them* before the Lord that they strive not about words to no profit, *but* to the subverting of the hearers. 15. Study to shew thyself approved unto God, a workman that needeth not to be ashamed, rightly dividing the word of truth. 16. But shun profane *and* vain babblings: for they will increase unto more ungodliness. 20. In a great house there are not only vessels of gold and of silver, but also of wood and of earth; and some to honour, and some to dishonour. 21. If a man therefore purge himself from these, he shall be a vessel unto honour, sanctified, and meet for the master's use, *and* prepared unto every good work. 22. Flee also youthful lusts: but follow righteousness, faith, charity, peace, with them that call on the Lord out of a pure heart. 23. But foolish and unlearned questions avoid, knowing that they do gender strifes. 24. And the servant of the Lord must not strive; but be gentle unto all *men*, apt to teach, patient, 25. In meekness instructing those that oppose themselves; if God peradventure will give them repentance to the acknowledging of the truth; 26. And *that* they may recover themselves out of the snare of the devil, who are taken captive by him at his will.

2 Tim. 3:14. Continue thou in the things which thou hast learned and hast been assured of, knowing of whom thou hast learned *them;* 16. All scripture *is* given by inspiration of God, and *is* profitable for doctrine, for reproof, for correction, for instruction in righteousness: 17. That the man of God may be perfect, throughly furnished unto all good works.

Tit. 1:5. For this cause left I thee in Crete, that thou shouldest set in order the things that are wanting, and ordain elders in every city, as I had appointed thee: 6. If any be blameless, the husband of one wife, having faithful children not accused of riot or unruly. 7. For a bishop must be blameless, as the steward of God; not selfwilled, not soon angry, [1 not given to wine,] no striker, not given to filthy lucre; 8. But a lover of hospitality, a lover of good men, sober, just, holy, temperate; 9. Holding fast the faithful word as he hath been taught, that he may be able by sound doctrine both to exhort and to convince the gainsayers. 13. Wherefore rebuke them sharply, that they may be sound in the faith; 14. Not giving heed to Jewish fables, and commandments of men, that turn from the truth.   [1 R. V. no brawler]

Tit. 2:1. Speak thou the things which become sound doctrine: 7. In all things shewing thyself a pattern of good works: in doctrine *shewing* uncorruptness, gravity, sincerity, 8. Sound speech, that cannot be condemned; that he that is of the contrary part may be ashamed, having no evil thing to say of you. 15. These things speak, and exhort, and rebuke with all authority. Let no man despise thee.

Tit. 3:1. Put them in mind to be subject to principalities and powers, to obey magistrates, to be ready to every good work, 2. To speak evil of no man, to be no brawlers, *but* gentle, shewing all meekness unto all men. 8. *This is* a faithful saying, and these things I will that thou affirm constantly, that they which have believed in God might be careful to maintain good works. These things are good and profitable unto men. 9. But avoid foolish questions, and genealogies, and contentions, and strivings about the law; for they are unprofitable and vain. [See Epistles to Timothy, and Titus, in full.]

Heb. 5:1. For every high priest taken from among men is ordained for men in things *pertaining* to God, that he may offer both gifts and sacrifices for sins: 2. Who can have compassion on the ignorant, and on them that are out of the way; for that he himself also is compassed with infirmity. 3. And by reason hereof he ought, as for the people, so also for himself, to offer for sins. 12. For when for the time ye ought to be teachers, ye have need that one teach you again which *be* the first principles of the oracles of God; and are become such as have need of milk, and not of strong meat. 13. For every one that useth milk *is* unskilful in the word of righteousness: for he is a babe. 14. But strong meat belongeth to them that are of full age, *even* those who by reason of use have their senses exercised to discern both good and evil.

Heb. 13:6. So that we may boldly say, The Lord *is* my helper, and I will not fear what man shall do unto me. 7. Remember them which have the rule over you, who have spoken unto you the word of God: whose faith follow, considering the end of *their* conversation. 9. Be not carried about with divers and strange doctrines. For *it is* a good thing that the heart be established with grace; not with meats, which have not profited them that have been occupied therein. 17. Obey them that have the rule over you, and submit yourselves: for they watch for your souls, as they that must give account, that they may do it with joy, and not with grief: for that *is* unprofitable for you.

Jas. 3:1. My brethren, be not many masters, knowing that we shall receive the greater condemnation. 13. Who *is* a wise man and endued with knowledge among you? let him shew out of a good conversation his works with meekness of wisdom. 16. For where envying and strife *is*, there *is* confusion and every evil work. 17. But the wisdom that is from above is first pure, then peaceable, gentle, *and* easy to be intreated, full of mercy and good fruits, without partiality, and without hypocrisy. 18. And the fruit of righteousness is sown in peace of them that make peace.

1 Pet. 4:10. As every man hath received the gift, *even so* minister the same one to another, as good stewards of the manifold grace of God. 11. If any man speak, *let him speak* as the oracles of God; if any man minister, *let him do it* as of the ability which God giveth: that God in all things may be glorified through Jesus Christ,

CHARGE DELIVERED TO: Num. 18:1. And the LORD said unto Aaron, Thou and thy sons and thy father's house with thee shall bear the iniquity of the sanctuary: and thou and thy sons with thee shall bear the iniquity of your priesthood. 2. And thy brethren also of the tribe of Levi, the tribe of thy father, bring thou with thee, that they may be joined unto thee, and minister unto thee: but thou and thy sons with thee *shall minister* before the tabernacle of witness. 3. And they shall keep thy charge, and the charge of all the tabernacle: only they shall not come nigh the vessels of the sanctuary and the altar, that neither they, nor ye also, die. 4. And they shall be joined unto thee, and keep the charge of the tabernacle of the congregation, for all the service of the tabernacle: and a stranger shall not come nigh unto you. 5. And ye shall keep the charge of the sanctuary, and the charge of the altar: that there be no wrath any more upon the children of Israel. 6. And I, behold, I have taken your brethren the Levites from among the children of Israel: to you *they are* given *as* a gift for the LORD, to do the service of the tabernacle of the congregation. 7. Therefore thou and thy sons with thee shall keep your priest's office for every thing of the altar, and within the vail; and ye shall serve: I have given your priest's office *unto you as* a service of gift:

Num. 27:18. And the LORD said unto Moses, Take thee Joshua the son of Nun, a man in whom *is* the spirit, and lay thine hand upon him; 19. And set him before Eleazar the priest, and before all the congregation; and give him a charge in their sight. 20. And thou shalt put *some* of thine honour upon him, that all the congregation of the children of Israel may be obedient. 21. And he shall stand before Eleazar the priest, who shall ask *counsel* for him after the judgment of Urim before the LORD: at his word shall they go out, and at his word they shall come in, *both* he, and all the children of Israel with him, even all the congregation. 22. And Moses did as the LORD commanded him: and he took Joshua, and set him before Eleazar the priest, and before all the congregation: 23. And he laid his hands upon him, and gave him a charge, as the LORD commanded by the hand of Moses.

Deut. 31:7. And Moses called unto Joshua, and said unto him in the sight of all Israel, Be strong and of a good courage: for thou must go with this people unto the land which the LORD hath sworn unto their fathers to give them; and thou shalt cause them to inherit it. 8. And the LORD, he *it is* that doth go before thee; he will be with thee, he will not fail thee, neither forsake thee: fear not, neither be dismayed. Deut. 31:14–23.

Josh. 1:1. Now after the death of Moses the servant of the LORD it came to pass, that the LORD spake unto Joshua the son of Nun, Moses' minister, saying, 2. Moses my servant is dead; now therefore arise, go over this Jordan, thou, and all this people, unto the land which I do give to them, *even* to the children of Israel. 3. Every place that the sole of your foot shall tread upon, that have I given unto you, as I said unto Moses. 4. From the wilderness and this Lebanon even unto the great river, the river Euphrates, all the land of the Hittites, and unto the great sea toward the going down of the sun, shall be your coast. 5. There shall not any man be able to stand before thee all the days of thy life: as I was with Moses, *so* I will be with thee: I will not fail thee, nor forsake thee. 6. Be strong and of a good courage: for unto this people shalt thou divide for an inheritance the land, which I sware unto their fathers to give them. 7. Only be thou strong and very courageous, that thou mayest observe to do according to all the law, which Moses my servant commanded thee: turn not from it *to* the right hand or *to* the left, that thou mayest prosper whithersoever thou goest. 8. This book of the law shall not depart out of thy mouth; but thou shalt meditate therein day and night, that thou mayest observe to do according to all that is written therein: for then thou shalt make thy way prosperous, and then thou shalt have good success. 9. Have not I commanded thee? Be strong and of a good courage; be not afraid, neither be thou dismayed: for the LORD thy God *is* with thee whithersoever thou goest.

Ezek. 3:4. And he said unto me, Son of man, go, get thee unto the house of Israel, and speak with my words unto them.

Matt. 10:5. These twelve Jesus sent forth, and commanded them, saying, Go not into the way of the Gentiles, and into *any* city of the Samaritans enter ye not: 6. But go rather to the lost sheep of the house of Israel. 7. And as ye go, preach, saying, The kingdom of heaven is at hand. 8. Heal the sick, cleanse the lepers, raise the dead, cast out devils: freely ye have received, freely give. 9. Provide neither gold, nor silver, nor brass in your purses, 10. Nor scrip for *your* journey, neither two coats, neither shoes, nor yet staves: for the workman is worthy of his meat. 11. And into whatsoever city or town ye shall enter, inquire who in it is worthy: and there abide till ye go thence. 12. And when ye come into an house, salute it. 13. And if the house be worthy, let your peace come upon it: but if it be not worthy, let your peace return to you. 14. And whosoever shall not receive you, nor hear your words, when ye depart out of that house or city, shake off the dust of your feet. 15. Verily I say unto you, It shall be more tolerable for the land of Sodom and Gomorrha in the day of judgment, than for that city. [Mark 6:11.] 16. Behold, I send you forth as sheep in the midst of wolves: be ye therefore wise as serpents, and harmless as doves. 17. But beware of men: for they will deliver you up to the councils, and they will scourge you in their synagogues; 18. And ye shall be brought before governors and kings for my sake, for a testimony against them and the Gentiles. 19. But when they deliver you up, take no thought how or what ye shall speak: for it shall be given you in that same hour what ye shall speak. 20. For it is not ye that speak, but the Spirit of your Father which speaketh in you. 21. And the brother shall deliver up the brother to death, and the father the child: and the children shall rise up against *their* parents, and cause them to be put to death. 22. And ye shall be hated of all *men* for my name's sake: but he that endureth to the end shall be saved. 23. But when they persecute you in this city, flee ye into another: for verily I say unto you, Ye shall not have gone over the cities of Israel, till the Son of man be come. 24. The disciple is not above *his* master, nor the servant above his lord. 25. It is enough for the disciple that he be as his master, and the servant as his lord. If they have called the master of the house Beelzebub, how much more *shall they call* them of his household? 26. Fear them not therefore: for there is nothing covered, that shall not be revealed; and hid, that shall not be known. 27. What I tell you in darkness, *that* speak ye in light: and what ye hear in the ear, *that* preach ye upon the housetops. 28. And fear not them which kill the body, but are not able to kill the soul: but rather fear him which is able to destroy both soul and body in hell. 29. Are not two sparrows sold for a farthing? and one of them shall not fall on the ground without your Father. 30. But the very hairs of your head are all numbered. 31. Fear ye not therefore, ye are of more value than many sparrows. 32. Whosoever therefore shall confess me before men, him will I confess also before my Father which is in heaven. 33. But whosoever shall deny me before men, him will I also deny before my Father which is in heaven. 34. Think not that I am come to send peace on earth: I came not to send peace, but a sword. 35. For I am come to set a man at variance against his father, and the daughter against her mother, and the daughter in law against her mother in law. 36. And a man's foes *shall be* they of his own household. 37. He that loveth father or mother more than

me is not worthy of me: and he that loveth son or daughter more than me is not worthy of me. 38. And he that taketh not his cross, and followeth after me, is not worthy of me. 39. He that findeth his life shall lose it: and he that loseth his life for my sake shall find it. 40. He that receiveth you receiveth me; and he that receiveth me receiveth him that sent me. 41. He that receiveth a prophet in the name of a prophet shall receive a prophet's reward; and he that receiveth a righteous man in the name of a righteous man shall receive a righteous man's reward. 42. And whosoever shall give to drink unto one of these little ones a cup of cold *water* only in the name of a disciple, verily I say unto you, he shall in no wise lose his reward.

Luke 10:1. After these things the Lord appointed other seventy also, and sent them two and two before his face into every city and place, whither he himself would come. 2. Therefore said he unto them, The harvest truly *is* great, but the labourers *are* few: pray ye therefore the Lord of the harvest, that he would send forth labourers into his harvest. 3. Go your ways: behold, I send you forth as lambs among wolves. 4. Carry neither purse, nor scrip, nor shoes: and salute no man by the way. 5. And into whatsoever house ye enter, first say, Peace *be* to this house. 6. And if the son of peace be there, your peace shall rest upon it: if not, it shall turn to you again. 7. And in the same house remain, eating and drinking such things as they give: for the labourer is worthy of his hire. Go not from house to house. 8. And into whatsoever city ye enter, and they receive you, eat such things as are set before you: 9. And heal the sick that are therein, and say unto them, The kingdom of God is come nigh unto you. 10. But into whatsoever city ye enter, and they receive you not, go your ways out into the streets of the same, and say, 11. Even the very dust of your city, which cleaveth on us, we do wipe off against you: notwithstanding, be ye sure of this, that the kingdom of God is come nigh unto you. 12. But I say unto you, that it shall be more tolerable in that day for Sodom, than for that city. 13. Woe unto thee, Chorazin! woe unto thee, Bethsaida! for if the mighty works had been done in Tyre and Sidon, which have been done in you, they had a great while ago repented, sitting in sackcloth and ashes. 14. But it shall be more tolerable for Tyre and Sidon at the judgment, than for you. 15. And thou, Capernaum, which art exalted to heaven, shalt be thrust down to hell. 16. He that heareth you heareth me; and he that despiseth you despiseth me; and he that despiseth me despiseth him that sent me.

1 Tim. 1:18. This charge I commit unto thee, son Timothy, according to the prophecies which went before on thee, that thou

by them mightest war a good warfare; 19. Holding faith, and a good conscience; which some having put away concerning faith have made shipwreck: 20. Of whom is Hymenæus and Alexander; whom I have delivered unto Satan, that they may learn not to blaspheme.

1 Tim. 2:1. I exhort therefore, that, first of all, supplications, prayers, intercessions, *and* giving of thanks, be made for all men; 2. For kings, and *for* all that are in authority; that we may lead a quiet and peaceable life in all godliness and honesty. 3. For this *is* good and acceptable in the sight of God our Saviour; 4. Who will have all men to be saved, and to come unto the knowledge of the truth. 5. For *there is* one God, and one mediator between God and men, the man Christ Jesus; 6. Who gave himself a ransom for all, to be testified in due time. 7. Whereunto I am ordained a preacher, and an apostle, (I speak the truth in Christ, *and* lie not;) a teacher of the Gentiles in faith and verity. 8. I will therefore that men pray every where, lifting up holy hands, without wrath and doubting. 9. In like manner also, that women adorn themselves in modest apparel, with shamefacedness and sobriety; not with braided hair, or gold, or pearls, or costly array; 10. But (which becometh women professing godliness) with good works. 11. Let the woman learn in silence with all subjection. 12. But I suffer not a woman to teach, nor to usurp authority over the man, but to be in silence. 13. For Adam was first formed, then Eve. 14. And Adam was not deceived, but the woman being deceived was in the transgression. 15. Notwithstanding she shall be saved in childbearing, if they continue in faith and charity and holiness with sobriety.

1 Tim. 3:1. This *is* a true saying, If a man desire the office of a bishop, he desireth a good work. 2. A bishop then must be blameless, the husband of one wife, vigilant, sober, of good behaviour, given to hospitality, apt to teach; 3. Not given to wine, no striker, not greedy of filthy lucre; but patient, not a brawler, not covetous; 4. One that ruleth well his own house, having his children in subjection with all gravity; 5. (For if a man know not how to rule his own house, how shall he take care of the church of God?) 6. Not a novice, lest being lifted up with pride he fall into the condemnation of the devil. 7. Moreover he must have a good report of them which are without: lest he fall into reproach and the snare of the devil. 8. Likewise *must* the deacons *be* grave, not doubletongued, not given to much wine, not greedy of filthy lucre; 9. Holding the mystery of the faith in a pure conscience. 10. And let these also first be proved; then let them use the office of a deacon, being *found* blameless. 11. Even so *must their* wives *be* grave, not slanderers, sober, faithful in all things. 12. Let

the deacons be the husbands of one wife, ruling their children and their own houses well. 13. For they that have used the office of a deacon well purchase to themselves a good degree, and great boldness in the faith which is in Christ Jesus. 14. These things write I unto thee, hoping to come unto thee shortly: 15. But if I tarry long, that thou mayest know how thou oughtest to behave thyself in the house of God, which is the church of the living God, the pillar and ground of the truth. 16. And without controversy great is the mystery of godliness: ¹God was manifest in the flesh, justified in the Spirit, seen of angels, preached unto the Gentiles, believed on in the world, received up into glory. [¹ R. V. He who]

1 Tim. 4:1. Now the Spirit speaketh expressly, that in the latter times some shall depart from the faith, giving heed to seducing spirits, and doctrines of devils; 2. Speaking lies in hypocrisy; having their conscience seared with a hot iron; 3. Forbidding to marry, *and commanding* to abstain from meats, which God hath created to be received with thanksgiving of them which believe and know the truth. 4. For every creature of God *is* good, and nothing to be refused, if it be received with thanksgiving: 5. For it is sanctified by the word of God and prayer. 6. If thou put the brethren in remembrance of these things, thou shalt be a good minister of Jesus Christ, nourished up in the words of faith and of good doctrine, whereunto thou hast attained. 7. But refuse profane and old wives' fables, and exercise thyself *rather* unto godliness. 8. For bodily exercise profiteth little: but godliness is profitable unto all things, having promise of the life that now is, and of that which is to come. 9. This *is* a faithful saying and worthy of all acceptation. 10. For therefore we both labour and suffer reproach, because we trust in the living God, who is the Saviour of all men, specially of those that believe. 11. These things command and teach. 12. Let no man despise thy youth; but be thou an example of the believers, in word, in conversation, in charity, in spirit, in faith, in purity. 13. Till I come, give attendance to reading, to exhortation, to doctrine. 14. Neglect not the gift that is in thee, which was given thee by prophecy, with the laying on of the hands of the presbytery. 15. Meditate upon these things; give thyself wholly to them: that thy profiting may appear to all. 16. Take heed unto thyself, and unto the doctrine; continue in them: for in doing this thou shalt both save thyself, and them that hear thee.

1 Tim. 5:1. Rebuke not an elder, but intreat *him* as a father; *and* the younger men as brethren: 2. The elder women as mothers; the younger as sisters, with all purity. 3. Honour widows that are widows indeed. 4. But if any widow have children or nephews, let them learn first to shew

piety at home, and to requite their parents: for that is good and acceptable before God. 5. Now she that is a widow indeed, and desolate, trusteth in God, and continueth in supplications and prayers night and day. 6. But she that liveth in pleasure is dead while she liveth. 7. And these things give in charge, that they may be blameless. 8. But if any provide not for his own, and specially for those of his own house, he hath denied the faith, and is worse than an infidel. 9. Let not a widow be taken into the number under threescore years old, having been the wife of one man, 10. Well reported of for good works; if she have brought up children, if she have lodged strangers, if she have washed the saints' feet, if she have relieved the afflicted, if she have diligently followed every good work. 11. But the younger widows refuse: for when they have begun to wax wanton against Christ, they will marry; 12. Having damnation, because they have cast off their first faith. 13. And withal they learn *to be* idle, wandering about from house to house; and not only idle, but tattlers also and busybodies, speaking things which they ought not. 14. I will therefore that the younger women marry, bear children, guide the house, give none occasion to the adversary to speak reproachfully. 15. For some are already turned aside after Satan. 16. If any man or woman that believeth have widows, let them relieve them, and let not the church be charged; that it may relieve them that are widows indeed. 17. Let the elders that rule well be counted worthy of double honour, especially they who labour in the word and doctrine. 18. For the scripture saith, Thou shalt not muzzle the ox that treadeth out the corn. And, The labourer *is* worthy of his reward. 19. Against an elder receive not an accusation, but before two or three witnesses. 20. Them that sin rebuke before all, that others also may fear. 21. I charge *thee* before God, and the Lord Jesus Christ, and the elect angels, that thou observe these things without preferring one before another, doing nothing by partiality. 22. Lay hands suddenly on no man, neither be partaker of other men's sins: keep thyself pure.

1 Tim. 6:1. Let as many servants as are under the yoke count their own masters worthy of all honour, that the name of God and *his* doctrine be not blasphemed. 2. And they that have believing masters, let them not despise *them*, because they are brethren; but rather do *them* service, because they are faithful and beloved, partakers of the benefit. These things teach and exhort. 3. If any man teach otherwise, and consent not to wholesome words, *even* the words of our Lord Jesus Christ, and to the doctrine which is according to godliness; 4. He is proud, knowing nothing, but doting about questions and strifes of words, whereof cometh envy, strife, railings, evil surmisings,

5. Perverse disputings of men of corrupt minds, and destitute of the truth, supposing that gain is godliness: from such withdraw thyself. 6. But godliness with contentment is great gain. 7. For we brought nothing into *this* world, *and it is* certain we can carry nothing out. 8. And having food and raiment let us be therewith content. 9. But they that will be rich fall into temptation and a snare, and *into* many foolish and hurtful lusts, which drown men in destruction and perdition. 10. For the love of money is the root of all evil: which while some coveted after, they have erred from the faith, and pierced themselves through with many sorrows. 11. But thou, O man of God, flee these things; and follow after righteousness, godliness, faith, love, patience, meekness. 12. Fight the good fight of faith, lay hold on eternal life, whereunto thou art also called, and hast professed a good profession before many witnesses. 13. I give thee charge in the sight of God, who quickeneth all things, and *before* Christ Jesus, who before Pontius Pilate witnessed a good confession; 14. That thou keep *this* commandment without spot, unrebukeable, until the appearing of our Lord Jesus Christ: 15. Which in his times he shall shew, *who is* the blessed and only Potentate, the King of kings, and Lord of lords; 16. Who only hath immortality, dwelling in the light which no man can approach unto; whom no man hath seen, nor can see: to whom *be* honour and power everlasting. Amen. 17. Charge them that are rich in this world, that they be not highminded, nor trust in uncertain riches, but in the living God, who giveth us richly all things to enjoy; 18. That they do good, that they be rich in good works, ready to distribute, willing to communicate; 19. Laying up in store for themselves a good foundation against the time to come, that they may lay hold on eternal life. 20. O Timothy, keep that which is committed to thy trust, avoiding profane *and* vain babblings, and oppositions of science falsely so called: 21. Which some professing have erred concerning the faith. Grace *be* with thee. Amen.

2 Tim. 1:6. Wherefore I put thee in remembrance that thou stir up the gift of God, which is in thee by the putting on of my hands. 7. For God hath not given us the spirit of fear; but of power, and of love, and of a sound mind. 8. Be not thou therefore ashamed of the testimony of our Lord, nor of me his prisoner: but be thou partaker of the afflictions of the gospel according to the power of God; 9. Who hath saved us, and called *us* with an holy calling, not according to our works, but according to his own purpose and grace, which was given us in Christ Jesus before the world began, 10. But is now made manifest by the appearing of our Saviour Jesus Christ, who hath abolished death, and hath brought

life and ¹immortality to light through the gospel: 11. Whereunto I am appointed a preacher, and an apostle, and a teacher of the Gentiles. 12. For the which cause I also suffer these things: nevertheless I am not ashamed: for I know whom I have believed, and am persuaded that he is able to keep that which I have committed unto him against that day. 13. Hold fast the form of sound words, which thou hast heard of me, in faith and love which is in Christ Jesus. [¹ R. V. incorruption]

2 Tim. 2:1. Thou therefore, my son, be strong in the grace that is in Christ Jesus. 2. And the things that thou hast heard of me among many witnesses, the same commit thou to faithful men, who shall be able to teach others also. 3. Thou therefore endure hardness, as a good soldier of Jesus Christ. 4. No man that warreth entangleth himself with the affairs of *this* life; that he may please him who hath chosen him to be a soldier. 5. And if a man also strive for masteries, *yet* is he not crowned, except he strive lawfully. 6. The husbandman that laboureth must be first partaker of the fruits. 7. Consider what I say; and the Lord give thee understanding in all things. 8. Remember that Jesus Christ of the seed of David was raised from the dead according to my gospel: 9. Wherein I suffer trouble, as an evil doer, *even* unto bonds; but the word of God is not bound. 10. Therefore I endure all things for the elect's sakes, that they may also obtain the salvation which is in Christ Jesus with eternal glory. 11. *It is* a faithful saying: For if we be dead with *him*, we shall also live with *him:* 12. If we suffer, we shall also reign with *him:* if we deny *him*, he also will deny us: 13. If we believe not, *yet* he abideth faithful: he cannot deny himself. 14. Of these things put *them* in remembrance, charging *them* before the Lord that they strive not about words to no profit, *but* to the subverting of the hearers. 15. Study to shew thyself approved unto God, a workman that needeth not to be ashamed, rightly dividing the word of truth. 16. But shun profane *and* vain babblings: for they will increase unto more ungodliness. 17. And their word will eat as doth a canker: of whom is Hymenæus and Philetus; 18. Who concerning the truth have erred, saying that the resurrection is past already; and overthrow the faith of some. 19. Nevertheless the foundation of God standeth sure, having this seal, The Lord knoweth them that are his. And, Let every one that nameth the name of Christ depart from iniquity. 20. But in a great house there are not only vessels of gold and of silver, but also of wood and of earth; and some to honour, and some to dishonour. 21. If a man therefore purge himself from these, he shall be a vessel unto honour, sanctified, and meet for the master's use, *and* prepared unto every good

work. 22. Flee also youthful lusts: but follow righteousness, faith, charity, peace, with them that call on the Lord out of a pure heart. 23. But foolish and unlearned questions avoid, knowing that they do gender strifes. 24. And the servant of the Lord must not strive; but be gentle unto all *men*, apt to teach, patient, 25. In meekness instructing those that oppose themselves; if God peradventure will give them repentance to the acknowledging of the truth; 26. And *that* they may recover themselves out of the snare of the devil, who are taken captive by him at his will.

2 Tim. 3:1. This know also, that in the last days perilous times shall come. 2. For men shall be lovers of their own selves, covetous, boasters, proud, blasphemers, disobedient to parents, unthankful, unholy, 3. Without natural affection, trucebreakers, false accusers, incontinent, fierce, despisers of those that are good, 4. Traitors, heady, highminded, lovers of pleasures more than lovers of God; 5. Having a form of godliness, but denying the power thereof: from such turn away. 6. For of this sort are they which creep into houses, and lead captive silly women laden with sins, led away with divers lusts, 7. Ever learning, and never able to come to the knowledge of the truth. 8. Now as Jannes and Jambres withstood Moses, so do these also resist the truth: men of corrupt minds, reprobate concerning the faith. 9. But they shall proceed no further: for their folly shall be manifest unto all *men*, as their's also was. 10. But thou hast fully known my doctrine, manner of life, purpose, faith, longsuffering, charity, patience, 11. Persecutions, afflictions, which came unto me at Antioch, at Iconium, at Lystra; what persecutions I endured: but out of *them* all the Lord delivered me. 12. Yea, and all that will live godly in Christ Jesus shall suffer persecution. 13. But evil men and seducers shall wax worse and worse, deceiving, and being deceived. 14. But continue thou in the things which thou hast learned and hast been assured of, knowing of whom thou hast learned *them;* 15. And that from a child thou hast known the holy scriptures, which are able to make thee wise unto salvation through faith which is in Christ Jesus. 16. All scripture *is* given by inspiration of God, and *is* profitable for doctrine, for reproof, for correction, for instruction in righteousness: 17. That the man of God may be perfect, throughly furnished unto all good works.

2 Tim. 4:1. I charge *thee* therefore before God, and the Lord Jesus Christ, who shall judge the quick and the dead at his appearing and his kingdom; 2. Preach the word; be instant in season, out of season; reprove, rebuke, exhort with all longsuffering and doctrine. 3. For the time will come when they will not endure sound doctrine; but after their own lusts shall they heap to

themselves teachers, having itching ears; 4. And they shall turn away *their* ears from the truth, and shall be turned unto fables. 5. But watch thou in all things, endure afflictions, do the work of an evangelist, make full proof of thy ministry. 6. For I am now ready to be offered, and the time of my departure is at hand. 7. I have fought a good fight, I have finished *my* course, I have kept the faith: 8. Henceforth there is laid up for me a crown of righteousness, which the Lord, the righteous judge, shall give me at that day: and not to me only, but unto all them also that love his appearing.

COURAGE OF: See COURAGE; REPROOF, FAITHFULNESS IN.

DUTIES OF: Ex. 4:12. Now therefore go, and I will be with thy mouth, and teach thee what thou shalt say.

Lev. 10:11. That ye may teach the children of Israel all the statutes which the LORD hath spoken unto them by the hand of Moses. *vs.* 8–11.

Josh. 1:8. This book of the law shall not depart out of thy mouth; but thou shalt meditate therein day and night, that thou mayest observe to do according to all that is written therein:

2 Kin. 17:27. Then the king of Assyria commanded, saying, Carry thither one of the priests whom ye brought from thence; and let them go and dwell there, and let him teach them the manner of the God of the land. 28. Then one of the priests whom they had carried away from Samaria came and dwelt in Beth-el, and taught them how they should fear the LORD.

2 Chr. 29:11. My sons, be not now negligent: for the LORD hath chosen you to stand before him, to serve him, and that ye should minister unto him, and burn incense.

Isa. 40:1. Comfort ye, comfort ye my people, saith your God. 2. Speak ye comfortably to Jerusalem, and cry unto her, that her warfare is accomplished, that her iniquity is pardoned: 3. The voice of him that crieth in the wilderness, Prepare ye the way of the LORD, make straight in the desert a highway for our God. 9. O Zion, that bringeth good tidings, get thee up into the high mountain; O Jerusalem, that bringeth good tidings, lift up thy voice with strength; lift *it* up, be not afraid; say unto the cities of Judah, Behold your God! [Nah. 1:15.] 11. He shall feed his flock like a shepherd: he shall gather the lambs with his arm, and carry *them* in his bosom, *and* shall gently lead those that are with young.

Isa. 52:11. Depart ye, depart ye, go ye out from thence, touch no unclean *thing;* go ye out of the midst of her; be ye clean, that bear the vessels of the LORD.

Isa. 57:14. And shall say, Cast ye up, cast ye up, prepare the way, take up the stumblingblock out of the way of my people.

Isa. 58:1. Cry aloud, spare not, lift up thy voice like a trumpet, and shew my people their transgression, and the house of Jacob their sins.

Isa. 62:6. I have set watchmen upon thy walls, O Jerusalem, *which* shall never hold their peace day nor night: ye that make mention of the LORD, keep not silence, 7. And give him no rest, till he establish, and till he make Jerusalem a praise in the earth.

Jer. 1:7. But the LORD said unto me, Say not, I *am* a child: for thou shalt go to all that I shall send thee, and whatsoever I command thee thou shalt speak. 8. Be not afraid of their faces: for I *am* with thee to deliver thee, saith the LORD. 17. Thou therefore gird up thy loins, and arise, and speak unto them all that I command thee: be not dismayed at their faces, lest I confound thee before them. 18. For, behold, I have made thee this day a defenced city, and an iron pillar, and brasen walls against the whole land, against the kings of Judah, against the princes thereof, against the priests thereof, and against the people of the land. 19. And they shall fight against thee; but they shall not prevail against thee; for I *am* with thee, saith the LORD, to deliver thee. Jer. 15:20,21.

Jer. 4:15. For a voice declareth from Dan, and publisheth affliction from mount Ephraim.

Jer. 6:27. I have set thee *for* a tower *and* a fortress among my people, that thou mayest know and try their way.

Jer. 15:19. Thus saith the LORD, If thou return, then will I bring thee again, *and* thou shalt stand before me: and if thou take forth the precious from the vile, thou shalt be as my mouth: let them return unto thee; but return not thou unto them.

Jer. 23:4. And I will set up shepherds over them which shall feed them: and they shall fear no more, nor be dismayed, neither shall they be lacking, saith the LORD. 22. But if they had stood in my counsel, and had caused my people to hear my words, then they should have turned them from their evil way, and from the evil of their doings. 28. The prophet that hath a dream, let him tell a dream; and he that hath my word, let him speak my word faithfully.

Jer. 26:2. Thus saith the LORD; Stand in the court of the LORD's house, and speak unto all the cities of Judah, which come to worship in the LORD's house, all the words that I command thee to speak unto them: diminish not a word:

Ezek. 2:6. And thou, son of man, be not afraid of them, neither be afraid of their words, though briers and thorns *be* with thee, and thou dost dwell among scorpions: be not afraid of their words, nor be dismayed at their looks, though they *be* a rebellious house. 7. And thou shalt speak my words unto them, whether they will hear, or whether they will forbear: for they *are* most rebellious. 8. But thou, son of man, hear what I say unto thee; Be not thou rebellious like that rebellious house: open thy mouth, and eat that I give thee.

Ezek. 3:8. Behold, I have made thy face strong against their faces, and thy forehead strong against their foreheads. 9. As an adamant harder than flint have I made thy forehead: fear them not, neither be dismayed at their looks, though they *be* a rebellious house. 10. Moreover he said unto me, Son of man, all my words that I shall speak unto thee receive in thine heart, and hear with thine ears. 17. Son of man, I have made thee a watchman unto the house of Israel: therefore hear the word at my mouth and give them warning from me. 18. When I say unto the wicked, Thou shalt surely die; and thou givest him not warning, nor speakest to warn the wicked from his wicked way, to save his life; the same wicked *man* shall die in his iniquity; but his blood will I require at thine hand. 19. Yet if thou warn the wicked, and he turn not from his wickedness, nor from his wicked way, he shall die in his iniquity; but thou hast delivered thy soul. 20. Again, When a righteous *man* doth turn from his righteousness, and commit iniquity, and I lay a stumblingblock before him, he shall die: because thou hast not given him warning, he shall die in his sin, and his righteousness which he hath done shall not be remembered; but his blood will I require at thine hand. 21. Nevertheless if thou warn the righteous *man*, that the righteous sin not, and he doth not sin, he shall surely live, because he is warned; also thou hast delivered thy soul. 27. But when I speak with thee, I will open thy mouth, and thou shalt say unto them, Thus saith the Lord GOD; He that heareth, let him hear; and he that forbeareth, let him forbear: for they *are* a rebellious house.

Ezek. 6:11. Thus saith the Lord GOD; Smite with thine hand, and stamp with thy foot, and say, Alas for all the evil abominations of the house of Israel!

Ezek. 33:1. Again the word of the LORD came unto me, saying, 2. Son of man, speak to the children of thy people, and say unto them, When I bring the sword upon a land, if the people of the land take a man of their coasts, and set him for their watchman: 3. If when he seeth the sword come upon the land, he blow the trumpet, and warn the people; 4. Then whosoever heareth the sound of the trumpet, and taketh not warning; if the sword come, and take him away, his blood shall be upon his own head. 5. He heard the sound of the trumpet, and took not warning; his blood shall be upon him. But he that taketh warning shall deliver his soul. 6. But if the watchman see the sword come, and blow not the trumpet, and the people be not warned; if the sword come, and take *any* person from among them, he is taken away in his iniquity; but his blood will I require at the watchman's hand. 7. So thou, O son of man, I have set thee a watchman unto the house of Israel; therefore thou shalt hear the word at my mouth, and warn them from me. 8. When I say unto the wicked, O wicked *man*, thou shalt surely die; if thou dost not speak to warn the wicked from his way, that wicked *man* shall die in his iniquity; but his blood will I require at thine hand. 9. Nevertheless, if thou warn the wicked of his way to turn from it; if he do not turn from his way, he shall die in his iniquity; but thou hast delivered thy soul.

Ezek. 34:2. Son of man, prophesy against the shepherds of Israel, prophesy, and say unto them, Thus saith the Lord GOD unto the shepherds; Woe *be* to the shepherds of Israel that do feed themselves! should not the shepherds feed the flocks? 3. Ye eat the fat, and ye clothe you with the wool, ye kill them that are fed; *but* ye feed not the flock. 4. The diseased have ye not strengthened, neither have ye healed that which was sick, neither have ye bound up *that which was* broken, neither have ye brought again that which was driven away, neither have ye sought that which was lost; but with force and with cruelty have ye ruled them. 5. And they were scattered, because *there is* no shepherd: and they became meat to all the beasts of the field, when they were scattered. 6. My sheep wandered through all the mountains, and upon every high hill: yea, my flock was scattered upon all the face of the earth, and none did search or seek *after them.* 7. Therefore, ye shepherds, hear the word of the LORD; 8. *As* I live, saith the Lord GOD, surely because my flock became a prey, and my flock became meat to every beast of the field, because *there was* no shepherd, neither did my shepherds search for my flock, but the shepherds fed themselves, and fed not my flock; 9. Therefore, O ye shepherds, hear the word of the LORD; 10. Thus saith the Lord GOD; Behold, I *am* against the shepherds; and I will require my flock at their hand, and cause them to cease from feeding the flock; neither shall the shepherds feed themselves any more; for I will deliver my flock from their mouth, that they may not be meat for them. 11. For thus saith the Lord GOD; Behold, I, *even* I, will both search my sheep, and seek them out. 12. As a shepherd seeketh out his flock in the day that he is among his sheep *that are* scattered; so will I seek out my sheep, and will deliver them out of all places where they have been scattered in the cloudy and dark day. 13. And I will bring them out from the people, and gather them from the countries, and will bring them to their own land, and feed them upon the mountains of Israel by the rivers, and in all the inhabited places of the country. 14. I will feed them in a good pasture, and upon the high mountains of Israel shall their fold be: there shall they lie in a good fold, and *in* a fat pasture shall they feed upon the mountains of Israel. 15. I will feed my flock, and I will cause them to lie down, saith the Lord GOD. 16. I will seek that which was lost, and bring again that which was driven away, and will bind up *that which was* broken, and will strengthen that which was sick: but I will destroy the fat and the strong; I will feed them with judgment. 17. And *as for* you, O my flock, thus saith the Lord GOD; Behold, I judge between cattle and cattle, between the rams and the he goats. 18. *Seemeth it* a small thing unto you to have eaten up the good pasture, but ye must tread down with your feet the residue of your pastures? and to have drunk of the deep waters, but ye must foul the residue with your feet? 19. And *as for* my flock, they eat that which ye have trodden with your feet; and they drink that which ye have fouled with your feet. 20. Therefore thus saith the Lord GOD unto them; Behold, I, *even* I, will judge between the fat cattle and between the lean cattle. 21. Because ye have thrust with side and with shoulder, and pushed all the diseased with your horns, till ye have scattered them abroad; 22. Therefore will I save my flock, and they shall no more be a prey; and I will judge between cattle and cattle. 23. And I will set up one shepherd over them, and he shall feed them, *even* my servant David; he shall feed them, and he shall be their shepherd. 24. And I the LORD will be their God, and my servant David a prince among them; I the LORD have spoken *it*. 25. And I will make with them a covenant of peace, and will cause the evil beasts to cease out of the land: and they shall dwell safely in the wilderness, and sleep in the woods. 26. And I will make them and the places round about my hill a blessing; and I will cause the shower to come down in his season; there shall be showers of blessing. 27. And the tree of the field shall yield her fruit, and the earth shall yield her increase, and they shall be safe in their land, and shall know that I *am* the LORD, when I have broken the bands of their yoke, and delivered them out of the hand of those that served themselves of them. 28. And they shall no more be a prey to the heathen, neither shall the beast of the land devour them; but they shall dwell safely, and none shall make *them* afraid. 29. And I will raise up for them a plant of renown, and they shall be no more consumed with hunger in the land, neither bear the shame of the heathen any more. 30. Thus shall they know that I the LORD their God *am* with them, and *that* they, *even* the house of Israel, *are* my people, saith the Lord GOD. 31. And ye my flock, the flock of my pasture, *are* men, *and* I *am* your God, saith the Lord GOD.

Ezek. 44:23. And they shall teach my people *the difference* between the holy and profane, and cause them to discern between the unclean and the clean.

Joel 1:13. Gird yourselves, and lament, ye priests: howl, ye ministers of the altar: come, lie all night in sackcloth, ye ministers of my God: for the meat offering and the drink offering is withholden from the house of your God. 14. Sanctify ye a fast, call a solemn assembly, gather the elders *and* all the inhabitants of the land *into* the house of the LORD your God, and cry unto the LORD, 15. Alas for the day! for the day of the LORD *is* at hand, and as a destruction from the Almighty shall it come.

Joel 2:17. Let the priests, the ministers of the LORD, weep between the porch and the altar, and let them say, Spare thy people, O LORD, and give not thine heritage to reproach, that the heathen should rule over them: wherefore should they say among the people, Where *is* their God?

Jonah 1:2. Arise, go to Nineveh, that great city, and cry against it; for their wickedness is come up before me.

Hab. 2:2. And the LORD answered me, and said, Write the vision, and make *it* plain upon tables, that he may run that readeth it.

Mal. 2:7. For the priest's lips should keep knowledge, and they should seek the law at his mouth: for he *is* the messenger of the LORD of hosts.

Matt. 7:6. Give not that which is holy unto the dogs, neither cast ye your pearls before swine, lest they trample them under their feet, and turn again and rend you.

Matt. 10:7. And as ye go, preach, saying, The kingdom of heaven is at hand. 8. Heal the sick, cleanse the lepers, raise the dead, cast out devils: freely ye have received, freely give. 11. Into whatsoever city or town ye shall enter, enquire who in it is worthy; and there abide till ye go thence. 12. And when ye come into an house, salute it. 13. And if the house be worthy, let your peace come upon it: but if it be not worthy, let your peace return to you. 16. Behold, I send you forth as sheep in the midst of wolves: be ye therefore wise as serpents, and harmless as doves. 25. It is enough for the disciple that he be as his master, and the servant as his lord. 27. What I tell you in darkness, *that* speak ye in light: and what ye hear in the ear, *that* preach ye upon the housetops. 28. And fear not them which kill the body, but are not able to kill the soul: but rather fear him which is able to destroy both soul and body in hell.

Matt. 18:5. And whoso shall receive one such little child in my name receiveth me. [Luke 9:48.] 6. But whoso shall offend one of these little ones which believe in me, it were better for him that a millstone were hanged about his neck, and *that* he were drowned in the depth of the sea. 18. Verily I say unto you, Whatsoever ye shall bind on earth shall be bound in heaven: and whatsoever ye shall loose on earth shall be loosed in heaven. chapter 16:19.

Matt. 20:25. But Jesus called them *unto* him, and said, Ye know that the princes of the Gentiles exercise dominion over them, and they that are great exercise authority upon them. 26. But it shall not be so among you: but whosoever will be great among you, let him be your minister; 27. And whosoever will be chief among you, let him be your servant: 28. Even as the Son of man came not to be ministered unto, but to minister, and to give his life a ransom for many. Mark 10:43-45.

Matt. 28:19. Go ye therefore, and teach all nations, baptizing them in the name of the Father, and of the Son, and of the Holy Ghost: 20. Teaching them to observe all things whatsoever I have commanded you: and, lo, I am with you alway, *even* unto the end of the world. Amen.

Luke 22:32. But I have prayed for thee, that thy faith fail not: and when thou art converted, strengthen thy brethren.

Luke 24:48. And ye are witnesses of these things.

John 3:34. For he whom God hath sent speaketh the words of God: for God giveth not the Spirit by measure *unto him*.

John 4:35. Say not ye, There are yet four months, and *then* cometh harvest? behold, I say unto you, Lift up your eyes, and look on the fields; for they are white already to harvest. 36. And he that reapeth receiveth wages, and gathereth fruit unto life eternal: that both he that soweth and he that reapeth may rejoice together. 37. And herein is that saying true, One soweth, and another reapeth. 38. I sent you to reap that whereon ye bestowed no labour: other men laboured, and ye are entered into their labours.

John 15:27. And ye also shall bear witness, because ye have been with me from the beginning.

John 20:23. Whose soever sins ye remit, they are remitted unto them; *and* whose soever *sins* ye retain, they are retained.

John 21:15. So when they had dined, Jesus saith to Simon Peter, Simon, *son* of Jonas, lovest thou me more than these? He saith unto him, Yea, Lord; thou knowest that I love thee. He saith unto him, Feed my lambs. 16. He saith to him again the second time, Simon, *son* of Jonas, lovest thou me? He saith unto him, Yea, Lord; thou knowest that I love thee. He saith unto him, Feed my sheep. 17. He saith unto him the third time, Simon, *son* of Jonas, lovest thou me? Peter was grieved because he said unto him the third time, Lovest thou me? And he said unto him, Lord, thou knowest all things; thou knowest that I love thee. Jesus saith unto him, Feed my sheep.

Acts 1:21. Wherefore of these men which have companied with us all the time that the Lord Jesus went in and out among us, 22. Beginning from the baptism of John, unto that same day that he was taken up from us, must one be ordained to be a witness with us of his resurrection.

Acts 5:20. Go, stand and speak in the temple to the people all the words of this life.

Acts 6:2. Then the twelve called the multitude of the disciples *unto them*, and said, It is not reason that we should leave the word of God, and serve tables. 4. But we will give ourselves continually to prayer, and to the ministry of the word.

Acts 10:42. And he commanded us to preach unto the people, and to testify that it is he which was ordained of God *to be* the Judge of quick and dead.

Acts 16:4. And as they went through the cities, they delivered them the decrees for to keep, that were ordained of the apostles and elders which were at Jerusalem.

Acts 18:9. Then spake the Lord to Paul in the night by a vision, Be not afraid, but speak, and hold not thy peace: 10. For I am with thee, and no man shall set on thee to hurt thee: for I have much people in this city.

Acts 20:28. Take heed therefore unto yourselves, and to all the flock, over the which the Holy Ghost hath made you overseers, to feed the church of God, which he hath purchased with his own blood.

Acts 22:15. For thou shalt be his witness unto all men of what thou hast seen and heard.

Acts 26:16. But rise, and stand upon thy feet: for I have appeared unto thee for this purpose, to make thee a minister and a witness both of these things which thou hast seen, and of those things in the which I will appear unto thee; 17. Delivering thee from the people, and *from* the Gentiles, unto whom now I send thee, 18. To open their eyes, *and* to turn *them* from darkness to light, and *from* the power of Satan unto God, that they may receive forgiveness of sins, and inheritance among them which are sanctified by faith that is in me.

Rom. 1:14. I am debtor both to the Greeks, and to the barbarians; both to the wise, and to the unwise. 15. So, as much as in me is, I am ready to preach the gospel to you that are at Rome also.

Rom. 12:6. Having then gifts differing according to the grace that is given to us, whether prophecy, *let us prophesy* according to the proportion of faith; 7. Or ministry, *let us wait* on *our* ministering: or he that teacheth, on teaching; 8. Or he that exhorteth, on exhortation: he that giveth, *let him do it* with simplicity; he that ruleth, with diligence; he that sheweth mercy, with cheerfulness. *vs.* 3-5.

1 Cor. 1:16. And I baptized also the household of Stephanas: besides, I know not whether I baptized any other.

1 Cor. 4:1. Let a man so account of us, as of the ministers of Christ, and stewards of the mysteries of God. 2. Moreover it is required in stewards, that a man be found faithful. 21. What will ye? shall I come unto you with a rod, or in love, and *in* the spirit of meekness?

1 Cor. 9:16. For though I preach the gospel, I have nothing to glory of: for necessity is laid upon me; yea, woe is unto me, if I preach not the gospel! 17. For if I do this thing willingly, I have a reward: but if against my will, a dispensation *of the gospel* is committed unto me.

2 Cor. 1:24. Not for that we have dominion over your faith, but are helpers of your joy: for by faith ye stand.

2 Cor. 4:1. Therefore, seeing we have this ministry, as we have received mercy, we faint not; 2. But have renounced the hidden things of dishonesty, not walking in craftiness, nor handling the word of God deceitfully; but by manifestation of the truth commending ourselves to every man's conscience in the sight of God. 5. For we preach not ourselves, but Christ Jesus the Lord; and ourselves your servants for Jesus' sake.

2 Cor. 5:14. For the love of Christ constraineth us; because we thus judge, that if one died for all, ¹then were all dead: 18. And all things *are* of God, who hath reconciled us to himself by Jesus Christ, and hath given to us the ministry of reconciliation; 20. Now then we are ambassadors for Christ, as though God did beseech *you* by us: we pray *you* in Christ's stead, be ye reconciled to God.   [¹ R. V. therefore all died;]

2 Cor. 6:3. Giving no offence in any thing, that the ministry be not blamed: 4. But in all *things* approving ourselves as the ministers of God, in much patience, in afflictions, in necessities, in distresses, 5. In stripes, in imprisonments, in tumults, in labours, in watchings, in fastings; 6. By pureness, by knowledge, by longsuffering, by kindness, by the Holy Ghost, by love unfeigned, 7. By the word of truth, by the power of God, by the armour of righteousness on the right hand and on the left, 8. By honour and dishonour, by evil report and good report: as deceivers, and *yet* true; 9. As unknown, and *yet* well known; as dying, and, behold, we live; as chastened, and not killed; 10. As sorrowful, yet alway rejoicing; as poor, yet making many rich; as having nothing, and *yet* possessing all things.

2 Cor. 7:4. Great *is* my boldness of speech toward you, great *is* my glorying of you: I am filled with comfort, I am exceeding joyful in all our tribulation. 5. For, when we were come into Macedonia, our flesh had no rest, but we were troubled on every side; without *were* fightings, within *were* fears. 6. Nevertheless God, that comforteth those that are cast down, comforted us by the coming of Titus; 7. And not by his coming only, but by the consolation wherewith he was comforted in you, when he told us your earnest desire, your mourning, your fervent mind toward me; so that I rejoiced the more. 8. For though I made you sorry with a letter, I do not repent, though I did repent: for I perceive that the same epistle hath made you sorry, though *it were* but

for a season. 9. Now I rejoice, not that ye were made sorry, but that ye sorrowed to repentance: for ye were made sorry after a godly manner, that ye might receive damage by us in nothing. 12. Wherefore, though I wrote unto you, *I did it* not for his cause that had done the wrong, nor for his cause that suffered wrong, but that our care for you in the sight of God might appear unto you. 15. And his inward affection is more abundant toward you, whilst he remembereth the obedience of you all, how with fear and trembling ye received him.

2 Cor. 8:23. Whether *any do enquire* of Titus, *he is* my partner and fellowhelper concerning you: or our brethren *be enquired of, they are* the messengers of the churches, *and* the glory of Christ.

2 Cor. 10:8. For though I should boast somewhat more of our authority, which the Lord hath given us for edification, and not for your destruction, I should not be ashamed:

2 Cor. 12:15. And I will very gladly spend and be spent for you; though the more abundantly I love you, the less I be loved. 19. Again, think ye that we excuse ourselves unto you? we speak before God in Christ: but *we do* all things, dearly beloved, for your edifying.

2 Cor. 13:2. I told you before, and foretell you, as if I were present, the second time; and being absent now I write to them which heretofore have sinned, and to all other, that, if I come again, I will not spare: 10. Therefore I write these things being absent, lest being present I should use sharpness, according to the power which the Lord hath given me to edification, and not to destruction.

Gal. 1:10. For do I now persuade men, or God? or do I seek to please men? for if I yet pleased men, I should not be the servant of Christ.

Eph. 3:8. Unto me, who am less than the least of all saints, is this grace given, that I should preach among the Gentiles the unsearchable riches of Christ; 9. And to make all *men* see what *is* the fellowship of the mystery, which from the beginning of the world hath been hid in God, who created all things ¹ by Jesus Christ: 10. To the intent that now unto the principalities and powers in heavenly *places* might be known by the church the manifold wisdom of God,   [¹ Omitted in R. V.]

Eph. 4:11. He gave some, apostles; and some, prophets; and some, evangelists; and some, pastors and teachers; 12. For the perfecting of the saints, for the work of the ministry, for the edifying of the body of Christ:

Eph. 6:20. For which I am an ambassador in bonds: that therein I may speak boldly, as I ought to speak.

Col. 4:17. Say to Archippus, Take heed to the ministry which thou hast received in the Lord, that thou fulfil it.

1 Thess. 2:4. But as we were allowed of

God to be put in trust with the gospel, even so we speak; not as pleasing men, but God, which trieth our hearts. 5. For neither at any time used we flattering words, as ye know, nor a cloke of covetousness; God *is* witness: 6. Nor of men sought we glory, neither of you, nor *yet* of others, when we might have been burdensome, as the apostles of Christ. 7. But we were gentle among you, even as a nurse cherisheth her children: 8. So being affectionately desirous of you, we were willing to have imparted unto you, not the gospel of God only, but also our own souls, because ye were dear unto us. 10. Ye *are* witnesses, and God *also*, how holily and justly and unblameably we behaved ourselves among you that believe: 11. As ye know how we exhorted and comforted and charged every one of you, as a father *doth* his children, 12. That ye would walk worthy of God, who hath called you unto his kingdom and glory.

1 Thess. 3:2. And sent Timotheus, our brother, and minister of God, and our fellowlabourer in the gospel of Christ, to establish you, and to comfort you concerning your faith:

1 Thess. 5:12. And we beseech you, brethren, to know them which labour among you, and are over you in the Lord, and admonish you;

2 Thess. 3:4. And we have confidence in the Lord touching you, that ye both do and will do the things which we command you.

1 Tim. 1:3. As I besought thee to abide still at Ephesus, when I went into Macedonia, that thou mightest charge some that they teach no other doctrine, 4. Neither give heed to fables and endless genealogies, which minister questions, rather than godly edifying which is in faith: *so do*. 11. According to the glorious gospel of the blessed God, which was committed to my trust. 18. This charge I commit unto thee, son Timothy, according to the prophecies which went before on thee, that thou by them mightest war a good warfare; 19. Holding faith, and a good conscience; which some having put away concerning faith have made shipwreck:

1 Tim. 2:7. Whereunto I am ordained a preacher, and an apostle, (I speak the truth in Christ, *and* lie not;) a teacher of the Gentiles in faith and verity.

1 Tim. 4:6. If thou put the brethren in remembrance of these things, thou shalt be a good minister of Jesus Christ, nourished up in the words of faith and of good doctrine, whereunto thou hast attained. 7. But refuse profane and old wives' fables, and exercise thyself *rather* unto godliness. 12. Let no man despise thy youth; but be thou an example of the believers, in word, in conversation, in charity, in spirit, in faith, in purity. 13. Till I come, give attendance to reading, to exhortation, to doctrine. 14. Neglect not the gift that is in thee, which was given thee by prophecy, with the lay-

ing on of the hands of the presbytery. 15. Meditate upon these things; give thyself wholly to them; that thy profiting may appear to all. 16. Take heed unto thyself, and unto the doctrine; continue in them: for in doing this thou shalt both save thyself, and them that hear thee.

1 Tim. 5:1. Rebuke not an elder, but intreat *him* as a father; *and* the younger men as brethren; 2. The elder women as mothers; the younger as sisters, with all purity. 3. Honour widows that are widows indeed. 7. And these things give in charge, that they may be blameless. 8. But if any provide not for his own, and specially for those of his own house, he hath denied the faith, and is worse than an infidel. 9. Let not a widow be taken into the number under threescore years old, having been the wife of one man. 10. Well reported of for good works; if she have brought up children, if she have lodged strangers, if she have washed the saints' feet, if she have relieved the afflicted, if she have diligently followed every good work. 11. But the younger widows refuse: 19. Against an elder receive not an accusation, but before two or three witnesses. 20. Them that sin rebuke before all, that others also may fear. 21. I charge *thee* before God, and the Lord Jesus Christ, and the elect angels, that thou observe these things without preferring one before another, doing nothing by partiality. 22. Lay hands suddenly on no man, neither be partaker of other men's sins: keep thyself pure.

1 Tim. 6:3. If any man teach otherwise, and consent not to wholesome words, *even* the words of our Lord Jesus Christ, and to the doctrine which is according to godliness; 4. He is proud, knowing nothing, but doting about questions and strifes of words, whereof cometh envy, strife, railings, evil surmisings, 10. For the love of money is the root of all evil: which while some coveted after, they have erred from the faith, and pierced themselves through with many sorrows. 11. But thou, O man of God, flee these things; and follow after righteousness, godliness, faith, love, patience, meekness. 12. Fight the good fight of faith, lay hold on eternal life, whereunto thou art also called, and hast professed a good profession before many witnesses. 13. I give thee charge in the sight of God, who quickeneth all things, and *before* Christ Jesus, who before Pontius Pilate witnessed a good confession; 14. That thou keep *this* commandment without spot, unrebukeable, until the appearing of our Lord Jesus Christ: 17. Charge them that are rich in this world, that they be not highminded, nor trust in uncertain riches, but in the living God, who giveth us richly all things to enjoy; 18. That they do good, that they be rich in good works, ready to distribute, willing to communicate; 19. Laying up in store for themselves a good foundation against the time to come, that they may lay hold on eternal life. 20. O

Timothy, keep that which is committed to thy trust, avoiding profane *and* vain babblings, and oppositions of science falsely so called: 21. Which some professing have erred concerning the faith.

2 Tim. 1:6. Wherefore I put thee in remembrance that thou stir up the gift of God, which is in thee by the putting on of my hands. 7. For God hath not given us the spirit of fear; but of power, and of love, and of a sound mind. 8. Be not thou therefore ashamed of the testimony of our Lord, nor of me his prisoner: but be thou partaker of the afflictions of the gospel according to the power of God;

2 Tim. 2:2. And the things that thou hast heard of me among many witnesses, the same commit thou to faithful men, who shall be able to teach others also. 3. Thou therefore endure hardness, as a good soldier of Jesus Christ. 4. No man that warreth entangleth himself with the affairs of *this* life; that he may please him who hath chosen him to be a soldier. 5. And if a man also strive for masteries, *yet* is he not crowned, except he strive lawfully. 6. The husbandman that laboureth must be first partaker of the fruits. 7. Consider what I say; and the Lord give thee understanding in all things. 14. Of these things put *them* in remembrance, charging *them* before the Lord that they strive not about words to no profit, *but* to the subverting of the hearers. 15. Study to shew thyself approved unto God, a workman that needeth not to be ashamed, rightly dividing the word' of truth. 16. But shun profane *and* vain babblings: for they will increase unto more ungodliness. 23. But foolish and unlearned questions avoid, knowing that they do gender strifes. 24. And the servant of the Lord must not strive; but be gentle unto all *men*, apt to teach, patient, 25. In meekness instructing those that oppose themselves: if God peradventure will give them repentance to the acknowledging of the truth;

2 Tim. 4:1. I charge *thee* therefore before God, and the Lord Jesus Christ, who shall judge the quick and the dead at his appearing and his kingdom; 2. Preach the word; be instant in season, out of season; reprove, rebuke, exhort with all longsuffering and doctrine. 5. But watch thou in all things, endure afflictions, do the work of an evangelist, make full proof of thy ministry.

1 Pet. 5:1. The elders which are among you I exhort, who am also an elder, . . . 2. Feed the flock of God which is among you, taking the oversight *thereof*, not by constraint, but willingly; not for filthy lucre, but of a ready mind; 3. Neither as being lords over *God's* heritage, but being ensamples to the flock. 4. And when the chief Shepherd shall appear, ye shall receive a crown of glory that' fadeth not away.

2 Pet. 1:12. Wherefore I will not be negli-

gent to put you always in remembrance of these things, though ye know *them*, and be established in the present truth. 13. Yea, I think it meet, as long as I am in this tabernacle, to stir you up by putting *you* in remembrance; 14. knowing that shortly I must put off *this* my tabernacle, even as our Lord Jesus Christ hath shewed me. 15. Moreover I will endeavour that ye may be able after my decease to have these things always in remembrance. 16. For we have not followed cunningly devised fables, when we made known unto you the power and coming of our Lord Jesus Christ, but were eyewitnesses of his majesty.

See CHARGE DELIVERED TO, above.

DUTIES OF THE CHURCH TO: Deut. 1:38. *But* Joshua the son of Nun, which standeth before thee, he shall go in thither: encourage him: for he shall cause Israel to inherit it.

Deut. 3:28. But charge Joshua, and encourage him, and strengthen him:

Deut. 12:19. Take heed to thyself that thou forsake not the Levite as long as thou livest upon the earth.

Deut. 31:7. And Moses called unto Joshua, and said unto him in the sight of all Israel, Be strong and of a good courage: for thou must go with this people unto the land which the LORD hath sworn unto their fathers to give them; and thou shalt cause them to inherit it.

1 Cor. 11:1. Be ye followers of me, even as I also *am* of Christ. 2. Now I praise you, brethren, that ye remember me in all things, and keep the ordinances, as I delivered *them* to you.

1 Cor. 16:15. I beseech you, brethren, (ye know the house of Stephanas, that it is the firstfruits of Achaia, and *that* they have addicted themselves to the ministry of the saints,) 16. That ye submit yourselves unto such, and to every one that helpeth with *us*, and laboureth.

Phil. 3:17. Brethren, be followers together of me, and mark them which walk so as ye have us for an ensample.

Col. 4:10. Aristarchus my fellowprisoner saluteth you, and Marcus, sister's son to Barnabas, (touching whom ye received commandments: if he come unto you, receive him;)

1 Thess. 5:12. And we beseech you, brethren, to know them which labour among you, and are over you in the Lord, and admonish you; 13. And to esteem them very highly in love for their work's sake.

Heb. 13:7. Remember them which have the rule over you, who have spoken unto you the word of God: whose faith follow, considering the end of *their* conversation. 17. Obey them that have the rule over you, and submit yourselves: for they watch for your souls, as they that must give account, that they may do it with joy, and not with grief: for that *is* unprofitable for you. 18. Pray for us: for we trust we have a good conscience, in all things willing to live honestly.

See Church, Duties of, to Ministers.

EMOLUMENTS OF: Num. 18:20. And the Lord spake unto Aaron, Thou shalt have no inheritance in their land, neither shalt thou have any part among them: I *am* thy part and thine inheritance among the children of Israel.

Deut. 10:9. Wherefore Levi hath no part nor inheritance with his brethren; the Lord *is* his inheritance, according as the Lord thy God promised him.

Deut. 14:27. And the Levite that *is* within thy gates; thou shalt not forsake him; for he hath no part nor inheritance with thee.

Deut. 18:1. The priests the Levites, *and* all the tribe of Levi, shall have no part nor inheritance with Israel: they shall eat the offerings of the Lord made by fire, and his inheritance. 2. Therefore shall they have no inheritance among their brethren: the Lord *is* their inheritance, as he hath said unto them.

Josh. 13:14. Only unto the tribe of Levi he gave none inheritance; the sacrifices of the Lord God of Israel made by fire *are* their inheritance, as he said unto them. 33. But unto the tribe of Levi Moses gave not *any* inheritance: the Lord God of Israel *was* their inheritance, as he said unto them.

Josh. 18:7. But the Levites have no part among you; for the priesthood of the Lord *is* their inheritance:

Jer. 31:14. And I will satiate the soul of the priests with fatness, and my people shall be satisfied with my goodness, saith the Lord.

Ezek. 44:28. And it shall be unto them for an inheritance: I *am* their inheritance: and ye shall give them no possession in Israel: I *am* their possession.

Matt. 10:9. Provide neither gold, nor silver, nor brass in your purses; 10. Nor scrip for *your* journey, neither two coats, neither shoes, nor yet staves: for the workman is worthy of his meat. Mark 6:8.

Luke 10:7. And in the same house remain, eating and drinking such things as they give: for the labourer is worthy of his hire. Go not from house to house. 8. And into whatsoever city ye enter, and they receive you, eat such things as are set before you:

Luke 22:35. And he said unto them, When I sent you without purse, and scrip, and shoes, lacked ye any thing? And they said, Nothing. 36. Then said he unto them, But now, he that hath a purse, let him take *it*, and likewise *his* scrip: and he that hath no sword, let him sell his garment, and buy one.

John 4:36. And he that reapeth receiveth wages, and gathereth fruit unto life eternal:

Acts 20:33. I have coveted no man's silver, or gold, or apparel. 34. Yea, ye yourselves know, that these hands have minis-

tered unto my necessities, and to them that were with me.

1 Cor. 9:3. Mine answer to them that do examine me is this, 4. Have we not power to eat and to drink? 7. Who goeth a warfare any time at his own charges? who planteth a vineyard, and eateth not of the fruit thereof? or who feedeth a flock, and eateth not of the milk of the flock? 8. Say I these things as a man? or saith not the law the same also? 9. For it is written in the law of Moses, Thou shalt not muzzle the mouth of the ox that treadeth out the corn. Doth God take care for oxen? 10. Or saith he *it* altogether for our sakes? For our sakes, no doubt, *this* is written: that he that ploweth should plow in hope; and that he that thresheth in hope should be partaker of his hope. 11. If we have sown unto you spiritual things, *is it* a great thing if we shall reap your carnal things? 12. If others be partakers of *this* power over you, *are* not we rather? Nevertheless we have not used this power; but suffer all things, lest we should hinder the gospel of Christ. 13. Do ye not know that they which minister about holy things live *of the things* of the temple? and they which wait at the altar are partakers with the altar? 14. Even so hath the Lord ordained that they which preach the gospel should live of the gospel. 15. But I have used none of these things: neither have I written these things, that it should be so done unto me: for *it were* better for me to die, than that any man should make my glorying void. 16. For though I preach the gospel, I have nothing to glory of: for necessity is laid upon me; yea, woe is unto me, if I preach not the gospel! 17. For if I do this thing willingly, I have a reward: but if against my will, a dispensation *of the gospel* is committed unto me. 18. What is my reward then? *Verily* that, when I preach the gospel, I may make the gospel of Christ without charge, that I abuse not my power in the gospel. 19. For though I be free from all *men*, yet have I made myself servant unto all, that I might gain the more. 20. And unto the Jews I became as a Jew, that I might gain the Jews; to them that are under the law, as under the law, that I might gain them that are under the law; 21. To them that are without law, as without law, (being not without law to God, but under the law to Christ,) that I might gain them that are without law. 22. To the weak became I as weak, that I might gain the weak: I am made all things to all *men*, that I might by all means save some. 23. And this I do for the gospel's sake, that I might be partaker thereof with *you*. *vs.* 1-6.

2 Cor. 11:7. Have I committed an offence in abasing myself that ye might be exalted, because I have preached to you the gospel of God freely? 8. I robbed other churches, taking wages *of them*, to do you service. 9. And when I was present with you, and wanted, I was chargeable to no man: for

that which was lacking to me the brethren which came from Macedonia supplied: and in all *things* I have kept myself from being burdensome unto you, and *so* will I keep *myself*. 10. As the truth of Christ is in me, no man shall stop me of this boasting in the regions of Achaia.

2 Cor. 12:13. For what is it wherein ye were inferior to other churches, except *it be* that I myself was not burdensome to you? forgive me this wrong. 14. Behold, the third time I am ready to come to you; and I will not be burdensome to you: for I seek not yours, but you: for the children ought not to lay up for the parents, but the parents for the children. 15. And I will very gladly spend and be spent for you; though the more abundantly I love you, the less I be loved. 16. But be it so, I did not burden you: nevertheless, being crafty, I caught you with guile. 17. Did I make a gain of you by any of them I sent unto you? 18. I desired Titus, and with *him* I sent a brother. Did Titus make a gain of you? walked we not in the same spirit? *walked we* not in the same steps?

Gal. 6:6. Let him that is taught in the word communicate unto him that teacheth in all good things.

Phil. 4:10. But I rejoiced in the Lord greatly, that now at the last your care of me hath flourished again; wherein ye were also careful, but ye lacked opportunity. 11. Not that I speak in respect of want: for I have learned, in whatsoever state I am, *therewith* to be content. 12. I know both how to be abased, and I know how to abound: every where and in all things I am instructed both to be full and to be hungry, both to abound and to suffer need. 13. I can do all things through Christ which strengtheneth me. 14. Notwithstanding ye have well done, that ye did communicate with my affliction. 15. Now ye Philippians know also, that in the beginning of the gospel, when I departed from Macedonia, no church communicated with me as concerning giving and receiving, but ye only. 16. For even in Thessalonica ye sent once and again unto my necessity. 17. Not because I desire a gift: but I desire fruit that may abound to your account. 18. But I have all, and abound: I am full, having received of Epaphroditus the things *which were sent* from you, an odour of a sweet smell, a sacrifice acceptable, wellpleasing to God.

1 Thess. 2:5. For neither at any time used we flattering words, as ye know, nor a cloke of covetousness; God *is* witness: 6. Nor of men sought we glory, neither of you, nor *yet* of others, when we might have been burdensome, as the apostles of Christ. 9. For ye remember, brethren, our labour and travail: for labouring night and day, because we would not be chargeable unto any of you, we preached unto you the gospel of God.

2 Thess. 3:7. For yourselves know how ye ought to follow us: for we behaved not ourselves disorderly among you; 8. Neither did we eat any man's bread for nought; but wrought with labour and travail night and day, that we might not be chargeable to any of you: 9. Not because we have not power, but to make ourselves an ensample unto you to follow us.

1 Tim. 5:18. For the scripture saith, Thou shalt not muzzle the ox that treadeth out the corn. And, The labourer *is* worthy of his reward.

3 John 7. Because that for his name's sake they went forth, taking nothing of the Gentiles.

See Priests; Levites; Emoluments of.

FAITHFUL: Instances of: Moses, Deut. 4:26; 30:19; Heb. 3:2,5. Micaiah, 2 Chr. 18: 12,13. Azariah, 2 Chr. 26:16-20. Balaam, Num. 22:18,38; 23:8,12; 24:12-14. Nathan, 2 Sam. 12:1-14. Isaiah, Isa. 22:4,5; 39:3-7. Jeremiah, Jer. 17:16; 26:1-15; 28; 37:9,10,16-18. John the Baptist, Matt. 3:2-12; Mark 6: 18-28; Luke 3:7-9,19. Peter, Acts 8:18-23. Paul, Acts 20:26,27; Col. 1:7. The apostles, Acts 3:12-26; 4:9-13,19,20,31; 5:21,29-32.

FALSE AND CORRUPT: Deut. 13:1. If there arise among you a prophet, or a dreamer of dreams, and giveth thee a sign or a wonder, 2. And the sign or the wonder come to pass, whereof he spake unto thee, saying, Let us go after other gods, which thou hast not known, and let us serve them; 3. Thou shalt not hearken unto the words of that prophet, or that dreamer of dreams: for the Lord your God proveth you, to know whether ye love the Lord your God with all your heart and with all your soul. 4. Ye shall walk after the Lord your God, and fear him, and keep his commandments, and obey his voice, and ye shall serve him, and cleave unto him. 5. And that prophet, or that dreamer of dreams, shall be put to death; because he hath spoken to turn *you* away from the Lord your God, which brought you out of the land of Egypt, and redeemed you out of the house of bondage, to thrust thee out of the way which the Lord thy God commanded thee to walk in. So shalt thou put the evil away from the midst of thee.

Deut. 18:20. The prophet, which shall presume to speak a word in my name, which I have not commanded him to speak, or that shall speak in the name of other gods, even that prophet shall die. 21. And if thou say in thine heart, How shall we know the word which the Lord hath not spoken? 22. When a prophet speaketh in the name of the Lord, if the thing follow not, nor come to pass, that *is* the thing which the Lord hath not spoken, *but* the prophet hath spoken it presumptuously: thou shalt not be afraid of him. Deut. 13:3,5.

1 Kin. 12:31. And he made an house of high places, and made priests of the lowest of the people, which were not of the sons of Levi.

2 Chr. 29:34. But the priests were too few,

so that they could not flay all the burnt offerings: wherefore their brethren the Levites did help them, till the work was ended, and until the *other* priests had sanctified themselves: for the Levites *were* more upright in heart to sanctify themselves than the priests.

2 Chr. 30:15. Then they killed the passover on the fourteenth *day* of the second month: and the priests and the Levites were ashamed, and sanctified themselves, and brought in the burnt offerings into the house of the LORD.

Neh. 13:29. Remember them, O my God, because they have defiled the priesthood, and the covenant of the priesthood, and of the Levites.

Prov. 19:27. Cease, my son, to hear the instruction *that causeth* to err from the words of knowledge.

Isa. 3:12. O my people, they which lead thee cause *thee* to err, and destroy the way of thy paths.

Isa. 5:20. Woe unto them that call evil good, and good evil; that put darkness for light, and light for darkness; and put bitter for sweet, and sweet for bitter!

Isa. 8:19. And when they shall say unto you, Seek unto them that have familiar spirits, and unto wizards that peep, and that mutter: should not a people seek unto their God? for the living to the dead? [*R. V.*, On behalf of the living should they seek unto the dead?] 20. To the law and to the testimony: if they speak not according to this word, *it is* because *there is* no light in them.

Isa. 9:14. Therefore the LORD will cut off from Israel head and tail, branch and rush, in one day. 15. The ancient and honourable, he *is* the head; and the prophet that teacheth lies, he *is* the tail. 16. For the leaders of this people cause *them* to err; and *they that are* led of them *are* destroyed.

Isa. 28:7. The priest and the prophet have erred through strong drink, they are swallowed up of wine, they are out of the way through strong drink; they err in vision, they stumble *in* judgment.

Isa. 29:10. The LORD hath poured out upon you the spirit of deep sleep, and hath closed your eyes: the prophets and your rulers, the seers hath he covered. 11. And the vision of all is become unto you as the words of a book that is sealed,

Isa. 30:10. Which say to the seers, See not; and to the prophets, Prophesy not unto us right things, speak unto us smooth things, prophesy deceits:

Isa. 43:27. Thy first father hath sinned, and thy teachers [*R. V.*, interpreters] have transgressed against me. 28. Therefore I have profaned the princes of the sanctuary, and have given Jacob to the curse, and Israel to reproaches.

Isa. 44:20. He feedeth on ashes: a deceived heart hath turned him aside, that he cannot deliver his soul, nor say, *Is there* not a lie in my right hand?

Isa. 56:10. His watchmen *are* blind: they are all ignorant, they *are* all dumb dogs, they cannot bark; sleeping, lying down, loving to slumber. 11. Yea, *they are* greedy dogs *which* can never have enough, and they *are* shepherds *that* cannot understand: they all look to their own way, every one for his gain, from his quarter. 12. Come ye, *say they*, I will fetch wine, and we will fill ourselves with strong drink;

Jer. 2:8. The priests said not, Where *is* the LORD? and they that handle the law knew me not: the pastors also transgressed against me, and the prophets prophesied by Baal, and walked after *things that do* not profit.

Jer. 5:30. A wonderful and horrible thing is committed in the land; 31. The prophets prophesy falsely, and the priests bear rule by their means; and my people love *to have it* so: *vs.* 13, 14.

Jer. 6:13. From the prophet even unto the priest every one dealeth falsely. 14. They have healed also the hurt *of the daughter* of my people slightly, saying, Peace, peace; when *there is* no peace. Jer. 8:10, 11.

Jer. 10:21. For the pastors are become brutish, and have not sought the LORD: therefore they shall not prosper, and all their flocks shall be scattered.

Jer. 12:10. Many pastors have destroyed my vineyard, they have trodden my portion under foot, they have made my pleasant portion a desolate wilderness.

Jer. 13:20. Lift up your eyes, and behold them that come from the north: where *is* the flock *that* was given thee, thy beautiful flock?

Jer. 14:13. Then said I, Ah, Lord God! behold the prophets say unto them, Ye shall not see the sword, neither shall ye have famine; but I will give you assured peace in this place. 14. Then the LORD said unto me, The prophets prophesy lies in my name: I sent them not, neither have I commanded them, neither spake unto them: they prophesy unto you a false vision and divination, and a thing of nought, and the deceit of their heart. 15. Therefore thus saith the LORD concerning the prophets that prophesy in my name, and I sent them not, yet they say, Sword and famine shall not be in this land: By sword and famine shall those prophets be consumed. 16. And the people to whom they prophesy shall be cast out in the streets of Jerusalem because of the famine and the sword; and they shall have none to bury them, them, their wives, nor their sons, nor their daughters: for I will pour their wickedness upon them.

Jer. 23:1. Woe be unto the pastors that destroy and scatter the sheep of my pasture! saith the LORD. 2. Therefore thus saith the LORD God of Israel against the pastors that feed my people; Ye have scattered my flock, and driven them away, and have not visited them: behold, I will visit upon you the evil of your doings, 11. Both prophet and priest are profane: yea, in my house have I found their wickedness, saith the LORD. 14. I have seen also in the prophets of Jerusalem an horrible thing: they commit adultery, and walk in lies: they strengthen also the hands of evildoers, that none doth return from his wickedness: they are all of them unto me as Sodom, and the inhabitants thereof as Gomorrah. 15. Therefore thus saith the LORD of hosts concerning the prophets; Behold, I will feed them with wormwood, and make them drink the water of gall: for from the prophets of Jerusalem is profaneness gone forth into all the land. 16. Thus saith the LORD of hosts, Hearken not unto the words of the prophets that prophesy unto you: they make you vain: they speak a vision of their own heart, *and* not out of the mouth of the LORD. 21. I have not sent these prophets, yet they ran: I have not spoken to them, yet they prophesied. 31. Behold, I *am* against the prophets, saith the LORD, that use their tongues, and say, He saith. 32. Behold, I *am* against them that prophesy false dreams, saith the LORD, and do tell them, and cause my people to err by their lies, and by their lightness; yet I sent them not, nor commanded them: therefore they shall not profit this people at all, saith the LORD. 36. The burden of the LORD shall ye mention no more: for every man's word shall be his burden; for ye have perverted the words of the living God, *vs.* 25-39; Jer. 27:9-18.

Jer. 48:10. Cursed *be* he that doeth the work of the LORD ¹ deceitfully,   [¹ R. V. negligently]

Jer. 50:6. My people hath been lost sheep: their shepherds have caused them to go astray, they have turned them away *on* the mountains: they have gone from mountain to hill, they have forgotten their resting-place.

Lam. 2:14. Thy prophets have seen vain and foolish things for thee: and they have not discovered thine iniquity, to turn away thy captivity;

Lam. 4:13. For the sins of her prophets, *and* the iniquities of her priests, that have shed the blood of the just in the midst of her, 14. They have wandered *as* blind *men* in the streets, they have polluted themselves with blood, so that men could not touch their garments.

Ezek. 13:2. Son of man, prophesy against the prophets of Israel that prophesy, and say thou unto them that prophesy out of their own hearts, Hear ye the word of the LORD; 3. Thus saith the Lord GOD; Woe unto the foolish prophets, that follow their own spirit, and have seen nothing! 4. O Israel, thy prophets are like the foxes in the deserts. 5. Ye have not gone up into the gaps, neither made up the hedge for the house of Israel to stand in the battle in the day of the LORD. 10. They have seduced my people, saying, Peace; and *there was* no peace; and one built up a wall, and, lo,

others daubed it with untempered *morter*: 11. Say unto them which daub *it* with untempered *morter*, that it shall fall: 16. The prophets of Israel which prophesy concerning Jerusalem, and which see visions of peace for her, and *there is* no peace, saith the Lord GOD. 17. Likewise, thou son of man, set thy face against the daughters of thy people, which prophesy out of their own heart; and prophesy thou against them, 18. And say, Thus saith the Lord GOD; Woe to the *women* that sew pillows to all armholes, and make kerchiefs upon the head of every stature to hunt souls! Will ye hunt the souls of my people, and will ye save the souls alive *that come* unto you? 19. Will ye pollute me among my people for handfuls of barley and for pieces of bread, to slay the souls that should not die, and to save the souls alive that should not live, by your lying to my people that hear *your* lies? 22. With lies ye have made the heart of the righteous sad, whom I have not made sad; and strengthened the hands of the wicked, that he should not return from his wicked way, by promising him life: *vs.* 1-23.

Ezek. 14:9. If the prophet be deceived when he hath spoken a thing, I the LORD have deceived that prophet, and I will stretch out my hand upon him, and will destroy him from the midst of my people Israel. 10. And they shall bear the punishment of their iniquity: the punishment of the prophet shall be even as the punishment of him that seeketh *unto him;*

Ezek. 22:25. *There is* a conspiracy of her prophets in the midst thereof, like a roaring lion ravening the prey; they have devoured souls; they have taken the treasure and precious things; they have made her many widows in the midst thereof. 26. Her priests have violated my law, and have profaned mine holy things: they have put no difference between the holy and profane, neither have they shewed *difference* between the unclean and the clean, and have hid their eyes from my sabbaths, and I am profaned among them. 28. Her prophets have daubed them with untempered *morter*, seeing vanity, and divining lies unto them, saying, Thus saith the Lord GOD, when the LORD hath not spoken.

Ezek. 34:2. Woe *be* to the shepherds of Israel that do feed themselves! should not the shepherds feed the flocks? 3. Ye eat the fat, and ye clothe you with the wool, ye kill them that are fed: *but* ye feed not the flock. 4. The diseased have ye not strengthened, neither have ye healed that which was sick, neither have ye bound up *that which was* broken, neither have ye brought again that which was driven away, neither have ye sought that which was lost; but with force and with cruelty have ye ruled them. 6. My flock was scattered upon all the face of the earth, and none did search or seek *after them.* 10. Behold, I *am* against the shepherds; and I will require my flock at their hand, and cause them to cease from feeding the flock; neither shall the shepherds feed themselves any more; for I will deliver my flock from their mouth, that they may not be meat for them. *vs.* 1-31.

Ezek. 44:8. Ye have not kept the charge of mine holy things: but ye have set keepers of my charge in my sanctuary for yourselves. 10. The Levites that are gone away far from me, . . . they shall even bear their iniquity.

Hos. 4:6. My people are destroyed for lack of knowledge: because thou hast rejected knowledge, I will also reject thee, that thou shalt be no priest to me: seeing thou hast forgotten the law of thy God, I will also forget thy children. 8. They eat up the sin of my people, and they set their heart on their iniquity. 9. And there shall be, like people, like priests: and I will punish them for their ways, and reward them their doings. *vs.* 10-13.

Hos. 5:1. Hear ye this, O priests; and hearken, ye house of Israel; and give ye ear, O house of the king; for judgment *is* toward you, because ye have been a snare on Mizpah, and a net spread upon Tabor.

Hos. 6:9. As troops of robbers wait for a man, *so* the company of priests murder in the way [1] by consent: for they commit lewdness. [1 R. V. toward Shechem: yea]

Hos. 9:8. The watchman of Ephraim *was* with my God: *but* the prophet *is* a snare of a fowler in all his ways, *and* hatred in the house of his God. *v.* 7.

Amos 2:11. I raised up of your sons for prophets, and of your young men for Nazarites. *Is it* not even thus, O ye children of Israel? saith the LORD. 12. But ye gave the Nazarites wine to drink; and commanded the prophets, saying, Prophesy not.

Mic. 2:11. If a man walking in the spirit and falsehood do lie, *saying*, I will prophesy unto thee of wine and of strong drink; he shall even be the prophet of this people.

Mic. 3:5. Thus saith the LORD concerning the prophets that make my people err, that bite with their teeth, and cry, Peace; and he that putteth not into their mouths, they even prepare war against him. 6. Therefore night *shall be* unto you, that ye shall not have a vision; and it shall be dark unto you, that ye shall not divine; and the sun shall go down over the prophets, and the day shall be dark over them. 7. Then shall the seers be ashamed, and the diviners confounded: yea, they shall all cover their lips; for *there is* no answer of God. 11. The heads thereof judge for reward, and the priests thereof teach for hire, and the prophets thereof divine for money: yet will they lean upon the LORD, and say, *Is* not the LORD among us? none evil can come upon us.

Zeph. 3:4. Her prophets *are* light *and* treacherous persons: her priests have polluted the sanctuary, they have done violence to the law.

Zech. 10:3. Mine anger was kindled against the shepherds, and I punished the goats: for the LORD of hosts hath visited his flock the house of Judah, and hath made them as his goodly horse in the battle.

Zech. 11:4. Thus saith the LORD my God; Feed the flock of the slaughter; 5. Whose possessors slay them, and hold themselves not guilty: and they that sell them say, Blessed *be* the LORD; for I am rich: and their own shepherds pity them not. 16. Lo, I will raise up a shepherd in the land, *which* shall not visit those that be cut off, neither shall seek the young one, nor heal that that is broken, nor feed that that standeth still: but he shall eat the flesh of the fat, and tear their claws in pieces. 17. Woe to the idol shepherd that leaveth the flock! the sword *shall be* upon his arm, and upon his right eye: his arm shall be clean dried up, and his right eye shall be utterly darkened.

Zech. 13:2. Saith the LORD of hosts, . . . I will cause the prophets and the unclean spirit to pass out of the land. 3. And it shall come to pass, *that* when any shall yet prophesy, then his father and his mother that begat him shall say unto him, Thou shalt not live; for thou speakest lies in the name of the LORD: and his father and his mother that begat him shall thrust him through when he prophesieth. 4. And it shall come to pass in that day, *that* the prophets shall be ashamed every one of his vision, when he hath prophesied; neither shall they wear a rough garment to deceive: 5. But he shall say, I *am* no prophet, I *am* an husbandman:

Mal. 1:6. If I *be* a master, where *is* my fear? saith the LORD of hosts unto you, O priests, that despise my name. And ye say, Wherein have we despised thy name? *vs.* 7-10.

Mal. 2:8. Ye are departed out of the way; ye have caused many to stumble at the law; ye have corrupted the covenant of Levi, saith the LORD of hosts. 9. Therefore have I also made you contemptible and base before all the people, according as ye have not kept my ways, but have been partial in the law. *vs.* 1-3.

Matt. 5:19. Whosoever therefore shall break one of these least commandments, and shall teach men so, he shall be called the least in the kingdom of heaven:

Matt. 7:15. Beware of false prophets, which come to you in sheep's clothing, but inwardly they are ravening wolves. 22. Many will say to me in that day, Lord, Lord, have we not prophesied in thy name? and in thy name have cast out devils? and in thy name done many wonderful works? 23. And then will I profess unto them, I never knew you: depart from me, ye that work iniquity.

Matt. 15:9. In vain they do worship me, teaching *for* doctrines the commandments of men. 13. Every plant, which my heavenly Father hath not planted, shall be rooted up. 14. Let them alone: they be blind leaders of the blind. And if the blind lead the blind, both shall fall into the ditch. Luke 6:39.

Matt. 20:20. Then came to him the mother of Zebedee's children with her sons, worshipping *him*, and desiring a certain thing of him. 21. And he said unto her, What wilt thou? She saith unto him, Grant that these my two sons may sit, the one on thy right hand, and the other on the left, in thy kingdom. 22. But Jesus answered and said, Ye know not what ye ask. Are ye able to drink of the cup that I shall drink of, and to be baptized with the baptism that I am baptized with? They say unto him, We are able. 23. And he saith unto them, Ye shall drink indeed of my cup, and be baptized with the baptism that I am baptized with: but to sit on my right hand, and on my left, is not mine to give, but *it shall be given to them* for whom it is prepared of my Father. 24. And when the ten heard *it*, they were moved with indignation against the two brethren. 25. But Jesus called them *unto him*, and said, Ye know that the princes of the Gentiles exercise dominion over them, and they that are great exercise authority upon them. 26. But it shall not be so among you: but whosoever will be great among you, let him be your minister; 27. And whosoever will be chief among you, let him be your servant: Mark 10:35–37; Luke 22:24.

Matt. 23:3. All therefore whatsoever they bid you observe, *that* observe and do; but do not ye after their works: for they say, and do not. 4. For they bind heavy burdens and grievous to be borne, and lay *them* on men's shoulders; but they *themselves* will not move them with one of their fingers. 13. Woe unto you, scribes and Pharisees, hypocrites! for ye shut up the kingdom of heaven against men: for ye neither go in *yourselves*, neither suffer ye them that are entering to go in.

Matt. 24:4. Take heed that no man deceive you. 5. For many shall come in my name, saying, I am Christ; and shall deceive many. 24. For there shall arise false Christs, and false prophets, and shall shew great signs and wonders; insomuch that, if *it were* possible, they shall deceive the very elect. *vs.* 11, 26, 48–51; Luke 21:8.

Mark 9:33. And he came to Capernaum: and being in the house he asked them, What was it that ye disputed among yourselves by the way? 34. But they held their peace: for by the way they had disputed among themselves, who *should be* the greatest. 35. And he sat down, and called the twelve, and saith unto them, If any man desire to be first, *the same* shall be last of all, and servant of all. Luke 9:46.

Mark 13:21. And then if any man shall say to you, Lo, here *is* Christ; or, lo, *he is* there; believe *him* not: 22. For false Christs and false prophets shall rise, and shall shew signs and wonders, to seduce, if *it were* possible, even the elect.

Luke 11:35. Take heed therefore that the light which is in thee be not darkness. 52. Woe unto you, lawyers! for ye have taken away the key of knowledge: ye entered not in yourselves, and them that were entering in ye hindered. *vs.* 46–51.

Luke 12:45. If that servant say in his heart, My lord delayeth his coming; and shall begin to beat the menservants and maidens, and to eat and drink, and to be drunken; 46. The lord of that servant will come in a day when he looketh not for *him*, and at an hour when he is not aware, and will cut him in sunder and will appoint him his portion with the unbelievers.

John 3:10. Art thou a master of Israel, and knowest not these things?

John 5:43. I am come in my Father's name, and ye receive me not: if another shall come in his own name, him ye will receive.

John 10:1. He that entereth not by the door into the sheepfold, but climbeth up some other way, the same is a thief and a robber. 5. A stranger will they not follow, but will flee from him: for they know not the voice of strangers. 8. All that ever came before me are thieves and robbers: but the sheep did not hear them. 10. The thief cometh not, but for to steal, and to kill, and to destroy: 12. He that is an hireling, and not the shepherd, whose own the sheep are not, seeth the wolf coming, and leaveth the sheep, and fleeth: and the wolf catcheth them, and scattereth the sheep. 13. The hireling fleeth, because he is an hireling, and careth not for the sheep.

Acts 20:29. For I know this, that after my departing shall grievous wolves enter in among you, not sparing the flock. 30. Also of your own selves shall men arise, speaking perverse things, to draw away disciples after them.

Rom. 2:19. Art confident that thou thyself art a guide of the blind, a light of them which are in darkness, 20. An instructor of the foolish, a teacher of babes, which hast the form of knowledge and of the truth in the law. 21. Thou therefore which teachest another, teachest thou not thyself? thou that preachest a man should not steal, dost thou steal? 22. Thou that sayest a man should not commit adultery, dost thou commit adultery? thou that abhorrest idols, dost thou commit sacrilege? 23. Thou that makest thy boast of the law, through breaking the law dishonourest thou God? 24. For the name of God is blasphemed among the Gentiles through you, as it is written. 25. For circumcision verily profiteth, if thou keep the law: but if thou be a breaker of the law, thy circumcision is made uncircumcision.

Rom. 16:17. Now I beseech you, brethren, mark them which cause divisions and offences contrary to the doctrine which ye have learned; and avoid them. 18. For they that are such serve not our Lord Jesus Christ, but their own belly; and by good words and fair speeches deceive the hearts of the simple.

1 Cor. 3:10. According to the grace of God which is given unto me, as a wise master-builder, I have laid the foundation, and another buildeth thereon. But let every man take heed how he buildeth thereupon. 11. For other foundation can no man lay than that is laid, which is Jesus Christ. 12. Now if any man build upon this foundation gold, silver, precious stones, wood, hay, stubble ; 13. Every man's work shall be made manifest : for the day shall declare it, because it shall be revealed by fire ; and the fire shall try every man's work of what sort it is. 14. If any man's work abide which he hath built thereupon, he shall receive a reward. 15. If any man's work shall be burned, he shall suffer loss: but he himself shall be saved ; yet so as by fire. 16. Know ye not that ye are the temple of God, and *that* the Spirit of God dwelleth in you? 21. Therefore let no man glory in men. *vs.* 1-4.

1 Cor. 11:18. I hear that there be divisions among you ; and I partly believe it. 19. For there must be also heresies among you, that they which are approved may be made manifest among you.

2 Cor. 2:17. We are not as many, which corrupt the word of God :

2 Cor. 11:3. I fear, lest by any means, as the serpent beguiled Eve through his subtilty, so your minds should be corrupted from the simplicity that is in Christ. 4. For if he that cometh preacheth another Jesus, whom we have not preached, or *if* ye receive another spirit, which ye have not received, or another gospel, which ye have not accepted, ye might well bear with *him.* 13. Such *are* false apostles, deceitful workers, transforming themselves into the apostles of Christ. 14. And no marvel ; for Satan himself is transformed into an angel of light. 15. Therefore *it is* no great thing if his ministers also be transformed as the ministers of righteousness ; whose end shall be according to their works. *vs.* 1-33.

Gal. 1:6. I marvel that ye are so soon removed from him that called you into the grace of Christ unto another gospel : 7. Which is not another ; but there be some that trouble you, and would pervert the gospel of Christ. 8. But though we, or an angel from heaven, preach any other gospel unto you than that which we have preached unto you, let him be accursed.

Gal. 5:10. He that troubleth you shall bear his judgment, whosoever he be.

Eph. 4:14. Be no more children, tossed to and fro, and carried about with every wind of doctrine, by the sleight of men, *and* cunning craftiness, whereby they lie in wait to deceive ;

Phil. 1:15. Some indeed preach Christ even of envy and strife ; and some also of good will : 16. The one preach Christ of contention, not sincerely, supposing to add affliction to my bonds :

Phil. 3:2. Beware of dogs, beware of evil workers, beware of the concision.

Col. 2:4. This I say, lest any man should beguile you with enticing words. 8. Beware lest any man spoil you through philosophy and vain deceit, after the tradition of men, after the rudiments of the world, and not after Christ. 18. Let no man beguile you of your reward in a voluntary humility and worshipping of angels, intruding into those things which he hath not seen, vainly puffed up by his fleshly mind, 19. And not holding the Head, from which all the body by joints and bands having nourishment ministered, and knit together, increaseth with the increase of God.

1 Tim. 1:3. I besought thee to abide still at Ephesus, when I went into Macedonia, that thou mightest charge some that they teach no other doctrine, 4. Neither give heed to fables and endless genealogies, which minister questions, rather than godly edifying which is in faith : *so do.* 5. Now the end of the commandment is charity out of a pure heart, and *of* a good conscience, and *of* faith unfeigned : 6. From which some having swerved have turned aside unto vain jangling ; 7. Desiring to be teachers of the law ; understanding neither what they say, nor whereof they affirm. 19. Holding faith and a good conscience ; which some having put away concerning faith have made shipwreck :

1 Tim. 4:1. Now the Spirit speaketh expressly, that in the latter times some shall depart from the faith, giving heed to seducing spirits, and doctrines of devils; 2. Speaking lies in hypocrisy ; having their conscience seared with a hot iron; 3. Forbidding to marry, *and commanding* to abstain from meats, 7. Refuse profane and old wives' fables, and exercise thyself *rather* unto godliness.

1 Tim. 6:3. If any man teach otherwise, and consent not to wholesome words, *even* the words of our Lord Jesus Christ, and to the doctrine which is according to godliness ; 4. He is proud, knowing nothing, but doting about questions and strifes of words, whereof cometh envy, strife, railings, evil surmisings, 5. Perverse disputings of men of corrupt minds, and destitute of the truth, supposing that [1] gain is godliness: from such withdraw thyself. 20. O Timothy, keep that which is committed to thy trust, avoiding profane *and* vain babblings, and oppositions of science falsely so called : 21. Which some professing have erred concerning the faith.

[1 R. V. godliness is a way of gain]

2 Tim. 2:14. Of these things put *them* in remembrance, charging *them* before the Lord that they strive not about words to no profit, *but* to the subverting of the hearers. 15. Study to shew thyself approved unto God, a workman that needeth not to be ashamed, rightly dividing the word of truth. 16. But shun profane *and* vain babblings: for they will increase unto more ungodliness. 17. And their word will eat as doth a canker: of whom is Hymenæus and Philetus; 18. Who concerning the truth have erred,

saying that the resurrection is past already; and overthrow the faith of some.

2 Tim. 3:6. Of this sort are they which creep into houses, and lead captive silly women laden with sins, led away with divers lusts, 7. Ever learning, and never able to come to the knowledge of the truth. 8. Now as Jannes and Jambres withstood Moses, so do these also resist the truth: men of corrupt minds, reprobate concerning the faith. 9. But they shall proceed no further: for their folly shall be manifest unto all men, as their's also was. 13. Evil men and seducers shall wax worse and worse, deceiving, and being deceived. 2 Tim. 4:3.

Tit. 1:10. There are many unruly and vain talkers and deceivers, specially they of the circumcision: 11. Whose mouths must be stopped, who subvert whole houses, teaching things which they ought not, for filthy lucre's sake. 12. One of themselves, even a prophet of their own, said, The Cretians are alway liars, evil beasts, slow bellies. 13. This witness is true. Wherefore rebuke them sharply, that they may be sound in the faith; 14. Not giving heed to Jewish fables, and commandments of men, that turn from the truth.

Tit. 3:10. A man that is an heretick after the first and second admonition reject; 11. Knowing that he that is such is subverted, and sinneth, being condemned of himself.

Heb. 13:9. Be not carried about with divers and strange doctrines.

2 Pet. 2:1. There were false prophets also among the people, even as there shall be false teachers among you, who privily shall bring in [1] damnable heresies, even denying the Lord that bought them, and bring upon themselves swift destruction. 2. And many shall follow their pernicious ways; by reason of whom the way of truth shall be evil spoken of. 3. And through covetousness shall they with feigned words make merchandise of you: whose judgment now of a long time lingereth not, and their [2] damnation slumbereth not. 13. Spots they are and blemishes, sporting themselves with their own deceivings while they feast with you; 14. Having eyes full of adultery, and that cannot cease from sin; beguiling unstable souls: an heart they have exercised with covetous practices; cursed children: 15. Which have forsaken the right way, and are gone astray, following the way of Balaam the son of Bosor, who loved the wages of unrighteousness; 16. But was rebuked for his iniquity: the dumb ass speaking with man's voice forbad the madness of the prophet. 17. These are wells without water, clouds that are carried with a tempest; to whom the mist of darkness is reserved for ever. 18. For when they speak great swelling words of vanity, they allure through the lusts of the flesh, through much wantonness, those that were clean escaped from them who live in error. 19. While they promise them liberty, they themselves are the servants of corruption: vs. 1–22.   [R. V. [1] destructive   [2] destruction]

2 Pet. 3:16. In which are some things hard to be understood, which they that are unlearned and unstable wrest, as they do also the other scriptures, unto their own destruction.

1 John 2:18. As ye have heard that antichrist shall come, even now are there many antichrists; whereby we know that it is the last time. 26. These things have I written unto you concerning them that seduce you.

1 John 4:1. Beloved, believe not every spirit, but try the spirits whether they are of God: because many false prophets are gone out into the world. 2. Hereby know ye the Spirit of God: Every spirit that confesseth that Jesus Christ is come in the flesh is of God: 3. And every spirit that confesseth not [1] that Jesus [1] Christ is come in the flesh is not of God: and this is that spirit of antichrist, whereof ye have heard that it should come; and even now already is it in the world. 5. They are of the world: therefore speak they of the world, and the world heareth them.   [[1] Omitted in R. V.]

2 John 7. Many deceivers are entered into the world, who confess not that Jesus Christ is come in the flesh. This is a deceiver and an antichrist. 10. If there come any unto you, and bring not this doctrine, receive him not into your house, neither bid him God speed: 11. For he that biddeth him God speed is partaker of his evil deeds.

3 John 10. Wherefore, if I come, I will remember his deeds which he doeth, prating against us with malicious words: and not content therewith, neither doth he himself receive the brethren, and forbiddeth them that would, and casteth them out of the church.

Jude 4. There are certain men crept in unawares, who were before of old ordained to this condemnation, ungodly men, turning the grace of our God into lasciviousness, and denying the only Lord God, and our Lord Jesus Christ. 11. Woe unto them! for they have gone in the way of Cain, and ran greedily after the error of Balaam for reward, and perished in the gainsaying of Core.

Rev. 2:1. Unto the angel of the church of Ephesus write; 2. I know thy works, and thy labour, and thy patience, and how thou canst not bear them which are evil: and thou hast tried them which say they are apostles, and are not, and hast found them liars: 12. And to the angel of the church in Pergamos write; These things saith he which hath the sharp sword with two edges; 14. But I have a few things against thee, because thou hast there them that hold the doctrine of Balaam, who taught Balac to cast a stumblingblock before the children of Israel, to eat things sacrificed unto idols, and to commit fornication. 15. So hast thou also them that hold the doctrine of the Nicolaitanes, which thing I hate. 18. And unto the angel of the church in Thyatira write; 20. Notwithstanding I have a few things against thee, because thou sufferest that woman Jezebel, which calleth herself a prophetess, to teach and to seduce my servants to commit fornication, and to eat things sacrificed unto idols. 21. And I gave her space to repent of her fornication; and she repented not. 22. Behold, I will cast her into a bed, and them that commit adultery with her into great tribulation, except they repent of their deeds. 23. And I will kill her children with death;

INSTANCES OF: Aaron, Num. 12:1–12. Nadab and Abihu, Lev. 10:1,2. Korah, Dathan, and Abiram, Num. 16. Eli's sons, 1 Sam. 2:12–17,22,25,28,29. Samuel's sons, 1 Sam. 8:1–3; 1 Chr. 6:28. The old prophet of Beth-el, 1 Kin. 13:11–32. Jonathan, Judg. 17:7–13; 18. Noadiah, Neh. 6:14. Priests under Jehoash, 2 Kin. 12:7; 2 Chr. 24:5,6; Hezekiah, 2 Chr. 30:3,5. Priests and Levites, Ezra 2: 61,62; 9:1,2; 10:18–24; Neh. 13:4–13,28,29; Zech. 7:5,6. Hananiah, Jer. 28. Jonah, Jonah 1:1– 6. Rulers in the temple, Matt. 16:6–12; 23: 16; Luke 12:1. Caiaphas, Matt. 26:2,3,57,63– 65; John 11:49–51; 18:14. Judas, Matt. 26:14– 16,21–25,47–50; 27:3–5; John 12:4–6; Acts 1: 18. Simon the sorcerer, Acts 8:9–11. Judaizing Christians, Acts 15:1; Gal. 3; 4; 5; 6. Diotrephes, 3 John 9. Elymas, Acts 13:6– 11. Hymenæus, 1 Tim. 1:20; 2 Tim. 2:17. Philetus, 2 Tim. 2:17,18.

HOSPITALITY TO: Woman of Zarephath to Elijah, 1 Kin. 17:10–16. The Shunammite to Elisha, 2 Kin. 4:8–10. The barbarians to Paul, Acts 28:1–10. Simon the tanner to Peter, Acts 9:43. The Philippian jailer, Acts 16:33,34. Aquila and Priscilla to Paul, Acts 18:3; to Apollos, Acts 18:26. Justus to Paul, Acts 18:7. Philip the evangelist to Paul, Acts 21:8–10.

ORDINATION OF: Of Matthias, Acts 1:26; of seven deacons, Acts 6:5,6; of Paul and Barnabas, Acts 13:3; Timothy, 1 Tim. 4:14. See PRIESTS; LEVITES.

PRAYER FOR, ENJOINED: Matt. 9:37. Then saith he unto his disciples, The harvest truly *is* plenteous, but the labourers *are* few; 38. Pray ye therefore the Lord of the harvest, that he will send forth labourers into his harvest. Luke 10:2.

Rom. 15:30. Now I beseech you, brethren, for the Lord Jesus Christ's sake, and for the love of the Spirit, that ye strive together with me in *your* prayers to God for me; 31. That I may be delivered from them that do not believe in Judæa; and that my service which *I have* for Jerusalem may be accepted of the saints; 32. That I may come unto you with joy by the will of God, and may with you be refreshed.

2 Cor. 1:11. Ye also helping together by prayer for us, that for the gift *bestowed* upon us by the means of many persons thanks may be given by many on our behalf.

Eph. 6:18. Praying always with all prayer and supplication in the Spirit, and watching thereunto with all perseverance and supplication for all saints; 19. And for me, that utterance may be given unto me, that I may

open my mouth boldly, to make known the mystery of the gospel, 20. For which I am an ambassador in bonds: that therein I may speak boldly, as I ought to speak.

Phil. 1:19. I know that this shall turn to my salvation through your prayer, and the supply of the Spirit of Jesus Christ,

Col. 4:2. Continue in prayer, and watch in the same with thanksgiving; 3. Withal praying also for us, that God would open unto us a door of utterance, to speak the mystery of Christ, for which I am also in bonds: 4. That I may make it manifest, as I ought to speak.

1 Thess. 5:25. Brethren, pray for us.

2 Thess. 3:1. Brethren, pray for us, that the word of the Lord may have *free* course, and be glorified, even as *it is* with you: 2. And that we may be delivered from unreasonable and wicked men: for all *men* have not faith.

Philem. 22. I trust that through your prayers I shall be given unto you.

Heb. 13:18. Pray for us: for we trust we have a good conscience, in all things willing to live honestly. 19. But I beseech *you* the rather to do this, that I may be restored to you the sooner.

PRAYER FOR, EXEMPLIFIED: 2 Chr. 6: 41. Let thy priests, O LORD God, be clothed with salvation, and let thy saints rejoice in goodness.

Psa. 132:9. Let thy priests be clothed with righteousness;

Acts 1:24. They prayed, and said, Thou, Lord, which knowest the hearts of all *men*, shew whether of these two thou hast chosen, 25. That he may take part of this ministry and apostleship, from which Judas by transgression fell, that he might go to his own place.

Acts 4:29. Now, Lord, behold their threatenings: and grant unto thy servants, that with all boldness they may speak thy word,

Acts 6:6. Whom they set before the apostles: and when they had prayed, they laid *their* hands on them.

Acts 12:5. Prayer was made without ceasing of the church unto God for him.

Acts 14:23. And when they had ordained them elders in every church, and had prayed with fasting, they commended them to the Lord, on whom they believed.

PROMISES TO, AND JOYS OF: 2 Sam. 23: 6. But *the sons* of Belial *shall be* all of them as thorns thrust away, because they cannot be taken with hands: 7. But the man *that* shall touch them must be fenced with iron and the staff of a spear; and they shall be utterly burned with fire in the *same* place.

Psa. 126:5. They that sow in tears shall reap in joy. 6. He that goeth forth and weepeth, bearing precious seed, shall doubtless come again with rejoicing, bringing his sheaves *with him*.

Jer. 1:7. But the LORD said unto me, Say not, I *am* a child: for thou shalt go to all that I shall send thee, and whatsoever I command thee thou shalt speak. 8. Be not afraid of their faces: for I *am* with thee to deliver thee, saith the Lord. 9. Then the Lord put forth his hand, and touched my mouth. And the Lord said unto me, Behold, I have put my words in thy mouth. 10. See, I have this day set thee over the nations and over the kingdoms, to root out, and to pull down, and to destroy, and to throw down, to build, and to plant. 17. Thou therefore gird up thy loins, and arise, and speak unto them all that I command thee: be not dismayed at their faces, lest I confound thee before them. 18. For, behold, I have made thee this day a defenced city, and an iron pillar, and brazen walls against the whole land, against the kings of Judah, against the princes thereof, against the priests thereof, and against the people of the land. 19. And they shall fight against thee; but they shall not prevail against thee; for I *am* with thee, saith the Lord, to deliver thee.

Jer. 20:11. But the Lord *is* with me as a mighty terrible one: therefore my persecutors shall stumble, and they shall not prevail: they shall be greatly ashamed; for they shall not prosper: *their* everlasting confusion shall never be forgotten.

Dan. 12:3. And they that be wise shall shine as the brightness of the firmament; and they that turn many to righteousness as the stars for ever and ever.

Matt. 10:28. And fear not them which kill the body, but are not able to kill the soul: but rather fear him which is able to destroy both soul and body in hell. 29. Are not two sparrows sold for a farthing? and one of them shall not fall on the ground without your Father. 30. But the very hairs of your head are all numbered. 31. Fear ye not therefore, ye are of more value than many sparrows.

Matt. 28:20. Lo, I am with you alway, *even* unto the end of the world. Amen.

Luke 12:11. And when they bring you unto the synagogues, and *unto* magistrates, and powers, take ye no thought how or what thing ye shall answer, or what ye shall say: 12. For the Holy Ghost shall teach you in the same hour what ye ought to say.

Luke 24:49. And, behold, I send the promise of my Father upon you: but tarry ye in the city of Jerusalem, until ye be endued with power from on high.

John 4:36. And he that reapeth receiveth wages, and gathereth fruit unto life eternal: that both he that soweth and he that reapeth may rejoice together. 37. And herein is that saying true, One soweth, and another reapeth. 38. I sent you to reap that whereon ye bestowed no labour: other men laboured, and ye are entered into their labours.

Acts 1:4. And, being assemble' together with *them*, commanded them that they should not depart from Jerusalem, but wait for the promise of the Father, which, *saith he*, ye have heard of me. 5. For John truly

baptized with water; but ye shall be baptized with the Holy Ghost not many days hence. 8. But ye shall receive power, after that the Holy Ghost is come upon you: and ye shall be witnesses unto me both in Jerusalem, and in all Judæa, and in Samaria, and unto the uttermost part of the earth.

1 Cor. 9:9. For it is written in the law of Moses, Thou shalt not muzzle the mouth of the ox that treadeth out the corn. Doth God take care for oxen? 10. Or saith he *it* altogether for our sakes? For our sakes, no doubt, *this* is written: that he that ploweth should plow in hope; and that he that thresheth in hope should be partaker of his hope.

2 Cor. 2:14. Now thanks *be* unto God, which always causeth us to triumph in Christ, and maketh manifest the savour of his knowledge by us in every place. 15. For we are unto God a sweet savour of Christ, in them that are saved, and in them that perish: 16. To the one *we are* the savour of death unto death; and to the other the savour of life unto life. And who *is* sufficient for these things?

2 Cor. 7:6. Nevertheless God, that comforteth those that are cast down, comforted us by the coming of Titus; 7. And not by his coming only, but by the consolation wherewith he was comforted in you, when he told us your earnest desire, your mourning, your fervent mind toward me; so that I rejoiced the more.

Phil. 2:16. Holding forth the word of life; that I may rejoice in the day of Christ,

1 Thess. 2:13. For this cause also thank we God without ceasing, because, when ye received the word of God which ye heard of us, ye received *it* not *as* the word of men, but as it is in truth, the word of God, which effectually worketh also in you that believe. 19. For what *is* our hope, or joy, or crown of rejoicing? *Are* not even ye in the presence of our Lord Jesus Christ at his coming? 20. For ye are our glory and joy.

1 Thess. 3:8. For now we live, if ye stand fast in the Lord. 9. For what thanks can we render to God again for you, for all the joy wherewith we joy for your sakes before our God;

3 John 4. I have no greater joy than to hear that my children walk in truth.

See Righteous, Promises to.

SUCCESS ATTENDING: Jonah, Jonah 1:5,6,9,14,16; 3:4–9. Apostles, Acts 2:1–4,41. Philip, Acts 8:6,8,12. Peter, Acts 9:32–35. Paul, Acts 13:16–43; 1 Cor. 4:15; 9:2; 15:11; 2 Cor. 3:2,3; 12:12; 13:4; Phil. 2:16; 1 Thess. 1:5. Apollos, Acts 18:24–28.

See Revivals.

TRIALS AND PERSECUTIONS OF: 1 Kin. 19:1. And Ahab told Jezebel all that Elijah had done, and withal how he had slain all the prophets with the sword. 2. Then Jezebel sent a messenger unto Elijah, saying, So let the gods do *to me*, and more also, if I make not thy life as the life of one of them by to morrow about this time. 3. And when he saw *that*, he arose, and went for his life, and came to Beer-sheba, which *belongeth* to Judah, and left his servant there. 4. But he himself went a day's journey into the wilderness, and came and sat down under a juniper tree: and he requested for himself that he might die; and said, It is enough; now, O Lord, take away my life; for I *am* not better than my fathers. 5. And as he lay and slept under a juniper tree, behold, then an angel touched him, and said unto him, Arise *and* eat. 6. And he looked, and, behold, *there was* a cake baken on the coals, and a cruse of water at his head. And he did eat and drink, and laid him down again. 7. And the angel of the Lord came again the second time, and touched him, and said, Arise *and* eat; because the journey *is* too great for thee. 8. And he arose, and did eat and drink, and went in the strength of that meat forty days and forty nights unto Horeb the mount of God. 9. And he came thither unto a cave, and lodged there: and, behold, the word of the Lord *came* to him, and he said unto him, What doest thou here, Elijah? 10. And he said, I have been very jealous for the Lord God of hosts: for the children of Israel have forsaken thy covenant, thrown down thine altars, and slain thy prophets with the sword; and I, *even* I only, am left; and they seek my life, to take it away.

Isa. 20:2. At the same time spake the Lord by Isaiah the son of Amoz, saying, Go and loose the sackcloth from off thy loins, and put off thy shoe from thy foot. And he did so, walking naked and barefoot. 3. And the Lord said, Like as my servant Isaiah hath walked naked and barefoot three years *for* a sign and wonder upon Egypt and upon Ethiopia;

Ezek. 24:15. Also the word of the Lord came unto me, saying, 16. Son of man, behold, I take away from thee the desire of thine eyes with a stroke: yet neither shalt thou mourn nor weep, neither shall thy tears run down. 17. Forbear to cry, make no mourning for the dead, bind the tire of thine head upon thee, and put on thy shoes upon thy feet, and cover not *thy* lips, and eat not the bread of men. 18. So I spake unto the people in the morning: and at even my wife died; and I did in the morning as I was commanded.

Hos. 1:2. And the Lord said to Hosea, Go, take unto thee a wife of whoredoms and children of whoredoms: for the land hath committed great whoredom, *departing* from the Lord.

Amos 5:10. They hate him that rebuketh in the gate, and they abhor him that speaketh uprightly.

Amos 7:10. Then Amaziah the priest of Beth-el sent to Jeroboam king of Israel, saying, Amos hath conspired against thee in the midst of the house of Israel: the land is not able to bear all his words. 11. For thus Amos saith, Jeroboam shall die by the sword, and Israel shall surely be led away captive out of their own land. 12. Also Amaziah said unto Amos, O thou seer, go, flee thee away into the land of Judah, and there eat bread, and prophesy there: 13. But prophesy not again any more at Beth-el: for it *is* the king's chapel, and it *is* the king's court. 14. Then answered Amos, and said to Amaziah, I *was* no prophet, neither *was* I a prophet's son; but I *was* an herdman, and a ¹ gatherer of sycomore ² fruit: 15. And the Lord took me as I followed the flock, and the Lord said unto me, Go, prophesy unto my people Israel. 16. Now therefore hear thou the word of the Lord: Thou sayest, Prophesy not against Israel, and drop not *thy word* against the house of Isaac. 17. Therefore thus saith the Lord; Thy wife shall be an harlot in the city, and thy sons and thy daughters shall fall by the sword, and thy land shall be divided by line; and thou shalt die in a polluted land: and Israel shall surely go into captivity forth of his land. [R. V. ¹ dresser ² trees]

Matt. 10:16. Behold, I send you forth as sheep in the midst of wolves: be ye therefore wise as serpents, and harmless as doves. 17. But beware of men: for they will deliver you up to the councils, and they will scourge you in their synagogues; 18. And ye shall be brought before governors and kings for my sake, for a testimony against them and the Gentiles. 19. But when they deliver you up, take no thought how or what ye shall speak: for it shall be given you in that same hour what ye shall speak. 20. For it is not ye that speak, but the Spirit of your Father which speaketh in you. 21. And the brother shall deliver up the brother to death, and the father the child: and the children shall rise up against *their* parents, and cause them to be put to death. 22. And ye shall be hated of all *men* for my name's sake: but he that endureth to the end shall be saved. 23. But when they persecute you in this city, flee ye into another: for verily I say unto you, Ye shall not have gone over the cities of Israel, till the Son of man be come. 24. The disciple is not above *his* master, nor the servant above his lord. 25. It is enough for the disciple that he be as his master, and the servant as his lord. If they have called the master of the house Beelzebub, how much more *shall they call* them of his household? [John 13:16.] 26. Fear them not therefore: for there is nothing covered, that shall not be revealed; and hid, that shall not be known. 27. What I tell you in darkness, *that* speak ye in light: and what ye hear in the ear, *that* preach ye upon the housetops.

Matt. 23:34. Wherefore, behold, I send unto you prophets, and wise men, and scribes: and *some* of them ye shall kill and crucify; and *some* of them shall ye scourge in your synagogues, and persecute *them* from city to city:

1 Cor. 2:1. And I, brethren, when I came to you, came not with excellency of speech or of wisdom, declaring unto you the testimony of God. 2. For I determined not to know any thing among you, save Jesus Christ, and him crucified. 3. And I was with you in weakness, and in fear, and in much trembling. 4. And my speech and my preaching *was* not with enticing words of man's wisdom, but in demonstration of the Spirit and of power:

1 Cor. 4:9. For I think that God hath set forth us the apostles last, as it were appointed to death: for we are made a spectacle unto the world, and to angels, and to men. 10. We *are* fools for Christ's sake, but ye *are* wise in Christ; we *are* weak, but ye *are* strong; ye *are* honourable, but we *are* despised. 11. Even unto this present hour we both hunger, and thirst, and are naked, and are buffeted, and have no certain dwelling-place; 12. And labour, working with our own hands: being reviled, we bless; being persecuted, we suffer it: 13. Being defamed, we intreat: we are made as the filth of the world, *and are* the offscouring of all things unto this day.

2 Cor. 6:4. But in all *things* approving ourselves as the ministers of God, in much patience, in afflictions, in necessities, in distresses, 5. In stripes, in imprisonments, in tumults, in labours, in watchings, in fastings; 6. By pureness, by knowledge, by longsuffering, by kindness, by the Holy Ghost, by love unfeigned, 7. By the word of truth, by the power of God, by the armour of righteousness on the right hand and on the left, 8. By honour and dishonour, by evil report and good report: as deceivers, and *yet* true; 9. As unknown, and *yet* well known; as dying, and, behold, we live; as chastened, and not killed; 10. As sorrowful, yet alway rejoicing; as poor, yet making many rich; as having nothing, and *yet* possessing all things.

2 Cor. 7:5. For, when we were come into Macedonia, our flesh had no rest, but we were troubled on every side; without *were* fightings, within *were* fears.

2 Cor. 11:23. In labours more abundant, in stripes above measure, in prisons more frequent, in deaths oft. 24. Of the Jews five times received I forty *stripes* save one. 25. Thrice was I beaten with rods, once was I stoned, thrice I suffered shipwreck, a night and a day I have been in the deep; 26. *In* journeyings often, *in* perils of waters, *in* perils of robbers, *in* perils by *mine own* countrymen, *in* perils by the heathen, *in* perils in the city, *in* perils in the wilderness, *in* perils in the sea, *in* perils among false brethren; 27. In weariness and painfulness, in watchings often, in hunger and thirst, in fastings often, in cold and nakedness. 28. Beside those things that are without, that which cometh upon me daily, the care of all the churches. 29. Who is weak, and I am not weak? who is offended, and I burn not?

30. If I must needs glory, I will glory of the things which concern mine infirmities. 31. The God and Father of our Lord Jesus Christ, which is blessed for evermore, knoweth that I lie not. 32. In Damascus the governor under Aretas the king kept the city of the Damascenes with a garrison, desirous to apprehend me: 33. And through a window in a basket was I let down by the wall, and escaped his hands.

2 Cor. 12:7. And lest I should be exalted above measure through the abundance of the revelations, there was given to me a thorn in the flesh, the messenger of Satan to buffet me, lest I should be exalted above measure. 8. For this thing I besought the Lord thrice, that it might depart from me. 9. And he said unto me, My grace is sufficient for thee: for my strength is made perfect in weakness. Most gladly therefore will I rather glory in my infirmities, that the power of Christ may rest upon me. 10. Therefore I take pleasure in infirmities, in reproaches, in necessities, in persecutions, in distresses for Christ's sake: for when I am weak, then am I strong. 11. I am become a fool in glorying; ye have compelled me: for I ought to have been commended of you: for in nothing am I behind the very chiefest apostles, though I be nothing. 12. Truly the signs of an apostle were wrought among you in all patience, in signs, and wonders, and mighty deeds.

Gal. 4:13. Ye know how through infirmity of the flesh I preached the gospel unto you at the first. 14. And my temptation which was in my flesh ye despised not, nor rejected; but received me as an angel of God, *even* as Christ Jesus.

Eph. 3:1. For this cause I Paul, the prisoner of Jesus Christ for you Gentiles, 13. Wherefore I desire that ye faint not at my tribulations for you, which is your glory.

Falsely Accused. See Accusation, False. See also Persecution.

Instances of Persecution: Micaiah, 1 Kin. 22:24–27. Hanani, 2 Chr. 16:10. Zechariah, 2 Chr. 24:20,21. The apostles, Acts 5:17–42. Peter, Acts 12:3–19. Paul, Acts 9:23–25, 29,30; 14:6–20; 16:11–40; 17:1–13; 20:3; 21:27–40; 22:18,21,24–30; 23:11–35; 24; 25; 26; 2 Cor. 11:31–33; Gal. 1:21–24; 2 Tim. 1:8,16; 2:9; 4: 16,17.

See Elijah; Jeremiah.

Zealous: Titus, 2 Cor. 8:16,17. Epaphroditus, Phil. 2:25–30. Epaphras, Col. 4:12,13. Tychicus, Col. 4:7. John, in his vision, Rev. 5:4,5.

See Zeal.

Minni, a district of Armenia, Jer. 51:27.

Minnith, a place E. of the Jordan, Judg. 11:33; Ezek. 27:17.

Minors, legal status of, Gal. 4:1,2.

See Orphan; Young Men.

Minority Report. See Reports.

Mint, Matt. 23:23; Luke 11:42.

MIRACLES. INDEX OF SUB-TOPICS: *Catalogue of,* p. 873; *Of Jesus in Chron-*

ological Order, p. 873; *Of the Disciples of Jesus*, p. 874; *Convincing Effect of*, p. 874; *Design of*, p. 876; *Miraculous Gifts of the Holy Ghost*, p. 881; *Miscellany of Minor Sub-Topics*, p. 881.

CATALOGUE OF, AND SUPERNATURAL EVENTS: Creation, Gen. 1. Flood, Gen. 7; 8. Confusion of tongues, Gen. 11:1-9. Fire on Abraham's sacrifice, Gen. 15:17. Conception of Isaac, Gen. 17:17; 18:12; 21:2. Destruction of Sodom, Gen. 19. Lot's wife turned to salt, Gen. 19:26. Closing of the wombs of Abimelech's household, Gen. 20: 17,18. Opening of Hagar's eyes, Gen. 21:19. Conception of Jacob and Esau, Gen. 25:21. Opening of Rachel's womb, Gen. 30:22. Flaming bush, Ex. 3:2. Transformation of Moses's rod into a serpent, Ex. 4:3,4,30; 7:10, 12. Moses's leprosy, Ex. 4:6,7,30. Plagues in Egypt, see PLAGUES. Pillar of cloud and fire, Ex. 13:21,22; 14:19,20. Passage of the Red Sea, Ex. 14:22. Destruction of Pharaoh and his army, Ex. 14:23-30. Sweetening the waters of Marah, Ex. 15:25. Manna, Ex. 16:4-31. Quails, Ex. 16:13. Defeat of Amalek, Ex. 17:9-13. Transfiguration of the face of Moses, Ex. 34:29-35. Water from the rock, Ex. 17:5,7. Thundering and lightning on Sinai, Ex. 19:16-20; 24:10,15-17; Deut. 4:33. Miriam's leprosy, Num.12:10-15. Judgment by fire, Num. 11:1-3. Destruction of Korah, Num. 16:31-35; Deut. 11:6,7. Plague, Num. 16:46-50. Aaron's rod buds, Num. 17:1-9. Waters from the rock in Kadesh, Num. 20:8-11. Scourge of serpents, Num. 21:6-9. Destruction of Nadab and Abihu, Lev. 10:1,2. Balaam's ass speaks, Num. 22:23-30. Preservation of Moses, Deut. 34:7. Jordan divided, Josh. 3:14-17; 4:16-18. Fall of Jericho, Josh. 6:20. Midianites destroyed, Judg. 7:16-22. Hail on the confederated kings, Josh. 10:11. Sun and moon stand still, Josh. 10:12-14. Dew on Gideon's fleece, Judg. 6:37-40. Samson's strength, Judg. 14:6; 16:3,29,30. Samson supplied with water, Judg. 15:19. Fall of Dagon, 1 Sam. 5:1-4. Cows return the ark, 1 Sam. 6:7-14. Hemorrhoids, 1 Sam. 5:9-12; 6:1-18. Destruction of the people of Beth-shemesh, 1 Sam. 6:19,20. Thunder, 1 Sam. 12:16-18. Destruction of Uzzah, 2 Sam. 6:1-8. Plague in Israel, 1 Chr. 21:14-26. Fire on the sacrifices of Aaron, Lev. 9:24; of Gideon, Judg. 6:21; of Manoah, Judg. 13:19,20; of Solomon, 2 Chr. 7:1; of Elijah, 1 Kin. 18:38. Jeroboam's hand withered, 1 Kin. 13: 3-6. Appearance of blood, 2 Kin. 3:20-22. Panic of the Syrians, 2 Kin. 7:6,7. Elijah is fed by ravens, 1 Kin. 17:6; by an angel, 1 Kin. 19:1-8; increases the widow's meal and oil, 1 Kin. 17:9-16; Luke 4:26; raises the widow's son, 1 Kin. 17:17-24. Rain in answer to Elijah's prayer, 1 Kin. 18:41-45. Elijah brings fire on Ahaziah's army, 2 Kin. 1:10-12; divides Jordan, 2 Kin. 2:8. Elijah's translation, 2 Kin. 2:11.

Elisha divides Jordan, 2 Kin. 2:14; sweetens the waters of Jericho, 2 Kin. 2:19-22;

increases a widow's oil, 2 Kin. 4:1-7; raises the Shunammite's child, 2 Kin. 4:18-37; renders harmless the poisoned pottage, 2 Kin. 4: 38-41; feeds one hundred men, 2 Kin. 4:42-44; cures Naaman, 2 Kin. 5:1-19; smites Gehazi with leprosy, 2 Kin. 5:26,27; causes the ax to float, 2 Kin. 6:6; reveals the counsel of the king of Syria, 2 Kin. 6:12; causes the eyes of his servant to be opened, 2 Kin. 6:17; smites with blindness the army of the king of Syria, 2 Kin. 6:18; the dead man restored to life, 2 Kin. 13:21.

Destruction of Sennacherib's army, 2 Kin. 19:35; Isa. 37:36; return of the shadow on the sun dial, 2 Kin. 20:9-11; Hezekiah's cure, Isa. 38:21; deliverance of Shadrach, Meshach, and Abed-nego, Dan. 3:23-27; of Daniel, Dan. 6:22; the sea calmed on Jonah being cast into it, Jonah 1:15; Jonah in the fish's belly, Jonah 1:17; 2:10; his gourd, Jonah 4:6,7.

Conception by Elisabeth, Luke 1:18,24,25; The incarnation of Jesus, Matt. 1:18-25; Luke 1:26-80. The appearance of the star of Bethlehem, Matt. 2:1-9. The deliverance of Jesus, Matt. 2:13-23.

OF JESUS, IN CHRONOLOGICAL ORDER: Water made wine, John 2:1-11.

Heals the nobleman's son, John 4:46-54.

Draught of fishes, Luke 5:1-11.

Heals the demoniac, Mark 1:23-26; Luke 4:33-36.

Heals Peter's mother-in-law, Matt. 8:14-17; Mark 1:29-31; Luke 4:38,39.

Cleanses the leper, Matt. 8:1-4; Mark 1:40-45; Luke 5:12-16.

Heals the paralytic, Matt. 9:1-8; Mark 2:1-12; Luke 5:17-26.

Healing of the impotent man, John 5:1-16. Restoring the withered hand, Matt. 12:9-13; Mark 3:1-5; Luke 6:6-11.

Restores the centurion's servant, Matt. 8: 5-13; Luke 7:1-10.

Raises the widow's son to life, Luke 7: 11-16.

Heals a demoniac, Matt. 12:22-37; Mark 3: 11; Luke 11:14,15.

Stills the tempest, Matt. 8:23-27; 14:32; Mark 4:35-41; Luke 8:22-25.

Casts devils out of two men of Gadara, Matt. 8:28-34; Mark 5:1-20; Luke 8:26-39.

Raises from the dead the daughter of Jairus, Matt. 9:18,19,23-26; Mark 5:22-24, 35-43; Luke 8:41,42,49-56.

Cures the woman with the issue of blood, Matt. 9:20-22; Mark 5:25-34; Luke 8:43-48.

Restores two blind men to sight, Matt. 9: 27-31.

Heals a demoniac, Matt. 9:32,33.

Feeds five thousand people, Matt. 14:15-21; Mark 6:35-44; Luke 9:12-17; John 6:5-14.

Walks on the sea, Matt. 14:22-33; Mark 6: 45-52; John 6:16-21.

Heals the daughter of the Syrophenician woman, Matt. 15:21-28; Mark 7:24-30.

Feeds four thousand people, Matt. 15:32-39; Mark 8:1-9.

Restores one deaf and dumb, Mark 7: 31-37.

Restores a blind man, Mark 8:22-26.

Restores lunatic child, Matt. 17:14-21; Mark 9:14-29; Luke 9:37-43.

Tribute money obtained from a fish's mouth, Matt. 17:24-27.

Restores ten lepers, Luke 17:11-19.

Opens the eyes of a man born blind, John 9.

Raises Lazarus from the dead, John 11:1-46.

Heals the woman with the spirit of infirmity, Luke 13:10-17.

Cures a man with dropsy, Luke 14:1-6.

Restores two blind men near Jericho, Matt. 20:29-34; Mark 10:46-52; Luke 18:35-43.

Curses a fig tree, Matt. 21:17-22; Mark 11:12-14,20-24.

Heals the ear of Malchus, Luke 22:49-51.

Second draught of fishes, John 21:6.

Not particularly described, see p. 700.

OF THE DISCIPLES OF JESUS: By the seventy, Luke 10:17-20; by other disciples, Mark 9:39; John 14:12; by the apostles, Acts 3:6,12,13,16; 4:10,30; 9:34,35; 16:18. Peter cures the sick, Acts 5:15,16; Æneas, Acts 9:34; raises Dorcas, Acts 9:40; causes the death of Ananias and Sapphira, Acts 5:5,10. Peter and John cure a lame man, Acts 3:2-11. Peter and other apostles delivered from prison, Acts 5:19-23; 12:6-11; 16:26. Philip carried away by the Spirit, Acts 8:39. Paul strikes Elymas with blindness, Acts 13:11; heals a cripple, Acts 14:10; casts out evil spirits, and cures sick, Acts 16:18; 19:11,12; 28:8,9; raises Eutychus to life, Acts 20:9-12; shakes a viper off his hand, Acts 28:5. Paul cured of blindness, Acts 9:3-6,17,18.

CONVINCING EFFECT OF: Ex. 4:28. And Moses told Aaron all the words of the LORD who had sent him, and all the signs which he had commanded him. 29. And Moses and Aaron went and gathered together all the elders of the children of Israel: 30. And Aaron spake all the words which the LORD had spoken unto Moses, and did the signs in the sight of the people. 31. And the people believed: and when they heard that the LORD had visited the children of Israel, and that he had looked upon their affliction, then they bowed their heads and worshipped.

Ex. 10:7. And Pharaoh's servants said unto him, How long shall this man be a snare unto us? let the men go, that they may serve the LORD their God: knowest thou not yet that Egypt is destroyed? 16. Then Pharaoh called for Moses and Aaron in haste; and he said, I have sinned against the LORD your God, and against you. 17. Now therefore forgive, I pray thee, my sin only this once, and intreat the LORD your God, that he may take away from me this death only.

Ex. 12:31. And he called for Moses and Aaron by night, and said, Rise up, *and* get you forth from among my people, both ye and the children of Israel; and go, serve the LORD, as ye have said. 32. Also take

your flocks and your herds, as ye have said, and be gone; and bless me also. 33. And the Egyptians were urgent upon the people, that they might send them out of the land in haste; for they said, We *be* all dead *men*.

Ex. 14:25. The Egyptians said, Let us flee from the face of Israel; for the LORD fighteth for them against the Egyptians. 31. And Israel saw that great work which the LORD did upon the Egyptians: and the people feared the LORD, and believed the LORD, and his servant Moses.

Judg. 6:17. If now I have found grace in thy sight, then shew me a sign that thou talkest with me. 18. Depart not hence, I pray thee, until I come unto thee, and bring forth my present, and set *it* before thee. And he said, I will tarry until thou come again. 19. And Gideon went in, and made ready a kid, and unleavened cakes of an ephah of flour: the flesh he put in a basket, and he put the broth in a pot, and brought *it* out unto him under the oak, and presented *it*. 20. And the angel of God said unto him, Take the flesh and the unleavened cakes, and lay *them* upon this rock, and pour out the broth. And he did so. 21. Then the angel of the LORD put forth the end of the staff that *was* in his hand, and touched the flesh and the unleavened cakes; and there rose up fire out of the rock, and consumed the flesh and the unleavened cakes. Then the angel of the LORD departed out of his sight. 22. And when Gideon perceived that he *was* an angel of the LORD, Gideon said, Alas, O Lord GOD! for because I have seen an angel of the LORD face to face. 36. And Gideon said unto God, If thou wilt save Israel by mine hand, as thou hast said, 37. Behold, I will put a fleece of wool in the floor; *and* if the dew be on the fleece only, and *it be* dry upon all the earth *beside*, then shall I know that thou wilt save Israel by mine hand, as thou hast said. 38. And it was so: for he rose up early on the morrow, and thrust the fleece together, and wringed the dew out of the fleece, a bowl full of water. 39. And Gideon said unto God, Let not thine anger be hot against me, and I will speak but this once: let me prove, I pray thee, but this once with the fleece; let it now be dry only upon the fleece, and upon all the ground let there be dew. 40. And God did so that night: for it was dry upon the fleece only, and there was dew on all the ground.

Judg. 7:1. Then Jerubbaal, who *is* Gideon, and all the people that *were* with him, rose up early, and pitched beside the well of Harod: so that the host of the Midianites were on the north side of them, by the hill of Moreh, in the valley.

Dan. 3:28. *Then* Nebuchadnezzar spake, and said, Blessed *be* the God of Shadrach, Meshach, and Abed-nego, who hath sent his angel, and delivered his servants that trusted in him, and have changed the king's word, and yielded their bodies, that they might not serve nor worship any god, except their own God. 29. Therefore I make a decree, That every people, nation, and language, which speak any thing amiss against the God of Shadrach, Meshach, and Abed-nego, shall be cut in pieces, and their houses shall be made a dunghill : because there is no other God that can deliver after this sort.

Dan. 4:2. I thought it good to shew the signs and wonders that the high God hath wrought toward me. 3. How great *are* his signs! and how mighty *are* his wonders! his kingdom *is* an everlasting kingdom, and his dominion *is* from generation to generation.

Luke 5:4. Now when he had left speaking, he said unto Simon, Launch out into the deep, and let down your nets for a draught. 5. And Simon answering said unto him, Master, we have toiled all the night, and have taken nothing: nevertheless at thy word I will let down the net. 6. And when they had this done, they inclosed a great multitude of fishes: and their net brake. 7. And they beckoned unto *their* partners, which were in the other ship, that they should come and help them. And they came, and filled both the ships, so that they began to sink. 8. When Simon Peter saw *it*, he fell down at Jesus' knees, saying, Depart from me; for I am a sinful man, O Lord. 9. For he was astonished, and all that were with him, at the draught of the fishes which they had taken: 10. And so *was* also James, and John, the sons of Zebedee, which were partners with Simon. And Jesus said unto Simon, Fear not; from henceforth thou shalt catch men. 11. And when they had brought their ships to land, they forsook all, and followed him.

John 2:11. This beginning of miracles did Jesus in Cana of Galilee, and manifested forth his glory; and his disciples believed on him. 22. When therefore he was risen from the dead, his disciples remembered that he had said this unto them ; and they believed the scripture, and the word which Jesus had said. 23. Now when he was in Jerusalem at the passover, in the feast *day*, many believed in his name, when they saw the miracles which he did.

John 4:48. Then said Jesus unto him, Except ye see signs and wonders, ye will not believe. 49. The nobleman saith unto him, Sir, come down ere my child die. 50. Jesus saith unto him, Go thy way; thy son liveth. And the man believed the word that Jesus had spoken unto him, and he went his way. 51. And as he was now going down, his servants met him, and told *him*, saying, Thy son liveth. 52. Then enquired he of them the hour when he began to amend. And they said unto him, Yesterday at the seventh hour the fever left him. 53. So the father knew that *it was* at the same hour, in the which Jesus said unto him, Thy son liveth: and himself believed, and his whole house.

John 7:31. And many of the people believed on him, and said, When Christ cometh, will he do more miracles than these which this *man* hath done?

John 11:43. And when he thus had spoken, he cried with a loud voice, Lazarus, come forth. 44. And he that was dead came forth, bound hand and foot with graveclothes: and his face was bound about with a napkin. Jesus saith unto them, Loose him, and let him go. 45. Then many of the Jews which came to Mary, and had seen the things which Jesus did, believed on him.

John 12:10. But the chief priests consulted that they might put Lazarus also to death; 11. Because that by reason of him many of the Jews went away, and believed on Jesus.

John 20:30. And many other signs truly did Jesus in the presence of his disciples, which are not written in this book: 31. But these are written, that ye might believe that Jesus is the Christ, the Son of God; and that believing ye might have life through his name.

Acts 8:6. And the people with one accord gave heed unto those things which Philip spake, hearing and seeing the miracles which he did.

Acts 9:32. And it came to pass, as Peter passed throughout all *quarters*, he came down also to the saints which dwelt at Lydda. 33. And there he found a certain man named Æneas, which had kept his bed eight years, and was sick of the palsy. 34. And Peter said unto him, Æneas, Jesus Christ maketh thee whole : arise, and make thy bed. And he arose immediately. 35. And all that dwelt at Lydda and Saron saw him, and turned to the Lord. 36. Now there was at Joppa a certain disciple named Tabitha, which by interpretation is called Dorcas: this woman was full of good works and almsdeeds which she did. 37. And it came to pass in those days, that she was sick, and died: whom when they had washed, they laid *her* in an upper chamber. 38. And forasmuch as Lydda was nigh to Joppa, and the disciples had heard that Peter was there, they sent unto him two men, desiring *him* that he would not delay to come to them. 39. Then Peter arose and went with them. When he was come, they brought him into the upper chamber: and all the widows stood by him weeping, and shewing the coats and garments which Dorcas made, while she was with them. 40. But Peter put them all forth, and kneeled down, and prayed; and turning *him* to the body said, Tabitha, arise. And she opened her eyes: and when she saw Peter, she sat up. 41. And he gave her *his* hand, and lifted her up, and when he had called the saints and widows, presented her alive. 42. And it was known throughout all Joppa; and many believed in the Lord.

Acts 13:8. But Elymas the scorcerer (for

so is his name by interpretation) withstood them, seeking to turn away the deputy from the faith. 9. Then Saul, (who also *is called* Paul,) filled with the Holy Ghost, set his eyes on him, 10. And said. O full of all subtilty and all mischief, *thou* child of the devil, *thou* enemy of all righteousness, wilt thou not cease to pervert the right ways of the Lord? 11. And now, behold, the hand of the Lord *is* upon thee, and thou shalt be blind, not seeing the sun for a season. And immediately there fell on him a mist and a darkness; and he went about seeking some to lead him by the hand. 12. Then the deputy, when he saw what was done, believed, being astonished at the doctrine of the Lord.

Acts 19:13. Then certain of the vagabond Jews, exorcists, took upon them to call over them which had evil spirits the name of the Lord Jesus, saying, We adjure you by Jesus whom Paul preacheth. 14. And there were seven sons of *one* Sceva, a Jew, *and* chief of the priests, which did so. 15. And the evil spirit answered and said, Jesus I know, and Paul I know; but who are ye? 16. And the man in whom the evil spirit was leaped on them, and overcame them, and prevailed against them, so that they fled out of that house naked and wounded. 17. And this was known to all the Jews and Greeks also dwelling at Ephesus; and fear fell on them all, and the name of the Lord Jesus was magnified. 18. And many that believed came, and confessed, and shewed their deeds.

Rom. 15:18. For I will not dare to speak of any of those things which Christ hath not wrought by me, to make the Gentiles obedient, by word and deed, 19. Through mighty signs and wonders, by the power of the Spirit of God; so that from Jerusalem, and round about unto Illyricum, I have fully preached the gospel of Christ.

See below, MIRACLES, DESIGN OF.

DESIGN OF: Ex. 3:19. And I am sure that the king of Egypt will not let you go, no, not by a mighty hand. 20. And I will stretch out my hand, and smite Egypt with all my wonders which I will do in the midst thereof: and after that he will let you go.

Ex. 4:2. And the LORD said unto him, What *is* that in thine hand? And he said, A rod. 3. And he said, Cast it on the ground. And he cast it on the ground, and it became a serpent; and Moses fled from before it. 4. And the LORD said unto Moses, Put forth thine hand, and take it by the tail. And he put forth his hand, and caught it, and it became a rod in his hand: 5. That they may believe that the LORD God of their fathers, the God of Abraham, the God of Isaac, and the God of Jacob, hath appeared unto thee. 6. And the LORD said furthermore unto him, Put now thine hand into thy bosom. And he put his hand into his bosom: and when he took it out, behold, his hand *was* leprous as snow. 7. And he said,

Put thine hand into thy bosom again. And he put his hand into his bosom again; and plucked it out of his bosom, and, behold, it was turned again as his *other* flesh. 8. And it shall come to pass, if they will not believe thee, neither hearken to the voice of the first sign, that they will believe the voice of the latter sign. 9. And it shall come to pass, if they will not believe also these two signs, neither hearken unto thy voice, that thou shalt take of the water of the river, and pour *it* upon the dry *land:* and the water which thou takest out of the river shall become blood upon the dry *land.*

Ex. 7:5. And the Egyptians shall know that I *am* the LORD, when I stretch forth mine hand upon Egypt, and bring out the children of Israel from among them. 17. Thus saith the LORD, In this thou shalt know that I *am* the LORD: behold, I will smite with the rod that *is* in mine hand upon the waters which *are* in the river, and they shall be turned to blood.

Ex. 8:8. Then Pharaoh called for Moses and Aaron, and said, Intreat the LORD, that he may take away the frogs from me, and from my people; and I will let the people go, that they may do sacrifice unto the LORD. 9. And Moses said unto Pharaoh, Glory over me: when shall I intreat for thee, and for thy servants, and for thy people, to destroy the frogs from thee and thy houses, *that* they may remain in the river only? 10. And he said, To morrow. And he said, *Be it* according to thy word: that thou mayest know that *there is* none like unto the LORD our God. 22. And I will sever in that day the land of Goshen, in which my people dwell, that no swarms *of flies* shall be there; to the end thou mayest know that I *am* the LORD in the midst of the earth.

Ex. 9:14. For I will at this time send all my plagues upon thine heart, and upon thy servants, and upon thy people; that thou mayest know that *there is* none like me in all the earth. 15. For now I will stretch out my hand, that I may smite thee and thy people with pestilence; and thou shalt be cut off from the earth. 16. And in very deed for this *cause* have I raised thee up, for to shew *in* thee my power; and that my name may be declared throughout all the earth. 29. And Moses said unto him, As soon as I am gone out of the city, I will spread abroad my hands unto the LORD: *and* the thunder shall cease, neither shall there be any more hail; that thou mayest know how that the earth *is* the LORD's.

Ex. 10:1. And the LORD said unto Moses, Go in unto Pharaoh: for I have hardened his heart, and the heart of his servants, that I might shew these my signs before him: 2. And that thou mayest tell in the ears of thy son, and of thy son's son, what things I have wrought in Egypt, and my signs which I have done among them; that ye may know how that I *am* the LORD. 16. Then

Pharaoh called for Moses and Aaron in haste; and he said, I have sinned against the LORD your God, and against you. 17. Now therefore forgive, I pray thee, my sin only this once, and intreat the LORD your God, that he may take away from me this death only.

Ex. 11:1. And the LORD said unto Moses, Yet will I bring one plague *more* upon Pharaoh, and upon Egypt; afterwards he will let you go hence: 7. But against any of the children of Israel shall not a dog move his tongue, against man or beast: that ye may know how that the LORD doth put a difference between the Egyptians and Israel. 8. And all these thy servants shall come down unto me, and bow down themselves unto me, saying, Get thee out, and all the people that follow thee: and after that I will go out. And he went out from Pharaoh in a great anger. 9. And the LORD said unto Moses, Pharaoh shall not hearken unto you; that my wonders may be multiplied in the land of Egypt.

Ex. 12:29. And it came to pass, that at midnight the LORD smote all the firstborn in the land of Egypt, from the firstborn of Pharaoh that sat on his throne unto the firstborn of the captive that *was* in the dungeon; and all the firstborn of cattle. 30. And Pharaoh rose up in the night, he, and all his servants, and all the Egyptians; and there was a great cry in Egypt; for *there was* not a house where *there was* not one dead. 31. And he called for Moses and Aaron by night, and said, Rise up, *and* get you forth from among my people, both ye and the children of Israel; and go, serve the LORD, as ye have said. 32. Also take your flocks and your herds, as ye have said, and be gone; and bless me also. 33. And the Egyptians were urgent upon the people, that they might send them out of the land in haste; for they said, We *be* all dead *men*.

Ex. 14:4. And I will harden Pharaoh's heart, that he shall follow after them; and I will be honoured upon Pharaoh, and upon all his host; that the Egyptians may know that I *am* the LORD. And they did so. 18. And the Egyptians shall know that I *am* the LORD, when I have gotten me honour upon Pharaoh, upon his chariots, and upon his horsemen. 24. And it came to pass, that in the morning watch the LORD looked unto the host of the Egyptians through the pillar of fire and of the cloud, and troubled the host of the Egyptians, 25. And took off their chariot wheels, that they drave them heavily: so that the Egyptians said, Let us flee from the face of Israel; for the LORD fighteth for them against the Egyptians. 31. And Israel saw that great work which the LORD did upon the Egyptians: and the people feared the LORD, and believed the LORD, and his servant Moses.

Ex. 16:4. Then said the LORD unto Moses, Behold, I will rain bread from heaven for you; and the people shall go out and gather a certain rate every day, that I may prove them, whether they will walk in my law, or no. 5. And it shall come to pass, that on the sixth day they shall prepare *that* which they bring in; and it shall be twice as much as they gather daily. 6. And Moses and Aaron said unto all the children of Israel, At even, then ye shall know that the LORD hath brought you out from the land of Egypt:

Ex. 19:4. Ye have seen what I did unto the Egyptians, and *how* I bare you on eagles' wings, and brought you unto myself. 5. Now therefore, if ye will obey my voice indeed, and keep my covenant, then ye shall be a peculiar treasure unto me above all people: for all the earth *is* mine: 9. And the LORD said unto Moses, Lo, I come unto thee in a thick cloud, that the people may hear when I speak with thee, and believe thee for ever.

Num. 14:11. And the LORD said unto Moses, How long will this people provoke me? and how long will it be ere they believe me, for all the signs which I have shewed among them?

Num. 16:28. And Moses said, Hereby ye shall know that the LORD hath sent me to do all these works; for *I have* not *done them* of mine own mind. 29. If these men die the common death of all men, or if they be visited after the visitation of all men; *then* the LORD hath not sent me. 30. But if the LORD make a new thing, and the earth open her mouth, and swallow them up, with all that *appertain* unto them, and they go down quick into the pit; then ye shall understand that these men have provoked the LORD. 31. And it came to pass, as he had made an end of speaking all these words, that the ground clave asunder that *was* under them: 32. And the earth opened her mouth, and swallowed them up, and their houses, and all the men that *appertained* unto Korah, and all *their* goods. 33. They, and all that *appertained* to them, went down alive into the pit, and the earth closed upon them: and they perished from among the congregation. 34. And all Israel that *were* round about them fled at the cry of them: for they said, Lest the earth swallow us up *also*. 35. And there came out a fire from the LORD, and consumed the two hundred and fifty men that offered incense.

Num. 17:1. And the LORD spake unto Moses, saying, 2. Speak unto the children of Israel, and take of every one of them a rod according to the house of *their* fathers, of all their princes according to the house of their fathers twelve rods: write thou every man's name upon his rod. 3. And thou shalt write Aaron's name upon the rod of Levi: for one rod *shall be* for the head of the house of their fathers. 4. And thou shalt lay them up in the tabernacle of the congregation before the testimony, where I will meet with you. 5. And it shall come to pass, *that* the man's rod, whom I shall choose, shall blossom: and I will make to cease from me the murmurings of the children of Israel, whereby they murmur against you. 6. And Moses spake unto the children of Israel, and every one of their princes gave him a rod apiece, for each prince one, according to their fathers' houses, *even* twelve rods: and the rod of Aaron *was* among their rods. 7. And Moses laid up the rods before the LORD in the tabernacle of witness. 8. And it came to pass, that on the morrow Moses went into the tabernacle of witness: and, behold, the rod of Aaron for the house of Levi was budded, and brought forth buds, and bloomed blossoms, and yielded almonds. 9. And Moses brought out all the rods from before the LORD unto all the children of Israel: and they looked, and took every man his rod. 10. And the LORD said unto Moses, Bring Aaron's rod again before the testimony, to be kept for a token against the rebels; and thou shalt quite take away their murmurings from me, that they die not. 11. And Moses did *so:* as the LORD commanded him, so did he. 12. And the children of Israel spake unto Moses, saying, Behold, we die, we perish, we all perish. 13. Whosoever cometh any thing near unto the tabernacle of the LORD shall die: shall we be consumed with dying?

Deut. 4:33. Did *ever* people hear the voice of God speaking out of the midst of the fire, as thou hast heard, and live? 34. Or hath God assayed to go *and* take him a nation from the midst of *another* nation, by temptations, by signs, and by wonders, and by war, and by a mighty hand, and by a stretched out arm, and by great terrors, according to all that the LORD your God did for you in Egypt before your eyes? 35. Unto thee it was shewed, that thou mightest know that the LORD he *is* God; *there is* none else beside him.

Deut. 11:1. Therefore thou shalt love the LORD thy God, and keep his charge, and his statutes, and his judgments, and his commandments, alway. 2. And know ye this day: for *I speak* not with your children which have not known, and which have not seen the chastisement of the LORD your God, his greatness, his mighty hand, and his stretched out arm, 3. And his miracles, and his acts, which he did in the midst of Egypt unto Pharaoh the king of Egypt, and unto all his land; [chapter 29:1-9.] 4. And what he did unto the army of Egypt, unto their horses, and to their chariots; how he made the water of the Red sea to overflow them as they pursued after you, and *how* the LORD hath destroyed them unto this day; 5. And what he did unto you in the wilderness, until ye came into this place; 6. And what he did unto Dathan and Abiram, the sons of Eliab, the son of Reuben: how the earth opened her mouth, and swallowed them up, and their households, and

their tents, and all the substance that *was* in their possession, in the midst of all Israel: 7. But your eyes have seen all the great acts of the LORD which he did. 8. Therefore shall ye keep all the commandments which I command you this day, that ye may be strong, and go in and possess the land, whither ye go to possess it;

Deut. 29:5. And I have led you forty years in the wilderness: your clothes are not waxen old upon you, and thy shoe is not waxen old upon thy foot. 6. Ye have not eaten bread, neither have ye drunk wine or strong drink: that ye might know that I *am* the LORD your God.

Josh. 2:9. And she said unto the men, I know that the LORD hath given you the land, and that your terror is fallen upon us, and that all the inhabitants of the land faint because of you. 10. For we have heard how the LORD dried up the water of the Red sea for you, when ye came out of Egypt; and what ye did unto the two kings of the Amorites, that *were* on the other side Jordan, Sihon and Og, whom ye utterly destroyed. 11. And as soon as we had heard *these things*, our hearts did melt, neither did there remain any more courage in any man, because of you: for the LORD your God, he *is* God in heaven above, and in earth beneath.

Josh. 3:10. And Joshua said, Hereby ye shall know that the living God *is* among you, and *that* he will without fail drive out from before you the Canaanites, and the Hittites, and the Hivites, and the Perizzites, and the Girgashites, and the Amorites, and the Jebusites. 11. Behold, the ark of the covenant of the Lord of all the earth passeth over before you into Jordan.

Josh. 4:23. For the LORD your God dried up the waters of Jordan from before you, until ye were passed over, as the LORD your God did to the Red sea, which he dried up from before us, until we were gone over: 24. That all the people of the earth might know the hand of the LORD, that it *is* mighty: that ye might fear the LORD your God for ever.

Josh. 5:1. And it came to pass, when all the kings of the Amorites, which *were* on the side of Jordan westward, and all the kings of the Canaanites, which *were* by the sea, heard that the LORD had dried up the waters of Jordan from before the children of Israel, until we were passed over, that their heart melted, neither was there spirit in them any more, because of the children of Israel.

Judg. 2:7. And the people served the LORD all the days of Joshua, and all the days of the elders that outlived Joshua, who had seen all the great works of the LORD, that he did for Israel.

1 Sam. 6:6. Wherefore then do ye harden your hearts, as the Egyptians and Pharaoh hardened their hearts? when he had wrought wonderfully among them, did they not let

the people go, and they departed? 7. Now therefore make a new cart, and take two milch kine, on which there hath come no yoke, and tie the kine to the cart, and bring their calves home from them: 8. And take the ark of the LORD, and lay it upon the cart; and put the jewels of gold, which ye return him *for* a trespass offering, in a coffer by the side thereof; and send it away, that it may go. 9. And see, if it goeth up by the way of his own coast to Beth-shemesh, *then* he hath done us this great evil: but if not, then we shall know that *it is* not his hand *that* smote us; it *was* a chance *that* happened to us. *vs.* 10–18.

1 Sam. 12:17. *Is it* not wheat harvest to day? I will call unto the LORD, and he shall send thunder and rain; that ye may perceive and see that your wickedness *is* great, which ye have done in the sight of the LORD, in asking you a king. 18. So Samuel called unto the LORD; and the LORD sent thunder and rain that day: and all the people greatly feared the LORD and Samuel.

1 Kin. 18:24. And call ye on the name of your gods, and I will call on the name of the LORD: and the God that answereth by fire, let him be God. And all the people answered and said, It is well spoken. 37. Hear me, O LORD, hear me, that this people may know that thou *art* the LORD God, and *that* thou hast turned their heart back again. 38. Then the fire of the LORD fell, and consumed the burnt sacrifice, and the wood, and the stones, and the dust, and licked up the water that *was* in the trench. 39. And when all the people saw *it*, they fell on their faces: and they said, The LORD, he *is* the God; the LORD, he *is* the God.

2 Kin. 5:14. Then went he down, and dipped himself seven times in Jordan, according to the saying of the man of God: and his flesh came again like unto the flesh of a little child, and he was clean. 15. And he returned to the man of God, he and all his company, and came, and stood before him: and he said, Behold, now I know that *there is* no God in all the earth, but in Israel: now therefore, I pray thee, take a blessing of thy servant.

2 Chr. 7:1. Now when Solomon had made an end of praying, the fire came down from heaven, and consumed the burnt offering and the sacrifices; and the glory of the LORD filled the house. 2. And the priests could not enter into the house of the LORD, because the glory of the LORD had filled the LORD's house. 3. And when all the children of Israel saw how the fire came down, and the glory of the LORD upon the house, they bowed themselves with their faces to the ground upon the pavement, and worshipped, and praised the LORD, *saying*, For *he is* good; for his mercy *endureth* for ever.

Psa. 78:10. They kept not the covenant of God, and refused to walk in his law; 11. And forgat his works, and his wonders that he had shewed them. 12. Marvellous things did he in the sight of their fathers, in the land of Egypt, *in* the field of Zoan. 13. He divided the sea, and caused them to pass through; and he made the waters to stand as an heap. 14. In the daytime also he led them with a cloud, and all the night with a light of fire. 15. He clave the rocks in the wilderness, and gave *them* drink as *out of* the great depths. 16. He brought streams also out of the rock, and caused waters to run down like rivers. 17. And they sinned yet more against him by provoking the most High in the wilderness. 18. And they tempted God in their heart by asking meat for their lust. 19. Yea, they spake against God; they said, Can God furnish a table in the wilderness? 20. Behold, he smote the rock, that the waters gushed out, and the streams overflowed; can he give bread also? can he provide flesh for his people? 21. Therefore the LORD heard *this*, and was wroth: so a fire was kindled against Jacob, and anger also came up against Israel; 22. Because they believed not in God, and trusted not in his salvation: 23. Though he had commanded the clouds from above, and opened the doors of heaven, 24. And had rained down manna upon them to eat, and had given them of the corn of heaven. 25. Man did eat angels' food: he sent them meat to the full. 26. He caused an east wind to blow in the heaven: and by his power he brought in the south wind. 27. He rained flesh also upon them as dust, and feathered fowls like as the sand of the sea: 28. And he let *it* fall in the midst of their camp, round about their habitations. 29. So they did eat, and were well filled: for he gave them their own desire; 30. They were not estranged from their lust. But while their meat *was* yet in their mouths, 31. The wrath of God came upon them, and slew the fattest of them, and smote down the chosen *men* of Israel. 32. For all this they sinned still, and believed not for his wondrous works.

Psa. 106:9. He rebuked the Red sea also, and it was dried up: so he led them through the depths, as through the wilderness. 10. And he saved them from the hand of him that hated *them*, and redeemed them from the hand of the enemy. 11. And the waters covered their enemies: there was not one of them left. 12. Then believed they his words; they sang his praise.

Jer. 32:20. Which hast set signs and wonders in the land of Egypt, *even* unto this day, and in Israel, and among *other* men; and hast made thee a name, as at this day;

Dan. 2:47. The king answered unto Daniel, and said, Of a truth *it is*, that your God *is* a God of gods, and a Lord of kings, and a revealer of secrets, seeing thou couldest reveal this secret.

Dan. 3:28. *Then* Nebuchadnezzar spake, and said, Blessed be the God of Shadrach, Meshach, and Abed-nego, who hath sent his angel, and delivered his servants that trusted in him, and have changed the king's word, and yielded their bodies, that they might not serve nor worship any god, except their own God. 29. Therefore I make a decree, That every people, nation, and language, which speak any thing amiss against the God of Shadrach, Meshach, and Abed-nego, shall be cut in pieces, and their houses shall be made a dunghill: because there is no other God that can deliver after this sort.

Dan. 6:20. And when he came to the den, he cried with a lamentable voice unto Daniel: *and* the king spake and said to Daniel, O Daniel, servant of the living God, is thy God, whom thou servest continually, able to deliver thee from the lions? 21. Then said Daniel unto the king, O king, live for ever. 22. My God hath sent his angel, and hath shut the lions' mouths, that they have not hurt me: forasmuch as before him innocency was found in me; and also before thee, O king, have I done no hurt. 23. Then was the king exceeding glad for him, and commanded that they should take Daniel up out of the den. So Daniel was taken up out of the den, and no manner of hurt was found upon him, because he believed in his God. 24. And the king commanded, and they brought those men which had accused Daniel, and they cast *them* into the den of lions, them, their children, and their wives; and the lions had the mastery of them, and brake all their bones in pieces or ever they came at the bottom of the den. 25. Then king Darius wrote unto all people, nations, and languages, that dwell in all the earth; Peace be multiplied unto you. 26. I make a decree, That in every dominion of my kingdom men tremble and fear before the God of Daniel: for he *is* the living God, and stedfast for ever, and his kingdom *that* which shall not be destroyed, and his dominion *shall be even* unto the end. 27. He delivereth and rescueth, and he worketh signs and wonders in heaven and in earth, who hath delivered Daniel from the power of the lions.

Jonah 1:14. Wherefore they cried unto the LORD, and said, We beseech thee, O LORD, we beseech thee, let us not perish for this man's life, and lay not upon us innocent blood: for thou, O LORD, hast done as it pleased thee. 15. So they took up Jonah, and cast him forth into the sea: and the sea ceased from her raging. 16. Then the men feared the LORD exceedingly, and offered a sacrifice unto the LORD, and made vows.

Zech. 2:9. For, behold, I will shake mine hand upon them, and they shall be a spoil to their servants: and ye shall know that the LORD of hosts hath sent me.

Matt. 4:3. And when the tempter came to him, he said, If thou be the Son of God, command that these stones be made bread. Luke 4:3,6.

Matt. 11:3. And said unto him, Art thou he that should come, or do we look for an-

other? 4. Jesus answered and said unto them, Go and shew John again those things which ye do hear and see: 5. The blind receive their sight, and the lame walk, the lepers are cleansed, and the deaf hear, the dead are raised up, and the poor have the gospel preached to them.

Mark 2:9. Whether is it easier to say to the sick of the palsy, *Thy* sins be forgiven thee; or to say, Arise, and take up thy bed, and walk? 10. But that ye may know that the Son of man hath power on earth to forgive sins, (he saith to the sick of the palsy,) 11. I say unto thee, Arise, and take up thy bed, and go thy way into thine house. 12. And immediately he arose, took up the bed, and went forth before them all; insomuch that they were all amazed, and glorified God, saying, We never saw it on this fashion. Luke 5:26.

Luke 18:42. And Jesus said unto him, Receive thy sight: thy faith hath saved thee. 43. And immediately he received his sight, and followed him, glorifying God: and all the people, when they saw *it*, gave praise unto God.

John 2:11. This beginning of miracles did Jesus in Cana of Galilee, and manifested forth his glory; and his disciples believed on him.

John 4:48. Then said Jesus unto him, Except ye see signs and wonders, ye will not believe.

John 5:36. But I have greater witness than *that* of John: for the works which the Father hath given me to finish, the same works that I do, bear witness of me, that the Father hath sent me.

John 9:3. Jesus answered, Neither hath this man sinned, nor his parents: but that the works of God should be made manifest in him.

John 11:4. When Jesus heard *that*, he said, This sickness is not unto death, but for the glory of God, that the Son of God might be glorified thereby. 40. Jesus saith unto her, Said I not unto thee, that, if thou wouldest believe, thou shouldest see the glory of God? 41. Then they took away the stone *from the place* where the dead was laid. And Jesus lifted up *his* eyes, and said, Father, I thank thee that thou hast heard me. 42. And I knew that thou hearest me always: but because of the people which stand by I said *it*, that they may believe that thou hast sent me.

Acts 2:22. Ye men of Israel, hear these words; Jesus of Nazareth, a man approved of God among you by miracles and wonders and signs, which God did by him in the midst of you, as ye yourselves also know:

Acts 3:1. Now Peter and John went up together into the temple at the hour of prayer, *being* the ninth *hour*. 2. And a certain man lame from his mother's womb was carried, whom they laid daily at the gate of the temple which is called Beautiful, to ask alms of them that entered into the temple;

3 Who seeing Peter and John about to go into the temple asked an alms. 4. And Peter, fastening his eyes upon him with John, said, Look on us. 5. And he gave heed unto them, expecting to receive something of them. 6. Then Peter said, Silver and gold have I none; but such as I have give I thee: In the name of Jesus Christ of Nazareth rise up and walk. 7. And he took him by the right hand, and lifted *him* up: and immediately his feet and ankle bones received strength. 8. And he leaping up stood, and walked, and entered with them into the temple, walking, and leaping, and praising God. 9. And all the people saw him walking and praising God: 10. And they knew that it was he which sat for alms at the Beautiful gate of the temple: and they were filled with wonder and amazement at that which had happened unto him.

Acts 4:21. For all *men* glorified God for that which was done. 22. For the man was above forty years old, on whom this miracle of healing was shewed.

1 Cor. 1:22. For the Jews require a sign, and the Greeks seek after wisdom:

MIRACULOUS GIFTS OF THE HOLY GHOST: Foretold, Isa. 35:4-6; Joel 2:28,29. Of different kinds, 1 Cor. 12:4-6. Enumerated, 1 Cor. 12:8-10,28. Christ was endued with, Matt. 12:28. Poured out on Pentecost, Acts 2:1-4. Communicated on preaching the gospel, Acts 10:44-46; by laying on of the apostles' hands, Acts 8:17,18; 19:6; for the confirmation of the gospel, Mark 16:20; Acts 14:3; Rom. 15:19; Heb. 2:4; for the edification of the church, 1 Cor. 12:7; 14:12,13. To be sought after, 1 Cor. 12:31; 14:1. Temporary nature of, 1 Cor. 13:8. Not to be neglected, 1 Tim. 4:14; 2 Tim. 1:6; or despised, 1 Thess. 5:20; or purchased, Acts 8:20.

MISCELLANY OF MINOR SUB-TOPICS: Called MARVELOUS THINGS, Psa. 78:12; MARVELOUS WORKS, Isa. 29:14; Psa. 105:5; SIGNS AND WONDERS, Jer. 32:21; John 4:48; 2 Cor. 12:12.

Performed through the power of God, John 3:2; Acts 14:3; 15:12; 19:11; of the Holy Ghost, Matt. 12:28; Rom. 15:19; 1 Cor. 12:9,10,28,30; in the name of Christ, Mark 16:17; Acts 3:16; 4:30. Faith required in those who perform, Matt. 17:20; 21:21; John 14:12· Acts 3:16; 6:8. Faith required in those for whom they were performed, Matt. 9:28; Mark 9:22-24; Acts 14:9. Power to work, given the disciples, Mark 3:14,15; 16:17,18,20. Demanded by unbelievers, Matt. 12:38,39; 16:1; Luke 11:16,29; 23:8. Alleged miracles performed by magicians, Ex. 7:10-12,22; 8:7; by other impostors, Matt. 7:22. Performed through the powers of evil, 2 Thess. 2:9; Rev. 16:14. Wrought in support of false religions, Deut. 13:1,2; by false christs, Matt. 24:24; by false prophets, Matt. 24:24; Rev. 19:20; by the Witch of En-dor, 1 Sam. 28:7-14; Simon Magus, Acts 8:9-11. Not to be regarded,

Deut. 13:3. Deceive the ungodly, 2 Thess. 2:10-12; Rev. 13:14; 19:20. A mark of apostasy, 2 Thess. 2:3,9; Rev. 13:13.

MIRE. FIGURATIVE: Psa. 40:2; 69:2.

MIRIAM, sister of Moses. Watches over Moses when he is in the ark, Ex. 2:4-8. Song of, after the destruction of Pharaoh and his army, Ex. 15:20,21; Mic. 6:4. Jealous of Moses, stricken with leprosy, healed on account of the intercession of Moses, Num. 12; Deut. 24:9. Dies and is buried at Kadesh, Num. 20:1.

MIRMA, a Benjamite, 1 Chr. 8:10.

MIRROR. Of brass, Job 37:18. Given by the Iraelitish women to be melted for the laver, Ex. 38:8.

FIGURATIVE: 1 Cor. 13:12; 2 Cor. 3:18; Jas. 1:23,24.

MISCEGENATION. Forbidden by Abraham, Gen. 24:3; Jacob, Gen. 28:1; Moses, Ex. 34:12-16; Deut 7:3,4; Joshua, Josh. 23:12. Reasons for prohibition, Ex. 34:16; Deut. 7:4; Josh. 23:12,13.

Results of, Judg. 3:6,7.

INSTANCES OF: Moses, Num. 12:1; Esau, Gen. 26:34,35; Israel, Num. 25:1,6-8; Judg. 3:5-8.

MISER, Eccl. 4:7,8.

MISGAB, an unknown place mentioned in Jer. 48:1.

MISHAEL. 1. A son of Uzziel, helps carry the bodies of Nadab and Abihu out of the camp, Ex. 6:22; Lev. 10:4.

2. A Jew who stood by Ezra when he read the law to the people, Neh. 8:4.

3. Called also MESHACH. One of three Hebrew children trained with Daniel at the court of Babylon, Dan. 1:6,7,11-20. Assists Daniel in interpreting Nebuchadnezzar's dream, Dan. 2:17-23. Cast into the fiery furnace, Dan. 3:13-30.

MISHAM, a Benjamite, 1 Chr. 8:12.

MISHEAL, called also MISHAL. A Levitical city, Josh. 19:26; 21:30.

MISHMA. 1. Son of Ishmael, Gen. 25:14; 1 Chr. 1:30.

2. Of the tribe of Simeon, 1 Chr. 4:25,26.

MISHMANNAH, a Gadite who joined David at Ziklag, 1 Chr. 12:10.

MISJUDGMENT. INSTANCES OF: Of the Reubenites and Gadites, Num. 32:1-33; Josh. 22:11-31. Of Hannah, 1 Sam. 1: 14-17.

See ACCUSATIONS, FALSE; UNCHARITABLENESS.

MISPERETH, called also MIZPAR. A Jew who returned with Zerubbabel from Babylon, Ezra 2:2; Neh. 7:7.

MISREPHOTH-MAIM, a city of E. Zidon, Josh. 11:8; 13:6.

MISSIONS. 2 Kin. 17:27. Then the king of Assyria commanded, saying, Carry thither one of the priests whom ye brought from thence; and let them go and dwell there, and let him teach them the manner of the God of the land. 28. Then one of the priests whom they had carried away from Samaria came and dwelt in Beth-el, and taught them how they should fear the LORD.

1 Chr. 16:23. Sing unto the LORD, all the earth; shew forth from day to day his salvation. 24. Declare his glory among the heathen; his marvellous works among all nations.

Psa. 18:49. Therefore will I give thanks unto thee, O LORD, among the heathen, and sing praises unto thy name.

Psa. 96:3. Declare his glory among the heathen, his wonders among all people. 10. Say among the heathen *that* the LORD reigneth: the world also shall be established that it shall not be moved: he shall judge the people righteously.

Isa. 43:6. I will say to the north, Give up; and to the south, Keep not back: bring my sons from far, and my daughters from the ends of the earth; 7. *Even* every one that is called by my name: for I have created him for my glory, I have formed him; yea, I have made him.

Jonah 3:1. And the word of the LORD came unto Jonah the second time, saying, 2. Arise, go unto Nineveh, that great city, and preach unto it the preaching that I bid thee. [chapters 1,2.] 3. So Jonah arose, and went unto Nineveh, according to the word of the LORD. Now Nineveh was an exceeding great city of three days' journey. 4. And Jonah began to enter into the city a day's journey, and he cried, and said, Yet forty days, and Nineveh shall be overthrown. 5. So the people of Nineveh believed God, and proclaimed a fast, and put on sackcloth, from the greatest of them even to the least of them. 6. For word came unto the king of Nineveh, and he arose from his throne, and he laid his robe from him, and covered *him* with sackcloth, and sat in ashes. 7. And he caused *it* to be proclaimed and published through Nineveh by the decree of the king and his nobles, saying, Let neither man nor beast, herd nor flock, taste any thing: let them not feed, nor drink water: 8. But let man and beast be covered with sackcloth, and cry mightily unto God: yea, let them turn every one from his evil way, and from the violence that *is* in their hands. 9. Who can tell *if* God will turn and repent, and turn away from his fierce anger, that we perish not?

Matt. 24:14. And this gospel of the kingdom shall be preached in all the world for a witness unto all nations; and then shall the end come.

Matt. 28:19. Go ye therefore, and teach all nations, baptizing them in the name of the Father, and of the Son, and of the Holy Ghost:

Mark 13:10. And the gospel must first be published among all nations.

Mark 16:15. And he said unto them, Go ye into all the world, and preach the gospel to every creature.

Luke 24:47. And that repentance and remission of sins should be preached in his name among all nations, beginning at Jeru-

salem. 48. And ye are witnesses of these things.

Acts 10:9. On the morrow, as they went on their journey, and drew nigh unto the city, Peter went up upon the housetop to pray about the sixth hour: 10. And he became very hungry, and would have eaten: but while they made ready, he fell into a trance, 11. And saw heaven opened, and a certain vessel descending unto him, as it had been a great sheet knit at the four corners, and let down to the earth: 12. Wherein were all manner of fourfooted beasts of the earth, and wild beasts, and creeping things, and fowls of the air. 13. And there came a voice to him, Rise, Peter; kill, and eat. 14. But Peter said, Not so, Lord; for I have never eaten any thing that is common or unclean. 15. And the voice *spake* unto him again the second time, What God hath cleansed, *that* call not thou common. 16. This was done thrice: and the vessel was received up again into heaven. 17. Now while Peter doubted in himself what this vision which he had seen should mean, behold, the men which were sent from Cornelius had made enquiry for Simon's house, and stood before the gate, 18. And called, and asked whether Simon, which was surnamed Peter, were lodged there. 19. While Peter thought on the vision, the Spirit said unto him, Behold, three men seek thee. 20. Arise therefore, and get thee down, and go with them, doubting nothing: for I have sent them.

Acts 13:2. As they ministered to the Lord, and fasted, the Holy Ghost said, Separate me Barnabas and Saul for the work whereunto I have called them. 3. And when they had fasted and prayed, and laid *their* hands on them, they sent *them* away. 4. So they, being sent forth by the Holy Ghost, departed unto Seleucia; and from thence they sailed to Cyprus. 47. For so hath the Lord commanded •us, *saying*, I have set thee to be a light of the Gentiles, that thou shouldest be for salvation unto the ends of the earth.

Acts 26:14. And when we were all fallen to the earth, I heard a voice speaking unto me, and saying in the Hebrew tongue, Saul, Saul, why persecutest thou me? *it is* hard for thee to kick against the pricks. 15. And I said, Who art thou, Lord? And he said, I am Jesus whom thou persecutest. 16. But rise, and stand upon thy feet: for I have appeared unto thee for this purpose, to make thee a minister and a witness both of these things which thou hast seen, and of those things in the which I will appear unto thee; 17. Delivering thee from the people, and *from* the Gentiles, unto whom now I send thee, 18. To open their eyes, *and* to turn *them* from darkness to light, and *from* the power of Satan unto God, that they may receive forgiveness of sins, and inheritance among them which are sanctified by faith that is in me.

1 Cor. 16:9. For a great door and effectual

is opened unto me, and *there are* many adversaries.

Rev. 14:6. And I saw another angel fly in the midst of heaven, having the everlasting gospel to preach unto them that dwell on the earth, and to every nation, and kindred, and tongue, and people, 7. Saying with a loud voice, Fear God, and give glory to him ; for the hour of his judgment is come : and worship him that made heaven, and earth, and the sea, and the fountains of waters.

Missionary Hymn, Psa. 96.

The first to do homage to the Messiah were heathen, Matt. 2:11.

See GENTILES, CALL OF ; HEATHEN ; JESUS, KING ; JESUS, KINGDOM OF, PROPHECIES CONCERNING.

MIST, Gen. 2:6; 2 Pet. 2:17.

MITE. About one-fifth of a cent, Mark 12:42. Widow's, Luke 21:2.

MITER, Ex. 28:4,36–39; 39:28–31; Ezek. 21:26 [*R.V.*].

MITHCAH, an encampment of the Israelites, Num. 33:28,29.

MITHREDATH. 1. Treasurer of Cyrus, Ezra 1:8.

2. A Persian officer who joined in writing a letter inimical to the Jews, Ezra 4:7.

MITYLENE. Capital of Lesbos. Paul visits, Acts 20:14,15.

MIZAR, a hill, Psa. 42:6.

MIZPAH. 1. A city allotted to Benjamin, Josh. 18:26. The Israelites assemble at, Judg. 20:1–3; and decree the penalty to be visited upon the Benjamites for their maltreatment of the Levite's concubine, Judg. 20:10. Assembled by Samuel that he might reprove them for their idolatry, 1 Sam. 7:5. Crown Saul king of Israel at, 1 Sam. 10:17–25. A judgment seat of Samuel, 1 Sam. 7:16. Walled by Asa, 1 Kin. 15:22; 2 Chr. 16:6. Temporarily the capital of the country after the children of Israel had been carried away captive, 2 Kin. 25:23,25; Jer. 40:6–15; 41:1–14. Captivity returned to, Neh. 3:7,15,19.

2. A valley near Lebanon, Josh. 11:3,8.

3. A city in Moab. David gives his parents to the care of the king of, 1 Sam. 22:3,4.

4. A city in the lowland of Judah, Josh. 15:38.

MIZPAR. See MISPERETH.

MIZRAIM, son of Ham, Gen. 10:6,13; 1 Chr. 1:8,11.

MIZZAH, son of Reuel, Gen. 36:13,17; 1 Chr. 1:37.

MNASON, a native and Christian of Cyprus who entertained Paul, Acts 21:16.

MOAB. 1. Son of Lot, Gen. 19:37.

2. Plains of. Israelites come in, Deut. 2:17,18. Military forces numbered in, Num. 26:3,63. The law rehearsed in, by Moses, Num. chapters 35,36; Deut. chapters 29–33. The Israelites renew their covenant in, Deut. 29:1. The land of promise allotted in, Josh. 13:32.

MOABITES. Descendants of Lot through his son Moab, Gen. 19:37. Called the people of Chemosh, Num. 21:29. The territory E. of Jordan, bounded on the N. by the river Arnon, Num. 21:13; Judg. 11:18. Children of Israel commanded not to distress the Moabites, Deut. 2:9. Refuse passage of Jephthah's army through their territory, Judg. 11:17,18. Balak was king of, Num. 22:4; calls for Baalam to curse Israel, Num. chapters 22–24; Josh. 24:9; Mic. 6:5. Are a snare to the Israelites, Num. 25:1–3; Ruth 1:4; 1 Kin. 11:1; 1 Chr. 8:8; Ezra 9:1,2; Neh. 13:23. Land of, not given to the Israelites as a possession, Deut. 2:9,29. David takes refuge among, from Saul, 1 Sam. 22:3,4. David conquers, 2 Sam. 8:2; 23:20; 1 Chr. 11:22; 18:2–11. Israelites had war with, 2 Kin. 3:5–27; 13:20; 24:2; 2 Chr. 20. Prophecies concerning judgments upon, Jer. 48.

MOADIAH, a priest, Neh. 12:17.

MOB, at Thessalonica, Acts 17:5; Jerusalem, Acts 21:28,30; Ephesus, Acts 19:29–40.

MOCKING. Ishmael mocks Sarah, Gen. 21:9. Elijah mocks the priests of Baal, 1 Kin. 18:27. Zedekiah mocks Micaiah, 1 Kin. 22:24. Children mock Elisha, 2 Kin. 2:23. The tormentors of Job mock, Job 15:12; 30:1. The persecutors of Jesus mock him, Matt. 26:67,68; 27:28–31,39–44; Mark 10:34; 14:65; 15:17–20,29–32; Luke 23:11; John 19:2,3,5; 1 Pet. 2:23. The Ammonites mock God, Ezek. 25:3. Tyre mocks Jerusalem, Ezek. 26:2. The obdurately wicked mock, Isa. 28:15,22; 2 Pet. 3:3.

See SCOFFING.

FIGURATIVE: Prov. 1:26.

MODESTY, of women, 1 Tim. 2:9. INSTANCES OF: Saul, 1 Sam. 9:21. Vashti, Esth. 1:11,12. Elihu, Job 32:4–7.

See HUMILITY.

MOLE, Lev. 11:30; Isa. 2:20.

MOLECH, called also MOLOCH and MILCOM. An idol of the Ammonites, Acts 7:43. Worshiped by the wives of Solomon, and by Solomon, 1 Kin. 11:1–8. Children sacrificed to, 2 Kin. 23:10; Jer. 32:35; 2 Kin. 16:3; 21:6; 2 Chr. 28:3; Isa. 57:5; Jer. 7:31; Ezek. 16:20,21; 20:26,31; 23:37,39; see Lev. 18:21; 20:2–5.

MOLDING. Job 28:2; Ezek. 24:11. Of images, Ex. 32:4,8; 34:17; Lev. 19:4; Deut. 9:12; pillars, 1 Kin. 7:15; laver, 1 Kin. 7:23; done in the plain of Jordan, 1 Kin. 7:46; 2 Chr. 4:17; mirrors, Job 37:18.

MONARCHY. Described by Samuel, 1 Sam. 8:11–18.

See GOVERNMENT ; KING.

MONEY. Silver used as, Gen. 17:12, 13,23,27; 20:16; 23:9,13; 31:15; 37:28; 42:25–35; 43:12–23; 44:1–8; 47:14–18; Ex. 12:44; 21:11,21,34,35; 22:7,17,25; 30:16; Lev. 22:11; 25:37,51; 27:15,18; Num. 3:48–51; 18:16; Deut. 2:6,28; 14:25,26; 21:14; 23:19; Judg. 5:19; 16:18; 17:4; 1 Kin. 21:2,6,15; 2 Kin. 5:26; 12:4, 7–16; 15:20; 22:7,9; 23:35; 2 Chr. 24:5,11,14; 34:9,14,17; Ezra 3:7; 7:17; Neh. 5:4,10,11; Esth. 4:7; Job 31:39; Psa. 15:5; Prov. 7:20; Eccl. 7:12; 10:19; Isa. 43:24; 52:3; 55:1,2; Jer.

32:9,10,25,44; Lam. 5:4; Mic. 3:11; Matt. 25:
18,27 (Argurion, Greek); 28:12,15; Mark 14:
11; Luke 9:3; 19:15,23; 22:5; Acts 7:16; 8:20.

Gold used as, Gen. 13:2; 24:35; 44:8, with
v. 1; 1 Chr. 21:25; Ezra 8:25-27; Isa. 13:17;
46:6; 60:9; Ezek. 7:19; 28:4; Matt. 2:11; 10:9;
Acts 3:6; 20:33; 1 Pet. 1:18.

Copper used as, Mark 6:8; 12:41.

Weighed, Gen. 23:16; 43:21; Job 28:15; Jer.
32:9,10; Zech. 11:12. Image on, Matt. 22:20,21.
Conscience, Judg. 17:2; Matt. 27:3,5. Atonement, Ex. 30:12-16; Lev. 5:15,16. Sin, 2 Kin.
12:16. Value of, varied corruptly, Amos 8:5.
Love of, the root of evil, 1 Tim. 6:10.

See FARTHING; GERAH; MITE; PENNY;
POUND; SHEKEL; SILVER; TALENT.

MONEY CHANGERS, Matt. 21:12;
Mark 11:15; John 2:15.

MONOPOLY. Of lands, Isa. 5:8; Mic.
2:2; by Pharaoh, Gen. 47:19-26; of food,
Prov. 11:26.

MONTH. Ancient use of, Gen. 7:11; 8:
4. Twelve months reckoned to a year, 1
Chr. 27:1-15.

1. Abib (April). The Jewish calendar began with, Ex. 12:2; 13:4; Deut. 16:1. Passover instituted and celebrated in, Ex. 12:1-
28; 23:15. Israelites left Egypt in, Ex. 13:4.
Tabernacle set up in, Ex. 40:2,17. Israelites
arrive at Zin in, Num. 20:1. Cross Jordan
in, Josh. 4:19. Jordan overflows in, 1 Chr.
12:15. Decree to put the Jews to death in,
Esth. 3:12. The death of Jesus in, Matt. 26;
27. After the captivity called Nisan, Neh.
2:1; Esth. 3:7.

2. Zif (May), 1 Kin. 6:1,37. Israel numbered in, Num. 1:1,18. Passover to be observed in, by the unclean and others who
could not observe it in the first month, Num.
9:10,11. Israel departed from the wilderness
of Zin in, Num. 10:11. Temple begun in, 1
Kin. 6:1; 2 Chr. 3:2. An irregular passover
celebrated in, 2 Chr. 30:1-27. Rebuilding
of the temple begun in, Ezra 3:8.

3. Sivan (June), Esth. 8:9. Asa renews
the covenant of himself and people in, 2
Chr. 15:10.

4. Tammuz (July). The number only
appears in the Bible. Jerusalem taken by
Nebuchadnezzar in, Jer. 39:2; 52:6,7.

5. Ab (August). Number only mentioned.
Aaron died on the first day of, Num. 33:38.
Temple destroyed in, 2 Kin. 25:8-10; Jer. 1:
3; 52:12-30. Ezra arrived at Jerusalem in,
Ezra 7:8,9.

6. Elul (September). Wall of Jerusalem
finished in, Neh. 6:15. Temple built in, Hag.
1:14,15.

7. Ethanim (October), 1 Kin. 8:2. Feasts
held in, Lev. 23:24,27; Neh. 8:13-15. Jubilee
proclaimed in, Lev. 25:9. Solomon's temple
dedicated in, 1 Kin. 8:2. Altar rebuilt and
offerings renewed in, Ezra 3:1,6.

8. Bul (November). The temple finished
in, 1 Kin. 6:38. Jeroboam's idolatrous feast
in, 1 Kin. 12:32,33; 1 Chr. 27:11.

9. Chisleu (December), Ezra 10:9; Jer. 36:
9,22; Zech. 7:1.

10. Tebeth (January), Esth. 2:16. Nebuchadnezzar besieges Jerusalem in, 2 Kin. 25:
1; Jer. 52:4.

11. Sebat (February), Zech. 1:7. Moses
probably died in, Deut. 1:3.

12. Adar (March), Esth. 3:7. Second temple finished in, Ezra 6:15. Feast of Purim in,
Esth. 9:1-26.

Months in prophecy, Rev. 11:2.

MONUMENT. See PILLAR.

MOON. Created by God, Gen. 1:16; Psa.
8:3; 136:7-9. Its light, Job 31:26; Eccl. 12:2;
Song 6:10; Jer. 31:35; 1 Cor. 15:41. Its influences, Deut. 33:14; Psa. 121:6. Seasons of
(months), Psa. 104:19. Joseph's dream concerning, Gen. 37:9. Stands still, Josh. 10:12,
13; Hab. 3:11. Worship of, forbidden, Deut.
4:19; 17:3. Worshiped, 2 Kin. 23:5; Job 31:
26,27; Jer. 7:18; 8:2; 44:17-19,25. No light of,
in heaven, Rev. 21:23. Darkening of, Job
25:5; Isa. 13:10; 24:23; Ezek. 32:7; Joel 2:10,
31; 3:15; Matt. 24:29; Mark 13:24; Luke 21:25;
Acts 2:20; Rev. 6:12; 8:12.

FIGURATIVE: Shining of, Isa. 30:26; 60:
19; Rev. 21:23.

SYMBOLICAL: Rev. 12:1.

FEAST OF THE NEW MOON: Num. 10:
10; 28:11-15; 1 Chr. 23:31; 2 Chr. 31:3; Ezra
3:5. Traffic at time of, prohibited, Amos 8:5.

MORAL AGENCY. See CONTINGEN-
CIES.

MORALITY. See DUTY OF MAN TO
MAN; INTEGRITY; NEIGHBOR.

MORAL LAW. See LAW.

MORDECAI. A Jewish captive in Persia, Esth. 2:5,6. Foster father of Esther,
Esth. 2:7. Informs Ahasuerus of a conspiracy against his life, and is rewarded, Esth.
2:21-23; Esth. 6:1-11. Promoted in Haman's
place, Esth. 8:1,2,15; 10:1-3. Intercedes with
Ahasuerus for the Jews; establishes the festival of Purim in commemoration of their
deliverance, Esth. 8; 9.

MOREH. 1. A plain near Shechem and
Gilgal, Gen. 12:6; Deut. 11:30.

2. A hill in the plain of Jezreel where the
Midianites encamped, Judg. 7:1,12.

MORIAH, the land of, Gen. 22:2; 2
Chr. 3:1.

MORTAR. 1. An instrument for pul-
verizing grains, Num. 11:8; Prov. 27:22.

See GRINDING; MILL.

2. A cement, Ex. 1:14. Slime used as, in
building tower of Babel, Gen. 11:3. Used to
plaster houses, Lev. 14:42,45. Untempered,
not enduring, Ezek. 13:10-15; 22:28. To be
trodden to make firm, Nah. 3:14.

FIGURATIVE: Isa. 41:25.

MORTGAGE, on land, Neh. 5:3.
See LAND.

MORTIFICATION. INSTANCES OF:
David's ambassadors, sent to Hanun, 2 Sam.
10:1-5. Judas, Matt. 27:3-5.

See HUMILITY.

MOSAIC LAW. See LAW.

MOSERA. An encampment of the Israelites where Aaron died, Deut. 10:6. Probably identical with MOSEROTH, below.

MOSEROTH, an encampment of the Israelites, Num. 33:30,31.

MOSES. A Levite and son of Amram, Ex. 2:1-4; 6:20; Acts 7:20; Heb. 11:23. Hidden in an ark, Ex. 2:3. Discovered and adopted by the daughter of Pharaoh, Ex. 2: 5-10. Learned in all the wisdom of Egypt, Acts 7:22. His loyalty to his race, Heb. 11: 24-26. Takes the life of an Egyptian; flees from Egypt; finds refuge among the Midianites, Ex. 2:11-22; Acts 7:24-29. Joins himself to Jethro, priest of Midian; marries his daughter Zipporah; has two sons, Ex. 2:15-22; 18:3,4. Is herdman for Jethro in the desert of Horeb, Ex. 3:1. Has the vision of the burning bush, Ex. 3:2-6. God reveals to him his purpose to deliver the Israelites and bring them into the land of Canaan, Ex. 3: 7-10. Commissioned as leader of the Israelites, Ex. 3:10-22; 6:13. His rod miraculously turned into a serpent, and his hand made leprous, and each restored, Ex. 4:1-9,28. With his wife and sons leaves Jethro to perform his mission, Ex. 4:18-20. His controversy with his wife on account of circumcision, Ex. 4:20-26. Meets Aaron in the wilderness, Ex. 4:27,28.

With Aaron assembles the leaders of Israel, Ex. 4:29-31. With Aaron goes before Pharaoh, in the name of Jehovah demands the liberties of his people, Ex. 5:1. Rejected by Pharaoh; hardships of the Israelites increased, Ex. 5. People murmur against Moses and Aaron, Ex. 5:20,21; 15:24; 16:2,3; 17:2,3; Num. 14:2-4; 16:41; 20:2-5; 21:4-6; Deut. 1:12,26-28. See ISRAEL. Receives comfort and assurance from the Lord, Ex. 6:1-8. Unbelief of the people, Ex. 6:9. Renews his appeal to Pharaoh, Ex. 6:11. Under divine direction brings plagues upon the land of Egypt, Ex. chapters 7-12. Secures the deliverance of the people and leads them out of Egypt, Ex. 13. Crosses the Red Sea; Pharaoh and his army are destroyed, Ex. 14. Composes a song for the children of Israel on their deliverance from Pharaoh, Ex. 15. Joined by his family in the wilderness, Ex. 18:1-12.

Institutes a system of government, Ex. 18:13-26; Num. 11:16-30; Deut. 1:9-18. Receives the law and ordains divers statutes. See LAW OF MOSES. Face of, transfigured, Ex. 34:29-35; 2 Cor. 3:13. Sets up the tabernacle. See TABERNACLE. Reproves Aaron for making the golden calf, Ex. 32:22,23; for irregularity in the offerings, Lev. 10:16-20. Jealousy of Aaron and Miriam toward, Num. 12. Rebellion of Korah, Dathan, and Abiram against, Num. 16. Appoints Joshua as his successor, Num. 27:22,23; Deut. 31:7,8,14,23; 34:9.

Not permitted to enter Canaan, but views the land from Mount Pisgah, Num. 27:12-14; Deut. 1:37; 3:23-29; 32:48-52; 34:1-8. Death and burial of, Num. 31:2; Deut. 32:50; 34:1-6. Body of, disputed over, Jude 9. One hundred and twenty years old at death, Deut. 31:2. Mourning for, thirty days in the plains of Moab, Deut. 34:8. His virility, Deut. 31:2; 34:7.

Present with Jesus on the mount of transfiguration, Matt. 17:3,4; Mark 9:4; Luke 9:30. Type of Christ, Deut. 18:15-18; Acts 3:22; 7:37.

BENEDICTIONS OF: Upon the people, Lev. 9:23; Num. 10:35,36; Deut. 1:11. Last benediction upon the twelve tribes, Deut. 33.

CHARACTER OF: Murmurings of, Ex. 5:22,23; Num. 11:10-15. Impatience of, Ex. 5:22,23; 6:12; 32:19; Num. 11:10-15; 16:15; 20:10; 31:14. Respected and feared, Ex. 33:8. Faith of, Num. 10:29; Deut. 9:1-3; Heb. 11:23-28. Called the man of God, Deut. 33:1. God spake to, as a man to his friend, Ex. 33:11. Magnified of God, Ex. 19:9; Num. 14:12-20; Deut. 9:13-29, with Ex. 32:30. Magnanimity of, toward Eldad and Medad, Num. 11:29. Meekness of, Ex. 14:13,14; 15:24,25; 16:2,3,7,8; Num. 12:3; 16:4-11. Obedience of, Ex. 7:6; 40:16,19,21. Unaspiring, Num. 14:12-20; Deut. 9:13-29, with Ex. 32:30.

INTERCESSORY PRAYERS OF: See INTERCESSION, INSTANCES OF; SOLICITED, INSTANCES OF; ANSWERED, INSTANCES OF.

MIRACLES OF: See MIRACLES.

PROPHECIES OF: Ex. 3:10; 4:5,11,12; 6: 13; 7:2; 17:16; 19:3-9; 33:11; Num. 11:17; 12: 7,8; 36:13; Deut. 1:3; 5:31; 18:15,18; 34:10,12; Hos. 12:13; Mark 7:9,10; Acts 7:37,38.

MOTE, a small particle, Matt. 7:3-5; Luke 6:41,42.

MOTH. An insect, Job 4:19; 27:18; Psa. 39:11. Destructive of garments, Job 13:28; Isa. 50:9; 51:8; Hos. 5:12.

FIGURATIVE: Matt. 6:19,20; Jas. 5:2.

MOTHER. Ex. 20:12. Honour thy father and thy mother: that thy days may be long upon the land which the LORD thy God giveth thee. Deut. 5:16; Matt. 15:4; 19:19; Mark 7:10; 10:19; Luke 18:20; Eph. 6:2.

Ex. 21:15. And he that smiteth his father, or his mother, shall be surely put to death. 17. And he that curseth his father, or his mother, shall surely be put to death.

Lev. 18:7. The nakedness of thy father, or the nakedness of thy mother, shalt thou not uncover: she *is* thy mother; thou shalt not uncover her nakedness.

Lev. 19:3. Ye shall fear every man his mother, and his father, and keep my sabbaths: I *am* the LORD your God.

Lev. 20:9. For every one that curseth his father or his mother shall be surely put to death: he hath cursed his father or his mother; his blood *shall be* upon him.

1 Kin. 19:20. And he left the oxen, and ran after Elijah, and said, Let me, I pray thee, kiss my father and my mother, and *then* I will follow thee.

Prov. 1:8. My son, hear the instruction of thy father, and forsake not the law of thy mother:

Prov. 6:20. My son, keep thy father's commandment, and forsake not the law of thy mother:

Prov. 10:1. A foolish son *is* the heaviness of his mother.

Prov. 15:20. A foolish man despiseth his mother.

Prov. 19:26. He that wasteth *his* father, *and* chaseth away *his* mother, *is* a son that causeth shame, and bringeth reproach.

Prov. 20:20. Whoso curseth his father or his mother, his lamp shall be put out in obscure darkness.

Prov. 23:22. Despise not thy mother when she is old. 23. Buy the truth, and sell *it* not; *also* wisdom, and instruction, and understanding. 24. The father of the righteous shall greatly rejoice: and he that begetteth a wise *child* shall have joy of him. 25. Thy father and thy mother shall be glad, and she that bare thee shall rejoice.

Prov. 28:24. Whoso robbeth his father or his mother, and saith, *It is* no transgression; the same *is* the companion of a destroyer.

Prov. 29:15. The rod and reproof give wisdom: but a child left *to himself* bringeth his mother to shame.

Prov. 30:11. *There is* a generation *that* curseth their father, and doth not bless their mother. 17. The eye *that* mocketh at *his* father, and despiseth to obey *his* mother, the ravens of the valley shall pick it out, and the young eagles shall eat it.

Matt. 10:37. He that loveth father or mother more than me is not worthy of me:

Matt. 15:4. For God commanded, saying, Honour thy father and mother: and, He that curseth father or mother, let him die the death. 5. But ye say, Whosoever shall say to *his* father or *his* mother, *It is* a gift, by whatsoever thou mightest be profited by me; 6. And honour not his father or his mother, *he shall be free.* Thus have ye made the commandment of God of none effect by your tradition. Mark 7:10-12.

2 Tim. 1:5. When I call to remembrance the unfeigned faith that is in thee, which dwelt first in thy grandmother Lois, and thy mother Eunice; and I am persuaded that in thee also.

See CHILDREN, DUTY OF; PARENTS.

MOTHER-IN-LAW. Matt. 10:35. Not to be defiled, Lev. 18:17; 20:14; Deut. 27:23. Beloved by Ruth, Ruth 1:14-17. Peter's, healed by Jesus, Mark 1:30,31.

MOTIVE. Ascribed to God, Psa. 106:8; Ezek. 36:21,22,32. Right, required, Matt. 6:1-18. Sinful, illustrated by Cain, Gen. 4:7; 1 John 3:12.

MISUNDERSTOOD: The tribes of Reuben and Gad, in asking inheritance E. of Jordan, Num. 32:1-33; when they built the memorial, Josh. 22:9-34. David's, by King Hanun, 2 Sam. 10:2,3; 1 Chr. 19:3,4. The king of Syria's, in sending presents to the king of Israel by Naaman, 2 Kin. 5:5-7. Job's in his righteousness, Job 1:9-11; 2:4,5.

MOTTO. See LEGEND.

MOUNTAIN. Melted, Psa. 97:5; Deut. 4:11; 5:23; Judg. 5:5; Isa. 64:1-3; Mic. 1:4; Nah. 1:5. Overturning and removing of,

Job 9:5; 14:18; 28:9; Ezek. 38:20. Abraham offers Isaac upon Mount Moriah, afterward called Mount Zion, the site of the temple, Gen. 22:2; see ZION. Horeb appointed as a place for the Israelites to worship, Ex. 3:12. Used for idolatrous worship, Deut. 12:2; 1 Sam. 10:5; 1 Kin. 14:23; Jer. 3:6; Hos. 4:13. Jesus tempted upon, Matt. 4:8; Luke 4:5. Jesus preaches from, Matt. 5:1. Jesus goes up into, for prayer, Matt. 14:23; Luke 6:12; 9:28; is transfigured upon, Matt. 17:1-9; Mark 9:2-10; Luke 9:28-36; meets his disciples on, after his resurrection, Matt. 28:16,17. Signals from, Isa. 13:2; 18:3; 30:17. Removed by faith, Matt. 17:20; 21:21; Mark 11:23. Burning mountains, see VOLCANO.

MOURNING. For the dead: Head uncovered, Lev. 10:6; 21:10; lying on ground, 2 Sam. 12:16; personal appearance neglected, 2 Sam. 14:2; cutting the flesh, Lev. 19:28; 21: 1-5; Deut. 14:1; Jer. 16:6,7; 41:5; lamentations, Gen. 50:10; Ex. 12:30; 1 Sam. 30:4; Jer. 22:18; Matt. 2:17,18; fasting, 1 Sam. 31:13; 2 Sam. 1:12; 3:35. Priests prohibited, except for nearest of kin, Lev. 21:1-11. For Nadab and Abihu forbidden, Lev. 10:6. Sexes separated in, Zech. 12:12,14.

Hired mourners, 2 Chr. 35:25; Eccl. 12:5; Jer. 9:17; Matt. 9:23.

Abraham mourned for Sarah, Gen. 23:2; Egyptians, for Jacob seventy days, Gen. 50: 1-3; Israelites, for Aaron thirty days, Num. 20:29.

David's lamentations over the death of Saul and his sons, 2 Sam. 1:17-27; the death of Abner, 2 Sam. 3:33,34; the death of Absalom, 2 Sam. 18:33.

Jeremiah and the singing men and singing women lament for Josiah, 2 Chr. 35:25.

For calamities and other sorrows: Rending the garments, Gen. 37:29,34; 44:13; Num. 14:6; Judg. 11:35; 2 Sam. 1:2,11; 3:31; 13:19, 31; 15:32; 2 Kin. 2:12; 5:8; 6:30; 11:14; 19:1; 22: 11,19; Ezra 9:3,5; Job 1:20; 2:12; Isa. 37:1; Jer. 41:5; Matt. 26:65; Acts 14:14. Wearing mourning dress, Gen. 38:14; 2 Sam. 14:2. See SACKCLOTH. Cutting or plucking off the hair and beard, Ezra 9:3; Jer. 7:29. See BALDNESS. Covering the head and face, 2 Sam. 15:30; 19:4; Esth. 6:12; Jer. 14:3,4; and the upper lip, Lev. 13:45; Ezek. 24:17,22; Mic. 3:7 [marg.]. Laying aside ornaments, Ex. 33:4,6. Walking barefoot, 2 Sam. 15:30; Isa. 20:2. Laying the hand on the head, 2 Sam. 13:19; Jer. 2:37. Ashes put on the head, Ezek. 27:30. Dust on the head, Josh. 7:6. Dressing in black, Jer. 14:2. Sitting on the ground, Isa. 3:26.

Caused ceremonial defilement, Num. 19: 11-16; 31:19; Lev. 21:1. Prevented offerings from being accepted, Deut. 26:14; Hos. 9:4.

See ELEGY.

MOUSE. Forbidden as food, Lev. 11:29; used as food, Isa. 66:17. Images of, 1 Sam. 6:4,5,11,18.

MOWING, Psa. 72:6; 90:6; 129:7; Amos 7:1.

MOZA. 1. A son of Caleb, 1 Chr. 2:46. 2. A Benjamite, 1 Chr. 8:36,37; 9:42,43.

MOZAH, a city of Benjamin, Josh. 18:26.

MUFFLER, Isa. 3:19.

MULBERRY TREE, 2 Sam. 5:23,24; Psa. 84:6 [marg.].

MULE. Uses of: For royal riders, 2 Sam. 13:29; 18:9; 1 Kin. 1:33,38; ridden by posts, Esth. 8:10,14; by saints in Isaiah's prophetic vision of the kingdom of Christ, Isa. 66:20; as pack animals, 2 Kin. 5:17; 1 Chr. 12:40. Tribute paid in, 1 Kin. 10:25. Used in barter, Ezek. 27:14; by the captivity in returning from Babylon, Ezra 2:66; Neh. 7: 68; in war, Zech. 14:15.

MUNITIONS, fortifications, Nah. 2:1.

MUPPIM, son of Benjamin, Gen. 46:21.

MURDER. See HOMICIDE.

MURMURING, of Israelites against Moses, Ex. 5:21; 15:24; 16:2,3; Num. 16:2,3,13, 14,41; 20:2–4.

AGAINST GOD: Ex. 5:22. And Moses returned unto the LORD, and said, Lord, wherefore hast thou *so* evil entreated this people? why *is* it *that* thou hast sent me? 23. For since I came to Pharaoh to speak in thy name, he hath done evil to this people; neither hast thou delivered thy people at all.

Ex. 16:8. And Moses said, *This shall be,* when the LORD shall give you in the evening flesh to eat, and in the morning bread to the full; for that the LORD heareth your murmurings which ye murmur against him: and what *are* we? your murmurings *are* not against us, but against the LORD. 12. I have heard the murmurings of the children of Israel: speak unto them, saying, At even ye shall eat flesh, and in the morning ye shall be filled with bread; and ye shall know that I *am* the LORD your God.

Num. 14:26. And the LORD spake unto Moses and unto Aaron, saying, 27. How long *shall I bear with* this evil congregation, which murmur against me? I have heard the murmurings of the children of Israel, which they murmur against me. 28. Say unto them, *As truly as* I live, saith the LORD, as ye have spoken in mine ears, so will I do to you: 29. Your carcases shall fall in this wilderness; and all that were numbered of you, according to your whole number, from twenty years old and upward, which have murmured against me, 30. Doubtless ye shall not come into the land, *concerning* which I sware to make you dwell therein, save Caleb the son of Jephunneh, and Joshua the son of Nun. 31. But your little ones, which ye said should be a prey, them will I bring in, and they shall know the land which ye have despised. 32. But *as for* you, your carcases, they shall fall in this wilderness. 33. And your children shall wander in the wilderness forty years, and bear your whoredoms, until your carcases be wasted in the wilderness. 34. After the number of the days in which ye searched the land, *even* forty days, each day for a year, shall

ye bear your iniquities, *even* forty years, and ye shall know my breach of promise. 35. I the LORD have said, I will surely do it unto all this evil congregation, that are gathered together against me: in this wilderness they shall be consumed, and there they shall die. 36. And the men, which Moses sent to search the land, who returned, and made all the congregation to murmur against him, by bringing up a slander upon the land, 37. Even those men that did bring up the evil report upon the land, died by the plague before the LORD. chapter 17:10,11.

Job 15:11. *Are* the consolations of God small with thee? is there any secret thing with thee? 12. Why doth thine heart carry thee away? and what do thy eyes wink at, 13. That thou turnest thy spirit against God, and lettest *such* words go out of thy mouth?

Job 33:12. Behold, *in* this thou art not just: I will answer thee, that God is greater than man. 13. Why dost thou strive against him? for he giveth not account of any of his matters.

Job 34:37. He addeth rebellion unto his sin, he clappeth *his hands* among us, and multiplieth his words against God.

Psa. 37:1. Fret not thyself because of evildoers, neither be thou envious against the workers of iniquity.

Psa. 44:9. But thou hast cast off, and put us to shame; and goest not forth with our armies. 10. Thou makest us to turn back from the enemy: and they which hate us spoil for themselves. 11. Thou hast given us like sheep *appointed* for meat; and hast scattered us among the heathen. 12. Thou sellest thy people for nought, and dost not increase *thy wealth* by their price. 13. Thou makest us a reproach to our neighbours, a scorn and a derision to them that are round about us. 14. Thou makest us a byword among the heathen, a shaking of the head among the people. 15. My confusion *is* continually before me, and the shame of my face hath covered me, 16. For the voice of him that reproacheth and blasphemeth; by reason of the enemy and avenger. 17. All this is come upon us; yet have we not forgotten thee, neither have we dealt falsely in thy covenant. 18. Our heart is not turned back, neither have our steps declined from thy way; 19. Though thou hast sore broken us in the place of dragons, and covered us with the shadow of death. 20. If we have forgotten the name of our God, or stretched out our hands to a strange god; 21. Shall not God search this out? for he knoweth the secrets of the heart. 22. Yea, for thy sake are we killed all the day long; we are counted as sheep for the slaughter. 23. Awake, why sleepest thou, O Lord? arise, cast *us* not off for ever. 24. Wherefore hidest thou thy face, *and* forgettest our affliction and our oppression? 25. For our soul is bowed down to the dust: our belly cleaveth unto the earth. 26. Arise for our help, and redeem us for thy mercies' sake.

Psa. 73:13. Verily I have cleansed my heart *in* vain, and washed my hands in innocency. 14. For all the day long have I been plagued, and chastened every morning. 15. If I say, I will speak thus; behold, I should offend *against* the generation of thy children. 16. When I thought to know this, it *was* too painful for me; 17. Until I went into the sanctuary of God; *then* understood I their end. 18. Surely thou didst set them in slippery places: thou castedst them down into destruction. 19. How are they *brought* into desolation, as in a moment! they are utterly consumed with terrors. 20. As a dream when *one* awaketh; *so,* O Lord, when thou awakest, thou shalt despise their image. 21. Thus my heart was grieved, and I was pricked in my reins. 22. So foolish *was* I, and ignorant: I was *as* a beast before thee.

Psa. 78:17. And they sinned yet more against him by provoking the most High in the wilderness. 18. And they tempted God in their heart by asking meat for their lust. 19. Yea, they spake against God; they said, Can God furnish a table in the wilderness? 20. Behold, he smote the rock, that the waters gushed out, and the streams overflowed; can he give bread also? can he provide flesh for his people? 21. Therefore the Lord heard *this,* and was wroth: so a fire was kindled against Jacob, and anger also came up against Israel;

Prov. 19:3. The foolishness of man perverteth his way: and his heart fretteth against the Lord.

Eccl. 7:10. Say not thou, What is *the cause* that the former days were better than these? for thou dost not enquire wisely concerning this.

Jer. 15:10. Woe is me, my mother, that thou hast borne me a man of strife and a man of contention to the whole earth! I have neither lent on usury, nor men have lent to me on usury; *yet* every one of them doth curse me.

Lam. 3:39. Wherefore doth a living man complain, a man for the punishment of his sins?

Mal. 3:14. Ye have said, It *is* vain to serve God: and what profit *is it* that we have kept his ordinance, and that we have walked mournfully before the Lord of hosts?

Luke 10:40. But Martha was cumbered about much serving, and came to him, and said, Lord, dost thou not care that my sister hath left me to serve alone? bid her therefore that she help me.

Rom. 9:19. Thou wilt say then unto me, Why doth he yet find fault? For who hath resisted his will? 20. Nay but, O man, who art thou that repliest against God? Shall the thing formed say to him that formed *it,* Why hast thou made me thus?

1 Cor. 10:10. Neither murmur ye, as some

of them also murmured, and were destroyed of the destroyer.

Phil. 2:14. Do all things without murmurings and disputings:

Jas. 5:9. Grudge not one against another, brethren, lest ye be condemned: behold, the judge standeth before the door.

Jude 16. These are murmurers, complainers, walking after their own lusts;

INSTANCES OF: Cain, Gen. 4:13,14. Rachel, Gen. 30:1. Moses, Ex. 5:22,23; Num. 11:11–15. Israelites, Ex. 5:21; 14:11,12; 15: 23,24; 16:2,3; 17:2,3; Num. 11:1–10,33; 14; 16: 41; 20:2–5; 21:5,6; Deut. 1:27,28; Psa. 106:24–26. Korah, Num. 16:8–11; Job, Job chapters 3; 6; 7; 9; 10; 13; 19; 23; 30. David, 2 Sam. 6:8; Psa. 116:10,11. Asaph, Psa. 73:3. Elijah, 1 Kin. 19:4,10. Solomon, Eccl. 2:17,18. Hezekiah, Isa. 38:10–18. Jeremiah, Jer. 20:14–18; Lam. 3. Jonah, Jonah 4. Jews, against Jesus, John 6:41–43,52.

See Doubt; Envy; Ingratitude. See also Contentment; Resignation.

MURRAIN, a plague of Egypt, Ex. 9: 3,6; Psa. 78:50 [marg.].

MUSHI, of the sons of Merari, Ex. 6:19; 1 Chr. 6:19,47.

MUSIC. Teachers of, 1 Chr. 15:22; 25:7,8; 2 Chr. 23:13. Physical effect of, on man, 1 Sam. 16:15,16,23. Discoursed during the offering of sacrifices, 2 Chr. 29:27,28. Precentor, Neh. 12:42. Chief musician, Neh. 12:42; Hab. 3:19. Chambers for musicians in the temple, in Ezekiel's vision, Ezek. 40: 44. In heaven, Rev. 5:8,9; 14:2,3; 15:2,3.

INSTRUMENTS OF: Invented by Jubal, Gen. 4:21; by David, 1 Chr. 23:5; 2 Chr. 7:6; 2 Chr. 29:26; Amos 6:5. Made by Solomon, 1 Kin. 10:12; 2 Chr. 9:11; Eccl. 2:8; by Tyrians, Ezek. 28:13.

Cornet, Dan. 3:5,7,10. See Trumpet.

Cymbal. See Cymbal.

Dulcimer, a double pipe, Dan. 3:5,10,15.

Flute, Dan. 3:5,7,10,15.

Gittith, a stringed instrument, Psalms 8, 81, 84 [titles].

Harp. See Harp.

Organ, probably composed of pipes furnishing a number of notes, Gen. 4:21; Job 21:12; 30:31; Psa. 150:4.

Pipe. See Pipe.

Psaltery. See Psaltery.

Sackbut, a harp, Dan. 3:5,7,10,15.

Tabret. See Timbrel.

Timbrel, a tambourine. See Timbrel.

Trumpet. See Trumpet.

Viol, a lyre, Isa. 5:12; 14:11; Amos 5:23; 6:5.

SYMBOLS USED IN: Alamoth. Literally *virgins.* A musical term which appears in 1 Chr. 15:20 and in the title of Psalm 46. It seems to indicate the rendering of the song by female voices, possibly soprano.

Al-taschith. It appears in the titles of Psalms 57, 58, 59, 75, and seems to have been used to indicate the kind of ode, or the kind of melody in which the ode should be sung.

HIGGAION. In Psa. 92:3, according to Gesenius, it signifies the murmuring tone of a harp, and hence that the music should be rendered in a plaintive manner. In Psa. 9:16, combined with "Selah," it may have been intended to indicate a pause in the vocal music while the instruments rendered an interlude. In Psa. 19:14, Mendelssohn translates it "meditation, thought." Hence that the music was to be rendered in a mode to promote devout meditation.

MAHALATH, MASCHIL, LEANNOTH. These terms are found in the titles of Psalm 53 and 88. Authorities grope in darkness as to their signification. They may indicate the instruments to be played or the melody to be sung.

MASCHIL. This musical sign occurs in the titles of Psalms 32, 42, 44, 45, 52, 53, 54, 55, 74, 78, 88, 89, 142. The meaning is obscure. But its signification where it occurs elsewhere than in the titles of Psalms is equivalent to the English word "instruction," or to become wise by instruction; hence Psa. 47:7, "Sing ye praises with understanding."

MICHTAM. A musical term in the titles of Psalms 16, 56, 57, 58–60. Luther interprets as "golden," that is, precious. Ewald interprets it as signifying a plaintive manner.

MUTH-LABBEN, in the title of Psalm 9. Authorities, ancient and modern, differ as to the probable signification. Gesenius and De Wette interpret it, "with the voice of virgins, by boys." Others derive the word from a different Hebrew root, and interpret it as indicating that the Psalm was a funeral ode.

NEGINAH and NEGINOTH appear in the titles of Psalms 4, 54, 55, 61, 67, and Hab. 3:19. Its use seems to have been to indicate that the song should be accompanied by stringed instruments.

NEHILOTH, in the title of Psalm 5. It seems to indicate, according to Gesenius, that when this Psalm was sung it was to be accompanied by wind instruments.

SELAH. This term appears frequently in the Psalms. Its use is not known. Possibly it signified a pause in the vocal music while an instrumental interlude or finale was rendered.

SHEMINITH, in the titles of Psalms 6 and 12, translated "eighth," probably indicates the measure, movement, or pitch.

SHIGGAION, in the title of Psalm 7, and its plural, SHIGIONOTH, in the title of Hab. 3, are supposed to have been musical terms to guide in rendering the song. At the close of the chapter the author refers the ode "to the chief musician, on my stringed instruments." The term may suggest the movement in interpreting the music set to it.

SHOSHANNIM and SHUSHAN-EDUTH, in the titles to Psalms 45, 60, 69, 80, seem to indicate the manner in which these Psalms were to be rendered. Kimchi, Tremellius, and Eichhorn render it "hexachorda," that is,

that in singing these Psalms instruments of six strings were to accompany.

UNCLASSIFIED SCRIPTURES RELATING TO : Gen. 31:27. Wherefore didst thou flee away secretly, and steal away from me : and didst not tell me, that I might have sent thee away with mirth, and with songs, with tabret, and with harp?

Ex. 15:1. Then sang Moses and the children of Israel this song unto the LORD, and spake, saying, I will sing unto the LORD, for he hath triumphed gloriously : the horse and his rider hath he thrown into the sea. [vs. 1–27.] 20. And Miriam the prophetess, the sister of Aaron, took a timbrel in her hand ; and all the women went out after her with timbrels and with dances. 21. And Miriam answered them, Sing ye to the LORD, for he hath triumphed gloriously ; the horse and his rider hath he thrown into the sea.

Num. 21:17. Then Israel sang this song, Spring up, O well ; sing ye unto it : 18. The princes digged the well, the nobles of the people digged it, by *the direction of* the lawgiver, with their staves. And from the wilderness *they went* to Mattanah : 19. And from Mattanah to Nahaliel : and from Nahaliel to Bamoth : 20. And from Bamoth *in* the valley, that *is* in the country of Moab, to the top of Pisgah, which looketh toward Jeshimon.

Judg. 5:1. Then sang Deborah and Barak the son of Abinoam on that day, saying, 2. Praise ye the LORD for the avenging of Israel, when the people willingly offered themselves. 3. Hear, O ye kings ; give ear, O ye princes ; I, *even* I, will sing unto the LORD ; I will sing *praise* to the LORD God of Israel. *vs.* 1–31.

Judg. 11:34. And Jephthah came to Mizpeh unto his house, and, behold, his daughter came out to meet him with timbrels and with dances : and she *was his* only child ; beside her he had neither son nor daughter.

1 Sam. 18:6. And it came to pass as they came, when David was returned from the slaughter of the Philistine, that the women came out of all cities of Israel, singing and dancing, to meet king Saul, with tabrets, with joy, and with instruments of musick. 7. And the women answered *one another* as they played, and said, Saul hath slain his thousands, and David his ten thousands.

2 Sam. 19:35. I *am* this day fourscore years old : . . . can I hear any more the voice of singing men and singing women?

1 Kin. 1:40. And all the people came up after him, and the people piped with pipes, and rejoiced with great joy, so that the earth rent with the sound of them.

1 Chr. 6:31. And these *are they* whom David set over the service of song in the house of the LORD, after that the ark had rest. 32. And they ministered before the dwelling place of the tabernacle of the congregation with singing, until Solomon had built the

house of the LORD in Jerusalem: and *then* they waited on their office according to their order.

1 Chr. 15:16. And David spake to the chief of the Levites to appoint their brethren *to be* the singers with instruments of musick, psalteries and harps and cymbals, sounding, by lifting up the voice with joy. 17. So the Levites appointed Heman the son of Joel; and of his brethren, Asaph the son of Berechiah; and of the sons of Merari their brethren, Ethan the son of Kushaiah; 18. And with them their brethren of the second *degree*, Zechariah, Ben, and Jaaziel, and Shemiramoth, and Jehiel, and Unni, Eliab, and Benaiah, and Maaseiah, and Mattithiah, and Elipheleh, and Mikneiah, and Obed-edom, and Jeiel, the porters. 19. So the singers, Heman, Asaph, and Ethan, *were appointed* to sound with cymbals of brass; 20. And Zechariah, and Aziel, and Shemiramoth, and Jehiel, and Unni, and Eliab, and Maaseiah, and Benaiah, with psalteries on Alamoth; 21. And Mattithiah, and Elipheleh, and Mikneiah, and Obed-edom, and Jeiel, and Azaziah, with harps on the Sheminith to excel. 22. And Chenaniah, chief of the Levites, *was* for song: he instructed about the song, because he *was* skilful. 24. And Shebaniah, and Jehoshaphat, and Nethaneel, and Amasai, and Zechariah, and Benaiah, and Eliezer, the priests, did blow with the trumpets before the ark of God: 27. And David *was* clothed with a robe of fine linen, and all the Levites that bare the ark, and the singers, and Chenaniah the master of the song with the singers: David also *had* upon him an ephod of linen. 28. Thus all Israel brought up the ark of the covenant of the LORD with shouting, and with sound of the cornet, and with trumpets, and with cymbals, making a noise with psalteries and harps.

1 Chr. 16:4. And he appointed *certain* of the Levites to minister before the ark of the LORD, and to record, and to thank and praise the LORD God of Israel: 5. Asaph the chief, and next to him Zechariah, Jeiel, and Shemiramoth, and Jehiel, Mattithiah, and Eliab, and Benaiah, and Obed-edom: and Jeiel with psalteries and harps; but Asaph made a sound with cymbals; 6. Benaiah also and Jahaziel the priests with trumpets continually before the ark of the covenant of God. 7. Then on that day David delivered first *this psalm* to thank the LORD into the hand of Asaph and his brethren. 8. Give thanks unto the LORD, call upon his name, make known his deeds among the people. 9. Sing unto him, sing psalms unto him, talk ye of all his wondrous works. 10. Glory ye in his holy name: let the heart of them rejoice that seek the LORD. 11. Seek the LORD and his strength, seek his face continually. 12. Remember his marvellous works that he hath done, his wonders, and the judgments of his mouth; 13. O ye seed of Israel his servant, ye children of Jacob, his chosen ones. 14. He *is* the LORD our God; his

judgments *are* in all the earth. 15. Be ye mindful always of his covenant; the word *which* he commanded to a thousand generations; 16. *Even of the covenant* which he made with Abraham, and of his oath unto Isaac; 17. And hath confirmed the same to Jacob for a law, *and* to Israel *for* an everlasting covenant, 18. Saying, Unto thee will I give the land of Canaan, the lot of your inheritance; 19. When ye were but few, even a few, and strangers in it. 20. And *when* they went from nation to nation, and from *one* kingdom to another people; 21. He suffered no man to do them wrong: yea, he reproved kings for their sakes, 22. *Saying*, Touch not mine anointed, and do my prophets no harm. 23. Sing unto the LORD, all the earth; shew forth from day to day his salvation. 24. Declare his glory among the heathen; his marvellous works among all nations. 25. For great *is* the LORD, and greatly to be praised: he also *is* to be feared above all gods. 26. For all the gods of the people *are* idols: but the LORD made the heavens. 27. Glory and honour *are* in his presence; strength and gladness *are* in his place. 28. Give unto the LORD, ye kindreds of the people, give unto the LORD glory and strength. 29. Give unto the LORD the glory *due* unto his name: bring an offering, and come before him: worship the LORD in the beauty of holiness. 30. Fear before him, all the earth: the world also shall be stable, that it be not moved. 31. Let the heavens be glad, and let the earth rejoice: and let *men* say among the nations, The LORD reigneth. 32. Let the sea roar, and the fulness thereof: let the fields rejoice, and all that *is* therein. 33. Then shall the trees of the wood sing out at the presence of the LORD, because he cometh to judge the earth. 34. O give thanks unto the LORD; for *he is* good; for his mercy *endureth* for ever. 35. And say ye, Save us, O God of our salvation, and gather us together, and deliver us from the heathen, that we may give thanks to thy holy name, *and* glory in thy praise. 36. Blessed *be* the LORD God of Israel for ever and ever. And all the people said, Amen, and praised the LORD. 37. So he left there before the ark of the covenant of the LORD Asaph and his brethren, to minister before the ark continually, as every day's work required: 38. And Obed-edom with their brethren, threescore and eight; Obed-edom also the son of Jeduthun and Hosah *to be* porters: 39. And Zadok the priest, and his brethren the priests, before the tabernacle of the LORD in the high place that *was* at Gibeon, 41. And with them Heman and Jeduthun, and the rest that were chosen, who were expressed by name, to give thanks to the LORD, because his mercy *endureth* for ever; 42. And with them Heman and Jeduthun with trumpets and cymbals for those that should make a sound, and with musical instruments of God.

1 Chr. 23:3. Now the Levites were numbered from the age of thirty years and upward: and their number by their polls, man by man, was thirty and eight thousand. 5. Four thousand *were* porters; and four thousand praised the LORD with the instruments which I made, *said David*, to praise *therewith*. 6. And David divided them into courses among the sons of Levi, *namely*, Gershon, Kohath, and Merari. 27. For by the last words of David the Levites *were* numbered from twenty years old and above: 30. And to stand every morning to thank and praise the LORD, and likewise at even;

1 Chr. 25:1. Moreover David and the captains of the host separated to the service of the sons of Asaph, and of Heman, and of Jeduthun, who should prophesy with harps, with psalteries, and with cymbals: and the number of the workmen according to their service was: [*vs.* 2–4.] 5. All these *were* the sons of Heman the king's seer in the words of God, to lift up the horn. And God gave to Heman fourteen sons and three daughters. 6. All these *were* under the hands of their father for song *in* the house of the LORD, with cymbals, psalteries, and harps, for the service of the house of God, according to the king's order to Asaph, Jeduthun, and Heman. 7. So the number of them, with their brethren that were instructed in the songs of the LORD, *even* all that were cunning, was two hundred fourscore and eight. 8. And they cast lots, ward against *ward*, as well the small as the great, the teacher as the scholar. *vs.* 9–31.

2 Chr. 5:12. Also the Levites *which were* the singers, all of them of Asaph, of Heman, of Jeduthun, with their sons and their brethren, *being* arrayed in white linen, having cymbals and psalteries and harps, stood at the east end of the altar, and with them an hundred and twenty priests sounding with trumpets: 13. It came even to pass, as the trumpeters and singers *were* as one, to make one sound to be heard in praising and thanking the LORD; and when they lifted up *their* voice with the trumpets and cymbals and instruments of musick, and praised the LORD, *saying*, For *he is* good; for his mercy *endureth* for ever: that *then* the house was filled with a cloud, *even* the house of the LORD;

2 Chr. 20:19. And the Levites, of the children of the Kohathites, and of the children of the Korhites, stood up to praise the LORD God of Israel with a loud voice on high. 21. And when he had consulted with the people, he appointed singers unto the LORD, and that should praise the beauty of holiness, as they went out before the army, and to say, Praise the LORD; for his mercy *endureth* for ever. 22. And when they began to sing and to praise, the LORD set ambushments against the children of Ammon, Moab, and mount Seir, which were come against Judah; and they were smitten. 28. And they came to Jerusalem with psalteries and harps and trumpets unto the house of the LORD.

2 Chr. 23:13. And she looked, and, behold, the king stood at his pillar at the entering in, and the princes and the trumpets by the king: and all the people of the land rejoiced, and sounded with trumpets, also the singers with instruments of musick, and such as taught to sing praise. Then Athaliah rent her clothes, and said, Treason, Treason. 18. Also Jehoiada appointed the offices of the house of the LORD by the hand of the priests the Levites, whom David had distributed in the house of the LORD, to offer the burnt offerings of the LORD, as *it is* written in the law of Moses, with rejoicing and with singing, *as it was ordained* by David.

2 Chr. 29:25. And he set the Levites in the house of the LORD with cymbals, with psalteries, and with harps, according to the commandment of David, and of Gad the king's seer, and Nathan the prophet: for *so was* the commandment of the LORD by his prophets. 26. And the Levites stood with the instruments of David, and the priests with the trumpets. 27. And Hezekiah commanded to offer the burnt offering upon the altar. And when the burnt offering began, the song of the LORD began *also* with the trumpets, and with the instruments *ordained* by David king of Israel. 28. And all the congregation worshipped, and the singers sang, and the trumpeters sounded: *and* all *this continued* until the burnt offering was finished.

2 Chr. 31:2. And Hezekiah appointed the courses of the priests and the Levites after their courses, every man according to his service, the priests and Levites for burnt offerings and for peace offerings, to minister, and to give thanks, and to praise in the gates of the tents of the LORD.

2 Chr. 35:15. And the singers the sons of Asaph *were* in their place, according to the commandment of David, and Asaph, and Heman, and Jeduthun the king's seer; and the porters *waited* at every gate; they might not depart from their service: for their brethren the Levites prepared for them. 25. And Jeremiah lamented for Josiah: and all the singing men and the singing women spake of Josiah in their lamentations to this day, and made them an ordinance in Israel: and, behold, they *are* written in the lamentations.

Ezra 2:64. The whole congregation together *was* forty and two thousand three hundred *and* threescore, 65. And *there were* among them two hundred singing men and singing women.

Ezra 3:10. And when the builders laid the foundation of the temple of the LORD, they set the priests in their apparel with trumpets, and the Levites the sons of Asaph with cymbals, to praise the LORD, after the ordinance of David king of Israel. 11. And they sang together by course in praising and giving thanks unto the LORD; because *he is* good, for his mercy *endureth* for ever toward Israel. And all the people shouted with a great shout, when they praised the Lord, because the foundation of the house of the Lord was laid.

Neh. 12:24. And the chief of the Levites: Hashabiah, Sherebiah, and Jeshua the son of Kadmiel, with their brethren over against them, to praise *and* to give thanks, according to the commandment of David the man of God, ward over against ward. 27. And at the dedication of the wall of Jerusalem they sought the Levites out of all their places, to bring them to Jerusalem, to keep the dedication with gladness, both with thanksgivings, and with singing, *with* cymbals, psalteries, and with harps. 28. And the sons of the singers gathered themselves together, both out of the plain country round about Jerusalem, and from the villages of Netophathi; 29. Also from the house of Gilgal, and out of the fields of Geba and Azmaveth: for the singers had builded them villages round about Jerusalem. 30. And the priests and the Levites purified themselves, and purified the people, and the gates, and the wall. 31. Then I brought up the princes of Judah upon the wall, and appointed two great *companies of them that gave* thanks, *whereof one* went on the right hand upon the wall toward the dung gate: *vs.* 32-47.

Job 21:12. They take the timbrel and harp, and rejoice at the sound of the organ.

Job 30:31. My harp also is *turned* to mourning, and my organ into the voice of them that weep.

Psa. 33:1. Rejoice in the Lord, O ye righteous: *for* praise is comely for the upright. 2. Praise the Lord with harp: sing unto him with the psaltery *and* an instrument of ten strings. 3. Sing unto him a new song; play skilfully with a loud noise. 4. For the word of the Lord *is* right; and all his works *are done* in truth.

Psa. 68:4. Sing unto God, sing praises to his name: extol him that rideth upon the heavens by his name JAH, and rejoice before him. 25. The singers went before, the players on instruments *followed* after; among *them were* the damsels playing with timbrels. 26. Bless ye God in the congregations, *even* the Lord, from the fountain of Israel. 32. Sing unto God, ye kingdoms of the earth; O sing praises unto the Lord; 33. To him that rideth upon the heavens of heavens, *which were* of old; lo, he doth send out his voice, *and that* a mighty voice. 34. Ascribe ye strength unto God: his excellency *is* over Israel, and his strength *is* in the clouds. 35. O God, *thou art* terrible out of thy holy places: the God of Israel *is* he that giveth strength and power unto *his* people. Blessed *be* God. *vs.* 1-35.

Psa. 81:1. Sing aloud unto God our strength: make a joyful noise unto the God of Jacob. 2. Take a psalm, and bring hith-

er the timbrel, the pleasant harp with the psaltery. 3. Blow up the trumpet in the new moon, in the time appointed, on our solemn feast day.

Psa. 87:7. As well the singers as the players on instruments *shall be there:* all my springs *are* in thee.

Psa. 92:1. *It is a* good *thing* to give thanks unto the Lord, and to sing praises unto thy name, O most High: 2. To shew forth thy lovingkindness in the morning, and thy faithfulness every night, 3. Upon an instrument of ten strings, and upon the psaltery; upon the harp with a solemn sound.

Psa. 95:1. O come, let us sing unto the Lord: let us make a joyful noise to the rock of our salvation. 2. Let us come before his presence with thanksgiving, and make a joyful noise unto him with psalms.

Psa. 98:1. O sing unto the Lord a new song; for he hath done marvellous things: his right hand, and his holy arm, hath gotten him the victory. 2. The Lord hath made known his salvation: his righteousness hath he openly shewed in the sight of the heathen. 3. He hath remembered his mercy and his truth toward the house of Israel: all the ends of the earth have seen the salvation of our God. 4. Make a joyful noise unto the Lord, all the earth: make a loud noise, and rejoice, and sing praise. 5. Sing unto the Lord with the harp; with the harp, and the voice of a psalm. 6. With trumpets and sound of cornet make a joyful noise before the Lord, the King. 7. Let the sea roar, and the fulness thereof; the world, and they that dwell therein. 8. Let the floods clap *their* hands: let the hills be joyful together.

Psa. 104:33. I will sing unto the Lord as long as I live: I will sing praise to my God while I have my being.

Psa. 105:2. Sing unto him, sing psalms unto him: talk ye of all his wondrous works.

Psa. 135:1. Praise ye the Lord. Praise ye the name of the Lord; praise *him*, O ye servants of the Lord. 2. Ye that stand in the house of the Lord, in the courts of the house of our God, 3. Praise the Lord; for the Lord *is* good: sing praises unto his name; for *it is* pleasant.

Psa. 137:1. By the rivers of Babylon, there we sat down, yea, we wept, when we remembered Zion. 2. We hanged our harps upon the willows in the midst thereof. 3. For there they that carried us away captive required of us a song; and they that wasted us *required of us* mirth, *saying*, Sing us *one* of the songs of Zion. 4. How shall we sing the Lord's song in a strange land? 5. If I forget thee, O Jerusalem, let my right hand forget *her cunning.* 6. If I do not remember thee, let my tongue cleave to the roof of my mouth; if I prefer not Jerusalem above my chief joy.

Psa. 144:9. I will sing a new song unto thee, O God: upon a psaltery *and* an instrument of ten strings will I sing praises unto thee.

Psa. 149:1. Praise ye the Lord. Sing unto the Lord a new song, *and* his praise in the congregation of saints. 2. Let Israel rejoice in him that made him: let the children of Zion be joyful in their King. 3. Let them praise his name in the dance: let them sing praises unto him with the timbrel and harp. 6. *Let* the high *praises* of God *be* in their mouth,

Psa. 150:1. Praise ye the Lord. Praise God in his sanctuary: praise him in the firmament of his power. 2. Praise him for his mighty acts: praise him according to his excellent greatness. 3. Praise him with the sound of the trumpet: praise him with the psaltery and harp. 4. Praise him with the timbrel and dance: praise him with stringed instruments and organs. 5. Praise him upon the loud cymbals: praise him upon the high sounding cymbals. 6. Let every thing that hath breath praise the Lord. Praise ye the Lord.

Prov. 25:20. *As* he that taketh away a garment in cold weather, *and as* vinegar upon nitre, so *is* he that singeth songs to an heavy heart.

Eccl. 2:8. I gat me men singers and women singers, and the delights of the sons of men, ¹ *as* musical instruments, and that of all sorts. [¹ R. V. concubines, very many]

Isa. 5:12. The harp, and the viol, the tabret, and pipe, and wine, are in their feasts:

Isa. 14:11. Thy pomp is brought down to the grave, *and* the noise of thy viols: the worm is spread under thee, and the worms cover thee.

Isa. 16:10. And gladness is taken away, and joy out of the plentiful field; and in the vineyards there shall be no singing, neither shall there be shouting: the treaders shall tread out no wine in *their* presses; I have made *their vintage* shouting to cease.

Isa. 23:16. Take an harp, go about the city, thou harlot that hast been forgotten; make sweet melody, sing many songs, that thou mayest be remembered.

Isa. 24:8. The mirth of tabrets ceaseth, the noise of them that rejoice endeth, the joy of the harp ceaseth. 9. They shall not drink wine with a song; strong drink shall be bitter to them that drink it.

Isa. 30:29. Ye shall have a song, as in the night *when* a holy solemnity is kept; and gladness of heart, as when one goeth with a pipe to come into the mountain of the Lord, to the mighty One of Israel. 32. And *in* every place where the grounded staff shall pass, which the Lord shall lay upon him, *it* shall be with tabrets and harps: and in battles of shaking will he fight with it. Jer. 31:4.

Ezek. 26:13. And I will cause the noise of thy songs to cease; and the sound of thy harps shall be no more heard.

Ezek. 33:32. And, lo, thou *art* unto them as a very lovely song of one that hath a pleasant voice, and can play well on an instrument: for they hear thy words, but they do them not.

Dan. 3:4. Then an herald cried aloud, To you it is commanded, O people, nations, and languages, 5. *That* at what time ye hear the sound of the cornet, flute, harp, sackbut, psaltery, dulcimer, and all kinds of musick, ye fall down and worship the golden image that Nebuchadnezzar the king hath set up: 6. And whoso falleth not down and worshippeth shall the same hour be cast into the midst of a burning fiery furnace. 7. Therefore at that time, when all the people heard the sound of the cornet, flute, harp, sackbut, psaltery, and all kinds of musick, all the people, the nations, and the languages, fell down *and* worshipped the golden image that Nebuchadnezzar the king had set up. *vs.* 10–16.

Amos 6:5. That chant to the sound of the viol, *and* invent to themselves instruments of musick, like David;

Amos 8:10. And I will turn your feasts into mourning, and all your songs into lamentation;

Matt. 9:23. And when Jesus came into the ruler's house, and saw the minstrels and the people making a noise,

Matt. 11:17. And saying, We have piped unto you, and ye have not danced; we have mourned unto you, and ye have not lamented.

Mark 14:26. And when they had sung an hymn, they went out into the mount of Olives.

1 Cor. 14:15. I will sing with the spirit, and I will sing with the understanding also.

Eph. 5:19. Speaking to yourselves in psalms and hymns and spiritual songs, singing and making melody in your heart to the Lord;

Col. 3:16. Let the word of Christ dwell in you richly in all wisdom; teaching and admonishing one another in psalms and hymns and spiritual songs, singing with grace in your hearts to the Lord.

Heb. 2:12. Saying, I will declare thy name unto my brethren, in the midst of the church will I sing praise unto thee.

Rev. 14:2. And I heard a voice from heaven, as the voice of many waters, and as the voice of a great thunder: and I heard the voice of harpers harping with their harps: 3. And they sung as it were a new song before the throne, and before the four beasts, and the elders: and no man could learn that song but the hundred *and* forty *and* four thousand, which were redeemed from the earth.

Rev. 18:22. And the voice of harpers, and musicians, and of pipers, and trumpeters, shall be heard no more at all in thee; and no craftsman, of whatsoever craft *he be*, shall be found any more in thee; and the sound of a millstone shall be heard no more at all in thee;

See PRAISE; PSALMS.

MUSTARD, Matt. 13:31,32; 17:20; Mark 4:30-33; Luke 13:19.

MUSTER, of troops, 1 Sam. 14:17; 2 Sam. 20:4; 1 Kin. 20:26; 2 Kin. 25:19; Isa. 13:4.

See ARMIES.

MUTH-LABBEN. See MUSIC.

MUTINY, Israelites against Moses, Num. 14:4.

See CONSPIRACY.

MYRA. A city of Lycia. Paul visits, Acts 27:5,6.

MYRRH, a fragrant gum. A product of the land of Canaan, Song 4:6,14; 5:1. One of the compounds in the sacred anointing oil, Ex. 30:23. Used as a perfume, Esth. 2:12; Psa. 45:8; Prov. 7:17; Song 3:6; 5:13. Brought by wise men as a present to Jesus, Matt. 2:11. Offered to Jesus on the cross, Mark 15:23. Used for embalming, John 19:39. Traffic in, Gen. 37:25; 43:11.

MYRTLE, Neh. 8:15; Isa. 41:19; 55:13; Zech. 1:8.

MYSIA. A province of Asia Minor. Paul visits, Acts 16:7,8.

MYSTERIES. OF REDEMPTION: Deut. 29:29. The secret *things belong* unto the LORD our God: but those *things which are* revealed *belong* unto us and to our children for ever, that *we* may do all the words of this law.

Job 15:8. Hast thou heard the secret of God? and dost thou restrain wisdom to thyself?

Psa. 25:14. The secret of the LORD *is* with them that fear him; and he will shew them his covenant.

Prov. 3:32. His secret *is* with the righteous.

Amos 3:7. Surely the Lord GOD will do nothing, but he revealeth his secret unto his servants the prophets.

Matt. 11:25. At that time Jesus answered and said, I thank thee, O Father, Lord of heaven and earth, because thou hast hid these things from the wise and prudent, and hast revealed them unto babes.

Matt. 13:11. It is given unto you to know the mysteries of the kingdom of heaven, but to them it is not given. 35. That it might be fulfilled which was spoken by the prophet, saying, I will open my mouth in parables; I will utter things which have been kept secret from the foundation of the world.

Mark 4:11. And he said unto them, Unto you it is given to know the mystery of the kingdom of God: but unto them that are without, all *these* things are done in parables:

Luke 8:10. And he said, Unto you it is given to know the mysteries of the kingdom of God: but to others in parables; that seeing they might not see, and hearing they might not understand.

John 3:8. The wind bloweth where it listeth, and thou hearest the sound thereof, but canst not tell whence it cometh, and whither it goeth: so is every one that is born of the Spirit. 9. Nicodemus answered and said unto him, How can these things be? 10. Jesus answered and said unto him, Art thou a master of Israel, and knowest not these things? 11. Verily, verily, I say unto thee, We speak that we do know, and testify that we have seen; and ye receive not our witness. 12. If I have told you earthly things, and ye believe not, how shall ye believe, if I tell you *of* heavenly things?

Rom. 16:25. Now to him that is of power to stablish you according to my gospel, and the preaching of Jesus Christ, according to the revelation of the mystery, which was kept secret since the world began, 26. But now is made manifest, and by the scriptures of the prophets, according to the commandment of the everlasting God, made known to all nations for the obedience of faith:

1 Cor. 2:7. But we speak the wisdom of God in a mystery, *even* the hidden *wisdom*, which God ordained before the world unto our glory: 8. Which none of the princes of this world knew: for had they known *it*, they would not have crucified the Lord of glory. 9. But as it is written, Eye hath not seen, nor ear heard, neither have entered into the heart of man, the things which God hath prepared for them that love him. 10. But God hath revealed *them* unto us by his Spirit: for the Spirit searcheth all things, yea, the deep things of God.

2 Cor. 3:12. Seeing then that we have such hope, we use great plainness of speech: 13. And not as Moses, *which* put a vail over his face, that the children of Israel could not stedfastly look to the end of that which is abolished: 14. But their minds were blinded: for until this day remaineth the same vail untaken away in the reading of the old testament; which *vail* is done away in Christ. 15. But even unto this day, when Moses is read, the vail is upon their heart. 16. Nevertheless when it shall turn to the Lord, the vail shall be taken away. 17. Now the Lord is that Spirit: and where the Spirit of the Lord *is*, there *is* liberty. 18. But we all, with open face beholding as in a glass the glory of the Lord, are changed into the same image from glory to glory, *even* as by the Spirit of the Lord.

Eph. 1:9. Having made known unto us the mystery of his will, according to his good pleasure which he hath purposed in himself: 10. That in the dispensation of the fulness of times he might gather together in one all things in Christ, both which are in heaven, and which are on earth; *even* in him:

Eph. 3:3. How that by revelation he made known unto me the mystery: (as I wrote afore in few words, 4. Whereby, when ye read, ye may understand my knowledge in the mystery of Christ) 5. Which in other ages was not made known unto the sons of men, as it is now revealed unto his holy apostles and prophets by the Spirit; 9. And to make all *men* see what *is* the fellowship of the mystery, which from the beginning of the world hath been hid in God, who created all things [1] by Jesus Christ : 18. May be able to comprehend with all saints what *is* the breadth, and length, and depth, and height ; 19. And to know the love of Christ, which passeth knowledge, that ye might be filled with all the fulness of God.   [1 Omitted in R. V.]

Eph. 6:19. And for me, that utterance may be given unto me, that I may open my mouth boldly, to make known the mystery of the gospel,

Col. 1:25. Wherof I am made a minister, according to the dispensation of God which is given to me for you, to fulfil the word of God ; 26. *Even* the mystery which hath been hid from ages and from generations, but now is made manifest to his saints : 27. To whom God would make known what *is* the riches of the glory of this mystery among the Gentiles; which is Christ in you, the hope of glory :

Col. 2:2. That their hearts might be comforted, being knit together in love, and unto all riches of the full assurance of understanding, [1] to the acknowledgement of the mystery of God, [2] and of the Father, and of Christ ;
[R. V. 1 that they may know   2 even Christ]

Col. 4:3. Withal praying also for us, that God would open unto us a door of utterance, to speak the mystery of Christ, for which I am also in bonds : 4. That I may make it manifest, as I ought to speak.

2 Thess. 2:7. For the mystery of iniquity doth already work : only he who now letteth *will let*, until he be taken out of the way.

1 Tim. 3:9. Holding the mystery of the faith in a pure conscience. 16. And without controversy great is the mystery of godliness : [1] God was manifest in the flesh, justified in the Spirit, seen of angels, preached unto the Gentiles, believed on in the world, received up into glory. [1 R. V. He who]

Heb. 5:11. Of whom we have many things to say, and hard to be uttered, seeing ye are dull of hearing.

1 Pet. 1:10. Of which salvation the prophets have enquired and searched diligently, who prophesied of the grace *that should come* unto you : 11. Searching what, or what manner of time the Spirit of Christ which was in them did signify, when it testified beforehand the sufferings of Christ, and the glory that should follow. 12. Unto whom it was revealed, that not unto themselves, but unto us they did minister the things, which are now reported unto you by them that have preached the gospel unto you with the Holy Ghost sent down from heaven; which things the angels desire to look into.

Rev. 10:7. But in the days of the voice of the seventh angel, when he shall begin to sound, the mystery of God should be finished, as he hath declared to his servants the prophets.

See SALVATION, PLAN OF.

N

NAAM, son of Caleb, 1 Chr. 4:15.

NAAMAH. 1. Sister of Tubal-cain, Gen. 4:22.

2. A wife of Solomon and mother of King Rehoboam, 1 Kin. 14:21,31; 2 Chr. 12:13.

3. A city of Judah, Josh. 15:41.

NAAMAN. 1. Son of Benjamin, Gen. 46:21.

2. Son of Bela, Num. 26:40; 1 Chr. 8:4.

3. Son of Ehud, 1 Chr. 8:7.

4. A Syrian general, healed of leprosy by Elisha, 2 Kin. 5:1-23; Luke 4:27.

NAARAH, a wife of Ashur, 1 Chr. 4:5,6.

NAARAI, called also PAARAI. One of David's heroes, 1 Chr. 11:37.

NAARAN, a city in the eastern limits of Ephraim, 1 Chr. 7:28.

NAARATH, a city on the southern boundary of Ephraim, Josh. 16:7.

NAASHON, called also NAASSON and NAHSHON. A captain of Judah's host, Ex. 6:23; Num. 1:7; 2:3; 7:12,17; 10:14. In the lineage of Christ, Matt. 1:4; Luke 3:32.

NABAL, husband of Abigail. History of, 1 Sam. 25:2-38.

NABOTH, a Jezreelite. His vineyard forcibly taken by Ahab; stoned at the instigation of Jezebel, 1 Kin. 21:1-19. His murder avenged, 2 Kin. 9:21-36.

NACHON, called also CHIDON. Uzzah slain at the threshing floor of, 2 Sam. 6:6,7; 1 Chr. 13:9.

NACHOR, an ancestor of Jesus, Luke 3:34.

NADAB. 1. Son of Aaron, Ex. 6:23. Called to Mount Sinai with Moses and Aaron to worship, Ex. 24:1,9,10. Set apart to priesthood, Ex. 28:1,4,40-43. Offers strange fire to God, and is destroyed, Lev. 10:1,2; Num. 3:4; 26:61. Is buried, Lev. 10:4,5. His father and brothers forbidden to mourn, Lev. 10:6,7.

2. Son and successor of Jeroboam, 1 Kin. 14:20. His wicked reign: murdered by Baasha, 1 Kin. 15:25-31.

3. Great-grandson of Jerahmeel, 1 Chr. 2: 28,30.

4. A Benjamite, 1 Chr. 8:30; 9:36.

NAGGE, an ancestor of Jesus, Luke 3:25.

NAHALIEL, a station of the Israelites, Num. 21:19.

NAHALLAL, called also NAHALAL and NAHALOL. A Levitical city, Josh. 19:15; 21: 35; Judg. 1:30.

NAHAM, brother of Hodiah, 1 Chr. 4:19.

NAHAMANI, a Jewish exile, Neh. 7:7.

NAHARAI, called also NAHARI. One of David's heroes, 2 Sam. 23:37; 1 Chr. 11:39.

NAHASH. 1. An Ammonite king. Defeated by Saul at Jabesh-gilead, 1 Sam.

11:1–11. Kindness of, to David, and death, 2 Sam. 10:1,2; 1 Chr. 19:1,2.

2. Probably identical with JESSE, 2 Sam. 17:25.

NAHATH. 1. Son of Reuel, Gen. 36:13, 17; 1 Chr. 1:37.

2. Called also TOAH and TOHU. A Levite, 1 Chr. 6:26,34; 1 Sam. 1:1.

3. A Levite and overseer of the sacred offerings, 2 Chr. 31:13.

NAHBI, a prince of Naphtali, and one of the twelve spies, Num. 13:14.

NAHOR. 1. Grandfather of Abraham, Gen. 11:22–26; 1 Chr. 1:26. In the lineage of Christ, Luke 3:34.

2. Brother of Abraham, Gen. 11:26; Josh. 24:2. Marriage and descendants of, Gen. 11:27,29; 22:20–24; 24:15,24.

NAHSHON. Son of Amminadab, Ex. 6: 23; Num. 1:7; 1 Chr. 2:10. Captain of the host of Judah, Num. 2:3; 10:14; 1 Chr. 2:10. Liberality of, Num. 7:12,17.

NAHUM, one of the minor prophets. Prophesies against the Assyrians; declares the majesty of God and his care for his people, Nah. 1. Foretells the destruction of Nineveh, Nah. chapters 2; 3.

NAIL. Isa. 41:7; Jer. 10:4. Made of iron, 1 Chr. 22:3; of gold, 2 Chr. 3:9. Jael kills Sisera with, Judg. 4:21.

FIGURATIVE: Ezra 9:8; Isa. 22:23,25; Zech. 10:4.

NAIN, a city in Galilee. Jesus restores to life a widow's son in, Luke 7:11.

NAIOTH, a place in Ramah, 1 Sam. 19: 18,19,22; 20:1.

NAME. Value of a good, Prov. 22:1; Eccl. 7:1. A new name given to persons who have spiritual adoption, Isa. 62:2. To Abraham, Gen. 17:5; Sarah, Gen. 17:15; Jacob, Gen. 32:28; Paul, Acts 13:9. Intercessional influence of the name of Jesus, see JESUS, IN HIS NAME.

SYMBOLICAL: Hos. 1:3,4,6,9; 2:1.

NAMES OF JESUS. See JESUS, NAMES OF.

NAOMI. Wife of Elimelech; mother-in-law of Ruth; dwelt in Moab; returns to Bethlehem; kinswoman of Boaz, Ruth chapters 1–4.

NAPHISH, called also NEPHISH. A son of Ishmael, Gen. 25:15; 1 Chr. 1:31.

NAPHTALI. 1. Son of Jacob and Bilhah, Gen. 30:7,8; 35:25. Jacob blesses, Gen. 49:21. Sons of, Gen. 46:24; 1 Chr. 7:13.

2. Tribe of. Census of, Num. 1:42,43; 26: 48–50. Position assigned to, in camp and march, Num. 2:25–31; 10:25–27. Moses's benediction on, Deut. 33:23. Inheritance of, Josh. 19:32–39; Judg. 1:33; Ezek. 48:3.

Defeat Sisera, Judg. 4:6,10; 5:18. Follow Gideon, Judg. 6:35; 7:23. Aid in conveying the ark to Jerusalem, Psa. 68:27. Military operations of, 1 Chr. 12:34,40; against, 1 Kin. 15:20; 2 Kin. 15:29; 2 Chr. 16:4.

Prophecies concerning, Isa. 9:1,2; Rev.7:6.

NAPHTUHIM, the inhabitants of central Egypt, Gen. 10:13; 1 Chr. 1:11.

NARCISSUS, a believer at Rome, Rom. 16:11.

NATHAN. 1. Son of David and Bathsheba, 2 Sam. 5:14; 1 Chr. 3:5; 14:4.

2. A prophet in the time of David. His message to David concerning the building of a temple, 2 Sam. 7:1–17; 1 Chr. 17:1–15. Reproves David for his adultery with Bathsheba and his murder of Uriah, 2 Sam. 12: 1–15. Gives Solomon the name Jedidiah, 2 Sam. 12:25. Assists Bath-sheba in securing to Solomon, her son, the succession to the throne, 1 Kin. 1:10–14,22–27. Assists in anointing Solomon, 1 Kin. 1:32–45.

Kept the chronicles, 1 Chr. 29:29; 2 Chr. 9:29. Assists David in the organization of the tabernacle, 2 Chr. 29:25.

NATHANAEL, becomes a disciple of Jesus, John 1:45–49; 21:2.

NATHAN-MELECH, an idolatrous chamberlain, 2 Kin. 23:11.

NATION. Sins of, Isa. 30:1,2. Chastised, Isa. 14:26,27; Jer. 5:29; 18:6–10; 25:12–33; Ezek. 2:3–5; 39:23,24; Dan. 7:9–12; 9:3–16; Hos. 7:12; Joel 1:1–20; Amos 9:9; Zeph. 3:6,8. Perish, Psa. 9:17; Isa. 60:12.

National adversity, prayer in, Judg. 21: 2–4; 2 Chr. 7:13,14; Psa. 74; Joel 2:12; lamented, Ezra 9; Neh. 1:4–11; Jer. 6:14; 8:11, 20,21; 9:1,2. See SIN, NATIONAL.

Prayer for, Psa. 85:1–7; Lam. 2:20–22; 5; Dan. 9:3–21.

Involved in sins of rulers, Gen. 20:4,9; 2 Sam. 24:10–17; 1 Chr. 21:7–17; of other individuals, as Achan, Josh. 7:1,11–26.

Peace of, Job 34:29; Psa. 33:12; 89:15–18. Promises of peace to, Lev. 26:6; 1 Kin. 2:33; 2 Kin. 20:19; 1 Chr. 22:9; Psa. 29:11; 46:9; 72:3,7; 128:6; Isa. 2:4; 14:4–7; 60:17,18; 65:25; Jer. 30:10; 50:34; Ezek. 34:25–28; Hos. 2:18; Mic. 4:3,4; Zech. 1:11; 3:10; 8:4,5; 9:10; 14:11. Prayer for peace, Jer. 29:7; 1 Tim. 2:1,2. Peace given by God, Josh. 21:44; 1 Chr. 22:18; 23:25; Psa. 147:13,14; Eccl. 3:8; Isa. 45:7. Instances of national peace, Josh. 14:15; Judg. 3:11,30; 1 Kin. 4:24,25. See WAR.

Righteousness exalteth, Prov. 14:34.

See GOVERNMENT; KING; RULERS.

NATURALIZATION, Acts 22:28; Eph. 2:12,19.

NATURAL RELIGION. See RELIGION, NATURAL.

NAUM, an ancestor of Jesus, Luke 3:25.

NAVIGATION, sounding in, Acts 27:28. See COMMERCE; MARINER; NAVY.

NAVEL, treatment of, at birth, Ezek. 16:4.

NAVY. Solomon's, 1 Kin. 9:26; Hiram's, 1 Kin. 10:11; of Chittim, Dan. 11:30,40. See COMMERCE; MARINER; NAVIGATION.

NAZARENE. See NAZARETH.

NAZARETH, a village in Galilee. Joseph and Mary dwell at, Matt. 2:23; Luke 1: 26,27,56; 2:4,39,51. Jesus from, Matt. 21:11; Mark 1:24; 10:47; Luke 4:34; 18:37; 24:19. People of, reject Jesus, Luke 4:16–30. Its name opprobrious, John 1:46.

NAZARITE. Law concerning, Num. 6: 1–21; Judg. 13:5. Character of, Lam. 4:7; Amos 2:11,12.

INSTANCES OF: Samson, Judg. 13:5,7; 16:17. Samuel, 1 Sam. 1:11. Rechabites, Jer. 35. John the Baptist, Matt. 11:18; Luke 1:15; 7:33.

NEAH, a city in Zebulun, Josh. 19:13.

NEAPOLIS, a seaport of Macedonia. Paul visits, Acts 16:11.

NEARIAH. 1. Son of Shemaiah,1 Chr. 3: 22,23.

2. A Simeonite captain, 1 Chr. 4:42.

NEBAIOTH, called also NEBAJOTH. Son of Ishmael, Gen. 25:13; 28:9; 36:3; 1 Chr. 1:29. Prophecies concerning, Isa. 60:7.

NEBALLAT, a town occupied by the Benjamites after the captivity, Neh. 11:34.

NEBAT, father of Jeroboam, 1 Kin. 11: 26; 12:2.

NEBO. 1. A city allotted to Reuben, Num. 32:3,38; 1 Chr. 5:8. Prophecies concerning, Isa. 15:2; Jer. 48:1,22.

2. A mountain range E. of the Jordan. Moses views Canaan from, Deut. 32:49,50; dies on, Deut. 34:1.

3. A city in Judah, Ezra 2:29; Neh. 7:33.

4. The ancestor of certain Jews, Ezra 10:43.

5. A Babylonian idol, Isa. 46:1.

NEBUCHADNEZZAR, called also NEBUCHADREZZAR. King of Babylon, Jer. 21:2. Empire of. See BABYLON. His administration, Dan. chapters 1–4. Conquests of: Of Jerusalem, 2 Kin. 24;25; 1 Chr. 6:15; 2 Chr. 36:5–21; Ezra 1:7; Jer. 39. Of Egypt, 2 Kin. 24:7; Jer. 46:2. Of Tyre, Ezek. 29:18. An instrument of God's judgments, Jer. 27:8. Prophecies concerning, Jer. 21:7,10; 22:25; 25:9; 27:6–9; 32:28; 43:10; 46:13; 49:30–33; Ezek. 26:7–12.

NEBUSHASBAN, a prince of Nebuchadnezzar, Jer. 39:13.

NEBUZAR-ADAN. Captain of the guard of King Nebuchadnezzar. Commands the Assyrian army which besieged Jerusalem and carried the inhabitants to Babylon, 2 Kin. 25:8–21; Jer. 39:9,10; 43:6; 52:12–30. Protects Jeremiah, Jer. 39:11–14; 40:1–5.

NECHO, king of Egypt, 2 Chr. 35:20,22; 36:4.

NECKLACE, [A. V., tablets, R. V., armlet], Ex. 35:22; Num. 31:50 [R.V., marg.].

NECROMANCY, Deut. 18:11; 26:14; Isa. 8:19; 29:4.

INSTANCE OF: The witch of En-dor, 1 Sam. 28:7–19.

See FAMILIAR SPIRITS ; SORCERY ; WITCH-CRAFT.

NEDABIAH, son of Jeconiah, 1 Chr. 3:18.

NEEDLE, Matt. 19:24; Mark 10:25; Luke 18:25.

NEEDLEWORK. See EMBROIDERY.

NEGINOTH. See MUSIC.

NEHEMIAH. 1. Son of Hachaliah, Neh. 1:1. Cupbearer of Artaxerxes, Neh. 1: 11; 2:1. Is grieved over the desolation of his country, Neh. 1. Is sent by the king to rebuild Jerusalem, Neh. 2:1–8. Register of the people whom he led from Babylon, Neh. 7; and of the priests and Levites, Neh. 12: 1–22. Rebuilds Jerusalem, Neh. chapters 2–6. His administration as ruler of the people, Neh. chapters 5; 6; 8; 9; 10; 11; 13.

2. Two Jews who returned to Jerusalem from exile, Ezra 2:2; Neh. 3:16; 7:7.

NEHILOTH. See MUSIC.

NEHUM, a chief exile, Neh. 7:7.

NEHUSHTA, wife of Jehoiakim, king of Judah, and mother of Jehoiachin, 2 Kin. 24:6,8.

NEHUSHTAN, the brazen serpent, 2 Kin. 18:4,

NEIEL, a landmark on the boundary of Asher, Josh. 19:27.

NEIGHBOR. Ex. 20:16. Thou shalt not bear false witness against thy neighbour.

Ex. 23:4. If thou meet thine enemy's ox or his ass going astray, thou shalt surely bring it back to him again. 5. If thou see the ass of him that hateth thee lying under his burden, and wouldest forbear to help him, thou shalt surely help with him.

Lev. 6:2. If a soul sin, and commit a trespass against the LORD, and lie unto his neighbour in that which was delivered him to keep, or in fellowship, or in a thing taken away by violence, or hath deceived his neighbour; 3. Or have found that which was lost, and lieth concerning it, and sweareth falsely ; in any of all these that a man doeth, sinning therein : 4. Then it shall be, because he hath sinned, and is guilty, that he shall restore that which he took violently away, or the thing which he has deceitfully gotten, or that which was delivered him to keep, or the lost thing which he found, 5. Or all that about which he hath sworn falsely; he shall even restore it in the principal, and shall add the fifth part more thereto, *and* give it unto him to whom it appertaineth, in the day of his trespass offering.

Lev. 19:13. Thou shalt not defraud thy neighbour, neither rob *him :* the wages of him that is hired shall not abide with thee all night until the morning. 16. Thou shalt not go up and down *as* a talebearer among thy people ; neither shalt thou stand against the blood of thy neighbour : I *am* the LORD. 17. Thou shalt not hate thy brother in thine heart : thou shalt in any wise rebuke thy neighbour, and not suffer sin upon him.

18. Thou shalt love thy neighbour as thyself : I *am* the LORD. Matt. 19:19; 22:39; Mark 12:31; Luke 10:27; Rom. 13:9; Gal. 5:14; Jas. 2:8.

Deut. 22:1. Thou shalt not see thy brother's ox or his sheep go astray, and hide thyself from them : thou shalt in any case bring them again unto thy brother. 2. And if thy brother *be* not nigh unto thee, or if thou know him not, then thou shalt bring it unto thine own house, and it shall be with thee until thy brother seek after it, and thou shalt restore it to him again. 3. In like manner shalt thou do with his ass ; and so snalt thou do with his raiment; and with all lost things of thy brother's, which he hath lost, and thou hast found, shalt thou do likewise: thou mayest not hide thyself. 4. Thou shalt not see thy brother's ass or his ox fall down by the way, and hide thyself from them: thou shalt surely help him lift *them* up again.

Psa. 15:1. Lord, who shall abide in thy tabernacle? who shall dwell in thy holy hill? 2. He that walketh uprightly, and worketh righteousness, and speaketh the truth in his heart. 3. *He that* backbiteth not with his tongue, nor doeth evil to his neighbour, nor taketh up a reproach against his neighbour.

Prov. 3:28. Say not unto thy neighbour, Go, and come again, and to morrow I will give; when thou hast it by thee. 29. Devise not evil against thy neighbour, seeing he dwelleth securely by thee.

Jer. 22:13. Woe unto him that buildeth his house by unrighteousness, and his chambers by wrong; *that* useth his neighbour's service without wages, and giveth him not for his work;

Isa. 58:6. *Is* not this the fast that I have chosen? to loose the bands of wickedness, to undo the heavy burdens, and to let the oppressed go free, and that ye break every yoke? 7. *Is it* not to deal thy bread to the hungry, and that thou bring the poor that are cast out to thy house? when thou seest the naked, that thou cover him; and that thou hide not thyself from thine own flesh? 8. Then shall thy light break forth as the morning, and thine health shall spring forth speedily: and thy righteousness shall go before thee: the glory of the LORD shall be thy rereward. 9. Then shalt thou call, and the LORD shall answer; thou shalt cry, and he shall say, Here I *am*. If thou take away from the midst of thee the yoke, the putting forth of the finger, and speaking vanity; 10. And *if* thou draw out thy soul to the hungry, and satisfy the afflicted soul: then shall thy light rise in obscurity, and thy darkness *be* as the noonday: 11. And the LORD shall guide thee continually, and satisfy thy soul in drought, and make fat thy bones: and thou shalt be like a watered garden, and like a spring of water, whose waters fail not. 12. And *they that shall be* of thee shall build the old waste places; thou shalt raise up the foundations of many generations; and thou shalt be called, The repairer of the breach, The restorer of paths to dwell in. 13. If thou turn away thy foot from the sabbath, *from* doing thy pleasure on my holy day; and call the sabbath a delight, the holy of the LORD, honourable; and shalt honour him, not doing thine own ways, nor finding thine own pleasure, nor speaking *thine own* words: 14. Then shalt thou delight thyself in the LORD; and I will cause thee to ride upon the high places of the earth, and feed thee with the heritage of Jacob thy father: for the mouth of the LORD hath spoken *it*.

Zech. 8:16. These *are* the things that ye shall do; Speak ye every man the truth to his neighbour; execute the judgment of truth and peace in your gates: 17. And let none of you imagine evil in your hearts against his neighbour; and love no false oath: for all these *are things* that I hate, saith the LORD.

Matt. 7:12. Therefore all things whatsoever ye would that men should do to you, do ye even so to them: for this is the law and the prophets.

Matt. 25:34. Then shall the King say unto them on his right hand, Come, ye blessed of my Father, inherit the kingdom prepared for you from the foundation of the world· 35. For I was an hungred, and ye gave me meat: I was thirsty, and ye gave me drink: I was a stranger, and ye took me in: 36. Naked, and ye clothed me: I was sick, and ye visited me: I was in prison, and ye came unto me. 37. Then shall the righteous answer him, saying, Lord, when saw we thee an hungred, and fed *thee*? or thirsty, and gave *thee* drink? 38. When saw we thee a stranger, and took *thee* in? or naked, and clothed *thee*? 39. Or when saw we thee sick, or in prison, and came unto thee? 40. And the King shall answer and say unto them, Verily I say unto you, Inasmuch as ye have done *it* unto one of the least of these my brethren, ye have done *it* unto me. 41. Then shall he say also unto them on the left hand, Depart from me, ye cursed, into everlasting fire, prepared for the devil and his angels: 42. For I was an hungred, and ye gave me no meat: I was thirsty, and ye gave me no drink: 43. I was a stranger, and ye took me not in: naked, and ye clothed me not: sick, and in prison, and ye visited me not. 44. Then shall they also answer him, saying, Lord, when saw we thee an hungred, or athirst, or a stranger, or naked, or sick, or in prison, and did not minister unto thee? 45. Then shall he answer them, saying, Verily I say unto you, Inasmuch as ye did *it* not to one of the least of these, ye did *it* not to me. 46. And these shall go away into everlasting punishment: but the righteous into life eternal.

Luke 10:25. And, behold, a certain lawyer stood up, and tempted him, saying, Master, what shall I do to inherit eternal life? 26. He said unto him, What is written in the law? how readest thou? 27. And he answering said, Thou shalt love the Lord thy God with all thy heart, and with all thy soul, and with all thy strength, and with all thy mind; and thy neighbour as thyself. 28. And he said unto him, Thou hast answered right: this do, and thou shalt live. 29. But he, willing to justify himself, said unto Jesus, And who is my neighbour? 30. And Jesus answering said, A certain *man* went down from Jerusalem to Jericho, and fell among thieves, who stripped him of his raiment, and wounded *him*, and departed, leaving *him* half dead. 31. And by chance there came down a certain priest that way: and when he saw him, he passed by on the other side. 32. And likewise a Levite, when he was at the place, came and looked *on him*, and passed by on the other side. 33. But a certain Samaritan, as he journeyed, came where he was: and when he saw him, he had compassion *on him*, 34. And went to *him*, and bound up his wounds, pouring in oil and wine, and set him on his own beast, and brought him to an inn, and took care of him. 35. And on the morrow when he departed, he took out two pence, and gave *them* to the host, and said unto him, Take care of him; and whatsoever thou spendest more, when I come again, I will repay thee. 36. Which now of these three, thinkest thou, was neighbour unto him that fell among the thieves? 37. And he said, He that shewed mercy on him. Then said Jesus unto him, Go, and do thou likewise.

Rom. 13:10. Love worketh no ill to his neighbour: therefore love *is* the fulfilling of the law.

Rom. 15:2. Let every one of us please *his* neighbour for *his* good to edification.

Gal. 6:10. As we have therefore opportunity, let us do good unto all *men*, especially unto them who are of the household of faith.

Heb. 13.3. Remember them that are in bonds, as bound with them; *and* them which suffer adversity, as being yourselves also in the body.

Jas. 2:8. If ye fulfil the royal law according to the scripture, Thou shalt love thy neighbour as thyself, ye do well: 9. But if ye have respect to persons, ye commit sin, and are convinced of the law as transgressors.

See DUTY; MAN.

NEKEB, a city in Naphtali, Josh. 19:33.

NEKODA, name of two Jewish exiles, Ezra 2:48,60; Neh. 7:50,62.

NEMUEL. 1. A Reubenite, Num. 26:9. 2. A son of Simeon, Num. 26:12; 1 Chr. 4:24.

NEOPHYTES, Mark 4:33; John 16:4,12; 1 Cor. 3:1,2; 8:9.

NEPHEG. 1. Son of Izhar, Ex. 6:21. 2. A son of David, 2 Sam. 5:15; 1 Chr. 3:7; 14:6.

NEPHISHESIM, a family of the Nephinim, Neh. 7:52.

NEPHTOAH, a stream between Judah and Benjamin, Josh. 15:9; 18:15.

NEPOTISM. Of Joseph, Gen. 47:11, 12. Of Saul, 1 Sam. 14:50. Of David, 2 Sam. 8:16; 19:13. Of Nehemiah, Neh. 7:2.

NER, father of Abner, 1 Sam. 14:50; of Kish, 1 Chr. 8:33; 9:39.

NEREUS, a Christian at Rome, Rom. 16:15.

NERGAL, an idol, 2 Kin. 17:30.

NERGAL-SHAREZER, the name of princes of Babylon, Jer. 39:3,13.

NERI, an ancestor of Jesus, Luke 3:27.

NERIAH, father of Baruch, Jer. 32:12.

NEST. Bird's, Num. 24:21; Matt. 8:20. Birds stir, Deut. 32:11.

NET. Of checker work, 1 Kin. 7:17. Hidden in a pit, Psa. 35:7,8. Set for birds, Prov. 1:17; wild animals, Isa. 51:20. Fish caught in, Matt. 4:18–21; 13:47; Luke 5:4; John 21:6–11.

See SNARE.

FIGURATIVE: Job 18:8; 19:6; Psa. 9:15; 10:9; 25:15; 31:4; 35:7,8; 57:6; 66:11; 140:5; 141: 10; Prov. 12:12; 29:5; Eccl. 7:26; 9:12; Isa. 19: 8; Ezek. 26:5,14; 47:10; Hos. 7:12.

NETHANEEL. 1. The prince of Issachar. Numbers the tribe, Num. 1:8. Captain of the host of Issachar, Num. 2:5; 10:15. Liberality of, for the tabernacle, Num. 7: 18–23.

2. A priest and doorkeeper for the ark, 1 Chr. 15:24.

3. A Levite, 1 Chr. 24:6.

4. Son of Obed-edom, and porter of the temple, 1 Chr. 26:4.

5. A prince sent by Jehoshaphat to teach the law in the cities of Judah, 2 Chr. 17:7.

6. A Levite, 2 Chr. 35:9.

7. A priest who divorced his Gentile wife, Ezra 10:22.

8. A priest, Neh. 12:21.

9. A Levite and musician, Neh. 12:36.

NETHANIAH. 1. Father of Ishmael, 2 Kin. 25:23,25; Jer. 40:8,14,15; 41:1,2,6,7,9–12.

2. A singer, and chief of the temple musicians, 1 Chr. 25:2,12.

3. A Levite appointed by Jehoshaphat to accompany the princes who were to teach the law in Judah, 2 Chr. 17:8.

4. Father of Jehudi, Jer. 36:14.

NETHINIM. Servants of the Levites, Ezra 8:20. Return from the captivity, 1 Chr. 9:2; Ezra 2:43,58,70; 7:7,24; 8:17; Neh. 3:26,31; 7:46,60,73; 10:28; 11:3,21.

NETOPHAH, a city in Judah, Ezra 2: 22; Neh. 7:26.

NETTLES, an obnoxious plant, Prov. 24:31; Isa. 34:13.

FIGURATIVE: Job 30:7; Hos. 9:6; Zeph. 2:9.

NEW CREATURE. See REGENERATION.

NEW MOON. Feast of, Num. 10:10; 28:11–15; 1 Chr. 23:31; 2 Chr. 31:3. Traffic at time of, suspended, Amos 8:5.

NEZIAH, one of the Nethinim, Ezra 2: 54; Neh. 7:56.

NEZIB, a city in Judah, Josh. 15:43.

NIBHAZ, an idol, 2 Kin. 17:31.

NIBSHAN, a city of Judah, Josh. 15:62.

NICANOR, a deacon of the church at Jerusalem, Acts 6:5.

NICODEMUS, a Jewish rabbi. Becomes a disciple of Jesus, John 3:1–10; 7:50–53; 19:39–42.

NICOLAITANES, Rev. 2:6,15.

NICOLAS, a proselyte of Antioch, and deacon of the church at Jerusalem, Acts 6:5,6.

NICOPOLIS, a city of Thrace. Paul lives in, Tit. 3:12.

NIGER, surname of Simeon, Acts 13:1.

NIGHT. Gen. 1:5,16,18. Meditations in,

Psa. 19:2; 77:6; 119:148; 139:11. Worship in, Psa. 134:1. Jesus prays all night, Luke 6:12. No night in heaven, Rev. 21:25; 22:5.

Divided into watches, Ex. 14:24; Judg. 7: 19; 1 Sam. 11:11; Neh. 12:9; Psa. 63:6; 119: 148; Lam. 2:19; Matt. 14:25; Luke 12:38. Divided into hours, Acts 23:23. Used figuratively, Isa. 15:1; 21:11,12; John 9:4; Rom. 13: 12; 1 Thess. 5:5.

NIGHT HAWK, forbidden as food, Lev. 11:16; Deut. 14:15.

NILE. Called THE RIVER, Isa. 11:15; 19: 5-10; Ezek. 29:4; Amos 8:8. Called SIHOR, Isa. 23:3; Jer. 2:18.

NIMRAH, a city in Gad, Num. 32:3.

NIMRIM, waters on the borders of Gad and Moab, Isa. 15:6; Jer. 48:34.

NIMROD, son of Cush. "A mighty hunter before the Lord," Gen. 10:8,9; 1 Chr. 1:10. Founder of Babylon. See BABYLON.

NIMSHI, father of Jehu, 2 Kin. 9:2,20.

NINEVEH. Capital of the Assyrian empire, Gen. 10:11,12. Contained a population of upwards of one hundred and twenty thousand when Jonah preached, Jonah 4:11. Extent of, Jonah 3:4. Sennacherib in, 2 Kin. 19:36,37; Isa. 37:37,38. Jonah preaches to, Jonah 1:1,2; 3. Nahum prophesies against, Nah. chapters 1-3; Zephaniah foretells the desolation of, Zeph. 2:13-15.

NISAN, the first month in the Jewish calendar. See MONTH.

NISROCH, an idol, 2 Kin. 19:36,37; Isa. 37:37,38.

NITRE, a chemical, Prov. 25:20 [soda, R. V., marg.]; Jer. 2:22 [lye, R. V.].

NO, a city on the Nile, Jer. 46:25; Ezek. 30:14-16; Nah. 3:8.

NOADIAH. 1. A Levite who assisted in weighing the silver, gold, and vessels of the temple brought back from Babylon, Ezra 8:33.

2. A false prophetess, Neh. 6:14.

NOAH. 1. Son of Lamech, Gen. 5:28,29. Builds an ark and saves his family from the flood, Gen. 6:14-22; 7;8; Matt. 24:38; Luke 17:27; Heb. 11:7; 1 Pet. 3:20. Builds an altar and offers sacrifices, Gen. 8:20,21. Receives the covenant from God that no flood should again visit the earth; the rainbow instituted as a token of the covenant, Gen. 8:20,22; 9:9-17. Intoxication of, and his curse upon Canaan, Gen. 9:20-27. His blessing upon Shem and Japheth, Gen. 9:26,27. Dies at the age of nine hundred and fifty years, Gen. 9:28,29.

2. A daughter of Zelophehad, special legislation in regard to the inheritance of, Num. 26:33; 27:1-7; 36; Josh. 17:3-7.

NOB. A city of Benjamin, Neh. 11:31,32. Called "the city of the priests," 1 Sam. 22: 19. Abode of Ahimelech, the priest, 1 Sam. 21:1; 22:11. Probable seat of the tabernacle in Saul's time, 1 Sam. 21:4,6,9. David flees to, and is aided by Ahimelech, 1 Sam. 21:1-9; 22:9,10. Destroyed by Saul, 2 Sam. 22:19. Prophecy concerning, Isa. 10:32.

NOBAH, an Israelite, Num. 32:42.

NOBLEMAN, John 4:46-53.

NOD, Cain dwelt in, Gen. 4:16.

NOGAH, son of David, 1 Chr. 3:7; 14:6.

NOHAH, son of Benjamin, 1 Chr. 8:2.

NOLLE PROSEQUI, of the complaint against Paul, Acts 18:12-17.

NONCONFORMITY. See CHURCH AND STATE; FORM; FORMALISM.

NOPH. A city of Egypt, Jer. 2:16. Prophecy against Jews in, Jer. 44. Prophecies against, Isa. 19:13; Jer. 46:13-19; Ezek. 30:13-16.

NOPHAH, a city of Sihon, Num. 21:30.

NOSE. Jewels for, Prov. 11:22; Isa. 3:21; Ezek. 16:12. Mutilated, Ezek. 23:25.

NURSE, Gen. 24:59; 35:8; Ex. 2:7; Ruth 4:16; 2 Kin. 11:2; Isa. 60:4; 1 Thess. 2:7. Careless, 2 Sam. 4:4.

NUT, Gen. 43:11; Song 6:11.

NYMPHAS. A christian of Laodicea. House of, used as a place of worship, Col. 4:15.

O

OAK, a tree. Grew in Palestine, Gen. 35:4. Absalom hung in the boughs of, 2 Sam. 18:9,14. Deborah buried under, Gen. 35:8. Oars made of, Ezek. 27:6.

FIGURATIVE: Amos 2:9.

OAR, Isa. 33:21; Ezek. 27:6,29.

OATH, a solemn qualification. Used in solemnizing covenants: Between Abraham and the king of Sodom, Gen. 14: 22,23; and Abimelech, Gen. 21:22,23; between Isaac and Abimelech, Gen. 26:26-29, 31. Abraham requires oath of his servant Eliezer, Gen. 24:2,3,9. Esau confirms the sale of his birthright by, Gen. 25:33. Jacob confirms the covenant between him and Laban by, Gen. 31:53; requires Joseph to swear that he would bury him with his fathers, Gen. 47:28-31. Joseph requires a like oath, Gen. 50:25. Rahab requires an oath from the spies, Josh. 2:12-14; 6:22. The Israelites confirm the covenant with the Hivites, Josh. 9:3-20. Moses covenants with Caleb by, Josh. 14:9. The elders of Gilead confirm their pledge to Jephthah by, Judg. 11:10. The Israelites swear in Mizpeh, Judg. 21:5. Ruth swears to Naomi, Ruth 1:17. Boaz swears to Ruth, Ruth 3:13. Saul swears to Jonathan, 1 Sam. 19:6. Jonathan and David confirm a covenant by, 1 Sam. 20:3,13-17. David swears to Saul, 1 Sam. 24:21,22; 2 Sam. 21:7. Saul swears to the witch of En-dor, 1 Sam. 28:10. David swears not to eat until the sun goes down, 2 Sam. 3:35. Joab confirms his word by, 2 Sam. 19: 7. David swears to Bath-sheba that Solomon shall be king, 1 Kin. 1:28, 29. Solomon confirms his word by, 1 Kin. 2:23; so also does Shimei, 1 Kin. 2:42. Elisha seals his vow to follow Elijah by, 2 Kin. 2:2. King of Samaria confirms his word with an, 2 Kin. 6:31. Gehazi confirms his lie by, 2 Kin. 5:20. Jehoida requires an oath from the rulers, 2 Kin. 11:4. Zedekiah violates, **2 Chr.**

36:13. Ezra requires, of the priests and Levites, Ezra 10:5,19; so also does Nehemiah, Neh. 5:12,13. Zedekiah swears to Jeremiah, Jer. 38:16. Gedaliah confirms his word by, Jer. 40:9. Peter confirms his denial of Jesus by, Mark 14:71.

ATTRIBUTED TO GOD: Gen. 22:16; Psa. 89:35; 95:11; 105:9; 132:11; Isa. 14:24; 45:23; Jer. 11:5; 22:5; 49:13; 51:14; Luke 1:73; Heb. 3:11,18; 4:3; 6:13,14,17; 7:21,28; Rev. 10:6.

UNCLASSIFIED SCRIPTURES RELATING TO: Ex. 20:7. Thou shalt not take the name of the LORD thy God in vain; for the LORD will not hold him guiltless that taketh his name in vain. Deut. 5:11.

Ex. 22:10. If a man deliver unto his neighbour an ass, or an ox, or a sheep, or any beast, to keep; and it die, or be hurt, or driven away, no man seeing *it*; 11. *Then* shall an oath of the LORD be between them both, that he hath not put his hand unto his neighbour's goods; and the owner of it shall accept *thereof*, and he shall not make *it* good.

Ex. 23:1. Thou shalt not raise a false report: put not thine hand with the wicked to be an unrighteous witness.

Lev. 6:2. If a soul sin, and commit a trespass against the LORD, and lie unto his neighbour in that which was delivered him to keep, or in fellowship, or in a thing taken away by violence, or hath deceived his neighbour; 3. Or have found that which was lost, and lieth concerning it, and sweareth falsely; in any of all these that a man doeth, sinning therein; 4. Then it shall be, because he hath sinned, and is guilty, that he shall restore that which he took violently away, or the thing which he hath deceitfully gotten, or that which was delivered him to keep, or the lost thing which he found, 5. Or all that about which he hath sworn falsely; he shall even restore it in the principal, and shall add the fifth part more thereto, *and* give it unto him to whom it appertaineth, in the day of his trespass offering.

Lev. 19:12. And ye shall not swear by my name falsely, neither shalt thou profane the name of thy God: I *am* the LORD.

Num. 5:19. And the priest shall charge her by an oath, and say unto the woman, If no man have lain with thee and if thou hast not gone aside to uncleanness *with another* instead of thy husband, be thou free from this bitter water that causeth the curse: 20. But if thou hast gone aside *to another* instead of thy husband, and if thou be defiled, and some man have lain with thee besides thine husband: 21. Then the priest shall charge the woman with an oath of cursing, and the priest shall say unto the woman, The LORD make thee a curse and an oath among thy people, when the LORD doth make thy thigh to rot, and thy belly to swell; 22. And this water that causeth the curse shall go into thy bowels, to make *thy* belly to swell, and *thy* thigh to rot: And

the woman shall say, Amen, amen. 23. And the priest shall write these curses in a book, and he shall blot *them* out with the bitter water; 24. And he shall cause the woman to drink the bitter water that causeth the curse: and the water that causeth the curse shall enter into her, *and become* bitter.

Deut. 6:13. Thou shalt fear the LORD thy God, and serve him, and shalt swear by his name. chapter 10:20.

1 Kin. 8:31. If any man trespass against his neighbour, and an oath be laid upon him to cause him to swear, and the oath come before thine altar in this house: 32. Then hear thou in heaven, and do, and judge thy servants, condemning the wicked, to bring his way upon his head; and justifying the righteous, to give him according to his righteousness.

Psa. 15:1. LORD, who shall abide in thy tabernacle? who shall dwell in thy holy hill? 2. He that walketh uprightly, and worketh righteousness, and speaketh the truth in his heart. 4. In whose eyes a vile person is contemned; but he honoureth them that fear the LORD. *He that* sweareth to *his own* hurt, and changeth not.

Eccl. 8:2. I *counsel thee* to keep the king's commandment, and *that* in regard of the oath of God.

Isa. 48:1. Hear ye this, O house of Jacob, which are called by the name of Israel, and are come forth out of the waters of Judah, which swear by the name of the LORD, and make mention of the God of Israel, *but* not in truth, nor in righteousness.

Jer. 4:2. And thou shalt swear, The LORD liveth, in truth, in judgment, and in righteousness; and the nations shall bless themselves in him, and in him shall they glory.

Jer. 5:2. And though they say, The LORD liveth; surely they swear falsely. 7. How shall I pardon thee for this? thy children have forsaken me, and sworn by *them that are* no gods:

Jer. 7:8. Behold, ye trust in lying words, that cannot profit. 9. Will ye steal, murder, and commit adultery, and swear falsely,

Jer. 12:16. And it shall come to pass, if they will diligently learn the ways of my people, to swear by my name, The LORD liveth, as they taught my people to swear by Baal; then shall they be built in the midst of my people.

Dan. 9:11. Yĕa, all Israel have transgressed thy law, even by departing, that they might not obey thy voice; therefore the curse is poured upon us, and the oath that *is* written in the law of Moses the servant of God, because we have sinned against him.

Dan. 12:7. And I heard the man clothed in linen, which *was* upon the waters of the river, when he held up his right hand and his left hand unto heaven, and sware by him that liveth for ever, that *it shall be* for a time, times, and an half; and when he shall have accomplished to scatter the power of the holy people, all these *things* shall be finished.

Hos. 4:15. Though thou, Israel, play the harlot, *yet* let not Judah offend; and come not ye unto Gilgal, neither go ye up to Beth-aven, nor swear, The LORD liveth.

Matt. 5:33. Ye have heard that it hath been said by them of old time, Thou shalt not forswear thyself, but shalt perform unto the Lord thine oaths: 34. But I say unto you, Swear not at all; neither by heaven; for it is God's throne: 35. Nor by the earth; for it is his footstool: neither by Jerusalem; for it is the city of the great King. 36. Neither shalt thou swear by thy head, because thou canst not make one hair white or black. 37. But let your communication be, Yea, yea; Nay, nay: for whatsoever is more than these cometh of evil.

Matt. 14:7. Whereupon he promised with an oath to give her whatsoever she would ask. 9. The king was sorry: nevertheless for the oath's sake, and them which sat with him at meat, he commanded *it* to be given *her*. *vs.* 3–12; Mark 6:26.

Matt. 23:18. Whosoever shall swear by the altar, it is nothing; but whosoever sweareth by the gift that is upon it, he is guilty. 19. *Ye* fools and blind: for whether *is* greater, the gift, or the altar that sanctifieth the gift? 20. Whoso therefore shall swear by the altar, sweareth by it, and by all things thereon. 21. And whoso shall swear by the temple, sweareth by it, and by him that dwelleth therein. 22. And he that shall swear by heaven, sweareth by the throne of God, and by him that sitteth thereon.

Matt. 26:63. The high priest answered and said unto him, I adjure thee by the living God, that thou tell us whether thou be the Christ, the Son of God.

Acts 23:12. And when it was day, certain of the Jews banded together, and bound themselves under a curse, saying that they would neither eat nor drink till they had killed Paul. 13. And they were more than forty which had made this conspiracy. 14. And they came to the chief priests and elders, and said, We have bound ourselves under a great curse, that we will eat nothing until we have slain Paul.

2 Cor. 1:23. Moreover I call God for a record upon my soul, that to spare you I came not as yet unto Corinth.

Gal. 1:20. Now the things which I write unto you, behold, before God, I lie not.

Heb. 6:16. For men verily swear by the greater: and an oath for confirmation *is* to them an end of all strife.

Jas. 5:12. But above all things, my brethren, swear not, neither by heaven, neither by the earth, neither by any other oath: but let your yea be yea; and *your* nay, nay; lest ye fall into condemnation.

Rev. 10:5. And the angel which I saw stand upon the sea and upon the earth lifted up his hand to heaven, 6. And sware by him that liveth for ever and ever, who created heaven, and the things that therein are, and the earth, and the things that therein are, and the sea, and the things which are therein, that there should be time no longer:

See COVENANT; FALSE WITNESS; GOD, PROFANING HIS NAME; PERJURY.

OBADIAH. 1. The governor of Ahab's house. Conceals in a cave one hundred prophets persecuted by Jezebel, 1 Kin. 18: 3,4. Meets Elijah and receives a commission from him, 1 Kin. 18:3–16.

2. Head of a family, 1 Chr. 3:21.

3. A descendant of Tola, 1 Chr. 7:3.

4. Son of Azel, 1 Chr. 8:38; 9:44.

5. A Levite, 1 Chr. 9:16.

6. A Gadite warrior who joined David at Ziklag, 1 Chr. 12:9.

7. Father of Ishmaiah, 1 Chr. 27:19.

8. A prince of Judah who instructed the people in the law, 2 Chr. 17:7–9.

9. A Levite. One of the overseers in the repairing of the temple by Josiah, 2 Chr. 34:12.

10. A descendant of Joab who returned from Babylon, Ezra 8:9.

11. A priest who sealed with Nehemiah a covenant to observe God's law, Neh. 10:5.

12. A gatekeeper of Jerusalem, under Nehemiah, Neh. 12:25.

13. A prophet who prophesied the destruction of Edom, Obad. 1.

OBAL, called also EBAL. A son of Joktan, Gen. 10:28; 1 Chr. 1:22.

OBDURACY. 2 Chr. 36:15. And the LORD God of their fathers sent to them by his messengers, rising up betimes, and sending; because he had compassion on his people, and on his dwelling place: 16. But they mocked the messengers of God, and despised his words, and misused his prophets, until the wrath of the LORD arose against his people, till *there was* no remedy.

Psa. 95:8. Harden not your heart, as in the provocation, *and* as *in* the day of temptation in the wilderness: 9. When your fathers tempted me, proved me, and saw my work. 10. Forty years long was I grieved with *this* generation, and said, It *is* a people that do err in their heart, and they have not known my ways: 11. Unto whom I sware in my wrath that they should not enter into my rest. Heb. 3:8,15; 4:7.

Prov. 1:24. Because I have called, and ye refused; I have stretched out my hand, and no man regarded; 25. But ye have set at nought all my counsel, and would none of my reproof: 26. I also will laugh at your calamity; I will mock when your fear cometh; 27. When your fear cometh as desolation, and your destruction cometh as a whirlwind; when distress and anguish cometh upon you. 28. Then shall they call upon me, but I will not answer; they shall seek me early, but they shall not find me: 29. For that they hated knowledge, and did not choose the fear of the LORD: 30. They would none of my counsel: they despised all my reproof. 31. Therefore shall they eat of the fruit of their own way, and be filled with their own devices.

Prov. 29:1. He, that being often reproved hardeneth *his* neck, shall suddenly be destroyed, and that without remedy.

Rev. 9:20. And the rest of the men which were not killed by these plagues yet repented not of the works of their hands, that they should not worship devils, and idols of gold, and silver, and brass, and stone, and of wood: which neither can see, nor hear, nor walk: 21. Neither repented they of their murders, nor of their sorceries, nor of their fornication, nor of their thefts.

See AFFLICTION, OBDURACY IN; IMPENITENCE; REPROBACY.

INSTANCES OF: The antediluvians, Gen. 6:3,5,7. Sodomites, Gen. 19:9,14. Pharaoh, Ex. 7:14,22,23; 8:15,19,32; 9:7,12,35; 10:20,28. Israelites, Num. 14:22. Sons of Eli, 1 Sam. 2:22–25.

OBED. 1. Son of Boaz and grandfather of David, Ruth 4:17–22; 1 Chr. 2:12; Matt. 1:5; Luke 3:32.

2. Son of Ephlal and grandson of Zabad, 1 Chr. 2:37,38.

3. One of David's heroes, 1 Chr. 11:47.

4. Son of Shemaiah. A gatekeeper of the temple, 1 Chr. 26:7.

5. Father of Azariah, 2 Chr. 23:1.

OBED-EDOM. 1. A Korhite Levite. Doorkeeper of the ark, 1 Chr. 15:18,24; 26:4–8. David leaves ark with, 2 Sam. 6:10; 1 Chr. 13:13,14. Ark removed from, 2 Sam. 6:12; 1 Chr. 15:25. Appointed to sound with harps, 1 Chr. 15:21. Appointed to minister before the ark, 1 Chr. 16:4,5,37,38.

2. A doorkeeper of the temple, 1 Chr. 16:38.

3. A conservator of the vessels of the temple in time of Amaziah, 2 Chr. 25:24.

OBEDIENCE. Gen. 18:19. For I know him, that he will command his children and his household after him, and they shall keep the way of the LORD, to do justice and judgment; that the LORD may bring upon Abraham that which he hath spoken of him.

Ex. 19:5. If ye will obey my voice indeed, and keep my covenant, then ye shall be a peculiar treasure unto me above all people:

Ex. 20:6. And shewing mercy unto thousands of them that love me, and keep my commandments. Deut. 5:10.

Ex. 24:7. And he took the book of the covenant, and read in the audience of the people: and they said, All that the LORD hath said will we do, and be obedient. Josh. 24:24.

Num. 9:23. At the commandment of the LORD they rested in the tents, and at the commandment of the LORD they journeyed: they kept the charge of the LORD, at the commandment of the LORD by the hand of Moses.

Num. 14:24. But my servant Caleb, because he had another spirit with him, and hath followed me fully, him will I bring into the land whereinto he went; and his seed shall possess it. Josh. 14:6–14.

Josh. 22:2. And said unto them, Ye have kept all that Moses the servant of the LORD commanded you, and have obeyed my voice in all that I commanded you:

1 Kin. 3:14. And if thou wilt walk in my ways, to keep my statutes and my commandments, as thy father David did walk, then I will lengthen thy days.

2 Kin. 18:6. For he clave to the LORD, *and* departed not from following him, but kept his commandments, which the LORD commanded Moses.

2 Kin. 21:8. Neither will I make the feet of Israel move any more out of the land which I gave their fathers; only if they will observe to do according to all that I have commanded them, and according to all the law that my servant Moses commanded them.

Neh. 1:5. I beseech thee, O LORD God of heaven, the great and terrible God, that keepeth covenant and mercy for them that love him and observe his commandments:

Psa. 1:2. But his delight *is* in the law of the LORD; and in his law doth he meditate day and night.

Psa. 18:44. As soon as they hear of me, they shall obey me: the strangers shall submit themselves unto me.

Psa. 25:10. All the paths of the LORD *are* mercy and truth unto such as keep his covenant and his testimonies.

Psa. 99:7. He spake unto them in the cloudy pillar: they kept his testimonies, and the ordinance *that* he gave them.

Psa. 103:17. The mercy of the LORD *is* from everlasting to everlasting upon them that fear him, and his righteousness unto children's children; 18. To such as keep his covenant, and to those that remember his commandments to do them. 20. Bless the LORD, ye his angels, that excel in strength, that do his commandments, hearkening unto the voice of his word. 21. Bless ye the LORD, all *ye* his hosts; *ye* ministers of his, that do his pleasure.

Psa. 111:10. The fear of the LORD *is* the beginning of wisdom: a good understanding have all they that do *his commandments*:

Psa. 112:1. Blessed *is* the man *that* feareth the LORD, *that* delighteth greatly in his commandments.

Psa. 119:2. Blessed *are* they that keep his testimonies, *and that* seek him with the whole heart. 4. Thou hast commanded *us* to keep thy precepts diligently. 5. O that my ways were directed to keep thy statutes! 6. Then shall I not be ashamed, when I have respect unto all thy commandments. 8. I will keep thy statutes: O forsake me not utterly. 10. With my whole heart have I sought thee: O let me not wander from thy commandments. 15. I will meditate in thy precepts, and have respect unto thy ways. 16. I will delight myself in thy statutes: I will not forget thy word. 22. Remove from me reproach and contempt; for I have kept thy testimonies. 30. I have chosen the way of truth: thy judgments have I laid *before me.* 31. I have stuck unto thy testimonies: O LORD, put me not to shame. 33. Teach me, O LORD, the way of thy statutes; and I shall keep it *unto* the end. 44. So shall I keep thy law continually for ever and ever. 45. I will walk at liberty: for I seek thy precepts. 55. I have remembered thy name, O LORD, in the night, and have kept thy law. 56. This I had, because I kept thy precepts. 59. I thought on my ways, and turned my feet unto thy testimonies. 60. I made haste, and delayed not to keep thy commandments. 72. The law of thy mouth *is* better unto me than thousands of gold and silver. 77. Let thy tender mercies come unto me, that I may live: for thy law *is* my delight. 87. They had almost consumed me upon earth; but I forsook not thy precepts. 97. O how love I thy law! it *is* my meditation all the day. 100. I understand more than the ancients, because I keep thy precepts. 101. I have refrained my feet from every evil way, that I might keep thy word. 102. I have not departed from thy judgments: for thou hast taught me. 104. Through thy precepts I get understanding: therefore I hate every false way. 105. Thy word *is* a lamp unto my feet, and a light unto my path. 106. I have sworn, and I will perform *it,* that I will keep thy righteous judgments. 109. My soul *is* continually in my hand: yet do I not forget thy law. 112. I have inclined mine heart to perform thy statutes alway, *even unto* the end. 129. Thy testimonies *are* wonderful: therefore doth my soul keep them. 166. LORD, I have hoped for thy salvation, and done thy commandments. 167. My soul hath kept thy testimonies; and I love them exceedingly. 168. I have kept thy precepts and thy testimonies: for all my ways *are* before thee.

Psa. 143:10. Teach me to do thy will; for thou *art* my God: thy spirit *is* good; lead me into the land of uprightness.

Prov. 1:33. But whoso hearkeneth unto me shall dwell safely, and shall be quiet from fear of evil.

Prov. 19:16. He that keepeth the commandment keepeth his own soul; *but* he that despiseth his ways shall die.

Prov. 28:7. Whoso keepeth the law *is* a wise son: but he that is a companion of riotous *men* shameth his father.

Isa. 1:19. If ye be willing and obedient, ye shall eat the good of the land: Jer. 7:23.

Ezek. 18:19. Yet say ye, Why? doth not the son bear the iniquity of the father? When the son hath done that which is lawful and right, *and* hath kept all my statutes, and hath done them, he shall surely live.

Ezek. 33:14. Again, when I say unto the wicked, Thou shalt surely die; if he turn from his sin, and do that which is lawful and right; 15. *If* the wicked restore the pledge, give again that he had robbed, walk in the statutes of life, without committing iniquity; he shall surely live, he shall not die. 16. None of his sins that he hath committed shall be mentioned unto him: he hath done that which is lawful and right; he shall surely live.

Dan. 7:27. And the kingdom and dominion, and the greatness of the kingdom under the whole heaven, shall be given to the people of the saints of the most High, whose kingdom *is* an everlasting kingdom, and all dominions shall serve and obey him.

Matt. 5:19. Whosoever therefore shall break one of these *least* commandments, and shall teach men so, he shall be called the least in the kingdom of heaven: but whosoever shall do and teach *them,* the same shall be called great in the kingdom of heaven.

Matt. 6:24. No man can serve two masters: for either he will hate the one, and love the other; or else he will hold to the one, and despise the other. Ye cannot serve God and mammon.

Matt. 9:9. And as Jesus passed forth from thence, he saw a man, named Matthew, sitting at the receipt of custom: and he saith unto him, Follow me. And he arose, and followed him. Mark 2:14.

Matt. 12:50. For whosoever shall do the will of my Father which is in heaven, the same is my brother, and sister, and mother.

Matt. 13:23. But he that received seed into the good ground is he that heareth the word, and understandeth *it;* which also beareth fruit, and bringeth forth, some an hundredfold, some sixty, some thirty. *v.* 8; Mark 4:20; Luke 8:15.

Matt. 25:20. And so he that had received five talents came and brought other five talents, saying, Lord, thou deliveredst unto me five talents: behold, I have gained beside them five talents more. 21. His lord said unto him, Well done, *thou* good and faithful servant: thou hast been faithful over a few things, I will make thee ruler over many things: enter thou into the joy of thy lord. 22. He also that had received two talents came and said, Lord, thou deliveredst unto me two talents: behold, I have gained two other talents beside them. 23. His lord said unto him, Well done, good and faithful servant; thou hast been faithful over a few things, I will make thee ruler over many things; enter thou into the joy of thy lord.

Mark 3:35. Whosoever shall do the will of God, the same is my brother, and my sister, and mother.

Luke 1:6. They were both righteous before God, walking in all the commandments and ordinances of the Lord blameless.

Luke 6:46. Why call ye me, Lord, Lord,

and do not the things which I say? 47. Whosoever cometh to me, and heareth my sayings, and doeth them, I will shew you to whom he is like: 48. He is like a man which built an house, and digged deep, and laid the foundation on a rock: and when the flood arose, the stream beat vehemently upon that house, and could not shake it: for it was founded upon a rock.

Luke 8:21. And he answered and said unto them, My mother and my brethren are these which hear the word of God, and do it.

Luke 11:12. ¹ Thy will be done, as in heaven, so 'n earth. [¹ Omitted in R.V.]

28. But he said, Yea rather, blessed *are* they that hear the word of God, and keep it.

Luke 12:37. Blessed *are* those servants, whom the lord when he cometh shall find watching: verily I say unto you, that he shall gird himself, and make them to sit down to meat, and will come forth and serve them. 38. And if he shall come in the second watch, or come in the third watch, and find *them* so, blessed are those servants.

John 8:28. Then said Jesus unto them, When ye have lifted up the Son of man, then shall ye know that I am *he*, and *that* I do nothing of myself; but as my Father hath taught me, I speak these things. 51. Verily, verily, I say unto you, If a man keep my saying, he shall never see death.

John 9:4. I must work the works of him that sent me, while it is day: the night cometh, when no man can work.

John 10:27. My sheep hear my voice, and I know them, and they follow me:

John 14:15. If ye love me, keep my commandments. 23. If a man love me, he will keep my words: and my Father will love him, and we will come unto him, and make our abode with him. 31. But that the world may know that I love the Father; and as the Father gave me commandment, even so I do.

John 15:10. If ye keep my commandments, ye shall abide in my love: even as I have kept my Father's commandments, and abide in his love. 14. Ye are my friends, if ye do whatsoever I command you. 16. Ye have not chosen me, but I have chosen you, and ordained you, that ye should go and bring forth fruit, and *that* your fruit should remain:

Acts 4:19. But Peter and John answered and said unto them, Whether it be right in the sight of God to hearken unto you more than unto God, judge ye.

Acts 5:29. Then Peter and the *other* apostles answered and said, We ought to obey God rather than men.

Rom. 6:17. But God be thanked, that ye were the servants of sin, but ye have obeyed from the heart that form of doctrine which was delivered you.

Eph. 2:10. We are his workmanship, created in Christ Jesus unto good works, which God hath before ordained that we should walk in them.

Phil. 2:12. Wherefore, my beloved, as ye have always obeyed, not as in my presence only, but now much more in my absence, work out your own salvation with fear and trembling.

Heb. 10:7. Then said I, Lo, I come (in the volume of the book it is written of me,) to do thy will, O God.

Jas. 2:10. Whosoever shall keep the whole law, and yet offend in one *point*, he is guilty of all. 11. For he that said, Do not commit adultery, said also, Do not kill. Now if thou commit no adultery, yet if thou kill, thou art become a transgressor of the law. 12. So speak ye, and so do, as they that shall be judged by the law of liberty.

1 Pet. 1:2. Elect according to the foreknowledge of God the Father, through sanctification of the Spirit, unto obedience and sprinkling of the blood of Jesus Christ: 14. As obedient children, not fashioning yourselves according to the former lusts in your ignorance:

1 John 2:3. Hereby we do know that we know him, if we keep his commandments. 4. He that saith, I know him, and keepeth not his commandments, is a liar, and the truth is not in him. 5. But whoso keepeth his word, in him verily is the love of God perfected: hereby know we that we are in him. 6. He that saith he abideth in him ought himself also so to walk, even as he walked. 17. He that doeth the will of God abideth for ever.

1 John 3:22. Whatsoever we ask, we receive of him, because we keep his commandments, and do those things that are pleasing in his sight. 24. He that keepeth his commandments dwelleth in him, and he in him.

1 John 5:2. By this we know that we love the children of God, when we love God, and keep his commandments. 3. This is the love of God, that we keep his commandments: and his commandments are not grievous.

2 John 6. This is love, that we walk after his commandments. This is the commandment, That, as ye have heard from the beginning, ye should walk in it. 9. Whosoever transgresseth, and abideth not in the doctrine of Christ, hath not God. He that abideth in the doctrine of Christ, he hath both the Father and the Son.

Rev. 12:17. And the dragon . . . went to make war with the remnant of her seed, which keep the commandments of God, and have the testimony of Jesus Christ.

Rev. 22:7. Behold, I come quickly: blessed *is* he that keepeth the sayings of the prophecy of this book. 14. Blessed *are* they that do his commandments, that they may have right to the tree of life, and may enter in through the gates into the city.

See BLESSINGS, CONTINGENT UPON OBEDIENCE.

ENJOINED: Gen. 17:9. And God said unto Abraham, Thou shalt keep my covenant therefore, thou, and thy seed after thee in their generations.

Ex. 23:22. But if thou shalt indeed obey his voice, and do all that I speak; then I will be an enemy unto thine enemies, and an adversary unto thine adversaries.

Lev. 19:36. I *am* the LORD your God, which brought you out of the land of Egypt. 37. Therefore shall ye observe all my statutes, and all my judgments, and do them: *v.* 19.

Lev. 20:8. Ye shall keep my statutes, and do them: I *am* the LORD which sanctify you. 22. Keep all my statutes, and all my judgments, and do them: that the land, whither I bring you to dwell therein, spue you not out. Lev. 22:31; Deut. 5:1,32.

Lev. 26:3. If ye walk in my statutes, and keep my commandments, and do them; 4. Then I will give you rain in due season, and the land shall yield her increase, and the trees of the field shall yield their fruit. 5. And your threshing shall reach unto the vintage, and the vintage shall reach unto the sowing time: and ye shall eat your bread to the full, and dwell in your land safely. 6. And I will give peace in the land, and ye shall lie down, and none shall make *you* afraid: and I will rid evil beasts out of the land, neither shall the sword go through your land. 7. And ye shall chase your enemies, and they shall fall before you by the sword. 8. And five of you shall chase an hundred, and an hundred of you shall put ten thousand to flight: and your enemies shall fall before you by the sword. 9. For I will have respect unto you, and make you fruitful, and multiply you, and establish my covenant with you. 10. And ye shall eat old store, and bring forth the old because of the new. 11. And I will set my tabernacle among you: and my soul shall not abhor you. 12. And I will walk among you, and will be your God, and ye shall be my people. 13. I *am* the LORD your God, which brought you forth out of the land of Egypt, that ye should not be their bondmen; and I have broken the bands of your yoke, and made you go upright.

Num. 15:38. Speak unto the children of Israel, and bid them that they make them fringes in the borders of their garments throughout their generations, and that they put upon the fringe of the borders a riband of blue: 39. And it shall be unto you for a fringe, that ye may look upon it, and remember all the commandments of the LORD, and do them; and that ye seek not after your own heart and your own eyes, after which ye use to go a whoring: 40. That ye may remember, and do all my commandments, and be holy unto your God.

Deut. 4:1. Now therefore hearken, O Israel, unto the statutes and unto the judgments, which I teach you, for to do *them*, that ye may live, and go in and possess the land which the LORD God of your fathers giveth you. 2. Ye shall not add unto the word which I command you, neither shall ye diminish *ought* from it, that ye may keep the commandments of the LORD your God which I command you. 5. Behold, I have taught you statutes and judgments, even as the LORD my God commanded me, that ye should do so in the land whither ye go to possess it. 6. Keep therefore and do *them;* for this *is* your wisdom and your understanding in the sight of the nations, which shall hear all these statutes, and say, Surely this great nation *is* a wise and understanding people. 9. Only take heed to thyself, and keep thy soul diligently, lest thou forget the things which thine eyes have seen, and lest they depart from thy heart all the days of thy life; but teach them thy sons, and thy sons' sons; 10. *Specially* the day that thou stoodest before the LORD thy God in Horeb, when the LORD said unto me, Gather me the people together, and I will make them hear my words, that they may learn to fear me all the days that they shall live upon the earth, and *that* they may teach their children. 39. Know therefore this day, and consider *it* in thine heart, that the LORD he *is* God in heaven above, and upon the earth beneath: *there is* none else. 40. Thou shalt keep therefore his statutes, and his commandments, which I command thee this day, that it may go well with thee, and with thy children after thee, and that thou mayest prolong *thy* days upon the earth, which the LORD thy God giveth thee, for ever. *vs.* 1–40.

Deut. 5:1. And Moses called all Israel, and said unto them, Hear, O Israel, the statutes and judgments, which I speak in your ears this day, that ye may learn them, and keep and do them. 32. Ye shall observe to do therefore as the LORD your God hath commanded you: ye shall not turn aside to the right hand or to the left. 33. Ye shall walk in all the ways which the LORD your God hath commanded you, that ye may live, and *that it may be* well with you, and *that* ye may prolong *your* days in the land which ye shall possess. *vs.* 1–33.

Deut. 6:1. Now these *are* the commandments, the statutes, and the judgments, which the LORD your God commanded to teach you, that ye might do *them* in the land whither ye go to possess it: 2. That thou mightest fear the LORD thy God, to keep all his statutes and his commandments, which I command thee, thou, and thy son, and thy son's son, all the days of thy life; and that thy days may be prolonged. 3. Hear therefore, O Israel, and observe to do *it;* that it may be well with thee, and that ye may increase mightily, as the LORD God of thy fathers hath promised thee, in the land that floweth with milk and honey. 4. Hear, O Israel: The LORD our God *is* one LORD: 5. And thou shalt love the LORD thy God with all thine heart, and with all thy soul, and with all thy might. 6. And these words, which I command thee this day, shall be in thine heart: 7. And thou shalt teach them diligently unto thy children, and shalt talk of them when thou sittest in thine house, and when thou walkest by the way, and when thou liest down, and when thou risest up. 8. And thou shalt bind them for a sign upon thine hand, and they shall be as frontlets between thine eyes. 9. And thou shalt write them upon the posts of thy house, and on thy gates. *vs.* 1-25.

Deut. 8:1. All the commandments which I command thee this day shall ye observe to do, that ye may live, and multiply, and go in and possess the land which the LORD sware unto your fathers. 2. And thou shalt remember all the way which the LORD thy God led thee these forty years in the wilderness, to humble thee, *and* to prove thee, to know what *was* in thine heart, whether thou wouldest keep his commandments, or no. 3. And he humbled thee, and suffered thee to hunger, and fed thee with manna, which thou knewest not, neither did thy fathers know; that he might make thee know that man doth not live by bread only, but by every *word* that proceedeth out of the mouth of the LORD doth man live. 4. Thy raiment waxed not old upon thee, neither did thy foot swell, these forty years. 5. Thou shalt also consider in thine heart, that, as a man chasteneth his son, *so* the LORD thy God chasteneth thee. 6. Therefore thou shalt keep the commandments of the LORD thy God, to walk in his ways, and to fear him. 11. Beware that thou forget not the LORD thy God, in not keeping his commandments, and his judgments, and his statutes, which I command thee this day: 12. Lest *when* thou hast eaten and art full, and hast built goodly houses, and dwelt *therein;* 13. And *when* thy herds and thy flocks multiply, and thy silver and thy gold is multiplied, and all that thou hast is multiplied; 14. Then thine heart be lifted up, and thou forget the LORD thy God, which brought thee forth out of the land of Egypt, from the house of bondage; 16. Who fed thee in the wilderness with manna, which thy fathers knew not, that he might humble thee, and that he might prove thee, to do thee good at thy latter end; 17. And thou say in thine heart, My power and the might of *mine* hand hath gotten me this wealth. 18. But thou shalt remember the LORD thy God: for *it is* he that giveth thee power to get wealth, that he may establish his covenant which he sware unto thy fathers, as *it is* this day. 19. And it shall be, if thou do at all forget the LORD thy God, and walk after other gods, and serve them, and worship them, I testify against you this day that ye shall surely perish. 20. As the nations which the LORD destroyeth before your face, so shall ye perish; because ye would not be obedient unto the voice of the LORD your God.

Deut. 10:12. And now, Israel, what doth the LORD thy God require of thee, but to fear the LORD thy God, to walk in all his ways, and to love him, and to serve the LORD thy God with all thy heart and with all thy soul, 13. To keep the commandments of the LORD, and his statutes, which I command thee this day for thy good?

Deut. 11:1. Therefore thou shalt love the LORD thy God, and keep his charge, and his statutes, and his judgments, and his commandments, alway. 2. And know ye this day: for *I speak* not with your children which have not known, and which have not seen the chastisement of the LORD your God, his greatness, his mighty hand, and his stretched out arm, 3. And his miracles, and his acts, which he did in the midst of Egypt unto Pharaoh the king of Egypt, and unto all his land; 8. Therefore shall ye keep all the commandments which I command you this day, that ye may be strong, and go in and possess the land, whither ye go to possess it; 9. And that ye may prolong *your* days in the land, which the LORD sware unto your fathers to give unto them and to their seed, a land that floweth with milk and honey. 13. And it shall come to pass, if ye shall hearken diligently unto my commandments which I command you this day, to love the LORD your God, and to serve him with all your heart and with all your soul, 14. That I will give *you* the rain of your land in his due season, the first rain and the latter rain, that thou mayest gather in thy corn, and thy wine, and thine oil. 15. And I will send grass in thy fields for thy cattle, that thou mayest eat and be full. 16. Take heed to yourselves, that your heart be not deceived, and ye turn aside, and serve other gods, and worship them; 17. And *then* the LORD's wrath be kindled against you, and he shut up the heaven, that there be no rain, and that the land yield not her fruit; and *lest* ye perish quickly from off the good land which the LORD giveth you. 18. Therefore shall ye lay up these my words in your heart and in your soul, and bind them for a sign upon your hand, that they may be as frontlets between your eyes. 19. And ye shall teach them your children, speaking of them when thou sittest in thine house, and when thou walkest by the way, when thou liest down, and when thou risest up. 20. And thou shalt write them upon the door posts of thine house, and upon thy gates: 21. That your days may be multiplied, and the days of your children, in the land which the LORD sware unto your fathers to give them, as the days of heaven upon the earth. 22. For if ye shall diligently keep all these commandments which I command you, to do them, to love the LORD your God, to walk in all his ways, and to cleave unto him; 23. Then will the LORD drive out all these nations from before you, and ye shall possess greater nations and mightier than yourselves. 24. Every place whereon the soles of your feet shall tread shall be your's: from the wilderness and Lebanon, from the river, the river Euphrates, even unto the uttermost sea shall your coast be. 25. There shall no man be able to stand before you : *for* the LORD your God shall lay the fear of you and the dread of you upon all the land that ye shall tread upon, as he hath said unto you. 26. Behold, I set before you this day a blessing and a curse; 27. A blessing, if ye obey the commandments of the LORD your God, which I command you this day : 28. And a curse, if ye will not obey the commandments of the LORD your God, but turn aside out of the way which I command you this day, to go after other gods, which ye have not known. 32. And ye shall observe to do all the statutes and judgments which I set before you this day.

Deut. 13:4. Ye shall walk after the LORD your God, and fear him, and keep his commandments, and obey his voice, and ye shall serve him, and cleave unto him.

Deut. 26:16. This day the LORD thy God hath commanded thee to do these statutes and judgments : thou shalt therefore keep and do them with all thine heart, and with all thy soul. 17. Thou hast avouched the LORD this day to be thy God, and to walk in his ways, and to keep his statutes, and his commandments, and his judgments, and to hearken unto his voice : 18. And the LORD hath avouched thee this day to be his peculiar people. as he hath promised thee, and that *thou* shouldest keep all his commandments ;

Deut. 27:1. And Moses with the elders of Israel commanded the people, saying, Keep all the commandments which I command you this day. 2. And it shall be on the day when ye shall pass over Jordan unto the land which the LORD thy God giveth thee, that thou shalt set thee up great stones, and plaister them with plaister : 3. And thou shalt write upon them all the words of this law, when thou art passed over, that thou mayest go in unto the land which the LORD thy God giveth thee, a land that floweth with milk and honey ; as the LORD God of thy fathers hath promised thee. 4. Therefore it shall be when ye be gone over Jordan, *that* ye shall set up these stones, which I command you this day, in mount Ebal, and thou shalt plaister them with plaister. 5. And there shalt thou build an altar unto the LORD thy God, an altar of stones: thou shalt not lift up *any* iron *tool* upon them. 6. Thou shalt build the altar of the LORD thy God of whole stones: and thou shalt offer burnt offerings thereon unto the LORD thy God : 7. And thou shalt offer peace offerings, and shalt eat there, and rejoice before the LORD thy God. 8. And thou shalt write upon the stones all the words of this law very plainly. 9. And Moses and the priests the Levites spake unto all Israel, saying, Take heed, and hearken, O Israel ; this day thou art become the people of the LORD thy God. 10. Thou shalt therefore obey the voice of the LORD thy God, and do his com-

mandments and his statutes, which I command thee this day.

Deut. 28:1. And it shall come to pass, if thou shalt hearken diligently unto the voice of the LORD thy God, to observe *and* to do all his commandments which I command thee this day, that the LORD thy God will set thee on high above all nations of the earth : 2. And all these blessings shall come on thee, and overtake thee, if thou shalt hearken unto the voice of the LORD thy God. 3. Blessed *shalt* thou *be* in the city, and blessed *shalt* thou *be* in the field. 4. Blessed *shall be* the fruit of thy body, and the fruit of thy ground, and the fruit of thy cattle, the increase of thy kine, and the flocks of thy sheep. 5. Blessed *shall be* thy basket and thy store. 6. Blessed *shalt* thou *be* when thou comest in, and blessed *shalt* thou *be* when thou goest out. 7. The LORD shall cause thine enemies that rise up against thee to be smitten before thy face : they shall come out against thee one way, and flee before thee seven ways. 8. The LORD shall command the blessing upon thee in thy storehouses, and in all that thou settest thine hand unto; and he shall bless thee in the land which the LORD thy God giveth thee. 9. The LORD shall establish thee an holy people unto himself, as he hath sworn unto thee, if thou shalt keep the commandments of the LORD thy God, and walk in his ways. 10. And all people of the earth shall see that thou art called by the name of the LORD ; and they shall be afraid of thee. 11. And the LORD shall make thee plenteous in goods, in the fruit of thy body, and in the fruit of thy cattle, and in the fruit of thy ground, in the land which the LORD sware unto thy fathers to give thee. 12. The LORD shall open unto thee his good treasure, the heaven to give the rain unto thy land in his season, and to bless all the work of thine hand : and thou shalt lend unto many nations, and thou shalt not borrow. 13. And the LORD shall make thee the head, and not the tail; and thou shalt be above only, and thou shalt not be beneath; if that thou hearken unto the commandments of the LORD thy God, which I command thee this day, to observe and to do *them:* 14. And thou shalt not go aside from any of the words which I command thee this day, *to* the right hand, or *to* the left, to go after other gods to serve them. 15. But it shall come to pass, if thou wilt not hearken unto the voice of the LORD thy God, to observe to do all his commandments and his statutes which I command thee this day ; that all these curses shall come upon thee, and overtake thee : 16. Cursed *shalt* thou *be* in the city, and cursed *shalt* thou *be* in the field. 17. Cursed *shall be* thy basket and thy store. 18. Cursed *shall be* the fruit of thy body, and the fruit of thy land, the increase of thy kine, and the flocks of thy sheep. 19. Cursed *shalt* thou *be* when thou comest in, and cursed *shalt* thou *be* when thou goest out. 20. The LORD shall send upon thee cursing, vexation, and rebuke, in all that thou settest thine hand unto for to do, until thou be destroyed, and until thou perish quickly; because of the wickedness of thy doings, whereby thou hast forsaken me. 21. The LORD shall make the pestilence cleave unto thee, until he have consumed thee from off the land, whither thou goest to possess it. 22. The LORD shall smite thee with a consumption, and with a fever, and with an inflammation, and with an extreme burning, and with the sword, and with blasting, and with mildew; and they shall pursue thee until thou perish. 23. And thy heaven that *is* over thy head shall be brass, and the earth that *is* under thee *shall be* iron. 24. The LORD shall make the rain of thy land powder and dust: from heaven shall it come down upon thee, until thou be destroyed. 25. The LORD shall cause thee to be smitten before thine enemies: thou shalt go out one way against them, and flee seven ways before them: and shalt be removed into all the kingdoms of the earth. 26. And thy carcase shall be meat unto all fowls of the air, and unto the beasts of the earth, and no man shall fray *them* away. 27. The LORD will smite thee with the botch of Egypt, and with the emerods, and with the scab, and with the itch, whereof thou canst not be healed. 28. The LORD shall smite thee with madness, and blindness, and astonishment of heart. 29. And thou shalt grope at noonday, as the blind gropeth in darkness, and thou shalt not prosper in thy ways: and thou shalt be only oppressed and spoiled evermore, and no man shall save *thee*. 30. Thou shalt betroth a wife, and another man shall lie with her: thou shalt build an house, and thou shalt not dwell therein: thou shalt plant a vineyard, and shalt not gather the grapes thereof. 31. Thine ox *shall be* slain before thine eyes, and thou shalt not eat thereof: thine ass *shall be* violently taken away from before thy face, and shall not be restored to thee: thy sheep *shall be* given unto thine enemies, and thou shalt have none to rescue *them*. 32. Thy sons and thy daughters *shall be* given unto another people, and thine eyes shall look, and fail *with longing* for them all the day long: and *there shall be* no might in thine hand. 33. The fruit of thy land, and all thy labours, shall a nation which thou knowest not eat up; and thou shalt be only oppressed and crushed alway: 34. So that thou shalt be mad for the sight of thine eyes which thou shalt see. 35. The LORD shall smite thee in the knees, and in the legs, with a sore botch that cannot be healed, from the sole of thy foot unto the top of thy head. 36. The LORD shall bring thee, and thy king which thou shalt set over thee, unto a nation which neither thou nor thy fathers have known; and there shalt thou serve other gods, wood and stone. 37. And thou shalt become an astonishment, a proverb, and a byword, among all nations whither the LORD shall lead thee. 38. Thou shalt carry much seed out into the field, and shalt gather *but* little in; for the locust shall consume it. 39. Thou shalt plant vineyards, and dress *them*, but shalt neither drink *of* the wine, nor gather *the grapes;* for the worms shall eat them. 40. Thou shalt have olive trees throughout all thy coasts, but thou shalt not anoint *thyself* with the oil; for thine olive shall cast *his fruit.* 41. Thou shalt beget sons and daughters, but thou shalt not enjoy them; for they shall go into captivity. 42. All thy trees and fruit of thy land shall the locust consume. 43. The stranger that *is* within thee shall get up above thee very high; and thou shalt come down very low. 44. He shall lend to thee, and thou shalt not lend to him: he shall be the head, and thou shalt be the tail. 45. Moreover all these curses shall come upon thee, and shall pursue thee, and overtake thee, till thou be destroyed; because thou hearkenedst not unto the voice of the LORD thy God, to keep his commandments and his statutes which he commanded thee. 46. And they shall be upon thee for a sign and for a wonder, and upon thy seed for ever. 47. Because thou servedst not the LORD thy God with joyfulness, and with gladness of heart, for the abundance of all *things;* 48. Therefore shalt thou serve thine enemies which the LORD shall send against thee, in hunger, and in thirst, and in nakedness, and in want of all *things:* and he shall put a yoke of iron upon thy neck, until he have destroyed thee. 49. The LORD shall bring a nation against thee from far, from the end of the earth, *as swift* as the eagle flieth: a nation whose tongue thou shalt not understand; 50. A nation of fierce countenance, which shall not regard the person of the old, nor shew favour to the young: 51. And he shall eat the fruit of thy cattle, and the fruit of thy land, until thou be destroyed: which *also* shall not leave thee *either* corn, wine, or oil, *or* the increase of thy kine, or flocks of thy sheep, until he have destroyed thee. 52. And he shall besiege thee in all thy gates, until thy high and fenced walls come down, wherein thou trustedst, throughout all thy land: and he shall besiege thee in all thy gates throughout all thy land, which the LORD thy God hath given thee. 53. And thou shalt eat the fruit of thine own body, the flesh of thy sons and of thy daughters, which the LORD thy God hath given thee, in the siege, and in the straitness, wherewith thine enemies shall distress thee: 54. *So that* the man *that is* tender among you, and very delicate, his eye shall be evil toward his brother, and toward the wife of his bosom, and toward the remnant of his children which he shall leave: 55. So that he will not give to any of them of the flesh of his children whom he shall eat: because he hath nothing left him in the siege, and in the straitness, wherewith thine enemies shall distress thee in all thy gates. 56. The tender and delicate woman among you, which would not adventure to set the sole of her foot upon the ground for delicateness and tenderness, her eye shall be evil toward the husband of her bosom, and toward her son, and toward her daughter, 57. And toward her young one that cometh out from between her feet, and toward her children which she shall bear : for she shall eat them for want of all *things* secretly in the siege and straitness, wherewith thine enemy shall distress thee in thy gates. 58. If thou wilt not observe to do all the words of this law that are written in this book, that thou mayest fear this glorious and fearful name, THE LORD THY GOD ; 59. Then the LORD will make thy plagues wonderful, and the plagues of thy seed, *even* great plagues, and of long continuance, and sore sicknesses, and of long continuance. 60. Moreover, he will bring upon thee all the diseases of Egypt, which thou wast afraid of ; and they shall cleave unto thee. 61. Also every sickness, and every plague, which *is* not written in the book of this law, them will the LORD bring upon thee, until thou be destroyed. 62. And ye shall be left few in number, whereas ye were as the stars of heaven for multitude ; because thou wouldest not obey the voice of the LORD thy God. 63. And it shall come to pass, *that* as the LORD rejoiced over you to do you good, and to multiply you ; so the LORD will rejoice over you to destroy you, and to bring you to nought ; and ye shall be plucked from off the land whither thou goest to possess it. 64. And the LORD shall scatter thee among all people, from the one end of the earth even unto tne other ; and there thou shalt serve other gods, which neither thou nor thy fathers have known, *even* wood and stone. 65. And among these nations shalt thou find no ease, neither shall the sole of thy foot have rest : but the LORD shall give thee there a trembling heart, and failing of eyes, and sorrow of mind : 66. And thy life shall hang in doubt before thee ; and thou shalt fear day and night, and shalt have none assurance of thy life : 67. In the morning thou shalt say, Would God it were even ! and at even thou shalt say, Would God it were morning ! for the fear of thine heart wherewith thou shalt fear, and for the sight of thine eyes which thou shalt see. 68. And the LORD shall bring thee into Egypt again with ships, by the way whereof I spake unto thee, Thou shalt see it no more again : and there ye shall be sold unto your enemies for bondmen and bondwomen, and no man shall buy *you*.

Deut. 32:46. And he [Moses] said unto them, Set your hearts unto all the words which I testify among you this day, which ye shall command your children to observe to do, all the words of this law.

Josh. 22:5. Take diligent heed to do the commandment and the law, which Moses the servant of the LORD charged you, to love the LORD your God, and to walk in all his ways, and to keep his commandments, and to cleave unto him, and to serve him with all your heart and with all your soul.

Josh. 23:6. Be ye therefore very courageous to keep and to do all that is written in the book of the law of Moses, that ye turn not aside therefrom *to* the right hand or *to* the left ; 7. That ye come not among these nations, these that remain among you ; neither make mention of the name of their gods, nor cause to swear *by them*, neither serve them, nor bow yourselves unto them :

Josh. 24:14. Fear the LORD, and serve him in sincerity and in truth : and put away the gods which your fathers served, . . . and serve ye the LORD. 15. If it seem evil unto you to serve the LORD, choose you this day whom ye will serve ;

1 Sam. 12:24. Only fear the LORD, and serve him in truth with all your heart : for consider how great *things* he hath done for you.

1 Sam. 15:22. Samuel said, Hath the LORD *as great* delight in burnt offerings and sacrifices, as in obeying the voice of the LORD ? Behold, to obey *is* better than sacrifice, *and* to hearken than the fat of rams.

2 Kin. 17:37. And the statutes, and the ordinances, and the law, and the commandment, which he wrote for you, ye shall observe to do for evermore ; and he shall not fear other gods. 38. And the covenant that I have made with you ye shall not forget ; neither shall ye fear other gods.

1 Chr. 16:15. Be ye mindful always of his covenant ; the word *which* he commanded to a thousand generations ;

1 Chr. 28:9. And thou, Solomon my son, know thou the God of thy father, and serve him with a perfect heart and with a willing mind : for the LORD searcheth all hearts, and understandeth all the imaginations of the thoughts : if thou seek him, he will be found of thee ; but if thou forsake him, he will cast thee off for ever. 10. Take heed now ; for the LORD hath chosen thee to build a house for the sanctuary : be strong, and do *it*. 20. And David said to Solomon his son, Be strong and of good courage, and do *it :* fear not, nor be dismayed, for the LORD God, *even* my God, *will be* with thee ; he will not fail thee, nor forsake thee, until thou hast finished all the work for the service of the house of the LORD.

Ezra 7:10. For Ezra had prepared his heart to seek the law of the LORD, and to do *it*, and to teach in Israel statutes and judgments. 23. Whatsoever is commanded by the God of heaven, let it be diligently done for the house of the God of heaven : for why should there be wrath against the realm of the king and his sons ?

Psa. 76:11. Vow, and pay unto the LORD your God : let all that be round about him bring presents unto him that ought to be feared.

Eccl. 12:13. Let us hear the conclusion of the whole matter : Fear God, and keep his commandments: for this *is* the whole *duty* of man.

Jer. 26:13. Therefore now amend your ways and your doings, and obey the voice of the LORD your God ; and the LORD will repent him of the evil that he hath pronounced against you.

Jer. 38:20. But Jeremiah said, They shall not deliver *thee.* Obey, I beseech thee, the voice of the LORD, which I speak unto thee : so it shall be well unto thee, and thy soul shall live.

Mal. 4:4. Remember ye the law of Moses my servant, which I commanded unto him in Horeb for all Israel, *with* the statutes and judgments.

Matt. 9:9. And as Jesus passed forth from thence, he saw a man, named Matthew, sitting at the receipt of custom : and he saith unto him, Follow me. And he arose and followed him. Mark 2:14.

Matt. 19:17. If thou wilt enter into life, keep the commandments. 29. And every one that hath forsaken houses, or brethren, or sisters, or father, or mother, or wife, or children, or lands, for my name's sake, shall receive an hundredfold, and shall inherit everlasting life.

John 12:26. If any man serve me, let him follow me ; and where I am, there shall also my servant be : if any man serve me, him will *my* Father honour.

John 13:17. If ye know these things, happy are ye if ye do them.

John 14:15. If ye love me, keep my commandments. 21. He that hath my commandments, and keepeth them, he it is that loveth me : and he that loveth me shall be loved of my Father, and I will love him, and will manifest myself to him.

Gal. 3:10. For as many as are of the works of the law are under the curse : for it is written, Cursed *is* every one that continueth not in all things which are written in the book of the law to do them. 12. And the law is not of faith : but, The man that doeth them shall live in them.

Gal. 5:3. I testify again to every man that is circumcised, that he is a debtor to do the whole law.

Eph. 4:1. I therefore, the prisoner of the Lord, beseech you that ye walk worthy of the vocation wherewith ye are called, 17. Henceforth walk not as other Gentiles walk, in the vanity of their mind,

Eph. 6:6. As the servants of Christ, doing the will of God from the heart; 7. With good will doing service, as to the Lord, and not to men: 8. Whatsoever good thing any man doeth, the same shall he receive of the Lord, whether *he be* bond or free.

Phil. 2:12. Wherefore, my beloved, as ye have always obeyed, not as in my presence only, but now much more in my absence,

work out your own salvation with fear and trembling.

1 Tim. 6:14. That thou keep *this* commandment without spot, unrebukeable, until the appearing of our Lord Jesus Christ : 18. That they do good, that they be rich in good works, ready to distribute, willing to communicate :

Heb. 13:16. To do good and to communicate forget not : for with such sacrifices God is well pleased.

Jas. 1:22. But be ye doers of the word, and not hearers only, deceiving your own selves. 23. For if any be a hearer of the word, and not a doer, he is like unto a man beholding his natural face in a glass : 24. For he beholdeth himself, and goeth his way, and straightway forgetteth what manner of man he was. 25. But whoso looketh into the perfect law of liberty, and continueth *therein*, he being not a forgetful hearer, but a doer of the w rk, this man shall be blessed in his deed.

See COMMANDMENTS ; DUTY ; LAW.

EXEMPLIFIED : Gen. 6:9. Noah was a just man, *and* perfect in his generations, *and* Noah walked with God.

Num. 9:23. At the commandment of the LORD they rested in the tents, and at the commandment of the LORD they journeyed : they kept the charge of the LORD, at the commandment of the LORD by the hand of Moses.

Num. 14:24. But my servant Caleb, because he hath another spirit with him, and hath followed me fully, him will I bring into the land whereinto he went ; and his seed shall possess it. Josh. 14:6-14.

2 Kin. 18:6. For he clave to the LORD, *and* departed not from following him, but kept his commandments, which the LORD commanded Moses.

2 Kin. 20:3. I beseech thee, O LORD, remember now how I have walked before thee in truth and with a perfect heart, and have done *that which is* good in thy sight.

2 Chr. 24:16. And they buried him in the city of David among the kings, because he had done good in Israel, both toward God, and toward his house.

2 Chr. 31:20. Thus did Hezekiah throughout all Judah, and wrought *that which was* good and right and truth before the LORD his God. 21. And in every work that he began in the service of the house of God, and in the law, and in the commandments, to seek his God, he did *it* with all his heart, and prospered.

Ezra 7:10. For Ezra had prepared his heart to seek the law of the LORD, and to do *it*, and to teach in Israel statutes and judgments.

Neh. 7:2. That I gave my brother Hanani, and Hananiah the ruler of the palace, charge over Jerusalem : for he *was* a faithful man, and feared God above many.

Job 1:8. And the LORD said unto Satan, Hast thou considered my servant Job, that *there is* none like him in the earth, a perfect and an upright man, one that feareth God, and escheweth evil?

Psa. 17:3. Thou hast proved mine heart; thou hast visited *me* in the night; thou hast tried me, *and* shalt find nothing; I am purposed *that* my mouth shall not transgress.

Psa. 26:3. Thy lovingkindness *is* before mine eyes: and I have walked in thy truth. 4. I have not sat with vain persons, neither will I go in with dissemblers. 5. I have hated the congregation of evil doers; and will not sit with the wicked. 6. I will wash mine hands in innocency: so will I compass thine altar, O Lord:

Psa. 99:7. He spake unto them in the cloudy pillar; they kept his testimonies, and the ordinance *that* he gave them.

Psa. 101:2. I will behave myself wisely in a perfect way. O when wilt thou come unto me? I will walk within my house with a perfect heart. 3. I will set no wicked thing before mine eyes: I hate the work of them that turn aside: *it* shall not cleave to me.

Psa. 106:30. Then stood up Phinehas, and executed judgment: and *so* the plague was stayed. 31. And that was counted unto him for righteousness unto all generations for evermore.

Psa. 119:30. I have chosen the way of truth: thy judgments have I laid *before* me. 31. I have stuck unto thy testimonies: O Lord, put me not to shame. 40. Behold, I have longed after thy precepts: quicken me in thy righteousness. 44. So shall I keep thy law continually for ever and ever. 45. And I will walk at liberty; for I seek thy precepts. 47. And I will delight myself in thy commandments, which I have loved. 48 My hands also will I lift up unto thy commandments, which I have loved; and I will meditate in thy statutes. 51. The proud have had me greatly in derision: *yet* have I not declined from thy law. 54. Thy statutes have been my songs in the house of my pilgrimage. 55. I have remembered thy name, O Lord, in the night, and have kept thy law. 56. This I had, because I kept thy precepts. 59. I thought on my ways, and turned my feet unto thy testimonies. 60. I made haste, and delayed not to keep thy commandments. 67. Before I was afflicted I went astray: but now have I kept thy word. 69. The proud have forged a lie against me: *but* I will keep thy precepts with *my* whole heart. 100. I understand more than the ancients, because I keep thy precepts. 101. I have refrained my feet from every evil way, that I might keep thy word. 102. I have not departed from thy judgments: for thou hast taught me. 105. Thy word *is* a lamp unto my feet, and a light unto my path. 106. I have sworn, and I will perform *it*, that I will keep thy righteous judgments. 110. The wicked have laid a snare for me: yet I erred not from thy precepts. 112. I have inclined mine heart to

perform thy statutes alway, *even unto* the end. 166. Lord, I have hoped for thy salvation, and done thy commandments. 167. My soul hath kept thy testimonies; and I love them exceedingly. 168. I have kept thy precepts and thy testimonies: for all my ways *are* before thee.

Acts 23:1. And Paul, earnestly beholding the council, said, Men *and* brethren, I have lived in all good conscience before God until this day.

Acts 24:16. And herein do I exercise myself, to have always a conscience void of offence toward God, and *toward* men.

Rom. 6:17. But God be thanked, that ['whereas, *R. V.*] ye were the servants of sin, . . . ye have obeyed from the heart that form of doctrine which was delivered you.

2 Cor. 1:12. For our rejoicing is this, the testimony of our conscience, that in simplicity and godly sincerity, not with fleshly wisdom, but by the grace of God, we have had our conversation in the world, and more abundantly to you-ward.

2 Cor. 6:3. Giving no offence in any thing, that the ministry be not blamed: 4. But in all *things* approving ourselves as the ministers of God, in much patience,

Phil. 3:7. But what things were gain to me, those I counted loss for Christ. 8. Yea doubtless, and I count all things *but* loss for the excellency of the knowledge of Christ Jesus my Lord: for whom I have suffered the loss of all things, and do count them *but* dung, that I may win Christ, 9. And be found in him, not having mine own righteousness, which is of the law, but that which is through the faith of Christ, the righteousness which is of God by faith: 10. That I may know him, and the power of his resurrection, and the fellowship of his sufferings, being made conformable unto his death; 11. If by any means I might attain unto the resurrection of the dead. 12. Not as though I had already attained, either were already perfect: but I follow after, if that I may apprehend that for which also I am apprehended of Christ Jesus. 13. Brethren, I count not myself to have apprehended: but *this* one thing *I do*, forgetting those things which are behind, and reaching forth unto those things which are before, 14. I press toward the mark for the prize of the high calling of God in Christ Jesus.

1 Thess. 1:9. For they themselves shew of us what manner of entering in we had unto you, and how ye turned to God from idols to serve the living and true God;

1 Thess. 2:10. Ye *are* witnesses, and God *also*, how holily and justly and unblameably we behaved ourselves among you that believe:

2 Tim. 1:3. I thank God, whom I serve from *my* forefathers with pure conscience,

Rev. 2:19. I know thy works, and charity, and service, and faith, and thy patience, and thy works; and the last *to be* more than the first.

Rev. 3:4. Thou hast a few names even in Sardis which have not defiled their garments; and they shall walk with me in white: for they are worthy.

Rev. 14:4. These are they which were not defiled with women; for they are virgins. These are they which follow the Lamb whithersoever he goeth. These were redeemed from among men, *being* the firstfruits unto God and to the Lamb. 5. And in their mouth was found no guile: for they are without fault before the throne of God.

See BLESSING, CONTINGENT UPON OBEDIENCE; COMMANDMENTS.

FILIAL: See CHILDREN.

INSTANCES OF: Noah, Gen. 6:9,22; 7:5; Heb. 11:7. Abraham, Gen. 12:1–4; 17:23; 21:4; 22:12; Neh. 9:8; Acts 7:3–8; Heb. 11:8–17; Jas. 2:21. Bethuel and Laban, Gen. 24:50. Jacob, Gen. 35:1,7. Moses, Num. 27:12–22; Heb. 3:2,3. Moses and Aaron, Ex. 7:6; 40:16,21,23,32. Israelites, Ex. 12:28; 32:25–29; 39:42,43; Num. 9:20,21; Deut. 33:9; Judg. 2:7; Psa. 99:7. Under the preaching of Haggai, Hag. 1:12.

Caleb, Deut. 1:36. Joshua, Josh. 10:40; 11:15. Reubenites, Josh. 22:2,3. Gideon, Judg. 6:25–28. David, 1 Sam. 18:14; 25:28; 1 Kin. 11:6,34; 15:5; 2 Chr. 29:2; Acts 13:22. Elisha, 1 Kin. 19:19–21. Hezekiah, 2 Kin. 18:6; 2 Chr. 31:20,21; Isa. 38:3. Josiah, 2 Kin. 22:2; 23:24,25. Asa, 2 Chr. 14:2. Jehoshaphat, 2 Chr. 17:3–6; 20:32; 22:9. Jehoiada, 2 Chr. 24:16. Uzziah, 2 Chr. 26:4,5. Jotham, 2 Chr. 27:2. Levites, 2 Chr. 29:34. Cyrus, 2 Chr. 36:22,23; Ezra 1:1–4. Ezra, Ezra 7:10. Hanani, Neh. 7:2. Job, Job 1:8. Daniel, Dan. 6:10. Three Hebrews, Dan. 3. Jonah, Jonah 3:3. Ninevites, Jonah 3:5–10.

Zacharias, Luke 1:6. Simeon, Luke 2:25. Joseph, Matt. 1:24; 2:14. Mary, Luke 1:38.

Jesus, Matt. 3:15; 26:39,42; Luke 22:42; John 4:32,34; 5:30; 12:49,50; 14:31; 17:4; Heb. 3:2.

John the Baptist, Matt. 3:15. John and James, Mark 1:19,20. Matthew, Matt. 9:9. Simon and Andrew, Mark 1:16–18. Levi, Mark 2:14. Nathanael, John 1:47. The rich young man, Matt. 19:20; Mark 10:19,20; Luke 18:21. The disciples, John 17:6. Cornelius, Acts 10:2. Paul, Acts 23:1; Acts 26:4,5; 2 Tim. 1:3.

TO CIVIL LAW: See CITIZEN.

OBIL, an Ishmaelite. Camel keeper for David, 1 Chr. 27:30.

OBJECT TEACHING. See INSTRUCTION.

OBLATION. See OFFERING.

OBLIGATION. A motive of obedience, Deut. 4:32–40; chapters 6–11; 26:16; 32:6; 1 Sam. 12:24; 1 Chr. 16:12; Rom. 2:4; 2 Cor. 5:15. Acknowledgment of, Psa. 116:12–14,17.

See DUTY.

OBLIQUITY, moral.

See DEPRAVITY.

OBOTH, a camping place of Israel in the forty years' wandering, Num. 21:10,11; 33:43,44.

OBSEQUIOUSNESS. INSTANCES OF: Abigail, 1 Sam. 25:23–31,41. Mephibosheth, 2 Sam. 9:8. The woman of Tekoah, 2 Sam. 14:4–20.

OBSTETRICS, Ezek. 16:4.

See MIDWIFE.

OCCULT SCIENCE. See SORCERY.

OCRAN, an Asherite and the father of Pagiel who numbers Israel, Num. 1:13; 2:27; 10:26.

ODED. 1. A prophet in Samaria, 2 Chr. 28:9.

2. Father of the prophet Azariah, 2 Chr. 15:1.

ODOR. See INCENSE; PERFUME.

OFFENSES. See TEMPTATION.

OFFERINGS. Offered at the door of the tabernacle, Lev. 1:3; 3:2; 17:4,8,9; of the temple, 2 Chr. 7:12; 1 Kin. 8:62; 12:27. All animal sacrifices must be eight days old or over, Lev. 22:27. Must be salted, Lev. 2:13; Ezek. 43:24; Mark 9:49; accompanied with leaven, Lev. 7:13; Amos 4:5; without leaven, Ex. 23:18; 34:25. Eaten, 1 Sam. 9:13. Ordinance relating to scapegoat, Lev. 16:7–26. Atonement for sin made by, see ATONEMENT.

[1 R. V. omits the reference to sacrifices.]

FIGURATIVE: Psa. 51:17; Jer. 33:11; Rom. 12:1; Phil. 4:18; Heb. 13:15.

ANIMAL SACRIFICES: A type of Christ, Psa. 40:6–8, with Heb. 10:1–14; Isa. 53:11,12, with Lev. 16:21; John 1:29; 1 Cor. 5:7; 2 Cor. 5:21; Eph. 5:2; Heb. 9:19–28; 10:1,11,12; 13:11–13; Rev. 5:6.

BURNT: Lev. 9:2. Its purpose was to make an atonement for sin, Lev. 1:4; 7. Ordinances concerning, Ex. 29:15–18; Lev. 1; 5:7–10; 6:9–13; 17:8,9; 23:18,26–37; Num. 15:24,25; 19:9; 28:26–31; 29. Accompanied by other offerings, Num. 15:3–16. Skins of, belonged to priests, Lev. 7:8. Offered daily, morning and evening, Gen. 15:17; Ex. 29:38–42; Lev. 6:20; Num. 28; 29:6; 1 Chr. 16:40; 2 Chr. 2:4; 13:11; Ezra 3:3; Ezek. 46:13–15. Music with, Num. 10:10.

DRINK: Libations of wine offered with the sacrifices, Gen. 35:14; Ex. 29:40,41; 30:9; Lev. 23:13,18; Num. 6:17; 15:24; 28:5–15,24–31; 29:6–11, 18–40; 2 Kin. 16:13; 1 Chr. 29:21; 2 Chr. 29:35; Ezra 7:17.

FREE WILL: Must be perfect, Lev. 22:17–25. To be eaten by priests, Lev. 7:11–18. With meat and drink offerings, Num. 15:1–16. Obligatory when signified in a vow, Deut. 16:10; 23:23.

HEAVE: Given to the priests' families as part of their emoluments, Lev. 10:14; Num. 5:9; 18:10–19,24. Consecrated by being elevated by the priest, Ex. 29:27. Consisted of the right thigh or hind quarter [*R. V.*], Ex. 29:27,28; Lev. 7:12–14, 32,34; 10:15; spoils, including captives and other articles of war, Num. 31:29,41. When offered, Lev. 7:12–14; Num. 6:20; 15:19–21. In certain instances this offering was brought to the tabernacle, or temple, Deut. 12:6,11,17,18. To be offered on taking possession of the land of Canaan, Num. 15: 18-21.

HUMAN SACRIFICES: Forbidden, Lev. 18:21; 20:2-5; Deut. 12:31. Offered by Abraham, Gen. 22:1-19; Heb. 11:17-19; by Canaanites, Deut. 12:31; Moabites, 2 Kin. 3:27. Israelites, 2 Kin. 16:3; 2 Chr. 28:3; 2 Kin. 23:10; Isa. 57:5; Jer. 7:31; 19:5; 32:35; Ezek. 16:20, 21; 20:26,31; 23:37,39; by the Sepharvites to idols, 2 Kin. 17:31. To demons, Psa. 106: 37,38; and to Baal, Jer. 19:5,6.

INSUFFICIENCY OF: Heb. 8:7. For if that first *covenant* had been faultless, then should no place have been sought for the second. 8. For finding fault with them, he saith, Behold, the days come, saith the Lord, when I will make a new covenant with the house of Israel and with the house of Judah: 9. Not according to the covenant that I made with their fathers in the day when I took them by the hand to lead them out of the land of Egypt; because they continued not in my covenant, and I regarded them not, saith the Lord. 10. For this *is* the covenant that I will make with the house of Israel after those days, saith the Lord; I will put my laws into their mind, and write them in their hearts: and I will be to them a God, and they shall be to me a people: 11. And they shall not teach every man his neighbour, and every man his brother, saying, Know the Lord: for all shall know me, from the least to the greatest. 12. For I will be merciful to their unrighteousness, and their sins and their iniquities will I remember no more. 13. In that he saith, A new *covenant*, he hath made the first old. Now that which decayeth and waxeth old *is* ready to vanish away.

Heb. 9:1. Then verily the first *covenant* had also ordinances of divine service, and a worldly sanctuary. 2. For there was a tabernacle made; the first, wherein *was* the candlestick, and the table, and the shewbread; which is called the sanctuary. 3. And after the second veil, the tabernacle which is called the Holiest of all: 4. Which had the golden censer, and the ark of the covenant overlaid round about with gold, wherein *was* the golden pot that had manna, and Aaron's rod that budded, and the tables of the covenant; 5. And over it the cherubims of glory shadowing the mercyseat; of which we cannot now speak particularly. 6. Now when these things were thus ordained, the priests went always into the first tabernacle, accomplishing the service *of God.* 7. But into the second *went* the high priest alone once every year, not without blood, which he offered for himself, and *for* the errors of the people: 8. The Holy Ghost this signifying, that the way into the holiest of all was not yet made manifest, while as the first tabernacle was yet standing: 9. Which *was* a figure for the time then present, in which were offered both gifts and sacrifices, that could not

make him that did the service perfect, as pertaining to the conscience; 10. *Which stood* only in meats and drinks, and divers washings, and carnal ordinances, imposed *on them* until the time of reformation. 11. But Christ being come an high priest of good things to come, by a greater and more perfect tabernacle, not made with hands, that is to say, not of this building; 12. Neither by the blood of goats and calves, but by his own blood he entered in once into the holy place, having obtained eternal redemption *for us.* 13. For if the blood of bulls and of goats, and the ashes of an heifer sprinkling the unclean, sanctifieth to the purifying of the flesh: 14. How much more shall the blood of Christ, who through the eternal Spirit offered himself without spot to God, purge your conscience from dead works to serve the living God? 15. And for this cause he is the mediator of the new testament, that by means of death, for the redemption of the transgressions *that were* under the first testament, they which are called might receive the promise of eternal inheritance.

Heb. 10:1. For the law having a shadow of good things to come, *and* not the very image of the things, can never with those sacrifices which they offered year by year continually make the comers thereunto perfect. 2. For then would they not have ceased to be offered? because that the worshippers once purged should have had no more conscience of sins. 3. But in those *sacrifices there is* a remembrance again *made* of sins every year. 4. For *it is* not possible that the blood of bulls and of goats should take away sins. 5. Wherefore when he cometh into the world, he saith, Sacrifice and offering thou wouldest not, but a body hast thou prepared me: 6. In burnt offerings and *sacrifices* for sin thou hast had no pleasure. 7. Then said I, Lo, I come (in the volume of the book it is written of me,) to do thy will, O God. 8. Above when he said, Sacrifice and offering and burnt offerings and *offering* for sin thou wouldest not, neither hadst pleasure *therein;* which are offered by the law; 9. Then said he, Lo, I come to do thy will, O God. He taketh away the first, that he may establish the second. 10. By the which will we are sanctified through the offering of the body of Jesus Christ once *for all.* 11. And every priest standeth daily ministering and offering oftentimes the same sacrifices, which can never take away sins: 12. But this man, after he had offered one sacrifice for sins for ever, sat down on the right hand of God; 13. Now where remission of these *is, there is* no more offering for sin. 19. Having therefore, brethren, boldness to enter into the holiest by the blood of Jesus, 20. By a new and living way, which he hath consecrated for us, through the veil that is to say, his flesh;

See ORDINANCE.

MEAT, OR MEAL: Ordinances concerning, Ex.29:40,41; 30:9; 40:29; Lev.2; 5:11,12; 6:14–23; 7:9–13,37; 9:17; 23:13,16,17; Num. 4:16; 5:15, 18,25,26; 8:8; 15:3–16,24; 18:9; 28:5,9,12,13,20, 21,26–31; 29:3,4,14. To be eaten in the holy place, Lev. 10:13; Num. 18:9,10. Offered with the sacrifices, Num. 15:3–16. Not mixed with leaven, Lev. 2:4,11; 6:14–18; 10:12,13; Num. 6:15,17. Storerooms for, in the temple reconstructed by Ezra, Neh. 12:44; 13:5,6; provided for in the vision of Ezekiel, Ezek. 42:13.

PEACE: Laws concerning, Ex. 29:19–22, 31; Lev. 7:11–15,18; 9:3,4,15–21; 23:19; Num. 6:14; 10:10.

SIN: Ordinances concerning, Ex. 29:10–14 with Heb. 13:11–13; Lev. 4; 5; 6:1–7,26–30; 9:1–21; 12:6–8; 14:19,22,31; 15:30; 23:19; Num. 6:10,11,14,16; 8:8,12; 15:27; 28:15,22–24,30; 29: 5,6,11,16–38. Temporary, Dan. 11:31: Heb. chapters 9,10.

SPECIAL SACRIFICES: In consecration of the altar, see ALTAR; of priests, see PRIESTS; of the temple, see TEMPLE, DEDICATION OF; for leprosy, see LEPROSY; for defilement, see DEFILEMENT.

THANK: Ordinances concerning, Lev. 7: 11–15; 22:29; Deut. 12:11,12.

TRESPASS: Ordinances concerning, Lev. 5; 6:1–7; 7:1–7; 14:10–22; 15:15,29,30; 19:21, 22; Num. 6:12; Ezra 10:19. To be eaten by the priests, Lev. 7:6,7; 14:13; Num. 18:9,10. Offered by idolaters, 1 Sam. 6:3,8,17,18. See SIN OFFERING, above.

UNAVAILING WHEN NOT ACCOMPANIED BY PIETY: 1 Sam. 15:22. And Samuel said, Hath the LORD *as great* delight in burnt offerings and sacrifices, as in obeying the voice of the LORD? Behold, to obey *is* better than sacrifice, *and* to hearken than the fat of rams.

Psa. 40:6. Sacrifice and offering thou didst not desire; mine ears hast thou opened: burnt offering and sin offering hast thou not required.

Psa. 50:8. I will not reprove thee for thy sacrifices or thy burnt offerings, *to have been* continually before me. 9. I will take no bullock out of thy house, *nor* he goats out of thy folds. 10. For every beast of the forest *is* mine, *and* the cattle upon a thousand hills. 11. I know all the fowls of the mountains: and the wild beasts of the field *are* mine. 12. If I were hungry, I would not tell thee: for the world *is* mine, and the fulness thereof. 13. Will I eat the flesh of bulls, or drink the blood of goats? 14. Offer unto God thanksgiving; and pay thy vows unto the most High:

Psa. 51:16. For thou desirest not sacrifice; else would I give *it:* thou delightest not in burnt offering. 17. The sacrifices of God *are* a broken spirit: a broken and a contrite heart, O God, thou wilt not despise.

Prov. 21:3. To do justice and judgment *is* more acceptable to the LORD than sacrifice. 27. The sacrifice of the wicked *is* abomination: how much more *when* he bringeth it with a wicked mind?

Isa. 1:11. To what purpose *is* the multitude of your sacrifices unto me? saith the LORD: I am full of the burnt offerings of rams, and the fat of fed beasts; and I delight not in the blood of bullocks, or of lambs, or of he goats. 12. When ye come to appear before me, who hath required this at your hand, to tread my courts? 13. Bring no more vain oblations: incense is an abomination unto me; the new moons and sabbaths, the calling of assemblies, I cannot away with; *it is* iniquity, even the solemn meeting. 14. Your new moons and your appointed feasts my soul hateth: they are a trouble unto me; I am weary to bear *them.*

Isa. 40:16. And Lebanon *is* not sufficient to burn, nor the beasts thereof sufficient for a burnt offering.

Isa. 66:3. He that killeth an ox *is as if* he slew a man; he that sacrificeth a lamb, *as if* he cut off a dog's neck; he that offereth an oblation, *as if he offered* swine's blood; he that burneth incense, *as if* he blessed an idol. Yea, they have chosen their own ways, and their soul delighteth in their abominations.

Jer. 6:20. To what purpose cometh there to me incense from Sheba, and the sweet cane from a far country? your burnt offerings *are* not acceptable, nor your sacrifices sweet unto me.

Jer. 7:21. Thus saith the LORD of hosts, the God of Israel; Put your burnt offerings unto your sacrifices, and eat flesh. 22. For I spake not unto your fathers, nor commanded them in the day that I brought them out of the land of Egypt, concerning burnt offerings or sacrifices: 23. But this thing commanded I them, saying, Obey my voice, and I will be your God, and ye shall be my people: and walk ye in all the ways that I have commanded you, that it may be well unto you.

Jer. 14:12. When they fast, I will not hear their cry; and when they offer burnt offering and an oblation, I will not accept them . but I will consume them by the sword, and by the famine, and by the pestilence.

Hos. 6:6. For I desired mercy, and not sacrifice; and the knowledge of God more than burnt offerings.

Hos. 8:13. They sacrifice flesh *for* the sacrifices of mine offerings, and eat *it;* but the LORD accepteth them not; now will he remember their iniquity, and visit their sins

Amos 5:21. I hate, I despise your feast days, and I will not smell in your solemn assemblies. 22. Though ye offer me burnt offerings and your meat offerings, I will not accept *them:* neither will I regard the peace offerings of your fat beasts. 23. Take thou away from me the noise of thy songs; for I will not hear the melody of thy viols. 24. But let judgment run down as waters, and righteousness as a mighty stream.

Mic. 6:6. Wherewith shall I come before the LORD, *and* bow myself before the high God? shall I come before him with burnt offerings, with calves of a year old? 7. Will the LORD be pleased with thousands of rams, *or* with ten thousands of rivers of oil? shall I give my firstborn *for* my transgression, the fruit of my body *for* the sin of my soul? 8. He hath shewed thee, O man, what *is* good; and what doth the LORD require of thee, but to do justly, and to love mercy, and to walk humbly with thy God?

Mark 12:33. And to love him with all the heart, and with all the understanding, and with all the soul, and with all the strength, and to love *his* neighbour as himself, is more than all whole burnt offerings and sacrifices.

VOW: Lev. 7:16,17; 22:17-25; Deut. 23: 21-23.

WAVE: Ordinances concerning, Ex. 29: 22,26-28; Lev. 7:29-34; 8:25-29; 9:19-21; 10: 14,15; 23:10,11,17-20; Num. 5:25; 6:19,20. Belonged to the priests, Ex. 29:26-28; Lev. 7:31,34; 8:29; 9:21; 23:20; Num. 18:11,18. To be eaten, Lev. 10:14,15; Num. 18:11,18,19,31.

WOOD: Fuel for the temple, Neh. 10:34; 13:31.

OFFICER. CIVIL: Chosen by the people, Deut. 1:13-16; appointed by kings, 2 Sam. 8:16-18; 20:23-26; 1 Kin. 4:1-19; 9:22; Ezra 7:25.

See GOVERNMENT; JUDGE; RULER.

ECCLESIASTICAL: See PRIEST; LEVITE; APOSTLE; ELDER; DEACON; MINISTER.

OG, king of Bashan. A man of gigantic stature, Num. 21:33; Deut. 3:11; Josh. 12:4; 13:12. Defeated and slain by Moses, Num. 21:33-35; Deut. 1:4; 3:1-7; 29:7; 31:4; Josh. 2: 10; 9:10; Psa. 135:10,11; 136:18-20. Land of, given to Gad, Reuben, and Manasseh, Num. 32:33; Deut. 3:8-17; 4:47-49; 29:7,8; Josh. 12: 4-6; 13:12,30,31; 1 Kin. 4:19; Neh. 9:22; Psa. 136:20,21.

OHAD, son of Simeon, Gen. 46:10; Ex. 6:15.

OHEL, son of Zerubbabel, 1 Chr. 3:20.

OIL. Sacred, Ex. 30:23-25; 31:11; 35:8, 15,28; 37:29; 39:38; Num. 4:16; 1 Chr. 9:30. Punishment for profaning, Ex. 30:31-33. Used for idols, Ezek. 23:41. Illuminating, for tabernacle, Ex. 25:6; 27:20; Lev. 24:2-4. For domestic use, Matt. 25:3. Used for food, Lev. 2:4,5; 14:10,21; Deut. 12:17; 1 Kin. 17: 12-16; Prov. 21:17; Ezek. 16:13; Hos. 2:5. For the head, Psa. 23:5; 105:15; Luke 7:46. For anointing kings, 1 Sam. 10:1; 16:1,13; 1 Kin. 1:39.

Tribute paid in, Hos. 12:1. Commerce in, 2 Kin. 4:1-7.

Petroleum [?] Job 29:6.

See ANOINTING; OINTMENT.

OINTMENT. NOT SACRED: 2 Kin. 20:13; Esth. 2:12; Eccl. 7:1; 10:1; Song 1:3; 4:10; Amos 6:6; Mark 14:3-5; John 12:3-5. The alabaster box of, Matt. 26:7.

SACRED: Formula for, Ex. 30:23-25. Uses of, Ex. 30:26-33. Compounded by Bezaleel, Ex. 37:1,29. See OIL, SACRED.

OLD AGE. Gen. 15:15. And thou shalt

go to thy fathers in peace; thou shalt be buried in a good old age.

Gen. 47:9. And Jacob said unto Pharaoh, The days of the years of my pilgrimage *are* an hundred and thirty years: few and evil have the days of the years of my life been, and have not attained unto the days of the years of the life of my fathers in the days of their pilgrimage.

Deut. 34:7. And Moses *was* an hundred and twenty years old when he died: his eye was not dim, nor his natural force abated.

2 Sam. 19:34. And Barzillai said unto the king, How long have I to live, that I should go up with the king unto Jerusalem? 35. I *am* this day fourscore years old: *and* can I discern between good and evil? can thy servant taste what I eat or what I drink? can I hear any more the voice of singing men and singing women? wherefore then should thy servant be yet a burden unto my lord the king? 36. Thy servant will go a little way over Jordan with the king: and why should the king recompense it me with such a reward? 37. Let thy servant, I pray thee, turn back again, that I may die in mine own city, *and be buried* by the grave of my father and of my mother.

1 Chr. 29:28. And he died in a good old age, full of days, riches, and honour: and Solomon his son reigned in his stead.

Job 5:26. Thou shalt come to *thy* grave in a full age, like as a shock of corn cometh in in his season.

Job 11:17. *Thine* age shall be clearer than the noonday; thou shalt shine forth, thou shalt be as the morning. Job 42:17.

Job 12:12. With the ancient *is* wisdom; and in length of days understanding.

Job 32:4. Now Elihu had waited till Job had spoken, because they *were* elder than he. 5. When Elihu saw that *there was* no answer in the mouth of *these* three men, then his wrath was kindled. 6. And Elihu the son of Barachel the Buzite answered and said, I *am* young, and ye *are* very old; wherefore I was afraid, and durst not shew you mine opinion. 7. I said, Days should speak, and multitude of years should teach wisdom. 8. But *there is* a spirit in man: and the inspiration of the Almighty giveth them understanding. 9. Great men are not *always* wise: neither do the aged understand judgment.

Psa. 71:9. Cast me not off in the time of old age; forsake me not when my strength faileth. 18. Now also when I am old and greyheaded, O God, forsake me not; until I have shewed thy strength unto *this* generation, *and* thy power to every one *that* is to come.

Psa. 90:10. The days of our years *are* threescore years and ten; and if by reason of strength *they be* fourscore years, yet *is* their strength labour and sorrow; for it is soon cut off, and we fly away.

Psa. 92:14. They shall still bring forth

fruit in old age; they shall be fat and flourishing;

Psa. 148:12. Both young men, and maidens; old men, and children: 13. Let them praise the name of the LORD:

Prov. 16:31. The hoary head *is* a crown of glory, *if* it be found in the way of righteousness.

Eccl. 6:3. If a man beget an hundred *children*, and live many years, so that the days of his years be many, and his soul be not filled with good, and also *that* he have no burial; I say, *that* an untimely birth *is* better than he. 6. Yea, though he live a thousand years twice *told*, yet hath he seen no good: do not all go to one place?

Eccl. 12:1. Remember now thy Creator in the days of thy youth, while the evil days come not, nor the years draw nigh, when thou shalt say, I have no pleasure in them; 2. While the sun, or the light, or the moon, or the stars, be not darkened, nor the clouds return after the rain: 3. In the day when the keepers of the house shall tremble, and the strong men shall bow themselves, and the grinders cease because they are few, and those that look out of the windows be darkened, 4. And the doors shall be shut in the streets, when the sound of the grinding is low, and he shall rise up at the voice of the bird, and all the daughters of musick shall be brought low; 5. Also *when* they shall be afraid of *that which is* high, and fears *shall be* in the way, and the almond tree shall flourish, and the grasshopper shall be a burden, and desire shall fail: because man goeth to his long home, and the mourners go about the streets: 6. Or ever the silver cord be loosed, or the golden bowl be broken, or the pitcher be broken at the fountain, or the wheel broken at the cistern. 7. Then shall the dust return to the earth as it was: and the spirit shall return unto God who gave it.

Isa. 46:4. *Even* to *your* old age I *am* he; and *even* to hoar hairs will I carry *you:* I have made, and I will bear; even I will carry, and will deliver *you.*

Luke 2:37. And she *was* a widow of about fourscore and four years, which departed not from the temple, but served *God* with fastings and prayers night and day.

Tit. 2:2. That the aged men be sober, grave, temperate, sound in faith, in charity, in patience. 3. The aged women likewise, that *they be* in behaviour as becometh holiness, not false accusers, not given to much wine, teachers of good things;

Philem. 9. Yet for love's sake I rather beseech *thee*, being such an one as Paul the aged, and now also a prisoner of Jesus Christ.

See LONGEVITY; INFIRMITIES.

OLIVE, a fruit tree. Branch of, brought by the dove to Noah's ark, Gen. 8:11. Common to the land of Canaan, Ex. 23:11; Deut. 6:11; 8:8; Israelites commanded to cultivate in the land of promise, Deut.

28:40. Branches of, used for booths, Neh. 8:15. Bears flowers, Job. 15:33. Precepts concerning gleaning the fruit of, Deut. 24: 20; Isa. 17:6. Cherubim made of the wood of, 1 Kin. 6:23,31-33. Fable of, Judg. 9:8.

FIGURATIVE: Of prosperity, Psa. 128:3. The wild, a figure of the Gentiles; the cultivated, of the Jews, Rom. 11:17-21,24.

SYMBOLICAL: Zech. 4:2-12; Rev. 11:4.

FRUIT OF: Oil extracted from, used as illuminating oil in the tabernacle, Ex. 39:37; Lev. 24:2; Zech. 4:12. See OIL.

OLIVES, Mount of. Called MOUNT OF CORRUPTION, 2 Kin. 23:13. [*R. V.*, marg., Mount of Olives]. East of Jerusalem. The highway to and from the east passed over it, 2 Sam. 15:30. Jesus' triumphant entry into Jerusalem by way of, Matt. 21:1; Mark 11:1; Luke 19:29,37. Jesus repairs to, Matt. 24:3; 26:30; Mark 13:3; 14:26; Luke 21:37; 22:39. Jesus makes his ascension from, Acts 1:12.

OLIVET. See OLIVES, MOUNT OF.

OLYMPAS, a believer at Rome, Rom. 16:15.

OMAR, son of Eliphaz, grandson of Esau, Gen. 36:11,15; 1 Chr. 1:36.

OMEGA, Alpha and Omega, the all-comprehensiveness of Christ, Rev. 1:8,11; 21:6; 22:13.

OMER, one-tenth part of an ephah. A dry measure containing, according to the Rabbins, two quarts, but according to Josephus, three and one-half quarts. Ex. 16: 16-18,36.

OMNIPOTENCE. See GOD, OMNIPOTENT; JESUS, OMNIPOTENCE OF.

OMNISCIENCE. See GOD, OMNISCIENT; JESUS, OMNISCIENCE OF.

OMRI. 1. King of Israel. Was commander of the army of Israel, and was proclaimed king by the army upon news of assassination of King Elah, 1 Kin. 16:16. Defeats his rival, Tibni, and establishes himself, 1 Kin. 16:17-22. Surrendered cities to king of Syria, 1 Kin. 20:34. Wicked reign and death of, 1 Kin. 16:23-28. Denounced by Micah, Mic. 6:16.

2. A son of Becher, grandson of Benjamin, 1 Chr. 7:8.

3. A descendant of Pharez, 1 Chr. 9:4.

4. Son of Michael, and ruler of tribe of Issachar in time of David, 1 Chr. 27:18.

ON. 1. Capital of lower Egypt, Gen. 41: 45; 46:20.

2. A leader of the Reubenites who rebelled against Moses, Num. 16:1.

ONAM, a son of Shobal, Gen. 36:23; 1 Chr. 1:40.

2. Son of Jerahmeel, 1 Chr. 2:26.28.

ONAN, son of Judah. Slain for his refusal to raise seed to his brother, Gen. 38: 4,8-10; 46:12: Num. 26:19; 1 Chr. 2:3.

ONESIMUS, a fugitive slave and convert of Paul, Col. 4:9; Philem. 10.

ONESIPHORUS, a Christian of Ephesus. 2 Tim. 1:16,17; 4:19.

ONION, Num. 11:5.

ONO, a town of Benjamim, 1 Chr. 8:12; Neh. 6:2; 11:35.

ONYCHA, a component of the sacred ointment, made from the shells of a species of mussel, possessing an odor, Ex. 30:34.

ONYX. Precious stone, Job 28:16; Ezek. 28:13. Used in erecting the temple, 1 Chr. 29:2. Seen in the foundations of the city of the New Jerusalem in John's apocalyptic vision, Rev. 21:20. Exported from Havilah, Gen. 2:12. Used in the breastplate, Ex. 28:9-12,20; 39:6,13. Contributed by Israelites for the priests' garments, Ex. 25:7; 35:9.

OPHEL, a gate in the wall of the city and the temple, 2 Chr. 27:3; 33:14; Neh. 3:26,27.

OPHIR. 1. Son of Joktan, Gen. 10:29; 1 Chr. 1:23.

2. A country celebrated for its gold and other valuable merchandise. Products of, used by Solomon and Hiram, 1 Kin. 9:28; 10:11; 2 Chr. 8:18; 9:10. Jehoshaphat sends ships to, which are wrecked, 1 Kin. 22:48. Gold of, proverbial for its fineness, 1 Chr. 29:4; Job 22:24; 28:16; Psa. 45:9; Isa. 13:12.

OPHNI, a town of the Benjamites, Josh. 18:24.

OPHRAH. 1. A city in Benjamin, Josh. 18:23; 1 Sam. 13:17. Possibly identical with EPHRAIN, 2 Chr. 13:19; and EPHRAIM, John 11:54.

2. A city in Manasseh, home of Gideon, Judg. 6:11,24; 8:27,32; 9:5.

3. Son of Meonothai. 1 Chr. 4:14.

OPINION, PUBLIC. Kings influenced by. See KINGS. Jesus inquires about, Matt. 16:13; Luke 9:18. Feared by Nicodemus, John 3:2; Joseph of Arimathæa, John 19:38; the parents of the man who was born blind, John 9:21,22; rulers, who believed in Jesus, but feared the Pharisees, John 12:42,43; chief priests, who feared to answer the questions of Jesus, Matt. 21:26; Mark 11:18,32; 12:12; and to further persecute the disciples, Acts 4:21; 5:26.

CONCESSIONS TO: By Paul, in circumcising Timothy, Acts 16:3. James and the Christian elders, who required Paul to observe certain rites, Acts 21:18-26. Disciples, who urged circumcision, Gal. 6:12. Peter and Barnabas with others, Gal. 2:11-14.

See PRUDENCE.

CORRUPT YIELDING TO: By Herod, in the case of John the Baptist, Mark 6:26; of Peter, Acts 12:3; by Peter, concerning Jesus, Matt. 26:69-75; by Pilate, Matt. 27:23-27; Mark 15:15; Luke 23:13-25; John 18:38,39; 19:4-16; by Felix and Festus, concerning Paul, Acts 24:27; 25:9.

OPPORTUNITY. THE MEASURE OF RESPONSIBILITY: Prov. 1:24. Because I have called, and ye refused; I have stretched out my hand, and no man regarded; 25. But ye have set at nought all my counsel, and would none of my reproof: 26. I also will laugh at your calamity; I will mock when your fear cometh; 27. When your fear cometh as desolation, and your de-

struction cometh as a whirlwind; when distress and anguish cometh upon you. 28. Then shall they call upon me, but I will not answer; they shall seek me early, but they shall not find me: 29. For that they hated knowledge, and did not choose the fear of the LORD: 30. They would none of my counsel: they despised all my reproof. 31. Therefore shall they eat of the fruit of their own way, and be filled with their own devices. 32. For the turning away of the simple shall slay them, and the prosperity of fools shall destroy them. 33. But whoso hearkeneth unto me shall dwell safely, and shall be quiet from fear of evil.

Jer. 8:20. The harvest is past, the summer is ended, and we are not saved.

Ezek. 3:19. Yet if thou warn the wicked, and he turn not from his wickedness, nor from his wicked way, he shall die in his iniquity; but thou hast delivered thy soul. chapter 33:1-17.

Hos. 5:6. They shall go with their flocks and with their herds to seek the LORD; but they shall not find *him;* he hath withdrawn himself from them.

Matt. 10:14. And whosoever shall not receive you, nor hear your words, when ye depart out of that house or city, shake off the dust of your feet. 15. Verily I say unto you, It shall be more tolerable for the land of Sodom and Gomorrha in the day of judgment, than for that city.

Matt. 11:20. Then began he to upbraid the cities wherein most of his mighty works were done, because they repented not: 21. Woe unto thee, Chorazin! woe unto thee, Bethsaida! for if the mighty works, which were done in you, had been done in Tyre and Sidon, they would have repented long ago in sackcloth and ashes. 22. But I say unto you, It shall be more tolerable for Tyre and Sidon at the day of judgment, than for you. 23. And thou, Capernaum, which art exalted unto heaven, shalt be brought down to hell: for if the mighty works, which have been done in thee, had been done in Sodom, it would have remained until this day. 24. But I say unto you, That it shall be more tolerable for the land of Sodom in the day of judgment, than for thee.

Matt. 23:34. Wherefore, behold, I send unto you prophets, and wise men, and scribes: and *some* of them ye shall kill and crucify; and *some* of them shall ye scourge in your synagogues, and persecute *them* from city to city: 35. That upon you may come all the righteous blood shed upon the earth, from the blood of righteous Abel unto the blood of Zacharias son of Barachias, whom ye slew between the temple and the altar. 36. Verily I say unto you, All these things shall come upon this generation. 37. O Jerusalem, Jerusalem, *thou* that killest the prophets, and stonest them which are sent unto thee, how often would I have gathered thy children together, even as a hen gathereth her chickens under *her* wings, and ye would not! 38. Behold, your house is left unto you desolate.

Matt. 25:1. Then shall the kingdom of heaven be likened unto ten virgins, which took their lamps, and went forth to meet the bridegroom. 2. And five of them were wise, and five *were* foolish. 3. They that *were* foolish took their lamps, and took no oil with them: 4. But the wise took oil in their vessels with their lamps. 5. While the bridegroom tarried, they all slumbered and slept. 6. And at midnight there was a cry made, Behold, the bridegroom cometh; go ye out to meet him. 7. Then all those virgins arose, and trimmed their lamps. 8. And the foolish said unto the wise, Give us of your oil; for our lamps are gone out. 9. But the wise answered, saying, *Not so;* lest there be not enough for us and you: but go ye rather to them that sell, and buy for yourselves. 10. And while they went to buy, the bridegroom came; and they that were ready went in with him to the marriage: and the door was shut. 11. Afterward came also the other virgins, saying, Lord, Lord, open to us. 12. But he answered and said, Verily I say unto you, I know you not. 13. Watch therefore, for ye know neither the day nor the hour wherein the Son of man cometh. 14. For *the kingdom of heaven is* as a man travelling into a far country, *who* called his own servants, and delivered unto them his goods. [Luke 19:12–27.] 15. And unto one he gave five talents, to another two, and to another one; to every man according to his several ability; and straightway took his journey. 16. Then he that had received the five talents went and traded with the same, and made *them* other five talents. 17. And likewise he that *had received* two, he also gained other two. 18. But he that had received one went and digged in the earth, and hid his lord's money. 19. After a long time the lord of those servants cometh, and reckoneth with them. 20. And so he that had received five talents came and brought other five talents, saying, Lord, thou deliveredst unto me five talents: behold, I have gained beside them five talents more. 21. His lord said unto him, Well done, *thou* good and faithful servant: thou hast been faithful over a few things, I will make thee ruler over many things: enter thou into the joy of thy lord. 22. He also that had received two talents came and said, Lord, thou deliveredst unto me two talents: behold, I have gained two other talents beside them. 23. His lord said unto him, Well done, good and faithful servant; thou hast been faithful over a few things, I will make thee ruler over many things: enter thou into the joy of thy lord. 24. Then he which had received the one talent came and said, Lord, I knew thee that thou art an hard man, reaping where thou hast not sown, and gathering where thou hast not strawed: 25. And I was afraid, and went and hid thy talent

in the earth: lo, *there* thou hast *that is* thine. 26. His lord answered and said unto him, *Thou* wicked and slothful servant, thou knewest that I reap where I sowed not, and gather where I have not strawed: 27. Thou oughtest therefore to have put my money to the exchangers, and *then* at my coming I should have received mine own with usury. 28. Take therefore the talent from him, and give *it* unto him which hath ten talents. 29. For unto every one that hath shall be given, and he shall have abundance: but from him that hath not shall be taken away even that which he hath. 30. And cast ye the unprofitable servant into outer darkness: there shall be weeping and gnashing of teeth. 31. When the Son of man shall come in his glory, and all the holy angels with him, then shall he sit upon the throne of his glory: 32. And before him shall be gathered all nations: and he shall separate them one from another, as a shepherd divideth *his* sheep from the goats: 33. And he shall set the sheep on his right hand, but the goats on the left. 34. Then shall the King say unto them on his right hand, Come, ye blessed of my Father, inherit the kingdom prepared for you from the foundation of the world: 35. For I was an hungred, and ye gave me meat: I was thirsty, and ye gave me drink: I was a stranger, and ye took me in: 36. Naked, and ye clothed me: I was sick, and ye visited me: I was in prison, and ye came unto me. 37. Then shall the righteous answer him, saying, Lord, when saw we thee an hungred, and fed *thee?* or thirsty, and gave *thee* drink? 38. When saw we thee a stranger, and took *thee* in? or naked, and clothed *thee?* 39. Or when saw we thee sick, or in prison, and came unto thee? 40. And the King shall answer and say unto them, Verily I say unto you, Inasmuch as ye have done *it* unto one of the least of these my brethren, ye have done *it* unto me. 41. Then shall he say also unto them on the left hand, Depart from me, ye cursed, into everlasting fire, prepared for the devil and his angels: 42. For I was an hungred, and ye gave me no meat: I was thirsty, and ye gave me no drink: 43. I was a stranger, and ye took me not in: naked, and ye clothed me not: sick, and in prison, and ye visited me not. 44. Then shall they also answer him, saying, Lord, when saw we thee an hungred, or athirst, or a stranger, or naked, or sick, or in prison, and did not minister unto thee? 45. Then shall he answer them, saying, Verily I say unto you, Inasmuch as ye did *it* not to one of the least of these, ye did *it* not to me. 46. And these shall go away into everlasting punishment: but the righteous into life eternal.

Luke 12:47. And that servant, which knew his lord's will, and prepared not *himself,* neither did according to his will, shall be beaten with many *stripes.*

Luke 13:25. When once the master of the

house is risen up, and hath shut to the door, and ye begin to stand without, and to knock at the door, saying, Lord, Lord, open unto us; and he shall answer and say unto you, I know you not whence ye are: 26. Then shall ye begin to say, We have eaten and drunk in thy presence, and thou hast taught in our streets. 27. But he shall say, I tell you, I know you not whence ye are; depart from me, all *ye* workers of iniquity. 28. There shall be weeping and gnashing of teeth, when ye shall see Abraham, and Isaac, and Jacob, and all the prophets, in the kingdom of God, and you *yourselves* thrust out.

Luke 14:16. Then said he unto him, A certain man made a great supper, and bade many: 17. And sent his servant at supper time to say to them that were bidden, Come; for all things are now ready. 18. And they all with one *consent* began to make excuse. The first said unto him, I have bought a piece of ground, and I must needs go and see it: I pray thee have me excused. 19. And another said, I have bought five yoke of oxen, and I go to prove them: I pray thee have me excused. 20. And another said, I have married a wife, and therefore I cannot come. 21. So that servant came, and shewed his lord these things. Then the master of the house being angry said to his servant, Go out quickly into the streets and lanes of the city, and bring in hither the poor, and the maimed, and the halt, and the blind. 22. And the servant said, Lord, it is done as thou hast commanded, and yet there is room. 23. And the lord said unto the servant, Go out into the highways and hedges, and compel *them* to come in, that my house may be filled. 24. For I say unto you, That none of those men which were bidden shall taste of my supper.

See JUDGMENT, ACCORDING TO OPPORTUNITY; RESPONSIBILITY.

OPPRESSION. God is a refuge from, Psa. 9:9. Prayers against, Psa. 17:9; 44:24; 119:121,134; Isa. 38:14. God's aid promised against, Psa. 12:5; 72:4,14; Jer. 50:34. God will judge, Psa. 103:6; Eccl. 5:8; Isa. 10; Jer. 22:17; Ezek. 22:7; Amos 4:1; Mic. 2:2; Mal.3:5; Jas. 5:4. National, God judges, Acts 7:7. National, relieved, Ex.3:9; Deut.26:7; Judg.2:14; 6; 7; 8; 10; 2 Kin.13; Isa.52:4.—*Bible Text-Book*.

INSTANCES OF: Of Hagar, by Sarah, Gen. 16:6. Of Israelites, by Egyptians, Ex. 1:10–22; 5. Rehoboam resolves to oppress the Israelites, 1 Kin. 12:14.

UNCLASSIFIED SCRIPTURES RELATING TO: Ex. 22:21. Thou shalt neither vex a stranger, nor oppress him: for ye were strangers in the land of Egypt. 22. Ye shall not afflict any widow, or fatherless child. 23. If thou afflict them in any wise, and they cry at all unto me, I will surely hear their cry; 24. And my wrath shall wax hot, and I will kill you with the sword; and your wives shall be widows, and your children fatherless.

Deut. 23:15. Thou shalt not deliver unto his master the servant which is escaped from his master unto thee: 16. He shall dwell with thee, *even* among you, in that place which he shall choose in one of thy gates, where it liketh him best: thou shalt not oppress him.

Deut. 24:14. Thou shalt not oppress an hired servant *that is* poor and needy, *whether he be* of thy brethren, or of thy strangers that *are* in thy land within thy gates: 15. At his day thou shalt give *him* his hire, neither shall the sun go down upon it; for he *is* poor, and setteth his heart upon it: lest he cry against thee unto the LORD, and it be sin unto thee.

Job 27:13. This *is* the portion of a wicked man with God, and the heritage of oppressors, *which* they shall receive of the Almighty. 14. If his children be multiplied, *it is* for the sword: and his offspring shall not be satisfied with bread. 15. Those that remain of him shall be buried in death: and his widows shall not weep. 16. Though he heap up silver as the dust, and prepare raiment as the clay; 17. He may prepare *it*, but the just shall put *it* on, and the innocent shall divide the silver. 18. He buildeth his house as a moth, and as a booth *that* the keeper maketh. 19. The rich man shall lie down, but he shall not be gathered: he openeth his eyes, and he *is* not. 20. Terrors take hold on him as waters, a tempest stealeth him away in the night. 21. The east wind carrieth him away, and he departeth: and as a storm hurleth him out of his place. 22. For *God* shall cast upon him, and not spare: he would fain flee out of his hand. 23. *Men* shall clap their hands at him, and shall hiss him out of his place.

Psa. 9:9. The LORD also will be a refuge for the oppressed, a refuge in times of trouble.

Psa. 10:17. LORD, thou hast heard the desire of the humble: thou wilt prepare their heart, thou wilt cause thine ear to hear: 18. To judge the fatherless and the oppressed, that the man of the earth may no more oppress.

Psa. 12:5. For the oppression of the poor, for the sighing of the needy, now will I arise, saith the LORD; I will set *him* in safety *from him that* puffeth at him.

Psa. 62:10. Trust not in oppression, and become not vain in robbery: if riches increase, set not your heart *upon them*.

Psa. 74:21. O let not the oppressed return ashamed: let the poor and needy praise thy name.

Psa. 119:134. Deliver me from the oppression of man: so will I keep thy precepts.

Prov. 3:31. Envy thou not the oppressor, and choose none of his ways.

Prov. 14:31. He that oppresseth the poor reproacheth his Maker: but he that honoureth him hath mercy on the poor. Prov. 22:16.

Prov. 22:22. Rob not the poor, because he *is* poor: neither oppress the afflicted in the gate:

Prov. 28:3. A poor man that oppresseth the poor *is like* a sweeping rain which leaveth no food.

Prov. 30:14. *There is* a generation, whose teeth *are as* swords, and their jaw teeth *as* knives, to devour the poor from off the earth, and the needy from *among* men.

Eccl. 4:1. So I returned, and considered all the oppressions that are done under the sun: and behold the tears of *such as were* oppressed, and they had no comforter; and on the side of their oppressors *there was* power; but they had no comforter.

Eccl. 5:8. If thou seest the oppression of the poor, and violent perverting of judgment and justice in a province, marvel not at the matter: for *he that is* higher than the highest regardeth; and *there be* higher than they.

Eccl. 7:7. Surely oppression maketh a wise man mad;

Isa. 1:17. Learn to do well; seek judgment, relieve the oppressed, judge the fatherless, plead for the widow.

Isa. 33:15. He that walketh righteously, and speaketh uprightly; he that despiseth the gain of oppressions, that shaketh his hands from holding of bribes, that stoppeth his ears from hearing of blood, and shutteth his eyes from seeing evil; 16. He shall dwell on high: his place of defence *shall be* the munitions of rocks: bread shall be given him; his waters *shall be* sure.

Isa. 58:6. *Is* not this the fast that I have chosen? to loose the bands of wickedness, to undo the heavy burdens, and to let the oppressed go free, and that ye break every yoke?

Jer. 21:12. O house of David, thus saith the LORD; Execute judgment in the morning, and deliver *him that is* spoiled out of the hand of the oppressor, lest my fury go out like fire, and burn that none can quench *it*, because of the evil of your doings.

Ezek. 22:29. The people of the land have used oppression, and exercised robbery, and have vexed the poor and needy: yea, they have oppressed the stranger wrongfully.

Ezek. 45:9. Thus saith the Lord GOD; Let it suffice you, O princes of Israel: remove violence and spoil, and execute judgment and justice, take away your exactions from my people, saith the Lord GOD.

Amos 5:11. Forasmuch therefore as your treading *is* upon the poor, and ye take from him burdens of wheat: ye have built houses of hewn stone, but ye shall not dwell in them; ye have planted pleasant vineyards, but ye shall not drink wine of them. 12. For I know your manifold transgressions and your mighty sins: they afflict the just, they take a bribe, and they turn aside the poor in the gate *from their right*.

Amos 8:4. Hear this, O ye that swallow up the needy, even to make the poor of the land to fail. 5. Saying, When will the new moon be gone, that we may sell corn? and the sabbath, that we may set forth wheat,

making the ephah small, and the shekel great, and falsifying the balances by deceit? 6. That we may buy the poor for silver, and the needy for a pair of shoes; *yea*, and sell the refuse of the wheat?

Mic. 2:1. Woe to them that devise iniquity, and work evil upon their beds! when the morning is light, they practise it, because it is in the power of their hand. 2. And they covet fields, and take *them* by violence; and houses, and take *them* away: so they oppress a man and his house, even a man and his heritage. 3. Therefore thus saith the LORD; Behold, against this family do I devise an evil, from which ye shall not remove your necks; neither shall ye go haughtily; for this time *is* evil. Isa. 5:8.

Hab. 2:5. Yea also, [1] because he transgresseth by wine, *he is* a proud man, neither keepeth at home, who enlargeth his desire as hell, and *is* as death, and cannot be satisfied, but gathereth unto him all nations, and heapeth unto him all people: 6. Shall not all these take up a parable against him, and a taunting proverb against him, and say, Woe to him that increaseth *that which is* not his! how long? and to him that ladeth himself with thick clay! 7. Shall they not rise up suddenly that shall bite thee, and awake that shall vex thee, and thou shalt be for booties unto them? 8. Because thou hast spoiled many nations, all the remnant of the people shall spoil thee; because of men's blood, and *for* the violence of the land, of the city, and of all that dwell therein. 9. Woe to him that coveteth an evil covetousness to his house, that he may set his nest on high, that he may be delivered from the power of evil! 10. Thou hast consulted shame to thy house by cutting off many people, and hast sinned *against* thy soul. 11. For the stone shall cry out of the wall, and the beam out of the timber shall answer it.

[1 R. V. wine is a treacherous dealer, a haughty]

Zech. 7:10. And oppress not the widow, nor the fatherless, the stranger, nor the poor; and let none of you imagine evil against his brother in your heart.

Matt. 23:2. The scribes and the Pharisees sit in Moses' seat: 3. All therefore whatsoever they bid you observe, *that* observe and do; but do not ye after their works: for they say, and do not. 4. For they bind heavy burdens and grievous to be borne, and lay *them* on men's shoulders; but they *themselves* will not move them with one of their fingers.

Jas. 2:6. Do not rich men oppress you, and draw you before the judgment seats?

ORACLE. The holy place, 1 Kin. 6:5; Psa. 28:2. The scriptures called oracles, Acts 7:38; Rom. 3:2; Heb. 5:12; 1 Pet. 4:11.

See TABERNACLE.

ORATOR, Isa. 3:3.

INSTANCES OF: Jonah, Jonah 3:4-10. The Apostles, Acts 2:1-41. Tertullus, Acts 24:1. Apollos, Acts 18:24-28.

ORDINANCE. A decree, Ex. 12:14, 24,

43; 13:10; 15:25; Num. 9:14; 10:8; 15:15; 18:8; Isa. 24:5; Mal. 4:4; Rom. 13:2; 1 Pet. 2:13.

INSUFFICIENCY OF, FOR SALVATION: Isa. 1:10. Hear the word of the LORD, ye rulers of Sodom; give ear unto the law of our God, ye people of Gomorrah. 11. To what purpose *is* the multitude of your sacrifices unto me? saith the LORD: I am full of the burnt offerings of rams, and the fat of fed beasts; and I delight not in the blood of bullocks, or of lambs, or of he goats. 12. When ye come to appear before me, who hath required this at your hand, to tread my courts? 13. Bring no more vain oblations; incense is an abomination unto me; the new moons and sabbaths, the calling of assemblies, I cannot away with; *it is* iniquity, even the solemn meeting. 14. Your new moons and your appointed feasts my soul hateth: they are a trouble unto me; I am weary to bear *them*. 15. And when ye spread forth your hands, I will hide mine eyes from you: yea, when ye make many prayers, I will not hear: your hands are full of blood. 16. Wash you, make you clean; put away the evil of your doings from before mine eyes; cease to do evil; 17. Learn to do well; seek judgment, relieve the oppressed, judge the fatherless, plead for the widow.

Gal. 5:6. For in Jesus Christ neither circumcision availeth any thing, nor uncircumcision; but faith which worketh by love.

Gal. 6:15. For in Christ Jesus neither circumcision availeth any thing, nor uncircumcision, but a new creature.

Eph. 2:15. Having abolished in his flesh the enmity, *even* the law of commandments *contained* in ordinances;

Col. 2:14. Blotting out the handwriting of ordinances that was against us, which was contrary to us, and took it out of the way, nailing it to his cross; 20. Wherefore if ye be dead with Christ from the rudiments of the world, why, as though living in the world, are ye subject to ordinances; 21. (Touch not, taste not, handle not; 22. Which all are to perish with the using;) after the commandments and doctrines of men? 23. Which things have indeed a shew of wisdom in will worship, and humility, and neglecting of the body; not in any honour to the satisfying of the flesh.

Heb. 9:1. Then verily the first *covenant* had also ordinances of divine service, and a worldly sanctuary. 8. The Holy Ghost this signifying, that the way into the holiest of all was not yet made manifest, while as the first tabernacle was yet standing: 9. Which *was* a figure for the time then present, in which were offered both gifts and sacrifices, that could not make him that did the service perfect, as pertaining to the conscience; 10. *Which stood* only in meats and drinks, and divers washings, and carnal ordinances, imposed *on them* until the time of reformation.

See FORM; FORMALISM.

ORDINATION, of priests, see PRIESTS; of ministers, see MINISTERS.

OREB. 1. A prince of Midian, overcome by Gideon and killed by the Ephraimites, Judg. 7:25; 8:3; Psa. 83:11.

2. A rock E. of the Jordan, where Oreb was slain, Judg. 7:25; Isa. 10:26.

OREN, son of Jerahmeel, 1 Chr. 2:25.

ORGAN. See MUSIC, INSTRUMENTS OF.

ORION, the constellation of, Job 9:9; 38:31; Isa. 13:10; Amos 5:8.

ORNAN. A Jebusite, 1 Chr. 21:15–25,28; 2 Chr. 3:1. Called ARAUNAH, 2 Sam. 24:16–25.

ORPAH, daughter-in-law of Naomi, Ruth 1:4,14.

ORPHAN. Ex. 22:22. Ye shall not afflict any widow, or fatherless child. 23. If thou afflict them in any wise, and they cry at all unto me, I will surely hear their cry; 24. And my wrath shall wax hot, and I will kill you with the sword; and your wives shall be widows, and your children fatherless.

Deut. 10:18. He doth execute the judgment of the fatherless and widow,

Deut. 14:28. At the end of three years thou shalt bring forth all the tithe of thine increase the same year, and shalt lay *it* up within thy gates: 29. And the Levite, (because he hath no part nor inheritance with thee,) and the stranger, and the fatherless, and the widow, which *are* within thy gates, shall come, and shall eat and be satisfied; that the LORD thy God may bless thee in all the work of thine hand which thou doest.

Deut. 16:11. And thou shalt rejoice before the LORD thy God, thou, and thy son, and thy daughter, and thy manservant, and thy maidservant, and the Levite that *is* within thy gates, and the stranger, and the fatherless, and the widow, that *are* among you, in the place which the LORD thy God hath chosen to place his name there. 14. And thou shalt rejoice in thy feast, thou, and thy son, and thy daughter, and thy manservant, and thy maidservant, and the Levite, the stranger, and the fatherless, and the widow, that *are* within thy gates.

Deut. 24:17. Thou shalt not pervert the judgment of the stranger, *nor* of the fatherless; nor take a widow's raiment to pledge: 18. But thou shalt remember that thou wast a bondman in Egypt, and the LORD thy God redeemed thee thence: therefore I command thee to do this thing. 19. When thou cuttest down thine harvest in thy field, and hast forgot a sheaf in the field, thou shalt not go again to fetch it: it shall be for the stranger, for the fatherless, and for the widow: that the LORD thy God may bless thee in all the work of thine hands. 20. When thou beatest thine olive tree, thou shalt not go over the boughs again: it shall be for the stranger, for the fatherless, and for the widow. 21. When thou gatherest the grapes of thy vineyard, thou shalt not glean *it* afterward: it shall be for the stranger, for the fatherless, and for the widow. 22. And thou shalt remember that thou wast a bondman in the land of Egypt: therefore I command thee to do this thing.

Deut. 26:12. When thou hast made an end of tithing all the tithes of thine increase the third year, *which is* the year of tithing, and hast given *it* unto the Levite, the stranger, the fatherless, and the widow, that they may eat within thy gates, and be filled; 13. Then thou shalt say before the LORD thy God, I have brought away the hallowed things out of *mine* house, and also have given them unto the Levite, and unto the stranger, to the fatherless, and to the widow, according to all thy commandments which thou hast commanded me: I have not transgressed thy commandments, neither have I forgotten *them*.

Deut. 27:19. Cursed *be* he that perverteth the judgment of the stranger, fatherless, and widow.

Job 6:27. Yea, ye overwhelm the fatherless, and ye dig *a pit* for your friend.

Job 22:9. Thou hast sent widows away empty, and the arms of the fatherless have been broken.

Job 24:3. They drive away the ass of the fatherless; they take the widow's ox for a pledge. 9. They pluck the fatherless from the breast, and take a pledge of the poor.

Job 29:12. Because I delivered the poor that cried, and the fatherless, and *him that had* none to help him. 13. The blessing of him that was ready to perish came upon me: and I caused the widow's heart to sing for joy.

Job 31:16. If I have withheld the poor from *their* desire, or have caused the eyes of the widow to fail; 17. Or have eaten my morsel myself alone, and the fatherless hath not eaten thereof; 18. (For from my youth he was brought up with me, as *with* a father, and I have guided her from my mother's womb;) 21. If I have lifted up my hand against the fatherless, when I saw my help in the gate:

Psa. 10:14. Thou art the helper of the fatherless. 17. LORD, thou hast heard the desire of the humble: thou wilt prepare their heart, thou wilt cause thine ear to hear: 18. To judge the fatherless and the oppressed, that the man of the earth may no more oppress.

Psa. 27:10. When my father and my mother forsake me, then the LORD will take me up.

Psa. 68:5. A father of the fatherless, and a judge of the widows, *is* God in his holy habitation.

Psa. 82:3. Defend the poor and fatherless: do justice to the afflicted and needy.

Psa. 94:6. They slay the widow and the stranger, and murder the fatherless.

Psa. 146:9. The LORD preserveth the strangers; he relieveth the fatherless and widow:

Prov. 23:10. Enter not into the fields of the fatherless: 11. For their redeemer *is* mighty; he shall plead their cause with thee.

Isa. 1:17. Learn to do well; seek judgment, relieve the oppressed, judge the fatherless, plead for the widow. 23. Thy princes *are* rebellious, . . . they judge not the fatherless, neither doth the cause of the widow come unto them.

Isa. 10:1. Woe unto them that decree unrighteous decrees, . . . 2. . . . *That* they may rob the fatherless!

Jer. 5:28. They are waxen fat, they shine: yea, they overpass the deeds of the wicked: they judge not the cause, the cause of the fatherless, yet they prosper; and the right of the needy do they not judge.

Jer. 7:6. *If* ye oppress not the stranger, the fatherless, . . . 7. Then will I cause you to dwell in this place, in the land that I gave to your fathers, for ever and ever.

Jer. 22:3. Thus saith the LORD; Execute ye judgment and righteousness, and deliver the spoiled out of the hand of the oppressor: and do no wrong, do no violence to the stranger, the fatherless,

Jer. 49:11. Leave thy fatherless children, I will preserve *them* alive;

Hos. 14:3. Neither will we say any more to the work of our hands, *Ye are* our gods: for in thee the fatherless findeth mercy.

Mal. 3:5. I will be a swift witness against . . . those that oppress the hireling in *his* wages, the widow, and the fatherless,

Jas. 1:27. Pure religion and undefiled before God and the Father is this, To visit the fatherless and widows in their affliction, *and* to keep himself unspotted from the world.

See ADOPTION; CHILDREN; WIDOW.

INSTANCES OF: Lot, Gen. 11:27,28. Daughters of Zelophehad, Num. 27:1–5. Jotham, Judg. 9:16–21. Mephibosheth, 2 Sam. 9:3. Joash, 2 Kin. 11:1–12. Esther, Esth. 2:7. A type of Zion in affliction, Lam. 5:3.

OSEE, Hoshea, so called, Rom. 9:25.

OSPREY, a carnivorous bird. Forbidden as food, Lev. 11:13; Deut. 14:12.

OSSIFRAGE, a carnivorous bird. Forbidden as food, Lev. 11:13; Deut. 14:12.

OSTENTATION, in prayer and alms-giving, Matt. 6:1; Prov. 25:14; 27:2.—*Bible Text Book.*

OSTRICHES, Job 39:13–18; Lam. 4:3; Isa. [*R. V.*] 13:21; 34:13; 43:20. The cry of, Mic. 1:8. In *A. V.* occurs the word owl, but in the *R. V.*, the word ostrich, Lev. 11:16; Deut. 14:15; Job 30:29; Isa. 43:20; Jer. 50:39; Mic. 1:8.

OTHNI, son of Shemaiah, 1 Chr. 26:7.

OTHNIEL, son of Kenaz and nephew of Caleb. Conquers Kirjath-sepher, and as reward secures Caleb's daughter to wife, Josh. 15:16–20; Judg. 1:12,13. Becomes deliverer and judge of Israel, Judg. 3:8–11. Death of, Judg. 3:11. Descendants of, 1 Chr. 4:13,14.

OUCHES, sockets, Ex. 28:11.

OVEN, for baking, Ex. 8:3; Lev. 2:4; 7:9; 11:35; 26:26.

See BREAD.

FIGURATIVE: Psa. 21:9; Hos. 7:4,6,7; Mal. 4:1; Matt. 6:30; Luke 12:28.

OVERCOMING. See PERSEVERANCE.

OVERSEER. Matt. 24:48,49.

See BISHOP.

OWL, a carnivorous bird. Unclean, Lev. 11:16,17; Deut. 14:16. In *R. V.* ostrich is substituted, Lev. 11:16; Deut. 14:15; Job 30:29; Isa. 13:21; 34:11,13; 43:20; Jer. 50:39; Mic. 1:8.

OX. See BULLOCK; CATTLE.

OZEM. 1. Son of Jesse, 1 Chr. 2:15.
2. Son of Jerahmeel, 1 Chr. 2:25.

OZIAS, a form given to the name of King Uzziah, Matt. 1:8,9.

See UZZIAH.

OZNI, son of Gad, Num. 26:16.

P

PAARAI. One of David's valiant men, 2 Sam. 23:35. Called NAARAI in 1 Chr. 11:37.

PACK ANIMALS, used for transporting army supplies, 1 Chr. 12:40.

PADAN-ARAM. See MESOPOTAMIA.

PADON, one of the Nethinim, Ezra 2:44; Neh. 7:47.

PAGIEL, son of Ocran and leader of the tribe of Asher at time of exodus, Num. 1:13; 2:27; 7:72,77; 10:26.

PAHATH-MOAB, the ancestor of an influential family of Judah, which returned to Jerusalem from the captivity, Ezra 2:6; 10:30; Neh. 3:11; 7:11.

PAI. A city in Edom, 1 Chr. 1:50. Called PAU in Gen. 36:39.

PAIN. Job 14:22. But his flesh upon him shall have pain, and his soul within him shall mourn.

Job 30:17. My bones are pierced in me in the night season: and my sinews take no rest. 18. By the great force *of my disease* is my garment changed: it bindeth me about as the collar of my coat.

Job 33:19. He is chastened also with pain upon his bed, and the multitude of his bones with strong *pain.*

Lam. 3:5. He hath builded against me, and compassed *me* with gall and travel.

Rev. 16:10. And the fifth angel poured out his vial upon the seat of the beast; and his kingdom was full of darkness; and they gnawed their tongues for pain,

Rev. 21:4. And God shall wipe away all tears from their eyes; and there shall be no more death, neither sorrow, nor crying, neither shall there be any more pain: for the former things are passed away.

See AFFLICTIONS.

PAINTING. Around the eyes, to enlarge their appearance, 2 Kin. 9:30; Jer. 4:30; Ezek. 23:40. Of rooms, Jer. 22:14. Of portraits, Ezek. 23:14.

See PICTURE.

PALACE. For kings, 1 Kin. 21:1; 2 Kin. 15:25; Jer. 49:27; Amos 1:12; Nah. 2:6. Of David, 2 Sam. 7:2. Of Solomon, 1 Kin. 7:1-12. At Babylon, Dan. 4:29; 5:5; 6:18. At Shushan, Neh. 1:1; Esth. 1:2; 7:7; Dan. 8:2. Archives kept in, Ezra 6:2. Proclamations issued from, Amos 3:9.

FIGURATIVE: Of a government, Amos 1:12; 2:2; Nah. 2:6.

PALAL. Son of Uzai. One of the workmen in rebuilding the walls of Jerusalem, Neh. 3:25.

PALE HORSE, symbol of death, Rev. 6:8.

PALESTINE. See CANAAN.

PALLU, called also PHALLU. Son of Reuben, Gen. 46:9; Ex. 6:14; Num. 26:5,8; 1 Chr. 5:3.

PALM TREE. Deborah judged Israel under, Judg. 4:5. Wood of, used in the temple, 1 Kin. 6:29,32,35; 2 Chr. 3:5. In the temple seen in the vision of Ezekiel, Ezek. 40:16; 41:18. Branches of, thrown in the way when Jesus made his triumphal entry into Jerusalem, John 12:13. Jericho was called the City of Palm Trees, Deut. 34:3.

FIGURATIVE: Of the prosperity of the righteous, Psa. 92:12. Used as a symbol of victory, Rev. 7:9.

PALMER-WORM, Joel 1:4; 2:25; Amos 4:9.

PALSY. See PARALYSIS.

PALTI, a chief Benjamite and one of the twelve spies sent into Canaan, Num. 13:9.

PALTIEL, a chief of Issachar and one of the committee of twelve appointed to divide Canaan among the tribes, Num. 34:26.

PAMPHYLIA. A province in Asia Minor. Men of, in Jerusalem, Acts 2:10. Paul goes to, Acts 13:13,14; 14:24. John, surnamed Mark, in, Acts 13:13; 15:38. Sea of, Acts 27:5.

PANIC. In armies, Lev. 26:17; Deut. 32:30; Josh. 23:10; Psa. 35:5. From God, Gen. 35:5; Ex. 15:14-16; Judg. 7:22; 1 Sam. 14:15-20; 2 Kin. 7:6,7; 2 Chr. 20:22,23.

See ARMIES.

PANTOMIME. By Isaiah, Isa. 20:2,3. By Ezekiel, Ezek. 4:1-8; 12:18. Agabus, Acts 21:11.

PAPER, 2 John 12.

See PARCHMENT.

PAPHOS. A city of Cyprus. Paul blinds a sorcerer in, Acts 13:6-13.

PAPYRUS. [*R. V.*, marg.] Ex. 2:3.

PARABLES. Of the trees, Judg. 9:8-15. Of the lamb, 2 Sam. 12:1-6. Of the woman of Tekoa, 2 Sam. 14:5-12. Of the garment rent in pieces, 1 Kin. 11:30-32. Of the prisoner of war, 1 Kin. 20:39-42. Of the thistle and cedar, 2 Kin. 14:9. Of a vine of Egypt, Psa. 80:8-16. Of the vineyard, Isa. 5:1-7; 27:2,3. Of the husbandman, Isa. 28:23-29. Of the skins filled with wine, Jer. 13:12-14. Of the vine, Ezek. 15; 17:5-10; 19:10-14. Of the two eagles, Ezek. 17. Of lions' whelps, Ezek. 19:1-9. Of Aholah and

Aholibah, Ezek. 23. The boiling pot, Ezek. 24:3-5. The gourd, Jonah 4:10,11. The sheet let down from heaven in Peter's vision, Acts 10:10-16. The two covenants, Gal. 4:22-31. The mercenary soldier, 2 Tim. 2:3,4. Husbandman, 2 Tim. 2:6. Furnished house, 2 Tim. 2:20,21. The athlete, 2 Tim. 2:5. Looking-glass, Jas. 1:23-25.

See JESUS, PARABLES OF; SYMBOLS; TYPES.

PARADISE, the place of the glorified spirits, Luke 23:43; 2 Cor. 12:4; Rev. 2:7.

See EDEN.

PARADOX. Prov. 13:7. There is that maketh himself rich, yet *hath* nothing: *there is* that maketh himself poor, yet *hath* great riches.

Matt. 10:39. He that findeth his life shall lose it: and he that loseth his life for my sake shall find it. chapter 16:25; Mark 8:35; Luke 17:33.

John 12:25. He that loveth his life shall lose it; and he that hateth his life in this world shall keep it unto life eternal.

1 Cor. 3:18. If any man among you seemeth to be wise in this world, let him become a fool, that he may be wise.

2 Cor. 6:4. But in all *things* approving ourselves as the ministers of God, 8. By honour and dishonour, by evil report and good report: as deceivers, and *yet* true; 9. As unknown, and *yet* well known; as dying, and, behold, we live; as chastened, and not killed; 10. As sorrowful, yet alway rejoicing; as poor, yet making many rich; as having nothing, and *yet* possessing all things.

2 Cor. 12:4. How that he was caught up into paradise, and heard unspeakable words, which it is not lawful for a man to utter. 10. Therefore I take pleasure in infirmities, in reproaches, in necessities, in persecutions, in distresses for Christ's sake: for when I am weak, then am I strong. 11. I am become a fool in glorying; ye have compelled me: for I ought to have been commended of you: for in nothing am I behind the very chiefest apostles, though I be nothing.

Eph. 3:17. That ye, being rooted and grounded in love, 18. May be able to comprehend with all saints what *is* the breadth, and length, and depth, and height; 19. And to know the love of Christ, which passeth knowledge.

Phil. 3:7. But what things were gain to me those I counted loss for Christ.

Rev. 21:18. And the building of the wall of it was *of* jasper: and the city *was* pure gold, like unto clear glass. 21. And the twelve gates *were* twelve pearls; every several gate was of one pearl: and the street of the city *was* pure gold, as it were transparent glass.

PARAH, a city in Benjamin, Josh. 18:23.

PARALYSIS. Cured by Jesus, Matt. 4:24; 8:6,13; 9:2,6; by Philip, Acts 8:7; Peter, Acts 9:33,34.

PARAN. Desert or wilderness of, Gen. 21:21; Num. 10:12; 12:16; 13:3,26; Deut. 1:1. Mountains of, Deut. 33:2; Hab. 3:3. Israelites encamp in, Num. 12:16. David takes refuge in, 1 Sam. 25:1. Hadad flees to, 1 Kin. 11:17,18.

PARCHMENT, 2 Tim. 4:13.

PARDON. OF SIN: See SIN, FORGIVENESS OF.

PARENTS. Covenant benefits of, entailed on children, Gen. 6:18; Ex. 20:6; Psa. 103:17. Curses entailed, Ex. 20:5; Lev. 20:5; Isa. 14:20; Jer. 9:14; Lam. 5:7; Ezek. 16:44, 45. Involved in children's wickedness, 1 Sam. 2:27-36; 4:10-22.

Partiality of: Isaac for Esau, Gen. 25:28; Rebekah for Jacob, Gen. 25:28; 27:6-17; Jacob for Joseph, Gen. 33:2; 37:3; 48:22; for Benjamin, Gen. 42:4. See PARTIALITY.

Parental affection exemplified: By Hagar, Gen. 21:15,16; Rebekah's mother, Gen. 24:55; Isaac and Rebekah, Gen. 25:28; Isaac, Gen. 27:26,27; Laban, Gen. 31:26-28; Jacob, Gen. 37:3,4; 42:4,38; 43:13,14; 45:26-28; 48:10,11; Moses's mother, Ex. 2; Naomi, Ruth 1:8,9; Hannah, 1 Sam. 2:19; David, 2 Sam. 12:18-23; 13:38,39; 14:1,33; 18:5,12,13,33; 19:1-6; Rizpah, 2 Sam. 21:10; the mother of the infant brought to Solomon by the harlots, 1 Kin. 3: 22-28; Mary, Matt. 12:46; Luke 2:48; John 2: 5; 19:25; Jairus, Mark 5:23; father of demoniac, Mark 9:24; nobleman, John 4:49.

Indulgent: Eli, 1 Sam. 2:27-36; 3:13,14; David, 1 Kin. 1:6.

Paternal blessings: Of Noah, Gen. 9:24-27; Abraham, Gen. 17:18; Isaac, Gen. 27:10-40; 28:3,4; Jacob, Gen. 48:15-20; 49:1-28.

Prayers in behalf of children: Of Hannah, 1 Sam. 1:27; David, 2 Sam. 7:25-29; 1 Chr. 17: 16-27; 2 Sam. 12:16; 1 Chr. 22:12; 29:19; Job, Job 1:5.

Paternal reproaches, Gen. 9:24,25; 49:3-7.

INFLUENCE OF: See INFLUENCE.

UNCLASSIFIED SCRIPTURES RELATING TO: Gen. 18:19. For I know him, that he will command his children and his household after him, and they shall keep the way of the LORD, to do justice and judgment; that the LORD may bring upon Abraham that which he hath spoken of him.

Ex. 10:2. And that thou mayest tell in the ears of thy son, and of thy son's son, what things I have wrought in Egypt, and my signs which I have done among them; that ye may know how that I *am* the LORD.

Ex. 12:26. And it shall come to pass, when your children shall say unto you, What mean ye by this service? 27. That ye shall say, It *is* the sacrifice of the LORD'S passover, who passed over the houses of the children of Israel in Egypt, when he smote the Egyptians, and delivered our houses. And the people bowed the head and worshipped.

Ex. 13:8. And thou shalt shew thy son in that day, saying, *This is done* because of that *which* the LORD did unto me when I came forth out of Egypt. 14. And it shall be when thy son asketh thee in time to come, saying, What *is* this? that thou shalt say unto him, By strength of hand the LORD brought us out from Egypt, from the house of bondage:

Ex. 20:5. Thou shalt not bow down thyself to them, nor serve them: for I the LORD thy God *am* a jealous God, visiting the iniquity of the fathers upon the children unto the third and fourth *generation* of them that hate me; [Lam. 5:7.] 10. But the seventh day *is* the sabbath of the LORD thy God: *in it* thou shalt not do any work, thou, nor thy son, nor thy daughter, thy manservant, nor thy maidservant, nor thy cattle, nor thy stranger that *is* within thy gates:

Ex. 21:17. And he that curseth his father, or his mother, shall surely be put to death.

Lev. 20:9. For every one that curseth his father or his mother shall be surely put to death: he hath cursed his father or his mother; his blood *shall be* upon him.

Lev. 23:3. Six days shall work be done: but the seventh day *is* the sabbath of rest, an holy convocation; ye shall do no work *therein:* it *is* the sabbath of the LORD in all your dwellings.

Deut. 4:9. Only take heed to thyself, and keep thy soul diligently, lest thou forget the things which thine eyes have seen, and lest they depart from thy heart all the days of thy life; but teach them thy sons, and thy sons' sons; 10. *Specially* the day that thou stoodest before the LORD thy God in Horeb, when the LORD said unto me, Gather me the people together, and I will make them hear my words, that they may learn to fear me all the days that they shall live upon the earth, and *that* they may teach their children.

Deut. 6:7. And thou shalt teach them diligently unto thy children, and shalt talk of them when thou sittest in thine house, and when thou walkest by the way, and when thou liest down, and when thou risest up. 20. *And* when thy son asketh thee in time to come, saying, What *mean* the testimonies, and the statutes, and the judgments, which the LORD our God hath commanded you? 21. Then thou shalt say unto thy son, We were Pharaoh's bondmen in Egypt; and the LORD brought us out of Egypt with a mighty hand: 22. And the LORD shewed signs and wonders, great and sore, upon Egypt, upon Pharaoh, and upon all his household, before our eyes: 23. And he brought us out from thence, that he might bring us in, to give us the land which he sware unto our fathers. 24. And the LORD commanded us to do all these statutes, to fear the LORD our God, for our good always, that he might preserve us alive, as *it is* at this day.

Deut. 11:18. Therefore shall ye lay up these my words in your heart and in your soul, and bind them for a sign upon your hand, that they may be as frontlets between

your eyes. 19. And ye shall teach them your children, speaking of them when thou sittest in thine house, and when thou walkest by the way, when thou liest down, and when thou risest up. 20. And thou shalt write them upon the door posts of thine house, and upon thy gates: 21. That your days may be multiplied, and the days of your children, in the land which the LORD sware unto your fathers to give them, as the days of heaven upon the earth.

Deut. 32:46. Set your hearts unto all the words which I testify among you this day, which ye shall command your children to observe to do, all the words of this law.

Psa. 78:5. For he established a testimony in Jacob, and appointed a law in Israel, which he commaned our fathers, that they should make them known to their children: 6. That the generation to come might know *them, even* the children *which* should be born; *who* should arise and declare *them* to their children:

Psa. 103:13. Like as a father pitieth *his* children, *so* the LORD pitieth them that fear him.

Prov. 3:12. Whom the LORD loveth he correcteth; even as a father the son *in whom* he delighteth.

Prov. 13:22. A good *man* leaveth an inheritance to his children's children: 24. He that spareth his rod hateth his son: but he that loveth him chasteneth him betimes.

Prov. 19:18. Chasten thy son while there is hope, and let not thy soul spare for his crying.

Prov. 22:6. Train up a child in the way he should go: and when he is old, he will not depart from it. 15. Foolishness *is* bound in the heart of a child; *but* the rod of correction shall drive it far from him.

Prov. 23:13. Withhold not correction from the child: for *if* thou beatest him with the rod, he shall not die. 14. Thou shalt beat him with the rod, and shalt deliver his soul from hell.

Prov. 27:11. My son, be wise, and make my heart glad, that I may answer him that reproacheth me.

Prov. 29:15. The rod and reproof give wisdom: but a child left *to himself* bringeth his mother to shame. 17. Correct thy son, and he shall give thee rest; yea, he shall give delight unto thy soul.

Prov. 31:28. Her children arise up, and call her blessed;

Isa. 38:19. The father to the children shall make known thy truth.

Isa. 49:15. Can a woman forget her sucking child, that she should not have compassion on the son of her womb?

Isa. 66:13. As one whom his mother comforteth, so will I comfort you;

Jer. 31:1. At the same time, saith the LORD, will I be the God of all the families of Israel, and they shall be my people.

Jer. 49:11. Leave thy fatherless children, I will preserve *them* alive;

Joel 1:3. Tell ye your children of it, and *let* your children *tell* their children, and their children another generation.

Mal. 4:6. He shall turn the heart of the fathers to the children, and the heart of the children to their fathers, lest I come and smite the earth with a curse.

Matt. 10:37. He that loveth son or daughter more than me is not worthy of me.

Luke 11:11. If a son shall ask bread of any of you that is a father, will ye give him a stone? or if *he ask* a fish, will he for a fish give him a serpent? 12. Or if he shall ask an egg, will he offer him a scorpion? 13. If ye then, being evil, know how to give good gifts unto your children: how much more shall *your* heavenly Father give the Holy Spirit to them that ask him?

2 Cor. 12:14. The children ought not to lay up for the parents, but the parents for the children.

Eph. 6:4. Fathers, provoke not your children to wrath : but bring them up in the nurture and admonition of the Lord.

Col. 3:21. Fathers, provoke not your children *to anger*, lest they be discouraged.

1 Thess. 2:11. Ye know how we exhorted and comforted and charged every one of you, as a father *doth* his children,

1 Tim. 3:4. One that ruleth well his own house, having his childen in subjection with all gravity ; 5. (For if a man know not how to rule his own house, how shall he take care of the church of God ?) 12. Let the deacons be the husbands of one wife, ruling their children and their own houses well.

1 Tim. 5:8. If any provide not for his own, and specially for those of his own house, he hath denied the faith, and is worse than an ¹ infidel.   [¹ R. V. unbeliever]

Tit. 1:6. If any be blameless, the husband of one wife, having faithful children not accused of riot or unruly.

Tit. 2:4. That they may teach the young women to be sober, to love their husbands, to love their children,

Heb. 12:7. If ye endure chastening, God dealeth with you as with sons; for what son is he whom the father chasteneth not ?

See CHILDREN ; INSTRUCTION.

PARLOR, 1 Sam. 9:22.

PARMASHTA, son of Haman, Esth. 9:9.

PARMENAS, one of the disciples, Acts 6:5.

PARNACH, father of Elizaphan, Num. 34:25.

PAROSH, called also PHAROSH. The ancestor of one of the families which returned to Jerusalem from captivity in Babylon, Ezra 2:3; 8:3; 10:25; Neh. 7:8; 10:14.

PARRICIDE, 2 Kin. 19:37; 2 Chr. 32:21; Isa. 37:38.

PARSHANDATHA, son of Haman, Esth. 9:7.

PARSIMONY. Of the Jews toward the temple, Hag. 1:2,4,6,9; toward God, Mal. 3:8,9. Of the disciples, when the oint-

ment was poured on Jesus, Matt. 26:8,9; John 12:4,5. Punishment of, Hag. 1:9–11.

See LIBERALITY.

PARTHIANS, the inhabitants of Parthia, a country northwest of Persia, Acts 2:9.

PARTIALITY. Among brethren forbidden, 1 Tim. 5:21. Of parents for particular children, see PARENTS. Its effect on other children, Gen. 37:4.

PARTICEPS CRIMINIS, 2 John 11.

See COLLUSION.

PARTNERSHIP, with God, 1 Cor. 3:7,9; 2 Cor. 6:1; Phil. 2:13.

See PROVIDENCE.

PARTRIDGE, 1 Sam. 26:20; Jer. 17:11.

PARUAH, father of Jehoshaphat, 1 Kin. 4:17.

PARVAIM, an unknown gold region, 2 Chr. 3:6.

PASACH, son of Japhlet, 1 Chr. 7:33.

PASCHAL LAMB. See PASSOVER.

PASSENGER. See COMMERCE.

PAS-DAMMIM. A battle between David and the Philistines, fought at, 1 Chr. 11:13. Called EPHES-DAMMIM in 1 Sam. 17:1.

PASEAH. 1. Called also PHASEAH. A son of Eshton, 1 Chr. 4:12.

2. Ancestor of a family which returned to Jerusalem from captivity in Babylon, Ezra 2:49; Neh. 7:51.

3. Father of Jehoiada, probably identical with preceding, Neh. 3:6.

PASHUR. 1. A priest, son of Malchiah, 1 Chr. 9:12. An influential man, and ancestor of an influential family, Jer. 21:1; 38:1; Ezra 2:38; 10:22; Neh. 7:41; 10:3; 11:12.

2. Son of Immer and governor of the temple. Beats and imprisons Jeremiah, Jer. 20:1–6.

3. Father of Gedaliah, who persecuted Jeremiah, Jer. 38:1.

PASSION, Acts 1:3.

See JESUS, SUFFERINGS OF.

PASSOVER. Institution of, Ex. 12:3–49; 23:15–18; 34:18; Lev. 23:4–8; Num. 9:2–5,13, 14; 28:16–25; Deut. 16:1–8,16; Psa. 81:3,5. Design of, Ex. 12:21–28.

Special passover, for those who were unclean, or on journey, to be held in second month, Num. 9:6–12; 2 Chr. 30:2–4. Lamb killed by Levites, for those who were ceremonially unclean, 2 Chr. 30:17; 35:3–11; Ezra 6:20. Strangers authorized to celebrate, Ex. 12:48,49; Num. 9:14.

Observed at place designated by God, Deut. 16:5–7; with unleavened bread, Ex. 12:8,15–20; 13:3,6; 23:15; Lev. 23:6; Num. 9:11; 28:17; Deut. 16:3,4; Mark 14:12; Luke 22:7; Acts 12:3; 1 Cor. 5:8. Penalty for neglecting to observe, Num. 9:13.

Reinstituted by Ezekiel, Ezek. 45:21–24.

Observation of, renewed by the Israelites on entering Canaan, Josh. 5:10,11; by Hezekiah, 2 Chr. 30:1; by Josiah, 2 Kin. 23:22,23; 2 Chr. 35:1,18; after return from captivity, Ezra 6:19,20. Observed by Jesus, Matt. 26: 17–20; Luke 22:15; John 2:13,23; 13. Jesus in the temple at time of, Luke 2:41–50.

Jesus crucified at time of, Matt. 26:2; Mark 14:1,2; John 18:28.   The lamb of, a type of Christ, 1 Cor. 5:7.   Lord's supper ordained at, Matt. 26:26–28; Mark 14:12–25; Luke 22: 7–20.

Prisoner released at, by the Romans, Matt. 27:15; Mark 15:6; Luke 23:16,17; John 18:39. Peter imprisoned at time of, Acts 12:3.

Christ called our passover, 1 Cor. 5:7.

See FEASTS.

PASSPORTS, given to Nehemiah, Neh. 2:7–9.

PASTOR, Jer. 22:22.

See SHEPHERD.

PATARA, a Lycian city in Asia Minor. Visited by Paul, Acts 21:1,2.

PATHROS, a part of Upper Egypt. Jewish captives in, Isa. 11:11; Jer. 44:1,15; Ezek. 29:14.   Prophecy against, Ezek. 30:14.

PATHRUSIM, a descendant of Mizraim and ancestor of the Philistines, Gen. 10:14; 1 Chr. 1:12.

PATIENCE. Psa. 37:7. Rest in the LORD, and wait patiently for him: fret not thyself because of him who prospereth in his way, because of the man who bringeth wicked devices to pass.   8. Cease from anger, and forsake wrath: fret not thyself in any wise to do evil.   9. For evildoers shall be cut off: but those that wait upon the LORD, they shall inherit the earth.

Prov. 15:18. A wrathful man stirreth up strife: but *he that is* slow to anger appeaseth strife.

Eccl. 7:8. The patient in spirit *is* better than the proud in spirit.   9. Be not hasty in thy spirit to be angry: for anger resteth in the bosom of fools.

Lam. 3:26. *It is* good that *a man* should both hope and quietly wait for the salvation of the LORD.   27. *It is* good for a man that he bear the yoke in his youth.

Luke 8:15. But that on the good ground are they, which in an honest and good heart, having heard the word, keep *it*, and bring forth fruit with patience.

Luke 21:19. In your patience ¹ possess ye your souls.   [¹ R. V. ye shall win your souls]

Rom. 2:7. To them who by patient continuance in well doing seek for glory and honour and immortality, eternal life:

Rom. 5:3. And not only *so*, but we glory in tribulations also; knowing that tribulation worketh patience;   4. And patience, experience; and experience, hope:

Rom. 8:25. But if we hope for that we see not, *then* do we with patience wait for *it*.

Rom. 12:12. Rejoicing in hope; patient in tribulation;

Rom. 15:4. For whatsoever things were written aforetime were written for our learning, that we through patience and comfort of the scriptures might have hope.   5. Now the God of patience and consolation grant you to be likeminded one toward another according to Christ Jesus:

1 Cor. 13:4. Charity suffereth long, *and* is kind; charity envieth not; charity vaunt-

eth not itself, is not puffed up,   5. Doth not behave itself unseemly, seeketh not ¹ her own, is not easily provoked, thinketh no evil;

[¹ R. V. its own, is not provoked, taketh not account of evil]

2 Cor. 6:4. But in all *things* approving ourselves as the ministers of God, in much patience, in afflictions, in necessities, in distresses,   5. In stripes, in imprisonments, in tumults, in labours, in watchings, in fastings;   6. By pureness, by knowledge, by longsuffering, by kindness,

2 Cor. 12:12. Truly the signs of an apostle were wrought among you in all patience, in signs, and wonders, and mighty deeds.

Gal. 6:9. And let us not be weary in well doing: for in due season we shall reap, if we faint not.

Eph. 4:1. I therefore, the prisoner of the Lord, beseech you that ye walk worthy of the vocation wherewith ye are called,   2. With all lowliness and meekness, with longsuffering, forbearing one another in love;

Col. 1:10. That ye might walk worthy of the Lord unto all pleasing, being fruitful in every good work, and increasing in the knowledge of God;   11. Strengthened with all might, according to his glorious power, unto all patience and longsuffering with joyfulness;

Col. 3:12. Put on therefore, as the elect of God, holy and beloved, bowels of mercies, kindness, humbleness of mind, meekness, longsuffering;   13. Forbearing one another, and forgiving one another, if any man have a quarrel against any: even as Christ forgave you, so also *do* ye.

1 Thess. 1:3. Remembering without ceasing your work of faith, and labour of love, and patience of hope in our Lord Jesus Christ, in the sight of God and our Father;

1 Thess. 5:14. Now we exhort you, brethren, . . . be patient toward all *men.*

2 Thess. 3:5. The Lord direct your hearts into the love of God, and into the ¹ patient waiting for Christ.   [¹ R. V. patience of]

1 Tim. 3:2. A bishop then must be blameless, the husband of one wife, vigilant, sober, of good behaviour, given to hospitality, apt to teach;   3. Not given to wine, no striker, not greedy of filthy lucre; but patient, not a brawler, not covetous;

1 Tim. 6:11. But thou, O man of God, flee these things; and follow after righteousness, godliness, faith, love, patience, meekness.

2 Tim. 2:24. The servant of the Lord must not strive; but be gentle unto all *men*, apt to teach, patient,   25. In meekness instructing those that oppose themselves.

Tit. 2:1. But speak thou the things which become sound doctrine: 2. That the aged men be . . . sound in faith, in charity, in patience.   9. *Exhort* servants to be obedient unto their own masters, *and* to please *them* well in all *things;* not answering again;

Heb. 6:12. That ye be not slothful, but followers of them who through faith and patience inherit the promises. 15. And so, after he had patiently endured, he obtained the promise.

Heb. 10:36. Ye have need of patience, that, after ye have done the will of God, ye might receive the promise.

Heb. 12:1. Wherefore seeing we also are compassed about with so great a cloud of witnesses, let us lay aside every weight, and the sin which doth so easily beset *us*, and let us run with patience the race that is set before us.

Jas. 1:3. Knowing *this*, that the trying of your faith worketh patience. 4. But let patience have *her* perfect work, that ye may be perfect and entire, wanting nothing. 19. Wherefore, my beloved brethren, let every man be swift to hear, slow to speak, slow to wrath:

Jas. 5:7. Be patient therefore, brethren, unto the coming of the Lord. Behold, the husbandman waiteth for the precious fruit of the earth, and hath long patience for it, until he receive the early and latter rain. 8. Be ye also patient; stablish your hearts: for the coming of the Lord draweth nigh.

1 Pet. 2:19. For this *is* thankworthy, if a man for conscience toward God endure grief, suffering wrongfully. 20. For what glory *is it*, if, when ye be buffeted for your faults, ye shall take it patiently? but if, when ye do well, and suffer *for it*, ye take it patiently, this *is* acceptable with God. 21. For even hereunto were ye called: because Christ also suffered for us, leaving us an example, that ye should follow his steps: 22. Who did no sin, neither was guile found in his mouth: 23. Who, when he was reviled, reviled not again; when he suffered, he threatened not;

2 Pet. 1:5. And beside this, giving all diligence, add to your faith virtue; and to virtue knowledge; 6. And to knowledge temperance; and to temperance patience; and to patience godliness;

Rev. 1:9. I John, who also am your brother, and companion in tribulation, and in the kingdom and patience of Jesus Christ,

Rev. 13:10. He that leadeth into captivity shall go into captivity: he that killeth with the sword must be killed with the sword. Here is the patience and the faith of the saints.

Rev. 14:12. Here is the patience of the saints: here *are* they that keep the commandments of God, and the faith of Jesus.

See kindred topics, LONGSUFFERING; MEEKNESS.

INSTANCES OF: Isaac toward the people of Gerar, Gen. 26:15-22. Moses, Ex. 16: 7,8. Job, Job 1:21; Jas. 5:11. David, Psa. 40:1. Simeon, Luke 2:25. Paul, 2 Tim. 3:10. Prophets, Jas. 5:10. The Thessalonians, 2 Thess. 1:4. The church at Ephesus, Rev. 2:2,3; and Thyatira, Rev. 2:19. John, Rev. 1:9.

PATMOS, an island in the Ægean Sea. John an exile on, Rev. 1:9.

PATRIARCH, head of a family, Acts 7:9.

PATRIARCHAL GOVERNMENT. See GOVERNMENT.

PATRICIDE, of Sennacherib, 2 Kin. 19:37; Isa. 37:38.

PATRIOTISM. Deut. 26:1. And it shall be, when thou *art* come in unto the land which the LORD thy God giveth thee *for* an inheritance, and possessest it, and dwellest therein; 2. That thou shalt take of the first of all the fruit of the earth, which thou shalt bring of thy land that the LORD thy God giveth thee, and shalt put *it* in a basket, and shalt go unto the place which the LORD thy God shall choose to place his name there. 3. And thou shalt go unto the priest that shall be in those days, and say unto him, I profess this day unto the LORD thy God, that I am come unto the country which the LORD sware unto our fathers for to give us. 4. And the priest shall take the basket out of thine hand, and set it down before the altar of the LORD thy God. 5. And thou shalt speak and say before the LORD thy God, A Syrian ready to perish *was* my father, and he went down into Egypt, and sojourned there with a few, and became there a nation, great, mighty, and populous: 6. And the Egyptians evil entreated us, and afflicted us, and laid upon us hard bondage. 7. And when we cried unto the LORD God of our fathers, the LORD heard our voice, and looked on our affliction, and our labour, and our oppression: 8. And the LORD brought us forth out of Egypt with a mighty hand, and with an outstretched arm, and with great terribleness, and with signs, and with wonders: 9. And he hath brought us into this place, and hath given us this land, *even* a land that floweth with milk and honey. 10. And now, behold, I have brought the firstfruits of the land, which thou, O LORD, hast given me. And thou shalt set it before the LORD thy God, and worship before the LORD thy God: 11. And thou shalt rejoice in every good *thing* which the LORD thy God hath given unto thee, and unto thine house, thou, and the Levite, and the stranger that *is* among you.

Judg. 5:1. Then sang Deborah and Barak the son of Abinoam on that day, saying, 2. Praise ye the LORD for the avenging of Israel, when the people willingly offered themselves. 3. Hear, O ye kings; give ear, O ye princes; I, *even* I, will sing unto the LORD; I will sing *praise* to the LORD God of Israel. 4. LORD, when thou wentest out of Seir, when thou marchedst out of the field of Edom, the earth trembled, and the heavens dropped, the clouds also dropped water. 5. The mountains melted from before the LORD, *even* that Sinai from before the LORD God of Israel. 6. In the days of Shamgar the son of Anath, in the days of Jael, the highways were unoccupied, and the travellers walked through byways,

7. *The inhabitants of* the villages ceased, they ceased in Israel, until that I Deborah arose, that I arose a mother in Israel. 8. They chose new gods; then *was* war in the gates: was there a shield or spear seen among forty thousand in Israel? 9. My heart *is* toward the governors of Israel, that offered themselves willingly among the people. Bless ye the LORD. 10. Speak, ye that ride on white asses, ye that sit in judgment, and walk by the way. 11. *They that are delivered* from the noise of archers in the places of drawing water, there shall they rehearse the righteous acts of the LORD, *even* the righteous acts *toward the inhabitants* of his villages in Israel: then shall the people of the LORD go down to the gates. 12. Awake, awake, Deborah: awake, awake, utter a song: arise, Barak, and lead thy captivity captive, thou son of Abinoam. 13. Then he made him that remaineth have dominion over the nobles among the people: the LORD made me have dominion over the mighty. 14. Out of Ephraim *was there* a root of them against Amalek; after thee, Benjamin, among thy people; out of Machir came down governors, and out of Zebulun they that handle the pen of the writer. 15. And the princes of Issachar *were* with Deborah; even Issachar, and also Barak: he was sent on foot into the valley. For the divisions of Reuben *there were* great thoughts of heart. 16. Why abodest thou among the sheepfolds, to hear the bleatings of the flocks? For the divisions of Reuben *there were* great searchings of heart. 17. Gilead abode beyond Jordan: and why did Dan remain in ships? Asher continued on the sea shore, and abode in his breaches. 18. Zebulun and Naphtali *were* a people *that* jeoparded their lives unto the death in the high places of the field. 19. The kings came *and* fought; then fought the kings of Canaan in Taanach by the waters of Megiddo; they took no gain of money. 20. They fought from heaven; the stars in their courses fought against Sisera. 21. The river of Kishon swept them away, that ancient river, the river Kishon. O my soul, thou hast trodden down strength. 22. Then were the horsehoofs broken by the means of the pransings, the pransings of their mighty ones. 23. Curse ye Meroz, said the angel of the LORD, curse ye bitterly the inhabitants thereof; because they came not to the help of the LORD, to the help of the LORD against the mighty. 24. Blessed above women shall Jael the wife of Heber the Kenite be: blessed shall she be above women in the tent. 25. He asked water, *and* she gave *him* milk; she brought forth butter in a lordly dish. 26. She put her hand to the nail, and her right hand to the workmen's hammer; and with the hammer she smote Sisera, she smote off his head, when she had pierced and stricken through his temples. 27. At her feet he bowed, he fell, he lay down: at her feet he bowed, he fell: where he bowed, there he fell down dead. 28. The mother of Sisera looked out at a window, and cried through the lattice, Why is his chariot *so* long in coming? why tarry the wheels of his chariots? 29. Her wise ladies answered her, yea, she returned answer to herself, 30. Have they not sped? have they *not* divided the prey; to every man a damsel *or* two; to Sisera a prey of divers colours, a prey of divers colours of needlework, of divers colours of needlework on both sides, *meet* for the necks of *them that take* the spoil? 31. So let all thine enemies perish, O LORD: but *let* them that love him *be* as the sun when he goeth forth in his might. And the land had rest forty years.

Psa. 51:18. Do good in thy good pleasure unto Zion: build thou the walls of Jerusalem.

Psa. 85:1. LORD, thou hast been favourable unto thy land: thou hast brought back the captivity of Jacob. 2. Thou hast forgiven the iniquity of thy people; thou hast covered all their sin. 3. Thou hast taken away all thy wrath: thou hast turned *thyself* from the fierceness of thine anger. 4. Turn us, O God of our salvation, and cause thine anger toward us to cease. 5. Wilt thou be angry with us for ever? wilt thou draw out thine anger to all generations? 6. Wilt thou not revive us again: that thy people may rejoice in thee? 7. Shew us thy mercy, O LORD, and grant us thy salvation. 8. I will hear what God the LORD will speak: for he will speak peace unto his people, and to his saints: but let them not turn again to folly. 9. Surely his salvation *is* nigh them that fear him; that glory may dwell in our land. 10. Mercy and truth are met together; and righteousness and peace have kissed *each other*. 11. Truth shall spring out of the earth; and righteousness shall look down from heaven. 12. Yea, the LORD shall give *that which is* good; and our land shall yield her increase. 13. Righteousness shall go before him; and shall set *us* in the way of his steps.

Psa. 122:6. Pray for the peace of Jerusalem: they shall prosper that love thee. 7. Peace be within thy walls, *and* prosperity within thy palaces.

Psa. 128:5. The LORD shall bless thee out of Zion: and thou shalt see the good of Jerusalem all the days of thy life. 6. Yea, thou shalt see thy children's children, *and* peace upon Israel.

Psa. 137:1. By the rivers of Babylon, there we sat down, yea, we wept, when we remembered Zion. 2. We hanged our harps upon the willows in the midst thereof. 3. For there they that carried us away captive required of us a song; and they that wasted us *required of us* mirth, *saying*, Sing us *one* of the songs of Zion. 4. How shall we sing the LORD's song in a strange land? 5. If I forget thee, O Jerusalem, let my right hand forget *her cunning.* 6. If I do not remember thee, let my tongue cleave to the roof of my mouth; if I prefer not Jerusalem above my chief joy.

Isa. 62:1. For Zion's sake will I not hold my peace, and for Jerusalem's sake I will not rest, until the righteousness thereof go 'orth as brightness, and the salvation thereof as a lamp *that* burneth.

Jer. 8:11. For they have healed the hurt of the daughter of my people slightly, saying, Peace, peace; when *there is* no peace. 21. For the hurt of the daughter of my people am I hurt; I am black; astonishment hath taken hold on me. 22. *Is there* no balm in Gilead? *is there* no physician there? why then is not the health of the daughter of my people recovered?

Jer. 9:1. Oh that my head were waters, and mine eyes a fountain of tears, that I might weep day and night for the slain of the daughter of my people! 2. Oh that I had in the wilderness a lodging place of wayfaring men; that I might leave my people, and go from them! for they *be* all adulterers, an assembly of treacherous men.

Lam. 5:1. Remember, O LORD, what is come upon us: consider, and behold our reproach. 2. Our inheritance is turned to strangers, our houses to aliens. 3. We are orphans and fatherless, our mothers *are* as widows. 4. We have drunken our water for money; our wood is sold unto us. 5. Our necks *are* under persecution: we labour, *and* have no rest. 6. We have given the hand *to* the Egyptians, *and to* the Assyrians, to be satisfied with bread. 7. Our fathers have sinned, and *are* not; and we have borne their iniquities. 8. Servants have ruled over us: *there is* none that doth deliver *us* out of their hand. 9. We gat our bread with *the peril of* our lives because of the sword of the wilderness. 10. Our skin was black like an oven because of the terrible famine. 11. They ravished the women in Zion, *and* the maids in the cities of Judah. 12. Princes are hanged up by their hand: the faces of elders were not honoured. 13. They took the young men to grind, and the children fell under the wood. 14. The elders have ceased from the gate, the young men from their musick. 15. The joy of our heart is ceased; our dance is turned into mourning. 16. The crown is fallen *from* our head: woe unto us, that we have sinned! 17. For this our heart is faint; for these *things* our eyes are dim. 18. Because of the mountain of Zion, which is desolate, the foxes walk upon it. 19. Thou, O LORD, remainest for ever; thy throne from generation to generation. 20. Wherefore dost thou forget us for ever, *and* forsake us so long time? 21. Turn thou us unto thee, O LORD, and we shall be turned; renew our days as of old. 22. But thou hast utterly rejected us; thou art very wroth against us.

See COUNTRY, LOVE OF.

INSTANCES OF: Moses, Heb. 11:24-26.

Deborah, Judg. 4; 5. The tribes of Zebulun and Naphtali, Judg. 5:18-20. Eli, 1 Sam. 4:17,18. Phinehas' wife, 1 Sam. 4:19-22. Joab, 2 Sam. 10:12. Uriah, 2 Sam. 11:11. Hadad, 1 Kin. 11:21,22. The lepers of Samaria, 2 Kin. 7:9. Nehemiah, Neh. 1:2,4-11; 2:3.

WANTING IN: The tribes of Reuben, Asher, and Dan, Judg. 5:15-17. Inhabitants of Meroz, Judg. 5:23; of Succoth and Penuel, Judg. 8:4-17.

PATROBAS, a believer at Rome, Rom. 16:14.

PATTERN, of the tabernacle, Heb. 8:5; 9:23.

See TABERNACLE.

PAU, called also PAI. A city of Edom. Gen. 36:39; 1 Chr. 1:50.

PAUL. Called also SAUL, Acts 8:1; 9:1; 13:9. Of the tribe of Benjamin, Rom. 11:1; Phil. 3:5. Personal appearance of, 2 Cor. 10: 1,10; 11:6. Born in Tarsus, Acts 9:11; 21:39; 22:3. Educated at Jerusalem in the school of Gamaliel, Acts 22:3; 26:4. A zealous Pharisee, Acts 22:3; 23:6; 26:5; 2 Cor. 11:22; Gal. 1:14; Phil. 3:5. A Roman, Acts 16:37; 22:25-28. Persecutes the Christians; present at, and gives consent to, the stoning of Stephen, Acts 7:58; 8:1,3; 9:1; 22:4. Sent to Damascus with letters for the arrest and return to Jerusalem of Christians, Acts 9: 1,2. His vision and conversion, Acts 9:3-22; 22:4-19; 26:9-15; 1 Cor. 9:1; 15:8; Gal. 1:13; 1 Tim. 1:12,13. Is baptized, Acts 9:18; 22:16. Called to be an apostle, Acts 22:14-21; 26:16-18; Rom. 1:1; 1 Cor. 1:1; 9:1,2; 15:9; Gal. 1:1, 15,16; Eph. 1:1; Col. 1:1; 1 Tim. 1:1; 2:7; 2 Tim. 1:1,11; Tit. 1:1,3. Preaches in Damascus, Acts 9:20,22. Is persecuted by the Jews, Acts 9:23. 24. Escapes by being let down from the wall in a basket; goes to Arabia, Gal. 1:17; Jerusalem, Acts 9:25,26; Gal. 1:18,19. Received by the disciples in Jerusalem, Acts 9:26-29. Goes to Cæsarea, Acts 9:30; 18:22. Sent unto the Gentiles, Acts 13:2,3,47,48; 22:17-21; Rom. 11:13; 15:16; Gal. 1:15-24. Has Barnabas as his companion, Acts 11:25,26. Teaches at Antioch one year, Acts 11:26. Conveys the contributions of the Christians in Antioch to the Christians in Jerusalem, Acts 11: 27-30. Returns with John to Antioch, Acts 12:25. Visits Seleucia, Acts 13:4; Cyprus, Acts 13:4. Preaches at Salamis, Acts 13:5; at Paphos, Acts 13:6. Sergius Paulus, deputy of the country, is a convert of, Acts 13:7-12. Contends with Elymas the sorcerer, Acts 13:6-12. Visits Perga in Pamphylia, Acts 13:13. John, a companion of. departs for Jerusalem, Acts 13:13. Visits Antioch in Pisidia, and preaches in the synagogue, Acts 13:14-41. His message received gladly by the Gentiles, Acts 13:42,49. Persecuted and expelled, Acts 13:50,51. Visits Iconium, and preaches to the Jews and Greeks; is persecuted; escapes to Lystra; goes to Derbe, Acts 14:1-6. Heals an impotent man, Acts 14:8-10. The people attempt to worship him, Acts 14:11-18. Is persecuted by certain Jews from Antioch and Iconium, and is stoned, Acts 14:19; 2 Cor. 11:25; 2 Tim. 3:11. Escapes to Derbe, where he preaches the gospel, and returns to Lystra, and to Iconium, and to Antioch, confirms the souls of the disciples, exhorts them to continue in the faith, and ordains elders, Acts 14:19-23. Revisits Pisidia, Pamphylia, Perga, Attalia, and Antioch, in Syria, where he abode, Acts 14:24-28. Contends with the Judaizing Christians against circumcision, Acts 15:1,2. Refers the question as to circumcision to the apostles and elders at Jerusalem, Acts 15:2,4. He declares to the apostles at Jerusalem the miracles and wonders God had wrought among the Gentiles by them, Acts 15:12. Returns to Antioch, accompanied by Barnabas, Judas, and Silas, with letters to the Gentiles, Acts 15: 22,25.

Makes his second tour of the churches, Acts 15:36. Chooses Silas as his companion, and passes through Syria and Cilicia, confirming the churches, Acts 15:36-41. Visits Lystra; circumcises Timothy, Acts 16:1-5. Goes through Phrygia and Galatia; is forbidden by the Holy Ghost to preach in Asia; visits Mysia; essays to go to Bithynia, but is restrained by the Spirit; goes to Troas, where he has a vision of a man saying, "Come over into Macedonia, and help us;" immediately proceeds to Macedonia, Acts 16:6-10. Visits Samothracia and Neopolis; comes to Philippi, the chief city of Macedonia; visits a place of prayer at the river side; preaches the word; the merchant, Lydia, of Thyatira, is converted and baptized, Acts 16:11-15. Reproves the soothsayer; causes the evil spirit to come out of the damsel who practises divination, Acts 16:16-18. Persecuted, beaten, and cast into prison with Silas; sings songs of praise in the prison; an earthquake shakes the prison; he preaches to the alarmed jailer, who believes, and is baptized with his household, Acts 16:19-34. Is released by the civil authorities on the ground of his being a Roman citizen, Acts 16:35-39; 2 Cor. 6:5; 11:25; 1 Thess. 2:2. Is received at the house of Lydia, Acts 16:40. Visits Amphipolis, and Apollonia, and Thessalonica, preaches in the synagogue, Acts 17:1-4. Is persecuted, Acts 17:5-9; 2 Thess. 1:1-4. Escapes to Berea by night; preaches in the synagogue; many honorable women, and men, not a few, believe, Acts 17:10-12. Persecuted by the Jews who come from Thessalonica; is conducted by the brethren to Athens, Acts 17: 13-15. Disputes on Mars' Hill with Grecians, Acts 17:16-34. Visits Corinth; dwells with Aquila and his wife, Priscilla, who were tentmakers; joins in their handicraft; reasons in the synagogue every Sabbath; is rejected of the Jews; turns to the Gentiles; makes his abode with Justus; continues there one year and six months, teaching the word of God, Acts 18:1-11. Persecuted by Jews, drawn before the deputy, charged with wicked lewdness; accusation dis-

missed; takes his leave after many days, and sails unto Syria, accompanied by Aquila and Priscilla, Acts 18:12-18. Visits Ephesus, where he leaves Aquila and Priscilla; enters into a synagogue, where he reasons with the Jews; starts on his return journey to Jerusalem; visits Cæsarea; goes over the country of Galatia and Phrygia, in order, strengthening the disciples, Acts 18:18-23. Returns to Ephesus; baptizes in the name of the Lord Jesus, and lays his hands upon the disciples, who are baptized with the Holy Ghost; preaches in the synagogue; remains in Ephesus for the space of two years; heals the sick, Acts 19:1-12. Reproves the exorcists; casts an evil spirit out of a man, and many believe, bringing their books of sorcery to be burned, Acts 19:13-20; 1 Cor. 16:8,9. Sends Timothy and Erastus into Macedonia, but remains himself in Asia for a season, Acts 19:21,22. The spread of the gospel through his preaching interferes with the makers of idols; he is persecuted, and a great uproar of the city is created; the town clerk appeases the people; dismisses the accusation against Paul, and disperses the people, Acts 19:23-41; 2 Cor. 1:8; 2 Tim. 4:14. Proceeds to Macedonia after confirming the churches in those parts; comes into Greece and abides three months; returns through Macedonia, accompanied by Sopater, Aristarchus, Secundus, Gaius, Timothy, Tychicus, and Trophimus, Acts 20:1-6. Visits Troas; preaches until break of day; restores to life the young man who fell from the window, Acts 20:6-12. Visits Assos, Mitylene, Chios, Samos, Trogyllium, and Miletus, hastening to Jerusalem, to be there at Pentecost, Acts 20:13-16. Sends for the elders of the church of Ephesus; rehearses to them how he had preached in Asia, and his temptations and afflictions testifying repentance toward God; declares he was going bound in spirit to Jerusalem; exhorts them to take heed to themselves and the flock over whom the Holy Ghost had made them overseers; kneels down and prays and takes his departure, Acts 20:17-38. Visits Coos, Rhodes, Patara; takes ship for Tyre; tarries at Tyre seven days; is brought on his way by the disciples to the outskirts of the city; kneels down and prays; takes ship; comes to Ptolemais; salutes the brethren, and abides one day, Acts 21:1-7. Departs for Cæsarea; enters the house of Philip, the Evangelist; is admonished by Agabus not to go to Jerusalem; proceeds nevertheless to Jerusalem, Acts 21:8-15. Is received by the brethren gladly; talks of the things that had been wrought among the Gentiles by his ministry; enters the temple; the people are stirred against him by Jews from Asia; an uproar is created; he is thrust out of the temple; the chief captain of the garrison interposes and arrests him, Acts 21:17-33. His defense, Acts 21:33-40; 22:1-21. Is confined in the castle, Acts 22:24-30. Is brought before the council; his defense, Acts 22:30; 23:1-5. Is returned to the castle, Acts 23:10. Is cheered by a vision, promising him that he shall bear witness in Rome, Acts 23:11. Jews conspire against his life, Acts 23:12-15. Thwarted by his nephew, Acts 23:16-22. Is escorted to Cæsarea by a military guard, Acts 23: 23-33. Is confined in Herod's Judgment Hall in Cæsarea, Acts 23:35. His trial before Felix, Acts 24. Remains in custody for two years, Acts 24:27. His trial before Festus, Acts 25:1-12. Appeals to Cæsar, Acts 25:10-12. His examination before Agrippa, Acts 25:13-27; 26. Is taken to Rome in custody of Julius, a centurion, and guard of soldiers; takes shipping, accompanied by other prisoners, and sails by way of the coasts of Asia; stops at Sidon, and at Myra, Acts 27:1-5. Transferred to a ship of Alexandria; sails by way of Cnidus, Crete, Salamis, and the Fair Havens, Acts 27:6-8. Predicts misfortune to the ship; his counsel not heeded, and the voyage resumed, Acts 27:9-13. The ship encounters a tempest; Paul encourages and comforts the officers and crew; the soldiers advise putting the prisoners to death; the centurion interferes, and all on board, consisting of two hundred and seventy-six souls, are saved, Acts 27:14-44. The ship is wrecked, and all on board take refuge on the island of Melita, Acts 27:14-44. Kind treatment by the inhabitants of the island, Acts 28:1,2. Is bitten by a viper and miraculously preserved, Acts 28:3-6. Heals the ruler's father and others, Acts 28:7-10. Is delayed in Melita three months; proceeds on the voyage; delays at Syracuse; sails by Rhegium and Puteoli; meets brethren who accompany him to Rome from Appii forum; arrives at Rome; is delivered to the captain of the guard; is permitted to dwell by himself in custody of a soldier, Acts 28:11-16. Calls the chief Jews together; states his situation; is kindly received; expounds the gospel; testifies to the kingdom of heaven, Acts 28: 17-29. Dwells two years in his own hired house, preaching and teaching, Acts 28:30,31.

Supports himself, Acts 18:3; 20:33-35. Sickness of, in Asia, 2 Cor. 1:8-11. His resolute determination to go to Jerusalem against the repeated admonition of the Holy Ghost, Acts 20:22,23; 21:4,10-14. Caught up to the third heavens, 2 Cor. 12:1-4. Has "a thorn in the flesh," 2 Cor. 12:7-9; Gal. 4:13,14. His independence of character, 1 Thess. 2:9; 2 Thess. 3:8. Persecutions of, 1 Thess. 2:2; Heb. 10:34. Persecutions endured by, see below. Zeal of, see ZEAL, OF PAUL.

PERSECUTIONS ENDURED BY: Acts 9:16. For I will shew him how great things he must suffer for my name's sake. 23. And after that many days were fulfilled, the Jews took counsel to kill him: 24. But their laying await was known of Saul. And they watched the gates day and night to kill him. 25. Then the disciples took him by night, and let *him* down by the wall in

a basket. 29. And he spake boldly in the name of the Lord Jesus, and disputed against the Grecians: but they went about to slay him.

Acts 16:19. And when her masters saw that the hope of their gains was gone, they caught Paul and Silas, and drew *them* into the marketplace unto the rulers, 20. And brought them to the magistrates, saying, These men, being Jews, do exceedingly trouble our city, 21. And teach customs, which are not lawful for us to receive, neither to observe, being Romans. 22. And the multitude rose up together against them: and the magistrates rent off their clothes, and commanded to beat *them*. 23. And when they had laid many stripes upon them, they cast *them* into prison, charging the jailor to keep them safely: 24. Who, having received such a charge, thrust them into the inner prison, and made their feet fast in the stocks. 25. At midnight Paul and Silas prayed, and sang praises unto God: and the prisoners heard them. *vs.* 2:24.

Acts 20:22. And now, behold, I go bound in the spirit unto Jerusalem, not knowing the things that shall befall me there: 23. Save that the Holy Ghost witnesseth in every city, saying that bonds and afflictions abide me. 24. But none of these things move me, neither count I my life dear unto myself, so that I might finish my course with joy, and the ministry, which I have received of the Lord Jesus, to testify the gospel of the grace of God.

Acts 21:13. What mean ye to weep and to break mine heart? for I am ready not to be bound only, but also to die at Jerusalem for the name of the Lord Jesus. 27. And when the seven days were almost ended, the Jews which were of Asia, when they saw him in the temple, stirred up all the people, and laid hands on him, 28. Crying out, Men of Israel, help: This is the man, that teacheth all *men* every where against the people, and the law, and this place: and further brought Greeks also into the temple, and hath polluted this holy place. 29. (For they had seen before with him in the city Trophimus an Ephesian, whom they supposed that Paul had brought into the temple.) 30. And all the city was moved, and the people ran together: and they took Paul, and drew him out of the temple: and forthwith the doors were shut. 31. And as they went about to kill him, tidings came unto the chief captain of the band, that all Jerusalem was in an uproar. 32. Who immediately took soldiers and centurions, and ran down unto them: and when they saw the chief captain and the soldiers, they left beating of Paul. 33. Then the chief captain came near, and took him, and commanded *him* to be bound with two chains; and demanded who he was, and what he had done.

Acts 22:22. And they gave him audience unto this word, and *then* lifted up their voices, and said, Away with such a *fellow* from the earth: for it is not fit that he should live. 23. And as they cried out, and cast off *their* clothes, and threw dust into the air, 24. The chief captain commanded him to be brought into the castle, and bade that he should be examined by scourging; that he might know wherefore they cried so against him.

Acts 23:10. And when there arose a great dissension, the chief captain, fearing lest Paul should have been pulled in pieces of them, commanded the soldiers to go down, and to take him by force from among them, and to bring *him* into the castle. 12. And when it was day, certain of the Jews banded together, and bound themselves under a curse, saying that they would neither eat nor drink till they had killed Paul. 13. And they were more than forty which had made this conspiracy. 14. And they came to the chief priests and elders, and said, We have bound ourselves under a great curse, that we will eat nothing until we have slain Paul. 15. Now therefore ye with the council signify to the chief captain that he bring him down unto you to morrow, as though ye would enquire something more perfectly concerning him: and we, or ever he come near, are ready to kill him.

Rom. 8:35. Who shall separate us from the love of Christ? *shall* tribulation, or distress, or persecution, or famine, or nakedness, or peril, or sword? 36. As it is written, For thy sake we are killed all the day long: we are accounted as sheep for the slaughter. 37. Nay, in all these things we are more than conquerors through him that loved us.

1 Cor. 4:9. For I think that God hath set forth us the apostles last, as it were appointed to death: for we are made a spectacle unto the world, and to angels, and to men. 11. Even unto this present hour we both hunger, and thirst, and are naked, and are buffeted, and have no certain dwelling-place; 12. And labour, working with our own hands: being reviled, we bless; being persecuted, we suffer it: 13. Being defamed, we intreat: we are made as the filth of the world, *and are* the offscouring of all things unto this day.

2 Cor. 1:8. For we would not, brethren, have you ignorant of our trouble which came to us in Asia, that we were pressed out of measure, above strength, insomuch that we despaired even of life: 9. But we had the sentence of death in ourselves, that we should not trust in ourselves, but in God which raiseth the dead: 10. Who delivered us from so great a death, and doth deliver: in whom we trust that he will yet deliver *us;*

2 Cor. 4:8. *We are* troubled on every side, yet not distressed; *we are* perplexed, but not in despair; 9. Persecuted, but not forsaken; cast down, but not destroyed; 10. Always bearing about in the body the dying of the Lord Jesus, that the life also of

Jesus might be made manifest in our body. 11. For we which live are alway delivered unto death for Jesus' sake, that the life also of Jesus might be made manifest in our mortal flesh. 12. So then death worketh in us, but life in you.

2 Cor. 6:4. But in all *things* approving ourselves as the ministers of God, in much patience, in afflictions, in necessities, in distresses, 5. In stripes, in imprisonments, in tumults, in labours, in watchings, in fastings; 8. By honour and dishonour, by evil report and good report: as deceivers, and *yet* true; 9. As unknown, and *yet* well known; as dying, and, behold, we live; as chastened, and not killed; 10. As sorrowful, yet alway rejoicing; as poor, yet making many rich; as having nothing, and *yet* possessing all things.

2 Cor. 11:23. Are they ministers of Christ? (I speak as a fool) I *am* more; in labours more abundant, in stripes above measure, in prisons more frequent, in deaths oft. 24. Of the Jews five times received I forty *stripes* save one. 25. Thrice was I beaten with rods, once was I stoned, thrice I suffered shipwreck, a night and a day I have been in the deep; 26. *In* journeyings often, *in* perils of waters, *in* perils of robbers, *in* perils by *mine own* countrymen, *in* perils by the heathen, *in* perils in the city, *in* perils in the wilderness, *in* perils in the sea, *in* perils among false brethren; 27. In weariness and painfulness, in watchings often, in hunger and thirst, in fastings often, in cold and nakedness. 32. In Damascus the governor under Aretas the king kept the city of the Damascenes with a garrison, desirous to apprehend me: 33. And through a window in a basket was I let down by the wall, and escaped his hands.

2 Cor. 12:10. Therefore I take pleasure in infirmities, in reproaches, in necessities, in persecutions, in distresses for Christ's sake: for when I am weak, then am I strong.

Gal. 5:11. And I, brethren, if I yet preach circumcision, why do I yet suffer persecution? then is the offence of the cross ceased.

Gal. 6:17. From henceforth let no man trouble me: for I bear in my body the marks of the Lord Jesus. 1 Thess. 3:4.

Phil. 1:30. Having the same conflict which ye saw in me, and now hear *to be* in me.

Phil. 2:17. Yea, and if I be offered upon the sacrifice and service of your faith, I joy, and rejoice with you all. 18. For the same cause also do ye joy, and rejoice with me.

Col. 1:24. Who now rejoice in my sufferings for you, and fill up that which is behind of the afflictions of Christ in my flesh for his body's sake, which is the church:

1 Thess. 2:2. Even after that we had suffered before, and were shamefully entreated, as ye know, at Philippi, we were bold in our God to speak unto you the gospel of God with much contention. 14. For ye also have suffered like things of your own countrymen, even as they *have* of the Jews:

15. Who both killed the Lord Jesus, and their own prophets, and have persecuted us:

2 Tim. 1:12. For the which cause I also suffer these things: nevertheless I am not ashamed: for I know whom I have believed, and am persuaded that he is able to keep that which I have committed unto him against that day.

2 Tim. 2:9. Wherein I suffer trouble, as an evil doer, *even* unto bonds; but the word of God is not bound. 10. Therefore I endure all things for the elect's sakes, that they may also obtain the salvation which is in Christ Jesus with eternal glory.

2 Tim. 3:11. Persecutions, afflictions, which came unto me at Antioch, at Iconium, at Lystra; what persecutions I endured: but out of *them* all the Lord delivered me. 12. Yea, and all that will live godly in Christ Jesus shall suffer persecution.

2 Tim. 4:16. At my first answer no man stood with me, but all *men* forsook me: *I pray God* that it may not be laid to their charge. 17. Notwithstanding the Lord stood with me, and strengthened me; that by me the preaching might be fully known, and *that* all the Gentiles might hear: and I was delivered out of the mouth of the lion.

PAVILION. See TABERNACLE.

PAWN, Ex. 22:26; Deut. 24:10-13,17; Job 24:3; Prov. 22:27; Ezek. 18:5,7,12; 33:15; Amos 2:8.

See SURETY.

PEACE. EXEMPLIFIED: By Abraham, Gen. 13:8,9; Abimelech, Gen. 26:29; Mordecai, Esth. 10:3; David, Psa. 120:7.

See CHARITABLENESS; NATION, PEACE OF.

SOCIAL: Gen. 45:24. So he sent his brethren away, and they departed: and he said unto them, See that ye fall not out by the way.

Lev. 26:6. And I will give peace in the land, and ye shall lie down, and none shall make *you* afraid: and I will rid evil beasts out of the land, neither shall the sword go through your land.

Job 5:23. For thou shalt be in league with the stones of the field: and the beasts of the field shall be at peace with thee. 24. And thou shalt know that thy tabernacle *shall be* in peace; and thou shalt visit thy habitation, and shalt not sin.

Psa. 34:14. Seek peace, and pursue it. 1 Pet. 3:11.

Psa. 120:6. My soul hath long dwelt with him that hateth peace. 7. I *am for* peace, but when I speak, they *are* for war.

Psa. 133:1. Behold, how good and how pleasant *it is* for brethren to dwell together in unity!

Prov. 12:20. To the counsellors of peace *is* joy.

Prov. 15:17. Better *is* a dinner of herbs where love is, than a stalled ox and hatred therewith.

Prov. 16:7. When a man's ways please the LORD, he maketh even his enemies to be at peace with him.

Prov. 17:1. Better *is* a dry morsel, and quietness therewith, than an house full of sacrifices *with* strife. 14. The beginning of strife *is as* when one letteth out water: therefore leave off contention, before it be meddled with.

Prov. 20:3. *It is* an honour for a man to cease from strife: but every fool will be meddling.

Eccl. 4:6. Better *is* an handful *with* quietness, than both the hands full *with* travail and vexation of spirit.

Isa. 2:4. He shall judge among the nations, and shall rebuke many people: and they shall beat their swords into plowshares, and their spears into pruninghooks: nation shall not lift up sword against nation, neither shall they learn war any more.

Isa. 45:7. I form the light, and create darkness: I make peace, and create evil: I the LORD do all these *things*.

Jer. 29:7. And seek the peace of the city whither I have caused you to be carried away captives, and pray unto the LORD for it: for in the peace thereof shall ye have peace.

Hos. 2:18. In that day will I make a covenant for them with the beasts of the field, and with the fowls of heaven, and *with* the creeping things of the ground: and I will break the bow and the sword and the battle out of the earth, and will make them to lie down safely.

Zech. 8:19. Love the truth and peace.

Matt. 5:9. Blessed *are* the peacemakers: for they shall be called the children of God.

Matt. 10:21. And the brother shall deliver up the brother to death, and the father the child: and the children shall rise up against *their* parents, and cause them to be put to death. 22. And ye shall be hated of all *men* for my name's sake: but he that endureth to the end shall be saved. 34. Think not that I am come to send peace on earth: I came not to send peace, but a sword. 35. For I am come to set a man at variance against his father, and the daughter against her mother, and the daughter in law against her mother in law. 36. And a man's foes *shall be* they of his own household.

Mark 9:50. Have peace one with another.

Luke 2:14. Glory to God in the highest, and on earth peace, good will toward men.

Acts 7:26. And the next day he shewed himself unto them as they strove, and would have set them at one again, saying, Sirs, ye are brethren; why do ye wrong one to another? 27. But he that did his neighbour wrong thrust him away, saying, Who made thee a ruler and a judge over us? 28. Wilt thou kill me, as thou didst the Egyptian yesterday? 29. Then fled Moses at this saying, and was a stranger in the land of Madian, where he begat two sons.

Acts 17:7. These all do contrary to the decrees of Cæsar, saying that there is another king, *one* Jesus. 8. And they troubled the people and the rulers of the city, when they heard these things. 9. And when they had taken security of Jason, and of the other, they let them go.

Rom. 12:18. If it be possible, as much as lieth in you, live peaceably with all men.

Rom. 14:19. Let us therefore follow after the things which make for peace, and things wherewith one may edify another.

1 Cor. 14:33. For God is not *the author* of confusion, but of peace, as in all churches of the saints.

2 Cor. 13:11. Be perfect, be of good comfort, be of one mind, live in peace;

Eph. 4:3. Endeavouring to keep the unity of the Spirit in the bond of peace.

1 Thess. 5:13. Be at peace among yourselves.

1 Tim. 2:2. That we may lead a quiet and peaceable life in all godliness and honesty.

2 Tim. 2:22. Follow righteousness, faith, charity, peace, with them that call on the Lord out of a pure heart.

Heb. 12:14. Follow peace with all *men*, and holiness, without which no man shall see the Lord:

Jas. 3:17. But the wisdom that is from above is first pure, then peaceable, gentle, *and* easy to be intreated, full of mercy and good fruits, without partiality, and without hypocrisy. 18. The fruit of righteousness is sown in peace of them that make peace.

1 Pet. 3:10. For he that will love life, and see good days, let him refrain his tongue from evil, and his lips that they speak no guile: 11. Let him eschew evil, and do good; let him seek peace, and ensue it.

SPIRITUAL: Job 22:21. Acquaint now thyself with him, and be at peace: thereby good shall come unto thee. 26. For then shalt thou have thy delight in the Almighty, and shalt lift up thy face unto God.

Job 34:29. When he giveth quietness, who then can make trouble?

Psa. 1:1. Blessed *is* the man that walketh not in the counsel of the ungodly, nor standeth in the way of sinners, nor sitteth in the seat of the scornful. 2. But his delight *is* in the law of the Lord; and in his law doth he meditate day and night.

Psa. 4:8. I will both lay me down in peace, and sleep: for thou, Lord, only makest me dwell in safety.

Psa. 17:15. As for me, I will behold thy face in righteousness: I shall be satisfied, when I awake, with thy likeness.

Psa. 25:12. What man *is* he that feareth the Lord? him shall he teach in the way *that* he shall choose. 13. His soul shall dwell at ease:

Psa. 29:11. The Lord will give strength unto his people; the Lord will bless his people with peace.

Psa. 37:4. Delight thyself also in the Lord; and he shall give thee the desires of thine heart. 11. The meek shall inherit the earth; and shall delight themselves in the abundance of peace. 37. Mark the perfect *man*, and behold the upright: for the end of *that* man *is* peace.

Psa. 73:25. Whom have I in heaven *but* thee? and *there is* none upon earth *that* I desire beside thee. 26. My flesh and my heart faileth: *but* God *is* the strength of my heart, and my portion for ever.

Psa. 85:8. I will hear what God the Lord will speak: for he will speak peace unto his people, and to his saints:

Psa. 119:165. Great peace have they which love thy law: and nothing shall offend them.

Psa. 125:1. They that trust in the Lord *shall be* as mount Zion, *which* cannot be removed, *but* abideth for ever. 5. As for such as turn aside unto their crooked ways, the Lord shall lead them forth with the workers of iniquity: *but* peace *shall be* upon Israel.

Prov. 3:17. Her ways *are* ways of pleasantness, and all her paths *are* peace. 24. When thou liest down, thou shalt not be afraid: yea, thou shalt lie down, and thy sleep shall be sweet. *vs.* 13–18.

Prov. 14:14. A good man *shall be satisfied* from himself.

Isa. 9:6. His name shall be called Wonderful, Counsellor, The mighty God, The everlasting Father, The Prince of Peace.

Isa. 11:6. The wolf also shall dwell with the lamb, and the leopard shall lie down with the kid; and the calf and the young lion and the fatling together; and a little child shall lead them. 7. And the cow and the bear shall feed; their young ones shall lie down together: and the lion shall eat straw like the ox. 8. And the sucking child shall play on the hole of the asp, and the weaned child shall put his hand on the cockatrice' den. 9. They shall not hurt nor destroy in all my holy mountain: for the earth shall be full of the knowledge of the Lord, as the waters cover the sea. 13. The envy also of Ephraim shall depart, and the adversaries of Judah shall be cut off: Ephraim shall not envy Judah, and Judah shall not vex Ephraim.

Isa. 12:1. And in that day thou shalt say, O Lord, I will praise thee: though thou wast angry with me, thine anger is turned away, and thou comfortedst me. 2. Behold, God *is* my salvation; I will trust, and not be afraid: for the Lord JEHOVAH *is* my strength and *my* song; he also is become my salvation.

Isa. 25:7. And he will destroy in this mountain the face of the covering cast over all people, and the vail that is spread over all nations. 8. He will swallow up death in victory; and the Lord God will wipe away tears from off all faces; and the rebuke of his people shall he take away from off all the earth: for the Lord hath spoken *it*.

Isa. 26:3. Thou wilt keep *him* in perfect peace, *whose* mind *is* stayed *on thee:* because he trusteth in thee. 12. Lord, thou wilt ordain peace for us: for thou also hast wrought all our works in us.

Isa. 27:5. Let him take hold of my strength,

that he may make peace with me; *and* he shall make peace with me.

Isa. 28:12. To whom he said, This *is* the rest *wherewith* ye may cause the weary to rest; and this *is* the refreshing·

Isa. 30:26. Moreover the light of the moon shall be as the light of the sun, and the light of the sun shall be sevenfold, as the light of seven days, in the day that the LORD bindeth up the breach of his people, and healeth the stroke of their wound.

Isa. 32:2. A man shall be as an hiding place from the wind, and a covert from the tempests; as rivers of water in a dry place, as the shadow of a great rock in a weary land. 17. The work of righteousness shall be peace; and the effect of righteousness quietness and assurance for ever. 18. And my people shall dwell in a peaceable habitation, and in sure dwellings, and in quiet resting places:

Isa. 48:18. O that thou hadst hearkened to my commandments! then had thy peace been as a river, and thy righteousness as the waves of the sea:

Isa. 53:5. The chastisement of our peace *was* upon him; and with his stripes we are healed.

Isa. 54:1. Sing, O barren, thou *that* didst not bear; break forth into singing, and cry aloud, thou *that* didst not travail with child: for more *are* the children of the desolate than the children of the married wife, saith the LORD. 10. For the mountains shall depart, and the hills be removed: but my kindness shall not depart from thee, neither shall the covenant of my peace be removed, saith the LORD that hath mercy on thee. 13. All thy children *shall be* taught of the LORD; and great *shall be* the peace of thy children.

Isa. 55:2. Wherefore do ye spend money for *that which is* not bread? and your labour for *that which* satisfieth not? hearken diligently unto me, and eat ye *that which is* good, and let your soul delight itself in fatness. 12. Ye shall go out with joy, and be led forth with peace: the mountains and the hills shall break forth before you into singing, and all the trees of the field shall clap *their* hands.

Isa. 57:1. The righteous perisheth, and no man layeth *it* to heart: and merciful men *are* taken away, none considering that the righteous is taken away from the evil *to come.* 2. He shall enter into peace: they shall rest in their beds, *each one* walking in his uprightness. 19. I create the fruit of the lips; Feace, peace to *him that is* far off, and to *him that is* near, saith the LORD; and I will heal him.

Isa. 60:20. Thy sun shall no more go down; neither shall thy moon withdraw itself: for the LORD shall be thine everlasting light, and the days of thy mourning shall be ended.

Jer. 33:6. Behold, I will bring it health and cure, and I will cure them, and will reveal unto them the abundance of peace and truth.

Ezek. 34:25. And I will make with them a covenant of peace,

Hag. 2:9. The glory of this latter house shall be greater than of the former, saith the LORD of hosts: and in this place will I give peace, saith the LORD of hosts.

Mal. 2:5. My covenant was with him of life and peace;

Luke 1:79. To give light to them that sit in darkness and *in* the shadow of death, to guide our feet into the way of peace.

Luke 2:14. Glory to God in the highest, and on earth peace, good will toward men. 29. Lord, now lettest thou thy servant depart in peace, according to thy word:

John 7:38. He that believeth on me, as the scripture hath said, out of his belly shall flow rivers of living water.

John 14:27. Peace I leave with you, my peace I give unto you: not as the world giveth, give I unto you. Let not your heart be troubled, neither let it be afraid.

John 16:33. These things I have spoken unto you, that in me ye might have peace.

John 20:19. Then the same day at evening, . . . came Jesus and stood in the midst, and saith unto them, Peace *be* unto you.

Acts 10:36. The word which *God* sent unto the children of Israel, preaching peace by Jesus Christ: (he is Lord of all:)

Rom. 2:10. Glory, honour, and peace, to every man that worketh good, to the Jew first, and also to the Gentile:

Rom. 5:1. Therefore being justified by faith, ¹ we have peace with God through our Lord Jesus Christ: [¹ R. V. let us]

Rom. 8:6. To be spiritually minded *is* life and peace.

Rom. 10:15. And how shall they preach, except they be sent? as it is written, How beautiful are the feet of them that ¹ preach the gospel of peace, and bring glad tidings of good things! [¹ Omitted in R. V.]

Rom. 14:17. The kingdom of God is not meat and drink; but righteousness, and peace, and joy in the Holy Ghost.

Rom. 15:13. Now the God of hope fill you with all joy and peace in believing, that ye may abound in hope, through the power of the Holy Ghost. 33. Now the God of peace *be* with you all.

Gal. 1:3. Grace *be* to you, and peace, from God our Father, and *from* the Lord Jesus Christ, 1 Cor. 1:3; 2 Cor. 1:2; 1 Thess. 1:1; 1 Tim. 1:2; 2 Tim. 1:2; Tit. 1:4; Philem. 3; Rev. 1:4.

Gal. 5:22. The fruit of the Spirit is love, joy, peace,

Eph. 2:14. For he is our peace, who hath made both one, and hath broken down the middle wall of partition *between us;* 15. Having abolished in his flesh the enmity, *even* the law of commandments *contained* in ordinances; for to make in himself of twain one new man, *so* making peace; 16. And that he might reconcile both unto God in one body by the cross, having slain the enmity thereby: 17. And came and preached peace to you which were afar off, and to them that were nigh.

Phil. 4:7. And the peace of God, which passeth all understanding, shall keep your hearts and minds through Christ Jesus. 9. Those things, which ye have both learned, and received, and heard, and seen in me, do: and the God of peace shall be with you.

Col. 1:20. And having made peace through the blood of his cross, by him to reconcile all things unto himself; by him, *I say*, whether *they be* things in earth, or things in heaven.

Col. 3:15. And let the peace of ¹ God rule in your hearts, to the which also ye are called in one body; and be ye thankful.   [¹ R. V. Christ]

2 Thess. 3:16. Now the Lord of peace himself give you peace always by all means.

See CHARITABLENESS; JOY; PRAISE.

PEACE OFFERINGS, Ex. 20:24; 24:5; Lev. 3:6; 7:11; 19:5. Offered by the princes, Num. 7:17; by Joshua, Josh. 8:31; by David, 2 Sam. 6:17; 24:25.

See OFFERINGS.

PEACOCK, 1 Kin. 10:22; 2 Chr. 9:21; Job 39:13.

PEARL, Job 28:18; Rev. 17:4; 18:12,16. "Pearl of great price," Matt. 13:46. Ornaments made of, 1 Tim. 2:9.

FIGURATIVE: Matt. 7:6. SYMBOLICAL: Rev. 21:21.

PEDAHEL, chief of Naphtali, Num. 34:28.

PEDAHZUR, father of Gamaliel, Num. 1:10; 2:20; 7:54,59; 10:23.

PEDAIAH. 1. Grandfather of King Josiah, 2 Kin. 23:36.

2. Father of Zerubbabel, 1 Chr. 3:18,19.

3. Father of Joel, 1 Chr. 27:20.

4. Son of Parosh, Neh. 3:25.

5. A Levite appointed as treasurer by Nehemiah, Neh. 8:4; 13:13.

6. A Benjamite, Neh. 11:7.

PEKAH, son of Remaliah. Captain of the army of Israel, 2 Kin. 15:25. Conspires against and assassinates King Pekahiah, 2 Kin. 15:25. Is made king of Israel, 2 Kin. 15:27. Victorious in war with Judah, 2 Chr. 28:5,6. Is plotted against and slain by Hoshea, 2 Kin. 15:30,31. Prophecies against, Isa. 7:1–16; 8:4–10.

PEKAHIAH, son of Menahem. King of Israel, 2 Kin. 15:22–26. Plotted against and slain by Pekah, 2 Kin. 15:25.

PEKOD, name for Chaldea, Jer. 50:21; Ezek. 23:23.

PELAIAH. 1. Son of Elioenai, 1 Chr. 3:24.

2. A Levite who assisted Ezra in instructing the people in the law, Neh. 8:7; 10:10.

PELALIAH, a priest, Neh. 11:12.

PELATIAH. 1. A son of Hananiah, of the family of David, 1 Chr. 3:21.

2. A Simeonite who was captain in an expedition against the Amalekites, 1 Chr. 4:42,43.

3. One of those who signed the covenant with Nehemiah, Neh. 10:22.

4. A prince against whom Ezekiel prophesied, and who fell dead at the close of the prophecy, Ezek. 11:1–13.

PELEG, son of Eber, Gen. 10:25; 11:16–19; 1 Chr. 1:19,25.

PELET. 1. Son of Jahdai, 1 Chr. 2:47.

2. Son of Azmaveth, 1 Chr. 12:3.

PELETH. 1. A Reubenite, Num. 16:1.

2. Son of Jonathan, 1 Chr. 2:33.

PELETHITES. A part of David's bodyguard, 1 Kin. 1:38; 2 Sam. 8:18; 20:7,23; 1 Chr. 18:17. Absalom's escort, 2 Sam. 15:18.

PELICAN, Lev. 11:18; Deut. 14:17; Psa. 102:6.

PELONITE. 1. An Ephraimite, 1 Chr. 11:27; 27:10.

2. An appellation of Ahijah the prophet, 1 Chr. 11:36.

PEN, Judg. 5:14; Psa. 45:1; Isa. 8:1; Jer. 8:8; 3 John 13. Made of iron, Job 19:24; Jer. 17:1.

PENALTY. See JUDGMENTS; PUNISHMENTS; SIN, PUNISHMENT OF; WICKED, PUNISHMENT OF.

PENIEL. See PENUEL.

PENITENCE. See REPENTANCE; SIN, CONFESSION OF

PENITENT. PROMISES TO: Lev. 26:40. If they shall confess their iniquity, and the iniquity of their fathers, with their trespass which they trespassed against me, and that also they have walked contrary unto me; 41. And *that* I also have walked contrary unto them, and have brought them into the land of their enemies; if then their uncircumcised hearts be humbled, and they then accept of the punishment of their iniquity: 42. Then will I remember my covenant with Jacob, and also my covenant with Isaac, and also my covenant with Abraham will I remember; and I will remember the land.

Num. 5:6. Speak unto the children of Israel, When a man or woman shall commit any sin that men commit, to do a trespass against the LORD, and that person be guilty; 7. Then they shall confess their sin which they have done: and he shall recompense his trespass with the principal thereof, and add unto it the fifth *part* thereof, and give *it* unto *him* against whom he hath trespassed.

Deut. 4:29. But if from thence thou shalt seek the LORD thy God, thou shalt find *him*, if thou seek him with all thy heart and with all thy soul. 30. When thou art in tribulation, and all these things are come upon thee, *even* in the latter days, if thou turn to the LORD thy God, and shalt be obedient unto his voice; 31. (For the LORD thy God *is* a merciful God;) he will not forsake thee, neither destroy thee, nor forget the covenant of thy fathers which he sware unto them.

Deut. 5:29. O that there were such an heart in them, that they would fear me, and keep all my commandments always, that it might be well with them, and with their children for ever!

Deut. 30:1. And it shall come to pass, when

all these things are come upon thee, the *blessing* and the curse, which I have set before thee, and thou shalt call *them* to mind among all the nations, whither the LORD thy God hath driven thee, 2. And shalt return unto the LORD thy God, and shalt obey his voice according to all that I command thee this day, thou and thy children, with all thine heart, and with all thy soul; 3. That then the LORD thy God will turn thy captivity, and have compassion upon thee, and will return and gather thee from all the nations, whither the LORD thy God hath scattered thee. 4. If *any* of thine be driven out unto the outmost *parts* of heaven, from thence will the LORD thy God gather thee, and from thence will he fetch thee: 5. And the LORD thy God will bring thee into the land which thy fathers possessed, and thou shalt possess it; and he will do thee good, and multiply thee above thy fathers. 6. And the LORD thy God will circumcise thine heart, and the heart of thy seed, to love the LORD thy God with all thine heart, and with all thy soul, that thou mayest live. 7. And the LORD thy God will put all these curses upon thine enemies, and on them that hate thee, which persecuted thee. 8. And thou shalt return and obey the voice of the LORD, and do all his commandments which I command thee this day. 9. And the LORD thy God will make thee plenteous in every work of thine hand, in the fruit of thy body, and in the fruit of thy cattle, and in the fruit of thy land, for good: for the LORD will again rejoice over thee for good, as he rejoiced over thy fathers: 10. If thou shalt hearken unto the voice of the LORD thy God, to keep his commandments and his statutes which are written in this book of the law, *and* if thou turn unto the LORD thy God with all thine heart, and with all thy soul.

2 Kin. 22:19. Because thine heart was tender, and thou hast humbled thyself before the LORD, when thou heardest what I spake against this place, and against the inhabitants thereof, that they should become a desolation and a curse, and hast rent thy clothes, and wept before me; I also have heard *thee*, saith the LORD.

1 Chr. 28:9. And thou, Solomon my son, know thou the God of thy father, and serve him with a perfect heart and with a willing mind: for the LORD searcheth all hearts, and understandeth all the imaginations of the thoughts: if thou seek him, he will be found of thee: but if thou forsake him, he will cast thee off for ever.

Job 22:23. If thou return to the Almighty, thou shalt be built up, thou shalt put away iniquity far from thy tabernacles. 24. Then shalt thou lay up gold as dust, and the *gold* of Ophir as the stones of the brooks. 25. Yea, the Almighty shall be thy defence, and thou shalt have plenty of silver. 26. For then shalt thou have thy delight in the Almighty, and shalt lift up thy face unto God. 27.

Thou shalt make thy prayer unto him, and he shall hear thee, and thou shalt pay thy vows. 28. Thou shalt also decree a thing, and it shall be established unto thee: and the light shall shine upon thy ways. 29. When *men* are cast down, then thou shalt say, *There is* lifting up; and he shall save the humble person.

Job 23:6. Will he plead against me with *his* great power? No; but he would put *strength* in me.

Job 33:26. He shall pray unto God, and he will be favourable unto him: and he shall see his face with joy: for he will render unto man his righteousness. 27. He looketh upon men, and *if any* say, I have sinned, and perverted *that which was* right, and it profited me not; 28. He will deliver his soul from going into the pit, and his life shall see the light.

Psa. 6:8. Depart from me, all ye workers of iniquity; for the LORD hath heard the voice of my weeping. 9. The LORD hath heard my supplication; the LORD will receive my prayer.

Psa. 9:10. And they that know thy name will put their trust in thee: for thou, LORD, hast not forsaken them that seek thee.

Psa. 22:26. The meek shall eat and be satisfied: they shall praise the LORD that seek him: your heart shall live for ever.

Psa. 24:3. Who shall ascend into the hill of the LORD? or who shall stand in his holy place? 4. He that hath clean hands, and a pure heart; who hath not lifted up his soul unto vanity, nor sworn deceitfully. 5. He shall receive the blessing from the LORD, and righteousness from the God of his salvation. 6. This *is* the generation of them that seek him, that seek thy face, O Jacob.

Psa. 32:5. I acknowledged my sin unto thee, and mine iniquity have I not hid. I said, I will confess my transgressions unto the LORD; and thou forgavest the iniquity of my sin. 6. For this shall every one that is godly pray unto thee in a time when thou mayest be found: surely in the floods of great waters they shall not come nigh unto him.

Psa. 34:18. The LORD *is* nigh unto them that are of a broken heart; and saveth such as be of a contrite spirit.

Psa. 51:17. The sacrifices of God *are* a broken spirit: a broken and a contrite heart, O God, thou wilt not despise.

Psa. 70:4. Let all those that seek thee rejoice and be glad in thee: and let such as love thy salvation say continually, Let God be magnified.

Psa. 90:14. O satisfy us early with thy mercy; that we may rejoice and be glad all our days. 15. Make us glad according to the days *wherein* thou hast afflicted us, *and* the years *wherein* we have seen evil.

Psa. 145:18. The LORD *is* nigh unto all them that call upon him, to all that call upon him in truth. 19. He will fulfil the desire of them that fear him: he also will hear their cry, and will save them.

Psa. 147:3. He healeth the broken in heart, and bindeth up their wounds.

Isa. 27:5. Let him take hold of my strength, *that* he may make peace with me; *and* he shall make peace with me.

Ezek. 18:21. If the wicked will turn from all his sins that he hath committed, and keep all my statutes, and do that which is lawful and right, he shall surely live, he shall not die. 22. All his transgressions that he hath committed, they shall not be mentioned unto him: in his righteousness that he hath done he shall live. 23. Have I any pleasure at all that the wicked should die? saith the Lord GOD: *and* not that he should return from his ways, and live? Ezek. 33:10-16.

Matt. 5:4. Blessed *are* they that mourn: for they shall be comforted.

Matt. 6:14. For if ye forgive men their trespasses, your heavenly Father will also forgive you: 15. But if ye forgive not men their trespasses, neither will your Father forgive your trespasses.

Matt. 7:7. Ask, and it shall be given you; seek, and ye shall find; knock, and it shall be opened unto you: [Luke 11:9-13.] 8. For every one that asketh receiveth; and he that seeketh findeth; and to him that knocketh it shall be opened. 9. Or what man is there of you, whom if his son ask bread, will he give him a stone? 10. Or if he ask a fish, will he give him a serpent? 11. If ye then, being evil, know how to give good gifts unto your children, how much more shall your Father which is in heaven give good things to them that ask him?

Matt. 11:28. Come unto me, all *ye* that labour and are heavy laden, and I will give you rest. 29. Take my yoke upon you, and learn of me; for I am meek and lowly in heart: and ye shall find rest unto your souls. 30. For my yoke *is* easy, and my burden is light.

Matt. 12:20. A bruised reed shall he not break, and smoking flax shall he not quench, till he send forth judgment unto victory. 31. Wherefore I say unto you, All manner of sin and blasphemy shall be forgiven unto men: but the blasphemy *against* the *Holy* Ghost shall not be forgiven unto men. Luke 12:10.

Matt. 18:11. ¹ For the Son of man is come to save that which was lost. Luke 19:10. [¹ Omitted in R. V.]

Luke 4:18. The Spirit of the Lord is upon me, because he hath anointed me to preach the gospel to the poor; he hath sent me to heal the brokenhearted, to preach deliverance to the captives, and recovering of sight to the blind, to set at liberty them that are bruised,

Luke 6:37. Judge not, and ye shall not be judged: condemn not, and ye shall not be condemned: forgive, and ye shall be forgiven:

Luke 15:4. What man of you, having a hundred sheep, if he lose one of them, doth not leave the ninety and nine in the wilderness, and go after that which is lost, until he find it? 5. And when he hath found *it*, he layeth *it* on his shoulders, rejoicing. 6. And when he cometh home, he calleth together *his* friends and neighbours, saying unto them, Rejoice with me; for I have found my sheep which was lost. 7. I say unto you, that likewise joy shall be in heaven over one sinner that repenteth, more than over ninety and nine just persons, which need no repentance. [Matt. 18:12-14.] 8. Either what woman having ten pieces of silver, if she lose one piece, doth not light a candle, and sweep the house, and seek diligently till she find it? 9. And when she hath found *it*, she calleth *her* friends and *her* neighbours together, saying, Rejoice with me; for I have found the piece which I had lost. 10. Likewise, I say unto you, there is joy in the presence of the angels of God over one sinner that repenteth. 11. And he said, A certain man had two sons: 12. And the younger of them said to *his* father, Father, give me the portion of goods that falleth *to me*. And he divided unto them *his* living. 13. And not many days after the younger son gathered all together, and took his journey into a far country, and there wasted his substance with riotous living. 14. And when he had spent all, there arose a mighty famine in that land; and he began to be in want. 15. And he went and joined himself to a citizen of that country; and he sent him into his fields to feed swine. 16. And he would fain have filled his belly with the husks that the swine did eat: and no man gave unto him. 17. And when he came to himself, he said, How many hired servants of my father's have bread enough and to spare, and I perish with hunger! 18. I will arise and go to my father, and will say unto him, Father, I have sinned against heaven, and before thee, 19. And am no more worthy to be called thy son: make me as one of thy hired servants. 20. And he arose, and came to his father. But when he was yet a great way off, his father saw him, and had compassion, and ran, and fell on his neck, and kissed him. 21. And the son said unto him, Father, I have sinned against heaven, and in thy sight, and am no more worthy to be called thy son. 22. But the father said to his servants, Bring forth the best robe, and put *it* on him; and put a ring on his hand, and shoes on *his* feet: 23. And bring hither the fatted calf, and kill *it;* and let us eat, and be merry: 24. For this my son was dead, and is alive again; he was lost, and is found. And they began to be merry. 25. Now his elder son was in the field: and as he came and drew nigh to the house, he heard musick and dancing. 26. And he called one of the servants, and asked what these things meant. 27. And he said unto him, Thy brother is come; and thy father hath killed the fatted calf, because he hath received him safe and sound. 28. And he was angry, and would not go in: therefore came his father out, and intreated him. 29. And he answering said to *his* father, Lo, these many years do I serve thee, neither transgressed I at any time thy commandment; and yet thou never gavest me a kid, that I might make merry with my friends: 30. But as soon as this thy son was come, which hath devoured thy living with harlots, thou hast killed for him the fatted calf. 31. And he said unto him, Son, thou art ever with me, and all that I have is thine. 32. It was meet that we should make merry, and be glad: for this thy brother was dead, and is alive again; and was lost, and is found.

Luke 18:10. Two men went up into the temple to pray; the one a Pharisee, and the other a publican. 11. The Pharisee stood and prayed thus with himself, God, I thank thee, that I am not as other men *are*, extortioners, unjust, adulterers, or even as this publican. 12. I fast twice in the week, I give tithes of all that I possess. 13. And the publican, standing afar off, would not lift up so much as *his* eyes unto heaven, but smote upon his breast, saying, God be merciful to me a sinner. 14. I tell you, this man went down to his house justified *rather* than the other: for every one that exalteth himself shall be abased; and he that humbleth himself shall be exalted.

John 6:37. Him that cometh to me, I will in no wise cast out.

John 10:9. I am the door: by me if any man enter in, he shall be saved, and shall go in and out, and find pasture.

Acts 13:38. Be it known unto you therefore, men *and* brethren, that through this man is preached unto you the forgiveness of sins: 39. And by him all that believe are justified from all things, from which ye could not be justified by the law of Moses.

Rom. 10:9. That if thou shalt confess with thy mouth the Lord Jesus, and shalt believe in thine heart that God hath raised him from the dead, thou shalt be saved. 10. For with the heart man believeth unto righteousness; and with the mouth confession is made unto salvation. 11. For the scripture saith, Whosoever believeth on him shall not be ashamed. 12. For there is no difference between the Jew and the Greek: for the same Lord over all is rich unto all that call upon him. 13. For whosoever shall call upon the name of the Lord shall be saved.

1 John 1:9. If we confess our sins, he is faithful and just to forgive us *our* sins, and to cleanse us from all unrighteousness.

See FORGIVENESS; REPENTANCE; SIN, CONFESSION OF. See also OBDURACY; REPROBACY.

PENKNIFE, Jer. 36:23.

PENINNAH, one of the wives of Elkanah, 1 Sam. 1:2.

PENNY. About seventeen cents, later fifteen cents, Matt. 18:28; Mark 6:37; 14:5;

Luke 7:41; 10:35. Roman, bore Cæsar's image, Matt. 22:19-21. A day's wages, Matt. 20:2-14.

PENSION, of Levites, 2 Chr. 31:16-18.

PENTECOST. Called FEAST OF WEEKS, Ex. 34:22; Deut. 16:10; FEAST OF HARVEST, Ex. 23:16; DAY OF FIRST FRUITS, Num. 28:26; DAY OF PENTECOST, Acts 2:1; 20:16; 1 Cor. 16:8.

Institution of, Ex. 23:16; 34:22; Lev. 23:15-21; Num. 28:26-31; Deut. 16:9-12,16.

Holy Ghost given to the apostles on the first day of, Acts 2.

See FEASTS.

PENURIOUSNESS. See PARSIMONY.

PENUEL. 1. Called also PENIEL. City built where Jacob wrestled with the angel, Gen. 32:31; Judg. 8:8,9,17; 1 Kin. 12:25.

2. Chief of Gedor, 1 Chr. 4:4.

3. A Benjamite, 1 Chr. 8:25.

PEOPLE, common. Heard Jesus gladly, Matt. 7:28; 9:8,33; 13:54; Mark 6:2.

PEOR, a mountain in Moab. Balak builds altars on, Num. 23:28-30.

PERESH, son of Machir, 1 Chr. 7:16.

PEREZ. See PHAREZ.

PEREZ-UZZA, place where the Lord smote Uzzah, 2 Sam. 6:8; 1 Chr. 13:11.

PERFECTION. Ascribed to Noah, Gen. 6:8,9; Jacob, Num. 23:21; David, 1 Kin. 11:4,6; Asa, 1 Kin. 15:14; Job, Job 1:1; Zacharias and Elizabeth, Luke 1:6; Nathanael, John 1:47.

UNCLASSIFIED SCRIPTURES RELATING TO: Gen. 17:1. And when Abram was ninety years old and nine, the LORD appeared to Abram, and said unto him, I *am* the Almighty God; walk before me, and be thou perfect.

Deut. 5:32. Ye shall observe to do therefore as the LORD your God hath commanded you: ye shall not turn aside to the right hand or to the left.

Deut. 18:13. Thou shalt be perfect with the LORD thy God.

Josh. 23:6. Be ye therefore very courageous to keep and to do all that is written in the book of the law of Moses, that ye turn not aside therefrom *to* the right hand or *to* the left;

1 Kin. 8:61. Let your heart therefore be perfect with the LORD our God, to walk in his statutes, and to keep his commandments, as at this day.

1 Chr. 28:9. And thou, Solomon my son, know thou the God of thy father, and serve him with a perfect heart and with a willing mind: for the LORD searcheth all hearts, and understandeth all the imaginations of the thoughts: if thou seek him, he will be found of thee; but if thou forsake him, he will cast thee off for ever.

1 Chr. 29:19. Give unto Solomon my son a perfect heart, to keep thy commandments, thy testimonies, and thy statutes,

2 Chr. 6:36. If they sin against thee, (for *there is* no man which sinneth not,) and thou be angry

Job 9:20. If I justify myself, mine own mouth shall condemn me: *if I say*, I *am* perfect, it shall also prove me perverse. 21. *Though* I *were* perfect, *yet* would I not know my soul: I would despise my life.

Psa. 18:32. *It is* God that girdeth me with strength, and maketh my way perfect.

Psa. 37:31. The law of his God *is* in his heart; none of his steps shall slide. 37. Mark the perfect *man*, and behold the upright: for the end of *that* man *is* peace.

Psa. 101:2. I will behave myself wisely in a perfect way. O when wilt thou come unto me? I will walk within my house with a perfect heart.

Psa. 106:3. Blessed *are* they that keep judgment, *and* he that doeth righteousness at all times.

Psa. 119:1. Blessed *are* the undefiled in the way, who walk in the law of the LORD. 2. Blessed *are* they that keep his testimonies, *and that* seek him with the whole heart. 3. They also do no iniquity: they walk in his ways. 6. Then shall I not be ashamed, when I have respect unto all thy commandments. 96. I have seen an end of all perfection: *but* thy commandment *is* exceeding broad.

Prov. 2:21. For the upright shall dwell in the land, and the perfect shall remain in it.

Eccl. 7:20. For *there is* not a just man upon earth, that doeth good, and sinneth not.

Matt. 5:6. Blessed *are* they which do hunger and thirst after righteousness: for they shall be filled.

48. Be ye therefore perfect, even as your Father which is in heaven is perfect.

Matt. 19:21. Jesus said unto him, If thou wilt be perfect, go *and* sell that thou hast, and give to the poor, and thou shalt have treasure in heaven: and come *and* follow me.

Luke 6:40. The disciple is not above his master: but every one that is perfect shall be as his master.

1 Cor. 2:6. Howbeit we speak wisdom among them that are perfect:

2 Cor. 7:1. Having therefore these promises, dearly beloved, let us cleanse ourselves from all filthiness of the flesh and spirit, perfecting holiness in the fear of God.

2 Cor. 13:9. For we are glad, when we are weak, and ye are strong: and this [1] also we wish, *even* your [2] perfection. 11. Be [3] perfect, be of good comfort, be of one mind, live in peace; and the God of love and peace shall be with you.

[R. V. [1] we also pray for   [2] perfecting   [3] perfected;]

Eph. 4:11. And he gave some, apostles; and some, prophets; and some, evangelists; and some, pastors and teachers: 12. For the perfecting of the saints, 13. Till we all come in the unity of the faith, and of the knowledge of the Son of God, unto a perfect man, unto the measure of the stature of the fulness of Christ:

Phil. 1:10. That ye may approve things that are excellent; that ye may be sin-

cere and without offence till the day of Christ;

Phil. 2:15. That ye may be blameless and harmless, the sons of God, without rebuke, in the midst of a crooked and perverse nation, among whom ye shine as lights in the world;

Phil. 3:12. Not as though I had already attained, either were already perfect: but I follow after, if that I may apprehend that for which also I am apprehended of Christ Jesus. 13. Brethren, I count not myself to have apprehended: but *this* one thing I *do*, forgetting those things which are behind, and reaching forth unto those things which are before, 14. I press toward the mark for the prize of the high calling of God in Christ Jesus. 15. Let us therefore, as many as be perfect, be thus minded: and if in any thing ye be otherwise minded, God shall reveal even this unto you.

Col. 1:21. And you, that were sometime alienated and enemies in *your* mind by wicked works, yet now hath he reconciled 22. In the body of his flesh through death, to present you holy and unblameable and unreproveable in his sight: 28. Whom we preach, warning every man, and teaching every man in all wisdom; that we may present every man perfect in Christ Jesus:

Col. 2:9. For in him dwelleth all the fulness of the Godhead bodily. 10. And ye are complete in him, which is the head of all principality and power: 11. In whom also ye are circumcised with the circumcision made without hands, in putting off the body of the sins of the flesh by the circumcision of Christ:

Col. 3:14. And above all these things *put on* charity, which is the bond of perfectness.

Col. 4:12. Epaphras, who is *one* of you, a servant of Christ, saluteth you, always labouring fervently for you in prayers, that ye may stand perfect and complete in all the will of God.

1 Thess. 3:10. Night and day praying exceedingly that we might see your face, and might perfect that which is lacking in your faith? 13. To the end he may stablish your hearts unblameable in holiness before God, even our Father, at the coming of our Lord Jesus Christ with all his saints.

2 Tim. 2:1. Thou therefore, my son, be strong in the grace that is in Christ Jesus.

2 Tim. 3:17. That the man of God may be perfect, throughly furnished unto all good works.

Heb. 6:1. Therefore leaving the principles of the doctrine of Christ, let us go on unto perfection;

Heb. 10:14. For by one offering he hath perfected for ever them that are sanctified.

Heb. 13:20. Now the God of peace, that brought again from the dead our Lord Jesus, that great shepherd of the sheep, through the blood of the everlasting covenant, 21. Make you perfect in every good work to do his will, working in you that which is well pleasing in his sight, through Jesus Christ; to whom *be* glory for ever and ever. Amen.

Jas. 1:4. But let patience have *her* perfect work, that ye may be perfect and entire, wanting nothing. 25. But whoso looketh into the perfect law of liberty, and continueth *therein*, he being not a forgetful hearer, but a doer of the work, this man shall be blessed in his deed.

Jas. 3:2. If any man offend not in word, the same *is* a perfect man, *and* able also to bridle the whole body.

1 Pet. 5:10. But the God of all grace, who hath called us unto his eternal glory by Christ Jesus, after that ye have suffered a while, make you perfect, stablish, strengthen, settle *you*.

1 John 2:5. But whoso keepeth his word, in him verily is the love of God perfected: hereby know we that we are in him.

1 John 3:6. Whosoever abideth in him sinneth not: whosoever sinneth hath not seen him, neither known him. 7. Little children, let no man deceive you: he that doeth righteousness is righteous, even as he is righteous. 8. He that committeth sin is of the devil: for the devil sinneth from the beginning. For this purpose the Son of God was manifested, that he might destroy the works of the devil. 9. Whosoever is born of God doth not commit sin; for his seed remaineth in him: and he cannot sin, because he is born of God. 10. In this the children of God are manifest, and the children of the devil: whosoever doeth not righteousness is not of God, neither he that loveth not his brother.

1 John 4:12. No man hath seen God at any time. If we love one another, God dwelleth in us, and his love is perfected in us.

1 John 5:18. We know that whosoever is born of God sinneth not; but he that is begotten of God keepeth himself, and that wicked one toucheth him not.

See GOD, PERFECTION OF; HOLINESS; SANCTIFICATION.

PERFIDY. See CONSPIRACY; HYPOCRISY; TREACHERY.

PERFUME. Prov. 27:9; Song 3:6; Isa. 57:9. Used in the tabernacle, Ex. 30:7; 35:28. Beds perfumed with myrrh, Prov. 7:17. Smelling bottles, translated "tablets" in *A. V.*, Isa. 3:20.

PERJURY. Lev. 6:2. If a soul sin, and commit a trespass against the LORD, and lie unto his neighbour in that which was delivered him to keep, or in fellowship, or in a thing taken away by violence, or hath deceived his neighbour; 3. Or have found that which was lost, and lieth concerning it, and sweareth falsely; in any of all these that a man doeth, sinning therein: 4. Then it shall be, because he hath sinned, and is guilty, that he shall restore that which he took violently away, or the thing which he

hath deceitfully gotten, or that which was delivered him to keep, or the lost thing which he found, 5. Or all that about which he hath sworn falsely; he shall even restore it in the principal, and shall add the fifth part more thereto, *and* give it unto him to whom it appertaineth, in the day of his trespass offering. 6. And he shall bring his trespass offering unto the LORD, a ram without blemish out of the flock, with thy estimation, for a trespass offering, unto the priest: 7. And the priest shall make an atonement for him before the LORD: and it shall be forgiven him for any thing of all that he hath done in trespassing therein.

Lev. 19:12. And ye shall not swear by my name falsely, neither shalt thou profane the name of thy God: I *am* the LORD.

Isa. 48:1. Hear ye this, O house of Jacob, which are called by the name of Israel, and are come forth out of the waters of Judah, which swear by the name of the LORD, and make mention of the God of Israel, *but* not in truth, nor in righteousness.

Jer. 5:2. And though they say, The LORD liveth; surely they swear falsely.

Jer. 7:9. Will ye steal, murder, and commit adultery, and swear falsely, and burn incense unto Baal, and walk after other gods whom ye know not;

Hos. 10:4. They have spoken words, swearing falsely in making a covenant: thus judgment springeth up as hemlock in the furrows of the field.

Zech. 5:4. I will bring it forth, saith the LORD of hosts, and it shall enter into the house of the thief, and into the house of him that sweareth falsely by my name: and it shall remain in the midst of his house, and shall consume it with the timber thereof and the stones thereof.

Zech. 8:17. And let none of you imagine evil in your hearts against his neighbour; and love no false oath: for all these *are* things that I hate, saith the LORD.

Mal. 3:5. And I will come near to you to judgment; and I will be a swift witness against the sorcerers, and against the adulterers, and against false swearers,

Matt. 5:33. Again, ye have heard that it hath been said by them of old time, Thou shalt not forswear thyself, but shalt perform unto the LORD thine oaths:

1 Tim. 1:9. Knowing this, that the law is not made for a righteous man, but for the lawless and disobedient, for the ungodly and for sinners, for unholy and profane, for murderers of fathers and murderers of mothers, for manslayers, 10. For whoremongers, for them that defile themselves with mankind, for menstealers, for liars, for perjured persons, and if there be any other thing that is contrary to sound doctrine;

See FALSEHOOD; FALSE WITNESS; OATH.

INSTANCES OF: Zedekiah, 2 Chr. 36:13. Witnesses against Naboth, 1 Kin. 21:8-13; David, Psa. 35:11; Jesus, Matt. 26:59; Mark 14:

56,57; Stephen, Acts 6:11,13,14. Peter, when he denied Jesus with an oath, Matt. 26:74; Mark 14:71.

PERGA, the capital of Pamphylia. Paul preaches in, Acts 13:13,14; 14:25.

PERGAMOS, a city of Mysia. One of the "seven churches" in, Rev. 1:11; 2:12–17.

PERIDA, one of the servants of Solomon. Descendants of, returned to Jerusalem from captivity in Babylon, Neh. 7:57. Called PERUDA in Ezra 2:55.

PERIZZITES. One of the seven nations in the land of Canaan, Gen. 13:7. Territory of, given to Abraham, Gen. 15:20; Ex. 3:8; 23:23. Doomed to destruction, Deut. 20:17. Not all destroyed; Israelites marry among, Judg. 3:5–7; Ezra 9:1,2.

See CANAANITES.

PERSECUTION. OF JESUS: Gen. 3: 15. I will put enmity between thee and the woman, and between thy seed and her seed; it shall bruise thy head, and thou shalt bruise his heel.

Psa. 2:1. Why do the heathen rage, and the people imagine a vain thing? 2. The kings of the earth set themselves, and the rulers take counsel together, against the LORD, and against his anointed, *saying*, 3. Let us break their bands asunder, and cast away their cords from us. 4. He that sitteth in the heavens shall laugh: the Lord shall have them in derision. 5. Then shall he speak unto them in his wrath, and vex them in his sore displeasure.

Psa. 22:1. My God, my God, why hast thou forsaken me? *why art thou so* far from helping me, *and from* the words of my roaring? 2. O my God, I cry in the daytime, but thou hearest not; and in the night season, and am not silent. 6. But I *am* a worm, and no man; a reproach of men, and despised of the people. 7. All they that see me laugh me to scorn: they shoot out the lip, they shake the head, *saying*, 8. He trusted on the LORD *that* he would deliver him: let him deliver him, seeing he delighted in him. 11. Be not far from me; for trouble *is* near; for *there is* none to help. 12. Many bulls have compassed me: strong *bulls* of Bashan have beset me round. 13. They gaped upon me *with* their mouths, *as* a ravening and a roaring lion. 14. I am poured out like water, and all my bones are out of joint: my heart is like wax; it is melted in the midst of my bowels. 15. My strength is dried up like a potsherd; and my tongue cleaveth to my jaws; and thou hast brought me into the dust of death. 16. For dogs have compassed me: the assembly of the wicked have inclosed me: they pierced my hands and my feet. 17. I may tell all my bones: they look *and* stare upon me. 18. They part my garments among them, and cast lots upon my vesture. 19. But be not thou far from me, O LORD: O my strength, haste thee to help me. 20. Deliver my soul from the sword; my darling from the power of the dog.

21. Save me from the lion's mouth: for thou hast heard me from the horns of the unicorns.

Psa. 69:7. For thy sake I have borne reproach; shame hath covered my face. 8. I am become a stranger unto my brethren, and an alien unto my mother's children. 9. For the zeal of thine house hath eaten me up; and the reproaches of them that reproached thee are fallen upon me. 20. Reproach hath broken my heart; and I am full of heaviness; and I looked *for some* to take pity, but *there was* none; and for comforters, but I found none. 21. They gave me also gall for my meat; and in my thirst they gave me vinegar to drink. 26. They persecute *him* whom thou hast smitten; and they talk to the grief of those whom thou hast wounded. *vs.* 1–21.

Psa. 109:25. I became also a reproach unto them: *when* they looked upon me they shaked their heads.

Isa. 49:7. Thus saith the LORD, the Redeemer of Israel, *and* his Holy One, to him whom man despiseth, to him whom the nation abhorreth, to a servant of rulers, Kings shall see and arise, princes also shall worship, because of the LORD that is faithful, *and* the Holy One of Israel, and he shall choose thee.

Isa. 50:6. I gave my back to the smiters, and my cheeks to them that plucked off the hair: I hid not my face from shame and spitting.

Isa. 52:14. As many were astonied at thee; his visage was so marred more than any man, and his form more than the sons of men:

Isa. 53:2. He shall grow up before him as a tender plant, and as a root out of a dry ground: he hath no form nor comeliness; and when we shall see him, *there is* no beauty that we should desire him. 3. He is despised and rejected of men; a man of sorrows, and acquainted with grief: and we hid as it were *our* faces from him; he was despised, and we esteemed him not. 4. Surely he hath borne our griefs, and carried our sorrows: yet we did esteem him stricken, smitten of God, and afflicted. 5. But he *was* wounded for our transgressions, *he was* bruised for our iniquities: the chastisement of our peace *was* upon him; and with his stripes we are healed. 7. He was oppressed, and he was afflicted, yet he opened not his mouth: he is brought as a lamb to the slaughter, and as a sheep before her shearers is dumb, so he openeth not his mouth. 8. He was taken from prison and from judgment: and who shall declare his generation? for he was cut off out of the land of the living: for the transgression of my people was he stricken. 9. And he made his grave with the wicked, and with the rich in his death; because he had done no violence, neither *was any* deceit in his mouth. 10. Yet it pleased the LORD to bruise him; he hath put *him* to grief:

Mic. 5:1. They shall smite the judge of Israel with a rod upon the cheek.

Matt. 2:13. And when they were departed, behold, the angel of the Lord appeareth to Joseph in a dream, saying, Arise, and take the young child and his mother, and flee into Egypt, and be thou there until I bring thee word: for Herod will seek the young child to destroy him.

Matt. 12:14. The Pharisees went out, and held a council against him, how they might destroy him. 24. When the Pharisees heard *it*, they said, This *fellow* doth not cast out devils, but by Beelzebub the prince of the devils. Mark 3:22; Luke 6:11; 11:15.

Matt. 16:1. The Pharisees also with the Sadducees came, and tempting desired him that he would shew them a sign from heaven.

Matt 26:3. Then assembled together the chief priests, and the scribes, and the elders of the people, unto the palace of the high priest, who was called Caiaphas, 4. And consulted that they might take Jesus by subtilty, and kill *him*. 14. Then one of the twelve, called Judas Iscariot, went unto the chief priests, 15. And said *unto them*, What will ye give me, and I will deliver him unto you? And they covenanted with him for thirty pieces of silver. 16. And from that time he sought opportunity to betray him. [Mark 14:1; 14:48.] 59. Now the chief priests, and elders, and all the council, sought false witness against Jesus, to put him to death;

Matt. 27:25. Then answered all the people, and said, His blood *be* on us, and on our children. 26. Then released he Barabbas unto them: and when he had scourged Jesus, he delivered *him* to be crucified. 27. Then the soldiers of the governor took Jesus into the common hall, and gathered unto him the whole band *of soldiers*. 28. And they stripped him, and put on him a scarlet robe. 29. And when they had platted a crown of thorns, they put *it* upon his head, and a reed in his right hand: and they bowed the knee before him, and mocked him, saying, Hail, King of the Jews! 30. And they spit upon him, and took the reed, and smote him on the head. 39. They that passed by reviled him, wagging their heads, 40. And saying, Thou that destroyest the temple, and buildest *it* in three days, save thyself. If thou be the Son of God, come down from the cross. 41. Likewise also the chief priests mocking *him*, with the scribes and elders, said, 42. He saved others; himself he cannot save. If he be the King of Israel, let him now come down from the cross, and we will believe him. 43. He trusted in God; let him deliver him now, if he will have him: for he said, I am the Son of God. 44. The thieves also, which were crucified with him, cast the same in his teeth. Mark 15; John 19.

Mark 3:6. And the Pharisees went forth, and straightway took counsel with the He-

(60)

rodians against him, how they might destroy him. 21. When his friends heard *of it*, they went out to lay hold on him: for they said, He is beside himself.

Mark 15:34. At the ninth hour Jesus cried with a loud voice, saying, Eloi, Eloi, lama sabachthani? which is, being interpreted, My God, my God, why hast thou forsaken me? with chapters 16; 17.

Luke 4:28. All they in the synagogue, when they heard these things, were filled with wrath, 29. And rose up, and thrust him out of the city, and led him unto the brow of the hill whereon their city was built, that they might cast him down headlong.

Luke 7:34. The Son of man is come eating and drinking; and ye say, Behold a gluttonous man, and a winebibber, a friend of publicans and sinners! Matt. 11:19.

Luke 11:53. The scribes and the Pharisees began to urge *him* vehemently, and to provoke him to speak of many things: 54. Laying wait for him, and seeking to catch something out of his mouth, that they might accuse him.

Luke 12:50. I have a baptism to be baptized with; and how am I straitened till it be accomplished! Matt. 20:22.

Luke 13:31. There came certain of the Pharisees, saying unto him, Get thee out, and depart hence: for Herod will kill thee.

Luke 19:14. His citizens hated him, and sent a message after him, saying, We will not have this *man* to reign over us. 47. The chief priests and the scribes and the chief of the people sought to destroy him, Mark 11:18.

Luke 20:20. They watched *him*, and sent forth spies, which should feign themselves just men, that they might take hold of his words, that so they might deliver him unto the power and authority of the governor. Matt. 22:15; Mark 12:13.

Luke 22:2. The chief priests and scribes sought how they might kill him; for they feared the people. 3. Then entered Satan into Judas surnamed Iscariot, being of the number of the twelve. 4. And he went his way, and communed with the chief priests and captains, how he might betray him unto them. 5. And they were glad, and covenanted to give him money. 52. Then Jesus said unto the chief priests, and captains of the temple, and the elders, which were come to him, Be ye come out, as against a thief, with swords and staves? 53. When I was daily with you in the temple, ye stretched forth no hands against me: but this is your hour, and the power of darkness. 63. The men that held Jesus mocked him, and smote *him*. 64. And when they had blindfolded him, they struck him on the face, and asked him, saying, Prophesy, who is it that smote thee? 65. And many other things blasphemously spake they against him. Matt. 26:67; Mark 14:65.

Luke 23:11. Herod with his men of war

set him at nought, and mocked *him*, and arrayed him in a gorgeous robe, and sent him again to Pilate. 23. They were instant with loud voices, requiring that he might be crucified. Mark 15:14.

John 5:16. Therefore did the Jews persecute Jesus, and sought to slay him, because he had done these things on the sabbath day.

John 7:1. After these things Jesus walked in Galilee: for he would not walk in Jewry, because the Jews sought to kill him. 7. The world cannot hate you; but me it hateth, because I testify of it, that the works thereof are evil. 19. Why go ye about to kill me? 20. The people answered and said, Thou hast a devil: who goeth about to kill thee? 30. Then they sought to take him: but no man laid hands on him, because his hour was not yet come. 32. The Pharisees heard that the people murmured such things concerning him: and the Pharisees and the chief priests sent officers to take him.

John 8:37. I know that ye are Abraham's seed; but ye seek to kill me, because my word hath no place in you. 40. Ye seek to kill me, a man that hath told you the truth, which I have heard of God: this did not Abraham. 48. Then answered the Jews, and said unto him, Say we not well that thou art a Samaritan, and hast a devil? 52. Now we know that thou hast a devil. 59. Then took they up stones to cast at him: John 10:31.

John 10:20. Many of them said, He hath a devil, and is mad; why hear ye him? 39. Therefore they sought again to take him: but he escaped out of their hand,

John 11:57. Now both the chief priests and the Pharisees had given a commandment, that, if any man knew where he were, he should shew *it*, that they might take him.

John 14:30. The prince of this world cometh, and hath nothing in me.

John 15:18. If the world hate you, ye know that it hated me before *it hated* you. 20. The servant is not greater than his lord. If they have persecuted me, they will also persecute you; 21. But all these things will they do unto you for my name's sake. 24. Now have they both seen and hated both me and my Father. 25. But *this cometh to pass*, that the word might be fulfilled that is written in their law, They hated me without a cause.

John 18:22. And when he had thus spoken, one of the officers which stood by struck Jesus with the palm of his hand, saying, Answerest thou the high priest so? 23. Jesus answered him, If I have spoken evil, bear witness of the evil: but if well, why smitest thou me? 29. Pilate then went out unto them, and said, What accusation bring ye against this man? 30. They answered and said unto him, If he were not a malefactor, we would not have delivered him up unto thee.

John 19:6. When the chief priests there-

fore and officers saw him, they cried out, saying, Crucify *him*, crucify *him*. Pilate saith unto them, Take ye him, and crucify *him*: for I find no fault in him. 15. They cried out, Away with *him*, away with *him*, crucify him.

Acts 2:23. Him, being delivered by the determinate counsel and foreknowledge of God, ye have taken, and by wicked hands have crucified and slain:

Acts 3:13. The God of Abraham, and of Isaac, and of Jacob, the God of our fathers, hath glorified his Son Jesus; whom ye delivered up, and denied him in the presence of Pilate, when he was determined to let *him* go. 14. But ye denied the Holy One and the Just, and desired a murderer to be granted unto you; 15. And killed the Prince of life, whom God hath raised from the dead; whereof we are witnesses.

Acts 4:27. For of a truth against thy holy child Jesus, whom thou hast anointed, both Herod, and Pontius Pilate, with the Gentiles, and the people of Israel, were gathered together,

Acts 7:52. Which of the prophets have not your fathers persecuted? and they have slain them which shewed before of the coming of the Just One; of whom ye have been now the betrayers and murderers:

Acts 13:27. For they that dwell at Jerusalem, and their rulers, because they knew him not, nor yet the voices of the prophets which are read every sabbath day, they have fulfilled *them* in condemning *him*. 28. And though they found no cause of death *in him*, yet desired they Pilate that he should be slain. 29. And when they had fulfilled all that was written of him, they took *him* down from the tree, and laid *him* in a sepulchre.

Heb. 12:2. Looking unto Jesus the author and finisher of *our* faith; who for the joy that was set before him endured the cross, despising the shame, and is set down at the right hand of the throne of God. 3. For consider him that endured such contradiction of sinners against himself, lest ye be wearied and faint in your minds.

1 Pet. 4:1. Forasmuch then as Christ hath suffered for us in the flesh, arm yourselves likewise with the same mind: for he that hath suffered in the flesh hath ceased from sin;

OF THE RIGHTEOUS: Gen. 49:23. The archers have sorely grieved him, and shot *at him*, and hated him:

Job 1:9. Then Satan answered the LORD, and said, Doth Job fear God for nought?

Job 2:4. And Satan answered the LORD, and said, Skin for skin, yea, all that a man hath will he give for his life. 5. But put forth thine hand now, and touch his bone and his flesh, and he will curse thee to thy face.

Job 12:4. I am *as* one mocked of his neighbour, who calleth upon God, and he answereth him: the just upright *man is* laughed to scorn. 5. He that is ready to slip with *his* feet *is as* a lamp despised in the thought of him that is at ease.

Psa. 11:2. For, lo, the wicked bend *their* bow, they make ready their arrow upon the string, that they may privily shoot at the upright in heart.

Psa. 37:32. The wicked watcheth the righteous, and seeketh to slay him.

Psa. 38:20. They also that render evil for good are mine adversaries; because I follow *the thing that* good *is*.

Psa. 42:3. My tears have been my meat day and night, while they continually say unto me, Where *is* thy God? 10. *As* with a sword in my bones, mine enemies reproach me; while they say daily unto me, Where *is* thy God?

Psa. 44:15. My confusion *is* continually before me, and the shame of my face hath covered me, 16. For the voice of him that reproacheth and blasphemeth; by reason of the enemy and avenger. 17. All this is come upon us; yet have we not forgotten thee, neither have we dealt falsely in thy covenant. 18. Our heart is not turned back, neither have our steps declined from thy way; 22. Yea, for thy sake are we killed all the day long; we are counted as sheep for the slaughter.

Psa. 56:5. Every day they wrest my words: all their thoughts *are* against me for evil.

Psa. 69:10. When I wept, *and chastened* my soul with fasting, that was to my reproach. 11. I made sackcloth also my garment; and I became a proverb to them. 12. They that sit in the gate speak against me; and I *was* the song of the drunkards.

Psa. 74:7. They have cast fire into thy sanctuary, they have defiled *by casting down* the dwelling place of thy name to the ground. 8. They said in their hearts, Let us destroy them together: they have burned up all the synagogues of God in the land.

Psa. 94:5. They break in pieces thy people, O LORD, and afflict thine heritage.

Psa. 119:51. The proud have had me greatly in derision: *yet* have I not declined from thy law. 61. The bands of the wicked have robbed me: *but* I have not forgotten thy law. 69. The proud have forged a lie against me: *but* I will keep thy precepts with *my* whole heart. 78. Let the proud be ashamed; for they dealt perversely with me without a cause: *but* I will meditate in thy precepts. 85. The proud have digged pits for me, which *are* not after thy law. 86. All thy commandments *are* faithful: they persecute me wrongfully; help thou me. 87. They had almost consumed me upon earth; but I forsook not thy precepts. 95. The wicked have waited for me to destroy me: *but* I will consider thy testimonies. 110. The wicked have laid a snare for me: yet I erred not from thy precepts. 157. Many

are my persecutors and mine enemies; *yet* do I not decline from thy testimonies. 161. Princes have persecuted me without a cause: but my heart standeth in awe of thy word.

Prov. 29:10. The bloodthirsty hate the upright: 27. *He that is* upright in the way *is* abomination to the wicked.

Isa. 26:20. Come, my people, enter thou into thy chambers, and shut thy doors about thee: hide thyself as it were for a little moment, until the indignation be overpast.

Isa. 29:20. For the terrible one is brought to nought, and the scorner is consumed, and all that watch for iniquity are cut off: 21. That make a man an offender for a word, and lay a snare for him that reproveth in the gate, and turn aside the just for a thing of nought.

Isa. 51:12. I, *even* I, *am* he that comforteth you: who *art* thou, that thou shouldest be afraid of a man *that* shall die, and of the son of man *which* shall be made *as* grass; 13. And forgettest the LORD thy maker, that hath stretched forth the heavens, and laid the foundations of the earth; and hast feared continually every day because of the fury of the oppressor, as if he were ready to destroy? and where *is* the fury of the oppressor?

Isa. 59:15. He *that* departeth from evil maketh himself a prey: and the LORD saw it, and it displeased him

Jer. 2:30. Your own sword hath devoured your prophets, like a destroying lion.

Jer. 11:19. I *was* like a lamb or an ox *that* is brought to the slaughter; and I knew not that they had devised devices against me, *saying*, Let us destroy the tree with the fruit thereof, and let us cut him off from the land of the living, that his name may be no more remembered.

Jer. 15:10. Woe is me, my mother, that thou hast borne me a man of strife and a man of contention to the whole earth! I have neither lent on usury, nor men have lent to me on usury; *yet* every one of them doth curse me.

Jer. 18:18. Then said they, Come, and let us devise devices against Jeremiah; . . . Come, and let us smite him with the tongue, and let us not give heed to any of his words.

Jer. 20:8. The word of the LORD was made a reproach unto me, and a derision, daily. *v.* 7.

Jer. 26:11. Then spake the priests and the prophets unto the princes and to all the people, saying, This man *is* worthy to die; for he hath prophesied against this city, as ye have heard with your ears. 12. Then spake Jeremiah unto all the princes and to all the people, saying, The LORD sent me to prophesy against this house and against this city all the words that ye have heard. 13. Therefore now amend your ways and your doings, and obey the voice of the LORD your God; and the LORD will repent him of the evil that he hath pronounced against you. 14. As for me behold, I *am* in your hand: do with me as seemeth good and meet unto you.

Jer. 50:7. All that found them have devoured them:

Amos 5:10. They hate him that rebuketh in the gate, and they abhor him that speaketh uprightly.

Hab. 1:13. *Thou art* of purer eyes than to behold evil, and canst not look on iniquity: wherefore lookest thou upon them that deal treacherously, *and* holdest thy tongue when the wicked devoureth *the man that is* more righteous than he?

Matt. 5:10. Blessed *are* they which are persecuted for righteousness' sake: for their's is the kingdom of heaven. 11. Blessed are ye, when *men* shall revile you, and persecute *you*, and shall say all manner of evil against you falsely, for my sake. 12. Rejoice, and be exceeding glad: for great *is* your reward in heaven: for so persecuted they the prophets which were before you. 44. But I say unto you, Love your enemies, bless them that curse you, do good to them that hate you, and pray for them which despitefully use you, and persecute you; Luke 6:26,27.

Matt. 10:16. I send you forth as sheep in the midst of wolves: be ye therefore wise as serpents, and harmless as doves. 17. But beware of men: for they will deliver you up to the councils, and they will scourge you in their synagogues; 18. And ye shall be brought before governors and kings for my sake, for a testimony against them and the Gentiles. 21. And the brother shall deliver up the brother to death, and the father the child: and the children shall rise up against *their* parents, and cause them to be put to death. 22. And ye shall be hated of all *men* for my name's sake: but he that endureth to the end shall be saved. 23. But when they persecute you in this city, flee ye into another: 28. Fear not them which kill the body, but are not able to kill the soul: but rather fear him which is able to destroy both soul and body in hell.

Matt. 20:22. But Jesus answered and said, Ye know not what ye ask. Are ye able to drink of the cup that I shall drink of, and to be baptized with the baptism that I am baptized with? They say unto him, We are able. 23. And he saith unto them, Ye shall drink indeed of my cup, and be baptized with the baptism that I am baptized with.

Matt. 23:34. Wherefore, behold, I send unto you prophets, and wise men, and scribes: and *some* of them ye shall kill and crucify; and *some* of them shall ye scourge in your synagogues, and persecute *them* from city to city: 35. That upon you may come all the righteous blood shed upon the earth, from the blood of righteous Abel unto the blood of Zacharias, son of Bara-

chias, whom ye slew between the temple and the altar.

Matt. 24:8. All these *are* the beginning of sorrows. 9. Then shall they deliver you up to be afflicted, and shall kill you: and ye shall be hated of all nations for my name's sake. 10. And then shall many be offended, and shall betray one another, and shall hate one another.

Mark 8:35. For whosoever will save his life shall lose it; but whosoever shall lose his life for my sake and the gospel's, the same shall save it. Luke 17:33.

Mark 9:42. And whosoever shall offend one of *these* little ones that believe in me, it is better for him that a millstone were hanged about his neck, and he were cast into the sea.

Mark 13:9. But take heed to yourselves: for they shall deliver you up to councils; and in the synagogues ye shall be beaten: and ye shall be brought before rulers and kings for my sake, for a testimony against them. 11. But when they shall lead *you*, and deliver you up, take no thought beforehand what ye shall speak, neither do ye premeditate: but whatsoever shall be given you in that hour, that speak ye: for it is not ye that speak, but the Holy Ghost. 12. Now the brother shall betray the brother to death, and the father the son; and children shall rise up against *their* parents, and shall cause them to be put to death. 13. And ye shall be hated of all *men* for my name's sake: but he that shall endure unto the end, the same shall be saved.

Luke 6:22. Blessed are ye, when men shall hate you, and when they shall separate you *from their company*, and shall reproach *you*, and cast out your name as evil, for the Son of man's sake. 23. Rejoice ye in that day, and leap for joy: for, behold, your reward *is* great in heaven: for in the like manner did their fathers unto the prophets.

Luke 21:12. But before all these, they shall lay their hands on you, and persecute *you*, delivering *you* up to the synagogues, and into prisons, being brought before kings and rulers for my name's sake. 13. And it shall turn to you for a testimony. 14. Settle *it* therefore in your hearts, not to meditate before what ye shall answer: 15. For I will give you a mouth and wisdom, which all your adversaries shall not be able to gainsay nor resist. 16. And ye shall be betrayed both by parents, and brethren, and kinsfolks, and friends: and *some* of you shall they cause to be put to death. 17. And ye shall be hated of all *men* for my name's sake. 18. But there shall not an hair of your head perish. 19. In your patience possess ye your souls.

John 12:42. Nevertheless among the chief rulers also many believed on him; but because of the Pharisees they did not confess *him*, lest they should be put out of the synagogue:

John 15:18. If the world hate you, ye know that it hated me before *it hated* you. 19. If ye were of the world, the world would love his own: but because ye are not of the world, but I have chosen you out of the world, therefore the world hateth you.

John 16:1. These things have I spoken unto you, that ye should not be offended. 2. They shall put you out of the synagogues: yea, the time cometh, that whosoever killeth you will think that he doeth God service.

John 17:14. I have given them thy word; and the world hath hated them, because they are not of the world, even as I am not of the world.

Acts 4:16. Saying, What shall we do to these men? for that indeed a notable miracle hath been done by them *is* manifest to all them that dwell in Jerusalem; and we cannot deny *it*. 17. But that it spread no further among the people, let us straitly threaten them, that they speak henceforth to no man in this name. 18. And they called them, and commanded them not to speak at all nor teach in the name of Jesus. 19. Peter and John answered and said unto them, Whether it be right in the sight of God to hearken unto you more than unto God, judge ye. 20. For we cannot but speak the things which we have seen and heard.

Acts 5:29. Then Peter and the *other* apostles answered and said, We ought to obey God rather than men. 40. And when they had called the apostles, and beaten *them*, they commanded that they should not speak in the name of Jesus, and let them go. 41. And they departed from the presence of the council, rejoicing that they were counted worthy to suffer shame for his name. 42. And daily in the temple, and in every house, they ceased not to teach and preach Jesus Christ.

Acts 7:52. Which of the prophets have not your fathers persecuted? and they have slain them which shewed before of the coming of the Just One; of whom ye have been now the betrayers and murderers:

Acts 8:4. They that were scatttered abroad went every where preaching the word.

Acts 28:22. But we desire to hear of thee what thou thinkest: for as concerning this sect, we know that every where it is spoken against.

Rom. 8:17. If so be that we suffer with *him*, that we may be also glorified together. 35. Who shall separate us from the love of Christ? *shall* tribulation, or distress, or persecution, or famine, or nakedness, or peril, or sword? 36. As it is written, For thy sake we are killed all the day long; we are accounted as sheep for the slaughter. 37. Nay, in all these things we are more than conquerors through him that loved us.

1 Cor. 4:9. I think that God hath set forth us the apostles last, as it were appointed to death: for we are made a spectacle unto the world, and to angels, and to men.

10. We *are* fools for Christ's sake, but ye *are* wise in Christ; we *are* weak, but ye *are* strong; ye *are* honourable, but we *are* despised. 11. Even unto this present hour we both hunger, and thirst, and are naked, and are buffeted, and have no certain dwellingplace; 12. And labour, working with our own hands: being reviled, we bless; being persecuted, we suffer it: 13. Being defamed, we intreat: we are made as the filth of the world, *and are* the offscouring of all things unto this day.

1 Cor. 13:3. Though I give my body to be burned, and have not charity, it profiteth me nothing.

2 Cor. 4:8. *We are* troubled on every side, yet not distressed; *we are* perplexed, but not in despair; 9. Persecuted, but not forsaken; cast down, but not destroyed; 10. Always bearing about in the body the dying of the Lord Jesus, that the life also of Jesus might be made manifest in our body. 11. For we which live are alway delivered unto death for Jesus' sake, that the life also of Jesus might be made manifest in our mortal flesh. 12. So then death worketh in us, but life in you.

2 Cor. 6:4. In all *things* approving ourselves as the ministers of God, in much patience, in afflictions, in necessities, in distresses, 5. In stripes, in imprisonments, in tumults, in labours, in watchings, in fastings; 8. By honour and dishonour, by evil report and good report: as deceivers, and *yet* true; 9. As unknown, and *yet* well known; as dying, and, behold, we live; as chastened, and not killed; 10. As sorrowful, yet alway rejoicing; as poor, yet making many rich; as having nothing, and *yet* possessing all things.

2 Cor. 11:23. In labours more abundant, in stripes above measure, in prisons more frequent, in deaths oft. 24. Of the Jews five times received I forty *stripes* save one. 25. Thrice was I beaten with rods, once was I stoned, thrice I suffered shipwreck, a night and a day I have been in the deep; 26. *In* journeyings often, *in* perils of waters, *in* perils of robbers, *in* perils by *mine own* countrymen, *in* perils by the heathen, *in* perils in the city, *in* perils in the wilderness, *in* perils in the sea, *in* perils among false brethren; 27. In weariness and painfulness, in watchings often, in hunger and thirst, in fastings often, in cold and nakedness.

2 Cor. 12:10. I take pleasure in infirmities, in reproaches, in necessities, in persecutions, in distresses for Christ's sake: for when I am weak, then am I strong.

Gal. 4:29. As then he that was born after the flesh persecuted him *that was born* after the Spirit, even so *it is* now.

Gal. 6:12. As many as desire to make a fair shew in the flesh, they constrain you to be circumcised; only lest they should suffer persecution for the cross of Christ. 17. I bear [1]in my body the marks of [2]the Lord Jesus. [R. V. [1]branded on [2]Omitted.]

Phil. 1:12. But I would ye should understand, brethren, that the things *which happened* unto me have fallen out rather unto the furtherance of the gospel; 13. So that my bonds in Christ are manifest in all the palace, and in all other *places;* 14. Many of the brethren in the Lord, waxing confident by my bonds, are much more bold to speak the word without fear. 28. In nothing terrified by your adversaries: which is to them an evident token of perdition, but to you of salvation, and that of God. 29. Unto you it is given in the behalf of Christ, not only to believe on him, but also to suffer for his sake;

Col. 1:24. Who now rejoice in my sufferings for you, and fill up that which is behind of the afflictions of Christ in my flesh for his body's sake, which is the church:

1 Thess. 1:6. And ye became followers of us, and of the Lord, having received the word in much affliction, with joy of the Holy Ghost:

1 Thess. 2:2. Even after that we had suffered before, and were shamefully entreated, as ye know, at Philippi, we were bold in our God to speak unto you the gospel of God with much contention. 14. For ye, brethren, became followers of the churches of God which in Judæa are in Christ Jesus: for ye also have suffered like things of your own countrymen, even as they *have* of the Jews: 15. Who both killed the Lord Jesus, and their own prophets, and have persecuted us; and they please not God, and are contrary to all men:

2 Thess. 1:4. So that we ourselves glory in you in the churches of God for your patience and faith in all your persecutions and tribulations that ye endure:

2 Tim. 1:8. Be not thou therefore ashamed of the testimony of our Lord, nor of me his prisoner: but be thou partaker of the afflictions of the gospel according to the power of God; 12. For the which cause I also suffer these things: nevertheless I am not ashamed:

2 Tim. 2:9. Wherein I suffer trouble, as an evil doer, *even* unto bonds; but the word of God is not bound. 10. Therefore I endure all things for the elect's sakes, that they may also obtain the salvation which is in Christ Jesus with eternal glory. 12. If we suffer, we shall also reign with *him:* if we deny *him,* he also will deny us:

2 Tim. 3:2. For men shall be lovers of their own selves, . . . 3. . . . Despisers of those that are good. 12. Yea, and all that will live godly in Christ Jesus shall suffer persecution.

2 Tim. 4:16. At my first answer no man stood with me, but all *men* forsook me: *I pray God* that it may not be laid to their charge. 17. Notwithstanding the Lord stood with me, and strengthened me; that by me the preaching might be fully known, and *that* all the Gentiles might hear: and I was delivered out of the mouth of the lion.

Heb. 10:32. Call to remembrance the former days, in which, after ye were illuminated, ye endured a great fight of afflictions; 33. Partly, whilst ye were made a gazingstock both by reproaches and afflictions; and partly, whilst ye became companions of them that were so used. 34. For ye had compassion of me in my bonds, and took joyfully the spoiling of your goods, knowing in yourselves that ye have in heaven a better and an enduring substance.

Heb. 11:25. Choosing rather to suffer affliction with the people of God, than to enjoy the pleasures of sin for a season; 26. Esteeming the reproach of Christ greater riches than the treasures in Egypt: for he had respect unto the recompence of the reward. 27. By faith he forsook Egypt, not fearing the wrath of the king: for he endured, as seeing him who is invisible. 33. Who through faith . . . stopped the mouths of lions, 34. Quenched the violence of fire, escaped the edge of the sword, out of weakness were made strong, 35. Others were tortured, not accepting deliverance; that they might obtain a better resurrection: 36. And others had trial of *cruel* mockings and scourgings, yea, moreover of bonds and imprisonment: 37. They were stoned, they were sawn asunder, were tempted, were slain with the sword: they wandered about in sheepskins and goatskins; being destitute, afflicted, tormented; 38. (Of whom the world was not worthy:) they wandered in deserts, and *in* mountains, and *in* dens and caves of the earth.

Heb. 12:3. Consider him that endured such contradiction of sinners against himself, lest ye be wearied and faint in your minds. 4. Ye have not yet resisted unto blood, striving against sin.

Heb. 13:13. Let us go forth therefore unto him without the camp, bearing his reproach.

Jas. 2:6. Do not rich men oppress you, and draw you before the judgment seats?

Jas. 5:6. Ye have condemned *and* killed the just; *and* he doth not resist you. 10. Take, my brethren, the prophets, who have spoken in the name of the Lord, for an example of suffering affliction, and of patience.

1 Pet. 3:14. But and if ye suffer for righteousness' sake, happy *are ye:* and be not afraid of their terror, neither be troubled; 16. Having a good conscience; that, whereas they speak evil of you, as of evildoers, they may be ashamed that falsely accuse your good conversation in Christ. 17. For *it is* better, if the will of God be so, that ye suffer for well doing, than for evil doing.

1 Pet. 4:3. We walked in lasciviousness, lusts, excess of wine, revellings, banquetings, and abominable idolatries: 4. Wherein they think it strange that ye run not with *them* to the same excess of riot, speaking evil of *you:* 12. Beloved, think it not strange concerning the fiery trial which is to try you, as though some strange thing happened unto you: 13. But rejoice, inasmuch as ye are partakers of Christ's sufferings; that, when his glory shall be revealed, ye may be glad also with exceeding joy. 14. If ye be reproached for the name of Christ, happy *are ye;* for the spirit of glory and of God resteth upon you: ¹ on their part he is evil spoken of, but on your part he is glorified. 16. If *any man suffer* as a Christian, let him not be ashamed; but let him glorify God on this behalf. 19. Let them that suffer according to the will of God commit the keeping of their souls *to him* in well doing, as unto a faithful Creator. 　　　　　[¹ Omitted in R. V.]

1 John 3:1. The world knoweth us not, because it knew him not. 13. Marvel not, my brethren, if the world hate you.

Rev. 2:3. Hast borne, and hast patience, and for my name's sake hast laboured, and hast not fainted. 10. Fear none of those things which thou shalt suffer: behold, the devil shall cast *some* of you into prison, that ye may be tried; and ye shall have tribulation ten days: be thou faithful unto death, and I will give thee a crown of life. 13. I know thy works, and where thou dwellest, *even* where Satan's seat *is:* and thou holdest fast my name, and hast not denied my faith, even in those days wherein Antipas *was* my faithful martyr, who was slain among you, where Satan dwelleth.

Rev. 6:9. And when he had opened the fifth seal, I saw under the altar the souls of them that were slain for the word of God, and for the testimony which they held: 10. And they cried with a loud voice, saying, How long, O Lord, holy and true, dost thou not judge and avenge our blood on them that dwell on the earth? 11. And white robes were given unto every one of them; and it was said unto them, that they should rest yet for a little season, until their fellowservants also and their brethren, that should be killed as they *were*, should be fulfilled.

Rev. 7:13. And one of the elders answered, saying unto me, What are these which are arrayed in white robes? and whence came they? 14. And I said unto him, Sir, thou knowest. And he said to me, These are they which came out of great tribulation, and have washed their robes, and made them white in the blood of the Lamb. 15. Therefore are they before the throne of God, and serve him day and night in his temple: and he that sitteth on the throne shall dwell among them. 16. They shall hunger no more, neither thirst any more; neither shall the sun light on them, nor any heat. 17. For the Lamb which is in the midst of the throne shall feed them, and shall lead them unto living fountains of waters: and God shall wipe away all tears from their eyes.

Rev. 12:11. They overcame him by the blood of the Lamb, and by the word of their testimony; and they loved not their lives unto the death.

Rev. 17:6. I saw the woman drunken with the blood of the saints, and with the blood of the martyrs of Jesus:

Rev. 20:4. *I saw* the souls of them that were beheaded for the witness of Jesus, and for the word of God, and which had not worshipped the beast, neither his image, neither had received *his* mark upon their foreheads, or in their hands; and they lived and reigned with Christ a thousand years. See PAUL.

A mode of divine chastisement, Lam. 1:3. Diffuses the gospel, Acts 8:1,4; 11:19-21; Phil. 1:12-14.

Prayer for deliverance from, Psa. 70:1-4; 83; 140:1,4; 142:6. Deliverance from, Psa. 124; 129:1,2.

INSTANCES OF: Of Abel, Gen. 4:8; Matt. 23: 35; 1 John 3:12. Of Lot, Gen. 19:9. Of Moses, Ex. 2:15; 17:4. Of David, Psa. 31:13; 59:1,2. Of prophets martyred by Jezebel, 1 Kin. 18:4. Of Gideon, Judg. 6:28-32. Of Elijah, 1 Kin. 18:10; 19; 2 Kin. 1:9; 2:23. Of Micaiah, 1 Kin. 22:26; 2 Chr. 18:26. Of Elisha, 2 Kin. 6:31. Of Hanani, 2 Chr. 16:10. Of Zachariah, 2 Chr. 24:21; Matt. 23:35. Of Job, Job 13:4-13; 16: 1-4; 17:2; 19:1-5; 30:1-10. Of Jeremiah, Jer. 15:10,15; 17:15-18; 18:18-23; 26; 32:2; 33:1; 36:26; 37; 38:1-6. Of Urijah, Jer. 26:23. Of prophets, Matt. 21:35,36. Of the three Hebrew children of the captivity, Dan. 3:8-23. Of Daniel, Dan. 6. Of the Jews, Ezra 4; Neh. 4. Of John the Baptist, Matt. 14:3-12. Of James, Acts 12:2. Of Simon, Mark 15:21. Of the disciples, John 9:22,34; 20:19. Of Lazarus, John 12:10. Of the apostles, Acts 4:3-18; 5:18-42; 12:1-19; Rev. 1:9. Of Stephen, Acts 6:9-15; 7. Of the church, Acts 8:1; 9:1-14; Gal. 1:13. Of Timothy, Heb. 13:23. Of John, Rev. 1:9. Of Antipas, Rev. 2:13. Of the church of Smyrna, Rev. 2:8-10. See PAUL.

PERSEVERANCE. 1 Chr. 16:11. Seek the LORD and his strength, seek his face continually.

Job 17:9. The righteous also shall hold on his way, and he that hath clean hands shall be stronger and stronger.

Psa. 37:24. Though he fall, he shall not be utterly cast down: for the LORD upholdeth *him with* his hand. 28. The LORD loveth judgment, and forsaketh not his saints; they are preserved for ever:

Psa. 73:24. Thou shalt guide me with thy counsel, and afterward receive me *to* glory.

Psa. 138:8. The LORD will perfect *that which* concerneth me:

Prov. 4:18. The path of the just *is* as the shining light, that shineth more and more unto the perfect day.

Jer. 32:40. I will make an everlasting covenant with them, that I will not turn away from them, to do them good; but I will put my fear in their hearts, that they shall not depart from me.

Hos. 12:6. Therefore turn thou to thy God: keep mercy and judgment, and wait on thy God continually.

Matt. 24:13. He that shall endure unto

the end, the same shall be saved. Matt. 10: 22; Mark 13:13.

Mark 4:3. Hearken; Behold, there went out a sower to sow: 4. And it came to pass, as he sowed, some fell by the way side, and the fowls of the air came and devoured it up. 5. And some fell on stony ground, where it had not much earth; and immediately it sprang up, because it had no depth of earth: 6. But when the sun was up, it was scorched; and because it had no root, it withered away. 7. And some fell among thorns, and the thorns grew up, and choked it, and it yielded no fruit. 8. And other fell on good ground, and did yield fruit that sprang up and increased; and brought forth, some thirty, and some sixty, and some an hundred.

Luke 10:42. But one thing is needful: and Mary hath chosen that good part, which shall not be taken away from her.

Luke 22:31. And the Lord said, Simon, Simon, behold, Satan hath desired *to have* you, that he may sift *you* as wheat: 32. But I have prayed for thee, that thy faith fail not:

John 6:37. All that the father giveth me shall come to me; and him that cometh to me I will in no wise cast out. 39. And this is the Father's will which hath sent me, that of all which he hath given me I should lose nothing, but should raise it up again at the last day. 40. And this is the will of him that sent me, that every one which seeth the Son, and believeth on him, may have everlasting life: and I will raise him up at the last day.

John 8:31. Then said Jesus to those Jews which believed on him, If ye continue in my word, *then* are ye my disciples indeed; 32. And ye shall know the truth, and the truth shall make you free.

John 10:28. I give unto them eternal life; and they shall never perish, neither shall any *man* pluck them out of my hand. 29. My Father, which gave *them* me, is greater than all; and no *man* is able to pluck *them* out of my Father's hand.

John 15:4. Abide in me, and I in you. As the branch cannot bear fruit of itself, except it abide in the vine; no more can ye, except ye abide in me. 5. I am the vine, ye *are* the branches: he that abideth in me, and I in him, the same bringeth forth much fruit: for without me ye can do nothing. 7. If ye abide in me, and my words abide in you, ye shall ask what ye will, and it shall be done unto you. 9. As the Father hath loved me, so have I loved you: continue ye in my love.

Acts 11:23. Who, when he came, and had seen the grace of God, was glad, and exhorted them all, that with purpose of heart they would cleave unto the Lord.

Acts 13:43. Now when the congregation was broken up, many of the Jews and religious proselytes followed Paul and Barnabas: who, speaking to them, persuaded them to continue in the grace of God.

Acts 14:21. And when they had preached the gospel to that city, and had taught many, they returned again to Lystra, and *to* Iconium, and Antioch, 22. Confirming the souls of the disciples, *and* exhorting them to continue in the faith, and that we must through much tribulation enter into the kingdom of God.

Rom. 2:6. Who will render to every man according to his deeds: 7. To them who by patient continuance in well doing seek for glory and honour and immortality, eternal life:

Rom. 8:30. Whom he did predestinate, them he also called: and whom he called, them he also justified: and whom he justified, them he also glorified. 33. Who shall lay any thing to the charge of God's elect? *It is* God that justifieth. 34. Who *is* he that condemneth? *It is* Christ that died, yea rather, that is risen again, who is even at the right hand of God, who also maketh intercession for us. 35. Who shall separate us from the love of Christ? *shall* tribulation, or distress, or persecution, or famine, or nakedness, or peril, or sword? 37. Nay, in all these things we are more than conquerors through him that loved us. 38. For I am persuaded, that neither death, nor life, nor angels, nor principalities, nor powers, nor things present, nor things to come, 39. Nor height, nor depth, nor any other creature, shall be able to separate us from the love of God, which is in Jesus Christ our Lord.

Rom. 11:29. For the gifts and calling of God *are* without repentance.

1 Cor. 1:8. Who shall also confirm you unto the end, *that ye may be* blameless in the day of our Lord Jesus Christ. 9. God *is* faithful, by whom ye were called unto the fellowship of his Son Jesus Christ our Lord.

1 Cor. 15:1. Moreover, brethren, I declare unto you the gospel which I preached unto you, which also ye have received, and wherein ye stand; 2. By which also ye are saved, if ye keep in memory what I preached unto you, unless ye have believed in vain. 58. Therefore, my beloved brethren, be ye stedfast, unmoveable, always abounding in the work of the Lord, forasmuch as ye know that your labour is not in vain in the Lord.

1 Cor. 16:13. Watch ye, stand fast in the faith, quit you like men, be strong.

2 Cor. 1:21. He which stablished us with you in Christ, and hath anointed us, *is* God; 22. Who hath also sealed us, and given the earnest of the Spirit in our hearts.

2 Cor. 5:9. Wherefore we labour, that, whether present or absent, we may be accepted of him. 15. He died for all, that they which live should not henceforth live unto themselves, but unto him which died for them, and rose again.

Gal. 5:1. Stand fast therefore in the liberty wherewith Christ hath made us free,

and be not entangled again with the yoke of bondage. 10. I have confidence in you through the Lord, that ye will be none otherwise minded:

Gal. 6:9. And let us not be weary in well doing: for in due season we shall reap, if we faint not.

Eph. 4:14. That we *henceforth* be no more children, tossed to and fro, and carried about with every wind of doctrine, by the sleight of men, *and* cunning craftiness, whereby they lie in wait to deceive;

Eph. 6:13. Wherefore take unto you the whole armour of God, that ye may be able to withstand in the evil day, and having done all, to stand. 18. Praying always with all prayer and supplication in the Spirit, and watching thereunto with all perseverance and supplication for all saints;

Phil. 1:6. Being confident of this very thing, that he which hath begun a good work in you will perform *it* until the day of Jesus Christ:

27. Let your conversation be as it becometh the gospel of Christ: that whether I come and see you, or else be absent, I may hear of your affairs, that ye stand fast in one spirit, with one mind striving together for the faith of the gospel;

Phil. 3:16. Nevertheless whereto we have already attained, let us walk by the same rule, let us mind the same thing.

Phil. 4:1. Stand fast in the Lord,

Col. 1:10. That ye might walk worthy of the Lord unto all pleasing, being fruitful in every good work, and increasing in the knowledge of God; 22. To present you holy and unblameable and unreproveable in his sight: 23. If ye continue in the faith grounded and settled, and *be* not moved away from the hope of the gospel,

Col. 2:7. Rooted and built up in him, and stablished in the faith,

1 Thess. 3:8. For now we live, if ye stand fast in the Lord. 13. To the end he may stablish your hearts unblameable in holiness before God,

1 Thess. 5:21. Prove all things; hold fast that which is good.

2 Thess. 2:15. Stand fast, and hold the traditions which ye have been taught, whether by word, or our epistle. 16. Now our Lord Jesus Christ himself, ... 17. Comfort your hearts, and stablish you in every good word and work.

2 Thess. 3:13. But ye, brethren, be not weary in well doing.

2 Tim. 1:12. I know whom I have believed, and am persuaded that he is able to keep that which I have committed unto him against that day. 13. Hold fast the form of sound words, which thou hast heard of me, in faith and love which is in Christ Jesus.

2 Tim. 2:1. Thou therefore, my son, be strong in the grace that is in Christ Jesus. 3. Endure hardness, as a good soldier of Jesus Christ. 12. If we suffer, we shall also

reign with *him:* if we deny *him*, he also will deny us:

2 Tim. 3:14. Continue thou in the things which thou hast learned and hast been assured of, knowing of whom thou hast learned *them;*

2 Tim. 4:18. The Lord shall deliver me from every evil work, and will preserve *me* unto his heavenly kingdom:

Tit. 1:9. Holding fast the faithful word as he hath been taught, that he may be able by sound doctrine both to exhort and to convince the gainsayers.

Heb. 2:1. Therefore we ought to give the more earnest heed to the things which we have heard, lest at any time we should let *them* slip.

Heb. 3:5. And Moses verily *was* faithful in all his house as a servant, for a testimony of those things which were to be spoken after; 6. But Christ as a son over his own house; whose house are we, if we hold fast the confidence and the rejoicing of the hope firm unto the end. 14. For we are made partakers of Christ, if we hold the beginning of our confidence stedfast unto the end;

Heb. 4:14. Seeing then that we have a great high priest, that is passed into the heavens, Jesus the Son of God, let us hold fast *our* profession.

Heb. 6:1. Leaving the principles of the doctrine of Christ, let us go on unto perfection; 11. And we desire that every one of you do shew the same diligence to the full assurance of hope unto the end: 12. That ye be not slothful, but followers of them who through faith and patience inherit the promises. 15. And so, after he had patiently endured, he obtained the promise. 17. Wherein God, willing more abundantly to shew unto the heirs of promise the immutability of his counsel, confirmed *it* by an oath: 18. That by two immutable things, in which *it was* impossible for God to lie, we might have a strong consolation, who have fled for refuge to lay hold upon the hope set before us:

Heb. 10:23. Let us hold fast the profession of *our* faith without wavering; (for he *is* faithful that promised;) 35. Cast not away therefore your confidence, which hath great recompence of reward. 36. For ye have need of patience, that, after ye have done the will of God, ye might receive the promise.

Heb. 12:1. Wherefore seeing we also are compassed about with so great a cloud of witnesses, let us lay aside every weight, and the sin which doth so easily beset *us*, and let us run with patience the race that is set before us, 2. Looking unto Jesus the author and finisher of *our* faith; who for the joy that was set before him endured the cross, despising the shame, and is set down at the right hand of the throne of God. 3. For consider him that endured such contradiction of sinners against himself, lest ye be wearied and faint in your minds. 4. Ye have not yet resisted unto blood, striving against sin. 5. And ye have forgotten the exhortation which speaketh unto you as unto children, My son, despise not thou the chastening of the Lord, nor faint when thou art rebuked of him. 6. For whom the Lord loveth he chasteneth, and scourgeth every son whom he receiveth. 7. If ye endure chastening, God dealeth with you as with sons; for what son is he whom the father chasteneth not? 8. But if ye be without chastisement, whereof all are partakers, then are ye bastards, and not sons. 9. Furthermore we have had fathers of our flesh which corrected *us*, and we gave *them* reverence: shall we not much rather be in subjection unto the Father of spirits, and live? 10. For they verily for a few days chastened *us* after their own pleasure; but he for *our* profit, that *we* might be partakers of his holiness. 11. Now no chastening for the present seemeth to be joyous, but grievous: nevertheless afterward it yieldeth the peaceable fruit of righteousness unto them which are exercised thereby. 12. Wherefore lift up the hands which hang down, and the feeble knees; 13. And make straight paths for your feet, lest that which is lame be turned out of the way; but let it rather be healed. 15. Looking diligently lest any man fail of the grace of God; lest any root of bitterness springing up trouble *you*, and thereby many be defiled;

Heb. 13:9. Be not carried about with divers and strange doctrines. For *it is* a good thing that the heart be established with grace; 13. Let us go forth therefore unto him without the camp, bearing his reproach.

Jas. 1:4. Let patience have *her* perfect work, that ye may be perfect and entire, wanting nothing. 12. Blessed *is* the man that endureth temptation: for when he is tried, he shall receive the crown of life, which the Lord hath promised to them that love him. 25. Whoso looketh into the perfect law of liberty, and continueth *therein*, he being not a forgetful hearer, but a doer of the work, this man shall be blessed in his deed.

Jas. 5:10. Take, my brethren, the prophets, who have spoken in the name of the Lord, for an example of suffering affliction, and of patience. 11. Behold we count them happy which endure. Ye have heard of the patience of Job, and have seen the end of the Lord; that the Lord is very pitiful, and of tender mercy.

1 Pet. 1:4. To an inheritance incorruptible, and undefiled, and that fadeth not away, reserved in heaven for you, 5. Who are kept by the power of God through faith unto salvation ready to be revealed in the last time. 6. Wherein ye greatly rejoice, though now for a season, if need be, ye are in heaviness through manifold temptations: 7. That the trial of your faith, being much more precious than of gold that perisheth, though it be tried with fire, might be found unto praise and honour and glory at the appearing of Jesus Christ:

1 Pet. 5:8. Be sober, be vigilant; because your adversary the devil, as a roaring lion, walketh about, seeking whom he may devour:

2 Pet. 1:10. Wherefore the rather, brethren, give diligence to make your calling and election sure: for if ye do these things, ye shall never fall: 11. For so an entrance shall be ministered unto you abundantly into the everlasting kingdom of our Lord and Saviour Jesus Christ.

2 Pet. 3:17. Ye therefore, beloved, seeing ye know *these things* before, beware lest ye also, being led away with the error of the wicked, fall from your own stedfastness. 18. But grow in grace, and *in* the knowledge of our Lord and Saviour Jesus Christ.

1 John 2:19. They went out from us, but they were not of us; for if they had been of us, they would *no doubt* have continued with us: but *they went out*, that they might be made manifest that they were not all of us. 27. The anointing which ye have received of him abideth in you, and ye need not that any man teach you: but as the same anointing teacheth you of all things, and is truth, and is no lie, and even as it hath taught you, ye shall abide in him.

Rev. 2:7. He that hath an ear, let him hear what the Spirit saith unto the churches; To him that overcometh will I give to eat of the tree of life, which is in the midst of the paradise of God. 10. Fear none of those things which thou shalt suffer: behold, the devil shall cast *some* of you into prison, that ye may be tried; and ye shall have tribulation ten days: be thou faithful unto death, and I will give thee a crown of life. 11. He that overcometh shall not be hurt of the second death. 17. To him that overcometh will I give to eat of the hidden manna, and will give him a white stone, and in the stone a new name written, which no man knoweth saving he that receiveth *it*. 25. But that which ye have *already* hold fast till I come. 26. And he that overcometh, and keepeth my works unto the end, to him will I give power over the nations: 27. And he shall rule them with a rod of iron; as the vessels of a potter shall they be broken to shivers: even as I received of my Father. 28. And I will give him the morning star.

Rev. 3:5. He that overcometh, the same shall be clothed in white raiment; and I will not blot out his name out of the book of life, but I will confess his name before my Father, and before his angels. 11. Behold, I come quickly: hold that fast which thou hast, that no man take thy crown. 12. Him that overcometh will I make a pillar in the temple of my God, and he shall go no more out: and I will write upon him the name of my God, and the name of the city of my God, *which is* new Jerusalem, which cometh down out of heaven from my God: 21. To him that overcometh will I grant to sit with me in my throne, even as I also overcame, and am set down with my Father in his throne.

Rev. 14:12. Here is the patience of the saints : here *are* they that keep the commandments of God, and the faith of Jesus.

Rev. 16:15. Behold, I come as a thief. Blessed *is* he that watcheth, and keepeth his garments, lest he walk naked, and they see his shame.

Rev. 21:7. He that overcometh shall inherit all things; and I will be his God, and he shall be my son. 8. But the fearful, and unbelieving, and the abominable, and murderers, and whoremongers, and sorcerers, and idolaters, and all liars, shall have their part in the lake which burneth with fire and brimstone: which is the second death.

Rev. 22:11. And he that is righteous, let him be righteous still: and he that is holy, let him be holy still.

See CHARACTER; INSTABILITY; STABILITY.

INSTANCES OF: Jacob, in prayer, Gen. 32:24-26. Caleb and Joshua, in representing the land of promise, Num. 14:24,38.

PERSIA. An empire which extended from India to Ethiopia, comprising one hundred and twenty-seven provinces, Esth. 1:1; Dan. 6:1. Government of, restricted by constitutional limitations, Esth. 8:8; Dan. 6: 8-12. Municipal governments in, provided with dual governors, Neh. 3:9,12,16-18. The princes advisory in matters of administration, Dan. 6:1-7. Status of women in, queen sat on the throne with the king, Neh. 2:6. Vashti divorced for refusing to appear before the king's courtiers, Esth. 1:10-22; 2:4.

Israel captive in, 2 Chr. 36:20; captivity foretold, Hos. 13:16. Men of, in the Tyrian army, Ezek. 27:10.

Rulers of: Ahasuerus, Esth. 1:3. Darius, Dan. 5:31; 6; 9:1. Artaxerxes I, Ezra 4:7-24. Artaxerxes II, Ezra 7; Neh. 2; 5:14. Cyrus, 2 Chr. 36:22,23; Ezra 1; 3:7; 4:3; 5:13,14,17; 6:3; Isa. 41:2,3; 44:28; 45:1-4,13; 46:11; 48:14,15. Princes of, Esth. 1:14.

System of justice, Ezra 7:25. Prophecies concerning, Isa. 13:17; 21:1-10; Jer. 49:34-39; 51:11-64; Ezek. 32:24,25; 38:5; Dan. 2:31-45; 5:28; 7; 8; 11:1-4.

See BABYLON; CHALDEA.

PERSIS, a Christian woman in Rome, Rom. 16:12.

PERSONAL CALL. See CALL, PERSONAL; MINISTERS, CALL OF.

PERSONIFICATION. Of wisdom, Prov. 1; 2:1-9; 8; 9. Of the church, Song chapters 1-8.

See PANTOMIME.

PERUDA, one of the servants of Solomon. Descendants of, return to Jerusalem from captivity in Babylon, Ezra 2:55. Called PERIDA in Neh. 7:57.

PESTILENCE. Sent as a judgment, Lev. 26:16,25. Sent upon the Egyptians, see EGYPT; PLAGUES.

PETER. Called also SIMON BAR-JONA and CEPHAS, Matt. 16:16-19; Mark 3:16; John 1:42. A fisherman, Matt. 4:18; Luke 5:1-7; John 21:3. Call of, Matt. 4:18-20; Mark 1: 16-18; Luke 5:1-11. His wife's mother healed, Matt. 8:14; Mark 1:29,30; Luke 4:38. An apostle, Matt. 10:2; 16:18,19; Mark 3:16; Luke 6:14: Acts 1:13. An evangelist, Mark 1:36,37. Confesses Jesus as Christ, Matt. 16:16-19; Mark 8:29; Luke 9:20; John 6:68, 69. His presumption in rebuking Jesus, Matt. 16:22,23; Mark 8:32,33; when the throng was pressing Jesus and the woman of infirmity touched him, Luke 8:45; in refusing to let Jesus wash his feet, John 13:6-11. Present at the healing of Jairus's daughter, Mark 5:37; Luke 8:51; at the transfiguration, Matt. 17:1-4; Mark 9:2-6; Luke 9:28-33; 2 Pet. 1:16-18; in Gethsemane, Matt. 26: 36-46; Mark 14:33-42; Luke 22:40-46. Seeks the interpretation of the parable of the steward, Luke 12:41; of the law of forgiveness, Matt. 18:21; of the law of defilement, Matt. 15:15; of the prophecy of Jesus concerning his second coming, Mark 13:3,4. Walks upon the water of the sea of Galilee, Matt. 14: 28-31. Sent with John to prepare the Passover, Luke 22:8. Calls attention to the withered fig tree, Mark 11:21. His perfidy foretold by Jesus, and his profession of fidelity, Matt. 26:33-35; Mark 14:29-31; Luke 22:31-34; John 13:36-38. Cuts off the ear of Malchus, Matt. 26:51; Mark 14:47; Luke 22: 50. Follows Jesus to the high priest's palace, Matt. 26:58; Mark 14:54; Luke 22:54; John 18:15. His denial of Jesus, and his repentance, Matt. 26:69-75; Mark 14:66-72; Luke 22:55-62; John 18:17,18,25-27. Visits the sepulcher, Luke 24:12; John 20:2-6. Jesus sends message to, after the resurrection, Mark 16:7. Jesus appears to, Luke 24:34; 1 Cor. 15:4,5. Present at the Sea of Tiberias when Jesus appeared to his disciples; leaps into the sea, and comes to land when Jesus is recognized, is commissioned to feed the flock of Christ, John 21:1-23. Abides in Jerusalem, Acts 1:13. His statement before the disciples concerning the death of Judas, and his recommendation that the vacancy in the apostleship be filled, Acts 1: 15-22. Preaches at Pentecost, Acts 2:14-40. Heals the impotent man in the portico of the temple, Acts 3. Accused by the council; his defense, Acts 4:1-23. Foretells the death of Ananias and Sapphira, Acts 5:1-11. Imprisoned and scourged; his defense before the council, Acts 5:17-42. Goes to Samaria, Acts 8:14. Prays for the baptism of the Holy Ghost, Acts 8:15-18. Rebukes Simon, the sorcerer, who desires to purchase like power, Acts 8:18-24. Returns to Jerusalem, Acts 8:25. Receives Paul, Gal. 1:18; 2:9. Visits Lydda; heals Æneas, Acts 9:32-34. Visits Joppa; dwells with Simon, the tanner; raises Dorcas from the dead, Acts 9:36-43. Has a vision of a sheet containing clean and unclean animals, Acts 10:9-16. Receives the servant of the centurion; goes to Cæsarea; preaches and baptizes the centurion and his household, Acts 10. Advocates, in the council of the apostles and elders, the preaching of the gospel to the Gentiles, Acts 11:1-18; 15:7-11. Imprisoned and delivered by an angel, Acts 12:3-19. Writes two epistles, 1 Pet. 1:1; 2 Pet. 1:1. Miracles of, see MIRACLES.

PETHAHIAH. 1. A priest in the reign of David, 1 Chr. 24:16.

2. A Levite who divorced his Gentile wife, Ezra 10:23. Probably identical with the one mentioned, Neh. 9:5.

3. A counselor of Artaxerxes, Neh. 11:24.

PETHOR, a city in Mesopotamia. Home of the prophet Balaam, Num. 22:5; Deut. 23:4.

PETHUEL, father of the prophet Joel, Joel 1:1.

PETITION. Right of, recognized by Pharaoh, Ex. 5:15-18; Israel, Num. 27:1-5; 32:1-5; 36:1-5; Josh. 17:4,14,16; 21:1,2; David, 1 Kin. 1:15-21; Rehoboam, 1 Kin. 12:1-17; 2 Chr. 10; Jehoram, 2 Kin. 8:3,6.

PETROLEUM. FIGURATIVE: Job 29:6.

PEULTHAI, a porter of the tabernacle, 1 Chr. 26:5.

PHALLU, called also PALLU. Son of Reuben, Gen. 46:9; Ex. 6:14; Num. 26:5,8; 1 Chr. 5:3.

PHALTI, called also PHALTIEL. Son-in-law of Saul, 1 Sam. 25:44; 2 Sam. 3:15,16.

PHALTIEL. See PHALTI.

PHARAOH. 1. King of Egypt at the time of Abraham, Gen. 12:14-20; Psa. 105:14.

2. Ruler of Egypt at the time of the famine. See EGYPT; ISRAELITES.

3. Ruler of Egypt at the time of the deliverance and exodus of the children of Israel. See ISRAELITES.

4. Father-in-law of Mered, 1 Chr. 4:18.

5. Ruler of Egypt at the time of David, 1 Kin. 11:17-22.

6. Father-in-law of Solomon, 1 Kin. 3:1; 9:16.

7. At the time of Hezekiah, 2 Kin. 18:21.

8. Pharaoh-nechoh. His invasion of Assyria, Josiah's death, 2 Kin. 23:29-35; 24:7; 2 Chr. 35:20-24; 36:3,4; Jer. 46:2; 47:1.

9. Pharaoh-hophra, Jer. 37:4-7; 44; Ezek. 17:15-17. Prophecies concerning, Jer. 44:30; 46:25,26; Ezek. 29; 30:21-26.

PHARES. See PHAREZ.

PHAREZ, called also PEREZ and PHARES. A twin son of Judah by Tamar, Gen. 38:29; 1 Chr. 2:4. Children of, Gen. 46:12; Num. 26:20,21; 1 Chr. 2:5; 9:4; return from the captivity, Neh. 11:4,6. In the lineage of Jesus, Matt. 1:3; Luke 3:33.

PHARISEES. A sect of the Jews, Acts 15:5. Doctrines of, Matt. 15:9; concerning the resurrection, Acts 23:6,8; association with publicans and sinners, Matt. 9:11-13. Traditions of, in regard to fasting, Matt. 9:14; Luke 18:12; the washing of hands, Matt. 15:1-3; Mark 7:1-15; the duties of children to parents, Matt. 15:4-9; the Sabbath, Matt. 12:2-8. Hypocrisy of, reproved by John, Matt. 3:7-10; by Jesus, Matt. 6:2-8,16-18; 15:1-9; 16:1-12; 21:33-46; 23:2-33; Luke 11:14-54; 12:1; 15:1-9. Reject John, Luke 7: 30; Christ, Matt. 12:38,39; 15:12; John 7:48. Come to Jesus with questions, Matt. 19:3; 22:15-22.

Minister to Jesus, Luke 7:36; 11:37; 14:1. Become disciples of Jesus, John 3:1; Acts 15:5; 22:3.

Paul a Pharisee, Acts 23:6; 26:5.

See HERODIANS; SADDUCEES.

PHAROSH, called also PAROSH. The ancestor of one of the families which returned to Jerusalem from captivity in Babylon, Ezra 2:3; 8:3; 10:25; Neh. 7:8; 10:14.

PHARPAR, a river of Damascus. Referred to by Naaman, 2 Kin. 5:12.

PHASEAH, called also PASEAH. Ancestor of a family which returned to Jerusalem from the captivity, Ezra 2:49; Neh. 3:6; 7:51.

PHEBE, a deaconess of the church at Cenchrea, Rom. 16:1.

PHENICE, a harbor of Crete, Acts 27: 12,13,21.

PHENICIA, called also PHENICE. Inhabitants of, descended from Canaan, Gen. 10:15,18,19. Called ZIDONIANS, Judg. 18:7; Ezek. 32:30. Jews from, hear Jesus, Mark 3:8. Paul visits the churches in, Acts 15:3; 21:2-4; 27:3.

PHICHOL, chief captain of the Philistines, Gen. 21:22,32; 26:26.

PHILADELPHIA, a city of Lydia. One of the "seven churches" at, Rev. 1:11; 3:7-13.

PHILANTHROPY, Isa. 58:6-12.

See ALMS; BENEFICENCE; CHARITABLENESS; LIBERALITY; NEIGHBOR; POOR.

PHILEMON, a Christian in Colosse. Paul's letter to, Philem. 1-25.

PHILETUS, an heretical teacher at Rome, 2 Tim. 2:17,18.

PHILIP. 1. Brother of Herod and husband of Herodias, Matt. 14:3; Mark 6:17; Luke 3:19.

2. Tetrarch of Iturea, Luke 3:1.

3. One of the seven deacons, Acts 6:5. Successfully preaches in Samaria, Acts 8:4-14. Expounds the scriptures to the Ethiopian eunuch whom he baptizes, Acts 8:27-38. Caught away by the Spirit to Azotus, preaches in the cities, and goes to Cæsarea, Acts 8:39,40. Abides at Cæsarea, and entertains Paul, Acts 21:8. Has four daughters, prophetesses, Acts 21:9,10.

4. One of the twelve apostles, Matt. 10:3; Mark 3:18; Luke 6:14; Acts 1:13. Call of, John 1:43. Brings Nathanael to Jesus, John 1:45-50. Assists in caring for the multitude whom Jesus miraculously feeds, John 6:5-7. Brings certain Greeks to Jesus who desire to see him, John 12:20-22. Asks Jesus to show the Father, John 14:8-13.

PHILIPPI, a city of Macedonia. Paul preaches in, Acts 16:12-40; 20:1-6; 1 Thess. 2:1,2. Contributes to the maintenance of Paul, Phil. 4:10-18. Paul sends Epaphroditus to, Phil. 2:25. Paul writes a letter to the Christians of, Phil. 1:1.

PHILISTIA, the sea coast in the W. of Dan and Simeon, Psa. 60:8; 87:4; 108:9.

PHILISTINES. Descendants of Mizraim, Gen. 10:14: 1 Chr. 1:12; Jer. 47:4; Amos 9:7. Called CHERETHITES, 1 Sam. 30: 14-16; Ezek. 25:16; Zeph. 2:5; CASLUHIM, Gen. 10:14; 1 Chr. 1:12; CAPHTORIM, Jer. 47:4; Amos 9:7. Territory of, Ex. 13:17; 23:31; Deut. 2:23; Josh. 13:3; 15:47; lords of, Josh. 13:3; Judg. 3:3; 16:5,30; 1 Sam. 5:8,11; 6:4,12; 7:7; 29:2,6,7.

Kings of: Abimelech I, Gen. 20; Abimelech II, Gen. 26; Achish, 1 Sam. 21:10-15; 27:2-12; 28:1,2; 29. Suffered to remain in Canaan, Judg. 3:3,4. Shamgar slays six hundred with an ox goad, Judg. 3:31. For their history during the leadership of Samson, see Judg. chapters 13-16. Defeat the Israelites; take the ark; suffer plagues, and return the ark, 1 Sam. chapters 4-6. Army of, 1 Sam. 13:5. Defeated by Samuel, 1 Sam. 7; by Saul and Jonathan, 1 Sam. 9:16; 13; 14. Their champion, Goliath, slain by David, 1 Sam. 17. David slays two hundred, 1 Sam. 18:22-30. David finds refuge among, 1 Sam. 27. Defeat the Israelites and slay Saul and his sons, 1 Sam. 31; 1 Chr. 10:1. Defeated by David, 2 Sam. 5:17-25; 23:9-16; 1 Chr. 14: 8-16. Pay tribute to Jehoshaphat, 2 Chr. 17:11. Defeated by Hezekiah, 2 Kin. 18:8. Prophecies against, Isa. 9:11,12; 14:29-31; Jer. 25:17-20; 47; Ezek. 25:15-17; Amos 1: 6-8; Zeph. 2:4-7; Zech. 9:5-7.

PHILOLOGUS, a disciple in Rome, Rom. 16:15.

PHILOSOPHY. The nature of things, Eccl. chapters 1-7. A philosophical disquisition on wisdom, Job. 28. Philosophical inductions and deductions relating to God and his providence, Job 5:8-20; 9; 10: 2-21; 12:6-24; 33:12-30; 37. Reveals the mysteries of providence, Prov. 25:2; Rom. 1:19,20. Is not sufficient for an adequate knowledge of God, 1 Cor. 1:21,22; or of salvation through the atonement of Jesus Christ, 1 Cor. 2:6-10. Employment of, was not Paul's method of preaching the gospel, 1 Cor. 1:17,19,21; 2:1-5,13. Greek schools of, Acts 17:18. Rabbinical, Col. 2:8,16-19; 1 Tim. 6:20.

See REASON; also GOD, UNCLASSIFIED SCRIPTURES RELATING TO.

PHINEHAS. 1. High priest, Ex. 6:25; 1 Chr. 6:4,50. Religious zeal of, Num. 25:7-15; Psa. 106:30. Chief of the Korahite Levites, 1 Chr. 9:19,20. Sent to sound the trumpets in the battle with the Midianites, Num. 31:6. A commissioner to the Israelites east of the Jordan, Josh. 22:13-32. Inheritance allotted to, Josh. 24:33. Mediator in behalf of the people, Judg. 20:28.

2. Son of Eli, 1 Sam. 1:3. Wickedness of, 1 Sam. 2:12-17,22-25,34. Slain in battle, 1 Sam. 4:4-11,17,19. Son of, 1 Sam. 14:3.

3. A priest, Ezra 8:33.

PHLEGON, a disciple in Rome, Rom. 16:14.

PHRYGIA, an inland province of Asia

Minor. People from, in Jerusalem, Acts 2:10. Paul in, Acts 16:6; 18:23.

PHURAH, a servant of Gideon, Judg. 7:10,11.

PHUT, called also PUT. 1. Son of Ham, Gen. 10:6; 1 Chr. 1:8.

2. The descendants of Phut, or the country inhabited by them, Ezek. 27:10; Nah. 3:9; Jer. 46:9 [marg.]; Ezek. 30:5 [marg.]; 38:5 [marg.].

PHUVAH, called also PUA and PUAH. Son of Issachar, Gen. 46:13; Num. 26:23; 1 Chr. 7:1. Descendants of, Num. 26:23.

PHYGELLUS, a Christian in Asia. Turns from Paul, 2 Tim. 1:15.

PHYLACTERY. A small box containing slips of parchment on which were written portions of the law, Ex. 13:9,16; Deut. 6:4-9; 11:18. Worn ostentatiously by the Jews, on the head and left arm, Matt. 23:5.

PHYSICIAN, 2 Chr. 16:12; Matt. 9:12; Mark 5:26; Luke 8:43. Proverbs about, Mark 2:17; Luke 4:23. Luke a physician, Col. 4:14.

FIGURATIVE: Job 13:4; Jer. 8:22; Luke 5:31.

PHYSIOGNOMY, character revealed in, Isa. 3:9.

See FACE.

PHYSIOLOGY, Job 10:11; Psa. 139:14-16; Prov. 14:30.

See ANATOMY; HYGIENE.

FIGURATIVE: Eph. 4:16; Col. 2:19.

PI-BESETH, a city in lower Egypt. Prophesied against by Ezekiel, Ezek. 30:17.

PICTURE, Lev. 26:1; Num. 33:52; Prov. 25:11; Isa. 2:16.

PIECE OF SILVER. See SILVER.

PIETY. See RELIGION.

PIGEON, used as sacrifice, Gen. 15:9; Lev. 1:14; 5:7; 12:8; 14:22; Luke 2:24.

See DOVE.

PI-HAHIROTH, the place on the W. shore of the Red Sea where Pharaoh overtook the Israelites, Ex. 14:2,9; Num. 33:7,8.

PILATE, PONTIUS. Roman governor of Judæa, Matt. 27:2; Luke 3:1. Causes slaughter of certain Galileans, Luke 13:1. Tries Jesus and orders his crucifixion, Matt. 27; Mark 15; Luke 23; John 18:28-40; 19; Acts 3:13; 4:27; 13:28; 1 Tim. 6:13. Allows Joseph of Arimathæa to take Jesus's body, Matt. 27:57,58; Mark 15:43-45; Luke 23:52; John 19:38.

PILDASH, son of Nahor, Gen. 22:22.

PILEHA, one of those who sealed the covenant with Nehemiah, Neh. 10:24.

PILLAR. Of Solomon's temple, 1 Kin. 7:13-22; 2 Kin. 25:17. Broken and carried to Babylon, 2 Kin. 25:13; Jer. 52:17,20,21. Of Solomon's palaces, 1 Kin. 7:6.

Used to mark roads, Jer. 31:21. Pillar of salt, Lot's wife turned to, Gen. 19:26; Luke 17:32. Monuments erected to commemorate events: By Jacob, his vision of angels, Gen. 28:18, with 31:13; 35:14; his covenant with Laban, Gen. 31:45; by Moses, the covenant between Jehovah and Israel, Ex. 24:4; by Joshua, the passing over Jordan, Josh.

4:1-9, with Deut. 27:2-6; Josh. 8:30; at Shechem, Josh. 24:25-27, with Judg. 9:6; by
Samuel, the discomfiture of the Philistines,
1 Sam. 7:12; by Absalom, to keep his
name in remembrance, 2 Sam. 18:18. As a
boundary, Josh. 15:6, with 18:17; a way-
mark, 1 Sam. 20:19; a landmark, 2 Sam.
20:8; 1 Kin. 1:9. Prophecy of one in Egypt,
Isa. 19:19. Monuments of idolatry, to be
destroyed, Deut. 12:3.

See CLOUD, PILLAR OF.

FIGURATIVE: Rev. 3:12.

PILLOW. 1. A cushion, Gen. 28:11,18; 1
Sam. 26:7,11,16.

2. A support for the head. Stones used
for, Gen. 28:11,18. Called bolster, 1 Sam.
26:7,11,12,16. Made of goats' hair, 1 Sam.
19:13,16. Jesus sleeps on, Mark 4:38.

FIGURATIVE: Of false teachers, Ezek.
13:18,20.

PILOT, Ezek. 27:8,27-29.

PILTAI, a priest who returned to Jerusalem from captivity in Babylon, Neh. 12:17.

PIN. See NAIL.

PINE, a tree, Neh. 8:15; Isa 41:19; 60:13.

PINNACLE, of temple, Matt. 4:5.

PINON, a leader of Edom, Gen. 36:41; 1
Chr. 1:52.

PIPE, a wind instrument of music.
Used in religious services, 1 Sam. 10:5; Isa.
30:29.

See MUSIC, INSTRUMENTS OF.

PIRAM, a king of the Amorites. Overcome and slain by Joshua, Josh. 10:3,16-18,
24-27.

PIRATHON. A place in the land of
Ephraim, Judg. 12:15. Men of, Judg. 12:13;
2 Sam. 23:30; 1 Chr. 11:31; 27:14.

PIRATHONITE. See PIRATHON.

PISGAH, a ridge or mountain E. of the
Jordan, opposite to Jericho. The Israelites
come to, Num. 21:20. A boundary of the
country assigned to the Reubenites and
Gadites, Deut. 3:17 [R. V.]; 4:49; Josh. 12:3
[R. V.]. Balaam prophesies on, Num. 23:14-
24. Moses views Palestine from, Deut. 3:27;
34:1-4.

PISIDIA, a province in Asia Minor.
Paul visits, Acts 13:14; 14:24.

PISON, one of the rivers of Eden, Gen.
2:11.

PISPAH, an Asherite, 1 Chr. 7:38.

PIT, Benaiah slays a lion in, 2 Sam.
23:20.

FIGURATIVE: Psa. 7:15,16; 40:2; 57:6;
69:15; 119:85; Prov. 23:27; 26:27; 28:10; Eccl.
10:8; Jer. 48:44. The bottomless pit, Rev.
9:1,2,11; 11:7; 17:8; 20:1,3.

PITCH. An opaque mineral used as a
plaster and cement, Isa. 34:9. Used by
Noah in the ark, Gen. 6:14. In making the
ark in which Moses was hidden, Ex. 2:3.

See BITUMEN.

PITCHER. Earthen. Lam. 4:2. Used
by Gideon in his battle with the Midianites,
Judg. 7:10-20.

PITHOM, a treasure city in lower
Egypt, Ex. 1:11.

PITHON, son of Micah, 1 Chr. 8:35; 9:41.

PITY. Of God, Isa. 63:9; Jas. 5:11. Of
Jesus, Mark 6:34; see JESUS, COMPASSION OF.
Not to be shown offenders, Deut. 7:16;
13:8; 19:13,21; 25:11,12.

See MERCY.

INSTANCES OF: The master of the impecunious servant, Matt. 18:27.

PLAGUE. As a judgment on the
Egyptians, Psa. 105; 135:8,9; Acts 7:36. The
plague of blood, Ex. 7:14-25: frogs, Ex.
8:1 15; lice, Ex. 8:16-19; flies, Ex. 8:20. On
cattle, Ex. 9:1-7. Of boils and blains, Ex.
9:8-12; hail, Ex. 9:18-34; locusts, Ex. 10:1-20;
darkness, Ex. 10:21-23. Death of the firstborn, Ex. 11:4-7; 12:17,29,30.

On the Israelites: On account of idolatry,
Ex. 32:35; after eating quail, Num. 11:33;
after refusing to enter the promised land,
Num. 14:37; after murmuring on account
of the destruction of Korah, Num. 16:41-50;
of serpents, Num. 21:6; for the sin of Peor,
Josh. 22:17; on account of David's sin, 2
Sam. 24:10-25.

On the Philistines, 1 Sam. 6:4,5.

Denounced as a judgment, Lev. 26:21;
Deut. 28:59. Foretold, Rev. 11:6; 15:1,6-8;
16; 22:18,19.

See JUDGMENTS; PESTILENCE.

PLAN OF SALVATION. See JESUS,
MISSION OF; REDEMPTION; SALVATION.

PLANE, a tool, Isa. 44:13.

PLANET. See ASTRONOMY; STARS.

PLANTS. See BOTANY.

PLASTER, Lev. 14:42,43,48; Deut. 27:2;
Dan. 5:5.

PLEADING, Deut. 17:8. Of the guilty,
Josh. 7:19-21. Jesus declined to plead, Matt.
26:62; Mark 15:2; Luke 23:3; John 18:33,34.
Prisoners required to plead, Acts 7:1.

See DEFENSE.

PLEASURE. WORLDLY: Job 20:12.
Though wickedness be sweet in his mouth,
though he hide it under his tongue; 13.
Though he spare it, and forsake it not; but
keep it still within his mouth: 14. *Yet* his
meat in his bowels is turned, *it is* the gall of
asps within him. 15. He hath swallowed
down riches, and he shall vomit them up
again: God shall cast them out of his belly.
16. He shall suck the poison of asps: the
viper's tongue shall slay him.

Job 21:12. They take the timbrel and harp,
and rejoice at the sound of the organ. 13.
They spend their days in wealth, and in a
moment go down to the grave.

Prov. 9:17. Stolen waters are sweet, and
bread *eaten* in secret is pleasant.

Prov. 15:21. Folly *is* joy to *him that is*
destitute of wisdom: but a man of understanding walketh uprightly.

Prov. 21:17. He that loveth pleasure *shall
be* a poor man: he that loveth wine and oil
shall not be rich.

Eccl. 1:17. I gave my heart to know wisdom, and to know madness and folly: I perceived that this also is vexation of spirit.

Eccl. 2:1. I said in mine heart, Go to now,

I will prove thee with mirth, therefore enjoy pleasure: and, behold, this also *is* vanity. 2. I said of laughter, *It is* mad: and of mirth, What doeth it? 3. I sought in mine heart to give myself unto wine, yet acquainting mine heart with wisdom; and to lay hold on folly, till I might see what *was* that good for the sons of men, which they should do under the heaven all the days of their life. 4. I made me great works; I builded me houses; I planted me vineyards: 5. I made me gardens and orchards, and I planted trees in them of all *kind of* fruits: 6. I made me pools of water, to water therewith the wood that bringeth forth trees: 7. I got *me* servants and maidens, and had servants born in my house; also I had great possessions of great and small cattle above all that were in Jerusalem before me: 8. I gathered me also silver and gold, and the peculiar treasure of kings and of the provinces: I gat me men singers and women singers, and the delights of the sons of men, *as* musical instruments, and that of all sorts. 9. So I was great, and increased more than all that were before me in Jerusalem: also my wisdom remained with me. 10. And whatsoever mine eyes desired I kept not from them, I withheld not my heart from any joy; for my heart rejoiced in all my labour: and this was my portion of all my labour. 11. Then I looked on all the works that my hands had wrought, and on the labour that I had laboured to do: and, behold, all *was* vanity and vexation of spirit, and *there was* no profit under the sun. 12. And I turned myself to behold wisdom, and madness, and folly: for what *can* the man *do* that cometh after the king? *even* that which hath been already done. 13. Then I saw that wisdom excelleth folly, as far as light excelleth darkness.

Isa. 5:11. Woe unto them that rise up early in the morning, *that* they may follow strong drink; that continue until night, *till* wine inflame them! 12. The harp and the viol, the tabret, and pipe, and wine, are in their feasts: but they regard not the work of the LORD, neither consider the operation of his hands.

Isa. 22:12. In that day did the Lord GOD of hosts call to weeping, and to mourning, and to baldness, and to girding with sackcloth: 13. Behold joy and gladness, slaying oxen, and killing sheep, eating flesh, and drinking wine: let us eat and drink; for to morrow we shall die.

Isa. 47:8. Therefore hear now this, *thou that art* given to pleasures, that dwellest carelessly, that sayest in thine heart, I *am,* and none else beside me; I shall not sit *as* a widow, neither shall I know the loss of children: 9. But these two *things* shall come to thee in a moment in one day, the loss of children, and widowhood: they shall come upon thee in their perfection for the multitude of thy sorceries, *and* for the great abundance of thine enchantments.

Amos 6:1. Woe to them *that are* at ease in Zion,

Luke 8:14. And that which fell among thorns are they, which, when they have heard, go forth, and are choked with cares and riches and pleasures of *this* life, and bring no fruit to perfection.

Rom. 1:32. Who knowing the judgment of God, that they which commit such things are worthy of death, not only do the same, but have pleasure in them that do them.

2 Thess. 2:12. That they all might be ¹ damned who believed not the truth, but had pleasure in unrighteousness.   [¹ R. V. judged]

1 Tim. 5:6. But she that liveth in pleasure is dead while she liveth.

2 Tim. 3:4. Traitors, heady, highminded, lovers of pleasures more than lovers of God:

Tit. 3:3. For we ourselves also were sometimes foolish, disobedient, deceived, serving divers lusts and pleasures, living in malice and envy, hateful, *and* hating one another.

Heb. 11:25. Choosing rather to suffer affliction with the people of God, than to enjoy the pleasures of sin for a season; 26. Esteeming the reproach of Christ greater riches than the treasures in Egypt: for he had respect unto the recompense of the reward.

2 Pet. 2:13. And shall receive the reward of unrighteousness, *as* they that count it pleasure to riot in the daytime.

See HAPPINESS; JOY; WORLDLINESS.

PLEDGE, Gen. 38:17-20. Creditor must not enter house of a debtor to take, Deut. 24:10-13.

See PAWN; SURETY.

PLEIADES, Job 9:9; 38:31; Amos 5:8.

PLOW. Shares of, sharpened by smiths of the Philistines, 1 Sam. 13:20. Used by Elisha with twelve yoke of oxen, 1 Kin. 19:19. By Job's servants, Job 1:14.

FIGURATIVE: Of afflictions, Psa. 129:3.

PLOWSHARE, Isa. 2:4; Joel 3:10; Mic. 4:3.

PLUMMET, Amos 7:7,8; Zech. 4:10.

FIGURATIVE: Isa. 28:17.

POCHERETH, the ancestor of a family which returned to Jerusalem from captivity in Babylon, Ezra 2:57; Neh. 7:59.

POET, Greek, Acts 17:28; Tit. 1:12.

See POETRY; PSALMS; SONGS.

POETRY. ACROSTIC: Psa. 25; 34; 37; 111; 112; 119; 145; Prov. 31:10-31; Lam. chapters 1-5.

DIDACTIC: Moses' song, Deut. 32. The Book of Job, the Proverbs, Solomon's Song, the books of prophecy. See PSALMS, DIDACTIC.

ELEGY: On the death of Saul, 2 Sam. 1:19-27. Of Abner, 2 Sam. 3:33,34. See ELEGY.

EPIC: Moses' song, Ex. 15:1-19. Miriam's song, Ex. 15:21. Song of Deborah, Judg. 5.

LYRICS, SACRED: Moses' and Miriam's songs, Ex. 15. Hannah's song, 1 Sam. 2:1-10. The song of Elizabeth, Luke 1:42-45. Of

Mary, Luke 1:46-55. Of Zacharias, Luke 1: 68-79. The Psalms, which see.

POLICY. See DIPLOMACY.

POLITICS, statecraft. **CORRUPTION IN:** Psa. 12:8; in the court of Ahasuerus, Esth. 3; of Darius, Dan. 6:4-15.

INSTANCES OF: Absalom, electioneering for the throne, 2 Sam. 15:2-6. Pilate, condemning Jesus to gratify popular clamor, Matt. 27:23-27; Mark 15:15; Luke 23:13-25; John 18:38,39; 19:4-13.

MINISTERS IN: Zadok the priest, a partisan of David, 2 Sam. 15:24-29. Nathan, the prophet, influences the selection of David's successor, 1 Kin. 1:11-40.

WOMEN IN: The wise woman of Abel, who saved the city through diplomacy, 2 Sam. 20:16-22. Bath-sheba, in securing the crown for Solomon, 1 Kin. 1:15-21. Herodias, in influencing the administration of Herod, Matt. 14:3-11; Mark 6:17-28. Mother of Zebedee's children, in seeking favor for her sons, Matt. 20:20-23.

For Influence in, see INFLUENCE, POLITICAL.

See DIPLOMACY; GOVERNMENT.

POLL TAX. See TAX.

POLYGAMY. Forbidden, Deut. 17:17; Lev. 18:18; Mal. 2:14,15; Matt. 19:4,5; Mark 10:2-8; 1 Tim. 3:2,12; Tit. 1:6. Authorized, 2 Sam. 12:8.

Tolerated, Ex. 21:10; 1 Sam. 1:2; 2 Chr. 24: 3. Practised, Job 27:15; by Lamech, Gen. 4:19; Abraham, Gen. 16; Esau, Gen. 26:34; 28:9; Jacob, Gen. 29:30; Ashur, 1 Chr. 4:5; Gideon, Judg. 8:30; Elkanah, 1 Sam. 1:2; David, 1 Sam. 25:39-44; 2 Sam. 3:2-5; 5:13; 1 Chr. 14:3. Solomon, 1 Kin. 11:1-8; Rehoboam, 2 Chr. 11:18-23; Abijah, 2 Chr. 13:21; Jehoram, 2 Chr. 21:14; Joash, 2 Chr. 24:3; Ahab, 2 Kin. 10:1; Jehoiachin, 2 Kin. 24:15; Belshazzar, Dan. 5:2; see 1 Chr. chapters 2-8; Hosea, Hos. 3:1,2. Mosaic law respecting the firstborn in, Deut. 21:15-17.

Sought by women, Isa. 4:1.

The evil effects of: Husband's favoritism in, Deut. 21:15-17; Jacob's, Gen. 29:30; 30:15; Elkanah's, 1 Sam. 1:5; Rehoboam's, 2 Chr. 11:21. Domestic infelicity, in Abraham's family, Gen. 16; 21:9-16; Jacob's, Gen. 29:30-34; 30:1-23; Elkanah's, 1 Sam. 1:4-7. Upon Solomon, 1 Kin. 11:4-8.

See CONCUBINAGE; MARRIAGE.

POLYTHEISM, Gen. 31:19; 35:2,4; Josh. 24:2,23; Judg. 2:13; 3:7; 10:16; 17:5; Jer. 2:28; 11:13; Dan. 4:8; 1 Cor. 8:5.

POMEGRANATE, a fruit. Abounded in the land of Canaan, 1 Sam. 14:2. Brought by the spies to show the fruitfulness of the land of Canaan, Num. 13:23. Figures of the fruits of, were embroidered on the ephod, Ex. 28:33,34; 39:24; carved on the pillars of the temple, 1 Kin. 7:18,20,42; Jer. 52:22,23. Wine made of, Song 8:2.

PONTIUS. See PILATE.

PONTUS. A province of Asia Minor, Acts 2:9; 1 Pet. 1:1. Aquila lived in, Acts 18:2.

POOL. Of Samaria, 1 Kin. 22:38; of Jerusalem, upper pool, 2 Kin. 18:17; Isa. 36: 2; lower pool, Isa. 22:9; Siloah, Neh. 3:15; John 9:7,11; of Heshbon, Song 7:4.

POOR. Atonement money of, uniform with that of the rich, Ex. 30:15. Inexpensive offerings of the impecunious, Lev. 5·7; 12:8; 14:21,22.

See ALMS; BENEFICENCE; LIBERALITY; ORPHANS; POVERTY; WIDOW. Also see RICH; RICHES.

UNCLASSIFIED SCRIPTURES RELATING TO: Ex. 23:3. Neither shalt thou countenance a poor man in his cause. 6. Thou shalt not wrest the judgment of thy poor in his cause.

Lev. 19:15. Ye shall do no unrighteousness in judgment: thou shalt not respect the person of the poor, nor honour the person of the mighty: *but* in righteousness shalt thou judge thy neighbour.

1 Sam. 2:7. The LORD maketh poor, and maketh rich: he bringeth low, and lifteth up.

Neh. 8:10. Then he said unto them, Go your way, eat the fat, and drink the sweet, and send portions unto them for whom nothing is prepared: for *this* day *is* holy unto our Lord: neither be ye sorry; for the joy of the LORD is your strength. 12. And all the people went their way to eat, and to drink, and to send portions, and to make great mirth, because they had understood the words that were declared unto them.

Job 29:11. When the ear heard *me*, then it blessed me; and when the eye saw *me*, it gave witness to me: 12. Because I delivered the poor that cried, and the fatherless, and *him that had* none to help him. 13. The blessing of him that was ready to perish came upon me: and I caused the widow's heart to sing for joy. 15. I was eyes to the blind, and feet *was* I to the lame. 16. I *was* a father to the poor: and the cause *which* I knew not I searched out.

Job 30:25. Did not I weep for him that was in trouble? was *not* my soul grieved for the poor?

Job 31:15. Did not he that made me in the womb make him? and did not one fashion us in the womb? 16. If I have withheld the poor from *their* desire, or have caused the eyes of the widow to fail; 17. Or have eaten my morsel myself alone, and the fatherless hath not eaten thereof; 18. (For from my youth he was brought up with me, as *with* a father, and I have guided her from my mother's womb;) 19. If I have seen any perish for want of clothing, or any poor without covering; 20. If his loins have not blessed me, and *if* he were *not* warmed with the fleece of my sheep; 21. If I have lifted up my hand against the fatherless, when I saw my help in the gate: 22. *Then* let mine arm fall from my shoulder blade, and mine arm be broken from the bone.

Job 34:19. *How much less to him* that accepteth not the persons of princes, nor regardeth the rich more than the poor? for they all *are* the work of his hands. Prov. 22:2.

Psa. 37:16. A little that a righteous man hath *is* better than the riches of many wicked.

Psa. 82:3. Defend the poor and fatherless: do justice to the afflicted and needy. 4. Deliver the poor and needy: rid *them* out of the hand of the wicked.

Psa. 109:16. Because that he remembered not to shew mercy, but persecuted the poor and needy man, that he might even slay the broken in heart.

Prov. 10:15. The rich man's wealth *is* his strong city : the destruction of the poor *is* their poverty.

Prov. 13:7. There is that maketh himself rich, yet *hath* nothing: *there is* that maketh himself poor, yet *hath* great riches. 8. The ransom of a man's life *are* his riches: but the poor heareth not rebuke. 23. Much food *is in* the tillage of the poor: but there is *that is* destroyed for want of judgment.

Prov. 14:20. The poor is hated even of his own neighbour: but the rich *hath* many friends.

21. He that despiseth his neighbour sinneth: but he that hath mercy on the poor, happy *is* he.

31. He that oppresseth the poor reproacheth his Maker: but he that honoureth him hath mercy on the poor.

Prov. 18:23. The poor useth intreaties; but the rich answereth roughly.

Prov. 19:1. Better *is* the poor that walketh in his integrity, than *he that is* perverse in his lips, and is a fool.

4. Wealth maketh many friends; but the poor is separated from his neighbour.

7. All the brethren of the poor do hate him: how much more do his friends go far from him? he pursueth *them with* words, *yet* they *are* wanting *to him.*

17. He that hath pity upon the poor lendeth unto the LORD; and that which he hath given will he pay him again.

22. A poor man *is* better than a liar.

Prov. 20:13. Love not sleep, lest thou come to poverty; open thine eyes, *and* thou shalt be satisfied with bread.

Prov. 21:13. Whoso stoppeth his ears at the cry of the poor, he also shall cry himself, but shall not be heard.

Prov. 22:2. The rich and poor meet together: the LORD *is* the maker of them all. 9. He that hath a bountiful eye shall be blessed; for he giveth of his bread to the poor.

Prov. 23:21. For the drunkard and the glutton shall come to poverty: and drowsiness shall clothe *a man* with rags.

Prov. 28:6. Better *is* the poor that walketh in his uprightness, than *he that is* perverse *in his* ways, though he *be* rich. 8. He that by usury and unjust gain increas-

eth his substance, he shall gather it for him that will pity the poor. 11. The rich man *is* wise in his own conceit; but the poor that hath understanding searcheth him out. 19. He that tilleth his land shall have plenty of bread : but he that followeth after vain *persons* shall have poverty enough.

Prov. 29:14. The king that faithfully judgeth the poor, his throne shall be established for ever.

Eccl. 4:6. Better *is* an handful *with* quietness, than both the hands full *with* travail and vexation of spirit. 13. Better *is* a poor and a wise child than an old and foolish king, who will no more be admonished.

Eccl. 6:8. For what hath the wise more than the fool? what hath the poor, that knoweth to walk before the living?

Eccl. 9:15. Now there was found in it a poor wise man, and he by his wisdom delivered the city; yet no man remembered that same poor man. 16. Then said I, Wisdom *is* better than strength: nevertheless the poor man's wisdom *is* despised, and his words are not heard.

Jer. 22:16. He judged the cause of the poor and needy; then *it was* well *with him: was* not this to know me? saith the LORD.

Ezek. 16:49. Behold, this was the iniquity of thy sister Sodom, pride, fulness of bread, and abundance of idleness was in her and in her daughters, neither did she strengthen the hand of the poor and needy.

Matt. 25:42. I was an hungred, and ye gave me no meat: I was thirsty, and ye gave me no drink: 45. Then shall he answer them, saying, Verily I say unto you, Inasmuch as ye did *it* not to one of the least of these, ye did *it* not to me.

Matt. 26:11. For ye have the poor always with you; but me ye have not always. Mark 14:7.

Mark 12:43. And he called *unto him* his disciples, and saith unto them, Verily I say unto you, That this poor widow hath cast more in, than all they which have cast into the treasury: 44. For all *they* did cast in of their abundance; but she of her want did cast in all that she had, *even* all her living.

Luke 6:35. Do good, and lend, hoping for nothing again; and your reward shall be great, and ye shall be the children of the Highest: for he is kind unto the unthankful and *to* the evil. *vs.* 30-34.

Luke 16:20. There was a certain beggar named Lazarus, which was laid at his gate, full of sores, 21. And desiring to be fed with the crumbs which fell from the rich man's table: moreover the dogs came and licked his sores.

John 12:6. This he said, not that he cared for the poor; but because he was a thief.

Jas. 1:9. Let the brother of low degree rejoice in that he is exalted: 10. But the rich, in that he is made low: because as the flower of the grass he shall pass away.

DUTY TO: Ex. 22:25. If thou lend money

to *any of* my people *that is* poor by thee, thou shalt not be to him as an usurer, neither shalt thou lay upon him usury. 26. If thou at all take thy neighbour's raiment to pledge, thou shalt deliver it unto him by that the sun goeth down: 27. For that *is* his covering only, it *is* his raiment for his skin: wherein shall he sleep? and it shall come to pass, when he crieth unto me, that I will hear; for I *am* gracious.

Ex. 23:11. But the seventh *year* thou shalt let it rest and lie still; that the poor of thy people may eat: and what they leave the beasts of the field shall eat. In like manner thou shalt deal with thy vineyard, *and* with thy oliveyard.

Lev. 19:9. And when ye reap the harvest of your land, thou shalt not wholly reap the corners of thy field, neither shalt thou gather the gleanings of thy harvest. 10. And thou shalt not glean thy vineyard, neither shalt thou gather *every* grape of thy vineyard; thou shalt leave them for the poor and stranger: I *am* the LORD your God. chapter 23:22.

Lev. 25:25. If thy brother be waxen poor, and hath sold away *some* of his possession, and if any of his kin come to redeem it, then shall he redeem that which his brother sold. 26. And if the man have none to redeem it, and himself be able to redeem it; 27. Then let him count the years of the sale thereof, and restore the overplus unto the man to whom he sold it; that he may return unto his possession. 28. But if he be not able to restore *it* to him, then that which is sold shall remain in the hand of him that hath bought it until the year of jubile: and in the jubile it shall go out, and he shall return unto his possession.

35. And if thy brother be waxen poor, and fallen in decay with thee; then thou shalt relieve him: *yea, though he be* a stranger, or a sojourner; that he may live with thee. 36. Take thou no usury of him, or increase: but fear thy God; that thy brother may live with thee. 37. Thou shalt not give him thy money upon usury, nor lend him thy victuals for increase. 39. And if thy brother *that dwelleth* by thee be waxen poor, and be sold unto thee; thou shalt not compel him to serve as a bondservant: 40. *But* as an hired servant, *and* as a sojourner, he shall be with thee, *and* shall serve thee up to the year of jubile; 41. And *then* shall he depart from thee, *both* he and his children with him, and shall return unto his own family, and unto the possession of his fathers shall he return. 42. For they *are* my servants, which I brought forth out of the land of Egypt: they shall not be sold as bondmen. 43. Thou shalt not rule over him with rigour; but shalt fear thy God.

Deut. 14:28. At the end of three years thou shalt bring forth all the tithe of thine increase the same year, and shalt lay *it* up within thy gates: 29. And the Levite, (because he hath no part nor inheritance with thee,)

and the stranger, and the fatherless, and the widow, which *are* within thy gates, shall come, and shall eat and be satisfied: that the LORD thy God may bless thee in all the work of thine hand which thou doest.

Deut. 15:2. And this *is* the manner of the release: Every creditor that lendeth *ought* unto his neighbour shall release *it;* he shall not exact *it* of his neighbour, or of his brother; because it is called the LORD's release. 3. Of a foreigner thou mayest exact *it again:* but *that* which is thine with thy brother thine hand shall release; 4. Save when there shall be no poor among you; for the LORD shall greatly bless thee in the land which the LORD thy God giveth thee *for* an inheritance to possess it: 5. Only if thou carefully hearken unto the voice of the LORD thy God, to observe to do all these commandments which I command thee this day. 6. For the LORD thy God blesseth thee, as he promised thee: and thou shalt lend unto many nations, but thou shalt not borrow; and thou shalt reign over many nations, but they shall not reign over thee. 7. If there be among you a poor man of one of thy brethren within any of thy gates in thy land which the LORD thy God giveth thee, thou shalt not harden thine heart, nor shut thine hand from thy poor brother: 8. But thou shalt open thine hand wide unto him, and shalt surely lend him sufficient for his need, *in that* which he wanteth. 9. Beware that there be not a thought in thy wicked heart, saying, The seventh year, the year of release, is at hand; and thine eye be evil against thy poor brother, and thou givest him nought; and he cry unto the LORD against thee, and it be sin unto thee. 10. Thou shalt surely give him, and thine heart shall not be grieved when thou givest unto him: because that for this thing the LORD thy God shall bless thee in all thy works, and in all that thou puttest thine hand unto. 11. For the poor shall never cease out of the land: therefore I command thee, saying, Thou shalt open thine hand wide unto thy brother, to thy poor, and to thy needy, in thy land. 12. *And* if thy brother, an Hebrew man, or an Hebrew woman, be sold unto thee, and serve thee six years; then in the seventh year thou shalt let him go free from thee. 13. And when thou sendest him out free from thee, thou shalt not let him go away empty: 14. Thou shalt furnish him liberally out of thy flock, and out of thy floor, and out of thy winepress: *of that* wherewith the LORD thy God hath blessed thee thou shalt give unto him.

Deut. 24:12. And if the man *be* poor, thou shalt not sleep with his pledge: 13. In any case thou shalt deliver him the pledge again when the sun goeth down, that he may sleep in his own raiment, and bless thee: and it shall be righteousness unto thee before the LORD thy God.

14. Thou shalt not oppress an hired servant *that is* poor and needy, *whether he be* of **thy**

brethren, or of thy strangers that *are* in thy land within thy gates: 15. At his day thou shalt give *him* his hire, neither shall the sun go down upon it; for he *is* poor, and setteth his heart upon it: lest he cry against thee unto the LORD, and it be sin unto thee. 16. The fathers shall not be put to death for the children, neither shall the children be put to death for the fathers: every man shall be put to death for his own sin.

17. Thou shalt not pervert the judgment of the stranger, *nor* of the fatherless; nor take a widow's raiment to pledge: 18. But thou shalt remember that thou wast a bondman in Egypt, and the LORD thy God redeemed thee thence: therefore I command thee to do this thing. 19. When thou cuttest down thine harvest in thy field, and hast forgot a sheaf in the field, thou shalt not go again to fetch it: it shall be for the stranger, for the fatherless, and for the widow: that the LORD thy God may bless thee in all the work of thine hands. 20. When thou beatest thine olive tree, thou shalt not go over the boughs again: it shall be for the stranger, for the fatherless, and for the widow. 21. When thou gatherest the grapes of thy vineyard, thou shalt not glean *it* afterward: it shall be for the stranger, for the fatherless, and for the widow.

Deut. 26:12. When thou hast made an end of tithing all the tithes of thine increase the third year, *which is* the year of tithing, and hast given *it* unto the Levite, the stranger, the fatherless, and the widow, that they may eat within thy gates, and be filled; 13. Then thou shalt say before the LORD thy God, I have brought away the hallowed things out of *mine* house, and also have given them unto the Levite, and unto the stranger, to the fatherless, and to the widow, according to all thy commandments which thou hast commanded me: I have not transgressed thy commandments, neither have I forgotten *them:*

Neh. 8:10. Then he said unto them, Go your way, eat the fat, and drink the sweet, and send portions unto them for whom nothing is prepared:

Psa. 37:21. The righteous sheweth mercy, and giveth. 26. *He is* ever merciful, and lendeth; and his seed *is* blessed.

Psa. 41:1. Blessed *is* he that considereth the poor: the LORD will deliver him in time of trouble. 2. The LORD will preserve him, and keep him alive; *and* he shall be blessed upon the earth: and thou wilt not deliver him unto the will of his enemies. 3. The LORD will strengthen him upon the bed of languishing: thou wilt make all his bed in his sickness.

Psa. 112:4. Unto the upright there ariseth light in the darkness: *he is* gracious, and full of compassion, and righteous. 5. A good man sheweth favour, and lendeth: 9. He hath dispersed, he hath given to the poor; his righteousness endureth for ever; his horn shall be exalted with honour.

Prov. 28:27. He that giveth unto the poor shall not lack: but he that hideth his eyes shall have many a curse.

Prov. 29:7. The righteous considereth the cause of the poor: *but* the wicked regardeth not to know *it.*

Prov. 31:9. Open thy mouth, judge righteously, and plead the cause of the poor and needy. 20. She stretcheth out her hand to the poor; yea, she reacheth forth her hands to the needy.

Isa. 1:17. Learn to do well: seek judgment, relieve the oppressed. judge the fatherless, plead for the widow.

Isa. 16:3. Take counsel, execute judgment; make thy shadow as the night in the midst of the noonday; hide the outcasts; bewray not him that wandereth. 4. Let mine outcasts dwell with thee, Moab; be thou a cover to them from the face of the spoiler:

Isa. 58:7. *Is it* not to deal thy bread to the hungry, and that thou bring the poor that are cast out to thy house? when thou seest the naked, that thou cover him; and that thou hide not thyself from thine own flesh? 10. And if thou draw out thy soul to the hungry, and satisfy the afflicted soul; then shall thy light rise in obscurity, and thy darkness *be* as the noon day:

Ezek. 18:7. And hath not oppressed any, . . . hath given his bread to the hungry, and hath covered the naked with a garment; *vs.* 16,17.

Dan. 4:27. Wherefore, O king, let my counsel be acceptable unto thee, and break off thy sins by righteousness, and thine iniquities by shewing mercy to the poor; if it may be a lengthening of thy tranquillity.

Zech. 7:10. Oppress not the widow, nor the fatherless, the stranger, nor the poor;

Matt. 5:42. Give to him that asketh thee, and from him that would borrow of thee turn not thou away. Luke 6:30.

Matt. 19:21. Jesus said unto him, If thou wilt be perfect, go *and* sell that thou hast, and give to the poor, and thou shalt have treasure in heaven: and come *and* follow me.

Matt. 25:35. I was an hungred, and ye gave me meat: I was thirsty, and ye gave me drink: I was a stranger, and ye took me in: 36. Naked, and ye clothed me: I was sick, and ye visited me: I was in prison, and ye came unto me.

Mark 14:7. For ye have the poor with you always, and whensoever ye will ye may do them good:

Luke 3:11. He that hath two coats, let him impart to him that hath none; and he that hath meat, let him do likewise.

Luke 11:41. Rather give alms of such things as ye have; and, behold, all things are clean unto you.

Luke 12:33. Sell that ye have, and give alms; provide yourselves bags which wax not old, a treasure in the heavens that faileth not, where no thief approacheth, neither moth corrupteth.

Luke 14:12. When thou makest a dinner or a supper, call not thy friends, nor thy brethren, neither thy kinsmen, nor *thy* rich neighbours; lest they also bid thee again, and a recompence be made thee. 13. But when thou makest a feast, call the poor, the maimed, the lame, the blind: 14. And thou shalt be blessed; for they cannot recompense thee: for thou shalt be recompensed at the resurrection of the just.

Luke 18:22. Yet lackest thou one thing: sell all that thou hast, and distribute unto the poor, and thou shalt have treasure in heaven: and come, follow me.

Luke 19:8. And Zacchæus stood, and said unto the Lord; Behold, Lord, the half of my goods I give to the poor; and if I have taken any thing from any man by false accusation, I restore *him* fourfold.

Acts 20:35. I have shewed you all things, how that so labouring ye ought to support the weak, and to remember the words of the Lord Jesus, how he said, It is more blessed to give than to receive.

Rom. 12:8. Or he that exhorteth, on exhortation: he that giveth, *let him do it* with ¹ simplicity; he that ruleth, with diligence; he that sheweth mercy, with cheerfulness. 13. Distributing to the necessity of saints; given to hospitality. 20. Therefore if thine enemy hunger, feed him; if he thirst, give him drink: ⁣⁣[¹ R. V. liberality]

1 Cor. 13:3. Though I bestow all my goods to feed *the poor*, . . . and have not charity, it profiteth me nothing.

1 Cor. 16:1. Now concerning the collection for the saints, as I have given order to the churches of Galatia, even so do ye. 2. Upon the first *day* of the week let every one of you lay by him in store, as ¹ *God* hath prospered him, that there be no gatherings when I come. ⁣⁣[¹ R. V. he may prosper]

2 Cor. 6:10. As poor, yet making many rich; as having nothing, and *yet* possessing all things.

2 Cor. 9:5. I thought it necessary to exhort the brethren, that they would go before unto you, and make up beforehand your bounty, whereof ye had notice before, that the same might be ready, as *a matter of* bounty, and not as *of* covetousness. 6. But this *I say*, He which soweth sparingly shall reap also sparingly; and he which soweth bountifully shall reap also bountifully. 7. Every man according as he purposeth in his heart, *so let him give;* not grudgingly, or of necessity: for God loveth a cheerful giver. *vs.* 1-15; 2 Cor. 8:9.

Gal. 2:10. Only *they would* that we should remember the poor; the same which I also was forward to do.

Gal. 6:10. As we have therefore opportunity, let us do good unto all *men*, especially unto them who are of the household of faith.

Eph. 4:28. But rather let him labour, working with *his* hands the thing which is good, that he may have to give to him that needeth.

1 Tim. 5:9. Let not a widow be taken into the number under threescore years old, having been the wife of one man, 10. Well reported of for good works; if she have brought up children, if she have lodged strangers, if she have washed the saints' feet, if she have relieved the afflicted, if she have diligently followed every good work. 16. If any man or woman that believeth have widows, let them relieve them, and let not the church be charged; that it may relieve them that are widows indeed.

Heb. 13:3. Remember them that are in bonds, as bound with them; *and* them which suffer adversity, as being yourselves also in the body.

Jas. 1:27. Pure religion and undefiled before God and the Father is this, To visit the fatherless and widows in their affliction,

Jas. 2:2. For if there come unto your assembly a man with a gold ring, in goodly apparel, and there come in also a poor man in vile raiment; 3. And ye have respect to him that weareth the gay clothing, and say unto him, Sit thou here in a good place; and say to the poor, Stand thou there, or sit here under my footstool: 4. Are ye not then partial in yourselves, and are become judges of evil thoughts? 5. Hearken, my beloved brethren, Hath not God chosen the poor of this world rich in faith, and heirs of the kingdom which he hath promised to them that love him? 6. But ye have despised the poor. Do not rich men oppress you, and draw you before the judgment seats? 7. Do not they blaspheme that worthy name by the which ye are called? 8. If ye fulfil the royal law according to the scripture, Thou shalt love thy neighbour as thyself, ye do well: 9. But if ye have respect to persons, ye commit sin, and are convinced of the law as transgressors. 15. If a brother or sister be naked, and destitute of daily food, 16. And one of you say unto them, Depart in peace, be *ye* warmed and filled; notwithstanding ye give them not those things which are needful to the body; what *doth it* profit?

Jas. 5:4. Behold, the hire of the labourers who have reaped down your fields, which is of you kept back by fraud, crieth: and the cries of them which have reaped are entered into the ears of the Lord of sabaoth.

1 John 3:17. Whoso hath this world's good, and seeth his brother have need, and shutteth up his bowels *of compassion* from him, how dwelleth the love of God in him? 18. My little children, let us not love in word, neither in tongue: but in deed and in truth. 19. And hereby we know that we are of the truth, and shall assure our hearts before him.

FIGURATIVE: Poor in spirit, Matt. 5:3, Luke 6:20; Isa. 66:2.

See CREDITOR; DEBTOR; EMPLOYEE; EMPLOYER; SERVANTS; WAGES.

GOD'S CARE OF: 1 Sam. 2:7. The LORD maketh poor, and maketh rich: he bringeth low, and lifteth up. 8. He raiseth up the poor out of the dust, *and* lifteth up the beggar from the dunghill, to set *them* among princes, and to make them inherit the throne of glory:

Job 5:15. He saveth the poor from the sword, from their mouth, and from the hand of the mighty. 16. So the poor hath hope, and iniquity stoppeth her mouth.

Job 31:15. Did not he that made me in the womb make him? and did not one fashion us in the womb?

Job 34:18. *Is it fit* to say to a king, *Thou art* wicked? *and* to princes, *Ye are* ungodly? 19. *How much less to him* that accepteth not the persons of princes, nor regardeth the rich more than the poor; for they all *are* the work of his hands. 28. So that they cause the cry of the poor to come unto him, and he heareth the cry of the afflicted.

Job 36:6. He preserveth not the life of the wicked: but giveth right to the poor. 15. He delivereth the poor in his affliction, and openeth their ears in oppression.

Psa. 9:18. The needy shall not alway be forgotten: the expectation of the poor shall *not* perish for ever.

Psa. 10:14. Thou hast seen *it;* for thou beholdest mischief and spite, to requite *it* with thy hand: the poor committeth himself unto thee;

Psa. 12:5. For the oppression of the poor, for the sighing of the needy, now will I arise, saith the LORD; I will set *him* in safety *from him that* puffeth at him.

Psa. 14:6. Ye have shamed the counsel of the poor, because the LORD *is* his refuge.

Psa. 34:6. This poor man cried, and the LORD heard *him*, and saved him out of all his troubles.

Psa. 35:10. All my bones shall say, LORD, who *is* like unto thee, which deliverest the poor from him that is too strong for him, yea, the poor and the needy from him that spoileth him?

Psa. 68:10. Thou, O God, hast prepared of thy goodness for the poor.

Psa. 69:33. For the LORD heareth the poor, and despiseth not his prisoners.

Psa. 72:2. He shall judge thy people with righteousness, and thy poor with judgment. 4. He shall judge the poor of the people, he shall save the children of the needy, and shall break in pieces the oppressor. 12. For he shall deliver the needy when he crieth; the poor also, and *him* that hath no helper. 13. He shall spare the poor and needy, and shall save the souls of the needy. 14. He shall redeem their soul from deceit and violence: and precious shall their blood be in his sight.

Psa. 74:21. O let not the oppressed return ashamed: let the poor and needy praise thy name.

Psa. 102:17. He will regard the prayer of the destitute, and not despise their prayer.

Psa. 107:9. For he satisfieth the longing soul, and filleth the hungry soul with goodness. 36. There he maketh the hungry to dwell, that they may prepare a city for habitation; 41. Yet setteth he the poor on high from affliction, and maketh *him* families like a flock.

Psa. 109:31. For he shall stand at the right hand of the poor, to save *him* from those that condemn his soul.

Psa. 113:7. He raiseth up the poor out of the dust, *and* lifteth the needy out of the dunghill; 8. That he may set *him* with princes, *even* with the princes of his people.

Psa. 132:15. I will abundantly bless her provision: I will satisfy her poor with bread.

Psa. 140:12. I know that the LORD will maintain the cause of the afflicted, *and* the right of the poor.

Psa. 146:5. Happy *is he* that *hath* the God of Jacob for his help, whose hope *is* in the LORD his God: 7. Which executeth judgment for the oppressed: which giveth food to the hungry.

Prov. 22:2. The rich and poor meet together: the LORD *is* the maker of them all. 22. Rob not the poor, because he *is* poor; neither oppress the afflicted in the gate: 23. For the LORD will plead their cause, and spoil the soul of those that spoiled them.

Prov. 29:13. The poor and the deceitful man meet together: the LORD lighteneth both their eyes.

Eccl. 5:8. If thou seest the oppression of the poor, and violent perverting of judgment and justice in a province, marvel not at the matter: for *he that is* higher than the highest regardeth; and *there be* higher than they.

Isa. 11:4. But with righteousness shall he judge the poor, and reprove with equity for the meek of the earth:

Isa. 14:30. The firstborn of the poor shall feed, and the needy shall lie down in safety: 32. The LORD hath founded Zion, and the poor of his people shall trust in it.

Isa. 25:4. For thou hast been a strength to the poor, a strength to the needy in his distress, a refuge from the storm, a shadow from the heat, when the blast of the terrible ones *is* as a storm *against* the wall.

Isa. 29:19. The meek also shall increase *their* joy in the LORD, and the poor among men shall rejoice in the Holy One of Israel.

Isa. 41:17. *When* the poor and needy seek water, and *there is* none, *and* their tongue faileth for thirst, I the LORD will hear them, *I* the God of Israel will not forsake them.

Jer. 20:13. Sing unto the LORD, praise ye the LORD: for he hath delivered the soul of the poor from the hand of evildoers.

Zeph. 3:12. I will also leave in the midst of thee an afflicted and poor people, and they shall trust in the name of the LORD.

Zech. 11:7. I will feed the flock of slaughter, *even* you, O poor of the flock.

Matt. 11:5. The blind receive their sight,

and the lame walk, the lepers are cleansed, and the deaf hear, the dead are raised up, and the poor have the gospel preached to them. Luke 7:22.

Luke 4:18. The Spirit of the Lord *is* upon me, because he hath anointed me to preach the gospel to the poor;

Luke 16:22. And it came to pass that the beggar died, and was carried by the angels into Abraham's bosom:

Jas. 2:5. Hearken, my beloved brethren, hath not God chosen the poor of this world rich in faith, and heirs of the kingdom which he hath promised to them that love him?

See God, Goodness of; Providence of.

KINDNESS TO: Instances of: To Ruth, Ruth 2:23; by Boaz, Ruth 2:14–16. To the Widow of Zarephath, 1 Kin.17:12–24. Prophet's widow, 2 Kin. 4:1–7. Jews, Esth. 9:22. By Job, Job 29:11–16; 31:16–21,38–40; the Temanites, Isa. 21:14; Nebuzar-adan, Jer. 39:10; the good Samaritan, Luke ˙10:33–35; Zacchæus, Luke 19:8; Christian churches, Acts 6:1; 11:29; Rom. 15:25,26; 2 Cor. 8:1–4; Dorcas, Acts 9:36; Cornelius, Acts 10:2,4; church at Antioch, Acts 11:29,30; Paul, Rom. 15:25; churches of Macedonia and Achaia, Rom. 15:26; 2 Cor. 8:1–5.

OPPRESSIONS OF: Neh. 5:1. And there was a great cry of the people and of their wives against their brethren the Jews. 2. For there were that said, We, our sons, and our daughters, *are* many : therefore we take up corn *for them*, that we may eat, and live. 3. *Some* also there were that said, We have mortgaged our lands, vineyards, and houses, that we might buy corn, because of the dearth. 4. There were also that said, We have borrowed money for the king's tribute, *and that upon* our lands and vineyards. 5. Yet now our flesh *is* as the flesh of our brethren, our children as their children : and, lo, we bring into bondage our sons and our daughters to be servants, and *some* of our daughters are brought into bondage *already :* neither *is it* in our power *to redeem them ;* for other men have our lands and vineyards. 6. And I was very angry when I heard their cry and these words. 7. Then I consulted with myself, and I rebuked the nobles, and the rulers, and said unto them, Ye exact usury, every one of his brother. And I set a great assembly against them. 8. And I said unto them, We, after our ability, have redeemed our brethren the Jews, which were sold unto the heathen ; and will ye even sell your brethren? or shall they be sold unto us? Then held they their peace, and found nothing *to answer.* 9. Also I said, It *is* not good that ye do : ought ye not to walk in the fear of our God because of the reproach of the heathen our enemies? 10. I likewise, *and* my brethren, and my servants, might exact of them money and corn : I pray you, let us leave off this usury. 11. Restore, I pray you, to them, even this day, their

lands, their vineyards, their oliveyards, and their houses, also the hundredth *part* of the money, and of the corn, the wine, and the oil, that ye exact of them. 12. Then said they, We will restore *them*, and will require nothing of them ; so will we do as thou sayest. Then I called the priests, and took an oath of them, that they should do according to this promise. 13. Also I shook my lap, and said, So God shake out every man from his house, and from his labour, that performeth not this promise, even thus be he shaken out, and emptied. And all the congregation said, Amen, and praised the Lord. And the people did according to this promise.

Job 20:19. Because he hath oppressed *and* hath forsaken the poor ; *because* he hath violently taken away an house which he builded not ; 20. Surely he shall not feel quietness in his belly, he shall not save of that which he desired. 21. There shall none of his meat be left ; therefore shall no man look for his goods.

Job 22:6. Thou hast taken a pledge from thy brother for nought, and stripped the naked of their clothing. 7. Thou hast not given water to the weary to drink, and thou hast withholden bread from the hungry. 9. Thou hast sent widows away empty, and the arms of the fatherless have been broken. 10. Therefore snares *are* round about thee, and sudden fear troubleth thee ; 11. Or darkness, *that* thou canst not see ; and abundance of waters cover thee.

Job. 24:4. They turn the needy out of the way : the poor of the earth hide themselves together. 7. They cause the naked to lodge without clothing, that *they have* no covering in the cold. 8. They are wet with the showers of the mountains, and embrace the rock for want of a shelter. 9. They pluck the fatherless from the breast, and take a pledge of the poor. 10. They cause *him* to go naked without clothing, and they take away the sheaf *from* the hungry ;

Psa. 10:2. The wicked in *his* pride doth persecute the poor : let them be taken in the devices that they have imagined. 8. He sitteth in the lurking places of the villages : in the secret places doth he murder the innocent : his eyes are privily set against the poor. 9. He lieth in wait secretly as a lion in his den : he lieth in wait to catch the poor : he doth catch the poor, when he draweth him into his net. 10. He croucheth, *and* humbleth himself, that the poor may fall by his strong ones.

Psa. 37:14. The wicked have drawn out the sword, and have bent their bow, to cast down the poor and needy,

Prov. 14:20. The poor is hated even of his own neighbour : but the rich *hath* many friends.

Prov. 17:5. Whoso mocketh the poor reproacheth his Maker : *and* he that is glad at calamities shall not be unpunished.

Prov. 19:7. All the brethren of the poor

do hate him : how much more do his friends go far from him ? he pursueth *them with* words, *yet* they *are* wanting *to him*.

Prov. 22:7. The rich ruleth over the poor, and the borrower *is* servant to the lender. 16. He that oppresseth the poor to increase his *riches, and* he that giveth to the rich, *shall* surely *come* to want.

Prov. 28:3. A poor man that oppresseth the poor *is like* a sweeping rain which leaveth no food. 15. *As* a roaring lion, and a ranging bear ; *so is* a wicked ruler over the poor people.

Prov. 30:14. *There is* a generation, whose teeth *are as* swords, and their jaw teeth *as* knives, to devour the poor from off the earth, and the needy from *among* men.

Eccl. 5:8. If thou seest the oppression of the poor, and violent perverting of judgment and justice in a province, marvel not at the matter : for *he that is* higher than the highest regardeth ; and *there be* higher than they.

Isa. 3:14. The LORD will enter into judgment with the ancients of his people, and the princes thereof : for ye have eaten up the vineyard ; the spoil of the poor *is* in your houses. 15. What mean ye *that* ye beat my people to pieces, and grind the faces of the poor ? saith the Lord GOD of hosts.

Isa. 10:1. Woe unto them that decree unrighteous decrees, and that write grievousness *which* they have prescribed ; 2. To turn aside the needy from judgment, and to take away the right from the poor of my people, that widows may be their prey, and *that* they may rob the fatherless !

Isa. 32:6. The vile person will speak villany, and his heart will work iniquity, . . . to make empty the soul of the hungry, and he will cause the drink of the thirsty to fail. 7. The instruments also of the churl *are* evil : he deviseth wicked devices to destroy the poor with lying words, even when the needy speaketh right.

Ezek. 18:12. Hath oppressed the poor and needy, hath spoiled by violence, hath not restored the pledge,

Ezek. 22:29. The people of the land have used oppression, and exercised robbery, and have vexed the poor and needy ; yea, they have oppressed the stranger wrongfully.

Amos 2:6. For three transgressions of Israel, and for four, I will not turn away *the punishment* thereof ; because they sold the righteous for silver, and the poor for a pair of shoes ; 7. That pant after the dust of the earth on the head of the poor, and turn aside the way of the meek ; . . . 8. And they lay *themselves* down upon clothes laid to pledge by every altar, and they drink the wine of the condemned *in* the house of their god.

Amos 4:1. Hear this word, ye kine of Bashan, that *are* in the mountain of Samaria, which oppress the poor, which crush the needy, which say to their masters, Bring, and let us drink. 2. The Lord GOD hath

sworn by his holiness, that, lo, the days shall come upon you, that he will take you away with hooks, and your posterity with fish-hooks.

Amos 5:11. As your treading *is* upon the poor, and ye take from him burdens of wheat : ye have built houses of hewn stone, but ye shall not dwell in them ; ye have planted pleasant vineyards, but ye shall not drink wine of them. 12. For I know your manifold transgressions and your mighty sins : they afflict the just, they take a bribe, and they turn aside the poor in the gate *from their right*.

Amos 8:4. Hear this, O ye that swallow up the needy, even to make the poor of the land to fail, 6. That we may buy the poor for silver, and the needy for a pair of shoes ;

Hab. 3:14. Thou didst strike through with his staves the head of his villages : they came out as a whirlwind to scatter me : their rejoicing *was* as to devour the poor secretly.

Jas. 2:6. But ye have despised the poor. See under sub-topic, DUTY TO.

INSTANCES OF : The widow's son, 2 Kin. 4:1-7.

See CREDITOR ; DEBTOR ; SERVANTS ; WAGES.

POPLAR, a tree, Gen. 30:37 ; Hos. 4:13.

POPULAR SINS, laws against, Ex. 23:2.

See SIN.

POPULARITY. INSTANCES OF : David, 2 Sam. 3:36. Absalom, 2 Sam. 15:2-6, 13. Job, Job 29.

PORATHA, son of Haman, Esth. 9:8.

PORCH. See TEMPLE.

PORCIUS. See FESTUS.

PORPOISE, Ex. 25:5 [marg., *R. V.*] ; 26:14 ; 36:19 ; 39:34.

PORTERS. Guards at the city gates, the doors of the king's palace, and doors of the temple, 1 Chr. 9:17-32 ; 2 Chr. 34:13 ; 35:15. Lodged round about the temple in order to be present for opening the doors, 1 Chr. 9:27. One-third were porters of the temple, 2 Chr. 23:4 ; one-third were porters of the king's house, 2 Chr. 23:5 ; one-third were porters of the gate of the foundation, 2 Chr. 23:5. They served, also, as porters of the gates of the walls, Neh. 12:25. They served in twenty-four courses, 1 Chr. 26:13-19. Their posts were determined by lot, 1 Chr. 24:31 ; 26:13-19.

POST. A bearer of message, Job 9:25 ; Jer. 51:31. Of Hezekiah, 2 Chr. 30:6,10 ; Ahasuerus, Esth. 3:13,15 ; 8:10,14.

POTIPHAR, an officer of Pharaoh. Joseph's master, Gen. 37:36 ; 39:1.

POTI-PHERAH, a priest of On. Joseph's father-in-law, Gen. 41:45,50 ; 46:20.

POTSHERD, fragment of earthenware, Job 2:8 ; Isa. 45:9.

POTTERY. Clay prepared for, by treading, Isa. 41:25. Vessels made of, Jer. 18:3,4. Place for manufacture of, outside the wall of Jerusalem, bought as a burying ground for the poor, Matt. 27:7-10.

FIGURATIVE: Isa. 64:8; Rom. 9:21. Of weakness, in the idol in Nebuchadnezzar's vision, Dan. 2:41.

POUND. The Hebrew word "maneh" is translated "pound," 1 Kin. 10:17; Ezra 2:69; Neh. 7:71,72, and is equivalent to about one pound, fourteen ounces. In John 12:3 the weight was equivalent to about twelve ounces. In Luke 19:13-25 the Greek word "mina" is translated "pound," and worth approximately nineteen dollars.

See MEASURE ; WEIGHTS.

POVERTY. Prov. 6:11. So shall thy poverty come as one that travelleth, and thy want as an armed man.

Prov. 10:15. The destruction of the poor *is* their poverty.

Prov. 15:16. Better *is* little with the fear of the LORD, than great treasure and trouble therewith.

Prov. 16:8. Better *is* a little with righteousness than great revenues without right. Eccl. 4:6.

Prov. 20:13. Love not sleep, lest thou come to poverty : open thine eyes, *and* thou shalt be satisfied with bread.

Prov. 23:21. For the drunkard and the glutton shall come to poverty : and drowsiness shall clothe *a man* with rags.

Prov. 24:33. *Yet* a little sleep, a little slumber, a little folding of the hands to sleep : 34. So shall thy poverty come as one that travelleth ; and thy want as an armed man.

Prov. 28:19. He that tilleth his land shall have plenty of bread : but he that followeth after vain *persons* shall have poverty enough.

Prov. 30:8. Give me neither poverty nor riches ; feed me with food convenient for me : 9. Or lest I be poor, and steal, and take the name of my God *in vain*.

See POOR, THE.

POWER. OF CHRIST: As the Son of God, is the power of God, John 5:17-19; 10:28-30; as man, is from the Father, Acts 10:38.

Described as supreme, Eph. 1:20,21; 1 Pet. 3:22; unlimited, Matt. 28:18; over all flesh, John 17:2; over all things, John 3:35; Eph. 1:22; glorious, 2 Thess. 1:9; everlasting, 1 Tim. 6:16. Is able to subdue all things, Phil. 3:21.

Exemplified in creation, John 1:3,10; Col. 1:16; upholding all things, Col. 1:17; Heb. 1:3; salvation, Isa. 63:1; Heb. 7:25; his teaching, Matt. 7:28,29; Luke 4:32; working miracles, Matt. 8:27; Luke 5:17; enabling others to work miracles, Matt. 10:1; Mark 16:17,18; Luke 10:17; forgiving sins, Matt. 9:6; Acts 5:31; giving spiritual life, John 5:21,25,26; giving eternal life, John 17:2; raising the dead, John 5:28,29; rising from the dead, John 2:19; 10:18; overcoming the world, John 16:33; overcoming Satan, Col. 2:15; Heb. 2:14; destroying the works of Satan, 1 John

3:8; ministers should make known, **2 Pet.** 1:16.

Saints made willing by, Psa. 110:3; succored by, Heb. 2:18; strengthened by, Phil. 4:13; 2 Tim. 4:17; preserved by, 2 Tim. 1:12; 4:18; bodies of, shall be changed by, Phil. 3:21; rests upon saints, 2 Cor. 12:9. Present in the assembly of saints, 1 Cor. 5:4. Shall be specially manifested at his second coming, Mark 13:26; 2 Pet. 1:16. Shall subdue all power, 1 Cor. 15:24. The wicked shall be destroyed by, Psa. 2:9; Isa. 11:4; 63:3; 2 Thess. 1:9.—*Bible Text-Book.*

See JESUS.

OF GOD: One of his attributes, Psa. 62:11. Expressed by the voice of God, Psa. 29:3, 5; 68:33; finger of God, Ex. 8:19; Psa. 8:3; hand of God, Ex. 9:3,15; Isa. 48:13; arm of God, Job 40:9; Isa. 52:10; thunder of his power, Job 26:14.

Described as great, Psa. 79:11; Nah. 1:3; strong, Psa. 89:13; 136:12; glorious, Ex. 15:6; Isa. 63:12; mighty, Job 9:4; Psa. 89:13; everlasting, Isa. 26:4; Rom. 1:20; sovereign, Rom. 9:21; effectual, Isa. 43:13; Eph. 3:7; irresistible, Deut. 32:39; Dan. 4:35; incomparable, Ex. 15:11,12; Deut. 3:24; Job 40:9; Psa. 89:8; unsearchable, Job 5:9; 9:10; incomprehensible, Job 26:14; Eccl. 3:11.

All things possible to, Matt. 19:26. Nothing too hard for, Gen. 18:14; Jer. 32:27. Can save by many or by few, 1 Sam. 14:6. Is the source of all strength, 1 Chr. 29:12; Psa. 68:35.

Exemplified in the creation, Psa. 102:25; Jer. 10:12; in establishing and governing all things, Psa. 65:6; 66:7; in the miracles of Christ, Luke 11:20; in the resurrection of Christ, 2 Cor. 13:4; Col. 2:12; in the resurrection of saints, 1 Cor. 6:14; in making the gospel effectual, Rom. 1:16; 1 Cor. 1:18,24; in delivering his people, Psa. 106:8; in the destruction of the wicked, Ex. 9:16; Rom. 9:22.

Saints long for exhibitions of, Psa. 63:1,2; have confidence in, Jer. 20:11; receive increase of grace by, 2 Cor. 9:8; strengthened by, Eph. 6:10; Col. 1:11; upheld by, Psa. 37:17; Isa. 41:10; supported in affliction by, 2 Cor. 6:7; 2 Tim. 1:8; delivered by, Neh. 1:10; Dan. 3:17; exalted by, Job 36:22; kept by, unto salvation, 1 Pet. 1:5. Exerted in behalf of saints, 1 Chr. 16:9. Works in and for saints, 2 Cor. 13:4; Eph. 1:19; 3:20. The faith of saints stands in, 1 Cor. 2:5.

Should be acknowledged, 1 Chr. 29:11; Isa. 33:13; pleaded in prayer, Psa. 79:11; Matt. 6:13; feared, Jer. 5:22; Matt. 10:28; magnified, Psa. 21:13; Jude 25. Efficiency of ministers is through, 1 Cor. 3:6-8; Gal. 2:8; Eph. 3:7. Is a ground of trust, Isa. 26:4; Rom. 4:21.

The wicked know not, Matt. 22:29; have against them, Ezra 8:22; shall be destroyed by, Luke 12:5. The heavenly host magnified, Rev. 4:11; 5:13; 11:17.—*Bible Text-Book.*

See GOD, OMNIPOTENT, POWER OF.

OF THE HOLY GHOST: Is the power of God, Matt. 12:28, with Luke 11:20. Christ commenced his ministry in, Luke 4:14. Christ wrought his miracles by, Matt. 12:28.

Exemplified in creation, Gen. 1:2; Job 26:13; Psa. 104:30; the conception of Christ, Luke 1:35; raising Christ from the dead, 1 Pet. 3:18; giving spiritual life, Ezek. 37:11-14, with Rom. 8:11; working miracles, Rom. 15:19; making the gospel efficacious, 1 Cor. 2:4; 1 Thess. 1:5; overcoming all difficulties, Zech. 4:6,7. Promised by the Father, Luke 24:49. Promised by Christ, Acts 1:8.

Saints upheld by, Psa. 51:12; strengthened by, Eph. 3:16; enabled to speak the truth boldly by, Mic. 3:8; Acts 6:5,10; 2 Tim. 1:7,8; helped in prayer by, Rom. 8:26; abound in hope by, Rom. 15:13. Qualifies ministers, Luke 24:49; Acts 1:8,9. God's word the instrument of, Eph. 6:17.—*Bible Text-Book.*

See HOLY SPIRIT.

SPIRITUAL: Gen. 32:28. And he said, Thy name shall be called no more Jacob, but Israel: for as a prince hast thou power with God and with men, and hast prevailed.

Isa. 40:29. He giveth power to the faint; and to *them that have* no might he increaseth strength. 30. Even the youths shall faint and be weary, and the young men shall utterly fall: 31. But they that wait upon the LORD shall renew *their* strength; they shall mount up with wings as eagles; they shall run, and not be weary; *and* they shall walk, and not faint.

Mark 9:29. And he said unto them, This kind can come forth by nothing, but by prayer 1 and fasting.   [1 Omitted in R. V.]

Luke 1:17. And he shall go before him in the spirit and power of Elias, to turn the hearts of the fathers to the children, and the disobedient to the wisdom of the just; to make ready a people prepared for the Lord.

Luke 4:32. And they were astonished at his doctrine: for his word was with power.

Luke 24:49. And, behold, I send the promise of my Father upon you: but tarry ye in the city of Jerusalem, until ye be endued with power from on high.

John 7:38. He that believeth on me, as the scripture hath said, out of his belly shall flow rivers of living water. 39. (But this spake he of the Spirit, which they that believe on him should receive: for the Holy Ghost was not yet *given;* because that Jesus was not yet glorified.)

Acts 1:8. But ye shall receive power, after that the Holy Ghost is come upon you: and ye shall be witnesses unto me both in Jerusalem, and in all Judæa, and in Samaria, and unto the uttermost part of the earth.

Acts 2:2. And suddenly there came a sound from heaven as of a rushing mighty wind, and it filled all the house where they were sitting. 3. And there appeared unto them cloven tongues like as of fire, and it sat upon each of them. 4. And they were all filled with the Holy Ghost, and began to speak with other tongues, as the Spirit gave them utterance.

Acts 6:8. And Stephen, full of faith and power, did great wonders and miracles among the people.

Eph. 1:19. And what *is* the exceeding greatness of his power to us-ward who believe, according to the working of his mighty power, 20. Which he wrought in Christ,

1 Cor. 1:24. But unto them which are called, both Jews and Greeks, Christ the power of God, and the wisdom of God. 25. Because the foolishness of God is wiser than men; and the weakness of God is stronger than men. 26. For ye see your calling, brethren, how that not many wise men after the flesh, not many mighty, not many noble, *are called:* 27. But God hath chosen the foolish things of the world to confound the wise; and God hath chosen the weak things of the world to confound the things which are mighty; 28. And base things of the world, and things which are despised, hath God chosen, *yea,* and things which are not, to bring to nought things that are:

1 Cor. 4:19. But I will come to you shortly, if the Lord will, and will know, not the speech of them which are puffed up, but the power. 20. For the kingdom of God *is* not in word, but in power.

2 Cor. 12:9. And he said unto me, My grace is sufficient for thee: for my strength is made perfect in weakness. Most gladly therefore will I rather glory in my infirmities, that the power of Christ may rest upon me.

1 Thess. 1:5. For our gospel came not unto you in word only, but also in power, and in the Holy Ghost, and in much assurance; as ye know what manner of men we were among you for your sake.

2 Tim. 1:7. For God hath not given us the spirit of fear; but of power, and of love, and of a sound mind.

Heb. 6:5. And have tasted the good word of God, and the powers of the world to come.

See HOLY SPIRIT.

PRAISE. Song of Moses, after the passage of the Red Sea, Ex. 15:1-19. Of Miriam, Ex. 15:21. Of Deborah, after defeating the Canaanites, Judg. 5. Of Hannah, 1 Sam. 2:1-10. Of David, celebrating his deliverance from the hand of Saul, 2 Sam. 22; on bring-ing the ark to Zion, 1 Chr. 16:8-36; at the close of his reign, 1 Chr. 29:10-19.

The chorus when Solomon brought the ark into the temple, 2 Chr. 5:13.

Psalms of, for God's goodness to Israel, Psalms 46; 48; 65; 66; 68; 76; 81; 85; 98; 105; 124; 126; 129; 135; 136. See printed scriptures below. For God's goodness to right-eous men, Psalms 23; 34; 36; 91; 100; 103; 107; 117; 121. See printed scriptures below. For God's goodness to individuals, Psalms 9; 18; 22; 30; 40; 75; 103; 108; 116; 118; 138; 144. For God's attributes, Psalms 8; 19; 22; 24; 29; 33; 47; 50; 65; 66; 76; 77; 92; 93; 95; 96; 97; 98; 99; 104; 111; 113; 114; 115; 134; 139; 147; 148; 150.

UNCLASSIFIED SCRIPTURES RELATING TO: Gen. 14:20. And blessed be the most high God, which hath delivered thine enemies into thy hand.

Ex. 15:1. Then sang Moses and the children of Israel this song unto the Lord, and spake, saying, I will sing unto the Lord, for he hath triumphed gloriously: the horse and his rider hath he thrown into the sea. 2. The Lord is my strength and song, and he is become my salvation: he is my God, and I will prepare him an habitation; my father's God, and I will exalt him.

Deut. 10:21. He is thy praise, and he is thy God, that hath done for thee these great and terrible things, which thine eyes have seen.

Judg. 5:3. Hear, O ye kings; give ear, O ye princes; I, even I, will sing unto the Lord; I will sing praise to the Lord God of Israel.

2 Sam. 22:4. I will call on the Lord, who is worthy to be praised: Psa. 18:3.

1 Chr. 16:31. Let the heavens be glad, and let the earth rejoice: and let men say among the nations, The Lord reigneth. 33. Then shall the trees of the wood sing out at the presence of the Lord, because he cometh to judge the earth. 34. O give thanks unto the Lord; for he is good; for his mercy endureth for ever. 36. Blessed be the Lord God of Israel for ever and ever. And all the people said, Amen, and praised the Lord.

1 Chr. 23:30. And to stand every morning to thank and, praise the Lord, and likewise at even;

2 Chr. 7:3. And when all the children of Israel saw how the fire came down, and the glory of the Lord upon the house, they bowed themselves with their faces to the ground upon the pavement, and worshipped, and praised the Lord, saying, For he is good; for his mercy endureth for ever.

Neh. 9:5. Then the Levites, Jeshua, and Kadmiel, Bani, Hashabniah, Sherebiah, Hodijah, Shebaniah, and Pethahiah, said, Stand up and bless the Lord your God for ever and ever: and blessed be thy glorious name, which is exalted above all blessing and praise. 6. Thou, even thou, art Lord alone; thou hast made heaven, the heaven of heavens, with all their host, the earth, and all things that are therein, the seas, and all that is therein, and thou preservest them all; and the host of heaven worshippeth thee.

Job 36:24. Remember that thou magnify his work, which men behold.

Psa. 7:17. I will praise the Lord according to his righteousness: and will sing praise to the name of the Lord most high.

Psa. 8:2. Out of the mouth of babes and sucklings hast thou ordained strength because of thine enemies, that thou mightest still the enemy and the avenger.

Psa. 9:11. Sing praises to the Lord, which dwelleth in Zion: declare among the people his doings.

Psa. 21:13. Be thou exalted, Lord, in thine own strength: so will we sing and praise thy power.

Psa. 22:22. I will declare thy name unto my brethren: in the midst of the congregation will I praise thee. 23. Ye that fear the Lord, praise him; all ye the seed of Jacob, glorify him; and fear him, all ye the seed of Israel. 25. My praise shall be of thee in the great congregation:

Psa. 24:7. Lift up your heads, O ye gates; and be ye lift up, ye everlasting doors; and the King of glory shall come in. 8. Who is this King of glory? The Lord strong and mighty, the Lord mighty in battle. 9. Lift up your heads, O ye gates; even lift them up, ye everlasting doors; and the King of glory shall come in. 10. Who is this King of glory? The Lord of hosts, he is the King of glory. Selah.

Psa. 26:12. In the congregations will I bless the Lord.

Psa. 28:6. Blessed be the Lord, because he hath heard the voice of my supplications. 7. The Lord is my strength and my shield; my heart trusted in him, and I am helped: therefore my heart greatly rejoiceth; and with my song will I praise him.

Psa. 30:4. Sing unto the Lord, O ye saints of his, and give thanks at the remembrance of his holiness. Psa. 97:12.

Psa. 32:11. Be glad in the Lord, and rejoice, ye righteous. and shout for joy, all ye that are upright in heart.

Psa. 33:1. Rejoice in the Lord, O ye righteous: for praise is comely for the upright. 2. Praise the Lord with harp: sing unto him with the psaltery and an instrument of ten strings. 3. Sing unto him a new song; play skilfully with a loud noise.

Psa. 34:1. I will bless the Lord at all times: his praise shall continually be in my mouth. 2. My soul shall make her boast in the Lord: the humble shall hear thereof, and be glad. 3. O magnify the Lord with me, and let us exalt his name together.

Psa. 35:18. I will give thee thanks in the great congregation: I will praise thee among much people. 28. My tongue shall speak of thy righteousness and of thy praise all the day long.

Psa. 41:13. Blessed be the Lord God of Israel from everlasting, and to everlasting.

Psa. 42:4. When I remember these things, I pour out my soul in me: for I had gone with the multitude, I went with them to the house of God, with the voice of joy and praise, with a multitude that kept holyday.

Psa. 43:3. O send out thy light and thy truth: let them lead me; let them bring me unto thy holy hill, and to thy tabernacles. 4. Then will I go unto the altar of God, unto God my exceeding joy: yea, upon the harp will I praise thee, O God my God.

Psa. 47:1. O clap your hands, all ye people; shout unto God with the voice of triumph. 6. Sing praises to God, sing praises: sing praises unto our King, sing praises. 7.

For God *is* the King of all the earth: sing ye praises with understanding.

Psa. 48:1. Great *is* the LORD, and greatly to be praised in the city of our God, *in* the mountain of his holiness.

Psa. 50:23. Whoso offereth praise glorifieth me:

Psa. 51:15. O Lord, open thou my lips; and my mouth shall shew forth thy praise.

Psa. 52:9. I will praise thee for ever, because thou hast done *it*: and I will wait on thy name; for *it is* good before thy saints.

Psa. 56:10. In God will I praise *his* word: in the LORD will I praise *his* word. 12. Thy vows *are* upon me, O God: I will render praises unto thee.

Psa. 57:7. My heart is fixed, O God, my heart is fixed: I will sing and give praise. 8. Awake up, my glory; awake, psaltery and harp: I *myself* will awake early. 9. I will praise thee, O Lord, among the people: I will sing unto thee among the nations. Psa. 108:1-3.

Psa. 61:8. So will I sing praise unto thy name for ever, that I may daily perform my vows.

Psa. 63:3. Because thy lovingkindness *is* better than life, my lips shall praise thee. 4. Thus will I bless thee while I live: I will lift up my hands in thy name. 5. My soul shall be satisfied as *with* marrow and fatness; and my mouth shall praise *thee* with joyful lips: 6. When I remember thee upon my bed, *and* meditate on thee in the *night* watches.

Psa. 65:1. Praise waiteth for thee, O God, in Sion: and unto thee shall the vow be performed.

Psa. 66:1. Make a joyful noise unto God, all ye lands: 2. Sing forth the honour of his name: make his praise glorious. 4. All the earth shall worship thee, and shall sing unto thee; they shall sing *to* thy name. 8. O bless our God, ye people, and make the voice of his praise to be heard:

Psa. 67:3. Let the people praise thee, O God; let all the people praise thee. 4. O let the nations be glad and sing for joy:

Psa. 68:4. Sing unto God, sing praises to his name: extol him that rideth upon the heavens by his name JAH, and rejoice before him. 26. Bless ye God in the congregations, *even* the Lord, from the fountain of Israel. 32. Sing unto God, ye kingdoms of the earth; O sing praises unto the Lord; Selah: 33. To him that rideth upon the heavens of heavens, *which were* of old; lo, he doth send out his voice, *and that* a mighty voice. 34. Ascribe ye strength unto God: his excellency *is* over Israel, and his strength *is* in the clouds.

Psa. 69:30. I will praise the name of God with a song, and will magnify him with thanksgiving. 34. Let the heaven and earth praise him, the seas, and every thing that moveth therein.

Psa. 70:4. Let all those that seek thee rejoice and be glad in thee: and let such as love thy salvation say continually, Let God be magnified.

Psa. 71:8. Let my mouth be filled *with* thy praise *and with* thy honour all the day. 14. But I will hope continually, and will yet praise thee more and more. 15. My mouth shall shew forth thy righteousness *and* thy salvation all the day; for I know not the numbers *thereof*. 22. I will also praise thee with the psaltery, *even* thy truth, O my God: unto thee will I sing with the harp, O thou Holy One of Israel.

Psa. 75:1. Unto thee, O God, do we give thanks, *unto thee* do we give thanks: for *that* thy name is near thy wondrous works declare.

Psa. 79:13. So we thy people and sheep of thy pasture will give thee thanks for ever: we will shew forth thy praise to all generations.

Psa. 81:1. Sing aloud unto God our strength: make a joyful noise unto the God of Jacob.

Psa. 84:4. Blessed *are* they that dwell in thy house: they will be still praising thee.

Psa. 86:12. I will praise thee, O Lord my God, with all my heart: and I will glorify thy name for evermore.

Psa. 89:5. And the heavens shall praise thy wonders, O LORD: thy faithfulness also in the congregation of the saints. 52. Blessed *be* the LORD for evermore. Amen, and Amen.

Psa. 92:1. *It is a* good *thing* to give thanks unto the LORD, and to sing praises unto thy name, O most High: 2. To shew forth thy lovingkindness in the morning, and thy faithfulness every night, 3. Upon an instrument of ten strings, and upon the psaltery; upon the harp with a solemn sound.

Psa. 95:1. O come, let us sing unto the LORD: let us make a joyful noise to the rock of our salvation. 2. Let us come before his presence with thanksgiving, and make a joyful noise unto him with psalms. 6. O come, let us worship and bow down: let us kneel before the LORD our maker. 7. For he *is* our God; and we *are* the people of his pasture, and the sheep of his hand.

Psa. 96:1. O sing unto the LORD a new song: sing unto the LORD, all the earth. 2. Sing unto the LORD, bless his name; shew forth his salvation from day to day. 3. Declare his glory among the heathen, his wonders among all people. 4. For the LORD *is* great, and greatly to be praised: 7. Give unto the LORD, O ye kindreds of the people, give unto the LORD glory and strength. 8. Give unto the LORD the glory *due unto* his name: bring an offering, and come into his courts. 9. O worship the LORD in the beauty of holiness: fear before him, all the earth.

Psa. 98:4. Make a joyful noise unto the LORD, all the earth: make a loud noise, and rejoice, and sing praise. 5. Sing unto the LORD with the harp; with the harp, and the voice of a psalm. 6. With trumpets and sound of cornet make a joyful noise before the LORD, the King.

Psa. 99:3. Let them praise thy great and terrible name; *for* it *is* holy. 5. Exalt ye the LORD our God, and worship at his footstool; *for* he *is* holy. 9. Exalt the LORD our God, and worship at his holy hill; for the LORD our God *is* holy.

Psa. 100:1. Make a joyful noise unto the LORD, all ye lands. 2. Serve the LORD with gladness: come before his presence with singing. 3. Know ye that the LORD he *is* God: *it is* he *that* hath made us, and not we ourselves; *we are* his people, and the sheep of his pasture. 4. Enter into his gates with thanksgiving, *and* into his courts with praise: be thankful unto him, *and* bless his name. 5. For the LORD *is* good; his mercy *is* everlasting; and his truth *endureth* to all generations.

Psa. 101:1. I will sing of mercy and judgment: unto thee, O LORD, will I sing.

Psa. 103:20. Bless the LORD, ye his angels, that excel in strength, that do his commandments, hearkening unto the voice of his word. 21. Bless ye the LORD, all *ye* his hosts; *ye* ministers of his, that do his pleasure. 22. Bless the LORD, all his works in all places of his dominion: bless the LORD, O my soul.

Psa. 104:33. I will sing unto the LORD as long as I live: I will sing praise to my God while I have my being. 34. My meditation of him shall be sweet: I will be glad in the LORD.

Psa. 105:1. Oh give thanks unto the LORD; call upon his name: make known his deeds among the people. 2. Sing unto him, sing psalms unto him: talk ye of all his wondrous works. 3. Glory ye in his holy name: let the heart of them rejoice that seek the LORD. 4. Seek the LORD, and his strength: seek his face evermore. 5. Remember his marvellous works that he hath done; his wonders, and the judgments of his mouth;

Psa. 106:1. Praise ye the LORD. O give thanks unto the LORD; for *he is* good: for his mercy *endureth* for ever. 48. Blessed *be* the LORD God of Israel from everlasting to everlasting: and let all the people say, Amen. Praise ye the LORD.

Psa. 107:8. Oh that *men* would praise the LORD *for* his goodness, and *for* his wonderful works to the children of men! [*vs.* 15, 21,31.] 9. For he satisfieth the longing soul, and filleth the hungry soul with goodness. 32. Let them exalt him also in the congregation of the people, and praise him in the assembly of the elders.

Psa. 109:30. I will greatly praise the LORD with my mouth; yea, I will praise him among the multitude.

Psa. 111:1. Praise ye the LORD. I will praise the LORD with *my* whole heart, in the assembly of the upright, and *in* the congregation. 10. His praise endureth for ever.

Psa. 113:1. Praise ye the LORD. Praise, O ye servants of the LORD, praise the name of the LORD. 2. Blessed be the name of the LORD from this time forth and for evermore.

Psa. 115:18. We will bless the LORD from this time forth and for evermore. Praise the LORD.

Psa. 116:12. What shall I render unto the LORD *for* all his benefits toward me? 13. I will take the cup of salvation, and call upon the name of the LORD. 14. I will pay my vows unto the LORD now in the presence of all his people. 17. I will offer to thee the sacrifice of thanksgiving, and will call upon the name of the LORD. 18. I will pay my vows unto the LORD now in the presence of all his people, 19. In the courts of the LORD's house, in the midst of thee, O Jerusalem. Praise ye the LORD.

Psa. 117:1. O praise the LORD, all ye nations: praise him, all ye people. 2. For his merciful kindness is great toward us: and the truth of the LORD *endureth* for ever. Praise ye the LORD.

Psa. 118:15. The voice of rejoicing and salvation *is* in the tabernacles of the righteous: 28. Thou *art* my God, and I will praise thee: *thou art* my God, I will exalt thee. 29. O give thanks unto the LORD; for *he is* good: for his mercy *endureth* for ever.

Psa. 119:7. I will praise thee with uprightness of heart, when I shall have learned thy righteous judgments. 62. At midnight I will rise to give thanks unto thee because of thy righteous judgments. 108. Accept, I beseech thee, the freewill offerings of my mouth, O LORD, and teach me thy judgments. 164. Seven times a day do I praise thee because of thy righteous judgments. 171. My lips shall utter praise, when thou hast taught me thy statutes. 172. My tongue shall speak of thy word: for all thy commandments *are* righteousness. 175. Let my soul live, and it shall praise thee; and let thy judgments help me.

Psa. 134:1. Behold, bless ye the LORD, all *ye* servants of the LORD, which by night stand in the house of the LORD. 2. Lift up your hands *in* the sanctuary, and bless the LORD.

Psa. 135:1. Praise ye the LORD. Praise ye the name of the LORD; praise *him*, O ye servants of the LORD. 2. Ye that stand in the house of the LORD, in the courts of the house of our God, 3. Praise the LORD; for the LORD *is* good: sing praises unto his name; for *it is* pleasant. 19. Bless the LORD, O house of Israel: bless the LORD, O house of Aaron: 20. Bless the LORD, O house of Levi: ye that fear the LORD, bless the LORD. 21. Blessed be the LORD out of Zion, which dwelleth at Jerusalem. Praise ye the LORD.

Psa. 136:2. O give thanks unto the God of gods: for his mercy *endureth* for ever. *vs.* 1-26.

Psa. 138:1. I will praise thee with my whole heart: before the gods I will sing praise unto thee. 2. I will worship toward thy holy temple, and praise thy name for thy lovingkindness and for thy truth:

Psa. 140:13. Surely the righteous shall give thanks unto thy name: the upright shall dwell in thy presence.

Psa. 144:1. Blessed *be* the LORD my strength, which teacheth my hands to war, *and* my fingers to fight: 2. My goodness, and my fortress; my high tower, and my deliverer; my shield, and *he* in whom I trust; who subdueth my people under me. 9. I will sing a new song unto thee, O God: upon a psaltery *and* an instrument of ten strings will I sing praises unto thee.

Psa. 145:1. I will extol thee, my God, O King; and I will bless thy name for ever and ever. 2. Every day will I bless thee; and I will praise thy name for ever and ever. 3. Great *is* the LORD, and greatly to be praised; and his greatness *is* unsearchable. 4. One generation shall praise thy works to another, and shall declare thy mighty acts. 5. I will speak of the glorious honour of thy majesty, and of thy wondrous works. 6. And *men* shall speak of the might of thy terrible acts: and I will declare thy greatness. 7. They shall abundantly utter the memory of thy great goodness, and shall sing of thy righteousness. 8. The LORD *is* gracious, and full of compassion; slow to anger, and of great mercy. 9. The LORD *is* good to all: and his tender mercies *are* over all his works. 10. All thy works shall praise thee, O LORD; and thy saints shall bless thee. 11. They shall speak of the glory of thy kingdom, and talk of thy power; 12. To make known to the sons of men his mighty acts, and the glorious majesty of his kingdom. 13. Thy kingdom *is* an everlasting kingdom, and thy dominion *endureth* throughout all generations. 14. The LORD upholdeth all that fall, and raiseth up all *those that be* bowed down. 15. The eyes of all wait upon thee; and thou givest them their meat in due season. 16. Thou openest thine hand, and satisfiest the desire of every living thing. 17. The LORD *is* righteous in all his ways, and holy in all his works. 18. The LORD *is* nigh unto all them that call upon him, to all that call upon him in truth. 19. He will fulfil the desire of them that fear him: he also will hear their cry, and will save them. 20. The LORD preserveth all them that love him: but all the wicked will he destroy. 21. My mouth shall speak the praise of the LORD: and let all flesh bless his holy name for ever and ever.

Psa. 146:1. Praise ye the LORD. Praise the LORD, O my soul. 2. While I live will I praise the LORD: I will sing praises unto my God while I have any being. 3. Put not your trust in princes, *nor* in the son of man, in whom *there is* no help. 4. His breath goeth forth, he returneth to his earth; in that very day his thoughts perish. 5. Happy *is* he that *hath* the God of Jacob for his help, whose hope *is* in the LORD his

God: 6. Which made heaven, and earth, the sea, and all that therein *is:* which keepeth truth for ever: 7. Which executeth judgment for the oppressed: which giveth food to the hungry. The LORD looseth the prisoners: 8. The LORD openeth *the eyes of* the blind: the LORD raiseth them that are bowed down: the LORD loveth the righteous: 9. The LORD preserveth the strangers: he relieveth the fatherless and widow: but the way of the wicked he turneth upside down. 10. The LORD shall reign for ever, *even* thy God, O Zion, unto all generations. Praise ye the LORD.

Psa. 147:1. Praise ye the LORD: for *it is* good to sing praises unto our God; for *it is* pleasant; *and* praise is comely. 2. The LORD doth build up Jerusalem: he gathereth together the outcasts of Israel. 3. He healeth the broken in heart, and bindeth up their wounds. 4. He telleth the number of the stars; he calleth them all by *their* names. 5. Great *is* our Lord, and of great power: his understanding *is* infinite. 6. The LORD lifteth up the meek: he casteth the wicked down to the ground. 7. Sing unto the LORD with thanksgiving; sing praise upon the harp unto our God: 8. Who covereth the heaven with clouds, who prepareth rain for the earth, who maketh grass to grow upon the mountains. 9. He giveth to the beast his food, *and* to the young ravens which cry. 10. He delighteth not in the strength of the horse: he taketh not pleasure in the legs of a man. 11. The LORD taketh pleasure in them that fear him, in those that hope in his mercy. 12. Praise the LORD, O Jerusalem; praise thy God, O Zion. 13. For he hath strengthened the bars of thy gates; he hath blessed thy children within thee. 14. He maketh peace *in* thy borders, *and* filleth thee with the finest of the wheat. 15. He sendest forth his commandment *upon* earth: his word runneth very swiftly. 16. He giveth snow like wool: he scattereth the hoar frost like ashes. 17. He casteth forth his ice like morsels: who can stand before his cold? 18. He sendeth out his word, and melteth them: he causeth his wind to blow, *and* the waters flow. 19. He sheweth his word unto Jacob, his statutes and his judgments unto Israel. 20. He hath not dealt so with any nation: and *as for his* judgments, they have not known them. Praise ye the LORD.

Psa. 148:1. Praise ye the LORD. Praise ye the LORD from the heavens: praise him in the heights. 2. Praise ye him, all his angels: praise ye him, all his hosts. 3. Praise ye him, sun and moon: praise him, all ye stars of light. 4. Praise him, ye heavens of heavens, and ye waters that *be* above the heavens. 5. Let them praise the name of the LORD: for he commanded, and they were created. 6. He hath also stablished them for ever and ever: he hath made a decree which shall not pass. 7. Praise the LORD from the earth, ye dragons, and all deeps: 8. Fire, and hail; snow, and vapour; stormy wind fulfilling his word: 9. Mountains, and all hills; fruitful trees, and all cedars: 10. Beasts, and all cattle; creeping things, and flying fowl: 11. Kings of the earth, and all people; princes, and all judges of the earth: 12. Both young men, and maidens; old men, and children: 13. Let them praise the name of the Lord: for his name alone is excellent; his glory is above the earth and heaven. 14. He also exalteth the horn of his people, the praise of all his saints; even of the children of Israel, a people near unto him. Praise ye the Lord.

Psa. 149:1. Praise ye the Lord. Sing unto the Lord a new song, and his praise in the congregation of saints. 2. Let Israel rejoice in him that made him: let the children of Zion be joyful in their King. 3. Let them praise his name in the dance: let them sing praises unto him with the timbrel and harp. 4. For the Lord taketh pleasure in his people: he will beautify the meek with salvation. 5. Let the saints be joyful in glory: let them sing aloud upon their beds. 6. Let the high praises of God be in their mouth, and a twoedged sword in their hand; 7. To execute vengeance upon the heathen, and punishments upon the people; 8. To bind their kings with chains, and their nobles with fetters of iron; 9. To execute upon them the judgment written: this honour have all his saints. Praise ye the Lord.

Psa. 150:1. Praise ye the Lord. Praise God in his sanctuary: praise him in the firmament of his power. 2. Praise him for his mighty acts: praise him according to his excellent greatness. 3. Praise him with the sound of the trumpet: praise him with the psaltery and harp. 4. Praise him with the timbrel and dance: praise him with stringed instruments and organs. 5. Praise him upon the loud cymbals: praise him upon the high sounding cymbals. 6. Let every thing that hath breath praise the Lord. Praise ye the Lord.

Isa. 12:1. And in that day thou shalt say, O Lord, I will praise thee: though thou wast angry with me, thine anger is turned away, and thou comfortedst me. 2. Behold, God is my salvation; I will trust, and not be afraid: for the Lord JEHOVAH is my strength and my song; he also is become my salvation. 3. Therefore with joy shall ye draw water out of the wells of salvation. 4. And in that day shall ye say, Praise the Lord, call upon his name, declare his doings among the people, make mention that his name is exalted. 5. Sing unto the Lord; for he hath done excellent things: this is known in all the earth. 6. Cry out and shout, thou inhabitant of Zion: for great is the Holy One of Israel in the midst of thee.

Isa. 24:14. They shall lift up their voice, they shall sing for the majesty of the Lord,

they shall cry aloud from the sea. 15. Wherefore glorify ye the Lord in the fires, even the name of the Lord God of Israel in the isles of the sea. 16. From the uttermost part of the earth have we heard songs, even glory to the righteous.

Isa. 25:1. O Lord, thou art my God; I will exalt thee, I will praise thy name; for thou hast done wonderful things; thy counsels of old are faithfulness and truth.

Isa. 35:10. The ransomed of the Lord shall return, and come to Zion with songs and everlasting joy upon their heads: they shall obtain joy and gladness, and sorrow and sighing shall flee away.

Isa. 38:18. For the grave cannot praise thee, death can not celebrate thee: they that go down into the pit cannot hope for thy truth. 19. The living, the living, he shall praise thee, as I do this day:

Isa. 42:10. Sing unto the Lord a new song, and his praise from the end of the earth, ye that go down to the sea, and all that is therein; the isles, and the inhabitants thereof. 11. Let the wilderness and the cities thereof lift up their voice, the villages that Kedar doth inhabit: let the inhabitants of the rock sing, let them shout from the top of the mountains. 12. Let them give glory unto the Lord, and declare his praise in the islands.

Isa. 43:21. This people have I formed for myself; they shall shew forth my praise.

Isa. 49:13. Sing, O heavens; and be joyful, O earth; and break forth into singing, O mountains: for the Lord hath comforted his people, and will have mercy upon his afflicted.

Isa. 51:3. For the Lord shall comfort Zion: he will comfort all her waste places; and he will make her wilderness like Eden, and her desert like the garden of the Lord; joy and gladness shall be found therein, thanksgiving, and the voice of melody.

Isa. 52:7. How beautiful upon the mountains are the feet of him that bringeth good tidings, that publisheth peace; that bringeth good tidings of good, that publisheth salvation; that saith unto Zion, Thy God reigneth! 8. Thy watchmen shall lift up the voice; with the voice together shall they sing: for they shall see eye to eye, when the Lord shall bring again Zion. 9. Break forth into joy, sing together, ye waste places of Jerusalem: for the Lord hath comforted his people, he hath redeemed Jerusalem. 10. The Lord hath made bare his holy arm in the eyes of all the nations; and all the ends of the earth shall see the salvation of our God.

Isa. 61:3. To appoint unto them that mourn in Zion, to give unto them beauty for ashes, the oil of joy for mourning, the garment of praise for the spirit of heaviness;

Jer. 31:7. Sing with gladness for Jacob, and shout among the chief of the nations: publish ye, praise ye, and say, O Lord, save thy people, the remnant of Israel.

Jer. 33:11. The voice of joy, and the voice of gladness, . . . the voice of them that shall say, Praise the LORD of hosts : for the LORD *is* good; for his mercy *endureth* for ever: *and* of them that shall bring the sacrifice of praise into the house of the LORD.

Dan. 2:20. Blessed be the name of God for ever and ever : for wisdom and might are his : 23. I thank thee, and praise thee, O thou God of my fathers, who hast given me wisdom and might, and hast made known unto me now what we desired of thee : for thou hast *now* made known unto us the king's matter.

Dan. 4:37. I Nebuchadnezzar praise and extol and honour the King of heaven, all whose works *are* truth, and his ways judgment :

Jonah 2:9. I will sacrifice unto thee with the voice of thanksgiving; I will pay *that* that I have vowed.

Matt. 26:30. When they had sung an hymn, they went out into the mount of Olives. Mark 14:26.

Luke 1:46. And Mary said, My soul doth magnify the Lord, 47. And my spirit hath rejoiced in God my Saviour. 48. For he hath regarded the low estate of his handmaiden : for, behold, from henceforth all generations shall call me blessed. 49. For he that is mighty hath done to me great things; and holy *is* his name. 50. And his mercy *is* on them that fear him from generation to generation. 51. He hath shewed strength with his arm; he hath scattered the proud in the imagination of their hearts. 52. He hath put down the mighty from *their* seats, and exalted them of low degree. 53. He hath filled the hungry with good things; and the rich he hath sent empty away. 54. He hath holpen his servant Israel, in remembrance of *his* mercy; 55. As he spake to our fathers, to Abraham, and to his seed for ever. 67. And his father Zacharias was filled with the Holy Ghost, and prophesied, saying, 68. Blessed *be* the Lord God of Israel; for he hath visited and redeemed his people, 69. And hath raised up an horn of salvation for us in the house of his servant David; 70. As he spake by the mouth of his holy prophets, which have been since the world began : 71. That we should be saved from our enemies, and from the hand of all that hate us; 72. To perform the mercy *promised* to our fathers, and to remember his holy covenant; 73. The oath which he sware to our father Abraham, 74. That he would grant unto us, that we being delivered out of the hand of our enemies might serve him without fear, 75. In holiness and righteousness before him, all the days of our life.

Luke 2:20. The shepherds returned, glorifying and praising God for all the things that they had heard and seen, as it was told unto them.

Luke 17:15. And one of them, when he saw that he was healed, turned back, and

with a loud voice glorified God, 16. And fell down on *his* face at his feet, giving him thanks : and he was a Samaritan.

Luke 19:37. And when he was come nigh, even now at the descent of the mount of Olives, the whole multitude of the disciples began to rejoice and praise God with a loud voice for all the mighty works that they had seen; 38. Saying, Blessed *be* the King that cometh in the name of the Lord : peace in heaven, and glory in the highest.

Luke 24:52. And they worshipped him, and returned to Jerusalem with great joy : 53. And were continually in the temple, praising and blessing God.

Acts 2:46. And they, continuing daily with one accord in the temple, and breaking bread from house to house, did eat their meat with gladness and singleness of heart, 47. Praising God, and having favour with all the people.

Acts 4:24. And when they heard that, they lifted up their voice to God with one accord, and said, Lord, thou *art* God, which hast made heaven, and earth, and the sea, and all that in them is :

Acts 16:25. At midnight Paul and Silas prayed, and sang praises unto God : and the prisoners heard them.

Rom. 11:36. For of him, and through him, and to him, *are* all things : to whom *be* glory for ever. Amen.

Rom. 16:27. To God only wise, *be* glory through Jesus Christ for ever.

1 Cor. 14:15. I will sing with the spirit, and I will sing with the understanding also.

1 Cor. 15:57. Thanks *be* to God, which giveth us the victory through our Lord Jesus Christ.

Eph. 1:3. Blessed *be* the God and Father of our Lord Jesus Christ, who hath blessed us with all spiritual blessings in heavenly *places* in Christ :

Eph. 3:20. Now unto him that is able to do exceeding abundantly above all that we ask or think, according to the power that worketh in us, 21. Unto him *be* glory in the church by Christ Jesus throughout all ages, world without end.

Eph. 5:19. Speaking to yourselves in psalms and hymns and spiritual songs, singing and making melody in your heart to the Lord;

Phil. 4:20. Now unto God and our Father *be* glory for ever and ever.

1 Tim. 1:17. Unto the King eternal, immortal, invisible, the only wise God, *be* honour and glory for ever and ever.

Heb. 2:12. I will declare thy name unto my brethren, in the midst of the church will I sing praise unto thee.

Heb. 13:15. By him therefore let us offer the sacrifice of praise to God continually, that is, the fruit of *our* lips giving thanks to his name.

Jas. 5:13. Is any [1] merry? let him sing [2] psalms.   [R. V. [1] cheerful   [2] praise]

1 Pet. 1:3. Blessed *be* the God and Father

of our Lord Jesus Christ, which, according to his abundant mercy, hath begotten us again unto a lively hope by the resurrection of Jesus Christ from the dead,

1 Pet. 2:9. But ye *are* a chosen generation, a royal priesthood, an holy nation, a peculiar people; that ye should shew forth the praises of him who hath called you out of darkness into his marvellous light:

1 Pet. 4:11. If any man speak, *let him speak* as the oracles of God; if any man minister, *let him do it* as of the ability which God giveth; that God in all things may be glorified through Jesus Christ: to whom be praise and dominion for ever and ever.

1 Pet. 5:11. To him *be* glory and dominion for ever and ever.   [Omitted in R. V.]

2 Pet. 3:18. But grow in grace, and *in* the knowledge of our Lord and Saviour Jesus Christ. To him *be* glory both now and for ever.

Jude 25. To the only wise God our Saviour, *be* glory and majesty, dominion and power, both now and ever.

Rev. 1:6. And hath made us kings and priests unto God and his Father; to him *be* glory and dominion for ever and ever.

Rev. 14:7. Saying with a loud voice, Fear God, and give glory to him; for the hour of his judgment is come: and worship him that made heaven, and earth, and the sea, and the fountains of waters.

IN HEAVEN: Neh. 9:6. Thou, *even* thou, *art* LORD alone; thou hast made heaven, the heaven of heavens, with all their host, the earth, and all *things* that *are* therein, the seas, and all *that is* therein, and thou preservest them all; and the host of heaven worshippeth thee.

Job 38:7. When the morning stars sang together, and all the sons of God shouted for joy?

Psa. 103:20. Bless the LORD, ye angels, that excel in strength, that do his commandments, hearkening unto the voice of his word. 21. Bless ye the LORD, all *ye* his hosts; *ye* ministers of his, that do his pleasure.

Psa. 148:2. Praise ye him, all his angels: praise ye him, all his hosts. 4. Praise him, ye heavens of heavens, and ye waters that *be* above the heavens.

Isa. 6:3. One cried unto another, and said, Holy, holy, holy, *is* the LORD of hosts: the whole earth *is* full of his glory.

Ezek. 3:12. Then the spirit took me up, and I heard behind me a voice of a great rushing, *saying*, Blessed *be* the glory of the LORD from his place.

Luke 2:13. Suddenly there was with the angel a multitude of the heavenly host praising God, and saying, 14. Glory to God in the highest, and on earth peace, good will toward men.

Luke 15:10. Likewise, I say unto you, there is joy in the presence of the angels of God over one sinner that repenteth. *v.* 7.

Rev. 1:6. Hath made us kings and priests unto God and his Father; to him *be* glory and dominion for ever and ever.

Rev. 4:8. They rest not day and night, saying, Holy, holy, holy, Lord God Almighty, which was, and is, and is to come. 9. And when those beasts give glory and honour and thanks to him that sat on the throne, who liveth for ever and ever, 10. The four and twenty elders fall down before him that sat on the throne, and worship him that liveth for ever and ever, and cast their crowns before the throne, saying, 11. Thou art worthy, O Lord, to receive glory and honour and power: for thou hast created all things, and for thy pleasure they are, and were created.

Rev. 5:9. They sung a new song, saying, Thou art worthy to take the book, and to open the seals thereof: for thou wast slain, and hast redeemed us to God by thy blood out of every kindred, and tongue, and people, and nation; 10. And hast made us unto our God kings and priests: and we shall reign on the earth. 11. I beheld, and I heard the voice of many angels round about the throne and the beasts and the elders: and the number of them was ten thousand times ten thousand, and thousands of thousands; 12. Saying with a loud voice, Worthy is the Lamb that was slain to receive power, and riches, and wisdom, and strength, and honour, and glory, and blessing. 13. And every creature which is in heaven, and on the earth, and under the earth, and such as are in the sea, and all that are in them, heard I saying, Blessing, and honour, and glory, and power, *be* unto him that sitteth upon the throne, and unto the Lamb for ever and ever. 14. And the four beasts said, Amen. And the four *and* twenty elders fell down and worshipped him that liveth for ever and ever.

Rev. 7:9. After this I beheld, and, lo, a great multitude, which no man could number, of all nations, and kindreds, and people, and tongues, stood before the throne, and before the Lamb, clothed with white robes, and palms in their hands; 10. And cried with a loud voice, saying, Salvation to our God which sitteth upon the throne, and unto the Lamb. 11. And all the angels stood round about the throne, and *about* the elders and the four beasts, and fell before the throne on their faces, and worshipped God, 12. Saying, Amen: Blessing, and glory, and wisdom, and thanksgiving, and honour, and power, and might, *be* unto our God for ever and ever. Amen.

Rev. 11:16. And the four and twenty elders, which sat before God on their seats, fell upon their faces, and worshipped God, 17. Saying, We give thee thanks, O Lord God Almighty, which art, and wast, and art to come; because thou hast taken to thee thy great power, and hast reigned.

Rev. 14:2. And I heard a voice from heaven, as the voice of many waters, and as the voice of a great thunder: and I heard the voice of harpers harping with their harps: 3. And they sung as it were a new song before the throne, and before the four beasts, and the elders: and no man could learn that song but the hundred *and* forty *and* four thousand, which were redeemed from the earth. Rev. 15:3. And they sing the song of Moses the servant of God, and the song of the Lamb, saying, Great and marvellous *are* thy works, Lord God Almighty; just and true *are* thy ways, thou King of saints. 4. Who shall not fear thee, O Lord, and glorify thy name? for *thou* only *art* holy: for all nations shall come and worship before thee; for thy judgments are made manifest. Rev. 19:1. And after these things I heard a great voice of much people in heaven, saying, Alleluia; Salvation, and glory, and honour, and power, unto the Lord our God: 2. For true and righteous *are* his judgments: for he hath judged the great whore, which did corrupt the earth with her fornication, and hath avenged the blood of his servants at her hand. 3. And again they said, Alleluia. And her smoke rose up for ever and ever. 4. And the four and twenty elders and the four beasts fell down and worshipped God that sat on the throne, saying, Amen; Alleluia. 5. And a voice came out of the throne, saying, Praise our God, all ye his servants, and ye that fear him, both small and great. 6. And I heard as it were the voice of a great multitude, and as the voice of many waters, and as the voice of mighty thunderings, saying, Alleluia: for the Lord God omnipotent reigneth. 7. Let us be glad and rejoice, and give honour to him: for the marriage of the Lamb is come, and his wife hath made herself ready.

PRAYER. INDEX OF SUB-TOPICS: *Miscellany of Minor Sub-Topics*, p. 977; *Unclassified Scriptures Relating to*, p. 978; *Answer to, Promised*, p. 979; *Answered*, p. 982; *Instances of Answered*, p. 983; *Confession in*, p. 984; *Importunity in*, p. 985; *Instances of Importunity in*, p. 988; *Intercessory*, p. 988; *Of the Wicked Not Heard*, p. 988; *Pleas Offered in*, p. 988; *Thanksgiving before Taking Food*, p. 991.

MISCELLANY OF MINOR SUB-TOPICS: Attitudes in, see WORSHIP. Prayer test proposed by Elijah, 1 Kin. 18:24-39.

Daily in the morning, Psa. 5:3; 88:13; 143:8; Isa. 33:2; twice daily, Psa. 88:1; thrice daily, Psa. 55:17; Dan. 6:10; all night, Luke 6:12; without ceasing, 1 Thess. 5:17.

Boldness in: Enjoined, Heb. 4:16. Exemplified by Abraham in his inquiry concerning Sodom, Gen. 18:23-32; by Moses, supplicating for assistance in delivering Israel, Ex. 33:12,18. Secret, Gen. 24:63; Matt. 6:6. Silent, Psa. 5:1. Weeping in, Ezra 10:1. In loud voice, satirized by Elijah, 1 Kin. 18:27. Long: Of Pharisees, Matt. 23:14; scribes,

Mark 12:40; Luke 20:47. Profuse, to be avoided, Eccl. 5:2; Matt. 6:7. Vain repetitions of, to be avoided, Matt. 6:7.

Tokens asked for, as assurance of answer: By Abraham's servant, Gen. 24:14. Gideon asks for a sign of dew on a fleece, Judg. 6:36-40.

Rebuked: Of Moses, at the Red Sea, Ex. 14:15, when he prayed to see Canaan, Deut. 3:23-27; of Joshua, Josh. 7:10.

Evils averted by, Jer. 26:19.

Unbelief in, Job. 21:15.

"Lord's Prayer," Matt. 6:9-13; Luke 11:2-4.

Answer to, withheld: Of Balaam, Deut. 23:5; Josh. 24:10; of Job, Job 30:20, with 42:12; of the Israelites, when attacked by the Amorites, Deut. 1:45. The prayer of Jesus, "Let this cup pass," Matt. 26:39,42,44, with *vs.* 45-75 and chapter 27.

Answer to, delayed, Psa. 22:1,2; 40:1; 80:4; 88:14; Jer. 42:7; Hab. 1:2; Luke 18:7.

Answer to, exceeds petition: Solomon asked wisdom; the answer included wisdom, riches, honour, and long life, 1 Kin. 3:7-14; 2 Chr. 1:10-12. The disciples prayed for Peter; the answer included Peter's deliverance, Acts 12:15, with *v*. 5.

Answer to, different from the request: Moses asked to be permitted to cross Jordan; the answer was permission to view the land of promise, Deut. 3:23-27. The Israelites lusted for the fleshpots of Egypt; the answer gave them flesh, but also leanness of soul, Psa. 106:14,15. Martha and Mary asked Jesus to come and heal their brother Lazarus; Jesus delayed, but raised Lazarus from the dead, John 11. Paul asked that the thorn in the flesh be removed; the answer was a promise of grace to endure it, 2 Cor. 12:8,9.

In Behalf of Nations. See NATIONS, PRAYER FOR.

Penitential: Of David, Psa. 51:1-17; the publican, Luke 18:13. See CONFESSION IN, below, and SIN, CONFESSION OF.

Imprecatory, Num. 16:15; 22:6-11; 23:7,8; 24:9,10; Deut. 11:29,30; 27:11-13; 33:11; Josh. 8:33,34; Judg. 16:28; 2 Sam. 16:10-12; Neh. 4:4,5; 5:13; Job 3:1-10; 27:7; Psa. 5:10; 6:10; 9:20; 10:2,15; 25:3; 28:4; 31:17,18; 35:4,8,26; 40:14,15; 54:5; 55:9,15; 56:7; 58:7; 59:5,11,15; 68:1,2; 69:23,24,27,28; 70:2,3; 71:13; 79:10,12; 83:13-17; 94:2; 109:7,9-20,28,29; 119:78,84; 129:5; 140:9,10; 143:12; 144:6; Jer. 11:20; 12:3; 15:15; 17:18; 18:21-23; 20:12; Lam. 1:22; 3:64-66; Gal. 1:8,9; 2 Tim. 4:14,15.

Submission in, exemplified by Jesus, Matt. 26:39; Mark 14:36; Luke 22:42; David, 2 Sam. 12:22,23; Job, Job 1:20,21.

Private, enjoined, Matt. 6:6.

Exemplified: By Lot, Gen. 19:20. Eliezer, Gen. 24:12. Jacob, Gen. 32:9-12. Gideon, Judg. 6:22,36,39. Hannah, 1 Sam. 1:10. David, 2 Sam. 7:18-29. Hezekiah, 2 Kin. 20:2. Isaiah, 2 Kin. 20:11. Manasseh, 2 Chr. 33:18,19. Ezra, Ezra 9:5,6. Nehemiah, Neh. 2:4. Jeremiah, Jer. 32:16-25. Daniel, Dan. 9:3,19. Jonah, Jonah 2:1. Habakkuk, Hab.

1:2. Anna, Luke 2:37. Jesus, Matt. 14:23; 26:36,39; Mark 1:35; Luke 9:18,29. Paul, Acts 9:11. Peter, Acts 9:40; 10:9. Cornelius, Acts 10:30.

Family: By Abraham, Gen. 12:5,8. Jacob, Gen. 35:3. Cornelius, Acts 10:2.

Social: Matt. 18:19; Acts 1:13,14; 16:25; 20:36; 21:5. Held in private houses, Acts 1:13,14; 12:12; in the temple, Acts 2:46; 3:1.

Of Jesus: In a mountain, Matt. 14:23; Mark 6:46; Luke 6:12; 9:28. In Gethsemane, Matt., 26:36; Mark 14:32; Luke 22:45. The Lord's prayer, Matt. 6:9; Luke 11:1. Before day, Mark 1:35. In distress, John 12:27; Heb. 5:7. In the wilderness, Luke 5:16. In behalf of Peter, Luke 22:31,32. For the Comforter, John 14:16. After the supper, John 17. Of the apostles: Acts 1:24,25.

To idols, 1 Kin. 18:26-29.

UNCLASSIFIED SCRIPTURES RELATING TO: Gen. 32:24. And Jacob was left alone; and there wrestled a man with him until the breaking of the day. 25. And when he saw that he prevailed not against him, he touched the hollow of his thigh; and the hollow of Jacob's thigh was out of joint, as he wrestled with him. 26. And he said, Let me go, for the day breaketh. And he said, I will not let thee go, except thou bless me. 27. And he said unto him, What *is* thy name? And he said, Jacob. 28. And he said, Thy name shall be called no more Jacob, but Israel: for as a prince hast thou power with God and with men, and hast prevailed. Hos. 12:4.

1 Chr. 16:11. Seek the Lord and his strength, seek his face continually. 35. And say ye, Save us, O God of our salvation, and gather us together, and deliver us from the heathen, that we may give thanks to thy holy name, *and* glory in thy praise.

2 Chr. 7:14. If my people, which are called by my name, shall humble themselves, and pray, and seek my face, and turn from their wicked ways; then will I hear from heaven, and will forgive their sin, and will heal their land.

Neh. 4:9. Nevertheless we made our prayer unto our God, and set a watch against them day and night, because of them.

Psa. 27:8. *When thou saidst,* Seek ye my face; my heart said unto thee, Thy face, Lord, will I seek.

Psa. 105:3. Glory ye in his holy name: let the heart of them rejoice that seek the Lord. 4. Seek the Lord, and his strength: seek his face evermore.

Psa. 145:18. The Lord *is* nigh unto all them that call upon him, to all that call upon him in truth.

Prov. 15:8. The sacrifice of the wicked *is* an abomination to the Lord: but the prayer of the upright *is* his delight.

Eccl. 5:2. Be not rash with thy mouth, and let not thine heart be hasty to utter *any* thing before God: for God *is* in heaven, and thou upon earth: therefore let thy words be few.

Isa. 55:6. Seek ye the Lord while he may be found, call ye upon him while he is near:

Lam. 3:41. Let us lift up our heart with *our* hands unto God in the heavens.

Zech. 12:10. I will pour upon the house of David, and upon the inhabitants of Jerusalem, the spirit of grace and of supplications: and they shall look upon me whom they have pierced, and they shall mourn for him, as one mourneth for *his* only *son*, and shall be in bitterness for him, as one that is in bitterness for *his* firstborn.

Matt. 6:5. When thou prayest, thou shalt not be as the hypocrites *are:* for they love to pray standing in the synagogues and in the corners of the streets, that they may be seen of men. Verily I say unto you, They have their reward. 6. But thou, when thou prayest, enter into thy closet, and when thou hast shut thy door, pray to thy Father which is in secret; and thy Father which seeth in secret shall reward thee openly. 7. But when ye pray, use not vain repetitions, as the heathen *do:* for they think that they shall be heard for their much speaking. 8. Be not ye therefore like unto them: for your Father knoweth what things ye have need of, before ye ask him. 9. After this manner therefore pray ye: Our Father which art in heaven, Hallowed be thy name. 10. Thy kingdom come. Thy will be done in earth, as *it is* in heaven. 11. Give us this day our daily bread. 12. And forgive us our debts, as we forgive our debtors. 13. And lead us not into temptation, but deliver us from evil: [1] For thine is the kingdom, and the power, and the glory, for ever. [1 Omitted in R. V.]

Matt. 7:7. Ask, and it shall be given you; seek, and ye shall find; knock, and it shall be opened unto you: 8. For every one that asketh receiveth; and he that seeketh findeth; and to him that knocketh it shall be opened. Matt. 21:22; Mark 11:24.

Mark 9:28. And when he was come into the house, his disciples asked him privately, Why could not we cast him out? 29. And he said unto them, This kind can come forth by nothing, but by prayer [1] and fasting. [1 Omitted in R. V.]

Luke 11:1. And it came to pass, that, as he was praying in a certain place, when he ceased, one of his disciples said unto him, Lord, teach us to pray, as John also taught his disciples. 2. And he said unto them, When ye pray, say, Our Father which art in heaven, Hallowed be thy name. Thy kingdom come. [1] Thy will be done, as in heaven, so in earth. 3. Give us day by day our daily bread. 4. And forgive us our sins; for we also forgive every one that is indebted to us. And lead us not into temptation; [1] but deliver us from evil. 5. And he said unto them, Which of you shall have a friend, and shall go unto him at midnight, and say unto him, Friend, lend me three loaves; 6. For a friend of mine in his journey is come to me, and I have nothing to set before him? 7. And he from within shall answer and say, Trouble me not: the door is now shut, and my children are with me in bed; I cannot rise and give thee. 8. I say unto you, Though he will not rise and give him, because he is his friend, yet because of his importunity he will rise and give him as many as he needeth. 9. And I say unto you, Ask, and it shall be given you; seek, and ye shall find; knock, and it shall be opened unto you. 10. For every one that asketh receiveth; and he that seeketh findeth; and to him that knocketh it shall be opened. 11. If a son shall ask bread of any of you that is a father, will he give him a stone? or if *he ask* a fish, will he for a fish give him a serpent? 12. Or if he shall ask an egg, will he offer him a scorpion? 13. If ye then, being evil, know how to give good gifts unto your children: how much more shall *your* heavenly Father give the Holy Spirit to them that ask him?

[1 Omitted in R. V.]

Luke 18:1. And he spake a parable unto them *to this end,* that men ought always *to* pray, and not to faint;

Rom. 8:26. Likewise the Spirit also helpeth our infirmities: for we know not what we should pray for as we ought: but the Spirit itself maketh intercession for us with groanings which cannot be uttered.

1 Cor. 14:15. I will pray with the spirit, and I will pray with the understanding also:

Eph. 3:11. According to the eternal purpose which he purposed in Christ Jesus our Lord: 12. In whom we have boldness and access with confidence by the faith of him.

Eph. 6:18. Praying always with all prayer and supplication in the Spirit, and watching thereunto with all perseverance and supplication for all saints; 19. And for me, that utterance may be given unto me, that I may open my mouth boldly, to make known the mystery of the gospel,

Phil. 4:6. Be careful for nothing; but in every thing by prayer and supplication with thanksgiving let your requests be made known unto God.

Col. 4:2. Continue in prayer, and watch in the same with thanksgiving;

1 Thess. 5:17. Pray without ceasing. 18. In every thing give thanks: for this is the will of God in Christ Jesus concerning you.

1 Tim. 2:8. I will therefore that men pray every where, lifting up holy hands, without wrath and doubting.

Heb. 4:16. Let us therefore come boldly unto the throne of grace, that we may obtain mercy, and find grace to help in time of need.

Jas. 5:16. The effectual fervent prayer of a righteous man availeth much.

Jude 20. But ye, beloved, building up yourselves on your most holy faith, praying in the Holy Ghost,

Rev. 5:8. And when he had taken the book, the four beasts and four *and* twenty elders fell down before the Lamb, having every one of them harps, and golden vials

full of odours, which are the prayers of saints.

Rev. 8:3. And another angel came and stood at the altar, having a golden censer; and there was given unto him much incense, that he should offer *it* with the prayers of all saints upon the golden altar which was before the throne. 4. And the smoke of the incense, *which came* with the prayers of the saints, ascended up before God out of the angel's hand.

ANSWER TO, PROMISED: Ex. 6:5. I have also heard the groaning of the children of Israel, whom the Egyptians keep in bondage; and I have remembered my covenant. Acts 7:34.

Ex. 22:23. If thou afflict them in any wise, and they cry at all unto me, I will surely hear their cry; 27. And it shall come to pass, when he crieth unto me, that I will hear; for I *am* gracious.

Ex. 33:17. And the LORD said unto Moses, I will do this thing also that thou hast spoken: for thou hast found grace in my sight, and I know thee by name. 18. And he said, I beseech thee, shew me thy glory. 19. And he said, I will make all my goodness pass before thee, and I will proclaim the name of the LORD before thee; and will be gracious to whom I will be gracious, and will shew mercy on whom I will shew mercy. 20. And he said, Thou canst not see my face: for there shall no man see me, and live.

Deut. 4:7. What nation *is there* so great, who *hath* God *so* nigh unto them, as the LORD our God *is* in all *things that* we call upon him *for?* 29. But if from thence thou shalt seek the LORD thy God, thou shalt find *him,* if thou seek him with all thy heart and with all thy soul. 30. When thou art in tribulation, and all these things are come upon thee, *even* in the latter days, if thou turn to the LORD thy God, and shalt be obedient unto his voice; 31. (For the LORD thy God *is* a merciful God;) he will not forsake thee, neither destroy thee, nor forget the covenant of thy fathers which he sware unto them.

1 Chr. 28:9. And thou, Solomon my son, know thou the God of thy father, and serve him with a perfect heart and with a willing mind: for the LORD searcheth all hearts, and understandeth all the imaginations of the thoughts: if thou seek him, he will be found of thee; but if thou forsake him, he will cast thee off for ever.

2 Chr. 7:13. If I shut up heaven that there be no rain, or if I command the locusts to devour the land, or if I send pestilence among my people; 14. If my people, which are called by my name, shall humble themselves, and pray, and seek my face, and turn from their wicked ways; then will I hear from heaven, and will forgive their sin, and will heal their land. 15. Now mine eyes shall be open, and mine ears attent unto the prayer *that is made* in this place. 1 Kin. 8:22-53; 2 Chr. **6.**

Job 8:5. If thou wouldest seek unto God betimes, and make thy supplication to the Almighty : 6. If thou *wert* pure and upright ; surely now he would awake for thee, and make the habitation of thy righteousness prosperous.

Job 12:4. I am *as* one mocked of his neighbour, who calleth upon God, and he answereth him :

Job 22:27. Thou shalt make thy prayer unto him, and he shall hear thee, and thou shalt pay thy vows.

Job 33:26. He shall pray unto God, and he will be favourable unto him : and he shall see his face with joy : for he will render unto man his righteousness.

Psa. 9:10. They that know thy name will put their trust in thee : for thou, LORD, hast not forsaken them that seek thee. 12. He forgetteth not the cry of the humble.

Psa. 10:17. LORD, thou hast heard the desire of the humble : thou wilt prepare their heart, thou wilt cause thine ear to hear :

Psa. 18:3. I will call upon the LORD, *who is worthy* to be praised : so shall I be saved from mine enemies.

Psa. 32:6. For this shall every one that is godly pray unto thee in a time when thou mayest be found : surely in the floods of great waters they shall not come nigh unto him.

Psa. 34:15. The eyes of the LORD *are* upon the righteous, and his ears *are open* unto their cry. 17. *The righteous* cry, and the LORD heareth, and delivereth them out of all their troubles.

Psa. 37:4. Delight thyself also in the LORD ; and he shall give thee the desires of thine heart. 5. Commit thy way unto the LORD ; trust also in him ; and he shall bring *it* to pass.

Psa. 38:15. In thee, O LORD, do I hope : thou wilt hear, O Lord my God.

Psa. 50:14. Offer unto God thanksgiving ; and pay thy vows unto the most High : 15. And call upon me in the day of trouble : I will deliver thee, and thou shalt glorify me.

Psa. 55:16. As for me, I will call upon God ; and the LORD shall save me. 17. Evening, and morning, and at noon, will I pray, and cry aloud : and he shall hear my voice.

Psa. 56:9. When I cry *unto thee*, then shall mine enemies turn back : this I know ; for God *is* for me.

Psa. 65:2. O thou that hearest prayer, unto thee shall all flesh come. 5. *By* terrible things in righteousness wilt thou answer us, O God of our salvation ; *who art* the confidence of all the ends of the earth, and of them that are afar off *upon* the sea :

Psa. 69:33. The LORD heareth the poor, and despiseth not his prisoners.

Psa. 81:10. Open thy mouth wide, and I will fill it.

Psa. 86:5. Thou, Lord, *art* good, and ready to forgive ; and plenteous in mercy unto all them that call upon thee. 6. Give ear, O LORD, unto my prayer ; and attend

to the voice of my supplications. 7. In the day of my trouble I will call upon thee : for thou wilt answer me.

Psa. 91:15. He shall call upon me, and I will answer him : I *will be* with him in trouble ; I will deliver him, and honour him.

Psa. 102:17. He will regard the prayer of the destitute, and not despise their prayer. 18. This shall be written for the generation to come : and the people which shall be created shall praise the LORD. 19. For he hath looked down from the height of his sanctuary ; from heaven did the LORD behold the earth ; 20. To hear the groaning of the prisoner ; to loose those that are appointed to death ;

Psa. 145:18. The LORD *is* nigh unto all them that call upon him, to all that call upon him in truth. 19. He will fulfil the desire of them that fear him : he also will hear their cry, and will save them.

Prov. 2:3. Yea, if thou criest after knowledge, *and* liftest up thy voice for understanding ; 5. Then shalt thou understand the fear of the LORD, and find the knowledge of God.

Prov. 3:6. In all thy ways acknowledge him, and he shall direct thy paths.

Prov. 10:24. The fear of the wicked, it shall come upon him : but the desire of the righteous shall be granted.

Prov. 15:8. The sacrifice of the wicked *is* an abomination to the LORD : but the prayer of the upright *is* his delight. 29. The LORD *is* far from the wicked : but he heareth the prayer of the righteous.

Prov. 16:1. The preparations of the heart in man, and the answer of the tongue, *is* from the LORD.

Isa. 19:20. And it shall be for a sign and for a witness unto the LORD of hosts in the land of Egypt : for they shall cry unto the LORD because of the oppressors, and he shall send them a saviour, and a great one, and he shall deliver them.

Isa. 30:19. For the people shall dwell in Zion at Jerusalem : thou shalt weep no more : he will be very gracious unto thee at the voice of thy cry ; when he shall hear it, he will answer thee.

Isa. 55:6. Seek ye the LORD while he may be found, call ye upon him while he is near :

Isa. 58:9. Then shalt thou call, and the LORD shall answer ; thou shalt cry, and he shall say, Here I *am*.

Isa. 65:24. It shall come to pass, that before they call, I will answer ; and while they are yet speaking, I will hear.

Jer. 29:12. Then shall ye call upon me, and ye shall go and pray unto me, and I will hearken unto you. 13. And ye shall seek me, and find *me*, when ye shall search for me with all your heart.

Jer. 31:9. They shall come with weeping, and with supplications will I lead them : I will cause them to walk by the rivers of waters in a straight way, wherein they shall not stumble :

Jer. 33:3. Call unto me, and I will answer thee, and shew thee great and mighty things, which thou knowest not.

Lam. 3:25. The Lord *is* good unto them that wait for him, to the soul *that* seeketh him.

Ezek. 36:37. Thus saith the Lord God; I will yet *for* this be enquired of by the house of Israel, to do *it* for them; I will increase them with men like a flock.

Joel 2:18. Then will the Lord be jealous for his land, and pity his people. 19. Yea, the Lord will answer and say unto his people, Behold, I will send you corn, and wine, and oil, and ye shall be satisfied therewith: and I will no more make you a reproach among the heathen: 32. And it shall come to pass, *that* whosoever shall call on the name of the Lord shall be delivered:

Amos 5:4. For thus saith the Lord unto the house of Israel, Seek ye me, and ye shall live: 5. But seek not Beth-el, nor enter into Gilgal, and pass not to Beer-sheba: for Gilgal shall surely go into captivity, and Beth-el shall come to nought. 6. Seek the Lord, and ye shall live;

Zeph. 2:3. Seek ye the Lord, all ye meek of the earth, which have wrought his judgment; seek righteousness, seek meekness: it may be ye shall be hid in the day of the Lord's anger.

Zech. 10:1. Ask ye of the Lord rain in the time of the latter rain; *so* the Lord shall make bright clouds, and give them showers of rain, to every one grass in the field. 6. And I will strengthen the house of Judah, and I will save the house of Joseph, and I will bring them again to place them; for I have mercy upon them: and they shall be as though I had not cast them off: for I *am* the Lord their God, and will hear them.

Zech. 13:9. They shall call on my name, and I will hear them: I will say, It *is* my people: and they shall say, The Lord *is* my God.

Matt. 6:5. When thou prayest, thou shalt not be as the hypocrites *are:* for they love to pray standing in the synagogues and in the corners of the streets, that they may be seen of men. Verily I say unto you, They have their reward. 6. But thou, when thou prayest, enter into thy closet, and when thou hast shut thy door, pray to thy Father which is in secret; and thy Father which seeth in secret shall reward thee openly. 7. But when ye pray, use not vain repetitions as the heathen *do:* for they think that they shall be heard for their much speaking. 8. Be not ye therefore like unto them: for your Father knoweth what things ye have need of, before ye ask him. 9. After this manner therefore pray ye: Our Father which art in heaven, Hallowed be thy name. *vs.* 9-13.

Matt. 7:7. Ask, and it shall be given you; seek, and ye shall find; knock, and it shall be opened unto you: 8. For every one that asketh receiveth; and he that seeketh find-

eth; and to him that knocketh it shall be opened. 9. Or what man is there of you, whom if his son ask bread, will he give him a stone? 10. Or if he ask a fish, will he give him a serpent? 11. If ye then, being evil, know how to give good gifts unto your children, how much more shall your Father which is in heaven give good things to them that ask him?

Matt. 18:19. Again I say unto you, That if two of you shall agree on earth as touching any thing that they shall ask, it shall be done for them of my Father which is in heaven. 20. For where two or three are gathered together in my name, there am I in the midst of them.

Matt. 21:22. All things, whatsoever ye shall ask in prayer, believing, ye shall receive.

Mark 11:24. Therefore I say unto you, What things soever ye desire, when ye pray, believe that ye receive *them*, and ye shall have *them*. 25. And when ye stand praying, forgive, if ye have ought against any: that your Father also which is in heaven may forgive you your trespasses.

Luke 11:13. If ye then, being evil, know how to give good gifts unto your children: how much more shall *your* heavenly Father give the Holy Spirit to them that ask him? *vs.* 5-12.

Luke 18:6. And the Lord said, Hear what the unjust judge saith. 7. And shall not God avenge his own elect, which cry day and night unto him, though he bear long with them? 8. I tell you that he will avenge them speedily. *vs.* 1-5.

Luke 21:36. Watch ye therefore, and pray always, that ye may be accounted worthy to escape all these things that shall come to pass, and to stand before the Son of man.

John 4:10. Jesus answered and said unto her, If thou knewest the gift of God, and who it is that saith to thee, Give me to drink; thou wouldest have asked of him, and he would have given thee living water. 23. The hour cometh, and now is, when the true worshippers shall worship the Father in spirit and in truth: for the Father seeketh such to worship him. 24. God *is* a Spirit: and they that worship him must worship *him* in spirit and in truth.

John 9:31. Now we know that God heareth not sinners: but if any man be a worshipper of God, and doeth his will, him he heareth.

John 14:13. Whatsoever ye shall ask in my name, that will I do, that the Father may be glorified in the Son. 14. If ye shall ask any thing in my name, I will do *it*.

John 15:7. If ye abide in me, and my words abide in you, ye shall ask what ye will, and it shall be done unto you. 16. Ye have not chosen me, but I have chosen you, and ordained you, that ye should go and bring forth fruit, and *that* your fruit should remain: that whatsoever ye shall ask of the Father in my name, he may give it you.

John 16:23. Whatsoever ye shall ask the Father in my name, he will give *it* you. 24. Hitherto have ye asked nothing in my name: ask, and ye shall receive, that your joy may be full. 26. At that day ye shall ask in my name: and I say not unto you, that I will pray the Father for you: 27. For the Father himself loveth you, because ye have loved me, and have believed that I came out from God.

Acts 22:16. And now why tarriest thou? arise, and be baptized, and wash away thy sins, calling on the name of the Lord.

Rom. 8:26. The Spirit also helpeth our infirmities: for we know not what we should pray for as we ought: but the Spirit itself maketh intercession for us with groanings which cannot be uttered.

Rom. 10:12. For there is no difference between the Jew and the Greek: for the same Lord over all is rich unto all that call upon him. 13. For whosoever shall call upon the name of the Lord shall be saved.

Eph. 2:18. For through him we both have access by one Spirit unto the Father.

Eph. 3:20. Now unto him that is able to do exceeding abundantly above all that we ask or think, according to the power that worketh in us,

Heb. 4:16. Let us therefore come boldly unto the throne of grace, that we may obtain mercy, and find grace to help in time of need.

Heb. 10:22. Let us draw near with a true heart in full assurance of faith, having our hearts sprinkled from an evil conscience, and our bodies washed with pure water. 23. Let us hold fast the profession of *our* faith without wavering; (for he *is* faithful that promised;)

Heb. 11:6. Without faith *it is* impossible to please *him:* for he that cometh to God must believe that he is, and *that* he is a rewarder of them that diligently seek him.

Jas. 1:5. If any of you lack wisdom, let him ask of God, that giveth to all *men* liberally, and upbraideth not; and it shall be given him. 6. But let him ask in faith, nothing wavering. For he that wavereth is like a wave of the sea driven with the wind and tossed. 7. For let not that man think that he shall receive any thing of the Lord.

Jas. 4:8. Draw nigh to God, and he will draw nigh to you. 10. Humble yourselves in the sight of the Lord, and he shall lift you up.

Jas. 5:16. Confess *your* faults one to another, and pray one for another, that ye may be healed. The effectual fervent prayer of a righteous man availeth much.

1 John 3:22. Whatsoever we ask, we receive of him, because we keep his commandments, and do those things that are pleasing in his sight.

1 John 5:14. This is the confidence that we have in him, that, if we ask any thing according to his will, he heareth us: 15. And if we know that he hear us, whatso-ever we ask, we know that we have the petitions that we desired of him.

ANSWERED: Job 34:28. So that they cause the cry of the poor to come unto him, and he heareth the cry of the afflicted.

Psa. 3:4. I cried unto the LORD with my voice, and he heard me out of his holy hill.

Psa. 4:1. Thou hast enlarged me *when I was* in distress; have mercy upon me, and hear my prayer.

Psa. 6:8. Depart from me, all ye workers of iniquity; for the LORD hath heard the voice of my weeping. 9. The LORD hath heard my supplication; the LORD will receive my prayer.

Psa. 18:6. In my distress I called upon the LORD, and cried unto my God: he heard my voice out of his temple, and my cry came before him, *even* into his ears. Psa. 120:1.

Psa. 21:2. Thou hast given him his heart's desire, and hast not withholden the request of his lips. 4. He asked life of thee, *and* thou gavest *it* him, *even* length of days for ever and ever.

Psa. 22:4. Our fathers trusted in thee: they trusted, and thou didst deliver them. 5. They cried unto thee, and were delivered: they trusted in thee, and were not confounded. 24. For he hath not despised nor abhorred the affliction of the afflicted; neither hath he hid his face from him; but when he cried unto him, he heard.

Psa. 28:6. Blessed *be* the LORD, because he hath heard the voice of my supplications.

Psa. 30:2. O LORD my God, I cried unto thee, and thou hast healed me. 3. O LORD, thou hast brought up my soul from the grave: thou hast kept me alive, that I should not go down to the pit.

Psa. 31:22. I said in my haste, I am cut off from before thine eyes: nevertheless thou heardest the voice of my supplications when I cried unto thee.

Psa. 34:4. I sought the LORD, and he heard me, and delivered me from all my fears. 5. They looked unto him, and were lightened: and their faces were not ashamed. 6. This poor man cried, and the LORD heard *him*, and saved him out of all his troubles.

Psa. 40:1. I waited patiently for the LORD: and he inclined unto me, and heard my cry.

Psa. 66:19. Verily God hath heard *me;* he hath attended to the voice of my prayer. 20. Blessed *be* God, which hath not turned away my prayer, nor his mercy from me.

Psa. 77:1. I cried unto God with my voice, *even* unto God with my voice; and he gave ear unto me. 2. In the day of my trouble I sought the Lord:

Psa. 81:7. Thou callest in trouble, and I delivered thee; I answered thee in the secret place of thunder:

Psa. 99:6. Moses and Aaron among his priests, and Samuel among them that call upon his name; they called upon the LORD, and he answered them. 7. He spake unto them in the cloudy pillar: they kept his testimonies, and the ordinance *that* he gave them. 8. Thou answeredst them, O LORD our God: thou wast a God that forgavest them, though thou tookest vengeance of their inventions.

Psa. 106:44. Nevertheless he regarded their affliction, when he heard their cry:

Psa. 107:6. They cried unto the LORD in their trouble, *and* he delivered them out of their distresses. 7. And he led them forth by the right way, that they might go to a city of habitation. *vs.* 13–20.

Psa. 116:1. I love the LORD, because he hath heard my voice *and* my supplications. 2. Because he hath inclined his ear unto me, therefore will I call upon *him* as long as I live.

Psa. 118:5. I called upon the LORD in distress: the LORD answered me, *and set me* in a large place. 21. I will praise thee: for thou hast heard me, and art become my salvation.

Psa. 119:26. I have declared my ways, and thou heardest me:

Psa. 138:3. In the day when I cried thou answeredst me, *and* strengthenedst me *with* strength in my soul.

Lam. 3:57. Thou drewest near in the day *that* I called upon thee: thou saidst, Fear not. 58. O Lord, thou hast pleaded the causes of my soul; thou hast redeemed my life.

Hos. 12:4. Yea, he had power over the angel, and prevailed: he wept, and made supplication unto him: he found him *in* Beth-el, and there he spake with us;

Jonah 2:1. Then Jonah prayed unto the LORD his God out of the fish's belly. 2. And said, I cried by reason of mine affliction unto the LORD, and he heard me; out of the belly of hell cried I, *and* thou heardest my voice. 7. When my soul fainted within me I remembered the LORD: and my prayer came in unto thee, into thine holy temple.

Luke 23:42. And he said unto Jesus, Lord, remember me when thou comest into thy kingdom. 43. And Jesus said unto him, Verily I say unto thee, To day shalt thou be with me in paradise.

Acts 4:31. When they had prayed, the place was shaken where they were assembled together; and they were all filled with the Holy Ghost, and they spake the word of God with boldness.

2 Cor. 12:8. For this thing I besought the Lord thrice, that it might depart from me. 9. And he said unto me, My grace is sufficient for thee: for my strength is made perfect in weakness.

Jas. 5:17. Elias was a man subject to like passions as we are, and he prayed earnestly that it might not rain: and it rained not on the earth by the space of three years and six months. 18. And he prayed again, and the heaven gave rain, and the earth brought forth her fruit.

INSTANCES OF ANSWERED: Cain, Gen. 4: 13–15. Abraham, for a son, Gen. 15; entreat-

ing for Sodom, Gen. 18:23–33; for Ishmael, Gen. 17:20; for Abimelech, Gen. 20:17. Hagar, for deliverance, Gen. 16:7-13. Abraham's servant, for guidance, Gen. 24: 12–52. Rebecca, concerning her pains in pregnancy, Gen. 25:22,23. Jacob, for deliverance from Esau, Gen. 32:9–32; 33:1–17. Moses, for help at the Red Sea, Ex. 14:15,16; at the waters of Marah, Ex. 15:25; at Horeb, Ex. 17:4–6; in the battle with the Amalekites, Ex. 17:8–14; concerning the murmuring of the Israelites for flesh, Num. 11:11-35; in behalf of Miriam's leprosy, Num. 12:13–15. Moses, Aaron, and Samuel, Psa. 99:6.

Israelites: for deliverance from bondage, Ex. 2:23–25; 3:7–10; Acts 7:34; from Pharaoh's army, Ex. 14:10–30; from the king of Mesopotamia, Judg. 3:9,15; Sisera, Judg. 4:3,23,24; 1 Sam. 12:9–11; Ammon, Judg. 10:6–18; 11:1–33; for God's favor under the reproofs of Azariah, 2 Chr. 15:1–15; from Babylonian bondage, Neh. 9:27.

Gideon, asking the token of dew, Judg. 6:36–40. Manoah, asking about Samson, Judg. 13:8,9. Samson, asking for strength, Judg. 16:28–30. Hannah, asking for a child, 1 Sam. 1:10–17,19,20. David, asking whether Keilah would be delivered into his hands, 1 Sam. 23:10–12; and Ziklag, 1 Sam. 30:8; whether he should go into Judah after Saul's death, 2 Sam. 2:1; whether he should go against the Philistines, 2 Sam. 5:19-25. David, in adversity, Psa. 118:5; 138:3. Solomon, asking wisdom, 1 Kin. 3:1-13; 9:2,3. Elijah, raising the widow's son, 1 Kin. 17: 22; asking fire on his sacrifice, 1 Kin. 18:36-38; rain, 1 Kin. 17:1; 18:1,42–45; Jas. 5:17. Elisha, leading the Syrian army, 2 Kin. 6:17-20. Jabez, asking for prosperity, 1 Chr. 4:10. Abijah, for victory over Jeroboam, 2 Chr. 13:14-18. Asa, for victory over Zerah, 2 Chr. 14:11–15. The people of Judah, 2 Chr. 15:15. Jehoshaphat, for victory over the Canaanites, 2 Chr. 18:31; 20:6-27. Jehoahaz, for victory over Hazael, 2 Kin. 13:4. Priests and Levites, when blessing the people, 2 Chr. 30:27. Hezekiah and Isaiah, for deliverance from Sennacherib, 2 Kin. 19:14-20; 2 Chr. 32:20-23; to save Hezekiah's life, 2 Kin. 20:1-7,11; 2 Chr. 32:24. Manasseh, for deliverance from the king of Babylon, 2 Chr. 33:13,19. Reubenites, for deliverance from the Hagarites, 1 Chr. 5:20. The Jews, returning from the captivity, Ezra 8:21,23. Ezekiel, to have the baking of his bread of affliction changed, Ezek. 4:12–15. Daniel, for the interpretation of Nebuchadnezzar's dream, Dan. 2:19–23; interceding for the people, Dan. 9:20–23; in a vision, Dan. 10: 12. Zacharias, for a son, Luke 1:13. The leper, for healing, Matt. 8:2,3; Mark 1:40-43; Luke 5:12,13. Centurion, for his servant, Matt. 8:5-13; Luke 7:3-10; John 4:50,51. Peter, asking that Tabitha be restored, Acts 9:40. The disciples, for Peter, Acts 12: 5–17. Paul, to be restored to health, 2 Cor. 1:9–11.

CONFESSION IN: Lev. 5:5. And it shall be, when he shall be guilty in one of these *things*, that he shall confess that he hath sinned in that *thing:*

Lev. 26:40. If they shall confess their iniquity, and the iniquity of their fathers, with their trespass which they trespassed against me, and that also they have walked contrary unto me;

Num. 5:6. Speak unto the children of Israel, When a man or woman shall commit any sin that men commit, to do a trespass against the LORD, and that person be guilty; 7. Then they shall confess their sin which they have done: *v. 5.*

Judg. 10:10. And the children of Israel cried unto the LORD, saying, We have sinned against thee, both because we have forsaken our God, and also served Baalim. 15. And the children of Israel said unto the LORD, We have sinned: do thou unto us whatsoever seemeth good unto thee; deliver us only, we pray thee, this day.

1 Sam. 12:10. And they cried unto the LORD, and said, We have sinned, because we have forsaken the LORD, and have served Baalim and Ashtaroth: but now deliver us out of the hand of our enemies, and we will serve thee.

1 Kin. 8:47. *Yet* if they shall bethink themselves in the land whither they were carried captives, and repent, and make supplication unto thee in the land of them that carried them captives, saying, We have sinned, and have done perversely, we have committed wickedness;

Ezra 9:6. And said, O my God, I am ashamed and blush to lift up my face to thee, my God: for our iniquities are increased over *our* head, and our trespass is grown up unto the heavens. 15. O LORD God of Israel, thou *art* righteous; for we remain yet escaped, as *it is* this day: behold, we *are* before thee in our trespasses: for we cannot stand before thee because of this.

Neh. 1:6. Let thine ear now be attentive, and thine eyes open, that thou mayest hear the prayer of thy servant, which I pray before thee now, day and night, for the children of Israel thy servants, and confess the sins of the children of Israel, which we have sinned against thee: both I and my father's house have sinned. 7. We have dealt very corruptly against thee, and have not kept the commandments, nor the statutes, nor the judgments, which thou commandest thy servant Moses.

Neh. 9:2. And the seed of Israel separated themselves from all strangers, and stood and confessed their sins, and the iniquities of their fathers. 33. Howbeit thou *art* just in all that is brought upon us; for thou hast done right, but we have done wickedly: 34. Neither have our kings, our princes, our priests, nor our fathers, kept thy law, nor hearkened unto thy commandments and thy testimonies, wherewith thou didst testify against them. 35. For they have not served thee in their kingdom, and in thy great goodness that thou gavest them, and in the large and fat land which thou gavest before them, neither turned they from their wicked works.

Job 7:20. I have sinned; what shall I do unto thee, O thou preserver of men? why hast thou set me as a mark against thee, so that I am a burden to myself?

Job 40:4. Behold, I am vile; what shall I answer thee? I will lay mine hand upon my mouth. 5. Once have I spoken; but I will not answer: yea, twice; but I will proceed no further.

Psa. 31:10. For my life is spent with grief, and my years with sighing: my strength faileth because of mine iniquity, and my bones are consumed.

Psa. 32:3. When I kept silence, my bones waxed old through my roaring all the day long. 5. I acknowledged my sin unto thee, and mine iniquity have I not hid. I said, I will confess my transgressions unto the LORD; and thou forgavest the iniquity of my sin.

Psa. 38:4. For mine iniquities are gone over mine head: as an heavy burden they are too heavy for me. 5. My wounds stink *and* are corrupt because of my foolishness. 6. I am troubled; I am bowed down greatly; I go mourning all the day long. 7. For my loins are filled with a loathsome *disease:* and *there is* no soundness in my flesh. 8. I am feeble and sore broken: I have roared by reason of the disquietness of my heart. 10. My heart panteth, my strength faileth me: as for the light of mine eyes, it also is gone from me. 18. For I will declare mine iniquity; I will be sorry for my sin.

Psa. 40:12. For innumerable evils have compassed me about: mine iniquities have taken hold upon me, so that I am not able to look up; they are more than the hairs of mine head: therefore my heart faileth me.

Psa. 51:3. For I acknowledge my transgressions: and my sin *is* ever before me. 4. Against thee, thee only, have I sinned, and done *this* evil in thy sight: that thou mightest be justified when thou speakest, *and* be clear when thou judgest.

Psa. 69:5. O God, thou knowest my foolishness; and my sins are not hid from thee.

Psa. 106: 6. We have sinned with our fathers, we have committed iniquity, we have done wickedly. 7. Our fathers understood not thy wonders in Egypt; they remembered not the multitude of thy mercies; but provoked *him* at the sea, *even* at the Red sea.

Psa. 119:176. I have gone astray like a lost sheep; seek thy servant; for I do not forget thy commandments.

Psa. 130:3. If thou, LORD, shouldest mark iniquities, O LORD, who shall stand?

Prov. 28:13. He that covereth his sins shall not prosper: but whoso confesseth and forsaketh *them* shall have mercy.

Isa. 6:5. Then said I, Woe *is* me! for I am

undone; because I *am* a man of unclean lips, and I dwell in the midst of a people of unclean lips: for mine eyes have seen the King, the LORD of hosts.

Isa. 59:12. For our transgressions are multiplied before thee, and our sins testify against us: for our transgressions *are* with us; and *as for* our iniquities, we know them; 13. In transgressing and lying against the LORD, and departing away from our God, speaking oppression and revolt, conceiving and uttering from the heart words of falsehood.

Jer. 3:13. Only acknowledge thine iniquity, that thou hast transgressed against the LORD thy God, and hast scattered thy ways to the strangers under every green tree, and ye have not obeyed my voice, saith the LORD. 25. We lie down in our shame, and our confusion covereth us: for we have sinned against the LORD our God, we and our fathers, from our youth even unto this day, and have not obeyed the voice of the LORD our God.

Jer. 14:7. O LORD, though our iniquities testify against us, do thou *it* for thy name's sake: for our backslidings are many; we have sinned against thee. 20. We acknowledge, O LORD, our wickedness, *and* the iniquity of our fathers: for we have sinned against thee.

Lam. 1:18. The LORD is righteous; for I have rebelled against his commandment: hear, I pray you, all people, and behold my sorrow: my virgins and my young men are gone into captivity.

Lam. 3:42. We have transgressed, and have rebelled: thou hast not pardoned.

Lam. 5:16. The crown is fallen *from* our head: woe unto us, that we have sinned!

Dan. 9:5. We have sinned, and have committed iniquity, and have done wickedly, and have rebelled, even by departing from thy precepts and from thy judgments: 6. Neither have we hearkened unto thy servants the prophets, which spake in thy name to our kings, our princes, and our fathers, and to all the people of the land. 7. O Lord, righteousness *belongeth* unto thee, but unto us confusion of faces, as at this day; to the men of Judah, and to the inhabitants of Jerusalem, and unto all Israel, *that are* near, and *that are* far off, through all the countries whither thou hast driven them, because of their trespass that they have trespassed against thee. 8. O Lord, to us *belongeth* confusion of face, to our kings, to our princes, and to our fathers, because we have sinned against thee. 9. To the Lord our God *belong* mercies and forgivenesses, though we have rebelled against him; 10. Neither have we obeyed the voice of the LORD our God, to walk in his laws, which he set before us by his servants the prophets. 11. Yea, all Israel have transgressed thy law, even by departing, that they might not obey thy voice; therefore the curse is poured upon us, and the oath that *is* written in the

law of Moses the servant of God, because we have sinned against him. 12. And he hath confirmed his words, which he spake against us, and against our judges that judged us, by bringing upon us a great evil: for under the whole heaven hath not been done as hath been done upon Jerusalem. 13. As *it is* written in the law of Moses, all this evil is come upon us: yet made we not our prayer before the LORD our God, that we might turn from our iniquities, and understand thy truth. 14. Therefore hath the LORD watched upon the evil, and brought it upon us: for the LORD our God *is* righteous in all his works which he doeth: for we obeyed not his voice. 15. And now, O Lord our God, that hast brought thy people forth out of the land of Egypt with a mighty hand, and hast gotten thee renown, as at this day; we have sinned, we have done wickedly.

IMPORTUNITY IN: Gen. 18:23. And Abraham drew near, and said, Wilt thou also destroy the righteous with the wicked? 24. Peradventure there be fifty righteous within the city: wilt thou also destroy and not spare the place for the fifty righteous that *are* therein? 25. That be far from thee to do after this manner, to slay the righteous with the wicked: and that the righteous should be as the wicked, that be far from thee: Shall not the Judge of all the earth do right? 26. And the LORD said, If I find in Sodom fifty righteous within the city, then I will spare all the place for their sakes. 27. And Abraham answered and said, Behold now, I have taken upon me to speak unto the Lord, which *am but* dust and ashes: 28. Peradventure there shall lack five of the fifty righteous: wilt thou destroy all the city for *lack of* five? And he said, If I find there forty and five, I will not destroy *it*. 29. And he spake unto him yet again, and said, Peradventure there shall be forty found there. And he said, I will not do *it* for forty's sake. 30. And he said *unto him*, Oh let not the Lord be angry, and I will speak: Peradventure there shall thirty be found there. And he said, I will not do *it*, if I find thirty there. 31. And he said, Behold now, I have taken upon me to speak unto the Lord: Peradventure there shall be twenty found there. And he said, I will not destroy *it* for twenty's sake. 32. And he said, Oh let not the Lord be angry, and I will speak yet but this once: Peradventure ten shall be found there.

Gen. 32:24. And Jacob was left alone; and there wrestled a man with him until the breaking of the day. 25. And when he saw that he prevailed not against him, he touched the hollow of his thigh; and the hollow of Jacob's thigh was out of joint, as he wrestled with him. 26. And he said, Let me go, for the day breaketh. And he said, I will not let thee go, except thou bless me. 27. And he said unto him, What *is* thy name? And he said, Jacob.

28. And he said, Thy name shall be called no more Jacob, but Israel: for as a prince hast thou power with God and with men, and hast prevailed. 29. And Jacob asked *him*, and said, Tell *me*, I pray thee, thy name. And he said, Wherefore *is it that* thou dost ask after my name? And he blessed him there.

Ex. 32:32. Yet now, if thou wilt forgive their sin—; and if not, blot me, I pray thee, out of thy book which thou hast written.

Deut. 9:25. Thus I fell down before the LORD forty days and forty nights, as I fell down *at the first;* because the LORD had said he would destroy you.

Judg. 6:36, And Gideon said unto God, If thou wilt save Israel by mine hand, as thou hast said, 37. Behold, I will put a fleece of wool in the floor; *and* if the dew be on the fleece only, and *it be* dry upon all the earth *beside*, then shall I know that thou wilt save Israel by mine hand, as thou hast said. 38. And it was so: for he rose up early on the morrow, and thrust the fleece together, and wringed the dew out of the fleece, a bowl full of water. 39. And Gideon said unto God, Let not thine anger be hot against me, and I will speak but this once: let me prove, I pray thee, but this once with the fleece; let it now be dry only upon the fleece, and upon all the ground let there be dew. 40. And God did so that night: for it was dry upon the fleece only, and there was dew on all the ground.

Judg. 16:28. Samson called unto the LORD, and said, O Lord GOD, remember me, I pray thee, and strengthen me, I pray thee, only this once, O God, that I may be at once avenged of the Philistines for my two eyes.

1 Sam. 1:10. She *was* in bitterness of soul, and prayed unto the LORD, and wept sore. 11. And she vowed a vow, and said, O LORD of hosts, if thou wilt indeed look on the affliction of thine handmaid, and remember me, and not forget thine handmaid, but wilt give unto thine handmaid a man child, then I will give him unto the LORD all the days of his life, and there shall no razor come upon his head.

1 Sam. 12:23. As for me, God forbid that I should sin against the LORD in ceasing to pray for you:

1 Kin. 8:22. And Solomon stood before the altar of the LORD in the presence of all the congregation of Israel, and spread forth his hands toward heaven: 23. And he said, LORD God of Israel, *there is* no God like thee, in heaven above, or on earth beneath, who keepest covenant and mercy with thy servants that walk before thee with all their heart: 24. Who hast kept with thy servant David my father that thou promisedst him: thou spakest also with thy mouth, and hast fulfilled *it* with thine hand, as *it is* this day. 25. Therefore now, LORD God of Israel, keep with thy servant David my father that thou prom-

isedst him, saying, There shall not fail thee a man in my sight to sit on the throne of Israel; so that thy children take heed to their way, that they walk before me as thou hast walked before me. 26. And now, O God of Israel, let thy word, I pray thee, be verified, which thou spakest unto thy servant David my father. 27. But will God indeed dwell on the earth? behold, the heaven and heaven of heavens cannot contain thee; how much less this house that I have builded? 28. Yet have thou respect unto the prayer of thy servant, and to his supplication, O LORD my God, to hearken unto the cry and to the prayer, which thy servant prayeth before thee to day: 29. That thine eyes may be open toward this house night and day, *even* toward the place of which thou hast said, My name shall be there: that thou mayest hearken unto the prayer which thy servant shall make toward this place. 30. And hearken thou to the supplication of thy servant, and of thy people Israel, when they shall pray toward this place: and hear thou in heaven thy dwelling place, and when thou hearest, forgive.

Ezra 9:5. At the evening sacrifice I arose up from my heaviness; and having rent my garment and my mantle, I fell upon my knees, and spread out my hands unto the LORD my God, 6. And said, O my God, I am ashamed and blush to lift up my face to thee, my God: for our iniquities are increased over *our* head, and our trespass is grown up unto the heavens.

Neh. 1:4. And it came to pass, when I heard these words, that I sat down and wept, and mourned *certain* days, and fasted, and prayed before the God of heaven, 5. And said, I beseech thee, O LORD God of heaven, the great and terrible God, that keepeth covenant and mercy for them that love him and observe his commandments: 6. Let thine ear now be attentive, and thine eyes open, that thou mayest hear the prayer of thy servant, which I pray before thee now, day and night, for the children of Israel thy servants, and confess the sins of the children of Israel, which we have sinned against thee: both I and my father's house have sinned.

Psa. 17:1. Hear the right, O LORD, attend unto my cry, give ear unto my prayer, *that goeth* not out of feigned lips. 6. I have called upon thee, for thou wilt hear me, O God: incline thine ear unto me, *and hear* my speech.

Psa. 22:1. My God, my God, why hast thou forsaken me? *why art thou so* far from helping me, *and from* the words of my roaring? 2. O my God, I cry in the daytime, but thou hearest not; and in the night season, and am not silent. 19. But be not thou far from me, O LORD: O my strength, haste thee to help me.

Psa. 28:1. Unto thee will I cry, O LORD my rock; be not silent to me: lest, *if thou* be silent to me, I become like them that go down into the pit. 2. Hear the voice of my supplications, when I cry unto thee, when I lift up my hands toward thy holy oracle.

Psa. 35:22. *This* thou hast seen, O LORD: keep not silence: O Lord, be not far from me. 23. Stir up thyself, and awake to my judgment, *even* unto my cause, my God and my Lord.

Psa. 55:1. Give ear to my prayer, O God; and hide not thyself from my supplication. 2. Attend unto me, and hear me: I mourn in my complaint, and make a noise; 16. As for me, I will call upon God; and the LORD shall save me. 17. Evening, and morning, and at noon, will I pray, and cry aloud: and he shall hear my voice.

Psa. 57:2. I will cry unto God most high; unto God that performeth *all things* for me.

Psa. 61:1. Hear my cry, O God; attend unto my prayer. 2. From the end of the earth will I cry unto thee, when my heart is overwhelmed: lead me to the rock *that* is higher than I.

Psa. 70:5. But I *am* poor and needy: make haste unto me, O God: thou *art* my help and my deliverer; O LORD, make no tarrying.

Psa. 86:3. Be merciful unto me, O Lord: for I cry unto thee daily. 6. Give ear, O LORD, unto my prayer; and attend to the voice of my supplications.

Psa. 88:1. O LORD God of my salvation, I have cried day *and* night before thee: 2. Let my prayer come before thee: incline thine ear unto my cry; 9. LORD, I have called daily upon thee, I have stretched out my hands unto thee. 13. But unto thee have I cried, O LORD; and in the morning shall my prayer prevent thee.

Psa. 102:1. Hear my prayer, O LORD, and let my cry come unto thee. 2. Hide not thy face from me in the day *when* I am in trouble; incline thine ear unto me: in the day *when* I call answer me speedily.

Psa. 119:58. I intreated thy favour with *my* whole heart: be merciful unto me according to thy word. 145. I cried with *my* whole heart; hear me, O LORD: I will keep thy statutes. 146. I cried unto thee; save me, and I shall keep thy testimonies. 147. I prevented the dawning of the morning, and cried: I hoped in thy word.

Psa. 130:1. Out of the depths have I cried unto thee, O LORD. 2. Lord, hear my voice: let thine ears be attentive to the voice of my supplications.

Psa. 141:1. LORD, I cry unto thee: make haste unto me; give ear unto my voice, when I cry unto thee. 2. Let my prayer be set forth before thee *as* incense; *and* the lifting up of my hands *as* the evening sacrifice.

Psa. 142:1. I cried unto the LORD with my voice; with my voice unto the LORD did I make my supplication. 2. I poured out my complaint before him; I shewed before him my trouble.

Isa. 38:2. Then Hezekiah turned his face toward the wall, and prayed unto the LORD, 3. And said, Remember now, O LORD, I beseech thee, how I have walked before thee in truth and with a perfect heart, and have done *that which is* good in thy sight. And Hezekiah wept sore.

Isa. 62:7. And give him no rest, till he establish, and till he make Jerusalem a praise in the earth.

Isa. 64:12. Wilt thou refrain thyself for these *things*, O LORD? wilt thou hold thy peace, and afflict us very sore?

Dan. 9:3. I set my face unto the Lord God, to seek by prayer and supplications, with fasting, and sackcloth, and ashes: 16. O Lord, according to all thy righteousness, I beseech thee, let thine anger and thy fury be turned away from thy city Jerusalem, thy holy mountain: because for our sins, and for the iniquities of our fathers, Jerusalem and thy people *are become* a reproach to all *that are* about us. 17. Now therefore, O our God, hear the prayer of thy servant, and his supplications, and cause thy face to shine upon thy sanctuary that is desolate, for the Lord's sake. 18. O my God, incline thine ear, and hear; open thine eyes, and behold our desolations, and the city which is called by thy name: for we do not present our supplications before thee for our righteousness, but for thy great mercies. 19. O Lord, hear; O Lord, forgive; O Lord, hearken and do; defer not, for thine own sake, O my God: for thy city and thy people are called by thy name.

Jonah 1:14. They cried unto the LORD, and said, We beseech thee, O LORD, we beseech thee, let us not perish for this man's life, and lay not upon us innocent blood:

Hab. 1:2. O LORD, how long shall I cry, and thou wilt not hear! *even* cry out unto thee *of* violence, and thou wilt not save!

Matt. 15:22. And, behold, a woman of Canaan came out of the same coasts, and cried unto him, saying, Have mercy on me, O Lord, *thou* son of David; my daughter is grievously vexed with a devil. 23. But he answered her not a word. And his disciples came and besought him, saying, Send her away; for she crieth after us. 24. But he answered and said, I am not sent but unto the lost sheep of the house of Israel. 25. Then came she and worshipped him, saying, Lord, help me. 26. But he answered and said, It is not meet to take the children's bread, and to cast *it* to dogs. 27. And she said, Truth, Lord: yet the dogs eat of the crumbs which fall from their masters' table. 28. Then Jesus answered and said unto her, O woman, great *is* thy faith: be it unto thee even as thou wilt. And her daughter was made whole from that very hour. Mark 7:25-29.

Luke 7:3. And when he heard of Jesus, he

sent unto him the elders of the Jews, beseeching him that he would come and heal his servant.

Luke 11:5. And he said unto them, Which of you shall have a friend, and shall go unto him at midnight, and say unto him, Friend, lend me three loaves; 6. For a friend of mine in his journey is come to me, and I have nothing to set before him? 7. And he from within shall answer and say, Trouble me not: the door is now shut and my children are with me in bed; I cannot rise and give thee. 8. I say unto you, Though he will not rise and give him, because he is his friend, yet because of his importunity he will rise and give him as many as he needeth.

Luke 18:1. And he spake a parable unto them *to this end*, that men ought always to pray, and not to faint; 2. Saying, There was in a city a judge, which feared not God, neither regarded man: 3. And there was a widow in that city; and she came unto him, saying, Avenge me of mine adversary. 4. And he would not for a while: but afterward he said within himself, Though I fear not God, nor regard man; 5. Yet because this widow troubleth me, I will avenge her, lest by her continual coming she weary me. 6. And the Lord said, Hear what the unjust judge saith. 7. And shall not God avenge his own elect, which cry day and night unto him, though he bear long with them?

Luke 22:44. And being in an agony he prayed more earnestly: and his sweat was as it were great drops of blood falling down to the ground.

Rom. 8:26. Likewise the Spirit also helpeth our infirmities: for we know not what we should pray for as we ought: but the Spirit itself maketh intercession for us with groanings which cannot be uttered.

2 Cor. 12:8. For this thing I besought the Lord thrice, that it might depart from me.

Eph. 6:18. Praying always with all prayer and supplication in the Spirit, and watching thereunto with all perseverance and supplication for all saints;

Heb. 5:7. Who in the days of his flesh, when he had offered up prayers and supplications with strong crying and tears unto him that was able to save him from death, and was heard in that he feared;

INSTANCES OF IMPORTUNITY IN: Jacob, Gen. 32:24–30. See above. Moses, Ex. 33:12–16; 34:9. Elijah, 1 Kin. 18:24–44. The two blind men of Jericho, Matt. 20:30,31; Mark 10:48; Luke 18:39. The Syrophenician woman, Matt. 15:22–28; Mark 7:25–30. The centurion, Matt. 8:5; Luke 7:3,4.

INTERCESSORY: See INTERCESSION; JESUS, MEDIATION OF.

OF THE WICKED NOT HEARD: See WICKED, PRAYER OF.

PLEAS OFFERED IN: Gen. 32:9. And Jacob said, O God of my father Abraham, and God of my father Isaac, the LORD which saidst unto me, Return unto thy country, and to thy kindred, and I will deal well with thee: 10. I am not worthy of the least of all the mercies, and of all the truth, which thou hast shewed unto thy servant; for with my staff I passed over this Jordan; and now I am become two bands. 11. Deliver me, I pray thee, from the hand of my brother, from the hand of Esau: for I fear him, lest he will come and smite me, *and* the mother with the children. 12. And thou saidst, I will surely do thee good, and make thy seed as the sand of the sea, which cannot be numbered for multitude.

Ex. 32:11. And Moses besought the LORD his God, and said, LORD, why doth thy wrath wax hot against thy people, which thou hast brought forth out of the land of Egypt with great power, and with a mighty hand? 12. Wherefore should the Egyptians speak, and say, For mischief did he bring them out, to slay them in the mountains, and to consume them from the face of the earth? Turn from thy fierce wrath, and repent of this evil against thy people. 13. Remember Abraham, Isaac, and Israel, thy servants, to whom thou swarest by thine own self, and saidst unto them, I will multiply your seed as the stars of heaven, and all this land that I have spoken of will I give unto your seed, and they shall inherit *it* for ever.

Ex. 33:13. Now therefore, I pray thee, if I have found grace in thy sight, shew me now thy way, that I may know thee, that I may find grace in thy sight: and consider that this nation *is* thy people.

Num. 14:13. Moses said unto the LORD, Then the Egyptians shall hear *it*, (for thou broughtest up this people in thy might from among them;) 14. And they will tell *it* to the inhabitants of this land: *for* they have heard that thou LORD *art* among this people, that thou LORD art seen face to face, and *that* thy cloud standeth over them, and *that* thou goest before them, by day time in a pillar of a cloud, and *in* a pillar of fire by night. 15. Now *if* thou shalt kill *all* this people as one man, then the nations which have heard the fame of thee will speak, saying, 16. Because the LORD was not able to bring this people into the land which he sware unto them, therefore he hath slain them in the wilderness. 17. I beseech thee, let the power of my Lord be great, according as thou hast spoken, saying, 18. The LORD *is* longsuffering, and of great mercy, forgiving iniquity and transgression, and by no means clearing *the guilty*, visiting the iniquity of the fathers upon the children unto the third and fourth *generation*.

Num. 16:22. And they fell upon their faces, and said, O God, the God of the spirits of all flesh, shall one man sin, and wilt thou be wroth with all the congregation?

Deut. 3:24. O Lord GOD, thou hast begun to shew thy servant thy greatness, and thy mighty hand: for what God *is there* in heaven or in earth, that can do according to

thy works, and according to thy might?
25. I pray thee, let me go over, and see the good land that *is* beyond Jordan,

Deut. 9:18. I fell down before the LORD, as at the first, forty days and forty nights: I did neither eat bread, nor drink water, because of all your sins which ye sinned, in doing wickedly in the sight of the LORD, to provoke him to anger. 25. Thus I fell down before the LORD forty days and forty nights, as I fell down *at the first;* because the LORD had said he would destroy you. 26. I prayed therefore unto the LORD, and said, O Lord GOD, destroy not thy people and thine inheritance, which thou hast redeemed through thy greatness, which thou hast brought forth out of Egypt with a mighty hand. 27. Remember thy servants, Abraham, Isaac, and Jacob; look not unto the stubbornness of this people, nor to their wickedness, nor to their sin: 28. Lest the land whence thou broughtest us out say, Because the LORD was not able to bring them into the land which he promised them, and because he hated them, he hath brought them out to slay them in the wilderness. 29. Yet they *are* thy people and thine inheritance, which thou broughtest out by thy mighty power and by thy stretched out arm.

Josh. 7:8. O Lord, what shall I say, when Israel turneth their backs before their enemies! 9. For the Canaanites and all the inhabitants of the land shall hear *of it,* and shall environ us round, and cut off our name from the earth: and what wilt thou do unto thy great name?

2 Sam. 7:25. And now, O LORD God, the word that thou hast spoken concerning thy servant, and concerning his house, establish *it* for ever, and do as thou hast said. 26. And let thy name be magnified for ever, saying, The LORD of hosts *is* the God over Israel: and let the house of thy servant David be established before thee. 27. For thou, O LORD of hosts, God of Israel, hast revealed to thy servant, saying, I will build thee an house: therefore hath thy servant found in his heart to pray this prayer unto thee. 28. And now, O Lord GOD, thou *art* that God, and thy words be true, and thou hast promised this goodness unto thy servant: 29. Therefore now let it please thee to bless the house of thy servant, that it may continue for ever before thee: for thou, O Lord GOD, hast spoken *it:* and with thy blessing let the house of thy servant be blessed for ever.

1 Kin. 8:25. Therefore now, LORD God of Israel, keep with thy servant David my father that thou promisedst him, saying, There shall not fail thee a man in my sight to sit on the throne of Israel; so that thy children take heed to their way, that they walk before me as thou hast walked before me. 26. And now, O God of Israel, let thy word, I pray thee, be verified, which thou spakest unto thy servant David my father. 59. And let these my words, wherewith I

have made supplication before the LORD, be nigh unto the LORD our God day and night, that he maintain the cause of his servant, and the cause of his people Israel at all times, as the matter shall require: 60. That all the people of the earth may know that the LORD *is* God, *and that there is* none else.

1 Kin. 18:36. And it came to pass at *the time of* the offering of the *evening* sacrifice, that Elijah the prophet came near, and said, LORD God of Abraham, Isaac, and of Israel, let it be known this day that thou *art* God in Israel, and *that* I *am* thy servant, and *that* I have done all these things at thy word. 37. Hear me, O LORD, hear me, that this people may know that thou *art* the LORD God, and *that* thou hast turned their heart back again.

2 Kin. 19:15. And Hezekiah prayed before the LORD, and said, O LORD God of Israel, which dwellest *between* the cherubims, thou art the God, *even* thou alone, of all the kingdoms of the earth; thou hast made heaven and earth. 16. LORD, bow down thine ear, and hear: open, LORD, thine eyes, and see: and hear the words of Sennacherib, which hath sent him to reproach the living God. 17. Of a truth, LORD, the kings of Assyria have destroyed the nations and their lands, 18. And have cast their gods into the fire: for they *were* no gods, but the work of men's hands, wood and stone: therefore they have destroyed them. 19. Now therefore, O LORD our God, I beseech thee, save thou us out of his hand, that all the kingdoms of the earth may know that thou *art* the LORD God, *even* thou only. Isa. 37:15-20.

2 Chr. 14:11. And Asa cried unto the LORD his God, and said, LORD, *it is* nothing with thee to help, whether with many, or with them that have no power: help us, O LORD our God; for we rest on thee, and in thy name we go against this multitude. O LORD, thou *art* our God; let not man prevail against thee.

Neh. 1:8. Remember, I beseech thee, the word that thou commandedst thy servant Moses, saying, *If* ye transgress, I will scatter you abroad among the nations: 9. But *if* ye turn unto me, and keep my commandments, and do them; though there were of you cast out unto the uttermost part of the heaven, *yet* will I gather them from thence, and will bring them unto the place that I have chosen to set my name there.

Neh. 9:32. Now therefore, our God, the great, the mighty, and the terrible God, who keepest covenant and mercy, let not all the trouble seem little before thee, that hath come upon us, on our kings, on our princes, and on our priests, and on our prophets, and on our fathers, and on all thy people, since the time of the kings of Assyria unto this day.

Psa. 4:1. Hear me when I call, O God of my righteousness: thou hast enlarged me *when I was* in distress; have mercy upon me, and hear my prayer.

Psa. 9:19. Arise, O LORD; let not man prevail: let the heathen be judged in thy sight. 20. Put them in fear, O LORD: *that* the nations may know themselves *to be but* men.

Psa. 25:6. Remember, O LORD, thy tender mercies and thy lovingkindnesses; for they *have been* ever of old.

Psa. 27:9. Hide not thy face *far* from me; put not thy servant away in anger: thou hast been my help; leave me not, neither forsake me, O God of my salvation.

Psa. 31:3. Thou *art* my rock and my fortress; therefore for thy name's sake lead me, and guide me.

Psa. 38:16. For I said, *Hear me*, lest *otherwise* they should rejoice over me: when my foot slippeth, they magnify *themselves* against me.

Psa. 69:6. Let not them that wait on thee, O Lord GOD of hosts, be ashamed for my sake: let not those that seek thee be confounded for my sake, O God of Israel. 13. But as for me, my prayer *is* unto thee, O LORD, *in* an acceptable time: O God, in the multitude of thy mercy hear me, in the truth of thy salvation. 16. For thy lovingkindness *is* good: turn unto me according to the multitude of thy tender mercies.

Psa. 71:18. Now also when I am old and grayheaded, O God, forsake me not; until I have shewed thy strength unto *this* generation, *and* thy power to every one *that* is to come.

Psa. 74:10. O God, how long shall the adversary reproach? shall the enemy blaspheme thy name for ever? 11. Why withdrawest thou thy hand, even thy right hand? pluck *it* out of thy bosom. 18. Remember this, *that* the enemy hath reproached, O LORD, and *that* the foolish people have blasphemed thy name. 20. Have respect unto the covenant: for the dark places of the earth are full of the habitations of cruelty. 21. O let not the oppressed return ashamed: let the poor and needy praise thy name. 22. Arise, O God, plead thine own cause: remember how the foolish man reproacheth thee daily. 23. Forget not the voice of thine enemies: the tumult of those that rise up against thee increaseth continually.

Psa. 79:10. Wherefore should the heathen say, Where *is* their God? let him be known among the heathen in our sight *by* the revenging of the blood of thy servants *which* is shed. 11. Let the sighing of the prisoner come before thee; according to the greatness of thy power preserve thou those that are appointed to die; 12. And render unto our neighbours sevenfold into their bosom their reproach, wherewith they have reproached thee, O Lord.

Psa. 83:1. Keep not thou silence, O God: hold not thy peace, and be not still, O God. 2. For, lo, thine enemies make a tumult: and they that hate thee have lifted up the head. 18. That *men* may know that thou,

whose name alone *is* JEHOVAH, *art* the most high over all the earth.

Psa. 86:1. Bow down thine ear, O LORD, hear me: for I *am* poor and needy. 2. Preserve my soul; for I *am* holy: O thou my God, save thy servant that trusteth in thee. 3. Be merciful unto me, O Lord: for I cry unto thee daily. 4. Rejoice the soul of thy servant: for unto thee, O Lord, do I lift up my soul. 5. For thou, Lord, *art* good, and ready to forgive; and plenteous in mercy unto all them that call upon thee. 17. Shew me a token for good; that they which hate me may see *it*, and be ashamed: because thou, LORD, hast holpen me, and comforted me.

Psa. 89:49. Lord, where *are* thy former lovingkindnesses, *which* thou swarest unto David in thy truth? 50. Remember, Lord, the reproach of thy servants; *how* I do bear in my bosom *the reproach of* all the mighty people; 51. Wherewith thine enemies have reproached, O LORD; wherewith they have reproached the footsteps of thine anointed.

Psa. 106:47. Save us, O LORD our God, and gather us from among the heathen, to give thanks unto thy holy name, *and* to triumph in thy praise.

Psa. 109:21. But do thou for me, O GOD the Lord, for thy name's sake: because thy mercy *is* good, deliver thou me. 22. For I *am* poor and needy, and my heart is wounded within me. 23. I am gone like the shadow when it declineth: I am tossed up and down as the locust. 24. My knees are weak through fasting; and my flesh faileth of fatness. 25. I became also a reproach unto them: *when* they looked upon me they shaked their heads. 26. Help me, O LORD my God: O save me according to thy mercy: 27. That they may know that this *is* thy hand; *that* thou, LORD, hast done it.

Psa. 115:1. Not unto us, O LORD, not unto us, but unto thy name give glory, for thy mercy, *and* for thy truth's sake. 2. Wherefore should the heathen say, Where *is* now their God?

Psa. 119:38. Stablish thy word unto thy servant, who *is devoted* to thy fear. 42. So shall I have wherewith to answer him that reproacheth me; for I trust in thy word. 43. And take not the word of truth utterly out of my mouth; for I have hoped in thy judgments. 49. Remember the word unto thy servant, upon which thou hast caused me to hope. 73. Thy hands have made me and fashioned me: give me understanding, that I may learn thy commandments. 94. I *am* thine, save me; for I have sought thy precepts. 116. Uphold me according unto thy word, that I may live: and let me not be ashamed of my hope. 124. Deal with thy servant according unto thy mercy, 145. I cried with *my* whole heart; hear me, O LORD: I will keep thy statutes. 146. I cried unto thee; save me, and I shall keep thy testimonies. 149. Hear my voice according unto thy lovingkindness: O LORD, quicken me according to thy judgment. 153. Consider mine affliction, and deliver me: for I do not forget thy law. 173. Let thine hand help me; for I have chosen thy precepts. 174. I have longed for thy salvation, O LORD; and thy law *is* my delight. 175. Let my soul live, and it shall praise thee; and let thy judgments help me. 176. I have gone astray like a lost sheep; seek thy servant; for I do not forget thy commandments.

Psa. 143:11. Quicken me, O LORD, for thy name's sake: for thy righteousness' sake bring my soul out of trouble. 12. And of thy mercy cut off mine enemies, and destroy all them that afflict my soul: for I *am* thy servant.

Isa. 63:17. O LORD, why hast thou made us to err from thy ways, *and* hardened our heart from thy fear? Return for thy servants' sake, the tribes of thine inheritance. 18. The people of thy holiness have possessed *it* but a little while: our adversaries have trodden down thy sanctuary. 19. We are *thine:* thou never barest rule over them; they were not called by thy name.

Jer. 14:21. Do not abhor *us*, for thy name's sake; do not disgrace the throne of thy glory: remember, break not thy covenant with us.

Jer. 18:20. Shall evil be recompensed for good? for they have digged a pit for my soul. Remember that I stood before thee to speak good for them, *and* to turn away thy wrath from them. 21. Therefore deliver up their children to the famine, and pour out their *blood* by the force of the sword; and let their wives be bereaved of their children, and *be* widows; and let their men be put to death; *let* their young men *be* slain by the sword in battle.

Lam. 3:56. Thou hast heard my voice: hide not thine ear at my breathing, at my cry. 57. Thou drewest near in the day *that* I called upon thee: thou saidst, Fear not. 58. O Lord, thou hast pleaded the causes of my soul; thou hast redeemed my life. 59. O LORD, thou hast seen my wrong: judge thou my cause. 60. Thou hast seen all their vengeance *and* all their imaginations against me. 61. Thou hast heard their reproach, O LORD, *and* all their imaginations against me; 62. The lips of those that rose up against me, and their device against me all the day. 63. Behold their sitting down, and their rising up; I *am* their musick.

Joel 2:17. Let the priests, the ministers of the LORD, weep between the porch and the altar, and let them say, Spare thy people, O LORD, and give not thine heritage to reproach, that the heathen should rule over them: wherefore should they say among the people, Where *is* their God?

THANKSGIVING AND, BEFORE TAKING FOOD: Josh. 9:14. And the men took of their victuals, and asked not *counsel* at the mouth of the LORD.

1 Sam. 9:13. As soon as ye be come into the city, ye shall straightway find him, before he go up to the high place to eat: for the people will not eat until he come, because he doth bless the sacrifice; *and* afterwards they eat that be bidden. Now therefore get you up; for about this time ye shall find him.

Matt. 14:19. And he commanded the multitude to sit down on the grass, and took the five loaves, and the two fishes, and looking up to heaven, he blessed, and brake, and gave the loaves to *his* disciples, and the disciples to the multitude. Mark 6:41; Luke 9:16; John 6:11,23.

Matt. 26:26. And as they were eating, Jesus took bread, and blessed *it*, and brake *it*, and gave *it* to the disciples, and said, Take, eat; this is my body. 27. And he took the cup, and gave thanks, and gave *it* to them, saying, Drink ye all of it; Mark 14:22,23; Luke 22:19; 1 Cor. 11:24.

Mark 8:6. And he commanded the people to sit down on the ground: and he took the seven loaves, and gave thanks, and brake, and gave to his disciples to set before *them;* and they did set *them* before the people. 7. And they had a few small fishes: and he blessed, and commanded to set them also before *them.* Matt. 15:36.

Acts 27:35. And when he had thus spoken, he took bread, and gave thanks to God in presence of them all: and when he had broken *it*, he began to eat.

Rom. 14:6. He that eateth, eateth to the Lord, for he giveth God thanks; and he that eateth not, to the Lord he eateth not, and giveth God thanks.

1 Cor. 10:30. For if I by grace be a partaker, why am I evil spoken of for that for which I give thanks? 31. Whether therefore ye eat, or drink, or whatsoever ye do, do all to the glory of God.

1 Tim. 4:3. Forbidding to marry, *and commanding* to abstain from meats, which God hath created to be received with thanksgiving of them which believe and know the truth. 4. For every creature of God *is* good, and nothing to be refused, if it be received with thanksgiving: 5. For it is sanctified by the word of God and prayer.

PRAYERFULNESS. Psa. 5:1. Give ear to my words, O LORD, consider my meditation. 2. Hearken unto the voice of my cry, my King, and my God: for unto thee will I pray. 3. My voice shalt thou hear in the morning, O LORD; in the morning will I direct *my prayer* unto thee, and will look up.

Psa. 42:8. *Yet* the LORD will command his lovingkindness in the daytime, and in the night his song *shall be* with me, *and* my prayer unto the God of my life.

Psa. 109:4. For my love they are my adversaries: but I *give myself unto* prayer.

Psa. 116:2. Because he hath inclined his

ear unto me, therefore will I call upon *him* as long as I live.

Dan. 6:10. Now when Daniel knew that the writing was signed, he went into his house; and his windows being open in his chamber toward Jerusalem, he kneeled upon his knees three times a day, and prayed, and gave thanks before his God, as he did aforetime.

Luke 2:37. She *was* a widow of about fourscore and four years, which departed not from the temple, but served *God* with fastings and prayers night and day.

Acts 6:4. But we will give ourselves continually to prayer, and to the ministry of the word.

Acts 10:2. A devout *man*, and one that feared God with all his house, which gave much alms to the people, and prayed to God alway. 9. On the morrow, as they went on their journey, and drew nigh unto the city, Peter went up upon the housetop to pray about the sixth hour :

Rom. 1:9. For God is my witness, whom I serve with my spirit in the gospel of his Son, that without ceasing I make mention of you always in my prayers ;

Rom. 12:12. Rejoicing in hope; patient in tribulation; continuing instant in prayer ;

Eph. 1:15. Wherefore I also, . . . 16. Cease not to give thanks for you, making mention of you in my prayers ;

Col. 1:9. For this cause we also, since the day we heard *it*, do not cease to pray for you, and to desire that ye might be filled with the knowledge of his will in all wisdom and spiritual understanding ;

1 Thess. 3:10. Night and day praying exceedingly that we might see ʸour face, and might perfect that which is lacking in your faith ?

1 Thess. 5:17. Pray without ceasing.

1 Tim. 5:5. Now she that is a widow indeed, and desolate, trusteth in God, and, continueth in supplications and prayers night and day.

2 Tim. 1:3. I thank God, whom I serve from *my* forefathers with pure conscience, that without ceasing I have remembrance of thee in my prayers night and day;

PRAYERLESSNESS. Job 15:4. Yea, thou castest off fear, and restrainest prayer before God.

Job 21:14. Therefore they say unto God, Depart from us; for we desire not the knowledge of thy ways. 15. What *is* the Almighty, that we should serve him ? and what profit should we have, if we pray unto him ?

Job 27:10. Will he delight himself in the Almighty ? will he always call upon God ?

Psa. 14:4. Have all the workers of iniquity no knowledge ? who eat up my people *as* they eat bread, and call not upon the LORD. Psa. 53:4.

Psa. 79:6. Pour out thy wrath upon the heathen that have not known thee, and

upon the kingdoms that have not called upon thy name.

Isa. 43:22. But thou hast not called upon me, O Jacob; but thou hast been weary of me, O Israel.

Isa. 64:7. *There is* none that calleth upon thy name, that stirreth up himself to take hold of thee :

Jer. 10:21. For the pastors are become brutish, and have not sought the LORD: therefore they shall not prosper, and all their flocks shall be scattered. 25. Pour out thy fury upon the heathen that know thee not, and upon the families that call not on thy name :

Dan. 9:13. As *it is* written in the law of Moses, all this evil is come upon us: yet made we not our prayer before the LORD our God, that we might turn from our iniquities, and understand thy truth.

Hos. 7:7. They are all hot as an oven, and have devoured their judges; all their kings are fallen : *there is* none among them that calleth uɲ me.

Jonah 1:6. So the shipmaster came to him, and said unto him, What meanest thou, O sleeper ? arise, call upon thy God, if so be that God will think upon us, that we perish not.

Zeph. 1:6. And them that are turned back from the LORD; and *those* that have not sought the LORD, nor enquired for him.

PREACHING, the act of exhorting, prophesying, reproving, teaching. Solomon called preacher, Eccl. 1:1,12. Noah called preacher, 2 Pet. 2:5. Sitting while, Matt. 5:1; Luke 4:20; 5:3. Moses, slow of speech, Ex. 4:10-12.

Repentance, the subject of John the Baptist's, Matt. 3:2; Mark 1:4,15; Luke 3:3; of Christ's, Matt. 4:17; Mark 1:15; the apostles, Mark 6:12. "The Gospel of the Kingdom of God," the subject of Christ's, Mark 1:14,15; 2:2; Luke 8:1. Christ crucified and risen, the burden of Paul's, Acts 17:3.

Effective: By Azariah, 2 Chr. 15:1-15; by Jonah, Jonah 3; by Peter and other apostles, Acts 2:14-41; by Philip, Acts 8: 5-12,27-38; by Paul, Acts 9:20; 13:16-43. See REVIVALS.

Impenitence under : Of Asa, 2 Chr. 16:7-10; Ahab, 2 Chr. 18:7-26; the Jews, Acts 13:46.

See OBDURACY. See also MINISTER ; CALL, PERSONAL.

UNCLASSIFIED SCRIPTURES RELATING TO : Matt. 11:25. At that time Jesus answered and said, I thank thee, O Father, Lord of heaven and earth, because thou hast hid these things from the wise and prudent, and hast revealed them unto babes. [Psa. 8:2.] 26. Even so, Father: for so it seemed good in thy sight. Luke 10:21.

1 Cor. 1:17. For Christ sent me not to baptize, but to preach the gospel: not with wisdom of words, lest the cross of Christ should be made of none effect. 18. For the

preaching of the cross is to them that perish foolishness; but unto us which are saved it is the power of God. 21. For after that in the wisdom of God the world by wisdom knew not God, it pleased God by the foolishness of preaching to save them that believe. 23. We preach Christ crucified, unto the Jews a stumblingblock, and unto the Greeks foolishness; 27. God hath chosen the foolish things of the world to confound the wise; and God hath chosen the weak things of the world to confound the things which are mighty; 28. And base things of the world, and things which are despised, hath God chosen, *yea*, and things which are not, to bring to nought things that are: 29. That no flesh should glory in his presence.

1 Cor. 2:1. And I, brethren, when I came to you, came not with excellency of speech or of wisdom, declaring unto you the testimony of God. 2. For I determined not to know any thing among you, save Jesus Christ, and him crucified. 3. And I was with you in weakness, and in fear, and in much trembling. 4. And my speech and my preaching *was* not with enticing words of man's wisdom, but in demonstration of the Spirit and of power: 5. That your faith should not stand in the wisdom of men, but in the power of God. 6. Howbeit we speak wisdom among them that are perfect: yet not the wisdom of this world, nor of the princes of this world, that come to nought: 7. But we speak the wisdom of God in a mystery, *even* the hidden *wisdom*, which God ordained before the world unto our glory: 8. Which none of the princes of this world knew: for had they known *it*, they would not have crucified the LORD of glory. 12. Now we have received, not the spirit of the world, but the spirit which is of God; that we might know the things that are freely given to us of God. 13. Which things also we speak, not in the words which man's wisdom teacheth, but which the Holy Ghost teacheth; comparing spiritual things with spiritual.

1 Cor. 14:1. Follow after charity, and desire spiritual *gifts*, but rather that ye may prophesy. 2. For he that speaketh in an *unknown* tongue speaketh not unto men, but unto God: for no man understandeth *him;* howbeit in the spirit he speaketh mysteries. 3. But he that prophesieth speaketh unto men *to* edification, and exhortation, and comfort. 4. He that speaketh in an *unknown* tongue edifieth himself; but he that prophesieth edifieth the church. 5. I would that ye all spake with tongues, but rather that ye prophesied: for greater *is* he that prophesieth than he that speaketh with tongues, except he interpret, that the church may receive edifying. 6. Now, brethren, if I come unto you speaking with tongues, what shall I profit you, except I shall speak to you either by revelation, or by knowledge, or by prophesying, or by doctrine? 7.

And even things without life giving sound, whether pipe or harp, except they give a distinction in the sounds, how shall it be known what is piped or harped? 8. For if the trumpet give an uncertain sound, who shall prepare himself to the battle? 9. So likewise ye, except ye utter by the tongue words easy to be understood, how shall it be known what is spoken? for ye shall speak into the air. 10. There are, it may be, so many kinds of voices in the world, and none of them *is* without signification. 11. Therefore if I know not the meaning of the voice, I shall be unto him that speaketh a barbarian, and he that speaketh *shall be* a barbarian unto me. 12. Even so ye, forasmuch as ye are zealous of spiritual *gifts*, seek that ye may excel to the edifying of the church. 13. Wherefore let him that speaketh in an *unknown* tongue pray that he may interpret. 14. For if I pray in an *unknown* tongue, my spirit prayeth, but my understanding is unfruitful. 15. What is it then? I will pray with the spirit, and I will pray with the understanding also: I will sing with the spirit, and I will sing with the understanding also. 16. Else when thou shalt bless with the spirit, how shall he that occupieth the room of the unlearned say Amen at thy giving of thanks, seeing he understandeth not what thou sayest? 17. For thou verily givest thanks well, but the other is not edified. 18. I thank my God, I speak with tongues more than ye all: 19. Yet in the church I had rather speak five words with my understanding, that *by my voice* I might teach others also, than ten thousand words in an *unknown* tongue. 20. Brethren, be not children in understanding: howbeit in malice be ye children, but in understanding be men. 24. But if all prophesy, and there come in one that believeth not, or *one* unlearned, he is convinced of all, he is judged of all: 25. And thus are the secrets of his heart made manifest; and so falling down on *his* face he will worship God, and report that God is in you of a truth.

2 Cor. 2:14. Now thanks *be* unto God, which always causeth us to triumph in Christ, and maketh manifest the savour of his knowledge by us in every place. 15. For we are unto God a sweet savour of Christ, in them that are saved, and in them that perish: 16. To the one *we are* the savour of death unto death; and to the other the savour of life unto life. And who *is* sufficient for these things?

2 Cor. 3:12. Seeing then that we have such hope, we use great plainness of speech: 13. And not as Moses, *which* put a vail over his face, that the children of Israel could not stedfastly look to the end of that which is abolished:

Col. 1:23. If ye continue in the faith grounded and settled, and *be* not moved away from the hope of the gospel, which ye have heard, *and* which was preached to every creature which is under heaven; whereof I Paul am made a minister; 24. Who now rejoice in my sufferings for you, and fill up that which is behind of the afflictions of Christ in my flesh for his body's sake, which is the church : 25. Whereof I am made a minister, according to the dispensation of God which is given to me for you, to fulfil the word of God ; 26. *Even* the mystery which hath been hid from ages and from generations, but now is made manifest to his saints : 27. To whom God would make known what *is* the riches of the glory of this mystery among the Gentiles ; which is Christ in you, the hope of glory : 28. Whom we preach, warning every man, and teaching every man in all wisdom; that we may present every man perfect in Christ Jesus : 29. Whereunto I also labour, striving according to his working, which worketh in me mightily.

1 Thess. 1:5. For our gospel came not unto you in word only, but also in power, and in the Holy Ghost,

1 Thess. 2:3. For our exhortation *was* not of deceit, nor of uncleanness, nor in guile : 4. But as we were allowed of God to be put in trust with the gospel, even so we speak; not as pleasing men, but God, which trieth our hearts. 5. For neither at any time used we flattering words, as ye know, nor a cloke of covetousness ; God *is* witness : 6. Nor of men sought we glory, neither of you, nor *yet* of others, when we might have been burdensome, as the apostles of Christ. 7. But we were gentle among you, even as a nurse cherisheth her children : 8. So being affectionately desirous of you, we were willing to have imparted unto you, not the gospel of God only, but also our own souls, because ye were dear unto us. 9. For ye remember, brethren, our labour and travail : for labouring night and day, because we would not be chargeable unto any of you, we preached unto you the gospel of God. 10. Ye *are* witnesses, and God *also*, how holily and justly and unblameably we behaved ourselves among you that believe : 11. As ye know how we exhorted and comforted and charged every one of you, as a father *doth* his children, 12. That ye would walk worthy of God, who hath called you unto his kingdom and glory.

1 Tim. 6:20. O Timothy, keep that which is committed to thy trust, avoiding profane *and* vain babblings, and oppositions of science falsely so called : 21. Which scme professing have erred concerning the faith.

2 Tim. 2:15. Study to shew thyself approved unto God, a workman that needeth not to be ashamed, rightly dividing the word of truth. 16. But shun profane *and* vain babblings :

Tit. 1:3. But hath in due times manifested his word through preaching, which is committed unto me according to the commandment of God our Saviour;

Tit. 3:8. *This is* a faithful saying, and these things I will that thou affirm constantly, that they which have believed in God might be careful to maintain good works. 9. But avoid foolish questions, and genealogies, and contentions, and strivings about the law; for they are unprofitable and vain.

PRECEPTS. See Commandments ; Law.

PRECIOUS STONES. See Stones.

PREDESTINATION. Gen. 21:12. In Isaac shall thy seed be called. 13. And also of the son of the bondwoman will I make a nation, because he *is* thy seed.

Ex. 9:16. And in very deed for this *cause* have I raised thee up, for to shew *in* thee my power; and that my name may be declared throughout all the earth.

Ex. 33:19. And he said, I will make all my goodness pass before thee, and I will proclaim the name of the Lord before thee; and will be gracious to whom I will be gracious, and will shew mercy on whom I will shew mercy.

Deut. 7:7. The Lord did not set his love upon you, nor choose you, because ye were more in number than any people ; for ye *were* the fewest of all people : 8. But because the Lord loved you, and because he would keep the oath which he had sworn unto your fathers, hath the Lord brought you out with a mighty hand, and redeemed you out of the house of bondmen, from the hand of Pharaoh king of Egypt.

Deut. 10:15. Only the Lord had a delight in thy fathers to love them, and he chose their seed after them, *even* you above all people, as *it is* this day. Deut. 4:37.

Deut. 32:8. When the Most High divided to the nations their inheritance, when he separated the sons of Adam, he set the bounds of the people according to the number of the children of Israel.

Josh. 11:20. For it was of the Lord to harden their hearts, that they should come against Israel in battle, that he might destroy them utterly, *and* that they might have no favour, but that he might destroy them, as the Lord commanded Moses.

1 Sam. 12:22. For the Lord will not forsake his people for his great name's sake : because it hath pleased the Lord to make you his people.

1 Kin. 12:15. Wherefore the king hearkened not unto the people ; for the cause was from the Lord, that he might perform his saying, which the Lord spake by Ahijah the Shilonite unto Jeroboam the son of Nebat.

1 Kin. 20:42. And he said unto him, Thus saith the Lord, Because thou hast let go out of *thy* hand a man whom I appointed to utter destruction, therefore thy life shall go for his life, and thy people for his people.

2 Kin. 19:25. Hast thou not heard long ago *how* I have done it, *and* of ancient times that I have formed it? now have I brought it to pass, that thou shouldest be to lay waste fenced cities *into* ruinous heaps.

2 Chr. 6:6. But I have chosen Jerusalem, that my name might be there; and have chosen David to be over my people Israel.

Job 23:13. But he *is* in one *mind*, and who can turn him? and *what* his soul desireth, even *that* he doeth. 14. For he performeth *the thing that is* appointed for me: and many such *things are* with him.

Psa. 33:12. Blessed *is* the nation whose God *is* the LORD; *and* the people *whom* he hath chosen for his own inheritance.

Psa. 65:4. Blessed *is the man whom* thou choosest, and causest to approach *unto thee, that* he may dwell in thy courts: we shall be satisfied with the goodness of thy house, *even* of thy holy temple.

Psa. 78:67. Moreover he refused the tabernacle of Joseph, and chose not the tribe of Ephraim: 68. But chose the tribe of Judah, the mount Zion which he loved. 70. He chose David also his servant, and took him from the sheepfolds: 71. From following the ewes great with young he brought him to feed Jacob his people, and Israel his inheritance. 72. So he fed them according to the integrity of his heart; and guided them by the skilfulness of his hands.

Psa. 105:17. He sent a man before them, *even* Joseph, *who* was sold for a servant: 18. Whose feet they hurt with fetters: he was laid in iron: 19. Until the time that his word came: the word of the LORD tried him. 20. The king sent and loosed him; *even* the ruler of the people, and let him go free. 21. He made him lord of his house, and ruler of all his substance: 22. To bind his princes at his pleasure; and teach his senators wisdom.

Psa. 135:4. For the LORD hath chosen Jacob unto himself, *and* Israel for his peculiar treasure.

Prov. 16:4. The LORD hath made all *things* for himself: yea, even the wicked for the day of evil.

Isa. 44:1. Yet now hear, O Jacob my servant; and Israel, whom I have chosen: 2. Thus saith the LORD that made thee, and formed thee from the womb, *which* will help thee; Fear not, O Jacob, my servant; and thou, Jesurun, whom I have chosen. 7. And who, as I, shall call, and shall declare it, and set it in order for me, since I appointed the ancient people? and the things that are coming, and shall come, let them shew unto them.

Jer. 1:4. Then the word of the LORD came unto me, saying, 5. Before I formed thee in the belly I knew thee; and before thou camest forth out of the womb I sanctified thee, *and* I ordained thee a prophet unto the nations.

Mal. 1:2. I have loved you, saith the LORD. Yet ye say, Wherein hast thou loved us? *Was* not Esau Jacob's brother? saith the LORD: yet I loved Jacob, 3. And I hated Esau, and laid his mountains and his heritage waste for the dragons of the wilderness.

Matt 11:25. At that time Jesus answered and said, I thank thee, O Father, Lord of heaven and earth, because thou hast hid these things from the wise and prudent, and hast revealed them unto babes. 26. Even so, Father: for so it seemed good in thy sight.

Matt. 20:16. So the last shall be first, and the first last: [1] for many be called, but few chosen. [chapter 22:14.] 23. And he saith unto them, Ye shall drink indeed of my cup, [1] and be baptized with the baptism that I am baptized with: but to sit on my right hand, and on my left, is not mine to give, but *it shall be given to them* for whom it is prepared of my Father.

[1 Omitted in R. V.]

Matt. 24:22. And except those days should be shortened, there should no flesh be saved: but for the elect's sake those days shall be shortened. [Mark 13:20.] 40. Then shall two be in the field; the one shall be taken, and the other left. *v.* 41; Luke 17:34-36.

Matt. 25:34. Then shall the King say unto them on his right hand, Come, ye blessed of my Father, inherit the kingdom prepared for you from the foundation of the world:

Mark 13:20. And except that the Lord had shortened those days, no flesh should be saved: but for the elect's sake, whom he hath chosen, he hath shortened the days. 22. For false Christs and false prophets shall rise, and shall shew signs and wonders, to seduce, if *it were* possible, even the elect.

Luke 4:25. But I tell you of a truth, many widows were in Israel in the days of Elias, when the heaven was shut up three years and six months, when great famine was throughout all the land; 26. But unto none of them was Elias sent, save unto Sarepta, *a city* of Sidon, unto a woman *that was* a widow. 27. And many lepers were in Israel in the time of Eliseus the prophet; and none of them was cleansed, saving Naaman the Syrian.

Luke 8:10. And he said, Unto you it is given to know the mysteries of the kingdom of God: but to others in parables; that seeing they might not see, and hearing they might not understand.

Luke 10:20. Notwithstanding in this rejoice not, that the spirits are subject unto you; but rather rejoice, because your names are written in heaven.

Luke 18:7. And shall not God avenge his own elect, which cry day and night unto him, though he bear long with them?

Luke 22:22. And truly the Son of man goeth, as it was determined: but woe unto that man by whom he is betrayed. Matt. 26:24; Mark. 14:21.

John 6:37. All that the Father giveth me shall come to me; and him that cometh to me I will in no wise cast out. 39. And this is the Father's will which hath sent me, that of all which he hath given me I should lose nothing, but should raise it up again at the last day. 44. No man can come to me, except the Father which hath sent me draw him: and I will raise him up at the last day. 45. It is written in the prophets, And they shall be all taught of God. Every man therefore that hath heard, and hath learned of the Father, cometh unto me.

John 15:16. Ye have not chosen me, but I have chosen you, and ordained you, that ye should go and bring forth fruit, and *that* your fruit should remain: that whatsoever ye shall ask of the Father in my name, he may give it you. 19. If ye were of the world, the world would love his own: but because ye are not of the world, but I have chosen you out of the world, therefore the world hateth you.

John 17:2. Thou hast given him power over all flesh, that he should give eternal life to as many as thou hast given him. 6. I have manifested thy name unto the men which thou gavest me out of the world: thine they were, and thou gavest them me; 9. I pray for them: I pray not for the world, but for them which thou hast given me; for they are thine.

John 21:23. Then went this saying abroad among the brethren, that that disciple should not die: yet Jesus said not unto him, He shall not die; but, If I will that he tarry till I come, what *is that* to thee?

Acts 1:7. And he said unto them, It is not for you to know the times or the seasons, which the Father hath put in his own power.

Acts 2:23. Him, being delivered by the determinate counsel and foreknowledge of God, ye have taken, and by wicked hands have crucified and slain: 39. For the promise is unto you, and to your children, and to all that are afar off, *even* as many as the Lord our God shall call. 47. And the Lord added to the church daily such as should be saved.

Acts 3:18. Those things, which God before had shewed by the mouth of all his prophets, that Christ should suffer, he hath so fulfilled.

Acts 4:28. For to do whatsoever thy hand and thy counsel determined before to be done.

Acts 13:48. And when the Gentiles heard this, they were glad, and glorified the word of the Lord: and as many as were ordained to eternal life believed.

Acts 17:26. And hath made of one blood all nations of men for to dwell on all the face of the earth, and hath determined the times before appointed, and the bounds of their habitation;

Acts 22:14. And he said, The God of our fathers hath chosen thee, that thou shouldest know his will, and see that Just One, and shouldest hear the voice of his mouth.

Rom. 1:6. Among whom are ye also the called of Jesus Christ:

Rom. 8:28. And we know that all things work together for good to them that love God, to them who are the called according to *his* purpose. 29. For whom he did foreknow, he also did predestinate *to be* con-

formed to the image of his Son, that he might be the firstborn among many brethren. 30. Moreover whom he did predestinate, them he also called: and whom he called, them he also justified: and whom he justified, them he also glorified. 33. Who shall lay any thing to the charge of God's elect?

Rom. 9:11 (For *the children* being not yet born, neither having done any good or evil, that the purpose of God according to election might stand, not of works, but of him that calleth;) 12. It was said unto her, The elder shall serve the younger. 13. As it is written, Jacob have I loved, but Esau have I hated. 14. What shall we say then? *Is there* unrighteousness with God? God forbid. 15. For he saith to Moses, I will have mercy on whom I will have mercy, and I will have compassion on whom I will have compassion. 16. So then *it is* not of him that willeth, nor of him that runneth, but of God that sheweth mercy. 17. For the scripture saith unto Pharaoh, Even for this same purpose have I raised thee up, that I might shew my power in thee, and that my name might be declared throughout all the earth. 18. Therefore hath he mercy on whom he will *have mercy*, and whom he will he hardeneth. [*vs.* 7-33.] 23. And that he might make known the riches of his glory on the vessels of mercy, which he had afore prepared unto glory. 24. Even us, whom he hath called, not of the Jews only, but also of the Gentiles? 27. Esaias also crieth concerning Israel, Though the number of the children of Israel be as the sand of the sea, a remnant shall be saved: 28. For he will finish the work, and cut *it* short in righteousness: because a short work will the Lord make upon the earth. 29. And as Esaias said before, Except the Lord of sabaoth had left us a seed, we had been as Sodoma, and been made like unto Gomorrha.

Rom. 11:5. Even so then at this present time also there is a remnant according to the election of grace. 7. What then? Israel hath not obtained that which he seeketh for; but the election hath obtained it, and the rest were blinded 8. (According as it is written, God hath given them the spirit of slumber, eyes that they should not see, and ears that they should not hear;) unto this day.

1 Cor. 1:26. For ye see your calling, brethren, how that not many wise men after the flesh, not many mighty, not many noble, *are called:* 27. But God hath chosen the foolish things of the world to confound the wise; and God hath chosen the weak things of the world to confound the things which are mighty; 28. And base things of the world, and things which are despised, hath God chosen, *yea,* and things which are not, to bring to nought things that are: 29. That no flesh should glory in his presence.

1 Cor. 2:7. But we speak the wisdom of God in a mystery, *even* the hidden *wisdom,* which God ordained before the world unto our glory:

Gal. 1:15. But when it pleased God, who separated me from my mother's womb, and called *me* by his grace,

Eph. 1:4. According as he hath chosen us in him before the foundation of the world, that we should be holy and without blame before him in love: 5. Having predestinated us unto the adoption of children by Jesus Christ to himself, according to the good pleasure of his will, 9. Having made known unto us the mystery of his will, according to his good pleasure which he hath purposed in himself: 10. That in the dispensation of the fulness of times he might gather together in one all things in Christ, both which are in heaven, and which are on earth; *even* in him: 11. In whom also we have obtained an inheritance, being predestinated according to the purpose of him who worketh all things after the counsel of his own will:

Eph. 2:10. For we are his workmanship, created in Christ Jesus unto good works, which God hath before ordained that we should walk in them.

Eph. 3:11. According to the eternal purpose which he purposed in Christ Jesus our Lord:

Col. 3:12. Put on therefore, as the elect of God, holy and beloved, bowels of mercies, kindness, humbleness of mind, meekness, longsuffering;

1 Thess. 1:4. Knowing, brethren ¹ beloved, your election ² of God.

[R. V. ¹ beloved of God   ² Omitted.]

1 Thess. 2:12. That ye would walk worthy of God, who hath called you unto his kingdom and glory.

2 Thess. 2:13. But we are bound to give thanks alway to God for you, brethren beloved of the Lord, because God hath from the beginning chosen you to salvation through sanctification of the Spirit and belief of the truth:

2 Tim. 1:9. Who hath saved us, and called *us* with an holy calling, not according to our works, but according to his own purpose and grace, which was given us in Christ Jesus before the world began,

Tit. 1:1. Paul, a servant of God, and an apostle of Jesus Christ, according to the faith of God's elect, and the acknowledging of the truth which is after godliness; 2. In hope of eternal life, which God, that cannot lie, promised before the world began;

Jas. 1:18. Of his own will begat he us with the word of truth, that we should be a kind of firstfruits of his creatures.

1 Pet. 1:2. Elect according to the foreknowledge of God the Father, through sanctification of the Spirit, unto obedience and sprinkling of the blood of Jesus Christ: 20. Who verily was foreordained before the foundation of the world, but was manifest in these last times for you,

2 Pet. 1:10. Wherefore the rather, brethren, give diligence to make your calling and election sure: for if ye do these things, ye shall never fall:

Jude 4. For there are certain men crept in unawares, who were before of old ordained to this condemnation, ungodly men, turning the grace of our God into lasciviousness, and denying the only Lord God, and our Lord Jesus Christ.

Rev. 13:8. All that dwell upon the earth shall worship him, whose names are not written in the book of life of the Lamb slain from the foundation of the world.

PRESCIENCE. See GOD, FOREKNOWLEDGE OF.

PRESENTS. To Abraham, by Pharaoh, Gen. 12:16; by Abimelech, Gen. 20:14. To Rebecca, Gen. 24:22. To Esau, Gen. 32:13–15. To prophets, 1 Kin. 14:3; 2 Kin. 4:42. To those in adversity, Job 42:10,11.

Betrothal, Gen. 24:53. Marriage, Esth. 2:18. Propitiatory, Gen. 32:20; 33:8–11; 1 Sam. 25: 27–35; Prov. 21:14. To confirm covenants, Gen. 21:28–30; 1 Sam. 18:3,4. Rewards of service, Dan. 5:7. Kings to kings, 2 Sam. 8:10; 1 Kin. 10:10,13; 15:18,19.

To corrupt courts, forbidden, Ex. 23:8; Deut. 16:19; 27:25; Isa. 5:23. See BRIBERY.

See LIBERALITY.

PRESUMPTION. Ex. 5:2. And Pharaoh said, Who *is* the LORD, that I should obey his voice to let Israel go? I know not the LORD, neither will I let Israel go.

Ex. 14:11. And they said unto Moses, Because *there were* no graves in Egypt, hast thou taken us away to die in the wilderness? wherefore hast thou dealt thus with us, to carry us forth out of Egypt? 12. *Is* not this the word that we did tell thee in Egypt, saying, Let us alone, that we may serve the Egyptians? For *it had been* better for us to serve the Egyptians, than that we should die in the wilderness.

Ex. 17:7. And he called the name of the place Massah, and Meribah, because of the chiding of the children of Israel, and because they tempted the LORD, saying, Is the LORD among us, or not?

Num. 15:30. But the soul that doeth *ought* presumptuously, *whether he be* born in the land, or a stranger, the same reproacheth the LORD; and that soul shall be cut off from among his people.

Num. 16:41. But on the morrow all the congregation of the children of Israel murmured against Moses and against Aaron, saying, Ye have killed the people of the LORD.

Num. 21:5. And the people spake against God, and against Moses, Wherefore have ye brought us up out of Egypt to die in the wilderness? for *there is* no bread, neither *is there any* water; and our soul loatheth this light bread.

Deut. 29:19. And it come to pass, when he heareth the words of this curse, that he bless himself in his heart, saying, I shall have peace, though I walk in the imagination of mine heart, to add drunkenness to thirst: 20. The LORD will not spare him, but then the anger of the LORD and his jealousy shall smoke against that man, and all the curses that are written in this book shall lie upon him, and the LORD shall blot out his name from under heaven.

1 Kin. 20:28. Thus saith the LORD, Because the Syrians have said, The LORD is God of the hills, but he is not God of the valleys, therefore will I deliver all this great multitude into thine hand, and ye shall know that I am the LORD.

1 Kin. 22:24. But Zedekiah the son of Chenaanah went near, and smote Micaiah on the cheek, and said, Which way went the Spirit of the LORD from me to speak unto thee?

Job 15:25. For he stretcheth out his hand against God, and strengtheneth himself against the Almighty.

Psa. 19:13. Keep back thy servant also from presumptuous sins; let them not have dominion over me: then shall I be upright, and I shall be innocent from the great transgression.

Psa. 131:1. LORD, my heart is not haughty, nor mine eyes lofty: neither do I exercise myself in great matters, or in things too high for me.

Prov. 18:12. Before destruction the heart of man is haughty, and before honour is humility. 13. He that answereth a matter before he heareth it, it is folly and shame unto him.

Prov. 25:6. Put not forth thyself in the presence of the king, and stand not in the place of great men: 7. For better it is that it be said unto thee, Come up hither; than that thou shouldest be put lower in the presence of the prince whom thine eyes have seen.

Isa. 5:18. Woe unto them that draw iniquity with cords of vanity, and sin as it were with a cart rope: 19. That say, Let him make speed, and hasten his work, that we may see it: and let the counsel of the Holy One of Israel draw nigh and come, that we may know it! 20. Woe unto them that call evil good, and good evil; that put darkness for light, and light for darkness; that put bitter for sweet, and sweet for bitter! 21. Woe unto them that are wise in their own eyes, and prudent in their own sight! 22. Woe unto them that are mighty to drink wine, and men of strength to mingle strong drink: 23. Which justify the wicked for reward, and take away the righteousness of the righteous from him! 24. Therefore as the fire devoureth the stubble, and the flame consumeth the chaff, so their root shall be as rottenness, and their blossom shall go up as dust: because they have cast away the law of the LORD of hosts, and despised the word of the Holy One of Israel. 25. Therefore is the anger of the LORD kindled against his people, and he hath stretched forth his hand against them, and hath smitten them: and the hills did tremble, and their carcases were torn in the midst of the streets. For all this his anger is not turned away, but his hand is stretched out still.

Isa. 10:15. Shall the ax boast itself against him that heweth therewith? or shall the saw magnify itself against him that shaketh it? as if the rod should shake itself against them that lift it up, or as if the staff should lift up itself, as if it were no wood.

Isa. 14:13. For thou hast said in thine heart, I will ascend into heaven, I will exalt my throne above the stars of God: I will sit also upon the mount of the congregation, in the sides of the north: 14. I will ascend above the heights of the clouds; I will be like the most High.

Isa. 28:14. Wherefore hear the word of the LORD, ye scornful men, that rule this people which is in Jerusalem. 15. Because ye have said, We have made a covenant with death, and with hell are we at agreement; when the overflowing scourge shall pass through, it shall not come unto us: for we have made lies our refuge, and under falsehood have we hid ourselves: 16. Therefore thus saith the Lord GOD, Behold, I lay in Zion for a foundation a stone, a tried stone, a precious corner stone, a sure foundation: he that believeth shall not make haste. 17. Judgment also will I lay to the line, and righteousness to the plummet: and the hail shall sweep away the refuge of lies, and the waters shall overflow the hiding place. 18. And your covenant with death shall be disannulled, and your agreement with hell shall not stand; when the overflowing scourge shall pass through, then ye shall be trodden down by it. 22. Now therefore be ye not mockers, lest your bands be made strong: for I have heard from the Lord GOD of hosts a consumption, even determined upon the whole earth.

Isa. 29:15. Woe unto them that seek deep to hide their counsel from the LORD, and their works are in the dark, and they say, Who seeth us? and who knoweth us? 16. Surely your turning of things upside down shall be esteemed as the potter's clay: for shall the work say of him that made it, He made me not? or shall the thing framed say of him that framed it, He had no understanding? 20. The scorner is consumed, and all that watch for iniquity are cut off:

Isa. 45:9. Woe unto him that striveth with his Maker! Let the potsherd strive with the potsherds of the earth. Shall the clay say to him that fashioneth it, What makest thou? or thy work, He hath no hands? 10. Woe unto him that saith unto his father, What begettest thou? or to the woman, What hast thou brought forth?

Isa. 58:3. Wherefore have we fasted, say they, and thou seest not? wherefore have we afflicted our soul, and thou takest no knowledge? Behold, in the day of your fast ye find pleasure, and exact all your labours.

Isa. 65:5. Which say, Stand by thyself,

come not near to me; for I am holier than thou.

Jer. 23:34. And *as for* the prophet, and the priest, and the people, that shall say, The burden of the LORD, I will even punish that man and his house.

Matt. 4:5. Then the devil taketh him up into the holy city, and setteth him on a pinnacle of the temple, 6. And saith unto him, If thou be the Son of God, cast thyself down: for it is written, He shall give his angels charge concerning thee: and in *their* hands they shall bear thee up, lest at any time thou dash thy foot against a stone. [Luke 4:9-11.] 7. Jesus said unto him, It is written again, Thou shalt not tempt the Lord thy God. Deut. 6:16.

Luke 12:18. And he said, This will I do: I will pull down my barns, and build greater; and there will I bestow all my fruits and my goods. 19. And I will say to my soul, Soul, thou hast much goods laid up for many years; take thine ease, eat, drink, *and* be merry. 20. But God said unto him, *Thou* fool, this night thy soul shall be required of thee: then whose shall those things be, which thou hast provided?

Luke 14:7. And he put forth a parable to those which were bidden, when he marked how they chose out the chief rooms; saying unto them, 8. When thou art bidden of any *man* to a wedding, sit not down in the highest room; lest a more honourable man than thou be bidden of him; 9. And he that bade thee and him come and say to thee, Give this man place; and thou begin with shame to take the lowest room. 10. But when thou art bidden, go and sit down in the lowest room; that when he that bade thee cometh, he may say unto thee, Friend, go up higher: then shalt thou have worship in the presence of them that sit at meat with thee. 11. For whosoever exalteth himself shall be abased; and he that humbleth himself shall be exalted.

Luke 18:11. The Pharisee stood and prayed thus with himself, God, I thank thee, that I am not as other men *are*, extortioners, unjust, adulterers, or even as this publican. 12. I fast twice in the week, I give tithes of all that I possess.

Rom. 1:32. Who knowing the judgment of God, that they which commit such things are worthy of death, not only do the same, but have pleasure in them that do them.

Rom. 9:20. Nay but, O man, who art thou that repliest against God? Shall the thing formed say to him that formed *it*, Why hast thou made me thus? 21. Hath not the potter power over the clay, of the same lump to make one vessel unto honour, and another unto dishonour?

1 Cor. 10:9. Neither let us tempt Christ, as some of them also tempted, and were destroyed of serpents. 10. Neither murmur ye, as some of them also murmured, and were destroyed of the destroyer. 11. Now all these things happened unto them for ensamples: and they are written for our admonition, upon whom the ends of the world are come. 12. Wherefore let him that thinketh he standeth take heed lest he fall.

2 Thess. 2:3. The son of perdition; 4. Who opposeth and exalteth himself above all that is called God, or that is worshipped; so that he as God sitteth in the temple of God, shewing himself that he is God.

Jas. 4:13. Go to now, ye that say, To day or to morrow we will go into such a city, and continue there a year, and buy and sell, and get gain: 14. Whereas ye know not what *shall be* on the morrow. For what *is* your life? It is even a vapour, that appeareth for a little time, and then vanisheth away. 15. For that ye *ought* to say, If the Lord will, we shall live, and do this, or that. 16. But now ye rejoice in your boastings: all such rejoicing is evil.

2 Pet. 2:10. But chiefly them that walk after the flesh in the lust of uncleanness, and despise government. Presumptuous *are they*, selfwilled, they are not afraid to speak evil of dignities. 11. Whereas angels, which are greater in power and might, bring not railing accusation against them before the Lord.

INSTANCES OF: Satan, when he said to Eve, "Ye shall not surely die," Gen. 3:1-5. Builders of Babel, Gen. 11:4. Abraham, in questioning about Sodom, Gen. 18:23-32. Moses, in upbraiding Jehovah, Num. 11:11-15,22. Nadab and Abihu, Lev. 10:1,2. Israelites, in ascending to the top of the hill against the Amalekites. Num. 14:44,45; murmuring at Meribah, Ex. 17:2,7; in reviling God, Mal. 1:6,7,12; 3:7,8,13. Korah, Dathan, and Abiram, Num. 16:3. Saul, in sacrificing, 1 Sam. 13:8-14; sparing the Amalekites, 1 Sam. 15:3,9-23. Men of Beth-shemesh, 1 Sam. 6:19. Uzzah, in steadying the ark, 2 Sam. 6:6,7. David's anger at Uzzah's death, 2 Sam. 6:8. David, in numbering Israel, 2 Sam. 24:1-17. Jeroboam, 1 Kin. 13:4. Ben-hadad, 1 Kin. 20:10. Uzziah, 2 Chr. 26:16. Sennacherib, 2 Chr. 32:13,14. Job, in cursing the day of his birth, Job 3; reproved by Eliphaz, Job 4: 5. Jonah, Jonah 4:1-8. Peter, in objecting to Jesus' statement that he must be killed, Matt. 16:21-23; Mark 8:32; in reflecting on his knowledge when he asked, amid a throng, who touched him, Luke 8:45; in objecting to Jesus washing his feet, John 13:8; in asking Jesus, "What shall this man do?" John 21:20-22. The disciples, in rebuking those who brought little children to Jesus. Matt. 19:13; Mark 10:13,14; Luke 18:15; in their indignation at the anointing of Jesus, Matt. 26:8,9; Mark 14:4,5; John 12:5. Reproving Jesus, John 7:3-5. James and John, in desiring to call down fire on the Samaritans, Luke 9:54. Those who reviled Jesus, Matt. 27:42,43; Mark 15:29-32. Theudas, Acts 5:36. Sons of Sceva, Acts 19:13,14. Diotrephes, 3 John 9.

See BLASPHEMY, which is presumption; MOCKING; PRIDE.

PRETORIUM, called also COMMON HALL, JUDGMENT HALL, and PALACE, Matt. 27:27; Mark 15:16; John 18:28,33; 19:9; Acts 23:35; Phil. 1:13.

PRIDE. Ex. 18:10. And Jethro said, ... 11. Now I know that the LORD *is* greater than all gods: for in the thing wherein they dealt proudly *he was* above them.

Lev. 26:19. I will break the pride of your power; and I will make your heaven as iron, and your earth as brass:

Deut. 8:11. Beware that thou forget not the LORD thy God, in not keeping his commandments, and his judgments, and his statutes, which I command thee this day: 12. Lest *when* thou hast eaten and art full, and hast built goodly houses, and dwelt *therein;* 13. And *when* thy herds and thy flocks multiply, and thy silver and thy gold is multiplied, and all that thou hast is multiplied; 14. Then thine heart be lifted up, and thou forget the LORD thy God, which brought thee forth out of the land of Egypt, from the house of bondage; 17. And thou say in thine heart, My power and the might of *mine* hand hath gotten me this wealth. 18. But thou shalt remember the LORD thy God: for *it is* he that giveth thee power to get wealth, that he may establish his covenant which he sware unto thy fathers, as *it is* this day. 19. And it shall be, if thou do at all forget the LORD thy God, and walk after other gods, and serve them, and worship them, I testify against you this day that ye shall surely perish. 20. As the nations which the LORD destroyeth before your face, so shall ye perish; because ye would not be obedient unto the voice of the LORD your God.

Judg. 9:14. Then said all the trees unto the bramble, Come thou, *and* reign over us. 15. And the bramble said unto the trees, If in truth ye anoint me king over you, *then* come *and* put your trust in my shadow: and if not, let fire come out of the bramble, and devour the cedars of Lebanon.

1 Sam. 2:3. Talk no more so exceeding proudly; let *not* arrogancy come out of your mouth: for the LORD *is* a God of knowledge, and by him actions are weighed. 4. The bows of the mighty men *are* broken, and they that stumbled are girded with strength. 5. *They that were* full have hired out themselves for bread;

1 Kin. 20:11. And the king of Israel answered and said, Tell *him,* Let not him that girdeth on *his harness* boast himself as he that putteth it off.

2 Kin. 14:9. And Jehoash the king of Israel sent to Amaziah king of Judah, saying, The thistle that *was* in Lebanon sent to the cedar that *was* in Lebanon, saying, Give thy daughter to my son to wife: and there passed by a wild beast that *was* in Lebanon, and trode down the thistle. 10. Thou hast indeed smitten Edom, and thine heart hath lifted thee up: glory *of this,* and tarry at home: for why shouldest thou

meddle to *thy* hurt, that thou shouldest fall, *even* thou, and Judah with thee? 2 Chr. 25:18,19.

Job 11:12. For vain man would be wise, though man be born *like* a wild ass's colt.

Job 12:2. No doubt but ye *are* the people, and wisdom shall die with you. 3. But I have understanding as well as you; I *am* not inferior to you: yea, who knoweth not such things as these?

Job 13:2. What ye know, *the same* do I know also: I *am* not inferior unto you. 5. O that ye would altogether hold your peace! and it should be your wisdom.

Job 15:1. Then answered Eliphaz the Temanite, and said, 2. Should a wise man utter vain knowledge, and fill his belly with the east wind? 3. Should he reason with unprofitable talk? or with speeches wherewith he can do no good? 4. Yea, thou castest off fear, and restrainest prayer before God. 5. For thy mouth uttereth thine iniquity, and thou choosest the tongue of the crafty. 6. Thine own mouth condemneth thee, and not I: yea, thine own lips testify against thee. 7. *Art* thou the first man *that* was born? or wast thou made before the hills? 8. Hast thou heard the secret of God? and dost thou restrain wisdom to thyself? 9. What knowest thou, that we know not? *what* understandest thou, which *is* not in us? 10. With us *are* both the grayheaded and very aged men, much elder than thy father. 11. *Are* the consolations of God small with thee? is there any secret thing with thee? 12. Why doth thine heart carry thee away? and what do thy eyes wink at, 13. That thou turnest thy spirit against God, and lettest *such* words go out of thy mouth?

Job 18:3. Wherefore are we counted as beasts, *and* reputed vile in your sight? 4. He teareth himself in his anger: shall the earth be forsaken for thee? and shall the rock be removed out of his place?

Job 21:31. Who shall declare his way to his face? and who shall repay him *what* he hath done? 32. Yet shall he be brought to the grave, and shall remain in the tomb.

Job 32:9. Great men are not *always* wise: neither do the aged understand judgment. 10. Therefore I said, Hearken to me; I also will shew mine opinion. 11. Behold, I waited for your words; I gave ear to your reasons, whilst ye searched out what to say. 12. Yea, I attended unto you, and, behold, *there was* none of you that convinced Job, *or* that answered his words: 13. Lest ye should say, We have found out wisdom: God thrusteth him down, not man.

Job 37:24. He respecteth not any *that are* wise of heart.

Psa. 9:20. Put them in fear, O LORD: *that* the nations may know themselves *to be but* men.

Psa. 10:2. The wicked in *his* pride doth persecute the poor: let them be taken in the devices that they have imagined. 3.

For the wicked boasteth of his heart's desire, and blesseth the covetous, *whom* the LORD abhorreth. 4. The wicked, through the pride of his countenance, will not seek *after God:* God *is* not in all his thoughts. 5. His ways are always grievous; thy judgments *are* far above out of his sight: *as for* all his enemies, he puffeth at them. 6. He hath said in his heart, I shall not be moved: for *I shall* never *be* in adversity. 11. He hath said in his heart, God hath forgotten: he hideth his face; he will never see *it*.

Psa. 12:3. The LORD shall cut off . . . the tongue that speaketh proud things : 4. Who have said, With our tongue will we prevail; our lips *are* our own: who *is* lord over us?

Psa. 18:27. Thou wilt save the afflicted people ; but wilt bring down high looks.

Psa. 31:23. The LORD preserveth the faithful, and plentifully rewardeth the proud doer.

Psa. 49:11. Their inward thought *is, that* their houses *shall continue* for ever, *and* their dwelling places to all generations; they call *their* lands after their own names.

Psa. 52:7. Lo, *this is* the man *that* made not God his strength ; but trusted in the abundance of his riches, *and* strengthened himself in his wickedness.

Psa. 73:6. Pride compasseth them about as a chain ; violence covereth them *as* a garment. 8. They are corrupt, and speak wickedly *concerning* oppression : they speak loftily. 9. They set their mouth against the heavens, and their tongue walketh through the earth.

Psa. 75:4. I said unto the fools, Deal not foolishly: and to the wicked, Lift not up the horn: 5. Lift not up your horn on high : speak *not with* a stiff neck. 6. For promotion *cometh* neither from the east, nor from the west, nor from the south.

Psa. 101:5. Him that hath an high look and a proud heart will not I suffer.

Psa. 119:21. Thou hast rebuked the proud *that are* cursed, which do err from thy commandments. 69. The proud have forged a lie against me : *but* I will keep thy precepts with *my* whole heart. 70. Their heart is as fat as grease; 78. Let the proud be ashamed; for they dealt perversely with me without a cause :

Psa. 138:6. Though the LORD *be* high, yet hath he respect unto the lowly : but the proud he knoweth afar off.

Prov. 3:34. Surely he scorneth the scorners : but he giveth grace unto the lowly.

Prov. 6:16. These six *things* doth the LORD hate : yea, seven *are* an abomination unto him : 17. A proud look, . . .

Prov. 8:13. Pride, and arrogancy, . . . do I hate.

Prov. 10:17. He *is in* the way of life that keepeth instruction: but he that refuseth reproof erreth.

Prov. 11:2. *When* pride cometh, then com-

eth shame : but with the lowly *is* wisdom. 12. He that is void of wisdom despiseth his neighbour :

Prov. 12:9. *He that is* despised, and hath a servant, *is* better than he that honoureth himself, and lacketh bread. 15. The way of a fool *is* right in his own eyes :

Prov. 13:10. Only by pride cometh contention :

Prov. 14:21. He that despiseth his neighbour sinneth :

Prov. 15:5. A fool despiseth his father's instruction : 10. Correction *is* grievous unto him that forsaketh the way : *and* he that hateth reproof shall die. 12. A scorner loveth not one that reproveth him : neither will he go unto the wise. 25. The LORD will destroy the house of the proud : 32. He that refuseth instruction despiseth his own soul :

Prov. 16:5. Every one *that is* proud in heart *is* an abomination to the LORD : *though* hand *join* in hand, he shall not be unpunished. 18. Pride *goeth* before destruction, and an haughty spirit before a fall. 19. Better *it is to be* of an humble spirit with the lowly, than to divide the spoil with the proud.

Prov. 17:19. He that exalteth his gate seeketh destruction.

Prov. 18:11. The rich man's wealth *is* his strong city, and as an high wall in his own conceit. 12. Before destruction the heart of man is haughty, and before honor *is* humility.

Prov. 20:6. Most men will proclaim every one his own goodness : but a faithful man who can find ?

Prov. 21:4. An high look, and a proud heart, . . . *is* sin. 24. Proud *and* haughty scorner *is* his name, who dealeth in proud wrath.

Prov. 25:14. Whoso boasteth himself of a false gift *is like* clouds and wind without rain. 27. *For men* to search their own glory *is not* glory.

Prov. 26:5. Answer a fool according to his folly, lest he be wise in his own conceit. 12. Seest thou a man wise in his own conceit ? *there is* more hope of a fool than of him. 16. The sluggard *is* wiser in his own conceit than seven men that can render a reason.

Prov. 27:2. Let another man praise thee, and not thine own mouth ; a stranger, and not thine own lips.

Prov. 28:11. The rich man *is* wise in his own conceit; but the poor that hath understanding searcheth him out. 25. He that is of a proud heart stirreth up strife :

Prov. 29:8. Scornful men bring a city into a snare : but wise *men* turn away wrath. 23. A man's pride shall bring him low : but honour shall uphold the humble in spirit.

Prov. 30:12. *There is* a generation *that are* pure in their own eyes, and *yet* is not washed from their filthiness. 13. *There is* a generation, O how lofty are their eyes! and their eyelids are lifted up.

Isa. 2:11. The lofty looks of man shall be humbled, and the haughtiness of men shall be bowed down, and the LORD alone shall be exalted in that day. 12. For the day of the LORD of hosts *shall be* upon every *one that is* proud and lofty, and upon every *one that is* lifted up; and he shall be brought low: 13. And upon all the cedars of Lebanon, *that are* high and lifted up, and upon all the oaks of Bashan, 14. And upon all the high mountains, and upon all the hills *that are* lifted up, 15. And upon every high tower, and upon every fenced wall, 16. And upon all the ships of Tarshish, and upon all pleasant pictures. 17. And the loftiness of man shall be bowed down, and the haughtiness of men shall be made low; and the LORD alone shall be exalted in that day.

Isa. 3:16. Moreover the LORD saith, Because the daughters of Zion are haughty, and walk with stretched forth necks and wanton eyes, walking and mincing *as* they go, and making a tinkling with their feet: 17. Therefore the Lord will smite with a scab the crown of the head of the daughters of Zion, and the LORD will discover their secret parts. 18. In that day the Lord will take away the bravery of *their* tinkling ornaments *about their feet*, and *their* cauls, and *their* round tires like the moon, 19. The chains, and the bracelets, and the mufflers, 20. The bonnets, and the ornaments of the legs, and the headbands, and the tablets, and the earrings, 21. The rings, and nose jewels, 22. The changeable suits of apparel, and the mantles, and the wimples, and the crisping pins, 23. The glasses, and the fine linen, and the hoods, and the vails. 24. And it shall come to pass, *that* instead of sweet smell there shall be stink; and instead of a girdle a rent; and instead of well set hair baldness; and instead of a stomacher a girding of sackcloth; *and* burning instead of beauty. 25. Thy men shall fall by the sword, and thy mighty in the war. 26. And her gates shall lament and mourn; and she *being* desolate shall sit upon the ground.

Isa. 5:8. Woe unto them that join house to house, *that* lay field to field, till *there be* no place, that they may be placed alone in the midst of the earth! 15. And the mean man shall be brought down, and the mighty man shall be humbled, and the eyes of the lofty shall be humbled:

Isa. 9:9. All the people shall know, *even* Ephraim, and the inhabitants of Samaria, that say in the pride and stoutness of heart, 10. The bricks are fallen down, but we will build with hewn stones; the sycomores are cut down, but we will change *them into* cedars.

Isa. 10:5. O Assyrian, the rod of mine anger, and the staff in their hand is mine indignation. 6. I will send him against an hypocritical nation, and against the people of my wrath will I give him a charge, to take the spoil, and to take the prey, and to tread them down like the mire of the streets. 7. Howbeit he meaneth not so, neither doth his heart think so; but *it is* in his heart to destroy and cut off nations not a few. 8. For he saith, *Are* not my princes altogether kings? 9. *Is* not Calno as Carchemish? *is* not Hamath as Arpad? *is* not Samaria as Damascus? 10. As my hand hath found the kingdoms of the idols, and whose graven images did excel them of Jerusalem and of Samaria; 11. Shall I not, as I have done unto Samaria and her idols, so do to Jerusalem and her idols? 12. Wherefore it shall come to pass, *that* when the Lord hath performed his whole work upon mount Zion and on Jerusalem, I will punish the fruit of the stout heart of the king of Assyria, and the glory of his high looks. 13. For he saith, By the strength of my hand I have done *it*, and by my wisdom; for I am prudent: and I have removed the bounds of the people, and have robbed their treasures, and I have put down the inhabitants like a valiant *man:* 14. And my hand hath found as a nest the riches of the people: and as one gathereth eggs *that are* left, have I gathered all the earth; and there was none that moved the wing, or opened the mouth, or peeped. 15. Shall the ax boast itself against him that heweth therewith? *or* shall the saw magnify itself against him that shaketh it? as if the rod should shake *itself* against them that lift it up, *or* as if the staff should lift up *itself, as if it were* no wood. 16. Therefore shall the Lord, the Lord of hosts, send among his fat ones leanness; and under his glory he shall kindle a burning like the burning of a fire.

Isa. 13:11. I will cause the arrogancy of the proud to cease, and will lay low the haughtiness of the terrible.

Isa. 14:12. How art thou fallen from heaven, O Lucifer, son of the morning! *how* art thou cut down to the ground, which didst weaken the nations! 13. For thou hast said in thine heart, I will ascend into heaven, I will exalt my throne above the stars of God: I will sit also upon the mount of the congregation, in the sides of the north: 14. I will ascend above the heights of the clouds; I will be like the most High. 15. Yet thou shalt be brought down to hell, to the sides of the pit. 16. They that see thee shall narrowly look upon thee, *and* consider thee, *saying, Is* this the man that made the earth to tremble, that did shake kingdoms;

Isa. 22:16. What hast thou here? and whom hast thou here, that thou hast hewed thee out a sepulchre here, *as* he that heweth him out a sepulchre on high, *and* that graveth an habitation for himself in a rock? 19. And I will drive thee from thy station, and from thy state shall he pull thee down.

Isa. 23:7. *Is* this your joyous *city*, whose antiquity *is* of ancient days? her own feet shall carry her afar off to sojourn. 9. The LORD of hosts hath purposed it, to stain the pride of all glory, *and* to bring into contempt all the honourable of the earth.

Isa. 24:4. The world languisheth *and* fadeth away, the haughty people of the earth do languish. 21. And it shall come to pass in that day, that the LORD shall punish the host of the high ones *that are* on high, and the kings of the earth upon the earth.

Isa. 26:5. He bringeth down them that dwell on high; the lofty city, he layeth it low; he layeth it low, *even* to the ground; he bringeth it *even* to the dust.

Isa. 28:3. The crown of pride, the drunkards of Ephraim, shall be trodden under feet:

Isa. 47:7. And thou saidst, I shall be a lady for ever: *so* that thou didst not lay these *things* to thy heart, neither didst remember the latter end of it. 8. Therefore hear now this, *thou that art* given to pleasures, that dwellest carelessly, that sayest in thine heart, I *am*, and none else beside me; I shall not sit *as* a widow, neither shall I know the loss of children: 9. But these two *things* shall come to thee in a moment in one day, the loss of children, and widowhood: they shall come upon thee in their perfection for the multitude of thy sorceries, *and* for the great abundance of thine enchantments. 10. For thou hast trusted in thy wickedness: thou hast said, None seeth me. Thy wisdom and thy knowledge, it hath perverted thee; and thou hast said in thine heart, I *am*, and none else beside me.

Jer. 9:23. Let not the wise *man* glory in his wisdom, neither let the mighty *man* glory in his might, let not the rich *man* glory in his riches: 24. But let him that glorieth glory in this, that he understandeth and knoweth me, that I *am* the LORD which exercise lovingkindness, judgment, and righteousness, in the earth: for in these *things* I delight, saith the LORD.

Jer. 13:9. After this manner will I mar the pride of Judah, and the great pride of Jerusalem. 15. Hear ye, and give ear; be not proud: for the LORD hath spoken. 17. But if ye will not hear it, my soul shall weep in secret places for *your* pride; and mine eye shall weep sore, and run down with tears, because the LORD'S flock is carried away captive.

Jer. 48:7. Because thou hast trusted in thy works and in thy treasures, thou shalt also be taken: 14. How say ye, We *are* mighty and strong men for the war? 15. Moab is spoiled, and gone up *out of* her cities, and his chosen young men are gone down to the slaughter, saith the King, whose name *is* the LORD of hosts. 29. We have heard the pride of Moab, (he is exceeding proud) his loftiness, and his arrogancy, and his pride, and the haughtiness of his heart. Isa. 16:6, 7.

Jer. 49:4. Wherefore gloriest thou in the valleys, thy flowing valley, O backsliding daughter? that trusted in her treasures, *saying*, Who shall come unto me? 16. Thy terribleness hath deceived thee, *and* the pride of thine heart, O thou that dwellest in the clefts of the rock, that holdest the height of the hill: though thou shouldest make thy nest as high as the eagle, I will bring thee down from thence, saith the LORD.

Jer. 50:31. I *am* against thee, *O thou* most proud, saith the Lord GOD of hosts: for thy day is come, the time *that* I will visit thee. 32. And the most proud shall stumble and fall, and none shall raise him up: and I will kindle a fire in his cities, and it shall devour all round about him.

Ezek. 16:56. Thy sister Sodom was not mentioned by thy mouth in the day of thy pride,

Ezek. 28:2. Son of man, say unto the prince of Tyrus, Thus saith the Lord GOD; Because thine heart *is* lifted up, and thou hast said, I *am* a God, I sit *in* the seat of God, in the midst of the seas; yet thou *art* a man, and not God, though thou set thine heart as the heart of God: 3. Behold, thou *art* wiser than Daniel; there is no secret that they can hide from thee: 4. With thy wisdom and with thine understanding thou hast gotten thee riches, and hast gotten gold and silver into thy treasures: 5. By thy great wisdom *and* by thy traffick hast thou increased thy riches, and thine heart is lifted up because of thy riches: 6. Therefore thus saith the Lord GOD; Because thou hast set thine heart as the heart of God; 7. Behold, therefore I will bring strangers upon thee, the terrible of the nations: and they shall draw their swords against the beauty of thy wisdom, and they shall defile thy brightness. 8. They shall bring thee down to the pit, and thou shalt die the deaths of *them that are* slain in the midst of the seas. 9. Wilt thou yet say before him that slayeth thee, I *am* God? but thou *shalt be* a man, and no God, in the hand of him that slayeth thee. 17. Thine heart was lifted up because of thy beauty, thou hast corrupted thy wisdom by reason of thy brightness: I will cast thee to the ground, I will lay thee before kings, that they may behold thee.

Ezek. 30:6. Thus saith the LORD; They also that uphold Egypt shall fall: and the pride of her power shall come down:

Ezek. 31:10. Because thou hast lifted up thyself in height, and he hath shot up his top among the thick boughs, and his heart is lifted up in his height; 11. I have therefore delivered him into the hand of the mighty one of the heathen; *vs.* 12-14.

Dan. 4:37. Now I Nebuchadnezzar praise and extol and honour the King of heaven, all whose works *are* truth, and his ways judgment: and those that walk in pride he is able to abase.

Dan. 11:45. He shall plant the tabernacles of his palace between the seas in the glorious holy mountain; yet he shall come to his end, and none shall help him.

Hos. 5:5. The pride of Israel doth testify to his face: therefore shall Israel and Ephraim fall in their iniquity; Judah also shall fall with them. Hos. 7:10.

Hos. 10:11. Ephraim *is as* an heifer *that is* taught, *and* loveth to tread out *the corn;* but I passed over upon her fair neck: I will make Ephraim to ride; Judah shall plow, *and* Jacob shall break his clods.

Obad. 3. The pride of thine heart hath deceived thee, thou that dwellest in the clefts of the rock, whose habitation *is* high; that saith in his heart, Who shall bring me down to the ground? 4. Though thou exalt *thyself* as the eagle, and though thou set thy nest among the stars, thence will I bring thee down, saith the LORD.

Nah. 3:19. *There is* no healing of thy bruise; thy wound is grievous: all that hear the bruit of thee shall clap the hands over thee; for upon whom hath not thy wickedness passed continually?

Hab. 2:4. His soul *which* is lifted up is not upright in him: but the just shall live by his faith. 5. Yea ¹ also, because he transgresseth by wine, *he is* a proud man, neither keepeth at home, who enlargeth his desire as hell, and *is* as death, and cannot be satisfied, but gathereth unto him all nations, and heapeth unto him all people: 9. Woe to him that coveteth an evil covetousness to his house, that he may set his nest on high, that he may be delivered from the power of evil!

[¹ R. V. moreover, wine is a treacherous dealer, a haughty

Zeph. 2:10. This shall they have for their pride, because they have reproached and magnified *themselves* against the people of the LORD of hosts. 15. This *is* the rejoicing city that dwelt carelessly, that said in her heart, I *am*, and *there is* none beside me: how is she become a desolation, a place for beasts to lie down in! every one that passeth by her shall hiss, *and* wag his hand.

Zeph. 3:11. In that day shalt thou not be ashamed for all thy doings, wherein thou hast transgressed against me: for then I will take away out of the midst of thee them that rejoice in thy pride, and thou shalt no more be haughty because of my holy mountain.

Mal. 4:1. Behold, the day cometh, that shall burn as an oven: and all the proud, yea, and all that do wickedly, shall be stubble: and the day that cometh shall burn them up, saith the LORD of hosts, that it shall leave them neither root nor branch.

Matt. 23:6. And love the uppermost rooms at feasts, and the chief seats in the synagogues, 7. And greetings in the markets, and to be called of men, Rabbi, Rabbi. 8. Be not ye called Rabbi: for one is your Master, *even* Christ; and all ye are brethren. 10. Neither be ye called masters: for one is your Master, *even* Christ. 11. But he that is greatest among you shall be your servant. 12. And whosoever shall exalt himself shall be abased; Matt. 20:26,27; Mark 10:43; Luke 9:46; 18:14.

Mark 7:21. For from within, out of the heart of men, proceed evil thoughts, . . . 22. . . . pride, foolishness:

Mark 12:38. Beware of the scribes, which love to go in long clothing, and *love* salutations in the marketplaces, 39. And the chief seats in the synagogues, and the uppermost rooms at feasts: Luke 20:45-47.

Luke 1:51. He hath scattered the proud in the imagination of their hearts. 52. He hath put down the mighty from *their* seats, and exalted them of low degree.

Luke 11:43. Woe unto you, Pharisees! for ye love the uppermost seats in the synagogues, and greetings in the markets.

Luke 14:8. When thou art bidden of any *man* to a wedding, sit not down in the highest room; lest a more honourable man than thou be bidden of him; 9. And he that bade thee and him come and say to thee, Give this man place; and thou begin with shame to take the lowest room.

Luke 20:46. Beware of the scribes, which desire to walk in long robes, and love greetings in the markets, and the highest seats in the synagogues, and the chief rooms at feasts. Matt. 23:6,7.

Rom. 1:22. Professing themselves to be wise, they became fools, 29. Being filled with all unrighteousness, . . . 30. . . . . proud, boasters.

Rom. 11:17. And if some of the branches be broken off, and thou, being a wild olive tree, wert graffed in among them, and with them partakest of the root and fatness of the olive tree; 18. Boast not against the branches. But if thou boast, thou bearest not the root, but the root thee. 19. Thou wilt say then, The branches were broken off, that I might be graffed in. 20. Well; because of unbelief they were broken off, and thou standest by faith. Be not highminded, but fear: 21. For if God spared not the natural branches, *take heed* lest he also spare not thee. 25. For I would not, brethren, that ye should be ignorant of this mystery, lest ye should be wise in your own conceits; that blindness in part is happened to Israel, until the fulness of the Gentiles be come in.

Rom. 12:3. I say, through the grace given unto me, to every man that is among you, not to think *of himself* more highly than he ought to think; but to think soberly, according as God hath dealt to every man the measure of faith. 16. Mind not high things, but condescend to men of low estate. Be not wise in your own conceits.

1 Cor. 1:29. No flesh should glory in his presence.

1 Cor. 3:18. Let no man deceive himself. If any man among you seemeth to be wise in this world, let him become a fool, that he may be wise.

1 Cor. 4:6. That ye might learn in us not to think *of men* above that which is written, that no one of you be puffed up for one against another. 7. For who maketh thee to differ *from another?* and what hast thou that thou didst not receive? now if thou didst receive *it*, why dost thou glory, as if thou hadst not received *it?* 8. Now

ye are full, now ye are rich, ye have reigned as kings without us: and I would to God ye did reign, that we also might reign with you. 10. We *are* fools for Christ's sake, but ye *are* wise in Christ; we *are* weak, but ye *are* strong; ye *are* honourable, but we *are* despised.

1 Cor. 5:2. Ye are puffed up, and have not rather mourned, that he that hath done this deed might be taken away from among you. 6. Your glorying *is* not good. Know ye not that a little leaven leaveneth the whole lump?

1 Cor. 8:1. Knowledge puffeth up, but charity edifieth. 2. If any man think that he knoweth any thing, he knoweth nothing yet as he ought to know.

1 Cor. 10:12. Wherefore let him that thinketh he standeth take heed lest he fall.

1 Cor. 13:4. Charity vaunteth not itself, is not puffed up.

1 Cor. 14:38. If any man be ignorant, let him be ignorant.

2 Cor. 10:5. Casting down imaginations, and every high thing that exalteth itself against the knowledge of God, and bringing into captivity every thought to the obedience of Christ; 12. We dare not make ourselves of the number, or compare ourselves with some that commend themselves: but they measuring themselves by themselves, and comparing themselves among themselves, are not wise. 18. Not he that commendeth himself is approved, but whom the Lord commendeth.

2 Cor. 12:7. And lest I should be exalted above measure through the abundance of the revelations, there was given to me a thorn in the flesh, the messenger of Satan to buffet me, lest I should be exalted above measure.

Gal. 6:3. If a man think himself to be something, when he is nothing, he deceiveth himself.

Eph. 4:17. This I say therefore, and testify in the Lord, that ye henceforth walk not as other Gentiles walk, in the vanity of their mind.

Phil. 2:3. *Let* nothing *be done* through strife or vainglory; but in lowliness of mind let each esteem other better than themselves.

1 Tim. 2:9. In like manner also, that women adorn themselves in modest apparel, with shamefacedness and sobriety; not with broided hair, or gold, or pearls, or costly array;

1 Tim. 3:6. Not a novice, lest being lifted up with pride he fall into the condemnation of the devil.

1 Tim. 6:3. If any man teach otherwise, and consent not to wholesome words, . . . 4. He is proud, knowing nothing, . . . 17. Charge them that are rich in this world, that they be not highminded.

2 Tim. 3:2. Men shall be lovers of their own selves, covetous, boasters, proud, . . . 4. Traitors, heady, highminded,

Jas. 3:1. My brethren, be not many masters, knowing that we shall receive the greater condemnation.

Jas. 4:6. Wherefore he saith, God resisteth the proud, but giveth grace unto the humble.

1 Pet. 5:3. Neither as being lords over *God's* heritage, but being ensamples to the flock. *v.* 5.

1 John 2:16. All that *is* in the world, the lust of the flesh, and the lust of the eyes, and the pride of life, is not of the Father, but is of the world.

Rev. 3:17. Because thou sayest, I am rich, and increased with goods, and have need of nothing; and knowest not that thou art wretched, and miserable, and poor, and blind, and naked: 18. I counsel thee to buy of me gold tried in the fire, that thou mayest be rich; and white raiment, that thou mayest be clothed, and *that* the shame of thy nakedness do not appear; and anoint thine eyes with eyesalve, that thou mayest see.

Rev. 18:7. How much she hath glorified herself, and lived deliciously, so much torment and sorrow give her: for she saith in her heart, I sit a queen, and am no widow, and shall see no sorrow. 8. Therefore shall her plagues come in one day, death, and mourning, and famine; and she shall be utterly burned with fire: for strong *is* the Lord God who judgeth her.

See RICH, THE.

INSTANCES OF: Ahithophel, 2 Sam. 17: 23. Naaman, refusing to wash in Jordan, 2 Kin. 5:11-13. Hezekiah, in displaying his resources, 2 Kin. 20:13; 2 Chr. 32:31; Isa. 39:2. Uzziah, 2 Chr. 26:16-19. Haman, Esth. 3:5; 5:11,13; 6:6; 7:10. Kings of Tyre, Ezek. 28:2. Nebuchadnezzar, Dan. 4:30-34; 5:20.

See AMBITION.

PRIEST. ANTEMOSAIC: Melchizedek, Gen. 14:18. Heb. 5:6,10,11; 6:20; 7:1-21. Jethro, Ex. 2:16. Priests in Israel before the giving of the law, Ex. 19:22,24. Called angel, Eccl. 5:6.

MOSAIC: Ex. 28:1-4; 29:9,44; Num. 3:10; 18:7; 1 Chr. 23:13. Hereditary descent of office, Ex. 27:21; 28:43; 29:9. Consecration of, Ex. 29:1-9,19-35; 40:12-16; Lev. 6:20-23; 8:6-35; Heb. 7:21. Is holy, Lev. 21:6,7; 22:9, 16. Ablutions of, Ex. 40:30-32; Lev. 16:24; see CONSECRATION OF, above. Must be without blemish, Lev. 21:17-23. Vestments of, Ex. 28:2-43; 39:1-29; Lev. 6:10,11; 8:13; Ezek. 44:17-19. Don vestments in temple, Ezek. 42:14; 44:19. Atonement for, Lev. 16:6,24; Ezek. 44:27. Defilement and purification of, Ezek. 44:25,26. Marriage of, Lev. 21:7-15; Ezek. 44:22. Chambers for, in temple, Ezek. 40:45,46. Exempt from tax, Ezra 7:24. Armed and organized for war at the time of the disaffection toward Saul, 1 Chr. 12:27,28. Beard and hair of, Ezek. 44:20.

Twenty-four courses of, 1 Chr. 24:1-19; 28:13,21; 2 Chr. 8:14; 31:2; 35:4,5; Ezra 2:

36–39; Neh. 13:30. Chosen by lot, Luke 1:8, 9,23.

Usurpations of office of, Num. 3:10; 16; 18: 7; 2 Chr. 26:18. Priests were appointed by Jeroboam who were not of the sons of Levi, 1 Kin. 12:31; 13:33.

See LEVITES; MINISTERS.

DUTIES OF: To offer sacrifices, Lev. 1: 4–17; 2:2,16; 3:5,11,13,16; 4:5–12,17,25,26,30–35; 1 Chr. 16:40; 2 Chr. 13:11; 29:34; 35:11–14; Ezra 6:20; Heb. 10:11; see OFFERINGS. To offer the first fruits, Lev. 23:10,11; Deut. 26:3,4. Pronounce benedictions, Num. 6:22–27; Deut. 21:5; 2 Chr. 30:27. Teach the law, Lev. 10:11; Deut. 24:8; 27:14; 31:9–13; 33:10; Jer. 2:8; Mal. 2:7. Light the lamps in the tabernacle, Ex. 27:20,21; 2 Chr. 13:11; Lev. 24:3,4. Keep the sacred fire always burning, Lev. 6:12,13. To furnish a quota of wood for the sanctuary, Neh. 10:34. Responsible for the sanctuary, Num. 4:5–15; 18:1,5,7. To act as scribes, Ezra 7:1–6; Neh. 8:9. Be present at and supervise the tithing, Neh. 10:38. Sound the trumpet in calling assemblies and in battle, Num. 10:2–10; 31:6; Josh. 6; 2 Chr. 13:12. Examine lepers, see LEPROSY. Purify the unclean, Lev. 15:31; see DEFILEMENT. Value things devoted, Lev. 27:8,12. Officiate in the holy place, Heb. 9:6. Chiefs of Levites, Num. 3:9,32; 4:19,28, 33; 1 Chr. 9:20. To act as magistrates, Num. 5:14–31; Deut. 17:8–13; 19:17; 21:5; 2 Chr. 19:8; Ezek. 44:23,24. To encourage the army on the eve of battle, Deut. 20: 2–4. Bear the ark through the Jordan, Josh. 3; 4:15–18; in battle, 1 Sam. 4:3–5.

EMOLUMENTS OF: No part of the land of Canaan allowed to, Num. 18:20; Deut. 10:9; 14:27; 18:1,2; Josh. 13:14,33; 14:3; 18:7; Ezek. 44:28. Provided with cities and suburbs, Lev. 25:32–34; Num. 35:2–8; Josh. 21: 1–4,13–19,41,42; 1 Chr. 6:57–60; Neh. 11: 3,20; Ezek. 45:1–6; 48:8–20. Own lands sanctified to the Lord, Lev. 27:21. Tithes of the tithes, Num. 18:8–18,26–32; Neh. 10:38. Part of the spoils of war, including captives, Num. 31:25–29. Firstfruits, Lev. 23:20; 24:9; Num. 18:12,13,17,18; Deut. 18:3–5; Neh. 10:36. Redemption money, Lev. 27:23; of firstborn, Num. 3:46–51; 18:15,16. Things devoted, Lev. 27:21; Num. 5:9,10; 18:14. Fines, Lev. 5:16; 22:14; Num. 5:8. Trespass money and other trespass offerings, Lev. 5:15,18; Num. 5:5–10; 18:9; 2 Kin. 12:16. The shewbread, Ex. 25:30; Lev. 24:5–9; 2 Chr. 2:4; 13:11; Neh. 10:33; Matt. 12:4; Heb. 9:2. Portions of sacrifices and offerings, Ex. 29:27–34; Lev. 2:2,3,9,10; 5:12,13,16; 6:15–18, 26; 7:6–10,31–34; 10:12–14; 14:12,13; Num. 6:19,20; 18:8–19; Deut. 18:3–5; 1; Sam.2:13,14; Ezek. 44:28–31; 45:1–4; 1 Cor. 9:13; 10:18.

Regulations by Hezekiah concerning emoluments, 2 Chr. 31:4–19. Portion of land allotted to. in redistribution in Ezekiel's vision, Ezek. 48:8–14. For sustenance of their families, Lev. 22:11–13; Num. 18:11,19.

FIGURATIVE: Ex. 19:6; Isa. 61:6; 1 Pet. 2:9; Rev. 1:6; 5:10; 20:6.

HIGH PRIEST: Moses did not denominate Aaron chief or high priest. The function he served was superior to that of other priests. The title appears after the institution of the office, Lev. 21:10–15; Num. 3:32. For qualifications, consecration, etc., see under the general topic above, PRIEST, MOSAIC INSTITUTION OF.

Vestments of, Ex. 28:2–43; 39:1–31; Lev. 8: 7–9. Respect due to, Acts 23:5.

DUTIES OF: Had charge of the sanctuary and altar, Num. 18:2,5,7. To offer sacrifices, Heb. 5:1; 8:3. To designate subordinate priests for duty, Num. 4:19; 1 Sam. 2: 36. To officiate in consecrations of Levites, Num. 8:11–21. To have charge of the treasury, 2 Kin. 12:10; 22:4; 2 Chr. 24:6–14; 34:9. To light the lamps of tabernacle, Ex. 27:20, 21; 30:8; Lev. 24:3,4; Num. 8:3. To burn incense, Ex. 30:7,8; 1 Sam. 2:28; 1 Chr. 23:13. To place shewbread on the table every Sabbath, Lev. 24:8. To offer for his own sins of ignorance, Lev. 4:3–12.

On the Day of Atonement, Ex. 30:10; Lev. 16; Heb. 5:3; 9:7,22,23.

Judicial, Num. 5:15; Deut. 17:8–13; 1 Sam. 4:18; Hos. 4:4; Matt. 26:3,50,57,62; Acts 5:21–28; 23:1–5. To number the people, Num. 1: 3. Officiate at choice of ruler, Num. 27: 18,19,21. Distribute spoils of war, Num. 31:26–29.

Emoluments of: See PRIEST, EMOLUMENTS OF, above.

A second priest, under the high priest, Num. 3:32; 4:16; 31:6; 1 Chr. 9:20; 2 Sam. 15:24; 2 Kin. 25:18; Luke 3:2.

MISCELLANEOUS FACTS CONCERNING: Loyal to Rehoboam at the time of the revolt of the ten tribes, 2 Chr. 11:13. Zeal of, in purging the temple, 2 Chr. 29:4–17. Wickedness of, 2 Chr. 36:14. Taken with the captivity to Babylon, Jer. 29:1. Return from the captivity, Ezra 1:5; 2:36–39,61, 70; 3:8; 7:7; 8:24–30; Neh. 7:39–42,63–73; 10:1–8; 12:1–7. Polluted by marrying idolatrous wives, Ezra 9:1,2; 10:5,18,19; Neh. 10:28. Restore the altar, and offer sacrifices, Ezra 3:1–7. Supervise the building of the temple, Ezra 3:8–13. Inquire of John the Baptist whether he were the Christ, John 1:19. Conspire to destroy Jesus, Matt. 26:3–5,14,15,47,51; Mark 14:10,11,43–47, 53–66; 15:1; Luke 22:1–6,50,54,66–71; 23:1,2; John 11:47; 19:15,16,18. Try and condemn Jesus, Matt. 26:57–68; 27:1,2; Mark 14:53–65; Luke 22:54–71; 23:13–24; John 18:15–32. Incite the people to ask that Barabbas be released and Jesus destroyed, Matt. 27:20; Mark 15:11; Luke 23:18. Persecute the disciples, Acts 22:5. Reprove and threaten Peter and John, Acts 4:6–21; 5:17–41. Try, condemn, and stone Stephen, Acts 6:12–15; 7. Paul brought before, Acts 22:30; 23:1–5. Many converts among, Acts 6:7.

Corrupt, Jer. 23:11,12; Ezek. 22:26; Luke 10:31. INSTANCES OF: Eli's sons, 1 Sam. 2: 12–17,22; of the captivity, Ezra 9:1,2; 10:18–22; Neh. 13:4–9,13,28,29.

Zealous, 1 Chr. 9:10–13. Priestly office performed by prophets, 1 Sam. 16:5.

PRIMOGENITURE. See FIRSTBORN; BIRTHRIGHT.

PRINCE OF PEACE. See JESUS.

PRINCESSES, taught in household duties, 2 Sam. 13:8,9.

PRISCA, a disciple in Ephesus, 2 Tim. 4:19.

PRISCILLA, wife of Aquila. A disciple at Corinth, Acts 18:1–3,18,19,26; Rom. 16:3,4; 1 Cor. 16:19; 2 Tim. 4:19.

PRISON, Gen. 39:20; 42:16–19; Lev. 24:12; Num. 15:34; Ezra 7:26; Jer. 52:11; Luke 23:19; Acts 4:3; 12:4,5. Public ward of, Acts 5:18. Cells of, Acts 16:24. Court of, Jer. 33:1. Dungeon in, see DUNGEON.

See IMPRISONMENT; PRISONERS.

PRISONERS. Joseph, Gen 39:20–23; 40; 41:1–44. Jeremiah, Jer. 38:6–28; 39:14. John the Baptist, Matt. 11:2; 14:3–12; Mark 6:17; Luke 3:20. Jesus, Matt. 26:47–75; 27; Mark 14:43–72; 15; Luke 22:47–71; 23; John 18:3–40; 19. Apostles, Acts 5:17–42. Peter, Acts 12:3–19. Paul, Acts 16:19–40; 21:27–40; 22–28 inclusive. Silas, Acts 16:19–40.

Required to labor, Judg. 16:21. Kept on bread and water of affliction, 1 Kin. 22:27; in chains, Acts 12:6; in stocks, Prov. 7:22; Jer. 29:26; Acts 16:24.

Confined in court of the palace, Jer. 32:2; house of the scribe, Jer. 37:15; house of captain of the guard, Gen. 40:3. Visited by friends, Matt. 11:2; Acts 24:23. Bound to soldiers, Acts 12:6,7.

Severe hardships of, mitigated, Jer. 37:20, 21. Cruelty to, Jer. 38:6· Lam. 3:53,54; see CAPTIVE. Keepers responsible for, Acts 12: 18,19. Tortured to extort self-criminating testimony, Acts 22:24. Scourged, Matt. 27: 26; Mark 15:15; Acts 16:23,33; 2 Cor. 6:5; 11: 23,24. Permitted to make defense, Acts 24: 10; 25:8,16; 26:1; 2 Tim. 4:16. Kindness to: By the prison keeper to Jeremiah, Jer. 38:7– 28; by Philippian jailer to Paul, Acts 16:33; by Felix, Acts 24:23; by Julius, the centurion, Acts 27:1,3; 28:16,30,31. To be visited and ministered to, Matt. 25:35–46. Released at feasts, Matt. 27:15–17; Mark 15:6; ¹ Luke 23:17; John 18:39. [¹ Omitted in R. V.]

OF WAR: Put to death, Josh. 10:16–27; 1 Sam. 15:33; 27:11; 2 Sam. 12:31; 2 Kin. 25:7; 1 Chr. 20:3; Hos. 13:16; Amos 1:13; Lam.3:34; by divine command, Num. 31:9,17. Thumbs and toes cut off, Judg. 1:6,7. Blinded, 2 Kin. 25:7. See CAPTIVE.

Consolations for, Psa. 69:33; 79:11; 102:19, 20; 146:7.

See CAPTIVE; IMPRISONMENT.

FIGURATIVE: Isa. 61:1; Luke 4:18.

PRIVILEGE. See JUDGMENT, ACCORDING TO OPPORTUNITY; RESPONSIBILITY.

PRIZE, a reward of merit, 1 Cor. 9:24.

FIGURATIVE: Phil. 3:14.

PROBATION, Rom. 5:4 [R. V.]. Adam on, Gen. 2:15–17; 3:3. Amorites, Gen. 15:16. Solomon, 1 Kin. 3:14; 9:4–9, with chapter 11:9–12. Taught in parables of the talents

and pounds, Matt. 25:14–30; Luke 19:12– 27; the fig tree, Luke 13:6–9; embezzling steward, Luke 16:1–12. Taught by Paul, Heb. 6.

None after death, Matt. 12:32; 25:10–13; 26:24. See PERSEVERANCE.

PROCHORUS, an early Christian deacon, Acts 6:5.

PROCLAMATION. Imperial, 2 Chr. 30:1–10; Esth. 1:22; 6:9; 8:10–14; Isa. 40:3,9. Dan. 3:4–7; 4:1; 5:29. Emancipation, 2 Chr. 36:23; Ezra 1:1–4.

PROCRASTINATION. Ex. 22:29. Thou shalt not delay *to offer* the first of thy ripe fruits, and of thy liquors: the firstborn of thy sons shalt thou give unto me.

Prov. 27:1. Boast not thyself of to morrow; for thou knowest not what a day may bring forth.

Ezek. 11:2. Then said he unto me, Son of man, these *are* the men that devise mischief, and give wicked counsel in this city: 3. Which say, *It is* not near; let us build houses: this *city is* the caldron, and we *be* the flesh.

Ezek.12:22. Son of man, what *is* that proverb *that* ye have in the land of Israel, saying, The days are prolonged, and every vision faileth? 27. Son of man, behold, *they of* the house of Israel say, The vision that he seeth *is* for many days *to come*, and he prophesieth of the times *that are* far off. 28. Therefore say unto them, Thus saith the Lord GOD; There shall none of my words be ¹ prolonged any more, but the word which I have spoken shall be ² done saith the Lord GOD. [R. V. ¹ deferred ² performed]

Matt. 8:21. And another of his disciples said unto him, Lord, suffer me first to go and bury my father. Luke 9:59,61.

Matt. 24:48. But and if that evil servant shall say in his heart, My lord delayeth his coming; 49. And shall begin to smite *his* fellowservants, and to eat and drink with the drunken; 50. The lord of that servant shall come in a day when he looketh not for *him*, and in an hour that he is not aware of, 51. And shall cut him asunder, and appoint *him* his portion with the hypocrites: there shall be weeping and gnashing of teeth.

Matt. 25:2. And five of them were wise, and five *were* foolish. 3. They that *were* foolish took their lamps, and took no oil with them: 4. But the wise took oil in their vessels with their lamps. 5. While the bridegroom tarried, they all slumbered and slept. 6. And at midnight there was a cry made, Behold, the bridegroom cometh; go ye out to meet him. 7. Then all those virgins arose, and trimmed their lamps. 8. And the foolish said unto the wise, Give us of your oil; for our lamps are gone out. 9. But the wise answered, saying, *Not so;* lest there be not enough for us and you: but go ye rather to them that sell, and buy for yourselves. 10. And while they went to buy, the bridegroom came; and they that were ready went in with him to the marriage: and the door was shut. 11. Afterward came also the other virgins, saying, Lord, Lord, open to us. 12. But he answered and said, Verily I say unto you, I know you not. 13. Watch therefore, for ye know neither the day nor the hour wherein the Son of man cometh.

Luke 9:59. And he said unto another, Follow me. But he said, Lord, suffer me first to go and bury my father. 60. Jesus said unto him, Let the dead bury their dead: but go thou and preach the kingdom of God. 61. And another also said, Lord, I will follow thee; but let me first go bid them farewell, which are at home at my house. 62. And Jesus said unto him, No man, having put his hand to the plough, and looking back, is fit for the kingdom of God.

Acts 24:25. And as he reasoned of righteousness, temperance, and judgment to come, Felix trembled, and answered, Go thy way for this time; when I have a convenient season, I will call for thee.

1 Thess. 5:2. For yourselves know perfectly that the day of the Lord so cometh as a thief in the night. 3. For when they shall say, Peace and safety; then sudden destruction cometh upon them, as travail upon a woman with child; and they shall not escape.

Heb. 3:7. Wherefore (as the Holy Ghost saith, To day if ye will hear his voice, 8. Harden not your hearts, as in the provocation, in the day of temptation in the wilderness: 9. When your fathers tempted me, proved me, and saw my works forty years. 10. Wherefore I was grieved with that generation, and said, They do alway err in *their* heart; and they have not known my ways. 11. So I sware in my wrath, They shall not enter into my rest.) 12. Take heed, brethren, lest there be in any of you an evil heart of unbelief, in departing from the living God. 13. But exhort one another daily, while it is called To day; lest any of you be hardened through the deceitfulness of sin. 14. For we are made partakers of Christ, if we hold the beginning of our confidence stedfast unto the end; 15. While it is said, To day if ye will hear his voice, harden not your hearts, as in the provocation. 16. For some, when they had heard, did provoke: howbeit not all that came out of Egypt by Moses. 17. But with whom was he grieved forty years? *was it* not with them that had sinned, whose carcases fell in the wilderness? 18. And to whom sware he that they should not enter into his rest, but to them that believed not? 19. So we see that they could not enter in because of unbelief. chapter 4:1-7.

See EXCUSES.

INSTANCES OF: Pharaoh, Ex. 8:10. Elisha, 1 Kin. 19:20,21. Esther, Esth. 5:8.

PRODIGALITY. See EXTRAVAGANCE; FRUGALITY; INDUSTRY.

PRODIGAL SON, Luke 15:11-32.

PROFANATION. See PROFANITY.

PROFANITY. See BLASPHEMY; OATH. Of the name of God, see GOD, under Miscellaneous Sub-topics; of the Sabbath, see SABBATH.

PROFESSION. False, Prov. 20:6; Hos. 8:2. Of faith in Jesus, see CONFESSION.

See TESTIMONY, RELIGIOUS.

PROGNOSTICATION, by astrologers, Isa. 47:13.

See PROPHECY; PROPHETS.

PROHIBITION, of the use of intoxicating liquors. To priests on duty, Lev. 10:9. To Nazarites, Num. 6:3,4.

See ABSTINENCE, TOTAL; COMMANDMENTS; DRUNKENNESS.

PROMISES. To the afflicted, see AFFLICTIONS, COMFORT IN; PSALMS. To backsliders, see BACKSLIDERS. To children, see CHILDREN. To orphans, see ORPHAN. To widows, see WIDOW. To penitents, see PENITENT. To the righteous, see RIGHTEOUS. To seekers, see SEEKERS, and other like subjects.

See also BLESSINGS, SPIRITUAL; GOD, GOODNESS OF; JESUS, COMPASSION OF, LOVE OF.

PROMOTION, Psa. 75:6,7; 78:70,71; 113:7,8. As a reward of merit, 1 Chr. 11·6.

INSTANCES OF: Abraham, Gen. 12:2. Joseph, from imprisoned slave to prince, Gen. 41:1-45. Moses, from exile to lawgiver, see MOSES. Aaron, from slave to high priest, see AARON. Saul, from obscurity to a scepter, see SAUL. David, from shepherd to throne, see DAVID. Jeroboam, from slave to throne, 1 Kin. 11:26-35. Baasha, "out of the dust" to throne, 1 Kin. 16:1,2. Daniel. from captive to premier, Dan. 2:48; see DANIEL. Shadrach, Meshach, and Abednego, Dan. 3:30.

PROPAGATION, of species, enjoined, Gen. 1:11,12,21-25,28; 9:1,7.

See BARRENNESS.

PROPERTY. IN REAL ESTATE: Gen. 23:17,18; 26:20. Rights in, violated, Gen. 21: 25-3; 26:18-22. Dedicated, Lev. 27:16-25. See LAND.

Dwellings. Alienated for debt, Lev. 25: 29,30; by absence, 2 Kin. 8:1-6; in villages, inalienable, Lev. 25:31-33. Dedicated, Lev. 27:14,15.

Confiscation of (Naboth's vineyard), 1 Kin. 21:15,16. Priests exempt from taxes, Gen. 47:22. Entail of, Num. 27:1-11; 36:1-9. Inherited, Eccl. 2:21. Landmarks of, not to be removed, Deut. 19:14; 27:17.

PERSONAL: Rights in, sacred, Ex. 20:17; Deut. 5:21. Laws concerning trespass of, and violence to, Ex. 21:28-36; 22:9; Deut. 23:25. Strayed, to be returned to owner, Lev. 6:3,4; Deut. 22:1-3. Hired, Ex. 22:14, 15; or loaned, Ex. 22:10-15. Sold for debt, Prov. 22:26-27; rights of redemption of, Jer. 32:7. Dedicated to God, redemption of, Lev. 27:9-13,26-33. In slaves, Ex. 21:4.

PROPHECY. Concerning Jesus, see JESUS. Concerning church, see CHURCH,

PROPHECIES CONCERNING. Relating to various countries, nations, and cities, see under their respective titles. Respecting individuals, see under their names.

Inspired, Isa. 28:22; Luke 1:70; 2 Tim. 3:16; 2 Pet. 1:21. "The word of the Lord came unto," etc.: To Elijah, 1 Kin. 17:8; 21:17,28; Isaiah, Isa. 2:1; 8:5; 13:1; 14:28; 38:4; Jeremiah, Jer. 1:4; 7:1; 11:1; 13:8; 16:1; 18:1; 25:1,2; 26:1; 27:1; 29:30; 30:1,4; 32:1,6,26; 33:1,19,23; 34:12; 35:12; 36:1; 37:6; 40:1; 43:8; 44:1; 46:1; 49:34; 50:1; Ezekiel, Ezek. 3:16; 6:1; 7:1; 11:14; 12:1,8,17,21; 13:1; 14:12; 15:1; 16:1; 17:1,11; 18:1; 20:45; 21:1,8,18; 22:1,17,23; 23:1; 24:1,15,20; 25:1; 26:1; 27:1; 28:1,11,20; 29:1, 17; 30:1,20; 31:1; 32:1,17; 33:1,23; 34:1; 35:1; 36:16; 37:15; 38:1; Amos, Amos 7:14,15; Jonah, Jonah 3:1; Haggai, Hag. 2:1,10,20; Zechariah, Zech. 1:7; 4:8; 6:9; 7:1,4,8; 8:1,18.

Publicly proclaimed, Jer. 11:6. Exemplified in pantomime, Ezek. 4; 5:1-4; Acts 21:11. Written by an amanuensis, Jer. 45:1; in books, Jer. 45:1; 51:60.

Proof of God's foreknowledge, Isa. 43:9. Sure fulfillment of, Ezek. 12:22-25,28; Hab. 2:3; Matt. 5:18; 24:35; Acts 13:27,29. Cessation of, Lam. 2:9.

Of apostasy, 1 John 2:18; Jude 17,18; false teachers, 2 Pet. 2:3. Tribulations of the righteous, Rev. 2:10.

CONCERNING THE MESSIAH, AND THE FULFILLMENT:

Gen. 12:3; 18:18; 22:18	Quoted in	Acts 3:25; Gal. 3:8.
Gen. 17:7,19; 22:16,17	"	Luke 1:55,72-74.
Deut. 18:15,18	"	Acts 3:22,23.
Psa. 2:1,2	"	Acts 4:25,26.
Psa. 2:7	"	Acts 13:33; Heb. 1:5; 5:5.
Psa. 8:2	"	Matt. 21:16.
Psa. 8:4-6	"	Heb. 2:6-8.
Psa. 16:8-11	"	Acts 2:25-28,31.
Psa. 16:10	"	Acts 13:35.
Psa. 22:1	"	Matt. 27:46; Mark 15:34.
Psa. 22:18	"	Matt. 27:35; Mark 15:24; Luke 23:34; John 19:24. [1 R. V. omits the reference to prophecy.]
Psa. 22:22	"	Heb. 2:12.
Psa. 31:5	"	Luke 23:46.
Psa. 41:9	"	John 13:18; Acts 1:16.
Psa. 45:6,7	"	Heb. 1:8,9.
Psa. 68:18	"	Eph. 4:8-10.
Psa. 69:21	"	Matt. 27:48; Mark 15:36; Luke 23:36; John 19:28,29.
Psa. 69:25; 109:8	"	Acts 1:20.
Psa. 95:7-11	"	Heb. 3:7-11; 4:3,5-7.
Psa. 102:25-27	"	Heb. 1:10-12.
Psa. 110:1	"	Matt. 22:44; Mark 12:36; Luke 20:42; Acts 2:34,35; Heb. 1:13.
Psa. 110:4	"	Heb. 5:6.
Psa. 118:22,23	"	Matt. 21:42; Mark 12:10,11; Luke 20:17; Acts 4:11.
Psa. 118:25,26	"	Matt. 21:9; Mark 11:9; John 12:13.
Psa. 132:11,17	"	Luke 1:69; Acts 2:30.
Isa. 7:14	"	Matt. 1:23.
Isa. 9:1,2	"	Matt. 4:15,16.
Isa. 9:7, with Dan. 7:14,27	"	Luke 1:32,33.
Isa. 11:10	"	Rom. 15:12.
Isa. 25:8	"	1 Cor. 15:54.
Isa. 59:20,21	"	Rom. 11:26,27.
Isa. 28:16	"	Rom. 9:33; 1 Pet. 2:6.
Isa. 40:3-5	"	Matt. 3:3; Mark 1:3; Luke 3:4-6.
Isa. 42:1-4	"	Matt. 12:17-21.
Isa. 49:6	"	Luke 2:32; Acts 13:47,48; 26:23.
Isa. 53:1	"	John 12:38; Rom. 10:16.
Isa. 53:3-6	"	Acts 26:22,23.
Isa. 53:4-6,11	"	1 Pet. 2:24,25.
Isa. 53:4	"	Matt. 8:17.
Isa. 53:9	"	1 Pet. 2:22.
Isa. 53:12	"	[1] Mark 15:28; Luke 22:37. [1 Omitted in R. V.]
Isa. 54:13	"	John 6:45.
Isa. 55:3	"	Acts 13:34.
Jer. 31:31-34	"	Heb. 8:8-12; 10:16,17.
Hos. 1:10	"	Rom. 9:26.
Hos. 2:23	"	Rom. 9:25; 1 Pet. 2:10.
Joel 2:28-32	"	Acts 2:16-21.
Amos 9:11,12	"	Acts 15:16,17.

Mic. 5:2	Quoted in	Matt. 2:5,6; John 7:42.
Hab. 1:5	"	Acts 13:40,41.
Hag. 2:6	"	Heb. 12:26.
Zech. 9:9	"	Matt. 21:4,5; John 12:14,15.
Zech. 11:13	"	Matt. 27:9,10.
Zech. 12:10	"	John 19:37.
Zech. 13:7	"	Matt. 26:31,56; Mark 14:27,50.
Mal. 3:1	"	Matt. 11:10; Mark 1:2; Luke 7:27.
Mal. 4:5,6	"	Matt. 11:13,14; 17:10–13; Mark 9:11–13; Luke 1:16,17.

See JESUS, PROPHECIES CONCERNING; PROPHETESS; PROPHETS.

MISCELLANEOUS, FULFILLED: The birth and zeal of Josiah, 1 Kin. 13:2; 2 Kin. 23:1–20. Death of the prophet of Judah, 1 Kin.13:21,22,24–30. Extinction of Jeroboam's house, 1 Kin. 14:5–17; of Baasha's house, 1 Kin.16:2,3,9–13. Concerning the rebuilding of Jericho, Josh.6:26; 1 Kin.16:34. The drought, foretold by Elijah, 1 Kin. 17:14. Destruction of Ben-hadad's army, 1 Kin. 20:13–30. The death of a man who refused to smite a prophet, 1 Kin. 20:35,36. The death of Ahab, 1 Kin. 20:42; 21:18–24; 22:31–38. The death of Ahaziah, 2 Kin. 1:3–17. Elijah's translation, 2 Kin. 2:3–11. Cannibalism among the children of Israel, Lev. 26:29; Deut. 28:53; 2 Kin. 6:28,29; Jer. 19:9; Lam. 4:10. The death of the Samaritan lord, 2 Kin. 7:2,19, 20. The end of the famine in Samaria, 2 Kin. 7:1–18. Jezebel's tragic death, 1 Kin. 21:23; 2 Kin. 9:10,33–37. The smiting of Syria by Joash, 2 Kin. 13:16–25. Conquests of Jeroboam, 2 Kin. 14:25–28. Four generations of Jehu to sit upon the throne of Israel, 2 Kin. 10:30, with 2 Kin. 15:12. Destruction of Sennacherib's army, and his death, 2 Kin. 19:6,7,20–37. The captivity of Judah, 2 Kin. 20:17,18; 24:10–16; 25:11–21. Concerning Christ, see JESUS, PROPHECIES CONCERNING. Also see above. Concerning John, Matt. 3:3. Rachel weeping for her children, Jer. 31:15; Matt. 2:17,18. Deliverance of Jeremiah, Jer. 39:15–18. Invasion of Judah by the Chaldeans, Hab. 1:6–11; fulfilled, 2 Kin. 25; 2 Chr. 36:17–21. Betrayal of Jesus by Judas, prophecy, Psa. 41:9; fulfillment, John 13:18; 18:1–9. Judas' self-destruction, Psa. 69:25; Acts 1:16,20; fulfilled, Matt. 27:5; Acts 1:16–20. Outpouring of the Holy Spirit, Joel 2:28,29; fulfilled, Acts 2: 16–21. Spiritual blindness of the Jews, Isa. 6:9; 29:13; fulfilled, Mark 7:6,7; Acts 28:25–27. Mission of Jesus, Psa. 68:18; fulfilled, Eph. 4:8,10; see JESUS, MISSION OF. Captivity of the Jews, Jer. 25:11,12; 29:10,14; 32:3–5; Dan. 9:2, with 2 Kin. 25:1–8; Ezra 1. Of the destruction of the ship in which Paul sailed, Acts 27:10,18–44.

PROPHETS. Called SEERS, 1 Sam. 9:19; 2 Sam. 15:27; 24:11; 2 Kin. 17:13; 1 Chr. 9:22; 29:29; 2 Chr. 9:29; 12:15; 29:30; Isa. 30:10; Mic. 3:7. Schools of, 1 Kin. 20:35; 2 Kin. 2: 3–15; 4:1,38; 9:1. Kept the chronicles, 1 Chr. 29:29; 2 Chr. 9:29; 12:15. Counsellors to kings, Isa. 37:2,3. Not honored in their own country, Matt. 13:57; Luke 4:24–27; John 4:44.

Inspired by angels, Zech. 1:9,13,14,19; Acts 7:53; Gal. 3:19; Heb. 2:2. Persecutions of, 2 Chr. 36:16; Amos 2:12. Martyrs, Jer. 2:30; Matt. 23:37; Mark 12:5; Luke 13:34; 1 Thess. 2:15; Heb. 11:37; Rev. 16:6.

EMOLUMENTS OF: Presents, 1 Sam. 9:7, 8; 1 Kin. 14:3; 2 Kin. 4:42; 8:8,9; Ezek. 13:19. Presents refused by, Num. 22:18; 1 Kin. 13: 7,8; 2 Kin. 5:5,16.

FALSE: 1 Kin. 13:18; Neh. 6:12; Jer. 23: 25–27,30–32; Lam.2:14. Admonitions to, Deut. 13:1–3. Denunciations against, Deut. 18:20; Jer. 14:15. Punishment of, Jer. 14:13–16; 20:6; 28:16,17; 29:32; Zech. 13:3.

INSTANCES OF: Noadiah, Neh. 6:14; four hundred in Samaria, 1 Kin. 22:6–12; 2 Chr. 18:5.

See MINISTERS, FALSE.

INSPIRATION OF: Gen. 40:8. And they said unto him, We have dreamed a dream, and *there is* no interpreter of it. And Joseph said unto them, *Do* not interpretations *belong* to God? tell me *them*, I pray you.

Gen. 41:16. And Joseph answered Pharaoh, saying, *It is* not in me: God shall give Pharaoh an answer of peace. 38. And Pharaoh said unto his servants, Can we find *such a one* as this *is*, a man in whom the Spirit of God *is?* 39. And Pharaoh said unto Joseph, Forasmuch as God hath shewed thee all this, *there is* none so discreet and wise as thou *art:*

Ex. 3:14. And God said unto Moses, I AM THAT I AM: and he said, Thus shalt thou say unto the children of Israel, I AM hath sent me unto you. 15. And God said moreover unto Moses, Thus shalt thou say unto the children of Israel, The LORD God of your fathers, the God of Abraham, the God of Isaac, and the God of Jacob, hath sent me unto you: this *is* my name for ever, and this *is* my memorial unto all generations.

Ex. 4:12. Now therefore go, and I will be with thy mouth, and teach thee what thou shalt say. 15. And thou shalt speak unto him, and put words in his mouth: and I will be with thy mouth, and with his mouth, and will teach you what ye shall do. 27. And the LORD said to Aaron, Go into the wilderness to meet Moses.

Ex. 6:13. And the LORD spake unto Moses and unto Aaron, and gave them a charge unto the children of Israel, and unto Pharaoh king of Egypt, to bring the children of Israel out of the land of Egypt. 29. I *am* the LORD: speak thou unto Pharaoh king of Egypt all that I say unto thee. Ex. 7:2.

Ex. 19:3. And Moses went up unto God, and the LORD called unto him out of the mountain, saying, Thus shalt thou say to the house of Jacob, and tell the children of Israel; 9. And the LORD said unto Moses, Lo, I come unto thee in a thick cloud, that the people may hear when I speak with thee, and believe thee for ever. 19. And when the voice of the trumpet sounded long, and waxed louder and louder, Moses spake, and God answered him by a voice.

Ex. 24:16. And the glory of the LORD abode upon mount Sinai, and the cloud covered it six days: and the seventh day he called unto Moses out of the midst of the cloud.

Ex. 25:22. And there I will meet with thee, and I will commune with thee from above the mercy seat, from between the two cherubims which *are* upon the ark of the testimony, of all *things* which I will give thee in commandment unto the children of Israel.

Ex. 33:9. *The LORD* talked with Moses. 11. And the LORD spake unto Moses face to face, as a man speaketh unto his friend.

Ex. 35:31. And he hath filled him with the spirit of God, in wisdom, in understanding, and in knowledge, and in all manner of workmanship; *v.* 35.

Num. 7:89. And when Moses was gone into the tabernacle of the congregation to speak with him, then he heard the voice of one speaking unto him from off the mercy seat that *was* upon the ark of testimony, from between the two cherubims: and he spake unto him. Lev. 1:1; Num. 1:1.

Num. 9:8. And Moses said unto them, Stand still, and I will hear what the LORD will command concerning you. *vs.* 9,10.

Num. 11:17. And I will come down and talk with thee there: and I will take of the spirit which *is* upon thee, and will put *it* upon them; and they shall bear the burden of the people with thee, that thou bear *it* not thyself alone. 25. And the LORD came down in a cloud, and spake unto him, and took of the spirit that *was* upon him, and gave *it* unto the seventy elders: and it came to pass, *that,* when the spirit rested upon them, they prophesied, and did not cease.

Num. 12:6. And he said, Hear now my words: If there be a prophet among you, *I* the LORD will make myself known unto him in a vision, *and* will speak unto him in a dream. 7. My servant Moses *is* not so, who *is* faithful in all mine house. 8. With him will I speak mouth to mouth, even apparently, and not in dark speeches; and the similitude of the LORD shall he behold: wherefore then were ye not afraid to speak against my servant Moses?

Num. 16:28. Moses said, Hereby ye shall know that the LORD hath sent me to do all these works; for *I have* not *done them* of mine own mind. 29. If these men die the common death of all men, or if they be visited after the visitation of all men; *then* the LORD hath not sent me.

Num. 22:18. If Balak would give me his house full of silver and gold, I cannot go beyond the word of the LORD my God, to do less or more. 38. And Balaam said unto Balak, Lo, I am come unto thee: have I now any power at all to say any thing? the word that God putteth in my mouth, that shall I speak.

Num. 23:5. And the LORD put a word in Balaam's mouth, and said, Return unto Balak, and thus thou shalt speak. 12. And he answered and said, Must I not take heed to speak that which the LORD hath put in my mouth? 20. Behold, I have received *commandment* to bless: and he hath blessed; and I cannot reverse it. 26. Told not I thee, saying, All that the LORD speaketh, that I must do?

Num. 24:2. And Balaam lifted up his eyes, and he saw Israel abiding *in his tents* according to their tribes; and the spirit of God came upon him. 3. And he took up his parable, and said, Balaam the son of Beor hath said, and the man whose eyes are open hath said: 4. He hath said, which heard the words of God, which saw the vision of the Almighty, falling *into a trance,* but having his eyes open: *vs.* 15,16.

Deut. 1:5. On this side Jordan, in the land of Moab, began Moses to declare this law, saying, 6. The LORD our God spake unto us in Horeb, saying, Ye have dwelt long enough in this mount:

Deut. 5:4. The LORD talked with you face to face in the mount out of the midst of the fire, 5. (I stood between the LORD and you at that time, to shew you the word of the LORD: for ye were afraid by reason of the fire, and went not up into the mount;) saying, 6. I *am* the LORD thy God, which brought thee out of the land of Egypt, from the house of bondage. 31. But as for thee, stand thou here by me, and I will speak unto thee all the commandments, and the statutes, and the judgments, which thou shalt teach them, that they may do *them* in the land which I give them to possess it.

Deut. 34:9. And Joshua the son of Nun was full of the spirit of wisdom; for Moses had laid his hands upon him: and the children of Israel hearkened unto him, and did as the LORD commanded Moses. 10. And there arose not a prophet since in Israel like unto Moses, whom the LORD knew face to face, 11. In all the signs and the wonders, which the LORD sent him to do in the land of Egypt to Pharaoh, and to all his servants, and to all his land,

Josh. 3:7. And the LORD said unto Joshua, This day will I begin to magnify thee in the sight of all Israel, that they may know that, as I was with Moses, *so* I will be with thee.

Judg. 6:7. And it came to pass, when the children of Israel cried unto the LORD because of the Midianites, 8. That the LORD sent a prophet unto the children of Israel, which said unto them, Thus saith the LORD God of Israel, I brought you up from Egypt, and brought you forth out of the house of bondage; 9. And I delivered you out of the hand of the Egyptians, and out of the hand of all that oppressed you, and drave them out from before you, and gave you their land; 10. And I said unto you, I *am* the LORD your God; fear not the gods of the Amorites, in whose land ye dwell: but ye have not obeyed my voice. 34. But the Spirit of the LORD came upon Gideon, and he blew a trumpet; Judg. 11:29; 1 Chr. 12:18.

Judg. 13:25. And the Spirit of the LORD began to move him [Samson] at times in the camp of Dan between Zorah and Eshtaol. Judg. 14:6,19.

1 Sam. 3:1. And the child Samuel ministered unto the LORD before Eli. And the word of the LORD was precious in those days; *there was* no open vision. 7. Samuel did not yet know the LORD, neither was the word of the LORD yet revealed unto him. 19. Samuel grew, and the LORD was with him, and did let none of his words fall to the ground. 20. And all Israel from Dan even to Beer-sheba knew that Samuel *was* established *to be* a prophet of the LORD. 21. And the LORD appeared again in Shiloh: for the LORD revealed himself to Samuel in Shiloh by the word of the LORD. *vs.* 4-10.

1 Sam. 9:6. Behold now, *there is* in this city a man of God, and *he is* an honourable man; all that he saith cometh surely to pass: 15. The LORD had told Samuel in his ear a day before Saul came, *vs.* 16-20.

1 Sam. 10:6. The Spirit of the LORD will come upon thee, and thou shalt prophesy with them, and shalt be turned into another man. 7. And let it be, when these signs are come unto thee, *that* thou do as occasion serve thee; for God *is* with thee. 10. And when they came thither to the hill, behold, a company of prophets met him; and the Spirit of God came upon him, and he prophesied among them.

1 Sam. 16:13. And the Spirit of the LORD came upon David from that day forward.

1 Sam. 19:20, And Saul sent messengers to take David: and when they saw the company of the prophets prophesying, and Samuel standing *as* appointed over them, the Spirit of God was upon the messengers of Saul, and they also prophesied. 23. And the Spirit of God was upon him also, and he went on, and prophesied, until he came to Naioth in Ramah. *v.* 24.

2 Sam. 7:4. And it came to pass that night, that the word of the LORD came unto Nathan, saying, *vs.* 3-7; 2 Sam. 12:1.

2 Sam. 23:2. The Spirit of the LORD spake by me, and his word *was* in my tongue. 3. The God of Israel said, the Rock of Israel spake to me, He that ruleth over men *must be* just, ruling in the fear of God. Acts 2:30.

1 Kin. 13:20. The word of the LORD came unto the prophet that brought him back:

1 Kin. 14:5. The LORD said unto Ahijah, Behold, the wife of Jeroboam cometh to ask a thing of thee for her son; for he *is* sick: thus and thus shalt thou say unto her:

1 Kin. 17:1. Elijah the Tishbite, . . . said unto Ahab, As the LORD God of Israel liveth, before whom I stand, there shall not be dew nor rain these years, but according to my word. 24. And the woman said to Elijah, Now by this I know that thou *art* a man of God, *and* that the word of the LORD in thy mouth *is* truth.

1 Kin. 18:36. Elijah the prophet came near, and said, LORD God . . . let it be known this day that thou *art* God in Israel, and *that* I *am* thy servant, and *that* I have done all these things at thy word. 46. And the hand of the LORD was on Elijah;

1 Kin. 19:9. And he came thither unto a cave, and lodged there; and, behold, the word of the LORD *came* to him, and he said unto him, What doest thou here, Elijah?

1 Kin. 22:14. And Micaiah said, As the LORD liveth, what the LORD saith unto me, that will I speak. 28. If thou return at all in peace, the LORD hath not spoken by me. And he said, Hearken, O people, every one of you. 2 Chr. 18:27.

2 Kin. 1:12. And Elijah answered and said unto them, If I *be* a man of God, let fire come down from heaven, and consume thee and thy fifty. And the fire of God came down from heaven, and consumed him and his fifty.

2 Kin. 2:9. Elisha said, I pray thee, let a double portion of thy spirit be upon me. 15. And when the sons of the prophets which *were* to view at Jericho saw him, they said, The spirit of Elijah doth rest on Elisha.

2 Kin. 3:11. But Jehoshaphat said, *Is there* not here a prophet of the LORD, that we may enquire of the LORD by him? And one of the king of Israel's servants answered and said, Here *is* Elisha the son of Shaphat, which poured water on the hands of Elijah. 12. And Jehoshaphat said, The word of the LORD is with him. 15. When the minstrel played, the hand of the LORD came upon him.

2 Kin. 4:27. The man of God said. Let her alone; for her soul *is* vexed within her: and the LORD hath hid *it* from me, and hath not told me.

2 Kin. 5:8. When Elisha the man of God had heard that the king of Israel had rent his clothes, that he sent to the king, saying, Wherefore hast thou rent thy clothes? let him come now to me, and he shall know that there is a prophet in Israel.

2 Kin. 6:8. Then the king of Syria warred against Israel, and took counsel with his servants, saying, In such and such a place *shall be* my camp. 9. And the man of God sent unto the king of Israel, saying, Beware that thou pass not such a place; for

thither the Syrians are come down. 10. And the king of Israel sent to the place which the man of God told him and warned him of, and saved himself there, not once nor twice. 11. Therefore the heart of the king of Syria was sore troubled for this thing; and he called his servants, and said unto them, Will ye not shew me which of us *is* for the king of Israel? 12. And one of his servants said, None, my lord, O king: but Elisha, the prophet that *is* in Israel, telleth the king of Israel the words that thou speakest in thy bedchamber. 17. And Elisha prayed, and said, LORD, I pray thee, open his eyes, that he may see. And the LORD opened the eyes of the young man; and he saw: and, behold, the mountain *was* full of horses and chariots of fire round about Elisha. 32. But Elisha sat in his house, and the elders sat with him; and *the king* sent a man from before him: but ere the messenger came to him, he said to the elders, See ye how this son of a murderer hath sent to take away mine head? look, when the messenger cometh, shut the door, and hold him fast at the door: *is* not the sound of his master's feet behind him?

2 Kin. 10:10. Know now that there shall fall unto the earth nothing of the word of the LORD, which the LORD spake concerning the house of Ahab: for the LORD hath done *that* which he spake by his servant Elijah.

1 Chr. 21:18. The angel of the LORD commanded Gad to say to David, that David should go up, and set up an altar unto the LORD in the threshingfloor of Ornan the Jebusite.

1 Chr. 28:11. David gave to Solomon . . . 12. . . . the pattern of all that he had by the spirit, 19. All *this, said David,* the LORD made me understand in writing by *his* hand upon me, *even* all the works of this pattern. Ex. 25:9; 26:30; 2 Chr. 8:14.

2 Chr. 20:14. Upon Jahaziel. . . came the Spirit of the LORD in the midst of the congregation; 2 Chr. 15:1; 24:20.

2 Chr. 26:5. And he sought God in the days of Zechariah, who had understanding in the visions of God:

2 Chr. 33:18. Now the rest of the acts of Manasseh, and his prayer unto his God, and the words of the seers that spake to him in the name of the LORD God of Israel, Ezra 5:1,2.

2 Chr. 36:12. He . . . humbled not himself before Jeremiah the prophet *speaking* from the mouth of the LORD. *v.* 15.

Neh. 9:30. Many years didst thou forbear them, and testifiedst against them by thy spirit in thy prophets:

Job 32:8. *There is* a spirit in man: and the inspiration of the Almighty giveth them understanding.

Job 33:14. God speaketh once, yea twice, *yet man* perceiveth it not. 15. In a dream, in a vision of the night, when deep sleep falleth upon men, in slumberings upon the bed; 16. Then he openeth the ears of men, and sealeth their instruction,

Psa. 103:7. He made known his ways unto Moses, his acts unto the children of Israel.

Isa. 6:1. I saw also the Lord sitting upon a throne, high and lifted up, and his train filled the temple. 8. I heard the voice of the Lord, saying, Whom shall I send, and who will go for us? Then said I, Here *am* I; send me. 9. And he said, Go, and tell this people, *vs.* 1–7.

Isa. 8:11. The LORD spake thus to me with a strong hand, and instructed me that I should not walk in the way of this people, saying,

Isa. 44:26. That confirmeth the word of his servant, and performeth the counsel of his messengers;

Isa. 63:11. Where *is* he that put his holy Spirit within him?

Jer. 1:1. The words of Jeremiah the son of Hilkiah, of the priests that *were* in Anathoth in the land of Benjamin: 2. To whom the word of the LORD came in the days of Josiah the son of Amon king of Judah, in the thirteenth year of his reign. chapters 2:1; 7:1; 11:1; 13:1–3; 16:1; 18:1; 24: 4; 26:1,12; 27:1,2; 29:30; 33:1; 34:1; Obad. 1:1; Jonah 1:1; Mic. 1:1; Zech. 1:1,7.

Jer. 1:4. Then the word of the LORD came unto me, saying, 5. Before I formed thee in the belly I knew thee; and before thou camest forth out of the womb I sanctified thee, *and* I ordained thee a prophet unto the nations. 6. Then said I, Ah, Lord GOD! behold, I cannot speak: for I *am* a child. 7. But the LORD said unto me, Say not, I *am* a child: for thou shalt go to all that I shall send thee, and whatsoever I command thee thou shalt speak. 8. Be not afraid of their faces: for I *am* with thee to deliver thee, saith the LORD. 9. Then the LORD put forth his hand, and touched my mouth. And the LORD said unto me, Behold, I have put my words in thy mouth. 10. See, I have this day set thee over the nations and over the kingdoms, to root out, and to pull down, and to destroy, and to throw down, to build, and to plant.

Jer. 7:25. Since the day that your fathers came forth out of the land of Egypt unto this day I have even sent unto you all my servants the prophets, daily rising up early and sending *them:* Jer. 25:3.

Jer. 11:18. The LORD hath given me knowledge *of it,* and I know *it:* then thou shewedst me their doings.

Jer. 20:9. I said, I will not make mention of him, nor speak any more in his name. But *his word* was in mine heart as a burning fire shut up in my bones, and I was weary with forbearing, and I could not *stay.*

Jer. 23:9. Mine heart within me is broken because of the prophets; all my bones shake; I am like a drunken man, and like a man whom wine hath overcome, because of the LORD, and because of the words of his holiness.

Jer. 26:2. Thus saith the LORD; Stand in the court of the LORD'S house, and speak unto all the cities of Judah, which come to worship in the LORD'S house, all the words that I command thee to speak unto them; diminish not a word:

Jer. 42:4. I will pray unto the LORD your God according to your words; and it shall come to pass, *that* whatsoever thing the LORD will answer you, I will declare *it* unto you; I will keep nothing back from you. 7. And it came to pass after ten days, that the word of the LORD came unto Jeremiah.

Ezek. 1:1. The heavens were opened, and I saw visions of God. 3. The word of the LORD came expressly unto Ezekiel . . . and the hand of the LORD was there upon him. 20. Whithersoever the spirit was to go, they went, thither *was their* spirit to go; and the wheels were lifted up over against them: for the spirit of the living creature *was* in the wheels.

Ezek. 2:1. I will speak unto thee. 2. And the spirit entered into me when he spake unto me. 4. I do send thee unto them; and thou shalt say unto them, Thus saith the Lord GOD. 5. And they, . . . yet shall know that there hath been a prophet among them.

Ezek. 3:10. Son of man, all my words that I shall speak unto thee receive in thine heart, and hear with thine ears. 11. And go, get thee to them of the captivity, unto the children of thy people, and speak unto them, and tell them, Thus saith the Lord GOD; whether they will hear, or whether they will forbear. 12. Then the spirit took me up, and I heard behind me a voice of a great rushing, *saying,* Blessed *be* the glory of the LORD from his place. 14. So the spirit lifted me up, and took me away, and I went in bitterness, in the heat of my spirit; but the hand of the LORD was strong upon me. 16. And it came to pass at the end of seven days, that the word of the LORD came unto me, saying, 17. Son of man, I have made thee a watchman unto the house of Israel: therefore hear the word at my mouth, and give them warning from me. 22. The hand of the LORD was there upon me; and he said unto me, Arise, go forth into the plain, and I will there talk with thee. 24. Then the spirit entered into me, and set me upon my feet, and spake with me. 27. But when I speak with thee, I will open thy mouth, and thou shalt say unto them, Thus saith the Lord GOD;

Ezek. 8:1. And it came to pass in the sixth year, in the sixth *month,* in the fifth *day* of the month, *as* I sat in mine house, and the elders of Judah sat before me, that the hand of the Lord GOD fell there upon me.

Ezek. 11:1. The spirit lifted me up, and brought me unto the east gate of the LORD'S house. 4. Therefore prophesy against them, prophesy, O son of man. 5. And the Spirit of the LORD fell upon me, and said unto me, Speak; Thus saith the LORD: 24. After-

wards the spirit took me up, and brought me in a vision by the Spirit of God into Chaldea, to them of the captivity.

Ezek. 33:22. The hand of the LORD was upon me in the evening, afore he that was escaped came; and had opened my mouth, until he came to me in the morning; and my mouth was opened, and I was no more dumb.

Ezek. 37:1. The hand of the LORD was upon me, and carried me out in the spirit of the LORD, and set me down in the midst of the valley which *was* full of bones,

Ezek. 40:1. The hand of the LORD was upon me, and brought me thither.

Ezek. 43:5. So the spirit took me up, and brought me into the inner court; and, behold, the glory of the LORD filled the house.

Dan. 1:17. As for these four children, God gave them knowledge and skill in all learning and wisdom: and Daniel had understanding in all visions and dreams.

Dan. 2:19. Then was the secret revealed unto Daniel in a night vision.

Dan. 7:16. I came near unto one of them that stood by, and asked him the truth of all this. So he told me, and made me know the interpretation of the things.

Dan. 8:16. I heard a man's voice, between *the banks of* Ulai, which called, and said, Gabriel, make this *man* to understand the vision.

Dan. 9:2. In the first year of his reign, I Daniel understood by books the number of the years, whereof the word of the LORD came to Jeremiah the prophet, that he would accomplish seventy years in the desolations of Jerusalem. 6. Neither have we hearkened unto thy servants the prophets, which spake in thy name to our kings, our princes, and our fathers, and to all the people of the land. 10. Neither have we obeyed the voice of the LORD our God, to walk in his laws, which he set before us by his servants the prophets. [*vs.* 1–21.] 22. And he informed *me,* and talked with me, and said, O Daniel, I am now come forth to give thee skill and understanding.

Dan. 10:7. And I Daniel alone saw the vision: for the men that were with me saw not the vision; but a great quaking fell upon them, so that they fled to hide themselves. 8. Therefore I was left alone, and saw this great vision, and there remained no strength in me: for my comeliness was turned in me into corruption, and I retained no strength. 9. Yet heard I the voice of his words: and when I heard the voice of his words, then was I in a deep sleep on my face, and my face toward the ground.

Hos. 1:1. The word of the LORD that came unto Hosea, *v.* 2.

Hos. 12:10. I have also spoken by the prophets, and I have multiplied visions, and used similitudes, by the ministry of the prophets.

Joel 2:28. It shall come to pass afterward, *that* I will pour out my spirit upon all flesh; and your sons and your daughters shall prophesy, your old men shall dream dreams, your young men shall see visions: 29. And also upon the servants and upon the handmaids in those days will I pour out my spirit.

Amos 3:7. Surely the Lord GOD will do nothing, but he revealeth his secret unto his servants the prophets. 8. The lion hath roared, who will not fear? the Lord GOD hath spoken, who can but prophesy?

Amos 7:7. Thus he shewed me: and, behold, the Lord stood upon a wall *made* by a plumbline, with a plumbline in his hand. 14. I *was* no prophet, neither *was* I a prophet's son; but I *was* an herdman, and a ¹gatherer of sycomore ²fruit: 15. And the LORD took me as I followed the flock, and the LORD said unto me, Go, prophesy unto my people Israel. [R. V. ¹dresser ²trees]

Amos 9:1. I saw the Lord standing upon the altar: and he said, Smite the lintel of the door, that the posts may shake: and cut them in the head, all of them; and I will slay the last of them with the sword: he that fleeth of them shall not flee away, and he that escapeth of them shall not be delivered.

Jonah 3:1. The word of the LORD came unto Jonah the second time, saying, 2. Arise, go unto Nineveh, that great city, and preach unto it the preaching that I bid thee.

Mic. 3:8. Truly I am full of power by the spirit of the LORD, and of judgment, and of might, to declare unto Jacob his trangression, and to Israel his sin.

Hab. 3:2. O LORD, I have heard thy speech, *and* was afraid: 16. When I heard, my belly trembled; my lips quivered at the voice: rottenness entered into my bones, and I trembled in myself, that I might rest in the day of trouble:

Hag. 1:13. Then spake Haggai the LORD's messenger in the LORD's message unto the people,

Zech. 2:9. For, behold, I will shake mine hand upon them, and they shall be a spoil to their servants: and ye shall know that the LORD of hosts hath sent me.

Zech. 7:12. Yea, they made their hearts *as* an adamant stone, lest they should hear the law, and the words which the LORD of hosts hath sent in his spirit by the former prophets: therefore came a great wrath from the LORD of hosts.

Mark 12:36. For David himself said by the Holy Ghost, The LORD said to my Lord, Sit thou on my right hand, till I make thine enemies thy footstool.

Luke 1:15. He shall be filled with the Holy Ghost, even from his mother's womb. 41. Elisabeth was filled with the Holy Ghost: 67. His father Zacharias was filled with the Holy Ghost, and prophesied, 70. He spake by the mouth of his holy prophets, which have been since the world began:

Luke 2:25. And, behold, there was a man in Jerusalem, whose name *was* Simeon; and the same man *was* just and devout, waiting for the consolation of Israel: and the Holy Ghost was upon him. 26. And it was revealed unto him by the Holy Ghost, that he should not see death, before he had seen the Lord's Christ. 27. And he came by the Spirit into the temple:

Luke 3:2. The word of God came unto John the son of Zacharias in the wilderness.

John 1:6. There was a man sent from God, whose name *was* John.

Acts 2:2. Suddenly there came a sound from heaven as of a rushing mighty wind, and it filled all the house where they were sitting. 3. And there appeared unto them cloven tongues like as of fire, and it sat upon each of them. 4. And they were all filled with the Holy Ghost, and began to speak with other tongues, as the Spirit gave them utterance.

Acts 3:18. Those things, which God before had shewed by the mouth of all his prophets, that Christ should suffer, he hath so fulfilled.

Acts 7:55. He, being full of the Holy Ghost, looked up stedfastly into heaven, and saw the glory of God, and Jesus standing on the right hand of God, *v.* 56.

Acts 8:29. Then the Spirit said unto Philip, Go near, and join thyself to this chariot. 39. And when they were come up out of the water, the Spirit of the Lord caught away Philip, that the eunuch saw him no more:

Acts 11:28. And there stood up one of them named Agabus, and signified by the spirit that there should be great dearth throughout all the world:

Acts 21:4. And finding disciples, we tarried there seven days: who said to Paul through the Spirit, that he should not go up to Jerusalem. 10. And as we tarried *there* many days, there came down from Judæa a certain prophet, named Agabus. 11. And when he was come unto us, he took Paul's girdle, and bound his own hands and feet, and said, Thus saith the Holy Ghost, So shall the Jews at Jerusalem bind the man that owneth this girdle, and shall deliver *him* into the hands of the Gentiles.

Acts 28:25. And when they agreed not among themselves, they departed, after that Paul had spoken one word, Well spake the Holy Ghost by Esaias the prophet unto our fathers,

Rom. 1:1. Paul, a servant of Jesus Christ, called *to be* an apostle, separated unto the gospel of God, 2. (Which he had promised afore by his prophets in the Holy Scriptures,)

1 Cor. 12:7. But the manifestation of the Spirit is given to every man to profit withal. 8. For to one is given by the Spirit the word of wisdom; to another the word of knowledge by the same Spirit; 9. To another faith by the same Spirit; to another the gifts of healing by the same Spirit; 10. To

another the working of miracles; to another prophecy; to another discerning of spirits; to another *divers* kinds of tongues; to another the interpretation of tongues: 11. But all these worketh that one and the self-same Spirit, dividing to every man severally as he will.

1 Cor. 14:32. The spirits of the prophets are subject to the prophets.

Heb. 1:1. God, who at sundry times and in divers manners spake in time past unto the fathers by the prophets,

Heb. 3:5. Moses verily *was* faithful in all his house, as a servant, for a testimony of those things which were to be spoken after;

Jas. 5:10. Take, my brethren, the prophets, who have spoken in the name of the Lord,

1 Pet. 1:10. Of which salvation the prophets have inquired and searched diligently, who prophesied of the grace *that should come* unto you: 11. Searching what, or what manner of time the Spirit of Christ which was in them did signify, when it testified beforehand the sufferings of Christ, and the glory that should follow.

2 Pet. 1:21. The prophecy came not in old time by the will of man: but holy men of God spake *as they were* moved by the Holy Ghost.

Jude 14. Enoch also, the seventh from Adam, prophesied of these, saying, Behold, the Lord cometh with ten thousands of his saints,

Rev. 2:7. He that hath an ear, let him hear what the Spirit saith unto the churches;

Rev. 10:7. As he hath declared to his servants, the prophets.

Rev. 14:13. I heard a voice from heaven saying unto me, Write, Blessed *are* the dead which die in the Lord from henceforth: Yea, saith the Spirit, that they may rest from their labours;

Rev. 22:6. And he said unto me, These sayings *are* faithful and true: and the Lord God of the holy prophets sent his angel to shew unto his servants the things which must shortly be done. 8. And I John saw these things, and heard *them*. And when I had heard and seen, I fell down to worship before the feet of the angel which shewed me these things.

See REVELATION; WORD OF GOD, INSPIRATION OF.

PROPHETESSES: Ezek. 13:17; Joel 2:28,29. Miriam, Ex. 15:20. Deborah, Judg. 4:4. Huldah, 2 Kin. 22:14. Noadiah, Neh. 6:14. Isaiah's wife, Isa. 8:3. Elizabeth, Luke 1:41-45. Anna, Luke 2:36-38. Daughters of Philip, Acts 21:9. Jezebel, Rev. 2:20.

See WOMEN.

PROPITIATION, Rom. 3:25; 5:1,10,11; 2 Cor. 5:18,19; Col. 1:20-22; 1 John 2:2; 4:10; Heb. 9:5. [*R. V.*, marg., reads, And over it the propitiatory.]

See ATONEMENT.

PROSPERITY. From God, Gen. 33:11; 49:24-26; Psa. 127:1; 128:1,2. Design of, Eccl. 7:14. Dangers of, Deut. 8:10-18; 31:20;

32:15; Jer. 5:7; Hos. 13:6. Evil effects of, Hos. 4:7. Pride in, 2 Chr. 32:25. Forgetfulness of God in, 2 Chr. 12:1; 26:16. The prosperous despise the unfortunate, Job 12:5.

Promised to the righteous, Job 22:23-27. Prudence in. Instances of: Joseph and Daniel, as deduced from their general conduct. See JOSEPH; DANIEL.

See BLESSINGS, TEMPORAL; RICH, THE; RICHES.

PROSTITUTION, lascivious. Forbidden, Lev. 19:29; Deut. 23:17.

See ADULTERY; LASCIVIOUSNESS.

"PROTRACTED MEETINGS," 1 Kin. 8:65; 2 Chr. 7:8-10; 30:23.

See REVIVALS.

PROUD. See PRIDE.

PROVERBS. Design of, Prov. 1:1-4. Written by Solomon, Prov. 1:1; 25:1.

MISCELLANY OF: 1 Sam. 10:12. Therefore it became a proverb, Is Saul also among the prophets?

1 Sam. 24:13. As saith the proverb of the ancients, Wickedness proceedeth from the wicked: but mine hand shall not be upon thee. 14. After whom is the king of Israel come out? after whom dost thou pursue? after a dead dog, after a flea.

2 Sam. 3:8. *Am* I a dog's head,

2 Sam. 20:18. Then she spake, saying, They were wont to speak in old time, saying, They shall surely ask *counsel* at Abel:

1 Kin. 20:11. And the king of Israel answered and said, Tell *him*, Let not him that girdeth on *his harness* boast himself as he that putteth it off.

Prov. 1:17. Surely in vain the net is spread in the sight of any bird.

Ezek. 12:22. Son of man, what *is* that proverb *that* ye have in the land of Israel, saying, The days are prolonged, and every vision faileth? 23. Tell them therefore, Thus saith the Lord GOD; I will make this proverb to cease, and they shall no more use it as a proverb in Israel; but say unto them, The days are at hand, and the effect of every vision.

Ezek. 16:44. Behold, every one that useth proverbs shall use *this* proverb against thee, saying, As *is* the mother, *so is* her daughter.

Ezek. 18:2. What mean ye, that ye use this proverb concerning the land of Israel, saying, The fathers have eaten sour grapes, and the children's teeth are set on edge? 3. *As* I live, saith the Lord GOD, ye shall not have *occasion* any more to use this proverb in Israel. [Jer. 31:29.] 4. Behold, all souls are mine; as the soul of the father, so also the soul of the son is mine: the soul that sinneth, it shall die.

Hos. 4:9. And there shall be, like people, like priest:

Matt. 12:33. The tree is known by *his* fruit. Luke 6:44.

Luke 4:23. And he said unto them, Ye will surely say unto me this [1] proverb, Physician, heal thyself:

[1 R. V. parable]

Luke 14:34. If the salt have lost his savour, wherewith shall it be seasoned?

John 1:46. Can there any good thing come out of Nazareth?

1 Cor. 15:33. Evil communications corrupt good manners.

Gal. 6:7. Whatsoever a man soweth, that shall he also reap.

See RIDDLE.

PROVIDENCE, OF GOD: See GOD, PROVIDENCE OF, AND OVERRULING INTERPOSITIONS OF.

PROXY, in priest's service, 2 Chr. 30:17.

See SUBSTITUTION; SUFFERINGS, VICARIOUS.

PRUDENCE. Job 34:3. The ear trieth words, as the mouth tasteth meat. 4. Let us choose to us judgment: let us know among ourselves what is good.

Psa. 39:1. I said, I will take heed to my ways, that I sin not with my tongue: I will keep my mouth with a bridle, while the wicked is before me.

Psa. 112:5. He will guide his affairs with discretion.

Prov. 6:1. My son, if thou be surety for thy friend, if thou hast stricken thy hand with a stranger, 2. Thou art snared with the words of thy mouth, thou art taken with the words of thy mouth.

Prov. 8:12. I wisdom dwell with prudence, and find out knowledge of witty inventions.

Prov. 11:13. A talebearer revealeth secrets: but he that is of a faithful spirit concealeth the 'matter. 15. He that is surety for a stranger shall smart for it: and he that hateth suretiship is sure. 29. The fool shall be servant to the wise of heart.

Prov. 12:8. A man shall be commended according to his wisdom: 16. A fool's wrath is presently known: but a prudent man covereth shame. 23. A prudent man concealeth knowledge: but the heart of fools proclaimeth foolishness.

Prov. 13:16. Every prudent man dealeth with knowledge: but a fool layeth open his folly.

Prov. 14:8. The wisdom of the prudent is to understand his way: 15. The simple believeth every word: but the prudent man looketh well to his going. 16. A wise man feareth, and departeth from evil: but the fool rageth, and is confident. 18 The simple inherit folly: but the prudent are crowned with knowledge.

Prov. 15:5. He that regardeth reproof is prudent. 22. Without counsel purposes are disappointed: but in the multitude of counsellors they are established.

Prov. 16:20. He that handleth a matter wisely shall find good: and whoso trusteth in the LORD, happy is he. 21. The wise in heart shall be called prudent:

Prov. 17:2. A wise servant shall have rule over a son that causeth shame, and shall have part of the inheritance among the brethren. 18. A man void of understanding striketh hands, and becometh surety in the presence of his friend.

Prov. 18:15. The heart of the prudent getteth knowledge; and the ear of the wise seeketh knowledge. 16. A man's gift maketh room for him, and bringeth him before great men.

Prov. 19:2. He that hasteth with his feet sinneth.

Prov. 20:5. Counsel in the heart of man is like deep water; but a man of understanding will draw it out. 16. Take his garment that is surety for a stranger: 18. Every purpose is established by counsel: and with good advice make war.

Prov. 21:5. The thoughts of the diligent tend only to plenteousness; but of every one that is hasty only to want. 20. There is treasure to be desired and oil in the dwelling of the wise; but a foolish man spendeth it up. 23. Whoso keepeth his mouth and his tongue keepeth his soul from troubles.

Prov. 22:3. A prudent man foreseeth the evil, and hideth himself: but the simple pass on, and are punished. 7. The rich ruleth over the poor, and the borrower is servant to the lender. 26. Be not thou one of them that strike hands, or of them that are sureties for debts. 27. If thou hast nothing to pay, why should he take away thy bed from under thee?

Prov. 23:1. When thou sittest to eat with a ruler, consider diligently what is before thee: 2. And put a knife to thy throat, if thou be a man given to appetite. 3. Be not desirous of his dainties: for they are deceitful meat. 9. Speak not in the ears of a fool: for he will despise the wisdom of thy words.

Prov. 24:6. By wise counsel thou shalt make thy war: and in multitude of counsellors there is safety. 27. Prepare thy work without, and make it fit for thyself in the field; and afterwards build thine house.

Prov. 25:8. Go not forth hastily to strive, lest thou know not what to do in the end thereof, when thy neighbour hath put thee to shame. 9. Debate thy cause with thy neighbour himself; and discover not a secret to another: 10. Lest he that heareth it put thee to shame, and thine infamy turn not away.

Prov. 26:4. Answer not a fool according to his folly, lest thou also be like unto him. 5. Answer a fool according to his folly, lest he be wise in his own conceit.

Prov. 27:12. A prudent man foreseeth the evil, and hideth himself:

Prov. 29:8. Scornful men bring a city into a snare: but wise men turn away wrath. 11. A fool uttereth all his mind: but a wise man keepeth it in till afterwards.

Eccl. 7:16. Be not righteous over much; neither make thyself over wise: why shouldest thou destroy thyself? 17. Be not over much wicked, neither be thou foolish: why shouldest thou die before thy time?

Eccl. 8:2. I counsel thee to keep the king's commandment, and that in regard of the oath of God. 3. Be not hasty to go out of his sight: stand not in an evil thing; for he doeth whatsoever pleaseth him.

Eccl. 10:1. Dead flies cause the ointment of the apothecary to send forth a stinking savour: *so doth* a little folly him that is in reputation for wisdom *and* honour. 10. If the iron be blunt, and he do not whet the edge, then must he put to more strength: but wisdom *is* profitable to direct.

Hos. 14:9. Who *is* wise, and he shall understand these *things?* prudent, and he shall know them? for the ways of the LORD *are* right, and the just shall walk in them: but the transgressors shall fall therein.

Amos 5:13. Therefore the prudent shall keep silence in that time; for it *is* an evil time.

Matt. 5:25. Agree with thine adversary quickly, whiles thou art in the way with him; lest at any time the adversary deliver thee to the judge, and the judge deliver thee to the officer, and thou be cast into prison. 26. Verily I say unto thee, Thou shalt by no means come out thence, till thou hast paid the uttermost farthing.

Matt. 7:6. Give not that which is holy unto the dogs, neither cast ye your pearls before swine, lest they trample them under their feet, and turn again and rend you.

Luke 14:28. Which of you, intending to build a tower, sitteth not down first, and counteth the cost, whether he have *sufficient* to finish it? 29. Lest haply, after he hath laid the foundation, and is not able to finish *it*, all that behold *it* begin to mock him, 30. Saying, This man began to build, and was not able to finish. 31. Or what king, going to make war against another king, sitteth not down first, and consulteth whether he be able with ten thousand to meet him that cometh against him with twenty thousand? 32. Or else, while the other is yet a great way off, he sendeth an ambassage, and desireth conditions of peace.

Rom. 14:16. Let not then your good be evil spoken of:

1 Cor. 6:12. All things are lawful unto me, but all things are not expedient: all things are lawful for me, but I will not be brought under the power of any. chapter 10:23.

1 Cor. 8:8. But meat commendeth us not to God: for neither, if we eat, are we the better; neither, if we eat not, are we the worse. 9. But take heed lest by any means this liberty of your's become a stumbling-block to them that are weak. 10. For if any man see thee which hast knowledge sit at meat in the idol's temple shall not the conscience of him which is weak be emboldened to eat those things which are offered to idols; 11. And through thy knowledge shall the weak brother perish, for whom Christ died? 12. But when ye sin so against the brethren, and wound their weak conscience, ye sin against Christ. 13. Wherefore, if meat make my brother to offend, I will eat no flesh while the world standeth, lest I make my brother to offend.

1 Cor. 10:25. Whatsoever is sold in the shambles, *that* eat, asking no question for conscience sake: 26. For the earth *is* the Lord's, and the fulness thereof. 27. If any of them that believe not bid you *to a feast*, and ye be disposed to go; whatsoever is set before you, eat, asking no question for conscience sake. 28. But if any man say unto you, This is offered in sacrifice unto idols, eat not for his sake that shewed it, and for conscience sake: ¹ for the earth *is* the Lord's, and the fulness thereof: 29. Conscience, I say, not thine own, but of the other: for why is my liberty judged of another *man's* conscience? 30. For if I by grace be a partaker, why am I evil spoken of for that for which I give thanks? 31. Whether therefore ye eat, or drink, or whatsoever ye do, do all to the glory of God. 32. Give none offence, neither to the Jews, nor to the Gentiles, nor to the church of God: 33. Even as I please all *men* in all *things*, not seeking mine own profit, but the *profit* of many, that they may be saved. [¹ Omitted in R. V.]

Col. 4:5. Walk in wisdom toward them that are without, redeeming the time.

Jas. 1:19. Wherefore, my beloved brethren, let every man be swift to hear, slow to speak, slow to wrath:

See DIPLOMACY; GENTLENESS; WISDOM.

INSTANCES OF: Jacob, in his conduct toward Esau, Gen. 32:3–21; toward his sons, after Dinah's defilement, Gen. 34:5,30. Joseph, in the affairs of Egypt, Gen. 41:33–57. Jethro's advice to Moses, Ex. 18:17–23. The Israelites, in the threatened war with the two and one-half tribes, Josh. 22:10–34. Saul, in not slaying the Jabesh-gileadites, 1 Sam. 11:13. David, in his conduct with Saul, 1 Sam. 18:5–30; in overthrowing Ahithophel's counsel, 2 Sam. 15:33–37. Abigail, in averting David's wrath, 1 Sam. 25: 18–31. Achish, in dismissing David, 1 Sam. 29. Elijah, in his flight from Jezebel, 1 Kin. 19:3,4. Rehoboam's counsellors, 1 Kin. 12:7. Jehoram, in suspecting a Syrian stratagem, 2 Kin. 7:12,13. Nehemiah, in conduct of affairs at Jerusalem, Neh. 2:12–16; 4:13–23. Daniel, Dan. 1:8–14. Certain elders of Israel, Jer. 26:17–23. Of Jesus, in charging those who were healed not to advertise his miracles, Matt. 9:30; 16:20; Mark 3:12; 5:43; 7:36; 8:30; 9:9; going to the feast secretly, John 7:10; in walking "no more openly," John 11:54; 12:36; in avoiding his enemies, Matt. 12:14–16; Mark 3:7; John 11:47–54. Joseph, in his conduct toward Mary, Matt. 1:19. Peter, in escaping Herod, Acts 12:17. Paul, in circumcising Timothy, Acts 16:3; in performing temple rites, Acts 21:20–26; in setting the Jewish sects on each other, Acts 23:6; avoiding suspicion in administering the gifts of the churches, 2 Cor. 8:20; his lack of, in his persistence in going to Jerusalem despite the warnings of the Spirit and his friends, Acts 20:22–25,37,38; 21:10–14; Paul and Barnabas, in escaping persecution, Acts 14:6; Paul and Silas, in escaping

from Berea, Acts 17:10–15. The town clerk of Ephesus, in averting a riot, Acts 19:29–41.
See DIPLOMACY.

PRUNING, Lev. 25:3,4; Isa. 5:6; 18:5; John 15:2–6. Pruninghook, Isa. 2:4; 18:5; Joel 3:10; Mic. 4:3.

PSALMS. Of Moses, celebrating the deliverance at the Red Sea, Ex. 15:1–19. Didactic songs composed by Moses, celebrating the providence, righteousness, and judgments of God, Deut. 32:1–43; Psa. 90. Song of Deborah, celebrating Israel's victory over Sisera, Judg. 5. Of Hannah, in thankfulness for a son, 1 Sam. 2:1–10. Of David, celebrating his deliverance, 2 Sam. 22; on the occasion of removing the ark, 1 Chr. 16:7–36; at the close of his reign, 2 Sam. 23:2–7; 1 Chr. 29:10–19. Of Isaiah, Isa. 12; 25; 26. Of Hezekiah, celebrating deliverance from death, Isa. 38:9–20. Of Mary, Luke 1:46–55. Elisabeth, Luke 1:42–45. Zacharias, Luke 1:68–79.

INDEX OF SUB-TOPICS: *Afflictions, p.* 1019; *Didactic, p.* 1038; *Historical, p.* 1052; *Imprecatory, p.* 1055; *Intercessional, p.* 1055; *Messianic, p.* 1057; *Penitential, p.*1057; *Praise, p.* 1059; *For God's Attributes, p.* 1059; *Prophetic, p.* 1067; *Thanksgiving, p.* 1072; *For God's Goodness to Israel, p.* 1072; *For God's Goodness to Good Men, p.* 1078; *For God's Mercies to Individuals, p.* 1082.

AFFLICTIONS:

PSALM 3.—*The security of God's protection.*

A PSALM OF DAVID, WHEN HE FLED FROM ABSALOM HIS SON.

1 LORD, how are they increased that trouble me! many *are* they that rise up against me.

2 Many *there be* which say of my soul, *There is* no help for him in God. Selah.

3 But thou, O LORD, *art* a shield for me; my glory, and the lifter up of mine head.

4 I cried unto the LORD with my voice, and he heard me out of his holy hill. Selah.

5 I laid me down and slept; I awaked; for the LORD sustained me.

6 I will not be afraid of ten thousands of people, that have set *themselves* against me round about.

7 Arise, O LORD; save me, O my God: for thou hast smitten all mine enemies *upon* the cheek bone; thou hast broken the teeth of the ungodly.

8 Salvation *belongeth* unto the LORD: thy blessing *is* upon thy people.   Selah.

PSALM 4.—1 *David prayeth for audience. 2 He reproveth and exhorteth his enemies. 6 Man's happiness is in God's favour.*

TO THE CHIEF MUSICIAN ON NEGINOTH, A PSALM OF DAVID.

1 Hear me when I call, O God of my righteousness: thou hast enlarged me *when I was* in distress; have mercy upon me, and hear my prayer.

2 O ye sons of men, how long *will ye turn* my glory into shame? *how long* will ye love vanity, *and* seek after leasing?   Selah.

3 But know that the LORD hath set apart him that is godly for himself: the LORD will hear when I call unto him.

4 Stand in awe, and sin not: commune with your own heart upon your bed, and be still.   Selah.

5 Offer the sacrifices of righteousness, and put your trust in the LORD.

6 *There be* many that say, Who will shew us *any* good? LORD, lift thou up the light of thy countenance upon us.

7 Thou hast put gladness in my heart, more than in the time *that* their corn and their wine increased.

8 I will both lay me down in peace, and sleep: for thou, LORD, only makest me dwell in safety.

PSALM 5.—1 *David prayeth, and professeth his study in prayer. 4 God favoureth not the wicked. 7 David, professing his faith, prayeth unto God to guide him, 10 to destroy his enemies, 11 and to preserve the godly.*

TO THE CHIEF MUSICIAN UPON NEHILOTH, A PSALM OF DAVID.

1 Give ear to my words, O LORD, consider my meditation.

2 Hearken unto the voice of my cry, my King, and my God: for unto thee will I pray.

3 My voice shalt thou hear in the morning, O LORD; in the morning will I direct *my prayer* unto thee, and will look up.

4 For thou *art* not a God that hath pleasure in wickedness: neither shall evil dwell with thee.

5 The foolish shall not stand in thy sight: thou hatest all workers of iniquity.

6 Thou shalt destroy them that speak leasing: the LORD will abhor the bloody and deceitful man.

7 But as for me, I will come *into* thy house in the multitude of thy mercy: *and* in thy fear will I worship toward thy holy temple.

8 Lead me, O LORD, in thy righteousness because of mine enemies; make thy way straight before my face.

9 For *there is* no faithfulness in their mouth; their inward part *is* very wickedness; their throat *is* an open sepulchre; they flatter with their tongue.

10 Destroy thou them, O God; let them fall by their own counsels; cast them out in the multitude of their transgressions; for they have rebelled against thee.

11 But let all those that put their trust in thee rejoice: let them ever shout for joy, because thou defendest them: let them also that love thy name be joyful in thee.

12 For thou, LORD, wilt bless the righteous; with favour wilt thou compass him as *with* a shield.

PSALM 7.—1 *David prayeth against the malice of his enemies, professing his innocency. 10 By faith he seeth his defence, and the destruction of his enemies.*

SHIGGAION OF DAVID, WHICH HE SANG UNTO THE LORD, CONCERNING THE WORDS OF CUSH THE BENJAMITE.

1 O LORD my God, in thee do I put my trust: save me from all them that persecute me, and deliver me:

2 Lest he tear my soul like a lion, rending *it* in pieces, while *there is* none to deliver.

3 O LORD my God, if I have done this; if there be iniquity in my hands;

4 If I have rewarded evil unto him that was at peace with me; (yea, I have delivered him that without cause is mine enemy :)

5 Let the enemy persecute my soul, and take *it;* yea, let him tread down my life upon the earth, and lay mine honour in the dust.   Selah.

6 Arise, O LORD, in thine anger, lift up thyself because of the rage of mine enemies: and awake for me *to* the judgment *that* thou hast commanded.

7 So shall the congregation of the people compass thee about: for their sakes therefore return thou on high.

8 The LORD shall judge the people: judge me, O LORD, according to my righteousness, and according to mine integrity *that is* in me.

9 Oh let the wickedness of the wicked come to an end; but establish the just: for the righteous God trieth the hearts and reins.

10 My defence *is* of God, which saveth the upright in heart.

11 God judgeth the righteous, and God is angry *with the wicked* every day.

12 If he turn not, he will whet his sword; he hath bent his bow, and made it ready.

13 He hath also prepared for him the instruments of death; he ordaineth his arrows against the persecutors.

14 Behold, he travaileth with iniquity, and hath conceived mischief, and brought forth falsehood.

15 He made a pit, and digged it, and is fallen into the ditch *which* he made.

16 His mischief shall return upon his own head, and his violent dealing shall come down upon his own pate.

17 I will praise the LORD according to his righteousness: and will sing praise to the name of the LORD most high.

PSALM 11.—*David encourageth himself in God against his enemies.* 4 *The providence and justice of God.*

To the chief Musician, A Psalm of David.

1 In the LORD put I my trust: how say ye to my soul, Flee *as* a bird to your mountain?

2 For, lo, the wicked bend *their* bow, they make ready their arrow upon the string, that they may privily shoot at the upright in heart.

3 If the foundations be destroyed, what can the righteous do?

4 The LORD *is* in his holy temple, the LORD's throne *is* in heaven: his eyes behold, his eyelids try, the children of men.

5 The LORD trieth the righteous: but the wicked and him that loveth violence his soul hateth.

6. Upon the wicked he shall rain snares, fire and brimstone, and an horrible tempest: *this shall be* the portion of their cup.

7 For the righteous LORD loveth righteousness; his countenance doth behold the upright.

PSALM 13.—1 *David complaineth of delay in help.* 3 *He prayeth for preventing grace.* 5 *He boasteth of divine mercy.*

To the chief Musician, A Psalm of David.

1 How long wilt thou forget me, O LORD? for ever? how long wilt thou hide thy face from me?

2 How long shall I take counsel in my soul, *having* sorrow in my heart daily? how long shall mine enemy be exalted over me?

3 Consider *and* hear me, O LORD my God: lighten mine eyes, lest I sleep the *sleep of* death;

4 Lest mine enemy say, I have prevailed against him; *and* those that trouble me rejoice when I am moved.

5 But I have trusted in thy mercy; my heart shall rejoice in thy salvation.

6 I will sing unto the LORD, because he hath dealt bountifully with me.

PSALM 16.—1 *David, in distrust of merits, and hatred of idolatry, fleeth to God for preservation.* 5 *He sheweth the hope of his calling, of the resurrection, and life everlasting.*

Michtam of David.

1 Preserve me, O God: for in thee do I put my trust.

2 *O my soul*, thou hast said unto the LORD, Thou *art* my Lord: my goodness *extendeth* not to thee;

3 *But* to the saints that *are* in the earth, and *to* the excellent, in whom *is* all my delight.

4 Their sorrows shall be multiplied *that* hasten *after* another *god:* their drink offerings of blood will I not offer, nor take up their names into my lips.

5 The LORD *is* the portion of mine inheritance and of my cup: thou maintainest my lot.

6 The lines are fallen unto me in pleasant *places;* yea. I have a goodly heritage.

7 I will bless the LORD, who hath given me counsel: my reins also instruct me in the night seasons.

8 I have set the LORD always before me: because *he is* at my right hand, I shall not be moved.

9 Therefore my heart is glad, and my glory rejoiceth: my flesh also shall rest in hope.

10 For thou wilt not leave my soul in hell; neither wilt thou suffer thine Holy One to see corruption.

11 Thou wilt shew me the path of life: in thy presence *is* fulness of joy; at thy right hand *there are* pleasures for evermore.

PSALM 17.—1 *David, in confidence of his integrity, craveth defence of God against his enemies.* 10 *He sheweth their pride, craft, and eagerness.* 13 *He prayeth against them in confidence of his hope.*

A Prayer of David.

1 Hear the right, O LORD, attend unto my cry, give ear unto my prayer, *that goeth* not out of feigned lips.

2 Let my sentence come forth from thy presence; let thine eyes behold the things that are equal.

3 Thou hast proved mine heart; thou hast visited *me* in the night; thou hast tried me, *and* shalt find nothing; I am purposed *that* my mouth shall not transgress.

4 Concerning the works of men, by the word of thy lips I have kept *me from* the paths of the destroyer.

5 Hold up my goings in thy paths, *that* my footsteps slip not.

6 I have called upon thee, for thou wilt hear me, O God: incline thine ear unto me, *and hear* my speech.

7 Shew thy marvellous lovingkindness, O thou that savest by thy right hand them which put their trust *in thee* from those that rise up *against them.*

8 Keep me as the apple of the eye, hide me under the shadow of thy wings,

9 From the wicked that oppress me, *from* my deadly enemies, *who* compass me about.

10 They are inclosed in their own fat: with their mouth they speak proudly.

11 They have now compassed us in our steps: they have set their eyes bowing down to the earth;

12 Like as a lion *that* is greedy of his prey, and as it were a young lion lurking in secret places.

13 Arise, O LORD, disappoint him, cast him down: deliver my soul from the wicked, *which is* thy sword:

14 From men *which are* thy hand, O LORD, from men of the world, *which have* their portion in *this* life, and whose belly thou fillest with thy hid *treasure:* they are full of children, and leave the rest of their *substance* to their babes.

15 As for me, I will behold thy face in righteousness: I shall be satisfied, when I awake, with thy likeness.

PSALM 22.—1 *David complaineth in great discourage-ment.* 9 *He prayeth in great distress.* 23 *He prais-eth God.*

To the chief Musician upon Aijeleth Shahar, A Psalm of David.

1 My God, my God, why hast thou for-saken me? *why art thou so* far from helping me, *and from* the words of my roaring?

2 O my God, I cry in the daytime, but thou hearest not; and in the night season, and am not silent.

3 But thou *art* holy, *O thou* that inhabit-est the praises of Israel.

4 Our fathers trusted in thee: they trusted, and thou didst deliver them.

5 They cried unto thee, and were deliv-ered: they trusted in thee, and were not confounded.

6 But I *am* a worm, and no man; a re-proach of men, and despised of the people.

7 All they that see me laugh me to scorn: they shoot out the lip, they shake the head, *saying,*

8 He trusted on the LORD *that* he would deliver him: let him deliver him, seeing he delighted in him.

9 But thou *art* he that took me out of the womb: thou didst make me hope *when I was* upon my mother's breasts.

10 I was cast upon thee from the womb: thou *art* my God from my mother's belly.

11 Be not far from me; for trouble *is* near; for *there is* none to help.

12 Many bulls have compassed me: strong *bulls* of Bashan have beset me round.

13 They gaped upon me *with* their mouths, *as* a ravening and a roaring lion.

14 I am poured out like water, and all my bones are out of joint: my heart is like wax; it is melted in the midst of my bowels.

15 My strength is dried up like a pot-sherd; and my tongue cleaveth to my jaws; and thou hast brought me into the dust of death.

16 For dogs have compassed me: the as-sembly of the wicked have inclosed me: they pierced my hands and my feet.

17 I may tell all my bones: they look *and* stare upon me.

18 They part my garments among them, and cast lots upon my vesture.

19 But be not thou far from me, O LORD: O my strength, haste thee to help me.

20 Deliver my soul from the sword; my darling from the power of the dog.

21 Save me from the lion's mouth: for thou hast heard me from the horns of the unicorns.

22 I will declare thy name unto my breth-ren: in the midst of the congregation will I praise thee.

23 Ye that fear the LORD, praise him; all ye the seed of Jacob, glorify him; and fear him, all ye the seed of Israel.

24 For he hath not despised nor abhorred the affliction of the afflicted; neither hath he hid his face from him; but when he cried unto him, he heard.

25 My praise *shall be* of thee in the great congregation: I will pay my vows before them that fear him.

26 The meek shall eat and be satisfied: they shall praise the LORD that seek him: your heart shall live for ever.

27 All the ends of the world shall remem-ber and turn unto the LORD: and all the kindreds of the nations shall worship before thee.

28 For the kingdom *is* the LORD'S: and he *is* the governor among the nations.

29 All *they that be* fat upon earth shall eat and worship: all they that go down to the dust shall bow before him: and none can keep alive his own soul.

30 A seed shall serve him; it shall be ac-counted to the Lord for a generation.

31 They shall come, and shall declare his righteousness unto a people that shall be born, that he hath done *this.*

PSALM 26.—*David resorteth unto God in confidence of his integrity.*

A Psalm of David.

1 Judge me, O LORD; for I have walked in mine integrity: I have trusted also in the LORD; *therefore* I shall not slide.

2 Examine me, O LORD, and prove me; try my reins and my heart.

3 For thy lovingkindness *is* before mine eyes: and I have walked in thy truth.

4 I have not sat with vain persons, neither will I go in with dissemblers.

5 I have hated the congregation of evil doers; and will not sit with the wicked.

6 I will wash mine hands in innocency: so will I compass thine altar, O LORD:

7 That I may publish with the voice of thanksgiving, and tell of all thy wondrous works.

8 LORD, I have loved the habitation of thy house, and the place where thine honour dwelleth.

9 Gather not my soul with sinners, nor my life with bloody men:

10 In whose hands *is* mischief, and their right hand is full of bribes.

11 But as for me, I will walk in mine in-tegrity: redeem me, and be merciful unto me.

12 My foot standeth in an even place: in the congregations will I bless the LORD.

PSALM 27.—1 *David sustaineth his faith by the power of God,* 4 *by his love to the service of God,* 9 *by prayer.*

A Psalm of David.

1 The LORD *is* my light and my salvation; whom shall I fear? the LORD *is* the strength of my life; of whom shall I be afraid?

2 When the wicked, *even* mine enemies and my foes, came upon me to eat up my flesh, they stumbled and fell.

3 Though an host should encamp against me, my heart shall not fear: though war should rise against me, in this *will* I *be* con-fident.

4 One *thing* have I desired of the LORD, that will I seek after; that I may dwell in the house of the LORD all the days of my life, to behold the beauty of the LORD, and to enquire in his temple.

5 For in the time of trouble he shall hide me in his pavilion: in the secret of his tabernacle shall he hide me; he shall set me up upon a rock.

6 And now shall mine head be lifted up above mine enemies round about me: therefore will I offer in his tabernacle sacrifices of joy; I will sing, yea, I will sing praises unto the LORD.

7 Hear, O LORD, *when* I cry with my voice: have mercy also upon me, and answer me.

8 *When thou saidst,* Seek ye my face; my heart said unto thee, Thy face, LORD, will I seek.

9 Hide not thy face *far* from me; put not thy servant away in anger: thou hast been my help; leave me not, neither forsake me, O God of my salvation.

10 When my father and my mother forsake me, then the LORD will take me up.

11 Teach me thy way, O LORD, and lead me in a plain path, because of mine enemies.

12 Deliver me not over unto the will of mine enemies: for false witnesses are risen up against me, and such as breathe out cruelty.

13 *I had fainted,* unless I had believed to see the goodness of the LORD in the land of the living.

14 Wait on the LORD: be of good courage, and he shall strengthen thine heart: wait, I say, on the LORD.

PSALM 28.—1 *David prayeth earnestly against his enemies.* 6 *He blesseth God.* 9 *He prayeth for the people.*

A PSALM OF DAVID.

1 Unto thee will I cry, O LORD my rock; be not silent to me: lest, *if* thou be silent to me, I become like them that go down into the pit.

2 Hear the voice of my supplications, when I cry unto thee, when I lift up my hands toward thy holy oracle.

3 Draw me not away with the wicked, and with the workers of iniquity, which speak peace to their neighbours, but mischief *is* in their hearts.

4 Give them according to their deeds, and according to the wickedness of their endeavours: give them after the work of their hands; render to them their desert.

5 Because they regard not the works of the LORD, nor the operation of his hands, he shall destroy them, and not build them up.

6 Blessed *be* the LORD, because he hath heard the voice of my supplications.

7 The LORD *is* my strength and my shield; my heart trusted in him, and I am helped: therefore my heart greatly rejoiceth; and with my song will I praise him.

8 The LORD *is* their strength, and he *is* the saving strength of his anointed.

9 Save thy people, and bless thine inheritance: feed them also, and lift them up for ever.

PSALM 31.—1 *David shewing his confidence in God craveth his help.* 7 *He rejoiceth in his mercy.* 9 *He prayeth in his calamity.* 19 *He praiseth God for his goodness.*

TO THE CHIEF MUSICIAN, A PSALM OF DAVID.

1 In thee, O LORD, do I put my trust; let me never be ashamed: deliver me in thy righteousness.

2 Bow down thine ear to me; deliver me speedily: be thou my strong rock, for an house of defence to save me.

3 For thou *art* my rock and my fortress; therefore for thy name's sake lead me, and guide me.

4 Pull me out of the net that they have laid privily for me: for thou *art* my strength.

5 Into thine hand I commit my spirit: thou hast redeemed me, O LORD God of truth.

6 I have hated them that regard lying vanities: but I trust in the LORD.

7 I will be glad and rejoice in thy mercy: for thou hast considered my trouble; thou hast known my soul in adversities;

8 And hast not shut me up into the hand of the enemy: thou hast set my feet in a large room.

9 Have mercy upon me, O LORD, for I am in trouble: mine eye is consumed with grief, *yea,* my soul and my belly.

10 For my life is spent with grief, and my years with sighing: my strength faileth because of mine iniquity, and my bones are consumed.

11 I was a reproach among all mine enemies, but especially among my neighbours, and a fear to mine acquaintance: they that did see me without fled from me.

12 I am forgotten as a dead man out of mind: I am like a broken vessel.

13 For I have heard the slander of many: fear *was* on every side: while they took counsel together against me, they devised to take away my life.

14 But I trusted in thee, O LORD: I said, Thou *art* my God.

15 My times *are* in thy hand: deliver me from the hand of mine enemies, and from them that persecute me.

16 Make thy face to shine upon thy servant: save me for thy mercies' sake.

17 Let me not be ashamed, O LORD; for I have called upon thee: let the wicked be ashamed, *and* let them be silent in the grave.

18 Let the lying lips be put to silence; which speak grievous things proudly and contemptuously against the righteous.

19 *Oh* how great *is* thy goodness, which thou hast laid up for them that fear thee; *which* thou hast wrought for them that trust in thee before the sons of men!

20 Thou shalt hide them in the secret of thy presence from the pride of man: thou shalt keep them secretly in a pavilion from the strife of tongues.

21 Blessed *be* the LORD: for he hath shewed me his marvellous kindness in a strong city.

22 For I said in my haste, I am cut off from before thine eyes: nevertheless thou heardest the voice of my supplications when I cried unto thee.

23 O love the LORD, all ye his saints: *for* the LORD preserveth the faithful, and plentifully rewardeth the proud doer.

24 Be of good courage, and he shall strengthen your heart, all ye that hope in the LORD.

PSALM 35.—1 *David prayeth for his own safety, and his enemies' confusion.* 11 *He complaineth of their wrongful dealing.* 22 *Thereby he inciteth God against them.*

A PSALM OF DAVID.

1 Plead *my* cause, O LORD, with them that strive with me: fight against them that fight against me.

2 Take hold of shield and buckler, and stand up for mine help.

3 Draw out also the spear, and stop *the way* against them that persecute me: say unto my soul, I *am* thy salvation.

4 Let them be confounded and put to shame that seek after my soul: let them be turned back and brought to confusion that devise my hurt.

5 Let them be as chaff before the wind: and let the angel of the LORD chase *them*.

6 Let their way be dark and slippery: and let the angel of the LORD persecute them.

7 For without cause have they hid for me their net *in* a pit, *which* without cause they have digged for my soul.

8 Let destruction come upon him at unawares; and let his net that he hath hid catch himself: into that very destruction let him fall.

9 And my soul shall be joyful in the LORD: it shall rejoice in his salvation.

10 All my bones shall say, LORD, who *is* like unto thee, which deliverest the poor from him that is too strong for him, yea, the poor and the needy from him that spoileth him?

11 False witnesses did rise up; they laid to my charge *things* that I knew not.

12 They rewarded me evil for good *to* the spoiling of my soul.

13 But as for me, when they were sick, my clothing *was* sackcloth: I humbled my soul with fasting; and my prayer returned into mine own bosom.

14 I behaved myself as though *he had been* my friend *or* brother: I bowed down heavily, as one that mourneth *for his* mother.

15 But in mine adversity they rejoiced, and gathered themselves together: *yea*, the abjects gathered themselves together against me, and I knew *it* not; they did tear *me*, and ceased not:

16 With hypocritical mockers in feasts, they gnashed upon me with their teeth.

17 Lord, how long wilt thou look on? rescue my soul from their destructions, my darling from the lions.

18 I will give thee thanks in the great congregation: I will praise thee among much people.

19 Let not them that are mine enemies wrongfully rejoice over me: *neither* let them wink with the eye that hate me without a cause.

20 For they speak not peace: but they devise deceitful matters against *them that are* quiet in the land.

21 Yea, they opened their mouth wide against me, *and* said, Aha, aha, our eye hath seen *it*.

22 *This* thou hast seen, O LORD: keep not silence: O Lord, be not far from me.

23 Stir up thyself, and awake to my judgment, *even* unto my cause, my God and my Lord.

24 Judge me, O LORD my God, according to thy righteousness; and let them not rejoice over me.

25 Let them not say in their hearts, Ah, so would we have it: let them not say, We have swallowed him up.

26 Let them be ashamed and brought to confusion together that rejoice at mine hurt: let them be clothed with shame and dishonour that magnify *themselves* against me.

27 Let them shout for joy, and be glad, that favour my righteous cause: yea, let them say continually, Let the LORD be magnified, which hath pleasure in the prosperity of his servant.

28 And my tongue shall speak of thy righteousness *and* of thy praise all the day long.

PSALM 41.—1 *God's care of the poor.* 4 *David complaineth of his enemies' treachery.* 10 *He fleeth to God for succour.*

TO THE CHIEF MUSICIAN, A PSALM OF DAVID.

1 Blessed *is* he that considereth the poor: the LORD will deliver him in time of trouble.

2 The LORD will preserve him, and keep him alive; *and* he shall be blessed upon the earth: and thou wilt not deliver him unto the will of his enemies.

3 The LORD will strengthen him upon the bed of languishing: thou wilt make all his bed in his sickness.

4 I said, LORD, be merciful unto me: heal my soul; for I have sinned against thee.

5 Mine enemies speak evil of me, When shall he die, and his name perish?

6 And if he come to see *me*, he speaketh vanity: his heart gathereth iniquity to itself; *when* he goeth abroad, he telleth *it*.

7 All that hate me whisper together against me: against me do they devise my hurt.

8 An evil disease, *say they*, cleaveth fast unto him: and *now* that he lieth he shall rise up no more.

9 Yea, mine own familiar friend, in whom

I trusted, which did eat of my bread, hath lifted up *his* heel against me.

10 But thou, O LORD, be merciful unto me, and raise me up, that I may requite them.

11 By this I know that thou favourest me, because mine enemy doth not triumph over me.

12 And as for me, thou upholdest me in mine integrity,' and settest me before thy face forever.

13 Blessed *be* the LORD God of Israel from everlasting, and to everlasting. Amen, and Amen.

PSALM 42.—1 *David's zeal to serve God in the temple.* 5 *He encourageth his soul to trust in God.*

To THE CHIEF MUSICIAN, MASCHIL, FOR THE SONS OF KORAH.

1 As the hart panteth after the water brooks, so panteth my soul after thee, O God.

2 My soul thirsteth for God, for the living God: when shall I come and appear before God?

3 My tears have been my meat day and night, while they continually say unto me, Where *is* thy God?

4 When I remember these *things*, I pour out my soul in me: for I had gone with the multitude, I went with them to the house of God, with the voice of joy and praise, with a multitude that kept holyday.

5 Why art thou cast down, O my soul? and *why* art thou disquieted in me? hope thou in God: for I shall yet praise him *for* the help of his countenance.

6 O my God, my soul is cast down within me: therefore will I remember thee from the land of Jordan, and of the Hermonites, from the hill Mizar.

7 Deep calleth unto deep at the noise of thy waterspouts: all thy waves and thy billows are gone over me.

8 *Yet* the LORD will command his lovingkindness in the daytime, and in the night his song *shall be* with me, *and* my prayer unto the God of my life.

9 I will say unto God my rock, Why hast thou forgotten me? why go I mourning because of the oppression of the enemy?

10 *As* with a sword in my bones, mine enemies reproach me; while they say daily unto me, Where *is* thy God?

11 Why art thou cast down, O my soul? and why art thou disquieted within me? hope thou in God: for I shall yet praise him, *who is* the health of my countenance, and my God.

PSALM 43.—1 *David, praying to be restored to the temple, promiseth to serve God joyfully.* 5 *He encourageth his soul to trust in God.*

1 Judge me, O God, and plead my cause against an ungodly nation: O deliver me from the deceitful and unjust man.

2 For thou *art* the God of my strength: why dost thou cast me off? why go I mourning because of the oppression of the enemy?

3 O send out thy light and thy truth: let them lead me; let them bring me unto thy holy hill, and to thy tabernacles.

4 Then will I go unto the altar of God, unto God my exceeding joy: yea, upon the harp will I praise thee, O God my God.

5 Why art thou cast down, O my soul? and why art thou disquieted within me? hope in God: for I shall yet praise him, *who is* the health of my countenance, and my God.

PSALM 44.—1 *The church, in memory of former favours,* 7 *complaineth of their present evils.* 17 *Professing her integrity,* 23 *she fervently prayeth for succour.*

To THE CHIEF MUSICIAN FOR THE SONS OF KORAH, MASCHIL.

1 We have heard with our ears, O God, our fathers have told us, *what* work thou didst in their days, in the times of old.

2 *How* thou didst drive out the heathen with thy hand, and plantedst them; *how* thou didst afflict the people, and cast them out.

3 For they got not the land in possession by their own sword, neither did their own arm save them: but thy right hand, and thine arm, and the light of thy countenance, because thou hadst a favour unto them.

4 Thou art my King, O God: command deliverances for Jacob.

5 Through thee will we push down our enemies: through thy name will we tread them under that rise up against us.

6 For I will not trust in my bow, neither shall my sword save me.

7 But thou hast saved us from our enemies, and hast put them to shame that hated us.

8 In God we boast all the day long, and praise thy name forever. Selah.

9 But thou hast cast off, and put us to shame; and goest not forth with our armies.

10 Thou makest us to turn back from the enemy: and they which hate us spoil for themselves.

11 Thou hast given us like sheep *appointed* for meat; and hast scattered us among the heathen.

12 Thou sellest thy people for nought, and dost not increase *thy wealth* by their price.

13 Thou makest us a reproach to our neighbours, a scorn and a derision to them that are round about us.

14 Thou makest us a byword among the heathen, a shaking of the head among the people.

15 My confusion *is* continually before me, and the shame of my face hath covered me,

16 For the voice of him that reproacheth and blasphemeth; by reason of the enemy and avenger.

17 All this is come upon us; yet have we not forgotten thee, neither have we dealt falsely in thy covenant.

18 Our heart is not turned back, neither have our steps declined from thy way;

19 Though thou hast sore broken us in the place of dragons, and covered us with the shadow of death.

20 If we have forgotten the name of our God, or stretched out our hands to a strange god;

21 Shall not God search this out? for he knoweth the secrets of the heart.

22 Yea, for thy sake are we killed all the day long; we are counted as sheep for the slaughter.

23 Awake, why sleepest thou, O Lord? arise, cast us not off for ever.

24 Wherefore hidest thou thy face, and forgettest our affliction and our oppression?

25 For our soul is bowed down to the dust: our belly cleaveth unto the earth.

26 Arise for our help, and redeem us for thy mercies' sake.

PSALM 54.—1 *David, complaining of the Ziphims, prayeth for salvation.* 4 *Upon his confidence in God's help he promiseth sacrifice.*

To the chief Musician on Neginoth, Maschil, A Psalm of David, when the Ziphims came and said to Saul, Doth not David hide himself with us?

1 Save me, O God, by thy name, and judge me by thy strength.

2 Hear my prayer, O God; give ear to the words of my mouth.

3 For strangers are risen up against me, and oppressors seek after my soul: they have not set God before them. Selah.

4 Behold, God *is* mine helper: the Lord *is* with them that uphold my soul.

5 He shall reward evil unto mine enemies: cut them off in thy truth.

6 I will freely sacrifice unto thee: I will praise thy name, O Lord; for *it is* good.

7 For he hath delivered me out of all trouble: and mine eye hath seen *his desire* upon mine enemies.

PSALM 55.—1 *David in his prayer complaineth of his fearful case.* 9 *He prayeth against his enemies, of whose wickedness and treachery he complaineth.* 16 *He comforteth himself in God's preservation of him, and confusion of his enemies.*

To the chief Musician on Neginoth, Maschil, A Psalm of David.

1 Give ear to my prayer, O God; and hide not thyself from my supplication.

2 Attend unto me, and hear me: I mourn in my complaint, and make a noise;

3 Because of the voice of the enemy, because of the oppression of the wicked: for they cast iniquity upon me, and in wrath they hate me.

4 My heart is sore pained within me: and the terrors of death are fallen upon me.

5 Fearfulness and trembling are come upon me, and horror hath overwhelmed me.

6 And I said, Oh that I had wings like a dove! *for then* would I fly away, and be at rest.

7 Lo, *then* would I wander far off, *and* remain in the wilderness. Selah.

8 I would hasten my escape from the windy storm *and* tempest.

9 Destroy, O Lord, *and* divide their tongues: for I have seen violence and strife in the city.

10 Day and night they go about it upon the walls thereof: mischief also and sorrow *are* in the midst of it.

11 Wickedness *is* in the midst thereof: deceit and guile depart not from her streets.

12 For *it was* not an enemy *that* reproached me; then I could have borne *it:* neither *was it* he that hated me *that* did magnify *himself* against me; then I would have hid myself from him:

13 But *it was* thou, a man mine equal, my guide, and mine acquaintance.

14 We took sweet counsel together, *and* walked unto the house of God in company.

15 Let death seize upon them, *and* let them go down quick into hell: for wickedness *is* in their dwellings, *and* among them.

16 As for me, I will call upon God; and the Lord shall save me.

17 Evening, and morning, and at noon, will I pray, and cry aloud: and he shall hear my voice.

18 He hath delivered my soul in peace from the battle *that was* against me: for there were many with me.

19 God shall hear, and afflict them, even he that abideth of old. Selah. Because they have no changes, therefore they fear not God.

20 He hath put forth his hands against such as be at peace with him: he hath broken his covenant.

21 *The words* of his mouth were smoother than butter, but war *was* in his heart: his words were softer than oil, yet *were* they drawn swords.

22 Cast thy burden upon the Lord, and he shall sustain thee: he shall never suffer the righteous to be moved.

23 But thou, O God, shalt bring them down into the pit of destruction: bloody and deceitful men shall not live out half their days; but I will trust in thee.

PSALM 56.—*David, praying to God in confidence of his word, complaineth of his enemies.* 9 *He professeth his confidence in God's word, and promiseth to praise him.*

To the chief Musician upon Jonathelem-rechokim, Michtam of David, when the Philistines took him in Gath.

1 Be merciful unto me, O God: for man would swallow me up; he fighting daily oppresseth me.

2 Mine enemies would daily swallow *me* up: for *they be* many that fight against me, O thou most High.

3 What time I am afraid, I will trust in thee.

4 In God I will praise his word, in God I have put my trust; I will not fear what flesh can do unto me.

5 Every day they wrest my words: all their thoughts *are* against me for evil.

6 They gather themselves together, they hide themselves, they mark my steps, when they wait for my soul.

7 Shall they escape by iniquity? in *thine* anger cast down the people, O God.

8 Thou tellest my wanderings: put thou my tears into thy bottle: *are they* not in thy book?

9 When I cry *unto thee*, then shall mine enemies turn back: this I know; for God *is* for me.

10 In God will I praise *his* word: in the LORD will I praise *his* word.

11 In God have I put my trust: I will not be afraid what man can do unto me.

12 Thy vows *are* upon me, O God: I will render praises unto thee.

13 For thou hast delivered my soul from death: *wilt* not *thou deliver* my feet from falling, that I may walk before God in the light of the living?

PSALM 57.—1 *David in prayer fleeing unto God complaineth of his dangerous case.* 7 *He encourageth himself to praise God.*

To the chief Musician, Al-taschith, Michtam of David, when he fled from Saul in the cave.

1 Be merciful unto me, O God, be merciful unto me: for my soul trusteth in thee: yea, in the shadow of thy wings will I make my refuge, until *these* calamities be overpast.

2 I will cry unto God most high; unto God that performeth *all things* for me.

3 He shall send from heaven, and save me *from* the reproach of him that would swallow me up. Selah. God shall send forth his mercy and his truth.

4 My soul *is* among lions: *and* I lie *even* among them that are set on fire, *even* the sons of men, whose teeth *are* spears and arrows, and their tongue a sharp sword.

5 Be thou exalted, O God, above the heavens: *let* thy glory *be* above all the earth.

6 They have prepared a net for my steps; my soul is bowed down: they have digged a pit before me, into the midst whereof they are fallen *themselves*. Selah.

7 My heart is fixed, O God, my heart is fixed: I will sing and give praise.

8 Awake up, my glory; awake, psaltery and harp: I *myself* will awake early.

9 I will praise thee, O Lord, among the people: I will sing unto thee among the nations.

10 For thy mercy *is* great unto the heavens, and thy truth unto the clouds.

11 Be thou exalted, O God, above the heavens: *let* thy glory *be* above all the earth.

PSALM 59.—1 *David prayeth to be delivered from his enemies.* 6 *He complaineth of their cruelty.* 8 *He trusteth in God.* 11 *He prayeth against them.* 16 *He praiseth God.*

To the chief Musician, Al-taschith, Michtam of David: when Saul sent, and they watched the house to kill him.

1 Deliver me from mine enemies, O my God: defend me from them that rise up against me

2 Deliver me from the workers of iniquity, and save me from bloody men.

3 For, lo, they lie in wait for my soul: the mighty are gathered against me; not *for* my transgression, nor *for* my sin, O LORD.

4 They run and prepare themselves without *my* fault: awake to help me, and behold.

5 Thou therefore, O LORD God of hosts, the God of Israel, awake to visit all the heathen: be not merciful to any wicked transgressors. Selah.

6 They return at evening: they make a noise like a dog, and go round about the city.

7 Behold, they belch out with their mouth: swords *are* in their lips: for who, *say they*, doth hear?

8 But thou, O LORD, shalt laugh at them; thou shalt have all the heathen in derision.

9 *Because of* his strength will I wait upon thee: for God *is* my defence.

10 The God of my mercy shall prevent me: God shall let me see *my desire* upon mine enemies.

11 Slay them not, lest my people forget: scatter them by thy power; and bring them down, O Lord our shield.

12 *For* the sin of their mouth *and* the words of their lips let them even be taken in their pride: and for cursing and lying *which* they speak.

13 Consume *them* in wrath, consume *them*, that they *may* not *be:* and let them know that God ruleth in Jacob unto the ends of the earth. Selah.

14 And at evening let them return; *and* let them make a noise like a dog, and go round about the city.

15 Let them wander up and down for meat, and grudge if they be not satisfied.

16 But I will sing of thy power; yea, I will sing aloud of thy mercy in the morning: for thou hast been my defence and refuge in the day of my trouble.

17 Unto thee, O my strength, will I sing: for God *is* my defence, *and* the God of my mercy.

PSALM 60.—1 *David, complaining to God of former judgment,* 4 *now, upon better hope, prayeth for deliverance.* 6 *Comforting himself in God's promises, he craveth that help whereon he trusteth.*

To the chief Musician upon Shushan-eduth, Michtam of David to teach; when he strove with Aram-naharaim, and with Aram-zobah, when Joab returned, and smote of Edom in the valley of salt twelve thousand.

1 O God, thou hast cast us off, thou hast scattered us, thou hast been displeased; O turn thyself to us again.

2 Thou hast made the earth to tremble; thou hast broken it: heal the breaches thereof; for it shaketh.

3 Thou hast shewed thy people hard things: thou hast made us to drink the wine of astonishment.

4 Thou hast given a banner to them that fear thee, that it may be displayed because of the truth. Selah.

5 That thy beloved may be delivered; save *with* thy right hand, and hear me.

6 God hath spoken in his holiness; I will rejoice, I will divide Shechem, and mete out the valley of Succoth.

7 Gilead *is* mine, and Manasseh *is* mine; Ephraim also *is* the strength of mine head; Judah *is* my lawgiver;

8 Moab *is* my washpot; over Edom will I cast out my shoe: Philistia, triumph thou because of me.

9 Who will bring me *into* the strong city? who will lead me into Edom?

10 *Wilt* not thou, O God, *which* hadst cast us off? and *thou*, O God, *which* didst not go out with our armies?

11 Give us help from trouble: for vain *is* the help of man.

12 Through God we shall do valiantly: for he *it is that* shall tread down our enemies.

PSALM 61.—1 *David fleeth to God upon his former experience.* 4 *He voweth perpetual service unto him, because of his promises.*

To the chief Musician upon Neginah, A Psalm of David.

1 Hear my cry, O God; attend unto my prayer.

2 From the end of the earth will I cry unto thee, when my heart is overwhelmed: lead me to the rock *that* is higher than I.

3 For thou hast been a shelter for me, *and* a strong tower from the enemy.

4 I will abide in thy tabernacle for ever: I will trust in the covert of thy wings. Selah.

5 For thou, O God, hast heard my vows: thou hast given *me* the heritage of those that fear thy name.

6 Thou wilt prolong the king's life: *and* his years as many generations.

7 He shall abide before God for ever: O prepare mercy and truth, *which* may preserve him.

8 So will I sing praise unto thy name for ever, that I may daily perform my vows.

PSALM 62.—1 *David professing his confidence in God discourageth his enemies.* 5 *In the same confidence he encourageth the godly.* 9 *No trust is to be put in worldly things.* 11 *Power and mercy belong to God.*

To the chief Musician, to Jeduthun, A Psalm of David.

1 Truly my soul waiteth upon God: from him *cometh* my salvation.

2 He only *is* my rock and my salvation; *he is* my defence; I shall not be greatly moved.

3 How long will ye imagine mischief against a man? ye shall be slain all of you: as a bowing wall *shall ye be, and as* a tottering fence.

4 They only consult to cast *him* down from his excellency: they delight in lies: they bless with their mouth, but they curse inwardly. Selah.

5 My soul, wait thou only upon God; for my expectation *is* from him.

6 He only *is* my rock and my salvation: *he is* my defence; I shall not be moved.

7 In God *is* my salvation and my glory: the rock of my strength, *and* my refuge, *is* in God.

8 Trust in him at all times; ye people, pour out your heart before him: God *is* a refuge for us. Selah.

9 Surely men of low degree *are* vanity, *and* men of high degree *are* a lie: to be laid in the balance, they *are* altogether *lighter* than vanity.

10 Trust not in oppression, and become not vain in robbery: if riches increase, set not your heart *upon them*.

11 God hath spoken once; twice have I heard this; that power *belongeth* unto God.

12 Also unto thee, O Lord, *belongeth* mercy: for thou renderest to every man according to his work.

PSALM 63.—1 *David's thirst for God.* 4 *His manner of blessing God.* 9 *His confidence of his enemies' destruction, and his own safety.*

A Psalm of David, when he was in the wilderness of Judah.

1 O God, thou *art* my God; early will I seek thee: my soul thirsteth for thee, my flesh longeth for thee in a dry and thirsty land, where no water is;

2 To see thy power and thy glory, so *as* I have seen thee in the sanctuary.

3 Because thy lovingkindness *is* better than life, my lips shall praise thee.

4 Thus will I bless thee while I live: I will lift up my hands in thy name.

5 My soul shall be satisfied as *with* marrow and fatness; and my mouth shall praise *thee* with joyful lips:

6 When I remember thee upon my bed, *and* meditate on thee in the *night* watches.

7 Because thou hast been my help, therefore in the shadow of thy wings will I rejoice.

8 My soul followeth hard after thee: thy right hand upholdeth me.

9 But those *that* seek my soul, to destroy *it*, shall go into the lower parts of the earth.

10 They shall fall by the sword: they shall be a portion for foxes.

11 But the king shall rejoice in God; every one that sweareth by him shall glory: but the mouth of them that speak lies shall be stopped.

PSALM 64.—1 *David prayeth for deliverance, complaining of his enemies.* 7 *He promiseth himself to see such an evident destruction of his enemies, as the righteous shall rejoice at it.*

To the chief Musician, A Psalm of David.

1 Hear my voice, O God, in my prayer: preserve my life from fear of the enemy.

2 Hide me from the secret counsel of the wicked; from the insurrection of the workers of iniquity:

3 Who whet their tongue like a sword, *and* bend *their bows to shoot* their arrows, *even* bitter words:

4 That they may shoot in secret at the perfect: suddenly do they shoot at him, and fear not.

5 They encourage themselves *in* an evil

matter: they commune of laying snares privily; they say, Who shall see them?

6 They search out iniquities; they accomplish a diligent search: both the inward *thought* of every one *of them*, and the heart, *is* deep.

7 But God shall shoot at them *with* an arrow; suddenly shall they be wounded.

8 So they shall make their own tongue to fall upon themselves: all that see them shall flee away.

9 And all men shall fear, and shall declare the work of God; for they shall wisely consider of his doing.

10 The righteous shall be glad in the LORD, and shall trust in him; and all the upright in heart shall glory.

PSALM 69.—1 *David complaineth of his affliction.* 13 *He prayeth for deliverance.* 22 *He devoteth his enemies to destruction.* 30 *He praiseth God with thanksgiving.*

To THE CHIEF MUSICIAN UPON SHOSHANNIM, A PSALM OF DAVID.

1 Save me, O God; for the waters are come in unto *my* soul.

2 I sink in deep mire, where *there is* no standing: I am come into deep waters, where the floods overflow me.

3 I am weary of my crying: my throat is dried: mine eyes fail while I wait for my God.

4 They that hate me without a cause are more than the hairs of mine head: they that would destroy me, *being* mine enemies wrongfully, are mighty: then I restored *that* which I took not away.

5 O God, thou knowest my foolishness; and my sins are not hid from thee.

6 Let not them that wait on thee, O Lord GOD of hosts, be ashamed for my sake: let not those that seek thee be confounded for my sake, O God of Israel.

7 Because for thy sake I have borne reproach; shame hath covered my face.

8 I am become a stranger unto my brethren, and an alien unto my mother's children.

9 For the zeal of thine house hath eaten me up; and the reproaches of them that reproached thee are fallen upon me.

10 When I wept, *and chastened* my soul with fasting, that was to my reproach.

11 I made sackcloth also my garment; and I became a proverb to them.

12 They that sit in the gate speak against me; and I *was* the song of the drunkards.

13 But as for me, my prayer *is* unto thee, O LORD, *in* an acceptable time: O God, in the multitude of thy mercy hear me, in the truth of thy salvation.

14 Deliver me out of the mire, and let me not sink: let me be delivered from them that hate me, and out of the deep waters.

15 Let not the waterflood overflow me, neither let the deep swallow me up, and let not the pit shut her mouth upon me.

16 Hear me, O LORD; for thy lovingkindness *is* good: turn unto me according to the multitude of thy tender mercies.

17 And hide not thy face from thy servant; for I am in trouble: hear me speedily.

18 Draw nigh unto my soul, *and* redeem it: deliver me because of mine enemies.

19 Thou hast known my reproach, and my shame, and my dishonour: mine adversaries *are* all before thee.

20 Reproach hath broken my heart; and I am full of heaviness: and I looked *for some* to take pity, but *there was* none; and for comforters, but I found none.

21 They gave me also gall for my meat; and in my thirst they gave me vinegar to drink.

22 Let their table become a snare before them: and *that which should have been* for *their* welfare, *let it become* a trap.

23 Let their eyes be darkened, that they see not; and make their loins continually to shake.

24 Pour out thine indignation upon them, and let thy wrathful anger take hold of them.

25 Let their habitation be desolate; *and* let none dwell in their tents.

26 For they persecute *him* whom thou hast smitten; and they talk to the grief of those whom thou hast wounded.

27 Add iniquity unto their iniquity: and let them not come into thy righteousness.

28 Let them be blotted out of the book of the living, and not be written with the righteous.

29 But I *am* poor and sorrowful: let thy salvation, O God, set me up on high.

30 I will praise the name of God with a song, and will magnify him with thanksgiving.

31 *This* also shall please the LORD better than an ox *or* bullock that hath horns and hoofs.

32 The humble shall see *this, and* be glad: and your heart shall live that seek God.

33 For the LORD heareth the poor, and despiseth not his prisoners.

34 Let the heaven and earth praise him, the seas, and every thing that moveth therein.

35 For God will save Zion, and will build the cities of Judah: that they may dwell there, and have it in possession.

36 The seed also of his servants shall inherit it: and they that love his name shall dwell therein.

PSALM 70.—*David soliciteth God to the speedy destruction of the wicked, and preservation of the godly.*

To THE CHIEF MUSICIAN, A PSALM OF DAVID, TO BRING TO REMEMBRANCE.

1 *Make haste*, O God, to deliver me; make haste to help me, O LORD.

2 Let them be ashamed and confounded that seek after my soul: let them be turned backward, and put to confusion, that desire my hurt.

3 Let them be turned back for a reward of their shame that say, Aha, aha.

4 Let all those that seek thee rejoice and be glad in thee: and let such as love thy

salvation say continually, Let God be magnified.

5 But I *am* poor and needy: make haste unto me, O God: thou *art* my help and my deliverer; O LORD, make no tarrying.

PSALM 71.—1 *David, in confidence of faith, and experience of God's favour, prayeth both for himself, and against the enemies of his soul.* 14 *He promiseth constancy.* 17 *He prayeth for perseverance.* 19 *He praiseth God, and promiseth to do it cheerfully.*

1 In thee, O LORD, do I put my trust: let me never be put to confusion.

2 Deliver me in thy righteousness, and cause me to escape: incline thine ear unto me, and save me.

3 Be thou my strong habitation, whereunto I may continually resort: thou hast given commandment to save me; for thou *art* my rock and my fortress.

4 Deliver me, O my God, out of the hand of the wicked, out of the hand of the unrighteous and cruel man.

5 For thou *art* my hope, O Lord GOD: *thou art* my trust from my youth.

6 By thee have I been holden up from the womb: thou art he that took me out of my mother's bowels: my praise *shall be* continually of thee.

7 I am as a wonder unto many; but thou *art* my strong refuge.

8 Let my mouth be filled *with* thy praise *and with* thy honour all the day.

9 Cast me not off in the time of old age; forsake me not when my strength faileth.

10 For mine enemies speak against me; and they that lay wait for my soul take counsel together,

11 Saying, God hath forsaken him: persecute and take him; for *there is* none to deliver *him.*

12 O God, be not far from me: O my God, make haste for my help.

13 Let them be confounded *and* consumed that are adversaries to my soul; let them be covered *with* reproach and dishonour that seek my hurt.

14 But I will hope continually, and will yet praise thee more and more.

15 My mouth shall shew forth thy righteousness *and* thy salvation all the day; for I know not the numbers *thereof.*

16 I will go in the strength of the Lord GOD: I will make mention of thy righteousness, *even* of thine only.

17 O God, thou hast taught me from my youth: and hitherto have I declared thy wondrous works.

18 Now also when I am old and greyheaded, O God, forsake me not; until I have shewed thy strength unto *this* generation, *and* thy power to every one *that* is to come.

19 Thy righteousness also, O God, *is* very high, who hast done great things: O God, who *is* like unto thee!

20 *Thou,* which hast shewed me great and sore troubles, shalt quicken me again,

and shalt bring me up again from the depths of the earth.

21 Thou shalt increase my greatness, and comfort me on every side.

22 I will also praise thee with the psaltery, *even* thy truth, O my God: unto thee will I sing with the harp, O thou Holy One of Israel.

23 My lips shall greatly rejoice when I sing unto thee; and my soul, which thou hast redeemed.

24 My tongue also shall talk of thy righteousness all the day long: for they are confounded, for they are brought unto shame, that seek my hurt.

PSALM 74.—1 *The prophet complaineth of the desolation of the sanctuary.* 10 *He moveth God to help in consideration of his power,* 18 *of his reproachful enemies, of his children, and of his covenant.*

MASCHIL OF ASAPH.

1 O God, why hast thou cast *us* off for ever? *why* doth thine anger smoke against the sheep of thy pasture?

2 Remember thy congregation, *which* thou hast purchased of old; the rod of thine inheritance, *which* thou hast redeemed; this mount Zion, wherein thou hast dwelt.

3 Lift up thy feet unto the perpetual desolations; *even* all *that* the enemy hath done wickedly in the sanctuary.

4 Thine enemies roar in the midst of thy congregations; they set up their ensigns *for* signs.

5 *A man* was famous according as he had lifted up axes upon the thick trees.

6 But now they break down the carved work thereof at once with axes and hammers.

7 They have cast fire into thy sanctuary, they have defiled *by casting down* the dwelling place of thy name to the ground.

8 They said in their hearts, Let us destroy them together: they have burned up all the synagogues of God in the land.

9 We see not our signs: *there is* no more any prophet: neither *is there* among us any that knoweth how long.

10 O God, how long shall the adversary reproach? shall the enemy blaspheme thy name for ever?

11 Why withdrawest thou thy hand, even thy right hand? pluck *it* out of thy bosom.

12 For God *is* my King of old, working salvation in the midst of the earth.

13 Thou didst divide the sea by thy strength: thou brakest the heads of the dragons in the waters.

14 Thou brakest the heads of leviathan in pieces, *and* gavest him *to be* meat to the people inhabiting the wilderness.

15 Thou didst cleave the fountain and the flood: thou driedst up mighty rivers.

16 The day *is* thine, the night also *is* thine: thou hast prepared the light and the sun.

17 Thou hast set all the borders of the earth: thou hast made summer and winter.

18 Remember this, *that* the enemy hath reproached, O LORD, and *that* the foolish people have blasphemed thy name.

19 O deliver not the soul of thy turtle-dove unto the multitude *of the wicked:* forget not the congregation of thy poor for ever.

20 Have respect unto the covenant: for the dark places of the earth are full of the habitations of cruelty.

21 O let not the oppressed return ashamed: let the poor and needy praise thy name.

22 Arise, O God, plead thine own cause: remember how the foolish man reproacheth thee daily.

23 Forget not the voice of thine enemies: the tumult of those that rise up against thee increaseth continually.

PSALM 77.—1 *The psalmist sheweth what fierce combat he had with diffidence.* 10 *The victory which he had by consideration of God's great and gracious works.*

TO THE CHIEF MUSICIAN, TO JEDUTHUN, A PSALM OF ASAPH.

1 I cried unto God with my voice, *even* unto God with my voice; and he gave ear unto me.

2 In the day of my trouble I sought the Lord: my sore ran in the night, and ceased not: my soul refused to be comforted.

3 I remembered God, and was troubled: I complained, and my spirit was overwhelmed. Selah.

4 Thou holdest mine eyes waking: I am so troubled that I cannot speak.

5 I have considered the days of old, the years of ancient times.

6 I call to remembrance my song in the night: I commune with mine own heart: and my spirit made diligent search.

7 Will the Lord cast off for ever? and will he be favourable no more?

8 Is his mercy clean gone for ever? doth *his* promise fail for evermore?

9 Hath God forgotten to be gracious? hath he in anger shut up his tender mercies? Selah.

10 And I said, This *is* my infirmity: *but I will remember* the years of the right hand of the most High.

11 I will remember the works of the LORD: surely I will remember thy wonders of old.

12 I will meditate also of all thy work, and talk of thy doings.

13 Thy way, O God, *is* in the sanctuary: who *is so* great a God as *our* God?

14 Thou *art* the God that doest wonders: thou hast declared thy strength among the people.

15 Thou hast with *thine* arm redeemed thy people, the sons of Jacob and Joseph. Selah.

16 The waters saw thee, O God, the waters saw thee; they were afraid: the depths also were troubled.

17 The clouds poured out water: the skies sent out a sound: thine arrows also went abroad.

18 The voice of thy thunder *was* in the heaven: the lightnings lightened the world: the earth trembled and shook.

19 Thy way *is* in the sea, and thy path in the great waters, and thy footsteps are not known.

20 Thou leddest thy people like a flock by the hand of Moses and Aaron.

PSALM 79.—1 *The psalmist complaineth of the desolation of Jerusalem.* 8 *He prayeth for deliverance,* 13 *and promiseth thankfulness.*

A PSALM OF ASAPH.

1 O God, the heathen are come into thine inheritance; thy holy temple have they defiled; they have laid Jerusalem on heaps.

2 The dead bodies of thy servants have they given *to be* meat unto the fowls of the heaven, the flesh of thy saints unto the beasts of the earth.

3 Their blood have they shed like water round about Jerusalem; and *there was* none to bury *them.*

4 We are become a reproach to our neighbours, a scorn and derision to them that are round about us.

5 How long, LORD? wilt thou be angry for ever? shall thy jealousy burn like fire?

6 Pour out thy wrath upon the heathen that have not known thee, and upon the kingdoms that have not called upon thy name.

7 For they have devoured Jacob, and laid waste his dwelling place.

8 O remember not against us former iniquities: let thy tender mercies speedily prevent us: for we are brought very low.

9 Help us, O God of our salvation, for the glory of thy name: and deliver us, and purge away our sins, for thy name's sake.

10 Wherefore should the heathen say, Where *is* their God? let him be known among the heathen in our sight *by* the revenging of the blood of thy servants *which is* shed.

11 Let the sighing of the prisoner come before thee; according to the greatness of thy power preserve thou those that are appointed to die:

12 And render unto our neighbours sevenfold into their bosom their reproach, wherewith they have reproached thee, O Lord.

13 So we thy people and sheep of thy pasture will give thee thanks for ever: we will shew forth thy praise to all generations.

PSALM 80.—1 *The psalmist in his prayer complaineth of the miseries of the church.* 8 *God's former favours are turned into judgments.* 14 *He prayeth for deliverance.*

TO THE CHIEF MUSICIAN UPON SHOSHANNIM-EDUTH, A PSALM OF ASAPH.

1 Give ear, O Shepherd of Israel, thou that leadest Joseph like a flock; thou that dwellest *between* the cherubims, shine forth.

2 Before Ephraim and Benjamin and Manasseh stir up thy strength, and come *and* save us.

3 Turn us again, O God, and cause thy face to shine; and we shall be saved.

4 O LORD God of hosts, how long wilt thou be angry against the prayer of thy people?

5 Thou feedest them with the bread of tears; and givest them tears to drink in great measure.

6 Thou makest us a strife unto our neighbours: and our enemies laugh among themselves.

7 Turn us again, O God of hosts, and cause thy face to shine; and we shall be saved.

8 Thou hast brought a vine out of Egypt: thou hast cast out the heathen, and planted it.

9 Thou preparedst *room* before it, and didst cause it to take deep root, and it filled the land.

10 The hills were covered with the shadow of it, and the boughs thereof *were like* the goodly cedars.

11 She sent out her boughs unto the sea, and her branches unto the river.

12 Why hast thou *then* broken down her hedges, so that all they which pass by the way do pluck her?

13 The boar out of the wood doth waste it, and the wild beast of the field doth devour it.

14 Return, we beseech thee, O God of hosts: look down from heaven, and behold, and visit this vine;

15 And the vineyard which thy right hand hath planted, and the branch *that* thou madest strong for thyself.

16 *It is* burned with fire, *it is* cut down: they perish at the rebuke of thy countenance.

17 Let thy hand be upon the man of thy right hand, upon the son of man *whom* thou madest strong for thyself.

18 So will not we go back from thee: quicken us, and we will call upon thy name.

19 Turn us again, O LORD God of hosts, cause thy face to shine; and we shall be saved.

PSALM 83.—1 *A complaint to God of the enemies' conspiracies.* 9 *A prayer against them that oppress the church.*

A SONG OR PSALM OF ASAPH.

1 Keep not thou silence, O God: hold not thy peace, and be not still, O God.

2 For, lo, thine enemies make a tumult: and they that hate thee have lifted up the head.

3 They have taken crafty counsel against thy people, and consulted against thy hidden ones.

4 They have said, Come, and let us cut them off from *being* a nation; that the name of Israel may be no more in remembrance.

5 For they have consulted together with one consent: they are confederate against thee:

6 The tabernacles of Edom, and the Ishmaelites; of Moab, and the Hagarenes;

7 Gebal, and Ammon, and Amalek; the Philistines with the inhabitants of Tyre;

8 Assur also is joined with them: they have holpen the children of Lot. Selah.

9 Do unto them as *unto* the Midianites; as *to* Sisera, as *to* Jabin, at the brook of Kison:

10 *Which* perished at En-dor: they became *as* dung for the earth.

11 Make their nobles like Oreb, and like Zeeb: yea, all their princes as Zebah, and as Zalmunna:

12 Who said, Let us take to ourselves the houses of God in possession.

13 O my God, make them like a wheel; as the stubble before the wind.

14 As the fire burneth a wood, and as the flame setteth the mountains on fire;

15 So persecute them with thy tempest, and make them afraid with thy storm.

16 Fill their faces with shame; that they may seek thy name, O LORD.

17 Let them be confounded and troubled forever; yea, let them be put to shame, and perish:

18 That *men* may know that thou, whose name alone *is* JEHOVAH, *art* the most high over all the earth.

PSALM 84.—1 *The prophet, longing for the communion of the sanctuary,* 4 *sheweth how blessed they are that dwell therein.* 8 *He prayeth to be restored unto it.*

TO THE CHIEF MUSICIAN UPON GITTITH, A PSALM FOR THE SONS OF KORAH.

1 How amiable *are* thy tabernacles, O LORD of hosts!

2 My soul longeth, yea, even fainteth for the courts of the LORD: my heart and my flesh crieth out for the living God.

3 Yea, the sparrow hath found an house, and the swallow a nest for herself, where she may lay her young, *even* thine altars, O LORD of hosts, my King, and my God.

4 Blessed *are* they that dwell in thy house: they will be still praising thee. Selah.

5 Blessed *is* the man whose strength *is* in thee; in whose heart *are* the ways *of* them.

6 *Who* passing through the valley of Baca make it a well; the rain also filleth the pools.

7 They go from strength to strength, *every one of them* in Zion appeareth before God.

8 O LORD God of hosts, hear my prayer: give ear, O God of Jacob. Selah.

9 Behold, O God our shield, and look upon the face of thine anointed.

10 For a day in thy courts *is* better than a thousand. I had rather be a doorkeeper in the house of my God, than to dwell in the tents of wickedness.

11 For the LORD God *is* a sun and shield: the LORD will give grace and glory: no good *thing* will he withhold from them that walk uprightly.

12 O LORD of hosts, blessed *is* the man that trusteth in thee.

PSALM 86.—1 *David strengtheneth his prayer by the conscience of his religion,* 5 *by the goodness and power of God.* 11 *He desireth the continuance of former grace.* 14 *Complaining of the proud, he craveth some token of God's goodness.*

A PRAYER OF DAVID.

1 Bow down thine ear, O LORD, hear me: for I *am* poor and needy.

2 Preserve my soul; for I *am* holy: O thou my God, save thy servant that trusteth in thee.

3 Be merciful unto me, O Lord: for I cry unto thee daily.

4 Rejoice the soul of thy servant: for unto thee, O Lord, do I lift up my soul.

5 For thou, Lord, *art* good, and ready to forgive; and plenteous in mercy unto all them that call upon thee.

6 Give ear, O LORD, unto my prayer; and attend to the voice of my supplications.

7 In the day of my trouble I will call upon thee: for thou wilt answer me.

8 Among the gods *there is* none like unto thee, O Lord; neither *are there any works* like unto thy works.

9 All nations whom thou hast made shall come and worship before thee, O Lord; and shall glorify thy name.

10 For thou *art* great, and doest wondrous things: thou *art* God alone.

11 Teach me thy way, O LORD; I will walk in thy truth: unite my heart to fear thy name.

12 I will praise thee, O Lord my God, with all my heart: and I will glorify thy name for evermore.

13 For great *is* thy mercy toward me: and thou hast delivered my soul from the lowest hell.

14 O God, the proud are risen against me, and the assemblies of violent *men* have sought after my soul; and have not set thee before them.

15 But thou, O Lord, *art* a God full of compassion, and gracious, longsuffering, and plenteous in mercy and truth.

16 O turn unto me, and have mercy upon me; give thy strength unto thy servant, and save the son of thine handmaid.

17 Shew me a token for good; that they which hate me may see *it,* and be ashamed: because thou, LORD, hast holpen me, and comforted me.

PSALM 88.—*A prayer containing a grievous complaint.*

A SONG OR PSALM FOR THE SONS OF KORAH, TO THE CHIEF MUSICIAN UPON MAHALATH LEANNOTH, MASCHIL OF HEMAN THE EZRAHITE.

1 O LORD God of my salvation, I have cried day *and* night before thee:

2 Let my prayer come before thee: incline thine ear unto my cry;

3 For my soul is full of troubles: and my life draweth nigh unto the grave.

4 I am counted with them that go down into the pit: I am as a man *that hath* no strength:

5 Free among the dead, like the slain that lie in the grave, whom thou rememberest

no more: and they are cut off from thy hand.

6 Thou hast laid me in the lowest pit, in darkness, in the deeps.

7 Thy wrath lieth hard upon me, and thou hast afflicted *me* with all thy waves. Selah.

8 Thou hast put away mine acquaintance far from me; thou hast made me an abomination unto them: *I am* shut up, and I cannot come forth.

9 Mine eye mourneth by reason of affliction: LORD, I have called daily upon thee, I have stretched out my hands unto thee.

10 Wilt thou shew wonders to the dead? shall the dead arise *and* praise thee? Selah.

11 Shall thy lovingkindness be declared in the grave? *or* thy faithfulness in destruction?

12 Shall thy wonders be known in the dark? and thy righteousness in the land of forgetfulness?

13 But unto thee have I cried, O LORD; and in the morning shall my prayer prevent thee.

14 LORD, why castest thou off my soul? *why* hidest thou thy face from me?

15 I *am* afflicted and ready to die from *my* youth up: *while* I suffer thy terrors I am distracted.

16 Thy fierce wrath goeth over me; thy terrors have cut me off.

17 They came round about me daily like water; they compassed me about together.

18 Lover and friend hast thou put far from me, *and* mine acquaintance into darkness.

PSALM 89.—1 *The psalmist praises God for his covenant,* 5 *for his wonderful power,* 15 *for the care of his church,* 19 *for his favour to the kingdom of David.* 38 *Then complaining of contrary events,* 46 *he expostulateth, prayeth, and blesseth God.*

MASCHIL OF ETHAN THE EZRAHITE.

1 I will sing of the mercies of the LORD forever: with my mouth will I make known thy faithfulness to all generations.

2 For I have said, Mercy shall be built up forever: thy faithfulness shalt thou establish in the very heavens.

3 I have made a covenant with my chosen, I have sworn unto David my servant,

4 Thy seed will I establish for ever, and build up thy throne to all generations. Selah.

5 And the heavens shall praise thy wonders, O LORD: thy faithfulness also in the congregation of the saints.

6 For who in the heaven can be compared unto the LORD? *who* among the sons of the mighty can be likened unto the LORD?

7 God is greatly to be feared in the assembly of the saints, and to be had in reverence of all *them that are* about him.

8 O LORD God of hosts, who *is* a strong LORD like unto thee? or to thy faithfulness round about thee?

9 Thou rulest the raging of the sea: when the waves thereof arise, thou stillest them.

10 Thou hast broken Rahab in pieces, as one that is slain; thou hast scattered thine enemies with thy strong arm.

11 The heavens *are* thine, the earth also *is* thine: *as for* the world and the fulness thereof, thou hast founded them.

12 The north and the south thou hast created them: Tabor and Hermon shall rejoice in thy name.

13 Thou hast a mighty arm: strong is thy hand, *and* high is thy right hand.

14 Justice and judgment *are* the habitation of thy throne: mercy and truth shall go before thy face.

15 Blessed *is* the people that know the joyful sound: they shall walk, O LORD, in the light of thy countenance.

16 In thy name shall they rejoice all the day: and in thy righteousness shall they be exalted.

17 For thou *art* the glory of their strength: and in thy favour our horn shall be exalted.

18 For the LORD *is* our defence; and the Holy One of Israel *is* our king.

19 Then thou spakest in vision to thy holy one, and saidst, I have laid help upon *one that is* mighty; I have exalted *one* chosen out of the people.

20 I have found David my servant; with my holy oil have I anointed him:

21 With whom my hand shall be established: mine arm also shall strengthen him.

22 The enemy shall not exact upon him; nor the son of wickedness afflict him.

23 And I will beat down his foes before his face, and plague them that hate him.

24 But my faithfulness and my mercy *shall be* with him: and in my name shall his horn be exalted.

25 I will set his hand also in the sea, and his right hand in the rivers.

26 He shall cry unto me, Thou *art* my father, my God, and the rock of my salvation.

27 Also I will make him *my* firstborn, higher than the kings of the earth.

28 My mercy will I keep for him for evermore, and my covenant shall stand fast with him.

29 His seed also will I make *to endure* for ever, and his throne as the days of heaven.

30 If his children forsake my law, and walk not in my judgments;

31 If they break my statutes, and keep not my commandments;

32 Then will I visit their transgression with the rod, and their iniquity with stripes.

33 Nevertheless my lovingkindness will I not utterly take from him, nor suffer my faithfulness to fail.

34 My covenant will I not break, nor alter the thing that is gone out of my lips.

35 Once have I sworn by my holiness that I will not lie unto David.

36 His seed shall endure for ever, and his throne as the sun before me.

37 It shall be established for ever as the moon, and *as* a faithful witness in heaven. Selah.

38 But thou hast cast off and abhorred, thou hast been wroth with thine anointed.

39 Thou hast made void the covenant of thy servant: thou hast profaned his crown *by casting it* to the ground.

40 Thou hast broken down all his hedges; thou hast brought his strong holds to ruin.

41 All that pass by the way spoil him: he is a reproach to his neighbours.

42 Thou hast set up the right hand of his adversaries; thou hast made all his enemies to rejoice.

43 Thou hast also turned the edge of his sword, and hast not made him to stand in the battle.

44 Thou hast made his glory to cease, and cast his throne down to the ground.

45 The days of his youth hast thou shortened: thou hast covered him with shame. Selah.

46 How long, LORD? wilt thou hide thyself for ever? shall thy wrath burn like fire?

47 Remember how short my time is: wherefore hast thou made all men in vain?

48 What man *is he that* liveth, and shall not see death? shall he deliver his soul from the hand of the grave? Selah.

49 Lord, where *are* thy former lovingkindnesses, *which* thou swarest unto David in thy truth?

50 Remember, Lord, the reproach of thy servants; *how* I do bear in my bosom *the reproach of* all the mighty people;

51 Wherewith thine enemies have reproached, O LORD; wherewith they have reproached the footsteps of thine anointed.

52 Blessed *be* the LORD for evermore. Amen, and Amen.

PSALM 94.—1 *The prophet, calling for justice, complaineth of tyranny and impiety.* 8 *He teacheth God's providence.* 12 *He sheweth the blessedness of affliction.* 16 *God is the defender of the afflicted.*

1 O LORD God, to whom vengeance belongeth; O God, to whom vengeance belongeth, shew thyself.

2 Lift up thyself, thou judge of the earth: render a reward to the proud.

3 LORD, how long shall the wicked, how long shall the wicked triumph?

4 *How long* shall they utter *and* speak hard things? *and* all the workers of iniquity boast themselves?

5 They break in pieces thy people, O LORD, and afflict thine heritage.

6 They slay the widow and the stranger, and murder the fatherless.

7 Yet they say, The LORD shall not see, neither shall the God of Jacob regard *it*.

8 Understand, ye brutish among the people: and *ye* fools, when will ye be wise?

9 He that planted the ear, shall he not hear? he that formed the eye, shall he not see?

10 He that chastiseth the heathen, shall not he correct? he that teacheth man knowledge, *shall not he know?*

11 The LORD knoweth the thoughts of man, that they *are* vanity.

12 Blessed *is* the man whom thou chastenest, O Lord, and teachest him out of thy law;

13 That thou mayest give him rest from the days of adversity, until the pit be digged for the wicked.

14 For the Lord will not cast off his people, neither will he forsake his inheritance.

15 But judgment shall return unto righteousness: and all the upright in heart shall follow it.

16 Who will rise up for me against the evildoers? *or* who will stand up for me against the workers of iniquity?

17 Unless the Lord *had been* my help, my soul had almost dwelt in silence.

18 When I said, My foot slippeth; thy mercy, O Lord, held me up.

19 In the multitude of my thoughts within me thy comforts delight my soul.

20 Shall the throne of iniquity have fellowship with thee, which frameth mischief by a law?

21 They gather themselves together against the soul of the righteous, and condemn the innocent blood.

22 But the Lord is my defence; and my God *is* the rock of my refuge.

23 And he shall bring upon them their own iniquity, and shall cut them off in their own wickedness; *yea*, the Lord our God shall cut them off.

PSALM 102.—1 *The prophet in his prayer maketh a grievous complaint.* 12 *He taketh comfort in the eternity and mercy of God.* 18 *The mercies of God are to be recorded.* 23 *He sustaineth his weakness by the unchangeableness of God.*

A PRAYER OF THE AFFLICTED, WHEN HE IS OVERWHELMED, AND POURETH OUT HIS COMPLAINT BEFORE THE LORD.

1 Hear my prayer, O Lord, and let my cry come unto thee.

2 Hide not thy face from me in the day *when* I am in trouble; incline thine ear unto me: in the day *when* I call answer me speedily.

3 For my days are consumed like smoke, and my bones are burned as an hearth.

4 My heart is smitten, and withered like grass; so that I forget to eat my bread.

5 By reason of the voice of my groaning my bones cleave to my skin.

6 I am like a pelican of the wilderness. I am like an owl of the desert.

7 I watch, and am as a sparrow alone upon the house top.

8 Mine enemies reproach me all the day; *and* they that are mad against me are sworn against me.

9 For I have eaten ashes like bread, and mingled my drink with weeping,

10 Because of thine indignation and thy wrath: for thou hast lifted me up, and cast me down.

11 My days *are* like a shadow that declineth; and I am withered like grass.

12 But thou, O Lord, shalt endure for ever; and thy remembrance unto all generations.

13 Thou shalt arise, *and* have mercy upon Zion: for the time to favour her, yea, the set time, is come.

14 For thy servants take pleasure in her stones, and favour the dust thereof.

15 So the heathen shall fear the name of the Lord, and all the kings of the earth thy glory.

16 When the Lord shall build up Zion, he shall appear in his glory.

17 He will regard the prayer of the destitute, and not despise their prayer.

18 This shall be written for the generation to come: and the people which shall be created shall praise the Lord.

19 For he hath looked down from the height of his sanctuary; from heaven did the Lord behold the earth;

20 To hear the groaning of the prisoner; to loose those that are appointed to death;

21 To declare the name of the Lord in Zion, and his praise in Jerusalem;

22 When the people are gathered together, and the kingdoms, to serve the Lord.

23 He weakened my strength in the way; he shortened my days.

24 I said, O my God, take me not away in the midst of my days: thy years *are* throughout all generations.

25 Of old hast thou laid the foundation of the earth: and the heavens *are* the work of thy hands.

26 They shall perish, but thou shalt endure: yea, all of them shall wax old like a garment; as a vesture shalt thou change them, and they shall be changed:

27 But thou *art* the same, and thy years shall have no end.

28 The children of thy servants shall continue, and their seed shall be established before thee.

PSALM 109.—*David, complaining of his slanderous enemies, under the person of Judas devoteth them.* 16 *He sheweth their sin.* 21 *Complaining of his own misery, he prayeth for help.* 29 *He promiseth thankfulness.*

TO THE CHIEF MUSICIAN, A PSALM OF DAVID.

1 Hold not thy peace, O God of my praise;

2 For the mouth of the wicked and the mouth of the deceitful are opened against me: they have spoken against me with a lying tongue.

3 They compassed me about also with words of hatred; and fought against me without a cause.

4 For my love they are my adversaries: but I *give myself unto* prayer.

5 And they have rewarded me evil for good, and hatred for my love.

6 Set thou a wicked man over him: and let Satan stand at his right hand.

7 When he shall be judged, let him be condemned: and let his prayer become sin.

8 Let his days be few; *and* let another take his office.

9 Let his children be fatherless, and his wife a widow.

10 Let his children be continually vaga-

bonds, and beg: let them seek *their bread* also out of their desolate places.

11 Let the extortioner catch all that he hath ; and let the strangers spoil his labour.

12 Let there be none to extend mercy unto him: neither let there be any to favour his fatherless children.

13 Let his posterity be cut off; *and* in the generation following let their name be blotted out.

14 Let the iniquity of his fathers be remembered with the LORD ; and let not the sin of his mother be blotted out.

15 Let them be before the LORD continually, that he may cut off the memory of them from the earth.

16 Because that he remembered not to shew mercy, but persecuted the poor and needy man, that he might even slay the broken in heart.

17 As he loved cursing, so let it come unto him : as he delighted not in blessing, so let it be far from him.

18 As he clothed himself with cursing like as with his garment, so let it come into his bowels like water, and like oil into his bones.

19 Let it be unto him as the garment *which* covereth him, and for a girdle wherewith he is girded continually.

20 *Let* this *be* the reward of mine adversaries from the LORD, and of them that speak evil against my soul.

21 But do thou for me, O GOD the Lord, for thy name's sake : because thy mercy *is* good, deliver thou me.

22 For I *am* poor and needy, and my heart is wounded within me.

23 I am gone like the shadow when it declineth: I am tossed up and down as the locust.

24 My knees are weak through fasting ; and my flesh faileth of fatness.

25 I became also a reproach unto them : *when* they looked upon me they shaked their heads.

26 Help me, O LORD my God : O save me according to thy mercy :

27 That they may know that this *is* thy hand ; *that* thou, LORD, hast done it.

28 Let them curse, but bless thou : when they arise, let them be ashamed ; but let thy servant rejoice.

29 Let mine adversaries be clothed with shame, and let them cover themselves with their own confusion, as with a mantle.

30 I will greatly praise the LORD with my mouth ; yea, I will praise him among the multitude.

31 For he shall stand at the right hand of the poor, to save *him* from those that condemn his soul.

PSALM 120.—1 *David prayeth against Doeg,* 3 *reproveth his tongue,* 5 *complaineth of his necessary conversation with the wicked.*

A SONG OF DEGREES.

1 In my distress I cried unto the LORD, and he heard me.

2 Deliver my soul, O LORD, from lying lips, *and* from a deceitful tongue.

3 What shall be given unto thee ? or what shall be done unto thee, thou false tongue ?

4 Sharp arrows of the mighty, with coals of juniper.

5 Woe is me, that I sojourn in Mesech, *that* I dwell in the tents of Kedar !

6 My soul hath long dwelt with him that hateth peace.

7 I *am for* peace : but when I speak, they *are* for war.

PSALM 123.—1 *The godly profess their confidence in God,* 3 *and pray to be delivered from contempt.*

A SONG OF DEGREES.

1 Unto thee lift I up mine eyes, O thou that dwellest in the heavens.

2 Behold, as the eyes of servants *look* unto the hand of their masters, *and* as the eyes of a maiden unto the hand of her mistress ; so our eyes *wait* upon the LORD our God, until that he have mercy upon us.

3 Have mercy upon us, O LORD, have mercy upon us : for we are exceedingly filled with contempt.

4 Our soul is exceedingly filled with the scorning of those that are at ease, *and* with the contempt of the proud.

PSALM 129.—1 *An exhortation to praise God for saving Israel in their great afflictions.* 5 *The haters of the church are cursed.*

A SONG OF DEGREES.

1 Many a time have they afflicted me from my youth, may Israel now say :

2 Many a time have they afflicted me from my youth : yet they have not prevailed against me.

3 The plowers plowed upon my back : they made long their furrows.

4 The LORD *is* righteous : he hath cut asunder the cords of the wicked.

5 Let them all be confounded and turned back that hate Zion.

6 Let them be as the grass *upon* the housetops, which withereth afore it groweth up :

7 Wherewith the mower filleth not his hand ; nor he that bindeth sheaves his bosom.

8 Neither do they which go by say, The blessing of the LORD *be* upon you : we bless you in the name of the LORD.

PSALM 137.—1 *The constancy of the Jews in captivity.* 7 *The prophet curseth Edom and Babel.*

1 By the rivers of Babylon, there we sat down, yea, we wept, when we remembered Zion.

2 We hanged our harps upon the willows in the midst thereof.

3 For there they that carried us away captive required of us a song ; and they that wasted us *required of us* mirth, *saying,* Sing us *one* of the songs of Zion.

4 How shall we sing the LORD's song in a strange land ?

5 If I forget thee, O Jerusalem, let my right hand forget *her cunning.*

6 If I do not remember thee, let my tongue cleave to the roof of my mouth ; if I prefer not Jerusalem above my chief joy.

7 Remember, O LORD, the children of

Edom in the day of Jerusalem; who said, Rase *it*, rase *it*, *even* to the foundation thereof.

8 O daughter of Babylon, who art to be destroyed; happy *shall he be*, that rewardeth thee as thou hast served us.

9 Happy *shall he be*, that taketh and dasheth thy little ones against the stones.

PSALM 140.—*David prayeth to be delivered from Saul and Doeg. 8 He prayeth against them. 12 He comforteth himself by confidence in God.*

To the chief Musician, A Psalm of David.

1 Deliver me, O Lord, from the evil man: preserve me from the violent man;

2 Which imagine mischiefs in *their* heart; continually are they gathered together *for* war.

3 They have sharpened their tongues like a serpent; adders' poison *is* under their lips. Selah.

4 Keep me, O Lord, from the hands of the wicked; preserve me from the violent man; who have purposed to overthrow my goings.

5 The proud have hid a snare for me, and cords; they have spread a net by the wayside; they have set gins for me. Selah.

6 I said unto the Lord, Thou *art* my God: hear the voice of my supplications, O Lord.

7 O God the Lord, the strength of my salvation, thou hast covered my head in the day of battle.

8 Grant not, O Lord, the desires of the wicked: further not his wicked device; *lest* they exalt themselves. Selah.

9 *As for* the head of those that compass me about, let the mischief of their own lips cover them.

10 Let burning coals fall upon them: let them be cast into the fire; into deep pits, that they rise not up again.

11 Let not an evil speaker be established in the earth: evil shall hunt the violent man to overthrow *him*.

12 I know that the Lord will maintain the cause of the afflicted, *and* the right of the poor.

13 Surely the righteous shall give thanks unto thy name: the upright shall dwell in thy presence.

PSALM 141.—*1 David prayeth that his suit may be acceptable, 3 his conscience sincere, 7 and his life safe from snares.*

A Psalm of David.

1 Lord, I cry unto thee: make haste unto me; give ear unto my voice, when I cry unto thee.

2 Let my prayer be set forth before thee *as* incense; *and* the lifting up of my hands *as* the evening sacrifice.

3 Set a watch, O Lord, before my mouth; keep the door of my lips.

4 Incline not my heart to *any* evil thing, to practise wicked works with men that work iniquity: and let me not eat of their dainties.

5 Let the righteous smite me; *it shall be* a kindness: and let him reprove me; *it*

shall be an excellent oil, *which* shall not break my head: for yet my prayer also *shall be* in their calamities.

6 When their judges are overthrown in stony places, they shall hear my words; for they are sweet.

7 Our bones are scattered at the grave's mouth, as when one cutteth and cleaveth *wood* upon the earth.

8 But mine eyes *are* unto thee, O God the Lord: in thee is my trust; leave not my soul destitute.

9 Keep me from the snares *which* they have laid for me, and the gins of the workers of iniquity.

10 Let the wicked fall into their own nets, whilst that I withal escape.

PSALM 142.—*David sheweth that in his trouble all his comfort was in prayer unto God.*

Maschil of David; A Prayer when he was in the cave.

1 I cried unto the Lord with my voice; with my voice unto the Lord did I make my supplication.

2 I poured out my complaint before him; I shewed before him my trouble.

3 When my spirit was overwhelmed within me, then thou knewest my path. In the way wherein I walked have they privily laid a snare for me.

4 I looked on *my* right hand, and beheld, but *there was* no man that would know me: refuge failed me; no man cared for my soul.

5 I cried unto thee, O Lord: I said, Thou *art* my refuge *and* my portion in the land of the living.

6 Attend unto my cry; for I am brought very low: deliver me from my persecutors; for they are stronger than I.

7 Bring my soul out of prison, that I may praise thy name: the righteous shall compass me about; for thou shalt deal bountifully with me.

PSALM 143.—*1 David prayeth for favour in judgment. 3 He complaineth of his griefs. 5 He strengtheneth his faith by meditation and prayer. 7 He prayeth for grace, 9 for deliverance, 10 for sanctification, 12 for destruction of his enemies.*

A Psalm of David.

1 Hear my prayer, O Lord, give ear to my supplications: in thy faithfulness answer me, *and* in thy righteousness.

2 And enter not into judgment with thy servant: for in thy sight shall no man living be justified.

3 For the enemy hath persecuted my soul; he hath smitten my life down to the ground; he hath made me to dwell in darkness, as those that have been long dead.

4 Therefore is my spirit overwhelmed within me; my heart within me is desolate.

5 I remember the days of old; I meditate on all thy works; I muse on the work of thy hands.

6 I stretch forth my hands unto thee: my soul *thirsteth* after thee, as a thirsty land. Selah.

7 Hear me speedily, O Lord: my spirit faileth: hide not thy face from me, lest I

be like unto them that go down into the pit.

8 Cause me to hear thy lovingkindness in the morning; for in thee do I trust: cause me to know the way wherein I should walk; for I lift up my soul unto thee.

9 Deliver me, O LORD, from mine enemies: I flee unto thee to hide me.

10 Teach me to do thy will; for thou *art* my God: thy spirit *is* good; lead me into the land of uprightness.

11 Quicken me, O LORD, for thy name's sake: for thy righteousness' sake bring my soul out of trouble.

12 And of thy mercy cut off mine enemies, and destroy all them that afflict my soul: for I *am* thy servant.

DIDACTIC:

PSALM 1.—1 *The happiness of the godly.* 4 *The unhappiness of the ungodly.*

1 Blessed *is* the man that walketh not in the counsel of the ungodly, nor standeth in the way of sinners, nor sitteth in the seat of the scornful.

2 But his delight *is* in the law of the LORD; and in his law doth he meditate day and night.

3 And he shall be like a tree planted by the rivers of water, that bringeth forth his fruit in his season; his leaf also shall not wither; and whatsoever he doeth shall prosper.

4 The ungodly *are* not so: but *are* like the chaff which the wind driveth away.

5 Therefore the ungodly shall not stand in the judgment, nor sinners in the congregation of the righteous.

6 For the LORD knoweth the way of the righteous: but the way of the ungodly shall perish.

PSALM 5.—1 *David prayeth, and professeth his study in prayer.* 4 *God favoureth not the wicked.* 7 *David, professing his faith, prayeth unto God to guide him,* 10 *to destroy his enemies,* 11 *and to preserve the godly.*

To THE CHIEF MUSICIAN UPON NEHILOTH, A PSALM OF DAVID.

1 Give ear to my words, O LORD, consider my meditation.

2 Hearken unto the voice of my cry, my King, and my God: for unto thee will I pray.

3 My voice shalt thou hear in the morning, O LORD; in the morning will I direct *my prayer* unto thee, and will look up.

4 For thou *art* not a God that hath pleasure in wickedness: neither shall evil dwell with thee.

5 The foolish shall not stand in thy sight: thou hatest all workers of iniquity.

6 Thou shalt destroy them that speak leasing: the LORD will abhor the bloody and deceitful man.

7 But as for me, I will come *into* thy house in the multitude of thy mercy: *and* in thy fear will I worship toward thy holy temple.

8 Lead me, O LORD, in thy righteousness because of mine enemies; make thy way straight before my face.

9 For *there is* no faithfulness in their mouth; their inward part *is* very wickedness; their throat *is* an open sepulchre; they flatter with their tongue.

10 Destroy thou them, O God; let them fall by their own counsels; cast them out in the multitude of their transgressions; for they have rebelled against thee.

11 But let all those that put their trust in thee rejoice: let them ever shout for joy, because thou defendest them: let them also that love thy name be joyful in thee.

12 For thou, LORD, wilt bless the righteous; with favour wilt thou compass him as *with* a shield.

PSALM 7.—1 *David prayeth against the malice of his enemies, professing his innocency.* 10 *By faith he seeth his defence, and the destruction of his enemies.*

SHIGGAION OF DAVID, WHICH HE SANG UNTO THE LORD, CONCERNING THE WORDS OF CUSH THE BENJAMITE.

1 O LORD my God, in thee do I put my trust: save me from all them that persecute me, and deliver me:

2 Lest he tear my soul like a lion, rending *it* in pieces, while *there is* none to deliver.

3 O LORD my God, if I have done this; if there be iniquity in my hands;

4 If I have rewarded evil unto him that was at peace with me; (yea, I have delivered him that without cause is mine enemy:)

5 Let the enemy persecute my soul, and take *it*; yea, let him tread down my life upon the earth, and lay mine honour in the dust. Selah.

6 Arise, O LORD, in thine anger, lift up thyself because of the rage of mine enemies: and awake for me *to* the judgment *that* thou hast commanded.

7 So shall the congregation of the people compass thee about: for their sakes therefore return thou on high.

8 The LORD shall judge the people: judge me, O LORD, according to my righteousness, and according to mine integrity *that is* in me.

9 Oh let the wickedness of the wicked come to an end; but establish the just: for the righteous God trieth the hearts and reins.

10 My defence *is* of God, which saveth the upright in heart.

11 God judgeth the righteous, and God is angry *with the wicked* every day.

12 If he turn not, he will whet his sword; he hath bent his bow, and made it ready.

13 He hath also prepared for him the instruments of death; he ordaineth his arrows against the persecutors.

14 Behold, he travaileth with iniquity, and hath conceived mischief, and brought forth falsehood.

15 He made a pit, and digged it, and is fallen into the ditch *which* he made.

16 His mischief shall return upon his own head, and his violent dealing shall come down upon his own pate.

17 I will praise the LORD according to his

righteousness: and will sing praise to the name of the LORD most high.

PSALM 9.—1 *David praiseth God for executing of judgment.* 11 *He inciteth others to praise him.* 13 *He prayeth that he may have cause to praise him.*

To the chief Musician upon Muthlabben, A Psalm of David.

1 I will praise *thee*, O LORD, with my whole heart; I will shew forth all thy marvellous works.

2 I will be glad and rejoice in thee: I will sing praise to thy name, O thou most High.

3 When mine enemies are turned back, they shall fall and perish at thy presence.

4 For thou hast maintained my right and my cause; thou satest in the throne judging right.

5 Thou hast rebuked the heathen, thou hast destroyed the wicked, thou hast put out their name for ever and ever.

6 O thou enemy, destructions are come to a perpetual end: and thou hast destroyed cities; their memorial is perished with them.

7 But the LORD shall endure for ever: he hath prepared his throne for judgment.

8 And he shall judge the world in righteousness, he shall minister judgment to the people in uprightness.

9 The LORD also will be a refuge for the oppressed, a refuge in times of trouble.

10 And they that know thy name will put their trust in thee: for thou, LORD, hast not forsaken them that seek thee.

11 Sing praises to the LORD, which dwelleth in Zion: declare among the people his doings.

12 When he maketh inquisition for blood, he remembereth them: he forgetteth not the cry of the humble.

13 Have mercy upon me, O LORD; consider my trouble *which I suffer* of them that hate me, thou that liftest me up from the gates of death:

14 That I may shew forth all thy praise in the gates of the daughter of Zion: I will rejoice in thy salvation.

15 The heathen are sunk down in the pit *that* they made: in the net which they hid is their own foot taken.

16 The LORD is known *by* the judgment *which* he executeth: the wicked is snared in the work of his own hands. Higgaion. Selah.

17 The wicked shall be turned into hell, *and* all the nations that forget God.

18 For the needy shall not alway be forgotten: the expectation of the poor shall *not* perish for ever.

19 Arise, O LORD; let not man prevail: let the heathen be judged in thy sight.

20 Put them in fear, O LORD: *that* the nations may know themselves *to be but* men. Selah.

PSALM 10.—1 *David complaineth to God of the outrage of the wicked.* 12 *He prayeth for remedy.* 16 *He professeth his confidence.*

1 Why standest thou afar off, O LORD? *why* hidest thou *thyself* in times of trouble?

2 The wicked in *his* pride doth persecute the poor: let them be taken in the devices that they have imagined.

3 For the wicked boasteth of his heart's desire, and blesseth the covetous, *whom* the LORD abhorreth.

4 The wicked, through the pride of his countenance, will not seek *after God:* God *is* not in all his thoughts.

5 His ways are always grievous; thy judgments *are* far above out of his sight: *as for* all his enemies, he puffeth at them.

6 He hath said in his heart, I shall not be moved: for *I shall* never *be* in adversity.

7 His mouth is full of cursing and deceit and fraud: under his tongue *is* mischief and vanity.

8 He sitteth in the lurking places of the villages: in the secret places doth he murder the innocent: his eyes are privily set against the poor.

9 He lieth in wait secretly as a lion in his den: he lieth in wait to catch the poor: he doth catch the poor, when he draweth him into his net.

10 He croucheth, *and* humbleth himself, that the poor may fall by his strong ones.

11 He hath said in his heart, God hath forgotten: he hideth his face; he will never see *it.*

12 Arise, O LORD; O God, lift up thine hand: forget not the humble.

13 Wherefore doth the wicked contemn God? he hath said in his heart, Thou wilt not require *it.*

14 Thou hast seen *it;* for thou beholdest mischief and spite, to requite *it* with thy hand: the poor committeth himself unto thee; thou art the helper of the fatherless.

15 Break thou the arm of the wicked and the evil *man:* seek out his wickedness *till* thou find none.

16 The LORD *is* King for ever and ever: the heathen are perished out of his land.

17 LORD, thou hast heard the desire of the humble: thou wilt prepare their heart, thou wilt cause thine ear to hear:

18 To judge the fatherless and the oppressed, that the man of the earth may no more oppress.

PSALM 11.—*David encourageth himself in God against his enemies.* 4 *The providence and justice of God.*

To the chief Musician, A Psalm of David.

1 In the LORD put I my trust: how say ye to my soul, Flee *as* a bird to your mountain?

2 For, lo, the wicked bend *their* bow, they make ready their arrow upon the string, that they may privily shoot at the upright in heart.

3 If the foundations be destroyed, what can the righteous do?

4 The LORD *is* in his holy temple, the LORD's throne *is* in heaven: his eyes behold, his eyelids try, the children of men.

5 The LORD trieth the righteous: but the

wicked and him that loveth violence his soul hateth.

6 Upon the wicked he shall rain snares, fire and brimstone, and an horrible tempest: *this shall be* the portion of their cup.

7 For the righteous LORD loveth righteousness; his countenance doth behold the upright.

PSALM 12.—1 *David, destitute of human comfort, craveth help of God.* 3 *He comforteth himself with God's judgments on the wicked, and confidence in God's tried promises.*

To THE CHIEF MUSICIAN UPON SHEMINITH, A PSALM OF DAVID.

1 Help, LORD; for the godly man ceaseth, for the faithful fail from among the children of men.

2 They speak vanity every one with his neighbour: *with* flattering lips *and* with a double heart do they speak.

3 The LORD shall cut off all flattering lips, *and* the tongue that speaketh proud things:

4 Who have said, With our tongue will we prevail; our lips *are* our own: who *is* lord over us?

5 For the oppression of the poor, for the sighing of the needy, now will I arise, saith the LORD; I will set *him* in safety *from him that* puffeth at him.

6 The words of the LORD *are* pure words: *as* silver tried in a furnace of earth, purified seven times.

7 Thou shalt keep them, O LORD, thou shalt preserve them from this generation for ever.

8 The wicked walk on every side, when the vilest men are exalted.

PSALM 14.—1 *David describeth the corruption of a natural man.* 4 *He convinceth the wicked by the light of their conscience.* 7 *He glorieth in the salvation of God.*

To THE CHIEF MUSICIAN, A PSALM OF DAVID.

1 The fool hath said in his heart, *There is* no God. They are corrupt, they have done abominable works, *there is* none that doeth good.

2 The LORD looked down from heaven upon the children of men, to see if there were any that did understand, *and* seek God.

3 They are all gone aside, they are *all* together become filthy: *there is* none that doeth good, no, not one.

4 Have all the workers of iniquity no knowledge? who eat up my people *as* they eat bread, and call not upon the LORD.

5 There were they in great fear: for God *is* in the generation of the righteous.

6 Ye have shamed the counsel of the poor, because the LORD *is* his refuge.

7 Oh that the salvation of Israel *were* come out of Zion! when the LORD bringeth back the captivity of his people, Jacob shall rejoice, *and* Israel shall be glad.

PSALM 15.—*David describeth a citizen of Zion.*

A PSALM OF DAVID.

1 LORD, who shall abide in thy tabernacle? who shall dwell in thy holy hill?

2 He that walketh uprightly, and worketh righteousness, and speaketh the truth in his heart.

3 *He that* backbiteth not with his tongue, nor doeth evil to his neighbour, nor taketh up a reproach against his neighbour.

4 In whose eyes a vile person is contemned; but he honoureth them that fear the LORD. *He that* sweareth to *his own* hurt, and changeth not.

5 *He that* putteth not out his money to usury, nor taketh reward against the innocent. He that doeth these *things* shall never be moved.

PSALM 17.—1 *David, in confidence of his integrity, craveth defence of God against his enemies.* 10 *He sheweth their pride, craft, and eagerness.* 13 *He prayeth against them in confidence of his hope.*

A PRAYER OF DAVID.

1 Hear the right, O LORD, attend unto my cry, give ear unto my prayer, *that goeth* not out of feigned lips.

2 Let my sentence come forth from thy presence; let thine eyes behold the things that are equal.

3 Thou hast proved mine heart; thou hast visited *me* in the night; thou hast tried me, *and* shalt find nothing; I am purposed *that* my mouth shall not transgress.

4 Concerning the works of men, by the word of thy lips I have kept *me from* the paths of the destroyer.

5 Hold up my goings in thy paths, *that* my footsteps slip not.

6 I have called upon thee, for thou wilt hear me, O God; incline thine ear unto me, *and hear* my speech.

7 Shew thy marvellous lovingkindness, O thou that savest by thy right hand them which put their trust *in thee* from those that rise up *against them.*

8 Keep me as the apple of the eye, hide me under the shadow of thy wings,

9 From the wicked that oppress me, *from* my deadly enemies, *who* compass me about.

10 They are inclosed in their own fat: with their mouth they speak proudly.

11 They have now compassed us in our steps: they have set their eyes bowing down to the earth;

12 Like as a lion *that* is greedy of his prey, and as it were a young lion lurking in secret places.

13 Arise, O LORD, disappoint him, cast him down: deliver my soul from the wicked, *which is* thy sword:

14 From men *which are* thy hand, O LORD, from men of the world, *which have* their portion in *this* life, and whose belly thou fillest with thy hid *treasure:* they are full of children, and leave the rest of their *substance* to their babes.

15 As for me, I will behold thy face in righteousness: I shall be satisfied, when I awake, with thy likeness.

PSALM 24.—1 *God's lordship in the world. The citizens of his spiritual kingdom.* 7 *An exhortation to receive him.*

A PSALM OF DAVID.

1 The earth *is* the LORD'S, and the fulness thereof; the world, and they that dwell therein.

2 For he hath founded it upon the seas, and established it upon the floods.

3 Who shall ascend into the hill of the LORD? or who shall stand in his holy place?

4 He that hath clean hands, and a pure heart; who hath not lifted up his soul unto vanity, nor sworn deceitfully.

5 He shall receive the blessing from the LORD, and righteousness from the God of his salvation.

6 This is the generation of them that seek him, that seek thy face, O Jacob. Selah.

7 Lift up your heads, O ye gates; and be ye lift up, ye everlasting doors; and the King of glory shall come in.

8 Who is this King of glory? The LORD strong and mighty, the LORD mighty in battle.

9 Lift up your heads, O ye gates; even lift them up, ye everlasting doors; and the King of glory shall come in.

10 Who is this King of glory? The LORD of hosts, he is the King of glory. Selah.

PSALM 25.—1 David's confidence in prayer. 7 He prayeth for remission of sins, 16 and for help in affliction.

A PSALM OF DAVID.

1 Unto thee, O LORD, do I lift up my soul.

2 O my God, I trust in thee: let me not be ashamed, let not mine enemies triumph over me.

3 Yea, let none that wait on thee be ashamed: let them be ashamed which transgress without cause.

4 Shew me thy ways, O LORD; teach me thy paths.

5 Lead me in thy truth, and teach me: for thou art the God of my salvation; on thee do I wait all the day.

6 Remember, O LORD, thy tender mercies and thy lovingkindnesses; for they have been ever of old.

7 Remember not the sins of my youth, nor my transgressions: according to thy mercy remember thou me for thy goodness' sake, O LORD.

8 Good and upright is the LORD: therefore will he teach sinners in the way.

9 The meek will he guide in judgment: and the meek will he teach his way.

10 All the paths of the LORD are mercy and truth unto such as keep his covenant and his testimonies.

11 For thy name's sake, O LORD, pardon mine iniquity; for it is great.

12 What man is he that feareth the LORD? him shall he teach in the way that he shall choose.

13 His soul shall dwell at ease; and his seed shall inherit the earth.

14 The secret of the LORD is with them that fear him; and he will shew them his covenant.

15 Mine eyes are ever toward the LORD; for he shall pluck my feet out of the net.

16 Turn thee unto me, and have mercy upon me; for I am desolate and afflicted.

17 The troubles of my heart are enlarged: O bring thou me out of my distresses.

18 Look upon mine affliction and my pain; and forgive all my sins.

19 Consider mine enemies; for they are many; and they hate me with cruel hatred.

20 O keep my soul, and deliver me: let me not be ashamed; for I put my trust in thee.

21 Let integrity and uprightness preserve me; for I wait on thee.

22 Redeem Israel, O God, out of all his troubles.

PSALM 32.—1 Blessedness consisteth in remission of sins. 3 Confession of sins giveth ease to the conscience. 8 God's promises bring joy.

A PSALM OF DAVID, MASCHIL.

1 Blessed is he whose transgression is forgiven, whose sin is covered.

2 Blessed is the man unto whom the LORD imputeth not iniquity, and in whose spirit there is no guile.

3 When I kept silence, my bones waxed old through my roaring all the day long.

4 For day and night thy hand was heavy upon me: my moisture is turned into the drought of summer. Selah.

5 I acknowledged my sin unto thee, and mine iniquity have I not hid. I said, I will confess my transgressions unto the LORD; and thou forgavest the iniquity of my sin. Selah.

6 For this shall every one that is godly pray unto thee in a time when thou mayest be found: surely in the floods of great waters they shall not come nigh unto him.

7 Thou art my hiding place; thou shalt preserve me from trouble; thou shalt compass me about with songs of deliverance. Selah.

8 I will instruct thee and teach thee in the way which thou shalt go: I will guide thee with mine eye.

9 Be ye not as the horse, or as the mule, which have no understanding: whose mouth must be held in with bit and bridle, lest they come near unto thee.

10 Many sorrows shall be to the wicked: but he that trusteth in the LORD, mercy shall compass him about.

11 Be glad in the LORD, and rejoice, ye righteous: and shout for joy, all ye that are upright in heart.

PSALM 34.—1 David praiseth God, and exhorteth others thereto by his experience. 8 They are blessed that trust in God. 11 He exhorteth to the fear of God. 15 The privileges of the righteous.

A PSALM OF DAVID, WHEN HE CHANGED HIS BEHAVIOUR BEFORE ABIMELECH; WHO DROVE HIM AWAY, AND HE DEPARTED.

1 I will bless the LORD at all times: his praise shall continually be in my mouth.

2 My soul shall make her boast in the LORD: the humble shall hear thereof, and be glad.

3 O magnify the LORD with me, and let us exalt his name together.

4 I sought the LORD, and he heard me, and delivered me from all my fears.

5 They looked unto him, and were lightened: and their faces were not ashamed.

6 This poor man cried, and the LORD heard *him*, and saved him out of all his troubles.

7 The angel of the LORD encampeth round about them that fear him, and delivereth them.

8 O taste and see that the LORD *is* good: blessed *is* the man *that* trusteth in him.

9 O fear the LORD, ye his saints: for *there is* no want to them that fear him.

10 The young lions do lack, and suffer hunger: but they that seek the LORD shall not want any good *thing*.

11 Come, ye children, hearken unto me: I will teach you the fear of the LORD.

12 What man *is he that* desireth life, *and* loveth *many* days, that he may see good?

13 Keep thy tongue from evil, and thy lips from speaking guile.

14 Depart from evil, and do good; seek peace, and pursue it.

15 The eyes of the LORD *are* upon the righteous, and his ears *are open* unto their cry.

16 The face of the LORD *is* against them that do evil, to cut off the remembrance of them from the earth.

17 *The righteous* cry, and the LORD heareth, and delivereth them out of all their troubles.

18 The LORD *is* nigh unto them that are of a broken heart; and saveth such as be of a contrite spirit.

19 Many *are* the afflictions of the righteous: but the LORD delivereth him out of them all.

20 He keepeth all his bones: not one of them is broken.

21 Evil shall slay the wicked: and they that hate the righteous shall be desolate.

22 The LORD redeemeth the soul of his servants: and none of them that trust in him shall be desolate.

PSALM 36.—1 *The grievous estate of the wicked.* 5 *The excellency of God's mercy.* 10 *David prayeth for favour to God's children.*

To THE CHIEF MUSICIAN, A PSALM OF DAVID THE SERVANT OF THE LORD.

1 The transgression of the wicked saith within my heart, *that there is* no fear of God before his eyes.

2 For he flattereth himself in his own eyes, until his iniquity be found to be hateful.

3 The words of his mouth *are* iniquity and deceit: he hath left off to be wise, *and* to do good.

4 He deviseth mischief upon his bed; he setteth himself in a way *that is* not good; he abhorreth not evil.

5 Thy mercy, O LORD, *is* in the heavens; *and* thy faithfulness *reacheth* unto the clouds.

6 Thy righteousness *is* like the great mountains; thy judgments *are* a great deep: O LORD, thou preservest man and beast.

7 How excellent *is* thy lovingkindness, O God! therefore the children of men put their trust under the shadow of thy wings.

8 They shall be abundantly satisfied with the fatness of thy house; and thou shalt make them drink of the river of thy pleasures.

9 For with thee *is* the fountain of life: in thy light shall we see light.

10 O continue thy lovingkindness unto them that know thee; and thy righteousness to the upright in heart.

11 Let not the foot of pride come against me, and let not the hand of the wicked remove me.

12 There are the workers of iniquity fallen: they are cast down, and shall not be able to rise.

PSALM 37.—*David persuadeth to patience and confidence in God, by the different estate of the godly and the wicked.*

A PSALM OF DAVID.

1 Fret not thyself because of evildoers, neither be thou envious against the workers of iniquity.

2 For they shall soon be cut down like the grass, and wither as the green herb.

3 Trust in the LORD, and do good; *so* shalt thou dwell in the land, and verily thou shalt be fed.

4 Delight thyself also in the LORD; and he shall give thee the desires of thine heart.

5 Commit thy way unto the LORD; trust also in him; and he shall bring *it* to pass.

6 And he shall bring forth thy righteousness as the light, and thy judgment as the noonday.

7 Rest in the LORD, and wait patiently for him: fret not thyself because of him who prospereth in his way, because of the man who bringeth wicked devices to pass.

8 Cease from anger, and forsake wrath: fret not thyself in any wise to do evil.

9 For evildoers shall be cut off: but those that wait upon the LORD, they shall inherit the earth.

10 For yet a little while, and the wicked *shall* not *be:* yea, thou shalt diligently consider his place, and it *shall* not *be.*

11 But the meek shall inherit the earth; and shall delight themselves in the abundance of peace.

12 The wicked plotteth against the just, and gnasheth upon him with his teeth.

13 The Lord shall laugh at him: for he seeth that his day is coming.

14 The wicked have drawn out the sword, and have bent their bow, to cast down the poor and needy, *and* to slay such as be of upright conversation.

15 Their sword shall enter into their own heart, and their bows shall be broken.

16 A little that a righteous man hath *is* better than the riches of many wicked.

17 For the arms of the wicked shall be broken: but the LORD upholdeth the righteous.

18 The LORD knoweth the days of the upright: and their inheritance shall be for ever.

19 They shall not be ashamed in the evil

time: and in the days of famine they shall be satisfied.

20 But the wicked shall perish, and the enemies of the LORD *shall be* as the fat of lambs: they shall consume; into smoke shall they consume away.

21 The wicked borroweth, and payeth not again: but the righteous sheweth mercy, and giveth.

22 For *such as be* blessed of him shall inherit the earth; and *they that be* cursed of him shall be cut off.

23 The steps of a *good* man are ordered by the LORD: and he delighteth in his way.

24 Though he fall, he shall not be utterly cast down: for the LORD upholdeth *him with* his hand.

25 I have been young, and *now* am old; yet have I not seen the righteous forsaken, nor his seed begging bread.

26 *He is* ever merciful, and lendeth; and his seed *is* blessed.

27 Depart from evil, and do good; and dwell for evermore.

28 For the LORD loveth judgment, and forsaketh not his saints; they are preserved for ever: but the seed of the wicked shall be cut off.

29 The righteous shall inherit the land, and dwell therein for ever.

30 The mouth of the righteous speaketh wisdom, and his tongue talketh of judgment.

31 The law of his God *is* in his heart; none of his steps shall slide.

32 The wicked watcheth the righteous, and seeketh to slay him.

33 The LORD will not leave him in his hand, nor condemn him when he is judged.

34 Wait on the LORD, and keep his way, and he shall exalt thee to inherit the land: when the wicked are cut off, thou shalt see it.

35 I have seen the wicked in great power, and spreading himself like a green bay tree.

36 Yet he passed away, and, lo, he *was* not: yea, I sought him, but he could not be found.

37 Mark the perfect *man*, and behold the upright: for the end of *that* man *is* peace.

38 But the transgressors shall be destroyed together: the end of the wicked shall be cut off.

39 But the salvation of the righteous *is* of the LORD: *he is* their strength in the time of trouble.

40 And the LORD shall help them, and deliver them: he shall deliver them from the wicked, and save them, because they trust in him.

PSALM 39.—1 *David's care of his thoughts.* 4 *The consideration of the brevity and vanity of life,* 7 *the reverence of God's judgments,* 10 *and prayer, are his bridles of impatiency.*

To THE CHIEF MUSICIAN, EVEN TO JEDUTHUN, A PSALM OF DAVID.

1 I said, I will take heed to my ways, that I sin not with my tongue: I will keep my mouth with a bridle, while the wicked is before me.

2 I was dumb with silence, I held my peace, *even* from good; and my sorrow was stirred.

3 My heart was hot within me, while I was musing the fire burned: *then* spake I with my tongue,

4 LORD, make me to know mine end, and the measure of my days, what it *is; that* I may know how frail I *am.*

5 Behold, thou hast made my days *as* an handbreadth; and mine age *is* as nothing before thee: verily every man at his best state *is* altogether vanity. Selah.

6 Surely every man walketh in a vain shew: surely they are disquieted in vain: he heapeth up *riches,* and knoweth not who shall gather them.

7 And now, Lord, what wait I for? my hope *is* in thee.

8 Deliver me from all my transgressions: make me not the reproach of the foolish.

9 I was dumb, I opened not my mouth; because thou didst *it.*

10 Remove thy stroke away from me: I am consumed by the blow of thine hand.

11 When thou with rebukes dost correct man for iniquity, thou makest his beauty to consume away like a moth: surely every man *is* vanity. Selah.

12 Hear my prayer, O LORD, and give ear unto my cry; hold not thy peace at my tears: for I *am* a stranger with thee, *and* a sojourner, as all my fathers *were.*

13 O spare me, that I may recover strength, before I go hence, and be no more.

PSALM 49.—1 *An earnest persuasion to build the faith of resurrection, not on worldly power, but on God.* 16 *Worldly prosperity is not to be admired.*

To THE CHIEF MUSICIAN, A PSALM FOR THE SONS OF KORAH.

1 Hear this, all *ye* people; give ear, all *ye* inhabitants of the world:

2 Both low and high, rich and poor, together.

3 My mouth shall speak of wisdom; and the meditation of my heart *shall be* of understanding.

4 I will incline mine ear to a parable: I will open my dark saying upon the harp.

5 Wherefore should I fear in the days of evil, *when* the iniquity of my heels shall compass me about?

6 They that trust in their wealth, and boast themselves in the multitude of their riches;

7 None *of them* can by any means redeem his brother, nor give to God a ransom for him:

8 (For the redemption of their soul *is* precious, and it ceaseth for ever:)

9 That he should still live for ever, *and* not see corruption.

10 For he seeth *that* wise men die, likewise the fool and the brutish person perish, and leave their wealth to others.

11 Their inward thought *is, that* their

houses *shall continue* for ever, *and* their dwelling places to all generations; they call *their* lands after their own names.

12 Nevertheless man *being* in honour abideth not: he is like the beasts *that* perish.

13 This their way *is* their folly: yet their posterity approve their sayings. Selah.

14 Like sheep they are laid in the grave; death shall feed on them; and the upright shall have dominion over them in the morning; and their beauty shall consume in the grave from their dwelling.

15 But God will redeem my soul from the power of the grave: for he shall receive me. Selah.

16 Be not thou afraid when one is made rich, when the glory of his house is increased;

17 For when he dieth he shall carry nothing away: his glory shall not descend after him.

18 Though while he lived he blessed his soul: and *men* will praise thee, when thou doest well to thyself.

19 He shall go to the generation of his fathers; they shall never see light.

20 Man *that is* in honour, and understandeth not, is like the beasts *that* perish.

PSALM 50.—1 *The majesty of God in the church.* 5 *His order to gather saints.* 7 *The pleasure of God is not in ceremonies,* 14 *but in sincerity of obedience.*

A PSALM OF ASAPH.

1 The mighty God, *even* the LORD, hath spoken, and called the earth from the rising of the sun unto the going down thereof.

2 Out of Zion, the perfection of beauty, God hath shined.

3 Our God shall come, and shall not keep silence: a fire shall devour before him, and it shall be very tempestuous round about him.

4 He shall call to the heavens from above, and to the earth, that he may judge his people.

5 Gather my saints together unto me; those that have made a covenant with me by sacrifice.

6 And the heavens shall declare his righteousness: for God *is* judge himself. Selah.

7 Hear, O my people, and I will speak; O Israel, and I will testify against thee: I *am* God, *even* thy God.

8 I will not reprove thee for thy sacrifices or thy burnt offerings, *to have been* continually before me.

9 I will take no bullock out of thy house, *nor* he goats out of thy folds.

10 For every beast of the forest *is* mine, *and* the cattle upon a thousand hills.

11 I know all the fowls of the mountains: and the wild beasts of the field *are* mine.

12 If I were hungry, I would not tell thee: for the world *is* mine, and the fulness thereof.

13 Will I eat the flesh of bulls, or drink the blood of goats?

14 Offer unto God thanksgiving; and pay thy vows unto the most High:

15 And call upon me in the day of trou-

ble: I will deliver thee, and thou shalt glorify me.

16 But unto the wicked God saith, What hast thou to do to declare my statutes, or *that* thou shouldest take my covenant in thy mouth?

17 Seeing thou hatest instruction, and castest my words behind thee.

18 When thou sawest a thief, then thou consentedst with him, and hast been partaker with adulterers.

19 Thou givest thy mouth to evil, and thy tongue frameth deceit.

20 Thou sittest *and* speakest against thy brother; thou slanderest thine own mother's son.

21 These *things* hast thou done, and I kept silence; thou thoughtest that I was altogether *such an one* as thyself: *but* I will reprove thee, and set *them* in order before thine eyes.

22 Now consider this, ye that forget God, lest I tear *you* in pieces, and *there be* none to deliver.

23 Whoso offereth praise glorifieth me: and to him that ordereth *his* conversation *aright* will I shew the salvation of God.

PSALM 52.—1 *David, condemning the spitefulness of Doeg, prophesieth his destruction.* 6 *The righteous shall rejoice at it.* 8 *David, upon his confidence in God's mercy, giveth thanks.*

To THE CHIEF MUSICIAN, MASCHIL, A PSALM OF DAVID, WHEN DOEG THE EDOMITE CAME AND TOLD SAUL, AND SAID UNTO HIM, DAVID IS COME TO THE HOUSE OF AHIMELECH.

1 Why boastest thou thyself in mischief, O mighty man? the goodness of God *endureth* continually.

2 Thy tongue deviseth mischiefs; like a sharp razor, working deceitfully.

3 Thou lovest evil more than good; *and* lying rather than to speak righteousness. Selah.

4 Thou lovest all devouring words, O *thou* deceitful tongue.

5 God shall likewise destroy thee for ever, he shall take thee away, and pluck thee out of *thy* dwelling place, and root thee out of the land of the living. Selah.

6 The righteous also shall see, and fear, and shall laugh at him:

7 Lo, *this is* the man *that* made not God his strength; but trusted in the abundance of his riches, *and* strengthened himself in his wickedness.

8 But I *am* like a green olive tree in the house of God: I trust in the mercy of God for ever and ever.

9 I will praise thee for ever, because thou hast done *it:* and I will wait on thy name; for *it is* good before thy saints.

PSALM 53.—1 *David describeth the corruption of a natural man.* 4 *He convinceth the wicked by the light of their own conscience.* 6 *He glorieth in the salvation of God.*

To THE CHIEF MUSICIAN UPON MAHALATH, MASCHIL, A PSALM OF DAVID.

1 The fool hath said in his heart, *There is* no God. Corrupt are they, and have done

abominable iniquity: *there is* none that doeth good.

2 God looked down from heaven upon the children of men, to see if there were *any* that did understand, that did seek God.

3 Every one of them is gone back: they are altogether become filthy; *there is* none that doeth good, no, not one.

4 Have the workers of iniquity no knowledge? who eat up my people *as* they eat bread: they have not called upon God.

5 There were they in great fear, *where* no fear was: for God hath scattered the bones of him that encampeth *against* thee: thou hast put *them* to shame, because God hath despised them.

6 Oh that the salvation of Israel *were* come out of Zion! When God bringeth back the captivity of his people, Jacob shall rejoice, *and* Israel shall be glad.

PSALM 58.—1 *David reproveth wicked judges,* 3 *describeth the nature of the wicked,* 6 *devoteth them to God's judgments,* 10 *whereat the righteous shall rejoice.*

To the chief Musician, Al-taschith, Michtam of David.

1 Do ye indeed speak righteousness, O congregation? do ye judge uprightly, O ye sons of men?

2 Yea, in heart ye work wickedness; ye weigh the violence of your hands in the earth.

3 The wicked are estranged from the womb: they go astray as soon as they be born, speaking lies.

4 Their poison *is* like the poison of a serpent: *they are* like the deaf adder *that* stoppeth her ear;

5 Which will not harken to the voice of charmers, charming never so wisely.

6 Break their teeth, O God, in their mouth: break out the great teeth of the young lions, O Lord.

7 Let them melt away as waters *which* run continually: *when* he bendeth *his bow to shoot* his arrows, let them be as cut in pieces.

8 As a snail *which* melteth, let *every one of them* pass away: *like* the untimely birth of a woman, *that* they may not see the sun.

9 Before your pots can feel the thorns, he shall take them away as with a whirlwind, both living, and in *his* wrath.

10 The righteous shall rejoice when he seeth the vengeance: he shall wash his feet in the blood of the wicked.

11 So that a man shall say, Verily *there is* a reward for the righteous: verily he is a God that judgeth in the earth.

PSALM 73.—1 *The prophet, prevailing in a temptation,* 2 *sheweth the occasion thereof, the prosperity of the wicked.* 13 *The wound given thereby, diffidence.* 15 *The victory over it, knowledge of God's purpose, in destroying of the wicked, and sustaining the righteous.*

A Psalm of Asaph.

1 Truly God *is* good to Israel, *even* to such as are of a clean heart.

2 But as for me, my feet were almost gone; my steps had well nigh slipped.

3 For I was envious at the foolish, *when* I saw the prosperity of the wicked.

4 For *there are* no bands in their death: but their strength *is* firm.

5 They *are* not in trouble *as other* men; neither are they plagued like *other* men.

6 Therefore pride compasseth them about as a chain; violence covereth them *as* a garment.

7 Their eyes stand out with fatness: they have more than heart could wish.

8 They are corrupt, and speak wickedly *concerning* oppression: they speak loftily.

9 They set their mouth against the heavens, and their tongue walketh through the earth.

10 Therefore his people return hither: and waters of a full *cup* are wrung out to them.

11 And they say, How doth God know? and is there knowledge in the most High?

12 Behold, these *are* the ungodly, who prosper in the world; they increase *in* riches.

13 Verily I have cleansed my heart *in* vain, and washed my hands in innocency.

14 For all the day long have I been plagued, and chastened every morning.

15 If I say, I will speak thus; behold, I should offend *against* the generation of thy children.

16 When I thought to know this, it *was* too painful for me;

17 Until I went into the sanctuary of God; *then* understood I their end.

18 Surely thou didst set them in slippery places: thou castedst them down into destruction.

19 How are they *brought* into desolation, as in a moment! they are utterly consumed with terrors.

20 As a dream when *one* awaketh; *so,* O Lord, when thou awakest, thou shalt despise their image.

21 Thus my heart was grieved, and I was pricked in my reins.

22 So foolish *was* I, and ignorant: I was *as* a beast before thee.

23 Nevertheless I *am* continually with thee: thou hast holden *me* by my right hand.

24 Thou shalt guide me with thy counsel, and afterward receive me *to* glory.

25 Whom have I in heaven *but thee?* and *there is* none upon earth *that* I desire beside thee.

26 My flesh and my heart faileth: *but* God *is* the strength of my heart, and my portion for ever.

27 For, lo, they that are far from thee shall perish: thou hast destroyed all them that go a whoring from thee.

28 But *it is* good for me to draw near to God: I have put my trust in the Lord God, that I may declare all thy works.

PSALM 75.—1 *The prophet praiseth God.* 2 *He promiseth to judge uprightly.* 4 *He rebuketh the proud by consideration of God's providence.* 9 *He praiseth God, and promiseth to execute justice.*

To the chief Musician, Al-taschith, A Psalm or Song of Asaph.

1 Unto thee, O God, do we give thanks, *unto thee* do we give thanks: for *that* thy name is near thy wondrous works declare.

2 When I shall receive the congregation I will judge uprightly.

3 The earth and all the inhabitants thereof are dissolved: I bear up the pillars of it. Selah.

4 I said unto the fools, Deal not foolishly: and to the wicked, Lift not up the horn:

5 Lift not up your horn on high: speak *not with* a stiff neck.

6 For promotion *cometh* neither from the east, nor from the west, nor from the south.

7 But God *is* the judge: he putteth down one, and setteth up another.

8 For in the hand of the Lord *there is* a cup, and the wine is red; it is full of mixture; and he poureth out of the same: but the dregs thereof, all the wicked of the earth shall wring *them* out, *and* drink *them*.

9 But I will declare for ever; I will sing praises to the God of Jacob.

10 All the horns of the wicked also will I cut off; *but* the horns of the righteous shall be exalted.

PSALM 82.—1 *The psalmist, having exhorted the judges,* 5 *and reproved their negligence,* 8 *prayeth God to judge.*

A Psalm of Asaph.

1 God standeth in the congregation of the mighty; he judgeth among the gods.

2 How long will ye judge unjustly, and accept the persons of the wicked? Selah.

3 Defend the poor and fatherless: do justice to the afflicted and needy.

4 Deliver the poor and needy: rid *them* out of the hand of the wicked.

5 They know not, neither will they understand; they walk on in darkness: all the foundations of the earth are out of course.

6 I have said, Ye *are* gods; and all of you *are* children of the most High.

7 But ye shall die like men, and fall like one of the princes.

8 Arise, O God, judge the earth: for thou shalt inherit all nations.

PSALM 84.—1 *The prophet, longing for the communion of the sanctuary,* 4 *sheweth how blessed they are that dwell therein.* 8 *He prayeth to be restored unto it.*

To the chief Musician upon Gittith, A Psalm for the sons of Korah.

1 How amiable *are* thy tabernacles, O Lord of hosts!

2 My soul longeth, yea, even fainteth for the courts of the Lord: my heart and my flesh crieth out for the living God.

3 Yea, the sparrow hath found an house, and the swallow a nest for herself, where she may lay her young, *even* thine altars, O Lord of hosts, my King, and my God.

4 Blessed *are* they that dwell in thy house: they will be still praising thee. Selah.

5 Blessed *is* the man whose strength *is* in thee; in whose heart *are* the ways *of them.*

6 *Who* passing through the valley of Baca make it a well; the rain also filleth the pools.

7 They go from strength to strength, *every one of them* in Zion appeareth before God.

8 O Lord God of hosts, hear my prayer: give ear, O God of Jacob. Selah.

9 Behold, O God our shield, and look upon the face of thine anointed.

10 For a day in thy courts *is* better than a thousand. I had rather be a doorkeeper in the house of my God, than to dwell in the tents of wickedness.

11 For the Lord God *is* a sun and shield: the Lord will give grace and glory: no good *thing* will he withhold from them that walk uprightly.

12 O Lord of hosts, blessed *is* the man that trusteth in thee.

PSALM 90.—1 *Moses, setting forth God's providence,* 3 *complaineth of human fragility,* 7 *divine chastisements,* 10 *and brevity of life.* 12 *He prayeth for the knowledge and sensible experience of God's good providence.*

A Prayer of Moses the man of God.

1 Lord, thou hast been our dwelling place in all generations.

2 Before the mountains were brought forth, or ever thou hadst formed the earth and the world, even from everlasting to everlasting, thou *art* God.

3 Thou turnest man to destruction; and sayest, Return, ye children of men.

4 For a thousand years in thy sight *are but* as yesterday when it is past, and *as* a watch in the night.

5 Thou carriest them away as with a flood; they are *as* a sleep: in the morning *they are* like grass *which* groweth up.

6 In the morning it flourisheth, and groweth up; in the evening it is cut down, and withereth.

7 For we are consumed by thine anger, and by thy wrath are we troubled.

8 Thou hast set our iniquities before thee, our secret *sins* in the light of thy countenance.

9 For all our days are passed away in thy wrath: we spend our years as a tale *that is told.*

10 The days of our years *are* threescore years and ten; and if by reason of strength *they be* fourscore years, yet *is* their strength labour and sorrow; for it is soon cut off, and we fly away.

11 Who knoweth the power of thine anger? even according to thy fear, *so is* thy wrath.

12 So teach *us* to number our days, that we may apply *our* hearts unto wisdom.

13 Return, O Lord, how long? and let it repent thee concerning thy servants.

14 O satisfy us early with thy mercy; that we may rejoice and be glad all our days.

15 Make us glad according to the days

wherein thou hast afflicted us, *and* the years *wherein* we have seen evil.

16 Let thy work appear unto thy servants, and thy glory unto their children.

17 And let the beauty of the LORD our God be upon us: and establish thou the work of our hands upon us; yea, the work of our hands establish thou it.

PSALM 91.—1 *The state of the godly.* 3 *Their safety.* 9 *Their habitation.* 11 *Their servants.* 14 *Their friend ; with the effects of them all.*

1 He that dwelleth in the secret place of the most High shall abide under the shadow of the Almighty.

2 I will say of the LORD, *He is* my refuge and my fortress: my God; in him will I trust.

3 Surely he shall deliver thee from the snare of the fowler, *and* from the noisome pestilence.

4 He shall cover thee with his feathers, and under his wings shalt thou trust: his truth *shall be thy* shield and buckler.

5 Thou shalt not be afraid for the terror by night; *nor* for the arrow *that* flieth by day;

6 *Nor* for the pestilence *that* walketh in darkness; *nor* for the destruction *that* wasteth at noonday.

7 A thousand shall fall at thy side, and ten thousand at thy right hand; *but* it shall not come nigh thee.

8 Only with thine eyes shalt thou behold and see the reward of the wicked.

9 Because thou hast made the LORD, *which is* my refuge, *even* the most High, thy habitation;

10 There shall no evil befall thee, neither shall any plague come nigh thy dwelling.

11 For he shall give his angels charge over thee, to keep thee in all thy ways.

12 They shall bear thee up in *their* hands, lest thou dash thy foot against a stone.

13 Thou shalt tread upon the lion and adder: the young lion and the dragon shalt thou trample under feet.

14 Because he hath set his love upon me, therefore will I deliver him: I will set him on high, because he hath known my name.

15 He shall call upon me, and I will answer him: I *will be* with him in trouble; I will deliver him, and honour him.

16 With long life will I satisfy him, and shew him my salvation.

PSALM 92.—1 *The prophet exhorteth to praise God,* 4 *for his great works,* 6 *for his judgments on the wicked,* 10 *and for his goodness to the godly.*

A PSALM OR SONG FOR THE SABBATH DAY.

1 *It is a* good *thing* to give thanks unto the LORD, and to sing praises unto thy name, O most High:

2 To shew forth thy lovingkindness in the morning, and thy faithfulness every night,

3 Upon an instrument of ten strings, and upon the psaltery; upon the harp with a solemn sound.

4 For thou, LORD, hast made me glad through thy work: I will triumph in the works of thy hands.

5 O LORD, how great are thy works! *and* thy thoughts are very deep.

6 A brutish man knoweth not; neither doth a fool understand this.

7 When the wicked spring as the grass, and when all the workers of iniquity do flourish; *it is* that they shall be destroyed for ever:

8 But thou, LORD, *art most* high for evermore.

9 For, lo, thine enemies, O LORD, for, lo, thine enemies shall perish; all the workers of iniquity shall be scattered.

10 But my horn shalt thou exalt like *the horn of* an unicorn: I shall be anointed with fresh oil.

11 Mine eye also shall see *my desire* on mine enemies, *and* mine ears shall hear *my desire* of the wicked that rise up against me.

12 The righteous shall flourish like the palm tree: he shall grow like a cedar in Lebanon.

13 Those that be planted in the house of the LORD shall flourish in the courts of our God.

14 They shall still bring forth fruit in old age; they shall be fat and flourishing;

15 To shew that the LORD *is* upright: *he is* my rock, and *there is* no unrighteousness in him.

PSALM 94.—1 *The prophet. calling for justice, complaineth of tyranny and impiety.* 8 *He teacheth God's providence.* 12 *He sheweth the blessedness of affliction.* 16 *God is the defender of the afflicted.*

1 O LORD God, to whom vengeance belongeth; O God, to whom vengeance belongeth, shew thyself.

2 Lift up thyself, thou judge of the earth: render a reward to the proud.

3 LORD, how long shall the wicked, how long shall the wicked triumph?

4 *How long* shall they utter *and* speak hard things? *and* all the workers of iniquity boast themselves?

5 They break in pieces thy people, O LORD, and afflict thine heritage.

6 They slay the widow and the stranger, and murder the fatherless.

7 Yet they say, The LORD shall not see, neither shall the God of Jacob regard *it*.

8 Understand, ye brutish among the people: and *ye* fools, when will ye be wise?

9 He that planted the ear, shall he not hear? he that formed the eye, shall he not see?

10 He that chastiseth the heathen, shall not he correct? he that teacheth man knowledge, *shall not he know?*

11 The LORD knoweth the thoughts of man, that they *are* vanity.

12 Blessed *is* the man whom thou chastenest, O LORD, and teachest him out of thy law;

13 That thou mayest give him rest from the days of adversity, until the pit be digged for the wicked.

14 For the LORD will not cast off his

people, neither will he forsake his inheritance.

15 But judgment shall return unto righteousness: and all the upright in heart shall follow it.

16 Who will rise up for me against the evildoers? or who will stand up for me against the workers of iniquity?

17 Unless the LORD *had been* my help, my soul had almost dwelt in silence.

18 When I said, My foot slippeth; thy mercy, O LORD, held me up.

19 In the multitude of my thoughts within me thy comforts delight my soul.

20 Shall the throne of iniquity have fellowship with thee, which frameth mischief by a law?

21 They gather themselves together against the soul of the righteous, and condemn the innocent blood.

22 But the LORD is my defence; and my God is the rock of my refuge.

23 And he shall bring upon them their own iniquity, and shall cut them off in their own wickedness; *yea*, the LORD our God shall cut them off.

PSALM 101.—*David maketh a vow and profession of godliness.*

A PSALM OF DAVID.

1 I will sing of mercy and judgment: unto thee, O LORD, will I sing.

2 I will behave myself wisely in a perfect way. O when wilt thou come unto me? I will walk within my house with a perfect heart.

3 I will set no wicked thing before mine eyes: I hate the work of them that turn aside, *it* shall not cleave to me.

4 A froward heart shall depart from me: I will not know a wicked *person*.

5 Whoso privily slandereth his neighbour, him will I cut off: him that hath an high look and a proud heart will not I suffer.

6 Mine eyes *shall be* upon the faithful of the land, that they may dwell with me: he that walketh in a perfect way, he shall serve me.

7 He that worketh deceit shall not dwell within my house: he that telleth lies shall not tarry in my sight.

8 I will early destroy all the wicked of the land; that I may cut off all wicked doers from the city of the LORD.

PSALM 112.—1 *Godliness hath the promises of this life,* 4 *and of the life to come.* 10 *The prosperity of the godly shall be an eyesore to the wicked.*

1 Praise ye the LORD. Blessed *is* the man *that* feareth the LORD, *that* delighteth greatly in his commandments.

2 His seed shall be mighty upon earth: the generation of the upright shall be blessed.

3 Wealth and riches *shall be* in his house: and his righteousness endureth for ever.

4 Unto the upright there ariseth light in the darkness: *he is* gracious, and full of compassion, and righteous.

5 A good man sheweth favour, and lendeth: he will guide his affairs with discretion.

6 Surely he shall not be moved for ever: the righteous shall be in everlasting remembrance.

7 He shall not be afraid of evil tidings: his heart is fixed, trusting in the LORD.

8 His heart *is* established, he shall not be afraid, until he see *his desire* upon his enemies.

9 He hath dispersed, he hath given to the poor; his righteousness endureth for ever; his horn shall be exalted with honour.

10 The wicked shall see *it*, and be grieved; he shall gnash with his teeth, and melt away: the desire of the wicked shall perish.

PSALM 119.—*This psalm containeth sundry prayers, praises, and professions of obedience.*

ALEPH.

1 Blessed *are* the undefiled in the way, who walk in the law of the LORD.

2 Blessed *are* they that keep his testimonies, *and that* seek him with the whole heart.

3 They also do no iniquity: they walk in his ways.

4 Thou hast commanded *us* to keep thy precepts diligently.

5 O that my ways were directed to keep thy statutes!

6 Then shall I not be ashamed, when I have respect unto all thy commandments.

7 I will praise thee with uprightness of heart, when I shall have learned thy righteous judgments.

8 I will keep thy statutes: O forsake me not utterly.

BETH.

9 Wherewithal shall a young man cleanse his way? by taking heed *thereto* according to thy word.

10 With my whole heart have I sought thee: O let me not wander from thy commandments.

11 Thy word have I hid in mine heart, that I might not sin against thee.

12 Blessed *art* thou, O LORD: teach me thy statutes.

13 With my lips have I declared all the judgments of thy mouth.

14 I have rejoiced in the way of thy testimonies, as *much as* in all riches.

15 I will meditate in thy precepts, and have respect unto thy ways.

16 I will delight myself in thy statutes. I will not forget thy word.

GIMEL.

17 Deal bountifully with thy servant, *that* I may live, and keep thy word.

18 Open thou mine eyes, that I may behold wondrous things out of thy law.

19 I *am* a stranger in the earth: hide not thy commandments from me.

20 My soul breaketh for the longing *that it hath* unto thy judgments at all times.

21 Thou hast rebuked the proud *that are*

cursed, which do err from thy commandments.

22 Remove from me reproach and contempt; for I have kept thy testimonies.

23 Princes also did sit *and* speak against me: *but* thy servant did meditate in thy statutes.

24 Thy testimonies also *are* my delight *and* my counsellors.

DALETH.

25 My soul cleaveth unto the dust: quicken thou me according to thy word.

26 I have declared my ways, and thou heardest me: teach me thy statutes.

27 Make me to understand the way of thy precepts: so shall I talk of thy wondrous works.

28 My soul melteth for heaviness: strengthen thou me according unto thy word.

29 Remove from me the way of lying: and grant me thy law graciously.

30 I have chosen the way of truth: thy judgments have I laid *before me.*

31 I have stuck unto thy testimonies: O LORD, put me not to shame.

32 I will run the way of thy commandments, when thou shalt enlarge my heart.

HE.

33 Teach me, O LORD, the way of thy statutes; and I shall keep it *unto* the end.

34 Give me understanding, and I shall keep thy law; yea, I shall observe it with *my* whole heart.

35 Make me to go in the path of thy commandments; for therein do I delight.

36 Incline my heart unto thy testimonies, and not to covetousness.

37 Turn away mine eyes from beholding vanity; *and* quicken thou me in thy way.

38 Stablish thy word unto thy servant, who *is devoted* to thy fear.

39 Turn away my reproach which I fear: for thy judgments *are* good.

40 Behold, I have longed after thy precepts: quicken me in thy righteousness.

VAU.

41 Let thy mercies come also unto me. O LORD, *even* thy salvation, according to thy word.

42 So shall I have wherewith to answer him that reproacheth me: for I trust in thy word.

43 And take not the word of truth utterly out of my mouth; for I have hoped in thy judgments.

44 So shall I keep thy law continually for ever and ever.

45 And I will walk at liberty: for I seek thy precepts.

46 I will speak of thy testimonies also before kings, and will not be ashamed.

47 And I will delight myself in thy commandments, which I have loved.

48 My hands also will I lift up unto thy commandments, which I have loved; and I will meditate in thy statutes.

ZAIN.

49 Remember the word unto thy servant, upon which thou hast caused me to hope.

50 This *is* my comfort in my affliction: for thy word hath quickened me.

51 The proud have had me greatly in derision: *yet* have I not declined from thy law.

52 I remembered thy judgments of old, O LORD; and have comforted myself.

53 Horror hath taken hold upon me because of the wicked that forsake thy law.

54 Thy statutes have been my songs in the house of my pilgrimage.

55 I have remembered thy name, O LORD, in the night, and have kept thy law.

56 This I had, because I kept thy precepts.

CHETH.

57 *Thou art* my portion, O LORD: I have said that I would keep thy words.

58 I intreated thy favour with *my* whole heart: be merciful unto me according to thy word.

59 I thought on my ways, and turned my feet unto thy testimonies.

60 I made haste, and delayed not to keep thy commandments.

61 The bands of the wicked have robbed me: *but* I have not forgotten thy law.

62 At midnight I will rise to give thanks unto thee because of thy righteous judgments.

63 I *am* a companion of all *them* that fear thee, and of them that keep thy precepts.

64 The earth, O LORD, is full of thy mercy: teach me thy statutes.

TETH.

65 Thou hast dealt well with thy servant, O LORD, according unto thy word.

66 Teach me good judgment and knowledge: for I have believed thy commandments.

67 Before I was afflicted I went astray: but now have I kept thy word.

68 Thou *art* good, and doest good; teach me thy statutes.

69 The proud have forged a lie against me: *but* I will keep thy precepts with *my* whole heart.

70 Their heart is as fat as grease; *but* I delight in thy law.

71 *It is* good for me that I have been afflicted; that I might learn thy statutes.

72 The law of thy mouth *is* better unto me than thousands of gold and silver.

JOD.

73 Thy hands have made me and fashioned me: give me understanding, that I may learn thy commandments.

74 They that fear thee will be glad when they see me; because I have hoped in thy word.

75 I know, O LORD, that thy judgments *are* right, and *that* thou in faithfulness hast afflicted me.

76 Let, I pray thee, thy merciful kindness be for my comfort, according to thy word unto thy servant.

77 Let thy tender mercies come unto me, that I may live: for thy law *is* my delight.

78 Let the proud be ashamed; for they dealt perversely with me without a cause: *but* I will meditate in thy precepts.

79 Let those that fear thee turn unto me, and those that have known thy testimonies.

80 Let my heart be sound in thy statutes; that I be not ashamed.

CAPH.

81 My soul fainteth for thy salvation: *but* I hope in thy word.

82 Mine eyes fail for thy word, saying, When wilt thou comfort me?

83 For I am become like a bottle in the smoke; *yet* do I not forget thy statutes.

84 How many *are* the days of thy servant? when wilt thou execute judgment on them that persecute me?

85 The proud have digged pits for me, which *are* not after thy law.

86 All thy commandments *are* faithful: they persecute me wrongfully; help thou me.

87 They had almost consumed me upon earth; but I forsook not thy precepts.

88 Quicken me after thy lovingkindness; so shall I keep the testimony of thy mouth.

LAMED.

89 For ever, O LORD, thy word is settled in heaven.

90 Thy faithfulness *is* unto all generations: thou hast established the earth, and it abideth.

91 They continue this day according to thine ordinances: for all *are* thy servants.

92 Unless thy law *had been* my delights, I should then have perished in mine affliction.

93 I will never forget thy precepts: for with them thou hast quickened me.

94 I *am* thine, save me; for I have sought thy precepts.

95 The wicked have waited for me to destroy me: *but* I will consider thy testimonies.

96 I have seen an end of all perfection: *but* thy commandment *is* exceeding broad.

MEM.

97 O how love I thy law! it *is* my meditation all the day.

98 Thou through thy commandments hast made me wiser than mine enemies: for they *are* ever with me.

99 I have more understanding than all my teachers: for thy testimonies *are* my meditation.

100 I understand more than the ancients, because I keep thy precepts.

101 I have refrained my feet from every evil way, that I might keep thy word.

102 I have not departed from thy judgments: for thou hast taught me.

103 How sweet are thy words unto my taste! *yea, sweeter* than honey to my mouth!

104 Through thy precepts I get understanding: therefore I hate every false way.

NUN.

105 Thy word *is* a lamp unto my feet, and a light unto my path.

106 I have sworn, and I will perform *it*, that I will keep thy righteous judgments.

107 I am afflicted very much: quicken me, O LORD, according unto thy word.

108 Accept, I beseech thee, the freewill offerings of my mouth, O LORD, and teach me thy judgments.

109 My soul *is* continually in my hand: yet do I not forget thy law.

110 The wicked have laid a snare for me: yet I erred not from thy precepts.

111 Thy testimonies have I taken as an heritage for ever: for they *are* the rejoicing of my heart.

112 I have inclined mine heart to perform thy statutes alway, *even unto* the end.

SAMECH.

113 I hate *vain* thoughts: but thy law do I love.

114 Thou *art* my hiding place and my shield: I hope in thy word.

115 Depart from me, ye evildoers: for I will keep the commandments of my God.

116 Uphold me according unto thy word, that I may live: and let me not be ashamed of my hope.

117 Hold thou me up, and I shall be safe: and I will have respect unto thy statutes continually.

118 Thou hast trodden down all them that err from thy statutes: for their deceit *is* falsehood.

119 Thou puttest away all the wicked of the earth *like* dross: therefore I love thy testimonies.

120 My flesh trembleth for fear of thee; and I am afraid of thy judgments.

AIN.

121 I have done judgment and justice: leave me not to mine oppressors.

122 Be surety for thy servant for good: let not the proud oppress me.

123 Mine eyes fail for thy salvation, and for the word of thy righteousness.

124 Deal with thy servant according unto thy mercy, and teach me thy statutes.

125 I *am* thy servant; give me understanding, that I may know thy testimonies.

126 *It is* time for *thee*, LORD, to work: *for* they have made void thy law.

127 Therefore I love thy commandments above gold; yea, above fine gold.

128 Therefore I esteem all *thy* precepts *concerning* all *things to be* right; *and* I hate every false way.

PE.

129 Thy testimonies *are* wonderful: therefore doth my soul keep them.

130 The entrance of thy words giveth light; it giveth understanding unto the simple.

131 I opened my mouth, and panted: for I longed for thy commandments.

132 Look thou upon me, and be merciful unto me, as thou usest to do unto those that love thy name.

133 Order my steps in thy word: and

let not any iniquity have dominion over me.

134 Deliver me from the oppression of man: so will I keep thy precepts.

135 Make thy face to shine upon thy servant; and teach me thy statutes.

136 Rivers of waters run down mine eyes, because they keep not thy law.

TZADDI.

137 Righteous *art* thou, O LORD, and upright *are* thy judgments.

138 Thy testimonies *that* thou hast commanded *are* righteous and very faithful.

139 My zeal hath consumed me, because mine enemies have forgotten thy words.

140 Thy word *is* very pure: therefore thy servant loveth it.

141 I *am* small and despised: *yet* do not I forget thy precepts.

142 Thy righteousness *is* an everlasting righteousness, and thy law *is* the truth.

143 Trouble and anguish have taken hold on me: *yet* thy commandments *are* my delights.

144 The righteousness of thy testimonies *is* everlasting: give me understanding, and I shall live.

KOPH.

145 I cried with *my* whole heart; hear me, O LORD: I will keep thy statutes.

146 I cried unto thee; save me, and I shall keep thy testimonies.

147 I prevented the dawning of the morning, and cried: I hoped in thy word.

148 Mine eyes prevent the *night* watches, that I might meditate in thy word.

149 Hear my voice according unto thy lovingkindness: O LORD, quicken me according to thy judgment.

150 They draw nigh that follow after mischief: they are far from thy law.

151 Thou *art* near, O LORD; and all thy commandments *are* truth.

152 Concerning thy testimonies, I have known of old that thou hast founded them for ever.

RESH.

153 Consider mine affliction, and deliver me: for I do not forget thy law.

154 Plead my cause, and deliver me: quicken me according to thy word.

155 Salvation *is* far from the wicked: for they seek not thy statutes.

156 Great *are* thy tender mercies, O LORD: quicken me according to thy judgments.

157 Many *are* my persecutors and mine enemies; *yet* do I not decline from thy testimonies.

158 I beheld the transgressors, and was grieved; because they kept not thy word.

159 Consider how I love thy precepts: quicken me, O LORD, according to thy lovingkindness.

160 Thy word *is* true *from* the beginning: and every one of thy righteous judgments *endureth* for ever.

SCHIN.

161 Princes have persecuted me without a cause: but my heart standeth in awe of thy word.

162 I rejoice at thy word, as one that findeth great spoil.

163 I hate and abhor lying: *but* thy law do I love.

164 Seven times a day do I praise thee because of thy righteous judgments.

165 Great peace have they which love thy law: and nothing shall offend them.

166 LORD, I have hoped for thy salvation, and done thy commandments.

167 My soul hath kept thy testimonies; and I love them exceedingly.

168 I have kept thy precepts and thy testimonies: for all my ways *are* before thee.

TAU.

169 Let my cry come near before thee, O LORD: give me understanding according to thy word.

170 Let my supplication come before thee: deliver me according to thy word.

171 My lips shall utter praise, when thou hast taught me thy statutes.

172 My tongue shall speak of thy word: for all thy commandments *are* righteousness.

173 Let thine hand help me; for I have chosen thy precepts.

174 I have longed for thy salvation, O LORD; and thy law *is* my delight.

175 Let my soul live, and it shall praise thee; and let thy judgments help me.

176 I have gone astray like a lost sheep; seek thy servant; for I do not forget thy commandments.

PSALM 121.—*The great safety of the godly, who put their trust in God's protection.*

A SONG OF DEGREES.

1 I will lift up mine eyes unto the hills, from whence cometh my help.

2 My help *cometh* from the LORD, which made heaven and earth.

3 He will not suffer thy foot to be moved: he that keepeth thee will not slumber.

4 Behold, he that keepeth Israel shall neither slumber nor sleep.

5 The LORD *is* thy keeper: the LORD *is* thy shade upon thy right hand.

6 The sun shall not smite thee by day, nor the moon by night.

7 The LORD shall preserve thee from all evil: he shall preserve thy soul.

8 The LORD shall preserve thy going out and thy coming in from this time forth, and even for evermore.

PSALM 125.—1 *The safety of such as trust in God.* 4 *A prayer for the godly, and against the wicked.*

A SONG OF DEGREES.

1 They that trust in the LORD *shall be* as mount Zion, *which* cannot be removed, *but* abideth for ever.

2 *As* the mountains *are* round about Jerusalem, so the LORD *is* round about his people from henceforth even for ever.

3 For the rod of the wicked shall not rest upon the lot of the righteous; lest the righteous put forth their hands unto iniquity.

4 Do good, O LORD, unto *those that be* good, and to *them that are* upright in their hearts.

5 As for such as turn aside unto their crooked ways, the LORD shall lead them forth with the workers of iniquity: *but* peace *shall be* upon Israel.

PSALM 127.—1 *The virtue of God's blessing.* 3 *Good children are his gift.*

A SONG OF DEGREES FOR SOLOMON.

1 Except the LORD build the house, they labour in vain that build it: except the LORD keep the city, the watchman waketh *but* in vain.

2 *It is* vain for you to rise up early, to sit up late, to eat the bread of sorrows: *for* so he giveth his beloved sleep.

3 Lo, children *are* an heritage of the LORD: *and* the fruit of the womb *is his* reward.

4 As arrows *are* in the hand of a mighty man; so *are* children of the youth.

5 Happy *is* the man that hath his quiver full of them: they shall not be ashamed, but they shall speak with the enemies in the gate.

PSALM 128.—*The sundry blessings which follow them that fear God.*

A SONG OF DEGREES.

1 Blessed *is* every one that feareth the LORD; that walketh in his ways.

2 For thou shalt eat the labour of thine hands: happy *shalt* thou *be*, and *it shall be* well with thee.

3 Thy wife *shall be* as a fruitful vine by the sides of thine house: thy children like olive plants round about thy table.

4 Behold, that thus shall the man be blessed that feareth the LORD.

5 The LORD shall bless thee out of Zion: and thou shalt see the good of Jerusalem all the days of thy life.

6 Yea, thou shalt see thy children's children, *and* peace upon Israel.

PSALM 131.—1 *David, professing his humility,* 3 *exhorteth Israel to hope in God.*

A SONG OF DEGREES OF DAVID.

1 LORD, my heart is not haughty, nor mine eyes lofty: neither do I exercise myself in great matters, or in things too high for me.

2 Surely I have behaved and quieted myself, as a child that is weaned of his mother: my soul *is* even as a weaned child.

3 Let Israel hope in the LORD from henceforth and for ever.

PSALM 133.—*The benefit of the communion of saints.*

A SONG OF DEGREES OF DAVID.

1 Behold, how good and how pleasant *it is* for brethren to dwell together in unity!

2 *It is* like the precious ointment upon the head, that ran down upon the beard, *even* Aaron's beard: that went down to the skirts of his garments;

3 As the dew of Hermon, *and as the dew*

that descended upon the mountains of Zion: for there the LORD commanded the blessing, *even* life for evermore.

HISTORICAL:

PSALM 78.—1 *An exhortation both to learn and to preach the law of God.* 9 *The story of God's wrath against the incredulous and disobedient.* 67 *The Israelites being rejected, God chose Judah, Zion, and David.*

MASCHIL OF ASAPH.

1 Give ear, O my people, *to* my law: incline your ears to the words of my mouth.

2 I will open my mouth in a parable: I will utter dark sayings of old:

3 Which we have heard and known, and our fathers have told us.

4 We will not hide *them* from their children, shewing to the generation to come the praises of the LORD, and his strength, and his wonderful works that he hath done.

5 For he established a testimony in Jacob, and appointed a law in Israel, which he commanded our fathers, that they should make them known to their children:

6 That the generation to come might know *them, even* the children *which* should be born; *who* should arise and declare *them* to their children:

7 That they might set their hope in God, and not forget the works of God, but keep his commandments:

8 And might not be as their fathers, a stubborn and rebellious generation; a generation *that* set not their heart aright, and whose spirit was not stedfast with God.

9 The children of Ephraim, *being* armed, *and* carrying bows, turned back in the day of battle.

10 They kept not the covenant of God, and refused to walk in his law;

11 And forgat his works, and his wonders that he had shewed them.

12 Marvellous things did he in the sight of their fathers, in the land of Egypt, *in* the field of Zoan.

13 He divided the sea, and caused them to pass through; and he made the waters to stand as an heap.

14 In the daytime also he led them with a cloud, and all the night with a light of fire.

15 He clave the rocks in the wilderness, and gave *them* drink as *out of* the great depths.

16 He brought streams also out of the rock, and caused waters to run down like rivers.

17 And they sinned yet more against him by provoking the most High in the wilderness.

18 And they tempted God in their heart by asking meat for their lust.

19 Yea, they spake against God: they said, Can God furnish a table in the wilderness?

20 Behold, he smote the rock, that the waters gushed out, and the streams overflowed; can he give bread also? can he provide flesh for his people?

21 Therefore the LORD heard *this*, and was wroth : so a fire was kindled against Jacob, and anger also came up against Israel;

22 Because they believed not in God, and trusted not in his salvation :

23 Though he had commanded the clouds from above, and opened the doors of heaven,

24 And had rained down manna upon them to eat; and had given them of the corn of heaven.

25 Man did eat angels' food : he sent them meat to the full.

26 He caused an east wind to blow in the heaven : and by his power he brought in the south wind.

27 He rained flesh also upon them as dust, and feathered fowls like as the sand of the sea :

28 And he let *it* fall in the midst of their camp, round about their habitations.

29 So they did eat, and were well filled : for he gave them their own desire ;

30 They were not estranged from their lust. But while their meat *was* yet in their mouths,

31 The wrath of God came upon them, and slew the fattest of them, and smote down the chosen *men* of Israel.

32 For all this they sinned still, and believed not for his wondrous works.

33 Therefore their days did he consume in vanity, and their years in trouble.

34 When he slew them, then they sought him : and they returned and enquired early after God.

35 And they remembered that God *was* their rock, and the high God their redeemer.

36 Nevertheless they did flatter him with their mouth, and they lied unto him with their tongues.

37 For their heart was not right with him, neither were they stedfast in his covenant.

38 But he, *being* full of compassion, forgave *their* iniquity, and destroyed *them* not : yea, many a time turned he his anger away, and did not stir up all his wrath.

39 For he remembered that they *were but* flesh ; a wind that passeth away, and cometh not again.

40 How oft did they provoke him in the wilderness, *and* grieve him in the desert !

41 Yea, they turned back and tempted God, and limited the Holy One of Israel.

42 They remembered not his hand, *nor* the day when he delivered them from the enemy.

43 How he had wrought his signs in Egypt, and his wonders in the field of Zoan :

44 And had turned their rivers into blood ; and their floods, that they could not drink.

45 He sent divers sorts of flies among them, which devoured them ; and frogs, which destroyed them.

46 He gave also their increase unto the caterpiller, and their labour unto the locust.

47 He destroyed their vines with hail, and their sycomore trees with frost.

48 He gave up their cattle also to the hail, and their flocks to hot thunderbolts.

49 He cast upon them the fierceness of his anger, wrath, and indignation, and trouble by sending evil angels *among them*.

50 He made a way to his anger; he spared not their soul from death, but gave their life over to the pestilence ;

51 And smote all the firstborn in Egypt ; the chief of *their* strength in the tabernacle of Ham :

52 But made his own people to go forth like sheep, and guided them in the wilderness like a flock.

53 And he led them on safely, so that they feared not : but the sea overwhelmed their enemies.

54 And he brought them to the border of his sanctuary, *even to* this mountain,*which* his right hand had purchased.

55 He cast out the heathen also before them, and divided them an inheritance by line, and made the tribes of Israel to dwell in their tents.

56 Yet they tempted and provoked the most high God, and kept not his testimonies :

57 But turned back, and dealt unfaithfully like their fathers: they were turned aside like a deceitful bow.

58 For they provoked him to anger with their high places, and moved him to jealousy with their graven images.

59 When God heard *this*, he was wroth, and greatly abhorred Israel :

60 So that he forsook the tabernacle of Shiloh, the tent *which* he placed among men ;

61 And delivered his strength into captivity, and his glory into the enemy's hand.

62 He gave his people over also unto the sword; and was wroth with his inheritance.

63 The fire consumed their young men ; and their maidens were not given to marriage.

64 Their priests fell by the sword; and their widows made no lamentation.

65 Then the Lord awaked as one out of sleep, *and* like a mighty man that shouteth by reason of wine.

66 And he smote his enemies in the hinder parts : he put them to a perpetual reproach.

67 Moreover he refused the tabernacle of Joseph, and chose not the tribe of Ephraim :

68 But chose the tribe of Judah, the mount Zion which he loved.

69 And he built his sanctuary like high *palaces*, like the earth which he hath established for ever.

70 He chose David also his servant, and took him from the sheepfolds :

71 From following the ewes great with young he brought him to feed Jacob his people, and Israel his inheritance.

72 So he fed them according to the integrity of his heart; and guided them by the skilfulness of his hands.

PSALM 105.—1 *An exhortation to praise God, and to seek out his works.* 7 *The story of God's providence over Abraham,* 16 *over Joseph,* 23 *over Jacob in Egypt.* 26 *over Moses delivering the Israelites,* 37 *over the Israelites brought out of Egypt, fed in the wilderness, and planted in Canaan.*

1 O give thanks unto the LORD; call upon his name: make known his deeds among the people.

2 Sing unto him, sing psalms unto him: talk ye of all his wondrous works.

3 Glory ye in his holy name: let the heart of them rejoice that seek the LORD.

4 Seek the LORD, and his strength: seek his face evermore.

5 Remember his marvellous works that he hath done; his wonders, and the judgments of his mouth;

6 O ye seed of Abraham his servant, ye children of Jacob his chosen.

7 He *is* the LORD our God: his judgments *are* in all the earth.

8 He hath remembered his covenant for ever, the word *which* be commanded to a thousand generations.

9 Which *covenant* he made with Abraham, and his oath unto Isaac;

10 And confirmed the same unto Jacob for a law, *and* to Israel *for* an everlasting covenant:

11 Saying, Unto thee will I give the land of Canaan, the lot of your inheritance:

12 When they were *but* a few men in number; yea, very few, and strangers in it.

13 When they went from one nation to another, from *one* kingdom to another people;

14 He suffered no man to do them wrong: yea, he reproved kings for their sakes;

15 *Saying,* Touch not mine anointed, and do my prophets no harm.

16 Moreover he called for a famine upon the land: he brake the whole staff of bread.

17 He sent a man before them, *even* Joseph, *who* was sold for a servant:

18 Whose feet they hurt with fetters: he was laid in iron:

19 Until the time that his word came: the word of the LORD tried him.

20 The king sent and loosed him; *even* the ruler of the people, and let him go free.

21 He made him lord of his house, and ruler of all his substance:

22 To bind his princes at his pleasure; and teach his senators wisdom.

23 Israel also came into Egypt; and Jacob sojourned in the land of Ham.

24 And he increased his people greatly; and made them stronger than their enemies.

25 He turned their heart to hate his people, to deal subtilly with his servants.

26 He sent Moses his servant; *and* Aaron whom he had chosen.

27 They shewed his signs among them, and wonders in the land of Ham.

28 He sent darkness, and made it dark; and they rebelled not against his word.

29 He turned their waters into blood, and slew their fish.

30 Their land brought forth frogs in abundance, in the chambers of their kings.

31 He spake, and there came divers sorts of flies, *and* lice in all their coasts.

32 He gave them hail for rain, *and* flaming fire in their land.

33 He smote their vines also and their fig trees; and brake the trees of their coasts.

34 He spake, and the locusts came, and caterpillers, and that without number,

35 And did eat up all the herbs in their land, and devoured the fruit of their ground.

36 He smote also all the firstborn in their land, the chief of all their strength.

37 He brought them forth also with silver and gold: and *there was* not one feeble *person* among their tribes.

38 Egypt was glad when they departed: for the fear of them fell upon them.

39 He spread a cloud for a covering; and fire to give light in the night.

40 *The people* asked, and he brought quails, and satisfied them with the bread of heaven.

41 He opened the rock, and the waters gushed out: they ran in the dry places *like* a river.

42 For he remembered his holy promise, *and* Abraham his servant.

43 And he brought forth his people with joy, *and* his chosen with gladness:

44 And gave them the lands of the heathen: and they inherited the labour of the people;

45 That they might observe his statutes, and keep his laws. Praise ye the LORD.

PSALM 106.—1 *The psalmist exhorteth to praise God.* 4 *He prayeth for pardon of sin, as God did with the fathers.* 7 *The story of the people's rebellion, and God's mercy.* 47 *He concludeth with prayer and praise.*

1 Praise ye the LORD. O give thanks unto the LORD; for *he is* good: for his mercy *endureth* forever.

2 Who can utter the mighty acts of the LORD? *who* can shew forth all his praise?

3 Blessed *are* they that keep judgment, *and* he that doeth righteousness at all times.

4 Remember me, O LORD, with the favour *that thou bearest unto* thy people: O visit me with thy salvation;

5 That I may see the good of thy chosen, that I may rejoice in the gladness of thy nation, that I may glory with thine inheritance.

6 We have sinned with our fathers, we have committed iniquity, we have done wickedly.

7 Our fathers understood not thy wonders in Egypt; they remembered not the multitude of thy mercies; but provoked *him* at the sea, *even* at the Red sea.

8 Nevertheless he saved them for his name's sake, that he might make his mighty power to be known.

9 He rebuked the Red sea also, and it was dried up: so he led them through the depths, as through the wilderness.

10 And he saved them from the hand of him that hated *them*, and redeemed them from the hand of the enemy.

11 And the waters covered their enemies: there was not one of them left.

12 Then believed they his words; they sang his praise.

13 They soon forgat his works; they waited not for his counsel:

14 But lusted exceedingly in the wilderness, and tempted God in the desert.

15 And he gave them their request; but sent leanness into their soul.

16 They envied Moses also in the camp, *and* Aaron the saint of the LORD.

17 The earth opened and swallowed up Dathan, and covered the company of Abiram.

18 And a fire was kindled in their company; the flame burned up the wicked.

19 They made a calf in Horeb, and worshipped the molten image.

20 Thus they changed their glory into the similitude of an ox that eateth grass.

21 They forgat God their saviour, which had done great things in Egypt;

22 Wondrous works in the land of Ham, *and* terrible things by the Red sea.

23 Therefore he said that he would destroy them, had not Moses his chosen stood before him in the breach, to turn away his wrath, lest he should destroy *them*.

24 Yea, they despised the pleasant land, they believed not his word:

25 But murmured in their tents, *and* hearkened not unto the voice of the LORD.

26 Therefore he lifted up his hand against them, to overthrow them in the wilderness:

27 To overthrow their seed also among the nations, and to scatter them in the lands.

28 They joined themselves also unto Baalpeor, and ate the sacrifices of the dead.

29 Thus they provoked *him* to anger with their inventions: and the plague brake in upon them.

30 Then stood up Phinehas, and executed judgment: and *so* the plague was stayed.

31 And that was counted unto him for righteousness unto all generations for evermore.

32 They angered *him* also at the waters of strife, so that it went ill with Moses for their sakes:

33 Because they provoked his spirit, so that he spake unadvisedly with his lips.

34 They did not destroy the nations, concerning whom the LORD commanded them:

35 But were mingled among the heathen, and learned their works.

36 And they served their idols: which were a snare unto them.

37 Yea, they sacrificed their sons and their daughters unto devils,

38 And shed innocent blood, *even* the blood of their sons and of their daughters,

whom they sacrificed unto the idols of Canaan: and the land was polluted with blood.

39 Thus were they defiled with their own works, and went a whoring with their own inventions.

40 Therefore was the wrath of the LORD kindled against his people, insomuch that he abhorred his own inheritance.

41 And he gave them into the hand of the heathen; and they that hated them ruled over them.

42 Their enemies also oppressed them, and they were brought into subjection under their hand.

43 Many times did he deliver them; but they provoked *him* with their counsel, and were brought low for their iniquity.

44 Nevertheless he regarded their affliction, when he heard their cry:

45 And he remembered for them his covenant, and repented according to the multitude of his mercies.

46 He made them also to be pitied of all those that carried them captives.

47 Save us, O LORD our God, and gather us from among the heathen, to give thanks unto thy holy name, *and* to triumph in thy praise.

48 Blessed *be* the LORD God of Israel from everlasting to everlasting: and let all the people say, Amen. Praise ye the LORD.

IMPRECATORY:

See PRAYER, IMPRECATORY.

INTERCESSIONAL:

PSALM 20.—1 *The church blesseth the king in his exploits.* 7 *Her confidence in God's succour.*

To THE CHIEF MUSICIAN, A PSALM OF DAVID.

1 The LORD hear thee in the day of trouble; the name of the God of Jacob defend thee;

2 Send thee help from the sanctuary, and strengthen thee out of Zion;

3 Remember all thy offerings, and accept thy burnt sacrifice; Selah.

4 Grant thee according to thine own heart, and fulfil all thy counsel.

5 We will rejoice in thy salvation, and in the name of our God we will set up *our* banners: the LORD fulfil all thy petitions.

6 Now know I that the LORD saveth his anointed, he will hear him from his holy heaven with the saving strength of his right hand.

7 Some *trust* in chariots, and some in horses: but we will remember the name of the LORD our God.

8 They are brought down and fallen: but we are risen, and stand upright.

9 Save, LORD: let the king hear us when we call.

PSALM 67.—*A prayer for the enlargement of God's kingdom,* 3 *to the joy of the people,* 6 *and the increase of God's blessings.*

To THE CHIEF MUSICIAN ON NEGINOTH, A PSALM OR SONG.

1 God be merciful unto us, and bless us; *and* cause his face to shine upon us; Selah.

2 That thy way may be known upon earth, thy saving health among all nations.

3 Let the people praise thee, O God; let all the people praise thee.

4 O let the nations be glad and sing for joy: for thou shalt judge the people righteously, and govern the nations upon earth. Selah.

5 Let the people praise thee, O God; let all the people praise thee.

6 *Then* shall the earth yield her increase; *and* God, *even* our own God, shall bless us.

7 God shall bless us; and all the ends of the earth shall fear him.

PSALM 122.—1 *David professeth his joy for the church,* 6 *and prayeth for the peace thereof.*

A SONG OF DEGREES OF DAVID.

1 I was glad when they said unto me, Let us go into the house of the LORD.

2 Our feet shall stand within thy gates, O Jerusalem.

3 Jerusalem is builded as a city that is compact together:

4 Whither the tribes go up, the tribes of the LORD, unto the testimony of Israel, to give thanks unto the name of the LORD.

5 For there are set thrones of judgment, the thrones of the house of David.

6 Pray for the peace of Jerusalem: they shall prosper that love thee.

7 Peace be within thy walls, *and* prosperity within thy palaces.

8 For my brethren and companions' sakes, I will now say, Peace *be* within thee.

9 Because of the house of the LORD our God I will seek thy good.

PSALM 132.—1 *David in his prayer commendeth unto God the religious care he had for the ark.* 8 *His prayer at the removing of the ark,* 11 *with a repetition of God's promises.*

A SONG OF DEGREES.

1 LORD, remember David, *and* all his afflictions:

2 How he sware unto the LORD, *and* vowed unto the mighty *God* of Jacob;

3 Surely I will not come into the tabernacle of my house, nor go up into my bed.

4 I will not give sleep to mine eyes, *or* slumber to mine eyelids,

5 Until I find out a place for the LORD, an habitation for the mighty *God* of Jacob.

6 Lo, we heard of it at Ephratah: we found it in the fields of the wood.

7 We will go into his tabernacles: we will worship at his footstool.

8 Arise, O LORD, into thy rest; thou, and the ark of thy strength.

9 Let thy priests be clothed with righteousness; and let thy saints shout for joy.

10 For thy servant David's sake turn not away the face of thine anointed.

11 The LORD hath sworn *in* truth unto David; he will not turn from it; Of the fruit of thy body will I set upon thy throne.

12 If thy children will keep my covenant and my testimony that I shall teach them, their children shall also sit upon thy throne for evermore.

13 For the LORD hath chosen Zion; he hath desired *it* for his habitation.

14 This *is* my rest for ever: here will I dwell; for I have desired it.

15 I will abundantly bless her provision: I will satisfy her poor with bread.

16 I will also clothe her priests with salvation: and her saints shall shout aloud for joy.

17 There will I make the horn of David to bud: I have ordained a lamp for mine anointed.

18 His enemies will I clothe with shame: but upon himself shall his crown flourish.

PSALM 144.—*David blesseth God for his mercy both to him and to man.* 5 *He prayeth that God would powerfully deliver him from his enemies.* 9 *He promiseth to praise God.* 11 *He prayeth for the happy state of the kingdom.*

A PSALM OF DAVID.

1 Blessed *be* the LORD my strength, which teacheth my hands to war, *and* my fingers to fight:

2 My goodness, and my fortress; my high tower, and my deliverer; my shield, and *he* in whom I trust; who subdueth my people under me.

3 LORD, what *is* man, that thou takest knowledge of him! *or* the son of man, that thou makest account of him!

4 Man.is like to vanity: his days *are* as a shadow that passeth away.

5 Bow thy heavens, O LORD, and come down: touch the mountains, and they shall smoke.

6 Cast forth lightning, and scatter them: shoot out thine arrows, and destroy them.

7 Send thine hand from above; rid me, and deliver me out of great waters, from the hand of strange children;

8 Whose mouth speaketh vanity, and their right hand *is* a right hand of falsehood.

9 I will sing a new song unto thee, O God: upon a psaltery *and* an instrument of ten strings will I sing praises unto thee.

10 *It is* he that giveth salvation unto kings: who delivereth David his servant from the hurtful sword.

11 Rid me, and deliver me from the hand of strange children, whose mouth speaketh vanity, and their right hand *is* a right hand of falsehood:

12 That our sons *may be* as plants grown up in their youth; *that* our daughters *may be* as corner stones, polished *after* the similitude of a palace:

13 *That* our garners *may be* full, affording all manner of store: *that* our sheep may bring forth thousands and ten thousands in our streets:

14 *That* our oxen *may be* strong to labour; *that there be* no breaking in, nor going out; that *there be* no complaining in our streets.

15 Happy *is that* people, that is in such a case: *yea,* happy *is that* people, whose God *is* the LORD.

MESSIANIC:

See JESUS, MESSIAH, MESSIANIC PSALMS.

PENITENTIAL:

PSALM 6.—1 *David's complaint in his sickness.* 8 *By faith he triumpheth over his enemies.*

TO THE CHIEF MUSICIAN ON NEGINOTH UPON SHEMI-NITH, A PSALM OF DAVID.

1 O LORD, rebuke me not in thine anger, neither chasten me in thy hot displeasure.

2 Have mercy upon me, O LORD: for I *am* weak: O LORD, heal me; for my bones are vexed.

3 My soul is also sore vexed: but thou, O LORD, how long?

4 Return, O LORD, deliver my soul: oh save me for thy mercies' sake.

5 For in death *there is* no remembrance of thee: in the grave who shall give thee thanks?

6 I am weary with my groaning; all the night make I my bed to swim; I water my couch with my tears.

7 Mine eye is consumed because of grief; it waxeth old because of all mine enemies.

8 Depart from me, all ye workers of iniquity; for the LORD hath heard the voice of my weeping.

9 The LORD hath heard my supplication; the LORD will receive my prayer.

10 Let all mine enemies be ashamed and sore vexed: let them return *and* be ashamed suddenly.

PSALM 25.—1 *David's confidence in prayer.* 7 *He prayeth for remission of sins,* 16 *and for help in affliction.*

A PSALM OF DAVID.

1 Unto thee, O LORD, do I lift up my soul.

2 O my God, I trust in thee: let me not be ashamed, let not mine enemies triumph over me.

3 Yea, let none that wait on thee be ashamed: let them be ashamed which transgress without cause.

4 Shew me thy ways, O LORD; teach me thy paths.

5 Lead me in thy truth, and teach me: for thou *art* the God of my salvation; on thee do I wait all the day.

6 Remember, O LORD, thy tender mercies and thy lovingkindnesses; for they *have been* ever of old.

7 Remember not the sins of my youth, nor my transgressions: according to thy mercy remember thou me for thy goodness' sake, O LORD.

8 Good and upright *is* the LORD: therefore will he teach sinners in the way.

9 The meek will he guide in judgment: and the meek will he teach his way.

10 All the paths of the LORD *are* mercy and truth unto such as keep his covenant and his testimonies.

11 For thy name's sake, O LORD, pardon mine iniquity; for it *is* great.

12 What man *is* he that feareth the LORD? him shall he teach in the way *that* he shall choose.

13 His soul shall dwell at ease: and his seed shall inherit the earth.

14 The secret of the LORD *is* with them that fear him; and he will shew them his covenant.

15 Mine eyes *are* ever toward the LORD; for he shall pluck my feet out of the net.

16 Turn thee unto me, and have mercy upon me; for I *am* desolate and afflicted.

17 The troubles of my heart are enlarged: *O* bring thou me out of my distresses.

18 Look upon mine affliction and my pain; and forgive all my sins.

19 Consider mine enemies; for they are many; and they hate me with cruel hatred.

20 O keep my soul, and deliver me: let me not be ashamed; for I put my trust in thee.

21 Let integrity and uprightness preserve me; for I wait on thee.

22 Redeem Israel, O God, out of all his troubles.

PSALM 32.—1 *Blessedness consisteth in remission of sins.* 3 *Confession of sins giveth ease to the conscience.* 8 *God's promises bring joy.*

A PSALM OF DAVID, MASCHIL.

1 Blessed *is he whose* transgression *is* forgiven, *whose* sin *is* covered.

2 Blessed *is* the man unto whom the LORD imputeth not iniquity, and in whose spirit *there is* no guile.

3 When I kept silence, my bones waxed old through my roaring all the day long.

4 For day and night thy hand was heavy upon me: my moisture is turned into the drought of summer. Selah.

5 I acknowledged my sin unto thee, and mine iniquity have I not hid. I said, I will confess my transgressions unto the LORD; and thou forgavest the iniquity of my sin. Selah.

6 For this shall every one that is godly pray unto thee in a time when thou mayest be found: surely in the floods of great waters they shall not come nigh unto him.

7 Thou *art* my hiding place; thou shalt preserve me from trouble; thou shalt compass me about with songs of deliverance. Selah.

8 I will instruct thee and teach thee in the way which thou shalt go: I will guide thee with mine eye.

9 Be not as the horse, *or* as the mule, *which* have no understanding: whose mouth must be held in with bit and bridle, lest they come near unto thee.

10 Many sorrows *shall be* to the wicked: but he that trusteth in the LORD, mercy shall compass him about.

11 Be glad in the LORD, and rejoice, ye righteous: and shout for joy, all *ye that are* upright in heart.

PSALM 38.—*David moveth God to take compassion of his pitiful case.*

A PSALM OF DAVID, TO BRING TO REMEMBRANCE.

1 O LORD, rebuke me not in thy wrath: neither chasten me in thy hot displeasure.

2 For thine arrows stick fast in me, and thy hand presseth me sore.

3 *There is* no soundness in my flesh because of thine anger; neither *is there any* rest in my bones because of my sin.

4 For mine iniquities are gone over mine head: as an heavy burden they are too heavy for me.

5 My wounds stink *and* are corrupt because of my foolishness.

6 I am troubled; I am bowed down greatly; I go mourning all the day long.

7 For my loins are filled with a loathsome *disease:* and *there is* no soundness in my flesh.

8 I am feeble and sore broken: I have roared by reason of the disquietness of my heart.

9 Lord, all my desire *is* before thee; and my groaning is not hid from thee.

10 My heart panteth, my strength faileth me: as for the light of mine eyes, it also is gone from me.

11 My lovers and my friends stand aloof from my sore; and my kinsmen stand afar off.

12 They also that seek after my life lay snares *for me:* and they that seek my hurt speak mischievous things, and imagine deceits all the day long.

13 But I, as a deaf *man,* heard not; and *I was* as a dumb man *that* openeth not his mouth.

14 Thus I was as a man that heareth not, and in whose mouth *are* no reproofs.

15 For in thee, O Lord, do I hope: thou wilt hear, O Lord my God.

16 For I said, *Hear me,* lest *otherwise* they should rejoice over me: when my foot slippeth, they magnify *themselves* against me.

17 For I *am ready* to halt, and my sorrow *is* continually before me.

18 For I will declare mine iniquity; I will be sorry for my sin.

19 But mine enemies *are* lively, *and* they are strong: and they that hate me wrongfully are multiplied.

20 They also that render evil for good are mine adversaries; because I follow *the thing that* good *is.*

21 Forsake me not, O Lord: O my God, be not far from me.

22 Make haste to help me, O Lord my salvation.

PSALM 51.—1 *David prayeth for remission of sins, whereof he maketh a deep confession.* 6 *He prayeth for sanctification.* 16 *God delighteth not in sacrifice, but in sincerity.* 18 *He prayeth for the church.*

To the chief Musician, A Psalm of David, when Nathan the prophet came unto him, after he had gone in to Bath-sheba.

1 Have mercy upon me, O God, according to thy lovingkindness: according unto the multitude of thy tender mercies blot out my transgressions.

2 Wash me throughly from mine iniquity, and cleanse me from my sin.

3 For I acknowledge my transgressions: and my sin *is* ever before me.

4 Against thee, thee only, have I sinned, and done *this* evil in thy sight: that thou mightest be justified when thou speakest, *and* be clear when thou judgest.

5 Behold, I was shapen in iniquity; and in sin did my mother conceive me.

6 Behold, thou desirest truth in the inward parts: and in the hidden *part* thou shalt make me to know wisdom.

7 Purge me with hyssop, and I shall be clean: wash me, and I shall be whiter than snow.

8 Make me to hear joy and gladness; *that* the bones *which* thou hast broken may rejoice.

9 Hide thy face from my sins, and blot out all mine iniquities.

10 Create in me a clean heart, O God; and renew a right spirit within me.

11 Cast me not away from thy presence; and take not thy holy spirit from me.

12 Restore unto me the joy of thy salvation; and uphold me *with thy* free spirit.

13 *Then* will I teach transgressors thy ways; and sinners shall be converted unto thee.

14 Deliver me from bloodguiltiness, O God, thou God of my salvation: *and* my tongue shall sing aloud of thy righteousness.

15 O Lord, open thou my lips; and my mouth shall shew forth thy praise.

16 For thou desirest not sacrifice; else would I give *it:* thou delightest not in burnt offering.

17 The sacrifices of God *are* a broken spirit: a broken and a contrite heart, O God, thou wilt not despise.

18 Do good in thy good pleasure unto Zion: build thou the walls of Jerusalem.

19 Then shalt thou be pleased with the sacrifices of righteousness, with burnt offering and whole burnt offering: then shall they offer bullocks upon thine altar.

PSALM 102.—1 *The prophet in his prayer maketh a grievous complaint.* 12 *He taketh comfort in the eternity and mercy of God.* 18 *The mercies of God are to be recorded.* 23 *He sustaineth his weakness by the unchangeableness of God.*

A Prayer of the afflicted, when he is overwhelmed, and poureth out his complaint before the Lord.

1 Hear my prayer, O Lord, and let my cry come unto thee.

2 Hide not thy face from me in the day *when* I am in trouble; incline thine ear unto me: in the day *when* I call answer me speedily.

3 For my days are consumed like smoke, and my bones are burned as an hearth.

4 My heart is smitten, and withered like grass; so that I forget to eat my bread.

5 By reason of the voice of my groaning my bones cleave to my skin.

6 I am like a pelican of the wilderness: I am like an owl of the desert.

7 I watch, and am as a sparrow alone upon the house top.

8 Mine enemies reproach me all the day:

and they that are mad against me are sworn against me.

9 For I have eaten ashes like bread, and mingled my drink with weeping,

10 Because of thine indignation and thy wrath: for thou hast lifted me up, and cast me down.

11 My days *are* like a shadow that declineth; and I am withered like grass.

12 But thou, O LORD, shalt endure for ever; and thy remembrance unto all generations.

13 Thou shalt arise, *and* have mercy upon Zion: for the time to favour her, yea, the set time, is come.

14 For thy servants take pleasure in her stones, and favour the dust thereof.

15 So the heathen shall fear the name of the LORD, and all the kings of the earth thy glory.

16 When the LORD shall build up Zion, he shall appear in his glory.

17 He will regard the prayer of the destitute, and not despise their prayer.

18 This shall be written for the generation to come: and the people which shall be created shall praise the LORD.

19 For he hath looked down from the height of his sanctuary; from heaven did the LORD behold the earth;

20 To hear the groaning of the prisoner; to loose those that are appointed to death;

21 To declare the name of the LORD in Zion, and his praise in Jerusalem;

22 When the people are gathered together, and the kingdoms, to serve the LORD.

23 He weakened my strength in the way; he shortened my days.

24 I said, O my God, take me not away in the midst of my days: thy years *are* throughout all generations.

25 Of old hast thou laid the foundation of the earth: and the heavens *are* the work of thy hands.

26 They shall perish, but thou shalt endure: yea, all of them shall wax old like a garment; as a vesture shalt thou change them, and they shall be changed:

27 But thou *art* the same, and thy years shall have no end.

28 The children of thy servants shall continue, and their seed shall be established before thee.

PSALM 130.—1 *The psalmist professeth his hope in prayer,* 5 *and his patience in hope.* 7 *He exhorteth Israel to hope in God.*

A SONG OF DEGREES.

1 Out of the depths have I cried unto thee. O LORD.

2 Lord, hear my voice: let thine ears be attentive to the voice of my supplications.

3 If thou, LORD, shouldest mark iniquities, O Lord, who shall stand?

4 But *there is* forgiveness with thee, that thou mayest be feared.

5 I wait for the LORD, my soul doth wait, and in his word do I hope.

6 My soul *waiteth* for the Lord more than they that watch for the morning: I *say, more than* they that watch for the morning.

7 Let Israel hope in the LORD: for with the LORD *there is* mercy, and with him *is* plenteous redemption.

8 And he shall redeem Israel from all his iniquities.

PSALM 143.—1 *David prayeth for favour in judgment.* 3 *He complaineth of his griefs.* 5 *He strengtheneth his faith by meditation and prayer.* 7 *He prayeth for grace,* 9 *for deliverance,* 10 *for sanctification,* 12 *for destruction of his enemies.*

A PSALM OF DAVID.

1 Hear my prayer, O LORD, give ear to my supplications: in thy faithfulness answer me, *and* in thy righteousness.

2 And enter not into judgment with thy servant: for in thy sight shall no man living be justified.

3 For the enemy hath persecuted my soul; he hath smitten my life down to the ground; he hath made me to dwell in darkness, as those that have been long dead.

4 Therefore is my spirit overwhelmed within me; my heart within me is desolate.

5 I remember the days of old; I meditate on all thy works; I muse on the work of thy hands.

6 I stretch forth my hands unto thee: my soul *thirsteth* after thee, as a thirsty land. Selah.

7 Hear me speedily, O LORD: my spirit faileth: hide not thy face from me, lest I be like unto them that go down into the pit.

8 Cause me to hear thy lovingkindness in the morning; for in thee do I trust: cause me to know the way wherein I should walk; for I lift up my soul unto thee.

9 Deliver me, O LORD, from mine enemies: I flee unto thee to hide me.

10 Teach me to do thy will; for thou *art* my God: thy spirit *is* good; lead me into the land of uprightness.

11 Quicken me, O LORD, for thy name's sake: for thy righteousness' sake bring my soul out of trouble.

12 And of thy mercy cut off mine enemies, and destroy all them that afflict my soul: for I *am* thy servant.

PRAISE:

FOR GOD'S ATTRIBUTES:

PSALM 8.—*God's glory is magnified by his works, and by his love to man.*

TO THE CHIEF MUSICIAN UPON GITTITH, A PSALM OF DAVID.

1 O LORD our Lord, how excellent *is* thy name in all the earth! who hast set thy glory above the heavens.

2 Out of the mouth of babes and sucklings hast thou ordained strength because of thine enemies, that thou mightest still the enemy and the avenger.

3 When I consider thy heavens, the work of thy fingers, the moon and the stars, which thou hast ordained;

4 What is man, that thou art mindful of him? and the son of man, that thou visitest him?

5 For thou hast made him a little lower than the angels, and hast crowned him with glory and honour.

6 Thou madest him to have dominion over the works of thy hands; thou hast put all *things* under his feet:

7 All sheep and oxen, yea, and the beasts of the field;

8 The fowl of the air, and the fish of the sea, *and whatsoever* passeth through the paths of the seas.

9 O LORD our Lord, how excellent *is* thy name in all the earth!

PSALM 19.—1 *The creatures shew God's glory.* 7 *The word his grace.* 12 *David prayeth for grace.*

To the chief Musician, A Psalm of David.

1 The heavens declare the glory of God; and the firmament sheweth his handywork.

2 Day unto day uttereth speech, and night unto night sheweth knowledge.

3 *There is* no speech nor language, *where* their voice is not heard.

4 Their line is gone out through all the earth, and their words to the end of the world. In them hath he set a tabernacle for the sun,

5 Which *is* as a bridegroom coming out of his chamber, *and* rejoiceth as a strong man to run a race.

6 His going forth *is* from the end of the heaven, and his circuit unto the ends of it: and there is nothing hid from the heat thereof.

7 The law of the LORD *is* perfect, converting the soul: the testimony of the LORD *is* sure, making wise the simple.

8 The statutes of the LORD *are* right, rejoicing the heart: the commandment of the LORD *is* pure, enlightening the eyes.

9 The fear of the LORD *is* clean, enduring for ever: the judgments of the LORD *are* true *and* righteous altogether.

10 More to be desired *are they* than gold, yea, than much fine gold: sweeter also than honey and the honeycomb.

11 Moreover by them is thy servant warned: *and* in keeping of them *there is* great reward.

12 Who can understand *his* errors? cleanse thou me from secret *faults.*

13 Keep back thy servant also from presumptuous *sins;* let them not have dominion over me: then shall I be upright, and I shall be innocent from the great transgression.

14 Let the words of my mouth, and the meditation of my heart, be acceptable in thy sight, O LORD, my strength, and my redeemer.

PSALM 24.—1 *God's lordship in the world.* 3 *The citizens of his spiritual kingdom.* 7 *An exhortation to receive him.*

A Psalm of David.

1 The earth *is* the LORD'S, and the fulness thereof; the world, and they that dwell therein.

2 For he hath founded it upon the seas, and established it upon the floods.

3 Who shall ascend into the hill of the LORD? or who shall stand in his holy place?

4 He that hath clean hands, and a pure heart; who hath not lifted up his soul unto vanity, nor sworn deceitfully.

5 He shall receive the blessing from the LORD, and righteousness from the God of his salvation.

6 This *is* the generation of them that seek him, that seek thy face, O Jacob. Selah.

7 Lift up your heads, O ye gates; and be ye lift up, ye everlasting doors; and the King of glory shall come in.

8 Who *is* this King of glory? The LORD strong and mighty, the LORD mighty in battle.

9 Lift up your heads, O ye gates; even lift *them* up, ye everlasting doors; and the King of glory shall come in.

10 Who is this King of glory? The LORD of hosts, he *is* the King of glory. Selah.

PSALM 29.—1 *David exhorteth princes to give glory to God,* 3 *by reason of his power,* 11 *and protection of his people.*

A Psalm of David.

1 Give unto the LORD, O ye mighty, give unto the LORD glory and strength.

2 Give unto the LORD the glory due unto his name; worship the LORD in the beauty of holiness.

3 The voice of the LORD *is* upon the waters: the God of glory thundereth: the LORD *is* upon many waters.

4 The voice of the LORD *is* powerful; the voice of the LORD *is* full of majesty.

5 The voice of the LORD breaketh the cedars; yea, the LORD breaketh the cedars of Lebanon.

6 He maketh them also to skip like a calf; Lebanon and Sirion like a young unicorn.

7 The voice of the LORD divideth the flames of fire.

8 The voice of the LORD shaketh the wilderness; the LORD shaketh the wilderness of Kadesh.

9 The voice of the LORD maketh the hinds to calve, and discovereth the forests: and in his temple doth every one speak of *his* glory.

10 The LORD sitteth upon the flood; yea, the LORD sitteth King for ever.

11 The LORD will give strength unto his people; the LORD will bless his people with peace.

PSALM 33.—1 *God is to be praised for his goodness,* 6 *for his power,* 12 *and for his providence.* 20 *Confidence is to be placed in God.*

1 Rejoice in the LORD, O ye righteous: *for* praise is comely for the upright.

2 Praise the LORD with harp: sing unto him with the psaltery *and* an instrument of ten strings.

3 Sing unto him a new song; play skilfully with a loud noise.

4 For the word of the LORD *is* right; and all his works *are done* in truth.

5 He loveth righteousness and judgment: the earth is full of the goodness of the LORD.

6 By the word of the LORD were the heavens made; and all the host of them by the breath of his mouth.

7 He gathereth the waters of the sea together as an heap: he layeth up the depth in storehouses.

8 Let all the earth fear the LORD: let all the inhabitants of the world stand in awe of him.

9 For he spake, and it was *done;* he commanded, and it stood fast.

10 The LORD bringeth the counsel of the heathen to nought: he maketh the devices of the people of none effect.

11 The counsel of the LORD standeth for ever, the thoughts of his heart to all generations.

12 Blessed *is* the nation whose God *is* the LORD; *and* the people *whom* he hath chosen for his own inheritance.

13 The LORD looketh from heaven; he beholdeth all the sons of men.

14 From the place of his habitation he looketh upon all the inhabitants of the earth.

15 He fashioneth their hearts alike; he considereth all their works.

16 There is no king saved by the multitude of an host: a mighty man is not delivered by much strength.

17 An horse *is* a vain thing for safety: neither shall he deliver *any* by his great strength.

18 Behold, the eye of the LORD *is* upon them that fear him, upon them that hope in his mercy;

19 To deliver their soul from death, and to keep them alive in famine.

20 Our soul waiteth for the LORD: he *is* our help and our shield.

21 For our heart shall rejoice in him, because we have trusted in his holy name.

22 Let thy mercy, O LORD, be upon us, according as we hope in thee.

PSALM 47.—*The nations are exhorted cheerfully to entertain the kingdom of Christ.*

To THE CHIEF MUSICIAN, A PSALM FOR THE SONS OF KORAH.

1 O clap your hands, all ye people; shout unto God with the voice of triumph.

2 For the LORD most high *is* terrible; *he is* a great King over all the earth.

3 He shall subdue the people under us, and the nations under our feet.

4 He shall choose our inheritance for us, the excellency of Jacob whom he loved. Selah.

5 God is gone up with a shout, the LORD with the sound of a trumpet.

6 Sing praises to God, sing praises: sing praises unto our King, sing praises.

7 For God *is* the King of all the earth: sing ye praises with understanding.

8 God reigneth over the heathen: God sitteth upon the throne of his holiness.

9 The princes of the people are gathered together, *even* the people of the God of Abraham: for the shields of the earth *belong* unto God: he is greatly exalted.

PSALM 50.—1 *The majesty of God in the church.* 5 *His order to gather saints.* 7 *The pleasure of God is not in ceremonies,* 14 *but in sincerity of obedience.*

A PSALM OF ASAPH.-

1 The mighty God, *even* the LORD, hath spoken, and called the earth from the rising of the sun unto the going down thereof.

2 Out of Zion, the perfection of beauty, God hath shined.

3 Our God shall come, and shall not keep silence: a fire shall devour before him, and it shall be very tempestuous round about him.

4 He shall call to the heavens from above, and to the earth, that he may judge his people.

5 Gather my saints together unto me; those that have made a covenant with me by sacrifice.

6 And the heavens shall declare his righteousness: for God *is* judge himself. Selah.

7 Hear, O my people, and I will speak; O Israel, and I will testify against thee: I *am* God, *even* thy God.

8 I will not reprove thee for thy sacrifices or thy burnt offerings, *to have been* continually before me.

9 I will take no bullock out of thy house, *nor* he goats out of thy folds.

10 For every beast of the forest *is* mine, *and* the cattle upon a thousand hills.

11 I know all the fowls of the mountains: and the wild beasts of the field *are* mine.

12 If I were hungry, I would not tell thee: for the world *is* mine, and the fulness thereof.

13 Will I eat the flesh of bulls, or drink the blood of goats?

14 Offer unto God thanksgiving; and pay thy vows unto the most High:

15 And call upon me in the day of trouble: I will deliver thee, and thou shalt glorify me.

16 But unto the wicked God saith, What hast thou to do to declare my statutes, or *that* thou shouldest take my covenant in thy mouth?

17 Seeing thou hatest instruction, and castest my words behind thee.

18 When thou sawest a thief, then thou consentedst with him, and hast been partaker with adulterers.

19 Thou givest thy mouth to evil, and thy tongue frameth deceit.

20 Thou sittest *and* speakest against thy brother; thou slanderest thine own mother's son.

21 These *things* hast thou done, and I kept silence; thou thoughtest that I was altogether *such an one* as thyself: *but* I will reprove thee, and set *them* in order before thine eyes.

22 Now consider this, ye that forget God, lest I tear *you* in pieces, and *there be* none to deliver.

23 Whoso offereth praise glorifieth me: and to him that ordereth *his* conversation *aright* will I shew the salvation of God.

PSALM 65.—1 *David praiseth God for his grace.* 4 *The blessedness of God's chosen by reasou of benefits.*

To the chief Musician, A Psalm and Song of David.

1 Praise waiteth for thee, O God, in Sion: and unto thee shall the vow be performed.

2 O thou that hearest prayer, unto thee shall all flesh come.

3 Iniquities prevail against me: *as for* our transgressions, thou shalt purge them away.

4 Blessed *is the man whom* thou choosest, and causest to approach *unto thee, that* he may dwell in thy courts: we shall be satisfied with the goodness of thy house, *even* of thy holy temple.

5 *By* terrible things in righteousness wilt thou answer us, O God of our salvation; *who art* the confidence of all the ends of the earth, and of them that are afar off *upon* the sea:

6 Which by his strength setteth fast the mountains; *being* girded with power.

7 Which stilleth the noise of the seas, the noise of their waves, and the tumult of the people.

8 They also that dwell in the uttermost parts are afraid at thy tokens: thou makest the outgoings of the morning and evening to rejoice.

9 Thou visitest the earth, and waterest it: thou greatly enrichest it with the river of God, *which* is full of water: thou preparest them corn, when thou hast so provided for it.

10 Thou waterest the ridges thereof abundantly: thou settlest the furrows thereof: thou makest it soft with showers: thou blessest the springing thereof.

11 Thou crownest the year with thy goodness; and thy paths drop fatness.

12 They drop *upon* the pastures of the wilderness: and the little hills rejoice on every side.

13 The pastures are clothed with flocks; the valleys also are covered over with corn; they shout for joy, they also sing.

PSALM 66.—*David exhorteth to praise God,* 5 *to observe his great works,* 8 *to bless him for his gracious benefits.* 12 *He voweth for himself religious service to God.* 16 *He declareth God's special goodness to himself.*

To the chief Musician, A Song or Psalm.

1 Make a joyful noise unto God, all ye lands:

2 Sing forth the honour of his name: make his praise glorious.

3 Say unto God, How terrible *art thou in* thy works! through the greatness of thy power shall thine enemies submit themselves unto thee.

4 All the earth shall worship thee, and shall sing unto thee; they shall sing *to* thy name. Selah.

5 Come and see the works of God: *he is*

terrible *in his* doing toward the children of men.

6 He turned the sea into dry *land:* they went through the flood on foot: there did we rejoice in him.

7 He ruleth by his power for ever; his eyes behold the nations: let not the rebellious exalt themselves. Selah.

8 O bless our God, ye people, and make the voice of his praise to be heard:

9 Which holdeth our soul in life, and suffereth not our feet to be moved.

10 For thou, O God, hast proved us: thou hast tried us, as silver is tried.

11 Thou broughtest us into the net; thou laidst affliction upon our loins.

12 Thou hast caused men to ride over our heads; we went through fire and through water: but thou broughtest us out into a wealthy *place.*

13 I will go into thy house with burnt offerings: I will pay thee my vows,

14 Which my lips have uttered, and my mouth hath spoken, when I was in trouble.

15 I will offer unto thee burnt sacrifices of fatlings, with the incense of rams; I will offer bullocks with goats. Selah.

16 Come *and* hear, all ye that fear God, and I will declare what he hath done for my soul.

17 I cried unto him with my mouth, and he was extolled with my tongue.

18 If I regard iniquity in my heart, the Lord will not hear *me:*

19 *But* verily God hath heard *me;* he hath attended to the voice of my prayer.

20 Blessed *be* God, which hath not turned away my prayer, nor his mercy from me.

PSALM 76.—1 *A declaration of God's majesty in the church.* 11 *An exhortation to serve him reverently.*

To the chief Musician on Neginoth, A Psalm or Song of Asaph.

1 In Judah *is* God known: his name *is* great in Israel.

2 In Salem also is his tabernacle, and his dwelling place in Zion.

3 There brake he the arrows of the bow, the shield, and the sword, and the battle. Selah.

4 Thou *art* more glorious *and* excellent than the mountains of prey.

5 The stouthearted are spoiled, they have slept their sleep: and none of the men of might have found their hands.

6 At thy rebuke, O God of Jacob, both the chariot and horse are cast into a dead sleep.

7 Thou, *even* thou, *art* to be feared: and who may stand in thy sight when once thou art angry?

8 Thou didst cause judgment to be heard from heaven; the earth feared, and was still,

9 When God arose to judgment, to save all the meek of the earth. Selah.

10 Surely the wrath of man shall praise thee: the remainder of wrath shalt thou restrain.

11 Vow, and pay unto the Lord your

God: let all that be round about him bring presents unto him that ought to be feared.

12 He shall cut off the spirit of princes: *he is* terrible to the kings of the earth.

PSALM 77.—1 *The psalmist sheweth what fierce combat he had with diffidence.* 10 *The victory which he had by consideration of God's great and gracious works.*

To the chief Musician, to Jeduthun, A Psalm of Asaph.

1 I cried unto God with my voice, *even* unto God with my voice; and he gave ear unto me.

2 In the day of my trouble I sought the Lord: my sore ran in the night, and ceased not: my soul refused to be comforted.

3 I remembered God, and was troubled: I complained, and my spirit was overwhelmed. Selah.

4 Thou holdest mine eyes waking: I am so troubled that I cannot speak.

5 I have considered the days of old, the years of ancient times.

6 I call to remembrance my song in the night: I commune with mine own heart: and my spirit made diligent search.

7 Will the Lord cast off for ever? and will he be favourable no more?

8 Is his mercy clean gone for ever? doth *his* promise fail for evermore?

9 Hath God forgotten to be gracious? hath he in anger shut up his tender mercies? Selah.

10 And I said, This *is* my infirmity: *but I will remember* the years of the right hand of the most High.

11 I will remember the works of the Lord: surely I will remember thy wonders of old.

12 I will meditate also of all thy work, and talk of thy doings.

13 Thy way, O God, *is* in the sanctuary: who *is so* great a God as *our* God?

14 Thou *art* the God that doest wonders: thou hast declared thy strength among the people.

15 Thou hast with *thine* arm redeemed thy people, the sons of Jacob and Joseph. Selah.

16 The waters saw thee, O God, the waters saw thee; they were afraid: the depths also were troubled.

17 The clouds poured out water: the skies sent out a sound: thine arrows also went abroad.

18 The voice of thy thunder *was* in the heaven: the lightnings lightened the world: the earth trembled and shook.

19 Thy way *is* in the sea, and thy path in the great waters, and thy footsteps are not known.

20 Thou leddest thy people like a flock by the hand of Moses and Aaron.

PSALM 93.—*The majesty, power, and holiness of Christ's kingdom.*

1 The Lord reigneth, he is clothed with majesty; the Lord is clothed with strength, *wherewith* he hath girded himself: the world also is stablished, that it cannot be moved.

2 Thy throne *is* established of old: thou *art* from everlasting.

3 The floods have lifted up, O Lord, the floods have lifted up their voice; the floods lift up their waves.

4 The Lord on high *is* mightier than the noise of many waters, *yea, than* the mighty waves of the sea.

5 Thy testimonies are very sure: holiness becometh thine house, O Lord, for ever.

PSALM 95.—1 *An exhortation to praise God,* 3 *for his greatness,* 6 *and for his goodness,* 8 *and not to tempt him.*

1 O come, let us sing unto the Lord: let us make a joyful noise to the rock of our salvation.

2 Let us come before his presence with thanksgiving, and make a joyful noise unto him with psalms.

3 For the Lord *is* a great God, and a great King above all gods.

4 In his hand *are* the deep places of the earth: the strength of the hills *is* his also.

5 The sea *is* his, and he made it: and his hands formed the dry *land*.

6 O come, let us worship and bow down: let us kneel before the Lord our maker.

7 For he *is* our God; and we *are* the people of his pasture, and the sheep of his hand. To day if ye will hear his voice,

8 Harden not your heart, as in the provocation, *and* as *in* the day of temptation in the wilderness:

9 When your fathers tempted me, proved me, and saw my work.

10 Forty years long was I grieved with *this* generation, and said, It *is* a people that do err in their heart, and they have not known my ways:

11 Unto whom I sware in my wrath that they should not enter into my rest.

PSALM 96.—1 *An exhortation to praise God,* 4 *for his greatness,* 8 *for his kingdom,* 11 *for his general judgment.*

1 O sing unto the Lord a new song: sing unto the Lord, all the earth.

2 Sing unto the Lord, bless his name; shew forth his salvation from day to day.

3 Declare his glory among the heathen, his wonders among all people.

4 For the Lord *is* great, and greatly to be praised: he *is* to be feared above all gods.

5 For all the gods of the nations *are* idols: but the Lord made the heavens.

6 Honour and majesty *are* before him: strength and beauty *are* in his sanctuary.

7 Give unto the Lord, O ye kindreds of the people, give unto the Lord glory and strength.

8 Give unto the Lord the glory *due unto* his name: bring an offering, and come into his courts.

9 O worship the Lord in the beauty of holiness: fear before him, all the earth.

10 Say among the heathen *that* the Lord reigneth: the world also shall be established that it shall not be moved: he shall judge the people righteously.

11 Let the heavens rejoice, and let the earth be glad; let the sea roar, and the fulness thereof.

12 Let the field be joyful, and all that *is* therein: then shall all the trees of the wood rejoice

13 Before the LORD: for he cometh, for he cometh to judge the earth: he shall judge the world with righteousness, and the people with his truth.

PSALM 97.—1 *The majesty of God's kingdom.* 7 *The church rejoiceth at God's judgments upon idolaters.* 10 *An exhortation to godliness and gladness.*

1 The LORD reigneth; let the earth rejoice; let the multitude of isles be glad *thereof.*

2 Clouds and darkness *are* round about him: righteousness and judgment *are* the habitation of his throne.

3 A fire goeth before him, and burneth up his enemies round about.

4 His lightnings enlightened the world: the earth saw, and trembled.

5 The hills melted like wax at the presence of the LORD, at the presence of the Lord of the whole earth.

6 The heavens declare his righteousness, and all the people see his glory.

7 Confounded be all they that serve graven images, that boast themselves of idols: worship him, all *ye* gods.

8 Zion heard, and was glad; and the daughters of Judah rejoiced because of thy judgments, O LORD.

9 For thou, LORD, *art* high above all the earth: thou art exalted far above all gods.

10 Ye that love the LORD, hate evil: he preserveth the souls of his saints; he delivereth them out of the hand of the wicked.

11 Light is sown for the righteous, and gladness for the upright in heart.

12 Rejoice in the LORD, ye righteous; and give thanks at the remembrance of his holiness.

PSALM 99.—1 *The prophet, setting forth the kingdom of God in Zion,* 5 *exhorteth all, by the example of forefathers, to worship God at his holy hill.*

1 The LORD reigneth; let the people tremble: he sitteth *between* the cherubims; let the earth be moved.

2 The LORD *is* great in Zion; and he *is* high above all the people.

3 Let them praise thy great and terrible name; *for* it *is* holy.

4 The king's strength also loveth judgment; thou dost establish equity, thou executest judgment and righteousness in Jacob.

5 Exalt ye the LORD our God, and worship at his footstool; *for* he *is* holy.

6 Moses and Aaron among his priests, and Samuel among them that call upon his name: they called upon the LORD, and he answered them

7 He spake unto them in the cloudy pillar: they kept his testimonies, and the ordinance *that* he gave them.

8 Thou answeredst them, O LORD our God: thou wast a God that forgavest them, though thou tookest vengeance of their inventions.

9 Exalt the LORD our God, and worship at his holy hill; for the LORD our God *is* holy.

PSALM 104.—1 *A meditation upon the mighty power,* 7 *and wonderful providence of God.* 31 *God's glory is eternal.* 33 *The prophet voweth perpetually to praise God.*

1 Bless the LORD, O my soul. O LORD my God, thou art very great; thou art clothed with honour and majesty.

2 Who coverest *thyself* with light as *with* a garment: who stretchest out the heavens like a curtain:

3 Who layeth the beams of his chambers in the waters: who maketh the clouds his chariot: who walketh upon the wings of the wind:

4 Who maketh his angels spirits; his ministers a flaming fire:

5 *Who* laid the foundations of the earth, *that* it should not be removed for ever.

6 Thou coveredst it with the deep as *with* a garment: the waters stood above the mountains.

7 At thy rebuke they fled; at the voice of thy thunder they hasted away.

8 They go up by the mountains; they go down by the valleys unto the place which thou hast founded for them.

9 Thou hast set a bound that they may not pass over; that they turn not again to cover the earth.

10 He sendeth the springs into the valleys, *which* run among the hills.

11 They give drink to every beast of the field: the wild asses quench their thirst.

12 By them shall the fowls of the heaven have their habitation, *which* sing among the branches.

13 He watereth the hills from his chambers: the earth is satisfied with the fruit of thy works.

14 He causeth the grass to grow for the cattle, and herb for the service of man: that he may bring forth food out of the earth;

15 And wine *that* maketh glad the heart of man, *and* oil to make *his* face to shine, and bread *which* strengtheneth man's heart.

16 The trees of the LORD are full *of sap;* the cedars of Lebanon, which he hath planted;

17 Where the birds make their nests: *as for* the stork, the fir trees *are* her house.

18 The high hills *are* a refuge for the wild goats; *and* the rocks for the conies.

19 He appointed the moon for seasons: the sun knoweth his going down.

20 Thou makest darkness, and it is night: wherein all the beasts of the forest do creep *forth.*

21 The young lions roar after their prey, and seek their meat from God.

22 The sun ariseth, they gather themselves together, and lay them down in their dens.

23 Man goeth forth unto his work and to his labour until the evening.

24 O LORD, how manifold are thy works! in wisdom hast thou made them all : the earth is full of thy riches.

25 *So is* this great and wide sea, wherein *are* things creeping innumerable, both small and great beasts.

26 There go the ships : *there is* that leviathan, *whom* thou hast made to play therein.

27 These wait all upon thee ; that thou mayest give *them* their meat in due season.

28 *That* thou givest them they gather : thou openest thine hand, they are filled with good.

29 Thou hidest thy face, they are troubled : thou takest away their breath, they die, and return to their dust.

30 Thou sendest forth thy spirit, they are created : and thou renewest the face of the earth.

31 The glory of the LORD shall endure for ever : the LORD shall rejoice in his works.

32 He looketh on the earth, and it trembleth : he toucheth the hills, and they smoke.

33 I will sing unto the LORD as long as I live : I will sing praise to my God while I have my being.

34 My meditation of him shall be sweet : I will be glad in the LORD.

35 Let the sinners be consumed out of the earth, and let the wicked be no more. Bless thou the LORD, O my soul. Praise ye the LORD.

PSALM 111.—1 *The psalmist by his example inciteth others to praise God for his glorious,* 5 *and gracious works.* 10 *The fear of God breedeth true wisdom.*

1 Praise ye the LORD. I will praise the LORD with *my* whole heart, in the assembly of the upright, and *in* the congregation.

2 The works of the LORD *are* great, sought out of all them that have pleasure therein.

3 His work *is* honourable and glorious : and his righteousness endureth for ever.

4 He hath made his wonderful works to be remembered : the LORD *is* gracious and full of compassion.

5 He hath given meat unto them that fear him : he will ever be mindful of his covenant.

6 He hath shewed his people the power of his works, that he may give them the heritage of the heathen.

7 The works of his hands *are* verity and judgment ; all his commandments *are* sure.

8 They stand fast for ever and ever, *and* are done in truth and uprightness.

9 He sent redemption unto his people : he hath commanded his covenant for ever : holy and reverend *is* his name.

10 The fear of the LORD *is* the beginning of wisdom. a good understanding have all they that do *his commandments :* his praise endureth for ever.

PSALM 113.—1 *An exhortation to praise God for his excellency,* 6 *for his mercy.*

1 Praise ye the LORD. Praise, O ye servants of the LORD, praise the name of the LORD.

2 Blessed be the name of the LORD from this time forth and for evermore.

3 From the rising of the sun unto the going down of the same the LORD's name *is* to be praised.

4 The LORD *is* high above all nations, *and* his glory above the heavens.

5 Who *is* like unto the LORD our God, who dwelleth on high,

6 Who humbleth *himself* to behold *the things that are* in heaven, and in the earth !

7 He raiseth up the poor out of the dust, *and* lifteth the needy out of the dunghill ;

8 That he may set *him* with princes, *even* with the princes of his people.

9 He maketh the barren woman to keep house, *and to be* a joyful mother of children. Praise ye the LORD.

PSALM 114.—*An exhortation, by the example of the dumb creatures, to fear God in his church.*

1 When Israel went out of Egypt, the house of Jacob from a people of strange language ;

2 Judah was his sanctuary, *and* Israel his dominion.

3 The sea saw *it*, and fled : Jordan was driven back.

4 The mountains skipped like rams, *and* the little hills like lambs.

5 What *ailed* thee, O thou sea, that thou fleddest ? thou Jordan, *that* thou wast driven back ?

6 Ye mountains, *that* ye skipped like rams : *and* ye little hills, like lambs ?

7 Tremble, thou earth, at the presence of the Lord, at the presence of the God of Jacob ;

8 Which turned the rock *into* a standing water, the flint into a fountain of waters.

PSALM 115.—1 *Because God is truly glorious,* 4 *and idols are vanity,* 9 *he exhorteth to confidence in God.* 12 *God is to be blessed for his blessings.*

1 Not unto us, O LORD, not unto us, but unto thy name give glory, for thy mercy, *and* for thy truth's sake.

2 Wherefore should the heathen say, Where *is* now their God ?

3 But our God *is* in the heavens : he hath done whatsoever he hath pleased.

4 Their idols *are* silver and gold, the work of men's hands.

5 They have mouths, but they speak not : eyes have they, but they see not :

6 They have ears, but they hear not : noses have they, but they smell not :

7 They have hands, but they handle not · feet have they, but they walk not : neither speak they through their throat.

8 They that make them are like unto them ; *so is* every one that trusteth in them.

9 O Israel, trust thou in the LORD : he *is* their help and their shield.

10 O house of Aaron, trust in the LORD : he *is* their help and their shield.

11 Ye that fear the LORD, trust in the LORD : he *is* their help and their shield.

12 The LORD hath been mindful of us : he

will bless *us;* he will bless the house of Israel; he will bless the house of Aaron.

13 He will bless them that fear the Lord, *both* small and great.

14 The Lord shall increase you more and more, you and your children.

15 Ye *are* blessed of the Lord which made heaven and earth.

16 The heaven, *even* the heavens, *are* the Lord's: but the earth hath he given to the children of men.

17 The dead praise not the Lord, neither any that go down into silence.

18 But we will bless the Lord from this time forth and for evermore. Praise the Lord.

PSALM 134.—*An exhortation to bless God.*
A Song of degrees.

1 Behold, bless ye the Lord, all *ye* servants of the Lord, which by night stand in the house of the Lord.

2 Lift up your hands *in* the sanctuary, and bless the Lord.

3 The Lord that made heaven and earth bless thee out of Zion.

PSALM 139.—1 *David praiseth God for his allseeing providence,* 17 *and for his infinite mercies.* 19 *He defieth the wicked.* 23 *He prayeth for sincerity.*

To the chief Musician, A Psalm of David.

1 O Lord, thou hast searched me, and known *me.*

2 Thou knowest my downsitting and mine uprising, thou understandest my thought afar off.

3 Thou compassest my path and my lying down, and art acquainted *with* all my ways.

4 For *there is* not a word in my tongue, *but,* lo, O Lord, thou knowest it altogether.

5 Thou hast beset me behind and before, and laid thine hand upon me.

6 *Such* knowledge *is* too wonderful for me; it is high, I cannot *attain* unto it.

7 Whither shall I go from thy spirit? or whither shall I flee from thy presence?

8 If I ascend up into heaven, thou *art* there: if I make my bed in hell, behold, thou *art there.*

9 *If* I take the wings of the morning, *and* dwell in the uttermost parts of the sea;

10 Even there shall thy hand lead me, and thy right hand shall hold me.

11 If I say, Surely the darkness shall cover me; even the night shall be light about me.

12 Yea, the darkness hideth not from thee; but the night shineth as the day: the darkness and the light *are* both alike *to thee.*

13 For thou hast possessed my reins: thou hast covered me in my mother's womb.

14 I will praise thee; for I am fearfully *and* wonderfully made: marvellous *are* thy works; and *that* my soul knoweth right well.

15 My substance was not hid from thee, when I was made in secret, *and* curiously wrought in the lowest parts of the earth.

16 Thine eyes did see my substance, yet being unperfect; and in thy book all *my*

members were written, *which* in continuance were fashioned, when *as yet there was* none of them.

17 How precious also are thy thoughts unto me, O God! how great is the sum of them!

18 *If* I should count them, they are more in number than the sand: when I awake, I am still with thee.

19 Surely thou wilt slay the wicked, O God: depart from me therefore, ye bloody men.

20 For they speak against thee wickedly, *and* thine enemies take *thy name* in vain.

21 Do not I hate them, O Lord, that hate thee? and am not I grieved with those that rise up against thee?

22 I hate them with perfect hatred: I count them mine enemies.

23 Search me, O God, and know my heart · try me, and know my thoughts:

24 And see if *there be any* wicked way in me, and lead me in the way everlasting.

PSALM 147.—1 *The prophet exhorteth to praise God for his care of the church,* 4 *his power,* 6 *and his mercy:* 7 *to praise him for his providence:* 12 *to praise him for his blessings upon the kingdom,* 15 *for his power over the meteors,* 19 *and for his ordinances in the church.*

1 Praise ye the Lord: for *it is* good to sing praises unto our God; for *it is* pleasant; *and* praise is comely.

2 The Lord doth build up Jerusalem: he gathereth together the outcasts of Israel.

3 He healeth the broken in heart, and bindeth up their wounds.

4 He telleth the number of the stars; he calleth them all by *their* names.

5 Great *is* our Lord, and of great power: his understanding *is* infinite.

6 The Lord lifteth up the meek: he casteth the wicked down to the ground.

7 Sing unto the Lord with thanksgiving; sing praise upon the harp unto our God:

8 Who covereth the heaven with clouds, who prepareth rain for the earth, who maketh grass to grow upon the mountains.

9 He giveth to the beast his food, *and* to the young ravens which cry.

10 He delighteth not in the strength of the horse: he taketh not pleasure in the legs of a man.

11 The Lord taketh pleasure in them that fear him, in those that hope in his mercy.

12 Praise the Lord, O Jerusalem; praise thy God, O Zion.

13 For he hath strengthened the bars of thy gates; he hath blessed thy children within thee.

14 He maketh peace *in* thy borders, *and* filleth thee with the finest of the wheat.

15 He sendeth forth his commandment *upon* earth: his word runneth very swiftly.

16 He giveth snow like wool: he scattereth the hoarfrost like ashes.

17 He casteth forth his ice like morsels: who can stand before his cold?

18 He sendeth out his word, and melteth

them: he causeth his wind to blow, *and* the waters flow.

19 He sheweth his word unto Jacob, his statutes and his judgments unto Israel.

20 He hath not dealt so with any nation: and *as for his* judgments, they have not known them. Praise ye the LORD.

PSALM 148.—1 *The psalmist exhorteth the celestial*, 7 *the terrestrial*, 11 *and the rational creatures to praise God.*

1 Praise ye the LORD. Praise ye the LORD from the heavens: praise him in the heights.

2 Praise ye him, all his angels: praise ye him, all his hosts.

3 Praise ye him, sun and moon: praise him, all ye stars of light.

4 Praise him, ye heavens of heavens, and ye waters that *be* above the heavens.

5 Let them praise the name of the LORD: for he commanded, and they were created.

6 He hath also stablished them for ever and ever: he hath made a decree which shall not pass.

7 Praise the LORD from the earth, ye dragons, and all deeps:

8 Fire, and hail; snow, and vapours; stormy wind fulfilling his word:

9 Mountains, and all hills; fruitful trees, and all cedars:

10 Beasts, and all cattle; creeping things, and flying fowl:

11 Kings of the earth, and all people; princes, and all judges of the earth:

12 Both young men, and maidens; old men, and children:

13 Let them praise the name of the LORD: for his name alone is excellent; his glory *is* above the earth and heaven.

14 He also exalteth the horn of his people, the praise of all his saints; *even* of the children of Israel, a people near unto him. Praise ye the LORD.

PSALM 150.—1 *An exhortation to praise God*, 3 *with all kind of instruments.*

1 Praise ye the LORD. Praise God in his sanctuary: praise him in the firmament of his power.

2 Praise him for his mighty acts: praise him according to his excellent greatness.

3 Praise him with the sound of the trumpet: praise him with the psaltery and harp.

4 Praise him with the timbrel and dance: praise him with stringed instruments and organs.

5 Praise him upon the loud cymbals: praise him upon the high sounding cymbals.

6 Let every thing that hath breath praise the LORD. Praise ye the LORD.

PROPHETIC:

PSALM 2.—1 *The kingdom of Christ.* 10 *Kings are exhorted to accept it.*

1 Why do the heathen rage, and the people imagine a vain thing?

2 The kings of the earth set themselves, and the rulers take counsel together, against the LORD, and against his anointed, *saying*,

3 Let us break their bands asunder, and cast away their cords from us.

4 He that sitteth in the heavens shall laugh: the Lord shall have them in derision.

5 Then shall he speak unto them in his wrath, and vex them in his sore displeasure.

6 Yet have I set my king upon my holy hill of Zion.

7 I will declare the decree: the LORD hath said unto me, Thou *art* my Son; this day have I begotten thee.

8 Ask of me, and I shall give *thee* the heathen *for* thine inheritance, and the uttermost parts of the earth *for* thy possession.

9 Thou shalt break them with a rod of iron; thou shalt dash them in pieces like a potter's vessel.

10 Be wise now therefore, O ye kings: be instructed, ye judges of the earth.

11 Serve the LORD with fear, and rejoice with trembling.

12 Kiss the Son, lest he be angry, and ye perish *from* the way, when his wrath is kindled but a little. Blessed *are* all they that put their trust in him.

PSALM 16.—1 *David, in distrust of merits, and hatred of idolatry, fleeth to God for preservation.* 5 *He sheweth the hope of his calling, of the resurrection, and life everlasting.*

MICHTAM OF DAVID.

1 Preserve me, O God: for in thee do I put my trust.

2 *O my soul,* thou hast said unto the LORD. Thou *art* my Lord: my goodness *extendeth* not to thee;

3 *But* to the saints that *are* in the earth, and *to* the excellent, in whom *is* all my delight.

4 Their sorrows shall be multiplied *that* hasten *after* another *god:* their drink offerings of blood will I not offer, nor take up their names into my lips.

5 The LORD *is* the portion of mine inheritance and of my cup: thou maintainest my lot.

6 The lines are fallen unto me in pleasant *places;* yea, I have a goodly heritage.

7 I will bless the LORD, who hath given me counsel: my reins also instruct me in the night seasons.

8 I have set the LORD always before me: because *he is* at my right hand, I shall not be moved.

9 Therefore my heart is glad, and my glory rejoiceth: my flesh also shall rest in hope.

10 For thou wilt not leave my soul in hell; neither wilt thou suffer thine Holy One to see corruption.

11 Thou wilt shew me the path of life: in thy presence *is* fulness of joy; at thy right hand *there are* pleasures for evermore.

PSALM 22.—1 *David complaineth in great discouragement.* 9 *He prayeth in great distress.* 23 *He praiseth God.*

TO THE CHIEF MUSICIAN UPON AIJELETH SHAHAR, A PSALM OF DAVID.

1 My God, my God, why hast thou forsaken me? *why art thou so* far from helping me, *and from* the words of my roaring?

2 O my God, I cry in the daytime, but thou hearest not; and in the night season, and am not silent.

3 But thou *art* holy, *O thou* that inhabitest the praises of Israel.

4 Our fathers trusted in thee: they trusted, and thou didst deliver them.

5 They cried unto thee, and were delivered: they trusted in thee, and were not confounded.

6 But I *am* a worm, and no man; a reproach of men, and despised of the people.

7 All they that see me laugh me to scorn: they shoot out the lip, they shake the head, *saying,*

8 He trusted on the LORD *that* he would deliver him · let him deliver him, seeing he delighted in him.

9 But thou *art* he that took me out of the womb: thou didst make me hope *when I was* upon my mother's breasts.

10 I was cast upon thee from the womb: thou *art* my God from my mother's belly.

11 Be not far from me; for trouble *is* near; for *there is* none to help.

12 Many bulls have compassed me: strong *bulls* of Bashan have beset me round.

13 They gaped upon me *with* their mouths, *as* a ravening and a roaring lion.

14 I am poured out like water, and all my bones are out of joint: my heart is like wax; it is melted in the midst of my bowels.

15 My strength is dried up like a potsherd; and my tongue cleaveth to my jaws; and thou hast brought me into the dust of death.

16 For dogs have compassed me: the assembly of the wicked have inclosed me: they pierced my hands and my feet.

17 I may tell all my bones: they look *and* stare upon me.

18 They part my garments among them, and cast lots upon my vesture.

19 But be not thou far from me, O LORD: O my strength, haste thee to help me.

20 Deliver my soul from the sword; my darling from the power of the dog.

21 Save me from the lion's mouth: for thou hast heard me from the horns of the unicorns.

22 I will declare thy name unto my brethren: in the midst of the congregation will I praise thee.

23 Ye that fear the LORD, praise him; all ye the seed of Jacob, glorify him; and fear him, all ye the seed of Israel.

24 For he hath not despised nor abhorred the affliction of the afflicted; neither hath he hid his face from him; but when he cried unto him, he heard.

25 My praise *shall be* of thee in the great congregation: I will pay my vows before them that fear him.

26 The meek shall eat and be satisfied: they shall praise the LORD that seek him: your heart shall live for ever.

27 All the ends of the world shall remember and turn unto the LORD: and all the kindreds of the nations shall worship before thee.

28 For the kingdom *is* the LORD's: and he *is* the governor among the nations.

29 All *they that be* fat upon earth shall eat and worship: all they that go down to the dust shall bow before him: and none can keep alive his own soul.

30 A seed shall serve him; it shall be accounted to the Lord for a generation.

31 They shall come, and shall declare his righteousness unto a people that shall be born, that he hath done *this.*

PSALM 40.—1 *The benefit of confidence in God.* 6 *Obedience is the best sacrifice.* 11 *The sense of David's evils inflameth his prayer.*

TO THE CHIEF MUSICIAN, A PSALM OF DAVID.

1 I waited patiently for the LORD; and he inclined unto me, and heard my cry.

2 He brought me up also out of an horrible pit, out of the miry clay, and set my feet upon a rock, *and* established my goings.

3 And he hath put a new song in my mouth, *even* praise unto our God: many shall see *it,* and fear, and shall trust in the LORD.

4. Blessed *is* that man that maketh the LORD his trust, and respecteth not the proud, nor such as turn aside to lies.

5 Many, O LORD my God, *are* thy wonderful works *which* thou hast done, and thy thoughts *which are* to us-ward: they cannot be reckoned up in order unto thee: *if* I would declare and speak *of them,* they are more than can be numbered.

6 Sacrifice and offering thou didst not desire; mine ears hast thou opened: burnt offering and sin offering hast thou not required.

7 Then said I, Lo, I come; in the volume of the book *it is* written of me,

8 I delight to do thy will, O my God: yea, thy law *is* within my heart.

9 I have preached righteousness in the great congregation: lo, I have not refrained my lips, O LORD, thou knowest.

10 I have not hid thy righteousness within my heart; I have declared thy faithfulness and thy salvation: I have not concealed thy lovingkindness and thy truth from the great congregation.

11 Withhold not thou thy tender mercies from me, O LORD: let thy lovingkindness and thy truth continually preserve me.

12 For innumerable evils have compassed me about: mine iniquities have taken hold upon me, so that I am not able to look up; they are more than the hairs of mine head: therefore my heart faileth me.

13 Be pleased, O LORD, to deliver me: O LORD, make haste to help me.

14 Let them be ashamed and confounded together that seek after my soul to destroy it; let them be driven backward and put to shame that wish me evil.

15 Let them be desolate for a reward of their shame that say unto me, Aha, aha.

16 Let all those that seek thee rejoice and

be glad in thee: let such as love thy salvation say continually, The LORD be magnified.

17 But I *am* poor and needy; *yet* the Lord thinketh upon me: thou *art* my help and my deliverer; make no tarrying, O my God.

PSALM 45.—1 *The majesty and grace of Christ's kingdom.* 10 *The duty of the church, and the benefits thereof.*

To THE CHIEF MUSICIAN UPON SHOSHANNIM, FOR THE SONS OF KORAH, MASCHIL, A SONG OF LOVES.

1 My heart is inditing a good matter: I speak of the things which I have made touching the king: my tongue *is* the pen of a ready writer.

2 Thou art fairer than the children of men: grace is poured into thy lips: therefore God hath blessed thee for ever.

3 Gird thy sword upon *thy* thigh, O *most* mighty, with thy glory and thy majesty.

4 And in thy majesty ride prosperously because of truth and meekness *and* righteousness; and thy right hand shall teach thee terrible things.

5 Thine arrows *are* sharp in the heart of the king's enemies; *whereby* the people fall under thee.

6 Thy throne, O God, *is* for ever and ever: the sceptre of thy kingdom *is* a right sceptre.

7 Thou lovest righteousness, and hatest wickedness: therefore God, thy God, hath anointed thee with the oil of gladness above thy fellows.

8 All thy garments *smell* of myrrh, and aloes, *and* cassia, out of the ivory palaces, whereby they have made thee glad.

9 Kings' daughters *were* among thy honourable women: upon thy right hand did stand the queen in gold of Ophir.

10 Hearken, O daughter, and consider, and incline thine ear; forget also thine own people, and thy father's house;

11 So shall the king greatly desire thy beauty: for he *is* thy Lord; and worship thou him.

12 And the daughter of Tyre *shall be there* with a gift; *even* the rich among the people shall intreat thy favour.

13 The king's daughter *is* all glorious within: her clothing *is* of wrought gold.

14 She shall be brought unto the king in raiment of needlework: the virgins her companions that follow her shall be brought unto thee.

15 With gladness and rejoicing shall they be brought: they shall enter into the king's palace.

16 Instead of thy fathers shall be thy children, whom thou mayest make princes in all the earth.

17 I will make thy name to be remembered in all generations: therefore shall the people praise thee for ever and ever.

PSALM 68.—1 *A prayer at the removing of the ark.* 4 *An exhortation to praise God for his mercies,* 7 *for his care of the church,* 19 *for his great works.*

To THE CHIEF MUSICIAN, A PSALM OR SONG OF DAVID.

1 Let God arise, let his enemies be scattered: let them also that hate him flee before him.

2 As smoke is driven away, *so* drive *them* away: as wax melteth before the fire, *so* let the wicked perish at the presence of God.

3 But let the righteous be glad; let them rejoice before God: yea, let them exceedingly rejoice.

4 Sing unto God, sing praises to his name: extol him that rideth upon the heavens by his name JAH, and rejoice before him.

5 A father of the fatherless, and a judge of the widows, *is* God in his holy habitation.

6 God setteth the solitary in families: he bringeth out those which are bound with chains: but the rebellious dwell in a dry *land.*

7 O God, when thou wentest forth before thy people, when thou didst march through the wilderness; Selah:

8 The earth shook, the heavens also dropped at the presence of God: *even* Sinai itself *was moved* at the presence of God, the God of Israel.

9 Thou, O God, didst send a plentiful rain, whereby thou didst confirm thine inheritance, when it was weary.

10 Thy congregation hath dwelt therein: thou, O God, hast prepared of thy goodness for the poor.

11 The Lord gave the word: great *was* the company of those that published *it.*

12 Kings of armies did flee apace: and she that tarried at home divided the spoil.

13 Though ye have lien among the pots, *yet shall ye be as* the wings of a dove covered with silver, and her feathers with yellow gold.

14 When the Almighty scattered kings in it, it was *white* as snow in Salmon.

15 The hill of God *is as* the hill of Bashan; an high hill *as* the hill of Bashan.

16 Why leap ye, ye high hills? *this is* the hill *which* God desireth to dwell in: yea, the LORD will dwell *in it* for ever.

17 The chariots of God *are* twenty thousand, *even* thousands of angels: the Lord *is* among them, *as in* Sinai, in the holy *place.*

18 Thou hast ascended on high, thou hast led captivity captive: thou hast received gifts for men; yea, *for* the rebellious also, that the LORD God might dwell *among them.*

19 Blessed *be* the Lord, *who* daily loadeth us *with benefits, even* the God of our salvation. Selah.

20 *He that is* our God *is* the God of salvation; and unto GOD the Lord *belong* the issues from death.

21 But God shall wound the head of his enemies, *and* the hairy scalp of such an one as goeth on still in his trespasses.

22 The Lord said, I will bring again from Bashan, I will bring *my people* again from the depths of the sea:

23 That thy foot may be dipped in the blood of *thine* enemies, *and* the tongue of thy dogs in the same.

24 They have seen thy goings, O God; *even* the goings of my God, my King, in the sanctuary.

25 The singers went before, the players on instruments *followed* after; among *them were* the damsels playing with timbrels.

26 Bless ye God in the congregations, *even* the Lord, from the fountain of Israel.

27 There *is* little Benjamin *with* their ruler, the princes of Judah *and* their council, the princes of Zebulun, *and* the princes of Naphtali.

28 Thy God hath commanded thy strength: strengthen, O God, that which thou hast wrought for us.

29 Because of thy temple at Jerusalem shall kings bring presents unto thee.

30 Rebuke the company of spearmen, the multitude of the bulls, with the calves of the people, *till every one* submit himself with pieces of silver: scatter thou the people *that* delight in war.

31 Princes shall come out of Egypt; Ethiopia shall soon stretch out her hands unto God.

32 Sing unto God, ye kingdoms of the earth; O sing praises unto the Lord; Selah:

33 To him that rideth upon the heavens of heavens, *which were* of old; lo, he doth send out his voice, *and that* a mighty voice.

34 Ascribe ye strength unto God: his excellency *is* over Israel, and his strength *is* in the clouds.

35 O God, *thou art* terrible out of thy holy places: the God of Israel *is* he that giveth strength and power unto *his* people. Blessed *be* God.

PSALM 69.—1 *David complaineth of his affliction.* 13 *He prayeth for deliverance.* 22 *He devoteth his enemies to destruction.* 30 *He praiseth God with thanksgiving.*

To the chief Musician upon Shoshannim, A Psalm of David.

1 Save me, O God; for the waters are come in unto *my* soul.

2 I sink in deep mire, where *there is* no standing: I am come into deep waters, where the floods overflow me.

3 I am weary of my crying: my throat is dried: mine eyes fail while I wait for my God.

4 They that hate me without a cause are more than the hairs of mine head: they that would destroy me, *being* mine enemies wrongfully, are mighty: then I restored *that* which I took not away.

5 O God, thou knowest my foolishness; and my sins are not hid from thee.

6 Let not them that wait on thee, O Lord God of hosts, be ashamed for my sake: let not those that seek thee be confounded for my sake, O God of Israel.

7 Because for thy sake I have borne reproach; shame hath covered my face.

8 I am become a stranger unto my brethren, and an alien unto my mother's children.

9 For the zeal of thine house hath eaten me up; and the reproaches of them that reproached thee are fallen upon me.

10 When I wept, *and chastened* my soul with fasting, that was to my reproach.

11 I made sackcloth also my garment; and I became a proverb to them.

12 They that sit in the gate speak against me; and I *was* the song of the drunkards.

13 But as for me, my prayer *is* unto thee, O Lord, *in* an acceptable time: O God, in the multitude of thy mercy hear me, in the truth of thy salvation.

14 Deliver me out of the mire, and let me not sink: let me be delivered from them that hate me, and out of the deep waters.

15 Let not the waterflood overflow me, neither let the deep swallow me up, and let not the pit shut her mouth upon me.

16 Hear me, O Lord; for thy lovingkindness *is* good: turn unto me according to the multitude of thy tender mercies.

17 And hide not thy face from thy servant; for I am in trouble: hear me speedily.

18 Draw nigh unto my soul, *and* redeem it: deliver me because of mine enemies.

19 Thou hast known my reproach, and my shame, and my dishonour: mine adversaries *are* all before thee.

20 Reproach hath broken my heart; and I am full of heaviness: and I looked *for some* to take pity, but *there was* none; and for comforters, but I found none.

21 They gave me also gall for my meat; and in my thirst they gave me vinegar to drink.

22 Let their table become a snare before them: and *that which should have been* for *their* welfare, *let it become* a trap.

23 Let their eyes be darkened, that they see not; and make their loins continually to shake.

24 Pour out thine indignation upon them, and let thy wrathful anger take hold of them.

25 Let their habitation be desolate; *and* let none dwell in their tents.

26 For they persecute *him* whom thou hast smitten; and they talk to the grief of those whom thou hast wounded.

27 Add iniquity unto their iniquity: and let them not come into thy righteousness.

28 Let them be blotted out of the book of the living, and not be written with the righteous.

29 But I *am* poor and sorrowful: let thy salvation, O God, set me up on high.

30 I will praise the name of God with a song, and will magnify him with thanksgiving.

31 *This* also shall please the Lord better than an ox *or* bullock that hath horns and hoofs.

32 The humble shall see *this, and* be glad: and your heart shall live that seek God.

33 For the Lord heareth the poor, and despiseth not his prisoners.

34 Let the heaven and earth praise him, the seas, and every thing that moveth therein.

35 For God will save Zion, and will build

the cities of Judah: that they may dwell there, and have it in possession.

36 The seed also of his servants shall inherit it: and they that love his name shall dwell therein.

PSALM 72.—1 *David, praying for Solomon, sheweth the goodness and glory of his, in type, and in truth, of Christ's kingdom.* 18 *He blesseth God.*

A PSALM FOR SOLOMON.

1 Give the king thy judgments, O God, and thy righteousness unto the king's son.

2 He shall judge thy people with righteousness, and thy poor with judgment.

3 The mountains shall bring peace to the people, and the little hills, by righteousness.

4 He shall judge the poor of the people, he shall save the children of the needy, and shall break in pieces the oppressor.

5 They shall fear thee as long as the sun and moon endure, throughout all generations.

6 He shall come down like rain upon the mown grass: as showers *that* water the earth.

7 In his days shall the righteous flourish; and abundance of peace so long as the moon endureth.

8 He shall have dominion also from sea to sea, and from the river unto the ends of the earth.

9 They that dwell in the wilderness shall bow before him; and his enemies shall lick the dust.

10 The kings of Tarshish and of the isles shall bring presents: the kings of Sheba and Seba shall offer gifts.

11 Yea, all kings shall fall down before him: all nations shall serve him.

12 For he shall deliver the needy when he crieth; the poor also, and *him* that hath no helper.

13 He shall spare the poor and needy, and shall save the souls of the needy.

14 He shall redeem their soul from deceit and violence: and precious shall their blood be in his sight.

15 And he shall live, and to him shall be given of the gold of Sheba: prayer also shall be made for him continually; *and* daily shall he be praised.

16 There shall be an handful of corn in the earth upon the top of the mountains: the fruit thereof shall shake like Lebanon: and *they* of the city shall flourish like grass of the earth.

17 His name shall endure for ever: his name shall be continued as long as the sun: and *men* shall be blessed in him: all nations shall call him blessed.

18 Blessed *be* the LORD God, the God of Israel, who only doeth wondrous things.

19 And blessed *be* his glorious name for ever: and let the whole earth be filled *with* his glory; Amen, and Amen.

20 The prayers of David the son of Jesse are ended.

PSALM 87.—1 *The nature and glory of the church.* 4 *The increase, honour, and comfort of the members thereof.*

A PSALM OR SONG FOR THE SONS OF KORAH.

1 His foundation *is* in the holy mountains.

2 The LORD loveth the gates of Zion more than all the dwellings of Jacob.

3 Glorious things are spoken of thee, O city of God. Selah.

4 I will make mention of Rahab and Babylon to them that know me: behold Philistia, and Tyre, with Ethiopia; this *man* was born there.

5 And of Zion it shall be said, This and that man was born in her: and the highest himself shall establish her.

6 The LORD shall count, when he writeth up the people, *that* this *man* was born there. Selah.

7 As well the singers as the players on instruments *shall be there:* all my springs *are* in thee.

PSALM 97.—1 *The majesty of God's kingdom.* 7 *The church rejoiceth at God's judgments upon idolaters.* 10 *An exhortation to godliness and gladness.*

1 The LORD reigneth; let the earth rejoice; let the multitude of isles be glad *thereof.*

2 Clouds and darkness *are* round about him: righteousness and judgment *are* the habitation of his throne.

3 A fire goeth before him, and burneth up his enemies round about.

4 His lightnings enlightened the world: the earth saw, and trembled.

5 The hills melted like wax at the presence of the LORD, at the presence of the Lord of the whole earth.

6 The heavens declare his righteousness, and all the people see his glory.

7 Confounded be all they that serve graven images, that boast themselves of idols: worship him, all *ye* gods.

8 Zion heard, and was glad; and the daughters of Judah rejoiced because of thy judgments, O LORD.

9 For thou, LORD, *art* high above all the earth: thou art exalted far above all gods.

10 Ye that love the LORD, hate evil: he preserveth the souls of his saints; he delivereth them out of the hand of the wicked.

11 Light is sown for the righteous, and gladness for the upright in heart.

12 Rejoice in the LORD, ye righteous; and give thanks at the remembrance of his holiness.

PSALM 110.—1 *The kingdom,* 4 *the priesthood,* 5 *the conquest,* 7 *and the passion of Christ.*

A PSALM OF DAVID.

1 The LORD said unto my Lord, Sit thou at my right hand, until I make thine enemies thy footstool.

2 The LORD shall send the rod of thy strength out of Zion: rule thou in the midst of thine enemies.

3 Thy people *shall be* willing in the day of thy power, in the beauties of holiness from

the womb of the morning : thou hast the dew of thy youth.

4 The LORD hath sworn, and will not repent, Thou *art* a priest for ever after the order of Melchizedek.

5 The Lord at thy right hand shall strike through kings in the day of his wrath.

6 He shall judge among the heathen, he shall fill *the places* with the dead bodies ; he shall wound the heads over many countries.

7 He shall drink of the brook in the way : therefore shall he lift up the head.

PSALM 118.—1 *An exhortation to praise God for his mercy. 5 The psalmist by his experience sheweth how good it is to trust in God. 19 Under the type of the psalmist the coming of Christ in his kingdom is expressed.*

1 O give thanks unto the LORD ; for *he is* good : because his mercy *endureth* for ever.

2 Let Israel now say, that his mercy *endureth* for ever.

3 Let the house of Aaron now say, that his mercy *endureth* for ever.

4 Let them now that fear the LORD say, that his mercy *endureth* for ever.

5 I called upon the LORD in distress : the LORD answered me, *and set me* in a large place.

6 The LORD *is* on my side ; I will not fear : what can man do unto me ?

7 The LORD taketh my part with them that help me : therefore shall I see *my desire* upon them that hate me.

8 *It is* better to trust in the LORD than to put confidence in man.

9 *It is* better to trust in the LORD than to put confidence in princes.

10 All nations compassed me about : but in the name of the LORD will I destroy them.

11 They compassed me about ; yea, they compassed me about : but in the name of the LORD I will destroy them.

12 They compassed me about like bees ; they are quenched as the fire of thorns : for in the name of the LORD I will destroy them.

13 Thou hast thrust sore at me that I might fall : but the LORD helped me.

14 The LORD *is* my strength and song, and is become my salvation.

15 The voice of rejoicing and salvation *is* in the tabernacles of the righteous : the right hand of the LORD doeth valiantly.

16 The right hand of the LORD is exalted : the right hand of the LORD doeth valiantly.

17 I shall not die, but live, and declare the works of the LORD.

18 The LORD hath chastened me sore : but he hath not given me over unto death.

19 Open to me the gates of righteousness : I will go into them, *and* I will praise the LORD :

20 This gate of the LORD, into which the righteous shall enter.

21 I will praise thee : for thou hast heard me, and art become my salvation.

22 The stone *which* the builders refused is become the head *stone* of the corner.

23 This is the LORD'S doing : it *is* marvellous in our eyes.

24 This *is* the day *which* the LORD hath made ; we will rejoice and be glad in it.

25 Save now, I beseech thee, O LORD : O LORD, I beseech thee, send now prosperity.

26 Blessed *be* he that cometh in the name of the LORD : we have blessed you out of the house of the LORD.

27 God *is* the LORD, which hath shewed us light : bind the sacrifice with cords, *even* unto the horns of the altar.

28 Thou *art* my God, and I will praise thee : *thou art* my God, I will exalt thee.

29 O give thanks unto the LORD ; for *he is* good : for his mercy *endureth* for ever.

THANKSGIVING :

FOR GOD'S GOODNESS TO ISRAEL ·

PSALM 21.—1 *A thanksgiving for victory. 7 Confidence of further success.*

To the chief MUSICIAN, A PSALM OF DAVID.

1 The king shall joy in thy strength, O LORD ; and in thy salvation how greatly shall he rejoice !

2 Thou hast given him his heart's desire, and hast not withholden the request of his lips. Selah.

3 For thou preventest him with the blessings of goodness : thou settest a crown of pure gold on his head.

4 He asked life of thee, *and* thou gavest *it* him, *even* length of days for ever and ever.

5 His glory *is* great in thy salvation : honour and majesty hast thou laid upon him.

6 For thou hast made him most blessed for ever : thou hast made him exceeding glad with thy countenance.

7 For the king trusteth in the LORD, and through the mercy of the most High he shall not be moved.

8 Thine hand shall find out all thine enemies : thy right hand shall find out those that hate thee.

9 Thou shalt make them as a fiery oven in the time of thine anger : the LORD shall swallow them up in his wrath, and the fire shall devour them.

10 Their fruit shalt thou destroy from the earth, and their seed from among the children of men.

11 For they intended evil against thee : they imagined a mischievous device, *which* they are not able *to perform*.

12 Therefore shalt thou make them turn their back, *when* thou shalt make ready *thine arrows* upon thy strings against the face of them.

13 Be thou exalted, LORD, in thine own strength : *so* will we sing and praise thy power.

PSALM 46.—1 *The confidence which the church hath in God. 8 An exhortation to behold it.*

To the chief MUSICIAN FOR THE SONS OF KORAH, A SONG UPON ALAMOTH.

1 God is our refuge and strength, a very present help in trouble.

2 Therefore will not we fear, though the earth be removed, and though the mountains be carried into the midst of the sea;

3 *Though* the waters thereof roar *and* be troubled, *though* the mountains shake with the swelling thereof. Selah.

4 *There is* a river, the streams whereof shall make glad the city of God, the holy *place* of the tabernacles of the most High.

5 God *is* in the midst of her; she shall not be moved: God shall help her, *and that* right early.

6 The heathen raged, the kingdoms were moved: he uttered his voice, the earth melted.

7 The LORD of hosts *is* with us; the God of Jacob *is* our refuge. Selah.

8 Come, behold the works of the LORD, what desolations he hath made in the earth.

9 He maketh wars to cease unto the end of the earth; he breaketh the bow, and cutteth the spear in sunder; he burneth the chariot in the fire.

10 Be still, and know that I *am* God: I will be exalted among the heathen, I will be exalted in the earth.

11 The LORD of hosts *is* with us; the God of Jacob *is* our refuge. Selah.

PSALM 48.—*The ornaments and privileges of the church.*

A SONG AND PSALM FOR THE SONS OF KORAH.

1 Great *is* the LORD, and greatly to be praised in the city of our God, *in* the mountain of his holiness.

2 Beautiful for situation, the joy of the whole earth, *is* mount Zion, *on* the sides of the north, the city of the great King.

3 God is known in her palaces for a refuge.

4 For, lo, the kings were assembled, they passed by together.

5 They saw *it, and* so they marvelled; they were troubled, *and* hasted away.

6 Fear took hold upon them there, *and* pain, as of a woman in travail.

7 Thou breakest the ships of Tarshish with an east wind.

8 As we have heard, so have we seen in the city of the LORD of hosts, in the city of our God: God will establish it for ever. Selah.

9 We have thought of thy lovingkindness, O God, in the midst of thy temple.

10 According to thy name, O God, so *is* thy praise unto the ends of the earth: thy right hand is full of righteousness.

11 Let mount Zion rejoice, let the daughters of Judah be glad, because of thy judgments.

12 Walk about Zion, and go round about her: tell the towers thereof.

13 Mark ye well her bulwarks, consider her palaces; that ye may tell *it* to the generation following.

14 For this God *is* our God for ever and ever: he will be our guide *even* unto death.

PSALM 65.—1 *David praiseth God for his grace.* 4 *The blessedness of God's chosen by reason of benefits.*

TO THE CHIEF MUSICIAN, A PSALM AND SONG OF DAVID.

1 Praise waiteth for thee, O God, in Sion: and unto thee shall the vow be performed.

2 O thou that hearest prayer, unto thee shall all flesh come.

3 Iniquities prevail against me: *as for* our transgressions, thou shalt purge them away.

4 Blessed *is the man whom* thou choosest, and causest to approach *unto thee, that* he may dwell in thy courts: we shall be satisfied with the goodness of thy house, *even* of thy holy temple.

5 *By* terrible things in righteousness wilt thou answer us, O God of our salvation; *who art* the confidence of all the ends of the earth, and of them that are afar off *upon* the sea:

6 Which by his strength setteth fast the mountains; *being* girded with power:

7 Which stilleth the noise of the seas, the noise of their waves, and the tumult of the people.

8 They also that dwell in the uttermost parts are afraid at thy tokens: thou makest the outgoings of the morning and evening to rejoice.

9 Thou visitest the earth, and waterest it: thou greatly enrichest it with the river of God, *which* is full of water: thou preparest them corn, when thou hast so provided for it.

10 Thou waterest the ridges thereof abundantly: thou settlest the furrows thereof: thou makest it soft with showers: thou blessest the springing thereof.

11 Thou crownest the year with thy goodness; and thy paths drop fatness.

12 They drop *upon* the pastures of the wilderness: and the little hills rejoice on every side.

13 The pastures are clothed with flocks; the valleys also are covered over with corn; they shout for joy, they also sing.

PSALM 66.—1 *David exhorteth to praise God,* 5 *to observe his great works,* 8 *to bless him for his gracious benefits.* 12 *He voweth for himself religious service to God.* 16 *He declareth God's special goodness to himself.*

TO THE CHIEF MUSICIAN, A SONG OR PSALM.

1 Make a joyful noise unto God, all ye lands:

2 Sing forth the honour of his name: make his praise glorious.

3 Say unto God, How terrible *art thou in* thy works! through the greatness of thy power shall thine enemies submit themselves unto thee.

4 All the earth shall worship thee, and shall sing unto thee; they shall sing *to* thy name. Selah.

5 Come and see the works of God: *he is* terrible *in his* doing toward the children of men.

6 He turned the sea into dry *land:* they went through the flood on foot: there did we rejoice in him.

7 He ruleth by his power forever; his eyes behold the nations: let not the rebellious exalt themselves. Selah.

8 O bless our God, ye people, and make the voice of his praise to be heard:

9 Which holdeth our soul in life, and suffereth not our feet to be moved.

10 For thou, O God, hast proved us: thou hast tried us, as silver is tried.

11 Thou broughtest us into the net; thou laidst affliction upon our loins.

12 Thou hast caused men to ride over our heads; we went through fire and through water: but thou broughtest us out into a wealthy *place*.

13 I will go into thy house with burnt offerings: I will pay thee my vows,

14 Which my lips have uttered, and my mouth hath spoken, when I was in trouble.

15 I will offer unto thee burnt sacrifices of fatlings, with the incense of rams; I will offer bullocks with goats. Selah.

16 Come *and* hear, all ye that fear God, and I will declare what he hath done for my soul.

17 I cried unto him with my mouth, and he was extolled with my tongue.

18 If I regard iniquity in my heart, the Lord will not hear *me:*

19 *But* verily God hath heard *me;* he hath attended to the voice of my prayer.

20 Blessed *be* God, which hath not turned away my prayer, nor his mercy from me.

PSALM 68.—1 *A prayer at the removing of the ark.* 4 *An exhortation to praise God for his mercies,* 7 *for his care of the church,* 19 *for his great works.*

To the chief Musician, A Psalm or Song of David.

1 Let God arise, let his enemies be scattered: let them also that hate him flee before him.

2 As smoke is driven away, *so* drive *them* away: as wax melteth before the fire, *so* let the wicked perish at the presence of God.

3 But let the righteous be glad; let them rejoice before God: yea, let them exceedingly rejoice.

4 Sing unto God, sing praises to his name: extol him that rideth upon the heavens by his name JAH, and rejoice before him.

5 A father of the fatherless, and a judge of the widows, *is* God in his holy habitation.

6 God setteth the solitary in families: he bringeth out those which are bound with chains: but the rebellious dwell in a dry *land*.

7 O God, when thou wentest forth before thy people, when thou didst march through the wilderness; Selah:

8 The earth shook, the heavens also dropped at the presence of God: *even* Sinai itself *was moved* at the presence of God, the God of Israel.

9 Thou, O God, didst send a plentiful rain, whereby thou didst confirm thine inheritance, when it was weary.

10 Thy congregation hath dwelt therein: thou, O God, hast prepared of thy goodness for the poor.

11 The Lord gave the word: great *was* the company of those that published *it*.

12 Kings of armies did flee apace: and she that tarried at home divided the spoil.

13 Though ye have lien among the pots, *yet shall ye be as* the wings of a dove covered with silver, and her feathers with yellow gold.

14 When the Almighty scattered kings in it, it was *white* as snow in Salmon.

15 The hill of God *is as* the hill of Bashan; an high hill *as* the hill of Bashan.

16 Why leap ye, ye high hills? *this is* the hill *which* God desireth to dwell in; yea, the Lord will dwell *in it* for ever.

17 The chariots of God *are* twenty thousand, *even* thousands of angels: the Lord *is* among them, *as in* Sinai, in the holy *place*.

18 Thou hast ascended on high, thou hast led captivity captive: thou hast received gifts from men; yea, *for* the rebellious also, that the Lord God might dwell *among them*.

19 Blessed *be* the Lord, *who* daily loadeth us *with benefits, even* the God of our salvation. Selah.

20 *He that is* our God *is* the God of salvation; and unto God the Lord *belong* the issues from death.

21 But God shall wound the head of his enemies, *and* the hairy scalp of such an one as goeth on still in his trespasses.

22 The Lord said, I will bring again from Bashan, I will bring *my people* again from the depths of the sea:

23 That thy foot may be dipped in the blood of *thine* enemies, *and* the tongue of thy dogs in the same.

24 They have seen thy goings, O God; *even* the goings of my God, my King, in the sanctuary.

25 The singers went before, the players on instruments *followed* after; among *them were* the damsels playing with timbrels.

26 Bless ye God in the congregations, *even* the Lord, from the fountain of Israel.

27 There *is* little Benjamin *with* their ruler, the princes of Judah *and* their council, the princes of Zebulun, *and* the princes of Naphtali.

28 Thy God hath commanded thy strength: strengthen, O God, that which thou hast wrought for us.

29 Because of thy temple at Jerusalem shall kings bring presents unto thee.

30 Rebuke the company of spearmen, the multitude of the bulls, with the calves of the people, *till every one* submit himself with pieces of silver: scatter thou the people *that* delight in war.

31 Princes shall come out of Egypt; Ethiopia shall soon stretch out her hands unto God.

32 Sing unto God, ye kingdoms of the earth; O sing praises unto the Lord; Selah:

33 To him that rideth upon the heavens

of heavens, *which were* of old; lo, he doth send out his voice, *and that* a mighty voice.

34 Ascribe ye strength unto God: his excellency *is* over Israel, and his strength *is* in the clouds.

35 O God, *thou art* terrible out of thy holy places: the God of Israel *is* he that giveth strength and power unto *his* people. Blessed *be* God.

PSALM 76.—1 *A declaration of God's majesty in the church.* 11 *An exhortation to serve him reverently.*

To the chief Musician on Neginoth, A Psalm or Song of Asaph.

1 In Judah *is* God known: his name *is* great in Israel.

2 In Salem also is his tabernacle, and his dwelling place in Zion.

3 There brake he the arrows of the bow, the shield, and the sword, and the battle. Selah.

4 Thou *art* more glorious *and* excellent than the mountains of prey.

5 The stouthearted are spoiled, they have slept their sleep: and none of the men of might have found their hands.

6 At thy rebuke, O God of Jacob, both the chariot and horse are cast into a dead sleep.

7 Thou, *even* thou, *art* to be feared: and who may stand in thy sight when once thou art angry?

8 Thou didst cause judgment to be heard from heaven; the earth feared, and was still,

9 When God arose to judgment, to save all the meek of the earth. Selah.

10 Surely the wrath of man shall praise thee: the remainder of wrath shalt thou restrain.

11 Vow, and pay unto the LORD your God: let all that be round about him bring presents unto him that ought to be feared.

12 He shall cut off the spirit of princes: *he is* terrible to the kings of the earth.

PSALM 81.—1 *An exhortation to a solemn praising of God.* 4 *God challengeth that duty by reason of his benefits.* 8 *God, exhorting to obedience, complaineth of their disobedience, which proveth their own hurt.*

To the chief Musician upon Gittith, A Psalm of Asaph.

1 Sing aloud unto God our strength: make a joyful noise unto the God of Jacob.

2 Take a psalm, and bring hither the timbrel, the pleasant harp with the psaltery.

3 Blow up the trumpet in the new moon, in the time appointed, on our solemn feast day.

4 For this *was* a statute for Israel, *and* a law of the God of Jacob.

5 This he ordained in Joseph *for* a testimony, when he went out through the land of Egypt: *where* I heard a language *that* I understood not.

6 I removed his shoulder from the burden: his hands were delivered from the pots.

7 Thou calledst in trouble, and I delivered thee; I answered thee in the secret place of thunder: I proved thee at the waters of Meribah. Selah.

8 Hear, O my people, and I will testify unto thee: O Israel, if thou wilt hearken unto me;

9 There shall no strange god be in thee; neither shalt thou worship any strange god.

10 I *am* the LORD thy God, which brought thee out of the land of Egypt: open thy mouth wide, and I will fill it.

11 But my people would not hearken to my voice; and Israel would none of me.

12 So I gave them up unto their own hearts' lust: *and* they walked in their own counsels.

13 Oh that my people had hearkened unto me, *and* Israel had walked in my ways!

14 I should soon have subdued their enemies, and turned my hand against their adversaries.

15 The haters of the LORD should have submitted themselves unto him: but their time should have endured for ever.

16 He should have fed them also with the finest of the wheat: and with honey out of the rock should I have satisfied thee.

PSALM 85.—1 *The psalmist, out of the experience of former mercies, prayeth for the continuance thereof.* 8 *He promiseth to wait thereon, out of confidence of God's goodness.*

To the chief Musician, A Psalm for the sons of Korah.

1 LORD, thou hast been favourable unto thy land: thou hast brought back the captivity of Jacob.

2 Thou hast forgiven the iniquity of thy people, thou hast covered all their sin. Selah.

3 Thou hast taken away all thy wrath: thou hast turned *thyself* from the fierceness of thine anger.

4 Turn us, O God of our salvation, and cause thine anger toward us to cease.

5 Wilt thou be angry with us for ever? wilt thou draw out thine anger to all generations?

6 Wilt thou not revive us again: that thy people may rejoice in thee?

7 Shew us thy mercy, O LORD, and grant us thy salvation.

8 I will hear what God the LORD will speak: for he will speak peace unto his people, and to his saints: but let them not turn again to folly.

9 Surely his salvation *is* nigh them that fear him; that glory may dwell in our land.

10 Mercy and truth are met together; righteousness and peace have kissed *each other*.

11 Truth shall spring out of the earth; and righteousness shall look down from heaven.

12 Yea, the LORD shall give *that which is* good; and our land shall yield her increase.

13 Righteousness shall go before him; and shall set *us* in the way of his steps.

PSALM 98.—1 *The psalmist exhorteth the Jews,* 4 *the Gentiles,* 7 *and all the creatures to praise God.*

A PSALM.

1 O sing unto the LORD a new song; for he hath done marvellous things: his right hand, and his holy arm, hath gotten him the victory.

2 The LORD hath made known his salvation: his righteousness hath he openly shewed in the sight of the heathen.

3 He hath remembered his mercy and his truth toward the house of Israel: all the ends of the earth have seen the salvation of our God.

4 Make a joyful noise unto the LORD, all the earth: make a loud noise, and rejoice, and sing praise.

5 Sing unto the LORD with the harp; with the harp, and the voice of a psalm.

6 With trumpets and sound of cornet make a joyful noise before the LORD, the King.

7 Let the sea roar, and the fulness thereof; the world, and they that dwell therein.

8 Let the floods clap *their* hands: let the hills be joyful together

9 Before the LORD; for he cometh to judge the earth: with righteousness shall he judge the world, and the people with equity.

PSALM 105.—1 *An exhortation to praise God, and to seek out his works.* 7 *The story of God's providence over Abraham,* 16 *over Joseph,* 23 *over Jacob in Egypt,* 26 *over Moses delivering the Israelites,* 37 *over the Israelites brought out of Egypt, fed in the wilderness, and planted in Canaan.*

1 O give thanks unto the LORD; call upon his name: make known his deeds among the people.

2 Sing unto him, sing psalms unto him: talk ye of all his wondrous works.

3 Glory ye in his holy name: let the heart of them rejoice that seek the LORD.

4 Seek the LORD, and his strength: seek his face evermore.

5 Remember his marvellous works that he hath done; his wonders, and the judgments of his mouth;

6 O ye seed of Abraham his servant, ye children of Jacob his chosen.

7 He *is* the LORD our God: his judgments *are* in all the earth.

8 He hath remembered his covenant for ever, the word *which* he commanded to a thousand generations.

9 Which *covenant* he made with Abraham, and his oath unto Isaac;

10 And confirmed the same unto Jacob for a law, *and* to Israel *for* an everlasting covenant:

11 Saying, Unto thee will I give the land of Canaan, the lot of your inheritance:

12 When they were *but* a few men in number; yea, very few, and strangers in it.

13 When they went from one nation to another, from *one* kingdom to another people;

14 He suffered no man to do them wrong: yea, he reproved kings for their sakes;

15 *Saying,* Touch not mine anointed, and do my prophets no harm.

16 Moreover he called for a famine upon the land: he brake the whole staff of bread.

17 He sent a man before them, *even* Joseph, *who* was sold for a servant:

18 Whose feet they hurt with fetters: he was laid in iron:

19 Until the time that his word came: the word of the LORD tried him.

20 The king sent and loosed him; *even* the ruler of the people, and let him go free.

21 He made him lord of his house, and ruler of all his substance:

22 To bind his princes at his pleasure; and teach his senators wisdom.

23 Israel also came into Egypt; and Jacob sojourned in the land of Ham.

24 And he increased his people greatly; and made them stronger than their enemies.

25 He turned their heart to hate his people, to deal subtilly with his servants.

26 He sent Moses his servant; *and* Aaron whom he had chosen.

27 They shewed his signs among them, and wonders in the land of Ham.

28 He sent darkness, and made it dark; and they rebelled not against his word.

29 He turned their waters into blood, and slew their fish.

30 Their land brought forth frogs in abundance, in the chambers of their kings.

31 He spake, and there came divers sorts of flies, *and* lice in all their coasts.

32 He gave them hail for rain, *and* flaming fire in their land.

33 He smote their vines also and their fig trees; and brake the trees of their coasts.

34 He spake, and the locusts came, and caterpillers, and that without number,

35 And did eat up all the herbs in their land, and devoured the fruit of their ground.

36 He smote also all the firstborn in their land, the chief of all their strength.

37 He brought them forth also with silver and gold: and *there was* not one feeble *person* among their tribes.

38 Egypt was glad when they departed: for the fear of them fell upon them.

39 He spread a cloud for a covering; and fire to give light in the night.

40 *The people* asked, and he brought quails, and satisfied them with the bread of heaven.

41 He opened the rock, and the waters gushed out; they ran in the dry places *like* a river.

42 For he remembered his holy promise, *and* Abraham his servant.

43 And he brought forth his people with joy, *and* his chosen with gladness:

44 And gave them the lands of the heathen: and they inherited the labour of the people;

45 That they might observe his statutes, and keep his laws. Praise ye the LORD.

PSALM 124.—*The church blesseth God for a miraculous deliverance.*

A Song of degrees of David.

1 If *it had not been* the LORD who was on our side, now may Israel say;

2 If *it had not been* the LORD who was on our side, when men rose up against us:

3 Then they had swallowed us up quick, when their wrath was kindled against us:

4 Then the waters had overwhelmed us, the stream had gone over our soul:

5 Then the proud waters had gone over our soul.

6 Blessed *be* the LORD, who hath not given us *as* a prey to their teeth.

7 Our soul is escaped as a bird out of the snare of the fowlers: the snare is broken, and we are escaped.

8 Our help *is* in the name of the LORD, who made heaven and earth.

PSALM 126.—1 *The church, celebrating her incredible return out of captivity,* 4 *prayeth for, and prophesieth the good success thereof.*

A Song of degrees.

1 When the LORD turned again the captivity of Zion, we were like them that dream.

2 Then was our mouth filled with laughter, and our tongue with singing: then said they among the heathen, The LORD hath done great things for them.

3 The LORD hath done great things for us; *whereof* we are glad.

4 Turn again our captivity, O LORD, as the streams in the south.

5 They that sow in tears shall reap in joy.

6 He that goeth forth and weepeth, bearing precious seed, shall doubtless come again with rejoicing, bringing his sheaves *with him.*

PSALM 129.—1 *An exhortation to praise God for saving Israel in their great afflictions.* 5 *The haters of the church are cursed.*

A Song of degrees.

1 Many a time have they afflicted me from my youth, may Israel now say:

2 Many a time have they afflicted me from my youth: yet they have not prevailed against me.

3 The plowers plowed upon my back: they made long their furrows.

4 The LORD *is* righteous: he hath cut asunder the cords of the wicked.

5 Let them all be confounded and turned back that hate Zion.

6 Let them be as the grass *upon* the housetops, which withereth afore it groweth up:

7 Wherewith the mower filleth not his hand; nor he that bindeth sheaves his bosom.

8 Neither do they which go by say, The blessing of the LORD *be* upon you: we bless you in the name of the LORD.

PSALM 135.—1 *An exhortation to praise God for his mercy,* 5 *for his power,* 8 *for his judgments.* 15 *The vanity of idols.* 19 *An exhortation to bless God.*

1 Praise ye the LORD. Praise ye the name of the LORD; praise *him*, O ye servants of the LORD.

2 Ye that stand in the house of the LORD, in the courts of the house of our God,

3 Praise the LORD; for the LORD *is* good: sing praises unto his name; for *it is* pleasant.

4 For the LORD hath chosen Jacob unto himself, *and* Israel for his peculiar treasure.

5 For I know that the LORD *is* great, and *that* our Lord *is* above all gods.

6 Whatsoever the LORD pleased, *that* did he in heaven, and in earth, in the seas, and all deep places.

7 He causeth the vapours to ascend from the ends of the earth; he maketh lightnings for the rain; he bringeth the wind out of his treasuries.

8 Who smote the firstborn of Egypt, both of man and beast.

9 *Who* sent tokens and wonders into the midst of thee, O Egypt, upon Pharaoh, and upon all his servants.

10 Who smote great nations, and slew mighty kings;

11 Sihon king of the Amorites, and Og king of Bashan, and all the kingdoms of Canaan:

12 And gave their land *for* an heritage, an heritage unto Israel his people.

13 Thy name, O LORD, *endureth* forever; *and* thy memorial, O LORD, throughout all generations.

14 For the LORD will judge his people, and he will repent himself concerning his servants.

15 The idols of the heathen *are* silver and gold, the work of men's hands.

16 They have mouths, but they speak not; eyes have they, but they see not;

17 They have ears, but they hear not; neither is there *any* breath in their mouths.

18 They that make them are like unto them: *so is* every one that trusteth in them.

19 Bless the LORD, O house of Israel: bless the LORD, O house of Aaron:

20 Bless the LORD, O house of Levi: ye that fear the LORD, bless the LORD.

21 Blessed be the LORD out of Zion, which dwelleth at Jerusalem. Praise ye the LORD.

PSALM 136.—*An exhortation to give thanks to God for particular mercies.*

1 O give thanks unto the LORD; for *he is* good: for his mercy *endureth* for ever.

2 O give thanks unto the God of gods: for his mercy *endureth* for ever.

3 O give thanks to the Lord of lords: for his mercy *endureth* for ever.

4 To him who alone doeth great wonders: for his mercy *endureth* for ever.

5 To him that by wisdom made the heavens: for his mercy *endureth* for ever.

6 To him that stretched out the earth above the waters: for his mercy *endureth* for ever.

7 To him that made great lights: for his mercy *endureth* for ever:

8 The sun to rule by day: for his mercy *endureth* for ever:

9 The moon and stars to rule by night: for his mercy *endureth* for ever.

10 To him that smote Egypt in their firstborn: for his mercy *endureth* for ever:

11 And brought out Israel from among them: for his mercy *endureth* for ever:

12 With a strong hand, and with a stretched out arm: for his mercy *endureth* for ever.

13 To him which divided the Red sea into parts: for his mercy *endureth* for ever:

14 And made Israel to pass through the midst of it: for his mercy *endureth* for ever:

15 But overthrew Pharaoh and his host in the Red sea: for his mercy *endureth* for ever.

16 To him which led his people through the wilderness: for his mercy *endureth* for ever.

17 To him which smote great kings: for his mercy *endureth* for ever:

18 And slew famous kings: for his mercy *endureth* for ever:

19 Sihon king of the Amorites: for his mercy *endureth* for ever:

20 And Og the king of Bashan: for his mercy *endureth* for ever:

21 And gave their land for an heritage: for his mercy *endureth* for ever:

22 *Even* an heritage unto Israel his servant: for his mercy *endureth* for ever.

23 Who remembered us in our low estate: for his mercy *endureth* for ever:

24 And hath redeemed us from our enemies: for his mercy *endureth* for ever.

25 Who giveth food to all flesh: for his mercy *endureth* for ever.

26 O give thanks unto the God of heaven: for his mercy *endureth* for ever.

PSALM 149.—1 *The prophet exhorteth to praise God for his love to the church,* 5 *and for that power which he hath given to the church.*

1 Praise ye the LORD. Sing unto the LORD a new song, *and* his praise in the congregation of saints.

2 Let Israel rejoice in him that made him: let the children of Zion be joyful in their King.

3 Let them praise his name in the dance: let them sing praises unto him with the timbrel and harp.

4 For the LORD taketh pleasure in his people: he will beautify the meek with salvation.

5 Let the saints be joyful in glory: let them sing aloud upon their beds.

6 *Let* the high *praises* of God *be* in their mouth, and a twoedged sword in their hand;

7 To execute vengeance upon the heathen, *and* punishments upon the people;

8 To bind their kings with chains, and their nobles with fetters of iron;

9 To execute upon them the judgment written: this honour have all his saints. Praise ye the LORD.

FOR GOD'S GOODNESS TO GOOD MEN:

PSALM 23.—*David's confidence in God's grace.*

A PSALM OF DAVID.

1 The LORD *is* my shepherd; I shall not want.

2 He maketh me to lie down in green pastures: he leadeth me beside the still waters.

3 He restoreth my soul: he leadeth me in the paths of righteousness for his name's sake.

4 Yea, though I walk through the valley of the shadow of death, I will fear no evil: for thou *art* with me; thy rod and thy staff they comfort me.

5 Thou preparest a table before me in the presence of mine enemies: thou anointest my head with oil; my cup runneth over.

6 Surely goodness and mercy shall follow me all the days of my life: and I will dwell in the house of the LORD for ever.

PSALM 34.—1 *David praiseth God, and exhorteth others thereto by his experience.* 8 *They are blessed that trust in God.* 11 *He exhorteth to the fear of God.* 15 *The privileges of the righteous.*

A PSALM OF DAVID, WHEN HE CHANGED HIS BEHAVIOUR BEFORE ABIMELECH; WHO DROVE HIM AWAY, AND HE DEPARTED.

1 I will bless the LORD at all times: his praise *shall* continually *be* in my mouth.

2 My soul shall make her boast in the LORD: the humble shall hear *thereof,* and be glad.

3 O magnify the LORD with me, and let us exalt his name together.

4 I sought the LORD, and he heard me, and delivered me from all my fears.

5 They looked unto him, and were lightened: and their faces were not ashamed.

6 This poor man cried, and the LORD heard *him,* and saved him out of all his troubles.

7 The angel of the LORD encampeth round about them that fear him, and delivereth them.

8 O taste and see that the LORD *is* good: blessed *is* the man *that* trusteth in him.

9 O fear the LORD, ye his saints: for *there is* no want to them that fear him.

10 The young lions do lack, and suffer hunger: but they that seek the LORD shall not want any good *thing.*

11 Come, ye children, hearken unto me: I will teach you the fear of the LORD.

12 What man *is he that* desireth life, *and* loveth *many* days, that he may see good?

13 Keep thy tongue from evil, and thy lips from speaking guile.

14 Depart from evil, and do good; seek peace, and pursue it.

15 The eyes of the LORD *are* upon the righteous, and his ears *are open* unto their cry.

16 The face of the LORD *is* against them that do evil, to cut off the remembrance of them from the earth.

17 *The righteous* cry, and the LORD heareth, and delivereth them out of all their troubles.

18 The LORD *is* nigh unto them that are of a broken heart; and saveth such as be of a contrite spirit.

19 Many *are* the afflictions of the righteous: but the LORD delivereth him out of them all.

20 He keepeth all his bones: not one of them is broken.

21 Evil shall slay the wicked: and they that hate the righteous shall be desolate.

22 The LORD redeemeth the soul of his servants: and none of them that trust in him shall be desolate.

PSALM 36.—1 *The grievous estate of the wicked.* 5 *The excellency of God's mercy.* 10 *David prayeth for favour to God's children.*

TO THE CHIEF MUSICIAN, A PSALM OF DAVID THE SERVANT OF THE LORD.

1 The transgression of the wicked saith within my heart, *that there is* no fear of God before his eyes.

2 For he flattereth himself in his own eyes, until his iniquity be found to be hateful.

3 The words of his mouth *are* iniquity and deceit: he hath left off to be wise, *and* to do good.

4 He deviseth mischief upon his bed; he setteth himself in a way *that is* not good; he abhorreth not evil.

5 Thy mercy, O LORD, *is* in the heavens; *and* thy faithfulness *reacheth* unto the clouds.

6 Thy righteousness *is* like the great mountains; thy judgments *are* a great deep: O LORD, thou preservest man and beast.

7 How excellent *is* thy lovingkindness, O God! therefore the children of men put their trust under the shadow of thy wings.

8 They shall be abundantly satisfied with the fatness of thy house; and thou shalt make them drink of the river of thy pleasures.

9 For with thee *is* the fountain of life: in thy light shall we see light.

10 O continue thy lovingkindness unto them that know thee; and thy righteousness to the upright in heart.

11 Let not the foot of pride come against me, and let not the hand of the wicked remove me.

12 There are the workers of iniquity fallen: they are cast down, and shall not be able to rise.

PSALM 91.—1 *The state of the godly.* 3 *Their safety.* 9 *Their habitation.* 11 *Their servants.* 14 *Their friend; with the effects of them all.*

1 He that dwelleth in the secret place of the most High shall abide under the shadow of the Almighty.

2 I will say of the LORD, *He is* my refuge and my fortress: my God; in him will I trust.

3 Surely he shall deliver thee from the snare of the fowler, *and* from the noisome pestilence.

4 He shall cover thee with his feathers, and under his wings shalt thou trust: his truth *shall be thy* shield and buckler.

5 Thou shalt not be afraid for the terror by night; *nor* for the arrow *that* flieth by day;

6 *Nor* for the pestilence *that* walketh in darkness; *nor* for the destruction *that* wasteth at noonday.

7 A thousand shall fall at thy side, and ten thousand at thy right hand; *but* it shall not come nigh thee.

8 Only with thine eyes shalt thou behold and see the reward of the wicked.

9 Because thou hast made the LORD, *which is* my refuge, *even* the most High, thy habitation;

10 There shall no evil befall thee, neither shall any plague come nigh thy dwelling.

11 For he shall give his angels charge over thee, to keep thee in all thy ways.

12 They shall bear thee up in *their* hands, lest thou dash thy foot against a stone.

13 Thou shalt tread upon the lion and adder: the young lion and the dragon shalt thou trample under feet.

14 Because he hath set his love upon me, therefore will I deliver him: I will set him on high, because he hath known my name.

15 He shall call upon me, and I will answer him: I *will be* with him in trouble; I will deliver him, and honour him.

16 With long life will I satisfy him, and shew him my salvation.

PSALM 100.—1 *An exhortation to praise God cheerfully,* 3 *for his greatness,* 4 *and for his power.*

A PSALM OF PRAISE.

1 Make a joyful noise unto the LORD, all ye lands.

2 Serve the LORD with gladness: come before his presence with singing.

3 Know ye that the LORD he *is* God: *it is* he *that* hath made us, and not we ourselves; *we are* his people, and the sheep of his pasture.

4 Enter into his gates with thanksgiving, *and* into his courts with praise: be thankful unto him, *and* bless his name.

5 For the LORD *is* good; his mercy *is* everlasting; and his truth *endureth* to all generations.

PSALM 103.—1 *An exhortation to bless God for his mercy,* 15 *and for the constancy thereof.*

A PSALM OF DAVID.

1 Bless the LORD, O my soul: and all that is within me, *bless* his holy name.

2 Bless the LORD, O my soul, and forget not all his benefits:

3 Who forgiveth all thine iniquities; who healeth all thy diseases;

4 Who redeemeth thy life from destruction; who crowneth thee with lovingkindness and tender mercies;

5 Who satisfieth thy mouth with good *things; so that* thy youth is renewed like the eagle's.

6 The LORD executeth righteousness and judgment for all that are oppressed.

7 He made known his ways unto Moses, his acts unto the children of Israel.

8 The LORD *is* merciful and gracious, slow to anger, and plenteous in mercy.

9 He will not always chide: neither will he keep *his anger* for ever.

10 He hath not dealt with us after our sins; nor rewarded us according to our iniquities.

11 For as the heaven is high above the earth, *so* great is his mercy toward them that fear him.

12 As far as the east is from the west, *so* far hath he removed our transgressions from us.

13 Like as a father pitieth *his* children, *so* the LORD pitieth them that fear him.

14 For he knoweth our frame; he remembereth that we *are* dust.

15 *As for* man, his days *are* as grass: as a flower of the field, so he flourisheth.

16 For the wind passeth over it, and it is gone; and the place thereof shall know it no more.

17 But the mercy of the LORD *is* from everlasting to everlasting upon them that fear him, and his righteousness unto children's children;

18 To such as keep his covenant, and to those that remember his commandments to do them.

19 The LORD hath prepared his throne in the heavens; and his kingdom ruleth over all.

20 Bless the LORD, ye his angels, that excel in strength, that do his commandments, hearkening unto the voice of his word.

21 Bless ye the LORD, all *ye* his hosts; *ye* ministers of his, that do his pleasure.

22 Bless the LORD, all his works in all places of his dominion: bless the LORD, O my soul.

PSALM 107.—1 *The psalmist exhorteth the redeemed, in praising God, to observe his manifold providence,* 4 *over travellers,* 10 *over captives,* 17 *over sick men,* 23 *over seamen,* 33 *and in divers varieties of life.*

1 O give thanks unto the LORD, for *he is* good: for his mercy *endureth* for ever.

2 Let the redeemed of the LORD say *so,* whom he hath redeemed from the hand of the enemy;

3 And gathered them out of the lands, from the east, and from the west, from the north, and from the south.

4 They wandered in the wilderness in a solitary way; they found no city to dwell in.

5 Hungry and thirsty, their soul fainted in them.

6 Then they cried unto the LORD in their trouble, *and* he delivered them out of their distresses.

7 And he led them forth by the right way, that they might go to a city of habitation.

8 Oh that *men* would praise the LORD *for* his goodness, and *for* his wonderful works to the children of men!

9 For he satisfieth the longing soul, and filleth the hungry soul with goodness.

10 Such as sit in darkness and in the shadow of death, *being* bound in affliction and iron;

11 Because they rebelled against the words of God, and contemned the counsel of the most High:

12 Therefore he brought down their heart with labour; they fell down, and *there was* none to help.

13 Then they cried unto the LORD in their trouble, *and* he saved them out of their distresses.

14 He brought them out of darkness and the shadow of death, and brake their bands in sunder.

15 Oh that *men* would praise the LORD *for* his goodness, and *for* his wonderful works to the children of men!

16 For he hath broken the gates of brass, and cut the bars of iron in sunder.

17 Fools because of their transgression, and because of their iniquities, are afflicted.

18 Their soul abhorreth all manner of meat; and they draw near unto the gates of death.

19 Then they cry unto the LORD in their trouble, *and* he saveth them out of their distresses.

20 He sent his word, and healed them, and delivered *them* from their destructions.

21 Oh that *men* would praise the LORD *for* his goodness, and *for* his wonderful works to the children of men!

22 And let them sacrifice the sacrifices of thanksgiving, and declare his works with rejoicing.

23 They that go down to the sea in ships, that do business in great waters;

24 These see the works of the LORD, and his wonders in the deep.

25 For he commandeth, and raiseth the stormy wind, which lifteth up the waves thereof.

26 They mount up to the heaven, they go down again to the depths: their soul is melted because of trouble.

27 They reel to and fro, and stagger like a drunken man, and are at their wit's end.

28 Then they cry unto the LORD in their trouble, and he bringeth them out of their distresses.

29 He maketh the storm a calm, so that the waves thereof are still.

30 Then are they glad because they be quiet; so he bringeth them unto their desired haven.

31 Oh that *men* would praise the LORD *for* his goodness, and *for* his wonderful works to the children of men!

32 Let them exalt him also in the congregation of the people, and praise him in the assembly of the elders.

33 He turneth rivers into a wilderness, and the watersprings into dry ground;

34 A fruitful land into barrenness, for the wickedness of them that dwell therein.

35 He turneth the wilderness into a standing water, and dry ground into watersprings.

36 And there he maketh the hungry to dwell, that they may prepare a city for habitation;

37 And sow the fields, and plant vineyards, which may yield fruits of increase.

38 He blesseth them also, so that they are multiplied greatly; and suffereth not their cattle to decrease.

39 Again, they are minished and brought low through oppression, affliction, and sorrow.

40 He poureth contempt upon princes, and causeth them to wander in the wilderness, *where there is* no way.

41 Yet setteth he the poor on high from affliction, and maketh *him* families like a flock.

42 The righteous shall see *it*, and rejoice: and all iniquity shall stop her mouth.

43 Whoso *is* wise, and will observe these *things*, even they shall understand the lovingkindness of the LORD.

PSALM 117.—*An exhortation to praise God for his mercy and truth.*

1 O praise the LORD, all ye nations: praise him, all ye people.

2 For his merciful kindness is great toward us: and the truth of the LORD *endureth* for ever. Praise ye the LORD.

PSALM 121.—*The great safety of the godly, who put their trust in God's protection.*

A SONG OF DEGREES.

1 I will lift up mine eyes unto the hills, from whence cometh my help.

2 My help *cometh* from the LORD, which made heaven and earth.

3 He will not suffer thy foot to be moved: he that keepeth thee will not slumber.

4 Behold, he that keepeth Israel shall neither slumber nor sleep.

5 The LORD *is* thy keeper: the LORD *is* thy shade upon thy right hand.

6 The sun shall not smite thee by day, nor the moon by night.

7 The LORD shall preserve thee from all evil: he shall preserve thy soul.

8 The LORD shall preserve thy going out and thy coming in from this time forth, and even for evermore.

PSALM 145.—1 *David praiseth God for his fame,* 8 *for his goodness,* 11 *for his kingdom,* 14 *for his providence,* 17 *for his saving mercy.*

DAVID'S PSALM OF PRAISE.

1 I will extol thee, my God, O king; and I will bless thy name for ever and ever.

2 Every day will I bless thee; and I will praise thy name for ever and ever.

3 Great *is* the LORD, and greatly to be praised; and his greatness *is* unsearchable.

4 One generation shall praise thy works to another, and shall declare thy mighty acts.

5 I will speak of the glorious honour of thy majesty, and of thy wondrous works.

6 And *men* shall speak of the might of thy terrible acts: and I will declare thy greatness.

7 They shall abundantly utter the memory of thy great goodness, and shall sing of thy righteousness.

8 The LORD *is* gracious, and full of compassion; slow to anger, and of great mercy.

9 The LORD *is* good to all: and his tender mercies *are* over all his works.

10 All thy works shall praise thee, O LORD; and thy saints shall bless thee.

11 They shall speak of the glory of thy kingdom, and talk of thy power;

12 To make known to the sons of men his mighty acts, and the glorious majesty of his kingdom.

13 Thy kingdom *is* an everlasting kingdom, and thy dominion *endureth* throughout all generations.

14 The LORD upholdeth all that fall, and raiseth up all *those that be* bowed down.

15 The eyes of all wait upon thee; and thou givest them their meat in due season.

16 Thou openest thine hand, and satisfiest the desire of every living thing.

17 The LORD *is* righteous in all his ways, and holy in all his works.

18 The LORD *is* nigh unto all them that call upon him, to all that call upon him in truth.

19 He will fulfil the desire of them that fear him: he also will hear their cry, and will save them.

20 The LORD preserveth all them that love him: but all the wicked will he destroy.

21 My mouth shall speak the praise of the LORD: and let all flesh bless his holy name for ever and ever.

PSALM 146.—1 *The psalmist voweth perpetual praises to God.* 3 *He exhorteth not to trust in man.* 5 *God, for his power, justice, mercy, and kingdom, is only worthy to be trusted.*

1 Praise ye the LORD. Praise the LORD, O my soul.

2 While I live will I praise the LORD: I will sing praises unto my God while I have any being.

3 Put not your trust in princes, *nor* in the son of man, in whom *there is* no help.

4 His breath goeth forth, he returneth to his earth; in that very day his thoughts perish.

5 Happy *is he* that *hath* the God of Jacob for his help, whose hope *is* in the LORD his God:

6 Which made heaven, and earth, the sea, and all that therein *is:* which keepeth truth for ever:

7 Which executeth judgment for the oppressed: which giveth food to the hungry. The LORD looseth the prisoners:

8 The LORD openeth *the eyes of* the blind: the LORD raiseth them that are bowed down: the LORD loveth the righteous:

9 The LORD preserveth the strangers; he relieveth the fatherless and widow: but the way of the wicked he turneth upside down.

10 The LORD shall reign for ever, *even* thy

God, O Zion, unto all generations. Praise ye the LORD.

FOR GOD'S MERCIES TO INDIVIDUALS:

PSALM 9.—1 *David praiseth God for executing of judgment.* 11 *He inciteth others to praise him.* 13 *He prayeth that he may have cause to praise him.*

To THE CHIEF MUSICIAN UPON MUTH-LABBEN, A PSALM OF DAVID.

1 I will praise *thee*, O LORD, with my whole heart; I will shew forth all thy marvellous works.

2 I will be glad and rejoice in thee: I will sing praise to thy name, O thou most High.

3 When mine enemies are turned back, they shall fall and perish at thy presence.

4 For thou hast maintained my right and my cause; thou satest in the throne judging right.

5 Thou hast rebuked the heathen, thou hast destroyed the wicked, thou hast put out their name for ever and ever.

6 O thou enemy, destructions are come to a perpetual end: and thou hast destroyed cities; their memorial is perished with them.

7 But the LORD shall endure for ever: he hath prepared his throne for judgment.

8 And he shall judge the world in righteousness, he shall minister judgment to the people in uprightness.

9 The LORD also will be a refuge for the oppressed, a refuge in times of trouble.

10 And they that know thy name will put their trust in thee: for thou, LORD, hast not forsaken them that seek thee.

11 Sing praises to the LORD, which dwelleth in Zion: declare among the people his doings.

12 When he maketh inquisition for blood, he remembereth them: he forgetteth not the cry of the humble.

13 Have mercy upon me, O LORD; consider my trouble *which I suffer* of them that hate me, thou that liftest me up from the gates of death:

14 That I may shew forth all thy praise in the gates of the daughter of Zion: I will rejoice in thy salvation.

15 The heathen are sunk down in the pit *that* they made: in the net which they hid is their own foot taken.

16 The LORD is known *by* the judgment *which* he executeth: the wicked is snared in the work of his own hands. Higgaion. Selah.

17 The wicked shall be turned into hell, *and* all the nations that forget God.

18 For the needy shall not alway be forgotten: the expectation of the poor shall *not* perish for ever.

19 Arise, O LORD; let not man prevail: let the heathen be judged in thy sight.

20 Put them in fear, O LORD: *that* the nations may know themselves *to be but* men. Selah.

PSALM 18.—*David praiseth God for his manifold and marvellous blessings.*

To THE CHIEF MUSICIAN, A PSALM OF DAVID, THE SERVANT OF THE LORD, WHO SPAKE UNTO THE LORD THE WORDS OF THIS SONG IN THE DAY THAT THE LORD DELIVERED HIM FROM THE HAND OF ALL HIS ENEMIES, AND FROM THE HAND OF SAUL: AND HE SAID,

1 I will love thee, O LORD, my strength.

2 The LORD *is* my rock, and my fortress, and my deliverer; my God, my strength, in whom I will trust; my buckler, and the horn of my salvation, *and* my high tower.

3 I will call upon the LORD, *who is worthy* to be praised: so shall I be saved from mine enemies.

4 The sorrows of death compassed me, and the floods of ungodly men made me afraid.

5 The sorrows of hell compassed me about: the snares of death prevented me.

6 In my distress I called upon the LORD, and cried unto my God: he heard my voice out of his temple, and my cry came before him, *even* into his ears.

7 Then the earth shook and trembled; the foundations also of the hills moved and were shaken, because he was wroth.

8 There went up a smoke out of his nostrils, and fire out of his mouth devoured: coals were kindled by it.

9 He bowed the heavens also, and came down: and darkness *was* under his feet.

10 And he rode upon a cherub, and did fly: yea, he did fly upon the wings of the wind.

11 He made darkness his secret place; his pavilion round about him *were* dark waters *and* thick clouds of the skies.

12 At the brightness *that was* before him his thick clouds passed, hail *stones* and coals of fire.

13 The LORD also thundered in the heavens, and the Highest gave his voice; hail *stones* and coals of fire.

14 Yea, he sent out his arrows, and scattered them; and he shot out lightnings, and discomfited them.

15 Then the channels of waters were seen, and the foundations of the world were discovered at thy rebuke, O LORD, at the blast of the breath of thy nostrils.

16 He sent from above, he took me, he drew me out of many waters.

17 He delivered me from my strong enemy, and from them which hated me: for they were too strong for me.

18 They prevented me in the day of my calamity: but the LORD was my stay.

19 He brought me forth also into a large place; he delivered me, because he delighted in me.

20 The LORD rewarded me according to my righteousness; according to the cleanness of my hands hath he recompensed me.

21 For I have kept the ways of the LORD, and have not wickedly departed from my God.

22 For all his judgments *were* before me, and I did not put away his statutes from me.

23 I was also upright before him, and I kept myself from mine iniquity.

24 Therefore hath the LORD recompensed me according to my righteousness, according to the cleanness of my hands in his eyesight.

25 With the merciful thou wilt shew thyself merciful; with an upright man thou wilt shew thyself upright;

26 With the pure thou wilt shew thyself pure; and with the froward thou wilt shew thyself froward.

27 For thou wilt save the afflicted people; but wilt bring down high looks.

28 For thou wilt light my candle: the LORD my God will enlighten my darkness.

29 For by thee I have run through a troop; and by my God have I leaped over a wall.

30 As for God, his way is perfect: the word of the LORD is tried: he is a buckler to all those that trust in him.

31 For who is God save the LORD? or who is a rock save our God?

32 It is God that girdeth me with strength, and maketh my way perfect.

33 He maketh my feet like hinds' feet, and setteth me upon my high places.

34 He teacheth my hands to war, so that a bow of steel is broken by mine arms.

35 Thou hast also given me the shield of thy salvation: and thy right hand hath holden me up, and thy gentleness hath made me great.

36 Thou hast enlarged my steps under me, that my feet did not slip.

37 I have pursued mine enemies, and overtaken them: neither did I turn again till they were consumed.

38 I have wounded them that they were not able to rise: they are fallen under my feet.

39 For thou hast girded me with strength unto the battle: thou hast subdued under me those that rose up against me.

40 Thou hast also given me the necks of mine enemies; that I might destroy them that hate me.

41 They cried, but there was none to save them: even unto the LORD, but he answered them not.

42 Then did I beat them small as the dust before the wind: I did cast them out as the dirt in the streets.

43 Thou hast delivered me from the strivings of the people; and thou hast made me the head of the heathen: a people whom I have not known shall serve me.

44 As soon as they hear of me, they shall obey me: the strangers shall submit themselves unto me.

45 The strangers shall fade away, and be afraid out of their close places.

46 The LORD liveth; and blessed be my rock; and let the God of my salvation be exalted.

47 It is God that avengeth me, and subdueth the people under me.

48 He delivereth me from mine enemies: yea, thou liftest me up above those that rise up against me: thou hast delivered me from the violent man.

49 Therefore will I give thanks unto thee, O LORD, among the heathen, and sing praises unto thy name.

50 Great deliverance giveth he to his king; and sheweth mercy to his anointed, to David, and to his seed for evermore.

PSALM 30.—1 David praiseth God for his deliverance. 4 He exhorteth others to praise him by example of God's dealing with him.

A PSALM AND SONG AT THE DEDICATION OF THE HOUSE OF DAVID.

1 I will extol thee, O LORD; for thou hast lifted me up, and hast not made my foes to rejoice over me.

2 O LORD my God, I cried unto thee, and thou hast healed me.

3 O LORD, thou hast brought up my soul from the grave: thou hast kept me alive, that I should not go down to the pit.

4 Sing unto the LORD, O ye saints of his, and give thanks at the remembrance of his holiness.

5 For his anger endureth but a moment; in his favour is life: weeping may endure for a night, but joy cometh in the morning.

6 And in my prosperity I said, I shall never be moved.

7 LORD, by thy favour thou hast made my mountain to stand strong: thou didst hide thy face, and I was troubled.

8 I cried to thee, O LORD; and unto the LORD I made supplication.

9 What profit is there in my blood, when I go down to the pit? Shall the dust praise thee? shall it declare thy truth?

10 Hear, O LORD, and have mercy upon me: LORD, be thou my helper.

11 Thou hast turned for me my mourning into dancing: thou hast put off my sackcloth, and girded me with gladness;

12 To the end that my glory may sing praise to thee, and not be silent. O LORD my God, I will give thanks unto thee for ever.

PSALM 34.—1 David praiseth God, and exhorteth others thereto by his experience. 8 They are blessed that trust in God. 11 He exhorteth to the fear of God. 15 The privileges of the righteous.

A PSALM OF DAVID, WHEN HE CHANGED HIS BEHAVIOUR BEFORE ABIMELECH; WHO DROVE HIM AWAY, AND HE DEPARTED.

1 I will bless the LORD at all times: his praise shall continually be in my mouth.

2 My soul shall make her boast in the LORD: the humble shall hear thereof, and be glad.

3 O magnify the LORD with me, and let us exalt his name together.

4 I sought the LORD, and he heard me, and delivered me from all my fears.

5 They looked unto him, and were lightened: and their faces were not ashamed.

6 This poor man cried, and the LORD heard him, and saved him out of all his troubles.

7 The angel of the LORD encampeth round

about them that fear him, and delivereth them.

8 O taste and see that the LORD *is* good: blessed *is* the man *that* trusteth in him.

9 O fear the LORD, ye his saints: for *there is* no want to them that fear him.

10 The young lions do lack, and suffer hunger: but they that seek the LORD shall not want any good *thing*.

11 Come, ye children, hearken unto me: I will teach you the fear of the LORD.

12 What man *is he that* desireth life, *and* loveth *many* days, that he may see good?

13 Keep thy tongue from evil, and thy lips from speaking guile.

14 Depart from evil, and do good; seek peace, and pursue it.

15 The eyes of the LORD *are* upon the righteous, and his ears *are open* unto their cry.

16 The face of the LORD *is* against them that do evil, to cut off the remembrance of them from the earth.

17 *The righteous* cry, and the LORD heareth, and delivereth them out of all their troubles.

18 The LORD *is* nigh unto them that are of a broken heart; and saveth such as be of a contrite spirit.

19 Many *are* the afflictions of the righteous: but the LORD delivereth him out of them all.

20 He keepeth all his bones: not one of them is broken.

21 Evil shall slay the wicked: and they that hate the righteous shall be desolate.

22 The LORD redeemeth the soul of his servants: and none of them that trust in him shall be desolate.

PSALM 40.—1 *The benefit of confidence in God. 6 Obedience is the best sacrifice. 11 The sense of David's evils inflameth his prayer.*

To the chief Musician, A Psalm of David.

1 I waited patiently for the LORD; and he inclined unto me, and heard my cry.

2 He brought me up also out of an horrible pit, out of the miry clay, and set my feet upon a rock, *and* established my goings.

3 And he hath put a new song in my mouth, *even* praise unto our God: many shall see *it*, and fear, and shall trust in the LORD.

4 Blessed *is* that man that maketh the LORD his trust, and respecteth not the proud, nor such as turn aside to lies.

5 Many, O LORD my God, *are* thy wonderful works *which* thou hast done, and thy thoughts *which are* to us-ward: they cannot be reckoned up in order unto thee: *if* I would declare and speak *of them*, they are more than can be numbered.

6 Sacrifice and offering thou didst not desire; mine ears hast thou opened: burnt offering and sin offering hast thou not required.

7 Then said I; Lo, I come: in the volume of the book *it is* written of me,

8 I delight to do thy will, O my God: yea, thy law *is* within my heart.

9 I have preached righteousness in the great congregation: lo, I have not refrained my lips, O LORD, thou knowest.

10 I have not hid thy righteousness within my heart; I have declared thy faithfulness and thy salvation: I have not concealed thy lovingkindness and thy truth from the great congregation.

11 Withhold not thou thy tender mercies from me, O LORD: let thy lovingkindness and thy truth continually preserve me.

12 For innumerable evils have compassed me about: mine iniquities have taken hold upon me, so that I am not able to look up; they are more than the hairs of mine head: therefore my heart faileth me.

13 Be pleased, O LORD, to deliver me: O LORD, make haste to help me.

14 Let them be ashamed and confounded together that seek after my soul to destroy it; let them be driven backward and put to shame that wish me evil.

15 Let them be desolate for a reward of their shame that say unto me, Aha, aha.

16 Let all those that seek thee rejoice and be glad in thee: let such as love thy salvation say continually, The LORD be magnified.

17 But I *am* poor and needy; *yet* the Lord thinketh upon me: thou *art* my help and my deliverer; make no tarrying, O my God.

PSALM 75.—1 *The prophet praiseth God. 2 He promiseth to judge uprightly. 4 He rebuketh the proud by consideration of God's providence. 9 He praiseth God, and promiseth to execute justice.*

To the chief Musician, Al-taschith, A Psalm or Song of Asaph.

1 Unto thee, O God, do we give thanks, *unto thee* do we give thanks: for *that* thy name is near thy wondrous works declare.

2 When I shall receive the congregation I will judge uprightly.

3 The earth and all the inhabitants thereof are dissolved: I bear up the pillars of it. Selah.

4 I said unto the fools, Deal not foolishly: and to the wicked, Lift not up the horn:

5 Lift not up your horn on high: speak *not with* a stiff neck.

6 For promotion *cometh* neither from the east, nor from the west, nor from the south.

7 But God *is* the judge: he putteth down one, and setteth up another.

8 For in the hand of the LORD *there is* a cup, and the wine is red; it is full of mixture; and he poureth out of the same: but the dregs thereof, all the wicked of the earth shall wring *them* out, *and* drink *them*.

9 But I will declare for ever; I will sing praises to the God of Jacob.

10 All the horns of the wicked also will I cut off; *but* the horns of the righteous shall be exalted.

PSALM 103.—1 *An exhortation to bless God for his mercy*, 15 *and for the constancy thereof.*

A PSALM OF DAVID.

1 Bless the LORD, O my soul: and all that is within me, *bless* his holy name.

2 Bless the LORD, O my soul, and forget not all his benefits:

3 Who forgiveth all thine iniquities; who healeth all thy diseases;

4 Who redeemeth thy life from destruction; who crowneth thee with lovingkindness and tender mercies;

5 Who satisfieth thy mouth with good *things; so that* thy youth is renewed like the eagle's.

6 The LORD executeth righteousness and judgment for all that are oppressed.

7 He made known his ways unto Moses, his acts unto the children of Israel.

8 The LORD *is* merciful and gracious, slow to anger, and plenteous in mercy.

9 He will not always chide: neither will he keep *his anger* for ever.

10 He hath not dealt with us after our sins; nor rewarded us according to our iniquities.

11 For as the heaven is high above the earth, *so* great is his mercy toward them that fear him.

12 As far as the east is from the west, *so* far hath he removed our transgressions from us.

13 Like as a father pitieth *his* children, *so* the LORD pitieth them that fear him.

14 For he knoweth our frame; he remembereth that we *are* dust.

15 *As for* man, his days *are* as grass: as a flower of the field, so he flourisheth.

16 For the wind passeth over it, and it is gone; and the place thereof shall know it no more.

17 But the mercy of the LORD *is* from everlasting to everlasting upon them that fear him, and his righteousness unto children's children;

18 To such as keep his covenant, and to those that remember his commandments to do them.

19 The LORD hath prepared his throne in the heavens; and his kingdom ruleth over all.

20 Bless the LORD, ye his angels, that excel in strength, that do his commandments, hearkening unto the voice of his word.

21 Bless ye the LORD, all *ye* his hosts; *ye* ministers of his, that do his pleasure.

22 Bless the LORD, all his works in all places of his dominion: bless the LORD, O my soul.

PSALM 108.—1 *David encourageth himself to praise God.* 5 *He prayeth for God's assistance according to his promise.* 11 *His confidence in God's help.*

A SONG OR PSALM OF DAVID.

1 O God, my heart is fixed; I will sing and give praise, even with my glory.

2 Awake, psaltery and harp: I *myself* will awake early.

3 I will praise thee, O LORD, among the people: and I will sing praises unto thee among the nations.

4 For thy mercy *is* great above the heavens: and thy truth *reacheth* unto the clouds.

5 Be thou exalted, O God, above the heavens: and thy glory above all the earth;

6 That thy beloved may be delivered: save *with* thy right hand, and answer me.

7 God hath spoken in his holiness; I will rejoice, I will divide Shechem, and mete out the valley of Succoth.

8 Gilead *is* mine; Manasseh *is* mine; Ephraim also *is* the strength of mine head; Judah *is* my lawgiver;

9 Moab *is* my washpot; over Edom will I cast out my shoe; over Philistia will I triumph.

10 Who will bring me into the strong city? who will lead me into Edom?

11 *Wilt* not *thou*, O God, *who* hast cast us off? and wilt not thou, O God, go forth with our hosts?

12 Give us help from trouble: for vain *is* the help of man.

13 Through God we shall do valiantly: for he *it is that* shall tread down our enemies.

PSALM 116.—1 *The psalmist professeth his love and duty to God for his deliverance.* 12 *He studieth to be thankful.*

1 I love the LORD, because he hath heard my voice *and* my supplications.

2 Because he hath inclined his ear unto me, therefore will I call upon *him* as long as I live.

3 The sorrows of death compassed me, and the pains of hell gat hold upon me: I found trouble and sorrow.

4 Then called I upon the name of the LORD; O LORD, I beseech thee, deliver my soul.

5 Gracious *is* the LORD, and righteous; yea, our God *is* merciful.

6 The LORD preserveth the simple: I was brought low, and he helped me.

7 Return unto thy rest, O my soul; for the LORD hath dealt bountifully with thee.

8 For thou hast delivered my soul from death, mine eyes from tears, *and* my feet from falling.

9 I will walk before the LORD in the land of the living.

10 I believed, therefore have I spoken: I was greatly afflicted:

11 I said in my haste, All men *are* liars.

12 What shall I render unto the LORD *for* all his benefits toward me?

13 I will take the cup of salvation, and call upon the name of the LORD.

14 I will pay my vows unto the LORD now in the presence of all his people.

15 Precious in the sight of the LORD *is* the death of his saints.

16 O LORD, truly I *am* thy servant; I *am* thy servant, *and* the son of thine handmaid: thou hast loosed my bonds.

17 I will offer to thee the sacrifice of

thanksgiving, and will call upon the name of the Lord.

18 I will pay my vows unto the Lord now in the presence of all his people,

19 In the courts of the Lord's house, in the midst of thee, O Jerusalem. Praise ye the Lord.

PSALM 118.—1 *An exhortation to praise God for his mercy.* 5 *The psalmist by his experience sheweth how good it is to trust in God.* 19 *Under the type of the psalmist the coming of Christ in his kingdom is expressed.*

1 O give thanks unto the Lord; for *he is* good: because his mercy *endureth* for ever.

2 Let Israel now say, that his mercy *endureth* for ever.

3 Let the house of Aaron now say, that his mercy *endureth* for ever.

4 Let them now that fear the Lord say, that his mercy *endureth* for ever.

5 I called upon the Lord in distress: the Lord answered me, *and set me* in a large place.

6 The Lord *is* on my side; I will not fear: what can man do unto me?

7 The Lord taketh my part with them that help me: therefore shall I see *my desire* upon them that hate me.

8 *It is* better to trust in the Lord than to put confidence in man.

9 *It is* better to trust in the Lord than to put confidence in princes.

10 All nations compassed me about: but in the name of the Lord will I destroy them.

11 They compassed me about; yea, they compassed me about: but in the name of the Lord I will destroy them.

12 They compassed me about like bees; they are quenched as the fire of thorns: for in the name of the Lord I will destroy them.

13 Thou hast thrust sore at me that I might fall: but the Lord helped me.

14 The Lord *is* my strength and song, and is become my salvation.

15 The voice of rejoicing and salvation *is* in the tabernacles of the righteous: the right hand of the Lord doeth valiantly.

16 The right hand of the Lord is exalted: the right hand of the Lord doeth valiantly.

17 I shall not die, but live, and declare the works of the Lord.

18 The Lord hath chastened me sore: but he hath not given me over unto death.

19 Open to me the gates of righteousness: I will go into them, *and* I will praise the Lord:

20 This gate of the Lord, into which the righteous shall enter.

21 I will praise thee: for thou hast heard me, and art become my salvation.

22 The stone *which* the builders refused is become the head *stone* of the corner.

23 This is the Lord's doing; it *is* marvellous in our eyes.

24 This *is* the day *which* the Lord hath made; we will rejoice and be glad in it.

25 Save now, I beseech thee, O Lord: O Lord, I beseech thee, send now prosperity.

26 Blessed *be* he that cometh in the name of the Lord: we have blessed you out of the house of the Lord.

27 God *is* the Lord, which hath shewed us light: bind the sacrifice with cords, *even* unto the horns of the altar.

28 Thou *art* my God, and I will praise thee: *thou art* my God, I will exalt thee.

29 O give thanks unto the Lord; for *he is* good: for his mercy *endureth* for ever.

PSALM 138.—1 *David praiseth God for the truth of his word.* 4 *He prophesieth that the kings of the earth shall praise God.* 7 *He professeth his confidence in God.*

A Psalm of David.

1 I will praise thee with my whole heart: before the gods will I sing praise unto thee.

2 I will worship toward thy holy temple, and praise thy name for thy lovingkindness and for thy truth: for thou hast magnified thy word above all thy name.

3 In the day when I cried thou answeredst me, *and* strengthenedst me *with* strength in my soul.

4 All the kings of the earth shall praise thee, O Lord, when they hear the words of thy mouth.

5 Yea, they shall sing in the ways of the Lord: for great *is* the glory of the Lord.

6 Though the Lord *be* high, yet hath he respect unto the lowly: but the proud he knoweth afar off.

7 Though I walk in the midst of trouble, thou wilt revive me: thou shalt stretch forth thine hand against the wrath of mine enemies, and thy right hand shall save me.

8 The Lord will perfect *that which* concerneth me: thy mercy, O Lord, *endureth* for ever: forsake not the works of thine own hands.

PSALM 144.—1 *David blesseth God for his mercy both to him and to man.* 5 *He prayeth that God would powerfully deliver him from his enemies.* 9 *He promiseth to praise God.* 11 *He prayeth for the happy state of the kingdom.*

A Psalm of David.

1 Blessed *be* the Lord my strength, which teacheth my hands to war, *and* my fingers to fight:

2 My goodness, and my fortress; my high tower, and my deliverer; my shield, and *he* in whom I trust; who subdueth my people under me.

3 Lord, what *is* man, that thou takest knowledge of him! *or* the son of man, that thou makest account of him!

4 Man is like to vanity: his days *are* as a shadow that passeth away.

5 Bow thy heavens, O Lord, and come down: touch the mountains, and they shall smoke.

6 Cast forth lightning, and scatter them: shoot out thine arrows, and destroy them.

7 Send thine hand from above; rid me,

and deliver me out of great waters, from the hand of strange children;

8 Whose mouth speaketh vanity, and their right hand *is* a right hand of falsehood.

9 I will sing a new song unto thee, O God: upon a psaltery *and* an instrument of ten strings will I sing praises unto thee.

10 *It is he* that giveth salvation unto kings: who delivereth David his servant from the hurtful sword.

11 Rid me, and deliver me from the hand of strange children, whose mouth speaketh vanity, and their right hand *is* a right hand of falsehood:

12 That our sons *may be* as plants grown up in their youth; *that* our daughters *may be* as corner stones, polished *after* the similitude of a palace:

13 *That* our garners *may be* full, affording all manner of store: *that* our sheep may bring forth thousands and ten thousands in our streets:

14 *That* our oxen *may be* strong to labour; *that there be* no breaking in, nor going out; that *there be* no complaining in our streets.

15 Happy *is that* people, that is in such a case: *yea*, happy *is that* people, whose God *is* the LORD.

PSALTERY, a harp. Used in religious services, 2 Sam. 6:5; 1 Chr. 13:8; 16:5; 25:1,5, 6; 2 Chr. 29:25; Psa. 33:2; 57:8; 71:22; 81:2; 92:3; 108:2; 144:9; 150:3; Rev. 5:8. At the dedication of the new wall when the captivity returned, Neh. 12:27. Used in idolatrous worship, Dan. 3:5,7,10,15.

See MUSIC, INSTRUMENTS OF.

PTOLEMAIS, a seaport in Asher, formerly called ACCHO, which see. Paul visits, Acts 21:7.

PUA. See PHUVAH.

PUAH. 1. A Hebrew midwife, Ex.1:15.

2. Father of Tola, Judg. 10:1.

3. See PHUVAH.

PUBLICANS, Roman tax collectors. Disreputable, Matt. 5:46,47; 9:11; 11:19; 18:17; 21:31; Luke 18:11. Repent under the preaching of John the Baptist, Matt. 21:32; Luke 3:12; 7:29. Matthew, the collector of Capernaum, becomes an apostle, Matt. 9:9; 10:3; Mark 2:14; Luke 5:27. Parable concerning, Luke 18:9-14. Zacchæus, chief among, receives Jesus into his house, Luke 19:2-10.

PUBLIUS, chief man in the island of Melita. Father of, healed by Paul, Acts 28:7,8.

PUDENS, a Christian in Rome, 2 Tim. 4:21.

PUL. 1. King of Assyria. Forced tribute from Menahem, king of Israel, 2 Kin. 15:19; 1 Chr. 5:26.

2. A place or tribe in Africa, Isa. 66:19.

PULPIT, Neh. 8:4; 2 Chr. 6:13.

PULSE, a sort of food, Dan. 1:12,16.

PUNISHMENT. DEATH PENALTY: Shall not be remitted, Num. 35:31. In the Mosaic law the death penalty was inflicted for murder, Gen. 9:5,6; Num. 35:16-21,30-

33; Deut. 17:6; adultery, Lev. 20:10; Deut. 22:24; incest, Lev. 20:11,12,14; bestiality, Ex. 22:19; Lev. 20:15,16; sodomy, Lev. 18: 22; 20:13; incontinence, Deut. 22:21-24; rape of a betrothed virgin, Deut. 22:25; perjury, Zech. 5:4; kidnapping, Ex. 21:16; Deut. 24: 7; upon a priest's daughter, who committed fornication, Lev. 21:9; for witchcraft, Ex. 22:18; offering human sacrifice, Lev. 20:2-5; for striking or cursing father or mother, Ex. 21:15,17; Lev. 20:9; disobedience to parents, Deut. 21:18-21; theft, Zech. 5:3,4; blasphemy, Lev. 24:11-14,16,23; for Sabbath desecration, Ex. 35:2; Num. 15:32-36; for prophesying falsely, or propagating false doctrines, Deut. 13:1-10; sacrificing to false gods, Ex. 22:20; refusing to abide by the decision of court, Deut. 17:12; for treason, 1 Kin. 2:25; Esth. 2:23; sedition, Acts 5:36,37.

MODES OF EXECUTION OF DEATH PENALTY: Burning, Gen. 38:24; Lev. 20:14; 21:9; Jer. 29:22; Ezek. 23:25; Dan. 3:19-23; stoning, Lev. 20:2,27; 24:14; Num. 14:10; 15:33-36; Deut. 13:10; 17:5; 22:21,24; Josh. 7:25; 1 Kin. 21:10; Ezek. 16:40; hanging, Gen. 40:22; Deut. 21:22,23; Josh. 8:29; beheading, Matt. 14:10; Mark 6:16,27,28; crucifixion, Matt. 27:35,38; Mark 15:24,27; Luke 23:33; the sword, Ex. 32:27,28; 1 Kin. 2:25,34,46; Acts 12:2.

Executed by the witnesses, Deut. 13:9; 17:7; Acts 7:58; by the congregation, Num. 15:35,36; Deut. 13:9.

Not inflicted on testimony of less than two witnesses, Num. 35:30; Deut. 17:6; 19:15.

MINOR OFFENSES: Punishable by scourging, Lev. 19:20; Deut. 22:18; 25:2,3; Prov. 17:10; 19:29; 20:30; Matt. 27:26; Mark 15:15; Luke 23:16; John 19:1; Acts 22:24,29; imprisonment, Gen. 39:20; 40; see PRISON. Confinement within limits, 1 Kin. 2:26,36-38.

ENTAILED: On children, Ex. 34:7; Jer. 31:29; Lam. 5:7; Ezek. 18:2,3.

See AFFLICTION, DESIGN OF; CHASTISEMENT; FINE; JUDGMENTS; RETALIATION; WICKED, PUNISHMENT OF.

ACCORDING TO DEEDS: Job 34:11. For the work of a man shall he render unto him, and cause every man to find according to *his* ways.

Psa. 62:12. Also unto thee, O Lord, *belongeth* mercy: for thou renderest to every man according to his work.

Prov. 12:14. The recompence of a man's hands shall be rendered unto him.

Prov. 24:12. If thou sayest, Behold, we knew it not; doth not he that pondereth the heart consider *it?* and he that keepeth thy soul, doth *not* he know *it?* and shall *not* he render to *every* man according to his works?

Isa. 59:18. According to *their* deeds, accordingly he will repay, fury to his adversaries, recompence to his enemies; to the islands he will repay recompence.

Jer. 17:10. I the LORD search the heart, *I* try the reins, even to give every man according to his ways, *and* according to the fruit of his doings.

Ezek. 7:3. Now *is* the end *come* upon thee, and I will send mine anger upon thee, and will judge thee according to thy ways, and will recompense upon thee all thine abominations. 27. I will do unto them after their way, and according to their deserts will I judge them; and they shall know that I *am* the LORD.

Ezek. 16:59. For thus saith the Lord GOD; I will even deal with thee as thou hast done, which hast despised the oath in breaking the covenant.

Ezek. 39:24. According to their uncleanness and according to their transgressions have I done unto them, and hid my face from them.

Zech. 1:6. Like as the LORD of hosts thought to do unto us, according to our ways, and according to our doings, so hath he dealt with us.

Matt. 5:22. But I say unto you, That whosoever is angry with his brother without a cause shall be in danger of the judgment: and whosoever shall say to his brother, Raca, shall be in danger of the council : but whosoever shall say, Thou fool, shall be in danger of hell fire.

Matt. 16:27. For the Son of man shall come in the glory of his Father with his angels; and then he shall reward every man according to his works.

Matt. 23:14. ¹ Woe unto you, scribes and Pharisees, hypocrites! for ye devour widows' houses, and for a pretence make long prayer: Therefore ye shall receive the greater damnation. Luke 20:47.

[¹ Omitted in R. V.]

Luke 12:47. And that servant, which knew his lord's will, and prepared not *himself*, neither did according to his will, shall be beaten with many *stripes*. 48. But he that knew not, and did commit things worthy of stripes, shall be beaten with few *stripes*. For unto whomsoever much is given, of him shall be much required : and to whom men have committed much, of him they will ask the more. See Parable of vineyard, Isa. 5:1-7; husbandman, Matt. 21:33-41; of the talents, Matt. 25:14-30.

See JUDGMENT, ACCORDING TO OPPORTUNITY AND WORKS.

DELAYED : Psa. 50:21. These *things* hast thou done, and I kept silence ; thou thoughtest that I was altogether *such an one* as thyself : *but* I will reprove thee, and set *them* in order before thine eyes.

Psa. 55:19. God shall hear, and afflict them, even he that abideth of old. Because they have no changes, therefore they fear not God.

Prov. 1:24. Because I have called, and ye refused ; I have stretched out my hand, and no man regarded ; 25. But ye have set at nought all my counsel, and would none of my reproof : 26. I also will laugh at your calamity ; I will mock when your fear cometh ; 27. When your fear cometh as desolation, and your destruction cometh as a whirlwind ; when distress

and anguish cometh upon you. 28. Then shall they call upon me, but I will not answer ; they shall seek me early, but they shall not find me : 29. For that they hated knowledge, and did not choose the fear of the LORD : 30. They would none of my counsel : they despised all my reproof. 31. Therefore shall they eat of the fruit of their own way, and be filled with their own devices.

Eccl. 8:11. Because sentence against an evil work is not executed speedily, therefore the heart of the sons of men is fully set in them to do evil. 12. Though a sinner do evil an hundred times, and his *days* be prolonged, yet surely I know that it shall be well with them that fear God, which fear before him : 13. But it shall not be well with the wicked, neither shall he prolong *his* days, *which are* as a shadow ; because he feareth not before God.

Hab. 1:2. O LORD, how long shall I cry, and thou wilt not hear ! *even* cry out unto thee *of* violence, and thou wilt not save ! 3. Why dost thou shew me iniquity, and cause *me* to behold grievance ? for spoiling and violence *are* before me : and there are *that* raise up strife and contention. 4. Therefore the law is slacked, and judgment doth never go forth : for the wicked doth compass about the righteous ; therefore wrong judgment proceedeth.

DESIGN OF : TO SECURE OBEDIENCE : Gen. 2:17. But of the tree of the knowledge of good and evil, thou shalt not eat of it : for in the day that thou eatest thereof thou shalt surely die.

Ex. 20:3. Thou shalt have no other gods before me. 4. Thou shalt not make unto thee any graven image, or any likeness *of any thing* that *is* in heaven above, or that *is* in the earth beneath, or that *is* in the water under the earth : 5. Thou shalt not bow down thyself to them, nor serve them : for I the LORD thy God *am* a jealous God, visiting the iniquity of the fathers upon the children unto the third and fourth *generation* of them that hate me :

Lev. 26:14. But if ye will not hearken unto me, and will not do all these commandments ; 15. And if ye shall despise my statutes, or if your soul abhor my judgments, so that ye will not do all my commandments, *but* that ye break my covenant : 16. I also will do this unto you ; I will even appoint over you terror, consumption, and the burning ague, that shall consume the eyes, and cause sorrow of heart : and ye shall sow your seed in vain, for your enemies shall eat it. 17. And I will set my face against you, and ye shall be slain before your enemies : they that hate you shall reign over you ; and ye shall flee when none pursueth you. 18. And if ye will not yet for all this hearken unto me, then I will punish you seven times more for your sins. 19. And I will break the pride of your power ; and I will make your heaven as iron, and your earth as brass: 20. And your strength shall be spent in vain: for your land shall not yield her increase, neither shall the trees of the land yield their fruits. 21. And if ye walk contrary unto me, and will not hearken unto me; I will bring seven times more plagues upon you according to your sins. 22. I will also send wild beasts among you, which shall rob you of your children, and destroy your cattle, and make you few in number; and your *high* ways shall be desolate. 23. And if ye will not be reformed by me by these things, but will walk contrary unto me; 24. Then will I also walk contrary unto you, and will punish you yet seven times for your sins. 25. And I will bring a sword upon you, that shall avenge the quarrel of *my* covenant: and when ye are gathered together within your cities, I will send the pestilence among you; and ye shall be delivered into the hand of the enemy. 26. *And* when I have broken the staff of your bread, ten women shall bake your bread in one oven, and they shall deliver *you* your bread again by weight: and ye shall eat, and not be satisfied. 27. And if ye will not for all this hearken unto me, but walk contrary unto me; 28. Then I will walk contrary unto you also in fury; and I, even I, will chastise you seven times for your sins. 29. And ye shall eat the flesh of your sons, and the flesh of your daughters shall ye eat. 30. And I will destroy your high places, and cut down your images, and cast your carcases upon the carcases of your idols, and my soul shall abhor you. 31. And I will make your cities waste, and bring your sanctuaries unto desolation, and I will not smell the savour of your sweet odours. 32. And I will bring the land into desolation: and your enemies which dwell therein shall be astonished at it. 33. And I will scatter you among the heathen, and will draw out a sword after you: and your land shall be desolate, and your cities waste. 34. Then shall the land enjoy her sabbaths, as long as it lieth desolate, and ye *be* in your enemies' land; *even* then shall the land rest, and enjoy her sabbaths. 35. As long as it lieth desolate it shall rest; because it did not rest in your sabbaths, when ye dwelt upon it. 36. And upon them that are left *alive* of you I will send a faintness into their hearts in the lands of their enemies; and the sound of a shaken leaf shall chase them; and they shall flee, as fleeing from a sword; and they shall fall when none pursueth. 37. And they shall fall one upon another, as it were before a sword, when none pursueth: and ye shall have no power to stand before your enemies. 38. And ye shall perish among the heathen, and the land of your enemies shall eat you up. 39. And they that are left of you shall pine away in their iniquity in your enemies' lands; and also in the iniquities of their fathers shall they pine away with them.

Deut. 13:10. And thou shalt stone him with stones, that he die; because he hath sought to thrust thee away from the LORD thy God, which brought thee out of the land of Egypt, from the house of bondage. 11. And all Israel shall hear, and fear, and shall do no more any such wickedness as this is among you.

Deut. 21:21. And all the men of his city shall stone him with stones, that he die: so shalt thou put evil away from among you: and all Israel shall hear, and fear. chapter 17:13; 19:20.

Prov. 19:25. Smite a scorner, and the simple will beware: and reprove one that hath understanding, *and* he will understand knowledge.

Prov. 21:11. When the scorner is punished, the simple is made wise:

Prov. 26:3. A whip for the horse, a bridle for the ass, and a rod for the fool's back.

See JUDGMENTS, DESIGN OF.

DIVINE: NO ESCAPE FROM: Job 11:20. But the eyes of the wicked shall fail, and they shall not escape, and their hope *shall be as* the giving up of the ghost.

Prov. 1:24. Because I have called, and ye refused; I have stretched out my hand, and no man regarded; 25. But ye have set at nought all my counsel, and would none of my reproof: 26. I also will laugh at your calamity; I will mock when your fear cometh; 27. When your fear cometh as a desolation, and your destruction cometh as a whirlwind: when distress and anguish cometh upon you. 28. Then shall they call upon me, but I will not answer; they shall seek me early, but they shall not find me: 29. For that they hated knowledge, and did not choose the fear of the LORD: 30. They would none of my counsel: they despised all my reproof. 31. Therefore shall they eat of the fruit of their own way, and be filled with their own devices.

Prov. 11:21. *Though* hand *join* in hand, the wicked shall not be unpunished:

Prov. 16:5. Every one *that is* proud in heart *is* an abomination to the LORD: *though* hand *join* in hand, he shall not be unpunished.

Prov. 29:1. He, that being often reproved hardeneth *his* neck, shall suddenly be destroyed, and that without remedy.

Jer. 11:11. Therefore thus saith the LORD, Behold, I will bring evil upon them, which they shall not be able to escape; and though they shall cry unto me, I will not hearken unto them.

Jer. 15:1. Then said the LORD unto me, Though Moses and Samuel stood before me, *yet* my mind *could* not *be* toward this people: cast *them* out of my sight, and let them go forth.

Jer. 25:28. And it shall be, if they refuse to take the cup at thine hand to drink, then shalt thou say unto them, Thus saith the LORD of hosts; Ye shall certainly drink.

29. For, lo, I begin to bring evil on the city which is called by my name, and should ye be utterly unpunished? Ye shall not be unpunished: for I will call for a sword upon all the inhabitants of the earth, saith the LORD of hosts.

Amos 2:14. Therefore the flight shall perish from the swift, and the strong shall not strengthen his force, neither shall the mighty deliver himself: 15. Neither shall he stand that handleth the bow; and *he that is* swift of foot shall not deliver *himself*: neither shall he that rideth the horse deliver himself. 16. And *he that is* courageous among the mighty shall flee away naked in that day, saith the LORD.

Zeph. 1:18. Neither their silver nor their gold shall be able to deliver them in the day of the LORD's wrath; but the whole land shall be devoured by the fire of his jealousy: for he shall make even a speedy riddance of all them that dwell in the land. Ezek. 7:19.

Matt. 10:28. And fear not them which kill the body, but are not able to kill the soul: but rather fear him which is able to destroy both soul and body in hell.

Matt. 23:33. *Ye* serpents, *ye* generation of vipers, how can ye escape the damnation of hell?

Rom. 2:3. Thinkest thou this, O man, that judgest them which do such things, and doest the same, that thou shalt escape the judgment of God?

Col. 3:25. He that doeth wrong shall receive for the wrong which he hath done: and there is no respect of persons.

Heb. 2:3. How shall we escape, if we neglect so great salvation;

Heb. 12:25. If they escaped not who refused him that spake on earth, much more *shall not* we *escape*, if we turn away from him that *speaketh* from heaven:

ETERNAL: Isa. 34:8. For *it is* the day of the LORD's vengeance, *and* the year of recompences for the controversy of Zion. 9. And the streams thereof shall be turned into pitch, and the dust thereof into brimstone, and the land thereof shall become burning pitch. 10. It shall not be quenched night nor day; the smoke thereof shall go up for ever: from generation to generation it shall lie waste; none shall pass through it for ever and ever.

Dan. 12:2. And many of them that sleep in the dust of the earth shall awake, some to everlasting life, and some to shame *and* everlasting contempt.

Matt. 3:12. He will burn up the chaff with unquenchable fire.

Matt. 10:28. And fear not them which kill the body, but are not able to kill the soul: but rather fear him which is able to destroy both soul and body in hell.

Matt. 18:8. Wherefore if thy hand or thy foot offend thee, cut them off, and cast *them* from thee: it is better for thee to enter into life halt or maimed, rather than having two hands or two feet to be cast into everlasting fire.

Matt. 25:41. Then shall he say also unto them on the left hand, Depart from me, ye cursed, into everlasting fire, prepared for the devil and his angels: 46. And these shall go away into everlasting punishment: but the righteous into life eternal.

Mark 3:29. But he that shall blaspheme against the Holy Ghost hath never forgiveness, but is [1] in danger of eternal [2] damnation:
[R. V. [1] guilty   [2] sin]

Luke 3:17. Whose fan *is* in his hand, and he will throughly purge his floor, and will gather the wheat into his garner; but the chaff he will burn with fire unquenchable.

John 5:29. And shall come forth; they that have done good, unto the resurrection of life; and they that have done evil, unto the resurrection of damnation.

Heb. 6:2. Of the doctrine of baptisms, and of laying on of hands, and of resurrection of the dead, and of eternal judgment.

Heb. 10:28. He that despised Moses' law died without mercy under two or three witnesses: 29. Of how much sorer punishment, suppose ye, shall he be thought worthy, who hath trodden under foot the Son of God, and hath counted the blood of the covenant, wherewith he was sanctified, an unholy thing, and hath done despite unto the Spirit of grace? 30. For we know him that hath said, Vengeance *belongeth* unto me, I will recompense, saith the Lord. And again, The Lord shall judge his people. 31. *It is* a fearful thing to fall into the hands of the living God.

Rev. 14:10. The same shall drink of the wine of the wrath of God, which is poured out without mixture into the cup of his indignation; and he shall be tormented with fire and brimstone in the presence of the holy angels, and in the presence of the Lamb: 11. And the smoke of their torment ascendeth up for ever and ever: and they have no rest day nor night, who worship the beast and his image, and whosoever receiveth the mark of his name.

Rev. 19:3. Her smoke rose up for ever and ever.

Rev. 20:10. The devil that deceived them was cast into the lake of fire and brimstone, where the beast and the false prophet *are*, and shall be tormented day and night for ever and ever.

See WICKED, PUNISHMENT OF.

PUNON, a city of Edom. A camping ground of the Israelites, in their forty years' wandering, Num. 33:42,43.

PUR, the lot, Esth. 3:7.
See PURIM.

PURIFICATION, sanitary and symbolical. For women before marriage, Esth. 2:12; after childbirth, Lev. 12:6–8; Luke 2:22; after menstruation, Lev. 15:19–33; 2 Sam. 11:4. Of the Jews before the passover, John 11:55. For those who have slain in battle, Num. 31:19–24. Of Levites, see below. Of lepers, see LEPROSY. By fire, for things that resist fire, Num. 31:23. By blood, Ex. 24:5–8; Lev. 14:6,7; Heb. 9: 12–14,19–22. By abstaining from sexual intercourse, Ex. 19:15. Washing in water parts of animal sacrifices, Lev. 1:9,13; 9:14; 2 Chr. 4:6. Penalty to be imposed upon those who do not observe the ordinances concerning, Lev. 7:20,21; Num. 19:13,20.

Water of, Num. 19:17–21; 31:23. Washing hands in water, symbolical of innocency, Deut. 21:6; Psa. 26:6; Matt. 27:24. Traditions of the elders concerning, Matt. 15:2; Mark 7:2–5,8,9; Luke 11:38. Of Paul, to show his fidelity to the law, Acts 21:24,26.

FIGURATIVE: Psa. 26:6; 51:7; Ezek. 36:25; Heb. 10:22.

See ABLUTION; DEFILEMENT; SANITATION.

SCRIPTURES RELATING TO: Gen. 35:2. Then Jacob said unto his household, and to all that *were* with him, . . . be clean, and change your garments:

Ex. 19:10. And the LORD said unto Moses, Go unto the people, and sanctify them to day and to morrow, and let them wash their clothes. 14. And Moses went down from the mount unto the people, and sanctified the people; and they washed their clothes.

Ex. 29:4. And Aaron and his sons thou shalt bring unto the door of the tabernacle of the congregation, and shalt wash them with water.

Ex. 30:18. Thou shalt also make a laver *of* brass, and his foot *also of* brass, to wash *withal:* and thou shalt put it between the tabernacle of the congregation and the altar, and thou shalt put water therein. 19. For Aaron and his sons shall wash their hands and their feet thereat: 20. When they go into the tabernacle of the congregation, they shall wash with water, that they die not; or when they come near to the altar to minister, to burn offering made by fire unto the LORD: 21. So they shall wash their hands and their feet, that they die not: and it shall be a statute for ever to them, *even* to him and to his seed throughout their generations.

Ex. 40:12. And thou shalt bring Aaron and his sons unto the door of the tabernacle of the congregation, and wash them with water. 30. And he set the laver between the tent of the congregation and the altar, and put water there, to wash *withal.* 31. And Moses and Aaron and his sons washed their hands and their feet thereat: 32. When they went into the tent of the congregation, and when they came near unto the altar, they washed; as the LORD commanded Moses.

Lev. 8:6. And Moses brought Aaron and his sons, and washed them with water.

Lev. 14:8. And he that is to be cleansed shall wash his clothes, and shave off all his hair, and wash himself in water, that he may be clean: and after that he shall come into the camp, and shall tarry abroad out of his tent seven days. 9. But it shall be on the seventh day, that he shall shave all his hair off his head and his beard and his eyebrows, even all his hair he shall shave off: and he shall wash his clothes, also he shall wash his flesh in water, and he shall be clean.

Lev. 15:4. Every bed, whereon he lieth that hath the issue, is unclean: and every thing, whereon he sitteth, shall be unclean. 5. And whosoever toucheth his bed shall wash his clothes, and bathe *himself* in water, and be unclean until the even. 6. And he that sitteth on *any* thing whereon he sat that hath the issue shall wash his clothes, and bathe *himself* in water, and be unclean until the even. 7. And he that toucheth the flesh of him that hath the issue shall wash his clothes, and bathe *himself* in water, and be unclean until the even. 8. And if he that hath the issue spit upon him that is clean; then he shall wash his clothes, and bathe *himself* in water, and be unclean until the even. 9. And what saddle soever he rideth upon that hath the issue shall be unclean. 10. And whosoever toucheth any thing that was under him shall be unclean until the even: and he that beareth *any of* those things shall wash his clothes, and bathe *himself* in water, and be unclean until the even. 11. And whomsoever he toucheth that hath the issue, and hath not rinsed his hands in water, he shall wash his clothes, and bathe *himself* in water, and be unclean until the even. 12. And the vessel of earth, that he toucheth which hath the issue, shall be broken: and every vessel of wood shall be rinsed in water. 13. And when he that hath an issue is cleansed of his issue; then he shall number to himself seven days for his cleansing, and wash his clothes, and bathe his flesh in running water, and shall be clean. 16. And if any man's seed of copulation go out from him, then he shall wash all his flesh in water, and be unclean until the even. 17. And every garment, and every skin, whereon is the seed of copulation, shall be washed with water, and be unclean until the even. 18. The woman also with whom man shall lie *with* seed of copulation, they shall *both* bathe *themselves* in water, and be unclean until the even. 19. And if a woman have an issue, *and* her issue in her flesh be blood, she shall be put apart seven days: and whosoever toucheth her shall be unclean until the even. 20. And every thing that she lieth upon in her separation shall be unclean: every thing also that she sitteth upon shall be unclean. 21. And whosoever toucheth her bed shall wash his clothes, and bathe *himself* in water, and be unclean until the even. 22. And whosoever toucheth any thing that she sat upon shall wash his clothes, and bathe *himself* in water, and be unclean until the even. 23. And if it *be* on *her* bed, or on any thing whereon she sitteth, when he toucheth it, he shall be unclean until the even. 24. And if any man lie with her at all, and her flowers be upon him, he shall be unclean seven days; and all the bed whereon he lieth shall be unclean. 25. And if a woman have an issue of her blood many days out of the time of her separation, or if it run beyond the time of her separation; all the days of the issue of her uncleanness shall be as the days of her separation: she *shall be* unclean. 26. Every bed whereon she lieth all the days of her issue shall be unto her as the bed of her separation: and whatsoever she sitteth upon shall be unclean, as the uncleanness of her separation. 27. And whosoever toucheth those things shall be unclean, and shall wash his clothes, and bathe *himself* in water, and be unclean until the even.

Lev. 16:4. He shall put on the holy linen coat, and he shall have the linen breeches upon his flesh, and shall be girded with a linen girdle, and with the linen mitre shall he be attired: these *are* holy garments; therefore shall he wash his flesh in water, and *so* put them on. 24. And he shall wash his flesh with water in the holy place, and put on his garments, and come forth, and offer his burnt offering, and the burnt offering of the people, and make an atonement for himself, and for the people. 26. And he that let go the goat for the scapegoat shall wash his clothes, and bathe his flesh in water, and afterward come into the camp. 28. And he that burneth them shall wash his clothes, and bathe his flesh in water, and afterward he shall come into the camp.

Lev. 17:15. And every soul that eateth that which died *of itself*, or that which was torn *with beasts, whether it be* one of your own country, or a stranger, he shall both wash his clothes, and bathe *himself* in water, and be unclean until the even: then shall he be clean.

Lev. 22:3. Say unto them, Whosoever *he be* of all your seed among your generations, that goeth unto the holy things, which the children of Israel hallow unto the LORD, having his uncleanness upon him, that soul shall be cut off from my presence: I *am* the LORD.

Num. 8:6. Take the Levites from among the children of Israel, and cleanse them. 7. And thus shalt thou do unto them, to cleanse them: Sprinkle water of purifying upon them, and let them shave all their flesh, and let them wash their clothes, and *so* make themselves clean. 21. And the Levites were purified, and they washed their clothes; and Aaron offered them *as* an offering before the LORD; and Aaron made an atonement for them to cleanse them.

Num. 19:7. Then the priest shall wash his clothes, and he shall bathe his flesh in water, and afterward he shall come into the camp, and the priest shall be unclean until the even. 8. And he that burneth her shall wash his clothes in water, and bathe his flesh in water, and shall be unclean until the even. 19. And on the seventh day he shall purify himself, and wash his clothes, and bathe himself in water, and shall be clean at even.

2 Chr. 4:6. He made also ten lavers, and put five on the right hand, and five on the left, to wash in them: such things as they offered for the burnt offering they washed in them; but the sea *was* for the priests to wash in.

Mark 7:2. And when they saw some of his disciples eat bread with defiled, that is to say, with unwashen, hands, they found fault. 3. For the Pharisees, and all the Jews, except they wash *their* hands oft, eat not, holding the tradition of the elders. 4. And *when they come* from the market, except they wash, they eat not. And many other things there be, which they have received to hold, *as* the washing of cups, and pots, brazen vessels, and of tables. 5. Then the Pharisees and scribes asked him, Why walk not thy disciples according to the tradition of the elders, but eat bread with unwashen hands? 6. He answered and said unto them, Well hath Esaias prophesied of you hypocrites, as it is written, This people honoureth me with *their* lips, but their heart is far from me. 7. Howbeit in vain do they worship me, teaching *for* doctrines the commandments of men. 8. For laying aside the commandment of God, ye hold the tradition of men, *as* the washing of pots and cups: and many other such like things ye do. 9. And he said unto them, Full well ye reject the commandment of God, that ye may keep your own tradition. Matt. 15:2.

Heb. 9:10. *Which stood* only in meats and drinks, and divers washings, and carnal ordinances, imposed *on them* until the time of reformation.

PURIM, a feast instituted to commemorate the deliverance of the Jews from the plot of Haman, Esth. 9:20-32.

PURITY. OF HEART: Psa. 19:8. The statutes of the LORD *are* right, rejoicing the heart: the commandment of the LORD *is* pure, enlightening the eyes. Psa. 12:6.

Psa. 24:3. Who shall ascend into the hill of the LORD? or who shall stand in his holy place? 4. He that hath clean hands, and a pure heart; who hath not lifted up his soul unto vanity, nor sworn deceitfully. 5. He shall receive the blessing from the LORD, and righteousness from the God of his salvation.

Psa. 51:7. Purge me with hyssop, and I shall be clean: wash me, and I shall be whiter than snow.

Psa. 65:3. Our transgressions, thou shalt purge them away.

Psa. 119:140. Thy word *is* very pure: therefore thy servant loveth it.

Prov. 15:26. *The words* of the pure *are* pleasant words.

Prov. 20:9. Who can say, I have made my heart clean, I am pure from my sin?

Prov. 21:8. The way of man *is* froward and strange: but *as for* the pure, his work *is* right.

Prov. 30:12. *There is* a generation *that are* pure in their own eyes, and *yet* is not washed from their filthiness.

Isa. 1:18. Though your sins be as scarlet, they shall be as white as snow; though they be red like crimson, they shall be as wool. 25. And I will turn my hand upon thee, and purely purge away thy dross, and take away all thy tin:

Isa. 6:7. And he laid *it* upon my mouth, and said, Lo, this hath touched thy lips; and thine iniquity is taken away, and thy sin purged.

Dan. 12:10. Many shall be purified, and made white, and tried; but the wicked shall do wickedly: and none of the wicked shall understand; but the wise shall understand.

Mic. 6:11. Shall I count *them* pure with the wicked balances, and with the bag of deceitful weights?

Mal. 3:2. But who may abide the day of his coming? and who shall stand when he appeareth? for he *is* like a refiner's fire, and like fullers' sope: 3. And he shall sit *as* a refiner and purifier of silver; and he shall purify the sons of Levi, and purge them as gold and silver, that they may offer unto the LORD an offering in righteousness.

Matt. 5:8. Blessed *are* the pure in heart: for they shall see God.

John 15:2. Every branch in me that beareth not fruit he taketh away: and every *branch* that beareth fruit, he purgeth it, that it may bring forth more fruit.

Phil. 4:8. Finally, brethren, whatsoever things are true, whatsoever things *are* honest, whatsoever things *are* just, whatsoever things *are* pure, whatsoever things *are* lovely, whatsoever things *are* of good report; if *there be* any virtue, and if *there be* any praise, think on these things.

1 Tim. 1:5. Now the end of the commandment is charity out of a pure heart, and *of* a good conscience, and *of* faith unfeigned:

1 Tim. 3:9. Holding the mystery of the faith in a pure conscience. 2 Tim. 1:3.

1 Tim. 5:22. Keep thyself pure.

2 Tim. 2:21. If a man therefore purge himself from these, he shall be a vessel unto honour, sanctified, and meet for the master's use, *and* prepared unto every good work. 22. Flee also youthful lusts: but follow righteousness, faith, charity, peace, with them that call on the Lord out of a pure heart.

Tit. 1:15. Unto the pure all things *are* pure.

Heb. 9:13. For if the blood of bulls and of goats, and the ashes of an heifer sprinkling the unclean, sanctifieth to the purifying of the flesh: 14. How much more shall the blood of Christ, who through the eternal Spirit offered himself without spot to God, purge your conscience from dead works to serve the living God?

Heb. 10:2. Worshippers once purged should have had no more conscience of sins.

Jas. 4:8. Cleanse *your* hands, ye sinners; and purify *your* hearts, ye doubleminded.

1 Pet. 1:22. Seeing ye have purified your souls in obeying the truth ¹through the Spirit

unto unfeigned love of the brethren, *see that ye* love one another with a pure heart fervently.   [¹ Omitted in R. V.]

1 John 3:3. And every man that hath this hope in him purifieth himself, even as he is pure.

For the symbolisms of purity, see ABLUTIONS; COLOR, WHITE; DEFILEMENT; PURIFICATION.

PURVEYOR, for Solomon, 1 Kin. 4:7–19,27.

PUT. See PHUT.

PUTEOLI, a seaport of Italy. Paul stays a week at, Acts 28:13,14.

PUTIEL, the father-in-law of Eleazar the priest, Ex. 6:25.

PYGARG, probably a species of antelope, Deut. 14:5.

Q

QUAIL. Miracle of, in the wilderness of Sin, Ex. 16:13; at Kibroth-hattaavah, Num. 11:31,32; Psa. 105:40.

QUARANTINE. See SANITATION, QUARANTINE.

QUARRIES, Judg. 3:19,26.

QUARTUS, a Christian in Corinth, Rom. 16:23.

QUATERNION, a squad of four soldiers, Acts 12:4.

QUEEN. The wife of a king, 1 Kin. 11:19. Crowned, Esth. 1:11; 2:17. Divorced, Esth. 1:10–22. Sits on the throne with the king, Neh. 2:6. Makes feasts for the women of the royal household, Esth. 1:9. Exerts an evil influence in public affairs, see JEZEBEL. Counsels the king, Dan. 5:10–12. Of Sheba visits Solomon, 1 Kin. 10:1–13. Candace, of Ethiopia, Acts 8:27.

The reigning sovereign, Athaliah. See ATHALIAH.

The moon called queen of heaven, Jer. 7:18; 44:7–19,25. Worshiped, see IDOLATRY.

QUICKENING. Of the church: By the Father, Psa. 71:20; 80:18; Rom. 4:17; 8:11; Eph. 2:1; 1 Tim. 6:13; by the Son, John 5:21; 1 Cor. 15:45; by the Holy Spirit, John 6:63; Rom. 8:11; 2 Cor. 3:6; 1 Pet. 3:18.—*Bible Text-Book.*

QUIVER, for arrows, Gen. 27:3; Isa. 22:6.

QUOTATIONS AND ALLUSIONS. IN THE NEW TESTAMENT FROM, AND TO, THE OLD TESTAMENT: Matt. 1:23. Behold, a virgin shall be with child, and shall bring forth a son, and they shall call his name Emmanuel, which being interpreted is, God with us. Isa. 7:14.

Matt 2:6. And thou Bethlehem, *in* the land of Juda, art not the least among the princes of Juda; for out of thee shall come a Governor, that shall rule my people Israel. Mic. 5:2.

15. Out of Egypt have I called my son. Hos. 11:1.

18. In Rama was there a voice heard, lamentation, and weeping, and great mourning, Rachel weeping *for* her children, and

would not be comforted, because they are not. Jer. 31:15.

Matt. 3:3. The voice of one crying in the wilderness, Prepare ye the way of the Lord, make his paths straight. Isa. 40:3.

Matt. 4:4. Man shall not live by bread alone, but by every word that proceedeth out of the mouth of God. Deut. 8:3; Luke 4:4.

6. He shall give his angels charge concerning thee: and in *their* hands they shall bear thee up, lest at any time thou dash thy foot against a stone. Psa. 91:11,12; Luke 4:10,11.

7. Jesus said unto him, It is written again, Thou shalt not tempt the Lord thy God. Deut. 6:16; Luke 4:12.

10. Thou shalt worship the Lord thy God, and him only shalt thou serve. Deut. 6:13; 10:20; Luke 4:8.

15. The land of Zabulon, and the land of Nephthalim, *by* the way of the sea, beyond Jordan, Galilee of the Gentiles; 16. The people which sat in darkness saw great light; and to them which sat in the region and shadow of death light is sprung up. Isa. 9:1,2; 42:7; Luke 2:32.

Matt. 5:5. Blessed *are* the meek: for they shall inherit the earth. Psa. 37:11.

21. Thou shalt not kill; and whosoever shall kill shall be in danger of the judgment: Ex. 20:13; Deut. 5:17.

27. Thou shalt not commit adultery: Ex. 20:14; Deut. 5:18.

31. Whosoever shall put away his wife, let him give her a writing of divorcement: Deut. 24:1; Matt. 19:7; Mark 10:4.

33. Thou shalt not forswear thyself, but shalt perform unto the Lord thine oaths: Ex. 20:7; Lev. 19:12; Deut. 5:11.

38. An eye for an eye, and a tooth for a tooth. Ex. 21:24.

43. Thou shalt love thy neighbour, and hate thine enemy. Lev. 19:18; Matt. 19:19; 22:39; Mark 12:31; Luke 10:27; Rom. 13:9; Gal. 5:14; Jas. 2:8.

Matt. 7:23. Depart from me, ye that work iniquity. Psa. 6:8.

Matt. 8:17. Himself took our infirmities, and bare *our* sicknesses. Isa. 53:4.

Matt. 9:13. I will have mercy, and not sacrifice: Matt. 12:7; Hos. 6:6.

Matt. 10:35. For I am come to set a man at variance against his father, and the daughter against her mother, and the daughter in law against her mother in law. Mic. 7:6; Mark 13:12; Luke 12:53.

Matt. 11:10. Behold, I send my messenger before thy face, which shall prepare thy way before thee. Mal. 3:1; Mark 1:2; Luke 7:27.

Matt. 12:18. Behold my servant, whom I have chosen; my beloved, in whom my soul is well pleased: I will put my spirit upon him, and he shall shew judgment to the Gentiles. 19. He shall not strive, nor cry; neither shall any man hear his voice in the streets. 20. A bruised reed shall he not break, and smoking flax shall he not quench, till he send forth judgment unto victory.

21. And in his name shall the Gentiles trust. Isa. 42:1–4.

Matt. 13:14. By hearing ye shall hear, and shall not understand; and seeing ye shall see, and shall not perceive: 15. For this people's heart is waxed gross, and *their* ears are dull of hearing, and their eyes they have closed; lest at any time they should see with *their* eyes, and hear with *their* ears, and should understand with *their* heart, and should be converted, and I should heal them. Isa. 6:9,10; Mark 4:12; 8:18; Luke 8:10; John 12:40; Acts 28:26,27.

35. I will open my mouth in parables; I will utter things which have been kept secret from the foundation of the world. Psa. 78:2.

Matt. 15:4. Honour thy father and mother: [Ex. 20:12.] He that [1] curseth father or mother, let him die the death. Ex. 21:17.

<small>[1 R. V. speaketh evil of]</small>

8. This people draweth nigh unto me with their mouth, and honoureth me with *their* lips; but their heart is far from me. 9. But in vain they do worship me, teaching *for* doctrines the commandments of men. Isa. 29:13.

Matt. 18:16. In the mouth of two or three witnesses every word may be established. Deut. 19:15; John 8:17; 2 Cor. 13:1.

Matt. 19:4. He which made *them* at the beginning made them male and female, Gen. 1:27.

5. For this cause shall a man leave father and mother, and shall cleave to his wife: and they twain shall be one flesh? Gen. 2:24; Deut. 24:1.

18. Thou shalt do no murder, Thou shalt not commit adultery, Thou shalt not steal, Thou shalt not bear false witness, 19. Honour thy father and *thy* mother: and, Thou shalt love thy neighbour as thyself. Ex. 20:12–16; Matt. 22:39; Luke 18:20; Col. 3:20.

Matt. 21:5. Tell ye the daughter of Sion, Behold, thy King cometh unto thee, meek, and sitting upon an ass, and a colt the foal of an ass. Zech. 9:9; John 12:15.

9. Blessed *is* he that cometh in the name of the Lord; Psa. 118:26; Mark 11:9; John 12:13.

13. My house shall be called the house of prayer; but ye have made it a den of thieves. Isa. 56:7; Jer. 7:11; Mark 11:17; Luke 19:46.

16. Out of the mouth of babes and sucklings thou hast perfected praise? Psa. 8:2.

33. There was a certain householder, which planted a vineyard, Isa. 5:1,2; Mark 12:2; Luke 20:9.

42. The stone which the builders rejected, the same is become the head of the corner: this is the Lord's doing, and it is marvellous in our eyes? Psa. 118:22,23; Mark 12:10; Luke 20:17; Acts 4:11; 1 Pet. 2:7.

Matt. 22:24. If a man die, having no children, his brother shall marry his wife, and raise up seed unto his brother. Deut. 25:5; Mark 12:19; Luke 20:28.

32. I am the God of Abraham, and the God of Isaac, and the God of Jacob? Ex. 3:6; Mark 12:26; Luke 20:37; Acts 7:32.

37. Thou shalt love the Lord thy God with

all thy heart, and with all thy soul, and with all thy mind. Deut. 6:5; Mark 12:29,30; Luke 10:27.

39. Thou shalt love thy neighbour as thyself. Lev. 19:18; Mark 12:31; Luke 10:27.

44. Sit thou on my right hand, till I make thine enemies thy footstool? Psa. 110:1; Mark 12:36; Luke 20:42,43; Acts 2:34,35; Heb. 1:13.

Matt. 23:39. Blessed *is* he that cometh in the name of the Lord. Psa. 118:26; Luke 13:35.

Matt. 24:15. The abomination of desolation, spoken of by Daniel the prophet, stand in the holy place. Dan. 9:27; Mark 13:14; Luke 21:20.

Matt. 26:31. I will smite the shepherd, and the sheep of the flock shall be scattered abroad. Zech. 13:7.

Matt. 27:9. And they took the thirty pieces of silver, the price of him that was valued, whom they of the children of Israel did value; 10. And gave them for the potter's field, as the Lord appointed me. Zech. 11:12,13.

35. ¹ They parted my garments among them, and upon my vesture did they cast lots. Psa. 22:18; John 19:24. [¹ Omitted in R. V.]

46. My God, my God, why hast thou forsaken me? Psa. 22:1.

Mark 1:2. Behold, I send my messenger before thy face, which shall prepare thy way before thee. Mal. 3:1; Luke 7:27.

3. Prepare ye the way of the Lord, make his paths straight. Isa. 40:3.

Mark 7:6. This people honoureth me with *their* lips, but their heart is far from me. 7. Howbeit in vain do they worship me, teaching *for* doctrines the commandments of men. Isa. 29:13.

10. Honour thy father and thy mother; and, Whoso curseth father or mother, let him die the death: Ex. 20:12; 21:17; Deut. 5:16.

Mark 9:48. Where their worm dieth not, and the fire is not quenched. Isa. 66:24.

Mark 10:6. God made them male and female. Gen. 1:27.

7. For this cause shall a man leave his father and mother, and cleave to his wife; 8. And they twain shall be one flesh: so then they are no more twain, but one flesh. Gen. 2.24.

19. Do not commit adultery, Do not kill, Do not steal, Do not bear false witness, Defraud not, Honour thy father and mother. Ex. 20:12–17; Deut. 5:16–20.

Mark 11:9. Hosanna; Blessed *is* he that cometh in the name of the Lord: Psa. 118:26.

Mark 12:29. The first of all the commandments *is*, Hear, O Israel; The Lord our God is one Lord: Deut. 6:4.

30. And thou shalt love the Lord thy God with all thy heart, and with all thy soul, and with all thy mind, and with all thy strength: this *is* the first commandment. Deut. 6:5.

31. Thou shalt love thy neighbour as thyself. There is none other commandment greater than these. Lev. 19:18.

Mark 14:27. I will smite the shepherd, and the sheep shall be scattered. Zech. 13:7.

Mark 15:28. ¹ And he was numbered with the transgressors. Isa. 53:12. [¹ Omitted in R. V.]

34. Eloi, Eloi, lama sabachthani? which is, being interpreted, My God, my God, why hast thou forsaken me? Psa. 22:1.

Luke 1:17. And he shall go before him in the spirit and power of Elias, to turn the hearts of the fathers to the children, and the disobedient to the wisdom of the just; to make ready a people prepared for the Lord. Mal. 4:6.

Mary's magnificat, Luke 1:46–54. Compare with 1 Sam. 2:1–11; Psa. 103:17; 113: 7,8; Isa. 41:8–14.

Luke 2:23. Every male that openeth the womb shall be called holy to the Lord; Ex. 13:2,12.

24. A pair of turtledoves, or two young pigeons. Lev. 12:8.

Luke 3:4. The voice of one crying in the wilderness, Prepare ye the way of the Lord, make his paths straight. 5. Every valley shall be filled, and every mountain and hill shall be brought low; and the crooked shall be made straight, and the rough ways *shall be* made smooth; 6. And all flesh shall see the salvation of God. Isa. 40:3–5.

Luke 4:18. He hath anointed me to preach the gospel to the poor; he hath sent me to heal the brokenhearted, to preach deliverance to the captives, and recovering of sight to the blind, to set at liberty them that are bruised, 19. To preach the acceptable year of the Lord. Isa. 61:1,2.

Luke 8:10. That seeing they might not see, and hearing they might not understand. Isa. 6:9.

Luke 22:37. And he was reckoned among the transgressors. Isa. 53:12.

Luke 23:30. Then shall they begin to say to the mountains, Fall on us; and to the hills, Cover us. Hos. 10:8.

46. He said, Father, into thy hands I commend my spirit: Psa. 31:5.

John 1:23. The voice of one crying in the wilderness, Make straight the way of the Lord. Isa. 40:3.

John 2:17. The zeal of thine house hath eaten me up. Psa. 69:9.

John 6:31. He gave them bread from heaven to eat. Psa. 78:24.

45. And they shall be all taught of God. Isa. 54:13.

John 7:38. The scripture hath said, out of his belly shall flow rivers of living water. [Not identified.]

42. Hath not the scripture said, That Christ cometh of the seed of David [Isa. 11:1; Jer. 23:5,6; 33:15], and out of the town of Bethlehem, where David was? Mic. 5:2.

John 10:34. I said, Ye are gods? Psa. 82:6.

John 12:38. Lord, who hath believed our report? and to whom hath the arm of the Lord been revealed? Isa. 53:1; Rom. 10:16.

40. He hath blinded their eyes, and hardened their heart; that they should not see with *their* eyes, nor understand with *their*

heart, and be converted, and I should heal them. Isa. 6:9,10.

John 13:18. He that eateth bread with me hath lifted up his heel against me. Psa. 41:9.

John 15:25. They hated me without a cause. Psa. 35:19; 69:4; 109:3; 119:161; Lam. 3:52.

John 19:24. They parted my raiment among them, and for my vesture they did cast lots. v. 29; Psa. 22:18.

36. A bone of him shall not be broken. Ex. 12:46; Psa. 34:20.

37. They shall look on him whom they pierced. Zech. 12:10.

Acts 1:20. Let his habitation be desolate, and let no man dwell therein: and his bishoprick let another take. Psa. 69:25; 109:8.

Acts 2:17. I will pour out of my Spirit upon all flesh: and your sons and your daughters shall prophesy, and your young men shall see visions, and your old men shall dream dreams: 18. And on my servants and on my handmaidens I will pour out in those days of my Spirit; and they shall prophesy: 19. And I will shew wonders in heaven above, and signs in the earth beneath; blood, and fire, and vapour of smoke: 20. The sun shall be turned into darkness, and the moon into blood, before that great and notable day of the Lord come: 21. And it shall come to pass, *that* whosoever shall call on the name of the Lord shall be saved. Joel 2:28–32; Rom. 10:13.

25. I foresaw the Lord always before my face, for he is on my right hand, that I should not be moved: 26. Therefore did my heart rejoice, and my tongue was glad; moreover also my flesh shall rest in hope: 27. Because thou wilt not leave my soul in hell, neither wilt thou suffer thine Holy One to see corruption. 28. Thou hast made known to me the ways of life; thou shalt make me full of joy with thy countenance. v. 31; Psa. 16:8–11.

Acts 3:22. A prophet shall the Lord your God raise up unto you of your brethren, like unto me; him shall ye hear in all things whatsoever he shall say unto you. 23. And it shall come to pass, *that* every soul, which will not hear that prophet, shall be destroyed from among the people. Deut. 18:15–19.

25. And in thy seed shall all the kindreds of the earth be blessed. Gen. 12:3,7; 22:18.

Acts 4:11. This is the stone which was set at nought of you builders, which is become the head of the corner. Psa. 118:22; Matt. 21:42; Mark 12:10; Luke 20:17.

25. Why did the heathen rage, and the people imagine vain things? 26. The kings of the earth stood up, and the rulers were gathered together against the Lord, and against his Christ. Psa. 2:1,2.

Acts 7:3. Get thee out of thy country, and from thy kindred, and come into the land which I shall shew thee. v. 5; Gen. 12:1,7; 13:15; 15:18.

6. And God spake on this wise, That his seed should sojourn in a strange land; and that

they should bring them into bondage, and entreat *them* evil four hundred years. 7. And the nation to whom they shall be in bondage will I judge, said God: and after that shall they come forth, and serve me in this place. Gen. 15:13,14.

9. And the patriarchs . . . sold Joseph into Egypt: but God was with him, 10. And delivered him out of all his afflictions, and gave him favour and wisdom. Gen. 37: 11,28; 39:3; 41:40,41.

11. Now there came a dearth over all the land of Egypt and Chanaan, and great affliction: and our fathers found no sustenance. Gen. 42.

13. And at the second *time* Joseph was made known to his brethren; 14. Then sent Joseph, and called his father Jacob to *him*, and all his kindred, threescore and fifteen souls. Gen. 45:1,16; 46:26,27.

15. So Jacob . . . died, he, and our fathers, 16. And were carried over into Sychem, and laid in the sepulchre that Abraham bought. Gen. 49:29–33; 50:1–13.

17. The people grew and multiplied in Egypt, 18. Till another king arose, which knew not Joseph. 19. The same dealt subtilly with our kindred, and evil entreated our fathers, so that they cast out their young children, to the end they might not live. Ex. 1.

20. In which time Moses was born, and was exceeding fair, and nourished up in his father's house three months: 21. And when he was cast out, Pharaoh's daughter took him up, and nourished him for her own son. Ex. 2:2,5–10.

23. And when he was full forty years old, it came into his heart to visit his brethren the children of Israel. 24. And seeing one *of them* suffer wrong, he defended *him*, and avenged him that was oppressed, and smote the Egyptian: *vs.* 25–29; Ex. 2:11–15.

26. And the next day he shewed himself unto them as they strove, and would have set them at one again, saying, Sirs, ye are brethren; why do ye wrong one to another? 27. But he that did his neighbour wrong thrust him away, saying, Who made thee a ruler and a judge over us? 28. Wilt thou kill me, as thou diddest the Egyptian yesterday? *vs.* 23–25,35; Ex. 2:11–15.

30. And when forty years were expired, there appeared to him in the wilderness of mount Sina an angel of the Lord in a flame of fire in a bush. Ex. 3:2.

31. When Moses saw *it*, he wondered at the sight: and as he drew near to behold *it*, the voice of the Lord came unto him. v. 32; Ex. 3:3–10; Mark 12:26.

33. Put off thy shoes from thy feet: for the place where thou standest is holy ground. 34. I have seen, I have seen the affliction of my people which is in Egypt, and I have heard their groaning, and am come down to deliver them. And now come, I will send thee into Egypt. Ex. 3:5–10.

36. He brought them out, after that he

had shewed wonders and signs in the land of Egypt, and in the Red sea, and in the wilderness forty years. Ex. chaps. 7-12.

37. A prophet shall the Lord your God raise up unto you of your brethren, like unto me; him shall ye hear. Deut. 18:15.

38. This is he . . . who received the lively oracles to give unto us: Ex. 19.

39. To whom our fathers would not obey, but thrust *him* from them, and in their hearts turned back again into Egypt, Num. 20:1-11.

40. Make us gods to go before us: for *as for* this Moses, which brought us out of the land of Egypt, we wot not what is become of him. Ex. 32:1-6,23.

42. O ye house of Israel, have ye offered to me slain beasts and sacrifices *by the space of* forty years in the wilderness? 43. Yea, ye took up the tabernacle of Moloch, and the star of your god Remphan, figures which ye made to worship them: and I will carry you away beyond Babylon. Amos 5:25-27.

44. Our fathers had the tabernacle of witness in the wilderness, Ex. 25:40; 26:30; Heb. 8:5.

46. Who found favour before God, and desired to find a tabernacle for the God of Jacob. 47. But Solomon built him an house. 1 Kin. 8:17-20.

49. Heaven *is* my throne, and earth *is* my footstool: what house will ye build me? saith the Lord: or what *is* the place of my rest? 50. Hath not my hand made all these things? Isa. 66:1,2.

Acts 8:32. He was led as a sheep to the slaughter; and like a lamb dumb before his shearer, so opened he not his mouth: 33. In his humiliation his judgment was taken away: and who shall declare his generation? for his life is taken from the earth. Isa. 53:7,8.

Acts 13:17. They dwelt as strangers in the land of Egypt, and with an high arm brought he them out of it. Ex. chaps.7-14; Deut.7:19.

18. Forty years suffered he their manners in the wilderness. Books of Exodus, Leviticus, Numbers, Deuteronomy.

19. And when he had destroyed seven nations in the land of Chanaan, he divided their land to them by lot. Book of Joshua.

22. I have found David the *son* of Jesse, a man after mine own heart, which shall fulfil all my will. Psa. 89:20; 1 Sam. 13:14.

33. Thou art my Son, this day have I begotten thee. Psa. 2:7.

34. I will give you the sure mercies of David. Isa. 55:3.

35. Thou shalt not suffer thine Holy One to see corruption. Psa. 16:10.

41. Behold, ye despisers, and wonder, and perish: for I work a work in your days, a work which ye shall in no wise believe, though a man declare it unto you. Hab. 1:5.

47. I have set thee to be a light of the Gentiles, that thou shouldest be for salvation unto the ends of the earth. Isa. 49:6.

Acts 15:16. After this I will return, and will build again the tabernacle of David, which is fallen down; and I will build again the ruins thereof, and I will set it up: 17. That the residue of men might seek after the Lord, and all the Gentiles, upon whom my name is called, saith the Lord, who doeth all these things. Amos 9:11,12.

Acts 23:5. Thou shalt not speak evil of the ruler of thy people. Ex. 22:28.

Rom. 1:17. The just shall live by faith. Hab. 2:4.

Rom. 2:24. The name of God is blasphemed among the Gentiles through you, Isa. 52:5.

Rom. 3:4. That thou mightest be justified in thy sayings, and mightest overcome when thou art judged. Psa. 51:4.

10. There is none righteous, no, not one: 11. There is none that understandeth, there is none that seeketh after God. 12. They are all gone out of the way, they are together become unprofitable; there is none that doeth good, no, not one. Psa. 14:1-3; Eccl. 7:20.

13. Their throat *is* an open sepulchre, with their tongues they have used deceit [Psa. 5:9]; the poison of asps *is* under their lips: Psa. 140:3.

14. Whose mouth *is* full of cursing and bitterness: Psa. 10:7.

15. Their feet *are* swift to shed blood: 16. Destruction and misery *are* in their ways: 17. And the way of peace have they not known: Isa. 59:7,8.

18. There is no fear of God before their eyes. Psa. 36:1.

Rom. 4:3. Abraham believed God, and it was counted unto him for righteousness. Gen. 15:6.

7. Blessed *are* they whose iniquities are forgiven, and whose sins are covered. 8. Blessed *is* the man to whom the Lord will not impute sin. Psa. 32:1,2.

17. I have made thee a father of many nations, Gen. 17:5.

18. So shall thy seed be. Gen. 15:5.

Rom. 7:7. I had not known sin, but by the law: for I had not known lust, except the law had said, Thou shalt not covet. Ex. 20:17.

Rom. 8:36. For thy sake we are killed all the day long; we are accounted as sheep for the slaughter. Psa. 44:22.

Rom. 9:7. In Isaac shall thy seed be called. Gen. 21:12.

9. At this time will I come, and Sarah shall have a son. Gen. 18:10.

12. The elder shall serve the younger. Gen. 25:23.

13. Jacob have I loved, but Esau have I hated. Mal. 1:2,3.

15. I will have mercy on whom I will have mercy, and I will have compassion on whom I will have compassion. Ex. 33:19.

17. Even for this same purpose have I raised thee up, that I might shew my power in thee, and that my name might be declared throughout all the earth. Ex. 9:16.

25. I will call them my people, which were not my people; and her beloved, which was not beloved. Hos. 2:23.

26. And it shall come to pass, *that* in the place where it was said unto them, Ye *are* not my people; there shall they be called the children of the living God. Hos. 1:10.

27. Though the number of the children of Israel be as the sand of the sea, a remnant shall be saved: 28. For he will finish the work, and cut *it* short in righteousness: because a short work will the Lord make upon the earth. Isa. 10:22,23.

29. Except the Lord of Sabaoth had left us a seed, we had been as Sodoma, and been made like unto Gomorrha. Isa. 1:9.

33. Behold, I lay in Sion a stumbling-stone and rock of offence: and whosoever believeth on him shall not be ashamed. Psa. 118:22; Isa. 8:14; 28:16; 1 Pet. 2:6,7.

Rom. 10:5. That the man which doeth those things shall live by them. Lev. 18:5.

6. But the righteousness which is of faith speaketh on this wise, Say not in thine heart, Who shall ascend into heaven? 7. Or, Who shall descend into the deep? 8. But what saith it? The word is nigh thee, *even* in thy mouth, and in thy heart: Deut. 30: 12–14.

13. For whosoever shall call upon the name of the Lord shall be saved. Joel 2:32.

15. How beautiful are the feet of them that preach the gospel of peace, and bring glad tidings of good things! Isa. 52:7.

16. For Esaias saith, Lord, who hath believed our report? Isa. 53:1.

18. Their sound went into all the earth, and their words unto the ends of the world. Psa. 19:4.

19. I will provoke you to jealousy by *them that are* no people, *and* by a foolish nation I will anger you. Deut. 32:21.

20. I was found of them that sought me not; I was made manifest unto them that asked not after me. 21. But to Israel he saith, All day long I have stretched forth my hands unto a disobedient and gainsaying people. Isa. 65:2.

Rom. 10:11. Whosoever believeth on him shall not be ashamed. Isa. 28:16.

Rom. 11:3. Lord, they have killed thy prophets, and digged down thine altars; and I am left alone, and they seek my life. 1 Kin. 19:14.

4. I have reserved to myself seven thousand men, who have not bowed the knee to *the image of* Baal. 1 Kin. 19:18.

8. God hath given them the spirit of slumber, eyes that they should not see, and ears that they should not hear; Isa. 6:9,10; 29:10; Ezek. 12:2.

9. Let their table be made a snare, and a trap, and a stumblingblock, and a recompence unto them: Psa. 69:22.

10. Let their eyes be darkened, that they may not see, and bow down their back alway. Psa. 69:23.

26. There shall come out of Sion the Deliverer, and shall turn away ungodliness from Jacob: 27. For this *is* my covenant unto them, when I shall take away their sins. Isa. 59:20,21; 27:9.

34. For who hath known the mind of the Lord? or who hath been his counsellor? Isa. 40:13.

Rom. 12:19. Vengeance *is* mine; I will repay, saith the Lord. Deut. 32:35; Heb. 10:30.

20. Therefore if thine enemy hunger, feed him; if he thirst, give him drink: for in so doing thou shalt heap coals of fire on his head. Prov. 25:21,22.

Rom. 13:9. For this, Thou shalt not commit adultery, Thou shalt not kill, Thou shalt not steal, Thou shalt not bear false witness, Thou shalt not covet; and if *there be* any other commandment, it is briefly comprehended in this saying, namely, Thou shalt love thy neighbour as thyself. Ex. 20: 13–17; Lev. 19:18; Deut. 5:16–21.

Rom. 14:11. *As* I live, saith the Lord, every knee shall bow to me, and every tongue shall confess to God. Isa. 45:23.

Rom. 15:3. The reproaches of them that reproached thee fell on me. Psa. 69:9.

9. For this cause I will confess to thee among the Gentiles, and sing unto thy name. 2 Sam. 22:50; Psa. 18:49.

10. Rejoice, ye Gentiles, with his people. Deut. 32:43.

11. Praise the Lord, all ye Gentiles; and laud him, all ye people. Psa. 117:1.

12. There shall be a root of Jesse, and he that shall rise to reign over the Gentiles; in him shall the Gentiles trust. Isa. 11:1,10.

21. To whom he was not spoken of, they shall see: and they that have not heard shall understand. Isa. 52:15.

1 Cor. 1:19. I will destroy the wisdom of the wise, and will bring to nothing the understanding of the prudent. Isa. 29:14.

31. He that glorieth, let him glory in the Lord. Jer. 9:24; 2 Cor. 10:17.

1 Cor. 2:9. Eye hath not seen, nor ear heard, neither have entered into the heart of man, the things which God hath prepared for them that love him. Isa. 64:4.

16. For who hath known the mind of the Lord, that he may instruct him? Isa. 40:13; Rom. 11:34.

1 Cor. 3:19. He taketh the wise in their own craftiness. Job 5:13.

20. The Lord knoweth the thoughts of the wise, that they are vain. Psa. 94:11.

1 Cor. 6:16. What! know ye not that he which is joined to an harlot is one body? for two, saith he, shall be one flesh. Gen. 2:24.

1 Cor. 9:9. Thou shalt not muzzle the mouth of the ox that treadeth out the corn. Deut. 25:4.

1 Cor. 10:7. The people sat down to eat and drink, and rose up to play. Ex. 32:6.

20. The things which the Gentiles sacrifice, they sacrifice to devils, and not to God: Deut. 32:17.

26. For the earth *is* the Lord's, and the fulness thereof. Psa. 24:1; 50:12.

1 Cor. 14:21. With *men of* other tongues and other lips will I speak unto this people;

and yet for all that will they not hear me, saith the Lord. Isa. 28:11,12.

1 Cor. 15:25. For he must reign, till he hath put all enemies under his feet. Psa. 110:1.

27. For he hath put all things under his feet. Psa. 8:6.

32. Let us eat and drink; for to morrow we die. Isa. 22:13.

45. The first man Adam was made a living soul: Gen. 2:7.

54. Death is swallowed up in victory. Isa. 25:8.

55. ¹ O death, where *is* thy sting? O grave, where *is* thy victory? Hos. 13:14.

¹¹ R. V. O death, where is thy victory? O death, where is thy sting?

2 Cor. 3:13. And not as Moses, *which* put a vail over his face, that the children of Israel could not stedfastly look to the end of that which is abolished. Ex. 34:33.

2 Cor. 4:13. I believed, and therefore have I spoken; Psa. 116:10.

2 Cor. 6:2. I have heard thee in a time accepted, and in the day of salvation have I succoured thee: Isa. 49:8.

16. I will dwell in them, and walk in *them;* and I will be their God, and they shall be my people. Lev. 26:11,12; Ezek. 37:27.

17. Wherefore come out from among them, and be ye separate, saith the Lord, and touch not the unclean *thing;* and I will receive you. Isa. 52:11,12.

18. And will be a Father unto you, and ye shall be my sons and daughters, saith the Lord Almighty. 2 Sam. 7:14.

2 Cor. 8:15. He that *had gathered* much had nothing over; and he that *had gathered* little had no lack. Ex. 16:18.

2 Cor. 9:9. He hath dispersed abroad; he hath given to the poor: his righteousness remaineth for ever. Psa. 112:9.

2 Cor. 13:1. In the mouth of two or three witnesses shall every word be established. Deut. 19:15.

Gal. 3:6. Even as Abraham believed God, and it was accounted to him for righteousness. Gen. 15:6.

8. In thee shall all nations be blessed. Gen. 12:3; 18:18.

10. Cursed *is* every one that continueth not in all things which are written in the book of the law to do them. Deut. 27:26.

11. The just shall live by faith. Hab. 2:4.

12. The man that doeth them shall live in them. Lev. 18:5.

13. Cursed *is* every one that hangeth on a tree: Deut. 21:23.

Gal. 4:27. Rejoice, thou barren that bearest not: break forth and cry, thou that travailest not: for the desolate hath many more children than she which hath an husband. Isa. 54:1.

30. Cast out the bondwoman and her son: Gen. 21:10.

Gal. 5:14. That the blessing of Abraham might come on the Gentiles through Jesus Christ; Lev. 19:18.

Eph. 4:8. When he ascended up on high,

he led captivity captive, and gave gifts unto men. Psa. 68:18.

25. Wherefore putting away lying, speak every man truth with his neighbour: Zech. 8:16.

26. Be ye angry, and sin not: Psa. 4:4.

Eph. 5:31. For this cause shall a man leave his father and mother, and shall be joined unto his wife, and they two shall be one flesh. Gen. 2:24.

Eph. 6:2. Honour thy father and mother; 3. That it may be well with thee, and thou mayest live long on the earth. Ex. 20:12; Deut. 5:16.

1 Tim. 5:18. Thou shalt not muzzle the ox that treadeth out the corn. [Deut. 25:4.] And, The labourer *is* worthy of his reward. Lev. 19:13; Deut. 24:14,15.

2 Tim. 2:19. The Lord knoweth them that are his. Num. 16.5.

Heb. 1:5. Thou art my son, this day have I begotten thee? [Psa. 2:7.] I will be to him a Father, and he shall be to me a Son? 2 Sam. 7:14.

6. And let all the angels of God worship him. Psa. 97:7.

7. Who maketh his angels spirits, and his ministers a flame of fire. Psa. 104:4.

8. Thy throne, O God, *is* for ever and ever: a sceptre of righteousness *is* the sceptre of thy kingdom. 9. Thou hast loved righteousness, and hated iniquity; therefore God, *even* thy God, hath anointed thee with the oil of gladness above thy fellows. Psa. 45:6,7.

10. Thou, Lord, in the beginning hast laid the foundation of the earth; and the heavens are the works of thine hands. 11. They shall perish; but thou remainest; and they all shall wax old as doth a garment; 12. And as a vesture shalt thou fold them up, and they shall be changed: but thou art the same, and thy years shall not fail. Psa. 102:25-27.

13. Sit on my right hand, until I make thine enemies thy footstool? Psa. 110:1.

Heb. 2:6. What is man, that thou art mindful of him? or the son of man, that thou visitest him? 7. Thou madest him a little lower than the angels; thou crownedst him with glory and honour, and didst set him over the works of thy hands: 8. Thou hast put all things in subjection under his feet. Psa. 8:4-6.

12. Saying, I will declare thy name unto my brethren, in the midst of the church will I sing praise unto thee. Psa. 22:22.

13. I will put my trust in him. And again, Behold I and the children which God hath given me. Isa. 8:17,18.

Heb. 3:2. Moses *was faithful* in all his house. Num. 12:7.

7. To day if ye will hear his voice, 8. Harden not your hearts, as in the provocation, in the day of temptation in the wilderness: 9. When your fathers tempted me, proved me, and saw my works forty years. 10. Wherefore I was grieved with that gen-

eration, and said, They do alway err in *their* heart; and they have not known my ways. Psa. 95:7–11; Heb. 4:7.

Heb. 4:3. As I have sworn in my wrath, if they shall enter into my rest : although the works were finished from the foundation of the world. Psa. 95:11.

4. God did rest the seventh day from all his works. Gen. 2:2; Ex. 20:11.

Heb. 5:5. Thou art my Son, to day have I begotten thee. Psa. 2:7.

6. Thou *art* a priest for ever after the order of Melchisedec. Heb. 6:20; 7:11,17,21; Psa. 110:4.

Heb. 6:14. Surely blessing I will bless thee, and multiplying I will multiply thee. Gen. 22:16,17.

Heb. 7:1. For this Melchisedec, . . . who met Abraham. Gen. 14:18–20.

Heb. 8:5. See, saith he, *that* thou make all things according to the pattern shewed to thee in the mount. Ex. 25:40; 26:30.

8. Behold, the days come, saith the Lord, when I will make a new covenant with the house of Israel and with the house of Judah : *vs.* 9–12; Jer. 31:31–34.

Heb. 9:20. This *is* the blood of the testament which God hath enjoined unto you. Ex. 24:8.

Heb. 10:5. Sacrifice and offering thou wouldest not, but a body hast thou prepared me : 6. In burnt offerings and *sacrifices* for sin thou hast had no pleasure. 7. Then said I, Lo, I come (in the volume of the book it is written of me,) to do thy will, O God. Psa. 40:6–8.

13. From henceforth expecting till his enemies be made his footstool. Psa. 110:1.

30. Vengeance *belongeth* unto me, I will recompense, saith the Lord. And again, The Lord shall judge his people. Deut. 32: 35,36.

38. Now the just shall live by faith : Hab. 2:3,4.

Heb. 11:3. The worlds were framed by the word of God, Psa. 33:6.

4. Abel offered unto God a more excellent sacrifice than Cain, Gen. 4:4.

5. Enoch was translated. Gen. 5:24.

7. Noah . . . prepared an ark. Gen. 6:22.

8. Abraham . . . obeyed; Gen. 12:1–5.

11. Sara herself received strength to conceive seed, and was delivered of a child when she was past age, Gen. 18:11,12; 21:2.

12. Therefore sprang there even of one, . . . *so many* as the stars of the sky in multitude, and as the sand which is by the sea shore innumerable. Gen. 22:17.

17. Abraham . . . offered up Isaac : Gen. 22:9,10.

18. In Isaac shall thy seed be called : Gen. 21:12.

20. Isaac blessed Jacob and Esau. Gen. 27:26–29.

21. Jacob . . . blessed both the sons of Joseph; Gen. 48:15–20.

22. Joseph . . . gave commandment concerning his bones. Gen. 50:25.

23. Moses . . . was hid three months of his parents, Ex. 2:2.

27. He forsook Egypt, Ex. 10:28,29.

28. He kept the passover, Ex. 12:21,27,28.

29. They passed through the Red sea. Ex. 14:22.

30. The walls of Jericho fell down, after they were compassed about seven days. Josh. 6. 20.

31. The harlot Rahab perished not. Josh. 6:23,25.

32. Time would fail me to tell of Gedeon, and *of* Barak, and *of* Samson, and *of* Jephthae ; *of* David also, and Samuel, and *of* the prophets : Judg. 4:10–17; 7; 11:32,33; 16:28–30; 1 Sam. 7:9–12; 19:8.

33. Who through faith subdued kingdoms, . . . stopped the mouths of lions, Dan. 6:22.

34. Quenched the violence of fire, Dan. 3:26.

35. Women received their dead raised to life again : 1 Kin. 17:17–23; 2 Kin. 4:32–37.

36. And others had . . . bonds and imprisonment : Gen. 39:20; Jer. 20:1–3.

37. They were stoned, 2 Chr. 24:20,21.

38. They wandered in deserts, and *in* mountains, and *in* dens and caves of the earth. 1 Kin. 18:4,13.

Heb. 12:5. My son, despise not thou the chastening of the Lord, nor faint when thou art rebuked of him : Prov. 3:11.

6. For whom the Lord loveth he chasteneth, and scourgeth every son whom he receiveth. Prov. 3:11,12.

16. Esau, who for one morsel of meat sold his birthright. Gen. 25:29–33.

18. For ye are not come unto the mount that might be touched, and that burned with fire, nor unto blackness, and darkness, and tempest, 19 And the sound of a trumpet, and the voice of words; which *voice* they that heard intreated that the word should not be spoken to them any more : Ex. 19:16; Deut. 4:11,12.

20. If so much as a beast touch the mountain, it shall be stoned, or thrust through with a dart : Ex. 19:13.

21. Moses said, I exceedingly fear and quake : Deut. 9:19.

26. Yet once more I shake not the earth only, but also heaven. Hag. 2:6.

Heb. 13:5. I will never leave thee, nor forsake thee. Deut. 31:6,8; Josh. 1:5.

6. The Lord *is* my helper, and I will not fear what man shall do unto me. Psa. 118:6.

15. By him therefore let us offer the sacrifice of praise to God continually, that is, the fruit of *our* lips giving thanks to his name. Hos. 14:2.

Jas. 2:8. Thou shalt love thy neighbour as thyself, Lev. 19:18.

11. Do not commit adultery, . . . Do not kill. Ex. 20:13,14; Deut. 5:18.

23. Abraham believed God, and it was imputed unto him for righteousness : Gen. 15:6.

Jas. 4:6. God resisteth the proud, but giveth grace unto the humble. Prov. 3:34.

1 Pet. 1:16. Be ye holy; for I am holy. Lev. 11:44; 19:2; 20:7.

24. For all flesh *is* as grass, and all the glory of man as the flower of grass. The grass withereth, and the flower thereof falleth away: 25. But the word of the Lord endureth for ever. Isa. 40:6-8.

1 Pet. 2:6. Behold, I lay in Sion a chief corner stone, elect, precious: and he that believeth on him shall not be confounded. *vs.* 7,8; Isa. 28:16.

7. The stone which the builders disallowed, the same is made the head of the corner, Psa. 118:22; Isa. 8:14.

9. A royal priesthood, an holy nation, Ex. 19:6; Deut. 14:2; Mal. 3:17.

22. Who did no sin, neither was guile found in his mouth: Isa. 53:9.

24. By whose stripes ye were healed. Isa. 53:4,5.

1 Pet. 3:6. Sara obeyed Abraham, calling him lord:

10. For he that will love life, and see good days, let him refrain his tongue from evil, and his lips that they speak no guile: 11. Let him eschew evil, and do good; let him seek peace, and ensue it. 12. For the eyes of the Lord *are* over the righteous, and his ears *are open* unto their prayers: but the face of the Lord *is* against them that do evil. Psa. 34:12-16.

15. Sanctify the Lord God in your hearts: Isa. 8:12,13.

1 Pet. 5:5. For God resisteth the proud, and giveth grace to the humble. Prov. 3:34.

2 Pet. 2:22. The dog *is* turned to his own vomit again; Prov. 26:11.

R.

RAAMAH. 1. Son of Cush, Gen. 10:7; 1 Chr. 1:9.

2. A place in Arabia, Ezek. 27:22.

RAAMIAH. One of those who returned to Jerusalem from captivity in Babylon, Neh. 7:7. Called REELAIAH in Ezra 2:2.

RAAMSES. See RAMESES.

RABBAH. 1. Called also RABBATH. A city E. of the Jordan, originally belonging to the Ammonites, Josh. 13:25. Bedstead of the giant Og kept at, Deut. 3:11. Taken by David, 2 Sam. 11:1; 12:26-31; 1 Chr. 20:1-3. Possessed again by the Ammonites; prophesied against, Jer. 49:2,3; Ezek. 21:20; 25:5; Amos 1:14.

2. A city in Judah, Josh. 15:60.

RABBATH. See RABBAH.

RABBI. The title of a teacher, Matt. 23: 7,8; John 3:2. Ostentatiously used by the Pharisees, Matt. 23:7. Used in addressing John, John 3:26; in addressing Jesus, John 1:38,49; 3:2; 6:25 [*R. V.*, Matt. 26:25,49; Mark 9:5; 11:21; 14:45; John 4:31; 9:2; 11:8]. Jesus called Rabboni, Mark 10:51 [*R. V.*]; John 20: 16. Forbidden by Jesus as a title to his disciples, Matt. 23:8.

RABBITH, a city in Issachar, Josh. 19:20.

RAB-MAG, an Assyrian prince, or, possibly, a second name given to Nergalsharezer, Jer. 39:3,13.

RABSARIS. 1. An Assyrian officer. Sent by Sennacherib against Jerusalem, 2 Kin. 18:17.

2. An Assyrian prince in time of Nebuchadnezzar, or, possibly, a second name given to Nebushasban, Jer. 39:3,13.

RAB-SHAKEH, an Assyrian officer. Sent by Sennacherib against Jerusalem; undertakes by a speech in the Jews' language to cause disloyalty to Hezekiah and a surrender of the city, 2 Kin. 18:17-36; 19: 4,8; Isa. 36; 37:4,8.

RACA, Matt. 5:22.

RACE. 1. Human. Unity of, Gen. 3:20; Mal. 2:10.

2. FOOT RACE. Figurative: Psa. 19:5; Eccl. 9:11; 1 Cor. 9:24; Gal. 5:7; Phil. 2:16; Heb. 12:1,2.

RACHAB. See RAHAB.

RACHAL, a city in Judah, 1 Sam. 30:29.

RACHEL, daughter of Laban and wife of Jacob. Meets Jacob at the well, Gen. 29: 9-12. Jacob serves Laban fourteen years to secure her for his wife, Gen. 29:15-30. Sterility of, Gen. 29:31. Her grief in consequence of her sterility; gives her maid to Jacob in order to secure children in her own name, Gen. 30:1-8,15,22-34. Later fecundity of; becomes the mother of Joseph, Gen. 30:22-25; of Benjamin, Gen. 35:16-18,24. Steals the household images of her father, Gen. 31:4,14-19,33-35. Her death and burial, Gen. 35:18-20; 48:7; 1 Sam. 10:2.

RADDAI, son of Jesse, 1 Chr. 2:14.

RAGAU, called also REU. Son of Peleg and ancestor of Jesus, Gen. 11:18-21; 1 Chr. 1:25; Luke 3:35.

RAGUEL, called also REUEL and JETHRO. Moses's father-in-law, Num. 10:29. See JETHRO.

RAHAB. 1. Called also RACHAB. A woman of Jericho. Assists the spies of Israel, Josh. 2. Is spared at the taking of Jericho, Josh. 6:17-25. Ancestor of Joseph, Matt. 1:5. Faith of, commended, Heb. 11:31; Jas. 2:25.

2. A symbolical name applied to Egypt, Psa. 87:4; 89:10; Isa. 30:7 [*R. V.*]; 51:9.

RAHAM, son of Shema, 1 Chr. 2:44.

RAILING, forbidden, 1 Cor. 5:11; 1 Tim. 6:4; 1 Pet. 3:9; 2 Pet. 2:11; Jude 9. See SLANDER; SPEAKING EVIL.

INSTANCES OF: 1 Sam. 25:14; 2 Sam. 16:7; Mark 15:29.—*Bible Text-Book.*

RAIMENT. See DRESS.

RAIN. Forty days of, at the time of the flood, Gen. 7:4,10-12,17-24. The plague of, upon Egypt, Ex. 9:22-26,33,34. Miraculously caused by Samuel, 1 Sam. 12:16-19; by Elijah, 1 Kin. 18:41-45. David delivered by, 2 Sam. 5:17-21; Isa. 28:21. North wind unfavorable to, Prov. 25:23. Withheld as judgment, Deut. 11:17; 28:24; 1 Kin. 8:35; 2 Chr. 7:13; Jer. 3:3; Amos 4:7; Zech. 14:17. The earth shall no more be destroyed by,

Gen. 9:8–17. Sent by God, Deut. 11:13,14; Job 37:6; Isa. 30:23; Jer. 5:24; 14:22. Contingent upon obedience, Lev. 26:3,4; Deut. 11:13,14. Prayer for, 1 Kin. 8:35,36; 2 Chr. 6:26,27. Answer to prayer for, promised, 2 Chr. 7:13,14; Zech. 10:1. Withheld, in answer to prayer, Jas. 5:17,18.

Rainy season in Palestine in the ninth month, corresponding to December, Ezra 10:9,13.

See METEOROLOGY.

FIGURATIVE: Psa. 72:6.

RAINBOW. A token that the earth shall no more be destroyed by flood, Gen. 9:8–16; Ezek. 1:28. Symbolical, Rev. 4:3; 10:1. See METEOROLOGY.

RAISIN, preserved grape. Given by Abigail to David, 1 Sam. 25:18. Given to the famishing Egyptian to revive him, 1 Sam 30:12. Given by Ziba to David, 2 Sam. 16:1. Given to David at Ziklag, 1 Chr. 12:40.

RAISING, from the dead, see DEAD; RESURRECTION.

RAKEM, a descendant of Machir, son of Manasseh, 1 Chr. 7:16.

RAKKATH, a city in Naphthali, Josh. 19:35.

RAKKON, a city in Dan, Josh. 19:46.

RAM. 1. Son of Hezron and an ancestor of Jesus, Ruth 4:19; 1 Chr. 2:9,10. Called ARAM, Matt. 1:3,4 ; Luke 3:33.

2. Son of Jerahmeel, 1 Chr. 2:25,27.

3. An ancestor, probably of Elihu, mentioned in Job 32:2.

4. A sheep. Skins of, used for the roof of the tabernacle, Ex. 26:14; 39:34. Seen in Daniel's vision, Dan. 8:3, 20. Used in sacrifice. See OFFERINGS.

Trumpets made of the horns of. See TRUMPETS.

RAMA. See RAMAH, 1.

RAMAH. 1. Called RAMA, Matt. 2:18. A city allotted to Benjamin, Josh. 18:25; Judg. 19:13. Attempted fortification of, by King Baasha; destruction of, by Asa, 1 Kin. 15:17–22; 2 Chr. 16:1–6. People of, return from the Babylonish captivity, Ezra 2:26; Neh. 7:30; 11:33. Jeremiah imprisoned in, Jer. 40:1. Prophecies concerning, Isa. 10: 29; Jer. 31:15; Hosea 5:8; Matt. 2:18.

2. A city of Asher, Josh. 19:29.

3. A city of Naphthali, Josh. 19:36.

4. Called also RAMATHAIM-ZOPHIM. A city in Mount Ephraim, Judg. 4:5; 1 Sam. 1:1. Home of Elkanah, 1 Sam. 1:1,19; 2:11; and of Samuel, 1 Sam. 1:19,20; 7:17; 8:4; 15:34; 16:13. David flees to, 1 Sam. 19:18. Samuel dies and was buried in, 1 Sam. 25:1; 28:3.

5. See RAMOTH-GILEAD.

RAMATH, a city of Simeon, Josh. 19:8.

RAMATHAIM-ZOPHIM. See RA-MAH, 4.

RAMATH-LEHI, place where Samson slew a thousand Philistines with the jawbone of an ass, Judg. 15:17.

RAMATH-MIZPEH, a town in Gad, Josh. 13:26.

RAMESES, called also RAAMSES. The district in Egypt inhabited by the Israelites, Gen. 47:11; Ex. 1:11; 12:37; Num. 33:3,5. City of, built by the Israelites as a treasure city for Pharaoh, Ex. 1:11.

RAMIAH, an Israelite in the time of Ezra. Had taken a strange wife, Ezra 10:25.

RAMOTH. 1. An Israelite in the time of Ezra. Had taken a strange wife, Ezra 10:29.

2. Called RAMATH OF THE SOUTH. A place probably in the south of Simeon, Josh. 19:8: 1 Sam. 30:27.

3. A city of Issachar, allotted to the Levites, 1 Chr. 6:73.

4. Ramoth in Gilead. See RAMOTH-GILEAD.

RAMOTH-GILEAD. Called also RA-MAH, 2 Kin. 8:29; 2 Chr. 22:6. A city of Gad, and a city of refuge, Deut. 4:43; Josh. 20:8; 1 Chr. 6:80. One of Solomon's commissaries at, 1 Kin. 4:13. In the possession of the Syrians, 1 Kin. 22:3. Besieged by Israel and Judah; Ahab slain at, 1 Kin. 22:29–36; 2 Chr. 18. Recovered by Joram; Joram wounded at, 2 Kin. 8:28,29; 9:14,15; 2 Chr. 22:5,6. Elisha anoints Jehu king at, 2 Kin. 9:1–6.

RANSOM. Of a man's life, Ex. 21:30; 30:12; Job 36:18; Psa. 49:7,8; Prov. 6:35; 13:8; Hos. 13:14.

FIGURATIVE: Job 33:24; Isa. 35:10; 51:10; Matt. 20:28; 1 Tim. 2:6.

See JESUS; SAVIOUR; REDEMPTION.

RAPE. Law imposes death penalty for, Deut. 22:25–27. Captives afflicted with, Isa. 13:16; Lam. 5:11; Zech. 14:2.

INSTANCES OF: Of the servant of a Levite, by Benjamites; tribe of Benjamin nearly exterminated by the army of the other tribes, as punishment for, Judg. 19: 22–30; 20:35. Of Tamar by Amnon; avenged in the death of Amnon at the hand of Absalom, Tamar's brother, 2 Sam. 13:6–29,32,33.

RAPHA. 1. Son of Benjamin, 1 Chr. 8:2.

2. Called also REPHAIAH. A descendant of Jonathan, 1 Chr. 8:37; 9:43.

3. An ancestor of certain Philistine warriors, 2 Sam. 21:16,20,22 [marg.]; 1 Chr. 20: 4,6,8 [marg.].

RAPHU, a Benjamite, Num. 13:9.

RASHNESS. Psa. 116:11. I said in my haste, All men are liars.

Prov. 14:29. He that is slow to wrath is of great understanding: but he that is hasty of spirit exalteth folly.

Prov. 19:2. He that hasteth with his feet sinneth.

Prov. 21:5. The thoughts of the diligent tend only to plenteousness; but of every one that is hasty only to want.

Prov. 25:8. Go not forth hastily to strive. lest thou know not what to do in the end thereof, when thy neighbour hath put thee to shame.

Prov. 29:20. Seest thou a man that is hasty in his words? there is more hope of a fool than of him.

Eccl. 5:2. Be not rash with thy mouth, and let not thine heart be hasty to utter *any* thing before God : for God *is* in heaven, and thou upon earth : therefore let thy words be few.

Eccl. 7:9. Be not hasty in thy spirit to be angry : for anger resteth in the bosom of fools.

INSTANCES OF : Moses, in slaying the Egyptian, Ex. 2:11,12; Acts 7:24,25. When he smote the rock, Num. 20:10-12. Jephtha's vow, Judg. 11:31-39. Israel's vow to destroy the Benjamites. Judg. 21:1-23. Uzzah, in steadying the ark, 2 Sam. 6:6,7. David, in his generosity to Ziba, 2 Sam. 16: 4; with chap. 19:26-29. Rehoboam, in forsaking the counsel of the old men, 1 Kin. 12:8-15. Josiah, in fighting against Necho, 2 Chr. 35:20-24. Naaman, in refusing to wash in Jordan, 2 Kin. 5:11,12. James and John, in desiring to call down fire on the Samaritans, Luke 9:54. Paul, in persisting in going to Jerusalem, against the repeated admonitions of the Holy Ghost, Acts 21:4,10-15. The centurion, in rejecting Paul's counsel, Acts 27:11.

RAVEN. A black carnivorous bird, Prov. 30:17; Song 5:11. Forbidden as food, Lev. 11:15; Deut. 14:14. Preserved by Noah in the ark, Gen. 8:7. Fed Elijah, 1 Kin. 17:4-6. Cared for by divine providence, Luke 12:24.

RAVISHMENT. See Rape.

RAZOR, Nazarite forbidden to use, Num. 6:5.

FIGURATIVE: Psa. 52:2; Isa. 7:20; Ezek. 5:1.

READING, taught, Deut. 6:9; 11:20.

READINGS, SELECT. JUDAH'S DEFENSE: Gen. 44:18. Then Judah came near unto him, and said, Oh my lord, let thy servant, I pray thee, speak a word in my lord's ears, and let not thine anger burn against thy servant : for thou *even* as Pharaoh. 19. My lord asked his servants, saying, Have ye a father, or a brother? 20. And we said unto my lord, We have a father, an old man, and a child of his old age, a little one; and his brother is dead, and he alone is left of his mother, and his father loveth him. 21. And thou saidst unto thy servants, Bring him down unto me, that I may set mine eyes upon him. 22. And we said unto my lord, The lad cannot leave his father : for *if* he should leave his father, *his father* would die. 23. And thou saidst unto thy servants, Except your youngest brother come down with you, ye shall see my face no more. 24. And it came to pass when we came up unto thy servant my father, we told him the words of my lord. 25. And our father said, Go again, *and* buy us a little food. 26. And we said, We cannot go down : if our youngest brother be with us, then will we go down : for we may not see the man's face, except our youngest brother *be* with us. 27. And thy servant my father said unto us, Ye know that my wife bare me two *sons :* 28. And the one went out from

me, and I said, Surely he is torn in pieces; and I saw him not since : 29. And if ye take this also from me, and mischief befall him, ye shall bring down my gray hairs with sorrow to the grave. 30. Now therefore when I come to thy servant my father, and the lad *be* not with us; seeing that his life is bound up in the lad's life; 31. It shall come to pass, when he seeth that the lad *is* not *with us*, that he will die : and thy servants shall bring down the gray hairs of thy servant our father with sorrow to the grave. 32. For thy servant became surety for the lad unto my father, saying, If I bring him not unto thee, then I shall bear the blame to my father for ever. 33. Now therefore, I pray thee, let thy servant abide instead of the lad a bondman to my lord ; and let the lad go up with his brethren. 34. For how shall I go up to my father, and the lad *be* not with me? lest peradventure I see the evil that shall come on my father.

JOSEPH REVEALING HIS IDENTITY : Gen. 45:1. Then Joseph could not refrain himself before all them that stood by him, and he cried, Cause every man to go out from me. And there stood no man with him, while Joseph made himself known unto his brethren. 2. And he wept aloud : and the Egyptians and the house of Pharaoh heard. 3. And Joseph said unto his brethren, I *am* Joseph ; doth my father yet live? And his brethren could not answer him ; for they were troubled at his presence. 4. And Joseph said unto his brethren, Come near to me, I pray you. And they came near. And he said, I *am* Joseph your brother, whom ye sold into Egypt. 5. Now therefore be not grieved, nor angry with yourselves, that ye sold me hither : for God did send me before you to preserve life. 6. For these two years *hath* the famine *been* in the land : and yet *there are* five years, in the which *there shall* neither *be* earing nor harvest. 7. And God sent me before you to preserve you a posterity in the earth, and to save your lives by a great deliverance. 8. So now *it was* not you *that* sent me hither, but God : and he hath made me a father to Pharaoh, and lord of all his house, and a ruler throughout all the land of Egypt. 9. Haste ye, and go up to my father, and say unto him, Thus saith thy son Joseph, God hath made me lord of all Egypt : come down unto me, tarry not : 10. And thou shalt dwell in the land of Goshen, and thou shalt be near unto me, thou, and thy children, and thy children's children, and thy flocks, and thy herds, and all that thou hast : 11. And there will I nourish thee ; for yet *there are* five years of famine ; lest thou, and thy household, and all that thou hast, come to poverty. 12. And, behold, your eyes see, and the eyes of my brother Benjamin, that *it is* my mouth that speaketh unto you. 13. And ye shall tell my father of all my glory in Egypt, and of all that ye have seen ; and ye shall haste and bring down my father hither. 14. And he fell upon his brother Benjamin's neck, and wept; and Benjamin wept upon his neck. 15. Moreover he kissed all his brethren, and wept upon them: and after that his brethren talked with him.

THE DELIVERANCE OF THE ISRAELITES FROM PHARAOH: Ex. 14:5. And it was told the king of Egypt that the people fled: and the heart of Pharaoh and of his servants was turned against the people, and they said, Why have we done this, that we have let Israel go from serving us? 6. And he made ready his chariot, and took his people with him: 7. And he took six hundred chosen chariots, and all the chariots of Egypt, and captains over every one of them. 8. And the LORD hardened the heart of Pharaoh king of Egypt, and he pursued after the children of Israel: and the children of Israel went out with an high hand. 9. But the Egyptians pursued after them, all the horses *and* chariots of Pharaoh, and his horsemen, and his army, and overtook them encamping by the sea, beside Pi-hahiroth, before Baal-zephon. 10. And when Pharaoh drew nigh, the children of Israel lifted up their eyes, and, behold, the Egyptians marched after them; and they were sore afraid: and the children of Israel cried out unto the LORD. 11. And they said unto Moses, Because *there were* no graves in Egypt, hast thou taken us away to die in the wilderness? wherefore hast thou dealt thus with us, to carry us forth out of Egypt? 12. *Is* not this the word that we did tell thee in Egypt, saying, Let us alone, that we may serve the Egyptians? For *it had been* better for us to serve the Egyptians, than that we should die in the wilderness. 13. And Moses said unto the people, Fear ye not, stand still, and see the salvation of the LORD, which he will shew to you to day: for the Egyptians whom ye have seen to day, ye shall see them again no more for ever. 14. The LORD shall fight for you, and ye shall hold your peace. 15. And the LORD said unto Moses, Wherefore criest thou unto me? speak unto the children of Israel, that they go forward: 16. But lift thou up thy rod, and stretch out thine hand over the sea, and divide it: and the children of Israel shall go on dry *ground* through the midst of the sea. 17. And I, behold, I will harden the hearts of the Egyptians, and they shall follow them: and I will get me honour upon Pharaoh, and upon all his host, upon his chariots, and upon his horsemen. 18. And the Egyptians shall know that I *am* the LORD, when I have gotten me honour upon Pharaoh, upon his chariots, and upon his horsemen. 19. And the angel of God, which went before the camp of Israel, removed and went behind them; and the pillar of the cloud went from before their face, and stood behind them: 20. And it came between the camp of the Egyptians and the camp of Israel; and it was a cloud and darkness *to them*, but it gave light by night

to these: so that the one came not near the other all the night. 21. And Moses stretched out his hand over the sea; and the LORD caused the sea to go *back* by a strong east wind all that night and made the sea dry *land*, and the waters were divided. 22. And the children of Israel went into the midst of the sea upon the dry *ground:* and the waters *were* a wall unto them on their right hand, and on their left. 23. And the Egyptians pursued, and went in after them to the midst of the sea, *even* all Pharaoh's horses, his chariots, and his horsemen. 24. And it came to pass, that in the morning watch the LORD looked unto the host of the Egyptians through the pillar of fire and of the cloud, and troubled the host of the Egyptians, 25. And took off their chariot wheels, that they drave them heavily: so that the Egyptians said, Let us flee from the face of Israel; for the LORD fighteth for them against the Egyptians. 26. And the LORD said unto Moses, Stretch out thine hand over the sea, that the waters may come again upon the Egyptians, upon their chariots, and upon their horsemen. 27. And Moses stretched forth his hand over the sea, and the sea returned to his strength when the morning appeared; and the Egyptians fled against it; and the LORD overthrew the Egyptians in the midst of the sea. 28. And the waters returned, and covered the chariots, and the horsemen, *and* all the host of Pharaoh that came into the sea after them; there remained not so much as one of them. 29. But the children of Israel walked upon dry *land* in the midst of the sea; and the waters *were* a wall unto them on their right hand, and on their left. 30. Thus the LORD saved Israel that day out of the hand of the Egyptians; and Israel saw the Egyptians dead upon the sea shore.

SONG OF MOSES WHEN PHARAOH AND HIS ARMY WERE OVERTHROWN: Ex. 15:1. Then sang Moses and the children of Israel this song unto the LORD, and spake, saying, I will sing unto the LORD, for he hath triumphed gloriously: the horse and his rider hath he thrown into the sea. 2. The LORD *is* my strength and song, and he is become my salvation: he *is* my God, and I will prepare him an habitation; my father's God, and I will exalt him. 3. The LORD *is* a man of war: the LORD *is* his name. 4. Pharaoh's chariots and his host hath he cast into the sea: his chosen captains also are drowned in the Red sea. 5. The depths have covered them: they sank into the bottom as a stone. 6. Thy right hand, O LORD, is become glorious in power: thy right hand, O LORD, hath dashed in pieces the enemy. 7. And in the greatness of thine excellency thou hast overthrown them that rose up against thee: thou sentest forth thy wrath, *which* consumed them as stubble. 8. And with the blast of thy nostrils the waters were gathered together, the floods stood upright as an heap, *and* the depths were congealed in the heart of the sea. 9. The enemy said, I will pursue, I will overtake, I will divide the spoil; my lust shall be satisfied upon them; I will draw my sword, my hand shall destroy them. 10. Thou didst blow with thy wind, the sea covered them: they sank as lead in the mighty waters. 11. Who *is* like unto thee, O LORD, among the gods? who *is* like thee, glorious in holiness, fearful *in* praises, doing wonders? 12. Thou stretchedst out thy right hand, the earth swallowed them. 13. Thou in thy mercy hast led forth the people *which* thou hast redeemed: thou hast guided *them* in thy strength unto thy holy habitation. 14. The people shall hear, *and* be afraid: sorrow shall take hold on the inhabitants of Palestina. 15. Then the dukes of Edom shall be amazed; the mighty men of Moab, trembling shall take hold upon them; all the inhabitants of Canaan shall melt away. 16. Fear and dread shall fall upon them; by the greatness of thine arm they shall be *as* still as a stone; till thy people pass over, O LORD, till the people pass over, *which* thou hast purchased. 17. Thou shalt bring them in, and plant them in the mountain of thine inheritance, *in* the place, O LORD, *which* thou hast made for thee to dwell in, *in* the Sanctuary, O Lord, *which* thy hands have established. 18. The LORD shall reign for ever and ever. 19. For the horse of Pharaoh went in with his chariots and with his horsemen into the sea, and the LORD brought again the waters of the sea upon them; but the children of Israel went on dry *land* in the midst of the sea.

DAVID'S LAMENT OVER ABSALOM: 2 Sam. 18:19. Then said Ahimaaz the son of Zadok, Let me now run, and bear the king tidings, how that the LORD hath avenged him of his enemies. 20. And Joab said unto him, Thou shalt not bear tidings this day, but thou shalt bear tidings another day: but this day thou shalt bear no tidings, because the king's son is dead. 21. Then said Joab to Cushi, Go tell the king what thou hast seen. And Cushi bowed himself unto Joab, and ran. 22. Then said Ahimaaz the son of Zadok yet again to Joab, But howsoever, let me, I pray thee, also run after Cushi. And Joab said, Wherefore wilt thou run, my son, seeing that thou hast no tidings ready? 23. But howsoever, *said he*, let me run. And he said unto him, Run. Then Ahimaaz ran by the way of the plain, and overran Cushi. 24. And David sat between the two gates: and the watchman went up to the roof over the gate unto the wall, and lifted up his eyes, and looked, and behold a man running alone. 25. And the watchman cried, and told the king. And the king said, If he *be* alone, *there is* tidings in his mouth. And he came apace, and drew near. 26. And the watchman saw another man running: and the watchman called unto the porter, and said, Behold *another* man run-

ning alone. And the king said, He also bringeth tidings. 27. And the watchman said, Me thinketh the running of the foremost is like the running of Ahimaaz the son of Zadok. And the king said, He *is* a good man, and cometh with good tidings. 28. And Ahimaaz called, and said unto the king, All is well. And he fell down to the earth upon his face before the king, and said, Blessed *be* the LORD thy God, which hath delivered up the men that lifted up their hand against my lord the king. 29. And the king said, Is the young man Absalom safe? And Ahimaaz answered, When Joab sent the king's servant, and *me* thy servant, I saw a great tumult, but I knew not what *it was*. 30. And the king said *unto him*, Turn aside, *and* stand here. And he turned aside, and stood still. 31. And, behold, Cushi came; and Cushi said, Tidings, my lord the king: for the LORD hath avenged thee this day of all them that rose up against thee. 32. And the king said unto Cushi, *Is* the young man Absalom safe? And Cushi, answered, The enemies of my lord the king, and all that rise against thee to do *thee* hurt, be as *that* young man *is*. 33. And the king was much moved, and went up to the chamber over the gate, and wept: and as he went, thus he said, O my son Absalom, my son, my son Absalom! would God I had died for thee, O Absalom, my son, my son!

LIGHTS AND SHADOWS: Ruth 1:1. Now it came to pass in the days when the judges ruled, that there was a famine in the land. And a certain man of Beth-lehem-judah went to sojourn in the country of Moab, he, and his wife, and his two sons. 2. And the name of the man *was* Elimelech, and the name of his wife Naomi, and the name of his two sons Mahlon and Chilion, Ephrathites of Beth-lehem-judah. And they came into the country of Moab, and continued there. 3. And Elimelech Naomi's husband died; and she was left, and her two sons. 4. And they took them wives of the women of Moab; the name of the one *was* Orpah, and the name of the other Ruth: and they dwelled there about ten years. 5. And Mahlon and Chilion died also both of them; and the woman was left of her two sons and her husband. 6. Then she arose with her daughters in law, that she might return from the country of Moab: for she had heard in the country of Moab how that the LORD had visited his people in giving them bread. 7. Wherefore she went forth out of the place where she was, and her two daughters in law with her; and they went on the way to return unto the land of Judah. 8. And Naomi said unto her two daughters in law, Go, return each to her mother's house: the LORD deal kindly with you, as ye have dealt with the dead, and with me. 9. The LORD grant you that ye may find rest, each *of you* in the house of her husband. Then she kissed them; and they lifted up their voice, and wept. 10. And they said unto her, Surely we will return with thee unto thy people. 11. And Naomi said, Turn again, my daughters: why will ye go with me? *are* there yet *any more* sons in my womb, that they may be your husbands? 12. Turn again, my daughters, go *your way;* for I am too old to have an husband. If I should say, I have hope, *if* I should have an husband also to night, and should also bear sons; 13. Would ye tarry for them till they were grown? would ye stay for them from having husbands? nay, my daughters; for it grieveth me much for your sakes that the hand of the LORD is gone out against me. 14. And they lifted up their voice, and wept again: and Orpah kissed her mother in law; but Ruth clave unto her. 15. And she said, Behold, thy sister in law is gone back unto her people, and unto her gods: return thou after thy sister in law. 16. And Ruth said, Intreat me not to leave thee, *or* to return from following after thee: for whither thou goest, I will go; and where thou lodgest, I will lodge: thy people *shall be* my people, and thy God my God: 17. Where thou diest, will I die, and there will I be buried: the LORD do so to me, and more also, *if ought* but death part thee and me. 18. When she saw that she was stedfastly minded to go with her, then she left speaking unto her. 19. So they two went until they came to Bethlehem. And it came to pass, when they were come to Beth-lehem, that all the city was moved about them, and they said, *Is* this Naomi? 20. And she said unto them, Call me not Naomi, call me Mara: for the Almighty hath dealt very bitterly with me. 21. I went out full, and the LORD hath brought me home again empty: why *then* call ye me Naomi, seeing the LORD hath testified against me, and the Almighty hath afflicted me? 22. So Naomi returned, and Ruth, the Moabitess, her daughter in law, with her, which returned out of the country of Moab: and they came to Beth-lehem in the beginning of barley harvest.

ELIJAH'S MIRACULOUS PRESERVATION : 1 Kin. 17:1.

And Elijah the Tishbite, *who was* of the inhabitants of Gilead, said unto Ahab, *As* the LORD God of Israel liveth, before whom I stand, there shall not be dew nor rain these years, but according to my word. 2. And the word of the LORD came unto him, saying, 3. Get thee hence, and turn thee eastward, and hide thyself by the brook Cherith, that *is* before Jordan. 4. And it shall be, *that* thou shalt drink of the brook; and I have commanded the ravens to feed thee there. 5. So he went and did according unto the word of the LORD: for he went and dwelt by the brook Cherith, that *is* before Jordan. 6. And the ravens brought him bread and flesh in the morning, and bread and flesh in the evening; and he drank of the brook. 7. And it came to pass after a while, that the brook dried up, because there had been no rain in the land. 8. And the word of the LORD came unto him, saying, 9. Arise, get thee to Zarephath, which *belongeth* to Zidon, and dwell there: behold, I have commanded a widow woman there to sustain thee. 10. So he arose and went to Zarephath. And when he came to the gate of the city, behold, the widow woman *was* there gathering of sticks: and he called to her, and said, Fetch me, I pray thee, a little water in a vessel, that I may drink. 11. And as she was going to fetch *it,* he called to her, and said, Bring me, I pray thee, a morsel of bread in thine hand. 12. And she said, *As* the LORD thy God liveth, I have not a cake, but an handful of meal in a barrel, and a little oil in a cruse: and, behold, I *am* gathering two sticks, that I may go in and dress it for me and my son, that we may eat it, and die. 13. And Elijah said unto her, Fear not; go *and* do as thou hast said: but make me thereof a little cake first, and bring *it* unto me, and after make for thee and for thy son. 14. For thus saith the LORD God of Israel, The barrel of meal shall not waste, neither shall the cruse of oil fail, until the day *that* the LORD sendeth rain upon the earth. 15. And she went and did according to the saying of Elijah: and she, and he, and her house, did eat *many* days. 16. *And* the barrel of meal wasted not, neither did the cruse of oil fail, according to the word of the LORD, which he spake by Elijah.

ELISHA AND THE WIDOW'S OIL : 2 Kin. 4:1.

Now there cried a certain woman of the wives of the sons of the prophets unto Elisha, saying, Thy servant my husband is dead; and thou knowest that thy servant did fear the LORD: and the creditor is come to take unto him my two sons to be bondmen. 2. And Elisha said unto her, What shall I do for thee? tell me, what hast thou in the house? And she said, Thine handmaid hath not any thing in the house, save a pot of oil. 3. Then he said, Go, borrow thee vessels abroad of all thy neighbours, *even* empty vessels; borrow not a few. 4. And when thou art come in, thou shalt shut the door upon thee and upon thy sons, and shalt pour out into all those vessels, and thou shalt set aside that which is full. 5. So she went from him, and shut the door upon her and upon her sons, who brought *the vessels* to her; and she poured out. 6. And it came to pass, when the vessels were full, that she said unto her son, Bring me yet a vessel. And he said unto her, *There is* not a vessel more. And the oil stayed. 7. Then she came and told the man of God. And he said, Go, sell the oil, and pay thy debt, and live thou and thy children of the rest.

NAAMAN THE LEPER : 2 Kin. 5:1.

Now Naaman, captain of the host of the king of Syria, was a great man with his master, and honourable, because by him the LORD had given deliverance unto Syria: he was also a mighty man in valour, *but he was* a leper. 2. And the Syrians had gone out by companies, and had brought away captive out of the land of Israel a little maid; and she waited on Naaman's wife. 3. And she said unto her mistress, Would God my lord *were* with the prophet that *is* in Samaria! for he would recover him of his leprosy. 4. And *one* went in, and told his lord, saying, Thus and thus said the maid that *is* of the land of Israel. 5. And the king of Syria said, Go to, go, and I will send a letter unto the king of Israel. And he departed, and took with him ten talents of silver, and six thousand *pieces* of gold, and ten changes of raiment. 6. And he brought the letter to the king of Israel, saying, Now, when this letter is come unto thee, behold, I have *therewith* sent Naaman my servant to thee, that thou mayest recover him of his leprosy. 7. And it came to pass, when the king of Israel had read the letter, that he rent his clothes, and said, *Am* I God, to kill and to make alive, that this man doth send unto me to recover a man of his leprosy? wherefore consider, I pray you, and see how he seeketh a quarrel against me. 8. And it was *so*, when Elisha the man of God had heard that the king of Israel had rent his clothes, that he sent to the king, saying, Wherefore hast thou rent thy clothes? let him come now to me, and he shall know that there is a prophet in Israel. 9. So Naaman came with his horses and with his chariot, and stood at the door of the house of Elisha. 10. And Elisha sent a messenger unto him, saying, Go and wash in Jordan seven times, and thy flesh shall come again to thee, and thou shalt be clean. 11. But Naaman was wroth, and went away, and said, Behold, I thought, He will surely come out to me, and stand, and call on the name of the LORD his God, and strike his hand over the place, and recover the leper. 12. *Are* not Abana and Pharpar, rivers of Damascus, better than all the waters of Israel? may I not wash in them, and be clean? So he turned and went away in a rage. 13. And his servants came near, and spake unto him, and said, My father, *if* the prophet had bid thee *do some* great thing, wouldest thou not have done *it?* how much rather then, when he saith to thee, Wash, and be clean? 14. Then went he down, and dipped himself seven times in Jordan, according to the saying of the man of God: and his flesh came again like unto the flesh of a little child, and he was clean.

ESTHER'S TRIUMPH: Esth. 4:1. When Mordecai perceived all that was done, Mordecai rent his clothes, and put on sackcloth with ashes, and went out into the midst of the city, and cried with a loud and a bitter cry; 2. And came even before the king's gate: for none *might* enter into the king's gate clothed with sackcloth. 3. And in every province, whithersoever the king's commandment and his decree came, *there*

was great mourning among the Jews, and fasting, and weeping, and wailing; and many lay in sackcloth and ashes. 4. So Esther's maids and her chamberlains came and told *it* her. Then was the queen exceedingly grieved; and she sent raiment to clothe Mordecai, and to take away his sackcloth from him: but he received *it* not. 5. Then called Esther for Hatach, *one* of the king's chamberlains, whom he had appointed to attend upon her, and gave him a commandment to Mordecai, to know what it *was*, and why it *was*. 6. So Hatach went forth to Mordecai unto the street of the city, which *was* before the king's gate. 7. And Mordecai told him of all that had happened unto him, and of the sum of the money that Haman had promised to pay to the king's treasuries for the Jews, to destroy them. 8. Also he gave him the copy of the writing of the decree that was given at Shushan to destroy them, to shew *it* unto Esther, and to declare *it* unto her, and to charge her that she should go in unto the king, to make supplication unto him, and to make request before him for her people. 9. And Hatach came and told Esther the words of Mordecai. 10. Again Esther spake unto Hatach, and gave him commandment unto Mordecai; 11. All the king's servants, and the people of the king's provinces, do know, that whosoever, whether man or woman, shall come unto the king into the inner court, who is not called, *there is* one law of his to put *him* to death, except such to whom the king shall hold out the golden sceptre, that he may live: but I have not been called to come in unto the king these thirty days. 12. And they told to Mordecai Esther's words. 13. Then Mordecai commanded to answer Esther, Think not with thyself that thou shalt escape in the king's house, more than all the Jews. 14. For if thou altogether holdest thy peace at this time, *then* shall there enlargement and deliverance arise to the Jews from another place; but thou and thy father's house shall be destroyed: and who knoweth whether thou art come to the kingdom for *such* a time as this? 15. Then Esther bade *them* return Mordecai *this answer*, 16. Go, gather together all the Jews that are present in Shushan, and fast ye for me, and neither eat nor drink three days, night or day: I also and my maidens will fast likewise; and so will I go in unto the king, which *is* not according to the law: and if I perish, I perish. 17. So Mordecai went his way, and did according to all that Esther had commanded him.

Esth. 7:1. So the king and Haman came to banquet with Esther the queen. 2. And the king said again unto Esther on the second day at the banquet of wine, What *is* thy petition, queen Esther? and it shall be granted thee: and what *is* thy request? and it shall be performed, *even* to the half of the kingdom.

3. Then Esther the queen answered and said, If I have found favour in thy sight, O king, and if it please the king, let my life be given me at my petition, and my people at my request: 4. For we are sold, I and my people, to be destroyed, to be slain, and to perish. But if we had been sold for bondmen and bondwomen, I had held my tongue, although the enemy could not countervail the king's damage. 5. Then the king Ahasuerus answered and said unto Esther the queen, Who is he, and where is he, that durst presume in his heart to do so? 6. And Esther said, The adversary and enemy *is* this wicked Haman. Then Haman was afraid before the king and the queen. 7. And the king arising from the banquet of wine in his wrath *went* into the palace garden: and Haman stood up to make request for his life to Esther the queen; for he saw that there was evil determined against him by the king. 8. Then the king returned out of the palace garden into the place of the banquet of wine; and Haman was fallen upon the bed whereon Esther *was*. Then said the king, Will he force the queen also before me in the house? As the word went out of the king's mouth, they covered Haman's face. 9. And Harbonah, one of the chamberlains, said before the king, Behold also, the gallows fifty cubits high, which Haman had made for Mordecai, who had spoken good for the king, standeth in the house of Haman. Then the king said, Hang him thereon. 10. So they hanged Haman on the gallows that he had prepared for Mordecai. Then was the king's wrath pacified.

THE BREVITY OF LIFE: Job 14:1. Man *that is* born of a woman *is* of few days, and full of trouble. 2. He cometh forth like a flower, and is cut down: he fleeth also as a shadow, and continueth not. 3. And dost thou open thine eyes upon such an one, and bringest me into judgment with thee? 4. Who can bring a clean *thing* out of an unclean? not one. 5. Seeing his days *are* determined, the number of his months *are* with thee, thou hast appointed his bounds that he cannot pass; 6. Turn from him, that he may rest, till he shall accomplish, as an hireling his day. 7. For there is hope of a tree, if it be cut down, that it will sprout again, and that the tender branch thereof will not cease. 8. Though the root thereof was old in the earth, and the stock thereof die in the ground; 9. *Yet* through the scent of water it will bud, and bring forth boughs like a plant. 10. But man dieth, and wasteth away: yea, man giveth up the ghost, and where *is* he?

NATURE'S TESTIMONY: Job 28:1. Surely there is a vein for the silver, and a place for gold *where* they fine *it.* 2. Iron is taken out of the earth, and brass *is* molten *out of* the stone. 3. He setteth an end to darkness, and searcheth out all perfection: the stones of darkness, and the shadow of death. 4. The flood breaketh out from the inhabitant; *even the waters* forgotten of the foot: they are dried up, they are gone away from men. 5. *As for* the earth, out of it cometh bread: and under it is turned up as it were fire. 6. The stones of it *are* the place of sapphires: and it hath dust of gold. 7. *There is* a path which no fowl knoweth, and which the vulture's eye hath not seen: 8. The lion's whelps have not trodden it, nor the fierce lion passed by it. 9. He putteth forth his hand upon the rock; he overturneth the mountains by the roots. 10. He cutteth out rivers among the rocks; and his eye seeth every precious thing. 11. He bindeth the floods from overflowing; and *the thing that is* hid bringeth he forth to light. 12. But where shall wisdom be found? and where *is* the place of understanding? 13. Man knoweth not the price thereof; neither is it found in the land of the living. 14. The depth saith, It *is* not in me: and the sea saith, *It is* not with me. 15. It cannot be gotten for gold, neither shall silver be weighed *for* the price thereof. 16. It cannot be valued with the gold of Ophir, with the precious onyx, or the sapphire. 17. The gold and the crystal cannot equal it: and the exchange of it *shall not be for* jewels of fine gold. 18. No mention shall be made of coral, or of pearls: for the price of wisdom *is* above rubies. 19. The topaz of Ethiopia shall not equal it, neither shall it be valued with pure gold. 20. Whence then cometh wisdom? and where *is* the place of understanding? 21. Seeing it is hid from the eyes of all living, and kept close from the fowls of the air. 22. Destruction and death say, We have heard the fame thereof with our ears. 23. God understandeth the way thereof, and he knoweth the place thereof. 24. For he looketh to the ends of the earth, *and* seeth under the whole heaven; 25. To make the weight for the winds; and he weigheth the waters by measure. 26. When he made a decree for the rain, and a way for the lightning of the thunder: 27. Then did he see it, and declare it; he prepared it, yea, and searched it out. 28. And unto man he said, Behold, the fear of the Lord, that *is* wisdom; and to depart from evil *is* understanding.

GOD'S CHALLENGE TO JOB: See Job 38, p. 430.

THE BEASTS OF THE FIELD: See Job 39, p. 430.

THE RIGHTEOUS AND THE WICKED IN CONTRAST: See Psa. 1, p. 1038.

THE TRIUMPHANT KING: See Psa. 2, p. 1067.

MAN IN NATURE: See Psa. 8, p. 1059.

MAN IN EXTREMITY: See Psa. 18:1–19, p. 1082.

CONFIDENCE IN GOD: See Psa. 23, p. 1078.

THE KING OF GLORY: See Psa. 24, p. 1040.

THE GLORY OF GOD: See Psa. 29, p. 1060.

OUR REFUGE: See Psa. 46, p. 1072.

THE MAJESTY OF GOD: See Psa.77:13-20, p. 1031.

THE JOY OF THE RIGHTEOUS: See Psa. 84, p. 1032.

THE STATE OF THE GODLY: See Psa. 91, p. 1047.

THE NEW SONG: See Psa. 98, p. 1076.

THE MAJESTY AND PROVIDENCE OF GOD: See Psa. 104, p. 1064.

IN CAPTIVITY: See Psa. 137, p. 1036.

THE OMNIPRESENCE OF GOD: See Psa. 139, p. 1066.

OLD AGE: Eccl. 12:1. Remember now thy Creator in the days of thy youth, while the evil days come not, nor the years draw nigh, when thou shalt say, I have no pleasure in them; 2. While the sun, or the light, or the moon, or the stars, be not darkened, nor the clouds return after the rain: 3. In the day when the keepers of the house shall tremble, and the strong men shall bow themselves and the grinders cease because they are few, and those that look out of the windows be darkened. 4. And the doors shall be shut in the streets, when the sound of the grinding is low, and he shall rise up at the voice of th bird, and all the daughters of musick shall be brought low; 5. Also *when* they shall be afraid of *that which* is high, and fears *shall be* in the way, and the almond tree shall flourish, and the grasshopper shall be a burden, and desire shall fail: because man goeth to his long home, and the mourners go about the streets; 6. Or ever the silver cord be loosed, or the golden bowl be broken, or the pitcher be broken at the fountain, or the wheel broken at the cistern. 7. Then shall the dust return to the earth as it was: and the spirit shall return unto God who gave it.

CHRIST'S KINGDOM FORESHADOWED: Isa. 35:1. The wilderness and the solitary place shall be glad for them; and the desert shall rejoice, and blossom as the rose. 2. It shall blossom abundantly, and rejoice even with joy and singing: the glory of Lebanon shall be given unto it, the excellency of Carmel and Sharon, they shall see the glory of the LORD, *and* the excellency of our God. 3. Strengthen ye the weak hands, and confirm the feeble knees. 4. Say to them *that are* of a fearful heart, Be strong, fear not: behold, your God will come *with* vengeance, *even* God *with* a recompence; he will come and save you. 5. Then the eyes of the blind shall be opened, and the ears of the deaf shall be unstopped. 6. Then shall the lame *man* leap as an hart, and the tongue of the dumb sing: for in the wilderness shall waters break out, and streams in the desert. 7. And the parched ground shall become a pool, and the thirsty land springs of water: in the habitation of dragons, where each lay, *shall be* grass with reeds and rushes. 8. And an highway shall be there, and a

way, and it shall be called The way of holiness; the unclean shall not pass over it; but it *shall be* for those: the wayfaring men, though fools, shall not err *therein.* 9. No lion shall be there, nor *any* ravenous beast shall go up thereon, it shall not be found there; but the redeemed shall walk *there:* 10. And the ransomed of the LORD shall return, and come to Zion with songs and everlasting joy upon their heads: they shall obtain joy and gladness, and sorrow and sighing shall flee away.

THE OMNIPOTENCE AND INCOMPARABLENESS OF GOD: Isa. 40:1. Comfort ye, comfort ye my people, saith your God. 2. Speak ye comfortably to Jerusalem, and cry unto her, that her warfare is accomplished, that her iniquity is pardoned: for she hath received of the LORD's hand double for all her sins. 3. The voice of him that crieth in the wilderness, Prepare ye the way of the LORD, make straight in the desert a highway for our God. 4. Every valley shall be exalted, and every mountain and hill shall be made low: and the crooked shall be made straight, and the rough places plain: 5. And the glory of the LORD shall be revealed, and all flesh shall see *it* together: for the mouth of the LORD hath spoken *it.* 6. The voice said, Cry. And he said, What shall I cry? All flesh *is* grass, and all the goodliness thereof *is* as the flower of the field: 7. The grass withereth, the flower fadeth: because the spirit of the LORD bloweth upon it: surely the people *is* grass. 8. The grass withereth, the flower fadeth: but the word of our God shall stand for ever. 9. O Zion, that bringest good tidings, get thee up into the high mountain; O Jerusalem, that bringest good things, lift up thy voice with strength; lift *it* up, be not afraid; say unto the cities of Judah, Behold your God! 10. Behold, the Lord GOD will come with strong *hand,* and his arm shall rule for him: behold, his reward *is* with him, and his work before him. 11. He shall feed his flock like a shepherd: he shall gather the lambs with his arm, and carry *them* in his bosom, *and* shall gently lead those that are with young. 12. Who hath measured the waters in the hollow of his hand, and meted out heaven with the span, and comprehended the dust of the earth in a measure, and weighed the mountains in scales, and the hills in a balance? 13. Who hath directed the Spirit of the LORD, or *being* his counsellor hath taught him? 14. With whom took he counsel, and *who* instructed him, and taught him in the path of judgment, and taught him knowledge, and shewed to him the way of understanding? 15. Behold, the nations *are* as a drop of a bucket, and are counted as the small dust of the balance: behold, he taketh up the isles as a very little thing. 16. And Lebanon *is* not sufficient to burn, nor the beasts thereof sufficient for a burnt offering. 17. All nations before him *are* as nothing; and they are counted to him less than nothing, and vanity. 18. To whom then will ye liken God? or what likeness will ye compare unto him? 19. The workman melteth a graven image, and the goldsmith spreadeth it over with gold, and casteth silver chains. 20. He that is so impoverished that he hath no oblation chooseth a tree that will not rot: he seeketh unto him a cunning workman to prepare a graven image, that shall not be moved. 21. Have ye not known? have ye not heard? hath it not been told you from the beginning? have ye not understood from the foundations of the earth? 22. It is he that sitteth upon the circle of the earth, and the inhabitants thereof are as grasshoppers; that stretcheth out the heavens as a curtain, and spreadeth them out as a tent to dwell in: 23. That bringeth the princes to nothing; he maketh the judges of the earth as vanity. 24. Yea, they shall not be planted; yea, they shall not be sown: yea, their stock shall not take root in the earth: and he shall also blow upon them, and they shall wither, and the whirlwind shall take them away as stubble. 25. To whom then will ye liken me, or shall I be equal? saith the Holy One. 26. Lift up your eyes on high, and behold who hath created these things, that bringeth out their host by number: he calleth them all by names by the greatness of his might, for that he is strong in power; not one faileth. 27. Why sayest thou, O Jacob, and speakest, O Israel, My way is hid from the LORD, and my judgment is passed over from my God? 28. Hast thou not known? hast thou not heard, that the everlasting God, the LORD, the Creator of the ends of the earth, fainteth not, neither is weary? there is no searching of his understanding. 29. He giveth power to the faint; and to them that have no might he increaseth strength. 30. Even the youths shall faint and be weary, and the young men shall utterly fall: 31. But they that wait upon the LORD shall renew their strength; they shall mount up with wings as eagles; they shall run, and not be weary; and they shall walk, and not faint.

THE WRATH OF GOD: Amos 9:1. I saw the Lord standing upon the altar: and he said, Smite the lintel of the door, that the posts may shake: and cut them in the head, all of them; and I will slay the last of them with the sword: he that fleeth of them shall not flee away, and he that escapeth of them shall not be delivered. 2. Though they dig into hell, thence shall mine hand take them; though they climb up to heaven, thence will I bring them down: 3. And though they hide themselves in the top of Carmel, I will search and take them out thence; and though they be hid from my sight in the bottom of the sea, thence will I command the serpent, and he shall bite them: 4. And though they go into captivity before their enemies, thence will I command the sword, and it shall slay them: and I will set mine

eyes upon them for evil, and not for good. 5. And the LORD GOD of hosts is he that toucheth the land, and it shall melt, and all that dwell therein shall mourn: and it shall rise up wholly like a flood; and shall be drowned, as by the flood of Egypt. 6. It is he that buildeth his stories in the heaven, and hath founded his troop in the earth; he that calleth for the waters of the sea, and poureth them out upon the face of the earth: The LORD is his name.

THE MAJESTY OF GOD: Hab. 3:3. God came from Teman, and the Holy One from mount Paran. Selah. His glory covered the heavens, and the earth was full of his praise. 4. And his brightness was as the light; he had horns coming out of his hand: and there was the hiding of his power. 5. Before him went the pestilence, and burning coals went forth at his feet. 6. He stood, and measured the earth: he beheld, and drove asunder the nations; and the everlasting mountains were scattered, the perpetual hills did bow: his ways are everlasting. 7. I saw the tents of Cushan in affliction: and the curtains of the land of Midian did tremble. 8. Was the LORD displeased against the rivers? was thine anger against the rivers? was thy wrath against the sea, that thou didst ride upon thine horses and thy chariots of salvation? 9. Thy bow was made quite naked, according to the oaths of the tribes, even thy word. Selah. Thou didst cleave the earth with rivers. 10. The mountains saw thee, and they trembled: the overflowing of the water passed by: the deep uttered his voice, and lifted up his hands on high. 11. The sun and moon stood still in their habitation: at the light of thine arrows they went, and at the shining of thy glittering spear. 12. Thou didst march through the land in indignation, thou didst thresh the heathen in anger. 13. Thou wentest forth for the salvation of thy people, even for salvation with thine anointed; thou woundedst the head out of the house of the wicked, by discovering the foundation unto the neck. Selah.

MARY'S MAGNIFICAT: Luke 1:46. And Mary said, My soul doth magnify the Lord, 47. And my spirit hath rejoiced in God my Saviour. 48. For he hath regarded the low estate of his handmaiden: for, behold, from henceforth all generations shall call me blessed. 49. For he that is mighty hath done to me great things; and holy is his name. 50. And his mercy is on them that fear him from generation to generation. 51. He hath shewed strength with his arm; he hath scattered the proud in the imagination of their hearts. 52. He hath put down the mighty from their seats, and exalted them of low degree. 53. He hath filled the hungry with good things; and the rich he hath sent empty away. 54. He hath holpen his servant Israel, in remembrance of his mercy; 55. As he spake to our fathers, to Abraham, and to his seed for ever. 56. And

Mary abode with her about three months, and returned to her own house.

THE PROPHETIC BLESSING OF ZACHARIAS: Luke 1:67. And his father Zacharias was filled with the Holy Ghost, and prophesied, saying, 68. Blessed *be* the Lord God of Israel; for he hath visited and redeemed his people, 69. And hath raised up an horn of salvation for us in the house of his servant David; 70. As he spake by the mouth of his holy prophets, which have been since the world began: 71. That we should be saved from our enemies, and from the hand of all that hate us; 72. To perform the mercy *promised* to our fathers, and to remember his holy covenant; 73. The oath which he sware to our father Abraham, 74. That he would grant unto us, that we being delivered out of the hand of our enemies might serve him without fear, 75. In holiness and righteousness before him, all the days of our life. 76. And thou, child, shalt be called the prophet of the Highest: for thou shalt go before the face of the Lord to prepare his ways; 77. To give knowledge of salvation unto his people by the remission of their sins, 78. Through the tender mercy of our God; whereby the day-spring from on high hath visited us, 79. To give light to them that sit in darkness and *in* the shadow of death, to guide our feet into the way of peace. 80. And the child grew, and waxed strong in spirit, and was in the deserts till the day of his shewing unto Israel.

THE BEATITUDES: Matt. 5:1. And seeing the multitudes, he went up into a mountain: and when he was set, his disciples came unto him: 2. And he opened his mouth, and taught them, saying, 3. Blessed *are* the poor in spirit: for their's is the kingdom of heaven. 4. Blessed *are* they that mourn: for they shall be comforted. 5. Blessed *are* the meek: for they shall inherit the earth. 6. Blessed *are* they which do hunger and thirst after righteousness: for they shall be filled. 7. Blessed *are* the merciful: for they shall obtain mercy. 8. Blessed *are* the pure in heart: for they shall see God. 9. Blessed *are* the peacemakers: for they shall be called the children of God. 10. Blessed *are* they which are persecuted for righteousness' sake: for their's is the kingdom of heaven. 11. Blessed are ye, when *men* shall revile you, and persecute *you*, and shall say all manner of evil against you falsely, for my sake. 12. Rejoice, and be exceeding glad: for great *is* your reward in heaven: for so persecuted they the prophets which were before you. 13. Ye are the salt of the earth: but if the salt have lost his savour, wherewith shall it be salted? it is thenceforth good for nothing, but to be cast out, and to be trodden under foot of men. 14. Ye are the light of the world. A city that is set on an hill cannot be hid. 15. Neither do men light a candle, and put it under a bushel, but on a candlestick; and it giveth

light unto all that are in the house. 16. Let your light so shine before men, that they may see your good works, and glorify your Father which is in heaven.

GOD'S PROVIDENCE: Matt. 6:26. Behold the fowls of the air: for they sow not, neither do they reap, nor gather into barns; yet your heavenly Father feedeth them. Are ye not much better than they? 27. Which of you by taking thought can add one cubit unto his stature? 28. And why take ye thought for raiment? Consider the lilies of the field, how they grow; they toil not, neither do they spin: 29. And yet I say unto you, That even Solomon in all his glory was not arrayed like one of these. 30. Wherefore, if God so clothe the grass of the field, which to day is, and to morrow is cast into the oven, *shall he* not much more *clothe* you, O ye of little faith? 31. Therefore take no thought, saying, What shall we eat? or, What shall we drink? or, Wherewithal shall we be clothed? 32. (For after all these things do the Gentiles seek:) for your heavenly Father knoweth that ye have need of all these things. 33. But seek ye first the kingdom of God, and his righteousness; and all these things shall be added unto you. 34. Take therefore no thought for the morrow: for the morrow shall take thought for the things of itself. Sufficient unto the day *is* the evil thereof.

WISE AND FOOLISH BUILDERS: Matt. 7:21. Not every one that saith unto me, Lord, Lord, shall enter into the kingdom of heaven; but he that doeth the will of my Father which is in heaven. 22. Many will say to me in that day, Lord, Lord, have we not prophesied in thy name? and in thy name have cast out devils? and in thy name done many wonderful works? 23. And then will I profess unto them, I never knew you: depart from me, ye that work iniquity. 24. Therefore whosoever heareth these sayings of mine, and doeth them, I will liken him unto a wise man, which built his house upon a rock: 25. And the rain descended, and the floods came, and the winds blew, and beat upon that house; and it fell not: for it was founded upon a rock. 26. And every one that heareth these sayings of mine, and doeth them not, shall be likened unto a foolish man, which built his house upon the sand: 27. And the rain descended, and the floods came, and the winds blew, and beat upon that house; and it fell: and great was the fall of it.

THE GOOD SAMARITAN: Luke 10:25. And, behold, a certain lawyer stood up, and tempted him, saying, Master, what shall I do to inherit eternal life? 26. He said unto him, What is written in the law? how readest thou? 27. And he answering said, Thou shalt love the Lord thy God with all thy heart, and with all thy soul, and with all thy strength, and with all thy mind; and thy neighbour as thyself. 28. And he said unto him, Thou hast answered right:

this do, and thou shalt live. 29. But he, willing to justify himself, said unto Jesus, And who is my neighbour? 30. And Jesus answering said, A certain *man* went down from Jerusalem to Jericho, and fell among thieves, which stripped him of his raiment, and wounded *him*, and departed, leaving *him* half dead. 31. And by chance there came down a certain priest that way: and when he saw him, he passed by on the other side. 32. And likewise a Levite, when he was at the place, came and looked *on him*, and passed by on the other side. 33. But a certain Samaritan, as he journeyed, came where he was: and when he saw him, he had compassion *on him*, 34. And went to *him*, and bound up his wounds, pouring in oil and wine, and set him on his own beast, and brought him to an inn, and took care of him. 35. And on the morrow when he departed, he took out two pence, and gave *them* to the host, and said unto him, Take care of him; and whatsoever thou spendest more, when I come again, I will repay thee. 36. Which now of these three, thinkest thou, was neighbour unto him that fell among the thieves? 37. And he said, He that shewed mercy on him. Then said Jesus unto him, Go, and do thou likewise.

THE PRODIGAL SON: Luke 15:11. And he said, A certain man had two sons: 12. And the younger of them said to *his* father, Father, give me the portion of goods that falleth *to me*. And he divided unto them *his* living. 13. And not many days after the younger son gathered all together, and took his journey into a far country, and there wasted his substance with riotous living. 14. And when he had spent all, there arose a mighty famine in that land; and he began to be in want. 15. And he went and joined himself to a citizen of that country; and he sent him into his fields to feed swine. 16. And he would fain have filled his belly with the husks that the swine did eat: and no man gave unto him. 17. And when he came to himself, he said, How many hired servants of my father's have bread enough and to spare, and I perish with hunger! 18. I will arise and go to my father, and will say unto him, Father, I have sinned against heaven, and before thee, 19. And am no more worthy to be called thy son: make me as one of thy hired servants. 20. And he arose, and came to his father. But when he was yet a great way off, his father saw him, and had compassion, and ran, and fell on his neck, and kissed him. 21. And the son said unto him, Father, I have sinned against heaven, and in thy sight, and am no more worthy to be called thy son. 22. But the father said to his servants, Bring forth the best robe, and put *it* on him; and put a ring on his hand, and shoes on *his* feet: 23. And bring hither the fatted calf, and kill *it;* and let us eat, and be merry: 24. For this my son was dead, and is alive again; he was lost, and is found. And they began to be merry. 25. Now his elder son was in the field: and as he came and drew nigh to the house, he heard musick and dancing. 26. And he called one of the servants, and asked what these things meant. 27. And he said unto him, Thy brother is come; and thy father hath killed the fatted calf, because he hath received him safe and sound. 28. And he was angry, and would not go in: therefore came his father out, and intreated him. 29. And he answering said to *his* father, Lo, these many years do I serve thee, neither transgressed I at any time thy commandment: and yet thou never gavest me a kid, that I might make merry with my friends: 30. But as soon as this thy son was come, which hath devoured thy living with harlots, thou hast killed for him the fatted calf. 31. And he said unto him, Son, thou art ever with me, and all that I have is thine. 32. It was meet that we should make merry, and be glad: for this thy brother was dead, and is alive again; and was lost, and is found.

THE RAISING OF LAZARUS: John 11:1. Now a certain *man* was sick, *named* Lazarus, of Bethany, the town of Mary and her sister Martha. 2. (It was *that* Mary which anointed the Lord with ointment, and wiped his feet with her hair, whose brother Lazarus was sick.) 3. Therefore his sisters sent unto him, saying, Lord, behold, he whom thou lovest is sick. 18. Now Bethany was nigh unto Jerusalem, about fifteen furlongs off: 19. And many of the Jews came to Martha and Mary, to comfort them concerning their brother. 20. Then Martha, as soon as she heard that Jesus was coming, went and met him: but Mary sat *still* in the house. 21. Then said Martha unto Jesus, Lord, if thou hadst been here, my brother had not died. 22. But I know, that even now, whatsoever thou wilt ask of God, God will give *it* thee. 23. Jesus saith unto her, Thy brother shall rise again. 24. Martha saith unto him, I know that he shall rise again in the resurrection at the last day. 25. Jesus said unto her, I am the resurrection, and the life: he that believeth in me, though he were dead, yet shall he live: 26. And whosoever liveth and believeth in me shall never die. Believest thou this? 27. She saith unto him, Yea, Lord: I believe that thou art the Christ, the Son of God, which should come into the world. 28. And when she had so said, she went her way, and called Mary her sister secretly, saying, The Master is come, and calleth for thee. 29. As soon as she heard *that*, she arose quickly, and came unto him. 30. Now Jesus was not yet come into the town, but was in that place where Martha met him. 31. The Jews then which were with her in the house, and comforted her, when they saw Mary, that she rose up hastily and went out, followed her, saying, She goeth unto the grave to weep there. 32. Then when Mary was come where Jesus was, and saw him, she fell down at his feet, saying unto him, Lord, if thou hadst been here, my brother had not died. 33. When Jesus therefore saw her weeping, and the Jews also weeping which came with her, he groaned in the spirit, and was troubled, 34. And said, Where have ye laid him? They said unto him, Lord, come and see. 35. Jesus wept. 36. Then said the Jews, Behold how he loved him! 37. And some of them said, Could not this man, which opened the eyes of the blind, have caused that even this man should not have died? 38. Jesus therefore again groaning in himself cometh to the grave. It was a cave, and a stone lay upon it. 39. Jesus said, Take ye away the stone. Martha, the sister of him that was dead, saith unto him, Lord, by this time he stinketh: for he hath been *dead* four days. 40. Jesus saith unto her, Said I not unto thee, that, if thou wouldest believe, thou shouldest see the glory of God? 41. Then they took away the stone *from the place* where the dead was laid. And Jesus lifted up *his* eyes, and said, Father, I thank thee that thou hast heard me. 42. And I knew that thou hearest me always: but because of the people which stand by I said *it*, that they may believe that thou hast sent me. 43. And when he thus had spoken, he cried with a loud voice, Lazarus, come forth. 44. And he that was dead came forth, bound hand and foot with graveclothes: and his face was bound about with a napkin. Jesus saith unto them, Loose him, and let him go. 45. Then many of the Jews which came to Mary, and had seen the things which Jesus did, believed on him. 46. But some of them went their ways to the Pharisees, and told them what things Jesus had done.

THE BETRAYAL: Luke 22:47. And while he yet spake, behold a multitude, and he that was called Judas, one of the twelve, went before them, and drew near unto Jesus to kiss him. 48. But Jesus said unto him, Judas, betrayest thou the Son of man with a kiss? 49. When they which were about him saw what would follow, they said unto him, Lord, shall we smite with the sword? 50. And one of them smote the servant of the high priest, and cut off his right ear. 51. And Jesus answered and said, Suffer ye thus far. And he touched his ear, and healed him. 52. Then Jesus said unto the chief priests, and captains of the temple, and the elders, which were come to him, Be ye come out, as against a thief, with swords and staves? 53. When I was daily with you in the temple, ye stretched forth no hands against me: but this is your hour, and the power of darkness. 54. Then took they him, and led *him*, and brought him into the high priest's house. And Peter followed afar off. 55. And when they had kindled a fire in the midst of the hall, and were set down together, Peter sat down among them. 56. But a certain maid beheld him as he sat by the fire, and earnestly

looked upon him, and said, This man was also with him. 57. And he denied him, saying, Woman, I know him not. 58. And after a little while another saw him, and said, Thou art also of them. And Peter said, Man, I am not. 59. And about the space of one hour after another confidently affirmed, saying, Of a truth this *fellow* also was with him: for he is a Galilæan. 60. And Peter said, Man, I know not what thou sayest. And immediately, while he yet spake, the cock crew. 61. And the Lord turned, and looked upon Peter. And Peter remembered the word of the Lord, how he had said unto him, Before the cock crow, thou shalt deny me thrice. 62. And Peter went out, and wept bitterly.

THE RESURRECTION: Luke 24:1. Now upon the first *day* of the week, very early in the morning, they came unto the sepulchre, bringing the spices which they had prepared, and certain *others* with them. 2. And they found the stone rolled away from the sepulchre. 3. And they entered in, and found not the body of the Lord Jesus. 4. And it came to pass, as they were much perplexed thereabout, behold, two men stood by them in shining garments: 5. And as they were afraid, and bowed down *their* faces to the earth, they said unto them, Why seek ye the living among the dead? 6. He is not here, but is risen: remember how he spake unto you when he was yet in Galilee, 7. Saying, The Son of man must be delivered into the hands of sinful men, and be crucified, and the third day rise again. 8. And they remembered his words, 9. And returned from the sepulchre, and told all these things unto the eleven, and to all the rest. 10. It was Mary Magdalene, and Joanna, and Mary *the mother* of James, and other *women that were* with them, which told these things unto the apostles. 11. And their words seemed to them as idle tales, and they believed them not. 12. Then arose Peter, and ran unto the sepulchre; and stooping down, he beheld the linen clothes laid by themselves, and departed, wondering in himself at that which was come to pass.

PETER AT PENTECOST: Acts. 2:1. And when the day of Pentecost was fully come, they were all with one accord in one place. 2. And suddenly there came a sound from heaven as of a rushing mighty wind, and it filled all the house where they were sitting. 3. And there appeared unto them cloven tongues like as of fire, and it sat upon each of them. 4. And they were all filled with the Holy Ghost, and began to speak with other tongues, as the Spirit gave them utterance. 5. And there were dwelling at Jerusalem Jews, devout men, out of every nation under heaven. 6. Now when this was noised abroad, the multitude came together, and were confounded, because that every man heard them speak in his own language. 7. And they were all amazed and marvelled, saying one to another, Behold, are not all these which speak Galilæans? 8. And how hear we every man in our own tongue, wherein we were born? 9. Parthians, and Medes, and Elamites, and the dwellers in Mesopotamia, and in Judæa, and Cappadocia, in Pontus, and Asia, 10. Phrygia, and Pamphylia, in Egypt, and in the parts of Libya about Cyrene, and strangers of Rome, Jews and proselytes, 11. Cretes and Arabians, we do hear them speak in our tongues the wonderful works of God. 12. And they were all amazed, and were in doubt, saying one to another, What meaneth this? 13. Others mocking said, These men are full of new wine, 14. But Peter, standing up with the eleven, lifted up his voice, and said unto them, Ye men of Judæa, and all *ye* that dwell at Jerusalem, be this known unto you, and hearken to my words: 15. For these are not drunken, as ye suppose, seeing it is *but* the third hour of the day. 16. But this is that which was spoken by the prophet Joel; 17. And it shall come to pass in the last days, saith God, I will pour out of my Spirit upon all flesh: and your sons and your daughters shall prophesy, and your young men shall see visions, and your old men shall dream dreams: 18. And on my servants and on my handmaidens I will pour out in those days of my Spirit; and they shall prophesy: 19. And I will shew wonders in heaven above, and signs in the earth beneath; blood, and fire, and vapour of smoke: 20. The sun shall be turned into darkness, and the moon into blood, before that great and notable day of the Lord come: 21. And it shall come to pass, *that* whosoever shall call on name of the Lord shall be saved. 22. Ye men of Israel, hear these words; Jesus of Nazareth, a man approved of God among you by miracles and wonders and signs, which God did by him in the midst of you, as ye yourselves also know: 23. Him, being delivered by the determinate counsel and foreknowledge of God, ye have taken, and by wicked hands have crucified and slain: 24. Whom God hath raised up, having loosed the pains of death: because it was not possible that he should be holden of it. 25. For David speaketh concerning him, I foresaw the Lord always before my face, for he is on my right hand, that I should not be moved. 26. Therefore did my heart rejoice, and my tongue was glad; moreover also my flesh shall rest in hope: 27. Because thou wilt not leave my soul in hell, neither wilt thou suffer thine Holy One to see corruption. 28. Thou hast made known to me the ways of life; thou shalt make me full of joy with thy countenance. 29. Men *and* brethren, let me freely speak unto you of the patriarch David, that he is both dead and buried, and his sepulchre is with us unto this day. 30. Therefore being a prophet, and knowing that God had sworn with an oath to him, that of the fruit of his loins, according to

the flesh, he would raise up Christ to sit on his throne; 31. He seeing this before spake of the resurrection of Christ, that his soul was not left in hell, neither his flesh did see corruption. 32. This Jesus hath God raised up, whereof we all are witnesses. 33. Therefore being by the right hand of God exalted, and having received of the Father the promise of the Holy Ghost, he hath shed forth this, which ye now see and hear. 34. For David is not ascended into the heavens: but he saith himself, The Lord said unto my Lord, Sit thou on my right hand, 35. Until I make thy foes thy footstool. 36. Therefore let all the house of Israel know assuredly, that God hath made that same Jesus, whom ye have crucified, both Lord and Christ.

STEPHEN'S DEFENSE: See p. 261.

PAUL AND SILAS IN PRISON: Acts 16:16. And it came to pass, as we went to prayer, a certain damsel possessed with a spirit of divination met us, which brought her masters much gain by soothsaying: 17. The same followed Paul and us, and cried, saying, These men are the servants of the most high God, which shew unto us the way of salvation. 18. And this did she many days. But Paul, being grieved, turned and said to the spirit, I command thee in the name of Jesus Christ to come out of her. And he came out the same hour. 19. And when her masters saw that the hope of their gains was gone, they caught Paul and Silas, and drew *them* into the marketplace unto the rulers, 20. And brought them to the magistrates, saying, These men, being Jews, do exceedingly trouble our city, 21. And teach customs, which are not lawful for us to receive, neither to observe, being Romans. 22. And the multitude rose up together against them: and the magistrates rent off their clothes, and commanded to beat *them*. 23. And when they had laid many stripes upon them, they cast *them* into prison, charging the jailor to keep them safely: 24. Who, having received such a charge, thrust them into the inner prison, and made their feet fast in the stocks. 25. And at midnight Paul and Silas prayed, and sang praises unto God: and the prisoners heard them. 26 And suddenly there was a great earthquake, so that the foundations of the prison were shaken: and immediately all the doors were opened, and every one's bands were loosed. 27. And the keeper of the prison awaking out of his sleep, and seeing the prison doors open, he drew out his sword, and would have killed himself, supposing that the prisoners had been fled. 28. But Paul cried with a loud voice, saying, Do thyself no harm: for we are all here. 29. Then he called for a light, and sprang in, and came trembling, and fell down before Paul and Silas, 30. And brought them out, and said, Sirs, what must I do to be saved? 31. And they said, Believe on the Lord Jesus Christ, and thou shalt be saved, and thy house. 32.

And they spake unto him the word of the Lord, and to all that were in his house. 33. And he took them the same hour of the night, and washed *their* stripes; and was baptized, he and all his, straightway. 34. And when he had brought them into his house, he set meat before them, and rejoiced, believing in God with all his house. 35. And when it was day, the magistrates sent the serjeants, saying, Let those men go. 36. And the keeper of the prison told this saying to Paul, The magistrates have sent to let you go: now therefore depart, and go in peace. 37. But Paul said unto them, They have beaten us openly uncondemned, being Romans, and have cast *us* into prison; and now do they thrust us out privily? nay verily; but let them come themselves and fetch us out. 38. And the serjeants told these words unto the magistrates: and they feared, when they heard that they were Romans. 39. And they came and besought them, and brought *them* out, and desired *them* to depart out of the city. 40. And they went out of the prison, and entered into *the house of* Lydia: and when they had seen the brethren, they comforted them, and departed.

PAUL ON MARS' HILL: Acts 17:22. Then Paul stood in the midst of Mars' hill, and said, *Ye* men of Athens, I perceive that in all things ye are too superstitious. 23. For as I passed by, and beheld your devotions, I found an altar with this inscription, TO THE UNKNOWN GOD. Whom therefore ye ignorantly worship, him declare I unto you. 24. God that made the world and all things therein, seeing that he is Lord of heaven and earth, dwelleth not in temples made with hands; 25. Neither is worshipped with men's hands, as though he needed any thing, seeing he giveth to all life, and breath, and all things; 26. And hath made of one blood all nations of men for to dwell on all the face of the earth, and hath determined the times before appointed, and the bounds of their habitation; 27. That they should seek the Lord, if haply they might feel after him, and find him, though he be not far from every one of us: 28. For in him we live, and move, and have our being; as certain also of your own poets have said, For we are also his offspring. 29. Forasmuch then as we are the offspring of God, we ought not to think that the Godhead is like unto gold, or silver, or stone, graven by art and man's device. 30. And the times of this ignorance God winked at; but now commandeth all men every where to repent: 31. Because he hath appointed a day, in the which he will judge the world in righteousness by *that* man whom he hath ordained; *whereof* he hath given assurance unto all *men*, in that he hath raised him from the dead.

PAUL BEFORE FELIX: Acts 24:1. And after five days Ananias the high priest descended with the elders, and *with* a certain orator *named* Tertullus, who informed the governor against Paul. 2. And when he was called forth, Tertullus began to accuse *him*, saying, Seeing that by thee we enjoy great quietness, and that very worthy deeds are done unto this nation by thy providence, 3. We accept *it* always, and in all places, most noble Felix, with all thankfulness. 4. Notwithstanding, that I be not further tedious unto thee, I pray thee that thou wouldest hear us of thy clemency a few words. 5. For we have found this man *a* pestilent *fellow*, and a mover of sedition among all the Jews throughout the world, and a ringleader of the sect of the Nazarenes: 6. Who also hath gone about to profane the temple: whom we took, and would have judged according to our law. 7. But the chief captain Lysias came *upon us*, and with great violence took *him* away out of our hands, 8. Commanding his accusers to come unto thee: by examining of whom thyself mayest take knowledge of all these things, whereof we accuse him. 9. And the Jews also assented, saying that these things were so. 10. Then Paul, after that the governor had beckoned unto him to speak, answered, Forasmuch as I know that thou hast been of many years a judge unto this nation, I do the more cheerfully answer for myself: 11. Because that thou mayest understand, that there are yet but twelve days since I went up to Jerusalem for to worship. 12. And they neither found me in the temple disputing with any man, neither raising up the people, neither in the synagogues, nor in the city: 13. Neither can they prove the things whereof they now accuse me. 14. But this I confess unto thee, that after the way which they call heresy, so worship I the God of my fathers, believing all things which are written in the law and in the prophets: 15. And have hope toward God, which they themselves also allow, that there shall be a resurrection of the dead, both of the just and unjust. 16. And herein do I exercise myself, to have always a conscience void of offence toward God, and *toward* men. 17. Now after many years I came to bring alms to my nation, and offerings. 18. Whereupon certain Jews from Asia found me purified in the temple, neither with multitude, nor with tumult. 19. Who ought to have been here before thee, and object, if they had ought against me. 20. Or else let these same *here* say, if they have found any evil doing in me, while I stood before the council, 21. Except it be for this one voice, that I cried standing among them, Touching the resurrection of the dead I am called in question by you this day. 22. And when Felix heard these things, having more perfect knowledge of *that* way, he deferred them, and said, When Lysias the chief captain shall come down, I will know the uttermost of your matter. 23. And he commanded a centurion to keep Paul, and to let *him* have liberty, and that he should forbid none of his acquaintance to minister or come unto him. 24. And after certain days, when Felix came with his wife Drusilla, which was a Jewess, he sent for Paul, and heard him concerning the faith in Christ. 25. And as he reasoned of righteousness, temperance, and judgment to come, Felix trembled, and answered, Go thy way for this time; when I have a convenient season, I will call for thee. 26. He hoped also that money should have been given him of Paul, that he might loose him: wherefore he sent for him the oftener, and communed with him. 27. But after two years Porcius Festus came into Felix' room: and Felix, willing to shew the Jews a pleasure, left Paul bound.

PAUL BEFORE AGRIPPA: See p. 262.

CHARITY: 1 Cor. 13:1. Though I speak with the tongues of men and of angels, and have not charity, I am become *as* sounding brass, or a tinkling cymbal. 2. And though I have *the gift of* prophecy, and understand all mysteries, and all knowledge; and though I have all faith, so that I could remove mountains, and have not charity, I am nothing. 3. And though I bestow all my goods to feed *the poor,* and though I give my body to be burned, and have not charity, it profiteth me nothing. 4. Charity suffereth long, *and* is kind; charity envieth not; charity vaunteth not itself, is not puffed up, 5. Doth not behave itself unseemly, seeketh not her own, is not easily provoked, thinketh no evil; 6. Rejoiceth not in iniquity, but rejoiceth in the truth; 7. Beareth all things, believeth all things, hopeth all things, endureth all things. 8. Charity never faileth: but whether *there be* prophecies, they shall fail; whether *there be* tongues, they shall cease; whether *there be* knowledge, it shall vanish away. 9. For we know in part, and we prophesy in part. 10. But when that which is perfect is come, then that which is in part shall be done away. 11. When I was a child, I spake as a child, I understood as a child, I thought as a child: but when I became a man, I put away childish things. 12. For now we see through a glass, darkly; but then face to face: now I know in part; but then shall I know even as also I am known. 13. And now abideth faith, hope, charity, these three; but the greatest of these *is* charity.

THE NEW HEAVEN AND THE NEW EARTH: Rev. 21:1. And I saw a new heaven and a new earth: for the first heaven and the first earth were passed away; and there was no more sea. 2. And I John saw the holy city, new Jerusalem, coming down from God out of heaven, prepared as a bride adorned for her husband. 3. And I heard a great voice out of heaven saying, Behold, the tabernacle of God *is* with men, and he will dwell with them, and they shall be his people, and God himself shall be with them, *and be*

their God. 4. And God shall wipe away all tears from their eyes; and there shall be no more death, neither sorrow, nor crying, neither shall there be any more pain: for the former things are passed away. 5. And he that sat upon the throne said, Behold, I make all things new. And he said unto me, Write: for these words are true and faithful. 6. And he said unto me, It is done. I am Alpha and Omega, the beginning and the end. I will give unto him that is athirst of the fountain of the water of life freely. 7. He that overcometh shall inherit all things; and I will be his God, and he shall be my son. 8. But the fearful, and unbelieving, and the abominable, and murderers, and whoremongers, and sorcerers, and idolaters, and all liars, shall have their part in the lake which burneth with fire and brimstone: which is the second death. 9. And there came unto me one of the seven angels which had the seven vials full of the seven last plagues, and talked with me, saying, Come hither, I will shew thee the bride, the Lamb's wife. 10. And he carried me away in the spirit to a great and high mountain, and shewed me that great city, the holy Jerusalem, descending out of heaven from God, 11. Having the glory of God: and her light *was* like unto a stone most precious, even like a jasper stone, clear as crystal; 12. And had a wall great and high, *and* had twelve gates, and at the gates twelve angels, and names written thereon, which are *the names* of the twelve tribes of the children of Israel: 13. On the east three gates; on the north three gates; on the south three gates; and on the west three gates. 14. And the wall of the city had twelve foundations, and in them the names of the twelve apostles of the Lamb. 15. And he that talked with me had a golden reed to measure the city, and the gates thereof, and the wall thereof. 16. And the city lieth foursquare, and the length is as large as the breadth: and he measured the city with the reed, twelve thousand furlongs. The length and the breadth and the height of it are equal. 17. And he measured the wall thereof, an hundred *and* forty *and* four cubits, *according to* the measure of a man, that is, of the angel. 18. And the building of the wall of it was *of* jasper: and the city *was* pure gold, like unto clear glass. 19. And the foundations of the wall of the city *were* garnished with all manner of precious stones. The first foundation *was* jasper; the second, sapphire; the third, a chalcedony; the fourth, an emerald; 20. The fifth, sardonyx; the sixth, sardius; the seventh, chrysolyte; the eighth, beryl; the ninth, a topaz; the tenth, a chrysoprasus; the eleventh, a jacinth; the twelfth, an amethyst. 21. And the twelve gates *were* twelve pearls; every several gate was of one pearl: and the street of the city *was* pure gold, as it were transparent glass. 22. And I saw no temple therein: for the Lord God Almighty and the Lamb are the temple of it. 23. And the city had no need of the sun, neither of the moon to shine in it: for the glory of God did lighten it, and the Lamb is the light thereof. 24. And the nations of them which are saved shall walk in the light of it: and the kings of the earth do bring their glory and honour into it. 25. And the gates of it shall not be shut at all by day: for there shall be no night there. 26. And they shall bring the glory and honour of the nations into it. 27. And there shall in no wise enter into it any thing that defileth, neither *whatsoever* worketh abomination, or *maketh* a lie: but they which are written in the Lamb's book of life.

THE RIVER OF LIFE: Rev. 22:1. And he shewed me a pure river of water of life, clear as crystal, proceeding out of the throne of God and of the Lamb. 2. In the midst of the street of it, and on either side of the river, *was there* the tree of life, which bare twelve *manner of* fruits, *and* yielded her fruit every month: and the leaves of the tree *were* for the healing of the nations. 3. And there shall be no more curse: but the throne of God and of the Lamb shall be in it; and his servants shall serve him: 4. And they shall see his face; and his name *shall be* in their foreheads. 5. And there shall be no night there; and they need no candle, neither light of the sun; for the Lord God giveth them light: and they shall reign for ever and ever. 6. And he said unto me, These sayings *are* faithful and true: and the Lord God of the holy prophets sent his angel to shew unto his servants the things which must shortly be done. 7. Behold, I come quickly: blessed *is* he that keepeth the sayings of the prophecy of this book. 8. And I John saw these things, and heard *them*. And when I had heard and seen, I fell down to worship before the feet of the angel which shewed me these things. 9. Then saith he unto me, See *thou do it* not: for I am thy fellow-servant, and of thy brethren the prophets, and of them which keep the sayings of this book: worship God. 10. And he saith unto me, Seal not the sayings of the prophecy of this book: for the time is at hand. 11. He that is unjust, let him be unjust still: and he which is filthy, let him be filthy still: and he that is righteous, let him be righteous still: and he that is holy, let him be holy still. 12. And, behold, I come quickly; and my reward *is* with me, to give every man according as his work shall be. 13. I am Alpha and Omega, the beginning and the end, the first and the last. 14. Blessed *are* they that do his commandments, that they may have right to the tree of life, and may enter in through the gates into the city. 15. For without *are* dogs, and sorcerers, and whoremongers,

and murderers, and idolaters, and whosoever loveth and maketh a lie. 16. I Jesus have sent mine angel to testify unto you these things in the churches. I am the root and the offspring of David, *and* the bright and morning star. 17. And the Spirit and the bride say, Come. And let him that heareth say, Come. And let him that is athirst come. And whosoever will, let him take the water of life freely. 18. For I testify unto every man that heareth the words of the prophecy of this book, If any man shall add unto these things, God shall add unto him the plagues that are written in this book: 19. And if any man shall take away from the words of the book of this prophecy, God shall take away his part out of the book of life, and out of the holy city, and *from* the things which are written in this book. 20. He which testifieth these things saith, Surely I come quickly. Amen. Even so, come, Lord Jesus. 21. The grace of our Lord Jesus Christ *be* with you all. Amen.

For other selections, see ELEGY, p. 336; PERSONIFICATION, p. 955.

REAIA, son of Micah, a Reubenite, 1 Chr. 5:5.

REAIAH. 1. A man of Judah, son of Shobal, 1 Chr. 4:2. Apparently called HAROEH, 1 Chr. 2:52.

2. Ancestor of a family which returned to Jerusalem from captivity in Babylon, Ezra 2:47; Neh. 7:50.

REAPING, Psa. 129:7. The ark of the Lord returned by the Philistines at the time of, 1 Sam. 6:13. Laws concerning gleaning at the time of, see GLEANING.

FIGURATIVE: Psa. 126:6; Hos. 10:12,13.

REASONING. With God, Job 13:3, 17–28. God reasons with men, Ex. 4:11; 20:5,11; Isa. 1:18; 5:3,4; 43:26; Hos. 4:1; Mic. 6:2.

Natural understanding, Dan. 4:36. To be applied to religion, 1 Cor. 10:15; 1 Pet. 3:15. Not a sufficient guide in human affairs, Deut. 12:8; Prov. 3:5; 14:12. Of the Pharisees, Luke 5:21,22; 20:5. Of Paul from the Scriptures, Acts 17:2; 18:4, 19; 24:25. The gospel cannot be explained by, 1 Cor. 1:18–28; 2:1–14.

See INVESTIGATION; PHILOSOPHY.

REBA, a king of Midian. Slain by the Israelites, Num. 31:8; Josh. 13:21.

REBECCA. See REBEKAH.

REBEKAH. Daughter of Bethuel, grandniece of Abraham, Gen. 22:20–23. Becomes Isaac's wife, Gen. 24:15–67; 25:20. Mother of Esau and Jacob, Gen. 25:21–28. Passes as Isaac's sister, Gen. 26:6–11. Displeased with Esau's wives, Gen. 26:34,35. Prompts Jacob to deceive Isaac, Gen. 27:5–29. Sends Jacob to Laban, Gen. 27:42–46. Burial place of, Gen. 49:31. Called REBECCA, Rom. 9:10.

REBELLION, treasonable, Prov. 17:11.

INSTANCES OF: Absalom, 2 Sam. chapters 15–18. Sheba, 2 Sam. 20. Revolt of the ten tribes, 1 Kin. 12:16–20; 2 Chr. 10; 13:5–12. See SIN.

RECHAB. 1. Son of Rimmon. Murders Ish-bosheth, son of Saul; put to death by David, 2 Sam. 4:5–12.

2. Father of Jehonadab, 2 Kin. 10:15,23; 1 Chr. 2:55; Jer. 35:6,8,16,19. Ancestor of the Rechabites, Jer. 35.

3. Father of Malchiah, Neh. 3:14.

RECHABITES. A family of Kenites descended from Rechab, through Jonadab, 1 Chr. 2:55; Jer. 35:6. Enjoined by Jonadab to drink no wine, Jer. 35:6. Adhere to the injunction of abstinence; perpetuation of the family promised as a reward, Jer. 35.

See ABSTINENCE, TOTAL; NAZARITES.

RECHAH, a city of unknown location, 1 Chr. 4:12.

RECIPROCITY, Rom. 15:27; 1 Cor. 9:11; Gal. 6:6.

RECONCILIATION. Between man and man, Matt. 5:23–26. Of Esau and Jacob, Gen. 33:4,11. Between Pilate and Herod, Luke 23:12.

BETWEEN GOD AND MAN: Lev. 8:15. And he slew it; and Moses took the blood, and put it upon the horns of the altar round about with his finger, and purified the altar, and poured the blood at the bottom of the altar, and sanctified it, to make reconciliation [R. V., atonement] upon it.

Ezek. 45:15. And one lamb out of the flock, out of two hundred, out of the fat pastures of Israel; for a meat offering, and for a burnt offering, and for peace offerings, to make reconciliation [R. V., atonement] for them, saith the Lord GOD.

Dan. 9:24. Seventy weeks are determined upon thy people and upon thy holy city, to finish the transgression, and to make an end of sins, and to make reconciliation for iniquity, and to bring in everlasting righteousness, and to seal up the vision and prophecy, and to anoint the Most Holy.

Rom. 5:1. Therefore being justified by faith, ¹ we have peace with God through our Lord Jesus Christ: 10. For if, when we were enemies, we were reconciled to God by the death of his Son; much more, being reconciled, we shall be saved by his life. [¹ R. V. let us]

Rom. 11:15. For if the casting away of them be the reconciling of the world, what shall the receiving of them be, but life from the dead?

2 Cor. 5:18. And all things are of God, who hath reconciled us to himself by Jesus Christ, and hath given to us the ministry of reconciliation; 19. To wit, that God was in Christ, reconciling the world unto himself, not imputing their trespasses unto them; and hath committed unto us the word of reconciliation. 20. Now then we are ambassadors for Christ, as though God did beseech you by us: we pray you in Christ's stead, be ye reconciled to God. 21. For he hath made him to be sin for us, who knew no sin; that we might be made the righteousness of God in him.

Eph. 2:15. Having abolished in his flesh the enmity, even the law of commandments contained in ordinances; for to make in himself of twain one new man, so making peace; 16. And that he might reconcile both unto God in one body by the cross, having slain the enmity thereby: 17. And came and preached peace to you which were afar off, and to them that were nigh. 18. For through him we both have access by one Spirit unto the Father.

Col. 1:20. And, having made peace through the blood of his cross, by him to reconcile all things unto himself; by him, I say, whether they be things in earth, or things in heaven. 21. And you, that were sometime alienated and enemies in your mind by wicked works, yet now hath he reconciled 22. In the body of his flesh through death, to present you holy and unblameable and unreproveable in his sight:

Heb. 2:17. Wherefore in all things it behoved him to be made like unto his brethren, that he might be a merciful and faithful high priest in things pertaining to God, to make reconciliation for the sins of the people.

See ATONEMENT; JESUS, MISSION OF; PROPITIATION; REDEMPTION.

RECONNOISSANCE. Of Jericho, Josh. 2:1–24; Beth-el, Judg. 1:23; Laish, Judg. 18:2–10.

RECORDER. See SCRIBE; SECRETARY.

RECREATION,* Jesus takes, from the fatigues of his ministry, Mark. 6:31,32; 7:24.

RED. See COLOR.

REDEMPTION. Of persons or property, Lev. 25:25–34; 27:2–13,14–33; Ruth 4: 3–10. Redemption money paid to priests, Num. 3:46–51. Of firstborn, see FIRSTBORN; of land, see JUBILEE.

OF OUR SOULS: Psa. 111:9. He sent redemption unto his people: he hath commanded his covenant for ever; holy and reverend is his name.

Psa. 130:7. Let Israel hope in the LORD: for with the LORD there is mercy, and with him is plenteous redemption.

Matt. 20:28. Even as the Son of man came not to be ministered unto, but to minister, and to give his life a ransom for many. Mark 10:45.

Luke 2:38. And she coming in that instant gave thanks likewise unto the Lord, and spake of him to all them that looked for redemption in Jerusalem.

Acts 20:28. Take heed therefore unto yourselves, and to all the flock, over the which the Holy Ghost hath made you overseers, to feed the church of God, which he hath purchased with his own blood.

Rom. 3:24. Being justified freely by his grace through the redemption that is in Christ Jesus: 25. Whom God hath set forth to be a propitiation through faith in his

---

* For a fuller development of the subject, study Sabbath, the numerous Mosaic feasts in which labor was prohibited, Jubilee, and Sabbatic year.

blood, to declare his righteousness for the remission of sins that are past, through the forbearance of God; 26. To declare, *I say*, at this time his righteousness: that he might be just, and the justifier of him which believeth in Jesus.

1 Cor. 1:30. But of him are ye in Christ Jesus, who of God is made unto us wisdom, and righteousness, and sanctification, and redemption:

1 Cor. 6:20. For ye are bought with a price: therefore glorify God in your body, and in your spirit, which are God's.

1 Cor. 7:23. Ye are bought with a price; be not ye the servants of men.

Gal. 1:4. Who gave himself for our sins, that he might deliver us from this present evil world, according to the will of God and our Father:

Gal. 2:20. I am crucified with Christ: nevertheless I live; yet not I, but Christ liveth in me: and the life which I now live in the flesh I live by the faith of the Son of God, who loved me, and gave himself for me.

Gal. 4:4. But when the fulness of the time was come, God sent forth his Son, made of a woman, made under the law, 5. To redeem them that were under the law, that we might receive the adoption of sons.

Eph. 1:7. In whom we have redemption through his blood, the forgiveness of sins, according to the riches of his grace;

Eph. 5:2. And walk in love, as Christ also hath loved us, and hath given himself for us an offering and a sacrifice to God for a sweetsmelling savour.

Col. 1:14. In whom we have redemption ¹through his blood, *even* the forgiveness of sins: 20. And, having made peace through the blood of his cross, by him to reconcile all things unto himself; by him, *I say*, whether *they be* things in earth, or things in heaven. 21. And you, that were sometime alienated and enemies in *your* mind by wicked works, yet now hath he reconciled 22. In the body of his flesh through death, to present you holy and unblameable and unreproveable in his sight: [¹ Omitted in R. V.]

1 Tim. 2:6. Who gave himself a ransom for all, to be testified in due time.

Tit. 2:14. Who gave himself for us, that he might redeem us from all iniquity, and purify unto himself a peculiar people, zealous of good works.

Heb. 9:12. Neither by the blood of goats and calves, but by his own blood he entered in once into the holy place, having obtained eternal redemption *for us.* 15. And for this cause he is the mediator of the new testament, that by means of death, for the redemption of the transgressions *that were* under the first testament, they which are called might receive the promise of eternal inheritance.

1 Pet. 1:18. Forasmuch as ye know that ye were not redeemed with corruptible things, *as* silver and gold, from your vain conver-

sation *received* by tradition from your fathers; 19. But with the precious blood of Christ, as of a lamb without blemish and without spot.

Rev. 5:9. And they sung a new song, saying, Thou art worthy to take the book, and to open the seals thereof: for thou wast slain, and hast redeemed us to God by thy blood out of every kindred, and tongue, and people, and nation; 10. And hast made us unto our God kings and priests: and we shall reign on the earth.

See ATONEMENT; RANSOM.

RED HEIFER, of purification, Num. 19.

RED SEA. The locusts which devastated Egypt destroyed in, Ex. 10:19. Israelites cross; Pharaoh and his army drowned in, Ex. 14; 15:1,4,11,19; Num. 33:8; Deut. 11:4; Josh. 2:10; 4:23; 24:6,7; Judg. 11:16; 2 Sam. 22:16; Neh. 9:9–11; Psa. 66:6; 78:13,53; 106:7–11,22; 136:13–15; Isa. 43:16,17; Acts 7:36; 1 Cor. 10:1,2; Heb. 11:29. Israelites camp by, Ex. 14:2,9; Num. 14:25; 21:4; 33:10,11; Deut. 1:40; 2:1–3. Boundary of the promised land, Ex. 23:31. Solomon builds ships on, 1 Kin. 9:26.

Wilderness of, Ex. 13:18.

REED. A water plant, Isa. 19:6,7; 35:7; Jer. 51:32. Used as a measuring device of six cubits, Ezek. 40:3–8; 41:8; 42:16–19; 45:1; Rev. 11:1; 21:15,16. Mockingly given to Jesus as a symbol of royalty, Matt. 27:29. Jesus smitten with, Matt. 27:30; Mark 15:19.

FIGURATIVE: Of weakness, 1 Kin. 14:15; 2 Kin. 18:21; Isa. 36:6; 42:3; Ezek. 29:6; Matt. 11:7; 12:20.

REELAIAH. A returned captive from Babylon, Ezra 2:2. Called RAAMIAH, Neh. 7:7.

REFINING, the process of eliminating by fire the dross of metals. Of gold, 1 Chr. 28:18. Of silver, 1 Chr. 29:4. Of wine, Isa. 25:6.

FIGURATIVE: Of the corrective judgments of God, Isa. 1:25; 48:10; Jer. 9:7; Zech. 13:9; Mal. 3:2,3. Of the purity of the word of God, Psa. 18:30; 119:140.

REFUGE. CITIES OF: From the avenger of blood, Ex. 21:13,14; Num. 35:11–32; Deut. 4:41–43; 19:2–13; Josh. 20:1–6. List of, Josh. 20:7–9. Roads made to, Deut. 19:3.

FIGURATIVE: Of Christ, Heb. 6:18.

REFUGEE SLAVES. Laws concerning, Deut. 23:15,16.

See SERVANT, BOND.

REGEM, son of Jahdai, 1 Chr. 2:47.

REGEM-MELECH, a captive sent as a messenger from the Jews in Babylon to Jerusalem, Zech. 7:2.

REGENCY, 1 Kin. 22:47; 2 Kin. 15:5.

REGENERATION.* Deut. 30:6. The LORD thy God will circumcise thine heart, and the heart of thy seed, to love the LORD thy God, with all thine heart, and with all thy soul, that thou mayest live. Deut. 29:4.

* Under this topic are collected those scriptures that relate to the change of affections, commonly denominated "conversion," "a new creature," "a new birth," etc.

1 Kin. 8:58. That he may incline our hearts unto him, to walk in all his ways, and to keep his commandments, and his statutes, and his judgments, which he commanded our fathers.

Psa. 36:9. With thee *is* the fountain of life: in thy light shall we see light.

Psa. 51:2. Wash me throughly from mine iniquity, and cleanse me from my sin. 7. Purge me with hyssop, and I shall be clean: wash me, and I shall be whiter than snow. 10. Create in me a clean heart, O God; and renew a right spirit within me.

Psa. 65:3. *As for* our transgressions, thou shalt purge them away.

Psa. 68:18. Thou hast ascended on high, thou hast led captivity captive: thou hast received gifts for men; yea, *for* the rebellious also, that the Lord God might dwell *among them*.

Psa. 87:4. I will make mention of Rahab and Babylon to them that know me: behold Philistia, and Tyre, with Ethiopia; this *man* was born there. 6. The Lord shall count, when he writeth up the people, *that* this *man* was born there.

Psa. 110:3. Thy people *shall be* willing in the day of thy power, in the beauties of holiness from the womb of the morning: thou hast the dew of thy youth.

Prov. 4:23. Keep thy heart with all diligence; for out of it *are* the issues of life.

Prov. 12:28. In the way of righteousness *is* life; and *in* the pathway *thereof there is* no death.

Prov. 14:27. The fear of the Lord *is* a fountain of life, to depart from the snares of death.

Prov. 16:1. The preparations of the heart in man, and the answer of the tongue, *is* from the Lord.

Isa. 1:16. Wash you, make you clean; put away the evil of your doings from before mine eyes; cease to do evil; 17. Learn to do well; seek judgment, relieve the oppressed, judge the fatherless, plead for the widow. 25. I will turn my hand upon thee, and purely purge away thy dross, and take away all thy tin:

Isa. 4:4. When the Lord shall have washed away the filth of the daughters of Zion, and shall have purged the blood of Jerusalem from the midst thereof, by the spirit of judgment, and by the spirit of burning.

Isa. 12:3. Therefore with joy shall ye draw water out of the wells of salvation.

Isa. 26:12. Lord, thou wilt ordain peace for us: for thou also hast wrought all our works in us.

Isa. 29:23. But when he seeth his children, the work of mine hands, in the midst of him, they shall sanctify my name, and sanctify the Holy One of Jacob, and shall fear the God of Israel.

Isa. 32:3. The eyes of them that see shall not be dim, and the ears of them that hear shall hearken. 4. The heart also of the rash shall understand knowledge, and the tongue of the stammerers shall be ready to speak plainly. 15. Until the spirit be poured upon us from on high, and the wilderness be a fruitful field, and the fruitful field be counted for a forest. 17. And the work of righteousness shall be peace; and the effect of righteousness quietness and assurance for ever.

Isa. 35:5. Then the eyes of the blind shall be opened, and the ears of the deaf shall be unstopped. 6. Then shall the lame *man* leap as an hart, and the tongue of the dumb sing:

Isa. 42:16. I will bring the blind by a way *that* they knew not; I will lead them in paths *that* they have not known: I will make darkness light before them, and crooked things straight.

Isa. 43:7. *Even* every one that is called by my name: for I have created him for my glory, I have formed him; yea, I have made him.

Isa. 44:3. I will pour water upon him that is thirsty, and floods upon the dry ground: I will pour my spirit upon thy seed, and my blessing upon thine offspring: 4. And they shall spring up *as* among the grass, as willows by the water courses. 5. One shall say, I *am* the Lord's; and another shall call *himself* by the name of Jacob; and another shall subscribe *with* his hand unto the Lord, and surname *himself* by the name of Israel.

Isa. 49:9. That thou mayest say to the prisoners, Go forth; to them that *are* in darkness, Shew yourselves.

Isa. 55:1. Ho, every one that thirsteth, come ye to the waters, and he that hath no money; come ye, buy, and eat; yea, come, buy wine and milk without money and without price. 2. Wherefore do ye spend money for *that which is* not bread? and your labour for *that which* satisfieth not? hearken diligently unto me, and eat ye *that which is* good, and let your soul delight itself in fatness. 3. Incline your ear, and come unto me: hear, and your soul shall live;

Jer. 13:23. Can the Ethiopian change his skin, or the leopard his spots? *then* may ye also do good, that are accustomed to do evil.

Jer. 17:13. O Lord, the hope of Israel, all that forsake thee shall be ashamed, *and* they that depart from me shall be written in the earth, because they have forsaken the Lord, the fountain of living waters. 14. Heal me, O Lord, and I shall be healed; save me, and I shall be saved: for thou *art* my praise.

Jer. 24:7. I will give them an heart to know me, that I *am* the Lord: and they shall be my people, and I will be their God: for they shall return unto me with their whole heart.

Jer. 31:3. The Lord hath appeared of old unto me, *saying*, Yea, I have loved thee with an everlasting love: therefore with lovingkindness have I drawn thee. 33. I will put my law in their inward parts, and write it in their hearts; and will be their God, and they shall be my people. 34. And they shall teach no more every man his neighbour, and every man his brother, saying, Know the LORD: for they shall all know me, from the least of them unto the greatest of them, saith the LORD: for I will forgive their iniquity, and I will remember their sin no more. Heb. 8:10,11.

Jer. 32:38. They shall be my people, and I will be their God: 39. And I will give them one heart, and one way, that they may fear me for ever, for the good of them, and of their children after them: 40. And I will make an everlasting covenant with them, that I will not turn away from them, to do them good; but I will put my fear in their hearts, that they shall not depart from me.

Jer. 33:6. Behold, I will bring it health and cure, and I will cure them, and will reveal unto them the abundance of peace and truth.

Ezek. 11:19. I will give them one heart, and I will put a new spirit within you; and I will take the stony heart out of their flesh, and will give them an heart of flesh: 20. That they may walk in my statutes, and keep mine ordinances, and do them: and they shall be my people, and I will be their God.

Ezek. 16:9. Then washed I thee with water; yea, I throughly washed away thy blood from thee, and I anointed thee with oil.

Ezek. 18:31. Cast away from you all your transgressions, whereby ye have transgressed; and make you a new heart and a new spirit: for why will ye die, O house of Israel?

Ezek. 36:26. A new heart also will I give you, and a new spirit will I put within you: and I will take away the stony heart out of your flesh, and I will give you an heart of flesh. [Ezek. 11:19.] 27. And I will put my spirit within you, and cause you to walk in my statutes, and ye shall keep my judgments, and do *them.* 29. I will also save you from all your uncleannesses:

Ezek. 37:1. The hand of the LORD was upon me, and carried me out in the spirit of the LORD, and set me down in the midst of the valley which *was* full of bones, 2. And caused me to pass by them round about: and, behold, *there were* very many in the open valley; and, lo, *they were* very dry. 3. And he said unto me, Son of man, can these bones live? And I answered, O Lord GOD, thou knowest. 4. Again he said unto me, Prophesy upon these bones, and say unto them, O ye dry bones, hear the word of the LORD. 5. Thus saith the Lord GOD unto these bones; Behold, I will cause breath to enter into you, and ye shall live: 6. And I will lay sinews upon you, and will bring up flesh upon you, and cover you with skin, and put breath in you, and ye

shall live; and ye shall know that I *am* the LORD. 7. So I prophesied as I was commanded: and as I prophesied, there was a noise, and behold a shaking, and the bones came together, bone to his bone. 8. And when I beheld, lo, the sinews and the flesh came up upon them, and the skin covered them above: but *there was* no breath in them. 9. Then said he unto me, Prophesy unto the wind, prophesy, son of man, and say to the wind, Thus saith the Lord GOD; Come from the four winds, O breath, and breathe upon these slain, that they may live. 10. So I prophesied as he commanded me, and the breath came into them, and they lived, and stood up upon their feet, an exceeding great army. 11. Then he said unto me, Son of man, these bones are the whole house of Israel: behold, they say, Our bones are dried, and our hope is lost: we are cut off for our parts. 12. Therefore prophesy and say unto them, Thus saith the Lord GOD; Behold, O my people, I will open your graves, and cause you to come up out of your graves, and bring you into the land of Israel. 13. And ye shall know that I *am* the LORD, when I have opened your graves, O my people, and brought you up out of your graves, 14. And shall put my spirit in you, and ye shall live, and I shall place you in your own land: then shall ye know that I the LORD have spoken *it,* and performed *it,* saith the LORD.

Ezek. 44:7. In that ye have brought *into my sanctuary* strangers, uncircumcised in heart, and uncircumcised in flesh, to be in my sanctuary, to pollute it, *even* my house, when ye offer my bread, the fat and the blood, and they have broken my covenant because of all your abominations. 9. Thus saith the Lord GOD; No stranger, uncircumcised in heart, nor uncircumcised in flesh, shall enter into my sanctuary, of any stranger that *is* among the children of Israel.

Zech. 12:10. And I will pour upon the house of David, and upon the inhabitants of Jerusalem, the spirit of grace and of supplications: and they shall look upon me whom they have pierced, and they shall mourn for him, as one mourneth for *his* only *son,* and shall be in bitterness for him, as one that is in bitterness for *his* firstborn.

Matt. 12:33. Either make the tree good, and his fruit good; or else make the tree corrupt, and his fruit corrupt: for the tree is known by *his* fruit. 34. O generation of vipers, how can ye, being evil, speak good things? for out of the abundance of the heart the mouth speaketh. 35. A good man out of the good treasure of the heart bringeth forth good things: and an evil man out of the evil treasure bringeth forth evil things. 43. When the unclean spirit is gone out of a man, he walketh through dry places, seeking rest, and findeth none. 44. Then he saith, I will return into my house from whence I came out; and when he is come, he findeth *it* empty, swept, and garnished.

Matt. 13:23. But he that received seed into the good ground is he that heareth the word, and understandeth *it;* which also beareth fruit, and bringeth forth, some an hundredfold, some sixty, some thirty. [Mark 4:20.] 33. The kingdom of heaven is like unto leaven, which a woman took, and hid in three measures of meal, till the whole was leavened. Luke 13:21.

Matt. 18:3. Except ye be converted, and become as little children, ye shall not enter into the kingdom of heaven. Mark 10;15; Luke 18:17.

Mark 4:26. And he said, So is the kingdom of God, as if a man should cast seed into the ground; 27. And should sleep, and rise night and day, and the seed should spring and grow up, he knoweth not how. 28. For the earth bringeth forth fruit of herself; first the blade, then the ear, after that the full corn in the ear. 29. But when the fruit is brought forth, immediately he putteth in the sickle, because the harvest is come.

Luke 1:16. Many of the children of Israel shall he turn to the Lord their God. 17. And he shall go before him in the spirit and power of Elias, to turn the hearts of the fathers to the children, and the disobedient to the wisdom of the just; to make ready a people prepared for the Lord.

Luke 8:35. Then they went out to see what was done; and came to Jesus, and found the man, out of whom the devils were departed, sitting at the feet of Jesus, clothed, and in his right mind: and they were afraid. 38. Now the man out of whom the devils were departed besought him that he might be with him: but Jesus sent him away, saying, 39. Return to thine own house, and shew how great things God hath done unto thee. And he went his way, and published throughout the whole city how great things Jesus had done unto him. Mark 5:19,20.

John 1:4. In him was life; and the life was the light of men. 13. Which were born, not of blood, nor of the will of the flesh, nor of the will of man, but of God. 16. And of his fulness have all we received, and grace for grace.

John 3:3. Jesus answered and said unto him, Verily, verily, I say unto thee, Except a man be born again, he cannot see the kingdom of God. 4. Nicodemus saith unto him, How can a man be born when he is old? can he enter the second time into his mother's womb, and be born? 5. Jesus answered, Verily, verily, I say unto thee, Except a man be born of water and *of* the Spirit, he cannot enter into the kingdom of God. 6. That which is born of the flesh is flesh; and that which is born of the Spirit is spirit. 7. Marvel not that I said unto thee, Ye must be born again. 8. The wind bloweth where it listeth, and thou hearest the sound thereof, but canst not tell whence it cometh, and whither it goeth: so is every one that is born of the Spirit.

John 4:10. Jesus answered and said unto her, If thou knewest the gift of God, and who it is that saith to thee, Give me to drink; thou wouldest have asked of him, and he would have given thee living water. 14. Whosoever drinketh of the water that I shall give him shall never thirst; but the water that I shall give him shall be in him a well of water springing up into everlasting life.

John 5:24. He that heareth my word, and believeth on him that sent me, hath everlasting life, and shall not come into condemnation; but is passed from death unto life.

John 6:44. No man can come to me, except the Father which hath sent me draw him: and I will raise him up at the last day. 45. It is written in the prophets, And they shall be all taught of God. Every man therefore that hath heard, and hath learned of the Father, cometh unto me. 47. Verily, verily, I say unto you, He that believeth on me hath everlasting life. 50. This is the bread which cometh down from heaven, that a man may eat thereof, and not die. 51. I am the living bread which came down from heaven: if any man eat of this bread, he shall live for ever: 57. As the living Father hath sent me, and I live by the Father: so he that eateth me, even he shall live by me.

John 8:12. I am the light of the world: he that followeth me shall not walk in darkness, but shall have the light of life. 32. And ye shall know the truth, and the truth shall make you free. 36. If the Son therefore shall make you free, ye shall be free indeed.

John 10:9. I am the door: by me if any man enter in, he shall be saved, and shall go in and out, and find pasture. 10. The thief cometh not, but for to steal, and to kill, and to destroy: I am come that they might have life, and that they might have *it* more abundantly.

John 13:8. Jesus answered him, If I wash thee not, thou hast no part with me.

John 15:1. I am the true vine, and my Father is the husbandman. 3. Now ye are clean through the word which I have spoken unto you.

John 17:2. As thou hast given him power over all flesh, that he should give eternal life to as many as thou hast given him.

Acts 2:38. Then Peter said unto them, Repent, and be baptized every one of you in the name of Jesus Christ for the remission of sins, and ye shall receive the gift of the Holy Ghost. 47. The Lord added to the church daily such as should be saved.

Acts 3:26. Unto you first God, having raised up his [1] Son Jesus, sent him to bless you, in turning away every one of you from his iniquities.   [1 R. V. Servant.]

Acts 11:17. Forasmuch then as God gave them the like gift as *he did* unto us, who believed on the Lord Jesus Christ; what was I, that I could withstand God? 21. The hand of the Lord was with them: and a great number believed, and turned unto the Lord.

Acts 15:9. Put no difference between us and them, purifying their hearts by faith.

Acts 16:14. A certain woman named Lydia, . . . whose heart the Lord opened, that she attended unto the things which were spoken of Paul.

Acts 21:19. When he had saluted them, he declared particularly what things God had wrought among the Gentiles by his ministry.

Acts 26:18. To open their eyes, *and* to turn *them* from darkness to light, and *from* the power of Satan unto God, that they may receive forgiveness of sins, and inheritance among them which are sanctified by faith that is in me.

Rom. 2:28. For he is not a Jew, which is one outwardly; neither *is that* circumcision, which is outward in the flesh: 29. But he *is* a Jew, which is one inwardly; and circumcision *is that* of the heart, in the spirit, *and* not in the letter; whose praise *is* not of men, but of God.

Rom. 6:3. Know ye not, that so many of us as were baptized into Jesus Christ were baptized into his death? 4. Therefore we are buried with him by baptism into death: that like as Christ was raised up from the dead by the glory of the Father, even so we also should walk in newness of life. 5. For if we have been planted together in the likeness of his death, we shall be also *in the likeness* of *his* resurrection: 6. Knowing this, that our old man is crucified with *him*, that the body of sin might be destroyed, that henceforth we should not serve sin. 7. For he that is dead is freed from sin. 8. Now if we be dead with Christ, we believe that we shall also live with him: 9. Knowing that Christ being raised from the dead dieth no more; death hath no more dominion over him. 10. For in that he died, he died unto sin once: but in that he liveth, he liveth unto God. 11. Likewise reckon ye also yourselves to be dead indeed unto sin, but alive unto God through Jesus Christ our Lord. 12. Let not sin therefore reign in your mortal body, that ye should obey it in the lusts thereof. 13. Neither yield ye your members *as* instruments of unrighteousness unto sin: but yield yourselves unto God, as those that are alive from the dead, and your members *as* instruments of righteousness unto God. 14. For sin shall not have dominion over you: for ye are not under the law, but under grace. 15. What then? shall we sin, because we are not under the law, but under grace? God forbid. 16. Know ye not, that to whom ye yield yourselves servants to obey, his servants ye are to whom ye obey; whether

of sin unto death, or of obedience unto righteousness? 17. But God be thanked, that ye were the servants of sin, but ye have obeyed from the heart that form of doctrine which was delivered you. 18. Being then made free from sin, ye became the servants of righteousness. 19. I speak after the manner of men because of the infirmity of your flesh: for as ye have yielded your members servants to uncleanness and to iniquity unto iniquity; even so now yield your members servants to righteousness unto holiness. 20. For when ye were the servants of sin, ye were free from righteousness. 21. What fruit had ye then in those things whereof ye are now ashamed? for the end of those things *is* death. 22. But now being made free from sin, and become servants to God, ye have your fruit unto holiness, and the end everlasting life. 23. For the wages of sin *is* death; but the gift of God *is* eternal life through Jesus Christ our Lord.

Rom. 7:6. Now we are delivered from the law, that being dead wherein we were held; that we should serve in newness of spirit, and not *in* the oldness of the letter. 24. O wretched man that I am! who shall deliver me from the body of this death? 25. I thank God through Jesus Christ our Lord.

Rom. 8:2. For the law of the Spirit of life in Christ Jesus hath made me free from the law of sin and death. 3. For what the law could not do, in that it was weak through the flesh, God sending his own Son in the likeness of sinful flesh, and for sin, condemned sin in the flesh: 4. That the righteousness of the law might be fulfilled in us, who walk not after the flesh, but after the Spirit. 5. For they that are after the flesh do mind the things of the flesh; but they that are after the Spirit the things of the Spirit. 6. For to be carnally minded *is* death; but to be spiritually minded *is* life and peace. 9. But ye are not in the flesh, but in the Spirit, if so be that the Spirit of God dwell in you. Now if any man have not the Spirit of Christ, he is none of his. 13. For if ye live after the flesh, ye shall die: but if ye through the Spirit do mortify the deeds of the body, ye shall live. 14. For as many as are led by the Spirit of God, they are the sons of God. 15. For ye have not received the spirit of bondage again to fear; but ye have received the Spirit of adoption, whereby we cry, Abba, Father. 16. The Spirit itself beareth witness with our spirit, that we are the children of God:

Rom. 12:2. Be not conformed to this world: but be ye transformed by the renewing of your mind, that ye may prove what *is* that good, and acceptable, and perfect, will of God.

Rom. 15:16. That I should be the minister of Jesus Christ to the Gentiles, ministering the gospel of God, that the offering up of the Gentiles might be acceptable, being sanctified by the Holy Ghost.

1 Cor. 1:9. God *is* faithful, by whom ye were called unto the fellowship of his Son Jesus Christ our Lord. 24. Unto them which are called, both Jews and Greeks, Christ the power of God, and the wisdom of God. 30. Of him are ye in Christ Jesus, who of God is made unto us wisdom, and righteousness, and sanctification, and redemption:

1 Cor. 2:12. We have received, not the spirit of the world, but the spirit which is of God; that we might know the things that are freely given to us of God. 14. The natural man receiveth not the things of the Spirit of God: for they are foolishness unto him: neither can he know *them*, because they are spiritually discerned. 15. But he that is spiritual judgeth all things, yet he himself is judged of no man. 16. For who hath known the mind of the Lord, that he may instruct him? But we have the mind of Christ.

1 Cor. 3:6. I have planted, Apollos watered; but God gave the increase. 7. So then neither is he that planteth any thing, neither he that watereth; but God that giveth the increase. 9. For we are labourers together with God: ye are God's husbandry, *ye are* God's building.

1 Cor. 6:11. But ye are washed, but ye are sanctified, but ye are justified in the name of the Lord Jesus, and by the Spirit of our God.

1 Cor. 12:6. And there are diversities of operations, but it is the same God which worketh all in all. 13. For by one Spirit are we all baptized into one body, whether *we be* Jews or Gentiles, whether *we be* bond or free; and have been all made to drink into one Spirit.

1 Cor. 15:10. By the grace of God I am what I am:

2 Cor. 1:21. Now he which stablisheth us with you in Christ, and hath anointed us, *is* God; 22. Who hath also sealed us, and given the earnest of the Spirit in our hearts.

2 Cor. 3:3. *Ye are* manifestly declared to be the epistle of Christ ministered by us, written not with ink, but with the Spirit of the living God; not in tables of stone, but in fleshy tables of the heart. 18. But we all, with open face beholding as in a glass the glory of the Lord, are changed into the same image from glory to glory, *even* as by the Spirit of the Lord.

2 Cor. 4:6. For God, who commanded the light to shine out of darkness, hath shined in our hearts, to *give* the light of the knowledge of the glory of God in the face of Jesus Christ.

2 Cor. 5:5. Now he that hath wrought us for the selfsame thing *is* God, who also hath given unto us the earnest of the Spirit. 17. If any man *be* in Christ, *he is* a new creature: old things are passed away; behold, all things are become new.

Gal. 2:20. I am crucified with Christ: nevertheless I live; yet not I, but Christ liveth in me: and the life which I now live in the flesh I live by the faith of the Son of God, who loved me, and gave himself for me.

Gal. 4:29. As then he that was born after the flesh persecuted him *that was born* after the Spirit, even so *it is* now.

Gal. 6:15. [1] In Christ Jesus neither circumcision availeth any thing, nor uncircumcision, but a new creature. [1 Omitted in R. V.]

Eph. 2:1. You *hath he quickened*, who were dead in trespasses and sins; 5. Even when we were dead in sins, hath quickened us together with Christ, (by grace ye are saved;) 6. And hath raised *us* up together, and made *us* sit together in heavenly *places* in Christ Jesus: 8. For by grace are ye saved through faith; and that not of yourselves: *it is* the gift of God: 10. We are his workmanship, created in Christ Jesus unto good works, which God hath before ordained that we should walk in them.

Eph. 4:7. Unto every one of us is given grace according to the measure of the gift of Christ. 8. Wherefore he saith, When he ascended up on high, he led captivity captive, and gave gifts unto men. 16. From whom the whole body fitly joined together and compacted by that which every joint supplieth, according to the effectual working in the measure of every part, maketh increase of the body unto the edifying of itself in love. 21. If so be that ye have heard him, and have been taught by him, as the truth is in Jesus: 22. That ye put off concerning the former conversation the old man, which is corrupt according to the deceitful lusts; 23. And be renewed in the spirit of your mind; 24. And that ye put on the new man, which after God is created in righteousness and true holiness.

Eph. 5:14. Awake thou that sleepest, and arise from the dead, and Christ shall give thee light.

Phil. 1:6. Being confident of this very thing, that he which hath begun a good work in you will perform *it* until the day of Jesus Christ:

Col. 2:11. In whom also ye are circumcised with the circumcision made without hands, in putting off the body of the sins of the flesh by the circumcision of Christ: 12. Buried with him in baptism, wherein also ye are risen with *him* through the faith of the operation of God, who hath raised him from the dead. 13. And you, being dead in your sins and the uncircumcision of your flesh, hath he quickened together with him, having forgiven you all trespasses;

Col. 3:9. Lie not one to another, seeing that ye have put off the old man with his deeds; 10. And have put on the new *man*, which is renewed in knowledge after the image of him that created him:

2 Thess. 2:13. But we are bound to give thanks alway to God for you, brethren beloved of the Lord, because God hath from the beginning chosen you to salvation through sanctification of the Spirit and belief of the truth:

Tit. 3:5. Not by works of righteousness which we have done, but according to his mercy he saved us, by the washing of regeneration, and renewing of the Holy Ghost; 6. Which he shed on us abundantly through Jesus Christ our Saviour;

Heb. 4:1. Let us therefore fear, lest, a promise being left *us* of entering into his rest, any of you should seem to come short of it. 2. For unto us was the gospel preached, as well as unto them: but the word preached did not profit them, not being mixed with faith in them that heard *it*. 3. For we which have believed do enter into rest, as he said, As I have sworn in my wrath, if they shall enter into my rest: although the works were finished from the foundation of the world. 4. For he spake in a certain place of the seventh *day* on this wise, And God did rest the seventh day from all his works. 5. And in this *place* again, If they shall enter into my rest. 6. Seeing therefore it remaineth that some must enter therein, and they to whom it was first preached entered not in because of unbelief: 7. Again, he limiteth a certain day, saying in David, To day, after so long a time; as it is said, To day if ye will hear his voice, harden not your hearts. 8. For if Jesus had given them rest, then would he not afterward have spoken of another day. 9. There remaineth therefore a rest to the people of God. 10. For he that is entered into his rest, he also hath ceased from his own works, as God *did* from his. 11. Let us labour therefore to enter into that rest, lest any man fall after the same example of unbelief. 12. For the word of God *is* quick, and powerful, and sharper than any twoedged sword, piercing even to the dividing asunder of soul and spirit, and of the joints and marrow, and *is* a discerner of the thoughts and intents of the heart.

Heb. 10:16. This *is* the covenant that I will make with them after those days, saith the Lord, I will put my laws into their hearts, and in their minds will I write them; 17. And their sins and iniquities will I remember no more. 22. Let us draw near with a true heart in full assurance of faith, having our hearts sprinkled from an evil conscience, and our bodies washed with pure water. 23. Let us hold fast the profession of *our* faith without wavering; (for he *is* faithful that promised;)

Jas. 1:18. Of his own will begat he us with the word of truth, that we should be a kind of firstfruits of his creatures.

Jas. 5:19. If any of you do err from the truth, and one convert him; 20. Let him know, that he which converteth the sinner from the error of his way shall save a soul from death, and shall hide a multitude of sins.

1 Pet. 1:2. Elect according to the foreknowledge of God the Father through sanctification of the Spirit, unto obedience and sprinkling of the blood of Jesus Christ: Grace unto you, and peace, be multiplied.

3. Blessed *be* the God and Father of our Lord Jesus Christ, which according to his abundant mercy hath begotten us again unto a lively hope by the resurrection of Jesus Christ from the dead, 22. Seeing ye have purified your souls in obeying the truth [1] through the Spirit unto unfeigned love of the brethren, *see that ye* love one another with a pure heart fervently: 23. Being born again not of corruptible seed, but of incorruptible, by the word of God, which liveth and abideth forever. [1 Omitted in R. V.]

1 Pet. 2:3. If so be ye have tasted that the Lord *is* gracious. 9. But ye *are* a chosen generation, a royal priesthood, an holy nation, a peculiar people; that ye should shew forth the praises of him who hath called you out of darkness into his marvellous light:

2 Pet. 1:3. His divine power hath given unto us all things that *pertain* unto life and godliness, through the knowledge of him that hath called us to glory and virtue: 4. Whereby are given unto us exceeding great and precious promises: that by these ye might be partakers of the divine nature, having escaped the corruption that is in the world through lust.

1 John 2:27. The anointing, which ye have received of him, abideth in you, and ye need not that any man teach you: but as the same anointing teacheth you of all things, and is truth, and is no lie, and even as it hath taught you, ye shall abide in him. 29. If ye know that he is righteous, ye know that every one that doeth righteousness is born of him.

1 John 3:9 Whosoever is born of God doth not commit sin; for his seed remaineth in him: and he cannot sin, because he is born of God. 14. We know that we have passed from death unto life, because we love the brethren.

1 John 4:7. Beloved, let us love one another: for love is of God; and every one that loveth is born of God, and knoweth God.

1 John 5:1. Whosoever believeth that Jesus is the Christ is born of God: and every one that loveth him that begat loveth him also that is begotten of him. 4. For whatsoever is born of God overcometh the world: and this is the victory that overcometh the world, *even* our faith. 5. Who is he that overcometh the world, but he that believeth that Jesus is the Son of God? 11. And this is the record, that God hath given to us eternal life, and this life is in his Son. 12. He that hath the Son hath life; *and* he that hath not the Son of God hath not life. 18. We know that whosoever is born of God sinneth not; but he that is begotten of God keepeth himself, and that wicked one toucheth him not.

See ATONEMENT; RECONCILIATION; REDEMPTION; SANCTIFICATION; SIN, FORGIVENESS OF.

INSTANCES OF: Jacob, Gen. 32:29. Saul, 1 Sam. 10:9. Saul of Tarsus, Acts 9:3–18. All righteous persons, see RIGHTEOUS.

REGICIDE. Of Ehud, Judg. 3:16–23. Of Saul, 2 Sam. 1:16. Of Ish-bosheth, 2 Sam. 4:5–8. Of Nadab, 1 Kin. 15:27–29. Of Elah, 1 Kin. 16:9–11. Of Joram, 2 Kin. 9:24. Of Ahaziah, 2 Kin. 9:27. Of Joash, 2 Kin. 12: 20,21. Of Amaziah, 2 Kin. 14:19,20. Of Zachariah, 2 Kin. 15:10. Of Shallum, 2 Kin. 15:14. Of Pekahiah, 2 Kin. 15:25. Of Pekah, 2 Kin. 15:30. Of Sennacherib, 2 Kin. 19:36, 37; Isa. 37:37,38.

See HOMICIDE.

REGISTRATION, of citizens, Isa. 4:3. See CENSUS.

REHABIAH, son of Eliezer, 1 Chr. 23:17; 24:21; 26:25.

REHOB. 1. Father of Hadadezer, king of Zobah, 2 Sam. 8:3,12.

2. A Levite who sealed the covenant with Nehemiah, Neh. 10:11.

3. A town in northern Palestine. The limit of the investigation made by the twelve spies, Num. 13:21. Possessed by the Syrians, 2 Sam. 10:6,8. Called BETH-REHOB, 2 Sam. 10:6.

4. An unlocated town of Asher, Josh. 19:28.

5. A Levitical city of Asher, Josh. 19:30; 21:31; 1 Chr. 6:75. Canaanites not driven from, Judg. 1:31.

REHOBOAM. Successor to Solomon as king, 1 Kin. 11:43; 2 Chr. 9:31. Refuses to reform abuses, 1 Kin. 12:1–15; 2 Chr. 10:1–15. Ten tribes, under leadership of Jeroboam, successfully revolt from, 1 Kin. 12:16–24; 2 Chr. 10:16–19; 11:1–4. Builds fortified cities; is temporarily prosperous, 2 Chr. 11:5–23. Invaded by king of Egypt and despoiled, 1 Kin. 14:25–28; 2 Chr. 12:1–12. Death of, 1 Kin. 14:31; 2 Chr. 12:16. Genealogy and descendants of, 1 Chr. 3; Matt. 1. Called ROBOAM, Matt. 1:7.

REHOBOTH. 1. A city built by Asshur, Gen. 10:11.

2. A city of the Edomites, Gen. 36:37; 1 Chr. 1:48.

3. The name given to a well dug by Isaac, Gen. 26:22.

REHUM. 1. A captive who returned to Jerusalem from Babylon, Ezra 2:2. Called NEHUM, Neh. 7:7.

2. A chancellor who wrote a letter to Artaxerxes, influencing him against the Jews, Ezra 4:8,9,17,23.

3. A Levite who repaired part of the wall of Jerusalem, Neh. 3:17.

4. A Jew of the exile who signed the covenant with Nehemiah, Neh. 10:25.

5. A priest who returned to Jerusalem from captivity in Babylon, Neh. 12:3.

REI, an Israelite loyal to David at the time of the usurpation of Adonijah, 1 Kin. 1:8.

REJECTION, of God, see GOD, REJECTED. Of Jesus, see JESUS, REJECTED.

REKEM. 1. A king of the Midianites, slain by the Israelites, Num. 31:8; Josh. 13:21.

2. A son of Hebron, 1 Chr. 2:43,44.

3. A city in Benjamin, Josh. 18:27.

RELEASE. YEAR OF: See JUBILEE, YEAR OF.

RELIGION. FALSE: Deut. 32:31–33. See IDOLATRY; INTOLERANCE; TEACHERS, FALSE.

FAMILY: See FAMILY.

NATIONAL: Supported by taxes, Ex. 30:11–16; 38:26. Priests supported by the State, 1 Kin. 18:19; 2 Chr. 11:13–15. Subverted by Jeroboam, 1 Kin. 12:26–33; 2 Chr. 11:13–15. Established by Jeroboam, 1 Kin. 12:26–33.

NATURAL: Job 12:7. But ask now the beasts, and they shall teach thee; and the fowls of the air, and they shall tell thee: 8. Or speak to the earth, and it shall teach thee; and the fishes of the sea shall declare unto thee. 9. Who knoweth not in all these that the hand of the LORD hath wrought this? 10. In whose hand is the soul of every living thing, and the breath of all mankind. 11. Doth not the ear try words? and the mouth taste his meat? 12. With the ancient is wisdom; and in length of days understanding. 13. With him is wisdom and strength, he hath counsel and understanding. 14. Behold, he breaketh down, and it cannot be built again; he shutteth up a man, and there can be no opening. 15. Behold, he withholdeth the waters, and they dry up: also he sendeth them out, and they overturn the earth. 16. With him is strength and wisdom: the deceived and the deceiver are his.

Job 35:10. But none saith, Where is God my maker, who giveth songs in the night; 11. Who teacheth us more than the beasts of the earth, and maketh us wiser than the fowls of heaven? 12. There they cry, but none giveth answer, because of the pride of evil men.

Job 37:1. At this also my heart trembleth, and is moved out of his place. 2. Hear attentively the noise of his voice, and the sound that goeth out of his mouth. 3. He directeth it under the whole heaven, and his lightning unto the ends of the earth. 4. After it a voice roareth: he thundereth with the voice of his excellency; and he will not stay them when his voice is heard. 5. God thundereth marvellously with his voice; great things doeth he, which we cannot comprehend. 6. For he saith to the snow, Be thou on the earth; likewise to the small rain, and to the great rain of his strength. 7. He sealeth up the hand of every man; that all men may know his work. 8. Then the beasts go into dens, and remain in their places. 9. Out of the south cometh the whirlwind: and cold out of the north. 10. By the breath of God frost is given: and the breadth of the waters is straitened. 11. Also by watering he wearieth the thick cloud: he scattereth his bright cloud: 12. And it is turned round about by his counsels: that they may do whatsoever he commandeth them upon the face of the world in the earth. 13. He causeth it to come, whether for correction, or for his land, or for mercy. 14. Hearken unto this, O Job: stand still, and consider the wondrous works of God. 15. Dost thou know when God disposed them, and caused the light of his cloud to shine? 16. Dost thou know the balancings of the clouds, the wondrous works of him which is perfect in knowledge? 17. How thy garments *are* warm, when he quieteth the earth by the south *wind?* 18. Hast thou with him spread out the sky, *which is* strong, *and* as a molten looking glass? 19. Teach us what we shall say unto him; *for* we cannot order *our* speech by reason of darkness. 20. Shall it be told him that I speak? if a man speak, surely he shall be swallowed up. 21. And now *men* see not the bright light which *is* in the clouds: but the wind passeth, and cleanseth them. 22. Fair weather cometh out of the north: with God *is* terrible majesty. 23. *Touching* the Almighty, we cannot find him out: *he is* excellent in power, and in judgment, and in plenty of justice: he will not afflict. 24. Men do therefore fear him: he respecteth not any *that are* wise of heart.

Psa. 8:1. O Lord our Lord, how excellent *is* thy name in all the earth! who hast set thy glory above the heavens. 2. Out of the mouth of babes and sucklings hast thou ordained strength because of thine enemies, that thou mightest still the enemy and the avenger. 3. When I consider thy heavens, the work of thy fingers, the moon and the stars, which thou hast ordained; 4. What is man, that thou art mindful of him? and the son of man, that thou visitest him? 5. For thou hast made him a little lower than the angels, and hast crowned him with glory and honour. 6. Thou madest him to have dominion over the works of thy hands; thou hast put all *things* under his feet: 7. All sheep and oxen, yea and the beasts of the field; 8. The fowl of the air, and the fish of the sea, *and whatsoever* passeth through the paths of the sea. 9. O Lord our Lord, how excellent *is* thy name in all the earth!

Psa. 19:1. The heavens declare the glory of God; and the firmament sheweth his handywork. 2. Day unto day uttereth speech, and night unto night sheweth knowledge. 3. *There is* no speech nor language, *where* their voice is not heard. 4. Their line is gone out through all the earth, and their words to the end of the world. In them hath he set a tabernacle for the sun, 5. Which *is* as a bridegroom coming out of his chamber, *and* rejoiceth as a strong man to run a race. 6. His going forth *is* from the end of the heaven, and his circuit unto the ends of it: and there is nothing hid from the heat thereof.

Acts 14:17. Nevertheless he left not himself without witness, in that he did good, and gave us rain from heaven, and fruitful seasons, filling our hearts with food and gladness.

Acts 17:23. For as I passed by, and beheld your devotions, I found an altar with this inscription, TO THE UNKNOWN GOD. Whom therefore ye ignorantly worship, him declare I unto you. 24. God that made the world and all things therein, seeing that he is Lord of heaven and earth, dwelleth not in temples made with hands; 25. Neither is worshipped with men's hands, as though he needed any thing, seeing he giveth to all life, and breath, and all things; 26. And hath made of one blood all nations of men for to dwell on all the face of the earth, and hath determined the times before appointed, and the bounds of their habitation; 27. That they should seek the Lord, if haply they might feel after him, and find him, though he be not far from every one of us: 28. For in him we live, and move, and have our being; as certain also of your own poets have said, For we are also his offspring.

Rom. 1:18. For the wrath of God is revealed from heaven against all ungodliness and unrighteousness of men, who hold the truth in unrighteousness; 19. Because that which may be known of God is manifest in them; for God hath shewed *it* unto them. 20. For the invisible things of him from the creation of the world are clearly seen, being understood by the things that are made, *even* his eternal power and Godhead; so that they are without excuse:

Rom. 10:16. But they have not all obeyed the gospel. For Esaias saith, Lord, who hath believed our report? 17. So then faith *cometh* by hearing, and hearing by the word of God. 18. But I say, Have they not heard? Yes verily, their sound went into all the earth, and their words unto the ends of the world.

See REVIVALS.

TRUE: Matt. 5:1. And seeing the multitudes, he went up into a mountain: and when he was set, his disciples came unto him: 2. And he opened his mouth, and taught them, saying, 3. Blessed *are* the poor in spirit: for their's is the kingdom of heaven. 4. Blessed are they that mourn: for they shall be comforted. 5. Blessed *are* the meek: for they shall inherit the earth. 6. Blessed *are* they which do hunger and thirst after righteousness: for they shall be filled. 7. Blessed *are* the merciful: for they shall obtain mercy. 8. Blessed *are* the pure in heart: for they shall see God. 9. Blessed *are* the peacemakers: for they shall be called the children of God. 10. Blessed *are* they which are persecuted for righteousness' sake: for their's is the kingdom of heaven. 11. Blessed are ye, when *men* shall revile you, and persecute *you*, and shall say all manner of evil against you falsely, for my sake. 12. Rejoice, and be exceeding glad: for great *is* your reward in heaven: for so persecuted they the prophets which were before you. 13. Ye are the salt of the earth: but if the salt have lost his savour, wherewith shall it be salted? it is thenceforth good for nothing, but to be cast out, and to be trodden under foot of men. 14. Ye are the light of the world. A city that is set on an hill cannot be hid. 15. Neither do men light a candle, and put it under a bushel, but on a candlestick; and it giveth light unto all that are in the house. 16. Let your light so shine before men, that they may see your good works, and glorify your Father which is in heaven. 17. Think not that I am come to destroy the law, or the prophets: I am not come to destroy, but to fulfil. 18. For verily I say unto you, Till heaven and earth pass, one jot or one tittle shall in no wise pass from the law, till all be fulfilled. 19. Whosoever therefore shall break one of these least commandments, and shall teach men so, he shall be called the least in the kingdom of heaven: but whosoever shall do and teach *them*, the same shall be called great in the kingdom of heaven. 20. For I say unto you, That except your righteousness shall exceed *the righteousness* of the scribes and Pharisees, ye shall in no case enter into the kingdom of heaven. 21. Ye have heard that it was said by them of old time, Thou shalt not kill; and whosoever shall kill shall be in danger of the judgment: 22. But I say unto you, That whosoever is angry with his brother without a cause shall be in danger of the judgment: and whosoever shall say to his brother, Raca, shall be in danger of the council: but whosoever shall say, Thou fool, shall be in danger of hell fire. 23. Therefore if thou bring thy gift to the altar, and there rememberest that thy brother hath ought against thee; 24. Leave there thy gift before the altar, and go thy way; first be reconciled to thy brother, and then come and offer thy gift. 25. Agree with thine adversary quickly, whiles thou art in the way with him; lest at any time the adversary deliver thee to the judge, and the judge deliver thee to the officer, and thou be cast into prison. 26. Verily I say unto thee, Thou shalt by no means come out thence, till thou hast paid the uttermost farthing. 27. Ye have heard that it was said by them of old time, Thou shalt not commit adultery: 28. But I say unto you, That whosoever looketh on a woman to lust after her hath committed adultery with her already in his heart. 29. And if thy right eye offend thee, pluck it out, and cast *it* from thee: for it is profitable for thee that one of thy members should perish, and not *that* thy whole body should be cast into hell. 30. And if thy right hand offend thee, cut it off, and cast *it* from thee: for it is profitable for thee that one of thy members should perish, and not *that* thy whole body should be cast into hell. 31. It hath been said, Whosoever shall put away his wife, let him give her a writing of divorcement: 32. But I say unto you, That whosoever shall put away his wife, saving for the cause of fornication, causeth her to commit adultery: and whosoever shall marry her that is divorced committeth adultery. 33. Again, ye have heard that it hath been said by them of old time, Thou shalt not forswear thyself, but shalt perform unto the Lord thine oaths: 34. But I say unto you, Swear not at all; neither by heaven; for it is God's throne: 35. Nor by the earth; for it is his footstool: neither by Jerusalem; for it is the city of the great King. 36. Neither shalt thou swear by thy head, because thou canst not make one hair white or black. 37. But let your communication be, Yea, yea; Nay, nay: for whatsoever is more than these cometh of evil. 38. Ye have heard that it hath been said, An eye for an eye, and a tooth for a tooth: 39. But I say unto you, That ye resist not evil: but whosoever shall smite thee on thy right cheek, turn to him the other also. 40. And if any man will sue thee at the law, and take away thy coat, let him have *thy* cloke also. 41. And whosoever shall compel thee to go a mile, go with him twain. 42. Give to him that asketh thee, and from him that would borrow of thee turn not thou away. 43. Ye have heard that it hath been said, Thou shalt love thy neighbour, and hate thine enemy. 44. But I say unto you, love your enemies, bless them that curse you, do good to them that hate you, and pray for them which despitefully use you, and persecute you; 45. That ye may be the children of your Father which is in heaven: for he maketh his sun to rise on the evil and on the good, and sendeth rain on the just and on the unjust. 46. For if ye love them which love you, what reward have ye? do not even the publicans the same? 47. And if ye salute your brethren only, what do ye more *than others?* do not even the publicans so? 48. Be ye therefore perfect, even as your Father which is in heaven is perfect.

Matt. 6:1. Take heed that ye do not your alms before men, to be seen of them: otherwise ye have no reward of your Father which is in heaven. 2. Therefore when thou doest *thine* alms, do not sound a trumpet before thee, as the hypocrites do in the synagogues and in the streets, that they may have glory of men. Verily I say unto you, They have their reward. 3. But when thou doest alms, let not thy left hand know what thy right hand doeth: 4. That thine alms may be in secret: and thy Father which seeth in secret himself shall reward thee openly. 5. And when thou prayest, thou shalt not be as the hypocrites *are:* for they love to pray standing in the synagogues and in the corners of the streets, that they may be seen of men. Verily I say unto you, They have their reward. 6. But thou, when thou prayest, enter into thy closet, and when thou hast shut thy door, pray to thy Father which is in secret; and thy Father which seeth in secret shall reward thee openly. 7. But when ye pray, use not vain repetitions, as the heathen *do:* for they think that they shall be heard for their much speaking. 8. Be not ye therefore like unto them: for your Father knoweth what things ye have need of, before ye ask him. 9. After this manner therefore pray ye: Our Father which art in heaven, Hallowed be thy name. 10. Thy kingdom come. Thy will be done in earth, as *it is* in heaven. 11. Give us this day our daily bread. 12. And forgive us our debts, as we forgive our debtors. 13. And lead us not into temptation, but deliver us from evil: For thine is the kingdom, and the power, and the glory, for ever. Amen. 14. For if ye forgive men their trespasses, your heavenly Father will also forgive you: 15. But if ye forgive not men their trespasses, neither will your Father forgive your trespasses. 16. Moreover when ye fast, be not, as the hypocrites, of a sad countenance: for they disfigure their faces, that they may appear unto men to fast. Verily I say unto you, They have their reward. 17. But thou, when thou fastest, anoint thine head, and wash thy face; 18. That thou appear not unto men to fast, but unto thy Father which is in secret: and thy Father, which seeth in secret, shall reward thee openly. 19. Lay not up for yourselves treasures upon earth, where moth and rust doth corrupt, and where thieves break through and steal: 20. But lay up for yourselves treasures in heaven, where neither moth nor rust doth corrupt, and where thieves do not break through nor steal: 21. For where your treasure is, there will your heart be also. 22. The light of the body is the eye: if therefore thine eye be single, thy whole body shall be full of light. 23. But if thine eye be evil, thy whole body shall be full of darkness. If therefore the light that is in thee be darkness, how great *is* that darkness! 24. No man can serve two masters: for either he will hate the one, and love the other; or else he will hold to the one, and despise the other. Ye cannot serve God and mammon. 25. Therefore I say unto you, Take no thought for your life, what ye shall eat, or what ye shall drink; nor yet for your body, what ye shall put on. Is not the life more than meat, and the body than raiment? 26. Behold the fowls of the air: for they sow not, neither do they reap, nor gather into barns; yet your heavenly Father feedeth them. Are ye not much better than they? 27. Which of you by taking thought can add one cubit unto his stature? 28. And why take ye thought for raiment? Consider the lilies of the field, how they grow; they toil not, neither do they spin: 29. And yet I say unto you, That even Solomon in all his glory was not arrayed like one of these. 30. Wherefore, if God so clothe the grass of the field, which to day is, and to morrow is cast into the oven, *shall he* not much more *clothe* you, O ye of little faith? 31. Therefore take no thought, saying, What shall we eat? or, What shall we drink? or, Where-

withal shall we be clothed? 32. (For after all these things do the Gentiles seek:) for your heavenly Father knoweth that ye have need of all these things. 33. But seek ye first the kingdom of God, and his righteousness; and all these things shall be added unto you. 34. Take therefore no thought for the morrow: for the morrow shall take thought for the things of itself. Sufficient unto the day *is* the evil thereof.

Matt. 7:1. Judge not, that ye be not judged. 2. For with what judgment ye judge, ye shall be judged: and with what measure ye mete, it shall be measured to you again. 3. And why beholdest thou the mote that is in thy brother's eye, but considerest not the beam that is in thine own eye? 4. Or how wilt thou say to thy brother, Let me pull out the mote out of thine eye; and, behold, a beam *is* in thine own eye? 5. Thou hypocrite, first cast out the beam out of thine own eye; and then shalt thou see clearly to cast out the mote out of thy brother's eye. 6. Give not that which is holy unto the dogs, neither cast ye your pearls before swine, lest they trample them under their feet, and turn again and rend you. 7. Ask, and it shall be given you; seek, and ye shall find; knock, and it shall be opened unto you: 8. For every one that asketh receiveth; and he that seeketh findeth; and to him that knocketh it shall be opened. 9. Or what man is there of you, whom if his son ask bread, will he give him a stone? 10. Or if he ask a fish, will he give him a serpent? 11. If ye then, being evil, know how to give good gifts unto your children, how much more shall your Father which is in heaven give good things to them that ask him? 12. Therefore all things whatsoever ye would that men should do to you, do ye even so to them: for this is the law and the prophets. 13. Enter ye in at the strait gate: for wide *is* the gate, and broad *is* the way, that leadeth to destruction, and many there be which go in thereat: 14. Because strait *is* the gate, and narrow *is* the way, which leadeth unto life, and few there be that find it. 15. Beware of false prophets, which come to you in sheep's clothing, but inwardly they are ravening wolves. 16. Ye shall know them by their fruits. Do men gather grapes of thorns, or figs of thistles? 17. Even so every good tree bringeth forth good fruit; but a corrupt tree bringeth forth evil fruit. 18. A good tree cannot bring forth evil fruit, neither *can* a corrupt tree bring forth good fruit. 19. Every tree that bringeth not forth good fruit is hewn down, and cast into the fire. 20. Wherefore by their fruits ye shall know them. 21. Not every one that saith unto me, Lord, Lord, shall enter into the kingdom of heaven; but he that doeth the will of my Father which is in heaven. 22. Many will say to me in that day, Lord, Lord, have we not prophesied in thy name? and in thy name have cast out devils? and in thy name done many wonderful works? 23. And then will I profess unto them, I never knew you: depart from me, ye that work iniquity. 24. Therefore whosoever heareth these sayings of mine, and doeth them, I will liken him unto a wise man, which built his house upon a rock: 25. And the rain descended, and the floods came, and the winds blew, and beat upon that house; and it fell not: for it was founded upon a rock. 26. And every one that heareth these sayings of mine, and doeth them not, shall be likened unto a foolish man, which built his house upon the sand: 27. And the rain descended, and the floods came, and the winds blew, and beat upon that house; and it fell: and great was the fall of it. 28. And it came to pass, when Jesus had ended these sayings, the people were astonished at his doctrine: 29. For he taught them as *one* having authority, and not as the scribes.

Matt. 22:36. Master, which *is* the great commandment in the law? 37. Jesus said unto him, Thou shalt love the Lord thy God with all thy heart, and with all thy soul, and with all thy mind. 38. This is the first and great commandment. 39. And the second *is* like unto it, Thou shalt love thy neighbour as thyself. 40. On these two commandments hang all the law and the prophets.

Acts 10:34. Then Peter opened *his* mouth, and said, Of a truth I perceive that God is no respecter of persons: 35. But in every nation he that feareth him, and worketh righteousness, is accepted with him.

Rom. 8:1. *There is* therefore now no condemnation to them which are in Christ Jesus, who walk not after the flesh, but after the Spirit. 2. For the law of the Spirit of life in Christ Jesus hath made me free from the law of sin and death. 3. For what the law could not do, in that it was weak through the flesh, God sending his own Son in the likeness of sinful flesh, and for sin, condemned sin in the flesh: 4. That the righteousness of the law might be fulfilled in us, who walk not after the flesh, but after the Spirit. 5. For they that are after the flesh do mind the things of the flesh; but they that are after the Spirit the things of the Spirit. 6. For to be carnally minded *is* death; but to be spiritually minded *is* life and peace. 7. Because the carnal mind *is* enmity against God: for it is not subject to the law of God, neither indeed can be. 8. So then they that are in the flesh cannot please God. 9. But ye are not in the flesh, but in the Spirit, if so be that the Spirit of God dwell in you. Now if any man have not the Spirit of Christ, he is none of his. 10. And if Christ *be* in you, the body *is* dead because of sin; but the Spirit *is* life because of righteousness. 11. But if the Spirit of him that raised up Jesus from the dead dwell in you, he that raised up Christ from the dead shall also

quicken your mortal bodies by his Spirit that dwelleth in you. 12. Therefore, brethren, we are debtors, not to the flesh, to live after the flesh. 13. For if ye live after the flesh, ye shall die: but if ye through the Spirit do mortify the deeds of the body, ye shall live. 14. For as many as are led by the Spirit of God, they are the sons of God. 15. For ye have not received the spirit of bondage again to fear; but ye have received the Spirit of adoption, whereby we cry, Abba, Father. 16. The Spirit itself beareth witness with our spirit, that we are the children of God: 17. And if children, then heirs; heirs of God, and joint-heirs with Christ; if so be that we suffer with *him*, that we may be also glorified together. 18. For I reckon that the sufferings of this present time *are* not worthy *to be compared* with the glory which shall be revealed in us.

Rom. 10:1. Brethren, my heart's desire and prayer to God for Israel is, that they might be saved. 2. For I bear them record that they have a zeal of God, but not according to knowledge. 3. For they being ignorant of God's righteousness, and going about to establish their own righteousness, have not submitted themselves unto the righteousness of God. 4. For Christ *is* the end of the law for righteousness to every one that believeth. 5. For Moses describeth the righteousness which is of the law, That the man which doeth those things shall live by them. 6. But the righteousness which is of faith speaketh on this wise, Say not in thine heart, Who shall ascend into heaven? (that is, to bring Christ down *from above:*) 7. Or, Who shall descend into the deep? (that is, to bring up Christ again from the dead.) 8. But what saith it? The word is nigh thee, *even* in thy mouth, and in thy heart: that is, the word of faith, which we preach; 9. That if thou shalt confess with thy mouth the Lord Jesus, and shalt believe in thine heart that God hath raised him from the dead, thou shalt be saved. 10. For with the heart man believeth unto righteousness; and with the mouth confession is made unto salvation. 11. For the scripture saith, Whosoever believeth on him shall not be ashamed. 12. For there is no difference between the Jew and the Greek: for the same Lord over all is rich unto all that call upon him. 13. For whosoever shall call upon the name of the Lord shall be saved.

Rom. 12:1. I beseech you therefore, brethren, by the mercies of God, that ye present your bodies a living sacrifice, holy, acceptable unto God, *which is* your reasonable service. 2. And be not conformed to this world: but be ye transformed by the renewing of your mind, that ye may prove what *is* that good, and acceptable, and perfect, will of God. 3. For I say, through the grace given unto me, to every man that is among you, not to think *of himself* more highly than he ought to think; but to think soberly, according as God hath dealt to every man the measure of faith. 4. For as we have many members in one body, and all members have not the same office: 5. So we, *being* many, are one body in Christ, and every one members one of another. 6. Having then gifts differing according to the grace that is given to us, whether prophecy, *let us prophesy* according to the proportion of faith; 7. Or ministry, *let us wait* on *our* ministering: or he that teacheth, on teaching; 8. Or he that exhorteth, on exhortation: he that giveth, *let him do it* with simplicity; he that ruleth, with diligence; he that sheweth mercy, with cheerfulness. 9. *Let* love be without dissimulation. Abhor that which is evil; cleave to that which is good. 10. *Be* kindly affectioned one to another with brotherly love; in honour preferring one another; 11. Not slothful in business; fervent in spirit; serving the Lord; 12. Rejoicing in hope; patient in tribulation; continuing instant in prayer; 13. Distributing to the necessity of saints; given to hospitality. 14. Bless them which persecute you: bless, and curse not. 15. Rejoice with them that do rejoice, and weep with them that weep. 16. *Be* of the same mind one toward another. Mind not high things, but condescend to men of low estate. Be not wise in your own conceits. 17. Recompense to no man evil for evil. Provide things honest in the sight of all men. 18. If it be possible, as much as lieth in you, live peaceably with all men. 19. Dearly beloved, avenge not yourselves, but *rather* give place unto wrath: for it is written, Vengeance *is* mine: I will repay, saith the Lord. 20. Therefore if thine enemy hunger, feed him; if he thirst, give him drink: for in so doing thou shalt heap coals of fire on his head. 21. Be not overcome of evil, but overcome evil with good.

1 Cor. 13:1. Though I speak with the tongues of men and of angels, and have not charity, I am become *as* sounding brass, or a tinkling cymbal. 2. And though I have *the gift of* prophecy, and understand all mysteries, and all knowledge; and though I have all faith, so that I could remove mountains, and have not charity, I am nothing. 3. And though I bestow all my goods to feed *the poor*, and though I give my body to be burned, and have not charity, it profiteth me nothing. 4. Charity suffereth long, *and* is kind; charity envieth not; charity vaunteth not itself, is not puffed up. 5. Doth not behave itself unseemly, seeketh not her own, is not easily provoked, thinketh no evil; 6. Rejoiceth not in iniquity, but rejoiceth in the truth; 7. Beareth all things, believeth all things, hopeth all things, endureth all things. 8. Charity never faileth: but whether *there be* prophecies, they shall fail; whether *there be* tongues, they shall cease; whether *there be* knowledge, it shall vanish away. 9. For we know in part, and we prophesy in part.

10. But when that which is perfect is come, then that which is in part shall be done away. 11. When I was a child, I spake as a child, I understood as a child, I thought as a child: but when I became a man, I put away childish things. 12. For now we see through a glass, darkly; but then face to face: now I know in part; but then shall I know even as also I am known. 13. And now abideth faith, hope, charity, these three; but the greatest of these *is* charity.

Gal. 5:22. But the fruit of the Spirit is love, joy, peace, longsuffering, gentleness, goodness, faith. 23. Meekness, temperance: against such there is no law. 24. And they that are Christ's have crucified the flesh with the affections and lusts. 25. If we live in the Spirit, let us also walk in the Spirit.

1 Thess. 5:15. See that none render evil for evil unto any *man;* but ever follow that which is good, both among yourselves, and to all *men.* 16. Rejoice evermore. 17. Pray without ceasing. 18. In everything give thanks: for this is the will of God in Christ Jesus concerning you. 19. Quench not the Spirit. 20. Despise not prophesyings. 21. Prove all things; hold fast that which is good. 22. Abstain from all appearance of evil. 23. And the very God of peace sanctify you wholly; and *I pray God* your whole spirit and soul and body be preserved blameless unto the coming of our Lord Jesus Christ.

Jas. 1:27. Pure religion and undefiled before God and the Father is this, To visit the fatherless and widows in their affliction, *and* to keep himself unspotted from the world.

Jas. 2:8. If ye fulfil the royal law according to the scripture, Thou shalt love thy neighbour as thyself, ye do well: 9. But if ye have respect to persons, ye commit sin, and are convinced of the law as transgressors. 10. For whosoever shall keep the whole law, and yet offend in one *point*, he is guilty of all. 11. For he that said. Do not commit adultery, said also, Do not kill. Now if thou commit no adultery, yet if thou kill, thou art become a transgressor of the law. 12. So speak ye, and so do, as they that shall be judged by the law of liberty. 13. For he shall have judgment without mercy, that hath shewed no mercy; and mercy rejoiceth against judgment. 14. What *doth it* profit, my brethren, though a man say he hath faith, and have not works? can faith save him? 15. If a brother or sister be naked, and destitute of daily food, 16. And one of you say unto them, Depart in peace, be ye warmed and filled; notwithstanding ye give them not those things which are needful to the body; what *doth it* profit? 17. Even so faith, if it hath not works, is dead, being alone. 18. Yea, a man may say, Thou hast faith, and I have works: shew me thy faith without thy works, and I will shew thee my faith by my works. 19. Thou believest that there is one God; thou doest well: the devils also believe, and tremble. 20. But wilt thou know, O vain man, that faith without works is dead? 21. Was not Abraham our father justified by works, when he had offered Isaac his son upon the altar? 22. Seest thou how faith wrought with his works, and by works was faith made perfect? 23. And the scripture was fulfilled which saith, Abraham believed God, and it was imputed unto him for righteousness: and he was called the Friend of God. 24. Ye see then how that by works a man is justified, and not by faith only. 25. Likewise also was not Rahab the harlot justified by works, when she had received the messengers, and had sent *them* out another way? 26. For as the body without the spirit is dead, so faith without works is dead also.

2 Pet. 1:5. And beside this, giving all diligence, add to your faith virtue; and to virtue knowledge; 6. And to knowledge temperance; and to temperance patience; and to patience godliness; 7. And to godliness brotherly kindness; and to brotherly kindness charity. 8. For if these things be in you, and abound, they make *you that ye shall* neither *be* barren nor unfruitful in the knowledge of our Lord Jesus Christ. 9. But he that lacketh these things is blind, and cannot see afar off, and hath forgotten that he was purged from his old sins.

Jude 20. But ye, beloved, building up yourselves on your most holy faith, praying in the Holy Ghost, 21. Keep yourselves in the love of God, looking for the mercy of our Lord Jesus Christ unto eternal life.

See BLESSINGS, SPIRITUAL; COMMANDMENTS; DUTY; GRACES; REGENERATION; REPENTANCE; SANCTIFICATION; SIN, FORGIVENESS OF.

INSTANCES OF CONSPICUOUSLY RELIGIOUS PERSONS: Abel, Gen. 4:4–8; Heb. 11:4. Noah, Gen. chapters 6–9. Abraham, Gen. 12:1–8; 15; 17; 18:22–33. Jacob, Gen. 28: 10–22; 32:24–32. Moses, Ex. 3:2–22; Deut. 32; 33. Jethro, Ex. 18:12. Joshua, Josh. 1. Gideon, Judg. 6; 7. Samuel, 1 Sam. 3. David, see PSALMS OF DAVID. Solomon, 1 Kin. 5:3–5; 2 Chr. 6. Jehu, 2 Kin. 10:16–30. Hezekiah, Isa. 18:3–7; 19:14–19. Jehoshaphat, 2 Chr. 17:3–9; 19;20. Jabez, 1 Chr. 4:9,10. Asa, 2 Chr. 14; 15. Josiah, 2 Kin. 22; 23. Daniel, Dan. 6:4–22. The three Hebrews, Dan. 3. Zacharias, Luke 1:13,67–79. Simeon, Luke 2:25–35. Anna, the prophetess, Luke 2:36,37. The centurion, Luke 7:1–10. Cornelius, Acts 10. Eunice and Lois, 2 Tim. 1:5.

See, for additional instances, each of the apostles, disciples, and JOHN, PAUL, PETER, STEPHEN; also each of the prophets.

REMALIAH, father of Pekah, king of Israel. 2 Kin. 15:25,27,30; 16:1,5; 2 Chr. 28:6; Isa. 7:1,4; 8:6.

REMMON. See RIMMON, 2.

REMMON - METHOAR. See RIMMON. 3.

REMORSE. Psa. 31:10. My life is spent with grief, and my years with sighing: my strength faileth because of mine iniquity. and my bones are consumed.

Psa. 38:2. Thine arrows stick fast in me, and thy hand presseth me sore. *3. There is* no soundness in my flesh because of thine anger; neither *is there any* rest in my bones because of my sin. 4. For mine iniquities are gone over mine head: as an heavy burden they are too heavy for me. 5. My wounds stink *and* are corrupt because of my foolishness. 6. I am troubled; I am bowed down greatly; I go mourning all the day long.

Psa. 51:1. Have mercy upon me, O God, according to thy lovingkindness: according unto the multitude of thy tender mercies blot out my transgressions. 2. Wash me throughly from mine iniquity, and cleanse me from my sin. 3. For I acknowledge my transgressions: and my sin *is* ever before me. 4. Against thee, thee only, have I sinned, and done *this* evil in thy sight: 7. Purge me with hyssop, and I shall be clean: wash me, and I shall be whiter than snow. 8. Make me to hear joy and gladness; *that* the bones *which* thou hast broken may rejoice. 9. Hide thy face from my sins, and blot out all mine iniquities. 10. Create in me a clean heart, O God; and renew a right spirit within me. 11. Cast me not away from thy presence; and take not thy holy spirit from me. 12. Restore unto me the joy of thy salvation; and uphold me *with thy* free spirit. 13. *Then* will I teach transgressors thy ways; and sinners shall be converted unto thee. 14. Deliver me from bloodguiltiness, O God, thou God of my salvation: *and* my tongue shall sing aloud of thy righteousness. 15. O Lord, open thou my lips; and my mouth shall shew forth thy praise. 16. For thou desirest not sacrifice; else would I give *it:* thou delightest not in burnt offering. 17. The sacrifices of God *are* a broken spirit: a broken and a contrite heart, O God, thou wilt not despise.

Prov. 1:25. But ye have set at nought all my counsel, and would none of my reproof: 26. I also will laugh at your calamity; I will mock when your fear cometh; 27. When your fear cometh as desolation, and your destruction cometh as a whirlwind; when distress and anguish cometh upon you.

Prov. 5:7. Hear me now therefore, O ye children, and depart not from the words of my mouth. 8. Remove thy way far from her, and come not nigh the door of her house: 9. Lest thou give thine honour unto others, and thy years unto the cruel: 10. Lest strangers be filled with thy wealth; and thy labours *be* in the house of a stranger; 11. And thou mourn at the last, when thy flesh and thy body are consumed, 12. And say, How have I hated instruction, and my heart despised reproof; 13. And have not obeyed the voice of my teachers, nor inclined mine ear to them that instructed me!

Prov. 28:1. The wicked flee when no man pursueth:

Isa. 2:19. And they shall go into the holes of the rocks, and into the caves of the earth, for fear of the LORD, and for the glory of his majesty, when he ariseth to shake terribly the earth. *v.* 21.

Isa. 6:5. Then said I, Woe *is* me! for I am undone; because I *am* a man of unclean lips, and I dwell in the midst of a people of unclean lips: for mine eyes have seen the King, the LORD of hosts.

Isa. 57:20. The wicked *are* like the troubled sea, when it cannot rest, whose waters cast up mire and dirt. 21. *There is* no peace, saith my God, to the wicked. Isa. 48:22.

Lam. 1:20. Behold, O LORD; for I *am* in distress; my bowels are troubled: mine heart is turned within me; for I have grievously rebelled:

Ezek. 7:16. But they that escape of them shall escape, and shall be on the mountains like doves of the valleys, all of them mourning, every one for his iniquity. 17. All hands shall be feeble, and all knees shall be weak *as* water. 18. They shall also gird *themselves* with sackcloth, and horror shall cover them; and shame *shall be* upon all faces, and baldness upon all their heads. 25. Destruction cometh; and they shall seek peace, and *there shall be* none. 26. Mischief shall come upon mischief, and rumour shall be upon rumour; then shall they seek a vision of the prophet; but the law shall perish from the priest, and counsel from the ancients.

Ezek. 33:10. Thus ye speak, saying, If our transgressions and our sins *be* upon us, and we pine away in them, how should we then live?

Luke 13:28. There shall be weeping and gnashing of teeth, when ye shall see Abraham, and Isaac, and Jacob, and all the prophets, in the kingdom of God, and you *yourselves* thrust out.

Acts 2:37. Now when they heard *this*, they were pricked in their heart, and said unto Peter and to the rest of the apostles, Men *and* brethren, what shall we do?

Acts 9:6. [1] He trembling and astonished said, Lord, what wilt thou have me to do?   [1 Omitted in R. V.]

1 John 3:20. If our heart condemn us, God is greater than our heart, and knoweth all things.

INSTANCES OF: David, Psa. 51. Peter, Matt. 26:75. Judas, Matt. 27:3-5.

See CONVICTION, OF SIN; PENITENTS; REPENTANCE; SIN, CONFESSION OF.

RENDING, of garments, a token of affliction, Gen. 37:29,34; Gen. 44:13; Num. 14:6; Judg. 11:35; 2 Sam. 1:2,11; 3:31; 13:19, 31; 15:32; 2 Kin. 2:12; 5:8; 6:30; 11:14; 19:1; 22:11,19; Ezra 9:3,5; Job 1:20; 2:12; Isa. 36: 22; 37:1; Jer. 41:5; Matt. 26:65; Acts 14:14.

FIGURATIVE: Joel 2:13. Symbol of rending of a kingdom, 1 Sam. 15:27,28.

RENTING, Land, Matt. 21:33-41; Luke 20:9-16. Houses, Acts 28:30.

REPENTANCE. Attributed to God, Gen. 6:6,7; Ex. 32:14; Deut. 32:36; Judg. 2:18; 1 Sam. 15:11,29,35; 2 Sam. 24:16; 1 Chr. 21:15; Psa. 106:45; 110:4; 135:14; Jer. 15:6; 18:8,10;

26:3; 42:10; Joel 2:13; Amos 7:3,6; Jonah 3:9, 10. The burden of the preaching of John the Baptist, Matt. 3; of Jesus, Matt. 4:17; Mark 1:15. Exhortation to, Prov. 1:23-33; Jer. 7:3,5; 26:3; Hos. 14:1-3; Amos 5:4-6; Matt. 3:2. Condition of God's favor, Lev. 26:40-42; 2 Chr. 7:14.

Unavailing to Israel, Num. 14:39-45; to Esau, Heb. 12:16,17.

UNCLASSIFIED SCRIPTURES RELATING TO: Lev. 26:40. If they shall confess their iniquity, and the iniquity of their fathers, with their trespass which they trespassed against me, and that also they have walked contrary unto me; 41. And *that* I also have walked contrary unto them, and have brought them into the land of their enemies; if then their uncircumcised hearts be humbled, and they then accept of the punishment of their iniquity: 42. Then will I remember my covenant . . . and I will remember the land.

Deut. 4:29. But if from thence thou shalt seek the LORD thy God, thou shalt find *him*, if thou seek him with all thy heart and with all thy soul. 30. When thou art in tribulation, and all these things are come upon thee, *even* in the latter days, if thou turn to the LORD thy God, and shalt be obedient unto his voice; 31. (For the LORD thy God *is* a merciful God;) he will not forsake thee, neither destroy thee, nor forget the covenant of thy fathers which he sware unto them.

Deut. 30:1. And it shall come to pass, when all these things are come upon thee, the blessing and the curse, which I have set before thee, and thou shalt call *them* to mind among all the nations, whither the LORD thy God hath driven thee, 2. And shalt return unto the LORD thy God, and shalt obey his voice according to all that I command thee this day, thou and thy children, with all thine heart, and with all thy soul; 3. That then the LORD thy God will turn thy captivity, and have compassion upon thee, and will return and gather thee from all the nations, whither the LORD thy God hath scattered thee. 8. And thou shalt return and obey the voice of the LORD, and do all his commandments which I command thee this day. 9. And the LORD thy God will make thee plenteous in every work of thine hand, in the fruit of thy body, and in the fruit of thy cattle, and in the fruit of thy land, for good: for the LORD will again rejoice over thee for good, as he rejoiced over thy fathers: 10. If thou shalt hearken unto the voice of the LORD thy God, to keep his commandments and his statutes which are written in this book of the law, *and* if thou turn unto the LORD thy God with all thine heart, and with all thy soul.

Deut. 32:29. O that they were wise, *that* they understood this, *that* they would consider their latter end!

1 Kin. 8:33. When thy people Israel be smitten down before the enemy, because

they have sinned against thee, and shall turn again to thee, and confess thy name, and pray, and make supplication unto thee in this house: 34. Then hear thou in heaven, and forgive the sin of thy people Israel, and bring them again unto the land which thou gavest unto their fathers. 35. When heaven is shut up, and there is no rain, because they have sinned against thee; if they pray toward this place, and confess thy name, and turn from their sin, when thou afflictest them: 36. Then hear thou in heaven, and forgive the sin of thy servants, and of thy people Israel, that thou teach them the good way wherein they should walk, and give rain upon thy land, which thou hast given to thy people for an inheritance. 37. If there be in the land famine, if there be pestilence, blasting, mildew, locust, or if there be caterpiller; if their enemy besiege them in the land of their cities; whatsoever plague, whatsoever sickness *there be;* 38. What prayer and supplication soever be *made* by any man, *or* by all thy people Israel, which shall know every man the plague of his own heart, and spread forth his hands toward this house: 39. Then hear thou in heaven thy dwelling place, and forgive, and do, and give to every man according to his ways, whose heart thou knowest; (for thou, *even* thou only, knowest the hearts of all the children of men ;) 40. That they may fear thee all the days that they live in the land which thou gavest unto our fathers. 41. Moreover concerning a stranger, that *is* not of thy people Israel, but cometh out of a far country for thy name's sake; 42. (For they shall hear of thy great name, and of thy strong hand, and of thy stretched out arm ;) when he shall come and pray toward this house; 43. Hear thou in heaven thy dwelling place, and do according to all that the stranger calleth to thee for: that all people of the earth may know thy name, to fear thee, as *do* thy people Israel; and that they may know that this house, which I have builded, is called by thy name. 44. If thy people go out to battle against their enemy, whithersoever thou shalt send them, and shall pray unto the LORD toward the city which thou hast chosen, and *toward* the house that I have built for thy name: 45. Then hear thou in heaven their prayer and their supplication, and maintain their cause. 46. If they sin against thee, (for *there is* no man that sinneth not,) and thou be angry with them, and deliver them to the enemy, so that they carry them away captives unto the land of the enemy, far or near: 47. *Yet* if they shall bethink themselves in the land whither they were carried captives, and repent, and make supplication unto thee in the land of them that carried them captives, saying, We have sinned, and have done perversely, we have committed wickedness; 48. And *so* return unto thee with all their heart, and with all their soul, in the land of their ene-

mies, which led them away captive, and pray unto thee toward their land, which thou gavest unto their fathers, the city which thou hast chosen, and the house which I have built for thy name : 49. Then hear thou their prayer and their supplication in heaven thy dwelling place, and maintain their cause, 50. And forgive thy people that have sinned against thee, and all their transgressions wherein they have transgressed against thee, and give them compassion before them who carried them captive, that they may have compassion on them :

2 Chr. 7:14. If my people, which are called by my name, shall humble themselves, and pray, and seek my face, and turn from their wicked ways; then will I hear from heaven, and will forgive their sin, and will heal their land. 2 Chr. 6:36–39.

2 Chr. 30:6. So the posts went with the letters from the king and his princes throughout all Israel and Judah, and according to the commandment of the king, saying, Ye children of Israel, turn again unto the LORD God of Abraham, Isaac, and Israel, and he will return to the remnant of you, that are escaped out of the hand of the kings of Assyria, 7. And be not ye like your fathers, and like your brethren, which trespassed against the LORD God of their fathers, *who* therefore gave them up to desolation, as ye see. 8. Now be ye not stiffnecked, as your fathers *were*, *but* yield yourselves unto the LORD, and enter into his sanctuary, which he hath sanctified for ever: and serve the LORD your God, that the fierceness of his wrath may turn away from you. 9. For if ye turn again unto the LORD, your brethren and your children *shall find* compassion before them that lead them captive, so that they shall come again into this land: for the LORD your God *is* gracious and merciful, and will not turn away *his* face from you, if ye return unto him.

Neh. 1:9. *If* ye turn unto me, and keep my commandments, and do them ; though there were of you cast out unto the uttermost part of the heaven, *yet* will I gather them from thence, and will bring them unto the place that I have chosen to set my name there.

Job 11:13. If thou prepare thine heart, and stretch out thine hands toward him ; 14. If iniquity *be* in thine hand, put it far away, and let not wickedness dwell in thy tabernacles. 15. For then shalt thou lift up thy face without spot ; yea, thou shalt be stedfast, and shalt not fear:

Job 22:23. If thou return to the Almighty, thou shalt be built up, thou shalt put away iniquity far from thy tabernacles.

Job 33:26. He shall pray unto God, and he will be favourable unto him: and he shall see his face with joy: for he will render unto man his righteousness. 27. He looketh upon men, and *if any* say, I have sinned, and perverted *that which was* right, and it profited me not; 28. He will deliver his soul from going into the pit, and his life shall see the light.

Job 34:31. Surely it is meet to be said unto God, I have borne *chastisement*, I will not offend *any more*: 32. *That which* I see not teach thou me: if I have done iniquity, I will do no more.

Job 36:10. He openeth also their ear to discipline, and commandeth that they return from iniquity.

Psa. 22:27. All the ends of the world shall remember, and turn unto the LORD:

Psa. 34:14. Depart from evil, and do good; seek peace, and pursue it. 18. The LORD *is* nigh unto them that are of a broken heart; and saveth such as be of a contrite spirit.

Psa. 51:17. The sacrifices of God *are* a broken spirit: a broken and a contrite heart, O God, thou wilt not despise.

Psa. 95:7. To day if ye will hear his voice, 8. Harden not your heart, as in the provocation, *and* as *in* the day of temptation in the wilderness:

Psa. 147:3. He healeth the broken in heart, and bindeth up their wounds.

Prov. 1:22. How long, ye simple ones, will ye love simplicity? and the scorners delight in their scorning, and fools hate knowledge? 23. Turn you at my reproof: behold, I will pour out my spirit unto you, I will make known my words unto you.

Prov. 9:6. Forsake the foolish, and live; and go in the way of understanding.

Prov. 28:13. He that covereth his sins shall not prosper: but whoso confesseth and forsaketh *them* shall have mercy.

Isa. 10:21. The remnant shall return, *even* the remnant of Jacob, unto the mighty God.

Isa. 22:12. In that day did the Lord GOD of hosts call to weeping, and to mourning, and to baldness, and to girding with sackcloth:

Isa. 31:6. Turn ye unto *him from* whom the children of Israel have deeply revolted.

Isa. 44:22. I have blotted out, as a thick cloud, thy transgressions, and, as a cloud, thy sins: return unto me; for I have redeemed thee.

Isa. 46:8. Remember this, and shew yourselves men: bring *it* again to mind, O ye transgressors.

Isa. 55:6. Seek ye the LORD while he may be found, call ye upon him while he is near: 7. Let the wicked forsake his way, and the unrighteous man his thoughts: and let him return unto the LORD, and he will have mercy upon him; and to our God, for he will abundantly pardon.

Isa. 57:15. For thus saith the high and lofty One that inhabiteth eternity, whose name *is* Holy; I dwell in the high and holy *place*, with him also *that is* of a contrite and humble spirit, to revive the spirit of the humble, and to revive the heart of the contrite ones.

Isa. 59:20. The Redeemer shall come to Zion, and unto them that turn from transgression in Jacob, saith the LORD.

Isa. 61:1. The Spirit of the Lord GOD *is* upon me; . . . he hath sent me to bind up the brokenhearted, to proclaim liberty to the captives, and the opening of the prison to *them that are* bound; 2. To proclaim the acceptable year of the LORD, . . . to comfort all that mourn;

Jer. 3:4. Wilt thou not from this time cry unto me, My father, thou *art* the guide of my youth? 12. Return, thou backsliding Israel, saith the LORD; *and* I will not cause mine anger to fall upon you: for I *am* merciful, saith the LORD, *and* I will not keep *anger* for ever. 13. Only acknowledge thine iniquity, that thou hast transgressed against the LORD thy God, and hast scattered thy ways to the strangers under every green tree, and ye have not obeyed my voice, saith the LORD. 14. Turn, O backsliding children, saith the LORD; for I am married unto you: and I will take you one of a city, and two of a family, and I will bring you to Zion: 19. I said, How shall I put thee among the children, and give thee a pleasant land, a goodly heritage of the hosts of nations? and I said, Thou shalt call me, My father; and shalt not turn away from me.

Jer. 4:1. If thou wilt return, O Israel, saith the LORD, return unto me: and if thou wilt put away thine abominations out of my sight, then shalt thou not remove. 2. And thou shalt swear, The LORD liveth, in truth, in judgment, and in righteousness; and the nations shall bless themselves in him, and in him shall they glory. 3. For thus saith the LORD to the men of Judah and Jerusalem, Break up your fallow ground, and sow not among thorns. 4. Circumcise yourselves to the LORD, and take away the foreskins of your heart, ye men of Judah and inhabitants of Jerusalem: lest my fury come forth like fire, and burn that none can quench *it*, because of the evil of your doings. [Deut. 10:16.] 14. O Jerusalem, wash thine heart from wickedness, that thou mayest be saved. How long shall thy vain thoughts lodge within thee?

Jer. 6:8. Be thou instructed, O Jerusalem, lest my soul depart from thee; lest I make thee desolate, a land not inhabited. 16. Thus saith the LORD, Stand ye in the ways, and see, and ask for the old paths, where *is* the good way, and walk therein, and ye shall find rest for your souls.

Jer. 7:5. For if ye throughly amend your ways and your doings; 7. Then will I cause you to dwell in this place, in the land that I gave to your fathers, for ever and ever.

Jer. 13:15. Hear ye, and give ear; be not proud: for the LORD hath spoken. 16. Give glory to the LORD your God, before he cause darkness, and before your feet stumble upon the dark mountains, and, while ye look for light, he turn it into the shadow of death, *and* make *it* gross darkness.

Jer. 18:8. If that nation, against whom I have pronounced, turn from their evil, I will repent of the evil that I thought to do unto them. 11. Now therefore go to, speak to the men of Judah, and to the inhabitants of Jerusalem, saying, Thus saith the Lord: Behold, I frame evil against you, and devise a device against you: return ye now every one from his evil way, and make your ways and your doings good.

Jer. 24:7. I will give them an heart to know me, that I *am* the Lord: and they shall be my people, and I will be their God: for they shall return unto me with their whole heart.

Jer. 25:5. Turn ye again now every one from his evil way, and from the evil of your doings, and dwell in the land that the Lord hath given unto you and to your fathers for ever and ever. Jer. 35:15.

Jer. 26:3. If so be they will hearken, and turn every man from his evil way, that I may repent me of the evil, which I purpose to do unto them because of the evil of their doings. 13. Therefore now amend your ways and your doings, and obey the voice of the Lord your God;

Jer. 31:9. They shall come with weeping, and with supplications will I lead them: I will cause them to walk by the rivers of waters in a straight way, wherein they shall not stumble: for I am a father to Israel, and Ephraim *is* my firstborn.

Jer. 36:3. It may be that the house of Judah will hear all the evil which I purpose to do unto them; that they may return every man from his evil way; that I may forgive their iniquity and their sin. 7. It may be they will present their supplication before the Lord, and will return every one from his evil way: for great *is* the anger and the fury that the Lord hath pronounced against this people.

Jer. 50:4. In those days, and in that time, saith the Lord, the children of Israel shall come, they and the children of Judah together, going and weeping: they shall go, and seek the Lord their God. 5. They shall ask the way to Zion with their faces thitherward, *saying*, Come, and let us join ourselves to the Lord in a perpetual covenant *that* shall not be forgotten.

Ezek. 7:16. But they that escape of them shall escape, and shall be on the mountains like doves of the valleys, all of them mourning, every one for his iniquity.

Ezek. 11:18. And they shall come thither, and they shall take away all the detestable things thereof and all the abominations thereof from thence. 19. And I will give them one heart, and I will put a new spirit within you; and I will take the stony heart out of their flesh, and will give them an heart of flesh: 20. That they may walk in my statutes, and keep mine ordinances, and do them: and they shall be my people, and I will be their God.

Ezek. 12:3. Therefore, thou son of man,

prepare thee stuff for removing, and remove by day in their sight; and thou shalt remove from thy place to another place in their sight: it may be they will consider, though they *be* a rebellious house.

Ezek. 14:6. Thus saith the Lord God: Repent, and turn *yourselves* from your idols; and turn away your faces from all your abominations.

Ezek. 16:61. Then thou shalt remember thy ways, and be ashamed, when thou shalt receive thy sisters, thine elder and thy younger: and I will give them unto thee for daughters, but not by thy covenant. 62. And I will establish my covenant with thee; and thou shalt know that I *am* the Lord: 63. That thou mayest remember, and be confounded, and never open thy mouth any more because of thy shame, when I am pacified toward thee for all that thou hast done, saith the Lord God.

Ezek. 18:21. If the wicked will turn from all his sins that he hath committed, and keep all my statutes, and do that which is lawful and right, he shall surely live, he shall not die. 22. All his transgressions that he hath committed, they shall not be mentioned unto him: in his righteousness that he hath done he shall live. 23. Have I any pleasure at all that the wicked should die? saith the Lord God: *and* not that he should return from his ways, and live? 27. Again, when the wicked *man* turneth away from his wickedness that he hath committed, and doeth that which is lawful and right, he shall save his soul alive. 28. Because he considereth, and turneth away from all his transgressions that he hath committed, he shall surely live, he shall not die. 30. Repent, and turn *yourselves* from all your transgressions; so iniquity shall not be your ruin. 31. Cast away from you all your transgressions, whereby ye have transgressed; and make you a new heart and a new spirit: for why will ye die, O house of Israel? *v.* 32.

Ezek. 20:43. There shall ye remember your ways, and all your doings, wherein ye have been defiled; and ye shall lothe yourselves in your own sight for all your evils that ye have committed. Ezek. 36:31.

Ezek. 33:10. Thus ye speak, saying, If our transgressions and our sins *be* upon us, and we pine away in them, how should we then live? 11. Say unto them, *As* I live, saith the Lord God, I have no pleasure in the death of the wicked; but that the wicked turn from his way and live: turn ye, turn ye from your evil ways; for why will ye die, O house of Israel? 12. Therefore, thou son of man, say unto the children of thy people, The righteousness of the righteous shall not deliver him in the day of his transgression: as for the wickedness of the wicked, he shall not fall thereby in the day that he turneth from his wickedness; *vs.* 14–16, 19.

Ezek. 37:23. Neither shall they defile

themselves any more with their idols, nor with their detestable things, nor with any of their transgressions: but I will save them out of all their dwellingplaces, wherein they have sinned, and will cleanse them: so shall they be my people, and I will be their God.

Dan. 4:27. Wherefore, O king, let my counsel be acceptable unto thee, and break off thy sins by righteousness, and thine iniquities by shewing mercy to the poor; if it may be a lengthening of thy tranquillity.

Hos. 2:7. And she shall follow after her lovers, but she shall not overtake them; and she shall seek them, but shall not find *them:* then shall she say, I will go and return to my first husband; for then *was it* better with me than now.

Hos. 3:5. Afterward shall the children of Israel return, and seek the LORD their God, and David their king; and shall fear the LORD and his goodness in the latter days.

Hos. 5:15. I will go *and* return to my place, till they acknowledge their offence, and seek my face: in their affliction they will seek me ¹ early.   [¹ R. V. earnestly]

Hos. 10:12. Sow to yourselves in righteousness, reap in mercy ; break up your fallow ground: for *it is* time to seek the LORD, till he come and rain righteousness upon you.

Hos. 12:6. Turn thou to thy God: keep mercy and judgment, and wait on thy God continually.

Hos. 14:1. O Israel, return unto the LORD thy God ; for thou hast fallen by thine iniquity.   2. Take with you words, and turn to the LORD: say unto him, Take away all iniquity, and receive *us* graciously : so will we render ¹ the calves of our lips.

[¹ R. V. as bullocks the offering of]

Joel 1:14. Sanctify ye a fast, call a solemn assembly, gather the elders *and* all the inhabitants of the land *into* the house of the LORD your God, and cry unto the LORD,

Joel 2:12. Therefore also now, saith the LORD, turn ye *even* to me with all your heart, and with fasting, and with weeping, and with mourning: 13. And rend your heart, and not your garments, and turn unto the LORD your God: for he *is* gracious and merciful, slow to anger, and of great kindness, and repenteth him of the evil.   15. Blow the trumpet in Zion, sanctify a fast, call a solemn assembly: 16. Gather the people, sanctify the congregation, assemble the elders, gather the children, and those that suck the breasts: let the bridegroom go forth of his chamber, and the bride out of her closet.   17. Let the priests, the ministers of the LORD, weep between the porch and the altar, and let them say, Spare thy people, O LORD, and give not thine heritage to reproach, that the heathen should rule over them: wherefore should they say among the people, Where *is* their God ? 18. Then will the LORD be jealous for his land, and pity his people.

Amos 4:12. Thus will I do unto thee, O Israel: *and* because I will do this unto thee, prepare to meet thy God, O Israel.

Amos 5:6. Seek the LORD, and ye shall live; 15. Hate the evil, and love the good, and establish judgment in the gate: it may be that the LORD God of hosts will be gracious.

Jonah 3:8. Let man and beast be covered with sackcloth, and cry mightily unto God: yea, let them turn every one from his evil way, and from the violence that *is* in their hands.   9. Who can tell *if* God will turn and repent, and turn away from his fierce anger, that we perish not ?

Hag. 1:7. Thus saith the LORD of hosts; Consider your ways.

Zech. 1:3. Turn ye unto me, saith the LORD of hosts, and I will turn unto you, saith the LORD of hosts.

Zech. 12:10. I will pour upon the house of David, and upon the inhabitants of Jerusalem, the spirit of grace and of supplications: and they shall look upon me whom they have pierced, and they shall mourn for him, as one mourneth for *his* only *son,* and shall be in bitterness for him, as one that is in bitterness for *his* firstborn.

Mal. 3:7. Return unto me, and I will return unto you, saith the LORD of hosts.

Matt. 3:2. Repent ye: for the kingdom of heaven is at hand.   7. O generation of vipers, who hath warned you to flee from the wrath to come ?   8. Bring forth therefore fruits meet for repentance:

Matt. 4:17. Jesus began to preach, and to say, Repent: for the kingdom of heaven is at hand.

Matt. 5:4. Blessed *are* they that mourn: for they shall be comforted.   Luke 6:21.

Matt. 9:13. But go ye and learn what *that* meaneth, I will have mercy, and not sacrifice: for I am not come to call the righteous, but sinners ¹ to repentance.   [¹ Omitted in R. V.]

Mark 1:4. John did baptize in the wilderness, and preach the baptism of repentance for the remission of sins.   15. Saying, The time is fulfilled, and the kingdom of God is at hand: repent ye, and believe the gospel.   Luke 3:3.

Mark 2:17. When Jesus heard *it,* he saith unto them, They that are whole have no need of the physician, but they that are sick: I came not to call the righteous, but sinners to repentance.

Mark 6:12. They went out, and preached that men should repent.

Luke 5:32. I came not to call the righteous, but sinners to repentance.

Luke 10:13. Woe unto thee, Chorazin! woe unto thee, Bethsaida! for if the mighty works had been done in Tyre and Sidon, which have been done in you, they had a great while ago repented, sitting in sackcloth and ashes.

Luke 13:1. There were present at that season some that told him of the Galilæans, whose blood Pilate had mingled with their sacrifices. 2. And Jesus answering said unto them, Suppose ye that these Galilæans were sinners above all the Galilæans, because they suffered such things? 3. I tell you, Nay: but, except ye repent, ye shall all likewise perish. 4. Or those eighteen, upon whom the tower in Siloam fell, and slew them, think ye that they were sinners above all men that dwelt in Jerusalem? 5. I tell you, Nay: but, except ye repent, ye shall all likewise perish.

Luke 15:7. I say unto you, that likewise joy shall be in heaven over one sinner that repenteth, more than over ninety and nine just persons, which need no repentance. *vs.* 1-10.

Luke 18:13. The publican, standing afar off, would not lift up so much as *his* eyes unto heaven, but smote upon his breast, saying, God be merciful to me a sinner. 14. I tell you, this man went down to his house justified *rather* than the other: for every one that exalteth himself shall be abased; and he that humbleth himself shall be exalted. *vs.* 10-14.

Luke 24:47. And that repentance and remission of sins should be preached in his name among all nations, beginning at Jerusalem.

Acts 2:38. Peter said unto them, Repent, and be baptized every one of you in the name of Jesus Christ for the remission of sins, and ye shall receive the gift of the Holy Ghost. 40. With many other words did he testify and exhort, saying, Save yourselves from this untoward generation.

Acts 3:19. Repent ye therefore, and be converted, that your sins may be blotted out when the times of refreshing shall come from the presence of the Lord;

Acts 5:31. Him hath God exalted with his right hand *to be* a Prince and a Saviour, for to give repentance to Israel, and forgiveness of sins.

Acts 8:22. Repent therefore of this thy wickedness, and pray God, if perhaps the thought of thine heart may be forgiven thee.

Acts 17:30. The times of this ignorance God winked at; but now commandeth all men every where to repent:

Acts 20:21. Testifying both to the Jews, and also to the Greeks, repentance toward God, and faith toward our Lord Jesus Christ.

Acts 26:20. But shewed first unto them of Damascus, and at Jerusalem, and throughout all the coasts of Judæa, and *then* to the Gentiles, that they should repent and turn to God, and do works meet for repentance.

Rom. 2:4. Or despisest thou the riches of his goodness and forbearance and longsuffering; not knowing that the goodness of God leadeth thee to repentance?

Rom. 11:23. They also, if they abide not still in unbelief, shall be graffed in: for God is able to graff them in again.

Rom. 14:11. *As* I live, saith the Lord, every knee shall bow to me, and every tongue shall confess to God.

Eph. 5:14. He saith, Awake thou that sleepest, and arise from the dead, and Christ shall give thee light.

2 Tim. 2:25. In meekness instructing those that oppose themselves; if God peradventure will give them repentance to the acknowledging of the truth;

Heb. 6:1. Therefore leaving the principles of the doctrine of Christ, let us go on unto perfection; not laying again the foundation of repentance from dead works, and of faith toward God,

Jas. 4:8. Draw nigh to God, and he will draw nigh to you. Cleanse *your* hands, *ye* sinners; and purify *your* hearts, *ye* double minded. 9. Be afflicted, and mourn, and weep: let your laughter be turned to mourning, and *your* joy to heaviness. 10. Humble yourselves in the sight of the Lord, and he shall lift you up.

1 John 1:9. If we confess our sins, he is faithful and just to forgive us *our* sins, and to cleanse us from all unrighteousness.

Rev. 2:5. Remember therefore from whence thou art fallen, and repent, and do the first works; or else I will come unto thee quickly, and will remove thy candlestick out of his place, except thou repent. 16. Repent; or else I will come unto thee quickly, and will fight against them with the sword of my mouth.

Rev. 3:2. Be watchful, and strengthen the things which remain, that are ready to die: for I have not found thy works perfect before God. 3. Remember therefore how thou hast received and heard, and hold fast, and repent. 19. As many as I love, I rebuke and chasten: be zealous therefore, and repent.

See CONVICTION; PENITENCE; REMORSE; SIN, CONFESSION OF; SIN, FORGIVENESS OF.

INSTANCES OF: Joseph's brethren, of their maltreatment of Joseph, Gen. 42:21; 50:17,18. Pharaoh, of his hardness of heart, Ex. 9:27; 10:16,17. Balaam, of his spiritual blindness, Num. 22:34, with *vs.* 24-35. Israelites, of worshiping the golden calf, Ex. 33: 3,4; of their murmuring on account of lack of bread and water, when the plague of fiery serpents came upon them, Num. 21:4-7; when rebuked by an angel for not expelling the Canaanites, Judg. 2:1-5; of their idolatry, when afflicted by the Philistines, Judg. 10:6-16: 1 Sam. 7:3-6; in asking for a king,1 Sam. 12:16-20; in the time of Asa, under the preaching of Azariah, 2 Chr. 15:1-15; under the preaching of Oded, 2 Chr. 28:9-15; under the influence of Hezekiah, 2 Chr. 30:11. Achan, of his theft, Josh. 7:20. Saul, at the reproof of Samuel for not destroying the Amalekites, 1 Sam. 15:24, with *vs.* 6-31. David, at the rebuke of Nathan, the prophet, of his sins of adultery and murder, 2 Sam. 12:11,13, with *vs.* 7-14. See PSALMS, PENITENTIAL. Rehoboam, when his kingdom was invaded, and Jerusalem besieged, 2 Chr. 12:1-12. Hezekiah, at the time of his sickness, 2 Chr. 32:26; when reproved by the prophet Micah, Jer. 26:18,19. Ahab, when reproved by Elijah for his idolatry, 1 Kin. 21:27, with vs. 17–29. Jehoahaz, 2 Kin. 13:4. Josiah, when he heard the law which had been discovered in the temple by Hilkiah, 2 Kin. 22:11–20. Manasseh, when he was carried captive to Babylon by the king of Assyria, 2 Chr. 33:12,13. The Jews of the captivity, at the dedication of the temple, Ezra 6:21; of their idolatrous marriages, Ezra 10; of their oppressive usury, Neh. 5:1–13; after hearing the law expounded by Ezra, Neh. 8:1–12; 9:1–3; under the preaching of Haggai, Hag. 1. Jonah, after his punishment, Jonah 2:2–9. The Ninevites, under the preaching of Jonah, Jonah 3:5–9. The Jews, under the preaching of John the Baptist, Matt. 3:6. The woman who anointed Jesus with oil, Luke 7:37–48. The disobedient son, Matt. 21:29. The prodigal son, Luke 15:17–21. Peter, of his denial of Jesus, Matt. 26:75; Mark 14:72; Luke 22:62. Judas, Matt. 27:3–5; Acts 1:16,18. The Ephesians, under the preaching of Paul, Acts 19:18.

EXEMPLIFIED: Num. 21:7. Therefore the people came to Moses, and said, We have sinned, for we have spoken against the LORD, and against thee; pray unto the LORD, that he take away the serpents from us. And Moses prayed for the people.

2 Sam. 24:10. David's heart smote him after that he had numbered the people. And David said unto the LORD, I have sinned greatly in that I have done; and now, I beseech thee, O LORD, take away the iniquity of thy servant; for I have done very foolishly. 17. And David spake unto the LORD when he saw the angel that smote the people, and said, Lo, I have sinned, and I have done wickedly: but these sheep, what have they done? let thine hand, I pray thee, be against me, and against my father's house. 1 Chr. 21:17.

2 Chr. 29:6. Our fathers have trespassed, and done that which was evil in the eyes of the LORD our God, and have forsaken him, and have turned away their faces from the habitation of the LORD, and turned their backs.

Ezra 9:4. Then were assembled unto me every one that trembled at the words of the God of Israel, because of the transgression of those that had been carried away; and I sat astonied until the evening sacrifices, 6. And said, O my God, I am ashamed and blush to lift up my face to thee, my God; for our iniquities are increased over our head, and our trespass is grown up unto the heavens. 10. Now, O our God, what shall we say after this? for we have forsaken thy commandments, 13. And after all that is come upon us for our evil deeds, and for our great trespass, seeing that thou our God hast punished us less than our iniquities deserve, and hast given us such deliverance as this; 14. Should we again break thy commandments, and join in affinity with the people of these abominations? wouldest not thou

be angry with us till thou hadst consumed us, so that there should be no remnant nor escaping?

Neh. 1:6. Let thine ear now be attentive, and thine eyes open, that thou mayest hear the prayer of thy servant, which I pray before thee now, day and night, for the children of Israel thy servants, and confess the sins of the children of Israel, which we have sinned against thee: both I and my father's house have sinned. 7. We have dealt very corruptly against thee, and have not kept the commandments, nor the statutes, nor the judgments, which thou commandedst thy servant Moses.

Neh. 9:33. Thou art just in all that is brought upon us; for thou hast done right, but we have done wickedly: 34. Neither have our kings, our princes, our priests, nor our fathers, kept thy law, nor hearkened unto thy commandments and thy testimonies, wherewith thou didst testify against them. 35. For they have not served thee in their kingdom, and in thy great goodness that thou gavest them, and in the large and fat land which thou gavest before them, neither turned they from their wicked works. vs. 16–37.

Job 7:20. I have sinned; what shall I do unto thee, O thou preserver of men? why hast thou set me as a mark against thee, so that I am a burden to myself?

Job 9:20. If I justify myself, mine own mouth shall condemn me: if I say, I am perfect, it shall also prove me perverse.

Job 13:23. How many are mine iniquities and sins? make me to know my transgression and my sin.

Job 40:4. Behold, I am vile; what shall I answer thee? I will lay mine hand upon my mouth.

Job 42:5. I have heard of thee by the hearing of the ear: but now mine eye seeth thee. 6. Wherefore I abhor myself, and repent in dust and ashes.

Psa. 32:5. I acknowledged my sin unto thee, and mine iniquity have I not hid. I said, I will confess my transgressions unto the LORD; and thou forgavest the iniquity of my sin.

Psa. 38:3. There is no soundness in my flesh because of thine anger; neither is there any rest in my bones because of my sin. 4. For mine iniquities are gone over mine head: as an heavy burden they are too heavy for me. 18. I will declare mine iniquity; I will be sorry for my sin.

Psa. 40:12. Mine iniquities have taken hold upon me, so that I am not able to look up; they are more than the hairs of mine head: therefore my heart faileth me.

Psa. 41:4. I said, LORD, be merciful unto me: heal my soul; for I have sinned against thee.

Psa. 51:1. Have mercy upon me, O God, according to thy lovingkindness: according unto the multitude of thy tender mercies blot out my transgressions. 2. Wash me throughly from mine iniquity, and cleanse me from my sin. 3. For I acknowledge my transgressions: and my sin *is* ever before me. 4. Against thee, thee only, have I sinned, and done *this* evil in thy sight: that thou mightest be justified when thou speakest, *and* be clear when thou judgest. 7. Purge me with hyssop, and I shall be clean: wash me, and I shall be whiter than snow. 8. Make me to hear joy and gladness; *that* the bones *which* thou hast broken may rejoice. 9. Hide thy face from my sins, and blot out all mine iniquities. 10. Create in me a clean heart, O God; and renew a right spirit within me. 11. Cast me not away from thy presence; and take not thy holy spirit from me. 12. Restore unto me the joy of thy salvation; and uphold me *with thy* free spirit. 13. *Then* will I teach transgressors thy ways; and sinners shall be converted unto thee. 14. Deliver me from bloodguiltiness, O God, thou God of my salvation: *and* my tongue shall sing aloud of thy righteousness. 15. O Lord, open thou my lips; and my mouth shall shew forth thy praise. 16. For thou desirest not sacrifice; else would I give *it:* thou delightest not in burnt offering. 17. The sacrifices of God *are* a broken spirit: a broken and a contrite heart, O God, thou wilt not despise.

Psa. 69:5. O God, thou knowest my foolishness; and my sins are not hid from thee. 10. When I wept, *and chastened* my soul with fasting, that was to my reproach.

Psa. 73:21. Thus my heart was grieved, and I was pricked in my reins. 22. So foolish *was* I, and ignorant:

Psa. 106:6. We have sinned with our fathers, we have committed iniquity, we have done wickedly.

Psa. 119:59. I thought on my ways, and turned my feet unto thy testimonies. 60. I made haste, and delayed not to keep thy commandments. 176. I have gone astray like a lost sheep;

Psa. 130:1. Out of the depths have I cried unto thee, O Lord. 2. Lord, hear my voice: let thine ears be attentive to the voice of my supplications. 3. If thou, Lord, shouldest mark iniquities, O Lord, who shall stand?

Isa. 6:5. Then said I, Woe *is* me! for I am undone; because I *am* a man of unclean lips, and I dwell in the midst of a people of unclean lips: for mine eyes have seen the King, the Lord of hosts.

Isa. 38:15. What shall I say? he hath both spoken unto me, and himself hath done *it:* I shall go softly all my years in the bitterness of my soul. 17. Behold, for peace I had great bitterness: but thou hast in love to my soul *delivered it* from the pit of corruption: for thou hast cast all my sins behind thy back.

Isa. 59:12. Our transgressions are multiplied before thee, and our sins testify against us: for our transgressions *are* with us; and *as for* our iniquities, we know them; *vs.* 13-15.

Isa. 64:5. Thou meetest him that rejoiceth and worketh righteousness, *those that* remember thee in thy ways: behold, thou **art** wroth; for we have sinned: in those is continuance, and we shall be saved. 6. But we are all as an unclean *thing*, and all our righteousnesses *are* as filthy rags; and we all do fade as a leaf; and our iniquities, like the wind, have taken us away. 7. And *there is* none that calleth upon thy name, that stirreth up himself to take hold of thee: for thou hast hid thy face from us, and hast consumed us, because of our iniquities.

Jer. 3:21. A voice was heard upon the high places, weeping *and* supplications of the children of Israel: for they have perverted their way, *and* they have forgotten the Lord their God. 22. Return, ye backsliding children, *and* I will heal your backslidings. Behold, we come unto thee; for thou art the Lord our God. 25. We lie down in our shame, and our confusion covereth us: for we have sinned against the Lord our God, we and our fathers, from our youth even unto this day, and have not obeyed the voice of the Lord our God.

Jer. 8:14. Why do we sit still? assemble yourselves, and let us enter into the defenced cities, and let us be silent there: for the Lord our God hath put us to silence, and given us water of gall to drink, because we have sinned againt the Lord.

Jer. 14:7. O Lord, though our iniquities testify against us, do thou *it* for thy name's sake: for our backslidings are many; we have sinned against thee. 20. We acknowledge, O Lord, our wickedness, *and* the iniquity of our fathers: for we have sinned against thee.

Jer. 31:18. I have surely heard Ephraim bemoaning himself *thus;* Thou hast chastised me, and I was chastised, as a bullock unaccustomed *to the yoke:* turn thou me, and I shall be turned; for thou *art* the Lord my God. 19. Surely after that I was turned, I repented; and after that I was instructed, I smote upon *my* thigh: I was ashamed, yea, even confounded, because I did bear the reproach of my youth.

Lam. 3:40. Let us search and try our ways, and turn again to the Lord. 41. Let us lift up our heart with *our* hands unto God in the heavens.

Dan. 9:5. We have sinned, and have committed iniquity, and have done wickedly, and have rebelled, even by departing from thy precepts, and from thy judgments: 6. Neither have we hearkened unto thy servants the prophets, which spake in thy name to our kings, our princes, and our fathers, and to all the people of the land. 7. O Lord, righteousness *belongeth* unto thee, but unto us confusion of faces, as at this day; to the men of Judah, and to the inhabitants of Jerusalem, and unto all Israel, *that are* near, and *that are* far off, through all the countries whither thou hast driven them, because of their trespass that they have trespassed against thee.

Dan. 10:12. Then said he unto me, Fear not, Daniel: for from the first day that thou didst set thine heart to understand, and to chasten thyself before thy God, thy words were heard, and I am come for thy words.

Hos. 6:1. Come, and let us return unto the LORD: for he hath torn, and he will heal us; he hath smitten, and he will bind us up.

Hos. 14:3. Asshur shall not save us; we will not ride upon horses: neither will we say any more to the work of our hands, *Ye are* our gods: for in thee the fatherless findeth mercy. 8. Ephraim *shall say*, What have I to do any more with idols?

Jonah 3:10. God saw their works, that they turned from their evil way; and God repented of the evil, that he had said that he would do unto them; and he did *it* not.

Mic. 7:9. I will bear the indignation of the LORD, because I have sinned against him, until he plead my cause, and execute judgment for me: he will bring me forth to the light, *and* I shall behold his righteousness.

Luke 15:17. And when he came to himself, he said, How many hired servants of my father's have bread enough, and to spare, and I perish with hunger! 18. I will arise and go to my father, and will say unto him, Father, I have sinned against heaven, and before thee, 19. And am no more worthy to be called thy son: make me as one of thy hired servants. 20. And he arose, and came to his father.

1 Cor. 15:9. I am the least of the apostles, that am not meet to be called an apostle, because I persecuted the church of God.

2 Cor. 7:9. Now I rejoice, not that ye were made sorry, but that ye sorrowed to repentance: for ye were made sorry after a godly manner, that ye might receive damage by us in nothing. 10. For godly sorrow worketh repentance to salvation not to be repented of: but the sorrow of the world worketh death. 11. For behold this selfsame thing, that ye sorrowed after a godly sort, what carefulness is wrought in you, yea, *what* clearing of yourselves, yea, *what* indignation, yea, *what* fear, yea, *what* vehement desire, yea, *what* zeal, yea, *what* revenge!

1 Pet. 2:25. Ye were as sheep going astray; but are now returned unto the Shepherd and Bishop of your souls.

See SIN, CONFESSION OF.

REPETITION. IN PRAYERS: See PRAYERS.

REPHAEL, a porter of the temple in the time of David, 1 Chr. 26:7.

REPHAH, a grandson of Ephraim, 1 Chr. 7:25.

REPHAIAH. 1. A descendant of David, 1 Chr. 3:21.

2. A Simeonite captain, 1 Chr. 4:42.

3. Son of Tola, of the tribe of Issachar, 1 Chr. 7:2.

4. A descendant of Jonathan, 1 Chr. 9:43. Called RAPHA, 1 Chr. 8:37.

5. Governor over half of Jerusalem in the time of Nehemiah, Neh. 3:9.

REPHAIM. 1. An ancient people of Palestine, of great stature, Gen. 14:5; 15:20; Deut. 2:11,20 [*R. V.*]; 3:11,13 [*R. V.*]; Josh. 12:4 [*R. V.*]; 13:12 [*R. V.*]; 17:15 [*R.V.*].

2. A valley. Boundary between Judah and Benjamin, Josh. 15:8 [*R. V.*]; 18:16 [*R. V.*]. Battle ground of David and the Philistines, 2 Sam. 5:18,22; 23:13; 1 Chr. 11:15; 14:9. Productiveness of, Isa. 17:5.

REPHIDIM, a camping-place of Israel in the forty years of wandering, Ex. 17:1,8; 19:2; Num. 33:14,15.

REPORTS. MAJORITY AND MINORITY: Of spies, Num. 13:26–33; 14:6–10.

REPROBACY. Gen. 6:5. And GOD saw that the wickedness of man *was* great in the earth, and *that* every imagination of the thoughts of his heart *was* only evil continually. 6. And it repented the LORD that he had made man on the earth, and it grieved him at his heart. 7. And the LORD said, I will destroy man whom I have created from the face of the earth; both man, and beast, and the creeping thing, and the fowls of the air; for it repenteth me that I have made them.

Gen. 19:13. For we will destroy this place, because the cry of them is waxen great before the face of the LORD; and the LORD hath sent us to destroy it.

Deut. 28:15. But it shall come to pass, if thou wilt not hearken unto the voice of the LORD thy God, to observe to do all his commandments and his statutes which I command thee this day; that all these curses shall come upon thee, and overtake thee: 16. Cursed *shalt* thou *be* in the city, and cursed *shalt* thou *be* in the field. 17. Cursed *shall be* thy basket and thy store. 18. Cursed *shall be* the fruit of thy body, and the fruit of thy land, the increase of thy kine, and the flocks of thy sheep. 19. Cursed *shalt* thou *be* when thou comest in, and cursed *shalt* thou *be* when thou goest out. 20. The LORD shall send upon thee cursing, vexation, and rebuke, in all that thou settest thine hand unto for to do, until thou be destroyed, and until thou perish quickly; because of the wickedness of thy doings, whereby thou hast forsaken me. 21. The LORD shall make the pestilence cleave unto thee, until he have consumed thee from off the land, whither thou goest to possess it. 22. The LORD shall smite thee with a consumption, and with a fever, and with an inflammation, and with an extreme burning, and with the sword, and with blasting, and with mildew; and they shall pursue thee until thou perish. 23. And thy heaven that *is* over thy head shall be brass, and the earth that *is* under thee *shall be* iron. 24. The LORD shall make the rain of thy land powder and dust: from heaven shall it come down upon thee, until thou be destroyed. 25. The LORD shall cause thee to be smitten before thine enemies: thou shalt go out one way against them, and flee seven ways before them : and shalt be removed into all the kingdoms of the earth. 26. And thy carcase shall be meat unto all fowls of the air, and unto the beasts of the earth, and no man shall fray *them* away. 27. The LORD will smite thee with the botch of Egypt, and with the emerods, and with the scab, and with the itch, whereof thou canst not be healed. 28. The LORD shall smite thee with madness, and blindness, and astonishment of heart: 29. And thou shalt grope at noonday, as the blind gropeth in darkness, and thou shalt not prosper in thy ways: and thou shalt be only oppressed and spoiled evermore, and no man shall save *thee*. 30. Thou shalt betroth a wife, and another man shall lie with her: thou shalt build an house, and thou shalt not dwell therein : thou shalt plant a vineyard, and shalt not gather the grapes thereof. 31. Thine ox *shall be* slain before thine eyes, and thou shalt not eat thereof: thine ass *shall be* violently taken away from before thy face, and shall not be restored to thee : thy sheep *shall be* given unto thine enemies, and thou shalt have none to rescue *them*. 32. Thy sons and thy daughters *shall be* given unto another people, and thine eyes shall look, and fail *with longing* for them all the day long: and *there shall be* no might in thine hand. 33. The fruit of thy land, and all thy labours, shall a nation which thou knowest not eat up ; and thou shalt be only oppressed and crushed alway : 34. So that thou shalt be mad for the sight of thine eyes which thou shalt see. 35. The LORD shall smite thee in the knees, and in the legs, with a sore botch that cannot be healed, from the sole of thy foot unto the top of thy head. 36. The LORD shall bring thee, and thy king which thou shalt set over thee, unto a nation which neither thou nor thy fathers have known ; and there shalt thou serve other gods, wood and stone. 37. And thou shalt become an astonishment, a proverb, and a byword, among all nations whither the LORD shall lead thee. 38. Thou shalt carry much seed out into the field, and shalt gather *but* little in ; for the locust shall consume it. 39. Thou shalt plant vineyards, and dress *them*, but shalt neither drink *of* the wine, nor gather *the grapes ;* for the worms shall eat them. 40. Thou shalt have olive trees throughout all thy coasts, but thou shalt not anoint *thyself* with the oil ; for thine olive shall cast *his fruit*. 41. Thou shalt beget sons and daughters, but thou shalt not enjoy them ; for they shall go into captivity. 42. All thy trees and fruit of thy land shall the locust consume. 43. The stranger that *is* within thee shall get up above thee very high ; and thou shalt come down very low. 44. He shall lend to thee, and thou shalt not lend to him : he shall be the head, and thou

shalt be the tail. 45. Moreover all these curses shall come upon thee, and shall pursue thee, and overtake thee, till thou be destroyed ; because thou hearkenedst not unto the voice of the LORD thy God, to keep his commandments and his statutes which he commanded thee : 46. And they shall be upon thee for a sign and for a wonder, and upon thy seed for ever. 47. Because thou servedst not the LORD thy God with joyfulness, and with gladness of heart, for the abundance of all *things ;* 48. Therefore shalt thou serve thine enemies which the LORD shall send against thee, in hunger, and in thirst, and in nakedness, and in want of all *things :* and he shall put a yoke of iron upon thy neck, until he have destroyed thee. 49. The LORD shall bring a nation against thee from far, from the end of the earth, *as swift* as the eagle flieth ; a nation whose tongue thou shalt not understand ; 50. A nation of fierce countenance, which shall not regard the person of the old, nor shew favour to the young : 51. And he shall eat the fruit of thy cattle, and the fruit of thy land, until thou be destroyed : which *also* shall not leave thee *either* corn, wine, or oil, *or* the increase of thy kine, or flocks of thy sheep, until he have destroyed thee. 52. And he shall besiege thee in all thy gates, until thy high and fenced walls come down, wherein thou trustedst, throughout all thy land : and he shall besiege thee in all thy gates throughout all thy land, which the LORD thy God hath given thee. 53. And thou shalt eat the fruit of thine own body, the flesh of thy sons and of thy daughters, which the LORD thy God hath given thee, in the siege, and in the straitness, wherewith thine enemies shall distress thee : 54. *So that* the man *that is* tender among you, and very delicate, his eye shall be evil toward his brother, and toward the wife of his bosom, and toward the remnant of his children which he shall leave : 55. So that he will not give to any of them of the flesh of his children whom he shall eat : because he hath nothing left him in the siege, and in the straitness, wherewith thine enemies shall distress thee in all thy gates. 56. The tender and delicate woman among you, which would not adventure to set the sole of her foot upon the ground for delicateness and tenderness, her eye shall be evil toward the husband of her bosom, and toward her son, and toward her daughter, 57. And toward her young one that cometh out from between her feet, and toward her children which she shall bear : for she shall eat them for want of all *things* secretly in the siege and straitness, wherewith thine enemy shall distress thee in thy gates. 58. If thou wilt not observe to do all the words of this law that are written in this book, that thou mayest fear this glorious and fearful name, THE LORD THY GOD ; 59. Then the LORD will make thy plagues wonderful, and the plagues of thy seed, *even* great plagues, and of long continuance, and sore sicknesses, and of long continuance. 60. Moreover he will bring upon thee all the diseases of Egypt, which thou wast afraid of; and they shall cleave unto thee. 61. Also every sickness, and every plague, which *is* not written in the book of this law, them will the LORD bring upon thee, until thou be destroyed. 62. And ye shall be left few in number, whereas ye were as the stars of heaven for multitude; because thou wouldest not obey the voice of the LORD thy God. 63. And it shall come to pass, *that* as the LORD rejoiced over you to do you good, and to multiply you; so the LORD will rejoice over you to destroy you, and to bring you to nought; and ye shall be plucked from off the land whither thou goest to possess it. 64. And the LORD shall scatter thee among all people, from the one end of the earth even unto the other; and there thou shalt serve other gods, which neither thou nor thy fathers have known, *even* wood and stone. 65. And among these nations shalt thou find no ease, neither shall the sole of thy foot have rest: but the LORD shall give thee there a trembling heart, and failing of eyes, and sorrow of mind: 66. And thy life shall hang in doubt before thee; and thou shalt fear day and night, and shalt have none assurance of thy life: 67. In the morning thou shalt say, Would God it were even! and at even thou shalt say, Would God it were morning! for the fear of thine heart wherewith thou shalt fear, and for the sight of thine eyes which thou shalt see. 68. And the LORD shall bring thee into Egypt again with ships, by the way whereof I spake unto thee, Thou shalt see it no more again: and there ye shall be sold unto your enemies for bondmen and bondwomen, and no man shall buy *you*.

Deut. 31:17. Then my anger shall be kindled against them in that day, and I will forsake them, and I will hide my face from them, and they shall be devoured, and many evils and troubles shall befall them; so that they will say in that day, Are not these evils come upon us, because our God *is* not among us? 18. And I will surely hide my face in that day for all the evils which they shall have wrought, in that they are turned unto other gods.

Psa. 81:11. But my people would not hearken to my voice; and Israel would none of me. 12. So I gave them up unto their own hearts' lust: *and* they walked in their own counsels.

Prov. 1:24. Because I have called, and ye refused; I have stretched out my hand, and no man regarded; 25. But ye have set at nought my counsel, and would none of my reproof: 26. I also will laugh at your calamity; I will mock when your fear cometh; 27. When your fear cometh as desolation, and your destruction cometh as a whirlwind; when distress and anguish cometh upon you. 28. Then shall they call upon me, but I will not answer; they shall seek me early, but they shall not find me:

Isa. 6:9. And he said, Go, and tell this people, Hear ye indeed, but understand not; and see ye indeed, but perceive not. 10. Make the heart of this people fat, and make their ears heavy, and shut their eyes; lest they see with their eyes, and hear with their ears, and understand with their heart, and convert, and be healed.

Isa. 22:12. And in that day did the Lord GOD of hosts call to weeping, and to mourning, and to baldness, and to girding with sackcloth: 13. And behold joy and gladness, slaying oxen, and killing sheep, eating flesh, and drinking wine: let us eat and drink; for to morrow we shall die. 14. And it was revealed in mine ears by the LORD of hosts, Surely this iniquity shall not be purged from you till ye die, saith the Lord GOD of hosts.

Isa. 28:13. But the word of the LORD was unto them precept upon precept, precept upon precept; line upon line, line upon line; here a little, *and* there a little; that they might go, and fall backward, and be broken, and snared, and taken.

Isa. 29:9. Stay yourselves, and wonder; cry ye out, and cry: they are drunken, but not with wine; they stagger, but not with strong drink. 10. For the LORD hath poured out upon you the spirit of deep sleep, and hath closed your eyes: the prophets and your rulers, the seers hath he covered. 11. And the vision of all is become unto you as the words of a book that is sealed, which *men* deliver to one that is learned, saying, Read this, I pray thee: and he saith, I cannot; for it *is* sealed: 12. And the book is delivered to him that is not learned, saying, Read this, I pray thee: and he saith, I am not learned.

Isa. 65:12. Therefore will I number you to the sword, and ye shall all bow down to the slaughter: because when I called, ye did not answer; when I spake, ye did not hear; but did evil before mine eyes, and did choose *that* wherein I delighted not.

Jer. 6:30. Reprobate silver shall *men* call them, because the LORD hath rejected them.

Jer. 7:16. Therefore pray not thou for this people, neither lift up cry nor prayer for them, neither make intercession to me: for I will not hear thee.

Jer. 15:1. Then said the LORD unto me, Though Moses and Samuel stood before me, *yet* my mind *could* not *be* toward this people: cast *them* out of my sight, and let them go forth.

Hos. 5:6. They shall go with their flocks and with their herds to seek the LORD; but they shall not find *him;* he hath withdrawn himself from them.

Matt. 13:14. And in them is fulfilled the prophecy of Esaias, which saith, By hearing ye shall hear, and shall not understand; and seeing ye shall see, and shall not perceive: 15. For this people's heart is waxed gross, and *their* ears are dull of hearing, and their eyes they have closed; lest at any time they should see with *their* eyes, and hear with *their* ears, and should understand with *their* heart, and should be converted, and I should heal them.

Matt. 15:14. Let them alone : they be blind leaders of the blind. And if the blind lead the blind, both shall fall into the ditch.

Matt. 25:8. And the foolish said unto the wise, Give us of your oil; for our lamps are gone out. 9. But the wise answered, saying, *Not so;* lest there be not enough for us and you : but go ye rather to them that sell, and buy for yourselves. 10. And while they went to buy, the bridegroom came; and they that were ready went in with him to the marriage : and the door was shut. 11. Afterward came also the other virgins, saying, Lord, Lord, open to us. 12. But he answered and said, Verily I say unto you, I know you not. 13. Watch therefore, for ye know neither the day nor the hour wherein the Son of man cometh.

Mark 3:29. But he that shall blaspheme against the Holy Ghost hath never forgiveness, but is ¹ in danger of eternal ² damnation.
[R. V. ¹ guilty ² sin]

Luke 13:24. Strive to enter in at the strait gate : for many, I say unto you, will seek to enter in, and shall not be able. 25. When once the master of the house is risen up, and hath shut to the door, and ye begin to stand without, and to knock at the door, saying Lord, Lord, open unto us; and he shall answer and say unto you, I know you not whence ye are : 26. Then shall ye begin to say, We have eaten and drunk in thy presence, and thou hast taught in our streets. 27. But he shall say, I tell you, I know you not whence ye are; depart from me, all *ye* workers of iniquity. 28. There shall be weeping and gnashing of teeth, when ye shall see Abraham, and Isaac, and Jacob, and all the prophets, in the kingdom of God, and you *yourselves* thrust out.

Luke 14:24. For I say unto you, That none of those men which were bidden shall taste of my supper.

John 10:26. But ye believe not, because ye are not of my sheep, as I said unto you.

John 17:12. While I was with them in the world, I kept them in thy name : those that thou gavest me I have kept, and none of them is lost, but the son of perdition; that the scripture might be fulfilled.

Rom. 9:21. Hath not the potter power over the clay, of the same lump to make one vessel unto honour, and another under dishonour ? 22. *What* if God, willing to shew *his* wrath, and to make his power known, endured with much longsuffering the vessels of wrath fitted to destruction ?

Rom. 11:7. What then ? Israel hath not obtained that which he seeketh for; but the election hath obtained it, and the rest were blinded 8. (According as it is written, God hath given them the spirit of slumber, eyes that they should not see, and ears that they should not hear;) unto this day. 17. And if some of the branches be broken off, and thou, being a wild olive tree, wert graffed in among them, and with them partakest of the root and fatness of the olive tree; 18. Boast not against the branches. But if thou boast, thou bearest not the root, but the root thee. 19. Thou wilt say then, The branches were broken off, that I might be graffed in. 20. Well; because of unbelief they were broken off, and thou standest by faith. Be not highminded, but fear :

2 Cor. 13:5. Examine yourselves, whether ye be in the faith; prove your own selves. Know ye not your own selves, how that Jesus Christ is in you, except ye be reprobates ? 6. But I trust that ye shall know that we are not reprobates. 7. Now I pray to God that ye do no evil; not that we should appear approved, but that ye should do that which is honest, though we be as reprobates.

2 Thess. 2:7. For the mystery of iniquity doth already work : only he who now letteth *will let,* until he be taken out of the way. 8. And then shall that Wicked be revealed, whom the Lord shall consume with the spirit of his mouth, and shall destroy with the brightness of his coming : 9. *Even him,* whose coming is after the working of Satan with all power and signs and lying wonders, 10. And with all deceivableness of unrighteousness in them that perish ; because they received not the love of the truth, that they might be saved. 11. And for this cause God shall send them strong delusion, that they should believe a lie : 12. That they all might be ¹ damned who believed not the truth, but had pleasure in unrighteousness. [¹ R. V. judged]

2 Tim. 3:8. Now as Jannes and Jambres withstood Moses, so do these also resist the truth : men of corrupt minds, reprobate concerning the faith.

Heb. 3:10. Wherefore I was grieved with that generation, and said, They do alway err in *their* heart; and they have not known my ways. 11. So I sware in my wrath, They shall not enter into my rest. 12. Take heed, brethren, lest there be in any of you an evil heart of unbelief, in departing from the living God. 17. But with whom was he grieved forty years ? *was it* not with them that had sinned, whose carcases fell in the wilderness ? 18. And to whom sware he that they should not enter into his rest, but to them that believed not ? 19. So we see that they could not enter in because of unbelief.

Heb. 6:4. For *it is* impossible for those who were once enlightened, and have tasted of the heavenly gift, and were made partakers of the Holy Ghost, 5. And have tasted the good word of God, and the powers of the world to come, 6. If they shall fall away, to renew them again unto repentance; seeing they crucify to themselves the Son of God afresh, and put *him* to an open shame. 7. For the earth which drinketh in the rain that cometh oft upon it, and bringeth forth herbs meet for them by whom it is dressed, receiveth blessing from God: 8. But that which beareth thorns and briers *is* rejected, and *is* nigh unto cursing; whose end *is* to be burned.

Heb. 10:26. For if we sin wilfully after that we have received the knowledge of the truth, there remaineth no more sacrifice for sins, 27. But a certain fearful looking for of judgment and fiery indignation, which shall devour the adversaries. 28. He that despised Moses' law died without mercy under two or three witnesses: 29. Of how much sorer punishment, suppose ye, shall he be thought worthy, who hath trodden under foot the Son of God, and hath counted the blood of the covenant, wherewith he was sanctified, an unholy thing, and hath done despite unto the Spirit of grace? 30. For we know him that hath said, Vengeance *belongeth* unto me, I will recompense, saith the Lord. And again, The Lord shall judge his people. 31. *It is* a fearful thing to fall into the hands of the living God.

Heb. 12:15. Looking diligently lest any man fail of the grace of God; lest any root of bitterness springing up trouble *you*, and thereby many be defiled; 16. Lest there *be* any fornicator, or profane person, as Esau, who for one morsel of meat sold his birthright. 17. For ye know how that afterward, when he would have inherited the blessing, he was rejected: for he found no place of repentance, though he sought it carefully with tears.

1 John 5:16. If any man see his brother sin a sin *which is* not unto death, he shall ask, and he shall give him life for them that sin not unto death. There is a sin unto death: I do not say that he shall pray for it.

Jude 4. For there are certain men crept in unawares, who were before of old ordained to this condemnation, ungodly men, turning the grace of our God into lasciviousness, and denying the only Lord God, and our Lord Jesus Christ. 5. I will therefore put you in remembrance, though ye once knew this, how that the Lord, having saved the people out of the land of Egypt, afterward destroyed them that believed not. 6. And the angels which kept not their first estate, but left their own habitation, he hath reserved in everlasting chains under darkness unto the judgment of the great day. 7. Even as Sodom and Gomorrha, and the cities about them in like manner, giving themselves over to fornication, and going after strange flesh, are set forth for an example, suffering the vengeance of eternal fire. 8. Likewise also these *filthy* dreamers defile the flesh, de-

spise dominion, and speak evil of dignities. 9. Yet Michael the archangel, when contending with the devil he disputed about the body of Moses, durst not bring against him a railing accusation, but said, The Lord rebuke thee. 10. But these speak evil of those things which they know not: but what they know naturally, as brute beasts, in those things they corrupt themselves. 11. Woe unto them! for they have gone in the way of Cain, and ran greedily after the error of Balaam for reward, and perished in the gainsaying of Core. 12. These are spots in your feasts of charity, when they feast with you, feeding themselves without fear: clouds *they are* without water, carried about of winds; trees whose fruit withereth, without fruit, twice dead, plucked up by the roots; 13. Raging waves of the sea, foaming out their own shame; wandering stars, to whom is reserved the blackness of darkness for ever.

Rev. 22:11. He that is unjust, let him be unjust still: and he which is filthy, let him be filthy still: and he that is righteous, let him be righteous still: and he that is holy, let him be holy still.

See OBDURACY.

INSTANCES OF: Israel, Num. 14:26-45; Deut. 1:42,43. Eli's house, 1 Sam. 3:14. Saul, 1 Sam. 15:23; 16:14; 18:12; 28:15.

REPRODUCTION. See PROPAGATION.

REPROOF. Lev. 19:17. Thou shalt in any wise rebuke thy neighbour, and not suffer sin upon him.

Psa. 141:5. Let the righteous smite me; *it shall be* a kindness: and let him reprove me; *it shall be* an excellent oil, *which* shall not break my head:

Prov. 9:7. He that reproveth a scorner getteth to himself shame: and he that rebuketh a wicked *man getteth* himself a blot. 8. Reprove not a scorner, lest he hate thee: rebuke a wise man, and he will love thee.

Prov. 10:17. He *is in* the way of life that keepeth instruction: but he that refuseth reproof erreth.

Prov. 12:1. Whoso loveth instruction loveth knowledge: but he that hateth reproof *is* brutish.

Prov. 13:18. Poverty and shame *shall be* to him that refuseth instruction: but he that regardeth reproof shall be honoured.

Prov. 15:5. A fool despiseth his father's instruction: but he that regardeth reproof is prudent. 10. Correction *is* grievous unto him that forsaketh the way: *and* he that hateth reproof shall die. 12. A scorner loveth not one that reproveth him: neither will he go unto the wise. 31. The ear that heareth the reproof of life abideth among the wise. 32. He that refuseth instruction despiseth his own soul: but he that heareth reproof getteth understanding,

Prov. 17:10. A reproof entereth more into a wise man than an hundred stripes into a fool.

Prov. 19:25. Smite a scorner, and the simple will beware: and reprove one that hath understanding, *and* he will understand knowledge.

Prov. 21:11. When the scorner is punished, the simple is made wise: and when the wise is instructed, he receiveth knowledge.

Prov. 25:12. *As* an earring of gold, and an ornament of fine gold, *so is* a wise reprover upon an obedient ear.

Prov. 26:5. Answer a fool according to his folly, lest he be wise in his own conceit.

Prov. 27:5. Open rebuke *is* better than secret love. 6. Faithful *are* the wounds of a friend;

Prov. 28:23. He that rebuketh a man afterwards shall find more favour than he that flattereth with the tongue.

Eccl. 7:5. *It is* better to hear the rebuke of the wise, than for a man to hear the song of fools.

Amos 5:10. They hate him that rebuketh in the gate, and they abhor him that speaketh uprightly.

Matt. 18:15. Moreover if thy brother shall trespass against thee, go and tell him his fault between thee and him alone: if he shall hear thee, thou hast gained thy brother. 16. But if he will not hear *thee*, *then* take with thee one or two more, that in the mouth of two or three witnesses every word may be established. 17. And if he shall neglect to hear them, tell *it* unto the church: but if he neglect to hear the church, let him be unto thee as an heathen man and a publican.

Luke 17:3. Take heed to yourselves: If thy brother trespass against thee, rebuke him; and if he repent, forgive him. 4. And if he trespass against thee seven times in a day, and seven times in a day turn again to thee, saying, I repent; thou shalt forgive him.

John 7:7. The world cannot hate you; but me it hateth, because I testify of it, that the works thereof are evil.

Gal. 4:16. Am I therefore become your enemy, because I tell you the truth?

Eph. 4:15. Speaking the truth in love, may grow up into him in all things, which is the head, *even* Christ:

Eph. 5:11. Have no fellowship with the unfruitful works of darkness, but rather reprove *them*. 13. All things that are reproved are made manifest by the light: for whatsoever doth make manifest is light.

Phil. 3:1. To write the same things to you, to me indeed *is* not grievous, but for you *it is* safe.

1 Thess. 5:14. Now we exhort you, brethren, warn them that are unruly, comfort the feebleminded. support the weak, be patient toward all *men*.

1 Tim. 5:1. Rebuke not an elder, but intreat *him* as a father; *and* the younger men as brethren; 2. The elder women as mothers; the younger as sisters, with all purity. 20. Them that sin rebuke before all, that others also may fear.

2 Tim. 4:2. Preach the word; be instant in season, out of season; reprove, rebuke, exhort with all longsuffering and doctrine.

Tit. 1:13. Wherefore rebuke them sharply, that they may be sound in the faith;

Heb. 3:13. Exhort one another daily, while it is called To day; lest any of you be hardened through the deceitfulness of sin.

Rev. 11:10. They that dwell upon the earth shall rejoice over them, and make merry, and shall send gifts one to another; because these two prophets tormented them that dwelt on the earth.

FAITHFULNESS IN: INSTANCES OF: Moses, of Pharaoh, Ex. 10:29; 11:8; of the Israelites, Ex. 16:6,7; 32:19-30; Num. 14:41; 20:10; 32:14; Deut. 1:12,26-43; 9:16-24; 29:2-4; 31:27-29; 32:15-18; of Eleazar, Lev. 10:16-18; of Korah, Num. 16:9-11. Israelites, of the two and one-half tribes, Josh. 22:15-20; of the tribe of Benjamin, Judg. 20:12,13. Samuel, of Saul, 1 Sam. 15:14-35. Jonathan, of Saul, 1 Sam. 19:4,5. Nathan, of David, 2 Sam. 12:1-9. Joab, of David, 2 Sam. 19:1-7; 24:3; 1 Chr. 21:3. The prophet Gad, of David, 2 Sam. 24:13. Shemaiah, of Rehoboam, 2 Chr. 12:5. A prophet of Judah, of Jeroboam, 1 Kin. 13:1-10; 2 Chr. 13:8-11. Elijah, of Ahab, 1 Kin. 18:18-21; 21:20-24; of Ahaziah, 2 Kin. 1. Micaiah, of Ahab, 1 Kin. 22:14-28. Elisha, of Jehoram, 2 Kin. 3:13,14; of Gehazi, 2 Kin. 5:26; of Hazael, 2 Kin. 8:11-13; of Jeroboam, 2 Kin. 13:19. Isaiah, of Hezekiah, 2 Kin. 20:17. Jehoash, of Jehoiada, 2 Kin. 12:7. Azariah, of Asa, 2 Chr. 15:2; of Uzziah, 2 Chr. 26:17,18. Hanani, of Asa, 2 Chr. 16:7-9. Jehu, of Jehoshaphat, 2 Chr. 19:2. Zechariah, of the princes of Judah, 2 Chr. 24:20. Oded, of the people of Samaria, 2 Chr. 28:9-11. Jeremiah, of the cities of Judah, Jer. 26:8-11. Ezra, of the men of Judah and Benjamin, Ezra 10:10. Nehemiah, of the Jews, Neh. 5:6-13; of the corruptions in the temple, and of the violation of the Sabbath, Neh. 13. Daniel, of Nebuchadnezzar, Dan. 4:27; of Belshazzar, Dan. 5:17-24. Amos, of the Israelites, Amos 7:12-17. Jesus, of the Jews: when Pharisees and Sadducees came to him desiring a sign, Matt. 16:1-4; Mark 8:11,12; of the scribes and Pharisees, Matt. 23; Luke 11:37-54; of the Pharisees, Luke 16; when they brought the woman to him who was taken in adultery, John 8:7. In his parables: Of the king's feast, Luke 14:16-24; of the two sons, Matt. 21:28-32; of the vineyard, Matt. 21:33-46; Mark 12:1-12; Luke 20:9-20; of the barren fig-tree, Luke 13:6-9; the withering of the fig tree, Matt. 21:17-20; Mark 11:12-14. John the Baptist, of the Jews, Matt. 3:7-12; Luke 3:7-9; of Herod, Matt. 14:3; Mark 6:17; Luke 3:19,20. Peter, of Simon, the sorcerer, Acts 8:20-23. Stephen, of the high priest, Acts 7:51-53. Paul, of Elymas, the sorcerer, Acts 13:9-11; of Ananias, the high priest, Acts 23:3. Paul and Silas, of the magistrates of Philippi, Acts 16:37–40.

DESPISED: By the Israelites, Num. 14: 9,10; Jer. 26:11. By Ahab, 1 Kin. 18:17; 21:20; 22:8. By Asa, 2 Chr. 16:10. By Herodias, Mark 6:18,19. By people of Nazareth, Luke 4:28,29. Jews, Acts 5:33; 7:54.

See REPROBACY.

REPUTATION, GOOD: Prov. 22:1; Eccl. 7:1.

See CHARACTER; NAME.

RESHEPH, grandson of Ephraim, 1 Chr. 7:25.

RESIGNATION. Job 5:17. Behold, happy *is* the man whom God correcteth: therefore despise not thou the chastening of the Almighty:

Job 34:31. Surely it is meet to be said unto God, I have borne *chastisement*, I will not offend *any more:*

Psa. 4:4. Stand in awe, and sin not, commune with your own heart upon your bed, and be still.

Psa. 46:10. Be still, and know that I *am* God:

Prov. 3:11. My son, despise not the chastening of the LORD; neither be weary of his correction:

Prov. 18:14. The spirit of a man will sustain his infirmity; but a wounded spirit who can bear?

Jer. 51:50. Ye that have escaped the sword, go away, stand not still: remember the LORD afar off, and let Jerusalem come into your mind.

Lam. 3:39. Wherefore doth a living man complain, a man for the punishment of his sins?

Mic. 6:9. The LORD's voice crieth unto the city, and *the man of* wisdom shall see thy name: hear ye the rod, and who hath appointed it.

Matt. 6:10. Thy will be done in earth, as *it is* in heaven. Luke 11:2.

Luke 21:19. In your patience ¹possess ye your souls.   [¹ R. V. ye shall win your souls]

Rom. 12:12. Rejoicing in hope; patient in tribulation; continuing instant in prayer;

Phil. 2:14. Do all things without murmurings and disputings:

Phil. 4:11. Not that I speak in respect of want: for I have learned, in whatsoever state I am, *therewith* to be content. 12. I know both how to be abased, and I know how to abound: every where and in all things I am instructed both to be full and to be hungry, both to abound and to suffer need. 13. I can do all things through Christ which strengtheneth me.

Col. 1:11. Strengthened with all might, according to his glorious power, unto all patience and longsuffering with joyfulness;

1 Thess. 3:3. That no man should be moved by these afflictions: for yourselves know that we are appointed thereunto.

2 Tim. 2:3. Thou therefore endure hardness, as a good soldier of Jesus Christ.

2 Tim. 4:5. But watch thou in all things, endure afflictions, do the work of an evangelist, make full proof of thy ministry.

Heb. 10:34. For ye had compassion of me in my bonds, and took joyfully the spoiling of your goods, knowing in yourselves that ye have in heaven a better and an enduring substance.

Heb. 12:3. Consider him that endured such contradiction of sinners against himself, lest ye be wearied and faint in your minds. 4. Ye have not yet resisted unto blood, striving against sin. 5. And ye have forgotten the exhortation which speaketh unto you as unto children, My son, despise not thou the chastening of the Lord, nor faint when thou art rebuked of him: 9. Furthermore we have had fathers of our flesh which corrected *us*, and we gave *them* reverence: shall we not much rather be in subjection unto the Father of spirits, and live? *vs.* 6–12.

Jas. 1:9. Let the brother of low degree rejoice in that he is exalted: 10. But the rich, in that he is made low: because as the flower of the grass he shall pass away.

Jas. 4:7. Submit yourselves therefore to God.

Jas. 5:13. Is any among you afflicted? let him pray. Is any merry? let him sing psalms.

1 Pet. 1:6. Wherein ye greatly rejoice, though now for a season, if need be, ye are in heaviness through manifold temptations:

1 Pet. 4:12. Beloved, think it not strange concerning the fiery trial which is to try you, as though some strange thing happened unto you: 13. But rejoice, inasmuch as ye are partakers of Christ's sufferings; that, when his glory shall be revealed, ye may be glad also with exceeding joy. 19. Wherefore let them that suffer according to the will of God commit the keeping of their souls *to him* in well doing, as unto a faithful Creator.

EXEMPLIFIED: Lev. 10:1. And Nadab and Abihu, the sons of Aaron, took either of them his censer, and put fire therein, and put incense thereon, and offered strange fire before the LORD, which he commanded them not. 2. And there went out fire from the LORD, and devoured them, and they died before the LORD. 3. Then Moses said unto Aaron, This *is it* that the LORD spake, saying, I will be sanctified in them that come nigh me, and before all the people I will be glorified. And Aaron held his peace.

Judg. 10:15. And the children of Israel said unto the LORD, We have sinned: do thou unto us whatsoever seemeth good unto thee; deliver us only, we pray thee, this day.

1 Sam. 3:18. And Samuel told him every whit, and hid nothing from him. And he said, It *is* the LORD: let him do what seemeth him good.

2 Sam. 12:23. Now he is dead, wherefore should I fast? can I bring him back again?

I shall go to him, but he shall not return to me.

2 Sam. 15:26. If he thus say, I have no delight in thee; behold, *here am* I, let him do to me as seemeth good unto him.

2 Sam. 16:10. And the king said, What have I to do with you, ye sons of Zeruiah? so let him curse, because the LORD hath said unto him, Curse David. Who shall then say, Wherefore hast thou done so? 11. And David said to Abishai, and to all his servants, Behold, my son, which came forth of my bowels, seeketh my life: how much more now *may this* Benjamite *do it?* let him alone, and let him curse; for the LORD hath bidden him.

2 Sam. 24:14. David said unto Gad, I am in a great strait: let us fall now into the hand of the LORD; for his mercies *are* great: and let me not fall into the hand of man.

2 Kin. 4:26. *Is it* well with the child? And she answered, *It is* well.

2 Kin. 20:19. Then said Hezekiah unto Isaiah, Good *is* the word of the LORD which thou hast spoken. And he said, *Is it* not *good*, if peace and truth be in my days? Isa. 39:8.

Neh. 9:33. Howbeit thou *art* just in all that is brought upon us; for thou hast done right, but we have done wickedly:

Esth. 4:16. Go, gather together all the Jews that are present in Shushan, and fast ye for me, and neither eat nor drink three days, night or day: I also and my maidens will fast likewise; and so will I go in unto the king, which *is* not according to the law: and if I perish, I perish.

Job 1:13. And there was a day when his sons and his daughters *were* eating and drinking wine in their eldest brother's house: 14. And there came a messenger unto Job, and said, The oxen were plowing, and the asses feeding beside them: 15. And the Sabeans fell *upon them*, and took them away; yea, they have slain the servants with the edge of the sword; and I only am escaped alone to tell thee. 16. While he *was* yet speaking, there came also another, and said, The fire of God is fallen from heaven, and hath burned up the sheep, and the servants, and consumed them; and I only am escaped alone to tell thee. 17. While he *was* yet speaking, there came also another, and said, The Chaldeans made out three bands, and fell upon the camels, and have carried them away, yea, and slain the servants with the edge of the sword; and I only am escaped to tell thee. 18. While he *was* yet speaking, there came also another, and said, Thy sons and thy daughters *were* eating and drinking wine in their eldest brother's house: 19. And, behold, there came a great wind from the wilderness, and smote the four corners of the house, and it fell upon the young men, and they are dead; and I only am escaped alone to tell thee. 20. Then Job arose, and rent his mantle, and shaved his head, and fell down upon the ground, and worshipped. 21. And said, Naked came I out of my mother's womb, and naked shall I return thither: the LORD gave, and the LORD hath taken away; blessed be the name of the LORD. 22. In all this Job sinned not, nor charged God foolishly.

Job 2:9. Then said his wife unto him, Dost thou still retain thine integrity? curse God, and die. 10. But he said unto her, Thou speakest as one of the foolish women speaketh. What? shall we receive good at the hand of God, and shall we not receive evil? In all this did not Job sin with his lips.

Psa. 39:9. I was dumb, I opened not my mouth; because thou didst *it*.

Psa. 103:10. He hath not dealt with us after our sins; nor rewarded us according to our iniquities.

Psa. 119:75. I know, O LORD, that thy judgments *are* right, and *that* thou in faithfulness hast afflicted me.

Jer. 10:19. Woe is me for my hurt! my wound is grievous: but I said, Truly this *is* a grief, and I must bear it.

Lam. 1:18. The LORD is righteous; for I have rebelled against his commandment:

Dan. 9:14. Therefore hath the LORD watched upon the evil, and brought it upon us: for the LORD our God *is* righteous in all his works which he doeth: for we obeyed not his voice.

Mic. 7:9. I will bear the indignation of the LORD, because I have sinned against him, until he plead my cause, and execute judgment for me: he will bring me forth to the light, *and* I shall behold his righteousness.

Matt. 26:39. And he went a little farther, and fell on his face, and prayed, saying, O my Father, if it be possible, let this cup pass from me: nevertheless not as I will, but as thou *wilt*. Mark 14:36; Luke 22:42.

Luke 23:40. But the other answering rebuked him, saying, Dost not thou fear God, seeing thou art in the same condemnation? 41. And we indeed justly; for we receive the due reward of our deeds: but this man hath done nothing amiss.

John 18:11. Then said Jesus unto Peter, Put up thy sword into the sheath: the cup which my Father hath given me, shall I not drink it?

Acts 7:59. And they stoned Stephen, calling upon *God*, and saying, Lord Jesus, receive my spirit. 60. And he kneeled down, and cried with a loud voice, Lord, lay not this sin to their charge.

Acts 21:14. When he would not be persuaded, we ceased, saying, The will of the Lord be done.

Rom. 5:3. We glory in tribulations also: knowing that tribulation worketh patience; 4. And patience, experience; and experience, hope: 5. And hope maketh not ashamed; because the love of God is shed abroad in our hearts by the Holy Ghost which is given unto us.

2 Cor. 6:9. As unknown, and *yet* well known; as dying, and, behold, we live; as chastened, and not killed; 10. As sorrowful, yet alway rejoicing; as poor, yet making many rich; as having nothing, and *yet* possessing all things. *vs.* 3–11.

2 Cor. 7:4. I am filled with comfort, I am exceeding joyful in all our tribulation.

Phil. 1:20. According to my earnest expectation and *my* hope, that in nothing I shall be ashamed, but *that* with all boldness, as always, *so* now also Christ shall be magnified in my body, whether *it be* by life, or by death. 21. For to me to live *is* Christ, and to die *is* gain. 22. But if I live in the flesh, this *is* the fruit of my labour: yet what I shall choose I wot not. 23. For I am in a strait betwixt two, having a desire to depart, and to be with Christ; which is far better: 24. Nevertheless to abide in the flesh *is* more needful for you.

2 Thess. 1:4. We ourselves glory in you in the churches of God for your patience and faith in all your persecutions and tribulations that ye endure:

2 Tim. 4:6. For I am now ready to be offered, and the time of my departure is at hand.

Jas. 5:11. Behold, we count them happy which endure. Ye have heard of the patience of Job, and have seen the end of the Lord; that the Lord is very pitiful, and of tender mercy.

See Affliction, Benefits of, Resignation in.

RESPECT. To the aged, Lev. 19:32. To rulers, Prov. 25:6. To a host, Luke 14:10. To one another, Rom. 12:10; Phil. 2:3; 1 Pet. 2:17.—*Bible Text-Book.*

RESPECT OF PERSONS, Prov. 24: 23; 28:21; Jas. 2:1–9. God does not have, Deut. 10:17; 2 Chr. 19:7; Job 31:13–15; 34:19; Acts 10:34; 15:9; Rom. 2:11,12; 10:12; Eph. 6:8,9; Col. 3:25; 1 Pet. 1:17.

See God, Justice of; Justice.

RESPONSIBILITY. Attempts to shift: Adam, Gen. 3:12,13; Eve, Gen. 3:13; Sarah, Gen. 16:5, with *v.* 2; Esau, Gen. 27:36, with Gen. 25:29–34; Aaron, Ex. 32:22–24; Saul, 1 Sam. 15:20,21; Pilate, Matt. 27:24. Assumed by the Jews for the death of Jesus, Matt. 27:25.

Personal, Ezek. 18:20,30; Matt. 12:37; John 9:41; 15:22–24; 1 Cor. 3:8,13–15; Gal. 6:5; Rev. 2:23.

ACCORDING TO PRIVILEGE: Ezek. 18:1. The word of the Lord came unto me again, saying, 2. What mean ye, that ye use this proverb concerning the land of Israel, saying, The fathers have eaten sour grapes, and the children's teeth are set on edge? 3. *As* I live, saith the Lord God, ye shall not have *occasion* any more to use this proverb in Israel. 4. Behold, all souls are mine; as the soul of the father, so also the soul of the son is mine: the soul that sinneth, it shall die. 5. But if a man be just, and do that which is lawful and right, 6. *And* hath

not eaten upon the mountains, neither hath lifted up his eyes to the idols of the house of Israel, neither hath defiled his neighbour's wife, neither hath come near to a menstruous woman, 7. And hath not oppressed any, *but* hath restored to the debtor his pledge, hath spoiled none by violence, hath given his bread to the hungry, and hath covered the naked with a garment; 8. He *that* hath not given forth upon usury, neither hath taken any increase, *that* hath withdrawn his hand from iniquity, hath executed true judgment between man and man, 9. Hath walked in my statutes, and hath kept my judgments, to deal truly; he *is* just, he shall surely live, saith the Lord God. 10. If he beget a son *that is* a robber, a shedder of blood, and *that* doeth the like to *any* one of these *things,* 11. And that doeth not any of those *duties,* but even hath eaten upon the mountains, and defiled his neighbour's wife, 12. Hath oppressed the poor and needy, hath spoiled by violence, hath not restored the pledge, and hath lifted up his eyes to the idols, hath committed abomination, 13. Hath given forth upon usury, and hath taken increase: shall he then live? he shall not live: he hath done all these abominations; he shall surely die; his blood shall be upon him. 14. Now, lo, *if* he beget a son, that seeth all his father's sins which he hath done, and considereth, and doeth not such like, 15. *That* hath not eaten upon the mountains, neither hath lifted up his eyes to the idols of the house of Israel, hath not defiled his neighbour's wife, 16. Neither hath oppressed any, hath not withholden the pledge, neither hath spoiled by violence, *but* hath given his bread to the hungry, and hath covered the naked with a garment, 17. *That* hath taken off his hand from the poor, *that* hath not received usury nor increase, hath executed my judgments, hath walked in my statutes; he shall not die for the iniquity of his father, he shall surely live. 18. *As for* his father, because he cruelly oppressed, spoiled his brother by violence, and did *that* which *is* not good among his people, lo, even he shall die in his iniquity. 19. Yet say ye, Why? doth not the son bear the iniquity of the father? When the son hath done that which is lawful and right, *and* hath kept all my statutes, and hath done them, he shall surely live. 20. The soul that sinneth, it shall die. The son shall not bear the iniquity of the father, neither shall the father bear the iniquity of the son: the righteousness of the righteous shall be upon him, and the wickedness of the wicked shall be upon him. 21. But if the wicked will turn from all his sins that he hath committed, and keep all my statutes, and do that which is lawful and right, he shall surely live, he shall not die. 22. All his transgressions that he hath committed, they shall not be mentioned unto him: in his righteousness that he hath done he shall live. 23. Have I any pleasure at all that the wicked should die? saith the Lord GOD: *and* not that he should return from his ways, and live? 24. But when the righteous turneth away from his righteousness, and committeth iniquity, *and* doeth according to all the abominations that the wicked *man* doeth, shall he live? All his righteousness that he hath done shall not be mentioned: in his trespass that he hath trespassed, and in his sin that he hath sinned, in them shall he die. 25. Yet ye say, The way of the Lord is not equal. Hear now, O house of Israel; Is not my way equal? are not your ways unequal? 26. When a righteous *man* turneth away from his righteousness, and committeth iniquity, and dieth in them; for his iniquity that he hath done shall he die. 27. Again, when the wicked *man* turneth away from his wickedness that he hath committed, and doeth that which is lawful and right, he shall save his soul alive. 28. Because he considereth, and turneth away from all his transgressions that he hath committed, he shall surely live, he shall not die. 29. Yet saith the house of Israel, The way of the Lord is not equal. O house of Israel, are not my ways equal? are not your ways unequal? 30. Therefore I will judge you, O house of Israel, every one according to his ways, saith the Lord GOD. Repent, and turn *yourselves* from all your transgressions; so iniquity shall not be your ruin.

Ezek. 33:1. Again the word of the LORD came unto me, saying, 2. Son of man, speak to the children of thy people, and say unto them, When I bring the sword upon a land, if the people of the land take a man of their coasts, and set him for their watchman: 3. If when he seeth the sword come upon the land, he blow the trumpet, and warn the people: 4. Then whosoever heareth the sound of the trumpet, and taketh not warning; if the sword come, and take him away, his blood shall be upon his own head. 5. He heard the sound of the trumpet, and took not warning; his blood shall be upon him. But he that taketh warning shall deliver his soul. 6. But if the watchman see the sword come, and blow not the trumpet, and the people be not warned; if the sword come, and take *any* person from among them, he is taken away in his iniquity; but his blood will I require at the watchman's hand. 7. So thou, O son of man, I have set thee a watchman unto the house of Israel; therefore thou shalt hear the word at my mouth, and warn them from me. 8. When I say unto the wicked, O wicked *man*, thou shalt surely die; if thou dost not speak to warn the wicked from his way, that wicked *man* shall die in his iniquity; but his blood will I require at thine hand. 9. Nevertheless, if thou warn the wicked of his way to turn from it; if he do not turn from his way, he shall die in his iniquity; but thou hast delivered thy soul. 10. Therefore, O thou son of man, speak

unto the house of Israel; Thus ye speak, saying, If our transgressions and our sins *be* upon us, and we pine away in them, how should we then live? 11. Say unto them, *As* I live, saith the Lord GOD, I have no pleasure in the death of the wicked; but that the wicked turn from his way and live: turn ye, turn ye from your evil ways; for why will ye die, O house of Israel? 12. Therefore, thou son of man, say unto the children of thy people, The righteousness of the righteous shall not deliver him in the day of his transgression: as for the wickedness of the wicked, he shall not fall thereby in the day that he turneth from his wickedness; neither shall the righteous be able to live for his *righteousness* in the day that he sinneth. 13. When I shall say to the righteous, *that* he shall surely live; if he trust to his own righteousness, and commit iniquity, all his righteousnesses shall not be remembered; but for his iniquity that he hath committed, he shall die for it. 14. Again, when I say unto the wicked, Thou shalt surely die; if he turn from his sin, and do that which is lawful and right; 15. *If* the wicked restore the pledge, give again that he had robbed, walk in the statutes of life, without committing iniquity; he shall surely live, he shall not die. 16. None of his sins that he hath committed shall be mentioned unto him: he hath done that which is lawful and right; he shall surely live. 17. Yet the children of thy people say, The way of the Lord is not equal: but as for them, their way is not equal. 18. When the righteous turneth from his righteousness, and committeth iniquity, he shall even die thereby. 19. But if the wicked turn from his wickedness, and do that which is lawful and right, he shall live thereby.

Matt. 10:11. And into whatsoever city or town ye shall enter, enquire who in it is worthy; and there abide till ye go thence. 12. And when ye come into an house, salute it. 13. And if the house be worthy, let your peace come upon it: but if it be not worthy, let your peace return to you. 14. And whosoever shall not receive you, nor hear your words, when ye depart out of that house or city, shake off the dust of your feet. 15. Verily I say unto you, It shall be more tolerable for the land of Sodom and Gomorrha in the day of judgment, than for that city. Luke 9:5; 10:10–15.

Matt. 11:20. Then began he to upbraid the cities wherein most of his mighty works were done, because they repented not: 21. Woe unto thee, Chorazin! woe unto thee, Bethsaida! for if the mighty works, which were done in you, had been done in Tyre and Sidon, they would have repented long ago in sackcloth and ashes. 22. But I say unto you, It shall be more tolerable for Tyre and Sidon at the day of judgment, than for you. 23. And thou, Capernaum, which art exalted unto heaven, shalt be brought down to hell: for if the mighty works, which have been done in thee, had been done in Sodom, it would have remained until this day. 24. But I say unto you, That it shall be more tolerable for the land of Sodom in the day of judgment, than for thee.

Matt. 12:41. The men of Nineveh shall rise in judgment with this generation, and shall condemn it: because they repented at the preaching of Jonas; and, behold, a greater than Jonas *is* here. 42. The queen of the south shall rise up in the judgment with this generation, and shall condemn it: for she came from the uttermost parts of the earth to hear the wisdom of Solomon; and, behold, a greater than Solomon *is* here. Luke 11:31,32.

Matt. 23:31. Wherefore ye be witnesses unto yourselves, that ye are the children of them which killed the prophets. 32. Fill ye up then the measure of your fathers. 33. Ye serpents, *ye* generation of vipers, how can ye escape the damnation of hell? 34. Wherefore, behold, I send unto you prophets, and wise men, and scribes: and *some* of them ye shall kill and crucify; and *some* of them shall ye scourge in your synagogues, and persecute *them* from city to city: 35. That upon you may come all the righteous blood shed upon the earth, from the blood of righteous Abel unto the blood of Zacharias son of Barachias, whom ye slew between the temple and the altar. Luke 11:49–51.

Matt. 25:14. For *the kingdom of heaven is* as a man travelling into a far country, *who* called his own servants, and delivered unto them his goods. 15. And unto one he gave five talents, to another two, and to another one; to every man according to his several ability; and straightway took his journey. 16. Then he that had received the five talents went and traded with the same, and made *them* other five talents. 17. And likewise he that *had received* two, he also gained other two. 18. But he that had received one went and digged in the earth, and hid his lord's money. 19. After a long time the lord of those servants cometh, and reckoneth with them. 20. And so he that had received five talents came and brought other five talents, saying, Lord, thou deliveredst unto me five talents: behold, I have gained beside them five talents more. 21. His lord said unto him, Well done, *thou* good and faithful servant: thou hast been faithful over a few things, I will make thee ruler over many things: enter thou into the joy of thy lord. 22. He also that had received two talents came and said, Lord, thou deliveredst unto me two talents: behold, I have gained two other talents beside them. 23. His lord said unto him, Well done, good and faithful servant; thou hast been faithful over a few things, I will make thee ruler over many things: enter thou into the joy of thy lord. 24. Then he which had received the

one talent came and said, Lord, I knew thee that thou art an hard man, reaping where thou hast not sown, and gathering where thou hast not strawed: 25. And I was afraid, and went and hid thy talent in the earth: lo, *there* thou hast *that is* thine. 26. His lord answered and said unto him, *Thou* wicked and slothful servant, thou knewest that I reap where I sowed not, and gather where I have not strawed: 27. Thou oughtest therefore to have put my money to the exchangers, and *then* at my coming I should have received mine own with usury. 28. Take therefore the talent from him, and give *it* unto him which hath ten talents. 29. For unto every one that hath shall be given, and he shall have abundance: but from him that hath not shall be taken away even that which he hath. 30. And cast ye the unprofitable servant into outer darkness: there shall be weeping and gnashing of teeth. Luke 19: 12–27.

Mark 6:11. And whosoever shall not receive you, nor hear you, when ye depart thence, shake off the dust under your feet for a testimony against them. [1] Verily I say unto you, It shall be more tolerable for Sodom and Gomorrha in the day of judgment, than for that city. [1 Omitted in R. V.]

Luke 13:6. He spake also this parable; A certain *man* had a fig tree planted in his vineyard; and he came and sought fruit thereon, and found none. 7. Then said he unto the dresser of his vineyard, Behold, these three years I come seeking fruit on this fig tree, and find none: cut it down; why cumbereth it the ground? 8. And he answering said unto him, Lord, let it alone this year also, till I shall dig about it, and dung *it:* 9. And if it bear fruit, *well:* and if not, *then* after that thou shalt cut it down.

Luke 21:1. And he looked up, and saw the rich men casting their gifts into the treasury. 2. And he saw also a certain poor widow casting in thither two mites. 3. And he said, Of a truth I say unto you, that this poor widow hath cast in more than they all: 4. For all these have of their abundance cast in unto the offerings of God: but she of her penury hath cast in all the living that she had.

John 3:18. He that believeth on him is not condemned: but he that believeth not is condemned already, because he hath not believed in the name of the only begotten Son of God. 19. And this is the condemnation, that light is come into the world, and men loved darkness rather than light, because their deeds were evil.

John 12:48. He that rejecteth me, and receiveth not my words, hath one that judgeth him: the word that I have spoken, the same shall judge him in the last day.

John 15:22. If I had not come and spoken unto them, they had not had sin: but now they have no cloke for their sin. 24. If I had not done among them the works which none other man did, they had not had sin : but now have they both seen and hated both me and my Father.

Acts 17:30. And the times of this ignorance God winked at; but now commandeth all men every where to repent : 31. Because he hath appointed a day, in the which he will judge the world in righteousness by *that* man whom he hath ordained ; *whereof* he hath given assurance unto all *men*, in that he hath raised him from the dead.

Rom. 12:3. For I say, through the grace given unto me, to every man that is among you, not to think *of himself* more highly than he ought to think ; but to think soberly, according as God hath dealt to every man the measure of faith. 6. Having then gifts differing according to the grace that is given to us, whether prophecy, *let us prophesy* according to the proportion of faith ; 7. Or ministry, *let us wait* on *our* ministering: or he that teacheth, on teaching ; 8. Or he that exhorteth, on exhortation: he that giveth, *let him do it* with simplicity ; he that ruleth, with diligence ; he that sheweth mercy, with cheerfulness.

Eph. 4:7. But unto every one of us is given grace according to the measure of the gift of Christ.

1 Tim. 6.20. O Timothy, keep that which is committed to thy trust,

See JUDGMENT ACCORDING TO OPPORTUNITY; PRIVILEGE.

RESPONSIVE RELIGIOUS SERVICE, Deut. 27:14–26.

REST. Divine institutions for, see SABBATH. Days of, Ex. 23:12; 34:21. The annual feasts added rest days, Lev. 23:7,8,21, 25,28,30,31,35,36; Num. 28:18,25,26; 29:1,7,12, 35. Recommended by Jesus, Mark 6:31,32, with Matt. 8:18,24.

HEAVENLY: 2 Thess. 1:7.

SPIRITUAL: Matt. 11:29; Heb. 4:1–11.

See PEACE, SPIRITUAL.

RESTITUTION. To be made for injury to life, limb, or property, Ex. 21:30–36; Lev. 24:18; for theft, Ex. 22:1–4; Prov. 6:30, 31; Ezek. 33:15; for dishonesty, Lev. 6:2–5; Num. 5:7; Job 20:18; Ezek. 33:15; Luke 19:8.

RESTORATION. Of the Jews, see ISRAELITES. Of all things, Acts 3:21; Rev. 21:1–5.

RESURRECTION. Job 14:12. Man lieth down, and riseth not : till the heavens *be* no more, they shall not awake, nor be raised out of their sleep. 13. O that thou wouldest hide me in the grave, that thou wouldest keep me secret, until thy wrath be past, that thou wouldest appoint me a set time, and remember me! 14. If a man die, shall he live *again?* all the days of my appointed time will I wait, till my change come. 15. Thou shalt call, and I will answer thee: thou wilt have a desire to the work of thine hands.

Job 19:25. I know *that* my redeemer liveth,

and *that* he shall stand at the latter *day* upon the earth : 26. And *though* after my skin *worms* destroy this *body*, yet in my flesh shall I see God : 27. Whom I shall see for myself, and mine eyes shall behold, and not another ; *though* my reins be consumed within me.

Psa. 16:9. Therefore my heart is glad, and my glory rejoiceth: my flesh also shall rest in hope. 10. For thou wilt not leave my soul in hell ; neither wilt thou suffer thine Holy One to see corruption.

Psa. 17:15. As for me, I will behold thy face in righteousness: I shall be satisfied, when I awake, with thy likeness.

Psa. 49:15. God will redeem my soul from the power of the grave: for he shall receive me.

Isa. 25:8. He will swallow up death [1] in victory ; and the Lord GOD will wipe away tears from off all faces; [1 R. V. for ever]

Isa. 26:19. Thy dead *men* shall live, *together with* my dead body shall they arise. Awake and sing, ye that dwell in dust : for thy dew *is as* the dew of herbs, and the earth shall cast out the dead.

Ezek. 37:1. The hand of the LORD was upon me, and carried me out in the spirit of the LORD, and set me down in the midst of the valley which *was* full of bones, 2. And caused me to pass by them round about : and, behold, *there were* very many in the open valley ; and, lo, *they were* very dry. 3. And he said unto me, Son of man, can these bones live ? And I answered, O Lord GOD, thou knowest. 4. Again he said unto me, Prophesy upon these bones, and say unto them, O ye dry bones, hear the word of the LORD. 5. Thus saith the Lord GOD unto these bones ; Behold, I will cause breath to enter into you, and ye shall live : 6. And I will lay sinews upon you, and will bring up flesh upon you, and cover you with skin, and put breath in you, and ye shall live: and ye shall know that I *am* the LORD. 7. So I prophesied as I was commanded : and as I prophesied, there was a noise, and behold a shaking, and the bones came together, bone to his bone. 8. And when I beheld, lo, the sinews and the flesh came up upon them, and the skin covered them above : but *there was* no breath in them. 9. Then said he unto me, Prophesy unto the wind, prophesy, son of man, and say to the wind, Thus saith the Lord GOD ; Come from the four winds, O breath, and breathe upon these slain, that they may live. 10. So I prophesied as he commanded me, and the breath came into them, and they lived, and stood up upon their feet, an exceeding great army. 11. Then he said unto me, Son of man, these bones are the whole house of Israel : behold, they say, Our bones are dried, and our hope is lost : we are cut off for our parts. 12. Therefore prophesy and say unto them, Thus saith the Lord GOD ; Behold, O my people, I will open your graves, and cause you to come up out of your graves, and bring you into the land of Israel. 13. And ye shall know that I *am* the LORD, when I have opened your graves, O my people, and brought you up out of your graves, 14. And shall put my spirit in you, and ye shall live, and I shall place you in your own land : then shall ye know that I the LORD have spoken *it*, and performed *it*, saith the LORD.

Dan. 12:2. Many of them that sleep in the dust of the earth shall awake, some to everlasting life, and some to shame *and* everlasting contempt. 3. And they that be wise shall shine as the brightness of the firmament; and they that turn many to righteousness as the stars for ever and ever. 13. Go thou thy way till the end *be :* for thou shalt rest, and stand in thy lot at the end of the days.

Hos. 13:14. I will ransom them from the power of the grave; I will redeem them from death: O death, I will be thy plagues; O grave, I will be thy destruction :

Matt. 22:23. The same day came to him the Sadducees, which say that there is no resurrection, and asked him, 24. Saying, Master, Moses said, If a man die, having no children, his brother shall marry his wife, and raise up seed unto his brother. 25. Now there were with us seven brethren: and the first, when he had married a wife, deceased, and, having no issue, left his wife unto his brother: 26. Likewise the second also, and the third, unto the seventh. 27. And last of all the woman died also. 28. Therefore in the resurrection whose wife shall she be of the seven? for they all had her. 29. Jesus answered and said unto them, Ye do err, not knowing the scriptures, nor the power of God. 30. For in the resurrection they neither marry, nor are given in marriage, but are as the angels of God in heaven. 31. But as touching the resurrection of the dead, have ye not read that which was spoken unto you by God, saying, 32. I am the God of Abraham, and the God of Isaac, and the God of Jacob? God is not the God of the dead, but of the living. Mark 12:18–27; Luke 20:27–37.

Matt. 24:31. And he shall send his angels with a great sound of a trumpet, and they shall gather together his elect from the four winds, from one end of heaven to the other.

Matt. 25:1. Then shall the kingdom of heaven be likened unto ten virgins, which took their lamps, and went forth to meet the bridegroom. 2. And five of them were wise, and five *were* foolish. 3. They that *were* foolish took their lamps, and took no oil with them: 4. But the wise took oil in their vessels with their lamps. 5. While the bridegroom tarried, they all slumbered and slept. 6. And at midnight there was a cry made, Behold, the bridegroom cometh; go ye out to meet him. 7. Then all those virgins arose, and trimmed their lamps. 8. And the foolish said unto the wise, Give us of your oil; for our lamps are gone out. 9. But the wise answered, saying, *Not so;* lest

there be not enough for us and you : but go ye rather to them that sell, and buy for yourselves. 10. And while they went to buy, the bridegroom came; and they that were ready went in with him to the marriage : and the door was shut. 11. Afterward came also the other virgins, saying, Lord, Lord, open to us. 12. But he answered and said, Verily I say unto you, I know you not. 13. Watch therefore, for ye know neither the day nor the hour wherein the Son of man cometh.

Matt. 27:52. The graves were opened; and many bodies of the saints which slept arose, 53. And came out of the graves after his resurrection, and went into the holy city, and appeared unto many.

Luke 14:14. And thou shalt be blessed; for they cannot recompense thee: for thou shalt be recompensed at the resurrection of the just.

Luke 20:35. They which shall be accounted worthy to obtain that world, and the resurrection from the dead, neither marry, nor are given in marriage: 36. Neither can they die any more : for they are equal unto the angels; and are the children of God, being the children of the resurrection. 37. Now that the dead are raised, even Moses shewed at the bush, when he calleth the Lord the God of Abraham, and the God of Isaac, and the God of Jacob. 38. For he is not a God of the dead, but of the living: for all live unto him. Matt. 22:30–32; Mark 12:25–27.

John 5:21. As the Father raiseth up the dead, and quickeneth *them;* even so the Son quickeneth whom he will. 25. Verily, verily, I say unto you, The hour is coming, and now is, when the dead shall hear the voice of the Son of God: and they that hear shall live. 28. Marvel not at this: for the hour is coming, in the which all that are in the graves shall hear his voice, 29. And shall come forth; they that have done good, unto the resurrection of life; and they that have done evil, unto the resurrection of damnation.

John 6:39. This is the Father's will which hath sent me, that of all which he hath given me I should lose nothing, but should raise it up again at the last day. 40. And this is the will of him that sent me, that every one which seeth the Son, and believeth on him, may have everlasting life: and I will raise him up at the last day. 44. No man can come to me, except the Father which hath sent me draw him: and I will raise him up at the last day. 54. Whoso eateth my flesh, and drinketh my blood, hath eternal life; and I will raise him up at the last day.

John 11:23. Jesus saith unto her, Thy brother shall rise again. 24. Martha saith unto him, I know that he shall rise again in the resurrection at the last day. 25. Jesus said unto her, I am the resurrection, and the life: he that believeth in me, though he ¹ were dead, yet shall he live :   [¹ R. V. die]

John 14:19. Yet a little while, and the world seeth me no more; but ye see me: because I live, ye shall live also.

Acts 2:26. Therefore did my heart rejoice, and my tongue was glad; moreover also my flesh shall rest in hope: 27. Because thou wilt not leave my soul in hell, neither wilt thou suffer thine Holy One to see corruption. 28. Thou hast made known to me the ways of life; thou shalt make me full of joy with thy countenance. 29. Men *and* brethren, let me freely speak unto you of the patriarch David, that he is both dead and buried, and his sepulchre is with us unto this day. 30. Therefore being a prophet, and knowing that God had sworn with an oath to him, that of the fruit of his loins, according to the flesh, he would raise up Christ to sit on his throne; 31. He seeing this before spake of the resurrection of Christ, that his soul was not left in hell, neither his flesh did see corruption.

Acts 4:1. The captain of the temple, and the Sadducees, came upon them, 2. Being grieved that they taught the people, and preached through Jesus the resurrection from the dead.

Acts 17:18. He preached unto them Jesus, and the resurrection. 32. When they heard of the resurrection of the dead, some mocked: and others said, We will hear thee again of this *matter*.

Acts 23:6. But when Paul perceived that the one part were Sadducees, and the other Pharisees, he cried out in the council, Men *and* brethren, I am a Pharisee, the son of a Pharisee: of the hope and resurrection of the dead I am called in question. 8. For the Sadducees say that there is no resurrection, neither angel, nor spirit: but the Pharisees confess both.

Acts 24:14. But this I confess unto thee, that after the way which they call heresy, so worship I the God of my fathers, believing all things which are written in the law and in the prophets: 15. And have hope toward God, which they themselves also allow, that there shall be a resurrection of the dead, both of the just and unjust.

Acts 26:6. I stand and am judged for the hope of the promise made of God unto our fathers: 7. Unto which *promise* our twelve tribes, instantly serving *God* day and night, hope to come. 8. Why should it be thought a thing incredible with you, that God should raise the dead?

Rom. 4:16. Abraham; who is the father of us all, 17. (As it is written, I have made thee a father of many nations,) before him whom he believed, *even* God, who quickeneth the dead, and calleth those things which be not as though they were. 18. Who against hope believed in hope, that he might become the father of many nations, according to that which was spoken, So shall thy seed be. 19. And being not weak in faith, he considered not his own body now dead, when he was about an hundred years old, neither yet the deadness of Sarah's womb: 20. He staggered not at the promise of God through unbelief; but was strong in faith, giving glory to God; 21. And being fully persuaded that, what he had promised, he was able also to perform.

Rom. 8:10. If Christ *be* in you, the body *is* dead because of sin; but the Spirit *is* life because of righteousness. 11. But if the Spirit of him that raised up Jesus from the dead dwell in you, he that raised up Christ from the dead shall also quicken your mortal bodies by his Spirit that dwelleth in you. 19. For the earnest expectation of the creature waiteth for the manifestation of the sons of God. 21. Because the creature itself also shall be delivered from the bondage of corruption into the glorious liberty of the children of God. 22. For we know that the whole creation groaneth and travaileth in pain together until now. 23. Not only *they*, but ourselves also, which have the firstfruits of the Spirit, even we ourselves groan within ourselves, waiting for the adoption, *to wit*, the redemption of our body.

1 Cor. 6:14. God hath both raised up the Lord, and will also raise up us by his own power.

1 Cor. 15:12. Now if Christ be preached that he rose from the dead, how say some among you that there is no resurrection of the dead? 13. But if there be no resurrection of the dead, then is Christ not risen: 14. And if Christ be not risen, then *is* our preaching vain, and your faith *is* also vain. 15. Yea, and we are found false witnesses of God; because we have testified of God that he raised up Christ: whom he raised not up, if so be that the dead rise not. 16. For if the dead rise not, then is not Christ raised: 17. And if Christ be not raised, your faith *is* vain; ye are yet in your sins. 18. Then they also which are fallen asleep in Christ are perished. 19. If in this life only we have hope in Christ, we are of all men most miserable. 20. But now is Christ risen from the dead, *and* become the firstfruits of them that slept. 21. For since by man *came* death, by man *came* also the resurrection of the dead. 22. For as in Adam all die, even so in Christ shall all be made alive. 23. But every man in his own order: Christ the firstfruits; afterward they that are Christ's at his coming. 24. Then *cometh* the end, when he shall have delivered up the kingdom to God, even the Father; when he shall have put down all rule and all authority and power. 25. For he must reign, till he hath put all enemies under his feet. 26. The last enemy *that* shall be destroyed *is* death. 27. For he hath put all things under his feet. But when he saith all things are put under *him*, *it is* manifest that he is excepted, which did put all things under him. 28. And when all things shall be subdued unto him,

then shall the Son also himself be subject unto him that put all things under him, that God may be all in all. 29. Else what shall they do which are baptized for the dead, if the dead rise not at all? why are they then baptized for the dead? 30. And why stand we in jeopardy every hour? 31. I protest by your rejoicing which I have in Christ Jesus our Lord, I die daily. 32. If after the manner of men I have fought with beasts at Ephesus, what advantageth it me, if the dead rise not? let us eat and drink; for to morrow we die. 35. But some *man* will say, How are the dead raised up? and with what body do they come? 36. *Thou* fool, that which thou sowest is not quickened, except it die: 37. And that which thou sowest, thou sowest not that body that shall be, but bare grain, it may chance of wheat, or of some other *grain*: 38. But God giveth it a body as it hath pleased him, and to every seed his own body. 39. All flesh *is* not the same flesh: but *there is* one *kind of* flesh of men, another flesh of beasts, another of fishes, *and* another of birds. 40. *There are* also celestial bodies, and bodies terrestrial: but the glory of the celestial *is* one, and the *glory* of the terrestrial *is* another. 41. *There is* one glory of the sun, and another glory of the moon, and another glory of the stars: for *one* star differeth from *another* star in glory. 42. So also *is* the resurrection of the dead. It is sown in corruption; it is raised in incorruption: 43. It is sown in dishonour; it is raised in glory: it is sown in weakness; it is raised in power: 44. It is sown a natural body; it is raised a spiritual body. There is a natural body, and there is a spiritual body. 45. And so it is written, The first man Adam was made a living soul; the last Adam *was made* a quickening spirit. 46. Howbeit that *was* not first which is spiritual, but that which is natural; and afterward that which is spiritual. 47. The first man *is* of the earth, earthy: the second man *is* the Lord from heaven. 48. As *is* the earthy, such *are* they also that are earthy: and as *is* the heavenly, such *are* they also that are heavenly. 49. And as we have borne the image of the earthy, we shall also bear the image of the heavenly. 50. Now this I say, brethren, that flesh and blood cannot inherit the kingdom of God; neither doth corruption inherit incorruption. 51. Behold, I shew you a mystery; We shall not all sleep, but we shall all be changed, 52. In a moment, in the twinkling of an eye, at the last trump: for the trumpet shall sound, and the dead shall be raised incorruptible, and we shall be changed. 53. For this corruptible must put on incorruption, and this mortal *must* put on immortality. 54. So when this corruptible shall have put on incorruption, and this mortal shall have put on immortality, then shall be brought to pass the saying that is written, Death is swallowed up in victory. 55. O death, where *is* thy sting? O grave, where *is* thy victory? 56. The sting of death *is* sin; and the strength of sin *is* the law. 57. But thanks *be* to God, which giveth us the victory through our Lord Jesus Christ.

2 Cor. 4:14. Knowing that he which raised up the Lord Jesus shall raise up us also by Jesus, and shall present *us* with you.

2 Cor. 5:1. For we know that if our earthly house of *this* tabernacle were dissolved, we have a building of God, an house not made with hands, eternal in the heavens. 2. For in this we groan, earnestly desiring to be clothed upon with our house which is from heaven: 3. If so be that being clothed we shall not be found naked. 4. For we that are in *this* tabernacle do groan, being burdened: not for that we would be unclothed, but clothed upon, that mortality might be swallowed up of life. 5. Now he that hath wrought us for the selfsame thing *is* God, who also hath given unto us the earnest of the Spirit.

Phil. 3:10. That I may know him, and the power of his resurrection, and the fellowship of his sufferings, being made conformable unto his death; 11. If by any means I might attain unto the resurrection of the dead. 21. Who shall change our vile body, that it may be fashioned like unto his glorious body, according to the working whereby he is able even to subdue all things unto himself.

1 Thess. 4:14. For if we believe that Jesus died and rose again, even so them also which sleep in Jesus will God bring with him. 16. For the Lord himself shall descend from heaven with a shout, with the voice of the archangel, and with the trump of God: and the dead in Christ shall rise first:

2 Tim. 1:10. But is now made manifest by the appearing of our Saviour Jesus Christ, who hath abolished death, and hath brought life and ¹immortality to light through the gospel: [¹ R. V. incorruption]

2 Tim. 2:18. Who concerning the truth have erred, saying that the resurrection is past already: and overthrow the faith of some.

Heb. 6:2. Of the doctrine of baptisms, and of laying on of hands, and of resurrection of the dead, and of eternal judgment.

Heb. 11:19. Accounting that God *was* able to raise *him* up, even from the dead; from whence also he received him in a figure. 35. Women received their dead raised to life again: and others were tortured, not accepting deliverance; that they might obtain a better resurrection:

Rev. 1:18. *I am* he that liveth, and was dead; and, behold, I am alive for evermore, Amen; and have the keys of hell and of death.

Rev. 20:4. And I saw thrones, and they sat upon them, and judgment was given unto them: and *I saw* the souls of them that were beheaded for the witness of Jesus, and for the word of God, and which had not worshipped the beast, neither his image, neither had received *his* mark upon their foreheads, or in their hands; and they lived and reigned with Christ a thousand years. 5. But the rest of the dead lived not again until the thousand years were finished. This *is* the first resurrection. 6. Blessed and holy *is* he that hath part in the first resurrection: on such the second death hath no power, but they shall be priests of God and of Christ, and shall reign with him a thousand years. 13. And the sea gave up the dead which were in it; and death and hell delivered up the dead which were in them: and they were judged every man according to their works.

See DEAD, RAISED; OF JESUS, see JESUS.

FIGURATIVE: Of regeneration, Rom. 6:4; Eph. 2:1,5,6; Col. 2:12; 3:1.

TYPIFIED: Isaac, Gen. 22:13, with Heb. 11:19. Jonah, Jonah 2:10, with Matt. 12:40.

SYMBOLICAL: Rev. 11:11.

RETALIATION. Ex. 21:23. And if *any* mischief follow, then thou shalt give life for life, 24. Eye for eye, tooth for tooth, hand for hand, foot for foot, 25. Burning for burning, wound for wound, stripe for stripe.

Lev. 19:18. Thou shalt not avenge, nor bear any grudge against the children of thy people, but thou shalt love thy neighbour as thyself: I *am* the LORD.

Lev. 24:17. And he that killeth any man shall surely be put to death. 18. And he that killeth a beast shall make it good; beast for beast. 19. And if a man cause a blemish in his neighbour; as he hath done, so shall it be done to him; 20. Breach for breach, eye for eye, tooth for tooth: as he hath caused a blemish in a man, so shall it be done to him *again*. 21. And he that killeth a beast, he shall restore it: and he that killeth a man, he shall be put to death. 22. Ye shall have one manner of law, as well for the stranger, as for one of your own country: for I *am* the LORD your God.

Deut. 19:19. Then shall ye do unto him, as he had thought to have done unto his brother: so shalt thou put the evil away from among you. 20. And those which remain shall hear, and fear, and shall henceforth commit no more any such evil among you. 21. And thine eye shall not pity; *but* life *shall* go for life, eye for eye, tooth for tooth, hand for hand, foot for foot.

Psa. 10:2. The wicked in *his* pride doth persecute the poor: let them be taken in the devices that they have imagined.

Prov. 20:22. Say not thou, I will recompense evil; *but* wait on the LORD, and he shall save thee.

Prov. 24:29. Say not, I will do so to him as he hath done to me: I will render to the man according to his work.

Prov. 26:27. Whoso diggeth a pit shall fall therein: and he that rolleth a stone, it will return upon him.

Isa. 33:1. Woe to thee that spoilest, and thou *wast* not spoiled; and dealest treacherously, and they dealt not treacherously with thee! when thou shalt cease to spoil, thou shalt be spoiled; *and* when thou shalt make an end to deal treacherously, they shall deal treacherously with thee.

Matt. 5:38. Ye have heard that it hath been said, An eye for an eye, and a tooth for a tooth: 39. But I say unto you, That ye resist not evil: but whosoever shall smite thee on thy right cheek, turn to him the other also. 40. And if any man will sue thee at the law, and take away thy coat, let him have *thy* cloke also. 41. And whosoever shall compel thee to go a mile, go with him twain. 42. Give to him that asketh thee, and from him that would borrow of thee turn not thou away. 43. Ye have heard that it hath been said, Thou shalt love thy neighbour, and hate thine enemy. 44. But I say unto you, Love your enemies, bless them that curse you, do good to them that hate you, and pray for them which despitefully use you, and persecute you;

Matt. 7:1. Judge not, that ye be not judged. 2. For with what judgment ye judge, ye shall be judged: and with what measure ye mete, it shall be measured to you again.

Luke 9:52. They went, and entered into a village of the Samaritans, to make ready for him. 53. And they did not receive him, because his face was as though he would go to Jerusalem. 54. And when his disciples James and John saw *this*, they said, Lord, wilt thou that we command fire to come down from heaven, and consume them, even as Elias did? 55. But he turned, and rebuked them, [1] and said, Ye know not what manner of spirit ye are of. 56. [1] For the Son of man is not come to destroy men's lives, but to save *them*.

[1 Omitted in R. V.]

Rom. 12:17. Recompense to no man evil for evil. 19. Dearly beloved, avenge not yourselves, but *rather* give place unto wrath: for it is written, Vengeance *is* mine; I will repay, saith the Lord.

1 Cor. 6:7. Now therefore there is utterly a fault among you, because ye go to law one with another. Why do ye not rather take wrong? why do ye not rather *suffer yourselves to* be defrauded? 8. Nay, ye do wrong, and defraud, and that *your* brethren.

1 Thess. 5:15. See that none render evil for evil unto any *man;* but ever follow that which is good, both among yourselves, and to all *men*.

1 Pet. 3:9. Not rendering evil for evil, or railing for railing: but contrariwise blessing; knowing that ye are thereunto called, that ye should inherit a blessing.

See AVENGER; HATRED; MALICE; REVENGE.

INSTANCES OF: Israelites on the Amalekites, Deut. 25:17-19, with 1 Sam. 15:1-9. Gideon on the princes of Succoth, Judg. 8:7,13-16; kings of Midian, Judg. 8:18-21;

Penuel, Judg. 8:8,17. Joab on Abner, 2 Sam. 3:27,30. David upon Michal, 2 Sam. 6:21-23; on Joab, 1 Kin. 2:5,6; Shimei, 1 Kin. 2:8,9. Jews on the Chaldeans, Esth. 9.

RETRIBUTION. See SIN, PUNISHMENT OF.

REU, son of Peleg and ancestor of Abraham, Gen. 11:18-21; 1 Chr. 1:25.

REUBEN. Son of Jacob, Gen. 29:32; 1 Chr. 2:1. Brings mandrakes to his mother, Gen. 30:14. Commits incest with one of his father's concubines, and, in consequence, forfeits the birthright, Gen. 35:22; 49:4; 1 Chr. 5:1. Adroitly seeks to save Joseph from the conspiracy of his brethren, Gen. 37:21-30; 42:22. Offers to become surety for Benjamin, Gen. 42:37. Jacob's prophetic benediction upon, Gen. 49:3,4. His children, Gen. 46:9; Ex. 6:14; 1 Chr. 5:3-6; Num. 16:1.

REUBENITES, the descendants of Reuben. Military enrollment of, at Sinai, Num. 1:20,21; in Moab, Num. 26:7. Place of, in camp and march, Num. 2:10. Standard of, Num. 10:18. Have their inheritance east of the Jordan, Num. 32; Deut. 3:1-20; Josh. 13:15-23; 18:7. Assist the other tribes in conquest of the region west of the Jordan, Josh. 1: 12-18; 22:1-6. Unite with the other tribes in building a monument to signify the unity of the tribes on the east of the Jordan with the tribes on the west of the river; monument misunderstood; the explanation and reconciliation, Josh. 22:10-34. Reproached by Deborah, Judg. 5:15,16. Taken captive into Assyria, 2 Kin. 15:29; 1 Chr. 5:26.
See ISRAEL.

REUEL. 1. Son of Esau, Gen. 36:4,10, 13,17; 1 Chr. 1:35,37.
2. Father-in-law of Moses, Ex. 2:18. Called also JETHRO and RAGUEL. See JETHRO.
3. Father of Eliasaph, Num. 2:14. Called DEUEL, Num. 1:14; 7:42,47; 10:20.
4. A Benjamite, 1 Chr. 9:8.

REUMAH, a concubine of Nahor, Gen. 22:24.

REVELATION. God reveals himself to Moses, Ex. 3:1-6,14; 6:1-3. The law is revealed, Ex. chapters 20-35; Lev. chapters 1-7; the pattern of the temple, 1 Chr. 28:11-19. The sonship of Jesus, Matt. 3:17; 16:17; 17:5.
See INSPIRATION; PROPHECY; PROPHET; WORD OF GOD, INSPIRATION OF.

REVENGE. Forbidden, Lev. 19:18; Prov. 24:29; Rom. 12:17,19; 1 Thess. 5:15; 1 Pet. 3:9. Jesus an example of forbearing, 1 Pet. 2:23. Rebuked by Jesus, Luke 9:54, 55. Inconsistent with a Christian spirit, Luke 9:55. Proceeds from a spiteful heart, Ezek. 25:15. Punishment for, Ezek. 25:15-17; Amos 1:11,12.

EXEMPLIFIED: By Simeon and Levi, Gen. 34:25. By Samson, Judg. 15:7,8; 16:28-30. By Joab, 2 Sam. 3:27. By Absalom, 2 Sam. 13:23-29. By Jezebel, 1 Kin. 19:2. By Ahab, 1 Kin. 22:27. By Haman, Esth. 3:8-15. By the Edomites, Ezek. 25:12. By the Philistines, Ezek. 25:15. By Herodias, Mark 6: 19-24. By James and John, Luke 9:54.

By the chief priests, Acts 5:33. By the Jews, Acts 7:54-59; 23:12.—*Bible Text-Book.*
See RETALIATION.

REVENUE, Solomon's, 2 Chr. 9:13,14.
See TAX.

REVERENCE. For God, Gen. 17:3; Ex. 3:5; 19:16-24; 34:29-35; Isa. 45:9. See FEAR OF GOD. For God's house, Lev. 19:30; 26:2. For ministers, 1 Sam. 16:4; Acts 28:10; 1 Cor. 16:18; Phil. 2:29; 1 Thess. 5:12,13; 1 Tim. 5:17; Heb. 13:7,17. See MINISTERS. For kings, 1 Sam. 24:6; 26:9,11; 2 Sam. 1:14; 16:21; Eccl. 10:20; 1 Pet. 2:17. See RULERS. For magistrates, Ex. 22:28; 2 Pet. 2:10; Jude 8. See RULERS. For parents, Ex. 20:12; Lev. 19:3; Isa. 45:10. See PARENTS. For the aged, Lev. 19:32; Job 32:4-7.

REVILING, of Jesus, Matt. 27:39-44.
See MOCKING.

REVIVALS. RELIGIOUS: Zech. 8:20-23. Prayer for, Hab. 3:2. Prophecies concerning, Isa. 32:15; Joel 2:28; Mic. 4:1-8; Hab. 3:2.
INSTANCES OF: Under Joshua, Josh. 5: 2-9; Samuel, 1 Sam. 7:1-6; Elijah, 1 Kin. 18: 17-40; Jehoash and Jehoiada, 2 Kin. chapters 11; 12; 2 Chr. chapters 23; 24; Hezekiah, 2 Kin. 18:1-7; 2 Chr. chapters 29-31; Josiah, 2 Kin. chapters 22; 23; 2 Chr. chapters 34; 35; Asa, 2 Chr. 14:2-5; 15:1-14; Manasseh, 2 Chr. 33:12-19. In Nineveh, Jonah 3:4-10. At Pentecost, and post-pentecostal times, Acts 2:1-42,46,47; 4:4; 5:14; 6:7; 9:35; 11:20,21; 12:24; 14:1; 19:17-20.
See RELIGION.

REVOLT, of the ten tribes, 1 Kin. 12:1-24.

REWARD. A MOTIVE TO FAITHFULNESS: Ex. 20:6. And shewing mercy unto thousands of them that love me, and keep my commandments. 12. Honour thy father and thy mother: that thy days may be long upon the land which the LORD thy God giveth thee. Eph. 6:1-3.

Lev. 25:18. Wherefore ye shall do my statutes, and keep my judgments, and do them; and ye shall dwell in the land in safety. 19. And the land shall yield her fruit, and ye shall eat your fill, and dwell therein in safety.

Lev. 26:3. If ye walk in my statutes, and keep my commandments, and do them; 4. Then I will give you rain in due season, and the land shall yield her increase, and the trees of the field shall yield their fruit. 5. And your threshing shall reach unto the vintage, and the vintage shall reach unto the sowing time: and ye shall eat your bread to the full, and dwell in your land safely. 6. And I will give peace in the land, and ye shall lie down, and none shall make *you* afraid : and I will rid evil beasts out of the land, neither shall the sword go through your land. 7. And ye shall chase your enemies, and they shall fall before you by the sword. 8. And five of you shall chase an hundred, and an hundred of you shall put ten thousand to flight : and your enemies shall fall before you by the sword. 9. For I will have respect unto you, and make you fruitful, and multiply you, and establish my covenant with you. 10. And ye shall eat old store, and bring forth the old because of the new. 11. And I will set my tabernacle. among you : and my soul shall not abhor you. 12. And I will walk among you, and will be your God, and ye shall be my people. 13. I *am* the LORD your God, which brought you forth out of the land of Egypt, that ye should not be their bondmen ; and I have broken the bands of your yoke, and made you go upright. *vs.* 14–39.

40. If they shall confess their iniquity, and the iniquity of their fathers, with their trespass which they trespassed against me, and that also they have walked contrary unto me; 41. And *that* I also have walked contrary unto them, and have brought them into the land of their enemies ; if then their uncircumcised hearts be humbled, and they then accept of the punishment of their iniquity : 42. Then will I remember my covenant with Jacob, and also my covenant with Isaac, and also my covenant with Abraham will I remember ; and I will remember the land. 43. The land also shall be left of them, and shall enjoy her sabbaths, while she lieth desolate without them : and they shall accept of the punishment of their iniquity : because, even because they despised my judgments, and because their soul abhorred my statutes. 44. And yet for all that, when they be in the land of their enemies, I will not cast them away, neither will I abhor them, to destroy them utterly, and to break my covenant with them : for I *am* the LORD their God. 45. But I will for their sakes remember the covenant of their ancestors, whom I brought forth out of the land of Egypt in the sight of the heathen, that I might be their God : I *am* the LORD.

Deut. 4:40. Thou shalt keep therefore his statutes, and his commandments, which I command thee this day, that it may go well with thee, and with thy children after thee, and that thou mayest prolong *thy* days upon the earth, which the LORD thy God giveth thee, for ever.

Deut. 6:3. Hear therefore, O Israel, and observe to do *it;* that it may be well with thee, and that ye may increase mightily, as the LORD God of thy fathers hath promised thee, in the land that floweth with milk and honey. *v.* 18.

Deut. 11:13. And it shall come to pass, if ye shall hearken diligently unto my commandments which I command you this day, to love the LORD your God, and to serve him with all your heart and with all your soul, 14. That I will give *you* the rain of your land in his due season, the first rain and the latter rain, that thou mayest gather in thy corn, and thy wine, and thine oil. 15. And I will send grass in thy fields for thy cattle, that thou mayest eat and be full. 16. Take heed to yourselves, that your

heart be not deceived, and ye turn aside, and serve other gods, and worship them ; 18. Therefore shall ye lay up these my words in your heart and in your soul, and bind them for a sign upon your hand, that they may be as frontlets between your eyes. 19. And ye shall teach them your children, speaking of them when thou sittest in thine house, and when thou walkest by the way, when thou liest down, and when thou risest up. 20. And thou shalt write them upon the door posts of thine house, and upon thy gates : 21. That your days may be multiplied, and the days of your children, in the land which the LORD sware unto your fathers to give them, as the days of heaven upon the earth. 26. Behold, I set before you this day a blessing and a curse ; 27. A blessing, if ye obey the commandments of the LORD your God, which I command you this day : 28. And a curse, if ye will not obey the commandments of the LORD your God, but turn aside out of the way which I command you this day, to go after other gods, which ye have not known. 29. And it shall come to pass, when the LORD thy God hath brought thee in unto the land whither thou goest to possess it, that thou shalt put the blessing upon mount Gerizim, and the curse upon mount Ebal. chapter 27:12–26; Josh. 8:33.

Deut. 15:9. Beware that there be not a thought in thy wicked heart, saying, The seventh year, the year of release, is at hand ; and thine eye be evil against thy poor brother, and thou givest him nought; and he cry unto the LORD against thee, and it be sin unto thee. 10. Thou shalt surely give him, and thine heart shall not be grieved when thou givest unto him : because that for this thing the LORD thy God shall bless thee in all thy works, and in all that thou puttest thine hand unto. 11. For the poor shall never cease out of the land : therefore I command thee, saying, Thou shalt open thine hand wide unto thy brother, to thy poor, and to thy needy, in thy land.

Deut. 22:7. *But* thou shalt in any wise let the dam go, and take the young to thee ; that it may be well with thee, and *that* thou mayest prolong *thy* days.

Deut. 24:19. When thou cuttest down thine harvest in thy field, and hast forgot a sheaf in the field, thou shalt not go again to fetch it : it shall be for the stranger, for the fatherless, and for the widow : that the LORD thy God may bless thee in all the work of thine hands.

Deut. 25:15. *But* thou shalt have a perfect and just weight, a perfect and just measure shalt thou have : that thy days may be lengthened in the land which the LORD thy God giveth thee.

Isa. 1:16. Wash you, make you clean : put away the evil of your doings from before mine eyes ; cease to do evil ; 17. Learn to do well ; seek judgment, relieve the oppressed, judge the fatherless, plead for the widow.

18. Come now, and let us reason together, saith the LORD: though your sins be as scarlet, they shall be as white as snow; though they be red like crimson, they shall be as wool. **19.** If ye be willing and obedient, ye shall eat the good of the land: **20.** But if ye refuse and rebel, ye shall be devoured with the sword: for the mouth of the LORD hath spoken *it.*

Isa. 3:10. Say ye to the righteous, that *it shall be* well *with him:* for they shall eat the fruit of their doings.

Isa. 40:10. Behold, the Lord GOD will come with strong *hand,* and his arm shall rule for him: behold, his reward *is* with him, and his work before him. **11.** He shall feed his flock like a shepherd: he shall gather the lambs with his arm, and carry *them* in his bosom, *and* shall gently lead those that are with young.

Jer. 22:3. Thus saith the LORD; Execute ye judgment and righteousness, and deliver the spoiled out of the hand of the oppressor: and do no wrong, do no violence to the stranger, the fatherless, nor the widow, neither shed innocent blood in this place. **4.** For if ye do this thing indeed, then shall there enter in by the gates of this house kings sitting upon the throne of David, riding in chariots and on horses, he, and his servants, and his people.   chapter 17:24–26.

Matt. 10:32. Whosoever therefore shall confess me before men, him will I confess also before my Father which is in heaven. Luke 12:8.

Matt. 16:24. Then said Jesus unto his disciples, If any *man* will come after me, let him deny himself, and take up his cross, and follow me. **25.** For whosoever will save his life shall lose it: and whosoever will lose his life for my sake shall find it. **26.** For what is a man profited, if he shall gain the whole world, and lose his own soul? or what shall a man give in exchange for his soul? **27.** For the Son of man shall come in the glory of his Father with his angels; and then he shall reward every man according to his works.

Matt. 20:1. For the kingdom of heaven is like unto a man *that is* an householder, which went out early in the morning to hire labourers into his vineyard. **2.** And when he had agreed with the labourers for a penny a day, he sent them into his vineyard. **3.** And he went out about the third hour, and saw others standing idle in the marketplace, **4.** And said unto them; Go ye also into the vineyard, and whatsoever is right I will give you. And they went their way. **5.** Again he went out about the sixth and ninth hour, and did likewise. **6.** And about the eleventh hour he went out, and found others standing idle, and saith unto them, Why stand ye here all the day idle? **7.** They say unto him, Because no man hath hired us. He saith unto them, Go ye also into the vineyard; ¹ and whatsoever is right, *that* shall ye receive. **8.** So when even was

come, the lord of the vineyard saith unto his steward, Call the labourers, and give them *their* hire, beginning from the last unto the first. **9.** And when they came that *were hired* about the eleventh hour, they received every man a penny. **10.** But when the first came, they supposed that they should have received more; and they likewise received every man a penny. **11.** And when they had received *it,* they murmured against the goodman of the house, **12.** Saying, These last have wrought *but* one hour, and thou hast made them equal unto us, which have borne the burden and heat of the day. **13.** But he answered one of them, and said, Friend, I do thee no wrong: didst not thou agree with me for a penny? **14.** Take *that* thine *is,* and go thy way: I will give unto this last, even as unto thee. **15.** Is it not lawful for me to do what I will with mine own? Is thine eye evil, because I am good? **16.** So the last shall be first, and the first last: ¹ for many be called, but few chosen.   [¹ Omitted in R. V.]

Matt. 25:34. Then shall the King say unto them on his right hand, Come, ye blessed of my Father, inherit the kingdom prepared for you from the foundation of the world: **35.** For I was an hungred, and ye gave me meat: I was thirsty, and ye gave me drink: I was a stranger, and ye took me in: **36.** Naked, and ye clothed me: I was sick, and ye visited me: I was in prison, and ye came unto me. **37.** Then shall the righteous answer him, saying, Lord, when saw we thee an hungred, and feed *thee?* or thirsty, and gave *thee* drink? **38.** When saw we thee a stranger, and took *thee* in? or naked, and clothed *thee?* **39.** Or when saw we thee sick, or in prison, and came unto thee? **40.** And the King shall answer and say unto them, Verily I say unto you, Inasmuch as ye have done *it* unto one of the least of these my brethren, ye have done *it* unto me. **41.** Then shall he say also unto them on the left hand, Depart from me, ye cursed, into everlasting fire, prepared for the devil and his angels: **42.** For I was an hungred, and ye gave me no meat: I was thirsty, and ye gave me no drink: **43.** I was a stranger, and ye took me not in: naked, and ye clothed me not: sick, and in prison, and ye visited me not. **44.** Then shall they also answer him, saying, Lord, when saw we thee an hungred, or athirst, or a stranger, or naked, or sick, or in prison, and did not minister unto thee? **45.** Then shall he answer them, saying, Verily I say unto you, Inasmuch as ye did *it* not to one of the least of these, ye did *it* not to me. **46.** And these shall go away into everlasting punishment: but the righteous into life eternal.

Mark 10:21. Then Jesus beholding him loved him, and said unto him, One thing thou lackest: go thy way, sell whatsoever thou hast, and give to the poor, and thou shalt have treasure in heaven: and come, take up the cross, and follow me.

Mark 13.13. And ye shall be hated of all *men* for my name's sake: but he that shall endure unto the end, the same shall be saved.

Luke 6:22. Blessed are ye, when men shall hate you, and when they shall separate you *from their company,* and shall reproach *you,* and cast out your name as evil, for the Son of man's sake. 23. Rejoice ye in that day, and leap for joy: for, behold, your reward *is* great in heaven: for in the like manner did their fathers unto the prophets. 35. But love ye your enemies, and do good, and lend, hoping for nothing again; and your reward shall be great, and ye shall be the children of the Highest: for he is kind unto the unthankful and *to* the evil.

Acts 26:18. To open their eyes, *and* to turn *them* from darkness to light, and *from* the power of Satan unto God, that they may receive forgiveness of sins, and inheritance among them which are sanctified by faith that is in me.

Rom. 2:10. But glory, honour, and peace, to every man that worketh good,

1 Cor. 3:8. Now he that planteth and he that watereth are one: and every man shall receive his own reward according to his own labour.

Heb. 10:34. For ye had compassion of me in my bonds, and took joyfully the spoiling of your goods, knowing in yourselves that ye have in heaven a better and an enduring substance.

36. For ye have need of patience, that, after ye have done the will of God, ye might receive the promise.

Heb. 11:26. Esteeming the reproach of Christ greater riches than the treasures in Egypt: for he had respect unto the recompence of the reward.

Heb. 12:1. Wherefore seeing we also are compassed about with so great a cloud of witnesses, let us lay aside every weight, and the sin which doth so easily beset *us,* and let us run with patience the race that is set before us, 2. Looking unto Jesus the author and finisher of *our* faith; who for the joy that was set before him endured the cross, despising the shame, and is set down at the right hand of the throne of God.

28. Wherefore we receiving a kingdom which cannot be moved, let us have grace, whereby we may serve God acceptably with reverence and godly fear:

1 Pet. 3:9. Not rendering evil for evil, or railing for railing: but contrariwise blessing; knowing that ye are thereunto called, that ye should inherit a blessing. 10. For he that will love life, and see good days, let him refrain his tongue from evil, and his lips that they speak no guile: 11. Let him eschew evil, and do good; let him seek peace, and ensue it. 12. For the eyes of the Lord *are* over the righteous, and his ears *are open* unto their prayers: but the face of the Lord *is* against them that do evil.

2 Pet. 1:10. Wherefore the rather, breth-

ren, give diligence to make your calling and election sure: for if ye do these things, ye shall never fall: 11. For so an entrance shall be ministered unto you abundantly into the everlasting kingdom of our Lord and Saviour Jesus Christ.

Rev. 2:10. Fear none of those things which thou shalt suffer: . . . and ye shall have tribulation ten days: be thou faithful unto death, and I will give thee a crown of life.

17. He that hath an ear, let him hear what the Spirit saith unto the churches; To him that overcometh will I give to eat of the hidden manna, and will give him a white stone, and in the stone a new name written, which no man knoweth saving he that receiveth *it.*

25. But that which ye have *already,* hold fast till I come. 26. And he that overcometh, and keepeth my works unto the end, to him will I give power over the nations: 27. And he shall rule them with a rod of iron; as the vessels of a potter shall they be broken to shivers: even as I received of my Father. 28. And I will give him the morning star.

Rev. 7:14. These are they which came out of great tribulation, and have washed their robes, and made them white in the blood of the Lamb. 15. Therefore are they before the throne of God, and serve him day and night in his temple: and he that sitteth on the throne shall dwell among them. 16. They shall hunger no more, neither thirst any more; neither shall the sun light on them, nor any heat. 17. For the Lamb which is in the midst of the throne shall feed them, and shall lead them unto living fountains of waters: and God shall wipe away all tears from their eyes.

Rev. 22:12. And, behold, I come quickly; and my reward *is* with me, to give every man according as his work shall be.

See BLESSING, CONTINGENT UPON OBEDIENCE; PUNISHMENTS; RIGHTEOUS, PROMISES TO; SIN, SEPARATES FROM GOD; WICKED, PUNISHMENT OF.

REZEPH, a city destroyed by the Assyrians, 2 Kin. 19:12; Isa. 37:12.

REZIA, an Asherite, 1 Chr. 7:39.

REZIN. 1. A king of Syria who harassed the kingdom of Judah, 2 Kin. 15:37; 16:5-9. Prophecy against, Isa. 7:1-9; 8:4-8; 9:11.

2. A returned Babylonian captive, Ezra 2:48; Neh. 7:50.

REZON, king of Damascus. An adversary of Solomon, 1 Kin. 11:23-25.

RHEGIUM, a city of Italy. Touched by Paul on the way to Rome, Acts 28:13.

RHESA, an ancestor of Jesus, Luke 3:27.

RHODA, a Christian girl in Jerusalem, Acts 12:13.

RHODES, an island visited by Paul, Acts 21:1.

RIBAI, a Benjamite. Father of Ittai, 2 Sam. 23:29; 1 Chr. 11:31.

RIBBAND, Num. 15:38.

RIBLAH. A border town of the promised land, Num. 34:10:11. King Jehoahaz overthrown in, by Pharaoh, 2 Kin. 23:33. Headquarters of Nebuchadnezzar in siege of Jerusalem, 2 Kin. 25:6,20,21; Jer. 39:5,6; 52:9,26.

RICH, THE: Neh. 5:1. And there was a great cry of the people and of their wives against their brethren the Jews. 2. For there were that said, We, our sons, and our daughters, *are* many: therefore we take up corn *for them*, that we may eat, and live. 3. *Some* also there were that said, We have mortgaged our lands, vineyards, and houses, that we might buy corn, because of the dearth. 4. There were also that said, We have borrowed money for the king's tribute, *and that upon* our lands and vineyards. 5. Yet now our flesh *is* as the flesh of our brethren, our children as their children: and, lo, we bring into bondage our sons and our daughters to be servants, and *some* of our daughters are brought unto bondage *already:* neither *is it* in our power *to redeem them;* for other men have our lands and vineyards. 6. And I was very angry when I heard their cry and these words. 7. Then I consulted with myself, and I rebuked the nobles, and the rulers, and said unto them, Ye exact usury, every one of his brother. And I set a great assembly against them. 8. And I said unto them, We after our ability have redeemed our brethren the Jews, which were sold unto the heathen; and will ye even sell your brethren? or shall they be sold unto us? Then held they their peace, and found nothing *to answer.* 9. Also I said, It *is* not good that ye do: ought ye not to walk in the fear of our God because of the reproach of the heathen our enemies? 10. I likewise, *and* my brethren, and my servants, might exact of them money and corn: I pray you, let us leave off this usury. 11. Restore, I pray you, to them, even this day, their lands, their vineyards, their oliveyards, and their houses, also the hundredth *part* of the money, and of the corn, the wine, and the oil, that ye exact of them. 12. Then said they, We will restore *them*, and will require nothing of them; so will we do as thou sayest. Then I called the priests, and took an oath of them, that they should do according to this promise. 13. Also I shook my lap, and said, So God shake out every man from his house, and from his labour, that performeth not this promise, even thus be he shaken out, and emptied. And all the congregation said, Amen, and praised the LORD. And the people did according to this promise.

Job 21:7. Wherefore do the wicked live, become old, yea, are mighty in power? 8. Their seed is established in their sight with them, and their offspring before their eyes. 9. Their houses *are* safe from fear, neither *is* the rod of God upon them. 10. Their bull gendereth, and faileth not: their cow calveth, and casteth not her calf. 11. They send

forth their little ones like a flock, and their children dance. 12. They take the timbrel and harp, and rejoice at the sound of the organ. 13. They spend their days in wealth, and in a moment go down to the grave. 14. Therefore they say unto God, Depart from us; for we desire not the knowledge of thy ways. 15. What *is* the Almighty, that we should serve him? and what profit should we have if we pray unto him?

Job 27:13. This *is* the portion of a wicked man with God, and the heritage of oppressors, *which* they shall receive of the Almighty. 14. If his children be multiplied, *it is* for the sword: and his offspring shall not be satisfied with bread. 15. Those that remain of him shall be buried in death: and his widows shall not weep. 16. Though he heap up silver as the dust, and prepare raiment as the clay; 17. He may prepare *it*, but the just shall put *it* on, and the innocent shall divide the silver. 18. He buildeth his house as a moth, and as a booth *that* the keeper maketh. 19. The rich man shall lie down, but he shall not be gathered: he openeth his eyes, and he is not. 20. Terrors take hold on him as waters, a tempest stealeth him away in the night. 21. The east wind carrieth him away, and he departeth: and as a storm hurleth him out of his place. 22. For *God* shall cast upon him, and not spare: he would fain flee out of his hand. 23. *Men* shall clap their hands at him, and shall hiss him out of his place.

Job 31:24. If I have made gold my hope, or have said to the fine gold, *Thou art* my confidence; 25. If I rejoiced because my wealth *was* great, and because mine hand had gotten much; 28. This also *were* an iniquity *to be punished by* the judge: for I should have denied the God *that is* above.

Psa. 49:16. Be not thou afraid when one is made rich, when the glory of his house is increased; 17. For when he dieth he shall carry nothing away: his glory shall not descend after him. 18. Though while he lived he blessed his soul:

Psa. 52:1. Why boastest thou thyself in mischief, O mighty man? the goodness of God *endureth* continually. 2. Thy tongue deviseth mischiefs; like a sharp razor, working deceitfully. 3. Thou lovest evil more than good; *and* lying rather than to speak righteousness. 4. Thou lovest all devouring words, O *thou* deceitful tongue. 5. God shall likewise destroy thee for ever, he shall take thee away, and pluck thee out of *thy* dwelling place, and root thee out of the land of the living. 6. The righteous also shall see, and fear, and shall laugh at him: 7. Lo, *this is* the man *that* made not God his strength; but trusted in the abundance of his riches, *and* strengthened himself in his wickedness.

Psa. 73:3. For I was envious at the foolish, *when* I saw the prosperity of the wicked. 4. For *there are* no bands in their death: but their strength *is* firm. 5. They *are* not in trouble *as other* men ; neither are they plagued like *other* men. 6. Therefore pride compasseth them about as a chain; violence covereth them *as* a garment. 7. Their eyes stand out with fatness : they have more than heart could wish. 8. They are corrupt, and speak wickedly *concerning* oppression : they speak loftily. 9. They set their mouth against the heavens, and their tongue walketh through the earth. 10. Therefore his people return hither : and waters of a full *cup* are wrung out to them. 11. And they say, How doth God know ? and is there knowledge in the most High ? 12. Behold, these *are* the ungodly, who prosper in the world; they increase *in* riches. 13. Verily I have cleansed my heart *in* vain, and washed my hands in innocency. 14. For all the day long have I been plagued, and chastened every morning. 15. If I say, I will speak thus ; behold, I should offend *against* the generation of thy children. 16. When I thought to know this, it *was* too painful for me ; 17. Until I went into the sanctuary of God ; *then* understood I their end. 18. Surely thou didst set them in slippery places : thou castedst them down into destruction. 19. How are they *brought* into desolation, as in a moment! they are utterly consumed with terrors. 20. As a dream when *one* awaketh ; *so*, O Lord, when thou awakest, thou shalt despise their image. 21. Thus my heart was grieved, and I was pricked in my reins. 22. So foolish *was* I, and ignorant: I was *as* a beast before thee.

Prov. 14:20. The poor is hated even of his own neighbour : but the rich *hath* many friends.

Prov. 18:11. The rich man's wealth *is* his strong city, and as an high wall in his own conceit. 23. The poor useth intreaties; but the rich answereth roughly.

Prov. 28:11. The rich man *is* wise in his own conceit; but the poor that hath understanding searcheth him out.

Eccl. 5:13. There is a sore evil *which* I have seen under the sun, *namely*, riches kept for the owners thereof to their hurt. 14. But those riches perish by evil travail: and he begetteth a son, and *there is* nothing in his hand.

19. Every man also to whom God hath given riches and wealth, and hath given him power to eat thereof, and to take his portion, and to rejoice in his labour; this *is* the gift of God. 20. For he shall not much remember the days of his life; because God answereth *him* in the 'joy of his heart.

Jer. 5:7. How shall I pardon thee for this ? thy children have forsaken me, and sworn by *them that are* no gods: when I had fed them to the full, they then committed adultery, and assembled themselves by troops in the harlots' houses. 8. They were *as* fed horses in the morning: every one neighed after his neighbour's wife. 9. Shall I not visit for these *things ?* saith the LORD : and

shall not my soul be avenged on such a nation as this ?

27. As a cage is full of birds, so *are* their houses full of deceit : therefore they are become great, and waxen rich. 28. They are waxen fat, they shine : yea, they overpass the deeds of the wicked : they judge not the cause, the cause of the fatherless, yet they prosper ; and the right of the needy do they not judge. 29. Shall I not visit for these *things ?* saith the LORD : shall not my soul be avenged on such a nation as this ?

Jer. 9:23. Thus saith the LORD, . . . let not the rich *man* glory in his riches :

Jer. 17:11. *As* the partridge sitteth *on eggs*, and hatcheth *them* not; *so* he that getteth riches, and not by right, shall leave them in the midst of his days, and at his end shall be a fool.

Jer. 22:13. Woe unto him that buildeth his house by unrighteousness, and his chambers by wrong; *that* useth his neighbour's service without wages, and giveth him not for his work; 14. That saith, I will build me a wide house and large chambers, and cutteth him out windows; and *it is* cieled with cedar, and painted with vermilion. 15. Shalt thou reign, because thou closest *thyself* in cedar ? did not thy father eat and drink, and do judgment and justice, *and* then *it was* well with him ? 16. He judged the cause of the poor and needy; then *it was* well *with him : was* not this to know me ? saith the LORD. 17. But thine eyes and thine heart *are* not but for thy covetousness, and for to shed innocent blood, and for oppression, and for violence, to do *it*. 18. Therefore thus saith the LORD concerning Jehoiakim the son of Josiah king of Judah; They shall not lament for him, *saying*, Ah my brother ! or, Ah sister ! they shall not lament for him, *saying*, Ah lord ! or, Ah his glory ! 19. He shall be buried with the burial of an ass, drawn and cast forth beyond the gates of Jerusalem.

Ezek. 7:19. They shall cast their silver in the streets, and their gold shall be removed : their silver and their gold shall not be able to deliver them in the day of the wrath of the LORD : they shall not satisfy their souls, neither fill their bowels : because it is the stumblingblock of their iniquity. Zeph. 1:18.

Ezek. 28:5. By thy great wisdom *and* by thy traffick hast thou increased thy riches, and thine heart is lifted up because of thy riches :

Amos 6:1. Woe to them *that are* at ease in Zion, and trust in the mountain of Samaria, *which are* named chief of the nations, to whom the house of Israel came ! 2. Pass ye unto Calneh, and see; and from thence go ye to Hamath the great : then go down to Gath of the Philistines : *be they* better than these kingdoms? or their border greater than your border ? 3. Ye that put far away the evil day, and cause the seat of violence to come near ; 4. That lie upon beds of ivory, and stretch themselves upon their couches, and eat the lambs out of the flock, and the calves out of the midst of the stall; 5. That chant to the sound of the viol, *and* invent to themselves instruments of music, like David; 6. That drink wine in bowls, and anoint themselves with the chief ointments: but they are not grieved for the affliction of Joseph.

Mic. 6:12. For the rich men thereof are full of violence, and the inhabitants thereof have spoken lies, and their tongue *is* deceitful in their mouth.

Zeph. 1:18. Neither their silver nor their gold shall be able to deliver them in the day of the LORD'S wrath;

Matt. 19:24. It is easier for a camel to go through the eye of a needle, than for a rich man to enter into the kingdom of God. *v.* 23; Luke 18:24,25.

Mark 10:17. And when he was gone forth into the way, there came one running, and kneeled to him, and asked him, Good Master, what shall I do that I may inherit eternal life? 18. And Jesus said unto him, Why callest thou me good? *there is* none good but one, *that is*, God. 19. Thou knowest the commandments, Do not commit adultery, Do not kill, Do not steal. Do not bear false witness, Defraud not, Honour thy father and mother. 20. And he answered and said unto him, Master, all these have I observed from my youth. 21. Then Jesus beholding him loved him, and said unto him, One thing thou lackest: go thy way, sell whatsoever thou hast, and give to the poor, and thou shalt have treasure in heaven: and come, take up the cross, and follow me. 22. And he was sad at that saying, and went away grieved: for he had great possessions. [Luke 18:22-26.] 23. And Jesus looked round about, and saith unto his disciples, How hardly shall they that have riches enter into the kingdom of God! [Matt. 19:23.] 24. And the disciples were astonished at his words. But Jesus answereth again, and saith unto them, Children, how hard is it for them that trust in riches to enter into the kingdom of God! 25. It is easier for a camel to go through the eye of a. needle, than for a rich man to enter into the kingdom of God. 26. And they were astonished out of measure, saying among themselves, Who then can be saved? 27. And Jesus looking upon them saith, With men *it is* impossible, but not with God: for with God all things are possible.

Luke 6:24. Woe unto you that are rich! for ye have received your consolation. 25. Woe unto you that are full! for ye shall hunger.

Luke 12:15. And he said unto them, Take heed, and beware of covetousness: for a man's life consisteth not in the abundance of the things which he possesseth. 16. And he spake a parable unto them, saying, The ground of a certain rich man brought forth plentifully: 17. And he thought within him-

self, saying, What shall I do, because I have no room where to bestow my fruits? 18. And he said, This will I do: I will pull down my barns, and build greater; and there will I bestow all my fruits and my goods. 19. And I will say to my soul, Soul, thou hast much goods laid up for many years; take thine ease, eat, drink, *and* be merry. 20. But God said unto him, *Thou* fool, this night thy soul shall be required of thee: then whose shall those things be, which thou hast provided? 21. So *is* he that layeth up treasure for himself, and is not rich toward God.

Luke 16:13. No servant can serve two masters: for either he will hate the one, and love the other; or else he will hold to the one, and despise the other. Ye cannot serve God and mammon. 14. And the Pharisees also, who were covetous, heard all these things: and they derided him. 19. There was a certain rich man, which was clothed in purple and fine linen, and fared sumptuously every day: 20. And there was a certain beggar named Lazarus, which was laid at his gate, full of sores, 21. And desiring to be fed with the crumbs which fell from the rich man's table: moreover the dogs came and licked his sores. 22. And it came to pass, that the beggar died, and was carried by the angels into Abraham's bosom: the rich man also died, and was buried; 23. And in hell he lift up his eyes, being in torments, and seeth Abraham afar off, and Lazarus in his bosom. 24. And he cried and said, Father Abraham, have mercy on me, and send Lazarus, that he may dip the tip of his finger in water, and cool my tongue; for I am tormented in this flame. 25. But Abraham said, Son, remember that thou in thy lifetime receivedst thy good things, and likewise Lazarus evil things: but now he is comforted, and thou art tormented. 26. And beside all this, between us and you there is a great gulf fixed: so that they which would pass from hence to you cannot; neither can they pass to us, that *would come* from thence.

1 Tim. 6:17. Charge them that are rich in this world, that they be not highminded, nor trust in uncertain riches, but in the living God, who giveth us richly all things to enjoy; 18. That they do good, that they be rich in good works, ready to distribute, willing to communicate; 19. Laying up in store for themselves a good foundation against the time to come, that they may lay hold on ¹ eternal life. [¹ R. V. the life which is life indeed]

Jas. 1:9. Let the brother of low degree rejoice in that he is exalted: 10. But the rich, in that he is made low: because as the flower of the grass he shall pass away. 11. For the sun is no sooner risen with a burning heat, but it withereth the grass, and the flower thereof falleth, and the grace of the fashion of it perisheth: so also shall the rich man fade away in his ways.

Jas. 5:1. Go to now, *ye* rich men, weep and

howl for your miseries that shall come upon *you*. 2. Your riches are corrupted, and your garments are motheaten. 3. Your gold and silver is cankered; and the rust of them shall be a witness against you, and shall eat your flesh as it were fire. Ye have heaped treasure together for the last days.

See RICHES.

INSTANCES OF: Abraham, Gen. 13:2; 24: 35. Solomon, 1 Kin. 10:23. Hezekiah, 2 Kin. 20:12–18. Job, Job 1:3. Joseph of Arimathæa, Matt. 27:57. Zacchæus, Luke 19:2.

RICHES. Deut. 6:10. And it shall be, when the LORD thy God shall have brought thee into the land which he sware unto thy fathers, to Abraham, to Isaac, and to Jacob, to give thee great and goodly cities, which thou buildedst not, 11. And houses full of all good *things*, which thou filledst not, and wells digged, which thou diggedst not, vineyards and olive trees, which thou plantedst not; when thou shalt have eaten and be full; 12. *Then* beware lest thou forget the LORD, which brought thee forth out of the land of Egypt, from the house of bondage.

Deut. 8:10. When thou hast eaten and art full, then thou shalt bless the LORD thy God for the good land which he hath given thee. 11. Beware that thou forget not the LORD thy God, in not keeping his commandments, and his judgments, and his statutes, which I command thee this day: 12. Lest *when* thou hast eaten and art full, and hast built goodly houses, and dwelt *therein;* 13. And *when* thy herds and thy flocks multiply, and thy silver and thy gold is multiplied, and all that thou hast is multiplied; 14. Then thine heart be lifted up, and thou forget the LORD thy God, which brought thee forth out of the land of Egypt, from the house of bondage; 15. Who led thee through that great and terrible wilderness, *wherein were* fiery serpents, and scorpions, and drought, where *there was* no water; who brought thee forth water out of the rock of flint; 16. Who fed thee in the wilderness with manna, which thy fathers knew not, that he might humble thee, and that he might prove thee, to do thee good at thy latter end; 17. And thou say in thine heart, My power and the might of *mine* hand hath gotten me this wealth. 18. But thou shalt remember the LORD thy God: for *it is* he that giveth thee power to get wealth, that he may establish his covenant which he sware unto thy fathers as *it is* this day.

Deut. 31:20. For when I shall have brought them into the land which I sware unto their fathers, that floweth with milk and honey; and they shall have eaten and filled themselves, and waxen fat; then will they turn unto other gods, and serve them, and provoke me, and break my covenant.

Deut. 32:15. But Jeshurun waxed fat, and kicked: thou art waxen fat, thou art grown thick, thou art covered *with fatness;* then he forsook God *which* made him, and lightly esteemed the Rock of his salvation.

1 Sam. 2:7. The LORD maketh poor, and maketh rich: he bringeth low, and lifteth up.

Psa. 37:16. A little that a righteous man hath *is* better than the riches of many wicked.

Prov. 10:2. Treasures of wickedness profit nothing: 22. The blessing of the LORD, it maketh rich, and he addeth no sorrow with it.

Prov. 11:4. Riches profit not in the day of wrath: but righteousness delivereth from death. 28. He that trusteth in his riches shall fall:

Prov. 13:7. There is that maketh himself rich, yet *hath* nothing: *there is* that maketh himself poor, yet *hath* great riches. 8. The ransom of a man's life *are* his riches: but the poor heareth not rebuke.

Prov. 14:24. The crown of the wise *is* their riches:

Prov. 15:6. In the house of the righteous *is* much treasure: but in the revenues of the wicked is trouble. 16. Better *is* little with the fear of the LORD than great treasure and trouble therewith. 17. Better *is* a dinner of herbs where love is, than a stalled ox and hatred therewith.

Prov. 16:8. Better *is* a little with righteousness than great revenues without right.

Prov. 19:4. Wealth maketh many friends; but the poor is separated from his neighbour.

Prov. 21:6. The getting of treasures by a lying tongue *is* a vanity tossed to and fro of them that seek death.

Prov. 23:4. Labour not to be rich: cease from thine own wisdom. 5. Wilt thou set thine eyes upon that which is not? for *riches* certainly make themselves wings; they fly away as an eagle toward heaven.

Prov. 27:23. Be thou diligent to know the state of thy flocks, *and* look well to thy herds. 24. For riches *are* not for ever: and doth the crown *endure* to every generation?

Prov. 28:8. He that by usury and unjust gain increaseth his substance, he shall gather it for him that will pity the poor. 20. A faithful man shall abound with blessings: but he that maketh haste to be rich shall not be innocent. 22. He that hasteth to be rich *hath* an evil eye, and considereth not that poverty shall come upon him.

Prov. 30:8. Give me neither poverty nor riches; feed me with food convenient for me: 9. Lest I be full, and deny *thee*, and say, Who *is* the LORD? or lest I be poor, and steal, and take the name of my God *in vain*.

Eccl. 5:9. Moreover the profit of the earth is for all: the king *himself* is served by the field. 10. He that loveth silver shall not be satisfied with silver; nor he that loveth abundance with increase: this *is* also vanity. 11. When goods increase, they are increased that eat them: and what good *is there* to the owners thereof, saving the beholding *of them* with their eyes? 12. The sleep of a labouring man *is* sweet, whether he eat little or much: but the abundance of the rich will not suffer him to sleep. 13. There is a sore evil *which* I have seen under the sun, *namely,* riches kept for the owners thereof to their hurt. 14. But those riches perish by evil travail: and he begetteth a son, and *there is* nothing in his hand. 15. As he came forth of his mother's womb, naked shall he return to go as he came, and shall take nothing of his labour, which he may carry away in his hand. 16. And this also *is* a sore evil, *that* in all points as he came, so shall he go: and what profit hath he that hath laboured for the wind? 17. All his days also he eateth in darkness, and *he hath* much sorrow and wrath with his sickness. 18. Behold *that* which I have seen: *it is* good and comely *for one* to eat and to drink, and to enjoy the good of all his labour that he taketh under the sun all the days of his life, which God giveth him: for it *is* his portion. 19. Every man also to whom God hath given riches and wealth, and hath given him power to eat thereof, and to take his portion, and to rejoice in his labour; this *is* the gift of God. 20. For he shall not much remember the days of his life; because God answereth *him* in the joy of his heart.

Eccl. 6:1. There is an evil which I have seen under the sun, and it *is* common among men: 2. A man to whom God hath given riches, wealth, and honour, so that he wanteth nothing for his soul of all that he desireth, yet God giveth him not power to eat thereof, but a stranger eateth it: this *is* vanity, and it *is* an evil disease.

Eccl. 7:11. Wisdom *is* good with an inheritance: and *by it there is* profit to them that see the sun. 12. For wisdom *is* a defence, and money *is* a defence: but the excellency of knowledge *is, that* wisdom giveth life to them that have it.

Eccl. 10:19. A feast is made for laughter, and wine maketh merry: but money answereth all *things.*

Isa. 5:8. Woe unto them that join house to house, *that* lay field to field, till *there be* no place, that they may be placed alone in the midst of the earth!

Jer. 48:36. Therefore mine heart shall sound for Moab like pipes, and mine heart shall sound like pipes for the men of Kirheres: because the riches *that* he hath gotten are perished.

Hos. 12:8. And Ephraim said, Yet I am become rich, I have found me out substance: *in* all my labours they shall find none iniquity in me that *were* sin.

Matt. 6:19. Lay not up for yourselves treasures upon earth, where moth and rust doth corrupt, and where thieves break through and steal: 20. But lay up for yourselves treasures in heaven, where neither moth nor rust doth corrupt, and where thieves do not break through nor steal: 21. For where your treasure is, there will your heart be also.

Matt. 13:22. He also that received seed among the thorns is he that heareth the word; and the care of this world, and the deceitfulness of riches, choke the word and he becometh unfruitful.

Matt. 19:16. And, behold, one came and said unto him, Good Master, what good thing shall I do, that I may have eternal life? 17. And he said unto him, Why callest thou me good? *there is* none good but one, *that is,* God: but if thou wilt enter into life, keep the commandments. 18. He saith unto him, Which? Jesus said, Thou shalt do no murder, Thou shalt not commit adultery, Thou shalt not steal, Thou shalt not bear false witness, 19. Honour thy father and *thy* mother: and, Thou shalt love thy neighbour as thyself. 20. The young man saith unto him, All these things have I kept from my youth up: what lack I yet? 21. Jesus said unto him, If thou wilt be perfect, go *and* sell that thou hast, and give to the poor, and thou shalt have treasure in heaven: and come *and* follow me. 22. But when the young man heard that saying, he went away sorrowful: for he had great possessions. 23. Then said Jesus unto his disciples, Verily I say unto you, That a rich man shall hardly enter into the kingdom of heaven. 24. And again I say unto you, It is easier for a camel to go through the eye of a needle, than for a rich man to enter into the kingdom of God. 25. When his disciples heard *it,* they were exceedingly amazed, saying, Who then can be saved? 26. But Jesus beheld *them,* and said unto them, With men this is impossible; but with God all things are possible. 27. Then answered Peter and said unto him, Behold, we have forsaken all, and followed thee; what shall we have therefore? 28. And Jesus said unto them, Verily I say unto you, That ye which have followed me, in the regeneration when the Son of man shall sit in the throne of his glory, ye also shall sit upon twelve thrones, judging the twelve tribes of Israel. 29. And every one that hath forsaken houses, or brethren, or sisters, or father, or mother, or wife, or children, or lands, for my name's sake, shall receive an hundredfold, and shall inherit everlasting life. Mark 10:17–25; Luke 18:18–25.

Mark 4:19. And the cares of this world, and the deceitfulness of riches, and the lusts of other things entering in, choke the word, and it becometh unfruitful.

Luke 12:15. Beware of covetousness: for a man's life consisteth not in the abundance of the things which he possesseth.

1 Tim. 6:4. He is proud, ... 5. . . . supposing that ¹ gain is godliness: from such withdraw thyself. 6. But godliness with contentment is great gain. 7. For we brought nothing into *this* world, *and it is* certain we can carry nothing out. 8. And having food and raiment let us be therewith content. 9. But they that will be rich fall into tempta-

tion and a snare, and *into* many foolish and hurtful lusts, which drown men in destruction and perdition. 10. For the love of money is the root of all evil: which while some coveted after, they have erred from the faith, and pierced themselves through with many sorrows. 11. But thou, O man of God, flee these things; and follow after righteousness, godliness, faith, love, patience, meekness. 17. Charge them that are rich in this world, that they be not highminded, nor trust in uncertain riches, but in the living God, who giveth us richly all things to enjoy; 18. That they do good, that they be rich in good works, ready to distribute, willing to communicate; 19. Laying up in store for themselves a good foundation against the time to come, that they may lay hold on ²eternal life.

[R. V. ¹ godliness is a way of gain]
² the life which is life indeed]

Jas. 2:6. Do not rich men oppress you, and draw you before the judgment seats? 7. Do not they blaspheme that worthy name by the which ye are called?

Jas. 5:1. Go to now, *ye* rich men, weep and howl for your miseries that shall come upon *you*. 2. Your riches are corrupted, and your garments are motheaten. 3. Your gold and silver is cankered; and the rust of them shall be a witness against you, and shall eat your flesh as it were fire. Ye have heaped treasure together for the last days. 4. Behold, the hire of the labourers who have reaped down your fields, which is of you kept back by fraud, crieth: and the cries of them which have reaped are entered into the ears of the Lord of sabaoth. 5. Ye have lived in pleasure on the earth, and been wanton; ye have nourished your hearts, as in a day of slaughter.

1 John 3:17. But whoso hath this world's good, and seeth his brother have need, and shutteth up his bowels *of compassion* from him, how dwelleth the love of God in him?

FIGURATIVE: Rev. 3:18.

See COVETOUSNESS; RICH.

RIDDLE. Used as a test of wit at Samson's feast, Judg. 14:12-18. By Agur, Prov. 30:15,16,18-31.

See PARABLE; PROVERBS.

RIGHTEOUS. INDEX OF SUB-TOPICS: *Miscellany of Minor Sub-Topics; Contrasted with the Wicked, p* 1166; *Described, p.* 1166; *Promises to, Expressed or Implied, p.* 1172.

MISCELLANY OF MINOR SUB-TOPICS: Compared with: The sun, Judg. 5:31; Matt. 13:43; stars, Dan. 12:3; lights, Matt. 5:14; Phil. 2:15; Mount Zion, Psa. 125:1,2; Lebanon, Hos. 14:5-7; treasure, Ex. 19:5; Psa. 135:4; jewels [*R. V.*, peculiar treasure], Mal. 3:17; gold, Job 23:10; Lam. 4:2; vessels of gold and silver, 2 Tim. 2:20; stones of a crown, Zech. 9:16; lively stones, 1 Pet. 2:5; babes, Matt. 11:25; 1 Pet. 2:2; little children, Matt. 18:3; 1 Cor. 14:20; obedient children, 1 Pet. 1:14; members of the body, 1 Cor. 12:20,27; soldiers, 2 Tim.

2:3,4; runners in a race, 1 Cor. 9:24; Heb. 12:1; wrestlers, 2 Tim. 2:5; good servants, Matt. 25:21; strangers and pilgrims, 1 Pet. 2:11; sheep, Psa. 78:52; Matt. 25:33; John 10; lambs, Isa. 40:11; John 21:15; calves of the stall, Mal. 4:2; lions, Prov. 28:1; Mic. 5:8; eagles, Psa. 103:5; Isa. 40:31; doves, Psa. 68:13; Isa. 60:8; thirsting deer, Psa. 42:1; good fishes, Matt. 13:48; dew and showers, Mic. 5:7; watered gardens, Isa. 58:11; unfailing springs, Isa. 58:11; vines, Song 6:11; Hos. 14:7; branches of a vine, John 15:2,4,5; pomegranates, Song 4:13; good figs, Jer. 24:2-7; lilies, Song 2:2; Hos. 14:5; willows by the water courses, Isa. 44:4; trees planted by rivers, Psa. 1:3; cedars in Lebanon, Psa. 92:12; palm trees, Psa. 92:12; green olive trees, Psa. 52:8; Hos. 14:6; fruitful trees, Psa. 1:3; Jer. 17:8; corn, Hos. 14:7; wheat, Matt. 3:12; 13: 29,30; salt, Matt. 5:13.—*Bible Text-Book.*

Access of, to God, Psa. 31:19,20; Isa. 12:6. Few, Matt. 7:14; 22:14. Relation of, to God, Lev. 20:24-26. Righteous and wicked, circumstances of, contrasted, Job 8; Psa. 17:14,15. See below.

At the judgment, see JUDGMENT, THE. Fellowship of, see FELLOWSHIP. Hatred toward, see PERSECUTIONS. Joy of, see JOY. Perseverance of, see PERSEVERANCE.

CONTRASTED WITH THE WICKED. See WICKED, DESCRIBED; WICKED, CONTRASTED WITH THE RIGHTEOUS.

DESCRIBED: Ex. 33:16. For wherein shall it be known here that I and thy people have found grace in thy sight? *is it* not in that thou goest with us? So shall we be separated, I and thy people, from all the people that *are* upon the face of the earth.

1 Sam. 13:14. But now thy kingdom shall not continue: the LORD hath sought him a man after his own heart, and the LORD hath commanded him *to be* captain over his people, because thou hast not kept *that* which the LORD commanded thee.

Ezra 10:3. Now therefore let us make a covenant with our God to put away all the wives, and such as are born of them, according to the counsel of my lord, and of those that tremble at the commandment of our God;

Psa. 1:1. Blessed *is* the man that walketh not in the counsel of the ungodly, nor standeth in the way of sinners, nor sitteth in the seat of the scornful. 2. But his delight *is* in the law of the LORD; and in his law doth he meditate day and night. 3. And he shall be like a tree planted by the rivers of water, that bringeth forth his fruit in his season; his leaf also shall not wither; and whatsoever he doeth shall prosper.

Psa. 4:3. But know that the LORD hath set apart him that is godly for himself:

Psa. 15:1. LORD, who shall abide in thy tabernacle? who shall dwell in thy holy hill? 2. He that walketh uprightly, and worketh righteousness, and speaketh the truth in his heart. 3. *He that* backbiteth not with his tongue, nor doeth evil to his neighbour, nor taketh up a reproach against his neighbour. 4. In whose eyes a vile person is contemned; but he honoureth them that fear the LORD. *He that* sweareth to *his own* hurt, and changeth not. 5. *He that* putteth not out his money to usury, nor taketh reward against the innocent.

Psa. 24:3. Who shall ascend into the hill of the LORD? or who shall stand in his holy place? 4. He that hath clean hands, and a pure heart; who hath not lifted up his soul unto vanity, nor sworn deceitfully. 5. He shall receive the blessing from the LORD, and righteousness from the God of his salvation.

Psa. 37:26. *He is* ever merciful, and lendeth; and his seed *is* blessed. 30. The mouth of the righteous speaketh wisdom, and his tongue talketh of judgment. 31. The law of his God *is* in his heart; none of his steps shall slide.

Psa. 64:10. The righteous shall be glad in the LORD, and shall trust in him; and all the upright in heart shall glory.

Psa. 84:7. They go from strength to strength, *every one of them* in Zion appeareth before God.

Psa. 87:5. Of Zion it shall be said, This and that man was born in her: and the highest himself shall establish her. 6. The LORD shall count, when he writeth up the people, *that* this man was born there.

Psa. 112:1. Blessed *is* the man *that* feareth the LORD, *that* delighteth greatly in his commandments. 2. His seed shall be mighty upon earth: the generation of the upright shall be blessed. 3. Wealth and riches *shall be* in his house: and his righteousness endureth for ever. 4. Unto the upright there ariseth light in the darkness: *he is* gracious, and full of compassion, and righteous. 5. A good man sheweth favour, and lendeth: he will guide his affairs with discretion. 6. Surely he shall not be moved for ever: the righteous shall be in everlasting remembrance. 7. He shall not be afraid of evil tidings: his heart is fixed, trusting in the LORD. 8. His heart *is* established, he shall not be afraid, until he see *his desire* upon his enemies. 9. He hath dispersed, he hath given to the poor; his righteousness endureth for ever; his horn shall be exalted with honour. 10. The wicked shall see *it*, and be grieved; he shall gnash with his teeth, and melt away: the desire of the wicked shall perish.

Psa. 119:1. Blessed *are* the undefiled in the way, who walk in the law of the LORD. 2. Blessed *are* they that keep his testimonies, *and that* seek him with the whole heart. 3. They also do no iniquity: they walk in his ways.

Prov. 2:9. Then shalt thou understand righteousness, and judgment, and equity; *yea*, every good path. 10. When wisdom entereth into thine heart, and knowledge is pleasant unto thy soul; 11. Discretion shall preserve thee, understanding shall keep

thee: 12. To deliver thee from the way of the evil *man*, from the man that speaketh froward things;

Prov. 4:18. But the path of the just *is* as the shining light, that shineth more and more unto the perfect day.

Prov. 13:5. A righteous *man* hateth lying:

Prov. 25:26. A righteous man falling down before the wicked *is as* a troubled fountain, and a corrupt spring.

Isa. 33:15. He that walketh righteously, and speaketh uprightly; he that despiseth the gain of oppressions, that shaketh his hands from holding of bribes, that stoppeth his ears from hearing of blood, and shutteth his eyes from seeing evil; 16. He shall dwell on high; his place of defence *shall be* the munitions of rocks: bread shall be given him; his waters *shall be* sure.

Isa. 51:1. Hearken to me, ye that follow after righteousness, ye that seek the LORD:

Isa. 54:13. And all thy children *shall be* taught of the LORD; and great *shall be* the peace of thy children.

Isa. 60:21. Thy people also *shall be* all righteous: they shall inherit the land for ever, the branch of my planting, the work of my hands, that I may be glorified.

Isa. 62:12. And they shall call them, The holy people, The redeemed of the LORD: and thou shalt be called, Sought out, A city not forsaken.

Isa. 63:8. For he said, Surely they *are* my people, children *that* will not lie: so he was their Saviour.

Jer. 31:12. Therefore they shall come and sing in the height of Zion, and shall flow together to the goodness of the LORD, for wheat, and for wine, and for oil, and for the young of the flock and of the herd: and their soul shall be as a watered garden; and they shall not sorrow any more at all. 13. Then shall the virgin rejoice in the dance, both young men and old together: for I will turn their mourning into joy, and will comfort them, and make them rejoice from their sorrow. 14. And I will satiate the soul of the priests with fatness, and my people shall be satisfied with my goodness, saith the LORD. 33. After those days, saith the LORD, I will put my law in their inward parts, and write it in their hearts; and will be their God, and they shall be my people. 34. And they shall teach no more every man his neighbour, and every man his brother, saying, Know the LORD: for they shall all know me, from the least of them unto the greatest of them, saith the LORD: for I will forgive their iniquity, and I will remember their sin no more.

Ezek. 18:5. But if a man be just, and do that which is lawful and right, 6. *And* hath not eaten upon the mountains, neither hath lifted up his eyes to the idols of the house of Israel, neither hath defiled his neighbour's wife, neither hath come near to a menstruous woman, 7. And hath not oppressed any, *but* hath restored to the debtor his pledge, hath spoiled none by violence, hath given his bread to the hungry, and hath covered the naked with a garment; 8. He *that* hath not given forth upon usury, neither hath taken any increase, *that* hath withdrawn his hand from iniquity, hath executed true judgment between man and man, 9. Hath walked in my statutes, and hath kept my judgments, to deal truly; he *is* just, he shall surely live, saith the Lord God.

Ezek. 44:9. Thus saith the Lord God; No stranger, uncircumcised in heart, nor uncircumcised in flesh, shall enter into my sanctuary, of any stranger that *is* among the children of Israel.

Zech. 3:2. The Lord rebuke thee, O Satan; even the Lord that hath chosen Jerusalem rebuke thee: *is* not this a brand plucked out of the fire? 7. Thus saith the Lord of hosts: If thou wilt walk in my ways, and if thou wilt keep my charge, then thou shalt also judge my house, and shalt also keep my courts, and I will give thee places to walk among these that stand by. 8. Hear now, O Joshua the high priest, thou, and thy fellows that sit before thee: for they *are* men wondered at:

Matt. 5:3. Blessed *are* the poor in spirit: for their's is the kingdom of heaven. 4. Blessed *are* they that mourn: for they shall be comforted. 5. Blessed *are* the meek: for they shall inherit the earth. 6. Blessed *are* they which do hunger and thirst after righteousness: for they shall be filled. 7. Blessed *are* the merciful: for they shall obtain mercy. 8. Blessed *are* the pure in heart: for they shall see God. 9. Blessed *are* the peacemakers: for they shall be called the children of God. 10. Blessed *are* they which are persecuted for righteousness' sake: for their's is the kingdom of heaven. 13. Ye are the salt of the earth: but if the salt have lost his savour, wherewith shall it be salted? it is thenceforth good for nothing, but to be cast out, and to be trodden under foot of men. 14. Ye are the light of the world. A city that is set on an hill cannot be hid. 15. Neither do men light a candle, and put it under a bushel, but on a candlestick; and it giveth light unto all that are in the house. 16. Let your light so shine before men, that they may see your good works, and glorify your Father which is in heaven.

Matt. 7:16. Ye shall know them by their fruits. Do men gather grapes of thorns, or figs of thistles? 17. Even so every good tree bringeth forth good fruit; but a corrupt tree bringeth forth evil fruit. 18. A good tree cannot bring forth evil fruit, neither *can* a corrupt tree bring forth good fruit. 19. Every tree that bringeth not forth good fruit is hewn down, and cast into the fire. 20. Wherefore by their fruits ye shall know them. 24. Therefore whosoever heareth these sayings of mine, and doeth them, I will liken him unto a wise man, which built his house upon a rock: 25. And the rain de-

scended, and the floods came, and the winds blew, and beat upon that house; and it fell not: for it was founded upon a rock. 26. And every one that heareth these sayings of mine, and doeth them not, shall be likened unto a foolish man, which built his house upon the sand: 27. And the rain descended, and the floods came, and the winds blew, and beat upon that house; and it fell: and great was the fall of it.

Matt. 12:50. For whosoever shall do the will of my Father which is in heaven, the same is my brother, and sister, and mother.

Matt. 13:23. But he that received seed into the good ground is he that heareth the word, and understandeth *it;* which also beareth fruit, and bringeth forth, some an hundredfold, some sixty, some thirty. 38. The field is the world; the good seed are the children of the kingdom; but the tares are the children of the wicked *one;*

Luke 6:45. A good man out of the good treasure of his heart bringeth forth that which is good; . . . for of the abundance of the heart his mouth speaketh.

Luke 18:16. But Jesus called them *unto him*, and said, Suffer little children to come unto me, and forbid them not: for of such is the kingdom of God. 17. Verily I say unto you, Whosoever shall not receive the kingdom of God as a little child shall in no wise enter therein. Matt. 19:14; Mark 10:14,15.

John 3:21. He that doeth truth cometh to the light, that his deeds may be made manifest, that they are wrought in God.

John 8:31. Then said Jesus to those Jews which believed on him, If ye continue in my word, *then* are ye my disciples indeed; 32. And ye shall know the truth, and the truth shall make you free. 39. Jesus saith unto them, If ye were Abraham's children, ye would do the works of Abraham. 42. If God were your Father, ye would love me: for I proceeded forth and came from God; 47. He that is of God heareth God's words: ye therefore hear *them* not, because ye are not of God.

John 10:4. And when he putteth forth his own sheep, he goeth before them, and the sheep follow him: for they know his voice. 5. And a stranger will they not follow, but will flee from him: for they know not the voice of strangers. 27. My sheep hear my voice, and I know them, and they follow me:

John 13:35. By this shall all *men* know that ye are my disciples, if ye have love one to another.

John 15:14. Ye are my friends, if ye do whatsoever I command you.

Acts 2:38. Then Peter said unto them, Repent, and be baptized every one of you in the name of Jesus Christ for the remission of sins, and ye shall receive the gift of the Holy Ghost. 47. The Lord added to the church daily such as should be saved.

Acts 8:36. The eunuch said, See, *here is* water; what doth hinder me to be baptized?

[1] 37. And Philip said, If thou believest with all thine heart, thou mayest. And he answered and said, I believe that Jesus Christ is the Son of God.

[1 Omitted in R. V.]

Acts 10:47. Can any man forbid water, that these should not be baptized, which have received the Holy Ghost as well as we?

Acts 11:23. Who, when he came, and had seen the grace of God, was glad, and exhorted them all, that with purpose of heart they would cleave unto the Lord. 24. For he was a good man, and full of the Holy Ghost and of faith: and much people was added unto the Lord.

Acts 18:7. And he departed thence, and entered into a certain *man's* house, named Justus, *one* that worshipped God, whose house joined hard to the synagogue. 8. And Crispus, the chief ruler of the synagogue, believed on the Lord with all his house; and many of the Corinthians hearing believed, and were baptized.

Rom. 1:6. Among whom are ye also the called of Jesus Christ: 7. To all that be in Rome, beloved of God, called *to be* saints:

Rom. 6:1. What shall we say then? Shall we continue in sin, that grace may abound? 2. God forbid. How shall we, that are dead to sin, live any longer therein? 3. Know ye not, that so many of us as were baptized into Jesus Christ were baptized into his death? 4. Therefore we are buried with him by baptism into death: that like as Christ was raised up from the dead by the glory of the Father, even so we also should walk in newness of life. 5. For if we have been planted together in the likeness of his death, we shall be also *in the likeness* of *his* resurrection: 6. Knowing this, that our old man is crucified with *him,* that the body of sin might be destroyed, that henceforth we should not serve sin. 7. For he that is dead is freed from sin. 8. Now if we be dead with Christ, we believe that we shall also live with him: 9. Knowing that Christ being raised from the dead dieth no more; death hath no more dominion over him. 10. For in that he died, he died unto sin once: but in that he liveth, he liveth unto God. 11. Likewise reckon ye also yourselves to be dead indeed unto sin, but alive unto God through Jesus Christ our Lord. 12. Let not sin therefore reign in your mortal body, that ye should obey it in the lusts thereof. 13. Neither yield ye your members *as* instruments of unrighteousness unto sin: but yield yourselves unto God, as those that are alive from the dead, and your members *as* instruments of righteousness unto God. 14. For sin shall not have dominion over you: for ye are not under the law, but under grace. 15. What then? shall we sin, because we are not under the law, but under grace? God forbid. 16. Know ye not, that to whom ye yield yourselves servants to obey, his servants ye are to whom ye obey; whether of sin unto death, or of obedience

unto righteousness? 17. But God be thanked, that ye were the servants of sin, but ye have obeyed from the heart that form of doctrine which was delivered you. 18. Being then made free from sin, ye became the servants of righteousness. 19. I speak after the manner of men because of the infirmity of your flesh: for as ye have yielded your members servants to uncleanness and to iniquity unto iniquity; even so now yield your members servants to righteousness unto holiness. 20. For when ye were the servants of sin, ye were free from righteousness. 21. What fruit had ye then in those things whereof ye are now ashamed? for the end of those things *is* death. 22. But now being made free from sin, and become servants to God, ye have your fruit unto holiness, and the end everlasting life. 23. For the wages of sin *is* death; but the gift of God *is* eternal life through Jesus Christ our Lord.

Rom. 8:5. For they that are after the flesh do mind the things of the flesh; but they that are after the Spirit the things of the Spirit. 6. For to be carnally minded *is* death; but to be spiritually minded *is* life and peace. 9. But ye are not in the flesh, but in the Spirit, if so be that the Spirit of God dwell in you. Now if any man have not the Spirit of Christ, he is none of his. 14. As many as are led by the Spirit of God, they are the sons of God. 15. For ye have not received the spirit of bondage again to fear; but ye have received the Spirit of adoption, whereby we cry, Abba, Father. 16. The Spirit itself beareth witness with our spirit, that we are the children of God: 29. For whom he did foreknow, he also did predestinate *to be* conformed to the image of his Son, that he might be the firstborn among many brethren. 35. Who shall separate us from the love of Christ? *shall* tribulation, or distress, or persecution, or famine, or nakedness, or peril, or sword? 36. As it is written, For thy sake we are killed all the day long; we are accounted as sheep for the slaughter. 37. Nay, in all these things we are more than conquerors through him that loved us. 38. For I am persuaded, that neither death, nor life, nor angels, nor principalities, nor powers, nor things present, nor things to come, 39. Nor height, nor depth, nor any other creature, shall be able to separate us from the love of God, which is in Christ Jesus our Lord.

Rom. 9:8. The children of the promise are counted for the seed.

Rom. 15:14. I myself also am persuaded of you, my brethren, that ye also are full of goodness, filled with all knowledge, able also to admonish one another.

Rom. 16:19. For your obedience is come abroad unto all *men.* I am glad therefore on your behalf: but yet I would have you wise unto that which is good, and simple concerning evil.

1 Cor. 1:2. Them that are sanctified in

Christ Jesus, called *to be* saints, with all that in every place call upon the name of Jesus Christ our Lord, both their's and our's: 26. For ye see your calling, brethren, how that not many wise men after the flesh, not many mighty, not many noble, *are called:* 27. But God hath chosen the foolish things of the world to confound the wise; and God hath chosen the weak things of the world to confound the things which are mighty; 30. But of him are ye in Christ Jesus, who of God is made unto us wisdom, and righteousness, and sanctification, and redemption:

1 Cor. 2:12. Now we have received, not the spirit of the world, but the spirit which is of God; that we might know the things that are freely given to us of God. 13. Which things also we speak, not in the words which man's wisdom teacheth, but which the Holy Ghost teacheth; comparing spiritual things with spiritual.

1 Cor. 6:9. Know ye not that the unrighteous shall not inherit the kingdom of God? Be not deceived: neither fornicators, nor idolaters, nor adulterers, nor effeminate, nor abusers of themselves with mankind, 10. Nor thieves, nor covetous, nor drunkards, nor revilers, nor extortioners, shall inherit the kingdom of God. 11. And such were some of you: but ye are washed, but ye are sanctified, but ye are justified in the name of the Lord Jesus, and by the Spirit of our God.

1 Cor. 15:48. As *is* the earthy, such *are* they also that are earthy: and as *is* the heavenly, such *are* they also that are heavenly. 49. And as we have borne the image of the earthy, we shall also bear the image of the heavenly.

2 Cor. 1:12. For our rejoicing is this, the testimony of our conscience, that in simplicity and godly sincerity, not with fleshly wisdom, but by the grace of God, we have had our conversation in the world, and more abundantly to you-ward.

2 Cor. 4:1. Therefore seeing we have this ministry, as we have received mercy, we faint not; 2. But have renounced the hidden things of dishonesty, not walking in craftiness, nor handling the word of God deceitfully; but by manifestation of the truth commending ourselves to every man's conscience in the sight of God.

2 Cor. 5:17. Therefore if any man *be* in Christ, *he is* a new creature: old things are passed away; behold, all things are become new. 21. For he hath made him *to be* sin for us, who knew no sin; that we might be made the righteousness of God in him.

Gal. 5:22. But the fruit of the Spirit is love, joy, peace, longsuffering, gentleness, goodness, ₁ faith, 23. Meekness, temperance: against such there is no law. 24. And they that are Christ's have crucified the flesh with the affections and lusts. 25. If we live in the Spirit, let us also walk in the Spirit. 26. Let us not be desirous of vain glory, provoking one another, envying one another.

Eph. 1:1. Paul, an apostle of Jesus Christ by the will of God, to the saints which are at Ephesus, and to the faithful in Christ Jesus: 4. According as he hath chosen us in him before the foundation of the world, that we should be holy and without blame before him in love: 5. Having predestinated us unto the adoption of children by Jesus Christ to himself, according to the good pleasure of his will, 6. To the praise of the glory of his grace, wherein he hath made us accepted in the beloved. 7. In whom we have redemption through his blood, the forgiveness of sins, according to the riches of his grace; [₁ R. V. faithfulness]

Eph. 2:1. And you *hath he quickened*, who were dead in trespasses and sins; 4. But God, who is rich in mercy, for his great love wherewith he loved us, 5. Even when we were dead in sins, hath quickened us together with Christ, (by grace ye are saved;) 6. And hath raised *us* up together, and made *us* sit together in heavenly *places* in Christ Jesus: 10. For we are his workmanship, created in Christ Jesus unto good works, which God hath before ordained that we should walk in them. 13. But now in Christ Jesus ye who sometimes were far off are made nigh by the blood of Christ. 14. For he is our peace, who hath made both one, and hath broken down the middle wall of partition *between us:* 19. Now therefore ye are no more strangers and foreigners, but fellowcitizens with the saints, and of the household of God; 20. And are built upon the foundation of the apostles and prophets, Jesus Christ himself being the chief corner *stone;* 21. In whom all the building fitly framed together groweth unto an holy temple in the Lord: 22. In whom ye also are builded together for an habitation of God through the Spirit.

Eph. 3:17. That Christ may dwell in your hearts by faith; that ye, being rooted and grounded in love, 18. May be able to comprehend with all saints what *is* the breadth, and length, and depth, and height; 19. And to know the love of Christ, which passeth knowledge, that ye might be filled with all the fulness of God.

Eph. 4:13. Till we all come in the unity of the faith, and of the knowledge of the Son of God, unto a perfect man, unto the measure of the stature of the fulness of Christ: 14. That we *henceforth* be no more children, tossed to and fro, and carried about with every wind of doctrine, by the sleight of men, *and* cunning craftiness, whereby they lie in wait to deceive; 15. But speaking the truth in love, may grow up into him in all things, which is the head, *even* Christ: 16. From whom the whole body fitly joined together and compacted by that which every joint supplieth, according to the effectual working in the measure of every part, maketh increase of the body unto the edifying of itself in love. 22. That ye put off concerning the former conversation the old man, which is corrupt according to the deceitful lusts; 23. And be renewed in the spirit of your mind; 24. And that ye put on the new man, which after God is created in righteousness and true holiness. 25. Wherefore putting away lying, speak every man truth with his neighbour: for we are members one of another. 26. Be ye angry, and sin not: let not the sun go down upon your wrath: 27. Neither give place to the devil. 28. Let him that stole steal no more: but rather let him labour, working with *his* hands the thing which is good, that he may have to give to him that needeth. 29. Let no corrupt communication proceed out of your mouth, but that which is good to the use of edifying, that it may minister grace unto the hearers. 30. And grieve not the holy Spirit of God, whereby ye are sealed unto the day of redemption. 31. Let all bitterness, and wrath, and anger, and clamour, and evil speaking, be put away from you, with all malice: 32. And be ye kind one to another, tenderhearted, forgiving one another, even as God for Christ's sake hath forgiven you.

Eph. 5:8. For ye were sometimes darkness, but now *are ye* light in the Lord: walk as children of light:

Phil. 2:15. That ye may be blameless and harmless, the sons of God, without rebuke, in the midst of a crooked and perverse nation, among whom ye shine as lights in the world;

Phil. 3:3. For we are the circumcision, which worship God in the spirit, and rejoice in Christ Jesus, and have no confidence in the flesh. 7. But what things were gain to me, those I counted loss for Christ. 8. Yea doubtless, and I count all things *but* loss for the excellency of the knowledge of Christ Jesus my Lord: for whom I have suffered the loss of all things, and do count them *but* dung, that I may win Christ, 9. And be found in him, not having mine own righteousness, which is of the law, but that which is through the faith of Christ, the righteousness which is of God by faith: 10. That I may know him, and the power of his resurrection, and the fellowship of his sufferings, being made conformable unto his death; 11. If by any means I might attain unto the resurrection of the dead.

Phil. 4:8. Whatsoever things are true, whatsoever things *are* honest, whatsoever things *are* just, whatsoever things *are* pure, whatsoever things *are* lovely, whatsoever things *are* of good report; if *there be* any virtue, and if *there be* any praise, think on these things.

Col. 1:9. For this cause we also, since the day we heard *it*, do not cease to pray for you, and to desire that ye might be filled with the knowledge of his will in all wisdom and spiritual understanding; 10. That ye might walk worthy of the Lord unto all pleasing, being fruitful in every good work, and increasing in the knowl-

edge of God; 11. Strengthened with all might, according to his glorious power, unto all patience and longsuffering with joyfulness; 12. Giving thanks unto the Father, which hath made us meet to be partakers of the inheritance of the saints in light: 13. Who hath delivered us from the power of darkness, and hath translated *us* into the kingdom of his dear Son:

Col. 2:7. Rooted and built up in him, and stablished in the faith, as ye have been taught, abounding therein with thanksgiving.

Col. 3:3. For ye are dead, and your life is hid with Christ in God.

1 Thess. 1:3. Remembering without ceasing your work of faith, and labour of love, and patience of hope in our Lord Jesus Christ, in the sight of God and our Father:

1 Thess. 5:4. But ye, brethren, are not in darkness, that that day should overtake you as a thief. 5. Ye are all the children of light, and the children of the day: we are not of the night, nor of darkness. 27. I charge you by the Lord that this epistle be read unto all the holy brethren.

2 Tim. 2:19. Let every one that nameth the name of Christ depart from iniquity. 21. If a man therefore purge himself from these, he shall be a vessel unto honour, sanctified, and meet for the master's use, *and* prepared unto every good work. 22. Flee also youthful lusts: but follow righteousness, faith, charity, peace, with them that call on the Lord out of a pure heart. 23. But foolish and unlearned questions avoid, knowing that they do gender strifes. 24. And the servant of the Lord must not strive; but be gentle unto all *men*, apt to teach, patient, 25. In meekness instructing those that oppose themselves;

Philem. 5. Hearing of thy love and faith, which thou hast toward the Lord Jesus, and toward all saints; 6. That the communication of thy faith may become effectual by the acknowledging of every good thing which is in you in Christ Jesus.

Heb. 3:1. Holy brethren, partakers of the heavenly calling, 6. But Christ . . . whose house are we, if we hold fast the confidence and the rejoicing of the hope firm unto the end.

1 Pet. 2:5. Ye also, as lively stones, are built up a spiritual house, an holy priesthood, to offer up spiritual sacrifices, acceptable to God by Jesus Christ. 9. But ye *are* a chosen generation, a royal priesthood, an holy nation, a peculiar people; that ye should shew forth the praises of him who hath called you out of darkness into his marvellous light: 10. Which in time past *were* not a people, but *are* now the people of God: which had not obtained mercy, but now have obtained mercy.

1 Pet. 4:1. Forasmuch then as Christ hath suffered for us in the flesh, arm yourselves likewise with the same mind: for he that hath suffered in the flesh hath ceased

from sin; 2. That he no longer should live the rest of *his* time in the flesh to the lusts of men, but to the will of God.

2 Pet. 1:1. Simon Peter, a servant and an apostle of Jesus Christ, to them that have obtained like precious faith with us through the righteousness of God and our Saviour Jesus Christ:

1 John 2:3. And hereby we do know that we know him, if we keep his commandments. 5. But whoso keepeth his word, in him verily is the love of God perfected: hereby know we that we are in him. 6. He that saith he abideth in him ought himself also so to walk, even as he walked. 12. I write unto you, little children, because your sins are forgiven you for his name's sake. 13. I write unto you, fathers, because ye have known him *that is* from the beginning. I write unto you, young men, because ye have overcome the wicked one. I write unto you, little children, because ye have known the Father. 14. I have written unto you, fathers, because ye have known him *that is* from the beginning. I have written unto you, young men, because ye are strong, and the word of God abideth in you, and ye have overcome the wicked one. 15. Love not the world, neither the things *that are* in the world.

1 John 3:2. Beloved, now are we the sons of God, and it doth not yet appear what we shall be: but we know that, when he shall appear, we shall be like him; for we shall see him as he is. 3. And every man that hath this hope in him purifieth himself, even as he is pure. 6. Whosoever abideth in him sinneth not: 7. Little children, let no man deceive you: he that doeth righteousness is righteous, even as he is righteous. 9. Whosoever is born of God doth not commit sin; for his seed remaineth in him: and he cannot sin, because he is born of God. 14. We know that we have passed from death unto life, because we love the brethren. He that loveth not *his* brother abideth in death. 18. My little children, let us not love in word, neither in tongue; but in deed and in truth. 19. And hereby we know that we are of the truth, and shall assure our hearts before him.

1 John 4:7. Beloved, let us love one another: for love is of God; and every one that loveth is born of God, and knoweth God.

1 John 5:1. Whosoever believeth that Jesus is the Christ is born of God; and every one that loveth him that begat loveth him also that is begotten of him.

2 John 9. He that abideth in the doctrine of Christ, he hath both the Father and the Son.

Rev. 1:6. And hath made us kings and priests unto God and his Father;

Rev. 14:4. These are they which were not defiled with women; for they are virgins. These are they which follow the Lamb whithersoever he goeth. These were re-

deemed from among men, *being* the first-fruits unto God and to the Lamb. 5. And in their mouth was found no guile: for they are without fault before the throne of God.

Rev. 17:14. He is Lord of lords, and King of kings: and they that are with him *are* called, and chosen, and faithful.

See Wicked, Described.

PROMISES TO, EXPRESSED OR IMPLIED: Gen. 15:1. After these things the word of the Lord came unto Abram in a vision, saying, Fear not, Abram: I *am* thy shield, *and* thy exceeding great reward.

Gen. 22:17. In blessing I will bless thee, and in multiplying I will multiply thy seed as the stars of the heaven, and as the sand which *is* upon the sea shore; and thy seed shall possess the gate of his enemies;

Ex. 23:22. But if thou shalt indeed obey his voice, and do all that I speak; then I will be an enemy unto thine enemies, and an adversary unto thine adversaries.

Lev. 26:5. And your threshing shall reach unto the vintage, and the vintage shall reach unto the sowing time: and ye shall eat your bread to the full, and dwell in your land safely. 6. And I will give peace in the land, and ye shall lie down, and none shall make *you* afraid: and I will rid evil beasts out of the land, neither shall the sword go through your land. 10. And ye shall eat old store, and bring forth the old because of the new.

Deut. 28:1. And it shall come to pass, if thou shalt hearken diligently unto the voice of the Lord thy God, to observe *and* to do all his commandments which I command thee this day, that the Lord thy God will set thee on high above all nations of the earth: 2. And all these blessings shall come on thee, and overtake thee, if thou shalt hearken unto the voice of the Lord thy God. 3. Blessed *shalt* thou *be* in the city, and blessed *shalt* thou *be* in the field. 4. Blessed *shall be* the fruit of thy body, and the fruit of thy ground, and the fruit of thy cattle, the increase of thy kine, and the flocks of thy sheep. 5. Blessed *shall be* thy basket and thy store. 6. Blessed *shalt* thou *be* when thou comest in, and blessed *shalt* thou *be* when thou goest out. 7. The Lord shall cause thine enemies that rise up against thee to be smitten before thy face: they shall come out against thee one way, and flee before thee seven ways. 8. The Lord shall command the blessing upon thee in thy storehouses, and in all that thou settest thine hand unto; and he shall bless thee in the land which the Lord thy God giveth thee. 9. The Lord shall establish thee an holy people unto himself, as he hath sworn unto thee, if thou shalt keep the commandments of the Lord thy God, and walk in his ways. 10. And all people of the earth shall see that thou art called by the name of the Lord; and they shall be afraid of thee. 11. And the Lord shall make thee plenteous in goods, in the fruit of thy body, and in the fruit of thy cattle, and in the fruit of thy ground, in the land which the LORD sware unto thy fathers to give thee. 12. The LORD shall open unto thee his good treasure, the heaven to give the rain unto thy land in his season, and to bless all the work of thine hand : and thou shalt lend unto many nations, and thou shalt not borrow. 13. And the LORD shall make thee the head, and not the tail; and thou shalt be above only, and thou shalt not be beneath; if that thou hearken unto the commandments of the LORD thy God, which I command thee this day, to observe and to do *them:*

Deut. 33:27. The eternal God *is thy* refuge, and underneath *are* the everlasting arms: and he shall thrust out the enemy from before thee; and shall say, Destroy *them.*

1 Sam. 2:9. He will keep the feet of his saints;

2 Chr. 16:9. For the eyes of the LORD run to and fro throughout the whole earth, to shew himself strong in the behalf of *them* whose heart *is* perfect toward him.

Ezra 8:22. The hand of our God *is* upon all them for good that seek him; but his power and his wrath *is* against all them that forsake him.

Job 5:11. To set up on high those that be low; that those which mourn may be exalted to safety. 12. He disappointeth the devices of the crafty, so that their hands cannot perform *their* enterprise. 13. He taketh the wise in their own craftiness: and the counsel of the froward is carried headlong. 14. They meet with darkness in the daytime, and grope in the noonday as in the night. 15. But he saveth the poor from the sword, from their mouth, and from the hand of the mighty. 16. So the poor hath hope, and iniquity stoppeth her mouth. 17. Behold, happy *is* the man whom God correcteth : therefore despise not thou the chastening of the Almighty: 18. For he maketh sore, and bindeth up: he woundeth, and his hands make whole. 19. He shall deliver thee in six troubles: yea, in seven there shall no evil touch thee. 20. In famine he shall redeem thee from death: and in war from the power of the sword. 21. Thou shalt be hid from the scourge of the tongue: neither shalt thou be afraid of destruction when it cometh. 22. At destruction and famine thou shalt laugh: neither shalt thou be afraid of the beasts of the earth. 23. For thou shalt be in league with the stones of the field : and the beasts of the field shall be at peace with thee. 24. And thou shalt know that thy tabernacle *shall be* in peace; and thou shalt visit thy habitation, and shalt not sin. 25. Thou shalt know also that thy seed *shall be* great, and thine offspring as the grass of the earth. 26. Thou shalt come to *thy* grave in a full age, like as a shock of corn cometh in in his season. 27. Lo this, we have searched it, so it *is;* hear it, and know thou *it* for thy good.

Job 8:4. If thy children have sinned against him, and he have cast them away for their transgression; 5. If thou wouldest seek unto God betimes, and make thy supplication to the Almighty; 6. If thou *wert* pure and upright; surely now he would awake for thee, and make the habitation of thy righteousness prosperous. 7. Though thy beginning was small, yet thy latter end should greatly increase.

20. Behold, God will not cast away a perfect *man*, neither will he help the evil doers: 21. Till he fill thy mouth with laughing, and thy lips with rejoicing.

Job 11:15. For then shalt thou lift up thy face without spot; yea, thou shalt be stedfast, and shalt not fear: 16. Because thou shalt forget *thy* misery, *and* remember *it* as waters *that* pass away: 17. And *thine* age shall be clearer than the noonday; thou shalt shine forth, thou shalt be as the morning. 18. And thou shalt be secure, because there is hope; yea, thou shalt dig *about* thee, *and* thou shalt take thy rest in safety. 19. Also thou shalt lie down, and none shall make *thee* afraid; yea, many shall make suit unto thee. 20. But the eyes of the wicked shall fail, and they shall not escape, and their hope *shall be as* the giving up of the ghost.

Job 22:21. Acquaint now thyself with him, and be at peace: thereby good shall come unto thee. 22. Receive, I pray thee, the law from his mouth, and lay up his words in thine heart. 23. If thou return to the Almighty, thou shalt be built up, thou shalt put away iniquity far from thy tabernacles. 24. Then shalt thou lay up gold as dust, and the *gold* of Ophir as the stones of the brooks. 25. Yea, the Almighty shall be thy defence, and thou shalt have plenty of silver. 26. For then shalt thou have thy delight in the Almighty, and shalt lift up thy face unto God. 27. Thou shalt make thy prayer unto him, and he shall hear thee, and thou shalt pay thy vows. 28. Thou shalt also decree a thing, and it shall be established unto thee: and the light shall shine upon thy ways. 29. When *men* are cast down, then thou shalt say, *There is* lifting up; and he shall save the humble person. 30. He shall deliver the island of the innocent: and it is delivered by the pureness of thine hands.

Job 36:7. He withdraweth not his eyes from the righteous: but with kings *are they* on the throne; yea, he doth establish them for ever, and they are exalted. 8. And if *they* be bound in fetters, *and* be holden in cords of affliction; 9. Then he sheweth them their work, and their transgressions that they have exceeded. 10. He openeth also their ear to discipline, and commandeth that they return from iniquity. 11. If they obey and serve *him*, they shall spend their days in prosperity, and their years in pleasures. 12. But if they obey not, they shall perish by the sword, and they shall die without knowledge.

Psa. 4:3. But know that the Lord hath set apart him that is godly for himself: the Lord will hear when I call unto him.

Psa. 5:12. For thou, Lord, wilt bless the righteous; with favour wilt thou compass him as *with* a shield.

Psa. 15:2. He that walketh uprightly, and worketh righteousness, and speaketh the truth in his heart. 3. *He that* backbiteth not with his tongue, nor doeth evil to his neighbour, nor taketh up a reproach against his neighbour. 4. In whose eyes a vile person is contemned; but he honoureth them that fear the Lord. *He that* sweareth to *his own* hurt, and changeth not. 5. *He that* putteth not out his money to usury, nor taketh reward against the innocent. He that doeth these *things* shall never be moved.

Psa. 23:6. Surely goodness and mercy shall follow me all the days of my life: and I will dwell in the house of the Lord for ever.

Psa. 25:10. All the paths of the Lord *are* mercy and truth unto such as keep his covenant and his testimonies. 11. For thy name's sake, O Lord, pardon mine iniquity; for it *is* great. 12. What man *is* he that feareth the Lord? him shall he teach in the way *that* he shall choose. 13. His soul shall dwell at ease; and his seed shall inherit the earth. 14. The secret of the Lord *is* with them that fear him; and he will shew them his covenant.

Psa. 28:8. The Lord *is* their strength, and he *is* the saving strength of his anointed.

Psa. 29:11. The Lord will give strength unto his people; the Lord will bless his people with peace.

Psa. 32:6. For this shall every one that is godly pray unto thee in a time when thou mayest be found: surely in the floods of great waters they shall not come nigh unto him. 7. Thou *art* my hiding place; thou shalt preserve me from trouble; thou shalt compass me about with songs of deliverance. 8. I will instruct thee and teach thee in the way which thou shalt go: I will guide thee with mine eye. 10. Many sorrows *shall be* to the wicked: but he that trusteth in the Lord, mercy shall compass him about.

Psa. 33:18. Behold, the eye of the Lord *is* upon them that fear him, upon them that hope in his mercy; 19. To deliver their soul from death, and to keep them alive in famine.

Psa. 34:9. O fear the Lord, ye his saints: for *there is* no want to them that fear him. 10. The young lions do lack, and suffer hunger: but they that seek the Lord shall not want any good *thing.* 15. The eyes of the Lord *are* upon the righteous, and his ears *are* open unto their cry. 17. *The righteous* cry, and the Lord heareth, and delivereth them out of all their troubles.

Psa. 37:3. Trust in the Lord, and do good; *so* shalt thou dwell in the land, and verily thou shalt be fed.

4. Delight thyself also in the Lord; and he shall give thee the desires of thine heart.

5. Commit thy way unto the Lord; trust also in him; and he shall bring *it* to pass.

9. For evil doers shall be cut off: but those that wait upon the Lord, they shall inherit the earth.

18. The Lord knoweth the days of the upright: and their inheritance shall be for ever.

23. The steps of a *good* man are ordered by the Lord: and he delighteth in his way. 24. Though he fall, he shall not be utterly cast down: for the Lord upholdeth *him with* his hand. 25. I have been young, and *now* am old; yet have I not seen the righteous forsaken, nor his seed begging bread. 26. *He is* ever merciful, and lendeth; and his seed *is* blessed.

27. Depart from evil and do good; and dwell for evermore. 28. For the Lord loveth judgment, and forsaketh not his saints; they are preserved for ever: but the seed of the wicked shall be cut off. 29. The righteous shall inherit the land, and dwell therein for ever. 34. Wait on the Lord, and keep his way, and he shall exalt thee to inherit the land: when the wicked are cut off, thou shalt see *it.*

Psa. 41:1. Blessed *is* he that considereth the poor: the Lord will deliver him in time of trouble. 2. The Lord will preserve him, and keep him alive; *and* he shall be blessed upon the earth: and thou wilt not deliver him unto the will of his enemies.

Psa. 50:15. Call upon me in the day of trouble: I will deliver thee, and thou shalt glorify me.

Psa. 55:22. Cast thy burden upon the Lord, and he shall sustain thee: he shall never suffer the righteous to be moved.

Psa. 58:11. So that a man shall say, Verily *there is* a reward for the righteous: verily he is a God that judgeth in the earth.

Psa. 62:8. Trust in him at all times; ye people, pour out your heart before him: God *is* a refuge for us.

Psa. 65:4. Blessed *is the man whom* thou choosest, and causest to approach *unto thee, that* he may dwell in thy courts: we shall be satisfied with the goodness of thy house, *even* of thy holy temple.

Psa. 73:24. Thou shalt guide me with thy counsel, and afterward receive me *to* glory.

Psa. 81:10. I *am* the Lord thy God, which brought thee out of the land of Egypt: open thy mouth wide, and I will fill it.

Psa. 84:11. For the Lord God *is* a sun and shield: the Lord will give grace and glory: no good *thing* will he withhold from them that walk uprightly.

Psa. 85:9. Surely his salvation *is* nigh them that fear him; that glory may dwell in our land.

Psa. 91:1. He that dwelleth in the secret place of the most High shall abide under the shadow of the Almighty.

3. Surely he shall deliver thee from the

snare of the fowler, *and* from the noisome pestilence. 4. He shall cover thee with his feathers, and under his wings shalt thou trust: his truth *shall be thy* shield and buckler. 5. Thou shalt not be afraid for the terror by night; *nor* for the arrow *that* flieth by day; 6. *Nor* for the pestilence *that* walketh in darkness; *nor* for the destruction *that* wasteth at noonday. 7. A thousand shall fall at thy side, and ten thousand at thy right hand; *but* it shall not come nigh thee. 9. Because thou hast made the LORD, *which is* my refuge, *even* the most High, thy habitation; 10. There shall no evil befall thee, neither shall any plague come nigh thy dwelling. 11. For he shall give his angels charge over thee, to keep thee in all thy ways. 12. They shall bear thee up in *their* hands, lest thou dash thy foot against a stone.

Psa. 94:17. Unless the LORD *had been* my help, my soul had almost dwelt in silence. 18. When I said, My foot slippeth; thy mercy, O LORD, held me up.

Psa. 97:10. He preserveth the souls of his saints; he delivereth them out of the hand of the wicked. 11. Light is sown for the righteous, and gladness for the upright in heart.

Psa. 111:5. He hath given meat unto them that fear him: he will ever be mindful of his covenant.

Psa. 112:6. Surely he shall not be moved for ever: the righteous shall be in everlasting remembrance.

Psa. 121:3. He will not suffer thy foot to be moved: he that keepeth thee will not slumber. 4. Behold, he that keepeth Israel shall neither slumber nor sleep. 5. The LORD *is* thy keeper: the LORD *is* thy shade upon thy right hand. 6. The sun shall not smite thee by day, nor the moon by night. 7. The LORD shall preserve thee from all evil: he shall preserve thy soul. 8. The LORD shall preserve thy going out and thy coming in from this time forth, and even for evermore.

Psa. 125:1. They that trust in the LORD *shall be* as mount Zion, *which* cannot be removed, *but* abideth for ever. 2. *As* the mountains *are* round about Jerusalem, so the LORD *is* round about his people from henceforth even for ever. 3. For the rod of the wicked shall not rest upon the lot of the righteous; lest the righteous put forth their hands unto iniquity.

Psa. 128:1. Blessed *is* every one that feareth the LORD; that walketh in his ways. 2. For thou shalt eat the labour of thine hands: happy *shalt* thou *be*, and *it shall be* well with thee. 3. Thy wife *shall be* as a fruitful vine by the sides of thine house: thy children like olive plants round about thy table. 4. Behold, that thus shall the man be blessed that feareth the LORD. 5. The LORD shall bless thee out of Zion: and thou shalt see the good of Jerusalem all the days of thy life. 6. Yea, thou shalt see thy children's children, *and* peace upon Israel.

Psa. 145:18. The LORD *is* nigh unto all them that call upon him, to all that call upon him in truth. 19. He will fulfil the desire of them that fear him: he also will hear their cry, and will save them. 20. The LORD preserveth all them that love him: but all the wicked will he destroy. 21. My mouth shall speak the praise of the LORD: and let all flesh bless his holy name for ever and ever.

Prov. 1:33. But whoso hearkeneth unto me shall dwell safely, and shall be quiet from fear of evil.

Prov. 2:21. The upright shall dwell in the land, and the perfect shall remain in it.

Prov. 3:1. My son, forget not my law; but let thine heart keep my commandments: 2. For length of days, and long life, and peace, shall they add to thee. 3. Let not mercy and truth forsake thee: bind them about thy neck; write them upon the table of thine heart: 4. So shalt thou find favour and good understanding in the sight of God and man.

5. Trust in the LORD with all thine heart; and lean not unto thine own understanding. 6. In all thy ways acknowledge him, and he shall direct thy paths.

7. Be not wise in thine own eyes: fear the LORD, and depart from evil. 8. It shall be health to thy navel, and marrow to thy bones. 9. Honour the LORD with thy substance, and with the firstfruits of all thine increase: 10. So shall thy barns be filled with plenty, and thy presses shall burst out with new wine.

25. Be not afraid of sudden fear, neither of the desolation of the wicked, when it cometh. 26. For the LORD shall be thy confidence, and shall keep thy foot from being taken.

Prov. 10:3. The LORD will not suffer the soul of the righteous to famish: but he casteth away the substance of the wicked.

Prov. 12:2. A good *man* obtaineth favour of the LORD:

Prov. 14:26. His children shall have a place of refuge.

Prov. 15:29. The LORD *is* far from the wicked: but he heareth the prayer of the righteous.

Prov. 16:7. When a man's ways please the LORD, he maketh even his enemies to be at peace with him.

Prov. 21:21. He that followeth after righteousness and mercy findeth life, righteousness, and honour.

Prov. 28:25. He that putteth his trust in the LORD shall be made fat.

Prov. 29:25. Whoso putteth his trust in the LORD shall be safe.

Eccl. 7:18. *It is* good that thou shouldest take hold of this; yea, also from this withdraw not thine hand: for he that feareth God shall come forth of them all.

Eccl. 8:5. Whoso keepeth the commandment shall feel no evil thing: and a wise man's heart discerneth both time and judgment.

Isa. 4:5. And the LORD will create upon every dwelling place of mount Zion, and upon her assemblies, a cloud and smoke by day, and the shining of a flaming fire by night: for upon all the glory *shall be* a defence. 6. And there shall be a tabernacle for a shadow in the daytime from the heat, and for a place of refuge, and for a covert from storm and from rain.

Isa. 11:6. The wolf also shall dwell with the lamb, and the leopard shall lie down with the kid; and the calf and the young lion and the fatling together: and a little child shall lead them. 7. And the cow and the bear shall feed; their young ones shall lie down together: and the lion shall eat straw like the ox. 8. And the sucking child shall play on the hole of the asp, and the weaned child shall put his hand on the cockatrice' den. 9. They shall not hurt nor destroy in all my holy mountain: for the earth shall be full of the knowledge of the LORD, as the waters cover the sea.

Isa. 25:8. He will swallow up death in victory; and the Lord GOD will wipe away tears from off all faces; and the rebuke of his people shall he take away from off all the earth: for the LORD hath spoken *it*.

Isa. 26:3. Thou wilt keep *him* in perfect peace, *whose* mind *is* stayed *on thee:* because he trusteth in thee.

Isa. 33:16. He shall dwell on high: his place of defence *shall be* the munitions of rocks: bread shall be given him; his waters *shall be* sure. 21. But there the glorious LORD *will be* unto us a place of broad rivers *and* streams: wherein shall go no galley with oars, neither shall gallant ship pass thereby. 22. For the LORD *is* our judge, the LORD *is* our lawgiver, the LORD *is* our King; he will save us. 24. And the inhabitant shall not say, I am sick: the people that dwell therein *shall be* forgiven *their* iniquity.

Isa. 35:10. And the ransomed of the LORD shall return, and come to Zion with songs and everlasting joy upon their heads: they shall obtain joy and gladness, and sorrow and sighing shall flee away.

Isa. 40:10. Behold, the Lord GOD will come with strong *hand*, and his arm shall rule for him: behold, his reward *is* with him, and his work before him. 11. He shall feed his flock like a shepherd: he shall gather the lambs with his arm, and carry *them* in his bosom, *and* shall gently lead those that are with young. 29. He giveth power to the faint; and to *them that have* no might he increaseth strength. 31. But they that wait upon the LORD shall renew *their* strength; they shall mount up with wings as eagles; they shall run, and not be weary; *and* they shall walk, and not faint.

Isa. 41:10. Fear thou not; for I *am* with thee: be not dismayed; for I *am* thy God: I will strengthen thee; yea, I will help thee; yea, I will uphold thee with the

right hand of my righteousness. 11. Behold, all they that were incensed against thee shall be ashamed and confounded: they shall be as nothing; and they that strive with thee shall perish. 13. For I the LORD thy God will hold thy right hand, saying unto thee, Fear not; I will help thee.

Isa. 43:2. When thou passest through the waters, I *will be* with thee; and through the rivers, they shall not overflow thee: when thou walkest through the fire, thou shalt not be burned; neither shall the flame kindle upon thee.

Isa. 44:2. Thus saith the LORD that made thee, and formed thee from the womb, *which* will help thee; Fear not, O Jacob, my servant; and thou, Jesurun, whom I have chosen. 3. For I will pour water upon him that is thirsty, and floods upon the dry ground: I will pour my spirit upon thy seed, and my blessing upon thine offspring:

Isa. 49:9. That thou mayest say to the prisoners, Go forth; to them that *are* in darkness, Shew yourselves. They shall feed in the ways, and their pastures *shall be* in all high places. 10. They shall not hunger nor thirst; neither shall the heat nor sun smite them: for he that hath mercy on them shall lead them, even by the springs of water shall he guide them. 11. And I will make all my mountains a way, and my highways shall be exalted. 12. Behold, these shall come from far: and, lo, these from the north and from the west; and these from the land of Sinim.

Isa. 50:7. For the Lord GOD will help me; therefore shall I not be confounded: therefore have I set my face like a flint, and I know that I shall not be ashamed. 8. *He is* near that justifieth me; who will contend with me? let us stand together: who *is* mine adversary? let him come near to me. 9. Behold, the Lord GOD will help me; who *is* he *that* shall condemn me? lo, they all shall wax old as a garment; the moth shall eat them up.

Isa. 51:11. Therefore the redeemed of the LORD shall return, and come with singing unto Zion; and everlasting joy *shall be* upon their head: they shall obtain gladness and joy; and sorrow and mourning shall flee away.

Isa. 54:14. In righteousness shalt thou be established: thou shalt be far from oppression; for thou shalt not fear: and from terror; for it shall not come near thee. 17. No weapon that is formed against thee shall prosper; and every tongue *that* shall rise against thee in judgment thou shalt condemn. This *is* the heritage of the servants of the LORD, and their righteousness *is* of me, saith the LORD. *v*. 1-16.

Isa. 56:2. Blessed *is* the man *that* doeth this, and the son of man *that* layeth hold on it; that keepeth the sabbath from polluting it, and keepeth his hand from doing any evil. 3. Neither let the son of the stranger, that hath joined himself to the Lord, speak, saying, The Lord hath utterly separated me from his people: neither let the eunuch say, Behold, I *am* a dry tree. 4. For thus saith the Lord unto the eunuchs that keep my sabbaths, and choose *the things* that please me, and take hold of my covenant; 5. Even unto them will I give in mine house and within my walls a place and a name better than of sons and of daughters: I will give them an everlasting name, that shall not be cut off. 6. Also the sons of the stranger, that join themselves to the Lord, to serve him, and to love the name of the Lord, to be his servants, every one that keepeth the sabbath from polluting it, and taketh hold of my covenant; 7. Even them will I bring to my holy mountain, and make them joyful in my house of prayer: their burnt offerings and their sacrifices *shall be* accepted upon mine altar; for mine house shall be called an house of prayer for all people. 8. The Lord God which gathereth the outcasts of Israel saith, Yet will I gather *others* to him, beside those that are gathered unto him.

Isa. 57:1. The righteous perisheth, and no man layeth *it* to heart: and merciful men *are* taken away, none considering that the righteous is taken away from the evil *to come.* 2. He shall enter into peace: they shall rest *in* their beds, *each one* walking in his uprightness.

Isa. 58:8. Then shall thy light break forth as the morning, and thine health shall spring forth speedily: and thy righteousness shall go before thee; the glory of the Lord shall be thy rereward. 9. Then shalt thou call, and the Lord shall answer; thou shalt cry, and he shall say, Here I *am.* If thou take away from the midst of thee the yoke, the putting forth of the finger, and speaking vanity; 10. And *if* thou draw out thy soul to the hungry, and satisfy the afflicted soul; then shall thy light rise in obscurity, and thy darkness *be* as the noonday; 11. And the Lord shall guide thee continually, and satisfy thy soul in drought, and make fat thy bones: and thou shalt be like a watered garden, and like a spring of water, whose waters fail not. 12. And *they that shall be* of thee shall build the old waste places: thou shalt raise up the foundations of many generations; and thou shalt be called, The repairer of the breach, The restorer of paths to dwell in. 13. If thou turn away thy foot from the sabbath, *from* doing thy pleasure on my holy day; and call the sabbath a delight, the holy of the Lord, honourable; and shalt honour him, not doing thine own ways, nor finding thine own pleasure, nor speaking *thine own* words: 14. Then shalt thou delight thyself in the Lord; and I will cause thee to ride upon the high places of the earth, and feed thee with the heritage of Jacob thy

father: for the mouth of the Lord hath spoken *it.*

Isa. 59:20. And the Redeemer shall come to Zion, and unto them that turn from transgression in Jacob, saith the Lord. 21. As for me, this *is* my covenant with them, saith the Lord; My spirit that *is* upon thee, and my words which I have put in thy mouth, shall not depart out of thy mouth, nor out of the mouth of thy seed, nor out of the mouth of thy seed's seed, saith the Lord, from henceforth and for ever.

Isa. 64:4. For since the beginning of the world *men* have not heard, nor perceived by the ear, neither hath the eye seen, O God, beside thee, *what* he hath prepared for him that waiteth for him.

Isa. 65:13. Therefore thus saith the Lord God, Behold, my servants shall eat, but ye shall be hungry: behold, my servants shall drink, but ye shall be thirsty: behold, my servants shall rejoice, but ye shall be ashamed: 14. Behold, my servants shall sing for joy of heart, but ye shall cry for sorrow of heart, and shall howl for vexation of spirit.

17. For, behold, I create new heavens and a new earth: and the former shall not be remembered, nor come into mind. 18. But be ye glad and rejoice for ever *in that* which I create: for, behold, I create Jerusalem a rejoicing, and her people a joy. 19. And I will rejoice in Jerusalem, and joy in my people: and the voice of weeping shall be no more heard in her, nor the voice of crying. 20. There shall be no more thence an infant of days, nor an old man that hath not filled his days: for the child shall die an hundred years old; but the sinner *being* an hundred years old shall be accursed. 21. And they shall build houses, and inhabit *them;* and they shall plant vineyards, and eat the fruit of them. 22. They shall not build, and another inhabit; they shall not plant, and another eat: for as the days of a tree *are* the days of my people, and mine elect shall long enjoy the work of their hands. 23. They shall not labour in vain, nor bring forth for trouble; for they *are* the seed of the blessed of the Lord, and their offspring with them. 24. And it shall come to pass, that before they call, I will answer; and while they are yet speaking, I will hear. 25. The wolf and the lamb shall feed together, and the lion shall eat straw like the bullock: and dust *shall be* the serpent's meat. They shall not hurt nor destroy in all my holy mountain, saith the Lord.

Isa. 66:13. As one whom his mother comforteth, so will I comfort you; and ye shall be comforted in Jerusalem. 14. And when ye see *this,* your heart shall rejoice, and your bones shall flourish like an herb: and the hand of the Lord shall be known toward his servants, and *his* indignation toward his enemies.

Jer. 17:7. Blessed *is* the man that trusteth in the Lord, and whose hope the Lord is. 8. For he shall be as a tree planted by the waters, and *that* spreadeth out her roots by the river, and shall not see when heat cometh, but her leaf shall be green; and shall not be careful in the year of drought, neither shall cease from yielding fruit.

Ezek. 18:5. But if a man be just, and do that which is lawful and right, 6. *And* hath not eaten upon the mountains, neither hath lifted up his eyes to the idols of the house of Israel, neither hath defiled his neighbour's wife, neither hath come near to a menstruous woman, 7. And hath not opposed any, *but* hath restored to the debtor his pledge, hath spoiled none by violence, hath given his bread to the hungry, and hath covered the naked with a garment; 8. He *that* hath not given forth upon usury, neither hath taken any increase, *that* hath withdrawn his hand from iniquity, hath executed true judgment between man and man, 9. Hath walked in my statutes, and hath kept my judgments, to deal truly; he *is* just, he shall surely live, saith the Lord God. 19. Yet say ye, Why? doth not the son bear the iniquity of the father? When the son hath done that which is lawful and right, *and* hath kept all my statutes, and hath done them, he shall surely live. 20. The soul that sinneth, it shall die. The son shall not bear the iniquity of the father, neither shall the father bear the iniquity of the son: the righteousness of the righteous shall be upon him, and the wickedness of the wicked shall be upon him.

Ezek. 34:11. For thus saith the Lord God; Behold, I, *even* I, will both search my sheep, and seek them out. 12. As a shepherd seeketh out his flock in the day that he is among his sheep *that are* scattered; so will I seek out my sheep, and will deliver them out of all places where they have been scattered in the cloudy and dark day. 13. And I will bring them out from the people, and gather them from the countries, and will bring them to their own land, and feed them upon the mountains of Israel by the rivers, and in all the inhabited places of the country. 14. I will feed them in a good pasture, and upon the high mountains of Israel shall their fold be: there shall they lie in a good fold, and *in* a fat pasture shall they feed upon the mountains of Israel. 15. I will feed my flock, and I will cause them to lie down, saith the Lord God. 16. I will seek that which was lost, and bring again that which was driven away, and will bind up *that which was* broken, and will strengthen that which was sick: but I will destroy the fat and the strong; I will feed them with judgment. 17. And *as for* you, O my flock, thus said the Lord God; Behold, I judge between cattle and cattle, between the rams and the he goats. 22. Therefore will I save my flock, and they

shall no more be a prey; and I will judge between cattle and cattle. 23. And I will set up one shepherd over them, and he shall feed them, *even* my servant David; he shall feed them, and he shall be their shepherd. 24. And I the Lord will be their God, and my servant David a prince among them; I the Lord have spoken *it*. 25. And I will make with them a covenant of peace, and will cause the evil beasts to cease out of the land: and they shall dwell safely in the wilderness, and sleep in the woods. 26. And I will make them and the places round about my hill a blessing; and I will cause the shower to come down in his season; there shall be showers of blessing. 27. And the tree of the field shall yield her fruit, and the earth shall yield her increase, and they shall be safe in their land, and shall know that I *am* the Lord, when I have broken the bands of their yoke, and delivered them out of the hand of those that served themselves of them. 28. And they shall no more be a prey to the heathen, neither shall the beast of the land devour them; but they shall dwell safely, and none shall make *them* afraid. 29. And I will raise up for them a plant of renown, and they shall be no more consumed with hunger in the land, neither bear the shame of the heathen any more. 30. Thus shall they know that I the Lord their God *am* with them, and *that* they, *even* the house of Israel, *are* my people, saith the Lord God. 31. And ye my flock, the flock of my pasture, *are* men, *and* I *am* your God, saith the Lord God.

Dan. 12:1. And at that time shall Michael stand up, the great prince which standeth for the children of thy people: and there shall be a time of trouble, such as never was since there was a nation *even* to that same time: and at that time thy people shall be delivered, every one that shall be found written in the book. 2. And many of them that sleep in the dust of the earth shall awake, some to everlasting life, and some to shame *and* everlasting contempt. 3. And they that be wise shall shine as the brightness of the firmament; and they that turn many to righteousness as the stars for ever and ever.

Hos. 6:3. Then shall we know, *if* we follow on to know the Lord: his going forth is prepared as the morning; and he shall come unto us as the rain, as the latter 1 *and* former rain unto the earth.   [1 R. V. rain that watereth]

Nah. 1:7. The Lord *is* good, a strong hold in the day of trouble; and he knoweth them that trust in him.

Hag. 1:13. Then spake Haggai the Lord's messenger in the Lord's message unto the people, saying, I *am* with you, saith the Lord.

Hag. 2:4. Yet now be strong, O Zerubbabel, saith the Lord; and be strong, O Joshua, son of Josedech, the high priest; and be strong, all ye people of the land, saith the Lord, and work: for I *am* with you, saith the LORD of hosts: 5. *According to* the word that I covenanted with you when ye came out of Egypt, so my spirit remaineth among you: fear ye not.

Zech. 3:7. Thus saith the LORD of hosts; If thou wilt walk in my ways, and if thou wilt keep my charge, then thou shalt also judge my house, and shalt also keep my courts, and I will give thee places to walk among these that stand by.

Mal. 3:16. Then they that feared the LORD spake often one to another: and the LORD hearkened, and heard *it*, and a book of remembrance was written before him for them that feared the LORD, and that thought upon his name. 17. And they shall be mine, saith the LORD of hosts, in that day when I make up my jewels; and I will spare them, as a man spareth his own son that serveth him. 18. Then shall ye return, and discern between the righteous and the wicked, between him that serveth God and him that serveth him not.

Mal. 4:2. But unto you that fear my name shall the Sun of righteousness arise with healing in his wings; and ye shall go forth, and grow up as calves of the stall. 3. And ye shall tread down the wicked; for they shall be ashes under the soles of your feet in the day that I shall do *this*, saith the LORD of hosts.

Matt. 5:3. Blessed *are* the poor in spirit: for their's is the kingdom of heaven.

4. Blessed *are* they that mourn: for they shall be comforted.

5. Blessed *are* the meek: for they shall inherit the earth.

6. Blessed *are* they which do hunger and thirst after righteousness: for they shall be filled.

7. Blessed *are* the merciful: for they shall obtain mercy.

8. Blessed *are* the pure in heart: for they shall see God.

9. Blessed *are* the peacemakers: for they shall be called the children of God.

10. Blessed *are* they which are persecuted for righteousness' sake: for their's is the kingdom of heaven.

11. Blessed are ye, when *men* shall revile you, and persecute *you*, and shall say all manner of evil against you falsely, for my sake.

12. Rejoice, and be exceeding glad: for great *is* your reward in heaven: for so persecuted they the prophets which were before you.

Matt. 7:7. Ask, and it shall be given you; seek, and ye shall find; knock, and it shall be opened unto you: 8. For every one that asketh receiveth; and he that seeketh findeth; and to him that knocketh it shall be opened. Luke 11:9,10.

Matt. 8:11. I say unto you, That many shall come from the east and west, and shall sit down with Abraham, and Isaac, and Jacob, in the kingdom of heaven.

Matt. 10:28. Fear not them which kill the body, but are not able to kill the soul: but rather fear him which is able to destroy both soul and body in hell. 29. Are not two sparrows sold for a farthing? and one of them shall not fall on the ground without your Father. 30. But the very hairs of your head are all numbered. 31. Fear ye not therefore, ye are of more value than many sparrows. 32. Whosoever therefore shall confess me before men, him will I confess also before my Father which is in heaven.

Matt. 13:43. Then shall the righteous shine forth as the sun in the kingdom of their Father.

Matt. 18:10. Take heed that ye despise not one of these little ones; for I say unto you, That in heaven their angels do always behold the face of my Father which is in heaven. 19. If two of you shall agree on earth as touching any thing that they shall ask, it shall be done for them of my Father which is in heaven. 20. For where two or three are gathered together in my name, there am I in the midst of them.

Matt. 24:21. Then shall be great tribulation, such as was not since the beginning of the world to this time, no, nor ever shall be. 22. And except those days should be shortened, there should no flesh be saved: but for the elect's sake those days shall be shortened.

Matt. 25:21. His lord said unto him, Well done, *thou* good and faithful servant: thou hast been faithful over a few things, I will make thee ruler over many things: enter thou into the joy of thy lord. Luke 19:16–21.

33. And he shall set the sheep on his right hand, but the goats on the left. 34. Then shall the King say unto them on his right hand, Come, ye blessed of my Father, inherit the kingdom prepared for you from the foundation of the world:

46. And these shall go away into everlasting punishment: but the righteous into life eternal.

Matt. 28:20. Lo, I am with you alway, *even* unto the end of the world.

Mark 3:35. For whosoever shall do the will of God, the same is my brother, and my sister, and mother.

Mark 8:35. For whosoever will save his life shall lose it; but whosoever shall lose his life for my sake and the gospel's, the same shall save it.

Mark 9:41. For whosoever shall give you a cup of water to drink in my name, because ye belong to Christ, verily I say unto you, he shall not lose his reward.

Mark 10:21. Then Jesus beholding him loved him, and said unto him, One thing thou lackest: go thy way, sell whatsoever thou hast, and give to the poor, and thou shalt have treasure in heaven: and come, take up the cross, and follow me.

29. And Jesus answered and said, Verily I say unto you, There is no man that hath left house, or brethren, or sisters, or father, or mother, or wife, or children, or lands,

for my sake, and the gospel's, [Matt. 19:29.] 30. But he shall receive an hundredfold now in this time, houses and brethren, and sisters, and mothers, and children, and lands, with persecutions; and in the world to come eternal life.

Mark 11:23. Whosoever shall say unto this mountain, Be thou removed, and be thou cast into the sea; and shall not doubt in his heart, but shall believe that those things which he saith shall come to pass; he shall have whatsoever he saith.   24. Therefore I say unto you, What things soever ye desire, when ye pray, believe that ye receive *them*, and ye shall have *them*.

Mark 13:13. Ye shall be hated of all *men* for my name's sake: but he that shall endure unto the end, the same shall be saved.

27. And then shall he send his angels, and shall gather together his elect from the four winds, from the uttermost part of the earth to the uttermost part of heaven.

Luke 3:17. Whose fan *is* in his hand, and he will throughly purge his floor, and will gather the wheat into his garner; Matt. 3:12.

Luke 6:20. And he lifted up his eyes on his disciples, and said, Blessed *be ye* poor: for your's is the kingdom of God. 21. Blessed *are ye* that hunger now: for ye shall be filled. Blessed *are ye* that weep now: for ye shall laugh.   22. Blessed are ye, when men shall hate you, and when they shall separate you *from their company*, and shall reproach *you*, and cast out your name as evil, for the Son of man's sake. 23. Rejoice ye in that day, and leap for joy: for, behold, your reward *is* great in heaven: for in the like manner did their fathers unto the prophets. Matt. 5:3–12.

Luke 10:20. Rather rejoice, because your names are written in heaven.

Luke 12:7. But even the very hairs of your head are all numbered. Fear not therefore: ye are of more value than many sparrows.   32. Fear not, little flock; for it is your Father's good pleasure to give you the kingdom.

Luke 16:22. That the beggar died, and was carried by the angels into Abraham's bosom: the rich man also died, and was buried;   23. And in hell he lift up his eyes, being in torments, and seeth Abraham afar off, and Lazarus in his bosom.   24. And he cried and said, Father Abraham, have mercy on me, and send Lazarus, that he may dip the tip of his finger in water, and cool my tongue; for I am tormented in this flame.   25. But Abraham said, Son, remember that thou in thy lifetime receivedst thy good things, and likewise Lazarus evil things: but now he is comforted, and thou art tormented.

Luke 18:29. And he said unto them, Verily I say unto you, There is no man that hath left house, or parents, or brethren, or wife, or children, for the kingdom of God's sake. 30. Who shall not receive manifold more in

this present time, and in the world to come life everlasting.

Luke 20:35. But they which shall be accounted worthy to obtain that world, and the resurrection from the dead, neither marry, nor are given in marriage: 36. Neither can they die any more: for they are equal unto the angels; and are the children of God, being the children of the resurrection.

Luke 21:18. But there shall not an hair of your head perish.   27. And then shall they see the Son of man coming in a cloud with power and great glory.   28. And when these things begin to come to pass, then look up, and lift up your heads; for your redemption draweth nigh.

Luke 22:29. I appoint unto you a kingdom, as my Father hath appointed unto me; 30. That ye may eat and drink at my table in my kingdom, and sit on thrones judging the twelve tribes of Israel.

Luke 23:43. Jesus said unto him, Verily I say unto thee, To day shalt thou be with me in paradise.

John 3:15. That whosoever believeth in him should not perish, but have eternal life.

16. For God so loved the world, that he gave his only begotten Son, that whosoever believeth in him should not perish, but have everlasting life.   17. For God sent not his Son into the world to condemn the world; but that the world through him might be saved.

18. He that believeth on him is not condemned: but he that believeth not is condemned already, because he hath not believed in the name of the only begotten Son of God.

36. He that believeth on the Son hath everlasting life:

John 4:14. But whosoever drinketh of the water that I shall give him shall never thirst; but the water that I shall give him shall be in him a well of water springing up into everlasting life.

John 5:24. He that heareth my word, and believeth on him that sent me, hath everlasting life, and shall not come into condemnation; but is passed from death unto life.

29. And shall come forth; they that have done good, unto the resurrection of life; and they that have done evil, unto the resurrection of damnation.

John 6:39. And this is the Father's will which hath sent me, that of all which he hath given me I should lose nothing, but should raise it up again at the last day. 40. And this is the will of him that sent me, that every one which seeth the Son, and believeth on him, may have everlasting life: and I will raise him up at the last day.

John 8:12. Then spake Jesus again unto them, saying, I am the light of the world: he that followeth me shall not walk in darkness, but shall have the light of life. 51. Verily, verily, I say unto you, If a man keep my saying, he shall never see death.

John 9:31. Now we know that God heareth not sinners: but if any man be a worshipper of God, and doeth his will, him he heareth.

John 10:27. My sheep hear my voice, and I know them, and they follow me: 28. And I give unto them eternal life; and they shall never perish, neither shall any *man* pluck them out of my hand. 29. My Father, which gave *them* me, is greater than all; and no *man* is able to pluck *them* out of my Father's hand.

John 12:25. He that loveth his life shall lose it; and he that hateth his life in this world shall keep it unto life eternal. 26. If any man serve me, let him follow me; and where I am, there shall also my servant be: if any man serve me, him will *my* Father honour.

John 13:36. Whither I go, thou canst not follow me now; but thou shalt follow me afterwards.

John 14:1. Let not your heart be troubled: ye believe in God, believe also in me. 2. In my Father's house are many mansions: if *it were* not *so*, I would have told you. I go to prepare a place for you. 3. And if I go and prepare a place for you, I will come again, and receive you unto myself; that where I am, *there* ye may be also.

12. Verily, verily, I say unto you, He that believeth on me, the works that I do shall he do also; and greater *works* than these shall he do; because I go unto my Father. 13. And whatsoever ye shall ask in my name, that will I do, that the Father may be glorified in the Son. 14. If ye shall ask any thing in my name, I will do *it*.

15. If ye love me, keep my commandments. 16. And I will pray the Father, and he shall give you another Comforter, that he may abide with you for ever; 17. *Even* the Spirit of truth; whom the world cannot receive, because it seeth him not, neither knoweth him: but ye know him; for he dwelleth with you, and shall be in you. 18. I will not leave you comfortless: I will come to you. 19. Yet a little while, and the world seeth me no more; but ye see me: because I live, ye shall live also. 20. At that day ye shall know that I *am* in my Father, and ye in me, and I in you. 21. He that hath my commandments, and keepeth them, he it is that loveth me: and he that loveth me shall be loved of my Father, and I will love him, and will manifest myself to him.

23. If a man love me, he will keep my words: and my Father will love him, and we will come unto him, and make our abode with him.

John 16:33. These things I have spoken unto you, that in me ye might have peace. In the world ye shall have tribulation: but be of good cheer; I have overcome the world.

John 17:2. As thou hast given him power over all flesh, that he should give eternal life to as many as thou hast given him. 22. And the glory which thou gavest me I have given them; that they may be one, even as we are one: 24. Father, I will that they also, whom thou hast given me, be with me where I am; that they may behold my glory, which thou hast given me: for thou lovedst me before the foundation of the world.

Acts 10:4. And he said unto him, Thy prayers and thine alms are come up for a memorial before God. 31. And said, Cornelius, thy prayer is heard, and thine alms are had in remembrance in the sight of God.

Acts 20:32. And now, brethren, I commend you to God, and to the word of his grace, which is able to build you up, and to give you an inheritance among all them which are sanctified.

Acts 26:18. To open their eyes, *and* to turn *them* from darkness to light, and *from* the power of Satan unto God, that they may receive forgiveness of sins, and inheritance among them which are sanctified by faith that is in me.

Rom. 2:7. To them who by patient continuance in well doing seek for glory and honour and immortality, eternal life: 10. But glory, honour, and peace, to every man that worketh good, to the Jew first, and also to the Gentile:

Rom. 5:9. Much more then, being now justified by his blood, we shall be saved from wrath through him. 10. For if, when we were enemies, we were reconciled to God by the death of his Son, much more, being reconciled, we shall be saved by his life. 11. And not only *so*, but we also joy in God through our Lord Jesus Christ, by whom we have now received the atonement. 17. They which receive abundance of grace and of the gift of righteousness shall reign in life by one, Jesus Christ.

Rom. 6:22. Being made free from sin, and become servants to God, ye have your fruit unto holiness, and the end everlasting life. 23. For the wages of sin *is* death; but the gift of God *is* eternal life through Jesus Christ our Lord.

Rom. 8:14. As many as are led by the Spirit of God, they are the sons of God. 15. For ye have not received the spirit of bondage again to fear; but ye have received the Spirit of adoption, whereby we cry, Abba, Father. 16. The Spirit itself beareth witness with our spirit, that we are the children of God: 17. And if children, then heirs; heirs of God, and joint-heirs with Christ; if so be that we suffer with *him*, that we may be also glorified together. 18. For I reckon that the sufferings of this present time *are* not worthy *to be compared* with the glory which shall be revealed in us.

28. And we know that all things work

together for good to them that love God, to them who are the called according to *his* purpose.

32. He that spared not his own Son, but delivered him up for us all, how shall he not with him also freely give us all things? 33. Who shall lay any thing to the charge of God's elect? *It is* God that justifieth. 34. Who *is* he that condemneth? *It is* Christ that died, yea rather, that is risen again, who is even at the right hand of God, who also maketh intercession for us. 35. Who shall separate us from the love of Christ? *shall* tribulation, or distress, or persecution, or famine, or nakedness, or peril, or sword? 36. As it is written, For thy sake we are killed all the day long; we are accounted as sheep for the slaughter. 37. Nay, in all these things we are more than conquerors through him that loved us. 38. For I am persuaded, that neither death, nor life, nor angels, nor principalities, nor powers, nor things present, nor things to come, 39. Nor height, nor depth, nor any other creature, shall be able to separate us from the love of God, which is in Christ Jesus our Lord.

Rom. 9:33. Behold, I lay in Sion a stumblingstone and rock of offence: and whosoever believeth on him shall not be ashamed.

Rom. 10:9. That if thou shalt confess with thy mouth the Lord Jesus, and shalt believe in thine heart that God hath raised him from the dead, thou shalt be saved. 11. For the scripture saith, Whosoever believeth on him shall not be ashamed. 12. For there is no difference between the Jew and the Greek: for the same Lord over all is rich unto all that call upon him. 13. For whosoever shall call upon the name of the Lord shall be saved.

Rom. 13:11. Knowing the time, that now *it is* high time to awake out of sleep: for now *is* our salvation nearer than when we believed.

1 Cor. 1:8. Who shall also confirm you unto the end, *that ye may be* blameless in the day of our Lord Jesus Christ. 9. God *is* faithful, by whom ye were called unto the fellowship of his Son Jesus Christ our Lord.

1 Cor. 2:9. Eye hath not seen, nor ear heard, neither have entered into the heart of man, the things which God hath prepared for them that love him.

1 Cor. 3:21. Let no man glory in men. For all things are your's; 22. Whether Paul, or Apollos, or Cephas, or the world, or life, or death, or things present, or things to come; all are your's; 23. And ye are Christ's; and Christ *is* God's.

1 Cor. 6:2. Do ye not know that the saints shall judge the world? and if the world shall be judged by you, are ye unworthy to judge the smallest matters? 3. Know ye not that we shall judge angels? how much more things that pertain to this life?

1 Cor. 8:3. But if any man love God, the same is known of him.

1 Cor. 13:10. When that which is perfect is come, then that which is in part shall be done away. 11. When I was a child, I spake as a child, I understood as a child, I thought as a child: but when I became a man, I put away childish things. 12. For now we see through a glass, darkly; but then face to face: now I know in part; but then shall I know even as also I am known.

1 Cor. 15:48. As *is* the earthy, such *are* they also that are earthy: and as *is* the heavenly, such *are* they also that are heavenly. 49. And as we have borne the image of the earthy, we shall also bear the image of the heavenly. 50. Now this I say, brethren, that flesh and blood cannot inherit the kingdom of God; neither doth corruption inherit incorruption. 51. Behold, I shew you a mystery; We shall not all sleep, but we shall all be changed, 52. In a moment, in the twinkling of an eye, at the last trump: for the trumpet shall sound, and the dead shall be raised incorruptible, and we shall be changed. 53. For this corruptible must put on incorruption, and this mortal *must* put on immortality. 54. So when this corruptible shall have put on incorruption, and this mortal shall have put on immortality, then shall be brought to pass the saying that is written, Death is swallowed up in victory. 55. O death, where *is* thy sting? O grave, where *is* thy victory? 56. The sting of death *is* sin; and the strength of sin *is* the law. 57. But thanks *be* to God, which giveth us the victory through our Lord Jesus Christ.

2 Cor. 1:20. All the promises of God in him *are* yea, and in him Amen, unto the glory of God by us. 21. Now he which stablisheth us with you in Christ, and hath anointed us, *is* God; 22. Who hath also sealed us, and given the earnest of the Spirit in our hearts.

2 Cor. 4:14. Knowing that he which raised up the Lord Jesus shall raise up us also by Jesus, and shall present *us* with you. 15. For all things *are* for your sakes, that the abundant grace might through the thanksgiving of many redound to the glory of God. 17. Our light affliction, which is but for a moment, worketh for us a far more exceeding *and* eternal weight of glory;

2 Cor. 7:1. Having therefore these promises, dearly beloved, let us cleanse ourselves from all filthiness of the flesh and spirit, perfecting holiness in the fear of God.

Gal. 3:29. If ye *be* Christ's, then are ye Abraham's seed, and heirs according to the promise.

Gal. 6:8. He that soweth to his flesh shall of the flesh reap corruption; but he that soweth to the Spirit shall of the Spirit reap life everlasting. 9. And let us not be weary in well doing: for in due season we shall reap, if we faint not.

Eph. 1:18. That ye may know what is the hope of his calling, and what the riches of the glory of his inheritance in the saints,

Eph. 2:7. That in the ages to come he might shew the exceeding riches of his grace in *his* kindness toward us through Christ Jesus.

Eph. 6:8. Knowing that whatsoever good thing any man doeth, the same shall he receive of the Lord, whether *he be* bond or free.

Phil. 4:7. And the peace of God, which passeth all understanding, shall keep your hearts and minds through Christ Jesus.

19. But my God shall supply all your need according to his riches in glory by Christ Jesus.

Col. 1:5. The hope which is laid up for you in heaven, whereof ye heard before in the word of the truth of the gospel; 12. Giving thanks unto the Father, which hath made us meet to be partakers of the inheritance of the saints in light:

Col. 3:4. When Christ, *who is* our life, shall appear, then shall ye also appear with him in glory. 24. Knowing that of the Lord ye shall receive the reward of the inheritance: for ye serve the Lord Christ.

1 Thess. 2:12. That ye would walk worthy of God, who hath called you unto his kingdom and glory.

1 Thess. 3:12. And the Lord make you to increase and abound in love one toward another, and toward all *men*, even as we *do* toward you: 13. To the end he may stablish your hearts unblameable in holiness before God, even our Father, at the coming of our Lord Jesus Christ with all his saints.

1 Thess. 4:15. For this we say unto you by the word of the Lord, that we which are alive *and* remain unto the coming of the Lord shall not prevent them which are asleep. 16. For the Lord himself shall descend from heaven with a shout, with the voice of the archangel, and with the trump of God: and the dead in Christ shall rise first: 17. Then we which are alive *and* remain shall be caught up together with them in the clouds, to meet the Lord in the air: and so shall we ever be with the Lord. 18. Wherefore comfort one another with these words.

1 Thess. 5:9. For God hath not appointed us to wrath, but to obtain salvation by our Lord Jesus Christ, 10. Who died for us, that, whether we wake or sleep, we should live together with him. 11. Wherefore comfort yourselves together, and edify one another, even as also ye do.

2 Thess. 1:5. *Which is* a manifest token of the righteous judgment of God, that ye may be counted worthy of the kingdom of God, for which ye also suffer: 6. Seeing *it is* a righteous thing with God to recompense tribulation to them that trouble you; 7. And to you who are troubled rest with us, when the Lord Jesus shall be revealed from heaven with his mighty angels.

2 Thess. 2:13. But we are bound to give thanks alway to God for you, brethren beloved of the Lord, because God hath from the beginning chosen you to salvation through sanctification of the Spirit and be-

lief of the truth: 14. Whereunto he called you by our gospel, to the obtaining of the glory of our Lord Jesus Christ.

1 Tim. 1:16. Howbeit for this cause I obtained mercy, that in me first Jesus Christ might shew forth all longsuffering, for a pattern to them which should hereafter believe on him to life everlasting.

1 Tim. 4:8. For bodily exercise profiteth little: but godliness is profitable unto all things, having promise of the life that now is, and of that which is to come.

2 Tim. 1:12. I know whom I have believed, and am persuaded that he is able to keep that which I have committed unto him against that day.

2 Tim. 2:10. Therefore I endure all things for the elect's sakes, that they may also obtain the salvation which is in Christ Jesus with eternal glory. 11. *It is* a faithful saying: For if we be dead with *him*, we shall also live with *him*: 12. If we suffer, we shall also reign with *him*: if we deny *him*, he also will deny us: 19. Nevertheless the foundation of God standeth sure, having this seal, The Lord knoweth them that are his. And, Let every one that nameth the name of Christ depart from iniquity.

2 Tim. 4:8. Henceforth there is laid up for me a crown of righteousness, which the Lord, the righteous judge, shall give me at that day: and not to me only, but unto all them also that love his appearing.

Tit. 2:11. For the grace of God that bringeth salvation hath appeared to all men, 12. Teaching us that, denying ungodliness and worldly lusts, we should live soberly, righteously, and godly, in this present world; 13. Looking for that blessed hope, and the glorious appearing of the great God and our Saviour Jesus Christ; 14. Who gave himself for us, that he might redeem us from all iniquity, and purify unto himself a peculiar people, zealous of good works.

Tit. 3:7. That being justified by his grace, we should be made heirs according to the hope of eternal life.

Heb. 1:14. Are they not all ministering spirits, sent forth to minister for them who shall be heirs of salvation?

Heb. 2:10. For it became him, for whom *are* all things, and by whom *are* all things, in bringing many sons unto glory, to make the captain of their salvation perfect through sufferings. 15. And deliver them who through fear of death were all their lifetime subject to bondage.

Heb. 4:9. There remaineth therefore a rest to the people of God. 15. For we have not an high priest which cannot be touched with the feeling of our infirmities; but was in all points tempted like as *we are*, *yet* without sin. 16. Let us therefore come boldly unto the throne of grace, that we may obtain mercy, and find grace to help in time of need.

Heb. 6:10. For God *is* not unrighteous to forget your work and labour of love, which ye have shewed toward his name, in that ye have ministered to the saints, and do minister. 16. For men verily swear by the greater: and an oath for confirmation *is* to them an end of all strife. 17. Wherein God, willing more abundantly to shew unto the heirs of promise the immutability of his counsel, confirmed *it* by an oath: 18. That by two immutable things, in which *it was* impossible for God to lie, we might have a strong consolation, who have fled for refuge to lay hold upon the hope set before us: 19. Which *hope* we have as an anchor of the soul, both sure and stedfast, and which entereth into that within the veil; 20. Whither the forerunner is for us entered, *even* Jesus, made an high priest for ever after the order of Melchisedec.

Heb. 9:15. And for this cause he is the mediator of the new testament, that by means of death, for the redemption of the transgressions *that were* under the first testament, they which are called might receive the promise of eternal inheritance. 28. So Christ was once offered to bear the sins of many; and unto them that look for him shall he appear the second time without sin unto salvation.

Heb. 10:34. For ye had compassion of me in my bonds, and took joyfully the spoiling of your goods, knowing in yourselves that ye have in heaven a better and an enduring substance. 35. Cast not away therefore your confidence, which hath great recompence of reward. 36. For ye have need of patience, that, after ye have done the will of God, ye might receive the promise.

Heb. 11:16. But now they desire a better *country,* that is, an heavenly: wherefore God is not ashamed to be called their God: for he hath prepared for them a city.

Heb. 12:22. But ye are come unto mount Sion, and unto the city of the living God the heavenly Jerusalem, and to an innumerable company of angels. 23. The general assembly and church of the firstborn, which are written in heaven, and to God the Judge of all, and to the spirits of just men made perfect, 28. Wherefore we receiving a kingdom which cannot be moved, let us have grace, whereby we may serve God acceptably with reverence and godly fear:

Heb. 13:5. *Let your* conversation *be* without covetousness; *and be* content with such things as ye have: for he hath said, I will never leave thee, nor forsake thee. 6. So that we may boldly say, the Lord *is* my helper, and I will not fear what man shall do unto me.

Jas. 1:5. If any of you lack wisdom, let him ask of God *that* giveth to all *men* liberally, and upbraideth not; and it shall be given him.

12. Blessed *is* the man that endureth temptation: for when he is tried, he shall receive the crown of life, which the Lord hath promised to them that love him.

25. But whoso looketh into the perfect law of liberty, and continueth *therein,* he being not a forgetful hearer, but a doer of the work, this man shall be blessed in his deed.

Jas. 2:5. Hearken, my beloved brethren, Hath not God chosen the poor of this world rich in faith, and heirs of the kingdom which he hath promised to them that love him?

Jas. 4:8. Draw nigh to God, and he will draw nigh to you.

1 Pet. 1:2. Elect according to the foreknowledge of God the Father, through sanctification of the Spirit, unto obedience and sprinkling of the blood of Jesus Christ: Grace unto you, and peace, be multiplied. 3. Blessed *be* the God and Father of our Lord Jesus Christ, which according to his abundant mercy hath begotten us again unto a lively hope by the resurrection of Jesus Christ from the dead, 4. To an inheritance incorruptible and undefiled, and that fadeth not away, reserved in heaven for you, 5. Who are kept by the power of God through faith unto salvation ready to be revealed in the last time.

1 Pet. 2:5. Ye also, as lively stones, are built up a spiritual house, an holy priesthood, to offer up spiritual sacrifices, acceptable to God by Jesus Christ. 6. Wherefore also it is contained in the scripture, Behold, I lay in Sion a chief corner stone, elect, precious: and he that believeth on him shall not be confounded. 9. But ye *are* a chosen generation, a royal priesthood, an holy nation, a peculiar people; that ye should shew forth the praises of him who hath called you out of darkness into his marvellous light: 10. Which in time past *were* not a people, but *are* now the people of God: which had not obtained mercy, but now have obtained mercy.

1 Pet. 3:9. Not rendering evil for evil, or railing for railing: but contrariwise blessing; knowing that ye are thereunto called, that ye should inherit a blessing. 10. For he that will love life, and see good days, let him refrain his tongue from evil, and his lips that they speak no guile: 11. Let him eschew evil, and do good; let him seek peace, and ensue it. 12. For the eyes of the Lord *are* over the righteous, and his ears *are* open unto their prayers: but the face of the Lord *is* against them that do evil.

1 Pet. 4:13. But rejoice, inasmuch as ye are partakers of Christ's sufferings; that, when his glory shall be revealed, ye may be glad also with exceeding joy.

1 Pet. 5:4. And when the chief Shepherd shall appear, ye shall receive a crown of glory that fadeth not away. 6. Humble yourselves therefore under the mighty hand of God, that he may exalt you in due time: 7. Casting all your care upon him; for he careth for you. 10. But the God of all

grace, who hath called us unto his eternal glory by Christ Jesus, after that ye have suffered a while, make you perfect, stablish, strengthen, settle *you*.

2 Pet. 1:4. Whereby are given unto us exceeding great and precious promises: that by these ye might be partakers of the divine nature, having escaped the corruption that is in the world through lust. 10. Wherefore the rather, brethren, give diligence to make your calling and election sure: for if ye do these things, ye shall never fall: 11. For so an entrance shall be ministered unto you abundantly into the everlasting kingdom of our Lord and Saviour Jesus Christ.

2 Pet. 2:9. The Lord knoweth how to deliver the godly out of temptations, and to reserve the unjust unto the day of judgment to be punished:

1 John 1:7. If we walk in the light, as he is in the light, we have fellowship one with another, and the blood of Jesus Christ his Son cleanseth us from all sin. 9. If we confess our sins, he is faithful and just to forgive us *our* sins, and to cleanse us from all unrighteousness.

1 John 2:17. And the world passeth away, and the lust thereof: but he that doeth the will of God abideth for ever. 25. And this is the promise that he hath promised us, *even* eternal life. 28. And now, little children, abide in him; that, when he shall appear, we may have confidence, and not be ashamed before him at his coming.

1 John 3:2. Beloved, now are we the sons of God, and it doth not yet appear what we shall be: but we know that, when he shall appear, we shall be like him; for we shall see him as he is. 22. And whatsoever we ask, we receive of him, because we keep his commandments, and do those things that are pleasing in his sight.

1 John 5:13. These things have I written unto you [1] that believe on the name of the Son of God; that ye may know that ye have eternal life, [2] and that ye may believe on the name of the Son of God. [R. V. ¹ Omitted. ² even unto you that]

Rev. 1:6. And hath made us kings and priests unto God and his Father; to him *be* glory and dominion for ever and ever.

Rev. 2:7. To him that overcometh will I give to eat of the tree of life, which is in the midst of the paradise of God. 10. Fear none of those things which thou shalt suffer: behold, the devil shall cast *some* of you into prison, that ye may be tried; and ye shall have tribulation ten days: be thou faithful unto death, and I will give thee a crown of life. 11. He that overcometh shall not be hurt of the second death. 17. To him that overcometh will I give to eat of the hidden manna, and will give him a white stone, and in the stone a new name written, which no man knoweth saving he that receiveth *it*. 26. And he that overcometh, and keepeth my works unto the end, to him will I give power over the nations. 27. And he shall rule them with a

rod of iron; as the vessels of a potter shall they be broken to shivers: even as I received of my Father. 28. And I will give him the morning star.

Rev. 3:4. Thou hast a few names even in Sardis which have not defiled their garments; and they shall walk with me in white: for they are worthy. 5. He that overcometh, the same shall be clothed in white raiment; and I will not blot out his name out of the book of life, but I will confess his name before my Father, and before his angels. 10. Because thou hast kept the word of my patience, I also will keep thee from the hour of temptation, which shall come upon all the world, to try them that dwell upon the earth. 12. Him that overcometh will I make a pillar in the temple of my God, and he shall go no more out: and I will write upon him the name of my God, and the name of the city of my God, *which is* new Jerusalem, which cometh down out of heaven from my God: and *I will write upon him* my new name. 21. To him that overcometh will I grant to sit with me in my throne, even as I also overcame, and am set down with my Father in his throne.

Rev. 7:3. Hurt not the earth, neither the sea, nor the trees, till we have sealed the servants of our God in their foreheads. 4. And I heard the number of them which were sealed: *and there were* sealed an hundred *and* forty *and* four thousand of all the tribes of the children of Israel. 9. After this I beheld, and, lo, a great multitude, which no man could number, of all nations, and kindreds, and people, and tongues, stood before the throne, and before the Lamb, clothed with white robes, and palms in their hands; 10. And cried with a loud voice, saying, Salvation to our God which sitteth upon the throne, and unto the Lamb. 11. And all the angels stood round about the throne, and *about* the elders and the four beasts, and fell before the throne on their faces, and worshipped God, 12. Saying, Amen: Blessing, and glory, and wisdom, and thanksgiving, and honour, and power, and might, *be* unto our God for ever and ever. Amen. 13. And one of the elders answered, saying unto me, What are these which are arrayed in white robes? and whence came they? 14. And I said unto him, Sir, thou knowest. And he said to me, These are they which came out of great tribulation, and have washed their robes, and made them white in the blood of the Lamb. 15. Therefore are they before the throne of God, and serve him day and night in his temple: and he that sitteth on the throne shall dwell among them. 16. They shall hunger no more, neither thirst any more; neither shall the sun light on them, nor any heat. 17. For the Lamb which is in the midst of the throne shall feed them, and shall lead them unto living fountains of waters: and God shall wipe away all tears from their eyes.

Rev. 11:12. And they heard a great voice from heaven saying unto them, Come up hither. And they ascended up to heaven in a cloud; and their enemies beheld them. 18. And the nations were angry, and thy wrath is come, and the time of the dead, that they should be judged, and that thou shouldest give reward unto thy servants the prophets, and to the saints, and them that fear thy name, small and great; and shouldest destroy them which destroy the earth.

Rev. 14:1. And I looked, and, lo, a Lamb stood on the mount Sion, and with him an hundred forty *and* four thousand, having his Father's name written in their foreheads. 2. And I heard a voice from heaven, as the voice of many waters, and as the voice of a great thunder: and I heard the voice of harpers harping with their harps: 3. And they sung as it were a new song before the throne, and before the four beasts, and the elders: and no man could learn that song but the hundred *and* forty *and* four thousand, which were redeemed from the earth. 4. These are they which were not defiled with women; for they are virgins. These are they which follow the Lamb whithersoever he goeth. These were redeemed from among men, *being* the first fruits unto God and to the Lamb. 5. And in their mouth was found no guile: for they are without fault before the throne of God. 13. And I heard a voice from heaven saying unto me, Write, Blessed *are* the dead which die in the Lord from henceforth: Yea, saith the Spirit, that they may rest from their labours; and their works do follow them.

Rev. 16:15. Behold, I come as a thief. Blessed *is* he that watcheth, and keepeth his garments, lest he walk naked, and they see his shame.

Rev. 20:4. And I saw thrones, and they sat upon them, and judgment was given unto them: and *I saw* the souls of them that were beheaded for the witness of Jesus, and for the word of God, and which had not worshipped the beast, neither his image, neither had received *his* mark upon their foreheads, or in their hands; and they lived and reigned with Christ a thousand years. 5. But the rest of the dead lived not again until the thousand years were finished. This *is* the first resurrection. 6. Blessed and holy *is* he that hath part in the first resurrection: on such the second death hath no power, but they shall be priests of God and of Christ, and shall reign with him a thousand years.

Rev. 21:3. And I heard a great voice out of heaven saying, Behold, the tabernacle of God *is* with men, and he will dwell with them, and they shall be his people, and God himself shall be with them, *and be* their God. 4. And God shall wipe away all tears from their eyes; and there shall be no more death, neither sorrow, nor crying,

neither shall there be any more pain: for the former things are passed away. 5. And he that sat upon the throne said, Behold, I make all things new. And he said unto me, Write: for these words are true and faithful. 6. And he said unto me, It is done. I am Alpha and Omega, the beginning and the end. I will give unto him that is athirst of the fountain of the water of life freely. 7. He that overcometh shall inherit all things; and I will be his God, and he shall be my son. 24. And the nations of them which are saved shall walk in the light of it: and the kings of the earth do bring their glory and honour into it.

Rev. 22:4. And they shall see his face; and his name *shall be* in their foreheads. 5. And there shall be no night there; and they need no candle, neither light of the sun; for the Lord God giveth them light: and they shall reign for ever and ever. 7. Behold, I come quickly: blessed *is* he that keepeth the sayings of the prophecy of this book. 12. And, behold, I come quickly; and my reward *is* with me, to give every man according as his work shall be. 14. Blessed *are* they that ¹do his commandments, that they may have right to the tree of life, and may enter in through the gates into the city.   [¹ R. V. wash their robes]

See ADOPTION; AFFLICTION, COMFORT IN; GOD, PRESERVER; GOD, PROVIDENCE OF.

For promises in particular, see BACKSLIDER; OBEDIENCE; PENITENT, PROMISES TO, etc., under such topics as may be desired.

UNITY OF, WITH CHRIST: John 6:56. He that eateth my flesh, and drinketh my blood, dwelleth in me, and I in him. *vs.* 51–57.

John 14:20. At that day ye shall know that I *am* in my Father, and ye in me, and I in you.

John 15:1. I am the true vine, and my Father is the husbandman. 2. Every branch in me that beareth not fruit he taketh away: and every *branch* that beareth fruit, he purgeth it, that it may bring forth more fruit. 3. Now ye are clean through the word which I have spoken unto you. 4. Abide in me, and I in you. As the branch cannot bear fruit of itself, except it abide in the vine; no more can ye, except ye abide in me. 5. I am the vine, ye *are* the branches: He that abideth in me, and I in him, the same bringeth forth much fruit: for without me ye can do nothing. 6. If a man abide not in me, he is cast forth as a branch, and is withered; and men gather them, and cast *them* into the fire, and they are burned. 7. If ye abide in me, and my words abide in you, ye shall ask what ye will, and it shall be done unto you. 8. Herein is my Father glorified, that ye bear much fruit; so shall ye be my disciples. 9. As the Father hath loved me, so have I loved you: continue ye in my love. 10. If ye keep my commandments, ye shall abide in my love; even as I have kept my Father's commandments, and abide in his love. 11. These things have I spoken unto you, that my joy might remain in you, and *that* your joy might be full. 19. If ye were of the world, the world would love his own : but because ye are not of the world, but I have chosen you out of the world, therefore the world hateth you.

John 17:21. That they all may be one; as thou, Father, *art* in me, and I in thee, that they also may be one in us: that the world may believe that thou hast sent me. 22. And the glory which thou gavest me I have given them; that they may be one, even as we are one: 23. I in them, and thou in me, that they may be made perfect in one; 26. And I have declared unto them thy name, and will declare *it:* that the love wherewith thou hast loved me may be in them, and I in them.

Rom. 8:1. *There is* therefore now no condemnation to them which are in Christ Jesus, [1] who walk not after the flesh, but after the Spirit. 10. And if Christ *be* in you, the body *is* dead because of sin; but the Spirit *is* life because of righteousness. [1 Omitted in R. V.]

Rom. 12:5. So we, *being* many, are one body in Christ, and every one members one of another.

1 Cor. 6:13. Now the body *is* not for fornication, but for the Lord : and the Lord for the body. 14. And God hath both raised up the Lord, and will also raise up us by his own power. 15. Know ye not that your bodies are the members of Christ? shall I then take the members of Christ, and make *them* the members of an harlot? God forbid. 16. What? know ye not that he which is joined to an harlot is one body? for two, saith he, shall be one flesh. 17. But he that is joined unto the Lord is one spirit. 18. Flee fornication. Every sin that a man doeth is without the body; but he that committeth fornication sinneth against his own body. 19. What? know ye not that your body is the temple of the Holy Ghost *which is* in you, which ye have of God, and ye are not your own? 20. For ye are bought with a price : therefore glorify God in your body, and in your spirit, which are God's.

1 Cor. 10:16. The cup of blessing which we bless, is it not the communion of the blood of Christ? The bread which we break, is it not the communion of the body of Christ? 17. For we *being* many are one bread, *and* one body: for we are all partakers of that one bread.

1 Cor. 12:12. For as the body is one, and hath many members, and all the members of that one body, being many, are one body: so also *is* Christ. 13. For by one Spirit are we all baptized into one body, whether *we be* Jews or Gentiles, whether *we be* bond or free; and have been all made to drink into one Spirit. 27. Now ye are the body of Christ, and members in particular.

2 Cor. 5:17. Therefore if any man *be* in Christ, *he is* a new creature: old things are passed away; behold, all things are become new. 21. For he hath made him *to be* sin for us, who knew no sin; that we might be made the righteousness of God in him.

2 Cor. 11:2. I have espoused you to one husband, that I may present *you as* a chaste virgin to Christ.

2 Cor. 13:5. Know ye not your own selves, how that Jesus Christ is in you, except ye be reprobates?

Gal. 2:20. I am crucified with Christ: nevertheless I live; yet not I, but Christ liveth in me: and the life which I now live in the flesh I live by the faith of the Son of God, who loved me, and gave himself for me.

Eph. 5:30. We are members of his body, of his flesh, and of his bones. 32. This is a great mystery: but I speak concerning Christ and the church.

Col. 1:27. To whom God would make known what *is* the riches of the glory of this mystery among the Gentiles; which is Christ in you, the hope of glory:

Col. 2:6. As ye have therefore received Christ Jesus the Lord, *so* walk ye in him; 7. Rooted and built up in him,

1 Pet. 4:13. Rejoice, inasmuch as ye are partakers of Christ's sufferings; that, when his glory shall be revealed, ye may be glad also with exceeding joy.

1 John 2:6. He that saith he abideth in him, ought himself also so to walk, even as he walked. 24. If that which ye have heard from the beginning shall remain in you, ye also shall continue in the Son, and in the Father. 28. Little children, abide in him; that, when he shall appear, we may have confidence, and not be ashamed before him at his coming.

1 John 3:6. Whosoever abideth in him sinneth not: 24. He that keepeth his commandments dwelleth in him, and he in him. And hereby we know that he abideth in us, by the Spirit which he hath given us.

1 John 4:13. Hereby know we that we dwell in him, and he in us, because he hath given us of his Spirit.

1 John 5:12. He that hath the Son hath life; *and* he that hath not the Son of God hath not life. 20. We are in him that is true, *even* in his Son Jesus Christ.

2 John 9. He that abideth in the doctrine of Christ, he hath both the Father and the Son.

Rev. 19:7. The marriage of the Lamb is come, and his wife hath made herself ready. 8. And to her was granted that she should be arrayed in fine linen, clean and white: for the fine linen is the righteousness of saints. 9. And he saith unto me, Write, Blessed *are* they which are called unto the marriage supper of the Lamb.

Rev. 21:9. The bride, the Lamb's wife.

See ADOPTION; COMMUNION; FELLOWSHIP.

RIGHTEOUSNESS. By faith, Gen. 15:6; Rom. 4:3,5,9,11,13,20,22,24. Garment of, Job 29:14; Matt. 22:11–14. Imputed on account of obedience, Deut. 6:25; Job 33:26.

FRUITS OF: Deut. 6:25. And it shall be our righteousness, if we observe to do all these commandments before the LORD our God, as he hath commanded us.

Josh. 22:31. And Phinehas the son of Eleazar the priest said unto the children of Reuben, and to the children of Gad, and to the children of Manasseh, This day we perceive that the LORD is among us, because ye have not committed this trespass against the LORD: now ye have delivered the children of Israel out of the hand of the LORD.

Psa. 1:3. And he shall be like a tree planted by the rivers of water, that bringeth forth his fruit in his season; his leaf also shall not wither; and whatsoever he doeth shall prosper.

Psa. 15:1. LORD, who shall abide in thy tabernacle? who shall dwell in thy holy hill? 2. He that walketh uprightly, and worketh righteousness, and speaketh the truth in his heart. 3. *He that* backbiteth not with his tongue, nor doeth evil to his neighbour, nor taketh up a reproach against his neighbour. 4. In whose eyes a vile person is contemned; but he honoureth them that fear the LORD. *He that* sweareth to *his own* hurt, and changeth not. 5. *He that* putteth not out his money to usury, nor taketh reward against the innocent. He that doeth these *things* shall never be moved.

Psa. 24:3. Who shall ascend into the hill of the LORD? or who shall stand in his holy place? 4. He that hath clean hands, and a pure heart; who hath not lifted up his soul unto vanity, nor sworn deceitfully. 5. He shall receive the blessing from the LORD, and righteousness from the God of his salvation.

Psa. 101:3. I will set no wicked thing before mine eyes: I hate the work of them that turn aside; *it* shall not cleave to me. 4. A froward heart shall depart from me: I will ¹ not know a wicked *person.*

[¹ R. V. know no evil thing]

Psa. 106:3. Blessed *are* they that keep judgment, *and* he that doeth righteousness at all times.

Psa. 112:4. Unto the upright there ariseth light in the darkness: *he is* gracious, and full of compassion, and righteous. 5. A good man sheweth favour, and lendeth: he will guide his affairs with discretion. 6. Surely he shall not be moved for ever: the righteous shall be in everlasting remembrance. 7. He shall not be afraid of evil tidings: his heart is fixed, trusting in the LORD. 8. His heart *is* established, he shall not be afraid,

Prov. 2:5. Then shalt thou understand the fear of the LORD, and find the knowledge of God. 6. For the LORD giveth wisdom: out of his mouth *cometh* knowledge and understanding. 7. He layeth up sound

wisdom for the righteous: *he is* a buckler to them that walk uprightly. 8. He keepeth the paths of judgment, and preserveth the way of his saints. 9. Then shalt thou understand righteousness, and judgment, and equity; *yea*, every good path. 10. When wisdom entereth into thine heart, and knowledge is pleasant unto thy soul; 11. Discretion shall preserve thee, understanding shall keep thee: 12. To deliver thee from the way of the evil *man*, from the man that speaketh froward things; 13. Who leave the paths of uprightness, to walk in the ways of darkness; 14. Who rejoice to do evil, *and* delight in the frowardness of the wicked; 15. Whose ways *are* crooked, and *they* froward in their paths: 16. To deliver thee from the strange woman, *even* from the stranger *which* flattereth with her words; 17. Which forsaketh the guide of her youth, and forgetteth the covenant of her God. 18. For her house inclineth unto death, and her paths unto the dead. 19. None that go unto her return again, neither take they hold of the paths of life. 20. That thou mayest walk in the way of good *men*, and keep the paths of the righteous.

Prov. 10:2. Treasures of wickedness profit nothing: but righteousness delivereth from death.

Prov. 11:5. The righteousness of the perfect shall direct his way: 6. The righteousness of the upright shall deliver them: 18. The wicked worketh a deceitful work: but to him that soweth righteousness *shall be* a sure reward. 19. As righteousness *tendeth* to life: so he that pursueth evil *pursueth it* to his own death. 30. The fruit of the righteous *is* a tree of life; and he that winneth souls *is* wise.

Prov. 12:28. In the way of righteousness *is* life; and *in* the pathway *thereof there is* no death. Prov. 10:16.

Prov. 13:6. Righteousness keepeth *him that is* upright in the way: but wickedness overthroweth the sinner.

Prov. 14:34. Righteousness exalteth a nation: but sin *is* a reproach to any people.

Prov. 21:3. To do justice and judgment *is* more acceptable to the LORD than sacrifice.

Prov. 29:7. The righteous considereth the cause of the poor: *but* the wicked regardeth not to know *it*.

Isa. 28:17. Judgment also will I lay to the line, and righteousness to the plummet: and the hail shall sweep away the refuge of lies, and the waters shall overflow the hiding place.

Isa. 32:16. Then judgment shall dwell in the wilderness, and righteousness remain in the fruitful field. 17. And the work of righteousness shall be peace; and the effect of righteousness quietness and assurance for ever. 18. And my people shall dwell in a peaceable habitation, and in sure dwellings, and in quiet resting places;

Isa. 33:15. He that walketh righteously, and speaketh uprightly; he that despiseth the gain of oppressions, that shaketh his hands from holding of bribes, that stoppeth his ears from hearing of blood, and shutteth his eyes from seeing evil; 16. He shall dwell on high: his place of defence *shall be* the munitions of rocks: bread shall be given him; his waters *shall be* sure. 17. Thine eyes shall see the king in his beauty: they shall behold the land that is very far off.

Isa. 55:12. For ye shall go out with joy, and be led forth with peace: the mountains and the hills shall break forth before you into singing, and all the trees of the field shall clap *their* hands. 13. Instead of the thorn shall come up the fir tree, and instead of the brier shall come up the myrtle tree: and it shall be to the LORD for a name, for an everlasting sign *that* shall not be cut off.

Isa. 58:6. *Is* not this the fast that I have chosen? to loose the bands of wickedness, to undo the heavy burdens, and to let the oppressed go free, and that ye break every yoke? 7. *Is it* not to deal thy bread to the hungry, and that thou bring the poor that are cast out to thy house? when thou seest the naked, that thou cover him; and that thou hide not thyself from thine own flesh? 8. Then shall thy light break forth as the morning, and thine health shall spring forth speedily: and thy righteousness shall go before thee; the glory of the LORD shall be thy rereward. 9. Then shalt thou call, and the LORD shall answer; thou shalt cry, and he shall say, Here I *am.* If thou take away from the midst of thee the yoke, the putting forth of the finger, and speaking vanity; 10. And *if* thou draw out thy soul to the hungry, and satisfy the afflicted soul; then shall thy light rise in obscurity, and thy darkness *be* as the noonday: 11. And the LORD shall guide thee continually, and satisfy thy soul in drought, and make fat thy bones: and thou shalt be like a watered garden, and like a spring of water, whose waters fail not. 12. And *they that shall be* of thee shall build the old waste places: thou shalt raise up the foundations of many generations; and thou shalt be called, The repairer of the breach, The restorer of paths to dwell in. 13. If thou turn away thy foot from the sabbath, *from* doing thy pleasure on my holy day; and call the sabbath a delight, the holy of the LORD, honourable; and shalt honour him, not doing thine own ways, nor finding thine own pleasure, nor speaking *thine own* words: 14. Then shalt thou delight thyself in the LORD; and I will cause thee to ride upon the high places of the earth, and feed thee with the heritage of Jacob thy father: for the mouth of the LORD hath spoken *it.*

Isa. 62:1. For Zion's sake will I not hold my peace, and for Jerusalem's sake I will not rest, until the righteousness thereof go forth as brightness, and the salvation thereof as a lamp *that* burneth.

Ezek. 18:5. But if a man be just, and do that which is lawful and right, 6. *And* hath not eaten upon the mountains, neither hath lifted up his eyes to the idols of the house of Israel, neither hath defiled his neighbour's wife, neither hath come near to a menstruous woman, 7. And hath not oppressed any, *but* hath restored to the debtor his pledge, hath spoiled none by violence, hath given his bread to the hungry, and hath covered the naked with a garment; 8. He *that* hath not given forth upon usury, neither hath taken any increase, *that* hath withdrawn his hand from iniquity, hath executed true judgment between man and man, 9. Hath walked in my statutes, and hath kept my judgments, to deal truly; he *is* just, he shall surely live, saith the Lord GOD.

Ezek. 33:15. *If* the wicked restore the pledge, give again that he had robbed, walk in the statutes of life, without committing iniquity; he shall surely live, he shall not die.

Dan. 12:3. And they that be wise shall shine as the brightness of the firmament: and they that turn many to righteousness as the stars for ever and ever.

Hos. 10:12. Sow to yourselves in righteousness, reap in mercy; break up your fallow ground: for *it is* time to seek the LORD, till he come and rain righteousness upon you.

Mal. 3:3. And he shall sit *as* a refiner and purifier of silver: and he shall purify the sons of Levi, and purge them as gold and silver, that they may offer unto the LORD an offering in righteousness.

Mal. 4:2. But unto you that fear my name shall the Sun of righteousness arise with healing in his wings;

Matt. 5:20. For I say unto you, That except your righteousness shall exceed *the righteousness* of the scribes and Pharisees, ye shall in no case enter into the kingdom of heaven.

Matt. 12:35. A good man out of the good treasure of the heart bringeth forth good things: and an evil man out of the evil treasure bringeth forth evil things.

Mark 3:33. And he answered them, saying, Who is my mother, or my brethren? 34. And he looked round about on them which sat about him, and said, Behold my mother and my brethren! 35. For whosoever shall do the will of God, the same is my brother, and my sister, and mother. Matt. 12:50.

Luke 3:10. And the people asked him, saying, What shall we do then? 11. He answereth and saith unto them, He that hath two coats, let him impart to him that hath none; and he that hath meat, let him do likewise. 12. Then came also publicans to be baptized, and said unto him, Master, what shall we do? 13. And he said unto them, Exact no more than that which is appointed you. 14. And the soldiers likewise demanded of him, saying, And what shall we do? And he said unto them, Do violence to no man, neither accuse *any* falsely; and be content with your wages.

Luke 8:15. That on the good ground are they, which in an honest and good heart, having heard the word, keep *it*, and bring forth fruit with patience.

John 3:21. But he that doeth truth cometh to the light, that his deeds may be made manifest, that they are wrought in God. 33. He that hath received his testimony hath set to his seal that God is true.

John 8:47. He that is of God heareth God's words: 49. Jesus answered, I have not a devil; but I honour my Father, and ye do dishonour me.

John 13:35. By this shall all *men* know that ye are my disciples, if ye have love one to another.

John 14:21. He that hath my commandments, and keepeth them, he it is that loveth me: and he that loveth me shall be loved of my Father, and I will love him, and will manifest myself to him. 22. Judas saith unto him, not Iscariot, Lord, how is it that thou wilt manifest thyself unto us, and not unto the world? 23. Jesus answered and said unto him, If a man love me, he will keep my words: and my Father will love him, and we will come unto him, and make our abode with him. 24. He that loveth me not keepeth not my sayings:

John 15:4. Abide in me, and I in you. As the branch cannot bear fruit of itself, except it abide in the vine; no more can ye, except ye abide in me. 5. I am the vine, ye *are* the branches: He that abideth in me, and I in him, the same bringeth forth much fruit: for without me ye can do nothing. 8. Herein is my Father glorified, that ye bear much fruit; so shall ye be my disciples. 12. This is my commandment, That ye love one another, as I have loved you.

Acts 9:36. Now there was at Joppa a certain disciple named Tabitha, which by interpretation is called Dorcas: this woman was full of good works and almsdeeds which she did.

Acts 11:29. Then the disciples, every man according to his ability, determined to send relief unto the brethren which dwelt in Judæa: 30. Which also they did, and sent it to the elders by the hands of Barnabas and Saul.

Acts 19:19. Many of them also which used curious arts brought their books together, and burned them before all *men:* and they counted the price of them, and found *it* fifty thousand *pieces* of silver.

Rom. 5:1. Therefore being justified by faith, ¹ we have peace with God through our Lord Jesus Christ: 2. By whom also we have accessby faith into this grace wherein we stand, and rejoice in hope of the glory of God. 3. And not only *so*, but we glory in tribulations also: knowing that tribulation worketh patience; 4. And patience, experience; and experience,

hope: 5. And hope maketh not ashamed; because the love of God is shed abroad in our hearts by the Holy Ghost which is given unto us. [¹ R. V. let us]

Rom. 6:19. I speak after the manner of men because of the infirmity of your flesh: for as ye have yielded your members servants to uncleanness and to iniquity unto iniquity: even so now yield your members servants to righteousness unto holiness. 20. For when ye were the servants of sin, ye were free from righteousness. 21. What fruit had ye then in those things whereof ye are now ashamed? for the end of those things *is* death. 22. But now being made free from sin, and become servants to God, ye have your fruit unto holiness, and the end everlasting life.

Rom. 7:4. Wherefore, my brethren, ye also are become dead to the law by the body of Christ; that ye should be married to another, *even* to him who is raised from the dead, that we should bring forth fruit unto God. 5. For when we were in the flesh, the motions of sins, which were by the law, did work in our members to bring forth fruit unto death. 6. But now we are delivered from the law, that being dead wherein we were held; that we should serve in newness of spirit, and not *in* the oldness of the letter.

Rom. 8:4. That the righteousness of the law might be fulfilled in us, who walk not after the flesh, but after the Spirit. 5. For they that are after the flesh do mind the things of the flesh; but they that are after the Spirit, the things of the Spirit. 6. For to be carnally minded *is* death; but to be spiritually minded *is* life and peace.

Rom. 14:17. For the kingdom of God is not meat and drink; but righteousness, and peace, and joy in the Holy Ghost. 18. For he that in these things serveth Christ *is* acceptable to God, and approved of men. 19. Let us therefore follow after the things which make for peace, and things wherewith one may edify another.

Rom. 15:1. We then that are strong ought to bear the infirmities of the weak, and not to please ourselves. 2. Let every one of us please *his* neighbour for *his* good to edification. 3. For even Christ pleased not himself: but, as it is written, The reproaches of them that reproached thee fell on me. 4. For whatsoever things were written aforetime were written for our learning, that we through patience and comfort of the scriptures might have hope. 5. Now the God of patience and consolation grant you to be likeminded one toward another according to Christ Jesus: 6. That ye may with one mind *and* and one mouth glorify God, even the Father of our Lord Jesus Christ. 7. Wherefore receive ye one another, as Christ also received us to the glory of God.

1 Cor. 4:19. But I will come to you shortly, if the Lord will, and will know, not the speech of them which are puffed up, but the

power. 20. For the kingdom of God *is* not in word, but in power.

1 Cor. 12:3. No man can say that Jesus is the Lord, but by the Holy Ghost.

1 Cor. 13:1. Though I speak with the tongues of men and of angels, and have not charity, I am become as sounding brass, or a tinkling cymbal. 2. And though I have *the gift of* prophecy, and understand all mysteries, and all knowledge; and though I have all faith, so that I could remove mountains, and have not charity, I am nothing. 3. And though I bestow all my goods to feed *the poor*, and though I give my body to be burned, and have not charity, it profiteth me nothing. 4. Charity suffereth long, *and* is kind; charity envieth not; charity vaunteth not itself, is not puffed up, 5. Doth not behave itself unseemly, seeketh not her own, is not easily provoked, thinketh no evil; 6. Rejoiceth not in iniquity, but rejoiceth in the truth; 7. Beareth all things, believeth all things, hopeth all things, endureth all things. 8. Charity never faileth: but whether *there be* prophecies, they shall fail; whether *there be* tongues, they shall cease; whether *there be* knowledge, it shall vanish away. 9. For we know in part, and we prophesy in part. 10. But when that which is perfect is come, then that which is in part shall be done away. 11. When I was a child, I spake as a child, I understood as a child, I thought as a child: but when I became a man, I put away childish things. 12. For now we see through a glass, darkly; but then face to face: now I know in part; but then shall I know even as also I am known. 13. And now abideth faith, hope, charity, these three; but the greatest of these *is* charity.

2 Cor. 5:17. Therefore if any man *be* in Christ, *he is* a new creature: old things are passed away; behold, all things are become new.

2 Cor. 7:10. For godly sorrow worketh repentance to salvation not to be repented of: but the sorrow of the world worketh death. 11. For behold this selfsame thing, that ye sorrowed after a godly sort, what carefulness it wrought in you, yea, *what* clearing of yourselves, yea, *what* indignation, yea, *what* fear, yea, *what* vehement desire, yea, *what* zeal, yea, *what* revenge! In all *things* ye have approved yourselves to be clear in this matter.

2 Cor. 9:10. Now he that ministereth seed to the sower both minister bread for *your* food, and multiply your seed sown, and increase the fruits of your righteousness;

2 Cor. 10:5. Casting down imaginations, and every high thing that exalteth itself against the knowledge of God, and bringing into captivity every thought to the obedience of Christ;

2 Cor. 13:5. Examine yourselves, whether ye be in the faith; prove your own selves. Know ye not your own selves, how that

Jesus Christ is in you, except ye be reprobates?

Gal. 4:6. And because ye are sons, God hath sent forth the Spirit of his Son into your hearts, crying, Abba, Father.

Gal. 5:22. But the fruit of the Spirit is love, joy, peace, longsuffering, gentleness, goodness, ¹faith, 23. Meekness, temperance: against such there is no law. [¹ R. V. faithfulness]

Gal. 6:7. Be not deceived; God is not mocked: for whatsoever a man soweth, that shall he also reap. 8. For he that soweth to his flesh shall of the flesh reap corruption; but he that soweth to the Spirit shall of the Spirit reap life everlasting.

Eph. 1:13. In whom ye also *trusted*, after that ye heard the word of truth, the gospel of your salvation: in whom also after that ye believed, ye were sealed with that holy Spirit of promise, 14. Which is the earnest of our inheritance until the redemption of the purchased possession, unto the praise of his glory.

Eph. 5:9. (For the fruit of the Spirit *is* in all goodness and righteousness and truth;)

Phil. 1:11. Being filled with the fruits of righteousness, which are by Jesus Christ, unto the glory and praise of God. 27. Only let your conversation be as it becometh the gospel of Christ: that whether I come and see you, or else be absent, I may hear of your affairs, that ye stand fast in one spirit, with one mind striving together for the faith of the gospel; 28. And in nothing terrified by your adversaries: which is to them an evident token of perdition, but to you of salvation, and that of God. 29. For unto you it is given in the behalf of Christ, not only to believe on him, but also to suffer for his sake;

Phil. 2:13. For it is God which worketh in you both to will and to do of *his* good pleasure.

Phil 3:12. Not as though I had already attained, either were already perfect: but I follow after, if that I may apprehend that for which also I am apprehended of Christ Jesus. 13. Brethren, I count not myself to have apprehended: but *this* one thing *I do*, forgetting those things which are behind, and reaching forth unto those things which are before, 14. I press toward the mark for the prize of the high calling of God in Christ Jesus.

Phil. 4:11. Not that I speak in respect of want: for I have learned, in whatsoever state I am, *therewith* to be content. 12. I know both how to be abased, and I know how to abound: every where and in all things I am instructed both to be full and to be hungry, both to abound and to suffer need. 13. I can do all things through Christ which strengtheneth me.

Col. 1:12. Giving thanks unto the Father, which hath made us meet to be partakers of the inheritance of the saints in light: 13. Who hath delivered us from the power of darkness, and hath translated *us* into the kingdom of his dear Son:

Col. 3:3. For ye are dead, and your life is hid with Christ in God. 5. Mortify therefore your members which are upon the earth; fornication, uncleanness, inordinate affection, evil concupiscence, and covetousness, which is idolatry: 9. Lie not one to another, seeing that ye have put off the old man with his deeds; 10. And have put on the new *man*, which is renewed in knowledge after the image of him that created him: 11. Where there is neither Greek nor Jew, circumcision nor uncircumcision, Barbarian, Scythian, bond *nor* free: but Christ *is* all, and in all. 12. Put on therefore, as the elect of God, holy and beloved, bowels of mercies, kindness, humbleness of mind, meekness, longsuffering; 13. Forbearing one another, and forgiving one another, if any man have a quarrel against any: even as Christ forgave you, so also *do* ye. 14. And above all these things *put on* charity, which is the bond of perfectness. 15. And let the peace of God rule in your hearts, to the which also ye are called in one body; and be ye thankful. 16. Let the word of Christ dwell in you richly in all wisdom; teaching and admonishing one another in psalms and hymns and spiritual songs, singing with grace in your hearts to the Lord. 17. And whatsoever ye do in word or deed, *do* all in the name of the Lord Jesus, giving thanks to God and the Father by him.

1 Thess. 1:3. Remembering without ceasing your work of faith, and labour of love, and patience of hope in our Lord Jesus Christ, in the sight of God and our Father; 9. They themselves shew of us what manner of entering in we had unto you, and how ye turned to God from idols to serve the living and true God; 10. And to wait for his Son from heaven, whom he raised from the dead, *even* Jesus, which delivered us from the wrath to come.

2 Thess. 1:3. We are bound to thank God always for you, brethren, as it is meet, because that your faith groweth exceedingly, and the charity of every one of you all toward each other aboundeth; 4. So that we ourselves glory in you in the churches of God, for your patience and faith in all your persecutions and tribulations that ye endure: 5. *Which is* a manifest token of the righteous judgment of God, that ye may be counted worthy of the kingdom of God, for which ye also suffer:

1 Tim. 2:9. In like manner also, that women adorn themselves in modest apparel, with shamefacedness and sobriety; not with broided hair, or gold, or pearls, or costly array; 10. But (which becometh women professing godliness) with good works.

1 Tim. 5:9. Let not a widow be taken into the number under threescore years old, having been the wife of one man, 10. Well reported of for good works; if she have brought up children, if she have lodged strangers, if she have washed the saints' feet, if she have relieved the afflicted, if she have diligently followed every good work.

2 Tim. 2:22. Flee also youthful lusts: but follow righteousness, faith, charity, peace, with them that call on the Lord out of a pure heart.

2 Tim. 4:6. For I am now ready to be offered, and the time of my departure is at hand. 7. I have fought a good fight, I have finished *my* course, I have kept the faith: 8. Henceforth there is laid up for me a crown of righteousness, which the Lord, the righteous judge, shall give me at that day: and not to me only, but unto all them also that love his appearing.

Tit. 2:2. That the aged men be sober, grave, temperate, sound in faith, in charity, in patience. 11. For the grace of God that bringeth salvation hath appeared to all men, 12. Teaching us that, denying ungodliness and worldly lusts, we should live soberly, righteously, and godly, in this present world:

Tit. 3:14. And let our's also learn to maintain good works for necessary uses, that they be not unfruitful.

Philem. 5. Hearing of thy love and faith, which thou hast toward the Lord Jesus, and toward all saints; 6. That the communication of thy faith may become effectual by the acknowledging of every good thing which is in you in Christ Jesus.

Jas. 1:27. Pure religion and undefiled before God and the Father is this, To visit the fatherless and widows in their affliction, *and* to keep himself unspotted from the world.

Jas. 2:14. What *doth it* profit, my brethren, though a man say he hath faith, and have not works? can faith save him? 15. If a brother or sister be naked, and destitute of daily food, 16. And one of you say unto them, Depart in peace, be *ye* warmed and filled; notwithstanding ye give them not those things which are needful to the body; what *doth it* profit? 17. Even so faith, if it hath not works, is dead, being alone. 18. Yea, a man may say, Thou hast faith, and I have works: shew me thy faith without thy works, and I will shew thee my faith by my works. 19. Thou believest that there is one God; thou doest well: the devils also believe and tremble. 20. But wilt thou know, O vain man, that faith without works is dead? 21. Was not Abraham our father justified by works, when he had offered Isaac his son upon the altar? 22. Seest thou how faith wrought with his works, and by works was faith made perfect? 23. And the scripture was fulfilled which saith, Abraham believed God, and it was imputed unto him for righteousness: and he was called the Friend of God. 24. Ye see then how that by works a man is justified, and not by faith only. 25. Likewise also was not Rahab the harlot justified by works, when she had received the messengers, and had sent *them* out another way ? 26. For as the body without the spirit is dead, so faith without works is dead also.

Jas. 3:11. Doth a fountain send forth at the same place sweet *water* and bitter ? 12. Can the fig tree, my brethren, bear olive berries ? either a vine, figs ? so *can* no fountain both yield salt water and fresh. 13. Who *is* a wise man and endued with knowledge among you ? let him shew out of a good conversation his works with meekness of wisdom. 14. But if ye have bitter envying and strife in your hearts, glory not, and lie not against the truth. 15. This wisdom descendeth not from above, but *is* earthly, sensual, devilish. 16. For where envying and strife *is*, there *is* confusion and every evil work. 17. But the wisdom that is from above is first pure, then peaceable, gentle, *and* easy to be intreated, full of mercy and good fruits, without partiality, and without hypocrisy. 18. And the fruit of righteousness is sown in peace of them that make peace.

1 Pet. 3:1. Likewise, ye wives, *be* in subjection to your own husbands; that, if any obey not the word, they also may without the word be won by the conversation of the wives; 2. While they behold your chaste conversation *coupled* with fear. 3. Whose adorning let it not be that outward *adorning* of plaiting the hair, and of wearing of gold, or of putting on of apparel; 4. But *let it be* the hidden man of the heart, in that which is not corruptible, *even the ornament* of a meek and quiet spirit, which is in the sight of God of great price. 5. For after this manner in the old time the holy women also, who trusted in God, adorned themselves, being in subjection unto their own husbands: 6. Even as Sara obeyed Abraham, calling him lord: whose daughters ye are, as long as ye do well, and are not afraid with any amazement. 7. Likewise, ye husbands, dwell with *them* according to knowledge, giving honour unto the wife, as unto the weaker vessel, and as being heirs together of the grace of life; that your prayers be not hindered. 8. Finally, *be ye* all of one mind, having compassion one of another, love as brethren, *be* pitiful, *be* courteous: 9. Not rendering evil for evil, or railing for railing: but contrariwise blessing; knowing that ye are thereunto called, that ye should inherit a blessing. 10. For he that will love life, and see good days, let him refrain his tongue from evil, and his lips that they speak no guile: 11. Let him eschew evil, and do good; let him seek peace, and ensue it. 14. But and if ye suffer for righteousness' sake, happy *are ye:*

1 Pet. 4:2. That he no longer should live the rest of *his* time in the flesh to the lusts of men, but to the will of God.

2 Pet. 1:5. And beside this, giving all diligence, add to your faith virtue; and to virtue knowledge; 6. And to knowledge temperance; and to temperance patience; and to patience godliness; 7. And to godliness brotherly kindness; and to brotherly kindness charity. 8. For if these things be in you, and abound, they make *you that ye shall* neither *be* barren nor unfruitful in the knowledge of our Lord Jesus Christ. 9. But he that lacketh these things is blind, and cannot see afar off, and hath forgotten that he was purged from his old sins.

1 John 2:3. And hereby we do know that we know him, if we keep his commandments. 4. He that saith, I know him, and keepeth not his commandments, is a liar, and the truth is not in him. 5. But whoso keepeth his word, in him verily is the love of God perfected : hereby know we that we are in him. 6. He that saith he abideth in him ought himself also so to walk, even as he walked. 10. He that loveth his brother abideth in the light, and there is none occasion of stumbling in him. 11. But he that hateth his brother is in darkness, and walketh in darkness, and knoweth not whither he goeth, because that darkness hath blinded his eyes. 24. Let that therefore abide in you, which ye have heard from the beginning. If that which ye have heard from the beginning shall remain in you, ye also shall continue in the Son, and in the Father. 29. If ye know that he is righteous, ye know that every one that doeth righteousness is born of him.

1 John 3:3. And every man that hath this hope in him purifieth himself, even as he is pure. 6. Whosoever abideth in him sinneth not : whosoever sinneth hath not seen him, neither known him. 7. He that doeth righteousness is righteous, even as he is righteous. 9. Whosoever is born of God doth not commit sin; for his seed remaineth in him: and he cannot sin, because he is born of God. 10. In this the children of God are manifest, and the children of the devil : whosoever doeth not righteousness is not of God, neither he that loveth not his brother. 11. For this is the message that ye heard from the beginning, that we should love one another. 14. We know that we have passed from death unto life, because we love the brethren. He that loveth not *his* brother abideth in death. 17. But whoso hath this world's good, and seeth his brother have need, and shutteth up his bowels *of compassion* from him, how dwelleth the love of God in him ? 18. My little children, let us not love in word, neither in tongue; but in deed and in truth. 19. And hereby we know that we are of the truth, and shall assure our hearts before him. 20. For if our heart condemn us, God is greater than our heart, and knoweth all things. 21. Beloved, if our heart condemn us not, *then* have we confidence toward God. 22. And whatsoever we ask, we receive of him, because we keep his commandments, and do those things that are pleasing in his sight. 23. And this is his commandment, That we

should believe on the name of his Son Jesus Christ, and love one another, as he gave us commandment. 24. And he that keepeth his commandments dwelleth in him, and he in him. And hereby we know that he abideth in us, by the Spirit which he hath given us.

1 John 4:4. Ye are of God, little children, and have overcome them : because greater is he that is in you, than he that is in the world. 5. They are of the world : therefore speak they of the world, and the world heareth them. 6. We are of God : he that knoweth God heareth us ; he that is not of God heareth not us. Hereby know we the spirit of truth, and the spirit of error. 7. Beloved, let us love one another : for love is of God ; and every one that loveth is born of God, and knoweth God. 8. He that loveth not knoweth not God ; for God is love. 9. In this was manifested the love of God toward us, because that God sent his only begotten Son into the world, that we might live through him. 10. Herein is love, not that we loved God, but that he loved us, and sent his Son *to be* the propitiation for our sins. 11. Beloved, if God so loved us, we ought also to love one another. 12. No man hath seen God at any time. If we love one another, God dwelleth in us, and his love is perfected in us. 13. Hereby know we that we dwell in him, and he in us, because he hath given us of his Spirit. 14. And we have seen and do testify that the Father sent the Son *to be* the Saviour of the world. 15. Whosoever shall confess that Jesus is the Son of God, God dwelleth in him, and he in God. 16. And we have known and believed the love that God hath to us. God is love : and he that dwelleth in love dwelleth in God, and God in him. 17. Herein is our love made perfect, that we may have boldness in the day of judgment : because as he is, so are we in this world. 18. There is no fear in love ; but perfect love casteth out fear : because fear hath torment. He that feareth is not made perfect in love. 19. We love him, because he first loved us. 20. If a man say, I love God, and hateth his brother, he is a liar : for he that loveth not his brother whom he hath seen, how can he love God whom he hath not seen ? 21. And this commandment have we from him, That he who loveth God love his brother also.

1 John 5:1. Whosoever believeth that Jesus is the Christ is born of God : and every one that loveth him that begat loveth him also that is begotten of him. 2. By this we know that we love the children of God, when we love God, and keep his commandments. 3. For this is the love of God, that we keep his commandments : and his commandments are not grievous. 4. For whatsoever is born of God overcometh the world : and this is the victory that overcometh the world, *even* our faith. 5. Who is he that overcometh the world, but he

that believeth that Jesus is the Son of God ? 10. He that believeth on the Son of God hath the witness in himself : he that believeth not God hath made him a liar ; because he believeth not the record that God gave of his son. 13. These things have I written unto you ¹ that believe on the name of the Son of God ; that ye may know that ye have eternal life, ² and that ye may believe on the name of the Son of God. 18. We know that whosoever is born of God sinneth not ; but he that is begotten of God keepeth himself, and that wicked one toucheth him not.

[R. V. ¹ Omitted.   ² even unto you that]

2 John 9. Whosoever transgresseth, and abideth not in the doctrine of Christ, hath not God. He that abideth in the doctrine of Christ, he hath both the Father and the Son.

3 John 11. Beloved, follow not that which is evil, but that which is good. He that doeth good is of God : but he that doeth evil hath not seen God.

Rev. 2:2. I know thy works, and thy labour, and thy patience, and how thou canst not bear them which are evil : and thou hast tried them which say they are apostles, and are not, and hast found them liars : 3. And hast borne, and hast patience, and for my name's sake hast laboured, and hast not fainted. 19. I know thy works, and charity, and service, and faith, and thy patience, and thy works ; and the last *to be* more than the first.

SYMBOLIZED : Ezek. 47:12 ; Rev. 22:2.

See SIN, FRUITS OF ; WORKS, GOOD.

RIMMON. 1. Father of the murderers of Ish-bosheth, 2 Sam. 4:2,5,9.

2. A city S. of Jerusalem, Zech. 14:10. Allotted to Judah, Josh. 15:32 ; Neh. 11:29 ; afterward to Simeon, Josh. 19:7 ; 1 Chr. 4: 32. Called REMMON, Josh. 19:7 ; and EN-RIM-MON, Neh. 11:29.

3. A city of Zebulun, 1 Chr. 6:77. Called REMMON-METHOAR, Josh. 19:13.

4. A rock in Benjamin, Judg. 20:45,47 ; 21:13.

5. A Syrian idol, 2 Kin. 5:18.

RIMMON-PAREZ, a camping place of the Israelites, Num. 33:19,20.

RING. Of gold, Num. 31:50. Worn as a badge of office, Gen. 41:42. Given as a token, Esth. 3:10,12 ; 8:2-10. Worn in the nose, Prov. 11:22 ; Isa. 3:21. Offerings of, to the tabernacle, Ex. 35:22 ; Num. 31:50.

RINNAH, a son of Shimon, 1 Chr. 4:20.

RIPHATH, a son of Gomer, Gen. 10:3 ; 1 Chr. 1:6.

RISING. EARLY: Prov. 31:15. For devotions, Psa. 5:3 ; 59:16 ; 63:1 ; 88:13 ; Song 7: 12 ; Isa. 26:9. Practised by the wicked. Prov. 27:14 ; Mic. 2:1 ; Zeph. 3:7 ; by drunkards, Isa. 5:11. Illustrates spiritual diligence, Rom. 13:11,12.

INSTANCES OF : Lot, Gen. 19:23. Abraham, Gen. 19:27 ; 21:14 ; 22:3. Isaac, Gen. 26:31. Abimelech, Gen. 20:8. Jacob, Gen. 28:18, 32:31. Laban, Gen. 31:55. Moses, Ex. 8:20 ;

9:13. Joshua, Josh. 3:1; 6:12,15; 7:16. Gideon, Judg. 6:38. Elkanah, 1 Sam. 1:19. Samuel, 1 Sam. 15:12. David, 1 Sam. 17:20. Mary, Mark 16:2; Luke 24:1. Apostles, Acts 5:21. See INDUSTRY.

LATE: Consequences of, Prov. 6:9-11; 24: 33,34.

See IDLENESS ; SLOTHFULNESS.

RISSAH, a camping place of the Israelites, Num. 33:21,22.

RITHMAH, a camping place of the Israelites, Num. 33:18,19.

RIVER. FIGURATIVE: Of salvation, Psa. 36:8; 46:4; Isa. 32:2; Ezek. 47:1-12; Rev. 22:1,2. Of grief, Psa. 119:136; Lam. 3:48.

RIZPAH. Concubine of Saul, 2 Sam. 3: 7. Guards the bodies of her sons hanged by command of David, 2 Sam. 21:8-11.

ROADS. Public highways, Deut. 2:27. From Gibeon to Beth-horon, Josh. 10:10. From Beth-el to Shechem, Judg. 21:19. From Judæa to Galilee, by way of Samaria, John 4:3-5,43. To the house of God, Judg. 20:31. To cities of refuge, Deut. 19:3. Built by rulers, Num. 20:17; 21:22.

FIGURATIVE: See HIGHWAYS.

ROBBERS, Prov. 1:11-16. Dens of, Jer. 7:11. Bands of, Hos. 6:9; 7:1.

See ROBBERY; THEFT.

ROBBERY. Forbidden, Lev. 19:13; Isa. 61:8. Punished with death, Ezek. 18:10,13. Forgiven, Ezek. 33:15.

INSTANCES OF: Judg. 9:25; Luke 10:30. See ROBBERS; THEFT.

ROBE. Of righteousness, 2 Chr. 6:41; Isa. 61:10; Rev. 6:11; 7:9,13. Parable of the man who was not dressed in a wedding garment, Matt. 22:11. See DRESS.

ROCK. Smitten by Moses for water, Deut. 8:15; Psa. 78:15,16,20. Houses in, Jer. 49:16; Obad. 3; Matt. 7:24,25. Oil from, Job 29:6; Deut. 32:13. Name of deity, Deut. 32:4.

FIGURATIVE: 2 Sam. 22:32,47; 23:3; Psa. 18:2; 31:2; 40:2; Isa. 17:10; 32:2; Matt. 16:18; 1 Cor. 10:4.

ROE. See DEER.

ROGELIM, the home of Barzillai, 2 Sam. 17:27; 19:31.

ROHGAH, son of Shamer, 1 Chr. 7:34.

ROLL, metallic table, Isa. 8:1. See BOOK.

ROMAMTI-EZER, son of Heman, 1 Chr. 25:4,31.

ROMAN EMPIRE. Ruled by Augustus Cæsar, Luke 2:1; Tiberius Cæsar, Luke 3:1; Claudius Cæsar, Acts 18:2; Nero, Phil. 4:22.* Citizenship in, by nativity, Acts 22: 28; by purchase, Acts 22:28. Rights of citizens, Acts 16:37; 22:25-29; of trial, Acts 25: 16; of appeal, Acts 25:10,21.

ROME, the capital of the Roman empire. Jews excluded from, by Claudius, Acts 18:2. Paul's visit to, see PAUL. Visited by Onesiphorus, 2 Tim. 1:16,17. Paul desires to preach in, Rom. 1:15. Abominations in, Rom. 1:18-32. Christians in, Rom. 16:5-17; Phil. 1:12-18; 4:22; 2 Tim. 4:21.

---

* See postscript to the Second Epistle of Paul to Timothy.

Paul's letter to the Christians in, Rom. 1: 7; testifies to them the gospel of Christ, Rom. 1:16; the condemnation of the Gentiles, Rom. 1:18; and the Jews, Rom. 2; God's judgment against all sin, Rom. 2:6; 3; justification by faith in Jesus Christ, Rom. 3:24; 4; 5; the faith of Abraham, Rom. 4; the fruits of faith, Rom. 5-7; the works of the flesh and the Spirit, Rom. 8; God's supreme power over all, Rom. 9; 11; the righteousness of the law and of faith, Rom. 10. Exhorted to humility, love, and good works, Rom. 12: to obey magistrates, Rom. 13; to mutual forbearance, Rom. 14; 15; requested to greet various brethren, Rom. 16.

ROOF. See HOUSE, ROOF OF.

ROPE. Threefold, Eccl. 4:12. Worn on the head as an emblem of servitude, 1 Kin. 20:31,32. Used in casting lots, Mic. 2:5.

FIGURATIVE: Of love, Hos. 11:4. Of affliction, Job 36:8. Of temptations, Psa. 140: 5; Prov. 5:22.

ROSE, Song 2:1; Isa. 35:1.

ROSH. 1. Son of Benjamin, Gen. 46:21. 2. An ancient people, Ezek. 38:2,3 [R. V.]; 39:1 [R. V.].

RUBY, Job 28:18; Prov. 20:15; 31:10; Lam. 4:7.

RUE, Luke 11:42.

RUFUS. Son of Simon, Mark 15:21. Probably identical with the RUFUS in Rom. 16:13.

RUHAMAH, a symbolic name of Israel, Hos. 2:1.

RULERS. Appointed and removed by God. See GOVERNMENT, GOD IN. Chastised, Dan. 4. See NATION.

Monarchical, see KINGS.

Patriarchal, Gen. 27:29,37. INSTANCES OF: Nimrod, Gen. 10:8-10. Abraham, Gen. 14: 13-24; 17:6; 21:21-32. Melchizedek, Gen. 14:18. Isaac, Gen. 26:26-31. Judah, Gen. 38:24. Heads of families, Ex. 6:14. Ishmael, Gen. 17:20. Esau, and the dukes of Edom, Gen. 36.

Theocratic. See GOVERNMENT.

CHARACTER AND QUALIFICATIONS OF: Gen. 41:33. Now therefore let Pharaoh look out a man discreet and wise, and set him over the land of Egypt.

Ex. 18:21. Moreover thou shalt provide out of all the people able men, such as fear God, men of truth, hating covetousness; and place such over them, to be rulers of thousands, and rulers of hundreds, rulers of fifties, and rulers of tens. 22. And let them judge the people at all seasons: and it shall be, that every great matter they shall bring unto thee, but every small matter they shall judge: so shall it be easier for thyself, and they shall bear the burden with thee.

Ex. 23:8. And thou shalt take no gift: for the gift blindeth the wise, and perverteth the words of the righteous.

Deut. 1:13. Take you wise men, and understanding, and known among your tribes, and I will make them rulers over you.

Deut. 16:18. Judges and officers shalt thou make thee in all thy gates, which the LORD thy God giveth thee, throughout thy tribes: and they shall judge the people with just judgment. 19. Thou shalt not wrest judgment; thou shalt not respect persons, neither take a gift: for a gift doth blind the eyes of the wise, and pervert the words of the righteous. 20. That which is altogether just shalt thou follow, that thou mayest live, and inherit the land which the LORD thy God giveth thee.

Deut. 27:19. Cursed *be* he that perverteth the judgment of the stranger, fatherless, and widow. And all the people shall say, Amen.

2 Sam. 23:3. The God of Israel said, the Rock of Israel spake to me, He that ruleth over men *must be* just, ruling in the fear of God. 4. And *he shall be* as the light of the morning, *when* the sun riseth, *even* a morning without clouds; *as* the tender grass *springing* out of the earth by clear shining after rain.

Ezra 7:25. And thou, Ezra, after the wisdom of thy God, that *is* in thine hand, set magistrates and judges, which may judge all the people that *are* beyond the river, all such as know the laws of thy God; and teach ye them that know *them* not.

Psa. 2:10. Be wise now therefore, O ye kings: be instructed, ye judges of the earth. 11. Serve the LORD with fear, and rejoice with trembling.

Psa. 72:1. Give the king thy judgments, O God, and thy righteousness unto the king's son. 2. He shall judge thy people with righteousness, and thy poor with judgment. 3. The mountains shall bring peace to the people, and the little hills, by righteousness. 4. He shall judge the poor of the people, he shall save the children of the needy, and shall break in pieces the oppressor. 5. They shall fear thee as long as the sun and moon endure, throughout all generations. 6. He shall come down like rain upon the mown grass: as showers *that* water the earth. 7. In his days shall the righteous flourish; and abundance of peace so long as the moon endureth. 8. He shall have dominion also from sea to sea, nd from the river unto the ends of the earth. 9. They that dwell in the wilderness shall bow before him; and his enemies shall lick the dust. 10. The kings of Tarshish and of the isles shall bring presents: the kings of Sheba and Seba shall offer gifts. 11. Yea, all kings shall fall down before him: all nations shall serve him. 12. For he shall deliver the needy when he crieth; the poor also, and *him* that hath no helper. 13. He shall spare the poor and needy, and shall save the souls of the needy. 14. He shall redeem their soul from deceit and violence: and precious shall their blood be in his sight. 15. And he shall live. and to him shall be given of the gold of Sheba: prayer also shall be made for him continually; *and* daily shall he be praised.

16. There shall be an handful of corn in the earth upon the top of the mountains; the fruit thereof shall shake like Lebanon: and *they* of the city shall flourish like grass of the earth. 17. His name shall endure for ever: his name shall be continued as long as the sun: and *men* shall be blessed in him: all nations shall call him blessed.

Prov. 16:10. A divine sentence *is* in the lips of the king: his mouth transgresseth not in judgment. 12. *It is* an abomination to kings to commit wickedness: for the throne is established by righteousness. 13. Righteous lips *are* the delight of kings; and they love him that speaketh right.

Prov. 17:7. Excellent speech becometh not a fool: much less do lying lips a prince.

Prov. 19:12. The king's wrath *is* as the roaring of a lion; but his favour *is* as dew upon the grass.

Prov. 20:8. A king that sitteth in the throne of judgment scattereth away all evil with his eyes. 26. A wise king scattereth the wicked, and bringeth the wheel over them. 28. Mercy and truth preserve the king: and his throne is upholden by mercy.

Prov. 21:1. The king's heart *is* in the hand of the LORD, *as* the rivers of water: he turneth it whithersoever he will.

Prov. 24:23. These *things* also *belong* to the wise. *It is* not good to have respect of persons in judgment. 24. He that saith unto the wicked, Thou *art* righteous; him shall the people curse, nations shall abhor him: 25. But to them that rebuke *him* shall be delight, and a good blessing shall come upon them. 26. *Every man* shall kiss *his* lips that giveth a right answer.

Prov. 25:2. *It is* the glory of God to conceal a thing: but the honour of kings *is* to search out a matter. 3. The heaven for height, and the earth for depth, and the heart of kings *is* unsearchable. 5. Take away the wicked *from* before the king, and his throne shall be established in righteousness.

Prov. 28:2. For the transgression of a land many *are* the princes thereof: but by a man of understanding *and* knowledge the state *thereof* shall be prolonged. 16. The prince that wanteth understanding *is* also a great oppressor: *but* he that hateth covetousness shall prolong *his* days.

Prov. 29:2. When the righteous are in authority, the people rejoice: but when the wicked beareth rule, the people mourn. 4. The king by judgment establisheth the land: but he that receiveth gifts overthroweth it. 14. The king that faithfully judgeth the poor, his throne shall be established for ever.

Prov. 31:4. *It is* not for kings, O Lemuel, *it is* not for kings to drink wine; nor for princes strong drink: 5. Lest they drink, and forget the law, and pervert the judgment of any of the afflicted. 8. Open thy mouth for the dumb in the cause of all such as are appointed to destruction. 9. Open thy mouth, judge righteously, and plead the cause of the poor and needy.

Eccl. 8:4. Where the word of a king *is, there is* power: and who may say unto him, What doest thou?

Eccl. 10:16. Woe to thee, O land, when thy king *is* a child, and thy princes eat in the morning! 17. Blessed *art* thou, O land, when thy king *is* the son of nobles, and thy princes eat in due season, for strength, and not for drunkenness!

Isa. 5:22. Woe unto *them that are* mighty to drink wine, and men of strength to mingle strong drink: 23. Which justify the wicked for reward, and take away the righteousness of the righteous from him!

Isa. 16:5. And in mercy shall the throne be established: and he shall sit upon it in truth in the tabernacle of David, judging, and seeking judgment, and hasting righteousness.

Isa. 28:6. And for a spirit of judgment to him that sitteth in judgment, and for strength to them that turn the battle to the gate.

Isa. 60:17. I will also make thy officers peace, and thine exactors righteousness.

Jer. 13:18. Say unto the king and to the queen, Humble yourselves, sit down: for your principalities shall come down, *even* the crown of your glory.

Rom. 12:8. Or he that exhorteth, on exhortation: he that giveth, *let him do it* with simplicity; he that ruleth, with diligence; he that sheweth mercy, with cheerfulness.

Rom. 13:1. Let every soul be subject unto the higher powers. For there is no power but of God: the powers that be are ordained of God. 2. Whosoever therefore resisteth the power, resisteth the ordinance of God: and they that resist shall receive to themselves damnation. 3. For rulers are not a terror to good works, but to the evil. Wilt thou then not be afraid of the power? do that which is good, and thou shalt have praise of the same: 4. For he is the minister of God to thee for good. But if thou do that which is evil, be afraid; for he beareth not the sword in vain: for he is the minister of God, a revenger to *execute* wrath upon him that doeth evil. 5. Wherefore *ye* must needs be subject, not only for wrath, but also for conscience' sake. 6. For for this cause pay ye tribute also: for they are God's ministers, attending continually upon this very thing. 7. Render therefore to all their dues: tribute to whom tribute *is due;* custom to whom custom; fear to whom fear; honour to whom honour.

1 Tim. 2:1. I exhort therefore, that, first of all, supplications, prayers, intercessions, *and* giving of thanks, be made for all men; 2. For kings, and *for* all that are in authority;

1 Pet. 2:13. Submit yourselves to every ordinance of man for the Lord's sake: whether it be to the king, as supreme; 14. Or unto governors, as unto them that are

sent by him for the punishment of evil doers, and for the praise of them that do well.

DUTIES OF: Ex. 18:16. When they have a matter, they come unto me; and I judge between one and another, and I do make *them* know the statutes of God, and his laws. 20. And thou shalt teach them ordinances and laws, and shalt shew them the way wherein they must walk, and the work that they must do. 21. Moreover thou shalt provide out of all the people able men, such as fear God, men of truth, hating covetousness; and place *such* over them, *to be* rulers of thousands, *and* rulers of hundreds, rulers of fifties, and rulers of tens:

Ex. 23:3. Neither shalt thou countenance a poor man in his cause. 6. Thou shall not wrest the judgment of thy poor in his cause. 7. Keep thee far from a false matter; and the innocent and righteous slay thou not: for I will not justify the wicked. 9. Also thou shalt not oppress a stranger: for ye know the heart of a stranger, seeing ye were strangers in the land of Egypt.

Lev. 19:15. Ye shall do no unrighteousness in judgment: thou shalt not respect the person of the poor, nor honour the person of the mighty: *but* in righteousness shalt thou judge thy neighbour.

Lev. 24:22. Ye shall have one manner of law, as well for the stranger, as for one of your own country: for I *am* the LORD your God.

Num. 27:16. Let the LORD, the God of the spirits of all flesh, set a man over the congregation, 17. Which may go out before them, and which may go in before them, and which may lead them out, and which may bring them in; that the congregation of the LORD be not as sheep which have no shepherd.

Deut. 1:16. And I charged your judges at that time, saying, Hear *the causes* between your brethren, and judge righteously between *every* man and his brother, and the stranger *that is* with him. 17. Ye shall not respect persons in judgment; *but* ye shall hear the small as well as the great; ye shall not be afraid of the face of man; for the judgment *is* God's:

Deut. 16:18. Judges and officers shalt thou make thee in all thy gates, which the LORD thy God giveth thee, throughout thy tribes: and they shall judge the people with just judgment. 19. Thou shalt not wrest judgment; thou shalt not respect persons, neither take a gift: for a gift doth blind the eyes of the wise, and pervert the words of the righteous. 20. That which is altogether just shalt thou follow, that thou mayest live, and inherit the land which the LORD thy God giveth thee.

Deut. 17:16. But he shall not multiply horses to himself, nor cause the people to return to Egypt, to the end that he should multiply horses: forasmuch as the LORD hath said unto you, Ye shall henceforth return no more that way. 17. Neither shall he multiply wives to himself, that his heart turn not away: neither shall he greatly multiply to himself silver and gold. 18. And it shall be, when he sitteth upon the throne of his kingdom, that he shall write him a copy of this law in a book out of *that which is* before the priests the Levites: 19. And it shall be with him, and he shall read therein all the days of his life: that he may learn to fear the LORD his God, to keep all the words of this law and these statutes, to do them: 20. That his heart be not lifted up above his brethren, and that he turn not aside from the commandment, *to* the right hand, or *to* the left: to the end that he may prolong *his* days in his ·kingdom, he, and his children, in the midst of Israel.

Deut. 19:18. And the judges shall make diligent inquisition: and, behold, *if* the witness *be* a false witness, *and* hath testified falsely against his brother; 19. Then shall ye do unto him, as he had thought to have done unto his brother: so shalt thou put the evil away from among you.

Deut. 24:16. The fathers shall not be put to death for the children, neither shall the children be put to death for the fathers: every man shall be put to death for his own sin.

Deut. 25:1. If there be a controversy between men, and they come unto judgment, that *the judges* may judge them; then they shall justify the righteous, and condemn the wicked.

Josh. 1:7. Only be thou strong and very courageous, that thou mayest observe to do according to all the law, which Moses my servant commanded thee: turn not from it *to* the right hand or *to* the left, that thou mayest prosper whithersoever thou goest. 8. This book of the law shall not depart out of thy mouth; but thou shalt meditate therein day and night, that thou mayest observe to do according to all that is written therein: for then thou shalt make thy way prosperous, and then thou shalt have good success.

2 Chr. 9:8. God loved Israel, to establish them for ever, therefore made he thee king over them, to do judgment and justice.

2 Chr. 19:6. And said to the judges, Take heed what ye do: for ye judge not for man, but for the LORD, who *is* with you in the judgment. 7. Wherefore now let the fear of the LORD be upon you; take heed and do *it:* for *there is* no iniquity with the LORD our God, nor respect of persons, nor taking of gifts.

Ezra 7:25. And thou, Ezra, after the wisdom of thy God, that *is* in thine hand, set magistrates and judges, which may judge all the people that *are* beyond the river, all such as know the laws of thy God; and teach ye them that know *them* not. 26. And whosoever will not do the law of thy God, and the law of the king, let judgment be executed speedily upon him, whether *it*

be unto death, or to banishment, or to confiscation of goods, or to imprisonment.

Psa. 82:2. How long will ye judge unjustly, and accept the persons of the wicked? 3. Defend the poor and fatherless: do justice to the afflicted and needy. 4. Deliver the poor and needy: rid *them* out of the hand of the wicked.

Psa. 148:11. Kings of the earth, and all people; princes, and all judges of the earth: 13. Let them praise the name of the LORD:

Isa. 58:6. *Is* not this the fast that I have chosen? to loose the bands of wickedness, to undo the heavy burdens, and to let the oppressed go free, and that ye break every yoke?

Jer. 22:1. Thus saith the LORD; Go down to the house of the king of Judah, and speak there this word, 2. And say, Hear the word of the LORD, O king of Judah, that sittest upon the throne of David, thou, and thy servants, and thy people that enter in by these gates: 3. Thus saith the LORD; Execute ye judgment and righteousness, and deliver the spoiled out of the hand of the oppressor: and do no wrong, do no violence to the stranger, the fatherless, nor the widow, neither shed innocent blood in this place. Jer. 21:12.

Zech. 7:9. Thus speaketh the LORD of hosts, saying, Execute true judgment, and shew mercy and compassions every man to his brother: 10. And oppress not the widow, nor the fatherless, the stranger, nor the poor; and let none of you imagine evil against his brother in your heart.

Zech. 8:16. These *are* the things that ye shall do; Speak ye every man the truth to his neighbour; execute the judgment of truth and peace in your gates:

Rom. 13:3. For rulers are not a terror to good works, but to the evil.

1 Tim. 2:2. For kings, and *for* all that are in authority; that we may lead a quiet and peaceable life in all godliness and honesty.

1 Pet. 2:14. Or unto governors, as unto them that are sent by him for the punishment of evildoers, and for the praise of them that do well.

RIGHTEOUS. INSTANCES OF: Pharaoh, in his treatment of Abraham, Gen. 12:15–20. Abimelech, in his treatment of Abraham, Gen. 20; of Isaac, Gen. 26:6–11. Joseph, in his conduct of the affairs of Egypt, Gen. 41:37–57. Pharaoh, in his treatment of Jacob and his family, Gen. 47:5–10; 50:1–6. Moses, in his administration of the affairs of the children of Israel, Num. 16:15. See GOVERNMENT, MOSAIC. Samuel, in not taking reward for judgment, 1 Sam. 12:3,4. Saul, after the defeat of the Ammonites, 1 Sam. 11:12,13. Solomon, in his judgment between the two women who claimed the same child, 1 Kin. 3:16–28; according to the testimony of the queen of Sheba, 1 Kin. 10:6–9. Asa, in abolishing sodomy and other abominations of idolatry, 1 Kin. 15:11–15: 2 Chr. 14:2–5. Jehoshaphat, in walking in the ways of the

Lord, 1 Kin. 22:41-46; 2 Chr. 17:3-10; 19; 20:3-30. Hezekiah, in his fear of the Lord, 2 Kin. 18:3; 20:1-11; 2 Chr. 30; 31. Josiah, in repairing the temple and in other good works, 2 Kin. 22; 23; 2 Chr. 34; 35. Cyrus, in emancipating the Jews, Ezra 1. Darius, in advancing the rebuilding of the temple, Ezra 6:1-12. Artaxerxes, in commissioning Ezra to restore the forms of worship at Jerusalem, Ezra 7; Neh. 2; 5:14. Nehemiah, Neh. chapters 4; 5. Daniel, see DANIEL. King of Nineveh, in repenting, and proclaiming a fast, Jonah 3:6-9.

WICKED: Gen. 15:13. Know of a surety that thy seed shall be a stranger in a land *that is* not their's, and shall serve them; and they shall afflict them four hundred years; 14. And also that nation, whom they shall serve, will I judge:

Ex. 3:9. The cry of the children of Israel is come unto me: and I have also seen the oppression wherewith the Egyptians oppress them.

Deut. 27:19. Cursed *be* he that perverteth the judgment of the stranger, fatherless, and widow.

1 Sam. 8:10. And Samuel told all the words of the LORD unto the people that asked of him a king. 11. And he said, This will be the manner of the king that shall reign over you: He will take your sons, and appoint *them* for himself, for his chariots, and *to be* his horsemen; and *some* shall run before his chariots. 12. And he will appoint him captains over thousands, and captains over fifties; and *will set them* to ear his ground, and to reap his harvest, and to make his instruments of war, and instruments of his chariots. 13. And he will take your daughters *to be* confectionaries, and *to be* cooks, and *to be* bakers. 14. And he will take your fields, and your vineyards, and your oliveyards, *even* the best *of them*, and give *them* to his servants. 15. And he will take the tenth of your seed, and of your vineyards, and give to his officers, and to his servants. 16. And he will take your menservants, and your maidservants, and your goodliest young men, and your asses, and put *them* to his work. 17. He will take the tenth of your sheep: and ye shall be his servants. 18. And ye shall cry out in that day because of your king which ye shall have chosen you;

2 Chr. 28:19. For the LORD brought Judah low because of Ahaz king of Israel; for he made Judah naked, and transgressed sore against the LORD.

Neh. 5:7. Then I consulted with myself, and I rebuked the nobles, and the rulers, and said unto them, Ye exact usury, every one of his brother. 8. And I said unto them, We after our ability have redeemed our brethren the Jews, which were sold unto the heathen; and will ye even sell your brethren? or shall they be sold unto us? Then held they their peace, and found nothing *to answer*. 9. Also I said, It *is* not good

that ye do: ought ye not to walk in the fear of our God because of the reproach of the heathen our enemies?

Neh. 9:34. Neither have our kings, our princes, our priests, nor our fathers, kept thy law, nor hearkened unto thy commandments and thy testimonies, wherewith thou didst testify against them. 35. For they have not served thee in their kingdom, and in thy great goodness that thou gavest them, and in the large and fat land which thou gavest before them, neither turned they from their wicked works. 36. Behold, we *are* servants this day, and *for* the land that thou gavest unto our fathers to eat the fruit thereof and the good thereof, behold, we *are* servants in it: 37. And it yieldeth much increase unto the kings whom thou hast set over us because of our sins: also they have dominion over our bodies, and over our cattle, at their pleasure, and we *are* in great distress.

Job 24:22. He draweth also the mighty with his power: he riseth up, and no *man* is sure of life. 24. They are exalted for a little while, but are gone and brought low; they are taken out of the way as all *other*, and cut off as the tops of the ears of corn.

Job 35:9. By reason of the multitude of oppressions they make *the oppressed* to cry: they cry out by reason of the arm of the mighty.

Psa. 10:17. LORD, thou hast heard the desire of the humble: thou wilt prepare their heart, thou wilt cause thine ear to hear: 18. To judge the fatherless and the oppressed, that the man of the earth may no more oppress.

Psa. 12:5. For the oppression of the poor, for the sighing of the needy, now will I arise, saith the LORD; I will set *him* in safety *from him that* puffeth at him. 8. The wicked walk on every side, when the vilest men are exalted.

Psa. 49:20. Man *that is* in honour, and understandeth not, is like the beasts *that* perish.

Psa. 58:1. Do ye judge uprightly, O ye sons of men? 2. Yea, in heart ye work wickedness; ye weigh the violence of your hands in the earth.

Psa. 82:2. How long will ye judge unjustly, and accept the persons of the wicked?

Psa. 94:20. Shall the throne of iniquity have fellowship with thee, which frameth mischief by a law? 21 They gather themselves together against the soul of the righteous, and condemn the innocent blood.

Psa. 110:5. The Lord at thy right hand shall strike through kings in the day of his wrath.

Prov. 17:15. He that justifieth the wicked, and he that condemneth the just, even they both *are* abomination to the LORD. 26. Also to punish the just *is* not good, *nor* to strike princes for equity.

Prov. 28:15. *As* a roaring lion, and a

ranging bear; *so is* a wicked ruler over the poor people. 16. The prince that wanteth understanding *is* also a great oppressor: *but* he that hateth coveteousness shall prolong *his* days. 28. When the wicked rise, men hide themselves: but when they perish, the righteous increase.

Prov. 29:2. When the righteous are in authority, the people rejoice: but when the wicked beareth rule, the people mourn. 4. The king by judgment establisheth the land: but he that receiveth gifts overthroweth it. 12. If a ruler hearken to lies, all his servants *are* wicked.

Prov. 30:21. For three *things* the earth is disquieted, and for four *which* it cannot bear: 22. For a servant when he reigneth; and a fool when he is filled with meat;

Eccl. 3:16. And moreover I saw under the sun the place of judgment, *that* wickedness *was* there; and the place of righteousness, *that* iniquity *was* there. 17. I said in mine heart, God shall judge the righteous and the wicked: for *there is* a time there for every purpose and for every work.

Eccl. 4:1. I returned, and considered all the oppressions that are done under the sun: and behold the tears of *such as were* oppressed, and they have no comforter; and on the side of their oppressors *there was* power; but they had no comforter. 13. Better *is* a poor and a wise child than an old and foolish king, who will no more be admonished. 14. For out of prison he cometh to reign; whereas also *he that is* born in his kingdom becometh poor.

Eccl. 5:8. If thou seest the oppression of the poor, and violent perverting of judgment and justice in a province, marvel not at the matter: for *he that is* higher than the highest regardeth; and *there be* higher than they.

Eccl. 8:9. All this have I seen, and applied my heart unto every work that is done under the sun: *there is* a time wherein one man ruleth over another to his own hurt.

Eccl. 10:5. There is an evil *which* I have seen under the sun, as an error *which* proceedeth from the ruler: 6. Folly is set in great dignity, and the rich sit in low place. 7. I have seen servants upon horses, and princes walking as servants upon the earth. 16. Woe to thee, O land, when thy king *is* a child, and thy princes eat in the morning! 17. Blessed *art* thou, O land, when thy king *is* the son of nobles, and thy princes eat in due season, for strength, and not for drunkenness!

Isa. 1:23. Thy princes *are* rebellious, and companions of thieves: every one loveth gifts, and followeth after rewards: they judge not the fatherless, neither doth the cause of the widow come unto them.

Isa. 3:12. *As for* my people, children *are* their oppressors, and women rule over them. O my people, they which lead thee cause *thee* to err, and destroy the way of thy paths. 14. The LORD will enter into judgment with the ancients of his people. and the princes thereof: for ye have eaten up the vineyard; the spoil of the poor *is* in your houses. 15. What mean ye *that* ye beat my people to pieces, and grind the faces of the poor? saith the Lord GOD of hosts.

Isa. 5:7. For the vineyard of the LORD of hosts *is* the house of Israel, and the men of Judah his pleasant plant: and he looked for judgment, but behold oppression; for righteousness, but behold a cry.

Isa. 10:1. Woe unto them that decree unrighteous decrees, and that write grievousness *which* they have prescribed; 2. To turn aside the needy from judgment, and to take away the right from the poor of my people, that widows may be their prey, and *that* they may rob the fatherless! 3. And what will ye do in the day of visitation, and in the desolation *which* shall come from far? to whom will ye flee for help? and where will ye leave your glory?

Isa. 14:5. The LORD hath broken the staff of the wicked, *and* the sceptre of the rulers. 6. He who smote the people in wrath with a continual stroke, he that ruled the nations in anger, is persecuted, *and* none hindereth. 19. But thou art cast out of thy grave like an abominable branch, *and as* the raiment of those that are slain, thrust through with a sword, that go down to the stones of the pit; as a carcase trodden under feet. 20. Thou shalt not be joined with them in burial, because thou hast destroyed thy land, *and* slain thy people: the seed of evildoers shall never be renowned. *vs.* 4–20.

Isa. 28:14. Wherefore hear the word of the LORD, ye scornful men, that rule this people which *is* in Jerusalem. 15. Because ye have said, We have made a covenant with death, and with hell are we at agreement; when the overflowing scourge shall pass through, it shall not come unto us: for we have made lies our refuge, and under falsehood have we hid ourselves:

Isa. 29:20. The terrible one is brought to nought, and the scorner is consumed, and all that watch for iniquity are cut off: 21. That make a man an offender for a word, and lay a snare for him that reproveth in the gate, and turn aside the just for a thing of nought.

Isa. 30:33. For Tophet *is* ordained of old; yea, for the king it is prepared; he hath made *it* deep *and* large: the pile thereof *is* fire and much wood; the breath of the LORD, like a stream of brimstone, doth kindle it.

Isa. 33:1. Woe to thee that spoilest, and thou *wast* not spoiled; and dealest treacherously, and they dealt not treacherously with thee! when thou shalt cease to spoil, thou shalt be spoiled; *and* when thou shalt make an end to deal treacherously, they shall deal treacherously with thee.

Isa. 40:23. That bringeth the princes to nothing; he maketh the judges of the earth as vanity.

Isa. 52:5. Now therefore, what have I here, saith the LORD, that my people is taken away for nought? they that rule over them make them to howl, saith the LORD;

Isa. 59:14. Judgment is turned away backward, and justice standeth afar off: for truth is fallen in the street, and equity cannot enter. 15. Yea, truth faileth; and he *that* departeth from evil maketh himself a prey: and the LORD saw *it*, and it displeased him that *there was* no judgment.

Jer. 5:28. They are waxen fat, they shine: yea, they overpass the deeds of the wicked: they judge not the cause, the cause of the fatherless, yet they prosper; and the right of the needy do they not judge. 29. Shall I not visit for these *things*? saith the LORD: shall not my soul be avenged on such a nation as this?

Ezek. 21:25. And thou, profane wicked prince of Israel, whose day is come, when iniquity *shall have* an end, 26. Thus saith the Lord GOD; Remove the diadem, and take off the crown:

Ezek. 22:6. Behold, the princes of Israel, every one were in thee to their power to shed blood. 27. Her princes in the midst thereof *are* like wolves ravening the prey, to shed blood, *and* to destroy souls, to get dishonest gain.

Ezek. 28:2. Son of man, say unto the prince of Tyrus, Thus saith the Lord GOD; Because thine heart *is* lifted up, and thou hast said, I *am* a God, I sit *in* the seat of God, in the midst of the seas; yet thou *art* a man, and not God, though thou set thine heart as the heart of God:

Ezek. 34:2. Woe *be* to the shepherds of Israel that do feed themselves! should not the shepherds feed the flocks? 3. Ye eat the fat, and ye clothe you with the wool, ye kill them that are fed: *but* ye feed not the flock. 4. The diseased have ye not strengthened, neither have ye healed that which was sick, neither have ye bound up *that which was* broken, neither have ye brought again that which was driven away, neither have ye sought that which was lost; but with force and with cruelty have ye ruled them. 7. Therefore, ye shepherds, hear the word of the LORD; 8. *As* I live, saith the Lord GOD, surely because my flock became a prey, and my flock became meat to every beast of the field, because *there was* no shepherd, neither did my shepherds search for my flock, but the shepherds fed themselves, and fed not my flock; 9. Therefore, O ye shepherds, hear the word of the LORD; 10. Thus saith the Lord GOD; Behold, I *am* against the shepherds; and I will require my flock at their hand, and cause them to cease from feeding the flock; neither shall the shepherds feed themselves any more: for I will deliver my flock from their mouth, that they may not be meat for them.

Ezek. 45:9. Thus saith the Lord GOD, Let it suffice you, O princes of Israel: remove violence and spoil, and execute judgment and justice, take away your exactions from my people, saith the Lord GOD.

Hos. 5:10. The princes of Judah were like them that remove the bound: *therefore* I will pour out my wrath upon them like water.

Hos. 7:3. They make the king glad with their wickedness, and the princes with their lies.

Hos. 10:7. *As for* Samaria, her king is cut off as the foam upon the water.

Amos 3:10. They know not to do right, saith the LORD, who store up violence and robbery in their palaces. 11. Therefore thus saith the Lord GOD; An adversary *there shall be* even round about the land; and he shall bring down thy strength from thee, and thy palaces shall be spoiled.

Amos 4:1. Hear this word, ye . . . which oppress the poor, which crush the needy, which say to their masters, Bring, and let us drink. 2. The Lord GOD hath sworn by his holiness, that, lo, the days shall come upon you, that he will take you away with hooks, and your posterity with fishhooks.

Amos 5:11. Forasmuch therefore as your treading *is* upon the poor, and ye take from him burdens of wheat: ye have built houses of hewn stone, but ye shall not dwell in them; ye have planted pleasant vineyards, but ye shall not drink wine of them. 12. For I know your manifold transgressions and your mighty sins: they afflict the just, they take a bribe, and they turn aside the poor in the gate *from their right.*

Amos 6:12. Shall horses run upon the rock? will *one* plow *there* with oxen? for ye have turned judgment into gall, and the fruit of righteousness into hemlock: 13. Ye which rejoice in a thing of nought, which say, Have we not taken to us horns by our own strength?

Mic. 3:1. Hear, I pray you, O heads of Jacob, and ye princes of the house of Israel; *Is it* not for you to know judgment? 2. Who hate the good, and love the evil; who pluck off their skin from off them, and their flesh from off their bones; 3. Who also eat the flesh of my people, and flay their skin from off them; and they break their bones, and chop them in pieces, as for the pot, and as flesh within the caldron. 9. Hear this, I pray you, ye heads of the house of Jacob, and princes of the house of Israel, that abhor judgment, and pervert all equity. 10. They build up Zion with blood, and Jerusalem with iniquity. 11. The heads thereof judge for reward, and the priests thereof teach for hire, and the prophets thereof divine for money: yet will they lean upon the LORD, and say, *Is* not the LORD among us? none evil can come upon us.

Mic. 7:3. That they may do evil with both hands earnestly, the prince asketh, and the judge *asketh* for a reward; and the great *man*, he uttereth his mischievous desire: so they wrap it up. 4. The best of them *is* as a brier: the most upright *is sharper* than a thorn hedge : the day of thy watchmen *and* thy visitation cometh ; now shall be their perplexity.

Hab. 1:4. Therefore the law is slacked, and judgment doth never go forth : for the wicked doth compass about the righteous ; therefore wrong judgment proceedeth.

Hab. 2:12. Woe to him that buildeth a town with blood, and stablisheth a city by iniquity ! *vs.* 5–13.

Zeph. 1:8. And it shall come to pass in the day of the LORD's sacrifice, that I will punish the princes, and the king's children, and all such as are clothed with strange apparel.

Zeph. 3:3. Her princes within her *are* roaring lions ; her judges *are* evening wolves ; they gnaw not the bones till the morrow.

Acts 23:3. Then said Paul unto him, God shall smite thee, *thou* whited wall : for sittest thou to judge me after the law, and commandest me to be smitten contrary to the law ?

Jas. 2:6. Do not rich men oppress you, and draw you before the judgment seats ? 9. If ye have respect to persons, ye commit sin, and are convinced of the law as transgressors.

INSTANCES OF : Potiphar, putting Joseph into prison. Gen. 39:20, with 40:15. Pharaoh, oppressing the Israelites, Ex. chapters, 1–11. Adoni-bezek, torturing seventy kings, Judg. 1:7. Abimelech, slaying his seventy brothers, Judg. 9:1–5. Eli's sons, desecrating the sacrifices, 1 Sam. 2:12–17; debauching themselves and the worshipers, 1 Sam. 2:22. Samuel's sons, taking bribes, 1 Sam. 8:1–5. Saul, sparing Agag and the best of the booty, 1 Sam. 15:8–35; in jealousy plotting against David. 1 Sam. 18:8–29; seeking to slay David, 1 Sam. 19; slaying Ahimelech and the priests, 1 Sam. 22:7–19. Hanun, maltreating David's servants, 2 Sam. 10:4; 1 Chr. 19:2–5. David, numbering Israel and Judah, 2 Sam. 24:1–9; 1 Chr. 21:1–7; 27:23, 24. Solomon, luxurious, and idolatrous, 1 Kin. 11:1–13; oppressing the people, 1 Kin. 12:4; 4:7–23. Rehoboam, making the yoke heavy, 1 Kin. 12:8–11; 2 Chr. 10:1–15. Jeroboam, perverting the true worship, 1 Kin. 12:26–33; 13:1–5; 14:16; exalting debased persons to the priesthood, 1 Kin. 12:31; 13:33; 2 Kin. 17:32; 2 Chr. 11:14,15; Ezek. 44:7, with Num. 3:10. Abijam, walking in the sins of Rehoboam, 1 Kin. 15:3. Nadab, walking in the ways of Jeroboam, 1 Kin. 15:26. Baasha, walking in the ways of Jeroboam, 1 Kin. 15:33,34. Asa, imprisoning the seer, and oppressing the people, 2 Chr. 16:10. Zimri, walking in the ways of Jeroboam, 1 Kin. 16:19. Omri, walking in the ways of Jeroboam, 1 Kin. 16:25–29. Ahab, serving Baal, 1 Kin. 16:30–33; 21:21–26; confiscating Naboth's vineyard, 1 Kin. 21, with 1 Sam. 8:14; 1 Kin. 22:38; 2 Kin. 9:26. Jehoram, cleaving to the sins of Jeroboam, 2 Kin. 3:2,3. Hazael, committing rapine, 2 Kin.

8:12; 10:32; 12:17; 13:3–7. Jehoram, walking in the ways of the kings of Israel, 2 Kin. 8:18; 2 Chr. 21:13. Jehu, departing not from the sins of Jeroboam, 2 Kin. 10:29. Jehoahaz, in following the sins of Jeroboam, 2 Kin. 13:1,2. Jehoash, in following the wicked example of Jeroboam, 2 Kin. 13:10, 11. Jeroboam II, not departing from the sins of Jeroboam, 2 Kin. 14:23,24. Zachariah, Menahem, Pekahiah, and Pekah, following the sins of Jeroboam, 2 Kin. 15:9,18,24, 28; conspiring against and slaying Pekahiah, 2 Kin. 15:25. Hoshea, who conspired against Pekah, 2 Kin. 15:30, in permitting Baal-worship, 2 Kin. 17:1,2,7–18. Ahaz, burning his children in idolatrous sacrifice, 2 Kin. 16:3; 2 Chr. 28:2–4. Manasseh, who committed the abominations of the heathen, 2 Kin. 21:1–17; 2 Chr. 33:2–7. Amon, who followed the evil example of Manasseh, 2 Kin. 21:19–22. Jehoahaz, who followed in the ways of his fathers, 2 Kin. 23:32. Jehoiakim, in walking in the ways of his fathers, 2 Kin. 23:37; and Jehoiachin, 2 Kin. 24:9. Zedekiah, following the evil example of Jehoiakim, 2 Kin. 24:19; 2 Chr. 36:12,13; and persecuting Jeremiah, Jer. 38:5,6. Joash, slaying Zechariah, 2 Chr. 24:2,17–25. Ahaziah, doing evil after the house of Ahab, 2 Chr. 22:1–9. Amaziah, worshiping the gods of Seir, 2 Chr. 25:14. Uzziah, invading the priest's office, 2 Chr. 26:16. Ahasuerus and Haman, decreeing the death of the Jews, Esth. 3. Nebuchadnezzar, commanding to destroy the wise men, Dan. 2:1–13; and committing the three Hebrews to the furnace, Dan. 3:1–23. Belshazzar, in drunkenness and committing sacrilege, Dan. 5:22, 23. Darius, in deifying himself, Dan. 6:7,9. The princes, conspiring against Daniel, Dan. 6:1–9. Herod the Great, slaying the children in Bethlehem, Matt. 2:16–18. Herod Antipas, in beheading John the Baptist, Matt. 14:1–11; in craftiness and tyranny, Luke 13:31,32; 23:6–15. Herod Agrippa, persecuting the church, Acts 12:1–19. Pilate, delivering Jesus for crucifixion, Matt. 27:11–26; Mark 15:15. Chief priests, elders, and all the council, seeking false witness against Jesus, Matt. 26:59. Ananias, commanding to smite Paul, Acts 23:2.

See GOVERNMENT ; JUDGES ; KINGS.

RUMAH, a city of unascertained location. Home of Jehoiakim's mother, 2 Kin. 23:36.

RUTH. The daughter-in-law of Naomi, Ruth 1:4. Her devotion to Naomi, Ruth 1:16,17, with verses 6–18. Goes to Bethlehem, Ruth 1:19,22. Gleaned in the field of Boaz, Ruth 2:3. Receives kindness from Boaz, Ruth 2:4–17; 3:15. Under Naomi's instructions claims from Boaz the duty of a kinsman, Ruth 3:1–9. Marries Boaz, Ruth 4:9–13. Becomes an ancestor of Jesus, Ruth 4:13, 21,22.

RYE [spelt, *R. V.*]. A small grain grown in Egypt, Ex. 9:32. Cultivated in Canaan, Isa. 28:25. Used in bread, Ezek. 4:9.

S

SABBATH. Signifying a rest period, Gen. 2:2,3; Lev. 23; 25; 26:34,35. Preparations for, Ex. 16:22; Matt. 27:62; Mark 15:42; Luke 23:54; John 19:31. Religious usages on, Gen. 2:3; Mark 6:2; Luke 4:16,31; 6:6; 13:10; Acts 13:14. Sacrifices on, Num. 28: 9,10; Ezek. 46:4,5.

UNCLASSIFIED SCRIPTURES RELATING TO: Gen. 2:2. On the seventh day God ended his work which he had made; and he rested on the seventh day from all his work which he had made. 3. And God blessed the seventh day, and sanctified it; because that in it he had rested from all his work which God created and made.

Ex. 16:5. And it shall come to pass, that on the sixth day they shall prepare *that* which they bring in; and it shall be twice as much as they gather daily. 23. This *is that* which the LORD hath said, To morrow *is* the rest of the holy sabbath unto the LORD: bake *that* which ye will bake *to day*, and seethe that ye will seethe; and that which remaineth over lay up for you to be kept until the morning. 24. And they laid it up till the morning, as Moses bade: and it did not stink, neither was there any worm therein. 25. And Moses said, Eat that to day; for to day *is* a sabbath unto the LORD: to day ye shall not find it in the field. 26. Six days ye shall gather it; but on the seventh day, *which is* the sabbath, in it there shall be none. 27. And it came to pass, *that* there went out *some* of the people on the seventh day for to gather, and they found none. 28. And the LORD said unto Moses, How long refuse ye to keep my commandments and my laws? 29. See, for that the LORD hath given you the sabbath, therefore he giveth you on the sixth day the bread of two days; abide ye every man in his place, let no man go out of his place on the seventh day. 30. So the people rested on the seventh day.

Ex. 20:8. Remember the sabbath day, to keep it holy. 9. Six days shalt thou labour, and do all thy work: 10. But the seventh day *is* the sabbath of the LORD thy God: *in it* thou shalt not do any work, thou, nor thy son, nor thy daughter, thy manservant, nor thy maidservant, nor thy cattle, nor thy stranger that *is* within thy gates: 11. For *in* six days the LORD made heaven and earth, the sea, and all that in them *is*, and rested the seventh day: wherefore the LORD blessed the sabbath day, and hallowed it.

Ex. 23:12. Six days thou shalt do thy work, and on the seventh day thou shalt rest: that thine ox and thine ass may rest, and the son of thy handmaid, and the stranger, may be refreshed.

Ex. 31:13. Speak thou also unto the children of Israel, saying, Verily my sabbaths ye shall keep: for it *is* a sign between me and you throughout your generations; that *ye* may know that I *am* the LORD that doth sanctify you. 14. Ye shall keep the sabbath therefore; for it *is* holy unto you: every one that defileth it shall surely be put to death: for whosoever doeth *any* work therein, that soul shall be cut off from among his people. 15. Six days may work be done; but in the seventh *is* the sabbath of rest, holy to the LORD: whosoever doeth *any* work in the sabbath day, he shall surely be put to death. 16. Wherefore the children of Israel shall keep the sabbath, to observe the sabbath throughout their generations, *for* a perpetual covenant. 17. It *is* a sign between me and the children of Israel for ever: for *in* six days the LORD made heaven and earth, and on the seventh day he rested, and was refreshed.

Ex. 34:21. Six days thou shalt work, but on the seventh day thou shalt rest: in earing time and in harvest thou shalt rest.

Ex. 35:2. Six days shall work be done, but on the seventh day there shall be to you an holy day, a sabbath of rest to the LORD: whosoever doeth work therein shall be put to death. 3. Ye shall kindle no fire throughout your habitations upon the sabbath day.

Lev. 19:3. Ye shall fear every man his mother, and his father, and keep my sabbaths: I *am* the LORD your God. 30. Ye shall keep my sabbaths, and reverence my sanctuary: I *am* the LORD.

Lev. 23:1. And the LORD spake unto Moses, saying, 2. Speak unto the children of Israel, and say unto them, *Concerning* the feasts of the LORD, which ye shall proclaim *to be* holy convocations, *even* these *are* my feasts. 3. Six days shall work be done: but the seventh day *is* the sabbath of rest, an holy convocation; ye shall do no work *therein:* it *is* the sabbath of the LORD in all your dwellings. 27. Also on the tenth *day* of this seventh month *there shall be* a day of atonement: it shall be an holy convocation unto you; and ye shall afflict your souls, and offer an offering made by fire unto the LORD. 28. And ye shall do no work in that same day: for it *is* a day of atonement, to make an atonement for you before the LORD your God. 29. For whatsoever soul *it be* that shall not be afflicted in that same day, he shall be cut off from among his people. 30. And whatsoever soul *it be* that doeth any work in that same day, the same soul will I destroy from among his people. 31. Ye shall do no manner of work: *it shall be* a statute for ever throughout your generations in all your dwellings. 32. It *shall be* unto you a sabbath of rest, and ye shall afflict your souls: in the ninth *day* of the month at even, from even unto even, shall ye celebrate your sabbath. Lev. 16:29-31.

Lev. 24:8. Every sabbath he shall set it in order before the LORD continually, *being taken* from the children of Israel by an everlasting covenant. 1 Chr. 9:32.

Lev. 26:2. Ye shall keep my sabbaths, and

reverence my sanctuary; I *am* the LORD. 34. Then shall the land enjoy her sabbaths, as long as it lieth desolate, and ye *be* in your enemies' land; *even* then shall the land rest, and enjoy her sabbaths. 35. As long as it lieth desolate it shall rest; because it did not rest in your sabbaths, when ye dwelt upon it.

Num. 15:32. And while the children of Israel were in the wilderness, they found a man that gathered sticks upon the sabbath day. 33. And they that found him gathering sticks brought him unto Moses and Aaron, and unto all the congregation. 34. And they put him in ward, because it was not declared what should be done to him. 35. And the LORD said unto Moses, The man shall be surely put to death: all the congregation shall stone him with stones without the camp. 36. And all the congregation brought him without the camp, and stoned him with stones, and he died; as the LORD commanded Moses.

Num. 28:9. And on the sabbath day two lambs of the first year without spot, and two tenth deals of flour *for* a meat offering, mingled with oil, and the drink offering thereof: 10. *This is* the burnt offering of every sabbath, beside the continual burnt offering, and his drink offering.

Deut. 5:12. Keep the sabbath day to sanctify it, as the LORD thy God hath commanded thee. 13. Six days thou shalt labour, and do all thy work: 14. But the seventh day *is* the sabbath of the LORD thy God: *in it* thou shalt not do any work, thou, nor thy son, nor thy daughter, nor thy manservant, nor thy maidservant, nor thine ox, nor thine ass, nor any of thy cattle, nor thy stranger that *is* within thy gates; that thy manservant and thy maidservant may rest as well as thou. 15. And remember that thou wast a servant in the land of Egypt, and *that* the LORD thy God brought thee out thence through a mighty hand and by a stretched out arm: therefore the LORD thy God commanded thee to keep the sabbath day.

2 Kin. 4:23. Wherefore wilt thou go to him to-day? *it is* neither new moon, nor sabbath.

2 Chr. 36:21. To fulfil the word of the LORD by the mouth of Jeremiah, until the land had enjoyed her sabbaths: *for* as long as she lay desolate she kept sabbath, to fulfil threescore and ten years.

Neh. 9:13. Thou camest down also upon mount Sinai, and spakest with them from heaven, and gavest them right judgments, and true laws, good statutes and commandments: 14. And madest known unto them thy holy sabbath,

Neh. 10:31. And *if* the people of the land bring ware or any victuals on the sabbath day to sell, *that* we would not buy it of them on the sabbath, or on the holy day:

Neh. 13:15. In those days saw I in Judah *some* treading wine presses on the sabbath, and bringing in sheaves, and lading asses;

as also wine, grapes, and figs, and all *manner of* burdens, which they brought into Jerusalem on the sabbath day: and I testified *against them* in the day wherein they sold victuals. 16. There dwelt men of Tyre also therein, which brought fish, and all manner of ware, and sold on the sabbath unto the children of Judah, and in Jerusalem. 17. Then I contended with the nobles of Judah, and said unto them, What evil thing *is* this that ye do, and profane the sabbath day? 18. Did not your fathers thus, and did not our God bring all this evil upon us, and upon this city? yet ye bring more wrath upon Israel by profaning the sabbath. 19. And it came to pass, that when the gates of Jerusalem began to be dark before the sabbath, I commanded that the gates should be shut, and charged that they should not be opened till after the sabbath: and *some* of my servants set I at the gates, *that* there should no burden be brought in on the sabbath day. 20. So the merchants and sellers of all kind of ware lodged without Jerusalem once or twice. 21. Then I testified against them, and said unto them, Why lodge ye about the wall? if ye do *so* again, I will lay hands on you. From that time forth came they no *more* on the sabbath. 22. And I commanded the Levites, that they should cleanse themselves, and *that* they should come *and* keep the gates, to sanctify the sabbath day.

[A Psalm *or* Song for the sabbath day.]

Psa. 92:1. *It is a* good *thing* to give thanks unto the LORD, and to sing praises unto thy name, O most High: 2. To shew forth thy lovingkindness in the morning, and thy faithfulness every night, 3. Upon an instrument of ten strings, and upon the psaltery; upon the harp with a solemn sound. 4. For thou, LORD, hast made me glad through thy work: I will triumph in the works of thy hands. 5. O LORD, how great are thy works! *and* thy thoughts are very deep. 6. A brutish man knoweth not; neither doth a fool understand this. 7. When the wicked spring as the grass, and when all the workers of iniquity do flourish; *it is* that they shall be destroyed for ever: 8. But thou, LORD, *art most* high for evermore. 9. For, lo, thine enemies, O LORD, for, lo, thine enemies shall perish; all the workers of iniquity shall be scattered. 10. But my horn shalt thou exalt like *the horn of* an unicorn: I shall be anointed with fresh oil. 11. Mine eye also shall see *my desire* on mine enemies, *and* mine ears shall hear *my desire* of the wicked that rise up against me. 12. The righteous shall flourish like the palm tree: he shall grow like a cedar in Lebanon. 13. Those that be planted in the house of the LORD shall flourish in the courts of our God. 14. They shall still bring forth fruit in old age; they shall be fat and flourishing; 15. To shew that the LORD *is* upright: *he is* my rock, and *there is* no unrighteousness in him.

Psa. 118:24. This *is* the day *which* the Lord hath made; we will rejoice and be glad in it.

Isa. 1:13. Bring no more vain oblations; incense is an abomination unto me; the new moons and sabbaths, the calling of assemblies, I cannot away with; *it is* iniquity, even the solemn meeting.

Isa. 56:2. Blessed *is* the man *that* doeth this, and the son of man *that* layeth hold on it; that keepeth the sabbath from polluting it, and keepeth his hand from doing any evil. 4. For thus saith the Lord unto the eunuchs that keep my sabbaths, and choose *the things* that please me, and take hold of my covenant; 5. Even unto them will I give in mine house and within my walls a place and a name better than of sons and of daughters: I will give them an everlasting name, that shall not be cut off. 6. Also the sons of the stranger, that join themselves to the Lord, to serve him, and to love the name of the Lord, to be his servants, every one that keepeth the sabbath from polluting it, and taketh hold of my covenant; 7. Even them will I bring to my holy mountain, and make them joyful in my house of prayer: their burnt offerings and their sacrifices *shall be* accepted upon mine altar; for mine house shall be called an house of prayer for all people.

Isa. 58:13. If thou turn away thy foot from the sabbath, *from* doing thy pleasure on my holy day; and call the sabbath a delight, the holy of the Lord, honourable; and shalt honour him, not doing thine own ways, nor finding thine own pleasure, nor speaking *thine own* words: 14. Then shalt thou delight thyself in the Lord; and I will cause thee to ride upon the high places of the earth, and feed thee with the heritage of Jacob thy father:

Isa. 66:23. And it shall come to pass, *that* from one new moon to another, and from one sabbath to another, shall all flesh come to worship before me, saith the Lord.

Jer. 17:21. Thus saith the Lord; Take heed to yourselves, and bear no burden on the sabbath day, nor bring *it* in by the gates of Jerusalem; 22. Neither carry forth a burden out of your houses on the sabbath day, neither do ye any work, but hallow ye the sabbath day, as I commanded your fathers. 24. And it shall come to pass, if ye diligently hearken unto me, saith the Lord, to bring in no burden through the gates of this city on the sabbath day, but hallow the sabbath day to do no work therein; 25. Then shall there enter into the gates of this city kings and princes sitting upon the throne of David, . . . 27. But if ye will not hearken unto me to hallow the sabbath day, and not to bear a burden, even entering in at the gates of Jerusalem on the sabbath day; then will I kindle a fire in the gates thereof, and it shall devour the palaces of Jerusalem, and it shall not be quenched.

Lam. 1:7. Jerusalem remembered in the days of her affliction and of her miseries all her pleasant things that she had in the days of old, when her people fell into the hand of the enemy, and none did help her: the adversaries saw her, *and* did mock at her [1] sabbaths. [1 R. V. desolations]

Lam. 2:6. And he hath violently taken away his tabernacle, as *if it were of* a garden: he hath destroyed his places of the assembly: the Lord hath caused the solemn feasts and sabbaths to be forgotten in Zion, and hath despised in the indignation of his anger the king and the priest.

Ezek. 20:12. Moreover also I gave them my sabbaths, to be a sign between me and them, that they might know that I *am* the Lord that sanctify them. 13. But the house of Israel rebelled against me in the wilderness: they walked not in my statutes, and they despised my judgments, which *if* a man do, he shall even live in them; and my sabbaths they greatly polluted: then I said, I would pour out my fury upon them in the wilderness, to consume them. 16. They despised my judgments, and walked not in my statutes, but polluted my sabbaths: for their heart went after their idols. *vs.* 20, 21, 24.

Ezek. 22:8. Thou hast despised mine holy things, and hast profaned my sabbaths.

Ezek. 23:38. They have defiled my sanctuary in the same day, and have profaned my sabbaths.

Ezek. 44:24. They shall hallow my sabbaths.

Ezek. 46:1. Thus saith the Lord God; The gate of the inner court that looketh toward the east shall be shut the six working days; but on the sabbath it shall be opened, 3. Likewise the people of the land shall worship at the door of this gate before the Lord in the sabbaths and in the new moons.

Hos. 2:11. I will also cause all her mirth to cease, her feast days, her new moons, and her sabbaths, and all her solemn feasts.

Amos 8:5. When will the new moon be gone, that we may sell corn? and the sabbath, that we may set forth wheat, making the ephah small, and the shekel great, and falsifying the balances by deceit?

Matt. 12:1. At that time Jesus went on the sabbath day through the corn; and his disciples were an hungred, and began to pluck the ears of corn, and to eat. 2. But when the Pharisees saw *it*, they said unto him, Behold, thy disciples do that which is not lawful to do upon the sabbath day. 3. But he said unto them, Have ye not read what David did, when he was an hungred, and they that were with him; 4. How he entered into the house of God, and did eat the shewbread, which was not lawful for him to eat, neither for them which were with him, but only for the priests? 5. Or have ye not read in the law, how that on the sabbath days the priests in the temple profane the sabbath, and are blameless? 6. But I say unto you, That in this place is *one* greater than the temple. 7. But if ye had known what *this* meaneth, I will have mercy, and not sacrifice, ye would not have condemned the guiltless. 8. For the Son of man is Lord even of the sabbath day. Mark 2:28.

10. And, behold, there was a man which had *his* hand withered. And they asked him, saying, Is it lawful to heal on the sabbath days? that they might accuse him. 11. And he said unto them, What man shall there be among you, that shall have one sheep, and if it fall into a pit on the sabbath day, will he not lay hold on it, and lift *it* out? 12. How much then is a man better than a sheep? Wherefore it is lawful to do well on the sabbath days. 13. Then saith he to the man, Stretch forth thine hand. And he stretched *it* forth; and it was restored whole, like as the other. Luke 6:1–10.

Matt. 24:20. But pray ye that your flight be not in the winter, neither on the sabbath day:

Mark 2:27. The sabbath was made for man, and not man for the sabbath: *v.* 28.

Mark 6:2. And when the sabbath day was come, he began to teach in the synagogue:

Mark 16:1. And when the sabbath was past, Mary Magdalene, and Mary the *mother* of James, and Salome, had bought sweet spices, that they might come and anoint him.

Luke 4:16. And he came to Nazareth, where he had been brought up: and, as his custom was, he went into the synagogue on the sabbath day, and stood up for to read. 31. And came down to Capernaum, a city of Galilee, and taught them on the sabbath days.

Luke 6:6. It came to pass also on another sabbath, that he entered into the synagogue and taught:

Luke 13:10. He was teaching in one of the synagogues on the sabbath. 11. And, behold, there was a woman which had a spirit of infirmity eighteen years, and was bowed together, and could in no wise lift up *herself*. 12. And when Jesus saw her, he called *her to him*, and said unto her, Woman, thou art loosed from thine infirmity. 13. And he laid *his* hands on her: and immediately she was made straight, and glorified God. 14. And the ruler of the synagogue answered with indignation, because that Jesus had healed on the sabbath day, and said unto the people, There are six days in which men ought to work: in them therefore come and be healed, and not on the sabbath day. 15. The Lord then answered him, and said, *Thou* hypocrite, doth not each one of you on the sabbath loose his ox or *his* ass from the stall, and lead *him* away to watering? 16. And ought not this woman, being a daughter of Abraham, whom Satan hath bound, lo, these eighteen years, be loosed from this bond on the sabbath day? 17. And when he had said these things, all his adversaries were ashamed:

Luke 14:1. And it came to pass, as he went into the house of one of the chief Pharisees to eat bread on the sabbath day, that they watched him. 2. And, behold, there was a certain man before him which had the dropsy. 3. And Jesus answering spake unto the lawyers and Pharisees, saying, Is it lawful to heal on the sabbath day? 4. And they held their peace. And he took *him*, and healed him, and let him go; 5. And answered them, saying, Which of you shall have an ass or an ox fallen into a pit, and will not straightway pull him out on the sabbath day? 6. And they could not answer him again to these things.

Luke 23:54. That day was the preparation, and the sabbath drew on. 56. And they returned, and prepared spices and ointments; and rested the sabbath day according to the commandment.

John 5:5. And a certain man was there, which had an infirmity thirty and eight years. 6. When Jesus saw him lie, and knew that he had been now a long time *in that case*, he saith unto him, Wilt thou be made whole? 7. The impotent man answered him, Sir, I have no man, when the water is troubled, to put me into the pool: but while I am coming, another steppeth down before me. 8. Jesus saith unto him, Rise, take up thy bed, and walk. 9. And immediately the man was made whole, and took up his bed, and walked: and on the same day was the sabbath. 10. The Jews therefore said unto him that was cured, It is the sabbath day: it is not lawful for thee to carry *thy* bed. 11. He answered them, He that made me whole, the same said unto me, Take up thy bed, and walk. 12. Then asked they him, What man is that which said unto thee, Take up thy bed, and walk? 13. And he that was healed wist not who it was: for Jesus had conveyed himself away, a multitude being in *that* place. 14. Afterward Jesus findeth him in the temple, and said unto him, Behold, thou art made whole: sin no more, lest a worse thing come unto thee.

John 7:21. Jesus answered and said unto them, I have done one work, and ye all marvel. 22. Moses therefore gave unto you circumcision; (not because it is of Moses, but of the fathers;) and ye on the sabbath day circumcise a man. 23. If a man on the sabbath day receive circumcision, that the law of Moses should not be broken; are ye angry at me, because I have made a man every whit whole on the sabbath day? 24. Judge not according to the appearance, but judge righteous judgment. chapter 9:1–34.

John 19:31. The Jews therefore, because it was the preparation, that the bodies should not remain upon the cross on the sabbath day, (for that sabbath day was an high day,) besought Pilate that their legs might be broken, and *that* they might be taken away.

Acts 13:14. They came to Antioch in Pisidia, and went into the synagogue on the sabbath day, and sat down. 27. For they that dwell at Jerusalem, and their rulers, because they knew him not, nor yet the voices of the prophets which are read every sabbath day, they have fulfilled *them* in condemning *him*. 42. And when the Jews were gone out of the synagogue, the Gentiles besought that these words might be preached to them the next sabbath. 44. And the next sabbath day came almost the whole city together to hear the word of God.

Acts 15:21. For Moses of old time hath in every city them that preach him, being read in the synagogues every sabbath day.

Acts 16:13. On the sabbath we went out of the city by a river side, where prayer was wont to be made; and we sat down, and spake unto the women which resorted *thither*.

Acts 17:2. And Paul, as his manner was, went in unto them, and three sabbath days reasoned with them out of the scriptures,

Acts 18:4. And he reasoned in the synagogue every sabbath, and persuaded the Jews and the Greeks.

Col. 2:16. Let no man therefore judge you in meat, or in drink, or in respect of an holyday, or of the new moon, or of the sabbath *days:*

Heb. 4:4. For he spake in a certain place of the seventh *day* on this wise, And God did rest the seventh day from all his works. *v. 9.*

OBSERVANCE OF: By Moses, Num. 15:32–34. By Nehemiah, Neh. 13:15,21. By the women preparing to embalm the body of Jesus, Luke 23:56. By Paul, Acts 13:14. By Disciples, Acts 16:13. By John, Rev. 1:10.

VIOLATIONS OF: INSTANCES OF: Gathering manna, Ex. 16:27. Gathering sticks, Num. 15:32. Men of Tyre, Neh. 13:16. Inhabitants of Jerusalem, Jer. 17:21–23.

CHRISTIAN SABBATH: First day of the week, Sunday. Mark 16:9. Now when *Jesus* was risen early the first *day* of the week, he appeared first to Mary Magdalene, Matt. 28:1,5,6,9.

John 20:19. Then the same day at evening, being the first *day* of the week, when the doors were shut where the disciples were assembled for fear of the Jews, came Jesus and stood in the midst, and saith unto them, Peace *be* unto you. [*vs.* 1,11–16.] 26. And after eight days again his disciples were within, and Thomas with them: *then* came Jesus, the doors being shut, and stood in the midst, and said, Peace *be* unto you.

Acts 20:7. And upon the first *day* of the week when the disciples came together to break bread, Paul preached unto them, ready to depart on the morrow; and continued his speech until midnight.

1 Cor. 16:2. Upon the first *day* of the week, let every one of you lay by him in store, as [1] *God* hath prospered him, that there be no gatherings when I come.   [1 R. V. he may prosper]

Rev. 1:10. I was in the Spirit on the Lord's day, and heard behind me a great voice, as of a trumpet,

SABBATH DAY'S JOURNEY, about two thousand paces, Acts 1:12.

SABBATIC YEAR, a rest recurring every seventh year. Called YEAR OF RELEASE, Deut. 15:9; 31:10. Ordinances concerning, Ex. 23:9–11; Lev. 25. Israelitish bondservants set free in, Ex. 21:2; Deut. 15:12; Jer. 34:14. Creditors required to release debtors in, Deut. 15:1–6,12–18; Neh. 10:31. Ordinances concerning instruction in the law during, Deut. 31:10–13; Neh. 8:18. Punishment to follow violation of the ordinances concerning, Lev. 26:34,35, with 32–41; Jer. 34:12–22.

See JUBILEE.

SABEANS. A people who invaded the land of Uz, Job 1:15; Isa. 43:3. Giants among, Isa. 45:14. Prophecies concerning, Isa. 43:3; Joel 3:8. Proverbial drunkards, Ezek. 23:42. [*R. V.*].

See SHEBA.

SABTA, called also SABTAH. Son of Cush, Gen. 10:7; 1 Chr. 1:9.

SABTECHA. Son of Cush, Gen. 10:7; 1 Chr. 1:9.

SACAR. 1. Father of Ahiam, 1 Chr. 11:35. Called SHARAR, 2 Sam. 23:33.

2. A Korhite. Son of Obed-edom, 1 Chr. 26:4.

SACKBUT, a stringed instrument of music, Dan. 3:5,7,10,15.

See MUSIC, INSTRUMENTS OF.

SACKCLOTH. A symbol of mourning, 1 Kin. 20:31,32; Job 16:15; Isa. 15:3; Jer. 4:8; 6:26; 49:3; Lam. 2:10; Ezek. 7:18; Dan. 9:3; Joel 1:8. Worn by Jacob when it was reported to him that Joseph had been devoured by wild beasts, Gen. 37:34. Animals covered with, at time of national mourning, Jonah 3:8.

See MOURNING.

SACRIFICES. FIGURATIVE: Isa. 34:6; Ezek. 39:17; Zeph. 1:7,8; Rom. 12:1; Phil. 2:17; 4:18. Of self-denial, Phil. 3:7,8. Of praise, Psa. 116:17; Jer. 33:11; Hos. 14:2; Heb. 13:15. Calves of the lips, signifying praise, Hos. 14:2.

See OFFERINGS.

SACRILEGE, profaning holy things. Forbidden, Lev. 19:8; 1 Cor. 3:17; Tit. 1:11; 1 Pet. 5:2.

INSTANCES OF: Esau sells his birthright, Gen. 25:33. Nadab and Abihu offer strange fire, Lev. 10:1–7; Num. 3:4. Of Uzzah, 2 Sam. 6:6,7. Of Uzziah, 2 Chr. 26:16–21. Of Korah and his company, Num. 16:40. Of the people of Beth-shemesh, 1 Sam. 6:19. Of Ahaz, 2 Chr. 28:24. Of money changers in the temple, Matt. 21:12,13; Luke 19:45; John 2:14–16. Of those who profaned the holy eucharist, 1 Cor. 11:29.

SADDUCEES, a sect of the Jews. Rebuked by John the Baptist, Matt. 3:7–9; Luke 3:7–9. Reject the doctrine of the resurrection, Matt. 22:23–34; Mark 12:18–27; Luke 20:27–40; Acts 23:7,8. Jesus warns his disciples against, Matt. 16:6–12. Persecute the apostles, Acts 4:1–3; 5:17–33.

SADOC, an ancestor of Joseph, Matt. 1:14.

SAILORS. See MARINERS.

SAINTS. See RIGHTEOUS.

SALAH, called also SALA and SHELAH. Son of Arphaxad and ancestor of Joseph, Gen. 10:24; 11:12–15; 1 Chr. 1:18,24; Luke 3:35.

SALAMIS, a city of Cyprus. Paul and Barnabas preach in, Acts 13:4,5.

SALATHIEL. See SHEALTIEL.

SALCAH, called also SALCHAH. A city of Gad, Deut. 3:10; Josh. 12:5; 13:11; 1 Chr. 5:11.

SALEM. See JERUSALEM.

SALIM, a city near to Ænon, John 3:23.

SALLAI. 1. A Benjamite dwelling in Jerusalem, Neh. 11:8.

2. A priest who returned to Jerusalem with Zerubbabel, Neh. 12:20. Called SALLU, Neh. 12:7.

SALLU. 1. A Benjamite. dwelling in Jerusalem, 1 Chr. 9:7; Neh. 11:7.

2. See SALLAI, 2.

SALMA. 1. Son of Caleb, 1 Chr. 2:51,54.

2. Called also SALMON. Father of Boaz, Ruth 4:20,21; 1 Chr. 2:11. In the lineage of Joseph, Matt. 1:4,5; Luke 3:32.

SALMON. 1. A hill, Psa. 68:14.

2. See SALMA, 2.

SALMONE, a promontory of Crete, Acts 27:7.

SALOME. Mother of James and John, Matt. 27:56, with Mark 15:40; 16:1. Asks Jesus to promote her sons, Matt. 20:20,21. Present at the cross, Mark 15:40; at the sepulchre, Mark 16:1,2.

SALT. Lot's wife turned into a pillar of, Gen. 19:26. The city of Salt, Josh. 15:62. The valley of salt, 2 Sam. 8:13; 2 Kin. 14:7. Salt sea, Gen. 14:3; Num. 34:12; Deut. 3:17; Josh. 3:16; 12:3; 15:2. Salt pits, Zeph. 2:9. All animal sacrifices were required to be seasoned with, Lev. 2:13; Ezra. 6:9; Ezek. 43:24; Mark 9:49. Used in ratifying covenants, Num. 18:19; 2 Chr. 13:5. Elisha casts, into the pool of Jericho, to purify it, 2 Kin. 2:20,21.

FIGURATIVE: Of the saving efficacy of the church, Matt. 5:13; Mark 9:49,50; Luke 14:34. Of wise conversation, Col. 4:6.

SALUTATIONS. By kissing, 2 Sam. 20:9; Matt. 26:49. By bowing, Gen. 18:2; 19:1,2; 23:7; 27:29; 33:3; 37:10; 41:43; 43:26,28; 49:8; 1 Sam. 25:23; 2 Sam. 18:28; 1 Kin. 1:16; Esth. 8:3; Matt. 2:11; Mark 5:22. Addresses in: " My lords," Gen. 19:2; "God be gracious unto thee, "Gen. 43: 29. "Peace," 1 Sam. 25:6. "Art thou in health, my brother ?" 2 Sam. 20:9. "Hail, Master," Matt. 26:49. "All hail," Matt. 28:9. "Peace to this house," Luke 10:5. "Peace unto you," John 20:21. From a master to his servants, "The Lord be with you," Ruth 2:4. Servants to their masters, "The Lord bless thee," Ruth 2:4. By letter, 1 Cor. 16:21; 2 Cor. 13:13; Col. 4:18; Phil. 4:21; 2 Thess. 3:17; 2 John 13; 3 John 14. To rulers, see KINGS. See MANNERS.

SALVATION.* ILLUSTRATED BY : A horn, Psa. 18:2; Luke 1:69; a tower, 2 Sam. 22: 51; a helmet, Isa. 59:17; Eph. 6:17; a shield, 2 Sam. 22:36; a lamp, Isa. 62:1; a cup, Psa. 116:13; clothing, 2 Chr. 6:41; Psa. 132:16; 149:4; Isa. 61:10; wells, Isa. 12:3; walls and bulwarks, Isa. 26:1; 60:18; chariots, Hab. 3:8; a victory, 1 Cor. 15:57.

Typified by the brazen serpent, Num. 21: 4–9, with John 3:14,15.—*Bible Text-Book.*

See ATONEMENT.

UNCLASSIFIED SCRIPTURES RELATING TO : Gen. 12:1. Now the LORD had said unto Abram, Get thee out of thy country, and from thy kindred, and from thy father's house, unto a land that I will shew thee: 3. . . . And in thee shall all families of the earth be blessed.

Ex. 15:2. The LORD *is* my strength and song, and he is become my salvation : he *is* my God, and I will prepare him an habitation ; my father's God, and I will exalt him.

Deut. 30:19. I call heaven and earth to record this day against you, *that* I have set before you life and death, blessing and cursing : therefore choose life, that both thou and thy seed may live : 20. That thou mayest love the LORD thy God, *and* that thou mayest obey his voice, and that thou mayest cleave unto him : for he *is* thy life, and the length of thy days :

Deut. 32:15. But Jeshurun waxed fat, and kicked ; thou art waxen fat, thou art grown thick, thou art covered *with fatness ;* then he forsook God *which* made him, and lightly esteemed the Rock of his salvation. Psa. 95:1.

2 Sam. 14:14. For we must needs die, and *are* as water spilt on the ground, which cannot be gathered up again ; neither doth God respect *any* person : yet doth he devise means, that his banished be not expelled from him.

1 Kin. 8:41. Moreover concerning a stranger, that *is* not of thy people Israel, but cometh out of a far country for thy name's sake ; 42. . . . when he shall come and pray toward this house ; 43. Hear thou in heaven thy dwelling place, and do according to all that the stranger calleth to thee for: that all people of the earth may know thy name, to fear thee, as *do* thy people Israel ;

1 Chr. 16:35. And say ye, Save us, O God of our salvation, and gather us together, and deliver us from the heathen, that we may give thanks to thy holy name, *and* glory in thy praise.

---

* Scriptures relating directly and remotely to a topic of the nature of this one, are difficult to separate accurately into sub-topics without giving space beyond reasonable limits. The plan of salvation, begun and completed, conditions of salvation, such as repentance, faith, perseverance, etc., suggest themselves in many passages, and a single verse frequently embraces a number of phases of the general subject. The author therefore has attempted only a partial analysis into sub-topics. He submits this collection of scriptures to enable the student to analyze for himself, according to the phase of the subject he may require.

2 Chr. 6:41. Let thy priests, O Lord God, be clothed with salvation, and let thy saints rejoice in goodness.

Psa. 3:8. Salvation *belongeth* unto the Lord: Psa. 37:39.

Psa. 36:8. They shall be abundantly satisfied with the fatness of thy house; and thou shalt make them drink of the river of thy pleasures. 9. For with thee *is* the fountain of life: in thy light shall we see light.

Psa. 46:4. *There is* a river, the streams whereof shall make glad the city of God, the holy *place* of the tabernacles of the most High.

Psa. 63:5. My soul shall be satisfied as *with* marrow and fatness; and my mouth shall praise *thee* with joyful lips: 6. When I remember thee upon my bed, *and* meditate on thee in the *night* watches.

Psa. 65:4. Blessed *is the man whom* thou choosest, and causest to approach *unto thee, that* he may dwell in thy courts: we shall be satisfied with the goodness of thy house, *even* of thy holy temple.

Psa. 68:18. Thou hast ascended on high, thou hast led captivity captive: thou hast received gifts for men; yea, *for* the rebellious also, that the Lord God might dwell *among them*. 19. Blessed *be* the Lord, *who* daily loadeth us *with benefits, even* the God of our salvation. 20. *He that is* our God *is* the God of salvation; and unto God *the* Lord *belong* the issues from death.

Psa. 86:13. Great *is* thy mercy toward me: and thou hast delivered my soul from the lowest hell.

Psa. 90:14. O satisfy us early with thy mercy; that we may rejoice and be glad all our days.

Psa. 91:16. With long life will I satisfy him, and shew him my salvation.

Psa. 98:2. The Lord hath made known his salvation: his righteousness hath he openly shewed in the sight of the heathen. 3. He hath remembered his mercy and his truth toward the house of Israel: all the ends of the earth have seen the salvation of our God.

Psa. 106:8. Nevertheless he saved them for his name's sake, that he might make his mighty power to be known.

Psa. 107:9. For he satisfieth the longing soul, and filleth the hungry soul with goodness.

Psa. 121:1. I will lift up mine eyes unto the hills, from whence cometh my help. 2. My help *cometh* from the Lord, which made heaven and earth. 3. He will not suffer thy foot to be moved: he that keepeth thee will not slumber. 4. Behold, he that keepeth Israel shall neither slumber nor sleep. 5. The Lord *is* thy keeper: the Lord *is* thy shade upon thy right hand. 6. The sun shall not smite thee by day, nor the moon by night. 7. The Lord shall preserve thee from all evil: he shall preserve thy soul. 8. The Lord shall preserve thy

going out and thy coming in from this time forth, and even for evermore.

Psa. 132:16. I will also clothe her priests with salvation: and her saints shall shout aloud for joy.

Prov. 1:20. Wisdom crieth without; she uttereth her voice in the streets: 21. She crieth in the chief place of concourse, in the openings of the gates: in the city she uttereth her words,

Prov. 8:1. Doth not wisdom cry? and understanding put forth her voice? 4. Unto you, O men, I call; and my voice *is* to the sons of man. 5. O ye simple, understand wisdom: and, ye fools, be ye of an understanding heart. *v.* 2,3.

Prov. 9:1. Wisdom hath builded her house, she hath hewn out her seven pillars: 2. She hath killed her beasts; she hath mingled her wine; she hath also furnished her table. 3. She hath sent forth her maidens: she crieth upon the highest places of the city. 4. Whoso *is* simple, let him turn in hither: as *for* him that wanteth understanding, she saith to him, 5. Come, eat of my bread, and drink of the wine *which* I have mingled. 6. Forsake the foolish, and live; and go in the way of understanding.

Isa. 1:18. Come now, and let us reason together, saith the Lord: Though your sins be as scarlet, they shall be as white as snow; though they be red like crimson, they shall be as wool.

Isa. 2:5. O house of Jacob, come ye, and let us walk in the light of the Lord.

Isa. 25:6. In this mountain shall the Lord of hosts make unto all people a feast of fat things, a feast of wines on the lees, of fat things full of marrow, of wines on the lees well refined. 7. And he will destroy in this mountain the face of the covering cast over all people, and the vail that is spread over all nations.

Isa. 29:18. In that day shall the deaf hear the words of the book, and the eyes of the blind shall see out of obscurity, and out of darkness. 19. The meek also shall increase *their* joy in the Lord, and the poor among men shall rejoice in the Holy One of Israel. 24. They also that erred in spirit shall come to understanding, and they that murmured shall learn doctrine.

Isa. 32:1. Behold, a king shall reign in righteousness, and princes shall rule in judgment. 2. And a man shall be as an hiding place from the wind, and a covert from the tempest; as rivers of water in a dry place, as the shadow of a great rock in a weary land. 3. And the eyes of them that see shall not be dim, and the ears of them that hear shall hearken. 4. The heart also of the rash shall understand knowledge, and the tongue of the stammerers shall be ready to speak plainly.

Isa. 35:8. An highway shall be there, and a way, and it shall be called The way of holiness; the unclean shall not pass over it;

but it *shall be* for those: the wayfaring men, though fools, shall not err *therein.*

Isa. 44:3. For I will pour water upon him that is thirsty, and floods upon the dry ground: I will pour my spirit upon thy seed, and my blessing upon thine offspring:

Isa. 45:17. *But* Israel shall be saved in the LORD with an everlasting salvation: ye shall not be ashamed nor confounded world without end.

Isa. 46:12. Hearken unto me, ye stout-hearted, that *are* far from righteousness: 13. I bring near my righteousness; it shall not be far off, and my salvation shall not tarry: and I will place salvation in Zion for Israel my glory.

Isa. 49:10. They shall not hunger nor thirst; neither shall the heat nor sun smite them: for he that hath mercy on them shall lead them, even by the springs of water shall he guide them. 11. And I will make all my mountains a way, and my highways shall be exalted.

Isa. 50:10. Who *is* among you that feareth the LORD, that obeyeth the voice of his servant, that walketh *in* darkness, and hath no light? let him trust in the name of the LORD, and stay upon his God.

Isa. 51:4. Hearken unto me, my people; and give ear unto me, O my nation: for a law shall proceed from me, and I will make my judgment to rest for a light of the people. 5. My righteousness *is* near; my salvation is gone forth, and mine arms shall judge the people; the isles shall wait upon me, and on mine arm shall they trust.

Isa. 52:10. The LORD hath made bare his holy arm in the eyes of all the nations; and all the ends of the earth shall see the salvation of our God. 15. So shall he sprinkle many nations; the kings shall shut their mouths at him: for *that* which had not been told them shall they see: and *that* which they had not heard shall they consider.

Isa. 55:1. Ho, every one that thirsteth, come ye to the waters, and he that hath no money; come ye, buy, and eat; yea, come, buy wine and milk without money and without price. 2. Wherefore do ye spend money for *that which is* not bread? and your labour for *that which* satisfieth not? hearken diligently unto me, and eat ye *that which is* good, and let your soul delight itself in fatness. 3. Incline your ear, and come unto me: hear, and your soul shall live: and I will make an everlasting covenant with you, *even* the sure mercies of David. 6. Seek ye the LORD while he may be found, call ye upon him while he is near: 7. Let the wicked forsake his way, and the unrighteous man his thoughts: and let him return unto the LORD, and he will have mercy upon him; and to our God, for he will abundantly pardon.

Isa. 56:1. Thus saith the LORD, Keep ye judgment, and do justice: for my salvation *is* near to come, and my righteousness to be revealed. 6. The sons of the stranger, that join themselves to the LORD, to serve him, and to love the name of the LORD, to be his servants, every one that keepeth the sabbath from polluting it, and taketh hold of my covenant; 7. Even them will I bring to my holy mountain, and make them joyful in my house of prayer: their burnt offerings and their sacrifices *shall be* accepted upon mine altar; for mine house shall be called an house of prayer for all people. 8. The Lord GOD which gathereth the outcasts of Israel saith, Yet will I gather *others* to him, beside those that are gathered unto him.

Isa. 57:18. I have seen his ways, and will heal him: I will lead him also, and restore comforts unto him and to his mourners 19. I create the fruit of the lips; Peace, peace to *him that is* far off, and to *him that is* near, saith the LORD; and I will heal him.

Isa. 61:1. The Spirit of the Lord GOD *is* upon me; because the LORD hath anointed me to preach good tidings unto the meek; he hath sent me to bind up the brokenhearted, to proclaim liberty to the captives, and the opening of the prison to *them that are* bound; 2. To proclaim the acceptable year of the LORD, and the day of vengeance of our God; to comfort all that mourn; 3. To appoint unto them that mourn in Zion, to give unto them beauty for ashes, the oil of joy for mourning, the garment of praise for the spirit of heaviness; that they might be called trees of righteousness, the planting of the LORD, that he might be glorified.

Isa. 63:9. In all their affliction he was afflicted, and the angel of his presence saved them: in his love and in his pity he redeemed them; and he bare them, and carried them all the days of old.

Jer. 3:23. Truly in vain *is salvation hoped for* from the hills, *and from* the multitude of mountains: truly in the LORD our God *is* the salvation of Israel.

Jer. 21:8. And unto this people thou shalt say, Thus saith the LORD; Behold, I set before you the way of life, and the way of death.

Ezek. 18:32. For I have no pleasure in the death of him that dieth, saith the Lord GOD: wherefore turn *yourselves,* and live ye.

Joel 2:32. And it shall come to pass, *that* whosoever shall call on the name of the LORD shall be delivered: for in mount Zion and in Jerusalem shall be deliverance, as the LORD hath said, and in the remnant whom the LORD shall call.

Amos 5:4. Thus saith the LORD unto the house of Israel, Seek ye me, and ye shall live:

Zech. 14:8. And it shall be in that day, *that* living waters shall go out from Jerusalem; half of them toward the former sea, and half of them toward the hinder sea: in summer and in winter shall it be.

Mal. 4:2. Unto you that fear my name shall the Sun of righteousness arise with healing in his wings;

Matt. 1:21. She shall bring forth a son, and thou shalt call his name JESUS: for he shall save his people from their sins. - '

Matt. 3:9. Think not to say within yourselves, We have Abraham to *our* father: for I say unto you, that God is able of these stones to raise up children unto Abraham.

Matt. 11:28. Come unto me, all *ye* that labour and are heavy laden, and I will give you rest. 29. Take my yoke upon you, and learn of me; for I am meek and lowly in heart: and ye shall find rest unto your souls. 30. For my yoke *is* easy, and my burden is light.

Matt. 18:14. Even so it is not the will of your Father which is in heaven, that one of these little ones should perish.

Matt. 21:31. Jesus saith unto them, Verily I say unto you, That the publicans and the harlots go into the kingdom of God before you.

Matt. 22:9. Go ye therefore into the highways, and as many as ye shall find, bid to the marriage. 10. So those servants went out into the highways, and gathered together all as many as they found, both bad and good: and the wedding was furnished with guests. 14. Many are called, but few *are* chosen.

Matt. 23:37. O Jerusalem, Jerusalem, *thou* that killest the prophets, and stonest them which are sent unto thee, how often would I have gathered thy children together, even as a hen gathereth her chickens under *her* wings, and ye would not!

Matt. 24:14. This gospel of the kingdom shall be preached in all the world for a witness unto all nations; and then shall the end come.

Mark 2:17. When Jesus heard *it*, he saith unto them, They that are whole have no need of the physician, but they that are sick: I came not to call the righteous, but sinners to repentance. Luke 5:31,32.

Mark 16:15. And he said unto them, Go ye into all the world, and preach the gospel to every creature. 16. He that believeth and is baptized shall be saved; Matt. 28:19.

Luke 2:10. And the angels said unto them, Fear not: for, behold, I bring you good tidings of great joy, which shall be to all people. 31. Which thou hast prepared before the face of all people; 32. A light to lighten the Gentiles, and the glory of thy people Israel.

Luke 3:6. And all flesh shall see the salvation of God.

Luke 7:47. Wherefore I say unto thee, her sins, which are many, are forgiven; for she loved much:

Luke 13:29. They shall come from the east, and *from* the west, and from the north, and *from* the south, and shall sit down in the kingdom of God. 30. And, behold, there are last which shall be first, and there are first which shall be last.

Luke 14:16. Then said he unto him, A certain man made a great supper, and bade many: 17. And sent his servant at supper time to say to them that were bidden, Come; for all things are now ready. 18. And they all with one *consent* began to make excuse. The first said unto him, I have bought a piece of ground, and I must needs go and see it: I pray thee have me excused. 19. And another said, I have bought five yoke of oxen, and I go to prove them: I pray thee have me excused. 20. And another said, I have married a wife, and therefore I cannot come. 21. So that servant came, and shewed his lord these things. Then the master of the house being angry said to his servant, Go out quickly into the streets and lanes of the city, and bring in hither the poor, and the maimed, and the halt, and the blind. 22. And the servant said, Lord, it is done as thou hast commanded, and yet there is room. 23. And the lord said unto the servant, Go out into the highways and hedges, and compel *them* to come in, that my house may be filled. 24. For I say unto you, That none of those men which were bidden shall taste of my supper.

Luke 15:2. And the Pharisees and scribes murmured, saying, This man receiveth sinners, and eateth with them. 4. What man of you, having an hundred sheep, if he lose one of them, doth not leave the ninety and nine in the wilderness, and go after that which is lost, until he find it? 5. And when he hath found *it*, he layeth *it* on his shoulders, rejoicing. 6. And when he cometh home, he calleth together *his* friends and neighbours, saying unto them, Rejoice with me; for I have found my sheep which was lost. 7. I say unto you, that likewise joy shall be in heaven over one sinner that repenteth, more than over ninety and nine just persons, which need no repentance. 8. Either what woman having ten pieces of silver, if she lose one piece, doth not light a candle, and sweep the house, and seek diligently till she find *it?* 9. And when she hath found *it*, she calleth *her* friends and *her* neighbours together, saying, Rejoice with me; for I have found the piece which I had lost. 10. Likewise, I say unto you, there is joy in the presence of the angels of God over one sinner that repenteth. 11. And he said, A certain man had two sons: 12. And the younger of them said to *his* father, Father, give me the portion of goods that falleth *to me.* And he divided unto them *his* living. 13. And not many days after the younger son gathered all together, and took his journey into a far country, and there wasted his substance with riotous living. 14. And when he had spent all, there arose a mighty famine in that land; and he began to be in want. 15. And he went and joined himself to a citizen of that country; and he sent him into his fields to feed swine. 16. And he would fain have filled his belly with the husks that the swine did eat: and no man gave unto him. 17. And when he came to himself, he said, How many hired servants of my father's have bread enough and to spare, and I perish with hunger! 18. I will arise and go to my father, and will say unto him, Father, I have sinned against heaven, and before thee, 19. And am no more worthy to be called thy son: make me as one of thy hired servants. 20. And he arose, and came to his father. But when he was yet a great way off, his father saw him, and had compassion, and ran, and fell on his neck, and kissed him. 21. And the son said unto him, Father, I have sinned against heaven, and in thy sight, and am no more worthy to be called thy son. 22. But the father said to his servants, Bring forth the best robe, and put *it* on him; and put a ring on his hand, and shoes on *his* feet: 23. And bring hither the fatted calf, and kill *it;* and let us eat, and be merry: 24. For this my son was dead, and is alive again; he was lost, and is found. And they began to be merry. 25. Now his elder son was in the field: and as he came and drew nigh to the house, he heard musick and dancing. 26. And he called one of the servants, and asked what these things meant. 27. And he said unto him, Thy brother is come; and thy father hath killed the fatted calf, because he hath received him safe and sound. 28. And he was angry, and would not go in: therefore came his father out, and intreated him. 29. And he answering said to *his* father, Lo, these many years do I serve thee, neither transgressed I at any time thy commandment: and yet thou never gavest me a kid, that I might make merry with my friends: 30. But as soon as this thy son was come, which hath devoured thy living with harlots, thou hast killed for him the fatted calf. 31. And he said unto him, Son, thou art ever with me, and all that I have is thine. 32. It was meet that we should make merry, and be glad: for this thy brother was dead, and is alive again; and was lost, and is found.

Luke 19:10. For the Son of man is come to seek and to save that which was lost.

Luke 24:47. That repentance and remission of sins should be preached in his name among all nations, beginning at Jerusalem.

John 1:7. The same came for a witness, to bear witness of the Light, that all *men* through him might believe.

John 3:14. And as Moses lifted up the serpent in the wilderness, even so must the Son of man be lifted up: 15. That whosoever believeth in him should not perish, but have eternal life. 16. For God so loved the world, that he gave his only begotten Son, that whosoever believeth in him should not perish, but have everlasting life. 17. For God sent not his Son into the world to condemn the world; but that the world through him might be saved.

John 4:14. But whosoever drinketh of the water that I shall give him shall never thirst; but the water that I shall give him shall be in him a well of water springing up into everlasting life. 22. Ye worship ye know not what: we know what we worship: for salvation is of the Jews.

John 5:40. Ye will not come to me, that ye might have life.

John 6:35. Jesus said unto them, I am the bread of life: he that cometh to me shall never hunger; and he that believeth on me shall never thirst. 37. All that the Father giveth me shall come to me; and him that cometh to me I will in no wise cast out.

John 7:37. In the last day, that great *day* of the feast, Jesus stood and cried, saying, If any man thirst, let him come unto me, and drink. 38. He that believeth on me, as the scripture hath said, out of his belly shall flow rivers of living water.

John 10:16. And other sheep I have, which are not of this fold: them also I must bring, and they shall hear my voice; and there shall be one fold, *and* one shepherd.

John 11:51. And this spake he not of himself: but being high priest that year, he prophesied that Jesus should die for that nation; 52. And not for that nation only, but that also he should gather together in one the children of God that were scattered abroad.

John 12:32. I, if I be lifted up from the earth, will draw all *men* unto me.

John 15:4. Abide in me, and I in you. As the branch cannot bear fruit of itself, except it abide in the vine; no more can ye, except ye abide in me. 5. I am the vine, ye *are* the branches: He that abideth in me, and I in him, the same bringeth forth much fruit: for without me ye can do nothing.

Acts 2:39. The promise is unto you, and to your children, and to all that are afar off, *even* as many as the Lord our God shall call.

Acts 4:12. Neither is there salvation in any other: for there is none other name under heaven given among men, whereby we must be saved.

Acts 5:20. Go, stand and speak in the temple to the people all the words of this life.

Acts 11:17. Forasmuch then as God gave them the like gift as *he did* unto us, who believed on the Lord Jesus Christ; what was I, that I could withstand God? 18. When they heard these things, they held their peace, and glorified God, saying, Then hath God also to the Gentiles granted repentance unto life.

Acts 13:26. Men *and* brethren, children of the stock of Abraham, and whosoever among you feareth God, to you is the word of this salvation sent. 38. Be it known unto you therefore, men *and* brethren, that through this man is preached unto you the forgiveness of sins: 39. And by him all that believe are justified from all things, from which ye could not be justified by the law of Moses. 47. For so hath the Lord commanded us, *saying*, I have set thee to be a light of the Gentiles, that thou shouldest be for salvation unto the ends of the earth.

Acts 15:7. And when there had been much disputing, Peter rose up, and said unto them, Men *and* brethren, ye know how that a good while ago God made choice among us, that the Gentiles by my mouth should hear the word of the gospel, and believe. 8. And God, which knoweth the hearts, bare them witness, giving them the Holy Ghost, even as *he did* unto us; 9. And put no difference between us and them, purifying their hearts by faith. 11. But we believe that through the grace of the Lord Jesus Christ we shall be saved,

Acts 16:17. The same followed Paul and us, and cried, saying, These men are the servants of the most high God, which shew unto us the way of salvation. 30. And brought them out, and said, Sirs, what must I do to be saved? 31. And they said, Believe on the Lord Jesus Christ, and thou shalt be saved, and thy house.

Acts 20:21. Testifying both to the Jews, and also to the Greeks, repentance toward God, and faith toward our Lord Jesus Christ.

Acts 28:28. Be it known therefore unto you, that the salvation of God is sent unto the Gentiles, and *that* they will hear it.

Rom. 1:5. By whom we have received grace and apostleship, for obedience to the faith among all nations, for his name: 14. I am debtor both to the Greeks, and to the Barbarians; both to the wise, and to the unwise. 16. For I am not ashamed of the gospel of Christ: for it is the power of God unto salvation to every one that believeth; to the Jew first, and also to the Greek. 17. For therein is the righteousness of God revealed from faith to faith: as it is written, The just shall live by faith.

Rom. 2:26. Therefore if the uncircumcision keep the righteousness of the law, shall not his uncircumcision be counted for circumcision?

Rom. 3:21. But now the righteousness of God without the law is manifested, being witnessed by the law and the prophets; 22. Even the righteousness of God *which is* by faith of Jesus Christ unto all and upon all them that believe; for there is no difference: 23. For all have sinned, and come short of the glory of God; 24. Being justified freely by his grace through the redemption that is in Christ Jesus: 25. Whom God hath set forth *to be* a propitiation through faith in his blood, to declare his righteousness for the remission of sins that are past, through the forbearance of God; 26. To declare, *I say*, at this time his righteousness: that he might be just, and the justifier of him which believeth in Jesus. 28. Therefore we conclude that a man is justified by faith without the deeds of the law. 29. *Is he* the God of the Jews only?

is he not also of the Gentiles? Yes, of the Gentiles also: 30. Seeing *it is* one God, which shall justify the circumcision by faith, and uncircumcision through faith.

Rom. 4:1. What shall we say then that Abraham our father, as pertaining to the flesh, hath found? 2. For if Abraham were justified by works, he hath *whereof* to glory; but not before God. 3. For what saith the scripture? Abraham believed God, and it was counted unto him for righteousness. 4. Now to him that worketh is the reward not reckoned of grace, but of debt. 5. But to him that worketh not, but believeth on him that justifieth the ungodly, his faith is counted for righteousness. 6. Even as David also describeth the blessedness of the man, unto whom God imputeth righteousness without works, 7. *Saying*, Blessed *are* they whose iniquities are forgiven, and whose sins are covered. 8. Blessed *is* the man to whom the Lord will not impute sin. 9. *Cometh* this blessedness then upon the circumcision *only*, or upon the uncircumcision also? for we say that faith was reckoned to Abraham for righteousness. 10. How was it then reckoned? when he was in circumcision, or in uncircumcision? Not in circumcision, but in uncircumcision. 11. And he received the sign of circumcision, a seal of the righteousness of the faith which *he had yet* being uncircumcised: that he might be the father of all them that believe, though they be not circumcised: that righteousness might be imputed unto them also: 12. And the father of circumcision to them who are not of the circumcision only, but who also walk in the steps of that faith of our father Abraham, which *he had* being *yet* uncircumcised. 13. For the promise, that he should be the heir of the world, *was* not to Abraham, or to his seed, through the law, but through the righteousness of faith. 14. For if they which are of the law *be* heirs, faith is made void, and the promise made of none effect: 15. Because the law worketh wrath: for where no law is, *there is* no transgression. 16. Therefore *it is* of faith, that *it might be* by grace; to the end the promise might be sure to all the seed; not to that only which is of the law, but to that also which is of the faith of Abraham; who is the father of us all, 17. (As it is written, I have made thee a father of many nations,) before him whom he believed, *even* God, who quickeneth the dead, and calleth those things which be not as though they were. 18. Who against hope believed in hope, that he might become the father of many nations, according to that which was spoken, So shall thy seed be. 19. And being not weak in faith, he considered not his own body now dead, when he was about an hundred years old, neither yet the deadness of Sarah's womb: 20. He staggered not at the promise of God through unbelief: but was strong in faith, giving glory to God; 21. And being fully persuaded that, what he had promised, he was able also to perform. 22. And therefore it was imputed to him for righteousness. 23. Now it was not written for his sake alone, that it was imputed to him; 24. But for us also, to whom it shall be imputed, if we believe on him that raised up Jesus our Lord from the dead; 25. Who was delivered for our offences, and was raised again for our justification.

Rom. 5:1. Therefore being justified by faith, ¹ we have peace with God through our Lord Jesus Christ: 2. By whom also we have access by faith into this grace wherein we stand, and rejoice in hope of the glory of God. *vs.* 15-21.   [¹ R. V. let us]

Rom. 7:24. O wretched man that I am! who shall deliver me from the body of this death? 25. I thank God through Jesus Christ our Lord.

Rom. 9:30. The Gentiles, which followed not after righteousness, have attained to righteousness, even the righteousness which is of faith. 31. But Israel, which followed after the law of righteousness, hath not attained to the law of righteousness. 32. Wherefore? Because *they sought it* not by faith, but as it were by the works of the law. For they stumbled at that stumblingstone; 33. As it is written, Behold, I lay in Sion a stumblingstone and rock of offence: and whosoever believeth on him shall not be ashamed.

Rom. 10:4. Christ *is* the end of the law for righteousness to every one that believeth. 8. The word is nigh thee, *even* in thy mouth, and in thy heart: that is, the word of faith, which we preach; 9. That if thou shalt confess with thy mouth the Lord Jesus, and shalt believe in thine heart that God hath raised him from the dead, thou shalt be saved. 10. For with the heart man believeth unto righteousness; and with the mouth confession is made unto salvation. 11. For the scripture saith, Whosoever believeth on him shall not be ashamed. 12. For there is no difference between the Jew and the Greek: for the same Lord over all is rich unto all that call upon him. 13. For whosoever shall call upon the name of the Lord shall be saved.

Rom. 11:6. And if by grace, then *is it* no more of works: otherwise grace is no more grace. But if *it be* of works, then is it no more grace: otherwise work is no more work. 11. I say then, Have they stumbled that they should fall? God forbid: but *rather* through their fall salvation *is come* unto the Gentiles, for to provoke them to jealousy. 12. Now if the fall of them *be* the riches of the world, and the diminishing of them the riches of the Gentiles; how much more their fulness? *vs.* 1-36.

Rom. 15:9. And that the Gentiles might glorify God for *his* mercy; as it is written, For this cause I will confess to thee among the Gentiles, and sing unto thy name. 16. That I should be the minister of Jesus Christ to the Gentiles, ministering the gospel of God, that the offering up of the Gentiles might be acceptable, being sanctified by the Holy Ghost.

1 Cor. 1:18. For the preaching of the cross is to them that perish, foolishness; but unto us which are saved, it is the power of God.

1 Cor. 6:11. And such were some of you: but ye are washed, but ye are sanctified, but ye are justified in the name of the Lord Jesus, and by the Spirit of our God.

2 Cor. 5:17. Therefore if any man *be* in Christ, *he is* a new creature: old things are passed away; behold, all things are become new. 20. Now then we are ambassadors for Christ, as though God did beseech *you* by us: we pray *you* in Christ's stead, be ye reconciled to God.

2 Cor. 6:1. We then, *as* workers together *with him*, beseech *you* also that ye receive not the grace of God in vain. 17. Wherefore come out from among them, and be ye separate, saith the Lord, and touch not the unclean *thing;* and I will receive you, 18. And will be a Father unto you, and ye shall be my sons and daughters, saith the Lord Almighty.

2 Cor. 7:10. For godly sorrow worketh repentance to salvation not to be repented of: but the sorrow of the world worketh death.

Gal. 1:4. Who gave himself for our sins, that he might deliver us from this present evil world, according to the will of God and our Father:

Gal. 2:16. Knowing that a man is not justified by the works of the law, but by the faith of Jesus Christ, even we have believed in Jesus Christ, that we might be justified by the faith of Christ, and not by the works of the law: for by the works of the law shall no flesh be justified.

Gal. 3:8. The scripture, foreseeing that God would justify the heathen through faith, preached before the gospel unto Abraham, *saying*, In thee shall all nations be blessed. 13. Christ hath redeemed us from the curse of the law, being made a curse for us: for it is written, Cursed *is* every one that hangeth on a tree: 14. That the blessing of Abraham might come on the Gentiles through Jesus Christ; that we might receive the promise of the Spirit through faith. 21. *Is* the law then against the promises of God? God forbid: for if there had been a law given which could have given life, verily righteousness should have been by the law. 26. For ye are all the children of God by faith in Christ Jesus. 27. For as many of you as have been baptized into Christ have put on Christ. 28. There is neither Jew nor Greek, there is neither bond nor free, there is neither male nor female: for ye are all one in Christ Jesus. *vs.* 1-28.

Eph. 1:9. Having made known unto us the mystery of his will, according to his good pleasure which he hath purposed in himself: 10. That in the dispensation of the fulness of times he might gather together in one all things in Christ, both which are in heaven, and which are on earth; *even* in him. 13. In whom ye also *trusted*, after that ye heard the word of truth, the gospel of your salvation: in whom also, after that ye believed, ye were sealed with that holy Spirit of promise,

Eph. 2:1. And you *hath he quickened*, who were dead in trespasses and sins; 3. And were by nature the children of wrath, even as others. 4. But God, who is rich in mercy, for his great love wherewith he loved us, 5. Even when we were dead in sins, hath quickened us together with Christ, (by grace ye are saved;) 8. By grace are ye saved through faith; and that not of yourselves; *it is* the gift of God: 9. Not of works, lest any man should boast. 14. For he is our peace, who hath made both one, and hath broken down the middle wall of partition *between us;* 15. Having abolished in his flesh the enmity, *even* the law of commandments *contained* in ordinances; for to make in himself of twain one new man, *so* making peace; 17. Preached peace to you which were afar off, and to them that were nigh.

Eph. 3:6. The Gentiles should be fellow-heirs, and of the same body, and partakers of his promise in Christ by the gospel: 9. To make all *men* see what *is* the [1] fellowship of the mystery, which from [2] the beginning of the world hath been hid in God, who created all things [3] by Jesus Christ:

[R. V. [1] dispensation   [2] all ages   [3] Omitted.]

Eph. 5:14. Wherefore he saith, Awake thou that sleepest, and arise from the dead, and Christ shall give thee light.

Phil. 2:12. Work out your own salvation with fear and trembling.

Phil. 3:7. But what things were gain to me, those I counted loss for Christ. 8. Yea doubtless, and I count all things *but* loss for the excellency of the knowledge of Christ Jesus my Lord: for whom I have suffered the loss of all things, and do count them *but* dung, that I may win Christ, 9. And be found in him, not having mine own right-eousness, which is of the law, but that which is through the faith of Christ, the righteous-ness which is of God by faith: 10. That I may know him, and the power of his resur-rection, and the fellowship of his sufferings, being made conformable unto his death; 11. If by any means I might attain unto the resurrection of the dead.

Col. 1:5. The word of the truth of the gos-pel; 6. Which is come unto you, as *it is* in all the world: 20. Having made peace through the blood of his cross, by him to reconcile all things unto himself; by him, *I say*, whether *they be* things in earth, or things in heaven. 21. And you, that were sometime alienated and enemies in *your* mind by wicked works, yet now hath he reconciled 22. In the body of his flesh through death, to present you holy and un-blameable and unreproveable in his sight: 23. If ye continue in the faith grounded and

settled, and *be* not moved away from the hope of the gospel, which ye have heard, *and* which was preached to every creature which is under heaven; 26. Even the mys-tery which hath been hid from ages and from generations, but now is made manifest to his saints: 27. To whom God would make known what *is* the riches of the glory of this mystery among the Gentiles; which is Christ in you, the hope of glory:

Col. 3:11. Where there is neither Greek nor Jew, circumcision nor uncircumcision, Barbarian, Scythian, bond *nor* free: but Christ *is* all, and in all.

1 Thess. 5:8. But let us, who are of the day, be sober, putting on the breastplate of faith and love; and for an helmet, the hope of salvation. 9. For God hath not appointed us to wrath, but to obtain salvation by our Lord Jesus Christ, 10. Who died for us, that, whether we wake or sleep, we should live together with him.

2 Thess. 2:13. God hath from the begin-ning chosen you to salvation through sanc-tification of the Spirit and belief of the truth: 14. Whereunto he called you by our gospel, to the obtaining of the glory of our Lord Jesus Christ.

1 Tim. 1:13. Who was before a blasphemer, and a persecutor, and injurious: but I ob-tained mercy, because I did *it* ignorantly in unbelief. 15. This *is* a faithful saying, and worthy of all acceptation, that Christ Jesus came into the world to save sinners; of whom I am chief. 16. Howbeit for this cause I obtained mercy, that in me first Jesus Christ might shew forth all longsuf-fering, for a pattern to them which should hereafter believe on him to life everlasting.

1 Tim. 2:3. For this *is* good and accept-able in the sight of God our Saviour; 4. Who will have all men to be saved, and to come unto the knowledge of the truth. 5. For *there is* one God, and one mediator be-tween God and men, the man Christ Jesus; 6. Who gave himself a ransom for all, to be testified in due time.

1 Tim. 4:10. For therefore we both labour and suffer reproach, because we trust in the living God, who is the Saviour of all men, specially of those that believe.

2 Tim. 1:9. Who hath saved us, and called *us* with an holy calling, not according to our works, but according to his own purpose and grace, which was given us in Christ Jesus be-fore the world began, 10. But is now made manifest by the appearing of our Saviour Jesus Christ, who hath abolished death, and hath brought life and [1] immortality to light through the gospel: [[1] R. V. incorruption]

2 Tim. 2:10. Therefore I endure all things for the elect's sakes, that they may also ob-tain the salvation which is in Christ Jesus with eternal glory.

2 Tim. 3:15. And that from a child thou hast known the holy scriptures, which are able to make thee wise unto salvation through faith which is in Christ Jesus.

Tit. 2:11. The grace of God that bringeth salvation hath appeared to all men,

Tit. 3:3. For we ourselves also were sometimes foolish, disobedient, deceived, serving divers lusts and pleasures, living in malice and envy, hateful, *and* hating one another. 4. But after that the kindness and love of God our Saviour toward man appeared, 5. Not by works of righteousness which we have done, but according to his mercy he saved us, by the washing of regeneration, and renewing of the Holy Ghost; 6. Which he shed on us abundantly through Jesus Christ our Saviour; 7. That being justified by his grace, we should be made heirs according to the hope of eternal life.

Heb. 1:14. Are they not all ministering spirits, sent forth to minister for them who shall be heirs of salvation?

Heb. 2:3. How shall we escape, if we neglect so great salvation; which at the first began to be spoken by the Lord, and was confirmed unto us by them that heard *him*; 10. For it became him, for whom *are* all things, and by whom *are* all things, in bringing many sons unto glory, to make the captain of their salvation perfect through sufferings.

Heb. 4:1. Let us therefore fear, lest, a promise being left *us* of entering into his rest, any of you should seem to come short of it. 2. For unto us was the gospel preached, as well as unto them: but the word preached did not profit them, not being mixed with faith in them that heard *it*. 3. For we which have believed do enter into rest, as he said, As I have sworn in my wrath, if they shall enter into my rest: although the works were finished from the foundation of the world. 4. For he spake in a certain place of the seventh *day* on this wise, And God did rest the seventh day from all his works. 5. And in this *place* again, If they shall enter into my rest. 6. Seeing therefore it remaineth that some must enter therein, and they to whom it was first preached entered not in because of unbelief: 7. Again, he limiteth a certain day, saying in David, To day, after so long a time; as it is said, To day if ye will hear his voice, harden not your hearts. 8. For if [1] Jesus had given them rest, then would he not afterward have spoken of another day. 9. There remaineth therefore a rest to the people of God. 10. For he that is entered into his rest, he also hath ceased from his own works, as God *did* from his.   [[1] R. V. Joshua]

Heb. 5:9. And being made perfect, he became the author of eternal salvation unto all them that obey him;

Heb. 7:25. Wherefore he is able also to save them to the uttermost that come unto God by him, seeing he ever liveth to make intercession for them.

Jas. 1:21. Wherefore lay apart all filthiness and superfluity of naughtiness, and receive with meekness the engrafted word, which is able to save your souls.

1 Pet. 1:5. Who are kept by the power of God through faith unto salvation ready to be revealed in the last time. 9. Receiving the end of your faith, *even* the salvation of *your* souls. 10. Of which salvation the prophets have inquired and searched diligently, who prophesied of the grace *that should come* unto you:

2 Pet. 3:9. The Lord is not slack concerning his promise, as some men count slackness; but is longsuffering to us-ward, not willing that any should perish, but that all should come to repentance. 15. And account *that* the longsuffering of our Lord *is* salvation;

1 John 2:25. This is the promise that he hath promised us, *even* eternal life.

1 John 4:9. In this was manifested the love of God toward us, because that God sent his only begotten Son into the world, that we might live through him. 10. Herein is love, not that we loved God, but that he loved us, and sent his Son *to be* the propitiation for our sins.

1 John 5:11. And this is the record, that God hath given to us eternal life, and this life is in his Son.

Jude 3. Beloved, when I gave all diligence to write unto you of the common salvation, it was needful for me to write unto you, and exhort *you* that ye should earnestly contend for the faith which was once delivered unto the saints.

Rev. 3:17. Because thou sayest, I am rich, and increased with goods, and have need of nothing; and knowest not that thou art wretched, and miserable, and poor, and blind, and naked: 18. I counsel thee to buy of me gold tried in the fire, that thou mayest be rich; and white raiment, that thou mayest be clothed, and *that* the shame of thy nakedness do not appear; and anoint thine eyes with eyesalve, that thou mayest see. 20. Behold, I stand at the door, and knock: if any man hear my voice, and open the door, I will come in to him, and will sup with him, and he with me.

Rev. 5:9. And they sung a new song, saying, Thou art worthy to take the book, and to open the seals thereof: for thou wast slain, and hast redeemed us to God by thy blood out of every kindred, and tongue, and people, and nation;

Rev. 7:9. After this I beheld, and, lo, a great multitude, which no man could number, of all nations, and kindreds, and people, and tongues, stood before the throne, and before the Lamb, clothed with white robes, and palms in their hands; 10. And cried with a loud voice, saying, Salvation to our God which sitteth upon the throne, and unto the Lamb.

Rev. 14:6. And I saw another angel fly in the midst of heaven, having the everlasting gospel to preach unto them that dwell on the earth, and to every nation, and kindred, and tongue, and people,

Rev. 21:6. I will give unto him that **is**

athirst of the fountain of the water of life freely.

Rev. 22:17. And the Spirit and the bride say, Come. And let him that heareth say, Come. And let him that is athirst come. And whosoever will, let him take the water of life freely.

See ADOPTION; REDEMPTION; REGENERATION; SANCTIFICATION.

CONDITIONS OF: Matt. 3:2. Repent ye: for the kingdom of heaven is at hand.

Matt. 18:3. And said, Verily I say unto you, Except ye be converted, and become as little children, ye shall not enter into the kingdom of heaven.

Matt. 19:16. And, behold, one came and said unto him, Good Master, what good thing shall I do, that I may have eternal life? 17. And he said unto him, Why callest thou me good? *there is* none good but one, *that is*, God: but if thou wilt enter into life, keep the commandments. 18. He saith unto him, Which? Jesus said, Thou shalt do no murder, Thou shalt not commit adultery, Thou shalt not steal, Thou shalt not bear false witness, 19. Honour thy father and *thy* mother: and, Thou shalt love thy neighbour as thyself. 20. The young man saith unto him, All these things have I kept from my youth up: what lack I yet? 21. Jesus said unto him, If thou wilt be perfect, go *and* sell that thou hast, and give to the poor, and thou shalt have treasure in heaven: and come *and* follow me. Luke 18: 18–26.

Matt. 24:13. But he that shall endure unto the end, the same shall be saved.

Mark 1:4. John did baptize in the wilderness, and preach the baptism of repentance for the remission of sins.

Luke 3:8. Bring forth therefore fruits worthy of repentance, and begin not to say within yourselves, We have Abraham to *our* father: for I say unto you, That God is able of these stones to raise up children unto Abraham.

Luke 14:25. And there went great multitudes with him: and he turned, and said unto them, 26. If any *man* come to me, and hate not his father, and mother, and wife, and children, and brethren, and sisters, yea, and his own life also, he cannot be my disciple. 27. And whosoever doth not bear his cross, and come after me, cannot be my disciple. 28. For which of you, intending to build a tower, sitteth not down first, and counteth the cost, whether he have *sufficient* to finish *it?* 29. Lest haply, after he hath laid the foundation, and is not able to finish *it*, all that behold *it* begin to mock him, 30. Saying, This man began to build, and was not able to finish. 31. Or what king, going to make war against another king, sitteth not down first, and consulteth whether he be able with ten thousand to meet him that cometh against him with twenty thousand? 32. Or else, while the other is yet a great way off, he sendeth an

ambassage, and desireth conditions of peace. 33. So likewise, whosoever he be of you that forsaketh not all that he hath, he cannot be my disciple.

John 3:3. Jesus answered and said unto him, Verily, verily, I say unto thee, Except a man be born again, he cannot see the kingdom of God. 4. Nicodemus saith unto him, How can a man be born when he is old? can he enter the second time into his mother's womb, and be born? 5. Jesus answered, Verily, verily I say unto thee, Except a man be born of water and *of* the Spirit, he cannot enter into the kingdom of God. 6. That which is born of the flesh is flesh; and that which is born of the Spirit is spirit. 7. Marvel not that I said unto thee, Ye must be born again. 8. The wind bloweth where it listeth, and thou hearest the sound thereof, but canst not tell whence it cometh, and whither it goeth: so is every one that is born of the Spirit. 9. Nicodemus answered and said unto him, How can these things be? 10. Jesus answered and said unto him, Art thou a master of Israel, and knowest not these things? 11. Verily, verily, I say unto thee, We speak that we do know, and testify that we have seen; and ye receive not our witness. 12. If I have told you earthly things, and ye believe not, how shall ye believe, if I tell you *of* heavenly things?

14. And as Moses lifted up the serpent in the wilderness, even so must the Son of man be lifted up: 15. That whosoever believeth in him should not perish, but have eternal life. 16. For God so loved the world, that he gave his only begotten Son, that whosoever believeth in him should not perish, but have everlasting life. 17. For God sent not his Son into the world to condemn the world; but that the world through him might be saved. 18. He that believeth on him is not condemned: but he that believeth not is condemned already, because he hath not believed in the name of the only begotten Son of God.

John 5:24. Verily, verily, I say unto you, He that heareth my word, and believeth on him that sent me, hath everlasting life, and shall not come into condemnation; but is passed from death unto life.

John 6:28. Then said they unto him, What shall we do, that we might work the works of God? 29. Jesus answered and said unto them, This is the work of God, that ye believe on him whom he hath sent.

47. Verily, verily, I say unto you, He that believeth on me hath everlasting life.

John 9:35. Jesus heard that they had cast him out; and when he had found him, he said unto him, Dost thou believe on the Son of God?

John 11:25. Jesus said unto her, I am the resurrection and the life: he that believeth in me, though he were dead, yet shall he live: 26. And whosoever liveth and believeth in me shall never die. Believest thou this?

John 12:36. While ye have light, believe in the light, that ye may be the children of light.

John 20:31. But these are written, that ye might believe that Jesus is the Christ, the Son of God; and that believing ye might have life through his name.

Acts 2:38. Then Peter said unto them, Repent, and be baptized every one of you in the name of Jesus Christ for the remission of sins, and ye shall receive the gift of the Holy Ghost.

Acts 3:19. Repent ye therefore, and be converted, that your sins may be blotted out, when the times of refreshing shall come from the presence of the Lord; 23. And it shall come to pass, *that* every soul, which will not hear that prophet, shall be destroyed from among the people.

See BLESSINGS, CONTINGENT UPON OBEDIENCE; FAITH; OBEDIENCE; REPENTANCE; PERSEVERANCE.

PLAN OF: Mark 4:11. And he said unto them, Unto you it is given to know the mystery of the kingdom of God: but unto them that are without, all *these* things are done in parables:

John 6:44. No man can come to me, except the Father which hath sent me draw him: and I will raise him up at the last day. *vs.* 37,65.

45. It is written in the prophets, And they shall be all taught of God. Every man therefore that hath heard, and hath learned of the Father, cometh unto me.

John 17:4. I have glorified thee on the earth: I have finished the work which thou gavest me to do.

John 18:11. Then said Jesus unto Peter, Put up thy sword into the sheath: the cup which my Father hath given me, shall I not drink it?

John 19:28. After this, Jesus knowing that all things were now accomplished, that the scripture might be fulfilled, saith, I thirst. 29. Now there was set a vessel full of vinegar: and they filled a spunge with vinegar, and put *it* upon hyssop, and put *it* to his mouth. 30. When Jesus therefore had received the vinegar, he said, It is finished: and he bowed his head, and gave up the ghost.

Acts 3:18. But those things, which God before had shewed by the mouth of all his prophets, that Christ should suffer, he hath so fulfilled.

Acts 17:3. Opening and alleging, that Christ must needs have suffered, and risen again from the dead; and that this Jesus, whom I preach unto you, is Christ.

Rom. 1:16. For I am not ashamed of the gospel of Christ: for it is the power of God unto salvation to every one that believeth; to the Jew first, and also to the Greek. 17. For therein is the righteousness of God revealed from faith to faith: as it is written, The just shall live by faith.

Rom. 10:3. For they being ignorant of God's righteousness, and going about to establish their own righteousness, have not submitted themselves unto the righteousness of God. 4. For Christ *is* the end of the law for righteousness to every one that believeth. 5. For Moses describeth the righteousness which is of the law, That the man which doeth those things shall live by them. 6. But the righteousness which is of faith speaketh on this wise, Say not in thine heart, Who shall ascend into heaven? (that is, to bring Christ down *from above:*) 7. Or, Who shall descend into the deep? (that is, to bring up Christ again from the dead.) 8. But what saith it? The word is nigh thee, *even* in thy mouth, and in thy heart: that is, the word of faith, which we preach; 9. That if thou shalt confess with thy mouth the Lord Jesus, and shalt believe in thine heart that God hath raised him from the dead, thou shalt be saved.

Rom. 16:25. Now to him that is of power to stablish you according to my gospel, and the preaching of Jesus Christ, according to the revelation of the mystery, which was kept secret since the world began, 26. But now is made manifest, and by the scriptures of the prophets, according to the commandment of the everlasting God, made known to all nations for the obedience of faith:

1 Cor. 1:21. For after that in the wisdom of God the world by wisdom knew not God, it pleased God by the foolishness of preaching to save them that believe. 22. For the Jews require a sign, and the Greeks seek after wisdom: 23. But we preach Christ crucified, unto the Jews a stumblingblock, and unto the Greeks foolishness; 24. But unto them which are called, both Jews and Greeks, Christ the power of God, and the wisdom of God. 25. Because the foolishness of God is wiser than men; and the weakness of God is stronger than men.

1 Cor. 2:7. But we speak the wisdom of God in a mystery, *even* the hidden *wisdom*, which God ordained before the world unto our glory: 8. Which none of the princes of this world knew: for had they known *it*, they would not have crucified the Lord of glory. 9. But as it is written, Eye hath not seen, nor ear heard, neither have entered into the heart of man, the things which God hath prepared for them that love him.

2 Cor. 5:18. And all things *are* of God, who hath reconciled us to himself by Jesus Christ, and hath given to us the ministry of reconciliation; 19. To wit, that God was in Christ, reconciling the world unto himself, not imputing their trespasses unto them; and hath committed unto us the word of reconciliation.

Gal. 4:4. But when the fulness of the time was come, God sent forth his Son, made of a woman, made under the law, 5. To redeem them that were under the law, that we might receive the adoption of sons.

Eph. 1:3. Blessed *be* the God and Father

of our Lord Jesus Christ, who hath blessed us with all spiritual blessings in heavenly *places* in Christ: 4. According as he hath chosen us in him before the foundation of the world, that we should be holy and without blame before him in love: 5. Having predestinated us unto the adoption of children by Jesus Christ to himself, according to the good pleasure of his will, 6. To the praise of the glory of his grace, wherein he hath made us accepted in the beloved: 7. In whom we have redemption through his blood, the forgiveness of sins, according to the riches of his grace; 8. Wherein he hath abounded toward us in all wisdom and prudence; 9. Having made known unto us the mystery of his will, according to his good pleasure which he hath purposed in himself: 10. That in the dispensation of the fulness of times he might gather together in one all things in Christ, both which are in heaven, and which are on earth; *even* in him: 11. In whom also we have obtained an inheritance, being predestinated according to the purpose of him who worketh all things after the counsel of his own will: 12. That we should be to the praise of his glory, who first trusted in Christ. 13. In whom ye also *trusted*, after that ye heard the word of truth, the gospel of your salvation: in whom also after that ye believed, ye were sealed with that Holy Spirit of promise, 14. Which is the earnest of our inheritance until the redemption of the purchased possession, unto the praise of his glory. 15. Wherefore I also, after I heard of your faith in the Lord Jesus, and love unto all the saints, 16. Cease not to give thanks for you, making mention of you in my prayers; 17. That the God of our Lord Jesus Christ, the Father of glory, may give unto you the spirit of wisdom and revelation in the knowledge of him: 18. The eyes of your understanding being enlightened; that ye may know what is the hope of his calling, and what the riches of the glory of his inheritance in the saints, 19. And what *is* the exceeding greatness of his power to us-ward who believe, according to the working of his mighty power, 20. Which he wrought in Christ, when he raised him from the dead, and set *him* at his own right hand in the heavenly *places*, 21. Far above all principality, and power, and might, and dominion, and every name that is named, not only in this world, but also in that which is to come: 22. And hath put all *things* under his feet, and gave him *to be* the head over all *things* to the church, 23. Which is his body, the fulness of him that filleth all in all.

Eph. 2:4. But God, who is rich in mercy, for his great love wherewith he loved us, 5. Even when we were dead in sins, hath quickened us together with Christ, (by grace ye are saved;) 6. And hath raised *us* up together, and made *us* sit together in heavenly *places* in Christ Jesus: 7. That in the ages to come he might shew the exceed-

ing riches of his grace in *his* kindness toward us through Christ Jesus. 8. For by grace are ye saved through faith; and that not of yourselves: *it is* the gift of God: 9. Not of works, lest any man should boast. 10. For we are his workmanship, created in Christ Jesus unto good works, which God hath before ordained that we should walk in them.

Eph. 3:1. For this cause I Paul, the prisoner of Jesus Christ for you Gentiles, 2. If ye have heard of the dispensation of the grace of God which is given me to you-ward: 3. How that by revelation he made known unto me the mystery; (as I wrote afore in few words, 4. Whereby, when ye read, ye may understand my knowledge in the mystery of Christ) 5. Which in other ages was not made known unto the sons of men, as it is now revealed unto his holy apostles and prophets by the Spirit; 6. That the Gentiles should be fellowheirs, and of the same body, and partakers of his promise in Christ by the gospel: 7. Whereof I was made a minister, according to the gift of the grace of God given unto me by the effectual working of his power. 8. Unto me, who am less than the least of all saints, is this grace given, that I should preach among the Gentiles the unsearchable riches of Christ; 9. And to make all *men* see what *is* the [1] fellowship of the mystery, which from [2] the beginning of the world hath been hid in God, who created all things [3] by Jesus Christ: 10. To the intent that now unto the principalities and powers in heavenly *places* might be known by the church the manifold wisdom of God, 11. According to the eternal purpose which he purposed in Christ Jesus our Lord:

[R. V. [1] dispensation [2] all ages [3] Omitted.]

Eph. 6:19. That utterance may be given unto me, that I may open my mouth boldly, to make known the mystery of the gospel,

Col. 1:19. For it pleased *the Father* that in him should all fulness dwell; 20. And, having made peace through the blood of his cross, by him to reconcile all things unto himself; by him, *I say*, whether *they be* things in earth, or things in heaven. 21. And you, that were sometime alienated and enemies in *your* mind by wicked works, yet now hath he reconciled 22. In the body of his flesh through death, to present you holy and unblameable and unreproveable in his sight: 23. If ye continue in the faith grounded and settled, and *be* not moved away from the hope of the gospel, which ye have heard, *and* which was preached to every creature which is under heaven; whereof I Paul am made a minister; 26. *Even* the mystery which hath been hid from ages and from generations, but now is made manifest to his saints: 27. To whom God would make known what *is* the riches of the glory of this mystery among the Gentiles; which is Christ in you, the hope of glory:

2 Thess. 2:13. But we are bound to give

thanks always to God for you, brethren beloved of the Lord, because God hath from the beginning chosen you to salvation through sanctification of the Spirit and belief of the truth : 14. Whereunto he called you by our gospel, to the obtaining of the glory of our Lord Jesus Christ.

1 Tim. 3:16. And without controversy great is the mystery of godliness : ¹ God was manifest in the flesh, justified in the Spirit, seen of angels, preached unto the Gentiles, believed on in the world, received up into glory.   [¹ R. V. He who]

2 Tim. 1:9. Who hath saved us, and called *us* with an holy calling, not according to our works, but according to his own purpose and grace, which was given us in Christ Jesus before the world began, 10. But is now made manifest by the appearing of our Saviour Jesus Christ, who hath abolished death, and hath brought life and ¹ immortality to light through the gospel :   [¹ R. V. incorruption]

Heb. 2:9. But we see Jesus, who was made a little lower than the angels for the suffering of death, crowned with glory and honour ; that he by the grace of God should taste death for every man. 10. For it became him, for whom *are* all things, and by whom *are* all things, in bringing many sons unto glory, to make the captain of their salvation perfect through sufferings. 14. Forasmuch then as the children are partakers of flesh and blood, he also himself likewise took part of the same ; that through death he might destroy him that had the power of death, that is, the devil ; 15. And deliver them who through fear of death were all their lifetime subject to bondage. 16. For verily he took not on *him the nature of* angels ; but he took on *him* the seed of Abraham. 17. Wherefore in all things it behoved him to be made like unto *his* brethren, that he might be a merciful and faithful high priest in things *pertaining* to God, to make reconciliation for the sins of the people. 18. For in that he himself hath suffered being tempted, he is able to succour them that are tempted.

Heb. 6:17. Wherein God, willing more abundantly to shew unto the heirs of promise the immutability of his counsel, confirmed *it* by an oath : 18. That by two immutable things, in which *it was* impossible for God to lie, we might have a strong consolation, who have fled for refuge to lay hold upon the hope set before us : 19. Which *hope* we have as an anchor of the soul, both sure and stedfast, and which entereth into that within the veil ; 20. Whither the forerunner is for us entered, *even* Jesus, made an high priest for ever after the order of Melchisedec.

Rev. 5:2. And I saw a strong angel proclaiming with a loud voice, Who is worthy to open the book, and to loose the seals thereof ? 3. And no man in heaven, nor in earth, neither under the earth, was able to open the book, neither to look thereon. 4.

And I wept much, because no man was found worthy to open and to read the book, neither to look thereon. 5. And one of the elders saith unto me, Weep not : behold, the Lion of the tribe of Juda, the Root of David, hath prevailed to open the book, and to loose the seven seals thereof.

Rev. 10:7. But in the days of the voice of the seventh angel, when he shall begin to sound, the mystery of God should be finished, as he hath declared to his servants the prophets.

See JESUS, MISSION OF ; REDEMPTION ; REGENERATION ; SANCTIFICATION ; SIN, FORGIVENESS OF.

SAMARIA. 1. City of, built by Omri, 1 Kin. 16:24. Capital of the kingdom of the ten tribes, 1 Kin. 16:29; 22:51; 2 Kin. 13:1,10; 15:8. Besieged by Ben-hadad, 1 Kin. 20; 2 Kin. 6:24–33; 7. The king of Syria is led into, by Elisha, who miraculously blinds him and his army, 2 Kin. 6:8–23. Ahab ruled in. See AHAB ; JEZEBEL. Besieged by Shalmaneser, king of Assyria, three years ; taken ; the people carried away to Halah and Habor, cities of the Medes, 2 Kin. 17:5,6; 18: 9–11. Idolatry of, 1 Kin. 16:32; 2 Kin. 13:6. Temple of, destroyed, 2 Kin. 10:17–28; 23:19. Paul and Barnabas preach in, Acts 15:3. Visited by Philip, Peter, and John, Acts 8: 5–25.

2. Country of, Isa. 7:9. Foreign colonies distributed among the cities of, by the king of Assyria, 2 Kin. 17:24–41; Ezra 4:9,10. Roads through, from Judæa into Galilee, Luke 17:11; John 4:3–8. Jesus journeys through, John 4:1–42; heals lepers in, Luke 17:11–19. The good Samaritan from, Luke 10: 33–35. No dealings between the Jews and the inhabitants of, John 4:9. Expect the Messiah, John 4:25. Disciples made from the inhabitants of, John 4:39–42; Acts 8:5–8,14–17,25. Jesus forbids the apostles to preach in the cities of, Matt. 10:5.

SAMGAR-NEBO, a prince of Babylon. At the siege of Jerusalem, Jer. 39:3.

SAMLAH, one of the ancient kings of Edom, Gen. 36:36,37; 1 Chr. 1:47,48.

SAMOS, an island in the Ægean Sea. Touched at by Paul, Acts 20:15.

SAMOTHRACIA, an island in the Ægean Sea. Touched at by Paul, Acts 16:11.

SAMSON. A judge of Israel, Judg. 16: 31. A Danite, son of Manoah ; miraculous birth of ; a Nazarite from his mother's womb ; the mother forbidden to drink wine or strong drink, or to eat any unclean thing during gestation, Judg. 13:2–7,24,25. Desires a Philistine woman for his wife ; slays a lion, Judg. 14:1–7. His marriage feast and the riddle propounded, Judg. 14:8–19. Slays thirty Philistines, Judg. 14:19. Wife of, estranged, Judg. 14:20; 15:1,2. Is avenged for the estrangement of his wife, Judg. 15: 3–8. His great strength, Judg. 15:7–14; Heb. 11:32. Slays a thousand Philistines with the jawbone of an ass, Judg. 15:13–17; Miraculously supplied with water, Judg. 15:18,19.

Cohabits with Delilah, an harlot; her machinations with the Philistines to overcome him, Judg. 16:1–20. Is blinded by the Philistines and confined to hard labor in prison; pulls down the pillars of the temple, meets his death and slays a multitude of his enemies, Judg. 16:21–31; Heb. 11:32.

SAMUEL. Miraculous birth of, 1 Sam. 1:7–20. Consecrated to God before his birth, 1 Sam. 1:11,22,24–28. His mother's song of thanksgiving, 1 Sam. 2:1–10. Ministered in the house of God, 1 Sam. 2:11,18,19. Blessed of God, 1 Sam. 2:21; 3:19. His vision concerning the house of Eli, 1 Sam. 3:1–18. A prophet of the Israelites, 1 Sam. 3:20,21; 4:1. A judge of Israel, his judgment seat at Beth-el, Gilgal, Mizpeh, and Ramah, 1 Sam. 7:15–17. Organizes the tabernacle service, 1 Chr. 9:22; 26:28; 2 Chr. 35:18. Israelites repent under his reproofs and admonitions, 1 Sam. 7:4–6. The Philistines defeated through his intercession and sacrifices, 1 Sam. 7:7–14. Makes his corrupt sons judges in Israel, 1 Sam. 8:1–3. People desire a king; he protests, 1 Sam. 8:4–22. Anoints Saul king of Israel, 1 Sam. 9; 10. Renews the kingdom of Saul, 1 Sam. 11:12–15. Reproves Saul; foretells that his kingdom shall not be established, 1 Sam. 13:11–15; 15. Anoints David to be king, 1 Sam. 16. Shelters David when escaping from Saul, 1 Sam. 19:18. Death of; the lament for him, 1 Sam. 25:1. Called up by the witch of Endor, 1 Sam. 28:3–20. His integrity as judge and ruler, 1 Sam. 12:1–5; Psa. 99:6; Jer. 15:1; Heb. 11:32. Chronicles of, 1 Chr. 29:29. Sons of, 1 Chr. 6:28,33. Called SHEMUEL, 1 Chr. 6:33.

SANBALLAT, an enemy of the Jews in rebuilding Jerusalem after the captivity, Neh. 2:10,19; 4; 6; 13:28.

SANCTIFICATION. Firstborn of Israelites sanctified, Ex. 13:2. All Israel sanctified, Ex. 19:10,14. Material things sanctified by anointing, Ex. 40:9–11. The Lord the sanctifier, Ex. 31:13; Lev. 20:8; 21:8; 22: 9. The altar sanctifies the gift, Ex. 29:37; 30:29. Tabernacle sanctified by God's presence, Ex. 29:43; 40:34,35.

UNCLASSIFIED SCRIPTURES RELATING TO: Ex. 31:13. Verily my sabbaths ye shall keep: for it *is* a sign between me and you throughout your generations; that *ye* may know that I *am* the LORD that doth sanctify you.

Ex. 33:16. For wherein shall it be known here that I and thy people have found grace in thy sight? *is it* not in that thou goest with us? so shall we be separated, I and thy people, from all the people that *are* upon the face of the earth.

Lev. 21:1. And the LORD said unto Moses, Speak unto the priests the sons of Aaron, and say unto them, There shall none be defiled for the dead among his people: 2. But for his kin, that is near unto him, *that is,* for his mother, and for his father, and for his son, and for his daughter, and for his

brother, 3. And for his sister a virgin, that is nigh unto him, which hath had no husband; for her may he be defiled. 4. *But* he shall not defile himself, *being* a chief man among his people, to profane himself. 5. They shall not make baldness upon their head, neither shall they shave off the corner of their beard, nor make any cuttings in their flesh. 6. They shall be holy unto their God, and not profane the name of their God: for the offerings of the LORD made by fire, *and* the bread of their God, they do offer: therefore they shall be holy. 7. They shall not take a wife *that is* a whore, or profane; neither shall they take a woman put away from her husband: for he *is* holy unto his God. 8. Thou shalt sanctify him therefore; for he offereth the bread of thy God: he shall be holy unto thee: for I the LORD, which sanctify you, *am* holy. 9. And the daughter of any priest, if she profane herself by playing the whore, she profaneth her father: she shall be burnt with fire. 10. And *he that is* the high priest among his brethren, upon whose head the anointing oil was poured, and that is consecrated to put on the garments, shall not uncover his head, nor rend his clothes; 11. Neither shall he go in to any dead body, nor defile himself for his father, or for his mother; 12. Neither shall he go out of the sanctuary, nor profane the sanctuary of his God; for the crown of the anointing oil of his God *is* upon him: I *am* the LORD. 13. And he shall take a wife in her virginity. 14. A widow, or a divorced woman, or profane, *or* an harlot, these shall he not take: but he shall take a virgin of his own people to wife. 15. Neither shall he profane his seed among his people: for I the LORD do sanctify him. 16. And the LORD spake unto Moses, saying, 17. Speak unto Aaron, saying, Whosoever *he be* of thy seed in their generations that hath *any* blemish, let him not approach to offer the bread of his God. 18. For whatsoever man *he be* that hath a blemish, he shall not approach: a blind man, or a lame, or he that hath a flat nose, or any thing superfluous, 19. Or a man that is brokenfooted, or brokenhanded, 20. Or crookbackt, or a dwarf, or that hath a blemish in his eye, or be scurvy, or scabbed, or hath his stones broken; 21. No man that hath a blemish of the seed of Aaron the priest shall come nigh to offer the offerings of the LORD made by fire: he hath a blemish; he shall not come nigh to offer the bread of his God. 22. He shall eat the bread of his God, *both* of the most holy, and of the holy. 23. Only he shall not go in unto the vail, nor come nigh unto the altar, because he hath a blemish; that he profane not my sanctuaries: for I the LORD do sanctify them.

Jer. 1:5. Before I formed thee in the belly I knew thee; and before thou camest forth out of the womb I sanctified thee, *and* I ordained thee a prophet unto the nations.

Ezek. 37:28. And the heathen shall know

that I the LORD do sanctify Israel, when my sanctuary shall be in the midst of them for evermore.

John 17:17. Sanctify them through thy truth: thy word is truth. 19: And for their sakes I sanctify myself, that they also might be sanctified through the truth.

Acts 26:17. I send thee, 18. To open their eyes, *and* to turn *them* from darkness to light, and *from* the power of Satan unto God, that they may receive forgiveness of sins, and inheritance among them which are sanctified by faith that is in me.

Rom. 15:16. That I should be the minister of Jesus Christ to the Gentiles, ministering the gospel of God, that the offering up of the Gentiles might be acceptable, being sanctified by the Holy Ghost.

1 Cor. 1:2. Unto the church of God which is at Corinth, to them that are sanctified in Christ Jesus, called *to be* saints. 30. But of him are ye in Christ Jesus, who of God is made unto us wisdom, and righteousness, and sanctification, and redemption:

1 Cor. 6:11. And such were some of you: but ye are washed, but ye are sanctified, but ye are justified in the name of the Lord Jesus, and by the Spirit of our God.

1 Cor. 13:1. Though I speak with the tongues of men and of angels, and have not charity, I am become *as* sounding brass, or a tinkling cymbal. 2. And though I have *the gift of* prophecy, and understand all mysteries, and all knowledge; and though I have all faith, so that I could remove mountains, and have not charity, I am nothing. 3. And though I bestow all my goods to feed *the poor*, and though I give my body to be burned, and have not charity, it profiteth me nothing. 4. Charity suffereth long, *and* is kind; charity envieth not; charity vaunteth not itself, is not puffed up, 5. Doth not behave itself unseemly, seeketh not her own, is not easily provoked, thinketh no evil; 6. Rejoiceth not in iniquity, but rejoiceth in the truth; 7. Beareth all things, believeth all things, hopeth all things, endureth all things. 8. Charity never faileth: but whether *there be* prophecies, they shall fail; whether *there be* tongues, they shall cease; whether *there be* knowledge, it shall vanish away. 9. For we know in part, and we prophesy in part. 10. But when that which is perfect is come, then that which is in part shall be done away. 11. When I was a child, I spake as a child, I understood as a child, I thought as a child: but when I became a man, I put away childish things. 12. For now we see through a glass, darkly; but then face to face: now I know in part; but then shall I know even as also I am known. 13. And now abideth faith, hope, charity, these three; but the greatest of these *is* charity.

2 Cor. 1:21. Now he which stablisheth us with you in Christ, and hath anointed us, *is* God: 22. Who hath also sealed us, and given the earnest of the Spirit in our hearts.

Gal. 2:20. I am crucified with Christ: nevertheless I live; yet not I, but Christ liveth in me: and the life which I now live in the flesh I live by the faith of the Son of God, who loved me, and gave himself for me.

Gal. 6:14. But God forbid that I should glory, save in the cross of our Lord Jesus Christ, by whom the world is crucified unto me, and I unto the world.

Eph. 1:3. Blessed *be* the God and Father of our Lord Jesus Christ, who hath blessed us with all spiritual blessings in heavenly *places* in Christ: 4. According as he hath chosen us in him before the foundation of the world, that we should be holy and without blame before him in love:

Eph. 3:19. And to know the love of Christ, which passeth knowledge, that ye might be filled with all the fulness of God.

Eph. 4:7. Unto every one of us is given grace according to the measure of the gift of Christ. 12. For the perfecting of the saints, for the work of the ministry, for the edifying of the body of Christ: 13. Till we all come in the unity of the faith, and of the knowledge of the Son of God, unto a perfect man, unto the measure of the stature of the fulness of Christ: 15. Speaking the truth in love, may grow up into him in all things, which is the head, *even* Christ: 16. From whom the whole body fitly joined together and compacted by that which every joint supplieth, according to the effectual working in the measure of every part, maketh increase of the body unto the edifying of itself in love.

Eph. 5:25. Husbands, love your wives, even as Christ also loved the church, and gave himself for it; 26. That he might sanctify and cleanse it with the washing of water by the word, 27. That he might present it to himself a glorious church, not having spot, or wrinkle, or any such thing; but that it should be holy and without blemish.

Col. 2:11. In whom also ye are circumcised with the circumcision made without hands, in putting off the body of the sins of the flesh by the circumcision of Christ:

1 Thess. 4:3. For this is the will of God, *even* your sanctification, that ye should abstain from fornication: 4. That every one of you should know how to possess his vessel in sanctification and honour;

1 Thess. 5:23. And the very God of peace sanctify you wholly; and *I pray God* your whole spirit and soul and body be preserved blameless unto the coming of our Lord Jesus Christ.

2 Thess. 2:13. God hath from the beginning chosen you to salvation through sanctification of the Spirit and belief of the truth: 14. Whereunto he called you by our gospel, to the obtaining of the glory of our Lord Jesus Christ.

2 Tim. 2:11. *It is* a faithful saying: For if we be dead with *him*, we shall also live with *him:* 21. If a man therefore purge himself from these, he shall be a vessel unto

honour, sanctified, and meet for the master's use, *and* prepared unto every good work.

Heb. 2:11. For both he that sanctifieth and they who are sanctified *are* all of one: for which cause he is not ashamed to call them brethren,

Heb. 9:14. How much more shall the blood of Christ, who through the eternal Spirit offered himself without spot to God, purge your conscience from dead works to serve the living God?

Heb. 10:10. By the which will we are sanctified through the offering of the body of Jesus Christ once *for all.* 14. For by one offering he hath perfected for ever them that are sanctified.

Heb. 12:10. For they verily for a few days chastened *us* after their own pleasure; but he for *our* profit, that *we* might be partakers of his holiness.

Heb. 13:12. Wherefore Jesus also, that he might sanctify the people with his own blood, suffered without the gate. 21. Make you perfect in every good work to do his will, working in you that which is well-pleasing in his sight, through Jesus Christ;

1 Pet. 1:2. Elect according to the foreknowledge of God the Father, through sanctification of the Spirit, unto obedience and sprinkling of the blood of Jesus Christ: Grace unto you, and peace, be multiplied.

2 Pet. 1:2. Grace and peace be multiplied unto you through the knowledge of God, and of Jesus our Lord, 3. According as his divine power hath given unto us all things that *pertain* unto life and godliness, through the knowledge of him that hath called us to glory and virtue: 4. Whereby are given unto us exceeding great and precious promises: that by these ye might be partakers of the divine nature, having escaped the corruption that is in the world through lust.

1 John 1:9. If we confess our sins, he is faithful and just to forgive us *our* sins, and to cleanse us from all unrighteousness.

Jude 1. Jude, the servant of Jesus Christ, and brother of James, to them that are sanctified by God the Father, and preserved in Jesus Christ, *and* called: 24. Now unto him that is able to keep you from falling, and to present *you* faultless before the presence of his glory with exceeding joy,

Rev. 7:14. These are they which came out of great tribulation, and have washed their robes, and made them white in the blood of the Lamb.

See HOLINESS; REGENERATION; REDEMPTION; SALVATION; SIN, FORGIVENESS OF.

SANCTUARY, the holy of holies. In the tabernacle, Heb. 9:2. Divine dwelling place, Ex. 25:8. Reverence for, Lev. 19:30; 26:2. In charge of high priest, Ex. 27:21; Lev. 24:3; Num. 18:5. The holy place in the temple, Lam. 2:7,20; Ezek. 42:20.

FIGURATIVE: Ezek. 11:16. Symbolical, Heb. 8:2,5.

See TABERNACLE; TEMPLE.

SANDAL. See SHOE.

SANHEDRIN. See GOVERNMENT.

SANITATION. CARCASES: Lev. 5:2. Or if a soul touch any unclean thing, whether *it be* a carcase of an unclean beast, or a carcase of unclean cattle, or the carcase of unclean creeping things, and *if* it be hidden from him; he also shall be unclean, and guilty.

Lev. 10:4. And Moses called Mishael and Elzaphan, the sons of Uzziel the uncle of Aaron, and said unto them, Come near, carry your brethren from before the sanctuary out of the camp. 5. So they went near, and carried them in their coats out of the camp; as Moses had said.

Lev. 11:24. And for these ye shall be unclean: whosoever toucheth the carcase of them shall b unclean until the even. 25. And whosoever beareth *ought* of the carcase of them shall wash his clothes, and be unclean until the even. 26. *The carcases* of every beast which divideth the hoof, and *is* not clovenfooted, nor cheweth the cud, *are* unclean unto you: every one that toucheth them shall be unclean. 27. And whatsoever goeth upon his paws, among all manner of beasts that go on *all* four, those *are* unclean unto you: whoso toucheth their carcase shall be unclean until the even. 28. And he that beareth the carcase of them shall wash his clothes, and be unclean until the even: they *are* unclean unto you. 31. These *are* unclean to you among all that creep: whosoever doth touch them, when they be dead, shall be unclean until the even. 32. And upon whatsoever *any* of them, when they are dead, doth fall, it shall be unclean; whether *it be* any vessel of wood, or raiment, or skin, or sack, whatsoever vessel *it be*, wherein *any* work is done, it must be put into water, and it shall be unclean until the even; so it shall be cleansed. 33. And every earthen vessel, whereinto *any* of them falleth, whatsoever *is* in it shall be unclean; and ye shall break it. 34. Of all meat which may be eaten, *that* on which *such* water cometh shall be unclean: and all drink that may be drunk in every *such* vessel shall be unclean. 35. And every *thing* whereupon *any part* of their carcase falleth shall be unclean; *whether it be* oven, or ranges for pots, they shall be broken down: *for* they *are* unclean, and shall be unclean unto you. 36. Nevertheless a fountain or pit, *wherein there is* plenty of water, shall be clean: but that which toucheth their carcase shall be unclean. 37. And if *any part* of their carcase fall upon any sowing seed which is to be sown, it *shall be* clean. 38. But if *any* water be put upon the seed, and *any part* of their carcase fall thereon, it *shall be* unclean unto you. 39. And if any beast, of which ye may eat, die; he that toucheth the carcase thereof shall be unclean until the even. 40. And he that eateth of the carcase of it shall wash his clothes, and be unclean until the even: he also that beareth the carcase of it shall wash his clothes, and be unclean until the even.

Lev. 22:4. And whoso toucheth any thing *that is* unclean *by* the dead, . . . 6. The soul which hath touched any such shall be unclean until even, and shall not eat of the holy things, unless he wash his flesh with water.

Num. 9:6. And there were certain men, who were defiled by the dead body of a man, that they could not keep the passover on that day : 10. Speak unto the children of Israel, saying, If any man of you or of your posterity shall be unclean by reason of a dead body, or *be* in a journey afar off, yet he shall keep the passover unto the LORD.

Num. 19:11. He that toucheth the dead body of any man shall be unclean seven days. 12. He shall purify himself with it on the third day, and on the seventh day he shall be clean : but if he purify not himself the third day, then the seventh day he shall not be clean. 13. Whosoever toucheth the dead body of any man that is dead, and purifieth not himself, defileth the tabernacle of the LORD ; and that soul shall be cut off from Israel : 14. This *is* the law, when a man dieth in a tent : all that come into the tent, and all that *is* in the tent, shall be unclean seven days. 15. And every open vessel, which hath no covering bound upon it, *is* unclean. 16. And whosoever toucheth one that is slain with a sword in the open fields, or a dead body, or a bone of a man, or a grave, shall be unclean seven days.

Num. 31:19. And do ye abide without the camp seven days : whosoever hath killed any person, and whosoever hath touched any slain, purify *both* yourselves and your captives on the third day, and on the seventh day.

Deut. 21:22. And if a man have committed a sin worthy of death, and he be to be put to death, and thou hang him on a tree : 23. His body shall not remain all night upon the tree, but thou shalt in any wise bury him that day ; (for he that is hanged *is* accursed of God ;) that thy land be not defiled, which the LORD thy God giveth thee *for* an inheritance.

CHILDBIRTH : Lev. 12:3. And in the eighth day the flesh of his foreskin shall be circumcised.

Ezek. 16:4. And *as for* thy nativity, in the day thou wast born thy navel was not cut, neither wast thou washed in water to supple *thee ;* thou wast not salted at all, nor swaddled at all.

CIRCUMCISION : See CIRCUMCISION.

CONTAGION : Lev. 5:2. Or if a soul touch any unclean thing, whether *it be* a carcase of an unclean beast, or a carcase of unclean cattle, or the carcase of unclean creeping things, and *if* it be hidden from him; he also shall be unclean, and guilty. 3. Or if he touch the uncleanness of man, whatsoever uncleanness *it be* that a man shall be defiled withal, and it be hid from him ; when he knoweth *of it*, then he shall be guilty.

Lev. 7:19. And the flesh that toucheth any unclean *thing* shall not be eaten ; it shall be burnt with fire : 21. Moreover the soul that shall touch any unclean *thing, as* the uncleanness of man, or *any* unclean beast, or any abominable unclean *thing*, and eat of the flesh of the sacrifice of peace offerings, which *pertain* unto the LORD, even that soul shall be cut off from his people.

Lev. 11:24. And for these ye shall be unclean : whosoever toucheth the carcase of them shall be unclean until the even. 25. And whosoever beareth *ought* of the carcase of them shall wash his clothes, and be unclean until the even. 26. *The carcases* of every beast which divideth the hoof, and *is* not clovenfooted, nor cheweth the cud, *are* unclean unto you : every one that toucheth them shall be unclean. 27. And whatsoever goeth upon his paws, among all manner of beasts that go on *all* four, those *are* unclean unto you : whoso toucheth their carcase shall be unclean until the even. 28. And he that beareth the carcase of them shall wash his clothes, and be unclean until the even : they *are* unclean unto you. 31. These *are* unclean to you among all that creep : whosoever doth touch them, when they be dead, shall be unclean until the even. 32. And upon whatsoever *any* of them, when they are dead, doth fall, it shall be unclean; whether *it be* any vessel of wood, or raiment, or skin, or sack, whatsoever vessel *it be*, wherein *any* work is done, it must be put into water, and it shall be unclean until the even ; so it shall be cleansed. 33. And every earthen vessel, whereinto *any* of them falleth, whatsoever *is* in it shall be unclean ; and ye shall break it. 34. Of all meat which may be eaten, *that* on which *such* water cometh shall be unclean : and all drink that may be drunk in every *such* vessel shall be unclean. 35. And every *thing* whereupon *any part* of their carcase falleth shall be unclean; *whether it be* oven, or ranges for pots, they shall be broken down : *for* they *are* unclean, and shall be unclean unto you. 36. Nevertheless a fountain or pit, *wherein there is* plenty of water, shall be clean : but that which toucheth their carcase shall be unclean. 37. And if *any part* of their carcase fall upon any sowing seed which is to be sown, it *shall be* clean. 38. But if *any* water be put upon the seed, and *any part* of their carcase fall thereon, it *shall be* unclean unto you. 39. And if any beast, of which ye may eat, die ; he that toucheth the carcase thereof shall be unclean until the even. 40. And he that eateth of the carcase of it shall wash his clothes, and be unclean until the even : he also that beareth the carcase of it shall wash his clothes, and be unclean until the even.

Lev. 13:2. When a man shall have in the skin of his flesh a rising, a scab, or bright spot, and it be in the skin of his flesh *like* the plague of leprosy ; then he shall be brought unto Aaron the priest, or unto one of his sons the priests: 3. And the priest shall look on the plague in the skin of the flesh: and *when* the hair in the plague is turned white, and the plague in sight *be* deeper than the skin of his flesh, it *is* a plague of leprosy: and the priest shall look on him, and pronounce him unclean. 4. If the bright spot *be* white in the skin of his flesh, and in sight *be* not deeper than the skin, and the hair thereof be not turned white; then the priest shall shut up *him that hath* the plague seven days: 5. And the priest shall look on him the seventh day: and, behold, *if* the plague in his sight be at a stay, *and* the plague spread not in the skin; then the priest shall shut him up seven days more: 6. And the priest shall look on him again the seventh day: and, behold, *if* the plague *be* somewhat dark, *and* the plague spread not in the skin, the priest shall pronounce him clean: it *is but* a scab: and he shall wash his clothes, and be clean. 7. But if the scab spread much abroad in the skin, after that he hath been seen of the priest for his cleansing, he shall be seen of the priest again: 8. And *if* the priest see that, behold, the scab spreadeth in the skin, then the priest shall pronounce him unclean: it *is* a leprosy. 9. When the plague of leprosy is in a man, then he shall be brought unto the priest; 10. And the priest shall see *him:* and, behold, *if* the rising *be* white in the skin, and it have turned the hair white, and *there be* quick raw flesh in the rising; 11. It *is* an old leprosy in the skin of his flesh, and the priest shall pronounce him unclean, and shall not shut him up: for he *is* unclean. 12. And if a leprosy break out abroad in the skin, and the leprosy cover all the skin of *him that hath* the plague from his head even to his foot, wheresoever the priest looketh; 13. Then the priest shall consider: and, behold, *if* the leprosy have covered all his flesh, he shall pronounce *him* clean *that hath* the plague: it is all turned white: he *is* clean. 14. But when raw flesh appeareth in him, he shall be unclean. 15. And the priest shall see the raw flesh, and pronounce him to be unclean: *for* the raw flesh *is* unclean: it *is* a leprosy. 16. Or if the raw flesh turn again, and be changed unto white, he shall come unto the priest; 17. And the priest shall see him: and, behold, *if* the plague be turned into white; then the priest shall pronounce *him* clean *that hath* the plague: he *is* clean. 18. The flesh also, in which, *even* in the skin thereof, was a boil, and is healed, 19. And in the place of the boil there be a white rising, or a bright spot, white, and somewhat reddish, and it be shewed to the priest; 20. And if, when the priest seeth it, behold, it *be* in sight lower than the skin, and the hair thereof be turned white; the priest shall pronounce him unclean: it *is* a plague of leprosy broken out of the boil. 21. But if the priest look on it, and, behold, *there be* no

white hairs therein, and *if* it *be* not lower than the skin, but *be* somewhat dark; then the priest shall shut him up seven days: 22. And if it spread much abroad in the skin, then the priest shall pronounce him unclean: it *is* a plague. 23. But if the bright spot stay in his place, *and* spread not, it *is* a burning boil; and the priest shall pronounce him clean. 24. Or if there be *any* flesh, in the skin whereof *there is* a hot burning, and the quick *flesh* that burneth have a white bright spot, somewhat reddish, or white; 25. Then the priest shall look upon it: and, behold, *if* the hair in the bright spot be turned white, and it *be in* sight deeper than the skin; it *is* a leprosy broken out of the burning: wherefore the priest shall pronounce him unclean: it *is* the plague of leprosy. 26. But if the priest look on it, and, behold, *there be* no white hair in the bright spot, and it *be* no lower than the *other* skin, but *be* somewhat dark; then the priest shall shut him up seven days: 27. And the priest shall look upon him the seventh day; *and* if it be spread much abroad in the skin, then the priest shall pronounce him unclean: it *is* the plague of leprosy. 28. And if the bright spot stay in his place, *and* spread not in the skin, but it *be* somewhat dark; it *is* a rising of the burning, and the priest shall pronounce him clean: for it *is* an inflammation of the burning. 29. If a man or woman have a plague upon the head or the beard; 30. Then the priest shall see the plague: and, behold, if it *be* in sight deeper than the skin; *and there be* in it a yellow thin hair; then the priest shall pronounce him unclean: it *is* a dry scall, *even* a leprosy upon the head or beard. 31. And if the priest look on the plague of the scall, and, behold, it *be* not in sight deeper than the skin, and *that there is* no black hair in it; then the priest shall shut up *him that hath* the plague of the scall seven days: 32. And in the seventh day the priest shall look on the plague: and, behold, *if* the scall spread not, and there be in it no yellow hair, and the scall *be* not in sight deeper than the skin; 33. He shall be shaven, but the scall shall he not shave; and the priest shall shut up *him that hath* the scall seven days more: 34. And in the seventh day the priest shall look on the scall: and, behold, *if* the scall be not spread in the skin, nor *be* in sight deeper than the skin; then the priest shall pronounce him clean: and he shall wash his clothes, and be clean. 35. But if the scall spread much in the skin after his cleansing; 36. Then the priest shall look on him: and, behold, if the scall be spread in the skin, the priest shall not seek for yellow hair; he *is* unclean. 37. But if the scall be in his sight at a stay, and *that* there is black hair grown up therein; the scall is healed, he *is* clean: and the priest shall pronounce him clean. 38. If a man also or a woman have in the skin of their flesh bright spots, *even* white bright spots; 39. Then the priest shall look: and, behold, *if* the bright spots in the skin of their flesh *be* darkish white; it *is* a freckled spot *that* groweth in the skin; he *is* clean. 40. And the man whose hair is fallen off his head, he *is* bald; *yet is* he clean. 41. And he that hath his hair fallen off from the part of his head toward his face, he *is* forehead bald; *yet is* he clean. 42. And if there be in the bald head, or bald forehead, a white reddish sore; it *is* a leprosy sprung up in his bald head, or his bald forehead. 43. Then the priest shall look upon it: and, behold, *if* the rising of the sore *be* white reddish in his bald head, or in his bald forehead, as the leprosy appeareth in the skin of the flesh; 44. He is a leprous man, he *is* unclean: the priest shall pronounce him utterly unclean; his plague *is* in his head. 45. And the leper in whom the plague *is*, his clothes shall be rent, and his head bare, and he shall put a covering upon his upper lip, and shall cry, Unclean, unclean. 46. All the days wherein the plague *shall be* in him he shall be defiled; he *is* unclean: he shall dwell alone; without the camp *shall* his habitation *be*. 47. The garment also that the plague of leprosy is in, *whether it be* a woollen garment, or a linen garment; 48. Whether *it be* in the warp, or woof; of linen, or of woollen; whether in a skin, or in any thing made of skin; 49. And if the plague be greenish or reddish in the garment, or in the skin, either in the warp, or in the woof, or in any thing of skin; it *is* a plague of leprosy, and shall be shewed unto the priest: 50. And the priest shall look upon the plague, and shut up *it that hath* the plague seven days: 51. And he shall look on the plague on the seventh day: if the plague be spread in the garment, either in the warp, or in the woof, or in a skin, *or* in any work that is made of skin; the plague *is* a fretting leprosy; it *is* unclean. 52. He shall therefore burn that garment, whether warp or woof, in woollen or in linen, or any thing of skin, wherein the plague is: for it *is* a fretting leprosy; it shall be burnt in the fire. 53. And if the priest shall look, and, behold, the plague be not spread in the garment, either in the warp, or in the woof, or in any thing of skin; 54. Then the priest shall command that they wash *the thing* wherein the plague *is*, and he shall shut it up seven days more: 55. And the priest shall look on the plague, after that it is washed: and, behold, *if* the plague have not changed his colour, and the plague be not spread; it *is* unclean; thou shalt burn it in the fire; it *is* fret inward, *whether* it *be* bare within or without. 56. And if the priest look, and, behold, the plague *be* somewhat dark after the washing of it; then he shall rend it out of the garment, or out of the skin, or out of the warp, or out of the woof: 57. And if it appear still in the garment, either in the warp, or in the woof, or in any thing of skin; it *is*

a spreading *plague:* thou shalt burn that wherein the plague *is* with fire. 58. And the garment, either warp, or woof, or whatsoever thing of skin *it be*, which thou shalt wash, if the plague be departed from them, then it shall be washed the second time, and shall be clean. 59. This *is* the law of the plague of leprosy in the garment of woollen or linen, either in the warp, or woof, or any thing of skins, to pronounce it clean, or to pronounce it unclean.

Lev. 14:2. This shall be the law of the leper in the day of his cleansing: He shall be brought unto the priest: 3. And the priest shall go forth out of the camp; and the priest shall look, and, behold, *if* the plague of leprosy be healed in the leper; 8. And he that is to be cleansed shall wash his clothes, and shave off all his hair, and wash himself in water, that he may be clean: and after that he shall come into the camp, and shall tarry abroad out of his tent seven days. 9. But it shall be on the seventh day, that he shall shave all his hair off his head and his beard and his eyebrows, even all his hair he shall shave off: and he shall wash his clothes, also he shall wash his flesh in water, and he shall be clean. 34. When ye be come into the land of Canaan, which I give to you for a possession, and I put the plague of leprosy in a house of the land of your possession; 35. And he that owneth the house shall come and tell the priest, saying, It seemeth to me *there is* as it were a plague in the house: 36. Then the priest shall command that they empty the house, before the priest go *into it* to see the plague, that all that *is* in the house be not made unclean: and afterward the priest shall go in to see the house: 37. And he shall look on the plague, and, behold, *if* the plague *be* in the walls of the house with hollow strakes, greenish or reddish, which in sight *are* lower than the wall; 38. Then the priest shall go out of the house to the door of the house, and shut up the house seven days: 39. And the priest shall come again the seventh day, and shall look: and, behold, *if* the plague be spread in the walls of the house; 40. Then the priest shall command that they take away the stones in which the plague *is*, and they shall cast them into an unclean place without the city: 41. And he shall cause the house to be scraped within round about, and they shall pour out the dust that they scrape off without the city into an unclean place: 42. And they shall take other stones, and put *them* in the place of those stones; and he shall take other mortar, and shall plaister the house. 43. And if the plague come again, and break out in the house, after that he hath taken away the stones, and after he hath scraped the house, and after it is plaistered; 44. Then the priest shall come and look, and, behold, *if* the plague be spread in the house, it *is* a fretting leprosy in the house: it *is* unclean. 45. And he shall break down the house, the stones of it, and the timber thereof, and all the morter of the house ; and he shall carry *them* forth out of the city into an unclean place. 46. Moreover he that goeth into the house all the while that it is shut up shall be unclean until the even. 47. And he that lieth in the house shall wash his clothes ; and he that eateth in the house shall wash his clothes. 48. And if the priest shall come in, and look *upon it,* and, behold, the plague hath not spread in the house, after the house was plaistered : then the priest shall pronounce the house clean, because the plague is healed. 54. This *is* the law for all manner of plague of leprosy, and scall, 55. And for the leprosy of a garment, and of a house, 56. And for a rising, and for a scab, and for a bright spot : 57. To teach when *it is* unclean, and when *it is* clean : this *is* the law of leprosy.

Lev. 15:2. When any man hath a running issue out of his flesh, *because of* his issue he *is* unclean. 3. And this shall be his uncleanness in his issue : whether his flesh run with his issue, or his flesh be stopped from his issue, it *is* his uncleanness. 4. Every bed, whereon he lieth that hath the issue, is unclean : and every thing, whereon he sitteth, shall be unclean. 5. And whosoever toucheth his bed shall wash his clothes, and bathe *himself* in water, and be unclean until the even. 6. And he that sitteth on *any* thing whereon he sat that hath the issue shall wash his clothes, and bathe *himself* in water, and be unclean until the even. 7. And he that toucheth the flesh of him that hath the issue shall wash his clothes, and bathe *himself* in water, and be unclean until the even. 8. And if he that hath the issue spit upon him that is clean ; then he shall wash his clothes, and bathe *himself* in water, and be unclean until the even. 9. And what saddle soever he rideth upon that hath the issue shall be unclean. 10. And whosoever toucheth any thing that was under him shall be unclean until the even : and he that beareth *any of* those things shall wash his clothes, and bathe *himself* in water, and be unclean until the even. 11. And whomsoever he toucheth that hath the issue, and hath not rinsed his hands in water, he shall wash his clothes, and bathe *himself* in water, and be unclean until the even. 12. And the vessel of earth, that he toucheth which hath the issue, shall be broken : and every vessel of wood shall be rinsed in water. 13. And when he that hath an issue is cleansed of his issue ; then he shall number to himself seven days for his cleansing, and wash his clothes, and bathe his flesh in running water, and shall be clean. 16. And if any man's seed of copulation go out from him, then he shall wash all his flesh in water, and be unclean until the even. 17. And every garment, and every skin, whereon is the seed of copulation, shall be washed with water, and be unclean until the even. 18. The woman also with whom man shall lie *with* seed of copulation, they shall *both* bathe

themselves in water, and be unclean until the even. 19. And if a woman have an issue, *and* her issue in her flesh be blood, she shall be put apart seven days : and whosoever toucheth her shall be unclean until the even. 20. And every thing that she lieth upon in her separation shall be unclean : every thing also that she sitteth upon shall be unclean. 21. And whosoever toucheth her bed shall wash his clothes, and bathe *himself* in water, and be unclean until the even. 22. And whosoever toucheth any thing that she sat upon shall wash his clothes, and bathe *himself* in water, and be unclean until the even. 23. And if it *be* on *her* bed, or on any thing whereon she sitteth, when he toucheth it, he shall be unclean until the even. 24. And if any man lie with her at all, and her flowers be upon him, he shall be unclean seven days ; and all the bed whereon he lieth shall be unclean. 25. And if a woman have an issue of her blood many days out of the time of her separation, or if it run beyond the time of her separation ; all the days of the issue of her uncleanness shall be as the days of her separation : she *shall be* unclean. 26. Every bed whereon she lieth all the days of her issue shall be unto her as the bed of her separation : and whatsoever she sitteth upon shall be unclean, as the uncleanness of her separation. 27. And whosoever toucheth those things shall be unclean, and shall wash his clothes, and bathe *himself* in water, and be unclean until the even. 28. But if she be cleansed of her issue, then she shall number to herself seven days, and after that she shall be clean. 31. Thus shall ye separate the children of Israel from their uncleanness ; that they die not in their uncleanness, when they defile my tabernacle that *is* among them. 32. This *is* the law of him that hath an issue, and *of him* whose seed goeth from him, and is defiled therewith ; 33. And of her that is sick of her flowers, and of him that hath an issue, of the man, and of the woman, and of him that lieth with her that is unclean.

Lev. 22:4. What man soever of the seed of Aaron *is* a leper, or hath a running issue ; he shall not eat of the holy things, until he be clean. And whoso toucheth any thing *that is* unclean *by* the dead, or a man whose seed goeth from him ; 5. Or whosoever toucheth any creeping thing, whereby he may be made unclean, or a man of whom he may take uncleanness, whatsoever uncleanness he hath ; 6. The soul which hath touched any such shall be unclean until even, and shall not eat of the holy things, unless he wash his flesh with water. 7. And when the sun is down, he shall be clean, and shall afterward eat of the holy things ; because it *is* his food. 8. That which dieth of itself, or is torn *with beasts,* he shall not eat to defile himself therewith :

Num. 5:2. Command the children of Israel, that they put out of the camp every leper, and every one that hath an issue, and whosoever is defiled by the dead : 3. Both male and female shall ye put out, without the camp shall ye put them ; that they defile not their camps, in the midst whereof I dwell. 4. And the children of Israel did so, and put them out without the camp :

Num. 9:6. And there were certain men, who were defiled by the dead body of a man, that they could not keep the passover on that day : 10. If any man of you or of your posterity shall be unclean by reason of a dead body, or *be* in a journey afar off, yet he shall keep the passover unto the LORD.

Num. 19:11. He that toucheth the dead body of any man shall be unclean seven days. 12. He shall purify himself with it on the third day, and on the seventh day he shall be clean : but if he purify not himself the third day, then the seventh day he shall not be clean. 13. Whosoever toucheth the dead body of any man that is dead, and purifieth not himself, defileth the tabernacle of the LORD ; and that soul shall be cut off from Israel : because the water of separation was not sprinkled upon him, he shall be unclean ; his uncleanness *is* yet upon him. 14. This *is* the law, when a man dieth in a tent : all that come into the tent, and all that *is* in the tent, shall be unclean seven days. 15. And every open vessel, which hath no covering bound upon it, *is* unclean. 16. And whosoever toucheth one that is slain with a sword in the open fields, or a dead body, or a bone of a man, or a grave, shall be unclean seven days. 22. And whatsoever the unclean *person* toucheth shall be unclean ; and the soul that toucheth *it* shall be unclean until even.

Num. 31:19. And do ye abide without the camp seven days: whosoever hath killed any person, and whosoever hath touched any slain, purify *both* yourselves and your captives on the third day, and on the seventh day. 20. And purify all *your* raiment, and all that is made of skins, and all work of goats' *hair*, and all things made of wood.

Deut. 23:10. If there be among you any man, that is not clean by reason of uncleanness that chanceth him by night, then shall he go abroad out of the camp, he shall not come within the camp : 11. But it shall be, when evening cometh on, he shall wash *himself* with water : and when the sun is down, he shall come into the camp *again*.

Deut. 24:8. Take heed in the plague of leprosy, that thou observe diligently, and do according to all that the priests the Levites shall teach you : as I commanded them, *so* ye shall observe to do.

DISINFECTION: Lev. 2:13. And every oblation of thy meat offering shalt thou season with salt ; neither shalt thou suffer the salt of the covenant of thy God to be lacking from thy meat offering : with all thine offerings thou shalt offer salt.

Lev. 7:19. And the flesh that toucheth any unclean *thing* shall not be eaten ; it shall be burnt with fire :

Lev. 11:24. And for these ye shall be unclean : whosoever toucheth the carcase of them shall be unclean until the even. 25. And whosoever beareth *ought* of the carcase of them shall wash his clothes, and be unclean until the even. 26. *The carcases* of every beast which divideth the hoof, and *is* not clovenfooted, nor cheweth the cud, *are* unclean unto you : every one that toucheth them shall be unclean. 27. And whatsoever goeth upon his paws, among all manner of beasts that go on *all* four, those *are* unclean unto you : whoso toucheth their carcase shall be unclean until the even. 28. And he that beareth the carcase of them shall wash his clothes, and be unclean until the even : they *are* unclean unto you. 29. These also *shall be* unclean unto you among the creeping things that creep upon the earth ; the weasel, and the mouse, and the tortoise after his kind, 30. And the ferret, and the chameleon, and the lizard, and the snail, and the mole. 31. These *are* unclean to you among all that creep : whosoever doth touch them, when they be dead, shall be unclean until the even. 32. And upon whatsoever *any* of them, when they are dead, doth fall, it shall be unclean ; whether *it be* any vessel of wood, or raiment, or skin, or sack, whatsoever vessel *it be*, wherein *any* work is done, it must be put into water, and it shall be unclean until the even ; so it shall be cleansed. 33. And every earthen vessel, whereinto *any* of them falleth, whatsoever *is* in it shall be unclean ; and ye shall break it. 34. Of all meat which may be eaten, *that* on which *such* water cometh shall be unclean : and all drink that may be drunk in every *such* vessel shall be unclean. 35. And every *thing* whereupon *any part* of their carcase falleth shall be unclean ; *whether it be* oven, or ranges for pots, they shall be broken down : *for* they *are* unclean, and shall be unclean unto you. 36. Nevertheless a fountain or pit, *wherein there is* plenty of water, shall be clean : but that which toucheth their carcase shall be unclean. 37. And if *any part* of their carcase fall upon any sowing seed which is to be sown, it *shall be* clean. 38. But if *any* water be put upon the seed, and *any part* of their carcase fall thereon, it *shall be* unclean unto you. 39. And if any beast, of which ye may eat, die ; he that toucheth the carcase thereof shall be unclean until the even. 40. And he that eateth of the carcase of it shall wash his clothes, and be unclean until the even : he also that beareth the carcase of it shall wash his clothes, and be unclean until the even.

Lev. 13:6. And the priest shall look on him again the seventh day : and, behold, *if* the plague *be* somewhat dark, *and* the plague spread not in the skin, the priest shall pronounce him clean : it *is but* a scab : and he shall wash his clothes, and be clean. 34. And in the seventh day the priest shall look on the scall : and, behold, *if* the scall be not spread in the skin, nor *be* in sight deeper than the skin; then the priest shall pronounce him clean: and he shall wash his clothes, and be clean. 47. The garment also that the plague of leprosy is in, *whether it be* a woollen garment, or a linen garment; 48. Whether *it be* in the warp, or woof; of linen, or of woollen; whether in a skin, or in any thing made of skin; 49. And if the plague be greenish or reddish in the garment, or in the skin, either in the warp, or in the woof, or in any thing of skin; it *is* a plague of leprosy, and shall be shewed unto the priest: 50. And the priest shall look upon the plague, and shut up *it that hath* the plague seven days; 51. And he shall look on the plague on the seventh day: if the plague be spread in the garment, either in the warp, or in the woof, or in a skin, *or* in any work that is made of skin; the plague *is* a fretting leprosy; it *is* unclean. 52. He shall therefore burn that garment, whether warp or woof, in woollen or in linen, or any thing of skin, wherein the plague is: for it *is* a fretting leprosy; it shall be burnt in the fire. 53. And if the priest shall look, and, behold, the plague be not spread in the garment, either in the warp, or in the woof, or in any thing of skin; 54. Then the priest shall command that they wash *the thing* wherein the plague *is*, and he shall shut it up seven days more: 55. And the priest shall look on the plague, after that it is washed: and, behold, *if* the plague have not changed his colour, and the plague be not spread; it *is* unclean; thou shalt burn it in the fire; it *is* fret inward, *whether* it *be* bare within or without. 56. And if the priest look, and, behold, the plague *be* somewhat dark after the washing of it; then he shall rend it out of the garment, or out of the skin, or out of the warp, or out of the woof: 57. And if it appear still in the garment, either in the warp, or in the woof, or in any thing of skin; it *is* a spreading *plague:* thou shalt burn that wherein the plague *is* with fire. 58. And the garment, either warp, or woof, or whatsoever thing of skin *it be*, which thou shalt wash, if the plague be departed from them, then it shall be washed the second time, and shall be clean. 59. This *is* the law of the plague of leprosy in a garment of woollen or linen, either in the warp, or woof, or any thing of skins, to pronounce it clean, or to pronounce it unclean.

Lev. 14:8. And he that is to be cleansed shall wash his clothes, and shave off all his hair, and wash himself in water, that he may be clean: and after that he shall come into the camp, and shall tarry abroad out of his tent seven days. 9. But it shall be on the seventh day, that he shall shave all his hair off his head and his beard and his eyebrows, even all his hair he shall shave off: and he shall wash his clothes, also he shall wash his flesh in water, and he shall be clean. 34. When ye be come into the land of Canaan, which I give to you for a possession, and I put the plague of leprosy in a house of the land of your possession ; 35. And he that owneth the house shall come and tell the priest, saying, It seemeth to me *there is* as it were a plague in the house: 36. Then the priest shall command that they empty the house, before the priest go *into it* to see the plague, that all that *is* in the house be not made unclean: and afterward the priest shall go in to see the house: 37. And he shall look on the plague, and, behold, *if* the plague *be* in the walls of the house with hollow strakes, greenish or reddish, which in sight *are* lower than the wall; 38. Then the priest shall go out of the house to the door of the house, and shut up the house seven days: 39. And the priest shall come again the seventh day, and shall look: and, behold, *if* the plague be spread in the walls of the house; 40. Then the priest shall command that they take away the stones in which the plague *is*, and they shall cast them into an unclean place without the city: 41. And he shall cause the house to be scraped within round about, and they shall pour out the dust that they scrape off without the city into an unclean place: 42. And they shall take other stones, and put *them* in the place of those stones; and he shall take other morter, and shall plaister the house. 43. And if the plague come again, and break out in the house, after that he hath taken away the stones, and after he hath scraped the house, and after it is plaistered; 44. Then the priest shall come and look, and, behold, *if* the plague be spread in the house, it *is* a fretting leprosy in the house: it *is* unclean. 45. And he shall break down the house, the stones of it, and the timber thereof, and all the morter of the house; and he shall carry *them* forth out of the city into an unclean place. 46. Moreover he that goeth into the house all the while that it is shut up shall be unclean until the even. 47. And he that lieth in the house shall wash his clothes; and he that eateth in the house shall wash his clothes. 48. And if the priest shall come in, and look *upon it*, and, behold, the plague hath not spread in the house, after the house was plaistered: then the priest shall pronounce the house clean, because the plague is healed. 54. This *is* the law for all manner of plague of leprosy, and scall, 55. And for the leprosy of a garment, and of a house, 56. And for a rising, and for a scab, and for a bright spot: 57. To teach when *it is* unclean, and when *it is* clean: this *is* the law of leprosy.

Lev. 15:2. When any man hath a running issue out of his flesh, *because of* his issue he *is* unclean. 3. And this shall be his uncleanness in his issue: whether his flesh run with his issue, or his flesh be stopped from his issue, it *is* his uncleanness. 4. Every bed, whereon he lieth that hath the issue, is unclean: and every thing, whereon he sitteth, shall be unclean. 5. And whosoever toucheth his bed shall wash his clothes, and bathe *himself* in water, and be unclean until the even. 6. And he that sitteth on *any* thing whereon he sat that hath the issue shall wash his clothes, and bathe *himself* in water, and be unclean until the even. 7. And he that toucheth the flesh of him that hath the issue shall wash his clothes, and bathe *himself* in water, and be unclean until the even. 8. And if he that hath the issue spit upon him that is clean; then he shall wash his clothes, and bathe *himself* in water, and be unclean until the even. 9. And what saddle soever he rideth upon that hath the issue shall be unclean. 10. And whosoever toucheth any thing that was under him shall be unclean until the even: and he that beareth *any of* those things shall wash his clothes, and bathe *himself* in water, and be unclean until the even. 11. And whomsoever he toucheth that hath the issue, and hath not rinsed his hands in water, he shall wash his clothes, and bathe *himself* in water, and be unclean until the even. 12. And the vessel of earth, that he toucheth which hath the issue, shall be broken: and every vessel of wood shall be rinsed in water. 13. And when he that hath an issue is cleansed of his issue; then he shall number to himself seven days for his cleansing, and wash his clothes, and bathe his flesh in running water, and shall be clean. 16. And if any man's seed of copulation go out from him, then he shall wash all his flesh in water, and be unclean until the even. 17. And every garment, and every skin, whereon is the seed of copulation, shall be washed with water, and be unclean until the even. 18. The woman also with whom man shall lie *with* seed of copulation, they shall *both* bathe *themselves* in water, and be unclean until the even. 19. And if a woman have an issue, *and* her issue in her flesh be blood, she shall be put apart seven days: and whosoever toucheth her shall be unclean until the even. 20. And every thing that she lieth upon in her separation shall be unclean: every thing also that she sitteth upon shall be unclean. 21. And whosoever toucheth her bed shall wash his clothes, and bathe *himself* in water, and be unclean until the even. 22. And whosoever toucheth any thing that she sat upon shall wash his clothes, and bathe *himself* in water, and be unclean until the even. 23. And if it *be* on *her* bed, or on any thing whereon she sitteth, when he toucheth it, he shall be unclean until the even. 24. And if any man lie with her at all, and her flowers be upon him, he shall be unclean seven days; and all the bed whereon he lieth shall be unclean. 25. And if a woman have an issue of her blood many days out of the time of her separation, or if it run beyond the time of her separation; all the days of the issue of her uncleanness shall be as the days of her separation: she *shall be* unclean. 26.

Every bed whereon she lieth all the days of her issue shall be unto her as the bed of her separation: and whatsoever she sitteth upon shall be unclean, as the uncleanness of her separation. 27. And whosoever toucheth those things shall be unclean, and shall wash his clothes, and bathe *himself* in water, and be unclean until the even. 28. But if she be cleansed of her issue, then she shall number to herself seven days, and after that she shall be clean.

Num. 31:19. And do ye abide without the camp seven days: whosoever hath killed any person, and whosoever hath touched any slain, purify *both* yourselves and your captives on the third day, and on the seventh day. 20. And purify all *your* raiment, and all that is made of skins, and all work of goats' *hair*, and all things made of wood. 22. Only the gold, and the silver, the brass, the iron, the tin, and the lead, 23. Every thing that may abide the fire, ye shall make *it* go through the fire, and it shall be clean: nevertheless it shall be purified with the water of separation: and all that abideth not the fire ye shall make go through the water. 24. And ye shall wash your clothes on the seventh day, and ye shall be clean, and afterward ye shall come into the camp.

See PURIFICATION.

FILTH, DISPOSITION OF: Ex. 29:14. But the flesh of the bullock, and his skin, and his dung, shalt thou burn with fire without the camp: it *is* a sin offering. 34. And if ought of the flesh of the consecrations, or of the bread, remain unto the morning, then thou shalt burn the remainder with fire: it shall not be eaten, because it *is* holy. Lev. 7:17; 19:6.

Lev. 4:11. And the skin of the bullock, and all his flesh, with his head, and with his legs, and his inwards, and his dung, 12. Even the whole bullock shall he carry forth without the camp unto a clean place, where the ashes are poured out, and burn him on the wood with fire: where the ashes are poured out shall he be burnt. *v.* 21.

Lev. 7:19. And the flesh that toucheth any unclean *thing* shall not be eaten; it shall be burnt with fire:

Lev. 8:17. But the bullock, and his hide, his flesh, and his dung, he burnt with fire without the camp; as the LORD commanded Moses. 32. And that which remaineth of the flesh and of the bread shall ye burn with fire.

Lev. 9:11. And the flesh and the hide he burnt with fire without the camp.

Lev. 16:27. And the bullock *for* the sin offering, and the goat *for* the sin offering, whose blood was brought in to make atonement in the holy *place*, shall *one* carry forth without the camp; and they shall burn in the fire their skins, and their flesh, and their dung. 28. And he that burneth them shall wash his clothes, and bathe his flesh in water, and afterward he shall come into the camp.

Deut. 23:12. Thou shalt have a place also without the camp, whither thou shalt go forth abroad: 13. And thou shalt have a paddle upon thy weapon; and it shall be, when thou wilt ease thyself abroad, thou shalt dig therewith, and shalt turn back and cover that which cometh from thee:

Heb. 13:11. For the bodies of those beasts, whose blood is brought into the sanctuary by the high priest for sin, are burned without the camp. Lev. 6:30.

FOOD: Lev. 3:17. *It shall be* a perpetual statute for your generations throughout all your dwellings, that ye eat neither fat nor blood.

Lev. 7:15. And the flesh of the sacrifice of his peace offerings for thanksgiving shall be eaten the same day that it is offered; he shall not leave any of it until the morning. 16. But if the sacrifice of his offering *be* a vow, or a voluntary offering, it shall be eaten the same day that he offereth his sacrifice: and on the morrow also the remainder of it shall be eaten: 17. But the remainder of the flesh of the sacrifice on the third day shall be burnt with fire. 18. And if *any* of the flesh of the sacrifice of his peace offerings be eaten at all on the third day, it shall not be accepted, neither shall it be imputed unto him that offereth it: it shall be an abomination, and the soul that eateth of it shall bear his iniquity. 19. And the flesh that toucheth any unclean *thing* shall not be eaten; it shall be burnt with fire: and as for the flesh, all that be clean shall eat thereof. 23. Ye shall eat no manner of fat, of ox, or of sheep, or of goat. 24. And the fat of the beast that dieth of itself, and the fat of that which is torn with beasts, may be used in any other use: but ye shall in no wise eat of it. 25. For whosoever eateth the fat of the beast, of which men offer an offering made by fire unto the LORD, even the soul that eateth *it* shall be cut off from his people. 26. Moreover ye shall eat no manner of blood, *whether it be* of fowl or of beast, in any of your dwellings. 27. Whatsoever soul *it be* that eateth any manner of blood, even that soul shall be cut off from his people.

Lev. 11:2. These *are* the beasts which ye shall eat among all the beasts that *are* on the earth. 3. Whatsoever parteth the hoof, and is clovenfooted, *and* cheweth the cud, among the beasts, that shall ye eat. 4. Nevertheless these shall ye not eat of them that chew the cud, or of them that divide the hoof: *as* the camel, because he cheweth the cud, but divideth not the hoof; he *is* unclean unto you. 5. And the coney, because he cheweth the cud, but divideth not the hoof; he *is* unclean unto you. 6. And the hare, because he cheweth the cud, but divideth not the hoof; he *is* unclean unto you. 7. And the swine, though he divide the hoof, and be clovenfooted, yet he cheweth not the cud; he *is* unclean to you. 8. Of their flesh shall ye not eat, and their car-

case shall ye not touch; they *are* unclean to you. 9. These shall ye eat of all that *are* in the waters: whatsoever hath fins and scales in the waters, in the seas, and in the rivers, them shall ye eat. 10. And all that have not fins and scales in the seas, and in the rivers, of all that move in the waters, and of any living thing which *is* in the waters, they *shall be* an abomination unto you: 11. They shall be even an abomination unto you; ye shall not eat of their flesh, but ye shall have their carcases in abomination. 12. Whatsoever hath no fins nor scales in the waters, that *shall be* an abomination unto you. 13. And these *are they which* ye shall have in abomination among the fowls: they shall not be eaten, they *are* an abomination: the eagle, and the ossifrage, and the ospray, 14. And the vulture, and the kite after his kind; 15. Every raven after his kind; 16. And the owl, and the night hawk, and the cuckow, and the hawk after his kind, 17. And the little owl, and the cormorant, and the great owl, 18. And the swan, and the pelican, and the gier eagle, 19. And the stork, the heron after her kind, and the lapwing, and the bat. 20. All fowls that creep, going upon *all* four, *shall be* an abomination unto you. 21. Yet these may ye eat of every flying creeping thing that goeth upon *all* four, which have legs above their feet, to leap withal upon the earth; 22. *Even* these of them ye may eat; the locust after his kind, and the bald locust after his kind, and the beetle after his kind, and the grasshopper after his kind. 23. But all *other* flying creeping things, which have four feet, *shall be* an abomination unto you. 26. *The carcases* of every beast which divideth the hoof, and *is* not clovenfooted, nor cheweth the cud, *are* unclean unto you: every one that toucheth them shall be unclean. 27. And whatsoever goeth upon his paws, among all manner of beasts that go on *all* four, those *are* unclean unto you: whoso toucheth their carcase shall be unclean until the even. 29. These also *shall be* unclean unto you among the creeping things that creep upon the earth; the weasel, and the mouse, and the tortoise after his kind, 30. And the ferret, and the chameleon, and the lizard, and the snail, and the mole. 31. These *are* unclean to you among all that creep: whosoever doth touch them, when they be dead, shall be unclean until the even. 32. And upon whatsoever *any* of them, when they are dead, doth fall, it shall be unclean; whether *it be* any vessel of wood, or raiment, or skin, or sack, whatsoever vessel *it be*, wherein *any* work is done, it must be put into water, and it shall be unclean until the even; so it shall be cleansed. 33. And every earthen vessel, whereunto *any* of them falleth, whatsoever *is* in it shall be unclean; and ye shall break it. 34. Of all meat which may be eaten, *that* on which such water cometh shall be unclean: and all drink that may be drunk in every *such* vessel shall be unclean. 35. And every *thing* whereupon *any part* of their carcase falleth shall be unclean; *whether it be* oven, or ranges for pots, they shall be broken down: *for* they *are* unclean, and shall be unclean unto you. 36. Nevertheless a fountain or pit, *wherein there is* plenty of water, shall be clean: but that which toucheth their carcase shall be unclean. 37. And if *any part* of their carcase fall upon any sowing seed which is to be sown, it *shall be* clean. 38. But if *any* water be put upon the seed, and *any part* of their carcase fall thereon, it *shall be* unclean unto you. 39. And if any beast, of which ye may eat, die; he that toucheth the carcase thereof shall be unclean until the even. 40. And he that eateth of the carcase of it shall wash his clothes, and be unclean until the even: he also that beareth the carcase of it shall wash his clothes, and be unclean until the even. 41. And every creeping thing that creepeth upon the earth *shall be* an abomination; it shall not be eaten. 42. Whatsoever goeth upon the belly, and whatsoever goeth upon *all* four, or whatsoever hath more feet among all creeping things that creep upon the earth, them ye shall not eat: for they *are* an abomination. 43. Ye shall not make yourselves abominable with any creeping thing that creepeth, neither shall ye make yourselves unclean with them, that ye should be defiled thereby. 46. This *is* the law of the beasts, and of the fowl, and of every living creature that moveth in the waters, and of every creature that creepeth upon the earth: 47. To make a difference between the unclean and the clean, and between the beast that may be eaten and the beast that may not be eaten.

Lev. 17:10. And whatsoever man *there be* of the house of Israel, or of the strangers that sojourn among you, that eateth any manner of blood; I will even set my face against that soul that eateth blood, and will cut him off from among his people. 11. For the life of the flesh *is* in the blood: and I have given it to you upon the altar to make an atonement for your souls: for it *is* the blood *that* maketh an atonement for the soul. 12. Therefore I said unto the children of Israel, No soul of you shall eat blood, neither shall any stranger that sojourneth among you eat blood. 13. And whatsoever man *there be* of the children of Israel, or of the strangers that sojourn among you, which hunteth and catcheth any beast or fowl that may be eaten; he shall even pour out the blood thereof, and cover it with dust. 14. For *it is* the life of all flesh; the blood of it *is* for the life thereof: therefore I said unto the children of Israel, Ye shall eat the blood of no manner of flesh: for the life of all flesh *is* the blood thereof: whosoever eateth it shall be cut off. 15. And every soul that eateth that which died *of itself*, or that which was torn *with beasts*, *whether it be* one of your own country, or

a stranger, he shall both wash his clothes, and bathe *himself* in water, and be unclean until the even: then shall he be clean.

Lev. 19:5. And if ye offer a sacrifice of peace offerings unto the LORD, ye shall offer it at your own will. 6. It shall be eaten the same day ye offer it, and on the morrow: and if ought remain until the third day, it shall be burnt in the fire. 7. And if it be eaten at all on the third day, it *is* abominable; it shall not be accepted. 8. Therefore *every one* that eateth it shall bear his iniquity, because he hath profaned the hallowed thing of the LORD: and that soul shall be cut off from among his people. 26. Ye shall not eat *any thing* with the blood:

Lev. 22:8. That which dieth of itself, or is torn *with beasts*, he shall not eat to defile himself therewith:

Deut. 12:16. Only ye shall not eat the blood; ye shall pour it upon the earth as water. 20. When the LORD thy God shall enlarge thy border, as he hath promised thee, and thou shalt say, I will eat flesh, because thy soul longeth to eat flesh; thou mayest eat flesh, whatsoever thy soul lusteth after. 21. If the place which the LORD thy God hath chosen to put his name there be too far from thee, then thou shalt kill of thy herd and of thy flock; which the LORD hath given thee, as I have commanded thee, and thou shalt eat in thy gates whatsoever thy soul lusteth after. 22. Even as the roebuck and the hart is eaten, so thou shalt eat them: the unclean and the clean shall eat *of* them alike. 23. Only be sure that thou eat not the blood: for the blood *is* the life; and thou mayest not eat the life with the flesh. 24. Thou shalt not eat it; thou shalt pour it upon the earth as water. 25. Thou shalt not eat it; that it may go well with thee, and with thy children after thee, when thou shalt do *that which is* right in the sight of the LORD. Deut. 15:22,23.

Deut. 14:3. Thou shalt not eat any abominable thing. 4. These *are* the beasts which ye shall eat: the ox, the sheep, and the goat, 5. The hart, and the roebuck, and the fallow deer, and the wild goat, and the pygarg, and the wild ox, and the chamois. 6. And every beast that parteth the hoof, and cleaveth the cleft into two claws, *and* cheweth the cud among the beasts, that ye shall eat. 7. Nevertheless these ye shall not eat of them that chew the cud, or of them that divide the cloven hoof; *as* the camel, and the hare, and the coney: for they chew the cud, but divide not the hoof; *therefore* they *are* unclean unto you. 8. And the swine, because it divideth the hoof, yet cheweth not the cud, it *is* unclean unto you: ye shall not eat of their flesh, nor touch their dead carcase. 9. These ye shall eat of all that *are* in the waters: all that have fins and scales shall ye eat: 10. And whatsoever hath not fins and scales ye may not eat; it *is* unclean unto you. 11. *Of* all clean birds ye shall eat. 12. But these *are they* of which ye shall not eat: the eagle, and the ossifrage, and the ospray, 13. And the glede, and the kite, and the vulture after his kind, 14. And every raven after his kind, 15. And the owl, and the night hawk, and the cuckow, and the hawk after his kind, 16. The little owl, and the great owl, and the swan, 17. And the pelican, and the gier eagle, and the cormorant, 18. And the stork, and the heron after her kind, and the lapwing, and the bat. 19. And every creeping thing that flieth *is* unclean unto you: they shall not be eaten. 20. *But of* all clean fowls ye may eat. 21. Ye shall not eat *of* any thing that dieth of itself: thou shalt give it unto the stranger that *is* in thy gates, that he may eat it; or thou mayest sell it unto an alien: for thou *art* an holy people unto the LORD thy God. Thou shalt not seethe a kid in his mother's milk. 26. And thou shalt bestow that money for whatsoever thy soul lusteth after, for oxen, or for sheep, or for wine, or for strong drink, or for whatsoever thy soul desireth: and thou shalt eat there before the LORD thy God, and thou shalt rejoice, thou, and thine household,

GLUTTONY, DISEASE RESULTING FROM: Num. 11:18. And say thou unto the people, Sanctify yourselves against to morrow, and ye shall eat flesh: for ye have wept in the ears of the LORD, saying, Who shall give us flesh to eat? for *it was* well with us in Egypt: therefore the LORD will give you flesh, and ye shall eat. 19. Ye shall not eat one day, nor two days, nor five days, neither ten days, nor twenty days; 20. *But* even a whole month, until it come out at your nostrils, and it be loathsome unto you: 31. And there went forth a wind from the LORD, and brought quails from the sea, and let *them* fall by the camp, as it were a day's journey on this side, and as it were a day's journey on the other side, round about the camp, and as it were two cubits *high* upon the face of the earth. 32. And the people stood up all that day, and all *that* night, and all the next day, and they gathered the quails: he that gathered least gathered ten homers: and they spread *them* all abroad for themselves round about the camp. 33. And while the flesh *was* yet between their teeth, ere it was chewed, the wrath of the LORD was kindled against the people, and the LORD smote the people with a very great plague.

PENALTIES CONCERNING: Deut. 28:15. But it shall come to pass, if thou wilt not hearken unto the voice of the LORD thy God, to observe to do all his commandments and his statutes which I command thee this day; that all these curses shall come upon thee, and overtake thee: 21. The LORD shall make the pestilence cleave unto thee, until he have consumed thee from off the land, whither thou goest to possess it. 22. The LORD shall smite thee with a consumption, **and** with a fever, and with an inflamma-

tion, and with an extreme burning, and with the sword, and with blasting, and with mildew; and they shall pursue thee until thou perish. 27. The LORD will smite thee with the botch of Egypt, and with the emerods, and with the scab, and with the itch, whereof thou canst not be healed. 35. The LORD shalt smite thee in the knees, and in the legs, with a sore botch that can not be healed, from the sole of thy foot unto the top of thy head. 45. Moreover all these curses shall come upon thee, and shall pursue thee, and overtake thee, till thou be destroyed; because thou hearkenedst not unto the voice of the LORD thy God, to keep his commandments and his statutes which he commanded thee: 59. Then the LORD will make thy plagues wonderful, and the plagues of thy seed, *even* great plagues, and of long continuance, and sore sicknesses, and of long continuance. 60. Moreover he will bring upon thee all the diseases of Egypt, which thou wast afraid of; and they shall cleave unto thee. 61. Also every sickness, and every plague, which *is* not written in the book of this law, them will the LORD bring upon thee, until thou be destroyed. 62. And ye shall be left few in number, whereas ye were as the stars of heaven for multitude; because thou wouldest not obey the voice of the LORD thy God.

QUARANTINE: Lev. 13:2. When a man shall have in the skin of his flesh a rising, a scab, or bright spot, and it be in the skin of his flesh *like* the plague of leprosy; then he shall be brought unto Aaron the priest, or unto one of his sons the priests: 3. And the priest shall look on the plague in the skin of the flesh: and *when* the hair in the plague is turned white, and the plague in sight *be* deeper than the skin of his flesh, it *is* a plague of leprosy: and the priest shall look on him, and pronounce him unclean. 4. If the bright spot *be* white in the skin of his flesh, and in sight *be* not deeper than the skin, and the hair thereof be not turned white; then the priest shall shut up *him that hath* the plague seven days: 5. And the priest shall look on him the seventh day: and, behold, *if* the plague in his sight be at a stay, *and* the plague spread not in the skin; then the priest shall shut him up seven days more: 31. And if the priest look on the plague of the scall, and, behold, it *be* not in sight deeper than the skin, and *that there is* no black hair in it; then the priest shall shut up *him that hath* the plague of the scall seven days: 32. And in the seventh day the priest shall look on the plague: and, behold, *if* the scall spread not, and there be in it no yellow hair, and the scall *be* not in sight deeper than the skin; 33. He shall be shaven, but the scall shall he not shave; and the priest shall shut up *him that hath* the scall seven days more: 45. And the leper in whom the plague *is*, his clothes shall be rent, and his head bare, and he shall put a covering upon his upper lip, and shall cry, Unclean, unclean. 46. All the days wherein the plague *shall be* in him he shall be defiled; he *is* unclean: he shall dwell alone; without the camp *shall* his habitation *be*.

Lev. 14:2. This shall be the law of the leper in the day of his cleansing: He shall be brought unto the priest: 3. And the priest shall go forth out of the camp; and the priest shall look, and, behold, *if* the plague of leprosy be healed in the leper; 8. And he that is to be cleansed shall wash his clothes, and shave off all his hair, and wash himself in water, that he may be clean: and after that he shall come into the camp, and shall tarry abroad out of his tent seven days. 34. When ye be come into the land of Canaan, which I give to you for a possession, and I put the plague of leprosy in a house of the land of your possession; 35. And he that owneth the house shall come and tell the priest, saying, It seemeth to me *there is* as it were a plague in the house: 36. Then the priest shall command that they empty the house, before the priest go *into it* to see the plague, that all that *is* in the house be not made unclean: and afterward the priest shall go in to see the house: 37. And he shall look on the plague, and, behold, *if* the plague *be* in the walls of the house with hollow strakes, greenish or reddish, which in sight *are* lower than the wall; 38. Then the priest shall go out of the house to the door of the house, and shut up the house seven days:

Lev. 15:19. And if a woman have an issue, *and* her issue in her flesh be blood, she shall be put apart seven days: and whosoever toucheth her shall be unclean until the even.

Num. 5:2. Command the children of Israel, that they put out of the camp every leper, and every one that hath an issue, and whosoever is defiled by the dead: 3. Both male and female shall ye put out, without the camp shall ye put them; that they defile not their camps, in the midst whereof I dwell.

Num. 31:11. And they took all the spoil, and all the prey, *both* of men and of beasts. 12. And they brought the captives, and the prey, and the spoil, unto Moses, and Eleazar the priest, and unto the congregation of the children of Israel, unto the camp at the plains of Moab, which *are* by Jordan *near* Jericho. 13. And Moses, and Eleazar the priest, and all the princes of the congregation, went forth to meet them without the camp. 14. And Moses was wroth with the officers of the host, *with* the captains over thousands, and captains over hundreds, which came from the battle. 15. And Moses said unto them, Have ye saved all the women alive? 16. Behold, these caused the children of Israel, through the counsel of Balaam, to commit trespass against the LORD in the matter of Peor, and there was a plague among the congregation of the LORD. 17. Now therefore kill

every male among the little ones, and kill every woman that hath known man by lying with him. 18. But all the women children, that have not known a man by lying with him, keep alive for yourselves. 19. And do ye abide without the camp seven days: whosoever hath killed any person, and whosoever hath touched any slain, purify *both* yourselves and your captives on the third day, and on the seventh day. 20. And purify all *your* raiment, and all that is made of skins, and all work of goats' *hair*, and all things made of wood.

Deut. 23:10. If there be among you any man, that is not clean by reason of uncleanness that chanceth him by night, then shall he go abroad out of the camp, he shall not come within the camp: 11. But it shall be, when evening cometh on, he shall wash *himself* with water: and when the sun is down, he shall come into the camp *again*.

INSTANCES OF: Num. 12:10. And the cloud departed from off the tabernacle; and, behold, Miriam *became* leprous, *white* as snow: and Aaron looked upon Miriam, and, behold, *she was* leprous. 14. And the LORD said unto Moses, If her father had but spit in her face, should she not be ashamed seven days? let her be shut out from the camp seven days, and after that let her be received in *again*. 15. And Miriam was shut out from the camp seven days: and the people journeyed not till Miriam was brought in *again*.

2 Kin. 7:3. And there were four leprous men at the entering in of the gate:

2 Kin. 15:5. And the LORD smote the king, so that he was a leper unto the day of his death, and dwelt in a several house. 2 Chr. 26:21.

Luke 17:12. And as he entered into a certain village, there met him ten men that were lepers, which stood afar off:

REST ENJOINED: Ex. 20:9. Six days shalt thou labour, and do all thy work: 10. But the seventh day *is* the sabbath of the LORD thy God: *in it* thou shalt not do any work, thou, nor thy son, nor thy daughter, thy manservant, nor thy maidservant, nor thy cattle, nor thy stranger that *is* within thy gates: 11. For *in* six days the LORD made heaven and earth, the sea, and all that in them *is*, and rested the seventh day: wherefore the LORD blessed the sabbath day, and hallowed it.

Ex. 31:13. Verily my sabbaths ye shall keep: for it *is* a sign between me and you throughout your generations; that *ye* may know that I *am* the LORD that doth sanctify you. 14. Ye shall keep the sabbath therefore; for it *is* holy unto you: every one that defileth it shall surely be put to death: for whosoever doeth *any* work therein, that soul shall be cut off from among his people. 15. Six days may work be done; but in the seventh *is* the sabbath of rest, holy to the LORD: whosoever doeth *any* work in the sabbath day, he shall surely be put to death. 16. Wherefore the children of Israel shall keep the sabbath, to observe the sabbath throughout their generations, *for* a perpetual covenant. 17. It *is* a sign between me and the children of Israel for ever: for *in* six days the LORD made heaven and earth, and on the seventh day he rested, and was refreshed.

Ex. 34:21. Six days thou shalt work, but on the seventh day thou shalt rest: in earing time and in harvest thou shalt rest. 22. And thou shalt observe the feast of weeks, of the firstfruits of wheat harvest, and the feast of ingathering at the year's end.

Ex. 35:2. Six days shall work be done, but on the seventh day there shall be to you an holy day, a sabbath of rest to the LORD: whosoever doeth work therein shall be put to death.

Lev. 23:3. Six days shall work be done: but the seventh day *is* the sabbath of rest, an holy convocation; ye shall do no work *therein:* it *is* the sabbath of the LORD in all your dwellings. 4. These *are* the feasts of the LORD, *even* holy convocations, which ye shall proclaim in their seasons. 5. In the fourteenth *day* of the first month at even *is* the LORD'S passover. 6. And on the fifteenth day of the same month *is* the feast of unleavened bread unto the LORD: seven days ye must eat unleavened bread. 7. In the first day ye shall have an holy convocation: ye shall do no servile work therein. 8. But ye shall offer an offering made by fire unto the LORD seven days: in the seventh day *is* an holy convocation: ye shall do no servile work *therein.* 24. In the seventh month, in the first *day* of the month, shall ye have a sabbath, a memorial of blowing of trumpets, an holy convocation. 25. Ye shall do no servile work *therein:* but ye shall offer an offering made by fire unto the LORD. 26. And the LORD spake unto Moses, saying, 27. Also on the tenth *day* of the seventh month *there shall be* a day of atonement: it shall be an holy convocation unto you; and ye shall afflict your souls; and offer an offering made by fire unto the LORD. 28. And ye shall do no work in that same day: for it *is* a day of atonement, to make an atonement for you before the LORD your God. 29. For whatsoever soul *it be* that shall not be afflicted in that same day, he shall be cut off from among his people. 30. And whatsoever soul *it be* that doeth any work in that same day, the same soul will I destroy from among his people. 31. Ye shall do no manner of work: *it shall be* a statute for ever throughout your generations in all your dwellings. 32. It *shall be* unto you a sabbath of rest, and ye shall afflict your souls: in the ninth *day* of the month at even, from even unto even, shall ye celebrate your sabbath. 33. And the LORD spake unto Moses, saying, 34. Speak unto the children of Israel, saying, The fifteenth day of this seventh

month *shall be* the feast of tabernacles *for* seven days unto the LORD. 35. On the first day *shall be* an holy convocation: ye shall do no servile work *therein.* 36. Seven days ye shall offer an offering made by fire unto the LORD: on the eighth day shall be an holy convocation unto you; and ye shall offer an offering made by fire unto the LORD: it *is* a solemn assembly; *and* ye shall do no servile work *therein.* 37. These *are* the feasts of the LORD, which ye shall proclaim *to be* holy convocations, to offer an offering made by fire unto the LORD, a burnt offering, and a meat offering, a sacrifice, and drink offerings, every thing upon his day: 38. Beside the sabbaths of the LORD, and beside your gifts, and beside all your vows, and beside all your freewill offerings, which ye give unto the LORD. 39. Also in the fifteenth day of the seventh month, when ye have gathered in the fruit of the land, ye shall keep a feast unto the LORD seven days: on the first day *shall be* a sabbath, and on the eighth day *shall be* a sabbath. 40. And ye shall take you on the first day the boughs of goodly trees, branches of palm trees, and the boughs of thick trees, and willows of the brook; and ye shall rejoice before the LORD your God seven days. 41. And ye shall keep it a feast unto the LORD seven days in the year. *It shall be* a statute for ever in your generations: ye shall celebrate it in the seventh month. 42. Ye shall dwell in the booths seven days; all that are Israelites born shall dwell in booths:

Lev. 25:2. When ye come into the land which I give you, then shall the land keep a sabbath unto the LORD. 3. Six years thou shalt sow thy field, and six years thou shalt prune thy vineyard, and gather in the fruit thereof; 4. But in the seventh year shall be a sabbath of rest unto the land, a sabbath for the LORD: thou shalt neither sow thy field, nor prune thy vineyard. 5. That which groweth of its own accord of thy harvest thou shalt not reap, neither gather the grapes of thy vine undressed: *for* it is a year of rest unto the land. 6. And the sabbath of the land shall be meat for you; for thee, and for thy servant, and for thy maid, and for thy hired servant, and for thy stranger that sojourneth with thee, 7. And for thy cattle, and for the beast that *are* in thy land, shall all the increase thereof be meat. 8. And thou shalt number seven sabbaths of years unto thee, seven times seven years; and the space of the seven sabbaths of years shall be unto thee forty and nine years. 9. Then shalt thou cause the trumpet of the jubile to sound on the tenth *day* of the seventh month, in the day of atonement shall ye make the trumpet sound throughout all your land. 10. And ye shall hallow the fiftieth year, and proclaim liberty throughout *all* the land unto all the inhabitants thereof: it shall be a jubile unto you; and ye shall return every man unto his possession, and ye shall return every man unto his family. 11. A jubile shall that fiftieth year be unto you: ye shall not sow, neither reap that which groweth of itself in it, nor gather *the grapes* in it of thy vine undressed. 12. For it *is* the jubile; it shall be holy unto you: ye shall eat the increase thereof out of the field.

Num. 9:2. Let the children of Israel also keep the passover at his appointed season. 3. In the fourteenth day of this month, at even, ye shall keep it in his appointed season: according to all the rites of it, and according to all the ceremonies thereof, shall ye keep it.

Num. 28:16. And in the fourteenth day of the first month *is* the passover of the LORD. 17. And in the fifteenth day of this month *is* the feast: seven days shall unleavened bread be eaten. 18. In the first day *shall be* an holy convocation; ye shall do no manner of servile work *therein:* 25. And on the seventh day ye shall have an holy convocation; ye shall do no servile work. 26. Also in the day of the firstfruits, when ye bring a new meat offering unto the LORD, after your weeks *be out*, ye shall have an holy convocation; ye shall do no servile work:

Num. 29:1. And in the seventh month, on the first *day* of the month, ye shall have an holy convocation; ye shall do no servile work: it is a day of blowing the trumpets unto you. 7. And ye shall have on the tenth *day* of this seventh month an holy convocation; and ye shall afflict your souls: ye shall not do any work *therein:*

Deut. 5:12. Keep the sabbath day to sanctify it, as the LORD thy God hath commanded thee. 13. Six days thou shalt labour, and do all thy work: 14. But the seventh day *is* the sabbath of the LORD thy God: *in it* thou shalt not do any work, thou, nor thy son, nor thy daughter, nor thy manservant, nor thy maidservant, nor thine ox, nor thine ass, nor any of thy cattle, nor thy stranger that *is* within thy gates; that thy manservant and thy maidservant may rest as well as thou.

See RECREATION; REST; SABBATH; SABBATIC YEAR.

UNCLEANNESS: Lev. 20:2. Whosoever *he be* of the children of Israel, or of the strangers that sojourn in Israel, that giveth *any* of his seed unto Molech; he shall surely be put to death: the people of the land shall stone him with stones. 3. And I will set my face against that man, and will cut him off from among his people; because he hath given of his seed unto Molech, to defile my sanctuary, and to profane my holy name. 4. And if the people of the land do any ways hide their eyes from the man, when he giveth of his seed unto Molech, and kill him not: 5. Then I will set my face against that man, and against his family, and will cut him off, and all that go a whoring after him, to commit whoredom with Molech,

from among their people. 6. And the soul that turneth after such as have familiar spirits, and after wizards, to go a whoring after them, I will even set my face against that soul, and will cut him off from among his people. 10. And the man that committeth adultery with *another* man's wife, *even he* that committeth adultery with his neighbour's wife, the adulterer and the adulteress shall surely be put to death. 11. And the man that lieth with his father's wife hath uncovered his father's nakedness: both of them shall surely be put to death, their blood *shall be* upon them. 12. And if a man lie with his daughter in law, both of them shall surely be put to death: they have wrought confusion; their blood *shall be* upon them. 13. If a man also lie with mankind, as he lieth with a woman, both of them have committed an abomination: they shall surely be put to death; their blood *shall be* upon them. 14. And if a man take a wife and her mother, it *is* wickedness: they shall be burnt with fire, both he and they; that there be no wickedness among you. 15. And if a man lie with a beast, he shall surely be put to death: and ye shall slay the beast. 16. And if a woman approach unto any beast, and lie down thereto, thou shalt kill the woman, and the beast: they shall surely be put to death; their blood *shall be* upon them. 17. And if a man shall take his sister, his father's daughter, or his mother's daughter, and see her nakedness, and she see his nakedness; it *is* a wicked thing; and they shall be cut off in the sight of their people: he hath uncovered his sister's nakedness; he shall bear his iniquity. 18. And if a man shall lie with a woman having her sickness, and shall uncover her nakedness; he hath discovered her fountain, and she hath uncovered the fountain of her blood; and both of them shall be cut off from among their people. 19. And thou shalt not uncover the nakedness of thy mother's sister, nor of thy father's sister: for he uncovereth his near kin: they shall bear their iniquity. 20. And if a man shall lie with his uncle's wife, he hath uncovered his uncle's nakedness: they shall bear their sin; they shall die childless. 21. And if a man shall take his brother's wife, it *is* an unclean thing: he hath uncovered his brother's nakedness; they shall be childless.

Deut. 27:20. Cursed *be* he that lieth with his father's wife; because he uncovereth his father's skirt. 21. Cursed *be* he that lieth with any manner of beast. 22. Cursed *be* he that lieth with his sister, the daughter of his father, or the daughter of his mother. 23. Cursed *be* he that lieth with his mother in law.

VENEREAL DISEASES: Lev. 15:2. When any man hath a running issue out of his flesh, *because of* his issue he *is* unclean. 3. And this shall be his uncleanness in his issue: whether his flesh run with his issue, or his flesh be stopped from his issue, it *is* his uncleanness. 4. Every bed, whereon he lieth that hath the issue, is unclean: and every thing, whereon he sitteth, shall be unclean. 5. And whosoever toucheth his bed shall wash his clothes, and bathe *himself* in water, and be unclean until the even. 6. And he that sitteth on *any* thing whereon he sat that hath the issue shall wash his clothes, and bathe *himself* in water, and be unclean until the even. 7. And he that toucheth the flesh of him that hath the issue shall wash his clothes, and bathe *himself* in water, and be unclean until the even. 8. And if he that hath the issue spit upon him that is clean; then he shall wash his clothes, and bathe *himself* in water, and be unclean until the even. 9. And what saddle soever he rideth upon that hath the issue shall be unclean. 10. And whosoever toucheth any thing that was under him shall be unclean until the even: and he that beareth *any of* those things shall wash his clothes, and bathe *himself* in water, and be unclean until the even. 11. And whomsoever he toucheth that hath the issue, and hath not rinsed his hands in water, he shall wash his clothes, and bathe *himself* in water, and be unclean until the even. 12. And the vessel of earth, that he toucheth which hath the issue, shall be broken: and every vessel of wood shall be rinsed in water. 13. And when he that hath an issue is cleansed of his issue; then he shall number to himself seven days for his cleansing, and wash his clothes, and bathe his flesh in running water, and shall be clean. 16. And if any man's seed of copulation go out from him then he shall wash all his flesh in water, and be unclean until the even. 17. And every garment, and every skin, whereon is the seed of copulation, shall be washed with water, and be unclean until the even. 18. The woman also with whom man shall lie *with* seed of copulation, they shall *both* bathe *themselves* in water, and be unclean until the even. 19. And if a woman have an issue, *and* her issue in her flesh be blood, she shall be put apart seven days: and whosoever toucheth her shall be unclean until the even. 20. And every thing that she lieth upon in her separation shall be unclean: every thing also that she sitteth upon shall be unclean. 21. And whosoever toucheth her bed shall wash his clothes, and bathe *himself* in water, and be unclean until the even. 22. And whosoever toucheth any thing that she sat upon shall wash his clothes, and bathe *himself* in water, and be unclean until the even. 23. And if it *be* on *her* bed, or on any thing whereon she sitteth, when he toucheth it, he shall be unclean until the even. 24. And if any man lie with her at all, and her flowers be upon him, he shall be unclean seven days; and all the bed whereon he lieth shall be unclean. 25. And if a woman have an issue of her blood many days out of the time of her separation, or if it run beyond the time of her separation; all the days of the issue of her uncleanness shall be as the days of her separation: she *shall be* unclean. 26. Every bed whereon she lieth all the days of her issue shall be unto her as the bed of her separation: and whatsoever she sitteth upon shall be unclean, as the uncleanness of her separation. 27. And whosoever toucheth those things shall be unclean, and shall wash his clothes, and bathe *himself* in water, and be unclean until the even. 28. But if she be cleansed of her issue, then she shall number to herself seven days, and after that she shall be clean. 31. Thus shall ye separate the children of Israel from their uncleanness; that they die not in their uncleanness, when they defile my tabernacle that *is* among them. 32. This *is* the law of him that hath an issue, and *of him* whose seed goeth from him, and is defiled therewith; 33. And of her that is sick of her flowers, and of him that hath an issue, of the man, and of the woman, and of him that lieth with her that is unclean.

Lev. 22:4. What man soever of the seed of Aaron *is* a leper, or hath a running issue; he shall not eat of the holy things, until he be clean. And whoso toucheth any thing *that is* unclean *by* the dead; or a man whose seed goeth from him; 6. The soul which hath touched any such shall be unclean until even, and shall not eat of the holy things, unless he wash his flesh with water.

WOMEN IN CHILDBIRTH: Lev. 12:2. If a woman have conceived seed, and born a man child: then she shall be unclean seven days; according to the days of the separation for her infirmity shall she be unclean. 4. And she shall then continue in the blood of her purifying three and thirty days; she shall touch no hallowed thing, nor come into the sanctuary, until the days of her purifying be fulfilled. 5. But if she bear a maid child, then she shall be unclean two weeks, as in her separation: and she shall continue in the blood of her purifying threescore and six days.

See ABLUTIONS; DEFILEMENT; LEPROSY; PURIFICATION; UNCLEANNESS.

SANSANNAH, a city of Judah, Josh. 15:31.

SAPH, called also SIPPAI. A Philistine giant, 2 Sam. 21:18; 1 Chr. 20:4.

SAPHIR, a city prophesied against by Micah, Mic. 1:11.

SAPPHIRA, wife of Ananias. Falsehood and death of, Acts 5:1-10.

SAPPHIRE. A precious stone, Job 28:6,16; Isa. 54:11; Ezek. 28:13. Set in the breastplate, Ex. 28:18. The color of the firmament, Ezek. 1:26. Seen in the foundation of the New Jerusalem in John's apocalyptic vision, Rev. 21:19.

SARAH. 1. Called also SARAI. Wife of Abraham, Gen. 11:29-31; 12:5. Near of kin to Abraham, Gen. 12:10–20; 20:12. Abraham represents her as his sister, and Abimelech, king of Gerar, takes her; she is restored to Abraham by means of a dream, Gen. 20:1–14. Is sterile; gives her maid, Hagar, to Abraham as a wife, Gen. 16:1–3. Her jealousy of Hagar, Gen. 16:4–6; 21:9–14. Her miraculous conception of Isaac, Gen. 17:15–21; 18:9–15. Name changed from Sarai to Sarah, Gen. 17:15. Gives birth to Isaac, Gen. 21:3,6–8. Death and burial of, Gen. 23; 25:10. Character of, Heb. 11:11; 1 Pet. 3:5,6.

2. See SERAH.

SARAPH, a descendant of Shelah, 1 Chr. 4:22.

SARCASM. INSTANCES OF: Cain's self-justifying argument when God asked him where Abel was, Gen. 4:9. Israelites reproaching Moses, Ex. 14:11. God reproaching Israel, Num. 11:20; Judg. 10:14. Balak reproaching Balaam, Num. 24:11. Joshua to descendants of Joseph, Josh. 17:15. By Jotham, Judg. 9:7–19; Samson, Judg. 14:18. The men of Jabesh to Nahash, 1 Sam. 11:10. Eliab to David, 1 Sam. 17:28. Elijah to the priests of Baal, 1 Kin. 18:27. David's reply to Michal's irony, 2 Sam. 6:21. Ahab's reply to Ben-hadad, 1 Kin. 20:11. Jehoash to Amaziah, 2 Kin. 14:9,10; 2 Chr. 25:18,19. Rabshakeh to Hezekiah, 2 Kin. 18:23,24. Sanballat's address to the army of Samaria, Neh. 4:2,3. Zophar to Job, Job 11:12. Job to Zophar, Job 12:2,3. Of Solomon, Prov. 26:16. The persecutors of Jesus, Matt. 27:28,29; Luke 23:11; John 19:2,3,5,15. Paul, 1 Tim. 4:7. Agrippa to Paul, Acts 26:28.

See IRONY; SATIRE.

SARDIS, a city in Asia. One of the seven churches in, Rev. 1:11; 3:1–4.

SARDITES, family of, Num. 26:26.

SARDIUS, a precious stone. In the breastplate, Ex. 28:17; 39:10. In the garden of Eden, Ezek. 28:13. Seen in John's apocalyptic vision of the foundation of the New Jerusalem, Rev. 21:20.

FIGURATIVE: Rev. 4:3.

SARDONYX, a precious stone.

FIGURATIVE: In the foundation of the heavenly city, Rev. 21:20.

SAREPTA. See ZAREPHATH.

SARGON, a king of Assyria, Isa. 20:1.

SARID, a city on the boundary of the tribe of Zebulun, Josh. 19:10,12.

SARON. See SHARON.

SARSECHIM, a prince of Babylon. Present at the taking of Jerusalem, Jer. 39:3.

SARUCH. See SERUG.

SATAN. Called Abaddon, Rev. 9:11; accuser of our brethren, Rev. 12:10; adversary, 1 Pet. 5:8; angel of the bottomless pit, Rev. 9:11; Apollyon, Rev. 9:11; Beelzebub, Matt. 12:24; Mark 3:22; Luke 11:15; Belial, 2 Cor. 6:15; the devil, Matt. 4:1; Luke 4:2,6; Rev. 20:2; enemy, Matt. 13:39; evil spirit, 1 Sam. 16:14; father of lies, John 8:44; gates of

hell, Matt. 16:18; great red dragon, Rev. 12:3; liar, John 8:44; lying spirit, 1 Kin. 22:22; murderer, John 8:44; old serpent, Rev. 12:9; 20:2; power of darkness, Col. 1:13; prince of this world, John 12:31; 14:30; 16:11; of devils, Matt. 12:24; of the power of the air, Eph. 2:2; ruler of the darkness of this world, Eph. 6:12; Satan, 1 Chr. 21:1; Job 1:6; John 13:27; Acts 5:3; 26:18; Rom. 16:20; serpent, Gen. 3:4,14; 2 Cor. 11:3; spirit that worketh in the children of disobedience, Eph. 2:2; tempter, Matt. 4:3; 1 Thess. 3:5; the god of this world, 2 Cor. 4:4; unclean spirit, Matt. 12:43; wicked one, Matt. 13:19,38.

Kingdom of, to be destroyed, 2 Sam. 23:6, 7, with context; Matt. 12:29; 13:30; Luke 11:21,22; 1 John 3:8. Synagogue of, Rev. 2:9; 3:9.

UNCLASSIFIED SCRIPTURES RELATING TO: Gen. 3:1. Now the serpent was more subtil than any beast of the field which the LORD God had made. And he said unto the woman, Yea, hath God said, Ye shall not eat of every tree of the garden? 4. And the serpent said unto the woman, Ye shall not surely die: 5. For God doth know that in the day ye eat thereof, then your eyes shall be opened, and ye shall be as gods, knowing good and evil. 14. And the LORD God said unto the serpent, Because thou hast done this, thou *art* cursed above all cattle, and above every beast of the field; upon thy belly shalt thou go, and dust shalt thou eat all the days of thy life: 15. And I will put enmity between thee and the woman, and between thy seed and her seed; it shall bruise thy head, and thou shalt bruise his heel.

1 Chr. 21:1. And Satan stood up against Israel, and provoked David to number Israel.

Job 1:6. Now there was a day when the sons of God came to present themselves before the LORD, and Satan came also among them. 7. And the LORD said unto Satan, Whence comest thou? Then Satan answered the LORD, and said, From going to and fro in the earth, and from walking up and down in it. 9. Then Satan answered the LORD, and said, Doth Job fear God for nought? 10. Hast not thou made an hedge about him, and about his house, and about all that he hath on every side? thou hast blessed the work of his hands, and his substance is increased in the land. 11. But put forth thine hand now, and touch all that he hath, and he will curse thee to thy face. 12. And the LORD said unto Satan, Behold, all that he hath *is* in thy power; only upon himself put not forth thine hand. So Satan went forth from the presence of the LORD.

Job 2:3. And the LORD said unto Satan, Hast thou considered my servant Job, that *there is* none like him in the earth, a perfect and an upright man, one that feareth God, and escheweth evil? and still he holdeth fast his integrity, although thou movedst me against him, to destroy him without cause. 4. And Satan answered the LORD, and said, Skin for skin, yea, all that a man hath will he give for his life. 5. But put forth thine hand now, and touch his bone and his flesh, and he will curse thee to thy face. 6. And the LORD said unto Satan, Behold, he *is* in thine hand; but save his life. 7. So went Satan forth from the presence of the LORD, and smote Job with sore boils from the sole of his foot unto his crown.

Job 9:24. The earth is given into the hand of the wicked: he covereth the faces of the judges thereof; if not, where, *and* who *is* he?

Psa. 109:6. Set thou a wicked man over him: and let Satan stand at his right hand.

Zech. 3:1. And he shewed me Joshua the high priest standing before the angel of the LORD, and Satan standing at his right hand to resist him. 2. And the LORD said unto Satan, The LORD rebuke thee, O Satan; even the LORD that hath chosen Jerusalem rebuke thee: *is* not this a brand plucked out of the fire?

Matt. 4:1. Then was Jesus led up of the spirit into the wilderness to be tempted of the devil. 2. And when he had fasted forty days and forty nights, he was afterward an hungred. 3. And when the tempter came to him, he said, If thou be the Son of God, command that these stones be made bread. 4. But he answered and said, It is written, Man shall not live by bread alone, but by every word that proceedeth out of the mouth of God. 5. Then the devil taketh him up into the holy city, and setteth him on a pinnacle of the temple, 6. And saith unto him, If thou be the Son of God, cast thyself down: for it is written, He shall give his angels charge concerning thee: and in *their* hands they shall bear thee up, lest at any time thou dash thy foot against a stone. 7. Jesus said unto him, It is written again, Thou shalt not tempt the Lord thy God. 8. Again, the devil taketh him up into an exceeding high mountain, and sheweth him all the kingdoms of the world, and the glory of them; 9. And saith unto him, All these things will I give thee, if thou wilt fall down and worship me. 10. Then saith Jesus unto him, Get thee hence, Satan: for it is written, Thou shalt worship the Lord thy God, and him only shalt thou serve. 11. Then the devil leaveth him, and, behold, angels came and ministered unto him. Mark 1:13; Luke 4:1–13.

Matt. 13:19. When any one heareth the word of the kingdom, and understandeth *it* not, then cometh the wicked *one*, and catcheth away that which was sown in his heart. [Mark 4:15; Luke 8:12.] 38. The field is the world; the good seed are the children of the kingdom; but the tares are the children of the wicked *one;* 39. The enemy that sowed them is the devil;

Matt. 25:41. Then shall he say also unto them on the left hand, Depart from me, ye

cursed, into everlasting fire, prepared for the devil and his angels:

Mark 3:22. And the scribes which came down from Jerusalem said, He hath Beelzebub, and by the prince of the devils casteth he out devils. 23. And he called them *unto him,* and said unto them in parables, How can Satan cast out Satan? 24. And if a kingdom be divided against itself, that kingdom cannot stand. 25. And if a house be divided against itself, that house cannot stand. 26. And if Satan rise up against himself, and be divided, he cannot stand, but hath an end. Matt. 9:34; Luke 11:15,18.

Luke 10:18. And he said unto them, I beheld Satan as lightning fall from heaven.

Luke 13:16. And ought not this woman, being a daughter of Abraham, whom Satan hath bound, lo, these eighteen years, be loosed from this bond on the sabbath day?

Luke 22:31. And the Lord said, Simon, Simon, behold, Satan hath desired *to have* you, that he may sift *you* as wheat: 53. When I was daily with you in the temple, ye stretched forth no hands against me: but this is your hour, and the power of darkness.

John 8:38. I speak that which I have seen with my Father: and ye do that which ye have seen with your father. 41. Ye do the deeds of your father. 44. Ye are of *your* father the devil, and the lusts of your father ye will do. He was a murderer from the beginning, and abode not in the truth, because there is no truth in him. When he speaketh a lie, he speaketh of his own: for he is a liar, and the father of it.

John 12:31. Now is the judgment of this world: now shall the prince of this world be cast out.

John 13:2. And supper being ended, the devil having now put into the heart of Judas Iscariot, Simon's *son,* to betray him; 27. After the sop Satan entered into him.

John 14:30. Hereafter I will not talk much with you: for the prince of this world cometh, and hath nothing in me.

John 16:11. Of judgment, because the prince of this world is judged.

Acts 5:3. But Peter said, Ananias, why hath Satan filled thine heart to lie to the Holy Ghost, and to keep back *part* of the price of the land?

Acts 13:10. And said, O full of all subtilty and all mischief, *thou* child of the devil, *thou* enemy of all righteousness, wilt thou not cease to pervert the right ways of the Lord?

Acts 26:18. To open their eyes, *and* to turn *them* from darkness to light, and *from* the power of Satan unto God, that they may receive forgiveness of sins, and inheritance among them which are sanctified by faith that is in me.

Rom. 16:20. And the God of peace shall bruise Satan under your feet shortly.

1 Cor. 7:5. Defraud ye not one the other, except *it be* with consent for a time. that ye may give yourselves to fasting and prayer;

and come together again, that Satan tempt you not for your incontinency.

2 Cor. 2:11. Lest Satan should get an advantage of us: for we are not ignorant of his devices.

2 Cor. 4:4. In whom the god of this world hath blinded the minds of them which believe not, lest the light of the glorious gospel of Christ, who is the image of God, should shine unto them.

2 Cor. 11:3. But I fear, lest by any means, as the serpent beguiled Eve through his subtilty, so your minds should be corrupted from the simplicity that is in Christ. 14. For Satan himself is transformed into an angel of light. 15. Therefore *it is* no great thing if his ministers also be transformed as the ministers of righteousness; whose end shall be according to their works.

2 Cor. 12:7. There was given to me a thorn in the flesh, the messenger of Satan to buffet me, lest I should be exalted above measure.

Eph. 2:2. Wherein in time past ye walked according to the course of this world, according to the prince of the power of the air, the spirit that now worketh in the children of disobedience:

Eph. 4:27. Neither give place to the devil.

Eph. 6:11. Put on the whole armour of God, that ye may be able to stand against the wiles of the devil. 12. For we wrestle not against flesh and blood, but against principalities, against powers, against the rulers of the darkness of this world, against spiritual wickedness in high *places*.

13. Wherefore take unto you the whole armour of God, that ye may be able to withstand in the evil day, and having done all, to stand. 14. Stand therefore, having your loins girt about with truth, and having on the breastplate of righteousness; 15. And your feet shod with the preparation of the gospel of peace; 16. Above all, taking the shield of faith, wherewith ye shall be able to quench all the fiery darts of the wicked.

Col. 1:13. Who hath delivered us from the power of darkness, and hath translated *us* into the kingdom of his dear Son:

Col. 2:15. Having spoiled principalities and powers, he made a shew of them openly, triumphing over them in it.

1 Thess. 2:18. Wherefore we would have come unto you, even I Paul, once and again; but Satan hindered us.

1 Thess. 3:5. For this cause, when I could no longer forbear, I sent to know your faith, lest by some means the tempter have tempted you, and our labour be in vain.

2 Thess. 2:9. *Even him*, whose coming is after the working of Satan with all power and signs and lying wonders.

1 Tim. 1:20. Of whom is Hymenæus and Alexander; whom I have delivered unto Satan, that they may learn not to blaspheme.

1 Tim. 3:6. Not a novice, lest being lifted up with pride he fall into the condemnation of the devil. 7. Moreover he must have a good report of them which are without; lest he fall into reproach and the snare of the devil.

1 Tim. 5:15. For some are already turned aside after Satan.

2 Tim. 2:26. And *that* they may recover themselves out of the snare of the devil, [1]who are taken captive by him at his will.

[U R. V. having been taken captive by the Lord's servant unto the will of God]

Heb. 2:14. Forasmuch then as the children are partakers of flesh and blood, he also himself likewise took part of the same; that through death he might destroy him that had the power of death, that is, the devil ;

Jas. 4:7. Resist the devil, and he will flee from you.

1 Pet. 5:8. Be sober, be vigilant; because your adversary the devil, as a roaring lion. walketh about, seeking whom he may devour: 9. Whom resist stedfast in the faith, knowing that the same afflictions are accomplished in your brethren that are in the world.

2 Pet. 2:4. For if God spared not the angels that sinned, but cast *them* down to hell, and delivered *them* into chains of darkness, to be reserved unto judgment;

1 John 2:13. I write unto you, young men, because ye have overcome the wicked one.

1 John 3:8. He that committeth sin is of the devil; for the devil sinneth from the beginning. For this purpose the Son of God was manifested, that he might destroy the works of the devil. 10. In this the children of God are manifest, and the children of the devil: 12. Not as Cain, *who* was of that wicked one, and slew his brother. And wherefore slew he him? Because his own works were evil, and his brother's righteous.

1 John 5:18. He that is begotten of God keepeth himself, and that wicked one toucheth him not.

Jude 6. And the angels which kept not their first estate, but left their own habitation, he hath reserved in everlasting chains under darkness unto the judgment of the great day. 9. Yet Michael the archangel, when contending with the devil he disputed about the body of Moses, durst not bring against him a railing accusation, but said, The Lord rebuke thee.

Rev. 2:9. *I know* the blasphemy of them which say they are Jews, and are not, but *are* the synagogue of Satan. [Rev. 3:9.] 10. Fear none of those things which thou shalt suffer: behold, the devil shall cast *some* of you into prison, that ye may be tried ; and ye shall have tribulation ten days: be thou faithful unto death, and I will give thee a crown of life. 13. I know thy works, and where thou dwellest, *even* where Satan's seat *is:* and thou holdest fast my name, and hast not denied my faith, even in those days wherein Antipas *was* my faithful martyr, who was slain among you, where Satan dwelleth. 24. But unto you I say, and unto the rest in Thyatira, as many as have not this doctrine, and which have not known the depths of Satan, as they speak;

Rev. 9:11. They had a king over them, *which is* the angel of the bottomless pit, whose name in the Hebrew tongue *is* Abaddon, but in the Greek tongue hath *his* name Apollyon.

Rev. 12:9. And the great dragon was cast out, that old serpent, called the Devil, and Satan, which deceiveth the whole world: he was cast out into the earth, and his angels were cast out with him. 10. And I heard a loud voice saying in heaven, Now is come salvation, and strength, and the kingdom of our God, and the power of his Christ: for the accuser of our brethren is cast down, which accused them before our God day and night. 11. And they overcame him by the blood of the Lamb, and by the word of their testimony; and they loved not their lives unto the death. 12. Therefore rejoice, *ye* heavens, and ye that dwell in them. Woe to the inhabiters of the earth and of the sea! for the devil is come down unto you, having great wrath, because he knoweth that he hath but a short time.

Rev. 20:1. I saw an angel come down from heaven, having the key of the bottomless pit and a great chain in his hand. 2. And he laid hold on the dragon, that old serpent, which is the Devil, and Satan, and bound him a thousand years, 3. And cast him into the bottomless pit, and shut him up, and set a seal upon him, that he should deceive the nations no more, till the thousand years should be fulfilled: and after that he must be loosed a little season. 7. And when the thousand years are expired, Satan shall be loosed out of his prison, 8. And shall go out to deceive the nations which are in the four quarters of the earth, Gog and Magog, to gather them together to battle: 10. And the devil that deceived them was cast into the lake of fire and brimstone, where the beast and the false prophet *are*, and shall be tormented day and night for ever and ever.

See DEMONS.

SATIRE. Hannah's song of exultation over Peninnah, 1 Sam. 2:1-10, with chapter 1:5-10. Of Jesus against hypocrites, Matt. 23:2-33; Mark 12:13-40; Luke 11:39-54.

See IRONY; SARCASM.

SATYR, a mythological creature, represented as half man and half goat, Lev. 17: 7 [*R. V.*, margin]; 2 Chr. 11:15 [*R. V.*, margin]; Isa. 13:21; 34:14.

SAUL. 1. Called also SHAUL. King of Edom, Gen. 36:37,38; 1 Chr. 1:48,49.

2. King of Israel. A Benjamite, son of Kish, 1 Sam. 9:1,2. Sons of, 1 Chr. 8:33. His personal appearance, 1 Sam. 9:2; 10:23. Made king of Israel, 1 Sam. 9; 10; 11:12-15; Hos. 13:11. Dwells at Gibeah of Saul, 1 Sam. 14: 2; 15:34; Isa. 10:29. Defeats the Philistines, 1 Sam. 13; 14:46,52. Smites the Amalekites, 1 Sam. 15. Is reproved by Samuel for

usurping the priestly functions, 1 Sam. 13: 11-14; for disobedience in not slaying the Amalekites; the loss of his kingdom foretold, 1 Sam. 15. Dedicates the spoils of war, 1 Sam. 15:21-25; 1 Chr. 26:28. Sends messengers to Jesse, asking that David be sent to him as musician and armor-bearer, 1 Sam. 16:17-23. Defeats the Philistines after Goliath is slain by David, 1 Sam. 17. His jealousy of David; gives his daughter, Michal, to David to be his wife; becomes David's enemy, 1 Sam. 18. Tries to slay David; Jonathan intercedes and incurs his father's displeasure; David's loyalty to him; Saul's repentance; prophesies, 1 Sam. 19. Hears Doeg against Ahimelech, and slays the priest and his family, 1 Sam. 22:9-19. Pursues David to the wilderness of Ziph; the Ziphites betray David to, 1 Sam. 23. Pursues David to En-gedi, 1 Sam. 24:1-6. His life saved by David, 1 Sam. 24:5-8. Saul's contrition for his bad faith, 1 Sam. 24:16-22. David is again betrayed to, by the Ziphites; Saul pursues him to the hill of Hachilah; his life spared again by David; his confession, and his blessing upon David, 1 Sam. 26. Slays the Gibeonites; crime avenged by the death of seven of his sons, 2 Sam. 21:1-9. His kingdom invaded by Philistines; seeks counsel of the witch of En-dor, who foretells his death, 1 Sam. 28:3-25; 29:1. Is defeated, and with his sons is slain, 1 Sam. 31; their bodies exposed in Beth-shan; rescued by the people of Jabesh and burned; bones of, buried under a tree at Jabesh, 1 Sam. 31, with 2 Sam. 1; 2; 1 Chr. 10. His death a judgment on account of his sins, 1 Chr. 10:13.

3. Of Tarsus. See PAUL.

SAVIOUR. See JESUS, SAVIOUR.

SAW. Used as an instrument of torture, 2 Sam. 12:31; Heb. 11:37; for cutting stone, 1 Kin. 7:9.

FIGURATIVE: Isa. 10:15.

SCAB, disease of the skin, Lev. 13:2,6-8; 14:56; 21:20; 22:22; Deut. 28:27; Isa. 3:17.

See DISEASE; SANITATION; SCURVY.

SCALES, fell from Paul's eyes, Acts 9:18.

FOR MEASURE. See BALANCES.

SCALL, a form of leprosy, Lev. 13:30.

See LEPROSY.

SCAPEBIRD, Lev. 14:4-7,53.

SCAPEGOAT, Lev. 16:7-10,20-34.

SCARLET. See COLOR.

SCEPTER. A wand used by kings to signify favor or disfavor to those who desired audience, Esth. 5:2; 8:4. A symbol of authority, Num. 24:17; Isa. 14:5. Made of gold, Esth. 4:11; of iron, Psa. 2:9; Rev. 2:27; 12:5.

FIGURATIVE: Gen. 49:10; Num. 24:17; Isa. 9:4.

SCEVA, a Jew of Ephesus, Acts 19:13-17.

SCHOOL. Of the prophets, at Naioth, 1 Sam. 19:20; Beth-el, 2 Kin. 2:3; Jericho, 2 Kin. 2:5,15; Gilgal, 2 Kin. 4:38; Jerusalem, probably, 2 Kin. 22:14; 2 Chr. 34:22. Crowded attendance at, 2 Kin. 6:1.

In the home, Deut. 4:9,10; 6:7,9; 11:19,20; Psa. 78:5-8. Bible school, Deut. 31:10-13.

State, 2 Chr. 17:7-9; Dan. 1:3-21. Of Gamaliel, Acts 5:34; 22:3. Of Tyrannus, Acts 19:9. Schoolmaster [tutor, *R. V.*], Gal. 3: 24,25.

See INSTRUCTION; PSALMS, DIDACTIC.

SCIENCE. Observations of, and deductions from, facts, Job 26:7-14; 28; Eccl. 1:13-17. So-called, false, 1 Tim. 6:20.

The key of knowledge, Luke 11:52; Rom. 2:20.

See GEOLOGY; ASTRONOMY; PHILOSOPHY.

SCOFFING: 2 Chr. 30:6. So the posts went with the letters from the king and his princes throughout all Israel and Judah, and according to the commandment of the king, saying, Ye children of Israel, turn again unto the LORD God of Abraham, Isaac, and Israel, and he will return to the remnant of you, that are escaped out of the hand of the kings of Assyria. 7. And be not ye like your fathers, and like your brethren, which trespassed against the LORD God of their fathers, *who* therefore gave them up to desolation, as ye see. 8. Now be ye not stiffnecked, as your fathers *were*, *but* yield yourselves unto the LORD, and enter into his sanctuary, which he hath sanctified for ever: and serve the LORD your God, that the fierceness of his wrath may turn away from you. 9. For if ye turn again unto the LORD, your brethren and your children *shall find* compassion before them that lead them captive, so that they shall come again into this land: for the LORD your God *is* gracious and merciful, and will not turn away *his* face from you, if ye return unto him. 10. So the posts passed from city to city through the country of Ephraim and Manasseh even unto Zebulun: but they laughed them to scorn, and mocked them.

2 Chr. 36:16. But they mocked the messengers of God, and despised his words, and misused his prophets, until the wrath of the LORD arose against his people, till *there was* no remedy.

Job 21:14. Therefore they say unto God, Depart from us; for we desire not the knowledge of thy ways. 15. What *is* the Almighty, that we should serve him? and what profit should we have, if we pray unto him?

Job 34:7. What man *is* like Job, *who* drinketh up scorning like water?

Psa. 1:1. Blessed *is* the man that walketh not in the counsel of the ungodly, nor standeth in the way of sinners, nor sitteth in the seat of the scornful.

Psa. 42:3. My tears have been my meat day and night, while they continually say unto me, Where *is* thy God? *v.* 10.

Psa. 73:11. They say, How doth God know? and is there knowledge in the most High?

Psa. 78:19. Yea, they spake against God; they said, Can God furnish a table in the wilderness? 20. Behold, he smote the rock, that the waters gushed out, and the streams overflowed; can he give bread also? can he provide flesh for his people?

Psa. 107:11. Because they rebelled against the words of God, and contemned the counsel of the most High: 12. Therefore he brought down their heart with labour; they fell down, and *there was* none to help.

Prov. 1:22. How long, ye simple ones, will ye love simplicity? and the scorners delight in their scorning, and fools hate knowledge? 25. But ye have set at nought all my counsel, and would none of my reproof:

Prov. 3:34. Surely he scorneth the scorners: but he giveth grace unto the lowly.

Prov. 9:12. If thou be wise, thou shalt be wise for thyself: but *if* thou scornest, thou alone shalt bear *it*.

Prov. 13:1. A wise son *heareth* his father's instruction: but a scorner heareth not rebuke.

Prov. 14:6. A scorner seeketh wisdom, and *findeth it* not: 9. Fools make a mock at sin:

Prov. 19:29. Judgments are prepared for scorners, and stripes for the back of fools.

Prov. 21:11. When the scorner is punished, the simple is made wise: 24. Proud *and* haughty scorner *is* his name, who dealeth in proud wrath.

Prov. 22:10. Cast out the scorner, and contention shall go out; yea, strife and reproach shall cease.

Prov. 24:9. The thought of foolishness *is* sin: and the scorner *is* an abomination to men.

Isa. 5:18. Woe unto them . . . 19. That say, Let him make speed, *and* hasten his work, that we may see *it:* and let the counsel of the Holy One of Israel draw nigh and come, that we may know *it!* 24. Therefore as the fire devoureth the stubble, and the flame consumeth the chaff, *so* their root shall be as rottenness, and their blossom shall go up as dust: because they have cast away the law of the LORD of hosts, and despised the word of the Holy One of Israel. 25. Therefore is the anger of the LORD kindled against his people, and he hath stretched forth his hand against them, and hath smitten them: and the hills did tremble,

Isa. 10:15. Shall the ax boast itself against him that heweth therewith? *or* shall the saw magnify itself against him that shaketh it? as if the rod should shake *itself* against them that lift it up, *or* as if the staff should lift up *itself*, *as if it were* no wood.

Isa. 29:20. For the terrible one is brought to nought, and the scorner is consumed, and all that watch for iniquity are cut off:

Isa. 57:4. Against whom do ye sport yourselves? against whom make ye a wide mouth, *and* draw out the tongue?

Jer. 17:15. Behold, they say unto me,

Where *is* the word of the LORD? let it come now.

Jer. 43:2. Then spake . . . all the proud men, saying unto Jeremiah, Thou speakest falsely: the LORD our God hath not sent thee to say, Go not into Egypt to sojourn there:

Lam. 1:7. Jerusalem remembered in the days of her affliction and of her miseries all her pleasant things that she had in the days of old, when her people fell into the hand of the enemy, and none did help her: the adversaries saw her, *and* did mock at her ¹ sabbaths.   [¹ R. V. desolations]

Ezek. 8:12. Then said he unto me, Son of man, hast thou seen what the ancients of the house of Israel do in the dark, every man in the chambers of his imagery? for they say, The LORD seeth us not; the LORD hath forsaken the earth.

Ezek. 9:9. The iniquity of the house of Israel and Judah *is* exceeding great, and the land is full of blood, and the city full of perverseness: for they say, The LORD hath forsaken the earth, and the LORD seeth not.

Ezek. 11:2. Then said he unto me, Son of man, these *are* the men that devise mischief, and give wicked counsel in this city: 3. Which say, *It is* not near; let us build houses: this *city is* the caldron, and we *be* the flesh.

Ezek. 12:22. Son of man, what *is* that proverb *that* ye have in the land of Israel, saying, The days are prolonged, and every vision faileth?

Ezek. 33:20. Yet ye say, The way of the Lord is not equal.

Hos. 7:5. In the day of our king the princes have made *him* sick with bottles of wine; he stretched out his hand with scorners.

Matt. 12:24. When the Pharisees heard *it*, they said, This *fellow* doth not cast out devils, but by Beelzebub the prince of the devils. Mark 3:22; Luke 11:15.

Luke 4:23. And he said unto them, Ye will surely say unto me this proverb, Physician, heal thyself: whatsoever we have heard done in Capernaum, do also here in thy country.

Luke 16:14. And the Pharisees also, who were covetous, heard all these things: and they derided him.

Acts 2:13. Others mocking said, These men are full of new wine.

Acts 13:45. But when the Jews saw the multitudes, they were filled with envy, and spake against those things which were spoken by Paul, contradicting and blaspheming.

Acts 17:18. Then certain philosophers of the Epicureans, and of the Stoicks, encountered him. And some said, What will this babbler say? other some, He seemeth to be a setter forth of strange gods: because he preached unto them Jesus, and the resurrection. 32. And when they heard of the resurrection of the dead, some mocked: and others said, We will hear thee again of this *matter*.

Heb. 10:29. Of how much sorer punishment, suppose ye, shall he be thought worthy, who hath trodden under foot the Son of God, and hath counted the blood of the covenant, wherewith he was sanctified, an unholy thing, and hath done despite unto the Spirit of grace?

2 Pet. 3:3. Knowing this first, that there shall come in the last days scoffers, walking after their own lusts, 4. And saying, Where is the promise of his coming? for since the fathers fell asleep, all things continue as *they were* from the beginning of the creation.

See HATRED; MALICE; UNBELIEF.

INSTANCES OF: Ishmael, Gen. 21:9. Children at Beth-el, 2 Kin. 2:23. Ephraim and Manasseh, 2 Chr. 30:10. Chiefs of Judah, 2 Chr. 36:16. Sanballat, Neh. 4:1. Enemies of Job, Job 30:1,9. Enemies of David, Psa. 35:15,16. Rulers of Israel, Isa. 28:14. Ammonites, Ezek. 25:3. Tyrians, Ezek. 26:2. Heathen, Ezek. 36:2, 3. Soldiers, Matt. 27:28-30; Luke 23:36. Chief priests, Matt. 27:41. Pharisees, Luke 16:14. The men who held Jesus, Luke 22:63,64. Herod, Luke 23:11. People and rulers, Luke 23:35. Some of the multitude, Acts 2:13. Athenians, Acts 17:32.

SCORPION. A venomous insect common in the wilderness through which children of Israel journeyed, Deut. 8:15. Power over, given to the seventy, Luke 10:19. Unfit for food, Luke 11:12. Sting of, in the tail, Rev. 9:10.

FIGURATIVE: Of enemies, Ezek. 2:6. Of cruelty, 1 Kin. 12:11,14.

SYMBOLICAL: Rev. 9:3,5,10.

SCOURGING, corporal punishment by stripes. Prescribed in the Mosaic law for fornication, Lev. 19:20; Deut. 22:18; for other offenses, Deut. 25:2. Forty stripes the maximum limit, Deut. 25:3. Fatal, Job 9:23; of servants avenged, Ex. 21:20. Foretold by Jesus as a persecution of the Christians, Matt. 10:17.

Of children, see CHILDREN, CORRECTION OF; PUNISHMENT.

INSTANCES OF: Of Jesus, Matt. 20:19; 27:26; Mark 15:15; John 19:1. Of Paul and Silas, Acts 16:23. Of Paul, Acts 21:32; 22:24; 2 Cor. 11:24,25. Of Sosthenes, Acts 18:17.

FIGURATIVE: Of the oppressions of rulers, 1 Kin. 12:11. Of the evil tongue, Job 5:21.

See ASSAULT AND BATTERY.

SCRIBE. A writer and transcriber of the law, 2 Sam. 8:17; 20:25; 1 Kin. 4:3; 2 Kin. 12:10; 18:37; 19:2; 1 Chr. 24:6; 27:32; Neh. 13:13; Jer. 36:12. King's secretary, 2 Kin. 12:10-12; 22:1-14; Esth. 3:12; 8:9. Mustering officer of the army, 2 Kin. 25:19; 2 Chr. 26:11. Instructors in the law, Matt. 7:29; 13:52; 17:10; 23:2,3. See LEVITES. Test Jesus with questions, bringing to Jesus a woman taken in adultery, John 8:3.

Members of the council, Matt. 2:4. Conspire against Jesus, Matt. 26:3,57; 27:41; Mark 14: 1; Luke 22:66. Hypocrisy of, reproved by Jesus, Matt. 5:20; 9:3; 12:38; 15:1; 16:21; 20: 18; 21:15.

SCRIPTURES. The word of God, Jer. 30:2. Interpreted by doctors, John 3: 10; 7:52. Inspired, 2 Tim. 3:16.

See WORD OF GOD.

SEA. Creation of, Gen. 1:9,10; Psa. 95:5; 148:4,5. Limits of, established by God, Psa. 1:9; Job 26:10; 38:8; Psa. 33:7; Jer. 5:22. Calmed by Jesus, Matt. 8:24–26; Mark 4:37–39. Jesus walked on, Matt. 14:25–31. Dead, to be given up by, at the resurrection, Rev. 20:13.

SYMBOLICAL: In Daniel's vision, Dan. 7: 2,3. In John's apocalyptic vision, Rev. 4:6; 8:8,9; 10:2,5,6,8; 13:1; 15:2; 16:3; 21:1.

SCURVY, Lev. 22:22.

See SCAB.

SCYTHIANS, Col. 3:11.

SEAL. 1. A stamp used for signifying documents. Given as a pledge, Gen. 38: 18. Engraved, Ex. 28:11,21,36; 39:6,14,30; 2 Tim. 2:19. Decrees signified by, 1 Kin. 21: 8; Esth. 8:8. Documents sealed with: Ahab's letter, 1 Kin. 21:8; covenants, Neh. 9:38; 10:1; Isa. 8:16; decrees, Esth. 8:8; Dan. 6:9; deeds, Jer. 32:10. Treasures secured by, Deut. 32:34. Lion's den made sure by, Dan. 6:17; sepulcher of Jesus, Matt. 27:66. Circumcision a seal of righteousness. Rom. 4:11.

FIGURATIVE: Of secrecy, Dan. 12:9; Rev. 5:1. Of certainty of divine approval, John 6:27; Rom. 15:28; 2 Cor. 1:22; Eph. 1:13; 4:30; Rev. 7:3,4.

2. An amphibious animal. Skins of, according to the Revised Version, were used as a covering of the tabernacle, Ex. 25:5; 26:14; 35:7,23; 36:19; 39:34; Num. 4:25.

SEAMEN. See MARINERS.

SEASONS, Gen. 1:14; 8:22; Psa. 104:19; Jer. 33:20; Dan. 2:21; Matt. 21:41; 24:32; Mark 12:2; Acts 1:7; 1 Thess. 5:1.

SEBA. 1. Son of Cush, Gen. 10:7; 1 Chr. 1:9.

2. A region in Ethiopia, Psa. 72:10; Isa. 43:3.

SEBAT, the eleventh month (February), Zech. 1:7.

SECOND DEATH, Rev. 20:14.

See WICKED, PUNISHMENT OF.

SECRET. Alms to be given in, Matt. 6:4. Prayer to be offered in, Matt. 6:6. Of others not to be divulged, Prov. 25:9; Matt. 18:15.

UNCLASSIFIED SCRIPTURES RELATING TO: Deut. 29:29. The secret *things belong* unto the LORD our God: but those *things which are* revealed *belong* unto us and to our children for ever, that *we* may do all the words of this law.

Deut. 31:21. I know their imagination which they go about, even now, before I have brought them into the land which I sware.

1 Sam. 16:7. But the LORD said unto Sam-

uel, Look not on his countenance, or on the height of his stature; because I have refused him: for *the* LORD *seeth* not as man seeth; for man looketh on the outward appearance, but the LORD looketh on the heart.

2 Sam. 7:20. And what can David say more unto thee? for thou, Lord GOD, knowest thy servant.

2 Kin. 19:27. But I know thy abode, and thy going out, and thy coming in,

Psa. 25:14. The secret of the LORD *is* with them that fear him; and he will shew them his covenant.

Psa. 44:21. Shall not God search this out? for he knoweth the secrets of the heart.

Psa. 90:8. Thou hast set our iniquities before thee, our secret *sins* in the light of thy countenance.

Eccl. 12:14. For God shall bring every work into judgment, with every secret thing, whether *it be* good, or whether *it be* evil.

Dan. 2:28. But there is a God in heaven that revealeth secrets,

47. The king answered unto Daniel, and said, Of a truth *it is,* that your God *is* a God of gods, and a Lord of kings, and a revealer of secrets, seeing thou couldest reveal this secret.

Amos 3:7. Surely the Lord GOD . . . revealeth his secret unto his servants the prophets.

Mark 4:22. For there is nothing hid, which shall not be manifested; neither was any thing kept secret, but that it should come abroad.

Luke 8:16. No man, when he hath lighted a candle, covereth it with a vessel, or putteth *it* under a bed; but setteth *it* on a candlestick, that they which enter in may see the light. 17. For nothing is secret, that shall not be made manifest; neither *any thing* hid, that shall not be known and come abroad.

Rom. 2:16. In the day when God shall judge the secrets of men by Jesus Christ according to my gospel.

1 Cor. 4:5. Therefore judge nothing before the time, until the Lord come, who both will bring to light the hidden things of darkness, and will make manifest the counsels of the heart: and then shall every man have praise of God.

Heb. 4:12. For the word of God *is* quick, and powerful, and sharper than any twoedged sword, piercing even to the dividing asunder of soul and spirit, and of the joints and marrow, and *is* a discerner of the thoughts and intents of the heart. 13. Neither is there any creature that is not manifest in his sight: but all things *are* naked and opened unto the eyes of him with whom we have to do.

See MYSTERY.

SECRETARY, 2 Sam. 8:17; 20:24; 1 Kin. 4:3; 2 Kin. 12:10–12; 18:18,37; 22:1–14; 1 Chr. 27:32; Esth. 3:12; 8:9. Military, 2 Kin. 25: 19; 2 Chr. 26:11.

See AMANUENSIS; SCRIBE.

SECUNDUS, a Thessalonian Christian. Accompanies Paul from Corinth, Acts 20:4–6.

SECURITY. FOR DEBT: See DEBT; SURETY.

FALSE: From the evils of sin. Promises peace and long life, Job 29:18. Is ignorant of God and truth, Psa. 10:4; 50:21. Trusts in lies, Isa. 28:15; Rev. 3:17. Is inconsiderate and forgetful, Isa. 47:7. Relies on earthly treasures, Jer. 49:4,16. Is deceived by pride, Obad. 3; Rev. 18:7. Puts off the evil day, Amos 6:3. Leads to increased guilt, Eccl. 8:11. Its refuges shall be scattered, Isa. 28:17. Ruin shall overtake it, Isa. 47:9; Amos 9:10.

God is against it, Jer. 21:13; Ezek. 39:6; Amos 6:1.—*Bible Text-Book.*

See CONFIDENCE, FALSE; SELF-DECEPTION; SELF-DELUSION.

SEDITION. Charged against Paul, Acts 24:5. How punished, Acts 5:36,37.

SEDUCTION, 2 Tim. 3:6,13. Laws concerning, Ex. 22:16,17; Deut. 22:23–29.

See RAPE.

INSTANCES OF: Of Dinah, Gen. 34:2. Tamar, 2 Sam. 13:1–14.

SEED. Every herb, tree, and grass, yields its own, Gen. 1:11,12,29. Each kind has its own body, 1 Cor. 15:38. Not to be mingled in sowing, Lev. 19:19; Deut. 22:9.

Parables concerning, Matt. 13; Luke 8.

Illustrative, Eccl. 11:6; Hos. 10:12; 2 Cor. 9:6; Gal. 6:7,8.

Sowing of, type of burial of the body, 1 Cor. 15:36–38.—*Bible Text-Book.*

SEEKERS. Gen. 49:18. I have waited for thy salvation, O LORD.

Deut. 4:29. But if from thence thou shalt seek the LORD thy God, thou shalt find *him*, if thou seek him with all thy heart and with all thy soul.

1 Chr. 16:11. Seek the LORD and his strength, seek his face continually.

1 Chr. 22:19. Now set your heart and your soul to seek the LORD your God;

1 Chr. 28:9. And thou, Solomon my son, know thou the God of thy father, and serve him with a perfect heart and with a willing mind: for the LORD searcheth all hearts, and understandeth all the imaginations of the thoughts: if thou seek him, he will be found of thee; but if thou forsake him, he will cast thee off for ever.

2 Chr. 11:16. And after them out of all the tribes of Israel such as set their hearts to seek the LORD God of Israel came to Jerusalem, to sacrifice unto the LORD God of their fathers.

2 Chr. 15:2. Hear ye me, Asa, and all Judah and Benjamin; The LORD *is* with you, while ye be with him; and if ye seek him, he will be found of you; but if ye forsake him, he will forsake you. 12. And they entered into a covenant to seek the LORD God of their fathers with all their heart and with all their soul; 13. That whosoever would not seek the LORD God

of Israel should be put to death, whether small or great, whether man or woman.

2 Chr. 26:5. And he sought God in the days of Zechariah, who had understanding in the visions of God: and as long as he sought the LORD, God made him to prosper.

2 Chr. 30:18. But Hezekiah prayed for them, saying, The good LORD pardon every one 19. *That* prepareth his heart to seek God, the LORD God of his fathers, though *he be* not *cleansed* according to the purification of the sanctuary.

2 Chr. 31:21. And in every work that he began in the service of the house of God, and in the law, and in the commandments, to seek his God, he did *it* with all his heart, and prospered.

Ezra 8:22. I was ashamed to require of the king a band of soldiers and horsemen to help us against the enemy in the way: because we had spoken unto the king, saying, The hand of our God *is* upon all them for good that seek him; but his power and his wrath *is* against all them that forsake him.

Job 5:8. I would seek unto God, and unto God would I commit my cause:

Job 8:5. If thou wouldest seek unto God betimes, and make thy supplication to the Almighty; 6. If thou *wert* pure and upright; surely now he would awake for thee, and make the habitation of thy righteousness prosperous.

Psa. 9:10. And they that know thy name will put their trust in thee: for thou, LORD, hast not forsaken them that seek thee.

Psa. 14:2. The LORD looked down from heaven upon the children of men, to see if there were any that did understand, *and* seek God.

Psa. 17:1. Hear the right, O LORD, attend unto my cry, give ear unto my prayer, *that goeth* not out of feigned lips. 2. Let my sentence come forth from thy presence; let thine eyes behold the things that are equal.

Psa. 22:26. They shall praise the LORD that seek him:

Psa. 24:3. Who shall ascend into the hill of the LORD? or who shall stand in his holy place? 4. He that hath clean hands, and a pure heart; who hath not lifted up his soul unto vanity, nor sworn deceitfully. 5. He shall receive the blessing from the LORD, and righteousness from the God of his salvation. 6. This *is* the generation of them that seek him, that seek thy face, O Jacob.

Psa. 25:5. Lead me in thy truth, and teach me: for thou *art* the God of my salvation; on thee do I wait all the day. 15. Mine eyes *are* ever toward the LORD; for he shall pluck my feet out of the net.

Psa. 27:4. One *thing* have I desired of the LORD, that will I seek after; that I may dwell in the house of the LORD all the days of my life, to behold the beauty of the LORD, and to inquire in his temple. 8. *When thou saidst*, Seek ye my face; my heart said unto thee, Thy face, LORD, will I seek.

14. Wait on the LORD: be of good courage, and he shall strengthen thine heart: wait, I say, on the LORD.

Psa. 33:20. Our soul waiteth for the LORD: he *is* our help and our shield.

Psa. 34:4. I sought the LORD, and he heard me, and delivered me from all my fears. 10. The young lions do lack, and suffer hunger: but they that seek the LORD shall not want any good *thing*.

Psa. 40:1. I waited patiently for the LORD; and he inclined unto me, and heard my cry. 2. He brought me up also out of an horrible pit, out of the miry clay, and set my feet upon a rock, *and* established my goings. 3. And he hath put a new song in my mouth. *even* praise unto our God: many shall see *it*, and fear, and shall trust in the LORD. 4. Blessed *is* that man that maketh the LORD his trust, and respecteth not the proud, nor such as turn aside to lies.

Psa. 42:1. As the hart panteth after the water brooks, so panteth my soul after thee, O God. 2. My soul thirsteth for God, for the living God: when shall I come and appear before God? 3. My tears have been my meat day and night, while they continually say unto me, Where *is* thy God? 4. When I remember these *things*, I pour out my soul in me: for I had gone with the multitude, I went with them to the house of God, with the voice of joy and praise, with a multitude that kept holyday.

Psa. 63:1. O God, thou *art* my God; early will I seek thee: my soul thirsteth for thee, my flesh longeth for thee in a dry and thirsty land, where no water is; 2. To see thy power and thy glory, so *as* I have seen thee in the sanctuary. 3. Because thy lovingkindness *is* better than life, my lips shall praise thee. 4. Thus will I bless thee while I live: I will lift up my hands in thy name. 5. My soul shall be satisfied as *with* marrow and fatness; and my mouth shall praise *thee* with joyful lips: 6. When I remember thee upon my bed, *and* meditate on thee in the *night* watches. 7. Because thou hast been my help, therefore in the shadow of thy wings will I rejoice. 8. My soul followeth hard after thee: thy right hand upholdeth me.

Psa. 69:32. The humble shall see *this*, *and* be glad: and your heart shall live that seek God.

Psa. 70:4. Let all those that seek thee rejoice and be glad in thee: and let such as love thy salvation say continually, Let God be magnified. 5. But I *am* poor and needy; make haste unto me, O God: thou *art* my help and my deliverer; O LORD, make no tarrying.

Psa. 77:1. I cried unto God with my voice, *even* unto God with my voice; and he gave ear unto me. 2. In the day of my trouble I sought the Lord: my sore ran in the night, and ceased not: my soul refused to be comforted. 3. I remembered God, and was troubled: I complained, and my spirit was overwhelmed. 4. Thou holdest mine eyes waking: I am so troubled that I cannot speak. 5. I have considered the days of old, the years of ancient times. 6. I call to remembrance my song in the night: I commune with mine own heart: and my spirit made diligent search. 7. Will the Lord cast off for ever? and will he be favourable no more? 8. Is his mercy clean gone for ever? doth *his* promise fail for evermore? 9. Hath God forgotten to be gracious? hath he in anger shut up his tender mercies?

Psa. 78:34. When he slew them, then they sought him: and they returned and inquired early after God.

Psa. 81:10. I *am* the LORD thy God, which brought thee out of the land of Egypt: open thy mouth wide, and I will fill it.

Psa. 83:16. Fill their faces with shame; that they may seek thy name, O LORD.

Psa. 84:2. My soul longeth, yea, even fainteth for the courts of the LORD: my heart and my flesh crieth out for the living God.

Psa. 105:4. Seek the LORD, and his strength: seek his face evermore.

Psa. 119:2. Blessed *are* they that keep his testimonies, *and that* seek him with the whole heart. 10. With my whole heart have I sought thee: O let me not wander from thy commandments.

Psa. 130:5. I wait for the LORD, my soul doth wait, and in his word do I hope. 6. My soul *waiteth* for the Lord more than they that watch for the morning: *I say*, *more than* they that watch for the morning.

Psa. 143:6. I stretch forth my hands unto thee: my soul *thirsteth* after thee, as a thirsty land.

Psa. 145:18. The LORD *is* nigh unto all them that call upon him, to all that call upon him in truth. 19. He will fulfil the desire of them that fear him: he also will hear their cry, and will save them.

Prov. 2:3. Yea, if thou criest after knowledge, *and* liftest up thy voice for understanding; 4. If thou seekest her as silver, and searchest for her as *for* hid treasures: 5. Then shalt thou understand the fear of the LORD, and find the knowledge of God.

Prov. 8:17. Those that seek me early shall find me. 34. Blessed *is* the man that heareth me, watching daily at my gates, waiting at the posts of my doors.

Prov. 28:5. They that seek the LORD understand all *things*.

Song 3:1. By night on my bed I sought him whom my soul loveth: I sought him, but I found him not. 2. I will rise now, and go about the city in the streets, and in the broad ways I will seek him whom my soul loveth: I sought him, but I found him not. 3. The watchmen that go about the city found me: *to whom I said*, Saw ye him whom my soul loveth? 4. *It was* but a little that I passed from them, but I found him whom my soul loveth: I held him, and would not let him go, until I had brought him into my mother's house, and into the chamber of her that conceived me.

Isa. 8:19. Should not a people seek unto their God? for the living to the dead?

Isa. 26:8. Yea, in the way of thy judgments, O Lord, have we waited for thee; the desire of *our* soul *is* to thy name, and to the remembrance of thee. 9. With my soul have I desired thee in the night; yea, with my spirit within me will I seek thee early:

Isa. 44:3. For I will pour water upon him that is thirsty, and floods upon the dry ground: I will pour my spirit upon thy seed, and my blessing upon thine offspring: 4. And they shall spring up *as* among the grass, as willows by the water courses.

Isa. 45:19. I have not spoken in secret, in a dark place of the earth: I said not unto the seed of Jacob, Seek ye me in vain: I the Lord speak righteousness, I declare things that are right. 22. Look unto me, and be ye saved, all the ends of the earth: for I *am* God, and *there is* none else.

Isa. 49:9. That thou mayest say to the prisoners, Go forth; to them that *are* in darkness, Shew yourselves. They shall feed in the ways, and their pastures *shall be* in all high places. 10. They shall not hunger nor thirst; neither shall the heat nor sun smite them: for he that hath mercy on them shall lead them, even by the springs of water shall he guide them. 11. And I will make all my mountains a way, and my highways shall be exalted. 12. Behold, these shall come from far: and, lo, these from the north and from the west; and these from the land of Sinim. 23. They shall not be ashamed that wait for me.

Isa. 51:1 Hearken to me, ye that follow after righteousness, ye that seek the Lord: look unto the rock *whence* ye are hewn, and to the hole of the pit *whence* ye are digged.

Isa. 55:6. Seek ye the Lord while he may be found, call ye upon him while he is near: 7. Let the wicked forsake his way, and the unrighteous man his thoughts: and let him return unto the Lord, and he will have mercy upon him; and to our God, for he will abundantly pardon.

Isa. 59:20. And the Redeemer shall come to Zion, and unto them that turn from transgression in Jacob, saith the Lord.

Isa. 61:1. The Spirit of the Lord God *is* upon me; because the Lord hath anointed me to preach good tidings unto the meek; he hath sent me to bind up the brokenhearted, to proclaim liberty to the captives, and the opening of the prison to *them that are* bound; 2. To proclaim the acceptable year of the Lord, and the day of vengeance of our God; to comfort all that mourn; 3. To appoint unto them that mourn in Zion, to give unto them beauty for ashes, the oil of joy for mourning, the garment of praise for the spirit of heaviness; that they might

be called trees of righteousness, the planting of the Lord, that he might be glorified.

Jer. 29:13. And ye shall seek me, and find *me*, when ye shall search for me with all your heart.

Jer. 42:3. That the Lord thy God may shew us the way wherein we may walk, and the thing that we may do.

Jer. 50:4. In those days, and in that time, saith the Lord, the children of Israel shall come, they and the children of Judah together, going and weeping: they shall go, and seek the Lord their God.

Lam. 3:25. The Lord *is* good unto them that wait for him, to the soul *that* seeketh him. 26. *It is* good that *a man* should both hope and quietly wait for the salvation of the Lord. 41. Let us lift up our heart with *our* hands unto God in the heavens.

Ezek. 18:21. But if the wicked will turn from all his sins that he hath committed, and keep all my statutes, and do that which is lawful and right, he shall surely live, he shall not die. 22. All his transgressions that he hath committed, they shall not be mentioned unto him: in his righteousness that he hath done he shall live. 23. Have I any pleasure at all that the wicked should die? saith the Lord God: *and* not that he should return from his ways, and live?

Dan. 9:3. I set my face unto the Lord God, to seek by prayer and supplications, with fasting, and sackcloth, and ashes:

Hos. 3:5. Afterward shall the children of Israel return, and seek the Lord their God, and David their king; and shall fear the Lord and his goodness in the latter days.

Hos. 5:15. I will go *and* return to my place, till they acknowledge their offence, and seek my face: in their affliction they will seek me [1 R. V. earnestly] early.

Hos. 10:12. *It is* time to seek the Lord, till he come and rain righteousness upon you.

Joel 2:12. Therefore also now, saith the Lord, turn ye *even* to me with all your heart, and with fasting, and with weeping, and with mourning: 13. And rend your heart, and not your garments, and turn unto the Lord your God: for he *is* gracious and merciful, slow to anger, and of great kindness, and repenteth him of the evil.

Amos 5:4. For thus saith the Lord unto the house of Israel, Seek ye me, and ye shall live: 5. But seek not Beth-el, nor enter into Gilgal, and pass not to Beer-sheba: for Gilgal shall surely go into captivity, and Beth-el shall come to nought. 6. Seek the Lord, and ye shall live; lest he break out like fire in the house of Joseph, and devour *it*, and *there be* none to quench *it* in Beth-el. 8. *Seek him* that maketh the seven stars and Orion, and turneth the shadow of death into the morning, and maketh the day dark with night: that calleth for the waters of the sea, and poureth them out upon the face of the earth: The Lord *is* his name: 14. Seek good, and not evil, that ye may live: and so the LORD, the God of hosts, shall be with you, as ye have spoken.

Amos 8:12. And they shall wander from sea to sea, and from the north even to the east, they shall run to and fro to seek the word of the LORD, and shall not find *it*.

Zeph. 2:3. Seek ye the LORD, all ye meek of the earth, which have wrought his judgment; seek righteousness. seek meekness: it may be ye shall be hid in the day of the LORD's anger.

Zech. 8:20. Thus saith the LORD of hosts; *It shall* yet *come to pass*, that there shall come people, and the inhabitants of many cities: 21. And the inhabitants of one *city* shall go to another, saying, Let us go speedily to pray before the LORD, and to seek the LORD of hosts: I will go also. 22. Yea, many people and strong nations shall come to seek the LORD of hosts in Jerusalem, and to pray before the LORD. 23. Thus saith the LORD of hosts; In those days *it shall come to pass*, that ten men shall take hold out of all languages of the nations, even shall take hold of the skirt of him that is a Jew, saying, We will go with you: for we have heard *that* God *is* with you.

Matt. 5:6. Blessed *are* they which do hunger and thirst after righteousness: for they shall be filled.

Matt. 6:33. But seek ye first the kingdom of God, and his righteousness; and all these things shall be added unto you.

Luke 6:21. Blessed *are ye* that hunger now: for ye shall be filled.

Luke 11:9. And I say unto you, Ask, and it shall be given you; seek, and ye shall find; knock, and it shall be opened unto you. [Matt. 7:7–12.] 10. For every one that asketh receiveth; and he that seeketh findeth; and to him that knocketh it shall be opened. 11. If a son shall ask bread of any of you that is a father, will he give him a stone? or if *he ask* a fish, will he for a fish give him a serpent? 12. Or if he shall ask an egg, will he offer him a scorpion? 13. If ye then, being evil, know how to give good gifts unto your children; how much more shall *your* heavenly Father give the Holy Spirit to them that ask him?

Luke 13:24. Strive to enter in at the strait gate: for many, I say unto you, will seek to enter in, and shall not be able.

Luke 14:26. If any *man* come to me, and hate not his father, and mother, and wife, and children, and brethren, and sisters, yea, and his own life also, he cannot be my disciple. 27. And whosoever doth not bear his cross, and come after me, cannot be my disciple. 28. For which of you, intending to build a tower, sitteth not down first, and counteth the cost, whether he have *sufficient* to finish *it?* 29. Lest haply, after he hath laid the foundation, and is not able to finish *it*, all that behold *it* begin to mock him, 30. Saying, This man began to build, and was not able to finish. 31. Or what king, going to make war against another king,

sitteth not down first, and consulteth whether he be able with ten thousand to meet him that cometh against him with twenty thousand? 32. Or else, while the other is yet a great way off, he sendeth an ambassage, and desireth conditions of peace. 33. So likewise, whosoever he be of you that forsaketh not all that he hath, he cannot be my disciple.

Luke 16:16. The law and the prophets *were* until John: since that time the kingdom of God is preached, and every man presseth into it.

John 6:37. All that the Father giveth me shall come to me; and him that cometh to me I will in no wise cast out.

Acts 2:21. And it shall come to pass, *that* whosoever shall call on the name of the Lord shall be saved.

Acts 17:27. That they should seek the Lord, if haply they might feel after him, and find him, though he be not far from every one of us:

Rom. 3:11. There is none that understandeth, there is none that seeketh after God.

Rom. 10:13. For whosoever shall call upon the name of the Lord shall be saved.

Heb. 7:25. Wherefore he is able also to save them to the uttermost that come unto God by him, seeing he ever liveth to make intercession for them.

Heb. 9:28. So Christ was once offered to bear the sins of many; and unto them that look for him shall he appear the second time without sin unto salvation.

Heb. 11:6. But without faith *it is* impossible to please *him:* for he that cometh to God must believe that he is, and *that* he is a rewarder of them that diligently seek him.

Jas. 4:8. Draw nigh to God, and he will draw nigh to you.

Rev. 3:20. Behold, I stand at the door, and knock: if any man hear my voice, and open the door, I will come in to him, and will sup with him, and he with me.

Rev. 21:6. I will give unto him that is athirst of the fountain of the water of life freely.

Rev. 22:17. And the Spirit and the bride say, Come. And let him that heareth say, Come. And let him that is athirst come. And whosoever will, let him take the water of life freely.

See BACKSLIDERS; PENITENTS; SIN, CONFESSION OF; FORGIVENESS OF.

INSTANCES OF: Asa, 2 Chr. 14:7. Jehoshaphat, 2 Chr. 17:3,4. Uzziah, 2 Chr. 26:5. Hezekiah, 2 Chr. 31:21. Josiah, 2 Chr. 34:3. Ezra, Ezra 7:10. David, Psa. 34:4. Daniel, Dan. 9:3,4. The Magi, Matt. 2:1,2.

See PENITENT; ZEAL.

SEER. See PROPHET.

SEGUB. 1. Son of Hiel, the rebuilder of Jericho, 1 Kin. 16:34.

2. Grandson of Judah, 1 Chr. 2:4,5,21,22.

SEIR. 1. A range of hills trending southwest from the Dead Sea, Deut. 1:2. Along the route from Horeb to Kadesh-barnea, Deut. 1:1,2. Children of Israel journey by, Deut. 1:2; 2:1; 33:2. Originally inhabited by Horites, Gen. 14:6; 36:20–30; Deut. 2:12; and later by the children of Esau after they destroyed the Horim, Deut. 2:12,22, with Gen. 32:3; 33:14,16; 36:8,9; Num. 24:18; Deut. 2:4,5. The southern boundary of the conquests of Joshua, Josh. 11:15–18.

2. A Horite chief, Gen. 36:20,21; 1 Chr. 1:38.

SEIRATH, a city of unknown location, Judg. 3:26.

SEIZIN, of real property.
See LAND.

SELA, called also SELAH. A city in Edom, 2 Kin. 14:7; Isa. 16:1.

SELA-HAMMAHLEKOTH, a rock in the wilderness of Maon, 1 Sam. 23:28.

SELED, a descendant of Jerahmeel, 1 Chr. 2:30.

SELEUCIA, a city of Syria, on the Mediterranean. Paul visits, Acts 13:4.

SELF-CONDEMNATION. 2 Sam. 24: 17. And David spake unto the LORD when he saw the angel that smote the people, and said, Lo, I have sinned, and I have done wickedly : but these sheep, what have they done? let thine hand, I pray thee, be against me, and against my father's house.

1 Kin. 8:31. If any man trespass against his neighbour, and an oath be laid upon him to cause him to swear, and the oath come before thine altar in this house : 32. Then hear thou in heaven, and do, and judge thy servants, condemning the wicked, to bring his way upon his head; and justifying the righteous, to give him according to his righteousness.

Job 9:20. If I justify myself, mine own mouth shall condemn me : if I say, I am perfect, it shall also prove me perverse.

Prov. 5:12. How have I hated instruction, and my heart despised reproof; 13. And have not obeyed the voice of my teachers, nor inclined mine ear to them that instructed me !

Matt. 23:31. Wherefore ye be witnesses unto yourselves, that ye are the children of them which killed the prophets.

Matt. 25:24. Then he which had received the one talent came and said, Lord, I knew thee that thou art an hard man, reaping where thou hast not sown, and gathering where thou hast not strawed : [Luke 19:21, 22.] 25. And I was afraid, and went and hid thy talent in the earth : lo, *there* thou hast *that is* thine. 26. His lord answered and said unto him, *Thou* wicked and slothful servant, thou knewest that I reap where I sowed not, and gather where I have not strawed : 27. Thou oughtest therefore to have put my money to the exchangers, and *then* at my coming I should have received mine own with usury.

Mark 12:1. And he began to speak unto them by parables. A *certain* man planted a vineyard, and set an hedge about *it*, and digged *a place for* the winefat, and built a tower, and let it out to husbandmen, and went into a far country. 2. And at the season he sent to the husbandmen a servant, that he might receive from the husbandmen of the fruit of the vineyard. 3. And they caught *him*, and beat him, and sent *him* away empty. 4. And again he sent unto them another servant; and at him they cast stones, and wounded *him* in the head, and sent *him* away shamefully handled. 5. And again he sent another; and him they killed, and many others; beating some, and killing some. 6. Having yet therefore one son, his wellbeloved, he sent him also last unto them, saying, They will reverence my son. 7. But those husbandmen said among themselves, This is the heir; come, let us kill him, and the inheritance shall be our's. 8. And they took him, and killed *him*, and cast *him* out of the vineyard. 9. What shall therefore the lord of the vineyard do? he will come and destroy the husbandmen, and will give the vineyard unto others. 10. And have ye not read this scripture; The stone which the builders rejected is become the head of the corner: 11. This was the Lord's doing, and it is marvellous in our eyes? 12. And they sought to lay hold on him, but feared the people : for they knew that he had spoken the parable against them : and they left him, and went their way. Matt. 21:33–41.

John 8:9. And they which heard *it*, being convicted by *their own* conscience, went out one by one, beginning at the eldest, *even* unto the last: and Jesus was left alone, and the woman standing in the midst.

Acts 22:24. The chief captain commanded him to be brought into the castle, and bade that he should be examined by scourging; that he might know wherefore they cried so against him.

Rom. 2:1. Therefore thou art inexcusable, O man, whosoever thou art that judgest: for wherein thou judgest another, thou condemnest thyself; for thou that judgest doest the same things.

See SELF-CRIMINATION; REMORSE; REPENTANCE.

INSTANCES OF: Achan, Josh. 7:19–25. David, 2 Sam. 12:5–7. Ahab, 1 Kin. 20: 39–42.

SELF-CONFIDENCE. See CONFIDENCE, FALSE.

SELF-CONTROL. Of Saul, 1 Sam. 10:27. Of David, 1 Sam. 24:1–15; 26:1–20. Of Jesus, Matt. 26:62,63; 27:12–14.

See ABSTINENCE, TOTAL; GRACES, CHRISTIAN; PATIENCE; TACT; also, RASHNESS.

SELF-CRIMINATION, Num. 5:11–27; 1 Kin. 8:31,32; Acts 22:24.

See SELF-CONDEMNATION.

INSTANCES OF: Achan, Josh. 7:19–25.

SELF-DECEPTION, Jas. 1:26.

See CONFIDENCE, FALSE; SECURITY, FALSE.

SELF-DEFENSE, accused heard in, Matt. 27:11–14; Mark 15:2–5; Luke 23:3; John 7:51; Acts 2:37–40; 22; 23; 24:10–21; 26.

SELF-DELUSION. A characteristic of the wicked, Psa. 49:18. Prosperity frequently leads to, Psa. 30:6; Hos. 12:8; Luke 12:17–19. Obstinate sinners often given up to, Psa. 81:11,12; Hos. 4:17; 2 Thess. 2:10,11.

Exhibited in thinking that: Our own ways are right, Prov. 14:12; we should adhere to established wicked practices, Jer. 44:17; we are pure, Prov. 30:12; we are better than others, Luke 18:11; we are rich in spiritual things, Rev. 3:17; we may have peace while in sin, Deut. 29:19; we are above adversity, Psa. 10:6; gifts entitle us to heaven, Matt. 7:21,22; privileges entitle us to heaven, Matt. 3:9; Luke 13:25,26; God will not punish our sins, Jer. 5:12; Christ will not come to judge, 2 Pet. 3:4; our lives will be prolonged, Isa. 56:12; Luke 12:19; Jas. 4:13.

Frequently persevered in to the last, Matt. 7:22; 25:11,12; Luke 13:24,25. Fatal consequences of, Matt. 7:23; 24:48–51; Luke 12:20; 1 Thess. 5:3.

EXEMPLIFIED: Ahab, 1 Kin. 20:27,34. Israelites, Hos. 12:8. Jews, John 8:33,41. Church of Laodicea, Rev. 3:17.—*Bible Text-Book.*

See CONFIDENCE, FALSE; SECURITY, FALSE.

SELF-DENIAL. Gen. 22:12. And he said, Lay not thine hand upon the lad, neither do thou any thing unto him: for now I know that thou fearest God, seeing thou hast not withheld thy son, thine only *son* from me. with *vs.* 1–12.

2 Sam. 24:24. And the king said unto Araunah, Nay; but I will surely buy *it* of thee at a price: neither will I offer burnt offerings unto the LORD my God of that which doth cost me nothing. So David bought the threshingfloor and the oxen for fifty shekels of silver.

Psa. 132:3. Surely I will not come into the tabernacle of my house, nor go up into my bed; 4. I will not give sleep to mine eyes, *or* slumber to mine eyelids, 5. Until I find out a place for the LORD, an habitation for the mighty *God* of Jacob.

Prov. 16:32. *He that is* slow to anger *is* better than the mighty; and he that ruleth his spirit than he that taketh a city.

Prov. 23:2. Put a knife to thy throat, if thou *be* a man given to appetite.

Dan. 10:3. I ate no pleasant bread, neither came flesh nor wine in my mouth, neither did I anoint myself at all, till three whole weeks were fulfilled.

Matt. 5:29. And if thy right eye offend thee, pluck it out, and cast *it* from thee: for it is profitable for thee that one of thy members should perish, and not *that* thy whole body should be cast into hell. 30. And if thy right hand offend thee, cut it off, and cast *it* from thee: for it is profitable for thee that one of thy members should perish, and not *that* thy whole body should be cast into hell. Mark 9:43.

Matt. 8:19. And a certain scribe came, and said unto him, Master, I will follow thee whithersoever thou goest. 20. And Jesus saith unto him, The foxes have holes, and the birds of the air *have* nests; but the Son of man hath not where to lay *his* head. [Luke 9:57,58.] 21. And another of his disciples said unto him, Lord, suffer me first to go and bury my father. 22. But Jesus said unto him, Follow me; and let the dead bury their dead. Luke 9:59,60.

Matt. 10:37. He that loveth father or mother more than me is not worthy of me: and he that loveth son or daughter more than me is not worthy of me. 38. And he that taketh not his cross, and followeth after me, is not worthy of me. 39. He that findeth his life shall lose it: and he that loseth his life for my sake shall find it.

Matt. 13:44. Again, the kingdom of heaven is like unto treasure hid in a field; the which when a man hath found, he hideth, and for joy thereof goeth and selleth all that he hath, and buyeth that field. 45. Again, the kingdom of heaven is like unto a merchant man, seeking goodly pearls: 46. Who, when he had found one pearl of great price, went and sold all that he had, and bought it.

Matt. 16:24. Then said Jesus unto his disciples, If any *man* will come after me, let him deny himself, and take up his cross, and follow me. 25. For whosoever will save his life shall lose it: and whosoever will lose his life for my sake shall find it. Mark 8:34,35; Luke 9:23,24.

Matt. 18:8. Wherefore if thy hand or thy foot offend thee, cut them off, and cast *them* from thee: it is better for thee to enter into life halt or maimed, rather than having two hands or two feet to be cast into everlasting fire. 9. And if thine eye offend thee, pluck it out, and cast *it* from thee: it is better for thee to enter into life with one eye, rather than having two eyes to be cast into hell fire. Mark 9:43.

Matt. 19:12. For there are some eunuchs, which were so born from *their* mother's womb: and there are some eunuchs, which were made eunuchs of men: and there be eunuchs, which have made themselves eunuchs for the kingdom of heaven's sake. He that is able to receive *it*, let him receive *it*. 21. Jesus said unto him, If thou wilt be perfect, go *and* sell that thou hast, and give to the poor, and thou shalt have treasure in heaven: and come *and* follow me. Luke 12:33.

Luke 5:11. And when they had brought their ships to land, they forsook all, and followed him. 27. And after these things he went forth, and saw a publican, named Levi, sitting at the receipt of custom: and he said unto him, Follow me. 28. And he left all, rose up, and followed him. Mark 2:14.

Luke 14:26. If any *man* come to me, and hate not his father, and mother, and wife, and children, and brethren, and sisters, yea, and his own life also, he cannot be my disciple. 27. And whosoever doth not bear his cross, and come after me, cannot be my disciple. 33. So likewise, whosoever he be of you that forsaketh not all that he hath, he cannot be my disciple. *vs.* 28–32.

Luke 18:27. And he said, The things which are impossible with men are possible with God. 28. Then Peter said, Lo, we have left all, and followed thee. 29. And he said unto them, Verily I say unto you, There is no man that hath left house, or parents, or brethren, or wife, or children, for the kingdom of God's sake, [Mark 10:29.] 30. Who shall not receive manifold more in this present time, and in the world to come life everlasting.

Luke 21:2. And he saw also a certain poor widow casting in thither two mites. 3. And he said, Of a truth I say unto you, that this poor widow hath cast in more than they all: 4. For all these have of their abundance cast in unto the offerings of God : but she of her penury hath cast in all the living that she had. Mark 12:43,44.

John 12:25. He that loveth his life shall lose it ; and he that hateth his life in this world shall keep it unto life eternal. Matt. 16:25; Mark 8:35.

Acts 20:22. And now, behold, I go bound in the spirit unto Jerusalem, not knowing the things that shall befall me there: 23. Save that the Holy Ghost witnesseth in every city, saying that bonds and afflictions abide me. 24. But none of these things move me, neither count I my life dear unto myself, so that I might finish my course with joy, and the ministry, which I have received of the Lord Jesus, to testify the gospel of the grace of God.

Acts 21:13. Then Paul answered, What mean ye to weep and to break mine heart? for I am ready not to be bound only, but also to die at Jerusalem for the name of the Lord Jesus.

Rom. 6:6. Knowing this, that our old man is crucified with *him*, that the body of sin might be destroyed, that henceforth we should not serve sin.

Rom. 8:12. Therefore, brethren, we are debtors, not to the flesh, to live after the flesh. 13. For if ye live after the flesh, ye shall die: but if ye through the Spirit do mortify the deeds of the body, ye shall live. 35. Who shall separate us from the love of Christ? *shall* tribulation, or distress, or persecution, or famine, or nakedness, or peril, or sword? 36. As it is written, For thy sake we are killed all the day long ; we are accounted as sheep for the slaughter.

Rom. 13:14. But put ye on the Lord Jesus Christ, and make not provision for the flesh, to *fulfil* the lusts *thereof*.

Rom. 14:1. Him that is weak in the faith receive ye, *but* not to doubtful disputations. 2. For one believeth that he may eat all things: another, who is weak, eateth herbs. 3. Let not him that eateth despise him that eateth not ; and let not him which eateth not judge him that eateth : for God hath received him. 4. Who art thou that judgest another man's servant? to his own master

he standeth or falleth. Yea, he shall be holden up: for God is able to make him stand. 5. One man esteemeth one day above another: another esteemeth every day *alike*. Let every man be fully persuaded in his own mind. 6. He that regardeth the day, regardeth *it* unto the Lord ; and he that regardeth not the day, to the Lord he doth not regard *it*. He that eateth, eateth to the Lord, for he giveth God thanks; and he that eateth not, to the Lord he eateth not, and giveth God thanks. 7. For none of us liveth to himself, and no man dieth to himself. 8. For whether we live, we live unto the Lord ; and whether we die, we die unto the Lord: whether we live therefore, or die, we are the Lord's. 9. For to this end Christ both died, and rose, and revived, that he might be Lord both of the dead and living. 10. But why dost thou judge thy brother? or why dost thou set at nought thy brother? for we shall all stand before the judgment seat of Christ. 11. For it is written, *As* I live, saith the Lord, every knee shall bow to me, and every tongue shall confess to God. 12. So then every one of us shall give account of himself to God. 13. Let us not therefore judge one another any more: but judge this rather, that no man put a stumblingblock or an occasion to fall in *his* brother's way. 14. I know, and am persuaded by the Lord Jesus, that *there is* nothing unclean of itself: but to him that esteemeth any thing to be unclean, to him *it is* unclean. 15. But if thy brother be grieved with *thy* meat, now walkest thou not charitably. Destroy not him with thy meat, for whom Christ died. 16. Let not then your good be evil spoken of : 17. For the kingdom of God is not meat and drink ; but righteousness, and peace, and joy in the Holy Ghost. 18. For he that in these things serveth Christ *is* acceptable to God, and approved of men. 19. Let us therefore follow after the things which make for peace, and things wherewith one may edify another. 20. For meat destroy not the work of God. All things indeed *are* pure ; but *it is* evil for that man who eateth with offence. 21. *It is* good neither to eat flesh, nor to drink wine, nor *any thing* whereby thy brother stumbleth, or is offended, or is made weak. 22. Hast thou faith? have *it* to thyself before God. Happy *is* he that condemneth not himself in that thing which he alloweth.

Rom. 15:1. We then that are strong ought to bear the infirmities of the weak, and not to please ourselves. 2. Let every one of us please *his* neighbour for *his* good to edification. 3. For even Christ pleased not himself ; but, as it is written, The reproaches of them that reproached thee fell on me. 4. For whatsoever things were written aforetime were written for our learning, that we through patience and comfort of the scriptures might have hope. 5. Now the **God** of patience and consolation grant you to be

1252 SELF-DENIAL.—INSTANCES OF.

likeminded one toward another according to Christ Jesus:

1 Cor. 6:12. All things are lawful unto me, but all things are not expedient: all things are lawful for me, but I will not be brought under the power of any.

1 Cor. 8:10. For if any man see thee which hast knowledge sit at meat in the idol's temple, shall not the conscience of him which is weak be emboldened to eat those things which are offered to idols; 11. And through thy knowledge shall the weak brother perish, for whom Christ died? 12. But when ye sin so against the brethren, and wound their weak conscience, ye sin against Christ. 13. Wherefore, if meat make my brother to offend, I will eat no flesh while the world standeth, lest I make my brother to offend.

1 Cor. 9:12. If others be partakers of this power over you, are not we rather? Nevertheless we have not used this power; but suffer all things, lest we should hinder the gospel of Christ. 15. I have used none of these things: neither have I written these things, that it should be so done unto me: for it were better for me to die, than that any man should make my glorying void. 18. What is my reward then? Verily that, when I preach the gospel, I may make the gospel of Christ without charge, that I abuse not my power in the gospel. 19. For though I be free from all men, yet have I made myself servant unto all, that I might gain the more. 23. This I do for the gospel's sake, that I might be partaker thereof with you. 25. Every man that striveth for the mastery is temperate in all things. Now they do it to obtain a corruptible crown; but we an incorruptible. 26. I therefore so run, not as uncertainly; so fight I, not as one that beateth the air: 27. But I keep under my body, and bring it into subjection: lest that by any means, when I have preached to others, I myself should be a castaway.

1 Cor. 10:23. All things are lawful for me, but all things are not expedient: all things are lawful for me, but all things edify not. 24. Let no man seek his own, but every man another's wealth.

2 Cor. 6:3. Giving no offence in any thing, that the ministry be not blamed:

Gal. 2:20. I am crucified with Christ: nevertheless I live: yet not I, but Christ liveth in me: and the life which I now live in the flesh I live by the faith of the Son of God, who loved me, and gave himself for me.

Gal. 5:16. This I say then, Walk in the Spirit, and ye shall not fulfil the lust of the flesh. 17. For the flesh lusteth against the Spirit, and the Spirit against the flesh: and these are contrary the one to the other: so that ye cannot do the things that ye would. 24. And they that are Christ's have crucified the flesh with the affections and lusts.

Gal. 6:14. But God forbid that I should glory, save in the cross of our Lord Jesus Christ, by whom the world is crucified unto me, and I unto the world.

Phil. 2:4. Look not every man on his own things, but every man also on the things of others. vs. 5–8.

Phil. 3:7. But what things were gain to me, those I counted loss for Christ. 8. Yea doubtless, and I count all things but loss for the excellency of the knowledge of Christ Jesus my Lord: for whom I have suffered the loss of all things, and do count them but dung, that I may win Christ, 9. And be found in him, not having mine own righteousness, which is of the law, but that which is through the faith of Christ, the righteousness which is of God by faith:

Col. 3:5. Mortify therefore your members which are upon the earth; fornication, uncleanness, inordinate affection, evil concupiscence, and coveteousness, which is idolatry:

2 Tim. 2:4. No man that warreth entangleth himself with the affairs of this life; that he may please him who hath chosen him to be a soldier.

Tit. 2:12. Teaching us that, denying ungodliness and worldly lusts, we should live soberly, righteously, and godly, in this present world;

Heb. 13:13. Let us go forth therefore unto him without the camp, bearing his reproach.

1 Pet. 2:11. Dearly beloved, I beseech you as strangers and pilgrims, abstain from fleshly lusts, which war against the soul; 12. Having your conversation honest among the Gentiles: that, whereas they speak against you as evildoers, they may by your good works, which they shall behold, glorify God in the day of visitation. 13. Submit yourselves to every ordinance of man for the Lord's sake: whether it be to the king, as supreme; 14. Or unto governors, as unto them that are sent by him for the punishment of evildoers, and for the praise of them that do well. 15. For so is the will of God, that with well doing ye may put to silence the ignorance of foolish men: 16. As free, and not using your liberty for a cloke of maliciousness, but as the servants of God.

1 Pet. 4:1. Forasmuch then as Christ hath suffered for us in the flesh, arm yourselves likewise with the same mind: for he that hath suffered in the flesh hath ceased from sin; 2. That he no longer should live the rest of his time in the flesh to the lusts of men, but to the will of God.

3 John 7. Because that for his name's sake they went forth, taking nothing of the Gentiles.

Rev. 12:11. And they overcame him by the blood of the Lamb, and by the word of their testimony; and they loved not their lives unto the death.

See CROSS; HUMILITY.

INSTANCES OF: Abraham, when he accorded to Lot, his junior, his preference of the land of Canaan, Gen. 13:9, with 17:8. Moses, in choosing rather to suffer affliction with the people of God than enjoy the pleasures of sin, Heb. 11:25; in taking no compensation from the Israelites for his services, Num. 16:15. Samuel, in his administration of justice, 1 Sam. 12:3,4. The widow of Zarephath, in sharing with Elijah the last of her sustenance, 1 Kin 17:12–15. Daniel, in his abstemiousness, Dan. 1:8; in refusing rewards from Belshazzar, Dan. 5:16,17. Esther, in risking her life for the deliverance of her people, Esth. 4:16. The Rechabites, in refusing to drink wine or strong drink, or even to plant vineyards. Jer. 35:6,7.

Peter and other apostles, in abandoning their vocations and following Jesus, Matt. 4: 20; 9:9; Mark 1:16–20; 2:14; Luke 5:11,27,28; in forsaking all and following Jesus, Matt. 19:27; Mark 10:28. The widow, who cast her all into the treasury, Luke 21:4. The early Christians, in having everything in common, Acts 2:44,45; 4:34. Joses, in selling his possessions, and giving all that he received to the apostles, Acts 4:36,37. Paul, in not counting even his life dear to himself, Acts 20:24; Phil. 3:7,8; in not coveting any man's silver or gold or apparel, Acts 20: 33; in laboring for his own support while he also taught, Acts 20:34,35; 1 Cor. 4:12: 10:33.

SELF-EXALTATION. Job 12:3. But I have understanding as well as you; I *am* not inferior to you: yea, who knoweth not such things as these?

Ezek. 31:10. Therefore thus saith the Lord God; Because thou hast lifted up thyself in height, and he hath shot up his top among the thick boughs, and his heart is lifted up in his height; 11. I have therefore delivered him into the hand of the mighty one of the heathen; he shall surely deal with him: I have driven him out for his wickedness. 12. And strangers, the terrible of the nations, have cut him off, and have left him: upon the mountains and in all the valleys his branches are fallen, and his boughs are broken by all the rivers of the land; and all the people of the earth are gone down from his shadow, and have left him. 13. Upon his ruin shall all the fowls of the heaven remain, and all the beasts of the field shall be upon his branches: 14. To the end that none of all the trees by the waters exalt themselves for their height, neither shoot up their top among the thick boughs, neither their trees stand up in their height, all that drink water: for they are all delivered unto death, to the nether parts of the earth, in the midst of the children of men, with them that go down to the pit.

Obad. 3. The pride of thine heart hath deceived thee, thou that dwellest in the clefts of the rock, whose habitation *is* high: that saith in his heart, Who shall bring me down to the ground? 4. Though thou exalt *thyself* as the eagle, and though thou set thy nest among the stars, thence will I bring thee down, saith the Lord.

Luke 14:7. And he put forth a parable to those which were bidden, when he marked how they chose out the chief rooms; saying unto them, 8. When thou art bidden of any *man* to a wedding, sit not down in the highest room; lest a more honourable man than thou be bidden of him; 9. And he that bade thee and him come and say to thee, Give this man place; and thou begin with shame to take the lowest room. 10. But when thou art bidden, go and sit down in the lowest room; that when he that bade thee cometh, he may say unto thee, Friend, go up higher: then shalt thou have worship in the presence of them that sit at meat with thee. 11. For whosoever exalteth himself shall be abased; and he that humbleth himself shall be exalted.

2 Cor. 10:5. Casting down imaginations, and every high thing that exalteth itself against the knowledge of God, and bringing into captivity every thought to the obedience of Christ: 17. But he that glorieth, let him glory in the Lord. 18. For not he that commendeth himself is approved, but whom the Lord commendeth.

Gal. 6:3. If a man think himself to be something, when he is nothing, he deceiveth himself.

2 Thess. 2:4. Who opposeth and exalteth himself above all that is called God, or that is worshipped; so that he as God sitteth in the temple of God, shewing himself that he is God.

See Pride; Selfishness; Self-Righteousness.

INSTANCES OF: Pharaoh, Ex. 9:17. Korah, Dathan, and Abiram, Num. 16:1-3. Sennacherib, 2 Chr. 32:9–19. Prince of Tyre, making himself God, Ezek. 28:2,9. Nebuchadnezzar, Dan. 4:30; 5:20. Belshazzar, Dan. 5:23. Simon the sorcerer, Acts 8:9. Herod, when defied by the people, Acts 12: 20–23.

SELF-EXAMINATION. Job 13:23. How many *are* mine iniquities and sins? make me to know my transgression and my sin.

Psa. 4:4. Stand in awe, and sin not: commune with your own heart upon your bed, and be still.

Psa. 19:12. Who can understand *his* errors? cleanse thou me from secret *faults*.

Psa. 26:2. Examine me, O Lord, and prove me; try my reins and my heart.

Psa. 77:6. I call to remembrance my song in the night: I commune with mine own heart: and my spirit made diligent search.

Psa. 119:59. I thought on my ways, and turned my feet unto thy testimonies.

Psa. 139:23. Search me, O God, and know my heart: try me, and know my thoughts: 24. And see if *there be any* wicked way in me, and lead me in the way everlasting.

Jer. 17:9. The heart *is* deceitful above all *things*, and desperately ˡ wicked: who can know it? [ᴸ R. V. sick]

Lam. 3:40. Let us search and try our ways, and turn again to the LORD.

Hag. 1:7. Thus saith the LORD of hosts; Consider your ways.

Matt. 26:22. And they were exceeding sorrowful, and began every one of them to say unto him, Lord, is it I? Mark 14:19.

1 Cor. 11:27. Wherefore whosoever shall eat this bread, and drink *this* cup of the Lord, unworthily, shall be guilty of the body and blood of the Lord. 28. But let a man examine himself, and so let him eat of *that* bread, and drink of *that* cup. 31. For if we would judge ourselves, we should not be judged.

2 Cor. 13:5. Examine yourselves, whether ye be in the faith; prove your own selves. Know ye not your own selves, how that Jesus Christ is in you, except ye be reprobates?

Gal. 6:3. For if a man think himself to be something, when he is nothing, he deceiveth himself. 4. But let every man prove his own work, and then shall he have rejoicing in himself alone, and not in another. 5. For every man shall bear his own burden.

See MEDITATION; REPENTANCE; SIN, CONFESSION OF.

SELF-INDULGENCE. INSTANCES OF: Solomon, Eccl. 2:10. The rich fool, Luke 12:16–20. Dives, Luke 16:19.

See GLUTTONY; IDLENESS; SLOTHFULNESS; also SELF-DENIAL.

SELFISHNESS. Gen. 4:9. And the LORD said unto Cain, Where *is* Abel thy brother? And he said, I know not: *Am* I my brother's keeper?

Num. 32:6. And Moses said unto the children of Gad and to the children of Reuben, Shall your brethren go to war, and shall ye sit here?

Psa. 38:11. My lovers and my friends stand aloof from my sore; and my kinsmen stand afar off.

Prov. 11:26. He that withholdeth corn, the people shall curse him: but blessing *shall be* upon the head of him that selleth *it*.

Prov. 18:17. *He that is* first in his own cause *seemeth* just; but his neighbour cometh and searcheth him.

Prov. 24:11. If thou forbear to deliver *them that are* drawn unto death, and *those that are* ready to be slain; 12. If thou sayest, Behold, we knew it not; doth not he that pondereth the heart consider *it?* and he that keepeth thy soul, doth *not* he know *it?* and shall *not* he render to *every* man according to his works?

Prov. 28:27. He that giveth unto the poor shall not lack: but he that hideth his eyes shall have many a curse.

Ezek. 34:18. *Seemeth it* a small thing unto you to have eaten up the good pasture, but ye must tread down with your feet the residue of your pastures? and to have drunk of the deep waters, but ye must foul the residue with your feet?

Mic. 3:11. The heads thereof judge for reward, and the priests thereof teach for hire, and the prophets thereof divine for money: yet will they lean upon the LORD, and say, *Is* not the LORD among us? none evil can come upon us.

Hag. 1:4. *Is it* time for you, O ye, to dwell in your cieled houses, and this house *lie* waste? 9. Ye looked for much, and, lo, *it came* to little; and when ye brought *it* home, I did blow upon it. Why? saith the LORD of hosts. Because of mine house that *is* waste, and ye run every man unto his own house. 10. Therefore the heaven over you is stayed from dew, and the earth is stayed *from* her fruit.

Zech. 7:6. When ye did eat, and when ye did drink, did not ye eat *for yourselves*, and drink *for yourselves?*

Mal. 1:10. Who *is there* even among you that would shut the doors *for nought?* neither do ye kindle *fire* on mine altar for nought.

Matt. 19:21. Jesus said unto him, If thou wilt be perfect, go *and* sell that thou hast, and give to the poor, and thou shalt have treasure in heaven: and come *and* follow me. 22. But when the young man heard that saying, he went away sorrowful: for he had great possessions.

Luke 6:32. If ye love them which love you, what thank have ye? for sinners also love those that love them. 33. And if ye do good to them which do good to you, what thank have ye? for sinners also do even the same. 34. And if ye lend *to them* of whom ye hope to receive, what thank have ye? for sinners also lend to sinners, to receive as much again.

Rom. 14:15. But if thy brother be grieved with *thy* meat, now walkest thou not charitably. Destroy not him with thy meat, for whom Christ died.

Rom. 15:1. We then that are strong ought to bear the infirmities of the weak, and not to please ourselves. 2. Let every one of us please *his* neighbour for *his* good to edification. 3. For even Christ pleased not himself;

1 Cor. 10:24. Let no man seek his own, but every man another's *wealth*.

2 Cor. 5:15. He died for all, that they which live should not henceforth live unto themselves, but unto him which died for them, and rose again.

Gal. 6:2. Bear ye one another's burdens, and so fulfil the law of Christ.

Phil. 2:4. Look not every man on his own things, but every man also on the things of others. 20. I have no man likeminded, who will naturally care for your state. 21. For all seek their own, not the things which are Jesus Christ's.

2 Tim. 3:2. For men shall be lovers of their own selves, covetous, boasters, proud, blasphemers, disobedient to parents, unthankful, unholy. 3. Without natural affection, trucebreakers, false accusers, incontinent,

fierce, despisers of those that are good, 4. Traitors, heady, highminded, lovers of pleasures more than lovers of God;

Jas. 2:15. If a brother or sister be naked, and destitute of daily food, 16. And one of you say unto them, Depart in peace, be *ye* warmed and filled; notwithstanding ye give them not those things which are needful to the body; what *doth it* profit?

1 John 3:17. Whoso hath this world's good, and seeth his brother have need, and shutteth up his bowels *of compassion* from him, how dwelleth the love of God in him?

See LIBERALITY; POOR; UNSELFISHNESS.

SELF-RIGHTEOUSNESS. Num. 16: 3. And they gathered themselves together against Moses and against Aaron, and said unto them, *Ye take* too much upon you, seeing all the congregation *are* holy, every one of them, and the LORD *is* among them: wherefore then lift ye up yourselves above the congregation of the LORD?

Deut. 9:4. Speak not thou in thine heart, after that the LORD thy God hath cast them out from before thee, saying, For my righteousness the LORD hath brought me in to possess this land: but for the wickedness of these nations the LORD doth drive them out from before thee. 5. Not for thy righteousness, or for the uprightness of thine heart, dost thou go to possess their land: but for the wickedness of these nations the LORD thy God doth drive them out from before thee, and that he may perform the word which the LORD sware unto thy fathers, Abraham, Isaac, and Jacob. 6. Understand therefore, that the LORD thy God giveth thee not this good land to possess it for thy righteousness; for thou *art* a stiffnecked people.

1 Sam. 2:9. He will keep the feet of his saints, and the wicked shall be silent in darkness; for by strength shall no man prevail.

Job 6:13. *Is* not my help in me? and is wisdom driven quite from me?

Job 11:4. For thou hast said, My doctrine *is* pure, and I am clean in thine eyes. 5. But oh that God would speak, and open his lips against thee; 6. And that he would shew thee the secrets of wisdom, that *they are* double to that which is! Know therefore that God exacteth of thee *less* than thine iniquity *deserveth.*

Job 12:2. No doubt but ye *are* the people, and wisdom shall die with you.

Job 13:3. Surely I would speak to the Almighty, and I desire to reason with God. 13. Hold your peace, let me alone, that I may speak, and let come on me what *will.* 15. Though he slay me, yet will I trust in him: but I will maintain mine own ways before him. 18. Behold now, I have ordered *my* cause; I know that I shall be justified. 19. Who *is* he *that* will plead with me? for now, if I hold my tongue, I shall give up the ghost.

Job 16:17. Not for *any* injustice in mine

hands: also my prayer *is* pure. 18. O earth, cover not thou my blood, and let my cry have no place.

Job 18:2. How long *will it be ere* ye make an end of words? mark, and afterwards we will speak. 3. Wherefore are we counted as beasts, *and* reputed vile in your sight? 4. He teareth himself in his anger: shall the earth be forsaken for thee? and shall the rock be removed out of his place?

Job 21:27. Behold, I know your thoughts, and the devices *which* ye wrongfully imagine against me. 28. For ye say, Where *is* the house of the prince? and where *are* the dwelling places of the wicked? 29. Have ye not asked them that go by the way? and do ye not know their tokens,

Job 22:2. Can a man be profitable unto God, as he that is wise may be profitable unto himself? 3. *Is it* any pleasure to the Almighty, that thou art righteous? or *is it* gain *to him*, that thou makest thy ways perfect?

Job 32:1. So these three men ceased to answer Job, because he *was* righteous in his own eyes. 2. Then was kindled the wrath of Elihu the son of Barachel the Buzite, of the kindred of Ram: against Job was his wrath kindled, because he justified himself rather than God.

Job 33:8. Surely thou hast spoken in mine hearing, and I have heard the voice of *thy* words, *saying,* 9. I am clean without transgression, I *am* innocent; neither *is there* iniquity in me.

Job 35:2. Thinkest thou this to be right, *that* thou saidst, My righteousness *is* more than God's? 7. If thou be righteous, what givest thou him? or what receiveth he of thine hand? 8. Thy wickedness *may hurt* a man as thou *art;* and thy righteousness *may profit* the son of man.

Psa. 10:5. His ways are always grievous. thy judgments *are* far above out of his sight: *as for* all his enemies, he puffeth at them. 6. He hath said in his heart, I shall not be moved: for *I shall* never *be* in adversity.

Prov. 12:15. The way of a fool *is* right in his own eyes: but he that hearkeneth unto counsel *is* wise.

Prov. 14:12. There is a way which seemeth right unto a man, but the end thereof *are* the ways of death.

Prov. 16:2. All the ways of a man *are* clean in his own eyes; but the LORD weigheth the spirits.

Prov. 20:6. Most men will proclaim every one his own goodness: but a faithful man who can find?

Prov. 21:2. Every way of a man *is* right in his own eyes: but the LORD pondereth the hearts.

Prov. 25:14. Whoso boasteth himself of a false gift *is like* clouds and wind without rain. 27. *It is* not good to eat much honey: so *for men* to search their own glory *is not* glory.

Prov. 26:12. Seest thou a man wise in his own conceit? *there is* more hope of a fool than of him.

Prov. 27:2. Let another man praise thee, and not thine own mouth; a stranger, and not thine own lips.

21. *As* the fining pot for silver, and the furnace for gold; so *is* a man to his praise.

Prov. 28:13. He that covereth his sins shall not prosper: but whoso confesseth and forsaketh *them* shall have mercy. 26. He that trusteth in his own heart is a fool: but whoso walketh wisely, he shall be delivered.

Prov. 30:12. *There is* a generation *that are* pure in their own eyes, and *yet* is not washed from their filthiness. 13. *There is* a generation, O how lofty are their eyes! and their eyelids are lifted up.

Isa. 5:21. Woe unto *them that are* wise in their own eyes, and prudent in their own sight!

Isa. 28:17. Judgment also will I lay to the line, and righteousness to the plummet: and the hail shall sweep away the refuge of lies, and the waters shall overflow the hiding place. 20. The bed is shorter than that *a man* can stretch himself *on it:* and the covering narrower than that he can wrap himself *in it.*

Isa. 47:7. And thou saidst, I shall be a lady for ever: *so* that thou didst not lay these *things* to thy heart, neither didst remember the latter end of it.

Isa. 50:11. Behold, all ye that kindle a fire, that compass *yourselves* about with sparks: walk in the light of your fire, and in the sparks *that* ye have kindled. This shall ye have of mine hand; ye shall lie down in sorrow.

Isa. 64:6. But we are all as an unclean *thing,* and all our righteousnesses *are* as filthy rags;

Isa. 65:3. A people that provoketh me to anger continually to my face; that sacrificeth in gardens, and burneth incense upon altars of brick; 4. Which remain among the graves, and lodge in the monuments, which eat swine's flesh, and broth of abominable *things is in* their vessels; 5. Which say, Stand by thyself, come not near to me; for I am holier than thou. These *are* a smoke in my nose, a fire that burneth all the day.

Jer. 2:13. For my people have committed two evils; they have forsaken me the fountain of living waters, *and* hewed them out cisterns, broken cisterns, that can hold no water. 22. For though thou wash thee with nitre [lye, *R. V.*], and take thee much sope, *yet* thine iniquity is marked before me, saith the Lord God. 23. How canst thou say, I am not polluted, I have not gone after Baalim? see thy way in the valley, know what thou hast done: 34. Also in thy skirts is found the blood of the souls of the poor innocents: I have not found it by secret search, but upon all these. 35.

Yet thou sayest, Because I am innocent, surely his anger shall turn from me. Behold, I will plead with thee, because thou sayest, I have not sinned.

Jer. 7:4. Trust ye not in lying words, saying, The temple of the Lord, The temple of the Lord, The temple of the Lord, *are* these.

Jer. 8:8. How do ye say, We *are* wise, and the law of the Lord *is* with us? Lo, certainly in vain made he *it;* the pen of the scribes *is* in vain.

Jer. 17:5. Thus saith the Lord; Cursed *be* the man that trusteth in man, and maketh flesh his arm, and whose heart departeth from the Lord.

Jer. 49:4. Wherefore gloriest thou in the valleys, thy flowing valley, O backsliding daughter? that trusted in her treasures, *saying,* Who shall come unto me? 16. Thy terribleness hath deceived thee, *and* the pride of thine heart, O thou that dwellest in the clefts of the rock, that holdest the height of the hill: though thou shouldest make thy nest as high as the eagle, I will bring thee down from thence, saith the Lord.

Ezek. 33:24. Son of man, they that inhabit those wastes of the land of Israel speak, saying, Abraham was one, and he inherited the land: but we *are* many; the land is given us for inheritance. 25. Wherefore say unto them, Thus saith the Lord God; Ye eat with the blood, and lift up your eyes toward your idols, and shed blood: and shall ye possess the land? 26. Ye stand upon your sword, ye work abomination, and ye defile every one his neighbour's wife: and shall ye possess the land?

Hos. 12:8. And Ephraim said, Yet I am become rich, I have found me out substance: *in* all my labours they shall find none iniquity in me that *were* sin.

Amos 6:13. Ye which rejoice in a thing of nought, which say, Have we not taken to us horns by our own strength?

Hab. 2:4. Behold, his soul *which* is lifted up is not upright in him: but the just shall live by his faith.

Zeph. 3:11. In that day shalt thou not be ashamed for all thy doings, wherein thou hast transgressed against me: for then I will take away out of the midst of thee them that rejoice in thy pride, and thou shalt no more be haughty because of my holy mountain.

Matt. 7:22. Many will say to me in that day, Lord, Lord, have we not prophesied in thy name? and in thy name have cast out devils? and in thy name done many wonderful works? 23. And then will I profess unto them, I never knew you: depart from me, ye that work iniquity.

Matt. 9:10. And it came to pass, as Jesus sat at meat in the house, behold, many publicans and sinners came and sat down with him and his disciples. 11. And when the Pharisees saw *it,* they said unto his disciples, Why eateth your Master with publicans and sinners? 12. But when Jesus heard *that*, he said unto them, They that be whole need not a physician, but they that are sick. 13. But go ye and learn what *that* meaneth, I will have mercy, and not sacrifice: for I am not come to call the righteous, but sinners to repentance. Mark 2:16; Luke 5:30.

Matt. 16:6. Take heed and beware of the leaven of the Pharisees and of the Sadducees. Mark 8:15.

Matt. 19:16. And, behold, one came and said unto him, Good Master, what good thing shall I do, that I may have eternal life? 17. And he said unto him, Why callest thou me good? *there is* none good but one, *that is*, God: but if thou wilt enter into life, keep the commandments. 18. He saith unto him, Which? Jesus said, Thou shalt do no murder, Thou shalt not commit adultery, Thou shalt not steal, Thou shalt not bear false witness, 19. Honour thy father and *thy* mother: and, Thou shalt love thy neighbour as thyself. 20. The young man saith unto him, All these things have I kept from my youth up: what lack I yet? 21. Jesus said unto him, If thou wilt be perfect, go *and* sell that thou hast, and give to the poor, and thou shalt have treasure in heaven: and come *and* follow me. 22. But when the young man heard that saying, he went away sorrowful: for he had great possessions. Mark 10:17–22; Luke 18:18–23.

Matt. 22:12. Friend, how camest thou in hither not having a wedding garment? And he was speechless. 13. Then said the king to the servants, Bind him hand and foot, and take him away, and cast *him* into outer darkness; there shall be weeping and gnashing of teeth.

Matt. 23:29. Woe unto you, scribes and Pharisees, hypocrites! because ye build the tombs of the prophets, and garnish the sepulchres of the righteous, 30. And say, If we had been in the days of our fathers, we would not have been partakers with them in the blood of the prophets. 31. Wherefore ye be witnesses unto yourselves, that ye are the children of them which killed the prophets.

Luke 7:36. And one of the Pharisees desired him that he would eat with him. And he went into the Pharisee's house, and sat down to meat. 37. And, behold, a woman in the city, which was a sinner, when she knew that *Jesus* sat at meat in the Pharisee's house, brought an alabaster box of ointment, 38. And stood at his feet behind *him* weeping, and began to wash his feet with tears, and did wipe *them* with the hairs of her head, and kissed his feet, and anointed *them* with the ointment. 39. Now when the Pharisee which had bidden him saw *it*, he spake within himself, saying, This man, if he were a prophet, would have known who and what manner of woman *this is* that toucheth him: for she is a sinner. 40. And Jesus answering said unto him, Simon, I have somewhat to say unto thee. And he saith, Master, say on. 41. There was a certain creditor which had two debtors: the one owed five hundred pence, and the other fifty. 42. And when they had nothing to pay, he frankly forgave them both. Tell me therefore, which of them will love him most? 43. Simon answered and said, I suppose that *he*, to whom he forgave most. And he said unto him, Thou hast rightly judged. 44. And he turned to the woman, and said unto Simon, Seest thou this woman? I entered into thine house, thou gavest me no water for my feet: but she hath washed my feet with tears, and wiped *them* with the hairs of her head. 45. Thou gavest me no kiss: but this woman since the time I came in hath not ceased to kiss my feet. 46. My head with oil thou didst not anoint: but this woman hath anointed my feet with ointment. 47. Wherefore I say unto thee, Her sins, which are many, are forgiven; for she loved much: but to whom little is forgiven, *the same* loveth little. 48. And he said unto her, Thy sins are forgiven. 49. And they that sat at meat with him began to say within themselves, Who is this that forgiveth sins also? 50. And he said to the woman, Thy faith hath saved thee; go in peace.

Luke 10:25. And, behold, a certain lawyer stood up, and tempted him, saying, Master, what shall I do to inherit eternal life? 26. He said unto him, What is written in the law? how readest thou? 27. And he answering said, Thou shalt love the Lord thy God with all thy heart, and with all thy soul, and with all thy strength, and with all thy mind; and thy neighbour as thyself. 28. And he said unto him, Thou hast answered right: this do, and thou shalt live. 29. But he, willing to justify himself, said unto Jesus, And who is my neighbour? 30. And Jesus answering said, A certain *man* went down from Jerusalem to Jericho, and fell among thieves, which stripped him of his raiment, and wounded *him*, and departed, leaving *him* half dead. 31. And by chance there came down a certain priest that way: and when he saw him, he passed by on the other side. 32. And likewise a Levite, when he was at the place, came and looked *on him*, and passed by on the other side. 33. But a certain Samaritan, as he journeyed, came where he was: and when he saw him, he had compassion *on him*, 34. And went to *him*, and bound up his wounds, pouring in oil and wine, and set him on his own beast, and brought him to an inn, and took care of him. 35. And on the morrow when he departed, he took out two pence, and gave *them* to the host, and said unto him, Take care of him; and whatsoever thou spendest more, when I come again, I will repay thee. 36. Which now of these three, thinkest thou, was neighbour unto him that fell among the thieves? 37. And he said, He that shewed mercy on him.

Then said Jesus unto him, Go, and do thou likewise.

Luke 15:2. The Pharisees and scribes murmured, saying, This man receiveth sinners, and eateth with them. 25. Now his elder son was in the field: and 'as he came and drew nigh to the house, he heard musick and dancing. 26. And he called one of the servants, and asked what these things meant. 27. And he said unto him, Thy brother is come; and thy father hath killed the fatted calf, because he hath received him safe and sound. 28. And he was angry, and would not go in: therefore came his father out, and intreated him. 29. And he answering said to *his* father, Lo, these many years do I serve thee, neither transgressed I at any time thy commandment: and yet thou never gavest me a kid, that I might make merry with my friends: 30. But as soon as this thy son was come, which hath devoured thy living with harlots, thou hast killed for him the fatted calf. 31. And he said unto him, Son, thou art ever with me, and all that I have is thine. 32. It was meet that we should make merry, and be glad: for this thy brother was dead, and is alive again; and was lost, and is found.

Luke 16:14. And the Pharisees also, who were covetous, heard all these things: and they derided him. 15. And he said unto them, Ye are they which justify yourselves before men; but God knoweth your hearts: for that which is highly esteemed among men is abomination in the sight of God.

Luke 18:9. And he spake this parable unto certain which trusted in themselves that they were righteous, and despised others: 10. Two men went up into the temple to pray; the one a Pharisee, and the other a publican. 11. The Pharisee stood and prayed thus with himself, God, I thank thee, that I am not as other men *are*, extortioners, unjust, adulterers, or even as this publican. 12. I fast twice in the week, I give tithes of all that I possess. 13. And the publican, standing afar off, would not lift up so much as *his* eyes unto heaven, but smote upon his breast, saying, God be merciful to me a sinner. 14. I tell you, this man went down to his house justified *rather* than the other: for every one that exalteth himself shall be abased; and he that humbleth himself shall be exalted.

John 9:34. They answered and said unto him, Thou wast altogether born in sins, and dost thou teach us? And they cast him out. 39. And Jesus said, For judgment I am come into this world, that they which see not might see; and that they which see might be made blind. 40. And *some* of the Pharisees which were with him heard these words, and said unto him, Are we blind also? 41. Jesus said unto them, If ye were blind, ye should have no sin: but now ye say, We see; therefore your sin remaineth.

Rom. 2:17. Behold, thou art called a Jew, and restest in the law, and makest thy boast of God, 18. And knowest *his* will, and approvest the things that are more excellent, being instructed out of the law; 19. And art confident that thou thyself art a guide of the blind, a light of them which are in darkness, 20. An instructor of the foolish, a teacher of babes, which hast the form of knowledge and of the truth in the law.

Rom. 3:27. Where *is* boasting then? It is excluded. By what law? of works? Nay: but by the law of faith.

Rom. 10:3. For they being ignorant of God's righteousness, and going about to establish their own righteousness, have not submitted themselves unto the righteousness of God.

Rom. 11:19. Thou wilt say then, The branches were broken off, that I might be graffed in. 20. Well; because of unbelief they were broken off, and thou standest by faith. Be not highminded, but fear: 21. For if God spared not the natural branches, *take heed* lest he also spare not thee.

2 Cor. 1:9. But we had the sentence of death in ourselves, that we should not trust in ourselves, but in God which raiseth the dead.

2 Cor. 10:17. But he that glorieth, let him glory in the Lord. 18. For not he that commendeth himself is approved, but whom the Lord commendeth.

Gal. 6:3. For if a man think himself to be something, when he is nothing, he deceiveth himself.

Rev. 3:17. Because thou sayest, I am rich, and increased with goods, and have need of nothing; and knowest not that thou art wretched, and miserable, and poor, and blind, and naked: 18. I counsel thee to buy of me gold tried in the fire, that thou mayest be rich; and white raiment, that thou mayest be clothed, and *that* the shame of thy nakedness do not appear; and anoint thine eyes with eyesalve, that thou mayest see.

See HYPOCRISY; SELF-EXALTATION.

INSTANCES OF: Saul, 1 Sam. 15:13-31. Young man, see above. Lawyer, see above. Pharisees, Luke 11:33-54; John 8:33-59; 9:28-34. Israel, Rom. 10:3. Church of Laodicea, Rev. 3:17.

SELF-WILL, stubbornness. Forbidden, 2 Chr. 30:8; Psa. 75:5. Proceeds from unbelief, 2 Kin. 17:14; pride, Neh. 9:16,29; an evil heart, Jer. 7:24. God knows, Isa. 48:4. Exhibited in refusing to hearken to God, Prov. 1:24; refusing to hearken to the messengers of God, 1 Sam. 8:19; Jer. 44:16; Zech. 7:11; refusing to walk in the ways of God, Neh. 9:17; Isa. 42:24; Psa. 78:10; refusing to hearken to parents, Deut. 21:18,19; refusing to receive correction, Deut. 21:18; Jer. 5:3; 7:28; rebelling against God, Deut. 31:27; Psa. 78:8; resisting the Holy Ghost, Acts 7:51; walking in the counsels of an evil heart, Jer. 7:24, with Jer. 23:17; hardening the neck, Neh. 9:16; hardening the heart, 2 Chr. 36:13; **going**

backward and not forward, Jer. 7:24; heinousness of, 1 Sam. 15:23.

Ministers should be without, Tit. 1:7; warn their people against, Heb. 3:7–12; pray that their people may be forgiven for, Ex. 34:9; Deut. 9:27. Characteristic of the wicked, Prov. 7:11; 2 Pet. 2:10. The wicked cease not from, Judg. 2:19. Punishment for, Deut. 21:21; Prov. 29:1.

Illustrated: Psa. 32:9; Jer. 31:18.

EXEMPLIFIED: Simeon and Levi, Gen. 49:6. Israelites, Ex. 32:9; Deut. 9:6,13. Saul, 1 Sam. 15:19–23. David, 2 Sam. 24:4. Josiah, 2 Chr. 35:22. Zedekiah, 2 Chr. 36:13.—*Bible Text-Book.*

See OBDURACY.

SEMACHIAH, son of Shemaiah, 1 Chr. 26:7.

SEMEI, an ancestor of Jesus, Luke 3:26.

SENAAH, a city of unknown location, Ezra 2:35; Neh. 7:38.

SENATE, the sanhedrin, Acts 5:21. Senator, an elder, Psa. 105:22.

See ELDER; GOVERNMENT.

SENEH, a rock protecting the garrison of the Philistines at Michmash, 1 Sam. 14:4.

SENIR. See SHENIR.

SENNACHERIB, king of Assyria. Invades Judah; lays siege to Jerusalem, but abandons the country and returns to Assyria, 2 Kin. 18:17–37; 19:8; 2 Chr. 32:1–23; Isa. 36:37. Death of, 2 Kin. 19:35–37; Isa. 37:36–38.

SENSUALITY. Eccl. 2:24. *There is* nothing better for a man, *than* that he should eat and drink, and *that* he should make his soul enjoy good in his labour. This also I saw, that it *was* from the hand of God.

Eccl. 8:15. Then I commended mirth, because a man hath no better thing under the sun, than to eat, and to drink, and to be merry: for that shall abide with him of his labour the days of his life, which God giveth him under the sun.

Eccl. 11:9. Rejoice, O young man, in thy youth; and let thy heart cheer thee in the days of thy youth, and walk in the ways of thine heart, and in the sight of thine eyes: but know thou, that for all these *things* God will bring thee into judgment.

Isa. 22:13. And behold joy and gladness, slaying oxen, and killing sheep, eating flesh, and drinking wine: let us eat and drink; for to morrow we shall die.

Isa. 56:12. Come ye, *say they,* I will fetch wine, and we will fill ourselves with strong drink; and to morrow shall be as this day, *and* much more abundant.

Luke 12:19. And I will say to my soul, Soul, thou hast much goods laid up for many years; take thine ease, eat, drink, *and* be merry. 20. But God said unto him, *Thou* fool, this night thy soul shall be required of thee: then whose shall those things be, which thou hast provided?

Luke 16:25. But Abraham said, Son, remember that thou in thy lifetime receivedst thy good things, and likewise Lazarus evil things: but now he is comforted, and thou art tormented.

1 Cor. 15:32. If after the manner of men I have fought with beasts at Ephesus, what advantageth it me, if the dead rise not? let us eat and drink; for to morrow we die. 33. Be not deceived: evil communications corrupt good manners.

Jas. 5:5. Ye have lived in pleasure on the earth, and been wanton; ye have nourished your hearts, as in a day of slaughter.

Jude 18. They told you there should be mockers in the last time, who should walk after their own ungodly lusts. 19. These be they who separate themselves, sensual, having not the Spirit.

See ADULTERY; DRUNKENNESS; FORNICATION; GLUTTONY; LASCIVIOUSNESS; SELF-INDULGENCE; SODOMY; also ABSTINENCE, TOTAL; CONTINENCE; SELF-DENIAL; TEMPERANCE.

SENTRY. See WATCHMAN.

SENUAH, father of Judah, a governor of Jerusalem, Neh. 11:9.

SEORIM, a governor of the temple, 1 Chr. 24:8.

SEPHAR, a mountain in Arabia, Gen. 10:30.

SEPHARAD, an unknown place, to which the inhabitants of Jerusalem were exiled, Obad. 20.

SEPHARVAIM, an Assyrian city, from which the king of Assyria colonized Samaria, 2 Kin. 17:24,31; 18:34; 19:13; Isa. 36: 19; 37:13.

SEPHARVITES, the people of Sepharvaim, 2 Kin. 17:31.

SEPULCHRE. See BURIAL.

SERAH, called also SARAH. Daughter of Asher, Gen. 46:17; Num. 26:46; 1 Chr. 7:30.

SERAIAH. 1. Called also SHEVA, SHISHA, and SHAVSHA. David's scribe, 2 Sam. 8:17; 20:25; 1 Kin. 4:3; 1 Chr. 18:16.

2. Chief priest at time of taking of Jerusalem, 2 Kin. 25:18. Father of Ezra, Ezra 7:1. Slain by Nebuchadnezzar, 2 Kin. 25:18–21; Jer. 52:24–27.

3. An Israelitish captain who surrendered to Gedaliah, 2 Kin. 25:23; Jer. 40:8.

4. Son of Kenaz, 1 Chr. 4:13,14.

5. A Simeonite, 1 Chr. 4:35.

6. A priest who returned from the Babylonian captivity, Ezra 2:2; Neh. 12:1,12. Called AZARIAH, Neh. 7:7.

7. One who sealed the covenant with Nehemiah, Neh. 10:2. Possibly identical with 6, above.

8. A ruler of the temple after the captivity, Neh. 11:11.

9. Son of Azriel. Commanded by king Jehoiakim to seize Jeremiah, Jer. 36:26.

10. A servant of Zedekiah, Jer. 51:59,61.

SERAPHIM, celestial beings, Isa. 6:2,6. See CHERUBIM.

SERED, son of Zebulun, Gen. 46:14; Num. 26:26.

SERGEANT, Acts 16:35,38.

SERGIUS PAULUS, a Roman deputy and convert of Paul, Acts 13:7–12.

SERMON. Of Jesus, "on the mount," Matt. 5:6;7; by the sea, Matt. 13:1–52; Mark 4:2–33.

See PREACHING; MINISTERS.

SERPENT. Satan appears in the form of, to Eve, Gen. 3:1–15; 2 Cor. 11:3. Subtlety of, Gen. 3:1; Eccl. 10:8; Matt. 10:16. Curse upon, Gen. 3:14,15; 49:17. Feeds upon the dust, Gen. 3:14; Isa. 65:25; Mic. 7:17. Unfit for food, Matt. 7:10. Venom of, Deut. 32:24,33; Job 20:16; Psa. 58:4; 140:3; Prov. 23:31,32; Acts 28:5,6. The staff of Moses transformed into, Ex. 4:3; 7:15. Fiery, sent as a plague upon the Israelites, Num. 21:6,7; Deut. 8:15; 1 Cor. 10:9. The wound of, miraculously healed by looking upon the brazen, set up by Moses, Num. 21:8,9. Charming of, Psa. 58:4,5; Eccl. 10:11; Jer. 8:17. Mentioned in Solomon's riddle. Prov. 30:19. Constriction of, Rev. 9:19. Sea serpent, Amos 9:3. The seventy endued with power over, Luke 10:19. The apostles given power over, Mark 16:18; Acts 28:5.

FIGURATIVE: Isa. 14:29; 30:6; 65:25.

SERUG. An ancestor of Abraham, Gen. 11:20–23; 1 Chr. 1:26. Called SARUCH, Luke 3:35.

SERVANT. Distinguished as bond servant, who was a slave, and hired servant.

BOND: Laws of Moses concerning, Ex. 21:1–11,20,21,26,27,32; Lev. 19:20–22; 25:6,10, 35–55; Deut. 15:12,14,18; 24:7. Manstealing forbidden, Deut. 21:10–14; 24:7; 1 Tim. 1:10; Rev. 18:13. Fugitive, not to be returned to master, Deut. 23:15,16. David erroneously supposed to be a fugitive slave, 1 Sam. 25:10. Instances of fugitive: Hagar, commanded by an angel to return to her mistress, Gen. 16:9. Sought by Shimei, 1 Kin. 2:39–41. Interceded for, by Paul, Philem. 10–21.

Rights of those born to a master, Gen. 14:14; 17:13,27; Ex. 21:4; Prov. 29:21; Eccl. 2:7; Jer. 2:14.

Bought and sold, Gen. 17:13,27; 37:28,36; 39:17; Deut. 28:68; Esth. 7:4; Ezek. 27:13; Joel 3:6; Amos 8:6; Rev. 18:13. Captives of war made, Deut. 20:14; 21:10–14; 2 Kin. 5:2; 2 Chr. 28:8,10; Lam. 5:13; captive bond servants shared by priests and Levites, Num. 31:28–47. Thieves punished by being made, Gen. 43:18; Ex. 22:3. Defaulting debtors made, Lev. 25:39; Matt. 18:25. Children of defaulting debtors sold for, 2 Kin. 4:1–7. Voluntary servitude of, Lev. 25:47; Deut. 15:16,17; Josh. 9:11–21. Given as dowry, Gen. 29:24, 29. Owned by priests, Lev. 22:11; Mark 14:66. Slaves owned slaves, 2 Sam. 9:10. The master might marry, or give in marriage, Ex. 21:7–10; Deut. 21:10–14; 1 Chr. 2:34,35. Taken in concubinage, Gen. 16:1,2,6; 30:3,9. Used as soldiers by Abraham, Gen. 14:14. Must be circumcised, Gen. 17:13,27; Ex.

12:44. Must enjoy religious privileges with the master's household, Deut. 12:12,18; 16:11, 14; 29:10,11. Must have rest on the sabbath, Ex. 20:10; 23:12; Deut. 5:14. Equal status of, with other disciples of Jesus, 1 Cor. 7:21, 22; 12:13; Gal. 3:28; Eph. 6:8. Kindness to, enjoined, Lev. 25:43; Eph. 6:9.

Bond service threatened, as a national punishment, for disobedience of Israel, Deut. 28:68; Joel 3:7,8. Degrading influences of bondage exemplified by cowardice, Ex. 14· 11,12; 16:3; Judg. 5:16–18,23.

Emancipation of, Ezra 1:1–4; Jer. 34:8–22; 1 Cor. 7:21. Freedmen called libertines. Acts 6:9.

Cruelty to: To Hagar, Gen. 16:1–21; Gal. 4: 22–31; to the Israelites, Ex. 1:8–22; 2:1–4; Acts 7:19,34. Sick, abandoned, 1 Sam. 30:13. Kindness to, by the centurion, Matt. 8:8–13; Luke 7:2–10; Paul, Philem. 1–21.

INSTANCES OF: Joseph, Gen. 37:26–28,36. Israelites, Ex. 1:10–22; 5:7–14; Deut. 6:12,21. Gibeonites, Josh. 9:22–27. Canaanites, 1 Kin. 9:21. Jews in Babylon, 2 Chr. 36:20. Esth. chapters 1–10. Emancipation of, 2 Chr. 36:23; Ezra 1:1–4.

FIGURATIVE: Lev. 25:42,55; Psa. 116:16; Matt. 24:45–51; Luke 12:35–48; 17:7–9; John 8:32–35; Rom. 6:16–22; 1 Cor. 4:1; 7:21–23; Gal. 5:13; 1 Pet. 2:16; 2 Pet. 2:19; Rev. 7:3.

INSTANCES OF GOOD: Joseph, Gen. 39:2–20; 41:9–57; Acts 7:10; Elisha, 2 Kin. 2:1–6. Servants of Abraham, Gen. 24; of Boaz, Ruth 2:4; of Jonathan, 1 Sam. 14:7; of Abigail, 1 Sam. 25:14–17; of David, 2 Sam. 12: 18; 15:15,21; of Ziba, 2 Sam. 9; of Naaman, 2 Kin. 5:2,3,13; of Nehemiah, Neh. 4:16,23; of centurion, Matt. 8:9; of Cornelius, Acts 10:7; Onesimus, Philem. 11. Servants in the parable of the pounds and talents, Matt. 25:14–23; Luke 19:12–19.

WICKED AND UNFAITHFUL. Jeroboam, 1 Kin. 11:26; Gehazi, 2 Kin. 5:20–27; Zimri, 1 Kin. 16:9,10; 2 Kin. 9:31; Onesimus, Philem. 11.

Of Abraham and Lot, Gen. 13:7. Of Abimelech, Gen. 21:25. Of Ziba, 2 Sam. 16: 1–4, with 2 Sam. 19:26,27. Of Absalom, 2 Sam. 13:28,29; 14:30. Of Shimei, 1 Kin. 2· 39. Of Joash, 2 Kin. 12:19–21. Of Amon, 2 Kin. 21:23. Of Job, Job 19:15,16. In the parable of the talents and pounds, Matt. 25:24–30; Luke 19:20–26. In the parable of the vineyard, Matt. 21:33–41; Mark 12· 1–9.

Conspiracy by. See CONSPIRACY.

UNCLASSIFIED SCRIPTURES RELATING TO: Gen. 16:6. But Abram said unto Sarai, Behold, thy maid *is* in thy hand; do to her as it pleaseth thee. And when Sarai dealt hardly with her, she fled from her face. 7. And the angel of the LORD found her by a fountain of water in the wilderness, by the fountain in the way to Shur. 8. And he said, Hagar, Sarai's maid, whence camest thou? and whither wilt thou go? And she said, I flee from the face of my mistress Sarai. 9. And the angel of the LORD said unto her, Return to thy mistress, and submit thyself under her hands.

Ex. 20:10. But the seventh day *is* the sabbath of the Lord thy God: *in it* thou shalt not do any work, thou, nor thy son, nor thy daughter, thy manservant, nor thy maidservant, nor thy cattle, nor thy stranger that *is* within thy gates. Deut. 5:14.

Neh. 5:8. And I said unto them, We, after our ability, have redeemed our brethren the Jews, which were sold unto the heathen; and will ye even sell your brethren? or shall they be sold unto us? Then held they their peace, and found nothing *to answer*.

Job 19:15. They that dwell in mine house, and my maids, count me for a stranger: I am an alien in their sight. 16. I called my servant, and he gave *me* no answer · I intreated him with my mouth.

Job 31:13. If I did despise the cause of my manservant or of my maidservant, when they contended with me; 14. What then shall I do when God riseth up? and when he visiteth, what shall I answer him?

Psa. 123:2. Behold, as the eyes of servants *look* unto the hand of their masters, *and* as the eyes of a maiden unto the hand of her mistress; so our eyes *wait* upon the Lord our God, until that he have mercy upon us.

Prov. 12:9. *He that is* despised, and hath a servant, *is* better than he that honoureth himself, and lacketh bread.

Prov. 13:17. A wicked messenger falleth into mischief: but a faithful ambassador *is* health.

Prov. 17:2. A wise servant shall have rule over a son that causeth shame, and shall have part of the inheritance among the brethren.

Prov. 19:10 Delight is not seemly for a fool; much less for a servant to have rule over princes.

Prov. 25:13. As the cold of snow in the time of harvest, *so is* a faithful messenger to them that send him: for he refresheth the soul of his masters.

Prov. 26:6. He that sendeth a message by the hand of a fool cutteth off the feet, *and* drinketh damage.

Prov. 27:18. Whoso keepeth the fig tree shall eat the fruit thereof: so he that waiteth on his master shall be honoured. 27. And *thou shalt have* goats' milk enough for thy food, for the food of thy household, and *for* the maintenance for thy maidens.

Prov. 29:19. A servant will not be corrected by words: for though he understand he will not answer.

21. He that delicately bringeth up his servant from a child shall have him become *his* son at the length.

Prov. 30:10. Accuse not a servant unto his master, lest he curse thee, and thou be found guilty. 21. For three *things* the earth is disquieted, and for four *which* it cannot bear: 22. For a servant when he

reigneth; and a fool when he is filled with meat; 23. For an odious *woman* when she is married; and an handmaid that is heir to her mistress.

Eccl. 7:21. Also take no heed unto all words that are spoken; lest thou hear thy servant curse thee:

Isa. 52:3. For thus saith the Lord, Ye have sold yourselves for nought; and ye shall be redeemed without money.

Jer. 22:13. Woe unto him that buildeth his house by unrighteousness, and his chambers by wrong; *that* useth his neighbour's service without wages, and giveth him not for his work;

Jer. 34:8. *This is* the word that came unto Jeremiah from the Lord, after that the king Zedekiah had made a covenant with all the people which *were* at Jerusalem, to proclaim liberty unto them; 9. That every man should let his manservant, and every man his maidservant, *being* an Hebrew or an Hebrewess, go free; that none should serve himself of them, *to wit*, of a Jew his brother. 10. Now when all the princes, and all the people, which had entered into the covenant, heard that every one should let his manservant, and every one his maidservant, go free, that none should serve themselves of them any more, then they obeyed, and let *them* go. 11. But afterward they turned, and caused the servants and the handmaids, whom they had let go free, to return, and brought them into subjection for servants and for handmaids. 12. Therefore the word of the Lord came to Jeremiah from the Lord, saying, 13. Thus saith the Lord, the God of Israel; I made a covenant with your fathers in the day that I brought them forth out of the land of Egypt, out of the house of bondmen, saying, 14. At the end of seven years let ye go every man his brother an Hebrew, which hath been sold unto thee; and when he hath served thee six years, thou shalt let him go free from thee: but your fathers hearkened not unto me, neither inclined their ear. 15. And ye were now turned, and had done right in my sight, in proclaiming liberty every man to his neighbour; and ye had made a covenant before me in the house which is called by my name: 16. But ye turned and polluted my name, and caused every man his servant, and every man his handmaid, whom he had set at liberty at their pleasure, to return, and brought them into subjection, to be unto you for servants and for handmaids. 17. Therefore thus saith the Lord; Ye have not hearkened unto me, in proclaiming liberty, every one to his brother, and every man to his neighbour: behold, I proclaim a liberty for you, saith the Lord, to the sword, to the pestilence, and to the famine; and I will make you to be removed into all the kingdoms of the earth.

Lam. 5:8. Servants have ruled over us: *there is* none that doth deliver *us* out of their hand.

Zeph. 1:9. In the same day also will I punish all those that leap on the threshold, which fill their masters' houses with violence and deceit.

Mal. 1:6. A son honoureth *his* father, and a servant his master :

Matt. 8:9. For I am a man under authority, having soldiers under me: and I say to this *man*, Go, and he goeth; and to another, Come, and he cometh ; and to my servant, Do this, and he doeth *it*.

Matt. 24:45. Who then is a faithful and wise servant, whom his lord hath made ruler over his household, to give them meat in due season ? 46. Blessed *is* that servant, whom his lord when he cometh shall find so doing. 47. Verily I say unto you, That he shall make him ruler over all his goods. 48. But and if that evil servant shall say in his heart, My lord delayeth his coming. 49. And shall begin to smite *his* fellow servants, and to eat and drink with the drunken; 50. The lord of that servant shall come in a day when he looketh not for *him*, and in an hour that he is not aware of, 51. And shall cut him asunder, and appoint *him* his portion with the hypocrites: there shall be weeping and gnashing of teeth.

Luke 12:35. Let your loins be girded about, and *your* lights burning; 36. And ye yourselves like unto men that wait for their lord, when he will return from the wedding; that when he cometh and knocketh, they may open unto him immediately. 37. Blessed *are* those servants, whom the lord when he cometh shall find watching : verily I say unto you, that he shall gird himself, and make them to sit down to meat, and will come forth and serve them. 38. And if he shall come in the second watch, or come in the third watch, and find *them* so, blessed are those servants. 39. And this know, that if the goodman of the house had known what hour the thief would come, he would have watched, and not have suffered his house to be broken through. 40. Be ye therefore ready also: for the Son of man cometh at an hour when ye think not. 41. Then Peter said unto him, Lord, speakest thou this parable unto us, or even to all ? 42. And the Lord said, Who then is that faithful and wise steward, whom *his* lord shall make ruler over his household, to give *them their* portion of meat in due season ? 43. Blessed *is* that servant, whom his lord when he cometh shall find so doing. 44. Of a truth I say unto you, that he will make him ruler over all that he hath. 45. But and if that servant say in his heart, My lord delayeth his coming; and shall begin to beat the menservants and maidens, and to eat and drink, and to be drunken; 46. The lord of that servant will come in a day when he looketh not for *him*, and at an hour when he is not aware, and will cut him in sunder, and will appoint him his portion with the unbelievers. 47. And

that servant, which knew his lord's will, and prepared not *himself*, neither did according to his will, shall be beaten with many *stripes*. 48. But he that knew not, and did commit things worthy of stripes, shall be beaten vith few *stripes*. For unto whomsoever much is given, of him shall be much required : and to whom men have committed much, of him they will ask the more.

Luke 16:1. And he said also unto his disciples, There was a certain rich man, which had a steward ; and the same was accused unto him that he had wasted his goods. 2. And he called him, and said unto him, How is it that I hear this of thee ? give an account of thy stewardship; for thou mayest be no longer steward. 3. Then the steward said within himself, What shall I do ? for my lord taketh away from me the stewardship : I cannot dig; to beg I am ashamed. 4. I am resolved what to do, that, when I am put out of the stewardship, they may receive me into their houses. 5. So he called every one of his lord's debtors *unto him*, and said unto the first, How much owest thou unto my lord ? 6. And he said, An hundred measures of oil. And he said unto him, Take thy bill, and sit down quickly, and write fifty. 7. Then said he to another, And how much owest thou ? And he said, An hundred measures of wheat. And he said unto him, Take thy bill, and write fourscore. 8. And the lord commended the unjust steward, because he had done wisely: for the children of this world are in their generation wiser than the children of light. 9. And I say unto you, Make to yourselves friends of the mammon of unrighteousness ; that, when ye fail, they may receive you into everlasting habitations. 10. He that is faithful in that which is least is faithful also in much: and he that is unjust in the least is unjust also in much. 11. If therefore ye have not been faithful in the unrighteous mammon, who will commit to your trust the true *riches ?* 12. And if ye have not been faithful in that which is another man's, who shall give you that which is your own ? 13. No servant can serve two masters : for either he will hate the one, and love the other ; or else he will hold to the one, and despise the other. Ye cannot serve God and mammon.

Luke 17:7. Which of you, having a servant plowing or feeding cattle, will say unto him by and by, when he is come from the field, Go and sit down to meat ? 8. And will not rather say unto him, Make ready wherewith I may sup, and gird thyself, and serve me, till I have eaten and drunken; and afterward thou shalt eat and drink ? 9. Doth he thank that servant because he did the things that were commanded him ? I trow not.

Luke 22:27. For whether *is* greater, he that sitteth at meat, or he that serveth ? *is* not he that sitteth at meat ? but I am among you as he that serveth.

John 13:16. Verily, verily, I say unto you, The servant is not greater than his lord; neither he that is sent greater than he that sent him. Matt. 10:24,25.

1 Cor. 4:2. Moreover it is required in stewards, that a man be found faithful.

1 Cor. 7:21. Art thou called *being* a servant? care not for it: but if thou mayest be made free, use *it* rather. 22. For he that is called in the Lord, *being* a servant, is the Lord's freeman: likewise also he that is called, *being* free, is Christ's servant. 23. Ye are bought with a price; be not ye the servants of men. 24. Brethren, let every man, wherein he is called, therein abide with God.

Eph. 6:5. Servants, be obedient to them that are *your* masters according to the flesh, with fear and trembling, in singleness of your heart, as unto Christ; 6. Not with eyeservice, as menpleasers; but as the servants of Christ, doing the will of God from the heart; 7. With good will doing service, as to the Lord, and not to men: 8. Knowing that whatsoever good thing any man doeth, the same shall he receive of the Lord, whether *he be* bond or free. 9. And, ye masters, do the same things unto them, forbearing threatening: knowing that your Master also is in heaven; neither is there respect of persons with him.

Col. 3:22. Servants, obey in all things *your* masters according to the flesh; not with eyeservice, as menpleasers; but in singleness of heart, fearing God: 23. And whatsoever ye do, do *it* heartily, as to the Lord, and not unto men; 24. Knowing that of the Lord ye shall receive the reward of the inheritance: for ye serve the Lord Christ. 25. But he that doeth wrong shall receive for the wrong which he hath done: and there is no respect of persons.

1 Tim. 6:1. Let as many servants as are under the yoke count their own masters worthy of all honour, that the name of God and *his* doctrine be not blasphemed. 2. And they that have believing masters, let them not despise *them*, because they are brethren; but rather do *them* service, because they are faithful and beloved, partakers of the benefit.

Tit. 2:9. *Exhort* servants to be obedient unto their own masters, *and* to please *them* well in all *things;* not answering again; 10. Not purloining, but shewing all good fidelity; that they may adorn the doctrine of God our Saviour in all things.

1 Pet. 2:18. Servants, *be* subject to *your* masters with all fear; not only to the good and gentle, but also to the froward. 19. For this *is* thankworthy, if a man for conscience toward God endure grief, suffering wrongfully. 20. For what glory *is it,* if, when ye be buffeted for your faults, ye shall take it patiently? but if, when ye do well, and suffer *for it,* ye take it patiently, this *is* acceptable with God.

See EMPLOYEE; EMPLOYER; MASTER.

HIRED: Jacob, Gen. 29:15; 30:26; reëmployed, Gen. 30:27-34; 31:6,7,41. Parable of laborers for a vineyard, Matt. 20:1-15; of the father of the prodigal son, Luke 15:17, 19. The prodigal, Luke 15:15-19.

Treatment of, more considerate than that accorded slaves, Lev. 25:53. Await employment in marketplace, Matt. 20:1-3. Wages paid in kind, Gen. 30:31,32; 2 Chr. 2:10; in money, Matt. 20:2.

UNCLASSIFIED SCRIPTURES RELATING TO: Lev. 19:13. Thou shalt not defraud thy neighbour, neither rob *him:* the wages of him that is hired shall not abide with thee all night until the morning.

Lev. 25:39. And if thy brother *that dwelleth* by thee be waxen poor, and be sold unto thee; thou shalt not compel him to serve as a bondservant: 40. *But* as an hired servant, *and* as a sojourner, he shall be with thee, *and* shall serve thee unto the year of jubile: 41. And *then* shall he depart from thee, *both* he and his children with him, and shall return unto his own family, and unto the possession of his fathers shall he return.

Deut. 24:14. Thou shalt not oppress an hired servant *that is* poor and needy, *whether he be* of thy brethren, or of thy strangers that *are* in thy land within thy gates: 15. At his day thou shalt give *him* his hire, neither shall the sun go down upon it; for he *is* poor, and setteth his heart upon it: lest he cry against thee unto the LORD, and it be sin unto thee.

Job 7:1. *Is there* not an appointed time to man upon earth? *are not* his days also like the days of an hireling? 2. As a servant earnestly desireth the shadow, and as a hireling looketh for *the reward of* his work:

Job 14:6. Turn from him, that he may rest, till he shall accomplish, as an hireling, his day.

Mal. 3:5. And I will come near to you to judgment; and I will be a swift witness against the sorcerers, and against the adulterers, and against false swearers, and against those that oppress the hireling in *his* wages,

Matt. 10:9. Provide neither gold, nor silver, nor brass in your purses, 10. Nor scrip for *your* journey, neither two coats, neither shoes, nor yet staves: for the workman is worthy of his meat. Luke 10:7.

Rom. 4:4. Now to him that worketh is the reward not reckoned of grace, but of debt.

Col. 4:1. Masters, give unto *your* servants that which is just and equal; knowing that ye also have a Master in heaven.

1 Tim. 5:18. For the scripture saith, Thou shalt not muzzle the ox that treadeth out the corn. And, The labourer *is* worthy of his reward.

Jas. 5:4. Behold, the hire of the labourers who have reaped down your fields, which is of you kept back by fraud, crieth: and the cries of them which have reaped are entered into the ears of the Lord of sabaoth.

See MASTERS; WAGES.

SERVICE. See ALTRUISM.

SETH. Son of Adam, Gen. 4:25,26; 5:3,8; 1 Chr. 1:1; Luke 3:38. Called SHETH, 1 Chr. 1:1.

SETHUR, one of the twelve spies, Num. 13:13.

SEVEN. Interesting facts concerning the number. **DAYS:** Week consists of, Gen. 2:3; Ex. 20:11; Deut. 5:13,14. Noah in the ark before the flood, Gen. 7:4,10; remains in the ark after sending forth the dove, Gen. 8:10,12. Mourning for Jacob lasted, Gen. 50:10; of Job, Job 2:13. The plague of bloody waters in Egypt lasted, Ex. 7:25. The Israelites compassed Jericho, Josh. 6:4. The passover lasted, Ex. 12:15. Saul directed by Samuel to tarry at Gilgal, awaiting the prophet's command, 1 Sam. 10:8; 13:8. The elders of Jabesh-gilead ask for a truce of, 1 Sam. 11:3. Dedication of the temple lasted double, 1 Kin. 8:65. Ezekiel sits by the river Chebar in astonishment, Ezek. 3:15. The feast of tabernacles lasted, Lev. 23:34,42. Consecration of priests and altars lasted, Ex. 29:30,35. Ezek. 43:25, 26. Defilements lasted, Lev. 12:2; 13:4. Fasts of, 1 Sam. 31:13; 2 Sam. 12:16,18,22. The firstborn of flocks and sheep shall remain with mother, before being offered, Ex. 22:30. The feast of Ahasuerus continued, Esth.1:5. Paul tarries at Tyre, Acts 21:4; at Puteoli, Acts 28:14.

WEEKS: In Daniel's vision concerning the coming of the Messiah, Dan. 9:25. Ten times, Dan. 9:24. The period between the Passover and the Pentecost, Lev. 23:15.

MONTHS: Holy convocations in the seventh month, Lev. 23:24-44; Num. 29; Ezek. 45:25.

YEARS: Jacob serves for each of his wives, Gen. 29:15-30. Of plenty, Gen. 41: 1-32,53. Famine lasted in Egypt, Gen. 41:1-32,54-56; in Canaan, 2 Sam. 24:13; 2 Kin. 8:1. Insanity of Nebuchadnezzar, Dan. 4:32. Seven times, the period between the jubilees, Lev. 25:8.

MISCELLANY OF SEVENS: Of clean beasts taken into the ark, Gen. 7:2. Abraham gives Abimelech seven lambs, Gen. 21:28. Rams and bullocks to the number of, required in sacrifices, Lev. 23:18; Num.23:1; 29: 32; 1 Chr. 15:26; Ezek. 45:23. Blood sprinkling seven times, Lev. 4:6; 14:7; oil, 14:16. Seven kine and seven ears of corn in Pharaoh's vision, Gen.41:2-7. The Israelites compassed Jericho seven times, on the seventh day sounding seven trumpets, Josh. 6:4. Elisha's servant looked seven times for appearance of rain, 1 Kin. 18:43. Naaman required to wash in Jordan seven times, 2 Kin. 5:10. Seven steps in the temple seen in Ezekiel's vision, Ezek. 40:22,26. The heat of Nebuchadnezzar's furnace intensified sevenfold, Dan. 3:19. The light of the sun intensified sevenfold, Isa. 30:26. The threat-

ened sevenfold punishment of Israel, Lev. 26:18-21. Silver purified seven times, Psa. 12:6. Worshiping seven times a day, Psa. 119:164. Seven chamberlains at the court of Ahasuerus, Esth. 1:10; seven princes, Esth. 1:14. Seven counsellors at the court of Artaxerxes, Ezra 7:14. Seven maidens given to Esther. Esth. 2:9. Symbolical of many sons, Ruth 4:15; 1 Sam. 2:5; Jer. 15:9; of liberality, Eccl. 11:1,2. Seven magi, Prov. 26:16. Seven women shall seek polygamous marriage, Isa. 4:1. Seven shepherds to be sent forth against Assyria, Mic. 5:5,6. Seven lamps and pipes, Zech. 4:2. Seven deacons in the apostolic church, Acts 6:3. Seven churches in Asia, Rev. 1:4,20. Seven seals, Rev. 5:1. Seven thunders, Rev. 10:3. Seven heads and seven crowns, Rev. 12:3; 13:1; 17:9. Seven kings, Rev. 17:10. Seven stars, Rev. 1:16,20; 3:1. Amos 5:8. Seven spirits, Rev. 1:4; 3:1; 4:5; 5:6. Seven eyes of the Lord, Zech. 3:9; 4:10; Rev. 5:6. Seven golden candlesticks, Rev. 1:12. Seven angels with seven trumpets, Rev. 8:2. Seven plagues, Rev. 15:1. Seven horns and seven eyes, Rev. 5:6. Seven angels with seven plagues, Rev. 15:6. Seven golden vials, Rev. 15:7. Scarlet colored beast having seven heads, Rev. 17:3,7.

SEVENEH, a city in Egypt, Ezek. 29:10 [R. V.]; 30:6 [R. V.]; A. V., SYENE.

SEVENTY. The senate of the Israelites composed of seventy elders, Ex. 24:1,9; Num. 11:16,24,25. Seventy disciples sent forth by Jesus, Luke 10:1-17. The Jews in captivity in Babylon seventy years, Jer. 25:11,12; 29:10; Dan. 9:2; Zech. 1:12; 7:5. See ISRAEL.

Seventy weeks in the vision of Daniel, Dan. 9:24.

SHAALABBIN. See SHAALBIM.

SHAALBIM. A city of Dan, Josh 19:42; Judg. 1:35. One of Solomon's commissary cities, 1 Kin. 4:9. Called SHAALABBIN, Josh. 19:42.

SHAAPH. 1. Son of Jahdai, 1 Chr. 2:47.

2. Son of Caleb, 1 Chr. 2:49.

SHAARAIM. 1. A city of Judah, called also SHARAIM, Josh. 15:36; 1 Sam. 17:52.

2. A city of Simeon, 1 Chr. 4:31.

SHAASHGAZ, a chamberlain of Ahasuerus, Esth. 2:14.

SHABBETHAI. 1. A Levite, assistant to Ezra, Ezra 10:15.

2. An expounder of the law, Neh. 8:7.

3. A chief Levite, attendant of the temple, Neh. 11:16.

SHACHIA, son of Shaharaim, 1 Chr. 8:10.

SHADRACH, called also HANANIAH. A Hebrew captive in Babylon, Dan. 1; 2: 17,49; 3.

SHAGE, father of Jonathan, one of David's guard, 1 Chr. 11:34.

SHAHARAIM, a Benjamite, 1 Chr. 8:8.

SHAHAZIMAH, a city in Issachar, Josh. 19:22.

SHALEM, Gen. 33:18. Translated "in peace" [R. V.].

SHALIM, a district of unknown location, 1 Sam. 9:4.

SHALISHA, a district bordering on Mount Ephraim, 1 Sam. 9:4.

SHALLECHETH, one of the gates of the temple, 1 Chr. 26:16.

SHALLUM. 1. King of Israel, 2 Kin. 15:10,13–15.

2. Husband of Huldah, the prophetess, 2 Kin. 22:14; 2 Chr. 34:22.

3. Son of Sisamai, 1 Chr. 2:40, 41.

4. See JEHOAHAZ, 3.

5. Grandson of Simeon, 1 Chr. 4:25.

6. Son of Zadok, 1 Chr. 6:12,13; Ezra 7:2.

Called MESHULLAM, 1 Chr. 9:11; Neh. 11:11.

7. See SHILLEM.

8. A chief porter of the temple, 1 Chr. 9:17,19,31.

9. Father of Jehizkiah, 2 Chr. 28:12.

10. The ancestor of a family of returned exiles, Ezra 2:42; Neh. 7:45.

11. A porter who put away his wife, Ezra 10:24.

12. A son of Bani, who put away his wife, Ezra 10:42.

13. A Jew who repaired a portion of the wall of Jerusalem, Neh. 3:12.

14. Uncle of Jeremiah, Jer. 32:7.

15. Father of Maaseiah, Jer. 35:4.

SHALLUN, a Jew who repaired a gate of Jerusalem, Neh. 3:15.

SHALMAI, one of the Nethinim, Ezra 2:46; Neh. 7:48.

SHALMAN. Identified by some authorities with Shalmaneser, Hos. 10:14. Other authorities disagree, and leave his identity uncertain.

SHALMANESER, king of Assyria. Overthrows the kingdom of Israel, 2 Kin. 17:3–6; 18:9–11.

SHAMA, one of David's heroes, 1 Chr. 11:44.

SHAMARIAH, son of Rehoboam, 2 Chr. 11:19.

SHAME. Jesus ashamed of those who deny him, Mark 8:38; Luke 9:26. Of Adam and Eve, Gen. 3:10. Destitute of, the Israelites when they worshiped the golden calf, Ex. 32:25; the unjust, Zeph. 3:5. Of the cross, Heb. 12:2.

SHAMER. 1. A Levite, father of Bani, 1 Chr. 6:46.

2. An Asherite, son of Heber, 1 Chr. 7:34. Called SHOMER, 1 Chr. 7:32.

SHAMGAR, a deliverer of Israel, Judg. 3:31; 5:6.

SHAMHUTH, one of David's captains, 1 Chr. 27:8.

SHAMIR. 1. A city in the mountains of Judah, Josh. 15:48.

2. A city in Mount Ephraim. Home and burial place of Tola, the judge, Judg. 10:1,2.

3. Son of Michah, a Levite, 1 Chr. 24:24.

SHAMMA, son of Zophah, an Asherite, 1 Chr. 7:37.

SHAMMAH. 1. Son of Reuel, Gen. 36: 13,17; 1 Chr. 1:37.

2. David's brother, 1 Sam. 16:9; 17:13. Called SHIMEAH, 2 Sam. 13:3,32; 21:21; SHIMMA, 1 Chr. 2:13; SHIMEA, 1 Chr. 20:7.

3. One of David's mighty men, son of Agee, 2 Sam. 23:11,12.

4. One of David's mighty men, 2 Sam. 23:25. Called SHAMMOTH, 1 Chr. 11:27.

5. A Hararite, one of David's mighty men, 2 Sam. 23:33.

SHAMMAI. 1. Son of Onam, 1 Chr. 2:28,32.

2. Father of Maon, 1 Chr. 2:44,45.

3. Son of Ezra, 1 Chr. 4:17.

SHAMMOTH. One of David's mighty men, 1 Chr. 11:27. Called SHAMMAH, 2 Sam. 23:25.

SHAMMUA. 1. The representative of Reuben among the twelve spies sent into Canaan, Num. 13:4.

2. See SHAMMUAH.

3. A Levite, father of Abda, Neh. 11:17. Called SHEMAIAH, 1 Chr. 9:16.

4. A priest, Neh. 12:18.

SHAMMUAH, son of David, 2 Sam. 5:14. Called SHIMEA, 1 Chr. 3:5; SHAMMUA, 1 Chr. 14:4.

SHAMSHERAI, son of Jeroham, 1 Chr. 8:26.

SHAPHAM, chief of Gad, 1 Chr. 5:12.

SHAPHAN. 1. A scribe of king Josiah, 2 Kin. 22:3–14; 2 Chr. 34:8–20. Father of Gemariah, Jer. 36:10–12.

2. Father of Ahikam and grandfather of Gedaliah, 2 Kin. 22:12; 25:22; 2 Chr. 34:20; Jer. 26:24; 39:14; 40:5,9,11; 41:2; 43:6.

3. Father of Elasah, Jer. 29:3.

4. Father of Jaazaniah, Ezek. 8:11.

SHAPHAT. 1. The representative of Simeon among the spies sent into Canaan, Num. 13:5.

2. Father of Elisha, 1 Kin. 19:16,19; 2 Kin. 3:11; 6:31.

3. Son of Shemaiah, 1 Chr. 3:22.

4. A Gadite, 1 Chr. 5:12.

5. Son of Adlai, 1 Chr. 27:29.

SHAPHER, a mountain, camping place of the Israelites in the desert, Num. 33:23,24.

SHARAI, a descendant of Bani, who put away his Gentile wife, Ezra 10:40.

SHARAIM. See SHAARAIM.

SHARAR. Father of Ahiam, 2 Sam. 23:33. Called SACAR, 1 Chr. 11:35.

SHAREZER. 1. Son of Sennacherib, 2 Kin. 19:37; Isa. 37:38.

2. [R. V.] A delegate to priests and prophets to consult as to a day of humiliation, Zech. 7:2. A. V., SHEREZER.

SHARON. 1. The maritime slope of Palestine north of Joppa. David's herds in, 1 Chr. 27:29. Roses and beauty of, Song 2:1; Isa. 33:9; 35:2; 65:10. Called SARON, Acts 9:35.

2. A place of unascertained location, 1 Chr. 5:16.

SHARUHEN, a city in Simeon, Josh. 19:6.

SHASHAI, a descendant of Bani, who put away his Gentile wife, Ezra 10:40.

SHASHAK, a Benjamite, 1 Chr. 8:14, 25.

SHAUL. 1. Son of Simeon, Gen. 46:10; Ex. 6:15; Num. 26:13; 1 Chr. 4:24.

2. An ancient king of Edom, 1 Chr. 1:48, 49. Called SAUL, Gen. 36:37.

3. Son of Uzziah, 1 Chr. 6:24.

SHAVEH, a valley. Called also "the king's dale," Gen. 14:17. Absalom's pillar in, 2 Sam. 18:18.

SHAVEH KIRIATHAIM, a valley in Moab, Gen. 14:5.

SHAVING. Forbidden to Nazarites, Num. 6:5; Judg. 13:5; to priests, Ezek. 44: 20.

See BEARD.

SHAVSHA. See SERAIAH, 1.

SHEAL, a descendant of Bani, who put away his Gentile wife, Ezra 10:29.

SHEALTIEL, called also SALATHIEL. Father of Zerubbabel and ancestor of Jesus, 1 Chr. 3:17; Ezra 3:2,8; 5:2; Neh. 12:1; Hag. 1:1,12,14; 2:2,23; Matt. 1:12; Luke 3:27.

SHEARIAH, son of Azel, 1 Chr. 8:38; 9:44.

SHEAR-JASHUB, a son of Isaiah, Isa. 7:3.

SHEBA. 1. Son of Raamah, Gen. 10:7; 1 Chr. 1:9.

2. Son of Joktan, Gen. 10:28; 1 Chr. 1: 22.

3. Son of Jokshan, Gen. 25:3; 1 Chr. 1: 32.

4. A Benjamite who led an insurrection against David, 2 Sam. 20.

5. A Gadite, 1 Chr. 5:13.

6. A city of Simeon, Josh. 19:2.

7. Queen of, visits Solomon, 1 Kin. 10:1–13; 2 Chr. 9:1–12. Kings of, bring gifts to Solomon, Psa. 72:10. Rich in gold, Psa. 72:15; incense, Jer. 6:20. Merchandise of, Ezek. 27:22,23; 38:13. Prophecies concerning the people of, coming into the kingdom of Messiah, Isa. 60:6.

See SABEANS.

SHEBAH, a name given by Isaac to a well, Gen. 26:33.

SHEBAM, a city of Reuben, Num. 32:3. Apparently called also SHIBMAH and SIBMAH. See SIBMAH.

SHEBANIAH. 1. A priest in the time of David, 1 Chr. 15:24.

2. A Levite who joined Nehemiah in covenant, Neh. 9:4,5; 10:10.

3. A priest who joined Nehemiah in covenant, Neh. 10:4; 12:14.

4. A Levite who joined Nehemiah in covenant, Neh. 10:12.

SHEBARIM, a place near Ai, Josh. 7:5.

SHEBER, a son of Caleb, 1 Chr. 2:48.

SHEBNA. 1. A scribe of Hezekiah, 2 Kin. 18:18,26,37; 19:2; Isa. 36:3,11,22; 37:2.

2. An official of the king, Isa. 22:15–19.

SHEBUEL. 1. Son of Gershom, 1 Chr. 23:16; 26:24. Called SHUBAEL, 1 Chr. 24:20.

2. A singer, son of Heman, 1 Chr. 25:4. Called SHUBAEL, 1 Chr. 25:20.

SHECANIAH. 1. A priest of the time of David, 1 Chr. 24:11.

2. A priest of the time of Hezekiah, 2 Chr. 31:15.

SHECHANIAH. 1. A descendant of David, 1 Chr. 3:21,22.

2. Two men whose descendants returned with Ezra from captivity in Babylon, Ezra 8:3,5.

3. A Jew who proposed to Ezra the putting away of Gentile wives, Ezra 10:2.

4. Father of Shemaiah, Neh. 3:29. Possibly identical with 1.

5. Father-in-law of Tobiah, Neh. 6:18.

6. A Levite who returned with Zerubbabel from captivity in Babylon, Neh. 12:3.

SHECHEM. 1. Called also SICHEM and SYCHEM, a district in the central part of the land of Canaan. Abraham dwells in, Gen. 12:6. Jacob buys a piece of ground in, and erects an altar, Gen. 33:18–20. The flocks and herds of Jacob kept in, Gen. 37:12–14. Joseph buried in, Josh. 24:32. Jacob buried in, Acts 7:16, with Gen. 50:13.

2. Called also SYCHAR, a city of refuge in Mount Ephraim, Josh. 20:7; 21:21; Judg. 21: 19. Joshua assembled the tribes of Israel at, with all their elders, chiefs, and judges, and presented them before the Lord, Josh. 24:1–28. Joshua buried at, Josh. 24:30–32. Abimelech made king at, Judg. 8:31; 9. Rehoboam crowned at, 1 Kin. 12:1. Destroyed by Abimelech, Judg. 9:45; rebuilt by Jeroboam, 1 Kin. 12:25. Men of, slain by Ishmael, Jer. 41:5. Jesus visits; disciples made in, John 4:1–42.

3. Son of Hamor; seduces Jacob's daughter; slain by Jacob's sons, Gen. 33:19; 34; Josh. 24:32; Judg. 9:28. Called SYCHEM, Acts 7:16.

4. Ancestor of the Shechemites, Num. 26: 31; Josh. 17:2.

5. Son of Shemidah, 1 Chr. 7:19.

SHECHEMITES, descendants of Shechem, Num. 26:31.

SHEDEUR, father of Elizur, Num. 1:5; 2:10; 7:30,35; 10:18.

SHEEP. Offered in sacrifice, by Abel, Gen. 4:4; by Noah, Gen. 8:20; by Abraham, Gen. 22:13. See OFFERINGS. Required in the Mosaic offerings, see OFFERINGS. The land of Bashan adapted to the raising of, Deut. 32:14; Bozrah, Mic. 2:12; Kedar, Ezek. 27:21; Nebaioth, Isa. 60:7; Sharon, Isa. 65:10. Jacob's management of, Gen. 30:32–40. Milk of, used for food, Deut. 32:14. Shearing of, Gen. 31:19; 38:12–17; Isa. 53:7; feasting at the time of shearing, 1 Sam. 25:11,36; 2 Sam. 13:23. First fleece of, belonged to priests and Levites, Deut. 18:4. Tribute paid in, 2 Kin. 3:4; 1 Chr. 5:21; 2 Chr. 17:11.

FIGURATIVE: 1 Chr. 21:17; Psa. 74:1,

Jer. 13:20. Of backsliders, Jer. 50:6. Of lost sinners, Matt. 9:36; 10:6. Of the righteous, Jer. 50:17; Ezek. 34; Matt. 26:31; Mark 14:27; John 10:1-16. Of the defenselessness of ministers, Matt. 10:16.

Parable of the lost, Matt. 18:11-13; Luke 15:4-7.

SHEEP GATE, an ancient gate of Jerusalem, Neh. 3:1,32; 12:39; John 5:2 [R. V.].

SHEEP MARKET. Of Jerusalem, John 5:2. Translated in R. V., "sheep gate."

SHEET, of Peter's vision, Acts 10:11.

SHEHARIAH, a Benjamite, 1 Chr. 8:26.

SHEKEL. A weight, equal to twenty gerahs, Ex. 30:13; Num. 3:47; Ezek. 45:12. Used to weigh silver, Josh. 7:21; Judg. 8:26; 17:2,3. Fractions of, used in currency, Ex. 30:13; 1 Sam. 9:8; Neh. 10:32. Used to weigh gold, Gen. 24:22; Num. 7:14,20-86; Josh. 7: 21; 1 Kin. 10:16; cinnamon, Ex. 30:23; hair, 2 Sam. 14:26; iron, 1 Sam. 17:7; myrrh, Ex. 30:23; rations, Ezek. 4:10. Fines paid in, Deut. 22:19,29. Fees paid in, 1 Sam. 9:8. Sanctuary revenues paid in, Ex. 30:13; Neh. 10:32. Of different standards: Of the sanctuary, Ex. 30:13; of the king's weight, 2 Sam. 14:26. Corrupted, Amos 8:5.

SHEKINAH, the visible sign of God's presence on the ark of testimony in the Holy of holies, Ex. 25:22; Lev. 16:2; 2 Sam. 6:2; 2 Kin. 19:14,15; Psa. 80:1; Isa. 37:16; Ezek. 9:3; 10:18; Heb. 9:5.

SHELAH. 1. Son of Judah, Gen. 38:5, 11,14,26; 46:12; Num. 26:20; 1 Chr. 2:3; 4:21.

2. See SALAH.

SHELANITES. Descendants of Shelah, Num. 26:20. Apparently called SHILONITES, 1 Chr. 9:5.

SHELEMIAH. 1. A porter of the tabernacle, 1 Chr. 26:14.

2. Name of two descendants of Bani who put away Gentile wives, Ezra 10:39,41.

3. Father of Hananiah, Neh. 3:30.

4. A priest made treasurer by Nehemiah, Neh. 13:13.

5. Son of Cushi, Jer. 36:14.

6. Son of Abdeel, commanded to seize Jeremiah, Jer. 36:26.

7. Father of Jehucal, Jer. 37:3; 38:1.

8. Father of Irijah, Jer. 37:13.

SHELEPH, son of Joktan, Gen. 10:26; 1 Chr. 1:20.

SHELESH, son of Helem, 1 Chr. 7:35.

SHELOMI, father of Ahihud, Num. 34:27.

SHELOMITH. 1. Mother of a blasphemer, Lev. 24:11.

2. Daughter of Zerubbabel, 1 Chr. 3:19.

3. Son of Shimei, 1 Chr. 23:9.

4. A son of Izhar, 1 Chr. 23:18. Called SHELOMOTH, 1 Chr. 24:22.

5. A descendant of Eliezer, 1 Chr. 26:25, 26,28.

6. A son or daughter of Rehoboam, 2 Chr. 11:20.

7. Ancestor of a family that returned with Ezra from captivity in Babylon, Ezra 8:10.

SHELOMOTH. See SHELOMITH, 4.

SHELUMIEL, son of Zurishaddai, and leader of Simeon in time of Moses, Num. 1: 6; 2:12; 7:36,41; 10:19.

SHEM, son of Noah. Preserved in the ark, Gen. 5:32; 6:10; 7:13; 9:18; 1 Chr. 1:4. His filial conduct, Gen. 9:23-27. Descendants of, Gen. 10:1,21-31; 11:10-29; 1 Chr. 1: 17-54. Called SEM, Luke 3:36.

SHEMA. 1. A city of Judah, Josh. 15: 26.

2. A son of Hebron, 1 Chr. 2:43,44.

3. Son of Joel, 1 Chr. 5:8. Called SHEMAIAH, 1 Chr. 5:4.

4. A Benjamite, 1 Chr. 8:13.

5. A man who stood at the right hand of Ezra when he read the law to the people, Neh. 8:4.

SHEMAAH, father of two of David's mighty men, 1 Chr. 12:3.

SHEMAIAH. 1. A prophet in the time of Rehoboam. Prevents Rehoboam from war with Jeroboam, 1 Kin. 12:22-24; 2 Chr. 11:2-4. Prophesies the punishment of Rehoboam by Shishak, king of Egypt, 2 Chr. 12:5,7. Writes chronicles, 2 Chr. 12:15.

2. A descendant of David, 1 Chr. 3:22.

3. A Simeonite, 1 Chr. 4:37.

4. Son of Joel. 1 Chr. 5:4. Called SHEMA, 1 Chr. 5:8.

5. A Merarite, 1 Chr. 9:14. In charge of the business of the temple in time of Nehemiah, Neh. 11:15,16.

6. Son of Galal, 1 Chr. 9:16. Called SHAMMUA, Neh. 11:17.

7. A chief Levite in time of David ; assisted in moving the ark from Obed-edom, 1 Chr. 15:8,11.

8. A Levite who assisted in the division of the priests, 1 Chr. 24:6.

9. A porter of the temple in time of David, 1 Chr. 26:4,6,7.

10. A Levite sent by Jehoshaphat to instruct the people in the law, 2 Chr. 17:8.

11. A Levite, son of Jeduthun, 2 Chr. 29:14.

12. A Levite, 2 Chr. 31:15.

13. A Levite who contributed largely for passover sacrifices, 2 Chr. 35:9.

14. A Jew who returned from Babylon with Ezra, Ezra 8:13.

15. A chief man with Ezra, Ezra 8:16.

16. A priest who put away his Gentile wife, Ezra 10:21.

17. An Israelite who put away his Gentile wife, Ezra 10:31.

18. Keeper of the east gate of Jerusalem in the time of Nehemiah, Neh. 3:29.

19. A false prophet in the time of Nehemiah, Neh. 6:10.

20. A priest who sealed the covenant with Nehemiah, Neh. 10:8.

21. A priest with Zerubbabel, Neh. 12:6,18.

22. A priest, Neh. 12:35.

23. The name of three men who celebrated the dedication of the new wall of Jerusalem, Neh. 12:34,36,42.

24. Father of the prophet Urijah, Jer. 26:20.

25. A false prophet, Jer. 29:24-32.

26. Father of Delaiah, Jer. 36:12.

SHEMARIAH. 1. One of David's mighty men, 1 Chr. 12:5.

2. Name of two Israelites who put away Gentile wives, Ezra 10:32,41.

SHEMEBER, king of Zeboim, Gen. 14:2.

SHEMER, owner of the site on which Samaria was built, 1 Kin. 16:24.

SHEMIDA, called also SHEMIDAH. Son of Gilead, Num. 26:32; Josh. 17:2; 1 Chr. 7:19.

SHEMINITH. See MUSIC.

SHEMIRAMOTH. 1. A Levite musician. 1 Chr. 15:18,20; 16:5.

2. A Levite sent by Jehoshaphat to instruct the people in the law, 2 Chr. 17:8.

SHEMUEL. 1. A Simeonite appointed on the committee to divide the land of Canaan, Num. 34:20.

2. See SAMUEL.

3. Head of a family in Issachar. 1 Chr. 7:2.

SHEN, a place of unknown location, 1 Sam. 7:12.

SHENAZAR, son of Jeconiah, 1 Chr. 3:18.

SHENIR, called also SENIR. Amorite name of Mount Hermon, Deut. 3:9; 1 Chr. 5:23; Song 4:8; Ezek. 27:5.

SHEOL. See HELL.

SHEPHAM, a place on the eastern boundary of the promised land, Num. 34:10,11.

SHEPHATIAH. 1. Son of David, 2 Sam. 3:4; 1 Chr. 3:3.

2. A Benjamite, father of Meshullam. 1 Chr. 9:8.

3. A valiant man who joined David at Ziklag, 1 Chr. 12:5.

4. A ruler of Simeon, 1 Chr. 27:16.

5. Son of Jehoshaphat, 2 Chr. 21:2.

6. The name of two men, ancestors of families which returned to Jersualem from captivity in Babylon, Ezra 2:4,57; 8:8; Neh. 7:9,59.

7. A descendant of Perez, Neh. 11:4.

8. An enemy of Jeremiah, Jer. 38:1,4.

SHEPHERD. One who cares for flocks, Gen. 31:38-40; Psa. 78:52,53; Jer. 31:10; Amos 3:12; Luke 2:8. David the, defends his flock against a lion and a bear, 1 Sam. 17:34,35. Causes the flock to rest, Psa. 23:2; Song 1:7; Jer. 33:12. Numbers the flock, Lev. 27:32; Jer. 33:13. Knows his flock by name, John 10:3-5. Keeps the sheep and goats apart, Matt. 25:32. Waters the flocks, Gen. 29: 2-10. Keeps the flocks in folds, Num. 32:16; 1 Sam. 24:3; 2 Sam. 7:8; John 10:1. Watch towers of, 2 Chr. 26:10; Mic. 4:8. Dogs of, Job 30:1. Was an abomination to the Egyptians, Gen. 46:34. Angels appeared to, Luke 2:8-20.

INSTANCES OF: Abel, Gen. 4:2. Rachel, Gen. 29:9. Daughters of Jethro, Ex. 2:16. Moses, Ex. 3:1. David, 1 Sam. 16:11; 2 Sam. 7:8; Psa. 78:70.

FIGURATIVE: Gen. 49:24. Of God's care, Psa. 23; 78:52; 80:1. Of prophets, priests, Levites, and civil authorities, Ezek. 34. Of Christ, Zech. 13:7; Matt. 26:31; John 10:1-16; Heb. 13:20; 1 Pet. 2:25. Name given to Jesus, Isa. 40:11; Mark 14:27; John 10:11; 1 Pet. 2:25; 5:4.

Name given to Cyrus, Isa. 44:28.

SHEPHI. See SHEPHO.

SHEPHO. Son of Shobal, Gen. 36:23. Called SHEPI, 1 Chr. 1:40.

SHEPHUPHAN, son of Bela, 1 Chr. 8:5.

SHERAH, daughter of Ephraim, 1 Chr. 7:24.

SHEREBIAH, a Levite assistant to Ezra, Ezra 8:18,24; Neh. 8:7; 9:4,5.

2. A Levite who sealed the covenant with Nehemiah, Neh. 10:12; 12:8,24.

SHERESH, son of Machir, 1 Chr. 7:16.

SHEREZER, a delegate to priests and prophets to consult as to a day of humiliation, Zech. 7:2. _R. V._, SHAREZER.

SHERIFF, Dan. 3:2,3.

SHESHACH, a symbolical name, apparently applied to Babylon, Jer. 25:26; 51:41.

SHESHAI, a son of Anak, Num. 13:22; Josh. 15:14; Judg. 1:10.

SHESHAN, a descendant of Jerahmeel, 1 Chr. 2:31,34,35.

SHESHBAZZAR, a name given, apparently, to Zerubbabel, Ezra 1:8,11; 5:14,16. See ZERUBBABEL.

SHETH. 1. Num. 24:17. Translated "tumult" [_R. V._].

2. See SETH.

SHETHAR, a prince of Persia, Esth. 1:14.

SHETHAR-BOZNAI, an official of the king of Persia, Ezra 5:3,6; 6:6,13.

SHEVA. 1. See SERAIAH, 1.

2. Son of Caleb, 1 Chr. 2:49.

SHEWBREAD, Heb. 9:2. Called HALLOWED BREAD, 1 Sam. 21:6. Ordinance concerning, Lev. 24:5-9. Required to be kept before the Lord continually, Ex. 25:30; 2 Chr. 2:4. Provided by a yearly _per capita_ tax, Neh. 10:32,33. Prepared by the Levites, 1 Chr. 9:32; 23:29. Unlawfully eaten by David, 1 Sam. 21:6; Matt. 12:3,4; Mark 2:25, 26; Luke 6:3,4. Placed on the table of shewbread, Ex. 40:22,23. See TABLE OF, below.

TABLE OF, Heb. 9:2. Ordinances concening, Ex. 25:23-28; 37:10-15. Its situation in the tabernacle, Ex. 26:35; 40:22. Furniture of, Ex. 25:29,30; 37:16; Num. 4:7. Consecration of, Ex. 30:26,27,29. How removed, Num. 4:7,15. For the temple, 1 Kin. 7:48, 50; 2 Chr. 4:19,22.

SHIBBOLETH, Judg. 12:6.

SHIBMAH. A city of Reuben, Num. 32: 38. Apparently called also SHEBAM and SIBMAH.

See SIBMAH.

SHICRON, a city of Judah, Josh. 15:11.

SHIELD, defensive armor. Different kinds of, designated as buckler, shield, target, Psa. 35:2; Ezek. 38:4. Used by Saul, 2 Sam. 1:21; by the Benjamites, 2 Chr. 14: 8; 17:17. Uzziah equipped the children of Israel with, 2 Chr. 26:14. Made of brass,

1 Kin. 14:27; of gold, 2 Sam. 8:7; 1 Kin. 10:16, 17; 2 Chr. 9:15,16; of wood, Ezek. 39:9,10; with bosses, Job 15:26. Stored in armories, 1 Kin. 10:17; 2 Chr. 11:12; 32:5,27; in the tabernacle, 2 Kin. 11:10; 2 Chr. 23:9. Covered when not in use, Isa. 22:6. Painted red, Nah. 2:3.

See ARMS.

FIGURATIVE: Of God's protection, Gen. 15:1; Deut. 33:29; 2 Sam. 22:3,36; Psa. 5:12; 18:2,35; 33:20; 59:11; 84:9,11; 89:18; Prov. 30: 5. Of God's truth, Psa. 91:4. Of an entire army, Jer. 46:3.

SHIGGAION, Psa. 7; Hab. 3:1.

See MUSIC.

SHIHON, a city in Issachar, Josh. 19:19.

SHIHOR. See SIHOR.

SHIHOR-LIBNATH, a place on the border of Asher, Josh. 19:26.

SHILHI, grandfather of Jehoshaphat, 1 Kin. 22:42; 2 Chr. 20:31.

SHILHIM, a city of Judah, Josh. 15:32.

SHILLEM, called also SHALLUM. Son of Naphtali, Gen. 46:24; Num. 26:49; 1 Chr. 7:13.

SHILOAH. A stream or pool, Isa. 8:6. Probably identical with SILOAH and SILOAM, which see.

SHILOH. 1. A name of Jesus, Gen. 49:10.

2. City of Ephraim, north of Beth-el, and on the highway from Beth-el to Shechem, Judg. 21:19. Tabernacle at, Josh. 18:1,8–10; Judg. 18:31; 21:19; 1 Sam. 1:3,9,21,24; 2:14; Psa. 78:60; Jer. 7:12. Seat of government during the time of Joshua, Josh. 21:1,2. The place of rendezvous for the tribes, Josh. 22: 9,12; Judg. 21:12. Eli dwelt at, 1 Sam. 1:9; 4:12,13; dies at, 1 Sam. 4:18. Ahijah the prophet dwells at, 1 Kin. 14:2. Devoted men from, slain by Ishmael, Jer. 41:5–9.

SHILONI, father of Zechariah, Neh. 11:5.

SHILONITE. 1. A man of Shiloh, 1 Kin. 11:29; 12:15; 15:29; 2 Chr. 9:29; 10:15.

2. Used, apparently, to denote a descendant of Shelah, 1 Chr. 9:5.

See SHELAMITES.

SHILSHAH, son of Zophah, 1 Chr. 7:37.

SHIMEA. 1. See SHAMMUAH.

2. See SHAMMAH, 2.

3. A Merarite Levite, 1 Chr. 6:30.

4. Grandfather of Asaph, 1 Chr. 6:39.

SHIMEAH. 1. A Benjamite, son of Mikloth, 1 Chr. 8:32. Called SHIMEAM, 1 Chr. 9:38.

2. See SHAMMAH, 2.

SHIMEAM. See SHIMEAH, 1.

SHIMEATH, mother of an assassin of King Joash, 2 Kin. 12:21; 2 Chr. 24:26.

SHIMEATHITES, a family of scribes, 1 Chr. 2:55.

SHIMEI. 1. Called also SHIMI. Son of Gershon, Ex. 6:17; Num. 3:18; 1 Chr. 6:17; 23:7,10.

2. A Benjamite. Curses David; David's magnanimity toward, 2 Sam. 16:5–13; 19:16–23, with 1 Kin. 2:36–46.

3. An officer of David, 1 Kin. 1:8.

4. One of Solomon's commissary officers, 1 Kin. 4:18.

5. Grandson of Jeconiah, 1 Chr. 3:19.

6. Son of Zacchur, 1 Chr. 4:26,27.

7. A Reubenite. Son of Gog, 1 Chr. 5:4.

8. A Merarite. Son of Libni, 1 Chr. 6:29.

9. A Gershonite. Son of Jahath, 1 Chr. 6:42.

10. Father of a family in Benjamin, 1 Chr. 8:21 [R. V.]. In A. V., called SHIMHI.

11. A Levite, 1 Chr. 23:9.

12. A leader of singers in time of David, 1 Chr. 25:17.

13. David's overseer of vineyards, 1 Chr. 27:27.

14. A son of Heman, 2 Chr. 29:14.

15. A Levite. Treasurer of tithes and offerings in time of Hezekiah, 2 Chr. 31:12,13.

16. A Levite who put away his Gentile wife, Ezra 10:23.

17. The name of two Israelites who put away Gentile wives, Ezra 10:33,38.

18. A Benjamite. Grandfather of Mordecai, Esth. 2:5.

19. The ancestor of a family, Zech. 12:13. Possibly identical with 1.

SHIMEON, an Israelite who put away his Gentile wife, Ezra 10:31.

SHIMHI, father of a family in Benjamin, 1 Chr. 8:21. In R. V., called SHIMEI.

SHIMI. See SHIMEI, 1.

SHIMMA. See SHAMMAH, 2.

SHIMON, a man of Judah, 1 Chr. 4:20.

SHIMRATH, son of Shimhi, 1 Chr. 8:21.

SHIMRI. 1. Head of a family in Simeon, 1 Chr. 4:37,38.

2. Father of one of David's mighty men, 1 Chr. 11:45.

3. A Merarite, 1 Chr. 26:10 [R. V.]. In A. V., called SIMRI.

4. A Levite in the time of Hezekiah, 2 Chr. 29:13.

SHIMRITH, a Moabitess. Mother of Jehozabad, murderer of King Joash, 2 Chr. 24:26. Called SHOMER, 2 Kin. 12:21.

SHIMROM. See SHIMRON.

SHIMRON. 1. Son of Issachar, Gen. 46:13; Num. 26:24. Called SHIMROM, 1 Chr. 7:1.

2. A city in Zebulun, Josh. 11:1; 19:15. See SHIMRON-MERON.

SHIMRONITES, the family of Shimron, Num. 26:24.

SHIMRON-MERON. A city conquered by Joshua, Josh. 12:20. Probably identical with SHIMRON, 2, which see.

SHIMSHAI, a scribe, Ezra 4:8,9,17,23.

SHINAB, king of Admah, Gen. 14:2.

SHINAR, land of. See BABYLON.

SHIP. Built by Noah, Gen. 6:13–22; by Solomon, 1 Kin. 9:26; 2 Chr. 8:17; by Jehoshaphat, 1 Kin. 22:48; 2 Chr. 20:35,36; of gopher wood, Gen. 6:14; of fir wood, Ezek. 27:5; of bulrushes, Isa. 18:2; sealed with pitch, Gen. 6:15. Equipped with helm, Jas. 3:4; rudder, Acts 27:40; tackling, Isa. 33:23; Acts 27:19;

sails, Isa. 33:23; Acts 27:1,9,17,40; sails embroidered, Ezek. 27:7; masts, Isa. 33:23; Ezek. 27:5; oars, Jonah 1:13; Mark 6:48; figurehead, Acts 28:11; anchor, Acts 27:29,30,40; Heb. 6:19; lifeboats, Acts 27:30,32.   Used in commerce, Acts 21:3; 27:10; in commerce with Tarshish, 1 Kin. 22:48; Isa. 60:9; Jonah 1:3; with Ophir, 1 Kin. 10:11; 2 Chr. 8:18; with Adramyttium, Acts 27:2; for passenger traffic, Isa. 60:9; Jonah 1:3; Acts 20:13; 27:2,37; 28:11; for ferriage, 2 Sam. 19:18. Repaired by calking, Ezek. 27:9.   Wrecked at Ezion-geber, 1 Kin. 22:48; 2 Chr. 20:35–37; at Melita, Acts 27:14,44.   Warships used by Chittim, Num. 24:24; Dan. 11:30.

See MARINERS.

SHIPHI, father of Ziza, 1 Chr. 4:37.

SHIPHRAH, a Hebrew midwife, Ex. 1:15.

SHIPHTAN, father of the representative of Ephraim on the committee which divided the promised land among the Israelites, Num. 34:24.

SHISHA.   See SERIAH, 1.

SHISHAK, king of Egypt.   Gives asylum to Jeroboam, 1 Kin. 11:40.   Spoils Jerusalem, 1 Kin. 14:25,26; 2 Chr. 12:2–9.

SHITRAI, a chief herder of David, 1 Chr. 27:29.

SHITTIM. 1. Called also ABEL-SHITTIM, Num. 33:49.   A camping place of Israel, Num. 25:1; 33:49.   Joshua sends spies from, Josh. 2:1.   Valley of, Joel 3:18.   Balaam prophesies in, Mic. 6:5.

2. Called also SHITTAH, a tree, the wood of which is fragrant.   Planted and cultivated, Isa. 41:19.   The ark of the covenant made of, Ex. 25:10; staves of the ark, Ex. 25:13; 38:6; boards in the tabernacle, Ex. 26:15–37; the altar of burnt offering, Ex. 38:1,6.

SHIZA, a Reubenite.   Father of one of David's mighty men, 1 Chr. 11:42.

SHOA, an unknown country or city, or a symbolical term, Ezek. 23:23.

SHOBAB. 1. Son of David, 2 Sam. 5:14; 1 Chr. 3:5; 14:4.

2. Son of Caleb, 1 Chr. 2:18.

SHOBACH. Captain of the host of Hadarezer.   Slain by David's army, 2 Sam. 10:16, 18.   Called SHOPHACH, 1 Chr. 19:16,18.

SHOBAI, a porter, whose descendants returned to Jerusalem with Zerubbabel, Ezra 2:42; Neh. 7:45.

SHOBAL. 1. Son of Seir, Gen. 36:20, 23.29; 1 Chr. 1:38,40.

2. Son of Caleb, 1 Chr. 2:50,52.

3. Son of Judah, 1 Chr. 4:1,2.

SHOBEK, a Jew who sealed the covenant with Nehemiah, Neh. 10:24.

SHOBI, son of Nahash.   Brought supplies to David in his flight from Absalom, 2 Sam. 17:27.

SHOCHO.   See SOCOH, 1.

SHOCHOH.   See SOCOH, 1.

SHOCO.   See SOCOH, 1.

SHOE.   Taken off on holy ground, Ex. 3:5; Josh. 5:15; Acts 7:33.   Put off in mourn-ing, Ezek. 24:17.   Of the children of Israel did not wax old, Deut. 29:5.   Loosed in token of refusal to observe the levirate marriage, Deut. 25:9; Ruth 4:7,8.   Poor sold for a pair of, Amos 2:6; 8:6.   Made of iron, Deut. 33:25; of badgers' skins, Ezek. 16:10; latchet of, Gen. 14:23; Isa. 5:27; Mark 1:7; loosing of, a humble service, Luke 3:16.

SHOHAM, a Merarite, 1 Chr. 24:27.

SHOMER. 1. See SHAMER, 2.

2. See SHIMRITH.

SHOPHACH.   See SHOBACH.

SHOPHAN, a city in Gad, Num. 32:35. *R. V.,* Atroth-shophan.

SHOSHANNIM, called also SHUSHAN, SHOSHANNIM-EDUTH.   A wind instrument, mentioned in the titles of Psalms 45,60,69,80. See MUSIC, INSTRUMENTS OF.

SHOUTING.   IN JOY AND PRAISE: 1 Chr. 15:28. Thus all Israel brought up the ark of the covenant of the LORD with shouting, and with sound of the cornet, and with trumpets, and with cymbals, making a noise with psalteries and harps.

2 Chr. 15:12. And they entered into a covenant to seek the LORD God of their fathers with all their heart and with all their soul; 13. That whosoever would not seek the LORD God of Israel should be put to death, whether small or great, whether man or woman. 14. And they sware unto the LORD with a loud voice, and with shouting, and with trumpets, and with cornets.

Ezra 3:11. And they sang together by course in praising and giving thanks unto the LORD; because *he is* good, for his mercy *endureth* for ever toward Israel.   And all the people shouted with a great shout, when they praised the LORD, because the foundation of the house of the LORD was laid.   12. But many of the priests and Levites and chief of the fathers, *who were* ancient men, that had seen the first house, when the foundation of this house was laid before their eyes, wept with a loud voice; and many shouted aloud for joy: 13. So that the people could not discern the noise of the shout of joy from the noise of the weeping of the people: for the people shouted with a loud shout, and the noise was heard afar off.

Psa. 5:11. But let all those that put their trust in thee rejoice: let them ever shout for joy, because thou defendest them: let them also that love thy name be joyful in thee.

Psa. 47:1. O clap your hands, all ye people; shout unto God with the voice of triumph.

Isa. 12:6. Cry out and shout, thou inhabitant of Zion: for great *is* the Holy One of Israel in the midst of thee.

Luke 17:15. And one of them, when he saw that he was healed, turned back, and with a loud voice glorified God,

Luke 19:37. And when he was come nigh, even now at the descent of the mount of Olives, the whole multitude of the disciples began to rejoice and praise God with a loud voice for all the mighty works that they had seen; 38. Saying, Blessed *be* the King that cometh in the name of the Lord: peace in heaven, and glory in the highest. 39. And some of the Pharisees from among the multitude said unto him, Master, rebuke thy disciples. 40. And he answered and said unto them, I tell you that, if these should hold their peace, the stones would immediately cry out. 41. And when he was come near, he beheld the city, and wept over it.

Acts 3:8. And he leaping up stood, and walked, and entered with them into the temple, walking, and leaping, and praising God. 9. And all the people saw him walking and praising God:

Rev. 5:12. Saying with a loud voice, Worthy is the Lamb that was slain to receive power, and riches, and wisdom, and strength, and honour, and glory, and blessing. 13. And every creature which is in heaven, and on the earth, and under the earth, and such as are in the sea, and all that are in them, heard I saying, Blessing, and honour, and glory, and power, *be* unto him that sitteth upon the throne, and unto the Lamb for ever and ever. 14. And the four beasts said, Amen. And the four *and* twenty elders fell down and worshipped him that liveth for ever and ever.

SHOVEL, a utensil in the tabernacle, Ex. 27:3; 38:3; Num. 4:14; temple, 1 Kin. 7: 40; Jer. 52:18.

SHRINE, an idolatrous symbol of the Temple of Diana, Acts 19:24.

SHUA. 1. A Canaanite and father-in-law of Judah, Gen. 38:2,12 [*R. V., A. V.* SHUAH]; 1 Chr. 2:3.

2. Daughter of Heber, 1 Chr. 7:32.

SHUAH. 1. Son of Abraham by his wife, or concubine, Keturah, Gen. 25:2; 1 Chr. 1:32.

2. Brother of Chelub, 1 Chr. 4:11.

SHUAL. 1. Son of Zophah, 1 Chr. 7:36.

2. A country of unknown location, 1 Sam. 13:17.

SHUBAEL. See SHEBUEL, 1 and 2.

SHUHAM. Son of Dan, Num. 26:42. Called HUSHIM, Gen. 46:23.

SHUNAMMITE. 1. A person from Shunem. Abishag, the damsel who nourished David, 1 Kin. 1:3; desired by Adonijah as wife, 1 Kin. 2:13-25.

2. A woman who gave hospitality to Elisha, and whose son he raised to life, 2 Kin. 4:8-37.

SHUNEM. A city allotted to the tribe of Issachar, Josh. 19:18. Elisha dwells at, with the Shunammite, 2 Kin. 4. A maid found in, to nourish David, 1 Kin. 1:3.

SHUNI, son of Gad, Gen. 46:16; Num. 26:15.

SHUPHAM, son of Benjamin, Num. 26:39.

SHUPPIM. 1. Son of Ir, 1 Chr. 7: 12,15.

2. A Levite, 1 Chr. 26:16.

SHUR, a wilderness southwest of Palestine, Gen. 16:7; 20:1; 25:18; Ex. 15:22; 1 Sam. 15:7; 27:8.

SHUSHAN. 1. Capital of the Medo-Persian empire, Esth. 1:2,3; 8:15.

2. King's palace at, Neh. 1:1; Esth. 1:2,5; 2:5,8; 4:8,16; 8:14,15; 9:11,15.

SHUSHAN-EDUTH. See MUSIC.

SHUTHELAH. 1. Son of Ephraim, Num. 26:35,36; 1 Chr. 7:20.

2. Son of Zabad, 1 Chr. 7:21.

SHUTTLE, Job 7:6.

SIA. See SIAHA.

SIAHA, called also SIA. One of the Nethinim, Ezra 2:44; Neh. 7:47.

SIBBECAI. See SIBBECHAI.

SIBBECHAI, called also SIBBECAI. A captain in David's army, 2 Sam. 21:18; 1 Chr. 11:29; 20:4; 27:11.

SIBMAH. A city of Reuben, Josh. 13: 19: Isa. 16:8,9; Jer. 48:32. Apparently called also SHEBAM, Num. 32:3; and SHIBMAH, Num. 32:38.

SIBRAIM, a city of Syria, Ezek. 47:16.

SICHEM. See SHECHEM.

SICK, THE: Visiting, Psa. 41:6. Visiting, a duty, Matt. 25:36,43; Jas. 1:27.

FIGURATIVE: Isa. 1:5,6; Hos. 5:13. See AFFLICTED; AFFLICTION.

SICKLE, an agricultural implement used for cutting grain, Deut. 23:25; Jer. 50: 16; Mark 4:29.

FIGURATIVE: Of the judgments of God, Joel 3:13; Rev. 14:14-19.

SICKNESS. See AFFLICTION; DISEASE.

SIDDIM, vale of, a valley of uncertain location. Scene of the defeat of the king of Sodom, Gen. 14:3,8,10.

SIDON. 1. Called also ZIDON. Son of Canaan, Gen. 10:15; 1 Chr. 1:13.

2. A city on the northern boundary of the Canaanites, Gen. 10:19. Designated by Jacob as the border of Zebulun, Gen. 49:13. Was on the northern boundary of Asher, Josh. 19:28; 2 Sam. 24:6. Belonged to the land of Israel according to promise, Josh. 13:6. Inhabitants of, dwelt in security and carelessness, Judg. 18:7. Israelites failed to make conquest of, Judg. 1:31; 3:3. The inhabitants of, contributed cedar for the first and second temple, 1 Kin. 5:6; 1 Chr. 22:4; Ezra 3:7. Solomon marries women of, 1 Kin. 11: 1. Ahab marries a woman of, 1 Kin. 16:31. People of, come to hear Jesus, Mark 3:8; Luke 6:17. Inhabitants of, offend Herod, Acts 12:20-23.

Commerce of, Isa. 23:2,4,12. Seamen of, Ezek. 27:8. Prophecies concerning, Jer. 25: 15-22; 27:3-11; 47:4; Ezek. 28:21-23; 32:30; Joel 3:4-8. Jesus visits the region of, and heals the daughter of the Syrophenician woman, Matt. 15:21-28; Mark 7:24-31. Visited by Paul, Acts 27:3.

SIEGE. Offer of peace must be made to the city before beginning, Deut. 20:10-12. Conducted by erecting embankments parallel to the walls of the besieged city, Deut. 20:19,20; Isa. 29:3; 37:33. Battering-rams used in, see BATTERING-RAMS. Distress of the inhabitants during, 2 Kin. 6:24–29; 25:3; Isa. 9:20; 36:12; Jer. 19:9. Cannibalism in, 2 Kin. 6:28,29.

INSTANCES OF : Of Jericho, Josh. 6. Rabbah, 2 Sam. 11:1; Abel, 2 Sam. 20:15; Gibbethon, 1 Kin. 15:27; Tirzah, 1 Kin. 16:17. Jerusalem, by the children of Judah, Judg. 1:8; by David, 2 Sam. 5:6,9; by Rezin, king of Syria, and Pekah, son of Remaliah, king of Israel, 2 Kin. 16:5; by Nebuchadnezzar, 2 Kin. 24:10,11; Dan. 1:1; 2 Kin. 25:1–3; Jer. 52; by Sennacherib, 2 Chr. 32:1–23. Samaria, 1 Kin. 20:1; 2 Kin. 6:24; 17:5; 18:9–11.

SIEVE. FIGURATIVE: Isa. 30:28; Amos 9:9; Luke 22:31.

SIGN. A miracle to confirm faith, Matt. 12:38; 16:4; 24:3,30; Mark 8:11,12; 13:4; John 2:11; 3:2; 4:48. Asked for by, and given to, Abraham, Gen. 15:8–17; Moses, Ex. 4:1–9; Gideon, Judg. 6:17,36–40; Hezekiah, 2 Kin. 20:8; Zacharias, Luke 1:18. Given to Jeroboam, 1 Kin. 13:3–5.

A token of coming events, Matt. 16:3,4; 24:3.

See MIRACLES.

SIGNAL, used in war, Isa. 18:3.

See ARMIES; ENSIGNS; TRUMPETS.

SIHON, king of the Amorites. His seat of government at Heshbon, Num. 21:26. The proverbial chant celebrating the victory of Sihon over the Moabites, Num. 21:26–30. Conquest of his kingdom by the Israelites, Num. 21:21–25; Deut. 2:24–37; 3:2,6,8.

SIHOR, called also SHIHOR. A river of Egypt, given by some authorities as the Nile, Josh. 13:3; 1 Chr. 13:5; Isa. 23:3. Jer. 2:18.

SILAS, called also SILVANUS. Sent to Paul, in Antioch, from Jerusalem, Acts 15: 22–34. Becomes Paul's companion, Acts 15:40,41; 2 Cor. 1:19; 1 Thess. 1:1; 2 Thess. 1:1. Imprisoned with Paul in Philippi, Acts 16:19–40. Driven, with Paul, from Thessalonica, Acts 17:4–10. Left by Paul at Berea, Acts 17:14. Rejoins Paul at Corinth, Acts 17:15; 18:5. Carries Peter's epistle to Asia Minor, 1 Pet. 5:12.

SILK. Wearing apparel made of, Prov. 31:22; Ezek. 16:10,13. Merchandise of, Rev. 18:12.

See COTTON; LINEN.

SILLA, a place of uncertain location, 2 Kin. 12:20.

SILOAH. See SILOAM.

SILOAM, called also SHILOAH and SILOAH. A pool in Jerusalem, Neh. 3:15; Isa. 8:6. Jesus directs the blind man, whom he healed, to wash in, John 9:1–11.

Tower of, in the wall of Jerusalem, falls and kills eighteen people, Luke 13:4.

SILVANUS. See SILAS.

SILVER. From Tarshish, Ezek. 27:12; Refining of, Prov. 17:3; 25:4; 26:23; Ezek. 22: 18–22; Jer. 6:29,30; Zech. 13:9; Mal. 3:3. See REFINING. Used for money, Gen. 13:2; 17:12; 20:16; 23:13–16; Amos 8:6; Matt. 10:9; 26:15; Mark 14:11; Acts 19:19. See MONEY. For

ornamentation of, and in the manufacture of, the utensils for the tabernacle, Ex. 26:19; 27:17; 35:24; 36:24; 38:25; Num. 7:13,19,25,31, 37,43,49,55,61,67,73,79,85; of the temple, 1 Chr. 28:14; 29:2–5; Ezra 5:14; 6:5; 8:26; Dan. 5:2. Cups made of, Gen. 44:2; trumpets, Num. 10:2; cords, Eccl. 12:6; chains, Isa. 40:19; shrines, Acts 19:24; idols, Ex. 20:23; Isa. 30:22; Hos. 13:2; baskets [*R. V.*], or filigree [marg., *R. V.*], Prov. 25:11; jewels, Song 1:11; see JEWELS; palace, Song 8:9.

Vessels of, Num. 7:85; 1 Kin. 10:25; 2 Sam. 8:10; 2 Kin. 12:13; 1 Chr. 18:10; 2 Chr. 24:14; Ezra 1:6; 5:14; 6:5; 8:26; Dan. 5:2; 11:8.

Abundance of, 1 Kin. 10:27; 1 Chr. 22:14; 29:2–7; 2 Chr. 1:15; Eccl. 2:8; Isa. 2:7. Dross from, Prov. 25:4; 26:23. Reprobate, Jer. 6: 30. Workers in, 2 Chr. 2:14; Acts 19:24. See SMITH.

See MONEY.

SYMBOLICAL : Dan. 2:32,35.

SILVERSMITH, Acts 19:24.

See SMITH.

SIMEON. 1. Son of Jacob, Gen. 29:33; 35:23; Ex. 1:1,2; 1 Chr. 2:1. With Levi avenges upon the Shechemites the seduction of Dinah, Gen. 34; 49:5–7. Jacob's denunciation of, Gen. 34:30; 49:5–7. Goes down into Egypt to buy corn; is bound by Joseph, and detained, Gen. 42:24,36; 43:23. His sons, Gen. 46:10; Ex. 6:15; 1 Chr. 4:24–37. Descendants of, Num. 26:12–14. See TRIBE OF, below.

2. TRIBE OF: Military enrollment of, at Sinai, Num. 1:22,23; 2:13; in the plains of Moab, Num. 26:14. Place of, in camp and march, Num. 2:12; 10:18,19. Inheritance allotted to, Josh. 19:1–9; Judg. 1:3–17; 1 Chr. 4:24–43. Stood on Mount Gerizim to bless at the time of the rehearsal of the law, Deut. 27:12. Joined with the people of Judah and Benjamin in the renewal of the passover, 2 Chr. 15:9, with *vs.* 1–15. Idolatry of, 2 Chr. 34:6, with *vs.* 1–7.

See ISRAEL.

3. A devout man in Jerusalem. Blesses Jesus in the temple, Luke 2:25–35.

4. An ancestor of Jesus, Luke 3:30.

5. A disciple. Called also NIGER, Acts 13:1.

6. Name given to Peter, Acts 15:14. See PETER.

SIMILITUDE, Hos. 12:10. See FIGURES: PARABLES: SYMBOLS; TYPES.

SIMON. 1. See PETER.

2. One of the twelve apostles. Called THE CANAANITE, Matt. 10:4; Mark 3:18; ZELOTES, Luke 6:15; Acts 1:13.

3. A brother of Jesus, Matt. 13:55; Mark 6:3.

4. A leper. Jesus dines with, Matt. 26:6; Mark 14:3.

5. A man of Cyrene. Compelled to carry Jesus' cross, Matt. 27:32; Mark 15:21; Luke 23:26.

6. A Pharisee. Jesus dines with, Luke 7:36–44.

7. The father of Judas Iscariot, John 6:71; 12:4; 13:2,26.

8. A sorcerer. Converted by Philip; rebuked by Peter, Acts 8:9-13,18-24.

9. A tanner. Peter lodges with, Acts 9:43; 10:6,17,32.

SIMONY, ecclesiastical corruption, Acts 8:18,19.

SIMRI. A Merarite, 1 Chr. 26:10. In R. V., called SHIMRI.

SIN. INDEX OF SUB-TOPICS: *Miscellany of Minor Sub-Topics,* p. 1273; *Unclassified Scriptures Relating to, Defining and Illustrating,* p. 1273; *Confession of,* p. 1275; *Consequences of, Entailed Upon Children,* p.1277; *Conviction of,* p. 1278; *Forgiveness of,* p.1278; *Fruits of,* p. 1280; *Known to God,* p. 1283; *Love of,* p. 1284; *National, Punishment of, with Instances of,* p. 1285; *Punishment of,* p. 1286; *Repugnant to God,* p. 1287; *Repugnant to the Righteous,* p. 1288; *Separates from God,* p. 1289.

MISCELLANY OF MINOR SUB-TOPICS: Paul's discussion of the responsibility for, Rom. chapters 2-9. Degrees in, Luke 7: 41-47; 12:47,48. Progressive, Deut. 29:19; 1 Kin. 16:31; Psa. 1:1; Isa. 5:18; 30:1; Jer. 9:3; 16:11,12; Hos. 13:2; 2 Tim. 3:13. Its progressiveness exemplified in Joseph's brethren, 1. Jealousy, Gen. 37:4. 2. Conspiracy, Gen. 37:18. 3. Murder, Gen. 37:20.

Sinfulness of, Job 22:5; Psa. 25:11; Isa. 1: 18; Rom. 7:13. Defiles, Psa. 51:2,7; Isa. 1:18; 1 John 1:7. See DEFILEMENT.

To be hated, Deut. 7:26; Psa. 119:113. Against the body, Eccl. 5:6. The besetting, Heb. 12:1. Little sins, Song. 2:15.

Unpardonable, Matt. 12:31; Mark 3:29; Luke 12:10; 1 John 5:16:17. Instances of unpardonable: Israel's, Num. 14:26-45; of Eli's house, 1 Sam. 3:14. See REPROBACY. No escape from the consequences of, Gen. 3:8-12; Isa. 28:18-22; Am. 9:1-4; Matt. 23:33; Heb. 2:3. See PUNISHMENT, NO ESCAPE FROM. Attempt to cover, vain, Isa. 29:15; 59:6. Secret sins, Psa. 19:12; 44:21; 64:2; 90:8; Eccl. 12:14; Ezek. 8:12; 11:5; Matt. 10:26; Luke 8:17; 12:2,3; John 3:20; Rom. 2:16; Eph. 5:12. Fools mock at, Prov. 14:9.

Against knowledge, Prov. 26:11; Luke 12:47; 48; John 9:41; 15:22; Rom. 1:21,32; 2:17-23; Heb. 10:26; Jas.4:17; 2 Pet. 2:21,22. See IGNORANCE, SINS OF. Not imputed to righteous, Psa. 32:2; ignorant, Rom. 5:13; redeemed, 2 Cor. 5:19.

Pleasures of, Job 20:12-16; 21:12,13; Luke 8:14. See PLEASURES, WORLDLY.

In believers a reproach to the Lord, 2 Sam. 12:14. None in heaven, Rev. 22:3,4.

UNCLASSIFIED SCRIPTURES RELATING TO, DEFINING AND ILLUSTRATING: Deut. 29:18. Lest there should be among you man, or woman, or family, or tribe, whose heart turneth away this day from the LORD our God, to go *and* serve the gods of these nations; lest there should be among you a root that beareth gall and wormwood;

2 Chr. 12:14. And he did evil, because he prepared not his heart to seek the LORD.

Job 14:4. Who can bring a clean *thing* out of an unclean? not one.

Job 22:5. *Is* not thy wickedness great? and thine iniquities infinite?

Psa. 25:11. For thy name's sake, O LORD, pardon mine iniquity; for it *is* great.

Psa. 95:10. Forty years long was I grieved with *this* generation, and said, It *is* a people that do err in their heart, and they have not known my ways:

Prov. 4:23. Keep thy heart with all diligence; for out of it *are* the issues of life.

Prov. 24:8. He that deviseth to do evil shall be called a mischievous person. 9. The thought of foolishness *is* sin: and the scorner *is* an abomination to men.

Eccl. 5:6. Suffer not thy mouth to cause thy flesh to sin; neither say thou before the angel, that it *was* an error: wherefore should God be angry at thy voice, and destroy the work of thine hands?

Isa. 1:6. From the sole of the foot even unto the head *there is* no soundness in it; *but* wounds, and bruises, and putrifying sores: they have not been closed, neither bound up, neither mollified with ointment. 18. Come now, and let us reason together, saith the LORD: though your sins be as scarlet, they shall be as white as snow; though they be red like crimson, they shall be as wool.

Isa. 44:20. He feedeth on ashes: a deceived heart hath turned him aside, that he cannot deliver his soul, nor say, *Is there* not a lie in my right hand?

Jer. 7:24. But they hearkened not, nor inclined their ear, but walked in the counsels *and* in the imagination of their evil heart, and went backward, and not forward.

Jer. 17:9. The heart *is* deceitful above all *things*, and desperately ꞁ wicked: who can know it? 　　　　　　　　[R. V. sick]

Ezek. 20:16. Because they despised my judgments, and walked not in my statutes, but polluted my sabbaths; for their heart went after their idols.

Matt. 5:28. But I say unto you, That whosoever looketh on a woman to lust after her hath committed adultery with her already in his heart.

Matt. 12:31. Wherefore I say unto you, All manner of sin and blasphemy shall be forgiven unto men: but the blasphemy *against* the *Holy* Ghost shall not be forgiven unto men. [Mark 3:29; Luke 12:10; 1 John 5:16,17.] 33. Either make the tree good, and his fruit good; or else make the tree corrupt, and his fruit corrupt: for the tree is known by his fruit. [Matt. 7:17,18.] 34. O generation of vipers, how can ye, being evil, speak good things? for out of the abundance of the heart the mouth speaketh. 35. A good man out of the good treasure of the heart bringeth forth good things: and an evil man out of the evil treasure bringeth forth evil things. Luke 6:45.

Matt. 13:24. Another parable put he forth unto them, saying, The kingdom of heaven is likened unto a man which sowed good seed in his field: 25. But while men slept, his enemy came and sowed tares among the wheat, and went his way. 38. The field is the world; the good seed are the children of the kingdom; but the tares are the children of the wicked one; 39. The enemy that sowed them is the devil; the harvest is the end of the world; and the reapers are the angels.

Matt. 15:2. Why do thy disciples transgress the tradition of the elders? for they wash not their hands when they eat bread. 3. But he answered and said unto them, Why do ye also transgress the commandment of God by your tradition? 4. For God commanded, saying, Honour thy father and mother; and, He that curseth father or m ther, let him die the death. 5. But ye say, Whosoever shall say to *his* father or *his* mother, It is a gift, by whatsoever thou mightest be profited by me; 6. And honour not his father or his mother, *he shall be free.* Thus have ye made the commandment of God of none effect by your tradition. 7. *Ye* hypocrites, well did Esaias prophesy of you, saying, 8. This people draweth nigh unto me with their mouth, and honoureth me with *their* lips; but their heart is far from me. 9. But in vain they do worship me, teaching *for* doctrines the commandments of men. 10. And he called the multitude, and said unto them, Hear, and understand: 11. Not that which goeth into the mouth defileth a man; but that which cometh out of the mouth, this defileth a man. 12. Then came his disciples, and said unto him, Knowest thou that the Pharisees were offended, after they heard this saying? 13. But he answered and said, Every plant, which my heavenly Father hath not planted, shall be rooted up. 14. Let them alone: they be blind leaders of the blind. And if the blind lead the blind, both shall fall into the ditch. 15. Then answered Peter and said unto him, Declare unto us this parable. 16. And Jesus said, Are ye also yet without understanding? 17. Do not ye yet understand, that whatsoever entereth in at the mouth goeth into the belly, and is cast out into the draught? 18. But those things which proceed out of the mouth come forth from the heart; and they defile the man. 19. For out of the heart proceed evil thoughts, murders, adulteries, fornications, thefts, false witness, blasphemies: 20. These are *the things* which defile a man: but to eat with unwashen hands defileth not a man.

John 8:34. Jesus answered them, Verily, verily, I say unto you, Whosoever committeth sin is the servant of sin. 44. Ye are of *your* father the devil, and the lusts of your father ye will do. He was a murderer from the beginning, and abode not in the truth, because there is no truth in him. When he speaketh a lie, he speaketh of his own; for he is a liar, and the father of it.

Rom. 5:12. Wherefore, as by one man sin entered into the world, and death by sin;

and so death passed upon all men, for that all have sinned: 13. (For until the law sin was in the world: but sin is not imputed when there is no law. 14. Nevertheless death reigned from Adam to Moses, even over them that had not sinned after the similitude of Adam's transgression, who is the figure of him that was to come. 15. But not as the offence, so also *is* the free gift. For if through the offence of one many be dead, much more the grace of God, and the gift by grace, *which is* by one man, Jesus Christ, hath abounded unto many. 16. And not as *it was* by one that sinned, *so is* the gift: for the judgment *was* by one to condemnation, but the free gift *is* of many offences unto justification. 17. For if by one man's offence death reigned by one; much more they which receive abundance of grace and of the gift of righteousness shall reign in life by one, Jesus Christ.) 18. Therefore, as by the offence of one *judgment came* upon all men to condemnation; even so by the righteousness of one *the free gift came* upon all men unto justification of life. 19. For as by one man's disobedience many were made sinners, so by the obedience of one shall many be made righteous. 20. Moreover the law entered, that the offence might abound. But where sin abounded, grace did much more abound: 21. That as sin hath reigned unto death, even so might grace reign through righteousness unto eternal life by Jesus Christ our Lord.

Rom. 7:7. What shall we say then? *Is* the law sin? God forbid. Nay, I had not known sin, but by the law: for I had not known lust, except the law had said, Thou shalt not covet. 13. Was then that which is good made death unto me? God forbid. But sin, that it might appear sin, working death in me by that which is good; that sin by the commandment might become exceeding sinful.

Rom. 14:23. And he that doubteth is damned if he eat, because *he eateth* not of faith: for whatsoever *is* not of faith is sin.

1 Cor. 5:6. Know ye not that a little leaven leaveneth the whole lump?

Eph. 2:1. You *hath he quickened,* who were dead in trespasses and sins; 2. Wherein in time past ye walked according to the course of this world, according to the prince of the power of the air, the spirit that now worketh in the children of disobedience:

Heb. 3:13. But exhort one another daily, while it is called To day; lest any of you be hardened through the deceitfulness of sin.

Heb. 12:15. Looking diligently lest any man fail of the grace of God; lest any root of bitterness springing up trouble *you,* and thereby many be defiled;

Jas. 1:14. But every man is tempted, when he is drawn away of his own lust, and enticed. 15. Then when lust hath conceived, it bringeth forth sin: and sin, when it is finished, bringeth forth death.

Jas. 2:10. For whosoever shall keep the

whole law, and yet offend in one *point*, he is guilty of all. 11. For he that said, Do not commit adultery, said also, Do not kill. Now if thou commit no adultery, yet if thou kill, thou art become a transgressor of the law.

Jas. 4:1. From whence *come* wars and fightings among you? *come they* not hence, *even* of your lusts that war in your members? 2. Ye lust, and have not: ye kill, and desire to have, and cannot obtain: ye fight and war, yet ye have not, because ye ask not. 3. Ye ask, and receive not, because ye ask amiss, that ye may consume *it* upon your lusts. 17. Therefore to him that knoweth to do good, and doeth *it* not, to him it is sin.

2 Pet. 1:4. That by these ye might be partakers of the divine nature, having escaped the corruption that is in the world through lust.

1 John 3:4. Whosoever committeth sin transgresseth also the law: for sin is the transgression of the law. 6. Whosoever abideth in him sinneth not: whosoever sinneth hath not seen him, neither known him. 8. He that committeth sin is of the devil; for the devil sinneth from the beginning. For this purpose the Son of God was manifested, that he might destroy the works of the devil. 9. Whosoever is born of God doth not commit sin; for his seed remaineth in him: and he cannot sin, because he is born of God. 10. In this the children of God are manifest, and the children of the devil: whosoever doeth not righteousness is not of God, neither he that loveth not his brother. 15. Whosoever hateth his brother is a murderer: and ye know that no murderer hath eternal life abiding in him.

1 John 5:17. All unrighteousness is sin:

For various phases of, and those kindred to, this topic, not found under this heading, see ATONEMENT; CONVICTION; DEPRAVITY; REGENERATION; REPENTANCE; REPROBACY; SALVATION; SANCTIFICATION; WICKED, THE, PUNISHMENT OF.

CONFESSION OF: Lev. 16:21. And Aaron shall lay both his hands upon the head of the live goat, and confess over him all the iniquities of the children of Israel, and all their transgressions in all their sins, putting them upon the head of the goat, and shall send *him* away by the hand of a fit man into the wilderness:

Num. 14:40. And they rose up early in the morning, and gat them up into the top of the mountain, saying, Lo, we *be here*, and will go up unto the place which the LORD hath promised: for we have sinned.

2 Sam. 24:10. And David's heart smote him after that he had numbered the people. And David said unto the LORD, I have sinned greatly in that I have done: and now, I beseech thee, O LORD, take away the iniquity of thy servant; for I have done very foolishly. 17. And David spake unto the LORD when he saw the angel that smote

the people, and said, Lo, I have sinned, and I have done wickedly: but these sheep, what have they done? let thine hand, I pray thee, be against me, and against my father's house. 1 Chr. 21:17.

2 Chr. 29:6. For our fathers have trespassed, and done *that which was* evil in the eyes of the LORD our God, and have forsaken him, and have turned away their faces from the habitation of the LORD, and turned *their* backs.

Ezra 9:4. Then were assembled unto me every one that trembled at the words of the God of Israel, because of the transgression of those that had been carried away; and I sat astonied until the evening sacrifice. 5. And at the evening sacrifice I arose up from my heaviness; and having rent my garment and my mantle, I fell upon my knees, and spread out my hands unto the LORD my God, 6. And said, O my God, I am ashamed and blush to lift up my face to thee, my God: for our iniquities are increased over *our* head, and our trespass is grown up unto the heavens. 7. Since the days of our fathers *have* we *been* in a great trespass unto this day; 10. And now, O our God, what shall we say after this? for we have forsaken thy commandments, 11 Which thou hast commanded by thy servants the prophets, saying, The land, unto which ye go to possess it, is an unclean land with the filthiness of the people of the lands, with their abominations, which have filled it from one end to another with their uncleanness. 12. Now therefore give not your daughters unto their sons, neither take their daughters unto your sons, nor seek their peace or their wealth for ever: that ye may be strong, and eat the good of the land, and leave *it* for an inheritance to your children for ever. 13. And after all that is come upon us for our evil deeds, and for our great trespass, seeing that thou our God hast punished us less than our iniquities *deserve*, and hast given us *such* deliverance as this; 14. Should we again break thy commandments, and join in affinity with the people of these abominations? wouldest not thou be angry with us till thou hadst consumed *us*, so that *there should be* no remnant nor escaping? 15. O LORD God of Israel, thou *art* righteous: for we remain yet escaped, as *it is* this day: behold, we *are* before thee in our trespasses: for we cannot stand before thee because of this.

Neh. 1:6. Let thine ear now be attentive, and thine eyes open, that thou mayest hear the prayer of thy servant, which I pray before thee now, day and night, for the children of Israel thy servants, and confess the sins of the children of Israel, which we have sinned against thee: both I and my father's house have sinned. 7. We have dealt very corruptly against thee, and have not kept the commandments, nor the statutes, nor the judgments, which thou commandedst thy servant Moses. *vs.* 8,9.

Neh. 9:2. And the seed of Israel separated themselves from all strangers, and stood and confessed their sins, and the iniquities of their fathers. 3. And they stood up in their place, and read in the book of the law of the Lord their God *one* fourth part of the day; and *another* fourth part they confessed, and worshipped the Lord their God. 33. Howbeit thou *art* just in all that is brought upon us; for thou hast done right, but we have done wickedly: 34. Neither have our kings, our princes, our priests, nor our fathers, kept thy law, nor hearkened unto thy commandments and thy testimonies, wherewith thou didst testify against them. 35. For they have not served thee in their kingdom, and in thy great goodness that thou gavest them, and in the large and fat land which thou gavest before them, neither turned they from their wicked works. *vs.* 5-38.

Job 7:20. I have sinned; what shall I do unto thee, O thou preserver of men?

Job 9:20. If I justify myself, mine own mouth shall condemn me: *if I say,* I *am* perfect, it shall also prove me perverse.

Job 13:23. How many *are* mine iniquities and sins? make me to know my transgression and my sin.

Job 40:4. Behold, I am vile; what shall I answer thee? I will lay mine hand upon my mouth.

Job 42:5. I have heard of thee by the hearing of the ear: but now mine eye seeth thee. 6. Wherefore I abhor *myself*, and repent in dust and ashes.

Psa. 32:5. I acknowledged my sin unto thee, and mine iniquity have I not hid. I said, I will confess my transgressions unto the Lord; and thou forgavest the iniquity of my sin.

Psa. 38:3. *There is* no soundness in my flesh because of thine anger; neither *is there any* rest in my bones because of my sin. 4. For mine iniquities are gone over mine head: as an heavy burden they are too heavy for me. 18. For I will declare mine iniquity; I will be sorry for my sin.

Psa. 40:11. Withhold not thou thy tender mercies from me, O Lord: let thy lovingkindness and thy truth continually preserve me. 12. For innumerable evils have compassed me about; mine iniquities have taken hold upon me, so that I am not able to look up; they are more than the hairs of mine head: therefore my heart faileth me.

Psa. 41:4. I said, Lord, be merciful unto me: heal my soul; for I have sinned against thee.

Psa. 51:2. Wash me throughly from mine iniquity, and cleanse me from my sin. 3. For I acknowledge my transgressions: and my sin *is* ever before me. 4. Against thee, thee only, have I sinned, and done *this* evil in thy sight: that thou mightest be justified when thou speakest, *and* be clear when thou judgest. 5. Behold, I was shapen in iniquity; and in sin did my mother conceive me.

Psa. 69:5. O God, thou knowest my foolishness; and my sins are not hid from thee.

Psa. 73:21. Thus my heart was grieved, and I was pricked in my reins. 22. So foolish *was* I, and ignorant: I was *as* a beast before thee.

Psa. 106:6. We have sinned with our fathers, we have committed iniquity, we have done wickedly.

Psa. 119:59. I thought on my ways, and turned my feet unto thy testimonies. 60. I made haste, and delayed not to keep thy commandments. 176. I have gone astray like a lost sheep; seek thy servant;

Psa. 130:3. If thou, Lord, shouldest mark iniquities, O Lord, who shall stand?

Isa. 6:5. Then said I, Woe *is* me! for I am undone; because I *am* a man of unclean lips, and I dwell in the midst of a people of unclean lips:

Isa. 26:13. O Lord our God, *other* lords beside thee have had dominion over us: *but* by thee only will we make mention of thy name.

Isa. 59:12. For our transgressions are multiplied before thee, and our sins testify against us: for our transgressions *are* with us; and *as for* our iniquities, we know them; 13. In transgressing and lying against the Lord, and departing away from our God, speaking oppression and revolt, conceiving and uttering from the heart words of falsehood. 14. And judgment is turned away backward, and justice standeth afar off: for truth is fallen in the street, and equity cannot enter. 15. Yea, truth faileth; and he *that* departeth from evil maketh himself a prey: and the Lord saw *it*, and it displeased him that *there was* no judgment.

Isa. 64:5. Thou meetest him that rejoiceth and worketh righteousness, *those that* remember thee in thy ways: behold, thou art wroth; for we have sinned: in those is continuance, and we shall be saved. 6. But we are all as an unclean *thing*, and all our righteousnesses *are* as filthy rags; and we all do fade as a leaf; and our iniquities, like the wind, have taken us away. 7. And *there is* none that calleth upon thy name, that stirreth up himself to take hold of thee: for thou hast hid thy face from us, and hast consumed us, because of our iniquities.

Jer. 3:21. A voice was heard upon the high places, weeping *and* supplications of the children of Israel: for they have perverted their way, *and* they have forgotten the Lord their God. 22. Return, ye backsliding children, *and* I will heal your backslidings. Behold, we come unto thee; for thou art the Lord our God. 25. We lie down in our shame, and our confusion covereth us: for we have sinned against the Lord our God, we and our fathers, from our youth even unto this day, and have not obeyed the voice of the Lord our God.

Jer. 8:14. Why do we sit still? assemble

yourselves, and let us enter into the defenced cities, and let us be silent there: for the LORD our God hath put us to silence, and given us water of gall to drink, because we have sinned against the LORD. 15. We looked for peace, but no good *came; and* for a time of health, and behold trouble!

Jer. 14:7. O LORD, though our iniquities testify against us, do thou *it* for thy name's sake: for our backslidings are many; we have sinned against thee. 20. We acknowledge, O LORD, our wickedness, *and* the iniquity of our fathers: for we have sinned against thee.

Jer. 31:18. I have surely heard Ephraim bemoaning himself *thus;* Thou hast chastised me, and I was chastised, as a bullock unaccustomed *to the yoke:* turn thou me, and I shall be turned; for thou *art* the LORD my God. 19. Surely after that I was turned, I repented; and after that I was instructed, I smote upon *my* thigh: I was ashamed, yea, even confounded, because I did bear the reproach of my youth.

Lam. 1:18. The LORD is righteous; for I have rebelled against his commandment: 20. Behold, O LORD; for I *am* in distress: my bowels are troubled; mine heart is turned within me; for I have grievously rebelled:

Lam. 3:40. Let us search and try our ways, and turn again to the LORD. 41. Let us lift up our heart with *our* hands unto God in the heavens. 42. We have transgressed and have rebelled: thou hast not pardoned.

Dan. 9:5. We have sinned, and have committed iniquity, and have done wickedly, and have rebelled, even by departing from thy precepts and from thy judgments: 6. Neither have we hearkened unto thy servants the prophets, which spake in thy name to our kings, our princes, and our fathers, and to all the people of the land. 8. O Lord, to us *belongeth* confusion of face, to our kings, to our princes, and to our fathers, because we have sinned against thee. 9. To the Lord our God *belong* mercies and forgivenesses, though we have rebelled against him; 10. Neither have we obeyed the voice of the LORD our God, to walk in his laws, which he set before us by his servants the prophets. 11. Yea, all Israel have transgressed thy law, even by departing, that they might not obey thy voice; 15. And now, O Lord our God, that hast brought thy people forth out of the land of Egypt with a mighty hand, and hast gotten thee renown, as at this day; we have sinned, we have done wickedly.

Luke 15:17. And when he came to himself, he said, How many hired servants of my father's have bread enough and to spare, and I perish with hunger! 18. I will arise, and go to my father, and will say unto him, Father, I have sinned against heaven, and before thee, 19. And am no more worthy to be called thy son: make

me as as one of thy hired servants. 20. And he arose, and came to his father. But when he was yet a great way off, his father saw him, and had compassion, and ran, and fell on his neck, and kissed him. 21. And the son said unto him, Father, I have sinned against heaven, and in thy sight, and am no more worthy to be called thy son.

1 Cor. 15:9. I am the least of the apostles, that am not meet to be called an apostle, because I persecuted the church of God.

Jas. 5:16. Confess *your* faults one to another, and pray one for another, that ye may be healed.

1 John 1:8. If we say that we have no sin, we deceive ourselves, and the truth is not in us. 9. If we confess our sins, he is faithful and just to forgive us *our* sins, and to cleanse us from all unrighteousness. 10. If we say that we have not sinned, we make him a liar, and his word is not in us.

CONSEQUENCES OF, ENTAILED UPON CHILDREN: Ex. 20:5. I the LORD thy God *am* a jealous God, visiting the iniquity of the fathers upon the children unto the third and fourth *generation* of them that hate me; Ex. 34:7.

Lev. 26:39. And they that are left of you shall pine away in their iniquity in your enemies' lands; and also in the iniquities of their fathers shall they pine away with them. *v.* 40.

Num. 14:33. And your children shall wander in the wilderness forty years, and bear your whoredoms, until your carcases be wasted in the wilderness.

Job 5:4. His children are far from safety, and they are crushed in the gate, neither *is there* any to deliver *them.*

Job 18:19. He shall neither have son nor nephew among his people, nor any remaining in his dwellings.

Job. 21:19. God layeth up his iniquity for his children: he rewardeth him, and he shall know *it.*

Psa. 21:10. Their fruit shalt thou destroy from the earth, and their seed from among the children of men.

Psa. 37:28. For the LORD loveth judgment, and forsaketh not his saints; they are preserved for ever: but the seed of the wicked shall be cut off.

Psa. 109:9. Let his children be fatherless, and his wife a widow. 10. Let his children be continually vagabonds, and beg; let them seek *their bread* also out of their desolate places.

Prov. 14:11. The house of the wicked shall be overthrown: but the tabernacle of the upright shall flourish.

Isa. 14:20. Thou shalt not be joined with them in burial, because thou hast destroyed thy land, *and* slain thy people: the seed of evildoers shall never be renowned. 21. Prepare slaughter for his children for the iniquity of their fathers, that they do not rise, nor possess the land, nor fill the face of the world with cities. 22. For I will rise up against them, saith the LORD of hosts, and cut off from Babylon the name, and remnant, and son, and nephew, saith the LORD.

Jer. 31:29. In those days they shall say no more. The fathers have eaten a sour grape, and the children's teeth are set on edge. 30. But every one shall die for his own iniquity: every man that eateth the sour grape, his teeth shall be set on edge.

Jer. 32:18. Thou shewest lovingkindness unto thousands, and recompensest the iniquity of the fathers into the bosom of their children after them : Isa. 65:7.

Lam. 5:7. Our fathers have sinned, *and are* not; and we have borne their iniquities.

Rom. 5:12. Wherefore, as by one man sin entered into the world, and death by sin; and so death passed upon all men, for that all have sinned: 13. (For until the law sin was in the world : but sin is not imputed when there is no law. 14. Nevertheless death reigned from Adam to Moses, even over them that had not sinned after the similitude of Adam's transgression, who is the figure of him that was to come. 15. But not as the offence, so also *is* the free gift. For if through the offence of one many be dead, much more the grace of God, and the gift by grace, *which is* by one man, Jesus Christ, hath abounded unto many. 16. And not as *it was* by one that sinned, *so is* the gift : for the judgment *was* by one to condemnation, but the free gift *is* of many offences unto justification. 17. For if by one man's offence death reigned by one; much more they which receive abundance of grace and of the gift of righteousness shall reign in life by one, Jesus Christ.) 18. Therefore as by the offence of one *judgment came* upon all men to condemnation; even so by the righteousness of one *the free gift came* upon all men unto justification of life. 19. For as by one man's disobedience many were made sinners, so by the obedience of one shall many be made righteous. 20. Moreover the law entered, that the offence might abound. But where sin abounded, grace did much more abound : 21. That as sin hath reigned unto death, even so might grace reign through righteousness unto eternal life by Jesus Christ our Lord.

See WICKED.

CONVICTION OF: See CONVICTION; REPENTANCE, INSTANCES OF.

FORGIVENESS OF: Ex. 34:6. And the LORD passed by before him, and proclaimed, The LORD, The LORD God, merciful and gracious, longsuffering, and abundant in goodness and truth, 7. Keeping mercy for thousands, forgiving iniquity and transgression and sin, Num. 14:18.

Lev. 4:20. And he shall do with the bullock as he did with the bullock for a sin offering, so shall he do with this: and the priest shall make an atonement for them, and it shall be forgiven them. 26. And he shall burn all his fat upon the altar, as the

fat of the sacrifice of peace offerings : and the priest shall make an atonement for him as concerning his sin, and it shall be forgiven him. *vs.* 31,35; Lev. 5:10–13; Num. 15:25.

Lev. 5:4. If a soul swear, pronouncing with *his* lips to do evil, or to do good, whatsoever *it be* that a man shall pronounce with an oath, and it be hid from him; when he knoweth *of it*, then he shall be guilty in one of these. 5. And it shall be, when he shall be guilty in one of these *things*, that he shall confess that he hath sinned in that *thing:* 6. And he shall bring his trespass offering unto the LORD for his sin which he hath sinned, a female from the flock, a lamb or a kid of the goats, for a sin offering; and the priest shall make an atonement for him concerning his sin. 7. And if he be not able to bring a lamb, then he shall bring for his trespass, which he hath committed, two turtledoves, or two young pigeons, unto the LORD; one for a sin offering, and the other for a burnt offering. 8. And he shall bring them unto the priest, who shall offer *that* which *is* for the sin offering first, and wring off his head from his neck, but shall not divide *it* asunder: 9. And he shall sprinkle of the blood of the sin offering upon the side of the altar; and the rest of the blood shall be wrung out at the bottom of the altar: it *is* a sin offering. 10. And he shall offer the second *for* a burnt offering, according to the manner : and the priest shall make an atonement for him for his sin which he hath sinned, and it shall be forgiven him.

Num. 14:20. And the LORD said, I have pardoned according to thy word :

2 Sam. 12:13. And David said unto Nathan, I have sinned against the LORD. And Nathan said unto David, The LORD also hath put away thy sin; thou shalt not die.

1 Kin. 8:33. When thy people Israel be smitten down before the enemy, because they have sinned against thee, and shall turn again to thee, and confess thy name, and pray, and make supplication unto thee in this house: 34. Then hear thou in heaven, and forgive the sin of thy people Israel, and bring them again unto the land which thou gavest unto their fathers. *vs.* 22–50.

Job 10:14. If I sin, then thou markest me, and thou wilt not acquit me from mine iniquity.

Psa. 19:12. Who can understand *his* errors ? cleanse thou me from secret *faults*.

Psa. 25:7. Remember not the sins of my youth, nor my transgressions: according to thy mercy remember thou me for thy goodness' sake, O LORD. 11. For thy name's sake, O LORD, pardon mine iniquity; for it *is* great. 18. Look upon mine affliction and my pain; and forgive all my sins.

Psa. 32:1. Blessed *is he whose* transgression *is* forgiven, *whose* sin *is* covered. 2. Blessed *is* the man unto whom the LORD imputeth not iniquity, and in whose spirit *there is* no guile. 5. I acknowledged my sin unto thee, and mine iniquity have I not hid. I said, I will confess my transgressions unto the LORD; and thou forgavest the iniquity of my sin.

Psa. 51:9. Hide thy face from my sins, and blot out all mine iniquities.

Psa. 65:3. Iniquities prevail against me: *as for* our transgressions, thou shalt purge them away.

Psa. 79:9. Help us, O God of our salvation, for the glory of thy name: and deliver us, and purge away our sins, for thy name's sake.

Psa. 85:2. Thou hast forgiven the iniquity of thy people, thou hast covered all their sin. 3. Thou hast taken away all thy wrath: thou hast turned *thyself* from the fierceness of thine anger.

Psa. 99:8. Thou answeredst them, O LORD our God: thou wast a God that forgavest them, though thou tookest vengeance of their inventions.

Psa. 103:12. As far as the east is from the west, *so* far hath he removed our transgressions from us.

Psa. 130:4. But *there is* forgiveness with thee that thou mayest be feared.

Isa. 1:18. Come now, and let us reason together, saith the LORD: though your sins be as scarlet, they shall be as white as snow; though they be red like crimson, they shall be as wool.

Isa. 6:6. Then flew one of the seraphims unto me, having a live coal in his hand, *which* he had taken with the tongs from off the altar: 7. And he laid *it* upon my mouth, and said, Lo, this hath touched thy lips; and thine iniquity is taken away, and thy sin purged.

Isa. 43:25. I, *even* I, *am* he that blotteth out thy transgressions for mine own sake, and will not remember thy sins. 26. Put me in remembrance: let us plead together: declare thou, that thou mayest be justified.

Isa. 44:21. Remember these, O Jacob and Israel; for thou *art* my servant: I have formed thee; thou *art* my servant: O Israel, thou shalt not be forgotten of me. 22. I have blotted out, as a thick cloud, thy transgressions, and, as a cloud, thy sins: return unto me; for I have redeemed thee.

Isa. 55:6. Seek ye the LORD while he may be found, call ye upon him while he is near: 7. Let the wicked forsake his way, and the unrighteous man his thoughts: and let him return unto the LORD, and he will have mercy upon him; and to our God, for he will abundantly pardon.

Jer. 2:22. For though thou wash thee with nitre [lye, *R. V.*], and take thee much sope, *yet* thine iniquity is marked before me, saith the Lord GOD.

Jer. 5:1. Run ye to and fro through the streets of Jerusalem, and see now, and know, and seek in the broad places thereof, if ye can find a man, if there be *any* that executeth judgment, that seeketh the truth;

and I will pardon it. 7. How shall I pardon thee for this? thy children have forsaken me, and sworn by *them that are* no gods: when I had fed them to the full, they then committed adultery, and assembled themselves by troops in the harlots' houses.

Jer. 31:34. And they shall teach no more every man his neighbour, and every man his brother, saying, Know the LORD: for they shall all know me, from the least of them unto the greatest of them, saith the LORD: for I will forgive their iniquity, and I will remember their sin no more.

Jer. 33:8. And I will cleanse them from all their iniquity, whereby they have sinned against me; and I will pardon all their iniquities, whereby they have sinned, and whereby they have transgressed against me.

Ezek. 33:14. Again, when I say unto the wicked, Thou shalt surely die; if he turn from his sin, and do that which is lawful and right; 15. *If* the wicked restore the pledge, give again that he had robbed, walk in the statutes of life, without committing iniquity; he shall surely live, he shall not die. [Chapter 18:21,22.] 16. None of his sins that he hath committed shall be mentioned unto him: he hath done that which is lawful and right; he shall surely live.

Matt. 1:21. And she shall bring forth a son, and thou shalt call his name JESUS: for he shall save his people from their sins.

Matt. 6:12. And forgive us our debts, as we forgive our debtors. 14. For if ye forgive men their trespasses, your heavenly Father will also forgive you: 15. But if ye forgive not men their trespasses, neither will your Father forgive your trespasses.

Matt. 18:23. Therefore is the kingdom of heaven likened unto a certain king, which would take account of his servants. 24. And when he had begun to reckon, one was brought unto him, which owed him ten thousand talents. 25. But forasmuch as he had not to pay, his lord commanded him to be sold, and his wife, and children, and all that he had, and payment to be made. 26. The servant therefore fell down, and worshipped him, saying, Lord, have patience with me, and I will pay thee all. 27. Then the lord of that servant was moved with compassion, and loosed him, and forgave him the debt.

Matt. 26:28. This is my blood of the new testament, which is shed for many for the remission of sins.

Mark 2:5. When Jesus saw their faith, he said unto the sick of the palsy, Son, thy sins be forgiven thee. 7. Why doth this *man* thus speak blasphemies? who can forgive sins but God only? Matt. 9:2,6; Luke 5:21,24.

Mark 3:28. Verily I say unto you, All sins shall be forgiven unto the sons of men, and blasphemies wherewith soever they shall blaspheme:

Mark 11:26. [1] But if ye do not forgive, neither will your Father which is in heaven forgive your trespasses. Matt. 18:35. [1 Omitted in R. V.]

Luke 3:3. And he came into all the country about Jordan, preaching the baptism of repentance for the remission of sins: Matt. 3:6.

Luke 24:47. That repentance and remission of sins should be preached in his name among all nations, beginning at Jerusalem.

John 8:11. Jesus said unto her, Neither do I condemn thee: go, and sin no more.

John 20:23. Whose soever sins ye remit, they are remitted unto them; *and* whose soever *sins* ye retain, they are retained.

Acts 2:38. Then Peter said unto them, Repent, and be baptized every one of you in the name of Jesus Christ for the remission of sins, and ye shall receive the gift of the Holy Ghost.

Acts 10:36. The word which *God* sent unto the children of Israel, preaching peace by Jesus Christ: (he is Lord of all:) 43. To him give all the prophets witness, that through his name whosoever believeth in him shall receive remission of sins.

Acts 13:38. Be it known unto you therefore, men *and* brethren, that through this man is preached unto you the forgiveness of sins: 39. And by him all that believe are justified from all things, from which ye could not be justified by the law of Moses.

Acts 26:16. Rise, and stand upon thy feet: for I have appeared unto thee for this purpose, to make thee a minister and a witness both of these things which thou hast seen, and of those things in the which I will appear unto thee; 17. Delivering thee from the people, and *from* the Gentiles, unto whom now I send thee, 18. To open their eyes, *and* to turn *them* from darkness to light, and *from* the power of Satan unto God, that they may receive forgiveness of sins, and inheritance among them which are sanctified by faith that is in me.

Rom. 4:7. Blessed *are* they whose iniquities are forgiven, and whose sins are covered. 8. Blessed *is* the man to whom the Lord will not impute sin.

Eph. 4:32. And be ye kind one to another, tenderhearted, forgiving one another, even as God for Christ's sake hath forgiven you.

Col. 2:13. And you, being dead in your sins and the uncircumcision of your flesh, hath he quickened together with him, having forgiven you all trespasses;

Heb. 8:12. I will be merciful to their unrighteousness, and their sins and their iniquities will I remember no more.

Heb. 9:22. Almost all things are by the law purged with blood; and without shedding of blood is no remission.

Heb. 10:2. For then would they not have ceased to be offered? because that the worshippers once purged should have had no more conscience of sins. 17. And their sins and iniquities will I remember no more. 18. Now where remission of these *is, there is* no more offering for sin.

Jas. 5:15. And the prayer of faith shall save the sick, and the Lord shall raise him up; and if he have committed sins, they shall be forgiven him. 20. Let him know, that he which converteth the sinner from the error of his way shall save a soul from death, and shall hide a multitude of sins.

1 John 1:7. If we walk in the light, as he is in the light, we have fellowship one with another, and the blood of Jesus Christ his Son cleanseth us from all sin. 9. If we confess our sins, he is faithful and just to forgive us *our* sins, and to cleanse us from all unrighteousness.

1 John 2:1. If any man sin, we have an advocate with the Father, Jesus Christ the righteous: 2. And he is the propitiation for our sins: and not for ours only, but also for *the sins of* the whole world. 12. I write unto you, little children, because your sins are forgiven you for his name's sake.

1 John 5:16. If any man see his brother sin a sin *which is* not unto death, he shall ask, and he shall give him life for them that sin not unto death. There is a sin unto death: I do not say that he shall pray for it. Matt. 12:31,32; Luke 12:10.

Rev. 1:5. And from Jesus Christ, *who is* the faithful witness, *and* the first begotten of the dead, and the prince of the kings of the earth. Unto him that loved us, and washed us from our sins in his own blood,

See ATONEMENT; CONVICTION; OFFERINGS; REPENTANCE.

FRUITS OF: Gen. 3:7. And the eyes of them both were opened, and they knew that they *were* naked; and they sewed fig leaves together, and made themselves aprons. 8. And they heard the voice of the LORD God walking in the garden in the cool of the day: and Adam and his wife hid themselves from the presence of the LORD God amongst the trees of the garden. 9. And the LORD God called unto Adam, and said unto him, Where *art* thou? 10. And he said, I heard thy voice in the garden, and I was afraid, because I *was* naked; and I hid myself. 11. And he said, Who told thee that thou *wast* naked? Hast thou eaten of the tree, whereof I commanded thee that thou shouldest not eat? 12. And the man said, The woman whom thou gavest *to be* with me, she gave me of the tree, and I did eat. 13. And the LORD God said unto the woman, What *is* this *that* thou hast done? And the woman said, The serpent beguiled me, and I did eat. 14. And the LORD God said unto the serpent, Because thou hast done this, thou *art* cursed above all cattle, and above every beast of the field; upon thy belly shalt thou go, and dust shalt thou eat all the days of thy life: 15. And I will put enmity between thee and the woman, and between thy seed and her seed; it shall bruise thy head, and thou shalt bruise his heel. 16. Unto the woman he said, I will greatly multiply thy sorrow and thy conception; in sorrow thou shalt bring forth children; and thy desire *shall be* to thy husband, and he shall rule over thee. 17. And unto Adam he said,

Because thou hast hearkened unto the voice of thy wife, and hast eaten of the tree, of which I commanded thee, saying, Thou shalt not eat of it: cursed *is* the ground for thy sake; in sorrow shalt thou eat *of* it all the days of thy life: 18. Thorns also and thistles shall it bring forth to thee; and thou shalt eat the herb of the field: 19. In the sweat of thy face shalt thou eat bread, till thou return unto the ground; for out of it wast thou taken: for dust thou *art*, and unto dust shalt thou return. 20. And Adam called his wife's name Eve; because she was the mother of all living. 21. Unto Adam also and to his wife did the LORD God make coats of skins, and clothed them. 22. And the LORD God said, Behold, the man is become as one of us, to know good and evil: and now, lest he put forth his hand, and take also of the tree of life, and eat, and live for ever: 23. Therefore the LORD God sent him forth from the garden of Eden, to till the ground from whence he was taken. 24. So he drove out the man; and he placed at the east of the garden of Eden Cherubims, and a flaming sword which turned every way, to keep the way of the tree of life.

Gen. 4:9. And the LORD said unto Cain, Where *is* Abel thy brother? And he said, I know not: *Am* I my brother's keeper? 10. And he said, What hast thou done? the voice of thy brother's blood crieth unto me from the ground. 11. And now *art* thou cursed from the earth, which hath opened her mouth to receive thy brother's blood from thy hand. 12. When thou tillest the ground, it shall not henceforth yield unto thee her strength; a fugitive and a vagabond shalt thou be in the earth. 13. And Cain said unto the LORD, My punishment *is* greater than I can bear. 14. Behold, thou hast driven me out this day from the face of the earth; and from thy face shall I be hid; and I shall be a fugitive and a vagabond in the earth; and it shall come to pass, *that* every one that findeth me shall slay me.

Gen. 6:5. And GOD saw that the wickedness of man *was* great in the earth, and *that* every imagination of the thoughts of his heart *was* only evil continually. 6. And it repented the LORD that he had made man on the earth, and it grieved him at his heart. 7. And the LORD said, I will destroy man whom I have created from the face of the earth; both man, and beast, and the creeping thing, and the fowls of the air; for it repenteth me that I have made them.

Deut. 29:18. Lest there should be among you a root that beareth gall and wormwood;

1 Kin. 13:33. After this thing Jeroboam returned not from his evil way, but made again of the lowest of the people priests of the high places: whosoever would, he consecrated him, and he became *one* of the priests of the high places. 34. And this thing became sin unto the house of Jeroboam, even to cut *it* off, and to destroy *it* from off the face of the earth.

Job 4:8. Even as I have seen, they that plow iniquity, and sow wickedness, reap the same.

Job 5:2. For wrath killeth the foolish man, and envy slayeth the silly one.

Job 13:26. For thou writest bitter things against me, and makest me to possess the iniquities of my youth.

Job 20:11. His bones are full [1 *of the sin* of] his youth, which shall lie down with him in the dust. [1 Omitted in R. V.]

Psa. 5:10. Destroy thou them, O God; let them fall by their own counsels; cast them out in the multitude of their transgressions; for they have rebelled against thee.

Psa. 9:15. The heathen are sunk down in the pit *that* they made: in the net which they hid is their own foot taken. 16. The LORD is known *by* the judgment *which* he executeth: the wicked is snared in the work of his own hands.

Psa. 10:2. The wicked in *his* pride doth persecute the poor: let them be taken in the devices that they have imagined.

Psa. 94:23. And he shall bring upon them their own iniquity, and shall cut them off in their own wickedness; *yea*, the LORD our God shall cut them off.

Psa. 141:10. Let the wicked fall into their own nets, whilst that I withal escape.

Prov. 1:31. Therefore shall they eat of the fruit of their own way, and be filled with their own devices.

Prov. 3:35. The wise shall inherit glory: but shame shall be the promotion of fools.

Prov. 5:22. His own iniquities shall take the wicked himself, and he shall be holden with the cords of his sins. 23. He shall die without instruction; and in the greatness of his folly he shall go astray.

Prov. 8:36. He that sinneth against me wrongeth his own soul: all they that hate me love death.

Prov. 10:24. The fear of the wicked, it shall come upon him: but the desire of the righteous shall be granted. 29. The way of the LORD *is* strength to the upright: but destruction *shall be* to the workers of iniquity. 30. The righteous shall never be removed: but the wicked shall not inhabit the earth. 31. The mouth of the just bringeth forth wisdom: but the froward tongue shall be cut out.

Prov. 11:5. The righteousness of the perfect shall direct his way: but the wicked shall fall by his own wickedness. 6. The righteousness of the upright shall deliver them: but transgressors shall be taken in *their own* naughtiness. 7. When a wicked man dieth, *his* expectation shall perish: and the hope of unjust *men* perisheth. 18. The wicked worketh a deceitful work: but to him that soweth righteousness *shall be* a sure reward. 19. As righteousness *tendeth* to life: so he that pursueth evil *pursueth it* to his own death. 27. He that diligently seeketh good procureth favour: but he that seeketh mischief, it shall come unto him.

29. He that troubleth his own house shall inherit the wind: and the fool *shall be* servant to the wise of heart.

Prov. 12:13. The wicked is snared by the transgression of *his* lips: but the just shall come out of trouble. 14. A man shall be satisfied with good by the fruit of *his* mouth: and the recompence of a man's hands shall be rendered unto him. 21. There shall no evil happen to the just: but the wicked shall be filled with mischief. 26. The righteous *is* more excellent than his neighbour: but the way of the wicked seduceth them.

Prov. 13:5. A righteous *man* hateth lying: but a wicked *man* is loathsome, and cometh to shame. 6. Righteousness keepeth *him that is* upright in the way: but wickedness overthroweth the sinner. 15. Good understanding giveth favour: but the way of transgressors *is* hard.

Prov. 22:8. He that soweth iniquity shall reap vanity: and the rod of his anger shall fail.

Prov. 27:8. As a bird that wandereth from her nest, so *is* a man that wandereth from his place.

Prov. 28:1. The wicked flee when no man pursueth:

Prov. 29:6. In the transgression of an evil man *there is* a snare: but the righteous doth sing and rejoice.

Prov. 30:20. Such *is* the way of an adulterous woman; she eateth, and wipeth her mouth, and saith. I have done no wickedness.

Isa. 3:9. The shew of their countenance doth witness against them; and they declare their sin as Sodom, they hide *it* not. Woe unto their soul! for they have rewarded evil unto themselves. 11. Woe unto the wicked! *it shall be* ill *with him:* for the reward of his hands shall be given him.

Isa. 9:18. Wickedness burneth as the fire: it shall devour the briers and thorns, and shall kindle in the thickets of the forest, and they shall mount up *like* the lifting up of smoke.

Isa. 14:21. Prepare slaughter for his children for the iniquity of their fathers; that they do not rise, nor possess the land, nor fill the face of the world with cities.

Isa. 50:11. Behold, all ye that kindle a fire, that compass *yourselves* about with sparks: walk in the light of your fire, and in the sparks *that* ye have kindled. This shall ye have of mine hand; ye shall lie down in sorrow.

Isa. 57:20. But the wicked *are* like the troubled sea, when it cannot rest, whose waters cast up mire and dirt. 21. *There is* no peace, saith my God, to the wicked.

Jer. 2:17. Hast thou not procured this unto thyself, in that thou hast forsaken the LORD thy God, when he led thee by the way? 19. Thine own wickedness shall correct thee, and thy backsliding shall reprove thee: know therefore and see that *it is* an evil *thing* and bitter, that thou hast for-

saken the LORD thy God, and that my fear *is* not in thee, saith the LORD God of hosts.

Jer. 4:18. Thy way and thy doings have procured these *things* unto thee; this *is* thy wickedness, because it is bitter, because it reacheth unto thine heart.

Jer. 5:25. Your iniquities have turned away these *things*, and your sins have withholden good *things* from you.

Jer. 7:19. Do they provoke me to anger? saith the LORD: *do they* not *provoke* themselves to the confusion of their own faces?

Jer. 14:16. They shall have none to bury them, them, their wives, nor their sons, nor their daughters: for I will pour their wickedness upon them.

Jer. 21:14. But I will punish you according to the fruit of your doings, saith the LORD: and I will kindle a fire in the forest thereof, and it shall devour all things round about it.

Ezek. 11:21. But as *for them* whose heart walketh after the heart of their detestable things and their abominations, I will recompense their way upon their own heads, saith the LORD. Ezek. 22:31.

Ezek. 23:31. Thou hast walked in the way of thy sister; therefore will I give her cup into thine hand. 32. Thus saith the Lord GOD; Thou shalt drink of thy sister's cup deep and large: thou shalt be laughed to scorn and had in derision; it containeth much. 33. Thou shalt be filled with drunkenness and sorrow, with the cup of astonishment and desolation, with the cup of thy sister Samaria. 34. Thou shalt even drink it and suck *it* out, and thou shalt break the sherds thereof, and pluck off thine own breasts: for I have spoken *it*, saith the Lord GOD. 35. Therefore thus saith the Lord GOD; Because thou hast forgotten me, and cast me behind thy back, therefore bear thou also thy lewdness and thy whoredoms.

Hos. 8:7. For they have sown the wind, and they shall reap the whirlwind: it hath no stalk: the bud shall yield no meal: if so be it yield, the strangers shall swallow it up.

Hos. 10:13. Ye have plowed wickedness, ye have reaped iniquity; ye have eaten the fruit of lies: because thou didst trust in thy way, in the multitude of thy mighty men.

Hos. 12:14. Ephraim provoked *him* to anger most bitterly: therefore shall he leave his blood upon him, and his reproach shall his Lord return unto him.

Hos. 13:9. O Israel, thou hast destroyed thyself; but in me *is* thine help.

Mic. 7:13. Notwithstanding the land shall be desolate because of them that dwell therein, for the fruit of their doings.

Mark 7:21. For from within, out of the heart of men, proceed evil thoughts, adulteries, fornications, murders, 22. Thefts, covetousness, wickedness, deceit, lasciviousness, an evil eye, blasphemy, pride, foolishness: 23. All these evil things come from within, and defile the man.

Acts 9:5. And he said. Who art thou, Lord? And the Lord said, I am Jesus whom thou persecutest: ¹ *it is* hard for thee to kick against the pricks. [¹ Omitted in R. V.]

Rom. 5:12. Wherefore, as by one man sin entered into the world, and death by sin; and so death passed upon all men, for that all have sinned: 13. (For until the law sin was in the world: but sin is not imputed when there is no law. 14. Nevertheless death reigned from Adam to Moses, even over them that had not sinned after the similitude of Adam's transgression, who is the figure of him that was to come. 15. But not as the offence, so also *is* the free gift. For if through the offence of one many be dead, much more the grace of God, and the gift by grace, *which is* by one man, Jesus Christ, hath abounded unto many. 16. And not as *it was* by one that sinned, *so is* the gift: for the judgment *was* by one to condemnation, but the free gift *is* of many offences unto justification. 17. For if by one man's offence death reigned by one; much more they which receive abundance of grace and of the gift of righteousness shall reign in life by one, Jesus Christ.) 18. Therefore as by the offence of one *judgment came* upon all men to condemnation; even so by the righteousness of one *the free gift came* upon all men unto justification of life. 19. For as by one man's disobedience many were made sinners, so by the obedience of one shall many be made righteous. 20. Moreover the law entered, that the offence might abound. But where sin abounded, grace did much more abound: 21. That as sin hath reigned unto death, even so might grace reign through righteousness unto eternal life by Jesus Christ our Lord.

Rom. 7:5. For when we were in the flesh, the motions of sins, which were by the law, did work in our members to bring forth fruit unto death.

1 Cor. 3:3. For ye are yet carnal: for whereas *there is* among you envying, and strife, and divisions, are ye not carnal, and walk as men?

1 Cor. 6:9. Know ye not that the unrighteous shall not inherit the kingdom of God? Be not deceived: neither fornicators, nor idolaters, nor adulterers, nor effeminate, nor abusers of themselves with mankind, 10. Nor thieves, nor covetous, nor drunkards, nor revilers, nor extortioners, shall inherit the kingdom of God. 11. And such were some of you: but ye are washed, but ye are sanctified, but ye are justified in the name of the Lord Jesus, and by the Spirit of our God.

Gal. 5:19: Now the works of the flesh are manifest, which are *these;* Adultery, fornication, uncleanness, lasciviousness, 20. Idolatry, witchcraft, hatred, variance, emulations, wrath, strife, seditions, heresies, 21. Envyings, murders, drunkenness, revellings, and such like: of the which I tell you before, as I have also told *you* in time past, that they which do such things shall not inherit the kingdom of God.

Gal. 6:7. Be not deceived; God is not mocked: for whatsoever a man soweth, that shall he also reap. 8. For he that soweth to his flesh shall of the flesh reap corruption; but he that soweth to the Spirit shall of the Spirit reap life everlasting.

1 Pet. 4:3. For the time past of *our* life may suffice us to have wrought the will of the Gentiles, when we walked in lasciviousness, lusts, excess of wine, revellings, banquetings, and abominable idolatries:

KNOWN TO GOD: Gen. 3:11. And he said, Who told thee that thou *wast* naked? Hast thou eaten of the tree, whereof I commanded thee that thou shouldest not eat?

Gen. 4:10. And he said, What hast thou done? the voice of thy brother's blood crieth unto me from the ground.

Gen. 18:13. The LORD said unto Abraham, Wherefore did Sarah laugh, saying, Shall I of a surety bear a child, which am old?

Ex. 16:8. And Moses said, *This shall be,* when the LORD shall give you in the evening flesh to eat, and in the morning bread to the full; for that the LORD heareth your murmurings which ye murmur against him: and what *are* we? your murmurings *are* not against us, but against the LORD. 9. And Moses spake unto Aaron, Say unto all the congregation of the children of Israel, Come near before the LORD: for he hath heard your murmurings. *v.* 12.

Num. 12:2. And they said, Hath the LORD indeed spoken only by Moses? hath he not spoken also by us? And the LORD heard *it.*

Num. 14:26. And the LORD spake unto Moses and unto Aaron, saying, 27. How long *shall I bear with* this evil congregation, which murmur against me? I have heard the murmurings of the children of Israel, which they murmur against me.

Deut. 1:34. And the LORD heard the voice of your words, and was wroth,

Deut. 31:21. This song shall testify against them as a witness; for it shall not be forgotten out of the mouths of their seed: for I know their imagination which they go about, even now, before I have brought them into the land which I sware.

Deut. 32:34. *Is* not this laid up in store with me, *and* sealed up among my treasures?

Job 10:14. If I sin, then thou markest me, and thou wilt not acquit me from mine iniquity. Josh. 7:10–15.

Job 11:11. For he knoweth vain men; he seeth wickedness also; will he not then consider *it?*

Job 13:27. Thou puttest my feet also in the stocks, and lookest narrowly unto all my paths; thou settest a print upon the heels of my feet.

Job 14:16. For now thou numberest my steps: dost thou not watch over my sin? 17. My transgression *is* sealed up in a bag, and thou sewest up mine iniquity.

Job 20:27. The heaven shall reveal his iniquity; and the earth shall rise up against him.

Job 34:21. For his eyes *are* upon the ways of man, and he seeth all his goings. 22. *There is* no darkness, nor shadow of death, where the workers of iniquity may hide themselves. 25. Therefore he knoweth their works, and he overturneth *them* in the night, so that they are destroyed. Job 24:23.

Psa. 44:20. If we have forgotten the name of our God, or stretched out our hands to a strange god; 21. Shall not God search this out? for he knoweth the secrets of the heart.

Psa. 69:5. O God, thou knowest my foolishness; and my sins are not hid from thee.

Psa. 90:8. Thou hast set our iniquities before thee, our secret *sins* in the light of thy countenance.

Psa. 94:11. The LORD knoweth the thoughts of man, that they *are* vanity.

Eccl. 5:8. If thou seest the oppression of the poor, and violent perverting of judgment and justice in a province, marvel not at the matter: for *he that is* higher than the highest regardeth; and *there be* higher than they.

Isa. 29:15. Woe unto them that seek deep to hide their counsel from the LORD, and their works are in the dark, and they say, Who seeth us? and who knoweth us?

Jer. 2:22. Though thou wash thee with nitre [lye, *R. V.*], and take thee much sope, *yet* thine iniquity is marked before me, saith the Lord GOD.

Jer. 16:17. For mine eyes *are* upon all their ways: they are not hid from my face, neither is their iniquity hid from mine eyes.

Jer. 29:23. Because they have committed villany in Israel, and have committed adultery with their neighbours' wives, and have spoken lying words in my name, which I have not commanded them; even I know, and *am* a witness, saith the LORD.

Ezek. 21:24. Therefore thus saith the Lord GOD; Because ye have made your iniquity to be remembered, in that your transgressions are discovered, so that in all your doings your sins do appear; because, *I say*, that ye are come to remembrance, ye shall be taken with the hand.

Hos. 5:3. I know Ephraim, and Israel is not hid from me: for now, O Ephraim, thou committest whoredom, *and* Israel is defiled.

Hos. 7:2. And they consider not in their hearts *that* I remember all their wickedness: now their own doings have beset them about; they are before my face.

Amos 5:12. For I know your manifold transgressions and your mighty sins: they afflict the just, they take a bribe, and they turn aside the poor in the gate *from their right*.

Amos 9:1. I saw the Lord standing upon the altar: and he said, Smite the lintel of the door, that the posts may shake: and cut them in the head, all of them; and I will slay the last of them with the sword: he that fleeth of them shall not flee away,

and he that escapeth of them shall not be delivered. 2. Though they dig into hell, thence shall mine hand take them; though they climb up to heaven, thence will I bring them down: 3. And though they hide themselves in the top of Carmel, I will search and take them out thence; and though they be hid from my sight in the bottom of the sea, thence will I command the serpent, and he shall bite them: 4. And though they go into captivity before their enemies, thence will I command the sword, and it shall slay them: and I will set mine eyes upon them for evil, and not for good. 8. Behold, the eyes of the Lord GOD *are* upon the sinful kingdom, and I will destroy it from off the face of the earth; saving that I will not utterly destroy the house of Jacob, saith the LORD.

Hab. 2:11. For the stone shall cry out of the wall, and the beam out of the timber shall answer it.

Mal. 2:14. Yet ye say, Wherefore? Because the LORD hath been witness between thee and the wife of thy youth, against whom thou hast dealt treacherously: yet *is* she thy companion, and the wife of thy covenant.

Matt. 10:26. Fear them not therefore: for there is nothing covered, that shall not be revealed; and hid, that shall not be known.

Matt. 22:18. But Jesus perceived their wickedness, and said, Why tempt ye me, *ye* hypocrites?

Matt. 26:46. Rise, let us be going: behold, he is at hand that doth betray me.

Luke 6:8. But he knew their thoughts, and said to the man which had the withered hand, Rise up, and stand forth in the midst.

John 4:17. The woman answered and said, I have no husband. Jesus said unto her, Thou hast well said, I have no husband: 18. For thou hast had five husbands; and he whom thou now hast is not thy husband: in that saidst thou truly. 19. The woman saith unto him, Sir, I perceive that thou art a prophet.

John 5:42. But I know you, that ye have not the love of God in you.

John 6:64. But there are some of you that believe not. For Jesus knew from the beginning who they were that believed not, and who should betray him.

John 13:11. For he knew who should betray him; therefore said he, Ye are not all clean.

Rev. 2:23. And I will kill her children with death; and all the churches shall know that I am he which searcheth the reins and hearts: and I will give unto every one of you according to your works.

See GOD, OMNISCIENT; JESUS, OMNISCIENCE OF.

LOVE OF: Job 15:16. How much more abominable and filthy *is* man, which drinketh iniquity like water?

Job. 20:12. Though wickedness be sweet

in his mouth, *though* he hide it under his tongue; 13. *Though* he spare it, and forsake it not; but keep it still within his mouth:

Prov. 2:14. Who rejoice to do evil, *and* delight in the frowardness of the wicked:

Prov. 4:17. For they eat the bread of wickedness, and drink the wine of violence.

Prov. 10:23. *It is* as sport to a fool to do mischief: but a man of understanding hath wisdom.

Prov. 16:30. He shutteth his eyes to devise froward things: moving his lips he bringeth evil to pass.

Prov. 26:11. As a dog returneth to his vomit, *so* a fool returneth to his folly.

Jer. 14:10. Thus saith the LORD unto this people, Thus have they loved to wander, they have not refrained their feet, therefore the LORD doth not accept them; he will now remember their iniquity, and visit their sins.

Ezek. 20:16. Because they despised my judgments, and walked not in my statutes, but polluted my sabbaths: for their heart went after their idols.

Hos. 4:8. They eat up the sin of my people, and they set their heart on their iniquity.

Hos. 9:10. I found Israel like grapes in the wilderness; I saw your fathers as the firstripe in the fig tree at her first time: *but* they went to Baal-peor, and separated themselves unto *that* shame; and *their* abominations were according as they loved.

Mic. 7:3. That they may do evil with both hands earnestly, the prince asketh, and the judge *asketh* for a reward: and the great *man*, he uttereth his mischievous desire: so they wrap it up.

John 3:19. And this is the condemnation, that light is come into the world, and men loved darkness rather than light, because their deeds were evil. 20. For every one that doeth evil hateth the light, neither cometh to the light, lest his deeds should be reproved.

John 12:43. For they loved the praise of men more than the praise of God.

1 Pet. 3:19. By which also he went and preached unto the spirits in prison; 20. Which sometime were disobedient, when once the longsuffering of God waited in the days of Noah, while the ark was a preparing, wherein few, that is, eight souls were saved by water.

2 Pet. 2:22. But it is happened unto them according to the true proverb, The dog *is* turned to his own vomit again: and the sow that was washed to her wallowing in the mire.

See REPROBACY; WICKED, DESCRIBED.

NATIONAL, PUNISHMENT OF: Gen. 6: 5. And GOD saw that the wickedness of man *was* great in the earth, and *that* every imagination of the thoughts of his heart *was* only evil continually. 6. And it repented the LORD that he had made man on the earth, and it grieved him at his heart. 7. And the LORD said, I will destroy man whom I have created from the face of the earth; both man, and beast, and the creeping thing, and the fowls of the air; for it repenteth me that I have made them.

Gen. 7:21. And all flesh died that moved upon the earth, both of fowl, and of cattle, and of beast, and of every creeping thing that creepeth upon the earth, and every man: 22. All in whose nostrils *was* the breath of life, of all that *was* in the dry *land*, died.

Lev. 26:14. But if ye will not hearken unto me, and will not do all these commandments; 15. And if ye shall despise my statutes, or if your soul abhor my judgments, so that ye will not do all my commandments, *but* that ye break my covenant: 16. I also will do this unto you; I will even appoint over you terror, consumption, and the burning ague, that shall consume the eyes, and cause sorrow of heart: and ye shall sow your seed in vain, for your enemies shall eat it. 17. And I will set my face against you, and ye shall be slain before your enemies: they that hate you shall reign over you; and ye shall flee when none pursueth you. 18. And if ye will not yet for all this hearken unto me, then I will punish you seven times more for your sins. 19. And I will break the pride of your power; and I will make your heaven as iron, and your earth as brass: 20. And your strength shall be spent in vain: for your land shall not yield her increase, neither shall the trees of the land yield their fruits. 21. And if ye walk contrary unto me, and will not hearken unto me; I will bring seven times more plagues upon you according to your sins. 22. I will also send wild beasts among you, which shall rob you of your children, and destroy your cattle, and make you few in number; and your *high* ways shall be desolate. 23. And if ye will not be reformed by me by these things, but will walk contrary unto me; 24. Then will I also walk contrary unto you, and will punish you yet seven times for your sins. 25. And I will bring a sword upon you, that shall avenge the quarrel of *my* covenant: and when ye are gathered together within your cities, I will send the pestilence among you; and ye shall be delivered into the hand of the enemy. 26. *And* when I have broken the staff of your bread, ten women shall bake your bread in one oven, and they shall deliver *you* your bread again by weight: and ye shall eat, and not be satisfied. 27. And if ye will not for all this hearken unto me, but walk contrary unto me; 28. Then I will walk contrary unto you also in fury; and I, even I, will chastise you seven times for your sins. 29. And ye shall eat the flesh of your sons, and the flesh of your daughters shall ye eat. 30. And I will destroy your high places, and cut down your images, and cast your carcases upon the carcases of your idols, and my soul shall abhor you. 31. And I will make your cities waste, and bring your sanctuaries unto desolation, and I will not smell the savour of your sweet odours. 32. And I will bring the land into desolation: and your enemies which dwell therein shall be astonished at it. 33. And I will scatter you among the heathen, and will draw out a sword after you: and your land shall be desolate, and your cities waste. 34. Then shall the land enjoy her sabbaths, as long as it lieth desolate, and ye *be* in your enemies' land; *even* then shall the land rest, and enjoy her sabbaths. 35. As long as it lieth desolate it shall rest; because it did not rest in your sabbaths, when ye dwelt upon it. 36. And upon them that are left *alive* of you I will send a faintness into their hearts in the lands of their enemies; and the sound of a shaken leaf shall chase them; and they shall flee, as fleeing from a sword; and they shall fall when none pursueth. 37. And they shall fall one upon another, as it were before a sword, when none pursueth: and ye shall have no power to stand before your enemies. 38. And ye shall perish among the heathen, and the land of your enemies shall eat you up.

Deut. 9:5. Not for thy righteousness, or for the uprightness of thine heart, dost thou go to possess their land: but for the wickedness of these nations the LORD thy God doth drive them out from before thee, and that he may perform the word which the LORD sware unto thy fathers, Abraham, Isaac, and Jacob.

Job 34:29. When he giveth quietness, who then can make trouble? and when he hideth *his* face, who then can behold him? whether *it be done* against a nation, or against a man only: 30. That the hypocrite reign not, lest the people be ensnared.

Isa. 19:4. And the Egyptians will I give over into the hand of a cruel lord; and a fierce king shall rule over them, saith the Lord, the LORD of hosts.

Jer. 12:17. But if they will not obey, I will utterly pluck up and destroy that nation, saith the LORD.

Jer. 25:31. A noise shall come *even* to the ends of the earth; for the LORD hath a controversy with the nations, he will plead with all flesh; he will give them *that are* wicked to the sword, saith the LORD. 32. Thus saith the LORD of hosts, Behold, evil shall go forth from nation to nation, and a great whirlwind shall be raised up from the coasts of the earth. 33. And the slain of the LORD shall be at that day from *one* end of the earth even unto the *other* end of the earth: they shall not be lamented, neither gathered, nor buried; they shall be dung upon the ground. 34. Howl, ye shepherds, and cry; and wallow yourselves *in the ashes*, ye principal of the flock: for the days of your slaughter and of your dispersions are accomplished; and ye shall fall like a

pleasant vessel. 35. And the shepherds shall have no way to flee, nor the principal of the flock to escape. 36. A voice of the cry of the shepherds, and an howling of the principal of the flock, *shall be heard:* for the LORD hath spoiled their pasture. 37. And the peaceable habitations are cut down because of the fierce anger of the LORD. 38. He hath forsaken his covert, as the lion: for their land is desolate because of the fierceness of the oppressor, and because of his fierce anger.

Jer. 46:28. Fear thou not, O Jacob my servant, saith the LORD: for I *am* with thee; for I will make a full end of all the nations whither I have driven thee: but I will not make a full end of thee, but correct thee in measure; yet will I not leave thee wholly unpunished.

Ezek. 16:49. Behold, this was the iniquity of thy sister Sodom, pride, fulness of bread, and abundance of idleness was in her and in her daughters, neither did she strengthen the hand of the poor and needy. 50. And they were haughty, and committed abomination before me: therefore I took them away as I saw *good*.

Jonah 1:2. Arise, go to Nineveh, that great city, and cry against it; for their wickedness is come up before me.

See GOVERNMENT; NATIONS.

INSTANCES OF: The Sodomites, Gen. 18:20. Egyptians, Ex. chapters 7-14; see EGYPT. Israelites, Lev. 26:14-39; Deut. 32:30; 2 Sam. 21:1; 24:1; 2 Kin. 24:3,4,20; 2 Chr. 36:21; Ezra 9; Neh. 9:36,37; Isa. 1:21-23; 3:4,8; 5; 59:1-15, Jer. 2; 5; 6; 9; 23; 30:11-15; Lam. 1:3,8,14; 4:6; Ezek. 2; 7; 22; 24:6-14; 28:18; 33:25,26; 36.16-20; 39:23,24; 44:4-14; Hos. 4:1-11; 6:8-10; 7:1-7; 13; Amos chapters 2; 5; Mic. 6; 7:2-6. Babylon, Jer. 50:45,46; 51; see BABYLON.

See also prophecies cited in the topics ASSYRIA; DAMASCUS; EDOM; ELAM; ETHIOPIA; PHILISTINES; SYRIA.

PUNISHMENT OF: Gen. 2:17. But of the tree of the knowledge of good and evil, thou shalt not eat of it: for in the day that thou eatest thereof thou shalt surely die.

Gen. 3:16. Unto the woman he said, I will greatly multiply thy sorrow and thy conception; in sorrow thou shalt bring forth children; and thy desire *shall be* to thy husband, and he shall rule over thee. 17. And unto Adam he said, Because thou hast hearkened unto the voice of thy wife, and hast eaten of the tree, of which I commanded thee, saying, Thou shalt not eat of it: cursed *is* the ground for thy sake; in ¹ sorrow shalt thou eat *of* it all the days of thy life; 18. Thorns also and thistles shall it bring forth to thee; and thou shalt eat the herb of the field; 19. In the sweat of thy face shalt thou eat bread, till thou return unto the ground; for out of it wast thou taken: for dust thou *art*, and unto dust shalt thou return.   ¹ R. V. toil]

Gen. 4:7. If thou doest well, shalt thou not be accepted? and if thou doest not well, **sin** lieth at the door.

Gen. 6:3. And the LORD said, My spirit shall not always strive with man, for that he also *is* flesh: 5. And GOD saw that the wickedness of man *was* great in the earth, and *that* every imagination of the thoughts of his heart *was* only evil continually. 6. And it repented the LORD that he had made man on the earth, and it grieved him at his heart. 7. And the LORD said, I will destroy man whom I have created from the face of the earth; both man, and beast, and the creeping thing, and the fowls of the air; for it repenteth me that I have made them.

Gen. 18:20. And the LORD said, Because the cry of Sodom and Gomorrah is great, and because their sin is very grievous;

Gen. 19:13. For we will destroy this place, because the cry of them is waxen great before the face of the LORD; and the LORD hath sent us to destroy it.

Ex. 32:33. And the LORD said unto Moses, Whosoever hath sinned against me, him will I blot out of my book. 34. Therefore now go, lead the people unto *the place* of which I have spoken unto thee: behold, mine Angel shall go before thee: nevertheless in the day when I visit I will visit their sin upon them.

Ex. 34:7. Keeping mercy for thousands, forgiving iniquity and transgression and sin, and that will by no means clear *the guilty;* visiting the iniquity of the fathers upon the children, and upon the children's children, unto the third and to the fourth *generation.*

Lev. 26:14. But if ye will not hearken unto me, and will not do all these commandments; 15. And if ye shall despise my statutes, or if your soul abhor my judgments, so that ye will not do all my commandments, *but* that ye break my covenant: 16. I also will do this unto you; I will even appoint over you terror, consumption, and the burning ague, that shall consume the eyes, and cause sorrow of heart: and ye shall sow your seed in vain, for your enemies shall eat it. 17. And I will set my face against you, and ye shall be slain before your enemies: they that hate you shall reign over you; and ye shall flee when none pursueth you. 18. And if ye will not yet for all this hearken unto me, then I will punish you seven times more for your sins. 19. And I will break the pride of your power; and I will make your heaven as iron, and your earth as brass: 20. And your strength shall be spent in vain: for your land shall not yield her increase, neither shall the trees of the land yield their fruits. 21. And if ye walk contrary unto me, and will not hearken unto me; I will bring seven times more plagues upon you according to your sins.

Num. 15:30. But the soul that doeth *ought* presumptuously, *whether he be* born in the land, or a stranger, the same reproacheth the LORD; and that soul shall be cut off from among his people. 31. Because he hath despised the word of the LORD, and hath bro-

ken his commandment, that soul shall utterly be cut off; his iniquity *shall be* upon him.

Num. 32:23. But if ye will not do so, behold, ye will have sinned against the LORD: and be sure your sin will find you out.

Job 21:17. How oft is the candle of the wicked put out! and *how oft* cometh their destruction upon them! *God* distributeth sorrows in his anger.

Psa. 95:10. Forty years long was I grieved with *this* generation, and said, It *is* a people that do err in their heart, and they have not known my ways: 11. Unto whom I sware in my wrath that they should not enter into my rest.

Jer. 44:2. Thus saith the LORD of hosts, the God of Israel; Ye have seen all the evil that I have brought upon Jerusalem, and upon all the cities of Judah; and, behold, this day they *are* a desolation, and no man dwelleth therein, 3. Because of their wickedness which they have committed to provoke me to anger, in that they went to burn incense, *and* to serve other gods, whom they knew not, *neither* they, ye, nor your fathers. 5. But they hearkened not, nor inclined their ear to turn from their wickedness, to burn no incense unto other gods. 6. Wherefore my fury and mine anger was poured forth, and was kindled in the cities of Judah and in the streets of Jerusalem; and they are wasted *and* desolate, as at this day.

See PUNISHMENT; WICKED, PUNISHMENT OF.

REPUGNANT TO GOD: Gen. 6:6. And it repented the LORD that he had made man on the earth, and it grieved him at his heart. 7. And the LORD said, I will destroy man whom I have created from the face of the earth; both man, and beast, and the creeping thing, and the fowls of the air; for it repenteth me that I have made them.

Num. 22:32. And the angel of the LORD said unto him, Wherefore hast thou smitten thine ass these three times? behold, I went out to withstand thee, because *thy* way is perverse before me:

Deut. 25:16. For all that do such things, *and* all that do unrighteously, *are* an abomination unto the LORD thy God.

Deut. 32:19. And when the LORD saw *it*, he abhorred *them*, because of the provoking of his sons, and of his daughters.

2 Sam. 11:27. And when the mourning was past, David sent and fetched her to his house, and she became his wife, and bare him a son. But the thing that David had done displeased the LORD.

1 Kin. 14:22. And Judah did evil in the sight of the LORD, and they provoked him to jealousy with their sins which they had committed, above all that their fathers had done.

Psa. 5:4. For thou *art* not a God that hath pleasure in wickedness: neither shall evil dwell with thee. 5. The foolish shall not stand in thy sight: thou hatest all workers of iniquity. 6. Thou shalt destroy them that speak leasing: the LORD will abhor the bloody and deceitful man.

Psa. 10:3. For the wicked boasteth of his heart's desire, and blesseth the covetous, *whom* the LORD abhorreth.

Psa. 11:5. The LORD trieth the righteous: but the wicked and him that loveth violence his soul hateth.

Psa. 78:59. When God heard *this*, he was wroth, and greatly abhorred Israel:

Psa. 95:10. Forty years long was I grieved with *this* generation, and said, It *is* a people that do err in their heart, and they have not known my ways:

Psa. 106:40. Therefore was the wrath of the LORD kindled against his people, insomuch that he abhorred his own inheritance.

Prov. 3:32. For the froward *is* abomination to the LORD: but his secret *is* with the righteous. Prov. 11:20.

Prov. 6:16. These six *things* doth the LORD hate: yea, seven *are* an abomination unto him: 17. A proud look, a lying tongue, and hands that shed innocent blood, 18. An heart that deviseth wicked imaginations, feet that be swift in running to mischief, 19. A false witness *that* speaketh lies, and he that soweth discord among brethren.

Prov. 15:8. The sacrifice of the wicked *is* an abomination to the LORD: but the prayer of the upright *is* his delight. 9. The way of the wicked *is* an abomination unto the LORD: but he loveth him that followeth after righteousness. 26. The thoughts of the wicked *are* an abomination to the LORD: but *the words* of the pure *are* pleasant words.

Prov. 21:27. The sacrifice of the wicked *is* abomination: how much more, *when* he bringeth it with a wicked mind?

Isa. 43:24. Thou hast bought me no sweet cane with money, neither hast thou filled me with the fat of thy sacrifices: but thou hast made me to serve with thy sins, thou hast wearied me with thine iniquities.

Jer. 25:7. Yet ye have not hearkened unto me, saith the LORD; that ye might provoke me to anger with the works of your hands to your own hurt.

Jer. 44:4. Howbeit I sent unto you all my servants the prophets, rising early and sending *them*, saying, Oh, do not this abominable thing that I hate. 21. The incense that ye burned in the cities of Judah, and in the streets of Jerusalem, ye, and your fathers, your kings, and your princes, and the people of the land, did not the LORD remember them, and came it *not* into his mind? 22. So that the LORD could no longer bear, because of the evil of your doings, *and* because of the abominations which ye have committed; therefore is your land a desolation, and an astonishment, and a curse, without an inhabitant, as at this day.

Hab. 1:13. *Thou art* of purer eyes than to behold evil, and canst not look on iniquity:

Zech. 8:17. And let none of you imagine evil in your hearts against his neighbour; and love no false oath: for all these *are things* that I hate, saith the LORD.

Luke 16:15. And he said unto them, Ye are they which justify yourselves before men; but God knoweth your hearts: for that which is highly esteemed among men is abomination in the sight of God.

Rev. 2:6. But this thou hast, that thou hatest the deeds of the Nicolaitanes, which I also hate. 15. So hast thou also them that hold the doctrine of the Nicolaitanes, which thing I hate.

See GOD, HOLINESS OF; HOLINESS.

REPUGNANT TO THE RIGHTEOUS: Gen. 39:7. And it came to pass after these things, that his master's wife cast her eyes upon Joseph; and she said, Lie with me. 8. But he refused, and said unto his master's wife, Behold, my master wotteth not what *is* with me in the house, and he hath committed all that he hath to my hand; 9. *There is* none greater in this house than I; neither hath he kept back any thing from me but thee, because thou *art* his wife: how then can I do this great wickedness, and sin against God?

Deut. 7:26. Neither shalt thou bring an abomination into thine house, lest thou be a cursed thing like it: *but* thou shalt utterly detest it, and thou shalt utterly abhor it; for it *is* a cursed thing.

Job 1:1. There was a man in the land of Uz, whose name *was* Job; and that man was perfect and upright, and one that feared God, and eschewed evil.

Job 21:16. Lo, their good *is* not in their hand: the counsel of the wicked is far from me.

Job 22:18. Yet he filled their houses with good *things:* but the counsel of the wicked is far from me.

Psa. 26:5. I have hated the congregation of evil doers; and will not sit with the wicked. 9. Gather not my soul with sinners, nor my life with bloody men:

Psa. 84:10. I had rather be a doorkeeper in the house of my God, than to dwell in the tents of wickedness.

Psa. 101:3. I will set no wicked thing before mine eyes: I hate the work of them that turn aside; *it* shall not cleave to me. 4. A froward heart shall depart from me: I will ¹ not know a wicked *person.* 7. He that worketh deceit shall not dwell within my house: he that telleth lies shall not tarry in my sight.   [¹ R. V. know no evil thing]

Psa. 119:104. Through thy precepts I get understanding: therefore I hate every false way. [*v.* 128.] 113. I hate *vain* thoughts: but thy law do I love. 163. I hate and abhor lying: *but* thy law do I love.

Psa. 120:2. Deliver my soul, O LORD, from lying lips, *and* from a deceitful tongue. 5. Woe is me, that I sojourn in Mesech, *that* I dwell in the tents of Kedar! 6. My soul hath long dwelt with him that hateth peace.

7. I *am for* peace: but when I speak, they *are* for war.

Psa. 139:19. Surely thou wilt slay the wicked, O God: depart from me therefore, ye bloody men. 20. For they speak against thee wickedly, *and* thine enemies take *thy name* in vain. 21. Do not I hate them, O LORD, that hate thee? and am not I grieved with those that rise up against thee? 22. I hate them with perfect hatred: I count them mine enemies.

Prov. 8:13. The fear of the LORD *is* to hate evil: pride, and arrogancy, and the evil way, and the froward mouth, do I hate.

Prov. 29:27. An unjust man *is* an abomination to the just: and *he that is* upright in the way *is* abomination to the wicked.

Jer. 9:2. Oh that I had in the wilderness a lodging place of wayfaring men; that I might leave my people, and go from them! for they *be* all adulterers, an assembly of treacherous men.

Rom. 7:15. For that which I do I allow not: for what I would, that do I not; but what I hate, that do I. 19. For the good that I would I do not: but the evil which I would not, that I do. 23. But I see another law in my members, warring against the law of my mind, and bringing me into captivity to the law of sin which is in my members. 24. O wretched man that I am! who shall deliver me from the body of this death?

2 Pet. 2:7. And delivered just Lot, vexed with the filthy conversation of the wicked: 8. (For that righteous man dwelling among them, in seeing and hearing, vexed *his* righteous soul from day to day with *their* unlawful deeds;)

Jude 23. And others save with fear, pulling *them* out of the fire; hating even the garment spotted by the flesh.

Rev. 2:2. I know thy works, and thy labour, and thy patience, and how thou canst not bear them which are evil: and thou hast tried them

See HOLINESS.

SEPARATES FROM GOD: Deut. 31:17. Then my anger shall be kindled against them in that day, and I will forsake them, and I will hide my face from them, and they shall be devoured, and many evils and troubles shall befall them; so that they will say in that day, Are not these evils come upon us, because our God *is* not among us? 18. And I will surely hide my face in that day for all the evils which they shall have wrought, in that they are turned unto other gods.

Josh. 7:12. Therefore the children of Israel could not stand before their enemies, *but* turned *their* backs before their enemies, because they were accursed: neither will I be with you any more, except ye destroy the accursed from among you.

2 Chr. 24:20. And the Spirit of God came upon Zechariah the son of Jehoiada the priest, which stood above the people, and

said unto them, Thus saith God, Why transgress ye the commandments of the LORD, that ye cannot prosper? because ye have forsaken the LORD, he hath also forsaken you.

Job 13:24. Wherefore hidest thou thy face, and holdest me for thine enemy?

Job 23:3. Oh that I knew where I might find him! *that* I might come *even* to his seat! 8. Behold, I go forward, but he *is* not *there;* and backward, but I cannot perceive him: 9. On the left hand, where he doth work, but I cannot behold *him:* he hideth himself on the right hand, that I cannot see *him:*

Psa. 78:59. When God heard *this,* he was wroth, and greatly abhorred Israel: 60. So that he forsook the tabernacle of Shiloh, the tent *which* he placed among men; 61. And delivered his strength into captivity, and his glory into the enemy's hand.

Isa. 59:1. Behold, the LORD's hand is not shortened, that it cannot save; neither his ear heavy, that it cannot hear: 2. But your iniquities have separated between you and your God, and your sins have hid *his* face from you, that he will not hear.

Isa. 64:7. And *there is* none that calleth upon thy name, that stirreth up himself to take hold of thee: for thou hast hid thy face from us, and hast consumed us, because of our iniquities.

Ezek. 23:18. So she discovered her whoredoms, and discovered her nakedness: then my mind was alienated from her, like as my mind was alienated from her sister.

Hos. 9:12. Though they bring up their children, yet will I bereave them, *that there shall* not *be* a man *left:* yea, woe also to them when I depart from them!

Amos 3:2. You only have I known of all the families of the earth: therefore I will punish you for all your iniquities. 3. Can two walk together, except they be agreed?

Mic. 3:4. Then shall they cry unto the LORD, but he will not hear them: he will even hide his face from them at that time, as they have behaved themselves ill in their doings.

Luke 13:27. But he shall say, I tell you, I know you not whence ye are; depart from me, all *ye* workers of iniquity. Matt. 7:23; 25:41.

Rom. 8:7. Because the carnal mind *is* enmity against God:

Heb. 12:14. Follow peace with all *men,* and holiness, without which no man shall see the Lord:

See GOD, HOLINESS OF; WICKED, PUNISHMENT OF.

SIN. 1. Desert of, a wilderness between Elim and Sinai. Children of Israel journey through, Ex. 16:1; murmur for bread in, Ex. 16:2; manna and quails given in, Ex. 16:4-36; numbered in, Num. 26:64.

2. A city of Egypt, Ezek. 30:15.

SINA. See SINAI.

SINAI. 1. A mountain in the peninsula

E. of Red Sea. Called also SINA-HORA. Children of Israel arrive at, in their wanderings in the wilderness, Ex. 16:1; 19:2; Deut. 1:2. The law delivered to Moses upon, Ex. 19:3-25; 20; 24:12-18; 32:15,16; 34: 2-4; Lev. 7:38; 25:1; 26:46; 27:34: Num. 3:1; Deut. 4:15; 5:26; 29:1; 33:2; Neh. 9:13; Psa. 68:8,17; Mal. 4:4; Acts 7:30,38.

    FIGURATIVE: Gal. 4:24,25.

    See HOREB; ISRAELITES.

    2. Wilderness of. Children of Israel journeyed in, Num. 10:12; kept the passover in, Num. 9:1-5; numbered in, Num. 26:64.

    SINCERITY. Does not exempt from guilt, Gen. 20. See IGNORANCE, SINS OF. Forgiveness of enemies must be sincere, Matt. 18:35. Servants must render honest service, Eph. 6:5-7. Whatsoever is done must be in, 1 Cor. 10:31. Jesus was an example of, 1 Pet. 2:22. Ministers should be examples of, Tit. 2:7. Opposed to fleshly wisdom, 2 Cor. 1:12.

    Should characterize our love to God, 2 Cor. 8:8,24; our love to Jesus, Eph. 6:24; our service to God, Josh. 24:14; our faith, 1 Tim. 1:5; our love to one another, Rom. 12:9; 1 Pet. 1:22; 1 John 3:18; our whole conduct, 2 Cor. 1:12; the preaching of the gospel, 2 Cor. 2:17; 1 Thess. 2:3-5.

    A characteristic of the doctrines of the gospel, 1 Pet. 2:2. The gospel sometimes preached without, Phil. 1:16. The wicked devoid of, Psa. 5:9; 55:21. Exhortations to, 1 Cor. 5:8; 1 Pet. 2:1. Prayer for, on behalf of others, Phil. 1:10. Blessedness of, Psa. 32:2.

    EXEMPLIFIED: By men of Zebulun, 1 Chr. 12:33. By Hezekiah, Isa. 38:3. By Nathanael, John 1:47. By Paul, 2 Cor. 1:12. By Timothy, 2 Tim. 1:5. By Lois and Eunice, 2 Tim. 1:5.

    SINEWS, Job 10:11; 30:17; Isa. 48:4; Ezek. 37:6,8.

    SINGERS. See MUSIC.

    SINGING. See MUSIC.

    SINIM, an unknown land, conjectured by some authorities to be China, Isa. 49:12.

    SINITES, a tribe of Canaanites, Gen. 10:17; 1 Chr. 1:15.

    SINLESSNESS. Psa. 119:3. They also do no iniquity: they walk in his ways.

    Acts 24:16. And herein do I exercise myself, to have always a conscience void of offence toward God, and *toward* men.

    Phil. 1:9. And this I pray, . . . 10. That ye may approve things that are excellent; that ye may be sincere and without offence till the day of Christ; 11. Being filled with the fruits of righteousness, which are by Jesus Christ, unto the glory and praise of God.

    1 Thess. 3:13. To the end he may stablish your hearts unblameable in holiness before God, even our Father, at the coming of our Lord Jesus Christ with all his saints.

    1 Thess. 5:23. And the very God of peace sanctify you wholly; and *I pray God* your whole spirit and soul and body be preserved

blameless unto the coming of our Lord Jesus Christ.

    1 Pet. 4:1. Forasmuch then as Christ hath suffered for us in the flesh, arm yourselves likewise with the same mind: for he that hath suffered in the flesh hath ceased from sin; 2. That he no longer should live the rest of *his* time in the flesh to the lusts of men, but to the will of God.

    1 John 1:8. If we say that we have no sin, we deceive ourselves, and the truth is not in us. 10. If we say that we have not sinned, we make him a liar, and his word is not in us.

    1 John 3:6. Whosoever abideth in him sinneth not: whosoever sinneth hath not seen him, neither known him. 9. Whosoever is born of God doth not commit sin; for his seed remaineth in him: and he cannot sin, because he is born of God.

    SIN MONEY, 2 Kin. 12:16.

    See CONSCIENCE MONEY.

    SINNER. See WICKED.

    SION. 1. A name of Mount Hermon, Deut. 4:48.

    2. See ZION.

    SIPHMOTH, a city of Judah, 1 Sam. 30:28.

    SIPPAI. A Philistine giant, 1 Chr. 20:4. Called SAPH, 2 Sam. 21:18.

    SIRAH, the name of a well, 2 Sam. 3:26.

    SIRION, Sidonian name of Mount Hermon, Deut. 3:9; Psa. 29:6.

    SISAMAI, son of Eleasah, 1 Chr. 2:40.

    SISERA. 1. Captain of a Canaanitish army, defeated by Barak; slain by Jael, Judg. 4; 5:20-31; 1 Sam. 12:9; Psa. 83:9.

    2. One of the Nethinim, Ezra 2:53; Neh. 7:55.

    SITNAH, a name given by Isaac to a well, Gen. 26:21.

    SIVAN, third month (June), Esth. 8:9.

    SKEPTICISM, Job 21:15; 22:17; Psa. 14:1; 53:1; Zeph. 1:12; Mal. 3:14. Of Pharaoh, Ex. 5:2. Of Thomas, John 20:25-28.

    See UNBELIEF.

    SKIN. Clothes of, Gen. 3:21. For covering the tabernacle, Ex. 25:5; Num. 4:8-14. Diseases of, Lev. 13:38,39; Deut. 28:27; Job 7:5. See BOILS; LEPROSY.

    SKIRT. See DRESS.

    SLANDER. Comes from the evil heart, Luke 6:45. Often arises from hatred, Psa. 109:3. Idleness leads to, 1 Tim. 5:13. The wicked addicted to, Psa. 50:20. Hypocrites addicted to, Prov. 11:9. A characteristic of the devil, Rev. 12:10. The wicked love, Psa. 52:4. They who indulge in, are fools, Prov. 10:18. Women warned against, Tit. 2:3. Ministers' wives should avoid, 1 Tim. 3:11. Christ was exposed to, Psa. 35:11; Matt. 26:60. Rulers exposed to, Jude 8. Ministers exposed to, Rom. 3:8; 2 Cor. 6:8. The nearest relations exposed to, Psa. 50:20. Saints exposed to, Psa. 38:12; 109:2; 1 Pet. 4:4.

    Saints should keep their tongues from, Psa. 34:13, with 1 Pet. 3:10; should lay aside,

Eph. 4:31; should be warned against. Tit. 3:1,2; should give no occasion for, 1 Pet. 2:12; 3:16; should return good for, 1 Cor 4:13; blessed in enduring, Matt. 5:11; characterized as avoiding, Psa. 15:1,3.

Should not be listened to, 1 Sam. 24:9; causes anger, Prov. 25:23 [R.V.].

Effects of: Separating friends, Prov. 16:28; 17:9; deadly wounds, Prov. 18:8; 26:22; strife, Prov. 26:20; discord among brethren, Prov. 6:19; murder, Psa. 31:13; Ezek. 22:9.

The tongue of, is a scourge, Job 5:21; is venomous, Psa. 140:3; Eccl. 10:11; is destructive, Prov. 11:9. End of, is mischievous madness, Eccl. 10:13. Men shall give account for, Matt. 12:36. Punishment for, Deut. 19: 16–21.—Bible Text-Book.

UNCLASSIFIED SCRIPTURES RELATING TO: Ex. 23:1. Thou shalt not raise a false report: put not thine hand with the wicked to be an unrighteous witness.

Deut. 22:13. If any man take a wife, and go in unto her, and hate her, 14. And give occasions of speech against her, and bring up an evil name upon her, and say, I took this woman, and when I came to her, I found her not a maid: 15. Then shall the father of the damsel, and her mother, take and bring forth the tokens of the damsel's virginity unto the elders of the city in the gate: 16. And the damsel's father shall say unto the elders, I gave my daughter unto this man to wife, and he hateth her; 17. And, lo, he hath given occasion of speech against her, saying, I found not thy daughter a maid; and yet these are the tokens of my daughter's virginity. And they shall spread the cloth before the elders of the city. 18. And the elders of that city shall take that man and chastise him; 19. And they shall amerce him in an hundred shekels of silver, and give them unto the father of the damsel, because he hath brought up an evil name upon a virgin of Israel: and she shall be his wife; he may not put her away all his days.

Job 5:21. Thou shalt be hid from the scourge of the tongue: neither shalt thou be afraid of destruction when it cometh.

Psa. 41:6. And if he come to see me, he speaketh vanity: his heart gathereth iniquity to itself; when he goeth abroad, he telleth it. 7. All that hate me whisper together against me: against me do they devise my hurt. 8. An evil disease, say they, cleaveth fast unto him: and now that he lieth he shall rise up no more. 9. Yea, mine own familiar friend, in whom I trusted, which did eat of my bread, hath lifted up his heel against me.

Psa. 50:20. Thou sittest and speakest against thy brother; thou slanderest thine own mother's son.

Psa. 101:5. Whoso privily slandereth his neighbour, him will I cut off:

Prov. 10:18. He that hideth hatred with lying lips, and he that uttereth a slander, is a fool.

Prov. 25:23. The north wind [1] driveth away rain: so doth [2] an angry countenance a backbiting tongue. [R. V. [1] bringeth forth [2] a backbiting tongue an angry countenance.]

Jer. 6:28. They are all grievous revolters, walking with slanders: they are brass and iron; they are all corrupters.

Jer. 9:4. Take ye heed every one of his neighbour, and trust ye not in any brother: for every brother will utterly supplant, and every neighbour will walk with slanders.

Rom. 1:29. Being filled with all unrighteousness, fornication, wickedness, covetousness, maliciousness; full of envy, murder, debate, deceit, malignity; whisperers, 30. Backbiters,

1 Cor. 4:13. Being defamed, we intreat:

1 Cor. 6:10. Nor thieves, nor covetous, nor drunkards, nor revilers, nor extortioners, shall inherit the kingdom of God.

2 Cor. 12:20. For I fear, lest, when I come, I shall not find you such as I would, and that I shall be found unto you such as ye would not: lest there be debates, envyings, wraths, strifes, backbitings, whisperings,

Jas. 4:11. Speak not evil one of another, brethren. He that speaketh evil of his brother, and judgeth his brother, speaketh evil of the law, and judgeth the law: but if thou judge the law, thou art not a doer of the law, but a judge.

1 Pet. 2:1. Wherefore laying aside all malice, and all guile, and hypocrisies, and envies, and all evil speakings,

2 Pet. 2:10. Presumptuous are they, self-willed, they are not afraid to speak evil of dignities.

INSTANCES OF: Joseph, by Potiphar's wife, Gen. 39:14–18. Land of Canaan misrepresented by the spies, Num. 14:36. Of Mephibosheth, by Ziba, 2 Sam. 16:3; 19:24–30. Of David, by his enemies, Psa. 31:13; 35:21; 41:5; 64:3; 140:3. Of Naboth, by Jezebel, 1 Kin. 21:9-14. Of Jeremiah, by the Jews, Jer. 18:18. Of Jesus, by the Jews falsely charging that he was a winebibber, Matt. 11:19; that he blasphemed, Mark 14: 64; John 5:18; that he had a devil, John 8:48,52; 10:20; that he was seditious, Luke 22:65; 23:5; that he was a king, Luke 23:2; John 18:37, with 19:1-5. Of Paul, see PAUL.

See ACCUSATION, FALSE; FALSE WITNESS; FALSEHOOD; SPEAKING EVIL.

SLAVERY. See SERVANT, BOND.

SLEEP. From God, Psa. 127:2. Of the sluggard, Prov. 6:9,10. Of Jesus, Matt. 8: 24; Mark 4:38; Luke 8:23. A symbol of death, Job 14:12; Matt. 9:24; Mark 5:39; Luke 8:52; John 11:11,12; 1 Thess. 4:14. See DEATH.

SLIME, a cement made of asphaltum. Valley of Siddim afforded, Gen. 14:10. Used at Babel, Gen. 11:3. Used in Noah's ark, Gen. 6:14; ark of Moses, Ex. 2:3. Inflammable. Isa. 34:9.

SLING. Used for throwing stones, Prov. 26:8. David slays Goliath with, 1 Sam. 17:

40–50. Dextrous use of, Judg. 20:16. Used in war, Judg. 20:16; 2 Kin. 3:25; 2 Chr. 26:14.

See ARMIES; ARMS.

SLOTHFULNESS. Prov. 6:6. Go to the ant, thou sluggard; consider her ways, and be wise: 7. Which having no guide, overseer, or ruler, 8. Provideth her meat in the summer, *and* gathereth her food in the harvest. 9. How long wilt thou sleep, O sluggard? when wilt thou arise out of thy sleep? 10. *Yet* a little sleep, a little slumber, a little folding of the hands to sleep: 11. So shall thy poverty come as one that travelleth, and thy want as an armed man.

Prov. 10:4. He becometh poor that dealeth *with* a slack hand: but the hand of the diligent maketh rich. 5. He that gathereth in summer *is* a wise son: *but* he that sleepeth in harvest *is* a son that causeth shame. 26. As vinegar to the teeth, and as smoke to the eyes, so *is* the sluggard to them that send him.

Prov. 12:24. The hand of the diligent shall bear rule: but the slothful shall be under tribute. 27. The slothful *man* roasteth not that which he took in hunting: but the substance of a diligent man *is* precious.

Prov. 13:4. The soul of the sluggard desireth, and *hath* nothing: but the soul of the diligent shall be made fat.

Prov. 15:19. The way of the slothful *man is* as an hedge of thorns: but the way of the righteous *is* made plain.

Prov. 18:9. He also that is slothful in his work is brother to him that is a great waster.

Prov. 19:15. Slothfulness casteth into a deep sleep; and an idle soul shall suffer hunger. 24. A slothful *man* hideth his hand in *his* bosom, and will not so much as bring it to his mouth again.

Prov. 20:4. The sluggard will not plough by reason of the cold; *therefore* shall he beg in harvest, and *have* nothing.

Prov. 21:25. The desire of the slothful killeth him; for his hands refuse to labour.

Prov. 23:21. For the drunkard and the glutton shall come to poverty: and drowsiness shall clothe *a man* with rags.

Prov. 24:30. I went by the field of the slothful, and by the vineyard of the man void of understanding; 31. And, lo, it was all grown over with thorns, *and* nettles had covered the face thereof, and the stone wall thereof was broken down. 32. Then I saw, *and* considered *it* well: I looked upon *it, and* received instruction. 33. *Yet* a little sleep, a little slumber, a little folding of the hands to sleep: 34. So shall thy poverty come *as* one that travelleth; and thy want as an armed man.

Prov. 26:13. The slothful *man* saith, There *is* a lion in the way; a lion *is* in the streets. [chapter 22:13.] 14. *As* the door turneth upon his hinges, so *doth* the slothful upon his bed. 15. The slothful hideth his hand in *his* bosom; it grieveth him to bring it again to his mouth. 16. The sluggard *is*

wiser in his own conceit than seven men that can render a reason.

Eccl. 10:18. By much slothfulness the building decayeth; and through idleness of the hands the house droppeth through.

Isa. 56:10. His watchmen *are* blind: they are all ignorant, they *are* all dumb dogs, they cannot bark; sleeping, lying down, loving to slumber.

Matt. 25:26. His lord answered and said unto him, *Thou* wicked and slothful servant, thou knewest that I reap where I sowed not, and gather where I have not strawed: 27. Thou oughtest therefore to have put my money to the exchangers, and *then* at my coming I should have received mine own with usury.

Rom. 12:11. Not slothful in business; fervent in spirit; serving the Lord;

2 Thess. 3:10. For even when we were with you, this we commanded you, that if any would not work, neither should he eat. 11. For we hear that there are some which walk among you disorderly, working not at all, but are busybodies. 12. Now them that are such we command and exhort by our Lord Jesus Christ, that with quietness they work, and eat their own bread.

Heb. 6:12. That ye be not slothful, but followers of them who through faith and patience inherit the promises.

See IDLENESS; INDUSTRY.

SLUGGARD. See IDLENESS.

SMITH, a worker in metals. Tubal-cain, Gen. 4:22. Bezaleel, Ex. 31:1–11. The Philistines, 1 Sam. 13:19. Jewish, carried captive to Babylon, 2 Kin. 24:14; Jer. 24:1. The manufacturers of idols, Isa. 41:7; 44:12. Genius of, from God, Ex. 31:3–5; 35:30–35; Isa. 54:16.

SMITING. See ASSAULT AND BATTERY.

SMOKE. FIGURATIVE: Isa. 6:4; Hos. 13:3.

SMYRNA, a city of Ionia. One of the "seven churches" in, Rev. 1:11; 2:8.

SNAIL, a crustacean. Forbidden as food, Lev. 11:30. Perishable, Psa. 58:8.

SNARE. Amos 3:5.

FIGURATIVE: Of the evils in life of the wicked, Job 18:8–10. Of the devices of the wicked to deceive the righteous, Psa. 91:3; Jer. 5:26.

See AMBUSH; CONSPIRACY; PIT.

SNOW. In Palestine, 2 Sam. 23:20. In Uz, Job 6:16; 9:30; 37:6. On mount Lebanon, Jer. 18:14.

FIGURATIVE: Of purity, Psa. 51:7; Isa. 1:18; Lam. 4:7.

SNUFFDISHES, in the tabernacle, Ex. 25:38.

SNUFFERS. Provided for the lamps in the temple, 1 Kin. 7:50; 2 Kin. 12:13; 25:14; Jer. 52:18.

SOAP, a washing compound, Jer. 2:22; Mal. 3:2.

SOBRIETY. Commanded, 1 Pet. 1:13; 5:8. The gospel designed to teach, Tit. 2:12. With watchfulness, 1 Thess. 5:6. With prayer, 1 Pet. 4:7. Required in ministers, 1 Tim. 3:2,3; Tit. 1:8; wives of ministers, 1 Tim. 3:11; aged men, Tit. 2:2; young men, Tit. 2:6; young women, Tit. 2:4; all saints, 1 Thess. 5:6,8. Women should exhibit in dress, 1 Tim. 2:9. We should estimate our character and talents with, Rom. 12:3. We should live in, Tit. 2:12. Motive for, 1 Pet. 4:7; 5:8.—*Bible Text-Book*.

See TEMPERANCE ; DRUNKENNESS.

SO, king of Egypt, 2 Kin. 17:4.

SOCHO, son of Heber, 1 Chr. 4:18.

SOCHOH. See SOCOH.

SOCOH. 1. Called also SHOCHO, SHOCHOH, SHOCO, SOCHOH. A city of Judah, Josh. 15:35; 1 Sam. 17:1. One of Solomon's commissaries in, 1 Kin. 4:10. Rebuilt and fortified by Rehoboam, 2 Chr. 11:7. Taken by Philistines, 2 Chr. 28:18.

2. A city in the mountains of Judah, Josh. 15:48.

SODI, a man of Zebulun, Num. 13:10.

SODOM, called also SODOMA. Situated in the plain of the Jordan, Gen. 13:10. The southeastern limit of the Canaanites, Gen. 10:19. Lot dwells at, Gen. 13:12. King of, joins other kings of the nations resisting the invasion of Chedorlaomer, Gen. 14:1–12. Wickedness of the inhabitants of, Gen. 13:13; 19:4–13; Deut. 32:32; Isa. 3:9; Jer. 23:14; Lam. 4:6; Ezek. 16:46,48,49; Jude 7. Abraham's intercession for, Gen. 18:16–33. Destroyed on account of the wickedness of the people, Gen. 19:1–29; Deut. 29:23; Isa. 13:19; Jer. 49:18; 50:40; Lam. 4:6; Amos 4:11; Zeph. 2:9; Matt. 10:15; Luke 17:29; Rom. 9:29; 2 Pet. 2:6.

FIGURATIVE : Of wickedness, Deut. 23:17; 32:32; Isa. 1:10; Ezek. 16:46–56.

SODOMITES, inhabitants of Sodom. Wickedness of, Gen. 19:4–14. Destroyed by fire as a judgment, Gen. 19:24,25. To be judged according to opportunity, Matt. 11:24; Luke 10:12. A proverbial term of reproach applied to those who practice sodomy, Deut. 23:17; 1 Kin. 14:24; 15:12; 22:46; 2 Kin. 23:7; Job 36:14 [marg.]. The word "harlot" in Gen. 38:21,22; Deut. 23:17; Hos. 4:14, is the translation of a Hebrew feminine form of the word translated elsewhere "sodomite." See SODOMY.

SODOMY, Gen. 19:5–8; Ex. 22:19; Lev. 18:22,23; 20:13,15,16; Deut. 23:17; 27:21; Judg. 19:22; 1 Kin. 14:24; 15:12; 22:46; 2 Kin. 23:7; Rom. 1:24,26,27; 1 Cor. 6:9; 1 Tim. 1:9,10. See SODOMITES.

SOLDERING, Isa. 41:7.

SOLDIERS. Military enrollment of Israel in the wilderness of Sinai, Num. 1; 2; in the plains of Moab, Num. 26. Levies of, in the ratio of one man to ten subject to duty, Judg. 20:10. Dressed in scarlet, Nah. 2:3. Cowards excused from duty as, Deut. 20:8; Judg. 7:3. Others exempt from service, Deut. 20:5–9; 24:5. Come to John, Luke 3:14. Mock Jesus, Matt. 27:27–31; Mark. 15:16–20; Luke 23:11,36,37. Officers concerned in the betrayal of Jesus, Luke 22:4. Crucified Jesus, Matt. 27:27,31–37; Mark 15:

16–24; John 19:23,24. Guard the sepulchre, Matt. 27:65; 28:11–15. Guard prisoners, Acts 12:4–6; 28:16. Maintain the peace, Acts 21:31–35. Their duty as sentinels, Acts 12:19. Perform escort duty, Acts 21:31–33,35; 22:24–28; 23:23,31–33; 27:1,31,42,43; 28:16.

FIGURATIVE : Of the divine protection, Isa. 59:16,17. Of the Christian, Eph. 6:11–17; 2 Tim. 2:3. Jesus called CAPTAIN [R. V., author] OF OUR SALVATION, Heb. 2:10.

See ARMIES.

SOLOMON. Son of David by Bathsheba, 2 Sam. 12:24; 1 Kin. 1:13,17,21. Named Jedidiah, by Nathan the prophet, 2 Sam. 12:24,25. Ancestor of Joseph, Matt. 1:6. Succeeds David to the throne of Israel, 1 Kin. 1:11–48; 2:12; 1 Chr. 23:1; 28; Eccl. 1:12. Anointed king a second time, 1 Chr. 29:22. His prayer for wisdom, and his vision, 1 Kin. 3:5–14; 2 Chr. 1:7–12. Covenant renewed in a vision after the dedication of the temple, 1 Kin. 9:1–9; 2 Chr. 7:12–22. His rigorous reign, 1 Kin. 2.

Builds the temple, 1 Kin. 5; 6; 9:10; 1 Chr. 6:10; 2 Chr. 2; 3; 4; 7:11; Jer. 52:20; Acts 7:45–47. Dedicates the temple, 1 Kin. 8; 2 Chr. 6. Renews the courses of the priests and Levites, and the forms of service according to the commandment of Moses and the regulations of David, 2 Chr. 8:12–16; 35:4; Neh. 12:45.

Builds his palace, 1 Kin. 3:1; 7:1,8; 9:10; 2 Chr. 7:11; 8:1; Eccl. 2:4; his house of the forest of Lebanon, 1 Kin. 7:2–7; for Pharaoh's daughter, 1 Kin. 7:8–12; 9:24; 2 Chr. 8:11; Eccl. 2:4. Ivory throne of, 1 Kin. 7:7; 10:18–20. Porches of judgment, 1 Kin. 7:7. Builds Millo, the wall of Jerusalem, the cities of Hazor, Megiddo, Gezer, Beth-horon, Baalath, Tadmor, store cities, and cities for chariots, and for cavalry, 1 Kin. 9:15–19; 2 Chr. 9:25. Provides an armory, 1 Kin. 10:16,17. Plants vineyards and orchards of all kinds of fruit trees; makes pools, Eccl. 2:4–6; imports apes and peacocks, 1 Kin. 10:22. Drinking vessels of his houses, 1 Kin. 10:21; 2 Chr. 9:20. Musicians and musical instruments of his court, 1 Kin. 10:12; 2 Chr. 9:11; Eccl. 2:8. The splendor of his court, 1 Kin. 10:5–9,12; 2 Chr. 9:3–8; Eccl. 2:9; Matt. 6:29; Luke 12:27.

Commerce of, 1 Kin. 9:28; 10:11,12,22,28, 29; 2 Chr. 1:16,17; 8:17,18; 9:13–22,28. Presents received by, 1 Kin. 10:10; 2 Chr. 9:9, 23,24. Is visited by the queen of Sheba, 1 Kin. 10:1–13; 2 Chr. 9:1–12. Wealth of, 1 Kin. 9; 10:10,14,15,23,27; 2 Chr. 1:15; 9:1,9, 13,24,27; Eccl. 1:16. Has seven hundred wives and three hundred concubines, 1 Kin. 11:3, with Deut. 17:17; their influence over him, 1 Kin. 11:4. Marries one of Pharaoh's daughters, 1 Kin. 3:1. Builds idolatrous temples, 1 Kin. 11:1–8; 2 Kin. 23:13. His idolatry, 1 Kin. 3:3,4; 2 Kin. 23:13; Neh. 13:26.

Extent of his dominions, 1 Kin. 4:21,24; 8:65; 2 Chr. 7:8; 9:26. Receives tribute, 1 Kin. 4:21; 9:21; 2 Chr. 8:8. Officers of, 1 Kin. 2:35; 4:1–19; 2 Chr. 8:9,10. His purveyors, 1 Kin. 4:7-19. Divides his kingdom into subsistence departments: the daily subsistence rate for his court, 1 Kin. 4:7-23, 27,28.

Military equipment of, 1 Kin. 4:26,28; 10:16, 17,26,28; 2 Chr. 1:14; 9:25, with Deut. 17:15,16. Cedes certain cities to Hiram, 1 Kin. 9:10-13; 2 Chr. 8:2. Wisdom and fame of, 1 Kin. 4: 29-34; 10:3,4,8,23,24; 1Chr. 29:24,25; 2 Chr. 9: 2-7,22,23; Eccl. 1:16; Matt. 12:42. Piety of, 1 Kin. 3:5-15; 4:29; 8. Beloved of God, 2 Sam. 12:24. Justice of, illustrated in his judgment of the two harlots, 1 Kin. 3:16-28. Oppressions of, 1 Kin. 12:4; 2 Chr. 10:4.

Reigns forty years, 2 Chr. 9:30. Death of, 2 Chr. 9:29-31.

Prophecies concerning, 2 Sam. 7:12-16; 1 Kin. 11:9-13; 1 Chr. 17:11-14; 28:6,7; Psa.132:11. A type of Christ, Psa. 45:2-17; 72.

SOLOMON'S PORCH, a part of the outer court of the temple, John 10:23; Acts 3:11; 5:12.

SON. FIGURATIVE: Of man's relation to God, Ex. 4:22.

See ADOPTION; GOD, FATHERHOOD OF; JESUS, SON OF GOD; JESUS, SON OF MAN.

SON-IN-LAW. Unjust, Jacob, Gen. 30: 37-42. Faithful, Peter, Mark 1:29,30; Luke 4:38.

SONG. Sung at the passover, Matt. 26: 30; Mark 14:26. Didactic, Deut. 32. See PSALMS, DIDACTIC. Impersonation of the church, Song chapters 1-8. Of Moses and the Lamb, Rev. 15:3,4. New, Psa. 33:3; 40:3. Prophetic, see PSALMS, PROPHETIC. Spiritual, singing of, enjoined, Eph. 5:19; Col. 3:16. Of praise, see PRAISE; PSALMS, PRAISE; PSALMS, THANKSGIVING; THANKFULNESS. Of redemption, Rev. 5:9,10. Of the redeemed, Rev. 14:2,3-5. Of thanksgiving, see THANKFULNESS; PSALMS, THANKSGIVING. War, Ex. 15:1-21; Num. 21:27-30; Judg. 5; 2 Sam. 1:19-27; 22. Solomon wrote one thousand and five, 1 Kin. 4:32.

See POETRY; PRAISE; PSALMS, THANKSGIVING.

SOOTHSAYER. See SORCERY.

SOPATER, a Christian of Berea, Acts 20:4.

SOPHERETH, a servant of Solomon, whose descendants returned from captivity to Jerusalem, Ezra 2:55; Neh. 7:57.

SORCERY, divination by an alleged assistance of evil spirits. Forbidden, Lev. 19: 26-28,31; 20:6; Deut. 18:9-14. Denounced, Isa. 8:19; Mal. 3:5.

Practised : By the Egyptians, Isa. 19:3,11, 12; by the magicians, Ex. 7:11,22; 8:7,18; by Balaam, Num. 22:6; 23:23, with chapters 22; 23; by Jezebel, 2 Kin. 9:22; by the Ninevites, Nah. 3:4,5; by the Babylonians, Isa. 47:9-13; Ezek. 21:21,22; Dan. 2:2,10,27; by Belshazzar, Dan. 5:7,15; by Simon Magus, Acts 8:9, 11; by Elymas, Acts 13:8; by the damsel at Philippi, Acts 16:16; by vagabond Jews, Acts 19:13; by sons of Sceva, Acts 19:14,15; by astrologers, Jer. 10:2; Mic. 3:6,7; by false

prophets, Jer. 14:14; 27:9; 29:8,9; Ezek. 13: 6-9; 22:28; Matt. 24:24.

To cease, Ezek. 12:23,24; 13:23; Mic. 5:12.

Messages of, false, Ezek. 21:29; Zech. 10:2; 2 Thess. 2:9. Diviners shall be confounded, Mic. 3:7. Belongs to the works of the flesh, Gal. 5:20. Wickedness of, 1 Sam. 15:23. Vainness of, Isa. 44:25. Punishment for, Ex.22:18; Lev. 20:27; Deut. 13:5. Divining by familiar spirits, Lev. 20:27; 1 Chr. 10:13; 2 Chr. 33:6; Isa. 8:19; 19:3; 29:4; by entrails, Ezek. 21:21; by images, 2 Kin. 23:24; Ezek. 21:21; by rods, Hos. 4:12.

Saul consulted the Witch of Endor, 1 Sam. 28:7-25.

Books of, destroyed, Acts 19:19.

SOREK, valley of, Judg. 16:4.

SORREL, a color, Zech. 1:8 [R. V.].

SORROW. God takes notice of Hagar's, Gen. 21:17-20; Israelites, Ex. 3:7-10.

For sin, 2 Cor. 7:10,11. See REPENTANCE; SIN, CONFESSION OF.

No sorrow in heaven, Rev. 21:4. "Sorrow and sighing shall flee away," Isa. 35:10.

Of Hannah, 1 Sam. 1:15. Of David for Absalom, 2 Sam. 18:33; 19:1-8. Of Mary and Martha, John 11:19-40. Jeremiah, Lam. 1: 12. Jesus, Isa. 53:11; Matt. 26:37-44; Mark 14:34-42; Luke 22:42-44.

From bereavement: Of Jacob for Joseph, Gen. 37:34,35; for Benjamin, Gen. 43:14.

Of the lost, Matt. 8:12; 13:42,50; 22:13; 24: 51; 25:30; Luke 13:28; 16:23. See WICKED, PUNISHMENT OF.

See AFFLICTION, BENEFITS OF, CONSOLATION IN, DESIGN OF, RESIGNATION IN; SUFFERING.

SOSIPATER, kinsman of Paul, Rom. 16:21.

SOSTHENES. 1. Chief ruler of the synagogue in Corinth, Acts 18:17.

2. A Christian with whom Paul wrote the first letter to the Corinthians, 1 Cor. 1:1.

SOTAI, a servant of Solomon whose descendants returned from captivity to Jerusalem, Ezra 2:55; Neh. 7:57.

SOUL. See SPIRIT; IMMORTALITY; MAN, A SPIRIT; RIGHTEOUS, FUTURE STATE OF; WICKED, PUNISHMENT OF.

SOUNDING, in navigation, Acts 27:28.

SOVEREIGNTY. Of God, see GOD, SOVEREIGN. Of Man, see MAN, DOMINION OF.

SOWER. Parable of the, Matt. 13:3-8; Mark 4:3-20; Luke 8:5-8. Sowing, Eccl. 11: 4; Isa. 28:25.

FIGURATIVE: Psa. 126:5; Prov. 11:18; Isa. 32:20; Hos. 8:7; 10:12; Gal. 6:7,8.

SPAIN, Paul purposes to visit, Rom. 15: 24,28.

SPAN, about nine or ten inches, Ex. 28: 16; 39:9.

SPARROW. Nests of, Psa. 84:3. Two, sold for a farthing, Matt. 10:29; Luke 12:6.

SPEAKING. EVIL: Ex. 22:28. Thou shalt not . . . curse the ruler of thy people. Job 19:18. Yea, young children despised me; I arose, and they spake against me. Psa. 10:7. His mouth is full of cursing and deceit and fraud: under his tongue *is* mischief and vanity. 8. He sitteth in the lurking places of the villages: in the secret places doth he murder the innocent: his eyes are privily set against the poor.

Psa. 12:3. The LORD shall cut off all flattering lips, *and* the tongue that speaketh proud things: 4. Who have said, With our tongue will we prevail; our lips *are* our own: who *is* lord over us?

Psa. 34:13. Keep thy tongue from evil, and thy lips from speaking guile.

Psa. 35:21. Yea, they opened their mouth wide against me, *and* said, Aha, aha, our eye hath seen *it.*

Psa. 41:5. Mine enemies speak evil of me, When shall he die, and his name perish? 6. And if he come to see *me,* he speaketh vanity: his heart gathereth iniquity to itself; *when* he goeth abroad, he telleth *it.* 7. All that hate me whisper together against me: against me do they devise my hurt. 8. An evil disease, *say they,* cleaveth fast unto him: and *now* that he lieth he shall rise up no more. 9. Yea, mine own familiar friend, in whom I trusted, which did eat of my bread, hath lifted up *his* heel against me.

Psa. 52:2. Thy tongue deviseth mischiefs; like a sharp razor, working deceitfully. 3. Thou lovest evil more than good; *and* lying rather than to speak righteousness. 4. Thou lovest all devouring words, O *thou* deceitful tongue.

Psa. 59:12. *For* the sin of their mouth *and* the words of their lips let them even be taken in their pride: and for cursing and lying *which* they speak.

Psa. 64:2. Hide me from the secret counsel of the wicked; from the insurrection of the workers of iniquity: 3. Who whet their tongue like a sword, *and* bend *their bows to shoot* their arrows, *even* bitter words: 4. That they may shoot in secret at the perfect: suddenly do they shoot at him, and fear not. 5. They encourage themselves *in* an evil manner: they commune of laying snares privily; they say, Who shall see them?

Psa. 69:12. They that sit in the gate speak against me; and I *was* the song of the drunkards. 26. For they persecute *him* whom thou hast smitten; and they talk to the grief of those whom thou hast wounded.

Psa. 70:3. Let them be turned back for a reward of their shame that say, Aha, aha.

Psa. 102:8. Mine enemies reproach me all the day; *and* they that are mad against me are sworn against me.

Psa. 106:33. Because they provoked his spirit, so that he spake unadvisedly with his lips.

Psa. 119:23. Princes also did sit *and* speak against me: *but* thy servant did meditate in thy statutes.

Psa. 120:1. In my distress I cried unto the LORD, and he heard me. 2. Deliver my soul, O LORD, from lying lips, *and* from a deceitful tongue. 3. What shall be given unto thee? or what shall be done unto thee, thou false tongue? 4. Sharp arrows of the mighty, with coals of juniper. 5. Woe is me, that I sojourn in Mesech, *that* I dwell in the tents of Kedar! 6. My soul hath long dwelt with him that hateth peace. 7. I *am for* peace: but when I speak, they *are* for war.

Psa. 140:3. They have sharpened their tongues like a serpent; adders' poison *is* under their lips. 11. Let not an evil speaker be established in the earth: evil shall hunt the violent man to overthrow *him.*

Prov. 4:24. Put away from thee a froward mouth, and perverse lips put far from thee.

Prov. 6:16. These six *things* doth the LORD hate: yea, seven *are* an abomination unto him: 17. A proud look, a lying tongue, and hands that shed innocent blood, 18. An heart that deviseth wicked imaginations, feet that be swift in running to mischief, 19. A false witness *that* speaketh lies, and he that soweth discord among brethren.

Prov. 8:13. The fear of the LORD *is* to hate evil: pride, and arrogancy, and the evil way, and the froward mouth, do I hate.

Prov. 10:11. The mouth of a righteous *man is* a well of life: but violence covereth the mouth of the wicked. 19. In the multitude of words there wanteth not sin: but he that refraineth his lips *is* wise. 31. The mouth of the just bringeth forth wisdom: but the froward tongue shall be cut out. 32. The lips of the righteous know what is acceptable: but the mouth of the wicked *speaketh* frowardness.

Prov. 11:11. By the blessing of the upright the city is exalted: but it is overthrown by the mouth of the wicked.

Prov. 12:5. The thoughts of the righteous *are* right: *but* the counsels of the wicked *are* deceit. 6. The words of the wicked *are* to lie in wait for blood: but the mouth of the upright shall deliver them. 13. The wicked is snared by the transgression of *his* lips: but the just shall come out of trouble. 17. *He that* speaketh truth shew-eth forth righteousness: but a false witness deceit. 18. There is that speaketh like the piercings of a sword: but the tongue of the wise *is* health. 19. The lip of truth shall be established for ever: but a lying tongue *is* but for a moment.

Prov. 13:3. He that keepeth his mouth keepeth his life: *but* he that openeth wide his lips shall have destruction.

Prov. 14:25. A true witness delivereth souls: but a deceitful *witness* speaketh lies.

Prov. 15:1. A soft answer turneth away wrath: but grievous words stir up anger. 4. A wholesome tongue *is* a tree of life: but perverseness therein *is* a breach in the spirit. 28. The heart of the righteous studieth to answer: but the mouth of the wicked pour-eth out evil things.

Prov. 16:27. An ungodly man diggeth up evil: and in his lips *there is* as a burning fire. 28. A froward man soweth strife: and a whisperer separateth chief friends.

Prov. 17:4. A wicked doer giveth heed to false lips; *and* a liar giveth ear to a naughty tongue. 9. He that covereth a transgression seeketh love; but he that repeateth a matter separateth *very* friends. 20. He that hath a froward heart findeth no good: and he that hath a perverse tongue falleth into mischief.

Prov. 18:8. The words of a talebearer *are* as wounds, and they go down into the innermost parts of the belly. 21. Death and life *are* in the power of the tongue: and they that love it shall eat the fruit thereof. 23. The poor useth intreaties; but the rich answereth roughly.

Prov. 19:1. Better *is* the poor that walketh in his integrity, than *he that is* perverse in his lips, and is a fool. 22. The desire of a man *is* his kindness: and a poor man *is* better than a liar. 28. An ungodly witness scorneth judgment: and the mouth of the wicked devoureth iniquity.

Prov. 24:2. For their heart studieth destruction, and their lips talk of mischief.

Prov. 25:23. The north wind ¹ driveth away rain: so *doth* ² an angry countenance a backbiting tongue. [R. V. ¹ bringeth forth ² a backbiting tongue an angry countenance.]

Prov. 26:20. Where no wood is, *there* the fire goeth out: so where *there is* no talebearer, the strife ceaseth. 21. As coals *are* to burning coals, and wood to fire; so *is* a contentious man to kindle strife. 22. The words of a talebearer *are* as wounds, and they go down into the innermost parts of the belly. 23. Burning lips and a wicked heart *are like* a potsherd covered with silver dross. 28. A lying tongue hateth *those that are* afflicted by it; and a flattering mouth worketh ruin.

Eccl. 7:22. For oftentimes also thine own heart knoweth that thou thyself likewise hast cursed others.

Eccl. 10:11. Surely the serpent will bite without enchantment; and a babbler is no better. 20. Curse not the king, no not in thy thought; and curse not the rich in thy bedchamber: for a bird of the air shall carry the voice, and that which hath wings shall tell the matter.

Isa. 6:5. Then said I, Woe *is* me! for I am undone; because I *am* a man of unclean lips, and I dwell in the midst of a people of unclean lips: for mine eyes have seen the King, the LORD of hosts.

Isa. 32:6. For the vile person will speak villany, and his heart will work iniquity, to practise hypocrisy, and to utter error against the LORD, to make empty the soul of the hungry, and he will cause the drink of the thirsty to fail. 7. The instruments also of the churl *are* evil: he deviseth wicked devices to destroy the poor with lying words, even when the needy speaketh right.

Jer. 20:10. For I heard the defaming of many, fear on every side. Report, *say they,* **and** we will report it. All my familiars

watched for my halting, *saying,* Peradventure he will be enticed, and we shall prevail against him, and we shall take our revenge on him.

Matt. 5:22. But I say unto you, That whosoever is angry with his brother without a cause shall be in danger of the judgment: and whosoever shall say to his brother, Raca, shall be in danger of the council: but whosoever shall say, Thou fool, shall be in danger of hell fire. 37. But let your communication be, Yea, yea; Nay, nay: for whatsoever is more than these cometh of evil.

Matt. 12:34. O generation of vipers, how can ye, being evil, speak good things? for out of the abundance of the heart the mouth speaketh. 35. A good man out of the good treasure of the heart bringeth forth good things: and an evil man out of the evil treasure bringeth forth evil things. [Luke 6: 45.] 36. But I say unto you, That every idle word that men shall speak, they shall give account thereof in the day of judgment. 37. For by thy words thou shalt be justified, and by thy words thou shalt be condemned.

Acts 23:5. Then said Paul, I wist not, brethren, that he was the high priest: for it is written, Thou shalt not speak evil of the ruler of thy people.

Rom. 1:29. Being filled with all unrighteousness, fornication, wickedness, covetousness, maliciousness; full of envy, murder, debate, deceit, malignity; whisperers, 30. Backbiters, haters of God, despiteful, proud, boasters,

Rom. 3:13. Their throat *is* an open sepulchre; with their tongues they have used deceit; the poison of asps *is* under their lips: 14. Whose mouth *is* full of cursing and bitterness:

1 Cor. 6:10. Nor thieves . . . nor revilers, nor extortioners, shall inherit the kingdom of God.

Eph. 4:25. Wherefore putting away lying, speak every man truth with his neighbour: for we are members one of another. 29. Let no corrupt communication proceed out of your mouth, but that which is good to the use of edifying, that it may minister grace unto the hearers. 31. Let all bitterness, and wrath, and anger, and clamour, and evil speaking, be put away from you, with all malice:

Eph. 5:4. Neither filthiness, nor foolish talking, nor jesting, which are not convenient: but rather giving of thanks.

Tit. 1:10. For there are many unruly and vain talkers and deceivers, specially they of the circumcision: 11. Whose mouths must be stopped, who subvert whole houses, teaching things which they ought not, for filthy lucre's sake.

Tit. 3:2. To speak evil of no man, to be no brawlers, *but* gentle, shewing all meekness unto all men.

Jas. 1:26. If any man among you seem to be religious, and bridleth not his tongue, out deceiveth his own heart, this man's religion *is* vain. *v.* 19.

Jas. 3:5. Even so the tongue is a little member, and boasteth great things. Behold, how great a matter a little fire kindleth! 6. And the tongue *is* a fire, a world of iniquity: so is the tongue among our members, that it defileth the whole body, and setteth on fire the course of nature; and it is set on fire of hell. 8. But the tongue can no man tame; *it is* an unruly evil, full of deadly poison. 9. Therewith bless we God, even the Father; and therewith curse we men, which are made after the similitude of God. 10. Out of the same mouth proceedeth blessing and cursing. My brethren, these things ought not so to be.

Jas. 4:11. Speak not evil one of another, brethren. He that speaketh evil of *his* brother, and judgeth his brother, speaketh evil of the law, and judgeth the law: but if thou judge the law, thou art not a doer of the law, but a judge.

1 Pet. 2:1. Wherefore laying aside all malice, . . . and all evil speakings,

1 Pet. 3:9. Not rendering evil for evil, or railing for railing: but contrariwise blessing; knowing that ye are thereunto called, that ye should inherit a blessing. 10. For he that will love life, and see good days, let him refrain his tongue from evil, and his lips that they speak no guile:

2 Pet. 2:7. And delivered just Lot, vexed with the filthy conversation of the wicked: 8. (For that righteous man dwelling among them, in seeing and hearing, vexed *his* righteous soul from day to day with *their* unlawful deeds:) 10. Presumptuous *are they,* selfwilled, they are not afraid to speak evil of dignities.

Jude 8. Likewise also these *filthy* dreamers defile the flesh, despise dominion, and speak evil of dignities. 10. But these speak evil of those things which they know not:

See ACCUSATION, FALSE; BLASPHEMY; BUSYBODY; FALSEHOOD; FLATTERY; SLANDER; TALEBEARER; UNCHARITABLENESS.

FOLLY IN: Job 13:5. O that ye would altogether hold your peace! and it should be your wisdom.

Job 16:3. Shall vain words have an end? or what emboldeneth thee that thou answerest? 4. I also could speak as ye *do:* if your soul were in my soul's stead, I could heap up words against you.

Job 38:2. Who *is* this that darkeneth counsel by words without knowledge?

Prov. 10:14. Wise *men* lay up knowledge: but the mouth of the foolish *is* near destruction.

Prov. 12:23. A prudent man concealeth knowledge: but the heart of fools proclaimeth foolishness.

Prov. 13:3. He that keepeth his mouth keepeth his life: *but* he that openeth wide his lips shall have destruction.

Prov. 14:3. In the mouth of the foolish *is*

a rod of pride: but the lips of the wise shall preserve them.

Prov. 15:2. The tongue of the wise useth knowledge aright: but the mouth of fools poureth out foolishness. 7. The lips of the wise disperse knowledge: but the heart of the foolish *doeth* not so. 14. The heart of him that hath understanding seeketh knowledge: but the mouth of fools feedeth on foolishness.

Prov. 18:6. A fool's lips enter into contention, and his mouth calleth for strokes. 7. A fool's mouth *is* his destruction, and his lips *are* the snare of his soul. 13. He that answereth a matter before he heareth *it,* it *is* folly and shame unto him.

Prov. 26:4. Answer not a fool according to his folly, lest thou also be like unto him. 7. The legs of the lame are not equal: so *is a* parable in the mouth of fools. 9. *As a* thorn goeth up into the hand of a drunkard, so *is* a parable in the mouth of fools.

Prov. 29:11. A fool uttereth all his mind: but a wise *man* keepeth it in till afterwards. 20. Seest thou a man *that is* hasty in his words? *there is* more hope of a fool than of him.

Prov. 30:10. Accuse not a servant unto his master, lest he curse thee, and thou be found guilty.

Eccl. 5:3. For a dream cometh through the multitude of business; and a fool's voice *is known* by multitude of words. 7. For in the multitude of dreams and many words *there are* also *divers* vanities: but fear thou God.

Eccl. 10:13. The beginning of the words of his mouth *is* foolishness: and the end of his talk *is* mischievous madness. 14. A fool also is full of words: a man cannot tell what shall be; and what shall be after him, who can tell him?

Matt. 12:36. But I say unto you, That every idle word that men shall speak, they shall give account thereof in the day of judgment. 37. For by thy words thou shalt be justified, and by thy words thou shalt be condemned.

Eph. 5:4. Neither filthiness, nor foolish talking, nor jesting, which are not convenient: but rather giving of thanks.

See FOOL.

WISDOM IN: Job 16:5. *But* I would strengthen you with my mouth, and the moving of my lips should assuage *your grief.*

Job 27:4. My lips shall not speak wickedness, nor my tongue utter deceit.

Psa. 15:1. LORD, who shall abide in thy tabernacle? who shall dwell in thy holy hill? 2. He that walketh uprightly, and worketh righteousness, and speaketh the truth in his heart. 3. *He that* backbiteth not with his tongue, nor doeth evil to his neighbour, nor taketh up a reproach against his neighbour.

Psa. 37:30. The mouth of the righteous speaketh wisdom, and his tongue talketh of judgment.

Psa. 39:1. I said, I will take heed to my

ways, that I sin not with my tongue: I will keep my mouth with a bridle, while the wicked is before me.

Psa. 50:23. Whoso offereth praise glorifieth me: and to him that ordereth *his* conversation *aright* will I shew the salvation of God.

Psa. 77:12. I will meditate also of all thy work, and talk of thy doings.

Psa. 119:13. With my lips have I declared all the judgments of thy mouth. 27. Make me to understand the way of thy precepts: so shall I talk of thy wondrous works. 46. I will speak of thy testimonies also before kings, and will not be ashamed. 54. Thy statutes have been my songs in the house of my pilgrimage. 172. My tongue shall speak of thy word: for all thy commandments *are* righteousness.

Psa. 141:3. Set a watch, O LORD, before my mouth: keep the door of my lips.

Psa. 145:5. I will speak of the glorious honour of thy majesty, and of thy wondrous works. 6. And *men* shall speak of the might of thy terrible acts: and I will declare thy greatness. 7. They shall abundantly utter the memory of thy great goodness, and shall sing of thy righteousness. 11. They shall speak of the glory of thy kingdom, and talk of thy power; 12. To make known to the sons of men his mighty acts, and the glorious majesty of his kingdom.

Prov. 10:11. The mouth of a righteous *man is* a well of life: but violence covereth the mouth of the wicked. 13. In the lips of him that hath understanding wisdom is found: but a rod *is* for the back of him that is void of understanding. 19. In the multitude of words there wanteth not sin: but he that refraineth his lips *is* wise. 20. The tongue of the just *is as* choice silver: the heart of the wicked *is* little worth. 21. The lips of the righteous feed many: but fools die for want of wisdom. 31. The mouth of the just bringeth forth wisdom: but the froward tongue shall be cut out. 32. The lips of the righteous know what is acceptable: but the mouth of the wicked *speaketh* frowardness.

Prov. 11:12. He that is void of wisdom despiseth his neighbour: but a man of understanding holdeth his peace. 13. A talebearer revealeth secrets: but he that is of a faithful spirit concealeth the matter. 14. Where no counsel *is*, the people fall: but in the multitude of counsellors *there is* safety.

Prov. 12:6. The words of the wicked *are* to lie in wait for blood: but the mouth of the upright shall deliver them. 14. A man shall be satisfied with good by the fruit of *his* mouth: and the recompence of a man's hands shall be rendered unto him. 16. A fool's wrath is presently known: but a prudent *man* covereth shame. 17. *He that* speaketh truth sheweth forth righteousness: but a false witness deceit. 18. There is that speaketh like the piercings of

a sword: but the tongue of the wise *is* health. 19. The lip of truth shall be established for ever: but a lying tongue *is* but for a moment. 20. Deceit *is* in the heart of them that imagine evil: but to the counsellors of peace *is* joy. 23. A prudent man concealeth knowledge: but the heart of fools proclaimeth foolishness.

Prov. 13:2. A man shall eat good by the fruit of *his* mouth: but the soul of the transgressors *shall eat* violence. 3. He that keepeth his mouth keepeth his life: but he that openeth wide his lips shall have destruction.

Prov. 14:3. In the mouth of the foolish *is* a rod of pride: but the lips of the wise shall preserve them.

Prov. 15:1. A soft answer turneth away wrath: but grievous words stir up anger. 2. The tongue of the wise useth knowledge aright: but the mouth of fools poureth out foolishness. 4. A wholesome tongue *is* a tree of life: but perverseness therein *is* a breach in the spirit. 7. The lips of the wise disperse knowledge: but the heart of the foolish *doeth* not so. 23. A man hath joy by the answer of his mouth: and a word *spoken* in due season, how good *is it!* 26. The thoughts of the wicked *are* an abomination to the LORD: but *the words* of the pure *are* pleasant words. 28. The heart of the righteous studieth to answer: but the mouth of the wicked poureth out evil things.

Prov. 16:21. The wise in heart shall be called prudent: and the sweetness of the lips increaseth learning. 23. The heart of the wise teacheth his mouth, and addeth learning to his lips. 24. Pleasant words *are as* an honeycomb, sweet to the soul, and health to the bones.

Prov. 17:7. Excellent speech becometh not a fool: much less do lying lips a prince. 27. He that hath knowledge spareth his words: *and* a man of understanding is of an excellent spirit. 28. Even a fool, when he holdeth his peace, is counted wise: *and* he that shutteth his lips *is* esteemed a man of understanding.

Prov. 18:4. The words of a man's mouth *are as* deep waters, *and* the wellspring of wisdom *as* a flowing brook. 20. A man's belly shall be satisfied with the fruit of his mouth: *and* with the increase of his lips shall he be filled.

Prov. 19:1. Better *is* the poor that walketh in his integrity, than *he that is* perverse in his lips, and is a fool.

Prov. 20:15. There is gold, and a multitude of rubies: but the lips of knowledge *are* a precious jewel.

Prov. 21:23. Whoso keepeth his mouth and his tongue keepeth his soul from troubles.

Prov. 22:11. He that loveth pureness of heart, *for* the grace of his lips the king *shall be* his friend.

Prov. 24:6. For by wise counsel thou shalt

make thy war: and in multitude of counsellors *there is* safety.

Prov. 25:11. A word fitly spoken *is like* apples of gold in pictures of silver. 15. By long forbearing is a prince persuaded, and a soft tongue breaketh the bone.

Prov. 26:5. Answer a fool according to his folly, lest he be wise in his own conceit.

Prov. 29:11. A fool uttereth all his mind, but a wise *man* keepeth it in till afterwards.

Prov. 31:26. She openeth her mouth with wisdom; and in her tongue *is* the law of kindness.

Eccl. 3:7. A time to rend, and a time to sew; a time to keep silence, and a time to speak;

Eccl. 9:17. The words of wise *men are* heard in quiet more than the cry of him that ruleth among fools.

Eccl. 10:12. The words of a wise man's mouth *are* gracious; but the lips of a fool will swallow up himself.

Eccl. 12:9. And moreover, because the preacher was wise, he still taught the people knowledge; yea, he gave good heed, and sought out, *and* set in order many proverbs. 10. The preacher sought to find out acceptable words: and *that which was* written *was* upright, *even* words of truth. 11. The words of the wise *are* as goads, and as nails fastened *by* the masters of assemblies, *which* are given from one shepherd.

Amos 5:13. Therefore the prudent shall keep silence in that time; for it *is* an evil time.

Zeph. 3:13. The remnant of Israel shall not do iniquity, nor speak lies; neither shall a deceitful tongue be found in their mouth: for they shall feed and lie down, and none shall make *them* afraid.

Zech. 8:16. These *are* the things that ye shall do: Speak ye every man the truth to his neighbour; execute the judgment of truth and peace in your gates:

Matt. 12:37. By thy words thou shalt be justified, and by thy words thou shalt be condemned.

Luke 6:45. A good man out of the good treasure of his heart bringeth forth that which is good; and an evil man out of the evil treasure of his heart bringeth forth that which is evil: for of the abundance of the heart his mouth speaketh. Matt. 12:35.

Eph. 4:22. That ye put off concerning the former conversation the old man, which is corrupt according to the deceitful lusts; 25. Wherefore putting away lying, speak every man truth with his neighbour: for we are members one of another. 29. Let no corrupt communication proceed out of your mouth, but that which is good to the use of edifying, that it may minister grace unto the hearers.

Phil. 1:27. Let your conversation be as it becometh the gospel of Christ:

Col. 4:6. Let your speech *be* alway with grace, seasoned with salt, that ye may know how ye ought to answer every man.

Jas. 1:19. Wherefore, my beloved brethren, let every man be swift to hear, slow to speak, slow to wrath: 26. If any man among you seem to be religious, and bridleth not his tongue, but deceiveth his own heart, this man's religion *is* vain.

Jas. 3:2. If any man offend not in word, the same *is* a perfect man, *and* able also to bridle the whole body. 13. Who *is* a wise man and endued with knowledge among you? let him shew out of a good conversation his works with meekness of wisdom.

1 Pet. 2:12. Having your conversation honest among the Gentiles: that, whereas they speak against you as evildoers, they may by *your* good works, which they shall behold, glorify God in the day of visitation.

1 Pet. 3:15. But sanctify the Lord God in your hearts: and *be* ready always to *give* an answer to every man that asketh you a reason of the hope that is in you with meekness and fear: 16. Having a good conscience; that, whereas they speak evil of you, as of evildoers, they may be ashamed that falsely accuse your good conversation in Christ.

Rev. 14:5. And in their mouth was found no guile: for they are without fault before the throne of God.

See WISDOM.

SPEAR, an implement of war. Spears and javelins differed in weight and size, but had similar uses. Goliath's, 1 Sam. 17:7. Saul's, 1 Sam. 18:10,11. Stored in the tabernacle, 2 Chr. 23:9. Changed into pruninghooks, Isa. 2:4; Mic. 4:3. Pruninghooks beat into, Joel 3:10. Plunged into Jesus' side, John 19:34; 20:27; Zech. 12:10; Rev. 1:7.

SPELT. See RYE.

SPERMATORRHEA, a disease of the genital organs, Lev. 15:16.

SPICES. In the formula for the sacred oil, Ex. 25:6; 35:8. Stores of, 2 Kin. 20:13. Used in the temple, 1 Chr. 9:29. Exported from Gilead, Gen. 37:25. Sent as a present by Jacob to Joseph, Gen. 43:11. Presented by the queen of Sheba to Solomon, 1 Kin. 10:2, 10. Sold in the markets of Tyre, Ezek. 27:22. Used in the embalming of Asa, 2 Chr. 16:14. Prepared for embalming the body of Jesus, Mark 16:1; Luke 23:56; 24:1; John 19:39,40.

SPIDER. Mentioned in one of Agur's riddles [*R. V.*, lizard], Prov. 30:28. Web of, figurative of the hope of the hypocrite, Job 8:14; Isa. 59:5.

SPIES, Gen. 42:9. Sent to investigate Canaan, Num. 13; Jaazer, Num. 21:32; Jericho, Josh. 2:1. Used by David, 1 Sam. 26:4; at the court of Absalom, 2 Sam. 15:10; 17:1-17. Pharisees acted as, Luke 20:20. In the church of Galatia, Gal. 2:4.

SPIKENARD. An aromatic plant, Song 4:13,14. Perfume prepared from, Song 1:12. A fragrant oil from, used in anointing, Mark 14:3; John 12:3.

SPINDLE, used in spinning, Prov. 31:19.

SPINNING, by hand, Ex. 35:25; Prov. 31:19.

SPIRIT, called inner man, Rom. 7:22; Eph. 3:16.

See ANGELS; DEMONS; GOD, A SPIRIT; HOLY SPIRIT; MAN, A SPIRIT; SATAN.

SPIRITUAL BLESSINGS. See BLESSINGS, SPIRITUAL; HOLY SPIRIT; SANCTIFICATION.

SPIRITUAL BLINDNESS. See BLINDNESS, SPIRITUAL.

SPIRITUAL DILIGENCE. See ZEAL.

SPIRITUALISM. See NECROMANCY; SORCERY.

SPIRITUALITY. Described as the great and enduring good, Luke 10:42; as love and devotion to God, Deut. 6:5; Josh. 22:5; 1 Kin. 8:23; Psa. 1:2; 51:6.

Brings peace, Isa. 26:3; Jer. 33:6; Rom. 8:6; 14:17; indifference to worldly good, 1 Cor. 7:29-31; Col. 3:1-3; thirst for heavenly blessings, Matt. 5:6; John 6:27.

Is produced by the indwelling of the Holy Spirit, John 14:16,17; Rom. 8:4.—*Bible Text-Book*.

SPIRITUAL PEACE. See JOY; PEACE.

SPITTING. In the face, as an indignity, Num. 12:14; Deut. 25:9; Job 30:10; Matt. 26:67; 27:30. Jesus used spittle in healing, Mark 7:33; 8:23.

SPOILS. Of war, Gen. 14:11,12; Num. 31:9,10; Deut. 2:35. Divided between the combatants and non-combatants of the Israelites, including priests and Levites, Num. 31:25-54; 1 Sam. 30:24. Dedicated to the Lord, 1 Sam. 15:15; 1 Chr. 26:27; 2 Chr. 15:11.

SPONGE, Matt. 27:48; Mark 15:36; John 19:29.

SPOONS. Of the tabernacle, Ex. 25:29; Num. 4:7; 7. Of the temple, 1 Kin. 7:50; 2 Chr. 4:22.

SPRING. 1. Season of, promised annual return of, Gen. 8:22. Described, Prov. 27: 25; Song 2:11-13.

2. Of water. Hot, Gen. 36:24 [*R. V.*].

FIGURATIVE: Corrupt, Prov. 25:26; Jas. 3:11.

See WELLS.

SPRINKLING. Of blood, Lev. 14:7, 51; 16:14; Heb. 9:13,19,21; 11:28; 12:24; 1 Pet. 1:2. See BLOOD. Of water, Num. 8:7; Ezek. 36:25; Heb. 9:19; 10:22.

STABILITY. OF CHARACTER: Psa. 57:7. My heart is fixed, O God, my heart is fixed: I will sing and give praise. Psa. 108:1; 112:7.

Matt. 10:22. And ye shall be hated of all *men* for my name's sake: but he that endureth to the end shall be saved. Matt. 24:13.

Mark 4:20. And these are they which are sown on good ground; such as hear the word, and receive *it*, and bring forth fruit, some thirtyfold, some sixty, and some an hundred.

1 Cor. 7:20. Let every man abide in the same calling wherein he was called.

1 Cor. 15:58. Therefore, my beloved brethren, be ye stedfast, unmoveable, always abounding in the work of the Lord, forasmuch as ye know that your labour is not in vain in the Lord.

2 Thess. 2:15. Therefore, brethren, stand fast, and hold the traditions which ye have been taught, whether by word, or our epistle.

2 Thess. 3:3. But the Lord is faithful, who shall stablish you, and keep *you* from evil.

Heb. 10:23. Let us hold fast the profession of *our* faith without wavering; (for he *is* faithful that promised;)

Heb. 13:9. Be not carried about with divers and strange doctrines. For *it is* a good thing that the heart be established with grace; not with meats, which have not profited them that have been occupied therein.

Jas. 1:23. For if any be a hearer of the word, and not a doer, he is like unto a man beholding his natural face in a glass: 24. For he beholdeth himself, and goeth his way, and straightway forgetteth what manner of man he was. 25. But whoso looketh into the perfect law of liberty, and continueth *therein*, he being not a forgetful hearer, but a doer of the work, this man shall be blessed in his deed.

Rev. 22:11. He that is unjust, let him be unjust still: and he which is filthy, let him be filthy still: and he that is righteous, let him be righteous still: and he that is holy, let him be holy still.

See CHARACTER; DECISION; PERSEVERANCE.

STACHYS, a Christian in Rome, Rom. 16:9.

STACTE, an unknown spice used in compounding the sacred perfume, Ex. 30:34.

STAIRS, of David, Neh. 3:15; 12:37.

STALL, for cattle, Prov. 15:17.

STAMMERING, Isa. 32:4; 33:19. Of Moses, Ex. 4:10.

STANDARD. An ensign used by each of the tribes of Israel in camp and march, Num. 1:52; 2:2. Banners used as, Psa. 20:5; Song 6:4,10. Used in war, Jer. 4:21. Used to direct the route to defensed cities, Jer. 4:6; to call attention to news, Jer. 50:2; 51:12.

See ARMIES; BANNER; ENSIGN.

FIGURATIVE: Isa. 49:22; 62:10; Jer. 4:6.

STARS. Created by God, Gen. 1:16; Job. 26:13; Psa. 8:3; 33:6; 136:7,9; Amos 5:8. Differ in splendor, 1 Cor. 15:41. Worship of, forbidden, Deut. 4:19. Worshiped, 2 Kin. 17:16; 21:3; 23:5; Jer. 19:13; Amos 5:26; Zeph. 1:5; Acts 7:42,43. Constellations of, Isa. 13:10; Orion, Job 9:9; Amos 5:8; serpent, Job 26:13. Planets, 2 Kin. 23:5; the morning star, Job 38:7; Rev. 2:28; 22:16. Darkening of, Job 9:7; Eccl. 12:2; Isa. 13:10; 34:4; Joel 2:10; 3:15; Rev. 8:11,12. Comets, Jude 13. Falling of, Dan. 8:10; Matt. 24:29; Mark 13: 25; Rev. 6:13; 8:10; 9:1; 12:4. Guides the wise men, Matt. 2:2,7,9,10.

FIGURATIVE: Of the deliverer, Num. 24:17. Seven stars of the seven churches, Rev. 1:16,20. Crown of twelve stars, Rev. 12:1. Of Jesus, Rev. 22:16.

STATE. See CHURCH and STATE; GOVERNMENT.

STATECRAFT. Wisdom in, Prov. 28:2. School in, Dan. 1:3–5. Skilled in. INSTANCES OF: Joseph, Gen. 47:15–26; Samuel, 1 Sam. 11:12–15; Nathan, 1 Kin. 1:11–14; Jeroboam, 1 Kin. 12:26–33; Daniel, see DANIEL.

See GOVERNMENT; KINGS; RULERS.

STAVES, used as weapons, Matt. 26:47; Mark 14:43.

SYMBOLICAL: Zech. 11:7–14.

STEADFASTNESS. See DECISION; PERSEVERANCE; STABILITY.

STEALING. See THEFT.

STEEL. Bows of, 2 Sam. 22:35; Job 20:24; Psa. 18:34. Strength of, Jer. 15:12. In each of the above references, the *R.V.* renders the translation "brass."

STEPHANAS, a Christian in Corinth, whose household Paul baptized, 1 Cor. 1:16; 16:15,17.

STEPHEN, a Christian martyr. Appointed one of the committee of seven to oversee the daily ministration, Acts 6:3,5,6. Faith and power of, Acts 6:5,8–10. False charges against, Acts 6:11–15. Defense of, Acts 7. See page 261. Stoned, Acts 7:54–60; 8:1; 22:20. Burial of, Acts 8:2. Gentle and forgiving spirit of, Acts 7:59,60.

STERILITY, of women. See BARRENNESS.

STEWARD, Gen. 15:2; 43:19; 1 Chr. 28:1; Luke 8:3.

FIGURATIVE: The faithful steward described, Luke 12:35–38,42. The unfaithful, described, Luke 16:1–8. See the parable of the pounds, Luke 19:12–27; of the talents, Matt. 25:14–30. Must be faithful, 1 Cor. 4:1,2; Tit. 1:7; 1 Pet. 4:10.

STICKS, used as cymbals, Ezek. 37:16.

STIFF-NECKED. See IMPENITENT; OBDURACY.

STOCKS. Feet fastened in, as a punishment, Job 13:27; 33:11; Prov. 7:22. In prisons, Jer. 20:2; Acts 16:24.

STOICISM. A Grecian philosophy, inculcating doctrines of severe morality, self-denials, and inconvenient services. Scripture analogies to: John the Baptist wears camel's hair and subsists on locusts and wild honey, Matt. 3:4; comes "neither eating nor drinking," Matt. 11:18; Luke 7:33. Jesus requires self-denials and crosses, Matt. 10:38,39; 16:24; Mark 8:34,35; Luke 9:23–26; 14:27; the subordination of natural affection, Matt. 10:37; Luke 14:26. Paul teaches that the "law of the mind" is at war with the "law of the members," Rom. 7:23, with *vs.* 14–24; that the body must be kept under, 1 Cor. 9:27; advises celibacy, 1 Cor. 7:1–9,25, 26,32,33,39,40.

School of, at Athens, Acts 17:18.

See ASCETICISM.

STOICS. See STOICISM; ASCETICISM.

STOMACHER, an article of dress, Isa. 3:24.

STONES. Commandments engraved upon, Ex. 24:12; 31:18; 34:1–4; Deut. 4:13; 5:22; 9:9–11; 10:1–3. The law of Moses written upon, Josh. 8:32. Houses built of, Isa. 9:10; Amos 5:11. Temple built of, 1 Kin. 5:17,18; 7:9–12; Matt. 24:2; Luke 19:44; 21:5,6. Prepared in the quarries, 1 Kin. 6:7. Hewn, Ex. 34:1; Deut. 10:1; 1 Kin. 5:17; 6:36; 7:9; 2 Kin. 12:12; 22:6; 1 Chr. 22:2; 2 Chr. 34:11; Lam. 3:9. Sawn, 1 Kin. 7:9. Hewers of, 1 Kin. 5:18; 2 Kin. 12:12; 1 Chr. 22:15.

City walls built of, Neh. 4:3. Memorial pillars of, Gen. 28:18–22; 31:45–52; Josh. 4:2–9,20–24; 24:25; 1 Sam 7:12. Great, as landmarks, Abel, 1 Sam. 6:18; Ezel, 1 Sam. 20:19; Zoheleth, 1 Kin. 1:9.

Cast upon accursed ground, 2 Kin. 3:19,25. Used in building altars, Josh. 8:31; for weighing, Lev. 19:36 [marg.]; for closing sepulchers, Matt. 27:60; Mark 15:46; 16:3. Sepulchers hewn in, Matt. 27:60; Mark 15:46; 16:3. Idols made of, Deut. 4:28; 28:36,64; 29:17; 2 Kin. 19:18; Isa. 37:19; Ezek. 20:32.

Great, in Solomon's temple, 1 Kin. 5:17, 18; 7:9–12. Magnificent, in Herod's, Mark 13:1. Skill in throwing, Judg. 20:16; 1 Chr. 12:2. See SLINGS.

See ADAMANT; CHALCEDONY; MARBLE; ONYX; PILLARS. See PRECIOUS, below.

FIGURATIVE: Gen. 49:24; Zech. 3:9. Of temptation, "stone of stumbling," Isa. 8:14; Rom. 9:33; 1 Pet. 2:8. Of Christ, "a tried stone," "a precious stone," "a sure foundation," Isa. 28:16; of Christ's rejection, the rejected corner stone, Psa. 118:22; Matt. 21:42–44; Mark 12:10; Luke 20:17,18; Acts 4:11; 1 Pet. 2:4; the true foundation, Isa. 28:16; Matt. 16:18; 1 Cor. 3:11; Eph. 2:20; Rev. 21:14. Of Christ, the water of life, 1 Cor. 10:4. Of the impenitent heart, Ezek. 36:26. Of the witness of the Spirit, the white stone, Rev. 2:17.

SYMBOLICAL: Of the kingdom of Christ, Dan. 2:34,45.

PRECIOUS: In the breastplate and ephod, Ex. 28:9–21; 39:6–14. Voluntary offerings of, by the Israelites for the breastplate and ephod, Ex. 35:27. Exported from Sheba, 1 Kin. 10:2,10; 2 Chr. 9:9,10; Ezek. 27:22; Ophir, 1 Kin. 10:11. Partial catalogue of, Ezek. 28:13. Seen in the foundation of the New Jerusalem in John's apocalyptic vision, Rev. 21:19,20.

In kings' crowns, 2 Sam. 12:30; 1 Chr. 20:2.

FIGURATIVE: Isa. 54:11,12.

See AGATE; AMETHYST; BERYL; CARBUNCLE; CHRYSOLITE; CHRYSOPRASUS; CORAL; CRYSTAL; DIAMOND; EMERALD; JACINTH; JASPER; LIGURE; RUBY; SAPPHIRE; SARDIUS; SARDONYX; TOPAZ.

STONING. Capital punishment by, Ex. 19:13; Deut. 13:10; 17:5; 22:21; Heb. 11:37. Instances of stoning: Sabbath breaker, Num. 15:36; Achan, Josh. 7:25; Naboth,

1 Kin. 21:13; Stephen, Acts 7:59; Paul, Acts 14:19; 2 Cor. 11:25.

See WITNESS.

STOOL, 2 Kin. 4:10.

FOOTSTOOL: FIGURATIVE: Of the earth, Isa. 66:1; Matt. 5:35; Acts 7:49; temple, 1 Chr. 28:2; Lam. 2:1; sanctuary, Psa. 99:5; 132:7; enemies of Jesus, Psa. 110:1; Matt. 22:44; Mark 12:36; Luke 20:43; Acts 2:35; Heb. 1:13.

STOREHOUSES. See TREASURE-HOUSES.

STORK. Forbidden as food, Lev. 11:19. Nest of, in fir trees, Psa. 104:17. Migratory, Jer. 8:7.

FIGURATIVE: Zech. 5:9.

STRAIGHT, name of a street in Damascus, Acts 9:11.

FIGURATIVE: Of righteousness, "straight paths," Isa. 40:3,4; Matt. 3:3; Heb. 12:13.

STRAIT GATE. Matt. 7:13,14; Luke 13:24.

STRANGERS. Mosaic law relating to: Authorized bondservice of, Lev. 25:44,45; usury of, Deut. 15:3; 23:20; sale to, of flesh of animals that had died, Deut. 14:21; forbid their being made kings over Israel, Deut. 17:15; their eating the passover, Ex. 12:43, 48; their eating things offered in sacrifice, Ex. 29:33; Lev. 22:10,12,25; their blaspheming, Lev. 24:16; their approaching the tabernacle, Num. 1:51; their eating blood, Lev. 17:10; injustice to, Ex. 12:49; Lev. 24:22; Num. 9:14; Deut. 1:16; Jer. 22:3; oppression of, forbidden, Ex. 22:21; Lev. 23:9; Deut. 24:14,17; 27:19; Jer. 22:3. Instances of oppression of, Ezek. 22:29; Mal. 3:5.

Required to observe the sabbath, Ex. 20:10; 23:12. Might offer oblations, Lev. 17:8; 22:18,19. Were buried in separate burial places, Matt. 27:7.

Kindness to, required, Lev. 19:33,34. Love of, enjoined, Deut. 10:18,19. Abhorrence of, forbidden, Deut. 23:7. Marriage with, forbidden, Deut. 25:5. Hospitality to, see HOSPITALITY.

See ALMS; HEATHEN; PROSELYTES.

STRANGLED, things dying by strangulation, forbidden as food, Acts 15:20,29; 21:25.

STRATEGY, in war, Gen. 14:14,15; 32:7,8; Josh. 8:3-25; Judg. 7:16-23; 20:29-43; 2 Sam. 15:32-34, with 17:7-14; Neh. 6; Isa. 15:1; Jer. 6:5.

See AMBUSHES; ARMIES.

STRAW. Used for provender, Gen. 24:32; Isa. 65:25; for brick, Ex. 5:7.

STRAY. Animals straying to be returned, Ex. 23:4; Deut. 22:1-3. Instance of animals straying, Kish's, 1 Sam. 9.

STRENGTH, a title given Jehovah, 1 Sam. 15:29. Spiritual, see POWER, SPIRITUAL.

STRIFE. Gen. 13:8. And Abram said unto Lot, Let there be no strife, I pray thee, between me and thee, and between my herdmen and thy herdmen; for we be brethren.

Gen. 45:24. So he sent his brethren away, and they departed: and he said unto them, See that ye fall not out by the way.

Deut. 1:12. How can I myself alone bear your cumbrance, and your burden, and your strife?

Psa. 31:20. Thou shalt hide them in the secret of thy presence from the pride of man: thou shalt keep them secretly in a pavilion from the strife of tongues.

Psa. 55:9. Destroy, O Lord, and divide their tongues: for I have seen violence and strife in the city.

Psa. 80:6. Thou makest us a strife unto our neighbours: and our enemies laugh among themselves.

Prov. 3:30. Strive not with a man without cause, if he have done thee no harm.

Prov. 6:12. A naughty person, a wicked man, walketh with a froward mouth. 13. He winketh with his eyes, he speaketh with his feet, he teacheth with his fingers; 14. Frowardness is in his heart, he deviseth mischief continually; he soweth discord. 16. These six things doth the LORD hate: yea, seven are an abomination unto him: 17. A proud look, a lying tongue, and hands that shed innocent blood, 18. An heart that deviseth wicked imaginations, feet that be swift in running to mischief, 19. A false witness that speaketh lies, and he that soweth discord among brethren.

Prov. 10:12. Hatred stirreth up strifes: but love covereth all sins.

Prov. 13:10. Only by pride cometh contention: but with the well advised is wisdom.

Prov. 15:18. A wrathful man stirreth up strife: but he that is slow to anger appeaseth strife.

Prov. 16:28. A froward man soweth strife: and a whisperer separateth chief friends.

Prov. 17:1. Better is a dry morsel, and quietness therewith, than an house full of sacrifices with strife. 14. The beginning of strife is as when one letteth out water: therefore leave off contention, before it be meddled with. 19. He loveth transgression that loveth strife: and he that exalteth his gate seeketh destruction.

Prov. 18:6. A fool's lips enter into contention, and his mouth calleth for strokes. 19. A brother offended is harder to be won than a strong city: and their contentions are like the bars of a castle.

Prov. 19:13. A foolish son is the calamity of his father: and the contentions of a wife are a continual dropping.

Prov. 20:3. It is an honour for a man to cease from strife: but every fool will be meddling.

Prov. 21:19. It is better to dwell in the wilderness, than with a contentious and an angry woman.

Prov. 22:10. Cast out the scorner, and contention shall go out; yea, strife and reproach shall cease.

Prov. 23:29. Who hath woe? who hath sorrow? who hath contentions? who hath babbling? who hath wounds without cause? who hath redness of eyes? 30. They that tarry long at the wine; they that go to seek mixed wine.

Prov. 25:8. Go not forth hastily to strive, lest *thou know not* what to do in the end thereof, when thy neighbour hath put thee to shame. 24. *It is* better to dwell in the corner of the housetop, than with a brawling woman and in a wide house.

Prov. 26:17. He that passeth by, *and* meddleth with strife *belonging* not to him, *is like* one that taketh a dog by the ears. 20. Where no wood is, *there* the fire goeth out: so where *there is* no talebearer, the strife ceaseth. 21. *As* coals *are* to burning coals, and wood to fire; so *is* a contentious man to kindle strife.

Prov. 27:15. A continual dropping in a very rainy day and a contentious woman are alike.

Prov. 28:25. He that is of a proud heart stirreth up strife:

Prov. 29:22. An angry man stirreth up strife, and a furious man aboundeth in transgression.

Prov. 30:33. Surely the churning of milk bringeth forth butter, and the wringing of the nose bringeth forth blood: so the forcing of wrath bringeth forth strife.

Isa. 41:11. Behold, all they that were incensed against thee shall be ashamed and confounded: they shall be as nothing; and they that strive with thee shall perish. 12. Thou shalt seek them, and shalt not find them, *even* them that contended with thee: they that war against thee shall be as nothing, and as a thing of nought.

Isa. 58:4. Behold, ye fast for strife and debate, and to smite with the fist of wickedness: ye shall not fast as *ye do this* day, to make your voice to be heard on high.

Hab. 1:3. Why dost thou shew me iniquity, and cause *me* to behold grievance? for spoiling and violence *are* before me: and there are *that* raise up strife and contention.

Matt. 5:25. Agree with thine adversary quickly, whiles thou art in the way with him; lest at any time the adversary deliver thee to the judge, and the judge deliver thee to the officer, and thou be cast into prison. 39. But I say unto you, That ye resist not evil: but whosoever shall smite thee on thy right cheek, turn to him the other also. 40. And if any man will sue thee at the law, and take away thy coat, let him have *thy* cloke also. 41. And whosoever shall compel thee to go a mile, go with him twain.

Matt. 10:34. Think not that I am come to send peace on earth: I came not to send peace, but a sword. 35. For I am come to set a man at variance against his father, and the daughter against her mother, and the daughter in law against her mother in law. 36. And a man's foes *shall be* they of his own household.

Matt. 12:25. And Jesus knew their thoughts, and said unto them, Every kingdom divided against itself is brought to des-

olation; and every city or house divided against itself shall not stand:

Matt. 18:15. Moreover if thy brother shall trespass against thee, go and tell him his fault between thee and him alone: if he shall hear thee, thou hast gained thy brother. 16. But if he will not hear *thee, then* take with thee one or two more, that in the mouth of two or three witnesses every word may be established. 17. And if he shall neglect to hear them, tell *it* unto the church: but if he neglect to hear the church, let him be unto thee as an heathen man and a publican.

Mark 3:24. And if a kingdom be divided against itself, that kingdom cannot stand. [Luke 11:17.] 25. And if a house be divided against itself, that house cannot stand.

Luke 12:51. Suppose ye that I am come to give peace on earth? I tell you, Nay; but rather division: 52. For from henceforth there shall be five in one house divided, three against two, and two against three. 53. The father shall be divided against the son, and the son against the father; the mother against the daughter, and the daughter against the mother; the mother in law against the daughter in law, and the daughter in law against her mother in law. 58. When thou goest with thine adversary to the magistrate, *as thou art* in the way, give diligence that thou mayest be delivered from him; lest he hale thee to the judge, and the judge deliver thee to the officer, and the officer cast thee into prison. 59. I tell thee, thou shalt not depart thence, till thou hast paid the very last mite.

Rom. 2:8. But unto them that are contentious, and do not obey the truth, but obey unrighteousness, indignation and wrath,

Rom. 12:18. If it be possible, as much as lieth in you, live peaceably with all men.

Rom. 13:13. Let us walk honestly, as in the day; . . . not in strife and envying.

Rom. 14:1. Him that is weak in the faith receive ye, *but* not to doubtful disputations. 19. Let us therefore follow after the things which make for peace, and things wherewith one may edify another. 21. *It is* good neither to eat flesh, nor to drink wine, nor *any thing* whereby thy brother stumbleth, or is offended, or is made weak.

Rom. 16:17. Now I beseech you, brethren, mark them which cause divisions and offences contrary to the doctrine which ye have learned; and avoid them. 18. For they that are such serve not our Lord Jesus Christ, but their own belly; and by good words and fair speeches deceive the hearts of the simple.

1 Cor. 1:10. I beseech you, brethren, by the name of our Lord Jesus Christ, that ye all speak the same thing, and *that* there be no divisions among you; but *that* ye be perfectly joined together in the same mind and in the same judgment. 11. For it hath been declared unto me of you, my brethren, by them *which are of the house* of Chloe, that

there are contentions among you. 12. Now this I say, that every one of you saith, I am of Paul; and I of Apollos; and I of Cephas; and I of Christ. 13. Is Christ divided? was Paul crucified for you? or were ye baptized in the name of Paul?

1 Cor. 3:1. I, brethren, could not speak unto you as unto spiritual, but as unto carnal, *even* as unto babes in Christ. 3. For ye are yet carnal: for whereas *there is* among you envying, and strife, and divisions, are ye not carnal, and walk as men? 4. For while one saith, I am of Paul; and another, I *am* of Apollos; are ye not carnal?

1 Cor. 4:6. And these things, brethren, I have in a figure transferred to myself and to Apollos for your sakes; that ye might learn in us not to think *of men* above that which is written, that no one of you be puffed up for one against another. 7. For who maketh thee to differ *from another?* and what hast thou that thou didst not receive? now if thou didst receive *it,* why dost thou glory, as if thou hadst not received *it?*

1 Cor. 6:1. Dare any of you, having a matter against another, go to law before the unjust, and not before the saints? 2. Do ye not know that the saints shall judge the world? and if the world shall be judged by you, are ye unworthy to judge the smallest matters? 3. Know ye not that we shall judge angels? how much more things that pertain to this life? 4. If then ye have judgments of things pertaining to this life, set them to judge who are least esteemed in the church. 5. I speak to your shame. Is it so, that there is not a wise man among you? no, not one that shall be able to judge between his brethren? 6. But brother goeth to law with brother, and that before the unbelievers. 7. Now therefore there is utterly a fault among you, because ye go to law one with another. Why do ye not rather take wrong? why do ye not rather *suffer yourselves to* be defrauded?

1 Cor. 11:16. But if any man seem to be contentious, we have no such custom, neither the churches of God. 17. Now in this that I declare *unto you* I praise *you* not, that ye come together not for the better, but for the worse. 18. For first of all, when ye come together in the church, I hear that there be divisions among you; and I partly believe it. 19. For there must be also heresies among you, that they which are approved may be made manifest among you.

2 Cor. 12:20. I fear, lest, when I come, I shall not find you such as I would, and *that* I shall be found unto you such as ye would not: lest *there be* debates, envyings, wraths, strifes, backbitings, whisperings, swellings, tumults:

Gal. 5:10. I have confidence in you through the Lord, that ye will be none otherwise minded: but he that troubleth you shall

bear his judgment, whosoever he be. 15. But if ye bite and devour one another, take heed that ye be not consumed one of another. 19. Now the works of the flesh are manifest, which are *these;* . . . 20. Idolatry, witchcraft, hatred, variance, emulations, wrath, strife, seditions, heresies, 21. Envyings, murders, drunkenness, revellings, and such like: of the which I tell you before, as I have also told *you* in time past, that they which do such things shall not inherit the kingdom of God.

Phil. 1:15. Some indeed preach Christ even of envy and strife; and some also of good will: 16. The one preach Christ of contention, not sincerely, supposing to add affliction to my bonds:

Phil. 2:3. *Let* nothing *be done* through strife or vainglory; but in lowliness of mind let each esteem other better than themselves. 14. Do all things without murmurings and disputings: 15. That ye may be blameless and harmless, the sons of God, without rebuke, in the midst of a crooked and perverse nation, among whom ye shine as lights in the world;

1 Tim. 1:5. Now the end of the commandment is charity out of a pure heart, and *of* a good conscience, and *of* faith unfeigned: 6. From which some having swerved have turned aside unto vain jangling; 7. Desiring to be teachers of the law; understanding neither what they say, nor whereof they affirm.

1 Tim. 2:8. I will therefore that men pray every where, lifting up holy hands, without wrath and doubting.

1 Tim. 3:2. A bishop then must be blameless, . . . 3. Not given to wine, no striker, not greedy of filthy lucre; but patient, not a brawler, not covetous;

1 Tim. 6:3. If any man teach otherwise, and consent not to wholesome words, *even* the words of our Lord Jesus Christ, and to the doctrine which is according to godliness; 4. He is proud, knowing nothing, but doting about questions and strifes of words, whereof cometh envy, strife, railings, evil surmisings, 5. Perverse disputings of men of corrupt minds, and destitute of the truth, supposing that [1 gain is godliness: from such withdraw thyself.] 20. O Timothy, keep that which is committed to thy trust, avoiding profane *and* vain babblings, and oppositions of science falsely so called: 21. Which some professing have erred concerning the faith. [1 R. V godliness is a way of gain]

2 Tim. 2:14. Of these things put *them* in remembrance, charging *them* before the Lord that they strive not about words to no profit, *but* to the subverting of the hearers. 23. But foolish and unlearned questions avoid, knowing that they do gender strifes. 24. And the servant of the Lord must not strive; but be gentle unto all *men,* apt to teach, patient, 25. In meekness instructing those that oppose themselves;

Tit. 3:1. Put them in mind . . . to be

ready to every good work, 2. To speak evil of no man, to be no brawlers, *but* gentle, shewing all meekness unto all men. 3. For we ourselves also were sometimes foolish, disobedient, deceived, serving divers lusts and pleasures, living in malice and envy, hateful, *and* hating one another. 9. But avoid foolish questions, and genealogies, and contentions, and strivings about the law; for they are unprofitable and vain.

Jas. 3:14. If ye have bitter envying and strife in your hearts, glory not, and lie not against the truth. 15. This wisdom descendeth not from above, but *is* earthly, sensual, devilish. 16. For where envying and strife *is*, there *is* confusion and every evil work.

Jas. 4:1. From whence *come* wars and fightings among you? *come they* not hence, *even* of your lusts that war in your members? 2. Ye lust, and have not: ye kill, and desire to have, and cannot obtain: ye fight and war, yet ye have not, because ye ask not.

See Anger; Envy; Jealousy; Malice.

INSTANCES OF: Between Abraham and Lot's herdmen, Gen. 13:6,7; Abimelech's, Gen. 21:25; Isaac's and those of Gerar, Gen. 26:20–22. Laban and Jacob, Gen. 31:36. Israelites, Deut. 1:12. Jephthah and his brethren, Judg. 11:2; and Ephraimites, Judg. 12:1–6. Israel and Judah, about David, 2 Sam. 19:41–43. Disciples, over who might be greatest, Mark 9:34; Luke 22:24. Jews, concerning Jesus, John 10:19. Christians at Antioch, about circumcision, Acts 15:2. Paul and Barnabas, about Mark, Acts 15:38,39. Pharisees and Sadducees, concerning the resurrection, Acts 23:7–10. Corinthians, 1 Cor. 1:11,12; 6:6.

STRIPES, inflicted on Paul, 2 Cor. 6:5; 11:23.

See Scourging.

STUBBLE. FIGURATIVE: Of the wicked, Ex. 15:7; Job 21:18; Psa. 83:13; Isa. 5:24; 40:24; 41:2; 47:14; Jer. 13:24; Joel 2:5; Nah. 1:10; Mal. 4:1.

STUBBORNNESS. See Obduracy.

STUDENTS. Poverty of, 2 Kin. 4:1. In state school, Dan. 1. In schools of the prophets, 1 Sam. 19:20; 1 Kin. 20:35; 2 Kin. 2:2,3,5,7,15; 4:1.

See Instruction; School.

STUMBLING. FIGURATIVE: Causes of, Psa. 69:6. Stone of, Isa. 8:14; Rom. 9:32, 33; 1 Pet. 2:8. Stumbling-block, Lev. 19:14; Psa. 119:165 [*R. V.*]; Isa. 57:14; Jer. 6:21; Ezek. 3:20; 7:19; 14:3,4,7; Zeph. 1:3; Luke 11: 52; Rom. 11:9; 14:13; 1 Cor. 1:23; 8:9–13; Rev. 2:14.

See Temptation.

SUAH, an Asherite. Son of Zophah, 1 Chr. 7:36.

SUBJECTS. See Citizen; Government; Patriotism; Rulers.

SUBMISSION. To authority: Jesus an example of, Matt. 26:39,42; Mark 14:36; Luke 22:42; Heb. 5:8.

Of Paul, 1 Cor. 16:7.

See Obedience.

SUBSTITUTION, Ex. 28:38. The offering for the offerer, Lev. 1:4; 16:21,22. The Levites for the firstborn of the Israelites, Num. 3:12,41,45; 8:18. The life of Ahab for that of Ben-hadad, 1 Kin. 20:42.

See Suffering, Vicarious.

SUBURBS, Num. 35:3–5; Josh. 14:4.

SUCCESSION. Of priests, irregularity in, Heb. 7:1–28. See Priests. Of kings, see Kings.

SUCCOTH. 1. A city probably east of the Jordan. Jacob builds a house in, Gen. 33:17. Allotted to Gad, Josh. 13:27. People of, punished by Gideon, Judg. 8:5–8,14–16. Located near the Jordan, 1 Kin. 7:46; 2 Chr. 4:17; Psa. 60:6; 108:7.

2. First camping place of the Israelites on leaving Rameses, Ex. 12:37; 13:20; Num. 33:5,6.

SUFFERING. FOR CHRIST: Acts 9: 16. For I will show him how great things he must suffer for my name's sake.

Rom. 8:17. And if children, then heirs; heirs of God, and joint-heirs with Christ; if so be that we suffer with *him*, that we may be also glorified together. 18. For I reckon that the sufferings of this present time *are* not worthy *to be compared* with the glory which shall be revealed in us. 19. For the earnest expectation of the creature waiteth for the manifestation of the sons of God. 20. For the creature was made subject to vanity, not willingly, but by reason of him who hath subjected *the same* in hope, 21. Because the creature itself also shall be delivered from the bondage of corruption into the glorious liberty of the children of God. 22. For we know that the whole creation groaneth and travaileth in pain together until now. 23. And not only *they*, but ourselves also, which have the firstfruits of the Spirit, even we ourselves groan within ourselves, waiting for the adoption, *to wit*, the redemption of our body. 26. Likewise the Spirit also helpeth our infirmities: for we know not what we should pray for as we ought: but the Spirit itself maketh intercession for us with groanings which cannot be uttered.

1 Cor. 4:12. And labour, working with our own hands: being reviled, we bless; being persecuted, we suffer it: 13. Being defamed, we intreat: we are made as the filth of the world, *and are* the offscouring of all things unto this day.

2 Cor. 1:7. And our hope of you *is* stedfast, knowing, that as ye are partakers of the sufferings, so *shall ye be* also of the consolation.

2 Cor. 4:11. For we which live are alway delivered unto death for Jesus' sake, that the life also of Jesus might be made manifest in our mortal flesh. 12. So then death worketh in us, but life in you. 13. We having the same spirit of faith, according as it is written, I believed, and therefore have I spoken; we also believe, and therefore speak; 14. Knowing that he which

raised up the Lord Jesus shall raise up us also by Jesus, and shall present *us* with you. 15. For all things *are* for your sakes, that the abundant grace might through the thanksgiving of many redound to the glory of God. 16. For which cause we faint not; but though our outward man perish, yet the inward *man* is renewed day by day. 17. For our light affliction, which is but for a moment, worketh for us a far more exceeding *and* eternal weight of glory; 18. While we look not at the things which are seen, but at the things which are not seen: for the things which are seen *are* temporal; but the things which are not seen *are* eternal.

Phil. 1:29. For unto you it is given in the behalf of Christ, not only to believe on him, but also to suffer for his sake;

Phil. 2:27. For indeed he was sick nigh unto death: but God had mercy on him; and not on him only, but on me also, lest I should have sorrow upon sorrow. 28. I sent him therefore the more carefully, that, when ye see him again, ye may rejoice, and that I may be the less sorrowful. 29. Receive him therefore in the Lord with all gladness; and hold such in reputation: 30. Because for the work of Christ he was nigh unto death, not regarding his life, to supply your lack of service toward me.

Phil. 3:10. That I may know him, and the power of his resurrection, and the fellowship of his sufferings, being made comformable unto his death.

Col. 1:24. Who now rejoice in my sufferings for you, and fill up that which is behind of the afflictions of Christ in my flesh for his body's sake, which is the church:

2 Thess. 1:4. So that we ourselves glory in you in the churches of God for your patience and faith in all your persecutions and tribulations that ye endure: 5. *Which is* a manifest token of the righteous judgment of God, that ye may be counted worthy of the kingdom of God, for which ye also suffer:

2 Tim. 2:12. If we suffer, we shall also reign with *him:*

Jas. 5:10. Take, my brethren, the prophets, who have spoken in the name of the Lord, for an example of suffering affliction, and of patience.

1 Pet. 4:13. But rejoice, inasmuch as ye are partakers of Christ's sufferings; that, when his glory shall be revealed, ye may be glad also with exceeding joy. 14. If ye be reproached for the name of Christ, happy *are ye;* for the spirit of glory and of God resteth upon you: [1] on their part he is evil spoken of, but on your part h[ ] is glorified.   [1 Omitted in R. V.]

1 Pet. 5:10. But the God of all grace, who hath called us unto his eternal glory by Christ Jesus, after that ye have suffered a while, make you perfect, stablish, strengthen, settle *you.*

See AFFLICTION; PERSECUTION.

OF CHRIST: Luke 24:46. Thus it is written, and thus it behoved Christ to suffer,

and to rise from the dead the third day: 47. And that repentance and remission of sins should be preached in his name among all nations, beginning at Jerusalem. *v.* 26.

John 6:51. I am the living bread which came down from heaven: if any man eat of this bread, he shall live for ever: and the bread that I will give is my flesh, which I will give for the life of the world.

John 10:11. I am the good shepherd: the good shepherd giveth his life for the sheep. 15. As the Father knoweth me, even so know I the Father: and I lay down my life for the sheep.

John 11:50. Nor consider that it is expedient for us, that one man should die for the people, and that the whole nation perish not. 51. And this spake he not of himself: but being high priest that year, he prophesied that Jesus should die for that nation; 52. And not for that nation only, but that also he should gather together in one the children of God that were scattered abroad.

Rom. 4:25. Who was delivered for our offences, and was raised again for our justification.

Rom. 5:6. For when we were yet without strength, in due time Christ died for the ungodly. 7. For scarcely for a righteous man will one die: yet peradventure for a good man some would even dare to die. 8. But God commendeth his love toward us, in that, while we were yet sinners, Christ died for us.

Rom. 14:15. But if thy brother be grieved with *thy* meat, now walkest thou not charitably. Destroy not him with thy meat, for whom Christ died.

1 Cor. 1:17. For Christ sent me not to baptize, but to preach the gospel: not with wisdom of words, lest the cross of Christ should be made of none effect. 18. For the preaching of the cross is to them that perish foolishness; but unto us which are saved it is the power of God. 23. But we preach Christ crucified, unto the Jews a stumblingblock, and unto the Greeks foolishness; 24. But unto them which are called, both Jews and Greeks, Christ the power of God, and the wisdom of God.

1 Cor. 8:11. And through thy knowledge shall the weak brother perish, for whom Christ died ?

1 Cor. 15:3. For I delivered unto you first of all that which I also received, how that Christ died for our sins according to the scriptures;

2 Cor. 5:14. For the love of Christ constraineth us; because we thus judge, that if one died for all, [1] then were all dead: 15. And *that* he died for all, that they which live should not henceforth live unto themselves, but unto him which died for them, and rose again.   [1 R. V. therefore all died;]

Gal. 1:4. Who gave himself for our sins, that he might deliver us from this present

evil world, according to the will of God and
our Father:

Gal. 2:20. I am crucified with Christ:
nevertheless I live; yet not I, but Christ
liveth in me: and the life which I now live
in the flesh I live by the faith of the Son of
God, who loved me, and gave himself for
me. 21. I do not frustrate the grace of
God: for if righteousness *come* by the law,
then Christ is dead in vain.

Eph. 5:2. And walk in love, as Christ also
hath loved us, and hath given himself for
us an offering and a sacrifice to God for a
sweetsmelling savour. 25. Christ also loved
the church, and gave himself for it;

1 Thess. 5:9. For God hath not appointed us
to wrath, but to obtain salvation by our
Lord Jesus Christ, 10. Who died for us,
that, whether we wake or sleep, we should
live together with him.

Heb. 2:9. But we see Jesus, who was made
a little lower than the angels for the suffering of death, crowned with glory and honour; that he by the grace of God should
taste death for every man. 10. For it became him, for whom *are* all things, and by
whom *are* all things, in bringing many sons
unto glory, to make the captain of their
salvation perfect through sufferings. 14.
Forasmuch then as the children are partakers of flesh and blood, he also himself likewise took part of the same; that through
death he might destroy him that had the
power of death, that is, the devil; 18. For
in that he himself hath suffered being
tempted, he is able to succour them that
are tempted.

Heb. 5:8. Though he were a Son, yet
learned he obedience by the things which
he suffered; 9. And being made perfect,
he became the author of eternal salvation
unto all them that obey him;

Heb. 9:15. For this cause he is the mediator of the new testament, that by means of
death, for the redemption of the transgressions *that were* under the first testament,
they which are called might receive the
promise of eternal inheritance. 16. For
where a testament *is*, there must also of
necessity be the death of the testator.

28. So Christ was once offered to bear the
sins of many; and unto them that look for
him shall he appear the second time without sin unto salvation.

Heb. 10:10. By the which will we are sanctified through the offering of the body of
Jesus Christ once *for all*.

18. Now where remission of these *is, there
is* no more offering for sin. 19. Having
therefore, brethren, boldness to enter into
the holiest by the blood of Jesus, 20. By a
new and living way, which he hath consecrated for us, through the veil, that is to
say, his flesh;

1 Pet. 2:21. For even hereunto were ye
called: because Christ also suffered for us,
leaving us an example, that ye should follow his steps: 24. Who his own self bare
our sins in his own body on the tree, that
we, being dead to sins, should live unto
righteousness: by whose stripes ye were
healed.

1 Pet. 3:18. For Christ also hath once suffered for sins, the just for the unjust, that he
might bring us to God, being put to death in
the flesh, but quickened by the Spirit:

1 Pet. 4:1. Forasmuch then as Christ hath
suffered for us in the flesh, arm yourselves
likewise with the same mind: for he that
hath suffered in the flesh hath ceased from
sin:

1 John 3:16. Hereby perceive we 1 the love
1 *of God*, because he laid down his life for us:
[1 Omitted in R. V.]

See ATONEMENT; JESUS, DEATH OF, DE-
SIGN OF HIS DEATH, SUFFERINGS OF.

VICARIOUS: Ex. 9:13. And the LORD said
unto Moses, Rise up early in the morning,
and stand before Pharaoh, and say unto him,
Thus saith the LORD God of the Hebrews,
Let my people go, that they may serve me.
14. For I will at this time send all my
plagues upon thine heart, and upon thy
servants, and upon thy people; that thou
mayest know that *there is* none like me in
all the earth. 15. For now I will stretch
out my hand, that I may smite thee and
thy people with pestilence; and thou shalt
be cut off from the earth. 16. And in very
deed for this *cause* have I raised thee up,
for to shew *in* thee my power; and that my
name may be declared throughout all the
earth.

John 15:13. Greater love hath no man than
this, that a man lay down his life for his
friends.

Rom. 9:3. For I could wish that myself
were accursed from Christ for my brethren,
my kinsmen according to the flesh:

1 Pet. 2:21. Christ also suffered for us,
leaving us an example, that ye should follow his steps:

1 John 3:16. We ought to lay down *our*
lives for the brethren.

See above, OF CHRIST.

INSTANCE OF: Goliath for the Philistines,
1 Sam. 17.

SUICIDE, Amos 9:2; Rev. 9:6. Temptation to, of Jesus, Matt. 4:5,6; Luke 4:9,10,11.
Of the Philippian jailer, Acts 16:27.

See DEATH, DESIRED.

INSTANCES OF: Samson, Judg. 16:29,30.
Saul and his armor-bearer, 1 Sam. 31:4,5: 1
Chr. 10:4,5. Ahithophel, 2 Sam. 17:23.
Zimri, 1 Kin. 16:18. Judas, Matt. 27:5; Acts
1:18.

SUING, Matt. 5:40. See CREDITORS;
DEBTORS.

SUKKIIMS, an African race. Invaded
Judah with Shishak, 2 Chr. 12:3.

SUMMER. Season of, promised while
the earth remains, Gen. 8:22. Cool rooms
for, Judg. 3:20,24; Amos 3:15. Fruits of, 2
Sam. 16:1,2; Isa. 16:9; 28:4; Jer. 40:10,12; 48:
32; Amos 8:1,2; Mic. 7:1. Drought of, Psa.
32:4. Given by God, Psa. 74:17. The time

for labor and harvest, Prov. 6:6–8; 10:5; 30: 25; Jer. 8:20. Snow in, Prov. 26:1. Threshing in, Dan. 2:35. Approach of, Matt. 24: 32; Mark 13:28; Luke 21:30.

FIGURATIVE: Jer. 8:20.

SUN. Created, Gen. 1:14–18; Psa. 74:16; 136:7; Jer. 31:35. Rising and setting of, Eccl. 1:5. Diurnal motion of, Psa. 19:4,6. Worship of, forbidden, Deut. 4:19; 17:3. Worshiped, Job 31:26–28; Jer. 8:2; Ezek. 6:4,6 [R. V.]; 8:16. Kings of Judah dedicate horses to, 2 Kin. 23:11.

Miracles concerning: Darkening of, Ex. 10:21–23; Isa. 5:30; 24:23; Ezek. 32:7; Joel 2: 10,31; 3:15; Amos 8:9; Mic. 3:6; Matt. 24:29; 27:45; Mark 13:24; 15:33; Luke 21:25; 23:44, 45; Acts 2:20; Rev. 6:12; 8:12; 9:2; 16:8. Stands still, Josh.10:12,13; Hab.3:11. Shadow of, goes back on Ahaz's dial, 2 Kin. 20:11; Isa. 38:8.

Does not shine in heaven, Rev. 21:23.

FIGURATIVE: Psa. 84:11; Mal. 4:2; Judg. 5:31; Isa. 30:26; 60:19,20; Jer. 15:9; Rev. 1:16; 12:1; 19:17.

SUN-DIAL, 2 Kin. 20:11; Isa. 38:8.

SUNSTROKE, 2 Kin. 4:19.

SUPEREROGATION, the doctrine of excessive and meritorious righteousness, Ezek. 33:12,13; Luke 17:10.

SUPERSCRIPTION, on the cross, Matt. 27:37; Mark 15:26; Luke 23:38; John 19:19.

SUPERSTITION, Acts 25:19 [R. V., RELIGION].

INSTANCES OF: Israelites, supposing that their defeat in battle with the Philistines was due to their not having brought with them the ark of the covenant, 1 Sam. 4:3, with vs. 10,11. Philistines, refusing to tread the threshold of the temple of Dagon after the image of Dagon had repeatedly fallen, 1 Sam. 5:5.

The belief of the Syrians concerning the help of the gods, 1 Kin. 20:23. Jews, attributing their calamities to having ceased offering sacrifices to the queen of heaven, Jer. 44:17–19. Nebuchadnezzar, supposing that the spirit of the gods was upon Daniel, Dan. 4:8,9. The sailors who cast Jonah into the sea, Jonah 1:4–16. The disciples, supposing they saw a spirit when Jesus came walking upon the sea, Matt. 14:26; Mark 6:49,50. Herod, imagining that John the Baptist had risen from the dead, Mark 6:14,16. The Gadarenes, on account of Jesus casting devils out of the Gadarene, Matt. 8:34. The disciples who were frightened at the appearance of Peter, Acts 12:14,15. The Ephesians, in their sorceries, Acts 19:13–19. The people of the island of Melita, in imagining Paul to be a god, Acts 28:6.

See IDOLATRY; SORCERY.

SUPPER. See FEASTS; EUCHARIST.

SUR, gate of the temple, 2 Kin. 11:6.

SURETY, Gen. 44:32; Ex. 22:26,27; Deut. 24:10–13; Prov. 6:1–5; 11:15; 17:18; 20:16; 22:26; 27:13; Ezek. 18:7,12; 33:15; Amos 2:8.

SURFEITING. See DRUNKENNESS; GLUTTONY.

SUSANCHITES, inhabitants of Samaria, Ezra 4:9,10.

SUSANNA, a woman who ministered to Jesus, Luke 8:3.

SUSI, a Manassite, Num. 13:11.

SUSPICION. See ACCUSATION; FALSE.

SWADDLE, of children, Job 38:9; Lam. 2:22; Ezek. 16:4; Luke 2:7,12.

SWALLOW. Builds its nest in the sanctuary, Psa. 84:3. Chattering of, figurative of the mourning of the afflicted, Isa. 38:14. Migration of, Jer. 8:7.

SWAN, forbidden as food, Lev. 11:18; Deut. 14:16.

SWEARING. See BLASPHEMY; GOD, NAME OF NOT TO BE PROFANED; OATH.

SWEAT, Gen. 3:19. An offense in the sanctuary, Ezek. 44:18. Of blood, Luke 22: 44.

SWEET INCENSE, made of spices, Ex. 25:6.

See INCENSE.

SWINE. Forbidden as food, Lev. 11:7; Deut. 14:8. Used for food, Isa. 65:4; 66:17; for sacrifice, Isa. 66:3. Wild boar, Psa. 80: 13. Jewels in the nose of, Prov. 11:22. Viciousness of, Matt. 7:6. Jesus sends devils into, Matt. 8:28–32; Mark 5:11–14; Luke 8:32,33. Feeding of, Luke 15:15,16. Sow returns to her wallow, 2 Pet. 2:22.

SWORD. Used by Gideon, Judg. 7:20; Goliath, 1 Sam 21:9; Peter, Matt. 26:51; John 18:10. David's army equipped with, 1 Chr. 21:5. To be beaten into plowshares, Isa. 2:4; Mic. 4:3. Made of plowshares Joel 3:10. Two-edged, Heb. 4:12; Rev. 1:16; 2:12.

FIGURATIVE: Of war, Gen. 27:40. Of judgments, Deut. 32:41; Psa. 17:13; Hos. 11: 6; Zech. 13:7. Of the malicious tongue, Psa. 57:4; Prov. 25:18.

SYMBOLICAL: Gen. 3:24; Josh. 5:13; Rev. 1:16.

SYCAMINE, a tree, Luke 17:6.

SYCHAR. See SHECHEM, 2.

SYCHEM. See SHECHEM, 1 and 3.

SYCAMORE, a tree. Abundant in the land of Canaan, 1 Kin. 10:27; 2 Chr. 1:15; 9:27; Isa. 9:10. Groves of, cared for, 1 Chr. 27:28. Destroyed by frost, Psa. 78:47. Care of, Amos 7:14 [R. V.]. Zacchæus climbs into, Luke 19:4.

SYENE, a city in Egypt, Ezek. 29:10; 30:6. [R. V., SEVENEH.]

SYMBOLS AND SIMILITUDES. Trees of life and knowledge, Gen. 2:9,17; 3: 3,24; Rev. 22:2. Rainbow, Gen. 9:12,13. Circumcision, of the covenant of Abraham, Gen. 17:11; Rom. 4:11. Passover, of the sparing of the firstborn, and of the atonement made by Christ, Ex. 12:3–28; 1 Cor. 5:7. Of the divine presence, the pillar of cloud, Ex. 13:21,22; 14:19,20; 19:9,16; thunder on Mount Sinai, Ex. 19:9,16. Darkness, of God's inscrutability, Ex. 20:21; Lev. 16:2; 1 Kin. 8:12; Psa. 18:11; 97:2; Heb. 12:18,19. The smitten rock, of Christ, Ex. 17:6; 1 Cor.

10:4. The sprinkled blood, of the covenant, Ex. 24:8. Wine, of the atoning blood, Matt. 26:27-29; Mark 14:23-25; Luke 22:17,18,20. The brazen serpent, of Christ, Num. 21:8,9; John 3:14.

Sacrificial animals, Gen. 15:8-11; John 1: 29,36. Waving the wave offering and heaving the heave offering, Ex. 29:24-28; Lev. 8:27-29; 9:21. The whole system of Mosaic rites, Heb. 9:9,10,18-23. Tabernacle, Psa. 15:1; Ezek. 37:27; Heb. 8:2,5; 9:1-12,23, 24. Sanctuary, Psa. 20:2. Canaan, of the spiritual rest, Heb. 3:11,12; 4:5.

Salt. Num. 18:19. Offering water to drink, Gen. 24:13-15,42-44. Lapping water, Judg. 7:4-8. Invitation to approach, 1 Sam. 14: 8-12. Bow-shot, by Jonathan, 1 Sam. 20: 21-37; by Joash, 2 Kin. 13:15-19. Men meeting Saul, 1 Sam. 10:2-7. Rain and thunder, 1 Sam. 12:16-18. Rent altar, 1 Kin. 13:3,5. Rending of the vail, Matt. 27:51; Mark 15: 38; Luke 23:45. Wounding, 1 Kin. 20:35-40. Praying toward the temple, 1 Kin. 8:29; Dan. 6:10. Harvest, 2 Kin. 19:29. Isaiah's children, Isa. 8:18. Nakedness, Isa. 20:2-4. Almond rod, Jer. 1:11. Sticks and staves, Ezek. 37:16,17; Zech. 11:7,10,11,14. Food, 2 Kin. 19:29; Isa. 37:30. Shadow on Ahaz's dial, 2 Kin. 20:8-11; Isa. 38:7,8. Cooking, Jer. 1: 13; Ezek. 4:9-15; 24:3-5. Girdle, Jer. 13:1-7; Acts 21:11. Bottles, Jer. 13:12; 19:1,2,10. Breaking of potter's vessel, Jer. 19. Good and bad figs, Jer. 24. Basket of fruit, Jer. 24:1-3; Amos 8:1,2. Wine, Jer. 25:15-17; Matt. 26:27; Mark 14:23; Luke 22:17. Yokes, Jer. 27:2,3; 28:10. Jeremiah's deeds of land, Jer. 32:1-16. Book cast into Euphrates, Jer. 51:63. Dumbness, Ezek. 3:26,27; 24: 27; 29:21; 33:22; Luke 1:20-22,62-64. Siege, Ezek. 4:1-3. Posture, Ezek. 4:4-8. Unclean food, Ezek. 4:9-17. Ezekiel's beard, Ezek. 5:1-4. Change of domicile, Ezek. 12:3-11. Eating bread with carefulness, Ezek. 12:17-20. Eating and drinking in fear, Ezek. 12:18. Vine, Ezek. 15:2; 19:10-14. Death, Ezek. 24:16-19. Boiling pot, Ezek. 24: 1-5. Mourning forbidden, Ezek. 24:15-18. Two sticks, Ezek. 37:15-28. Handwriting on the wall, Dan. 5:5,6,16-28. Plumb line, Amos 7:7,8. Marrying a whore, Hos. 1:2-9; 3:1-4. Roll, Zech. 5:2-4. Ephah, Zech. 5: 6-11. Jonas, Matt. 16:4; Luke 11:29,30. Star in the east, Matt. 2:2. Smitten rock, 1 Cor. 10:4; Ex. 17:6. Salt, Col. 4:6. Bread, Matt. 26:26; Mark 14:22; Luke 22:19. Childhood, Matt. 18:3; Mark 10:14,15; Luke 18:16,17. Manna, John 6:31-58.

OF THE HOLY SPIRIT: WATER, John 3:5; 7:38,39; cleansing by, Ezek. 16:9; 36:25; Eph. 5:26; Heb. 10:22; vivifying, Psa. 1:3; Isa. 27:3,6; 44:3,4; 58:11.

FIRE, Matt. 3:11; purifying, Isa. 4:4; Mal. 3:2,3; illuminating, Ex. 13:21; Psa. 78:14; searching, Zeph. 1:12, with 1 Cor. 2:10.

WIND, Song 4:16; incomprehensible, John 3:8; 1 Cor. 12:11; powerful, 1 Kin. 19:11, with Acts 2:2; sensible in its effects, John 3:8; reviving, Ezek. 37:9,10,14.

OIL, Psa. 45:7; healing, Isa. 1:6; Luke 10:34; Rev. 18:13; comforting, Isa. 61:3; Heb. 1:9; illuminating, Zech. 4:2,3,11-13; Matt. 25:3,4; 1 John 2:20,27; consecrating, Ex. 29:7; 30:30; Isa. 61:1.

RAIN AND DEW, Psa. 72:6; fertilizing, Ezek. 34:26,27; Hos. 6:3; 10:12; 14:5; refreshing, Psa. 68:9; Isa. 18:4; abundant, Psa. 133:3; imperceptible, 2 Sam. 17:12, with Mark 4:26-28.

A DOVE, Matt. 3:16.

A VOICE, Isa. 6:8; speaking, Matt. 10:20; guiding, Isa. 30:21, with John 16:13; warning, Heb. 3:7-11.

A SEAL, Rev. 7:2; impressing, Job 38:14, with 2 Cor. 3:18; earnest, Eph. 1:13,14; 4:30; 2 Cor. 1:22.

CLOVEN TONGUES, Acts 2:3,6,11.

Ablutions, a symbol of purity, see ABLUTIONS; PURIFICATIONS. For symbolisms of color, see COLORS. See also ALLEGORY; INSTRUCTION BY SYMBOLS; INSTRUCTION, OF CHILDREN; INSTRUCTION, IN RELIGION.

SYMPATHY. Job 2:11. Now when Job's three friends heard of all this evil that was come upon him, they came every one from his own place; Eliphaz the Temanite, and Bildad the Shuhite, and Zophar the Naamathite: for they had made an appointment together to come to mourn with him and to comfort him. 12. And when they lifted up their eyes afar off, and knew him not, they lifted up their voice, and wept; and they rent every one his mantle, and sprinkled dust upon their heads toward heaven. 13. So they sat down with him upon the ground seven days and seven nights, and none spake a word unto him: for they saw that *his* grief was very great.

Job 6:14. To him that is afflicted pity *should be shewed* from his friend; but he forsaketh the fear of the Almighty.

Job 22:29. When *men* are cast down, then thou shalt say, *There is* lifting up; and he shall save the humble person.

Eccl. 7:2. *It is* better to go to the house of mourning, than to go to the house of feasting: for that *is* the end of all men; and the living will lay *it* to his heart.

Phil. 2:1. If *there be* therefore any consolation in Christ, if any comfort of love, if any fellowship of the Spirit, if any bowels and mercies, 2. Fulfil ye my joy, that ye be likeminded, having the same love, *being* of one accord, of one mind.

Jas. 1:27. Pure religion and undefiled before God and the Father is this, To visit the fatherless and widows in their affliction, *and* to keep himself unspotted from the world.

1 Pet. 3:8. *Be* pitiful,

See AFFLICTED; AFFLICTIONS; JESUS, COMPASSION OF; PITY.

SYNAGOGUE. 1. Primarily an assembly, Acts 13:43 [*R.V.*]; Jas. 2:2 [*R.V.*]. Constitutes a court of justice, Luke 12:11; Acts 9:2. Had powers of criminal courts, Matt. 10:17; Matt. 23:34; Acts 22:19; 26:11;

of ecclesiastical courts, John 9:22,34; 12:42; 16:2.

2. Place of assembly. Scriptures read and expounded in, Neh. 8:1–8; 9:3,5; Matt. 4:23; 9:35; 13:54; Mark 1:39; Luke 4:15–33; 13:10; John 18:20; Acts 9:20; 13:5–44; 14:1; 15: 21; 17:2,10; 18:4,19,26.

In Jerusalem, Acts 6:9; Damascus, Acts 9:2.20; other cities, Acts 14:1; 17:1,10; 18: 4. Built by Jairus, Luke 7:5. Jesus performed healing in, Matt. 12:9–13; Luke 13:11–14. Alms given in, Matt. 6:2.

Of Satan, Rev. 2:9; 3:9.

See CHURCH.

SYNTYCHE, a Christian woman in Philippi, Phil. 4:2.

SYRACUSE, a city of Sicily. Paul visits, Acts 28:12.

SYRIA, highlands lying between the river Euphrates and the Mediterranean Sea. Called ARAM, from the son of Shem, Gen. 10:22,23; Num. 23:7; 1 Chr. 1:17; 2:23. In the time of Abraham it seems to have embraced the region between the rivers Tigris and Euphrates, Gen. 24:10, with chapter 25:20, including Padan-aram, Gen.25:20; 28:5.

Minor kingdoms within the region: Aram-zobah, called also ZOBAH and ZOBA, 1 Sam. 14:47; 2 Sam. 8:3; 10:6,8; 1 Kin. 11:23; 1 Chr. 18:5,9; 19:6; Psa. 60 [title]; Geshur, 2 Sam. 15:8; Aram-rehob, called also BETH-REHOB, 2 Sam. 10:6,8; Damascus, 2 Sam. 8:5,6; 1 Chr. 18:5,6; Hamath, 2 Sam. 8:9,10.

Conquest of: By David, 2 Sam. 8:3–13; by Jeroboam, 2 Kin. 14:25,28; by Tiglath-pileser, king of Assyria, 2 Kin. 16:7–9; 18:33,34. People of, colonized in Samaria by the king of Assyria, 2 Kin. 17:24. Confederate with Nebuchadnezzar, 2 Kin. 24:2; Jer. 39:5.

The Roman province of, included the land of Canaan, Luke 2:2,3; and Phenicia, Mark 7:26; Acts 21:3. The fame of Jesus extended over, Matt. 4:24.

Paul goes to, with letters to apprehend the Christians; is converted and begins his evangelistic ministry, Acts 9:1–31. See PAUL.

Paul preaches in, Acts 15:41; 18:18; 21:3; Gal. 1:21. Damascus, the capital of, see DAMASCUS.

Wars between, and the kingdoms of Judah and Israel, see ISRAEL. Prophecies concerning, Isa. 7:8–16; 8:4–7; 17:1–3; Jer. 1:15; 49:23–27; Amos 1:3–5; Zech. 9:1.

SYRIA-MAACHAH, called also MAACHAH. A small kingdom, 1 Chr. 19:6. See MAACHAH, 10.

SYROPHENICIAN, the nationality of a woman whose daughter was cured by Jesus, Matt. 15:21–28; Mark 7:24–30.

T

TAANACH, called also TANACH. A city conquered by Joshua, Josh. 12:21. Allotted to Manasseh, Josh. 17:11; 1 Chr. 7:29. Canaanites not driven from, Josh. 17:12; Judg.

1:27. Assigned to the Levites, Josh. 21:25. The scene of Barak's victory, Judg. 5:19. One of Solomon's commissaries at, 1 Kin. 4:12.

TAANATH-SHILOH, a city of Ephraim, Josh. 16:6.

TABBAOTH, one of the Nethinim, Ezra 2:43; Neh. 7:46.

TABBATH, a place of uncertain location, Judg. 7:22.

TABEAL, father of one whom the kings of Syria and Israel sought to make king in Judah instead of Ahaz, Isa. 7:6. [R. V., TABEEL.]

TABEEL. 1. A Persian official in Samaria, Ezra 4:7.

2. See TABEAL.

TABERAH, a place in the wilderness where the Israelites were punished for their murmuring, Num. 11:3; Deut. 9:22.

TABERNACLE. One existed before Moses received the pattern authorized on Mount Sinai, Ex. 33:7–11. The one instituted by Moses was called SANCTUARY, Ex. 25:8; TABERNACLE [A. V.], TENT OF MEETING [R. V.], Ex 27:21; TABERNACLE [A. V.], TENT [R. V.], Ex. 33:7; 2 Chr. 5:5; OF TESTIMONY, Ex. 38:21; Num. 1:50; TENT OF TESTIMONY [R. V.], Num. 17:7,8; 2 Chr. 24:6; TEMPLE OF THE LORD, 1 Sam. 1:9; 3:3; HOUSE OF THE LORD, Josh. 6:24.

Pattern of, revealed to Moses, Ex. 25:9; 26: 30; 39:32,42,43; Acts 7:44; Heb. 8:5. Materials for, voluntarily offered, Ex. 25:1–8; 35: 4–29; 36:3–7. Value of the substance contributed for, Ex. 38:24–31. Workmen who constructed it were inspired, Ex. 31:1–11; 35:30–35.

Description of: Frame, Ex. 26:15–37; 36: 20–38. Outer covering, Ex. 25:5; 26:7–14; 36:14–19. Second covering, Ex. 25:5; 26:14; 35:7,23; 36:19; 39:34. Curtains of, Ex. 26:1–14,31–37; 27:9–16; 35:15,17; 36:8–19,35,37; Court of, Ex. 27:9–17; 38:9–16,18; 40:8,33.

Holy place of, Ex. 26:31–37; 40:22–26; Heb. 9:2–6,8. The most holy place, Ex. 26: 33–35; 40:20,21; Heb. 9:3–5,7,8.

Furniture of, Ex. 25:10–40; 27:1–8,19; 37; 38:1–8. See ALTAR; ARK; CANDLESTICK; CHERUBIM; LAVER; MERCY SEAT; SHEW-BREAD.

Completed, Ex. 39:32. Dedicated, Num. 7. Sanctified, Ex. 29:43; 40:9–16; Num. 7:1. Anointed with holy oil, Ex. 30:25,26; Lev. 8:10; Num. 7:1. Sprinkled with blood, Lev. 16:15–20; Heb. 9:21,23. Filled with the cloud of glory, Ex. 40:34–38.

How prepared for removal during the journeyings of the Israelites, Num. 1:51; 4: 5–15. How and by whom carried, Num. 4: 5–33; 7:6–9. Strangers forbidden to enter, Num. 1:51. Duties of the Levites concerning, see LEVITES. Defilement of, punished, Lev. 15:31; Num. 19:13,20; Ezek. 5:11; 23:38. Duties of the priests in relation to, see PRIESTS. Israelites worship at, Num. 10:3; 16:19,42,43; 20:6; 25:6; 1 Sam. 2:22; Psa. 27: 4. Offerings brought to, Lev. 17:4; Num.

31:54; Deut. 12:5,6,11-14. Causes tried at, Deut. 12:5,6,11-14.

Tribes encamped around, while in the wilderness, Num. 2. All males required to appear before, three times each year, Ex. 23:17. Tabernacle tax, Ex. 30:11-16.

Carried in front of the children of Israel in the line of march, Num. 10:33-36; Josh. 3:3-6. The Lord reveals himself at, Lev. 1: 1; Num. 1:1; 7:89; 12:4-10; Deut. 31:14,15.

Pitched at Gilgal, Josh. 4:18,19; at Shiloh, Josh. 18:1; 19:51; Judg. 18:31; 20:18,26, 27; 21:19; 1 Sam. 2:14; 4:3,4; Jer. 7:12,14; at Nob, 1 Sam. 21:1-6; at Gibeon, 1 Chr. 21:29. Renewed by David, and pitched on Mount Zion, 1 Chr. 15:1; 16:1,2; 2 Chr. 1:4. Solomon offers sacrifice at, 2 Chr. 1:3-6. Brought to the temple by Solomon, 2 Chr. 5:5, with 1 Kin. 8:1,4,5.

Symbol of spiritual things, Psa. 15:1; Heb. 8:2,5; 9:1-12,24.

See LEVITES; PRIESTS; TEMPLE.

TABERNACLES, FEAST OF, called also FEAST OF INGATHERING. Instituted, Ex. 23:16; 34:22; Lev. 23:34-43; Num. 29:12-40; Deut. 16:13-16. Design of, Lev. 23:42, 43. The law read in connection with, every seventh year, Deut. 31:10-12; Neh. 8:18.

Observance of, after the captivity, Ezra 3:4; Neh. 8:14-18; by Jesus, John 7:2,14. Observance of, omitted, Neh. 8:17. Penalty for not observing, Zech. 14:16-19.

Jeroboam institutes an idolatrous feast to correspond to, in the eighth month, 1 Kin. 12:32,33; 1 Chr. 27:11.

TABITHA, a Christian woman in Joppa. Restored to life by Peter, Acts 9:36-41.

TABLE. 1. An article of furniture, Judg. 1:7; 1 Sam. 20:29,34; 2 Kin. 4:10; John 2:15. Made of silver, 1 Chr. 28:16.

FIGURATIVE: Of the altar, Mal. 1:7,12; of the Lord's supper, 1 Cor. 10:21; of idolatrous feasts, 1 Cor. 10:21; of charities, Acts 6:2.

2. Of shewbread, see SHEWBREAD, TABLE OF.

3. Of testimony, Ex. 31:18; 32:15; 34:29. The commandments engraved upon, Ex. 20:3-17; 24:12; Deut. 4:13; 5:4-22; 9:10; Hos. 8:12; broken, Ex. 24:12; 31:18; 32:15-19; Deut. 4:13; 9:9-11,17. A second set engraved, Ex. 34:1; Deut. 10:1-4. Placed in the ark, Deut. 10:5; 1 Kin. 8:9; Heb. 9:4.

4. A slab on which inscriptions were made, Isa. 30:8; Hab. 2:2; Luke 1:63.

FIGURATIVE: Prov. 3:3; Jer. 17:1; 2 Cor. 3:3.

TABOR. 1. A mountain on the border of Issachar, Josh. 19:22; Judg. 8:18; Psa. 89:12; Jer. 46:18; Hos. 5:1. Assembling place of Barak's army, Judg. 4:6,12,14.

2. A plain [R. V.. " oak "] of unknown location, 1 Sam. 10:3.

3. A Levitical city in Zebulun, 1 Chr. 6:77. See CHISLOTH-TABOR.

TABRET. See TIMBREL.

TABRIMON, father of Ben-hadad, 1 Kin. 15:18.

TACT, Prov. 15:1; 25:15. In preaching, 1 Cor. 9:19-22; 2 Cor. 12:6. Of Gideon, Judg. 8:1-3. Of Saul, in managing malcontents, 1 Sam. 10:27; 11:7,12-15. Nabal's wife, 1 Sam. 25:18-37. In David's popular methods: in mourning for Abner, 2 Sam. 3:28-37; in organizing the temple music, 1 Chr. 15:16-24; in securing popular consent to bringing the ark to Jerusalem, 1 Chr. 13:1-4. Joab's trick in obtaining David's consent to the return of Absalom, 2 Sam. 14:1-22. The wise woman of Abel, 2 Sam. 20:16-22. Solomon, in arbitrating between the harlots, 1 Kin. 3:24-28.

Mordecai, in concealing Esther's nationality, Esth. 2:10. Esther, in placating the king, Esth. chapters 5-7. Paul, in circumcising Timothy, Acts 16:3; in turning the preaching of adversaries to account, Phil. 1:10-22; in stimulating benevolent giving, 2 Cor. 8:1-8; 9:1-5; in arraying the two religious factions of the Jews against each other when he was in trouble, Acts 23:6-10. The town clerk of Ephesus, Acts 19:35-41. The church council at Jerusalem, Acts 21: 20-25.

TACTICS. See ARMIES; STRATEGY.

TADMOR, a city built in the wilderness by Solomon, 1 Kin. 9:18; 2 Chr. 8:4.

TAHAN. 1. Son of Ephraim, Num. 26:35.

2. A descendant of Ephraim, 1 Chr. 7:25.

TAHAPANES. See TAHPANHES.

TAHATH. 1. A camping place of the Israelites, Num. 33:26,27.

2. A Kohathite, 1 Chr. 6:24,37.

3. The name of two Ephraimites, 1 Chr. 7:20.

TAHPANHES, called also TAHAPANES and TEHAPHNEHES. A city in Egypt, Jer. 2:16; 43:7-9; 44:1; 46:14; Ezek. 30:18.

TAHPENES, a queen of Egypt, 1 Kin. 11:19,20.

TAHREA. Son of Micah, 1 Chr. 9:41. Called TAREA, 1 Chr. 8:35.

TAHTIM-HODSHI, an unknown place, 2 Sam. 24:6.

TAILORING, Ex. 31:2,3,6,10; 39:1.

TALEBEARER. Lev. 19:16. Thou shalt not go up and down as a talebearer among thy people: neither shalt thou stand against the blood of thy neighbour; I am the LORD.

Psa. 15:1. LORD, who shall abide in thy tabernacle? who shall dwell in thy holy hill? 2. He that walketh uprightly, and worketh righteousness, and speaketh the truth in his heart. 3. He that backbiteth not with his tongue, nor doeth evil to his neighbour, nor taketh up a reproach against his neighbour.

Prov. 11:13. A talebearer revealeth secrets: but he that is of a faithful spirit concealeth the matter.

Prov. 16:28. A froward man soweth strife: and a whisperer separateth chief friends.

Prov. 17:9. He that repeateth a matter separateth very friends.

Prov. 18:8. The words of a talebearer are

as wounds, and they go down into the innermost parts of the belly.

Prov. 20:19. He that goeth about *as* a talebearer revealeth secrets: therefore meddle not with him that flattereth with his lips.

Prov. 26:20. Where no wood is, *there* the fire goeth out: so where *there is* no talebearer, the strife ceaseth. 21. *As* coals *are* to burning coals, and wood to fire; so *is* a contentious man to kindle strife. 22. The words of a talebearer *are* as wounds, and they go down into the innermost parts of the belly.

1 Tim. 5:11. But the younger widows refuse: for when they have begun to wax wanton against Christ, they will marry; 13. And withal they learn *to be* idle, wandering about from house to house; and not only idle, but tattlers also and busybodies, speaking things which they ought not.

See BUSYBODY; SLANDER; SPEAKING, EVIL.

INSTANCES OF: Joseph, Gen. 37:2. Israelites, 2 Sam. 3:23. Tobiah, Neh. 6.

TALENT, 1 Kin. 9:14,28; 10:10,14. A weight equal to three thousand shekels— about one hundred and twenty-five pounds, Ex. 38:25,26. Value of, of gold, about six thousand pounds, or twenty-nine thousand one hundred dollars; of silver, four hundred pounds, or one thousand nine hundred and forty dollars. Parables of the, Matt. 18:24; 25:15,28.

TALKING, with God, see COMMUNION.

TALMAI. 1. A son of Anak, Num. 13: 22; Josh. 15:14; Judg. 1:10.

2. King of Geshur, 2 Sam. 3:3; 13:37; 1 Chr. 3:2.

TALMON. A porter of the temple, 1 Chr. 9:17. Family of, return from captivity with Zerubbabel, Ezra 2:42; Neh. 7:45; 11:19; 12:25.

TAMAH. One of the Nethinim, Neh. 7:55. Called THAMAH, Ezra 2:53.

TAMAR. 1. Wife of the sons of Judah, Gen. 38:6–24; Ruth 4:12; 1 Chr. 2:4. Called THAMAR, Matt. 1:3.

2. Daughter of David, 2 Sam. 13:1–32; 1 Chr. 3:9.

3. Daughter of Absalom, 2 Sam. 14:27.

4. A city of unknown location, Ezek. 47: 19; 48:28.

TAMBOURINE. See TIMBREL.

TAMMUZ, a Syrian idol, Ezek. 8:14.

TANACH. See TAANACH.

TANHUMETH, father of Seraiah, 2 Kin. 25:23; Jer. 40:8.

TANNING, Acts 9:43; 10:5,6.

TANTALIZING, 1 Sam. 1:6,7; 1 Kin. 18:27.

TAPESTRY, Prov. 7:16; 31:22. Of the tabernacle, Ex. 26:1–14,31–37; 27:9–17; 36:8– 18. Gold thread woven in, Ex. 39:3. In palaces, Esth. 1:6; Song 1:5. In groves, 2 Kin. 23:7.

See CURTAINS; EMBROIDERY.

TAPHATH, daughter of Solomon, 1 Kin. 4:11.

TAPPUAH. 1. A city of Judah, Josh. 12:17; 15:34.

2. A city in Ephraim, Josh. 16:8; 17:8.

3. Son of Hebron, 1 Chr. 2:43.

TARAH, a camping place of the Israelites, Num. 33:27,28.

TARALAH, a city in Benjamin, Josh. 18:27.

TAREA. A son of Micah, 1 Chr. 8:35. Called TAHREA, 1 Chr. 9:41.

TARES, parable of, Matt. 13:24–30,38– 42.

TARGET, a defensive article of armor. Used by spearmen, 2 Chr. 14:8. Made of brass, 1 Sam. 17:6; of gold, 1 Kin. 10:16; 2 Chr. 9:15.

See SHIELD.

TARIFF. See DUTY.

TARPELITES, an Assyrian tribe. Colonists in Samaria, Ezra 4:9.

TARSHISH. 1. Son of Javan, Gen. 10: 4; 1 Chr. 1:7.

2. Called also THARSHISH. Probably Spain, Gen. 10:4,5; Psa. 72:10; Isa. 66:19. Solomon makes valuable imports from, 1 Kin. 10:22; 2 Chr. 9:21. Commerce and wealth of, 1 Kin. 10:22; 22:48; 2 Chr. 9:21; 20:36; Psa. 48:7; Isa. 2:16; 23:1–14; 60:9; Jer. 10:9; Ezek. 27:12,25; 38:13. Jonah would flee to, Jonah 1:3; 4:2. Prophecies concerning, Psa. 72:10; Isa. 2:16; 23:1–14; 60:9; 66:19.

3. Son of Bilhan, 1 Chr. 7:10 [*R. V.*]. [*A. V.*, THARSHISH.]

4. A Persian prince, Esth. 1:14.

TARSUS, capital of Cilicia, in Asia Minor. Paul's birthplace, Acts 9:11; 21:39; 22:3. Paul sent to, from Jerusalem, to avoid assassination, Acts 9:30. Paul brought from, by Barnabas, Acts 11:25,26.

TARTAK, an Assyrian idol, 2 Kin. 17:31.

TARTAN, an Assyrian general, 2 Kin. 18:17; Isa. 20:1.

TASKMASTERS, Ex. 5:13,14. See MASTERS; OPPRESSION; SERVANTS.

TASTE, the sense of, lost; 2 Sam. 19:35.

TATNAI, a Persian governor in Samaria, Ezra 5:3,6; 6:6,13.

TATTLER. See TALEBEARER.

TATTOOING, forbidden, Lev. 19:28.

TAVERNS. See THREE TAVERNS.

TAX. Poll, Ex. 30:11–16; 38:26; Neh. 10: 32; Luke 2:1. Jesus pays, Matt. 17:24–27.

Land, Gen. 41:34,48; 2 Kin. 23:35. Land mortgaged for, Neh. 5:3,4. Priests exempted from, Gen. 47:26; Ezra 7:24. Paid in grain, Amos 5:11; 7:1; in provisions, 1 Kin. 4:7–28.

Personal, 1 Kin. 9:15; 2 Kin. 15:19,20; 23: 35. Resisted by Israelites, 1 Kin. 12:18; 2 Chr. 10:18. World-wide, levied by Cæsar. The *R. V.* changes the reading to enrolled instead of taxed, Luke 2:1–3. Collectors of, 2 Sam. 20:24; 1 Kin. 4:6; Isa. 33:18; Dan. 11: 20; Mark 2:14; Luke 3:13; 5:27; unpopular, Matt. 5:46; 9:11; 11:19; 18:17; 21:31; Luke 18: 11; stoned, 2 Chr. 10:18.

TEACHERS. Samuel, head of school of prophets, 1 Sam. 19:20. Elisha, head of, at Gilgal, 2 Kin. 4:38.

See INSTRUCTION; JESUS, TEACHER; MINISTERS, DUTIES OF.

FALSE: Admonition against, Deut. 13:1-3; Matt. 5:19; 7:15; 15:2-20; 23:2-33; Luke 11:38-52.

See MINISTERS, FALSE.

TEACHING. See INSTRUCTION; MINISTERS, DUTIES OF.

TEARS, Psa. 6:6; 39:12; 42:3. Observed by God, Psa. 56:8; Isa. 38:3-5. Wiped away, Rev. 7:17. None in heaven, Rev. 21:4.

FIGURATIVE: Psa. 80:5.

TEBAH, son of Nahor, Gen. 22:24.

TEBALIAH, son of Hosah, 1 Chr. 26:11.

TEBETH, the tenth month (January), Esth. 2:16; Ezek. 29:1.

TECHNICALITIES, legal, Matt. 12:2, 10; Luke 6:2,7.

TEETH, Prov. 10:26. Gnashing of, Psa. 112:10; Lam. 2:16; Matt. 8:12; 13:42,50; 22:13; 24:51; 25:30; Mark 9:18; Luke 13:28.

TEHAPHNEHES. See TAHPANHES.

TEHINNAH, son of Eshton, 1 Chr. 4:12.

TEIL TREE, Isa. 6:13.

TEKEL, Dan. 5:25,27.

TEKOA. 1. Son of Ashur, 1 Chr. 2:24; 4:5. Some authorities interpret these passages to mean that Ashur colonized the town of Tekoah.

2. See TEKOAH.

TEKOAH, called also TEKOA. A city in Judah, 2 Chr. 11:6. Home of the woman who interceded for Absalom, 2 Sam. 14:2,4,9. Rebuilt by Rehoboam, 2 Chr. 11:6. Desert of, 2 Chr. 20:20. People of, work on the new wall of Jerusalem, Neh. 3:5,27. Prophecy concerning, Jer. 6:1. Home of Amos, Amos 1:1.

See TEKOA.

TEL-ABIB, residence of Jewish captives in Babylonia, Ezek. 3:15.

TELAH, son of Rephah, 1 Chr. 7:25.

TELAIM, a place of unknown location, 1 Sam. 15:4.

TELASSAR, called also THELASAR. A city or district conquered by the Assyrians, 2 Kin. 19:12; Isa. 37:12.

TELEM. 1. A city of Judah, Josh. 15:24.

2. A porter who put away his Gentile wife, Ezra 10:24.

TEL-HARSA, called also TEL-HARESHA. A place in Babylonia, Ezra 2:59; Neh. 7:61.

TEL-MELAH, a place in Babylonia, Ezra 2:59; Neh. 7:61.

TEMA. 1. Son of Ishmael, Gen. 25:15; 1 Chr. 1:30.

2. A people of Arabia, probably descendant from Tema, Ishmael's son, Job 6:19; Isa. 21:14; Jer. 25:23.

TEMAN. 1. Son of Eliphaz, Gen. 36:11, 15,42; 1 Chr. 1:36,53.

2. Called also TEMANI and TEMANITES. A people supposed to be descended from Teman, son of Eliphaz, Gen. 36:34; Job 2:11. Prophecies concerning, Jer. 49:7; Ezek. 25:13; Amos 1:12; Obad. 9; Hab. 3:3.

TEMANI. See TEMAN.

TEMANITE. See TEMAN.

TEMENI, son of Ashur, 1 Chr. 4:6.

TEMPER. See ANGER; MALICE; SELF-CONTROL.

TEMPERANCE. Esth. 1:7. And they gave *them* drink in vessels of gold, (the vessels being diverse one from another,) and royal wine in abundance, according to the state of the king. 8. And the drinking *was* according to the law; none did compel: for so the king had appointed to all the officers of his house, that they should do according to every man's pleasure.

Prov. 23:1. When thou sittest to eat with a ruler, consider diligently what *is* before thee: 2. And put a knife to thy throat, if thou *be* a man given to appetite. 3. Be not desirous of his dainties: for they *are* deceitful meat.

Prov. 25:16. Hast thou found honey? eat so much as is sufficient for thee, lest thou be filled therewith, and vomit it.

Dan. 1:8. But Daniel purposed in his heart that he would not defile himself with the portion of the king's meat, nor with the wine which he drank: therefore he requested of the prince of the eunuchs that he might not defile himself. 12. Prove thy servants, I beseech thee, ten days; and let them give us pulse to eat, and water to drink. 13. Then let our countenances be looked upon before thee, and the countenance of the children that eat of the portion of the king's meat: and as thou seest, deal with thy servants. 14. So he consented to them in this matter, and proved them ten days. 15. And at the end of ten days their countenances appeared fairer and fatter in flesh than all the children which did eat the portion of the king's meat. 16. Thus Melzar took away the portion of their meat, and the wine that they should drink; and gave them pulse.

Rom. 13:14. But put ye on the Lord Jesus Christ, and make not provision for the flesh, to *fulfil* the lusts *thereof*.

1 Cor. 9:25. Every man that striveth for the mastery is temperate in all things. Now they *do it* to obtain a corruptible crown; but we an incorruptible. 27. But I keep under my body, and bring *it* into subjection: lest that by any means, when I have preached to others, I myself should be a castaway.

Phil. 4:5. Let your ¹ moderation be known unto all men.   [¹ R. V. forbearance]

1 Thess. 5:6. Therefore let us not sleep, as *do* others; but let us watch and be sober. 7. For they that sleep sleep in the night; and they that be drunken are drunken in the night. 8. But let us, who are of the day, be sober, putting on the breastplate of faith and love; and for an helmet, the hope of salvation.

1 Tim. 3:2. A bishop then must be blameless, the husband of one wife, vigilant, sober, of good behaviour, given to hospitality, apt to teach; 3. Not given to wine, [Tit. 1:7,8.] 8. Likewise *must* the deacons *be* grave,

not doubletongued, not given to much wine, not greedy of filthy lucre;

Tit. 2:2. That the aged men be sober, grave, temperate, sound in faith, in charity, in patience. 3. The aged women likewise, that *they be* in behaviour as becometh holiness, not false accusers, not given to much wine, teachers of good things; 12. Teaching us that, denying ungodliness and worldly lusts, we should live soberly, righteously, and godly, in this present world;

2 Pet. 1:5. And beside this, giving all diligence, add to your faith virtue; and to virtue knowledge; 6. And to knowledge temperance;

See ABSTINENCE; DRUNKENNESS; WINE.

TEMPLE. SOLOMON'S: Called also TEMPLE OF THE LORD, 2 Kin. 11:10; HOLY TEMPLE, Psa. 79:1; HOLY HOUSE, 1 Chr. 29:3; HOUSE OF GOD, 1 Chr. 29:2; 2 Chr. 23:9; HOUSE OF THE LORD, 2 Chr. 23:5,12; Jer. 28:5; FATHER'S HOUSE, John 2:16; HOUSE OF THE GOD OF JACOB, Isa. 2:3; HOUSE OF MY GLORY, Isa. 60:7; HOUSE OF PRAYER, Isa. 56:7; Matt. 21:13; HOUSE OF SACRIFICE, 2 Chr. 7:12; HOUSE OF THEIR SANCTUARY, 2 Chr. 36:17; HOLY AND BEAUTIFUL HOUSE, Isa. 64:11; HOLY MOUNT, Isa. 27:13; MOUNTAIN OF THE LORD'S HOUSE, Isa. 2:2; PALACE, 1 Chr. 29:1, 19; SANCTUARY, 2 Chr. 20:8; TABERNACLE OF WITNESS, 2 Chr. 24:6; ZION, Psa. 20:2; 48:12; 74:2; 87:2; Isa. 2:3.

Greatness of, 2 Chr. 2:5,6. Beauty of, Isa. 64:11. Holiness of, 1 Kin. 8:10; 9:3; Lam. 1: 10; Matt. 23:17; John 2:14–16.

David undertakes the building of, 2 Sam. 7:2,3; 1 Chr. 22:7; 28:2; Psa. 132:2–5; Acts 7:46; forbidden of God because he was a man of war, 2 Sam. 7:4–12; 1 Kin. 5:3; 1 Chr. 22:8; 28:3. Not asked for by God, 2 Sam. 7:7. The building of, committed to Solomon, 2 Sam. 7:13. David makes preparation for, 1 Chr. 22; 28:14–18; 29:1-5; 2 Chr. 3:1; 5:1. Built by Solomon, Acts 7:47. Solomon makes levies of men for the building of, 1 Kin. 5:13–16; 2 Chr. 2:2, 17,18.

Materials for, furnished by Hiram, 1 Kin. 5:8–18. Pattern and building of, 1 Kin. 6; 7:13–51; 1 Chr. 28:11–19; 2 Chr. 3; 4; Acts 7:47. Time when begun, 1 Kin. 6:1,37; 2 Chr. 3:2; finished, 1 Kin. 6:38. Site of, 1 Chr. 21:28–30; 22:1; 2 Chr. 3:1; where Abraham offered Isaac, Gen. 22:2,4.

Materials prepared for, 1 Kin. 5:17, 18. No tools used in the erection of, 1 Kin. 6:7. Foundations of, 1 Kin. 5:17,18; Luke 21:5.

Apartments and furnishings of: Oracle, or holy of holies, in, 1 Kin. 6:19,20; 8:6. Called MOST HOLY HOUSE, 2 Chr. 3:8; INNER HOUSE, 1 Kin. 6:27; HOLIEST OF ALL, Heb. 9:3. Description of, 1 Kin. 6:16,19–35; 2 Chr. 3:8–14; 4:22. Gold used in, 2 Chr. 3:8–10. Contents of the holy of holies: ark, 1 Kin. 6:19; 8:6; 2 Chr. 5:2–10; see ARK; cherubims, 1 Kin. 6:23–28; 2 Chr. 3:10–13; 5:7,8. See ARK; CHERUBIM; VAIL; MERCY SEAT.

Holy place, 1 Kin. 8:8,10. Called the GREATER HOUSE, 2 Chr. 3:5; TEMPLE, 1 Kin. 6:17. Description of, 1 Kin. 6:15–18; 2 Chr. 3:3,5-7,14–17. Contents of the holy place: The table of shewbread, 1 Kin. 7:48; 2 Chr. 29:18. See SHEWBREAD, TABLE OF. Other tables of gold and silver, 1 Chr. 28:16; 2 Chr. 4:18,19. Candlesticks and their utensils, 1 Kin. 7:49,50; 1 Chr. 28:15; 2 Chr. 4:7,20–22. See CANDLESTICK. Altar of incense and its furniture, 1 Kin. 6:20; 7:48,50; 1 Chr. 28:17,18; 2 Chr. 4:19,22. See ALTAR OF INCENSE.

Porch of, called PORCH OF THE LORD, 2 Chr. 15:8. Dimensions of, 1 Kin. 6:3; 2 Chr. 3:4. Doors of, 2 Chr. 29:7. Overlaid with gold, 2 Chr. 3:4. Pillars of, 1 Kin. 7: 15–22; 2 Kin. 11:14; 23:3; 25:17; 2 Chr. 3:15–17; 4:12,13.

Chambers of, 1 Kin. 6:5–10; 2 Kin. 11:2,3. Offerings brought to, Neh. 10:37-39. Treasuries in, see TREASURE.

Courts of: Of the priests, 2 Chr. 4:9; inner, 1 Kin. 6:36; surrounded by rows of stones and cedar beams, 1 Kin. 6:36; 7:12. Contents of the courts: Altar of burnt offering, 2 Chr. 15:8; see ALTAR; the brazen sea, 1 Kin. 7:23–37,44,46; 2 Chr. 4:2–5, 10; ten lavers, 1 Kin. 7:38–46; 2 Chr. 4:6. Great court of, 2 Chr. 4:9; Jer. 19:14; 26:2. Covered place for the Sabbath and king's entry, 2 Kin. 16:18.

Gates of: Higher gate, 2 Kin. 15:35; new gate, Jer. 26:10; 36:10; beautiful gate, Acts 3:2; eastern gate, closed on working days, open on the Sabbath, Ezek. 46:1,12. Gifts received at, 2 Chr. 24:8–11.

Uses of the temple: A dwelling place of the Lord, 1 Kin. 8:10,11,13; 9:3; 2 Kin. 21:7; 1 Chr. 29:1; 2 Chr. 5:13,14; 7:1-3,16; Ezek. 10:3,4; Mic. 1:2; to contain the ark of the covenant, 1 Kin. 8:21; for the offering of sweet incense, 2 Chr. 2:4; for the continual shewbread and the burnt offerings, 2 Chr. 2:4; for prayer and worship, 1 Kin. 8; 2 Kin. 19:14,15; 2 Chr. 30:27; Isa. 27:13; 56:7; Jer. 7:2; 26:2; Ezek 46:2,3,9; Zech. 7:2, 3; 8: 21,22; Mark 11:17; Luke 1:10; 2:37; 18:10; Acts 3:1; 22:17; prayer made toward, 1 Kin. 8:38; Dan. 6:10; Jonah 2:4; for an armory, 2 Kin. 11:10; 2 Chr. 23:9,10; for refuge, 2 Kin. 11:15; Neh. 6:10,11.

Facts about: Dedication of, 1 Kin. 8; 2 Chr. 5; 6; 7; services in, organized by David, 1 Chr. 15:16; 23:24. Pillaged by Shishak, 1 Kin. 14:25,26; by Jehoash, king of Israel, 2 Kin. 14:14. Repaired by Jehoash, king of Judah, 2 Kin. 12:4–14; 2 Chr. 24:7–14; by Josiah, 2 Kin. 22:3–7; 2 Chr. 34:8–13. Ahaz changes the pattern of the altar in, 2 Kin. 16:10–17. Purified by Hezekiah, 2 Chr. 29: 15–19. Converted into an idolatrous shrine by Manasseh, 2 Kin. 21:4–7; 2 Chr. 33:4–7. Treasures of, used in the purchase of peace: By Asa, from Ben-hadad, 1 Kin. 15:18; by Jehoash, king of Judah, from Hazael, 2 Kin. 12:18; by Hezekiah, from the king of Assyria, 2 Kin. 18:15,16. Ezekiel's vision concerning, Ezek. 8:16. Jews swore by, Matt. 23:16–22.

Destroyed by Nebuchadnezzar, and the valuable contents carried to Babylon, 2 Kin. 24:13; 25:9–17; 2 Chr. 36:7,19; Psa. 79:1; Isa. 64:11; Jer. 27:16,19–22; 28:3; 52:13,17–23; Lam. 2:7; 4:1; Ezra 1:7. Vessels of, used by Belshazzar, Dan. 5:2,3.

Destruction of, foretold, Isa. 66:6; Jer. 27:18–22; Ezek. 7:22,25; Matt. 24:2; Mark 13:2.

Restoration of, ordered by Cyrus, Ezra 1:7–11.

THE SECOND: Restored by Zerubbabel, Ezra 1; 2:68,69; 3:2–13; 4; 5:2–17; 6:3–5; Neh. 7:70–72; Isa. 44:28; Hag. 2:3. Building of, suspended, Ezra 4; resumed, Ezra 4:24; 5; 6; Hag. 1:2–9; 2:15; Zech. 8:9; finished, Ezra 6:14,15; dedicated, Ezra 6:15–18. Artaxerxes' favorable action toward, Ezra 7:11–28; 8:25–34.

Prophecies of its restoration, Isa. 44:28; Dan. 8:13,14; Hag. 1; 2; Zech. 1:16; 4:8–10; 6:12–15; 8:9–15; Mal. 3:1.

EZEKIEL'S VISION OF: Ezek. 37:26,28; chapters 40–48.

HEROD'S: Forty-six years in building, John 2:20. Goodly stones of, Mark 13:1; Luke 21:5. Magnificence of, Matt. 24:1. Beautiful gate of, Acts 3:10. Solomon's porch, John 10:23; Acts 3:11; 5:12. Treasury of, Mark 12:41–44. Zacharias, officiating priest in, has a vision of an angel; receives promise of a son, Luke 1:5–23, with *vs.* 57–64. Jesus brought to, according to the law and custom, Luke 2:21–39; Simeon blesses Jesus in, Luke 2:25–35; Anna, the prophetess, dwells in, Luke 2:36,37. Jesus in, when a youth, Luke 2:46; taken to the pinnacle of, in his temptation, Matt. 4:5–7; Luke 4:9–12; teaches in, Mark 11:27–33; 12: 35–44; 14:49; John 5:14–47; 7:14–28; 8; 10:23–38: 18:20; performs miracles in, Matt. 21:14, 15; drives money changers from, Matt. 21: 12,13; Mark 11:15–17; Luke 19:45,46; John 2:15,16.

Captains of, Luke 22:52; Acts 4:1; 5:24,26. Judas casts down the pieces of silver in, Matt. 27:5.

Vail of, rent at the time of the crucifixion, Matt. 27:51. The disciples worship in, after the resurrection, Luke 24:53; Acts 2:46; 3:1. Peter heals the lame man at the gate of, Acts 3:1–16. Disciples preach in, Acts 5:20, 21,42. Paul's vision in, Acts 22:17–21. Paul observes the rights of, Acts 21:26–30; is apprehended in, Acts 21:33.

Prophecies concerning its destruction, by Daniel, Dan. 8:11–15; 11:30,31. Jesus foretells the destruction of, Matt. 24; Mark 13:2; Luke 21:6.

FIGURATIVE: Of the body of Jesus, Matt. 26:61; 27:40; John 2:19. Of the indwelling of God, 1 Cor. 3:16,17; 2 Cor. 6:16. Of the Church, Eph. 2:21; 2 Thess. 2:4; Rev. 3:12. Of the kingdom of Christ, Rev. 11; 14:15,17. Of Christ, the head of the Church, sending forth the forces of righteousness

against the powers of evil, Rev. 15:5–8; 16: 1–17.

IDOLATROUS: Of Dagon, at Ashdod, 1 Sam. 5:2; of the calves, at Beth-el, 1 Kin. 12: 31,33; of Rimmon, at Damascus, 2 Kin. 5:18; of Baal, at Samaria, 2 Kin. 10:21,27; at Babylon, 2 Chr. 36:7; Dan. 1:2; of Diana, at Ephesus, Acts 19:27.

Trophies stored in, 1 Sam. 31:10; 1 Chr. 10:9,10; Dan. 1:2.

See TABERNACLE.

TEMPORAL BLESSINGS. See BLESSINGS.

TEMPTATION. Gen. 3:1. Now the serpent was more subtil than any beast of the field which the LORD God had made. And he said unto the woman, Yea, hath God said, Ye shall not eat of every tree of the garden? 2. And the woman said unto the serpent, We may eat of the fruit of the trees of the garden: 3. But of the fruit of the tree which *is* in the midst of the garden, God hath said, Ye shall not eat of it, neither shall ye touch it, lest ye die. 4. And the serpent said unto the woman, Ye shall not surely die: 5. For God doth know that in the day ye eat thereof, then your eyes shall be opened, and ye shall be as gods, knowing good and evil. 6. And when the woman saw that the tree *was* good for food, and that it *was* pleasant to the eyes, and a tree to be desired to make *one* wise, she took of the fruit thereof, and did eat, and gave also unto her husband with her; and he did eat. 7. And the eyes of them both were opened, and they knew that they *were* naked; and they sewed fig leaves together, and made themselves aprons. 8. And they heard the voice of the LORD God walking in the garden in the cool of the day: and Adam and his wife hid themselves from the presence of the LORD God amongst the trees of the garden. 9. And the LORD God called unto Adam, and said unto him, Where *art* thou? 10. And he said, I heard thy voice in the garden, and I was afraid, because I *was* naked; and I hid myself. 11. And he said, Who told thee that thou *wast* naked? Hast thou eaten of the tree, whereof I commanded thee that thou shouldest not eat? 12. And the man said, The woman whom thou gavest *to be* with me, she gave me of the tree, and I did eat. 13. And the LORD God said unto the woman, What *is* this *that* thou hast done? And the woman said, The serpent beguiled me, and I did eat.

Gen. 20:6. And God said unto him in a dream, Yea, I know that thou didst this in the integrity of thy heart; for I also withheld thee from sinning against me: therefore suffered I thee not to touch her.

Ex. 34:12. Take heed to thyself, lest thou make a covenant with the inhabitants of the land whither thou goest, lest it be for a snare in the midst of thee: *vs.* 13–16.

Deut. 7:25. The graven images of their gods shall ye burn with fire: thou shalt not desire the silver or gold *that is* on them, nor take *it* unto thee, lest thou be snared therein: for it *is* an abomination to the LORD thy God.

Deut. 8:11. Beware that thou forget not the LORD thy God, in not keeping his commandments, and his judgments, and his statutes, which I command thee this day: 12. Lest *when* thou hast eaten and art full, and hast built goodly houses, and dwelt *therein;* 13. And *when* thy herds and thy flocks multiply, and thy silver and thy gold is multiplied, and all that thou hast is multiplied; 14. Then thine heart be lifted up, and thou forget the LORD thy God, which brought thee forth out of the land of Egypt, from the house of bondage; 17. And thou say in thine heart, My power and the might of *mine* hand hath gotten me this wealth. 18. But thou shalt remember the LORD thy God: for *it is* he that giveth thee power to get wealth, that he may establish his covenant which he sware unto thy fathers, as *it is* this day.

Deut. 13:3. Thou shalt not hearken unto the words of that prophet, or that dreamer of dreams: for the LORD your God proveth you, to know whether ye love the LORD your God with all your heart and with all your soul.

1 Chr. 21:1. And Satan stood up against Israel, and provoked David to number Israel.

2 Chr. 32:30. And Hezekiah prospered in all his works. 31. Howbeit in *the business of* the ambassadors of the princes of Babylon, who sent unto him to enquire of the wonder that was *done* in the land, God left him, to try him, that he might know all *that was* in his heart.

Psa. 119:165. Great peace have they which love thy law: and nothing shall offend them.

Prov. 1:10. My son, if sinners entice thee, consent thou not. 11. If they say, Come with us, let us lay wait for blood, let us lurk privily for the innocent without cause: 12. Let us swallow them up alive as the grave; and whole, as those that go down into the pit: 13. We shall find all precious substance, we shall fill our houses with spoil: 14. Cast in thy lot among us; let us all have one purse: 15. My son, walk not thou in the way with them; refrain thy foot from their path: 16. For their feet run to evil, and make haste to shed blood. 17. Surely in vain the net is spread in the sight of any bird.

Prov. 2:10. When wisdom entereth into thine heart, and knowledge is pleasant unto thy soul; 11. Discretion shall preserve thee, understanding shall keep thee: 12. To deliver thee from the way of the evil *man*, from the man that speaketh froward things; 16. To deliver thee from the strange woman, *even* from the stranger *which* flattereth with her words;

Prov. 4:14. Enter not into the path of the wicked, and go not in the way of evil *men.*

15. Avoid it, pass not by it, turn from it, and pass away.

Prov. 5:6. Lest thou shouldest ponder the path of life, her ways are moveable, *that* thou canst not know *them.* 7. Hear me now therefore, O ye children, and depart not from the words of my mouth. 8. Remove thy way far from her, and come not nigh the door of her house: 9. Lest thou give thine honour unto others, and thy years unto the cruel: 10. Lest strangers be filled with thy wealth; and thy labours *be* in the house of a stranger; 11. And thou mourn at the last, when thy flesh and thy body are consumed, 12. And say, How have I hated instruction, and my heart despised reproof; 13. And have not obeyed the voice of my teachers, nor inclined mine ear to them that instructed me! 14. I was almost in all evil in the midst of the congregation and assembly. 15. Drink waters out of thine own cistern, and running waters out of thine own well. 16. Let thy fountains be dispersed abroad, *and* rivers of waters in the streets. 17. Let them be only thine own, and not strangers' with thee. 18. Let thy fountain be blessed: and rejoice with the wife of thy youth. 19. *Let her be as* the loving hind and pleasant roe; let her breasts satisfy thee at all times; and be thou ravished always with her love. 20. And why wilt thou, my son, be ravished with a strange woman, and embrace the bosom of a stranger? 21. For the ways of man *are* before the eyes of the LORD, and he pondereth all his goings.

Prov. 6:27. Can a man take fire in his bosom, and his clothes not be burned? 28. Can one go upon hot coals, and his feet not be burned?

Prov. 7:7. I discerned among the youths, a young man void of understanding, 8. Passing through the street near her corner; and he went the way to her house, 9. In the twilight, in the evening, in the black and dark night: 10. And, behold, there met him a woman *with* the attire of an harlot, and subtil of heart. 11. (She *is* loud and stubborn; her feet abide not in her house: 12. Now *is she* without, now in the streets, and lieth in wait at every corner.) 13. So she caught him, and kissed him, *and* with an impudent face said unto him, 14. *I have* peace offerings with me; this day have I paid my vows. 15. Therefore came I forth to meet thee, diligently to seek thy face, and I have found thee. 16. I have decked my bed with coverings of tapestry, with carved *works*, with fine linen of Egypt. 17. I have perfumed my bed with myrrh, aloes, and cinnamon. 18. Come, let us take our fill of love until the morning: let us solace ourselves with loves. 19. For the goodman *is* not at home, he is gone a long journey: 20. He hath taken a bag of money with him, *and* will come home at the day appointed. 21. With her much fair speech she caused him to yield, with the flattering of her lips she forced him. 22. He goeth after her straightway, as an ox goeth to the slaughter, or as a fool to the correction of the stocks; 23. Till a dart strike through his liver; as a bird hasteth to the snare, and knoweth not that it *is* for his life.

Prov. 9:15. To call passengers who go right on their ways: 16. Whoso *is* simple, let him turn in hither: and *as for* him that wanteth understanding, she saith to him, 17. Stolen waters are sweet, and bread *eaten* in secret is pleasant.

Prov. 12:26. The righteous *is* more excellent than his neighbour: but the way of the wicked seduceth them.

Prov. 14:27. The fear of the LORD *is* a fountain of life, to depart from the snares of death. Prov. 13:14.

Prov. 16:29. A violent man enticeth his neighbour, and leadeth him into the way *that is* not good.

Prov. 19:27. Cease, my son, to hear the instruction *that causeth* to err from the words of knowledge.

Prov. 28:10. Whoso causeth the righteous to go astray in an evil way, he shall fall himself into his own pit: but the upright shall have good *things* in possession.

Eccl. 7:26. And I find more bitter than death the woman, whose heart *is* snares and nets, *and* her hands *as* bands: whoso pleaseth God shall escape from her; but the sinner shall be taken by her.

Isa. 33:15. He that walketh righteously, and speaketh uprightly; he that despiseth the gain of oppressions, that shaketh his hands from holding of bribes, that stoppeth his ears from hearing of blood, and shutteth his eyes from seeing evil; 16. He shall dwell on high: his place of defence *shall be* the munitions of rocks: bread shall be given him; his waters *shall be* sure.

Jer. 2:24. A wild ass used to the wilderness, *that* snuffeth up the wind at her pleasure; in her occasion who can turn her away? all they that seek her will not weary themselves; in her month they shall find her. 25. Withhold thy foot from being unshod, and thy throat from thirst: but thou saidst, There is no hope: no; for I have loved strangers, and after them will I go.

Jer. 35:5. And I set before the sons of the house of the Rechabites pots full of wine, and cups, and I said unto them, Drink ye wine. 6. But they said, We will drink no wine: for Jonadab the son of Rechab our father commanded us, saying, Ye shall drink no wine, *neither* ye, nor your sons for ever: 7. Neither shall ye build house, nor sow seed, nor plant vineyard, nor have *any:* but all your days ye shall dwell in tents; that ye may live many days in the land where ye *be* strangers.

Hos. 7:5. In the day of our king the princes have made *him* sick with bottles of wine; he stretched out his hand with scorners.

Amos 2:12. But ye gave the Nazarites wine to drink; and commanded the prophets, saying, Prophesy not.

Matt. 4:1. Then was Jesus led up of the spirit into the wilderness to be tempted of the devil. 2. And when he had fasted forty days and forty nights, he was afterward an hungred. 3. And when the tempter came to him, he said, If thou be the Son of God, command that these stones be made bread. 4. But he answered and said, It is written, Man shall not live by bread alone, but by every word that proceedeth out of the mouth of God. 5. Then the devil taketh him up into the holy city, and setteth him on a pinnacle of the temple, 6. And saith unto him, If thou be the Son of God, cast thyself down: for it is written, He shall give his angels charge concerning thee: and in *their* hands they shall bear thee up, lest at any time thou dash thy foot against a stone. 7. Jesus said unto him, It is written again, Thou shalt not tempt the Lord thy God. 8. Again, the devil taketh him up into an exceeding high mountain, and sheweth him all the kingdoms of the world, and the glory of them; 9. And saith unto him, All these things will I give thee, if thou wilt fall down and worship me. 10. Then saith Jesus unto him, Get thee hence, Satan: for it is written, Thou shalt worship the Lord thy God, and him only shalt thou serve. 11. Then the devil leaveth him, and, behold, angels came and ministered unto him. Luke 4:1–13.

Matt. 5:19. Whosoever therefore shall break one of these least commandments, and shall teach men so, he shall be called the least in the kingdom of heaven:

Matt. 12:45. Then goeth he, and taketh with himself seven other spirits more wicked than himself, and they enter in and dwell there: and the last *state* of that man is worse than the first. Even so shall it be also unto this wicked generation.

Matt. 13:22. He also that received seed among the thorns is he that heareth the word; and the care of this world, and the deceitfulness of riches, choke the word, and he becometh unfruitful. Luke 8:13,14.

Matt. 18:6. But whoso shall offend [cause to stumble, *R. V.*] one of these little ones which believe in me, it were better for him that a millstone were hanged about his neck, and *that* he were drowned in the depth of the sea. 7. Woe unto the world because of offences [occasions of stumbling, *R. V.*]! for it must needs be that offences come; but woe to that man by whom the offence [occasion, *R. V.*] cometh! 8. Wherefore if thy hand or thy foot offend thee [causeth thee to stumble, *R. V.*], cut them off, and cast *them* from thee: it is better for thee to enter into life halt or maimed, rather than having two hands or two feet to be cast into everlasting fire. 9. And if thine eye offend thee [causeth thee to stumble, *R. V.*], pluck it out, and cast *it* from thee: it is better for thee to enter into life with one eye, rather than having two eyes to be cast into hell fire.

Matt. 26:31. Then saith Jesus unto them, All ye shall be offended because of me this night: for it is written, I will smite the shepherd, and the sheep of the flock shall be scattered abroad. 41. Watch and pray, that ye enter not into temptation: the spirit indeed *is* willing, but the flesh *is* weak. Luke 22:40.

Mark 4:15. And these are they by the way side, where the word is sown; but when they have heard, Satan cometh immediately, and taketh away the word that was sown in their hearts. 17. And have no root in themselves, and so endure but for a time: afterward, when affliction or persecution ariseth for the word's sake, immediately they are offended [stumble, *R. V.*].

Mark 10:21. Then Jesus beholding him loved him, and said unto him, One thing thou lackest: go thy way, sell whatsoever thou hast, and give to the poor, and thou shalt have treasure in heaven: and come, take up the cross, and follow me. 22. And he was sad at that saying, and went away grieved: for he had great possessions. 23. And Jesus looked round about, and saith unto his disciples, How hardly shall they that have riches enter into the kingdom of God! 24. And the disciples were astonished at his words. But Jesus answereth again, and saith unto them, Children, how hard is it for them that trust in riches to enter into the kingdom of God! 25. It is easier for a camel to go through the eye of a needle, than for a rich man to enter into the kingdom of God.

Mark 13:21. And then if any man shall say to you, Lo, here *is* Christ; or, Lo, *he is* there; believe *him* not: 22. For false Christs and false prophets shall rise, and shall shew signs and wonders, to seduce, if *it were* possible, even the elect.

Luke 11:4. And forgive us our sins; for we also forgive every one that is indebted to us. And lead us not into temptation; ¹ but deliver us from evil.   [¹ Omitted in R. V.]

Luke 22:3. Then entered Satan into Judas surnamed Iscariot, being of the number of the twelve. 31. And the Lord said, Simon, Simon, behold, Satan hath desired *to have* you, that he may sift *you* as wheat: 32. But I have prayed for thee, that thy faith fail not: and when thou art converted, strengthen thy brethren. 46. And said unto them, Why sleep ye? rise and pray, lest ye enter into temptation. Mark 14:38.

John 16:1. These things have I spoken unto you, that ye should not be offended [made to stumble, *R. V.*]. 2. They shall put you out of the synagogues: yea, the time cometh, that whosoever killeth you will think that he doeth God service.

Rom. 6:12. Let not sin therefore reign in your mortal body, that ye should obey it in the lusts thereof. 13. Neither yield ye your members *as* instruments of unrighteousness

unto sin: but yield yourselves unto God, as those that are alive from the dead, and your members *as* instruments of righteousness unto God. 14. For sin shall not have dominion over you: for ye are not under the law, but under grace.

Rom. 7:5. For when we were in the flesh, the motions of sins, which were by the law, did work in our members to bring forth fruit unto death.

Rom. 8:35. Who shall separate us from the love of Christ? *shall* tribulation, or distress, or persecution, or famine, or nakedness, or peril, or sword? 36. As it is written, For thy sake we are killed all the day long; we are accounted as sheep for the slaughter. 37. Nay, in all these things we are more than conquerors through him that loved us. 38. For I am persuaded, that neither death, nor life, nor angels, nor principalities, nor powers, nor things present, nor things to come, 39. Nor height, nor depth, nor any other creature, shall be able to separate us from the love of God, which is in Christ Jesus our Lord.

Rom. 12:21. Be not overcome of evil, but overcome evil with good.

Rom. 14:13. Let us not therefore judge one another any more: but judge this rather, that no man put a stumblingblock or an occasion to fall in *his* brother's way. 15. But if thy brother be grieved with *thy* meat, now walkest thou not charitably. Destroy not him with thy meat, for whom Christ died. 21. *It is* good neither to eat flesh, nor to drink wine, nor *any thing* whereby thy brother stumbleth, ¹ or is offended, or is made weak.   [¹ Omitted in R. V.]

1 Cor. 7:5. Defraud ye not one the other, except *it be* with consent for a time, that ye may give yourselves to fasting and prayer; and come together again, that Satan tempt you not for [because of, *R. V.*] your incontinency.

1 Cor. 8:9. But take heed lest by any means this liberty of yours become a stumblingblock to them that are weak. 10. For if any man see thee which hast knowledge sit at meat in the idol's temple, shall not the conscience of him which is weak be emboldened to eat those things which are offered to idols; 11. And through thy knowledge shall the weak brother perish, for whom Christ died? 12. But when ye sin so against the brethren, and wound their weak conscience, ye sin against Christ. 13. Wherefore, if meat make my brother to offend, I will eat no flesh while the world standeth, lest I make my brother to offend.

1 Cor. 10:13. There hath no temptation taken you but such as ¹ is common to man: but God *is* faithful, who will not suffer you to be tempted above that ye are able; but will with the temptation also make a way to escape, that ye may be able to bear it.
                          [¹ R. V. man can bear]

28. But if any man say unto you, This is offered in sacrifice ¹ unto idols, eat not for his

sake that shewed it, and for conscience sake: ¹ for the earth *is* the Lord's, and the fulness thereof: 29. Conscience, I say, not thine own, but of the other: for why is my liberty judged of another *man's* conscience? 30. For if I by grace be a partaker, why am I evil spoken of for that for which I give thanks? 31. Whether therefore ye eat, or drink, or whatsoever ye do, do all to the glory of God. 32. Give none offence, neither to the Jews, nor to the Gentiles, nor to the church of God: [¹ Omitted in R. V.]

2 Cor. 2:11. Lest Satan should get an advantage of us: for we are not ignorant of his devices.

2 Cor. 11:3. But I fear, lest by any means, as the serpent beguiled Eve through his subtilty, so your minds should be corrupted from the simplicity that is in Christ. 14. And no marvel; for Satan himself is transformed into an angel of light. 15. Therefore *it is* no great thing if his ministers also be transformed as the ministers of righteousness; whose end shall be according to their works.

2 Cor. 12:7. And lest I should be exalted above measure through the abundance of the revelations, there was given to me a thorn in the flesh, the messenger of Satan to buffet me, lest I should be exalted above measure. Gal. 4:14.

Gal. 5:17. For the flesh lusteth against the Spirit, and the Spirit against the flesh: and these are contrary the one to the other: so that ye cannot do the things that ye would.

Eph. 4:27. Neither give place to the devil.

Eph. 6:11. Put on the whole armour of God, that ye may be able to stand against the wiles of the devil. 13. Wherefore take unto you the whole armour of God, that ye may be able to withstand in the evil day, and having done all, to stand. 14. Stand therefore, having your loins girt about with truth, and having on the breastplate of righteousness; 15. And your feet shod with the preparation of the gospel of peace; 16. Above all, taking the shield of faith, wherewith ye shall be able to quench all the fiery darts of the wicked. 17. And take the helmet of salvation, and the sword of the Spirit, which is the word of God:

1 Thess. 3:5. For this cause, when I could no longer forbear, I sent to know your faith, lest by some means the tempter have tempted you, and our labour be in vain.

1 Tim. 5:15. For some are already turned aside after Satan.

1 Tim. 6:9. But they that will be rich fall into temptation and a snare, and *into* many foolish and hurtful lusts, which drown men in destruction and perdition. 10. For the love of money is the root of all evil: which while some coveted after, they have erred from the faith, and pierced themselves through with many sorrows.

2 Tim. 3:13. But evil men and seducers shall wax worse and worse, deceiving, and being deceived.

Heb. 2:18. In that he himself hath suffered being tempted, he is able to succour them that are tempted.

Heb. 4:15. For we have not an high priest which cannot be touched with the feeling of our infirmities; but was in all points tempted like as *we are*, *yet* without sin.

Heb. 12:3. Consider him that endured such contradiction of sinners against himself, lest ye be wearied and faint in your minds. 4. Ye have not yet resisted unto blood, striving against sin.

Jas. 1:2. My brethren, count it all joy when ye fall into divers temptations; 3. Knowing *this*, that the trying of your faith worketh patience. 4. But let patience have *her* perfect work, that ye may be perfect and entire, wanting nothing. 12. Blessed *is* the man that endureth temptation: for when he ¹ is tried, he shall receive the crown of life, which the Lord hath promised to them that love him. 13. Let no man say when he is tempted, I am tempted of God: for God cannot be tempted with evil, neither tempteth he any man: 14. But every man is tempted, when he is drawn away of his own lust, and enticed. 15. Then when lust hath conceived, it bringeth forth sin: and sin, when it is finished, bringeth forth death. 16. Do not err, my beloved brethren.

[¹ R. V. hath been approved]

Jas. 4:7. Resist the devil, and he will flee from you.

1 Pet. 1:6. Wherein ye greatly rejoice, though now for a season, if need be, ye are in heaviness through manifold temptations: 7. That the trial of your faith, being much more precious than of gold that perisheth, though it be tried with fire, might be found unto praise and honour and glory at the appearing of Jesus Christ:

1 Pet. 4:12. Beloved, think it not strange concerning the fiery trial which is to try you, as though some strange thing happened unto you:

1 Pet. 5:8. Be sober, be vigilant; because your adversary the devil, as a roaring lion, walketh about, seeking whom he may devour: 9. Whom resist stedfast in the faith, knowing that the same afflictions are accomplished in your brethren that are in the world.

2 Pet. 2:9. The Lord knoweth how to deliver the godly out of temptations, and to reserve the unjust unto the day of judgment to be punished:

18. For when they speak great swelling *words* of vanity, they allure through the lusts of the flesh, *through much* wantonness, those that were clean escaped from them who live in error.

2 Pet. 3:17. Ye therefore, beloved, seeing ye know *these things* before, beware lest ye also, being led away with the error of the wicked, fall from your own stedfastness.

1 John 2:16. For all that *is* in the world, the lust of the flesh, and the lust of the eyes, and the pride of life, is not of the Father, but is of the world. 26. These *things*

have I written unto you concerning them that seduce you.

1 John 4:4. Ye are of God, little children, and have overcome them: because greater is he that is in you, than he that is in the world.

Rev. 3:10. Because thou hast kept the word of my patience, I also will keep thee from the hour of temptation, which shall come upon all the world, to try them that dwell upon the earth.

Rev. 12:10. And I heard a loud voice saying in heaven, Now is come salvation, and strength, and the kingdom of our God, and the power of his Christ: for the accuser of our brethren is cast down, which accused them before our God day and night. 11. And they overcame him by the blood of the Lamb, and by the word of their testimony; and they loved not their lives unto the death. 17. And the dragon was wroth with the woman, and went to make war with the remnant of her seed, which keep the commandments of God, and have the testimony of Jesus Christ.

See DEMONS; FAITH, TRIAL OF; SATAN.

A TEST: Gen. 22:1. And it came to pass after these things, that God did tempt Abraham, and said unto him, Abraham: and he said, Behold, *here I am. vs.* 2–14; Heb. 11:17.

Deut. 8:2. And thou shalt remember all the way which the LORD thy God led thee these forty years in the wilderness, to humble thee, *and* to prove thee, to know what *was* in thine heart, whether thou wouldest keep his commandments, or no. 5. Thou shalt also consider in thine heart, that, as a man chasteneth his son, *so* the LORD thy God chasteneth thee.

Deut 13:1. If . . . a prophet, or a dreamer of dreams . . . giveth thee a sign or a wonder, 2. And the sign or the wonder come to pass, whereof he spake unto thee, saying, Let us go after other gods, which thou hast not known, and let us serve them; 3. Thou shalt not hearken unto the words of that prophet, or that dreamer of dreams: for the LORD your God proveth you, to know whether ye love the LORD your God with all your heart and with all your soul.

2 Chr. 32:31. Howbeit in *the business of* the ambassadors of the princes of Babylon, who sent unto him to enquire of the wonder that was *done* in the land, God left him [Hezekiah], to try him, that he might know all *that was* in his heart.

Job 1:8. And the LORD said unto Satan, Hast thou considered my servant Job, that *there is* none like him in the earth, a perfect and an upright man, one that feareth God, and escheweth evil? 9. Then Satan answered the LORD, and said, Doth Job fear God for nought? 10. Hast not thou made an hedge about him, and about his house, and about all that he hath on every side? thou hast blessed the work of his hands,

and his substance is increased in the land. 11. But put forth thine hand now, and touch all that he hath, and he will curse thee to thy face. 12. And the LORD said unto Satan, Behold, all that he hath *is* in thy power; only upon himself put not forth thine hand. So Satan went forth from the presence of the LORD. 13. And there was a day when his sons and his daughters *were* eating and drinking wine in their eldest brother's house: 14. And there came a messenger unto Job, and said, The oxen were plowing, and the asses feeding beside them: 15. And the Sabeans fell *upon them*, and took them away; yea, they have slain the servants with the edge of the sword; and I only am escaped alone to tell thee. 16. While he *was* yet speaking, there came also another, and said, The fire of God is fallen from heaven, and hath burned up the sheep, and the servants, and consumed them; and I only am escaped alone to tell thee. 17. While he *was* yet speaking, there came also another, and said, The Chaldeans made out three bands, and fell upon the camels, and have carried them away, yea, and slain the servants with the edge of the sword; and I only am escaped alone to tell thee. 18. While he *was* yet speaking, there came also another, and said, Thy sons and thy daughters *were* eating and drinking wine in their eldest brother's house: 19. And, behold, there came a great wind from the wilderness, and smote the four corners of the house, and it fell upon the young men, and they are dead; and I only am escaped alone to tell thee. 20. Then Job arose, and rent his mantle, and shaved his head, and fell down upon the ground, and worshipped, 21. And said, Naked came I out of my mother's womb, and naked shall I return thither: the LORD gave, and the LORD hath taken away; blessed be the name of the LORD. 22. In all this Job sinned not, nor charged God foolishly.

Job 2:3. And the LORD said unto Satan, Hast thou considered my servant Job, that *there is* none like him in the earth, a perfect and an upright man, one that feareth God, and escheweth evil? and still he holdeth fast his integrity, although thou movedst me against him, to destroy him without cause. 4. And Satan answered the LORD, and said, Skin for skin, yea, all that a man hath will he give for his life. 5. But put forth thine hand now, and touch his bone and his flesh, and he will curse thee to thy face. 6. And the LORD said unto Satan, Behold, he *is* in thine hand; but save his life. 7. So went Satan forth from the presence of the LORD, and smote Job with sore boils from the sole of his foot unto his crown. 8. And he took him a potsherd to scrape himself withal; and he sat down among the ashes. 9. Then said his wife unto him, Dost thou still retain thine integrity? curse God, and die. 10. But he said unto her, Thou speakest as one of the foolish women speaketh. What? shall we receive good at the hand of God, and shall we not receive evil? In all this did not Job sin with his lips. Psa. 66:10. For thou, O God, hast proved us: thou hast tried us, as silver is tried. 11. Thou broughtest us into the net; thou laidst affliction upon our loins. 12. Thou hast caused men to ride over our heads; we went through fire and through water: but thou broughtest us out into a wealthy *place*. 13. I will go into thy house with burnt offerings: I will pay thee my vows.

Dan. 12:10. Many shall be purified, and made white, and ¹ tried; but the wicked shall do wickedly: and none of the wicked shall understand; but the wise shall understand.

[¹ R. V. be refined]

Zech. 13:9. And I will bring the third part through the fire, and will refine them as silver is refined, and will try them as gold is tried:

Jas. 1:2. My brethren, count it all joy when ye fall into divers temptations; 3. Knowing *this*, that the trying of your faith worketh patience. 12. Blessed *is* the man that endureth temptation: for when he ² is tried, he shall receive the crown of life, which the Lord hath promised to them that love him.

[² R. V. hath been approved]

1 Pet. 1:6. Wherein ye greatly rejoice, though now for a season, if need be, ye are in heaviness through manifold temptations: 7. That the trial of your faith, being much more precious than of gold that perisheth, though it be tried with fire, might be found unto praise and honour and glory at the appearing of Jesus Christ:

See AFFLICTION, DESIGN OF; FAITH, TRIAL OF.

LEADING INTO: Prayer against being led into, Matt. 6:13; Luke 22:40. INSTANCES OF: Abraham leads Pharaoh, Gen. 12:18,19; Abimelech, Gen. 20:9. Balak tempts Balaam, Num. 22; 23; 24. The old prophet of Beth-el, the prophet of Judah, 1 Kin. 13:15–19. Gideon leads Israel into sin, Judg. 8:27. Jeroboam leads Israel into, 1 Kin. 15:30.

See RESISTANCE TO; YIELDING TO, below.

RESISTANCE TO: Gen. 39:7. And it came to pass after these things, that his master's wife cast her eyes upon Joseph; and she said, Lie with me. 8. But he refused, and said unto his master's wife, Behold, my master wotteth not what *is* with me in the house, and he hath committed all that he hath to my hand; 9. *There is* none greater in this house than I; neither hath he kept back any thing from me but thee, because thou *art* his wife: how then can I do this great wickedness, and sin against God? 10. And it came to pass, as she spake to Joseph day by day, that he hearkened not unto her, to lie by her, *or* to be with her.

Neh. 4:9. Nevertheless we made our prayer unto our God, and set a watch against them day and night, because of them.

Job 31:1. I made a covenant with mine eyes; why then should I think upon a maid? 5. If I have walked with vanity, or if my foot hath hasted to deceit; 6. Let me be weighed in an even balance, that God may know mine integrity. 7. If my step hath turned out of the way, and mine heart walked after mine eyes, and if any blot hath cleaved to mine hands; 8. *Then* let me sow, and let another eat; yea, let my offspring be rooted out. 9. If mine heart have been deceived by a woman, or *if* I have laid wait at my neighbour's door; 10. *Then* let my wife grind unto another, and let others bow down upon her. 11. For this *is* an heinous crime; yea, it *is* an iniquity *to be punished by* the judges. 12. For it *is* a fire *that* consumeth to destruction, and would root out all mine increase. 13. If I did despise the cause of my manservant or of my maidservant, when they contended with me; 14. What then shall I do when God riseth up? and when he visiteth, what shall I answer him? 15. Did not he that made me in the womb make him? and did not one fashion us in the womb? 16. If I have withheld the poor from *their* desire, or have caused the eyes of the widow to fail; 17. Or have eaten my morsel myself alone, and the fatherless hath not eaten thereof; 19. If I have seen any perish for want of clothing, or any poor without covering; 20. If his loins have not blessed me, and *if* he were *not* warmed with the fleece of my sheep; 21. If I have lifted up my hand against the fatherless, when I saw my help in the gate: 22. *Then* let mine arm fall from my shoulder blade, and mine arm be broken from the bone. 23. For destruction *from* God *was* a terror to me, and by reason of his highness I could not endure. 24. If I have made gold my hope, or have said to the fine gold, *Thou art* my confidence; 25. If I rejoiced because my wealth *was* great, and because mine hand had gotten much; 26. If I beheld the sun when it shined, or the moon walking *in* brightness; 27. And my heart hath been secretly enticed, or my mouth hath kissed my hand: 28. This also *were* an iniquity *to be punished by* the judge: for I should have denied the God *that is* above. 29. If I rejoiced at the destruction of him that hated me, or lifted up myself when evil found him: 30. Neither have I suffered my mouth to sin by wishing a curse to his soul. 31. If the men of my tabernacle said not, Oh that we had of his flesh! we cannot be satisfied. 32. The stranger did not lodge in the street: *but* I opened my doors to the traveller. 33. If I covered my transgressions as Adam, by hiding mine iniquity in my bosom: 34. Did I fear a great multitude, or did the contempt of families terrify me, that I kept silence, *and* went not out of the door? 38. If my land cry against me, or that the furrows likewise thereof complain; 39. If I have eaten the fruits thereof without money, or have caused the owners thereof to lose their life: 40. Let thistles grow instead of wheat, and cockle instead of barley.

Psa. 17:4. Concerning the works of men, by the word of thy lips I have kept *me from* the paths of the destroyer.

Psa. 73:2. But as for me, my feet were almost gone; my steps had well nigh slipped. 3. For I was envious at the foolish, *when* I saw the prosperity of the wicked. 4. For *there are* no bands in their death: but their strength *is* firm. 5. They *are* not in trouble *as other* men; neither are they plagued like *other* men. 6. Therefore pride compasseth them about as a chain; violence covereth them *as* a garment. 7. Their eyes stand out with fatness: they have more than heart could wish. 8. They are corrupt, and speak wickedly *concerning* oppression: they speak loftily. 9. They set their mouth against the heavens, and their tongue walketh through the earth. 10. Therefore his people return hither: and waters of a full *cup* are wrung out to them. 11. And they say, How doth God know? and is there knowledge in the most High? 12. Behold, these *are* the ungodly, who prosper in the world; they increase *in* riches. 13. Verily I have cleansed my heart *in* vain, and washed my hands in innocency. 14. For all the day long have I been plagued, and chastened every morning. 15. If I say, I will speak thus; behold, I should offend *against* the generation of thy children. 16. When I thought to know this, it *was* too painful for me; 17. Until I went into the sanctuary of God; *then* understood I their end. 18. Surely thou didst set them in slippery places: thou castedst them down into destruction. 19. How are they *brought* into desolation, as in a moment! they are utterly consumed with terrors. 20. As a dream when *one* awaketh; *so*, O Lord, when thou awakest, thou shalt despise their image. 21. Thus my heart was grieved, and I was pricked in my reins. 22. So foolish *was* I, and ignorant: I was *as* a beast before thee. 23. Nevertheless I *am* continually with thee: thou hast holden *me* by my right hand. 24. Thou shalt guide me with thy counsel, and afterward receive me *to* glory. 25. Whom have I in heaven *but thee?* and *there is* none upon earth *that* I desire beside thee. 26. My flesh and my heart faileth: *but* God *is* the strength of my heart, and my portion for ever.

Psa. 94:17. Unless the LORD *had been* my help, my soul had almost dwelt in silence. 18. When I said, My foot slippeth; thy mercy, O LORD, held me up.

Psa. 119:101. I have refrained my feet from every evil way, that I might keep thy word. 110. The wicked have laid a snare for me: yet I erred not from thy precepts.

Amos 4:12. Therefore thus will I do unto thee, O Israel: *and* because I will do this unto thee, prepare to meet thy God, O Israel.

Matt. 4:1. Then was Jesus led up of the spirit into the wilderness to be tempted of the devil. 2. And when he had fasted forty days and forty nights, he was afterward an hungred. 3. And when the tempter came to him, he said, If thou be the Son of God, command that these stones be made bread. 4. But he answered and said, It is written, Man shall not live by bread alone, but by every word that proceedeth out of the mouth of God. 5. Then the devil taketh him up into the holy city, and sitteth him on a pinnacle of the temple, 6. And saith unto him, If thou be the Son of God, cast thyself down: for it is written, He shall give his angels charge concerning thee: and in *their* hands they shall bear thee up, lest at any time thou dash thy foot against a stone. 7. Jesus said unto him, It is written again, Thou shalt not tempt the Lord thy God. 8. Again, the devil taketh him up into an exceeding high mountain, and sheweth him all the kingdoms of the world, and the glory of them; 9. And saith unto him, All these things will I give thee, if thou wilt fall down and worship me. 10. Then saith Jesus unto him, Get thee hence, Satan: for it is written, Thou shalt worship the Lord thy God, and him only shalt thou serve. 11. Then the devil leaveth him, and, behold, angels came and ministered unto him. Luke 4:1–13.

Matt. 24:42. Watch therefore, for ye know not what hour your Lord doth come. 43. But know this, that if the goodman of the house had known in what watch the thief would come, he would have watched, and would not have suffered his house to be broken up. 44. Therefore be ye also ready: for in such an hour as ye think not the Son of man cometh.

Matt. 25:13. Watch therefore, for ye know neither the day nor the hour wherein the Son of man cometh.

Matt. 26:38. Then saith he unto them, My soul is exceeding sorrowful, even unto death: tarry ye here, and watch with me. 39. And he went a little further, and fell on his face, and prayed, saying, O my Father, if it be possible, let this cup pass from me: nevertheless not as I will, but as thou *wilt.* 40. And he cometh unto the disciples, and findeth them asleep, and saith unto Peter, What, could ye not watch with me one hour? 41. Watch and pray, that ye enter not into temptation: the spirit indeed *is* willing, but the flesh *is* weak. 42. He went away again the second time, and prayed, saying, O my Father, if this cup may not pass away from me, except I drink it, thy will be done.

Mark 13:33. Take ye heed, watch and pray: for ye know not when the time is. 34. *For the Son of man is* as a man taking a far journey, who left his house, and gave authority to his servants, and to every man his work, and commanded the porter to watch. 35. Watch ye therefore; for ye know not when the master of the house cometh, at even, or at midnight, or at the cockcrowing, or in the morning: 36. Lest coming suddenly he find you sleeping. 37. And what I say unto you, I say unto all, Watch.

Mark 14:37. And he cometh, and findeth them sleeping, and saith unto Peter, Simon, sleepest thou? couldest not thou watch one hour? 38. Watch ye, and pray, lest ye enter into temptation: the spirit truly *is* ready; but the flesh *is* weak.

Luke 12:35. Let your loins be girded about, and *your* lights burning; 36. And ye yourselves like unto men that wait for their lord, when he will return from the wedding; that when he cometh and knocketh, they may open unto him immediately. 37. Blessed *are* those servants, whom the lord when he cometh shall find watching: verily I say unto you, that he shall gird himself, and make them to sit down to meat, and will come forth and serve them. 38. And if he shall come in the second watch, or come in the third watch, and find *them* so, blessed are those servants.

Luke 21:33. Heaven and earth shall pass away; but my words shall not pass away. 34. And take heed to yourselves, lest at any time your hearts be overcharged with surfeiting, and drunkenness, and cares of this life, and *so* that day come upon you unawares. 35. For as a snare shall it come on all them that dwell on the face of the whole earth. 36. Watch ye therefore, and pray always, that ye may be accounted worthy to escape all these things that shall come to pass, and to stand before the Son of man.

1 Cor. 16:13. Watch ye, stand fast in the faith, quit you like men, be strong.

1 Pet. 4:7. But the end of all things is at hand: be ye therefore sober, and watch unto prayer.

Rev. 3:2. Be watchful, and strengthen the things which remain, that are ready to die: for I have not found thy works perfect before God. 3. Remember therefore how thou hast received and heard, and hold fast, and repent. If therefore thou shalt not watch, I will come on thee as a thief, and thou shalt not know what hour I will come upon thee.

INSTANCES OF: Joseph resists the temptation to commit adultery, Gen. 39:7-12. Balaam, in refusing to curse the children of Israel, Num. 22:7-18; 24:12,13. The prophet of Judah, 1 Kin. 13:7-9. Micaiah, 1 Kin. 22: 13-28. Job, Job 1:6-21; 2:4-10. Rechabites, Jer. 35. David, to injure Saul, 1 Sam. 26:5-25. The people of Jerusalem, not to trust Jehovah, 2 Kin. 18:30-36. Jesus, Matt. 4:1-11.

YIELDING TO: INSTANCES OF: Adam and Eve, Gen. 3:1-19. Sarah, to lie, Gen. 12: 13; 18:13-15; 20:13. Isaac, to lie, Gen. 26:7. Jacob, to defraud Esau, Gen. 27:6-13. Balaam, Num. 22:15-22; 2 Pet. 2:15. Achan, Josh. 7:21. David, to commit adultery, 2 Sam. 11:2-5; to number Israel, 1 Chr. 21. Solomon, to become an idolater through the influences of his wives, 1 Kin. 11:4; Neh. 13: 26. The prophet of Judah, 1 Kin. 13:11-19.

Hezekiah, 2 Kin. 20:12-20; Isa. 39:1-4,6,7 Peter, Matt. 26:69-74; Mark 14:67-71; Luke 22:55-60.

TEN, used for an indefinite number, Gen. 31:7; Lev. 26:26; Num. 14:22; Zech. 8: 23.

TEN COMMANDMENTS. See COMMANDMENTS.

TENANTS, evicted, Matt. 21:41; Mark 12:9; Luke 20:16.

TENT. Used for dwelling, Gen. 4:20; by Noah, Gen. 9:21; by Abraham, Gen. 12: 8; 13:18; 18:1; by Lot, Gen. 13:5; by Moses, Ex. 18:7; by children of Israel, Num. 24:5,6; 2 Sam. 20:1; 1 Kin. 12:16; by the Midianites; Judg. 6:5; by Cushites, Hab. 3:7; by Arabians, Isa. 13:20; by shepherds, Isa. 38:12; Jer. 6:3. Women had tents apart from men. Gen 24:67; 31:33. Used for cattle, 2 Chr. 14: 15. Manufacture of, Acts 18:3. Used as a place of worship, see TABERNACLE.

TERAH. Father of Abraham, Gen. 11: 24-32. Was an idolater, Josh. 24:2. Called THARA, Luke 3:34.

TERAPHIM, household idols. Used by Laban, stolen by Rachael, Gen. 31:19,30-35; by Micah, stolen by the Danites, Judg. 17:5; 18:14,17-20. Condemned and disposed of by Jacob, Gen. 35:2-4, with Gen. 31:35-39. Destroyed by Josiah, see IDOLS.

TERESH, a Persian chamberlain. Plotted against Ahasuerus, Esth. 2:21-23; 6:2.

TERTIUS, Paul's amanuensis in writing the book of Romans, Rom. 16:22.

TERTULLUS, accuser of Paul before Felix, Acts 24:1,2.

TESTAMENT. A will, Heb. 9:16-18. The new [*R. V.*, covenant], Matt. 26:28; Mark 14:24; Luke 22:20; 1 Cor. 11:25.

See COVENANT.

TESTIMONY. LEGAL: See EVIDENCE; WITNESSES. Ark of, see ARK.

RELIGIOUS: 1 Chr. 16:8. Give thanks unto the LORD, call upon his name, make known his deeds among the people. 9. Sing unto him, sing psalms unto him, talk ye of all his wondrous works.

Psa. 9:11. Sing praises to the LORD, which dwelleth in Zion: declare among the people his doings.

Psa. 18:49. Therefore will I give thanks unto thee, O LORD, among the heathen, and sing praises unto thy name.

Psa. 26:6. I will wash mine hands in innocency: so will I compass thine altar, O LORD: 7. That I may publish with the voice of thanksgiving, and tell of all thy wondrous works.

Psa. 119:27. Make me to understand the way of thy precepts: so shall I [1] talk of thy wondrous works. 172. My tongue shall speak of thy word: for all thy commandments *are* righteousness. [1 R. V. meditate]

Psa. 145:11. They shall speak of the glory of thy kingdom, and talk of thy power; 12. To make known to the sons of men his mighty acts, and the glorious majesty of his kingdom.

Isa. 12:4. And in that day shall ye say, Praise the LORD, call upon his name, declare his doings among the people, make mention that his name is exalted. 5. Sing unto the LORD; for he hath done excellent things: this *is* known in all the earth. 6. Cry out and shout, thou inhabitant of Zion: for great *is* the Holy One of Israel in the midst of thee.

Isa. 32:4. The heart also of the rash shall understand knowledge, and the tongue of the stammerers shall be ready to speak plainly.

Isa. 43:10. Ye *are* my witnesses, saith the LORD, and my servant whom I have chosen: that ye may know and believe me, and understand that I *am* he: before me there was no God formed, neither shall there be after me. chapter 44:8.

Isa. 45:24. Surely, shall *one* say, in the LORD have I righteousness and strength: *even* to him shall *men* come: and all that are incensed against him shall be ashamed.

Jer. 51:10. The LORD hath brought forth our righteousness: come, and let us declare in Zion the work of the LORD our God.

Mark 4:21. And he said unto them, Is a candle brought to be put under a bushel, or under a bed? and not to be set on a candlestick? Matt. 5:15; Luke 8:16.

Mark 5:16. And they that saw *it* told them how it befell to him that was possessed with the devil, and *also* concerning the swine. 19. Howbeit Jesus suffered him not, but saith unto him, Go home to thy friends, and tell them how great things the Lord hath done for thee, and hath had compassion on thee. 20. And he departed, and began to publish in Decapolis how great things Jesus had done for him: and all *men* did marvel.

Luke 8:38. Now the man out of whom the devils were departed besought him that he might be with him: but Jesus sent him away, saying, 39. Return to thine own house, and shew how great things God hath done unto thee. And he went his way, and published throughout the whole city how great things Jesus had done unto him.

Luke 12:8. Also I say unto you, Whosoever shall confess me before men, him shall the Son of man also confess before the angels of God: 9. But he that denieth me before men shall be denied before the angels of God. Matt. 10:32.

Luke 24:48. And ye are witnesses of these things.

John 4:28. The woman then left her waterpot, and went her way into the city, and saith to the men, 29. Come, see a man, which told me all things that ever I did: is not this the Christ? 30. Then they went out of the city, and came unto him. 39. And many of the Samaritans of that city believed on him for the saying of the woman, which testified, He told me all that ever I did. 41. And many more believed because of his own word; 42. And said unto the woman, Now we believe, not because of

thy saying: for we have heard *him* ourselves, and know that this is indeed the Christ, the Saviour of the world.

John 15:27. And ye also shall bear witness, because ye have been with me from the beginning.

Acts 1:8. But ye shall receive power, after that the Holy Ghost is come upon you: and ye shall be witnesses unto me both in Jerusalem, and in all Judæa, and in Samaria, and unto the uttermost part of the earth. 22. Beginning from the baptism of John, unto that same day that he was taken up from us, must one be ordained to be a witness with us of his resurrection.

Rom. 10:9. That if thou shalt confess with thy mouth the Lord Jesus, and shalt believe in thine heart that God hath raised him from the dead, thou shalt be saved. 10. For with the heart man believeth unto righteousness; and with the mouth confession is made unto salvation.

1 Cor. 1:5. That in every thing ye are enriched by him, in all utterance, and *in* all knowledge; 6. Even as the testimony of Christ was confirmed in you:

1 Cor. 12:3. Wherefore I give you to understand, that no man speaking by the Spirit of God calleth Jesus accursed: and *that* no man can say that Jesus is the Lord, but by the Holy Ghost.

1 Cor. 13:1. Though I speak with the tongues of men and of angels, and have not charity, I am become *as* sounding brass, or a tinkling cymbal.

Eph. 5:19. Speaking to yourselves in psalms and hymns and spiritual songs, singing and making melody in your heart to the Lord;

Phil. 3:7. But what things were gain to me, those I counted loss for Christ. 8. Yea doubtless, and I count all things *but* loss for the excellency of the knowledge of Christ Jesus my Lord: for whom I have suffered the loss of all things, and do count them *but* dung, that I may win Christ, 9. And be found in him, not having mine own righteousness, which is of the law, but that which is through the faith of Christ, the righteousness which is of God by faith: 10. That I may know him, and the power of his resurrection, and the fellowship of his sufferings, being made conformable unto his death; 11. If by any means I might attain unto the resurrection of the dead. 12. Not as though I had already attained, either were already perfect: but I follow after, if that I may apprehend that for which also I am apprehended of Christ Jesus. 13. Brethren, I count not myself to have apprehended: but *this* one thing *I do*, forgetting those things which are behind, and reaching forth unto those things which are before, 14. I press toward the mark for the prize of the high calling of God in Christ Jesus.

1 Tim. 6:12. Fight the good fight of faith, lay hold on eternal life, whereunto thou art also called, and hast professed a good pro-

fession before many witnesses. 13. I give thee charge in the sight of God, who quickeneth all things, and *before* Christ Jesus, who before Pontius Pilate witnessed a good confession;

2 Tim. 1:8. Be not thou therefore ashamed of the testimony of our Lord, nor of me his prisoner: but be thou partaker of the afflictions of the gospel according to the power of God;

Heb. 2:3. How shall we escape, if we neglect so great salvation; which at the first began to be spoken by the Lord, and was confirmed unto us by them that heard *him;* 12. I will declare thy name unto my brethren, in the midst of the church will I sing praise unto thee.

1 Pet. 3:15. But sanctify the Lord God in your hearts: and *be* ready always to *give* an answer to every man that asketh you a reason of the hope that is in you with meekness and fear:

1 Pet. 5:1. The elders which are among you I exhort, who am also an elder, and a witness of the sufferings of Christ, and also a partaker of the glory that shall be revealed:

Rev. 12:11. And they overcame him by the blood of the Lamb, and by the word of their testimony; and they loved not their lives unto the death.

See CONFESSION.

RELIGIOUS, EXEMPLIFIED: Job 19:25. For I know *that* my redeemer liveth, and *that* he shall stand at the latter *day* upon the earth: 26. And *though* after my skin *worms* destroy this *body,* yet in my flesh shall I see God: 27. Whom I shall see for myself, and mine eyes shall behold, and not another; *though* my reins be consumed within me.

Psa. 16:5. The LORD *is* the portion of mine inheritance and of my cup: thou maintainest my lot. 6. The lines are fallen unto me in pleasant *places;* yea, I have a goodly heritage. 7. I will bless the LORD, who hath given me counsel: my reins also instruct me in the night seasons. 8. I have set the LORD always before me: because *he is* at my right hand, I shall not be moved. 9. Therefore my heart is glad, and my glory rejoiceth: my flesh also shall rest in hope.

Psa. 18:2. The LORD *is* my rock, and my fortress, and my deliverer; my God, my strength, in whom I will trust; my buckler, and the horn of my salvation, *and* my high tower. 3. I will call upon the LORD, *who is worthy* to be praised: so shall I be saved from mine enemies.

35. Thou hast also given me the shield of thy salvation: and thy right hand hath holden me up, and thy gentleness hath made me great. 36. Thou hast enlarged my steps under me, that my feet did not slip.

Psa. 22:22. I will declare thy name unto my brethren: in the midst of the congregation will I praise thee.

Psa. 23:1. The LORD *is* my shepherd; I shall not want. 2. He maketh me to lie down in green pastures: he leadeth me beside the still waters. 3. He restoreth my soul: he leadeth me in the paths of righteousness for his name's sake. 4. Yea, though I walk through the valley of the shadow of death, I will fear no evil: for thou *art* with me; thy rod and thy staff they comfort me. 5. Thou preparest a table before me in the presence of mine enemies: thou anointest my head with oil; my cup runneth over. 6. Surely goodness and mercy shall follow me all the days of my life: and I will dwell in the house of the LORD for ever.

Psa. 26:12. My foot standeth in an even place: in the congregations will I bless the LORD.

Psa. 27:1. The LORD *is* my light and my salvation; whom shall I fear? the LORD *is* the strength of my life; of whom shall I be afraid? 2. When the wicked, *even* mine enemies and my foes, came upon me to eat up my flesh, they stumbled and fell. 3. Though an host should encamp against me, my heart shall not fear: though war should rise against me, in this *will* I *be* confident. 4. One *thing* have I desired of the LORD, that will I seek after; that I may dwell in the house of the LORD all the days of my life, to behold the beauty of the LORD, and to enquire in his temple. 5. For in the time of trouble he shall hide me in his pavilion: in the secret of his tabernacle shall he hide me; he shall set me up upon a rock. 6. And now shall mine head be lifted up above mine enemies round about me: therefore will I offer in his tabernacle sacrifices of joy; I will sing, yea, I will sing praises unto the LORD. 13. *I had fainted,* unless I had believed to see the goodness of the LORD in the land of the living.

Psa. 28:6. Blessed *be* the LORD, because he hath heard the voice of my supplications. 7. The LORD *is* my strength and my shield: my heart trusted in him, and I am helped: therefore my heart greatly rejoiceth; and with my song will I praise him. 8. The LORD *is* their strength, and he *is* the saving strength of his anointed.

Psa. 30:1. I will extol thee, O LORD; for thou hast lifted me up, and hast not made my foes to rejoice over me. 2. O LORD my God, I cried unto thee, and thou hast healed me. 3. O LORD, thou hast brought up my soul from the grave: thou hast kept me alive, that I should not go down to the pit. 4. Sing unto the LORD, O ye saints of his, and give thanks at the remembrance of his holiness. 5. For his anger *endureth but* a moment; in his favour *is* life: weeping may endure for a night, but joy *cometh* in the morning. 6. And in my prosperity I said, I shall never be moved.

Psa. 34:1. I will bless the LORD at all times: his praise *shall* continually *be* in my mouth. 2. My soul shall make her boast in the LORD: the humble shall hear *thereof,* and be glad. 3. O magnify the LORD with me, and let us exalt his name together. 4. I sought the Lord, and he heard me, and delivered me from all my fears. 8. O taste and see that the Lord *is* good: blessed *is* the man *that* trusteth in him. 9. O fear the Lord, ye his saints: for *there is* no want to them that fear him.

Psa. 35:28. And my tongue shall speak of thy righteousness *and* of thy praise all the day long.

Psa. 40:1. I waited patiently for the Lord; and he inclined unto me, and heard my cry. 2. He brought me up also out of an horrible pit, out of the miry clay, and set my feet upon a rock, *and* established my goings. 3. And he hath put a new song in my mouth, *even* praise unto our God: many shall see *it*, and fear, and shall trust in the Lord. 9. I have preached righteousness in the great congregation: lo, I have not refrained my lips, O Lord, thou knowest.

Psa. 54:7. For he hath delivered me out of all trouble:

Psa. 57:7. My heart is fixed, O God, my heart is fixed: I will sing and give praise. 8. Awake up, my glory; awake, psaltery and harp: I *myself* will awake early. 9. I will praise thee, O Lord, among the people: I will sing unto thee among the nations.

Psa. 62:1. Truly my soul waiteth upon God: from him *cometh* my salvation. 2. He only *is* my rock and my salvation; *he is* my defence; I shall not be greatly moved.

Psa. 66:16. Come *and* hear, all ye that fear God, and I will declare what he hath done for my soul. 17. I cried unto him with my mouth, and he was extolled with my tongue. 18. If I regard iniquity in my heart, the Lord will not hear *me:* 19. *But* verily God hath heard *me;* he hath attended to the voice of my prayer. 20. Blessed *be* God, which hath not turned away my prayer, nor his mercy from me.

Psa. 71:15. My mouth shall shew forth thy righteousness *and* thy salvation all the day; for I know not the numbers *thereof.* 16. I will go in the strength of the Lord God: I will make mention of thy righteousness, *even* of thine only. 17. O God, thou hast taught me from my youth: and hitherto have I declared thy wondrous works. 18. Now also when I am old and greyheaded, O God, forsake me not; until I have shewed thy strength unto *this* generation, *and* thy power to every one *that* is to come. 24. My tongue also shall talk of thy righteousness all the day long: for they are confounded, for they are brought unto shame, that seek my hurt.

Psa. 73:23. Nevertheless I *am* continually with thee: thou hast holden *me* by my right hand. 24. Thou shalt guide me with thy counsel, and afterward receive me *to* glory. 25. Whom have I in heaven *but thee?* and *there is* none upon earth *that* I desire beside thee. 26. My flesh and my heart faileth: *but* God *is* the strength of my heart, and my portion for ever. 28. But *it is* good

for me to draw near to God: I have put my trust in the Lord God, that I may declare all thy works.

Psa. 77:12. I will meditate also of all thy work, and talk of thy doings.

Psa. 89:1. I will sing of the mercies of the Lord for ever: with my mouth will I make known thy faithfulness to all generations.

Psa. 91:2. I will say of the Lord, *He is* my refuge and my fortress: my God; in him will I trust. 3. Surely he shall deliver thee from the snare of the fowler, *and* from the noisome pestilence. 4. He shall cover thee with his feathers, and under his wings shalt thou trust: his truth *shall be thy* shield and buckler. 5. Thou shalt not be afraid for the terror by night; *nor* for the arrow *that* flieth by day; 6. *Nor* for the pestilence *that* walketh in darkness; *nor* for the destruction *that* wasteth at noonday. 7. A thousand shall fall at thy side, and ten thousand at thy right hand; *but* it shall not come nigh thee. 8. Only with thine eyes shalt thou behold and see the reward of the wicked. 9. Because thou hast made the Lord, *which is* my refuge, *even* the most High, thy habitation; 10. There shall no evil befall thee, neither shall any plague come nigh thy dwelling. 11. For he shall give his angels charge over thee, to keep thee in all thy ways. 12. They shall bear thee up in *their* hands, lest thou dash thy foot against a stone. 13. Thou shalt tread upon the lion and adder: the young lion and the dragon shalt thou trample under feet.

Psa. 116:1. I love the Lord, because he hath heard my voice *and* my supplications. 2. Because he hath inclined his ear unto me, therefore will I call upon *him* as long as I live. 3. The sorrows of death compassed me, and the pains of hell gat hold upon me: I found trouble and sorrow. 4. Then called I upon the name of the Lord; O Lord, I beseech thee, deliver my soul. 5. Gracious *is* the Lord, and righteous; yea, our God *is* merciful. 6. The Lord preserveth the simple: I was brought low, and he helped me. 7. Return unto thy rest, O my soul; for the Lord hath dealt bountifully with thee. 8. For thou hast delivered my soul from death, mine eyes from tears, *and* my feet from falling. 9. I will walk before the Lord in the land of the living. 10. I believed, therefore have I spoken: I was greatly afflicted: 11. I said in my haste, All men *are* liars. 12. What shall I render unto the Lord *for* all his benefits toward me? 13. I will take the cup of salvation, and call upon the name of the Lord. 14. I will pay my vows unto the Lord now in the presence of all his people.

Psa. 119:13. With my lips have I declared all the judgments of thy mouth. 26. I have declared my ways, and thou heardest me: teach me thy statutes. 27. Make me to understand the way of thy precepts: so shall I talk of thy wondrous works. 46. I will speak of thy testimonies also before kings, and will not be ashamed. 67. Before I was afflicted I went astray: but now have I kept thy word. 71. *It is* good for me that I have been afflicted; that I might learn thy statutes.

Psa. 145:4. One generation shall praise thy works to another, and shall declare thy mighty acts. 5. I will speak of the glorious honour of thy majesty, and of thy wondrous works. 6. And *men* shall speak of the might of thy terrible acts: and I will declare thy greatness. 7. They shall abundantly utter the memory of thy great goodness, and shall sing of thy righteousness. 10. All thy works shall praise thee, O LORD; and thy saints shall bless thee. 11. They shall speak of the glory of thy kingdom, and talk of thy power; 12. To make known to the sons of men his mighty acts, and the glorious majesty of his kingdom.

Dan. 4:1. Nebuchadnezzar the king, unto all people, nations, and languages, that dwell in all the earth; Peace be multiplied unto you. 2. I thought it good to shew the signs and wonders that the high God hath wrought toward me. 3. How great *are* his signs! and how mighty *are* his wonders! his kingdom *is* an everlasting kingdom, and his dominion *is* from generation to generation.

34. And at the end of the days I Nebuchadnezzar lifted up mine eyes unto heaven, and mine understanding returned unto me, and I blessed the most High, and I praised and honoured him that liveth for ever, whose dominion *is* an everlasting dominion, and his kingdom *is* from generation to generation: 35. And all the inhabitants of the earth *are* reputed as nothing: and he doeth according to his will in the army of heaven, and *among* the inhabitants of the earth: and none can stay his hand, or say unto him, What doest thou? 36. At the same time my reason returned unto me; and for the glory of my kingdom, mine honour and brightness returned unto me; and my counsellors and my lords sought unto me; and I was established in my kingdom, and excellent majesty was added unto me. 37. Now I Nebuchadnezzar praise and extol and honour the King of heaven, all whose works *are* truth, and his ways judgment: and those that walk in pride he is able to abase. *vs.* 1–37.

John 9:17. They say unto the blind man again, What sayest thou of him, that he hath opened thine eyes? He said, He is a prophet. 30. The man answered and said unto them, Why herein is a marvellous thing, that ye know not from whence he is, and *yet* he hath opened mine eyes. 31. Now we know that God heareth not sinners: but if any man be a worshipper of God, and doeth his will, him he heareth. 32. Since the world began was it not heard that any man opened the eyes of one that was born blind. 33. If this man were not of God, he could do nothing.

Acts 2:4. And they were all filled with the Holy Ghost, and began to speak with other tongues, as the the the Spirit gave them utterance. 5. And there were dwelling at Jerusalem Jews, devout men, out of every nation under heaven. 6. Now when this was noised abroad, the multitude came together, and were confounded, because that every man heard them speak in his own language. 7. And they were all amazed and marvelled. saying one to another, Behold, are not all these which speak Galilæans? 8. And how hear we every man in our own tongue. wherein we were born? 9. Parthians, and Medes, and Elamites, and the dwellers in Mesopotamia, and in Judæa, and Cappadocia, in Pontus, and Asia, 10. Phrygia, and Pamphylia, in Egypt, and in the parts of Libya about Cyrene, and strangers of Rome, Jews and proselytes, 11. Cretes and Arabians, we do hear them speak in our tongues the wonderful works of God.

Acts 3:15. And killed the Prince of life, whom God hath raised from the dead; whereof we are witnesses.

Acts 4:18. And they called them, and commanded them not to speak at all nor teach in the name of Jesus. 19. But Peter and John answered and said unto them, Whether it be right in the sight of God to hearken unto you more than unto God, judge ye. 20. For we cannot but speak the things which we have seen and heard.

Acts 5:31. Him hath God exalted with his right hand *to be* a Prince and a Saviour, for to give repentance to Israel, and forgiveness of sins. 32. And we are his witnesses of these things; and *so is* also the Holy Ghost, whom God hath given to them that obey him.

Acts 13:31. And he was seen many days of them which came up with him from Galilee to Jerusalem, who are his witnesses unto the people.

Acts 26:12. Whereupon as I went to Damascus with authority and commission from the chief priest, 13. At midday, O king, I saw in the way a light from heaven, above the brightness of the sun, shining round about me and them which journeyed with me. 14. And when we were all fallen to the earth, I heard a voice speaking unto me, and saying in the Hebrew tongue, Saul, Saul, why persecutest thou me? *it is* hard for thee to kick against the pricks. 15. And I said, Who art thou, Lord? And he said, I am Jesus whom thou persecutest. 16. But rise, and stand upon thy feet: for I have appeared unto thee for this purpose, to make thee a minister and a witness both of these things which thou hast seen, and of those things in the which I will appear unto thee; 17. Delivering thee from the people, and *from* the Gentiles, unto whom now I send thee, 18. To open their eyes, *and* to turn *them* from darkness to light, and *from* the power of Satan unto God, that they may receive forgiveness of sins, and

inheritance among them which are sanctified by faith that is in me. 19. Whereupon, O
king Agrippa, I was not disobedient unto the
heavenly vision: 20. But shewed first unto
them of Damascus, and at Jerusalem, and
throughout all the coasts of Judæa, and *then*
to the Gentiles, that they should repent and
turn to God, and do works meet for repentance. 21. For these causes the Jews caught
me in the temple, and went about to kill
me. 22. Having therefore obtained help of
God, I continue unto this day, witnessing
both to small and great, saying none other
things than those which the prophets and
Moses did say should come: 23. That Christ
should suffer, *and* that he should be the
first that should rise from the dead, and
should shew light unto the people, and to
the Gentiles. Acts 22.

1 Cor. 15:15. Yea, and we are found false
witnesses of God; because we have testified
of God that he raised up Christ: whom he
raised not up, if so be that the dead rise not.

2 Cor. 4:13. We having the same spirit of
faith, according as it is written, I believed,
and therefore have I spoken; we also believe, and therefore speak; 14. Knowing
that he which raised up the Lord Jesus
shall raise up us also by Jesus, and shall present *us* with you.

2 Cor. 5:1. For we know that if our earthly
house of *this* tabernacle were dissolved, we
have a building of God, an house not made
with hands, eternal in the heavens.

Gal. 2:20. I am crucified with Christ: nevertheless I live; yet not I, but Christ liveth
in me: and the life which I now live in the
flesh I live by the faith of the Son of God,
who loved me, and gave himself for me.

Phil. 3:4. Though I might also have confidence in the flesh. If any other man thinketh that he hath whereof he might trust in
the flesh, I more: 5. Circumcised the eighth
day, of the stock of Israel, *of* the tribe of
Benjamin, an Hebrew of the Hebrews; as
touching the law, a Pharisee; 6. Concerning zeal, persecuting the church; touching
the righteousness which is in the law, blameless. 7. But what things were gain to me,
those I counted loss for Christ. 8. Yea
doubtless, and I count all things *but* loss
for the excellency of the knowledge of Christ
Jesus my Lord: for whom I have suffered
the loss of all things, and do count them
but dung, that I may win Christ, 9. And
be found in him, not having mine own
righteousness, which is of the law, but that
which is through the faith of Christ, the
righteousness which is of God by faith: 10.
That I may know him, and the power of
his resurrection, and the fellowship of his
sufferings, being made conformable unto
his death; 11. If by any means I might attain unto the resurrection of the dead. 12.
Not as though I had already attained, either
were already perfect: but I follow after, if
that I may apprehend that for which also I
am apprehended of Christ Jesus. 13. Breth-

ren, I count not myself to have apprehended:
but *this* one thing I *do*, forgetting those
things which are behind, and reaching forth
unto those things which are before, 14. I
press toward the mark for the prize of the
high calling of God in Christ Jesus.

2 Tim. 1:12. For the which cause I also
suffer these things: nevertheless I am not
ashamed: for I know whom I have believed, and am persuaded that he is able to
keep that which I have committed unto
him against that day.

2 Tim. 4:7. I have fought a good fight, I
have finished *my* course, I have kept the
faith: 8. Henceforth there is laid up for
me a crown of righteousness, which the
Lord, the righteous judge, shall give me at
that day: and not to me only, but unto all
them also that love his appearing.

Tit. 1:1. Paul, a servant of God, and an
apostle of Jesus Christ, according to the
faith of God's elect, and the acknowledging
of the truth which is after godliness; 2. In
hope of eternal life, which God, that cannot
lie, promised before the world began;

Tit. 3:3. For we ourselves also were sometimes foolish, disobedient, deceived, serving
divers lusts and pleasures, living in malice
and envy, hateful, *and* hating one another.
4. But after that the kindness and love of
God our Saviour toward man appeared, 5.
Not by works of righteousness which we
have done, but according to his mercy he
saved us, by the washing of regeneration,
and renewing of the Holy Ghost; 6. Which
he shed on us abundantly through Jesus
Christ our Saviour; 7. That being justified
by his grace, we should be made heirs according to the hope of eternal life.

1 Pet. 5:12. I have written briefly, exhorting, and testifying that this is the true
grace of God wherein ye stand.

2 Pet. 1:16. For we have not followed cunningly devised fables, when we made known
unto you the power and coming of our
Lord Jesus Christ, but were eyewitnesses
of his majesty.

1 John 1:1. That which was from the beginning, which we have heard, which we
have seen with our eyes, which we have
looked upon, and our hands have handled,
of the Word of life; 2. (For the life was
manifested, and we have seen *it*, and bear
witness, and shew unto you that eternal life,
which was with the Father, and was manifested unto us;) 3. That which we have
seen and heard declare we unto you, that
ye also may have fellowship with us: and
truly our fellowship *is* with the Father,
and with his Son Jesus Christ. 4. And
these things write we unto you, that your
joy may be full.

TETRARCH, a Roman ruler, Matt. 14:1.

THADDÆUS, one of the twelve apostles, Matt. 10:3; Mark 3:18.

THAHASH, son of Nahor, Gen. 22:24.

THAMAH, called also, TAMAH. One of
the Nethinim, Ezra 2:53; Neh. 7:55.

THAMAR. See TAMAR, 1.

THANKFULNESS. Jesus set an example of, Matt. 11:25; 26:27; John 11:41. The heavenly host engage in, Rev. 4:9; 7:11, 12; 11:16,17. Commanded, Psa. 50:14.

Should be offered to God, Psa. 50:14; to Christ, 1 Tim 1:12; through Christ, Rom. 1:8; Col. 3:17; Heb. 13:15; in the name of Christ, Eph. 5:20; in behalf of ministers, 2 Cor. 1:11; in private worship, Dan. 6:10; in public worship, Psa. 35:18; in everything, 1 Thess. 5:18; upon the completion of great undertakings, Neh. 12:31,40; before taking food, John 6:11; Acts 27:35; always, Eph. 1:16; 5:20; 1 Thess. 1:2; as the remembrance of God's holiness, Psa. 30:4; 97:12; for the goodness and mercy of God, Psa. 106:1; 107:1; 136:1-3; for the gift of Christ, 2 Cor. 9:15; for Christ's power and reign, Rev. 11:17; for the reception and effectual working of the word of God in others, 1 Thess. 2:13; for deliverance through Christ, from indwelling sin, Rom. 7:23-25; for victory over death and the grave, 1 Cor. 15:57; for wisdom and might, Dan.2:23; for the triumph of the gospel, 2 Cor. 2:14; for the conversion of others, Rom. 6:17; for faith exhibited by others, Rom. 1:8; 2 Thess. 1:3; for love exhibited by others, 2 Thess. 1:3; for the grace bestowed on others, 1 Cor. 1:4; Phil. 1:3-5; Col. 1:3-6; for the zeal exhibited by others, 2 Cor. 8:16; for nearness of God's presence, Psa. 75:1; for appointment to the ministry, 1 Tim. 1:12; for willingness to offer our property for God's service, 1 Chr. 29:6-14; for the supply of our bodily wants, Rom. 14:6,7; 1 Tim. 4:3,4; for all men, 1 Tim. 2:1; for all things, 2 Cor. 9:11; Eph. 5:20.

Should be accompanied by intercession for others, 1 Tim. 2:1; 2 Tim. 1:3; Philem. 4. Should always accompany prayer, Neh. 11:17; Phil. 4:6; Col. 4:2. Should always accompany praise, Psa. 92:1; Heb. 13:15. Expressed in psalms, 1 Chr. 16:7. Ministers appointed to offer, in public, 1 Chr. 16:4,7; 23:30; 2 Chr. 31:2.

Saints exhorted to, Psa. 105:1; Col. 3:15; resolve to offer, Psa. 18:49; 30:12; habitually offer, Dan. 6:10; offer sacrifices of, Psa. 116: 17; abound in the faith with, Col. 2:7; magnify God by, Psa. 69:30; come before God with, Psa. 95:2; should enter God's gates with, Psa. 100:4. Of hypocrites, full of boasting, Luke 18:11. The wicked averse to, Rom. 1:21.

EXEMPLIFIED: David, 1 Chr. 29:13. Levites, 2 Chr. 5:12,13. Daniel, Dan. 2:23. Jonah, Jonah 2:9. Simeon, Luke 2:28. Anna, Luke 2:38. Paul, Acts 28:15.—*Bible Text-Book.*

ENJOINED: Gen. 35:1. And God said unto Jacob, Arise, go up to Beth-el, and dwell there: and make there an altar unto God, that appeared unto thee when thou fleddest from the face of Esau thy brother.

Ex. 12:14. And this day shall be unto you for a memorial; and ye shall keep it a feast to the LORD throughout your generations;

ye shall keep it a feast by an ordinance for ever. 17. And ye shall observe *the feast of* unleavened bread; for in this selfsame day have I brought your armies out of the land of Egypt: therefore shall ye observe this day in your generations by an ordinance for ever. 42. It *is* a night to be much observed unto the LORD for bringing them out from the land of Egypt: this *is* that night of the LORD to be observed of all the children of Israel in their generations.

Ex. 13:3. And Moses said unto the people, Remember this day, in which ye came out from Egypt, out of the house of bondage: for by strength of hand the LORD brought you out from this *place:* there shall no leavened bread be eaten. 8. And thou shalt shew thy son in that day, saying, *This is done* because of that *which* the LORD did unto me when I came forth out of Egypt. 9. And it shall be for a sign unto thee upon thine hand, and for a memorial between thine eyes, that the LORD's law may be in thy mouth: for with a strong hand hath the LORD brought thee out of Egypt. 10. Thou shalt therefore keep this ordinance in his season from year to year. 14. And it shall be when thy son asketh thee in time to come, saying, What *is* this? that thou shalt say unto him, By strength of hand the LORD brought us out from Egypt, from the house of bondage: 15. And it came to pass, when Pharaoh would hardly let us go, that the LORD slew all the firstborn in the land of Egypt, both the firstborn of man, and the firstborn of beast: therefore I sacrifice to the LORD all that openeth the matrix, being males; but all the firstborn of my children I redeem. 16. And it shall be for a token upon thine hand, and for frontlets between thine eyes: for by strength of hand the LORD brought us forth out of Egypt.

Ex. 16:32. And Moses said, This *is* the thing which the LORD commandeth, Fill an omer of it to be kept for your generations; that they may see the bread wherewith I have fed you in the wilderness, when I brought you forth from the land of Egypt.

Ex. 34:26. The first of the firstfruits of thy land thou shalt bring unto the house of the LORD thy God.

Lev. 19:24. But in the fourth year all the fruit thereof shall be holy to praise the LORD *withal.*

Lev. 23:14. And ye shall eat neither bread, nor parched corn, nor green ears, until the selfsame day that ye have brought an offering unto your God: *it shall be* a statute for ever throughout your generations in all your dwellings.

Deut. 12:18. But thou must eat them before the LORD thy God in the place which the LORD thy God shall choose, thou, and thy son, and thy daughter, and thy manservant, and thy maidservant, and the Levite that *is* within thy gates: and thou shalt rejoice before the LORD thy God in all that thou puttest thine hands unto.

Deut. 16:9. Seven weeks shalt thou number unto thee: begin to number the seven weeks from *such time as* thou beginnest *to put* the sickle to the corn. 10. And thou shalt keep the feast of weeks unto the LORD thy God with a tribute of a freewill offering of thine hand, which thou shalt give *unto the LORD thy God*, according as the LORD thy God hath blessed thee: 11. And thou shalt rejoice before the LORD thy God, thou, and thy son, and thy daughter, and thy manservant, and thy maidservant, and the Levite that *is* within thy gates, and the stranger, and the fatherless, and the widow, that *are* among you, in the place which the LORD thy God hath chosen to place his name there. 12. And thou shalt remember that thou wast a bondman in Egypt: and thou shalt observe and do these statutes. 13. Thou shalt observe the feast of tabernacles seven days, after that thou hast gathered in thy corn and thy wine: 14. And thou shalt rejoice in thy feast, thou, and thy son, and thy daughter, and thy manservant, and thy maidservant, and the Levite, the stranger, and the fatherless, and the widow, that *are* within thy gates. 15. Seven days shalt thou keep a solemn feast unto the LORD thy God in the place which the LORD shall choose: because the LORD thy God shall bless thee in all thine increase, and in all the works of thine hands, therefore thou shalt surely rejoice.

Deut. 26:10. I have brought the firstfruits of the land, which thou, O LORD, hast given me. And thou shalt set it before the LORD thy God, and worship before the LORD thy God:

Judg. 5:11. *They that are delivered* from the noise of archers in the places of drawing water, there shall they rehearse the righteous acts of the LORD, *even* the righteous acts *toward the inhabitants* of his villages in Israel: then shall the people of the LORD go down to the gates.

Psa. 48:11. Let mount Zion rejoice, let the daughters of Judah be glad, because of thy judgments.

Psa. 50:14. Offer unto God thanksgiving; and pay thy vows unto the most High: 15. And call upon me in the day of trouble: I will deliver thee, and thou shalt glorify me.

Psa. 98:1. O sing unto the LORD a new song; for he hath done marvellous things: his right hand, and his holy arm, hath gotten him the victory.

Psa. 105:1. O give thanks unto the LORD; call upon his name: make known his deeds among the people. 5. Remember his marvellous works that he hath done; his wonders, and the judgments of his mouth; 42. For he remembered his holy promise, *and* Abraham his servant. 43. And he brought forth his people with joy, *and* his chosen with gladness: 44. And gave them the

lands of the heathen: and they inherited the labour of the people; 45. That they might observe his statutes, and keep his laws. Praise ye the LORD. *vs.* 1–45.

Psa. 106:1. Praise ye the LORD. O give thanks unto the LORD; for *he is* good: for his mercy *endureth* for ever.

Psa. 107:1. O give thanks unto the LORD, for *he is* good: for his mercy *endureth* for ever. 2. Let the redeemed of the LORD say *so*, whom he hath redeemed from the hand of the enemy; 15. Oh that *men* would praise the LORD *for* his goodness, and *for* his wonderful works to the children of men! 22. And let them sacrifice the sacrifices of thanksgiving, and declare his works with rejoicing. 42. The righteous shall see *it*, and rejoice: and all iniquity shall stop her mouth. 43. Whoso *is* wise, and will observe these *things*, even they shall understand the lovingkindness of the LORD.

Psa. 118:1. O give thanks unto the LORD; for *he is* good: because his mercy *endureth* for ever. 4. Let them now that fear the LORD say, that his mercy *endureth* for ever.

Prov. 3:9. Honour the LORD with thy substance, and with the firstfruits of all thine increase: 10. So shall thy barns be filled with plenty, and thy presses shall burst out with new wine.

Eccl. 7:14. In the day of prosperity be joyful, but in the day of adversity consider: God also hath set the one over against the other, to the end that man should find nothing after him.

Isa. 48:20. Go ye forth of Babylon, flee ye from the Chaldeans, with a voice of singing declare ye, tell this, utter it *even* to the end of the earth; say ye, The LORD hath redeemed his servant Jacob.

Joel 2:26. And ye shall eat in plenty, and be satisfied, and praise the name of the LORD your God, that hath dealt wondrously with you: and my people shall never be ashamed.

Rom. 2:4. Or despisest thou the riches of his goodness and forbearance and longsuffering; not knowing that the goodness of God leadeth thee to repentance?

Rom. 15:27. For if the Gentiles have been made partakers of their spiritual things, their duty is also to minister unto them in carnal things.

Eph. 5:4. Neither filthiness, nor foolish talking, nor jesting, which are not convenient: but rather giving of thanks. 19. Speaking to yourselves in psalms and hymns and spiritual songs, singing and making melody in your heart to the Lord; 20. Giving thanks always for all things unto God and the Father in the name of our Lord Jesus Christ;

Phil. 4:6. Be careful for nothing; but in every thing by prayer and supplication with thanksgiving let your requests be made known unto God.

Col. 1:12. Giving thanks unto the Father, which hath made us meet to be partakers of the inheritance of the saints in light:

Col. 2:7. Rooted and built up in him, and stablished in the faith, as ye have been taught, abounding therein with thanksgiving.

Col. 3:15. And let the peace of God rule in your hearts, to the which also ye are called in one body; and be ye thankful. 16. Let the word of Christ dwell in you richly in all wisdom; teaching and admonishing one another in psalms and hymns and spiritual songs, singing with grace in your hearts to the Lord. 17. And whatsoever ye do in word or deed, *do* all in the name of the Lord Jesus, giving thanks to God and the Father by him.

Col. 4:2. Continue in prayer, and watch in the same with thanksgiving;

1 Thess. 5:18. In every thing give thanks: for this is the will of God in Christ Jesus concerning you.

1 Tim. 2:1. I exhort therefore, that, first of all, supplications, prayers, intercessions, *and* giving of thanks, be made for all men;

1 Tim. 4:3. Forbidding to marry, *and commanding* to abstain from meats, which God hath created to be received with thanksgiving of them which believe and know the truth. 4. For every creature of God *is* good, and nothing to be refused, if it be received with thanksgiving: 5. For it is sanctified by the word of God and prayer.

Heb. 13:15. By him therefore let us offer the sacrifice of praise to God continually, that is, the fruit of *our* lips giving thanks to his name.

Jas. 1:9. Let the brother of low degree rejoice in that he is exalted:

See JOY; PRAISE; PSALMS.

EXEMPLIFIED: Gen. 32:10. I am not worthy of the least of all the mercies, and of all the truth, which thou hast shewed unto thy servant; for with my staff I passed over this Jordan; and now I am become two bands.

Gen. 48:11. And Israel said unto Joseph, I had not thought to see thy face: and, lo, God hath shewed me also thy seed. 15. And he blessed Joseph, and said, God, before whom my fathers Abraham and Isaac did walk, the God which fed me all my life long unto this day, 16. The Angel which redeemed me from all evil, bless the lads; and let my name be named on them, and the name of my fathers Abraham and Isaac: and let them grow into a multitude in the midst of the earth.

Ex. 15:1. Then sang Moses and the children of Israel this song unto the LORD, and spake, saying, I will sing unto the LORD, for he hath triumphed gloriously: the horse and his rider hath he thrown into the sea. 2. The LORD *is* my strength and song, and he is become my salvation: he *is* my God, and I will prepare him an habitation; my father's God, and I will exalt him. 3. The LORD *is*

a man of war: the LORD *is* his name. 4. Pharaoh's chariots and his host hath he cast into the sea: his chosen captains also are drowned in the Red sea. 5. The depths have covered them: they sank into the bottom as a stone. 6. Thy right hand, O LORD, is become glorious in power: thy right hand, O LORD, hath dashed in pieces the enemy. 7. And in the greatness of thine excellency thou hast overthrown them that rose up against thee: thou sentest forth thy wrath, *which* consumed them as stubble. 8. And with the blast of thy nostrils the waters were gathered together, the floods stood upright as an heap, *and* the depths were congealed in the heart of the sea. 9. The enemy said, I will pursue, I will overtake, I will divide the spoil; my lust shall be satisfied upon them; I will draw my sword, my hand shall destroy them. 10. Thou didst blow with thy wind, the sea covered them: they sank as lead in the mighty waters. 11. Who *is* like unto thee, O LORD, among the gods? who *is* like thee, glorious in holiness, fearful *in* praises, doing wonders? 12. Thou stretchedst out thy right hand, the earth swallowed them. 13. Thou in thy mercy hast led forth the people *which* thou hast redeemed: thou hast guided *them* in thy strength unto thy holy habitation. 14. The people shall hear, *and* be afraid: sorrow shall take hold on the inhabitants of Palestina. 15. Then the dukes of Edom shall be amazed; the mighty men of Moab, trembling shall take hold upon them; all the inhabitants of Canaan shall melt away. 16. Fear and dread shall fall upon them; by the greatness of thine arm they shall be *as* still as a stone; till thy people pass over, O LORD, till the people pass over, *which* thou hast purchased. 17. Thou shalt bring them in, and plant them in the mountain of thine inheritance, *in* the place, O LORD, *which* thou hast made for thee to dwell in, *in* the Sanctuary, O Lord, *which* thy hands have established. 18. The LORD shall reign for ever and ever. 19. For the horse of Pharaoh went in with his chariots and with his horsemen into the sea, and the LORD brought again the waters of the sea upon them; but the children of Israel went on dry *land* in the midst of the sea. 20. And Miriam the prophetess, the sister of Aaron, took a timbrel in her hand; and all the women went out after her with timbrels and with dances. 21. And Miriam answered them, Sing ye to the LORD, for he hath triumphed gloriously; the horse and his rider hath he thrown into the sea.

Num. 21:17. Then Israel sang this song, Spring up, O well; sing ye unto it: 18. The princes digged the well, the nobles of the people digged it, by *the direction of* the lawgiver, with their staves.

1 Kin. 8:56. Blessed *be* the LORD, that hath given rest unto his people Israel, according to all that he promised: there hath not failed one word of all his good promise,

1 Chr. 29:14. All things *come* of thee, and of thine own have we given thee.

Ezra 7:27. Blessed *be* the LORD God of our fathers, which hath put *such a thing* as this in the king's heart, to beautify the house of the LORD, which *is* in Jerusalem.

Psa. 9:1. I will praise *thee*, O LORD, with my whole heart; I will shew forth all thy marvellous works. 2. I will be glad and rejoice in thee: I will sing praise to thy name, O thou most High. 4. For thou hast maintained my right and my cause; thou satest in the throne judging right.

Psa. 13:6. I will sing unto the LORD, because he hath dealt bountifully with me.

Psa. 22:23. Ye that fear the LORD, praise him; all ye the seed of Jacob, glorify him; and fear him, all ye the seed of Israel. 24. For he hath not despised nor abhorred the affliction of the afflicted; neither hath he hid his face from him; but when he cried unto him, he heard. 25. My praise *shall be* of thee in the great congregation: I will pay my vows before them that fear him.

Psa. 26:7. That I may publish with the voice of thanksgiving, and tell of all thy wondrous works.

Psa. 28:7. The LORD *is* my strength and my shield; my heart trusted in him, and I am helped : therefore my heart greatly rejoiceth; and with my song will I praise him.

Psa. 30:1. I will extol thee, O LORD; for thou hast lifted me up, and hast not made my foes to rejoice over me. 3. O LORD, thou hast brought up my soul from the grave : thou hast kept me alive, that I should not go down to the pit. 11. Thou hast turned for me my mourning into dancing : thou hast put off my sackcloth, and girded me with gladness; 12. To the end that *my* glory may sing praise to thee, and not be silent. O LORD my God, I will give thanks unto thee for ever.

Psa. 31:7. I will be glad and rejoice in thy mercy: for thou hast considered my trouble; thou hast known my soul in adversities; 21. Blessed *be* the LORD : for he hath shewed me his marvellous kindness in a strong city.

Psa. 35:9. My soul shall be joyful in the LORD : it shall rejoice in his salvation. 10. All my bones shall say, LORD, who *is* like unto thee, which deliverest the poor from him that is too strong for him, yea, the poor and the needy from him that spoileth him ? 18. I will give thee thanks in the great congregation : I will praise thee among much people.

Psa. 40:2. He brought me up also out of an horrible pit, out of the miry clay, and set my feet upon a rock, *and* established my goings. 3. And he hath put a new song in my mouth, *even* praise unto our God : many shall see *it*, and fear, and shall trust in the LORD. 5. Many, O LORD my God, *are* thy wonderful works *which* thou hast done, and thy thoughts *which are* to us-ward : they cannot be reckoned up in

order unto thee: *if* I would declare and speak *of them*, they are more than can be numbered.

Psa. 41:11. By this I know that thou favourest me, because mine enemy doth not triumph over me. 12. And as for me, thou upholdest me in mine integrity, and settest me before thy face for ever.

Psa. 44:7. But thou hast saved us from our enemies, and hast put them to shame that hated us. 8. In God we boast all the day long, and praise thy name for ever.

Psa. 54:6. I will freely sacrifice unto thee : I will praise thy name, O LORD; for *it is* good. 7. For he hath delivered me out of all trouble :

Psa. 56:12. Thy vows *are* upon me, O God: I will render praises unto thee. 13. For thou hast delivered my soul from death :

Psa. 59:16. I will sing of thy power ; yea, I will sing aloud of thy mercy in the morning : for thou hast been my defence and refuge in the day of my trouble. 17. Unto thee, O my strength, will I sing: for God *is* my defence, *and* the God of my mercy.

Psa. 66:8. O bless our God, ye people, and make the voice of his praise to be heard : 9. Which holdeth our soul in life, and suffereth not our feet to be moved. 12. Thou broughtest us out into a wealthy *place*. 13. I will go into thy house with burnt offerings: I will pay thee my vows, 14. Which my lips have uttered, and my mouth hath spoken, when I was in trouble. 15. I will offer unto thee burnt sacrifices of fatlings, with the incense of rams; I will offer bullocks with goats. 16. Come *and* hear, all ye that fear God, and I will declare what he hath done for my soul. 20. Blessed *be* God, which hath not turned away my prayer, nor his mercy from me.

Psa. 68:19. Blessed *be* the Lord, *who* daily loadeth us *with benefits, even* the God of our salvation.

Psa. 71:15. My mouth shall shew forth thy righteousness *and* thy salvation all the day; for I know not the numbers *thereof*. 23. My lips shall greatly rejoice when I sing unto thee; and my soul, which thou hast redeemed. 24. My tongue also shall talk of thy righteousness all the day long :

Psa. 79:13. We thy people and sheep of thy pasture will give thee thanks for ever : we will shew forth thy praise to all generations.

Psa. 89:1. I will sing of the mercies of the LORD for ever: with my mouth will I make known thy faithfulness to all generations.

Psa. 92:1. *It is a* good *thing* to give thanks unto the LORD, and to sing praises unto thy name, O most High : 2. To shew forth thy lovingkindness in the morning, and thy faithfulness every night. 4. For thou, LORD, hast made me glad through thy work : I will triumph in the works of thy hands.

Psa. 98:1. O sing unto the LORD a new

song; for he hath done marvellous things: his right hand, and his holy arm, hath gotten him the victory.

Psa. 100:4. Enter into his gates with thanksgiving, *and* into his courts with praise: be thankful unto him, *and* bless his name.

Psa. 102:18. This shall be written for the generation to come: and the people which shall be created shall praise the LORD. 19. For he hath looked down from the height of his sanctuary; from heaven did the LORD behold the earth; 20. To hear the groaning of the prisoner; to loose those that are appointed to death;

Psa 104:1. Bless the LORD. O my soul. O LORD my God, thou art very great; thou art clothed with honour and majesty.

Psa. 116:12. What shall I render unto the LORD *for* all his benefits toward me? 13. I will take the cup of salvation, and call upon the name of the LORD. 14. I will pay my vows unto the LORD now in the presence of all his people. 17. I will offer to thee the sacrifice of thanksgiving, and will call upon the name of the LORD.

Psa. 119:65. Thou hast dealt well with thy servant, O LORD, according unto thy word. 108. Accept, I beseech thee, the freewill offerings of my mouth, O LORD, and teach me thy judgments.

Psa. 136:1. O give thanks unto the LORD; for *he is* good: for his mercy *endureth* for ever. 2. O give thanks unto the God of gods: for his mercy *endureth* for ever. 3. O give thanks to the Lord of lords: for his mercy *endureth* for ever. 4. To him who alone doeth great wonders: for his mercy *endureth* for ever. 5. To him that by wisdom made the heavens: for his mercy *endureth* for ever. 6. To him that stretched out the earth above the waters: for his mercy *endureth* for ever. 7. To him that made great lights: for his mercy *endureth* for ever: 8. The sun to rule by day: for his mercy *endureth* for ever. 9. The moon and stars to rule by night: for his mercy *endureth* for ever. 10. To him that smote Egypt in their firstborn: for his mercy *endureth* for ever: 11. And brought out Israel from among them: for his mercy *endureth* for ever. 12. With a strong hand, and with a stretched out arm: for his mercy *endureth* for ever. 13. To him which divided the Red sea into parts: for his mercy *endureth* for ever: 14. And made Israel to pass through the midst of it: for his mercy *endureth* for ever: 15. But overthrew Pharaoh and his hosts in the Red sea: for his mercy *endureth* for ever. 16. To him which led his people through the wilderness: for his mercy *endureth* for ever. 17. To him which smote great kings: for his mercy *endureth* for ever: 18. And slew famous kings: for his mercy *endureth* for ever: 19. Sihon king of the Amorites: for his mercy *endureth* for ever: 20. And Og the king of Bashan: for his

mercy *endureth* for ever: 21. And gave their land for an heritage: for his mercy *endureth* for ever: 22. *Even* an heritage unto Israel his servant: for his mercy *endureth* for ever. 23. Who remembered us in our low estate: for his mercy *endureth* for ever: 24. And hath redeemed us from our enemies: for his mercy *endureth* for ever. 25. Who giveth food to all flesh: for his mercy *endureth* for ever. 26. O give thanks unto the God of heaven: for his mercy *endureth* for ever.

Isa. 63:7. I will mention the lovingkindnesses of the LORD, *and* the praises of the LORD, according to all that the LORD hath bestowed on us, and the great goodness toward the house of Israel, which he hath bestowed on them according to his mercies, and according to the multitude of his lovingkindnesses.

Dan. 2:23. I thank thee, and praise thee, O thou God of my fathers, who hast given me wisdom and might, and hast made known unto me now what we desired of thee: for thou hast *now* made known unto us the king's matter.

Dan. 4:2. I thought it good to shew the signs and wonders that the high God hath wrought toward me. 34. And at the end of the days I Nebuchadnezzar lifted up mine eyes unto heaven, and mine understanding returned unto me, and I blessed the most High, and I praised and honoured him that liveth for ever, whose dominion *is* an everlasting dominion, and his kingdom *is* from generation to generation:

Dan. 6:22. My God hath sent his angel, and hath shut the lions' mouths, that they have not hurt me:

Acts 2:46. They, continuing daily with one accord in the temple, and breaking bread from house to house, did eat their meat with gladness and singleness of heart, 47. Praising God, and having favour with all the people.

Acts 28:15. And from thence, when the brethren heard of us, they came to meet us as far as Appii forum, and The three taverns: whom when Paul saw, he thanked God, and took courage.

Rom. 14:6. He that eateth, eateth to the Lord, for he giveth God thanks; and he that eateth not, to the Lord he eateth not, and giveth God thanks.

Col. 1:3. We give thanks to God and the Father of our Lord Jesus Christ, praying always for you,

1 Tim. 1:12. I thank Christ Jesus our Lord, who hath enabled me, for that he counted me faithful, putting me into the ministry;

See JOY; PRAISE; PSALMS; WORSHIP.

OF MAN TO MAN. The Israelites, to Joshua, Josh. 19:49,50. The spies, to Rahab, Josh. 6:22-25. Saul, to the Kenites, 1 Sam. 15:6. Naomi, to Boaz, Ruth 2:19,20. David, to the men of Jabesh-gilead, 2 Sam. 2:5-7; to Hanun, 2 Sam. 10:2; to Barzillai, 1 Kin.

2:7. Paul, to Phebe, Rom. 16:1–4; to Ones-iphorus, 2 Tim. 1:16–18. The people of Melita, to Paul, Acts 28:10.

TO GOD: Instances of: Of Eve, Gen. 4:1,25. Of Noah, Gen. 8:20. Of Melchizedek, Gen. 14:20. Of Lot, Gen. 19:19. Of Sarah, Gen. 21:6,7. Of Abraham, Gen. 12:7; 13:4. Of Abraham's servant, Gen. 24:27,35. Of Isaac, Gen. 26:22. Of Leah, Gen. 29:32–35. Of Rachel, Gen. 30:6. Of Jacob, Gen. 31:42; 35:3,7. Of Joseph, Gen. 41:51,52. Of Moses, Ex. 15:1–19. Of Miriam, Ex. 15:20–22. Of Jethro, Ex. 18:10. Of Israel, Ex. 4:31; Num. 21:17; 31:49–54; 1 Chr. 29:22. Of Deborah, Judg. 5. Of Hannah, 1 Sam. 1:27,28. Of Samuel, 1 Sam. 7:12. Of David, 2 Sam. 6:21. See Psalms, above. Of the Queen of Sheba, 1 Kin. 10:9. Of Hiram, 2 Chr. 2:12. Of Jehoshaphat's army, 2 Chr. 20:27,28. Of the Levites, Neh. 9:4–38. Of the Jews, Neh. 12:43. Of the mariners, Jonah 1:16. Of the shepherds, Luke 2:20. Those whom Jesus healed: The man with palsy, Luke 5:25; the healed demoniac, Luke 8:39; the woman bent with infirmity, Luke 13:13; one of the ten lepers whom Jesus healed, Luke 17:15,16; blind Bartimæus, Luke 18:43; Mark 10:46–52; the centurion for his son, John 4:53. The lame man healed by Peter, Acts 3:8. Before taking food, by Jesus, Matt. 14:19; Mark 8:6,7; Paul, Acts, 27:35.

See Praise; Prayer Before Taking Food.

THANK OFFERINGS. See Offerings.

THANKSGIVING. See Praise; Thankfulness.

THARA. See Tarah.

THARSHISH. 1. Son of Bilhan, 1 Chr. 7:10. [R. V., Tarshish.]

2. See Tarshish, 2.

THEATER, Acts 19:29,31.

THEBEZ, a city, in besieging which Abimelech was slain, Judg. 9:50–56; 2 Sam. 11:21.

THEFT AND THIEVES. Ex. 20:15. Thou shalt not steal. Deut. 5:19; Matt. 19:18; Luke 18:20; Rom. 13:9.

Ex. 21:16. And he that stealeth a man, and selleth him, or if he be found in his hand, he shall surely be put to death.

Ex. 22:1. If a man shall steal an ox, or a sheep, and kill it, or sell it; he shall restore five oxen for an ox, and four sheep for a sheep. 2. If a thief be found breaking up, and be smitten that he die, *there shall* no blood *be shed* for him. 3. If the sun be risen upon him, *there shall be* blood *shed* for him; *for* he should make full restitution; if he have nothing, then he shall be sold for his theft. 4. If the theft be certainly found in his hand alive, whether it be ox, or ass, or sheep; he shall restore double. 10. If a man deliver unto his neighbour an ass, or an ox, or a sheep, or any beast, to keep; and it die, or be hurt, or driven away, no man seeing *it:* 11. *Then* shall an oath of the Lord be between them

both, that he hath not put his hand unto his neighbour's goods; and the owner of it shall accept *thereof*, and he shall not make *it* good. 12. And if it be stolen from him, he shall make restitution unto the owner thereof. 13. If it be torn in pieces, *then* let him bring it *for* witness, *and* he shall not make good that which was torn. 14. And if a man borrow *ought* of his neighbour, and it be hurt, or die, the owner thereof *being* not with it, he shall surely make *it* good. 15. *But* if the owner thereof *be* with it, he shall not make *it* good; if it *be* an hired *thing*, it came for his hire.

Lev. 6:2. If a soul sin, and commit a trespass against the Lord, and lie unto his neighbour in that which was delivered him to keep, or in fellowship, or in a thing taken away by violence, or hath deceived his neighbour; 3. Or have found that which was lost, and lieth concerning it, and sweareth falsely; in any of all these that a man doeth, sinning therein: 4. Then it shall be, because he hath sinned, and is guilty, that he shall restore that which he took violently away, or the thing which he hath deceitfully gotten, or that which was delivered him to keep, or the lost thing which he found, 5. Or all that about which he hath sworn falsely; he shall even restore it in the principal, and shall add the fifth part more thereto, *and* give it unto him to whom it appertaineth, in the day of his trespass offering. 6. And he shall bring his trespass offering unto the Lord, a ram without blemish out of the flock, with thy estimation, for a trespass offering, unto the priest: 7. And the priest shall make an atonement for him before the Lord: and it shall be forgiven him for any thing of all that he hath done in trespassing therein.

Lev. 19:11. Ye shall not steal, neither deal falsely, 13. Thou shalt not defraud thy neighbour, neither rob *him:*

Deut. 23:24. When thou comest into thy neighbour's vineyard, then thou mayest eat grapes thy fill at thine own pleasure; but thou shalt not put *any* in thy vessel. 25. When thou comest into the standing corn of thy neighbour, then thou mayest pluck the ears with thine hand; but thou shalt not move a sickle unto thy neighbour's standing corn.

Psa. 50:18. When thou sawest a thief, then thou consentedst with him,

Psa. 62:10. Trust not in oppression, and become not vain in robbery:

Psa. 119:61. The bands of the wicked have robbed me:

Prov. 6:30. *Men* do not despise a thief, if he steal to satisfy his soul when he is hungry; 31. But *if* he be found, he shall restore sevenfold; he shall give all the substance of his house.

Prov. 21:7. The robbery of the wicked shall destroy them;

Isa. 61:8. For I the Lord love judgment, I hate robbery for burnt offering;

Jer. 2:26. As the thief is ashamed when he is found, so is the house of Israel ashamed;

Jer. 7:9. Will ye steal, murder, and commit adultery, and swear falsely, and burn incense unto Baal, and walk after other gods whom ye know not; 10. And come and stand before me in this house, which is called by my name, and say, We are delivered to do all these abominations?

Ezek. 22:29. The people of the land have used oppression, and exercised robbery, and have vexed the poor and needy: yea, they have oppressed the stranger wrongfully.

Hos. 4:1. Hear the word of the Lord, ye children of Israel: for the Lord hath a controversy with the inhabitants of the land, because *there is* no truth, nor mercy, nor knowledge of God in the land. 2. By swearing, and lying, and killing, and stealing, and committing adultery, they break out, and blood toucheth blood.

Nah. 3:1. Woe to the bloody city! it *is* all full of lies *and* robbery;

Zech. 5:3. Then said he unto me, This *is* the curse that goeth forth over the face of the whole earth: for every one that stealeth shall be cut off *as* on this side according to it: and every one that sweareth shall be cut off *as* on that side according to it.

Matt. 6:19. Lay not up for yourselves treasures upon earth, where moth and rust doth corrupt, and where thieves break through and steal: 20. But lay up for yourselves treasures in heaven, where neither moth nor rust doth corrupt, and where thieves do not break through nor steal:

Matt. 15:19. For out of the heart proceed evil thoughts, murders, adulteries, fornications, thefts, Mark 7:21,22.

Mark 11:17. Is it not written, My house shall be called of all nations the house of prayer? but ye have made it a den of thieves. Matt. 21:13; Luke 19:45,46.

Mark 15:27. And with him they crucify two thieves; the one on his right hand, and the other on his left. Matt. 27:38,44.

John 10:1. Verily, verily, I say unto you, He that entereth not by the door into the sheepfold, but climbeth up some other way, the same is a thief and a robber.

Rom. 2:21. Thou therefore which teachest another, teachest thou not thyself? thou that preachest a man should not steal, dost thou steal?

1 Cor. 6:8. Nay, ye do wrong, and defraud, and that *your* brethren. 10. Nor thieves, nor covetous, . . . nor extortioners, shall inherit the kingdom of God.

Eph. 4:28. Let him that stole steal no more: but rather let him labour, working with *his* hands the thing which is good, that he may have to give to him that needeth.

Tit. 2:10. Not purloining, but shewing all good fidelity; that they may adorn the doctrine of God our Saviour in all things.

1 Pet. 4:15. But let none of you suffer as a murderer, or *as* a thief, or *as* an evil-doer, or as a busybody in other men's matters.

Rev. 3:3. If therefore thou shalt not watch, I will come on thee as a thief, and thou shalt not know what hour I will come upon thee.

Rev. 9:21. Neither repented they of their murders, nor of their sorceries, nor of their fornication, nor of their thefts.

See Dishonesty.

FIGURATIVE: Obad. 5.

INSTANCES OF: By Rachel, of the household gods, Gen. 31:19,34,35. Achan, Josh 7:11. Micah, Judg. 17:2. The spies of Laish, Judg. 18:14–27; Judas, John 12:6.

THELASAR, called also Telassar. A city or district conquered by the Assyrians, 2 Kin. 19:12; Isa. 37:12.

THEOCRACY. Established, Ex. 19:8; 24:3,7; Deut. 5:25–29; 33:2–5; Judg. 8:23; 1 Sam. 12:12. Rejected by Israel, 1 Sam. 8:7, 19; 10:19; 2 Chr. 13:8.

See God, Sovereign; Government.

THEOLOGY. See God.

THEOPHILUS, a Christian to whom Luke addressed the books of Luke and Acts, Luke 1:3; Acts 1:1.

THESSALONIANS. See Thessalonica.

THESSALONICA, a city of Macedonia. Paul visits, Acts 17:1; Phil. 4:16. People of, persecute Paul, Acts 17:5–8,11,13. Men of, accompany Paul, Acts 20:4; 27:2. Paul writes to Christians in, 1 Thess. 1:1; 2 Thess. 1:1. Demas goes to, 2 Tim. 4:10.

THEUDAS, a Jewish insurrectionist, Acts 5:36.

THIMNATHAH, a city in Dan, Josh. 19:43.

THIRST, figurative of the ardent desire of the devout mind, Psa. 42:1–4; 63:1; 143:6; Isa. 55:1; Amos 8:11–13; Matt. 5:6; John 4: 14,15; 7:37; Rev. 21:6; 22:17.

See Desire, Spiritual; Diligence; Hunger, Spiritual; Zeal.

THISTLE. A noxious plant, Gen. 3:18; Job 31:40; Hos. 10:8. Parables of, 2 Kin. 14:9; 2 Chr. 25:18; Matt. 7:16.

THOMAS, called Didymus. One of the twelve apostles, Matt. 10:3; Mark 3:18; Luke 6:15. Present at the raising of Lazarus, John 11:16. Asks Jesus the way to the Father's house, John 14:5. Absent when Jesus first appeared to the disciples after the resurrection, John 20:24. Skepticism of, John 20:25. Sees Jesus after the resurrection, John 20:26–29; 21:1,2. Dwells with the other apostles in Jerusalem, Acts 1:13,14. Loyalty of, to Jesus, John 11:16; 20:28.

THORN. The ground cursed with, Gen. 3:18. Used as an awl, Job 41:2; for fuel, Psa. 58:9; 118:12; Eccl. 7:6. Hedges formed of, Hos. 2:6; Mic. 7:4. Crown of, mockingly put on Jesus' head, Matt. 27:29; Mark 15:17; John 19:2,5.

FIGURATIVE: Of afflictions, Num. 33:

55; 2 Cor. 12:7. Of the adversities of the wicked, Prov. 22:5. Of the evils that spring from the heart to choke the truth, Matt. 13: 7,22.

THREE TAVERNS, a town in Italy. Roman Christians meet Paul in, Acts 28:15.

THRESHING. By beating, Ruth 2:17; by treading, Deut. 25:4; Isa. 25:10; Hos. 10:11; 1 Cor. 9:9; 1 Tim. 5:18. With instruments of wood, 2 Sam. 24:22; of iron, Amos 1:3; with a cart wheel, Isa. 28:27,28. Floors for, Gen. 50:10,11; Judg. 6:37; Ruth 3:2–14; 1 Sam. 23:1; 2 Sam. 6:6; Hos. 9:2; Joel 2:24. Floor of Araunah bought by David for a place of sacrifice, 2 Sam. 24:16–25. Floor for, in barns, 2 Kin. 6:27.

THRONE. Of Pharaoh, Gen. 41:40; Ex. 11:5. Of David, 1 Kin. 2:12,24; Psa. 132:11, 12; Isa. 9:7; Jer. 13:13; 17:25; Luke 1:32. Of Solomon, 1 Kin. 2:19; 2 Chr. 9:17–19. Of ivory, 1 Kin. 10:18–20. Of Solomon, called THE THRONE OF THE LORD, 1 Chr. 29:23. Of Herod, Acts 12:21. Of Israel, 1 Kin. 8: 20; 10:9; 2 Chr. 6:10.

Abdicated by David, 1 Kin. 1:32–40.

FIGURATIVE: Anthropomorphic use of: Of God, 2 Chr. 18:18; Psa. 9:4,7; 11:4; 47:8; 89:14; 97:2; 103:19; Isa. 6:1; 66:1; Matt. 5:34; 23:22; Heb. 8:1; 12:2; Rev. 14:3,5; of Christ, Matt. 19:28; 25:31; Acts 2:30; Rev. 1:4; 3:21; 4:2–10; 7:9–17; 19:4; 21:5; 22:3.

THUMB. Blood put on, in consecration, Ex. 29:20; Lev. 8:23; in purification, Lev. 14: 14,25. Oil put on, Lev. 14:17,28. Of prisoners cut off, Judg. 1:6,7. See HAND.

THUMMIM. See URIM.

THUNDER. Sent as a plague upon the Egyptians, Ex. 9:23-34; the Philistines, in battle with the children of Israel, 1 Sam. 7: 10. Sent as a judgment, Isa. 29:6. On Sinai, Ex. 19:16; Psa. 77:18; Heb. 12:18,19. A token of divine anger, 1 Sam 12:17,18. A manifestation of divine power, Job 26:14; Psa. 77:18. Sons of Zebedee called sons of, Mark 3:17.

THYATIRA. Home of Lydia, a convert of Paul, Acts 16:14. John given a message for, Rev. 1:11; 2:18,24.

THYINE, an aromatic wood, Rev. 18:12.

TIBERIAS. 1. A city on the Sea of Galilee, John 6:23.

2. Sea of, a name given to the Sea of Galilee, John 6:1; 21:1. See GALILEE, 2.

TIBERIUS CÆSAR, emperor of Rome, Luke 3:1.

TIBHATH, a city conquered by David, 1 Chr. 18:8.

TIBNI, chosen by half of Israel to be king; death of, 1 Kin. 16:21,22.

TIDAL, king of nations [R. V., Goiim], Gen. 14:1,9.

TIGLATH-PILESER, called also TILGATH-PILNESER, king of Assyria. Invades Israel; carries part of the people captive to Assyria, 2 Kin. 15:29; 1 Chr. 5:6,26. Forms an alliance with Ahaz; captures Damascus, 2 Kin. 16:7–10; 2 Chr. 28:19–21.

TIKVAH. 1. Called also TIKVATH,

father of Shallum, 2 Kin. 22:14; 2 Chr. 34:22.

2. Father of Jahaziah, Ezra 10:15.

TILE, brick, Ezek. 4:1; Luke 5:19.

TILGATH-PILNESER. See TIGLATH-PILESER.

TILON, son of Shimon, 1 Chr. 4:20.

TIMÆUS, father of a blind man cured by Jesus, Mark 10:46.

TIMBREL, called also TABRET, an instrument of music of the tambourine sort. Used by Miriam, Ex. 15:20; by Jephthah's daughter, Judg. 11:34. Used in religious service, 2 Sam. 6:5; 1 Chr. 13:8; Psa. 68:25; 81:2; 149:3; 150:4. Used in dances, Job 21:12. See MUSIC, INSTRUMENTS OF.

TIME. Beginning of, Gen. 1:1,14. Epochs of: Before the flood, Josh. 24:2. The exodus, Ex. 19:1; 40:17; 1 Kin. 6:1. Daniel's reckoning of time, and times, and half times, Dan. 7:25; 12:7.

Indicated by a sundial, 2 Kin. 20:9–11; Isa. 38:8. Division of, into watches, Ex. 14:24; 1 Sam. 11:11; Matt. 14:25; Mark 6:48.

One day as a thousand years, 2 Pet. 3:8. Fullness of, Gal. 4:4; Eph. 1:10. End of, Job 26:10; Rev. 10:6.

TIMNA. 1. Concubine of Eliphaz, Gen. 36:12.

2. Daughter of Seir, Gen. 36:22; 1 Chr. 1:39.

3. Son of Eliphaz, 1 Chr. 1:36.

TIMNAH. 1. A duke of Edom, Gen. 36:40; 1 Chr. 1:51.

2. A city in Judah, Josh. 15:10; 2 Chr. 28:18.

3. A city in the mountains of Judah, Josh. 15:57.

TIMNATH. 1. A city given by some authorities as identical with TIMNAH, 2, Gen. 38:12–14.

2. Home of Samson's wife, Judg. 14:1,2,5; 15:6. Believed by some authorities to be identical with the preceding.

TIMNATH-HERES. See TIMNATH-SERAH.

TIMNATH-SERAH, a city, called also TIMNATH-HERES. Given to Joshua, Josh. 19:50. Joshua buried in, Josh. 24:30; Judg. 2:9.

TIMON, a member of the committee of seven appointed to supervise the daily ministration, Acts 6:5.

TIMOTHY, called also TIMOTHEUS, the companion of Paul. Parentage of, Acts 16:1. Reputation and Christian faith of, Acts 16:2; 1 Cor. 4:17; 16:10; 2 Tim. 1:5; 3:15. Circumcised; becomes Paul's companion, Acts 16:3; 1 Thess. 3:2. Left by Paul at Berea, Acts 17:14. Rejoins Paul at Corinth, Acts 17:15; 18:5. Sent into Macedonia, Acts 19:22. Rejoined by Paul; accompanies Paul to Asia, Acts 20:1–4. Sends salutation to the Romans, Rom. 16:21. Sent to the Corinthians, 1 Cor. 4:17; 16:10,11; see postscript to 1 Corinthians. Preaches to the Corinthians, 2 Cor. 1:19. Sent to the Philippians, Phil. 2:19,23. Sent to the Thessalonians, 1 Thess.

3:2,6. Left by Paul in Ephesus, 1 Tim. 1:3.

Confined with Paul in Rome, Phil. 2:19–23; Philem. 1; Heb. 13:23; with the postscripts to Philippians, Philemon, and Hebrews.

Ordained bishop of the Ephesians, see postscript to 2 Timothy. Joins Paul in the Epistle to the Philippians, Phil. 1:1; to the Colossians, Col. 1:1,2; to the Thessalonians, 1 Thess. 1:1; 2 Thess. 1:1; to Philemon, Philem. 1. Acts as Paul's amanuensis in writing the first letter to the Corinthians, see postscript to 1 Corinthians; in writing the letter to the Hebrews, see postscript to Hebrews.

Zeal of, Phil. 2:19–22; 1 Tim. 6:12. Power of, 1 Tim. 4:14; 2 Tim. 1:6. Paul's love for, 1 Cor. 4:17; Phil. 2:22; 1 Tim. 1:2,18; 2 Tim. 1:2–4. Paul writes to, 1 Tim. 1:1,2; 2 Tim. 1:1,2.

TIN, Num. 31:22; Ezek. 22:18,20; 27:12.

TIPHSAH. 1. A city on the Euphrates, 1 Kin. 4:24.

2. A city of unknown location, 2 Kin. 15:16.

TIRAS, son of Japheth, Gen. 10:2; 1 Chr. 1:5.

TIRE, a headdress, Isa. 3:18; Ezek. 24:17.

TIRHAKAH, a king of Ethiopia, 2 Kin. 19:9; Isa. 37:9.

TIRHANAH, son of Caleb, 1 Chr. 2:48.

TIRIA, son of Jehaleleel, 1 Chr. 4:16.

TIRSHATHA, a title of Persian governors, Ezra 2:63; Neh. 7:65,70; 8:9.

TIRZAH. 1. A daughter of Zelophehad, Num. 26:33; 36:11; Josh. 17:3. Special legislation in regard to the inheritance of, Num. 27:1–11; 36; Josh. 17:3,4.

2. A city of Canaan. Captured by Joshua, Josh. 12:24. Becomes the residence of the kings of Israel, 1 Kin. 14:17; 15:21,33; 16:6,8, 9,15,17,23. Royal residence moved from, 1 Kin. 16:23,24. Base of military operations of Menahem, 2 Kin. 15:14,16. Beauty of, Song 6:4.

TITHES. Paid by Abraham to Melchizedek, Gen. 14:20; Heb. 7:2–6. Jacob vows a tenth of all his property to God, Gen. 28:22.

Mosaic laws instituting, Lev. 27:30–33; Num. 18:21–24; Deut. 12:6,7,17 19; 14:22–29; 26:12–15. Customs relating to, Neh. 10:37,38; Amos 4:4; Heb. 7:5–9. Tithe of tithes for priests, Num. 18:26; Neh. 10:38. Stored in the temple, Neh. 10:38,39; 12:44; 13:5,12; 2 Chr. 31:11,12; Mal. 3:10.

Payment of, resumed in Hezekiah's reign, 2 Chr. 31:5–10. Under Nehemiah, Neh. 13:12. Withheld, Neh. 13:10; Mal. 3:8.

Customary in later times, Matt. 23:23; Luke 11:42;18:12. Observed by idolaters, Amos 4:4,5.

See ALMS; BENEFICENCE; GIVING; LIBERALITY; TAX.

TITLE, to real estate. See LAND.

TITUS, a Greek companion of Paul. Paul's love for, 2 Cor. 2:13; 7:6,7,13,14; 8:23; Tit. 1:4. With Paul in Macedonia, 2 Cor. 7:5,6; see postscript to 2 Corinthians.

Affection of, for the Corinthians, 2 Cor. 7:15. Sent to Corinth, 2 Cor. 8:6,16–22; 12:17,18. Character of, 2 Cor. 12:18. Paul's amanuensis in writing to the Corinthians, see postscript to 2 Corinthians. Accompanies Paul to Jerusalem, Gal. 2:1–3. Compare Acts 15:1–29. Left by Paul in Crete, Tit. 1:5; to rejoin him in Nicopolis, Tit. 3:12. Ordained bishop of the Cretians, see postscript to Titus. Paul writes to, Tit. 1:1–4. With Paul in Rome, 2 Tim. 4:10, with postscript to 2 Timothy. Goes to Dalmatia, 2 Tim. 4:10.

TOAH. See NAHATH, 2.

TOB, a district in Syria, Judg. 11:3,5. Called ISH-TOB, 2 Sam. 10:6,8.

TOB-ADONIJAH. A Levite sent by Jehoshaphat to instruct the people in the law, 2 Chr. 17:8.

TOBIAH. 1. Ancestor of a family of Babylonian captives, Ezra 2:60; Neh. 7:62.

2. An enemy of the Jews in the time of Nehemiah. Opposes the rebuilding of the wall of Jerusalem, Neh. 2:10,19; 4:3,7,8. Conspires to injure and intimidate Nehemiah, Neh. 6:1–14,19. Subverts nobles of Judah, Neh. 6:17,18. Allies himself with Eliashib, the priest, Neh. 13:4–9.

TOBIJAH. 1. A Levite sent by Jehoshaphat to instruct the people in the law, 2 Chr. 17:8.

2. A captive in Babylon, Zech. 6:10,14.

TOCHEN, a city in Simeon, 1 Chr. 4:32.

TOE. Anointed in consecration, Ex. 29:20; Lev. 8:23,24: in purification, Lev. 14:14,17,25,28. Of prisoners of war cut off, Judg. 1:6,7. Six, on each foot, 2 Sam. 21:20; 1 Chr. 20:6.

TOGARMAH. Son of Gomer, Gen. 10:3; 1 Chr. 1:6. Descendants of, Ezek. 27:14; 38:6.

TOHU. See NAHATH, 2.

TOI, called also TOU. King of Hamath, 2 Sam. 8:9,10; 1 Chr. 18:9,10.

TOLA. 1. Son of Issachar, Gen. 46:13; Num. 26:23; 1 Chr. 7:1,2.

2. A judge of Israel, Judg. 10:1,2.

TOKEN. A sign, Ex. 3:12. Sun and moon for time and seasons, Gen. 1:14. The mark of Cain, Gen. 4:15. Rainbow, that the world might no more be destroyed by a flood, Gen. 9:12–17. Circumcision, of the covenant of Abraham, Gen. 17:11. Presents, Gen. 21:27, 30. Miracles of Moses, of the divine authority of his missions, Ex. 4:1–9. Blood of the pascal lamb, Ex. 12:13. The Passover, Ex. 13:9. Consecration of the firstborn, Ex. 13:14–16. The Sabbath, Ex. 31:13,17; a fringe, Num. 15:38–40. Scarlet thread, Josh. 2:18,21. Cover of the altar, Num. 16:38–40. Aaron's rod, Num. 17:10. Memorial stones, Josh. 4:2–9. Dew on Gideon's fleece, Judg. 6:36–40. Prayer for tokens of mercy, Psa. 86:17.

See MIRACLES.

TOLAD. See ELTOLAD.

TOLERATION, religious, Mic. 4:4,5; Mark 9:38–40; Luke 9:49,50; Acts 17:11; 28:31; Rom. 14; 1 Cor. 10:28–32.

See INTOLERANCE.

TOLL. See TRIBUTE; TAX.

TOMB. See BURIAL.

TOMBSTONE, at Rachel's grave, Gen. 35:20.

See PILLARS.

TONGS. Ex. 25:38; Num. 4:9; 1 Kin. 7:49.

TONGUE. Language, Gen. 10:5,20; Isa. 66:18; Rev. 7:9. Confusion of, Gen. 11:1-9. Gift of, Acts 2:1-18,33; 10:46; 19:6; 1 Cor. 12:10, 28,30; 14.

Loquacious, Prov. 10:8,19. Restrained by wisdom, Prov. 17:27; 21:23; Eccl. 3:7. Hasty, Prov. 29:20.

An evil, see SPEAKING, EVIL; SLANDER.

TONGUES, the miraculous gift of the early Christians, 1 Cor. 12:10,28,30; 13:8; 14:2-19,21-28,39.

TOOLS. See IMPLEMENTS.

TOPAZ. A precious stone, Ezek. 28:13; Rev. 21:20. In the breastplate, Ex. 28:17; 39:10. Ethiopian, celebrated, Job 28:19.

TOPHEL, a place in the wilderness of Sinai, Deut. 1:1.

TOPHET, called also TOPHETH. A place in the valley of the sons of Hinnom, 2 Kin. 23:10. Jewish children passed through the fire to Molech in, 2 Kin. 23:10; Jer. 7:31,32; 19:6,11-14; 32:35. See also 2 Chr. 28:3; 33:6. Destroyed by Josiah, 2 Kin. 23:10. Horror of, Isa. 30:33.

TOPOGRAPHY, of Canaan, Josh. 13: 15-33; 15; 18:9.

TORMENTS, of the wicked, Luke 16: 23-28; Rev. 14:10,11.

See WICKED, PUNISHMENT OF.

TORTOISE, Lev. 11:29.

TOTAL ABSTINENCE. See ABSTINENCE.

TOU. See TOI.

TOW, Judg. 16:9; Isa. 1:31.

See FLAX.

TOWEL, John 13:4,5.

TOWER. Of Babel, Gen. 11:1-9. Of Edar, Gen. 35:21. Of Penuel, Judg. 8:8,9, 17. Of Shechem, Judg. 9:46,49. Of Meah, Neh. 3:1; 12:39. Of Hananeel, Neh. 3:1; 12: 39; Jer. 31:38; Zech. 14:10. Of David, Song 4:4. Of Syene, Ezek. 29:10. Of Siloam, Luke 13:4. In the walls of Jerusalem, 2 Chr. 26:9; 32:5; Neh. 12:38,39. Of other cities. 2 Chr. 14:7.

In the desert, 2 Chr. 26:10. For watchmen or sentinels, 2 Kin. 9:17; 18:8. As fortress, Matt. 21:33.

Parable of, Luke 14:28,29.

See FORTS.

FIGURATIVE: Of divine protection, 2 Sam. 22:3,51; Psa. 18:2; 61:3; 144:2; Prov. 18:10.

TOWN. See CITY.

TOWN CLERK, Acts 19:35.

TRACHONITIS, a part of the tetrarchy of Philip, Luke 3:1.

TRADE. 1. Occupation. See under name of each trade.

2. Commerce. See COMMERCE.

TRADITION, the decisions and minor

precepts taught by Paul, 1 Cor. 11:2 [R.V.]; 2 Thess. 2:15; 3:6.

Commandments of men, Matt. 12:1-8; 15: 2-6; Mark 7:3-9; Luke 6:1-11; Col. 2:8; 1 Pet. 1:18. Not authoritative, Matt. 15:3-20; 1 Tim. 1:4; 4:7.

TRAFFIC, suspended on the Sabbath, Neh. 13:15-22.

TRAITOR. Judas, Matt. 26:14-16,46-50; Mark 14:10,11,43-45; Luke 22:3-6,21-23,47,48; John 13:2,27-30; 18:2-8,13.

See TREASON.

TRAMP, Prov. 6:11 [R.V. marg.].

TRANCE. Of Balaam, Num. 24:4,16. Of Peter, Acts 10:10. Of Paul, Acts 22:17.

TRANSFIGURATION. Of Moses, Ex. 34:29-35. Of Jesus, Matt. 17:2-9; Mark 9:2-10; Luke 9:29-36; 2 Pet. 1:16-18. Of Stephen, Acts 6:15.

TRANSLATION. Of Enoch, Gen. 5: 24; Heb. 11:5. Of Elijah, 2 Kin. 2:1-12. Of Jesus, Mark 16:19; Luke 24:51; Acts 1:9-11. Desired by Paul, 2 Cor. 5:4.

TRAP, Josh. 23:13; Job 18:10; Jer. 5:26.

TREACHERY, Jer. 9:8. Of Rahab to her people, Josh. 2. Of the man of Beth-el, Judg. 1:24,25. Of Jael, Judg. 4:18-21. Of Shechemites, Judg. 9:23. Of Joab, 2 Sam. 3: 26,27. Of Baanah and Rechab, 2 Sam. 4:6. Of David to Uriah, 2 Sam. 11. Of Joab to Amasa, 2 Sam. 20:9,10. Of Jehu, 2 Kin. 10:18-28. Of the enemies of Nehemiah, Neh. 6.

See CONSPIRACY; TREASON.

TREASON. INSTANCES OF: Of Aaron and Miriam against Moses, Num. 12: 1-11. Of Korah, Dathan, and Abiram against Moses and Aaron, Num. 16:1-33. Of Rahab against Jericho, Josh. 2. Of the betrayer of Beth-el, Judg. 1:24,25. Of the Shechemites against Abimelech, Judg. 9:22-25. Of the Ephraimites against Jephthah, Judg. 12:1-4. Of the Israelites against Saul, 1 Sam. 10:27; against Rehoboam, 1 Kin. 12: 16-19. Of the Egyptian servant against the Amalekites, 1 Sam. 30:15,16. Of Abner against Ish-bosheth, 2 Sam. 3:6-21. Of Jehoiada against Athaliah, 2 Kin. 11:14-16. Of Absalom against his father, see ABSALOM.

Death penalty for, Esth. 2:23.

Jesus falsely accused of, Matt. 27:11,29,30; Luke 23:2,3,38; John 19:12,14,15,19. Paul falsely accused of, Acts 17:7.

David's amnesty of the traitors, 2 Sam. 19:16-23; to Amasa, 2 Sam. 19:13.

See CONSPIRACY; TREACHERY.

TREASURE. 1. A thing of highly estimated value. Money, Gen. 42:25,27,28,35; 43:23, with vs. 18,21,22. Precious stones. 1 Chr. 29:8.

Jesus forbids the hoarding of, Matt. 6:19; 19:21; Luke 12:33. Hidden, Matt. 13:44.

FIGURATIVE: Of the graces of the spirit, Prov. 21:20; Isa. 33:6. Of spiritual understanding, Matt. 13:52; Col. 2:3. Of the object of the affections, Matt. 6:21; Luke 12: 34. Of spiritual calling, 2 Cor. 4:6,7.

Gospel called, 2 Cor. 4:7. Parable of, Matt. 13:44.

TREASURE CITIES, built for the storage of the king's substance, Ex. 1:11; 1 Kin. 9:19; 2 Chr. 8:4,6.

TREASURE-HOUSES. Of kings, 2 Kin. 20:13; 1 Chr. 27:25; 2 Chr. 32:27,28; Ezra 1:7,8; Esth. 3:9. Records preserved in, Ezra 5:17; 6:1. Treasurers in charge of, Ezra 7:20,21.

Heathen temples used for, Dan. 1:2.

Tabernacle used for, Num. 31:54; Josh. 6:19,24. Solomon's temple used for, 1 Kin. 7:51; 2 Kin. 12:4-14,18; 22:4,5; 1 Chr. 28:11, 12; Matt. 27:6; Mark 12:41,43; Luke 21:1; John 8:20. Under the charge of the Levites, 1 Chr. 26:20. Chambers provided in the temple for various kinds of offerings, Neh. 10:38,39; 13:5,9,12; Mal. 3:10. Priests and Levites in charge of, 1 Chr. 9:26; 26:20-28; Neh. 12:44; 13:13.

TREATY. Between nations : Israelites and Gibeonites, Josh. 9:3-15; Judah and Syria, 1 Kin. 15:19. Cession of territory by, 1 Kin. 9:10-14; 20:34. Sacredness of, Josh. 9:16-21, with chapter 2:8-21.

Reciprocity, 1 Kin. 5:1-12. With idolatrous nations forbidden, Ex. 34:12,15.

TREE. Of life, Gen. 2:9; 3:22,24; Rev. 22:14. Of knowledge, Gen. 2:9,17; 3:3-6,11, 12,17.

FIGURATIVE: Psa. 1:3; Jer. 17:8.

SYMBOLICAL. Dan. 4:10-12.

TRESPASS. Ex. 22:9. Of an ox, Ex. 21:28-36. Of a brother, Matt. 18:15-18. Luke 17:3,4. Creditor shall not enter debtor's house to take a pledge, Deut. 24:10.

Trespass offering, see OFFERINGS.

TRIAL. Before court, Lev. 24:10-14. Right of, John 7:51; Acts 16:37-39; 22:25-30.

See COURT; JUSTICE; PRISONERS.

OF FAITH: See FAITH; TEMPTATION.

TRIBULATION, John 16:33.

See AFFLICTION; SUFFERING.

TRIBUTE. From conquered nations, Josh. 16:10; Judg. 1:30-33; 2 Kin. 15:19; 23: 35; Matt. 17:24-27; 22:15-22; Luke 2:1-5. By Arabians to Solomon, 2 Chr. 9:14; to Jehoshaphat, 2 Chr. 17:11.

See DUTY; TAX.

TRINITY. THE HOLY: Gen. 1:26. And God said, Let us make man in our image, after our likeness :

Gen. 3:22. And the LORD God said, Behold, the man is become as one of us, to know good and evil :

Isa. 6:3. And one cried unto another, and said, Holy, holy, holy, is the LORD of hosts : the whole earth is full of his glory. 8. Also I heard the voice of the Lord, saying, Whom shall I send, and who will go for us ?

Isa. 11:2. The spirit of the LORD shall rest upon him, . . . 3. And shall make him of quick understanding in the fear of the LORD :

Isa. 42:1. Behold my servant, whom I uphold ; mine elect, in whom my soul delight-

eth; I have put my spirit upon him : Matt. 12:18.

Isa. 48:16. Come ye near unto me, hear ye this ; I have not spoken in secret from the beginning ; from the time that it was, there am I: and now the Lord GOD, and his Spirit, hath sent me.

Isa. 61:1. The Spirit of the Lord GOD is upon me ; because the LORD hath anointed me to preach good tidings unto the meek ; he hath sent me to bind up the brokenhearted, to proclaim liberty to the captives, and the opening of the prison to them that are bound ; [Luke 4:18.] 2. To proclaim the acceptable year of the LORD, and the day of vengeance of our God ; to comfort all that mourn ; 3. To appoint unto them that mourn in Zion, to give unto them beauty for ashes, the oil of joy for mourning, the garment of praise for the spirit of heaviness ; that they might be called trees of righteousness, the planting of the LORD, that he might be glorified.

Isa. 63:9. In all their affliction he was afflicted, and the angel of his presence saved them : . . . 10. But they rebelled, and vexed his holy Spirit :

Matt. 1:18. Now the birth of Jesus Christ was on this wise : When as his mother Mary was espoused to Joseph, before they came together, she was found with child of the Holy Ghost. 20. The angel of the Lord appeared unto him in a dream, saying, Joseph, thou son of David, fear not to take unto thee Mary thy wife : for that which is conceived in her is of the Holy Ghost.

Matt. 3:11. He that cometh after me is mightier than I, whose shoes I am not worthy to bear : he shall baptize you with the Holy Ghost, and with fire : Mark 1:8; Luke 3:16.

Matt. 12:28. But if I cast out devils by the Spirit of God, then the kingdom of God is come unto you.

Matt. 28:19. Go ye therefore, and teach all nations, baptizing them in the name of the Father, and of the Son, and of the Holy Ghost :

Luke 1:35. The angel answered and said unto her, The Holy Ghost shall come upon thee, and the power of the Highest shall overshadow thee ; therefore also that holy thing which shall be born of thee shall be called the Son of God.

Luke 3:22. The Holy Ghost descended in a bodily shape like a dove upon him, and a voice came from heaven, which said, Thou art my beloved Son ; in thee I am well pleased. Matt. 3:16.

Luke 4:1. Jesus being full of the Holy Ghost returned from Jordan, and was led by the Spirit into the wilderness, 14. Jesus returned in the power of the Spirit into Galilee :

John 1:32. And John bare record, saying, I saw the Spirit descending from heaven like a dove, and it abode upon him. 33. And I knew him not : but he that sent me to baptize with water, the same said unto me, Upon whom thou shalt see the Spirit descending, and remaining on him, the same is he which baptizeth with the Holy Ghost.

John 3:34. For he whom God hath sent speaketh the words of God : for God giveth not the Spirit by measure *unto him.* 35. The Father loveth the Son, and hath given all things into his hand.

John 7:39. (But this spake he of the Spirit, which they that believe on him should receive: for the Holy Ghost was not yet *given;* because that Jesus was not yet glorified.)

John 14:16. And I will pray the Father, and he shall give you another Comforter, that he may abide with you for ever; 17. *Even* the Spirit of truth; whom the world cannot receive, because it seeth him not, neither knoweth him: but ye know him; for he dwelleth with you, and shall be in you. 26. But the Comforter, *which is* the Holy Ghost, whom the Father will send in my name, he shall teach you all things, and bring all things to your remembrance, whatsover I have said unto you.

John 15:26. When the Comforter is come, whom I will send unto you from the Father, *even* the Spirit of truth, which proceedeth from the Father, he shall testify of me :

John 16:7. It is expedient for you that I go away: for if I go not away, the Comforter will not come unto you; but if I depart, I will send him unto you. 13. Howbeit when he, the Spirit of truth, is come, he will guide you into all truth: for he shall not speak of himself; but whatsoever he shall hear, *that* shall he speak: and he will shew you things to come. 14. He shall glorify me: for he shall receive of mine, and shall shew *it* unto you. 15. All things that the Father hath are mine: therefore said I, that he shall take of mine, and shall shew *it* unto you.

John 20:22. He breathed on *them,* and saith unto them, Receive ye the Holy Ghost:

Acts 1:2. Until the day in which he was taken up, after that he through the Holy Ghost had given commandments unto the apostles whom he had chosen: 4. That they should not depart from Jerusalem, but wait for the promise of the Father, which, *saith he,* ye have heard of me. 5. For John truly baptized with water; but ye shall be baptized with the Holy Ghost not many days hence.

Acts 2:33. Therefore being by the right hand of God exalted, and having received of the Father the promise of the Holy Ghost, he hath shed forth this, which ye now see and hear.

Acts 10:36. The word which *God* sent unto the children of Israel, preaching peace by Jesus Christ: (he is Lord of all:) 37. That word, *I say,* ye know, which was published throughout all Judæa, and began from Galilee, after the baptism which John preached; 38. How God anointed Jesus of Nazareth with the Holy Ghost and with

power: who went about doing good, and healing all that were oppressed of the devil; for God was with him.

Rom. 1:3. Concerning his Son Jesus Christ our Lord, which was made of the seed of David according to the flesh; 4. And declared *to be* the Son of God with power, according to the spirit of holiness, by the resurrection from the dead:

Rom. 8:9. But ye are not in the flesh, but in the Spirit, if so be that the Spirit of God dwell in you. Now if any man have not the Spirit of Christ, he is none of his. 10. And if Christ *be* in you, the body *is* dead because of sin; but the Spirit *is* life because of righteousness. 11. But if the Spirit of him that raised up Jesus from the dead dwell in you, he that raised up Christ from the dead shall also quicken your mortal bodies by his Spirit that dwelleth in you. 26. Likewise the Spirit also helpeth our infirmities: for we know not what we should pray for as we ought: but the Spirit itself maketh intercession for us with groanings which cannot be uttered. 27. And he that searcheth the hearts knoweth what *is* the mind of the Spirit, because he maketh intercession for the saints according to *the will of* God.

1 Cor. 2:10. But God hath revealed *them* unto us by his Spirit: for the Spirit searcheth all things, yea, the deep things of God. 11. For what man knoweth the things of a man, save the spirit of man which is in him? even so the things of God knoweth no man, but the Spirit of God.

1 Cor. 6:19. What ? know ye not that your body is the temple of the Holy Ghost *which is* in you, which ye have of God, and ye are not your own ?

1 Cor. 8:6. But to us *there is but* one God, the Father, of whom *are* all things, and we in him; and one Lord Jesus Christ, by whom *are* all things, and we by him.

1 Cor. 12:3. Wherefore I give you to understand, that no man speaking by the Spirit of God calleth Jesus accursed: and *that* no man can say that Jesus is the Lord, but by the Holy Ghost. 4. Now there are diversities of gifts, but the same Spirit. 5. And there are differences of administrations, but the same Lord. 6. And there are diversities of operations, but it is the same God which worketh all in all.

2 Cor. 1:21. Now he which stablisheth us with you in Christ, and hath anointed us, *is* God; 22. Who hath also sealed us, and given the earnest of the Spirit in our hearts. 2 Cor. 5:5.

2 Cor. 3:17. The Lord is that Spirit: and where the Spirit of the Lord *is,* there *is* liberty.

2 Cor. 13:14. The grace of the Lord Jesus Christ, and the love of God, and the communion of the Holy Ghost. *be* with you all.

Gal. 4:4. But when the fulness of the time was come, God sent forth his Son, made of a woman, made under the law, 6. And because ye are sons, God hath sent forth the Spirit of his Son into your hearts, crying, Abba, Father.

Phil. 1:19. For I know that this shall turn to my salvation through your prayer, and the supply of the Spirit of Jesus Christ,

Col. 2:2. That their hearts might be comforted, being knit together in love, and unto all riches of the full assurance of understanding, 1 to the acknowledgement of the mystery of God, and of the Father, and of Christ ;
[1 R. V. that they may know the mystery of God, even Christ,]

2 Thess. 2:13. But we are bound to give thanks alway to God for you, brethren beloved of the Lord, because God hath from the beginning chosen you to salvation through sanctification of the Spirit and belief of the truth : 14. Whereunto he called you by our gospel, to the obtaining of the glory of our Lord Jesus Christ. 16. Now our Lord Jesus Christ himself, and God, even our Father, which hath loved us, and hath given *us* everlasting consolation and good hope through grace,

1 Tim. 3:16. And without controversy great is the mystery of godliness : 1 God was manifest in the flesh, justified in the Spirit, seen of angels, preached unto the Gentiles, believed on in the world, received up into glory.   [1 R. V. He who]

Tit. 3:4. But after that the kindness and love of God our Saviour toward man appeared, 5. Not by works of righteousness which we have done, but according to his mercy he saved us, by the washing of regeneration, and renewing of the Holy Ghost ; 6. Which he shed on us abundantly through Jesus Christ our Saviour ;

Heb. 9:14. How much more shall the blood of Christ, who through the eternal Spirit offered himself without spot to God, purge your conscience from dead works to serve the living God ?

1 Pet. 1:2. Elect according to the foreknowledge of God the Father, through sanctification of the Spirit, unto obedience and sprinkling of the blood of Jesus Christ :

1 Pet. 3:18. Christ also hath once suffered for sins, the just for the unjust, that he might bring us to God, being put to death in the flesh, but quickened by the Spirit :

1 John 5:6. This is he that came by water and blood, *even* Jesus Christ ; . . . And it is the Spirit that beareth witness, because the Spirit is truth. 1 7. There are three that bear record in heaven, the Father, the Word, and the Holy Ghost : and these three are one. '
[1 Omitted in R. V.]

Rev. 4:8. And the four beasts had each of them six wings about *him ;* and *they were* full of eyes within : and they rest not day and night, saying, Holy, holy, holy, Lord God Almighty, which was, and is, and is to come.

See GOD ; HOLY GHOST ; JESUS.

TROAS, a seaport of Mysia, in Asia Minor. Paul visits, Acts 16:8,11; 20:5,6; 2 Cor. 2:12; 2 Tim. 4:13.

TROGYLLIUM, a town and promontory in Caria. of Asia Minor. Visited by Paul, Acts 20:115.   [1 R. V. omits Trogyllium.]

TROPHIES, Goliath's head and armor, 1 Sam. 17:54; 21:9; Saul's, 1 Sam. 31:8–10. Placed in temples, see TEMPLES.

TROPHIMUS, an Ephesian companion of Paul. Accompanies Paul from Greece to Asia, Acts 20:4. With Paul in Jerusalem ; made the occasion of an attack on Paul, Acts 21:27–30. Left ill at Miletus, 2 Tim. 4:20.

TROUBLE. BORROWING : Matt. 6:25. Take no thought [Be not anxious, *R. V.*] for your life, what ye shall eat, or what ye shall drink ; nor yet for your body, what ye shall put on. Is not the life more than meat, and the body than raiment ? 26 Behold the fowls of the air : for they sow not, neither do they reap, nor gather into barns ; yet your heavenly Father feedeth them. Are ye not much better than they ? 27. Which of you by taking thought [being anxious, *R. V.*] can add one cubit unto his stature ? 28. And why take ye thought for raiment ? Consider the lilies of the field, how they grow ; they toil not, neither do they spin : 29. And yet I say unto you, That even Solomon in all his glory was not arrayed like one of these. 30. Wherefore, if God so clothe the grass of the field, which to day is, and to morrow is cast into the oven, *shall he* not much more *clothe* you, O ye of little faith ? 31. Therefore take no thought [Be not therefore anxious, *R. V.*], saying, What shall we eat ? or, What shall we drink ? or Wherewithal shall we be clothed ? 32. (For after all these things do the Gentiles seek :) for your heavenly Father knoweth that ye have need of all these things. 33. But seek ye first the kingdom of God, and his righteousness ; and all these things shall be added unto you. 34. Take therefore no thought [Be not therefore anxious, *R. V.*] for the morrow : for the morrow shall take thought for the things of itself. Sufficient unto the day *is* the evil thereof.

Mark 5:35. While he yet spake, there came from the ruler of the synagogue's *house certain* which said, Thy daughter is dead : why troublest thou the Master any further ? 36. As soon as Jesus heard the word that was spoken, he saith unto the ruler of the synagogue, Be not afraid, only believe.

John 14:1. Let not your heart be troubled : ye believe in God, believe also in me.

John 16:6. But because I have said these things unto you, sorrow hath filled your heart. 7. Nevertheless I tell you the truth ; It is expedient for you that I go away : for if I go not away, the Comforter will not come unto you ; but if I depart, I will send him unto you.

Phil. 4:6. Be careful for nothing [In nothing be anxious, *R. V.*] ;

1 Pet. 5:7. Casting all your care [anxiety, *R. V.*] upon him ; for he careth for you.

See AFFLICTION ; SUFFERING.

INSTANCES OF : Israelites at the Red Sea, Ex. 14:10-12; about water, Ex. 15:23-25; 17:2,3; Num. 20:1-13; food, Ex. 16:2,3; Num. 11:4-33. When Moses tarried in the mount, Ex. 32:1. When the spies brought their adverse report, Num. 13:28,29,31-33; 14:1-4, with *vs*.4-12. Elijah, under the juniper tree and in the cave, 1 Kin. 19:4-15. The disciples, as to how the multitude could be fed, Matt. 14:15; Mark 6:37; in the tempest, when Jesus was asleep in the ship, Matt. 8:23-26; Mark 4:36-39; Luke 8:22-24; when Jesus was crucified, Luke 24:4-9,24-31,36-40. Mary at the sepulchre; John 20:11-17. The people in the shipwreck, Acts 27:22-25,30-36.

TRUCE, in battle, 2 Sam. 2:26-31.

TRUMPET. Made of ram's horn, Josh. 6:4-6,8,13; of silver, Num. 10:2. Uses of, prescribed by Moses, Num. 10:1-10. Used in war, Job 39:24,25; Jer. 4:19; 6:1,17; 42:14; 51:27; Ezek. 7:14; Amos 2:2; 3:6; Zeph. 1:16; 1 Cor. 14:8. To summon soldiers, by Phinehas, Num. 31:6; by Ehud, Judg. 3:27; by Gideon, Judg. 6:34; by Saul, 1 Sam. 15:3; by Joab, 2 Sam. 2:28; 18:16; 20:22; by Absalom, 2 Sam. 15:10; by Sheba, 2 Sam. 20:1; by Nehemiah, Neh. 4:18,20. By Gideon's soldiers, Judg. 7:8-22. In war, of Abijah, 2 Chr. 13:12,14. In the siege of Jericho, Josh. 6:4-20.

Sounded in time of danger, Ezek. 33:3-6; Joel 2:1.

Used at Sinai, Ex. 19:13-19; 20:18; Heb. 12:19; on the great day of atonement, Isa. 27:13; at the jubilee, Lev. 25:9; at the bringing up of the ark, 2 Sam. 6:5,15; 1 Chr. 13:8; 15:28; the anointing of kings, 1 Kin. 1:34,39; 2 Kin. 9:13; 11:14; dedication of Solomon's temple, 2 Chr. 5:12,13; 7:6; in worship, 1 Chr. 15:24; 16:42; 25:5; Psa. 81:3,4; at Jehoshaphat's triumph, 2 Chr. 20:28; at the foundation of the second temple, Ezra 3:10,11; at the dedication of the wall, Neh. 12:35,41.

FIGURATIVE : Isa. 27:13; Ezek. 33:3; Joel 2:1; Zech. 9:14; Matt. 6:2.

SYMBOLICAL : Matt. 24:31; 1 Cor. 15:52; 1 Thess. 4:16; Rev. 1:10; 4:1; 8; 9:1-14; 10:7; 11:15.

See MUSIC, INSTRUMENTS OF.

TRUMPETS, FEAST OF : When and how observed, Lev. 23:24,25; Num. 29:1-6. Celebrated after the captivity with joy, Neh. 8:2,9-12.

See FEASTS.

TRUST. See FAITH.

TRUSTEE. Mosaic law concerning, Ex. 22:7-13; Lev. 6:2-7. The parable of the pounds, Matt. 25:14-28; Luke 19:12-27.

See STEWARD.

TRUTH. Saints should worship God in, John 4:24, with Psa. 145:18; serve God in, Josh. 24:14; 1 Sam. 12:24; walk before God in, 1 Kin. 2:4; 2 Kin. 20:3; keep religious feasts with, 1 Cor. 5:8; esteem, as inestimable, Prov. 23:23; love, Zech. 8:19; rejoice in, 1 Cor. 13:6; speak, to one another, Zech.

8:16; Eph. 4:25; execute judgment with, Zech. 8:16; meditate upon, Phil. 4:8; bind, about the neck, Prov. 3:3; write, upon the tables of the heart, Prov. 3:3.

The fruit of the Spirit is in, Eph. 5:9.

Ministers should speak, 2 Cor. 12:6; Gal. 4:16; teach in, 1 Tim. 2:7; approve themselves by, 2 Cor. 6:7,8.

Magistrates should be men of, Ex. 18:21.

Kings are preserved by, Prov. 20:28.

They who speak, show forth righteousness, Prov. 12:17; are the delight of God, Prov. 12:22.

The wicked destitute of, Hos. 4:1; speak not, Jer. 9:5; uphold not, Isa. 59:14,15; plead not for, Isa. 59:4; are not valiant for, Jer. 9:3; punished for want of, Jer. 9:5,9; Hos. 4:1,3.

The gospel as, came by Christ, John 1:17. Is in Christ, 1 Tim 2:7. John bare witness to, John 5:33. Is according to godliness, Tit. 1:1. Is sanctifying, John 17:17,19. Is purifying, 1 Pet. 1:22. Is part of the Christian armor, Eph. 6:14. Revealed abundantly to saints, Jer. 33:6. Abides continually with saints, 2 John 2. Should be acknowledged, 2 Tim. 2:25. Should be believed, 2 Thess. 2:12,13; 1 Tim. 4:3. Should be obeyed, Rom. 2:8; Gal. 3:1. Should be loved, 2 Thess. 2:10. Should be manifested, 2 Cor. 4:2. Should be rightly divided, 2 Tim. 2:15. The wicked turn away from, 2 Tim. 4:4. The wicked resist, 2 Tim. 3:8. The wicked destitute of, 1 Tim. 6:5. The Church is the pillar and ground of, 1 Tim. 3:15. The devil is devoid of, John 8:44.—*Bible Text-Book.*

OF GOD : Is one of his attributes, Deut. 32:4; Isa. 65:16; he keeps, forever, Psa. 146:6; abundant, Ex. 34:6; inviolable, Num. 23:19; Tit. 1:2; enduring to all generations, Psa. 100:5. Exhibited in his ways, Rev. 15:3; works, Psa. 33:4; 111:7; Dan. 4:37; judicial statutes, Psa. 19:9; word, Psa. 119:160; John 17:17: fulfillment of promises in Christ, 2 Cor. 1:20; fulfillment of his covenant, Mic. 7:20; dealings with saints, Psa. 25:10; deliverance of saints, Psa. 57:3; punishment of the wicked, Rev. 16:7. Is a shield and buckler to saints, Psa. 91:4. We should confide in, Psa. 31:5; Tit. 1:2. Plead in prayer, Psa. 89:49. Pray for its manifestation to ourselves, 2 Chr. 6:17. Pray for its exhibition to others, 2 Sam. 2:6. Make known, to others, Isa. 38:19. Magnify, Psa. 71:22; 138:2. Is denied by the devil, Gen. 3:4,5; the self-righteous, 1 John 1:10; unbelievers, 1 John 5:10.—*Bible Text-Book.*

UNCLASSIFIED SCRIPTURES RELATING TO : Ex. 34:6. And the LORD passed by before him, and proclaimed, The LORD, The LORD God, merciful and gracious, longsuffering, and abundant in goodness and truth.

Deut. 32:4. All his ways *are* judgment: a God of truth and without iniquity, just and right *is* he.

Psa. 31:5. Thou hast redeemed me, O LORD God of truth.

Psa. 33:4. For the word of the LORD *is* right; and all his works *are done* in truth.

Psa. 40:10. I have not concealed thy lovingkindness and thy truth from the great congregation.

Psa. 51:6. Behold, thou desirest truth in the inward parts:

Psa. 57:3. God shall send forth his mercy and his truth. 10. For thy mercy *is* great unto the heavens, and thy truth unto the clouds.

Psa. 85:10. Mercy and truth are met together; righteousness and peace have kissed *each other*. 11. Truth shall spring out of the earth; and righteousness shall look down from heaven.

Psa. 86:15. But thou, O Lord, *art* a God full of compassion, and gracious, longsuffering, and plenteous in mercy and truth.

Psa. 89:14. Justice and judgment *are* the habitation of thy throne: mercy and truth shall go before thy face.

Psa. 96:13. He shall judge the world with righteousness, and the people with his truth.

Psa. 98:3. He hath remembered his mercy and his truth toward the house of Israel:

Psa. 100:5. For the Lord *is* good; his mercy *is* everlasting; and his truth *endureth* to all generations.

Psa. 108:4. For thy mercy *is* great above the heavens: and thy truth *reacheth* unto the clouds.

Prov. 12:19. The lip of truth shall be established for ever: but a lying tongue *is* but for a moment.

Prov. 16:13. Righteous lips *are* the delight of kings; and they love him that speaketh right.

Isa. 25:1. O Lord, thou *art* my God; I will exalt thee, I will praise thy name; for thou hast done wonderful *things; thy* counsels of old *are* faithfulness *and* truth.

Isa. 59:14. Truth is fallen in the street, and equity cannot enter. 15. Yea, truth faileth;

Isa. 65:16. That he who blesseth himself in the earth shall bless himself in the God of truth: and he that sweareth in the earth shall swear by the God of truth;

Jer. 5:3. O Lord, *are* not thine eyes upon the truth?

Dan. 4:37. Now I Nebuchadnezzar praise and extol and honour the King of heaven, all whose works *are* truth, and his ways judgment:

Dan. 10:21. But I will shew thee that which is noted in the scripture of truth:

Mic. 7:20. Thou wilt perform the truth to Jacob, *and* the mercy to Abraham, which thou hast sworn unto our fathers from the days of old.

John 1:14. And the Word was made flesh, and dwelt among us, (and we beheld his glory, the glory as of the only begotten of the Father,) full of grace and truth.

John 8:31. Then said Jesus to those Jews which believed on him, If ye continue in my word, *then* are ye my disciples indeed; 32. And ye shall know the truth, and the truth shall make you free.

John 14:6. Jesus saith unto him, I am the way, the truth, and the life: 17. The Spirit of truth;

John 16:13. Howbeit when he, the Spirit of truth, is come, he will guide you into all truth:

John 17:17. Sanctify them through thy truth: thy word is truth. 19. And for their sakes I sanctify myself, that they also might be sanctified through the truth.

John 18:37. Pilate therefore said unto him, Art thou a king then? Jesus answered, Thou sayest that I am a king. To this end was I born, and for this cause came I into the world, that I should bear witness unto the truth. Every one that is of the truth heareth my voice. 38. Pilate saith unto him, What is truth? And when he had said this, he went out again unto the Jews, and saith unto them, I find in him no fault *at all.*

Rom. 2:2. But we are sure that the judgment of God is according to truth against them which commit such things.

TRYPHENA, a Christian woman in Rome, Rom. 16:12.

TRYPHOSA, a Christian woman in Rome, Rom. 16:12.

TUBAL, son of Japheth, Gen. 10:2; 1 Chr. 1:5. Descendants of, become a nation, Isa. 66:19; Ezek. 27:13; 32:26; 38:2,3; 39:1.

TUBAL-CAIN, the inventor of edge tools, Gen. 4:22.

TUMOR, a morbid swelling. *R. V.* 1 Sam. 5:6,9,12; 6:4,5,11,17.

See Boil.

TURTLEDOVE. See Dove.

TUTOR, 2 Kin. 10:1; Acts 22:3; Gal. 4:1,2.

TWINS. Jacob and Esau, Gen. 25:24-26. Pharez and Zarah, Gen. 38:27-30.

TYCHICUS, an Asian companion of Paul. Accompanies Paul from Greece to Asia, Acts 20:4. With Paul in Nicopolis, Tit. 3:12, with postscript to Titus. With Paul in Rome, Eph. 6:21,22; Col. 4:7,8, with postscripts to Ephesians and Colossians. Paul's amanuensis in writing to the Ephesians and Colossians, see the postscripts to Ephesians and Colossians. Sent to Ephesus, Eph. 6:21,22; 2 Tim. 4:12. Sent to Colosse, Col. 4:7,8.

TYPES. MISCELLANEOUS: Bride, a type of the Church, Rev. 21:2,9; 22:17. The sanctuary a type of the heavenly sanctuary, Ex. 40:2,24; Heb. 8:2,5; 9:1-12. The saving of Noah and his family, of the salvation through the gospel, 1 Pet. 3:20,21.

Defilement a type of sin, see Defilement; Purification. Leaven a type of sin, see Leaven. Ablutions were, see Ablutions.

See Allegory; Parables; Symbols.

OF THE SAVIOUR: Col. 2:17; Heb. 9:7-15,18-28; 10:1-10. High priest, typical of the mediatorship, Ex. 28:1,12,29,30,38; Lev. 16:15; Zech. 6:12,13, with Heb.5; 8:2; 10:21. The institutions ordained by Moses,

Matt. 26:54; Luke 24:25-27,44-47; Col. 2:14-17; Heb. 10:1-14. The sacrifices, Lev. 4: 2,3,12; Heb. 9:7-15,18-25; 10:1-22,29; 13:11-13; 1 Pet. 1:19; Rev. 5:6. The morning and evening sacrifice, John 1:29,36. The red heifer, Num. 19:2-6, with Heb. 9:13,14. The paschal lamb, 1 Cor. 5:7. The brazen altar, Ex. 27:1,2, with Heb. 13:10. The laver of brass, Ex. 30:18-20, with Zech. 13:1; Eph. 5: 26,27. Mercy seat, Ex. 25:17-22, with Heb. 4:16. The veil, Ex. 40:21; 2 Chr. 3:14, with Heb. 10:20. Manna, John 6:32-35; 1 Cor. 10: 3. Cities of refuge, Num. 35:6, with Heb. 6:18. Brazen serpent, Num. 21:9; John 3: 14,15. Tree of life, Gen. 2:9, with John 1:4; Rev. 22:2.

Adam, Rom. 5:14; 1 Cor. 15:45. Abel, Gen. 4:8,10, with Heb. 12:24. Noah, Gen. 5:29, with 2 Cor. 1:5. Melchizedek, Heb. 7:1-17. Moses, Deut. 18:15,18; Acts 3:20,22; 7:37; Heb. 3:2-6. David, 2 Sam. 8:15; Psa. 89:19, 20; Ezek. 37:24; Phil. 2:9. Eliakim, Isa. 22:20-22; Rev. 3:7. Jonah, Jonah 1:17, with Matt. 12:40.

TYRANNUS, an Ephesian. Paul taught in the school of, for two years, Acts 19: 9,10.

TYRANNY. See Government, Tyrannical.

TYRE. 1. Kingdom of. Hiram, king of, 1 Kin. 5:1; 2 Chr. 2:3. Sends material to David for his palace, 2 Chr. 2:3. Men and materials sent from, to Solomon, for the erection of the temple and his castles, 1 Kin. 5:1-11; 9:10,11; 2 Chr. 2:3-16.

See Hiram.

2. City of. Situated on the shore of the Mediterranean. On the northern boundary of Asher, Josh. 19:29. Pleasant site of, Hos. 9:13. Fortified, Josh. 19:29; 2 Sam. 24:7. Commerce of, 1 Kin. 9:26-28; 10:11; Isa. 23; Ezek. 27; 28:1-19; Zech. 9:2; Acts 21:3. Merchants of, Isa. 23:8. Antiquity of, Isa. 23:7. Riches of, Isa. 23:8; Zech. 9:3. Besieged by Nebuchadnezzar, Ezek. 26:7; 29:18.

Jesus goes to the coasts of, Matt. 15:21. Heals the daughter of the Syrophenician woman near, Matt. 15:21-28; Mark 7:24-31. Multitudes from, come to hear Jesus, and to be healed of their diseases, Mark 3:8; Luke 6:17. Herod's hostility toward, Acts 12:20-23. Paul visits, Acts 21:3-7.

To be judged according to its opportunity and privileges, Matt. 11:21,22; Luke 10:13,14.

Prophecies relating to, Psa. 45:12; 87:4; Isa. 23; Jer. 25:22; 27:1-11; 47:4; Ezek. chapters 26-28; Joel 3:4-8; Amos 1:9,10; Zech. 9: 2-4.

U

UCAL, a man mentioned only in Prov. 30:1.

UEL, an Israelite who put away his Gentile wife, Ezra 10:34.

ULAI, a river of Chaldea, Dan. 8:2,16.

ULAM. 1. Son of Sheresh, 1 Chr. 7:16, 17.

2. Son of Eshek, 1 Chr. 8:39,40.

ULLA, an Asherite, 1 Chr. 7:39.

UMMAH, a city of Asher, Josh. 19:30.

UNBELIEF. Ex. 4:1. And Moses answered and said, But, behold, they will not believe me, nor hearken unto my voice: for they will say, The Lord hath not appeared unto thee.

Num. 11:21. And Moses said, The people, among whom I *am, are* six hundred thousand footmen; and thou hast said, I will give them flesh, that they may eat a whole month. 22. Shall the flocks and the herds be slain for them, to suffice them? or shall all the fish of the sea be gathered together for them, to suffice them? 23. And the Lord said unto Moses, Is the Lord's hand waxed short? thou shalt see now whether my word shall come to pass unto thee or not.

Num 20:12. And the Lord spake unto Moses and Aaron, Because ye believed me not, to sanctify me in the eyes of the children of Israel, therefore ye shall not bring this congregation into the land which I have given them. 13. This *is* the water of Meribah; because the children of Israel strove with the Lord, and he was sanctified in them.

Psa. 78:19. Yea, they spake against God; they said, Can God furnish a table in the wilderness? 21. Therefore the Lord heard *this,* and was wroth: so a fire was kindled against Jacob, and anger also came up against Israel; 22. Because they believed not in God, and trusted not in his salvation:

32. For all this they sinned still, and believed not for his wondrous works.

Psa. 95:8. Harden not your heart, as in the provocation, *and* as *in* the day of temptation in the wilderness: 9. When your fathers tempted me, proved me, and saw my work. 10. Forty years long was I grieved with *this* generation, and said, It *is* a people that do err in their heart, and they have not known my ways: 11. Unto whom I sware in my wrath that they should not enter into my rest.

Psa. 106:7. Our fathers understood not thy wonders in Egypt; they remembered not the multitude of thy mercies; but provoked *him* at the sea, *even* at the Red sea. 24. Yea, they despised the pleasant land, they believed not his word:

Isa. 7:9. If ye will not believe, surely ye shall not be established.

Isa. 53:1. Who hath believed our report? and to whom is the arm of the Lord revealed? [John 12:38.] 2. For he shall grow up before him as a tender plant, and as a root out of a dry ground: he hath no form nor comeliness; and when we shall see him, *there is* no beauty that we should desire him. 3. He is despised and rejected of men: a man of sorrows, and acquainted with grief: and we hid as it were *our* faces from him; he was despised, and we esteemed him not.

Isa. 58:3. Wherefore have we fasted, *say, they,* and thou seest not? *wherefore* have we afflicted our soul, and thou takest no knowledge? Behold, in the day of your fast ye find pleasure, and exact all your labours.

Jer. 5:12. They have belied the LORD, and said, It is not he; neither shall evil come upon us; neither shall we see sword nor famine: 13. And the prophets shall become wind, and the word is not in them: thus shall it be done unto them. 14. Wherefore thus saith the LORD God of hosts, Because ye speak this word, behold, I will make my words in thy mouth fire, and this people wood, and it shall devour them.

Mal. 1:2. I have loved you, saith the LORD. Yet ye say, Wherein hast thou loved us? 7. Ye offer polluted bread upon mine altar; and ye say, Wherein have we polluted thee? In that ye say, The table of the LORD is contemptible.

Matt. 10:14. Whosoever shall not receive you, nor hear your words, when ye depart out of that house or city, shake off the dust of your feet. 15. Verily I say unto you, It shall be more tolerable for the land of Sodom and Gomorrha in the day of judgment, than for that city.

Matt. 11:16. Whereunto shall I liken this generation? It is like unto children sitting in the markets, and calling unto their fellows, 17. And saying, We have piped unto you, and ye have not danced; we have mourned unto you, and ye have not lamented. 18. For John came neither eating nor drinking, and they say, He hath a devil. 19. The Son of man came eating and drinking, and they say, Behold, a man gluttonous, and a winebibber, a friend of publicans and sinners. Luke 7:31–35.

Matt. 13:13. Therefore speak I to them in parables: because they seeing see not; and hearing they hear not, neither do they understand. 14. And in them is fulfilled the prophecy of Esaias, which saith, By hearing ye shall hear, and shall not understand; and seeing ye shall see, and shall not perceive: 15. For this people's heart is waxed gross, and their ears are dull of hearing, and their eyes they have closed; lest at any time they should see with their eyes, and hear with their ears, and should understand with their heart, and should be converted, and I should heal them. [Isa. 6:9,10.] 58. And he did not many mighty works there because of their unbelief.

Matt. 17:17. Then Jesus answered and said, O faithless and perverse generation, how long shall I be with you? how long shall I suffer you? bring him hither to me. 19. Then came the disciples to Jesus apart, and said, Why could not we cast him out? 20. And Jesus said unto them, Because of your ¹ unbelief: for verily I say unto you, If ye have faith as a grain of mustard seed, ye shall say unto this mountain, Remove hence to yonder place; and it shall remove; and nothing shall be impossible unto you. [¹ R. V. little faith]

Matt. 21:32. John came unto you in the way of righteousness, and ye believed him not; but the publicans and the harlots believed him: and ye, when ye had seen it, repented not afterward, that ye might believe him.

Mark 6:2. Many hearing him were astonished, saying, From whence hath this man these things? and what wisdom is this which is given unto him, that even such mighty works are wrought by his hands? 3. Is not this the carpenter, the son of Mary, the brother of James, and Joses, and of Juda, and Simon? and are not his sisters here with us? And they were offended at him. 4. But Jesus said unto them, A prophet is not without honour, but in his own country, and among his own kin, and in his own house. 5. And he could there do no mighty work, save that he laid his hands upon a few sick folk, and healed them. 6. And he marvelled because of their unbelief.

Mark 9:24. And straightway the father of the child cried out, and said with tears, Lord, I believe; help thou mine unbelief.

Mark 16:14. Afterward he appeared unto the eleven as they sat at meat, and upbraided them with their unbelief and hardness of heart, because they believed not them which had seen him after he was risen. 16. He that believeth and is baptized shall be saved; but he that believeth not shall be ¹ damned. [¹ R. V. condemned]

Luke 8:12. Those by the wayside are they that hear; then cometh the devil, and taketh away the word out of their hearts, lest they should believe and be saved. 18. Take heed therefore how ye hear: for whosoever hath, to him shall be given; and whosoever hath not, from him shall be taken even that which he seemeth to have. Mark 4:24,25.

Luke 10:16. He that heareth you heareth me; and he that despiseth you despiseth me; and he that despiseth me despiseth him that sent me.

Luke 12:46. The lord of that servant will come in a day when he looketh not for him, and at an hour when he is not aware, and will cut him in sunder, and will appoint him his portion with the unbelievers.

Luke 13:34. O Jerusalem, Jerusalem, which killest the prophets, and stonest them that are sent unto thee; how often would I have gathered thy children together, as a hen doth gather her brood under her wings, and ye would not!

Luke 14:16. Then said he unto him, A certain man made a great supper, and bade many: 17. And sent his servant at supper time to say to them that were bidden, Come; for all things are now ready. 18. And they all with one consent began to make excuse. The first said unto him, I have bought a piece of ground, and I must needs go and see it: I pray thee have me excused. 19. And another said, I have bought five yoke of oxen, and I go to prove them: I pray thee have me excused. 20. And another said, I have married a wife, and therefore I cannot come. 21. So that servant came, and shewed his lord these things. Then the master of the house being angry said to his servant, Go out quickly into the streets and lanes of the city, and bring in hither the poor, and the maimed, and the halt, and the blind. 22. And the servant said, Lord, it is done as thou hast commanded, and yet there is room. 23. And the lord said unto the servant, Go out into the highways and hedges, and compel *them* to come in, that my house may be filled. 24. For I say unto you, That none of those men which were bidden shall taste of my supper.

Luke 16:31. And he said unto him, If they hear not Moses and the prophets, neither will they be persuaded, though one rose from the dead.

Luke 18:8. When the Son of man cometh, shall he find faith on the earth?

Luke 19:41. And when he was come near, he beheld the city, and wept over it, 42. Saying, If thou hadst known, even thou, at least in this thy day, the things *which belong* unto thy peace! but now they are hid from thine eyes.

Luke 22:67. Art thou the Christ? tell us. And he said unto them, If I tell you, ye will not believe:

Luke 24:11. And their words seemed to them as idle tales, and they believed them not. 21. But we trusted that it had been he which should have redeemed Israel: and beside all this, to day is the third day since these things were done. 25. Then he said unto them, O fools, and slow of heart to believe all that the prophets have spoken: 26. Ought not Christ to have suffered these things, and to enter into his glory? 36. And as they thus spake, Jesus himself stood in the midst of them, and saith unto them, Peace *be* unto you. 37. But they were terrified and affrighted, and supposed that they had seen a spirit. 38. And he said unto them, Why are ye troubled? and why do thoughts arise in your hearts? 39. Behold my hands and my feet, that it is I myself: handle me, and see; for a spirit hath not flesh and bones, as ye see me have. 40. And when he had thus spoken, he shewed them *his* hands and *his* feet. 41. And while they yet believed not for joy, and wondered, he said unto them, Have ye here any meat? 42. And they gave him a piece of a broiled fish, and of an honeycomb. 43. And he took *it*, and did eat before them. 44. And he said unto them, These *are* the words which I spake unto you, while I was yet with you, that all things must be fulfilled, which were written in the law of Moses, and *in* the prophets, and *in* the psalms, concerning me. 45. Then opened he their understanding, that they might understand the scriptures,

John 1:10. He was in the world, and the world was made by him, and the world knew kim not. 11. He came unto his own, and his own received him not.

John 3:7. Marvel not that I said unto thee, Ye must be born again. 11. Verily, verily, I say unto thee, We speak that we do know, and testify that we have seen; and ye receive not our witness. 12. If I have told you earthly things, and ye believe not, how shall ye believe, if I tell you *of* heavenly things? 18. He that believeth on him is not condemned: but he that believeth not is condemned already, because he hath not believed in the name of the only begotten Son of God. 32. And what he hath seen and heard, that he testifieth; and no man receiveth his testimony. 36. He that believeth on the Son hath everlasting life: and he that [1] believeth not the Son shall not see life; but the wrath of God abideth on him.   [1 R. V. obeyeth]

John 4:48. Then said Jesus unto him, Except ye see signs and wonders, ye will not believe.

John 5:38. And ye have not his word abiding in you: for whom he hath sent, him ye believe not. 40. And ye will not come to me, that ye might have life. 43. I am come in my Father's name, and ye receive me not: if another shall come in his own name, him ye will receive. 44. How can ye believe, which receive honour one of another, and seek not the honour that *cometh* from God only? 46. For had ye believed Moses, ye would have believed me: for he wrote of me. 47. But if ye believe not his writings, how shall ye believe my words?

John 6:36. But I said unto you, That ye also have seen me, and believe not. 60. Many therefore of his disciples, when they had heard *this*, said, This is an hard saying; who can hear it? 61. When Jesus knew in himself that his disciples murmured at it, he said unto them, Doth this offend you? 62. *What* and if ye shall see the Son of man ascend up where he was before? 64. But there are some of you that believe not. For Jesus knew from the beginning who they were that believed not, and who should betray him. 66. From that *time* many of his disciples went back, and walked no more with him. 70. Jesus answered them, Have not I chosen you twelve, and one of you is a devil? 71. He spake of Judas Iscariot *the son* of Simon: for he it was that should betray him, being one of the twelve.

John 8:24. I said therefore unto you, that ye shall die in your sins: for if ye believe not that I am *he*, ye shall die in your sins. 45. And because I tell *you* the truth, ye believe me not. 46. Which of you convinceth me of sin? And if I say the truth, why do ye not believe me? 47. He that is of God heareth God's words: ye therefore hear *them* not, because ye are not of God. 52. Then said the Jews unto him, Now we know that thou hast a devil. Abraham is dead, and the prophets; and thou sayest, If a man keep my saying, he shall never taste of death. 53. Art thou greater than our father Abraham, which is dead? and the prophets are dead: whom makest thou thyself?

John 10:25. Jesus answered them, I told you, and ye believed not: the works that I do in my Father's name, they bear witness of me. 26. But ye believe not, because ye are not of my sheep, as I said unto you. 37. If I do not the works of my Father, believe me not. 38. But if I do, though ye believe not me, believe the works: that ye may know. and believe, that the Father *is* in me, and I in him.

John 12:37. But though he had done so many miracles before them, yet they believed not on him: 39. Therefore they could not believe, because that Esaias said again, 40. He hath blinded their eyes, and hardened their heart; that they should not see with *their* eyes, nor understand with *their* heart, and be converted, and I should heal them. 47. If any man hear my words, and believe not, I judge him not: for I came not to judge the world, but to save the world. 48. He that rejecteth me, and receiveth not my words, hath one that judgeth him: the word that I have spoken, the same shall judge him in the last day.

John 14:17. *Even* the Spirit of truth; whom the world cannot receive, because it seeth him not, neither knoweth him: but ye know him; for he dwelleth with you, and shall be in you.

John 16:8. And when he is come, he will reprove the world . . . 9. Of sin, because they believe not on me;

John 20:27. Then saith he to Thomas, Reach hither thy finger, and behold my hands; and reach hither thy hand, and thrust *it* into my side: and be not faithless, but believing.

Acts 13:40. Beware therefore, lest that come upon you, which is spoken of in the prophets; 41. Behold, ye despisers, and wonder, and perish: for I work a work in your days, a work which ye shall in no wise believe, though a man declare it unto you.

Acts 19:9. But when divers were hardened, and believed not, but spake evil of that way before the multitude, he departed from them,

Acts 22:18. And saw him saying unto me, Make haste, and get thee quickly out of Jerusalem: for they will not receive thy testimony concerning me.

Acts 28:24. And some believed the things which were spoken, and some believed not.

Rom. 1:18. The wrath of God is revealed from heaven ·against all ungodliness and unrighteousness of men, who hold the truth in unrighteousness:

Rom. 3:3. For what if some did not believe? shall their unbelief make the faith of God without effect?

Rom. 4:20. He staggered not at the promise of God through unbelief: but was strong in faith, giving glory to God;

Rom. 9:31. But Israel, which followed after the law of righteousness, hath not attained to the law of righteousness. 32. Wherefore? Because *they sought it* not by faith, but as it were by the works of the law.

Rom. 10:6. But the righteousness which is of faith speaketh on this wise, Say not in thine heart, Who shall ascend into heaven? (that is, to bring Christ down *from above:*) 7. Or, Who shall descend into the deep? (that is, to bring up Christ again from the dead.) 14. How then shall they call on him in whom they have not believed? and how shall they believe in him of whom they have not heard? 16. But they have not all obeyed the gospel. For Esaias saith, Lord, who hath believed our report? 21. But to Israel he saith, All day long I have stretched forth my hands unto a disobedient and gainsaying people.

Rom. 11:20. Well; because of unbelief they [the branches] were broken off, and thou standest by faith. Be not highminded, but fear: 30. For as ye in times past 1 have not believed God, yet have now obtained mercy 2 through their unbelief: 31. Even so have these also now 3 not believed, that through your mercy they also may obtain mercy. 32. For God hath 4 concluded them all in unbelief, that he might have mercy upon all.

[R. V. 1 were disobedient to 2 by their disobedience 3 been disobedient 4 shut up all unto disobedience]

Rom. 14:23. He that doubteth is damned if he eat, because *he eateth* not of faith: for whatsoever *is* not of faith is sin.

1 Cor. 1:18. For the preaching of the cross is to them that perish foolishness; but unto us which are saved it is the power of God. 22. The Jews require a sign, and the Greeks seek after wisdom: 23. But we preach Christ crucified, unto the Jews a stumblingblock, and unto the Greeks foolishness;

1 Cor. 2:14. But the natural man receiveth not the things of the Spirit of God: for they are foolishness unto him: neither can he know *them*, because they are spiritually discerned.

1 Cor. 14:22. Wherefore tongues are for a sign, not to them that believe, but to them that believe not: but prophesying *serveth* not for them that believe not, but for them which believe.

2 Cor. 6:14. Be ye not unequally yoked together with unbelievers: for what fellowship hath righteousness with unrighteousness? and what communion hath light with darkness? 15. And what concord hath Christ with Belial? or what part hath he that believeth with an infidel? 16. And what agreement hath the temple of God with idols? for ye are the temple of the living God; as God hath said, I will dwell in them, and walk in *them;* and I will be their God, and they shall be my people.

2 Thess. 2:11. And for this cause God shall send them strong delusion, that they should

believe a lie: 12. That they all might be [1]damned who believe not the truth, but had [1]leasure in unrighteousness.   [1 R. V. judged]

2 Thess. 3:2. And that we may be delivered from unreasonable and wicked men: for all *men* have not faith.

1 Tim. 1:13. Who was before a blasphemer, and a persecutor, and injurious: but I obtained mercy, because I did *it* ignorantly in unbelief.

2 Tim. 2:13. If we believe not, *yet* he abideth faithful: he cannot deny himself.

Tit. 1:15. Unto the pure all things *are* pure: but unto them that are defiled and unbelieving *is* nothing pure; but even their mind and conscience is defiled.

Heb. 3:12. Take heed, brethren, lest there be in any of you an evil heart of unbelief, in departing from the living God. 16. Some, when they had heard, did provoke: howbeit not all that came out of Egypt by Moses. 17. But with whom was he grieved forty years? *was it* not with them that had sinned, whose carcases fell in the wilderness? 18. And to whom sware he that they should not enter into his rest, but to them that [1]believed not? 19. So we see that they could not enter in because of unbelief.   [1 R. V. were disobedient]

Heb. 4:1. Let us therefore fear, lest, a promise being left *us* of entering into his rest, any of you should seem to come short of it. 2. For unto us was the gospel preached, as well as unto them: but the word preached did not profit them, not being mixed with faith in them that heard *it*. 3. For we which have believed do enter into rest, as he said, As I have sworn in my wrath, if they shall enter into my rest: although the works were finished from the foundation of the world. 6. Seeing therefore it remaineth that some must enter therein, and they to whom it was first preached entered not in because of [1]unbelief: 11. Let us labour . . . to enter into that rest, lest any man fall after the same example of [1]unbelief.   [1 R. V. disobedience]

Heb. 11:6. But without faith *it is* impossible to please *him:* for he that cometh to God must believe that he is, and *that* he is a rewarder of them that diligently seek him. 31. By faith the harlot Rahab perished not with them that [1]believed not, when she had received the spies with peace.   [1 R. V. were disobedient, having]

Heb. 12:25. See that ye refuse not him that speaketh. For if they escaped not who refused him that spake on earth, much more *shall not* we *escape*, if we turn away from him that *speaketh* from heaven:

Jas. 1:6. But let him ask in faith, nothing [1]wavering. For he that [2]wavereth is like a wave of the sea driven with the wind and tossed. 7. For let not that man think that he shall receive any thing of the Lord.

[R. V. [1]doubting   [2]doubteth]

1 Pet. 2:7. Unto you therefore which believe *he is* precious: but unto them which be disobedient, the stone which the builders disallowed, the same is made the head of the corner, 8. And a stone of stumbling, and a rock of offence, *even to them* which stumble at the word, being disobedient:

2 Pet. 3:4. Where is the promise of his coming? for since the fathers fell asleep, all things continue as *they were* from the beginning of the creation.

1 John 2:22. Who is a liar but he that denieth that Jesus is the Christ? He is antichrist, that denieth the Father and the Son. 23. Whosoever denieth the Son, the same hath not the Father:

1 John 4:3. Every spirit that confesseth not [1]that Jesus [1]Christ is come in the flesh is not of God: and this is that *spirit* of antichrist, whereof ye have heard that it should come; and even now already is it in the world.

[1 Omitted in R. V.]

1 John 5:10. He that believeth on the Son of God hath the witness in himself: he that believeth not God hath made him a liar; because he believeth not the record that God gave of his Son. 12. He that hath the Son hath life; *and* he that hath not the Son of God hath not life.

Jude 5. I will therefore put you in remembrance, though ye once knew this, how that the Lord, having saved the people out of the land of Egypt, afterward destroyed them that believed not.

Rev. 21:8. But the fearful, and unbelieving, and the abominable, . . . shall have their part in the lake which burneth with fire and brimstone: which is the second death.

INSTANCES OF: Eve, Gen. 3:4–6. Moses and Aaron, Num. 20:12. Israelites, Deut. 9:23; 2 Kin. 17:14; Psa. 78. Naaman, 2 Kin. 5:12. Samaritan lord, 2 Kin. 7:2. Disciples, Matt. 17:17; Luke 24:11,25. Zacharias, Luke 1:20. Chief priests, Luke 22:67. The Jews, Mark 1:45; 2:6–11; 8:11,12; 15:29–32; John 5:38,40,43,46,47. Disciples, Matt. 17:20; Mark 4:38,40; Luke 24:41–45. Brethren of Christ, John 7:5. Thomas, John 20:25. Jews of Iconium, Acts 14:2. Thessalonian Jews, Acts 17:5. Jews in Jerusalem, Rom. 15:31. Ephesians, Acts 19:9. Saul, 1 Tim. 1:13. People of Jericho, Heb. 11:31.

UNCHARITABLENESS. Isa. 29:20. The terrible one is brought to nought, and the scorner is consumed, and all that watch for iniquity are cut off: 21. That make a man an offender for a word, and lay a snare for him that reproveth in the gate, and turn aside the just for a thing of nought.

Matt. 7:1. Judge not, that ye be not judged. 2. For with what judgment ye judge, ye shall be judged: and with what measure ye mete, it shall be measured to you again. 3. And why beholdest thou the mote that is in thy brother's eye, but considerest not the beam that is in thine own eye? 4. Or how wilt thou say to thy brother, Let me pull out the mote out of thine eye; and, behold, a beam *is* in thine own eye? 5. Thou hypocrite, first cast out the beam out of thine own eye; and then shalt thou see clearly to cast out the mote out of thy brother's eye. Luke 6:37–42.

Luke 12:57. Yea, and why even of yourselves judge ye not what is right?

John 7:24. Judge not according to the appearance, but judge righteous judgment.

John 8:7. So when they continued asking him, he lifted up himself, and said unto them, He that is without sin among you, let him first cast a stone at her.

Rom. 2:1. Therefore thou art inexcusable, O man, whosoever thou art that judgest: for wherein thou judgest another, thou condemnest thyself; for thou that judgest doest the same things.

Rom. 14:1. Him that is weak in the faith receive ye, *but* not to doubtful disputations. 2. For one believeth that he may eat all things: another, who is weak, eateth herbs. 3. Let not him that eateth despise him that eateth not; and let not him which eateth not judge him that eateth: for God hath received him. 4. Who art thou that judgest another man's servant? to his own master he standeth or falleth. Yea, he shall be holden up: for God is able to make him stand. 5. One man esteemeth one day above another: another esteemeth every day *alike*. Let every man be fully persuaded in his own mind. 6. He that regardeth the day, regardeth *it* unto the Lord; and he that regardeth not the day, to the Lord he doth not regard *it*. He that eateth, eateth to the Lord, for he giveth God thanks; and he that eateth not, to the Lord he eateth not, and giveth God thanks. 7. For none of us liveth to himself, and no man dieth to himself. 8. For whether we live, we live unto the Lord; and whether we die, we die unto the Lord: whether we live therefore, or die, we are the Lord's. 9. For to this end Christ both died, and rose, and revived, that he might be Lord both of the dead and living. 10. But why dost thou judge thy brother? or why dost thou set at nought thy brother? for we shall all stand before the judgment seat of Christ. 11. For it is written, *As* I live, saith the Lord, every knee shall bow to me, and every tongue shall confess to God. 12. So then every one of us shall give account of himself to God. 13. Let us not therefore judge one another any more: but judge this rather, that no man put a stumblingblock or an occasion to fall in *his* brother's way. 14. I know, and am persuaded by the Lord Jesus, that *there is* nothing unclean of itself: but to him that esteemeth any thing to be unclean, to him *it is* unclean. 15. But if thy brother be grieved with *thy* meat, now walkest thou not charitably. Destroy not him with thy meat, for whom Christ died.

1 Cor. 4:3. But with me it is a very small thing that I should be judged of you, or of man's judgment: yea, I judge not mine own self. 4. For I know nothing ᴵby my self; yet am I not hereby justified: but he that judgeth me is the Lord. 5. Therefore judge nothing before the time, until the Lord come, who both will bring to light the hidden things of darkness, and will make manifest the counsels of the hearts· and then shall every man have praise of God. 7. For who maketh thee to differ *from another?* and what hast thou that thou didst not receive? now if thou didst receive *it*, why dost thou glory, as if thou hadst not received *it?*   [ᴵ R. V. against]

1 Cor. 13:1. Though I speak with the tongues of men and of angels, and have not charity, I am become *as* sounding brass, or a tinkling cymbal. 2. And though I have *the gift of* prophecy, and understand all mysteries, and all knowledge; and though I have all faith, so that I could remove mountains, and have not charity, I am nothing. 3. And though I bestow all my goods to feed *the poor*, and though I give my body to be burned, and have not charity, it profiteth me nothing. 4. Charity suffereth long, *and* is kind; charity envieth not; charity vaunteth not itself, is not puffed up, 5. Doth not behave itself unseemly, seeketh not her own, is not easily provoked, thinketh no evil; 6. Rejoiceth not in iniquity, but rejoiceth in the truth;

Jas. 4:11. Speak not evil one of another, brethren. He that speaketh evil of *his* brother, and judgeth his brother, speaketh evil of the law, and judgeth the law: but if thou judge the law, thou art not a doer of the law, but a judge. 12. There is one lawgiver, who is able to save and to destroy: who art thou that judgest another?

See ACCUSATION, FALSE; CHARITABLENESS; SLANDER; SPEAKING, EVIL; TALEBEARER.

INSTANCES OF: The Israelites toward Moses, charging him with having made them abhorred by the Egyptians, Ex. 5:21; charging him with bringing them out of Egypt to die, Ex. 14:11,12; in murmuring against Moses, see MURMURING, INSTANCES OF.

The tribes west of Jordan toward the two and a half tribes, Num. 32:1-33; Josh. 22:11-31. Of Eli toward Hannah, 1 Sam. 1:14-17.

Eliab toward David, charging him with presumption, when he offered to fight Goliath, 1 Sam. 17:28. Princes of Ammon toward David, when he sent commissioners to convey his sympathy to Hanun, 2 Sam. 10:3. Bildad toward Job, Job 8. Eliphaz toward Job, Job 15; 22; 42:7,8. Zophar toward Job, Job 11:1-6; 20. Nathanael, when he said, "Can any good thing come out of Nazareth," John 1:46. The Jews, charging Paul with teaching contrary to the law and against the temple. Acts 21:28.

UNCIRCUMCISION, Eph. 2:11. Uncircumcised heart, Ezek. 28:10; 44:7,9.

UNCLEAN, creatures designated as such, Lev. 11; Deut. 14.

See UNCLEANNESS.

UNCLEANNESS, Lev. 5:2,3; 7:20,21; 17:15; 21:1-15; 22:2-8; Num. 5:2,3; 9:6-11; 19; 31:19; Deut. 23.10,11.

See ABLUTIONS; DEFILEMENT; PURIFICA-TION; SANITATION.

UNCTION. FIGURATIVE: 1 John 2: 20,27.

See ANOINTING.

UNFAITHFULNESS. Prov. 24:11. If thou forbear to deliver *them that are* drawn unto death, and *those that are* ready to be slain; 12. If thou sayest, Behold, we knew it not; doth not he that pondereth the heart consider *it?* and he that keepeth thy soul, doth *not* he know *it?* and shall *not* he render to *every* man according to his works?

Isa. 5:1. Now will I sing to my wellbeloved a song of my beloved touching his vineyard. My wellbeloved hath a vineyard in a very fruitful hill: 2. And he fenced it, and gathered out the stones thereof, and planted it with the choicest vine, and built a tower in the midst of it, and also made a winepress therein: and he looked that it should bring forth grapes, and it brought forth wild grapes. 3. And now, O inhabitants of Jerusalem, and men of Judah, judge, I pray you, betwixt me and my vineyard. 4. What could have been done more to my vineyard, that I have not done in it? wherefore, when I looked that it should bring forth grapes, brought it forth wild grapes? 5. And now go to; I will tell you what I will do to my vineyard: I will take away the hedge thereof, and it shall be eaten up; *and* break down the wall thereof, and it shall be trodden down: 6. And I will lay it waste: it shall not be pruned, nor digged; but there shall come up briers and thorns: I will also command the clouds that they rain no rain upon it. 7. For the vineyard of the LORD of hosts *is* the house of Israel, and the men of Judah his pleasant plant: and he looked for judgment, but behold oppression; for righteousness, but behold a cry.

Hos. 10:1. Israel *is* an empty vine, he bringeth forth fruit unto himself: according to the multitude of his fruit he hath increased the altars; according to the goodness of his land they have made goodly images. 2. Their heart is divided; now shall they be found faulty: he shall break down their altars, he shall spoil their images.

Matt. 3:10. Now also the ax is laid unto the root of the trees: therefore every tree which bringeth not forth good fruit is hewn down, and cast into the fire.

Matt. 13:12. Whosoever hath, to him shall be given, and he shall have more abundance: but whosoever hath not, from him shall be taken away even that he hath.

Matt. 21:19. And when he saw a fig tree in the way, he came to it, and found nothing thereon, but leaves only, and said unto it, Let no fruit grow on thee henceforward for ever. And presently the fig tree withered away. 20. And when the disciples saw *it,* they marvelled, saying, How soon is the fig tree withered away! Mark 11:13,14.

33. Hear another parable: There was a certain householder, which planted a vineyard, and hedged it round about, and digged a winepress in it, and built a tower, and let it out to husbandmen, and went into a far country: 34. And when the time of the fruit drew near, he sent his servants to the husbandmen, that they might receive the fruits of it. 35. And the husbandmen took his servants, and beat one, and killed another, and stoned another. 36. Again, he sent other servants more than the first: and they did unto them likewise. 37. But last of all he sent unto them his son, saying, They will reverence my son. 38. But when the husbandmen saw the son, they said among themselves, This is the heir; come, let us kill him, and let us seize on his inheritance. 39. And they caught him, and cast *him* out of the vineyard, and slew *him.* 40. When the lord therefore of the vineyard cometh, what will he do unto those husbandmen? 41. They say unto him, He will miserably destroy those wicked men, and will let out *his* vineyard unto other husbandmen, which shall render him the fruits in their seasons. 42. Jesus saith unto them, Did ye never read in the scriptures, The stone which the builders rejected, the same is become the head of the corner: this is the Lord's doing, and it is marvellous in our eyes? 43. Therefore say I unto you, The kingdom of God shall be taken from you, and given to a nation bringing forth the fruits thereof. Mark 12:1–9.

Matt. 25:8. And the foolish said unto the wise, Give us of your oil; for our lamps are gone out. 9. But the wise answered, saying, *Not so;* lest there be not enough for us and you: but go ye rather to them that sell, and buy for yourselves. 10. And while they went to buy, the bridegroom came; and they that were ready went in with him to the marriage: and the door was shut. 11. Afterward came also the other virgins, saying, Lord, Lord, open to us. 12. But he answered and said, Verily I say unto you, I know you not. 13. Watch therefore, for ye know neither the day nor the hour wherein the Son of man cometh. *vs.* 1–13.

24. Then he which had received the one talent came and said, Lord, I knew thee that thou art an hard man, reaping where thou hast not sown, and gathering where thou hast not strawed: 25. And I was afraid, and went and hid thy talent in the earth: lo, *there* thou hast *that is* thine. 26. His lord answered and said unto him, *Thou* wicked and slothful servant, thou knewest that I reap where I sowed not, and gather where I have not strawed: 27. Thou oughtest therefore to have put my money to the exchangers, and *then* at my coming I should have received mine own with usury. 28. Take therefore the talent from him, and give *it* unto him which hath ten talents. 29. For unto every one that hath shall be given, and he shall have abundance: but from him that hath not shall be taken away even that which he hath.

30. And cast ye the unprofitable servant into outer darkness: there shall be weeping and gnashing of teeth. *vs.* 14–30; Luke 19:12–27.

41. Then shall he say also unto them on the left hand, Depart from me, ye cursed, into everlasting fire, prepared for the devil and his angels: 42. For I was an hungred, and ye gave me no meat: I was thirsty, and ye gave me no drink: 43. I was a stranger, and ye took me not in: naked, and ye clothed me not: sick, and in prison, and ye visited me not. 44. Then shall they also answer him, saying, Lord, when saw we thee an hungred, or athirst, or a stranger, or naked, or sick, or in prison, and did not minister unto thee? 45. Then shall he answer them, saying, Verily I say unto you, Inasmuch as ye did *it* not to one of the least of these, ye did *it* not to me. 46. And these shall go away into everlasting punishment: but the righteous into life eternal. *vs.* 31–46.

Luke 13:6. He spake also this parable; A certain *man* had a fig tree planted in his vineyard; and he came and sought fruit thereon, and found none. 7. Then said he unto the dresser of his vineyard, Behold, these three years I come seeking fruit on this fig tree, and find none: cut it down; why cumbereth it the ground? 8. And he answering said unto him, Lord, let it alone this year also, till I shall dig about it, and dung *it:* 9. And if it bear fruit, *well:* and if not, *then* after that thou shalt cut it down.

John 15:2. Every branch in me that beareth not fruit he taketh away: and every *branch* that beareth fruit, be purgeth it, that it may bring forth more fruit.

2 Pet. 1:8. For if these things be in you, and abound, they make *you that ye shall* neither *be* barren nor unfruitful in the knowledge of our Lord Jesus Christ. 9. But he that lacketh these things is blind, and cannot see afar off, and hath forgotten that he was purged from his old sins.

See SIN, FRUITS OF ; UNFRUITFULNESS. See also RIGHTEOUSNESS, FRUITS OF.

OF FRIENDS: See FRIENDS, FALSE.

UNFRUITFULNESS. Isa. 5:2. And he fenced it, and gathered out the stones thereof, and planted it with the choicest vine, and built a tower in the midst of it, and also made a winepress therein: and he looked that it should bring forth grapes, and it brought forth wild grapes.

Matt. 3:10. And now also the ax is laid unto the root of the trees: therefore every tree which bringeth not forth good fruit is hewn down, and cast into the fire. Luke 3:9.

Matt. 7:19. Every tree that bringeth not forth good fruit is hewn down, and cast into the fire.

Matt. 13:4. And when he sowed, some *seeds* fell by the way side, and the fowls came and devoured them up: 5. Some fell upon stony places, where they had not much earth: and forthwith they sprung up, because they had no deepness of earth:

6. And when the sun was up, they were scorched; and because they had no root, they withered away. 7. And some fell among thorns; and the thorns sprung up, and choked them:

Matt. 21:19. And when he saw a fig tree in the way, he came to it, and found nothing thereon, but leaves only, and said unto it, Let no fruit grow on thee henceforward for ever. And presently the fig tree withered away. 20. And when the disciples saw *it,* they marvelled, saying, How soon is the fig tree withered away. Mark 11:13.

Luke 13:6. He spake also this parable; A certain *man* had a fig tree planted in his vineyard; and he came and sought fruit thereon, and found none. 7. Then said he unto the dresser of his vineyard, Behold, these three years I come seeking fruit on this fig tree, and find none: cut it down; why cumbereth it the ground? 8. And he answering said unto him, Lord, let it alone this year also, till I shall dig about it, and dung *it:* 9. And if it bear fruit, *well:* and if not, *then* after that thou shalt cut it down.

John 15:2. Every branch in me that beareth not fruit he taketh away: and every *branch* that beareth fruit, he purgeth it, that it may bring forth more fruit. 4. Abide in me, and I in you. As the branch cannot bear fruit of itself, except it abide in the vine; no more can ye, except ye abide in me. 6. If a man abide not in me, he is cast forth as a branch, and is withered: and men gather them, and cast *them* into the fire, and they are burned.

See SIN, FRUITS OF; UNFAITHFULNESS. See also RIGHTEOUSNESS, FRUITS OF.

UNICORN [wild ox, *R. V.*]. Intractable, Job 39:9–12. Horned, Deut. 33:17; Psa. 22:21; 92:10. Great strength of, Num. 23:22; 24:8; Job 39:9–12. Agile, Psa. 29:6.

FIGURATIVE: Of the judgments of God, Isa. 34:7.

UNION, advantages of, Prov. 15:22; Eccl. 4:9–12.

OF THE RIGHTEOUS: See UNITY, OF THE RIGHTEOUS; of the righteous with Christ, see RIGHTEOUS, UNITY OF, WITH CHRIST.

UNITY. OF THE GODHEAD: See GOD, UNITY OF.

OF THE RIGHTEOUS: Psa. 133:1. Behold, how good and how pleasant *it is* for brethren to dwell together in unity !

Isa. 52:8. Thy watchmen shall lift up the voice; with the voice together shall they sing: for they shall see eye to eye, when the LORD shall bring again Zion.

Matt. 23:8. But be not ye called Rabbi: for one is your Master, *even* Christ; and all ye are brethren.

Acts 4:32. The multitude of them that believed were of one heart and of one soul: neither said any *of them* that ought of the things which he possessed was his own; but they had all things common.

Rom. 12:16. *Be* of the same mind one toward another.

Rom. 14:19. Let us therefore follow after the things which make for peace, and things wherewith one may edify another.

Rom. 15:5. Now the God of patience and consolation grant you to be likeminded one toward another, according to Christ Jesus: 6. That ye may with one mind *and* one mouth glorify God, even the Father of our Lord Jesus Christ.

1 Cor. 1:10. Now I beseech you, brethren, by the name of our Lord Jesus Christ, that ye all speak the same thing, and *that* there be no divisions among you; but *that* ye be perfectly joined together in the same mind and in the same judgment.

2 Cor. 13:11. Be perfect, be of good comfort, be of one mind, live in peace; and the God of love and peace shall be with you.

Eph. 4:3. Endeavouring to keep the unity of the Spirit in the bond of peace.

Phil 1:27. Only let your conversation be as it becometh the gospel of Christ: that whether I come and see you, or else be absent, I may hear of your affairs, that ye stand fast in one spirit, with one mind striving together for the faith of the gospel;

Phil. 2:2. Fulfil ye my joy, that ye be likeminded, having the same love, *being* of one accord, of one mind.

Phil. 3:16. Let us walk by the same rule, let us mind the same thing. 17. Brethren, be followers together of me, and mark them which walk so as ye have us for an ensample.

1 Pet. 3:8. Finally, *be ye* all of one mind, having compassion one of another, love as brethren, *be* pitiful, *be* courteous:

See COMMUNION; FELLOWSHIP.

UNLEAVENED BREAD. See BREAD; PASSOVER.

UNNI. 1. A musician in the time of David, 1 Chr. 15:18,20.

2. A Levite in the time of Nehemiah, Neh. 12:9. [*R. V.*, UNNO.]

UNNO. See UNNI, 2.

UNPARDONABLE SIN, 2 Kin. 24:4; Matt. 12:31,32; Luke 12:10; Heb. 6:4-6; 1 John 5:16.

See OBDURACY; REPROBACY.

INSTANCES OF: Israel, Num. 14:26-45. Eli's house, 1 Sam. 3:14.

UNSELFISHNESS. Rom. 12:10. *Be* kindly affectioned one to another with brotherly love; in honour preferring one another;

Rom. 15:1. We then that are strong ought to bear the infirmities of the weak, and not to please ourselves. 2. Let every one of us please *his* neighbour for *his* good to edification. 3. For even Christ pleased not himself; but, as it is written, The reproaches of them that reproached thee fell on me.

1 Cor. 9:19. For though I be free from all *men*, yet have I made myself servant unto all, that I might gain the more. 20. And unto the Jews I became as a Jew, that I might gain the Jews; to them that are un-

der the law, as under the law, that I might gain them that are under the law; 21. To them that are without law, as without law, (being not without law to God, but under the law to Christ,) that I might gain them that are without law. 22. To the weak became I as weak, that I might gain the weak: I am made all things to all *men*, that I might by all means save some. 23. And this I do for the gospel's sake, that I might be partaker thereof with *you*.

1 Cor. 10:24. Let no man seek his own, but every man another's *wealth*. 33. Even as I please all *men* in all *things*, not seeking mine own profit, but the *profit* of many, that they may be saved.

1 Cor. 13:4. Charity suffereth long, *and* is kind; charity envieth not; charity vaunteth not itself, is not puffed up, 5. Doth not behave itself unseemly, seeketh not her own, is not easily provoked, thinketh no evil;

2 Cor. 5:14. For the love of Christ constraineth us; because we thus judge, that if one died for all, ¹ then were all dead: 15. And *that* he died for all, that they which live should not henceforth live unto themselves, but unto him which died for them, and rose again. [¹ R. V. therefore all died;]

2 Cor. 8:9. For ye know the grace of our Lord Jesus Christ, that, though he was rich, yet for your sakes he became poor, that ye through his poverty might be rich.

Phil. 2:3. *Let* nothing *be done* through strife or vainglory; but in lowliness of mind let each esteem other better than themselves. 4. Look not every man on his own things, but every man also on the things of others.

Jas. 2:8. If ye fulfil the royal law according to the scripture, Thou shalt love thy neighbour as thyself, ye do well:

INSTANCES OF: Abraham, Gen. 13:9; 14: 23,24. King of Sodom, Gen. 14:21. Children of Heth, Gen. 23:6,11. Judah, Gen. 44:33,34. Moses, Num. 11:29; 14:12-19. Gideon, Judg. 8:22,23. Saul, 1 Sam. 11:12,13. Jonathan, 1 Sam. 23:17,18. David, 1 Sam. 24:17; 2 Sam. 15:19,20; 23:16,17; 1 Chr. 21:17; Psa. 69:6. Araunah, 2 Sam. 24:22-24. Nehemiah, Neh. 5:14-18. Jews, Esth. 9:15. Daniel, Dan. 5: 17. Jonah, Jonah 1:12,13. Joseph, Matt. 1: 19. The disciples, Acts 4:34,35. Priscilla and Aquila, Rom. 16:3,4. Paul, 1 Cor. 10: 33; Phil. 1:18; 4:17; 2 Thess. 3:8. Philemon, Philem. 13,14.

See CHARITABLENESS; FELLOWSHIP; FRATERNITY; SELFISHNESS.

UPHARSIN, divided, Dan. 5:25,28.

UPHAZ, a country famous for gold, Jer. 10:9; Dan. 10:5.

See OPHIR.

UPRIGHTNESS. See RIGHTEOUSNESS.

UR. 1. Abraham's native place, Gen. 11: 27,28. Abraham leaves, Gen. 11:31; 15:7; Neh. 9:7.

2. Father of one of David's mighty men, 1 Chr. 11:35.

URBANE, a Christian in Rome, Rom. 16:9.

URIAH. 1. One of David's mighty men, 2 Sam. 23:39; 1 Chr. 11:41. David's adultery with the wife of, 2 Sam. 11:2–5; 1 Kin. 15:5. Summoned from seat of war by David, 2 Sam. 11:6–13. Noble spirit of, 2 Sam. 11: 11. David compasses the death of, 2 Sam.11: 14–25. David marries the widow of, 2 Sam. 11:26,27. Called URIAS, Matt. 1:6.

2. A priest. The father of Meremoth, Ezra 8:33. Called URIJAH, Neh. 3:4,21; but in *R. V.*, URIAH.

3. See URIJAH, 3.

4. A priest. Witness to one of Isaiah's prophecies, Isa. 8:2. Probably identical with Urijah, 2 Kin. 16:10. See URIJAH, 1.

URIAS. See URIAH, 1.

URIEL. 1. A Levite. Son of Tahath, 1 Chr. 6:24.

2. A Levite. Assisted in moving the ark, 1 Chr. 15:5,11,12.

3. Grandfather of King Abijah, 2 Chr. 13:2.

URIJAH. 1. A priest in the time of Ahaz. Builds a new altar for Ahaz, 2 Kin. 16:10–16. Probably identical with Uriah, witness to a prophecy of Isaiah, Isa. 8:2.

2. See URIAH, 2.

3. A priest. Assistant to Ezra, Neh. 8:4. Called in *R. V.*, URIAH.

4. A prophet in the time of Jehoiakim. Prophesies against Judah, Jer. 26:20. Fled to Egypt; taken; slain by Jehoiakim, Jer. 26:21–23.

URIM AND THUMMIM, signifying light and perfection. In the breastplate, Ex. 28:30; Lev. 8:8. Eleazar to ask counsel for Joshua, after the judgment of, Num. 27: 21. Priests only might interpret, Deut. 33: 8; Ezra 2:63; Neh. 7:65. Israelites consult, Judg. 1:1; 20:18,23. Withheld answer from King Saul, 1 Sam. 28:6.

USURPATION. OF POLITICAL FUNC-TIONS: By Absalom, 2 Sam. 15:1–12. By Adonijah, 1 Kin. 1:5–9. By Baasha, 1 Kin. 15:27,28. By Zimri, 1 Kin. 16:9,10. By Jehu, 2 Kin. 9:11–37. By Athaliah, 2 Kin. 11:1–16. By Shallum, 2 Kin. 15:10.

IN ECCLESIASTICAL AFFAIRS: By Saul, in assuming priestly functions, 1 Sam. 13:8–14. By Solomon, in thrusting Abiathar out of the priesthood, 1 Kin. 2:26,27. By Uzziah, in assuming priestly offices, 2 Chr. 26:16–21. By Ahaz, 2 Kin. 16:12,13.

See CHURCH AND STATE, STATE SUPERIOR TO THE CHURCH; GOVERNMENT, ECCLESIAS-TICAL.

OF EXECUTIVE POWER: In ordering Naboth's death and confiscation of his vine-yard, 1 Kin. 21:7–19. In the scheme of Joseph to dispossess the Egyptians of their real and personal property, Gen. 47:13–26. Of Pharaoh, making bondservants of the Israelites, Ex. 1:9–22. Moses accused of, Num. 16:3.

USURY, interest, not necessarily unrea-sonable exaction, but all income from loans. Forbidden, Ex. 22:25; Lev. 25:35–37; Deut. 23:19; Psa. 15:5; Prov. 28:8; Jer. 15:10; Ezek. 18:8,13,17; 22:12. Exaction of, rebuked, Neh.

5:1–13. Authorized, of strangers, Deut. 23: 20. Exacted by Jews, Ezek. 22:12.

Just men innocent of the vice of requir-ing. Ezek. 18:8.

See INTEREST : MONEY.

UTHAI. 1. Son of Ammihud, 1 Chr. 9:4.

2. Son of Bigvai. Returned from Babylon with Ezra, Ezra 8:14.

UZ. 1. Son of Aram, Gen. 10:23; 1 Chr. 1:17.

2. Son of Nahor, Gen. 22:21 [*R. V.*]. In *A. V.*, called HUZ.

3. Son of Dishan, Gen. 36:28; 1 Chr. 1:42.

4. A country of unknown location. Home of Job, Job 1:1. Prophecies concerning, Jer. 25:20; Lam. 4:21.

UZAI, father of Palal, Neh. 3:25.

UZAL, son of Joktan, Gen. 10:27; 1 Chr. 1:21.

UZZA. 1. See UZZAH, 1.

2. Proprietor of the burial place of kings Manasseh and Amon, 2 Kin. 21:18,26.

3. Son of Shimei, 1 Chr. 6:29. In *R. V.*, called UZZAH.

4. Son of Ehud, 1 Chr. 8:7.

5. One of the Nethinim, Ezra 2:49; Neh. 7:51.

UZZAH. 1. Called also UZZA, son of Abinadab. Driver of the cart in moving the ark, 2 Sam. 6:3; 1 Chr. 13:7. Stricken dead for touching the ark, 2 Sam. 6:6–8; 1 Chr. 13:9–11.

2. See UZZA, 2.

UZZEN-SHERAH, a city of unknown location, 1 Chr. 7:24.

UZZI. 1. A priest. Son of Bukki, 1 Chr. 6:5,6,51; Ezra 7:4.

2. Grandson of Issachar, 1 Chr. 7:2,3.

3. Grandson of Benjamin, 1 Chr. 7:7.

4. Son of Michri, 1 Chr. 9:8.

5. An overseer of the Levites, Neh. 11:22.

6. A priest in the time of Nehemiah, Neh. 12:19,42.

UZZIA, one of David's mighty men, 1 Chr. 11:44.

UZZIAH. 1. Called AZARIAH. King of Judah, 2 Kin. 14:21; 15:1,2; 2 Chr. 26:1.3. Rebuilds Elath, 2 Kin. 14:22; 2 Chr. 26:2. Reigns righteously, 2 Kin. 15:3; 2 Chr. 26:4, 5. Defeats the Philistines, 2 Chr. 26:6,7. Takes tribute from the Ammonites; strengthens the kingdom, 2 Chr. 26:8. Strengthens the fortifications of Jerusalem, 2 Chr. 26:9. Promotes cattle raising and agriculture, 2 Chr. 26:10. Military establish-ment of, 2 Chr. 26:11–15. Is presumptuous in burning incense; stricken with leprosy ; quarantined, 2 Chr. 26:16–21; 2 Kin. 15:5. Jotham regent during quarantine of, 2 Kin. 15:5; 2 Chr. 26:21. Death of, 2 Kin. 15:7; 2 Chr. 26:23. History of, written by Isaiah, 2 Chr. 26:22; Isa. 1:1. Earthquake in the reign of, Amos 1:1; Zech. 14:5.

2. Son of Uriel, 1 Chr. 6:24.

3. Father of Jehonathan, 1 Chr. 27:25.

4. A priest. Puts away his Gentile wife, Ezra 10:21.

5. Father of Athaiah, Neh. 11:4.

UZZIEL. 1. A son of Kohath, Ex. 6:18, 22; Lev. 10:4.

2. A Simeonite captain, 1 Chr. 4:42.

3. Son of Bela, 1 Chr. 7:7.

4. One of David's musicians, 1 Chr. 25:4.

5. A Levite. Son of Jeduthun, 2 Chr. 29:14.

6. A goldsmith. Aided in repairing the walls of Jerusalem, Neh. 3:8.

V

VAIL. 1. Hangings used in the tabernacle to divide the holy of holies from the holy place. Called the second veil, Heb. 6:19; 9:3. Ordinances prescribing, Ex. 26: 31-33. Made by Bezaleel and Aholiab, Ex. 36:35,36. See VEIL.

2. A covering for the ark, Ex. 35:12; 39:34; 40:21; Num. 4:5.

3. Of the temple, 2 Chr. 3:14. Rent at the time of the crucifixion of Jesus, Matt. 27:51; Mark 15:38; Luke 23:45.

FIGURATIVE: Heb. 10:20.

VAJEZATHA, son of Haman, Esth. 9:9.

VALOR. See COURAGE.

VANIAH, an Israelite. Puts away his Gentile wife, Ezra 10:36.

VANITY. A consequence of the fall, Rom. 8:20. Every man is, Psa. 39:11. Every state of man is, Psa. 62:9. Man at his best estate is, Psa. 39:5. Man is like to, Psa. 144:4. The thoughts of man are, Psa. 94:11. The days of man are, Job 7:16; Eccl. 6:12. Childhood and youth are, Eccl. 11:10. The beauty of man is, Psa. 39:11; Prov. 31:30. The help of man is, Psa. 60:11; Lam. 4:17. Man's own righteousness is, Isa. 57:12. Worldly wisdom is, Eccl. 2:15,21; 1 Cor. 3:20. Worldly pleasure is, Eccl. 2:1. Worldly anxiety is, Psa. 39:6; 127:2. Worldly labor is, Eccl. 2:11; 4:4. Worldly enjoyment is, Eccl. 2:3,10,11. Worldly possessions are, Eccl. 2:4-11. Treasures of wickedness are, Prov. 10:2. Heaping up riches is, Eccl. 2:26; 4:8. Love of riches is, Eccl. 5:10. Unblessed riches are, Eccl. 6:2. Riches gotten by falsehood are, Prov. 21:6. All earthly things are, Eccl. 1:2. Foolish questions are, 1 Tim. 1:6,7; 6:20; 2 Tim. 2:14,16; Tit. 3:9. The conduct of the ungodly is, 1 Pet. 1:18. The religion of hypocrites is, Jas. 1:26. The worship of the wicked is, Isa. 1:13; Matt. 6:7. Lying words are, Jer. 7:8. False teaching is but, Jer. 23:32. Mere external religion is, 1 Tim. 4:8; Heb. 13:9. Almsgiving without charity is, 1 Cor. 13:3. Faith without works is, Jas. 2:14. Idolatry is, 2 Kin. 17:15; Psa. 31:6; Isa. 44:9,10; Jer. 10:8; 18:15. Wealth gotten by, diminishes, Prov. 13:11.

Saints hate the thoughts of, Psa. 119:113; pray to be kept from, Psa. 119:37; Prov. 30:8; avoid, Psa. 24:4; avoid those given to, Psa. 26:4.

The wicked especially characterized by, Job 11:11; though full of, affect to be wise, Job 11:12; love, Psa. 4:2; imagine, Psa. 2:1; Acts 4:25; Rom. 1:21; devise, Psa. 36:4

[see marg.]; speak, Psa. 10:7; 12:2; 41:6; count God's service as, Job 21:15; Mal. 3:14; allure others by words of, 2 Pet. 2:18; walk after, Jer. 2:5; walk in, Psa. 39:6; Eph. 4:17; inherit, Jer. 16:19; reap, Prov. 22:8; Jer. 12:13; judicially given up to, Psa. 78:33; Isa. 57:13.

Fools follow those given to, Prov. 12:11. Following those given to, leads to poverty, Prov. 28:19. All should know and acknowledge, Deut. 4:35.—*Bible Text-Book.*

See PRIDE.

VASHNI. See JOEL, 1.

VASHTI, wife of king Ahasuerus. Put away for refusing to exhibit herself at a royal banquet, Esth. 1:9-22; 2:1,4,17.

VEDAN. A place whose merchants traded with Tyre, Ezek. 27:19 [*R. V.*]. In *A. V.*, called DAN.

VEGETARIANS, persons who eat no flesh, Rom. 14:2.

VEGETATION. Created the third day, Gen. 1:11; 2:5. For food, Gen. 1:29,30.

VEIL. Worn by Rebekah, Gen. 24:65; by Tamar, Gen. 38:14,19; by Moses, to screen his face when he descended from Mount Sinai, Ex. 34:33,35; 2 Cor. 3:13-16.

See DRESS; VAIL; WIMPLE.

VENERATION, for parents, Gen. 48: 15,16.

See OLD AGE; PARENTS; REVERENCE.

VENGEANCE, belongs to God, Psa. 94:1; Rom. 12:19.

INSTANCE OF: Sons of Jacob on Hamor and Shechem, Gen. 34:20-31.

See JUDGMENTS; REVENGE; RETALIATION.

VENTRILOQUISM, Isa. 29:4. Divination by, Acts 16:16.

VERDICT, against Jesus, Matt. 26:66; 27:24-26; Mark 15:15; Luke 23:24; John 19:16.

See COURTS.

VERMILION, a color, Jer. 22:14; Ezek. 23:14.

See COLOR.

VESTMENTS. Of priests, see PRIESTS.

VICARIOUS. DEATH: The ram for Isaac, Gen. 22:13. Jesus for sinners, see JESUS, DEATH OF, MISSION OF, SUFFERINGS OF.

See ATONEMENT; SUFFERINGS, VICARIOUS: JESUS, SAVIOUR.

VICEGERENCY. Of Elisha, in miraculously rewarding the Shunammite, 2 Kin. 4:16,17; in cursing Gehazi, 2 Kin. 5:27. Of the apostles, Matt. 16:19; 18:18; John 20:23.

VIGILANCE. INSTANCE OF: King of Jericho, Josh. 2:1-3.

See WATCHMAN.

VICTORIES. In battle, from God, Psa. 55:18; 76:5,6. Celebrated in song, Judg. 5; 2 Sam. 22; by women, 1 Sam, 18: 6,7; 2 Sam. 1:20.

See ARMIES; WAR, GOD IN.

VINE. Degeneracy of, Jer. 2:21. Fable of, Judg. 9:12,13. Pruned, Isa. 5:6; John 15:1-5. Parables of, Psa. 80:8-14; Ezek. 17: 6-10; 19:10-14.

SYMBOLICAL, John 15:1-5

See VINEYARD.

VINEGAR, a sour wine. Forbidden to Nazarites, Num. 6:3. Used with food, Ruth 2:14; Psa. 69:21; Prov. 10:26; 25:20. Offered to Christ on the cross, Matt. 27:34, 48; John 19:29, with Mark 15:23.

VINEYARD. Cottages [*R. V.*, booths] in, Isa. 1:8. Towers in, Isa. 5:2; Matt. 21:33; Mark 12:1. Winepress in, Isa. 5:2. Pools in, Eccl. 2:4,6. Leased, Song 8:11,12; Isa. 7: 23; Matt. 21:33-39. Of kings, 1 Chr. 27:26-28. Neglected, Prov. 24:30,31. Plain of the, Judg. 11:33.

Parables of, Isa. 5:1-7; 27:2,3; Jer. 12:10; Matt. 20:1-16; 21:28-31,33-41; Luke 13:6-9.

See VINE; WINE. Also see ABSTINENCE.

VIOL, an instrument of music, Isa. 5:12.

See MUSIC, INSTRUMENTS OF; PSALTERY.

VIPER. A serpent, Job 20:16; Isa. 30:6; 59:5. Fastens on Paul's hand, Acts 28:3.

See SERPENT.

FIGURATIVE: Matt. 3:7; 23:33; Luke 3:7.

VIRGIN. Proofs of, Deut. 22:13-21. Dowry of, Ex. 22:17. Character of, to be protected, Deut. 22:17-21,23,24. Betrothal of, a quasi marriage, Deut. 22:23,24. Distinguishing apparel of, 2 Sam. 13:18. Priests might marry none but, Lev. 21:14. Mourn in the temple, Lam. 1:4; 2:10. Virginity of, bewailed, Judg. 11:37-39. Parable of the wise and foolish, Matt. 25:1-13. Mother of Jesus a, Isa. 7:14; Matt. 1:23; Luke 1:27. Advised by Paul not to marry, 1 Cor. 7.

FIGURATIVE: Of the Church, Isa. 62:5; Jer. 14:17; 31:4,13; 2 Cor. 11:2. Of personal purity, 1 Cor. 7:25,37; Rev. 14:4.

VIRGINITY. See VIRGIN.

VIRTUE. Power [*R. V.*], Luke 6:19; 8: 46. Excellence, Phil. 4:8; 2 Pet. 1:5.

See CHASTITY; CONTINENCE; COURAGE.

VISION, a mode of revelation, Num. 12:6; 1 Sam. 3:1; 2 Chr. 26:5; Psa. 89:19; Prov. 29:18; Jer. 14:14; 23:16; Dan 1:17; Hos. 12:10; Joel 2:28; Obad. 1; Hab. 2:2; Acts 2:17.

Of Abraham, concerning his descendants, Gen. 15:1-17. Of Jacob, of the ladder with ascending and descending angels, Gen. 28: 12; at Beer-sheba, Gen. 46:2. Of Joshua, of the captain of the Lord's host, Josh. 5:13-15. Of Moses, of the burning bush, Ex. 3:2; of the glory of God, Ex. 24:9-11; 33:18-23.

Of the Israelites, of the manifestation of the glory of God, Ex. 24:10,17; Heb. 12:18-21. Of Balaam, in a trance, see BALAAM. Of Elisha, at the translation of Elijah, 2 Kin. 2:11. Of Elisha's servant, of the chariots of the Lord, 2 Kin. 6:17. Of Micaiah, of the defeat of the Israelites; of the Lord on his throne; and of a lying spirit, 1 Kin. 22:17-23; 2 Chr. 18:16-22. Of David, of the angel of the Lord by the threshing floor of Ornan, 1 Chr. 21:15-18. Of Job, of a spirit, Job 4:12-16. Of Isaiah, of the Lord and his glory in the temple, Isa. 6; of the valley of vision, Isa. 22. Of Jeremiah, of an almond rod, Jer. 1:11; of the seething pot, Jer. 1:13.

Of Ezekiel, of the glory of God, Ezek. 1:3, 12-14; 23; of the roll, Ezek. 2:9; of the man

of fire, Ezek. 8; 9; of the coals of fire, Ezek. 10:1-7; of the dry bones, Ezek. 37:1-14; of the city and temple, Ezek. chapters 40-48; of the waters, Ezek. 47:1-12.

Of Daniel, of the four beasts, Dan. 7; of the Ancient of days, Dan. 7:9-27; of the ram and the he goat, Dan. 8; of the angel, Dan. 10.

Of Amos, of grasshoppers, Amos 7:1,2; of fire, Amos 7:4; of a plumb line, Amos 7:7,8; of summer fruit, Amos 8:1,2; of the temple, Amos 9:1.

Of Zechariah, of horses, Zech. 1:8-11; of horns and carpenters, Zech. 1:18-21; of the high priest, Zech. 3:1-5; of the golden candlestick, Zech. 4; of the flying roll, Zech. 5:1-4; of the mountains and chariots, Zech. 6:1-8.

Of Zacharias, in the temple, Luke 1:13-22. Of John the Baptist, at the baptism of Jesus, Matt. 3:16; Mark 1:10; Luke 3:22; John 1:32-34. Peter, James, and John, of the transfiguration of Jesus and the appearance of Moses and Elijah, Matt. 17:1-9; Luke 9:28-36. Of the people, of the tongues of fire at Pentecost, Acts 2:2,3. Of Stephen, of Christ, Acts 7:55,56. Of Paul, of Christ, on the way to Damascus, Acts 9:3-6; 1 Cor. 9:1; of Ananias, Acts 9:12; of a man of Macedonia, saying, "Come over into Macedonia, and help us," Acts 16:9; in Corinth, Acts 18:9,10; in a trance, Acts 22:17-21; of paradise, 2 Cor. 12:1-4. Of Ananias, of Christ, Acts 9: 10-12. Of Cornelius, the centurion, of an angel, Acts 10:3. Of Peter, of the sheet let down from heaven, Acts 10:9-18.

Of John on the Isle of Patmos, the Book of Revelation.

Of Christ and the golden candlesticks, Rev. 1:10-20; the open door, Rev. 4:1; a rainbow and throne, Rev. 4:2,3; twenty-four elders, Rev. 4:4; seven lamps, Rev. 4:5; sea of glass, Rev. 4:6; four living creatures, Rev. 4:6-8; book with seven seals, Rev. 5: 1-5; golden vials, Rev. 5:8; of the six seals, Rev. 6; four horses, Rev. 6:2-8; earthquake and celestial phenomena, Rev. 6:12-14; four angels, Rev. 7:1; sealing of the one hundred and forty-four thousand, Rev. 7:2-8; of the seventh seal and seven angels, Rev. chapters 8-11; of the censer, Rev. 8:5; hail and fire, Rev. 8:7; mountain cast into the sea, Rev. 8:8,9; falling star, Rev. 8:10,11; 9:1; the third part of sun and moon and stars darkened, Rev. 8:12; bottomless pit, Rev. 9:2; locusts, Rev. 9:3-11; four angels loosed from the Euphrates, Rev. 9:14; army of horsemen, Rev. 9:16-19; angel having a book, Rev. 10:1-10; seven thunders, Rev. 10:3,4; measurement of the temple, Rev. 11:1,2; two witnesses, Rev. 11:3-12; court of the Gentiles, Rev. 11:2; two olive trees and two candlesticks, Rev. 11:4; the beast out of the bottomless pit, Rev. 11:7; fall of the city, Rev. 11:13; second and third woes, Rev. 11:14; a woman clothed with the sun; birth of the man child, Rev. 12; a red dragon, Rev. 12:3-17;

war in heaven, Rev. 12:7-9; the beast rising out of the sea, Rev. 13:1-10; the beast coming out of the earth, Rev. 13:11-18; the Lamb on Mount Zion, Rev. 14:1-5; the angel having the everlasting gospel, Rev. 14:6,7; the angel proclaiming the fall of Babylon, Rev. 14:8-13; the Son of man with a sickle, Rev. 14:14-16; angel reaping the harvest, Rev. 14:14-20; angel coming out of the temple, Rev. 14:17-19; an angel having power over fire, Rev. 14:18; the vine and the winepress, Rev. 14:18-20; angels with the seven last plagues, Rev. 15; sea of glass, Rev. 15:2; temple opened, Rev. 15:5; the plague upon the men who had the mark of the beast, Rev. 16:2; sea turned into blood, Rev. 16:3; the seven angels with the seven vials of the wrath of God, Rev. 16; 17; destruction of Babylon, Rev. 18; of the multitude praising, Rev. 19:1-9; of him who is faithful and true riding a white horse, Rev. 19:11-16; angel in the sun, Rev. 19:17-21; Satan bound a thousand years, Rev. 20:1-3; thrones of judgment, and the resurrection, and the loosing of Satan, Rev. 20:1-10; great white throne, Rev. 20:11; opening of the book of life, Rev. 20:12; death and hell, Rev. 20:14; New Jerusalem, Rev. 21; river of life, Rev. 22:1; tree of life, Rev. 22:2.

See DREAM.

VISITORS. See GUESTS.

VOICE. OF GOD: Ezek. 1:24,28; 10:5; John 5:37; 12:28-30; Acts 7:31; 9:4,7; 26:14,15. See ANTHROPOMORPHISMS.

VOLCANOES, Deut 4:11; 5:23; Judg. 5:5; Psa. 97:5; 104:32; 144:5; Isa. 34:9,10; 64: 1-3; Jer. 51:25; Mic. 1:4; Nah. 1:5,6.

See EARTHQUAKE ; MOUNTAIN.

VOLUPTUOUSNESS. See LASCIVIOUSNESS; SENSUALITY.

VOPHSI, father of Nahbi, Num. 13:14.

VOWS. Mosaic laws concerning, Lev. 23:37,38; Num. 29:39. Must be voluntary, see below. Must be performed, see below. Estimation of the redemption price of things offered in vows, to be made by the priest, according to age and sex of the person making the offering, Lev. 27:1-13. The redemption price of the offering of real estate, to be valued by the priest, Lev. 27: 14,15; of a field, Lev. 27:16-25.

Edible things offered in, to be eaten the same day they were offered, Lev. 7:16-18. Things offered in, to be brought to the tabernacle or temple, Deut. 12:6,11,17,18,26; belonged to the priests, Num. 18:14.

Rash: By Jephthah, in consecration of his daughter as a sacrifice, if his campaign against the Ammonites were successful, Judg. 11:29-40; the Israelites, to destroy the Benjamites, Judg. 21:5,6, with chapters 20; 21.

Things forbidden to be offered in : Receipts of the whore and price of a dog, Deut. 23:18; a minor, of himself, Mark 7:11-13.

UNCLASSIFIED SCRIPTURES RELATING TO : Gen. 28:20. And Jacob vowed a vow, saying, If God will be with me, and

will keep me in this way that I go, and will give me bread to eat, and raiment to put on, 21. So that I come again to my father's house in peace : then shall the LORD be my God. Gen. 31:13.

Lev. 5:4. Or if a soul swear, pronouncing with *his* lips to do evil, or to do good, whatsoever *it be* that a man shall pronounce with an oath, and it be hid from him; when he knoweth *of it,* then he shall be guilty in one of these. 5. And it shall be, when he shall be guilty in one of these *things,* that he shall confess that he hath sinned in that *thing:* 6. And he shall bring his trespass offering unto the LORD for his sin which he hath sinned, a female from the flock, a lamb or a kid of the goats, for a sin offering; and the priest shall make an atonement for him concerning his sin. 7. And if he be not able to bring a lamb, then he shall bring for his trespass, which he hath committed, two turtledoves, or two young pigeons, unto the LORD; one for a sin offering, and the other for a burnt offering. 8. And he shall bring them unto the priest, who shall offer *that* which *is* for the sin offering first, and wring off his head from his neck, but shall not divide *it* asunder: 9. And he shall sprinkle of the blood of the sin offering upon the side of the altar; and the rest of the blood shall be wrung out at the bottom of the altar: it *is* a sin offering. 10. And he shall offer the second *for* a burnt offering, according to the manner; and the priest shall make an atonement for him for his sin which he hath sinned, and it shall be forgiven him. 11. But if he be not able to bring two turtledoves, or two young pigeons, then he that sinned shall bring for his offering the tenth part of an ephah of fine flour for a sin offering; he shall put no oil upon it, neither shall he put *any* frankincense thereon: for it *is* a sin offering. 12. Then shall he bring it to the priest, and the priest shall take his handful of it, *even* a memorial thereof, and burn *it* on the altar, according to the offerings made by fire unto the LORD: it *is* a sin offering. 13. And the priest shall make an atonement for him as touching his sin that he hath sinned in one of these, and it shall be forgiven him: and *the remnant* shall be the priest's, as a meat offering.

Lev. 22:18. Speak unto Aaron, and to his sons, and unto all the children of Israel, and say unto them, Whatsoever *he be* of the house of Israel, or of the strangers in Israel, that will offer his oblation for all his vows, and for all his freewill offerings, which they will offer unto the LORD for a burnt offering; 19. *Ye shall offer* at your own will a male without blemish, of the beeves, of the sheep, or of the goats. 20. *But* whatsoever hath a blemish, *that* shall ye not offer : for it shall not be acceptable for you. 21. And whosoever offereth a sacrifice of peace offerings unto the LORD to accomplish *his* vow, or a freewill offering in beeves or sheep, it shall be perfect to be accepted; there shall be no blemish therein. 22. Blind, or broken, or maimed, or having a wen, or scurvy, or scabbed, ye shall not offer these unto the Lord, nor make an offering by fire of them upon the altar unto the Lord. 23. Either a bullock or a lamb that hath any thing superfluous or lacking in his parts, that mayest thou offer *for* a freewill offering; but for a vow it shall not be accepted. 24. Ye shall not offer unto the Lord that which is bruised, or crushed, or broken, or cut; neither shall ye make *any offering thereof* in your land. 25. Neither from a stranger's hand shall ye offer the bread of your God of any of these; because their corruption *is* in them, *and* blemishes *be* in them: they shall not be accepted for you.

Num. 15:2. Speak unto the children of Israel, and say unto them, When ye be come into the land of your habitations, which I give unto you, 3. And will make an offering by fire unto the Lord, . . . sacrifice in performing a vow, or in a freewill offering, . . . a sweet savour unto the Lord, of the herd, or of the flock: 4. Then shall he that offereth his offering unto the Lord bring a meat offering of a tenth deal of flour mingled with the fourth *part* of an hin of oil. 5. And the fourth *part* of an hin of wine for a drink offering shalt thou prepare with the burnt offering or sacrifice, for one lamb. 6. Or for a ram, thou shalt prepare *for* a meat offering two tenth deals of flour mingled with the third *part* of an hin of oil. 7. And for a drink offering thou shalt offer the third *part* of an hin of wine, *for* a sweet savour unto the Lord. 8. And when thou preparest a bullock *for* a burnt offering, or *for* a sacrifice in performing a vow, or peace offerings unto the Lord: 9. Then shall he bring with a bullock a meat offering of three tenth deals of flour mingled with half an hin of oil. 10. And thou shalt bring for a drink offering half an hin of wine, *for* an offering made by fire, of a sweet savour unto the Lord. 11. Thus shall it be done for one bullock, or for one ram, or for a lamb, or a kid. 12. According to the number that ye shall prepare, so shall ye do to every one according to their number. 13. All that are born of the country shall do these things after this manner, in offering an offering made by fire, of a sweet savour unto the Lord. 14. And if a stranger sojourn with you, or whosoever *be* among you in your generations, and will offer an offering made by fire, of a sweet savour unto the Lord; as ye do, so he shall do. 15. One ordinance *shall be both* for you of the congregation, and also for the stranger that sojourneth *with you*, an ordinance for ever in your generations: as ye *are*, so shall the stranger be before the Lord. 16. One law and one manner shall be for you, and for the stranger that sojourneth with you.

Num. 30:2. If a man vow a vow unto the Lord, or swear an oath to bind his soul with a bond; he shall not break his word, he shall do according to all that proceedeth out of his mouth. 3. If a woman also vow a vow unto the Lord, and bind *herself* by a bond, *being* in her father's house in her youth; 4. And her father hear her vow, and her bond wherewith she hath bound her soul, and her father shall hold his peace at her: then all her vows shall stand, and every bond wherewith she hath bound her soul shall stand. 5. But if her father disallow her in the day that he heareth; not any of her vows, or of her bonds wherewith she hath bound her soul, shall stand: and the Lord shall forgive her, because her father disallowed her. 6. And if she had at all an husband, when she vowed, or uttered ought out of her lips, wherewith she bound her soul; 7. And her husband heard *it*, and held his peace at her in the day that he heard *it:* then her vows shall stand, and her bonds wherewith she bound her soul shall stand. 8. But if her husband disallowed her on the day that he heard *it;* then he shall make her vow which she vowed, and that which she uttered with her lips, wherewith she bound her soul, of none effect: and the Lord shall forgive her. 9. But every vow of a widow, and of her that is divorced, wherewith they have bound their souls, shall stand against her. 10. And if she vowed in her husband's house, or bound her soul by a bond with an oath; 11. And her husband heard *it*, and held his peace at her, *and* disallowed her not: then all her vows shall stand, and every bond wherewith she bound her soul shall stand. 12. But if her husband hath utterly made them void on the day he heard *them; then* whatsoever proceeded out of her lips concerning her vows, or concerning the bond of her soul, shall not stand: her husband hath made them void; and the Lord shall forgive her. 13. Every vow, and every binding oath to afflict the soul, her husband may establish it, or her husband may make it void. 14. But if her husband altogether hold his peace at her from day to day; then he establisheth all her vows, or all her bonds, which *are* upon her: he confirmeth them, because he held his peace at her in the day that he heard *them*. 15. But if he shall any ways make them void after that he hath heard *them;* then he shall bear her iniquity. 16. These *are* the statutes, which the Lord commanded Moses, between a man and his wife, between the father and his daughter, *being yet* in her youth in her father's house. *v. 1.*

Deut. 23:18. Thou shalt not bring the hire of a whore, or the price of a dog, into the house of the Lord thy God for any vow: for even both these *are* abomination unto the Lord thy God. 21. When thou shalt vow a vow unto the Lord thy God, thou shalt not slack to pay it: for the Lord thy God will surely require it of thee; and it would be sin in thee. 22. But if thou shalt forbear to vow, it shall be no sin in thee. 23. That which is gone out of thy lips thou shalt keep and perform; *even* a freewill offering, according as thou hast vowed unto the LORD thy God, which thou hast promised with thy mouth.

Job 22:27. Thou shalt make thy prayer unto him, and he shall hear thee, and thou shalt pay thy vows.

Psa. 22:25. My praise *shall be* of thee in the great congregation: I will pay my vows before them that fear him.

Psa. 50:14. Offer unto God thanksgiving; and pay thy vows unto the most High: 15. And call upon me in the day of trouble: I will deliver thee, and thou shalt glorify me.

Psa. 56:12. Thy vows *are* upon me, O God: I will render praises unto thee.

Psa. 61:5. Thou, O God, hast heard my vows: 8. So will I sing praise unto thy name for ever, that I may daily perform my vows.

Psa. 65:1. Praise waiteth for thee, O God, in Sion: and unto thee shall the vow be performed.

Psa. 66:13. I will go into thy house with burnt offerings: I will pay thee my vows, 14. Which my lips have uttered, and my mouth hath spoken, when I was in trouble.

Psa. 76:11. Vow, and pay unto the LORD your God: let all that be round about him bring presents unto him that ought to be feared.

Psa. 116:14. I will pay my vows unto the LORD now in the presence of all his people. 15. Precious in the sight of the LORD *is* the death of his saints. 16. O LORD, truly I *am* thy servant; I *am* thy servant, *and* the son of thine handmaid: thou hast loosed my bonds. 17. I will offer to thee the sacrifice of thanksgiving, and will call upon the name of the LORD. 18. I will pay my vows unto the LORD now in the presence of all his people, 19. In the courts of the LORD's house, in the midst of thee, O Jerusalem. Praise ye the LORD.

Prov. 20:25. *It is* a snare to the man *who* devoureth *that which is* holy, and after vows to make enquiry.

Eccl. 5:4. When thou vowest a vow unto God, defer not to pay it; for *he hath* no pleasure in fools: pay that which thou hast vowed. 5. Better *is it* that thou shouldest not vow, than that thou shouldest vow and not pay. 6. Suffer not thy mouth to cause thy flesh to sin; neither say thou before the angel, that it *was* an error: wherefore should God be angry at thy voice, and destroy the work of thine hands?

Jonah 2:9. But I will sacrifice unto thee with the voice of thanksgiving; I will pay *that* that I have vowed. Salvation *is* of the LORD.

Nah. 1:15. Behold upon the mountains the feet of him that bringeth good tidings, that publisheth peace! O Judah, keep thy solemn feasts, perform thy vows: for the wicked shall no more pass through thee; he is utterly cut off.

See CONTRACT; COVENANT.

INSTANCES OF: Of Jacob, see above, Gen. 28:20–22. Of the mother of Micah, in the dedication of silver for the making of an idol, Judg. 17:2,3. Of Hannah, to consecrate unto the Lord the child for which she prayed, 1 Sam. 1:11, with *vs.* 27,28. Of Elkanah, 1 Sam. 1:21. Of Absalom, 2 Sam. 15:7,8. Of Job, not to entertain thoughts of fornication, Job 31:1. Of David, Psa. 132:2. Of Ananias and Sapphira, in the dedication of the proceeds of the sale of their land, Acts 5:1–11. Of the Jews, to slay Paul, Acts 23: 12–15. Of Jephthah, and of the Israelites, see RASH VOWS, above.

See NAZARITE.

VULTURE. A carnivorous bird, Lev. 11:14; Deut. 14:13. In *R.V.*, translated falcon, Job 28:7, and kite, Isa. 34:15.

W

WAFER, Ex. 29:23; Num. 6:19.

WAGES. Of Jacob, Gen. 29:15–30; 30: 28–34; 31:7,41. Parable concerning, Matt. 20:1–15.

See MASTER; SERVANT.

UNCLASSIFIED SCRIPTURES RELATING TO: Lev. 19:13. Thou shalt not defraud thy neighbour, neither rob *him:* the wages of him that is hired shall not abide with thee all night until the morning.

Deut. 24:14. Thou shalt not oppress an hired servant *that is* poor and needy, *whether he be* of thy brethren, or of thy strangers that *are* in thy land within thy gates: 15. At his day thou shalt give *him* his hire, neither shall the sun go down upon it; for he *is* poor, and setteth his heart upon it: lest he cry against thee unto the LORD, and it be sin unto thee.

Deut. 25:4. Thou shalt not muzzle the ox when he treadeth out *the corn.*

Jer. 22:13. Woe unto him that buildeth his house by unrighteousness, and his chambers by wrong; *that* useth his neighbour's service without wages, and giveth him not for his work;

Hag. 1:6. Ye have sown much, and bring in little; ye eat, but ye have not enough; ye drink, but ye are not filled with drink; ye clothe you, but there is none warm; and he that earneth wages, earneth wages *to put it* into a bag with holes.

Mal. 3:5. And I will come near to you to judgment; and I will be a swift witness . . . against those that oppress the hireling in *his* wages, the widow, and the fatherless, and that turn aside the stranger *from his right*, and fear not me, saith the LORD of hosts.

Luke 3:14. And the soldiers likewise demanded of him, saying, And what shall we do? And he said unto them, . . . be content with your wages.

Luke 10:7. For the labourer is worthy of his hire. Matt. 10:10.

Rom. 4:4. Now to him that worketh is the reward not reckoned of grace, but of debt.

Rom. 6:23. For the wages of sin *is* death; but the gift of God *is* eternal life through Jesus Christ our Lord.

Col. 4:1. Masters, give unto *your* servants that which is just and equal; knowing that ye also have a Master in heaven.

Jas. 5:4. Behold, the hire of the labourers who have reaped down your fields, which is of you kept back by fraud, crieth: and the cries of them which have reaped are entered into the ears of the Lord of sabaoth.

WAGON, Gen. 45:19,27; Num. 7:3-9. See CART.

WAILING, of the wicked, Matt. 13:42.

WAITING. Upon God: As the God of providence Jer. 14:22; as the God of salvation, Psa. 25:5; as the giver of all temporal blessings, Psa. 104:27,28; 145:15,16.

For mercy, Psa. 123:2; pardon, Psa. 39:7, 8; the consolation of Israel, Luke 2:25; salvation, Gen. 49:18; Psa. 62:1,2; guidance and teaching, Psa. 25:5; protection, Psa. 33: 20; 59:9,10; the fulfillment of his word, Hab. 2:3; the fulfillment of his promises, Acts 1:4; hope of righteousness by faith, Gal. 5:5; coming of Christ, 1 Cor. 1:7; 1 Thess. 1:10. Is good, Psa. 52:9. God calls us to, Zeph. 3: 8. Exhortations and encouragements to, Psa. 27:14; 37:7; Hos. 12:6.

Should be with the soul, Psa. 62:1,5; with earnest desire, Psa. 130:6; with patience, Psa. 37:7; 40:1; with resignation, Lam. 3:26; with hope in his word, Psa. 130:5; with full confidence, Mic. 7:7; continually, Hos. 12:6; all the day, Psa. 25:5; specially in adversity, Psa. 59:1-9; Isa. 8:17; in the way of his judgments, Isa. 26:8. Saints resolve on, Psa. 52:9; 59:9. Saints have expectation from, Psa. 62:5. Saints plead, in prayer, Psa. 25: 21; Isa. 33:2. The patience of saints often tried in, Psa. 69:3.

They who engage in, wait upon him only, Psa. 62:5; are heard, Psa. 40:1; are blessed, Isa. 30:18; Dan. 12:12; experience his goodness, Lam. 3:25; shall not be ashamed, Psa. 25:3; Isa. 49:23; shall renew their strength, Isa. 40:31; shall inherit the earth, Psa. 37:9; shall be saved, Prov. 20:22; Isa. 25:9; shall rejoice in salvation, Isa. 25:9; shall receive the glorious things prepared by God for them, Isa. 64:4. Predicted of the Gentiles, Isa. 42:4; 60:9. Illustrated, Psa. 123:2; Luke 12:36; Jas. 5:7.

EXEMPLIFIED: Jacob, Gen. 49:18; David, Psa. 39:7; Isaiah, Isa. 8:17; Micah, Mic. 7:7; Joseph, Mark 15:43. — *Bible Text-Book.*

WALKING. With God: According to his commands, Deut. 5:33; Psa. 1; Jer. 7:23; in his ways, Deut. 28:9; Josh. 22:5; in the old paths, Jer. 6:16; as taught by him, 1 Kin. 8: 36; Isa. 2:3; 30:21; uprightly, Prov. 2:7; in his statutes and judgments, Ezek. 37:24; in newness of life, Rom. 6:4; not after the flesh, but after the Spirit, Rom. 8:1; Gal. 5:16; honestly, as in the day, Rom. 13:13; by faith,

not by sight, 2 Cor. 5:7; in love, following Christ, Eph. 5:2; worthy of the Lord, Col. 1: 10; in Christ, Col. 2:6; by the gospel rule, Phil. 3:16; in the light, as God is, 1 John 1:7; in white raiment, Rev. 3:4; in the light of heaven, Rev. 21:24.

INSTANCES OF: Enoch, Gen. 5:24; Noah, Gen. 6:9.—*Bible Text-Book.*

WALLS, of the cities. Of Bashan, destroyed by the Israelites, Deut. 3:5,6. Of Jericho, Josh. 2:15; 6. Of Jerusalem, see JERUSALEM. Of Babylon, Jer. 51:44; broad, Jer. 51:58. Of Beth-shan, 1 Sam. 31:10. Of Rabbah, 2 Sam. 11:20. Of Abel, 2 Sam. 20: 15,21.

Houses built upon, Josh. 2:15. Double, 2 Kin. 25:4; Isa. 22:11. Sentinels on, see WATCHMAN.

FIGURATIVE: Of the new Jerusalem, Rev. 21:12,14,17-21.

WAR. Divine approval of, 2 Sam. 22:35. Civil, Judg. 12:1-6; 20; 2 Sam. 2:12-31; 3:1; 20; 1 Kin. 14:30; 16:21; Isa. 19:2; forbidden, 2 Chr. 11:4; averted, Josh. 22:11-34. Enemy harangued by general of opposing side, 2 Kin. 18:19-36; 2 Chr. 13:4-12. Of extermination, Num. 31:7-17; Deut. 2:33,34; 3:6; 20: 13-18; Josh. 6:21,24; 8:24,25; 10:2-40; 11:11-23; 1 Sam. 15:3-9; 27:8-11.

God in, Ex. 14:13,14; Deut. 1:30; 3:21,22; 7:17-24; 20:1,4; 31:6-8,23; 32:29,30; Josh. 1:1, 5-7,9; Judg. 1:2; 6:16; 7:9; 11:29; 1 Sam. 17: 45-47; 19:5; 30:7,8; 2 Sam. 5:22-24; 22:18; 1 Kin. 20:28; Psa. 18:34; 76:3; Jer. 46:15; Amos 5:8,9; Zech.10:5. God uses, as a judgment, Ex. 23:24; Lev. 26:17,31-39; Deut. 28:25-68; 32:30; Judg. 2:14; 2 Kin. 15:37; 1 Chr. 5:22,26; 21:12; 2 Chr. 12:1-12; 15:6; 24: 23,24; 33:11; 36; Job 19:29; Psa.44:9-16; 60:1-3; 105:25; Isa. 5:1-8,25-30; 9:8-12; 13:3,4,9; 19:2; 34:2-6; 43:28; 45:7; Jer. 12:7,12; 46:15-17,21; 47:6,7; 48:10; 49:5; 50:25; Ezek. 23:22-25; Amos 3:6; 4:11; Zeph. 1:7-18; Zech. 8:10; 14:2.

Repugnant to God, 1 Chr. 22:8,9; Psa. 68: 30; 120:6,7; Rev. 13:10. God sends panic in, Ex. 15:14-16; threatens defeat in, Deut. 32: 25; 1 Sam. 2:10; 2 Chr. 18:12-16; Isa. 30:15-17; Ezek. 15:6-8; 21:9-17; inflicts defeat in, Josh. 7:12,13; 2 Chr. 12:5-8; 24:23,24; Psa. 76:3; 78:66; 79:10; Isa. 5:25; Jer. 46:15,16.

Counsels of, Josh. 22:10-34; Judg. 7:10,11; 2 Sam. 16:20; 17:1-15; Psa. 48:4-7; Prov. 11:14; 20:18. Wisdom required in, Prov. 21:22; 24:6; Eccl. 9:14-18; Luke 14:31,32.

Tumult of, Amos 2:2. Slain in, neglected, Isa. 14:19; 18:6. Evils of, 2 Sam. 2:26; Psa. 46:8; 79:1-3; 137:9; Isa. 3:5,25,26; 5:29,30; 6:11,12; 9:5,19-21; 13:15,16; 15; 16:9, 10; 18:6; 19:2-16; 32:13,14; 33:8,9; 34:7-15; Jer. 4:19-31; 5:16,17; 6:24-26; 7:33,34; 8:16,17; 9:10-21; 10:20; 13:14; 14:18; 15:8,9; 19:7-9; 25:33; 46:3-12; 47:3; 48:28,33; 51:30-58; Lam. chapters 1-5; Ezek. 33:27; 39:17-19; Hos. 10: 14; 13:16; Joel 2:2-10; Amos 1:13; 6:9,10; 8:3; Nah. 2:10; 3:3,10; Zech. 14:2; Luke 21:20-26; Rev. 19:17,18.

To cease, Psa. 46:9; Isa. 2:4; Mic. 4:3.

Wars and rumors of, Matt. 24:6; Mark 13:7; Luke 21:9.

See ARMIES; ARMS; FORT; SOLDIERS; STRATEGY; TOWER; WATCHMAN.

FIGURATIVE: Warfare of saints: Is not after the flesh, 2 Cor. 10:3. Is a good warfare, 1 Tim. 1:18,19. Called the good fight of faith, 1 Tim. 6:12.

Is ·against the devil, Gen. 3:15; 2 Cor. 2:11; Eph. 6:12; Jas. 4:7; 1 Pet. 5:8; Rev. 12:17; the flesh, Rom. 7:23; 1 Cor. 9:25–27; 2 Cor. 12:7; Gal. 5:17; 1 Pet. 2:11; enemies, Psa. 38:19; 56:2; 59:3; the world, John 16:33; 1 John 5:4,5; death, 1 Cor. 15:26, with Heb. 2:14,15.

Often arises from the opposition of friends or relatives, Mic. 7:6; Matt. 10:35,36. To be carried on under Christ, as our Captain, Heb. 2:10; under the Lord's banner, Psa. 60:4; with faith, 1 Tim. 1:18,19; with a good conscience, 1 Tim. 1:18,19; with steadfastness in the faith, 1 Cor. 16:13; 1 Pet. 5:9, with Heb. 10:23; with earnestness, Jude 3; with watchfulness, 1 Cor. 16:13; 1 Pet. 5:8; with sobriety, 1 Thess. 5:6; 1 Pet 5:8; with endurance of hardness, 2 Tim. 2:3,10; with self-denial, 1 Cor. 9:25–27; with confidence in God, Psa. 27:1–3; with prayer, Psa. 35:1–3; Eph. 6:18; without earthly entanglements, 2 Tim. 2:4. Mere professors do not maintain, Jer. 9:3.

Saints are all engaged in, Phil. 1:30; must stand firm in, Eph. 6:13,14; exhorted to diligence in, 1 Tim. 6:12; Jude 3; encouraged in, Isa. 41:11,12; 51:12; Mic. 7:8; 1 John 4:4; helped by God in, Psa. 118:13; Isa. 41:13, 14; protected by God in, Psa. 140:7; comforted by God in, 2 Cor. 7:5,6; strengthened by God in, Psa. 20:2; 27:14; Isa. 41:10; strengthened by Christ in, 2 Cor. 12:9; 2 Tim. 4:17; delivered by Christ in, 2 Tim. 4:18; thank God for victory in, Rom. 7:25; 1 Cor. 15:57.

Armor for: a girdle of truth, Eph. 6:14; the breastplate of righteousness, Eph. 6:14; preparation of the gospel, Eph. 6:15; shield of faith, Eph. 6:16; helmet of salvation, Eph. 6:17; 1 Thess. 5:8; sword of the Spirit, Eph. 6:17; called armor of God, Eph. 6:11; called armor of righteousness, 2 Cor. 6:7; called armor of light, Rom. 13:12; not carnal, 2 Cor. 10:4; mighty through God, 2 Cor. 10:4,5; the whole, is required, Eph. 6:13; must be put on, Rom. 13:12; Eph. 6:11; to be on right hand and left, 2 Cor. 6:7.

Victory in, is from God, 1 Cor 15:57; 2 Cor. 2:14; through Christ, Rom. 7:25; 1 Cor. 15:57; 2 Cor. 12:9; Rev. 12:11; by faith, Heb. 11:33–37; 1 John 5:4,5; over the devil, Rom. 16:20; 1 John 2:14; over the flesh, Rom. 7:24, 25; Gal. 5:24; over the world, 1 John 5:4,5; over all that exalts itself, 2 Cor. 10:5; over death and the grave, Isa. 25:8; 26:19; Hos. 13:14; 1 Cor. 15:54,55; triumphant, Rom. 8:37; 2 Cor. 10:5.

They who overcome in, shall eat of the hidden manna, Rev. 2:17; eat of the tree of life, Rev. 2:7; be clothed in white raiment, Rev. 3:5; be pillars in the temple of God,

Rev. 3:12; sit with Christ in his throne, Rev. 3:21; have a white stone, and in it a new name written, Rev. 2:17; have power over the nations, Rev. 2:26; have the name of God written upon them by Christ, Rev. 3:12; have God as their God, Rev. 21:7; have the morning star, Rev. 2:28; inherit all things, Rev. 21:7; be confessed by Christ before God the Father, Rev. 3:5; be sons of God, Rev. 21:7; not be hurt by the second death, Rev. 2:11; not have their names blotted out of the book of life, Rev. 3:5.

Symbolized by a red horse, Rev. 6:4.

IN HEAVEN: SYMBOLICAL, Rev. 12:7.

WARFARE. See WAR. Spiritual, see FIGURATIVE, under WAR.

WARNING. See WICKED, WARNED.

WASHING. Of hands, a token of innocency, Deut. 21:6; Psa. 26:6; 73:13; Matt. 27:24.

See ABLUTION; PURIFICATION.

FIGURATIVE: Of regeneration, Psa. 51: 7; Prov. 30:12; Isa. 1:16; 4:4; Zech. 13:1; 1 Cor. 6:11; Eph. 5:26; Tit. 3:5.

WATCH, a division of time, see NIGHT TIME.

WATCHFULNESS. Ex. 23:13. And in all *things* that I have said unto you be circumspect: and make no mention of the name of other gods, neither let it be heard out of thy mouth.

Ex. 34:12. Take heed to thyself, lest thou make a covenant with the inhabitants of the land whither thou goest, lest it be for a snare in the midst of thee:

Deut. 4:9. Only take heed to thyself, and keep thy soul diligently, lest thou forget the things which thine eyes have seen, and lest they depart from thy heart all the days of thy life: but teach them thy sons, and thy sons' sons: 23. Take heed unto yourselves, lest ye forget the covenant of the LORD your God, which he made with you, and make you a graven image, *or* the likeness of any *thing*, which the LORD thy God hath forbidden thee.

Deut. 11:16. Take heed to yourselves, that your heart be not deceived, and ye turn aside, and serve other gods, and worship them;

Deut. 12:13. Take heed to thyself that thou offer not thy burnt offerings in every place that thou seest:

Deut. 27:9. And Moses and the priests the Levites spake unto all Israel, saying, Take heed, and hearken, O Israel; this day thou art become the people of the LORD thy God.

Josh. 22:5. But take diligent heed to do the commandment and the law, which Moses the servant of the LORD charged you, to love the LORD your God, and to walk in all his ways, and to keep his commandments, and to cleave unto him, and to serve him with all your heart and with all your soul. Deut. 6:17.

Josh. 23:11. Take good heed therefore unto yourselves, that ye love the LORD your God.

1 Kin. 2:3. And keep the charge of the LORD thy God, to walk in his ways, to keep his statutes, and his commandments, and his judgments, and his testimonies, as it is written in the law of Moses, that thou mayest prosper in all that thou doest, and withersoever thou turnest thyself:

1 Kin. 8:25. So that thy children take heed to their way, that they walk before me as thou hast walked before me. 1 Kin. 2:4.

2 Chr. 19:7. Wherefore now let the fear of the LORD be upon you; take heed and do *it:* for *there is* no iniquity with the LORD our God, nor respect of persons, nor taking of gifts.

Neh. 4:9. Nevertheless we made our prayer unto our God, and set a watch against them day and night, because of them.

Job 36:18. Because *there is* wrath, *beware* lest he take thee away with *his* stroke: then a great ransom cannot deliver thee. 19. Will he esteem thy riches? *no,* not gold, nor all the forces of strength. 20. Desire not the night, when people are cut off in their place. 21. Take heed, regard not iniquity: for this hast thou chosen rather than affliction.

Psa. 39:1. I said, I will take heed to my ways, that I sin not with my tongue: I will keep my mouth with a bridle, while the wicked is before me.

Psa. 102:7. I watch, and am as a sparrow alone upon the housetop.

Psa. 119:9. Wherewithal shall a young man cleanse his way? by taking heed *thereto* according to thy word.

Psa. 141:3. Set a watch, O LORD, before my mouth; keep the door of my lips.

Prov. 4:23. Keep thy heart with all diligence; for out of it *are* the issues of life. 25. Let thine eyes look right on, and let thine eyelids look straight before thee. 26. Ponder the path of thy feet, and let all thy ways be established.

Prov. 8:34. Blessed *is* the man that heareth me, watching daily at my gates, waiting at the posts of my doors.

Prov. 16:17. The highway of the upright *is* to depart from evil: he that keepeth his way preserveth his soul.

Prov. 28:26. He that trusteth in his own heart is a fool: but whoso walketh wisely, he shall be delivered.

Nah. 2:1. He that dasheth in pieces is come up before thy face: keep the munition, watch the way, make *thy* loins strong, fortify *thy* power mightily.

Hab. 2:1. I will stand upon my watch, and set me upon the tower, and will watch to see what he will say unto me, and what I shall answer when I am reproved.

Mal. 2:15. Therefore take heed to your spirit,

Matt. 6:1. Take heed that ye do not your alms before men, to be seen of them: otherwise ye have no reward of your Father which is in heaven.

Matt. 16:6. Then Jesus said unto them, Take heed and beware of the leaven of the Pharisees and of the Sadducees.

Matt. 18:10. Take heed that ye despise not one of these little ones; for I say unto you, That in heaven their angels do always behold the face of my Father which is in heaven.

Matt. 24:4. And Jesus answered and said unto them, Take heed that no man deceive you.

Matt. 25:13. Watch therefore, for ye know neither the day nor the hour wherein the Son of man cometh.

Matt. 26:40. And he cometh unto the disciples, and findeth them asleep, and saith unto Peter, What, could ye not watch with me one hour? 41. Watch and pray, that ye enter not into temptation: the spirit indeed *is* willing, but the flesh *is* weak.

Mark 4:24. And he said unto them, Take heed what ye hear: with what measure ye mete, it shall be measured to you: and unto you that hear shall more be given. Luke 8:18.

Mark 13:9. But take heed to yourselves: for they shall deliver you up to councils; and in the synagogues ye shall be beaten: and ye shall be brought before rulers and kings for my sake, for a testimony against them. [*vs.* 10-20.] 21. And then if any man shall say to you, Lo, here *is* Christ; or, lo, *he is* there; believe *him* not: 22. For false Christs and false prophets shall rise, and shall shew signs and wonders, to seduce, if *it were* possible, even the elect. 23. But take ye heed: behold, I have foretold you all things. 32. But of that day and *that* hour knoweth no man, no, not the angels which are in heaven, neither the Son, but the Father. 33. Take ye heed, watch and pray: for ye know not when the time is. 34. *For the son of man is* as a man taking a far journey, who left his house, and gave authority to his servants, and to every man his work, and commanded the porter to watch. 35. Watch ye therefore: for ye know not when the master of the house cometh, at even, or at midnight, or at the cockcrowing, or in the morning: 36. Lest coming suddenly he find you sleeping. 37. And what I say unto you I say unto all, Watch. Matt. 24:42-51; Luke 21:8-36.

Luke 11:35. Take heed therefore that the light which is in thee be not darkness.

Luke 12:15. And he said unto them, Take heed, and beware of covetousness: for a man's life consisteth not in the abundance of the things which he possesseth. 35. Let your loins be girded about, and *your* lights burning; 36. And ye yourselves like unto men that wait for their lord, when he will return from the wedding; that when he cometh and knocketh, they may open unto him immediately. 37. Blessed *are* those servants, whom the lord when he cometh shall find watching: verily I say unto you, that he shall gird himself, and make them to sit down to meat, and will come forth and serve them. 38. And if he shall come in the second watch, or come in the third watch, and find *them* so, blessed are those servants. 39. And this know, that if the goodman of the house had known what hour the thief would come, he would have watched, and not have suffered his house to be broken through. 40. Be ye therefore ready also: for the Son of man cometh at an hour when ye think not. Matt. 24:42–47; Mark 13:33–37.

Acts 20:28. Take heed therefore unto yourselves, and to all the flock, over the which the Holy Ghost hath made you overseers, to feed the church of God, which he hath purchased with his own blood. 29. For I know this, that after my departing shall grievous wolves enter in among you, not sparing the flock. 30. Also of your own selves shall men arise, speaking perverse things, to draw away disciples after them. 31. Therefore watch, and remember, that by the space of three years I ceased not to warn every one night and day with tears.

Rom. 11:21. For if God spared not the natural branches, *take heed* lest he also spare not thee.

Rom. 13:11. And that, knowing the time, that now *it is* high time to awake out of sleep: for now *is* our salvation nearer that when we believed.

1 Cor. 7:29. But this I say, brethren, the time *is* short: it remaineth, that both they that have wives be as though they had none; 30. And they that weep, as though they wept not; and they that rejoice, as though they rejoiced not; and they that buy, as though they possessed not; 31. And they that use this world, as not abusing *it:* for the fashion of this world passeth away.

1 Cor. 9:27. But I keep under my body, and bring *it* into subjection: lest that by any means, when I have preached to others, I myself should be a castaway.

1 Cor. 10:12. Wherefore let him that thinketh he standeth take heed lest he fall.

1 Cor. 11:28. But let a man examine himself, and so let him eat of *that* bread, and drink of *that* cup.

1 Cor. 16:13. Watch ye, stand fast in the faith, quit you like men,

Gal. 6:1. Brethren, if a man be overtaken in a fault, ye which are spiritual, restore such an one in the spirit of meekness; considering thyself, lest thou also be tempted.

Eph. 5:15. See then that ye walk circumspectly, not as fools, but as wise,

Eph. 6:18. Praying always with all prayer and supplication in the Spirit, and watching thereunto with all perseverance and supplication for all saints;

Phil. 3:2. Beware of dogs, beware of evil workers, beware of the concision.

Phil. 4:5. The Lord *is* at hand.

Col. 4:2. Continue in prayer, and watch **in the** same with thanksgiving; 17. Take

heed to the ministry which thou hast received in the Lord, that thou fulfil it.

1 Thess. 5:4. But ye, brethren, are not in darkness, that that day should overtake you as a thief. 6. Therefore let us not sleep, as *do* others; but let us watch and be sober. 21. Prove all things; hold fast that which is good.

1 Tim. 4:16. Take heed unto thyself, and unto the doctrine; continue in them: for in doing this thou shalt both save thyself, and them that hear thee.

2 Tim. 4:5. But watch thou in all things, endure afflictions, do the work of an evangelist, make full proof of thy ministry.

Heb. 2:1. Therefore we ought to give the more earnest heed to the things which we have heard, lest at any time we should let *them* slip.

Heb. 3:12. Take heed, brethren, lest there be in any of you an evil heart of unbelief, in departing from the living God.

Heb. 12:15. Looking diligently lest any man fail of the grace of God; lest any root of bitterness springing up trouble *you,* and thereby many be defiled;

1 Pet. 1:13. Wherefore gird up the loins of your mind, be sober, and hope to the end for the grace that is to be brought unto you at the revelation of Jesus Christ; 17. And if ye call on the Father, who without respect of persons judgeth according to every man's work, pass the time of your sojourning *here* in fear:

1 Pet. 4:7. The end of all things is at hand: be ye therefore sober, and watch unto prayer.

1 Pet. 5:8. Be sober, be vigilant; because your adversary the devil, as a roaring lion, walketh about, seeking whom he may devour:

2 Pet. 1:19. We have also a more sure word of prophecy; whereunto ye do well that ye take heed, as unto a light that shineth in a dark place, until the day dawn, and the day star arise in your hearts:

2 Pet. 3:17. Ye therefore, beloved, seeing ye know *these things* before, beware lest ye also, being led away with the error of the wicked, fall from your own stedfastness.

1 John 5:18. We know that whosoever is born of God sinneth not; but he that is begotten of God keepeth himself, and that wicked one toucheth him not.

2 John 8. Look to yourselves, that we lose not those things which we have wrought, but that we receive a full reward.

Jude 20. But ye, beloved, building up yourselves on your most holy faith, praying in the Holy Ghost, 21. Keep yourselves in the love of God, looking for the mercy of our Lord Jesus Christ unto eternal life.

Rev. 3:2. Be watchful, and strengthen the things which remain, that are ready to die: for I have not found thy works perfect before God. 3. Remember therefore how thou hast received and heard, and hold fast, and repent. If therefore thou shalt not watch, I will come on thee as a thief, and thou shalt not know what hour I will come upon thee. 11. Behold, I come quickly : hold that fast which thou hast, that no man take thy crown.

Rev. 16:15. Behold, I come as a thief. Blessed *is* he that watcheth, and keepeth his garments, lest he walk naked, and they see his shame.

See TEMPTATION.

WATCHMAN, a sentinel. On the walls of cities, Song 3:3; 5:7; of Jerusalem, 2 Sam. 13:34; 18:24,25; Neh. 4:9; 7:3; Isa. 52:8; 62:6; of Babylon, Jer. 51:12. On towers, 2 Kin. 9:17; 2 Chr. 20:24; Isa. 21:5-12; Jer. 31:6. At the gates of the temple, 2 Kin. 11:6,7. Alarm of, given by trumpets, Ezek. 33:3-6. Unfaithfulness in the discharge of duty of, punished by death, Ezek. 33:6; Matt. 28:14; Acts 12:19.

WATER. Creation of, Psa. 148:4,5. Covered the whole earth, Gen. 1:9. Daily allowance of, Ezek. 4:11. City waterworks, 2 Kin. 20:20. Vision of, by Ezekiel, Ezek. 47:1-5. Of separation, Num. 19:2-22. Libation of, 1 Sam. 7:6. Irrigation with, see IRRIGATION. Miraculously supplied to the Israelites, Ex. 17:1,6; Num. 20:11; to Samson, Judg. 15:19; to Jehoshaphat's army, 2 Kin. 3: 16-20. Purified by Elisha, 2 Kin. 2:19-22. Red Sea divided, Ex. 14:21,22; the river Jordan, Josh. 3:14-17; 2 Kin. 2:6-8,14. Jesus walks on, Matt. 14:25. Changed to wine, John 2:1-11; to blood, Rev. 16:3-5.

FIGURATIVE: Water of life, John 4:14; 7:37-39; Rev. 21:6; 22:17. Of affliction, 2 Sam. 22:17; Psa. 69:1; Isa. 30:20; 43:2. Of salvation, Isa. 12:3; 49:10; 55:1; Ezek. 36:25; John 4:10; 7:38. Domestic love, Prov. 5:15.

SYMBOLICAL: Isa. 8:7; Rev. 8:11; 12:15; 16:4; 17:1,15.

WAX, Psa. 22:14; 68:2; 97:5; Mic. 1:4.

WAY. FIGURATIVE: Of holiness, Psa. 16:11; Isa. 35:8,9; Jer. 6:16; Hos. 14:9. Of righteousness, narrow, Matt. 7:14. Of sin, broad, Matt. 7:13. Jesus the, John 14:6; Heb. 9:8. Doctrines taught by Christ, Acts 9:2; 19:23; 22:4; 24:14,22.

WEALTH. See RICHES.

WEAPONS. See ARMOR ; ARMS.

WEASEL, Lev. 11:29.

WEATHER. Signs of, Matt. 16:2,3. Sayings concerning, Job 37:9,17,22.

See METEOROLOGY.

WEAVING, Isa. 19:9; 38:12. Bezaleel skilled in, Ex. 35:35. Wrought by women, 2 Kin. 23:7. Of the ephod, Ex. 28:32; 39:22. Of coats, Ex. 39:27.

Weaver's shuttle, Job 7:6; beam, Judg. 16:14; 2 Sam. 21:19; 1 Chr. 11:23.

WEDDING. See MARRIAGE.

WEEDING, Matt. 13:28.

WEEPING, Rom. 12:15; 1 Cor. 7:30. In perdition, Matt. 8:12; 22:13; 24:51; 25:30. None in heaven, Rev. 7:17. Penitential, Jer. 50:4; Joel 2:12. Instances of penitential : The Israelites, Judg. 2:4,5. Peter, Matt. 26: 75; Mark 14:72; Luke 22:62. While doing

good, Psa. 126:5,6. For others, Jer. 9:1. On account of tribulation, Jer. 22:10; Amos 5: 16,17.

INSTANCES OF: Of Abraham for Sarah, Gen. 23:2. Of Esau, Gen. 27:38. Of Jacob and Esau, Gen. 33:4. Of Jacob, Gen. 37:35. Of Joseph, Gen. 42:24; 43:30; 45:2,14; 46:29; 50: 1,17. Of Hannah, 1 Sam. 1:7. Of Jonathan and David, 1 Sam. 20:41. Of David, 2 Sam. 1:17; 3:32; 13:36; 15:23,30; 18:33. Of Hezekiah, 2 Kin. 20:3; Isa. 38:3. Of Jesus, over Jerusalem, Luke 19:41; at the grave of Lazarus, John 11:35. Of Mary, when she washed the feet of Jesus, Luke 7:38; John 11:2,33. Of Mary Magdalene, John 20:11. Of Paul, Acts 20:19; Phil. 3:18.

WEIGHTS, must be just, Lev. 19:35, 36; Deut. 25:13-15; Prov. 11:1; 16:11; 20:10,23; Mic. 6:10,11.

See MEASURE.

WELLS. The occasion of feuds : Between Abraham and Abimelech, Gen. 21: 25-30; between Isaac and Abimelech, Gen. 26:15-22,32,33. Of Jacob, John 4:6. Of Solomon, Eccl. 2:6. Of Uzziah, 2 Chr. 26: 10. Of Hezekiah, see GIHON. At Haran, Gen. 24:16.

FIGURATIVE: Of salvation, Isa. 12:3; John 4:14. Without water, Jer. 15:18; 2 Pet. 2:17.

See SPRING.

WEN, a tumor, Lev. 22:22.

WHALE. Created, Gen. 1:21. Called sea monster, in the *R. V.*, Job 7:12.

See DRAGON.

WHEAT, Rev. 6:6. Grown in Palestine, 1 Kin. 5:11; Psa. 81:16; 147:14. Offerings of, Num. 18:12. Prophecy of the sale of a measure of, for a penny, Rev. 6:6.

Parables of, Matt. 13:25; Luke 16:7. Winnowing of, Matt. 3:12; Luke 3:17. Ground in a mortar, Prov. 27:22. Chaff of, Jer. 23: 28; Matt. 3:12; Luke 3:17. Growth of, figurative of vicarious death, John 12:24.

FIGURATIVE: Of God's mercy, Psa. 81: 16; 147:14. Of self-righteousness, Jer. 12:13.

WHEEL. Potter's, Jer. 18:3.

FIGURATIVE: Prov. 20:26; Eccl. 12:6.

SYMBOLICAL: Ezek. 1:15-21; 3:13; 10:9-19; 11:22.

WHIP, 1 Kin. 12:11; Prov. 26:3; Nah.3:2.

WHITE. See COLOR.

WHIRLWIND. Destructive, Prov. 1: 27. From the south in the land of Uz, Job 37:9; in the valley of the Euphrates, Isa. 21: 1; in the land of Canaan, Zech. 9:14. From the north, Ezek. 1:4. Elijah translated in, 2 Kin. 2:1,11. God answered Job in, Job 38:1.

See METEOROLOGY.

FIGURATIVE: Of the judgment of God, Jer. 23:19; 30:23. Of the fruits of unrighteousness, Hos. 8:7. Of divine judgments, Ezek. 1:4.

WHISPER. See BUSYBODY ; SLANDER; TALEBEARER.

WHISPERER, a slanderer, Rom. 1:29; 2 Cor. 12:20.

See SLANDER ; SPEAKING, EVIL.

WHORE, revenues of, not to be brought to the sanctuary, Deut. 23:18.

See HARLOT.

WHOREDOM, licentious rites of, in idolatrous worship, Lev. 19:29; Deut. 31:16; Judg. 2:17; 2 Kin. 9:22.

See IDOLATRY.

FIGURATIVE: Ezek. 16; 23; Rev. 17: 1-6.

WHOREMONGER, Rev. 21:8; 22:15.

See ADULTERY ; SENSUALITY.

WICKED. Compared with : Abominable branches, Isa. 14:19; ashes under the feet, Mal. 4:3; bad fishes, Matt. 13:48; beasts, Psa. 49:12; 2 Pet. 2:12; the blind, Zeph. 1: 17; Matt. 15:14; brass and iron, Jer. 6: 28; Ezek. 22:18; briers and thorns, Isa. 55: 13; Ezek. 2:6; bulls of Bashan, Psa. 22:12; carcases trodden under feet, Isa. 14:19; chaff, Job 21:18; Psa. 1:4; Matt. 3:12; clouds without water, Jude 12; corn blasted, 2 Kin. 19:26; corrupt trees, Luke 6:43; deaf adders, Psa. 58:4; dogs, Prov. 26:11; Matt. 7:6; 2 Pet. 2:22; dross, Psa. 119:119; Ezek. 22: 18,19; early dew that passeth away, Hos. 13:3; evil figs, Jer. 24:8; fading oaks, Isa. 1:30; fiery oven, Psa. 21:9; Hos. 7:4; fire of thorns, Psa. 118:12; fools building upon sand, Matt. 7:26; fuel of fire, Isa. 9:19; garden without water, Isa. 1:30; goats, Matt. 25:32; grass, Psa. 37:2; 92:7; grass on the housetop, 2 Kin. 19:26; green bay tree, Psa. 37:35; green herbs, Psa. 37:2; heath in the desert, Jer. 17:6; horses rushing into the battle, Jer. 8:6; idols, Psa. 115:8; lions greedy of prey, Psa. 17:12; melting wax, Psa. 68:2; morning clouds, Hos. 13:3; moth-eaten garments, Isa. 50:9; 51:8; passing whirlwinds, Prov. 10:25; potsherds, Prov. 26:23; raging waves of the sea, Jude 13; reprobate silver, Jer. 6:30; scorpions, Ezek. 2:6; serpents, Psa. 58:4; Matt. 23:33; smoke, Hos. 13:3; stony ground, Matt. 13:5; stubble, Job 21:18; Mal. 4:1; swine, Matt. 7:6; 2 Pet. 2:22; tares, Matt. 13:38; troubled sea, Isa. 57:20; visions of the night, Job 20:8; wandering stars, Jude 13; wayward children, Matt. 11:16; wells without water, 2 Pet. 2:17; wheels, Psa. 83:13; whited sepulchers, Matt. 23:27; wild ass's colts, Job 11: 12.—*Bible Text-Book.*

God is angry with, Psa. 5:5,6; 7:11; Rom. 9:13; 1 Cor. 10:5. Spirit of God withdrawn from, Gen. 6:3; Hos. 4:17-19; Rom. 1:24,26, 28. Hate the righteous, Matt. 5:11,12; Luke 6:22,23. Worship of, offensive to God, Psa. 50:16,17; Isa. 1:10-15.

Present and future state of the wicked and righteous contrasted, Job 8; Psa. 49. See below.

Prosperity of, Job 5:3-5; 12:6; 15:21,23,27, 29; 20:5,22; 21:7-13; Psa. 37:1,35,36; 49:10-15; 73:3-22; 92:6,7; Eccl. 8:12,13; Jer. 12:1,2; Hab. 1:3,4,13-17; Mal. 3:15. Hate reproof, 1 Kin. 22:8; 2 Chr. 18:7. God's mercy to, Job 33:14-30; love for, Deut. 5:29; 32:29; Matt. 18:11-14; John 3:16,17; Rom. 5:8; 1 John 3:16; 4:9,10. Dread God, Job 18:11.

Eliphaz's exhortation to, Job 22:21-30. Temporal punishment of, Job 27:13-23; 15:20-35; 18:5-21; 20:5-29; 21:7-33; 24:2-24; Jer. 5:25; Ezek. 11:10; 12:19,20; Zech. 14:17-19. False hope of, Job 8:13-18.

Gospel invitation to, illustrated by the parables of the householder, Matt. 20:1-16; and marriage supper, Matt. 22:1-14.

Warned, Jer. 7:13-15,23-25; 25:4-6; 26:2-7, 12,13; 29:17-19; Ezek. 33:8; Dan. 4:4-27; 5:4-29; Zeph. 2:1,2; Luke 3:7-9; 1 Cor. 10:11; Jude 4-7; Rev. 3:1-3,16-19. Terrors of, at the judgment, Rev. 1:7. Death of, Psa. 49:14, 73:4.

See IMPENITENCE ; OBDURACY ; PENITENCE ; REPROBACY ; SEEKERS ; SIN, CONFESSION OF.

CONTRASTED WITH THE RIGHTEOUS: Psa. 1:1. Blessed *is* the man that walketh not in the counsel of the ungodly, nor standeth in the way of sinners, nor sitteth in the seat of the scornful. 2. But his delight *is* in the law of the LORD; and in his law doth he meditate day and night. 3. And he shall be like a tree planted by the rivers of water, that bringeth forth his fruit in his season ; his leaf also shall not wither ; and whatsoever he doeth shall prosper. 4. The ungodly *are* not so : but *are* like the chaff which the wind driveth away. 5. Therefore the ungodly shall not stand in the judgment, nor sinners in the congregation of the righteous. 6. For the LORD knoweth the way of the righteous : but the way of the ungodly shall perish.

Psa. 11:5. The LORD trieth the righteous : but the wicked and him that loveth violence his soul hateth.

Psa. 17:14. From men *which are* thy hand, O LORD, from men of the world, *which have* their portion in *this* life, and whose belly thou fillest with thy hid *treasure :* they are full of children, and leave the rest of their *substance* to their babes. 15. As for me, I will behold thy face in righteousness : I shall be satisfied, when I awake, with thy likeness.

Psa. 32:10. Many sorrows *shall be* to the wicked : but he that trusteth in the LORD, mercy shall compass him about.

Psa. 37:17. For the arms of the wicked shall be broken : but the LORD upholdeth the righteous. 18. The LORD knoweth the days of the upright : and their inheritance shall be for ever. 19. They shall not be ashamed in the evil time : and in the days of famine they shall be satisfied. 20. But the wicked shall perish, and the enemies of the LORD *shall be* as the fat of lambs : they shall consume ; into smoke shall they consume away. 21. The wicked borroweth, and payeth not again : but the righteous sheweth mercy, and giveth. 22. For *such as be* blessed of him shall inherit the earth ; and *they that be* cursed of him shall be cut off. 37. Mark the perfect *man,* and behold the upright : for the end of *that* man *is* peace. 38. But the transgressors shall be destroyed together: the end of the wicked shall be cut off.

Psa. 68:6. God setteth the solitary in families: he bringeth out those which are bound with chains: but the rebellious dwell in a dry *land*.

Psa. 73:1. Truly God *is* good to Israel, *even* to such as are of a clean heart. 2. But as for me, my feet were almost gone; my steps had well nigh slipped. 3. For I was envious at the foolish, *when* I saw the prosperity of the wicked. 4. For *there are* no bands in their death: but their strength *is* firm. 5. They *are* not in trouble *as other* men; neither are they plagued like *other* men. 6. Therefore pride compasseth them about as a chain; violence covereth them *as* a garment. 7. Their eyes stand out with fatness: they have more than heart could wish. 8. They are corrupt, and speak wickedly *concerning* oppression: they speak loftily. 9. They set their mouth against the heavens, and their tongue walketh through the earth. 10. Therefore his people return hither: and waters of a full *cup* are wrung out to them. 11. And they say, How doth God know? and is there knowledge in the most High? 12. Behold, these *are* the ungodly, who prosper in the world; they increase *in* riches. 13. Verily I have cleansed my heart *in* vain, and washed my hands in innocency. 14. For all the day long have I been plagued, and chastened every morning. 15. If I say, I will speak thus; behold, I should offend *against* the generation of thy children. 16. When I thought to know this, it *was* too painful for me; 17. Until I went into the sanctuary of God; *then* understood I their end. 18. Surely thou didst set them in slippery places: thou castedst them down into destruction. 19. How are they *brought* into desolation, as in a moment! they are utterly consumed with terrors. 20. As a dream when *one* awaketh; *so*, O Lord, when thou awakest, thou shalt despise their image. 21. Thus my heart was grieved, and I was pricked in my reins. 22. So foolish *was* I, and ignorant: I was *as* a beast before thee. 23. Nevertheless I *am* continually with thee: thou hast holden *me* by my right hand. 24. Thou shalt guide me with thy counsel, and afterward receive me *to* glory. 25. Whom have I in heaven *but thee?* and *there is* none upon earth *that* I desire beside thee. 26. My flesh and my heart faileth: *but* God *is* the strength of my heart, and my portion for ever. 27. For, lo, they that are far from thee shall perish: thou hast destroyed all them that go a whoring from thee. 28. But *it is* good for me to draw near to God: I have put my trust in the Lord GOD, that I may declare all thy works.

Psa. 75:10. All the horns of the wicked also will I cut off; *but* the horns of the righteous shall be exalted.

Psa. 91:7. A thousand shall fall at thy side, and ten thousand at thy right hand; *but* it shall not come nigh thee. 8. Only with thine eyes shalt thou behold and see the reward of the wicked.

Psa. 107:33. He turneth rivers into a wilderness, and the watersprings into dry ground; 34. A fruitful land into barrenness, for the wickedness of them that dwell therein. 35. He turneth the wilderness into a standing water, and dry ground into watersprings. 36. And there he maketh the hungry to dwell, that they may prepare a city for habitation; 37. And sow the fields, and plant vineyards, which may yield fruits of increase. 38. He blesseth them also, so that they are multiplied greatly; and suffereth not their cattle to decrease.

Psa. 125:5. As for such as turn aside unto their crooked ways, the LORD shall lead them forth with the workers of iniquity: *but* peace *shall be* upon Israel.

Prov. 10:6. Blessings *are* upon the head of the just: but violence covereth the mouth of the wicked. 9. He that walketh uprightly walketh surely: but he that perverteth his ways shall be known. 21. The lips of the righteous feed many: but fools die for want of wisdom. 23. *It is* as sport to a fool to do mischief: but a man of understanding hath wisdom. 24. The fear of the wicked, it shall come upon him: but the desire of the righteous shall be granted. 25. As the whirlwind passeth, so *is* the wicked no *more:* but the righteous *is* an everlasting foundation. 28. The hope of the righteous *shall be* gladness: but the expectation of the wicked shall perish. 29. The way of the LORD *is* strength to the upright: but destruction *shall be* to the workers of iniquity. 30. The righteous shall never be removed: but the wicked shall not inhabit the earth. 32. The lips of the righteous know what is acceptable: but the mouth of the wicked *speaketh* frowardness.

Prov. 11:3. The integrity of the upright shall guide them: but the perverseness of transgressors shall destroy them. 5. The righteousness of the perfect shall direct his way: but the wicked shall fall by his own wickedness. 6. The righteousness of the upright shall deliver them: but transgressors shall be taken in *their own* naughtiness. 8. The righteous is delivered out of trouble, and the wicked cometh in his stead. 10. When it goeth well with the righteous, the city rejoiceth: and when the wicked perish, *there is* shouting. 11. By the blessing of the upright the city is exalted: but it is overthrown by the mouth of the wicked. 18. The wicked worketh a deceitful work: but to him that soweth righteousness *shall be* a sure reward. 19. As righteousness *tendeth* to life: so he that pursueth evil *pursueth it* to his own death. 20. They that are of a froward heart *are* abomination to the LORD: but *such as are* upright in *their* way *are* his delight. 21. *Though* hand *join* in hand, the wicked shall not be unpunished: but the seed of the righteous shall be delivered. 23. The desire of the righteous *is* only good: *but* the expectation of the wicked *is* wrath. 31. Behold, the righteous shall be recompensed in the earth: much more the wicked and the sinner.

Prov. 12:3. A man shall not be established by wickedness: but the root of the righteous shall not be moved. 5. The thoughts of the righteous *are* right: *but* the counsels of the wicked *are* deceit. 6. The words of the wicked *are* to lie in wait for blood: but the mouth of the upright shall deliver them. 7. The wicked are overthrown, and *are* not: but the house of the righteous shall stand. 13. The wicked is snared by the transgression of *his* lips: but the just shall come out of trouble. 21. There shall no evil happen to the just: but the wicked shall be filled with mischief. 26. The righteous *is* more excellent than his neighbour: but the way of the wicked seduceth them.

Prov. 13:6. Righteousness keepeth *him that is* upright in the way: but wickedness overthroweth the sinner. 13. Whoso despiseth the word shall be destroyed: but he that feareth the commandment shall be rewarded. 17. A wicked messenger falleth into mischief: but a faithful ambassador *is* health. 21. Evil pursueth sinners: but to the righteous good shall be repaid.

Prov. 14:19. The evil bow before the good; and the wicked at the gates of the righteous. 22. Do they not err that devise evil? but mercy and truth *shall be* to them that devise good. 32. The wicked is driven away in his wickedness: but the righteous hath hope in his death.

Prov. 15:6. In the house of the righteous *is* much treasure: but in the revenues of the wicked is trouble.

Prov. 21:18. The wicked *shall be* a ransom for the righteous, and the transgressor for the upright. 26. He coveteth greedily all the day long: but the righteous giveth and spareth not.

Prov. 22:5. Thorns *and* snares *are* in the way of the froward: he that doth keep his soul shall be far from them.

Prov. 28:1. The wicked flee when no man pursueth: but the righteous are bold as a lion. 4. They that forsake the law praise the wicked: but such as keep the law contend with them. 5. Evil men understand not judgment: but they that seek the LORD understand all *things*. 13. He that covereth his sins shall not prosper: but whoso confesseth and forsaketh *them* shall have mercy. 14. Happy *is* the man that feareth alway: but he that hardeneth his heart shall fall into mischief. 18. Whoso walketh uprightly shall be saved: but *he that is* perverse *in his* ways shall fall at once.

Isa. 32:1. Behold, a king shall reign in righteousness, and princes shall rule in judgment. 2. And a man shall be as an hiding place from the wind, and a covert from the tempest; as rivers of water in a dry place, as the shadow of a great rock in a weary land. 3. And the eyes of them that see shall not be dim, and the ears of them that hear shall hearken. 4. The heart also of the rash shall understand knowledge, and the tongue of the stammerers shall be ready to speak plainly. 5. The vile person shall be no more called liberal, nor the churl said *to be* bountiful. 6. For the vile person will speak villany, and his heart will work iniquity, to practise hypocrisy, and to utter error against the LORD, to make empty the soul of the hungry, and he will cause the drink of the thirsty to fail. 7. The instruments also of the churl *are* evil: he deviseth wicked devices to destroy the poor with lying words, even when the needy speaketh right. 8. But the liberal deviseth liberal things; and by liberal things shall he stand.

Isa. 65:13. Therefore thus saith the Lord GOD, Behold, my servants shall eat, but ye shall be hungry: behold, my servants shall drink, but ye shall be thirsty: behold, my servants shall rejoice, but ye shall be ashamed: 14. Behold, my servants shall sing for joy of heart, but ye shall cry for sorrow of heart, and shall howl for vexation of spirit.

Mal. 3:18. Then shall ye return, and discern between the righteous and the wicked, between him that serveth God and him that serveth him not.

Rom. 2:7. To them who by patient continuance in well doing seek for glory and honour and immortality, eternal life: 8. But unto them that are contentious, and do not obey the truth, but obey unrighteousness, indignation and wrath, 9. Tribulation and anguish, upon every soul of man that doeth evil, of the Jew first, and also of the Gentile; 10. But glory, honour, and peace, to every man that worketh good, to the Jew first, and also to the Gentile:

Eph. 2:12. That at that time ye were without Christ, being aliens from the commonwealth of Israel, and strangers from the covenants of promise, having no hope, and without God in the world: 13. But now in Christ Jesus ye who sometimes were far off are made nigh by the blood of Christ. 14. For he is our peace, who hath made both one, and hath broken down the middle wall of partition *between us;*

Phil. 2:15. That ye may be blameless and harmless, the sons of God, without rebuke, in the midst of a crooked and perverse nation, among whom ye shine as lights in the world;

1 Thess. 5:5. Ye are all the children of light, and the children of the day: we are not of the night, nor of darkness. 6. Therefore let us not sleep, as *do* others; but let us watch and be sober. 7. For they that sleep sleep in the night; and they that be drunken are drunken in the night. 8. But let us, who are of the day, be sober, putting on the

breastplace of faith and love; and for an helmet, the hope of salvation.

Tit. 1:15. Unto the pure all things *are* pure: but unto them that are defiled and unbelieving *is* nothing pure; but even their mind and conscience is defiled.

1 Pet. 4:17. For the time *is come* that judgment must begin at the house of God: and if *it* first *begin* at us, what shall the end *be* of them that obey not the gospel of God? 18. And if the righteous scarcely be saved, where shall the ungodly and the sinner appear?

1 John 1:6. If we say that we have fellowship with him, and walk in darkness, we lie, and do not the truth: 7. But if we walk in the light, as he is in the light, we have fellowship one with another, and the blood of Jesus Christ his Son cleanseth us from all sin.

1 John 3:3. And every man that hath this hope in him purifieth himself, even as he is pure. 4. Whosoever committeth sin transgresseth also the law: for sin is the transgression of the law. 5. And ye know that he was manifested to take away our sins; and in him is no sin. 6. Whosoever abideth in him sinneth not: whosoever sinneth hath not seen him, neither known him. 7. Little children, let no man deceive you: he that doeth righteousness is righteous, even as he is righteous. 8. He that committeth sin is of the devil; for the devil sinneth from the beginning. For this purpose the Son of God was manifested, that he might destroy the works of the devil. 9. Whosoever is born of God doth not commit sin; for his seed remaineth in him: and he cannot sin, because he is born of God. 10. In this the children of God are manifest, and the children of the devil: whosoever doeth not righteousness is not of God, neither he that loveth not his brother. 11. For this is the message that ye heard from the beginning, that we should love one another. 12. Not as Cain, *who* was of that wicked one, and slew his brother. And wherefore slew he him? Because his own works were evil, and his brother's righteous. 13. Marvel not, my brethren, if the world hate you. 14. We know that we have passed from death unto life, because we love the brethren. He that loveth not *his* brother abideth in death. 15. Whosoever hateth his brother is a murderer: and ye know that no murderer hath eternal life abiding in him. 16. Hereby perceive we the love [1 *of God*], because he laid down his life for us: and we ought to lay down *our* lives for the brethren. 17. But whoso hath this world's good, and seeth his brother have need, and shutteth up his bowels of *compassion* from him, how dwelleth the love of God in him? [1 Omitted in R. V.]

DESCRIBED: Gen. 13:13. But the men of Sodom *were* wicked and sinners before the LORD exceedingly.

Gen. 18:20. And the LORD said, Because the cry of Sodom and Gomorrah is great, and because their sin is very grievous;

Lev. 18:25. The land is defiled: therefore I do visit the iniquity thereof upon it, and the land itself vomiteth out her inhabitants.

Deut. 9:13. The LORD spake unto me, saying, I have seen this people, and, behold, it *is* a stiffnecked people: 24. Ye have been rebellious against the LORD from the day that I knew you.

Deut. 32:10. He found him in a desert land, and in the waste howling wilderness; he led him about, he instructed him, he kept him as the apple of his eye. 32. Their vine *is* of the vine of Sodom, and of the fields of Gomorrah: their grapes *are* grapes of gall, their clusters *are* bitter: 33. Their wine *is* the poison of dragons, and the cruel venom of asps.

1 Sam. 24:13. As saith the proverb of the ancients, Wickedness proceedeth from the wicked: but mine hand shall not be upon thee.

1 Kin. 21:20. And Ahab said to Elijah, Hast thou found me, O mine enemy? And he answered, I have found *thee:* because thou hast sold thyself to work evil in the sight of the LORD.

2 Chr. 28:10. And now ye purpose to keep under the children of Judah and Jerusalem for bondmen and bondwomen unto you: *but are there* not with you, even with you, sins against the LORD your God? 22. In the time of his distress did he trespass yet more against the LORD: this *is that* king Ahaz.

Ezra 9:11. Which thou hast commanded by thy servants the prophets, saying, The land, unto which ye go to possess it, is an unclean land with the filthiness of the people of the lands, with their abominations, which have filled it from one end to another with their uncleanness.

Job 14:4. Who can bring a clean *thing* out of an unclean? not one.

Job 15:16. How much more abominable and filthy *is* man, which drinketh iniquity like water? 20. The wicked man travaileth with pain all *his* days, and the number of years is hidden to the oppressor. 21. A dreadful sound *is* in his ears: in prosperity the destroyer shall come upon him. 22. He believeth not that he shall return out of darkness, and he is waited for of the sword. 23. He wandereth abroad for bread, *saying,* Where *is it?* he knoweth that the day of darkness is ready at his hand. 24. Trouble and anguish shall make him afraid; they shall prevail against him, as a king ready to the battle. 25. For he stretcheth out his hand against God, and strengtheneth himself against the Almighty. 26. He runneth upon him, *even* on *his* neck, upon the thick bosses of his bucklers: 27. Because he covereth his face with his fatness, and maketh collops of fat on *his* flanks. 28. And he dwelleth in desolate cities, *and* in houses which no man inhabiteth, which are ready to become heaps. 29. He shall not be rich, neither shall his substance continue, neither shall he prolong the perfection thereof upon the earth. 30. He shall not depart out of darkness; the flame shall dry up his branches, and by the breath of his mouth shall he go away. 31. Let not him that is deceived trust in vanity: for vanity shall be his recompence. 32. It shall be accomplished before his time, and his branch shall not be green. 33. He shall shake off his unripe grape as the vine, and shall cast off his flower as the olive. 34. For the congregation of hypocrites *shall be* desolate, and fire shall consume the tabernacles of bribery. 35. They conceive mischief, and bring forth vanity, and their belly prepareth deceit.

Job 20:12. Though wickedness be sweet in his mouth, *though* he hide it under his tongue; 13. *Though* he spare it, and forsake it not; but keep it still within his mouth:

Job 22:5. *Is* not thy wickedness great? and thine iniquities infinite?

Job 24:2. *Some* remove the landmarks; they violently take away flocks, and feed *thereof*. 3. They drive away the ass of the fatherless, they take the widow's ox for a pledge. 4. They turn the needy out of the way: the poor of the earth hide themselves together. 5. Behold, *as* wild asses in the desert, go they forth to their work; rising betimes for a prey: the wilderness *yieldeth* food for them *and* for *their* children. 6. They reap *every one* his corn in the field: and they gather the vintage of the wicked. 7. They cause the naked to lodge without clothing, that *they have* no covering in the cold. 8. They are wet with the showers of the mountains, and embrace the rock for want of a shelter. 9. They pluck the fatherless from the breast, and take a pledge of the poor. 10. They cause *him* to go naked without clothing, and they take away the sheaf *from* the hungry; 11. *Which* make oil within their walls, *and* tread *their* winepresses, and suffer thirst. 12. Men groan from out of the city, and the soul of the wounded crieth out: yet God layeth not folly *to them*. 13. They are of those that rebel against the light; they know not the ways thereof, nor abide in the paths thereof. 14. The murderer rising with the light killeth the poor and needy, and in the night is as a thief. 15. The eye also of the adulterer waiteth for the twilight, saying, No eye shall see me: and disguiseth *his* face. 16. In the dark they dig through houses, *which* they had marked for themselves in the daytime: they know not the light. 17. For the morning *is* to them even as the shadow of death: if *one* know *them, they are in* the terrors of the shadow of death. 18. He *is* swift as the waters; their portion is cursed in the earth: he beholdeth not the way of the vineyards. 19. Drought and heat consume the snow waters; *so doth* the grave *those which* have sinned. 20. The womb shall

forget him; the worm shall feed sweetly on him; he shall be no more remembered; and wickedness shall be broken as a tree. 21. He evil entreateth the barren *that* beareth not: and doeth not good to the widow. 22. He draweth also the mighty with his power: he riseth up, and no *man* is sure of life. 23. *Though* it be given him *to be* in safety, whereon he resteth; yet his eyes *are* upon their ways. 24. They are exalted for a little while, but are gone and brought low; they are taken out of the way as all *other*, and cut off as the tops of the ears of corn.

Psa. 5:9. For *there is* no faithfulness in their mouth; their inward part *is* very wickedness; their throat *is* an open sepulchre; they flatter with their tongue.

Psa. 7:14. Behold, he travaileth with iniquity, and hath conceived mischief, and brought forth falsehood. 15. He made a pit, and digged it, and is fallen into the ditch *which* he made. 16. His mischief shall return upon his own head, and his violent dealing shall come down upon his own pate.

Psa. 10:4. The wicked, ¹ through the pride of his countenance, ² will not ³ seek *after God:* ⁴ God *is* not in all his thoughts. 5. His ways are always grievous; thy judgments *are* far above out of his sight: *as for* all his enemies, he puffeth at them. 6. He hath said in his heart, I shall not be moved: for *I shall* never *be* in adversity. 7. His mouth is full of cursing and deceit and fraud: under his tongue *is* mischief and vanity. 8. He sitteth in the lurking places of the villages: in the secret places doth he murder the innocent: his eyes are privily set against the poor. 9. He lieth in wait secretly as a lion in his den: he lieth in wait to catch the poor: he doth catch the poor, when he draweth him into his net. 10. He croucheth, *and* humbleth himself, that the poor may fall by his strong ones. 11. He hath said in his heart, God hath forgotten: he hideth his face; he will never see *it*.

[R. V. ¹ in ² *saith*, He ³ require it. ⁴ All his thoughts are, There is no God.]

Psa. 36:1. The transgression of the wicked saith within my heart, *that there is* no fear of God before his eyes. 2. For he flattereth himself in his own eyes, until his iniquity be found to be hateful. 3. The words of his mouth *are* iniquity and deceit: he hath left off to be wise, *and* to do good. 4. He deviseth mischief upon his bed; he setteth himself in a way *that is* not good; he abhorreth not evil.

Psa. 37:12. The wicked plotteth against the just, and gnasheth upon him with his teeth.

Psa. 49:20. Man *that is* in honour, and understandeth not, is like the beasts *that* perish.

Psa. 50:17. Seeing thou hatest instruction, and castest my words behind thee. 18. When thou sawest a thief, then thou consentedst with him, and hast been partaker with adulterers. 19. Thou givest thy mouth to evil, and thy tongue frameth deceit. 20. Thou sittest *and* speakest against thy brother; thou slanderest thine own mother's son.

Psa. 52:1. Why boastest thou thyself in mischief, O mighty man? the goodness of God *endureth* continually. 2. Thy tongue deviseth mischiefs; like a sharp razor, working deceitfully. 3. Thou lovest evil more than good; *and* lying rather than to speak righteousness. 4. Thou lovest all devouring words, O *thou* deceitful tongue.

Psa. 53:1. The fool hath said in his heart, *There is* no God. Corrupt are they, and have done abominable iniquity: *there is* none that doeth good. 2. God looked down from heaven upon the children of men, to see if there were *any* that did understand, that did seek God. 3. Every one of them is gone back: they are altogether become filthy; *there is* none that doeth good, no, not one. 4. Have the workers of iniquity no knowledge? who eat up my people *as* they eat bread: they have not called upon God. 5. There were they in great fear, *where* no fear was: for God hath scattered the bones of him that encampeth *against* thee: thou hast put *them* to shame, because God hath despised them.

Psa. 58:3. The wicked are estranged from the womb: they go astray as soon as they be born, speaking lies. 4. Their poison *is* like the poison of a serpent: *they are* like the deaf adder *that* stoppeth her ear; 5. Which will not hearken to the voice of charmers, charming never so wisely.

Psa. 59:6. They return at evening: they make a noise like a dog, and go round about the city. 7. Behold, they belch out with their mouth: swords *are* in their lips: for who, *say they*, doth hear?

Psa. 64:3. Who whet their tongue like a sword, *and* bend *their bows to shoot* their arrows, *even* bitter words: 4. That they may shoot in secret at the perfect: suddenly do they shoot at him, and fear not. 5. They encourage themselves *in* an evil matter: they commune of laying snares privily; they say, Who shall see them? 6. They search out iniquities; they accomplish a diligent search: both the inward *thought* of every one *of them*, and the heart, *is* deep.

Psa. 73:4. For *there are* no bands in their death: but their strength *is* firm. 5. They *are* not in trouble *as other* men; neither are they plagued like *other* men. 6. Therefore pride compasseth them about as a chain; violence covereth them *as* a garment. 7. Their eyes stand out with fatness: they have more than heart could wish. 8. They are corrupt, and speak wickedly *concerning* oppression: they speak loftily. 9. They set their mouth against the heavens, and their tongue walketh through the earth. 10. Therefore his people return hither: and waters of a full *cup* are wrung out to them. 11. And they say, How doth God know? and is there knowledge in the most High? 12. Behold, these *are* the ungodly, who

prosper in the world; they increase *in* riches.

Psa. 94:3. LORD, how long shall the wicked, how long shall the wicked triumph? 4. *How long* shall they utter *and* speak hard things? *and* all the workers of iniquity boast themselves? 5. They break in pieces thy people, O LORD, and afflict thine heritage. 6. They slay the widow and the stranger, and murder the fatherless. 7. Yet they say, The LORD shall not see, neither shall the God of Jacob regard *it.* 8. Understand, ye brutish among the people: and *ye* fools, when will ye be wise?

Psa. 119:155. Salvation *is* far from the wicked: for they seek not thy statutes.

Prov. 1:29. They hated knowledge, and did not choose the fear of the LORD: 30. They would none of my counsel: they despised all my reproof.

Prov. 2:12. To deliver thee from the way of the evil *man*, from the man that speaketh froward things; 13. Who leave the paths of uprightness, to walk in the ways of darkness: 14. Who rejoice to do evil, *and* delight in the frowardness of the wicked; 15. Whose ways *are* crooked, and *they* froward in their paths: 16. To deliver thee from the strange woman, *even* from the stranger *which* flattereth with her words; 17. Which forsaketh the guide of her youth, and forgetteth the covenant of her God. 18. For her house inclineth unto death, and her paths unto the dead. 19. None that go unto her return again, neither take they hold of the paths of life.

Prov. 4:16. They sleep not, except they have done mischief; and their sleep is taken away, unless they cause *some* to fall.

Prov. 6:12. A naughty person, a wicked man, walketh with a froward mouth. 13. He winketh with his eyes, he speaketh with his feet, he teacheth with his fingers; 14. Frowardness *is* in his heart, he deviseth mischief continually; he soweth discord. 15. Therefore shall his calamity come suddenly; suddenly shall he be broken without remedy.

Prov. 10:23. *It is* as sport to a fool to do mischief: but a man of understanding hath wisdom.

Prov. 13:19. *It is* abomination to fools to depart from evil.

Prov. 14:9. Fools make a mock at sin:

Prov. 15:9. The way of the wicked *is* an abomination unto the LORD: but he loveth him that followeth after righteousness. 10. Correction *is* grievous unto him that forsaketh the way; *and* he that hateth reproof shall die.

Prov. 27:22. Though thou shouldest bray a fool in a mortar among wheat with a pestle, *yet* will not his foolishness depart from him.

Prov. 28:4. They that forsake the law praise the wicked: but such as keep the law contend with them.

Eccl. 3:18. I said in mine heart concerning

the estate of the sons of men, that God might manifest them, and that they might see that they themselves are beasts.

Eccl. 8:11. Because sentence against an evil work is not executed speedily, therefore the heart of the sons of men is fully set in them to do evil.

Isa. 1:4. Ah sinful nation, a people laden with iniquity, a seed of evildoers, children that are corrupters: they have forsaken the LORD, they have provoked the Holy One of Israel unto anger, they are gone away backward. 5. Why should ye be stricken any more? ye will revolt more and more: the whole head is sick, and the whole heart faint. 6. From the sole of the foot even unto the head *there is* no soundness in it; *but* wounds, and bruises, and putrifying sores: they have not been closed, neither bound up, neither mollified with ointment.

Isa. 3:9. The shew of their countenance doth witness against them; and they declare their sin as Sodom, they hide *it* not.

Isa. 5:11. Woe unto them that rise up early in the morning, *that* they may follow strong drink: that continue until night, *till* wine inflame them! 12. And the harp, and the viol, the tabret, and pipe, and wine, are in their feasts: but they regard not the work of the LORD, neither consider the operation of his hands. 18. Woe unto them that draw iniquity with cords of vanity, and sin as it were with a cart rope: 19. That say, Let him make speed, *and* hasten his work, that we may see *it:* and let the counsel of the Holy One of Israel draw nigh and come, that we may know *it!* 20. Woe unto them that call evil good, and good evil: that put darkness for light, and light for darkness; that put bitter for sweet, and sweet for bitter! 21. Woe unto *them that are* wise in their own eyes, and prudent in their own sight! 22. Woe unto *them that are* mighty to drink wine, and men of strength to mingle strong drink: 23. Which justify the wicked for reward, and take away the righteousness of the righteous from him! 24. Therefore as the fire devoureth the stubble, and the flame consumeth the chaff, *so* their root shall be as rottenness, and their blossom shall go up as dust: because they have cast away the law of the LORD of hosts, and despised the word of the Holy One of Israel. 25. Therefore is the anger of the LORD kindled against his people, and he hath stretched forth his hand against them, and hath smitten them: and the hills did tremble, and their carcases *were* torn in the midst of the streets. For all this his anger is not turned away, but his hand *is* stretched out still.

Isa. 26:10. Let favour be shewed to the wicked, *yet* will he not learn righteousness; in the land of uprightness will he deal unjustly, and will not behold the majesty of the LORD. 11. LORD, *when* thy hand is lifted up, they will not see: *but* they shall see, and be ashamed for *their* envy at the

people; yea, the fire of thine enemies shall devour them.

Isa. 30:1. Woe to the rebellious children, saith the LORD, that take counsel, but not of me; and that cover with a covering, but not of my spirit, that they may add sin to sin: 9. This *is* a rebellious people; lying children, children *that* will not hear the law of the LORD: 10. Which say to the seers, See not; and to the prophets, Prophesy not unto us right things, speak unto us smooth things, prophesy deceits: 11. Get you out of the way, turn aside out of the path, cause the Holy One of Israel to cease from before us.

Isa. 32:6. For the vile person will speak villany, and his heart will work iniquity, to practise hypocrisy, and to utter error against the LORD, to make empty the soul of the hungry, and he will cause the drink of the thirsty to fail. 7. The instruments also of the churl *are* evil; he deviseth wicked devices to destroy the poor with lying words, even when the needy speaketh right.

Isa. 57:20. The wicked *are* like the troubled sea, when it cannot rest, whose waters cast up mire and dirt. 21. *There is* no peace, saith my God, to the wicked.

Isa. 59:2. But your iniquities have separated between you and your God, and your sins have hid *his* face from you, that he will not hear. 3. For your hands are defiled with blood, and your fingers with iniquity: your lips have spoken lies, your tongue hath muttered perverseness. 4. None calleth for justice, nor *any* pleadeth for truth: they trust in vanity, and speak lies; they conceive mischief, and bring forth iniquity. 5. They hatch cockatrice' eggs, and weave the spider's web: he that eateth of their eggs dieth, and that which is crushed breaketh out into a viper. 6. Their webs shall not become garments, neither shall they cover themselves with their works: their works *are* works of iniquity, and the act of violence *is* in their hands. 7. Their feet run to evil, and they make haste to shed innocent blood: their thoughts *are* thoughts of iniquity; wasting and destruction *are* in their paths. 8. The way of peace they know not; and *there is* no judgment in their goings: they have made them crooked paths: whosoever goeth therein shall not know peace.

Isa. 63:19. We are *thine:* thou never barest rule over them; they were not called by thy name.

Jer. 2:22. For though thou wash thee with ¹nitre, and take thee much sope, *yet* thine iniquity is marked before me, saith the Lord GOD. 23. How canst thou say, I am not polluted, I have not gone after Baalim? see thy way in the valley, know what thou hast done: *thou art* a swift dromedary traversing her ways; 24. A wild ass used to the wilderness, *that* snuffeth up the wind at her pleasure; in her occasion who can turn her away? all they that seek her will not weary themselves; in her month they shall find her. 25. Withhold thy foot from being unshod, and thy throat from thirst: but thou saidst, There is no hope: no; for I have loved strangers, and after them will I go. [¹ R. V. lye]

Jer. 3:5. Behold, thou hast spoken and done evil things as thou couldest.

Jer. 4:22. My people *is* foolish, they have not known me; they *are* sottish children, and they have none understanding: they *are* wise to do evil, but to do good they have no knowledge.

Jer. 5:4. Therefore I said, Surely these *are* poor; they are foolish: for they know not the way of the LORD, *nor* the judgment of their God. 5. I will get me unto the great men, and will speak unto them; for they have known the way of the LORD, *and* the judgment of their God: but these have altogether broken the yoke, *and* burst the bonds. 26. For among my people are found wicked *men:* they lay wait, as he that setteth snares; they set a trap, they catch men. 27. As a cage is full of birds, so *are* their houses full of deceit: therefore they are become great, and waxen rich. 28. They are waxen fat, they shine: yea, they overpass the deeds of the wicked: they judge not the cause, the cause of the fatherless, yet they prosper; and the right of the needy do they not judge.

Jer. 6:7. As a fountain casteth out her waters, so she casteth out her wickedness: violence and spoil is heard in her; before me continually *is* grief and wounds. 15. Were they ashamed when they had committed abomination? nay, they were not at all ashamed, neither could they blush: therefore they shall fall among them that fall: at the time *that* I visit them they shall be cast down, saith the LORD. Jer. 8:12.

Jer. 8:6. I hearkened and heard, *but* they spake not aright: no man repented him of his wickedness, saying, What have I done? every one turned to his course, as the horse rusheth into the battle.

Jer. 9:3. They bend their tongues *like* their bow *for* lies: but they are not valiant for the truth upon the earth; for they proceed from evil to evil, and they know not me, saith the LORD. 4. Take ye heed every one of his neighbour, and trust ye not in any brother: for every brother will utterly supplant, and every neighbour will walk with slanders. 5. And they will deceive every one his neighbour and will not speak the truth: they have taught their tongue to speak lies, *and* weary themselves to commit iniquity. 6. Thine habitation *is* in the midst of deceit; through deceit they refuse to know me, saith the LORD.

Jer. 11:8. Yet they obeyed not, nor inclined their ear, but walked every one in the imagination of their evil heart: 15. What hath my beloved to do in mine house, *seeing* she hath wrought lewdness with many, and the holy flesh is passed from

thee? when thou doest evil, then thou rejoicest.

Jer. 13:10. This evil people, which refuse to hear my words, which walk in the imagination of their heart, and walk after other gods, to serve them, and to worship them, shall even be as this girdle, which is good for nothing.

Jer. 14:10. Thus saith the LORD unto this people, Thus have they loved to wander, they have not refrained their feet, therefore the LORD doth not accept them;

Jer. 17:1. The sin of Judah *is* written with a pen of iron, *and* with the point of a diamond; *it is* graven upon the table of their heart, and upon the horns of your altars;

Jer. 30:12. For thus saith the LORD, Thy bruise *is* incurable, *and* thy wound *is* grievous. 13. *There is* none to plead thy cause, that thou mayest be bound up: thou hast no healing medicines. 14. All thy lovers have forgotten thee; they seek thee not; for I have wounded thee with the wound of an enemy, with the chastisement of a cruel one, for the multitude of thine iniquity; *because* thy sins were increased. 15. Why criest thou for thine affliction? thy sorrow *is* incurable for the multitude of thine iniquity: *because* thy sins were increased, I have done these things unto thee.

Ezek. 3:7. But the house of Israel will not hearken unto thee; for they will not hearken unto me: for all the house of Israel *are* impudent and hardhearted.

Ezek. 11:12. And ye shall know that I *am* the LORD: for ye have not walked in my statutes, neither executed my judgments, but have done after the manners of the heathen that *are* round about you.

Ezek. 16:47. Yet hast thou not walked after their ways, nor done after their abominations: but, as *if that were* a very little *thing*, thou wast corrupted more than they in all thy ways.

Ezek. 20:16. Because they despised my judgments, and walked not in my statutes, but polluted my sabbaths: for their heart went after their idols.

Hos. 4:8. They eat up the sin of my people, and they set their heart on their iniquity.

Hos. 7:3. They make the king glad with their wickedness, and the princes with their lies. 9. Strangers have devoured his strength, and he knoweth *it* not: yea, gray hairs are here and there upon him, yet he knoweth not.

Hos. 9:10. I found Israel like grapes in the wilderness; I saw your fathers as the firstripe in the fig tree at her first time: *but* they went to Baal-peor, and separated themselves unto *that* shame; and *their* abominations were according as they loved.

Hos. 13:12. The iniquity of Ephraim *is* bound up; his sin *is* hid.

Amos 5:10. They hate him that rebuketh in the gate, and they abhor him that speaketh uprightly.

Mic. 3:1. And I said, Hear, I pray you, O

heads of Jacob, and ye princes of the house of Israel; *Is it* not for you to know judgment? 2. Who hate the good, and love the evil;

Mic. 7:2. The good *man* is perished out of the earth: and *there is* none upright among men: they all lie in wait for blood; they hunt every man his brother with a net. 3. That they may do evil with both hands earnestly, the prince asketh, and the judge *asketh* for a reward; and the great *man*, he uttereth his mischievous desire: so they wrap it up. 4. The best of them *is* as a brier: the most upright *is sharper* than a thorn hedge:

Zeph. 3:5. The unjust knoweth no shame. 7. I said, Surely thou wilt fear me, thou wilt receive instruction; so their dwelling should not be cut off, howsoever I punished them: but they rose early, *and* corrupted all their doings.

Hag. 2:14. So *is* this people, and so *is* this nation before me, saith the Lord; and so *is* every work of their hands; and that which they offer there *is* unclean.

Matt. 4:16. The people which sat in darkness saw great light; and to them which sat in the region and shadow of death light is sprung up.

Matt. 6:23. But if thine eye be evil, thy whole body shall be full of darkness. If therefore the light that is in thee be darkness, how great *is* that darkness!

Matt. 18:11. ¹For the Son of man is come to save that which was lost.   [¹Omitted in R. V.]

Mark 4:11. Unto them that are without, all *these* things are done in parables:

Luke 1:79. Them that sit in darkness and *in* the shadow of death,

Luke 19:10. The Son of man is come to seek and to save that which was lost.

John 3:18. He that believeth not is condemned already, because he hath not believed in the name of the only begotten Son of God. 19. And this is the condemnation, that light is come into the world, and men loved darkness rather than light, because their deeds were evil. 20. For every one that doeth evil hateth the light, neither cometh to the light, lest his deeds should be reproved.

John 5:42. But I know you, that ye have not the love of God in you.

John 8:34. Jesus answered them, Verily, verily, I say unto you, Whosoever committeth sin is the servant of sin. 44. Ye are of *your* father the devil, and the lusts of your father ye will do.

Acts 8:21. Thou hast neither part nor lot in this matter: for thy heart is not right in the sight of God. 23. For I perceive that thou art in the gall of bitterness, and *in* the bond of iniquity.

Acts 13:10. O full of all subtilty and all mischief, *thou* child of the devil, *thou* enemy of all righteousness, wilt thou not cease to pervert the right ways of the Lord?

Rom. 1:20. So that they are without excuse: 21. Because that, when they knew God, they glorified *him* not as God, neither were thankful; but became vain in their imaginations, and their foolish heart was darkened. 22. Professing themselves to be wise, they became fools, 23. And changed the glory of the uncorruptible God into an image made like to corruptible man, and to birds, and fourfooted beasts, and creeping things. 24. Wherefore God also gave them up to uncleanness through the lusts of their own hearts, to dishonour their own bodies between themselves: 25. Who changed the truth of God into a lie, and worshipped and served the creature more than the Creator, who is blessed for ever. Amen. 26. For this cause God gave them up unto vile affections: for even their women did change the natural use into that which is against nature: 27. And likewise also the men, leaving the natural use of the woman, burned in their lust one toward another; men with men working that which is unseemly, and receiving in themselves that recompence of their error which was meet. 28. And even as they did not like to retain God in *their* knowledge, God gave them over to a reprobate mind, to do those things which are not convenient; 29. Being filled with all unrighteousnes, fornication, wickedness, covetousness, maliciousness; full of envy, murder, debate, deceit, malignity; whisperers, 30. Backbiters, haters of God, despiteful, proud, boasters, inventors of evil things, disobedient to parents, 31. Without understanding, covenantbreakers, without natural affection, implacable, unmerciful: 32. Who knowing the judgment of God, that they which commit such things are worthy of death, not only do the same, but have pleasure in them that do them.

Rom. 2:8. Contentious, and do not obey the truth, but obey unrighteousness,

Rom. 3:10. As it is written, There is none righteous, no, not one: 11. There is none that understandeth, there is none that seeketh after God. 12. They are all gone out of the way, they are together become unprofitable; there is none that doeth good, no, not one. 13. Their throat *is* an open sepulchre; with their tongues they have used deceit; the poison of asps *is* under their lips: 14. Whose mouth *is* full of cursing and bitterness: 15. Their feet *are* swift to shed blood: 16. Destruction and misery *are* in their ways: 17. And the way of peace have they not known: 18. There is no fear of God before their eyes.

Rom. 8:5. For they that are after the flesh do mind the things of the flesh; 7. Because the carnal mind *is* enmity against God: for it is not subject to the law of God, neither indeed can be. 8. So then they that are in the flesh cannot please God.

Rom. 9:8. They which are the children of the flesh, these *are* not the children of God:

Eph. 2:1. And you *hath he quickened*, who were dead in trespasses and sins; 2. Wherein in time past ye walked according to the course of this world, according to the prince of the power of the air, the spirit that now worketh in the children of disobedience: 3. Among whom also we all had our conversation in times past in the lusts of our flesh, fulfilling the desires of the flesh and of the mind; and were by nature the children of wrath, even as others. 12. At that time ye were without Christ, being aliens from the commonwealth of Israel, and strangers from the covenants of promise, having no hope, and without God in the world:

Eph. 4:17. Gentiles walk, in the vanity of their mind, 18. Having the understanding darkened, being alienated from the life of God through the ignorance that is in them, because of the blindness of their heart: 19. Who being past feeling have given themselves over unto lasciviousness, to work all uncleanness with greediness.

Eph. 5:11. And have no fellowship with the unfruitful works of darkness, but rather reprove *them*. 12. For it is a shame even to speak of those things which are done of them in secret.

Phil. 2:15. A crooked and perverse nation, among whom ye shine as lights in the world;

Col. 1:21. Alienated and enemies in *your* mind by wicked works.

1 Thess. 5:7. They that sleep sleep in the night; and they that be drunken are drunken in the night.

2 Thess. 1:8. Them that know not God, and that obey not the gospel of our Lord Jesus Christ:

1 Tim. 1:9. Knowing this, that the law is not made for a righteous man, but for the lawless and disobedient, for the ungodly and for sinners, for unholy and profane, for murderers of fathers and murderers of mothers, for manslayers, 10. For whoremongers, for them that defile themselves with mankind, for menstealers, for liars, for perjured persons, and if there be any other thing that is contrary to sound doctrine;

2 Tim. 3:2. For men shall be lovers of their own selves, covetous, boasters, proud, ¹ blasphemers, disobedient to parents, unthankful, unholy. 3. Without natural affection, trucebreakers, false accusers, incontinent, fierce, despisers of those that are good, 4. Traitors, heady, highminded, lovers of pleasures more than lovers of God; 5. Having a form of godliness, but denying the power thereof: from such turn away. 6. For of this sort are they which creep into houses, and lead captive silly women laden with sins, led away with divers lusts. 7. Ever learning, and never able to come to the knowledge of the truth. 8. Now as Jannes and Jambres withstood Moses, so do these also resist the truth: men of cor-

rupt minds, reprobate concerning the faith. 9. But they shall proceed no further: for their folly shall be manifest unto all *men*, as their's also was. 10. But thou hast fully known my doctrine, manner of life, purpose, faith, longsuffering, charity, patience, 11. Persecutions, afflictions, which came unto me at Antioch, at Iconium, at Lystra; what persecutions I endured: but out of *them* all the Lord delivered me. 12. Yea, and all that will live godly in Christ Jesus shall suffer persecution. 13. But evil men and seducers shall wax worse and worse, deceiving, and being deceived. [¹ R. V. railers]

Tit. 1:15. Unto the pure all things *are* pure: but unto them that are defiled and unbelieving *is* nothing pure; but even their mind and conscience is defiled. 16. They profess that they know God; but in works they deny *him*, being abominable, and disobedient, and unto every good work reprobate.

Tit. 3:3. For we ourselves also were sometimes foolish, disobedient, deceived, serving divers lusts and pleasures, living in malice and envy, hateful, *and* hating one another.

2 Pet. 2:10. But chiefly them that walk after the flesh in the lust of uncleanness, and despise government. Presumptuous *are they*, selfwilled, they are not afraid to speak evil of dignities. 12. But these, as natural brute beasts, made to be taken and destroyed, speak evil of the things that they understand not; and shall utterly perish in their own corruption: 13. And shall receive the reward of unrighteousness, *as* they that count it pleasure to riot in the daytime. Spots *they are* and blemishes, sporting themselves with their own deceivings while they feast with you; 14. Having eyes full of adultery, and that cannot cease from sin; beguiling unstable souls: an heart they have exercised with covetous practices; cursed children: 15. Which have forsaken the right way, and are gone astray, following the way of Balaam *the son* of Bosor, who loved the wages of unrighteousness; 16. But was rebuked for his iniquity: the dumb ass speaking with man's voice forbade the madness of the prophet. 17. These are wells without water, clouds that are carried with a tempest; to whom the mist of darkness is reserved for ever. 18. For when they speak great swelling *words* of vanity, they allure through the lusts of the flesh, *through much* wantonness, those that were clean escaped from them who live in error. 19. While they promise them liberty, they themselves are the servants of corruption: for of whom a man is overcome, of the same is he brought in bondage.

1 John 3:8. He that committeth sin is of the devil; for the devil sinneth from the beginning. For this purpose the Son of God was manifested, that he might destroy the works of the devil. 10. In this the children of God are manifest and the children of the devil: whosoever doeth not righteousness is

not of God, neither he that loveth not his brother. 14. We know that we have passed from death unto life, because we love the brethren. He that loveth not *his* brother abideth in death. 15. Whosoever hateth his brother is a murderer : and ye know that no murderer hath eternal life abiding in him.

Jude 12. These are spots in your feasts of charity, when they feast with you, feeding themselves without fear : clouds *they are* without water, carried about of winds ; trees whose fruit withereth, without fruit, twice dead, plucked up by the roots ; 13. Raging waves of the sea, foaming out their own shame ; wandering stars, to whom is reserved the blackness of darkness for ever.

Rev. 3:17. Because thou sayest, I am rich, and increased with goods, and have need of nothing ; and knowest not that thou art wretched, and miserable, and poor, and blind, and naked : 18. I counsel thee to buy of me gold tried in the fire, that thou mayest be rich ; and white raiment, that thou mayest be clothed, and *that* the shame of thy nakedness do not appear ; and anoint thine eyes with eyesalve, that thou mayest see.

PRAYER OF: Deut. 1:45. And ye returned and wept before the LORD ; but the LORD would not hearken to your voice, nor give ear unto you.

Deut. 3:26. But the LORD was wroth with me for your sakes, and would not hear me : and the LORD said unto me, Let it suffice thee ; speak no more unto me of this matter.

2 Sam. 22:42. They looked, but *there was* none to save ; *even* unto the LORD, but he answered them not.

Job 27:9. Will God hear his cry when trouble cometh upon him ?

Job 35:12. There they cry, but none giveth answer, because of the pride of evil men. 13. Surely God will not hear vanity, neither will the Almighty regard it.

Psa. 18:41. They cried, but *there was* none to save *them; even* unto the LORD, but he answered them not.

Psa. 66:18. If I regard iniquity in my heart, the Lord will not hear me :

Prov. 1:24. Because I have called, and ye refused ; I have stretched out my hand, and no man regarded ; 25. But ye have set at nought all my counsel, and would none of my reproof : 26. I also will laugh at your calamity ; I will mock when your fear cometh ; 27. When your fear cometh as desolation, and your destruction cometh as a whirlwind ; when distress and anguish cometh upon you. 28. Then shall they call upon me, but I will not answer ; they shall seek me early, but they shall not find me :

Prov. 15:8. The sacrifice of the wicked *is* an abomination to the LORD : but the prayer of the upright *is* his delight. 29. The LORD *is* far from the wicked : but he heareth the prayer of the righteous.

Prov. 21:13. Whoso stoppeth his ears at the cry of the poor, he also shall cry himself, but shall not be heard. 27. The sacrifice of the wicked *is* abomination : how much more, *when* he bringeth it with a wicked mind ?

Prov. 28:9. He that turneth away his ear from hearing the law, even his prayer *shall be* abomination.

Isa. 1:15. And when ye spread forth your hands, I will hide mine eyes from you : yea, when ye make many prayers, I will not hear : your hands are full of blood.

Isa. 45:19. I said not unto the seed of Jacob, Seek ye me in vain :

Isa. 59:2. But your iniquities have separated between you and your God, and your sins have hid *his* face from you, that he will not hear.

Jer. 11:11. Therefore thus saith the LORD, Behold, I will bring evil upon them, which they shall not be able to escape ; and though they shall cry unto me, I will not hearken unto them.

Jer. 14:12. When they fast, I will not hear their cry ; and when they offer burnt offering and an oblation, I will not accept them : but I will consume them by the sword, and by the famine, and by the pestilence.

Jer. 15:1. Then said the LORD unto me, Though Moses and Samuel stood before me, *yet* my mind *could* not *be* toward this people : cast *them* out of my sight, and let them go forth.

Jer. 18:17. I will scatter them as with an east wind before the enemy ; I will [1]shew them the back, and not the face, in the day of their calamity.   [1 R. V. look upon their]

Lam. 3:8. Also when I cry and shout, he shutteth out my prayer. 44. Thou hast covered thyself with a cloud, that *our* prayer should not pass through.

Ezek. 8:18. Therefore will I also deal in fury : mine eye shall not spare, neither will I have pity : and though they cry in mine ears with a loud voice, *yet* will I not hear them.

Ezek. 20:3. Son of man, speak unto the elders of Israel, and say unto them, Thus saith the Lord GOD ; Are ye come to enquire of me ? *As* I live, saith the Lord GOD, I will not be enquired of by you. 31. For when ye offer your gifts, when ye make your sons to pass through the fire, ye pollute yourselves with all your idols, even unto this day : and shall I be enquired of by you, O house of Israel ? *As* I live, saith the Lord GOD, I will not be enquired of by you.

Hos. 5:6. They shall go with their flocks and with their herds to seek the LORD ; but they shall not find *him ;* he hath withdrawn himself from them.

Mic. 3:4. Then shall they cry unto the LORD, but he will not hear them : he will even hide his face from them at that time, as they have behaved themselves ill in their doings.

Zech. 7:12. Yea, they made their hearts *as* an adamant stone, lest they should hear the law, and the words which the LORD of hosts hath sent in his spirit by the former prophets: therefore came a great wrath from the LORD of hosts. 13. Therefore it is come to pass, *that* as he cried, and they would not hear; so they cried, and I would not hear, saith the LORD of hosts:

Mal. 1:9. And now, I pray you, beseech God that he will be gracious unto us: this hath been by your means: will he regard your persons? saith the LORD of hosts.

Mal. 2:11. Judah hath dealt treacherously, and an abomination is committed in Israel and in Jerusalem; for Judah hath profaned the holiness of the LORD which he loved, and hath married the daughter of a strange god. 12. The LORD will cut off the man that doeth this, the master and the scholar, out of the tabernacles of Jacob, and him that offereth an offering unto the LORD of hosts. 13. And this have ye done again, covering the altar of the LORD with tears, with weeping, and with crying out, insomuch that he regardeth not the offering any more, or receiveth *it* with good will at your hand.

John 9:31. Now we know that God heareth not sinners: but if any man be a worshipper of God, and doeth his will, him he heareth.

Jas. 1:6. But let him ask in faith, nothing wavering. For he that wavereth is like a wave of the sea driven with the wind and tossed. 7. For let not that man think that he shall receive any thing of the Lord.

Jas. 4:3. Ye ask, and receive not, because ye ask amiss, that ye may consume *it* upon your lusts.

1 Pet. 3:7. Likewise, ye husbands, dwell with *them* according to knowledge, giving honour unto the wife, as unto the weaker vessel, and as being heirs together of the grace of life; that your prayers be not hindered.

PUNISHMENT OF: Gen. 2:17. But of the tree of the knowledge of good and evil, thou shalt not eat of it: for in the day that thou eatest thereof thou shalt surely die.

Gen. 3:16. Unto the woman he said, I will greatly multiply thy sorrow and thy conception; in sorrow thou shalt bring forth children; and thy desire *shall be* to thy husband, and he shall rule over thee. 17. And unto Adam he said, Because thou hast hearkened unto the voice of thy wife, and hast eaten of the tree, of which I commanded thee, saying, Thou shalt not eat of it: cursed *is* the ground for thy sake; in ¹ sorrow shalt thou eat *of* it all the days of thy life; 18. Thorns also and thistles shall it bring forth to thee; and thou shalt eat the herb of the field; 19. In the sweat of thy face shalt thou eat bread, till thou return unto the ground; for out of it wast thou taken: for dust thou *art*, and unto dust shalt thou return. [¹ R. V. toil]

Gen. 4:7. If thou doest well, shalt thou not be accepted? and if thou doest not well, sin lieth at the door.

Gen. 6:3. And the LORD said, My spirit shall not always strive with man, for that he also *is* flesh: 7. And the LORD said, I will destroy man whom I have created from the face of the earth; both man, and beast, and the creeping thing, and the fowls of the air; for it repenteth me that I have made them. 12. And God looked upon the earth, and, behold, it was corrupt; for all flesh had corrupted his way upon the earth. 13. And God said unto Noah, The end of all flesh is come before me; for the earth is filled with violence through them; and, behold, I will destroy them with the earth.

Ex. 20:5. I the LORD thy God *am* a jealous God, visiting the iniquity of the fathers upon the children unto the third and fourth *generation* of them that hate me; Ex. 34:7.

Ex. 32:33. And the LORD said unto Moses, Whosoever hath sinned against me, him will I blot out of my book. 34. Therefore now go, lead the people unto *the place* of which I have spoken unto thee: behold, mine Angel shall go before thee: nevertheless in the day when I visit I will visit their sin upon them. 35. And the LORD plagued the people, because they made the calf, which Aaron made.

Lev. 26:14. But if ye will not hearken unto me, and will not do all these commandments; 16. I also will do this unto you; I will even appoint over you terror, consumption, and the burning ague, that shall consume the eyes, and cause sorrow of heart: and ye shall sow your seed in vain, for your enemies shall eat it. 17. And I will set my face against you, and ye shall be slain before your enemies: they that hate you shall reign over you; and ye shall flee when none pursueth you. 18. And if ye will not yet for all this hearken unto me, then I will punish you seven times more for your sins. *vs.* 18–39.

Num. 15:31. Because he hath despised the word of the LORD, and hath broken his commandment, that soul shall utterly be cut off; his iniquity *shall be* upon him.

Num. 32:23. If ye will not do so, behold, ye have sinned against the LORD: and be sure your sin will find you out.

Deut. 7:9. Know therefore that the LORD thy God, he *is* God, . . . 10. And repayeth them that hate him to their face, to destroy them: he will not be slack to him that hateth him, he will repay him to his face.

Deut. 11:26. Behold, I set before you this day a blessing and a curse; 28. A curse, if ye will not obey the commandments of the LORD your God,

Deut. 28:20. The LORD shall send upon thee cursing, vexation, and rebuke, in all that thou settest thine hand for to do, until thou be destroyed, and until thou perish quickly; because of the wickedness of thy doings, whereby thou hast forsaken me. *vs.* 15–68.

Deut. 30:15. See, I have set before thee this day life and good, and death and evil; 19. I call heaven and earth to record this day against you, *that* I have set before you life and death, blessing and cursing: therefore choose life, that both thou and thy seed may live:

Deut. 31:29. For I know that after my death ye will utterly corrupt *yourselves*, and turn aside from the way which I have commanded you; and evil will befall you in the latter days; because ye will do evil in the sight of the LORD, to provoke him to anger through the work of your hands.

1 Sam. 3:11. And the LORD said to Samuel, Behold, I will do a thing in Israel, at which both the ears of every one that heareth it shall tingle. 12. In that day I will perform against Eli all *things* which I have spoken concerning his house: when I begin, I will also make an end. 13. For I have told him that I will judge his house for ever for the iniquity which he knoweth; because his sons made themselves vile, and he restrained them not. 14. And therefore I have sworn unto the house of Eli, that the iniquity of Eli's house shall not be purged with sacrifice nor offering for ever.

1 Sam. 12:25. If ye shall still do wickedly, ye shall be consumed, both ye and your king.

2 Sam. 3:39. And I *am* this day weak, though anointed king; and these men the sons of Zeruiah *be* too hard for me: the LORD shall reward the doer of evil according to his wickedness.

2 Sam. 7:14. If he commit iniquity, I will chasten him with the rod of men, and with the stripes of the children of men:

2 Sam. 22:27. With the pure thou wilt shew thyself pure; and with the froward thou wilt shew thyself unsavoury. 28. And the afflicted people thou wilt save: but thine eyes *are* upon the haughty, *that* thou mayest bring *them* down. Psa. 18:26,27.

2 Sam. 23:6. But *the sons* of Belial *shall be* all of them as thorns thrust away, because they cannot be taken with hands: 7. But the man *that* shall touch them must be fenced with iron and the staff of a spear; and they shall be utterly burned with fire in the *same* place.

1 Kin. 21:20. And Ahab said to Elijah, Hast thou found me, O mine enemy? And he answered, I have found *thee:* because thou hast sold thyself to work evil in the sight of the LORD. 21. Behold, I will bring evil upon thee, and will take away thy posterity,

1 Chr. 10:13. So Saul died for his transgression which he committed against the LORD, *even* against the word of the LORD, which he kept not, and also for asking *counsel* of *one that had* a familiar spirit, to enquire *of it:* 14. And enquired not of the LORD: therefore he slew him, and turned the kingdom unto David the son of Jesse.

1 Chr. 15:13. For because ye *did it* not at the first, the LORD our God made a breach upon us, for that we sought him not after the due order.

1 Chr. 28:9. If thou forsake him, he will cast thee off for ever.

2 Chr. 15:2. The LORD *is* with you, while ye be with him; and if ye seek him, he will be found of you; but if ye forsake him, he will forsake you.

Job 4:8. Even as I have seen, they that plow iniquity, and sow wickedness, reap the same. 9. By the blast of God they perish, and by the breath of his nostrils are they consumed.

Job 5:3. I have seen the foolish taking root: but suddenly I cursed his habitation. 14. They meet with darkness in the daytime, and grope in the noonday as in the night.

Job 8:20. Behold, God will not cast away a perfect *man*, neither will he help the evil doers: 22. They that hate thee shall be clothed with shame; and the dwelling place of the wicked shall come to nought.

Job 10:14. If I sin, then thou markest me, and thou wilt not acquit me from mine iniquity. 15. If I be wicked, woe unto me;

Job 11:20. The eyes of the wicked shall fail, and they shall not escape, and their hope *shall be as* the giving up of the ghost.

Job 15:20. The wicked man travaileth with pain all *his* days, and the number of years is hidden to the oppressor. 21. A dreadful sound *is* in his ears: in prosperity the destroyer shall come upon him. 22. He believeth not that he shall return out of darkness, and he is waited for of the sword. 23. He wandereth abroad for bread, *saying*, Where *is it?* he knoweth that the day of darkness is ready at his hand. 24. Trouble and anguish shall make him afraid; they shall prevail against him, as a king ready to the battle. *vs.* 28-30.

Job 18:5. Yea, the light of the wicked shall be put out, and the spark of his fire shall not shine. 6. The light shall be dark in his tabernacle, and his candle shall be put out with him. 7. The steps of his strength shall be straitened, and his own counsel shall cast him down. 8. For he is cast into a net by his own feet, and he walketh upon a snare. 9. The gin shall take *him* by the heel, *and* the robber shall prevail against him. 10. The snare *is* laid for him in the ground, and a trap for him in the way. 11. Terrors shall make him afraid on every side, and shall drive him to his feet. 12. His strength shall be hungerbitten, and destruction *shall be* ready at his side. 13. It shall devour the strength of his skin: *even* the firstborn of death shall devour his strength. 14. His confidence shall be rooted out of his tabernacle, and it shall bring him to the king of terrors. 15. It shall dwell in his tabernacle, because *it is* none of his: brimstone shall be scattered upon his habitation. 16. His roots shall be dried up beneath, and above shall his branch be cut off. 17. His remembrance shall perish from the earth, and he shall have no name in the street. 18. He shall be driven from light into darkness, and chased out of the world. 19. He shall neither have son nor nephew among his people, nor any remaining in his dwellings. 20. They that come after *him* shall be astonied at his day, as they that went before were affrighted. 21. Surely such *are* the dwellings of the wicked, and this *is* the place *of him that* knoweth not God.

Job 19:29. Be ye afraid of the sword: for wrath *bringeth* the punishments of the sword, that ye may know *there is* a judgment.

Job 20:5. That the triumphing of the wicked *is* short, and the joy of the hypocrite *but* for a moment? 6. Though his excellency mount up to the heavens, and his head reach unto the clouds; 7. *Yet* he shall perish for ever like his own dung: they which have seen him shall say, Where *is* he? 8. He shall fly away as a dream, and shall not be found: yea, he shall be chased away as a vision of the night. 9. The eye also *which* saw him shall *see him* no more; neither shall his place any more behold him. 10. His children shall seek to please the poor, and his hands shall restore their goods. 11. His bones are full *of the sin* of his youth, which shall lie down with him in the dust. 12. Though wickedness be sweet in his mouth, *though* he hide it under his tongue; 13. *Though* he spare it, and forsake it not, but keep it still within' his mouth; 14. *Yet* his meat in his bowels is turned, *it is* the gall of asps within him. 15. He hath swallowed down riches, and he shall vomit them up again: God shall cast them out of his belly. 16. He shall suck the poison of asps: the viper's tongue shall slay him. 17. He shall not see the rivers, the floods, the brooks of honey and butter. 18. That which he laboured for shall he restore, and shall not swallow *it* down: according to *his* substance *shall* the restitution *be,* and he shall not rejoice *therein.* 19. Because he hath oppressed *and* hath forsaken the poor; *because* he hath violently taken away an house which he builded not; 20. Surely he shall not feel quietness in his belly, he shall not save of that which he desired. 21. There shall none of his meat be left; therefore shall no man look for his goods. 22. In the fulness of his sufficiency he shall be in straits: every hand of the wicked shall come upon him. 23. *When* he is about to fill his belly, *God* shall cast the fury of his wrath upon him, and shall rain *it* upon him while he is eating. 24. He shall flee from the iron weapon, *and* the bow of steel shall strike him through. 25. It is drawn, and cometh out of the body; yea, the glittering sword cometh out of his gall: terrors *are* upon him. 26. All darkness *shall be* hid in his secret places: a fire not blown shall consume him; it shall go ill with him that is left in his tabernacle.

27. The heaven shall reveal his iniquity; and the earth shall rise up against him. 28. The increase of his house shall depart, *and his goods* shall flow away in the day of his wrath. 29. This *is* the portion of a wicked man from God, and the heritage appointed unto him by God.

Job 21:7. Wherefore do the wicked live, become old, yea, are mighty in power? 8. Their seed is established in their sight with them, and their offspring before their eyes. 9. Their houses *are* safe from fear, neither *is* the rod of God upon them. 10. Their bull gendereth, and faileth not; their cow calveth, and casteth not her calf. 11. They send forth their little ones like a flock, and their children dance. 12. They take the timbrel and harp, and rejoice at the sound of the organ. 13. They spend their days in wealth, and in a moment go down to the grave. 14. Therefore they say unto God, Depart from us; for we desire not the knowledge of thy ways. 15. What *is* the Almighty, that we should serve him? and what profit should we have, if we pray unto him? 16. Lo, their good *is* not in their hand: the counsel of the wicked is far from me. 17. How oft is the candle of the wicked put out! and *how oft* cometh their destruction upon them! *God* distributeth sorrows in his anger. 18. They are as stubble before the wind, and as chaff that the storm carrieth away. 19. God layeth up his iniquity for his children: he rewardeth him, and he shall know *it.* 20. His eyes shall see his destruction, and he shall drink of the wrath of the Almighty. 21. For what pleasure *hath* he in his house after him, when the number of his months is cut off in the midst? 22. Shall *any* teach God knowledge? seeing he judgeth those that are high. 23. One dieth in his full strength, being wholly at ease and quiet. 24. His breasts are full of milk, and his bones are moistened with marrow. 25. And another dieth in the bitterness of his soul, and never eateth with pleasure. 26. They shall lie down alike in the dust, and the worms shall cover them. 27. Behold, I know your thoughts, and the devices *which* ye wrongfully imagine against me. 28. For ye say, Where *is* the house of the prince? and where *are* the dwellingplaces of the wicked? 29. Have ye not asked them that go by the way? and do ye not know their tokens, 30. That the wicked is reserved to the day of destruction? they shall be brought forth to the day of wrath. 31. Who shall declare his way to his face? and who shall repay him *what* he hath done? 32 Yet shall he be brought to the grave, and shall remain in the tomb. 33. The clods of the valley shall be sweet unto him, and every man shall draw after him, as *there are* innumerable before him.

Job 27:8. For what *is* the hope of the hypocrite, though he hath gained, when God taketh away his soul? 9. Will God hear his cry when trouble cometh upon him? 10. Will he delight himself in the Almighty? will he always call upon God? 11. I will teach you by the hand of God: *that* which *is* with the Almighty will I not conceal. 12. Behold, all ye yourselves have seen *it;* why then are ye thus altogether vain? 13. This *is* the portion of a wicked man with God, and the heritage of oppressors, *which* they shall receive of the Almighty. 14. If his children be multiplied, *it is* for the sword: and his offspring shall not be satisfied with bread. 15. Those that remain of him shall be buried in death: and his widows shall not weep. 16. Though he heap up silver as the dust, and prepare raiment as the clay; 17. He may prepare *it,* but the just shall put *it* on, and the innocent shall divide the silver. 18. He buildeth his house as a moth, and as a booth *that* the keeper maketh. 19. The rich man shall lie down, but he shall not be gathered: he openeth his eyes, and he *is* not. 20. Terrors take hold on him as waters, a tempest stealeth him away in the night. 21. The east wind carrieth him away, and he departeth: and as a storm hurleth him out of his place. 22. For *God* shall cast upon him, and not spare: he would fain flee out of his hand. 23. *Men* shall clap their hands at him, and shall hiss him out of his place.

Job 31:3. *Is* not destruction to the wicked? and a strange *punishment* to the workers of iniquity?

Job 34:22. *There is* no darkness, nor shadow of death, where the workers of iniquity may hide themselves.

Job 36:12. But if they obey not, they shall perish by the sword, and they shall die without knowledge. 17. Thou hast fulfilled the judgment of the wicked: judgment and justice take hold *on thee.*

Psa. 1:4. The ungodly *are* not so: but *are* like the chaff which the wind driveth away. 5. Therefore the ungodly shall not stand in the judgment, nor sinners in the congregation of the righteous. 6. For the LORD knoweth the way of the righteous: but the way of the ungodly shall perish.

Psa. 2:4. He that sitteth in the heavens shall laugh: the Lord shall have them in derision. 5. Then shall he speak unto them in his wrath, and vex them in his sore displeasure. 9. Thou shalt break them with a rod of iron; thou shalt dash them in pieces like a potter's vessel.

Psa. 3:7. Thou hast broken the teeth of the ungodly.

Psa. 5:5. The foolish shall not stand in thy sight: thou hatest all workers of iniquity.

Psa. 7:11. God judgeth the righteous, and God is angry *with the wicked* every day. 12. If he turn not, he will whet his sword; he hath bent his bow, and made it ready. 13. He hath also prepared for him the instruments of death; he ordaineth his arrows against the persecutors.

Psa. 9:5. Thou hast rebuked the heathen, thou hast destroyed the wicked, thou hast put out their name for ever and ever. 17. The wicked shall be turned into hell, *and* all the nations that forget God.

Psa. 10:15. Break thou the arm of the wicked and the evil *man:* seek out his wickedness *till* thou find none.

Psa. 11:6. Upon the wicked he shall rain snares, fire and brimstone, and an horrible tempest: *this shall be* the portion of their cup.

Psa. 18:14. Yea, he sent out his arrows, and scattered them; and he shot out lightnings, and discomfited them.

Psa. 21:9. Thou shalt make them as a fiery oven in the time of thine anger: the LORD shall swallow them up in his wrath, and the fire shall devour them. 10. Their fruit shalt thou destroy from the earth, and their seed from among the children of men.

Psa. 28:4. Give them according to their deeds, and according to the wickedness of their endeavours: give them after the work of their hands; render to them their desert. 5. Because they regard not the works of the LORD, nor the operation of his hands, he shall destroy them, and not build them up.

Psa. 32:10. Many sorrows *shall be* to the wicked:

Psa. 34:16. The face of the LORD *is* against them that do evil, to cut off the remembrance of them from the earth. 21. Evil shall slay the wicked: and they that hate the righteous shall be desolate.

Psa. 36:12. There are the workers of iniquity fallen: they are cast down, and shall not be able to rise.

Psa. 37:1. Fret not thyself because of evil doers, neither be thou envious against the workers of iniquity. 2. For they shall soon be cut down like the grass, and wither as the green herb. 9. For evildoers shall be cut off: but those that wait upon the LORD, they shall inherit the earth. 10. For yet a little while, and the wicked *shall* not *be:* yea, thou shalt diligently consider his place, and it *shall* not *be.* 17. The arms of the wicked shall be broken: 20. The wicked shall perish, and the enemies of the LORD *shall be* as the fat of lambs: they shall consume; into smoke shall they consume away. 22. *They that be* cursed of him shall be cut off. 34. Wait on the LORD, and keep his way, and he shall exalt thee to inherit the land: when the wicked are cut off, thou shalt see *it.* 35. I have seen the wicked in great power, and spreading himself like a green bay tree. 36. Yet he passed away, and, lo, he *was* not: yea, I sought him, but he could not be found. 37. Mark the perfect *man,* and behold the upright: for the end of *that* man *is* peace. 38. But the transgressors shall be destroyed together: the end of the wicked shall be cut off. *vs.* 13–22.

Psa. 39:11. When thou with rebukes dost correct man for iniquity, thou makest his beauty to consume away like a moth:

Psa. 50:22. Now consider this, ye that forget God, lest I tear *you* in pieces, and *there be* none to deliver.

Psa. 52:5. God shall likewise destroy thee for ever, he shall take thee away, and pluck thee out of *thy* dwelling place, and root thee out of the land of the living.

Psa. 55:19. God shall hear, and afflict them, even he that abideth of old. 23. But thou, O God, shalt bring them down into the pit of destruction: bloody and deceitful men shall not live out half their days; but I will trust in thee.

Psa. 56:7. Shall they escape by iniquity? in *thine* anger cast down the people, O God.

Psa. 58:6. Break their teeth, O God, in their mouth: break out the great teeth of the young lions, O LORD. 7. Let them melt away as waters *which* run continually: *when* he bendeth *his bow to shoot* his arrows, let them be as cut in pieces. 8. As a snail *which* melteth, let *every one of them* pass away: *like* the untimely birth of a woman, *that* they may not see the sun. 9. Before your pots can feel the thorns, he shall take them away as with a whirlwind, both living, and in *his* wrath.

Psa. 59:5. Thou therefore, O LORD God of hosts, the God of Israel, awake to visit all the heathen: be not merciful to any wicked transgressors. 8. But thou, O LORD, shalt laugh at them: thou shalt have all the heathen in derision.

Psa. 62:3. How long will ye imagine mischief against a man? ye shall be slain all of you: as a bowing wall *shall ye be, and as a* tottering fence.

Psa. 64:7. But God shall shoot at them *with* an arrow; suddenly shall they be wounded. 8. So they shall make their own tongue to fall upon themselves: all that see them shall flee away.

Psa. 68:1. Let God arise, let his enemies be scattered: let them also that hate him flee before him. 2. As smoke is driven away, *so* drive *them* away: as wax melteth before the fire, *so* let the wicked perish at the presence of God. 6. God setteth the solitary in families: he bringeth out those which are bound with chains: but the rebellious dwell in a dry *land*. 21. God shall wound the head of his enemies, *and* the hairy scalp of such an one as goeth on still in his trespasses.

Psa. 73:2. But as for me, my feet were almost gone; my steps had well nigh slipped. 3. For I was envious at the foolish, *when I* saw the prosperity of the wicked. 4. For *there are* no bands in their death: but their strength *is* firm. 5. They *are* not in trouble *as other* men; neither are they plagued like *other* men. 6. Therefore pride compasseth them about as a chain; violence covereth them *as a* garment. 7. Their eyes stand out with fatness they have more than heart could wish. 8. They are corrupt, and speak wickedly *concerning* oppression: they speak loftily. 9. They set their mouth

against the heavens, and their tongue walketh through the earth. 10. Therefore his people return hither: and waters of a full *cup* are wrung out to them. 11. And they say, How doth God know? and is there knowledge in the most High? 12. Behold, these *are* the ungodly, who prosper in the world; they increase *in* riches. 13. Verily I have cleansed my heart *in* vain, and washed my hands in innocency. 14. For all the day long have I been plagued, and chastened every morning. 15. If I say, I will speak thus; behold, I should offend *against* the generation of thy children. 16. When I thought to know this, it *was* too painful for me; 17. Until I went into the sanctuary of God; *then* understood I their end. 18. Surely thou didst set them in slippery places: thou castedst them down into destruction. 19. How are they *brought* into desolation, as in a moment! they are utterly consumed with terrors. 20. As a dream when *one* awaketh; *so,* O Lord, when thou awakest, thou shalt despise their image. 21. Thus my heart was grieved, and I was pricked in my reins. 27. For, lo, they that are far from thee shall perish: thou hast destroyed all them that go a whoring from thee.

Psa. 75:8. In the hand of the LORD *there is* a cup, and the wine is red; it is full of mixture; and he poureth out of the same: but the dregs thereof, all the wicked of the earth shall wring *them* out, *and* drink *them*. 10. All the horns of the wicked also will I cut off;

Psa. 78:49. He cast upon them the fierceness of his anger, wrath, and indignation, and trouble, by sending evil angels *among them*. 50. He made a way to his anger; he spared not their soul from death, but gave their life over to the pestilence; *vs.* 1–67.

Psa. 89:10. Thou hast broken Rahab in pieces, as one that is slain; thou hast scattered thine enemies with thy strong arm. 31. If they break my statutes, and keep not my commandments; 32. Then will I visit their transgression with the rod, and their iniquity with stripes.

Psa. 91:8. Only with thine eyes shalt thou behold and see the reward of the wicked.

Psa. 92:7. When the wicked spring as the grass, and when all the workers of iniquity do flourish; *it is* that they shall be destroyed for ever: 9. For, lo, thine enemies, O LORD, for, lo, thine enemies shall perish; all the workers of iniquity shall be scattered.

Psa. 94:13. That thou mayest give him rest from the days of adversity, until the pit be digged for the wicked. 23. And he shall bring upon them their own iniquity, and shall cut them off in their own wickedness; *yea,* the LORD our God shall cut them off.

Psa. 97:3. A fire goeth before him, and burneth up his enemies round about.

Psa. 101:8. I will early destroy all the wicked of the land; that I may cut off all wicked doers from the city of the LORD.

Psa. 104:35. Let the sinners be consumed out of the earth, and let the wicked be no more.

Psa. 106:18. And a fire was kindled in their company; the flame burned up the wicked. 43. They provoked *him* with their counsel, and were brought low for their iniquity.

Psa. 107:17. Fools because of their transgression, and because of their iniquities, are afflicted. 33. He turneth rivers into a wilderness, and the watersprings into dry ground; 34. A fruitful land into barrenness; for the wickedness of them that dwell therein.

Psa. 109:6. Set thou a wicked man over him: and let Satan stand at his right hand. 7. When he shall be judged, let him be condemned: and let his prayer become sin. 8. Let his days be few; *and* let another take his office. 9. Let his children be fatherless, and his wife a widow. 10. Let his children be continually vagabonds, and beg: let them seek *their bread* also out of their desolate places. 11. Let the extortioner catch all that he hath; and let the strangers spoil his labour. 12. Let there be none to extend mercy unto him: neither let there be any to favour his fatherless children. 13. Let his posterity be cut off; *and* in the generation following let their name be blotted out. 14. Let the iniquity of his fathers be remembered with the LORD; and let not the sin of his mother be blotted out. 15. Let them be before the LORD continually, that he may cut off the memory of them from the earth. 16. Because that he remembered not to shew mercy, but persecuted the poor and needy man, that he might even slay the broken in heart. 17. As he loved cursing, so let it come unto him: as he delighted not in blessing, so let it be far from him. 18. As he clothed himself with cursing like as with his garment, so let it come into his bowels like water, and like oil into his bones. 19. Let it be unto him as the garment *which* covereth him, and for a girdle wherewith he is girded continually.

Psa. 119:21. Thou hast rebuked the proud *that are* cursed, which do err from thy commandments. 118. Thou hast trodden down all them that err from thy statutes: for their deceit *is* falsehood. 119. Thou puttest away all the wicked of the earth *like* dross: 155. Salvation *is* far from the wicked: for they seek not thy statutes.

Psa. 129:4. The LORD *is* righteous: he hath cut asunder the cords of the wicked.

Psa. 139:19. Surely thou wilt slay the wicked, O God: depart from me therefore, ye bloody men.

Psa. 145:20. The LORD preserveth all them that love him: but all the wicked will he destroy.

Psa. 146:9. The LORD preserveth the stran-gers; he relieveth the fatherless and widow: but the way of the wicked he turneth upside down.

Psa. 147:6. The LORD lifteth up the meek: he casteth the wicked down to the ground.

Prov. 2:22. But the wicked shall be cut off from the earth, and the transgressors shall be rooted out of it.

Prov. 3:33. The curse of the LORD *is* in the house of the wicked:

Prov. 6:12. A naughty person, a wicked man, walketh with a froward mouth. 13. He winketh with his eyes, he speaketh with his feet, he teacheth with his fingers; 14. Frowardness *is* in his heart, he deviseth mischief continually; he soweth discord. 15. Therefore shall his calamity come suddenly; suddenly shall he be broken without remedy.

Prov. 10:3. The LORD will not suffer the soul of the righteous to famish: but he casteth away the substance of the wicked. 6. Blessings *are* upon the head of the just: but violence covereth the mouth of the wicked. 7. The memory of the just *is* blessed: but the name of the wicked shall rot. 8. The wise in heart will receive commandments: but a prating fool shall fall. 14. Wise *men* lay up knowledge: but the mouth of the foolish *is* near destruction. 24. The fear of the wicked, it shall come upon him: but the desire of the righteous shall be granted. 25. As the whirlwind passeth, so *is* the wicked no *more:* but the righteous *is* an everlasting foundation. 27. The fear of the LORD prolongeth days: but the years of the wicked shall be shortened. 28. The hope of the righteous *shall be* gladness: but the expectation of the wicked shall perish. 29. The way of the LORD *is* strength to the upright: but destruction *shall be* to the workers of iniquity. 30. The righteous shall never be removed: but the wicked shall not inhabit the earth. 31. The mouth of the just bringeth forth wisdom: but the froward tongue shall be cut out.

Prov. 11:3. The integrity of the upright shall guide them: but the perverseness of transgressors shall destroy them. 5. The righteousness of the perfect shall direct his way: but the wicked shall fall by his own wickedness. 6. The righteousness of the upright shall deliver them: but transgressors shall be taken in *their own* naughtiness. 7. When a wicked man dieth, *his* expectation shall perish: and the hope of unjust *men* perisheth. 8. The righteous is delivered out of trouble, and the wicked cometh in his stead. 19. As righteousness *tendeth* to life; so he that pursueth evil *pursueth it* to his own death. 21. *Though* hand *join* in hand, the wicked shall not be unpunished: but the seed of the righteous shall be delivered. 23. The desire of the righteous *is* only good: *but* the expectation of the wicked *is* wrath. 31. Behold, the righteous shall be recompensed in the earth: much more the wicked and the sinner.

Prov. 12:2. A good *man* obtaineth favour of the LORD: but a man of wicked devices will he condemn. 3. A man shall not be established by wickedness: but the root of the righteous shall not be moved. 7. The wicked are overthrown, and *are* not: but the house of the righteous shall stand.

Prov. 13:2. A man shall eat good by the fruit of *his* mouth: but the soul of the transgressors *shall eat* violence. 5. A righteous *man* hateth lying: but a wicked *man* is loathsome, and cometh to shame. 6. Righteousness keepeth *him that is* upright in the way: but wickedness overthroweth the sinner. 9. The light of the righteous rejoiceth: but the lamp of the wicked shall be put out. 21. Evil pursueth sinners: but to the righteous good shall be repayed. 25. The righteous eateth to the satisfying of his soul: but the belly of the wicked shall want.

Prov. 14:12. There is a way which seemeth right unto a man, but the end thereof *are* the ways of death. [Prov. 16:25.] 19. The evil bow before the good; and the wicked at the gates of the righteous. 32. The wicked is driven away in his wickedness:

Prov. 16:4. The LORD hath made all *things* for himself: yea, even the wicked for the day of evil. 5. Every one *that is* proud in heart *is* an abomination to the LORD: *though* hand *join* in hand, he shall not be unpunished.

Prov. 18:3. When the wicked cometh, *then* cometh also contempt, and with ignominy reproach.

Prov. 19:16. He that keepeth the commandment keepeth his own soul; *but* he that despiseth his ways shall die.

Prov. 21:12. The righteous *man* wisely considereth the house of the wicked: *but* God overthroweth the wicked for *their* wickedness. 15. *It is* joy to the just to do judgment: but destruction *shall be* to the workers of iniquity. 16. The man that wandereth out of the way of understanding shall remain in the congregation of the dead.

Prov. 22:5. Thorns *and* snares *are* in the way of the froward: he that doth keep his soul shall be far from them. 23. For the LORD will plead their cause, and spoil the soul of those that spoiled them.

Prov. 24:20. There shall be no reward to the evil *man;* the candle of the wicked shall be put out. 22. Their calamity shall rise suddenly; and who knoweth the ruin of them both?

Prov. 26:10. The great *God* that formed all *things* both rewardeth the fool, and rewardeth transgressors.

Prov. 28:14. Happy *is* the man that feareth alway: but he that hardeneth his heart shall fall into mischief. 18. Whoso walketh uprightly shall be saved: but *he that is* perverse *in his* ways shall fall at once.

Prov. 29:1. He, that being often reproved hardeneth *his* neck, shall suddenly be destroyed, and that without remedy. 16.

When the wicked are multiplied, transgression increaseth: but the righteous shall see their fall.

Eccl. 2:26. For *God* giveth to a man that *is* good in his sight wisdom, and knowledge, and joy: but to the sinner he giveth travail, to gather and to heap up, that he may give to *him that is* good before God.

Eccl. 7:17. Be not over much wicked, neither be thou foolish: why shouldest thou die before thy time?

Eccl. 8:12. Though a sinner do evil an hundred times, and his *days* be prolonged, yet surely I know that it shall be well with them that fear God, which fear before him: 13. It shall not be well with the wicked, neither shall he prolong *his* days, *which are* as a shadow; because he feareth not before God.

Isa. 3:11. Woe unto the wicked! *it shall be* ill *with him:* for the reward of his hands shall be given him.

Isa. 5:11. Woe unto them that rise up early in the morning, *that* they may follow strong drink; that continue until night, *till* wine inflame them! 12. And the harp, and the viol, the tabret, and pipe, and wine, are in their feasts: but they regard not the work of the LORD, neither consider the operation of his hands. 13. Therefore my people are gone into captivity, because *they have* no knowledge: and their honourable men *are* famished, and their multitude dried up with thirst. 14. Therefore hell hath enlarged herself, and opened her mouth without measure: and their glory, and their multitude, and their pomp, and he that rejoiceth, shall descend into it. 24. As the fire devoureth the stubble, and the flame consumeth the chaff, *so* their root shall be as rottenness, and their blossom shall go up as dust:

Isa. 9:18. For wickedness burneth as the fire: it shall devour the briers and thorns, and shall kindle in the thickets of the forest, and they shall mount up *like* the lifting up of smoke.

Isa. 10:3. What will ye do in the day of visitation, and in the desolation *which* shall come from far? to whom will ye flee for help? and where will ye leave your glory?

Isa. 11:4. But with righteousness shall he judge the poor, and reprove with equity for the meek of the earth: and he shall smite the earth with a rod of his mouth, and with the breath of his lips shall he slay the wicked.

Isa. 13:9. Behold, the day of the LORD cometh, cruel both with wrath and fierce anger, to lay the land desolate: and he shall destroy the sinners thereof out of it. 11. And I will punish the world for *their* evil, and the wicked for their iniquity; and I will cause the arrogancy of the proud to cease, and will lay low the haughtiness of the terrible.

Isa. 24:17. Fear, and the pit, and the snare, *are* upon thee, O inhabitant of the earth. 18. And it shall come to pass, *that* he who fleeth from the noise of the fear shall fall into the pit; and he that cometh up out of the midst of the pit shall be taken in the snare: for the windows from on high are open, and the foundations of the earth do shake.

Isa. 26:21. For, behold, the LORD cometh out of his place to punish the inhabitants of the earth for their iniquity: the earth also shall disclose her blood, and shall no more cover her slain.

Isa. 28:18. And your covenant with death shall be disannulled, and your agreement with hell shall not stand; when the overflowing scourge shall pass through, then ye shall be trodden down by it. 19. From the time that it goeth forth it shall take you: for morning by morning shall it pass over, by day and by night: and it shall be a vexation only to understand the report. 20. For the bed is shorter than that a man can stretch himself on it: and the covering narrower than that he can wrap himself in it. 21. For the LORD shall rise up as in mount Perazim, he shall be wroth as in the valley of Gibeon, that he may do his work, his strange work; and bring to pass his act, his strange act. 22. Now therefore be ye not mockers, lest your bands be made strong: for I have heard from the Lord GOD of hosts a consumption, even determined upon the whole earth.

Isa. 33:11. Ye shall conceive chaff, ye shall bring forth stubble: your breath, as fire, shall devour you. 12. And the people shall be as the burnings of lime: as thorns cut up shall they be burned in the fire. 14. The sinners in Zion are afraid; fearfulness hath surprised the hypocrites. Who among us shall dwell with the devouring fire? who among us shall dwell with everlasting burnings?

Isa. 40:2. Speak ye comfortably to Jerusalem, and cry unto her, that her warfare is accomplished, that her iniquity is pardoned: for she hath received of the LORD's hand double for all her sins. Jer. 16:18.

Isa. 48:22. There is no peace, saith the LORD, unto the wicked.

Isa. 50:11. This shall ye have of mine hand; ye shall lie down in sorrow.

Isa. 57:20. But the wicked are like the troubled sea, when it cannot rest, whose waters cast up mire and dirt. 21. There is no peace, saith my God, to the wicked.

Isa. 64:5. Behold, thou art wroth; for we have sinned: in those is continuance, and we shall be saved. 6. But we are all as an unclean thing, and all our righteousnesses are as filthy rags; and we all do fade as a leaf; and our iniquities, like the wind, have taken us away. 7. And there is none that calleth upon thy name, that stirreth up himself to take hold of thee: for thou hast hid thy face from us, and hast consumed us, because of our iniquities.

Isa. 65:12. Therefore will I number you to the sword, and ye shall all bow down to

the slaughter: because when I called, ye did not answer; when I spake, ye did not hear; but did evil before mine eyes, and did choose that wherein I delighted not. 13. Therefore thus saith the Lord GOD, Behold, my servants shall eat, but ye shall be hungry: behold, my servants shall drink, but ye shall be thirsty: behold, my servants shall rejoice, but ye shall be ashamed: 14. Behold, my servants shall sing for joy of heart, but ye shall cry for sorrow of heart, and shall howl for vexation of spirit.

Jer. 8:12. Were they ashamed when they had committed abomination? nay, they were not at all ashamed, neither could they blush: therefore shall they fall among them that fall: in the time of their visitation they shall be cast down, saith the LORD. 13. I will surely consume them, saith the LORD: there shall be no grapes on the vine, nor figs on the fig tree, and the leaf shall fade; and the things that I have given them shall pass away from them. 14. Why do we sit still? assemble yourselves, and let us enter into the defenced cities, and let us be silent there: for the LORD our God hath put us to silence, and given us water of gall to drink, because we have sinned against the LORD. 20. The harvest is past, the summer is ended, and we are not saved. 21. For the hurt of the daughter of my people am I hurt; I am black; astonishment hath taken hold on me. 22. Is there no balm in Gilead; is there no physician there? why then is not the health of the daughter of my people recovered?

Jer. 9:1. Oh that my head were waters, and mine eyes a fountain of tears, that I might weep day and night for the slain of the daughter of my people!

Jer. 13:14. And I will dash them one against another, even the fathers and the sons together, saith the LORD: I will not pity, nor spare, nor have mercy, but destroy them. 16. Give glory to the LORD your God, before he cause darkness, and before your feet stumble upon the dark mountains, and, while ye look for light, he turn it into the shadow of death, and make it gross darkness. 22. And if thou say in thine heart, Wherefore come these things upon me? For the greatness of thine iniquity are thy skirts discovered, and thy heels made bare.

Jer. 14:10. Thus saith the LORD unto this people, Thus have they loved to wander, they have not refrained their feet, therefore the LORD doth not accept them; he will now remember their iniquity, and visit their sins. 12. When they fast, I will not hear their cry; and when they offer burnt offering and an oblation, I will not accept them: but I will consume them by the sword, and by the famine, and by the pestilence.

Jer. 21:14. But I will punish you according to the fruit of your doings, saith the

LORD: and I will kindle a fire in the forest thereof, and it shall devour all things round about it.

Jer. 25:31. A noise shall come *even* to the ends of the earth; for the LORD hath a controversy with the nations, he will plead with all flesh; he will give them *that are* wicked to the sword, saith the LORD.

Jer. 36:31. And I will punish him and his seed and his servants for their iniquity; and I will bring upon them, and upon the inhabitants of Jerusalem, and upon the men of Judah, all the evil that I have pronounced against them; but they hearkened not.

Jer. 44:23. Because ye have burned incense, and because ye have sinned against the LORD, and have not obeyed the voice of the LORD, nor walked in his law, nor in his statutes, nor in his testimonies; therefore this evil is happened unto you, as at this day.

Jer. 49:12. For thus saith the LORD; Behold, they whose judgment *was* not to drink of the cup have assuredly drunken; and *art* thou he *that* shall altogether go unpunished? thou shalt not go unpunished, but thou shalt surely drink *of it*.

Lam. 3:39. Wherefore doth a living man complain, a man for the punishment of his sins?

Lam. 4:22. The punishment of thine iniquity is accomplished, O daughter of Zion;

Lam. 5:16. The crown is fallen *from* our head: woe unto us, that we have sinned! 17. For this our heart is faint; for these *things* our eyes are dim.

Ezek. 3:18. When I say unto the wicked, Thou shalt surely die; and thou givest him not warning, nor speakest to warn the wicked from his wicked way, to save his life; the same wicked *man* shall die in his iniquity; but his blood will I require at thine hand. 19. Yet if thou warn the wicked, and he turn not from his wickedness, nor from his wicked way, he shall die in his iniquity; but thou hast delivered thy soul. 20. Again, When a righteous *man* doth turn from his righteousness, and commit iniquity, and I lay a stumblingblock before him, he shall die: because thou hast not given him warning, he shall die in his sin, and his righteousness which he hath done shall not be remembered; but his blood will I require at thine hand.

Ezek. 5:4. Then take of them again, and cast them into the midst of the fire, and burn them in the fire; *for* thereof shall a fire come forth into all the house of Israel. 8. Therefore thus saith the Lord GOD; Behold, I, even I, *am* against thee, and will execute judgments in the midst of thee in the sight of the nations. 9. And I will do in thee that which I have not done, and whereunto I will not do any more the like, because of all thine abominations. 10. Therefore the fathers shall eat the sons in the midst of thee, and the sons shall eat their fathers; and I will execute judgments in thee, and the whole remnant of thee will I scatter into all the winds. 11. Wherefore, *as* I live, saith the Lord GOD; Surely, because thou hast defiled my sanctuary with all thy detestable things, and with all thine abominations, therefore will I also diminish *thee;* neither shall mine eye spare, neither will I have any pity. 12. A third part of thee shall die with the pestilence, and with famine shall they be consumed in the midst of thee: and a third part shall fall by the sword round about thee; and I will scatter a third part into all the winds, and I will draw out a sword after them. 13. Thus shall mine anger be accomplished, and I will cause my fury to rest upon them, and I will be comforted: and they shall know that I the LORD have spoken *it* in my zeal, when I have accomplished my fury in them. 14. Moreover I will make thee waste, and a reproach among the nations that *are* round about thee, in the sight of all that pass by. 15. So it shall be a reproach and a taunt, an instruction and an astonishment unto the nations that *are* round about thee, when I shall execute judgments in thee in anger and in fury and in furious rebukes. I the LORD have spoken *it*. 16. When I shall send upon them the evil arrows of famine, which shall be for *their* destruction, *and* which I will send to destroy you: and I will increase the famine upon you, and will break your staff of bread: 17. So will I send upon you famine and evil beasts, and they shall bereave thee; and pestilence and blood shall pass through thee; and I will bring the sword upon thee. I the LORD have spoken *it*.

Ezek. 7:4. Mine eyes shall not spare thee, neither will I have pity: but I will recompense thy ways upon thee, and thine abominations shall be in the midst of thee: and ye shall know that I *am* the LORD. 5. Thus saith the Lord GOD; An evil, an only evil, behold, is come. 6. An end is come, the end is come: it watcheth for thee; behold, it is come.

Ezek. 9:5. And to the others he said in mine hearing, Go ye after him through the city, and smite: let not your eye spare, neither have ye pity: 6. Slay utterly old *and* young, both maids, and little children, and women: but come not near any man upon whom *is* the mark; and begin at my sanctuary. Then they began at the ancient men which *were* before the house. 7. And he said unto them, Defile the house, and fill the courts with the slain: go ye forth. And they went forth, and slew in the city. 10. And as for me also, mine eye shall not spare, neither will I have pity, *but* I will recompense their way upon their head.

Ezek. 11:21. But *as for them* whose heart walketh after the heart of their detestable things and their abominations, I will recompense their way upon their own heads, saith the Lord GOD.

Ezek. 18:1. The word of the Lord came unto me again, saying, 2. What mean ye, that ye use this proverb concerning the land of Israel, saying, The fathers have eaten sour grapes, and the children's teeth are set on edge? 3. As I live, saith the Lord God, ye shall not have *occasion* any more to use this proverb in Israel. 4. Behold, all souls are mine; as the soul of the father, so also the soul of the son is mine: the soul that sinneth, it shall die. 5. But if a man be just, and do that which is lawful and right, 6. And hath not eaten upon the mountains, neither hath lifted up his eyes to the idols of the house of Israel, neither hath defiled his neighbour's wife, neither hath come near to a menstruous woman, 7. And hath not oppressed any, *but* hath restored to the debtor his pledge, hath spoiled none by violence, hath given his bread to the hungry, and hath covered the naked with a garment; 8. He *that* hath not given forth upon usury, neither hath taken any increase, *that* hath withdrawn his hand from iniquity, hath executed true judgment between man and man, 9. Hath walked in my statutes, and hath kept my judgments, to deal truly; he *is* just, he shall surely live, saith the Lord God. 10. If he beget a son *that is* a robber, a shedder of blood, and *that* doeth the like to *any* one of these *things*, 11. And that doeth not any of those *duties*, but even hath eaten upon the mountains, and defiled his neighbour's wife, 12. Hath oppressed the poor and needy, hath spoiled by violence, hath not restored the pledge, and hath lifted up his eyes to the idols, hath committed abomination, 13. Hath given forth upon usury, and hath taken increase: shall he then live? he shall not live: he hath done all these abominations; he shall surely die; his blood shall be upon him. 14. Now, lo, *if* he beget a son, that seeth all his father's sins which he hath done, and considereth, and doeth not such like, 15. *That* hath not eaten upon the mountains, neither hath lifted up his eyes to the idols of the house of Israel, hath not defiled his neighbour's wife, 16. Neither hath oppressed any, hath not withholden the pledge, neither hath spoiled by violence, *but* hath given his bread to the hungry, and hath covered the naked with a garment, 17. *That* hath taken off his hand from the poor, *that* hath not received usury nor increase, hath executed my judgments, hath walked in my statutes; he shall not die for the iniquity of his father, he shall surely live. 18. As *for* his father, because he cruelly oppressed, spoiled his brother by violence, and did *that* which *is* not good among his people, lo, even he shall die in his iniquity. 19. Yet say ye, Why? doth not the son bear the iniquity of the father? When the son hath done that which is lawful and right, *and* hath kept all my statutes, and hath done them, he shall surely live.

20. The soul that sinneth, it shall die. The son shall not bear the iniquity of the father, neither shall the father bear the iniquity of the son: the righteousness of the righteous shall be upon him, and the wickedness of the wicked shall be upon him. 21. But if the wicked will turn from all his sins that he hath committed, and keep all my statutes, and do that which is lawful and right, he shall surely live, he shall not die. 22. All his transgressions that he hath committed, they shall not be mentioned unto him: in his righteousness that he hath done he shall live. 23. Have I any pleasure at all that the wicked should die? saith the Lord God: *and* not that he should return from his ways, and live? 24. But when the righteous turneth away from his righteousness, and committeth iniquity, *and* doeth according to all the abominations that the wicked *man* doeth, shall he live? All his righteousness that he hath done shall not be mentioned: in his trespass that he hath trespassed, and in his sin that he hath sinned, in them shall he die. 25. Yet ye say, The way of the Lord is not equal. Hear now, O house of Israel; Is not my way equal? are not your ways unequal? 26. When a righteous *man* turneth away from his righteousness, and committeth iniquity, and dieth in them; for his iniquity that he hath done shall he die. 27. Again, when the wicked *man* turneth away from his wickedness that he hath committed, and doeth that which is lawful and right, he shall save his soul alive. 28. Because he considereth, and turneth away from all his transgressions that he hath committed, he shall surely live, he shall not die. 29. Yet saith the house of Israel, The way of the Lord is not equal. O house of Israel, are not my ways equal? are not your ways unequal? 30. Therefore I will judge you, O house of Israel, every one according to his ways, saith the Lord God. Repent, and turn *yourselves* from all your transgressions; so iniquity shall not be your ruin. 31. Cast away from you all your transgressions, whereby ye have transgressed; and make you a new heart and a new spirit: for why will ye die, O house of Israel? 32. For I have no pleasure in the death of him that dieth, saith the Lord God: wherefore turn *yourselves*, and live ye.

Ezek. 20:8. But they rebelled against me, and would not hearken unto me: they did not every man cast away the abominations of their eyes, neither did they forsake the idols of Egypt: then I said, I will pour out my fury upon them, to accomplish my anger against them in the midst of the land of Egypt.

Ezek. 22:14. Can thine heart endure, or can thine hands be strong, in the days that I shall deal with thee? 20. As they gather silver, and brass, and iron, and lead, and tin, into the midst of the furnace, to blow the fire upon it, to melt *it;* so will I gather *you* in mine anger and in my fury, and I will leave *you there,* and melt you. 21. Yea, I will gather you, and blow upon you in the fire of my wrath, and ye shall be melted in the midst thereof. 31. Therefore have I poured out mine indignation upon them; I have consumed them with the fire of my wrath: their own way have I recompensed upon their heads, saith the Lord God.

Ezek. 24:13. In thy filthiness *is* lewdness: because I have purged thee, and thou wast not purged, thou shalt not be purged from thy filthiness any more, till I have caused my fury to rest upon thee. 14. I the Lord have spoken *it:* it shall come to pass, and I will do *it;* I will not go back, neither will I spare, neither will I repent; according to thy ways, and according to thy doings, shall they judge thee, saith the Lord God.

Ezek. 25:7. Behold, therefore I will stretch out mine hand upon thee, and will deliver thee for a spoil to the heathen; and I will cut thee off from the people, and I will cause thee to perish out of the countries: I will destroy thee; and thou shalt know that I *am* the Lord.

Ezek. 33:7. So thou, O son of man, I have set thee a watchman unto the house of Israel; therefore thou shalt hear the word at my mouth, and warn them from me. 8. When I say unto the wicked, O wicked *man,* thou shalt surely die; if thou dost not speak to warn the wicked from his way, that wicked *man* shall die in his iniquity; but his blood will I require at thine hand. 9. Nevertheless, if thou warn the wicked of his way to turn from it; if he do not turn from his way, he shall die in his iniquity; but thou hast delivered thy soul. 10. Therefore, O thou son of man, speak unto the house of Israel; Thus ye speak, saying, If our transgressions and our sins *be* upon us, and we pine away in them, how should we then live? 11. Say unto them, *As* I live, saith the Lord God, I have no pleasure in the death of the wicked; but that the wicked turn from his way and live: turn ye, turn ye from your evil ways; for why will ye die, O house of Israel? 12. Therefore, thou son of man, say unto the children of thy people, The righteousness of the righteous shall not deliver him in the day of his transgression: as for the wickedness of the wicked, he shall not fall thereby in the day that he turneth from his wickedness; neither shall the righteous be able to live for his *righteousness* in the day that he sinneth. 13. When I shall say to the righteous, *that* he shall surely live; if he trust to his own righteousness, and commit iniquity, all his righteousnesses shall not be remembered; but for his iniquity that he hath committed, he shall die for it. 14. Again, when I say unto the wicked, Thou shalt surely die; if he turn from his sin, and do that which is lawful and right; 15. *If* the wicked restore the pledge, give again that he had robbed, walk in the statutes of life, without committing iniquity; he shall surely live, he shall not die. 16. None of his sins that he hath committed shall be mentioned unto him: he hath done that which is lawful and right; he shall surely live. 17. Yet the children of thy people say, The way of the Lord is not equal: but as for them, their way is not equal. 18. When the righteous turneth from his righteousness, and committeth iniquity, he shall even die thereby. 19. But if the wicked turn from his wickedness, and do that which is lawful and right, he shall live thereby. 20. Yet ye say, The way of the Lord is not equal. O ye house of Israel, I will judge you every one after his ways.

Dan. 12:2. And many of them that sleep in the dust of the earth shall awake, some to everlasting life, and some to shame *and* everlasting contempt.

Hos. 2:9. Therefore will I return, and take away my corn in the time thereof, and my wine in the season thereof, and will recover my wool and my flax *given* to cover her nakedness. 10. And now will I discover her lewdness in the sight of her lovers, and none shall deliver her out of mine hand. 11. I will also cause all her mirth to cease, her feast days, her new moons, and her sabbaths, and all her solemn feasts. 12. And I will destroy her vines and her fig trees, whereof she hath said, These *are* my rewards that my lovers have given me: and I will make them a forest, and the beasts of the field shall eat them. 13. And I will visit upon her the days of Baalim, wherein she burned incense to them, and she decked herself with her earrings and her jewels, and she went after her lovers, and forgat me, saith the Lord.

Hos. 5:4. They will not frame their doings to turn unto their God: for the spirit of whoredoms *is* in the midst of them, and they have not known the Lord. 5. And the pride of Israel doth testify to his face: therefore shall Israel and Ephraim fall in their iniquity; Judah also shall fall with them. 6. They shall go with their flocks and with their herds to seek the Lord; but they shall not find *him;* he hath withdrawn himself from them. 9. Ephraim shall be desolate in the day of rebuke: among the tribes of Israel have I made known that which shall surely be.

Hos. 7:12. When they shall go, I will spread my net upon them; I will bring them down as the fowls of the heaven; I will chastise them, as their congregation hath heard. 13. Woe unto them! for they have fled from me: destruction unto them! because they have transgressed against me: though I have redeemed them, yet they have spoken lies against me.

Hos. 9:7. The days of visitation are come, the days of recompence are come; Israel shall know *it:* the prophet *is* a fool, the spiritual man *is* mad, for the multitude of thine iniquity, and the great hatred. 9. They have deeply corrupted *themselves*, as in the days of Gibeah : *therefore* he will remember their iniquity, he will visit their sins. 15. All their wickedness *is* in Gilgal : for there I hated them : for the wickedness of their doings I will drive them out of mine house, I will love them no more : all their princes *are* revolters.

Hos. 10:8. They shall say to the mountains, Cover us ; and to the hills, Fall on us. Luke 23:30; Rev. 6:16; 9:6.

Hos. 12:2. The LORD hath also a controversy with Judah, and will punish Jacob according to his ways ; according to his doings will he recompense him. 14. Ephraim provoked *him* to anger most bitterly : therefore shall he leave his blood upon him, and his reproach shall his Lord return unto him.

Hos. 13:1. When Ephraim spake trembling, he exalted himself in Israel ; but when he offended in Baal, he died. 3. Therefore they shall be as the morning cloud, and as the early dew that passeth away, as the chaff *that* is driven with the whirlwind out of the floor, and as the smoke out of the chimney.

Hos. 14:9. Who *is* wise, and he shall understand these *things?* prudent, and he shall know them? for the ways of the LORD *are* right, and the just shall walk in them : but the transgressors shall fall therein.

Joel 2:1. Blow ye the trumpet in Zion, and sound an alarm in my holy mountain : let all the inhabitants of the land tremble : for the day of the LORD cometh, for *it is* nigh at hand ; 2. A day of darkness and of gloominess, a day of clouds and of thick darkness, as the morning spread upon the mountains : a great people and a strong ; there hath not been ever the like, neither shall be any more after it, *even* to the years of many generations.

Joel 3:13. Put ye in the sickle, for the harvest is ripe : come, get you down ; for the press is full, the fats overflow ; for their wickedness *is* great. 14. Multitudes, multitudes in the valley of decision : for the day of the LORD *is* near in the valley of decision. 15. The sun and the moon shall be darkened, and the stars shall withdraw their shining. 16. The LORD also shall roar out of Zion, and utter his voice from Jerusalem ; and the heavens and the earth shall shake : but the LORD *will be* the hope of his people, and the strength of the children of Israel.

Amos 3:2. I will punish you for all your iniquities.

Amos 5:18. Woe unto you that desire the day of the LORD! to what end *is* it for you? the day of the LORD *is* darkness, and not light. 19. As if a man did flee from a lion, and a bear met him ; or went into the house, and leaned his hand on the wall, and a serpent bit him. 20. *Shall* not the day of the LORD *be* darkness, and not light? even very dark, and no brightness in it?

Amos 8:14. They that swear by the sin of Samaria, and say, Thy god, O Dan, liveth ; and, The manner of Beer-sheba liveth ; even they shall fall, and never rise up again.

Amos 9:1. I saw the Lord standing upon the altar : and he said, Smite the lintel of the door, that the posts may shake : and cut them in the head, all of them ; and I will slay the last of them with the sword : he that fleeth of them shall not flee away, and he that escapeth of them shall not be delivered. 2. Though they dig into hell, thence shall mine hand take them ; though they climb up to heaven, thence will I bring them down : 3. And though they hide themselves in the top of Carmel, I will search and take them out thence ; and though they be hid from my sight in the bottom of the sea, thence will I command the serpent, and he shall bite them : 4. And though they go into captivity before their enemies, thence will I command the sword, and it shall slay them : and I will set mine eyes upon them for evil, and not for good. 5. And the Lord GOD of hosts *is* he that toucheth the land, and it shall melt, and all that dwell therein shall mourn : and it shall rise up wholly like a flood ; and shall be drowned, as *by* the flood of Egypt. 10. All the sinners of my people shall die by the sword, which say, The evil shall not overtake nor prevent us.

Jonah 3:9. Who can tell *if* God will turn and repent, and turn away from his fierce anger, that we perish not?

Mic. 2:3. Therefore thus saith the LORD ; Behold, against this family do I devise an evil, from which ye shall not remove your necks ; neither shall ye go haughtily : for this time *is* evil.

Mic. 6:13. Therefore also will I make *thee* sick in smiting thee, in making *thee* desolate because of thy sins.

Nah. 1:2. God *is* jealous, and the LORD revengeth ; the LORD revengeth, and *is* furious ; the LORD will take vengeance on his adversaries, and he reserveth *wrath* for his enemies. 8. But with an overrunning flood he will make an utter end of the place thereof, and darkness shall pursue his enemies. 9. What do ye imagine against the LORD? he will make an utter end : affliction shall not rise up the second time. 10. For while *they be* folden together *as* thorns, and while they are drunken *as* drunkards, they shall be devoured as stubble fully dry.

Zeph. 1:12. And it shall come to pass at that time, *that* I will search Jerusalem with candles, and punish the men that are settled on their lees : that say in their heart, The LORD will not do good, neither will he do evil. 13. Therefore their goods shall become a booty, and their houses a desolation : they shall also build houses, but not inhabit *them* ; and they shall plant vineyards, but not drink the wine thereof. 14. The great day of the LORD *is* near, *it is* near, and hasteth greatly, *even* the voice of the day of the LORD : the mighty man shall cry there bitterly. 15. That day *is* a day of wrath, a day of trouble and distress, a day of wasteness and desolation, a day of darkness and gloominess, a day of clouds and thick darkness, 16. A day of the trumpet and alarm against the fenced cities, and against the high towers. 17. And I will bring distress upon men, that they shall walk like blind men, because they have sinned against the LORD: and their blood shall be poured out as dust, and their flesh as the dung. 18. Neither their silver nor their gold shall be able to deliver them in the day of the LORD's wrath; but the whole land shall be devoured by the fire of his jealousy: for he shall make even a speedy riddance of all them that dwell in the land.

Zech. 5:2. And he said unto me, What seest thou? And I answered, I see a flying roll; the length thereof *is* twenty cubits, and the breadth thereof ten cubits. 3. Then said he unto me, This *is* the curse that goeth forth over the face of the whole earth: for every one that stealeth shall be cut off *as* on this side according to it; and every one that sweareth shall be cut off *as* on that side according to it. 4. I will bring it forth, saith the LORD of hosts, and it shall enter into the house of the thief, and into the house of him that sweareth falsely by my name: and it shall remain in the midst of his house, and shall consume it with the timber thereof and the stones thereof.

Mal. 3:17. And they shall be mine, saith the LORD of hosts, in that day when I make up my jewels; and I will spare them, as a man spareth his own son that serveth him. 18. Then shall ye return, and discern between the righteous and the wicked, between him that serveth God and him that serveth him not.

Mal. 4:1. For, behold, the day cometh, that shall burn as an oven; and all the proud, yea, and all that do wickedly, shall be stubble: and the day that cometh shall burn them up, saith the LORD of hosts, that it shall leave them neither root nor branch.

Matt. 3:7. But when he saw many of the Pharisees and Sadducees come to his baptism, he said unto them, O generation of vipers, who hath warned you to flee from the wrath to come? [Luke 3:7.] 10. And now also the ax is laid unto the root of the trees: therefore every tree which bringeth not forth good fruit is hewn down, and cast into the fire. [Matt. 7:19; Luke 13:7,9.] 12. Whose fan *is* in his hand, and he will throughly purge his floor, and gather his wheat into the garner; but he will burn up the chaff with unquenchable fire. Luke 3:17.

Matt. 5:19. Whosoever therefore shall break one of these least commandments, and shall teach men so, he shall be called the least in the kingdom of heaven. *vs.* 20–30.

Matt. 7:13. Enter ye in at the strait gate: for wide *is* the gate, and broad *is* the way, that leadeth to destruction, and many there be which go in thereat: [Luke 13:24.] 26. And every one that heareth these sayings of mine, and doeth them not, shall be likened unto a foolish man, which built his house upon the sand: 27. And the rain descended, and the floods came, and the winds blew, and beat upon that house; and it fell: and great was the fall of it. Luke 6:49.

Matt. 8:12. But the children of the kingdom shall be cast out into outer darkness: there shall be weeping and gnashing of teeth.

Matt. 10:28. And fear not them which kill the body, but are not able to kill the soul: but rather fear him which is able to destroy both soul and body in hell. [Luke 12:4,5.] 33. But whosoever shall deny me before men, him will I also deny before my Father which is in heaven. Mark 8:38; Luke 9:26.

Matt. 11:23. And thou, Capernaum, which art exalted unto heaven, shalt be brought down to hell:

Matt. 13:12. For whosoever hath, to him shall be given, and he shall have more abundance: but whosoever hath not, from him shall be taken away even that he hath. [Mark 4:25; Luke 8:18; 19:26.] 13. Therefore speak I to them in parables: because they seeing see not; and hearing they hear not, neither do they understand. 14. And in them is fulfilled the prophecy of Esaias, which saith, By hearing ye shall hear, and shall not understand; and seeing ye shall see, and shall not perceive: 15. For this people's heart is waxed gross, and *their* ears are dull of hearing, and their eyes they have closed; lest at any time they should see with *their* eyes, and hear with *their* ears, and should understand with *their* heart, and should be converted, and I should heal them. [Mark 4:12; John 12:40.] 30. Let both grow together until the harvest: and in the time of harvest I will say to the reapers, Gather ye together first the tares, and bind them in bundles to burn them: but gather the wheat into my barn. 38. The field is the world; the good seed are the children of the kingdom; but the tares are the children of the wicked one; 39. The enemy that sowed them is the devil; the harvest is the end of the world; and the reapers are the angels. 40. As therefore the tares are gathered and burned in the fire; so shall it be in the end of this world. 41. The Son of man shall send forth his angels, and they shall gather out of his kingdom all things that offend, and them which do iniquity; 42. And shall cast them into a furnace of fire: there shall be wailing and gnashing of teeth. 49. So shall it be at the end of the world: the angels shall come forth, and sever the wicked from among the just, 50. And shall cast them into the furnace of fire: there shall be wailing and gnashing of teeth.

Matt. 15:13. He answered and said, Every plant, which my heavenly Father hath not planted, shall be rooted up. John 15:2.

Matt. 18:7. Woe unto the world because of offences! for it must needs be that offences come; but woe to that man by whom the offence cometh! 8. Wherefore if thy hand or thy foot offend thee, cut them off, and cast *them* from thee: it is better for thee to enter into life halt or maimed, rather than having two hands or two feet to be cast into everlasting fire. 9. And if thine eye offend thee, pluck it out, and cast *it* from thee: it is better for thee to enter into life with one eye, rather than having two eyes to be cast into hell fire. [Mark 9:43.] 34. And his lord was wroth, and delivered him to the tormentors, till he should pay all that was due unto him. 35. So likewise shall my heavenly Father do also unto you, if ye from your hearts forgive not every one his brother their trespasses. ¹ Mark 11:26.   [¹ Omitted in R. V.]

Matt. 21:41. They say unto him, He will miserably destroy those wicked men, and will let out *his* vineyard unto other husbandmen, which shall render him the fruits in their seasons. [Mark 12:1–9.] 44. And whosoever shall fall on this stone shall be broken: but on whomsoever it shall fall, it will grind him to powder. Luke 20:18.

Matt. 22:13. Then said the king to the servants, Bind him hand and foot, and take him away, and cast *him* into outer darkness; there shall be weeping and gnashing of teeth. Matt. 8:12.

Matt. 23:33. *Ye* serpents, *ye* generation of vipers, how can ye escape the ¹ damnation of hell? Matt. 12:34.   [¹ R. V. judgment]

Matt. 24:50. The lord of that servant shall come in a day when he looketh not for *him*, and in an hour that he is not aware of, 51. And shall cut him asunder, and appoint *him* his portion with the hypocrites: there shall be weeping and gnashing of teeth. Luke 12:46, 47.

Matt. 25:30. And cast ye the unprofitable servant into outer darkness: there shall be weeping and gnashing of teeth. 32. And before him shall be gathered all nations: and he shall separate them one from another, as a shepherd divideth *his* sheep from the goats: 33. And he shall set the sheep on his right hand, but the goats on the left. 41. Then shall he say also unto them on the left hand, Depart from me, ye cursed, into everlasting fire, prepared for the devil and his angels: 46. And these shall go away into everlasting punishment: but the righteous into life eternal.

Matt. 26:24. The Son of man goeth as it is written of him: but woe unto that man by whom the Son of man is betrayed! it had been good for that man if he had not been born. Mark 14:21; Luke 22:22.

Mark 12:40. Which devour widows' houses, and for a pretence make long prayers: these shall receive greater ¹ damnation.

[¹ R. V. condemnation]

Mark 16:16. He that believeth not shall be ¹ damned.   [¹ R. V. condemned]

Luke 9:24. For whosoever will save his life shall lose it: but whosoever will lose his life for my sake, the same shall save it. 25. For what is a man advantaged, if he gain the whole world, and lose himself, or be cast away? Matt. 16:26; Mark 8:36.

Luke 13:3. Except ye repent, ye shall all likewise perish. [v. 5.] 6. He spake also this parable; A certain *man* had a fig tree planted in his vineyard; and he came and sought fruit thereon, and found none. 7. Then said he unto the dresser of his vineyard, Behold, these three years I come seeking fruit on this fig tree, and find none: cut it down; why cumbereth it the ground? [Matt. 21:19.] 27. But he shall say, I tell you, I know you not whence ye are; depart from me, all *ye* workers of iniquity. 28. There shall be weeping and gnashing of teeth, when ye shall see Abraham, and Isaac, and Jacob, and all the prophets, in the kingdom of God, and you *yourselves* thrust out. Matt. 7:23.

Luke 16:22. And it came to pass, that the beggar died, and was carried by the angels into Abraham's bosom: the rich man also died, and was buried; 23. And in hell he lift up his eyes, being in torments, and seeth Abraham afar off, and Lazarus in his bosom. 24. And he cried and said, Father Abraham, have mercy on me, and send Lazarus, that he may dip the tip of his finger in water, and cool my tongue; for I am tormented in this flame. 25. But Abraham said, Son, remember that thou in thy lifetime receivedst thy good things, and likewise Lazarus evil things: but now he is comforted, and thou art tormented. 26. And beside all this, between us and you there is a great gulf fixed: so that they which would pass from hence to you cannot; neither can they pass to us, that *would come* from thence. 27. Then he said, I pray thee therefore, father, that thou wouldest send him to my father's house: 28. For I have five brethren; that he may testify unto them, lest they also come into this place of torment.

Luke 17:1. It is impossible but that offences will come: but woe *unto him*, through whom they come! 2. It were better for him that a millstone were hanged about his neck, and he cast into the sea, than that he should offend one of these little ones.

Luke 19:27. But those mine enemies, which would not that I should reign over them, bring hither, and slay *them* before me.

Luke 23:30. Then shall they begin to say to the mountains, Fall on us; and to the hills, Cover us. [Isa. 2:19.] 31. For if they do these things in a green tree, what shall be done in the dry?

John 3:15. That whosoever ¹ believeth in him ² should not perish, but have eternal life. 16. For God so loved the world, that he gave his only begotten Son, that whosoever believeth in him should not perish, but have everlasting life. 18. He that believeth on him is not condemned: but he that believeth not is condemned already, because he hath not believed in the name of the only begotten Son of God. 36. He that believeth on the Son hath everlasting life: and he that believeth not the Son shall not see life; but the wrath of God abideth on him.

[R. V. ¹believeth may   ²Omitted.]

John 5:14. Afterward Jesus findeth him in the temple, and said unto him, Behold, thou art made whole: sin no more, lest a worse thing come unto thee.

29. And shall come forth; they that have done good, unto the resurrection of life; and they that have done evil, unto the resurrection of damnation [judgment, R. V.].

John 7:34. Ye shall seek me, and shall not find me: and where I am, thither ye cannot come.   John 8:21.

John 17:12. While I was with them in the world, I kept them in thy name: those that thou gavest me I have kept, and none of them is lost, but the son of perdition; that the scripture might be fulfilled.

Acts 1:18. Now this man purchased a field with the reward of iniquity; and falling headlong, he burst asunder in the midst, and all his bowels gushed out.   25. That he may take part of this ministry and apostleship, from which Judas by transgression fell, that he might go to his own place.

Acts 3:23. And it shall come to pass, that every soul, which will not hear that prophet, shall be destroyed from among the people.

Rom. 1:18. For the wrath of God is revealed from heaven against all ungodliness and unrighteousness of men, who hold the truth in unrighteousness;

Rom. 2:5. But after thy hardness and impenitent heart treasurest up unto thyself wrath against the day of wrath and revelation of the righteous judgment of God; 8. But unto them that are contentious, and do not obey the truth, but obey unrighteousness, indignation and wrath, 9. Tribulation and anguish, upon every soul of man that doeth evil, 12. For as many as have sinned without law shall also perish without law: and as many as have sinned in the law shall be judged by the law;

Rom. 5:12. Wherefore, as by one man sin entered into the world, and death by sin; and so death passed upon all men, for that all have sinned: 21. That as sin hath reigned unto death, even so might grace reign through righteousness unto eternal life by Jesus Christ our Lord.

Rom. 6:16. Know ye not, that to whom ye yield yourselves servants to obey, his servants ye are to whom ye obey; whether of sin unto death, or of obedience unto righteousness? 21. What fruit had ye then in those things whereof ye are now ashamed? for the end of those things is death.

Rom. 8:2. For the law of the Spirit of life in Christ Jesus hath made me free from the law of sin and death. 6. For to be carnally minded is death; but to be spiritually minded is life and peace. 7. Because the carnal

mind is enmity against God: for it is not subject to the law of God, neither indeed can be. 13. For if ye live after the flesh, ye shall die: but if ye through the Spirit do mortify the deeds of the body, ye shall live.

Rom. 9:22. What if God, willing to shew his wrath, and to make his power known, endureth with much longsuffering the vessels of wrath fitted to destruction:

Rom. 11:22. Behold . . . the goodness and severity of God: on them which fell, severity;

Rom. 14:23. And he that doubteth is ¹damned if he eat, because he eateth not of faith: for whatsoever is not of faith is sin.

[¹ R. V. condemned]

1 Cor. 3:17. If any man defile the temple of God, him shall God destroy; for the temple of God is holy, which temple ye are.

1 Cor. 5:5. To deliver such an one unto Satan for the destruction of the flesh, that the spirit may be saved in the day of the Lord Jesus.   13. But them that are without God judgeth. Therefore put away from among yourselves that wicked person.

1 Cor. 6:9. Know ye not that the unrighteous shall not inherit the kingdom of God? Be not deceived: neither fornicators, nor idolaters, nor adulterers, nor effeminate, nor abusers of themselves with mankind, 10. Nor thieves, nor covetous, nor drunkards, nor revilers, nor extortioners, shall inherit the kingdom of God.

1 Cor. 9:27. But I keep under my body, and bring it into subjection: lest that by any means, when I have preached to others, I myself should be a castaway.

1 Cor. 10:5. But with many of them God was not well pleased: for they were overthrown in the wilderness. 6. Now these things were our examples, to the intent we should not lust after evil things, as they also lusted. 7. Neither be ye idolaters, as were some of them; as it is written, The people sat down to eat and drink, and rose up to play. 8. Neither let us commit fornication, as some of them committed, and fell in one day three and twenty thousand. 9. Neither let us tempt Christ, as some of them also tempted, and were destroyed of serpents. 10. Neither murmur ye, as some of them also murmured, and were destroyed of the destroyer. 11. Now all these things happened unto them for ensamples: and they are written for our admonition, upon whom the ends of the world are come.

1 Cor. 15:21. For since by man came death, by man came also the resurrection of the dead. 22. For as in Adam all die, even so in Christ shall all be made alive.

2 Cor. 7:10. The sorrow of the world worketh death.

Gal. 3:10. For as many as are of the works of the law are under the curse: for it is written, Cursed is every one that continueth not in all things which are written in the book of the law to do them.

Gal. 5:19. Now the works of the flesh are manifest, which are these; Adultery, fornication, uncleanness, lasciviousness, 20. Idolatry, witchcraft, hatred, variance, emulations, wrath, strife, seditions, heresies, 21. Envyings, murders, drunkenness, revellings, and such like: of the which I tell you before, as I have also told *you* in the time past, that they which do such things shall not inherit the kingdom of God.

Gal. 6:8. For he that soweth to his flesh shall of the flesh reap corruption;

Eph. 5:5. For this ye know, that no whoremonger, nor unclean person, nor covetous man, who is an idolater, hath any inheritance in the kingdom of Christ and of God. 6. Let no man deceive you with vain words: for because of these things cometh the wrath of God upon the children of disobedience.

Phil. 3:18. (For many walk, of whom I have told you often, and now tell you even weeping, *that they are* the enemies of the cross of Christ: 19. Whose end *is* destruction, whose God *is their* belly, and *whose* glory *is* in their shame, who mind earthly things.)

Col. 3:25. But he that doeth wrong shall receive for the wrong which he hath done: and there is no respect of persons.

1 Thess. 1:10. And to wait for his Son from heaven, whom he raised from the dead, *even* Jesus, which delivered us from the wrath to come.

1 Thess. 5:3. When they shall say, Peace and safety; then sudden destruction cometh upon them, as travail upon a woman with child; and they shall not escape. Isa. 13:8.

2 Thess. 1:5. *Which is* a manifest token of the righteous judgment of God, that ye may be counted worthy of the kingdom of God, for which ye also suffer: 6. Seeing *it is* a righteous thing with God to recompense tribulation to them that trouble you; 7. And to you who are troubled rest with us, when the Lord Jesus shall be revealed from heaven with his mighty angels, 8. In flaming fire taking vengeance on them that know not God, and that obey not the gospel of our Lord Jesus Christ: 9. Who shall be punished with everlasting destruction from the presence of the Lord, and from the glory of his power;

2 Thess. 2:8. And then shall that Wicked be revealed, whom the Lord shall consume with the spirit of his mouth, and shall destroy with the brightness of his coming: 9. *Even him,* whose coming is after the working of Satan with all power and signs and lying wonders, 10. And with all deceivableness of unrighteousness in them that perish; because they received not the love of the truth, that they might be saved.

1 Tim. 1:20 Of whom is Hymenæus and Alexander; whom I have delivered unto Satan, that they may learn not to blaspheme.

1 Tim. 5:24. Some men's sins are open beforehand, going before to judgment; and some *men* they follow after.

2 Tim. 2:12. If we suffer, we shall also reign with *him:* if we deny *him,* he also will deny us: 13. If we believe not, *yet* he abideth faithful: he cannot deny himself.

Heb. 2:2. For if the word spoken by angels was stedfast, and every transgression and disobedience received a just recompence of reward; 3. How shall we escape, if we neglect so great salvation;

Heb. 6:8. That which beareth thorns and briers *is* rejected, and *is* nigh unto cursing: whose end *is* to be burned.

Heb. 10:27. But a certain fearful looking for of judgment and fiery indignation, which shall devour the adversaries. 28. He that despised Moses' law died without mercy under two or three witnesses: 29. Of how much sorer punishment, suppose ye, shall he be thought worthy, who hath trodden under foot the Son of God, and hath counted the blood of the covenant, wherewith he was sanctified, an unholy thing, and hath done despite unto the Spirit of grace? 30. For we know him that hath said, Vengeance *belongeth* unto me, I will recompense, saith the Lord. And again, The Lord shall judge his people. 31. *It is* a fearful thing to fall into the hands of the living God.

Jas. 1:14. But every man is tempted, when he is drawn away of his own lust, and enticed. 15. Then when lust hath conceived, it bringeth forth sin: and sin, when it is finished, bringeth forth death.

Jas. 5:1. Go to now, *ye* rich men, weep and howl for your miseries that shall come upon *you.* 2. Your riches are corrupted, and your garments are motheaten. 3. Your gold and silver is cankered; and the rust of them shall be a witness against you, and shall eat your flesh as it were fire. Ye have heaped treasure together for the last days. 20. Let him know, that he which converteth the sinner from the error of his way shall save a soul from death, and shall hide a multitude of sins.

1 Pet. 3:12. The face of the Lord *is* against them that do evil.

1 Pet. 4:17. For the time *is come* that judgment must begin at the house of God: and if *it* first *begin* at us, what shall the end *be* of them that obey not the gospel of God? 18. And if the righteous scarcely be saved, where shall the ungodly and the sinner appear?

2 Pet. 2:3. And through covetousness shall they with feigned words make merchandise of you: whose judgment now of a long time lingereth not, and their [1] damnation slumbereth not. 4. For if God spared not the angels that sinned, but cast *them* down to hell, and delivered *them* into chains of darkness, to be reserved unto judgment; 5. And spared not the old world, but saved Noah the eighth *person,* a preacher of righteousness, bringing in the flood upon the world of the ungodly; 6. And turning the cities of Sodom and Gomorrha into ashes condemned *them* with an overthrow, mak-

ing *them* an ensample unto those that after should live ungodly; 7 And delivered just Lot, vexed with the filthy conversation of the wicked: 8. (For that righteous man dwelling among them, in seeing and hearing, vexed *his* righteous soul from day to day with *their* unlawful deeds;) 9. The Lord knoweth how to deliver the godly out of temptations, and to reserve the unjust unto the day of judgment to be punished: 12. But these, as natural brute beasts, made to be taken and destroyed, speak evil of the things that they understand not; and shall utterly perish in their own corruption; 13. And shall receive the reward of unrighteousness, *as* they that count it pleasure to riot in the daytime. Spots *they are* and blemishes, sporting themselves with their own deceivings while they feast with you; 14. Having eyes full of adultery, and that cannot cease from sin: beguiling unstable souls: an heart they have exercised with covetous practices; cursed children: 15. Which have forsaken the right way, and are gone astray, following the way of Balaam *the son* of Bosor, who loved the wages of unrighteousness; 16. But was rebuked for his iniquity: the dumb ass speaking with man's voice forbade the madness of the prophet. 17. These are wells without water, clouds that are carried with a tempest; to whom the mist of darkness is reserved for ever. [1 R. V. destruction]

1 John 3:14. We know that we have passed from death unto life, because we love the brethren. He that loveth not *his* brother abideth in death. 15. Whosoever hateth his brother is a murderer: and ye know that no murderer hath eternal life abiding in him.

Jude 5. I will therefore put you in remembrance, though ye once knew this, how that the Lord, having saved the people out of the land of Egypt, afterward destroyed them that believed not. 6. And the angels which kept not their first estate, but left their own habitation, he hath reserved in everlasting chains under darkness unto the judgment of the great day. 7. Even as Sodom and Gomorrha, and the cities about them in like manner, giving themselves over to fornication, and going after strange flesh, are set forth for an example, suffering the vengeance of eternal fire. 11. Woe unto them! for they have gone in the way of Cain, and ran greedily after the error of Balaam for reward, and perished in the gainsaying of Core. 12. These are spots in your feasts of charity, when they feast with you, feeding themselves without fear: clouds *they are* without water, carried about of winds; trees whose fruit withereth, without fruit, twice dead, plucked up by the roots; 13. Raging waves of the sea, foaming out their own shame; wandering stars, to whom is reserved the blackness of darkness for ever. 14. And Enoch also, the seventh from

Adam, prophesied of these, saying, Behold, the Lord cometh with ten thousand of his saints, 15. To execute judgment upon all, and to convince all that are ungodly among them of all their ungodly deeds which they have ungodly committed, and of all their hard *speeches* which ungodly sinners have spoken against him.

Rev. 2:22. Behold, I will cast her into a bed, and them that commit adultery with her into great tribulation, except they repent of their deeds. 23. And I will kill her children with death; and all the churches shall know that I am he which searcheth the reins and hearts: and I will give unto every one of you according to your works.

Rev. 3:3. If therefore thou shalt not watch, I will come on thee as a thief, and thou shalt not know what hour I will come upon thee.

Rev. 6:15. And the kings of the earth, and the great men, and the rich men, and the chief captains, and the mighty men, and every bondman, and every free man, hid themselves in the dens and in the rocks of the mountains; 16. And said to the mountains and rocks, Fall on us, and hide us from the face of him that sitteth on the throne, and from the wrath of the Lamb: 17. For the great day of his wrath is come; and who shall be able to stand?

Rev. 9:4. And it was commanded them that they should not hurt the grass of the earth, neither any green thing, neither any tree; but only those men which have not the seal of God in their foreheads. 5. And to them it was given that they should not kill them, but that they should be tormented five months: and their torment *was* as the torment of a scorpion, when he striketh a man. 6. And in those days shall men seek death, and shall not find it; and shall desire to die, and death shall flee from them. 15. And the four angels were loosed, which were prepared for an hour, and a day, and a month, and a year, for to slay the third part of men. 18. By these three was the third part of men killed, by the fire, and by the smoke, and by the brimstone, which issued out of their mouths.

Rev. 11:18. And the nations were angry, and thy wrath is come, and the time of the dead, that they should be judged, and that thou shouldest give reward unto thy servants the prophets, and to the saints, and them that fear thy name, small and great; and shouldest destroy them which destroy the earth.

Rev. 14:9. And the third angel followed them, saying with a loud voice, If any man worship the beast and his image, and receive *his* mark in his forehead, or in his hand, 10. The same shall drink of the wine of the wrath of God, which is poured out without mixture into the cup of his indignation; and he shall be tormented with fire and brimstone in the presence of the holy angels, and in the presence of the

Lamb: 11. And the smoke of their torment ascendeth up for ever and ever: and they have no rest day nor night, who worship the beast and his image, and whosoever receiveth the mark of his name.

Rev. 16:2. And the first went, and poured out his vial upon the earth; and there fell a noisome and grievous sore upon the men which had the mark of the beast, and *upon* them which worshipped his image. 3. And the second angel poured out his vial upon the sea; and it became as the blood of a dead *man:* and every living soul died in the sea. 4. And the third angel poured out his vial upon the rivers and fountains of waters; and they became blood. 5. And I heard the angel of the waters say, Thou art righteous, O Lord, which art, and wast, and shalt be, because thou hast judged thus. 6. For they have shed the blood of saints and prophets, and thou hast given them blood to drink; for they are worthy. 7. And I heard another out of the altar say, Even so, Lord God Almighty, true and righteous *are* thy judgments. 8. And the fourth angel poured out his vial upon the sun; and power was given unto him to scorch men with fire. 9. And men were scorched with great heat, and blasphemed the name of God, which hath power over these plagues: and they repented not to give him glory. 10. And the fifth angel poured out his vial upon the seat of the beast; and his kingdom was full of darkness; and they gnawed their tongues for pain, 11. And blasphemed the God of heaven because of their pains and their sores, and repented not of their deeds. 12. And the sixth angel poured out his vial upon the great river Euphrates; and the water thereof was dried up, that the way of the kings of the east might be prepared. 13. And I saw three unclean spirits like frogs *come* out of the mouth of the dragon, and out of the mouth of the beast, and out of the mouth of the false prophet. 14. For they are the spirits of devils, working miracles, *which* go forth unto the kings of the earth and of the whole world, to gather them to the battle of that great day of God Almighty. 15. Behold, I come as a thief. Blessed *is* he that watcheth, and keepeth his garments, lest he walk naked, and they see his shame. 16. And he gathered them together into a place called in the Hebrew tongue Armageddon. 17. And the seventh angel poured out his vial into the air; and there came a great voice out of the temple of heaven, from the throne, saying, It is done. 18. And there were voices, and thunders, and lightnings; and there was a great earthquake, such as was not since men were upon the earth, so mighty an earthquake, *and* so great. 19. And the great city was divided into three parts, and the cities of the nations fell: and great Babylon came in remembrance before God, to give unto her the cup of the wine of the fierceness of his wrath. 20. And every island fled away, and the mountains were not found. 21. And there fell upon men a great hail out of heaven, *every stone* about the weight of a talent: and men blasphemed God because of the plague of the hail; for the plague thereof was exceeding great.

Rev. 18:5. For her sins have reached unto heaven, and God hath remembered her iniquities.

Rev. 19:15. And out of his mouth goeth a sharp sword, that with it he should smite the nations: and he shall rule them with a rod of iron: and he treadeth the winepress of the fierceness and wrath of Almighty God. 17. And I saw an angel standing in the sun; and he cried with a loud voice, saying to all the fowls that fly in the midst of heaven, Come and gather yourselves together unto the supper of the great God; 18. That ye may eat the flesh of kings, and the flesh of captains, and the flesh of mighty men, and the flesh of horses, and of them that sit on them, and the flesh of all *men*, *both* free and bond, both small and great. 19. And I saw the beast, and the kings of the earth, and their armies, gathered together to make war against him that sat on the horse, and against his army. 20. And the beast was taken, and with him the false prophet that wrought miracles before him, with which he deceived them that had received the mark of the beast, and them that worshipped his image. These both were cast alive into a lake of fire burning with brimstone. 21. And the remnant were slain with the sword of him that sat upon the horse, which *sword* proceeded out of his mouth: and all the fowls were filled with their flesh.

Rev. 20:10. And the devil that deceived them was cast into the lake of fire and brimstone, where the beast and the false prophet *are*, and shall be tormented day and night for ever and ever. 15. And whosoever was not found written in the book of life was cast into the lake of fire.

Rev. 21:8. But the fearful, and unbelieving, and the abominable, and murderers, and whoremongers, and sorcerers, and idolaters, and all liars, shall have their part in the lake which burneth with fire and brimstone: which is the second death. 27. There shall in no wise enter into it any thing that defileth, neither *whatsoever* worketh abomination, or *maketh* a lie:

Rev. 22:19. And if any man shall take away from the words of the book of this prophecy, God shall take away his part out of the ¹ book of life, and out of the holy city, and *from* the things which are written in this book.   [¹ R. V. tree]

See JUDGMENTS; HELL; PUNISHMENT.

WIDOW. Vows of, binding, Num. 30:9. When daughters of priests, to be supported by their fathers, Lev. 22:13. Priests forbidden to marry, Lev. 21:14. Marriage of, authorized, Rom. 7:3; 1 Cor. 7:39. Widows' dower, see DOWRY.

UNCLASSIFIED SCRIPTURES RELATING TO: Ex. 22:22. Ye shall not afflict any widow, or fatherless child. 23. If thou afflict them in any wise, and they cry at all unto me, I will surely hear their cry; 24. And my wrath shall wax hot, and I will kill you with the sword; and your wives shall be widows, and your children fatherless.

Deut. 10:18. He doth execute the judgment of the fatherless and widow, and loveth the stranger, in giving him food and raiment.

Deut. 14:28. At the end of three years thou shalt bring forth all the tithe of thine increase the same year, and shalt lay it up within thy gates: 29. And the Levite, (because he hath no part nor inheritance with thee,) and the stranger, and the fatherless, and the widow, which are within thy gates, shall come, and shall eat and be satisfied; that the LORD thy God may bless thee in all the work of thine hand which thou doest.

Deut. 16:11. And thou shalt rejoice before the LORD thy God, thou, and thy son, and thy daughter, and thy manservant, and thy maidservant, and the Levite that is within thy gates, and the stranger, and the fatherless, and the widow, that are among you, in the place which the LORD thy God hath chosen to place his name there. 12. And thou shalt remember that thou wast a bondman in Egypt: and thou shalt observe and do these statutes. 13. Thou shalt observe the feast of tabernacles seven days, after that thou hast gathered in thy corn and thy wine: 14. And thou shalt rejoice in thy feast, thou, and thy son, and thy daughter, and thy manservant, and thy maidservant, and the Levite, the stranger, and the fatherless, and the widow, that are within thy gates.

Deut. 24:17. Thou shalt not pervert the judgment of the stranger nor of the fatherless; nor take a widow's raiment to pledge: 19. When thou cuttest down thine harvest in thy field, and hast forgot a sheaf in the field, thou shalt not go again to fetch it: it shall be for the stranger, for the fatherless, and for the widow: that the LORD thy God may bless thee in all the work of thine hands. 20. When thou beatest thine olive tree, thou shalt not go over the boughs again: it shall be for the stranger, for the fatherless, and for the widow. 21. When thou gatherest the grapes of thy vineyard, thou shalt not glean it afterward: it shall be for the stranger, for the fatherless, and for the widow.

Deut. 25:5. If brethren dwell together, and one of them die, and have no child, the wife of the dead shall not marry without unto a stranger: her husband's brother shall go in unto her, and take her to him to wife, and perform the duty of an husband's brother unto her. 6. And it shall be, that the firstborn which she beareth shall succeed in the name of his brother which is dead, that his name be not put out of Israel. 7. And if the man like not to take his brother's wife, then let his brother's wife go up to the gate unto the elders, and say, My husband's brother refuseth to raise up unto his brother a name in Israel, he will not perform the duty of my husband's brother. 8. Then the elders of his city shall call him, and speak unto him: and if he stand to it, and say, I like not to take her; 9. Then shall his brother's wife come unto him in the presence of the elders, and loose his shoe from off his foot, and spit in his face, and shall answer and say, So shall it be done unto that man that will not build up his brother's house. 10. And his name shall be called in Israel, The house of him that hath his shoe loosed.

Deut. 27:19. Cursed be he that perverteth the judgment of the stranger, fatherless, and widow:

Job 22:5. Is not thy wickedness great? and thine iniquities infinite? 9. Thou hast sent widows away empty,

Job 24:3. They take the widow's ox for a pledge. 21. He evil entreateth the barren that beareth not, and doeth not good to the widow.

Job 29:13. I caused the widow's heart to sing for joy.

Job 31:16. If I have withheld the poor from their desire, or have caused the eyes of the widow to fail; 22. Then let mine arm fall from my shoulder blade, and mine arm be broken from the bone.

Psa. 68:5. A father of the fatherless, and a judge of the widows, is God in his holy habitation.

Psa. 94:6. They slay the widow and the stranger, and murder the fatherless.

Psa. 146:9. The LORD preserveth the stranger; he relieveth the fatherless and widow:

Prov. 15:25. The LORD . . . will establish the border of the widow.

Isa. 1:17. Plead for the widow. 23. Thy princes are rebellious, and companions of thieves: every one loveth gifts, and followeth after rewards: they judge not the fatherless, neither doth the cause of the widow come unto them. Ezek. 22:7.

Isa. 10:1. Woe unto them that decree unrighteous decrees, . . . 2. To turn aside the needy from judgment, and to take away the right from the poor of my people, that widows may be their prey, and that they may rob the fatherless!

Jer. 7:6. If ye oppress not the stranger, the fatherless, and the widow, . . . 7. Then will I cause you to dwell in this place, in the land that I gave to your fathers, for ever and ever.

Jer. 22:3. Do no wrong, do no violence to the stranger, the fatherless, nor the widow,

Jer. 49:11. Let thy widows trust in me.

Zech. 7:10. Oppress not the widow,

Mal. 3:5. . . . And I will be a swift witness . . . against those that oppress the hireling in *his* wages, the widow,

Matt. 23:14. [1] Woe unto you, scribes and Pharisees, hypocrites! for ye devour widows' houses. Mark 12:40; Luke 20:47.   [1 Omitted in R. V.]

Acts 6:1. . . . There arose a murmuring of the Grecians against the Hebrews, because their widows were neglected in the daily ministration.

1 Tim. 5:3. Honour widows that are widows indeed. 4. But if any widow have children or nephews, let them learn first to shew piety at home, and to requite their parents: for that is good and acceptable before God. 5. Now she that is a widow indeed, and desolate, trusteth in God, and continueth in supplications and prayers night and day. 6. But she that liveth in pleasure is dead while she liveth. 9. Let not a widow be taken into the number under threescore years old, having been the wife of one man, 10. Well reported of for good works; if she have brought up children, if she have lodged strangers, if she have washed the saints' feet, if she have relieved the afflicted, if she have diligently followed every good work. 11. But the younger widows refuse: for when they have begun to wax wanton against Christ, they will marry; 12. Having damnation, because they have cast off their first faith. 16. If any man or woman that believeth have widows, let them relieve them, and let not the church be charged: that it may relieve them that are widows indeed.

Jas. 1:27. Pure religion and undefiled before God and the Father is this, To visit the fatherless and widows in their affliction, *and* to keep himself unspotted from the world.

INSTANCES OF: Naomi, Ruth 1:3. Ruth, Ruth chapters 1–4. The widow of Zarephath, who sustained Elijah during a famine, 1 Kin. 17. The woman whose sons Elisha saved from being sold for debt, 2 Kin. 4:1–7. Anna, Luke 2:36,37. The woman who gave two mites in the temple, Mark 12:41–44; Luke 21:2; of Nain, whose only son Jesus raised from the dead, Luke 7: 11–15.

See WOMAN: MARRIAGE, LEVIRATE.

WIFE. Called DESIRE OF THE EYES, Ezek. 24:16. HELP, Gen. 2:18,20. FRUITFUL VINE, Psa.128:3. The judgment denounced against Eve, Gen. 3:16. Relation of, to husband, Gen. 2:18,23,24; 1 Cor. 11:3–12. Domestic duties of, Gen. 18:6; Prov. 31:13–27. Beloved, by Isaac, Gen. 24:67; by Jacob, Gen. 29:30. Hated, Gen. 29:31–33. Loyal, Gen. 31:14–16. Unfaithful, Num. 5:14–31; Potiphar's, Gen. 39:7; Bath-sheba, 2 Sam. 11:2–5. Contentious, Zipporah, Ex. 4:25. See UNCLASSIFIED SCRIPTURES, below. Idolatrous, Solomon's wives, 1 Kin. 11:4–8; Neh. 13:26; Jezebel, 1 Kin. 21; 2 Kin. 9:30–37. Incorruptible, Vashti, Esth. 1:10–22. Tactful, Abigail, 1 Sam. 25:3,14–42.

·Bought, Gen. 29; Ex. 21:7–11; Ruth 4:10.

Gotten by violence, Judg. 21. Procured, Gen. 24; 34:4–10; 38:6.

Vows of, Num. 30:6–16.

See DIVORCE; MARRIAGE; VIRGIN.

UNCLASSIFIED SCRIPTURES RELATING TO: Gen. 2:18. And the LORD God said, *It is* not good that the man should be alone; I will make him an help meet for him. 23. And Adam said, This *is* now bone of my bones, and flesh of my flesh: she shall be called Woman, because she was taken out of Man. 24. Therefore shall a man leave his father and his mother, and shall cleave unto his wife: and they shall be one flesh.

Gen. 3:16. Unto the woman he said, I will greatly multiply thy sorrow and thy conception; in sorrow thou shalt bring forth children; and thy desire *shall be* to thy husband, and he shall rule over thee.

Esth. 1:20. And when the king's decree which he shall make shall be published throughout all his empire, (for it is great,) all the wives shall give to their husbands honour, both to great and small. 21. And the king did according to the word of Memucan: 22. For he sent letters into all the king's provinces, into every province according to the writing thereof, and to every people after their language, that every man should bear rule in his own house, and that *it* should be published according to the language of every people.

Psa. 128:3. Thy wife *shall be* as a fruitful vine by the sides of thine house: thy children like olive plants round about thy table. 4. Behold, that thus shall the man be blessed that feareth the LORD.

Prov. 12:4. A virtuous woman *is* a crown to her husband: but she that maketh ashamed *is* as rottenness in his bones.

Prov. 14:1. Every wise woman buildeth her house: but the foolish plucketh it down with her hands.

Prov. 18:22. *Whoso* findeth a wife findeth a good *thing*, and obtaineth favour of the LORD.

Prov. 19:13. The contentions of a wife *are* a continual dropping. 14. And a prudent wife *is* from the LORD.

Prov. 25:24. *It is* better to dwell in the corner of the housetop, than with a brawling woman and in a wide house. Prov. 21:9, 19.

Prov. 30:21. For three *things* the earth is disquieted, and for four *which* it cannot bear: 22. For a servant when he reigneth; and a fool when he is filled with meat; 23. For an odious *woman* when she is married; and an handmaid that is heir to her mistress.

Prov. 31:10. Who can find a virtuous woman? for her price *is* far above rubies. 11. The heart of her husband doth safely trust in her, so that he shall have no need of spoil. 12. She will do him good and not evil all the days of her life. 13. She seeketh wool, and flax, and worketh willingly with her hands. 14. She is like the merchants' ships; she bringeth her food from afar. 15. She riseth also while it is yet night, and giveth meat to her household, and a portion to her maidens. 16. She considereth a field, and buyeth it: with the fruit of her hands she planteth a vineyard. 17. She girdeth her loins with strength, and strengtheneth her arms. 18. She perceiveth that her merchandise *is* good: her candle goeth not out by night. 19. She layeth her hands to the spindle, and her hands hold the distaff. 20. She stretcheth out her hand to the poor; yea, she reacheth forth her hands to the needy. 21. She is not afraid of the snow for her household: for all her household *are* clothed with scarlet. 22. She maketh herself coverings of tapestry; her clothing *is* silk and purple. 23. Her husband is known in the gates, when he sitteth among the elders of the land. 24. She maketh fine linen, and selleth *it;* and delivereth girdles unto the merchant. 25. Strength and honour *are* her clothing; and she shall rejoice in time to come. 26. She openeth her mouth with wisdom; and in her tongue *is* the law of kindness. 27. She looketh well to the ways of her household, and eateth not the bread of idleness. 28. Her children arise up, and call her blessed; her husband *also*, and he praiseth her. 29. Many daughters have done virtuously, but thou excellest them all. 30. Favour *is* deceitful, and beauty *is* vain: *but* a woman *that* feareth the LORD, she shall be praised. 31. Give her of the fruit of her hands; and let her own works praise her in the gates.

1 Cor. 7:2. Nevertheless, *to avoid* fornication, let every man have his own wife, and let every woman have her own husband. 3. Let the husband render unto the wife due benevolence: and likewise also the wife unto the husband. 4. The wife hath not power of her own body, but the husband: and likewise also the husband hath not power of his own body, but the wife. 5. Defraud ye not one the other, except *it be* with consent for a time, that ye may give yourselves to fasting and prayer; and come together again, that Satan tempt you not for your incontinency. 6. But I speak this by permission, *and* not of commandment. 10. And unto the married I command, *yet* not I, but the Lord, Let not the wife depart from *her* husband: 11. But and if she depart, let her remain unmarried, or be reconciled to *her* husband: and let not the husband put away *his* wife. 12. But to the rest speak I, not the Lord: If any brother hath a wife that believeth not, and she be pleased to dwell with him, let him not put her away. 13. And the woman which hath an husband that believeth not, and if he be pleased to dwell with her, let her not leave him. 14. For the unbelieving husband is sanctified by the wife, and the unbelieving wife is sanctified by the husband: else were your children unclean; but now are they

holy. 16. For what knowest thou, O wife, whether thou shalt save *thy* husband? or how knowest thou, O man, whether thou shalt save *thy* wife? 27. Art thou bound unto a wife? seek not to be loosed. Art thou loosed from a wife? seek not a wife. 28. But and if thou marry, thou hast not sinned; and if a virgin marry, she hath not sinned. Nevertheless such shall have trouble in the flesh: but I spare you. 29. But this I say, brethren, the time *is* short: it remaineth, that both they that have wives be as though they had none; 32. But I would have you without carefulness. He that is unmarried careth for the things that belong to the Lord, how he may please the Lord: 33. But he that is married careth for the things that are of the world, how he may please *his* wife. 34. There is difference *also* between a wife and a virgin. The unmarried woman careth for the things of the Lord, that she may be holy both in body and in spirit: but she that is married careth for the things of the world, how she may please *her* husband. 38. So then he that giveth *her* in marriage doeth well; but he that giveth *her* not in marriage doeth better. 39. The wife is bound by the law as long as her husband liveth; but if her husband be dead, she is at liberty to be married to whom she will; only in the Lord. 40. But she is happier if she so abide, after my judgment: and I think also that I have the Spirit of God.

1 Cor. 11:3. But I would have you know, that . . . the head of the woman *is* the man; 7. But the woman is the glory of the man. 8. For the man is not of the woman; but the woman of the man. 9. Neither was the man created for the woman; but the woman for the man. 11. Nevertheless neither is the man without the woman, neither the woman without the man, in the Lord. 12. For as the woman *is* of the man, even so *is* the man also by the woman; but all things of God.

1 Cor. 14:34. Let your women keep silence in the churches: for it is not permitted unto them to speak; but *they are commanded* to be under obedience, as also saith the law. 35. And if they will learn any thing, let them ask their husbands at home: for it is a shame for women to speak in church.

Eph. 5:22. Wives, submit yourselves unto your own husbands, as unto the Lord. 23. For the husband is the head of the wife, even as Christ is the head of the church: and he is the saviour of the body. 24. Therefore as the church is subject unto Christ, so *let* the wives *be* to their own husbands in every thing. 25. Husbands, love your wives, even as Christ also loved the church, and gave himself for it; 28. So ought men to love their wives as their own bodies. He that loveth his wife loveth himself. 31. For this cause shall a man leave his father and mother, and shall be joined unto his wife, and they two shall be one flesh. 33. Nevertheless let every one of you in particular so love his wife even as himself; and the wife *see* that she reverence *her* husband.

Col. 3:18. Wives, submit yourselves unto your own husbands, as it is fit in the Lord. 19. Husbands, love *your* wives, and be not bitter against them.

1 Tim. 3:11. Even so *must* ¹*their* wives *be* grave, not slanderers, ²sober, faithful in all things.　　　　　　[R. V. ¹ women　²temperate]

1 Tim. 5:9. Let not a widow be taken into the number under threescore years old, having been the wife of one man,　10. Well reported of for good works; if she have brought up children, if she have lodged strangers, if she have washed the saints' feet, if she have relieved the afflicted, if she have diligently followed every good work.　14. I will therefore that the younger women marry, bear children, guide the house, give none occasion to the adversary to speak reproachfully.

Tit. 2:3. The aged women likewise, that *they be* in behaviour as becometh holiness, not false accusers, not given to much wine, teachers of good things;　4. That they may teach the young women to be sober, to love their husbands, to love their children,　5. *To be* discreet, chaste, keepers at home, good, obedient to their own husbands, that the word of God be not blasphemed.

1 Pet. 3:1. Likewise, ye wives, *be* in subjection to your own husbands; that, if any obey not the word, they also may without the word be won by the conversation of the wives;　2. While they behold your chaste ¹ conversation, *coupled* with fear.　3. Whose adorning let it not be that outward *adorning* of plaiting the hair, and of wearing of gold, or of putting on of apparel:　4. But *let it be* the hidden man of the heart, in that which is not corruptible, *even the ornament* of a meek and quiet spirit, which is in the sight of God of great price.　5. For after this manner in the old time the holy women also, who trusted in God, adorned themselves, being in subjection unto their own husbands:　6. Even as Sara obeyed Abraham, calling him lord: whose daughters ye are as long as ye do well, and are not afraid with any amazement.　7. Likewise, ye husbands, dwell with *them* according to knowledge, giving honour unto the wife, as unto the weaker vessel, and as being heirs together of the grace of life; that your prayers be not hindered.　　　[¹ R. V. behavior]

See HUSBAND; PARENTS; WIDOW; WOMEN.

WILDERNESS. Wandering of the Israelites in, see ISRAEL, page 643.　Typical of the sinner's state, Deut. 32:10.　Jesus' temptation in, Matt. 4:1; Mark 1:12,13; Luke 4:1. See DESERT.

WILL. THE MENTAL FACULTY : Freedom of, recognized by God, Gen. 4:6-10. Deut. 5:29; 1 Kin. 20:42; Isa. 1:18-20; 43:26; Jer. 36:3,7; John 7:17.

See BLESSINGS, CONTINGENT ON OBEDIENCE; CHOICE; CONTINGENCY.

OF GOD, THE SUPREME RULE OF DUTY : Matt. 12:50. For whosoever shall do the will of my Father which is in heaven, the same is my brother, and sister, and mother.　Mark 3:35.

Matt. 26:39. And he went a little farther, and fell on his face, and prayed, saying, O my Father, if it be possible, let this cup pass from me: nevertheless not as I will, but as thou *wilt*.　[Mark 14:36; Luke 22:42.] 42. He went away again the second time, and prayed, saying, O my Father, if this cup may not pass away from me, except I drink it, thy will be done.

Luke 11:2. And he said unto them, When ye pray, say, Our Father which art in heaven, Hallowed be thy name.　Thy kingdom come.　¹ Thy will be done, as in heaven, so in earth.　Matt. 6:10.　　　[¹ Omitted in R. V.]

John 4:34. Jesus saith unto them, My meat is to do the will of him that sent me, and to finish his work.

John 5:30. I can of mine own self do nothing: as I hear, I judge: and my judgment is just; because I seek not mine own will, but the will of the Father which hath sent me.

John 6:38. For I came down from heaven, not to do mine own will, but the will of him that sent me.　39. And this is the Father's will which hath sent me, that of all which he hath given me I should lose nothing, but should raise it up again at the last day.　40. And this is the will of him that sent me, that every one which seeth the Son, and believeth on him, may have everlasting life: and I will raise him up at the last day.

Acts 18:21. But bade them farewell, saying, I must by all means keep this feast that cometh in Jerusalem: but I will return again unto you, if God will.

Rom. 12:2. And be not conformed to this world: but be ye transformed by the renewing of your mind, that ye may prove what *is* that good, and acceptable, and perfect, will of God.

Rom. 15:32. That I may come unto you with joy by the will of God, and may with you be refreshed.

1 Cor. 4:19. But I will come to you shortly, if the Lord will, and will know, not the speech of them which are puffed up, but the power.

1 Cor. 16:7. For I will not see you now by the way; but I trust to tarry awhile with you, if the Lord permit.

Heb. 6:3. And this will we do, if God permit.

See AGENCY.

A TESTAMENT : Of Abraham, Gen. 25:5,6. Jacob, Gen. 48; 49.　David, 1 Kin. 2:1-9.　Jehoshaphat, 2 Chr. 21:3.　May not be annulled, Gal. 3:15.　In force after death only, Heb. 9:16,17.

See TESTAMENT.

WILLFULNESS. See OBDURACY; SELF-WILL.

WILLOW, Lev. 23:40; Psa. 137:2; Ezek. 17:5.

FIGURATIVE: Isa. 44:4.

WIMPLE, Isa. 3:22.

WIND, blasting, 2 Kin. 19:7,35.

East: Hot and blasting in Egypt, Gen. 41:6; in the valley of the Euphrates, Ezek. 19:12; in Canaan, Hos. 13:15; Luke 12:55; at Nineveh, Jonah 4:8; tempestuous in Uz, Job 27:21.

West: Took away the plague of locusts from the land of Egypt, Ex. 10:19.

North: Free from humidity in Canaan, Prov. 25:23.

South: Soothing, Job 37:17; tempestuous, Job 37:9; purifying, Job 37:21.

FIGURATIVE: Hos. 4:19. Of the judgments of God, Jer. 22:22; Hos. 13:15; Matt. 7:25. Of the Spirit, John 3:8. Of heresy, Eph. 4:14.

WINDOW, Gen. 6:16; 26:8; Josh. 2:15, 21; 1 Kin. 6:4; Ezek. 40:16–36; Acts 20:9.

WINE. Made from grapes, Gen.40:11; 49: 11; Isa. 25:6; Jer. 40:10,12; from pomegranates, Song 8:2. Kept in jars, Jer. 13:12 [*R.V.*]; 48:12 [*R.V.*]; in skins [*R.V.*], Josh. 9:4,13; Job 32:19; Matt. 9:17; Luke 5:37,38; in bottles, Josh. 9:4,13; Job 32:19; Jer. 13:12; 48:12; Matt. 9: 17; Luke 5:37,38. Cellars for, 1 Chr. 27:27. New, Hag. 1:11. Old, Luke 5:39.

Medicinal use of, Prov. 31:6,7; recommended by Paul to Timothy, 1 Tim. 5:23. Used at meals, Matt. 26:27–29; Mark 14:23. Made by Jesus at the marriage feast in Cana, John 2:9,10. Sacramental use of, Matt. 26: 27–29; Luke 22:17–20.

Forbidden to priests while on duty, Lev. 10:9; Ezek.44:21; to Nazarites, Num. 6:2,3; see NAZARITE. Abstinence from, of Daniel, Dan. 1:5,8,16; 10:3; of courtiers of Ahasuerus, Esth.1:8; of Timothy, 1 Tim. 5:23. Samson's mother forbidden to drink, Judg. 13:4,5. Forbidden to kings, Prov. 31:4. Denied to the Israelites in the wilderness, that they might know that the Lord was their God, Deut. 29:6. Offered with sacrifices, Ex. 29:40; Lev. 23:13; Num. 15:5,10; 28:7,14. Given by Melchizedek to Abraham, Gen.14: 18. Fermented, Lev. 10:9; Num. 6:3; 28:7; Deut. 14:26; 29:6; Prov. 23:31,32; Mark 2:22. Refined, Isa. 25:6; Jer. 48:11. Of staggering [*R.V.*], Psa. 60:3. Inflames the eyes, Gen. 49:12. Commerce in, Rev. 18:13. Banquets of, Esth. 5:6. Given to Jesus at the crucifixion, Matt. 27:48; Mark 15:23; Luke 23:36; John 19:29. Intoxication from the use of, Psa. 104:15; Prov. 4:17.

INSTANCES OF INTOXICATION FROM: Noah, Gen. 9:21; Lot, Gen. 19:32; Joseph and his brethren, Gen. 43:34; Nabal, 1 Sam. 25:36; Amnon, 2 Sam. 13:28,29; Ahasuerus, Esth. 1:10; kings of Israel, Hos. 7:5; falsely charged against the disciples, Acts 2:13.

FIGURATIVE: Of the divine judgments. Psa. 60:3; 75:8; Jer. 51:7. Of the joy of wisdom, Prov. 9:2,5. Of the joys of religion, Isa. 25:6; 55:1; Joel 2:19. Of abominations, Rev. 14:8; 16:19.

SYMBOLICAL: Of the blood of Jesus, Matt. 26:28; Mark 14:23,24; Luke 22:20; John 6: 53–56.

UNCLASSIFIED SCRIPTURES RELATING TO: Deut. 14:26. And thou shalt bestow that money for whatsoever thy soul lusteth after, for oxen, or for sheep, or for wine, or for strong drink, or for whatsoever thy soul desireth: and thou shalt eat there before the LORD thy God, and thou shalt rejoice, thou, and thine household,

Deut. 33:28. Israel then shall dwell in safety alone: the fountain of Jacob *shall be* upon a land of corn and wine; also his heavens shall drop down dew.

2 Kin. 18:32. Until I come and take you away to a land like your own land, a land of corn and wine, a land of bread and vineyards, a land of oil olive and of honey, that ye may live, and not die: and hearken not unto Hezekiah, when he persuadeth you, saying, The LORD will deliver us.

2 Chr. 32:28. Storehouses also for the increase of corn, and wine, and oil: and stalls for all manner of beasts, and cotes for flocks.

Neh. 10:39. For the children of Israel and the children of Levi shall bring the offering of the corn, of the new wine, and the oil, unto the chambers, where *are* the vessels of the sanctuary, and the priests that minister, and the porters, and the singers: and we will not forsake the house of our God.

Psa. 4:7. Thou hast put gladness in my heart, more than in the time *that* their corn and their wine increased.

Psa. 104:14. He causeth the grass to grow for the cattle, and herb for the service of man: that he may bring forth food out of the earth; 15. And wine *that* maketh glad the heart of man, *and* oil to make *his* face to shine, and bread *which* strengtheneth man's heart.

Prov. 31:6. Give strong drink unto him that is ready to perish, and wine unto those that be of heavy hearts. 7. Let him drink, and forget his poverty, and remember his misery no more.

Eccl. 2:3. I sought in mine heart to give myself unto wine, yet acquainting mine heart with wisdom; and to lay hold on folly, till I might see what *was* that good for the sons of men, which they should do under the heaven all the days of their life. 11. Then I looked on all the works that my hand had wrought, and on the labour that I had laboured to do: and, behold, all *was* vanity and vexation of spirit, and *there was* no profit under the sun.

Isa. 56:12. Come ye, *say they,* I will fetch wine, and we will fill ourselves with strong drink; and to morrow shall be as this day, *and* much more abundant.

Hos. 2:8. For she did not know that I gave her corn, and wine, and oil, and multiplied her silver and gold, *which* they prepared for Baal. 22. And the earth shall ¹ hear the corn, and the wine, and the oil; and they shall ¹ hear Jezreel.　[¹ R. V. answer]

Hos. 7:14. And they have not cried unto me with their heart, when they howled upon their beds: they assemble themselves for corn and wine, *and* they rebel against me.

Joel 1:5. Awake, ye drunkards, and weep; and howl, all ye drinkers of wine, because of the new wine; for it is cut off from your mouth.

Joel 2:24. And the floors shall be full of wheat, and the fats shall overflow with wine and oil.

Joel 3:3. And they have cast lots for my people; and have given a boy for an harlot, and sold a girl for wine, that they might drink.

Amos 6:6. That drink wine in bowls, and anoint themselves with the chief ointments: but they are not grieved for the affliction of Joseph.

Hab. 2:5. Yea ¹ also, because he transgresseth by wine, *he is* a proud man, neither keepeth at home, who enlargeth his desire as hell, and *is* as death, and cannot be satisfied, but gathereth unto him all nations, and heapeth unto him all people:

[R. V. moreover, wine is a treacherous dealer, a haughty]

Hag. 1:11. And I called for a drought upon the land, and upon the mountains, and upon the corn, and upon the new wine, and upon the oil, and upon *that* which the ground bringeth forth, and upon men, and upon cattle, and upon all the labour of the hands.

Zech. 9:17. For how great *is* his goodness, and how great *is* his beauty! corn shall make the young men cheerful, and new wine the maids.

Zech. 10:7. And *they of* Ephraim shall be like a mighty *man*, and their heart shall rejoice as through wine:

1 Tim. 5:23. Drink no longer water, but use a little wine for thy stomach's sake and thine often infirmities.

See Vine; Vineyard.

ADMONITIONS AGAINST THE USE OF:
Lev. 10:9. Do not drink wine nor strong drink, thou, nor thy sons with thee, when ye go into the tabernacle of the congregation, lest ye die: *it shall be* a statute for ever throughout your generations.

Num. 6:3. He shall separate *himself* from wine and strong drink, and shall drink no vinegar of wine, or vinegar of strong drink, neither shall he drink any liquor of grapes, nor eat moist grapes, or dried.

Judg. 13:4. Now therefore beware, I pray thee, and drink not wine nor strong drink, and eat not any unclean *thing:*

Prov. 20:1. Wine *is* a mocker, strong drink *is* raging: and whosoever is deceived thereby is not wise.

Prov. 21:17. He that loveth pleasure *shall be* a poor man: he that loveth wine and oil shall not be rich.

Prov. 23:29. Who hath woe? who hath sorrow? who hath contentions? who hath babbling? who hath wounds without cause? who hath redness of eyes? 30. They that tarry long at the wine; they that go to seek mixed wine. 31. Look not thou upon the wine when it is red, when it giveth his colour in the cup, *when* it moveth itself aright. 32. At the last it biteth like a serpent, and stingeth like an adder.

Prov. 31:4. *It is* not for kings, O Lemuel, *it is* not for kings to drink wine; nor for princes strong drink: 5. Lest they drink, and forget the law, and pervert the judgment of any of the afflicted.

Isa. 5:11. Woe unto them that rise up early in the morning, *that* they may follow strong drink　that continue until night, *till* wine inflame them! 22. Woe unto *them that are* mighty to drink wine, and men of strength to mingle strong drink:

Isa. 24:9. They shall not drink wine with a song; strong drink shall be bitter to them that drink it.

Isa. 28:1. Woe to the crown of pride, to the drunkards of Ephraim, whose glorious beauty *is* a fading flower, which *are* on the head of the fat valleys of them that are overcome with wine! 3. The crown of pride, the drunkards of Ephraim, shall be trodden under feet: 7. But they also have erred through wine, and through strong drink are out of the way: the priest and the prophet have erred through strong drink,

Jer. 23:9. Mine heart within me is broken because of the prophets; all my bones shake; I am like a drunken man, and like a man whom wine hath overcome, because of the LORD, and because of the words of his holiness.

Jer. 35:2. Go unto the house of the Rechabites, and speak unto them, and bring them into the house of the LORD, into one of the chambers, and give them wine to drink. 3. Then I took Jaazaniah the son of Jeremiah, the son of Habaziniah, and his brethren, and all his sons, and the whole house of the Rechabites; 4. And I brought them into the house of the LORD, into the chamber of the sons of Hanan, the son of Igdaliah, a man of God, which *was* by the chamber of the princes, which *was* above the chamber of Maaseiah the son of Shallum, the keeper of the door: 5. And I set before the sons of the house of the Rechabites pots full of wine, and cups, and I said unto them, Drink ye wine. 6. But they said, We will drink no wine: for Jonadab the son of Rechab our father commanded us, saying, Ye shall drink no wine, *neither* ye, nor your sons for ever. 7. Neither shall ye build house, nor sow seed, nor plant vineyard, nor have *any:* but all your days ye shall dwell in tents; that ye may live many days in the land where ye *be* strangers. 8. Thus have we obeyed the voice of Jonadab the son of Rechab our father in all that he hath charged us, to drink no wine all our days, we, our wives, our sons, nor our daughters; 9. Nor to build houses for us to dwell in; neither have we vineyard, nor field, nor seed: 10. But we have dwelt in tents, and have obeyed, and done according to all that Jonadab our father commanded us. 14. The words of Jonadab the son of Rechab, that he commanded his sons not to drink wine, are performed; for unto this day they drink none, but obey their father's commandment: notwithstanding I have spoken unto you, rising early and speaking; but ye hearkened not unto me. 18. And Jeremiah said unto the house of the Rechabites, Thus saith the Lord of hosts, the God of Israel; Because ye have obeyed the commandment of Jonadab your father, and kept all his precepts, and done according unto all that he hath commanded you: 19. Therefore thus saith the Lord of hosts, the God of Israel; Jonadab the son of Rechab shall not want a man to stand before me for ever.

Ezek. 44:21. Neither shall any priest drink wine when they enter into the inner court.

Hos. 4:11. Whoredom and wine and new wine take away the heart.

Luke 1:15. For he shall be great in the sight of the Lord, and shall drink neither wine nor strong drink; and he shall be filled with the Holy Ghost, even from his mother's womb.

Rom. 14:21. It is good neither to eat flesh, nor to drink wine, nor any thing whereby thy brother stumbleth, 1 or is offended, or is made weak.   [1 Omitted in R. V.]

Eph. 5:18. And be not drunk with wine, wherein is excess; but be filled with the Spirit.

Tit. 2:3. The aged women likewise, that they be in behaviour as becometh holiness, not false accusers, not given to much wine, teachers of good things.

See ABSTINENCE; DRUNKENNESS.

WINEBIBBER, Jesus falsely accused of being a, Matt. 11:19; Luke 7:34.

WINE PRESS, Num. 18:27,30; Deut. 15:14; Judg. 6:11. In vineyards, Isa. 5:2; Matt. 21:33; Mark 12:1. Trodden with joy and shouting, Jer. 48:33.

FIGURATIVE: Treading the, of the sufferings of Christ, Isa. 63:2,3; of the judgments of God, Lam. 1:15; Rev. 14:19,20.

WINNOWING, of grain, Ruth 3:2; Isa. 30:24; Matt. 3:12.

WINTER. Annual return of, shall never cease, Gen. 8:22. Plowing in, in Canaan, Prov. 20:4 [marg.]. Rainy season in, in Canaan, Song 2:11. Shipping suspended in, on the Mediterranean Sea, Acts 27:12; 28:11. Paul remains one, at Nicopolis, Tit. 3:12. Summer and winter houses, Jer. 36:22; Amos 3:15.

See METEOROLOGY.

WISDOM. Of Joseph, Gen. 41:16,25-39; Acts 7:10. Of Moses, Acts 7:22. Of Bezaleel, Ex. 31:3-5; 35:31-35; 36:1. Of Aholiab, Ex. 31:6; 35:34,35; 36:1; of other skilled artisans, Ex. 36:2; of women, Ex. 35:26. Of Hiram, 1 Kin. 7:14; 2 Chr. 2:14. Of Solo-

mon, 1 Kin. 3:12,16-28; 4:29-34; 5:12; 10:24. Of Ethan, Heman, Chalcol, and Darda, 1 Kin. 4:31. Of the princes of Issachar, 1 Chr. 12:32. Of Ezra, Ezra 7:25. Of Daniel, Dan. 1:17; 5:14. Of Paul, 2 Pet. 3:15. Of the Magi, Matt. 2:1-12.

SPIRITUAL: UNCLASSIFIED SCRIPTURES RELATING TO: Deut. 32:29. O that they were wise, that they understood this, that they would consider their latter end!

Job 5:27. Lo this, we have searched it, so it is; hear it, and know thou it for thy good.

Job 8:8. For enquire, I pray thee, of the former age, and prepare thyself to the search of their fathers: 10. Shall not they teach thee, and tell thee, and utter words out of their heart?

Job 12:2. No doubt but ye are the people, and wisdom shall die with you. 3. But I have understanding as well as you; I am not inferior to you: yea, who knoweth not such things as these? 7. But ask now the beasts, and they shall teach thee; and the fowls of the air, and they shall tell thee: 8. Or speak to the earth, and it shall teach thee: and the fishes of the sea shall declare unto thee. 9. Who knoweth not in all these that the hand of the Lord hath wrought this? 10. In whose hand is the soul of every living thing, and the breath of all mankind. 11. Doth not the ear try words? and the mouth taste his meat? 12. With the ancient is wisdom; and in length of days understanding. 13. With him is wisdom and strength, he hath counsel and understanding. 16. With him is strength and wisdom: the deceived and the deceiver are his. 17. He leadeth counsellors away spoiled, and maketh the judges fools. 22. He discovereth deep things out of darkness, and bringeth out to light the shadow of death.

Job 28:12. But where shall wisdom be found? and where is the place of understanding? 13. Man knoweth not the price thereof; neither is it found in the land of the living. 14. The depth saith, It is not in me: and the sea saith, It is not with me. 15. It cannot be gotten for gold, neither shall silver be weighed for the price thereof. 16. It cannot be valued with the gold of Ophir, with the precious onyx, or the sapphire. 17. The gold and the crystal cannot equal it: and the exchange of it shall not be for jewels of fine gold. 18. No mention shall be made of coral, or of pearls: for the price of wisdom is above rubies. 19. The topaz of Ethiopia shall not equal it, neither shall it be valued with pure gold. 20. Whence then cometh wisdom? and where is the place of understanding? 21. Seeing it is hid from the eyes of all living, and kept close from the fowls of the air. 22. Destruction and death say, We have heard the fame thereof with our ears. 23. God understandeth the way thereof, and he knoweth the place thereof. 24. For he looketh to the ends of the earth, and seeth under the whole heaven: 25. To make the weight for the winds; and he weigheth the waters by measure. 26. When he made a decree for the rain, and a way for the lightning of the thunder: 27. Then did he see it, and declare it; he prepared it, yea, and searched it out. 28. And unto man he said, Behold, the fear of the Lord, that *is* wisdom; and to depart from evil *is* understanding.

Job 32:9. Great men are not *always* wise: neither do the aged understand judgment.

Job 42:5. I have heard of thee by the hearing of the ear: but now mine eye seeth thee.

Psa. 2:10. Be wise now therefore, O ye kings: be instructed, ye judges of the earth.

Psa. 9:10. And they that know thy name will put their trust in thee: for thou, Lord, hast not forsaken them that seek thee.

Psa. 76:1. In Judah *is* God known: his name *is* great in Israel.

Psa. 107:43. Whoso *is* wise, and will observe these *things*, even they shall understand the lovingkindness of the Lord.

Psa. 111:10. The fear of the Lord *is* the beginning of wisdom: a good understanding have all they that do *his commandments*:

Prov. 1:5. A wise *man* will hear, and will increase learning; and a man of understanding shall attain unto wise counsel: 7. The fear of the Lord *is* the beginning of knowledge: *but* fools despise wisdom and instruction. 20. Wisdom crieth without; she uttereth her voice in the streets: 21. She crieth in the chief place of concourse, in the openings of the gates: in the city she uttereth her words, *saying*, 22. How long, ye simple ones, will ye love simplicity? and the scorners delight in their scorning, and fools hate knowledge? 23. Turn you at my reproof: behold, I will pour out my spirit unto you, I will make known my words unto you. 24. Because I have called, and ye refused; I have stretched out my hand, and no man regarded; 25. But ye have set at nought all my counsel, and would none of my reproof: 26. I also will laugh at your calamity; I will mock when your fear cometh; 27. When your fear cometh as desolation, and your destruction cometh as a whirlwind; when distress and anguish cometh upon you. 28. Then shall they call upon me, but I will not answer; they shall seek me early, but they shall not find me: 29. For that they hated knowledge, and did not choose the fear of the Lord: 30. They would none of my counsel: they despised all my reproof. 31. Therefore shall they eat of the fruit of their own way, and be filled with their own devices. 32. For the turning away of the simple shall slay them, and the prosperity of fools shall destroy them. 33. But whoso hearkeneth unto me shall dwell safely, and shall be quiet from fear of evil.

Prov. 2:1. My son, if thou wilt receive my words, and hide my commandments with thee; 2. So that thou incline thine ear unto wisdom, *and* apply thine heart to understanding; 3. Yea, if thou criest after knowledge, *and* liftest up thy voice for understanding; 4. If thou seekest her as silver, and searchest for her as *for* hid treasures; 5. Then shalt thou understand the fear of the Lord, and find the knowledge of God. 6. For the Lord giveth wisdom: out of his mouth *cometh* knowledge and understanding. 7. He layeth up sound wisdom for the righteous: *he is* a buckler to them that walk uprightly. 8. He keepeth the paths of judgment, and preserveth the way of his saints. 9. Then shalt thou understand righteousness, and judgment, and equity; *yea*, every good path. 10. When wisdom entereth into thine heart, and knowledge is pleasant unto thy soul; 11. Discretion shall preserve thee, understanding shall keep thee: 12. To deliver thee from the way of the evil *man*, from the man that speaketh froward things; 13. Who leave the paths of uprightness, to walk in the ways of darkness; 14. Who rejoice to do evil, *and* delight in the frowardness of the wicked; 15. Whose ways *are* crooked, and *they* froward in their paths: 16. To deliver thee from the strange woman, *even* from the stranger *which* flattereth with her words; 17. Which forsaketh the guide of her youth, and forgetteth the covenant of her God. 18. For her house inclineth unto death, and her paths unto the dead. 19. None that go unto her return again, neither take they hold of the paths of life. 20. That thou mayest walk in the way of good *men*, and keep the paths of the righteous.

Prov. 3:13. Happy *is* the man *that* findeth wisdom, and the man *that* getteth understanding. 14. For the merchandise of it *is* better than the merchandise of silver, and the gain thereof than fine gold. 15. She *is* more precious than rubies: and all the things thou canst desire are not to be compared unto her. 16. Length of days *is* in her right hand; *and* in her left hand riches and honour. 17. Her ways *are* ways of pleasantness, and all her paths *are* peace. 18. She *is* a tree of life to them that lay hold upon her: and happy *is every one* that retaineth her. 19. The Lord by wisdom hath founded the earth; by understanding hath he established the heavens. 20. By his knowledge the depths are broken up, and the clouds drop down the dew. 21. My son, let not them depart from thine eyes: keep sound wisdom and discretion: 22. So shall they be life unto thy soul, and grace to thy neck. 23. Then shalt thou walk in thy ways safely, and thy foot shall not stumble. 24. When thou liest down, thou shalt not be afraid: yea, thou shalt lie down, and thy sleep shall be sweet. 25. Be not afraid of sudden fear, neither of the desolation of the wicked, when it cometh. 26. For the Lord shall be thy confidence, and shall keep thy foot from being taken. 34. Surely he scorneth the scorners: but he giveth grace unto the lowly. 35. The wise shall inherit glory:

but shame shall be the promotion of fools.

Prov. 4:4. He taught me also, and said unto me, Let thine heart retain my words: keep my commandments, and live. 5. Get wisdom, get understanding: forget *it* not; neither decline from the words of my mouth. 6. Forsake her not, and she shall preserve thee: love her, and she shall keep thee. 7. Wisdom *is* the principal thing; *therefore* get wisdom: and with all thy getting get understanding. 8. Exalt her, and she shall promote thee: she shall bring thee to honour, when thou dost embrace her. 9. She shall give to thine head an ornament of grace: a crown of glory shall she deliver to thee: 10. Hear, O my son, and receive my sayings; and the years of thy life shall be many. 11. I have taught thee in the way of wisdom; I have led thee in right paths. 12. When thou goest, thy steps shall not be straitened; and when thou runnest, thou shalt not stumble. 13. Take fast hold of instruction; let *her* not go: keep her; for she *is* thy life. 18. But the path of the just *is* as the shining light, that shineth more and more unto the perfect day. 19. The way of the wicked *is* as darkness: they know not at what they stumble. 20. My son, attend to my words; incline thine ear unto my sayings. 21. Let them not depart from thine eyes; keep them in the mids'. of thine heart. 22. For they *are* life unto those that find them, and health to all their flesh.

Prov. 5:12. And say, How have I hated instruction, and my heart despised reproof;

Prov. 7:2. Keep my commandments, and live; and my law as the apple of thine eye. 3. Bind them upon thy fingers, write them upon the table of thine heart. 4. Say unto wisdom, Thou *art* my sister; and call understanding *thy* kinswoman:

Prov. 8:1. Doth not wisdom cry? and understanding put forth her voice? 2. She standeth in the top of high places, by the way in the places of the paths. 3. She crieth at the gates, at the entry of the city, at the coming in at the doors: 4. Unto you, O men, I call; and my voice *is* to the sons of man. 5. O ye simple, understand wisdom: and, ye fools, be ye of an understanding heart. 6. Hear; for I will speak of excellent things; and the opening of my lips *shall be* right things. 7. For my mouth shall speak truth; and wickedness *is* an abomination to my lips. 8. All the words of my mouth *are* in righteousness; *there is* nothing froward or perverse in them. 9. They *are* all plain to him that understandeth, and right to them that find knowledge. 10. Receive my instruction, and not silver; and knowledge rather than choice gold. 11. For wisdom *is* better than rubies; and all the things that may be desired are not to be compared to it. 12. I wisdom dwell with prudence, and find out knowledge of witty inventions. 13. The fear of the LORD *is* to hate evil: pride, and arrogancy, and the evil way, and the froward mouth, do I hate. 14. Counsel *is* mine, and sound wisdom: I *am* understanding; I have strength. 15. By me kings reign, and princes decree justice. 16. By me princes rule, and nobles, *even* all the judges of the earth. 17. I love them that love me; and those that seek me early shall find me. 18. Riches and honour *are* with me; *yea*, durable riches and righteousness. 19. My fruit *is* better than gold, yea, than fine gold; and my revenue than choice silver. 20. I lead in the way of righteousness, in the midst of the paths of judgment: 21. That I may cause those that love me to inherit substance; and I will fill their treasures. 22. The LORD possessed me in the beginning of his way, before his works of old. 23. I was set up from everlasting, from the beginning, or ever the earth was. 24. When *there were* no depths, I was brought forth; when *there were* no fountains abounding with water. 25. Before the mountains were settled, before the hills was I brought forth: 26. While as yet he had not made the earth, nor the fields, nor the highest part of the dust of the world. 27. When he prepared the heavens, I *was* there: when he set a compass upon the face of the depth: 28. When he established the clouds above: when he strengthened the fountains of the deep: 29. When he gave to the sea his decree, that the waters should not pass his commandment: when he appointed the foundations of the earth: 30. Then I was by him, *as* one brought up *with him:* and I was daily *his* delight, rejoicing always before him; 31. Rejoicing in the habitable part of his earth; and my delights *were* with the sons of men. 32. Now therefore hearken unto me, O ye children: for blessed *are they that* keep my ways. 33. Hear instruction, and be wise, and refuse it not. 34. Blessed *is* the man that heareth me, watching daily at my gates, waiting at the posts of my doors. 35. For whoso findeth me findeth life, and shall obtain favour of the LORD. 36. But he that sinneth against me wrongeth his own soul: all they that hate me love death.

Prov. 9:1. Wisdom hath builded her house, she hath hewn out her seven pillars: 2. She hath killed her beasts; she hath mingled her wine; she hath also furnished her table. 3. She hath sent forth her maidens: she crieth upon the highest places of the city, 4. Whoso *is* simple, let him turn in hither: *as for* him that wanteth understanding, she saith to him, 5. Come, eat of my bread, and drink of the wine *which* I have mingled. 6. Forsake the foolish, and live; and go in the way of understanding. 9. Give *instruction* to a wise *man*, and he will be yet wiser: teach a just *man*, and he will increase in learning. 10. The fear of the LORD *is* the beginning of wisdom: and the knowledge of the holy *is* understanding. 11. By me thy days shall be multiplied, and the years of thy life shall be increased. 12. If thou be wise, thou shalt be wise for thyself: but *if* thou scornest, thou alone shalt bear *it*.

Prov. 10:8. The wise in heart will receive commandments: but a prating fool shall fall. 13. In the lips of him that hath understanding wisdom is found: but a rod *is* for the back of him that is void of understanding. 14. Wise *men* lay up knowledge: but the mouth of the foolish *is* near destruction. 21. The lips of the righteous feed many: but fools die for want of wisdom. 23. *It is* as sport to a fool to do mischief: but a man of understanding hath wisdom.

Prov. 11:12. He that is void of wisdom despiseth his neighbour: but a man of understanding holdeth his peace. *v.* 9.

Prov. 12:1. Whoso loveth instruction loveth knowledge: but he that hateth reproof *is* brutish. 8. A man shall be commended according to his wisdom: but he that is of a perverse heart shall be despised. 15. The way of a fool *is* right in his own eyes: but he that hearkeneth unto counsel *is* wise.

Prov. 13:14. The law of the wise *is* a fountain of life, to depart from the snares of death. 15. Good understanding giveth favour: but the way of transgressors *is* hard. 16. Every prudent *man* dealeth with knowledge: but a fool layeth open *his* folly. Prov. 14:18.

Prov. 14:6. A scorner seeketh wisdom, and *findeth it* not: but knowledge *is* easy unto him that understandeth. 7. Go from the presence of a foolish man, when thou perceivest not *in him* the lips of knowledge. 8. The wisdom of the prudent *is* to understand his way: but the folly of fools *is* deceit. 16. A wise *man* feareth, and departeth from evil: but the fool rageth, and is confident. 33. Wisdom resteth in the heart of him that hath understanding: but *that which is* in the midst of fools is made known.

Prov. 15:7. The lips of the wise disperse knowledge: but the heart of the foolish *doeth* not so. [*v.* 2.] 14. The heart of him that hath understanding seeketh knowledge: but the mouth of fools feedeth on foolishness. 33 The fear of the LORD *is* the instruction of wisdom; and before honour *is* humility.

Prov. 16:16. How much better *is it* to get wisdom than gold! and to get understanding rather to be chosen than silver! 20. He that handleth a matter wisely shall find good: and whoso trusteth in the LORD, happy *is* he. 21. The wise in heart shall be called prudent: and the sweetness of the lips increaseth learning. 22. Understanding *is* a wellspring of life unto him that hath it: but the instruction of fools *is* folly. 23. The heart of the wise teacheth his mouth, and addeth learning to his lips. 24. Pleasant words *are as* an honeycomb, sweet to the soul, and health to the bones.

Prov. 17:10. A reproof entereth more into a wise man than an hundred stripes into a fool. 24. Wisdom *is* before him that hath understanding: but the eyes of a fool *are* in the ends of the earth.

Prov. 18:15. The heart of the prudent getteth knowledge; and the ear of the wise seeketh knowledge.

Prov. 19:8. He that getteth wisdom loveth his own soul: he that keepeth understanding shall find good. 20. Hear counsel, and receive instruction, that thou mayest be wise in thy latter end.

Prov. 21:11. When the scorner is punished, the simple is made wise: and when the wise is instructed, he receiveth knowledge.

Prov. 22:17. Bow down thine ear, and hear the words of the wise, and apply thine heart unto my knowledge. 18. For *it is* a pleasant thing if thou keep them within thee; they shall withal be fitted in thy lips. 19. That thy trust may be in the LORD, I have made known to thee this day, even to thee. 20. Have not I written to thee excellent things in counsels and knowledge, 21. That I might make thee know the certainty of the words of truth; that thou mightest answer the words of truth to them that send unto thee?

Prov. 23:12. Apply thine heart unto instruction, and thine ears to the words of knowledge. 19. Hear thou, my son, and be wise, and guide thine heart in the way. 23. Buy the truth, and sell *it* not; *also* wisdom, and instruction, and understanding.

Prov. 24:13. My son, eat thou honey, because *it is* good; and the honeycomb, *which is* sweet to thy taste: 14. So *shall* the knowledge of wisdom *be* unto thy soul: when thou hast found *it*, then there shall be a reward, and thy expectation shall not be cut off.

Prov. 28:5. Evil men understand not judgment: but they that seek the LORD understand all *things*. 7. Whoso keepeth the law *is* a wise son: but he that is a companion of riotous *men* shameth his father. Prov. 29:3.

Eccl. 8:1. Who *is* as the wise *man?* and who knoweth the interpretation of a thing? a man's wisdom maketh his face to shine, and the boldness of his face shall be changed. 5. Whoso keepeth the commandment shall feel no evil thing: and a wise man's heart discerneth both time and judgment.

Eccl. 9:13. This wisdom have I seen also under the sun, and it *seemed* great unto me: 14. *There was* a little city, and few men within it; and there came a great king against it, and besieged it, and built great bulwarks against it: 15. Now there was found in it a poor wise man, and he by his wisdom delivered the city; yet no man remembered that same poor man. 16. Then said I, Wisdom *is* better than strength: nevertheless the poor man's wisdom *is* despised, and his words are not heard. 17. The words of wise *men are* heard in quiet more than the cry of him that ruleth among fools. 18. Wisdom *is* better than weapons of war: but one sinner destroyeth much good.

Eccl. 10:12. The words of a wise man's mouth *are* gracious; but the lips of a fool will swallow up himself.

Eccl. 12:11. The words of the wise *are* as goads, and as nails fastened *by* the masters of assemblies, *which* are given from one shepherd.

Isa. 2:3. And many people shall go and say, Come ye, and let us go up to the mountain of the LORD, to the house of the God of Jacob; and he will teach us of his ways, and we will walk in his paths: for out of Zion shall go forth the law, and the word of the LORD from Jerusalem.

Isa. 11:9. They shall not hurt nor destroy in all my holy mountain: for the earth shall be full of the knowledge of the LORD, as the waters cover the sea.

Isa. 29:24. They also that erred in spirit shall come to understanding, and they that murmured shall learn doctrine.

Isa. 33:6. Wisdom and knowledge shall be the stability of thy times, *and* strength of salvation: the fear of the LORD *is* his treasure.

Jer. 9:23. Thus saith the LORD, Let not the wise *man* glory in his wisdom, neither let the mighty *man* glory in his might, let not the rich *man* glory in his riches: 24. But let him that glorieth glory in this, that he understandeth and knoweth me, that I *am* the LORD which exercise lovingkindness, judgment, and righteousness, in the earth: for in these *things* I delight, saith the LORD.

Jer. 31:34. And they shall teach no more every man his neighbour, and every man his brother, saying, Know the LORD: for they shall all know me, from the least of them unto the greatest of them, saith the LORD: for I will forgive their iniquity, and I will remember their sin no more.

Dan. 11:32. And such as do wickedly against the covenant shall he corrupt by flatteries: but the people that do know their God shall be strong, and do *exploits*. 33. And they that understand among the people shall instruct many:

Dan. 12:3. And they that be wise shall shine as the brightness of the firmament; and they that turn many to righteousness as the stars for ever and ever. 4. But thou, O Daniel, shut up the words, and seal the book, *even* to the time of the end: many shall run to and fro, and knowledge shall be increased. 10. Many shall ¹ be purified, and ² made white, and ³ tried; but the wicked shall do wickedly: and none of the wicked shall understand: but the wise shall understand.

[R. V. ¹ purify themselves ² make themselves ³ be refined]

Hos. 6:3. Then shall we know, *if* we follow on to know the LORD: his going forth is prepared as the morning; and he shall come unto us as the rain, as the latter *and* former rain unto the earth. 6. For I desired mercy, and not sacrifice; and the knowledge of God more than burnt offerings.

Hos. 14:9. Who *is* wise, and he shall understand these *things?* prudent, and he shall know them? for the ways of the LORD *are* right, and the just shall walk in them:

Matt. 6:22. The light of the body is the eye: if therefore thine eye be single, thy whole body shall be full of light. 23. But if thine eye be evil, thy whole body shall be full of darkness. If therefore the light that is in thee be darkness, how great *is* that darkness! Luke 11:34–36.

Matt. 7:24. Therefore whosoever heareth these sayings of mine, and doeth them, I will liken him unto a wise man, which built his house upon a rock: 25. And the rain descended, and the floods came. and the winds blew, and beat upon that house; and it fell not: for it was founded upon a rock.

Matt. 11:19. But wisdom is justified of her children. Luke 7:35.

Matt. 25:1. Then shall the kingdom of heaven be likened unto ten virgins, which took their lamps, and went forth to meet the bridegroom. 2. And five of them were wise, and five *were* foolish. 3. They that *were* foolish took their lamps, and took no oil with them: 4. But the wise took oil in their vessels with their lamps. 5. While the bridegroom tarried, they all slumbered and slept. 6. And at midnight there was a cry made, Behold, the bridegroom cometh; go ye out to meet him. 7. Then all those virgins arose, and trimmed their lamps. 8. And the foolish said unto the wise, Give us of your oil; for our lamps are gone out. 9. But the wise answered, saying, *Not so;* lest there be not enough for us and you: but go ye rather to them that sell, and buy for yourselves. 10. And while they went to buy, the bridegroom came; and they that were ready went in with him to the marriage: and the door was shut. 11. Afterward came also the other virgins, saying, Lord, Lord, open to us. 12. But he answered and said, Verily I say unto you, I know you not. 13. Watch therefore. for ye know neither the day nor the hour wherein the Son of man cometh.

Mark 12:32. And the scribe said unto him, Well, Master, thou hast said the truth: for there is one God; and there is none other but he: 33. And to love him with all the heart, and with all the understanding, and with all the soul, and with all the strength, and to love *his* neighbour as himself, is more than all whole burnt offerings and sacrifices. 34. And when Jesus saw that he answered discreetly, he said unto him, Thou art not far from the kingdom of God. And no man after that durst ask him *any question.*

Luke 1:17. And he shall go before him in the spirit and power of Elias, to turn the hearts of the fathers to the children, and the disobedient to the wisdom of the just; to make ready a people prepared for the Lord.

John 7:17. If any man will do his will, he shall know of the doctrine, whether it be of God, or *whether* I speak of myself.

John 8:32. Ye shall know the truth, and the truth shall make you free.

John 10:4. When he putteth forth his own sheep, he goeth before them, and the sheep follow him : for they know his voice. 14. I am the good shepherd, and know my *sheep*, and am known of mine.

John 17:3. This is life eternal, that they might know thee the only true God, and Jesus Christ, whom thou has sent. 7. Now they have known that all things whatsoever thou hast given me are of thee. 8. For I have given unto them the words which thou gavest me: and they have received *them*, and have known surely that I came out from thee, and they have believed that thou didst send me. 25. O righteous Father, the world hath not known thee : but I have known thee, and these have known that thou hast sent me.

Acts 6:10. And they were not able to resist the wisdom and the spirit by which he spake.

Rom. 15:14. I myself also am persuaded of you, my brethren, that ye also are full of goodness, filled with all knowledge, able also to admonish one another.

Rom. 16:19. For your obedience is come abroad unto all *men*. I am glad therefore on your behalf : but yet I would have you wise unto that which is good, and simple concerning evil.

1 Cor. 2:6. Howbeit we speak wisdom among them that are perfect : yet not the wisdom of this world, nor of the princes of this world, that come to nought : 7. But we speak the wisdom of God in a mystery, *even* the hidden *wisdom*, which God ordained before the world unto our glory : 8. Which none of the princes of this world knew for had they known *it*, they would not have crucified the Lord of glory. 9. But as it is written, Eye hath not seen, nor ear heard, neither have entered into the heart of man, the things which God hath prepared for them that love him. 10. But God hath revealed *them* unto us by his Spirit : for the Spirit searcheth all things, yea, the deep things of God. 11. For what man knoweth the things of a man, save the spirit of man which is in him ? even so the things of God knoweth no man, but the Spirit of God. 12. Now we have received, not the spirit of the world, but the spirit which is of God ; that we might know the things that are freely given to us of God. 13. Which things also we speak, not in the words which man's wisdom teacheth, but which the Holy Ghost teacheth ; comparing spiritual things with spiritual. 14. But the natural man receiveth not the things of the Spirit of God : for they are foolishness unto him : neither can he know *them*, because they are spiritually discerned. 15. But he that is spiritual judgeth all things, yet he

himself is judged of no man. 16. For who hath known the mind of the Lord, that he may instruct him ? But we have the mind of Christ.

1 Cor. 3:18. Let no man deceive himself. If any man among you seemeth to be wise in this world, let him become a fool, that he may be wise.

1 Cor. 8:3. But if any man love God, the same is known of him.

1 Cor. 13:11. When I was a child, I spake as a child, I understood as a child, I thought as a child : but when I became a man, I put away childish things.

1 Cor. 14:20. Brethren, be not children in understanding : howbeit in malice be ye children, but in understanding be men.

2 Cor. 2:11. Lest Satan should get an advantage of us : for we are not ignorant of his devices.

2 Cor. 8:7. Therefore, as ye abound in every *thing*, *in* faith, and utterance, and knowledge, and *in* all diligence, and *in* your love to us, *see* that ye abound in this grace also.

Gal. 4:9. But now, after that ye have known God, or rather are known of God, how turn ye again to the weak and beggarly elements, whereunto ye desire again to be in bondage ?

Eph. 4:11. And he gave some, apostles; and some, prophets ; and some, evangelists; and some, pastors and teachers; 12. For the perfecting of the saints, for the work of the ministry, for the edifying of the body of Christ : 13. Till we all come in the unity of the faith, and of the knowledge of the Son of God, unto a perfect man, unto the measure of the stature of the fulness of Christ :

Eph. 5:15. See then that ye walk circumspectly, not as fools, but as wise, 16. Redeeming the time, because the days are evil. 17. Wherefore be ye not unwise, but understanding what the will of the Lord *is*.

Phil. 3:7. But what things were gain to me, those I counted loss for Christ. 8. Yea doubtless, and I count all things *but* loss for the excellency of the knowledge of Christ Jesus my Lord : 10. That I may know him, and the power of his resurrection, and the fellowship of his sufferings, being made conformable unto his death ;

Col. 3:10. And have put on the new *man*, which is renewed in knowledge after the image of him that created him : 16. Let the word of Christ dwell in you richly in all wisdom ; teaching and admonishing one another in psalms and hymns and spiritual songs, singing with grace in your hearts to the Lord.

1 Thess. 5:4. Ye, brethren, are not in darkness, that that day should overtake you as a thief. 5. Ye are all the children of light, and the children of the day : we are not of the night, nor of darkness.

1 Tim. 2:4. Who will have all men to be saved, and to come unto the knowledge of the truth.

2 Tim. 3:15. And that from a child thou hast known the holy scriptures, which are able to make thee wise unto salvation through faith which is in Christ Jesus.

Jas. 3:13. Who *is* a wise man and endued with knowledge among you? let him shew out of a good conversation his works with meekness of wisdom.

1 John 4:6. We are of God. he that knoweth God heareth us; he that is not of God heareth not us. Hereby know we the spirit of truth, and the spirit of error.

See KNOWLEDGE; SPEAKING, WISDOM IN.

SPIRITUAL, FROM GOD: Ex. 4:11. And the LORD said unto him, Who hath made man's mouth? or who maketh the dumb, or deaf, or the seeing, or the blind? have not I the LORD? 12. Now therefore go, and I will be with thy mouth, and teach thee what thou shalt say.

Ex. 8:9. And Moses said unto Pharaoh, Glory over me: when shall I intreat for thee, and for thy servants, and for thy people, to destroy the frogs from thee and thy houses, *that* they may remain in the river only? 10. And he said, To morrow. And he said, *Be it* according to thy word: that thou mayest know that *there is* none like unto the LORD our God.

Deut. 4:5. Behold, I have taught you statutes and judgments, even as the LORD my God commanded me, that ye should do so in the land whither ye go to possess it. 6. Keep therefore and do *them;* for this *is* your wisdom and your understanding in the sight of the nations, which shall hear all these statutes, and say, Surely this great nation *is* a wise and understanding people. 35. Unto thee it was shewed, that thou mightest know that the LORD he *is* God; *there is* none else beside him. 36. Out of heaven he made thee to hear his voice, that he might instruct thee: and upon earth he shewed thee his great fire; and thou heardest his words out of the midst of the fire.

Deut. 29:4. Yet the LORD hath not given you an heart to perceive, and eyes to see, and ears to hear, unto this day.

1 Chr. 22:12. Only the LORD give thee wisdom and understanding, and give thee charge concerning Israel, that thou mayest keep the law of the LORD thy God.

Neh. 9:20. Thou gavest also thy good spirit to instruct them, and withheldest not thy manna from their mouth, and gavest them water for their thirst.

Job 4:3. Behold, thou hast instructed many, and thou hast strengthened the weak hands.

Job 11:5. But oh that God would speak, and open his lips against thee; 6. And that he would shew thee the secrets of wisdom, that *they are* double to that which is!

Job 22:21. Acquaint now thyself with him, and be at peace: thereby good shall come unto thee. 22. Receive, I pray thee,

the law from his mouth, and lay up his words in thine heart.

Job 32:7. I said, Days should speak, and multitude of years should teach wisdom. 8. But *there is* a spirit in man: and the inspiration of the Almighty giveth them understanding.

Job 33:16. Then he openeth the ears of men, and sealeth their instruction,

Job 35:10. But none saith, Where *is* God my maker, who giveth songs in the night; 11. Who teacheth us more than the beasts of the earth, and maketh us wiser than the fowls of heaven?

Job 36:22. Behold, God exalteth by his power: who teacheth like him?

Job 38:36. Who hath put wisdom in the inward parts? or who hath given understanding to the heart? 37. Who can number the clouds in wisdom? or who can stay the bottles of heaven,

Psa. 16:7. I will bless the LORD, who hath given me counsel: my reins also instruct me in the night seasons.

Psa. 19:1. The heavens declare the glory of God; and the firmament sheweth his handywork. 2. Day unto day uttereth speech, and night unto night sheweth knowledge.

Psa. 25:8. Good and upright *is* the LORD: therefore will he teach sinners in the way. 9. The meek will he guide in judgment: and the meek will he teach his way. 12. What man *is* he that feareth the LORD? him shall he teach in the way *that* he shall choose. 14. The secret of the LORD *is* with them that fear him; and he will shew them his covenant.

Psa. 32:8. I will instruct thee and teach thee in the way which thou shalt go: I will guide thee with mine eye.

Psa. 36:9. For with thee *is* the fountain of life: in thy light shall we see light.

Psa. 51:6. Behold, thou desirest truth in the inward parts: and in the hidden *part* thou shalt make me to know wisdom.

Psa. 71:17. O God, thou hast taught me from my youth: and hitherto have I declared thy wondrous works.

Psa. 94:12. Blessed *is* the man whom thou chastenest, O LORD, and teachest him out of thy law;

Psa. 112:4. Unto the upright there ariseth light in the darkness: *he is* gracious, and full of compassion, and righteous.

Psa. 119:130. The entrance of thy words giveth light; it giveth understanding unto the simple.

Prov. 1:23. Turn you at my reproof: behold, I will pour out my spirit unto you, I will make known my words unto you.

Prov. 2:6. For the LORD giveth wisdom: out of his mouth *cometh* knowledge and understanding. 7. He layeth up sound wisdom for the righteous: *he is* a buckler to them that walk uprightly.

Prov. 3:5. Trust in the LORD with all thine heart; and lean not unto thine own understanding. 6. In all thy ways acknowledge him, and he shall direct thy paths.

Eccl. 2:26. For *God* giveth to a man that *is* good in his sight wisdom, and knowledge, and joy:

Isa. 11:1. And there shall come forth a rod out of the stem of Jesse, and a Branch shall grow out of his roots: 2. And the spirit of the LORD shall rest upon him, the spirit of wisdom and understanding, the spirit of counsel and might, the spirit of knowledge and of the fear of the LORD; 3. And shall make him of quick understanding in the fear of the LORD: and he shall not judge after the sight of his eyes, neither reprove after the hearing of his ears:

Isa. 30:21. And thine ears shall hear a word behind thee, saying, This *is* the way, walk ye in it, when ye turn to the right hand, and when ye turn to the left.

Isa. 42:6. I the LORD have called thee in righteousness, and will hold thine hand, and will keep thee, and give thee for a covenant of the people, for a light of the Gentiles; 7. To open the blind eyes, to bring out the prisoners from the prison, *and* them that sit in darkness out of the prison house. 16. And I will bring the blind by a way *that* they knew not; I will lead them in paths *that* they have not known: I will make darkness light before them, and crooked things straight. These things will I do unto them, and not forsake them.

Isa. 48:17. Thus saith the LORD, thy Redeemer, the Holy One of Israel; I *am* the LORD thy God which teacheth thee to profit, which leadeth thee by the way *that* thou shouldest go.

Isa. 54:13. And all thy children *shall be* taught of the LORD; and great *shall be* the peace of thy children.

Jer. 24:7. And I will give them an heart to know me, that I *am* the LORD: and they shall be my people, and I will be their God: for they shall return unto me with their whole heart.

Dan. 1:17. As for these four children, God gave them knowledge and skill in all learning and wisdom: and Daniel had understanding in all visions and dreams.

Dan. 2:20. Daniel answered and said, Blessed be the name of God for ever and ever: for wisdom and might are his: 21. And he changeth the times and the seasons: he removeth kings, and setteth up kings: he giveth wisdom unto the wise, and knowledge to them that know understanding: 22. He revealeth the deep and secret things: he knoweth what *is* in the darkness, and the light dwelleth with him. 23. I thank thee, and praise thee, O thou God of my fathers, who hast given me wisdom and might, and hast made known unto me now what we desired of thee: for thou hast *now* made known unto us the king's matter.

Matt. 11:25. At that time Jesus answered and said, I thank thee, O Father, Lord of heaven and earth, because thou hast hid these things from the wise and prudent, and hast revealed them unto babes. 26. Even so, Father: for so it seemed good in thy sight. 27. All things are delivered unto me of my Father: and no man knoweth the Son, but the Father; neither knoweth any man the Father, save the Son, and *he* to whomsoever the Son will reveal *him*.

Matt. 13:11. He answered and said unto them, Because it is given unto you to know the mysteries of the kingdom of heaven, but to them it is not given.

Matt. 16:16. And Simon Peter answered and said, Thou art the Christ, the Son of the living God. 17. And Jesus answered and said unto him, Blessed art thou, Simon Barjona: for flesh and blood hath not revealed *it* unto thee, but my Father which is in heaven.

Luke 1:76. And thou, child, shalt be called the prophet of the Highest: for thou shalt go before the face of the Lord to prepare his ways; 77. To give knowledge of salvation unto his people by the remission of their sins, 78. Through the tender mercy of our God; whereby the dayspring from on high hath visited us. 79. To give light to them that sit in darkness and *in* the shadow of death, to guide our feet into the way of peace.

Luke 12:11. And when they bring you unto the synagogues, and *unto* magistrates, and powers, take ye no thought how or what thing ye shall answer, or what ye shall say: 12. For the Holy Ghost shall teach you in the same hour what ye ought to say.

Luke 21:15. I will give you a mouth and wisdom, which all your adversaries shall not be able to gainsay nor resist.

Luke 24:32. And they said one to another, Did not our heart burn within us, while he talked with us by the way, and while he opened to us the scriptures? 45. Then opened he their understanding, that they might understand the scriptures.

John 1:1. In the beginning was the Word, and the Word was with God, and the Word was God. 4. In him was life; and the life was the light of men. 5. And the light shineth in darkness; and the darkness comprehended it not. 7. The same came for a witness, to bear witness of the Light, that all *men* through him might believe. 8. He was not that Light, but *was sent* to bear witness of that Light. 9. *That* was the true Light, which lighteth every man that cometh into the world. 17. The law was given by Moses, *but* grace and truth came by Jesus Christ.

John 6:45. It is written in the prophets, And they shall be all taught of God. Every man therefore that hath heard.

and hath learned of the Father, cometh unto me.

John 8:12. Then spake Jesus again unto them, saying, I am the light of the world: he that followeth me shall not walk in darkness, but shall have the light of life. 31. Then said Jesus to those Jews which believed on him, If ye continue in my word, *then* are ye my disciples indeed; 32. And ye shall know the truth, and the truth shall make you free.

John 9:5. As long as I am in the world, I am the light of the world. 39. And Jesus said, For judgment I am come into this world, that they which see not might see; and that they which see might be made blind.

John 12:46. I am come a light into the world, that whosoever believeth on me should not abide in darkness.

John 14:7. If ye had known me, ye should have known my Father also: and from henceforth ye know him, and have seen him.

John 16:13. Howbeit when he, the Spirit of truth, is come, he will guide you into all truth: for he shall not speak of himself; but whatsoever he shall hear, *that* shall he speak: and he will shew you things to come. 14. He shall glorify me: for he shall receive of mine, and shall shew *it* unto you.

John 17:6. I have manifested thy name unto the men which thou gavest me out of the world: thine they were, and thou gavest them me; and they have kept thy word. 26. And I have declared unto them thy name, and will declare *it:* that the love wherewith thou hast loved me may be in them, and I in them.

John 18:37. To this end was I born, and for this cause came I into the world, that I should bear witness unto the truth. Every one that is of the truth heareth my voice.

Rom. 1:19. Because that which may be known of God is manifest in them; for God hath shewed *it* unto them. 20. For the invisible things of him from the creation of the world are clearly seen, being understood by the things that are made, *even* his eternal power and Godhead;

1 Cor. 1:30. But of him are ye in Christ Jesus, who of God is made unto us wisdom, and righteousness, and sanctification, and redemption;

1 Cor. 2:9. But as it is written, Eye hath not seen, nor ear heard, neither have entered into the heart of man, the things which God hath prepared for them that love him. 10. But God hath revealed *them* unto us by his Spirit: for the Spirit searcheth all things, yea, the deep things of God. 11. For what man knoweth the things of a man, save the spirit of man which is in him? even so the things of God knoweth no man, but the Spirit of God. 12. Now we have received, not the spirit of the world, but the spirit which is of God; that we might know the things that are freely given to us of God. 13. Which things also we speak, not in the words which man's wisdom teacheth, but which the Holy Ghost teacheth; comparing spiritual things with spiritual. 14. But the natural man receiveth not the things of the Spirit of God: for they are foolishness unto him: neither can he know *them,* because they are spiritually discerned.

1 Cor. 12:8. For to one is given by the Spirit the word of wisdom; to another the word of knowledge by the same Spirit;

2 Cor. 4:6. God, who commanded the light to shine out of darkness, hath shined in our hearts, to *give* the light of the knowledge of the glory of God in the face of Jesus Christ.

Phil. 3:15. Let us therefore, as many as be perfect, be thus minded: and if in any thing ye be otherwise minded, God shall reveal even this unto you.

Col. 1:26. *Even* the mystery which hath been hid from ages and from generations, but now is made manifest to his saints: 27. To whom God would make known what *is* the riches of the glory of this mystery among the Gentiles; which is Christ in you, the hope of glory: 28. Whom we preach, warning every man, and teaching every man in all wisdom;

2 Tim. 1:7. God hath not given us the spirit of fear; but of power, and of love, and of a sound mind.

Jas. 3:17. But the wisdom that is from above is first pure, then peaceable, gentle, *and* easy to be intreated, full of mercy and good fruits, without partiality, and without hypocrisy.

2 Pet. 1:2. Grace and peace be multiplied unto you through the knowledge of God, and of Jesus our Lord, 3. According as his divine power hath given unto us all things that *pertain* unto life and godliness, through the knowledge of him that hath called us to glory and virtue: 4. Whereby are given unto us exceeding great and precious promises: that by these ye might be partakers of the divine nature, having escaped the corruption that is in the world through lust. 5. And beside this, giving all diligence, add to your faith virtue; and to virtue knowledge; 8. If these things be in you, and abound, they make *you that ye shall* neither *be* barren nor unfruitful in the knowledge of our Lord Jesus Christ. 12. Wherefore I will not be negligent to put you always in remembrance of these things, though ye know *them,* and be established in the present truth.

2 Pet. 3:18. But grow in grace, and *in* the knowledge of our Lord and Saviour Jesus Christ.

1 John 2:20. But ye have an unction from the Holy One, and ye know all things. 27. The anointing which ye have received of him abideth in you, and ye need not that

any man teach you; but as the same anointing teacheth you of all things, and is truth, and is no lie, and even as it hath taught you, ye shall abide in him.

1 John 5:20. And we know that the Son of God is come, and hath given us an understanding, that we may know him that is true, and we are in him that is true, *even* in his Son Jesus Christ.

See GOD, WISDOM OF.

PRAYER FOR SPIRITUAL: Num. 27:21. And he shall stand before Eleazar the priest, who shall ask *counsel* for him after the judgment of Urim before the LORD: at his word shall they go out, and at his word they shall come in, *both* he, and all the children of Israel with him, even all the congregation.

Judg. 20:18. And the children of Israel arose, and went up to the house of God, and asked counsel of God,

1 Kin. 3:7. And now, O LORD my God, thou hast made thy servant king instead of David my father: and I *am but* a little child: I know not *how* to go out or come in. 9. Give therefore thy servant an understanding heart to judge thy people, that I may discern between good and bad: for who is able to judge this thy so great a people? 2 Chr. 1:10.

1 Kin. 8:36. Then hear thou in heaven, and forgive the sin of thy servants, and of thy people Israel, that thou teach them the good way wherein they should walk,

Job 34:32. *That which* I see not teach thou me: if I have done iniquity, I will do no more.

Psa. 5:8. Lead me, O LORD, in thy righteousness because of mine enemies; make thy ways straight before my face.

Psa. 25:4. Shew me thy ways, O LORD; teach me thy paths. 5. Lead me in thy truth, and teach me: for thou *art* the God of my salvation: on thee do I wait all the day.

Psa. 27:11. Teach me thy way, O LORD, and lead me in a plain path, because of mine enemies.

Psa. 31:3. For thou *art* my rock and my fortress: therefore for thy name's sake lead me, and guide me.

Psa. 39:4. LORD, make me to know mine end, and the measure of my days, what *it is; that* I may know how frail I *am.*

Psa. 43:3. O send out thy light and thy truth: let them lead me; let them bring me unto thy holy hill, and to thy tabernacles.

Psa. 86:11. Teach me thy way, O LORD; I will walk in thy truth: unite my heart to fear thy name.

Psa. 90:12. So teach *us* to number our days, that we may apply *our* hearts unto wisdom.

Psa. 119:12. Blessed *art* thou, O LORD: teach me thy statutes. 18. Open thou mine eyes, that I may behold wondrous things out of thy law. 19. I *am* a stranger in the earth: hide not thy commandments from me. 26. I have declared my ways, and

thou heardest me: teach me thy statutes. 27. Make me to understand the way of thy precepts: so shall I talk of thy wondrous works. 33. Teach me, O LORD, the way of thy statutes; and I shall keep it *unto* the end. 34. Give me understanding, and I shall keep thy law; yea, I shall observe it with *my* whole heart. 66. Teach me good judgment and knowledge: for I have believed thy commandments. 68. Thou *art* good, and doest good; teach me thy statutes. 73. Thy hands have made me and fashioned me: give me understanding, that I may learn thy commandments. 80. Let my heart be sound in thy statutes; that I be not ashamed. 124. Deal with thy servant according unto thy mercy, and teach me thy statutes. 125. I *am* thy servant; give me understanding, that I may know thy testimonies. 135. Make thy face to shine upon thy servant; and teach me thy statutes. 144. The righteousness of thy testimonies *is* everlasting: give me understanding, and I shall live. 169. Let my cry come near before thee, O LORD: give me understanding according to thy word. 171. My lips shall utter praise, when thou hast taught me thy statutes.

Psa. 139:24. And see if *there be any* wicked way in me, and lead me in the way everlasting.

Eph. 1:16. Making mention of you in my prayers; 17. That the God of our Lord Jesus Christ, the Father of glory, may give unto you the spirit of wisdom and revelation in the knowledge of him: 18. The eyes of your understanding being enlightened; that ye may know what is the hope of his calling, and what the riches of the glory of his inheritance in the saints, 19. And what *is* the exceeding greatness of his power to us-ward who believe, according to the working of his mighty power.

Eph. 3:14. For this cause I bow my knees unto the Father of our Lord Jesus Christ, 15. Of whom the whole family in heaven and earth is named, 16. That he would grant you, according to the riches of his glory, to be strengthened with might by his Spirit in the inner man; 17. That Christ may dwell in your hearts by faith; that ye, being rooted and grounded in love, 18. May be able to comprehend with all saints what *is* the breadth, and length, and depth, and height; 19. And to know the love of Christ, which passeth knowledge, that ye might be filled with all the fulness of God.

Eph. 6:18. Praying always with all prayer and supplication in the Spirit, and watching thereunto with all perseverance and supplication for all saints; 19. And for me, that utterance may be given unto me, that I may open my mouth boldly, to make known the mystery of the gospel, 20. For which I am an ambassador in bonds: that therein I may speak boldly, as I ought to speak.

Phil. 1:9. And this I pray, that your love

may abound yet more and more in knowledge and *in* all judgment; 10. That ye may approve things that are excellent; that ye may be sincere and without offence till the day of Christ;

Col. 1:9. For this cause we also, since the day we heard *it*, do not cease to pray for you, and to desire that ye might be filled with the knowledge of his will in all wisdom and spiritual understanding; 10. That ye might walk worthy of the Lord unto all pleasing, being fruitful in every good work, and increasing in the knowledge of God;

Col. 2:1. For I would that ye knew what great conflict I have for you, and *for* them at Laodicea, and *for* as many as have not seen my face in the flesh; 2. That their hearts might be comforted, being knit together in love, and unto all riches of the full assurance of understanding, to the acknowledgement of the mystery of God, and of the Father, and of Christ; 3. In whom are hid all the treasures of wisdom and knowledge.

Col. 4:2. Continue in prayer, and watch in the same with thanksgiving; 3. Withal praying also for us, that God would open unto us a door of utterance, to speak the mystery of Christ, for which I am also in bonds; 4. That I may make it manifest, as I ought to speak.

2 Tim. 2:7. Consider what I say; and the Lord give thee understanding in all things.

Jas. 1:5. If any of you lack wisdom, let him ask of God, that giveth to all *men* liberally, and upraideth not; and it shall be given him.

See DESIRE, SPIRITUAL.

WORLDLY: Gen. 3:6. And when the woman saw that the tree *was* good for food, and that it *was* pleasant to the eyes, and a tree to be desired to make *one* wise, she took of the fruit thereof, and did eat, and gave also unto her husband with her; and he did eat. 7. And the eyes of them both were opened, and they knew that they *were* naked; and they sewed fig leaves together, and made themselves aprons.

Job 4:18. Behold, he put no trust in his servants; and his angels he charged with folly: 19. How much less *in* them that dwell in houses of clay, whose foundation *is* in the dust, *which* are crushed before the moth? 20. They are destroyed from morning to evening: they perish for ever without any regarding *it*. 21. Doth not their excellency *which is* in them go away? they die, even without wisdom.

Job 5:13. He taketh the wise in their own craftiness: and the counsel of the froward is carried headlong.

Job 11:2. Should not the multitude of words be answered? and should a man full of talk be justified? 12. For vain man would be wise, though man be born *like* a wild ass's colt.

Job 37:24. Men do therefore fear him: he respecteth not any *that are* wise of heart.

Prov. 3:7. Be not wise in thine own eyes: fear the LORD, and depart from evil.

Prov. 15:21. Folly *is* joy to *him that is* destitute of wisdom: but a man of understanding walketh uprightly. 22. Without counsel purposes are disappointed: but in the multitude of counsellors they are established.

Prov. 16:25. There is a way that seemeth right unto a man, but the end thereof *are* the ways of death.

Prov. 17:2. A wise servant shall have rule over a son that causeth shame, and shall have part of the inheritance among the brethren. 10. A reproof entereth more into a wise man than an hundred stripes into a fool.

Prov. 18:1. Through desire a man, having separated himself, seeketh *and* intermeddleth with all wisdom.

Prov. 20:18. *Every* purpose is established by counsel: and with good advice make war.

Prov. 21:20. *There is* treasure to be desired and oil in the dwelling of the wise; but a foolish man spendeth it up. 22. A wise *man* scaleth the city of the mighty, and casteth down the strength of the confidence thereof. 30. *There is* no wisdom nor understanding nor counsel against the LORD.

Prov. 24:3. Through wisdom is an house builded; and by understanding it is established: 4. And by knowledge shall the chambers be filled with all precious and pleasant riches. 5. A wise man *is* strong; yea, a man of knowledge increaseth strength. 6. For by wise counsel thou shalt make thy war: and in multitude of counsellors *there is* safety. 7. Wisdom *is* too high for a fool: he openeth not his mouth in the gate.

Prov. 28:11. The rich man *is* wise in his own conceit; but the poor that hath understanding searcheth him out.

Eccl. 1:18. In much wisdom *is* much grief: and he that increaseth knowledge increaseth sorrow.

Eccl. 2:1. I said in mine heart, Go to now, I will prove thee with mirth; therefore enjoy pleasure: and, behold, this also *is* vanity. 2. I said of laughter, *It is* mad: and of mirth, What doeth it? 3. I sought in mine heart to give myself unto wine, yet acquainting mine heart with wisdom; and to lay hold on folly, till I might see what *was* that good for the sons of men, which they should do under the heaven all the days of their life. 4. I made me great works; I builded me houses; I planted me vineyards: 5. I made me gardens and orchards, and I planted trees in them of all *kind of* fruits: 6. I made me pools of water, to water therewith the wood that bringeth forth trees: 7. I got *me* servants and maidens, and had servants born in my house; also I had great possessions of great and small cattle above all that were in Jerusalem before me: 8. I gathered me also silver and gold, and the peculiar treasure of kings and of the provinces: I gat me men singers and women singers, and the delights of the sons of men, *as* musical instruments, and that of all sorts. 9. So I was great, and increased more than all that were before me in Jerusalem: also my wisdom remained with me. 10. And whatsoever mine eyes desired I kept not from them, I withheld not my heart from any joy; for my heart rejoiced in all my labour: and this was my portion of all my labour. 11. Then I looked on all the works that my hands had wrought, and on the labour that I had laboured to do: and, behold, all *was* vanity and vexation of spirit, and *there was* no profit under the sun. 12. And I turned myself to behold wisdom, and madness, and folly: for what *can* the man *do* that cometh after the king? *even* that which hath been already done. 13. Then I saw that wisdom excelleth folly, as far as light excelleth darkness. 14. The wise man's eyes *are* in his head; but the fool walketh in darkness: and I myself perceived also that one event happeneth to them all. 15. Then said I in my heart, As it happeneth to the fool, so it happeneth even to me; and why was I then more wise? Then I said in my heart, that this also *is* vanity. 16. For *there is* no remembrance of the wise more than of the fool for ever; seeing that which now *is* in the days to come shall all be forgotten. And how dieth the wise *man?* as the fool. 17. Therefore I hated life; because the work that is wrought under the sun *is* grievous unto me: for all *is* vanity and vexation of spirit. 18. Yea, I hated all my labour which I had taken under the sun: because I should leave it unto the man that shall be after me. 19. And who knoweth whether he shall be a wise *man* or a fool? yet shall he have rule over all my labour wherein I have laboured, and wherein I have shewed myself wise under the sun. This *is* also vanity. 20. Therefore I went about to cause my heart to despair of all the labour which I took under the sun. 21. For there *is* a man whose labour *is* in wisdom, and in knowledge, and in equity; yet to a man that hath not laboured therein shall he leave it *for* his portion. This also *is* vanity and a great evil. 22. For what hath man of all his labour, and of the vexation of his heart, wherein he hath laboured under the sun? 23. For all his days *are* sorrows, and his travail grief; yea, his heart taketh not rest in the night. This is also vanity. 24. *There is* nothing better for a man, *than* that he should eat and drink, and *that* he should make his soul enjoy good in his labour. This also I saw, that it *was* from the hand of God. 25. For who can eat, or who else

can hasten *hereunto*, more than I? 26. For *God* giveth to a man that *is* good in his sight wisdom, and knowledge, and joy: but to the sinner he giveth travail, to gather and to heap up, that he may give to *him that is* good before God. This also *is* vanity and vexation of spirit.

Eccl. 7:11. Wisdom *is* good with an inheritance: and *by it there is* profit to them that see the sun. 12. For wisdom *is* a defence, *and* money *is* a defence; but the excellency of knowledge *is, that* wisdom giveth life to them that have it. 13. Consider the work of God: for who can make *that* straight, which he hath made crooked? 16. Be not righteous over much; neither make thyself over wise: why shouldest thou destroy thyself? 17. Be not over much wicked, neither be thou foolish: why shouldest thou die before thy time? 18. *It is* good that thou shouldest take hold of this; yea, also from this withdraw not thine hand: for he that feareth God shall come forth of them all. 19. Wisdom strengtheneth the wise more than ten mighty *men* which are in the city. 20. For *there is* not a just man upon earth, that doeth good, and sinneth not. 21. Also take no heed unto all words that are spoken; lest thou hear thy servant curse thee: 22. For oftentimes also thine own heart knoweth that thou thyself likewise hast cursed others. 23. All this have I proved by wisdom: I said, I will be wise; but it *was* far from me. 24. That which is far off, and exceeding deep, who can find it out? 25. I applied mine heart to know, and to search, and to seek out wisdom, and the reason *of things*, and to know the wickedness of folly, even of foolishness *and* madness:

Eccl. 8:1. Who *is* as the wise *man?* and who knoweth the interpretation of a thing? a man's wisdom maketh his face to shine, and the boldness of his face shall be changed. 16. When I applied mine heart to know wisdom, and to see the business that is done upon the earth: (for also *there is that* neither day nor night seeth sleep with his eyes:) 17. Then I beheld all the work of God, that a man cannot find out the work that is done under the sun: because though a man labour to seek *it* out, yet he shall not find *it;* yea farther; though a wise *man* think to know *it*, yet shall he not be able to find *it*.

Eccl. 10:2. A wise man's heart *is* at his right hand; but a fool's heart at his left. 3. Yea also, when he that is a fool walketh by the way, his wisdom faileth *him*, and he saith to every one *that* he *is* a fool. 10. If the iron be blunt, and he do not whet the edge, then must he put to more strength: but wisdom *is* profitable to direct.

Isa. 5:21. Woe unto *them that are* wise in their own eyes, and prudent in their own sight!

Isa. 28:24. Doth the plowman plow all day

to sow? doth he open and break the clods of his ground? 25. When he hath made plain the face thereof, doth he not cast abroad the fitches, and scatter the cummin, and cast in the principal wheat and the appointed barley and the rie in their place? 26. For his God doth instruct him to discretion, *and* doth teach him. 27. For the fitches are not threshed with a threshing instrument, neither is a cart wheel turned about upon the cummin; but the fitches are beaten out with a staff, and the cummin with a rod. 28. Bread *corn* is bruised; because he will not ever be threshing it, nor break it *with* the wheel of his cart, nor bruise it *with* his horsemen. 29. This also cometh forth from the LORD of hosts, *which* is wonderful in counsel, *and* excellent in working.

Isa. 29:14. Therefore, behold, I will proceed to do a marvellous work among this people, *even* a marvellous work and a wonder: for the wisdom of their wise *men* shall perish, and the understanding of their prudent *men* shall be hid. 15. Woe unto them that seek deep to hide their counsel from the LORD and their works are in the dark, and they say, Who seeth us? and who knoweth us? 16. Surely your turning of things upside down shall be esteemed as the potter's clay: for shall the work say of him that made it, He made me not? or shall the thing framed say of him that framed it, He had no understanding?

Isa. 47:10. For thou hast trusted in thy wickedness: thou hast said, None seeth me. Thy wisdom and thy knowledge, it hath perverted thee; and thou hast said in thine heart, I *am*, and none else beside me. 11. Therefore shall evil come upon thee;

Jer. 8:7. Yea, the stork in the heaven knoweth her appointed times; and the turtle and the crane and the swallow observe the time of their coming; but my people know not the judgment of the LORD. 8. How do ye say, We *are* wise, and the law of the LORD *is* with us? Lo, certainly in vain made he *it;* the pen of the scribes *is* in vain. 9. The wise *men* are ashamed, they are dismayed and taken: lo, they have rejected the word of the LORD; and what wisdom *is* in them?

Jer. 9:23. Thus saith the LORD, Let not the wise *man* glory in his wisdom, neither let the mighty *man* glory in his might, let not the rich *man* glory in his riches: 24. But let him that glorieth glory in this, that he understandeth and knoweth me, that I *am* the LORD which exercise lovingkindness, judgment, and righteousness, in the earth: for in these *things* I delight, saith the LORD.

Jer. 49:7. Concerning Edom, thus saith the LORD of hosts; *Is* wisdom no more in Teman? is counsel perished from the prudent? is their wisdom vanished!

Matt. 6:23. But if thine eye be evil, thy whole body shall be full of darkness. If therefore the light that is in thee be darkness, how great *is* that darkness!

Matt. 7:24. Therefore whosoever heareth these sayings of mine, and doeth them, I will liken him unto a wise man, which built his house upon a rock: 25. And the rain descended, and the floods came, and the winds blew, and beat upon that house; and it fell not: for it was founded upon a rock. 26. And every one that heareth these sayings of mine, and doeth them not, shall be likened unto a foolish man, which built his house upon the sand: 27. And the rain descended, and the floods came, and the winds blew, and beat upon that house; and it fell: and great was the fall of it.

Matt. 11:25. At that time Jesus answered and said, I thank thee. O Father, Lord of heaven and earth, because thou hast hid these things from the wise and prudent, and hast revealed them unto babes. Luke 10:21.

Luke 16:8. And the lord commended the unjust steward, because he had done wisely: for the children of this world are in their generation wiser than the children of light.

Rom. 1:21. Because that, when they knew God, they glorified *him* not as God, neither were thankful; but became vain in their imaginations, and their foolish heart was darkened. 22. Professing themselves to be wise, they became fools, 23. And changed the glory of the uncorruptible God into an image made like to corruptible man, and to birds, and fourfooted beasts, and creeping things.

1 Cor. 1:17. For Christ sent me not to baptize, but to preach the gospel: not with wisdom of words, lest the cross of Christ should be made of none effect. 18. For the preaching of the cross is to them that perish foolishness; but unto us which are saved it is the power of God. 19. For it is written, I will destroy the wisdom of the wise, and will bring to nothing the understanding of the prudent. 20. Where *is* the wise? where *is* the scribe? where *is* the disputer of this world? hath not God made foolish the wisdom of this world? 21. For after that in the wisdom of God the world by wisdom knew not God, it pleased God by the foolishness of preaching to save them that believe. 22. For the Jews require a sign, and the Greeks seek after wisdom: 23. But we preach Christ crucified, unto the Jews a stumblingblock, and unto the Greeks foolishness; 24. But unto them which are called, both Jews and Greeks, Christ the power of God, and the wisdom of God. 25. Because the foolishness of God is wiser than men; and the weakness of God is stronger than men. 26. For ye see your calling, brethren, how that not many wise men after the flesh, not many mighty, not many noble, *are called:*

1 Cor. 2:1. And I, brethren, when I came

to you, came not with excellency of speech or of wisdom, declaring unto you the testimony of God. 2. For I determined not to know any thing among you, save Jesus Christ, and him crucified. 3. And I was with you in weakness, and in fear, and in much trembling. 4. And my speech and my preaching *was* not with enticing words of man's wisdom, but in demonstration of the Spirit and of power: 5. That your faith should not stand in the wisdom of men, but in the power of God. 6. Howbeit we speak wisdom among them that are perfect: yet not the wisdom of this world, nor of the princes of this world, that come to nought: 7. But we speak the wisdom of God in a mystery, *even* the hidden *wisdom*, which God ordained before the world unto our glory: 8. Which none of the princes of this world knew: for had they known *it*, they would not have crucified the Lord of glory. 9. But as it is written, Eye hath not seen, nor ear heard, neither have entered into the heart of man, the things which God hath prepared for them that love him. 10. But God hath revealed *them* unto us by his Spirit: for the Spirit searcheth all things, yea, the deep things of God. 11. For what man knoweth the things of a man, save the spirit of man which is in him? even so the things of God knoweth no man, but the Spirit of God. 12. Now we have received, not the spirit of the world, but the spirit which is of God; that we might know the things that are freely given to us of God. 13. Which things also we speak, not in the words which man's wisdom teacheth, but which the Holy Ghost teacheth; comparing spiritual things with spiritual. 14. But the natural man receiveth not the things of the Spirit of God: for they are foolishness unto him: neither can he know *them*, because they are spiritually designed.

1 Cor. 3:18. Let no man deceive himself. If any man among you seemeth to be wise in this world, let him become a fool, that he may be wise. 19. For the wisdom of this world is foolishness with God. For it is written, He taketh the wise in their own craftiness. 20. And again, The Lord knoweth the thoughts of the wise, that they are vain.

1 Cor. 8:1. Knowledge puffeth up, but charity edifieth. 2. And if any man think that he knoweth any thing, he knoweth nothing yet as he ought to know.

2 Cor. 1:12. For our rejoicing is this, the testimony of our conscience, that in simplicity and godly sincerity, not with fleshly wisdom, but by the grace of God, we have had our conversation in the world, and more abundantly to you-ward.

Col. 2:8. Beware lest any man spoil you through philosophy and vain deceit, after the tradition of men, after the rudiments of the world, and not after Christ.

1 Tim. 6:20. O Timothy, keep that which is committed to thy trust, avoiding pro-

fane *and* vain babblings, and oppositions of science falsely so called: 21. Which some professing have erred concerning the faith.

See KNOWLEDGE.

WISE MEN. Of Egypt, Gen. 41:8,24; Ex. 7:11. Solomon, 1 Kin. 4:29–34. Of Babylon, Dan. 4:18; 5:8. Of the East, Matt. 2:1–12.

See WISDOM.

WITCHCRAFT. Law concerning, Ex. 22:18; Lev. 19:31; 20:6,27. Witch of Endor, 1 Sam. 28:7–25. Witches destroyed, 1 Sam. 28:3,9.

See SORCERY.

WITNESS, Lev. 5:1; Prov. 18:17. Qualified by oath, Ex. 22:11; Num. 5:19,21; 1 Kin. 8:31,32; by laying hands on the accused, Lev. 24:14. Two necessary to establish a fact, Num. 35:30; Deut. 17:6; 19:15; Matt. 18:16; John 8:17; 2 Cor. 13:1; 1 Tim. 5:19; Heb. 10:28. Required to cast the first stone in executing sentence, Deut. 13:9; 17:5–7; Acts 7:58.

To the transfer of land, Gen. 21:25–30; 23:11,16–18; Ruth 4:1–9; Jer. 32:9–12,25,44. To marriage, Ruth 4:10,11; Isa. 8:2,3. Incorruptible, Psa. 15:4. Corrupted by money, Matt. 28:11–15; Acts 6:11,13.

FIGURATIVE: Of instruction in righteousness, Rev. 11:3.

See COURTS; EVIDENCE; FALSEHOOD; FALSE WITNESS; HOLY SPIRIT; TESTIMONY; TESTIMONY, RELIGIOUS.

WIZARD. See SORCERY.

WOLF, ravenous, Gen. 49:27; Jer. 5:6; Ezek. 22:27; Zeph. 3:3; John 10:12.

FIGURATIVE: Of the enemies of the righteous, Matt. 7:15; 10:16; John 10:12; Acts 20:29. Of the reconciling power of the gospel, Isa. 11:6.

WOMEN. Creation of, Gen. 1:27; 2:21,22. Named, Gen. 2:23. Fall of, and curse upon, Gen. 3:1–16; 2 Cor. 11:3; 1 Tim. 2:14. Promise to, Gen. 3:15.

Had separate apartments in dwellings, Gen. 24:67; 31:33; Esth. 2:9,11. Veiled the face, Gen. 24:65; see VAIL.

Vows of, Num. 30:3–16. When jealously charged with infidelity, guilt or innocence to be determined by trial, Num. 5:12–31.

Took part in ancient worship, Ex. 15:20, 21; 38:8; 1 Sam. 2:22; in choir, 1 Chr. 25:5,6; Ezra 2:65; Neh. 7:67. Worshiped in separate compartments, Ex. 38:8; 1 Sam. 2:22. Consecrated jewels to tabernacle, Ex. 35:22; mirrors, Ex. 38:8. Required to attend reading of the law, Deut. 31:12; Josh 8:35.

Purifications of: After menstruation, Lev. 15:19–33; 2 Sam. 11:4; childbirth, Lev. 12; Luke 2:22. Difference in ceremonies made between male and female children, Lev. 12.

Religious privileges of, among early Christians, Acts 1:14; 12:12,13; 1 Cor. 11:5; 14:34; 1 Tim. 2:11.

Domestic duties of, Gen. 18:6; Prov. 31:15–19; Matt. 24:41. Cooked, Gen. 18:6; spun, Ex. 35:25,26; 1 Sam. 2:19; Prov. 31:19–24; embroidered, Prov. 31:22. Made garments,

Acts 9:39. Gleaned, Ruth 2:8. Kept vine-yards, Song 1:6. Tended flocks and herds, Gen. 24:11,13,14,19,20; 29:9; Ex. 2:16. Worked in fields. Isa. 27:11; Ezek. 26:6,8. Was doorkeeper, Matt. 26:69; John 18:16,17; Acts 12:13,14.

Forbidden to wear men's costume, Deut. 22:5. Wore hair long, 1 Cor. 11:5-15. Rules for dress of Christian, 1 Tim. 2:9,10; 1 Pet. 3:3,4. Ornaments of, Isa. 3:16-23.

Weaker than men, 1 Pet. 3:7. Are timid, Isa. 19:16; Jer. 50:37; 51:30; Nah. 3:13; affectionate, 2 Sam. 1:26; tender to her offspring, Isa. 49:15; Lam. 4:10; mirthsome, Judg. 11:34; 21:21; Jer. 31:13; Zech. 9:17; courteous to strangers, Gen. 24:17. Could not marry without consent of parents, Gen. 24:3,4; 34:6; Ex. 22:17. Not to be given in marriage considered a calamity, Judg. 11:37; Psa. 78:63; Isa. 4:1. Taken captive, Num. 31:9,15,17,18,35; Lam. 1:18; Ezek. 30:17,18. Shrewd, 2 Sam. 20:16-22.

Punishment to be inflicted on men for seducing, when betrothed, Deut. 22:23-27. Punishment for seducing, when not betrothed, Ex. 22:16,17; Deut. 22:28,29. Treated with cruelty in war, Deut. 32:25; Lam. 2:21; 5:11.

Virtuous, held in high estimation, Ruth 3:11; Prov. 31:10-30.

Fond of self-indulgence, Isa. 32:9-11; of ornaments, Jer. 2:32. Subtle and deceitful, Prov. 6:24-29,32-35; 7:6-27; Eccl. 7:26. Silly, and easily led into error, 2 Tim. 3:6. Zealous in promoting superstition and idolatry, Jer. 7:18; Ezek. 13:17,23. Active in instigating iniquity, Num. 31:15,16; 1 Kin. 21:25; Neh. 13:26. Guilty of sodomy, 2 Kin. 23:7; Rom. 1:26.

As rulers, Isa. 3:12; Deborah, Judg. 4:4; Athaliah, 2 Kin. 11:1-16; 2 Chr. 22:2,3,10-12; Queen of Sheba, 1 Kin. 10:1-13; Candace, Acts 8:27; Persian queen sat on throne with the king, Neh. 2:6. Patriotic: Miriam, Ex. 15:20; Deborah, Judg. 5; women of Israel, 1 Sam. 18:6; of the Philistines, 2 Sam. 1:20. Aid in defensive operations, Judg. 9:53.

As poets: Miriam, Ex. 15:21; Deborah, Judg. 5; Hannah, 1 Sam. 2:1-10; Elisabeth, Luke 1:42-45; Mary, Luke 1:46-55.

As prophets: Miriam, Ex. 15:20,21; Mic. 6:4; Deborah, Judg. 4:4,5; Huldah, 2 Kin. 22:14-20; 2 Chr. 34:22-28; Noadiah, Neh. 6:14; Anna, Luke 2:36-38; Philip's daughters, Acts 21:9. False prophets, Ezek. 13:17-23.

In business, Prov. 31:14-18,24. Property rights of: In inheritance, Num. 27:1-11; 36; Josh. 17:3-6; Job 42:15; to sell real estate, Ruth 4:3-9.

Sold for husband's debts, Matt. 18:25.

First to sin, Gen. 3:6. Last at the cross, Matt. 27:55,56; Mark 15:40,41. First at the sepulcher, Mark 15:46,47; 16:1-6; Luke 23:27,28,49,55,56; 24:1-10. First to whom the risen Lord appeared, Mark 16:9; John 20:14-18.

Converted by preaching of Paul, Acts 16:14,15; 17:4,12,34.

Social status of: In Persia, Esth. 1:10-22; Dan. 5:1-12; in Roman customs, Acts 24:24; 25:13,23; 26:30.

UNCLASSIFIED SCRIPTURES RELATING TO: Gen 2:18. And the LORD God said, It is not good that the man should be alone; I will make him an help meet for him. 21. And the LORD God caused a deep sleep to fall upon Adam, and he slept: and he took one of his ribs, and closed up the flesh instead thereof; 22. And the rib, which the LORD God had taken from man, made he a woman, and brought her unto the man. 23. And Adam said, This is now bone of my bones, and flesh of my flesh: she shall be called Woman, because she was taken out of Man. 24. Therefore shall a man leave his father and his mother, and shall cleave unto his wife: and they shall be one flesh.

Gen. 3:16. Unto the woman he said, I will greatly multiply thy sorrow and thy conception; in sorrow thou shalt bring forth children; and thy desire shall be to thy husband, and he shall rule over thee.

Esth. 1:20. And when the king's decree which he shall make shall be published throughout all his empire, (for it is great,) all the wives shall give to their husbands honour, both to great and small. 21. And the king did according to the word of Memucan: 22. For he sent letters into all the king's provinces, into every province . . . and to every people after their language, that every man should bear rule in his own house,

Psa. 68:11. The Lord gave the word: [1] great was the company of those that published it.

[1 R. V. the women that publish the tidings are a great host]

Prov. 11:16. A gracious woman retaineth honour: 22. As a jewel of gold in a swine's snout, so is a fair woman which is without discretion.

Prov. 12:4. A virtuous woman is a crown to her husband: but she that maketh ashamed is as rottenness in his bones.

Prov. 14:1. Every wise woman buildeth her house: but the foolish plucketh it down with her hands.

Prov. 18:22. Whoso findeth a wife findeth a good thing, and obtaineth favour of the LORD.

Prov. 19:13. The contentions of a wife are a continual dropping. 14. House and riches are the inheritance of fathers: and a prudent wife is from the LORD.

Prov. 21:9. It is better to dwell in a corner of the housetop, than with a brawling woman in a wide house. 19. It is better to dwell in the wilderness, than with a contentious and an angry woman. Prov. 25:24.

Prov. 27:15. A continual dropping in a very rainy day and a contentious woman are alike. 16. Whosoever hideth her hideth the wind, and the ointment of his right hand, which bewrayeth itself.

Prov. 30:21. For three things the earth is

disquieted, and for four *which* it cannot bear: 22. For a servant when he reigneth; and a fool when he is filled with meat; 23. For an odious *woman* when she is married; and an handmaid that is heir to her mistress.

Prov. 31:10. Who can find a virtuous woman? for her price *is* far above rubies. 11. The heart of her husband doth safely trust in her, so that he shall have no need of spoil. 12. She will do him good and not evil all the days of her life. 13. She seeketh wool, and flax, and worketh willingly with her hands. 14. She is like the merchants' ships; she bringeth her food from afar. 15. She riseth also while it is yet night, and giveth meat to her household, and a portion to her maidens. 16. She considereth a field, and buyeth it: with the fruit of her hands she planteth a vineyard. 17. She girdeth her loins with strength, and strengtheneth her arms. 18. She perceiveth that her merchandise *is* good: her candle goeth not out by night. 19. She layeth her hands to the spindle, and her hands hold the distaff. 20. She stretcheth out her hand to the poor; yea, she reacheth forth her hands to the needy. 21. She is not afraid of the snow for her household: for all her household *are* clothed with scarlet. 22. She maketh herself coverings of tapestry; her clothing *is* silk and purple. 23. Her husband is known in the gates, when he sitteth among the elders of the land. 24. She maketh fine linen, and selleth *it;* and delivereth girdles unto the merchant. 25. Strength and honour *are* her clothing; and she shall rejoice in time to come. 26. She openeth her mouth with wisdom; and in her tongue *is* the law of kindness. 27. She looketh well to the ways of her household, and eateth not the bread of idleness. 28. Her children arise up, and call her blessed; her husband *also*, and he praiseth her. 29. Many daughters have done virtuously, but thou excellest them all. 30. Favour *is* deceitful, and beauty *is* vain: *but* a woman *that* feareth the LORD, she shall be praised. 31. Give her of the fruit of her hands; and let her own works praise her in the gates.

Eccl. 7:26. And I find more bitter than death the woman, whose heart *is* snares and nets, *and* her hands *as* bands: whoso pleaseth God shall escape from her; but the sinner shall be taken by her. 27. Behold, this have I found, saith the preacher, *counting* one by one, to find out the account: 28. Which yet my soul seeketh, but I find not: one man among a thousand have I found; but a woman among all those have I not found.

Isa. 3:16. Moreover the LORD saith, Because the daughters of Zion are haughty, and walk with stretched forth necks and wanton eyes, walking and mincing *as* they go, and making a tinkling with their feet: 17. Therefore the Lord will smite with a scab the crown of the head of the daughters

of Zion, and the LORD will discover their secret parts. 18. In that day the Lord will take away the bravery of *their* tinkling ornaments *about their feet*, and *their* cauls, and *their* round tires like the moon. 19. The chains, and the bracelets, and the mufflers, 20. The bonnets, and the ornaments of the legs, and the headbands, and the tablets, and the earrings, 21. The rings, and nose jewels, 22. The changeable suits of apparel, and the mantles, and the wimples, and the crisping pins, 23. The glasses, and the fine linen, and the hoods, and the vails. 24. And it shall come to pass, *that* instead of sweet smell there shall be stink; and instead of a girdle a rent; and instead of well set hair baldness; and instead of a stomacher a girding of sackcloth; *and* burning instead of beauty.

Isa. 32:9. Rise up, ye women that are at ease; hear my voice, ye careless daughters; give ear unto my speech. 10. Many days and years shall ye be troubled, ye careless women: for the vintage shall fail, the gathering shall not come. 11. Tremble, ye women that are at ease; be troubled, ye careless ones: strip you, and make you bare, and gird *sackcloth* upon *your* loins. 12. They shall lament for the teats, for the pleasant fields, for the fruitful vine.

Ezek. 13:17. Likewise, thou son of man, set thy face against the daughters of thy people, which prophesy out of their own heart; and prophesy thou against them. 18. And say, Thus saith the Lord GOD; Woe to the *women* that sew pillows to all armholes, and make kerchiefs upon the head of every stature to hunt souls! Will ye hunt the souls of my people, and will ye save the souls alive *that come* unto you? 19. And will ye pollute me among my people for handfuls of barley and for pieces of bread, to slay the souls that should not die, and to save the souls alive that should not live, by your lying to my people that hear *your* lies? 20. Wherefore thus saith the Lord GOD; Behold, I *am* against your pillows, wherewith ye there hunt the souls to make *them* fly, and I will tear them from your arms, and will let the souls go, *even* the souls that ye hunt to make *them* fly. 21. Your kerchiefs also will I tear, and deliver my people out of your hand, and they shall be no more in your hand to be hunted; and ye shall know that I *am* the LORD. 22. Because with lies ye have made the heart of the righteous sad, whom I have not made sad; and strengthened the hands of the wicked, that he should not return from his wicked way, by promising him life: 23. Therefore ye shall see no more vanity, nor divine divinations: for I will deliver my people out of your hand: and ye shall know that I *am* the LORD.

1 Cor. 11:3. But I would have you know, that the head of every man is Christ; and the head of the woman *is* the man; and the head of Christ *is* God. 4. Every man pray-

ing or prophesying, having *his* head covered, dishonoureth his head. 5. But every woman that prayeth or prophesieth with *her* head uncovered dishonoureth her head : for that is even all one as if she were shaven. 6. For if the woman be not covered, let her also be shorn : but if it be a shame for a woman to be shorn or shaven, let her be covered. 7. For a man indeed ought not to cover *his* head, forasmuch as he is the image and glory of God : but the woman is the glory of the man. 8. For the man is not of the woman ; but the woman of the man. 9. Neither was the man created for the woman ; but the woman for the man. 10. For this cause ought the woman to have power on *her* head because of the angels. 11. Nevertheless neither is the man without the woman, neither the woman without the man, in the Lord. 12. For as the woman *is* of the man, even so *is* the man also by the woman ; but all things of God. 13. Judge in yourselves : is it comely that a woman pray unto God uncovered ? 14. Doth not even nature itself teach you, that, if a man have long hair, it is a shame unto him ? 15. But if a woman have long hair, it is a glory to her : for *her* hair is given her for a covering.

1 Cor. 14:34. Let your women keep silence in the churches : for it is not permitted unto them to speak ; but *they are commanded* to be under obedience, as also saith the law. 35. And if they will learn any thing, let them ask their husbands at home : for it is a shame for women to speak in the church.

1 Tim. 2:9. In like manner also, that women adorn themselves in modest apparel, with shamefacedness and sobriety ; not with broided hair, or gold, or pearls, or costly array ; 10. But (which becometh women professing godliness) with good works. 11. Let the woman learn in silence with all subjection. 12. But I suffer not a woman to teach, nor to usurp authority over the man, but to be in silence. 13. For Adam was first formed, then Eve. 14. And Adam was not deceived, but the woman being deceived was in the transgression. 15. Notwithstanding she shall be saved in childbearing, if they continue in faith and charity and holiness with sobriety. Psa. 68:11, *R. V.*

1 Tim. 3:11. Even so *must their* wives *be* grave, not slanderous, sober, faithful in all things.

1 Tim. 5:1. Rebuke not an elder, but intreat *him* as a father ; *and* the younger men as brethren ; 2. The elder women as mothers ; the younger as sisters, with all purity. 3. Honour widows that are widows indeed. 4. But if any widow have children or nephews, let them learn first to show piety at home, and to requite their parents : for that is good and acceptable before God. 5. Now she that is a widow indeed, and desolate, trusteth in God, and continueth in supplications and prayers night and day. 6. But she that liveth in pleasure is dead while she

liveth. 7. And these things give in charge, that they may be blameless. 8. But if any provide not for his own, and specially for those of his own house, he hath denied the faith, and is worse than an infidel. 9. Let not a widow be taken into the number under threescore years old, having been the wife of one man, 10. Well reported of for good works ; if she have brought up children, if she have lodged strangers, if she have washed the saints' feet, if she have relieved the afflicted, if she have diligently followed every good work. 11. But the younger widows refuse : for when they have begun to wax wanton against Christ, they will marry ; 12. Having damnation, because they have cast off their first faith. 13. And withal they learn *to be* idle, wandering about from house to house ; and not only idle, but tattlers also and busybodies, speaking things which they ought not. 14. I will therefore that the younger women marry, bear children, guide the house, give none occasion to the adversary to speak reproachfully. 15. For some are already turned aside after Satan. 16. If any man or woman that believeth have widows, let them relieve them, and let not the church be charged ; that it may relieve them that are widows indeed.

2 Tim. 3:6. For of this sort are they which creep into houses, and lead captive silly women laden with sins, led away with divers lusts, 7. Ever learning, and never able to come to the knowledge of the truth.

Tit. 2:3. The aged women likewise, that *they be* in behaviour as becometh holiness, not false accusers, not given to much wine, teachers of good things ; 4. That they may teach the young women to be sober, to love their husbands, to love their children, 5. *To be* discreet, chaste, keepers at home, good, obedient to their own husbands, that the word of God be not blasphemed.

See WIDOW ; WIFE.

See also HUSBANDS ; PARENTS.

GOOD : INSTANCES OF : Deborah, a judge, prophetess, and military leader, Judg. 4; 5. Mother of Samson, Judg. 13:23. Naomi, Ruth 1; 2; 3:1. Ruth, Ruth 1:4,14–22, and chapters 2–4. Hannah, the mother of Samuel, 1 Sam. 1:9–18,24–28. Widow of Zarephath, who fed Elijah during the famine, 1 Kin. 17:8–24. The Shunammite, who gave hospitality to Elisha, 2 Kin. 4:8–38. Vashti, Esth. 1:11,12. Esther, Esth. 4:15–17. Mary, Luke 1:26–38. Elisabeth, Luke 1:6,41–45. Anna, Luke 2:37. The widow who cast her mite into the treasury, Mark 12:41–44; Luke 21:2–4. Mary and Martha, Mark 14:3–9; Luke 10:42; John 11:5. Mary Magdalene, Mark 16:1; Luke 8:2; John 20:1, 2,11–16. Pilate's wife, Matt. 27:19. Dorcas, Acts 9:36. Lydia, Acts 16:14. Priscilla, Acts 18:26. Phebe, Rom. 16:1,2. Julia, Rom. 16:15. Mary, Rom. 16:6. Lois and Eunice, 2 Tim. 1:5. Philippians, Phil. 4:3.

FIGURATIVE : Of the church of Christ,

Psa. 45:2-15; Gal. 4:26; Rev. 12:1. Of saints, Matt. 25:1-4; 2 Cor. 11:2; Rev. 14:4.

WICKED: 2 Kin. 9:30-37; 23:7; Jer. 44:15-19,25; Ezek. 8:14; Rom. 1:26. Zeal of, in licentious practices of idolatry, 2 Kin. 23:7; Hos. 4:13,14. Guileful and licentious, Prov. 2:16-19; 5:3-20; 6:24-29,32-35; 7:6-27; Eccl. 7:26; Ezek. 16:32. Commits forgery, 1 Kin. 21:8. Silly and wayward, 2 Tim. 3:6.

INSTANCES OF: Eve, in yielding to temptation and seducing her husband, Gen. 3:6; 1 Tim. 2:14. Sarah, in her jealousy and malice toward Hagar, Gen. 21:9-11, with vs. 12-21. Lot's wife, in her rebellion against her situation, and against the destruction of Sodom, Gen. 19:26; Luke 17:32. The daughters of Lot, in their incestuous lust, Gen. 19:31-38. Rebekah, in her partiality for Jacob, and her sharp practice to secure for him Isaac's blessing, Gen. 27:11-17. Rachel, in her jealousy of Leah, Gen. 30:1; in stealing images, 31:19,34. Leah, in her imitation of Rachel in the matter of children, Gen. 30:9-18. Dinah, in her fornication, Gen. 34:1,2. Tamar, in her adultery, Gen. 38:14-24. Potiphar's wife, in her lascivious lust and slander against Joseph, Gen. 39:7-20. Zipporah, in her persecution of Moses on account of his religious obligations, Ex. 4:25,26. Miriam, in her sedition with Aaron against Moses, Num. 12. Rahab, in her harlotry, Josh. 2:1. Delilah, in her conspiracy against Samson, Judg. 16:4-20. Peninnah, the wife of Elkanah, in her jealous taunting of Hannah, 1 Sam. 1:4-8. The Midianitish woman in the camp of Israel, taken in adultery, Num. 25:6-8. Michal, in her derision of David's religious zeal, 2 Sam. 6:16,20-23. Bath-sheba, in her adultery, in becoming the wife of her husband's murderer, 2 Sam. 11:4,5,27; 12:9,10. Solomon's wives, in their idolatrous and wicked influence over Solomon, 1 Kin. 11:1-11; Neh. 13:26. Jezebel, in her persecution and destruction of the prophets of the Lord, 1 Kin. 18:4,13; in her persecution of Elijah, 1 Kin. 19:2; in her conspiracy against Naboth, to despoil him of his vineyard, 1 Kin. 21:1-16; in her evil counsels to, and influence over, Ahab, 1 Kin. 21:25, with vs. 17-27, and 2 Kin. 9:30-37. The cannibal mothers of Samaria, 2 Kin. 6: 28,29. Athaliah, in destroying the royal household and usurping the throne, 2 Kin. 11:1-16; 2 Chr. 22:10,12; 23:12-15. The sodomites of Judah, 2 Kin. 23:7. Noadiah, a false prophetess, in troubling the Jews when they were restoring Jerusalem, Neh. 6:14. Haman's wife, in counseling him to hang Mordecai, Esth. 5:14; 6:13. Job's wife, in counseling him to curse God, Job 2:9; 19:17. The idolatrous wives of Hosea, Hos. 1:2,3; 3:1. Herodias, in her incestuous marriage with Herod, Matt. 14:3,4; Mark 6:17-19; Luke 3:19; compassing the death of John the Baptist, Matt. 14:6-11; Mark 6:24-28. The daughter of Herodias, in her complicity with her mother in securing the death of John the Baptist, Matt. 14:8; Mark 6:18-28. Sap-

phira, in her blasphemous falsehood, Acts 5:2-10. The woman taken in adultery and brought to Jesus in the temple, John 8:1-11.

FIGURATIVE: Of backsliding, Jer. 6:2; Rev. 17:4,18. Of the wicked, Isa. 32:9,11; Matt. 25:1-13.

SYMBOLICAL: Of wickedness, Zech. 5:7,8; Rev. 17; 19:2.

See WIFE.

WONDERFUL, a name of the Messiah, Isa. 9:6. See Judg. 13:18.

See JESUS, NAMES OF.

WOOL. Used for clothing, Lev. 13:47-52,59; Prov. 31:13; Ezek. 34:3; 44:17. Prohibited in the priest's temple dress, Ezek. 44:17. Mixing of, with other fabrics forbidden, Lev. 19:19; Deut. 22:11. Fleece of, Judg. 6:37. First fleece of, belonged to the priests, Deut. 18:4.

WORD, a title of Jesus, John 1:1,14; 1 John 5:7; Rev. 19:13.

See JESUS, NAMES OF.

WORD OF GOD. Called BOOK, Psa. 40:7; Rev. 22:19; BOOK OF THE LORD, Isa. 34:16; BOOK OF THE LAW, Neh. 8:3; Gal. 3:10; GOOD WORD OF GOD, Heb. 6:5; HOLY SCRIPTURES, Rom. 1:2; 2 Tim. 3:15; LAW OF THE LORD, Psa. 1:2; Isa. 30:9; ORACLES OF GOD, Rom. 3:2; 1 Pet. 4:11; SCRIPTURES, 1 Cor. 15:3; SCRIPTURES OF TRUTH, Dan. 10:21; SWORD OF THE SPIRIT, Eph. 6:17; THE WORD, Jas. 1:21-23; 1 Pet. 2:2; WORD OF GOD, Luke 11:28; Heb. 4:12; WORD OF CHRIST, Col. 3:16; WORD OF LIFE, Phil. 2:16; WORD OF TRUTH, 2 Tim. 2:15; Jas. 1:18.

Likened to seed, Matt. 13:3-8,18-23,37,38; Mark 4:3-20,26-32; Luke 8:5-15; to a two-edged sword, Heb. 4:12.

To be read publicly, Deut. 31:11-13; Josh. 8:33-35; 2 Kin. 23:2; 2 Chr. 17:7-9; Neh. 8:1-8,13,18; Jer. 36:6; Acts 13:15,27; Col. 4:16; 1 Thess. 5:27. The people stood and responded by saying, "Amen," Neh. 8:5,6; Ex. 24:7; Deut. 27:12-26. Expounded, Neh. 8:8; by Jesus, Luke 4:16-27; 24:27,45. Searched, Acts 17:11. Searching of, enjoined, John 5: 39; 7:52. Texts of, to be written on doorposts, Deut. 6:9; 11:20. Not to be added to, or taken from, Deut. 4:2; 12:32; Rev. 22:18,19. Conviction of sin from reading, 2 Kin. 22: 9-13; 2 Chr. 17:7-10; 34.

Fulfilled by Jesus, Matt. 5:17; Luke 24:27; John 19:24. Testify of Jesus, John 5:39; Acts 10:43; 18:28; 1 Cor. 15:3. See JESUS, PROPHECIES CONCERNING. Taught by the apostles, Acts 2; 3; 8:32,35; 13:27; 17:2; 18:24; 28:23. The standard of the judgment, John 12:48; Rom. 2:16. Not to be handled deceitfully, 2 Cor. 4:2.

UNCLASSIFIED SCRIPTURES RELATING TO: Ex. 13:9. And it shall be for a sign unto thee upon thine hand, and for a memorial between thine eyes, that the LORD's law may be in thy mouth: for with a strong hand hath the LORD brought thee out of Egypt.

Ex. 19:9. And the LORD said unto Moses, Lo, I come unto thee in a thick cloud, that the people may hear when I speak with thee, and believe thee for ever. And Moses told the words of the people unto the LORD.

Ex. 24:3. And Moses came and told the people all the words of the LORD, and all the judgments: and all the people answered with one voice, and said, All the words which the LORD hath said will we do. 4. And Moses wrote all the words of the LORD,

Deut. 4:2. Ye shall not add unto the word which I command you, neither shall ye diminish *ought* from it, that ye may keep the commandments of the LORD your God which I command you. [Deut. 12:32.] 5. Behold, I have taught you statutes and judgments, even as the LORD my God commanded me, that ye should do so in the land whither ye go to possess it. 6. Keep therefore and do *them;* for this *is* your wisdom and your understanding in the sight of the nations, which shall hear all these statutes, and say, Surely this great nation *is* a wise and understanding people. 8. And what nation *is there so* great, that hath statutes and judgments *so* righteous as all this law, which I set before you this day? 10. *Specially* the day that thou stoodest before the LORD thy God in Horeb, when the LORD said unto me, Gather me the people together, and I will make them hear my words, that they may learn to fear me all the days that they shall live upon the earth, and *that* they may teach their children. 14. And the LORD commanded me at that time to teach you statutes and judgments, that ye might do them in the land whither ye go over to possess it.

Deut. 6:6. And these words, which I command thee this day, shall be in thine heart: 7. And thou shalt teach them diligently unto thy children, and shalt talk of them when thou sittest in thine house, and when thou walkest by the way, and when thou liest down, and when thou risest up. 8. And thou shalt bind them for a sign upon thine hand, and they shall be as frontlets between thine eyes. 9. And thou shalt write them upon the posts of thy house, and on thy gates. Deut. 11:18–21.

Deut. 8:3. And he humbled thee, and suffered thee to hunger, and fed thee with manna, which thou knewest not, neither did thy fathers know: that he might make thee know that man doth not live by bread only, but by every *word* that proceedeth out of the mouth of the LORD doth man live. Matt. 4:4.

Deut. 17:18. And it shall be, when he sitteth upon the throne of his kingdom, that he shall write him a copy of this law in a book out of *that which is* before the priests the Levites: 19. And it shall be with him, and he shall read therein all the days of his life: that he may learn to fear the LORD his God, to keep all the words of this law and these statutes, to do them:

Deut. 27:2. And it shall be on the day when ye shall pass over Jordan unto the land which the LORD thy God giveth thee, that thou shalt set thee up great stones, and plaister them with plaister: 3. And thou shalt write upon them all the words of this law, when thou art passed over, that thou mayest go in unto the land which the LORD thy God giveth thee, a land that floweth with milk and honey; as the LORD God of thy fathers hath promised thee. 8. And thou shalt write upon the stones all the words of this law very plainly.

Deut. 29:29. The secret *things belong* unto the LORD our God: but those *things which are* revealed *belong* unto us and to our children for ever, that *we* may do all the words of this law.

Deut. 30:11. For this commandment which I command thee this day, it *is* not hidden from thee, neither *is* it far off. 12. It *is* not in heaven, that thou shouldest say, Who shall go up for us to heaven, and bring it unto us, that we may hear it, and do it? 13. Neither *is* it beyond the sea, that thou shouldest say, Who shall go over the sea for us, and bring it unto us, that we may hear it, and do it? 14. But the word *is* very nigh unto thee, in thy mouth, and in thy heart, that thou mayest do it.

Deut. 31:9. And Moses wrote this law, and delivered it unto the priests the sons of Levi, which bare the ark of the covenant of the LORD, and unto all the elders of Israel. 10. And Moses commanded them, saying, At the end of *every* seven years, in the solemnity of the year of release, in the feast of tabernacles, 11. When all Israel is come to appear before the LORD thy God in the place which he shall choose, thou shalt read this law before all Israel in their hearing. 12. Gather the people together, men, and women, and children, and thy stranger that *is* within thy gates, that they may hear, and that they may learn, and fear the LORD your God, and observe to do all the words of this law: 13. And *that* their children, which have not known *any thing*, may hear, and learn to fear the LORD your God, as long as ye live in the land whither ye go over Jordan to possess it.

19. Now therefore write ye this song for you, and teach it the children of Israel: put it in their mouths, that this song may be a witness for me against the children of Israel. 21. And it shall come to pass, when many evils and troubles are befallen them, that this song shall testify against them as a witness; for it shall not be forgotten out of the mouths of their seed: for I know their imagination which they go about, even now, before I have brought them into the land which I sware.

26. Take this book of the law, and put it in the side of the ark of the covenant of the LORD your God, that it may be there for a witness against thee.

Josh. 1:8. This book of the law shall not depart out of thy mouth; but thou shalt meditate therein day and night, that thou mayest observe to do according to all that is written therein: for then thou shalt make thy way prosperous, and then thou shalt have good success.

Josh. 3:9. And Joshua said unto the children of Israel, Come hither, and hear the words of the Lord your God.

Josh. 8:32. And he wrote there upon the stones a copy of the law of Moses, which he wrote in the presence of the children of Israel. 33. And all Israel, and their elders, and officers, and their judges, stood on this side the ark and on that side before the priests the Levites, which bare the ark of the covenant of the Lord, as well the stranger, as he that was born among them; half of them over against mount Gerizim, and half of them over against mount Ebal; as Moses the servant of the Lord had commanded before, that they should bless the people of Israel. 34. And afterward he read all the words of the law, the blessings and cursings, according to all that is written in the book of the law. 35. There was not a word of all that Moses commanded, which Joshua read not before all the congregation of Israel, with the women, and the little ones, and the strangers that were conversant among them.

2 Sam. 22:31. As for God, his way is perfect; the word of the Lord is tried: Psa. 18:30.

1 Chr. 16:15. Be ye mindful always of his covenant; the word which he commanded to a thousand generations;

2 Chr. 15:3. Now for a long season Israel hath been without the true God, and without a teaching priest, and without law.

Job 22:22. Receive, I pray thee, the law from his mouth, and lay up his words in thine heart.

Job 23:12. Neither have I gone back from the commandment of his lips; I have esteemed the words of his mouth more than my necessary food.

Psa. 1:2. But his delight is in the law of the Lord; and in his law doth he meditate day and night.

Psa. 12:6. The words of the Lord are pure words: as silver tried in a furnace of earth, purified seven times.

Psa. 17:4. Concerning the works of men, by the word of thy lips I have kept me from the paths of the destroyer.

Psa. 19:7. The law of the Lord is perfect, converting the soul: the testimony of the Lord is sure, making wise the simple. 8. The statutes of the Lord are right, rejoicing the heart: the commandment of the Lord is pure, enlightening the eyes. 9. The fear of the Lord is clean, enduring for ever: the judgments of the Lord are true and righteous altogether. 10. More to be desired are they than gold, yea, than much fine gold: sweeter also than honey and the honeycomb. 11. Moreover by them is thy servant warned: and in keeping of them there is great reward.

Psa. 33:4. For the word of the Lord is right; 6. By the word of the Lord were the heavens made; and all the host of them by the breath of his mouth.

Psa. 37:31. The law of his God is in his heart; none of his steps shall slide.

Psa. 40:8. I delight to do thy will, O my God: yea, thy law is within my heart.

Psa. 43:3. O send out thy light and thy truth: let them lead me; let them bring me unto thy holy hill, and to thy tabernacles.

Psa. 56:4. In God I will praise his word, in God I have put my trust;

Psa. 78:1. Give ear, O my people, to my law: incline your ears to the words of my mouth. 7. That they might set their hope in God, and not forget the works of God, but keep his commandments: 8. And might not be as their fathers, a stubborn and rebellious generation; a generation that set not their heart aright, and whose spirit was not stedfast with God.

Psa. 85:8. I will hear what God the Lord will speak: for he will speak peace unto his people, and to his saints: but let them not turn again to folly.

Psa. 93:5. Thy testimonies are very sure: holiness becometh thine house, O Lord, for ever.

Psa. 94:12. Blessed is the man whom thou chastenest, O Lord, and teachest him out of thy law;

Psa. 102:18. This shall be written for the generation to come: and the people which shall be created shall praise the Lord.

Psa. 107:19. Then they cry unto the Lord in their trouble, and he saveth them out of their distresses. 20. He sent his word, and healed them, and delivered them from their destructions.

Psa. 111:7. The works of his hands are verity and judgment; all his commandments are sure. 8. They stand fast for ever and ever, and are done in truth and uprightness.

Psa. 119:9. Wherewithal shall a young man cleanse his way? by taking heed thereto according to thy word. 11. Thy word have I hid in mine heart, that I might not sin against thee. 12. Blessed art thou, O Lord: teach me thy statutes. 14. I have rejoiced in the way of thy testimonies, as much as in all riches. 15. I will meditate in thy precepts, and have respect unto thy ways. 16. I will delight myself in thy statutes: I will not forget thy word. 18. Open thou mine eyes, that I may behold wondrous things out of thy law. 19. I am a stranger in the earth: hide not thy commandments from me. 20. My soul breaketh for the longing that it hath unto thy judgments at all times. [v. 40.] 23. Princes also did sit and speak against me: but thy servant did meditate in thy statutes. 24. Thy testimonies also are my delight and my counsellors. 25. My soul cleaveth unto the dust: quicken thou me according to thy word. 28. My soul melteth for heaviness: strengthen thou me according unto thy word. 30. I have chosen the way of truth: thy judgments have I laid *before me.* 31. I have stuck unto thy testimonies: O Lord, put me not to shame. 33. Teach me, O Lord, the way of thy statutes; and I shall keep it *unto* the end. 35. Make me to go in the path of thy commandments; for therein do I delight. 41. Let thy mercies come also unto me, O Lord, *even* thy salvation, according to thy word. 45. And I will walk at liberty: for I seek thy precepts. 46. I will speak of thy testimonies also before kings, and will not be ashamed. 47. And I will delight myself in thy commandments, which I have loved. 48. My hands also will I lift up unto thy commandments, which I have loved; and I will meditate in thy statutes. 49. Remember the word unto thy servant, upon which thou hast caused me to hope. 50. This *is* my comfort in my affliction: for thy word hath quickened me. 51. The proud have had me greatly in derision: *yet* have I not declined from thy law. 52. I remember thy judgments of old, O Lord; and have comforted myself. 54. Thy statutes have been my songs in the house of my pilgrimage. 61. The bands of the wicked have robbed me: *but* I have not forgotten thy law. 66. Teach me good judgment and knowledge: for I have believed thy commandments. 67. Before I was afflicted I went astray: but now have I kept thy word. 70. Their heart is as fat as grease; *but* I delight in thy law. 72. The law of thy mouth *is* better unto me than thousands of gold and silver. 74. They that fear thee will be glad when they see me; because I have hoped in thy word. [*v.* 147.] 76. Let, I pray thee, thy merciful kindness be for my comfort, according to thy word unto thy servant. 77. Let thy tender mercies come unto me, that I may live: for thy law *is* my delight. 78. Let the proud be ashamed; for they dealt perversely with me without a cause: *but* I will meditate in thy precepts. 81. My soul fainteth for thy salvation: *but* I hope in thy word. [*v.* 147]. 82. Mine eyes fail for thy word, saying, When wilt thou comfort me? 83. For I am become like a bottle in the smoke; *yet* do I not forget thy statutes. 86. All thy commandments *are* faithful: they persecute me wrongfully; help thou me. 89. For ever, O Lord, thy word is settled in heaven. 92. Unless thy law *had been* my delights, I should then have perished in mine affliction. 93. I will never forget thy precepts: for with them thou hast quickened me. 96. I have seen an end of all perfection: *but* thy commandment *is* exceeding broad. 97. O how love I thy law! it *is* my meditation all the day. 98. Thou through thy commandments hast made me wiser than mine enemies: for they *are* ever with me. 99. I have more understanding than all my teachers: for thy testimonies *are* my meditation. 100. I understand more

than the ancients, because I keep thy precepts. 103. How sweet are thy words unto my taste! *yea, sweeter* than honey to my mouth! 104. Through thy precepts I get understanding: therefore I hate every false way. 105. Thy word *is* a lamp unto my feet, and a light unto my path. 109. My soul *is* continually in my hand: yet do I not forget thy law. 111. Thy testimonies have I taken as an heritage for ever: for they *are* the rejoicing of my heart. 113. I hate *vain* thoughts: but thy law do I love. 115. Depart from me, ye evildoers: for I will keep the commandments of my God. 119. Thou puttest away all the wicked of the earth *like* dross: therefore I love thy testimonies. 127. Therefore I love thy commandments above gold; yea, above fine gold. 128. Therefore I esteem all *thy* precepts *concerning* all *things to be* right; *and* I hate every false way. 129. Thy testimonies *are* wonderful: therefore doth my soul keep them. 130. The entrance of thy words giveth light: it giveth understanding unto the simple. 131. I opened my mouth, and panted: for I longed for thy commandments. 133. Order my steps in thy word: 138. Thy testimonies *that* thou hast commanded *are* righteous and very faithful. 140. Thy word *is* very pure: therefore thy servant loveth it. 141. I *am* small and despised: *yet* do not I forget thy precepts. 142. Thy righteousness *is* an everlasting righteousness, and thy law *is* the truth. 143. Trouble and anguish have taken hold on me: *yet* thy commandments *are* my delights. 144. The righteousness of thy testimonies *is* everlasting: give me understanding, and I shall live. 148. Mine eyes prevent the *night* watches, that I might meditate in thy word. 151. Thou *art* near, O Lord; and all thy commandments *are* truth. 152. Concerning thy testimonies, I have known of old that thou hast founded them for ever. 153. Consider mine affliction, and deliver me: for I do not forget thy law. 157. Many *are* my persecutors and mine enemies; *yet* do I not decline from thy testimonies. 158. I beheld the transgressors, and was grieved; because they kept not thy word. 159. Consider how I love thy precepts: quicken me, O Lord, according to thy lovingkindness. 160. Thy word *is* true *from* the beginning: and every one of thy righteous judgments *endureth* for ever. 161. Princes have persecuted me without a cause: but my heart standeth in awe of thy word. 162. I rejoice at thy word, as one that findeth great spoil. 163. I hate and abhor lying: *but* thy law do I love. 165. Great peace have they which love thy law: and nothing shall offend them. 167. My soul hath kept thy testimonies; and I love them exceedingly. 172. My tongue shall speak of thy word: for all thy commandments *are* righteousness. 173. Let thine hand help me; for I have chosen thy precepts. 174. I have longed for thy salvation, O Lord; and thy law is my delight.

Psa. 138:2. I will worship toward thy holy temple, and praise thy name for thy lovingkindness and for thy truth: for thou hast magnified thy word above all thy name.

Psa. 147:15. He sendeth forth his commandment upon earth: his word runneth very swiftly. 19. He sheweth his word unto Jacob, his statutes and his judgments unto Israel. v. 20.

Prov. 6:20. My son, keep thy father's commandment, and forsake not the law of thy mother: 21. Bind them continually upon thine heart, and tie them about thy neck. 22. When thou goest, it shall lead thee; when thou sleepest, it shall keep thee; and when thou awakest, it shall talk with thee. 23. For the commandment is a lamp; and the law is light; and reproofs of instruction are the way of life:

Prov. 22:21. That I might make thee know the certainty of the words of truth; that thou mightest answer the words of truth to them that send unto thee?

Prov. 30:5. Every word of God is pure: he is a shield unto them that put their trust in him. 6. Add thou not unto his words, lest he reprove thee, and thou be found a liar.

Eccl. 5:1. Keep thy foot when thou goest to the house of God, and be more ready to hear, than to give the sacrifice of fools: for they consider not that they do evil.

Eccl. 12:10. The preacher sought to find out acceptable words: and that which was written was upright, even words of truth. 11. The words of the wise are as goads, and as nails fastened by the masters of assemblies, which are given from one shepherd.

Isa. 2:3. And many people shall go and say, Come ye, and let us go up to the mountain of the Lord, to the house of the God of Jacob; and he will teach us of his ways, and we will walk in his paths: for out of Zion shall go forth the law, and the word of the Lord from Jerusalem.

Isa. 8:16. Bind up the testimony, seal the law among my disciples. 20. To the law and to the testimony: if they speak not according to this word, it is because there is no light in them.

Isa. 28:13. But the word of the Lord was unto them precept upon precept, precept upon precept; line upon line, line upon line: here a little, and there a little; that they might go, and fall backward, and be broken, and snared, and taken.

Isa. 30:21. And thine ears shall hear a word behind thee, saying, This is the way, walk ye in it, when ye turn to the right hand, and when ye turn to the left.

Isa. 34:16. Seek ye out of the book of the Lord, and read: no one of these shall fail, none shall want her mate: for my mouth it hath commanded, and his spirit it hath gathered them.

Isa. 40:8. The grass withereth, the flower fadeth: but the word of our God shall stand for ever.

Isa. 51:7. Hearken unto me, ye that know righteousness, the people in whose heart is my law;

Isa. 55:10. For as the rain cometh down, and the snow from heaven, and returneth not thither, but watereth the earth, and maketh it bring forth and bud, that it may give seed to the sower, and bread to the eater: 11. So shall my word be that goeth forth out of my mouth: it shall not return unto me void, but it shall accomplish that which I please, and it shall prosper in the thing whereto I sent it.

Jer. 8:9. The wise men are ashamed, they are dismayed and taken: lo, they have rejected the word of the Lord; and what wisdom is in them?

Jer. 13:15. Hear ye, and give ear; be not proud: for the Lord hath spoken.

Jer. 15:16. Thy words were found, and I did eat them; and thy word was unto me the joy and rejoicing of mine heart: for I am called by thy name, O Lord God of hosts.

Jer. 22:29. O earth, earth, earth, hear the word of the Lord.

Jer. 23:28. The prophet that hath a dream, let him tell a dream; and he that hath my word, let him speak my word faithfully. What is the chaff to the wheat? saith the Lord.   29. Is not my word like as a fire? saith the Lord; and like a hammer that breaketh the rock in pieces? 36. And the burden of the Lord shall ye mention no more: for every man's word shall be his burden; for ye have perverted the words of the living God, of the Lord of hosts our God.

Ezek. 3:3. And he said unto me, Son of man, cause thy belly to eat, and fill thy bowels with this roll that I give thee.   Then did I eat it; and it was in my mouth as honey for sweetness. 10. Moreover he said unto me, Son of man, all my words that I shall speak unto thee receive in thine heart, and hear with thine ears.

Ezek. 44:5. And the Lord said unto me, Son of man, mark well, and behold with thine eyes, and hear with thine ears all that I say unto thee concerning all the ordinances of the house of the Lord, and all the laws thereof;

Dan. 10:21. But I will shew thee that which is noted in the scripture of truth:

Dan 12:4. But thou, O Daniel, shut up the words, and seal the book, even to the time of the end: many shall run to and fro, and knowledge shall be increased. [Dan. 8:26.] 9. And he said, Go thy way, Daniel: for the words are closed up and sealed till the time of the end.

Hos. 6:5. Therefore have I hewed them by the prophets; I have slain them by the words of my mouth: and thy judgments are as the light that goeth forth.

Amos 8:11. Behold, the days come, saith

the Lord God, that I will send a famine in the land, not a famine of bread, nor a thirst for water, but of hearing the words of the Lord: 12. And they shall wander from sea to sea, and from the north even to the east, they shall run to and fro to seek the word of the Lord, and shall not find *it.* 13. In that day shall the fair virgins and young men faint for thirst.

Mic. 2:7. O *thou that art* named the house of Jacob, is the spirit of the Lord straitened? *are* these his doings? do not my words do good to him that walketh uprightly?

Hab. 2:2. And the Lord answered me, and said, Write the vision, and make *it* plain upon tables, that he may run that readeth it.

Zech. 7:7. *Should ye* not *hear* the words which the Lord hath cried by the former prophets, when Jerusalem was inhabited and in prosperity,

Matt. 5:17. Think not that I am come to destroy the law, or the prophets: I am not come to destroy, but to fulfil.

Matt. 7:24. Therefore whosoever heareth these sayings of mine, and doeth them, I will liken him unto a wise man, which built his house upon a rock: 25. And the rain descended, and the floods came, and the winds blew, and beat upon that house; and it fell not: for it was founded upon a rock. Luke 6:47,48.

Matt. 11:13. For all the prophets and the law prophesied until John. 15. He that hath ears to hear, let him hear.

Matt. 13:23. But he that received seed into the good ground is he that heareth the word, and understandeth *it;* which also beareth fruit, and bringeth forth, some an hundredfold, some sixty, some thirty. Mark 4:20; Luke 8:15.

33. Another parable spake he unto them; The kingdom of heaven is like unto leaven, which a woman took, and hid in three measures of meal, till the whole was leavened. Luke 13:21.

Matt. 15:3. But he answered and said unto them, Why do ye also transgress the commandment of God by your tradition? 9. But in vain they do worship me, teaching *for* doctrines the commandments of men.

Matt. 22:29. Ye do err, not knowing the scriptures, nor the power of God.

Mark 1:15. The time is fulfilled, and the kingdom of God is at hand: repent ye, and believe the Gospel.

Mark 7:9. And he said unto them, Full well ye reject the commandment of God, that ye may keep your own tradition. 13. Making the word of God of none effect through your tradition, which ye have delivered:

Mark 12:24. And Jesus answering said unto them, Do ye not therefore err, because ye know not the scriptures, neither the power of God?

Mark 13:31. Heaven and earth shall pass away, but my words shall not pass away.

Luke 1:37. For no word from God shall be void of power. [R.V.]

Luke 4:22. And all bare him witness, and wondered at the gracious words which proceeded out of his mouth.

Luke 8:11. Now the parable is this: The seed is the word of God. 12. Those by the way side are they that hear; then cometh the devil, and taketh away the word out of their hearts, lest they should believe and be saved. 13. They on the rock *are they*, which, when they hear, receive the word with joy; and these have no root, which for a while believe, and in time of temptation fall away. 14. And that which fell among thorns are they, which, when they have heard, go forth, and are choked with cares and riches and pleasures of *this* life, and bring no fruit to perfection. 15. But that on the good ground are they, which in an honest and good heart, having heard the word, keep *it*, and bring forth fruit with patience.

Luke 11:28. But he said, Yea rather, blessed *are* they that hear the word of God, and keep it.

Luke 16:17. And it is easier for heaven and earth to pass, than one tittle of the law to fail. 29. Abraham saith unto him, They have Moses and the prophets; let them hear them. 31. And he said unto him, If they hear not Moses and the prophets, neither will they be persuaded, though one rose from the dead.

Luke 24:32. And they said one to another, Did not our heart burn within us, while he talked with us by the way, and while he opened to us the scriptures? 45. Then opened he their understanding, that they might understand the scriptures,

John 2:22. When therefore he was risen from the dead, his disciples remembered that he had said this unto them; and they believed the scripture, and the word which Jesus had said.

John 5:24. Verily, verily, I say unto you, He that heareth my word, and believeth on him that sent me, hath everlasting life, and shall not come into condemnation; but is passed from death unto life. 39. Search the scriptures [Ye search the scriptures, R.V.]; for in them ye think ye have eternal life: and they are they which testify of me.

John 6:63. It is the spirit that quickeneth; the flesh profiteth nothing: the words that I speak unto you, *they* are spirit, and *they* are life.

John 8:31. Then said Jesus to those Jews which believed on him, If ye continue in my word, *then* are ye my disciples indeed; 32. And ye shall know the truth, and the truth shall make you free.

John 10:35. If he called them gods, unto whom the word of God came, and the scripture cannot be broken;

John 15:3. Now ye are clean through the word which I have spoken unto you.

John 17:8. For I have given unto them

the words which thou gavest me; and they have received *them*, and have known surely that I came out from thee, and they have believed that thou didst send me. [*v.* 14.] 17. Sanctify them through thy truth: thy word is truth.   19. And for their sakes I sanctify myself, that they also might be sanctified through the truth.   20. Neither pray I for these alone, but for them also which shall believe on me through their word;

John 20:31. But these are written, that ye might believe that Jesus is the Christ, the Son of God; and that believing ye might have life through his name.

Acts 10:15. And the voice *spake* unto him again the second time, What God hath cleansed, *that* call not thou common.

Acts 17:11. These were more noble than those in Thessalonica, in that they received the word with all readiness of mind, and searched the scriptures daily, whether those things were so.

Acts 20:32. And now, brethren, I commend you to God, and to the word of his grace, which is able to build you up, and to give you an inheritance among all them which are sanctified.

Acts 26:18. To open their eyes, *and* to turn *them* from darkness to light, and *from* the power of Satan unto God, that they may receive forgiveness of sins, and inheritance among them which are sanctified by faith that is in me.   22. Having therefore obtained help of God, I continue unto this day, witnessing both to small and great, saying none other things than those which the prophets and Moses did say should come:

Rom. 3:1. What advantage then hath the Jew? or what profit *is there* of circumcision?   2. Much every way: chiefly, because that unto them were committed the oracles of God.

Rom. 4:23. Now it was not written for his sake alone, that it was imputed to him; 24. But for us also, to whom it shall be imputed, if we believe on him that raised up Jesus our Lord from the dead;

Rom. 6:17. But God be thanked, that ye were the servants of sin, but ye have obeyed from the heart that form of doctrine which was delivered you.

Rom. 9:4. Who are Israelites; to whom *pertaineth* the adoption, and the glory, and the covenants, and the giving of the law, and the service *of God*, and the promises; 6. Not as though the word of God hath taken none effect.

Rom. 10:17. So then faith *cometh* by hearing, and hearing by the word of 1 God.   [1 R. V. Christ]

Rom. 12:2. And be not conformed to this world: but be ye transformed by the renewing of your mind, that ye may prove what *is* that good, and acceptable, and perfect, will of God.

Rom. 15:4. For whatsoever things were written aforetime were written for our learn-ing, that we through patience and comfort of the scriptures might have hope.

Rom. 16:26. But now is made manifest, and by the scriptures of the prophets, according to the commandment of the ever-lasting God, made known to all nations for the obedience of faith:

1 Cor. 2:13. Which things also we speak, not in the words which man's wisdom teacheth, but which the Holy Ghost teacheth; comparing spiritual things with spiritual.

1 Cor. 7:6. But I speak this by permission, *and* not of commandment.   10. And unto the married I command, *yet* not I, but the Lord, Let not the wife depart from *her* husband: 12. But to the rest speak I, not the Lord: 2 Cor. 8:10.

1 Cor. 9:10. Or saith he *it* altogether for our sakes? For our sakes, no doubt, *this* is written: that he that ploweth should plow in hope; and that he that thresheth in hope should be partaker of his hope.

1 Cor. 10:11. Now all these things happened unto them for ensamples: and they are written for our admonition, upon whom the ends of the world are come.

1 Cor. 11:2. Now I praise you, brethren, that ye remember me in all things, and keep the ordinances, as I delivered *them* to you.

1 Cor. 15:3. For I delivered unto you first of all that which I also received, how that Christ died for our sins according to the scriptures;

2 Cor. 2:17. For we are not as many, which corrupt the word of God: but as of sincerity, but as of God, in the sight of God speak we in Christ.

2 Cor. 3:6. Who also hath made us able ministers of the new testament; not of the letter, but of the spirit: for the letter killeth, but the spirit giveth life.

Gal. 1:8. But though we, or an angel from heaven, preach any other gospel unto you than that which we have preached unto you, let him be accursed.   [*v.* 9.] 11. But I certify you, brethren, that the gospel which was preached of me is not after man.   12. For I neither received it of man, neither was I taught *it*, but by the revelation of Jesus Christ.

Eph. 1:12. That we should be to the praise of his glory, who first trusted in Christ. 13. In whom ye also *trusted*, after that ye heard the word of truth, the gospel of your salvation:

Eph. 3:3. By revelation he made known unto me the mystery; (as I wrote afore in few words;   4. Whereby, when ye read, ye may understand my knowledge in the mystery of Christ,)   5. Which in other ages was not made known unto the sons of man, as it is now revealed unto his holy apostles and prophets by the Spirit;

Eph. 5:26. That he might sanctify and cleanse it with the washing of water by the word,

Eph. 6:17. And take the helmet of salvation, and the sword of the Spirit, which is the word of God:

Phil. 2:16. Holding forth the word of life;

Col. 1:5. For the hope which is laid up for you in heaven, whereof ye heard before in the word of the truth of the gospel;

Col. 3:16. Let the word of Christ dwell in you richly in all wisdom; teaching and admonishing one another in psalms and hymns and spiritual songs, singing with grace in your hearts to the Lord.

1 Thess. 1:5. Our gospel came not unto you in word only, but also in power, and in the Holy Ghost, and in much assurance; 8. For from you sounded out the word of the Lord not only in Macedonia and Achaia, but also in every place your faith to God-ward is spread abroad;

1 Thess. 2:13. For this cause also thank we God without ceasing, because, when ye received the word of God which ye heard of us, ye received it not as the word of men, but as it is in truth, the word of God, which effectually worketh also in you that believe.

1 Thess. 4:1. Furthermore then we beseech you, brethren, and exhort you by the Lord Jesus, that as ye have received of us how ye ought to walk and to please God, so ye would abound more and more. 2. For ye know what commandments we gave you by the Lord Jesus.

1 Thess. 5:20. Despise not prophesyings.

2 Thess. 2:14. Whereunto he called you by our gospel, to the obtaining of the glory of our Lord Jesus Christ. 15. Therefore, brethren, stand fast, and hold the traditions which ye have been taught, whether by word, or our epistle.

1 Tim. 4:5. For it is sanctified by the word of God and prayer. 6. If thou put the brethren in remembrance of these things, thou shalt be a good minister of Jesus Christ, nourished up in the words of faith and of good doctrine, whereunto thou hast attained.

1 Tim. 6:3. If any man teach otherwise, and consent not to wholesome words, even the words of our Lord Jesus Christ, and to the doctrine which is according to godliness; 4. He is proud, knowing nothing, but doting about questions and strifes of words, whereof cometh envy, strife, railings, evil surmisings,

2 Tim. 1:13. Hold fast the form of sound words, which thou hast heard of me, in faith and love which is in Christ Jesus.

2 Tim. 2:8. Remember that Jesus Christ of the seed of David was raised from the dead according to my gospel: 9. Wherein I suffer trouble, as an evil doer, even unto bonds; but the word of God is not bound. 15. Study to shew thyself approved unto God, a workman that needeth not to be ashamed, rightly dividing the word of truth.

2 Tim. 3:15. And that from a child thou hast known the holy scriptures, which are able to make thee wise unto salvation through faith which is in Christ Jesus. 16. ¹ All scripture is given by inspiraiton of God, and is profitable for doctrine, for reproof, for correction, for instruction in righteousness: 17. That the man of God may be perfect, throughly furnished unto all good works.

[¹ R. V. Every scripture inspired of God is also profitable for teaching, for reproof, for correction, for instruction which is in righteousness]

Heb. 1:1. God, who at sundry times and in divers manners spake in time past unto the fathers by the prophets, 2. Hath in these last days spoken unto us by his Son, whom he hath appointed heir of all things, by whom also he made the worlds;

Heb. 2:1. Therefore we ought to give the more earnest heed to the things which we have heard, lest at any time we should let them slip. 2. For if the word spoken by angels was stedfast, and every transgression and disobedience received a just recompence of reward: 3. How shall we escape, if we neglect so great salvation; which at the first began to be spoken by the Lord, and was confirmed unto us by them that heard him;

Heb. 4:2. Unto us was the gospel preached, as well as unto them: but the word preached did not profit them, not being mixed with faith in them that heard it. 12. The word of God is quick, and powerful, and sharper than any twoedged sword, piercing even to the dividing asunder of soul and spirit, and of the joints and marrow, and is a discerner of the thoughts and intents of the heart.

Heb. 6:5. And have tasted the good word of God, and the powers of the world to come,

Heb. 10:7. Then said I, Lo, I come (in the volume of the book it is written of me,) to do thy will, O God.

Heb. 10:28. He that despised Moses' law died without mercy under two or three witnesses:

Heb. 11:3. Through faith we understand that the worlds were framed by the word of God, so that things which are seen were not made of things which do appear.

Jas. 1:18. Of his own will begat he us with the word of truth, that we should be a kind of firstfruits of his creatures. 19. Wherefore, my beloved brethren, let every man be swift to hear, slow to speak, slow to wrath: 21. Wherefore lay apart all filthiness and superfluity of naughtiness, and receive with meekness the engrafted word, which is able to save your souls. 22. But be ye doers of the word, and not hearers only, deceiving your own selves. 23. For if any be a hearer of the word, and not a doer, he is like unto a man beholding his natural face in a glass: 24. For he beholdeth himself, and goeth his way, and straightway forgetteth what manner of man he was. 25. But whoso looketh into the perfect law of liberty, and continueth therein, he being not a forgetful hearer, but a doer of the work, this man shall be blessed in his deed.

1 Pet. 1:23. Being born again, not of corruptible seed, but of incorruptible, by the word of God, which liveth and abideth for ever. 24. For all flesh *is* as grass, and all the glory of man as the flower of grass. The grass withereth, and the flower thereof falleth away: 25. But the word of the Lord endureth for ever. And this is the word which by the gospel is preached unto you.

1 Pet. 2:2. As newborn babes, desire the sincere milk of the word, that ye may grow thereby: 3. If so be ye have tasted that the Lord *is* gracious.

2 Pet. 1:4. Whereby are given unto us exceeding great and precious promises: that by these ye might be partakers of the divine nature, having escaped the corruption that is in the world through lust. 19. We have also a more sure word of prophecy; whereunto ye do well that ye take heed, as unto a light that shineth in a dark place, until the day dawn, and the day star arise in your hearts: 20. Knowing this first, that no prophecy of the scripture is of any private interpretation. 21. For the prophecy came not in old time by the will of man: but holy men of God spake *as they were* moved by the Holy Ghost.

2 Pet. 3:1. This second epistle, beloved, I now write unto you; in *both* which I stir up your pure minds by way of remembrance: 2. That ye may be mindful of the words which were spoken before by the holy prophets, and of the commandment of us the apostles of the Lord and Saviour: 15. And account *that* the longsuffering of our Lord *is* salvation; even as our beloved brother Paul also according to the wisdom given unto him hath written unto you; 16. As also in all *his* epistles, speaking in them of these things; in which are some things hard to be understood, which they that are unlearned and unstable wrest, as *they do* also the other scriptures, unto their own destruction.

1 John 1:4. And these things write we unto you, that your joy may be full. 5. This then is the message which we have heard of him, and declare unto you, that God is light, and in him is no darkness at all.

1 John 2:7. Brethren, I write no new commandment unto you, but an old commandment which ye had from the beginning. The old commandment is the word which ye have heard from the beginning. 8. Again, a new commandment I write unto you, which thing is true in him and in you: because the darkness is past, and the true light now shineth. 12. I write unto you, little children, because your sins are forgiven you for his name's sake. 14. I have written unto you, fathers, because ye have known him *that is* from the beginning. I have written unto you, young men, because ye are strong, and the word of God abideth

in you, and ye have overcome the wicked one. 21. I have not written unto you because ye know not the truth, but because ye know it, and that no lie is of the truth.

1 John 5:11. And this is the record, that God hath given to us eternal life, and this life is in his Son. 13. These things have I written unto you [1] that believe on the name of the Son of God; that ye may know that ye have eternal life, [2] and that ye may believe on the name of the Son of God.

Jude 3. Beloved, when I gave all diligence to write unto you of the common salvation, it was needful for me to write unto you, and exhort *you* that ye should earnestly contend for the faith which was once delivered unto the saints. 17. But, beloved, remember ye the words which were spoken before of the apostles of our Lord Jesus Christ;

Rev. 1:2. Who bare record of the word of God, and of the testimony of Jesus Christ, and of all things that he saw. 3. Blessed *is* he that readeth, and they that hear the words of this prophecy, and keep those things which are written therein: for the time *is* at hand.

Rev. 22:18. For I testify unto every man that heareth the words of the prophecy of this book, If any man shall add unto these things, God shall add unto him the plagues that are written in this book: 19. And if any man shall take away from the words of the book of this prophecy, God shall take away his part out of the book of life, and out of the holy city, and *from* the things which are written in this book.

See COMMANDMENTS.

INSPIRATION OF: Ex. 19:7. And Moses came and called for the elders of the people, and laid before their faces all these words which the LORD commanded him.

Ex. 20:1. And God spake all these words,

Ex. 24:4. And Moses wrote all the words of the LORD, 12. And the LORD said unto Moses, Come up to me into the mount, and be there: and I will give thee tables of stone, and a law, and commandments which I have written; that thou mayest teach them.

Ex. 25:21. And thou shalt put the mercy seat above upon the ark; and in the ark thou shalt put the testimony that I shall give thee.

Ex. 31:18. And he gave unto Moses, when he had made an end of communing with him upon mount Sinai, two tables of testimony, tables of stone, written with the finger of God.

Ex. 32:16. And the tables *were* the work of God, and the writing *was* the writing of God, graven upon the tables.

Ex. 34:27. And the LORD said unto Moses, Write thou these words: for after the tenor of these words I have made a covenant with thee and with Israel. 32. And afterward all the children of Israel came nigh: and he gave them in commandment all that the LORD had spoken with him in mount Sinai.

Lev. 26:46. These *are* the statutes and judgments and laws, which the LORD made between him and the children of Israel in mount Sinai by the hand of Moses.

Deut. 4:5. Behold, I have taught you statutes and judgments, even as the LORD my God commanded me, that ye should do so in the land whither ye go to possess it. *v.* 14.

Deut. 11:18. Therefore shall ye lay up these my words in your heart and in your soul, and bind them for a sign upon your hand, that they may be as frontlets between your eyes.

Deut. 31:19. Now therefore write ye this song for you, and teach it the children of Israel: put it in their mouths, that this song may be as witness for me against the children of Israel. 22. Moses therefore wrote the song the same day, and taught it the children of Israel.

2 Kin. 17:13. Yet the LORD testified against Israel, and against Judah, by all the prophets, *and by* all the seers, saying, Turn ye from your evil ways, and keep my commandments *and* my statutes, according to all the law which I commanded your fathers, and which I sent to you by my servants the prophets.

2 Chr. 33:18. Now the rest of the acts of Manasseh, and his prayer unto his God, and the words of the seers that spake to him in the name of the LORD God of Israel, behold, they *are written* in the book of the kings of Israel.

Job 23:12. Neither have I gone back from the commandment of his lips; I have esteemed the words of his mouth more than my necessary *food.*

Psa. 78:5. For he established a testimony in Jacob, and appointed a law in Israel, which he commanded our fathers, that they should make them known to their children:

Psa. 99:7. He spake unto them in the cloudy pillar: they kept his testimonies, and the ordinance *that* he gave them.

Psa. 147:19. He sheweth his word unto Jacob, his statutes and his judgments unto Israel.

Eccl. 12:11. The words of the wise *are* as goads, and as nails fastened *by* the masters of assemblies, *which* are given from one shepherd.

Isa. 30:12. Wherefore thus saith the Holy One of Israel, Because ye despise this word, and trust in oppression and perverseness, and stay thereon: 13. Therefore this iniquity shall be to you as a breach ready to fall, swelling out in a high wall, whose breaking cometh suddenly at an instant.

Isa. 34:16. Seek ye out of the book of the LORD, and read: no one of these shall fail, none shall want her mate: for my mouth it hath commanded, and his spirit it hath gathered them.

Isa. 59:21. As for me, this *is* my covenant with them, saith the LORD; My spirit that *is* upon thee, and my words which I have put in thy mouth, shall not depart out of thy mouth, nor out of the mouth of thy seed, nor out of the mouth of thy seed's seed, saith the LORD, from henceforth and for ever.

Jer. 30:2. Thus speaketh the LORD God of Israel, saying, Write thee all the words that I have spoken unto thee in a book.

Jer. 36:1. This word came unto Jeremiah from the LORD, saying, 2. Take thee a roll of a book, and write therein all the words that I have spoken unto thee 27. Then the word of the LORD came to Jeremiah, after that the king had burned the roll, and the words which Baruch wrote at the mouth of Jeremiah, saying, 28. Take thee again another roll, and write in it all the former words that were in the first roll, which Jehoiakim the king of Judah hath burned. 32. Then took Jeremiah another roll, and gave it to Baruch the scribe, the son of Neriah; who wrote therein from the mouth of Jeremiah all the words of the book which Jehoiakim king of Judah had burned in the fire: and there were added besides unto them many like words. Jer. 51:59-64.

Ezek. 11:25. Then I spake unto them of the captivity all the things that the LORD had shewed me.

Dan. 10:21. But I will shew thee that which is noted in the scripture of truth:

Hos. 8:12. [1] I have written to him the great things of my law, *but* they were counted as a strange thing.

[1 R. V. Though I write for him my law in ten thousand precepts, they are]

Zech. 7:12. Yea, they made their hearts *as* an adamant stone, lest they should hear the law, and the words which the LORD of hosts hath sent in his spirit by the former prophets:

Matt. 22:31. But as touching the resurrection of the dead, have ye not read that which was spoken unto you by God, saying, 32. I am the God of Abraham, and the God of Isaac, and the God of Jacob?

Luke 1:1. Forasmuch as many have taken in hand to set forth in order a declaration of those things which are most surely believed among us, 2. Even as they delivered them unto us, which from the beginning were eyewitnesses, and ministers of the word; 3. It seemed good to me also, having had perfect understanding of all things from the very first, to write unto thee in order, most excellent Theophilus, 4. That thou mightest know the certainty of those things, wherein thou hast been instructed. 68. Blessed *be* the Lord God of Israel; for he hath visited and redeemed his people, 69. And hath raised up an horn of salvation for us in the house of his servant David; 70. As he spake by the mouth of his holy prophets, which have been since the world began: 71. That we should be saved from our enemies, and from the hand of all that hate us; 72. To perform the mercy *prom-*

ised to our fathers, and to remember his holy covenant; 73. The oath which he sware to our father Abraham,

Acts 1:16. Men *and* brethren, this scripture must needs have been fulfilled, which the Holy Ghost by the mouth of David spake before concerning Judas, which was guide to them that took Jesus.

Acts 28:25. And when they agreed not among themselves, they departed, after that Paul had spoken one word, Well spake the Holy Ghost by Esaias the prophet unto our fathers,

Rom. 3:1. What advantage then hath the Jew? or what profit *is there* of circumcision? 2. Much every way: chiefly, because that unto them were committed the oracles of God. Heb. 5:12.

1 Cor. 2:12. Now we have received, not the spirit of the world, but the spirit which is of God; that we might know the things that are freely given to us of God. 13. Which things also we speak, not in the words which man's wisdom teacheth, but which the Holy Ghost teacheth; comparing spiritual things with spiritual.

1 Cor. 7:10. And unto the married I command, *yet* not I, but the Lord, Let not the wife depart from *her* husband:

1 Cor. 14:37. If any man think himself to be a prophet, or spiritual, let him acknowledge that the things that I write unto you are the commandments of the Lord.

Eph. 6:17. And take the helmet of salvation, and the sword of the Spirit, which is the word of God:

Col. 3:16. Let the word of Christ dwell in you richly in all wisdom; teaching and admonishing one another in psalms and hymns and spiritual songs, singing with grace in your hearts to the Lord.

1 Thess. 2:13. For this cause also thank we God without ceasing, because, when ye received the word of God which ye heard of us, ye received *it* not *as* the word of men, but as it is in truth, the word of God, which effectually worketh also in you that believe.

1 Thess. 4:1. Furthermore then we beseech you, brethren, and exhort *you* by the Lord Jesus, that as ye have received of us how ye ought to walk and to please God, *so* ye would abound more and more. 2. For ye know what commandments we gave you by the Lord Jesus. 3. For this is the will of God, *even* your sanctification, that ye should abstain from fornication:

1 Tim. 6:3. If any man teach otherwise, and consent not to wholesome words, *even* the words of our Lord Jesus Christ, and to the doctrine which is according to godliness; 4. He is proud, knowing nothing, but doting about questions and strifes of words, whereof cometh envy, strife, railings, evil surmisings, 5. Perverse disputings of men of corrupt minds, and destitute of the truth, supposing that [1] gain is godliness: **from such withdraw thyself.**

[1 R. V. godliness is a way of gain]

2 Tim. 3:16. [1] All scripture *is* given by inspiration of God, and *is* profitable for doctrine, for reproof, for correction, for instruction in righteousness: 17. That the man of God may be perfect, throughly furnished unto all good works.

[1 R. V. Every scripture inspired of God *is* also profitable for teaching, for reproof, for correction, for instruction which is in righteousness]

Heb. 1:1. God, who at sundry times and in divers manners spake in time past unto the fathers by the prophets, 2 Hath in these last days spoken unto us by *his* Son, whom he hath appointed heir of all things, by whom also he made the worlds:

Heb. 3:7. Wherefore as the Holy Ghost saith, To day if ye will hear his voice, 8. Harden not your hearts, as in the provocation, in the day of temptation in the wilderness:

Heb. 4:12. For the word of God *is* quick, and powerful, and sharper than any two edged sword, piercing even to the dividing asunder of soul and spirit, and of the joints and marrow, and *is* a discerner of the thoughts and intents of the heart.

1 Pet. 1:11. Searching what, or what manner of time the Spirit of Christ which was in them did signify, when it testified beforehand the sufferings of Christ, and the glory that should follow. 12. Unto whom it was revealed, that not unto themselves, but unto us they did minister the things, which are now reported unto you by them that have preached the gospel unto you with the Holy Ghost sent down from heaven; which things the angels desire to look into.

2 Pet. 1:21. For the prophecy came not in old time by the will of man: but holy men of God spake *as they were* moved by the Holy Ghost.

2 Pet. 3:2. That we may be mindful of the words which were spoken before by the holy prophets, and of the commandment of us the apostles of the Lord and Saviour: 15. And account *that* the longsuffering of our Lord *is* salvation; even as our beloved brother Paul also according to the wisdom given unto him hath written unto you;

1 John 1:1. That which was from the beginning, which we have heard, which we have seen with our eyes, which we have looked upon, and our hands have handled, of the Word of life; 2. (For the life was manifested, and we have seen *it*, and bear witness, and shew unto you that eternal life, which was with the Father, and was manifested unto us;) 3. That which we have seen and heard declare we unto you, that ye also may have fellowship with us: and truly our fellowship *is* with the Father, and with his Son Jesus Christ. 4. And these things write we unto you, that your joy may be full. 5. This then is the message which we have heard of him, and declare unto you, that God is light, and in him is no darkness at all.

Rev. 1:1. The Revelation of Jesus Christ,

which God gave unto him, to shew unto his servants things which must shortly come to pass; and he sent and signified *it* by his angel unto his servant John: 2. Who bare record of the word of God, and of the testimony of Jesus Christ, and of all things that he saw. 11. I am Alpha and Omega, the first and the last: and, What thou seest, write in a book, and send *it* unto the seven churches which are in Asia; 17. And he laid his right hand upon me, saying unto me, Fear not; I am the first and the last: 18. *I am* he that liveth, and was dead; and, behold, I am alive for evermore, Amen; and have the keys of hell and of death. 19. Write the things which thou hast seen, and the things which are, and the things which shall be hereafter;

Rev. 2:7. He that hath an ear, let him hear what the Spirit saith unto the churches;

Rev. 19:10. And I fell at his feet to worship him. And he said unto me, See *thou do it* not: I am thy fellowservant, and of thy brethren that have the testimony of Jesus: worship God: for the testimony of Jesus is the spirit of prophecy.

Rev. 22:6. And he said unto me, These sayings *are* faithful and true: and the Lord God of the holy prophets sent his angel to shew unto his servants the things which must shortly be done. 7. Behold, I come quickly: blessed *is* he that keepeth the sayings of the prophecy of this book. 8. And I John saw these things, and heard *them.*

UNBELIEF IN: Psa. 50:16. But unto the wicked God saith, What hast thou to do to declare my statutes, or *that* thou shouldest take my covenant in thy mouth? 17. Seeing thou hatest instruction, and castest my words behind thee.

Prov. 1:29. For that they hated knowledge, and did not choose the fear of the LORD: 30. They would none of my counsel: they despised all my reproof.

Prov. 13:13. Whoso despiseth the word shall be destroyed: but he that feareth the commandment shall be rewarded.

Isa. 5:24. Therefore as the fire devoureth the stubble, and the flame consumeth the chaff, *so* their root shall be as rottenness, and their blossom shall go up as dust: because they have cast away the law of the LORD of hosts, and despised the word of the Holy One of Israel.

Isa. 28:9. Whom shall he teach knowledge? and whom shall he make to understand doctrine? *them that are* weaned from the milk, *and* drawn from the breasts. 10. For precept *must be* upon precept, precept upon precept; line upon line, line upon line; here a little, *and* there a little: 11. For with stammering lips and another tongue will he speak to this people. 12. To whom he said, This *is* the rest *wherewith* ye may cause the weary to rest; and this *is* the refreshing: yet they would not hear. 13. But the word of the LORD was unto them precept upon precept, precept upon precept;

line upon line, line upon line; here a little, *and* there a little; that they might go, and fall backward, and be broken, and snared, and taken. 14. Wherefore hear the word of the LORD, ye scornful men, that rule this people which *is* in Jerusalem.

Isa. 30:9. That this *is* a rebellious people, lying children, children *that* will not hear the law of the LORD: 10. Which say to the seers, See not; and to the prophets, Prophesy not unto us right things, speak unto us smooth things, prophesy deceits: 11. Get you out of the way, turn aside out of the path, cause the Holy One of Israel to cease from before us.

Isa. 53:1. Who hath believed our report? and to whom is the arm of the LORD revealed?

Jer. 6:10. To whom shall I speak, and give warning, that they may hear? behold, their ear *is* uncircumcised, and they cannot hearken: behold, the word of the LORD is unto them a reproach; they have no delight in it.

Jer. 8:9. The wise *men* are ashamed, they are dismayed and taken: lo, they have rejected the word of the LORD; and what wisdom *is* in them?

Hos. 8:12. [1] I have written to him the great things of my law, *but* they were counted as a strange thing.

[1 R. V. Though I write for him my law in ten thousand precepts, they are]

Amos 2:12. But ye gave the Nazarites wine to drink; and commanded the prophets, saying, Prophesy not.

Mic. 2:6. Prophesy ye not, *say they to them that* prophesy: they shall not prophesy to them, *that* they shall not take shame.

Luke 16:31. And he said unto him, If they hear not Moses and the prophets, neither will they be persuaded, though one rose from the dead.

Luke 24:25. Then he said unto them, O fools, and slow of heart to believe all that the prophets have spoken:

John 3:20. For every one that doeth evil hateth the light, neither cometh to the light, lest his deeds should be reproved.

John 5:46. For had ye believed Moses, ye would have believed me: for he wrote of me. 47. But if ye believe not his writings, how shall ye believe my words?

John 8:37. I know that ye are Abraham's seed; but ye seek to kill me, because my word hath no place in you. 45. And because I tell *you* the truth, ye believe me not.

1 Cor. 1:18. For the preaching of the cross is to them that perish foolishness; but unto us which are saved it is the power of God. 22. For the Jews require a sign, and the Greeks seek after wisdom: 23. But we preach Christ crucified, unto the Jews a stumblingblock, and unto the Greeks foolishness;

2 Tim. 3:8. Now as Jannes and Jambres withstood Moses, so do these also resist the truth: men of corrupt minds, reprobate concerning the faith.

2 Tim. 4:3. For the time will come when they will not endure sound doctrine; but after their own lusts shall they heap to themselves teachers, having itching ears; 4. And they shall turn away *their* ears from the truth, and shall be turned unto fables.

1 Pet. 2:8. And a stone of stumbling, and a rock of offence, *even to them* which stumble at the word, being disobedient: whereunto also they were appointed.

2 Pet. 3:15. And account *that* the longsuffering of our Lord *is* salvation; even as our beloved brother Paul also according to the wisdom given unto him hath written unto you; 16. As also in all *his* epistles, speaking in them of these things; in which are some things hard to be understood, which they that are unlearned and unstable wrest, as *they do* also the other scriptures, unto their own destruction.

Rev. 22:19. And if any man shall take away from the words of the book of this prophecy, God shall take away his part out of the book of life, and out of the holy city, and *from* the things which are written in this book.

WORDS. Of Jesus: Gracious, Luke 4:22; spirit and life, John 6:63; eternal life, John 6:68; shall judge, John 12:47,48. Of the wise: As goads, and as nails well fastened, Eccl. 12: 11; gracious, Eccl. 10:12. Spoken in season, Prov. 15:23; Isa. 50:4. Fitly spoken, like apples of gold in filigree of silver, Prov. 25: 11. Of the perfect man, gentle, Jas. 3:2.

Should be acceptable to God, Psa. 19:14.

Of the teacher, should be plain, 1 Cor. 14: 9,19. Unprofitable, to be avoided, 2 Tim. 2:14. Unspeakable, heard by Paul in paradise, 2 Cor. 12:4. Vain, not to be regarded, Ex. 5:9; Eph. 5:6; like a tempest, Job 8:2. Without knowledge, darken counsel, Job 38:2. Idle, account must be given for in the day of judgment, Matt. 12:36,37. Hasty, folly of, Prov. 29:20. In a multitude of, is sin, Prov. 10:19. Fool known by the multitude of, Eccl. 5:3; will swallow himself, Eccl. 10:12-14. Seditious, deceive the simple, Rom. 16:18. Deceitful, are a snare to him who utters them, Prov. 6:2. Of the hypocrite, softer than oil, Psa. 55:21. Of the talebearer, wounds to the soul, Prov. 18:8.

See BUSYBODY; SLANDER; SPEAKING, EVIL; TALEBEARER.

WORK. See INDUSTRY; LABOR.

WORKS. GOOD: Jesus an example of, John 10:32; Acts 10:38. Holy women should manifest, 1 Tim. 2:10; 5:10. God remembers, Neh. 13:14, with Heb. 6:9,10. Shall be brought into judgment, Eccl. 12:14, with 2 Cor. 5:10. In the judgment, will be an evidence of faith, Matt. 25:34-40, with Jas. 2:14-20. Ministers should be patterns of, Tit. 2:7. Ministers should exhort to, 1 Tim. 6:17,18; Tit. 3:1,8,14. God is glorified by, John 15:8. Designed to lead others to glorify God, Matt. 5:16; 1 Pet. 2:12. A blessing attends, Jas. 1:25. Of the righteous, are manifest, 1 Tim. 5:25.

Parables relating to: The talents and pounds, Matt. 25:14-29; Luke 19:12-27; of the laborers in the vineyard, Matt. 20:11-15; the two sons, Matt. 21:28-31; of the barren fig tree, Luke 13:6-9.

UNCLASSIFIED SCRIPTURES RELATING TO: Deut. 6:25. And it shall be our righteousness, if we observe to do all these commandments before the LORD our God, as he hath commanded us.

Deut 24:13. In any case thou shalt deliver him the pledge again when the sun goeth down, that he may sleep in his own raiment, and bless thee: and it shall be righteousness unto thee before the LORD thy God.

Neh. 13:14. Remember me, O my God, concerning this, and wipe not out my good deeds that I have done for the house of my God, and for the offices thereof. chapter 5:19.

Job 30:25. Did not I weep for him that was in trouble? was *not* my soul grieved for the poor?

Psa. 37:3. Trust in the LORD, and do good; *so* shalt thou dwell in the land, and verily thou shalt be fed.

Psa. 90:17. And let the beauty of the LORD our God be upon us: and establish thou the work of our hands upon us; yea, the work of our hands establish thou it.

Psa. 106:30. Then stood up Phinehas, and executed judgment: and *so* the plague was stayed. 31. And that was counted unto him for righteousness unto all generations for evermore.

Jer. 22:15. Shalt thou reign, because thou closest *thyself* in cedar? did not thy father eat and drink, and do judgment and justice, *and* then *it was* well with him? 16. He judged the cause of the poor and needy; then *it was* well *with him:* was not this to know me? saith the LORD.

Ezek. 14:14. Though these three men, Noah, Daniel, and Job, were in it, they should deliver *but* their own souls by their righteousness, saith the Lord GOD. *v.* 20.

Ezek. 18:5. But if a man be just, and do that which is lawful and right, 6. *And* hath not eaten upon the mountains, neither hath lifted up his eyes to the idols of the house of Israel, neither hath defiled his neighbour's wife, neither hath come near to a menstruous woman, 7. And hath not oppressed any, *but* hath restored to the debtor his pledge, hath spoiled none by violence, hath given his bread to the hungry, and hath covered the naked with a garment; 8. He *that* hath not given forth upon usury, neither hath taken any increase, *that* hath withdrawn his hand from iniquity, hath executed true judgment between man and man, 9. Hath walked in my statutes, and hath kept my judgments, to deal truly; he *is* just, he shall surely live, saith the Lord GOD.

Matt. 3:8. Bring forth therefore fruits meet for repentance:

Matt. 6:1. Take heed that ye do not your alms before men, to be seen of them: otherwise ye have no reward of your Father which is in heaven. 2. Therefore when thou doest *thine* alms, do not sound a trumpet before thee, as the hypocrites do in the synagogues and in the streets, that they may have glory of men. Verily I say unto you, They have their reward. 3. But when thou doest alms, let not thy left hand know what thy right hand doeth. 4. That thine alms may be in secret: and thy Father which seeth in secret himself shall reward thee openly.

Matt. 10:42. And whosoever shall give to drink unto one of these little ones a cup of cold *water* only in the name of a disciple, verily I say unto you, he shall in no wise lose his reward.

Matt. 18:5. And whoso shall receive one such little child in my name receiveth me.

Matt. 19:16. And, behold, one came and said unto him, Good Master, what good thing shall I do, that I may have eternal life? 17. And he said unto him, Why callest thou me good? *there is* none good but one, *that is,* God: but if thou wilt enter into life, keep the commandments. [Mark 10:17; Luke 10:25.] 18. He saith unto him, Which? Jesus said, Thou shalt do no murder, Thou shalt not commit adultery, Thou shalt not steal, Thou shalt not bear false witness, 19. Honour thy father and *thy* mother: and, Thou shalt love thy neighbour as thyself. 20. The young man saith unto him, All these things have I kept from my youth up: what lack I yet? 21. Jesus said unto him, If thou wilt be perfect, go *and* sell that thou hast, and give to the poor, and thou shalt have treasure in heaven: and come *and* follow me.

Matt. 25:34. Then shall the King say unto them on his right hand, Come, ye blessed of my Father, inherit the kingdom prepared for you from the foundation of the world: 35. For I was an hungred, and ye gave me meat: I was thirsty, and ye gave me drink: I was a stranger, and ye took me in: 36. Naked, and ye clothed me: I was sick, and ye visited me: I was in prison, and ye came unto me. 37. Then shall the righteous answer him, saying, Lord, when saw we thee an hungred, and fed *thee?* or thirsty, and gave *thee* drink? 38. When saw we thee a stranger, and took *thee* in? or naked, and clothed *thee?* 39. Or when saw we thee sick, or in prison, and came unto thee? 40. And the King shall answer and say unto them, Verily I say unto you, Inasmuch as ye have done *it* unto one of the least of these my brethren, ye have done *it* unto me. 41. Then shall he say also unto them on the left hand, Depart from me, ye cursed, into everlasting fire, prepared for the devil and his angels: 42. For I was an hungred, and ye gave me no meat: I was thirsty, and ye gave me no drink: 43. I was a stranger, and ye took me not in: naked, and ye clothed me not:

sick, and in prison, and ye visited me not. 44. Then shall they also answer him, saying, Lord, when saw we thee an hungred, or athirst, or a stranger, or naked, or sick, or in prison, and did not minister unto thee? 45. Then shall he answer them, saying, Verily I say unto you, Inasmuch as ye did *it* not to one of the least of these, ye did *it* not to me. 46. And these shall go away into everlasting punishment: but the righteous into life eternal.

John 3:21. But he that doeth truth cometh to the light, that his deeds may be made manifest, that they are wrought in God.

John 15:2. Every branch in me that beareth not fruit he taketh away: and every *branch* that beareth fruit, he purgeth it, that it may bring forth more fruit. 3. Now ye are clean through the word which I have spoken unto you. 4. Abide in me, and I in you. As the branch cannot bear fruit of itself, except it abide in the vine; no more can ye, except ye abide in me. 5. I am the vine, ye *are* the branches. He that abideth in me, and I in him, the same bringeth forth much fruit: for without me ye can do nothing. 6. If a man abide not in me, he is cast forth as a branch, and is withered; and men gather them, and cast *them* into the fire, and they are burned. 7. If ye abide in me, and my words abide in you, ye shall ask what ye will, and it shall be done unto you. 8. Herein is my Father glorified, that ye bear much fruit; so shall ye be my disciples. 14. Ye are my friends, if ye do whatsoever I command you.

Acts 10:4. And when he looked on him, he was afraid, and said, What is it, Lord? And he said unto him, Thy prayers and thine alms are come up for a memorial before God. 38. How God anointed Jesus of Nazareth with the Holy Ghost and with power: who went about doing good, and healing all that were oppressed of the devil; for God was with him.

Rom. 2:13. (For not the hearers of the law *are* just before God, but the doers of the law shall be justified.

1 Cor. 3:6. I have planted, Apollos watered; but God gave the increase. 7. So then neither is he that planteth any thing, neither he that watereth; but God that giveth the increase. 8. Now he that planteth and he that watereth are one: and every man shall receive his own reward according to his own labour. 9. For we are labourers together with God: ye are God's husbandry, *ye are* God's building.

2 Cor. 9:8. And God *is* able to make all grace abound toward you; that ye, always having all sufficiency in all *things,* may abound to every good work:

Gal. 6:4. But let every man prove his own work, and then shall he have rejoicing in himself alone, and not in another.

Eph. 2:10. For we are his workmanship, created in Christ Jesus unto good works, which God hath before ordained that we should walk in them.

Phil. 1:11. Being filled with the fruits of righteousness, which are by Jesus Christ, unto the glory and praise of God.

Phil. 2:13. It is God which worketh in you both to will and to do of *his* good pleasure.

Col. 1:10. That ye might walk worthy of the Lord unto all pleasing, being fruitful in every good work, and increasing in the knowledge of God;

Col. 3:12. Put on therefore, as the elect of God, holy and beloved, bowels of mercies, kindness, humbleness of mind, meekness, longsuffering; 13. Forbearing one another, and forgiving one another, if any man have a quarrel against any: even as Christ forgave you, so also *do* ye. 14. And above all these things *put on* charity, which is the bond of perfectness. 17. And whatsoever ye do in word or deed, *do* all in the name of the Lord Jesus, giving thanks to God and the Father by him.

1 Thess. 1:3. Remembering without ceasing your work of faith, and labour of love, and patience of hope in our Lord Jesus Christ, in the sight of God and our Father; 7. So that ye were ensamples to all that believe in Macedonia and Achaia. 8. For from you sounded out the word of the Lord not only in Macedonia and Achaia, but also in every place your faith to God-ward is spread abroad; so that we need not to speak any thing.

2 Thess. 2:17. Comfort your hearts, and stablish you in every good word and work.

1 Tim. 2:10. But (which becometh women professing godliness) with good works.

1 Tim. 5:9. Let not a widow be taken into the number under threescore years old, having been the wife of one man, 10. Well reported of for good works; if she have brought up children, if she have lodged strangers, if she have washed the saints' feet, if she have relieved the afflicted, if she have diligently followed every good work.

1 Tim. 6:18. That they do good, that they be rich in good works, ready to distribute, willing to communicate; 19. Laying up in store for themselves a good foundation against the time to come, that they may lay hold on [1] eternal life. [1 R. V. the life which is life indeed]

2 Tim. 2:21. If a man therefore purge himself from these, he shall be a vessel unto honour, sanctified, and meet for the master's use, *and* prepared unto every good work.

2 Tim. 3:16. [1] All scripture *is* given by inspiration of God, and *is* profitable for doctrine, for reproof, for correction, for instruction in righteousness: 17. That the man of God may be perfect, throughly furnished unto all good works.

[1 R. V. Every scripture inspired of God *is* also profitable for teaching, for reproof, for correction, for instruction which is in righteousness]

Tit. 2:14. Who gave himself for us, that he might redeem us from all iniquity, and purify unto himself a peculiar people, zealous of good works.

Tit. 3:1. Put them in mind to be subject to principalities and powers, to obey magistrates, to be ready to every good work, 2. To speak evil of no man, to be no brawlers, *but* gentle, shewing all meekness unto all men. 8. *This is* a faithful saying, and these things I will that thou affirm constantly, that they which have believed in God might be careful to maintain good works. These things are good and profitable unto men. 14. And let our's also learn to maintain good works for necessary uses, that they be not unfruitful.

Heb. 6:10. For God *is* not unrighteous to forget your work and labour of love, which ye have shewed toward his name, in that ye have ministered to the saints, and do minister.

Heb. 10:24. And let us consider one another to provoke unto love and to good works:

Heb. 13:21. Make you perfect in every good work to do his will, working in you that which is wellpleasing in his sight, through Jesus Christ; to whom *be* glory for ever and ever.

Jas. 1:22. But be ye doers of the word, and not hearers only, deceiving your own selves. 23. For if any be a hearer of the word, and not a doer, he is like unto a man beholding his natural face in a glass: 24. For he beholdeth himself, and goeth his way, and straightway forgetteth what manner of man he was. 25. But whoso looketh into the perfect law of liberty, and continueth *therein*, he being not a forgetful hearer, but a doer of the work, this man shall be blessed in his deed. 26. If any man among you seem to be religious, and bridleth not his tongue, but deceiveth his own heart, this man's religion *is* vain. 27. Pure religion and undefiled before God and the Father is this, To visit the fatherless and widows in their affliction, *and* to keep himself unspotted from the world.

Jas. 3:13. Who *is* a wise man and endued with knowledge among you? let him shew out of a good conversation his works with meekness of wisdom. 17. But the wisdom that is from above is first pure, then peaceable, gentle, *and* easy to be intreated, full of mercy and good fruits, without partiality, and without hypocrisy. 18. And the fruit of righteousness is sown in peace of them that make peace.

Rev. 14:13. And I heard a voice from heaven saying unto me, Write, Blessed *are* the dead which die in the Lord from henceforth: Yea, saith the Spirit, that they may rest from their labours; and their works do follow them.

Rev. 22:14. Blessed *are* they that [1] do his commandments, that they may have right to the tree of life, and may enter in through the gates into the city. [1 R. V. wash their robes]

INSUFFICIENCY OF, FOR SALVATION:
Psa. 49:7. None *of them* can by any means redeem his brother, nor give to God a ransom

for him: 8. (For the redemption of their soul *is* precious, and it ceaseth for ever:)

Psa. 127:1. Except the LORD build the house, they labour in vain that build it: except the LORD keep the city, the watchman waketh *but* in vain. 2. *It is* vain for you to rise up early, to sit up late, to eat the bread of sorrows: *for* so he giveth his beloved sleep.

Eccl. 1:14. I have seen all the works that are done under the sun; and, behold, all *is* vanity and vexation of spirit.

Isa. 43:26. Put me in remembrance: let us plead together: declare thou, that thou mayest be justified.

Isa. 57:12. I will declare thy righteousness, and thy works; for they shall not profit thee.

Isa. 64:6. But we are all as an unclean *thing*, and all our righteousnesses *are* as filthy rags; and we all do fade as a leaf; and our iniquities, like the wind, have taken us away.

Ezek. 7:19. They shall cast their silver in the streets, and their gold shall be removed: their silver and their gold shall not be able to deliver them in the day of the wrath of the LORD: they shall not satisfy their souls, neither fill their bowels: because it is the stumblingblock of their iniquity.

Ezek. 33:12. Therefore, thou son of man, say unto the children of thy people, The righteousness of the righteous shall not deliver him in the day of his transgression: as for the wickedness of the wicked, he shall not fall thereby in the day that he turneth from his wickedness; neither shall the righteous be able to live for his *righteousness* in the day that he sinneth. 13. When I shall say to the righteous, *that* he shall surely live; if he trust to his own righteousness, and commit iniquity, all his righteousnesses shall not be remembered; but for his iniquity that he hath committed, he shall die for it. 14. Again, when I say unto the wicked, Thou shalt surely die; if he turn from his sin, and do that which is lawful and right; 15. *If* the wicked restore the pledge, give again that he had robbed, walk in the statutes of life, without committing iniquity; he shall surely live, he shall not die. 16. None of his sins that he hath committed shall be mentioned unto him: he hath done that which is lawful and right; he shall surely live. 17. Yet the children of thy people say, The way of the Lord is not equal: but as for them, their way is not equal. 18. When the righteous turneth from his righteousness, and committeth iniquity, he shall even die thereby. 19. But if the wicked turn from his wickedness, and do that which is lawful and right, he shall live thereby.

Dan. 9:18. O my God, incline thine ear, and hear; open thine eyes, and behold our desolations, and the city which is called by thy name: for we do not present our supplications before thee for our righteousnesses, but for thy great mercies.

Matt. 5:20. For I say unto you, That except your righteousness shall exceed *the righteousness* of the scribes and Pharisees, ye shall in no case enter into the kingdom of heaven.

Luke 17:7. But which of you, having a servant plowing or feeding cattle, will say unto him by and by, when he is come from the field, Go and sit down to meat? 8. And will not rather say unto him, Make ready wherewith I may sup, and gird thyself, and serve me, till I have eaten and drunken; and afterward thou shalt eat and drink? 9. Doth he thank that servant because he did the things that were commanded him? I trow not. 10. So likewise ye, when ye shall have done all those things which are commanded you, say, We are unprofitable servants: we have done that which was our duty to do.

Luke 18:9. And he spake this parable unto certain which trusted in themselves that they were righteous, and despised others: 10. Two men went up into the temple to pray; the one a Pharisee, and the other a publican. 11. The Pharisee stood and prayed thus with himself, God, I thank thee, that I am not as other men *are*, extortioners, unjust, adulterers, or even as this publican. 12. I fast twice in the week, I give tithes of all that I possess. 13. And the publican, standing afar off, would not lift up so much as *his* eyes unto heaven, but smote upon his breast, saying, God be merciful to me a sinner. 14. I tell you, this man went down to his house justified *rather* than the other: for every one that exalteth himself shall be abased; and he that humbleth himself shall be exalted.

Acts 13:39. And by him all that believe are justified from all things, from which ye could not be justified by the law of Moses.

Rom. 3:20. Therefore by the deeds of the law there shall no flesh be justified in his sight: for by the law *is* the knowledge of sin. 21. But now the righteousness of God without the law is manifested, being witnessed by the law and the prophets; 22. Even the righteousness of God *which is* by faith of Jesus Christ unto all and upon all them that believe: for there is no difference: 23. For all have sinned, and come short of the glory of God; 24. Being justified freely by his grace through the redemption that is in Christ Jesus: 25. Whom God hath set forth *to be* a propitiation through faith in his blood, to declare his righteousness for the remission of sins that are past, through the forbearance of God; 26. To declare, *I say*, at this time his righteousness: that he might be just, and the justifier of him which believeth in Jesus. 27. Where *is* boasting then? It is excluded. By what law? of works? Nay: but by the law of faith. 28. Therefore we conclude that a man is justified by faith without the deeds of the law. 29. *Is he* the God of the Jews only? *is he* not also of the Gentiles? Yes, of the Gentiles also: 30. Seeing *it is* one God, which shall justify the circumcision by faith, and uncircumcision through faith. 31. Do we then make void the law through faith? God forbid: yea, we establish the law.

Rom. 4:1. What shall we say then that Abraham our father, as pertaining to the flesh, hath found? 2. For if Abraham were justified by works, he hath *whereof* to glory; but not before God. 3. For what saith the scripture? Abraham believed God, and it was counted unto him for righteousness. 4. Now to him that worketh is the reward not reckoned of grace, but of debt. 5. But to him that worketh not, but believeth on him that justifieth the ungodly, his faith is counted for righteousness. 6. Even as David also describeth the blessedness of the man, unto whom God imputeth righteousness without works, 7. *Saying*, Blessed *are* they whose iniquities are forgiven, and whose sins are covered. 8. Blessed *is* the man to whom the Lord will not impute sin. *vs.* 9–22.

Rom. 8:3. For what the law could not do, in that it was weak through the flesh, God sending his own Son in the likeness of sinful flesh, and for sin, condemned sin in the flesh:

Rom. 9:16. So then *it is* not of him that willeth, nor of him that runneth, but of God that sheweth mercy. 31. But Israel, which followed after the law of righteousness, hath not attained to the law of righteousness. 32. Wherefore? Because *they sought it* not by faith, but as it were by the works of the law.

Rom. 11:6. If by grace, then *is it* no more of works: otherwise grace is no more grace. But if *it be* of works, then is it no more grace: otherwise work is no more work.

1 Cor. 13:1. Though I speak with the tongues of men and of angels, and have not charity, I am become *as* sounding brass, or a tinkling cymbal. 2. And though I have *the gift of* prophecy, and understand all mysteries, and all knowledge; and though I have all faith, so that I could remove mountains, and have not charity, I am nothing. 3. And though I bestow all my goods to feed *the poor*, and though I give my body to be burned, and have not charity, it profiteth me nothing.

Gal. 2:16. Knowing that a man is not justified by the works of the law, but by the faith of Jesus Christ, even we have believed in Jesus Christ, that we might be justified by the faith of Christ, and not by the works of the law: for by the works of the law shall no flesh be justified. 19. I through the law am dead to the law, that I might live unto God. 21. I do not frustrate the grace of God: for if righteousness *come* by the law, then Christ is dead in vain.

Gal. 3:10. As many as are of the works of the law are under the curse: for it is written, Cursed *is* every one that continueth

not in all things which are written in the book of the law to do them. 11. But that no man is justified by the law in the sight of God, *it is* evident: for, The just shall live by faith. 12. And the law is not of faith: but, The man that doeth them shall live in them. 21. *Is* the law then against the promises of God? God forbid: for if there had been a law given which could have given life, verily righteousness should have been by the law. *vs.* 1–29.

Gal. 4:9. After that ye have known God, or rather are known of God, how turn ye again to the weak and beggarly elements, whereunto ye desire again to be in bondage? 10. Ye observe days, and months, and times, and years. 11. I am afraid of you, lest I have bestowed upon you labour in vain.

Gal. 5:2. Behold, I Paul say unto you, that if ye be circumcised, Christ shall profit you nothing. 4. Christ is become of no effect unto you, whosoever of you are justified by the law; ye are fallen from grace. 6. For in Jesus Christ neither circumcision availeth any thing, nor uncircumcision; but faith which worketh by love. 18. But if ye be led of the Spirit, ye are not under the law.

Gal. 6:15. For ¹ in Christ Jesus neither circumcision availeth any thing, nor uncircumcision, but a new creature.   [¹ Omitted in R. V.]

Eph. 2:8. For by grace are ye saved through faith; and that not of yourselves: *it is* the gift of God: 9. Not of works, lest any man should boast.

Phil. 3:3. For we are the circumcision, which worship God in the spirit, and rejoice in Christ Jesus, and have no confidence in the flesh. 4. Though I might also have confidence in the flesh. If any other man thinketh that he hath whereof he might trust in the flesh, I more: 5. Circumcised the eighth day, of the stock of Israel, *of* the tribe of Benjamin, an Hebrew of the Hebrews; as touching the law, a Pharisee; 6. Concerning zeal, persecuting the church; touching the righteousness which is in the law, blameless. 7. But what things were gain to me, those I counted loss for Christ. 8. Yea doubtless, and I count all things *but* loss for the excellency of the knowledge of Christ Jesus my Lord: for whom I have suffered the loss of all things, and do count them *but* dung, that I may win Christ, 9. And be found in him, not having mine own righteousness, which is of the law, but that which is through the faith of Christ, the righteousness which is of God by faith:

Col. 2:20. Wherefore if ye be dead with Christ from the rudiments of the world, why, as though living in the world, are ye subject to ordinances, 21. (Touch not; taste not; handle not; 22. Which all are to perish with the using;) after the commandments and doctrines of men? 23. Which things have indeed a shew of wisdom in will worship, and humility, and neglecting of the body; not in any honour to the satisfying of the flesh.

2 Tim. 1:9. Who hath saved us, and called *us* with an holy calling, not according to our works, but according to his own purpose and grace, which was given us in Christ Jesus

Tit. 3:4. But after that the kindness and love of God our Saviour toward man appeared, 5. Not by works of righteousness which we have done, but according to his mercy he saved us, by the washing of regeneration, and renewing of the Holy Ghost;

Heb. 4:3. For we which have believed do enter into rest, as he said, As I have sworn in my wrath, if they shall enter into my rest: although the works were finished from the foundation of the world. 4. For he spake in a certain place of the seventh *day* on this wise, And God did rest the seventh day from all his works. 5. And in this *place* again, If they shall enter into my rest. 6. Seeing therefore it remaineth that some must enter therein, and they to whom it was first preached entered not in because of unbelief: 7. Again, he limiteth a certain day, saying in David, To day, after so long a time; as it is said, To day if ye will hear his voice, harden not your hearts. 8. For if Jesus had given them rest, then would he not afterward have spoken of another day. 9. There remaineth therefore a rest to the people of God. 10. For he that is entered into his rest, he also hath ceased from his own works, as God *did* from his.

Heb. 6:1. Therefore leaving the principles of the doctrine of Christ, let us go on unto perfection; not laying again the foundation of repentance from dead works, and of faith toward God. 2. Of the doctrine of baptisms, and of laying on of hands, and of resurrection of the dead, and of eternal judgment.

Heb. 9:1. Then verily the first *covenant* had also ordinances of divine service, and a worldly sanctuary. 2. For there was a tabernacle made; the first, wherein *was* the candlestick, and the table, and the shewbread; which is called the sanctuary. 3. And after the second veil, the tabernacle which is called the holiest of all; 4. Which had the golden censer, and the ark of the covenant overlaid round about with gold, wherein *was* the golden pot that had manna, and Aaron's rod that budded, and the tables of the covenant; 5. And over it the cherubims of glory shadowing the mercyseat; of which we cannot now speak particularly. 6. Now when these things were thus ordained, the priests went always into the first tabernacle, accomplishing the service *of God.* 7. But into the second *went* the high priest alone once every year, not without blood, which he offered for himself, and *for* the errors of the people: 8. The Holy Ghost this signifying, that the way into the holiest of all was not yet made manifest, while as the first tabernacle was yet standing: 9. Which *was* a figure for the time then present, in which were offered both gifts and sacrifices, that could not make him that did the service perfect, as pertaining to the conscience; 10. *Which stood* only in meats and drinks, and divers washings, and carnal ordinances, imposed *on them* until the time of reformation. 11. But Christ being come an high priest of good things to come, by a greater and more perfect tabernacle, not made with hands, that is to say, not of this building; 12. Neither by the blood of goats and calves, but by his own blood he entered in once into the holy place, having obtained eternal redemption *for us.* 13. For if the blood of bulls and of goats, and the ashes of an heifer sprinkling the unclean, sanctifieth to the purifying of the flesh: 14. How much more shall the blood of Christ, who through the eternal Spirit offered himself without spot to God, purge your conscience from dead works to serve the living God?

Jas. 2:10. Whosoever shall keep the whole law, and yet offend in one *point*, he is guilty of all. 11. For he that said, Do not commit adultery, said also, Do not kill. Now if thou commit no adultery, yet if thou kill, thou art become a transgressor of the law.

OF GOD: See GOD, WORKS OF.

WORLD. See EARTH.

WORLDLINESS. 1 Sam. 8:19. Nevertheless the people refused to obey the voice of Samuel; and they said, Nay; but we will have a king over us; 20. That we also may be like all the nations;

Job 20:4. Knowest thou *not* this of old, since man was placed upon earth, 5. That the triumphing of the wicked *is* short, and the joy of the hypocrite *but* for a moment? 6. Though his excellency mount up to the heavens, and his head reach unto the clouds; 7. *Yet* he shall perish for ever like his own dung: they which have seen him shall say, Where *is* he? 8. He shall fly away as a dream, and shall not be found: yea, he shall be chased away as a vision of the night. 9. The eye also *which* saw him shall *see him* no more; neither shall his place any more behold him. 10. His children shall seek to please the poor, and his hands shall restore their goods. 11. His bones are full *of the sin* of his youth, which shall lie down with him in the dust. 12. Though wickedness be sweet in his mouth, *though* he hide it under his tongue; 13. *Though* he spare it, and forsake it not; but keep it still within his mouth: 14. *Yet* his meat in his bowels is turned, *it is* the gall of asps within him. 15. He hath swallowed down riches, and he shall vomit them up again: God shall cast them out of his belly. 16. He shall suck the poison of asps: the viper's tongue shall slay him. 17. He shall not see the rivers, the floods, the brooks of honey and butter. 18. That which he laboured for shall he restore, and shall not swallow *it* down: according to *his* substance *shall* the restitution *be,* and he shall not rejoice *therein.* 19. Because he hath oppressed *and* hath forsaken the poor; *because* he hath violently taken away an house which he builded not; 20. Surely he shall not feel quietness in his belly, he shall not save of that which he desired. 21. There shall none of his meat be left; therefore shall no man look for his goods. 22. In the fulness of his sufficiency he shall be in straits: every hand of the wicked shall come upon him. 23. *When* he is about to fill his belly, *God* shall cast the fury of his wrath upon him, and shall rain *it* upon him while he is eating. 24. He shall flee from the iron weapon, *and* the bow of steel shall strike him through. 25. It is drawn, and cometh out of the body; yea, the glittering sword cometh out of his gall: terrors *are* upon him. 26. All darkness *shall be* hid in his secret places: a fire not blown shall consume him; it shall go ill with him that is left in his tabernacle. 27. The heaven shall reveal his iniquity; and the earth shall rise up against him. 28. The increase of his house shall depart, *and his goods* shall flow away in the day of his wrath. 29. This *is* the portion of a wicked man from God, and the heritage appointed unto him by God.

Job 21:11. They send forth their little ones like a flock, and their children dance. 12. They take the timbrel and harp, and rejoice at the sound of the organ. 13. They spend their days in wealth, and in a moment go down to the grave. 14. Therefore they say unto God, Depart from us, for we desire not the knowledge of thy ways. 15. What *is* the Almighty, that we should serve him? and what profit should we have, if we pray unto him?

Psa. 49:16. Be not thou afraid when one is made rich, when the glory of his house is increased; 17. For when he dieth he shall carry nothing away: his glory shall not descend after him. 18. Though while he lived he blessed his soul: and *men* will praise thee, when thou doest well to thyself.

Psa. 73:2. But as for me, my feet were almost gone; my steps had well nigh slipped. 3. For I was envious at the foolish, *when* I saw the prosperity of the wicked. 4. For *there are* no bands in their death: but their strength *is* firm. 5. They *are* not in trouble *as other* men; neither are they plagued like *other* men. 6. Therefore pride compasseth them about as a chain; violence covereth them *as* a garment. 7. Their eyes stand out with fatness: they have more than heart could wish. 8. They are corrupt, and speak wickedly *concerning* oppression: they speak loftily. 9. They set their mouth against the heavens, and their tongue walketh through the earth. 10. Therefore his people return hither: and waters of a full *cup* are wrung out to them. 11. And they say, How doth God know? and is there knowledge in the most High? 12. Behold, these *are* the ungodly,

who prosper in the world; they increase *in* riches. 13. Verily I have cleansed my heart *in* vain, and washed my hands in innocency. 14. For all the day long have I been plagued, and chastened every morning. 15. If I say, I will speak thus; behold, I should offend *against* the generation of thy children. 16. When I thought to know this, it *was* too painful for me; 17. Until I went into the sanctuary of God; *then* understood I their end. 18. Surely thou didst set them in slippery places: thou castedst them down into destruction. 19. How are they *brought* into desolation, as in a moment! they are utterly consumed with terrors. 20. As a dream when *one* awaketh; *so,* O Lord, when thou awakest, thou shalt despise their image. 21. Thus my heart was grieved, and I was pricked in my reins. 22. So foolish *was* I, and ignorant: I was *as* a beast before thee.

Prov. 14:12. There is a way which seemeth right unto a man, but the end thereof *are* the ways of death. 13. Even in laughter the heart is sorrowful; and the end of that mirth *is* heaviness.

Prov. 15:21. Folly *is* joy to *him that is* destitute of wisdom: but a man of understanding walketh uprightly.

Prov. 21:17. He that loveth pleasure *shall be* a poor man: he that loveth wine and oil shall not be rich.

Prov. 23:20. Be not among winebibbers; among riotous eaters of flesh: 21. For the drunkard and the glutton shall come to poverty: and drowsiness shall clothe *a man* with rags.

Prov. 27:1. Boast not thyself of to morrow; for thou knowest not what a day may bring forth. 7. The full soul loatheth an honeycomb; but to the hungry soul every bitter thing is sweet.

Eccl. 1:8. All things *are* full of labour; man cannot utter *it:* the eye is not satisfied with seeing, nor the ear filled with hearing.

Eccl. 2:1. I said in mine heart, Go to now, I will prove thee with mirth, therefore enjoy pleasure: and, behold, this also *is* vanity. 2. I said of laughter, *It is* mad: and of mirth, What doeth it? 3. I sought in mine heart to give myself unto wine, yet acquainting mine heart with wisdom; and to lay hold on folly, till I might see what *was* that good for the sons of men, which they should do under the heaven all the days of their life. 4. I made me great works; I builded me houses; I planted me vineyards: 5. I made me gardens and orchards, and I planted trees in them of all *kind of* fruits: 6. I made me pools of water, to water therewith the wood that bringeth forth trees: 7. I got *me* servants and maidens, and had servants born in my house; also I had great possessions of great and small cattle above all that were in Jerusalem before me: 8. I gathered me also silver and gold, and the peculiar treasure of kings and of the provinces: I gat me men singers and women singers, and the delights of the sons of men, *as* musical instruments, and that of all sorts. 9. So I was great, and increased more than all that were before me in Jerusalem: also my wisdom remained with me. 10. And whatsoever mine eyes desired I kept not from them, I withheld not my heart from any joy; for my heart rejoiced in all my labour: and this was my portion of all my labour. 11. Then I looked on all the works that my hands had wrought, and on the labour that I had laboured to do: and, behold, all *was* vanity and vexation of spirit, and *there was* no profit under the sun. 12. And I turned myself to behold wisdom, and madness, and folly: for what *can* the man *do* that cometh after the king? *even* that which hath been already done.

Eccl. 6:11. Seeing there be many things that increase vanity, what *is* man the better? 12. For who knoweth what *is* good for man in *this* life, all the days of his vain life which he spendeth as a shadow? for who can tell a man what shall be after him under the sun?

Eccl. 8:15. Then I commended mirth, because a man hath no better thing under the sun, than to eat, and to drink, and to be merry: for that shall abide with him of his labour the days of his life, which God giveth him under the sun. 16. When I applied mine heart to know wisdom, and to see the business that is done upon the earth: (for also *there is that* neither day nor night seeth sleep with his eyes:) 17. Then I beheld all the work of God, that a man cannot find out the work that is done under the sun: because though a man labour to seek *it* out, yet he shall not find *it;* yea farther; though a wise *man* think to know *it*, yet shall he not be able to find *it*.

Eccl. 10:19. A feast is made for laughter, and wine maketh merry: but money answereth all *things*.

Eccl. 11:9. Rejoice, O young man, in thy youth; and let thy heart cheer thee in the days of thy youth, and walk in the ways of thine heart, and in the sight of thine eyes: but know thou, that for all these *things* God will bring thee into judgment. 10. Therefore remove sorrow from thy heart, and put away evil from thy flesh: for childhood and youth *are* vanity.

Isa. 22:12. And in that day did the Lord GOD of hosts call to weeping, and to mourning, and to baldness, and to girding with sackcloth: 13. And behold joy and gladness, slaying oxen, and killing sheep, eating flesh, and drinking wine: let us eat and drink; for to morrow we shall die.

Isa. 24:7. The new wine mourneth, the vine languisheth, all the merryhearted do sigh. 8. The mirth of tabrets ceaseth, the noise of them that rejoice endeth, the joy of the harp ceaseth. 9. They shall not drink wine with a song; strong drink shall be bitter to them that drink it. 10. The city

of confusion is broken down: every house is shut up, that no man may come in. 11. *There is* a crying for wine in the streets; all joy is darkened, the mirth of the land is gone.

Isa. 28:4. And the glorious beauty, which *is* on the head of the fat valley, shall be a fading flower, *and* as the hasty fruit before the summer; which *when* he that looketh upon it seeth, while it is yet in his hand he eateth it up.

Isa. 32:9. Rise up, ye women that are at ease; hear my voice, ye careless daughters; give ear unto my speech. 10. Many days and years shall ye be troubled, ye careless women: for the vintage shall fail, the gathering shall not come. 11. Tremble, ye women that are at ease; be troubled, ye careless ones: strip you, and make you bare, and gird *sackcloth* upon *your* loins.

Isa. 47:7. And thou saidst, I shall be a lady for ever: *so* that thou didst not lay these *things* to thy heart, neither didst remember the latter end of it. 8. Therefore hear now this, *thou that art* given to pleasures, that dwellest carelessly, that sayest in thine heart, I *am*, and none else beside me; I shall not sit *as* a widow, neither shall I know the loss of children: 9. But these two *things* shall come to thee in a moment in one day, the loss of children, and widowhood: they shall come upon thee in their perfection for the multitude of thy sorceries, *and* for the great abundance of thine enchantments.

Hos. 9:1. Rejoice not, O Israel, for joy, as *other* people: for thou hast gone a whoring from thy God, thou hast loved a reward upon every cornfloor. 11. *As for* Ephraim, their glory shall fly away like a bird, from the birth, and from the womb, and from the conception. 13. Ephraim, as I saw Tyrus, *is* planted in a pleasant place: but Ephraim shall bring forth his children to the murderer.

Amos 6:3. Ye that put far away the evil day, and cause the seat of violence to come near; 4. That lie upon beds of ivory, and stretch themselves upon their couches, and eat the lambs out of the flock, and the calves out of the midst of the stall; 5. That chant to the sound of the viol, *and* invent to themselves instruments of musick, like David; 6. That drink wine in bowls, and anoint themselves with the chief ointments: but they are not grieved for the affliction of Joseph. 7. Therefore now shall they go captive with the first that go captive, and the banquet of them that stretched themselves shall be removed.

Amos 8:10. And I will turn your feasts into mourning, and all your songs into lamentation; and I will bring up sackcloth upon all loins, and baldness upon every head; and I will make it as the mourning of an only *son*, and the end thereof as a bitter day.

Mic. 2:10. Arise ye, and depart; for this

is not *your* rest: because it is polluted, it shall destroy *you*, even with a sore destruction.

Mic. 6:14. Thou shalt eat, but not be satisfied; and thy casting down *shall be* in the midst of thee; and thou shalt take hold, but shalt not deliver; and *that* which thou deliverest will I give up to the sword.

Hag. 1:6. Ye have sown much, and bring in little; ye eat, but ye have not enough; ye drink, but ye are not filled with drink; ye clothe you, but there is none warm; and he that earneth wages earneth wages *to put it* into a bag with holes.

Matt. 6:25. Therefore I say unto you, ¹ Take no thought for your life, what ye shall eat, or what ye shall drink; nor yet for your body, what ye shall put on. Is not the life more than meat, and the body than raiment? 26. Behold the fowls of the air: for they sow not, neither do they reap, nor gather into barns; yet your heavenly Father feedeth them. Are ye not much better than they? 27. Which of you by ²taking thought can add one cubit unto his stature? 28. And why ³take ye thought for raiment? Consider the lilies of the field, how they grow; they toil not, neither do they spin: 29. And yet I say unto you, That even Solomon in all his glory was not arrayed like one of these. 30. Wherefore, if God so clothe the grass of the field, which to day is, and to morrow is cast into the oven, *shall he* not much more *clothe* you, O ye of little faith? 31. ⁴Therefore take no thought, saying, What shall we eat? or, What shall we drink? or, Wherewithal shall we be clothed? 32. (For after all these things do the Gentiles seek:) for your heavenly Father knoweth that ye have need of all these things. 33. But seek ye first the kingdom of God, and his righteousness; and all these things shall be added unto you. 34. ⁴Take therefore no thought for the morrow: for the morrow ⁵ shall take thought for the things of itself. Sufficient unto the day *is* the evil thereof.

[R. V. ¹ Be not anxious   ² being anxious ³ are ye anxious concerning ⁴ Be not therefore anxious ⁵ will be anxious for]

Matt. 10:39. He that findeth his life shall lose it: and he that loseth his life for my sake shall find it. Matt. 16:25; Mark 8:35; Luke 17:33; John 12:25.

Matt. 16:26. For what is a man profited, if he shall gain the whole world, and lose his own soul? or what shall a man give in exchange for his soul? Mark 8:36,37.

Matt. 18:1. At the same time came the disciples unto Jesus, saying, Who is the greatest in the kingdom of heaven? 2. And Jesus called a little child unto him, and set him in the midst of them, 3. And said, Verily I say unto you, Except ye be converted, and become as little children, ye shall not enter into the kingdom of heaven. 4. Whosoever therefore shall humble himself as this little child, the same is greatest in the kingdom of heaven. Luke 9:46-48; **Mark** 9:33-36.

Matt. 24:38. For as in the days that were before the flood they were eating and drinking, marrying and giving in marriage, until the day that Noe entered into the ark, 39. And knew not until the flood came, and took them all away; so shall also the coming of the Son of man be. Luke 17:26-29.

Luke 8:14. And that which fell among thorns are they, which, when they have heard, go forth, and are choked with cares and riches and pleasures of *this* life, and bring no fruit to perfection. Matt. 13:22; Mark 4:19.

Luke 12:19. And I will say to my soul, Soul, thou hast much goods laid up for many years; take thine ease, eat, drink, *and* be merry.

Luke 14:17. And sent his servant at supper time to say to them that were bidden, Come; for all things are now ready. 18. And they all with one *consent* began to make excuse. The first said unto him, I have bought a piece of ground, and I must needs go and see it: I pray thee have me excused. 19. And another said, I have bought five yoke of oxen, and I go to prove them: I pray thee have me excused. 20. And another said, I have married a wife, and therefore I cannot come. 21. So that servant came, and shewed his lord these things. Then the master of the house being angry said to his servant, Go out quickly into the streets and lanes of the city, and bring in hither the poor, and the maimed, and the halt, and the blind. 22. And the servant said, Lord, it is done as thou hast commanded, and yet there is room. 23. And the lord said unto the servant, Go out into the highways and hedges, and compel *them* to come in, that my house may be filled. 24. For I say unto you, That none of those men which were bidden shall taste of my supper. Matt. 22:2-6.

Luke 16:1. And he said also unto his disciples, There was a certain rich man, which had a steward; and the same was accused unto him that he had wasted his goods. 2. And he called him, and said unto him, How is it that I hear this of thee? give an account of thy stewardship: for thou mayest be no longer steward. 3. Then the steward said within himself, What shall I do? for my lord taketh away from me the stewardship: I cannot dig, to beg I am ashamed. 4. I am resolved what to do, that, when I am put out of the stewardship, they may receive me into their houses. 5. So he called every one of his lord's debtors *unto him*, and said unto the first, How much owest thou unto my lord? 6. And he said, An hundred measures of oil. And he said unto him, Take thy bill, and sit down quickly, and write fifty. 7. Then said he to another, And how much owest thou? And he said, An hundred measures of wheat. And he said unto him, Take thy bill, and write fourscore. 8. And the lord commended the unjust steward, because he had done wisely: for the children of this world are in their generation wiser than the children of light. 9. And I say unto you, Make to yourselves friends of the mammon of unrighteousness; that, when ye fail, they may receive you into everlasting habitations. 10. He that is faithful in that which is least is faithful also in much: and he that is unjust in the least is unjust also in much. 11. If therefore ye have not been faithful in the unrighteous mammon, who will commit to your trust the true *riches?* 12. And if ye have not been faithful in that which is another man's, who shall give you that which is your own? 13. No servant can serve two masters: for either he will hate the one, and love the other; or else he will hold to the one, and despise the other. Ye cannot serve God and mammon. 19. There was a certain rich man, which was clothed in purple and fine linen, and fared sumptuously every day: 20. And there was a certain beggar named Lazarus, which was laid at his gate, full of sores, 21. And desiring to be fed with the crumbs which fell from the rich man's table: moreover the dogs came and licked his sores. 22. And it came to pass, that the beggar died, and was carried by the angels into Abraham's bosom: the rich man also died, and was buried: 23. And in hell he lift up his eyes, being in torments, and seeth Abraham afar off, and Lazarus in his bosom. 24. And he cried and said, Father Abraham, have mercy on me, and send Lazarus, that he may dip the tip of his finger in water, and cool my tongue; for I am tormented in this flame. 25. But Abraham said, Son, remember that thou in thy lifetime receivedst thy good things, and likewise Lazarus evil things: but now he is comforted, and thou art tormented.

Luke 21:34. And take heed to yourselves, lest at any time your hearts be overcharged with surfeiting, and drunkenness, and cares of this life, and *so* that day come upon you unawares.

John 5:44. How can ye believe, which receive honour one of another, and seek not the honour that *cometh* from God only?

John 12:43. For they loved the praise of men more than the praise of God.

John 15:19. If ye were of the world, the world would love his own: but because ye are not of the world, but I have chosen you out of the world, therefore the world hateth you.

Rom. 12:2. And be not conformed to this world: but be ye transformed by the renewing of your mind, that ye may prove what *is* that good, and acceptable, and perfect, will of God.

1 Cor. 7:29. But this I say, brethren, the time *is* short: it remaineth, that both they that have wives be as though they had none; 30. And they that weep, as though they wept not; and they that rejoice, as though

they rejoiced not; and they that buy, as though they possessed not; 31. And they that use this world, as not abusing *it:* for the fashion of this world passeth away.

1 Cor. 10:6. Now these things were our examples, to the intent we should not lust after evil things, as they also lusted.

1 Cor. 15:32. If after the manner of men I have fought with beasts at Ephesus, what advantageth it me, if the dead rise not? let us eat and drink; for to morrow we die.

Phil. 3:18. (For many walk, of whom I have told you often, and now tell you even weeping, *that they are* the enemies of the cross of Christ: 19. Whose end *is* destruction, whose God *is their* belly, and *whose* glory *is* in their shame, who mind earthly things.)

Col. 3:2. Set your affection on things above, not on things on the earth. 5. Mortify therefore your members which are upon the earth; fornication, uncleanness, inordinate affection, evil concupiscence, and covetousness, which is idolatry:

1 Tim. 5:6. But she that liveth in pleasure is dead while she liveth.

2 Tim. 2:4. No man that warreth entangleth himself with the affairs of *this* life; that he may please him who hath chosen him to be a soldier. 22. Flee also youthful lusts: but follow righteousness, faith, charity, peace, with them that call on the Lord out of a pure heart.

2 Tim. 3:2. For men shall be lovers of their own selves, covetous, boasters, proud, blasphemers, disobedient to parents, unthankful, unholy, 3. Without natural affection, trucebreakers, false accusers, incontinent, fierce, despisers of those that are good, 4. Traitors, heady, highminded, lovers of pleasures more than lovers of God; 5. Having a form of godliness, but denying the power thereof: from such turn away. 6. For of this sort are they which creep into houses, and lead captive silly women laden with sins, led away with divers lusts, 7. Ever learning, and never able to come to the knowledge of the truth.

Tit. 2:12. Teaching us that, denying ungodliness and worldly lusts, we should live soberly, righteously, and godly, in this present world:

Tit. 3:3. For we ourselves also were sometimes foolish, disobedient, deceived, serving divers lusts and pleasures, living in malice and envy, hateful, *and* hating one another.

Heb. 11:24. By faith Moses, when he was come to years, refused to be called the son of Pharaoh's daughter, 25. Choosing rather to suffer affliction with the people of God, than to enjoy the pleasures of sin for a season; 26. Esteeming the reproach of Christ greater riches than the treasures in Egypt: for he had respect unto the recompence of the reward.

Jas. 2:1. My brethren, have not the faith of our Lord Jesus Christ, *the Lord* of glory, with respect of persons. 2. For if there come into your assembly a man with a gold ring, in goodly apparel, and there come in also a poor man in vile raiment; 3. And ye have respect to him that weareth the gay clothing, and say unto him, Sit thou here in a good place; and say to the poor, Stand thou there, or sit here under my footstool: 4. Are ye not then partial in yourselves, and are become judges of evil thoughts?

Jas. 4:4. Ye adulterers and adulteresses, know ye not that the friendship of the world is enmity with God? whosoever therefore will be a friend of the world is the enemy of God. 9. Be afflicted, and mourn, and weep: let your laughter be turned to mourning, and *your* joy to heaviness.

Jas. 5:5. Ye have lived in pleasure on the earth, and been wanton; ye have nourished your hearts, as in a day of slaughter.

1 Pet. 1:14. As obedient children, not fashioning yourselves according to the former lusts in your ignorance: 24. For all flesh *is* as grass, and all the glory of man as the flower of grass. The grass withereth, and the flower thereof falleth away:

1 Pet. 2:11. Dearly beloved, I beseech *you* as strangers and pilgrims, abstain from fleshly lusts, which war against the soul;

1 Pet. 4:3. For the time past of *our* life may suffice us to have wrought the will of the Gentiles, when we walked in lasciviousness, lusts, excess of wine, revellings, banquetings, and abominable idolatries: 4. Wherein they think it strange that ye run not with *them* to the same excess of riot, speaking evil of *you:*

2 Pet. 2:12. But these, as natural brute beasts, made to be taken and destroyed, speak evil of the things that they understand not; and shall utterly perish in their own corruption; 13. And shall receive the reward of unrighteousness, *as* they that count it pleasure to riot in the day time. Spots *they are* and blemishes, sporting themselves with their own deceivings while they feast with you; 14. Having eyes full of adultery, and that cannot cease from sin; beguiling unstable souls: an heart they have exercised with covetous practices; cursed children: 15. Which have forsaken the right way, and are gone astray, following the way of Balaam *the son* of Bosor, who loved the wages of unrighteousness; 18. For when they speak great swelling *words* of vanity, they allure through the lusts of the flesh, *through much* wantonness, those that were clean escaped from them who live in error.

1 John 2:15. Love not the world, neither the things *that are* in the world. If any man love the world, the love of the Father is not in him. 16. For all that *is* in the world, the lust of the flesh, and the lust of the eyes, and the pride of life, is not of the Father, but is of the world. 17. And the world passeth away, and the lust thereof: but he that doeth the will of God abideth for ever.

Jude 11. Woe unto them! for they have gone in the way of Cain, and ran greedily after the error of Balaam for reward, and perished in the gainsaying of Core. 12. These are spots in your feasts of charity, when they feast with you, feeding themselves without fear: clouds *they are* without water, carried about of winds; trees whose fruit withereth, without fruit, twice dead, plucked up by the roots; 13. Raging waves of the sea, foaming out their own shame; wandering stars, to whom is reserved the blackness of darkness for ever. 16. These are murmurers, complainers, walking after their own lusts; and their mouth speaketh great swelling *words*, having men's persons in admiration because of advantage. 19. These be they who separate themselves, sensual, having not the Spirit.

See COVETOUSNESS; PLEASURES; RICHES.

INSTANCES OF: Esau, Gen. 25:30–34; Heb. 12:16. Jacob, Gen. 25:31–34; 27:36; 30: 37–43. Judah, Gen. 37:26,27. Israelites, Num. 11:33,34; Psa. 78:18,29–31. Balaam, 2 Pet. 2:15; Jude 11, with Num. 22; 23; 24. Eli's sons, 1 Sam. 2:12–17. Gehazi, 2 Kin. 5:21–27. Herod, Matt. 14:6,7. Cretians, Tit. 1:12.

WORM, Ex. 16:20,24; Jonah 4:7. Herod eaten of, Acts 12:23.

FIGURATIVE: Job 25:6; Isa. 41:14; 66:24. Of remorse, Mark 9:44,46,48. *vs.* 44, 46 omitted in *R. V.*

WORMWOOD, a bitter plant, Deut. 29:18.

FIGURATIVE: Deut. 29:18; Prov. 5:4; Jer. 9:15; 23:15; Lam. 3:19.

SYMBOLICAL, Rev. 8:11.

WORSHIP, to be rendered to God only, Ex. 20:3; Deut. 5:7; 6:13; Matt. 4:10; Luke 4:8; Acts 10:26; 14:15; Col. 2:18; Rev. 19:10; 22:8.

Of Jesus, see JESUS, WORSHIP OF.

Acceptable to God, Gen. 4:4; 8:21. Of the wicked rejected, Gen. 4:5,7. See PRAYER, OF THE WICKED. "Iniquity of the holy things," Ex. 28:38. Public, in the temple, Jer. 26:2; Luke 18:10; 24:53. David's ordinances for, 1 Chr. chapters 23–26. Family, Deut. 16:11,14; of Abraham, Gen. 12:7,8; 13: 4,18; of Jacob, Gen. 35:2,3; of Job, Job 1:5; of the Philippian jailer, Acts 16:34. In private homes, Acts 1:13,14; 5:42; 12:12; 20:7–9; Rom. 16:5; 1 Cor. 16:19; Col. 4:15; Philem. 2. In the night, Isa. 30:29; Acts 16:25. Jesus prays a whole night, Luke 6:12.

Attitudes in: Bowing, Ex. 34:8; 2 Chr. 20: 18. Prostration, Gen. 17:3; Mark 3:11.

Prayer in, see PRAYER.

God's presence in, Lev. 19:30; Psa. 77:13; 84:4; Isa. 56:7; Heb. 10:25.

Loved by his people, Psa. 27:4; 84:1–3,10; Zech. 8:21.

Benedictions pronounced, see BENEDICTIONS.

The whole nation required to assemble for, including men, women, children, servants, and strangers, Deut. 16:11; 31:11-13; in Mount Gerizim and Mount Ebal, Josh. 8:32-35. The word of God read in public assemblies, Ex. 24:7; Deut. 27:12-26; 31:11-13; Josh. 8:33-35; 2 Kin. 23:1-3; Neh. 8:1-8,13-18; Matt. 21:23; Luke 4:16,17.

Of angels, forbidden, Rev. 19:10; 22:8,9.

See Afflictions, Prayer in ; Blasphemy; Children; Church; Consecration; Dedication; Idolatry; Instruction, in Religion; Levites; Minister; Music; Offering; Praise; Prayer; Preaching; Priest; Psalms; Religion; Sacrilege; Servant; Stranger; Tabernacle; Temple; Thanksgiving; Women; Word of God; Young Men.

UNCLASSIFIED SCRIPTURES RELATING TO: Gen. 35:2. Then Jacob said unto his household, and to all that were with him, Put away the strange gods that are among you, and be clean, and change your garments: 3. And let us arise, and go up to Beth-el; and I will make there an altar unto God, who answered me in the day of my distress, and was with me in the way which I went.

Ex. 3:5. And he said, Draw not nigh hither: put off thy shoes from off thy feet, for the place whereon thou standest is holy ground. [Josh. 5:15.] 6. Moreover he said, I am the God of thy father, the God of Abraham, the God of Isaac, and the God of Jacob. And Moses hid his face; for he was afraid to look upon God.

Ex. 5:1. And afterward Moses and Aaron went in, and told Pharaoh, Thus saith the Lord God of Israel, Let my people go, that they may hold a feast unto me in the wilderness.

Ex. 15:2. The Lord is my strength and song, and he is become my salvation: he is my God, and I will prepare him an habitation; my father's God, and I will exalt him.

Ex. 19:10. And the Lord said unto Moses, Go unto the people, and sanctify them to day and to morrow, and let them wash their clothes, 11. And be ready against the third day: for the third day the Lord will come down in the sight of all the people upon mount Sinai. 12. And thou shalt set bounds unto the people round about, saying, Take heed to yourselves, that ye go not up into the mount, or touch the border of it: whosoever toucheth the mount shall be surely put to death: 13. There shall not an hand touch it, but he shall surely be stoned, or shot through; whether it be beast or man, it shall not live: when the trumpet soundeth long, they shall come up to the mount. 21. And the Lord said unto Moses, Go down, charge the people, lest they break through unto the Lord to gaze, and many of them perish. 22. And let the priests also, which come near to the Lord, sanctify themselves, lest the Lord break forth upon them. 23. And Moses said unto the Lord,

The people cannot come up to mount Sinai: for thou chargedst us, saying, Set bounds about the mount, and sanctify it. 24. And the Lord said unto him, Away, get thee down, and thou shalt come up, thou, and Aaron with thee: but let not the priests and the people break through to come up unto the Lord, lest he break forth upon them.

Ex. 20:24. An altar of earth thou shalt make unto me, and shalt sacrifice thereon thy burnt offerings, and thy peace offerings, thy sheep, and thine oxen: in all places where I record my name I will come unto thee, and I will bless thee. 25. And if thou wilt make me an altar of stone, thou shalt not build it of hewn stone: for if thou lift up thy tool upon it, thou hast polluted it. 26. Neither shalt thou go up by steps unto mine altar, that thy nakedness be not discovered thereon.

Ex. 24:1. And he said unto Moses, Come up unto the Lord, thou, and Aaron, Nadab, and Abihu, and seventy of the elders of Israel; and worship ye afar off. 2. And Moses alone shall come near the Lord: but they shall not come nigh; neither shall the people go up with him.

Ex. 25:8. And let them make me a sanctuary; that I may dwell among them. 22. And there I will meet with thee, and I will commune with thee from above the mercy seat, and from between the two cherubims which are upon the ark of the testimony, of all things which I will give thee in commandment unto the children of Israel. Num. 17:4.

Ex. 28:34. A golden bell and a pomegranate, a golden bell and a pomegranate, upon the hem of the robe round about. 35. And it shall be upon Aaron to minister: and his sound shall be heard when he goeth in unto the holy place before the Lord, and when he cometh out, that he die not.

Ex. 29:43. And there I will meet with the children of Israel, and the tabernacle shall be sanctified by my glory. Ex. 40:34,35.

Ex. 30:19. For Aaron and his sons shall wash their hands and their feet thereat: 20. When they go into the tabernacle of the congregation, they shall wash with water, that they die not; or when they come near to the altar to minister, to burn offering made by fire unto the Lord: 21. So they shall wash their hands and their feet, that they die not: and it shall be a statute for ever to them, even to him and to his seed throughout their generations.

Ex. 34:8. And Moses made haste, and bowed his head toward the earth, and worshipped.

Lev. 10:3. Then Moses said unto Aaron, This is it that the Lord spake, saying, I will be sanctified in them that come nigh me, and before all the people I will be glorified. And Aaron held his peace.

Lev. 16:2. And the Lord said unto Moses. Speak unto Aaron thy brother, that he come not at all times into the holy place within the vail before the mercy seat, which *is* upon the ark; that he die not: for I will appear in the cloud upon the mercy seat.

2 Kin. 17:36. But the LORD, who brought you up out of the land of Egypt with great power and a stretched out arm, him shall ye fear, and him shall ye worship, and to him shall ye do sacrifice.

1 Chr. 16:29. Give unto the LORD the glory *due* unto his name: bring an offering, and come before him: worship the LORD in the beauty of holiness. Psa. 29:2.

2 Chr. 5:13. It came even to pass, as the trumpeters and singers *were* as one, to make one sound to be heard in praising and thanking the LORD; and when they lifted up *their* voice with the trumpets and cymbals and instruments of musick, and praised the LORD, *saying,* For *he is* good; for his mercy *endureth* for ever: that *then* the house was filled with a cloud, *even* the house of the LORD; 14. So that the priests could not stand to minister by reason of the cloud: for the glory of the LORD had filled the house of God. 1 Kin. 8:3–11.

2 Chr. 7:1. Now when Solomon had made an end of praying, the fire came down from heaven, and consumed the burnt offering and the sacrifices; and the glory of the LORD filled the house.

2 Chr. 30:27. Then the priests the Levites arose and blessed the people: and their voice was heard, and their prayer came *up* to his holy dwelling place, *even* unto heaven.

Ezra 3:10. And when the builders laid the foundation of the temple of the LORD, they set the priests in their apparel with trumpets, and the Levites the sons of Asaph with cymbals, to praise the LORD, after the ordinance of David king of Israel. 11. And they sang together by course in praising and giving thanks unto the LORD; because *he is* good **for** his mercy *endureth* for ever toward Israel. And all the people shouted with a great shout, when they praised the LORD, because the foundation of the house of the LORD was laid. 12. But many of the priests and Levites and chief of the fathers, *who were* ancient men, that had seen the first house, when the foundation of this house was laid before their eyes, wept with a loud voice; and many shouted aloud for joy: 13. So that the people could not discern the noise of the shout of joy from the noise of the weeping of the people: for the people shouted with a loud shout, and the noise was heard afar off.

Neh. 10:39. For the children of Israel and the children of Levi shall bring the offering of the corn, of the new wine, and the oil, unto the chambers, where *are* the vessels of the sanctuary, and the priests that minister, and the porters, and the singers: and we will not forsake the house of our God.

Psa. 5:7. But as for me, I will come *into* thy house in the multitude of thy mercy:

and in thy fear will I worship toward thy holy temple.

Psa. 22:22. I will declare thy name unto my brethren: in the midst of the congregation will I praise thee.

Psa. 24:3. Who shall ascend into the hill of the LORD? or who shall stand in his holy place? 4. He that hath clean hands, and a pure heart; who hath not lifted up his soul unto vanity, nor sworn deceitfully. 5. He shall receive the blessing from the LORD, and righteousness from the God of his salvation. 6. This *is* the generation of them that seek him, that seek thy face, O Jacob.

Psa. 26:6. I will wash mine hands in innocency: so will I compass thine altar, O LORD; 7. That I may publish with the voice of thanksgiving, and tell of all thy wondrous works. 8. LORD, I have loved the habitation of thy house, and the place where thine honour dwelleth.

Psa. 27:4. One *thing* have I desired of the LORD, that will I seek after; that I may dwell in the house of the LORD all the days of my life, to behold the beauty of the LORD, and to enquire in his temple.

Psa. 29:2. Give unto the LORD the glory due unto his name; worship the LORD in the beauty of holiness.

Psa. 35:18. I will give thee thanks in the great congregation: I will praise thee among much people.

Psa. 36:8. They shall be abundantly satisfied with the fatness of thy house; and thou shalt make them drink of the river of thy pleasures.

Psa. 42:4. When I remember these *things,* I pour out my soul in me: for I had gone with the multitude, I went with them to the house of God, with the voice of joy and praise, with a multitude that kept holyday.

Psa. 48:9. We have thought of thy lovingkindness, O God, in the midst of thy temple.

Psa. 51:19. Then shalt thou be pleased with the sacrifices of righteousness, with burnt offering and whole burnt offering: then shall they offer bullocks upon thine altar.

Psa. 55:14. We took sweet counsel together, *and* walked unto the house of God in company.

Psa. 63:1. O God, thou *art* my God; early will I seek thee: my soul thirsteth for thee, my flesh longeth for thee in a dry and thirsty land, where no water is; 2. To see thy power and thy glory, so *as* I have seen thee in the sanctuary.

Psa. 65:4. Blessed *is the man whom* thou choosest, and causest to approach *unto thee,* *that* he may dwell in thy courts: we shall be satisfied with the goodness of thy house, *even* of thy holy temple.

Psa. 66:4. All the earth shall worship thee, and shall sing unto thee; they shall sing *to* thy name. 13. I will go into thy house with burnt offerings: I will pay thee my vows, 14. Which my lips have uttered, and my mouth hath spoken, when I was in trouble.

Psa. 77:13. Thy way, O God, *is* in the sanctuary: who *is so* great a God as *our* God?

Psa. 84:1. How amiable *are* thy tabernacles, O LORD of hosts! 2. My soul longeth, yea, even fainteth for the courts of the LORD: my heart and my flesh crieth out for the living God. 3. Yea, the sparrow hath found an house, and the swallow a nest for herself, where she may lay her young, *even* thine altars, O LORD of hosts, my King, and my God. 4. Blessed *are* they that dwell in thy house: they will be still praising thee. 10. For a day in thy courts *is* better than a thousand. I had rather be a doorkeeper in the house of my God, than to dwell in the tents of wickedness.

Psa. 89:7. God is greatly to be feared in the assembly of the saints, and to be had in reverence of all *them that are* about him.

Psa. 92:13. Those that be planted in the house of the LORD shall flourish in the courts of our God. 14. They shall still bring forth fruit in old age; they shall be fat and flourishing;

Psa. 93:5. Thy testimonies are very sure: holiness becometh thine house, O LORD, for ever.

Psa. 95:6. O come, let us worship and bow down: let us kneel before the LORD our maker.

Psa. 98:2. The LORD hath made known his salvation: his righteousness hath he openly shewed in the sight of the heathen. 3. He hath remembered his mercy and his truth toward the house of Israel:

Psa. 100:1. Make a joyful noise unto the LORD, all ye lands. 2. Serve the LORD with gladness: come before his presence with singing. 3. Know ye that the LORD he *is* God: *it is* he *that* hath made us, and not we ourselves; *we are* his people, and the sheep of his pasture. 4. Enter into his gates with thanksgiving, *and* into his courts with praise: be thankful unto him, *and* bless his name.

Psa 103:1. Bless the LORD, O my soul: and all that is within me, *bless* his holy name. 2. Bless the LORD, O my soul, and forget not all his benefits: 3. Who forgiveth all thine iniquities; who healeth all thy diseases; 4. Who redeemeth thy life from destruction; who crowneth thee with lovingkindness and tender mercies;

Psa. 107:6. Then they cried unto the LORD in their trouble, *and* he delivered them out of their distresses. 7. And he led them forth by the right way, that they might go to a city of habitation. 8. Oh that *men* would praise the LORD *for* his goodness, and *for* his wonderful works to the children of men! 32. Let them exalt him also in the congregation of the people, and praise him in the assembly of the elders.

Psa. 116:12. What shall I render unto the LORD *for* all his benefits toward me? 13.

I will take the cup of salvation, and call upon the name of the LORD. 14. I will pay my vows unto the LORD now in the presence of all his people. 17. I will offer to thee the sacrifice of thanksgiving, and will call upon the name of the LORD.

Psa. 118:18. The LORD hath chastened me sore: but he hath not given me over unto death. 19. Open to me the gates of righteousness: I will go into them, *and* I will praise the LORD:

Psa. 119:108. Accept, I beseech thee, the freewill offerings of my mouth, O LORD, and teach me thy judgments.

Psa. 122:1. I was glad when they said unto me, Let us go into the house of the LORD.

Psa. 126:1. When the LORD turned again the captivity of Zion, we were like them that dream. 2. Then was our mouth filled with laughter, and our tongue with singing: then said they among the heathen, The LORD hath done great things for them. 3. The LORD hath done great things for us; *whereof* we are glad.

Psa. 132:7. We will go into his tabernacles: we will worship at his footstool. 13. For the LORD hath chosen Zion; he hath desired *it* for his habitation. 14. This *is* my rest for ever: here will I dwell; for I have desired it.

Psa. 138:2. I will worship toward thy holy temple, and praise thy name for thy lovingkindness and for thy truth: for thou hast magnified thy word above all thy name.

Psa. 149:1. Sing unto the LORD a new song, *and* his praise in the congregation of saints.

Eccl. 5:1. Keep thy foot when thou goest to the house of God, and be more ready to hear, than to give the sacrifice of fools: for they consider not that they do evil. 2. Be not rash with thy mouth, and let not thine heart be hasty to utter *any* thing before God: for God *is* in heaven, and thou upon earth: therefore let thy words be few.

Isa. 1:11. To what purpose *is* the multitude of your sacrifices unto me? saith the LORD: I am full of the burnt offerings of rams, and the fat of fed beasts; and I delight not in the blood of bullocks, or of lambs, or of he goats. 12. When ye come to appear before me, who hath required this at your hand, to tread my courts? 13. Bring no more vain oblations; incense is an abomination unto me; the new moons and sabbaths, the calling of assemblies, I cannot away with; *it is* iniquity, even the solemn meeting. 14. Your new moons and your appointed feasts my soul hateth: they are a trouble unto me; I am weary to bear *them.* 15. And when ye spread forth your hands, I will hide mine eyes from you: yea, when ye make many prayers, I will not hear: your hands are full of blood.

Isa. 2:3. And many people shall go and say, Come ye, and let us go up to the mountain of the LORD, to the house of the God of Jacob; and he will teach us of his ways, and

(91)

we will walk in his paths: for out of Zion shall go forth the law, and the word of the LORD from Jerusalem. Mic. 4:2.

Isa. 4:5. And the LORD will create upon every dwelling place of mount Zion, and upon her assemblies, a cloud and smoke by day, and the shining of a flaming fire by night: for upon all the glory *shall be* a defence.

Isa. 12:5. Sing unto the LORD; for he hath done excellent things: this *is* known in all the earth. 6. Cry out and shout, thou inhabitant of Zion: for great *is* the Holy One of Israel in the midst of thee.

Isa. 25:9. And it shall be said in that day, Lo, this *is* our God; we have waited for him, and he will save us: this *is* the LORD; we have waited for him, we will be glad and rejoice in his salvation.

Isa. 29:13. Wherefore the Lord said, Forasmuch as this people draw near *me* with their mouth, and with their lips do honour me, but have removed their heart far from me, and their fear toward me is taught by the precept of men: 14. Therefore, behold, I will proceed to do a marvellous work among this people, *even* a marvellous work and a wonder: for the wisdom of their wise *men* shall perish, and the understanding of their prudent *men* shall be hid. 15. Woe unto them that seek deep to hide their counsel from the LORD, and their works are in the dark, and they say, Who seeth us? and who knoweth us? 16. Surely your turning of things upside down shall be esteemed as the potter's clay:

Isa. 30:29. Ye shall have a song, as in the night *when* a holy solemnity is kept; and gladness of heart, as when one goeth with a pipe to come into the mountain of the LORD, to the mighty One of Israel.

Isa. 38:20. The LORD *was ready* to save me: therefore we will sing my songs to the stringed instruments all the days of our life in the house of the LORD.

Isa. 40:31. But they that wait upon the LORD shall renew *their* strength; they shall mount up with wings as eagles; they shall run, and not be weary; *and* they shall walk, and not faint.

Isa. 43:22. But thou hast not called upon me, O Jacob; but thou hast been weary of me, O Israel. 23. Thou hast not brought me the small cattle of thy burnt offerings; neither hast thou honoured me with thy sacrifices. I have not caused thee to serve with an offering, nor wearied thee with incense. 24. Thou hast bought me no sweet cane with money, neither hast thou filled me with the fat of thy sacrifices: but thou hast made me to serve with thy sins, thou hast wearied me with thine iniquities.

Isa. 49:13. Sing, O heavens; and be joyful, O earth; and break forth into singing, O mountains: for the LORD hath comforted his people and will have mercy upon his afflicted.

Isa. 52:9. Break forth into joy, sing together, ye waste places of Jerusalem: for the LORD hath comforted his people, he hath redeemed Jerusalem.

Isa. 56:6. Also the sons of the stranger, that join themselves to the LORD, to serve him, and to love the name of the LORD, to be his servants, every one that keepeth the sabbath from polluting it, and taketh hold of my covenant; 7. Even them will I bring to my holy mountain, and make them joyful in my house of prayer: their burnt offerings and their sacrifices *shall be* accepted upon mine altar; for mine house shall be called an house of prayer for all people.

Isa. 66:1. Thus saith the LORD, The heaven *is* my throne, and the earth *is* my footstool: where *is* the house that ye build unto me? and where *is* the place of my rest? 2. For all those *things* hath mine hand made, and all those *things* have been, saith the LORD: but to this *man* will I look, *even to him that is* poor and of a contrite spirit, and trembleth at my word.

Jer. 31:11. For the LORD hath redeemed Jacob, and ransomed him from the hand of *him that was* stronger than he. 12. Therefore they shall come and sing in the height of Zion, and shall flow together to the goodness of the LORD, for wheat, and for wine, and for oil, and for the young of the flock and of the herd: and their soul shall be as a watered garden; and they shall not sorrow any more at all.

Ezek. 22:8. Thou hast despised mine holy things, and hast profaned my sabbaths.

Hos. 6:6. For I desired mercy, and not sacrifice; and the knowledge of God more than burnt offerings.

Amos 5:21. I hate, I despise your feast days, and I will not smell in your solemn assemblies. 22. Though ye offer me burnt offerings and your meat offerings, I will not accept *them:* neither will I regard the peace offerings of your fat beasts. 23. Take thou away from me the noise of thy songs; for I will not hear the melody of thy viols. 24. But let judgment run down as waters, and righteousness as a mighty stream.

Hab. 2:20. The LORD *is* in his holy temple: let all the earth keep silence before him.

Zeph. 3:18. I will gather *them that are* sorrowful for the solemn assembly, *who* are of thee, *to whom* the reproach of it *was* a burden.

Zech. 8:21. The inhabitants of one *city* shall go to another, saying, Let us go speedily to pray before the LORD, and to seek the LORD of hosts: I will go also. 22. Yea, many people and strong nations shall come to seek the LORD of hosts in Jerusalem, and to pray before the LORD.

Mal. 3:3. And he shall sit *as* a refiner and purifier of silver: and he shall purify the sons of Levi, and purge them as gold and silver, that they may offer unto the LORD an offering in righteousness. 4. Then shall the offering of Judah and Jerusalem be pleasant unto the LORD, as in the days of old, and as in former years.

Matt. 18:19. Again I say unto you, That if two of you shall agree on earth as touching any thing that they shall ask, it shall be done for them of my Father which is in heaven. 20. For where two or three are gathered together in my name, there am I in the midst of them.

Luke 4:8. Thou shalt worship the Lord thy God, and him only shalt thou serve.

John 4:23. The hour cometh, and now is, when the true worshippers shall worship the Father in spirit and in truth: for the Father seeketh such to worship him. 24. God is a Spirit: and they that worship him must worship *him* in spirit and in truth.

Acts 2:1. When the day of Pentecost was fully come, they were all with one accord in one place. 2. And suddenly there came a sound from heaven as of a rushing mighty wind, and it filled all the house where they were sitting. 3. And there appeared unto them cloven tongues like as of fire, and it sat upon each of them. 4. And they were all filled with the Holy Ghost, and began to speak with other tongues, as the Spirit gave them utterance.

Acts 17:24. God that made the world and all things therein, seeing that he is Lord of heaven and earth, dwelleth not in temples made with hands; 25. Neither is worshipped with men's hands, as though he needed any thing, seeing he giveth to all life, and breath, and all things;

1 Cor. 11:13. Judge in yourselves: is it comely that a woman pray unto God uncovered? 20. When ye come together therefore into one place, *this* is not to eat the Lord's supper. 21. For in eating every one taketh before *other* his own supper: and one is hungry, and another is drunken. 22. What? have ye not houses to eat and drink in? or despise ye the church of God, and shame them that have not? What shall I say to you? shall I praise you in this? I praise *you* not.

1 Cor. 14:15. What is it then? I will pray with the spirit, and I will pray with the understanding also: I will sing with the spirit, and I will sing with the understanding also. 16. Else when thou shalt bless with the spirit, how shall he that occupieth the room of the unlearned say Amen at thy giving of thanks, seeing he understandeth not what thou sayest? 17. For thou verily givest thanks well, but the other is not edified.

Phil. 3:3. For we are the circumcision, which worship God in the spirit, and rejoice in Christ Jesus, and have no confidence in the flesh.

1 Tim. 2:8. I will therefore that men pray every where, lifting up holy hands, without wrath and doubting.

Heb. 10:25. Not forsaking the assembling of ourselves together, as the manner of some *is*; but exhorting *one another*: and so much the more, as ye see the day approaching.

Heb. 12:28. Wherefore we receiving a kingdom which cannot be moved, let us have grace, whereby we may serve God acceptably with reverence and godly fear:

1 Pet. 2:5. Ye also, as lively stones, be built up a spiritual house, an holy priesthood, to offer up spiritual sacrifices, acceptable to God by Jesus Christ.

Rev. 11:1. And there was given me a reed like unto a rod: and the angel stood, saying, Rise, and measure the temple of God, and the altar, and them that worship therein.

Rev. 14:6. And I saw another angel fly in the midst of heaven, having the everlasting gospel to preach unto them that dwell on the earth, and to every nation, and kindred, and tongue, and people, 7. Saying with a loud voice, Fear God, and give glory to him; for the hour of his judgment is come: and worship him that made heaven, and earth, and the sea, and the fountains of waters.

Rev. 15:4. Who shall not fear thee, O Lord, and glorify thy name? for *thou* only *art* holy: for all nations shall come and worship before thee; for thy judgments are made manifest.

See PRAISE; PRAYER; THANKFULNESS.

ENJOINED: Gen. 35:1. And God said unto Jacob, Arise, go up to Beth-el, and dwell there: and make there an altar unto God, that appeared unto thee when thou fleddest from the face of Esau thy brother.

Ex. 23:17. Three times in the year all thy males shall appear before the Lord GOD. [Ex. 34:23.] 18. Thou shalt not offer the blood of my sacrifice with leavened bread; neither shall the fat of my sacrifice remain until the morning.

Deut. 12:5. But unto the place which the LORD your God shall choose out of all your tribes to put his name there, *even* unto his habitation shall ye seek, and thither thou shalt come: 6. And thither ye shall bring your burnt offerings, and your sacrifices, and your tithes, and heave offerings of your hand, and your vows, and your freewill offerings, and the firstlings of your herds and of your flocks: 7. And there ye shall eat before the LORD your God, and ye shall rejoice in all that ye put your hand unto, ye and your households, wherein the LORD thy God hath blessed thee. 11. Then there shall be a place which the LORD your God shall choose to cause his name to dwell there; thither shall ye bring all that I command you; your burnt offerings, and your sacrifices, your tithes, and the heave offering of your hand, and all your choice vows which ye vow unto the LORD: 12. And ye shall rejoice before the LORD your God, ye, and your sons, and your daughters, and your menservants, and your maidservants, and the Levite that *is* within your gates;

Deut. 16:6. But at the place which the

LORD thy God shall choose to place his name in, there thou shalt sacrifice the passover at even, at the going down of the sun, at the season that thou camest forth out of Egypt. 7. And thou shalt roast and eat *it* in the place which the LORD thy God shall choose: and thou shalt turn in the morning, and go unto thy tents. 8. Six days thou shalt eat unleavened bread: and on the seventh day *shall be* a solemn assembly to the LORD thy God: thou shalt do no work *therein.*

Deut. 31:11. When all Israel is come to appear before the LORD thy God in the place which he shall choose, thou shalt read this law before all Israel in their hearing. 12. Gather the people together, men, and women, and children, and thy stranger that *is* within thy gates, that they may hear, and that they may learn, and fear the LORD your God, and observe to do all the words of this law: 13. And *that* their children, which have not known *any thing,* may hear, and learn to fear the LORD your God, as long as ye live in the land whither ye go over Jordan to possess it.

Deut. 33:19. They shall call the people unto the mountain; there they shall offer sacrifices of righteousness: for they shall suck *of* the abundance of the seas, and *of* treasures hid in the sand.

2 Kin. 17:36. But the LORD, who brought you up out of the land of Egypt with great power and a stretched out arm, him shall ye fear, and him shall ye worship, and to him shall ye do sacrifice.

Psa. 45:11. So shall the king greatly desire thy beauty: for he *is* thy Lord; and worship thou him.

Psa. 76:11. Vow, and pay unto the LORD your God: let all that be round about him bring presents unto him that ought to be feared.

Psa. 96:8. Give unto the LORD the glory *due unto* his name: bring an offering, and come into his courts. 9. O worship the LORD in the beauty of holiness: fear before him, all the earth.

Psa. 97:7. Confounded be all they that serve graven images, that boast themselves of idols: worship him, all *ye* gods.

Psa. 99:5. Exalt ye the LORD our God, and worship at his footstool; *for* he *is* holy.

Joel 1:14. Sanctify ye a fast, call a solemn assembly, gather the elders *and* all the inhabitants of the land *into* the house of the LORD your God, and cry unto the LORD. 15. Alas for the day! for the day of the LORD *is* at hand, and as a destruction from the Almighty shall it come.

Joel 2:15. Blow the trumpet in Zion, sanctify a fast, call a solemn assembly: 16. Gather the people, sanctify the congregation, assemble the elders, gather the children, and those that suck the breasts: let the bridegroom go forth of his chamber, and the bride out of her closet. 17. Let the priests, the ministers of the LORD, weep between the porch and the altar, and let them say, Spare thy people, O LORD, and give not thine heritage to reproach, that the heathen should rule over them: wherefore should they say among the people, Where *is* their God?

Nah. 1:15. Behold upon the mountains the feet of him that bringeth good tidings, that publisheth peace! O Judah, keep thy solemn feasts, perform thy vows: for the wicked shall no more pass through thee; he is utterly cut off.

Hag. 1:8. Go up to the mountain, and bring wood, and build the house; and I will take pleasure in it, and I will be glorified, saith the LORD.

Zech. 14:16. And it shall come to pass, *that* every one that is left of all the nations which came against Jerusalem shall even go up from year to year to worship the King, the LORD of hosts, and to keep the feast of tabernacles. 17. And it shall be, *that* whoso will not come up of *all* the families of the earth unto Jerusalem to worship the King, the LORD of hosts, even upon them shall be no rain. 18. And if the family of Egypt go not up, and come not, that *have* no *rain;* there shall be the plague, wherewith the LORD will smite the heathen that come not up to keep the feast of tabernacles.

Matt. 8:4. And Jesus saith unto him, See thou tell no man: but go thy way, shew thyself to the priest, and offer the gift that Moses commanded, for a testimony unto them. Mark 1:44; Luke 5:14.

Heb. 10:25. Not forsaking the assembling of ourselves together, as the manner of some *is;* but exhorting *one another:* and so much the more, as ye see the day approaching.

Rev. 14:7. Saying with a loud voice, Fear God, and give glory to him; for the hour of his judgment is come: and worship him that made heaven, and earth, and the sea, and the fountains of waters.

Rev. 19:10. And I fell at his feet to worship him. And he said unto me, See *thou do it* not: I am thy fellowservant, and of thy brethren that have the testimony of Jesus: worship God: for the testimony of Jesus is the spirit of prophecy.

WOUNDS, treatment of, Prov. 20:30; Isa. 1:6; Luke 10:34.

WRATH. See ANGER; GOD, ANGER OF.

WRESTLING. FIGURATIVE: Gen. 30:8; 32:24,25; Eph. 6:12.

WRITING. Copyists were called scribes. See SCRIBES.

See BOOKS; ENGRAVING; INK; INKHORN; LETTERS; PEN; TABLES OF STONE.

Y

YARN, 1 Kin. 10:28; 2 Chr. 1:16. See WEAVING.

YEAR, Gen. 1:14. Divided into months, Ex. 12:2; Num. 10:10; 28:11. See MONTHS.

Annual feasts, Lev. 25:5. See FEASTS.

Redemption of houses sold, limited to one, Lev. 25:29,30. Land to rest one, in seven, Lev. 25:5. Of release, Deut. 15:9.

Age computed by: Of Abraham, Gen. 25:7; of Jacob, Gen. 47:9. See LONGEVITY.

A thousand, with the Lord as one day, Psa. 90:4; 2 Pet. 3:8. Satan to be bound a thousand, Rev. 20:2-4,7.

See JUBILEE, YEAR OF; MILLENNIUM; TIME.

YOKE. FIGURATIVE: Lev. 26:13; Isa. 9:4; 10:27; Jer. 2:20; 5:5; 28:2,4,10; 30:8; Lam. 1:14; 3:27; Matt. 11:29,30; Acts 15:10.

YOUNG MEN. Ex. 24:3. And Moses came and told the people all the words of the LORD, and all the judgments: and all the people answered with one voice, and said, All the words which the LORD hath said will we do. 4. And Moses wrote all the words of the LORD, and rose up early in the morning, and builded an altar under the hill, and twelve pillars, according to the twelve tribes of Israel. 5. And he sent young men of the children of Israel, which offered burnt offerings, and sacrificed peace offerings of oxen unto the LORD.

1 Kin. 12:6. And king Rehoboam consulted with the old men, that stood before Solomon his father while he yet lived, and said, How do ye advise that I may answer this people? 7. And they spake unto him, saying, If thou wilt be a servant unto this people this day, and wilt serve them, and answer them, and speak good words to them, then they will be thy servants for ever. 8. But he forsook the counsel of the old men, which they had given him, and consulted with the young men that were grown up with him, *and* which stood before him: 9. And he said unto them, What counsel give ye that we may answer this people, who have spoken to me, saying, Make the yoke which thy father did put upon us lighter? 10. And the young men that were grown up with him spake unto him, saying, Thus shalt thou speak unto this people that spake unto thee, saying, Thy father made our yoke heavy, but make thou *it* lighter unto us; thus shalt thou say unto them, My little *finger* shall be thicker than my father's loins. 11. And now whereas my father did lade you with a heavy yoke, I will add to your yoke: my father hath chastised you with whips, but I will chastise you with scorpions. 12. So Jeroboam and all the people came to Rehoboam the third day, as the king had appointed, saying, Come to me again the third day. 13. And the king answered the people roughly, and forsook the old men's counsel that they gave him; 14. And spake to them after the counsel of the young men, saying, My father made your yoke heavy, and I will add to your yoke: my father *also* chastised you with whips, but I will chastise you with scorpions. 15. Wherefore the king hearkened not unto the people; for the cause

was from the LORD, that he might perform his saying, which the LORD spake by Ahijah the Shilonite unto Jeroboam the son of Nebat. 2 Chr. 10:8.

Psa. 119:9. Wherewithal shall a young man cleanse his way? by taking heed *thereto* according to thy word.

Psa. 148:12. Both young men, and maidens; old men, and children: 13. Let them praise the name of the LORD: for his name alone is excellent; his glory *is* above the earth and heaven.

Prov. 1:1. The proverbs of Solomon the son of David, king of Israel; 2. To know wisdom and instruction; to perceive the words of understanding; 3. To receive the instruction of wisdom, justice, and judgment, and equity; 4. To give subtilty to the simple, to the young man knowledge and discretion. 5. A wise *man* will hear, and will increase learning; and a man of understanding shall attain unto wise counsels: 6. To understand a proverb, and the interpretation; the words of the wise, and their dark sayings. 7. The fear of the LORD *is* the beginning of knowledge: *but* fools despise wisdom and instruction. 8. My son, hear the instruction of thy father, and forsake not the law of thy mother: 9. For they *shall be* an ornament of grace unto thy head, and chains about thy neck. 10. My son, if sinners entice thee, consent thou not. 11. If they say, Come with us, let us lay wait for blood, let us lurk privily for the innocent without cause: 12. Let us swallow them up alive as the grave; and whole, as those that go down into the pit: 13. We shall find all precious substance, we shall fill our houses with spoil: 14. Cast in thy lot among us; let us all have one purse: 15. My son, walk not thou in the way with them; refrain thy foot from their path: 16. For their feet run to evil, and make haste to shed blood. 17. Surely in vain the net is spread in the sight of any bird. 18. And they lay wait for their *own* blood; they lurk privily for their *own* lives. 19. So *are* the ways of every one that is greedy of gain; *which* taketh away the life of the owners thereof. 20. Wisdom crieth without; she uttereth her voice in the streets: 21. She crieth in the chief place of concourse, in the openings of the gates: in the city she uttereth her words, *saying*, 22. How long, ye simple ones, will ye love simplicity? and the scorners delight in their scorning, and fools hate knowledge? 23. Turn you at my reproof: behold, I will pour out my spirit unto you, I will make known my words unto you. 24. Because I have called, and ye refused; I have stretched out my hand, and no man regarded; 25. But ye have set at nought all my counsel, and would none of my reproof: 26. I also will laugh at your calamity; I will mock when your fear cometh; 27. When your fear cometh as desolation, and your destruction cometh as a whirlwind; when distress and anguish cometh upon you. 28. Then shall they call upon me, but I will not answer; they shall seek me early, but they shall not find me: 29. For that they hated knowledge, and did not choose the fear of the LORD: 30. They would none of my counsel: they despised all my reproof. 31. Therefore shall they eat of the fruit of their own way, and be filled with their own devices. 32. For the turning away of the simple shall slay them, and the prosperity of fools shall destroy them. 33. But whoso hearkeneth unto me shall dwell safely, and shall be quiet from fear of evil.

Prov. 2:1. My son, if thou wilt receive my words, and hide my commandments with thee; 2. So that thou incline thine ear unto wisdom, *and* apply thine heart to understanding; 3. Yea, if thou criest after knowledge, *and* liftest up thy voice for understanding; 4. If thou seekest her as silver, and searchest for her as *for* hid treasures; 5. Then shalt thou understand the fear of the LORD, and find the knowledge of God. 6. For the LORD giveth wisdom: out of his mouth *cometh* knowledge and understanding. 7. He layeth up sound wisdom for the righteous: *he is* a buckler to them that walk uprightly. 8. He keepeth the paths of judgment, and preserveth the way of his saints. 9. Then shalt thou understand righteousness, and judgment, and equity; *yea*, every good path. 10. When wisdom entereth into thine heart, and knowledge is pleasant unto thy soul; 11. Discretion shall preserve thee, understanding shall keep thee: 12. To deliver thee from the way of the evil *man*, from the man that speaketh froward things; 13. Who leave the paths of uprightness, to walk in the ways of darkness; 14. Who rejoice to do evil, *and* delight in the frowardness of the wicked; 15. Whose ways *are* crooked, and *they* froward in their paths: 16. To deliver thee from the strange woman, *even* from the stranger *which* flattereth with her words; 17. Which forsaketh the guide of her youth, and forgetteth the covenant of her God. 18. For her house inclineth unto death, and her paths unto the dead. 19. None that go unto her return again, neither take they hold of the paths of life. 20. That thou mayest walk in the way of good *men*, and keep the paths of the righteous. 21. For the upright shall dwell in the land, and the perfect shall remain in it. 22. But the wicked shall be cut off from the earth, and the transgressors shall be rooted out of it.

Prov. 3:1. My son, forget not my law; but let thine heart keep my commandments: 2. For length of days, and long life, and peace, shall they add to thee. 3. Let not mercy and truth forsake thee: bind them about thy neck; write them upon the table of thine heart: 4. So shalt thou find favour and good understanding in the sight of God and man.

5. Trust in the LORD with all thine heart; and lean not unto thine own understanding. 6. In all thy ways acknowledge him, and he shall direct thy paths. 7. Be not wise in thine own eyes: fear the LORD, and depart from evil. 8. It shall be health to thy navel, and marrow to thy bones. 9. Honour the LORD with thy substance, and with the firstfruits of all thine increase: 10. So shall thy barns be filled with plenty, and thy presses shall burst out with new wine. 11. My son, despise not the chastening of the LORD; neither be weary of his correction: 12. For whom the LORD loveth he correcteth; even as a father the son *in whom* he delighteth. 13. Happy *is* the man *that* findeth wisdom, and the man *that* getteth understanding. 14. For the merchandise of it *is* better than the merchandise of silver, and the gain thereof than fine gold. 15. She *is* more precious than rubies: and all the things thou canst desire are not to be compared unto her. 16. Length of days *is* in her right hand; *and* in her left hand riches and honour. 17. Her ways *are* ways of pleasantness, and all her paths *are* peace. 18. She *is* a tree of life to them that lay hold upon her: and happy *is every one* that retaineth her. 19. The LORD by wisdom hath founded the earth; by understanding hath he established the heavens. 20. By his knowledge the depths are broken up, and the clouds drop down the dew. 21. My son, let not them depart from thine eyes: keep sound wisdom and discretion: 22. So shall they be life unto thy soul, and grace to thy neck. 23. Then shalt thou walk in thy way safely, and thy foot shall not stumble. 24. When thou liest down, thou shalt not be afraid: yea, thou shalt lie down, and thy sleep shall be sweet. 25. Be not afraid of sudden fear, neither of the desolation of the wicked, when it cometh. 26. For the LORD shall be thy confidence, and shall keep thy foot from being taken. 27. Withhold not good from them to whom it is due, when it is in the power of thine hand to do *it*. 28. Say not unto thy neighbour, Go, and come again, and to morrow I will give; when thou hast it by thee. 29. Devise not evil against thy neighbour, seeing he dwelleth securely by thee. 30. Strive not with a man without cause, if he have done thee no harm. 31. Envy thou not the oppressor, and choose none of his ways. 32. For the froward *is* abomination to the LORD: but his secret *is* with the righteous. 33. The curse of the LORD *is* in the house of the wicked: but he blesseth the habitation of the just. 34. Surely he scorneth the scorners: but he giveth grace unto the lowly. 35. The wise shall inherit glory: but shame shall be the promotion of fools.

Prov. 4:1. Hear, ye children, the instruction of a father, and attend to know understanding. 2. For I give you good doctrine, forsake ye not my law. 3. For I was my father's son, tender and only *beloved* in the sight of my mother. 4. He taught me also, and said unto me, Let thine heart retain my words: keep my commandments, and live. 5. Get wisdom, get understanding: forget *it* not; neither decline from the words of my mouth. 6. Forsake her not, and she shall preserve thee: love her, and she shall keep thee. 7. Wisdom *is* the principal thing; *therefore* get wisdom: and with all thy getting get understanding. 8. Exalt her, and she shall promote thee: she shall bring thee to honour, when thou dost embrace her. 9. She shall give to thine head an ornament of grace: a crown of glory shall she deliver to thee. 10. Hear, O my son, and receive my sayings; and the years of thy life shall be many. 11. I have taught thee in the way of wisdom; I have led thee in right paths. 12. When thou goest, thy steps shall not be straitened; and when thou runnest, thou shalt not stumble. 13. Take fast hold of instruction; let *her* not go: keep her; for she *is* thy life. 14. Enter not into the path of the wicked, and go not in the way of evil *men*. 15. Avoid it, pass not by it, turn from it, and pass away. 16. For they sleep not, except they have done mischief; and their sleep is taken away, unless they cause *some* to fall. 17. For they eat the bread of wickedness, and drink the wine of violence. 18. But the path of the just *is* as the shining light, that shineth more and more unto the perfect day. 19. The way of the wicked *is* as darkness: they know not at what they stumble. 20. My son, attend to my words; incline thine ear unto my sayings. 21. Let them not depart from thine eyes; keep them in the midst of thine heart. 22. For they *are* life unto those that find them, and health to all their flesh. 23. Keep thy heart with all diligence; for out of it *are* the issues of life. 24. Put away from thee a froward mouth, and perverse lips put far from thee. 25. Let thine eyes look right on, and let thine eyelids look straight before thee. 26. Ponder the path of thy feet, and let all thy ways be established. 27. Turn not to the right hand nor to the left: remove thy foot from evil.

Prov. 5:1. My son, attend unto my wisdom, *and* bow thine ear to my understanding: 2. That thou mayest regard discretion, and *that* thy lips may keep knowledge. 3. For the lips of a strange woman drop *as* an honeycomb, and her mouth *is* smoother than oil: 4. But her end is bitter as wormwood, sharp as a twoedged sword. 5. Her feet go down to death; her steps take hold on hell. 6. Lest thou shouldest ponder the path of life, her ways are moveable, *that* thou canst not know *them*. 7. Hear me now therefore, O ye children, and depart not from the words of my mouth. 8. Remove thy way far from her, and come not nigh the door of her house: 9. Lest thou give thine honour unto others, and thy years unto the cruel: 10. Lest strangers be filled with thy wealth; and

thy labours *be* in the house of a stranger; 11. And thou mourn at the last, when thy flesh and thy body are consumed, 12. And say, How have I hated instruction, and my heart despised reproof; 13. And have not obeyed the voice of my teachers, nor inclined mine ear to them that instructed me! 14. I was almost in all evil in the midst of the congregation and assembly. 15. Drink waters out of thine own cistern, and running waters out of thine own well. 16. Let thy fountains be dispersed abroad, *and* rivers of waters in the streets. 17. Let them be only thine own, and not strangers' with thee. 18. Let thy fountain be blessed: and rejoice with the wife of thy youth. 19. *Let her be as* the loving hind and pleasant roe; let her breasts satisfy thee at all times; and be thou ravished always with her love. 20. And why wilt thou, my son, be ravished with a strange woman, and embrace the bosom of a stranger? 21. For the ways of man *are* before the eyes of the LORD, and he pondereth all his goings. 22. His own iniquities shall take the wicked himself, and he shall be holden with the cords of his sins. 23. He shall die without instruction; and in the greatness of his folly he shall go astray. Prov. 31:1-3.

Prov. 6:1. My son, if thou be surety for thy friend, *if* thou hast stricken thy hand with a stranger, 2. Thou art snared with the words of thy mouth, thou art taken with the words of thy mouth. 3. Do this now, my son, and deliver thyself, when thou art come into the hand of thy friend; go, humble thyself, and make sure thy friend. 4. Give not sleep to thine eyes, nor slumber to thine eyelids. 5. Deliver thyself as a roe from the hand *of the hunter*, and as a bird from the hand of the fowler. 6. Go to the ant, thou sluggard; consider her ways, and be wise: 7. Which having no guide, overseer, or ruler, 8. Provideth her meat in the summer, *and* gathereth her food in the harvest. 9. How long wilt thou sleep, O sluggard? when wilt thou arise out of thy sleep? 10. *Yet* a little sleep, a little slumber, a little folding of the hands to sleep: 11. So shall thy poverty come as one that travelleth, and thy want as an armed man. 12. A naughty person, a wicked man, walketh with a froward mouth. 13. He winketh with his eyes, he speaketh with his feet, he teacheth with his fingers; 14. Frowardness *is* in his heart, he deviseth mischief continually; he soweth discord. 15. Therefore shall his calamity come suddenly; suddenly shall he be broken without remedy. 16. These six *things* doth the LORD hate; yea, seven *are* an abomination unto him: 17. A proud look, a lying tongue, and hands that shed innocent blood, 18. An heart that deviseth wicked imaginations, feet that be swift in running to mischief, 19. A false witness *that* speaketh lies, and he that soweth discord among brethren. 20. My son, keep thy father's commandment, and forsake not the law of thy mother: 21. Bind them continually upon thine heart, *and* tie them about thy neck. 22. When thou goest, it shall lead thee; when thou sleepest, it shall keep thee; and *when* thou awakest, it shall talk with thee. 23. For the commandment *is* a lamp; and the law *is* light; and reproofs of instruction *are* the way of life: 24. To keep thee from the evil woman, from the flattery of the tongue of a strange woman. 25. Lust not after her beauty in thine heart; neither let her take thee with her eyelids. 26. For by means of a whorish woman *a man is brought* to a piece of bread: and the adulteress will hunt for the precious life. 27. Can a man take fire in his bosom, and his clothes not be burned? 28. Can one go upon hot coals, and his feet not be burned? 29. So he that goeth in to his neighbour's wife; whosoever toucheth her shall not be innocent. 30. *Men* do not despise a thief, if he steal to satisfy his soul when he is hungry; 31. But *if* he be found, he shall restore sevenfold; he shall give all the substance of his house. 32. *But* whoso committeth adultery with a woman lacketh understanding: he *that* doeth it destroyeth his own soul. 33. A wound and dishonour shall he get; and his reproach shall not be wiped away. 34. For jealousy is the rage of a man: therefore he will not spare in the day of vengeance. 35. He will not regard any ransom; neither will he rest content, though thou givest many gifts.

Prov. 7:1. My son, keep my words, and lay up my commandments with thee. 2. Keep my commandments, and live; and my law as the apple of thine eye. 3. Bind them upon thy fingers, write them upon the table of thine heart. 4. Say unto wisdom, Thou *art* my sister; and call understanding *thy* kinswoman: 5. That they may keep thee from the strange woman, from the stranger *which* flattereth with her words. 6. For at the window of my house I looked through my casement, 7. And beheld among the simple ones, I discerned among the youths, a young man void of understanding, 8. Passing through the street near her corner; and he went the way to her house, 9. In the twilight, in the evening, in the black and dark night: 10. And, behold, there met him a woman *with* the attire of an harlot, and subtil of heart. 11. (She *is* loud and stubborn; her feet abide not in her house: 12. Now *is she* without, now in the streets, and lieth in wait at every corner.) 13. So she caught him, and kissed him, *and* with an impudent face said unto him, 14. *I have* peace offerings with me; this day have I paid my vows. 15. Therefore came I forth to meet thee, diligently to seek thy face, and I have found thee. 16. I have decked my bed with coverings of tapestry, with carved *works*, with fine linen of Egypt. 17. I have perfumed my bed with myrrh, aloes, and

cinnamon. 18. Come, let us take our fill of love until the morning: let us solace ourselves with loves. 19. For the goodman *is* not at home, he is gone a long journey: 20. He hath taken a bag of money with him, *and* will come home at the day appointed. 21. With her much fair speech she caused him to yield, with the flattering of her lips she forced him. 22. He goeth after her straightway, as an ox goeth to the slaughter, or as a fool to the correction of the stocks; 23. Till a dart strike through his liver; as a bird hasteth to the snare, and knoweth not that it *is* for his life. 24. Hearken unto me now therefore, O ye children, and attend to the words of my mouth. 25. Let not thine heart decline to her ways, go not astray in her paths. 26. For she hath cast down many wounded: yea, many strong *men* have been slain by her. 27. Her house *is* the way to hell, going down to the chambers of death.

Prov. 10:1. A wise son maketh a glad father: but a foolish son *is* the heaviness of his mother.

Prov. 13:1. A wise son *heareth* his father's instruction: but a scorner heareth not rebuke.

Prov. 15:5. A fool despiseth his father's instruction: but he that regardeth reproof is prudent. 20. A wise son maketh a glad father: but a foolish man despiseth his mother.

Prov. 17:2. A wise servant shall have rule over a son that causeth shame, and shall have part of the inheritance among the brethren. 25. A foolish son *is* a grief to his father, and bitterness to her that bare him.

Prov. 19:13. A foolish son *is* the calamity of his father: 26. He that wasteth *his* father, *and* chaseth away *his* mother, *is* a son that causeth shame, and bringeth reproach. 27. Cease, my son, to hear the instruction *that causeth* to err from the words of knowledge.

Prov. 20:29. The glory of young men *is* their strength: and the beauty of old men *is* the gray head.

Prov. 23:15. My son, if thine heart be wise, my heart shall rejoice, even mine. 16. Yea, my reins shall rejoice, when thy lips speak right things. 17. Let not thine heart envy sinners: but *be thou* in the fear of the LORD all the day long. 18. For surely there is an end; and thine expectation shall not be cut off. 19. Hear thou, my son, and be wise, and guide thine heart in the way. 20. Be not among winebibbers; among riotous eaters of flesh: 21. For the drunkard and the glutton shall come to poverty: and drowsiness shall clothe *a man* with rags. 22. Hearken unto thy father that begat thee, and despise not thy mother when she is old. 23. Buy the truth, and sell *it* not; *also* wisdom, and instruction, and understanding. 24. The father of the righteous shall greatly rejoice: and he that begetteth a wise *child* shall have joy of him. 25. Thy father and thy mother shall be glad, and she that bare thee shall rejoice. 26. My son, give me thine heart, and let thine eyes observe my ways. 27. For a whore *is* a deep ditch; and a strange woman *is* a narrow pit. 28. She also lieth in wait as *for* a prey, and increaseth the transgressors among men. 29. Who hath woe? who hath sorrow? who hath contentions? who hath babbling? who hath wounds without cause? who hath redness of eyes? 30. They that tarry long at the wine; they that go to seek mixed wine. 31. Look not thou upon the wine when it is red, when it giveth his colour in the cup, *when* it moveth itself aright. 32. At the last it biteth like a serpent, and stingeth like an adder. 33. Thine eyes shall behold strange women, and thine heart shall utter perverse things. 34. Yea, thou shalt be as he that lieth down in the midst of the sea, or as he that lieth upon the top of a mast. 35. They have stricken me, *shalt thou say, and* I was not sick; they have beaten me, *and* I felt *it* not; when shall I awake? I will seek it yet again.

Prov. 24:1. Be not thou envious against evil men, neither desire to be with them. 2. For their heart studieth destruction, and their lips talk of mischief. 3. Through wisdom is an house builded; and by understanding it is established: 4. And by knowledge shall the chambers be filled with all precious and pleasant riches. 5. A wise man *is* strong; yea, a man of knowledge increaseth strength. 6. For by wise counsel thou shalt make thy war: and in multitude of counsellors *there is* safety. 7. Wisdom *is* too high for a fool: he openeth not his mouth in the gate. 8. He that deviseth to do evil shall be called a mischievous person. 9. The thought of foolishness *is* sin: and the scorner *is* an abomination to men. 10. *If* thou faint in the day of adversity, thy strength *is* small. 11. If thou forbear to deliver *them that are* drawn unto death, and *those that are* ready to be slain; 12. If thou sayest, Behold, we knew it not; doth not he that pondereth the heart consider *it?* and he that keepeth thy soul, doth *not* he know *it?* and shall *not* he render to *every* man according to his works? 13. My son, eat thou honey, because *it is* good; and the honeycomb, *which is* sweet to thy taste: 14. So *shall* the knowledge of wisdom *be* unto thy soul: when thou hast found *it*, then there shall be a reward, and thy expectation shall not be cut off. 15. Lay not wait, O wicked *man*, against the dwelling of the righteous; spoil not his resting place: 16. For a just *man* falleth seven times, and riseth up again: but the wicked shall fall into mischief. 17. Rejoice not when thine enemy falleth, and let not thine heart be glad when he stumbleth: 18. Lest the LORD see *it*, and it displease him, and he turn away his wrath from him. 19. Fret not thyself because of evil *men*,

neither be thou envious at the wicked: 20. For there shall be no reward to the evil *man;* the candle of the wicked shall be put out. 21. My son, fear thou the LORD and the king: *and* meddle not with them that are given to change: 22. For their calamity shall rise suddenly; and who knoweth the ruin of them both? 23. These *things* also *belong* to the wise. *It is* not good to have respect of persons in judgment. 24. He that saith unto the wicked, Thou *art* righteous; him shall the people curse, nations shall abhor him: 25. But to them that rebuke *him* shall be delight, and a good blessing shall come upon them. 26. *Every man* shall kiss *his* lips that giveth a right answer. 27. Prepare thy work without, and make it fit for thyself in the field; and afterwards build thine house. 28. Be not a witness against thy neighbour without cause; and deceive *not* with thy lips. 29. Say not, I will do so to him as he hath done to me: I will render to the man according to his work. 30. I went by the field of the slothful, and by the vineyard of the man void of understanding; 31. And, lo, it *was* all grown over with thorns, *and* nettles had covered the face thereof, and the stone wall thereof was broken down. 32. Then I saw, *and* considered *it* well: I looked upon *it*, *and* received instruction. 33. *Yet* a little sleep, a little slumber, a little folding of the hands to sleep: 34. So shall thy poverty come *as* one that travelleth; and thy want as an armed man.

Prov. 27:11. My son, be wise, and make my heart glad, that I may answer him that reproacheth me.

Prov. 28:7. Whoso keepeth the law *is* a wise son: but he that is a companion of riotous *men* shameth his father.

Prov. 29:3. Whoso loveth wisdom rejoiceth his father: but he that keepeth company with harlots spendeth *his* substance.

Jer. 22:18. Therefore thus saith the LORD concerning Jehoiakim the son of Josiah king of Judah; They shall not lament for him, *saying*, Ah my brother! or, Ah sister! they shall not lament for him, *saying*, Ah lord! or, Ah his glory! 19. He shall be buried with the burial of an ass, drawn and cast forth beyond the gates of Jerusalem. 20. Go up to Lebanon, and cry; and lift up thy voice in Bashan, and cry from the passages: for all thy lovers are destroyed. 21. I spake unto thee in thy prosperity; *but* thou saidst, I will not hear. This *hath been* thy manner from thy youth, that thou obeyedst not my voice.

Matt. 19:16. And, behold, one came and said unto him, Good Master, what good thing shall I do, that I may have eternal life? 17. And he said unto him, Why callest thou me good? *there is* none good but one, *that is*, God: but if thou wilt enter into life, keep the commandments. 18. He saith unto him, Which? Jesus said, Thou shalt do no murder, Thou shalt not commit adultery, Thou shalt not steal, Thou shalt not bear false witness. 19. Honour thy father and *thy* mother: and, Thou shalt love thy neighbour as thyself. 20. The young man saith unto him, All these things have I kept from my youth up: what lack I yet? 21. Jesus said unto him, If thou wilt be perfect, go *and* sell that thou hast, and give to the poor, and thou shalt have treasure in heaven: and come *and* follow me. 22. But when the young man heard that saying, he went away sorrowful: for he had great possessions. Mark 10:17-22; Luke 18:18-23.

Luke 15:11. And he said, A certain man had two sons: 12. And the younger of them said to *his* father, Father, give me the portion of goods that falleth *to me*. And he divided unto them *his* living. 13. And not many days after the younger son gathered all together, and took his journey into a far country, and there wasted his substance with riotous living. 14. And when he had spent all, there arose a mighty famine in that land; and he began to be in want. 15. And he went and joined himself to a citizen of that country; and he sent him into his fields to feed swine. 16. And he would fain have filled his belly with the husks that the swine did eat: and no man gave unto him. 17. And when he came to himself, he said, How many hired servants of my father's have bread enough and to spare, and I perish with hunger! 18. I will arise and go to my father, and will say unto him, Father, I have sinned against heaven, and before thee. 19. And am no more worthy to be called thy son: make me as one of thy hired servants. 20. And he arose, and came to his father. But when he was yet a great way off, his father saw him, and had compassion, and ran, and fell on his neck, and kissed him. 21. And the son said unto him, Father, I have sinned against heaven, and in thy sight, and am no more worthy to be called thy son. 22. But the father said to his servants, Bring forth the best robe, and put *it* on him; and put a ring on his hand, and shoes on *his* feet: 23. And bring hither the fatted calf, and kill *it*; and let us eat, and be merry: 24. For this my son was dead, and is alive again; he was lost, and is found. And they began to be merry. 25. Now his elder son was in the field: and as he came and drew nigh to the house, he heard musick and dancing. 26. And he called one of the servants, and asked what these things meant. 27. And he said unto him, Thy brother is come; and thy father hath killed the fatted calf, because he hath received him safe and sound. 28. And he was angry, and would not go in: therefore came his father out, and intreated him. 29. And he answering said to *his* father, Lo, these many years do I serve thee, neither transgressed I at any time thy commandment; and yet thou never gavest me a

kid, that I might make merry with my friends: 30. But as soon as this thy son was come, which hath devoured thy living with harlots, thou hast killed for him the fatted calf. 31. And he said unto him, Son, thou art ever with me, and all that I have is thine. 32. It was meet that we should make merry, and be glad: for this thy brother was dead, and is alive again; and was lost, and is found.

1 Tim. 4:12. Let no man despise thy youth; but be thou an example of the believers, in word, in conversation, in charity, in spirit, in faith, in purity.

2 Tim. 2:22. Flee also youthful lusts: but follow righteousness, faith, charity, peace, with them that call on the Lord out of a pure heart. 23. But foolish and unlearned questions avoid, knowing that they do gender strifes.

Tit. 2:6. Young men likewise exhort to be sober minded.

Heb. 11:24. By faith Moses, when he was come to years, refused to be called the son of Pharaoh's daughter; 25. Choosing rather to suffer affliction with the people of God, than to enjoy the pleasures of sin for a season; 26. Esteeming the reproach of Christ greater riches than the treasures in Egypt: for he had respect unto the recompence of the reward.

1 John 2:13. I write unto you, young men, because ye have overcome the wicked one. I write unto you, little children, because ye have known the Father. 14. I have written unto you, fathers, because ye have known him *that is* from the beginning. I have written unto you, young men, because ye are strong, and the word of God abideth in you, and ye have overcome the wicked one. 15. Love not the world, neither the things *that are* in the world. If any man love the world, the love of the Father is not in him. 16. For all that *is* in the world, the lust of the flesh, and the lust of the eyes, and the pride of life, is not of the Father, but is of the world. 17. And the world passeth away, and the lust thereof: but he that doeth the will of God abideth for ever.

INSTANCES OF RELIGIOUS: See JOSEPH, JOSHUA. SAMUEL, DAVID, SOLOMON, URIAH. The rich young man, Matt. 19:16-22; Mark 10:17-22; Luke 18:18-23.

See CHILDREN; PARENTS.

Z

ZAANAIM, called also ZAANANNIM. A plain near Kedesh, Josh. 19:33; Judg. 4:11.

ZAANAN, called also ZENAN. A place of uncertain location. Josh. 15:37; Mic. 1:11.

ZAANANNIM. See ZAANAIM.

ZAAVAN, called also ZAVAN. A son of Ezer. Gen. 36:27; 1 Chr. 1:42.

ZABAD. 1. Son of Nathan. 1 Chr. 2:36,37. 2. An Ephraimite, 1 Chr. 7:21. 3. One of David's valiant men, 1 Chr. 11:41.

4. An assassin of King Joash, 2 Chr. 24:26; 25:3,4. Called JOZACHAR in 2 Kin. 12:21.

5. Three Israelites who divorced their Gentile wives, Ezra 10:27,33,43.

ZABBAI. 1. Son of Bebai, Ezra 10:28.

2. Father of Baruch, Neh. 3:20.

ZABBUD, a returned exile, Ezra 8:14.

ZABDI. 1. Father of Carmi, Josh. 7:1, 17,18.

2. A Benjamite, 1 Chr. 8:19.

3. David's storekeeper, 1 Chr. 27:27.

4. Son of Asaph, Neh. 11:17.

ZABDIEL. 1. Father of Jashobeam, 1 Chr. 27:2.

2. An overseer of one hundred and twenty-eight mighty men of valor, who dwelt in Jerusalem, Neh. 11:14.

ZABUD, a chief officer of Solomon, 1 Kin. 4:5.

ZABULON. See ZEBULUN.

ZACCAI, a Jew whose descendants returned from exile, Ezra 2:9; Neh. 7:14.

ZACCHÆUS, a collector of tribute in Jericho. Entertains Jesus, Luke 19:1-10.

ZACCHUR. A Simeonite, 1 Chr. 4:26. See ZACCUR.

ZACCUR. 1. A Reubenite, Num. 13:4.

2. Called also ZACCHUR, which see.

3. A Merarite, 1 Chr. 24:27.

4. Son of Asaph, 1 Chr. 25:2,10; Neh. 12:35.

5. Son of Imri, Neh. 3:2.

ZACHARIAH. 1. Son of Jeroboam, and last of the house of Jehu, 2 Kin. 10:30; 14:29; 15:8-12.

2. Grandfather of Hezekiah, 2 Kin. 18:2; 2 Chr. 29:1.

ZACHARIAS. 1. A man slain by the Jews. Referred to by Jesus, Matt. 23:35; Luke 11:51.

2. Father of John the Baptist, Luke 1:5-80; 3:2. See ELISABETH; JOHN THE BAPTIST.

ZACHER. A Benjamite, 1 Chr. 8:31. Called ZECHARIAH in 1 Chr. 9:37.

ZADOK. 1. High priest in time of David's reign, 2 Sam. 19:11; 20:25; 1 Chr. 15:11; 16:39. Removes the ark from Jerusalem at the time of Absalom's usurpation; returns with it at David's command, 2 Sam. 15:24-36; 17:15,17-21. Stands aloof from Adonijah at the time of his attempted usurpation, 1 Kin. 1:8, 26. Summoned by David to anoint Solomon, 1 Kin. 1:32-40,44,45. Performs the function of high priest after Abiathar was deposed by Solomon, 1 Kin. 2:35; 1 Chr.29:22.

2. Father of Jerusha, 2 Kin. 15:33; 2 Chr. 27:1.

3. Son of Ahitub, 1 Chr. 6:12.

4. A man of valor, 1 Chr. 12:28.

5. Son of Baana, Neh. 3:4.

6. A priest, Neh. 3:29.

7. A returned exile, Neh. 10:21.

8. Son of Meraioth, Neh. 11:11.

9. A treasurer of the temple, Neh. 13:13.

ZAHAM, grandson of Solomon, 2 Chr. 11:19.

ZAIR, a city in Edom, 2 Kin. 8:21.

ZALAPH, father of Hanun, Neh. 3:30.

ZALMON. 1. Called also SALMON, probably. A hill in Samaria, Judg. 9:48; Psa. 68:14.

2. One of David's warriors, 2 Sam. 23:28.

ZALMONAH, one of the camping places of Israel, Num. 33:41,42.

ZALMUNNA, king of Midian, Judg. 8: 5-21; Psa. 83:11.

ZAMZUMMIMS, called also ZUZIMS. A race of giants, Gen. 14:5; Deut. 2:20,21.

ZANOAH. 1. A city of western Judah, Josh. 15:34; Neh. 3:13; 11:30.

2. A city of eastern Judah, Josh. 15:56.

3. A descendant of Caleb, 1 Chr. 4:18.

ZAPHNATH-PAANEAH, a name given to Joseph by Pharaoh, Gen. 41:45.

ZAPHON, a city in Gad, Josh. 13:27.

ZARA, called also ZARAH. Son of Judah, Matt. 1:3.

ZARAH, called also ZERAH and ZARA. Son of Judah and Tamar, Gen. 38:30; 46:12; Num. 26:20; 1 Chr. 2:4,6; Neh. 11:24.

ZAREAH, a city of Judah, Neh. 11:29. See ZORAH.

ZARED, called also ZERED. A brook, Num. 21:12; Deut. 2:13,14.

ZAREPHATH, a city between Tyre and Sidon. Elijah performs two miracles in, 1 Kin. 17:8-24. Called SAREPTA in Luke 4:26.

ZARETAN, probably identical with ZARTANAH and ZARTHAN. A city of uncertain location, Josh. 3:16; 1 Kin. 4:12; 7:46.

ZARETH-SHAHAR, a city in Reuben, Josh. 13:19.

ZATTHU. See ZATTU.

ZATTU. 1. One whose descendants returned with Zerubbabel, Ezra 2:8; 10:27; Neh. 7:13.

2. Probably identical with ZATTHU. One who sealed the covenant with Nehemiah, Neh. 10:14.

ZAVAN. See ZAAVAN.

ZAZA, son of Jonathan, 1 Chr. 2:33.

ZEAL, RELIGIOUS. Josh. 24:15. And if it seem evil unto you to serve the LORD, choose you this day whom ye will serve; whether the gods which your fathers served that *were* on the other side of the flood, or the gods of the Amorites, in whose land ye dwell: but as for me and my house, we will serve the LORD. 16. And the people answered and said, God forbid that we should forsake the LORD, to serve other gods;

2 Sam. 24:24. And the king said unto Araunah, Nay; but I will surely buy *it* of thee at a price: neither will I offer burnt offerings unto the LORD my God of that which doth cost me nothing. So David bought the threshingfloor and the oxen for fifty shekels of silver. 25. And David built there an altar unto the LORD, and offered burnt offerings and peace offerings.

1 Kin. 9:4. And if thou wilt walk before me, as David thy father walked, in integrity of heart, and in uprightness, to do according to all that I have commanded thee, *and* wilt keep my statutes and my judgments:

1 Kin. 15:14. Nevertheless Asa's heart was perfect with the LORD all his days.

1 Chr. 29:17. In the uprightness of mine heart I have willingly offered all these things: and now have I seen with joy thy people, which are present here, to offer willingly unto thee.

2 Chr. 15:15. And all Judah rejoiced at the oath: for they had sworn with all their heart, and sought him with their whole desire; and he was found of them: and the LORD gave them rest round about.

2 Chr. 19:3. Nevertheless there are good things found in thee, in that thou hast taken away the groves out of the land, and hast prepared thine heart to seek God.

Ezra 7:23. Whatsoever is commanded by the God of heaven, let it be diligently done for the house of the God of heaven: for why should there be wrath against the realm of the king and his sons?

Job 16:19. Also now, behold, my witness is in heaven, and my record is on high.

Psa. 42:1. As the hart panteth after the water brooks, so panteth my soul after thee, O God. 2. My soul thirsteth for God, for the living God: when shall I come and appear before God?

Psa. 60:4. Thou hast given a banner to them that fear thee, that it may be displayed because of the truth.

Psa. 96:2. Sing unto the LORD, bless his name; shew forth his salvation from day to day. 3. Declare his glory among the heathen, his wonders among all people. 10. Say among the heathen that the LORD reigneth:

Psa. 119:139. My zeal hath consumed me, because mine enemies have forgotten thy words.

Prov. 11:30. The fruit of the righteous is a tree of life; and he that winneth souls is wise.

Eccl. 9:10. Whatsoever thy hand findeth to do, do it with thy might; for there is no work, nor device, nor knowledge, nor wisdom, in the grave, whither thou goest.

Isa. 58:12. They that shall be of thee shall build the old waste places: thou shalt raise up the foundations of many generations; and thou shalt be called, The repairer of the breach, The restorer of paths to dwell in.

Isa. 60:1. Arise, shine; for thy light is come, and the glory of the LORD is risen upon thee.

Isa. 62:6. I have set watchmen upon thy walls, O Jerusalem, which shall never hold their peace day nor night: ye that make mention of the LORD keep not silence, 7. And give him no rest, till he establish, and till he make Jerusalem a praise in the earth.

Dan. 12:3. They that be wise shall shine as the brightness of the firmament; and they that turn many to righteousness as the stars for ever and ever.

Mic. 5:7. The remnant of Jacob shall be in the midst of many people as a dew from the LORD, as the showers upon the grass, that tarrieth not for man, nor waiteth for the sons of men.

Hab. 2:2. And the LORD answered me, and said, Write the vision, and make it plain upon tables, that he may run that readeth it.

Hag. 2:4. Be strong, O Zerubbabel, saith the LORD; and be strong, O Joshua, son of Josedech, the high priest; and be strong, all ye people of the land, saith the LORD, and work: for I am with you, saith the LORD of hosts: 5. According to the word that I covenanted with you when ye came out of Egypt, so my spirit remaineth among you: fear ye not.

Zech. 14:20. In that day shall there be upon the bells of the horses, HOLINESS UNTO THE LORD; and the pots in the LORD's house shall be like the bowls before the altar. 21. Yea, every pot in Jerusalem and in Judah shall be holiness unto the LORD of hosts: and all they that sacrifice shall come and take of them, and seethe therein: and in that day there shall be no more the Canaanite in the house of the LORD of hosts.

Matt. 5:13. Ye are the salt of the earth: but if the salt have lost his savour, wherewith shall it be salted? it is thenceforth good for nothing, but to be cast out, and to be trodden under foot of men. 14. Ye are the light of the world. A city that is set on an hill cannot be hid. 15. Neither do men light a candle, and put it under a bushel, but on a candlestick; and it giveth light unto all that are in the house. 16. Let your light so shine before men, that they may see your good works, and glorify your Father which is in heaven. Mark 4:21,22; Luke 8:16,17.

Luke 22:32. But I have prayed for thee, that thy faith fail not: and when thou art converted, strengthen thy brethren. 33. And he said unto him, Lord, I am ready to go with thee, both into prison, and to death.

John 6:27. Labour not for the meat which perisheth, but for that meat which endureth unto everlasting life, which the Son of man shall give unto you:

John 9:4. I must work the works of him that sent me, while it is day: the night cometh, when no man can work.

Acts 10:42. He commanded us to preach unto the people, and to testify that it is he which was ordained of God to be the Judge of quick and dead.

Acts 26:29. And Paul said, I would to God, that not only thou, but also all that hear me this day, were both almost, and altogether such as I am, except these bonds.

Rom. 1:8. First, I thank my God through Jesus Christ for you all, that your faith is spoken of throughout the whole world. 9. For God is my witness, whom I serve with my spirit in the gospel of his Son, that without ceasing I make mention of you always in my prayers;

Rom. 7:22. I delight in the law of God after the inward man:

Rom. 12:11. Not slothful in business; fervent in spirit; serving the Lord;

1 Cor. 5:8. Let us keep the feast, not with old leaven, neither with the leaven of malice and wickedness; but with the unleavened *bread* of sincerity and truth.

1 Cor. 7:29. But this I say, brethren, the time *is* short: it remaineth, that both they that have wives be as though they had none; 30. And they that weep, as though they wept not; and they that rejoice, as though they rejoiced not; and they that buy, as though they possessed not; 31. And they that use this world, as not abusing *it:* for the fashion of this world passeth away. 32. But I would have you without carefulness. He that is unmarried careth for the things that belong to the Lord, how he may please the Lord: 33. But he that is married careth for the things that are of the world, how he may please *his* wife. 34. There is difference *also* between a wife and a virgin. The unmarried woman careth for the things of the Lord, that she may be holy both in body and in spirit: but she that is married careth for the things of the world, how she may please *her* husband.

1 Cor. 13:3. And though I bestow all my goods to feed *the poor,* and though I give my body to be burned, and have not charity, it profiteth me nothing.

1 Cor. 14:12. Even so ye, forasmuch as ye are zealous of spiritual *gifts,* seek that ye may excel to the edifying of the church.

1 Cor. 15:58. Therefore, my beloved brethren, be ye stedfast, unmoveable, always abounding in the work of the Lord, forasmuch as ye know that your labour is not in vain in the Lord.

2 Cor. 4:8. *We are* troubled on every side, yet not distressed; *we are* perplexed, but not in despair; 9. Persecuted, but not forsaken; cast down, but not destroyed; 10. Always bearing about in the body the dying of the Lord Jesus, that the life also of Jesus might be made manifest in our body. 13. We having the same spirit of faith, according as it is written, I believed, and therefore have I spoken; we also believe, and therefore speak; 16. For which cause we faint not; but though our outward man perish, yet the inward *man* is renewed day by day. 17. For our light affliction, which is but for a moment, worketh for us a far more exceeding *and* eternal weight of glory; 18. While we look not at the things which are seen, but at the things which are not seen: for the things which are seen *are* temporal; but the things which are not seen *are* eternal.

2 Cor. 7:11. For behold this selfsame thing, that ye sorrowed after a godly sort, what carefulness it wrought in you, yea, *what* clearing of yourselves, yea, *what* indignation, yea, *what* fear, yea, *what* vehement desire, yea, *what* zeal, yea, *what* revenge! In all *things* ye have approved yourselves to be clear in this matter.

2 Cor. 9:2. For I know the forwardness of your mind, for which I boast of you to them of Macedonia, that Achaia was ready a year ago; and your zeal hath provoked very many.

Gal. 4:18. But *it is* good to be zealously affected always in *a* good *thing,*

Gal. 6:9. Let us not be weary in well doing: for in due season we shall reap, if we faint not. 2 Thess. 3:13.

Eph. 5:15. See then that ye walk circumspectly, not as fools, but as wise, 16. Redeeming the time, because the days are evil.

Eph. 6:14. Stand therefore, having your loins girt about with truth, and having on the breastplate of righteousness; 15. And your feet shod with the preparation of the gospel of peace; 16. Above all, taking the shield of faith, wherewith ye shall be able to quench all the fiery darts of the wicked. 17. And take the helmet of salvation, and the sword of the Spirit, which is the word of God: 18. Praying always with all prayer and supplication in the Spirit, and watching thereunto with all perseverance and supplication for all saints; 19. And for me, that utterance may be given unto me, that I may open my mouth boldly, to make known the mystery of the gospel, 20. For which I am an ambassador in bonds: that therein I may speak boldly, as I ought to speak.

Phil. 1:27. Only let your conversation be as it becometh the gospel of Christ: that whether I come and see you, or else be absent, I may hear of your affairs, that ye stand fast in one spirit, with one mind striving together for the faith of the gospel; 28. And in nothing terrified by your adversaries: which is to them an evident token of perdition, but to you of salvation, and that of God.

Phil. 2:15. That ye may be blameless and harmless, the sons of God, without rebuke, in the midst of a crooked and perverse nation, among whom ye shine as lights in the world;

Phil. 3:4. Though I might also have confidence in the flesh. If any other man thinketh that he hath whereof he might trust in the flesh, I more: 5. Circumcised the eighth day, of the stock of Israel, *of* the tribe of Benjamin, an Hebrew of the Hebrews; as touching the law, a Pharisee; 6. Concerning zeal, persecuting the church; touching the righteousness which is in the law, blameless. 7. But what things were gain to me, those I counted loss for Christ. 8. Yea doubtless, and I count all things *but* loss for the excellency of the knowledge of Christ Jesus my Lord: for whom I have suffered the loss of all things, and do count them *but* dung, that I may win Christ, 9. And be found in him, not having mine own righteousness, which is of the law, but that which is through the faith of Christ, the righteousness which is of God by faith: 10. That I may know him, and the power of his resurrection, and the fellowship of his sufferings, being made conformable unto his death; 11. If by any means I might attain unto the resurrection of the dead. 12. Not as though I had already attained, either were already perfect; but I follow after, if that I may apprehend that for which also I am apprehended of Christ Jesus. 13. Brethren, I count not myself to have apprehended: but *this* one thing *I do*, forgetting those things which are behind, and reaching forth unto those things which are before, 14. I press toward the mark for the prize of the high calling of God in Christ Jesus. 20. For our conversation is in heaven; from whence also we look for the Saviour, the Lord Jesus Christ:

Col. 4:5. Walk in wisdom toward them that are without, redeeming the time.

Tit. 2:14. Who gave himself for us, that he might redeem us from all iniquity, and purify unto himself a peculiar people, zealous of good works.

Tit. 3:1. Put them in mind to be subject to principalities and powers, to obey magistrates, to be ready to every good work,

Heb. 10:34. For ye had compassion of me in my bonds, and took joyfully the spoiling of your goods, knowing in yourselves that ye have in heaven a better and an enduring substance.

Heb. 11:15. And truly, if they had been mindful of that *country* from whence they came out, they might have had opportunity to have returned. 16. But now they desire a better *country*, that is, an heavenly: wherefore God is not ashamed to be called their God: for he hath prepared for them a city. 24. By faith Moses, when he was come to years, refused to be called the son of Pharaoh's daughter; 25. Choosing rather to suffer affliction with the people of God, than to enjoy the pleasures of sin for a season; 26. Esteeming the reproach of Christ greater riches than the treasures in Egypt: for he had respect unto the recompence of the reward. 27. By faith he forsook Egypt, not fearing the wrath of the king: for he endured, as seeing him who is invisible.

Heb. 13:13. Let us go forth therefore unto him without the camp, bearing his reproach. 14. For here have we no continuing city, but we seek one to come. 15. By him therefore let us offer the sacrifice of praise to God continually, that is, the fruit of *our* lips giving thanks to his name.

Jas. 5:19. Brethren, if any of you do err from the truth, and one convert him; 20. Let him know, that he which converteth the sinner from the error of his way shall save a soul from death, and shall hide a multitude of sins.

1 Pet. 2:2. As newborn babes, desire the sincere milk of the word, that ye may grow thereby:

2 Pet. 3:14. Wherefore, beloved, seeing that ye look for such things, be diligent that ye may be found of him in peace, without spot, and blameless. 2 Pet. 1:10,11.

Jude 3. It was needful for me to write unto you, and exhort *you* that ye should earnestly contend for the faith which was once delivered unto the saints. 22. Of some have compassion, making a difference: 23. And others save with fear, pulling *them* out of the fire; hating even the garment spotted by the flesh.

Rev. 3:19. As many as I love, I rebuke and chasten: be zealous therefore, and repent.

Rev. 5:4. And I wept much, because no man was found worthy to open and to read the book, neither to look thereon. 5. And one of the elders saith unto me, Weep not: behold, the Lion of the tribe of Juda, the Root of David, hath prevailed to open the book, and to loose the seven seals thereof.

Rev. 22:17. The Spirit and the bride say, Come. And let him that heareth say, Come.

EXEMPLIFIED: Ex. 32:31. Oh, this people have sinned a great sin, and have made them gods of gold. 32. Yet now, if thou wilt forgive their sin—; and if not, blot me, I pray thee, out of thy book which thou hast written.

Num. 10:29. We are journeying unto the place of which the LORD said, I will give it you: come thou with us, and we will do thee good: for the LORD hath spoken good concerning Israel.

Num. 11:29. Enviest thou for my sake? would God that all the LORD's people were prophets, *and* that the LORD would put his spirit upon them!

Deut. 9:18. I fell down before the LORD, as at the first, forty days and forty nights: I did neither eat bread, nor drink water, because of all your sins which ye sinned, in doing wickedly in the sight of the LORD, to provoke him to anger. *v.* 19.

Josh. 24:14. Now therefore fear the LORD, and serve him in sincerity and in truth; and put away the gods which your fathers served on the other side of the flood, and in Egypt; and serve ye the LORD. 15. And if it seem evil unto you to serve the LORD, choose you this day whom ye will serve; whether the gods which your fathers served that *were* on the other side of the flood, or the gods of the Amorites, in whose land ye dwell: but as for me and my house, we will serve the LORD. 16. And the people answered and said, God forbid that we should forsake the LORD, to serve other gods;

1 Sam. 17:26. And David spake to the men that stood by him, saying, What shall be done to the man that killeth this Philistine, and taketh away the reproach from Israel? for who *is* this uncircumcised Philistine, that he should defy the armies of the living God?

1 Kin. 8:43. Hear thou in heaven thy dwelling place, and do according to all that the stranger calleth to thee for: that all people of the earth may know thy name, to fear thee, as *do* thy people Israel; *v.* 42; 2 Chr. 6:33.

1 Kin 22:14. And Micaiah said, *As* the LORD liveth, what the LORD saith unto me, that will I speak.

Job 6:10. I have not concealed the words of the Holy One.

Psa. 40:7. Then said I, Lo, I come: in the

volume of the book *it is* written of me, 8. I delight to do thy will, O my God : yea, thy law *is* within my heart. 9. I have preached righteousness in the great congregation : lo, I have not refrained my lips, O Lord, thou knowest. 10. I have not hid thy righteousness within my heart; I have declared thy faithfulness and thy salvation : I have not concealed thy lovingkindness and thy truth from the great congregation.

Psa. 51:13. *Then* will I teach trangressors thy ways; and sinners shall be converted unto thee.

Psa. 69:7. Because for thy sake I have borne reproach; shame hath covered my face. 8. I am become a stranger unto my brethren, and an alien unto my mother's children. 9. For the zeal of thine house hath eaten me up; and the reproaches of them that reproached thee are fallen upon me.

Psa. 71:17. O God, thou hast taught me from my youth : and hitherto have I declared thy wondrous works. 18. Now also, when I am old and greyheaded, O God, forsake me not, until I have shewed thy strength unto *this* generation, *and* thy power to every one *that* is to come.

Psa. 94:16. Who will rise up for me against the evildoers ? *or* who will stand up for me against the workers of iniquity ?

Psa. 101:8. I will early destroy all the wicked of the land ; that I may cut off all wicked doers from the city of the Lord.

Psa. 119:53. Horror hath taken hold upon me because of the wicked that forsake thy law. 126. *It is* time for *thee*, Lord, to work : *for* they have made void thy law. 136. Rivers of waters run down mine eyes, because they keep not thy law. 139. My zeal hath consumed me, because mine enemies have forgotten thy words. 158. I beheld the transgressors, and was grieved ; because they kept not thy word. Psa. 9:19,20; 74:10,18–23; 115:1,2.

Prov. 28:4. They that forsake the law praise the wicked : but such as keep the law contend with them.

Eccl. 12:9. Moreover, because the preacher was wise, he still taught the people knowledge ; yea, he gave good heed, and sought out, *and* set in order many proverbs. 10. The preacher sought to find out acceptable words : and *that which was* written *was* upright, *even* words of truth.

Isa. 2:3. And many people shall go and say, Come ye, and let us go up to the mountain of the Lord, to the house of the God of Jacob ; and he will teach us of his ways, and we will walk in his paths : for out of Zion shall go forth the law, and the word of the Lord from Jerusalem. 5. O house of Jacob, come ye, and let us walk in the light of the Lord.

Isa. 6:8. I heard the voice of the Lord, saying, Whom shall I send, and who will go for us ? Then said I, Here *am* I ; send me.

Isa. 59:17. He put on righteousness as a breastplate, and an helmet of salvation upon his head ; and he put on the garments of vengeance *for* clothing, and was clad with zeal as a cloke.

Isa. 62:1. For Zion's sake will I not hold my peace, and for Jerusalem's sake I will not rest, until the righteousness thereof go forth as brightness, and the salvation thereof as a lamp *that* burneth.

Jer. 9:1. Oh that my head were waters, and mine eyes a fountain of tears, that I might weep day and night for the slain of the daughter of my people ! 2. Oh that I had in the wilderness a lodging place of wayfaring men ; that I might leave my people, and go from them ! for they *be* all adulterers, an assembly of treacherous men. 3. And they bend their tongues *like* their bow *for* lies : but they are not valiant for the truth upon the earth ; for they proceed from evil to evil, and they know not me, saith the Lord.

Jer. 13:17. If ye will not hear it, my soul shall weep in secret places for *your* pride ; and mine eye shall weep sore, and run down with tears, because the Lord's flock is carried away captive.

Jer. 17:16. As for me, I have not hastened from *being* a pastor to follow thee : neither have I desired the woeful day : thou knowest : that which came out of my lips was *right* before thee.

Jer. 18:20. Remember that I stood before thee to speak good for them, *and* to turn away thy wrath from them.

Jer. 20:9. Then I said, I will not make mention of him, nor speak any more in his name. But *his word* was in mine heart as a burning fire shut up in my bones, and I was weary with forbearing, and I could not *stay*. Jer. 26:12–15.

Ezek. 9:4. And the Lord said unto him, Go through the midst of the city, through the midst of Jerusalem, and set a mark upon the foreheads of the men that sigh and that cry for all the abominations that be done in the midst thereof.

Ezek. 44:15. But the priests the Levites, the sons of Zadok, that kept the charge of my sanctuary when the children of Israel went astray from me, they shall come near to me to minister unto me,

Dan. 3:17. If it be *so*, our God whom we serve is able to deliver us from the burning fiery furnace, and he will deliver *us* out of thine hand, O king. 18. But if not, be it known unto thee, O king, that we will not serve thy gods, nor worship the golden image which thou hast set up.

Mic. 3:8. Truly I am full of power by the spirit of the Lord, and of judgment, and of might, to declare unto Jacob his transgression, and to Israel his sin.

Mic. 7:1. Woe is me ! for I am as when they have gathered the summer fruits, as the grapegleanings of the vintage : *there is* no cluster to eat : my soul desired the firstripe fruit. 2. The good *man* is perished out of the earth : and *there is* none upright among men : they all lie in wait for blood ;

they hunt every man his brother with a net.

Hab. 1:2. O Lord, how long shall I cry, and thou wilt not hear! *even* cry out unto thee *of* violence, and thou wilt not save! *vs.* 3,4.

Mark 5:20. And he departed, and began to publish in Decapolis how great things Jesus had done for him: and all *men* did marvel. *v.* 19.

Mark 6:6. And he marvelled because of their unbelief. And he went round about the villages, teaching.

Mark 14:29. But Peter said unto him, Although all shall be offended, yet *will* not I. 30. And Jesus saith unto him, Verily I say unto thee, That this day, *even* in this night, before the cock crow twice, thou shalt deny me thrice. 31. But he spake the more vehemently, If I should die with thee, I will not deny thee in any wise. Likewise also said they all.

Mark 16:20. They went forth, and preached every where, the Lord working with *them*, and confirming the work with signs following.

Luke 1:16. Many of the children of Israel shall he turn to the Lord their God. 17. And he shall go before him in the spirit and power of Elias, to turn the hearts of the fathers to the children, and the disobedient to the wisdom of the just; to make ready a people prepared for the Lord. *v.* 15.

Luke 19:41. When he was come near, he beheld the city, and wept over it, *v.* 42; Matt. 23:37.

John 1:40. One of the two which heard John *speak*, and followed him, was Andrew, Simon Peter's brother. 41. He first findeth his own brother Simon, and saith unto him, We have found the Messias, which is, being interpreted, the Christ. 42. And he brought him to Jesus. 45. Philip findeth Nathanael, and saith unto him, We have found him, of whom Moses in the law, and the prophets, did write, Jesus of Nazareth, the son of Joseph. 46. And Nathanael said unto him, Can there any good thing come out of Nazareth? Philip saith unto him, Come and see.

John 4:34. Jesus saith unto them, My meat is to do the will of him that sent me, and to finish his work. 35. Say not ye, There are yet four months, and *then* cometh harvest? behold, I say unto you, Lift up your eyes, and look on the fields; for they are white already to harvest.

Acts 4:13. When they saw the boldness of Peter and John, and perceived that they were unlearned and ignorant men, they marvelled; and they took knowledge of them, that they had been with Jesus. 18. And they called them, and commanded them not to speak at all nor teach in the name of Jesus. 19. But Peter and John answered and said unto them, Whether it be right in the sight of God to hearken unto you more than unto God, judge ye. 20. For we

cannot but speak the things which we have seen and heard. 31. And when they had prayed, the place was shaken where they were assembled together; and they were all filled with the Holy Ghost, and they spake the word of God with boldness. 33. With great power gave the apostles witness of the resurrection of the Lord Jesus: and great grace was upon them all. *vs.* 2,8–12.

Acts 5:42. And daily in the temple, and in every house, they ceased not to teach and preach Jesus Christ. *vs.* 21,25,29–32.

Acts 6:4. But we will give ourselves continually to prayer, and to the ministry of the word. 10. And they were not able to resist the wisdom and the spirit by which he spake.

Acts 8:4. Therefore they that were scattered abroad went every where preaching the word. 35. Philip opened his mouth, and began at the same scripture, and preached unto him Jesus. *vs.* 12,25,30,40; Acts 11:19,20, 24,26.

Acts 18:25. This man was instructed in the way of the Lord; and being fervent in the spirit, he spake and talked diligently the things of the Lord, knowing only the baptism of John. 26. And he began to speak boldly in the synagogue: whom when Aquila and Priscilla had heard, they took him unto *them*, and expounded unto him the way of God more perfectly. 27. And when he was disposed to pass into Achaia, the brethren wrote, exhorting the disciples to receive him: who, when he was come, helped them much which had believed through grace: 28. For he mightily convinced the Jews, *and that* publickly, shewing by the scriptures that Jesus was Christ. *v.* 24.

Rom. 1:11. I long to see you, that I may impart unto you some spiritual gift, to the end ye may be established;

Rom. 9:1. I say the truth in Christ, I lie not, my conscience also bearing me witness in the Holy Ghost, 2. That I have great heaviness and continual sorrow in my heart. 3. For I could wish that myself were accursed from Christ for my brethren, my kinsmen according to the flesh:

Rom. 10:1. Brethren, my heart's desire and prayer to God for Israel is, that they might be saved.

Rom. 15:18. For I will not dare to speak of any of those things which Christ hath not wrought by me, to make the Gentiles obedient, by word and deed, 19. Through mighty signs and wonders, by the power of the Spirit of God; so that from Jerusalem, and round about unto Illyricum, I have fully preached the gospel of Christ. 20. Yea, so have I strived to preach the gospel, not where Christ was named, lest I should build upon another man's foundation: 21. But as it is written, To whom he was not spoken of, they shall see: and they that have not heard shall understand.

2 Cor. 5:9. Wherefore we labour, that, whether present or absent, we may be accepted of him.

2 Cor. 6:11. O *ye* Corinthians, our mouth is open unto you, our heart is enlarged.

2 Cor. 8:1. Moreover, brethren, we do you to wit of the grace of God bestowed on the churches of Macedonia; 2. How that in a great trial of affliction the abundance of their joy and their deep poverty abounded unto the riches of their liberality. 3. For to *their* power, I bear record, yea, and beyond *their* power *they were* willing of themselves; 4. Praying us with much intreaty that we would receive the gift, and *take upon us* the fellowship of the ministering to the saints. 5. And *this they did*, not as we hoped, but first gave their own selves to the Lord, and unto us by the will of God. 16. But thanks *be* to God, which put the same earnest care into the heart of Titus for you. 17. For indeed he accepted the exhortation; but being more forward, of his own accord he went unto you. 18. We have sent with him the brother, whose praise *is* in the gospel throughout all the churches.

2 Cor. 12:20. For I fear, lest, when I come, I shall not find you such as I would, and *that* I shall be found unto you such as ye would not: 21. *And* lest, when I come again, my God will humble me among you, and *that* I shall bewail many which have sinned already, and have not repented

Eph. 4:26. Be ye angry, and sin not: let not the sun go down upon your wrath: *vs.* 25,32.

Phil. 1:14. Many of the brethren in the Lord, waxing confident by my bonds, are much more bold to speak the word without fear. *vs.* 12–18.

Phil. 2:22. Ye know the proof of him [Timotheus], that, as a son with the father, he hath served with me in the gospel. 26. He [Epaphroditus] longed after you all, and was full of heaviness, because that ye had heard that he had been sick. 30. For the work of Christ he was nigh unto death, not regarding his life, to supply your lack of service toward me. 1 Cor. 16:10.

Phil. 4:3. I intreat thee also, true yokefellow, help those women which laboured with me in the gospel, with Clement also, and *with* other my fellowlabourers, whose names *are* in the book of life.

Col. 4:7. All my state shall Tychicus declare unto you, *who is* a beloved brother, and a faithful minister and fellowservant in the Lord: 8. Whom I have sent unto you for the same purpose, that he might know your estate, and comfort your hearts; 9. With Onesimus, a faithful and beloved brother, who is *one* of you. They shall make known unto you all things which *are done* here. 10. Aristarchus my fellowprisoner saluteth you, and Marcus, sister's son to Barnabas, (touching whom ye received commandments: if he come unto you, receive him;) 11. And Jesus, which is called Justus, who are of the circumcision. These only *are my* fellowworkers unto the kingdom of God, which have been a comfort unto me. Col. 1:7; Eph. 6:21.

1 Thess. 1:2. We give thanks to God always

for you all, making mention of you in our prayers; 3. Remembering without ceasing your work of faith, and labour of love, and patience of hope in our Lord Jesus Christ, in the sight of God and our Father; 4. Knowing, brethren beloved, your election of God. 5. For our gospel came not unto you in word only, but also in power, and in the Holy Ghost, and in much assurance; as ye know what manner of men we were among you for your sake. 6. And ye became followers of us, and of the Lord, having received the word in much affliction, with joy of the Holy Ghost: 7. So that ye were ensamples to all that believe in Macedonia and Achaia. 8. For from you sounded out the word of the Lord not only in Macedonia and Achaia, but also in every place your faith to God-ward is spread abroad; so that we need not to speak any thing.

1 Thess. 3:1. Wherefore when we could no longer forbear, we thought it good to be left at Athens alone; 2. And sent Timotheus, our brother, and minister of God, and our fellowlabourer in the gospel of Christ, to establish you, and to comfort you concerning your faith:

2 Pet. 1:12: I will not be negligent to put you always in remembrance of these things, though ye know *them*, and be established in the present truth. 13. Yea, I think it meet, as long as I am in this tabernacle, to stir you up by putting *you* in remembrance: 15. Moreover I will endeavour that ye may be able after my decease to have these things always in remembrance.

2 Pet. 2:4. For if God spared not the angels that sinned, but cast *them* down to hell, and delivered *them* into chains of darkness, to be reserved unto judgment; 5. And spared not the old world, but saved Noah the eighth *person*, a preacher of righteousness, bringing in the flood upon the world of the ungodly;

3 John 4. I have no greater joy than to hear that my children walk in truth. 5. Beloved, thou doest faithfully whatsoever thou doest to the brethren, and to strangers; 6. Which have borne witness of thy charity before the church: whom if thou bring forward on their journey after a godly sort, thou shalt do well: 7. Because that for his name's sake they went forth, taking nothing of the Gentiles.

Jude 3. Beloved, when I gave all diligence to write unto you of the common salvation, it was needful for me to write unto you, and exhort *you* that ye should earnestly contend for the faith which was once delivered unto the saints.

Rev. 3:19. As many as I love, I rebuke and chasten: be zealous therefore, and repent.

INSTANCES OF: Moses, Ex. 2:12; 11:8; 32:19,20. Phinehas, Num. 25:7–13; Psa. 106: 30. Joshua, Num. 11:27–29; Josh. 7:6; 8:28, 29; Gideon, Judg. 6:11–32. Jephthah, Judg. 11:30,31,34–39. Samuel, 1 Sam. 12:23; 15: 11,35; 16:1. Saul, 1 Sam. 14:38–44. David,

2 Sam. 6; 7:2; 8:11,12. Elijah, 1 Kin. 19:10. Obadiah, 1 Kin. 18:3,4. Jehoash, 2 Kin. 12: 2-16. Jehu, 2 Kin. 9; 10. Jehoiada, 2 Kin. 11:4-17; 2 Chr. 23:1-17. Asa, 1 Kin. 15:11-15; 2 Chr. 14:1-5,15. Jehoshaphat, 2 Chr. 17:3-10; 19. Hezekiah, 2 Chr. 30;31; Isa. 37: 1. Josiah, 2 Kin. 22; 23; 2 Chr. 34:3-7,29-33. Priests, 1 Chr. 9:13; Ezra 8:17,18. Ezra, Ezra 7:10; 9; 10. Nehemiah, Neh. 4;5;'8; 13:7-9,15-28. Jeremiah, Jer. 25:3,4. Shepherds, Luke 2:17,18. Anna, Luke 2:38. Andrew and Philip, John 1:41-46. Two blind men proclaiming the miracle of healing, contrary to the injunction of Jesus, Matt. 9:30,31. The restored leper, Mark 1:44,45. The healed deaf mute, Mark 7:36. Peter rebuking Jesus, Matt. 16:22. Samaritan woman, John 4:28-30,39. Peter, Acts 2:14-40; 3:12-26. John, see JOHN THE BAPTIST. Paul and Barnabas, Acts 11:22-26; 14:14,15. Phebe, Rom. 16:1,2. Ephesians, Rev. 2:2,3,6.

See JESUS, ZEAL OF; also, EXEMPLIFIED BY PAUL, below.

EXEMPLIFIED BY PAUL: Acts 9:20. Straightway he preached Christ in the synagogues, that he is the Son of God. *vs.* 20-29.

Acts 14:22. Confirming the souls of the disciples, *and* exhorting them to continue in the faith, and that we must through much tribulation enter into the kingdom of God. *vs.* 1-28.

Acts 15:26. Men that have hazarded their lives for the name of our Lord Jesus Christ. *vs.* 30-36,41.

Acts 16:31. They said, Believe on the Lord Jesus Christ, and thou shalt be saved, and thy house. 32. And they spake unto him the word of the Lord, and to all that were in his house. *vs.* 10,13,17.

Acts 17:2. Paul, as his manner was, went in unto them, and three sabbath days reasoned with them out of the scriptures, 3. Opening and alleging, that Christ must needs have suffered, and risen again from the dead; and that this Jesus, whom I preach unto you, is Christ. 16. His spirit was stirred in him, when he saw the city wholly given to idolatry. 17. Therefore disputed he in the synagogue with the Jews, and with the devout persons, and in the market daily with them that met with him. *vs.* 22-31.

Acts 18:5. Paul was pressed in the spirit, and testified to the Jews *that* Jesus *was* Christ. 6. And when they opposed themselves, and blasphemed, he shook *his* raiment, and said unto them, Your blood *be* upon your own heads; I *am* clean: from henceforth I will go unto the Gentiles. *vs.* 4,19,23; Acts 13:16-52'.

Acts 20:18. I have been with you at all seasons, 19. Serving the Lord with all humility of mind, and with many tears, and temptations, which befell me by the lying in wait of the Jews: 20. *And* how I kept back nothing that was profitable *unto you*, but have shewed you, and have taught you publickly, and from house to house, 21. Testi-

fying both to the Jews, and also to the Greeks, repentance toward God, and faith toward our Lord Jesus Christ. 22. Now, behold, I go bound in the spirit unto Jerusalem, not knowing the things that shall befall me there: 23. Save that the Holy Ghost witnesseth in every city, saying that bonds and afflictions abide me. 24. But none of these things move me, neither count I my life dear unto myself, so that I might finish my course with joy, and the ministry, which I have received of the Lord Jesus, to testify the gospel of the grace of God. 26. Wherefore I take you to record this day, that I *am* pure from the blood of all *men.* 27. For I have not shunned to declare unto you all the counsel of God. 31. Therefore watch, and remember, that by the space of three years I ceased not to warn every one night and day with tears. 33. I have coveted no man's silver, or gold, or apparel. 34. Yea, ye yourselves know, that these hands have ministered unto my necessities, and to them that were with me. *vs.* 7,25; Acts 19:8-10,21; 21:13.

Acts 24:25. He reasoned of righteousness, temperance, and judgment to come, *vs.* 14-25.

Acts 26:19. I was not disobedient unto the heavenly vision: 20. But shewed first unto them of Damascus, and at Jerusalem, and throughout all the coasts of Judæa, and *then* to the Gentiles, that they should repent and turn to God, and do works meet for repentance. 22. Having therefore obtained help of God, I continue unto this day, witnessing both to small and great, saying none other things than those which the prophets and Moses did say should come: 23. That Christ should suffer, *and* that he should be the first that should rise from the dead, and should shew light unto the people, and to the Gentiles. 29. Paul said, I would to God, that not only thou, but also all that hear me this day, were both almost, and altogether such as I am, except these bonds. *vs.* 1-29.

Acts 28:23. When they had appointed him a day, there came many to him into *his* lodging; to whom he expounded and testified the kingdom of God, persuading them concerning Jesus, both out of the law of Moses, and *out of* the prophets, from morning till evening. 30. Paul dwelt two whole years in his own hired house, and received all that came in unto him, 31. Preaching the kingdom of God, and teaching those things which concern the Lord Jesus Christ, with all confidence, *vs.* 24-28.

Rom. 1:1. Paul, a servant of Jesus Christ, called *to be* an apostle, separated unto the gospel of God, 14. I am debtor both to the Greeks, and to the Barbarians; both to the wise, and to the unwise. 15. So, as much as in me is, I am ready to preach the gospel to you that are at Rome also. *vs.* 9-13.

Rom. 9:1. I say the truth in Christ, I lie not, my conscience also bearing me witness in the Holy Ghost. 2. That I have great heaviness and continual sorrow in my heart.

3. For I could wish that myself were accursed from Christ for my brethren, my kinsmen according to the flesh:

Rom. 10:1. Brethren, my heart's desire and prayer to God for Israel is, that they might be saved. Rom. 11:13,14.

Rom. 15:19. From Jerusalem, and round about unto Illyricum, I have fully preached the gospel of Christ. 20. Yea, so have I strived to preach the gospel, not where Christ was named, lest I should build upon another man's foundation: *vs.* 15–32; 2 Cor. 10:14–16.

1 Cor. 1:17. Christ sent me not to baptize, but to preach the gospel: not with wisdom of words, lest the cross of Christ should be made of none effect. 23. We preach Christ crucified, unto the Jews a stumblingblock, and unto the Greeks foolishness;

1 Cor. 2:1. I, brethren, when I came to you, came not with excellency of speech or of wisdom, declaring unto you the testimony of God. 2. For I determined not to know any thing among you, save Jesus Christ, and him crucified. 3. And I was with you in weakness, and in fear, and in much trembling. 4. And my speech and my preaching *was* not with enticing words of man's wisdom, but in demonstration of the Spirit and of power. 13. Which things also we speak, not in the words which man's wisdom teacheth, but which the Holy Ghost teacheth; comparing spiritual things with spiritual. *vs.* 6,7.

1 Cor. 3:1. I, brethren, could not speak unto you as unto spiritual, but as unto carnal, *even* as unto babes in Christ. 2. I have fed you with milk, and not with meat: for hitherto ye were not able *to bear it*, neither yet now are ye able. *vs.* 5–7.

1 Cor. 4:12. Labour, working with our own hands: being reviled, we bless; being persecuted, we suffer it: 13. Being defamed, we intreat: we are made as the filth of the world, *and are* the offscouring of all things unto this day. *vs.* 1–21.

1 Cor. 9:16. Though I preach the gospel, I have nothing to glory of: for necessity is laid upon me; yea, woe is unto me, if I preach not the gospel! 18. What is my reward then? *Verily* that, when I preach the gospel, I may make the gospel of Christ without charge, that I abuse not my power in the gospel. 19. Though I be free from all *men*, yet have I made myself servant unto all, that I might gain the more. 22. To the weak became I as weak, that I might gain the weak: I am made all things to all *men*, that I might by all means save some. 23. And this I do for the gospel's sake. 27. I keep under my body, and bring *it* into subjection: lest that by any means, when I have preached to others, I myself should be a castaway. *vs.* 12,15,17, 20,21.

1 Cor. 10:33. I please all *men* in all *things*, not seeking mine own profit, but the *profit* of many, that they may be saved.

1 Cor. 11:1. Be ye followers of me, even as I also *am* of Christ.

1 Cor. 13:1. Though I speak with the tongues of men and of angels, and have not charity, I am become *as* sounding brass, or a tinkling cymbal.

1 Cor. 15:3. I delivered unto you first of all that which I also received, how that Christ died for our sins according to the scriptures; 10. By the grace of God I am what I am: and his grace which *was bestowed* upon me was not in vain; but I laboured more abundantly than they all: yet not I, but the grace of God which was with me. 11. Whether *it were* I or they, so we preach, and so ye believed. 31. I protest by your rejoicing which I have in Christ Jesus our Lord, I die daily. *vs.* 1–32.

2 Cor. 1:12. Our rejoicing is this, the testimony of our conscience, that in simplicity and godly sincerity, not with fleshly wisdom, but by the grace of God, we have had our conversation in the world, and more abundantly to you-ward. *vs.* 15–19,24.

2 Cor. 2:17. We are not as many, which corrupt the word of God: but as of sincerity, but as of God, in the sight of God speak we in Christ. *vs.* 12–16.

2 Cor. 3:6. Who also hath made us able ministers of the new testament; not of the letter, but of the spirit: for the letter killeth, but the spirit giveth life. 12. Seeing then that we have such hope, we use great plainness of speech:

2 Cor. 4:1. Seeing we have this ministry, as we have received mercy, we faint not; 2. But have renounced the hidden things of dishonesty, not walking in craftiness, nor handling the word of God deceitfully; but by manifestation of the truth commending ourselves to every man's conscience in the sight of God. 5. We preach not ourselves, but Christ Jesus the Lord; and ourselves your servants for Jesus' sake. 13. We having the same spirit of faith, according as it is written, I believed, and therefore have I spoken; we also believe, and therefore speak. *vs.* 8–15.

2 Cor. 5:11. Knowing therefore the terror of the Lord, we persuade men; but we are made manifest unto God; and I trust also are made manifest in your consciences. 13. Whether we be beside ourselves, *it is* to God: or whether we be sober, *it is* for your cause. 14. For the love of Christ constraineth us; because we thus judge, that if one died for all, then were all dead: 20. We are ambassadors for Christ, as though God did beseech *you* by us: we pray *you* in Christ's stead, be ye reconciled to God. *v.* 18.

2 Cor. 6:3. Giving no offence in any thing, that the ministry be not blamed. 4. In all *things* approving ourselves as the ministers of God, in much patience, in afflictions, in necessities, in distresses, 5. In stripes, in imprisonments, in tumults, in labours, in watchings, in fastings: 6. By pureness, by knowledge, by longsuffering, by kindness, by the Holy Ghost, by love unfeigned, 7. By the word of truth, by the power of God, by

the armour of righteousness on the right hand and on the left, *vs.* 8–10.

2 Cor. 7:2. Receive us; we have wronged no man, we have corrupted no man, we have defrauded no man.

2 Cor. 10:3. Though we walk in the flesh, we do not war after the flesh:

2 Cor. 11:9. And when I was present with you, and wanted, I was chargeable to no man: for that which was lacking to me the brethren which came from Macedonia supplied: and in all *things* I have kept myself from being burdensome unto you, and *so* will I keep *myself*. *vs.* 7,12.

22. Are they Hebrews? so *am* I. Are they Israelites? so *am* I. Are they the seed of Abraham? so *am* I. 23. Are they ministers of Christ? (I speak as a fool) I *am* more; in labours more abundant, in stripes above measure, in prisons more frequent, in deaths oft. 24. Of the Jews five times received I forty *stripes* save one. 25. Thrice was I beaten with rods, once was I stoned, thrice I suffered shipwreck, a night and a day I have been in the deep; 26. *In* journeyings often, *in* perils of waters, *in* perils of robbers, *in* perils by *mine own* countrymen, *in* perils by the heathen, *in* perils in the city, *in* perils in the wilderness, *in* perils in the sea, *in* perils among false brethren; 27. In weariness and painfulness, in watchings often, in hunger and thirst, in fastings often, in cold and nakedness. 28. Beside those things that are without, that which cometh upon me daily, the care of all the churches. 29. Who is weak, and I am not weak? who is offended, and I burn not? 30. If I must needs glory, I will glory of the things which concern mine infirmities. 31. The God and Father of our Lord Jesus Christ, which is blessed for evermore, knoweth that I lie not. 32. In Damascus the governor under Aretas the king kept the city of the Damascenes with a garrison, desirous to apprehend me: 33. And through a window in a basket was I let down by the wall, and escaped his hands.

2 Cor. 12:10. I take pleasure in infirmities, in reproaches, in necessities, in persecutions, in distresses for Christ's sake: 14. I will not be burdensome to you: for I seek not your's, but you: 15. I will very gladly spend and be spent for you; though the more abundantly I love you, the less I be loved. 21. Lest, when I come again, my God will humble me among you, and *that* I shall bewail many which have sinned already, and have not repented *vs.* 17–19.

2 Cor. 13:8. We can do nothing against the truth, but for the truth. *vs.* 6–9.

Gal. 1:10. Do I now persuade men, or God? or do I seek to please men? for if I yet pleased men, I should not be the servant of Christ. 15. When it pleased God, who separated me from my mother's womb, and called *me* by his grace, 16. To reveal his Son in me, that I might preach him among the heathen; immediately I conferred not with flesh and blood:

Gal. 2:2. I went up by revelation, and communicated unto them that gospel which I preach among the Gentiles, but privately to them which were of reputation, lest by any means I should run, or had run, in vain. Gal. 3:1.

Gal. 4:19. My little children, of whom I travail in birth again until Christ be formed in you, *v.* 11.

Gal. 5:11. I, brethren, if I yet preach circumcision, why do I yet suffer persecution? then is the offence of the cross ceased.

Eph. 6:20. For which I am an ambassador in bonds: that therein I may speak boldly, as I ought to speak. *v.* 17; Phil. 1:17; 4:11, 12,17.

Phil. 1:18. What then? notwithstanding, every way, whether in pretence, or in truth, Christ is preached; and I therein do rejoice, yea, and will rejoice. 20. According to my earnest expectation and *my* hope, that in nothing I shall be ashamed, but *that* with all boldness, as always, *so* now also Christ shall be magnified in my body, whether *it be* by life, or by death. 24. To abide in the flesh *is* more needful for you. 25. And having this confidence, I know that I shall abide and continue with you all for your furtherance and joy of faith; 27. That whether I come and see you, or else be absent, I may hear of your affairs, that ye stand fast in one spirit, with one mind striving together for the faith of the gospel; *vs.* 22,23; Phil. 2:16,17.

Phil. 3:4. Though I might also have confidence in the flesh. If any other man thinketh that he hath whereof he might trust in the flesh, I more: 5. Circumcised the eighth day, of the stock of Israel, *of* the tribe of Benjamin, an Hebrew of the Hebrews; as touching the law, a Pharisee; 6. Concerning zeal, persecuting the church; touching the righteousness which is in the law, blameless. 7. But what things were gain to me, those I counted loss for Christ. 8. Yea doubtless, and I count all things *but* loss for the excellency of the knowledge of Christ Jesus my Lord: for whom I have suffered the loss of all things, and do count them *but* dung, that I may win Christ. 9. And be found in him, not having mine own righteousness, which is of the law, but that which is through the faith of Christ, the righteousness which is of God by faith: 10. That I may know him, and the power of his resurrection, and the fellowship of his sufferings, being made conformable unto his death; 11. If by any means I might attain unto the resurrection of the dead. 12. Not as though I had already attained, either were already perfect: but I follow after, if that I may apprehend that for which also I am apprehended of Christ Jesus. 13. Brethren, I count not myself to have apprehended: but *this* one thing *I do*, forgetting those things which are behind, and reaching forth unto those things which are before, 14. I press toward the mark for the prize of the high calling of

God in Christ Jesus. 15. Let us therefore, as many as be perfect, be thus minded : and if in any thing ye be otherwise minded, God shall reveal even this unto you. 16. Nevertheless, whereto we have already attained, let us walk by the same rule, let us mind the same thing.

Col. 1:28. Whom we preach, warning every man, and teaching every man in all wisdom ; that we may present every man perfect in Christ Jesus. 29. I also labour, striving according to his working, which worketh in me mightily. v. 24.

Col. 2:1. I would that ye knew what great conflict I have for you, and for them at Laodicea, and for as many as have not seen my face in the flesh ;

1 Thess.1:5. Ye know what manner of men we were among you for your sake. 6. And ye became followers of us, and of the Lord,

1 Thess. 2:2. Even after that we had suffered before, and were shamefully entreated, as ye know, at Philippi, we were bold in our God to speak unto you the gospel of God with much contention. 3. Our exhortation was not of deceit, nor of uncleanness, nor in guile : 4. As we were allowed of God to be put in trust with the gospel, even so we speak ; not as pleasing men, but God, which trieth our hearts. 5. For neither at any time used we flattering words, as ye know, nor a cloke of covetousness; God is witness : 6. Nor of men sought we glory, neither of you, nor yet of others, when we might have been burdensome, as the apostles of Christ. 8. Being affectionately desirous of you, we were willing to have imparted unto you, not the gospel of God only, but also our own souls, because ye were dear unto us. 9. For ye remember, brethren, our labour and travail : for labouring night and day, because we would not be chargeable unto any of you, we preached unto you the gospel of God. 10. Ye are witnesses, and God also, how holily and justly and unblameably we behaved ourselves among you that believe : 11. Ye know how we exhorted and comforted and charged every one of you, as a father doth his children, 2 Tim. 1:3,7,11–13.

2 Thess. 3:7. Yourselves know how ye ought to follow us : for we behaved not ourselves disorderly among you ; 8. Neither did we eat any man's bread for nought; but wrought with labour and travail night and day, that we might not be chargeable to any of you : 9. Not because we have not power, but to make ourselves an ensample unto you to follow us. Phil. 3:17.

1 Tim. 4:10. We both labour and suffer reproach, because we trust in the living God, 2 Tim. 2:9,10.

2 Tim. 3:10. Thou hast fully known my doctrine, manner of life, purpose, faith, longsuffering, charity, patience. 11. Persecutions, afflictions, which came unto me at Antioch, at Iconium, at Lystra; what per-

secutions I endured : but out of them all the Lord delivered me.

Heb. 13:18. Pray for us : for we trust we have a good conscience, in all things willing to live honestly.

WITHOUT KNOWLEDGE : Eccl. 7:16. Be not righteous over much ; neither make thyself over wise : why shouldest thou destroy thyself ?

Matt. 8:19. And a certain scribe came, and said unto him, Master, I will follow thee whithersoever thou goest. 20. And Jesus saith unto him, The foxes have holes, and the birds of the air have nests ; but the Son of man hath not where to lay his head. Luke 9:57,58.

John 16:2. They shall put you out of the synagogues : yea, the time cometh, that whosoever killeth you will think that he doeth God service.

Acts 21:20. And when they heard it, they glorified the Lord, and said unto him, Thou seest, brother, how many thousands of Jews there are which believe; and they are all zealous of the law.

Rom. 10:2. For I bear them record that they have a zeal of God, but not according to knowledge. 3. For they being ignorant of God's righteousness, and going about to establish their own righteousness, have not submitted themselves unto the righteousness of God.

Gal. 1:13. For ye have heard of my conversation in time past in the Jews' religion, how that beyond measure I persecuted the church of God, and wasted it : 14. And profited in the Jews' religion above many my equals in mine own nation, being exceedingly zealous of the traditions of my fathers.

Gal. 4:17. They zealously affect you, but not well; yea, they would exclude you, that ye might affect them.

Phil. 1:15. Some indeed preach Christ even of envy and strife; and some also of good will : 16. The one preach Christ of contention, not sincerely, supposing to add affliction to my bonds : 17. But the other of love, knowing that I am set for the defence of the gospel. 18. What then ? notwithstanding, every way, whether in pretence, or in truth, Christ is preached ; and I therein do rejoice, yea, and will rejoice.

IN PUNISHING THE WICKED : Moses and Levites, Ex. 32:20,26–29; Phinehas, Num. 25:11–13; Psa. 106:30,31. Israelites, Josh. 22:11–20; Judg. 20. Samuel, 1 Sam. 15:33. David, 2 Sam. 1:14; 4:9–12. Elijah, 1 Kin. 18:40. Jehu, 2 Kin. 10:15–28. Jehoiada, 2 Kin. 11:18. Josiah, 2 Kin. 23:20.

IN REPROVING INIQUITY : See REPROOF, FAITHFULNESS IN.

ZEBADIAH. 1. Two Benjamites, 1 Chr. 8:15,17.

2. An Israelite who joined David at Ziklag, 1 Chr. 12:7.

3. A Korhite porter in the temple, 1 Chr. 26:2.

4. Son of Asahel, 1 Chr. 27:7.

5. An itinerant Levite teacher, 2 Chr. 17:8.

6. Son of Ishmael and counselor of the king, 2 Chr. 19:11.

7. Son of Shephaniah, Ezra 8:8.

8. A priest who defiled himself by marrying an idolatrous woman, Ezra 10:20.

ZEBAH, king of Midian, Judg. 8:5–21; Psa. 83:11.

ZEBAIM, a place the exact location of which is unknown, Ezra 2:57; Neh. 7:59.

ZEBEDEE, father of James and John, Matt. 4:21; 20:20; 27:56; Mark 1:20.

ZEBINA, son of Nebo, Ezra 10:43.

ZEBOIM. 1. Called also ZEBOIIM. One of the cities in the valley of Siddim, Gen. 10:19; 14:2,8; Deut. 29:23; Hos. 11:8.

2. A city and valley in Benjamin, 1 Sam. 13:18; Neh. 11:34.

ZEBUDAH, wife of Josiah, king of Judah, 2 Kin. 23:36.

ZEBUL, an officer of Abimelech, Judg. 9:28–41.

ZEBULUN. 1. Son of Jacob and Leah, Gen. 30:20; 35:23; 46:14; 49:13; Ex. 1:3; 1 Chr. 2:1. Descendants of, Gen. 46:14; Num. 26: 26,27. Called also ZABULUN.

2. Tribe of. Place of, in march and camp, Num. 2:3,7; 10:14,16. Territory awarded to, Gen. 49:13; Josh. 19:10–16; Matt. 4:13. Aboriginal inhabitants of the territory of, not expelled, Judg. 1:30. Levitical cities of, Josh. 21:34,35; 1 Chr. 6:77. Moses' benediction upon, Deut. 33:18,19. Loyalty of, in resisting the enemies of Israel: with Barak against Sisera, Judg. 4:6,10; 5:14,18; with Gideon against the Midianites, Judg. 6:35; with David when made king over Israel, 1 Chr. 12:33,38–40. Joins with Hezekiah in renewing the passover, 2 Chr. 30:11,18. Conquest of, by Tiglath-pileser; carried to Assyria into captivity, 2 Kin. 15:29; Isa. 9:1. Jesus dwelt in the land of, Matt. 4:15. Twelve thousand sealed, Rev. 7:8.

See ISRAEL.

ZECHARIAH. 1. A Reubenite,1 Chr. 5:7.

2. Three Levites in the days of David, 1 Chr. 9:21; 15:18,20,24; 16:5; 26:2,14.

3. A Benjamite, 1 Chr. 9:37. Called ZACHER in 1 Chr. 8:31.

4. Two Kohathites, 1 Chr. 24:25; 2 Chr. 34:12.

5. A Merarite porter in the temple, 1 Chr. 26:11.

6. Father of Iddo, 1 Chr. 27:21.

7. A prince sent by Jehoshaphat along with priests and Levites to teach in the cities, 2 Chr. 17:7.

8. A Levite, and father of Jahaziel, 2 Chr. 20:14.

9. Son of Jehoshaphat, 2 Chr. 21:2.

10. High priest, and son or grandson of Jehoiada. Put to death for prophesying against Jerusalem, 2 Chr. 24:20–22,25; Matt. 23:35; Luke 11:51.

11. A prophet in the reign of Uzziah, 2 Chr. 26:5.

12. A ruler of the temple, 2 Chr. 35:8.

13. The prophet. Son of Berechiah, Zech. 2:4. Prophesied in the reign of Darius, Ezra 4:24; 5:1; 6:14; Zech. 1:1,7; 7:1. Probably the priest mentioned in Neh. 12:16.

14. Two chiefs who returned with Ezra, Ezra 8:3,11,16.

15. Name of various Jews after the captivity, Ezra 10:26; Neh. 8:4; 11:4,5,12; 12:16.

16. A priest and temple musician, Neh. 12:35,41.

17. Perhaps identical with 11, above, Isa. 8:2.

18. A Levite in the reign of Hezekiah, 2 Chr. 29:13.

19. See ZACHARIAH.

ZEDAD, a place near Hamath, Num. 34: 8; Ezek. 47:15.

ZEDEKIAH. 1. Made king of Judah by Nebuchadnezzar, 2 Kin. 24:17,18; 1 Chr. 3:15; 2 Chr. 36:10; Jer. 37:1. Throws off his allegiance to Nebuchadnezzar, 2 Kin. 24:20; 2 Chr. 36:13; Jer. 52:3; Ezek. 17:12–21. Forms an alliance with the king of Egypt, Ezek. 17: 11–18. The allegiance denounced by Jeremiah, 2 Chr. 36:12; Jer. 21; 24:8–10; 27:12–22; 32:3–5; 34; 37:7–10,17; 38:14–28; by Ezekiel, Ezek. 12:10–16; 17:12–21. Imprisons Jeremiah on account of his denunciations, Jer. 32:2,3; 37:15–21; 38:5–28. Seeks the intercession of Jeremiah with God in his behalf, Jer. 21:1–3; 37:3; 38:14–27. Wicked reign of, 2 Kin. 24:19,20; 2 Chr. 36:12,13; Jer. 37:2; 38: 5,19,24–26; 52:2. Nebuchadnezzar destroys the city and temple, takes him captive to Babylon, blinds his eyes, slays his sons, 2 Kin. 25:1–10; 2 Chr. 36:17–20; Jer. 1:3; 32:1,2; 39:1–10; 51:59; 52:4–30.

2. Grandson of Jehoiakim, 1 Chr. 3:16.

3. A false prophet, Jer. 29:21–23.

4. A prince of Judah, Jer. 36:12.

5. A false prophet. Prophesies to Ahab victory over the Syrians, instead of defeat, 1 Kin. 22:11; 2 Chr. 18:10. Smites Micaiah, the true prophet, 1 Kin. 22:24; 2 Chr. 18:23.

ZEEB, a prince of Midian, Judg. 7:25; 8:3; Psa. 83:11.

ZELAH, a city in Benjamin. Saul buried in, Josh. 18:28; 2 Sam. 21:14.

ZELEK, an Ammonite, 2 Sam. 23:37; 1 Chr. 11:39.

ZELOPHEHAD, grandson of Gilead. His daughters petition for his inheritance, Num. 27:1–11; 36; Josh. 17:3–6; 1 Chr. 7:15.

ZELOTES. See SIMON.

ZELZAH, a city of Benjamin,1 Sam. 10:2.

ZEMARAIM. 1. A city of Benjamin, Josh. 18:22.

2. A part of Mount Ephraim, 2 Chr. 13:4.

ZEMARITES, a tribe descended from Canaan, Gen 10:18; 1 Chr. 1:16.

ZEMIRA, a son of Becher, 1 Chr. 7:8.

ZENAN, a city of Judah, Josh. 15:37.

ZENAS, a Christian believer and lawyer, Tit. 3:13.

ZEPHANIAH. 1. A priest in the reign of Zedekiah, king of Judah. Sent by the king to Jeremiah with a message soliciting the prophet's intercession and prayers, Jer

21:1,2. Shows Jeremiah the false prophet's letter, Jer. 29:25-29. Taken to Riblah and slain, 2 Kin. 25:18-21; Jer. 52:24-27.

2. A Kohathite, 1 Chr. 6:36.

3. A prophet in the days of Josiah, Zeph. 1:1.

4. Father of Josiah, Zech. 6:10,14.

ZEPHATH. A Canaanitish city, Judg. 1:17. See HORMAH.

ZEPHATHAH, a valley W. of Judah, 2 Chr. 14:10.

ZEPHI. See ZEPHO.

ZEPHO, called also ZEPHI. Son of Eliphaz, Gen. 36:11,15; 1 Chr. 1:36.

ZEPHON, son of Gad, Num. 26:15.

ZER, a city in Naphtali, Josh. 19:35.

ZERAH. 1. Son of Reuel, Gen. 36:13,17; 1 Chr. 1:37.

2. Father of Jobab, Gen. 36:33; 1 Chr. 1:44.

3. See ZARAH.

4. Son of Simeon, Num. 26:13; 1 Chr. 4:24.

5. A Gershonite, 1 Chr. 6:21.

6. A Levite, 1 Chr. 6:41.

7. King of Ethiopia, 2 Chr. 14:9-15.

ZERAHIAH. 1. An ancestor of Ezra, 1 Chr. 6:6,51; Ezra 7:4.

2. Father of Elihoenai, Ezra 8:4.

ZERED. See ZARED.

ZEREDA, a city or district of Ephraim, 1 Kin. 11:26.

ZEREDATHAH, in Manasseh, 2 Chr. 4:17.

ZERERATH, a district of uncertain location, Judg. 7:22.

ZERESH, wife of Haman, Esth. 5:10-14; 6:13.

ZERETH, son of Ashur, 1 Chr. 4:7.

ZERI, son of Jeduthun, 1 Chr. 25:3.

ZEROR, father of Abiel, 1 Sam. 9:1.

ZERUAH, mother of Jeroboam, 1 Kin. 11:26.

ZERUBBABEL, called also SHESH-BAZZAR. Directs the rebuilding of the altar and temple after his return from captivity in Babylon, Ezra 3:2-8; 4:2,3; 5:2,14-16; Hag. 1:12-14. Leads the emancipated Jews back from Babylon, Ezra 1:8-11; 2; Neh. 12. Appoints the Levites to inaugurate the rebuilding of the temple, Ezra 3:2-8. Prophecies relating to, Hag. 2:2; Zech. 4:6-10. Called ZOROBABEL in the genealogy of Joseph, Matt. 1:12; Luke 3:27.

ZERUIAH. Sister of David, 1 Chr. 2:16. Mother of three of David's great soldiers, 1 Chr. 2:16; 2 Sam. 2:18; 3:39; 16:9-11; 17:25.

ZETHAM, a son of Laadan, 1 Chr. 23:8; 26:22.

ZETHAN, son of Bilhan, 1 Chr. 7:10.

ZETHAR, one of the seven chamberlains of the king of Persia, Esth. 1:10.

ZIA, a Gadite, 1 Chr. 5:13.

ZIBA, Saul's servant. His fidelity to Mephibosheth, 2 Sam. 9; to David, 2 Sam. 16:1-4; 19:17,26-29.

ZIBEON. 1. A Hivite, Gen. 36:2,14.

2. Son of Seir, Gen. 36:20,24,29; 1 Chr. 1: 38,40.

ZIBIA, a Benjamite, 1 Chr. 8:9.

ZIBIAH, wife of Ahaziah, 2 Kin. 12:1; 2 Chr. 24:1.

ZICHRI. 1. Son of Izhar, Ex. 6:21.

2. Three Benjamites, 1 Chr. 8:19,23,27.

3. A Levite, 1 Chr. 9:15.

4. Two chiefs in the days of David, 1 Chr. 26:25; 27:16.

5. Father of Amasiah, 2 Chr. 17:16.

6. Father of Elishaphat, 2 Chr. 23:1.

7. An Ephraimite, 2 Chr. 28:7.

8. Father of Joel, Neh. 11:9.

9. A priest, Neh. 12:17.

ZIDDIM, a city in Naphtali, Josh. 19:35.

ZIDKIJAH, a chief prince of the exiles who returned to Jerusalem, Neh. 10:1.

ZIDON. See SIDON.

ZIF, second month (May), 1 Kin. 6:1,37.

ZIHA. 1. One of the Nethinim, Ezra 2:43; Neh. 7:46.

2. A ruler of the Nethinim, Neh. 11:21.

ZIKLAG. A city within the territory allotted to the tribe of Judah, Josh. 15:31. Reallotted to the tribe of Simeon, Josh. 19:5. David dwells at, 1 Sam. 27:5,6; 2 Sam. 1:1; 1 Chr. 12:1. Amalekites destroy, 1 Sam. 30. Inhabited by the returned exiles of Judah, Neh. 11:28.

ZILLAH, wife of Lamech, Gen. 4:19,22,23.

ZILPAH. Leah's handmaid, Gen. 29:24. Mother of Gad and Asher by Jacob. Gen. 30:9-13; 35:26; 37:2; 46:18.

ZILTHAI. 1. A Benjamite, 1 Chr. 8:20.

2. A captain of Manasseh, 1 Chr. 12:20.

ZIMMAH. 1. A son of Jahath, 1 Chr. 6:20.

2. Two Gershonites, 1 Chr. 6:42; 2 Chr. 29:12.

ZIMRAN, son of Abraham, Gen. 25:2; 1 Chr. 1:32.

ZIMRI. 1. A chief of Simeon, Num. 25: 6-8,14.

2. King of Israel, 1 Kin. 16:9-20; 2 Kin. 9:31.

3. Son of Zerah, 1 Chr. 2:6.

4. A Benjamite, 1 Chr. 8:36; 9:42.

5. An unknown place, Jer. 25:25.

ZIN, a desert S. of Judah, Num. 13:21; 20:1; 27:14; 33:36; 34:3,4; Deut. 32:51; Josh. 15:1,3.

ZINA. A son of Shimei, 1 Chr. 23:10. Called ZIZAH in v. 11.

ZION, called also SION, stronghold of Jerusalem. Taken from the Jebusites by David, 2 Sam. 5:6-9; 1 Chr. 11:5-7. Called thereafter "the city of David," 2 Sam. 5:7, 9; 6:12,16; 1 Kin. 8:1; 1 Chr. 11:5,7; 15:1,29; 2 Chr. 5:2. Ark of the covenant placed in, 2 Sam. 6:12,16; 1 Kin. 8:1; 1 Chr. 15:1,29; 2 Chr. 5:2; removed from, to Solomon's temple on Mount Moriah, 1 Kin. 8:1; 2 Chr. 5:2, with 2 Chr. 3:1.

Collectively, the place, the forms, and the assemblies of Israelitish worship, 2 Kin. 19:21,31; Psa. 9:11; 48:2,11,12; 74:2; 132:13; 137:1; Isa. 35:10; 40:9; 49:14; 51:16; 52:1,2,7,8; 60:14; 62:1,11; Jer. 31:6; 50:5; Lam. 1:4; Joel 2:1,15; Matt. 21:5; John 12:15; Rom. 9:33; 11:26; 1 Pet. 2:6. Name of, applied to Jerusalem, Psa. 87:2,5; 149:2; Song 3:11; Isa. 33: 14,20; Jer. 9:19; 30:17; Zech. 9:13. Called the city of God, Psa. 87:2,3; Isa. 60:14. Restoration of, promised, Isa. 51:3,11,16; 52:1, 2,7,8; 59:20; 60:14; Obad.17,21; Zeph. 3:14,16; Zech. 1:14,17; 2:7,10; 8:2,3; 9:9,13. Name of, applied to the city of the redeemed, Heb. 12:22; Rev. 14:1.

See CHURCH; JERUSALEM.

ZIOR, a city in Judah, Josh. 15:54.

ZIPH. 1. Two cities of Judah, Josh. 15: 24,55; 1 Sam. 23:14,15,24; 26:2; 2 Chr. 11:8.

2. Grandson of Caleb, 1 Chr. 2:42.

3. Son of Jehaleleel, 1 Chr. 4:16.

ZIPHAH, a son of Jehaleleel, 1 Chr. 4:16.

ZIPHION. A son of Gad, Gen. 46:16. Called ZEPHON in Num. 26:15.

ZIPHRON, a place in the N. of Palestine, Num. 34:9.

ZIPPOR, father of Balak, Num. 22:2,4, 10,16; 23:18; Josh. 24:9.

ZIPPORAH. Wife of Moses, Ex. 2:16–22. Reproaches Moses, Ex. 4:25,26. Separates from Moses, is brought again to him by her father, Ex. 18:2–6. Miriam and Aaron upbraid Moses concerning, Num. 12:1.

ZITHRI, a son of Uzziel, Ex. 6:22.

ZIZ, a pass in Judah, 2 Chr. 20:16.

ZIZA. 1. A Simeonite, 1 Chr. 4:37.

2. Son of Rehoboam, 2 Chr. 11:20.

ZIZAH. A Gershonite, 1 Chr. 23:11. Called ZINA in *v.* 10.

ZOAN, a city in Egypt. Built seven years after Hebron in the land of Canaan, Num. 13:22. Prophecies concerning, Ezek. 30:14. Wise men from, were counselors of Pharaoh, Isa. 19:11,13. Princes of, Isa. 30:4.

ZOAR. A city of the Moabites, near the Jordan, Gen. 13:10. Territory of, Deut. 34:3; Isa. 15:5; Jer. 48:34. King of, fought against Chedorlaomer, Gen. 14:2,8. Not destroyed with Sodom and Gomorrah, Gen. 19:20–23,30.

ZOBA. See ZOBAH.

ZOBAH, called also ZOBA; ARAM-ZO-BAH; HAMATH-ZOBAH. A kingdom in the N. of Palestine, 1 Sam. 14:47. Conquest of, by David, 2 Sam. 8:3–8,12; 1 Kin. 11:23,24; 1 Chr.

18:2–9. Its inhabitants mercenaries of the Ammonites against David, 2 Sam. 10:6–19; 1 Chr. 19:6–19. David writes a psalm after the conquest of, see title of Psa. 60. Invaded by Solomon, 2 Chr. 8:3.

ZODIAC, signs of, Job 38:32 [*R. V.* marg.].

ZOBEBAH, daughter of Coz, 1 Chr. 4:8.

ZOHAR. 1. Father of Ephron, Gen. 23: 8; 25:9.

2. Son of Simeon, Gen. 46:10; Ex. 6:15.

ZOHELETH, a stone near En-rogel, 1 Kin. 1:9.

ZOHETH, son of Ishi, 1 Chr. 4:20.

ZOPHAH, son of Helem, 1 Chr. 7:35,36.

ZOPHAI, son of Elkanah, 1 Chr. 6:26.

ZOPHAR, one of Job's three friends, Job 2:11; 11; 20; 42:7–9.

ZOPHIM. 1. A place on the top of Pisgah, Num. 23:14.

2. A city on Mount Ephraim, 1 Sam. 1:1.

ZORAH, called also ZAREAH and ZO-REAH. A city of Dan or Judah, Josh. 15:33; 19:41. The city of Samson, Judg. 13:2,24,25; 16:31. Representatives of the tribe of Dan sent from, to spy out the land with a view to its conquest, Judg. 18. Fortified by Rehoboam, 2 Chr. 11:10. Repeopled after the captivity, Neh. 11:29.

ZOROBABEL, called also ZERUBBABEL and SHESHBAZZAR. An ancestor of Joseph, Matt. 1:12,13; Luke 3:27.

See ZERUBBABEL.

ZUAR, father of Nethaneel, Num. 1:8; 2:5; 7:18,23; 10:15.

ZUPH. 1. A Kohathite, 1 Sam. 1:1; 1 Chr. 6:35.

2. A district northwest of Jerusalem, 1 Sam. 9:5.

ZUR. 1. A prince of Midian, Num. 25:15, 18; 31:8; Josh. 13:21.

2. A Benjamite, 1 Chr. 8:30; 9:36.

ZURIEL, a Merarite, Num. 3:35.

ZURISHADDAI, father of Shelumiel, Num. 1:6; 2:12; 7:36,41; 10:19.

ZUZIMS. See ZAMZUMMIMS.

INDEX

Showing the pages and columns in which each verse of Scripture occurs in this work. Inasmuch as many verses and series of verses contain numerous subjects, it is the purpose of this index to guide the student to the various pages where each verse has been quoted or cited, thus enabling him to ascertain what subjects each verse or series of verses contains, and with what Scriptures it is grouped.

The book and chapter stand by themselves, causing a break in the matter in the columns. The left-hand column of figures indicates the verses of the chapter. The figures following the verse numbers indicate the page or pages where the verse has been quoted or cited. The small superior figures indicate the columns in which the verse has been quoted or cited. The small superior figure one (^{1}) indicates that the verse is in the first column, and the superior figure two (^{2}) indicates that the verse is in the second column.

The parenthesis is used to show that the verse which it follows, instead of standing alone, as it does where it is not in parentheses, is the initial verse of a series of verses.

The star (*) indicates that the verse which it follows is contained in one or more of the citations above it (in the same chapter), which are included in parentheses. For instance, Gen. 1:16, below, has a star following the verse number (16). This indicates that this verse is included in the references inclosed in the parentheses following verse 1, (1–31), for, of course, 1–31 includes verse 16. It is also included, for the same reason, in the parenthetical references (14–17) and (14–18) following verse 14.

GENESIS, 556^1.

Verse

Genesis.1.

1 268^1, 268^1 (1–31), 330^2, 434^2,548^2, 548^2, 667^1, 873^1 (1–31), 1336^2.
2* 275^2, 434^2, 562^1, 969^1.
3* 434^2, 798^1 (3–5).
4* 434^2.
5* 275^2, 278^2, 434^2, 899^2.
6* 330^2, 398^2 (6–8), 434^2.
7* 330^2, 434^2.
8* 278^2, 434^2.
9* 246^2, 421^2, 434^2, 778^1, 1244^1, 1363^1.
10* 246^2, 421^2, 434^2, 515^1, 1244^1.
11* 410^2, 434^2, 534^2, 1008^2, 1245^1, 1354^2.
12* 410^2, 434^2, 1008^2, 1245^1.
13* 278^2, 434^2.
14* 398^2 (14–17), 434^2, 1244^1, 1308^1 (14–18), 1336^2, 1337^2, 1444^2.
15* 434^2.
16* 434^2, 884^2, 899^2, 1300^2.
17* 434^2.
18* 434^2, 515^1, 899^2.
19* 278^2, 434^2.
20* 115^2 (20–30), 398^2, 399^1 (20–22), 434^2.
21* 435^1, 515^1, 1008^2 (21–25), 1363^2.
22* 107^2, 435^1.
23* 278^2, 435^1.
24* 68^2, 435^1.
25* 68^2, 435^1, 515^1.
26* 12^1 (26–28), 12^1 (26–30), 115^2 270^1, 347^2 (26–28), 435^1, 438^1, 600^1, 710^1, 817^2, 818^1, 818^2, 1339^1.
27* 410^2, 435^1, 438^1, 600^1, 817^2, 818^1, 1094^2, 1095^1, 1412^2.
28* 107^2, 115^2, 410^2, 435^1, 818^2, 1008^2.
29* 400^2, 410^2, 493^2, 554^1, 1245^1, 1354^2.
30* 68^2, 128^1, 400^2, 493^2, 554^1, 1354^2.
31* 278^2, 435^1.

Genesis 2.

1 59^1, 59^1, 268^1 (1–25), 435^1, 435^1 (1–25), 548^2.
2* 70^1, 71^1, 278^2, 435^1, 1100^1, 1203^1, 1203^1.
3* 70^1, 71^1, 435^1, 665^2, 1203^1, 1203^1, 1264^1.
4* 435^1.
5* 835^1, 1354^2.
6* 835^1, 883^1.
7* 12^1, 144^2, 328^2, 435^1, 438^1, 534^2, 793^2, 796^2, 817^2, 1099^1.
8* 332^2 (8–17).
9* 534^2, 776^1, 793^2, 1308^2, 1339^1, 1339^1, 1344^1.
10*
11* 517^1, 541^1, 958^1.
12* 106^1, 517^1, 918^1.
13* 273^1, 424^2.
14* 80^1, 347^2, 555^2.

Verse

15* 49^2, 610^1, 1007^1 (15–17).
16* 12^1 (16–25), 246^2, 263^2, 374^2, 493^2.
17* 246^2, 263^2, 280^2, 374^2, 776^1, 1088^2, 1286^2, 1308^2, 1339^1, 1375^1.
18* 1394^1, 1394^1, 1394^2, 1413^2.
19* 68^2, 70^1, 534^2, 818^2.
20* 68^2, 818^2, 1394^1.
21* 347^2 (21–24), 1412^2, 1413^2.
22* 1412^2, 1413^2.
23* 347^2, 379^2, 582^2, 822^2, 1394^2, 1412^2, 1413^2.
24* 379^2, 582^2, 822^2, 1094^2, 1095^1, 1098^2, 1099^2, 1394^1, 1391^2, 1413^2.
25* 622^1.

Genesis 3.

1 12^1 (1–24), 268^1 (1–5), 347^2 (1–24), 374^2, 517^2 (1–24), 611^1, 616^1 (1–5), 999^2 (1–5), 1238^2, 1260^1 (1–15), 1260^1, 1315^2, 1323^1 (1–19), 1412^2 (1–16).
2* 374^2, 1315^2.
3* 246^2, 374^2, 1007^1, 1308^2, 1315^2, 1339^1 (3–6).
4* 298^1, 374^2, 377^2, 611^1, 1238^2, 1238^2, 1315^2, 1342^2, 1348^2 (4–6).
5* 56^2, 374^2, 377^2, 1238^2, 1315^2, 1342^2.
6* 56^2, 267^1, 272^1, 318^1 (6–11), 374^2, 616^1, 810^2, 1315^2, 1409^1, 1413^1, 1416^1.
7* 243^1, 326^2, 345^1, 347^2, 374^2, 397^2, 622^1 (7–11), 1280^2, 1315^2, 1409^1.
8* 71^1, 243^1, 251^1 (8–10), 345^1, 374^2, 387^1 (8–13), 427^2 (8–21), 1280^2, 1315^2.
9* 345^1, 374^2, 1280^2, 1315^2.
10* 345^1, 374^2, 1265^1, 1280^2, 1315^2.
11* 345^1, 374^2, 1280^2, 1283^2, 1315^2, 1339^1.
12* 267^1, 352^1, 374^2, 377^2, 1149^1, 1280^2, 1315^2, 1339^1.
13* 352^2, 374^2, 377^2, 1149^1, 1149^1, 1280^2, 1315^2.
14* 68^2, 272^1, 374^2, 766^2, 1238^2, 1238^2, 1260^1, 1260^1, 1280^2.
15* 49^1, 272^1, 272^1 (15–19), 347^2, 374^2, 659^2, 661^2, 671^1, 673^1, 704^2, 712^1, 766^2, 813^1, 944^1, 1238^2, 1260^1, 1280^2, 1360^1, 1412^2.
16* 20^2 (16–19), 20^2, 116^1, 347^2, 374^2, 379^2, 766^2, 1280^2, 1286^2, 1375^1, 1394^1, 1394^2, 1413^2.
17* 20^2, 272^1, 330^2, 374^2, 534^2, 766^2 (17–19), 1280^2, 1286^2, 1339^1, 1375^1.
18* 272^1, 330^2, 374^2, 1281^1, 1286^2, 1335^1, 1335^2, 1375^1.
19* 49^2, 252^2, 280^1, 280^2, 328^2, 374^2, 534^2, 776^2, 1281^1, 1286^2, 1308^1, 1375^1.
20* 12^1 (20–24), 347^2, 1101^2, 1281^1.
21* 326^2, 347^2, 785^2, 1281^1, 1290^2.
22* 102^2 (22–24), 776^1, 793^2, 1281^1, 1339^1, 1339^1.

Verse

23* 49^2, 328^2, 332^2, 534^2, 1281^1.
24* 59^2, 166^2, 332^2, 793^2, 1281^1, 1308^2, 1308^2, 1339^1.

Genesis 4.

1 7^2 (1–15), 12^1, 147^1, 167^2, 347^2, 1334^1.
2* 12^1, 49^2, 49^2, 70^1, 70^1, 347^2, 1268^1.
3* 70^1, 70^1, 70^1, 147^1 (3–15), 826^1 (3–8).
4* 68^2, 70^1, 85^2, 244^1 (4–7), 313^2(4–8), 1100^1, 1132^1 (4–8), 1266^2, 1438^2.
5* 64^2 (5–8), 253^1, 649^2, 1438^2.
6* 63^2, 649^2, 1396^1 (6–10).
7* 246^2, 398^2, 763^1, 886^1, 1286^2, 1375^1, 1438^2.
8* 408^2, 571^1, 640^2, 649^2, 817^1, 951^2, 1344^1.
9* 345^1, 377^2, 569^2, 1238^1, 1254^1, 1281^1.
10* 345^1, 569^2, 1281^1, 1283^2, 1344^1.
11* 272^1 (11–16), 345^1, 569^2, 572^2 (11–15), 766^2 (11–15), 1281^1.
12* 569^2, 1281^1.
13* 166^2, 250^1, 312^2, 572^1, 888^2, 983^1 (13–15), 1281^1.
14* 88^2, 102^2, 166^2, 312^2, 572^1, 888^2, 1281^1.
15* 88^2, 572^1, 1337^2.
16* 147^1, 332^2, 413^2 (16–22), 900^2.
17* 147^1, 204^2, 342^2, 342^2.
18* 147^1, 342^2, 640^2, 777^2 (18–24), 832^2, 838^1.
19* 11^2 (19–23), 960^1, 1463^2.
20* 70^1 (20–22), 70^1 (20–22), 77^2, 647^1, 1323^2.
21* 77^2, 77^2, 539^2, 640^2, 755^1, 888^2, 888^2.
22* 77^2, 77^2, 144^1, 144^1, 640^2, 640^2, 827^2, 829^1, 895^2, 1292^2, 1343^2, 1463^2.
23* 571^1, 1463^2.
24* 88^2, 571^2.
25 7^2, 12^1, 167^2, 347^2, 1264^1, 1334^1.
26 70^1, 342^2, 1264^1.

Genesis 5.

1 12^1 (1–5), 141^2, 413^2 (1–32), 435^1 438^1, 600^1, 817^2.
2* 435^1, 438^1, 817^2.
3* 347^2, 554^1, 1264^1.
4* 347^2.
5* 12^1, 800^2.
6* 342^2 (6–11).
7 413^2.
8* 800^2, 1264^1.
9* 147^1 (9–15).
10* 413^2.
11* 800^2.
12* 812^2 (12–17).
13 413^2.
14* 800^2.
15* 649^1.
16* 649^1.

Verse

7* 255^2, 749^3, 849^1, 860^2, 885^1.

8* 255^2, 360^2, 453^1, 849^2, 885^1, 1100^2.

9* 141^2, 527^1, 626^2, 781^1, 1006^1 (9-13), 1417^2.

10* 626^2, 781^1 (10-13), 1207^2, 1207^2 (10-13), 1242^1 (10-13), 1311^1 (10-13), 1417^2.

11* 389^2, 626^2, 1416^2 (11-13), 1417^2, 1439^1 (11-13), 1439^1 (11-13), 1444^1.

12* 170^1, 389^2, 626^2, 1412^2, 1417^2, 1444^1.

13* 170^1, 389^2, 626^2, 1417^2, 1444^1.

14* 148^2, 286^2, 427^2, 849^2 (14-23), 885^1, 1311^1.

15* 210^2, 286^2, 427^2, 1311^1.

16* 98^2, 280^1, 286^2, 395^1, 593^1 (16-21), 618^1, 1364^1.

17* 20^2, 34^2, 98^2, 395^1, 568^2, 1143^1, 1289^1.

18* 98^2, 568^2, 1143^1, 1289^1.

19* 98^2, 286^2, 628^1, 1417^2, 1425^1.

20* 98^2, 1016^1, 1164^1.

21* 98^2, 286^2, 465^1, 543^2, 1244^1 1283^2, 1417^2.

22* 99^1, 255^2, 286^2, 1425^1.

23* 99^1, 148^2, 255^2, 286^2, 360^2, 643^2, 749^2, 885^1, 1359^2.

24* 99^1, 141^2, 286^2.

25* 99^1, 286^2.

26* 74^2, 75^1, 99^1, 141^2, 287^1, 781^1, 1417^2.

27* 99^1, 287^1, 1146^2 (27-29), 1258^2.

28* 99^1, 287^1, 527^1.

29* 99^1, 287^1, 593^1, 1376^1.

30* 99^1, 287^1.

Deuteronomy 32.

1 287^1, 628^1, 843^2, 883^1 (1-52), 959^2 (1-52), 1019^1 (1-43), 1294^1 (1-52).

2* 287^1, 628^1, 843^2.

3* 287^1, 628^1, 844^1.

4* 287^1, 441^1, 456^2, 461^1, 481^1, 512^2, 515^1, 628^1, 1195^1, 1342^2, 1342^2.

5* 12^2, 99^1, 159^1, 287^1, 443^2, 628^1.

6* 12^2, 99^1, 159^1, 159^1, 287^1, 438^2, 443^2, 618^1, 628^1, 913^1.

7* 287^1, 579^1, 628^1.

8* 12^1, 287^1, 318^2, 330^2, 509^2, 628^1, 994^2.

9* 177^1, 177^1, 177^2, 287^1, 471^1, 628^1.

10* 287^1, 305^2, 455^2, 471^1, 487^2, 628^1, 1367^2, 1396^1.

11* 68^2, 287^1, 330^2, 330^2, 330^2, 471^1, 494^2, 628^1, 899^1.

12* 111^1, 287^1, 455^2, 471^1, 481^1, 494^2, 628^1.

13* 129^1, 287^1, 400^1, 494^2, 573^2, 618^1, 628^1, 1195^1.

14* 105^2, 129^1, 146^2, 287^1, 400^1, 427^1, 494^2, 628^1, 773^2, 839^1, 839^1, 1266^2, 1266^2.

15* 71^2, 93^1, 99^1, 287^1, 438^2, 506^2, 515^2, 593^1 (15-26), 611^2, 618^1, 628^1, 654^1, 1016^2, 1146^2 (15-18), 1164^1, 1208^2.

16* 9^2, 93^1, 287^2, 460^1, 628^1, 649^1.

17* 93^1, 287^2, 305^1, 628^2, 1098^2.

18* 93^1, 99^1, 287^2, 438^2, 618^1, 628^2, 712^2.

19* 93^1, 287^2, 628^2, 766^2 (19-43), 1287^2.

20* 93^1, 287^2, 628^2.

21* 65^2, 93^1, 194^2, 287^2, 415^1, 460^1, 628^2, 649^1, 681^1, 1098^1.

22* 65^2, 93^1, 287^2, 398^2, 552^1, 628^2.

23* 77^2, 93^1, 287^2, 628^2.

24* 93^1, 287^2, 628^2, 1260^1.

25* 93^1, 287^2, 628^2, 1359^2, 1413^1.

26* 93^1, 96^2, 287^2, 628^2.

27* 93^1, 287^2, 628^2.

28* 93^1, 96^2, 134^1, 287^2, 628^2.

29* 93^1, 96^2, 134^1, 283^2, 287^2, 475^1, 628^2, 1133^2, 1359^2, 1364^1, 1399^2.

30* 93^1, 267^2, 287^2, 568^1, 628^2, 924^2, 1286^2, 1359^2, 1359^2.

31* 287^2, 506^2, 628^2, 1126^2 (31-33).

32* 287^2, 517^2, 534^2, 628^2, 813^1, 1293^1, 1293^1, 1367^2.

33* 79^1, 79^1, 287^2, 326^1, 628^2, 813^2, 1132^1, 1260^1, 1367^2.

Verse

34* 287^2, 628^2, 1244^1, 1283^2.

35* 287^2, 461^1, 628^2, 1098^2, 1100^1.

36* 287^2, 475^1, 628^2, 1100^1, 1133^1.

37* 287^2, 595^1, 628^2.

38* 288^1, 383^1, 592^2, 595^1, 628^2.

39* 37^2, 281^2, 288^1, 481^1, 482^1, 506^2, 509^2, 629^1, 796^2, 968^2.

40* 288^1, 439^2, 509^1, 629^1, 796^2.

41* 288^1, 509^2, 629^1, 1308^2.

42* 77^2, 288^1, 509^2, 629^1.

43* 288^1, 475^1, 509^2, 629^1, 1098^2.

44* 288^1, 576^1, 629^1.

45* 288^1, 629^1.

46* 216^1, 288^1, 629^1, 910^1, 926^2.

47* 216^1, 288^1, 494^2, 629^1.

48* 288^1, 885^1 (48-52).

49* 115^1, 288^1, 897^1.

50* 7^1, 288^1, 575^2, 885^1, 897^1.

51* 288^1, 1463^2.

52* 288^1.

Deuteronomy 33.

1 107^2 (1-29), 288^1, 642^2 (1-29), 840^2, 883^1 (1-29), 885^2 (1-29), 885^2.

2* 59^1, 61^1, 77^1, 288^1, 449^1, 781^1, 781^1, 781^1 (2-4), 925^2, 1249^1, 1290^1, 1335^2 (2-5).

3* 288^1, 390^2, 469^2, 471^1.

4* 288^1.

5* 288^1, 654^1.

6* 288^2, 638^2 (6-17).

7* 288^2, 757^1.

8* 288^2, 1353^1.

9* 288^2, 788^1, 913^1.

10* 288^2, 608^2, 781^1, 788^1, 788^1, 1006^1.

11* 133^2, 288^2, 977^2.

12* 288^2, 469^2, 471^1, 487^2.

13* 133^2, 288^2, 313^1, 344^1 (13-17), 749^2 (13-17), 821^2 (13-17).

14* 133^2, 288^2, 884^2.

15* 133^2, 288^2, 330^2.

16* 133^2, 288^2.

17* 288^2, 1351^2.

18* 288^2, 646^2, 1462^1.

19* 288^2, 646^2, 1444^1, 1462^1.

20* 288^2, 411^1.

21* 288^2.

22* 274^2, 288^2.

23* 288^2, 453^1, 896^1.

24* 78^2, 133^2, 288^2.

25* 78^2, 125^1, 144^1, 289^1, 487^2, 506^2 (25-29), 1270^2.

26* 289^1, 449^1, 482^1, 487^2, 654^1.

27* 29^1, 75^1, 125^1, 289^1, 439^2, 482^1, 487^2, 1173^1.

28* 252^1, 289^1, 488^1, 1397^2.

29* 289^1, 488^1, 506^2, 538^1, 1269^1.

Deuteronomy 34.

1 274^2, 289^1, 424^2, 643^2 (1-12), 652^1, 885^1 (1-8), 885^1 (1-6), 897^1, 958^1 (1-4).

2* 289^1.

3* 289^1, 652^1, 924^2, 1464^1.

4* 289^1.

5* 289^1.

6* 113^2, 289^1.

7* 614^2, 643^1, 800^2, 873^1, 885^2, 916^2.

8* 885^2.

9* 537^2, 623^1, 749^2, 749^2, 885^1, 1011^2.

10* 885^2, 1011^2.

11* 1011^2.

12* 885^2.

JOSHUA, 556^1.

Joshua 1.

1 148^2, 231^1 (1-9), 255^2 (1-9), 750^1 (1-18), 849^2, 1132^1 (1-18), 1359^2.

2* 148^2, 849^2.

3* 148^2, 849^2.

4* 149^1, 151^1, 151^1, 347^1, 556^1, 556^1, 785^2, 830^1, 849^2.

5* 149^1, 360^2 (5-9), 453^1, 749^2, 750^1 (5-9), 849^2, 1100^2, 1359^2 (5-7).

6* 149^1, 849^2.

7* 149^1, 300^1, 849^2, 1198^1.

8* 123^1, 129^1, 149^1, 494^2, 829^2, 849^2, 854^1, 1198^1, 1417^2.

Verse

9* 149^1, 360^2, 453^1, 749^2, 849^2, 1359^2.

10*

11*

12* 821^2 (12-15), 1157^1 (12-18).

13*

14*

15*

16* 206^1 (16-18), 750^1 (16-18), 810^1 (16-18).

17*

18*

Joshua 2.

1 76^1 (1-24), 577^2 (1-16), 652^1 (1-24), 750^1 (1-24), 1101^2 (1-24), 1118^2 (1-24), 1270^1, 1299^2, 1338^2 (1-24), 1338^2 (1-24), 1354^2 (1-3), 1416^1.

2*

3* 539^2 (3-6).

4* 378^1 (4-6).

5* 412^2.

6* 400^1, 578^1, 774^2 (6-16).

7* 412^2, 749^1.

8* 578^1, 1339^1 (8-21).

9* 368^2, 878^2.

10* 878^2, 916^1, 1119^2.

11* 268^1, 368^2, 486^1, 509^2, 878^2.

12* 900^2 (12-14).

13*

14*

15* 577^2, 1359^2, 1359^2, 1397^1.

16*

17*

18* 1337^2.

19*

20*

21* 422^2, 1337^2, 1397^1.

22*

23*

24* 368^2.

Joshua 3.

1 643^2, 749^1 (1-17), 750^1 (1-17), 1006^1 (1-17), 1195^1.

2*

3* 1311^1 (3-6).

4*

5*

6* 75^1.

7* 749^2, 1011^2.

8*

9* 1418^1.

10* 577^2, 425^1, 878^2.

11* 509^2, 509^2, 878^2.

12*

13*

14* 75^1, 873^1 (14-17), 1363^1 (14-17).

15* 749^1.

16* 12^1, 280^1, 1208^1, 1451^2.

17*

Joshua 4.

1 627^1 (1-11), 643^2 (1-24), 749^1 (1-24), 750^1 (1-24), 958^1 (1-9).

2* 1301^2 (2-9), 1337^2 (2-9).

3*

4*

5*

6*

7* 74^2.

8*

9*

10*

11* 75^1.

12* 411^2, 821^2.

13* 411^2, 821^2.

14*

15* 1006^1 (15-18).

16* 873^1 (16-18).

17*

18*

19* 8^1, 424^2, 424^2 (19-24), 624^2 (19-24), 884^1, 1311^1.

20* 1301^2 (20-24).

21*

22*

23* 878^2, 1119^2.

24* 383^2, 482^2, 537^2, 878^2.

Joshua 5.

1 57^2, 151^1, 268^1, 643^2 (1-15), 749^1, 750^1 (1-15), 878^2.

Verse
3* 1451¹.
4* 1451¹.
5* 76¹, 76¹, 76¹, 76¹, 76².
6* 76², 273², 344¹.
7* 344¹, 369¹ (7-10).
8* 482².
9* 482².
10* 64².
11* 152¹, 333¹, 748¹.
12* 152¹, 333¹, 572¹, **748¹.**
13* 113¹.
14* 73², 1202².
15* 594¹.
16* 608².
17* 650¹ (17-24).
18* 1000², 1238¹, 1335².
19* 542² 1000², 1238¹.
20*
21* 113² (21-23).
22*
23* 52¹, 344², 645¹, 653¹, **653².**
24* 577², 653², 903¹.
25*
26* 141².
27* 73², 96¹, 244².
28* 652²

2 Chronicles 26.

1 645² (1-23), 1353².
2* 334¹, 1353².
3* 649², 1353².
4* 913¹, 1353².
5* 123², 133² (5-15), 247², 502² (5-15), 913¹, 1013¹, 1245², 1248², 1353², 1355¹, 1462¹.
6* 78², 412², 647¹, 1353².
7* 57¹, 74¹, 535¹, 82 , 1353².
8* 57¹, 1353².
9* 76¹, 653², 1338¹, 1353².
10* 49², 49², 153², 406², 531¹, 534², 653², 775¹, 1268¹, 1338¹, 1353², 1363².
11* 76² (11-15), 537¹, 651¹, 811², 1243², 1244², 1353² (11-15).
12*
13*
14* 74², 553², 1268², 1292¹.
15* 76¹, 146¹, 342², 406², 618², 640², 1353².
16* 204¹ (16-21), 542² 609¹ (16-21), 618², 862² (16-20), 999², 1005² (16-19), 1016², 1202², 1207² (16-21), 1353¹ (16-21), 1353² (16-21).
17* 314¹ (17-20), 1146².
18* 7¹, 176¹, 1006¹, 1146².
19* 20² (19-21), 64².
20* 787².
21* 176¹, 750¹ (21-23), 787², 787², 1234², 1353².
22* 141², 641², 775¹, 1353².
23* 787², 1353².

2 Chronicles 27.

1 645² (1-9), 653², 750¹ (1-9), 750¹ (1-9), 1451¹.
2* 99¹, 913¹.
3* 653², 918¹.
4* 153².
5* 57¹, 105¹, 252¹, 828¹.
6* 123², 133², 502².
7* 141².
8*
9*

2 Chronicles 28.

1 52¹ (1-27), 645² (1-27).
2* 90², 1202² (2-4).
3* 556¹, 592², 883², 914¹, 1338¹.
4*
5* 20² (5-8), 938¹.
6* 938¹, 1132¹.
7* 90², 338², 652¹ (7-15), 775¹, 811², 840², 1463².
8* 1260¹.
9* 63², 913², 1138² (9-15), 1146² (9-11).
10* 1260¹, 1367².
11*
12* 55², 90¹, 112¹, 536¹, 650¹, 747², 834², 1265¹.
13* **834².**
14*

Verse
15* 69², 79¹.
16* 53², 76².
17* 333¹.
18* 53¹, 113², 413¹, 425¹, 1293¹, 1336².
19* 1199¹, 1336¹ (19-21).
20* 76².
21* 53².
22* 20², 40¹, 594², 1367².
23* 40¹, 593², 594².
24* 1207².
25*
26* 141².
27*

2 Chronicles 29.

1 7², 555¹, 555¹ (1-36), 617¹ (1-36), 645² (1-36), 793¹ (1-36), 1157² (1-36), 1451¹.
2* 555¹, 913¹.
3*
4* 653¹, 1006² (4-17).
5* 176¹, 176¹.
6* 99¹, 1139¹, 1275².
7* 1314².
8* 99¹.
9*
10* 301².
11* 843¹, 854¹.
12* 7², 55², 332², 649², 746², 747², 775², 788¹ (12-36), 812², 1463², 1269², 1462².
13* 78¹ (13-30), 338¹, 651², 827¹, 1269², 1462².
14* 650¹, 1267², 1269², 1354¹.
15* 176¹, 1314² (15-19).
16* 157², 773².
17*
18* 54¹ (18-24), 1314².
19* 52¹.
20*
21* 176¹.
22*
23*
24*
25* 273², 411², 539², 891², 896², 1087¹.
26* 278², 640², 888², 891².
27* 278¹ (27-30), 888², 891².
28* 888², 891².
29*
30* 78¹, 754², 1010¹.
31*
32*
33*
34* 404², 862², 913¹, 1006¹.
35* 913².
36* 754².

2 Chronicles 30.

1 308² (1-10), 555¹ (1-27), 617¹ (1-27), 645² (1-27), 793¹ (1-12), 821² (1-27), 884¹ (1-27), 927² (1-27), 1007² (1-10), 1157² (1-27), 1199¹ (1-27), 1458¹ (1-27).
2* 102¹ (2-12), 404², 774², 927² (2-4).
3* 404², 869¹.
4* 404².
5* 404², 869¹.
6* 611², 967², 1134², 1242¹.
7* 349², 1134², 1242¹.
8* 176¹, 1134², 1242¹, 1258².
9* 96², 123², 475², 495¹, 1134², 1242¹.
10* 611², 967², 1242¹, 1243².
11* 78², 1138², 1462¹.
12*
13*
14* 591², 592².
15* 863¹.
16*
17* 404², 927², 1017¹.
18* 344¹, 405¹, 636¹, 644² (18-26), 646², 1245², 1462¹.
19* 176¹, 405¹, 542¹, 636¹, 1245².
20* 405¹.
21* 390² (21-26), 754².
22* 788¹.
23* 754², 1016².
24*
25*
26* 754².
27* 176¹, 544², 983², 1006¹, 1314², 1440¹.

Verse
2 Chronicles 31.

1 344¹, 555¹ (1-21), 555¹, 617¹ (1-21), 645² (1-21), 793¹ (1-10), 1157² (1-21), 1199¹ (1-21), 1458¹ (1-21).
2* 204¹ (2-19), 555¹ (2-21), 891², 1005², 1329¹.
3* 884², 899².
4* 1006¹ (4-19).
5* 276², 399¹, 1337¹ (5-10).
6*
7*
8*
9*
10* 52², 90¹, 123², 129², 495¹.
11* 788¹ (11-19), 1337¹.
12* 240², 1269², 1337¹.
13* 78¹, 90¹, 90¹, 107¹, 240², 337¹, 642², 650¹, 755¹, 812², 896¹, 1269².
14* 409¹, 604², 776¹.
15* 55² (15-19), 332², 654¹, 840², 1266², 1267².
16* 174², 788² (16-18), 941² (16-18).
17*
18*
19*
20* 555¹, 911², 913¹.
21* 313², 555¹, 793¹, 911², 913¹, 1245², 1248².

2 Chronicles 32.

1 80¹ (1-33), 555¹ (1-33), 645² (1-33), 653² (1-33), 1259¹ (1-23), 1272¹ (1-23).
2*
3* 653².
4* 157², 555¹, 653², 773².
5* 840², 1269¹, 1338¹.
6*
7* 255², 360², 363¹.
8* 255², 360², 363¹.
9* 777², 1253² (9-19).
10*
11*
12* 608².
13* 999².
14* 999².
15* 611².
16* 611² (16-19).
17*
18* 746¹.
19* 117¹.
20* 983² (20-23).
21* 60², 174², 502², **927¹.**
22* 455², 502².
23*
24* 555¹, 983².
25* 28², 555¹, 618², 1016².
26* 28², 555¹, 1138², 1269¹.
27* 555¹ (27-30), 1339¹.
28* 775¹, 1339¹, 1397².
29* 133², 502², 775¹.
30* 555¹, 653², 1316¹.
31* 55², 555¹, 640², 1005², 1316¹, 1320¹.
32* 141², 555¹, 641², 775¹.
33* 146², 555¹.

2 Chronicles 33.

1 645² (1-20), 821² (1-20).
2* 204¹ (2-9), 1202² (2-7).
3* 90², 555¹, 592².
4* 1314² (4-7)
5* 592².
6* 556¹, 592², 1294², 1338¹.
7* 176¹.
8*
9* 615².
10* 608².
11* 91¹, 397², 766², 1359².
12* 28¹, 28², 40², 502², 617¹ (12-19), 1139¹, 1157² (12-19).
13* 28¹, 40², 502², 983², 1139¹.
14* 399¹, 555¹, 653², 918¹.
15* 176¹, 204¹ (15-17), 591².
16* 54¹, 793¹.
17* 555².
18* 141², 141², 977², 1013¹, **1425¹.**
19* 141², 977², 983².
20* 645² (20-25).
21* 57² (21-25).

Verse
19* 780^1.
20*
21* 115^2 (21-23), 206^1 (21-23), 206^2, 244^2 (21-23), 810^1 (21-23), 884^2 (21-23), 1323^2 (21-23).
22* 345^2.
23* 412^1, 1087^2, 1338^2.

Esther 3.

1 528^1 (1-15), 536^2, 536^2 (1-15), 536^2 (1-15), 645^2 (1-15), 775^1, 826^2 (1-15), 840^1, 960^1 (1-15), 1202^1 (1-15), 1260^2 (1-15).
2* 303^2, 568^2, 775^1.
3* 303^2.
4*
5* 64^2, 568^2, 817^1 (5-15), 1005^2.
6*
7* 12^1, 91^2 (7-15), 801^1, 884^1, 884^2, 1090^1.
8* 378^2, 1157^1 (8-15).
9* 145^2, 1339^1.
10* 536^2, 1194^2.
11*
12* 884^1, 1194^2, 1243^2, 1244^2.
13* 812^2, 967^2.
14*
15* 967^2.

Esther 4.

1 78^2, 345^2 (1-17), 528^1 (1-17), 536^2 (1-17), 645^2 (1-17), 1107^1, 1260^2 (1-17).
2* 1107^1.
3* 78^2, 1107^1.
4* 158^2, 1107^2.
5* 158^2, 540^2, 1107^2.
6* 540^2, 1107^2.
7* 883^2, 1107^2.
8* 256^1, 1107^2, 1271^2.
9* 540^2, 1107^2.
10* 540^2, 1107^2.
11* 1107^2, 1241^2.
12* 1107^2.
13* 1107^2.
14* 369^1, 1107^2.
15* 1107^2, 1415^2 (15-17).
16* 47^2, 256^1, 303^2, 381^2, 1107^2, 1148^1, 1253^1, 1271^2.
17* 1107^2.

Esther 5.

1 256^1 (1-14), 345^2 (1-14), 536^2 (1-14), 645^2 (1-14), 774^2 (1-8), 1260^2 (1-14), 1311^2 (1-14).
2* 1241^2.
3*
4*
5*
6* 390^2, 775^1, 1397^1.
7*
8* 610^1, 1008^1.
9* 56^2(9-13), 538^1 (9-11), 817^1(9-14).
10* 1463^1 (10-14).
11* 1005^2.
12*
13* 343^2, 538^1, 1005^2.
14* 412^1, 1416^1.

Esther 6.

1 141^2, 207^1, 256^1 (1-14), 345^2 (1-14), 503^1 (1-12), 536^2 (1-14), 622^2, 645^2 (1-14), 775^1, 884^2 (1-11), 1260^2 (1-14), 1311^2 (1-14).
2* 115^2, 207^1, 1323^2.
3* 207^1.
4* 207^1, 412^1.
5* 207^1.
6* 56^2 (6-9), 207^1, 1005^2.
7* 207^1.
8* 207^1, 271^1, 326^2, 775^1.
9* 207^1, 1007^2.
10* 207^2.
11* 207^2.
12* 886^2.
13* 1416^1, 1463^1.
14*

Esther 7.

1 256^1 (1-10), 345^2 (1-10), 536^2 (1-10), 645^2 (1-10), 1107^1, 1260^2 (1-10), 1311^2 (1-10).

Verse
2* 775^1, 1107^2.
3* 1108^1.
4* 1108^1, 1260^1.
5* 1108^1.
6* 1108^1.
7* 64^2, 390^2, 924^2, 1108^1.
8* 1108^1.
9* 412^1, 539^1, 1108^1.
10* 412^1, 503^1, 537^2, 572^2, 754^2 1005^2, 1108^1.

Esther 8.

1 240^1, 345^2 (1-17), 536^2 (1-17), 645^2 (1-17), 775^1, 840^1 (1-17), 884^2, 884^2 (1-17), 1260^2 (1-17).
2* 775^1, 884^2, 1194^2 (2-10).
3* 1208^1.
4* 1241^2.
5* 536^2.
6*
7*
8* 91^2, 775^1, 955^1, 1244^1, 1244^1.
9* 91^2, 610^1, 884^1, 1243^2, 1244^2, 1290^2.
10* 150^2, 327^1, 812^2, 887^1, 967^2, 1007^2 (10-14).
11*
12* 12^1.
13*
14* 150^2, 887^1, 967^2, 1271^2.
15* 213^1, 271^1, 517^1, 754^2, 775^1, 799^1, 884^2, 1271^2, 1271^2.
16* 754^2.
17* 390^2.

Esther 9.

1 12^1, 345^2 (1-32), 503^1, 536^2 (1-32), 645^2 (1-32), 840^2 (1-32), 884^2 (1-26), 884^2 (1-32), 1157^1 (1-32), 1260^2 (1-32).
2*
3*
4*
5*
6*
7* 79^1, 273^2, 927^1.
8* 12^1, 74^2, 967^2.
9* 74^2, 74^2, 927^1, 1354^1.
10* 536^2.
11* 1271^2.
12*
13* 412^1.
14*
15* 1271^2, 1352^2.
16*
17* 390^2 (17-19).
18*
19*
20* 1092^1 (20-32).
21*
22* 966^1.
23*
24* 536^2, 801^1.
25* 412^1, 503^1.
26*
27*
28*
29*
30* 91^2.
31*
32* 141^2.

Esther 10.

1 884^2 (1-3), 1260^2 (1-3).
2*
3* 775^1, 840^1, 935^1.

JOB, 959^2.

Job 1.

1 39^1 (1-22), 373^2 (1-22), 505^2 (1-22), 747^1, 747^1, 941^2, 1288^2, 1353^2.
2*
3* 150^2, 747^1, 1164^1.
4*
5* 57^2, 171^1, 318^2, 379^2, 634^1, 747^1, 925^2, 1438^2.
6* 1238^2, 1238^2, 1323^1 (6-21).
7* 1238^2.
8* 386^2, 747^1, 911^2, 913^1, 1320^1.

Verse
9* 11^2, 377^2, 493^2 (9-12), 886^1 (9-11), 946^2, 1238^2, 1320^1.
10* 11^2, 133^2, 377^2, 488^1, 502^2, 550^2, 1238^2, 1320^1.
11* 1238^2, 1320^2.
12* 1238^2, 1320^2.
13* 747^1 (13-19), 1148^1, 1320^2.
14* 959^2, 1148^1, 1320^2.
15* 1148^1, 1207^2, 1320^2.
16* 1148^1, 1320^2.
17* 76^1, 150^2, 1148^1, 1320^2.
18* 111^2, 838^1, 1148^1, 1320^2.
19* 111^2, 838^1, 1148^1, 1320^2.
20* 111^2, 326^2, 747^1 (20-22), 822^1, 886^2, 977^2, 1133^1, 1148^1, 1320^2.
21* 38^1, 47^2, 111^2, 168^1, 282^1, 374^1, 939^1, 977^2, 1148^1, 1320^2.
22* 47^2, 374^1, 1148^2, 1320^2.

Job 2.

1 39^1 (1-13), 373^2 (1-13), 505^2 (1-13).
2*
3* 303^2, 747^1, 1238^2, 1320^2.
4* 11^2, 377^2, 886^1, 946^2, 1239^1, 1320^2, 1323^1 (4-10).
5* 11^2, 377^2, 886^1, 946^2, 1239^1, 1320^2.
6* 493^2, 1239^1, 1320^2.
7* 141^1, 747^1 (7-10), 1239^1, 1320^2.
8* 78^2, 141^1, 967^2, 1320^2.
9* 20^2, 120^1, 374^1, 1148^2, 1320^2, 1416^1.
10* 47^2, 374^1, 747^1, 747^1, 1148^2, 1320^2.
11* 115^2 (11-13), 236^1, 337^2, 410^1 (11-13), 747^1 (11-13), 1309^2, 1313^1, 1464^2.
12* 328^2, 822^1, 886^2, 1133^1, 1309^2.
13* 1264^1, 1309^2.

Job 3.

1 21^1, 116^1 (1-26), 280^2 (1-26), 311^1, 323^1 (1-26), 747^1 (1-26), 793^2 (1-26), 888^2 (1-26), 977^2 (1-10), 999^2 (1-26).
2* 21^1, 311^1.
3* 21^1, 311^1.
4* 21^1, 311^1.
5* 21^1, 212^1, 311^1.
6* 21^1, 311^1.
7* 21^1, 311^1.
8* 21^1, 311^1.
9* 21^1, 311^1.
10* 21^1, 311^1.
11* 21^1, 311^1.
12* 21^1, 311^1.
13* 21^1, 279^1, 280^2, 311^1.
14* 21^1, 279^1, 311^1.
15* 21^1, 279^1, 311^1.
16* 21^1, 279^1, 311^1.
17* 21^1, 279^1, 280^2, 311^1, 546^1.
18* 21^1, 279^1, 281^1, 311^1.
19* 21^1, 279^1, 281^1, 311^1, 505^2 (19-23).
20* 21^1, 311^1.
21* 21^1, 311^1.
22* 21^1, 311^1.
23* 21^1, 311^1.
24* 21^1, 311^1.
25* 21^1, 311^1.
26* 21^1, 311^1.

Job 4.

1 337^2 (1-21), 544^2 (1-21), 747^1 (1-21), 999^2 (1-21).
2*
3* 323^1, 1405^1.
4* 323^1.
5* 37^1, 323^1.
6* 323^1.
7* 363^1, 488^1.
8* 20^2, 363^1, 1281^1, 1376^2.
9* 120^1, 144^2, 363^1, 1376^2.
10* 363^1, 799^2.
11* 363^1.
12* 326^1 (12-21), 363^1, 1355^1 (12-16).
13* 363^1.
14* 363^1.
15* 61^1, 363^1.
16* 61^1, 363^1.
17* 61^1, 305^2, 363^1, 456^1, 461^1, 600^2, 817^2, 820^1.

Verse
18* 61^1, 63^2, 305^2, 363^1, 456^2, 600^2, 819^2, 819^2, 1409^1.
19* 61^1, 141^1, 209^1, 305^2, 363^1, 456^2, 534^2, 600^2, 794^1, 819^2, 819^2, 820^1, 885^2, 1409^1.
20* 363^1, 600^2, 794^1, 820^1, 1409^1.
21* 290^1, 363^1, 600^2, 794^1, 820^1, 1409^1.

Job 5.

1 337^2 (1-27), 747^1 (1-27), 999^2 (1-27).
2* 63^2, 342^2, 1281^2.
3* 342^2, 1364^1 (3-5), 1376^2.
4* 1277^2.
5*
6* 20^2, 21^1, 26^1, 29^1, 38^1, 369^1 (6-27), 495^2.
7* 20^2, 21^1, 26^1, 29^1, 495^2.
8* 26^1, 29^1, 363^1, 427^2, 495^2, 514^1, 957^1 (8-20), 1245^2.
9* 26^1, 29^1, 363^1, 427^2, 482^2, 495^2, 514^1, 968^2.
10* 26^1, 29^1, 129^2, 427^2, 495^2.
11* 26^1, 29^1, 427^2, 488^1, 495^2, 578^2, 1173^1.
12* 29^1, 427^2, 503^2, 1173^1.
13* 29^1, 427^2, 503^2, 1098^2, 1173^1, 1409^1.
14* 29^1, 427^2, 1173^1, 1376^2.
15* 29^1, 427^2, 965^1, 1173^1.
16* 29^1, 427^2, 965^1, 1173^1.
17* 20^2, 21^1, 26^2, 29^1, 38^1, 46^2, 163^2, 427^2, 538^1, 1147^1, 1173^1.
18* 21^1, 29^1, 38^1, 427^2, 488^1, 538^1, 1173^1.
19* 427^2, 1173^1, 488^1, 538^1, 1173^1.
20* 29^1, 381^2, 427^2, 488^1, 538^1, 1173^1.
21* 29^1, 488^1, 538^1, 1173^1, 1243^2, 1291^1, 1301^1.
22* 29^1, 488^2 (22-24), 538^1, 1173^1.
23* 29^2, 538^1, 935^1, 1173^1.
24* 29^2, 495^2, 538^1, 557^1, 935^1, 1173^1.
25* 29^2, 167^1, 495^2, 538^1, 1173^1.
26* 29^2, 495^2, 538^1, 800^1, 916^2, 1173^1.
27* 29^2, 538^1, 1173^1, 1399^2.

Job 6.

1 21^1, 747^1 (1-30), 888^2 (1-30).
2* 21^1, 102^1.
3* 21^2.
4* 21^2, 38^1, 77^2.
5* 21^2, 79^1.
6* 21^2.
7* 21^2.
8* 21^2, 280^2 (8-11).
9* 21^2.
10* 21^2, 456^2, 1454^2.
11* 21^2.
12* 21^2.
13* 21^2, 1255^1.
14* 19^2, 21^2, 409^1, 1309^2.
15* 21^2, 298^1, 409^1.
16* 21^2, 591^1, 1292^2.
17* 21^2.
18* 21^2.
19* 21^2, 1313^1.
20* 21^2.
21* 21^2.
22* 21^2.
23* 21^2.
24* 21^2.
25* 21^2.
26* 21^2.
27* 21^2, 923^1.
28* 21^2.
29* 21^2.
30* 21^2.

Job 7.

1 280^2 (1-3), 281^1, 339^2, 747^1 (1-21), 793^2 (1-3), 888^2 (1-21), 1263^2.
2* 21^2, 339^2, 1263^2.
3* 21^2, 339^2.
4* 21^2.
5* 21^2, 1290^2.
6* 21^2, 794^1, 1271^2, 1363^1.
7* 794^1.
8* 281^1, 794^1.
9* 281^1, 552^1, 794^1.
10* 281^1, 794^1.

Verse
11*
12* 1363^2.
13*
14*
15* 280^2.
16* 280^2, 1354^1.
17* 469^2, 581^1, 794^1.
18* 581^1.
19*
20* 984^2, 1139^2, 1276^1.
21* 280^1, 281^1.

Job 8.

1 115^2, 544^2 (1-22), 747^1 (1-22), 1166^2 (1-22), 1349^2 (1-22), 1364^1 (1-22).
2* 1428^1.
3* 461^1.
4* 1173^2.
5* 980^1, 1173^2, 1245^2.
6* 495^2, 980^1, 1173^2, 1245^2.
7* 495^2, 1173^2.
8* 556^1 (8-10), 1399^2.
9* 595^1, 794^1.
10* 1399^2.
11* 399^1, 516^1.
12* 403^2, 516^1.
13* 159^1, 403^2, 403^2, 516^1, 575^1, 584^2, 1364^2 (13-18).
14* 584^2, 1299^2.
15* 584^2.
16*
17*
18*
19*
20* 495^2, 1173^2, 1376^2.
21* 495^2, 750^2, 1173^2.
22* 1376^2.

Job 9.

1 515^2 (1-35), 747^1 (1-35), 888^2 (1-35), 957^1 (1-35).
2* 305^2, 427^2, 604^2.
3* 305^2, 427^2.
4* 427^2, 482^2, 514^2, 542^2, 604^2, 968^2.
5* 427^2, 482^2, 886^2.
6* 81^1, 330^2, 332^1, 427^2, 482^2.
7* 81^1, 428^1, 482^2, 835^1, 1300^2.
8* 81^1, 428^1, 435^2, 549^1.
9* 74^2, 81^1, 244^2, 428^1, 435^2, 922^2, 959^2, 1300^2.
10* 428^1, 482^2, 514^1, 968^2.
11* 428^1, 459^2.
12* 38^1, 428^1, 482^2, 510^1.
13* 428^1, 482^2.
14* 428^1, 581^1.
15* 428^1, 461^2, 581^1.
16* 37^1, 117^1, 323^1, 428^1.
17* 37^1, 117^1, 323^1, 428^1.
18* 22^1, 37^1, 117^1, 323^1, 428^1.
19* 37^1, 323^1, 428^1, 482^2.
20* 37^1, 305^2, 323^1, 428^1, 942^1, 1139^2, 1249^1, 1276^1.
21* 37^1, 323^1, 428^1, 942^1.
22* 37^1, 38^1, 323^1, 428^1.
23* 37^1, 323^1, 428^1, 1243^2.
24* 37^1, 428^1, 1239^1.
25* 37^1, 428^1, 794^1, 967^2.
26* 37^1, 330^2, 428^1, 794^1.
27* 37^1, 428^1.
28* 37^1, 428^1, 461^2.
29* 37^1, 305^2, 428^1.
30* 37^1, 305^2, 428^1, 1292^2.
31* 37^1, 305^2, 428^1.
32* 37^2, 428^1, 449^1, 634^1.
33* 37^2, 278^2, 428^1, 449^1, 634^1, 703^2.
34* 37^2, 117^1, 428^1.
35* 37^2, 117^1, 428^1.

Job 10.

1 280^2, 888^2 (1-22).
2* 40^2, 117^1, 428^1, 817^2, 957^1 (2-21).
3* 117^1, 428^1, 435^2, 817^2.
4* 117^1, 428^1.
5* 117^1, 428^1.
6* 117^1, 428^1.
7* 117^1, 428^2, 482^2, 629^2.
8* 38^1, 428^2, 435^2, 438^2, 817^2.
9* 40^2, 428^2, 438^2, 794^1, 817^2.
10* 166^1, 400^1, 428^2.
11* 59^1, 428^2, 438^2, 957^2, 1290^1.
12* 363^1, 428^2, 438^2, 453^1, 488^1, 531^1.

Verse
13* 428^2.
14* 428^2, 1278^2, 1283^2, 1376^2.
15* 40^2, 428^2, 504^2, 581^1, 1376^2.
16* 428^2, 582^2.
17* 428^2.
18* 428^2, 793^2 (18-20).
19*
20* 212^1, 794^1.
21* 212^1, 281^1, 794^1.
22* 212^1, 281^1.

Job 11.

1 544^2 (1-20), 747^1 (1-20), 1349^2 (1-6), 1464^1 (1-20).
2* 1409^1.
3*
4* 1255^1.
5* 1255^1, 1405^1.
6* 476^1, 1255^1, 1405^1.
7* 458^2, 514^1, 595^2.
8* 458^2, 514^1, 552^1, 596^1.
9* 458^2, 514^1.
10* 38^1, 482^2.
11* 465^1, 543^2, 1283^2, 1354^1.
12* 305^2, 596^1, 1000^2, 1238^1, 1354^1, 1364^1, 1409^1.
13* 1134^2.
14* 1134^2.
15* 1134^2, 1173^2.
16* 29^2, 1173^2.
17* 29^2, 495^2, 916^2, 1173^2.
18* 29^2, 488^2, 495^2, 1173^2.
19* 29^2, 488^2, 495^2, 1173^2.
20* 237^2, 575^1, 1089^2, 1173^2, 1376^2.

Job 12.

1 747^1 (1-25).
2* 641^1, 1000^2, 1238^1, 1255^1, 1399^2.
3* 1000^2, 1238^1, 1253^1, 1399^2.
4* 946^2, 980^1.
5* 22^1, 39^1, 947^1, 1016^2.
6* 504^2, 957^1 (6-24), 1364^1.
7* 68^2, 82^1, 308^2 (7-11), 428^2, 435^2, 1126^2, 1399^2.
8* 68^2, 82^1, 421^2, 428^2, 435^2, 1126^2, 1399^2.
9* 82^1, 421^2, 428^2, 435^2, 510^1, 1126^2, 1399^2.
10* 82^1, 428^2, 438^2, 510^1, 1126^2, 1399^2.
11* 82^1, 428^2, 1126^2, 1399^2.
12* 82^1, 428^2, 916^2, 1126^2, 1399^2.
13* 82^1, 428^2, 465^2, 514^2, 1126^2, 1399^2.
14* 38^1, 82^1, 428^2, 482^2, 1126^2.
15* 38^1, 82^1, 428^2, 482^2, 1126^2.
16* 38^1, 82^1, 428^2, 465^2, 482^2, 510^1, 514^2, 1126^2, 1399^2.
17* 38^1, 82^1, 428^2, 510^1, 1399^2.
18* 38^1, 82^1, 428^2, 428^2.
19* 38^1, 82^1, 428^2.
20* 38^1, 82^1, 428^2.
21* 38^1, 82^1.
22* 38^1, 82^1, 465^2, 1399^2.
23* 38^1, 82^1, 129^2, 495^2.
24* 38^1, 82^1.
25* 38^1, 82^1.

Job 13.

1 747^1 (1-28), 888^2 (1-28).
2* 1000^2.
3* 1117^2, 1255^1.
4* 375^2, 951^2 (4-13), 957^2.
5* 1000^2, 1297^1
6*
7* 117^1.
8* 117^1.
9* 117^1.
10*
11* 449^1.
12* 794^1.
13* 1255^1.
14*
15* 46^2, 47^2, 363^1, 630^1, 1255^1.
16* 363^1, 584^2.
17* 1117^2 (17-28).
18* 630^1, 1255^1.
19* 1255^1.
20*
21* 40^2, 389^2.
22*

Verse

23* 48^1 (23-25), 554^2, 933^2, 1007^1, 1114^2, 1243^2.
24* 608^2, 933^2, 1007^1, 1007^1, 1114^2, 1301^1.
25* 381^1, 753^2, 754^2, 933^2, 975^2, 978^1, 1114^2, 1488^2.
26* 332^1, 381^1, 493^2 (26-39), 874^1, 1114^2.
27* 249^2 (27-34), 268^1, 381^1, 648^1 (27-34), 1114^2, 1307^2.
28* 381^1, 1114^2.
29* 251^1, 381^1, 1114^2.
30* 251^1, 251^2, 381^1, 1114^2, 1213^1.
31* 370^1, 373^1 (31-34), 379^2 (31-34), 381^1, 704^1, 731^2, 1114^2, 1213^1, 1458^1.
32* 381^1, 1114^2, 1458^1.
33* 103^2, 381^1, 869^1, 1007^1, 1007^1, 1115^1.
34* 367^1, 381^1, 753^2, 869^1, 1115^1, 1488^2.
35* 812^1, 932^1 (35-39), 1115^1, 1260^1.
36* 1115^1.
37* 106^1, 205^2, 931^2, 1115^1, 1147^1 (37-40), 1195^1, 1339^1 (37-39).
38* 812^1, 1115^1, 1260^1.
39* 1115^1.
40* 811^2, 932^1, 1115^1.

Acts 17.

1 57^2, 71^2, 781^1 (1-3), 872^2 (1-13), 932^1 (1-4), 932^1 (1-9), 1310^1, 1335^2.
2* 86^1, 534^2 (2-4), 699^2, 727^2, 1117^2, 1207^1, 1310^1, 1416^1, 1458^1.
3* 86^1, 699^2, 727^2, 742^1, 992^2, 1218^1, 1458^1.
4* 249^2, 393^2, 413^2, 1272^1 (4-10), 1413^2.
5* 342^2, 378^2 (5-7), 379^1 (5-7), 640^2, 649^1, 817^1, 883^2, 1335^2 (5-8), 1348^2.
6* 649^1.
7* 11^2, 610^1, 649^1, 935^2, 1338^2.
8* 935^2.
9* 141^2, 649^1, 936^1.
10* 111^2, 932^1 (10-12), 1019^1 (10-15), 1310^1, 1310^1.
11* 1335^2, 1337^2, 1416^2, 1422^1.
12* 249^2, 534^2, 1413^2.
13* 111^2, 640^2, 932^1 (13-15), 1335^2.
14* 1272^1, 1336^2.
15* 82^2 (15-34), 1272^1, 1336^2.
16* 413^2, 593^2, 932^1 (16-34), 1458^1.
17* 413^2, 1458^1.
18* 91^1, 344^2, 614^2, 957^1, 1154^1, 1243^1, 1301^1.
19* 74^2, 272^1 (19-21), 825^2 (19-34).
20*
21* 592^2.
22* 414^1, 595^2, 1115^1, 1458^1 (22-31).
23* 54^1, 137^2, 414^1, 595^2, 597^1, 1115^1, 1127^2.
24* 414^1, 437^1, 439^1, 480^2, 486^2, 509^1, 512^1, 1115^1, 1127^2, 1443^1.
25* 144^2, 414^1, 437^2, 439^1, 509^1, 512^1, 797^1, 1115^1, 1127^2, 1443^1.
26* 414^1, 437^2, 439^1, 512^2, 797^1, 819^1, 996^1, 1115^1, 1127^2.
27* 414^1, 480^2, 486^2, 1115^1, 1127^2, 1248^2.
28* 439^1, 480^2, 486^2, 493^1, 534^2, 797^1, 959^2, 1115^1, 1127^2.
29* 439^1, 512^2, 595^2, 1115^1.
30* 468^2, 479^2, 597^1, 1115^1, 1138^1, 1152^2.
31* 464^1, 506^1, 672^2, 676^1, 727^2, 762^1, 1115^1, 1152^2.
32* 614^2, 1154^1, 1243^1, 1243^2.
33*
34* 274^2, 313^2, 534^2, 1413^2.

Acts 18.

1 11^2 (1-28), 74^1 (1-3), 252^1 (1-28), 932^1 (1-11), 1007^1 (1-3).
2* 102^2, 209^1, 646^2, 960^1, 1195^1, 1195^1.
3* 77^2, 611^1, 869^1, 933^1, 1323^2.
4* 420^1, 781^1, 1117^2, 1207^1, 1310^1, 1310^1, 1458^1.
5* 236^2, 420^1, 722^1, 1272^1, 1336^2, 1458^1.

Verse

6* 147^1, 420^1, 722^1, 841^1, 1458^1.
7* 772^2, 869^1, 1169^1.
8* 103^2, 271^1, 373^1, 373^1, 379^2, 381^2, 1169^1.
9* 657^1, 857^2, 1355^2.
10* 857^2, 1355^2.
11*
12* 114^2, 244^2, 308^2, 412^1 (12-17), 766^2, 900^2 (12-17), 932^2 (12-18).
13* 114^2, 555^1, 610^1, 640^2.
14* 610^1 (14-16).
15*
16*
17* 106^1, 534^2, 1243^1, 1294^2.
18* 74^1, 158^1, 343^2 (18-28), 932^2 (18-23), 1007^1, 1310^1.
19* 74^1, 343^2 (19-21), 1007^1, 1117^2, 1310^1, 1458^1.
20*
21* 390^2, 653^1, 1396^2.
22* 71^1, 203^1, 931^2.
23* 411^2, 957^2, 1458^1.
24* 53^1, 71^2 (24-28), 870^2 (24-28), 921^2 (24-28), 1416^2, 1456^2.
25* 103^2, 313^2, 1456^2.
26* 74^1, 781^1, 869^1, 1007^1, 1310^1, 1415^2, 1456^2.
27* 1456^2.
28* 1416^2, 1456^2.

Acts 19.

1 71^2, 79^1 (1-41), 252^1, 343^2 (1-41), 932^2 (1-12).
2* 104^2, 137^2, 565^1.
3* 103^1, 565^1.
4* 103^1, 103^2, 237^1, 565^1, 703^1, 747^2.
5* 103^2, 237^1, 565^1.
6* 104^2, 161^1, 537^2, 565^1, 778^1, 881^1, 1338^1.
7*
8* 1458^2 (8-10).
9* 534^1, 1242^1, 1344^1, 1347^1, 1348^2.
10* 1344^1.
11* 537^2, 874^1, 881^1.
12* 305^1, 537^2, 874^1.
13* 305^1 (13-16), 343^2 (13-16), 704^2, 876^1, 932^2 (13-20), 999^2, 1241^2 (13-17), 1294^1, 1308^1 (13-19).
14* 876^1, 999^2, 1294^1.
15* 305^1, 876^1, 1294^1.
16* 876^1.
17* 425^2, 876^1.
18* 876^1, 1139^1.
19* 141^2, 141^2, 1190^1, 1272^1, 1294^2.
20*
21* 11^2, 390^2, 932^1, 1458^2.
22* 344^2, 812^1, 841^2, 932^1, 1336^2.
23* 812^1, 932^2 (23-41), 1363^1.
24* 267^1, 305^1 (24-38), 313^1, 591^2, 1271^1, 1272^2, 1272^2, 1272^2.
25* 591^2.
26*
27* 267^1, 313^1, 1315^2.
28* 313^1.
29* 74^2, 411^2, 883^2 (29-40), 1019^1 (29-41), 1334^1.
30*
31* 1334^1.
32*
33* 53^1.
34*
35* 204^2, 205^2 (35-41), 209^2, 313^1, 768^2, 1311^2 (35-41), 1338^1.
36* 205^2, 205^2.
37* 206^1.
38* 206^1, 308^2.
39* 206^1.
40*
41*

Acts 20.

1 812^1 (1-6), 932^2 (1-6), 956^2 (1-6), 1336^2 (1-4).
2*
3* 872^2.
4* 74^2, 79^1, 111^2, 308^2, 411^2, 1245^1 (4-6), 1294^1, 1335^2, 1341^2, 1343^2.
5* 810^1, 1341^2.
6* 390^2, 810^1, 932^2 (6-12), 1341^2.
7* 144^2, 347^1, 1207^1, 1438^2 (7-9), 1458^2.
8* 578^1.

Verse

9* 278^2 (9-12), 347^2 (9-11), 874^1 (9-12), 1397^1.
10*
11*
12*
13 79^2, 932^2 (13-16), 1270^1.
14* 79^2, 883^1.
15* 175^1, 839^1, 883^1, 1220^2, **1341^2**.
16* 79^1, 343^2 (16-38), 390^2, 941^2.
17* 188^2, 335^1, 839^1 (17-38), 841^1 (17-38), 932^2 (17-38).
18* 1458^1.
19* 1363^2, 1458^1.
20* 1458^1.
21* 370^1, 704^1, **1138^1**, 1213^1, 1458^1.
22* 160^1 (22-24), 256^1 (22-24), 754^2 (22-24), 845^2, 933^1, 933^2, 1018^2 (22-25), 1251^1, 1458^1.
23* 20^2, 845^2, 933^1, 933^2, 1251^1, 1458^2.
24* 20^2, 518^1, 519^2, 842^2, 845^2, 933^2, 1251^1, 1253^1, 1458^2.
25* 1458^2.
26* 807^1, 841^1, 862^2, 1458^2.
27* 807^1, 841^1, 862^2, 1458^2.
28* 85^2, 86^1, 116^1, 139^2, 177^1, 177^2, 181^1, 188^2, 335^1, 565^1, 662^2, 665^2, 666^2, 737^1, 841^1, 857^2, 1118^2, 1362^1.
29* 335^1, 866^2, 1362^1, 1412^2.
30* 335^1, 866^2, 1362^1.
31* 335^1, 807^1, 1362^1, 1458^2.
32* 127^1, 335^1, 519^2, 602^1, 621^1, **638^2** 1181^2, 1422^1.
33* 54^2 (33-35), 517^1, 611^1, 861^1, 884^1, 933^1 (33-35), 1253^1, 1458^2.
34* 611^1, 861^1, 1253^1, 1458^2.
35* 352^1, 393^2, 774^1, 777^1, 792^2, 964^1, 1253^1.
36* 978^1.
37* 775^2, 841^1, 1018^2.
38* 841^1, 1018^2.

Acts 21.

1 252^1, 810^1 (1-18), **928^1**, 932^2 (1-7), 1160^2.
2* 230^1, 928^1, 956^2 (2-4).
3* 273^2, 1270^1, 1310^1, 1310^1, 1344^1, 1344^1 (3-7).
4* 314^1, 318^1, 933^1, 1015^2, 1103^1, 1264^1.
5* 841^1, 978^1.
6* 841^1.
7* 11^1, 1087^1.
8* 147^1, 869^1 (8-10), 932^2 (8-15), 956^2.
9* 956^2, 1016^1, 1413^1.
10* 48^1, 318^1 (10-14), 933^1 (10-14), 956^2, 1015^2, 1018^2 (10-14), 1103^1 (10-15).
11* 425^1, 924^1, 1009^2, 1015^2, 1309^1.
12*
13* 160^1, 803^1, 933^1, 1251^1, 1458^2.
14* 48^1, 160^1, 1148^2.
15*
16* 273^2, 883^1.
17* 932^2 (17-33).
18* 335^1, 648^2, 918^1 (18-26).
19* 648^2, 1123^1.
20* 115^2 (20-25), 145^2, 314^1 (20-25), 646^1, 757^1 (20-25), 783^1, 832^1 (20-26), 1018^2 (20-26), 1311^2 (20-25), 1461^2.
21* 783^1, 1293^2 (21-35).
22*
23* 783^1.
24* 408^2 (24-31), 541^2, 783^1, 1091^1.
25* 188^2, 783^1, 1302^1.
26* 1091^1, 1315^1 (26-30).
27* 79^1, 872^2 (27-40), 933^2, 1007^1 (27-40), 1241^2 (27-30).
28* 11^2, 115^2, 176^1, 640^2 (28-31), 883^2, 933^2, 1349^2.
29* 115^2, 933^2.
30* 77^1, 883^2, 933^2.
31* 209^1 (31-40), 933^2, 1293^2 (31-33).
32* 76^2, 106^1, 158^1, 933^2, 1243^2.
33* 158^1, 932^2 (33-40), 933^2, 1315^1.
34* 153^2, 653^1.
35* 1293^2.
36*
37* 153^2, 778^1.

The Bible: Book for All Time

*I*s there a God?

What is he like?

Why was mankind created in the first place?

Why is man so noble, yet so weak and sinful, all at the same time? What can be done about it? How should people behave?

Does history have any meaning? Is it heading anywhere?

Because the Bible grapples with these basic questions man has always asked himself, it has fascinated him for 2,000 years and more. This is why it is the most influential and widely read book in human history.

The Bible, actually a collection of sixty-six small books, tells of the rise and fall of ancient nations and the clash of armies. It tells about kings and plain people, heroes and villains. It contains history and theology, poetry and songs, philosophy and letters. It contains strange dream-visions, wise sayings, and some seemingly dull collections of court records, family trees, and religious rules. It contains some of the greatest literature man has produced. All of it is directed to the relationship between man and God.

"In the beginning . . ." Opening with those famous first words of GENESIS, the Bible asserts immediately that an all-powerful personal God created the heavens and this earth. The climax of this creative explosion was man, made in God's "image." But God did not create man as a robot. He gave him the dignity—and the peril—of free will. The first three chapters of GENESIS tell us that in the Garden of Eden the ancestors of the human race, Adam and Eve, commit the first sin against God by eating fruit God has forbidden them to eat. Much of the remaining 1,186 chapters of the Bible deals with how this breach between man and God was healed.

At first the breach was widened to the breaking point as the descendants of Adam and Eve multiplied on the face of the earth. Misusing his God-given free will, man had fallen into the ways of sin. God was sorry that he had made man and decided to destroy him. So he sent the flood that was survived only by the good man Noah, his family, and the animals they took into the ark.

After this prehistoric beginning the Old Testament focuses upon the Hebrews or, as they were later known, Israelites. In non-biblical history they were a rather obscure group, but in religious history they proved to be the instrument for God's dealings with man. Their national literature, the Old Testament, is unique among the ethnic writings of ancient civilizations. Such writings of other nations are sanitized; the rulers are flawless and their armies never seem to lose a battle.

The Old Testament, on the other hand, is most candid in showing the dark side of man. Yet it also holds him in higher esteem than many other books. The leaders of Israel are portrayed realistically as flesh-and-blood men combining greatness with moral weakness. Then come the prophets, their voices ringing like trumpets in the land. These spokesmen for God appear continually to announce God's judgment and to jerk the nation and its leaders back to righteousness.

God as revealed to the Hebrews is not only unique in his moral demands and in his oneness (monotheism). He is also unique in the lengths to which he goes to redeem his people, the Hebrews (or Israelites), and, through them, all of sin-stained mankind. This is why theologians call the Bible "salvation history."

The long pageant of God's mercy may be said to begin nearly 4,000 years ago, when God made a covenant with Abraham. GENESIS records that he told Abraham to migrate to Canaan from Mesopotamia a little before the era of the great Hammurabi, who compiled the famous code of laws. "I will make of thee a great nation, and I will bless thee," God said, ". . . and in thee shall all the families of the earth be blessed." Here God makes it plain for first time that the Hebrews are to bring the blessing of their God to all mankind. And God's covenant makes Abraham the founder of the Hebrew nation.

An instance in which man's evil is turned to good use appears in the drama of Abraham's great-grandson, Joseph. Joseph's envious brothers sell him into slavery and traders take him to Egypt. Eventually, after he interprets Pharaoh's dreams to mean famine and urges him to store food, Joseph becomes prime minister there and offers a haven for his family when the famine comes also to Canaan. In this way God arranges for the children of Israel (Hebrews) to move to Egypt under favorable circumstances. But centuries later the Pharaohs had reduced the Israelites to slavery, setting the stage for the book of EXODUS.

God's help came in the person of Moses, the nation's greatest leader. God appears to him in a burning bush and tells him to return to Egypt from his exile in Midian, and to lead his people back to freedom in Canaan, a land flowing with milk and honey. Moses and his brother Aaron went to see the Pharaoh, but the Pharaoh wouldn't let the children of Israel go. Then Moses, with God's power acting through him, performs miracles to show how powerful is the God of Israel; and Moses brings plagues, pestilence, and disaster to Egypt. But each time Pharaoh's heart is hardened and he refuses to let the children of Israel go.

Finally God tells the children of Israel, through Moses, to mark their doorposts with the blood of a spotless lamb. That night, while the Israelites eat roast lamb, as God has directed, the angel of death strikes Egypt. He passes over the houses of the Israelites, which are marked with lamb's blood, but kills the firstborn of the Egyptians, even the firstborn of Pharaoh himself. This is more than even Pharaoh can bear. He summons Moses in the night and gives him permission for the Israelites to leave Egypt. To this day, the Jews celebrate the Passover each spring with a seder feast of lamb.

After leaving Egypt the children of Israel wander in the wilderness for forty years. During this journey God meets Moses on Mount Sinai and, in effect, tells the Israelites what sin is. He spells out his laws in detail, beginning with the Ten Commandments, which are the foundation of modern morality. The laws continue through the book of LEVITICUS, a virtual handbook for priests.

The many sacrifices and ceremonies told about in LEVITICUS seem strange to us today. But in ancient times the sacrifices were important, for they helped people realize how serious it is to disobey God's rules for living. Moses frequently reminded the people that their God was holy, which means "absolutely good," and that they must be holy too. The sins of the people were laid on the lamb without blemish offered in sacrifice, which brought God's forgiveness. Nevertheless, as NUMBERS tells us, the errant Israelites continue to fall into sin at times and even into rebellion against God's chosen leader, Moses.

At the end of his life Moses addresses the people, summarizing the history and laws of the exodus from Egypt. He emphasizes love toward God and toward one's neighbors. This address, as the book of DEUTERONOMY, completes the first five books of the Old Testment, called the Pentateuch or, by Jews, the Torah (Law).

But Moses is destined to die before the Israelites enter the land of Canaan. Before he does, God gives him a glimpse of the promised land from the top of a mountain. The honor and responsibility for leading the Israelites into Canaan fell to Joshua, the son of Nun, chosen by God as Moses had been. The book of JOSHUA tells how God delivered the land of Canaan to the armies of Israel.

But the Israelites had trouble achieving peace in their new land. JUDGES tells how the new settlers survived during the next two centuries in a loose confederation of tribes. They were often tempted to forsake the true God in favor of the pagan fertility gods of the Canaanites. Whenever they committed this sin, God would allow enemy armies to beat the Israelites down until they repented of their disobedience.

After all the blood and fury of these war stories, the love story of RUTH comes as a pleasant interlude. Once again God shows that his purposes extend beyond his chosen nation. Ruth is a girl from Moab. The Moabites are distant relatives of the Israelites, as are today's Arabs. She turns from Moab's false religion to worship the God of the Israelites. Eventually she comes to marry the wealthy Boaz. Thus she becomes the great-grandmother of the great King David.

In Hebrew history family trees are important. They look backward to the family of the patriarch, Abraham, and ahead to the Messiah who, prophets declare, will come from the family of David. Ruth, the Moabitess, as the wife of Boaz, the Israelite, is an ancestress of David and, therefore, of the Messiah. Thus the coming of the Messiah is seen as having meaning for other nations.

Eventually the twelve tribes of Israel were drawn together in a government by monarchy, as recorded in I and II SAMUEL. In these two books and those just following are some of the most exciting reading in the Bible. The tempestuous personality of the first king, Saul, brings a clash of rivalry with the shepherd-soldier, David, who eventually succeeds Saul as king. At one point David even forms a private army, turning a mixed-up bunch of unhappy, rebellious men into a strong, skillful band of warriors. At another point David shows great skill in staying out of the way of Saul, who is pursuing him with 3,000 of the finest fighting men in the kingdom.

The Bible frankly records not only King David's greatness, but also his sinfulness. He commits adultery with a married woman, Bathsheba. He ships her husband, Uriah the Hittite, to the hottest part of the battle lines so that he will be killed. Nathan confronts David with this crime by telling him a parable about a pitiless rich man. David says angrily that the man deserves to die. Nathan thunders, "You are the man."

The principal message of David's reign also comes from Nathan. David wants to build a "house" (temple) for God. But God says, through Nathan, that he will give David a "house," meaning a family or dynasty: "And thy house and thy kingdom shall be established for ever before thee; thy throne shall be established for ever." The subsequent woes of the kingdom made this promise seem a mockery. But the throne God was talking about was the spiritual throne he was preparing for the Messiah.

A golden age for Israel, politically at least, comes in I KINGS with the reign of David's son, Solomon. He was Israel's wisest, richest, and perhaps most foolish king. For diplomatic reasons Solomon made marriages with women from other nations. His foreign wives corrupted the worship of the one God by bringing pagan religions to the court. Because of this sinfulness and because of the high taxes required to keep the lavish court going, ten of the twelve tribes revolted after Solomon's death and formed the Northern Kingdom (Israel) about 930 B.C. The other two tribes became the Southern Kingdom (Judah).

The ten tribes may have escaped high taxes, but they certainly didn't escape sin. Throughout its sad history, lasting two centuries, the Northern Kingdom tried to mix worship of the true God with various pagan beliefs. But God demanded absolute loyalty.

The climax of the conflict between gods comes on Mount Carmel. There the prophet Elijah taunts the priests of the fertility god, Baal, whose worship involved ritual prostitution and even child sacrifice. "If the LORD is God, follow him; but if Baal, then follow him," Elijah challenges them. Baal's priests fail to command fire to light a stack of wood, laid to roast a bullock. Then at Elijah's word, the Lord God of Abraham sends fire and burns the wood. God's victory over Baal saves the true worship for the time being.

But the effect of Elijah's demonstration is short lived. The Northern Kingdom again falls into sinfulness, combining false worship with a crude lack of social justice. This moral emptiness is assailed by the first two prophets whose words were collected in book form, Amos and Hosea. Their caustic social comments are as timely as tomorrow morning's newspaper. Hosea's prophecies are especially telling, because his own wife was unfaithful. In the depth of her disgrace he takes her back. Hosea uses this personal tragedy as an allegory to show God's forgiveness of his wayward people.

The fall of the Northern Kingdom, described in II KINGS, came in about 722 B.C. II KINGS also traces the history of the Southern Kingdom until the Israelites are conquered and taken into exile in Babylon in the sixth century B.C. I and II CHRONICLES give another account of David's reign and then continue the history of the Southern Kingdom to its fall. They ignore the Northern Kingdom.

In times of defeat and disaster the prophets were there. The overriding personality of the last days of the Southern Kingdom is the prophet Jeremiah, whose dramatic biography and poetic prophecies are recorded in the book that bears his name. Jeremiah was a leader in the religious reform movement under King Josiah. But as the kingdom later declined, he predicted accurately that it would be crushed by Babylon. This brought trouble. Viewed as a subversive, he was thrown into a dungeon. The king even burned one of his writings. After his imprisonment he fled to Egypt.

At the depth of the nation's despair, the LAMENTATIONS, a dirge for the Holy City of Jerusalem, was written—perhaps by Jeremiah himself. Jeremiah's later prophecies, however, carry a message of hope: a faithful remnant from the family of David will again return to the Holy Land. From this remnant God will raise up a king, the "righteous Branch," who will be called "The LORD our righteousness." Again, intimations of a Messiah who would save mankind.

Hope, along with recrimination, also comes from another source during the exile in Babylon: the prophet Ezekiel, known for his weird visions. Like Jeremiah, he preached that Jerusalem had fallen because of the wickedness of its people. But he offered hope that Jerusalem would be regained if the people would only obey God's laws. When the Persians defeated the Babylonians the Israelites were permitted to return to their homeland, beginning in about 538 B.C. They could again worship in the Temple, as Ezekiel had prophesied. This period is described in EZRA and NEHEMIAH. The story of Esther and the apocalyptic visions of Daniel also occur in this Persian era.

If the Israelites often fell away from God, they also had many periods of nearness to God as reflected in PSALMS, a national hymnal of praise and prayer to God. PSALMS is one of the world's most beautiful collections of poems. They were written in many circumstances by many individuals; about half of them are attributed to King David.

Much western poetry achieves rhythm by the regular succession of long and short syllables and by end-rhymes. In Hebrew poetry rhythm depends on a parallelism of ideas, as in the following typical example:

> The LORD is my light and my salvation: whom shall I fear? The LORD is the strength of my life; of whom shall I be afraid?

In others, such as Psalm 150, the rhythmic phrase "praise him" punctuates the poem, almost like the beat of a drum. Like most of the Old Testament books, PSALMS also contains important foreshadowings of the Messiah and is quoted seventeen times in the New Testament as referring to Jesus Christ.

PROVERBS is different from the other books of the Old Testament. It is a collection of wise sayings, many of them famous. Many of them come from King Solomon. Here are two of the most familiar:

> A good name is rather to be chosen than great riches, and loving favour rather than silver or gold. (PROVERBS 22:1)

> A soft answer turneth away wrath: but grievous words stir up anger. (PROVERBS 15:1)

JOB, the greatest philosophical drama preserved from ancient times, deals with a great question: the mystery of man's suffering under a loving God. The dramatic form is also used in SONG OF SOLOMON, a lovely book that glorifies married love and depicts sexual love as a gift from God when it follows his laws. Others see this book as showing allegorically God's love for the Church. Philosophy comes again in ECCLESIASTES. This book was written by a man who had evidently tried everything the world had to offer yet was still lonely and unsatisfied. His advice: "Fear God, and keep his commandments: for this is the whole duty of man. For God shall bring every work into judgment, with every secret thing, whether it be good, or whether it be evil."

The prophets hold center stage in the last twelve books of the Old Testament. These are the "minor" prophets, so called because their books are shorter than those of the "major" prophets. Their work appeared over a span of three centuries or more. Here we find JONAH, the most reluctant missionary in history. God makes him preach redemption to the Ninevites, whom he hated, showing him that God's mercy extends beyond the nation of Israel. MICAH prophesies that the coming Messiah will be born in Bethlehem. AMOS, another minor prophet, exhorts the people to righteousness and right actions under God. The other minor prophets are HOSEA, JOEL, OBADIAH, NAHUM, HABAKKUK, ZEPHANIAH, HAGGAI, ZECHARIAH, and MALACHI.

The book that best binds the Old Testament to the New is the book of ISAIAH. Isaiah was an eighth-century B.C. prophet whose remarkable vision included many details about the Messiah, through whom Israel would become a light to all nations. He predicted the birth of one who would be called Immanuel, which means "God with us."

Several passages provide radiant descriptions of the Messiah's kingdom, full of joy, justice, and peace. One of the best known is "For unto us a child is born, unto us a son is given: and the government shall be upon his shoulder . . ." These words, together with other Old Testament prophecies, are the subject of Handel's oratorio, "The Messiah," one of the world's great pieces of music.

Along with these grand visions, however, Isaiah strikes a more solemn note in foretelling the coming of one described as a "man of sorrows" who would be rejected by men: "But he was wounded for our transgressions, he was bruised for our iniquities: the chastisement of our peace was upon him: and with his stripes we are healed. All we like sheep have gone astray; we have turned every one to his own way; and the LORD has laid on him the iniquity of us all."

This seeming contradiction—a universal King and a suffering Servant—is resolved within the unique life of Jesus Christ, as recorded in the four GOSPELS, MATTHEW, MARK, LUKE, and JOHN. Only gradually during his life did Jesus' followers come to realize that his kingdom is spiritual and that he would not be a warlike Messiah who would establish a free Jewish state and throw off the Roman yoke. His full authority over the earth would come only at the "end of the world," as pictured in the visions of REVELATION, which closes the New Testament.

Before Jesus was raised from his tomb and appeared to his disciples in his resurrected body, his execution on the cross seemed a crushing defeat. But God was using mankind's evil to bring about the greatest example of his redeeming love for sinful man. The death of Jesus was the climax of a long history of blood sacrifice on Jewish altars. Unlike the repeated offering of the sacrificial lamb on which the sins of the people were laid, as the Son of God his death was effective once and for all. As Isaiah had written, one man's punishment atones for the sins of all mankind.

With this firm belief and this dynamic message, the Christian movement soon spread throughout the Roman Empire, as related in ACTS, the first book of church history. The chief strategist for carrying Christianity outside the Jewish nation was Paul. He was a former Pharisee and persecutor of Christians who was converted to Christianity after seeing a vision of Christ while traveling to Damascus.

Reading the letters (epistles) of Paul, Peter, James, John, and Jude is like having these fathers of the church talk to you about Jesus and his meaning for us. Of the 21 letters included in the New Testament, 13 are from

Paul. Many were letters of instruction to the new missionary churches: ROMANS, I and II CORINTHIANS, GALATIANS, EPHESIANS, PHILIPPIANS, COLOSSIANS, and I and II THESSALONIANS. The others were to individuals: I and II TIMOTHY, TITUS, and PHILEMON. The New Testament also includes the epistle to the HEBREWS and the letters of JAMES; I and II PETER; I, II, and III JOHN; and JUDE.

In the epistle to the ROMANS, written about 25 years after Jesus' earthly life ended, Paul explains the meaning of Jesus' death on the cross. He says that God is righteous and all men are sinful, so that all men, Jews and Gentiles alike, are condemned by divine justice despite their best human efforts. God has solved this problem through a free gift, the sacrificial death of his Son, Jesus Christ, which pays for the sins of all who believe in him. Thus man can be fully reunited with God and regain what was lost through Adam's sin. The great seventeenth-century poet, John Milton, opens his epic *Paradise Lost* with this link between GENESIS and Jesus, telling

> Of man's first disobedience, and the fruit
> Of that forbidden tree, whose mortal taste

Brought death into the world, and all our woe
With the loss of Eden, till one greater Man
Restore us, and regain the blissful Seat. . . .

Thus we see the New Testament as the fulfillment of the Old Testament. We see the life and death and resurrection of Jesus as the ultimate events in the great story of redemption from sin. As the opening of the epistle to the HEBREWS puts it:

"God who at sundry times and in divers manners spake in time past unto the fathers by the prophets, Hath in these last days spoken unto us by his Son, whom he hath appointed heir of all things, by whom he made the worlds; who being the brightness of his glory, and the express image of his person, and upholding all things by the word of his power, when he had by himself purged our sins, sat down on the right hand of the Majesty on high."

Below is a list of references that will help you find the Bible passages you most want to read. You will find more about the four Gospels and the life of Jesus in the first article.

Great Bible Chapters

Questions about God and Man

The ancient words sped through silent, starry space with the speed of light:

"In the beginning God created the heaven and the earth. And the earth was without form, and void; and darkness was upon the face of the deep. And the Spirit of God moved upon the face of the waters."

On that hushed Christmas Eve three American astronauts were orbiting the moon, man's first small leap into the limitless universe. Their flight represented a technological achievement far beyond anything man had done before. Yet as they read from GENESIS and the audience on earth listened, the words seemed neither old-fashioned nor absurd. On the contrary, they seemed just right. Coming from the three men out in space, these familiar words seemed to bring everyone a little closer to the wonder of creation.

The three astronauts represented the vanguard of science, searching out the secrets of the moon. Yet beyond them, beyond all science, lies mystery. The wonder of creation, the wonder of the universe, the wonder of life—these raise questions about God. Certainly it was their sensing a superior creative force behind the universe that led these men to choose the words of GENESIS as their message to the world from space.

Who Is God?

When we consider the awesome majesty of his works, it is difficult to realize that the God of the Bible is not some impossibly distant deity, but a Father who has chosen to reveal himself to man. He reveals himself in nature, which he created, in the mind and heart, and in the Bible, the written record of his activities in history.

The writers of the Old Testament describe a God who loves and disciplines his chosen people, the Israelites, like an affectionate and rather strict parent. He is a God of love, holiness, and justice. When the Israel-

ites sin, as they often did, he punishes them. When they repent and mend their ways, he forgives them.

The most important revelation of God is in the New Testament, through the life, personality, teachings, and works of Jesus. Indeed, the Apostle John declares that Jesus was God in visible, tangent form. During his life Jesus' followers gradually realized that he was the promised Messiah, or the Christ, the Son of the living God. According to the Fourth Gospel Jesus told them "I and my Father are one." This could only mean that God was there in the person of a flesh-and-blood man.

God also exists as the Holy Spirit. Although the Spirit is eternal (and is described in the Bible as having other attributes of God), Jesus promised that the Holy Spirit would come as a special gift to the church after his own earthly life was completed. This happened on Pentecost, the founding day of the church, a day marked with strange events and a moving evangelistic sermon.

The Gospel according to Matthew closes with Jesus' command to his followers to baptize all peoples "in the name of the Father, and of the Son, and of the Holy Ghost." To explain this New Testament extension of Israel's idea of "one God" (monotheism) later theologians used the word "Trinity" for one God mysteriously existing in three personalities. Modern writers have used other images, such as the three facets of the same triangle, or water existing as ice, liquid, or vapor.

Who Is Man?

According to GENESIS, man is God's most important creation—a creation, not just an accidental combination of chemicals. Man is created in God's image, capable of reason and given free will. It was free will that first got man into trouble with God. Adam and Eve chose to disobey God by eating the fruit he had forbidden them to eat. It is this capacity to sin that has kept man in frequent conflict with God ever since. God has given man free will, but holds him responsible for making the right decisions. God's laws enable man to determine what is right and what is sinful.

And God made man ruler of the earth, as he told Adam and Noah. The fish of the sea, the fowls of the air, and all living things are for man's benefit. It can be assumed that the natural resources of the earth, such as oil, minerals, stone, and the like, may also be used to benefit man. Since man is the ruler over all, it is up to him to see that both the living things and the natural resources are used wisely and economically.

Man's God-given ability to reason, his science, his art, his literature, have made him what he is today. Man in society has not been wholly successful, for there are millions of people in the world dying of starvation and preventable diseases. Nor has he been able to achieve a society wholly obedient to God's laws.

How Does Man Find God?

You might think that the Bible would begin by proving that God exists. Instead, it shows God immediately at work, in the creation. It tells us that the world had a beginning, but there is no hint that God did. He simply exists —he is forever. From ancient times philosophers have tried to prove or disprove the existence of God, but the Bible doesn't. From its very beginning the Bible presumes faith.

Faith in God is not blind acceptance of something not proved. Very few scientific discoveries are made without faith. A scientist observes, for example, behavior in an atom that indicates the presence of a previously unknown particle. He sets up a hypothesis that affirms the existence of this new particle. This is an act of faith; and it may lead to many months of testing to prove or disprove the hypothesis. If he finds the particle, his faith is justified. Without faith he would never know, would never discover the particle.

The same principle applies to faith in God. Our hypothesis is the existence of God the Father, the Son, and the Holy Spirit, the Son having been born of a virgin, having died to redeem mankind from sin, and having been resurrected from the dead. Our evidence is the account of God's actions in the Bible and the witness of hundreds of millions of Christians, some of whom suffered torture and death for their faith.

To test this hypothesis we must place our faith in it with all our hearts and minds. If this act of faith works for us, then our hypothesis is true. There is no simple test, however. God manifests himself in many ways in our lives. We may have a vivid awareness of his presence, a sense of his love working through us to bring love to others, a peaceful feeling of redemption from sin, a secure feeling that our lives are being guided by God. With an act of faith each of us can discover God for himself. Without faith we can never discover him.

The writer of the Epistle to the HEBREWS sums up faith as "evidence of things not seen." There will always be some mystery about God that our faith must bridge.

What Is Jesus to Us?

The reason for Jesus' appearance on earth goes back to the very beginning of the Bible. From the first sin of Adam and Eve, man's wrongdoing had built a fence between himself and God. Since God is perfectly good and man was always sinning, how could God and man be reconciled? The Bible says that to be really fair God should have punished man for his sins, and the punishment for sin is death.

This is the problem that Jesus came to earth to solve. One of the Bible's most-quoted verses explains, "God so loved the world that he gave his only begotten Son, that whosoever believeth in him should not perish but have everlasting life." What God did was send Jesus, a sinless person, to die in our place. Our sins were laid on him just as, in earlier times, the sins of the Israelites were laid on the lamb in ritual sacrifice. By taking our punishment on himself, Jesus saved us from being punished.

Thus, by his death Jesus redeemed us from sin. By rising again he triumphs over both sin and death. If we accept him as our Lord and Saviour his strength will undergird our lives. The

Bible concludes that because Jesus rose again, those who believe in him will also have eternal life, not only after death, but a newly born life that begins now.

In his Epistle to the COLOSSIANS, Paul describes Jesus as man's "hope of glory" who "made peace through the blood of his cross" in order to reconcile us to God.

Why Does God Allow Suffering?

Perhaps the greatest trial for faith is the puzzle of why evil and suffering exist. If God is all-powerful and loves mankind, as the Bible teaches, why does he permit the good to suffer and the evil to prosper, as so often happens? Why does he permit poverty and illness and war, which destroy innocent and guilty alike?

This puzzle is the theme of the anonymous book of JOB, one of the great masterpieces of ancient literature. God allows Satan to test Job's faith by taking away this good man's wealth, his children, and finally his health. Most of the book consists of Job's poetic agonies, for the philosophical problem proved to be more painful than pain itself. His friends were no help. They simply concluded that he was being punished for some great sins he had committed. But the simplistic view that virtue is always rewarded would never square with the undeserved suffering of Jesus, the only sinless man that ever lived.

Jesus himself offered a key to part of the riddle when he said that our heavenly Father "maketh his sun to rise on the evil and on the good, and sends rain on the just and on the unjust." Reason, free will, and a bounteous environment are gifts from God to all men, good and bad alike, to use as they wish. But man is sinful; and, in consequence, the society he creates includes many injustices. The poor, the underprivileged, the war victims, and the criminal all arise out of this imperfect society. But they are man's responsibility, not God's.

There are glimpses of loving purpose even in the ills and misfortunes of life. Pain, a common mode of suffering, is needed to warn us when we touch a hot stove or when we have appendicitis. Gravity, which causes a disabled plane to crash, is necessary to hold us on our planet and to keep the elements of the universe in balance. Unhappiness is simply the dark side of our capacity to feel happiness. The need to work for a living enables us to fulfill our abilities and saves us from becoming a race of jellyfish.

Yet the puzzle is not completely solved, for we still do not fully understand God's purpose. But we can safely put our trust in his love. The Apostle Paul says, "I reckon that the sufferings of this present time are not worthy to be compared with the glory which shall be revealed to us."

What Is Prayer?

The inevitable result of faith in a personal God is the desire to communicate with him. To the Christian, whose God desires to share himself, prayer is not a mysterious abracadabra, but a personal, respectful communication. Paul advises in PHILIPPIANS, "Be careful for nothing, but in every thing, by prayer and supplication with thanksgiving, let your requests be made known unto God. And the peace of God, which passeth all understanding, shall keep your hearts and minds through Christ Jesus."

Whatever the other results, peace of mind is the product of prayer. Jesus taught that unlimited power is available through the prayers of those who believe that God is willing to answer. Yet he himself, though asking God to prevent his crucifixion, concluded "nevertheless, not my will, but thine, be done." God hears our prayers but in his infinite wisdom does not always answer them as we prefer. And we should not limit ourselves to praying only when we want something. The Bible includes many prayers of confession, of thanks, and of pure praise to God.

How Shall a Christian Live?

The Bible is also vitally concerned with what God requires of the person to whom he freely offers salvation. And the Bible provides directions on how to live and what to do in today's world. Sometimes this is in the form of specific rules, and sometimes in the form of principles which are applied daily through the help of the Holy Spirit.

Jesus and the biblical writers were

Jews, and that meant that they obeyed a series of laws that God gave to the Hebrews while they wandered in the wilderness. Jesus said that all these various laws could be summarized in a few words: "Thou shalt love the Lord, thy God, with all thy heart, and with all thy soul, and with all thy mind. This is the first and great commandment. And the second is like unto it, Thou shalt love thy neighbor as thyself. On these two commandments hang all the law and the prophets."

The Ten Commandments given by God on Mount Sinai are the center of divine law. God begins by forbidding the worship of any other gods, or idols, or the misuse of his name. Then he commands that one day a week be kept "holy," and that children "honor" their parents. Finally God forbids killing (meaning murder, in modern terminology), adultery, stealing, speaking in "false witness" (lying), and lust for a neighbor's wife or possessions.

Jesus also said that a person can break any of the commandments in thought as well as deed. If a man looks on a woman in lust he has committed adultery in his heart.

The Old Testament includes numerous laws which Christians are not expected to follow. With Jesus Christ's sacrifice, the need for the Hebrew priesthood and the ritual sacrifices disappeared, so many of the detailed rules no longer apply. But the basic principles of Old Testament law remain valid.

What Is Love?

Love is the heart of the Christian lifestyle, yet many Christians do not really know how to define it. Jesus said that we must love not only those easy to love, but everyone—thieves, dope addicts, drunkards, even our enemies. Obviously this is not romantic love, as in the movies. It is not some sort of sentimental, sticky, or sensual feeling, but a matter of discipline that often puts the Christian at odds with society. It involves a loving concern that leads the Christian to help all those who need help. This can only be done by being so open to God that his love works through us.

Jesus teaches that doing good is vitally important. But Paul warns us that good works alone won't put us right

with God. It takes God's grace and man's faith to do that. Yet faith alone is not enough. James tells us that "Faith, if it hath not works, is dead." Jesus put unusual emphasis on the motive behind actions. Because pride is a basic human sin, Jesus scorned acts of charity or piety done for show.

What about Sex and Marriage?

Jesus and his disciples followed the strict Jewish tradition that limited sexual relations to marriage. In Jewish life generally men had little contact with women outside marriage. The Bible freely accepts sex as a gift of God, unlike some non-biblical religions that regard bodily existence as evil in itself. It provides rules for sex not to limit human happiness, but because in God's design happiness and fulfillment in sexual activity involves commitment and consideration for other people. Sex can't be just a matter of gratifying one person's desires. Christians practice chastity out of love for God and other people, not just because they fear venereal disease or pregnancy out of wedlock. By putting sex within marriage, God also establishes a firm family unit in which children can be raised and in which couples can grow old sharing mutual love.

God created the first woman because "it is not good that man should be alone." After Eve joined Adam the Bible said, "Therefore shall a man leave his father and his mother, and shall cleave unto his wife; and they shall be one flesh." There are two balancing aspects of marriage: companionship and sexual fulfillment. The first makes marriage possible and the second makes marriage distinct from all other human relationships.

What about Race Relations?

To explain one of the two main points of the Law, "Love thy neighbor," Jesus told the story of the good Samaritan. The Samaritans were regarded as inferior by the Jews because they were of a different religion and race. Yet in the story the Samaritan is the hero, the real neighbor, because he helps a Jew whose countrymen were indifferent to his plight.

This shows pointedly what Jesus thinks about disliking or mistreating people who are different in ethnic background, skin color, or religion. In GENESIS God created all men in one human family. Paul makes this a major doctrine in his famous sermon on Mars' Hill in Athens, Greece. Some people in the early church showed their dislike of people who were "different." So Paul wrote that we "are all one in Christ Jesus."

What about Our Environment?

When God made the world, he handed it over to man to take care of for him. But instead we have destroyed much of it through selfishness and thoughtlessness. In the process we have cut down huge forests, littered the landscape, poured sewage and waste into our rivers, made it difficult for wild animals to live, and even begun to imperil our own existence. The remedy is a recovery of a sense of humility before the Creator and his creation, as in PSALM 104, and learning to use the resources of the earth he has given us with wisdom and economy.

What about Our Nation?

Jesus said we should "render unto Caesar the things which are Caesar's" and Peter urges us to pray for those in positions of authority. This means more than the grudging payment of taxes or obedience to the laws. It also means we have a responsibility to take part in government and to do what we can to bring it closer to the teachings of Jesus Christ.

Our first loyalty is to God, and not to our country. Nazi Germany showed tragically that a nation and its leaders can become pagan idols. God has established human governments to keep evil under control and encourage good. But sometimes governments don't do this and occasionally they even oppose God. In deciding whether a government must be disobeyed, though, a man must beware of his own delusions, selfishness, and pride.

What about War?

When Jesus told his followers to turn the other cheek and love their enemies, did this rule out war? Christians have been divided on the answer to this question for hundreds of years.

On the one hand, Jesus gave high praise to a Roman centurion and Paul assented to the nation's use of the sword.

On the other hand, Jesus called his disciples to be peacemakers, and these words cannot be dismissed lightly. The biblical idea of peacemaking is not merely to call a truce, but rather to make whole that which had been chaotic, to harmonize discords. Such peacemaking starts within the individual himself, integrating his own personality, but then it spreads, affecting his family, his community, his nation, and his world.

As Jesus predicted, international sabre-rattling will always be a din in our ears, but the Christian who renders his portion to God as well as to Caesar must always be an instrument of peace.

What about Mind-Benders?

While it may be popular to use mind-benders like alcohol and drugs, the Christian must be guided by the Bible. By getting drunk or "high" on alcohol or drugs we distort the personality that God gave us. Some suppose that these chemicals help people get better acquainted with each other, but they often have the reverse effect—making us think only of ourselves. When you get high you take yourself into a little world of your own, with no room in it for others. Besides that, people whose minds are artificially askew can inflict mental or physical damage on other people. Drunken drivers often cause accidents.

God has given us the things of this world to use for good purposes. When we let something become our master, as alcohol and drugs—and smoking—can do, even if it is only temporarily, we fail God and ourselves. He wants us to be the master of what he has given us and not the slave.

How to Enjoy the Good Life?

The early Christians made every waking minute count, and ACTS tells us of the dramatic results. Whether the work is religious or not, whether it is a humble vocation or one with high prestige, the Bible gives it dignity. Paul advises, "Whatsoever ye do, do it heartily as unto the Lord." A job well done pleases God and the worker as well. So we should make the most of the tasks and the abilities God gives us. And as Christians we should also make sure that society provides meaningful work for every person.

In a beautiful section of his Epistle to the PHILIPPIANS, Paul says that we should fix our minds on "whatsoever things are true, whatsoever things are honest, whatsoever things are just, whatsoever things are pure, whatsoever things are lovely . . ." God is pleased by the things in culture that are true and beautiful, in music, the arts, or literature, and it is right to take pleasure in them. God has given men the ability to create these things so that they might be enjoyed.

What about the Church?

In the Bible, the family of God begins with Adam and Eve and eventually includes the Israelites who descended from Abraham. The surprising climax comes with Jesus Christ and a new kind of family that encompasses all peoples. This family—or fellowship—is called the Church, and everything in the New Testament from ACTS onward tells about it.

In modern times, institutions—particularly any that go back as far as 2,000 years—are open to question. However, the Bible teaches that Christianity is not just a private affair. The Christian growth necessary to deal with problems like sex, drugs, and race relations comes partly through the fellowship of those who believe in Jesus. New Testament history shows that the Christian community soon included all sorts of people: young and old, rich and poor, male and female, members of various racial and ethnic groups. The community was not a cozy cell of like-minded, carbon-copied people, but a lively collection of many individuals who shared the same faith in Christ.

Things did not always run smoothly. There were arguments over beliefs and over personalities. In 1 CORINTHIANS Paul writes to an early mission church disturbed by factionalism, and tempted by the vices of Corinth, a cosmopolitan port city. And in EPHESIANS Paul describes the essential quality of unity: "There is one body and one Spirit, even as ye are called in one hope of your calling; one Lord, one faith, one baptism, one God and Father of all, who is above all, and through all, and in you all." However, unity is not to be sought at the expense of truth. The Epistles of II PETER, I, II, and III JOHN, and JUDE advocate discipline to safeguard the purity of Christian beliefs.

Baptism and the Lord's Supper (also called the Communion or Eucharist) are two Church observances commanded by Christ in the Gospels. Today churches call them sacraments or ordinances.

Baptism is a kind of initiation ceremony, parallel to the circumcision of Jews. Through it you enter the Church family. Water is used to show that you have been washed free of sin by the death and resurrection of Jesus.

While baptism takes place only once in a Christian's life, the Lord's Supper is a repeated observance of the church. The last time Jesus celebrated the Passover supper with his disciples he began this observance, which he called a "new covenant." Since that time Christians have remembered Jesus' death in the Supper and have on this occasion given joyous thanks for his resurrection.

These two ceremonies are part of Christian worship. The word "worship" means "to honor according to worth." So Christians gather together regularly to honor God in their worship. The writer to the HEBREWS warned his readers not to forsake "the assembling of ourselves together." This is a good warning for Christians today.

Another mark of Christian fellowship from its earliest days has been organized charity. Many of the noblest charitable and educational institutions of the world today were begun by the Christian Church.

The Church has also been a missionary force. Jesus' last words on earth are often called the Great Commission: "Go ye therefore, and teach all nations. . . ." So the Church began by telling its message energetically to everyone who would listen. Wherever they went the early Christians insisted that belief in Jesus was essential, for they remembered that he himself had said: "I am the way, the truth, and the life: no man cometh unto the Father, but by me."

Where Is History Heading?

The Bible teaches that one day Jesus Christ will return. When Jesus ascended into heaven at the end of his life on earth, his disciples were reminded, "This same Jesus . . . shall so come in like manner as ye have seen him go into heaven." The coming of Jesus is the central teaching of some of Paul's letters, and the last book of the Bible, REVELATION, ends with Christ's words, "Surely I come quickly," and John's response, "Even so, come, Lord Jesus."

When this will happen no one knows, but the New Testament repeatedly reminds us to live the kind of life that would prepare us to meet Jesus at any moment without shame. The New Testament tells us that if our lives are committed fully to God, we need not flinch, but should look forward to such a meeting with joy.

The Bible, then, is like a great drama in which God is at work before history, during history, and in the climax of history. Life on earth is preparation for eternity. And God allows man on earth to decide whether he wants to spend his eternity with God or apart from him. Man's free-will decision here has eternal repercussions.

In the future Christ's Kingdom will be fully established. In the book of REVELATION, which presents a vision of these coming events, heavenly voices announce the time when "The kingdoms of this world are become the kingdoms of our Lord, and of his Christ; and he shall reign for ever and ever."

What the Bible Teaches About . . .

God:

The Creation Story
"In the beginning God" — Genesis 1

The Creation of Man
In the image of God — Genesis 2

A Vision of God's Holiness
"Holy, holy, holy" — Isaiah 6

How God answered Job
"Where were you, Job" — Job 38–41

God Without Equal
The greatness of the Creator — Isaiah 40

Psalm of Amazement
"What is man?" — Psalm 8

Sin and Redemption:

The First Sin
"Hath God said?" — Genesis 3

Psalm of Confession
"Have mercy on me" — Psalm 51

God's Promise to His People
"Because the Lord loves you" — Deuteronomy 7:6–8:10

The Suffering Servant
"All we like sheep" — Isaiah 53

Nicodemus at Night
"For God so loved the world" — John 3

All Have Sinned
The answer is faith — Romans 3:10–25

The Importance of the Resurrection
Is faith in vain? — I Corinthians 15:1–28

Redemption from the World
Saved by God's grace — Ephesians 2:1–10